PRONUNCIATION KEY

The symbol (′), as in **moth·er** (mŭth′ər), is used to mark primary stress; the syllable preceding it is pronounced with greater prominence than the other syllables in the word. The symbol (′), as in **grand·moth·er** (gränd′mŭth′ər), is used to mark secondary stress; a syllable marked for secondary stress is pronounced with less prominence than the one marked (′) but with more prominence than those bearing no stress mark at all.

ă	act, bat	**m**	my, him	ŭ	up, love
ā	able, cape	**n**	now, on	ū	use, cute
â	air, dare	**ng**	sing, England	û	urge, burn
ä	art, calm				
		ŏ	box, hot	**v**	voice, live
b	back, rub	ō	over, no	**w**	west, away
ch	chief, beach	ô	order, ball	**y**	yes, young
d	do, bed	**oi**	oil, joy	**z**	zeal, lazy, those
ĕ	ebb, set	o͝o	book, put	**zh**	vision, measure
ē	equal, bee	o͞o	ooze, rule		
		ou	out, loud	ə	occurs only in un-
f	fit, puff				accented syllables
g	give, beg				and indicates the
h	hit, hear	**p**	page, stop		sound of
ĭ	if, big	**r**	read, cry		a *in* alone
ī	ice, bite	**s**	see, miss		e *in* system
		sh	shoe, push		i *in* easily
j	just, edge	**t**	ten, bit		o *in* gallop
k	kept, make	**th**	thin, path		u *in* circus
l	low, all	**t͟h**	that, other		

FOREIGN SOUNDS

à as in French *ami* [a vowel intermediate in quality between the ă of *cat* and the ä of *calm*, but closer to the former]

KH as in German *ach;* Scottish *loch* [a consonant made by bringing the tongue into the position for *k*, as in *key, coo,* while pronouncing a strong *h*]

N [a symbol used to indicate nasalized vowels as in *bon*. There are four such vowels in French, found in *un bon vin blanc* (œn bōn văn blän)]

œ as in French *feu;* German *schön* [a vowel made with the lips rounded in position for ō as in *over,* while trying to say ā as in *able*]

Y as in French *tu;* German *über* [a vowel made with the lips rounded in position for o͞o as in *ooze,* while trying to say ē as in *easy*]

THE
AMERICAN COLLEGE
ENCYCLOPEDIC
DICTIONARY

———

VOLUME I

THE
AMERICAN COLLEGE
ENCYCLOPEDIC
DICTIONARY

Edited by

CLARENCE L. BARNHART

An accurate, authoritative,
comprehensive dictionary, to which, during years
of preparation, more than 355 recognized
authorities contributed the best
of modern scholarship

VOLUME I

Chicago

SPENCER PRESS, Inc.
1955

TO

EDWARD L. THORNDIKE

AND

LEONARD BLOOMFIELD

Contents

VOLUME I

VOLUME II

GENERAL INTRODUCTION

The Modern Library Dictionary is a record of the English language prepared by more than 350 scholars, specialists, and editors to meet the essential needs of the reader, speaker, and writer who want to know the meaning of a word, how to pronounce it, how to spell it, its history, or some important fact of usage. The first abridged dictionary to be prepared by a staff larger than is usually assembled for an unabridged dictionary, the MLD is the latest record of current usage made by any dictionary staff since World War II. This fact alone justifies publishing this new dictionary.

The MLD, however, differs from other similar dictionaries in many important particulars. Linguists have made significant advances in the study of language and psychologists have developed techniques of presenting facts which have been neglected by dictionary-makers who base the dictionaries they prepare today on the same general principles they used one hundred years ago. In order to insure that the MLD would be carefully planned in accordance with the current knowledge of scholars in the various fields of language study, we secured the services of a distinguished editorial board, representing the fields of general linguistics, psychology, phonetics, usage, and etymology. This board laid down certain general principles, formulated in accordance with the findings of modern scholarship, which the sixteen special editors followed.

This dictionary records the usage of the speakers and writers of our language; no dictionary founded on the methods of modern scholarship can prescribe as to usage; it can only inform on the basis of the facts of usage. A good dictionary is a guide to usage much as a good map tells you the nature of the terrain over which you may want to travel. It is not the function of the dictionary-maker to tell you how to speak, any more than it is the function of the mapmaker to move rivers or rearrange mountains or fill in lakes. A dictionary should tell you what is commonly accepted usage and wherein different classes of speakers or regions differ in their use of the language. We have taken special pains to give an accurate record of the distribution of usage (*Colloq.*, *Slang*, *Brit.*, *U.S.*, etc.) so far as we can determine it; a committee of five special editors who are experts in the study of levels of usage and dialect distribution have recorded their observations in the MLD. This is the first time that a dictionary has attempted such an undertaking, the principles of which are explained by Charles C. Fries on page xxix and by Allen Walker Read on page xxx.

New techniques have been worked out for the selection of information to go into the MLD. It is necessary to select from the hundreds of thousands of words in the language and over a million possible definitions the meanings that will be most needed by a person of wide reading. At the same time it is essential that the basic vocabularies of all the special fields of knowledge should be covered. To select the words and meanings needed by the general user we utilized the Lorge-Thorndike Semantic Count which measures the occurrences of various meanings in the general

vocabulary. By using this count, which is based upon a reading of modern standard literature, we have been able to select the important meanings needed by the reader of today and to have some statistical assurance of the occurrence of the meanings. This count has also been of considerable importance in the arrangement of meanings, since it has enabled us to determine with some certainty which are the common meanings and to put them first. The uses of this count are explained by Irving Lorge on page xxiii.

The selection of the basic vocabularies of various special fields has been a more difficult matter; here the usage of today is important. The only satisfactory way to get current usage in special fields is to go directly to the users of the special vocabularies. With the aid of librarians and of the specialists themselves, we divided knowledge systematically into various narrow fields and secured experts in each field. By utilizing the services of experts in this fashion, we have been able to record the usage of today. It is not enough to read and record usage from books and magazines—although this is important—since any reading must be a very inadequate sampling of the current vocabulary. By going directly to the specialists who know and use the words, however, we have been able to speed up by many years the recording of current usage. We have also made certain that relevant and basic facts needed today are included in the definitions. Such a group of specialists has two functions, then: (1) to make sure that we include basic current terms; (2) to check the accuracy of the facts in the definitions themselves.

The pronunciations in the MLD are represented by a system which gives only forty-four symbols for the 251 common spellings of sounds in the language. This system has proved useful in the training of radio speakers, since it focuses attention on the pronunciation instead of on the spelling; it utilizes the traditional textbook key so far as possible, but takes one symbol from the International Phonetic Alphabet—the standard alphabet used by phoneticians everywhere. By the use of this symbol (ə) we have been able to avoid cluttering the key with a dozen additional symbols based on spelling instead of on sound and to give natural pronunciations in cultivated use rather than the artificial pronunciations so common in existing dictionaries. Variant pronunciations common in extensive regions of the country or used by large groups of people are recorded. Any pronunciation in this dictionary is a good pronunciation and may be safely used. If the second or third pronunciation is your natural pronunciation, it is the one to use. In pronunciation, as in vocabulary, we are a record of usage. For a fuller explanation of the principles of pronunciation, see the preface by W. Cabell Greet on page xxiv.

So far as synonym studies and lists are concerned the MLD differs from similar dictionaries in keying studies and lists to the definitions. Realization of the fact that different words are not synonymous in their entirety but only in certain relatively narrow areas of meaning will lead to a more precise use of words. For example, *unqualified* and *utter* are synonyms of *absolute* in the meaning "free from limitation or restriction"; *complete* and *perfect*, however, are synonyms of *absolute* in the meaning "free from imperfection." For other areas of meaning of *absolute*, other synonyms exist; it is all-important to settle first on the common or core meaning of the synonyms to be distinguished, discriminate carefully among them, and give examples illustrating the use of the synonymous words. Clear examples are almost as important as the discriminations; we have been especially careful to provide illustrative examples for each synonym. We have also placed synonym studies under the well-known word, since it is more likely that the writer will go from the well-known word to the unknown or unfamiliar one. For a further explanation of the principles of handling synonyms and antonyms see the preface by Miles L. Hanley on page xxvii.

The most important fact to learn about the etymology of a word is whether it is a native word or borrowed one. We differ from other dictionaries in immediately indicating this fact. We employ a method of presentation of etymologies which enables the user of the dictionary to read etymologies with a more precise idea of the development of the word. In general, the treatment of the etymologies has been conservative, but a survey of research in this field has been made, and the reader will find many new etymologies recorded here for the first time, particularly of Americanisms, words derived from the American Indian languages, and words from the Romance languages. The preface on etymologies by Kemp Malone, explaining the system carefully and in detail, is on page xxv.

All facts have been arranged in the easiest possible fashion for the user. All entries are in one alphabetical list; the reader will not have to look in a half dozen lists to find an entry. All inflected forms of verbs, nouns, etc., in which the stem is changed in any way by the addition of a suffix have been entered in this dictionary; so have all foreign plurals and all regular plurals likely to be confused with irregular plurals. All definitions are numbered. Central or common meanings are put first. By using different kinds of type for different kinds of information, we have been able to distinguish clearly between main and secondary entries and between definitions and illustrative phrases. The type page has been specially designed so that the user can quickly find the entry for which he is looking.

By putting proper names in the main vocabulary list we have been able to apply the same standards of defining to proper names that we do to the common vocabulary. We have tried to give the most significant facts about each person or place having importance today. Data have been checked against the most recent and reliable sources available and are presented in a clear, readily intelligible manner.

The illustrations have been chosen as aids to the definitions. We have avoided picturing common birds, flowers, and fishes that can be of value only when shown in color or in magnified detail. Captions explaining the illustrations, as under *abacus*, are also designed to supplement the definitions. Actual sizes of animals are given instead of ratios of reduction which the user must figure out and usually doesn't. There are over three hundred spot maps throughout the dictionary giving locations of historically important places (as *Acadia*), places that are hard to find in current atlases (as *Alaska Highway*), and places of literary interest (as *Sherwood Forest*).

The editor, the special editors, the office staff, and the special consultants have had available for their use two outstanding products of American lexicography: *The Century Dictionary* and *The New Century Dictionary*. We were also fortunate in being able to secure the right from the University of Chicago Press to use definitions and sentences from *The Dictionary of American English* (1944).

It is impossible adequately to thank all who have helped in the cooperative project of writing this dictionary, but I am specially grateful to Mr. Jess Stein for his efficient management of the staff and his many editorial suggestions which have materially improved the book. Two editors at Random House, Mr. Robert N. Linscott and Mr. Saxe Commins, have given helpful counsel and support whenever needed. To them I am deeply indebted. Finally, I express my appreciation to Messrs. Bennett A. Cerf, Robert K. Haas, and Donald S. Klopfer for the opportunity to edit a modern dictionary based on present-day scholarship.

Clarence L. Barnhart

SPECIAL CONSULTANTS

ACCOUNTING—See under *COMMERCE:* Accounting, Bookkeeping, and Business Statistics.

ACOUSTICS—See under *PHYSICS.*

AERONAUTICS—See under *APPLIED SCIENCE.*

AGRICULTURE—See under *APPLIED SCIENCE:* Agricultural Machinery; Agriculture; see under *BOTANY:* Grasses; North Temperate Edible Vegetables; North Temperate Fruits, Plant Propagation, and Nursery Practice; Plant Genetics; Tropical Edible Plants; see under *ZOOLOGY:* Beef and Dual-Purpose Cattle; Dairy Cattle and Dairying; Poultry; Sheep and Goats; Stockbreeding and Horses; Swine; see under *THERAPEUTICS:* Veterinary Science.

ALGAE—See under *BOTANY.*

ANATOMY, PHYSIOLOGY, AND EMBRYOLOGY

Brain and Nervous System, Sensory Organs

THEODORE C. RUCH, Professor of Physiology (Chairman of Department), School of Medicine, University of Washington (Au., *Bibliographia primatologica*).

Circulatory System

R. BURTON-OPITZ, Lecturer in Physiology, Columbia University; Consulting Cardiologist.

Comparative Anatomy

DANIEL P. QUIRING, Associate Professor of Biology, Western Reserve University; Head of Anatomical Division, Cleveland Clinic Foundation.

Dental Structure and Dentistry

MOSES DIAMOND, Associate Professor, Department of Anatomy, College of Physicians and Surgeons, Columbia University.

Embryology

EMIL WITSCHI, Professor of Zoölogy, Embryology, and Endocrinology, State University of Iowa (Au., *Sex Deviations, Inversions and Parabiosis*).

Endocrinology

EARL A. DENNIS, Professor of Biology, American University.

Gastro-intestinal System

ALFRED E. WILHELMI, Assistant Professor of Physiological Chemistry, School of Medicine, Yale University.

General Anatomical Terms

L. F. NIMS, Associate Professor of Physiology, Yale University.

Genito-urinary System

EDWARD A. BOYDEN, Professor of Anatomy (Chairman of Department), University of Minnesota (Managing Editor, *Anatomical Record*).

Histology and Cytology

CHARLES WRIGHT HOOKER, Associate Professor of Anatomy, School of Medicine, Yale University.

Major Body Parts

NORMAND L. HOERR, Professor of Anatomy, Western Reserve University.

Muscular System

EDWARD A. BOYDEN. See: Genito-urinary System.

Physiological Processes

ALBERT TYLER, Assistant Professor of Embryology, California Institute of Technology.

Respiratory System

L. F. NIMS. See: General Anatomical Terms.

Skeletal Structure

G. KASTEN TALLMADGE, Associate Professor of Anatomy, School of Medicine, Marquette University.

E. J. CAREY, Dean of the School of Medicine and Professor of Anatomy, Marquette University (Au., *Studies in Anatomy*) (Deceased).

ANIMAL HUSBANDRY—See under *ZOOLOGY:* Beef and Dual-purpose Cattle; Dairy Cattle and Dairying; Poultry; Sheep and Goats; Stockbreeding and Horses; Swine; see under *THERAPEUTICS:* Veterinary Science.

ANTHROPOLOGY

Archaeology

ALFRED V. KIDDER, Chairman, Division of Historical Research, Carnegie Institute of Washington (Au., *Introduction to Southwestern Archaeology; Basketmaker Caves in Northeastern Arizona*).

Cultural Anthropology

RALPH LINTON, Professor of Anthropology, Yale University (Au., *The Study of Man; The Material Culture of the Marquesas Islands; Cultural Background of Personality*).

Ethnology: American Indian Tribes

C. F. VOEGELIN, Professor of Anthropology, Indiana University (Ed., *International Journal of American Linguistics*; au., *Tubatulabal Grammar*).

Ethnology: General

A. L. KROEBER, Professor Emeritus of Anthropology, University of California (Au., *Cultural and Natural Areas; Configurations of Culture Growth; Anthropology*).

Physical Anthropology

WILTON M. KROGMAN, Professor of Physical Anthropology, University of Pennsylvania (Au., *Physical Anthropology of the Seminole Indians of Oklahoma; Growth of Man*).

APPLIED SCIENCE

Aeronautics

ALEXANDER KLEMIN, Aeronautical Consultant; formerly, Guggenheim Research Professor of Aeronautical Engineering, New York University; Aviation Editor, *Scientific American;* Helicopter Editor, *Aero Digest.*

Agricultural Machinery

R. I. SHAWL, Professor of Farm Machinery, University of Illinois.

Agriculture

W. A. ALBRECHT, Professor of Soils (Chairman of Department), University of Missouri.

Automobiles

RAY F. KUNS, Au., *Automotive Essentials; Automotive Service; Auto-Mechanics;* formerly, Editor of *Automotive Digest* and Principal of Automotive High School of Cincinnati.

Ceramics

R. K. HURSH, Professor of Ceramic Engineering, University of Illinois.

Civil Engineering

CHARLES H. NORRIS, Associate Professor of Structural Engineering, Massachusetts Institute of Technology.

Coke and Petroleum Industries

E. DeGOLYER, Senior Partner, DeGolyer and Mac-Naughton, Consulting Geologists and Engineers; formerly, Professor of Geology, University of Texas, and Director of American Petroleum Institute; Associate Editor, *Journal of Economic Geology.*

Electrical Devices

NORMAN L. TOWLE, Professor of Electrical Engineering (Head of Department), The Cooper Union School of Engineering.

Electronics

W. L. EVERITT, Professor of Electrical Engineering (Head of Department), University of Illinois; formerly, Director of Operational Research, Office Chief Signal Officer, United States War Department; Past President, Institute of Radio Engineers.

G. H. FETT, Professor of Electrical Engineering, University of Illinois.

Foundry and Ferrous Metallurgy

C. W. MORISETTE, Instructor, Milwaukee Vocational School.

General and Nonferrous Metallurgy

ALFRED BORNEMANN, Associate Professor of Chemical Engineering, Stevens Institute of Technology; Director, Peirce Metals Laboratory.

Glass Industries

S. R. SCHOLES, Glass Technologist and Dean, New York State College of Ceramics, Alfred University (Au., *Modern Glass Practice;* editor, *Glass Industry Handbook*).

Horse-drawn Vehicles

CARL W. MITMAN, Head Curator, Department of Engineering and Industries, United States National Museum (Au., *An Outline Development of Highway Travel; Beginning of Mechanical Transport Era in America*).

Mining

R. D. PARKS, Associate Professor of Mineral Industry, Massachusetts Institute of Technology (Co-au., *Mine Examination and Valuation*).

Photography

C. B. NEBLETTE, Supervisor of Department of Photographic Technology, Rochester Institute of Technology.

Plumbing

G. W. FARNDALE, Instructor, Milwaukee Vocational School.

Railroads

C. J. CORLISS, Section Manager, Public Relations Office, Association of American Railroads.

Surveying

A. J. BONE, Associate Professor of Highway and Airport Engineering, Massachusetts Institute of Technology.

Telegraphy and Telephony

K. S. JOHNSON, Transmission Standards Engineer, Bell Telephone Laboratories, Inc.

ARCHAEOLOGY—See under *ANTHROPOLOGY*; see under *HISTORY*: Ancient History.

ARCHITECTURE

Construction

FRED N. SEVERUD, Consulting Engineer.

Decorative Treatment

KENNETH J CONANT, Professor of Architecture, Harvard University.

General and Stylistic Terms

RICHARD KRAUTHEIMER, Professor of Art, Vassar College.

Miscellaneous Terms

HENRY WRIGHT, Managing Editor, *Architectural Forum*.

Structure

TALBOT F. HAMLIN, Professor of Architecture, Columbia University (Au., *Architecture through the Ages; Greek Revival Architecture in America; Architecture, an Art for All Men*)

ARMOR—See under *MILITARY TERMS*.

ARTS

Dance

ANATOLE CHUJOY, Editor, *Dance News.*

Decorative Arts

EDWIN J. HIPKISS, Curator of Department of Decorative Arts of Europe and America, Boston Museum of Fine Arts.

Engraving Techniques

A. HYATT MAYOR, Curator of Prints, Metropolitan Museum of Art.

General and Stylistic Terms

DIMITRI TSELOS, Associate Professor of Fine Arts, Institute of Fine Arts, New York University.

Motion Pictures

WILLARD VAN DYKE, Motion Picture Director and Producer; Partner in Affiliated Film Producers, Inc.

Painting and Graphic Arts

HARRY B. WEHLE, Curator of Paintings, Metropolitan Museum of Art.

Sculpture

WILLIAM ZORACH, Sculptor; Instructor of Sculpture, Art Students' League (Au., *Zorach Explains Sculpture*).

Theater

EDWARD C. COLE, Associate Professor and Production Manager, Department of Drama, School of the Fine Arts, Yale University.

ASTRONOMY

Astronomical Instruments

CHARLES A. FEDERER, JR., Editor, *Sky and Telescope.*

Astrophysics

OTTO STRUVE, Andrew McLeish Distinguished Service Professor of Astrophysics, University of Chicago; Honorary Director, Yerkes and McDonald Observatories (Former Editor, *Astrophysical Journal*).

Celestial Mechanics

DIRK BROUWER, Professor of Astronomy and Director of Observatory, Yale University (Editor, *Astronomical Journal*).

General Terms

NEWTON LACY PIERCE, Associate Professor of Astronomy, Princeton University.

The Solar System

SETH B. NICHOLSON, Astronomer, Mount Wilson Observatory (Editor, *Publications of the Astronomical Society of the Pacific*).

Stellar Astronomy

WILLIAM W. MORGAN, Professor of Astronomy, Yerkes Observatory, University of Chicago.

ATHLETICS—See under *SPORTS AND GAMES*: Baseball, Boxing, Football, and General Terms; Basketball, Swimming, and Gymnastics; Golf, Tennis, and Track.

AUTOMOBILES—See under *APPLIED SCIENCE*.

BACTERIOLOGY—See under *BOTANY*: Bacteria.

BANKING—See under *COMMERCE*: Banking, Credit, and Foreign Exchange.

BIBLE—See under *RELIGION*.

BIOCHEMISTRY—See under *CHEMISTRY*.

BIOLOGY—See *ANATOMY, PHYSIOLOGY, AND EMBRYOLOGY; BOTANY; ZOOLOGY*.

BIRDS—See under *ZOOLOGY*: Ornithology.

BOOKKEEPING—See under *COMMERCE*: Accounting, Bookkeeping, and Business Statistics.

BOTANY

Algae

GILBERT M. SMITH, Professor of Botany, Stanford University (Au., *Freshwater Algae of United States; Cryptogamic Botany; Marine Algae of the Monterey Peninsula, California*; co-au., *A Textbook of General Botany*).

Angiosperms

LEON CROIZAT, Ministerio de Agricultura y Cria, Caracas, Venezuela; formerly, Staff Member of Arnold Arboretum, Harvard University.

Bacteria

MARIO MOLLARI, Professor of Bacteriology and Immunology (Chairman of Department), Georgetown University.

Bryophytes

HENRY S. CONARD, Research Professor, State University of Iowa; Professor of Botany (Retired), Grinnell College.

Fungi

H. M. FITZPATRICK, Professor of Mycology, Cornell University (Au., *The Lower Fungi; Phycomycetes*).

Grasses

MASON A. HEIN, Senior Agronomist, United States Department of Agriculture, Division of Forage Crops and Diseases, Plant Industry Station, Beltsville, Maryland.

Gymnosperms

JOHN T. BUCHHOLZ, Professor of Botany, University of Illinois.

Medicinal Plants

ELMER H. WIRTH, Professor of Pharmacognosy and Pharmacology, College of Pharmacy, University of Illinois; Director, University of Illinois Drug Plant Experiment Station.

Nomenclature

ALBERT F. HILL. See: Plants of Economic Use.

North Temperate Edible Vegetables

H. C. THOMPSON, Professor of Vegetable Crops (Head of Department), Cornell University (Au., *Vegetable Crops; Sweet Potato Production and Marketing; Asparagus Production*).

North Temperate Fruits, Plant Propagation, and Nursery Practice

H. B. TUKEY, Professor of Horticulture (Head of Department), Michigan State College (Au., *The Pear and Its Culture*; contributing editor, *American Nurseryman; Scientific Monthly*).

Ornamental Flowering Plants

CHARLES H. CONNORS, Professor of Ornamental Horticulture, Rutgers University; Head of Department of Ornamental Horticulture, New Jersey State Agricultural Experiment Station.

Ornamental Woody Plants

DONALD WYMAN, Horticulturist, Arnold Arboretum, Harvard University.

Plant Anatomy

H. E. HAYWARD, Director and Senior Plant Anatomist, U.S. Regional Salinity Laboratory, Bureau of Plant Industry, Soils and Agricultural Engineering, United States Department of Agriculture, Riverside, California (Au., *The Structure of Economic Plants*).

Plant Ecology

PAUL B. SEARS, Professor of Botany, Oberlin College (Au., *Life and Environment*).

Plant Genetics

DONALD FORSHA JONES, Head of Department of Genetics, Connecticut Agricultural Experiment Station.

Plant Physiology

JAMES BONNER, Professor of Biology, California Institute of Technology.

Plants of Economic Use

ALBERT F. HILL, Research Fellow, Botanical Museum of Harvard University (Au., *Economic Botany*).

Pteridophytes

C. A. WEATHERBY, Research Associate, Gray Herbarium, Harvard University.

Tropical Edible Plants

ROBERT WILLARD HODGSON, Professor of Sub-tropical Horticulture, University of California; Assistant Dean, College of Agriculture, Los Angeles.

BUILDING TRADES

Carpentry

DeWITT T HUNT, Professor of Industrial Arts Education (Head, Department of Industrial Arts Education and Engineering Shopwork), Oklahoma Agricultural and Mechanical College.

Masonry and Bricklaying, Painting and Plastering

HENRY P. ADAMS, Professor of Industrial Arts Education (Director of School of Technical Training), Oklahoma Agricultural and Mechanical College.

Structural Elements and Materials

VERNON C. GRESHAM, Associate Professor of Industrial Arts and Director of Vocational Training, Tennessee Polytechnic Institute; Educational Specialist, USNR Publications Project, Naval Gun Factory, Washington, D. C.

CARD, DICE, AND PARLOR GAMES — See under *SPORTS AND GAMES.*

CARTOGRAPHY — See under *GEOGRAPHY:* General Geography and Cartography.

CERAMICS — See under *APPLIED SCIENCE.*

CHEMISTRY

Biochemistry

RUDOLPH J. ANDERSON, Professor of Chemistry, Yale University (Member of Editorial Board, *Journal of Biological Chemistry*)

Chemical Apparatus

W. T. READ, Chief of Research Section of the National Roster of Scientific and Specialized Personnel; Dean of School of Chemistry, Rutgers University, 1930–43 (Au., *Industrial Chemistry*).

Chemical Formulas

A. H. BLATT. See: Organic Chemistry.

Chemical Industries

DONALD BROUGHTON, Assistant Professor of Chemical Engineering, Massachusetts Institute of Technology.

The Elements

H. S. BOOTH, Professor of Chemistry (Chairman of Department), Western Reserve University (Editor, *Inorganic Syntheses, Vol. I*).

General Chemical Terms

LEE F. SUPPLE, Professor of Organic Chemistry, Illinois Institute of Technology.

Inorganic Compounds

ROBERT D. FOWLER, Professor of Chemistry (Chairman of Department), Johns Hopkins University.

Inorganic Radicals

HUBERT N. ALYEA, Associate Professor of Chemistry, Princeton University.

Organic Chemistry

L. F. AUDRIETH, Professor of Inorganic Chemistry, University of Illinois.

A. H. BLATT, Associate Professor of Chemistry, Queens College.

CHARLES D. HURD, Professor of Chemistry, Northwestern University (Member Editorial Board, *Journal of Organic Chemistry*).

R. A. PENNEMAN, Research Fellow, University of Illinois.

Physical Chemistry

FRANK T. GUCKER, JR., Professor of Chemistry (Chairman of Department), Indiana University.

Selection of Terms

LOUIS SATTLER, Associate Professor of Chemistry, Brooklyn College; Research Chemist, New York Sugar Trade Laboratory.

CHESS AND CHECKERS — See under *SPORTS AND GAMES.*

CIVIL ENGINEERING — See under *APPLIED SCIENCE.*

CLOTHING — See under *HOME ECONOMICS.*

COINS

Current Money and Coinage

F. LELAND HOWARD, Assistant Director, United States Mint.

Numismatics and Older Monetary Units

SYDNEY P NOE, formerly, Secretary, Librarian, and Editor of the Publications of The American Numismatic Society; Curator, Museum of The American Numismatic Society.

COLOR — See under *PHYSICS.*

COMMERCE

Accounting, Bookkeeping, and Business Statistics

MARTIN LEE BLACK, JR., Professor of Accounting, Duke University.

Banking, Credit, and Foreign Exchange

CHARLES R. WHITTLESEY, Professor of Finance and Economics (Chairman of Department), University of Pennsylvania (Au., *National Interest and International Cartels; International Monetary Issues*).

Bonds and Stocks

HARRY G. GUTHMANN, Professor of Finance, Northwestern University (Au., *The Analysis of Financial Statements;* co-au., *Corporate Financial Policy; Investment Principles and Practices*).

Corporations

JAMES C. DONBRIGHT, Professor of Finance, Columbia University (Au., *Public Utilities and the National Power Policies; Railroad Capitalization; Valuation of Property;* co-au. *The Holding Company*).

Import and Export

J. S. DAVIS, Professor of Economic Research and Director of Food Research Institute, Stanford University.

Insurance

S. S. HUEBNER, Professor of Insurance and Commerce, University of Pennsylvania; President, American College of Life Underwriters; Chairman, Board of Trustees of American Institute for Property and Liability Underwriters, Inc. (Au., *State Insurance;* co-au., *Life Insurance and Investment*).

Labor

WILLIAM M. LEISERSON, Visiting Professor of Politica Economy, Johns Hopkins University; Former Member of National Labor Relations Board; Former Chairman of National Mediation Board (Au., *Right and Wrong in Labor Relations*).

Transportation

C. O. RUGGLES, Professor of Public Utility Management and Regulation, Harvard University (Au., *Terminal Charges at United States Ports; Problems in Public Utility Economics and Management*).

Wholesale and Retail Marketing

PAUL D. CONVERSE, Professor of Marketing, University of Illinois (Au., *Marketing Methods and Policies; Selling Policies; Essentials of Distribution; Elements of Marketing;* co-au., *Introduction to Marketing*).

COOKERY — See under *HOME ECONOMICS:* Food.

CORPORATIONS — See under *COMMERCE.*

CRANIOMETRY AND CRANIOLOGY — See under *ANTHROPOLOGY:* Physical Anthropology.

CRYSTALLOGRAPHY — See under *GEOLOGY.*

DANCE — See under *ARTS.*

DENTISTRY — See under *ANATOMY, PHYSIOLOGY, AND EMBRYOLOGY:* Dental Structure and Dentistry.

DERMATOLOGY — See under *THERAPEUTICS.*

DOGS — See under *ZOOLOGY.*

DRAMA — See under *LITERATURE;* see under *ARTS:* Theater.

ECOLOGY — See under *BOTANY:* Plant Ecology; see under *ZOOLOGY:* Animal Ecology.

ECONOMICS — See under *COMMERCE:* Banking, Credit, and Foreign Exchange; Import and Export; Insurance; Labor; Wholesale and Retail Marketing; see under *GOVERNMENT:* Political Economy.

EDUCATION

Administration

DONALD P. COTTRELL, Dean, College of Education, Ohio State University; formerly, Professor of Education and Executive Director of Horace Mann-Lincoln School of Teachers College, Columbia University (Co-au., *Redirecting Teacher Education*).

Comparative and Foreign Education

I. L. KANDEL, Professor Emeritus of Education, Teachers College, Columbia University (Au., *Intellectual Cooperation: National and International; Conflicting Theories of Education; History of Secondary Education; Comparative Education; Essays in Comparative Education; The Classics in Germany, England, and France*; editor, *Educational Yearbook of the International Institute*).

Higher Education

JOHN DALE RUSSELL, Director, Division of Higher Education, United States Office of Education; formerly, Professor of Education and Dean of Students, Division of Social Sciences, University of Chicago.

Philosophy of Education

EDGAR W. KNIGHT, Kenan Professor of Education, University of North Carolina (Au., *Twenty Centuries of Education; Education in the United States; Public Education in the South; Reports on European Education; What College Presidents Say; Henry Harrisse on Collegiate Education*; co-au., *Culture in the South; The Graduate School; Research and Publications*).

Tests and Measurements—See under *PSYCHOLOGY*.

ELECTRICAL DEVICES—See under *APPLIED SCIENCE*.

ELECTRICITY AND MAGNETISM—See under *PHYSICS*.

ELECTRONICS—See under *APPLIED SCIENCE*.

EMBRYOLOGY—See under *ANATOMY, PHYSIOLOGY, AND EMBRYOLOGY*; see under *ZOOLOGY*: Animal Embryology.

ETHICS—See under *PHILOSOPHY*.

ETHNOLOGY—See under *ANTHROPOLOGY*.

FISHES—See under *ZOOLOGY*: Ichthyology.

FOOD—See under *HOME ECONOMICS*.

FUNGI—See under *BOTANY*.

FURNITURE AND FURNISHINGS—See under *HOME ECONOMICS*.

GEMS AND JEWELRY—See under *GEOLOGY*.

GENETICS—See under *ZOOLOGY*; see under *BOTANY*: Plant Genetics.

GEOGRAPHY

General Geography and Cartography

RICHARD HARTSHORNE, Professor of Geography, University of Wisconsin (Au., *The Nature of Geography*).

Oceanography

HARRY AARON MARMER, Assistant Chief of Division of Tides and Currents, United States Coast and Geodetic Survey (Au., *Tides and Currents in New York Harbor; Coastal Currents Along the Pacific Coast of the United States; The Sea; The Tide*).

Physical Geography

ROBERT BOWMAN, Professor of Geography, State University of Iowa.

Selection of Maps

ARTHUR H. ROBINSON, Assistant Professor of Geography, University of Wisconsin.

ROBERT L. REYNOLDS, Professor of History, University of Wisconsin.

Statistical Data

HENRY J. DUBESTER, Chief, Census Library Project, Library of Congress.

GEOLOGY

Crystallography

CLIFFORD FRONDEL, Associate Professor of Mineralogy, Harvard University (Co-au., *Dana's System of Mineralogy, 7th ed.*).

Gems and Jewelry

FREDERICK H. POUGH, Curator of Physical Geology and Mineralogy, American Museum of Natural History.

Mineralogy: General Mineralogical Terms

S. JAMES SHAND, Newberry Professor of Geology, Columbia University.

Mineralogy: Mineral Names

MICHAEL FLEISCHER, Senior Geochemist, United States Geological Survey, Washington, D. C. (Associate Editor, *American Mineralogist*; assistant editor, *Chemical Abstracts*).

Paleontology

JOHN ERIC HILL, Assistant Curator of Mammals, American Museum of Natural History (Deceased).

Petrology: General Petrological Terms

KENNETH K. LANDES, Professor of Geology (Chairman of Department), University of Michigan.

Petrology: Igneous Rocks

CORNELIUS S HURLBUT, JR., Associate Professor of Mineralogy, Harvard University.

Petrology: Metamorphic and Sedimentary Rocks

S. JAMES SHAND. See: Mineralogy: General Mineralogical Terms.

Physical Geology

KIRTLEY F. MATHER, Professor of Geology, Harvard University; formerly, Geologist, United States Geological Survey (Au., *Old Mother Earth; Sons of the Earth*; co-au., *A Source Book in Geology*)

Stratigraphy

RAYMOND C. MOORE, Professor of Geology, University of Kansas; Chairman, American Commission of Stratigraphic Nomenclature; Geologist, United States Geological Survey; State Geologist of Kansas (Au., *Historical Geology*).

GLASS INDUSTRIES—See under *APPLIED SCIENCE*.

GOVERNMENT

Comparative Government: England

R. K. GOOCH, Professor of Political Science, University of Virginia (Au., *The Government of England*; editor, *Source Book on the Government of England*).

Comparative Government: Europe

NORMAN L. HILL, Professor of Political Science, Nebraska University (Au., *Claims to Territory*; co-au., *The Background of European Governments*).

International Law and Diplomacy

PITMAN B. POTTER, Grozier Professor of International Law (Chairman of Department), American University (Managing Editor, *American Journal of International Law*; au., *Introduction to the Study of International Organization; The Wal Wal Arbitration*).

International Relations

W. E. DIEZ, Associate Professor of Government, University of Rochester.

Legislation

ALPHEUS THOMAS MASON, McCormick Professor of Jurisprudence, Princeton University (Au., *The Brandeis Way: A Case Study in the Workings of Democracy; Bureaucracy Convicts Itself: The Ballinger-Pinchot Controversy; Brandeis: A Free Man's Life*).

Local and State Government

AUSTIN F. MACDONALD, Professor of Political Science, University of California (Au., *American State Government and Administration; American City Government and Administration*).

National Government

ARTHUR N. HOLCOMBE, Eaton Professor of the Science of Government, Harvard University (Au., *The Middle Classes in American Politics; The Chinese Revolution; The Foundations of the Modern Commonwealth*).

Political Economy

ALVIN H. HANSEN, Lucius N. Littauer Professor of Political Economy, Harvard University (Co-au., *Principles of Economics*; au., *America's Role in the World Economy; Fiscal Policy and Business Cycles; Economic Stabilization in an Unbalanced World; Economic Policy and Full Employment*).

Political Parties

V. O. KEY, JR., Professor of Political Science, Johns Hopkins University.

Political Theory

R. M. MacIVER, Lieber Professor of Political Philosophy and Sociology, Columbia University (Au., *Toward an Abiding Peace; Social Causation; Society: A Textbook of Sociology; The Web of Government*).

GRAMMAR—See under *LINGUISTICS*: Morphology.

GRASSES—See under *BOTANY*.

GYNECOLOGY—See under *THERAPEUTICS*.

HERALDRY

CHARLES K. BOLTON, Au., *Bolton's American Armory*; formerly, Associate Professor, Simmons College, and Librarian, Boston Athenaeum.

HISTORY

Ancient History

A. E. R. BOAK, Richard Hudson Professor of Ancient History (formerly, Chairman of Department), University of Michigan (Au., *History of Rome to 565 A.D.*).

The British Empire

PAUL ALEXANDER KNAPLUND, Professor of History (Chairman of Department), University of Wisconsin (Au., *Gladstone and Britain's Imperial Policy; Gladstone's Foreign Policy; The British Empire, 1817–1939*).

China and Japan

OWEN LATTIMORE, Lecturer and Director of Walter Hines Page School of International Relations, Johns Hopkins University; formerly, Political Advisor to General Chiang Kai-shek, 1941–42; Deputy Director of Pacific Operations, Office of War Information (Au., *Solution in Asia*).

England to 1689

WILLIAM EDWARD LUNT, Walter D. and Edith M. L. Scull Professor of English Constitutional History, Haverford College (Au., *History of England; Financial Relations of the Papacy with England to 1327*; associate editor, *American Historical Review*).

England from 1689

ARTHUR H. BASYE, Professor of History, Dartmouth College.

France

ARTHUR L. DUNHAM, Professor of History, University of Michigan.

Italy

MARY LUCILLE SHAY, Assistant Professor of History, University of Illinois.

Medieval History

SIDNEY R. PACKARD, Professor of History, Smith College (Au., *Europe and the Church under Innocent III*).

Middle and Near Eastern History

ALBERT HOWE LYBYER, Professor Emeritus of History, University of Illinois (Au., *The Government of the Ottoman Empire in the Time of Suleiman the Magnificent*).

Modern European History

DWIGHT ERWIN LEE, Professor of Modern European History, Clark University (Au., *Great Britain and the Cyprus Convention Policy of 1878; Ten Years: The World on the Way to War, 1930–40*).

Russia

SIR BERNARD PARES, formerly, Professor of Russian History, Language, and Literature, and Director of the School of Slavonic and East European Studies, University of London; Visiting Professor of History, Sarah Lawrence College (Au., *History of Russia; The Fall of the Russian Monarchy; Russia and the Peace*).

Spain and Latin America

C. H. HARING, Robert Woods Bliss Professor of Latin-American History and Economics, Harvard University (Au., *Trade and Navigation Between Spain and the Indies in the Time of the Hapsburgs; The Spanish Empire in America*).

United States

WILLIAM B. HESSELTINE, Professor of History, University of Wisconsin (Au., *Ulysses S. Grant, Politician; The South in American History*).

HOME ECONOMICS

Clothing

MARY EVANS, Professor of Home Economics, Teachers College, Columbia University (Au., *Costume Silhouettes; Costume Throughout the Ages; Draping and Dress Design; How to Make Historic American Costumes*).

Food

MYRNA JOHNSTON, Director, Better Foods and Home Equipment Departments, *Better Homes and Gardens*.

JEAN GUTHRIE DUMONT, Former Director, Better Foods and Home Equipment Departments, *Better Homes and Gardens*.

Furniture and Furnishings

RUTH A. FOLGER, Associate Professor of Fine Arts (Head of Department), Russell Sage College.

Textiles

GRACE G. DENNY, Professor of Home Economics, University of Washington (Au., *Fabrics*).

HOROLOGY—See under *MACHINES AND MACHINERY*.

HORTICULTURE—See under *BOTANY*: North Temperate Edible Vegetables; North Temperate Fruits, Plant Propagation, and Nursery Practice; Ornamental Flowering Plants; Ornamental Woody Plants; Tropical Edible Plants.

HUNTING AND FISHING—See under *SPORTS AND GAMES*.

HYDRAULICS AND HYDRAULIC ENGINEERING—See under *PHYSICS*.

INSECTS—See under *ZOOLOGY*: Entomology.

INSURANCE—See under *COMMERCE*.

INTERNATIONAL LAW—See under *GOVERNMENT*: International Law and Diplomacy; see under *LAW*: International and Military Law.

JEWELRY—See under *GEOLOGY*: Gems and Jewelry.

JOURNALISM—See under *LITERATURE*.

LABOR—See under *COMMERCE*.

LAW

Attorney and Client Relationship

ELLIOTT E. CHEATHAM, Professor of Law, Columbia University (Au., *Cases and Materials on the Legal Profession*).

Business and Membership Organizations

HENRY WINTHROP BALLANTINE, Professor of Law, University of California (Au., *Problems in Law; Law of Corporations*).

Contracts

LON L. FULLER, Professor of Law, Harvard University (Au., *The Law in Quest of Itself*).

Conveyancing

W. BARTON LEACH, Professor of Law, Harvard University.

Copyright, Patent, and Trademark Law

HORACE G. BALL, Au., *The Law of Copyright and Literary Property*.

Criminal Law

LIVINGSTON HALL, Professor of Law (Vice Dean, Law School) Harvard University (Co-au., *Cases on Criminal Law*).

Decedents' Estates

MAX RHEINSTEIN, Max Pam Professor of Comparative Law, University of Chicago (Au., *Cases and Materials on Decedents' Estates*).

Domestic Relations and Persons

ALBERT CHARLES JACOBS, Provost and Professor of Law, Columbia University (Au., *Cases and Materials on Domestic Relations; Cases and Materials on Landlord and Tenant*).

English and Scottish Law

JOHN P. DAWSON, Professor of Law, University of Michigan.

Evidence

CHARLES T. McCORMICK, Dean and Professor of Law, School of Law, University of Texas (Au., *Handbook on Law of Damages; Cases and Materials on the Law of Evidence; Cases and Materials on Law of Damages; co-au., Texas Law of Evidence; Cases and Materials on Federal Courts*).

Fiduciaries and Insolvent Estates

AUSTIN W. SCOTT, Dane Professor of Law, Harvard University (Au., *The Law of Trusts*).

International and Military Law

EARLE H. KETCHAM, Professor of Political Science, Syracuse University.

Judges and Courts

EDSON R. SUNDERLAND, Professor of Law and Legal Research, University of Michigan (Au., *Cases on Code Pleading; Cases on Common Law Pleading; Cases on Trial and Appellate Practice; Cases on Judicial Administration*).

Maritime Law

HOBART COFFEY, Professor of Law and Director of the Law Library, University of Michigan.

Penology

EDWIN H. SUTHERLAND, Professor of Sociology (Head of Department), Indiana University; formerly, President, Indiana University Institute of Criminal Law and Criminology (Au., *Principles of Criminology; The Professional Thief*).

Personal Property

HORACE E. WHITESIDE, Professor of Law, Cornell University.

Procedure

GEORGE H. DESSION, Professor of Law, Yale University; formerly, Special Assistant to Attorney General, Anti-Trust Division, United States Department of Justice; Member, Advisory Committee on Rules of Criminal Procedure, United States Supreme Court.

Quasi-judicial Public Offices

KENNETH C. SEARS, Professor of Law, University of Chicago (Au., *Cases on Administrative Law*; co-au., *May on Crimes, 4th ed.*).

Real Property

RICHARD R. POWELL, Dwight Professor of Law, Columbia University (Au., *Law of Property Future Interests; Trusts*).

Roman and Civil Law

MAX RADIN, John Henry Boalt Professor of Law, University of California (Au., *Handbook of Roman Law; Handbook of Anglo-American Legal History*).

Torts

PHILIP MECHEM, Professor of Law, University of Iowa (Au., *Cases on Agency*; co-au., *Cases on Wills*).

LEGISLATION—See under *GOVERNMENT*.

LIBRARY SCIENCE—See under *LITERATURE*.

LINGUISTICS

General

BERNARD BLOCH, Professor of Linguistics, Yale University (Assistant Editor, *Linguistic Atlas of New England*; co-au., *Outline of Linguistic Analysis*; editor, *Language*).

ALBERT H. MARCKWARDT, Professor of English, University of Michigan (Au., *Introduction to the English Language*; *Scribner Handbook of English*).

Phonetics and Phonemics

W. FREEMAN TWADDELL, Professor of Linguistics, Brown University.

Semitic-Hamitic Languages (Special Review)

ZELLIG S. HARRIS, Professor of Linguistics, University of Pennsylvania (Au., *Development of the Canaanite Dialects; Grammar of the Phoenician Language*; editor, *Journal of the American Oriental Society*).

Speech

KARL R. WALLACE, Professor of Speech (Head of Department), University of Illinois (Editor, *Quarterly Journal of Speech*).

LITERATURE

Classical Myths and Legends in Literature

DOUGLAS BUSH, Professor of English, Harvard University (Au., *Mythology and the Renaissance Tradition in English Poetry; Mythology and the Romantic Tradition in English Poetry*).

Drama

ARTHUR H. QUINN, John Welsh Centennial Emeritus Professor of History and English Literature, University of Pennsylvania (Au., *History of American Drama from the Beginning to the Civil War; History of American Drama from the Civil War to the Present Day*).

General Terms in Literature

GEORGE W. SHERBURN, Professor of English Literature (Chairman, Division of Modern Languages), Harvard University.

Journalism

FRANK LUTHER MOTT, Dean of School of Journalism, University of Missouri (Au., *A History of American Magazines; American Journalism: A History; Jefferson and the Press*).

Library Science

NATHANIEL STEWART, Associate, School of Library Service, Columbia University; formerly, Chief of Card Division, Library of Congress, Washington, D. C.

Proper Names

JOSEPH WOOD KRUTCH, Brander Matthews Professor of Dramatic Literature, Columbia University.

Prosody

DONALD A. STAUFFER, Professor of English (Chairman of Department), Princeton University (Au., *The Nature of Poetry*; editor, *The Intent of the Critic*).

LOGIC—See under *PHILOSOPHY*.

MACHINES AND MACHINERY

Air Machines and Refrigeration

H. G. VENEMANN, Professor of Refrigeration, Purdue University (Au., *Refrigeration Theory and Applications*).

Boilers and Furnaces

ROBERT P. KOLB, Professor of Heat-Power Engineering, Worcester Polytechnic Institute.

Horology

WARREN TeRONDE, Instructor, Milwaukee Vocational School.

Internal Combustion Engines

HAROLD C. HERRMANN, Instructor, Milwaukee Vocational School.

Machine Shop Tools and Practice

W. N. LATHROP, Supervisor of Trade and Industry, Milwaukee Vocational School.

MAMMALS—See under *ZOOLOGY:* Mammalogy.

MATHEMATICS

Algebra

A. ADRIAN ALBERT, Professor of Mathematics, University of Chicago (Editor, *Transactions of the American Mathematical Society*).

Analytic Geometry

FRANCIS D. MURNAGHAN, Professor of Applied Mathematics, Johns Hopkins University (Editor, *American Journal of Mathematics*).

Calculus and Function Theory

M. R. HESTENES, Professor of Mathematics, University of California.

General Terms in Mathematics

R. G. SANGER, Professor of Mathematics (Chairman of Department), Kansas State College of Agriculture and Applied Science.

Number Theory and Arithmetic

D. H. LEHMER, Associate Professor of Mathematics, University of California.

Statistics

SAMUEL S. WILKS, Professor of Mathematical Statistics, Princeton University (Editor, *Annals of Mathematical Statistics*).

Synthetic Geometry

S. B. MYERS, Associate Professor of Mathematics, University of Michigan (Associate Editor, *American Journal of Mathematics*).

MEASURES—See under *WEIGHTS AND MEASURES*.

MECHANICS—See under *PHYSICS*.

MEDICINE—See under *THERAPEUTICS*.

METALLURGY—See under *APPLIED SCIENCE:* Foundry and Ferrous Metallurgy; General and Nonferrous Metallurgy.

METAPHYSICS—See under *PHILOSOPHY*.

METEOROLOGY—See under *PHYSICS*.

MICROSCOPY—See under *ZOOLOGY*.

MILITARY TERMS

Air Warfare, Cutting and Thrusting Weapons, Subsistence

S. L. A. MARSHALL, Military Critic, *Detroit News*; Colonel, G.S.C.; Chief Historian, European Theater of Operations (Au., *Blitzkrieg; Armies on Wheels; Men Against Fire*).

Armor, Obsolete Weapons and Firearms

STEPHEN V. GRANCSAY, Curator of Arms and Armor, Metropolitan Museum of Art.

Artillery and Gunnery

RICHARD ERNEST DUPUY, Colonel, Field Artillery, U.S.A.; Bureau of Public Relations, War Department.

Equipment, Organization, and Tactics

JOSEPH INGHAM GREENE, Colonel, Infantry, U.S.A., Retired; Editor, *Infantry Journal*.

Explosives and Fortifications

WILLIAM FRANCIS HEAVEY, Colonel, Corps of Engineers, U.S.A.; District Engineer of New York District.

MINERALOGY—See under *GEOLOGY*.

MINING—See under *APPLIED SCIENCE*.

MOTION PICTURES—See under *ARTS*.

MUSIC

General Terms in Music

JAMES H. HALL, Professor of the History and Criticism of Music, Oberlin College.

Harmony

WALTER PISTON, Professor of Music, Harvard University; Composer (Au., *Harmony; Harmonic Analysis; Counterpoint*).

Jazz

WILLIAM RUSSELL, President, American Music Records.

Musical Forms

OTTO LUENING, Associate Professor (Chairman of Department), Barnard College, Columbia University; Composer; formerly, Chairman of Music Department, Bennington College.

Musical Instruments: Ancient

EMANUEL WINTERNITZ, Keeper of Collections of Musical Instruments, Head of Music Department, Metropolitan Museum of Art; Lecturer in Music, Columbia University.

Musical Instruments: Modern

CURT SACHS, Visiting Professor of Music, Graduate School of Arts and Sciences, New York University; Music Consultant, New York Public Library (Au., *The History of Musical Instruments*).

Notation

CARL DEIS, Music Editor-in-Chief, G. Schirmer, Inc.; Composer.

Proper Names

FREDERICK JACOBI, Teacher of Composition, Juilliard School of Music; Composer.

ROSS LEE FINNEY, Professor of Music, Smith College; Composer.

MYTHS AND LEGENDS

General

STITH THOMPSON, Professor of English and Folklore, Indiana University (Au., *Our Heritage of World Literature; Motif-Index of Folk-Literature; The Folktale*).

Greek Legends

WHITNEY J. OATES, Ewing Professor of Greek, Princeton University.

Greek Myths

GILBERT HIGHET, Professor of Greek and Latin, Columbia University (Translator, *Paideia, The Ideals of Greek Culture*).

Medieval and Arthurian Myths

JOHN WEBSTER SPARGO, Professor of English, Northwestern University (Au., *Chaucer's Shipman's Tale; Juridical Folklore in England*).

Roman Legends and Myths

GEORGE E. DUCKWORTH, Giger Professor of Classics, Princeton University.

NAUTICAL AND NAVAL TERMS

Boats and Inland Vessels

WENDELL P. ROOP, Captain (Retired), U.S.N.; Swarthmore College.

General Seamanship and Gear

HERBERT L. STONE, President, Yachting Publishing Company; Editor, *Yachting*.

Nautical Science

GEORGE S. BRYAN, Rear Admiral (Retired), U.S.N.; Hydrographer of the Navy, 1938–1946; International Correspondence Schools.

Ships and Ship Repair

THOMAS B. RICHEY, Rear Admiral (Retired), U.S.N.; attached to Joint Chiefs of Staff, Washington, D. C., 1943–45.

NEUROLOGY—See under THERAPEUTICS: Brain and Nervous Pathology.

NUMISMATICS—See under COINS.

OCEANOGRAPHY—See under GEOGRAPHY.

OPHTHALMOLOGY—See under THERAPEUTICS.

OPTICS—See under PHYSICS: Geometric Optics; Light and Light Measurements.

PAINTING AND GRAPHIC ARTS—See under ARTS.

PALEONTOLOGY—See under GEOLOGY.

PARASITOLOGY—See under ZOOLOGY.

PATHOLOGY—See under THERAPEUTICS: Blood and Heart Pathology; Brain and Nervous Pathology; Deformities and Skeletal Pathology; Digestive Pathology; General Pathology.

PETROLEUM INDUSTRIES—See under APPLIED SCIENCE: Coke and Petroleum Industries.

PETROLOGY—See under GEOLOGY.

PHARMACOLOGY—See under THERAPEUTICS.

PHILATELY

WINTHROP S. BOGGS, Director, The Philatelic Foundation (Au., *The Postage Stamps and Postal History of Canada*).

PHILOSOPHY

Ethics

T. V SMITH, Professor of Philosophy, University of Chicago (Au., *Democracy and Dictatorship; The Democratic Way of Life*; editor, *International Journal of Ethics*).

General

RICHARD P. McKEON, Professor of Greek and Philosophy (formerly, Dean of Division of Humanities), University of Chicago (Au., *The Philosophy of Spinoza*; co-au., *Studies in the History of Ideas, Vol. III*; editor and translator, *Selections from Medieval Philosophers*; editor, *The Basic Works of Aristotle*).

Logic

ERNEST NAGEL, Professor of Philosophy, Columbia University (Au., *Principles of the Theory of Probability*; co-au., *Introduction to Logic and Scientific Method*; co-editor, *Journal of Philosophy*).

Metaphysics

R. W. SELLARS, Professor of Philosophy, University of Michigan (Au., *Critical Realism; Principles and Problems of Philosophy; The Philosophy of Physical Realism*).

PHONETICS AND PHONEMICS—See under LINGUISTICS.

PHOTOGRAPHY—See under APPLIED SCIENCE.

PHYSICS

Acoustics

LEONARD O. OLSEN, Associate Professor of Physics, Case School of Applied Science.

Color

M. LUCKIESH, Director of Lighting Research Laboratory, Lamp Department, General Electric Company (Au., *Light; Vision and Seeing; Color and Colors; The Science of Seeing; Torch of Civilization; Reading as a Visual Task*).

Electricity and Magnetism

NORMAN E. GILBERT, Professor Emeritus of Physics, Dartmouth College; Visiting Professor of Physics, Rollins College (Au., *Electricity and Magnetism*).

General Terms in Physics

DUANE ROLLER, Professor of Physics, Wabash College (Co-au., *Mechanics; Molecular Physics; Heat and Sound; Laboratory Manual of Physics*; editor, *American Journal of Physics*).

Geometric Optics

P. G. NUTTING, Former Consulting Engineer in Charge of Research, Westinghouse Electric and Manufacturing Company; formerly, Geophysicist, United States Geological Survey.

Heat and Thermodynamics

J. M. CORK, Professor of Physics, University of Michigan (Au., *Pyrometry, Heat, Radioactivity and Nuclear Physics*).

Hydraulics and Hydraulic Engineering

HUNTER ROUSE, Professor of Fluid Mechanics, State University of Iowa; Director, Iowa Institute of Hydraulic Research (Au., *Fluid Mechanics for Hydraulic Engineers; Elementary Mechanics of Fluids*).

Light and Light Measurements

WILLIAM W. WATSON, Professor of Physics (Chairman of Department), Yale University.

Mechanics

GUSTAV G. FREYGANG, Professor of Mechanics, Stevens Institute of Technology.

Meteorology
MICHAEL FERENCE, Associate Professor of Physics and Meteorology, University of Chicago (Associate Editor, *Journal of Meteorology*).

Pneumatics and Aerodynamics
FREDERICK K. TEICHMANN, Professor of Aeronautical Engineering (Chairman of Department), New York University (Au., *Airplane Design Manual*).

Radiation and Nuclear Physics
I. I. RABI, Professor of Physics (Executive Officer), Columbia University; Staff Member and Associate Director of Radiation Laboratory, Massachusetts Institute of Technology.

HENRY M. FOLEY, Associate in Physics, Columbia University

PHYSIOLOGY—See under *ANATOMY, PHYSIOLOGY, AND EMBRYOLOGY.*

PLUMBING—See under *APPLIED SCIENCE.*

POLITICAL ECONOMY—See under *GOVERNMENT.*

POLITICAL THEORY—See under *GOVERNMENT.*

PRINTING
Presswork
AUGUSTUS E. GIEGENGACK, The Public Printer, Government Printing Office, Washington, D.C.

Typography
BRUCE ROGERS, Printer and Book Designer; formerly, Printing Adviser to the Cambridge University Press and the Harvard University Press (Co-au., *Paragraphs on Printing*).

PROSODY—See under *LITERATURE.*

PSYCHIATRY—See under *THERAPEUTICS.*

PSYCHOLOGY
General Psychological Processes
G. W. ALLPORT, Professor of Psychology, Harvard University (Au., *Personality—A Psychological Interpretation*).

Personality Traits and Their Expression
GARDNER MURPHY, Professor of Psychology, College of the City of New York (Au., *Personality; Experimental Social Psychology; Historical Introduction to Modern Psychology;* co-au., *Approaches to Personality*).

Psychoanalysis
LAWRENCE S. KUBIE, Associate Neurologist, Neurological Institute, Columbia University; Clinical Professor of Psychiatry, School of Medicine, Yale University (Au., *Practical Aspects of Psychoanalysis*).

Tests and Measurements
LEWIS M. TERMAN, Professor Emeritus of Psychology (Executive Head, Department of Psychology), Stanford University (Au., *The Stanford Revision of the Binet-Simon Intelligence Scale; Genetic Studies of Genius;* co-au., *Measuring Intelligence;* editor, *The Measurement and Adjustment Series*).

RADIO—See under *APPLIED SCIENCE:* Electronics.

RAILROADS—See under *APPLIED SCIENCE.*

REAL PROPERTY—See under *LAW.*

REFRIGERATION—See under *MACHINES AND MACHINERY:* Air Machines and Refrigeration.

RELIGION
Anglicanism
REV. WALTER RUSSELL BOWIE, Dean of Students and Professor of Practical Theology, Union Theological Seminary; Member, American Standard Bible Revision Committee (Associate editor, *The Interpreter's Bible;* au., *The Story of the Bible; The Master, the Life of Jesus Christ*).

The Bible: Apocrypha and General Terms
EDGAR J. GOODSPEED, Distinguished Service Professor Emeritus of Biblical and Patristic Greek, University of Chicago; Member, American Standard Bible Revision Committee (Au., *The Apocrypha, An American Translation; The Story of the Apocrypha*).

The Bible: New Testament
FREDERICK C. GRANT, Professor of Biblical Theology, Union Theological Seminary; Member, American Standard Bible Revision Committee (Au., *The Growth of the Gospels; The Earliest Gospel; The Economic Background of the Gospels*).

The Bible: Old Testament
JAMES MUILENBURG, Professor of Hebrew and Cognate Languages, Union Theological Seminary; Member, American Standard Bible Revision Committee.

Buddhism, Hinduism, Mohammedanism, and the Persian Religion
ROBERT E. HUME, Professor Emeritus of History of Religions, Union Theological Seminary (Au., *The World's Living Religions; Treasure House of the Living Religions;* translator, *Thirteen Principal Upanishads*).

Christian Theology
ALBERT C. KNUDSON, Dean Emeritus and Professor Emeritus of Systematic Theology, Boston University.

General Theology
A. EUSTACE HAYDON, Professor Emeritus of History of Religions (Chairman, Department of Comparative Religion), University of Chicago (Au., *Biography of the Gods; Man's Search for the Good Life; The Quest of the Ages*).

Greek Orthodox Church
REV. E. D. TSOUKALAS, Assistant Dean, Greek Orthodox Theological School.

Judaism
H. A. WOLFSON, Professor of Hebrew Literature and Philosophy, Harvard University (Au., *The Philosophy of Spinoza; Philo: Foundations of Religious Philosophy in Judaism, Christianity, and Islam*).

Mormonism
L. H. CREER, Professor of History (Head of Department), University of Utah (Contributor, "Mormonism," *Encyclopedia of Social Sciences;* au., *Utah and the Nation*).

Protestantism
H. RICHARD NIEBUHR, Professor of Christian Ethics, Divinity School, Yale University (Au., *The Kingdom of God in America; The Meaning of Revelation*).

Roman Catholicism: Church Calendar, Orders and Ranks, Vestments
REV. VINCENT L. KENNEDY, Professor of Greek, St. Michael's College; Professor of History of Christian Worship, Institute of Medieval Studies, University of Toronto.

Roman Catholicism: Dogma
RT. REV. MSGR. FULTON J. SHEEN, Associate Professor of Philosophy, Catholic University of America.

Roman Catholicism: General Terms
RT. REV. MSGR. JOHN FEARNS, President, St. Joseph's Seminary, Dunwoodie, N. Y.

REPTILES—See under *ZOOLOGY:* Reptiles and Amphibians.

SCULPTURE—See under *ARTS.*

SHIPS—See under *NAUTICAL AND NAVAL TERMS.*

SOCIOLOGY
HERBERT BLUMER, Professor of Sociology, University of Chicago (Editor, *American Journal of Sociology*).

SPEECH—See under *LINGUISTICS.*

SPORTS AND GAMES
Baseball, Boxing, Football, and General Terms
ARCH WARD, Sports Editor, *Chicago Tribune.*
EDWARD PRELL, Assistant Sports Editor, *Chicago Tribune.*

Basketball, Swimming, and Gymnastics
AUGUSTA W. NEIDHARDT, Associate Professor of Physical Education (Chairman of Department), Hunter College.

Card, Dice, and Parlor Games
ALBERT A. OSTROW, Au., *The Complete Card Player.*

Chess and Checkers
FRED REINFELD, Chess Editor, David McKay Company.

Golf, Tennis, and Track
RICHARD F. VAUGHAN, Athletic Coach, Princeton University; formerly, Staff Writer, *Life* magazine.

Hunting and Fishing
J. P. CUENIN, Outdoor Sports Writer, *San Francisco Examiner.*

Miscellaneous
MARTY BERG, Editor, *Sports-Week.*

STAMP COLLECTING—See *PHILATELY.*

STATISTICS—See under *MATHEMATICS.*

STOCKBREEDING—See under *ZOOLOGY:* Stockbreeding and Horses.

STRATIGRAPHY—See under *GEOLOGY.*

SURGERY—See under *THERAPEUTICS.*

SURVEYING—See under *APPLIED SCIENCE.*

TELEGRAPHY AND TELEPHONY—See under *APPLIED SCIENCE.*

TEXTILES—See under *HOME ECONOMICS.*

THEATER—See under *ARTS;* see under *LITERATURE:* Drama.

THEOLOGY—See under *RELIGION:* Christian Theology; General Theology.

THERAPEUTICS

Blood and Heart Pathology
H. ROSS MAGEE, Internist, New York City; formerly, Associate in Medicine, Mayo Clinic and Mayo Foundation.

Brain and Nervous Pathology
GEORGE B. HASSIN, Professor Emeritus of Neurology, College of Medicine, University of Illinois (Chief Editor, *Journal of Neuropathology and Experimental Neurology*).

Curative Processes
J. C. MEAKINS, Dean of Faculty of Medicine, Professor of Medicine, McGill University

Deformities and Skeletal Pathology
ARTHUR STEINDLER, Professor of Orthopedics, State University of Iowa.

Dermatology
U. J. WILE, Professor of Dermatology and Syphilology, University of Michigan; Chief Medical Consultant, United States Public Health Service.

Digestive Pathology
ALFRED E. WILHELMI, Assistant Professor of Physiological Chemistry, School of Medicine, Yale University.

Fevers
E. V. COWDRY, Professor of Anatomy, Washington University; Director of Research, Barnard Free Skin and Cancer Hospital (Au., *Textbook of Histology; Microscopic Technique*).

General Pathology
J. FURTH, Professor of Pathology, Medical College, Cornell University.

Gynecology
J. NOVAK, Clinical Professor of Gynecology, Columbia University.

Medical Instruments
MORRIS I. GERNER, Chester, New York; formerly, Assistant Surgeon, Third Auxiliary Surgical Group, A.U.S.

Medical Substances
CARL F. SCHMIDT, Professor of Pharmacology, University of Pennsylvania.

Miscellaneous Diseases
GEORGE F. DICK, Professor of Medicine (Chairman of Department), University of Chicago.

Ophthalmology
ARTHUR GERARD DeVOE, Associate in Ophthalmology, College of Physicians and Surgeons, Columbia University.

Pharmacology
M. H. SEEVERS, Professor of Pharmacology (Chairman of Department), University of Michigan.

Psychiatry
NOLAN D. C. LEWIS, Director, New York Psychiatric Institute and Hospital; Professor of Psychiatry, Columbia University (Au., *History of Psychiatric Achievement;* managing editor, *Journal of Nervous and Mental Disease; Psychoanalytic Review; Monograph Series*).

Surgery
HENRY NELSON HARKINS, Professor of Surgery (Executive Officer of Department), University of Washington; formerly, Associate Professor of Surgery, Johns Hopkins University (Au., *The Treatment of Burns;* editor, *Quarterly Review of Surgery*).

Trauma
MARK M. RAVITCH, Associate Professor of Surgery, Johns Hopkins University.

Tumors and Pustular Disorders
N. C. FOOT, Professor of Surgical Pathology, Cornell University; Surgical Pathologist, New York Hospital.

Veterinary Science
WILLIAM A. HAGAN, Dean of New York State Veterinary College, Cornell University (Au., *The Infectious Diseases of Domestic Animals*).

THERMODYNAMICS—See under *PHYSICS:* Heat and Thermodynamics.

TRANSPORTATION—See under *APPLIED SCIENCE:* Aeronautics; Automobiles; Horse-drawn Vehicles; Railroads; see under *COMMERCE;* see under *NAUTICAL AND NAVAL TERMS.*

TYPOGRAPHY—See under *PRINTING.*

VETERINARY SCIENCE—See under *THERAPEUTICS.*

WEIGHTS AND MEASURES
LEWIS V. JUDSON, Senior Physicist, National Bureau of Standards.

WINES, SPIRITS, AND BEER
HAROLD J. GROSSMAN, Au., *Grossman's Guide to Wines, Spirits, and Beer.*

ZOOLOGY

Animal Ecology
RALPH BUCHSBAUM, Assistant Professor of Zoölogy, University of Chicago (Au., *Animals Without Backbones*).

Animal Embryology
JERRY J. KOLLROS, Assistant Professor of Zoölogy, State University of Iowa.

Arachnids
A. M. CHICKERING, Professor of Biology (Chairman, Division of Science and Mathematics), Albion College.

Beef and Dual-purpose Cattle
W. H. BLACK, Senior Animal Husbandman in Charge of Beef and Dual-purpose Cattle Investigations, Bureau of Animal Industry, Agricultural Research Administration, United States Department of Agriculture.

Classification
WILLIAM C. SCHROEDER, Associate Curator of Fishes, Museum of Comparative Zoölogy, Harvard University; Business Manager, Oceanographic Institution, Woods Hole Massachusetts.

Crustaceans
J. H WELSH, Associate Professor of Biology, Harvard University.

Dairy Cattle and Dairying
O. E. REED, Chief of Bureau of Dairy Industry, United States Department of Agriculture.

Dogs
LEONARD WHITTLESEY GOSS, Professor of Veterinary Pathology, Ohio State University.

Entomology: General Entomological Terms
R. E. SNODGRASS, Collaborator in Entomology, United States Department of Agriculture (Au., *Principles of Insect Morphology; Insects, Their Ways and Means of Living*).

Entomology: Insect Names
C. H. SEEVERS, Research Associate, Chicago Natural History Museum; Professor of Biology, Roosevelt College of Chicago.

Evolution
EDWIN G. CONKLIN, Professor Emeritus of Biology, Princeton University (Co-editor, *Biological Bulletin; Journal of Experimental Zoology; Genetics;* au., *The Mechanism of Evolution*).

General Biological Terms
JAMES A. MULLEN, Assistant Professor of Biology, Fordham University.

Genetics
E. W. LINDSTROM, Professor of Genetics (Head of Department), Dean of Graduate College, Iowa State College.

Ichthyology: Fish Names
CARL L. HUBBS, Professor of Biology, The Scripps Institution of Oceanography, University of California; Member of the Editorial Board, *The American Naturalist* (Co-au., *The Improvement of Lakes for Fishing; Guide to the Fishes of the Great Lakes and Tributary Waters*).

Ichthyology: General Ichthyological Terms
LOREN P. WOODS, Curator of Fishes, Chicago Natural History Museum.

Ichthyology: Salt-water Food Fish

GEORGE S. MYERS, Professor of Biology, Stanford University; Curator, Zoölogical Collections, Natural History Museum (Editor, *Stanford Ichthyological Bulletin*).

Ichthyology: Tropical Marine Fish

SAMUEL F. HILDEBRAND, Senior Ichthyologist, Fish and Wildlife Service, Division of Fishes, National Museum, Washington, D.C. (Au., *A Descriptive Catalog of the Shore Fishes of Peru*; co-au., *Marine Fishes of Panama*).

Lower Invertebrates

L. H. HYMAN, Research Associate in Invertebrates, American Museum of Natural History.

Mammalogy: African Mammals and Primates

JOHN ERIC HILL, Assistant Curator of Mammals, American Museum of Natural History (Deceased).

Mammalogy: Anatomy and General Mammalogical Terms

WILLIAM K. GREGORY, Curator Emeritus, Department of Comparative Anatomy and Fishes, American Museum of Natural History; Da Costa Professor Emeritus of Vertebrate Paleontology, Columbia University (Au., *The Orders of the Mammals*).

Mammalogy: Asiatic, European, and South American Mammals

GEORGE H. H. TATE, Curator of Mammals, American Museum of Natural History.

Mammalogy: North American and European Mammals

W. J. HAMILTON, Jr., Professor of Zoölogy, Cornell University (Au., *American Mammals; Mammals of the Eastern United States*).

Microscopy

RUDOLF T. KEMPTON, Professor of Zoölogy (Chairman of Department), Vassar College; Teaching Staff in Physiology, Marine Biological Laboratory, Woods Hole, Massachusetts (Au., *Laboratory Manual for Comparative Anatomy*).

Myriapods

R. V. CHAMBERLIN, Professor of Zoölogy (Head of Division of Biology), University of Utah (Au., *The Myriapoda of the Australian Region; Lithobiida of North America*; editor, *University of Utah Biological Series*).

Nomenclature and Sizes in Picture Captions

COLIN C. SANBORN, Curator of Mammalogy, Chicago Natural History Museum.

Ornithology: African, Asiatic, South American, and Mexican Birds

HERBERT FRIEDMANN, Curator of Birds, United States National Museum (Au., *Birds Collected by the Childs Frick Expedition in Ethiopia and Kenya Colony; Birds of North and Middle America*).

Ornithology: Anatomy and General Ornithological Terms

ALEXANDER WETMORE, Secretary, Smithsonian Institution; Director, United States National Museum (Au., *The Migration of Birds; Systematic Classification for Birds of the World; Fossil Birds of North America*).

Ornithology: North American and European Birds

GEORGE M. SUTTON, Curator, Division of Birds, Museum of Zoölogy, University of Michigan (Contributing Editor, *Audubon Magazine*).

Parasitology

ASA C. CHANDLER, Professor of Biology, Rice Institute; formerly, Special Consultant, United States Public Health Service (Au., *Introduction to Parasitology*).

Poultry

THEODORE C. BYERLY, Senior Poultry Husbandman in Charge of Poultry Husbandry Investigations, United States Agricultural Research Center, Division of Animal Husbandry, Beltsville, Maryland, United States Department of Agriculture.

Reptiles and Amphibians

KARL PATTERSON SCHMIDT, Chief Curator of Zoölogy, Chicago Natural History Museum (Au., *Homes and Habits of Wild Animals*; co-au., *Field Book of Snakes*).

Sheep and Goats

D. A. SPENCER, Senior Animal Husbandman in Charge of Sheep, Goat, and Animal Fiber Investigations, Agricultural Research Administration, United States Department of Agriculture.

Stockbreeding and Horses

RALPH W PHILLIPS, Head, Animal Industry Branch, Agriculture Division, Food and Agriculture Organization of the United Nations; formerly, Senior Animal Husbandman in Charge of Genetics Investigations, Bureau of Animal Industries, United States Department of Agriculture (Editor, *Journal of Animal Science*).

Swine

JOHN H. ZELLER, Senior Animal Husbandman in Charge of Swine Investigations, United States Agricultural Research Center, Beltsville, Maryland, United States Department of Agriculture.

EDITORIAL STAFF

MANAGING EDITOR: Jess Stein

EDITORS: Rosemary Barnsdall Blackmon, Harriet Cassell, William A. Frankel, Kiyoko Hosoura, Dimmes McDowell, Merle E. Severy

ASSOCIATE EDITORS: Elizabeth J. Denning, Elizabeth Gedney, William J. Gedney, Cecil P. Golann, Martha L. Huot, Babette Keeler, Frederick S. Pease, Jr., Constance Stark, Burton D. Thiel, John S. Wasley, Ralph Weiman

EDITORIAL ASSISTANTS: Noreen E. Barron, Emmy Bloch, Leonore Crary, Mary Ellis, Mary E. Fallon, Henry Florman, Frances Halsey, Walter Heartsill, Philip Krapp, David A. Lawson, Ellen Nelson, N. Bryce Nelson, Alma Nespital, Nancy Rayfiel, Herbert Rowen, Thomas R. Royston, Phyllis Ruckgaber, Priscilla Smith, Dorothy R. Thelander, Abraham Waisglass, Mabel Wilcox

RESEARCH ASSISTANTS: Doris Alexander, Rodney W. Alexander, John C. Brunner, William Cannastra, Emily Cloud, Elizabeth Diez, Norman Hoss, Joseph Kaplan, Arthur Kohlenberg, Lawrence Krader, Herbert J. Landar, Evelyn Leverah, Leon F. Schwartz, Anne Thomson

OFFICE ASSISTANTS: Grace Bergh, Lorraine Binder, John Brothers, Jean Connors, Natalie Firstenberg, Gerald Gottlieb, Shirley Heckel, Mary Hodge, Sally Horan, Paul Kessler, Eleanor Morse, Ruth Rosoff, Evelyn Smith, Marjorie Waldo, Evelyn Wexler, Luise Wickel, Florence Woolf

ARTISTS: Leon Pray, Thomas Voter, Edward Willms

SPECIAL ACKNOWLEDGMENTS

GEORGE O. CURME, Professor Emeritus of Germanic Philology, Northwestern University
WILLIAM ETKIN, Department of Biology, College of the City of New York
RICHMOND Y. HATHORN, Department of Greek and Latin, Columbia University
CHARLES HOCKETT, Assistant Professor of Linguistics, Cornell University
MARTIN JOOS, Associate Professor of German, University of Wisconsin
JOHN KEPKE, New York City
SAMUEL LIEBERMAN, Department of Classical Languages, Queens College
W. ROSS MARVIN, Editor in Chief, World Book Company
BERNARD MATTSON, Department of History, Evanston Township High School
NORMAN McQUOWN, Assistant Professor of Anthropology, University of Chicago
HAROLD RASHKIS, Department of Psychology, University of Pennsylvania
ELIZABETH SCANLAN, Department of Speech, Queens College
JOEL SHOR, Clinical Psychologist, Department of Health, Yale University
S. STEPHENSON SMITH, Department of English, New York University
WILLIAM B. S. SMITH, Advisory Editor, Columbia University Press
GEORGE L. TRAGER, Professor of Linguistics, University of Oklahoma
MORRIS WINOKUR, Department of Biology, College of the City of New York

SELECTION OF ENTRIES AND DEFINITIONS: Irving Lorge

The intricate architecture of a dictionary rests on the basic blueprint of the entries that are defined, illustrated, explained, and clarified. The selection of the words, names, places for inclusion in a dictionary must consider how and why a person goes to a dictionary. He goes to find the meaning of words such as *aorist*, or the preferred spelling of words such as *enclose*, or the pronunciation of words such as *stupefacient*. He also goes to find the location of places such as *Pohai* or the significance of names such as *Marie Antoinette*. Such a list of possible uses of the dictionary may, of course, be extended and amplified.

A dictionary, therefore, must include within it those words, names, pronunciations, and other facts that the user is likely to need for meaning, spelling, pronunciation, significant fact, or location.

The primary consideration in the selection of entries, therefore, is the specification of words, places, names, and borrowings from other languages that should be included. A reasonable rule would be to include all words that are likely to be read. No one can quarrel with so sagacious a principle. The difficulty is how to put it into practice. If a tabulation were made of every word printed in every book, a master list could be prepared. Then the lexicographer would have a basis for selecting the words to be defined. No such master list exists. There are, however, word counts which have been made of *samples* of printed materials. The most recent word count is based on the tabulation of the frequency of occurrence of each different word in about twenty-five million running words of text. Such a count provides the listing of the words appearing most frequently in printed materials, i.e. in novels, essays, textbooks, monographs, pamphlets, magazines and in business and social letters. In this count[1] are listed the 30,000 words including names of places, people, and characters which were most frequently found.

Words such as *boycott*, *brummagem*, and *macadam* have been incorporated in the stock of English words although they were originally the names of people or places. The reader, however, will find many illustrations of the uses of names or places in factual or metaphoric reference. References to *Paul* or *Moses*, to *Confucius* or *Aristotle*, to *Robin Hood* or *Robinson Crusoe*, to *Galileo* or *Magellan*, to *Bach* or *Kant*, to *Lincoln* or *Roosevelt*, to *Ford* or *Edison*, to *Shaw* or *Wells*, or to *Balzac* or *Zola* need explanation just as much as do references to the words of the language. For names of these persons and characters as well as for the names of places, a dictionary should include significant material about the facts and achievements that will give the reference adequate meaning.

The lexicographer may be reasonably certain that all (or most) of the words in a list of the most frequent 30,000 words will occur in the reading of high school and college students and literate adults. Such a list, however, has defects: first, it cannot include the new words that are added to the stock of the language; second, it does not include the large technical vocabulary that is needed in the specialized study of the humanities, the social studies, and the sciences.

A list of the most frequently occurring words, therefore, must be supplemented by the judgment of specialists in all fields of practice and knowledge. The final list of entries, therefore, is based not only on such facts about word frequency as are available, but, more, on the judgment of hundreds of experts in all fields from astronomy through zoölogy. All in all, more than 350 experts indicated what words, names, places should be defined or explained. Thus, words like *ant lion*, *Antofagasta*, *Antoinette*, *Antoninus*, *antonomasia*, *antre*, and *antrum* are added to *antlered*, *anvil*, *anxious*, and *any*. The master list for this dictionary included more than 200,000 basic entries.

When the list of entries was established, the next problem was the selection of senses to be defined. Most of the words that occur with great frequency are words used in many different senses. The word *point*, for instance, means a sharp end, an extremity, a period, a size of type, a location, a score, an electrical contact, a kind of lace, and many other things. Trained editors who specialized in recognizing the distinction among the meanings of words found that 1100 separate occurrences of the word *point* were used in 55 different senses. Other words were even more startling in the variety of senses: the editors distinguished 109 different meanings of the word *run*. The available knowledge about word frequency and the expert judgment of specialists is as essential in choosing the senses to be defined as in choosing the basic entry to be included. The variety of different senses of a homograph has been recognized by all who read or write. So far only one count of the frequency of the occurrence of different senses or meanings has been made. Professors Lorge and Thorndike, with the aid of a staff of 270 persons, counted the frequency of the occurrence of different meanings of a sample of about four and a half million words in context.[2]

This dictionary has utilized the semantic count to select the different senses of a homograph for definition. The word *style*, for instance, is given with eighteen different senses. These eighteen senses include those which were found and discriminated as different by the semanticists; to these senses were added those suggested by the experts in botany and zoölogy. Not only is the sense given by definition, it is also explained, elucidated and illustrated to help the reader to make the distinction. Thus, sense 13, **Old Style** or **New Style** is more than a definition; and sense 14 is pictured for clarity. The word *appeal* is another illustration of the multi-meaning character of common words. The dictionary distinguishes ten different senses which were recognized as different by semantic specialists. These distinctions of *appeal*, further, are clarified by the explanation of the synonyms of the word.

This dictionary, therefore, is based on the accumulated facts about which words are likely to occur in the reading and listening of high school and college students and of literate adults in general. To those words which have been found in the printed materials that people read has been added the scientific and technical vocabulary of business, art, and industry and of the humanities, the social studies, and the sciences. Moreover, the dictionary has combined the facts about the frequency of the occurrence of different meanings that were tabulated by scholars with the judgments of experts in choosing the senses of each word that were to be discriminated and clarified. As such, the dictionary utilizes the last forty years of scholarship in vocabulary selection and discrimination in the choice of senses of words to be defined, and in the selection of names of persons, places, and characters to be described or explained.

[1] Thorndike, Edward L. and Lorge, Irving. *The Teacher's Word Book of 30,000 Words*, New York: Bureau of Publications, Teachers College, Columbia University, 1944, 274 + xii pp.

[2] Lorge, Irving. "The English Semantic Count," *Teachers College Record*, Vol. 39, 65–77: October, 1937.

Lorge, Irving and Thorndike, Edward L. *A Semantic Count of English Words*, New York: The Institute of Educational Research, Teachers College, Columbia University, 1938. [Hectographed; approximately 1200 pages.]

PRONUNCIATION: W. Cabell Greet

Correct pronunciation is one of the many kinds of information that Americans expect to find in their dictionaries. If we may judge from the usual absence of pronunciation in general encyclopedias and technical handbooks, pronunciation may be the distinguishing mark of the American or encyclopedic dictionary. This statement is extravagant and humorous, but whatever else we may find in our dictionaries—and over the years they have approached encyclopedias in breadth of learning—we are certain to find pronunciation; whereas in other reference books and indexes of particular fields of knowledge pronunciation is ordinarily excluded. Their compilers have dedicated themselves to assisting the practitioners, the writers, and the printers of the science or art: meaning and spelling take all their care, as if we were still living in a world where mass communication was entirely a matter of the printing press without radio and phonograph. But the American dictionary! How often have hard-pressed broadcasters blessed the happy result of our "dictionary wars" of the last century. The competing dictionaries have got larger and larger. Everything with a name—and everything known has a name—animal, vegetable, mineral, personal, geographical, supernatural—is more likely than not to appear in an American dictionary, and there it is pronounced. This practice has been justified, for in our time the spoken word, as in the classical past of Greece and Rome and Elizabethan England, has become quite as important as the written word. Rhetoric, which once meant oratory, was used by our fathers and grandfathers to mean the rules of written composition. But the new rhetoric, of the printed page as well as of radio, is based more on the sounds and rhythms of speech than upon visual patterns. Pronunciation is important.

American spelling is phonetic. That is to say, the letters of our alphabet stand for sounds, and when they are arranged in certain patterns they "spell out" words for people who know how to "read English." But the phonetic principles of American spelling must provide for so many exceptions and the position of the accent is so uncertain, that when we are faced with a new word, or when we hear a strange pronunciation, we ask that the dictionary supplement the conventional spelling of English by marking the accents and indicating the sounds by unequivocal and independent letters and symbols.

The uncertainties of English spelling are due to the remarkable conservatism of the spelling tradition that accompanied an equally remarkable disposition to change in pronunciation. Many explanations have been suggested. Without doubt the unbroken length of the tradition is of the greatest importance. More than seven hundred years divide Orm, an orthographer of the twelfth century, and the spelling reformers who were backed by Andrew Carnegie and encouraged by Theodore Roosevelt. It is no wonder that old rules have survived, as is shown by the table of English spellings on page xl, where 44 sounds are represented by 251 spellings. There have been no social strains, internal or external, sufficient to break the scribal tradition of English. Sufficient changes were made to keep the spelling from chaos. The machine was tinkered with to keep it running. Good people are always fearful that language may become unintelligible, but that, as a matter of fact, is what never seems to happen so long as there are active speakers and writers. They may occasionally mislead one another, but a minimum degree of intelligibility sufficient to the pressing needs of society the users of a language always provide, no matter how careless they seem as pronouncers and spellers. And so, as there has always been an England—if so many centuries may pass muster for "always"—there will always be an England and the English language and its curious ways of spelling until disaster overtakes us, perhaps bringing in its wake orthographic improvements. The new American scene was able to simplify pounds, shillings, and pence, but even in America the spelling tradition has been cultivated with loving and stubborn care.

In bold black type this dictionary presents the conventional spelling. In most instances this will suggest the pronunciation, but on the chance that the user may wish confirmation of his supposition or additional information, a pronunciation is added in a simple phonetic alphabet, auxiliary to the conventional spelling and subject always to the speech ways that are standard in the major regions. For instance, as in all American dictionaries, *r* after vowels is included in the phonetic respelling but without the expectation or desire that southern and northeastern Americans should change their pronunciation of words like *farther*. The symbol schwa (ə) is used for vowels, however spelled conventionally, which with lack of stress tend to lose their distinctive values and to merge, more or less, in a common centralized sound like the *a* of *about*

or the *i* of *sensible*. The symbol schwa is not a command to utter this undistinguished vowel where you fancy you pronounce one of more definite character. It is, however, a sign, placed by a sincere and conscientious staff of phoneticians, that the vowel of this syllable, when uttered in connected discourse, has less than the full values indicated by breve (˘) and macron (−). Occasionally one is in doubt whether the reduced vowel is a kind of *uh*-sound or an enfeebled *ih*, *eh*, or *oh*. Such uncertainty is difficult to resolve because of many varieties of pronunciation and shifting stresses and because of the shortness and the lax quality of the sounds. But the symbol schwa (ə) may be taken as a sign supplementary to the spelling. It signifies that a vowel is reduced in strength, relaxed, and dulled to a degree that may vary with speakers and circumstances. It matters not whether one pronounces the word *added*, ad′ihd or ad′uhd (this transcription and the opinion are my own), but it is essential for intelligibility that the vowel of the last syllable be "reduced, relaxed, and dulled"; otherwise someone may think that Ad is dead. Particularly in these days of radio we must realize that unstressed and therefore reduced vowels are a respectable and essential element in the English language. No broadcaster is so tedious, annoying, and difficult to understand, as he who "overpronounces," stressing syllables and preserving vowels that are neglected in idiomatic and correct English speech.

Inferior teaching in the first grade has sometimes been responsible for a mistaken idea of correct English. The child points out, "Thee boy has ay pen— . . ." and hesitates. The teacher adds, "c i l spells 'sil'—pen′ -sil′." By imitating other speakers the child learns to say "thuh boi′ haz uh pen′səl," but an unfortunate experience of the schoolroom may persist in the erroneous notion that "correct English" is something artificial and apart. And in the past many dictionaries have willy-nilly encouraged the error by giving the pronunciation of a word when isolated, as in a list, instead of the pronunciation when it is joined with other words in discourse. The pronunciation of *a* as a single word is (ā), but as one of a group of words it is "uh." This simple illustration does not illustrate the complexity of the problem for the makers of dictionaries, because the user, having encountered a difficult word in a phrase, nevertheless looks it up in isolation. What pronunciation shall he be given, for instance, of *Roosevelt* or *government?* It is the practice of this dictionary to give a conservative pronunciation of the word per se, and to indicate by the use of schwa and by additional transcriptions, if necessary, some of the striking changes that may take place in speech. This middle course may grieve young radicals and old conservatives, but it is hoped that it will please the judicious.

The use of schwa and attention to actual speech make these pronunciations exceedingly practical as well as correct. But the symbols are not themselves sound nor are they convertible into sound except through the minds and the linguistic habits of individuals. The most efficient indication of pronunciation, in black on white, is the sound track of talking motion pictures. It is really a translation of sound into corresponding values of another medium, because the outlines or the shades of black on white can be reconverted into sound with a predetermined percentage of loss or error. It is possible, though it would be expensive, to construct a machine which would give you, on the pressing of keys in code, the pronunciation of each and every word of this dictionary in, if you wish, the voice of Mickey Mouse or Clark Gable or any other notable who might be willing to record the tens of thousands of words. The advantage would be a lifelike reproduction of sound. A disadvantage might be that the pronunciation would be personal and individual. A dictionary phonetic-transcription is after all general, not individual, abstract, not personal. Perhaps this is as it should be. The American people, like the British, have shown remarkable resistance to every movement towards establishing a dictatorship of speech. Pronunciations and voices may wax and wane in popular acceptance.

In selecting pronunciations, the staff of the American College Dictionary have exercised due care under the circumstances. As I have elsewhere described the procedure, "Without seeking to impair any citizen's right to be his own professor of English, we look for what is national, contemporary, and reputable." This is our standard of correctness, and pronunciations which do not meet it are clearly labeled. The authority of a dictionary is based completely upon the actual speech and writing of the community of effective citizens, with admiration for those skilled in the arts and with respect for those who do but save the nation.

TREATMENT OF ETYMOLOGIES:
Kemp Malone

Scientific investigation into the origin and history of words has never been more active than it is at the present time. English etymologists in particular have been busy, and their researches have cleared up many points once enigmatic or wrongly set forth. Our etymological staff have taken due account of the learned publications in this field, and in a number of cases have made contributions of their own. They have provided in this dictionary a presentation of etymologies which is up to date in form and substance. Outmoded and pre-scientific terms like *Anglo-Saxon*, *Teutonic*, and *Zend* have been avoided, and the reader will find, instead, the terminology now usual in linguistic science. The terms used are duly defined in the dictionary proper.

The treatment of the etymological material is conservative. The use of hypothetical or reconstructed forms has, in general, been avoided, and where such forms appear, they are marked with an asterisk. The origin of many words is put down as "uncertain" or "unknown," and plausible but doubtful etymologies are given (if at all) with a question mark. Rival explanations have been carefully weighed and, if the balance seemed even, both alternatives have been included. In sum, the etymologies here set down present, in succinct form, the fruits of scholarly research, old and new, on the origins of English words.

Extreme brevity of presentation commonly marks the etymologies given in a college dictionary. In this dictionary, too, limitations of space have made brevity needful, but the etymological treatment remains remarkably full, and is combined with an exactness of detail rarely found even in unabridged dictionaries. The method of presentation used is described in the paragraphs which follow.

METHOD OF PRESENTATION

The etymological part of a word entry is normally the final section of the entry proper; it is set off from the rest of the entry by square brackets. In some cases, where the entry word needs two etymologies (thus, one for the noun, one for the verb, if noun and verb have been treated in a single entry), each etymology will be found at the end of the definition group to which it applies.

The etymology begins with some indication of the age of the word in English. This item of information is not etymological, strictly speaking, and might have been given elsewhere in the entry, but it has proved convenient to include it in the etymological part. If the word was current in English in the Middle Ages (before A.D. 1500), it is marked ME (Middle English); if the word was current in the early Middle Ages (before A.D. 1100), it is marked OE (Old English). Thus, the etymological part of the entry **guilt** reads: [ME *gilt*, OE *gylt* offense]. If the modern written form (spelling) of the word was already in use in Middle English, it is not repeated after "ME." Thus, for **name** we have: [ME; OE *nama*, . . .]. Here the semicolon marks the fact that ME and Modern English agree in the spelling of the word. If the Old English spelling likewise agrees with the one now current, the entry word is not repeated at all in the etymology. Thus, for **god** we have: [ME and OE, . . .]. If the word does not occur in English before the 16th century, no indication of its date is set down; this want of indication serves to mark the word as postmedieval.

NATIVE WORDS

Next comes the etymology proper. The fundamental distinction here is that between native words and words of foreign origin. The etymology of a native word like *guilt* or *god* is comparatively simple: after giving the oldest recorded form (if it differs from the current form), one lists the cognates; that is, the words in kindred tongues that correspond both formally and semantically. The etymological part of the word entry **god** reads: [ME and OE, c. D *god*, G *gott*, Icel. *godh*, Goth. *guth*]. This means that *god* occurs in Middle English and Old English, and that it is cognate with Dutch *god*, German *gott*, Icelandic *godh*, and Gothic *guth*. Not all the cognates are listed, of course. Thus, the Danish cognate *gud* is here omitted, and in most cases only one or two cognates can be given, for want of space. The etymology of *guilt* (given above) includes no cognates for the simple reason that none exist; this word occurs in English only, the kindred languages having no words with which *guilt* can be etymologically connected.

Most native words lack the simplicity of *guilt* and *god*. Even so, however, their etymology can usually be pre-

sented in a line, or less. Only now and then is more space required, as it is with **godsend**: [earlier *God's send*, var. (under influence of SEND, V.) of *God's sond* or *sand*, OE *sond*, *sand* message, service]. Here a mere analysis into *god* and *send* would have been insufficient. In many composite words, however, such an analysis meets every etymological need. Often, indeed, the word explains itself, so to speak. Thus, the structure of the adjective *godly* is evident, and the reader in search of etymological explanations need only take the word apart and look up its elements *god* and *-ly* in the dictionary. For this reason the entry **godly**, and many like entries, have no etymological section.

FOREIGN WORDS

The etymology of words of foreign origin takes up more space, on the average, **if** only because the language of origin must be specified. Moreover, many such words got into English, not directly from the tongues to which they were native, but through other tongues, and the etymology usually gives the intermediate stages as well as the ultimate source, so far as these can be determined. The word **heroine** is one of the simpler examples: [t. L, t. Gk., der. *hêrōs* hero]. This means that the English word was taken from Latin, and that the Latin word had been taken from Greek, in both cases without change in spelling; further, that the Greek word was derived from the corresponding masculine word. The etymology of **honorary**, too, is simple: [t. L: m.s. *honōrārius* relating to honor]. This means that *honorary* was taken (into English) from Latin; more precisely, that the English form of the word is a modification of the stem of the Latin form. The technical term *stem* (abbreviated s.) is defined in the entry **stem** of this dictionary, and is used accordingly in the etymologies. The stem of Latin *honōrārius* is *honōrāri-* (the *-us* is an inflectional ending that marks the form as nominative, singular, and masculine). The Latin word was not taken into English in its stem form, however, but in a modification (m.) of that form required by a rule of English spelling; the letter *i* is not permitted at the end of a word and in this position is regularly replaced by *y*. In accordance with this rule we write *honorarium* but *honorary*, and the English word-form *honorary* is explained, in our etymology above, as m.s. (that is, a modification of the stem) of L *honōrārius*. The colon in the etymology makes a division between the general statement of origin (namely, that the word was taken from Latin) and the particulars which explain the precise written form of the English word.

The colon is also used in etymologies like that of **biceps**: [t. L: two-headed]. Here the English word and its Latin etymon agree in written form but differ in meaning. In English the word is a noun, used to name a muscle with a double attachment; in Latin, it is an adjective with no particular reference to muscles, though applicable enough to a muscle thought of as two-headed. In such cases the meaning of the etymon is set after the colon. In cases like **inspector**, however, no gloss is needed, and the etymological part of the entry reads simply: [t. L]. This etymology might have been expanded by reference to the entries INSPECT and -OR, where further etymological information is given, but space is precious and the user of the dictionary may be trusted to make for himself this analysis of **inspector**.

CROSS REFERENCES

References to other entries are made by printing the entry word in small capitals. Thus, the etymology of **mischance** reads: [ME *meschance*, t. OF: m. *mescheance*. See MIS-[1], CHANCE]. Here, at the end of the etymology, the reader is referred to two other entries, MIS- and CHANCE, where he will find further etymological information. In this case the reference takes the form "see MIS-, CHANCE." But a mere gloss, if printed in small capitals, serves also as an entry reference. There are two such references in the etymology of **interregnum**: [t. L, f. *inter-* INTER- + *regnum* REIGN]. This etymological statement means that *interregnum* was taken from Latin, and that the Latin word was formed from *inter-* and *regnum*, both the meaning and the etymology of which may be found by consulting the entries INTER- and REIGN in this dictionary. The repetition here may seem needless, but is actually needful, because one must distinguish between Latin and English, even though the word forms are the same. In the sequence "*inter-* INTER-" the first form is Latin; the second, its English gloss.

FORMATIONS

Many English words were not taken, as such, from a foreign tongue but were made by putting together words or word elements of foreign origin, and therefore have a distinctly foreign look. Thus, the learned term **homeomorphism** looks like a Greek word because its parts are Greek in origin. Its etymology reads: [f. m.s. Gk. *homoiómorphos* of like form + -ISM]. This means that the word was formed from a modification of the stem of Greek *homoiómorphos* plus the English word element *-ism*, itself of Greek origin. In this dictionary such words are carefully distinguished from words actually taken from a foreign language. The reader will note that the etymology begins with the abbreviation f. (formed from), not with t. (taken from).

REPLACEMENT

Another important feature of the English vocabulary is brought out in the etymologies by the abbreviation r. (replacing). The etymology of **horizon** serves for illustration: [t. L, t. Gk.: bounding circle, horizon, prop. ppr., bounding; r. ME *orizonte*, t. OF]. The modern form of the word, which agrees with the Latin and Greek etymon, replaced a medieval form taken from Old French. This change marks part of a process of Latinization which the English language underwent during the Renaissance, a process which has continued, in various ways, to the present day. One result of it has been to reduce greatly the number of French words in the English vocabulary, replacing them by the corresponding Latin or Greek words. In this dictionary systematic account has been taken of such replacements.

DESCENT VS. ADOPTION

The etymology of words taken from French and the other Romance languages makes special problems of presentation because of the very fact that these words can usually be traced back to Latin, the language out of which all the Romance languages grew. The Romance vocabulary is made up, in part, of words Latin by descent, having been handed down from generation to generation while spoken Latin was becoming Romance. In this dictionary such words are said to go back to Latin (abbreviated g. L). In the same way a native English word might go back to Germanic, but since such words are rarely traced back, in the etymologies, to Germanic times (for want of records), this parallel is of little practical importance here. Most of the Romance words of Latin origin, however, like the corresponding words in English, German, and other European languages, were simply taken from Latin by learned men at various times and added to the vernacular vocabulary. Such words are of course marked t. L, not g. L, in the etymologies. The two etymologies which follow illustrate the difference between the two kinds of Romance words of Latin origin:

ire   [ME, t. OF, t. L: m. *īra*]
isle   [ME *isle, ile*, t. OF, g. L *insula*]

SCANDINAVIAN WORDS

The English vocabulary includes many words of Scandinavian origin, most of them taken into English in the 10th and 11th centuries, though rarely recorded until Middle English times and often without record even then. It is usually impossible to say which particular Scandinavian language they came from. In such cases the etymology specifies Scandinavian origin and gives a pertinent form from some Scandinavian tongue, usually Icelandic, the classical language of the North. We illustrate with **bulk**: [ME *bolke* heap, t. Scand.; cf. Icel. *bulki* heap, cargo]. A like difficulty arises with many Romance words of Germanic origin, and the etymology of these is given in a like form.

DERIVATIVES

The expression "derived from" (abbreviated der.) is used in the etymologies in its strict or narrow sense only. Thus, it appears in the etymology of **jaundice**: [ME *jaunes, jaundis*, t. OF: m. *jaunisse*, der. *jaune* yellow, g. L *galbinus* greenish-yellow]. Here we are told that Old French *jaunisse* was derived from *jaune*. The derivative was made by adding to the basic word *jaune* the noun suffix *-isse* -ICE, but this is left unexplained in the etymology, its obviousness being taken for granted. The reader

will not find "der." used loosely in an etymology, to signify mere origin or the like. Thus, the etymology just given does not say that the English word *jaundice* was derived from French, or from Old French.

COMBINING FORMS

Most English words are composite; that is, they were made by putting together other words or word elements. In composition a word may have a special form, different from the one it has when used alone. In the etymologies of this dictionary such a special form is called a combining form (abbreviated comb. form). A familiar example is *thir-*, the combining form of *three*, as in *thirteen* and *thirty*. The numeral *ten* has two combining forms: *-teen*, as in *thirteen* (3 plus 10), and *-ty*, as in *thirty* (3 times 10). Other native words have combining forms, of course, but by far the greatest number of such forms are of classical (Latin and Greek) origin. These classical combining forms have a special interest for the historical linguist. Thus, the initial combining forms usually end in a vowel, often identical with the stem vowel of prehistoric times. In the classical period the vowel with which most prehistoric stems ended had become, functionally, a part (or the whole) of the inflectional ending, and was no longer treated as belonging to the stem. In an uninflected combining form, however, the old stem vowel may be kept as such. It must be added that these forms, even in classical times, tended to end in *o*, irrespective of etymology, and this tendency is still more marked in modern formations. The vowel *i* was also favored in this position. In this dictionary many combining forms have entries of their own, and the others used in English words are duly identified in the etymologies. The same holds for the prefixes, the suffixes, and even the inflectional endings of English.

BLENDS

Many English words, though a very small proportion of the whole, are compounds of a special kind, technically known as blends (abbreviated b.). They usually have the appearance of simple words because of the way in which they were put together. An example is the word *boost*, a blend of *boom* and *hoist*. Each of the sources of a blend contributes something to the final product, but the contribution may be small. If a whole word as such enters into a compound, that compound is not a blend. In origin, the blend is usually slangy and jocular, but blends often become serious and respectable members of linguistic society. The importance of this method of making words was first brought out by the American scholar Louise Pound in her book on the subject. In this dictionary a number of words are etymologized as blends, and a few of these etymologies are new.

TRANSLITERATIONS

The forms given in the etymologies reproduce the spelling of the originals, with certain conventional changes. Letters not in the modern English alphabet are not used, but ligatures like æ and marks like the tilde are kept. The letter yogh of Middle English is represented by *y* or *gh*, according to its phonetic value. Old and Middle English thorn and eth are replaced by *th*, but for obvious phonetic reasons the treatment of the corresponding Icelandic letters is different, thorn being represented by *th*, eth by *dh*. Old English and Icelandic long vowels are marked with a macron, but Middle English long vowels are left unmarked. In general, long vowels are marked in ancient word forms. In marking Latin quantities, Harper's dictionary has been followed. Greek quantities have been conformed to Liddell and Scott. The transliterations from languages which do not use the Latin alphabet are conventional, and need no further comment here.

ABBREVIATIONS

In the course of the discussion above, some of the abbreviations used in the etymologies have been explained. Many other abbreviations are used, of course, but these are too familiar to need explanation. A key to all the abbreviations will be found on the inside of each cover, and a shorter key, giving only the most frequent abbreviations, appears at the bottom of every other page. By the use of abbreviation it has proved possible to present in limited space a substantial amount of etymological information with clarity and precision. It is hoped that the reader will find the presentation convenient and informative.

SYNONYMS AND ANTONYMS: Miles L. Hanley

I. WHAT ARE SYNONYMS?

Early writers referred to synonyms as words of identical meaning. To be sure, there have been groups of words in English which, for a period of time, could be considered synonymous in this oldest and strictest sense. But, like other languages, English has had what is known as *semantic change*, affecting the meanings of words. Many words, while usually keeping earlier meanings, have developed new ones; together with figurative uses, specialized uses, and differences of various other kinds. English has also borrowed freely from the languages with which it has come in contact; and when words have been borrowed, the meaning of any corresponding English terms, or that of the borrowed terms, or both, has commonly been changed. For example, at the time when the word *animal*—already widely known as a Latin word—was adopted into English, there was the native word *deer*, which had the same meaning. But after *animal* had come in as the general term, the word *deer* developed the specialized meaning of "a horned beast." Between words originally identical in meaning, therefore, differences, great and small, have developed, in one of their senses or in several.

That a word may now be truly synonymous with another word or words in some meanings but not in others, needs little proof. *Steal, rob,* and *pilfer* are quite clearly synonymous in the sense of "to take away that which belongs to another." They are quite as clearly not synonymous in the sense of "to move quietly or furtively," another of the meanings of *steal*. Thus, the college student who wrote "The sun came pilfering through the leaves," was making the mistake of considering these synonyms as identical in all their meanings.

Important as semantic change is, a discussion of it is not practical here; obviously we must consider words according to their current meanings and uses. We can, however, take some account of it in our definition of synonyms: THOSE WORDS ARE SYNONYMS FOR ONE ANOTHER WHICH HAVE THE SAME, OR A VERY SIMILAR, GENERAL MEANING, THOUGH ONE OR MORE OF THEIR OTHER MEANINGS MAY DIFFER MORE OR LESS WIDELY.

II. WHY STUDY SYNONYMS?

"To consider synonymous words *identical* is fatal to accuracy; to forget that they are *similar*, to some extent *equivalent*, and sometimes *interchangeable* is destructive of freedom and variety." This statement (*Standard Dictionary*, 1894), which remains one of the best on the subject, points to some of the principal values in studying synonyms.

If one becomes aware of distinctions commonly (sometimes even unconsciously) made between similar words, he has added to his understanding of those words. If his attention is also drawn to some of the *ways* of distinguishing between words, and to some of the *kinds of differences* between words in some ways similar, he then has the equipment for gaining an understanding of further words which he may encounter.

One can be said truly to have enlarged his vocabulary only with those words which he can use with precision and with judgment. A corollary of the statements preceding is, then, that by studying synonyms one may learn not to use undiscriminatingly words which he does not understand, lest, in his attempts to be elegant, he succeed only in being ridiculous.

Discriminated studies of synonyms, especially, therefore, can be of assistance if one has such purposes as: (1) gaining freedom and ease in speaking and writing, (2) gaining a sense of appropriateness which will encourage careful discrimination, and (3) acquiring accuracy and precision in the use of words.

III. PRINCIPLES OF SELECTION OF SYNONYMS

A partial treatment of all possible synonyms, or a full treatment of even a part of all possible synonyms, would require volumes devoted exclusively to the subject. A chosen vocabulary of synonyms must necessarily be limited according to some principle or principles of selection.

In this book, lists of synonymous words have been provided where it was thought that these would be useful in throwing further light on the meaning, or meanings, of entry words of high frequency. The lists are in addition to, and exclusive of, words given in definitions and in the studies. Such lists were to serve not only as "finding lists," but to encourage further exploration into the meanings of the head word.

In the discriminated studies, however, the first con-sideration was frequency of use. In the past, just as the earliest English dictionaries were lists of "hard words," words of a literary tinge or words considered particularly difficult were likely to be selected for such study. Or those might be chosen which would be used in "elegant" conversation (Mrs. Thrale, *British Synonymy*, 1794). But a modern reference book cannot anticipate the infinite variety of needs that individual readers may have; only a word list chosen on the basis of frequency has a chance of being frequently useful to many.

It is, moreover, the frequently used, long-established word, which has developed the great variety of meanings. And it is here that the general reader needs help. For example, in what contexts is "little" more appropriate than "small"? When and why is "small" to be preferred?

It is only fair to say, at this point, that there are still many unsolved problems in determining frequency. The work of Thorndike, Lorge, Buckingham, Dolch, Zipf, and others, as well as the writer's own *Word Index of James Joyce's Ulysses*, has revealed many useful facts. But so far, the choice of material for the study of frequency has necessarily been limited, and to a degree distorted, the findings. Most of the material studied has been either literary or at least written; no account has been taken of the differences between vocabularies in oral and written materials. Much of the material has not been concerned with current usage, and until recently there has been no separation according to levels of formality, informality, etc.; or of parts of speech (when a single form may be used as noun and verb or as noun and adjective) though one part of speech may account for all but a small percentage of the occurrences, leaving the other part of speech a rare word; or of the different definitions of any word (some uses being out of fashion so that only one or two may account for all or most of a fairly high frequency).

An outstanding advantage of the ACD is the extensive use that has been made of the semantic word count of Drs. Irving Lorge and Edward L. Thorndike. In this, the classifications and subdivisions of the great Oxford English Dictionary have been used in showing the relative frequency of various uses of a word. With this help we have been able to build on the studies and analyses made by some of our most distinguished English scholars over a period of more than seventy years.

Insofar as frequency has been established, we have used it as our first principle. Almost all the words selected for study are from Thorndike's first 10,000, and well up in frequency as indicated in *The Teacher's Word Book of 30,000 Words*, by Thorndike and Lorge.

Other principles were used to a lesser degree. Some of them follow:

1. We have chosen words with which general readers have difficulty; that is, some of the words often inquired about in newspaper columns, radio programs, college classes, and the like.

2. We have attempted to state concisely the distinctions between some words confused with one another and mistakenly thought to be synonyms, in such a way that the preferred usages will be clear.

3. We have taken into account the kinds of difficulty which persons learning English have; such studies as *judicious, judicial* are intended to be useful to this group of readers.

4. We have included a few examples from required readings in literature, which students need to understand.

5. Some of the words traditionally included in any treatment of synonyms have, of course, been considered.

6. A few groups needed to illustrate important principles (see Section V) have been added.

IV. METHOD OF TREATMENT OF SYNONYMS

In the synonym studies, the words discriminated have been limited to groups which have a considerable area of meaning in common. In order that the core meaning might be clear and might be stated in each study, the number of words compared in a study has been kept small—usually three or four, though sometimes only two, and only in a few instances five or more.

A study has practically always been placed under the entry of highest frequency, unless for a special reason (as *ado*, important for occurrence in literature; or *await*, a contrast with the modern form) it has seemed desirable to call greater attention to a word now less frequently used.

To call attention to the fact that the same word may have a number of different meanings; that other words may be its synonyms in one sense but not in another; and that a frequently used sense of one word may be a synonym for a less frequent one of another word, we have keyed each study to a particular sense of a word. With the other definitions of each word easily available, the reader may compare the other senses of the words as he wishes, and discover whatever additional area of synonymy there is. In some cases, different definitions of the same word are closely related in meaning—so closely at times that a number had to be arbitrarily assigned to the study—but in other cases the differences are great (as for example, *brazen*, "of brass," and *brazen*, "bold"). The hope is to lead the reader to consider the *various* definitions of a word and not merely to take the first one or two, if it has several. To examine all the meanings is essential to finding one which fits a context; and the habit is essential in learning to use unfamiliar synonyms discriminatingly—or even to discover which of the meanings are synonymous (the No. 1 definition of one word may be synonymous with the No. 5 of another word, but not with the first four).

In each study we give first a statement of the idea that the words have in common, to show how they are alike. We then go on to show how they differ, by giving the distinctive characteristics of each word. Sometimes it is felt that little more than a comparison of definitions is necessary—a first step in any discrimination. But various methods have been used to illustrate a variety of differences (see Section V).

In most cases, examples in context have been given, not to limit use by a single idiomatic example, but to illustrate an accepted use. It would have been possible to use literary, especially poetic, quotations for many of the examples; but it has seemed wiser not to do so, since the poet or literary artist frequently finds an original, striking, or suggestive use which, in itself properly memorable, would be usable only rarely in everyday life. Therefore, the examples are expressions that are, or could be, found in ordinary conversation or writing. In a few instances, it has been possible to use all of the discriminated words in a single context, to show how the use of each word produces some difference in the meaning.

V. POINTS ILLUSTRATED IN THE SYNONYM STUDIES

We have tried to illustrate various ways in which words may be discriminated, or ways in which "words that mean the same thing" may differ to the degree that they must be discriminated. A common question is, "What is the difference between this word and that one?" Some of the differences we have illustrated are the following:
1. Between general and specific.
2. Between shades of meaning.
3. In emphasis.
4. In implication.
5. In application.
6. In connotation.
7. In emotional effect.
8. In levels of usage.
9. Between literary and colloquial usage.
10. Effects of prefixes and suffixes.
11. In idiom.
12. In British and American usage.
13. Between borrowed and native words.
14. Between literal and figurative uses.
15. Between concrete and abstract uses.
16. Between technical (or occupational) uses and popular uses.
17. In aspect of action.
18. Between local or provincial usages and general usage.

VI. WHAT ARE ANTONYMS?

When, in 1867, C. J. Smith coined the term *antonym*, he meant it to be used in the sense of "counter-term" (such as "non-x" for "x"), a name already well known. *Antonym*, however, has since his time been variously interpreted.

As with *synonym*, the strictest interpretation has turned out to be too strict. If the strictest sense, "word of (completely) contradictory meaning," were adopted, most English words would not have antonyms. This is true, in any case, of scientific words, most of which are monosemantic. But it is perfectly obvious that, for a very large percentage of the nonscientific words, there are other words which offer a sharp contrast to at least some of the aspects or meanings.

Even such an unpromising word as *man*, for example, may be contrasted with other words which most emphatically do not mean the same thing as *man: woman* (different sex); *boy* (different age); *officer* (different rank), etc. Naturally this process could not be carried to the extreme of saying that all words not *man* are its antonyms because they differ from it in some respect. As with synonyms, there must first be some basis of likeness in classification; that is, for *man* the antonyms must be those referring to human beings, or at least to something living; an antonym for *black* should be the name of a color; for *anger* should be the name of an emotion, and the like. Perhaps, however, this likeness in classification may be taken for granted.

Since there are, as yet, many unsolved problems concerning antonyms, trying to give a definition is very difficult. A narrow definition is unsatisfactory; but a broad one must have limitations. A tentative statement might be made as follows: AN ANTONYM IS A WORD WHICH EXPRESSES THE OPPOSITE OR THE NEGATIVE OF ONE OR MORE OF THE MEANINGS OF ANOTHER WORD.

The number of antonyms which any word can have is not limited to one. Indeed, most words which would have antonyms at all would have several, and some words have great numbers. In this book we have not attempted to give as many antonyms as possible (either for any word or in total). As with synonyms, we have keyed antonyms to specific meanings of entry words, and have usually given only one antonym; but that one a word whose usual meaning is in sharp contrast to the sense of the entry word indicated.

We have, in general, omitted antonyms which are simply the entry word plus or minus such prefixes as *un-*, *in-*, *non-*, and *ir-*, *il-*, or the suffix *-less*. These should be considered as taken for granted. We have also omitted antonyms when a definition carries the words "the opposite of —" or "not —."

VII. OF WHAT VALUE ARE ANTONYMS?

Antonyms have here been given, in many instances, for entry words used in synonym studies; but they have also been given for several hundred words not connected with the studies. Like synonyms, antonyms throw light on the meaning of entry words; for the understanding of a word, often what it is *not* is as important as what it *is*. In fact, the contrast in the antonym often clarifies the meaning of the entry word and sharpens it far beyond the definition, particularly when the antonym is the better known of the two words.

A few antonyms of lower frequency have been included, again to encourage further exploration by the reader; but most of the antonyms given are words of high frequency. However, in the selection of antonyms, effectiveness of contrast was the main principle of choice. An interesting result was that the same word sometimes seemed to be the most satisfactory antonym for one meaning of each of a number of other words which themselves were not close synonyms.

The outstanding conclusion of a considerable amount of study is that antonyms are not of value for their own sakes in the same way that synonyms are. It would probably not be worth while to make discriminated studies of antonyms; but it is eminently worth while to select antonyms discriminatingly for separate definitions, —that is, for different senses of a word. We have made a beginning of thus discriminating antonyms, in order to demonstrate the possibilities. We have not carried out this feature elaborately, but have given a sufficient number of instances to establish the principle that antonyms, carefully selected, keyed to separate meanings, have a considerably enhanced value in aiding the understanding of entry words.

See also "A Dictionary of Synonyms and
Antonyms," page 3, Volume II

USAGE LEVELS AND DIALECT
DISTRIBUTION: Charles C. Fries

Even a very superficial examination of the language practices of native speakers of English will reveal many differences in those practices from person to person. A hasty glance at the materials gathered for the *Linguistic Atlas of New England* will not only confirm the impression one receives from casually listening to the speech of those who talk English but will furnish convincing evidence that the differences of usage among native speakers of English are much greater and much more intricate than is usually believed. These differences of English usage occur not only in matters of vocabulary but also in matters of grammar and especially in matters of pronunciation. It is these differences in the practice of those who speak English that give rise to the many discussions concerning our language and often send students and others to our dictionaries for the information necessary to understand these differences. Ever since the publication of Samuel Johnson's *English Dictionary* in 1755 the "dictionary" has been looked to and consulted as the "authority" concerning the acceptability of words and the proper use of word meanings. "What does *the* dictionary say?" occurs as the common question in all our disputes concerning our language—as if there were but one dictionary with ultimate authority and as if the statements recorded in any dictionary were valid for all time. Those who ask "What does the dictionary say?" practically never inquire concerning the publication date of the particular dictionary consulted or the qualifications of those who have produced it. The desire for an easily accessible "authority" on the part of the general public has created an enormous market for many cheap dictionaries, often produced by unscrupulous publishers who have achieved cheapness by reprinting old dictionary materials upon which the copyright has expired—adding, of course, a few of the well-known new words in order to give the appearance of being up-to-date.

ATTITUDES TOWARD USAGE DIFFERENCES

Part of the difficulty lies in the common and traditional view of the differences of English usage. Often it is assumed that there exist in any language only two kinds of words, word meanings, and pronunciations:—those that are correct and proper and those that are incorrect or mistakes. The "mistakes" are thought to be derived by ignorance and carelessness from the correct or proper uses. It is assumed also that the separation and labeling of the mistakes is a simple process and that grammarians and lexicographers have llong ago made the proper decisions and the results of their work need only be preserved and made known to succeeding generations. It is assumed that all dictionaries will incorporate these "accepted" decisions and therefore there is no reason to inquire concerning the qualifications of the editors of a new dictionary or even the means employed to make the assignment of usage labels valid.

NECESSITY OF RECORDING USAGE

From the point of view of modern linguistic science these common naïve assumptions concerning the differences of usage in English must be discarded. They belong to a pre-scientific period in the study of language—to an age that still believes the earth to be flat and denies the circulation of the blood. The modern dictionary editor who is aware of the principles and methods of the modern scientific study of language and of the accumulations of knowledge concerning our language built up by the patient study of many scholars, cannot in honesty follow the easy path of copying the usage labels as they are attached to words and word meanings in former dictionaries. He cannot, as Samuel Johnson often did, condemn words and word meanings in accord with his special prejudices. Johnson, in spite of the fact that his quotations show the word *excepting* is used by Dryden and Collier, condemns it with the label "an improper word." In similar fashion he attaches the label "low words" to *budge, fun,* and *clever,* although his own quotations give examples of these words from Shakespeare and from Moore, from Addison, Pope, and Arbuthnot.

Constant change—in pronunciation, in grammatical structure, in word meanings, and in the words themselves—is, as far as we know, the normal condition of every language spoken by a living people. The careful study of these changes by the rigorous techniques developed by linguistic science has given us linguistic history. A hundred years of scholarly work has gone into establishing the details of the history of the English language and has forced us to turn away from the methods of

"authority" as they are represented in Samuel Johnson's *Dictionary* and its successors. It has demanded the patient recording of the facts of usage as the language is and has been employed by the hosts of speakers of English in this country and in the other countries where English is the language in which the major affairs of the people are conducted. The editor of a modern dictionary is thus confronted with a wide range of constantly changing differences in English usage that cannot be easily separated into correct and proper forms on the one hand and mistakes on the other. These changes in usage render the older dictionaries inaccurate and make necessary continually new examinations of the status of the words and word meanings in English. A dictionary can be an "authority" only in the sense in which a book of chemistry or of physics or of botany can be an "authority"—by the accuracy and the completeness of its record of the observed facts of the field examined, in accord with the latest principles and techniques of the particular science. Older "authorities" in the uses of words are thus superseded by those which incorporate the latest results of the more scientific investigations in the English language.

REGIONAL DIFFERENCES

In the matter of English usage it is not always possible to define precisely the boundaries within which a word or a word meaning is used or recognized. The facilities of travel have so developed in modern times that many speakers of English hear constantly the language of those from other geographical areas. And the radio has brought into even the most secluded communities the speech of all sections of the country. This mixing of speech forms from various geographical areas is not by any means limited to the upper classes.

"I knowed you wasn't Oklahomy folks. You talk queer kinda—That ain't no blame, you understan'."
"Ever'body says words different," said Ivy. "Arkansas folks says 'em different, and Oklahomy folks says 'em different. And we seen a lady from Massachusetts, an' she said 'em differentest of all. Couldn' hardly make out what she was sayin'."
(J. Steinbeck, *The Grapes of Wrath,* p. 168.)

In the great mass of differences of usage that appear in the practice of English speakers, however, some words and word meanings and some pronunciations are in common use in special parts of the English-speaking world and appear much less frequently or never in other areas. For these this dictionary marks the geographical areas of special use. Some of the areas thus indicated within this country are New England, the old South, and the Southwest for such words as the following: *selectman, sharpie, levee*[1] (def. 1), *granny* (def. 4), *corn pone, alamo, chaps, chuck wagon* (see the definitions of these words).

British usage differs from the usage of the United States in such words as *lift* (def. 21), *navvy, lorry* (def. 1), *petrol* (def. 1), *gorse* (see the definitions of these words, and the preface by A. W. Read on "British and American Usage," page xxx).

And Australia has its particular words and word meanings, as *paddock* (def. 3), *swag*[2] (def. 2), *billabong, billy* (def. 3) (see the definitions of these words).

Many words and word meanings are characteristic of certain fields of human activity. Each trade and occupation and sport has its technical vocabulary. Some of this technical vocabulary consists of special words used only in science, art, trade, or sport, such as *Binet test, electrode, binnacle, chiaroscuro, silo, forward pass* (see the definitions of these words).

Much of these technical vocabularies, however, consists of special meanings and uses of words that are employed generally in the language. The *field* in baseball has a special sense, as does *sacrifice, run, hit, out, plate, pitcher.* In the preparation and marketing of alcoholic beverages, the words *proof, dry, mash,* and *smooth* are used with special meanings.

"LEVELS" OF USAGE

Most frequently, however, discussions of language center upon what are often called the "levels" of usage. Some words and word meanings are frequently called "slang." The term "slang" has suffered such a wide extension of its signification and has been applied to so many varieties of words that it is extremely difficult to draw the line between what is slang and what is not. The difference between slang and not-slang does not rest in the meanings of the words themselves. To say that a man is "recalcitrant" is using an acceptable and somewhat learned word; to call him "a kicker" in the same situation is using slang, although the meanings are similar. Some clipped words, as *gent*, are often regarded as slang; others, such as *piano*, *phone*, and *cello*, are not slang. Slang cannot be defined in terms of either the forms or the strict meanings of the words themselves; it can, however, be characterized in terms of the suggested feelings accompanying certain words—their connotations rather than their denotations. Flippant humor marks the expressions we call slang. Some examples are *Java* (def. 3), *ice* (def. 8), *croak* (def. 4), *hangout*, *corking* (see the definitions of these words).

Some expressions appear only in poetry. They suggest then those circumstances in which they usually occur. Others are now found only in the written material of books. To mark them "*Poetic*" and "*Literary*" serves to record the special areas in which they are commonly used. Some examples are: *gloaming*, *e'er*, *lidless* (def. 3), *naught* (def. 2), *scarce* (def. 4) (see the definitions of these words).

Many expressions occur primarily in conversation rather than in formal writing. The occasions for their use are chiefly conversational situations. These are marked "*Colloq.*" Even teachers of English frequently misunderstand the application of the label *Colloquial* in our best dictionaries. Some confuse it with *localism* and think of the words and constructions marked "colloquial" as peculiarities of speaking which are characteristic of a particular locality. Others feel that some stigma attaches to the label "*Colloquial*" and would strive to avoid as incorrect (or as of a low level) all words so marked. The word *colloquial*, however, as used to label words and phrases in a modern scientifically edited dictionary has no such meaning. It is used to mark those words and constructions whose range of use is primarily that of the polite conversation of cultivated people, of their familiar letters and informal speeches, as distinct from those words and constructions which are common also in formal writing. The usage of our better magazines and of public addresses generally has, during the past generation, moved away from the formal and literary toward the colloquial.

Some words and expressions occur primarily in the language of those without much conventional education. These expressions are often called "illiterate" or "vulgar English," and are considered "incorrect." As a matter of fact, many of these expressions are survivals from an older period of the language and are "incorrect" only in the sense that they do not occur in the usage of standard English—the practice of the socially accepted, those who are carrying on the important affairs of English-speaking people. Much of the language spoken by the uneducated is the same as that of the polite conversation of cultivated people and also duplicates the expressions of formal literary discourse. The usage labels in a dictionary attempt to mark only those expressions that are peculiar to a particular type or dialect of English. If one ignores the differences that characterize the various geographical areas and the differences of the separate fields of human

activity, of trades and vocations and sports, the situation may be roughly represented by the following diagram:

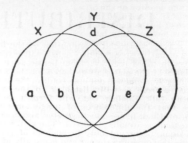

The three circles X, Y, Z, represent the three sets of language habits indicated above.

X—formal literary English, the words, the expressions, and the structures one finds in serious books.

Y—colloquial English, the words, expressions, and the structures of the informal but polite conversation of cultivated people.

Z—illiterate English, the words, the expressions, and the structures of the language of the uneducated.

b, c, and e represent the overlappings of the three types of English.

c—that which is common to all three: formal literary English, colloquial English, and illiterate English.

b—that which is common to both formal literary English and colloquial English.

e—that which is common to both colloquial English and illiterate English.

a, d, and f represent those portions of each type of English that are peculiar to that particular set of language habits.

The following is a list of some of the other usage labels used in this dictionary with typical examples under each of the particular words and expressions to which each label is assigned.

Archaic: impose (def. 8), hugger-mugger (def. 2), glister (def. 1), lief (def. 2), angle² (def. 3).

Colloq.: angel (def. 6), brass tacks, fizzle (def. 2), flimflam, goner.

Humorous: celestial (def. 5), human (def. 4).

Obs.: loblolly boy, lust (def. 5), flittermouse, **murther**, drugget (def. 2).

Obsolesc.: saloon (def. 6), regimen (def. 5).

Rare: image (def. 17), impassionate, faulty **(def. 2)**, instancy (def. 2), genial¹ (def. 3).

Scot.: chap¹ (def. 5), laird, hag² (def. 1), icker.

Scot. and N. Eng.: unco, kirk (def. 1), ilk (def. 2), **braw**, bairn.

South African: laager, kraal (def. 3).

U.S.: chain lightning, challenge (def. 14), **biscuit (def. 1)**, boss (def. 2), quilting bee.

BRITISH AND AMERICAN USAGE:
Allen Walker Read

The passengers on the Mayflower, we may assume, were not troubled with problems of British and American usage. These came as a result of natural linguistic developments, on both sides of the ocean, in succeeding centuries. But so much cultural interchange between England and America has regularly taken place that the lines of linguistic division have never been clear-cut nor easily marked. However, most speakers of English recognize that certain expressions have their chief currency in one country or the other; and we have attempted to mark such currency more systematically and thoroughly than has been done in any previous dictionary.

Our criterion has been current usage. Thus the country of origin is not relevant to our marking. Words like *blizzard*, *jingoism*, *O. K.*, or *teetotaler* are well known either as Americanisms or Briticisms in origin, but they have now come to be used wherever English is spoken, and a regional label for them belongs only in a historical dictionary.

An unscientific attitude towards language has often in the past interfered with an impartial consideration of regional variation. Many people have regarded the "standard" language as the prime, original form and any deviation from it as a degenerate, deteriorated form. But the contrary is the case: the "standard" form of English developed, by means of social and commercial prestige, out

of a multiplicity of dialects. The old, mistaken view has often influenced the attitude toward Americanisms, and most Americans themselves had a "colonial" attitude in language until very recent years. For their part, many Englishmen have assumed that their form of English is the only one with validity, and such a thing as a "Briticism" is impossible—it is simply "English." But in this dictionary, where normal usage is our all-important guide, we have taken an impartial, scientific view: if the frequency or incidence of a word is greater in one region of the English-speaking world than in another, it is a fact that deserves to be recorded. Our symbols *Brit.* and *U. S.* thus have a basis of an informal statistical type. The *Brit.* or *U. S.* is not a "stigma" but a record of current usage, as accurate as we can determine it.

Americans have always adopted British expressions with very little reluctance. A few terms, such as *dustman*, *lift*, *petrol*, *tram*, *treacle*, etc., are conspicuously British, often used to identify the "stage Englishman"; and Americans, except for a few avowed Anglophiles, tend to avoid these. But if a British expression does not get strongly identified as such, Americans adopt it with little hesitation. Englishmen have been somewhat more cautious in adopting American expressions, but even here a constant borrowing has been going on for generations. The symbols *Brit.* and *U. S.* cannot be taken in any "absolute" sense, for exceptions are sure to be found. Sometimes, when usage is much divided, and only a preponderance will be found in one country or the other, the labels *Chiefly Brit.* and *Chiefly U. S.* are used. Some matters of currency are taken care of in the definition, and the word or meaning therefore is not specially labeled. If a political or social institution is described as being "in Great Britain" or "in U. S.," or if the range of a plant or animal is given in the definition, no further label is needed.

The graphic reflection of words (or spelling) sometimes differs between England and America, and typically British spellings are so labeled in this work. The *-our* and *-re* endings, rather than *-or* and *-er*, often find favor in England, and in the derived forms of a two-syllabled word the final consonant is there doubled even when the accent is on the first syllable, as in *travel, travelled, travelling,* or *counsel, counselled, counselling.* Other typical British forms are *cheque, connexion, jewellery, gaol, kerb, pyjamas,* etc.

Most British-American differences occur in the language of everyday life rather than on literary levels, and one can sometimes read long passages of solid discussion in books or newspapers in both England and America without coming on distinctive peculiarities of language. But whenever they are found they should be an object of the lexicographer's comment, and we have paid particular attention in this work to such material.

GUIDE TO USAGE: Harrison Platt, Jr.

WHAT IS GOOD USAGE?

People who lack confidence in their knowledge of good English would like to have each spelling, pronunciation, meaning, and grammatical usage decided for them, once and for all, so that they could know that one is right and another wrong. They feel uncertain when choices are clearly permissible. Partly because they would like to have a fixed standard to settle all questions of usage, they come to believe that one exists and operates, and constantly repeat judgments and rules without examining the basis for them.

But if a fixed standard does exist, it must have a basis. Let us examine some of the possible bases for a rigid standard of good English.

The appeal to immemorial custom and history will not support a fixed standard. The whole history of the language has been one of change. No one would want to outlaw all innovations since *Beowulf*, and it is more than questionable that the language of Chaucer would suit today's needs as well as the speech we use. A word or a construction has no special virtue merely because it is old.

Only in a police state, rigidly controlled, could a fixed standard of correctness rest on a "supreme authority." In the United States we would want to know who is to pick the authority. Moreover, if the judgments of an authority ran counter to the speech habits of many people, its rulings would be ignored. This is indicated by the experience of some countries in which a single central authority to "reform" or control the language has been tried. When the French Academy was set up in the time of Cardinal Richelieu, one of its functions was supervision of the language. The Academy issued dictionaries and from time to time ruled on questions of grammar, spelling, and the like which were submitted to its judgment. Although the Academy has no doubt had some influence on the French language, dialects have continued to flourish in the provinces, a rich and varied slang has never ceased being born in Paris and throughout the country, and even the literary language has evolved very largely without reference to the fiats of the Academy.

In spelling, pronunciation, meaning, and grammar, then, one looks in vain for a fixed standard or for an ultimate authority. Does this mean that there is no standard of good English and that one way of using the language is no better and no worse than any other? Not at all. There are two standards which can be safely followed.

(1) The purpose of language is communication—not communication in a void but communication between the writer or speaker and his audience. The personality and background of the writer or speaker must be taken into account. The way he expresses himself should be in keeping with his nature and background. It should be natural to him, to his habits of speech and thought. It should be as far as possible suitable to his audience. It should take into account their probable knowledge of what he is speaking about, their acquaintance with the concepts and vocabulary of his subject, their ability to follow abstract discussion or their need for illustration, example and explanation. Finally, the way he expresses himself should be adapted to his subject matter. An incident at a ball game requires a different sort of exposition from an explanation of atomic fission. A doctor discussing a problem of nutrition would properly use a different vocabulary, a different sentence structure, and a different approach to his subject if he were addressing, respectively, a convention of doctors, a parent-teacher association, and a class of fourth-grade pupils. That English is good English which communicates well the thought of a given speaker to a given audience. Change the thought, the speaker, or the audience, and the same mode of expression might be extremely bad. The measure of English is the effectiveness of its communication, and this in turn depends on its appropriateness to the subject, the speaker, and the audience.

(2) The second measure of language is social, not functional. People are accustomed to make judgments on the basis of language, just as they do on the basis of clothes and manners. A tuxedo is not better than slacks and sport shirt, it is simply more formal. One is suitable for certain occasions, the others for other occasions. In both formal and informal dress a reasonable degree of neatness and care is expected. It is the same with language.

Writing *thier* for *their* or *her's* for *hers* or saying *it ain't* for *it isn't* does not seriously interfere with communication, but it makes the writer or speaker look ignorant. Noticeably inappropriate mixtures of formal, polysyllabic vocabulary with slang or casual, informal phrases permit the same sort of adverse judgments that wearing a violently colored shirt with otherwise formal dress would. This principle is easy to apply to many language situations.

English has many levels. Communication on any level may be adequate, yet the speaker or writer may be unwilling to let others place him on a particular level because of his use of language. The test here, as before, is appropriateness.

In sum, we may say that English usage is never just good. It is good in respect to a particular situation, speaker, and audience. If it is appropriate to all three, and if it is effective in communication, it is good.

What, in the light of these remarks, is the rôle of a dictionary in settling questions of pronunciation or meaning or grammar? It is *not* a legislating authority on good English. It attempts to record what usage at any time actually is. Insofar as possible, it points out divided usage. It indicates regional variations of pronunciation or meaning wherever practical. It points out meanings and uses peculiar to a trade, profession, or special activity. It suggests the levels on which certain words or usages are appropriate. A dictionary such as this, based on a realistic sampling of usage, furnishes the information necessary for a sound judgment of what is good English in a given situation. To this extent the dictionary is an authority, and beyond this authority should not go.

SECTION I. WRITTEN ENGLISH

PUNCTUATION

Since English no longer uses more than a handful of inflectional endings (such as are still found in German nouns or French verbs), the relation between the words of a sentence is indicated by their order. Yet there is a great flexibility in word order. In spoken English the rise and fall of the voice, the natural pauses in speaking group the words in their proper relation to one another. In written English this grouping must be indicated by the various marks of punctuation.

In the nineteenth century, writers tended to write long, somewhat formal sentences. In order to guide the reader through the intricate patterns of these long sentences, they ordinarily used much more punctuation than is common today. Modern writers tend toward short sentences, approximating the informality of everyday speech.

The amount of punctuation should vary with the length and complexity of the writer's sentences. Excessive punctuation interferes with ready reading just as much as too little punctuation. Words and punctuation should combine to bring meaning. Any system of punctuation that calls for a particular mark of punctuation regardless of the length and difficulty of the sentence is mechanical and unlikely to produce in practice an easily read or "good" style. The proper punctuation is an integral part of writing a sentence just as the proper arrangement of the words is.

Here is the place for a useful bit of advice. If a sentence is very difficult to punctuate so as to make the meaning clear, the chances are that the arrangement of words and ideas is at fault. The writer will do better if he rearranges his word order instead of wrestling with his punctuation.

A badly worded sentence cannot be made clear by any punctuation.

Grammars and handbooks of English give many rules of punctuation. These are useful for certain arbitrary customs, such as the use of apostrophes, quotation marks, and hyphens. For all the marks indicating pauses they are not very helpful. The difficulty is not so much in deciding what mark to use in a recognized and well understood situation (as the rulemakers seem to think) but in recognizing a situation that will benefit by punctuation. In the great variety of English sentences, long and short, complicated or simple, these situations are not always clear-cut and require judgment on the writer's part.

On the other hand, there are only a few kinds of punctuation situations. To learn them and learn what to do with them is within the reach of anyone.

ENDING SENTENCES

The sentence is the common unit of thought and language. At the end of a spoken sentence the voice usually drops and always makes a complete pause. In the written language this full stop has to be indicated by punctuation.

STATEMENTS. Most sentences are statements. They may be a single statement like the one just before this, or they may consist of two or more *very closely related in thought*, like this one. The full stop at the end of a statement is commonly indicated by a period (.). Any sentence in this paragraph will serve as an example.

QUESTIONS. If the sentence consists of a question instead of a statement, the full stop at the end is commonly indicated by a question mark (?):

Who owns this book?

Polite orders or requests are often put in question form: Sometimes no question is intended, as in the following:

Will you pass the bread, please.

The writer can use either a period or a question mark, depending on whether he feels there is a real question intended.

EXCLAMATIONS. An exclamation, whether long or short, even a single word, is closed by an exclamation point (!). Single words or characteristic phrasings offer no problem:

Gosh! What a beautiful day!

The degree of feeling or excitement will determine the proper close of sentences like the following:

Get out of here! (or) Get out of here.

An excessive number of exclamatory sentences often bothers readers. They should be used with caution for this reason.

INTERRUPTED THOUGHT. Especially in narrative, a writer sometimes has to deal with a sentence not entirely completed. A sentence broken off abruptly by an interruption may be closed off with a long (2-em) dash:

"Oh, the train doesn't leave for five——"
"All aboard," shouted the conductor.

If a thought is allowed to trail off unfinished, many writers close the sentence with an ellipsis (. . .).

If a writer knows when he has finished a sentence, the best choice of punctuation is not much of a problem. The knowledge that he has finished it is sometimes less simple than it seems.

PUNCTUATION TO SEPARATE

Within the sentence it is necessary to separate, with punctuation, groups of words which might otherwise run together and cause confusion.

MAIN CLAUSES. One of the major categories of sentence elements that should be kept distinct is that of main clauses in compound or in compound complex sentences. Main clauses are grammatically exactly like sentences. Where two or more are very closely related in thought, they are frequently joined together in a single sentence, sometimes with a conjunction between, sometimes with none. Although they are joined, they are not merged.

The old rule taught in most schools called for a semicolon between main clauses if there was no conjunction or if there was interior punctuation within either clause. If there was a conjunction between the clauses, it and a comma were sufficient to separate the clauses. To use a comma when a semicolon was called for, or no punctuation when the rule prescribed a comma, was regarded as a high crime against good English and branded the transgressor, to quote more than one textbook, as "deficient in sentence sense." The offense was called a comma fault, comma blunder, or, among the relatively charitable, a run-on sentence.

A close examination of the actual practice of publishers in current books and magazines will show that these rules are not observed with any regularity. In some magazines there will not be a single semicolon on a close-packed

page. If a writer habitually uses a maximum of punctuation, if he writes long, involved clauses, he very frequently does use semicolons to separate them. But if he normally employs a minimum of punctuation and if his clauses are rather short and easily followed, he is likely to separate his clauses with a comma or, if a conjunction is present, by no punctuation at all.

The punctuation to be used depends on the writer's usual method of punctuation and on the length and difficulty of the particular sentence under consideration. Examples follow:

HEAVY OR FORMAL PUNCTUATION

With the abundance of the sea and the lush growth all around, poverty is no spur; and the native will work, if he will work at all, only at tasks which amuse him.

Battleships without air cover were proved fatally vulnerable; their preëminence was gone.

LIGHT OR INFORMAL PUNCTUATION

He could forgive, he could not forget.

She stumbled against him and his arms went around her.

Compound verbs within the same clause are sometimes separated but need not be if the sentence is clearly written and easily followed:

He swung the car into the side road and gradually eased down the accelerator.

COORDINATE ELEMENTS. Many sentences contain series of coördinate (equal and similar) elements. They may be nouns, verbs, adjectives, adverbs, phrases, or clauses. If conjunctions (*and, or,* or the like) are used between them, no punctuation is ordinarily used to separate them. If, however, conjunctions are omitted entirely or used only between the last two elements, they are commonly separated by punctuation. If the elements in the series are simple and contain no internal punctuation, commas are ordinarily used. If commas lead to confusion because of internal punctuation, semicolons are used.

When a conjunction appears between the last two elements of a series, usage is divided on whether there should also be punctuation here. As in compound sentences, the answer is in the general system of punctuation being used. If heavy punctuation is the established system, the last two elements of a series should be separated by punctuation, regardless of the presence of the conjunction. If light punctuation is used elsewhere, the punctuation is omitted between the last two elements of a series:

The flag is red, white (,) and blue.
The group consisted of Charles White, the pianist; Willis Twyford, the trap drummer; Elmer Smith, on trumpet (;) and Bill Stone, guitar.
(In the last example, without the semicolons the quartet might be thought of as a sextet.)
Running, blocking, kicking (,) and passing with deadly precision, Young did as he pleased in the second half.
During the long, hot afternoons we splashed in the cool, green, sun-speckled water of the lake.

SUBORDINATE PHRASES OR CLAUSES. Usage is divided as to separating a phrase or a clause preceding a main clause. Again the question of heavy or light punctuation enters in. If the phrase or clause is short and closely related to the main clause, many writers prefer to omit a comma. If the phrase or clause is long or not very closely related to the main clause, as this one is, it is commonly separated from the main clause by a comma. This is a question of judgment, and the writer can decide whether punctuation would make his sentence clearer.

When words are brought together so as to form an apparent phrase not called for by the meaning, they should always be separated by punctuation, usually a comma:

Inside, Norah was weeping as she washed the dishes.
(A reader not guided by the comma might read: *Inside Norah.*)
To Frances, North seemed an old man.
(A reader not guided by the comma might read: *To Frances North.*)

QUOTATIONS. A quotation is separated from its introductory clause by a colon or a comma. If the quotation is long or formally introduced, most writers use a colon:

The President spoke as follows:

In informal quotation, such as dialogue in a story, a comma is the common mark:

Becky answered, "I'm staying right here."

PUNCTUATION TO SET OFF

A child beginning to form sentences frequently succeeds in getting only a single, uncomplicated idea into each one. The result is the primer sentence: I see the dog. The dog is black. It has a curly tail. The next step is to join the three sentences together with *and's* between. The adult mind combines, producing a simple sentence: I see the black dog with a curly tail.

NONRESTRICTIVE PHRASES OR CLAUSES. Frequently a writer wants to add extra information not essential to the central meaning of the sentence. For example, the clause *who is six* does not affect the central meaning of the following sentence:

My niece, *who is six*, almost never cries.

Any word, phrase, or clause thus added to a sentence should be set off by a mark of punctuation *at beginning and end*. If the added information is very loosely related to the sentence, parentheses might be used to set it off. Obviously two marks are required, one at the beginning and one at the close of the added material:

Leningrad (*formerly called Petrograd*) was under siege for months.

Slightly more closely related information would be set off by paired dashes or commas, more commonly by commas. Again the punctuation requires two marks unless one would fall at the beginning or end of the sentence:

Lester Eaker—*a full-blooded Indian*—was the fastest man on the squad.
The radio, *which was playing softly*, filled in the pause.

RESTRICTIVE PHRASES OR CLAUSES. The sense is the best test of whether information is essential to the main meaning of the sentence. If a writer is in doubt, he can read the sentence with the questionable phrase or clause omitted:

People *who mutilate books* should not be allowed library privileges.
People . . . should not be allowed library privileges.

Obviously the writer of the original sentence did not mean that all people should be forbidden the use of the library, but only those few who mutilate books. The omission of the clause changes the main meaning of the sentence. It is therefore essential and should not be set off.

The third baseman, *who was left-handed*, came to bat.
The third baseman . . . came to bat.

The information that the batter was left-handed is not essential. Its omission does not change the main meaning. It should therefore be set off.

Look for additional, nonessential information in situations like the following:

Mary, I want you to clean your room. And you, *Tom*, should cut the grass.
Mr. Elkins, *the football coach*, was very popular with the boys.
The common automobile, *not the airplane*, is the most dangerous form of transportation.
Most of the climbers—*all but three*—turned back when the fog closed down.
It might be added, *incidentally*, that the rumor had no foundation.
Isak Dinesen's *Seven Gothic Tales* (*published by Random House*) is a remarkable book of short stories.

Although parentheses, paired dashes, or commas serve the same purpose and may be used to set off added but nonessential information, parentheses and dashes often make a break or pause too strong to suit the situation. Commas are by far the most widely used and the most satisfactory for this purpose. There is a prejudice against the use of many dashes held by publishers because they believe a page speckled with dashes is unsightly, and held by teachers because students unable to decide whether to use a comma or a semicolon compromise on a dash, again and again.

STYLES OF PUNCTUATION

Throughout the whole discussion of punctuation a conclusion has been emerging more and more clearly. Usage is almost everywhere divided, but this fact does not mean that there is no standard. In philosophical writing, thoughtful political or economic analysis, and the like, authors are aiming at fine distinctions, carefully weighed judgments. Their sentences are frequently long and much qualified. They tend, therefore, to punctuate heavily to help the reader through their complex thought. The norm in this sort of writing is rather heavy, rather formal punctuation. It should be consistently maintained.

On the other hand, the aim of the mystery story, the news magazine, the light novel is rapid, effortless reading. Sentences are usually rather simple in structure, short and informal. They need little punctuation and would merely be slowed down if more were put in. Publishers offering this sort of fare try to keep punctuation to its minimum essentials.

The aims of writers and publishers of all sorts are clarity and suitability to the general style. If these two aims are achieved, consistently, the punctuation is good.

The use of the apostrophe, the hyphen, and quotation marks is to a great extent formalized, not subject to judgment, although divided usage will be found here too. The principal uses of these marks are discussed below.

THE APOSTROPHE

POSSESSIVE FORMS. The most common use of the apostrophe is in spelling the possessive forms of nouns and some pronouns. If the word ends with any sound except that of *s* (or sometimes *sh* or *z*), the possessive is formed by the addition of *'s*. If the word ends with the sound of *s* (or sometimes *sh* or *z*), the possessive is formed by the addition of ' alone:

Ending not in *s*	Ending in *s*
girl's	companies'
nobody's	conscience'
men's	several horses'

Because most singulars do not end in *s* and form the possessive by adding *'s*, many writers feel uncomfortable when they form the possessive of a singular ending in *s* merely by the addition of '. There is a growing tendency to add an extra *s* to such words, especially when they consist of a single syllable. The extra *s* then provides an extra syllable and differentiates the sound of the possessive from the simple form:

Tom *Jones's* house instead of Tom *Jones'* house.
The *moss's* color instead of the *moss'* color.

Possessives of the personal pronouns do *not* take the apostrophe:

my, mine	our, ours
your, yours	your, yours
her, hers	their, theirs
his	whose
its	

The possessive is used not only in its obvious function but in such phrases as: two *hours'* work, a *week's* trip.

OMISSION. The apostrophe is also used to show the omission of one or more letters in contractions: *he'll*, *I'm*, *it's* [*it is*], *can't*. In quoted dialogue or speech, an apostrophe indicates a speaker's omission of sounds represented by the conventional spelling of the word, for instance: the state of *No'th* Carolina.

PLURAL OF NUMBERS, ETC. An apostrophe is generally used in forming the plural of numbers, letters, or words thought of as words:

two *e's*	the *1890's*
four *6's*	the last two *the's*

PLURAL OF ABBREVIATIONS. Initials used as abbreviations are often treated the same way:

two GI's

THE HYPHEN

The hyphen is regularly used when a word has to be broken at the end of a line to show that the remainder of the word is to follow on the next line. A word should be broken only between syllables: *port-able*, *run-ning*, *dis-pense*.

It is bad printing or typing practice to carry over a syllable of only two letters and virtually forbidden to carry over a single letter. It is equally forbidden to leave a single letter at the end of a line. Never break: *e-lapse*, *read-y*, *e-rase*. Avoid breaking: *real-ly*, *el-bow*, *du-ly*.

The hyphen is also used in a variety of compounds. Here usage is divided violently. A *half-finished* building stands beside a *half finished* building. *Slow-moving* traffic flows along with *slow moving* traffic. A *drug-store* clerk works in a *drug store* called The Evans Drugstore. Some publishers prefer to bring compounds into single words without space or hyphen. A wag once said of *Time Magazine*, "*Time* abhors the hyphen." Other publishers simply follow the usage of a given dictionary. Others prefer wherever possible to break compounds into two words. Choose a system and try to be consistent.

The hyphen is sometimes used between a prefix ending with a vowel and a root beginning with the same vowel (*re-enter*, *co-operate*). Many writers prefer to write *reënter* and *coöperate* or *reenter* and *cooperate*. Again, usage is violently divided.

A hyphen is used when a prefix added would make confusion with another word:

Re-cover a chair but *recover* from an illness.
He decided to *re-turn* the bacon but *return* postage guaranteed.

A hyphen is used between a prefix and a proper name:

pro-Republican	anti-Russian

Compound numerals between twenty-one and ninety-nine and fractions are usually hyphenated:

one hundred and thirty-one   three-quarters

Some writers now omit this hyphen.

QUOTATIONS

In a piece of writing, words spoken by someone other than the author, directly quoted, are usually marked as quotation. Indirectly quoted words are not so marked:

DIRECT: President Coolidge said, "I do not choose to run."

INDIRECT: President Coolidge said that he did not choose to run.

Material is quoted or it is not; there can be no compromise between direct and indirect quotation.

The indication of quotation follows no logic but custom, and the system is arbitrary. Short quotations are usually marked off by quotation marks placed at the beginning and end of the actual quotation. If the quotation is interrupted (for example, by *he said*), the interruption makes a new end and beginning which should be marked off by quotation marks:

"Won't you come to dinner?" he asked. "Come straight from the office."

In the United States quotations are usually indicated by double quotes (like those used above) and quotations within quotations are marked off by single quotes. ('These are single quotes.') In England the opposite system is used. Some publishers of American books and magazines use the English system. Either method is clear, and many book designers claim that the single quotes give a less speckled appearance

The position of quotation marks in relation to other punctuation is ruled by a rather rigid custom in the United States, although the usage in England, equally fixed, is different. In the United States final quotes follow a period or a comma:

" . . . the greatest of these is charity."
The better class of pickers are "blanket stiffs," men who own their own bedding.

Final quotes precede semicolons or colons:

"Divided we fall"; this truth illustrates itself day by day.

These two rules were built up in deference to the esthetic feelings of a generation or two of typesetters.

The position of final quotes in relation to exclamation points, question marks, or dashes is determined by meaning. The test is the same for all three. If a question mark, for example, belongs with the quotation but not with the whole sentence, it goes inside final quotes:

The sentry called, "Who goes there?"

If it goes with the whole sentence, it should be placed outside the final quotes:

Who can say without vanity, "I am an honest man"?

Dashes usually come inside final quotes, but the meaning is the test.

Long quotations are often printed in a different type or with wider margins or with the lines closer together than the main text, to indicate quotation. If this method is followed, no quotation marks are used. It is much used where a number of rather long passages must be quoted, particularly in serious nonfiction.

If a quotation of two or more paragraphs is marked off by quotation marks, beginning quotes are usually placed at the beginning of each paragraph but no final quotes are written until the end of the quotation is reached.

Long or formal quotations are often marked off from their introductory sentences by colons. Short, informal quotations, such as the dialogue in a story, are usually marked off by a comma. Very short quotations, one or two words, require no punctuation.

FORMAL: The Secretary of State spoke as follows: " . . .
INFORMAL: "Hollywood," he said, "always reminds me of a stage set."
VERY SHORT: He said "No." (or) He said *No* (or) *no*.

Titles of songs, stories, chapters of a book, poems, magazines, plays, motion pictures, operas, and so forth are usually written in quotes. Titles of books are sometimes put in quotes although they are more commonly put in italics.

CAPITALIZATION

Although there is considerable variation in the use of capital letters in many situations, copyreaders and compositors have worked out rules for their own use, and for the most part capitalization follows well defined conventions. Some of the commoner conventions are as follows:

1. Capitalize the first word of each sentence; also the beginning of a word or phrase standing independently, like a sentence.

2. Capitalize the beginning of each line of poetry or conventional verse:

The steed bit his master;
How came this to pass?
He heard the good pastor
Cry, "All flesh is grass."
—ANON.

Exception: Some modern poetry is written without capitals or only with such capitals as prose would have.

3. Capitalize proper nouns and adjectives:

George Washington   French
the United States   Germanic
Elizabeth   New England

4. The German *von* and Dutch *van* in proper names are commonly not printed with a capital when part of a name, but usage varies:

Paul von Hindenburg   Vincent van Gogh

5. The French particles *de* and *du* and the Italian *di* and *da* are commonly written in lower case when they are preceded by a first name or title. Without title or first name, the particle is sometimes dropped, sometimes capitalized. One American newspaper's style book adds: "Except De Gaulle, which is always capped."

Marquis de Lafayette   Count de Mirabeau
[De] Lafayette   [De] Mirabeau

In English or American names these particles are commonly capitalized in all positions:

William De Morgan   Lee De Forest
De Morgan   De Forest

6. Do not capitalize words made from proper nouns now having a special meaning distinct from the proper name:

antimacassar   china
pasteurize   macadam

7. Capitalize recognized geographical names:

Ohio River   Strait of Juan de Fuca
Cascade Mountains   Gulf of Mexico

8. Capitalize the following when they follow a single proper name and are written in the singular:

Butte   Gap   Peninsula
Canyon   Glacier   Plateau
County (in U.S.)   Harbor   Range
Creek   Head   River
Delta   Ocean   Valley

For example, the *Sacramento River*, but the *Tennessee and Cumberland rivers.*

9. Capitalize the following in the singular and plural when they follow a proper name:

Hill   Mountain
Island   Narrows

10. Capitalize in the singular whether placed before or after the name. Capitalize in the plural when they come before the name and sometimes following a single name:

Bay   Military Camp   Shoal
Cape   Lake   Point
Desert   Mount   Strait
Gulf   Peak   Sea
Isle   Plain   Zone

For example, *Lakes George and Champlain* but *Malheur and Goose lakes.* Contrast *Muscle Shoals.*

11. Capitalize compass directions when they designate particular regions, also the nicknames or special names for regions or districts:

East Tennessee   the South
Middle Atlantic States   the Near East
the Hub   Upper Michigan

Exceptions: Do not capitalize merely directional parts of states or countries:

eastern Washington   southern Indiana

12. Capitalize the names of streets, parks, buildings, etc.:

Forty-second Street   Central Park
Merchandise Mart   Palmolive Building

Exceptions: Do not capitalize such categories of buildings as *library, post office,* or *museum,* written without a proper name, unless local custom makes the classification equivalent to a proper name.

13. Capitalize the names of political parties, alliances, movements, classes, religious groups, etc.:

Democratic party   Royalist Spain
Labor party   Axis powers
Republicans   Soviet Russia
Protestants   Negroes

14. Capitalize divisions, departments, and offices of

government, when the official name is used. Do not capitalize incomplete or roundabout designations:

Department of Commerce
Circuit Court of Marion County
Bureau of Labor Statistics
Congress (United States)
Senate (United States)
House of Burgesses
United States Army (but army doctor)
Board of Aldermen
the council
the lower house (of Congress)
the bureau
the legislature

15. Capitalize the names of wars, battles, treaties, and important events:

Revolutionary War	Black Death
Congress of Vienna	War of 1812

Do not capitalize *war* or *treaty* when used without the distinguishing name.

16. Capitalize the numeral used with kings, dynasties, or organizations. Numerals preceding the name are ordinarily spelled out; those following the name are commonly put in Roman numerals:

Nineteenth Amendment	Third Army
Forty-eighth Congress	Henry IV

17. Capitalize titles of rank or honor, military or civil, academic degrees, decorations, etc., when written with the name, and all titles of honor or rank when used for specific persons in place of the name:

General Bradley
the Senator from Ohio (but a senator)
Nicholas Murray Butler, Doctor of Letters
the Earl of Rochester
King George
the Archbishop of Canterbury

18. Capitalization of the titles of books, plays, articles, pieces of music, and so forth is handled in two ways. The commoner method is to capitalize all main words (the nouns, verbs, adjectives, and adverbs) as well as the first word. The Library of Congress style, however, until recently called for the capitalization of only the first word and any proper nouns or adjectives appearing in the title.

The Gem of the Prairie
Mourning Becomes Electra

Titles of chapters in a book, and references to parts of a specific book, such as *Bibliography*, *Index*, or *Table of Contents*, are commonly capitalized.

In references to the names of newspapers and periodicals, an initial article need not be capitalized or treated as part of the title:

The story was reprinted in the *Reader's Digest*.

19. Capitalize the first word of a direct quotation:

An aide reported, "The left wing is being driven back in confusion."

20. Capitalize the first person singular pronoun in the nominative: I. None of the other pronouns are capitalized.

21. Capitalize personifications:

Darwin drew a picture of Nature red in tooth and claw.
The Senator talked grandly of Industry as a mother holding twin children, Labor and Capital, on her capacious lap.

22. Capitalize the various names of God or of the Christian Trinity, both nouns and adjectives, and also pronouns clearly referring to the Deity:

the Savior	the Word	Jĕhovah
the Messiah	the Son	Yahweh
the Almighty	the Virgin Mary	Holy Ghost

23. In expressions of time, A.M. and P.M. are usually set in small capitals without space between them:

9:40 A.M.	12:00 M. (noon)	6:10 P.M.
12:00 P.M. (midnight)	A.D. 1491	42 B.C.

SECTION II. CORRESPONDENCE

Every business letter performs a double function. The original carries a message to its recipient. The carbon copy, retained in the sender's files, serves as an automatic record. Since either the original or the carbon may be referred to long afterward, both must contain all the information that will then be required.

In addition to the material in the letter proper, the letter must contain the name and address of the recipient (necessary for the file copy) and the name and address of the sender (necessary for reply to the original) as well as the date of writing and often other information.

Certain more or less standardized forms have been worked out for furnishing this information briefly and with a minimum of typing effort, clearly and with an attractive appearance. Within these broad conventions each company or organization works out and employs its own preferred style for all correspondence. A newcomer can familiarize himself with an organization's house style by a few minutes' study of the correspondence files.

Most letters today are variations of the block style because it permits a stenographer to get out a maximum of work in a minimum of time. Brief descriptions of the principal variations will follow a discussion of the standard block style.

HEADING

On plain paper the heading consists of the sender's address and the date of writing. It is commonly placed so as to align with the right margin of the body of the letter, at least two inches below the top of the sheet. Each line should be started directly below the line above so as to form a block:

8096 Whiteside Drive
Detroit 16, Michigan
November 23, 1947

No punctuation is required at the end of a line.

On a letterhead the sender's address is printed and only the date need be typed in. It is placed so as to end in alignment with the right margin of the letter proper, usually about four spaces below the head but lower down if the letter is short. Sometimes the date is centered below the head.

INSIDE ADDRESS

The inside address should contain the recipient's name and full address. The state is commonly written on the same line as the city. Each line is aligned with the left margin of the letter proper. It is usually placed four spaces below the heading but a little lower if the letter is short.

In letters addressed to an individual some business organizations prefer to have the inside address appear at the end of the letter, two to four spaces below the signature. This position is also useful for personal typewritten correspondence of which a carbon is to be kept. It gets the formal information into the carbon but it avoids a formal look at the opening.

In addressing an individual with a long title the following forms are convenient:

Mr. John Jackson, Chairman
Committee on International
Commerce
Mr. John Jackson
Chairman of the Committee on
International Commerce

Frequently people are proud of a military rank, an honorary title, or a doctor's degree. They will appreciate the accurate use of rank or title. Dr. and Mr. are regular abbreviations. Abbreviations of other titles may be used, but it is more courteous to write them out in full. However, some college professors and nonmedical doctors prefer not to use the title. When the recipient's preference is known it should always be followed.

SALUTATION

Beginning at the left margin, usually two spaces below the inside address, in a letter to a single individual write Dear Sir: Dear Madam: Dear Mr. (or Mrs. or Miss) ————:. A woman whose marital status is unknown to the writer should always be addressed as Miss. In a letter to an organization, corporation, company, or group of any kind begin Gentlemen: . . . . After any of these it is conventional to use a colon.

Some letters addressed to an organization or company may be directed to the attention of a particular individual or official. This may be done as follows:

Attention of the Sales Manager (or)
Attention: Sales Manager
Attention of Mr. Wilbur M. Schwartz (or)
Attention: Mr. Wilbur M. Schwartz

The line is usually placed between the inside address and the salutation, with two spaces above and below. It is sometimes written on the same line with the salutation placed so as to end in alignment with the right-hand margin. To bring it to the immediate notice of the recipient, it is sometimes underlined. Even though the letter is directed to the attention of a single person, since it is addressed to an organization the proper salutation remains Gentlemen:.

The proper arrangement of inside address, direction of attention, and salutation is as follows:

Stamford Brass Co., Inc.
516 Little Street
Stamford 4, Connecticut
Attention: Advertising Manager
Gentlemen:

Some companies and organizations regularly indicate the subject of the letter to follow. A special place for a brief statement of the subject is provided on some letterheads. On plain paper it is usually centered on the same line as the salutation or two spaces below it:

Nonpareil Woolens
Woonsocket 2, R. I.
Gentlemen: Subject: *Insurance*

The body of the letter follows, typed in single space with double space between paragraphs. Each line begins at the left margin without indentation.

COMPLIMENTARY CLOSE

In formal business correspondence the complimentary close is limited to *Yours truly*, or variations of it such as *Very truly yours*, or, if the letter is addressed to a person of high reputation or office, *Respectfully yours*. Any of these phrases is followed by a comma.

A few conservative writers cling to the old form, now rapidly dropping out of use, in which the final sentence of the body of the letter is run into the complimentary close in the following manner:

Hoping to hear from you soon, I remain
                    Very truly yours,

The complimentary close should be set two spaces below the body of the letter. It is usually begun at the center or very slightly to the right of center.

SIGNATURE

The signature of a letter is handled in a variety of ways. If the firm name is used, it should be typed in full, two spaces below the complimentary close. Below it, or below the complimentary close if no firm name is used, space is left for the longhand signature of the writer. Below the space is typed the writer's position, often preceded by his typewritten name. It may be arranged in block or in an oblique form as the writer prefers:

(1) Yours truly,   (2) Yours truly,
    Richard Smith   Richard Smith
    Sales Manager   Sales Manager

(3) Yours truly,
    ACME MANUFACTURING COMPANY

    Richard Smith
    Sales Manager

(4) Yours truly,
    ACME MANUFACTURING COMPANY

        Richard Smith
        Sales Manager

When the writer has a personal friendship with the recipient of the letter, he need not restrict himself to the formal phrase. He is free to avail himself of any of the closing phrases of personal correspondence.

In order to identify the writer of the letter and the stenographer, it is customary to put the initials of the writer, followed by those of the stenographer, in the lower left-hand corner: RLS/J or RLS/AJ. If any enclosures are to be made, *Encl.* or *Enclosures* (3) is added directly below these initials as a reminder to the person who puts the letter in its envelope.

ADDRESS ON ENVELOPE

The address should start at or near the center. Double spacing is preferred. Arrangement may be either block or oblique. Where zone numbers are provided, they should be written after the name of the city. The Post Office prefers to have the state written on a separate line. If the address requires more than four lines, the least essential information, such as the room number in a building, should be written separately in the left-hand corner of the envelope.

SPECIAL LETTERS

Occasionally it is necessary to write to an official of the city, state, or national government, to a college president, a dignitary of the Roman Catholic Church, or the like. If the writer happens to be intimately acquainted with the recipient, he can write as he likes. Here is a list:

U. S. SENATOR
Name: The Hon. Horace Dana
Address: United States Senate, Washington, D. C.
Salutation: My dear Senator: (or, less formal)
                    Dear Mr. Dana:
Close: Yours very truly,

CONGRESSMAN
Name: The Hon. Horace Dana
Address: United States House of Representatives, Washington, D. C.
Salutation: Dear Sir: (or, less formal) **Dear Mr. Dana:**
Close: Yours very truly,

CABINET MEMBER
Name: The Secretary of the Interior
Address: Washington, D. C.
Salutation: Dear Mr. Secretary:
Close: Yours very truly,

PRESIDENT OF THE UNITED STATES
Name: The President
Address: Washington, D. C.
Salutation: Sir: (or, less formal) Dear Mr. President:
Close: Yours very truly,

GOVERNOR OF A STATE
Name: The Hon. Warren Dewey
Address: Governor's Office (or State House or Executive Mansion), state capital, state
Salutation: Dear Sir:
Close: Yours very truly,

MAYOR
Name: The Hon. Richard Farley
Address: Mayor's Office, city, state
Salutation: Dear Sir: (or, less formal) **Dear Mr. Mayor:**
Close: Yours very truly,

JUDGE
Name: The Hon. Frank Murphy
Address: United States Supreme Court, Washington, D. C.
Salutation: Dear Sir:
Close: Yours very truly,

FOREIGN AMBASSADOR
Name: His Excellency the Brazilian **Ambassador**
Address: Washington, D. C.
Salutation: Dear Mr. Ambassador:
Close: Yours very truly,

FOREIGN CONSUL
Name: The British Consul
Address: street, city, state
Salutation: Dear Mr. Consul:
Close: Yours very truly,

BISHOP
Name: The Rt. Rev. James Trenton, D. D.
Address: Bishop of Portland, Portland, Oregon
Salutation: Sir: (or) Right Reverend Bishop:
Close: Yours sincerely, or Very truly yours,
        Sincerely yours in Christ, should be used by a Catholic writer.

PARISH PRIEST
Name: The Rev. John Kelly
Address: Rector of St. —————'s Church, street and number, city, state.
Salutation: Dear Reverend Father: (or) Reverend and dear Father:
Close: Sincerely yours,   Very truly yours,

VARIATIONS IN STYLE

There are many variations of style. Stenographers should remember that no single style has any special claim to correctness and that a style different from that which they were taught in business school or which they used in a preceding job is not therefore to be condemned. Within limits, each part of the letter may be arranged to suit the preference of the writer.

Block Indented is about as much used as block. It is the same as block except that the first line of each paragraph is indented five spaces or more.

Extreme Block is an ultra-modern arrangement. Heading, inside address, salutation, complimentary close, and signature are all aligned with the left margin of the letter proper. Because the carriage of the typewriter is always thrown clear over, it is quick and easy for the typist. The extreme block is, however, open to the objection that its balance is likely to be too heavy on the left.

Oblique is a legacy of the handwritten letter. In this style the heading, the inside address, and the signature are arranged with each successive line several spaces to the right of the line above. Because this style puts a heavy burden on the stenographer and mistakes in spacing are likely to occur, the use of it has almost disappeared.

SECTION III. PREPARATION OF COPY FOR THE TYPESETTER OR PUBLISHER

GENERAL NOTES

In the event that a piece of writing is to be printed, the writer wants his manuscript in proper form before he sends it in. To prepare a manuscript so as to cause a minimum of resetting and correction, the writer must begin at a point before the final typing of the manuscript is made.

If the manuscript is to go directly to the typesetter, it will have no editing after it leaves the hands of the author. The writer should study similar publications and note details of punctuation, capitalization, the use of italics or quotes for titles, a useful arrangement of footnote material, if any, and so forth. Before the final draft is typed, he should put his manuscript in the form he has decided to adopt.

If the manuscript is to be published in a magazine or book put out by a regular publisher, he should study the publisher's preferred style and, as far as he can, make his own manuscript conform to it. He should also expect that the publisher will have his copy gone over and altered where it fails to conform to the publisher's regular style.

With the rough draft of the manuscript corrected, the final typing is the next step. *It is simple common sense always to make at least one carbon, usually two.* Many a manuscript has gone astray in the mail, or been lost or burned up in a fire. Frequently, too, the publisher or typesetter has a question that requires reference to the text, and if the writer has no text handy he is in an embarrassing position.

The final typing should be double-spaced on one side of regular 8½″ x 11″ typewriter paper. Margins should be ample, at least an inch and a half at the top and left, at least an inch at the right and bottom. A black typewriter ribbon and fresh carbon paper help to make both original and carbons easily read. Everyone who has to read and handle manuscript appreciates the use of opaque paper.

If corrections are necessary, they should be made neatly and clearly. If an addition is too long to be written clearly between the typed lines, it may be written in the margin and a guide line drawn to the point of insertion. If the corrections on any page destroy legibility, or even impair it, the page should be retyped.

FOOTNOTES AND BIBLIOGRAPHY

A writer often has to make use of the work of other men in the field. Although his combination of ideas may be new and his conclusions original, he is obliged to these earlier men for part of his material. It is no more than courtesy for him to acknowledge the obligation. It is also fair dealing with the reader to let him know the path by which the writer has come to the position he takes in his article. For both reasons the writer should acknowledge his sources.

In formal papers, theses, monographs, dissertations, articles in the learned journals, it is necessary to cite the sources for each important fact or idea in a footnote. The style of footnote varies somewhat in different fields of study and in different journals. A writer knowing that his work is to be published in a certain journal should study its style and prepare his footnotes in accordance with its practices.

In informal papers, popular books, or magazine articles, the source of an idea may be worked into the text:

> Bob Casey in *Battle Below* makes you realize that the plumbing on a submarine is not simple to handle and the beginner needs an operational chart.

In an informal article, the source may be indicated in a parenthesis in the text:

> Gertrude Stein makes Edmund Wilson uneasy (see *Axel's Castle*) because she always carries an idea to its logical—or illogical—extremity.

The writer will have little difficulty in determining what needs to be footnoted, whether the footnotes are inserted informally in the text or arranged at the bottom of the page or at the end of a chapter. Any direct quotation is the most obvious. If the quotation is from material in copyright, permission of the copyright owner must be shown. If the copyright owner prescribes a form of credit, it must be followed word for word. If not, the usual footnote form may be employed. If a summary of another writer's facts or ideas is presented, it should be acknowledged. Figures, dates, opinions, and interpretations should also be credited to their source.

In scholarly work employing a good many notes each footnote is numbered, often for a chapter, occasionally for each page. In books very lightly footnoted, a footnote may be indicated by an asterisk, a dagger, or other symbols. The reference number or symbol is placed slightly above the line at the exact spot where acknowledgment should be made.

For a book, a citation should include the author, title, place of publication, the publisher (sometimes omitted), the date of publication, the volume number (if any), and the pages cited. For an article, a citation should include the author, the title, the publication, the date, volume, and pages cited:

[1]Otto Eisenschiml and Ralph Newman, *The American Iliad* (Indianapolis: The Bobbs-Merrill Co., 1947), 472–474.

[9]W. L. Jenks, "Patrick Sinclair, Builder of Fort Mackinac," *Michigan Historical Collections,* XXXIX (Lansing, 1915), 61–85.

FOOTNOTE FORM

Footnotes are so stylized and so varied that no short summary will include all the problems that the writer may face. The most important features of the footnote can, however, be indicated. The author, not the title, comes first. The title of a book follows in italics if printed, underlined if in typescript. The title of an article in a periodical or a chapter in a book is put in quotation marks, and the title of the periodical or book is put in italics in type or underlined in typescript.

The first time a book is mentioned the facts of publication are given, the city and year (and the publisher between the city and year, if the writer prefers). The first time an article in a periodical is cited, the year is given, the volume number in Roman numerals, and the pages in Arabic numbers.

For later references to the same sources, short forms can be used. When not more than one work by the same author is being used, the author's last name and a page reference are enough:

[6]Eisenschiml and Newman, 613.

If several works by the same author are cited, the author's name and a shortened title and page reference suffice:

[3]Chateaubriand, *Atala*, 123.

When two references to the same work follow in sequence, the second may use *ibid.* (meaning *in the same place*) instead of author and shortened title.

Quoted passages are commonly quoted exactly, letter for letter and punctuation mark for punctuation mark, even down to errors and misprints. If the writer wants to disclaim responsibility for errors in the original, he can insert in brackets the Latin word *sic* (meaning *thus in the original*). If he is quoting a quotation, he can indicate the fact in a footnote and put off responsibility for the accuracy of his quotation on his actual source:

[2]John Dryden, *Mac Flecknoe*, quoted in W. H. Auden, *The Oxford Book of Light Verse* (Oxford, 1938), 195.

ABBREVIATIONS

Abbreviations in footnotes are conventional. In old books most of the abbreviations represent Latin words. Many of these are being replaced by English words.

cf. (meaning *compare*) sometimes used instead of *see.*

infra (meaning *below*) referring to something discussed later.

op. cit. (*opere citato* meaning *the work cited*).

passim (meaning *here and there, in various passages*) used for scattered references.

supra (meaning *above*) referring to something previously discussed.

vide (meaning *see*) now largely replaced by *see.*

In recent books the following abbreviations are likely to occur:

c. or *ca.* (*circa* meaning *about*) used with dates not exactly ascertainable.

ed. meaning *edited by* or *edition* (4th ed.)

f. meaning *one following page* (47 f.)

ff. meaning *following pages* (287 ff.)

n.d. meaning *no date.* This is used when the date of publication cannot be found.

n.p. meaning *no place.* This is used when the place of publication cannot be found.

p. meaning *page.*

pp. meaning *pages.* If page references are consistently indicated in Arabic numbers and volumes in Roman numerals, the words *volume* and *page* or their abbreviations can be safely omitted.

tr. meaning *translator* or *translated by.*

vol. meaning *volume* or *volumes.* See note under *pp.* above.

Several styles of punctuation are used in footnotes. No one is necessarily better than another. It is important to choose a style which can be followed consistently.

BIBLIOGRAPHY

A bibliography following a piece of writing is a convenient record for the reader of the books, articles, and other items drawn on by the writer for material. Bibliographies vary from formal listings to informal notes written in ordinary sentence form, mentioning and commenting on books and articles that might be of interest to the reader. Such notes are suitable for a popular work with a minimum of footnoting in its body. For a scholarly work a formal bibliography is required. This will supply compactly a complete list of the items drawn on for material, arranged for ready reference but not for reading.

For the informal bibliographical note, no style is prescribed. The only requirement is that each work referred to be adequately identified.

In the formal bibliography the following information should be included: author (last name first, followed by first name or initials), exact title in full, and the facts of publication, sometimes followed by a very brief criticism or characterization. As in footnotes, book titles are put in italics when printed, underlined in typescript. Titles of magazine articles, chapters of books, and the like are put in quotation marks; titles of magazines or newspapers in italics or underlined.

Styles of punctuation within each entry vary. Sometimes the three main parts are punctuated by periods, sometimes by commas. The important point is to use consistent punctuation throughout the bibliography. The name of the publisher may be left out or included between the place of publication and the date. Some typical entries follow:

Howe, Will D. *Charles Lamb and His Friends.* Indianapolis: The Bobbs-Merrill Company, 1944.

Asquith, Henry Herbert, *The Genesis of the War*, New York, 1923.

Cousins, Norman, "Bystanders Are Not Innocent," *The Saturday Review of Literature*, Aug. 2, 1947, Vol. XXX, No. 31, pp. 7–9.

Palmer, Mary B. "Experiment in Health," *Harper's Magazine*, Vol. 194 (May, 1947), 427–32.

The items of the bibliography are commonly arranged alphabetically by authors. If a book or article has no author, it may be alphabetized according to the first main word of its title. If two or more books by the same author are listed, for all those after the first a long dash can be substituted for the author's name.

PROOFREADER'S MARKS AND PROOFREADING

The common marks used by proofreaders and typesetters are listed and illustrated here. If the writer feels the slightest doubt of his ability to make clear his intention with them, he can write on the margin a brief note to the typesetter, explaining precisely what he wants done.

After a piece of writing is set in type, proofs are pulled and sent to the author for correction or approval. Usually the proofs are galleys, long sheets equal to a little more than three pages of an ordinary book. Each galley represents a heavy tray of metal at the typesetter's, and any change in the proof must be duplicated in the type itself.

When the original manuscript was set in type, the typesetter read each line of the manuscript, word for word, and transcribed it. When the corrected galleys go back to the typesetter so that the type can be made to correspond with the amended galleys, the typesetter does not read them. He looks only at the margins. Any correction not clearly marked outside the type area will be ignored. All corrections should be made in the margins and leader lines drawn to the precise spot.

PROOFREADER'S MARKS

⋏	Insert comma	⌄2	Superscript (number specified)
⌄'	Insert apostrophe		
⌄⌄	Insert quotation marks	⌃2	Subscript (number specified)
⊙	Insert period		
⊝	Insert colon	#	Insert space
;/	Insert semicolon	hr#	Hair space between letters
?/	Insert question mark	↧	Push down space
=/	Insert hyphen	⊏	Move to left
⊥/M	One-em dash	⊐	Move to right
2/m	Two-em dash	⊔	Lower
en	En dash	⊓	Elevate
⌇⌇⌇⌇	Ellipsis (If preceded by a period there will be 4 dots.)	X	Broken letter
		⌒	Ligature (A͡Esop)
		ⓈⓅ	Spell out (U.S.)
ℐ	Delete	stet	Let it stand (some day)
◡	Close up	wf	Wrong font
ℐ	Delete and close up	bf	Set in boldface type
℥	Reverse; upside-down	rom	Set in roman type
⋀	Insert (caret)	ital	Set in italic type
¶	Paragraph	sc	Small capitals
no¶	No paragraph; run in	caps	Capitals
tr	Transpose (their only is)	lc	Set in lower case
=	Align	ld>	Insert lead between lines

EXPLANATORY NOTES

Material in this dictionary has been arranged in the order considered to be the most convenient for the user. All items in the dictionary are in one alphabetical list: words of the common vocabulary, names of persons, geographical names, abbreviations, foreign words and phrases, etc.

Similarly, all information within a vocabulary entry has been arranged for the convenience of the user. In general, information about spelling and pronunciation comes first, meanings next, etymologies and synonyms last. The sequence of material in the entries is as follows:

   I. the entry word or words.
   II. the pronunciation.
   III. the parts of speech.
   IV. the inflected forms.
   V. the restrictive label.
   VI. the definition or definitions, including subentries and idiomatic phrases.
   VII. variant spellings.
   VIII. etymology.
   IX. run-on (or, undefined derivative) entries.
   X. synonym lists and studies.
   XI. antonym lists.

Abbreviations used in this dictionary have been limited as far as possible to familiar ones. All abbreviations used appear in their individual alphabetical places in the dictionary itself.

I. ENTRY WORD OR WORDS.

(A) The entry word appears in large boldface type at the left, slightly further into the left margin than the usual line of the text. (Example: **guard**)

(B) Syllables are separated by a centered dot, while entries of two or more words have open spaces between the words. (Example: **guarantee**)

(C) Syllabication is not shown in phrases unless the individual words are not separately entered.

(D) Each foreign word and phrase is always followed by a label indicating the language of the word or phrase. (Example: **anno Domini**)

(E) Separate entries are made for all words which, though spelled identically, are of completely unrelated derivation; in such cases, each entry word is followed by a small superscript number. (Example: **gum**[1] and **gum**[2])

II. PRONUNCIATION.

(A) The pronunciation follows the entry word, within parentheses. (Example: **grow**)

(B) The first pronunciation shown is, as a rule, the form in widest general use.

(C) Variations preferred in some sections of the country, in British usage, or by any other substantial group of speakers of the language are shown, usually with only the variant syllable or syllables isolated, to focus the reader's attention on the point or points of difference.

(D) Pronunciations are generally given for run-on entries, unless the pronunciation is easily ascertained from the combination of the main entry and the suffix. (Example: **guardedly**)

A full key to the pronunciation system appears inside both the front and back covers of this dictionary. In addition, for ready reference, an abbreviated pronunciation key appears at the bottom of each right-hand page.

III. PARTS OF SPEECH.

(A) The pronunciation is followed by an abbreviation in italics, indicating the part of speech of the entry word.

(B) If the entry word is used in more than one grammatical form, an italicized abbreviation indicating the part of speech precedes each set of definitions to which it refers.

IV. INFLECTED FORMS.

(A) If an entry word has irregularly inflected forms (any form not formed by the simple addition of the suffix to the main entry), the summary of these forms is given immediately after the pronunciation.

(B) If a word has variant inflected forms, these variants are shown. (Example: **grovel**)

(C) Regularly inflected forms, not generally shown, include:

   (1) Nouns forming a plural merely by the addition of *-s* or *-es*, such as *dog* (*dogs*) or *class* (*classes*);

   (2) Verbs forming the past tense by adding *-ed*, such as *halt* (*halted*);

   (3) Verbs forming the present tense by adding *-s* or *-es*, such as *talk* (*talks*) or *smash* (*smashes*);

   (4) Verbs forming the present participle by adding *-ing*, such as *walk* (*walking*).

Regular forms are given when necessary, however, for clarity, or the avoidance of confusion.

(D) In the case of inflected forms of verbs, if two forms are shown, the first represents the past tense and the past participle, while the second represents the present participle.

(E) If three inflected forms of verbs are shown, the first represents the past tense, the second the past participle, and the third the present participle.

(F) If necessary, variants of inflected forms are labeled as to level of usage or dialect distribution.

V. RESTRICTIVE LABELS.

(A) Entries that are limited in usage as to level, region time, or subject, are marked with such labels as: *Colloq.*, *Slang*, *Brit.*, *Western U. S.*, *Obs.*, *Archaic. Electronics*, *Psychiatry*, etc.

(B) If the restrictive label applies to the entire entry, it appears before the first part of speech label. (Example: **grouch**)

(C) If the restrictive label applies to only one part of speech, it appears after that part of speech label but before the definition numbers.

(D) If the restrictive label applies only to one definition, it appears after the definition number but before the definition itself. (Example: **grub**, def. 3)

VI. DEFINITIONS.

(A) Definitions are individually numbered; numbers appear in a single sequence without regard to part of speech. The central meaning of each part of speech is put first; usually this is also the commonest meaning. The usual order after the central meaning is: figurative or transferred meanings, specialized meanings, general meanings, obsolete, archaic, or rare meanings. This order, however, has been broken whenever it is desirable to group related meanings together and for other reasons.

(B) In some cases in which two definitions are very closely related, usually within the same field of information, they are marked with boldface letters of the alphabet under the same definition number.

(C) If a meaning occurs with both capitalized and lowercase forms, an indication of this is given at the beginning of the definition. (Example: **Guernsey**, def. 2)

(D) Special effort has been made to indicate unique grammatical context wherever possible. Thus, the customary prepositional forms following certain words are often shown. (Example: **gulp**, def. 2)

(E) Idiomatic phrases, etc., are often shown in secondary boldface under main entries. Such subentries are usually placed under the difficult or key word. Noun phrases, in general, have been given separate main entries. (Example: **ground**)

VII. VARIANT SPELLINGS.

Definitions always appear under the commonest spelling of a word.

(A) Less common variants merely cross-refer to the more common ones.

(B) At the end of the definitions of the most common spellings, the variants are usually shown.

(C) Variants are often labeled as to usage, either within specific fields (as *Law*) or within specific levels, regions, or times (as *Colloq.*, *Brit.*, *Archaic*, etc.).

VIII. ETYMOLOGIES.

Etymologies appear in square brackets after the definition or definitions of the entry.

A full key to the etymology appears inside both the front and back of this dictionary, and a short abbreviated key appears at the bottom of every left-hand page.

IX. RUN-ON ENTRIES.

Words which are simple derivatives of the main entry, and which present no meaning problem, are run on after the etymology, or (if there is no etymology) after the last definition in the entry. Such entries appear in secondary boldface type. They are syllabicated and pronounced (or only stressed, if no pronunciation is needed), and followed by an indication of their grammatical form.

X. SYNONYMS.

(A) Studies discriminating between synonyms appear with numbers corresponding to the definitions involved. These studies have been placed under the commonest of the synonyms under discussion, and cross references are placed under the other terms.

(B) At the end of certain entries, lists of synonyms appear, each list being preceded by a number indicating the particular definition to which that list applies. In these lists, semicolons have been used to set off clusters of words with slightly different facets of meaning within the same general definitions.

XI. ANTONYMS.

Lists of antonyms are shown throughout the book, preceded by a number indicating the definition to which the antonym list refers.

TABLE OF COMMON ENGLISH SPELLINGS

The most frequent spelling or spellings of each sound, shown in boldface italics, are related below to the phonetic symbols of the American College Dictionary (ACD) and the International Phonetic Alphabet (IPA).

ACD Symbol	IPA Symbol	Spellings	Examples
ă	æ	*a*, ai	hat, plaid
ā	eɪ, e	*a*, ai, ao, au, ay, ea, eh, ei, ey	ate, rain, gaol, gauge, ray, steak, eh, veil, obey
â	ɛ:	*a*, ai, ay, e, ea, ei	dare, chair, prayer, there, wear, their
ä	ɑ	*a*, e, ea	father, sergeant, hearth
b	b	*b*, bb	bed, hobby
ch	tʃ	*ch*, tch, te, ti, tu	chief, catch, righteous, question, natural
d	d	*d*, dd, ed	do, ladder, pulled
ĕ	ɛ	a, ae, ai, ay, *e*, ea, ei, eo, ie, oe, u	any, aesthetic, said, says, ebb, leather, heifer, leopard, friend, foetid, bury
ē	i	ae, ay, *e*, ea, *ee*, ei, eo, ey, i, ie, oe	Caesar, quay, equal, team, see, deceive, people, key, machine, field, amoeba
f	f	*f*, ff, gh, ph	feed, muffin, tough, physics
g	g	*g*, gg, gh, gu, gue	give, egg, ghost, guard, demagogue
h	h	*h*, wh	hit, who
ĭ	ɪ	e, ee, *i*, ie, o, u, ui, y	England, been, if, sieve, women, busy, build, hymn
ī	aɪ	ai, ay, ei, ey, *i*, ie, uy, y, ye	aisle, aye, height, eye, ice, tie, buy, sky, lye
j	dʒ	ch, d, dg, dge, di, g, gg, *j*	Greenwich, graduate, judgment, bridge, soldier, magic, exaggerate, just
k	k	*c*, cc, cch, ch, ck, cq, cque, cu, gh, *k*, qu	car, account, bacchanal, character, back, acquaint, sacque, biscuit, kill, liquor
l	l	*l*, ll	live, call
m	m	chm, gm, lm, *m*, mb, mm, mn	drachm, paradigm, calm, more, limb, hammer, hymn
n	n	gn, kn, *n*, nn, pn	gnat, knife, not, runner, pneumatic
ng	ŋ	n, *ng*, ngue	pink, ring, tongue
ŏ	ɒ	a, *o*	wander, box
ō	oʊ, o	au, eau, eo, ew, *o*, oa, oe, oh, oo, ou, ow	hautboy, beau, yeoman, sew, note, road, toe, oh, brooch, soul, flow
ô	ɔ	*a*, ah, al, au, aw, *o*, oa, ou	tall, Utah, talk, fault, raw, order, broad, fought
ōō	u	eu, ew, o, oe, *oo*, ou, u, ue, ui	maneuver, grew, move, canoe, ooze, troupe, rule, flue, fruit
ŏŏ	ʊ	o, *oo*, ou, *u*	wolf, look, should, pull
oi	ɔɪ	*oi*, oy	oil, toy
ou	aʊ	*ou*, ough, *ow*	out, bough, brow
p	p	*p*, pp	pen, stopper
r	r	*r*, rh, rr	red, rhythm, carrot
s	s	c, ce, *s*, sc, sch, ss	city, mice, see, scene, schism, loss
sh	ʃ	ce, ch, ci, psh, s, sch, sci, se, *sh*, si, ss, ssi, ti	ocean, machine, special, pshaw, sugar, schist, conscience, nauseous, ship, mansion, tissue, mission, mention
t	t	ed, ght, *t*, th, tt	talked, bought, toe, thyme, bottom
th	θ	th	thin
ŧħ	ð	th, the	then, bathe
ŭ	ʌ	o, oe, oo, ou, *u*	son, does, flood, couple, cup
ū	ju, ɪu	eau, eu, eue, ew, ieu, iew, *u*, ue, ui, yu, yew, you	beauty, feud, queue, few, adieu, view, use, cue, suit, yule, yew, you
ûr	ɜr, ɜ	*er*, ear, ir, or, our, *ur*, yr	term, learn, thirst, worm, courage, hurt, myrtle
v	v	f, ph, *v*, vv	of, Stephen, visit, flivver
w	w	o, u, *w*	choir, quiet, well
y	j	g, i, j, *y*	lorgnette, union, hallelujah, yet
z	z	s, sc, ss, x, *z*, zz	has, discern, scissors, Xerxes, zone, dazzle
zh	ʒ	g, s, *si*, z, zi	garage, measure, division, azure, brazier
ə	ə	*a*, ai, *e*, ei, eo, *i*, ia, *o*, oi, ou, *u*	alone, mountain, system, mullein, dungeon, easily, parliament, gallop, porpoise, curious, circus
ər	ər, ɚ	ar, *er*, ir, or, our, ur, yr	liar, father, elixir, labor, labour, augur, martyr

A DICTIONARY
OF THE
ENGLISH LANGUAGE

A

A, a (ā), *n., pl.* **A's** or **As, a's** or **as. 1.** the first letter of the English alphabet. **2.** *U.S.* the highest mark for school or college work. **3.** *Music.* **a.** the sixth tone in the scale of C major, or the first in the relative minor scale of A minor. **b.** a written or printed note indicating this tone. **c.** a string, key, or pipe tuned to this note. **d.** (in the fixed system of solmization) the sixth tone of the scale, called **la. 4. from A to Z,** from beginning to end.

a¹ (ā; *unstressed* ə), *adj. or indef. article.* a doublet of **an** used before words beginning with consonant sounds to mean: **1.** some (indefinite singular referring to one individual of a class): *a man, a house, a star.* **2.** another: *he is a Cicero in eloquence.* **3.** one: *two of a kind, a thousand.* **4.** any (a single): *not a one.* **5.** indefinite plural: *a few, a great many.* [ME, phonetic var. of AN]

a² (ā; *unstressed* ə), *adj. or indef. article.* each; every: *three times a day.* [orig. *a*, prep., OE *an, on,* confused with the indefinite article. See A-¹]

a³ (ə), *prep. Colloq. or Dial.* of: *cloth a gold.* [OE *of* of]

a', (ä, ô), *adj. Scot.* all: *for a' that.* Also, **a.**

a-¹, a reduced form of Old English prep. *on,* meaning "on," "in," "into," "to," "towards," preserved before a noun in a prepositional phrase, forming a predicate adjective or an adverbial element, as in *afoot, abed, ashore, apart, aside,* and in archaic and dialectal use before a present participle in *-ing,* as in *to set the bells aringing.* [ME and late OE *a-,* var. of OE *an, on* at, on. See ON]

a-², a reduced form of Old English *of,* as in *akin, afresh, anew.* [ME *a-,* OE *of* (prep.) off, of]

a-³, an old point-action prefix, not referring to an act as a whole, but only to the beginning or end: *she awoke* (became awake), *they abided by these conclusions* (remained faithful to the end). [OE *ā-;* in some cases confused with OF *a-* (g. L *ad-* AD-) and erroneously refashioned after supposed L analogies, as in *a(l)lay*]

a-⁴, var. of ab- before *m, p* and *v,* as in *amove, aperient, avert.* [ME *a-,* t. F, g. L *ab-;* or t. L, reduced form of *ab-.* See AB-]

a-⁵, var. of ad-, used: (1) before *sc, sp, st* as in *ascend.* (2) in words of French derivation (often with the sense of increase, addition), as in *amass.* [ME *a-,* t. F, g. L *ad-,* or assimilated forms of *ad-,* such as *ab-, ac-, af-,* etc.; or t. L, reduced form of *ad-* AD-]

a-⁶, var. of an-¹ before consonants, as in *achromatic.* [t. Gk., called alpha privative, before vowels *an-;* akin to L *in-* not, E UN-¹]

A, 1. *Chem.* argon. **2.** *Physics.* angstrom unit.

a., 1. about. **2.** acre; acres. **3.** adjective. **4.** *Baseball.* assists.

A-1, A one.

AAA, *U.S.* **1.** Agricultural Adjustment Administration. **2.** Anti-aircraft Artillery.

A.A.A.L., American Academy of Arts and Letters.

A.A.A.S., American Association for the Advancement of Science.

Aa·chen (ä'kən: *Ger.* ä'кнən). *n.* a city in western Germany: taken by U.S. forces, Oct., 1944. 162,164 (1939). French, **Aix-la-Chapelle.**

AAF, *U.S.* Army Air Forces.

Aal·borg (ôl'bôr), *n.* a seaport in N Denmark. 81,084 (1945).

Aalst (älst), *n.* Flemish name of Alost.

aard·vark (ärd'värk'), *n.* a large, nocturnal, burrowing mammal of Africa, subsisting largely on termites, and having a long, extensile tongue, claws, and conspicuously long ears. There is only one genus, *Oryc-*

Aardvark, *Orycteropus afer*
(Overall length 5 to 6 ft.;
tail 2 to 2½ ft.)

teropus, constituting a separate order, *Tubulidentata.* [t. S Afr. D, f. m. *aarde* earth + *vark* pig]

aard·wolf (ärd'woolf'), *n.* a striped, hyenalike African mammal, *Protoles cristatus,* that feeds largely on insects. [t. S Afr. D, f. m. *aarde* earth + *wolf* wolf]

Aar·hus (ôr'hōōs'), *n.* a seaport in Denmark, in E Jutland. 137,722 (1945).

Aar·on (âr'ən), *n.* the first high priest of the Hebrews and the brother of Moses. Exodus 4:14.

Aar·on·ic (â rŏn'ĭk), *adj.* **1.** pertaining to Aaron. **2.** pertaining or belonging to the Jewish priestly order. **3.** levitical; ecclesiastical. **4.** of the second or lesser order of priesthood among the Mormons. Also, **Aa·ron'-i·cal** (esp. def. 3).

A.A.U.P., American Association of University Professors.

Ab (äb, ăb), *n.* (in the Jewish calendar) the eleventh month of the year.

ab-, a prefix meaning "off," "away," "from," as in *abduct, abjure.* Also, **abs-, a-⁴.** [t. L, repr. *ab,* prep., from, away; akin to Gk. *apó,* Skt. *ápa* from]

Ab, *Chem.* alabamine.

ab., 1. about. **2.** *Baseball.* (times) at bat.

A.B., 1. (L *Artium Baccalaureus*) Bachelor of Arts. **2.** able-bodied (seaman).

a·ba (ä'bə), *n.* a sleeveless outer garment, worn by Arabs. [t. Ar.: m. *'ubā'a*]

a·ba·ca (ä/bä kä/), *n.* **1.** a Philippine plant, *Musa textilis.* **2.** the fiber of this plant, used in making hemp.

a·back (ə băk'), *adv.* **1. taken aback, a.** suddenly disconcerted. **b.** (of a ship) caught by the wind so as to press the sails back against the mast. **c.** (of sails) caught by a wind on the forward surface. **2.** with the wind blowing against the forward side of a sail or sails, instead of the after side. **3.** back against the mast, as sails, or with sails so placed. **4.** toward the back. [ME *abak,* OE *on,* prep., + *bæc* on or to the back]

ab·a·cus (ăb'ə kəs), *n., pl.* **-cuses, -ci** (-sī'). **1.** a contrivance for calculating, consisting of beads or balls strung on wires or rods set in a frame. **2.** *Archit.* a slab forming the top of the capital of a column. See diag. under **column.** [t. L, t. Gk.: m. *ábax*]

Chinese abacus:
(Each vertical column = one
integer: each bead in group A
= 5 when lowered; each bead
in group B = 1 when raised;
value of this setting is
203,691,500)

A·bad·don (ə băd'ən), *n.* **1.** the place of destruction; the depth of hell. **2.** Apollyon. Rev. 9:11. [Heb.: destruction]

a·baft (ə băft', ə bäft'), *Naut.* —*prep.* **1.** in the rear of; behind. —*adv.* **2.** at or toward the stern; aft. [ME, f. A-¹ + *baft,* OE *bæftan, be æftan.* See BY, AFT]

ab·a·lo·ne (ăb/ə lō'nĭ), *n.* a large snail of the genus *Haliotis* having a bowllike shell bearing a row of respiratory holes. The flesh is used for food and the shell for ornament and mother-of-pearl objects. [t. Sp.]

a·ban·don¹ (ə băn'dən), *v.t.* **1.** to leave completely and finally; forsake utterly: *to abandon one's home.* **2.** to give up all concern in: *to abandon the cares of empire.* **3.** to give up the control of: *to abandon a city to a conqueror.* **4.** to yield (oneself) unrestrainedly: *to abandon oneself to grief.* **5.** *Law.* to cast away or leave (one's property) with no intention to reclaim it, thereby making the property available for appropriation by any person. **6.** to relinquish (insured property) to the underwriter in case of partial loss, thus enabling the insured to claim a total loss. **7.** *Obs.* to banish. [ME *abandone(n),* t. OF: m. *abandoner,* der. phrase *a bandon* under one's jurisdiction] —**a·ban'don·er,** *n.* —**a·ban'don·ment,** *n.* —**Syn. 2.** ABANDON, RELINQUISH, RENOUNCE mean to give up all concern in something. ABANDON means to give up (or

---

ăct, āble, dâre, ärt; ĕbb, ēqual; ĭf, īce; hŏt, ōver, ôrder, oil, bŏok, ōōze, out; ŭp, ūse, ûrge; ə = a in alone; ch, chief; g, give; ng, ring; sh, shoe; th, thin; ŧħ, that; zh, vision. See the full key on inside cover. b., blend of, blended; c., cognate with; d., dialect, dialectal; der., derived from; f., formed from; g., going back to; m., modification of; r., replacing; s., stem of; t., taken from; ?, perhaps. See the full key on inside cover.

discontinue any further) interest in something, because of discouragement, weariness, distaste, or the like: *to abandon one's efforts.* RELINQUISH implies being (or feeling) compelled to give up something one would prefer to keep: *to relinquish a long-cherished desire.* RENOUNCE implies making (and perhaps formally stating) a voluntary decision to give something up: *to renounce worldly pleasures.* See also desert[2]. 3. give up, yield, surrender, resign, waive, abdicate —Ant. 3. keep.

a·ban·don[2] (ə băn′dən; *Fr.* à bäṉ dôṉ′), *n.* a giving up to natural impulses; freedom from constraint or conventionality: *to do something with abandon.* [t. F]

a·ban·doned (ə băn′dənd), *adj.* 1. forsaken. 2. unrestrained. 3. shamelessly and recklessly wicked. —Syn. 3. See immoral.

à bas (à bä′), *French.* down with (the person or thing named)!

a·base (ə bās′), *v.t.*, abased, abasing. 1. to reduce or lower, as in rank, office, estimation; humble; degrade. 2. *Archaic.* to lower; bring down. [b. BASE[2] and ME *abesse*(n) (t. OF: m. *abaissier,* f. a- A-[5]+ *baissier* lower, ult. der. LL *bassus* low)] —a·base′ment, *n.* —a·bas′er, *n.*

a·bash (ə băsh′), *v.t.* to destroy the self-possession of; make ashamed or embarrassed: *stand or feel abashed.* [ME *abashe*(n), t. AF: m. *abaïss-,* var. of OF *esbaïss-,* s. *esbaïr* astonish] —a·bash′ment, *n.*

a·bate (ə bāt′), *v.,* abated, abating. —*v.t.* 1. to reduce in amount, intensity, etc.; lessen; diminish: *to abate a tax, one's enthusiasm, etc.* 2. *Law.* to put an end to or suppress (a nuisance); suspend or extinguish (an action); annul (a writ). 3. to deduct or subtract. 4. to omit. —*v.i.* 5. to decrease or become less in strength or violence: *the storm has abated.* 6. *Obs. except Law.* to fail; become void. [ME *abate*(n), t. OF: m. *abatre,* f. a- A-[5]+ *batre* beat] —a·bat′a·ble, *adj.* —a·bat′er, *Law.* a·ba′tor, *n.* —Ant.5. increase, intensify.

a·bate·ment (ə bāt′mənt), *n.* 1. alleviation; mitigation. 2. suppression or termination: *abatement of a nuisance.* 3. *Law.* a. a wrongful entry on land made by a stranger, after the owner's death and before the owner's heir or devisee has obtained possession. b. a decrease in the legacies of a will when the assets of an estate are insufficient to pay all general legacies in full.

ab·a·tis (ăb′ə tĭs; *Mil.* ăb′ə tē′), *n.* an obstacle of trees with bent or sharpened branches directed toward the enemy, and now often interlaced with barbed wire. [t. F; akin to ABATE]

ab·at·toir (ăb′ə twär′), *n.* a slaughterhouse. [t. F]

ab·ax·i·al (ăb ăk′sĭ əl), *adj.* away from the axis: *the abaxial surface of a leaf.* [t. AB- + L *axi*(s) axle + -AL[1]]

ab·ba·cy (ăb′ə sĭ), *n., pl.* -cies. 1. an abbot's office, rights, privileges, or jurisdiction. 2. the period of office of an abbot. [var. of ME *abbatie,* t. LL: m. *abbātia*]

Ab·bas·side (ə băs′īd, ăb′ə sīd′), *n.* a caliph of the dynasty which ruled at Bagdad, A.D. 750 to 1258, claiming descent from Abbas, uncle of Mohammed.

ab·ba·tial (ə bā′shəl), *adj.* of or pertaining to an abbot, abbess, or abbey. [t. LL: s. *abbātiālis*]

ab·bé (ăb′ā; *Fr.* à bĕ′), *n.* (esp. in France) 1. an abbot. 2. any ecclesiastic, esp. one who has no other title. [F]

ab·bess (ăb′ĭs), *n.* the female superior of a convent, regularly in the same religious orders in which monks are governed by an abbot. [ME *abbesse,* t. OF, s. LL *abbātissa*]

ab·bey (ăb′ĭ), *n., pl.* -beys. 1. the religious body or establishment under an abbot or abbess; a monastery or convent. 2. the monastic buildings. 3. the church of an abbey. 4. the Abbey, *Brit.* Westminster Abbey. 5. *Brit.* a country residence that was formerly an abbatial house: *Newstead Abbey.* [ME *abbeye,* t. OF: m. *abaie,* g. LL *abbātia*]

Abbey Theatre, a theater in Dublin associated with the Irish National Theatre Society (founded 1901) and the dramas of Synge, Yeats, and Lady Gregory.

ab·bot (ăb′ət), *n.* the head or superior of a monastery. [ME, var. of ME and OE *abbad,* t. LL: m.s. *abbās,* t. LGk., t. Aram.: m. *abbā* father] —ab′bot·ship′, *n.*

Ab·bot (ăb′ət), *n.* Charles Greeley, born 1872, U.S. astrophysicist.

Ab·bots·ford (ăb′əts fərd), *n.* Sir Walter Scott's residence from 1812 to 1832, near Melrose, in SE Scotland.

abbr., abbreviation. Also, abbrev.

ab·bre·vi·ate (ə brē′vĭ āt′), *v.t.,* -ated, -ating. to make briefer; make shorter by contraction or omission: *to abbreviate "foot" to "ft."* [t. L: m.s. *abbreviātus,* pp.] —ab·bre′vi·a′tor, *n.* —Syn. See shorten.

ab·bre·vi·a·tion (ə brē′vĭ ā′shən), *n.* 1. a shortened or contracted form of a word or phrase, used as a symbol for the whole. 2. reduction in length; abridgment. 3. *Music.* any of several signs or symbols used to abbreviate musical notation, as those indicating the repetition of a phrase or a note. [t. L: s. *abbreviātio*]

ABC (ā′bē′sē′), *n.* 1. the main or the basic facts, principles, etc. (of any subject). 2. ABC's.

ABC's (ā′bē′sēz′), *n.pl.* the alphabet.

Abd-el Krim (ăb′dĕl krēm′), *n.* born c1883, Riff leader of a native revolt in Morocco, 1921–26.

Ab·di·as (ăb dī′əs), *n.* (in the Douay Bible) Obadiah.

ab·di·cate (ăb′də kāt′), *v.,* -cated, -cating. —*v.i.* 1. to renounce a throne or some claim; relinquish a right, power, or trust. —*v.t.* 2. to give up or renounce (office, duties, authority, etc.), esp. in a voluntary, public, or formal manner. [t. L: m.s. *abdicātus,* pp.] —ab·di·ca-

ble (ăb′də kə bəl), *adj.* —ab′di·ca′tive, *adj.* —ab′di·ca′tor, *n.*

ab·di·ca·tion (ăb′də kā′shən), *n.* act of abdicating; renunciation, esp. of sovereign power.

ab·do·men (ăb′də mən, ăb dō′-), *n.* 1. that part of the body of a mammal between the thorax and the pelvis; the visceral cavity containing most of the digestive organs; the belly. 2. (in vertebrates below mammals) a region of the body corresponding to but not coincident with the human abdomen. 3. *Entomol.* the posterior section of the body of an arthropod, behind the thorax or the cephalothorax. See diag. under insect. [t. L]

ab·dom·i·nal (ăb dŏm′ə nəl), *adj.* of, in, or on the abdomen: *abdominal muscles.* —ab·dom′i·nal·ly, *adv.*

ab·dom·i·nous (ăb dŏm′ə nəs), *adj.* potbellied.

ab·duce (ăb dūs′, -dōōs′), *v.t.,* -duced, -ducing. *Physiol.* to draw away or aside, as by the action of a muscle. [t. L: m.s. *abdūcere*]

ab·du·cent (ăb dū′sənt, -dōō′-), *adj.* *Physiol.* drawing away (applied to muscles, etc.).

ab·duct (ăb dŭkt′), *v.t.* 1. to carry off surreptitiously or by force, esp. to kidnap. 2. *Physiol.* to draw away from the original position (opposed to *adduct*). [t. L: s. *abductus,* pp.] —ab·duc′tion, *n.* —ab·duc′tor, *n.*

Ab·dul-Ha·mid II (ăb′dōōl hä mēd′). 1842–1918, sultan of Turkey, 1876–1909.

a·beam (ə bēm′), *adv.* *Naut.* at right angles to the keel of a ship; directly opposite the middle part of a ship.

a·be·ce·dar·i·an (ā′bĭ′sĭ dâr′ĭ ən), *n.* 1. a pupil who is learning the letters of the alphabet. 2. a beginner. —*adj.* 3. alphabetical. 4. primary; rudimentary. [f. s. ML *abecedārius* ABCD book + -AN]

a·be·ce·da·ry (ā′bĭ sē′də rĭ), *n., pl.* -ries. *adj.* abecedarian.

a·bed (ə bĕd′), *adv.* 1. in bed. 2. confined to bed.

A·bed·ne·go (ə bĕd′nĭ gō′), *n.* See Shadrach.

A·bel (ā′bəl), *n.* *Bible.* the second son of Adam and Eve, slain by his brother, Cain. Gen. 4.

Ab·é·lard (ăb′ə lärd′; *Fr.* à bĕ lär′), *n.* Pierre (pyĕr), (*Peter Abelard*) 1079–1142, French scholastic philosopher, teacher, and theologian. His love affair with Héloïse is one of the famous romances of history.

a·bele (ə bēl′, ā′bəl), *n.* the white poplar tree, *Populus alba.* [t. D: m. *abeel,* t. OF: m. *abel,* g. LL *albellus,* dim. of L *albus* white]

a·bel·mosk (ā′bəl mŏsk′), *n.* a malvaceous plant, *Hibiscus Abelmoschus,* of warm countries, cultivated for its musky seed, which is used in perfumery, etc. [t. NL: m. s. *Abelmoschus,* t. Ar.: m. *ḥabb el-mosk* grain of musk]

Ab·er·deen (ăb′ər dēn′), *n.* 1. Also, Ab·er·deen·shire (ăb′ər dēn′shĭr, -shər). a county in NE Scotland. 320,200 pop. (est. 1946); 1974 sq. mi. 2. its county seat: a seaport. 178,200 (est. 1946). 3. a seaport in W Washington. 19,653 (1950). 4. a city in NE South Dakota. 21,051 (1950). —Ab·er·do·ni·an (ăb′ər dō′nĭ ən), *adj., n.*

Aberdeen An·gus (ăng′gəs), one of a breed of hornless beef cattle with smooth black hair, originally bred in Scotland.

A·ber·glau·be (ä′bər glou′bə), *n.* *German.* belief beyond what is justified by experience and knowledge.

ab·er·rant (ăb ĕr′ənt), *adj.* 1. straying from the right or usual course. 2. deviating from the ordinary or normal type. [t. L: s. *aberrans,* ppr.] —ab·er′rance, ab·er′ran·cy, *n.*

ab·er·ra·tion (ăb′ə rā′shən), *n.* 1. act of wandering from the usual way or normal course. 2. deviation from truth or moral rectitude. 3. lapse from a sound mental state. 4. *Astron.* apparent displacement of a heavenly body, due to the joint effect of the motion of the rays of light proceeding from it and the motion of the earth. 5. *Optics.* any disturbance of the rays of a pencil of light such that they can no longer be brought to a sharp focus or form a clear image. [t. L: s. *aberrātio*]

a·bet (ə bĕt′), *v.t.,* abetted, abetting. to encourage or countenance (to aid or approval (used chiefly in a bad sense): *to abet evildoers, to abet a crime or offense.* [ME *abbette*(n), t. OF: m. *abeter,* f. a- A-[5] + *beter* (t. Scand.; cf. Icel. *beita* cause to bite. See BAIT)] —a·bet′ment, *n.*

a·bet·tor (ə bĕt′ər), *n.* one who abets. Also, a·bet′ter.

ab ex·tra (ăb ĕk′strə), *Latin.* from the outside.

a·bey·ance (ə bā′əns), *n.* 1. temporary inactivity or suspension. 2. a state of waiting for the ascertainment of the person entitled to ownership: *an estate in abeyance.* [t. AF: m. *abeiance* expectation, der. OF *abeer* gape after, f. a- A-[5] + *baer* gape, g. LL *badāre*]

a·bey·ant (ə bā′ənt), *adj.* in abeyance.

ab·hor (ăb hôr′), *v.t.,* -horred, -horring. to regard with repugnance; loathe or abominate. [late ME, t. L: m. s. *abhorrēre*] —ab·hor′rer, *n.* —Syn. See hate.

ab·hor·rence (ăb hŏr′əns, -hôr′-), *n.* 1. a feeling of extreme aversion. 2. something detested.

ab·hor·rent (ăb hŏr′ənt, -hôr′-), *adj.* 1. feeling horror (fol. by *of*): *abhorrent of excess.* 2. utterly opposed (fol. by *to*): *abhorrent to reason.* 3. exciting horror; detestable. 4. remote in character (fol. by *from*): *abhorrent from the principles of law.* —ab·hor′rent·ly, *adv.*

a·bid·ance (ə bī′dəns), *n.* 1. act of abiding. 2. conformity (fol. by *by*): *abidance by rules.*

a·bide (ə bīd′), *v.,* abode or abided, abiding. —*v.i.* 1. to remain; continue; stay: *abide with me.* 2. to dwell; reside. 3. to continue in a certain condition; remain steadfast or faithful. **4. abide by, a.** to stand by: *to abide by a friend.* **b.** to await or accept the consequences of: *to abide by the event.* —*v.t.* **5.** to wait for. **6.** to stand one's ground against; await or sustain defiantly. **7.** *Colloq.* to put up with; tolerate: *I can't abide such people.* **8.** to pay the price or penalty of; suffer for. [ME *abide(n)*, OE *ābīdan.* See A-³. In def. 8 confused with ABY] —**a·bid′er,** *n.*

a·bid·ing (ə bī′dĭng), *adj.* continuing; steadfast: *an abiding faith.* —**a·bid′ing·ly,** *adv.* —**a·bid′ing·ness,** *n.*

ab·i·et·ic acid (ăb′ĭ ĕt′ĭk), a yellow crystalline acid, $C_{19}H_{29}COOH$, derived from the resin of a species of pine, used in driers, varnishes, and soaps. [f. s. L *abiēs* fir + -IC + ACID]

ab·i·gail (ăb′ə gāl′), *n.* a lady's maid. [from *Abigail*, the "waiting gentlewoman," in Beaumont and Fletcher's *The Scornful Lady.* See also 1 Sam. 25:23–42]

Ab·i·lene (ăb′ə lēn′), *n.* a city in central Texas. 45,570 (1950).

a·bil·i·ty (ə bĭl′ə tĭ), *n.*, *pl.* **-ties. 1.** power or capacity to do or act in any relation. **2.** competence in any occupation or field of action, from the possession of capacity, skill, means, or other qualification. **3.** (*pl.*) talents; mental gifts or endowments. [ME *(h)abilite*, t. F, t. L: m.s. *habilitas*; r. ME *ablete*, t. OF] —**Syn. 1.** capability; proficiency, expertness, dexterity. **2.** ABILITY, FACULTY, TALENT denote mental qualifications or powers. ABILITY is a general word for mental power, native or acquired, enabling one to do things well: *a person of great ability, ability in mathematics.* FACULTY denotes a natural ability for a particular kind of action: *a faculty of saying what he means.* TALENT is often used to mean a native ability or aptitude in a special field: *a talent for music or art.*

ab in·i·ti·o (ăb ĭ nĭsh′ĭ ō′), *Latin.* from the beginning.

ab in·tra (ăb ĭn′trə), *Latin.* from inside; from within.

ab·i·o·gen·e·sis (ăb′ĭ ō jĕn′ə sĭs), *n. Biol.* the (hypothetical) production of living things from inanimate matter; spontaneous generation. [f. A-⁶ + BIO- + GENESIS] —**ab·i·og·e·nist** (ăb′ĭ ŏj′ə nĭst), *n.*

ab·i·o·gen·et·ic (ăb′ĭ ō jə nĕt′ĭk), *adj. Biol.* of or pertaining to abiogenesis. —**ab·i·o·ge·net′i·cal·ly,** *adv.*

ab·ir·ri·tant (ăb ĭr′ə tənt), *Pathol.* —*n.* **1.** a soothing agent. —*adj.* **2.** allaying irritability.

ab·ir·ri·tate (ăb ĭr′ə tāt′), *v.t.,* **-tated, -tating.** *Med.* to make less irritable. —**ab·ir′ri·ta′tion,** *n.*

ab·ject (ăb′jĕkt, ăb jĕkt′), *adj.* **1.** utterly humiliating or disheartening: *abject poverty.* **2.** contemptible; despicable: *an abject liar.* **3.** *Obs.* cast aside. [ME, t. L: s. *abjectus*, pp., thrown away] —**ab·jec′tion,** *n.* —**ab·ject·ly** (ăb jĕkt′lĭ, ăb′jĕkt lĭ), *adv.* —**ab·ject′ness,** *n.*

ab·ju·ra·tion (ăb′jŏŏ rā′shən), *n.* act of abjuring; renunciation upon oath.

ab·jure (ăb jŏŏr′), *v.t.,* **-jured, -juring. 1.** to renounce or repudiate; retract, esp. with solemnity: *to abjure one's errors.* **2.** to renounce upon oath; forswear: *to abjure allegiance.* [t. L: m.s. *abjurāre*] —**ab·jur′a·to·ry,** *adj.* —**ab·jur′er,** *n.*

Ab·kha·zi·a (ăb hä′sĭ ä′), *n.* an autonomous republic in the SW Soviet Union, on the E coast of the Black Sea. 200,500 pop. (1926); 3360 sq. mi. *Cap.:* Sukhum. Also, **Ab·kha′si·a.**

abl., ablative.

ab·lac·tate (ăb lăk′tāt), *v.t.,* **-tated, -tating.** to wean. [t. L: m. s. *ablactātus*, pp.] —**ab′lac·ta′tion,** *n.*

ab·la·tion (ăb lā′shən), *n.* removal, esp. of organs, abnormal growths, or harmful substances, from the body by mechanical means, as by surgery. [t. L: s. *ablātio* a carrying away]

ab·la·tive (ăb′lə tĭv), *Gram.* —*adj.* **1.** (in some inflected languages) denoting a case which has among its functions the indication of place from which, place in which, manner, means, instrument, agent, etc. —*n.* **2.** the ablative case. **3.** a word in that case, as *Troiā* in Latin *Æneas came from Troiā.* "Aeneas came from Troy." [t. L: m. s. *ablātivus* of removal; r. late ME *ablatif*, t. F]

ablative absolute, (in Latin grammar) a construction not dependent upon any other part of the sentence, consisting of a noun and a participle, noun and adjective, or two nouns, in which both members are in the ablative case, as Latin *viā factā,* "the road having been made."

ab·laut (ăb′lout, ăb′-; *Ger.* äp′lout), *n. Gram.* **1.** regular change in the internal structure of roots, particularly in the vowel, showing alteration in function and meaning. **2.** such change in Indo-European languages, as in English *sing, sang, sung, song;* gradation. [t. G: f. *ab* off + *laut* sound]

a·blaze (ə blāz′), *adv.* **1.** on fire. —*adj.* **2.** gleaming. **3.** excited; eagerly desirous. **4.** very angry.

a·ble (ā′bəl), *adj.,* **abler, ablest. 1.** having sufficient power, strength, or qualifications; qualified: *a man able to perform military service.* **2.** having unusual intellectual qualifications: *an able minister.* **3.** showing talent or knowledge: *an able speech.* [ME, t. OF, g. L *habilis* easy to handle, fit] —**Syn. 1.** ABLE, CAPABLE, COMPETENT all mean possessing adequate power for doing something. ABLE implies power equal to effort required: *able to finish in time.* CAPABLE implies power to meet or fulfill ordinary, usual requirements: *a capable workman.* COMPETENT suggests power to meet demands in a completely satisfactory manner: *a competent nurse.* **2.** talented, accomplished, gifted; skilled, clever.

-able, a suffix used to form adjectives, esp. from verbs,

to denote ability, liability, tendency, worthiness, or likelihood, as in *teachable, perishable, obtainable,* but also attached to other parts of speech (esp. nouns) as in *objectionable, peaceable,* and even verb phrases, as in *come-at-able.* Many of these adjectives, such as *durable, tolerable,* have been borrowed directly from Latin or French, in which language they were already compounded. However, **-able** is attached freely (now usually with passive force) to stems of any origin. Also, **-ble, -ible.** [ME, t. OF, g. s. L *-ābilis*]

a·ble-bod·ied (ā′bəl bŏd′ĭd), *adj.* physically competent.

able-bodied seaman, an experienced seaman who has passed certain tests in the practice of seamanship.

ab·le·gate (ăb′lĭ gāt′), *n.* a papal envoy to a newly appointed dignitary.

a·blins (ā′blĭnz), *adv. Scot.* perhaps. Also, **aiblins.**

a·bloom (ə blōōm′), *adv., adj.* in blossom.

ab·lu·ent (ăb′lōō ənt), *adj.* **1.** cleansing. —*n.* **2.** a cleansing agent; a detergent. [t. L: m.s. *abluens*, ppr.]

ab·lu·tion (ăb lōō′shən), *n.* **1.** a cleansing with water or other liquid, as in ceremonial purification. **2.** the liquid used. [ME, t. L: s. *ablūtio*] —**ab·lu′tion·ar·y,** *adj.*

a·bly (ā′blĭ), *adv.* in an able manner; competently.

ab·ne·gate (ăb′nə gāt′), *v.t.,* **-gated, -gating.** to refuse or deny to oneself; reject; renounce. [t. L: m.s. *abnegātus*, pp.] —**ab′ne·ga′tion,** *n.* —**ab′ne·ga′tor,** *n.*

ab·nor·mal (ăb nôr′məl), *adj.* not conforming to rule; deviating from the type or standard. [f. s. L *abnormis* irregular + -AL¹; r. *anormal*, t. F, t. ML: s. *anormalus*, for L *anōmalus,* t. Gk.: m. *anōmalos.* See ANOMALOUS] —**ab·nor′mal·ly,** *adv.* —**Syn.** anomalous, aberrant, peculiar; exceptional, unusual; odd. See **irregular.**

ab·nor·mal·i·ty (ăb′nôr măl′ə tĭ), *n., pl.* **-ties. 1.** an abnormal thing, happening, or feature. **2.** deviation from the standard, rule, or type; irregularity.

abnormal psychology, the study of mental phenomena, behavior patterns, etc., of individuals who deviate widely from the average.

ab·nor·mi·ty (ăb nôr′mə tĭ), *n., pl.* **-ties. 1.** abnormality; irregularity. **2.** malformation; monstrosity.

Å·bo (ō′bōō), *n.* Swedish name of **Turku.**

a·board (ə bōrd′), *adv.* **1.** on board; on or in a ship, railroad car, etc. (in England applied esp. to ships, but in the U.S. also applied to railroad cars, buses, etc.). **2.** alongside. —*prep.* **3.** on board of.

a·bode (ə bōd′), *n.* **1.** a dwelling place; a habitation. **2.** continuance in a place; sojourn; stay. —*v.* **3.** pt. and pp. of **abide.** [ME *abood,* OE *ābād,* p.t. of *ābīdan* ABIDE]

a·bol·ish (ə bŏl′ĭsh), *v.t.* to do away with; put an end to; annul or make void; destroy: *to abolish slavery.* [t. F: m. *aboliss-,* s. *abolir* make perish, g. s. L *abolescere* perish] —**a·bol′ish·a·ble,** *adj.* —**a·bol′ish·er,** *n.* —**a·bol′ish·ment,** *n.* —**Syn.** suppress; annihilate; exterminate. ABOLISH, ERADICATE, STAMP OUT mean to do away completely with something. To ABOLISH is to cause to cease, often by a summary order: *to abolish a requirement.* STAMP OUT, stronger though less formal, implies forcibly making an end to something considered undesirable or harmful: *to stamp out the opium traffic.* ERADICATE (literally, to tear out by the roots), a formal word, suggests extirpation, leaving no vestige or trace: *to eradicate the dandelions in the lawn.*

ab·o·li·tion (ăb′ə lĭsh′ən), *n.* **1.** utter destruction; annulment; abrogation: *the abolition of laws, customs, debts,* etc. **2.** the legal extinction of Negro slavery. [t. L: s. *abolitio*] —**ab′o·li·tion·ar·y,** *adj.* —**ab′o·li·tion·ist,** *n.*

ab·o·li·tion·ism (ăb′ə lĭsh′ən ĭz′əm), *n.* the principle or policy of abolition, esp. of Negro slavery.

ab·o·ma·sum (ăb′ə mā′səm), *n.* the fourth or true stomach of cud-chewing animals, lying next to the omasum. Also, **ab·o·ma·sus** (ăb′ə mā′səs). [t. NL, f. L *ab-* AB- + *omāsum* bullock's tripe]

A-bomb (ā′bŏm′), *n.* atomic bomb.

a·bom·i·na·ble (ə bŏm′ə nə bəl), *adj.* detestable; loathsome. [ME, t. F, t. L: m.s. *abōmināblilis*] —**a·bom′i·na·ble·ness,** *n.* —**a·bom′i·na·bly,** *adv.*

a·bom·i·nate (ə bŏm′ə nāt′), *v.t.,* **-nated, -nating. 1.** to regard with intense aversion; abhor. **2.** to dislike strongly. [t. L: m.s. *abōminātus*, pp., having deprecated as an ill omen] —**a·bom′i·na′tor,** *n.* —**Syn. 1.** See **hate.**

a·bom·i·na·tion (ə bŏm′ə nā′shən), *n.* **1.** an object greatly disliked or abhorred. **2.** intense aversion; detestation. **3.** a detestable action; a shameful vice.

ab·o·rig·i·nal (ăb′ə rĭj′ə nəl), *adj.* **1.** pertaining to aborigines; primitive: *aboriginal customs.* **2.** original; native; indigenous. —*n.* **3.** an aborigine. —**ab′o·rig′i·nal·i·ty,** *n.* —**ab′o·rig′i·nal·ly,** *adv.*

ab o·ri·gi·ne (ăb ō rĭj′ə nē′), *Latin.* from the very first; from the source or origin.

ab·o·rig·i·nes (ăb′ə rĭj′ə nēz′), *n., pl.* of **aborigine. 1.** the primitive inhabitants of a country; the people living in a country at the earliest period. **2.** the original fauna or flora of a region. [t. L, der. *ab orīgine* from the beginning]

a·bort (ə bôrt′), *v.i.* **1.** to miscarry. **2.** to develop incompletely, remaining in a rudimentary state or degenerating. **3.** *Mil. Slang.* to fail to complete a mission. [t. L: s. *abortus*, pp., having miscarried]

a·bor·ti·cide¹ (ə bôr′tə sīd′), *n.* destruction of a fetus in the uterus; feticide. [f. s. L *abortus* miscarriage + -(I)CIDE²]

a·bor·ti·cide² (ə bôr'tə sīd'), *n.* an abortifacient. [f. s. L *abortus* miscarriage + -(I)CIDE¹]

a·bor·ti·fa·cient (ə bôr'tə fā'shənt), *adj.* 1. causing abortion. —*n.* 2. something used to produce abortion. [f. s. L *abortus* miscarriage + -(I)FACIENT]

a·bor·tion (ə bôr'shən), *n.* 1. the expulsion of a human fetus before it is viable (within the first 28 weeks of pregnancy). 2. an immature and not viable birth product; miscarriage. 3. *Biol.* the arrested development of an embryo or an organ at its (more or less) early stage. 4. anything which fails in its progress before it is matured or perfected, as a design or project. [t. L: s. *abortio* miscarriage] —**a·bor'tion·al**, *adj.*

a·bor·tion·ist (ə bôr'shən ĭst), *n.* one who produces or aims to produce a criminal abortion, esp. one who makes a practice of so doing.

a·bor·tive (ə bôr'tĭv), *adj.* 1. failing to succeed; miscarrying: *an abortive scheme.* 2. born prematurely. 3. imperfectly developed; rudimentary. 4. *Med.* **a.** producing or intended to produce abortion; abortifacient. **b.** acting to halt progress of a disease. 5. *Pathol.* (of the course of a disease) short and mild without the commonly pronounced clinical symptoms. —**a·bor'tive·ly**, *adv.* —**a·bor'tive·ness**, *n.*

A·bou·kir (ä'boo kēr'), *n.* Abukir.

a·bou·li·a (ə boo'lĭə), *n.* abulia. —**a·bou'lic**, *adj.*

a·bound (ə bound'), *v.i.* 1. to be in great plenty; be very prevalent: *the discontent which abounds in the world.* 2. to be rich (fol. by *in*): *some languages abound in figurative expressions.* 3. to be filled; teem (fol. by *with*): *the ship abounds with rats.* [ME *abounde(n)*, t. OF: m. *abunder*, g. L *abundāre*] —**a·bound'ing**, *adj.*

a·bout (ə bout'), *prep.* 1. of; concerning; in regard to: *to talk about secrets.* 2. connected with: *instructions about the work.* 3. somewhere near or in: *he is about the house.* 4. near; close to: *about my height.* 5. on every side of; around: *the railing about the tower.* 6. on or near (one's person): *they had lost all they had about them.* 7. on the point of (fol. by an infinitive): *about to leave.* 8. here and there in or on: *wander about the place.* 9. *Archaic.* concerned with; engaged in doing. —*adv.* 10. near in time, number, degree, etc.; approximately: *about a hundred miles.* 11. *Colloq.* nearly; almost: *about ready.* 12. nearby: *he is somewhere about.* 13. on every side; in every direction: *look about.* 14. half round; in the reverse direction: *to spin about.* 15. to and fro; here and there: *move furniture about.* 16. in rotation or succession; alternately: *turn about is fair play.* 17. on the move: *be up and about.* 18. *Archaic.* around. [ME; OE *abūtan*, var. of *onbūtan*, *on būtan* on the outside (of)]

about face, *U.S.* the military command to face to the rear in a prescribed manner while standing. Also, *Brit.*, **about turn.**

a·bout-face (*n.* ə bout'fās'; *v.* ə bout'fās'), *n., v.,* **-faced, -facing.** —*n.* 1. a complete, sudden change in position, principle, attitude, etc. —*v.i.* 2. to turn in the opposite direction.

a·bout-ship (ə bout'shĭp'), *v.i.* *Naut.* to tack a ship.

a·bove (ə bŭv'), *adv.* 1. in or to a higher place; overhead: *the blue sky above.* 2. higher in rank or power: *appeal to the courts above.* 3. before in order, esp. in a book or writing: *from what has been said above.* 4. in heaven. —*prep.* 5. in or to a higher place than: *fly above the earth.* 6. more in quantity or number than: *the weight is above a ton.* 7. superior to: *above mean actions.* —*adj.* 8. said, mentioned, or written above; foregoing: *the above explanation.* —*n.* 9. **the above,** that which was said, mentioned, or written above. [ME; OE *abufan*, f. A-¹ + *bufan* above]

a·bove·board (ə bŭv'bôrd'), *adv., adj.* in open sight; without tricks or disguise: *an honest man deals aboveboard; his actions are open and aboveboard.*

ab o·vo (ăb ō'vō), from the beginning. [L: from the egg]

ab·ra·ca·dab·ra (ăb'rə kə dăb'rə), *n.* 1. a mystical word used in incantations, or written in triangular form as a charm on an amulet. 2. any word charm or empty jingle of words. 3. gibberish; nonsense. [t. L]

a·bra·dant (ə brā'dənt), *adj.* 1. having the property or quality of abrading. —*n.* 2. an abrasive.

a·brade (ə brād'), *v.t., v.i.,* **abraded, abrading.** to wear off or down by friction; scrape off. [t. L: m. s. *abrādere* scrape off] —**a·brad'er**, *n.*

A·bra·ham (ā'brə hăm', -həm), *n.* *Bible.* the first of the great patriarchs, father of Isaac, and traditional founder of the Hebrew people. Gen. 11–25. [t. Heb.]

a·bran·chi·ate (ā brăng'kĭ ĭt, -āt'), *adj.* *Zool.* without gills. Also, **a·bran·chi·al** (ā brăng'kĭ əl). [f. A-⁶ + s. Gk. *bránchia* gills + -ATE¹]

a·bra·sion (ə brā'zhən), *n.* 1. the result of rubbing or abrading; an abraded spot or place. 2. act or process of abrading. [t. L: s. *abrāsio* a scraping off]

a·bra·sive (ə brā'sĭv, -zĭv), *n.* 1. any material or substance used for grinding, polishing, lapping, etc., as emery or sand. —*adj.* 2. tending to produce abrasion.

ab·re·act (ăb'rĭ ăkt'), *v.t.* *Psychoanal.* to remove by abreaction.

ab·re·ac·tion (ăb'rĭ ăk'shən), *n.* *Psychoanal.* the release of psychic tension through verbalizing or acting out an adequate resolution of a repressed traumatic experience, with the appropriate emotion or affect. [f. AB- + REACTION. Cf. G *abreagierung*]

a·breast (ə brĕst'), *adv., adj.* 1. side by side. 2. along-

side in progress or attainment; equally advanced (fol. by *of* or *with*): *to keep abreast of the times in science.*

a·bridge (ə brĭj'), *v.t.,* **abridged, abridging.** 1. to shorten by condensation or omission, or both; rewrite or reconstruct on a smaller scale. 2. to lessen; diminish. 3. to deprive; cut off. [ME *abrege(n)*, t. OF: m. *abreger*, g. L *abbreviāre* shorten] —**a·bridg'a·ble,** esp. *Brit.* **a·bridge/a·ble,** *adj.* —**a·bridged'**, *adj.* —**a·bridg'er**, *n.* —**Syn.** 1. cut down; epitomize; condense. See **shorten.** 2. contract. 3. curtail. —**Ant.** 1. lengthen. 2. expand.

a·bridg·ment (ə brĭj'mənt), *n.* 1. a condensation, as of a book; a reproduction of anything in reduced or condensed form. 2. act of abridging. 3. state of being abridged. Also, esp. *Brit.*, **a·bridge'ment.**

a·broach (ə brōch'), *adv.* 1. broached. 2. **set abroach, a.** to cause (a cask, a barrel, etc.) to flow or to let out liquor. **b.** to give rise to; spread abroad.

a·broad (ə brôd'), *adv.* 1. in a foreign country or countries: *to live abroad.* 2. out of doors: *the owl ventures abroad at night.* 3. astir; in circulation: *rumors of disaster are abroad.* 4. broadly; widely. 5. wide of the truth. [ME *a brood;* f. A-¹ + BROAD. Cf. E *at large*]

ab·ro·gate (ăb'rə gāt'), *v.t.,* **-gated, -gating.** to abolish summarily; annul by an authoritative act; repeal: *to abrogate a law.* [t. L: m. s. *abrogātus*, pp.] —**ab,ro·ga·ble** (ăb'rə gə bəl), *adj.* —**ab'ro·ga'tion**, *n.* —**ab'ro·ga'tive**, *adj.* —**ab'ro·ga'tor**, *n.*

ab·rupt (ə brŭpt'), *adj.* 1. terminating or changing suddenly: *an abrupt turn in a road.* 2. sudden; unceremonious: *an abrupt entrance.* 3. lacking in continuity; having sudden transitions from one subject to another: *an abrupt literary style.* 4. steep; precipitous: *an abrupt descent.* 5. *Bot.* truncate. [t. L: m. s. *abruptus*, pp., broken off] —**ab·rupt'ly**, *adv.* —**ab·rupt'ness**, *n.* —**Syn.** 1. See **sudden.**

ab·rup·tion (ə brŭp'shən), *n.* a sudden breaking off.

A·bruz·zi (ä broot'tsē), *n.* **Duke of the,** (Prince Luigi Amedeo of Savoy-Aosta) 1873–1933, Italian naval officer, mountain climber, and arctic explorer.

abs-, var. of *ab-* before *c, q, t,* as in *abscond, absterge.*

Ab·sa·lom (ăb'sə ləm), *n.* *Bible.* third son of David, who rebelled against his father and was slain. II Sam. 13–19.

ab·scess (ăb'sĕs), *n.* a localized collection of pus in the tissues of the body, often accompanied by swelling and inflammation and often caused by bacteria. [t. L: s. *abscessus* a going away] —**ab'scessed**, *adj.*

ab·scis·sa (ăb sĭs'ə), *n., pl.* **-scissas, -scissae** (-sĭs'ē). *Math.* (in plane Cartesian coördinates) the x-coördinate of a point, i.e., its horizontal distance from the y-axis measured parallel to the x-axis. [t. L: short for *līnea abscissa* line cut off]

ab·scis·sion (ăb sĭzh'ən, -sĭsh'-), *n.* act of cutting off; sudden termination. [t. L: s. *abscissio*]

Abscissa: P, any point; AP or OB, abscissa of P; XX, axis of abscissa; YY, axis of the ordinate

ab·scond (ăb skŏnd'), *v.i.* to depart in a sudden and secret manner, esp. to avoid legal process. [t. L: s. *abscondere* put away] —**ab·scond'er**, *n.*

ab·sence (ăb'səns), *n.* 1. state of being away: *speak ill of no one in his absence.* 2. period of being away: *an absence of several weeks.* 3. lack: *the absence of proof.* [ME, t. F, t. L: m. s. *absentia*]

absence of mind, absent-mindedness.

ab·sent (*adj.* ăb'sənt; *v.* ăb sĕnt'), *adj.* 1. not in a certain place at a given time; away (opposed to *present*). 2. lacking: *revenge is absent from his mind.* 3. absentminded. —*v.t.* 4. to take or keep (oneself) away: *to absent oneself from home.* [ME, t. L: *absens*, ppr.] —**ab·sen·ta·tion** (ăb'sən tā'shən), *n.* —**ab·sent'er**, *n.* —**ab'sent·ness**, *n.*

ab·sen·tee (ăb'sən tē'), *n.* 1. one who is absent. 2. one who withdraws from his country, office, post, duty, etc. —**ab'sen·tee'ism**, *n.*

absentee landlord, an owner, investor, or incumbent who lives in a place, region, or country other than that from which he draws his income.

ab·sent·ly (ăb'sənt lĭ), *adv.* inattentively.

ab·sent-mind·ed (ăb'sənt mīn'dĭd), *adj.* forgetful of one's immediate surroundings; preoccupied. —**ab'sent-mind'ed·ly**, *adv.* —**ab'sent-mind'ed·ness**, *n.* —**Syn.** ABSENT-MINDED, ABSTRACTED, OBLIVIOUS all mean inattentive to immediate surroundings. ABSENT-MINDED suggests an unintentional wandering of the mind from the present: *an absent-minded professor.* ABSTRACTED implies that the mind has been drawn away from the immediate present by reflection upon some engrossing subject: *wearing an abstracted air.* OBLIVIOUS implies absorption in some thought which causes one to be completely forgetful of or unaware of his surroundings: *oblivious of danger.*

absent without leave, away from military duties without permission, but without the intention of deserting (usually used in the abbreviation A.W.O.L.).

ab·sinthe (ăb'sĭnth), *n.* 1. a strong, bitter, green-colored, aromatic liqueur, 68 per cent alcohol, made with wormwood and other herbs, having a pronounced licorice flavor. 2. wormwood (defs. 1, 3). 3. *U.S.* sagebrush. Also, **ab'sinth.** [t. F, t. L: m. s. *absinthium*, t. Gk.: m. *apsinthion* wormwood] —**ab·sin'thi·al, ab·sin'thi·an**, *adj.*

ab·sinth·ism (ăb′sĭn thĭz′əm), n. a morbid condition due to the excessive use of absinthe.

ab·so·lute (ăb′sə lo͞ot′), adj. 1. free from imperfection; complete; perfect: *absolute liberty.* 2. not mixed; pure. 3. free from restriction or limitation; unqualified: *absolute command.* 4. arbitrary or despotic: *an absolute monarchy.* 5. viewed independently; not comparative or relative: *absolute position.* 6. positive: *absolute in opinion.* 7. *Gram.* a. syntactically independent; not grammatically connected with any other element in the sentence, as *It being Sunday* in *It being Sunday, the family went to church.* b. (of a transitive verb) used with no object expressed, as *to give* in *the solicitors for the community chest asked him to give.* c. (of an adjective) having its noun understood, not expressed, as *poor* in *the poor are always with us.* d. characterizing the phonetic or phonemic form of a word or phrase occurring by itself, not influenced by surrounding forms (distinguished from *sandhi form*). Example: "not" in "is not" as opposed to "isn't," or "will" in "they will" as opposed to "they'll." 8. *Physics.* a. as nearly independent as possible of arbitrary standards or of properties of special substances or systems: *absolute zero of temperature.* b. pertaining to a system of units based on some primary units, esp. units of length, mass, and time: *cgs units are absolute units.* c. pertaining to a measurement based on an absolute zero or unit: *absolute pressure.* —*n.* 9. **the absolute, a.** that which is free from any restriction, or is unconditioned; the ultimate ground of all things. b. that which is independent of some or all relations. c. that which is perfect or complete. [ME, t. L: m. s. *absolūtus*, pp., loosened from] **—ab′so·lute′ness,** n.

—**Syn.** 2. sheer. 3. ABSOLUTE, UNQUALIFIED, UTTER al. mean unmodified. ABSOLUTE implies an unquestionable finality: *an absolute coward.* UNQUALIFIED means without reservations or conditions: *an unqualified success.* UTTER expresses totality or entirety: *an utter failure.*

absolute alcohol, ethyl alcohol containing not more than one per cent by weight of water.

ab·so·lute·ly (ăb′sə lo͞ot′lĭ; *emphatic* ăb′sə lo͞ot′lĭ), *adv.* 1. completely; wholly. 2. positively. 3. (of a transitive verb) without an object.

absolute majority, (in England) over half, as *majority* alone can mean plurality.

absolute music, music whose patterns in sound are not illustrative of or dependent upon a text or program.

absolute pitch, *Music.* 1. the exact pitch of a tone in terms of vibration per second. 2. the ability to sing or recognize the pitch of a tone by ear.

absolute zero, the lowest possible temperature which the nature of matter admits, or that temperature at which the particles whose motion constitutes heat would be at rest, being a hypothetical point 273 degrees below the zero of the centigrade scale. Cf. **absolute** (def. 8a).

ab·so·lu·tion (ăb′sə lo͞o′shən), n. 1. act of absolving; release from consequences, obligations, or penalties. 2. state of being absolved. 3. *Rom. Cath. Theol.* a a remission of sin or of the punishment due to sin, which the priest, on the ground of authority received from Christ, makes in the sacrament of penance. b. the formula declaring such remission. 4. *Prot. Theol.* a declaration or assurance of divine forgiveness to penitent believers, made after confession of sins. [t. L: s. *absolūtio* an acquittal; r. ME *absolucioun*, t. F]

ab·so·lut·ism (ăb′sə lo͞o tĭz′əm), n. 1. the principle or the exercise of absolute power in government. 2. *Philos.* the doctrine of an absolute or nonrelative being. **—ab′so·lut′ist,** n. **—ab′so·lu·tis′tic,** adj.

ab·so·lu·to·ry (ăb sŏl′yə tōr′ĭ), adj. giving absolution.

ab·solve (ăb sŏlv′, -zŏlv′), v.t., **-solved, -solving.** 1. to free from the consequences or penalties attaching to action (fol. by *from*): *to absolve one from moral blame.* 2. to set free or release, as from some duty, obligation, or responsibility (fol. by *from*): *absolved from his oath.* 3. to grant pardon for. 4. *Eccles.* a. to grant or pronounce remission of sins to. b. to remit (sin). c. to declare (censure, as excommunication) removed. [t. L: m. s. *absolvere* loosen from] **—ab·solv′a·ble,** adj. **—ab·sol′vent,** adj., n. **—ab·solv′er,** n.

—**Syn.** 1. ABSOLVE, ACQUIT, EXONERATE mean to free from blame. ABSOLVE is a general word for this idea. To ACQUIT is to release from a specific and usually formal accusation: *the court must acquit the accused if there is enough evidence of innocence.* To EXONERATE is to consider a person clear of blame or consequences for an act (even when the act is admitted), or to justify him for having done it: *to exonerate one for a crime committed in self-defense.* 2. liberate; exempt. —**Ant.** 1. blame.

ab·so·nant (ăb′sə nənt), adj. discordant (fol. by *from* or *to*). [f. AB- + s. L *sonans,* ppr., sounding]

ab·sorb (ăb sôrb′, -zôrb′), v.t. 1. to swallow up the identity or individuality of: *the empire absorbed all the small states.* 2. to engross wholly: *absorbed in a book.* 3. to suck up or drink in (liquids): *a sponge absorbs water.* 4. to take up or receive in by chemical or molecular action: *carbonic acid is formed when water absorbs carbon dioxide.* 5. to take in without echo or recoil: *to absorb sound.* 6. *Obs.* to swallow up. [t. L: s. *absorbēre*] **—ab·sorb′a·ble,** adj. **—ab·sorb′a·bil′i·ty,** n. **—ab·sorb′er,** n. **—Syn.** 1. assimilate, consume, engulf.

ab·sorbed (ăb sôrbd′, -zôrbd′), adj. engrossed; preoccupied. **—ab·sorb·ed·ly** (ăb sôr′bĭd lĭ, -zôr′-), *adv.* **—ab·sorb′ed·ness,** n.

ab·sor·be·fa·cient (ăb sôr′bə fā′shənt, -zôr′-), *adj.* causing absorption. [f. L *absorbē(re)* absorb + -FACIENT]

ab·sorb·ent (ăb sôr′bənt, -zôr′-), adj. 1. capable of absorbing; performing the function of absorption. —*n.* 2. a thing that absorbs. **—ab·sorb′en·cy,** n.

absorbent cotton, raw cotton for surgical dressings and toilet purposes which has had its natural wax chemically removed.

ab·sorb·ing (ăb sôr′bĭng, -zôr′-), adj. engrossing: *an absorbing pursuit.* **—ab·sorb′ing·ly,** *adv.*

ab·sorp·tion (ăb sôrp′shən, -zôrp′-), n. 1. assimilation: *the absorption of small farms into one big one.* 2. passage of substances to the blood, lymph, and cells, as from the alimentary canal (e.g., digested foods) or from the tissues. 3. a taking in or reception by molecular or chemical action: *absorption of gases, light, heat, etc.* 4. preoccupation. [t. L: s. *absorptio*] **—ab·sorp′tive,** adj. **—ab·sorp′tive·ness,** n.

absorption coefficient, *Optics.* a constant of any material giving its absorption power for light passing through it.

ab·sorp·tiv·i·ty (ăb′sôrp tĭv′ə tĭ, -zôrp-), n. *Physics.* the ratio between the radiation absorbed by a surface and the total energy striking the surface.

ab·stain (ăb stān′), v.i. to refrain voluntarily, esp. from doing or enjoying something (fol. by *from*): *abstain from using intoxicating liquor.* [ME *absteine(n),* t. F: m. *abstenir,* r. OF *astenir,* g. L *abstinēre*] **—ab·stain′er,** n. **—Syn.** forbear; desist, cease.

ab·ste·mi·ous (ăb stē′mĭ əs), adj. 1. sparing in diet; moderate in the use of food and drink; temperate. 2. characterized by abstinence: *an abstemious life.* 3. sparing: *an abstemious diet.* [t. L: m. *abstēmius*] **—ab·ste′mi·ous·ly,** adv. **—ab·ste′mi·ous·ness,** n.

ab·sten·tion (ăb stĕn′shən), n. a holding off or refraining; abstinence from action. [f. s. L *abstentus,* pp., abstained + -ION] **—ab·sten′tious,** adj.

ab·sterge (ăb stûrj′), v.t., **-sterged, -sterging.** 1. *Med.* to purge. 2. to make clean by wiping. [t. L: m. s. *abstergēre* wipe off]

ab·ster·gent (ăb stûr′jənt), adj. 1. cleansing; detergent. —*n.* 2. a cleansing agent; a detergent, as soap.

ab·ster·sion (ăb stûr′shən), n. act of absterging.

ab·ster·sive (ăb stûr′sĭv), adj. abstergent. **—ab·ster′sive·ness,** n.

ab·sti·nence (ăb′stə nəns), n. 1. forbearance from any indulgence of appetite, esp. from the use of alcoholic liquors: *total abstinence.* 2. self-restraint; forbearance. 3. *Eccles.* the refraining from certain kinds of food on certain days, as from flesh on Fridays. Also, **ab′sti·nen·cy.** [ME *abstynens,* t. L: m. s. *abstinentia*] **—ab′sti·nent,** adj. **—ab′sti·nent·ly,** adv. **—Syn.** 1. abstemiousness; moderation, temperance.

ab·stract (adj. ăb′străkt, ăb străkt′; n. ăb′străkt; v. ăb străkt′ *for 10–13,* ăb′străkt *for 14*), adj. 1. conceived apart from matter and from special cases: *an abstract number.* 2. theoretical; not applied: *abstract science.* 3. difficult to understand; abstruse: *abstract speculations.* 4. of or pertaining to nonrepresentational art; using only lines, colors, generalized or geometrical forms, etc. —*n.* 5. a summary of a statement, document, speech, etc. 6. that which concentrates in itself the essential qualities of anything more extensive or more general, or of several things; essence. 7. an idea or term considered apart from some material basis or object. 8. **the abstract,** the ideal. 9. **in the abstract,** without reference to special circumstances or particular applications. —*v.t.* 10. to draw or take away; remove. 11. to withdraw or divert (the attention). 12. to steal. 13. to consider as a general object apart from special circumstances: *to abstract the notions of time, of space, or of matter.* 14. to summarize. [t. L: s. *abstractus,* pp., drawn away] **—ab·stract′er,** n. **—ab·stract′ly,** adv. **—ab′stract·ness,** n.

ab·stract·ed (ăb străk′tĭd), adj. lost in thought; preoccupied. **—ab·stract′ed·ly,** adv. **—ab·stract′ed·ness,** n. —**Syn.** See absent-minded.

ab·strac·tion (ăb străk′shən), n. 1. an abstract or general idea or term. 2. an idea which cannot lead to any practical result; something visionary. 3. act of considering something as a general object apart from special circumstances. 4. act of taking away or separating; withdrawal: *the sensation of cold is due to the abstraction of heat from our bodies.* 5. absent-mindedness; reverie. 6. *Fine Arts.* a. a work of art (**pure abstraction**) using lines, shapes, and colors without reference to natural objects. b. a work of art (**near abstraction**) retaining representational characteristics but expressing them through geometrical or generalized forms. [t. L: s. *abstractio*]

ab·strac·tive (ăb străk′tĭv), adj. 1. having the power of abstracting. 2. pertaining to an epitome or summary.

abstract noun, *Gram.* 1. a noun having an abstract (as opposed to concrete) meaning, as *dread.* 2. a noun made with an abstract suffix, as *witness.*

abstract of title, *Law.* an outline history of the title to a parcel of real estate, showing the original grant, subsequent conveyances, mortgages, etc.

ab·stric·tion (ăb strĭk′shən), n. *Bot.* a method of spore formation in which successive portions of the sporophore are cut off through the growth of septa. [f. AB- + L *strictio* a drawing together]

ab·struse (ăb strōōs′), *adj.* **1.** difficult to understand; esoteric: *abstruse questions.* **2.** *Obs.* hidden. [t. L: m. s. *abstrūsus*, pp., concealed] —**ab·struse′ly**, *adv.* —**ab·struse′ness**, *n.*

ab·surd (ăb sûrd′, -zûrd′), *adj.* contrary to reason or common sense; obviously false or foolish; logically contradictory; ridiculous: *an absurd statement.* [t. L: s. *absurdus*] —**ab·surd′ly**, *adv.* —**ab·surd′ness**, *n.*
—**Syn.** ABSURD, RIDICULOUS, PREPOSTEROUS all mean inconsistent with reason or common sense. ABSURD means glaringly opposed to manifest truth or reason: *an absurd claim.* RIDICULOUS implies that something is fit only to be laughed at, perhaps contemptuously or derisively: *a ridiculous suggestion.* PREPOSTEROUS implies an amazing extreme of foolishness: *a preposterous proposal.*

ab·surd·i·ty (ăb sûr′də tĭ, -zûr′-), *n., pl.* **-ties. 1.** state or quality of being absurd. **2.** something absurd.

A·bu-Bek·r (ə bōō′běk′ər), *n.* A.D. 573–634, first caliph of Mecca, A.D. 632–634; Mohammed's father-in-law and successor.

A·bu·kir (ä′bōō kēr′), *n.* a bay of the Mediterranean, in N Egypt: "Battle of the Nile," 1798. Also, **Aboukir.**

a·bu·li·a (ə bū′lǐ ə), *n. Psychiatry.* a form of mental derangement in which volition is impaired or lost. Also, **aboulia.** [t. Gk.: m. *aboulía* ill counsel] —**a·bu′lic**, *adj.*

a·bun·dance (ə bŭn′dəns), *n.* **1.** an overflowing quantity or supply: *an abundance of grain.* **2.** overflowing fullness: *abundance of the heart.* **3.** affluence; wealth. [ME, t. OF, g. L *abundantia*] —**Syn. 1.** copiousness, profusion. See **plenty.**

a·bun·dant (ə bŭn′dənt), *adj.* **1.** present in great quantity; fully sufficient: *an abundant supply.* **2.** possessing in great quantity; abounding (fol. by *in*): *a river abundant in salmon.* [ME, t. OF, g. s. L *abundans*, ppr.] —**a·bun′dant·ly**, *adv.* —**Syn.** plentiful, copious, profuse, overflowing.

ab ur·be con·di·ta (ăb ûr′bĭ kŏn′də tə), *Latin.* from the founding of the city (Rome, ab. 753 B.C.). *Abbr.:* A.U.C. The year 360 A.U.C. would be the 360th year after the founding of Rome.

a·buse (*v.* ə būz′; *n.* ə būs′), *v.*, **abused, abusing,** *n.* —*v.t.* **1.** to use wrongly or improperly; misuse: *to abuse rights or authority.* **2.** to do wrong to; act injuriously toward: *to abuse one's wife.* **3.** to revile; malign. **4.** *Archaic.* to deceive. [ME *abuse(n)*, t. F: m. *abuser*, ult. der. L *abūsus*, pp., having used up]
—*n.* **5.** wrong or improper use; misuse: *the abuse of privileges.* **6.** insulting language. **7.** ill-treatment of a person. **8.** a corrupt practice or custom; an offense: *the abuses of bad government.* **9.** *Archaic.* deception. [t. F: m. *abus*, t. L: s. *abūsus* a wasting, misuse] —**a·bus′er**, *n.*
—**Syn. 2.** ill-use, maltreat. **3.** vilify, vituperate, berate, upbraid. **6.** ABUSE, CENSURE, INVECTIVE all mean strongly expressed disapproval. ABUSE implies an outburst of harsh and scathing words against another (often one who is defenseless): *abuse directed against an opponent.* CENSURE implies blame, adverse criticism, or hostile condemnation: *severe censure of acts showing bad judgment.* INVECTIVE applies to strong but formal denunciation in speech or print, often in the public interest: *invective against graft.*

a·bu·sive (ə bū′sǐv), *adj.* **1.** using harsh words or ill treatment: *an abusive author.* **2.** characterized by or containing abuse: *an abusive satire.* **3.** wrongly used, corrupt: *an abusive exercise of power.* [t. L: m. s. *abūsivus*] —**a·bu′sive·ly**, *adv.* —**a·bu′sive·ness**, *n.*

a·but (ə bŭt′), *v.i.*, **abutted, abutting.** to be adjacent to (often fol. by *on, upon,* or *against*): *this piece of land abuts upon a street.* [ME *abutte(n)* t. OF: coalescence of *abouter* join end to end (der. a- A-⁵ + *bout* end) and *abuter* make contact with one end (der. a- A-⁵ + *but* end)]

a·bu·ti·lon (ə bū′tə lŏn′), *n.* any plant of the malvaceous genus *Abutilon,* esp. the flowering maple. [t. NL, t. Ar.: m. *aubūṭīlūn*]

a·but·ment (ə bŭt′mənt), *n.* **1.** that on which something abuts, as the part of a pier which receives the thrust of an arch; a part for sustaining or resisting pressure, as the part of a bridge pier exposed to the force of the current or of floating ice, or the structure supporting the shore ends of a bridge and restraining the embankment which supports the approaches. **2.** the place where projecting parts meet; junction.

a·but·ter (ə bŭt′ər), *n.* *U.S.* an owner of adjacent land.

a·by (ə bī′), *v.t., pt. and pp.* **abought.** *Archaic.* to pay the penalty of. Also, **a·bye′.** [ME *abye(n)*, OE *ābyg*- s. *ābycgan,* f. ā- A-³ + *bycgan* buy]

Abutment: A, Arch abutment; B, Current abutment

A·by·dos (ə bī′dŏs), *n.* **1.** an ancient ruined city in central Egypt: temples and tombs. **2.** an ancient town in N W Asia Minor, at the narrowest part of the Hellespont. See **Hero and Leander.**

a·bysm (ə bĭz′əm), *n.* an abyss. [ME *abi(s)me,* t. OF, g. VL *abyssimus,* superl. of L *abyssus* ABYSS]

a·bys·mal (ə bĭz′məl), *adj.* of or like an abyss; immeasurable: *abysmal ignorance.* —**a·bys′mal·ly**, *adv.*

a·byss (ə bĭs′), *n.* **1.** a bottomless gulf; any deep, immeasurable space. **2.** anything profound and unfathomable: *the abyss of time.* **3.** the bottomless pit; hell. [t. L: s. *abyssus,* t. Gk.: m. *ábyssos* without bottom]

a·byss·al (ə bĭs′əl), *adj.* **1.** abysmal. **2.** of or pertaining to the lowest depths of the ocean.

Ab·ys·sin·i·a (ăb′ə sĭn′ĭ ə), *n.* Ethiopia (def. 1). —**Ab·ys·sin′i·an**, *adj., n.*

ac-, var. of ad- (by assimilation) before *c* and *qu,* as in *accede, acquire,* etc.

-ac, an adjective suffix meaning "pertaining to," as in *elegiac, cardiac.* [repr. Gk. adj. suffix -*akos,* whence L -*acus,* F -*aque*]

Ac, *Chem.* actinium.

AC, 1. Air Corps. **2.** *Chem.* hydrocyanic acid.

A.C., *Elect.* alternating current. Also, **a.c.**

a·ca·cia (ə kā′shə), *n.* **1.** any tree or shrub of the mimosaceous genus *Acacia,* native in warm regions. **2.** one of several other plants, as the locust tree. **3.** gum arabic. [t. L, t. Gk.: m. *akakía* a thorny Egyptian tree]

Ac·a·deme (ăk′ə dēm′), *n. Poetic.* **1.** the Academy of Athens. **2.** (*l.c.*) any place of instruction.

ac·a·dem·ic (ăk′ə děm′ĭk), *adj.* **1.** pertaining to an advanced institution of learning, as a college, university, or academy; relating to higher education. **2.** *U.S.* pertaining to the classical, mathematical, and general literary departments of a college or university, as distinguished from the professional and scientific departments. **3.** theoretical; not practical. **4.** conforming to set rules and traditions; conventional. —*n.* **5.** a member of a college or university. —**Syn. 4.** See **formal.**

ac·a·dem·i·cal (ăk′ə děm′ə kəl), *adj.* **1.** academic. —*n.* **2.** (*pl.*) cap and gown. —**ac·a·dem′i·cal·ly**, *adv.*

academic freedom, freedom of a teacher to discuss social, economic, or political problems without interference from school or public officials.

a·cad·e·mi·cian (ə kăd′ə mĭsh′ən, ăk′ə də-), *n.* a member of a society for promoting literature, art, or science.

ac·a·dem·i·cism (ăk′ə děm′ə sĭz′əm), *n.* traditionalism or conventionalism in art, literature, etc.

a·cad·e·mism (ə kăd′ə mĭz′əm), *n.* **1.** academicism. **2.** *Philos.* the doctrines of the school founded by Plato.

a·cad·e·my (ə kăd′ə mĭ), *n., pl.* **-mies. 1.** a secondary school, esp. a private one. **2.** a school for instruction in a particular art or science: *a military academy.* **3.** an association or institution for the promotion of literature, science, or art: *the Academy of Arts and Letters.* **4.** the **Academy, a.** the French Academy. **b.** (in England) the Royal Academy. **c.** the public grove in Athens, in which Plato taught. **d.** the Platonic school of philosophy. [t. L: m.s. *academīa,* t. Gk.: m. *Akadḗmeia* (der. *Akádēmos,* an Attic hero)]

A·ca·di·a (ə kā′dĭ ə), *n.* a former French colony in SE Canada: ceded to Great Britain, 1713. French, **A·ca·die** (á kà dē′).

A·ca·di·an (ə kā′dĭ ən), *adj.* **1.** of or pertaining to Acadia or its inhabitants. —*n.* **2.** Also, *Dial.,* **Cajun, Cajian.** a native or inhabitant of Acadia, or one of the descendants of these in Louisiana.

Acadia, c1605–1713

ac·a·leph (ăk′ə lěf′), *n.* one of the *Acalephae,* a group of coelenterate marine animals including the sea nettles and jellyfishes. Also, **ac·a·lephe** (ăk′ə lěf′). [t. NL: s. *Acalēpha,* t. Gk.: m. *akalēphē* nettle]

ac·an·tha·ceous (ăk′ən thā′shəs), *adj.* **1.** having prickly growths. **2.** belonging to the *Acanthaceae,* or acanthus family of plants.

acantho-, *Bot.* a word element meaning "thorn," or "thorny." Also, before vowels, **acanth-.** [t. Gk.: m. *akantho-,* comb. form of *ákantha* thorn]

a·can·tho·ceph·a·lan (ə kăn′thə sĕf′ə lən), *n.* any of the worms belonging to a phylum or class of internal parasitic worms, *Acanthocephala,* having a protrusile proboscis covered with recurved hooks and a hollow body without digestive tract, found in the intestine of vertebrates.

ac·an·tho·di·an (ăk′ən thō′dĭ ən), *n.* a spiny-finned sharklike fish of the late Silurian and Devonian.

a·can·thoid (ə kăn′thoid), *adj.* spiny; spinous.

ac·an·thop·ter·yg·i·an (ăk′ən thŏp′tə rĭj′ĭ ən), *adj.* **1.** belonging or pertaining to the *Acanthopterygii,* the group of fishes with spiny fins, as the bass and perch. —*n.* **2.** an acanthopterygian fish. [f. ACANTHO- + s. Gk. *pterýgion* fin + -AN]

a·can·thous (ə kăn′thəs), *adj.* spinous.

a·can·thus (ə kăn′thəs), *n., pl.* **-thuses, -thi** (-thī). **1.** a plant of the genus *Acanthus,* of the Mediterranean regions, with large spiny or toothed leaves. **2.** an architectural ornament resembling the leaves of this plant, as in the Corinthian capital. [t. L, t. Gk.: m. *ákanthos* a thorny tree]

Acanthus: A, Leaf of plant, *Acanthus mollis;* B, Architectural ornament, front and side view

a cap·pel·la (ä′ kə pěl′ə; *It.* ä′ käp pěl′lä), *Music.* **1.** without instrumental accompaniment. **2.** in the style of church or chapel music. [It.]

A·ca·pul·co (ä′kä pōōl′kō), *n.* a seaport in SW Mexico. 9943 (1940).

ac·a·ri·a·sis (ăk′ə rī′ə sĭs), *n.* **1.** infestation with acarids, esp. mites. **2.** a skin disease caused by such infestation. [f. m. Gk. *ákar(i)* mite + -IASIS]

---

b., blend of, blended; c., cognate with; d., dialect, dialectal; der., derived from; f., formed from; g., going back to; m., modification of; r., replacing; s., stem of; t., taken from; ?, perhaps. See the full key on inside cover.

ac·a·rid (ăk′ə rĭd), *n.* any animal belonging to the *Acari* (or *Acarida*), an order of arachnids including the mites, ticks, etc. [f. m. Gk. *ăkar(i)* mite + -ɪᴅ²]

a·car·i·dan (ə kăr′ə dən), *adj.* 1. belonging to the acarids. —*n.* 2. an acarid.

ac·a·roid (ăk′ə roid′), *adj.* resembling an acarid.

acaroid gum, a red resin exuded from the trunk of the liliaceous Australian grass tree, *Xanthorrhoea hastilis*, and other species. Also, **acaroid resin.**

a·car·pel·ous (ā kär′pəl əs), *adj. Bot.* having no carpels. Also, **a·car′pel·lous.**

a·car·pous (ā kär′pəs), *adj. Bot.* not producing fruit; sterile; barren. [t. Gk.: m. *ăkarpos* without fruit]

ac·a·rus (ăk′ə rəs), *n., pl.* -ri (-rī′). an animal of the genus *Acarus*; a mite. [t. L, t. Gk.: m. *ăkari*]

ac·a·ta·lec·tic (ā kăt′ə lĕk′tĭk), Pros. —*adj.* 1. not catalectic; complete. —*n.* 2. a verse having the complete number of syllables in the last foot. See example under **catalectic.**

a·cau·dal (ā kô′dəl), *adj. Zool.* tailless; anurous. Also, **a·cau·date** (ā kô′dāt).

ac·au·les·cent (ăk′ô lĕs′ənt), *adj. Bot.* not caulescent; stemless; without visible stem. Also, **a·cau·line** (ā kô′lĭn, -lĭn), **a·cau·lose** (ā kô′lōs), **a·cau·lous** (ā kô′ləs). —**ac′au·les·cence,** *n.*

acc., 1. account. 2. accusative.

Ac·cad (ăk′ad, ä′käd), *n.* Akkad.

ac·cede (ăk sēd′), *v.i.* -ceded, -ceding. 1. to give consent; agree; yield: *to accede to terms.* 2. to attain, as an office or dignity; arrive at (fol. by *to*): *to accede to the throne.* 3. *Internat. Law.* to become a party (*to*), as a nation signing a treaty. [t. L: m. s. *accēdere* go to] —**ac·ced′ence,** *n.* —**ac·ced′er,** *n.*

accel., accelerando.

ac·cel·er·an·do (ăk sĕl′ə rän′dō; *It.* ät chĕ′lĕ rän′dô), *adv., adj. Music.* gradually increasing in speed. [It.]

ac·cel·er·ant (ăk sĕl′ər ənt), *n. Chem.* accelerator.

ac·cel·er·ate (ăk sĕl′ə rāt′), *v.* -ated, -ating. —*v.t.* 1. to cause to move or advance faster: *accelerate growth.* 2. to help to bring about more speedily than would otherwise have been the case: *to accelerate the fall of a government.* 3. to increase or otherwise change the velocity of (a body) or the rate of (motion); cause to undergo acceleration. —*v.i.* 4. to become faster; increase in speed. [t. L: m.s. *accelerātus,* pp.]

ac·cel·er·a·tion (ăk sĕl′ə rā′shən), *n.* 1. act of accelerating; increase of speed or velocity. 2. a change in velocity. 3. the time rate of change in velocity.

acceleration of gravity, the acceleration of a falling body due to gravity which is a little more than 32 feet per second, per second, at sea level, and which varies with latitude and altitude: represented by the letter *g*.

ac·cel·er·a·tive (ăk sĕl′ə rā′tĭv), *adj.* tending to accelerate; increasing the velocity (*of*). Also, **ac·cel·er·a·to·ry** (ăk sĕl′ər ə tôr′ĭ).

ac·cel·er·a·tor (ăk sĕl′ə rā′tər), *n.* 1. one that accelerates. 2. *Auto.* a device for opening and closing the throttle, esp. when operated by the foot. 3. *Photog.* any substance, device, or the like, that shortens the time of exposure or development. 4. *Chem.* **a.** any substance that increases the speed of a chemical change. **b.** any chemical which increases the rate of vulcanization of rubber. 5. *Anat.* any muscle, nerve, or activating substance that quickens a movement.

ac·cel·er·om·e·ter (ăk sĕl′ə rŏm′ə tər), *n.* an instrument used for measuring acceleration, used in aircraft.

ac·cent (*n.* ăk′sĕnt; *v.* ăk′sĕnt, ăk sĕnt′), *n.* 1. the distinctive character of a vowel or syllable determined by its degree or pattern of stress or musical tone. 2. any one of the degrees or patterns of stress used in a particular language as essential features of vowels, syllables, or words: *primary accent, falling accent, sentence accent.* 3. a mark indicating stress, musical tone, or vowel quality. In English the accent mark (′) is used to indicate the syllable which is stressed. French has three accent marks, the acute (′), the grave (\), and the circumflex (^), which indicate vowel quality (or sometimes merely distinguish meaning, as *la* "the" and *là* "there"). 4. *Pros.* **a.** regularly recurring stress. **b.** a mark indicating stress or some other distinction in pronunciation or value. 5. any one of the musical tones or melodies used in a particular language as essential features of vowels or syllables. 6. characteristic style of pronunciation: *foreign accent.* 7. *Music.* **a.** stress or emphasis given to certain notes. **b.** a mark denoting this. **c.** stress or emphasis regularly recurring as a feature of rhythm. 8. *Math., etc.* a mark, or one of a number of marks, placed after a letter or figure: **a.** to distinguish similar quantities which differ in value, as in b′, b′′, b′′′, etc. (called *b prime, b second, b third,* etc. respectively). **b.** to indicate a particular unit or measure, as feet (′) or inches (′′): 5′3′′, meaning *5 feet, 3 inches;* or as minutes (′) or seconds (′′) of time or a degree: 18′25′′, meaning *18 minutes, 25 seconds.* **c.** to indicate the operation of differentiation in calculus. 9. words or tones expressive of some emotion. 10. (*pl.*) *Poetic.* words; language. 11. distinctive character or tone. —*v.t.* 12. to pronounce (a vowel, syllable, or word) with one of the distinctive accents of the language, esp. with a stress accent. 13. to mark with a written accent or accents: *to accent a word to indicate its pronunciation.* 14. to emphasize; accentuate. [t. L: s. *accentus* tone]

ac·cen·tu·al (ăk sĕn′chōō əl), *adj.* 1. pertaining to accent; rhythmical. 2. *Pros.* of, pertaining to, or characterized by syllabic accent (distinguished from *quantitative*). —**ac·cen′tu·al·ly,** *adv.*

ac·cen·tu·ate (ăk sĕn′chōō āt′), *v.t.* -ated, -ating. 1. to emphasize. 2. to mark or pronounce with an accent. [t. ML: m. s. *accentuātus,* pp.] —**ac·cen′tu·a′tion,** *n.*

ac·cept (ăk sĕpt′), *v.t.* 1. to take or receive (something offered); receive with approval or favor: *his proposal was accepted.* 2. to admit and agree to; accede or assent to: *to accept a treaty, an excuse, etc.* 3. to take with formal acknowledgment of responsibility or consequences: *to accept office.* 4. to accommodate oneself to: *accept the situation.* 5. to believe: *to accept a fact.* 6. to receive as to meaning; understand. 7. *Com.* to acknowledge, by signature, as calling for payment, and thus to agree to pay, as a draft. 8. (in a deliberative body) to receive as an adequate performance of the duty with which an officer or a committee has been charged; receive for further action: *the report of the committee was accepted.* —*v.i.* 9. to accept an invitation, gift, position, etc. (sometimes fol. by *of*). [ME *accept(en),* t. L: m. *acceptāre,* freq. of *accipere* take] —**ac·cept′er,** *esp. in Com.* **ac·cep′tor,** *n.*

ac·cept·a·ble (ăk sĕp′tə bəl), *adj.* 1. capable or worthy of being accepted. 2. pleasing to the receiver; agreeable; welcome. —**ac·cept′a·bil′i·ty, ac·cept′a·ble·ness,** *n.* —**ac·cept′a·bly,** *adv.*

ac·cept·ance (ăk sĕp′təns), *n.* 1. act of taking or receiving something offered. 2. favorable reception; favor. 3. act of assenting or believing: *acceptance of a theory.* 4. fact or state of being accepted or acceptable. 5. *Com.* **a.** an engagement to pay an order, draft, or bill of exchange when it becomes due, as by the person on whom it is drawn. **b.** an order, draft, etc., which a person has accepted as calling for payment and has thus promised to pay: *a trade acceptance.*

acceptance sampling, a procedure by which a decision is made to accept or reject a lot of articles on the basis of the results of the inspection of one or more samples of articles from the lot.

ac·cept·ant (ăk sĕp′tənt), *adj.* accepting; receptive.

ac·cep·ta·tion (ăk′sĕp tā′shən), *n.* 1. favorable regard. 2. belief. 3. usual or received meaning.

ac·cept·ed (ăk sĕp′tĭd), *adj.* approved.

ac·cess (ăk′sĕs), *n.* 1. act or privilege of coming to; admittance; approach: *to gain access to a person.* 2. approachability; accessibility: *the house is difficult of access.* 3. way or means of approach. 4. *Theol.* approach to God through Jesus Christ. Eph. 2:18. 5. an attack, as of disease. 6. sudden outburst of passion. 7. accession. [ME, t. L: s. *accessus* approach]

ac·ces·sa·ry (ăk sĕs′ər ĭ), *n., pl.* -ries, *adj. Chiefly Law.* accessory. —**ac·ces′sa·ri·ly,** *adv.* —**ac·ces′sa·ri·ness,** *n.*

ac·ces·si·ble (ăk sĕs′ə bəl), *adj.* 1. easy of access; approachable. 2. attainable: *accessible evidence.* 3. open to the influence of (fol. by *to*): *accessible to bribery.* —**ac·ces′si·bil′i·ty,** *n.* —**ac·ces′si·bly,** *adv.*

ac·ces·sion (ăk sĕsh′ən), *n.* 1. act of coming into the possession of a right, dignity, office, etc.: *accession to the throne.* 2. an increase by something added: *an accession of territory.* 3. something added. 4. *Law.* addition to property by growth or improvement. 5. consent: *accession to a demand.* 6. *Internat. Law.* formal acceptance of a treaty, international convention, or other agreement between states. 7. act of coming near; approach. [t. L: s. *accessio* increase] —**ac·ces′sion·al,** *adj.*

ac·ces·so·ri·al (ăk′sə sôr′ĭ əl), *adj.* accessory.

ac·ces·so·ry (ăk sĕs′ər ĭ), *n., pl.* -ries, *adj.* —*n.* 1. a subordinate part or object; something added or attached for convenience, attractiveness, etc., such as a spotlight, heater, rear-vision mirror, etc., for an automobile. 2. *Law.* one who, without being present at its commission, is guilty of aiding or abetting another who commits a felony: **an accessory before the fact** is not present when the act is done; **an accessory after the fact** knowingly conceals or assists another who has committed a felony. —*adj.* 3. contributing to a general effect; subsidiary: *accessory sounds in music.* 4. *Law.* giving aid as an accessory. 5. *Petrog.* denoting minerals present in relatively small amounts in a rock, and not mentioned in its definition, as zircon in granite. Also, *esp. Law,* **accessary.** [t. LL: m. s. *accessōrius*] —**ac·ces′so·ri·ly,** *adv.* —**ac·ces′so·ri·ness,** *n.* —Syn. 1. See addition.

ac·ciac·ca·tu·ra (ät chäk′kä tōō′rä), *n. Music.* 1. a short appoggiatura. 2. a short grace note one half step below, and struck at the same time with, a principal note. [It.]

ac·ci·dence (ăk′sə dəns), *n.* 1. the rudiments of any subject. 2. *Gram.* **a.** that part of morphology dealing with inflection. **b.** an inflected form of a word. **c.** a property shown by such inflection. [var. of *accidents,* pl. of *accident* (def. 5), or t. L: m. s. *accidentia,* neut. pl. of *accidens,* ppr., striking, happening as if fem. noun]

Acciaccatura (def. 2)
A, Grace note; B, Principal note

ac·ci·dent (ăk′sə dənt), *n.* 1. an undesirable or unfortunate happening; casualty; mishap. 2. anything that happens unexpectedly, without design, or by chance. 3. the operation of chance: *I was there by accident.* 4. a nonessential circumstance; occasional characteristic. **5.** *Gram.* an inflectional variation of a word, as *them* (an inflected form of *they*). **6.** *Geol.* an irregularity, generally on a small scale, on a surface, the explanation for which is not readily apparent. [ME, t. L: s. *accidens*, ppr., happening] —**Syn. 1.** mischance, misfortune, disaster, calamity, catastrophe.

ac·ci·den·tal (ăk/sə děn/təl), *adj.* **1.** happening by chance or accident, or unexpectedly: *an accidental meeting.* **2.** nonessential; incidental; subsidiary: *accidental benefits.* **3.** *Music.* relating to or indicating sharps, flats, or naturals. —*n.* **4.** a nonessential or subsidiary circumstance or feature. **5.** *Music.* a sign placed before a note indicating a change of its pitch. —**ac/ci·den/tal·ly,** *adv.* —**ac/ci·den/tal·ness,** *n.*
—**Syn. 1.** ACCIDENTAL, CASUAL, FORTUITOUS all describe something outside the usual course of events. ACCIDENTAL implies occurring unexpectedly or by chance: *an accidental blow.* CASUAL describes a passing event of slight importance: *a casual reference.* FORTUITOUS is applied to events occurring without known cause: *a fortuitous shower of meteors.*

ac·cip·i·ter (ăk sĭp/ə tər), *n.*, *pl.* **-tres** (-trēz/). any bird of the subfamily *Accipitrinae* and genus *Accipiter*, which comprises short-winged, long-tailed hawks. [t. L]

ac·cip·i·tral (ăk sĭp/ə trəl), *adj.* accipitrine.

ac·cip·i·trine (ăk sĭp/ə trĭn, -trīn/), *adj.* **1.** belonging to the *Accipitridae*, a hawk family. **2.** raptorial; like or related to the birds of prey.

ac·claim (ə klām/), *v.t.* **1.** to salute with words or sounds of joy or approval; applaud. **2.** to announce or proclaim by acclamation. —*v.i.* **3.** to make acclamation; applaud. —*n.* **4.** act of acclaiming; applause; shout of applause. [t. L: m. s. *acclāmāre*] —**ac·claim/er,** *n.*

ac·cla·ma·tion (ăk/lə mā/shən), *n.* **1.** a shout or other demonstration of welcome, good will, or applause. **2.** act of acclaiming. **3.** (in parliamentary procedure) an oral vote, often unanimous, usually taken after the sense of a meeting is clear and unmistakable. —**ac·clam·a·to·ry** (ə klăm/ə tōr/ĭ), *adj.*

ac·cli·mate (ə klī/mĭt, ăk/lə māt/), *v.t.*, *v.i.*, **-mated, -mating.** *Chiefly U.S.* to habituate or become habituated to a new climate or environment. [t. F: m.s. *acclimater*, der. à to + *climat* climate] —**ac·cli·mat·a·ble** (ə klī/mĭt ə bəl), *adj.* —**ac·cli·ma·tion** (ăk/lə mā/shən), *n.*

ac·cli·ma·tize (ə klī/mə tīz/), *v.t.*, *v.i.*, **-tized, -tizing.** *Chiefly Brit.* to acclimate. —**ac·cli·ma·tiz/a·ble,** *adj.* —**ac·cli·ma·ti·za/tion,** *n.* —**ac·cli·ma·tiz/er,** *n.*

ac·cliv·i·ty (ə klĭv/ə tĭ), *n.*, *pl.* **-ties.** an upward slope, as of ground; an ascent (opposed to *declivity*). [t. L: m. s. *acclīvitas* steepness]

ac·co·lade (ăk/ə lād/, -lād/), *n.* **1.** a ceremony used in conferring knighthood, consisting at one time of an embrace, and afterward of giving the candidate a light blow upon the shoulder with the flat of a sword. **2.** the blow itself. **3.** any award; honor. **4.** *Music.* a brace joining several staves. [t. F, t. It.: m. *accollata*, prop. fem. pp. of *accollare* embrace about the neck; r. ME *acolee*, t. OF]

ac·com·mo·date (ə kŏm/ə dāt/), *v.*, **-dated, -dating.** —*v.t.* **1.** to do a kindness or a favor to; oblige: *to accommodate a friend.* **2.** to provide suitably; supply (fol. by *with*): *to accommodate a friend with money.* **3.** to provide with room and sometimes with food and entertainment. **4.** to make suitable or consistent; adapt: *to accommodate oneself to circumstances.* **5.** to bring into harmony; adjust; reconcile: *to accommodate differences.* **6.** to furnish with accommodations. —*v.i.* **7.** to become or be conformable; act conformably; agree. [t. L: m.s. *accommodātus*, pp., suited] —**ac·com/mo·da/tor,** *n.* —**Syn. 1.** serve, aid, assist. See **oblige. 6.** See **contain.**

ac·com·mo·dat·ing (ə kŏm/ə dā/tĭng), *adj.* easy to deal with; obliging. —**ac·com/mo·dat/ing·ly,** *adv.*

ac·com·mo·da·tion (ə kŏm/ə dā/shən), *n.* **1.** act of accommodating; state or process of being accommodated; adaptation. **2.** adjustment of differences; reconciliation. **3.** *Sociol.* a process of mutual adaptation between persons or social groups, usually through eliminating or lessening of factors of hostility. **4.** anything which supplies a want; a convenience. **5.** (*chiefly pl.*) lodging, or food and lodging. **6.** readiness to aid others; obligingness. **7.** *U.S.* a loan or pecuniary favor. **8.** *Physiol.* the automatic adjustment by which the eye adapts itself to distinct vision at different distances. **9.** an accommodation bill, draft, note, etc.

accommodation bill, draft, note, etc. *U.S.* a bill, draft, note, etc., drawn, accepted, or endorsed by one person for another without consideration, to enable the second person to obtain credit or raise money.

accommodation ladder, a ladder or stairway hung from a ship's side to connect with boats below.

ac·com·mo·da·tive (ə kŏm/ə dā/tĭv), *adj.* tending to accommodate; adaptive. —**ac·com/mo·da/tive·ness,** *n.*

ac·com·pa·ni·ment (ə kŭm/pə nĭ mənt, ə kŭmp/nĭ-), *n.* **1.** something incidental or added for ornament, symmetry, etc. **2.** *Music.* any subsidiary part or parts added to a solo or concerted composition to enhance the effect.

ac·com·pa·nist (ə kŭm/pə nĭst, ə kŭmp/nĭst), *n.* *Music.* one who plays an accompaniment. Also, **accompanyist.**

ac·com·pa·ny (ə kŭm/pə nĭ), *v.t.*, **-nied, -nying. 1.** to go along or in company with; join in action: *to accompany a friend on a walk.* **2.** to be or exist in company with: *thunder accompanies lightning.* **3.** to put in company with; cause to be or go along; associate (fol. by *with*): *he accompanied his speech with gestures.* **4.** *Music.* to play or sing an accompaniment to. [ME *accompanye(n)*, t. F: m. *accompagner*, der. à to + *compagne* COMPANION] —**ac·com/pa·ni·er,** *n.*
—**Syn. 1.** ACCOMPANY, ATTEND, CONVOY, ESCORT mean to go along with someone (or something). TO ACCOMPANY is to go along as an associate on equal terms: *to accompany a friend on a shopping trip.* ATTEND implies going along with, usually to render service or perform duties: *to attend one's employer on a business trip.* To CONVOY is to accompany (especially ships) with an armed guard, for protection: *to convoy a fleet of merchant vessels.* To ESCORT is to accompany in order to protect, guard, honor, or show courtesy: *to escort a visiting dignitary.*

ac·com·pa·ny·ist (ə kŭm/pə nĭ ĭst), *n.* accompanist.

ac·com·plice (ə kŏm/plĭs), *n.* an associate in a crime; partner in wrongdoing. [f. A¹ + COMPLICE]

ac·com·plish (ə kŏm/plĭsh), *v.t.* **1.** to bring to pass; carry out; perform; finish: *to accomplish one's mission.* **2.** to complete (a distance or period of time). **3.** to make complete; equip perfectly. [ME *accomplice(n)*, t. OF: m. *acompliss-*, s. *acomplir*, g. LL *accomplēre*] —**ac·com/plish·a·ble,** *adj.* —**ac·com/plish·er,** *n.* —**Syn. 1.** complete, fulfill; execute. See **do.**

ac·com·plished (ə kŏm/plĭsht), *adj.* **1.** completed; effected: *an accomplished fact.* **2.** perfected; expert: *an accomplished scholar.* **3.** perfected in the graces and attainments of polite society.

ac·com·plish·ment (ə kŏm/plĭsh mənt), *n.* **1.** act of carrying into effect; fulfillment: *the accomplishment of our desires.* **2.** anything accomplished; achievement: *the accomplishments of scientists.* **3.** (*often pl.*) an acquired art or grace; polite attainment. —**Syn. 1.** completion.

ac·compt (ə kount/), *n.*, *v.i.*, *v.t.* *Archaic.* account.

ac·cord (ə kôrd/), *v.i.* **1.** to be in correspondence or harmony; agree. —*v.t.* **2.** to make to agree or correspond; adapt. **3.** to grant; concede: *to accord due praise.* **4.** *Archaic.* to settle; reconcile. —*n.* **5.** just correspondence of things; harmony of relation. **6.** a harmonious union of sounds. **7.** consent or concurrence of opinions or wills; agreement. **8.** an international agreement; settlement of questions outstanding between nations. **9.** **of one's own accord,** voluntarily. [t. LL: s. *accordāre*; r. ME *acorde(n)*, t. OF: m. *acorder*] —**ac·cord/a·ble,** *adj.* —**ac·cord/er,** *n.* —**Syn. 1.** See **agree.**

ac·cord·ance (ə kôr/dəns), *n.* **1.** agreement; conformity. **2.** act of according.

ac·cord·ant (ə kôr/dənt), *adj.* agreeing; conformable. —**ac·cord/ant·ly,** *adv.*

ac·cord·ing (ə kôr/dĭng), *adv.* **1. according to, a.** in accordance with: *according to his judgment.* **b.** proportionately. **c.** on the authority of; as stated by. **2. according as,** conformably or proportionately as. —*adj.* **3.** agreeing.

ac·cord·ing·ly (ə kôr/dĭng lĭ), *adv.* **1.** in accordance; correspondingly. **2.** in due course; therefore; so. —**Syn. 1, 2.** consequently, hence, thus. See **therefore.**

ac·cor·di·on (ə kôr/dĭ ən), *n.* **1.** a portable, keyed, bellowslike wind instrument sounded by means of metallic reeds. —*adj.* **2.** having folds like the bellows of an accordion. [f. ACCORD + -ION] —**ac·cor/di·on·ist,** *n.* Boy playing an accordion

ac·cost (ə kŏst/, ə kôst/), *v.t.* **1.** to approach, esp. with a greeting or remark. —*n.* **2.** greeting; salutation. [t. F: s. *accoster*, g. LL *accostāre* put side by side]

ac·couche·ment (ə kōōsh/mənt; *Fr.* å kōōsh måN/), *n.* *French.* period of confinement in childbirth.

ac·cou·cheur (ăk/ōō shûr/; *Fr.* å kōō shœr/), *n.* *French.* a man who acts as a midwife.

ac·count (ə kount/), *n.* **1.** a verbal or written recital of particular transactions and events; narrative: *an account of everything as it happened.* **2.** an explanatory statement of conduct, as to a superior. **3.** a statement of reasons, causes, etc., explaining some event. **4.** reason; consideration (prec. by *on*): *on all accounts.* **5.** consequence; importance: *things of no account.* **6.** estimation; judgment: *to take into account.* **7.** profit; advantage: *to turn anything to account.* **8. on account of, a.** because of; by reason of. **b.** for the sake of. **9.** a statement of pecuniary transactions. **10.** *Bookkeeping.* **a.** a formal record of the debits and credits relating to the person named (or caption placed) at the head of the ledger account. **b.** a balance of a specified period's receipts and expenditures. [ME *acount(e)*, t. OF: m. *acont*, *acunt*, later *acompt*, f. à to + *cont*, g. LL *comptum*, L *computum* calculation]
—*v.i.* **11.** to give an explanation (fol. by *for*): *to account for the accident.* **12.** to answer concerning one's conduct, duties, etc. (fol. by *for*): *to account for shortages.* **13.** to render an account, esp. of money. **14.** to cause death, capture, etc. (fol. by *for*). —*v.t.* **15.** to count; consider as: *I account myself well paid.* **16.** to assign or impute (fol. by *to*). [ME *acunte(n)*, t. OF: m. *acunter*, g. LL *accomptāre*] —**Syn. 1.** See **narrative.**

ac·count·a·ble (ə koun/tə bəl), *adj.* **1.** liable to be called to account; responsible. **2.** that can be explained. —**ac·count/a·bil/i·ty, ac·count/a·ble·ness,** *n.* —**ac·count/a·bly,** *adv.*

---

ac·count·an·cy (ə koun′tən sĭ), *n.* the art or practice of an accountant.

ac·count·ant (ə koun′tənt), *n.* a person whose profession is inspecting and auditing business accounts. —**ac·count′ant·ship′**, *n.*

ac·count·ing (ə koun′tĭng), *n.* the theory and system of setting up, maintaining, and auditing the books of a firm; the art of analyzing the financial position and operating results of a business house from a study of its sales, purchases, overhead, etc. (distinguished from *bookkeeping* in that a bookkeeper only makes the proper entries in books set up to the accountant's plan).

ac·cou·ple·ment (ə kŭp′əl mənt), *n.* **1.** act of coupling. **2.** that which couples, esp. (in building) a tie or brace. [t. F, der. *accoupler*, der. *a* to + *couple* COUPLE]

ac·cou·ter (ə kōō′tər), *v.t.* to equip or array, esp. with military accouterments. Also, *Brit.*, **ac·cou′tre**. [t. F: m. s. *accoutrer*]

ac·cou·ter·ments (ə kōō′tər mənts), *n.pl.* **1.** equipage; trappings. **2.** the equipment of a soldier except arms and clothing. Also, *Brit.*, **ac·cou′tre·ments**.

Ac·cra (ăk′rə; *native* ə krä′), *n.* a seaport in British West Africa: the capital of Gold Coast. 72,977 (est. 1937). Also, **Akkra**. See map under **Gold Coast**.

ac·cred·it (ə krĕd′ĭt), *v.t.* **1.** to ascribe or attribute to (fol. by *with*): *he was accredited with having said it.* **2.** to attribute; consider as belonging to: *a discovery accredited to Edison.* **3.** to send with credentials: *to accred´t an envoy.* **4.** to certify as meeting official requirements: *to accredit a school.* **5.** to bring into credit; invest with credit or authority. **6.** to believe. [t. F: s. *accréditer*]

ac·crete (ə krēt′), *v.*, **-creted**, **-creting**, *adj.* —*v.i.* **1.** to grow together; adhere (fol. by *to*). —*v.t.* **2.** to add as by growth. —*adj.* **3.** *Bot.* grown together. [t. L: m. s. *accrētus*, pp., increased]

ac·cre·tion (ə krē′shən), *n.* **1.** an increase by natural growth or by gradual external addition; growth in size or extent. **2.** the result of this process. **3.** an extraneous addition: *the last part of the legend is a later accretion.* **4.** the growing together of separate parts into a single whole. **5.** *Law.* increase of property by gradual additions caused by acts of nature, as of land by alluvion. **6.** *Pathol.* conglomeration; piling up of substance. [t. L: s. *accrētio*] —**ac·cre′tive**, *adj.*

ac·cru·al (ə krōō′əl), *n.* **1.** act or process of accruing. **2.** something accrued; accretion.

ac·crue (ə krōō′), *v.i.*, **-crued**, **-cruing**. **1.** to happen or result as a natural growth; arise in due course; come or fall as an addition or increment. **2.** *Law.* to become a present and enforceable right or demand. [der. *accrue*, obs. n., t. F, orig. fem. pp. of *accroître* increase, g. L *accrescere*] **ac·crue′ment**, *n.*

accrued interest, the amount of interest accumulated at a given time but not yet paid (or received).

acct., account.

ac·cul·tur·a·tion (ə kŭl′chə rā′shən), *n.* *Sociol.* the process and result of adopting the culture traits of another group.

ac·cum·bent (ə kŭm′bənt), *adj.* **1.** reclining: *accumbent posture.* **2.** *Bot.* lying against something. [t. L: m. s. *accumbens*, ppr.] —**ac·cum′ben·cy**, *n.*

ac·cu·mu·late (ə kū′myə lāt′), *v.*, **-lated**, **-lating**. —*v.t.* **1.** to heap up; gather as into a mass; collect: *to accumulate wealth.* —*v.i.* **2.** to grow into a heap or mass; form an increasing quantity: *public evils accumulate.* [t. L: m. s. *accumulātus*, pp., heaped up]

ac·cu·mu·la·tion (ə kū′myə lā′shən), *n.* **1.** a collecting together. **2.** that which is accumulated. **3.** growth by continuous additions, as of interest to principal.

ac·cu·mu·la·tive (ə kū′myə lā′tĭv), *adj.* tending to or arising from accumulation; cumulative. —**ac·cu′mu·la·tive·ly**, *adv.* —**ac·cu′mu·la·tive·ness**, *n.*

ac·cu·mu·la·tor (ə kū′myə lā′tər), *n.* **1.** one that accumulates. **2.** *Brit.* a storage battery. [t. L]

ac·cu·ra·cy (ăk′yə rə sĭ), *n.* condition or quality of being accurate; precision or exactness; correctness.

ac·cu·rate (ăk′yər ĭt), *adj.* in exact conformity to truth, to a standard or rule, or to a model; free from error or defect: *an accurate typist.* [t. L: m. s. *accūrātus*, pp., exact, cared for] —**ac′cu·rate·ly**, *adv.* —**ac′cu·rate·ness**, *n.* —Syn. See **correct**.

ac·curs·ed (ə kûr′sĭd, ə kûrst′), *adj.* **1.** subject to a curse; ruined. **2.** worthy of curses; detestable. Also, **ac·curst** (ə kûrst′). —**ac·curs·ed·ly** (ə kûr′sĭd lĭ), *adv.* —**ac·curs′ed·ness**, *n.*

ac·cu·sa·tion (ăk′yŏŏ zā′shən), *n.* **1.** a charge of wrongdoing; imputation of guilt or blame. **2.** the specific offense charged: *the accusation is murder.* **3.** act of accusing or charging. Also, **ac·cus·al** (ə kū′zəl). [t. L: s. *accūsātio*]

ac·cu·sa·ti·val (ə kū′zə tī′vəl), *adj.* pertaining to the accusative case.

ac·cu·sa·tive (ə kū′zə tĭv), *adj.* **1.** (in Greek, Latin, and English grammar) denoting in Latin and Greek by means of its form, in English by means of its form or its position, a case which has as one of its chief functions the indication of the direct object of a finite verb, as in "the boy loves the girl." **2.** similar to such a case form in function or meaning. —*n.* **3.** the accusative case. **4.** a word in that case: *Latin "puellam" may be spoken of as an accusative.* **5.** a form or construction of similar meaning. [t. L: m.s. *accūsātīvus*, trans. of Gk. (*ptōsis*) *aitiātikē*

pertaining to that which is caused] —**ac·cu′sa·tive·ly.** *adv.*

ac·cu·sa·to·ri·al (ə kū′zə tōr′ĭ əl), *adj.* pertaining to an accuser. —**ac·cu′sa·to·ri·al·ly**, *adv.*

ac·cu·sa·to·ry (ə kū′zə tōr′ĭ), *adj.* containing an accusation; accusing: *he looked at the jury with an accusatory expression.*

ac·cuse (ə kūz′), *v.t.*, **-cused**, **-cusing**. **1.** to bring a charge against; impute with the fault or crime of. **2.** to blame. [t. L: m. s. *accūsāre* accuse, blame; r. ME *acuse*, t. OF] —**ac·cus′er**, *n.* —**ac·cus′ing·ly**, *adv.* —Syn. **1.** arraign, indict; incriminate; impeach.

ac·cus·tom (ə kŭs′təm), *v.t.* to familiarize by custom or use; habituate: *to accustom oneself to cold weather.* [late ME *acustume(n)*, t. OF: m. *acostumer*, der. *a* to + *costume* custom]

ac·cus·tomed (ə kŭs′təmd), *adj.* **1.** customary; habitual: *in their accustomed manner.* **2.** in the habit of: *accustomed to doing good.* —**ac·cus′tomed·ness**, *n.*

ace (ās), *n.* **1.** a single spot or mark on a card or die. **2.** a card or die marked with a single spot. **3.** (in tennis, badminton, etc.) **a.** a serve which the opponent fails to touch. **b.** the point thus scored. **4.** a very small quantity, amount, or degree; a particle: *within an ace of winning.* **5.** a highly skilled person; an adept: *an ace at tap dancing.* **6.** a fighter pilot officially credited with shooting down five or more enemy airplanes. —*adj.* **7.** excellent; first in quality; outstanding. [ME *ac*, t. OF, g. L, supposedly t. d. Gk., var. of Gk. *heîs* one]

-acea, *Zool.* a suffix of (Latin) names of classes and orders of animals, as in *Crustacea*. [t. L, neut. pl. of *-āceus*. See -ACEOUS]

-aceae, *Bot.* a suffix of (Latin) names of families of plants, as in *Rosaceae*. [t. L, fem. pl. of *-āceus*. See -ACEOUS]

A·cel·da·ma (ə sĕl′də mə), *n.* **1.** the "field of blood," near Jerusalem, purchased with the bribe Judas took for betraying Jesus. Matt. 27:8; Acts 1:19. **2.** any place of slaughter. [t. L, t. Gk.: m. *Akeldamá*, t. Aram.: m. *hagal damā*]

a·cen·tric (ā sĕn′trĭk), *adj.* not centered; having no center.

-aceous, a suffix of adjectives used in scientific terminology, as in *cretaceous*, *herbaceous*, and in adjectives derived from *-aceu*, *-aceae*. [t. L: m. *-āceus* of the nature of]

a·ceph·a·lous (ā sĕf′ə ləs), *adj.* **1.** headless; lacking a distinct head. **2.** without a leader. [t. LL: m. *acephalus*, t. Gk.: m. *aképhalos*]

a·ce·quia (ə sā′kyə; *Sp.* ä sē′kyä), *n.* *Southwestern U.S.* an irrigation ditch. [t. Sp.]

ac·er·bate (*v.* ăs′ər bāt′; *adj.* ə sûr′bĭt), *v.*, **-bated**, **-bating**, *adj.* —*v.t.* **1.** to make sour or bitter. **2.** to exasperate. —*adj.* **3.** embittered. [t. L: m. s. *acerbātus*, pp.]

a·cer·bi·ty (ə sûr′bə tĭ), *n.*, *pl.* **-ties**. **1.** sourness, with roughness or astringency of taste. **2.** harshness or severity, as of temper or expression. [t. F: m. *acerbité*, t. L: m. s. *acerbitas*]

ac·er·ose (ăs′ə rōs′), *adj.* *Bot.* needle-shaped, as the leaves of the pine. Also, **ac·er·ate** (ăs′ər ĭt, -ə rāt′), **ac·er·ous** (ăs′er əs). [t. L: m.s. *acerōsus*, der. *acus* chaff, but confused with *acus* needle]

a·cer·vate (ə sûr′vĭt, -vāt), *adj.* *Bot.* heaped; growing in heaps, or in closely compacted clusters. [t. L: m. s. *acervātus*, pp., heaped] —**a·cer′vate·ly**, *adv.*

a·ces·cent (ə sĕs′ənt), *adj.* turning sour; slightly sour; acidulous. [t. L: m. s. *acescens*, ppr.] —**a·ces′cence**, **a·ces′cen·cy**, *n.*

acet-, var. of *aceto-*, used before vowels, as in *acetal*.

ac·e·tab·u·lum (ăs′ə tăb′yə ləm), *n.*, *pl.* **-la** (-lə). *Anat.* the socket in the hipbone which receives the head of the thighbone. [t. L: vinegar cup, saucer] —**ac′e·tab′u·lar**, *adj.*

ac·e·tal (ăs′ə tăl′), *n.* **1.** a colorless, volatile fluid, $C_6H_{14}O_2$, used as a hypnotic or solvent. **2.** (*pl.*) a class of compounds of aldehydes or ketones with alcohols.

ac·et·al·de·hyde (ăs′ə tăl′də hīd′), *n.* a volatile, colorless, aromatic liquid, CH_3CHO, used commercially in the silvering of mirrors and in organic synthesis.

ac·et·am·ide (ăs′ə tăm′īd, -ĭd; ə sĕt′ə mīd′, -mĭd), *n.* *Chem.* the amide of acetic acid, a white crystalline solid, CH_3CONH_2, melting at 80°C. Also, **ac·et·am·id** (ăs′ə tăm′ĭd, ə sĕt′ə mĭd). [f. ACET(YL) + AMIDE]

ac·et·an·i·lide (ăs′ə tăn′ə lĭd′, -lĭd), *n.* an organic compound, C_8H_9ON, derived by the action of glacial acetic acid upon aniline, used as a remedy for fever, headache, rheumatism, etc., and in the lacquer industry. Also, **ac·et·an·i·lid** (ăs′ə tăn′ə lĭd). [f. ACET(YL) + ANIL(INE) + -IDE]

ac·e·tate (ăs′ə tāt′), *n.* *Chem.* a salt or ester of acetic acid. [f. ACET- + -ATE²] —**ac′e·tat′ed**, *adj.*

acetate rayon, a rayon made from the acetic ester of cellulose, differing from viscose rayon in having a greater strength when wet and in being more sensitive to high temperature.

a·ce·tic (ə sē′tĭk, ə sĕt′ĭk), *adj.* pertaining to, derived from, or producing vinegar or acetic acid.

acetic acid, a colorless liquid, CH_3COOH, the essential constituent of vinegar, used in the manufacture of acetate rayon and the production of numerous esters used as solvents and flavoring agents.

ăct, āble, dâre, ärt; ĕbb, ēqual; ĭf, īce; hŏt, ōver, ôrder, oil, bŏŏk, ōōze, out; ŭp, ūse, ûrge; ə = a in alone; ch, chief; g, give; ng, ring; sh, shoe; th, thin; ŧħ, that; zh, vision. See the full key on inside cover.

acetic anhydride, a colorless, pungent fluid, $(CH_3.CO)_2O$, the anhydride of acetic acid, used as a re-agent and in the production of plastics, film, and fabrics derived from cellulose.

a·cet·i·fy (əsĕt′əfī′), v.t., v.i., **-fied, -fying.** to turn into vinegar; make or become acetous. [f. ACET- + -(I)FY] **—a·cet′i·fi·ca′tion,** n. **—a·cet′i·fi′er,** n.

aceto-, a word element indicating the presence of acetic acid or the radical acetyl. Also, **acet-.** [comb. form repr. L acētum vinegar]

ac·e·tone (ăs′ətōn′), n. a colorless, volatile, inflammable liquid, $(CH_3)_2CO$, formed in the distillation of acetates, etc., used as a solvent and in smokeless powders, varnishes, etc. [f. ACET- + -ONE]

ac·e·tous (ăs′ətəs, əsē′-), adj. **1.** containing or producing acetic acid. **2.** sour; vinegary. Also, **ac·e·tose** (ăs′ətōs′). [t. LL: m. s. acetōsus]

ac·e·tum (əsē′təm), n. a preparation made with vinegar or dilute acetic acid as the solvent. [t. L: vinegar]

ac·e·tyl (ăs′ətĭl), n. Chem. a radical, CH_3CO, in acetic acid. [f. ACET- + -YL] **—ac·e·tyl′ic,** adj.

a·cet·y·late (əsĕt′əlāt′), v.t., **-lated, -lating.** Chem. to combine (a compound) with one or more acetyl groups. **—a·cet′y·la′tion,** n.

ac·e·tyl·cho·line (ăs′ətĭlkō′lēn, -kŏl′ēn, -ĭn), n. an alkaline organic compound, $C_7H_{17}O_3N$, prepared from ergot, and used medicinally to decrease the blood pressure or to set up peristalsis.

a·cet·y·lene (əsĕt′əlēn′), n. a colorless gas, C_2H_2, prepared by the action of water on calcium carbide, used in metal welding and cutting, as an illuminant, etc.

acetylene series, Chem. a series of unsaturated aliphatic hydrocarbons containing a triple bond and having the general formula C_nH_{2n-2}.

ac·e·tyl·sal·i·cyl·ic acid (ăs′ətĭl săl′əsĭl′ĭk, əsē′təl-), aspirin.

ace·y·deuc·y (ā′sĭdū′sĭ, -dōō′-), n. a form of backgammon.

A·chae·an (əkē′ən), adj. **1.** of Achaia or the Achaeans. **2.** Greek. —n. **3.** an inhabitant of Achaia. **4.** a Greek. Also, **A·cha·ian** (əkā′ən, əkī′-). [f. s. L Achaeus (t. Gk.: m. Achaiós) + -AN]

Achaean League, a political confederation of Achaean and other Greek cities, 281–146 B.C.

A·cha·ia (əkā′ə, əkī′ə), n. an ancient country in S Greece, on the Gulf of Corinth. Also, **A·chae·a** (əkē′ə). See map under **Attica.**

A·cha·tes (əkā′tēz), n. **1.** (in Vergil's Aeneid) the companion and friend of Aeneas. **2.** a faithful comrade.

ache (āk), v., **ached, aching,** n. —v.i. **1.** to suffer pain; have or be in continued pain: his whole body ached. **2.** Colloq. to be eager; yearn; long. [pseudo-Gk. sp. of ake, ME aken, OE acan] —n. **3.** pain of some duration, in opposition to sudden twinges or spasmodic pain. [ME; OE æce, der. acan] **—ach′ing·ly,** adv. **—Syn. 3.** See **pain.**

Ach·e·lo·us (ăk′əlō′əs), n. Gk. Myth. a river god, defeated by Hercules in a struggle over Deianira.

a·chene (əkēn′), n. Bot. a small, dry, hard, one-seeded, indehiscent fruit. Also, **akene.** [t. NL: m. s. achaenium, f. Gk. a- A-[6] + m. s. Gk. chainein gape + -ium -IUM] **—a·che·ni·al** (əkē′nĭəl), adj.

Ach·er·on (ăk′ərŏn′), n. **1.** Gk. and Rom. Myth. a river in Hades, over which Charon ferried the souls of the dead. **2.** the lower world; hell.

Ach·e·son (ăch′əsən), n. **Dean Gooderham,** born 1893, U.S. Secretary of State since 1949.

à che·val (à shə vàl′), French. by horse; on horseback.

a·chieve (əchēv′), v., **achieved, achieving.** —v.t. **1.** to bring to a successful end; carry through; accomplish. **2.** to bring about, as by effort; gain or obtain: to achieve victory. —v.i. **3.** to accomplish some enterprise; bring about a result intended. [ME acheve(n), t. F: m. achever, der. phrase (venir) à chief = LL ad caput venīre bring to a head] **—a·chiev′a·ble,** adj. **—a·chiev′er,** n. **—Syn.** consummate, complete; effect, execute. See **do. 2.** attain, realize, win.

a·chieve·ment (əchēv′mənt), n. **1.** something accomplished, esp. by valor, boldness, or superior ability; a great or heroic deed. **2.** act of achieving; accomplishment: the achievement of one's object. **—Syn. 1.** ACHIEVEMENT, EXPLOIT, FEAT are terms for a noteworthy act. ACHIEVEMENT connotes final accomplishment of something noteworthy, after much effort and often in spite of obstacles and discouragements: a scientific achievement. EXPLOIT connotes boldness, bravery, and usually ingenuity: the famous exploit of an aviator. FEAT connotes the performance of something difficult, generally demanding skill and strength: a feat of horsemanship.

achievement age, Psychol. the average age at which any given score is made on an achievement test. Cf. **achievement quotient.**

achievement quotient, Psychol. educational age divided by actual age. Thus, a child of 10 years whose educational achievement equals that of the average 12-year-old has an achievement quotient of 1.2 (commonly expressed as 120). Abbr.: A.Q.

achievement test, Psychol. a test designed to measure the results of learning or teaching, as contrasted with tests of native ability or aptitude.

A·chil·les (əkĭl′ēz), n. Gk. Legend. the hero of Homer's Iliad, the greatest Greek warrior in the Trojan war, who came to be the ideal of Greek manhood. According to legend, he died when Paris wounded him in the heel, where alone he was vulnerable. **—Ach·il·le·an** (ăk′əlē′ən), adj.

Achilles' heel, a vulnerable spot.

Achilles' tendon, Anat. the tendon joining the calf muscles to the heelbone.

a·chlam·y·date (ăklăm′ədāt′, -dĭt), adj. Zool. not chlamydate; having no mantle or pallium.

ach·la·myd·e·ous (ăk′ləmĭd′Yəs), adj. Bot. not chlamydeous; having no floral envelope. [f. A-[6] + s. Gk. chlamýs cloak + -EOUS]

ach·ro·mat·ic (ăk′rəmăt′Yk), adj. **1.** Optics. free from color due to the decomposition of light in chromatic aberration. **2.** Biol. **a.** containing or consisting of achromatin. **b.** resisting dyes. **3.** Music. without accidentals or changes in key. [f. s. Gk. achrōmatos colorless + -IC] **—ach′ro·mat′i·cal·ly,** adv.

a·chro·ma·tin (ākrō′mətĭn), n. Biol. that portion of the nucleus of a cell which is less highly colored by staining agents than the rest of the cell.

a·chro·ma·tism (ākrō′mətĭz′əm), n. freedom from chromatic aberration. Also, **a·chro·ma·tic·i·ty** (ā krō′ mətĭs′ə tĭ).

a·chro·ma·tize (ākrō′mətīz′), v.t., **-tized, -tizing.** to make achromatic; deprive of color.

a·chro·ma·tous (ākrō′mətəs), adj. without color; of a lighter color than normal. [t. Gk.: m. achrōmatos]

a·chro·mic (ākrō′mĭk), adj. colorless; without coloring matter. Also, **a·chro′mous.** [f. A-[6] + m. Gk. chrōma color + -IC]

a·cic·u·la (əsĭk′yələ), n., pl. **-lae** (-lē′). a needle-shaped part or process; a spine, bristle, or needlelike crystal. [t. L, dim. of acus needle]

a·cic·u·lar (əsĭk′yələr), adj. needle-shaped. **—a·cic′u·lar·ly,** adv.

a·cic·u·late (əsĭk′yəlĭt, -lāt′), adj. **1.** having aciculae. **2.** marked as with needle scratches. **3.** needle-shaped; acicular. Also, **a·cic′u·lat′ed.**

a·cic·u·lum (əsĭk′yələm), n., pl. **-lums, -la** (-lə). **1.** an acicula. **2.** Zool. one of the slender sharp stylets embedded in the parapodia of some annelids, as the Polychaeta. [erroneous var. of ACICULA]

ac·id (ăs′ĭd), n. **1.** Chem. a compound (usually having a sour taste and capable of neutralizing alkalis and reddening blue litmus paper) containing hydrogen which can be replaced by a metal or an electropositive radical to form a salt. Acids are proton donors, and yield hydronium ions in water solution. **2.** a substance with a sour taste. —adj. **3.** Chem. **a.** belonging or pertaining to acids or the anhydrides of acids. **b.** having only a part of the hydrogen of an acid replaced by a metal or its equivalent: an acid phosphate, etc. **4.** tasting like vinegar: acid fruits. **5.** sour; sharp; ill-tempered: an acid remark, wit, etc. **6.** Petrog. containing much silica. [t. L: s. acidus sour] **—ac′id·ly,** adv. **—ac′id·ness,** n. **—Syn. 5.** ACID, ASTRINGENT are terms used figuratively of wit or humor. ACID suggests a sharp, biting, or ill-natured quality: an acid joke about an opponent. ASTRINGENT connotes severity but usually also a bracing quality, as of something applied with curative intent: much-needed astringent criticism.

ac·id-fast (ăs′ĭd făst′, -fäst′), adj. resistant to decoloring by acid after staining.

ac·id-form·ing (ăs′ĭd fôr′mĭng), adj. **1.** yielding acid in chemical reaction; acidic. **2.** (of food) containing a large amount of acid ash after complete oxidation.

a·cid·ic (əsĭd′ĭk), adj. **1.** Petrog. containing a large amount of silica. **2.** acid-forming (def. 1).

a·cid·i·fy (əsĭd′əfī′), v.t., v.i., **-fied, -fying.** to make or become acid; convert into an acid. [f. ACID + -(I)FY] **—a·cid′i·fi′a·ble,** adj. **—a·cid′i·fi·ca′tion,** n. **—a·cid′i·fi′er,** n.

a·cid·i·ty (əsĭd′ətĭ), n., pl. **-ties. 1.** quality of being acid. **2.** sourness; tartness. **3.** excessive acid quality, as of the gastric juice.

ac·i·do·phil (ăs′ədəfĭl′, əsĭd′ə-), n. Biol. a cell or cell constituent with selective affinity for acid dyes.

ac·i·doph·i·lus (ăs′ədŏf′ələs), n. See **lactobacillus.**

acidophilus milk, a fermented milk which alters the bacterial content of the intestines. The fermenting bacteria are Lactobacilli acidophili.

ac·i·do·sis (ăs′ədō′sĭs), n. Pathol. poisoning by acids forming within the body under morbid conditions. [irreg. f. ACID + -OSIS] **—ac·i·dot·ic** (ăs′ədŏt′ĭk), adj.

acid soil, a soil of acid reaction, or having predominance of hydrogen ions, tasting sour in solution.

acid test, a critical test; final analysis.

a·cid·u·late (əsĭj′əlāt′), v.t., **-lated, -lating. 1.** to make somewhat acid. **2.** to sour; embitter. **—a·cid′u·la′tion,** n.

a·cid·u·lous (əsĭj′ələs), adj. **1.** slightly sour. **2.** sharp; caustic. **3.** subacid. [t. L: m. acidulus, dim. of acidus]

ac·i·er·ate (ăs′ĭərāt′), v.t., **-ated, -ating.** to convert (iron) into steel. [f. F acier steel + -ATE[1]] **—ac′i·er·a′tion,** n.

ac·i·form (ăs′əfôrm′), adj. needle-shaped; acicular. [f. L ac(us) needle + -(I)FORM]

ac·i·nac·i·form (ăs′ənăs′əfôrm′), adj. Bot. scimitar-shaped, as a leaf. [f. s. L acinaces short sword (t. Gk.: m. akinákēs) + -(I)FORM]

a·cin·i·form (əsĭn′əfôrm′), adj. **1.** clustered like grapes. **2.** acinous. [f. s. L acinus grape + -(I)FORM]

Acinaciform leaf

b., blend of, blended; c., cognate with; d., dialect, dialectal; der., derived from; f., formed from; g., going back to; m., modification of; r., replacing; s., stem of; t., taken from; ?, perhaps. See the full key on inside cover.

ac·i·nous (ăs/ə nəs), *adj.* consisting of acini. Also, **ac·i·nose** (ăs/ə nōs/). [t. L: m. s. *acinōsus* like grapes]

ac·i·nus (ăs/ə nəs), *n., pl.* **-ni** (-nī/). **1.** *Bot.* one of the small drupelets or berries of an aggregate baccate fruit, as the blackberry, etc. **2.** a berry, as a grape, currant, etc. **3.** *Anat.* **a.** a minute rounded lobule. **b.** the smallest secreting portion of a gland. [t. L: berry, grape]

-acious, an adjective suffix made by adding **-ous** to nouns ending in **-acity** (the *-ty* being dropped), as *audacious*.

-acity, a suffix for nouns denoting quality and the like. [t. F: m. *-acité*, t. L: m. s. *-ācitas*, or directly t. L]

ack-ack (ăk/ăk/), *n.* *Slang.* **1.** anti-aircraft fire. **2.** anti-aircraft arms. [used by Brit. radio operators for A. A. (anti-aircraft)]

ac·knowl·edge (ăk nŏl/Yj), *v.t.*, **-edged, -edging. 1.** to admit to be real or true; recognize the existence, truth, or fact of: *to acknowledge belief in God.* **2.** to express recognition or realization of: *to acknowledge an acquaintance by bowing.* **3.** to recognize the authority or claims of: *to acknowledge his right to vote.* **4.** to indicate appreciation or gratitude for. **5.** to admit or certify the receipt of: *to acknowledge a letter.* **6.** *Law.* to own as binding or of legal force: *to acknowledge a deed.* [b. obs. *acknow* (OE *oncnāwan* confess) and *knowledge*, v., admit] **—ac·knowl/edg·a·ble**, *adj.* **—ac·knowl/edg·er**, *n.*
—Syn. 1. ACKNOWLEDGE, ADMIT, CONFESS agree in the idea of declaring something to be true. ACKNOWLEDGE implies making a statement reluctantly, often about something previously denied: *to acknowledge a fault.* ADMIT especially implies acknowledging something under pressure: *to admit a charge.* CONFESS usually means stating somewhat formally an admission of wrongdoing, crime, or shortcoming: *to confess guilt, to an inability to understand.* **—Ant. 1.** deny.

ac·knowl·edg·ment (ăk nŏl/Yj mənt), *n.* **1.** act of acknowledging or admitting. **2.** a recognition of the existence or truth of anything: *the acknowledgment of a sovereign power.* **3.** an expression of appreciation. **4.** a thing done or given in appreciation or gratitude. **5.** *Law.* **a.** declaration by a person before an official that he executed a legal document. **b.** an official certificate of a formal acknowledging. Also, *esp.* Brit., **ac·knowl/edge·ment.**

a·clin·ic (ā klĭn/Yk), *adj.* free from inclination or dip of the magnetic needle (applied to an imaginary line near the equator). [f. m.s. Gk. *aklinēs* not bending + -ic]

ac·me (ăk/mY), *n.* the highest point. [t. Gk.: m. *akmē*]

ac·ne (ăk/nY), *n.* an inflammatory disease of the sebaceous glands, characterized by an eruption (often pustular) of the skin, esp. of the face. [orig. uncert.]

ac·node (ăk/nōd), *n.* *Math.* a double point belonging to a curve, but separated from other real points of the curve. [f. s. L *acus* needle + NODE] **—ac·no/dal**, *adj.*

a·cock (ə kŏk/), *adv., adj.* in a cocked position.

ac·o·lyte (ăk/ə līt/), *n.* **1.** an altar attendant of minor rank; altar boy. **2.** *Rom. Cath. Ch.* a member of the highest of the four minor orders, ranking next below a subdeacon. **3.** an attendant; an assistant. [ME *acolyt*, t. ML: m. s. *acolitus*, t. Gk.: m. *akolouthos* follower]

A·con·ca·gua (ä/kŏn kä/gwä), *n.* a mountain in W Argentina, in the Andes: the highest peak in the Western Hemisphere. 23,003 ft.

ac·o·nite (ăk/ə nīt/), *n.* **1.** any plant of the ranunculaceous genus *Aconitum*, including plants with poisonous and medicinal properties, as monkshood or wolfsbane. **2.** an extract or tincture made from the root of any of these plants. Also, **ac·o·ni·tum** (ăk/ə nī/təm). [t. L: m.s. *aconītum*, t. Gk.: m. *akónīton*] **—ac·o·nit·ic** (ăk/ə nĭt/Yk), *adj.*

a·corn (ā/kôrn, ā/kərn), *n.* the fruit of the oak, a nut in a hardened scaly cup. [d. ME *acorne*, r. ME *akern*, OE *æcern*, c. Icel. *akarn*]

a·cot·y·le·don (ā/kŏt ə lē/dən, ā kŏt/-), *n.* *Bot.* a plant without cotyledons. [f. A-⁶ + COTYLEDON] **—a·cot·y·le·don·ous** (ā/kŏt ə lē/dən əs, -lĕd/ən əs, ā kŏt/-), *adj.*

a·cous·tic (ə kōōs/tYk or, *esp.* Brit., ə kous/-), *adj.* **1.** Also, **a·cous/ti·cal.** pertaining to the sense or organs of hearing, or to the science of sound. **—n. 2.** a remedy for deafness or imperfect hearing. [t. F: m. *acoustique*, t. Gk.: m.s. *akoustikós*] **—a·cous/ti·cal·ly**, *adv.*

ac·ous·ti·cian (ăk/ōō stYsh/ən or, *esp.* Brit., ăk/ou-), *n.* an acoustic engineer.

a·cous·tics (ə kōōs/tYks or, *esp.* Brit., ə kous/-), *n.* **1.** *Physics.* the science of sound. **2.** (*construed as pl.*) acoustic properties, as of an auditorium. [pl. of ACOUSTIC. See -ICS]

à cou·vert (á kōō vĕr/), French. under cover.

ac·quaint (ə kwānt/), *v.t.* **1.** to make more or less familiar or conversant (fol. by *with*): *to acquaint him with our plan.* **2.** to furnish with knowledge; inform: *to acquaint a friend with one's efforts.* [ME *acointe(n)*, t. OF: m. *acointer*, t. gL *adcognitare* make known]

ac·quaint·ance (ə kwān/təns), *n.* **1.** a person (or persons) known to one, esp. a person with whom one is not on terms of great intimacy. **2.** state of being acquainted; personal knowledge. **—ac·quaint/ance·ship/**, *n.*
—Syn. 1. ACQUAINTANCE, ASSOCIATE, COMPANION, FRIEND refer to a person with whom one is in contact. An ACQUAINTANCE is someone recognized by sight or someone known though not intimately: *a casual acquaintance.* An ASSOCIATE is a person who is often in one's company, usually because of some work, enterprise, or pursuit in common: *a business associate.* A COMPANION is a person who shares one's activities, fate, or condition: *a traveling companion, companion in despair.* A FRIEND is a person with whom one is on intimate

terms and for whom one feels a warm affection: *a trusted friend.* **2.** association, familiarity, intimacy.

ac·quaint·ed (ə kwān/tYd), *adj.* having personal knowledge; informed (fol. by *with*): *acquainted with law.*

ac·qui·esce (ăk/wY ĕs/), *v.i.*, **-esced, -escing.** to assent tacitly; comply quietly; agree; consent (often fol. by *in*): *to acquiesce in an opinion.* [t. F: m.s. *acquiescer*, t. L: m. *acquiescere*] **—ac/qui·esc/ing·ly**, *adv.*

ac·qui·es·cence (ăk/wY ĕs/əns), *n.* **1.** act or condition of acquiescing or giving tacit assent; a silent submission, or submission with apparent consent. **2.** *Law.* such neglect to take legal proceedings in opposition to a matter as implies consent thereto.

ac·qui·es·cent (ăk/wY ĕs/ənt), *adj.* disposed to acquiesce or yield; submissive. **—ac/qui·es/cent·ly**, *adv.*

ac·quire (ə kwīr/), *v.t.*, **-quired, -quiring. 1.** to come into possession of; get as one's own: *to acquire property, a title, etc.* **2.** to gain for oneself through one's actions or efforts: *to acquire learning, a reputation, etc.* [t. L: m.s. *acquīrere*; r. ME *acquere(n)*, t. OF: m. *acquerre*] **—ac·quir/a·ble**, *adj.* **—ac·quir/er**, *n.* **—Syn. 1.** obtain, procure, secure; win, earn; attain. See **get.**

acquired characters, *Biol.* characters that are the results of environment, use, or disuse, rather than of heredity. Also, **acquired characteristics.**

ac·quire·ment (ə kwīr/mənt), *n.* **1.** act of acquiring, esp. the gaining of knowledge or mental attributes. **2.** (*often pl.*) that which is acquired; attainment.

ac·qui·si·tion (ăk/wə zYsh/ən), *n.* **1.** act of acquiring or gaining possession: *the acquisition of property.* **2.** something acquired: *a valued acquisition.* [t. L: s. *acquisītio*]

ac·quis·i·tive (ə kwĭz/ə tĭv), *adj.* tending to make acquisitions; fond of acquiring: *an acquisitive society.* **—ac·quis/i·tive·ly**, *adv.* **—ac·quis/i·tive·ness**, *n.*

ac·quit (ə kwĭt/), *v.t.*, **-quitted, -quitting. 1.** to relieve from a charge of fault or crime; pronounce not guilty (fol. by *of*). **2.** to release or discharge (a person) from an obligation. **3.** to settle (a debt, obligation, claim, etc.). **4. acquit oneself, a.** to behave; bear or conduct oneself: *he acquitted himself well in battle.* **b.** to clear oneself: *he acquitted himself of suspicion.* [ME *aquite(n)*, t. OF: m. *aquiter.* See AD-, QUIT] **—ac·quit/ter**, *n.* **—Syn. 1.** See **absolve.**

ac·quit·tal (ə kwĭt/əl), *n.* **1.** act of acquitting; discharge. **2.** state of being acquitted; release. **3.** discharge of an obligation or a debt. **4.** *Law.* judicial deliverance from a criminal charge on a verdict or finding of not guilty.

ac·quit·tance (ə kwĭt/əns), *n.* **1.** act of acquitting. **2.** discharge of or from debt or obligation. **3.** a receipt or quittance.

a·cre (ā/kər), *n.* **1.** a common variable unit of land measure, now equal in the U.S. and Great Britain to 43,560 sq. ft. or ¹/₆₄₀ sq. mile. **2.** (*pl.*) fields or land in general. **3.** (*pl.*) *Colloq.* large quantities. **4.** *Obs.* an open plowed or sowed field. [ME *aker*, OE *æcer*, c. G *acker*]

A·cre (ä/kər, ā/kər), *n.* a seaport in NW Israel: captured during the Third Crusade by Richard the Lion-Hearted, 1191. 12,360 (est. 1944).

a·cre·age (ā/kər Yj), *n.* acres collectively; extent in acres.

a·cred (ā/kərd), *adj.* having acres; landed.

a·cre-foot (ā/kər fŏŏt/), *n.* a unit of volume of water in irrigation, the amount covering one acre to a depth of one foot (43,560 cubic feet).

a·cre-inch (ā/kər Ynch/), *n.* one twelfth of an acre-foot.

ac·rid (ăk/rYd), *adj.* **1.** sharp or biting to the taste; bitterly pungent; irritating. **2.** violent; stinging: *acrid remarks.* [f. s. L *ācer* sharp + -ID⁴] **—a·crid/i·ty**, **ac/rid·ness**, *n.* **—ac/rid·ly**, *adv.*

ac·ri·dine (ăk/rə dēn/, -dĭn), *n.* a crystalline substance, $C_{13}H_9N$, part of the anthracene fraction of coal tar. It occurs as needle-shaped crystals and is a source of synthetic dyes and drugs.

ac·ri·fla·vine (ăk/rə flā/vYn, -vēn), *n.* a derivative of acridine, $C_{14}H_{14}N_3Cl$, used as a disinfectant and an antiseptic; trypaflavine.

ac·ri·mo·ni·ous (ăk/rə mō/nY əs), *adj.* caustic; stinging; bitter; virulent: *an acrimonious answer.* **—ac/ri·mo/ni·ous·ly**, *adv.* **—ac/ri·mo/ni·ous·ness**, *n.*

ac·ri·mo·ny (ăk/rə mō/nY), *n., pl.* **-nies.** sharpness or severity of temper; bitterness of expression proceeding from anger or ill nature. [t. L: m. s. *ācrimōnia*]

acro-, a word element meaning "tip," "top," "apex," or "edge," as in *acrogen.* Also, before vowels, **acr-.** [t. Gk.: m. *akro-*, comb. form of *ákros* at the top or end]

ac·ro·bat (ăk/rə băt/), *n.* **1.** a skilled performer who can walk on a tightrope, perform on a trapeze, or do other similar feats. **2.** one who makes striking changes of opinion, as in politics, etc. [t. F: m. *acrobate*, t. Gk.: m. s. *akróbatos* walking on tiptoe] **—ac/ro·bat/ic**, *adj.* **—ac/ro·bat/i·cal·ly**, *adv.*

ac·ro·bat·ics (ăk/rə băt/Yks), *n. pl.* **1.** the feats of an acrobat; gymnastics. **2.** skilled tricks like those of an acrobat. Also, **ac/ro·bat/ism.**

ac·ro·car·pous (ăk/rə kär/pəs), *adj.* *Bot.* having the fruit at the end of the primary axis.

ac·ro·dont (ăk/rə dŏnt/), *adj.* *Anat., Zool.* **1.** with rootless teeth fastened to the alveolar ridge of the jaws. **2.** with sharp tips on the crowns of the cheek teeth.

ac·ro·drome (ăk/rə drōm/), *adj.* *Bot.* running to a point: said of a nervation with the nerves terminating in, or curving inward to, the point of a leaf. Also, **a·crod·ro·mous** (ə krŏd/rə məs).

ac·ro·gen (ăk′rə jən), *n.* *Bot.* a flowerless plant growing at the apex only, as ferns and mosses. —**ac·ro·gen·ic** (ăk′rə jĕn′ĭk), **a·crog·e·nous** (ə krŏj′ə nəs), *adj.* —**a·crog′e·nous·ly,** *adv.*

a·cro·le·in (ə krō′lĭ ĭn), *n.* *Chem.* a yellowish. pungent liquid, acrylic aldehyde, C_3H_4O, obtained in the decomposition of glycerol. [f. ACR(ID) + L *olē(re)* smell + -IN²]

ac·ro·lith (ăk′rə lĭth), *n.* a sculptured figure having only the head and extremities made of marble or other stone. [t. L: s. *acrolithus,* t. Gk.: m. *akrōlithos*]

ac·ro·me·gal·ic (ăk′rō mə găl′ĭk), *adj.* 1. pertaining to or suffering from acromegaly. —*n.* 2. a person suffering from acromegaly.

ac·ro·meg·a·ly (ăk′rō mĕg′ə lĭ), *n.* *Pathol.* a chronic nervous disease characterized by enlargement of the head, feet, hands, and sometimes the chest extremities and other structures, due to dysfunction of the pituitary gland. [t. F: m. *acromégalie.* See ACRO-, MEGALO-]

a·cro·mi·on (ə krō′mĭ ŏn), *n.,* *pl.* **-mia** (-mĭ ə). *Anat.* the outward end of the spine of the scapula or shoulder blade. See diag. under **shoulder.** [t. NL, t. Gk.: m. *akrōmion*] —**a·cro′mi·al,** *adj.*

a·cron·i·cal (ə krŏn′ə kəl), *adj.* occurring at sunset, as the rising or setting of a star. Also, **a·cron′y·cal.** [f. m.s. Gk. *akrŏnychos* at nightfall + -AL¹]

ac·ro·nym (ăk′rə nĭm), *n.* a word formed from the initial letters of other words, as *WAC* (from *Women's Army Corps*) or *loran* (from *long range navigation*). [f. ACR(O)- + m. Gk. *ŏnyma* name (Doric), modeled on HOMONYM]

a·crop·e·tal (ə krŏp′ə təl), *adj.* *Bot.* (of an inflorescence) developing upwards, toward the apex.

ac·ro·pho·bi·a (ăk′rə fō′bĭ ə), *n.* *Psychiatry.* a pathological dread of high places.

a·crop·o·lis (ə krŏp′ə lĭs), *n.* 1. the citadel of an ancient Greek city. 2. **the Acropolis,** the citadel of Athens. [t. L, t. Gk.: m. *akrópolis* the upper city]

ac·ro·spire (ăk′rə spīr′), *n.* *Bot.* the first sprout appearing in the germination of grain; the developed plumule of the seed. [f. ACRO- + SPIRE¹]

a·cross (ə krôs′, ə krŏs′), *prep.* 1. from side to side of: *a bridge across a river.* 2. on the other side of: *across the sea.* 3. so as to meet or fall in with: *we came across our friends.* —*adv.* 4. *U.S.* from one side to another: *I came across in a steamer.* 5. *U.S.* on the other side: *we'll soon be across.* 6. crosswise: *with arms across.* 7. *U.S. Colloq.* so as to pay or own up: *come across.* [f. A-¹ + CROSS]

a·cros·tic (ə krôs′tĭk, ə krŏs′-), *n.* 1. a series of lines or verses in which the first, last, or other particular letters form a word, phrase, the alphabet, etc. —*adj.* 2. of or forming an acrostic. [t. L: m. s. *acrostichis,* t. Gk.: m. *akrostichis.* See ACRO-, STICHIC] —**a·cros′ti·cal·ly,** *adv.*

ac·ro·tism (ăk′rə tĭz′əm), *n.* *Pathol.* absence or weakness of the pulse. [f. A-⁶ + m.s. Gk. *krŏtos* a beat + -ISM] —**a·crot′ic** (ə krŏt′ĭk), *adj.*

ac·ryl (ăk′rĭl), *n.* *Chem.* the hypothetical radical of the allyl series, C_3H_3O. [f. ACR(OLEIN) + -YL]

a·cryl·ic acids (ə krĭl′ĭk), *Chem.* a series of acids derived from the alkenes, with the general formula, $C_nH_{2n-2}O_2$.

acrylic esters, *Chem.* the series of esters derived from the acrylic acids.

acrylic resins, *Chem.* the group of thermoplastic resins formed by polymerizing the esters or amides of acrylic acid, used chiefly when transparency is desired. Lucite and plexiglass are in this group.

act (ăkt), *n.* 1. anything done or performed; a doing; deed. 2. the process of doing: *caught in the act.* 3. a decree, edict, law, statute, judgment, resolve, or award: *an act of Parliament or of Congress.* 4. a deed or instrument recording a transaction. 5. one of the main divisions of a play or opera. 6. an individual performance forming part of a variety show, radio program, etc. —*v.i.* 7. to do something; exert energy or force; be employed or operative: *his mind acts sluggishly.* 8. to be employed or operate in a particular way; perform specific duties or functions: *to act as chairman.* 9. to produce effect; perform a function: *the medicine failed to act.* 10. to behave: *to act well under pressure.* 11. to pretend. 12. to perform as an actor: *did she ever act on the stage?* 13. to be capable of being acted on the stage: *his plays don't act well.* 14. to serve or substitute (fol. by *for*). 15. **act on** or **upon, a.** to act in accordance with; follow: *he acted upon my suggestion.* **b.** to affect: *alcohol acts on the brain.* —*v.t.* 16. to represent (a fictitious or historical character) with one's person: *to act Macbeth.* 17. to feign; counterfeit: *to act outraged virtue.* 18. to behave as: *he acted the fool.* 19. *Obs.* to actuate. [ME, t. L: s. *actum* a thing done, and s. *actus* a doing] —**Syn.** 1. feat, exploit; achievement; transaction. See **action.**

act·a·ble (ăk′tə bəl), *adj.* 1. capable of being acted (on the stage). 2. capable of being carried out in practice. —**act′a·bil′i·ty,** *n.*

Ac·tae·on (ăk tē′ən), *n.* *Class. Legend.* a hunter, who, having seen Artemis (Diana) bathing, was changed by her into a stag.

actg., acting.

ACTH (ā′sē′tē′āch′), *n.* a hormone extracted from the pituitary glands of hogs, which stimulates the activity of the cortical substance of human adrenal glands. It is especially effective against rheumatic fever, rheumatoid arthritis, and various allergic disorders. [initials of *adreno-cortico-tropic hormone*]

ac·tin (ăk′tən), *n.* *Biochem.* a globulin present in muscle plasma which, in connection with myosin, plays an important role in muscle contraction.

ac·ti·nal (ăk′tə nəl, ăk tī′-), *adj.* *Zool.* having tentacles or rays. —**ac′ti·nal·ly,** *adv.*

act·ing (ăk′tĭng), *adj.* 1. serving temporarily; substitute: *acting governor.* 2. that acts; functioning. 3. provided with stage directions; designed to be used for performance: *an acting version of a play.*

ac·tin·i·a (ăk tĭn′ĭ ə), *n.,* *pl.* **-tiniae** (-tĭn′ĭ ē′). a sea anemone of the genus *Actinia.*

ac·tin·ic (ăk tĭn′ĭk), *adj.* 1. pertaining to actinism. 2. (of radiation) chemically active. —**ac·tin′i·cal·ly,** *adv.*

actinic rays, light of shorter wave lengths (violet and ultraviolet) which produces photochemical effects.

ac·tin·i·form (ăk tĭn′ə fôrm′), *adj.* *Zool.* having a radiate form.

ac·tin·ism (ăk′tən ĭz′əm), *n.* the action or the property of radiant energy of producing chemical change.

ac·tin·i·um (ăk tĭn′ĭ əm), *n.* *Chem.* a radioactive chemical element, an isotope of mesothorium occurring in pitchblende, and resembling the rare earths in chemical behavior and valence. *Symbol:* Ac; *at. no.:* 89; *at. wt.:* 227; radioactive half life 13.5 years. [f. ACTINO- + -IUM]

actino-, 1. *Chem.* a word element used in compounds relating to actinism or actinic activity, as in *actinotherapy.* 2. *Zool.* a word element used in compounds relating to chambered structures, as in *actinoid.* Also, **actin-.** [t. Gk.: m. *aktīno-,* comb. form of *aktís* ray]

ac·tin·o·gram (ăk tĭn′ə grăm′), *n.* a record made by an actinograph.

ac·tin·o·graph (ăk tĭn′ə grăf′, -gräf′), *n.* a recording actinometer. —**ac·tin′o·graph′ic,** *adj.*

ac·ti·nog·ra·phy (ăk′tə nŏg′rə fĭ), *n.* the recording of actinic power by the actinograph.

ac·ti·noid (ăk′tə noid′), *adj.* raylike; radiate.

ac·tin·o·lite (ăk tĭn′ə līt′), *n.* a variety of amphibole, occurring in greenish bladed crystals or in masses.

ac·ti·nom·e·ter (ăk′tə nŏm′ə tər), *n.* an instrument for measuring the intensity of radiation, whether by the chemical effects or otherwise.

ac·ti·nom·e·try (ăk′tə nŏm′ə trĭ), *n.* measurement of the intensity of radiation. —**ac·ti·no·met·ric** (ăk′tə nō mĕt′rĭk), **ac·ti·no·met′ri·cal,** *adj.*

ac·ti·no·mor·phic (ăk′tə nō môr′fĭk), *adj.* 1. having radial symmetry. 2. *Bot.* (of certain flowers, as the buttercup) divisible vertically into similar halves by each of a number of planes. Also, **ac·ti·no·mor′phous.**

ac·ti·no·my·cete (ăk′tə nō′mī sēt′), *n.* any member of the *Actinomycetes,* a group of microorganisms commonly regarded as filamentous bacteria.

ac·ti·no·my·co·sis (ăk′tə nō′mī kō′sĭs), *n.* *Vet. Sci., Med.* an infectious, inflammatory disease of cattle and other animals and of man, due to certain parasites and causing lumpy, often suppurating tumors, esp. about the jaws. —**ac·ti·no·my·cot·ic** (ăk′tə nō′mī kŏt′ĭk), *adj.*

ac·ti·non (ăk′tə nŏn′), *n.* *Chem.* an inert gas, an isotope of radon. It is a member of the actinium series of radioactive elements. *Symbol:* An; *at. no.:* 86; *at. wt.:* 219.

ac·ti·no·zo·an (ăk′tə nə zō′ən), *n., adj. Zool.* anthozoan.

ac·tion (ăk′shən), *n.* 1. process or state of acting or of being active: *the machine is not now in action.* 2. something done; an act; deed. 3. (*pl.*) habitual or usual acts; conduct. 4. energetic activity. 5. an exertion of power or force: *the action of wind upon a ship's sails.* 6. *Physiol,* a change in organs, tissues, or cells leading to performance of a function, as in muscular contraction. 7. way or manner of moving: *the action of a machine, or* (chiefly British) *of a horse.* 8. the mechanism by which something is operated, as that of a breechloading rifle or a piano. 9. a small battle. 10. military and naval combat. 11. *Poetry and Drama.* the main subject or story, as distinguished from an incidental episode. 12. *Drama.* **a.** one of the three unities. See **unity** (def. 11). **b.** an event or happening that is part of a dramatic plot: *the action of a scene, a bit of action.* 13. the gestures or deportment of an actor or speaker. 14. *Fine Arts.* the appearance of animation, movement, or passion given to figures by their attitude, position, or expression. 15. *Law.* **a.** a proceeding instituted by one party against another. **b.** the right of bringing it. **c. take action,** to commence legal proceedings. [t. L: s. *actio;* r. ME *accioun,* t. OF] —**ac′tion·less,** *adj.* —**Syn.** 2. ACTION, ACT both mean something done. ACTION applies esp. to the doing, ACT to the result of the doing. An ACTION usually lasts through some time and consists of more than one act: *to take action on a petition.* An ACT is single and of slight duration: *an act of kindness.* 9. See **battle¹.**

ac·tion·a·ble (ăk′shən ə bəl), *adj.* 1. furnishing ground for a law suit. 2. liable to a law suit. —**ac′tion·a·bly,** *adv.*

Ac·ti·um (ăk′tĭ əm, -shī′-), *n.* a promontory in NW ancient Greece: Antony and Cleopatra were defeated by Agrippa in a naval battle near here, 31 B.C.

ac·ti·vate (ăk′tə vāt′), *v.t.,* **-vated, -vating.** 1. to make active. 2. *Physics.* to render radioactive. 3. to aerate (sewage) as a purification measure. 4. *Chem.* **a.** to make more active: *to activate carbon, a catalyst, molecules.* **b.** to hasten (reactions) by various means, such as heating. 5. *U.S. Army* to place (a military unit) in an active status by assigning to it officers, enlisted men, and all necessary equipment for war strength and training for war service. —**ac′ti·va′tion,** *n.*

ac·ti·va·tor (ăk′tə vā′tər) *n.* a catalyst.

---

b., blend of, blended; c., cognate with; d., dialect, dialectal; der., derived from; f., formed from; g., going back to; m., modification of; r., replacing; s., stem of; t., taken from; ?, perhaps. See the full key on inside cover.

ac·tive (ăk′tĭv), *adj.* **1.** in a state of action; in actual progress or motion: *active hostilities.* **2.** constantly engaged in action; busy: *an active life.* **3.** having the power of quick motion; nimble: *an active animal.* **4.** moving in considerable volume; brisk; lively: *an active market.* **5.** causing change; capable of exerting influence: *active treason.* **6.** *Gram.* denoting a voice of verb inflection, in which the subject is represented as performing the action expressed by the verb (opposed to *passive*). For example: In English, *he writes the letter* (active); *the letter was written* (passive). **7.** requiring action; practical: *the intellectual and the active mental powers.* **8.** (of a volcano) in eruption. **9.** *Accounting.* profitable; busy: *active accounts* (ones having current transactions). **10.** interest-bearing: *active paper.* **11.** *Med.* acting quickly; producing immediate effects: *active remedies.* —*n.* **12.** *Gram.* **a.** the active voice. **b.** a form or construction in that voice. [t. L: m.s. *actīvus*; r. ME *actif*, t. F] —**ac′tive·ly,** *adv.* —**ac′tive·ness,** *n.*
—**Syn.** **1.** acting; working; operative. **2.** ACTIVE, ENERGETIC, STRENUOUS, VIGOROUS imply a liveliness and briskness in accomplishing something. ACTIVE suggests quickness and diligence as opposed to laziness or dilatory methods: *an active and useful person.* ENERGETIC suggests forceful and intense, sometimes nervous, activity: *conducting an energetic campaign.* STRENUOUS implies eager and zealous activity with a sense of urgency: *making a strenuous effort.* VIGOROUS suggests strong, effective activity: *using vigorous measures to accomplish an end.* **3.** agile, sprightly.
active duty, *Mil.* **1.** the status of full duty: *on active duty.* **2.** full duty.
active immunity, immunity achieved by the manufacture of antibodies within the organism.
active service, **1.** *U.S. Army.* state of being on full duty with full pay. **2.** the performance of military duty in the field in time of war.
ac·tiv·ist (ăk′tə vĭst′), *n.* an especially zealous worker, as in a political cause. —**ac′ti·vism′,** *n.*
ac·tiv·i·ty (ăk tĭv′ə tĭ), *n., pl.* **-ties.** **1.** state of action; doing. **2.** quality of acting promptly; energy. **3.** a specific deed or action; sphere of action: *social activities.* **4.** an exercise of energy or force; an active movement or operation. **5.** liveliness; agility.
act of God, *Law.* a direct, sudden, and irresistible action of natural forces, such as could not humanly have been foreseen or prevented.
act of war, an illegal act of aggression by a country against another with which it is nominally at peace.
ac·tor (ăk′tər), *n.* **1.** one who represents fictitious or historical characters in a play, motion picture, broadcast, etc. **2.** one who acts; doer. [t. L]
ac·tress (ăk′trĭs), *n.* a female actor.
Acts of the Apostles, the fifth book in the New Testament. Also, **Acts.**
ac·tu·al (ăk′chŏŏ əl), *adj.* **1.** existing in act or fact; real. **2.** now existing; present: *the actual position of the moon.* **3.** *Obs.* exhibited in action. [t. LL: s. *actuālis* active, practical; r. ME *actuel*, t. OF] —**ac′tu·al·ness,** *n.* —**Syn.** **1.** true, genuine. See **real.**
actual grace, *Rom. Cath. Ch.* supernatural help given by God to enlighten the mind and strengthen the will to do good and avoid evil.
ac·tu·al·i·ty (ăk′chŏŏ ăl′ə tĭ), *n., pl.* **-ties.** **1.** actual existence; reality. **2.** (*pl.*) actual conditions or circumstances; facts: *he had no choice but to adjust himself to the actualities of life.*
ac·tu·al·ize (ăk′chŏŏ ə līz′), *v.t.,* **-ized, -izing.** to make actual; realize in action or fact. —**ac′tu·al·i·za′tion,** *n.*
ac·tu·al·ly (ăk′chŏŏ ə lĭ), *adv.* as an actual or existing fact; really.
actual sin, *Theol.* the sin of an individual, as contrasted with original sin.
ac·tu·ar·y (ăk′chŏŏ ĕr′ĭ), *n., pl.* **-aries. 1.** *Insurance.* an officer who computes risks, rates, and the like according to probabilities indicated by recorded facts. **2.** (formerly) a registrar or clerk. [t. L: m. s. *actuārius*] —**ac·tu·ar·i·al** (ăk′chŏŏ âr′ĭ əl), *adj.* —**ac′tu·ar′i·al·ly,** *adv.*
ac·tu·ate (ăk′chŏŏ āt′), *v.t.,* **-ated, -ating. 1.** to incite to action: *actuated by selfish motives.* **2.** to put into action. [t. ML: m. s. *actuātus,* pp.] —**ac′tu·a′tion,** *n.* —**ac′tu·a′tor,** *n.*
ac·u·ate (ăk′yŏŏ ĭt, -āt′), *adj.* sharpened; pointed. [t. ML: m.s. *acuātus,* pp.]
a·cu·i·ty (ə kū′ə tĭ), *n.* sharpness; acuteness: *acuity of vision.* [t. L: m.s. *acuitas*]
a·cu·le·ate (ə kū′lĭ ĭt, -āt′), *adj.* **1.** *Biol.* having or denoting any sharp-pointed structure. **2.** having a slender ovipositor or sting, as the *Hymenoptera.* **3.** pointed; stinging. Also, **a·cu′le·at·ed.** [t. L: m.s. *acūleātus* prickly]
a·cu·men (ə kū′mən), *n.* quickness of perception; mental acuteness; keen insight. [t. L]
a·cu·mi·nate (*adj.* ə kū′mə nĭt, -nāt′; *v.* ə kū′mə nāt′), *adj., v.,* **-nated, -nating.** —*adj.* **1.** *Bot., Zool., etc.* pointed; tapering to a point. —*v.t.* **2.** to make sharp or keen. [t. L: m.s. *acūminātus,* pp.] —**a·cu′mi·na′tion,** *n.*
a·cute (ə kūt′), *adj.* **1.** sharp at the end; ending in a point (opposed to *blunt* or *obtuse*). **2.** sharp in effect; intense; poignant: *acute sorrow.* **3.** severe; crucial: *an acute shortage.* **4.** brief and severe, as disease (opposed to *chronic*). **5.** sharp or penetrating in intellect, insight, or percep-

tion: *an acute observer.* **6.** having quick sensibility; susceptible to slight impressions: *acute eyesight.* **7.** high in pitch, as sound (opposed to *grave*). **8.** *Geom., etc.* (of an angle) less than 90°. See diag. under **angle. 9.** *Gram.* designating or having a particular accent (′) indicating **a.** (orig.) a raised pitch (as in ancient Greek). **b.** (later) stress (as in the Spanish *adiós*), quality of sound (as in the French *résumé*), vowel length (as in Hungarian), etc. —*n.* **10.** the acute accent. [t. L: m.s. *acūtus,* pp., sharpened] —**a·cute′ly,** *adv.* —**a·cute′ness,** *n.*
—**Syn.** **5.** keen, astute, discerning, perspicacious; sharp-witted. ACUTE, PENETRATING, SHREWD imply a keenness of understanding, perception, or insight. ACUTE suggests particularly a clearness of perception and a realization of related meanings: *an acute intellect.* PENETRATING adds the idea of depth of perception and a realization of implications: *a wise and penetrating judgment.* SHREWD adds the idea of knowing how to apply practically (or to one's own advantage) what one perceives and understands: *wary and shrewd.*
-acy, a suffix of nouns of quality, state, office, etc., many of which accompany adjectives in -*acious* or nouns or adjectives in -*ate,* as in *efficacy, fallacy,* etc., *advocacy, primacy,* etc., *accuracy, delicacy,* etc. [repr. L -*ācia,* -*ātia,* and Gk. -*āteia*]
a·cy·clic (ā sī′klĭk, ā sĭk′lĭk), *adj. Bot.* not cyclic; not arranged in whorls. [f. A-⁶ + CYCLIC]
ad¹ (ăd), *n. Colloq.* advertisement.
ad² (ăd), *n. Tennis.* advantage (def. 5).
ad-, a prefix of direction, tendency, and addition, attached chiefly to stems not found as words themselves, as in *advert, advent.* Also, **ac-, af-, ag-, al-, an-, ap-, ar-, as-, at-,** and **a-⁵.** [t. L, repr. *ad,* prep., to, toward, at, about]
-ad, **1.** a suffix forming nouns denoting a collection of a certain number, as in *triad.* **2.** a suffix found in words and names proper to Greek myth, as in *dryad, Pleiad.* **3.** a literary suffix used in titles imitating *Iliad,* as in *Dunciad.* [repr. Gk. -*áda,* acc. (nom. -*ás*)]
A.D., (L *anno Domini*) in the year of our Lord; since Christ was born. From 20 B.C. to A.D. 50 is 71 years.
a·dac·ty·lous (ā dăk′tə ləs), *adj. Zool.* without fingers or toes. [f. A-⁶ + DACTYL +-OUS]
ad·age (ăd′ĭj), *n.* a proverb. [t. F, t. L: m.s. *adagium*]
a·da·gio (ə dä′jō, -zhУ ō′; *It.* ä dä′jō), *adv., adj., n., pl.* **-gios.** *Music, etc.* **1.** in a leisurely manner; slowly. —*adj.* **2.** slow. —*n.* **3.** an adagio movement or piece. [It.]
Ad·am (ăd′əm), *n.* **1.** the name of the first man, the progenitor of the human race. Genesis 2:7. **2. the old Adam,** the evil inherent in man. —**A·dam·ic** (ə dăm′ĭk), *adj.*
Ad·am (ăd′əm), *n.* **1. James,** 1730–94, and his brother, **Robert,** 1728–92, British architects and furniture designers in the classic manner. —*adj.* **2.** (of furniture) pertaining to or in the style of these two brothers.
Ad·am-and-Eve (ăd′əm ənd ēv′), *n. U.S.* the putty-root (plant).
ad·a·mant (ăd′ə mănt′ *or, esp. Brit.,* -mənt), *n.* **1.** (in ancient times) some impenetrably hard substance, variously identified later as the diamond or loadstone. **2.** any impenetrably hard substance. —*adj.* **3.** hard as adamant; adamantine. **4.** hard-hearted. [t. L: s. *adamas,* t. Gk.; r. ME *adamaunt,* t. OF; and OE *athamans* (repr. LL var. of *adamas*)]
ad·a·man·tine (ăd′ə măn′tĭn, -tēn, -tīn), *adj.* **1.** impenetrable. **2.** like a diamond in luster.
Ad·am·ite (ăd′ə mīt′), *n.* **1.** a descendant of Adam; a human being. **2.** a nudist. —**Ad·am·i·tic** (ău′ə mĭt′-ĭk), *adj.*
Ad·ams (ăd′əmz), *n.* **1. Charles Francis,** 1807–86, U.S. statesman: minister to Great Britain, 1861–68 (son of John Quincy Adams). **2. Franklin Pierce,** ("F.P.A.") born 1881, U.S. author and columnist. **3. Henry (Brooks),** 1838–1918, U.S. historian, writer, and teacher (son of Charles Francis Adams). **4. James Truslow** (trŭs′lō), 1878–1949, U.S. historian. **5. John,** 1735–1826, second president of the U.S., 1797–1801; leader in the American Revolution. **6. John Quincy** (kwĭn′sĭ), 1767–1848, sixth president of the U.S., 1825–1829; secretary of state, 1817–25 (son of John Adams). **7. Maude,** (*Maude Kiskadden*) born 1872, U.S. actress. **8. Samuel,** 1722–1803, leader in the American Revolution. **9. Samuel Hopkins,** born 1871, U.S. writer.
Ad·ams (ăd′əmz), *n.* **Mount, 1.** a peak in SW Washington, in the Cascade Range. 12,470 ft. **2.** a peak in N New Hampshire, in the White Mountains. 5805 ft.
Adam's ale, *Colloq.* water.
Adam's apple, a projection of the thyroid cartilage at the front of the (male) throat.
ad·ams·ite (ăd′əmz īt′), *n.* a yellow irritant smoke, containing a form of arsenic that is poisonous, used as a harassing agent. Symbol: DM. [named after Major Roger *Adams,* U.S. soldier (born 1889), who invented it. See -ITE¹]
Ad·am's-nee·dle (ăd′əmz nē′dəl), *n. U.S.* a species of yucca, *Yucca filamentosa,* much cultivated for ornament.
A·da·na (ä′dä nä′), *n.* a city in S Turkey. 88,119 (1940).
a·dapt (ə dăpt′), *v.t.* to make suitable to requirements; adjust or modify fittingly. [t. L: s. *adaptāre*] —**Syn.** fit, accommodate, suit, compose, reconcile. See **adjust.**
a·dapt·a·ble (ə dăp′tə bəl), *adj.* **1.** capable of being adapted. **2.** able to adapt oneself easily to new conditions. —**a·dapt′a·bil′i·ty, a·dapt′a·ble·ness,** *n.*

ad·ap·ta·tion (ăd/əp tā/shən), *n*. **1.** act of adapting. **2.** state of being adapted; adjustment. **3.** something produced by adapting. **4.** *Biol.* **a.** alteration in the structure or function of organisms which fits them to survive and multiply in a changed environment. **b.** a form or structure modified to fit changed environment. **5.** *Physiol.* the response of sensory receptor organs, as those of vision, touch, temperature, olfaction, audition, and pain, to changed, constantly applied, environmental conditions. **6.** Also, **a·dap·tion** (ə dăp/shən). *Sociol.* a slow, usually unconscious modification of individual and social activity in adjustment to cultural surroundings. —**ad/ap·ta/tion·al,** *adj.*

a·dapt·er (ə dăp/tər), *n*. **1.** one that adapts. **2.** a device for fitting together parts having different sizes or designs. **3.** an accessory to convert a machine, tool, etc., to a new or modified use. Also, **a·dap/tor.**

a·dap·tive (ə dăp/tĭv), *adj.* serving to adapt; showing adaptation. *adaptive coloring of a chameleon.* —**a·dap/tive·ly,** *adv.* —**a·dap/tive·ness,** *n*.

A·dar (ə där/), *n*. (in the Jewish calendar) the sixth month of the year. [Heb.]

ad a·stra per a·spe·ra (ăd ăs/trə pər ăs/pə rə), *Latin.* to the stars through difficulties (motto of Kansas).

ad·ax·i·al (ăd ăk/sĭ əl), *adj. Bot.* situated on the side toward the axis. [f. AD- + L *axi(s)* axle + -AL¹]

A.D.C., aide-de-camp.

ad cap·tan·dum (**vul·gus**) (ăd kăp tăn/dəm vŭl/gəs), *Latin.* in order to please (the mob); emotional.

add (ăd), *v.t.* **1.** to unite or join, so as to increase the number, quantity, size, or importance: *to add another stone to the pile.* **2.** to find the sum of (often fol. by *up*). **3.** to say or write further. **4.** to include (fol. by *in*). —*v.i.* **5.** to perform the arithmetical operation of addition. **6.** to be or serve as an addition (fol. by *to*): *to add to one's grief.* **7.** to make the desired or expected total (fol. by *up*): *these figures don't add up.* [ME *adde(n)*, t. L: m. *addere*] —**add/a·ble, add/i·ble,** *adj.* —**add/er,** *n*. —**Syn. 1.** append; attach.

Ad·dams (ăd/əmz), *n.* **Jane,** 1860–1935, U.S. social worker and writer.

ad·dax (ăd/ăks), *n.* a large, pale-colored antelope, *Addax nasomaculatus,* of North Africa, with loosely spiral horns. [t. L; of African orig.]

added line, *Music.* a leger line. See illus. under **leger line.**

ad·dend (ăd/ĕnd, ə dĕnd/), *n. Math.* summand.

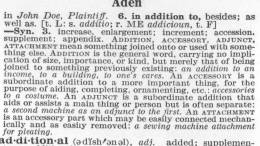
Addax, *Addax nasomaculatus* (3 ft. high at the shoulder, 6 ft. long, horns 3 or 4 ft. long)

ad·den·dum (ə dĕn/dəm), *n., pl.* **-da** (-də). **1.** a thing to be added; an addition. **2.** an appendix to a book. **3.** *Mach.* **a.** that part of a tooth which projects beyond the pitch circle or pitch line of a toothed wheel or rack. **b.** Also, **addendum circle.** an imaginary circle touching the ends of the teeth of a toothed wheel. [t. L, neut. ger. of *addere* add]

ad·der (ăd/ər), *n.* **1.** the common European viper, *Vipera berus,* a small venomous snake, widespread in northern Eurasia. **2.** any of various other snakes, venomous or harmless, resembling the viper. [var. of ME *nadder* (*a nadder* being taken as *an adder*), OE *nædre*]

ad·der's-mouth (ăd/ərz mouth/), *n.* U.S. **1.** either of two small terrestrial orchids, *Malaxis monophyllos* and *M. unifolia,* natives of North America, bearing minute white or greenish flowers. **2.** any of the delicate North American orchids of the genus *Pogonia.*

ad·der's-tongue (ăd/ərz tŭng/), *n.* **1.** a fern of the genus *Ophioglossum,* with a fruiting spike. **2.** *U.S.* the American species of dogtooth violet.

ad·dict (*n.* ăd/ĭkt; *v.* ə dĭkt/), *n.* **1.** one who is addicted to a practice or habit: *a drug addict.* —*v.t.* **2.** to give (oneself) over, as to a habit or pursuit; apply or devote habitually (fol. by *to*): *addict oneself to science.* [t. L: s. *addictus,* pp., adjudged, devoted]

ad·dict·ed (ə dĭk/tĭd), *adj.* devoted or given up (to a practice or habit) (fol. by *to*): *addicted to the drug habit.* —**ad·dict/ed·ness,** *n*.

ad·dic·tion (ə dĭk/shən), *n.* state of being given up to some habit, practice, or pursuit, esp. to narcotics.

Ad·dis A·ba·ba (ăd/dĭs ä/bə bä/), the capital of Ethiopia, in the central part. 300,000 (est. 1936).

Ad·di·son (ăd/ə sən), *n.* **Joseph,** 1672–1719, British essayist and poet. —**Ad·di·so·ni·an** (ăd/ə sō/nĭ ən), *adj.*

Addison's disease, *Pathol.* a disease characterized by asthenia, low blood pressure, and a brownish coloration of the skin, due to disturbance of the suprarenal glands. [named after T. *Addison,* British physician (1793–1860), who first described it]

ad·dit·a·ment (ə dĭt/ə mənt), *n.* something added; an addition. [t. L: s. *additamentum*]

ad·di·tion (ə dĭsh/ən), *n.* **1.** act or process of adding or uniting. **2.** the process of uniting two or more numbers into one sum, denoted by the symbol +. **3.** the result of adding; anything added. **4.** *U.S.* wings, rooms, etc., added to a building, or abutting land added to real estate already owned. **5.** *Obs. except Law.* a particularizing designation added to a person's name, as *Plaintiff*

in *John Doe, Plaintiff.* **6. in addition to,** besides; as well as. [t. L: s. *additio*; r. ME *addicioun,* t. F]

—**Syn. 3.** increase, enlargement; increment; accession, supplement; appendix. ADDITION, ACCESSORY, ADJUNCT, ATTACHMENT mean something joined onto or used with something else. ADDITION is the general word, carrying no implication of size, importance, or kind, but merely that of being joined to something previously existing: *an addition to an income, to a building, to one's cares.* An ACCESSORY is a subordinate addition to a more important thing, for the purpose of aiding, completing, ornamenting, etc.: *accessories to a costume.* An ADJUNCT is a subordinate addition that aids or assists a main thing or person but is often separate: *a second machine as an adjunct to the first.* An ATTACHMENT is an accessory part which may be easily connected mechanically and as easily removed: *a sewing machine attachment for pleating.*

ad·di·tion·al (ə dĭsh/ən əl), *adj.* added; supplementary: *additional information.* —**ad·di/tion·al·ly,** *adv.*

ad·di·tive (ăd/ə tĭv), *adj.* to be added; of the nature of an addition; characterized by addition: *an additive process.* [t. L: m.s. *additivus*] —**ad/di·tive·ly,** *adv.*

ad·dle (ăd/əl), *v.,* **-dled, -dling,** *adj.* —*v.t., v.i.* **1.** to make or become muddled or confused. **2.** to make or become spoiled or rotten, as eggs. —*adj.* **3.** mentally confused; muddled, as in the combinations, **ad/dle-brained/, ad/dle-head/ed. 4.** rotten: *addle eggs.* [OE *adela* liquid filth, c. MLG *adele* mud]

ad·dress (*n.* ə drĕs/, ăd/rĕs; *v.* ə drĕs/), *n., v.,* **-dressed** or **-drest, -dressing.** —*n.* **1.** a formal speech or writing directed to a person or a group of persons: *an address on current problems.* **2.** a direction as to name and residence inscribed on a letter, etc. **3.** a place where a person lives or may be reached. **4.** manner of speaking to persons; personal bearing in conversation. **5.** skillful management; ready skill: *to handle a matter with address.* **6.** *Govt.* a request to the executive by the legislature to remove a judge for unfitness. **7.** (*usually pl.*) attentions paid by a lover; courtship. **8.** (*usually cap.*) the reply to the King's speech in the English parliament. **9.** *Obs.* preparation. —*v.t.* **10.** to direct speech or writing to: *to address an assembly, how does one address the governor?* **11.** to direct to the ear or attention: *to address a warning to someone.* **12.** to apply in speech (used reflexively, fol. by *to*): *he addressed himself to the chairman.* **13.** to direct for delivery; put a direction on: *to address a letter.* **14.** *Com.* to consign or entrust to the care of another, as agent or factor. **15.** to direct the energy or force of (used reflexively fol. by *to*): *he addressed himself to the work in hand.* **16.** to pay court to; woo; court. **17.** *Golf.* to adjust and apply the club to (the ball) in preparing for a stroke. **18.** *Obs. except in Golf.* to give direction to; aim. **19.** *Obs.* to prepare. —*v.i.* **20.** *Obs.* to make an appeal. **21.** *Obs.* to make preparations. [ME *addresse(n),* t. F: m. *adresser,* earlier *adrecier,* ult. der. L *ad* to + *directus* straight] —**ad·dress/er, ad·dres/sor,** *n.* —**Syn. 1.** discourse, lecture. See **speech. 5.** adroitness, dexterity; cleverness, ingenuity; tact.

ad·dress·ee (ə drĕ sē/, ăd/rĕ-), *n.* U.S. one to whom anything is addressed.

ad·dres·so·graph (ə drĕs/ə grăf/, -gräf/), *n.* **1.** a machine that prints addresses upon envelopes, etc., from stencils. **2.** (*cap.*) a trademark for this machine.

ad·duce (ə dūs/, ə dōōs/), *v.t.,* **-duced, -ducing.** to bring forward in argument; cite as pertinent or conclusive: *to adduce reasons.* [t. L: m.s. *addūcere* lead to] —**ad·duce/a·ble, ad·duc/i·ble,** *adj.* —**ad·duc/er,** *n*.

ad·du·cent (ə dū/sənt, ə dōō/-), *adj. Physiol.* drawing toward; adducting (applied to muscles, etc.). [t. L: s. *addūcens,* ppr., leading to]

ad·duct (ə dŭkt/), *v.t. Physiol.* to draw toward the main axis (opposed to *abduct*). [t. L: s. *adductus,* pp., led to] —**ad·duc/tive,** *adj.* —**ad·duc/tor,** *n*.

ad·duc·tion (ə dŭk/shən), *n.* **1.** *Physiol.* the action of the adductor or adducent muscles. **2.** act of adducing.

Ade (ād), *n.* **George,** 1866–1944, U. S. humorist.

-ade¹, 1. a suffix found in nouns denoting action or process, product or result of action, person or persons acting, often irregularly attached, as in *blockade, escapade, masquerade.* **2.** a noun suffix indicating a drink made of a particular fruit, as in *orangeade.* [t. F, t. Pr.: m. *-ada,* g. L *-āta;* in some words -ADE is for Sp. and Pg. *-ado,* It. *-ato,* g. L *-ātus*]

-ade², a collective suffix like **-ad** (def. 1), as in *decade.* [t. F, t. Gk.: m. *-ada* (acc.), *-ás* (nom.)]

Ad·e·laide (ăd/ə lād/), *n.* a city in S Australia: the capital of the state of South Australia. 350,000 (with suburbs, est. 1941).

a·demp·tion (ə dĕmp/shən), *n. Law.* the failure of a specific legacy because the subject matter no longer belongs to the testator's estate at his death. [t. L: s. *ademptio*]

A·den (ä/dən, ā/-), *n.* **1.** a British protectorate in SW Arabia. ab. 600,000 pop.; ab. 112,-000 sq. mi. **2.** a British colony adjoining this protectorate. 45,992 pop. (1931); 77 sq. mi. **3.** the capital of this protectorate and colony: a seaport. ab. 33,000. **4.** Gulf of, an arm of the Arabian Sea between the E tip of Africa and the Arabian peninsula.

Aden (defs. 1, 2)

ad·e·nal·gi·a (ăd'ə năl'jĭ'ə), n. Pathol. pain in a gland.

ad·e·nine (ăd'ə nĭn, -nēn', -nĭn'), n. an alkaloid, C₅H₅N₅, obtained from purine, found as a component of nucleic acid in such organs as the pancreas, spleen, etc.

adeno-, Anat. a word element meaning "gland." Also, before vowels, **aden-**. [t. Gk., comb. form of adēn]

ad·e·noid (ăd'ə noid'), n. 1. (usually pl.) an enlarged mass of lymphoid tissue in the upper pharynx, as in children, often preventing nasal breathing. —adj. 2. Also, **ad'e·noi'dal**. pertaining to the lymphatic glands. [t. Gk.: m.s. adenoeidēs glandular]

ad·e·noid·ec·to·my (ăd'ə noi dĕk'tə mĭ), n., pl. **-mies.** Surg. the operation of removing the adenoids.

ad·e·no·ma (ăd'ə nō'mə), n., pl. **-mata** (-mə tə), **-mas.** Pathol. 1. a tumor originating in a gland. 2. a tumor of glandlike structure. —**ad·e·nom·a·tous** (ăd'ə nŏm'ə təs, -nō'mə-), adj.

ad·ept (n. ăd'ĕpt, ə dĕpt'; adj. ə dĕpt'), n. 1. one who has attained proficiency; one fully skilled in anything. —adj. 2. well-skilled; proficient. [t. L: s. adeptus, pp., having attained] —**a·dept'ly**, adv. —**a·dept'ness**, n.

ad·e·qua·cy (ăd'ə kwə sĭ), n. state or quality of being adequate; a sufficiency for a particular purpose.

ad·e·quate (ăd'ə kwĭt), adj. 1. equal to the requirement or occasion; commensurate; fully sufficient, suitable, or fit (often fol. by to). 2. Law. reasonably sufficient for starting legal action: adequate grounds. [t. L: m.s. adaequātus, pp., equalized] —**ad'e·quate·ly**, adv. —**ad'e·quate·ness**, n. —**Syn. 1.** satisfactory; capable.

à deux (à dœ'), French. of or for two; two at a time.

ad ex·tre·mum (ăd ĕks trē'məm), Latin. to the extreme; at last; finally.

ad fin., (L ad finem) to, toward, or at the end.

ad glo·ri·am (ăd glôr'ĭ ăm'), Latin. 1. for glory. 2. (ironically) for nothing.

ad·here (ăd hĭr'), v.i., **-hered**, **-hering.** 1. to stick fast; cleave; cling (fol. by to). 2. to be devoted; be attached as a follower or upholder (fol. by to): to adhere to a party, a leader, a church, a creed, etc. 3. to hold closely or firmly (fol. by to): to adhere to a plan. 4. Obs. to be consistent. [t. L: m.s. adhaerēre] —**ad·her'er**, n. —**Syn. 1.** See **stick.**

ad·her·ence (ăd hĭr'əns), n. 1. quality of adhering; fidelity; steady attachment: adherence to a party, rigid adherence to rules. 2. act or state of adhering; adhesion.

ad·her·ent (ăd hĭr'ənt), n. 1. one who follows or upholds a leader, cause, etc.; supporter; follower (fol. by of). —adj. 2. sticking; clinging; adhering. 3. Bot. adnate. 4. Gram. standing before a noun. —**ad·her'ent·ly**, adv. —**Syn. 1.** See **follower.**

ad·he·sion (ăd hē'zhən), n. 1. act or state of adhering, or of being united: the adhesion of parts united by growth. 2. steady attachment of the mind or feelings; adherence. 3. assent; concurrence. 4. Physics. the molecular force exerted across the surface of contact between unlike liquids and solids which resists their separation. 5. Pathol. a. the abnormal union of adjacent tissues due to inflammation. b. the fibrous tissue so involved. [t. L: m.s. adhaesio]

ad·he·sive (ăd hē'sĭv), adj. 1. clinging; tenacious; sticking fast. 2. gummed: adhesive tape. —n. 3. adhesive plaster. —**ad·he'sive·ly**, adv. —**ad·he'sive·ness**, n.

adhesive plaster, cotton or other fabric coated with an adhesive preparation, used for covering slight cuts, etc., on the skin.

ad·hib·it (ăd hĭb'ĭt), v.t. 1. to take or let in; admit. 2. to use or apply. 3. Rare. to attach. [t. L: s. adhibitus, pp., applied] —**ad·hi·bi'tion** (ăd'hə bĭsh'ən), n.

ad hoc (ăd hŏk'), Latin. for this (special purpose); with respect to this (subject or thing).

ad ho·mi·nem (ăd hŏm'ə nĕm'), Latin. to the man; personal. An argument ad hominem appeals to a person's prejudices or special interests instead of to his intellect.

ad·i·a·bat·ic (ăd'ĭ ə băt'ĭk, ā'dĭ-), adj. Physics, Chem. without change in heat content (distinguished from isothermal). [f. s. Gk. adiábatos impassable + -ic] —**ad'i·a·bat'i·cal·ly**, adv.

ad·i·aph·o·rous (ăd'ĭ ăf'ə rəs), adj. doing neither good nor harm, as a medicine. [t. Gk.: m. adiáphoros]

ad·i·a·ther·man·cy (ăd'ĭ ə thûr'mən sĭ), n. Physics. inability to transmit heat radiation. —**ad'i·a·ther'ma·nous**, adj.

a·dieu (ə dū', ə dōō'; Fr. à dyœ'), interj., n., pl. **adieus**, **adieux** (ə dūz', ə dōōz'; Fr. à dyœ'). —interj. 1. good-by; farewell. —n. 2. act of taking one's leave; a farewell. [ME, t. F, g. L ad Deum (I commend you) to God]

A·di·ge (ä'dē jĕ), n. a river in N Italy, flowing SE to the Adriatic. ab. 220 mi.

ad inf., ad infinitum.

ad in·fi·ni·tum (ăd ĭn'fə nī'təm), Latin. to infinity; endlessly; without limit.

ad int., ad interim.

ad in·te·rim (ăd ĭn'tə rĭm), Latin. in the meantime.

a·dios (ä dyôs'), interj. Spanish. good-by; farewell.

ad·i·po·cere (ăd'ə pō sĭr'), n. a waxy substance sometimes formed from dead animal bodies in moist burial places or under water. [f. adipo- (comb. form repr. L adeps fat) + m. L cēra wax] —**ad·i·poc·er·ous** (ăd'ə pŏs'ər əs), adj.

ad·i·pose (ăd'ə pōs'), adj. 1. fatty; consisting of, resembling, or having relation to fat: adipose tissue.

—n. 2. animal fat stored in the fatty tissue of the body. [t. NL: m.s. adipōsus fatty, der. L adeps fat] —**ad'i·pose'ness**, **ad·i·pos·i·ty** (ăd'ə pŏs'ə tĭ), n.

adipose fin, Ichthyol. a finlike projection, fleshy and lacking rays, behind the dorsal fin.

Ad·i·ron·dack Mountains (ăd'ə rŏn'dăk), a mountain range in NE New York: a part of the Appalachian system. Highest peak, Mt. Marcy, 5344 ft. Also, **Adirondacks.**

ad·it (ăd'ĭt), n. 1. an entrance or a passage. 2. Mining. a nearly horizontal passage leading into a mine. 3. access. [t. L: s. aditus approach]

adj., 1. adjective. 2. adjourned. 3. adjunct. 4. Banking. adjustment. 5. adjutant.

ad·ja·cen·cy (ə jā'sən sĭ), n., pl. **-cies.** 1. state of being adjacent; proximity. 2. (usually pl.) that which is adjacent.

ad·ja·cent (ə jā'sənt), adj. lying near, close, or contiguous; adjoining; neighboring: a field adjacent to the highway. [t. L: s. adjacens, ppr.] —**ad·ja'cent·ly**, adv. —**Syn.** abutting, bordering. See **adjoining.**

adjacent angles, Geom. two angles having the same vertex and having a common side between them.

ad·jec·tive (ăj'ĭk tĭv), n. 1. Gram. a. one of the major form classes, or parts of speech, of many languages, comprising words used to qualify or limit a noun. b. such a word, as wise in a wise ruler, or in he is wise. c. any word or phrase of similar function or meaning. —adj. 2. Gram. pertaining to an adjective; functioning as an adjective; adjectival: the adjective use of a noun. 3. not able to stand alone; dependent. 4. Law. concerning methods of enforcement of legal rights, as pleading and practice (opposed to substantive). 5. Dyeing. (of colors) requiring a mordant or the like to render them permanent (opposed to substantive). [t. L: m.s. adjectīvus] —**ad·jec·ti·val** (ăj'ĭk tī'vəl, ăj'ĭk tĭ vəl), adj. —**ad'jec·ti'val·ly, ad'jec·tive·ly**, adv.

ad·join (ə join'), v.t. 1. to be in connection or contact with; abut on: his house adjoins the lake. —v.i. 2. to lie or be next, or in contact. [ME ajoine(n), t. OF: m. adjoindre, g. L adjungere join to]

ad·join·ing (ə joi'nĭng), adj. bordering; contiguous: the adjoining room. —**Syn.** ADJOINING, ADJACENT, BORDERING all mean near or close to something. ADJACENT implies being near by or next to: adjacent angles. ADJOINING implies touching, having a common point or line: an adjoining yard. BORDERING means having a common boundary with: Ohio is a State bordering on Indiana.

ad·journ (ə jûrn'), v.t. 1. to suspend the meeting of, as a public or private body, to a future day or to another place: adjourn the court. 2. to defer or postpone to a future meeting of the same body: the court adjourned consideration of the question. 3. to put off; defer; postpone. —v.i. 4. to postpone, suspend, or transfer proceedings. [ME ajourne(n), t. OF: m. ajorner, g. LL adjurnāre fix a day]

ad·journ·ment (ə jûrn'mənt), n. 1. act of adjourning. 2. state or period of being adjourned.

adjt., adjutant.

ad·judge (ə jŭj'), v.t., **-judged**, **-judging.** 1. to pronounce formally; decree: the will was adjudged void. 2. to award judicially; assign: the prize was adjudged to him. 3. to decide by a judicial opinion or sentence: to adjudge a case. 4. to sentence or condemn: he was adjudged to die. 5. to deem; consider: it was adjudged wise to avoid war. [ME ajuge(n), t. OF: m. ajugier, g. L adjūdicāre]

ad·ju·di·cate (ə jōō'də kāt'), v., **-cated, -cating.** —v.t. 1. to pronounce or decree by judicial sentence; settle judicially; pass judgment on; to determine an issue or dispute judicially. —v.i. 2. to sit in judgment (fol. by upon). [t. L: m. s. adjūdicātus, pp.] —**ad·ju'di·ca'tive**, adj. —**ad·ju'di·ca'tor**, n.

ad·ju·di·ca·tion (ə jōō'də kā'shən), n. 1. act of adjudicating. 2. Law. a. act of a court in making an order, judgment, or decree. b. a judicial decision or sentence.

ad·junct (ăj'ŭngkt), n. 1. something added to another thing but not essentially a part of it. 2. a person joined to another in some duty or service; an assistant. 3. Gram. a qualifying form, word, phrase, etc., depending on some other form, word, phrase, etc. —adj. 4. joined to a thing or person, esp. subordinately; associated; auxiliary. [t. L: s. adjunctus, pp.] —**Syn. 1.** See **addition.**

ad·junc·tive (ə jŭngk'tĭv), adj. forming an adjunct. —**ad·junc'tive·ly**, adv.

ad·jure (ə jōōr'), v.t., **-jured, -juring.** 1. to charge, bind, or command, earnestly and solemnly, often under oath or the threat of a curse. 2. to entreat or request earnestly. [ME adjure(n), t. L: m. adjūrāre] —**ad·ju·ra·tion** (ăj'ōō rā'shən), n. —**ad·jur·a·to·ry** (ə jōōr'ə tōr'ĭ), adj. —**ad·jur'er, ad·ju'ror**, n.

ad·just (ə jŭst'), v.t. 1. to fit, as one thing to another; make correspondent or conformable; adapt; accommodate: to adjust things to a standard. 2. to put in working order; regulate; bring to a proper state or position: to adjust an instrument. 3. to settle or bring to a satisfactory state, so that parties are agreed in the result: to adjust differences. 4. Insurance. to fix (the sum to be paid on a claim); settle (a claim). 5. to systematize. 6. Mil. to correct the elevation and deflection of (a gun). —v.i. 7. to adapt oneself; become adapted. [t. F (obs.): s. adjuster, t. ML: m. adjūstāre, erroneous Latinization of OF *ajouster*, g. LL *adjuxtāre*] —**ad·just′a·ble**, *adj.* —**ad·just′a·bly**, *adv.* —**ad·just′er, ad·jus′tor**, *n.* —**Syn. 2.** ADJUST, ADAPT, ALTER in their literal meanings imply making necessary or desirable changes (as in position, shape, and the like). To ADJUST is to move into proper position for use: *to adjust the eyepiece of a telescope.* To ADAPT is to make a change in character, to make something useful in a new way: *to adapt a paper clip for a hairpin.* To ALTER is to change the appearance but not the use: *to alter the height of a table.* 3. arrange; rectify; reconcile.

ad·just·a·ble pitch, *Aeron.* (of a propeller) having blades whose pitch can be changed while the propeller is stationary to suit various conditions of flight.

ad·just·ment (ə jŭst′mənt), *n.* 1. act of adjusting; act of adapting to a given purpose. 2. state of being adjusted; orderly relation of parts or elements. 3. a means of adjusting: *the adjustment of a microscope.* 4. *Sociol.* a process of fitting individual or collective patterns of activity to other such patterns made with some awareness or purposefulness. 5. *Insurance.* act of ascertaining the amount of indemnity which the party insured is entitled to receive under the policy, and settling the claim. 6. a settlement of a disputed account or claim.

ad·ju·tant (ăj′ə tənt), *n.* 1. *Mil.* a staff officer who assists the commanding officer to issue orders. 2. *Brit.* an executive officer. 3. an assistant. 4. the adjutant bird. [t. L: s. *adjūtans*, ppr., aiding] —**ad′ju·tan·cy**, *n.*

adjutant bird, a large East Indian stork, *Leptoptilus dubius.* Also, **adjutant crane, adjutant stork.**

adjutant general, *pl.* **adjutants general. 1.** *U.S. Army.* **a.** a member of the Adjutant General's Department, from which adjutants for higher command are assigned. **b. the Adjutant General,** the chief administrative officer of the Army. **2.** a high (often highest) officer of the National Guard of a State or Territory.

ad·ju·vant (ăj′ə vənt), *adj.* 1. serving to help or assist. —*n.* 2. a person or thing aiding or helping. 3. *Med.* whatever aids in removing or preventing a disease, esp. a substance added to a prescription to aid the operation of the main ingredient. [t. L: s. *adjuvans*, ppr.]

Ad·ler (ăd′lər), *n.* 1. Alfred, 1870–1937, Austrian psychiatrist and psychologist. 2. Felix, 1851–1933, U.S. educator, reformer, and writer.

ad-lib (ăd lĭb′), *v.i., v.t.,* **-libbed, -libbing.** *Colloq.* to improvise, as notes, words, or business, during rehearsal or performance. [v. use of AD LIB.]

ad lib., ad libitum.

ad lib·i·tum (ăd lĭb′ə təm), *Latin.* at pleasure; to any extent; without restriction: used in music to indicate that the manner of performance of a passage is left to the discretion of the performer. *Abbr.:* ad lib.

ad lit·te·ram (ăd lĭt′ə răm′), *Latin.* to the letter; exactly. One cites an author *verbatim* and *ad litteram.*

ad loc., (L *ad locum*) at or to the place.

Adm., 1. Admiral. **2.** Admiralty.

ad ma·jo·rem De·i glo·ri·am (ăd mə jōr′ĕm dē′ī glōr′ĭ ăm′), *Latin.* for the greater glory of God (motto of the Jesuit order).

ad·meas·ure (ăd mĕzh′ər), *v.t.,* **-ured, -uring.** to measure off or out; apportion. [f. AD- + MEASURE; r. ME *amesure*, t. OF: m. *amesurer*, g. LL *admēnsūrāre*]

ad·meas·ure·ment (ăd mĕzh′ər mənt), *n.* 1. process of measuring. 2. number, dimensions, or measure of anything. 3. apportionment.

Ad·me·tus (ăd mē′təs), *n. Gk. Legend.* a Thessalian king, one of the Argonauts and husband of Alcestis.

ad·min·i·cle (ăd mĭn′ə kəl), *n.* an aid; auxiliary. [t. L: m.s. *adminiculum* a prop] —**ad·mi·nic·u·lar** (ăd′mə nĭk′yə lər), *adj.*

ad·min·is·ter (ăd mĭn′əs tər), *v.* 1. to manage (affairs, a government, etc.); have executive charge of: *to administer laws.* 2. to bring into use or operation; dispense: *to administer justice.* 3. to make application of; give: *to administer medicine.* 4. to tender or impose: *to administer an oath.* 5. *Law.* to manage or dispose of, as a decedent's estate by an executor or administrator, or a trust estate by a trustee. —*v.i.* 6. to contribute assistance; bring aid or supplies (fol. by *to*): *to administer to the needs of the poor.* 7. to perform the duties of an administrator. [t. L: m.s. *administrāre*; r. ME *amynistre*, t. OF: m. *aministrer*] —**ad·min·is·tra·ble** (ăd mĭn′əs trə bəl), *adj.* —**ad·min·is·trant** (ăd mĭn′əs trənt), *adj., n.* —**Syn. 1.** conduct, control. See **rule.** 3. dispense; apply.

ad·min·is·trate (ăd mĭn′ə strāt′), *v.t.,* **-trated, -trating.** *U.S.* to administer.

ad·min·is·tra·tion (ăd mĭn′ə strā′shən), *n.* 1. the conducting of any office or employment; direction; management. 2. the function of a political state in exercising its governmental duties. 3. the duty or duties of an administrator, specif., the executive functions of government, both general and local, which are neither legislative nor judicial. 4. the executive officers, collectively. 5. *U.S.* their period of service. 6. *U.S.* any body of men entrusted with executive or administrative powers. 7. *Law.* management of a decedent estate by an executor or administrator, or of a trust estate by a trustee. 8. act of dispensing, esp. formally: *administration of the sacraments.* 9. act of tendering: *the administration of an oath.* 10. the applying of a medicine, etc.

ad·min·is·tra·tive (ăd mĭn′ə strā′tĭv), *adj.* pertaining to administration; executive: *administrative ability, problems, etc.* —**ad·min·is·tra′tive·ly**, *adv.*

ad·min·is·tra·tor (ăd mĭn′ə strā′tər), *n.* 1. one who directs or manages affairs of any kind. 2. a person with a talent for managing or organizing. 3. *Law.* a person appointed by a court to take charge of the estate of a decedent, but not appointed in the decedent's will. [t. L] —**ad·min·is·tra′tor·ship′**, *n.*

ad·min·is·tra·trix (ăd mĭn′ə strā′trĭks, ăd′mĭn ə-), *n., pl.* **-istratrices** (-ə strā′trə sēz′, -ə strə trī′sēz). *Law.* a female administrator.

ad·mi·ra·ble (ăd′mə rə bəl), *adj.* worthy of admiration; exciting approval, reverence, or affection; excellent. [t. L: m.s. *admīrābilis*] —**ad′mi·ra·ble·ness**, *n.* —**ad′mi·ra·bly**, *adv.* —**Syn.** estimable, praiseworthy.

ad·mi·ral (ăd′mərəl), *n.* 1. the commander in chief of a fleet. 2. a naval officer of the highest rank. 3. a naval officer of a high rank. The grades in the U. S. Navy are: fleet admiral, admiral, vice-admiral, and rear admiral. 4. the flagship of an admiral. 5. *Brit.* a master who directs a fishing fleet. 6. any of various handsome butterflies, as the **red admiral** (*Vanessa atalanta*). [var. of ME *amiral*, t. OF, t. Ar: m. *amīr al* (chief of) in various phrases, e.g. *amīr al baḥr* commander of the sea; var. *admiral* arose by assoc. with L *admīrābilis* admirable, etc.] —**ad′mi·ral·ship′**, *n.*

ad·mi·ral·ty (ăd′mərəl tĭ), *n., pl.* **-ties**, *adj.* —*n.* 1. the office or jurisdiction of an admiral. 2. the officials or the department of state having charge of naval affairs, as in Great Britain. 3. maritime law. 4. a tribunal administering it. 5. **the Admiralty,** the official building, at London, of the British commissioners for naval affairs. —*adj.* 6. pertaining to the sea: *admiralty law.*

Admiralty Islands, a group of islands in the SW Pacific, N of New Guinea: under Australian administration. 13,450 pop. (1940); ab. 800 sq. mi.

Admiralty Range, a mountain range in Antarctica, NW of the Ross Sea.

ad·mi·ra·tion (ăd′mə rā′shən), *n.* 1. a feeling of wonder, pleasure, and approbation. 2. act of looking on or contemplating with pleasure: *admiration of a pretty girl.* 3. an object of wonder or approbation: *she was the admiration of everyone.* 4. *Archaic.* wonder. —**Syn.** 1. approval; esteem; veneration.

ad·mire (ăd mīr′), *v.,* **-mired, -miring.** —*v.t.* 1. to regard with wonder, pleasure, and approbation. 2. to regard with wonder or surprise (now usually ironical or sarcastic): *I admire your audacity.* —*v.i.* 3. to feel or express admiration. 4. *U.S. or Dial.* to like or desire (to do something). [t. L: m. s *admīrārī* wonder at] —**ad·mir′er**, *n.* —**ad·mir′ing·ly**, *adv.* —**Syn. 1.** esteem; revere, venerate.

ad·mis·si·ble (ăd mĭs′ə bəl), *adj.* 1. that may be allowed or conceded; allowable. 2. capable or worthy of being admitted. —**ad·mis′si·bil′i·ty, ad·mis′si·ble·ness**, *n.* —**ad·mis′si·bly**, *adv.*

ad·mis·sion (ăd mĭsh′ən), *n.* 1. act of allowing to enter; entrance afforded by permission, by provision or existence of means, or by the removal of obstacles: *the admission of aliens into a country.* 2. power or permission to enter: *to grant a person admission.* 3. the price paid for entrance, as to a theater, etc. 4. act or condition of being received or accepted in a position or office; appointment: *admission to the practice of law.* 5. confession of a charge, an error, or a crime; acknowledgment: *his admission of the theft solved the mystery.* 6. an acknowledgment of the truth of something. 7. a point or statement admitted; concession. [t. L: s. *admissio*] —**Syn. 1.** See **entrance.**

Admission Day, *U.S.* a legal holiday in some States commemorating the day of their admission into the Union: Feb. 14 in Arizona, Sept. 9 in California, and Oct. 31 in Nevada.

ad·mis·sive (ăd mĭs′ĭv), *adj.* tending to admit.

ad·mit (ăd mĭt′), *v.,* **-mitted, -mitting.** —*v.t.* 1. to allow to enter; grant or afford entrance to: *to admit a student to college.* 2. to give right or means of entrance to. 3. *U.S.* to permit to exercise a certain function or privilege: *admitted to the bar.* 4. to permit; allow. 5. to allow as valid: *to admit the force of an argument.* 6. to have capacity for the admission of at one time: *this passage admits two abreast.* 7. to acknowledge; confess: *he admitted his guilt.* 8. to grant in argument; concede: *the fact is admitted.* —*v.i.* 9. to permit entrance; to give access: *this key admits to the garden.* 10. to grant opportunity or permission (fol. by *of*): *circumstances do not admit of this.* [t. L: m. s. *admittere*; r. late ME *amitte(n),* t. F] —**ad·mit′ter**, *n.* —**Syn. 7.** own; avow. See **acknowledge.**

ad·mit·tance (ăd mĭt′əns), *n.* 1. permission to enter; the power or right of entrance: *admittance into the church.* 2. act of admitting. 3. actual entrance. 4. *Elect.* the reciprocal of impedance. —**Syn. 1.** See **entrance.**

ad·mit·ted·ly (ăd mĭt′ĭd lĭ), *adv.* by acknowledgment; confessedly: *he was admittedly the one who had lost the documents.*

ad·mix (ăd mĭks′), *v.t., v.i.* to mingle with or add to something else. [back formation from ME *admixt*, t. L: s. *admixtus*, pp., mingled with]

ad·mix·ture (ăd mĭks′chər), *n.* 1. act of mixing. 2. state of being mixed. 3. anything added; any alien element or ingredient.

ad·mon·ish (ăd·mŏn′ĭsh), *v.t.* **1.** to counsel against something; caution or advise. **2.** to notify of or reprove for a fault, esp. mildly: *to admonish someone as a brother.* **3.** to recall or incite to duty; remind: *to admonish someone about his obligations.* [back formation from ADMONITION; r. ME *amonesten,* t. OF] —**ad·mon′ish·er,** *n.* —**ad·mon′ish·ing·ly,** *adv.* —**ad·mon′ish·ment,** *n.* —**Syn. 1.** See **warn. 2.** rebuke, censure.

ad·mo·ni·tion (ăd′mə·nĭsh′ən), *n.* act of admonishing; counsel or advice; gentle reproof; caution. [t. L: s. *admonitio;* r. ME *amonicioun,* t. OF]

ad·mon·i·tor (ăd·mŏn′ə·tər), *n.* an admonisher. [t. L]

ad·mon·i·to·ry (ăd·mŏn′ə·tōr′ĭ), *adj.* tending or serving to admonish: *an admonitory gesture.*

ad·nate (ăd′nāt), *adj. Bot., Zool., etc.* grown fast to something; congenitally attached. [t. L: m. s. *adnātus* born to]

ad·na·tion (ăd·nā′shən), *n.* adnate condition.

ad nau·se·am (ăd nô′shĭ·ăm′,·sĭ·), *Latin.* to a sickening or disgusting extent.

ad·noun (ăd′noun′), *n.* **1.** *Gram.* an adjective in its substantival use: *the useful.* The more common term is *adjective used as a noun.* —*adj.* **2.** *Rare.* adjective. [f. AD- + NOUN, modeled on ADVERB] —**ad·nom·i·nal** (ăd nŏm′ə nəl), *adj.*

a·do (ə·dōō′), *n.* activity; bustle; fuss. [d. ME *ado, at do* to do]
—**Syn.** ADO, TO-DO, COMMOTION, STIR, TUMULT suggest a great deal of fuss and noise. ADO implies a confused bustle of activity, a considerable emotional upset, and a great deal of talking: *Much Ado About Nothing.* TO-DO, now more commonly used, may mean merely excitement and noise, and may be pleasant or unpleasant: *a great to-do over a movie star.* COMMOTION suggests a noisy confusion and babble: *commotion at the scene of an accident.* STIR suggests excitement and noise, with a hint of emotional cause: *the report was followed by a tremendous stir in the city.* TUMULT suggests disorder with noise and violence: *a tumult as the mob stormed the Bastille.*

a·do·be (ə·dō′bĭ), *n.* **1.** the sun-dried brick in common use in countries having little rainfall. **2.** a yellow silt or clay, deposited by rivers, used to make bricks. **3.** a building constructed of adobe. **4.** a dark, heavy soil, containing clay. [t. Sp.]

adobe flat, a plain consisting of adobe deposited by short-lived rainfall or thaw streams, usually having a smooth or unmarked surface.

ad·o·les·cence (ăd′ə·lĕs′əns), *n.* **1.** the transition period between puberty (boyhood or girlhood) and adult stages of development; youth. It extends from about 14 to 25 years of age in man, and from 12 to 21 in woman. **2.** quality or state of being adolescent; youthfulness. Also, **ad′o·les′cen·cy.**

ad·o·les·cent (ăd′ə·lĕs′ənt), *adj.* **1.** growing to manhood or womanhood; youthful. **2.** having the characteristics of adolescence or of an adolescent. —*n.* **3.** an adolescent person. [t. L: s. *adolescens,* ppr.]

A·don·ic (ə·dŏn′ĭk), *adj.* **1.** *Pros.* noting a verse consisting of a dactyl (– ‿ ‿) followed by a spondee (– –) or trochee (– ‿). **2.** of Adonis. —*n.* **3.** *Pros.* an Adonic verse or line. [t. ML: s. *adonicus*]

A·do·nis (ə·dō′nĭs or, *esp. for 2,* ə·dŏn′ĭs), *n.* **1.** *Gk. Myth.* a favorite of Aphrodite, slain by a wild boar, but permitted by Zeus to pass four months every year in the lower world with Persephone, four with Aphrodite, and four wherever else he chose. In another account he spent half the year on earth and thus symbolically represented the vegetation cycle. **2.** a very handsome young man.

a·dopt (ə·dŏpt′), *v.t.* **1.** to choose for or take to oneself; make one's own by selection or assent: *to adopt a name or idea.* **2.** to take as one's own child, specif. by a formal legal act. **3.** to vote to accept: *the House adopted the report.* **4.** to take or receive into any kind of new relationship: *to adopt a person as an heir.* **5.** *Brit.* to nominate (a candidate) for political office. [t. L: s. *adoptāre*] —**a·dopt′a·ble,** *adj.* —**a·dopt′er,** *n.* —**a·dop′tion,** *n.*

a·dop·tive (ə·dŏp′tĭv), *adj.* **1.** *Brit.* related by adoption: *an adoptive father or son.* **2.** tending to adopt. —**a·dop′tive·ly,** *adv.*

a·dor·a·ble (ə·dōr′ə·bəl), *adj.* **1.** worthy of being adored. **2.** *Colloq.* arousing strong liking. —**a·dor′a·ble·ness, a·dor·a·bil′i·ty,** *n.* —**a·dor′a·bly,** *adv.*

ad·o·ra·tion (ăd′ə·rā′shən), *n.* **1.** act of paying honor, as to a divine being; worship. **2.** reverent homage. **3.** fervent and devoted love.

a·dore (ə·dōr′), *v.,* **adored, adoring.** —*v.t.* **1.** to regard with the utmost esteem, love, and respect; honor. **2.** to pay divine honor to; worship: *to be adored as gods.* **3.** *Colloq.* to like greatly. —*v.i.* **4.** to worship [t. LL: m.s. *adorāre* worship, L address; r. ME *aoure(n),* t. OF: m. *ao(u)rer*] —**a·dor′er,** *n.* —**a·dor′ing,** *adj.* —**a·dor′ing·ly,** *adv.* —**Syn. 1.** reverence, revere, venerate.

a·dorn (ə·dôrn′), *v.t.* **1.** to make pleasing or more attractive; embellish; add luster to: *the piety which adorns his character.* **2.** to increase or lend beauty to, as by dress or ornaments; decorate: *garlands of flowers adorning her hair.* [t. L: s. *adornāre;* r. ME *aourne,* t. OF: m. *ao(u)rner*] —**a·dorn′er,** *n.* —**a·dorn′ing·ly,** *adv.* —**Syn. 2.** beautify; deck, bedeck.

a·dorn·ment (ə·dôrn′mənt), *n.* **1.** ornament: *the adornments and furnishings of a room.* **2.** an adorning; ornamentation: *personal adornment.*

a·down (ə·doun′), *adv., prep. Poetic.* down.

ad pa·tres (ăd pā′trēz), *Latin.* to (his) fathers; dead.

ad quem (ăd kwĕm′), *Latin.* at or to which; the goal.

A·dras·tus (ə·drăs′təs), *n. Gk. Legend.* a king of Argos and leader of the Seven against Thebes (which see).

ad rem (ăd rĕm′), *Latin.* to the matter or thing. To reply *ad rem* is to keep to the subject being considered.

ad·re·nal (ə·drē′nəl), *Anat., Zool.* —*adj.* **1.** situated near or on the kidneys; suprarenal. **2.** of or produced by the adrenal glands. —*n.* **3.** one of the adrenal glands. [f. AD- + s. L *rēnēs* kidneys + -AL[1]]

ad·re·nal·ec·to·my (ə·drē′nə·lĕk′tə·mĭ), *n., pl.* **-mies.** *Surg.* the removal of one or both adrenal glands.

adrenal glands, *Anat., Zool.* a pair of ductless glands, located above the kidneys, which secrete at least two hormones, adrenalin and cortin.

ad·ren·al·in (ə·drĕn′əl·ĭn), *n.* **1.** a white crystalline drug, $C_9H_{13}NO_3$, purified from the suprarenal secretion of animals and used to speed heart action, contract blood vessels, etc.; epinephrine. **2.** (*cap.*) a trademark for this drug. Also, **a·dren·al·ine** (ə·drĕn′əl·ĭn, -ə·lēn′).

Adrianople. A.D. 378

A·dri·an (ā′drĭ·ən), *n.* **1.** name of six popes, esp. **Adrian I,** died A.D. 795, pope from A.D.772–795, and **Adrian IV,** c1100–1159, pope from 1154–1159, the only Englishman ever to become pope. **2.** Hadrian. **3.** Edgar Douglas, born 1889, British physiologist.

A·dri·an·o·ple (ā′drĭ·ə·nō′pəl), *n.* a city in European Turkey. 45,680 (1940). Turkish, **Edirne.** See map just above.

A·dri·at·ic Sea (ā′drĭ·ăt′-ĭk), an arm of the Mediterranean between Italy and Yugoslavia. ab. 500 mi. long.

a·drift (ə·drĭft′), *adv., adj.* **1.** not fastened by any kind of moorings; at the mercy of winds and currents. **2.** swayed by any chance impulse. [f. A-[1] + DRIFT]

a·droit (ə·droit′), *adj.* expert in the use of the hand or mind; possessing readiness of resource; ingenious. [t. F, der. phrase *à droit* rightly, *droit* g. L *dīrectus* straight] —**a·droit′ly,** *adv.* —**a·droit′ness,** *n.* —**Syn.** dexterous; skillful, clever; deft.

à droite (à drwăt′), *French.* to the right.

ad·sci·ti·tious (ăd′sə·tĭsh′əs), *adj.* added or derived from without; supplemental; additional. [f. s. L *adscītus,* pp., derived + -ITIOUS]

ad·script (ăd′skrĭpt), *adj.* written after (distinguished from *subscript*). [t. L: s. *adscriptus,* pp.]

ad·scrip·tion (ăd·skrĭp′shən), *n.* ascription.

ad·sorb (ăd·sôrb′), *v.t.* to gather (a gas, liquid, or dissolved substance) on a surface in a condensed layer, as when charcoal adsorbs gases. [f. AD- + s. L *sorbēre* suck in] —**ad·sorb′ent,** *adj., n.* —**ad·sorp·tion** (ăd·sôrp′shən), *n.* —**ad·sorp′tive,** *adj., n.*

ad·su·ki bean (ăd·sōō′kĭ, -zōō′-), a kind of bean, *Phaseolus angularis,* extensively grown in parts of Asia and to a limited degree in the U. S. Also, **adzuki bean.** [t. Jap.: m. *adzuki*]

ad·u·lar·i·a (ăj′ə·lâr′ĭ·ə), *n. Mineral.* a transparent or translucent variety of orthoclase, often pearly or opalescent, as the moonstone. [named after the *Adula* mountain group in Switzerland. See -ARIA]

ad·u·late (ăj′ə·lāt′), *v.t.,* **-lated, -lating.** to show pretended or undiscriminating devotion to; flatter servilely. [t. L: m. s. *adūlāta,* pp.] —**ad·u·la′tion,** *n.* —**ad′u·la·tor,** *n.* —**ad·u·la·to·ry** (ăj′ə·lə·tōr′ĭ), *adj.*

a·dult (ə·dŭlt′, ăd′ŭlt), *adj.* **1.** having attained full size and strength; grown up; mature: *an adult person, animal, or plant.* **2.** pertaining to or designed for adults: *adult education.* —*n.* **3.** a person who is grown up or of age. **4.** a full-grown animal or plant. **5.** *Common Law.* a designation of a person who has attained 21 years of age. **6.** *Civil Law.* a male after attaining 14, or a female after attaining 12, years of age. [t. L: s. *adultus,* pp.] —**a·dult′hood,** *n.* —**a·dult′ness,** *n.*

a·dul·ter·ant (ə·dŭl′tər·ənt), *n.* **1.** a substance used for adulterating. —*adj.* **2.** adulterating.

a·dul·ter·ate (*v.* ə·dŭl′tər·āt′; *adj.* ə·dŭl′tər·ĭt, -ə·rāt′), *v.,* **-ated, -ating.** —*v.t.* **1.** to debase by adding inferior materials or elements; make impure by admixture; use cheaper, inferior, or less desirable goods in the production or marketing of (any professedly genuine article): *to adulterate food.* —*adj.* **2.** adulterated. **3.** adulterous. [t. L: m. s. *adulterātus,* pp., defiled] —**a·dul′ter·a′tor,** *n.*

a·dul·ter·a·tion (ə·dŭl′tə·rā′shən), *n.* **1.** act or process of adulterating. **2.** state of being adulterated. **3.** something adulterated.

a·dul·ter·er (ə·dŭl′tər·ər), *n.* a person, esp. a man, guilty of adultery. —**a·dul·ter·ess** (ə·dŭl′tər·ĭs, -trĭs), *n.fem.*

a·dul·ter·ine (ə·dŭl′tər·ĭn, -tə·rīn′), *adj.* **1.** characterized by adulteration; spurious. **2.** born of adultery. **3.** of or involving adultery. [t. L: m.s. *adulterīnus*]

a·dul·ter·ous (ə dŭl′tər əs), *adj.* **1.** characterized by or given to adultery; illicit. **2.** spurious. **—a·dul′ter·ous·ly,** *adv.*

a·dul·ter·y (ə dŭl′tə rĭ), *n., pl.* **-teries.** voluntary sexual intercourse between a married person and any other than the lawful spouse. [t. L: m.s. *adulterium;* r. ME *avoutrie,* t. OF]

ad·um·bral (ăd ŭm′brəl), *adj.* shadowy; shady.

ad·um·brate (ăd ŭm′brāt, ăd′əm brāt′), *v.t.,* **-brated, -brating. 1.** to give a faint shadow or resemblance of; outline or shadow forth. **2.** to foreshadow; prefigure. **3.** to darken or conceal partially; overshadow. [t. L: m. s. *adumbrātus,* pp., shadowed] **—ad′um·bra′tion,** *n.*

ad·um·bra·tive (ăd ŭm′brə tĭv), *adj.* shadowing forth; indicative. **—ad·um′bra·tive·ly,** *adv.*

a·dunc (ə dŭngk′), *adj.* curved inward; hooked. Also, **a·dun·cous** (ə dŭng′kəs). [t. L: s. *aduncus* crooked]

a·dust (ə dŭst′), *adj.* **1.** dried or darkened as by heat; burned; scorched. **2.** atrabilious; sallow; gloomy. [t. L: s. *adūstus,* pp.]

ad u·trum·que pa·ra·tus (ăd ū trŭm′kwĭ pə rā′təs), *Latin.* ready for either alternative.

A·du·wa (ä′dŏŏ wä′), *n.* a town in N Ethiopia: the Ethiopians defeated the Italians here, 1896. ab. 6000.

adv., 1. adverb. **2.** adverbial. **3.** adverbially. **4.** advertisement. **5.** ad valorem.

ad val., ad valorem.

ad va·lo·rem (ăd və lōr′ĕm), in proportion to the value. An *ad valorem* duty charged on goods entering a country is fixed at a percentage of the customs value as stated on the invoice. [t. L]

ad·vance (ăd văns′, -väns′), *v.,* **-vanced, -vancing,** *n., adj.* **—***v.t.* **1.** to move or bring forward in place: *the troops were advanced to the new position.* **2.** to bring to view or notice; propose: *to advance an argument.* **3.** to improve; further: *to advance one's interests.* **4.** to raise in rank; promote. **5.** to raise in rate: *to advance the price.* **6.** to bring forward in time; accelerate: *to advance growth.* **7.** to supply beforehand; furnish on credit, or before goods are delivered or work is done. **8.** to furnish as part of a stock or fund. **9.** to supply or pay in expectation of reimbursement: *to advance money on loan.* **10.** *Archaic.* to raise, as a banner. **—***v.i.* **11.** to move or go forward; proceed: *the troops advanced.* **12.** to improve or make progress; grow: *to advance in knowledge or rank.* **13.** to increase in quantity, value, price, etc.: *stocks advanced three points.* **—***n.* **14.** a moving forward; progress in space: *advance to the sea.* **15.** advancement; promotion: *an advance in rank.* **16.** a step forward; actual progress in any course of action: *the advance of knowledge.* **17.** (*usually pl.*) an effort to bring about acquaintance, accord, understanding, etc. **18.** addition to price; rise in price: *an advance on cottons.* **19.** *Com.* **a.** a giving beforehand; a furnishing of something before an equivalent is received. **b.** the money or goods thus furnished. **20.** *U.S.* the leading body of an army. **21.** *Mil.* (formerly) the order or a signal to advance. **22. in advance, a.** before; in front. **b.** beforehand; ahead of time: *he insisted on paying his rent in advance.* **—***adj.* **23.** going before: *the advance section of a train.* **24.** made or given in advance: *an advance payment.* **25.** issued in advance: *an advance copy.* **26.** having gone beyond others or beyond the average. [ME *avaunce(n)* t. OF: m. *avancier,* g. LL *abanteāre,* der. *abante* (f. *ab + ante*) from before] **—ad·vanc′er,** *n.* **—Syn. 2.** adduce; propound; offer. **5.** increase. **6.** quicken, hasten, speed up. **11.** ADVANCE, MOVE ON, PROCEED all imply movement forward. ADVANCE applies to forward movement, esp. toward an objective: *to advance to a platform.* PROCEED emphasizes movement as from one place to another, and often implies continuing after a halt: *to proceed on one's journey.* MOVE ON, a more informal expression, is similar in meaning to PROCEED; it does not, however, imply a definite goal: *the crowd was told to move on.* **12.** thrive, flourish; prosper. **13.** rise. **17.** overture; proposal.

ad·vanced (ăd vănst′, -vänst′), *adj.* **1.** placed in advance: *with foot advanced.* **2.** far on in progress: *beyond the average: an advanced class in French.* **3.** far on in time: *an advanced age.*

advanced standing, acceptance by a college of credits which a student has earned in another school.

advance guard, a body of troops going before the main force to clear the way, guard against surprise, etc.

ad·vance·ment (ăd văns′mənt, -väns′-), *n.* **1.** act of moving forward. **2.** promotion in rank or standing; preferment: *his hopes of advancement failed.* **3.** *Law.* money or property given during his lifetime by a person subsequently dying intestate and deducted from the intestate share of the recipient.

ad·van·tage (ăd văn′tĭj, -vän′-), *n., v.,* **-taged, -taging.** **—***n.* **1.** any state, circumstance, opportunity, or means specially favorable to success, interest, or any desired end: *the advantage of a good education.* **2.** benefit; gain; profit: *it is to his advantage.* **3.** superiority or ascendancy (often fol. by *over* or *of*): *to have the advantage of age.* **4.** a position of superiority (often fol. by *over* or *of*): *don't let him get the advantage of us.* **5.** *Tennis.* the first point scored after deuce, or the resulting state of the score; vantage. **6. take advantage of, a.** to make use of: *to take advantage of an opportunity.* **b.** to impose upon: *to take advantage of someone.* **7. to advantage,** with good effect; advantageously. **—***v.t.* **8.** to be of service to; yield profit or gain to; benefit. [ME *avantage,*

t. OF, der. *avant* before, forward, g. LL *abante.* See ADVANCE]
—Syn. 2. ADVANTAGE, BENEFIT, PROFIT all mean something that is of use or value. ADVANTAGE is anything that places one in an improved position, esp. in coping with competition or difficulties: *it is to one's advantage to have traveled widely.* BENEFIT is anything that promotes the welfare or improves the state of a person or group: *a benefit to society.* PROFIT is any valuable, useful, or helpful gain: *profit from trade or experience.*

ad·van·ta·geous (ăd′vən tā′jəs), *adj.* of advantage; furnishing convenience or opportunity; profitable; useful; beneficial: *an advantageous position.* **—ad′van·ta′geous·ly,** *adv.* **—ad′van·ta′geous·ness,** *n.*

ad·vec·tion (ăd vĕk′shən), *n.* **1.** the transfer of heat by horizontal movements of air; horizontal convection. **2.** the movement of air horizontally. [t. L: s. *advectio* a carrying]

ad·vent (ăd′vĕnt), *n.* **1.** a coming into place, view, or being; arrival: *the advent of death.* **2.** (*cap. or l.c.*) the coming of Christ into the world. **3.** (*cap.*) a season (including four Sundays) preceding Christmas, commemorative of Christ's coming. **4. Second Advent,** the second coming of Christ to establish a personal reign upon the earth as its king. [ME, t. L: s. *adventus* arrival]

Ad·vent·ist (ăd′vĕn tĭst, ăd vĕn′-), *n.* a member of any of certain Christian denominations which maintain that the second coming of Christ is near at hand; Second Adventist. Cf. **Millerite. —Ad′vent·ism,** *n.*

ad·ven·ti·tious (ăd′vən tĭsh′əs), *adj.* **1.** accidentally or casually acquired; added extrinsically; foreign. **2.** *Bot., Zool.* appearing in an abnormal or unusual position or place, as a root. [t. L: m. *adventīcius* coming from abroad] **—ad′ven·ti′tious·ly,** *adv.* **—ad′ven·ti′tious·ness,** *n.*

ad·ven·tive (ăd vĕn′tĭv), *Bot., Zool.* **—***adj.* **1.** not native, as exotic plants or animals. **—***n.* **2.** an adventive plant or animal.

Advent Sunday, the first Sunday in Advent, being the Sunday nearest to St. Andrew's Day (Nov. 30).

ad·ven·ture (ăd vĕn′chər), *n., v.,* **-tured, -turing. —***n.* **1.** an undertaking of uncertain outcome; a hazardous enterprise. **2.** an exciting experience. **3.** participation in exciting undertakings or enterprises: *the spirit of adventure.* **4.** a commercial or financial speculation of any kind; a venture. **5.** *Obs.* peril; danger. **6.** *Obs.* chance. **—***v.t.* **7.** to risk or hazard. **8.** to take the chance of; dare. **9.** to venture to say or utter: *to adventure an opinion.* **—***v.i.* **10.** to take the risk involved. **11.** to venture. [ME *aventure,* t. OF, g. L *adventūra,* future p., (sc. *rēs*) (a thing) about to happen]

ad·ven·tur·er (ăd vĕn′chər ər), *n.* **1.** one who adventures. **2.** a seeker of fortune in daring enterprises; a soldier of fortune. **3.** one who undertakes any great commercial risk; a speculator. **4.** a seeker of fortune by underhand or equivocal means.

ad·ven·ture·some (ăd vĕn′chər səm), *adj.* bold; daring; adventurous.

ad·ven·tur·ess (ăd vĕn′chər ĭs), *n.* **1.** a female adventurer. **2.** a woman who schemes to win social position, money, etc., by equivocal methods.

ad·ven·tur·ism (ăd vĕn′chə rĭz′əm), *n.* defiance of accepted standards of behavior.

ad·ven·tur·ous (ăd vĕn′chər əs), *adj.* **1.** inclined or willing to engage in adventures. **2.** attended with risk; requiring courage: *an adventurous undertaking.* **—ad·ven′tur·ous·ly,** *adv.* **—ad·ven′tur·ous·ness,** *n.* **—Syn. 1.** daring, venturous, venturesome.

ad·verb (ăd′vûrb), *n.* **1.** one of the major form classes or "parts of speech," comprising words used to qualify or limit a verb, a verbal noun (also, in Latin, English, and some other languages, an adjective or another adverb), or an adverbial phrase or clause. An adverbial element expresses some relation of place, time, manner, attendant circumstance, degree, cause, inference, result, condition, exception, concession, purpose, or means. **2.** such a word, as *well* in English *she sings well.* **3.** any word or phrase of similar function or meaning. [earlier *adverbe,* t. L: m. s. *adverbium*] **—ad·ver·bi·al** (ădvûr′bĭ əl), *adj.* **—ad·ver′bi·al·ly,** *adv.* **—ad′verb·less,** *adj.*

ad ver·bum (ăd vûr′bəm), *Latin.* to the word; exact in wording according to an original.

ad·ver·sar·y (ăd′vər sĕr′ĭ), *n., pl.* **-saries. 1.** an unfriendly opponent. **2.** an opponent in a contest; a contestant. **3. the Adversary,** the Devil; Satan. [ME *adversarie,* t. L: m. *adversārius*]
—Syn. 1. ADVERSARY, ANTAGONIST mean a person, a group, or a personified force, contending against another. ADVERSARY suggests an enemy who fights determinedly, continuously, and relentlessly: *a formidable adversary.* ANTAGONIST suggests one who, in hostile spirit, opposes another, often in a particular contest or struggle: *a duel with an antagonist.* **—Ant. 1.** ally, supporter.

ad·ver·sa·tive (ăd vûr′sə tĭv), *adj.* **1.** expressing contrariety, opposition, or antithesis: "but" *is an adversative conjunction.* **—***n.* **2.** an adversative word or proposition. [t. LL: m. s. *adversātīvus*] **—ad·ver′sa·tive·ly,** *adv.*

ad·verse (ăd vûrs′, ăd′vûrs), *adj.* **1.** antagonistic in purpose or effect: *adverse criticism, adverse to slavery.* **2.** opposing one's interests or desire: *adverse fate, fortune, influences, or circumstances.* **3.** being or acting in a contrary direction; opposed or opposing: *adverse winds.* **4.** opposite; confronting: *the adverse page.* **5.** *Bot.* turned toward the axis, as a leaf. [ME, t. L: m. *adversus,* pp.,

turned against, turned towards] —ad·verse′ly, adv.
—ad·verse′ness, n. —Syn. 1. hostile, inimical. 2. unfavorable; unlucky, disastrous. See contrary.

ad·ver·si·ty (ăd vûr′sə tĭ), n., pl. -ties. 1. adverse
fortune or fate; a condition marked by misfortune, calamity, or distress: his struggles with adversity. 2. an unfortunate event or circumstance: the prosperities and adversities of this life. [ME adversite, t. L: m. adversitas
opposition] —Syn. 2. See affliction.

ad·vert¹ (ăd vûrt′), v.i. 1. to make a remark or remarks (about or in relation to); refer (fol. by to): he
adverted briefly to the occurrences of the day. 2. to turn
the attention (fol. by to). [t. L: s. advertere turn to; r.
ME averte(n), t. OF: m. avertir]

ad·vert² (ăd′vərt), n. Brit. Colloq. advertisement.

ad·vert·ent (ăd vûr′tənt), adj. attentive; heedful.
—ad·vert′ence, ad·vert′en·cy, n. —ad·vert′ent·ly,
adv.

ad·ver·tise (ăd′vər tīz′, ăd′vər tīz′), v., -tised, -tising.
—v.t. 1. to give information to the public concerning;
make public announcement of, by publication in periodicals, by printed bills, by broadcasting over the radio,
etc.: to advertise a reward. 2. to praise the good qualities
of, in order to induce the public to buy or invest in.
3. to give notice, advice, or information to; inform: I ad-
vertised him of my intention. 4. Obs. to admonish; warn.
—v.i. 5. to ask (for) by placing an advertisement in a
newspaper, magazine, etc., or by broadcasting over the
radio: to advertise for a house to rent. Also, ad′ver·tize′.
[ME advertise(n), t. MF: m. advertiss-, s. advertir, t. L:
m. advertere. See ADVERT¹, -ISE] —ad′ver·tis′er, ad′-
ver·tiz′er, n.

ad·ver·tise·ment (ăd′vər tīz′mənt, ăd vûr′tĭs mənt,
-tĭz-), n. 1. a printed announcement, as of goods for
sale, in a newspaper, magazine, etc. 2. a public notice,
esp. in print. Also, ad′ver·tize′ment. [ME, t. MF: m.
advertissement]

ad·ver·tis·ing (ăd′vər tī′zĭng), n. 1. act or practice
of bringing anything, as one's wants or one's business,
into public notice, esp. by paid announcements in periodicals, on billboards, etc., or on the radio: to secure
customers by advertising. 2. paid announcements; advertisements. 3. the profession of designing and writing
advertisements. Also, ad′ver·tiz′ing.

ad·vice (ăd vīs′), n. 1. an opinion recommended, or
offered, as worthy to be followed: I shall act on your advice. 2. a communication, esp. from a distance, containing information: advice from abroad. [late ME advyse, t.
MF: m. advis opinion, f. L: ad- AD- + s. vīsum, pp. neut.,
what seems best; r. ME avis, t. OF]
—Syn. 1. admonition ADVICE, COUNSEL are suggestions
given by a (presumably) wiser or more highly trained person
to one considered in need of guidance. ADVICE is a practical
recommendation as to action or conduct: advice about purchasing land. COUNSEL is weighty and serious advice, given
after careful deliberation: counsel about one's career. 2. information, news, tidings; report.

ad·vis·a·ble (ăd vī′zə bəl), adj. 1. proper to be advised or to be recommended. 2. open to or desirous of
advice. —ad·vis′a·bil′i·ty, ad·vis′a·ble·ness, n.
—ad·vis′a·bly, adv. —Syn. 1. expedient, politic,
proper, prudent, sensible.

ad·vise (ăd vīz′), v., -vised, -vising. —v.t. 1. to give
counsel to; offer an opinion to, as worthy or expedient to
be followed: I advise you to be cautious. 2. to recommend
as wise, prudent, etc.: he advised secrecy. 3. to give (a
person, etc.) information or notice (fol. by of): the merchants were advised of the risk. —v.i. 4. to take counsel
(fol. by with): I shall advise with my friends. 5. to offer
counsel; give advice: I shall act as you advise. [t. LL:
m.s. advīsāre; r. ME avise(n), t. OF] —Syn. 1. admonish, caution. See warn. 3. inform, notify, apprise.
4. consult, confer.

ad·vised (ăd vīzd′), adj. 1. considered: now chiefly in
ill-advised or well-advised. 2. informed: kept thoroughly
advised. —ad·vis·ed·ness (ăd vī′zĭd nĭs), n.

ad·vis·ed·ly (ăd vī′zĭd lĭ), adv. after due consideration; deliberately.

ad·vise·ment (ăd vīz′mənt), n. careful deliberation;
consultation: the application was taken under advisement.

ad·vis·er (ăd vī′zər), n. 1. one who gives advice.
2. Educ. a teacher who helps students select their course
of studies, etc. Also, ad·vi′sor.

ad·vi·so·ry (ăd vī′zə rĭ), adj. of, or giving, advice;
having power to advise: an advisory council.

ad·vo·ca·cy (ăd′və kə sĭ), n. act of pleading for, supporting, or recommending; active espousal.

ad·vo·cate (v. ăd′və kāt′; n. ăd′və kĭt, -kāt′), v.,
-cated, -cating. —v.t. 1. to plead in favor of; support or urge by argument; recommend publicly: he advocated isolationism. —n. 2. one who defends, vindi-
cates, or espouses a cause by argument; an upholder; a
defender (fol. by of): an advocate of peace. 3. one who
pleads for or in behalf of another; intercessor. 4. Chiefly
Scot., sometimes English, and formerly U.S. one who
pleads the cause of another in a court of law. [t. L: m. s.
advocātus (prop. pp.) one summoned to help another (in
legal case); r. ME avocat, t. OF] —ad′vo·ca′tor, n.

ad·vo·ca·tion (ăd′və kā′shən), n. 1. Law. the calling
of an action before itself by a superior (papal or Scottish)
court. 2. Obs. advocacy. 3. Obs. act of summoning.

ad·voc·a·to·ry (ăd vŏk′ə tōr′ĭ), adj. of an advocate
or his functions.

ad·vo·ca·tus di·a·bo·li (ăd′və kā′təs dī ăb′ə lī′), Medieval Latin. 1. the devil's advocate. 2. an adverse
critic, esp. of what is deemed good; a detractor.

ad·vow·son (ăd vou′zən), n. Eng. Law. the right of
presentation to a benefice. [t. AF; r. ME avoweson, t.
OF: m. avoeson, g. L advocātio]

advt., advertisement.

ad·y·na·mi·a (ăd′ə nā′mĭ ə), n. Pathol. weakness; debility; asthenia. [t. Gk.]

ad·y·nam·ic (ăd′ə năm′ĭk, ā/dī-), adj. Pathol. lacking
strength; asthenic.

ad·y·tum (ăd′ə təm), n., pl. -ta (-tə). 1. (in ancient worship) a sacred place which the public might not enter; an
inner shrine. 2. the most sacred or re-
served part of any place of worship. [t.
L, t. Gk.: m. ádyton not to be entered]

adz (ădz), n. a heavy chisellike steel
tool fastened at right angles to a wooden
handle, used to remove surplus material,
etc. Also, adze. [ME adese, OE adesa]

ad·zu·ki bean (ăd zōō′kĭ), adsuki
bean.

ae¹ (ā), adj. Scot. one.

ae² or æ, 1. a digraph or ligature appearing in Latin and Latinized Greek
words. In English words of Latin or
Greek origin, ae is now usually reduced to e, except
generally in proper names (Caesar), in words belonging
to Roman or Greek antiquities (aegis), and in modern
words of scientific or technical use (aecium). 2. an early
English ligature representing a vowel sound like the a in
modern bad. The long æ continued in use until about
1250, but was finally replaced by e. The short æ was
given up by 1150, being replaced usually by a but sometimes by e.

ae-. For words with initial ae-, see also e-.

Æ, pen name of George William Russell. Also, A.E.

ae., (L aetatis) at the age of; aged.

Ae·a·cus (ē′ə kəs), n. Gk. Myth. a son of Zeus; grandfather of Achilles and a judge in the lower world. Cf.
Minos, Rhadamanthus.

ae·ci·al stage (ē′shĭ əl), Bot. the part of the life
cycle of the rust fungi in which aecia are formed.

ae·cid·i·al stage (ē sĭd′ĭ əl), Bot. the part of the life
cycle of the rust fungi in which aecidia are formed.

ae·cid·i·um (ē sĭd′ĭ əm), n., pl. -cidia (-sĭd′ĭ ə). Bot. an
aecium in which the spores are always formed in
chains and enclosed in a cup-shaped peridium, as in the
form genus Aecidium. [NL dim. of Gk. aikía injury]

ae·ci·o·spore (ē′sĭ ə spōr′), n. Bot. a spore borne by
an aecium.

ae·ci·um (ē′shĭ əm, ē′sĭ-), n., pl. -cia (-shĭ ə, -sĭ ə). Bot.
the sorus of rust fungi which arises from the haploid
mycelium, commonly accompanied by spermogonia and
bearing chainlike or stalked spores. [t. NL: f. m.s. Gk.
aikía an injurious effect + -ium -IUM] —ae·ci·al
(ē′shĭ əl), adj.

a·ë·des (ā ē′dēz), n. 1. the mosquito, Aëdes aegypti,
which transmits yellow fever and dengue. 2. any mosquito of the genus Aëdes. [t. NL, t. Gk: unpleasant]

ae·dile (ē′dīl), n. (in ancient Rome) one of a board of
magistrates in charge of public buildings, streets, markets, games, etc. Also, edile. [t. L: m. s. aedīlis] —ae′-
dile·ship′, n.

Ae·ë·tes (ē ē′tēz), n. Gk. Legend. a king of Colchis,
father of Medea, and custodian of the Golden Fleece.

A.E.F., American Expeditionary Forces.

Ae·ge·an (ē jē′ən), adj. denoting or pertaining to the
civilization which preceded the historic Hellenic period
and which flourished in vari-
ous islands in, and lands adjacent to, the Aegean Sea, as
Crete, Argolis, etc. [f. m. s.
L Aegaeus (t. Gk.: m.
Aigaîos) + -AN]

Aegean Islands, Greek
islands of the Aegean Sea, including the Dodecanese, Cyclades, and Sporades groups.

Aegean Sea, an arm of the
Mediterranean between
Greece and Asia Minor. ab.
350 mi. long; ab. 200 mi. wide.

Ae·geus (ē′jōōs, ē′jĭ əs), n.
Gk. Legend. king of Athens and father of Theseus.

Ae·gi·na (ē jī′nə), n. 1. Gulf of, a gulf in SE Greece.
2. an island in this gulf. 12,028 pop. (1940); 32 sq. mi.
3. a seaport on this island. 6909 (1940).

Ae·gir (ā′gĭr, ē′jĭr), n. Scand. Myth. the sea god, the
husband of Ran. [t. Icel.]

ae·gis (ē′jĭs), n. 1. Gk. Myth. a. the shield of Zeus.
b. the shield lent by Zeus to other deities, esp. Athene.
2. protection; sponsorship: under the imperial aegis. Also,
egis. [t. L, t. Gk.: m. aigís, lit., a goatskin]

Ae·gis·thus (ē jĭs′thəs), n. Gk. Legend. the cousin of
Agamemnon. He seduced Clytemnestra in the absence
of her husband, Agamemnon, and was later slain by her
son, Orestes.

Ae·gos·pot·a·mi (ē′gəs pŏt′ə mī′), n. a creek in ancient Thrace, flowing into the Hellespont: near its mouth
the Athenian fleet was defeated by Lysander, 405 B.C.
leading to the termination of the Peloponnesian War.

Ae·gyp·tus (ē̇·jĭp′təs), n. Gk. Legend. a king of Egypt and twin brother of Danaus.

Æl·fric (ăl′frĭk), n. ("Ælfric Grammaticus") A.D. c955–c1020, British abbot and writer.

-aemia, var. of **-emia**, as in toxaemia.

Ae·ne·as (ĭ·nē′əs), n. Class. Myth. the son of Anchises and Aphrodite (Venus): a Trojan hero, who became the founder of Rome. See **Aeneid**. [t. L, t. Gk.: m. Aineias]

Ae·ne·id (ĭ·nē′ĭd), n. a Latin epic poem by Vergil, reciting the adventures of Aeneas after the fall of Troy.

a·ë·ne·ous (ā·ē′nĭ·əs), adj. bronze-colored. [t. L: m. aēneus brazen]

Ae·o·li·an (ē·ō′lĭ·ən), adj. 1. belonging to a branch of the Greek race named from Aeolus, the legendary founder; Aeolic. —n. 2. a member of one of the three great divisions of the ancient Greek race, the two other divisions being the Dorian and the Ionian. 3. Aeolic. Also, **Eolian**. [f. m.s. Gk. Aioleús Aeolus + -AN]

Ae·o·li·an (ē·ō′lĭ·ən), adj. 1. pertaining to Aeolus, or to the winds in general. 2. (l.c.) due to atmospheric action; wind-blown. [f. m.s. Gk. Aíolos Aeolus + -IAN]

aeolian harp, a box over which are stretched a number of strings of equal length, tuned in unison and sounded by the wind. Also, **aeolian lyre**.

Ae·ol·ic (ē·ŏl′ĭk), n. 1. the dialect of Greek spoken by the Aeolians. —adj. 2. Aeolian[1]. Also, **Eolic**.

ae·o·li·pile (ē·ŏl′ə·pīl′), n. an instrument consisting essentially of a round vessel rotated by the force of steam generated within and escaping through bent arms. Also, **ae·ol′i·pyle′**. [t. L: m. s. aeolīpila, orig. Aeolī pila ball of Aeolus, or Aeolī pylae doorway of Aeolus]

Ae·o·lis (ē′ə·lĭs), n. an ancient coastal region and Greek colony in NW Asia Minor.

ae·o·lo·trop·ic (ē′ə·lō·trŏp′ĭk), adj. Physics. not isotropic; anisotropic. [f. m. Gk. aiólo(s) changeful + -TROPIC] —**ae·o·lot·ro·py** (ē′ə·lŏt′rə·pĭ), **ae·o·lot·ro·pism** (ē′ə·lŏt′rə·pĭz′əm), n.

Ae·o·lus (ē′ə·ləs), n. Gk. Myth. the ruler of the winds.

ae·on (ē′ən, ē′ŏn), n. 1. an indefinitely long period of time; an age. 2. (in the Gnostic doctrine) one of a class of powers or beings conceived as emanating from the Supreme Being and performing various functions in the operations of the universe. 3. Geol. eon. [t. L, t. Gk.: m. aiōn lifetime, age]

ae·o·ni·an (ē·ō′nĭ·ən), adj. eternal. [f. m. s. Gk. aiōnios age-long + -AN]

aer-, var. of **aero-** before vowels. Also, **aër-**.

aer·ate (âr′āt, ā′ə·rāt′), v.t., **-ated**, **-ating**. 1. to expose to the free action of the air: to aerate milk in order to remove odors. 2. to charge or treat with air or a gas, esp. with carbon dioxide. 3. Physiol. to expose (a medium or tissue) to air, as in the oxygenation of the blood in respiration. [f. AER- + -ATE[1]] —**aer·a′tion**, n.

aer·a·tor (âr′ā·tər, ā′ə·rā′tər), n. 1. an apparatus for aerating water or other fluids. 2. a contrivance for fumigating wheat and other grain, to bleach it and destroy fungi and insects.

aer·i·al (adj. âr′ĭ·əl, ā·ĭr′ĭ·əl; n. âr′ĭ·əl), adj. 1. of, in, or produced by the air: aerial currents. 2. inhabiting or frequenting the air: aerial creatures. 3. reaching far into the air; high; lofty: aerial spires. 4. partaking of the nature of air; airy: aerial beings. 5. unsubstantial; visionary: aerial fancies. 6. having a light and graceful beauty; ethereal: aerial music. 7. Biol. growing in the air, as the adventitious roots of some trees. See illus. under **banyan**. 8. pertaining to or used for, against, or in aircraft. —n. 9. Radio. an antenna. [f. s. L aērius airy (t. Gk.: m. āérios) + -AL[1]] —**aer′i·al·ly**, adv.

aer·i·al·ist (âr′ĭ·əl·ĭst, ā·ĭr′ĭ·əl-), n. a trapeze artist.

aer·i·al·i·ty (âr′ĭ·ăl′ə·tĭ, ā·ĭr′-), n. unsubstantiality.

aerial perspective, that branch of perspective which considers the variations of light, shade, and color in objects delineated, according to their distances, the quality of light falling on them, and the medium through which they are seen.

aer·ie (âr′ĭ, ĭr′ĭ), n. 1. the nest of a bird of prey, as an eagle or a hawk. 2. a lofty nest of any large bird. 3. the brood in the nest; the young of a bird of prey. 4. Archaic. children. 5. an elevated habitation or situation. Also, **aery**, **eyrie**, **eyry**. [t. ML: m. aeria, t. OF: m. aire, g. L ārea (see AREA) or L ātrium ATRIUM]

aer·if·er·ous (â·rĭf′ər·əs), adj. conveying air, as the bronchial tubes. [f. AER- + -(I)FEROUS]

aer·i·fi·ca·tion (âr′ə·fə·kā′shən, ā·ĭr′-), n. 1. act of combining with air. 2. state of being filled with air.

aer·i·form (âr′ə·fôrm′, ā·ĭr′-), adj. 1. having the form or nature of air; gaseous. 2. unsubstantial; unreal.

aer·i·fy (âr′ə·fī′, ā·ĭr′-), v.t. **-fied**, **-fying**. 1. to aerate. 2. to make aeriform; convert into vapor.

aer·o (âr′ō), adj. 1. of or for aircraft. 2. of aeronautics.

aero-, a word element meaning: 1. air; atmosphere. 2. gas. 3. airplane. Also, **aër-**. [t. Gk., comb. form of āēr air]

aer·obe (âr′ōb), n. a bacterium or other microörganism whose existence requires, or is not destroyed by, the presence of free oxygen (opposed to anaerobe). [t. NL: m. aerobia, f. Gk.: aēro- AERO- + m. bíos life]

aer·o·bee (âr′ə·bĭ′), n. a recently developed rocket, capable of attaining an altitude of 100 miles and a speed of 3000 miles an hour, used mainly for carrying scientific recording instruments.

aer·o·bic (â·rō′bĭk), adj. 1. (of organisms or tissues) requiring, or not destroyed by, the presence of free oxygen. 2. pertaining to or caused by the presence of oxygen: aerobic respiration. —**aer·o′bi·cal·ly**, adv.

aer·o·bi·um (â·rō′bĭ·əm), n., pl. **-bia** (-bĭ·ə). aerobe.

aer·o·do·net·ics (âr′ō·dō·nĕt′ĭks), n. the study of gliding or soaring flight; the science dealing with gliding craft. [f. s. Gk. aerodónetos air-tossed + -ICS]

aer·o·drome (âr′ə·drōm′), n. Chiefly Brit. an airdrome.

aer·o·dy·nam·ics (âr′ō·dī·năm′ĭks, -dĭ-), n. the science that treats of the motion of the air and other gases, or of their properties and mechanical effects when in motion. —**aer′o·dy·nam′ic**, adj.

aer·o·dyne (âr′ə·dīn′), n. any heavier-than-air craft.

aer·o·em·bo·lism (âr′ō·ĕm′bə·lĭz′əm), n. a morbid condition caused by substantial decrease in atmospheric pressure, as in high-altitude flying, and characterized by the formation of nitrogen bubbles in the blood, pains in the lungs, etc. Cf. **bends** and **caisson disease**.

aer·o·gram (âr′ə·grăm′), n. 1. a radiogram. 2. a message carried by aircraft.

aer·og·ra·phy (â·rŏg′rə·fĭ), n. description of the air or atmosphere. —**aer·og′ra·pher**, n. —**aer·o·graph·ic** (âr′ə·grăf′ĭk), **aer′o·graph′i·cal**, adj.

aer·o·lite (âr′ə·līt′), n. a meteorite consisting mainly of stony matter. Also, **aer·o·lith** (âr′ə·lĭth). —**aer·o·lit·ic** (âr′ə·lĭt′ĭk), adj.

aer·ol·o·gy (â·rŏl′ə·jĭ), n. the study of the properties of air and of the atmosphere. —**aer·o·log·ic** (âr′ə·lŏj′ĭk), **aer′o·log′i·cal**, adj. —**aer·ol′o·gist**, n.

aer·o·ma·rine (âr′ō·mə·rēn′), adj. Aeron. relating to navigation of aircraft above the ocean.

aer·o·me·chan·ic (âr′ō·mə·kăn′ĭk·), n. 1. an aviation mechanic. —adj. 2. of or pertaining to aeromechanics.

aer·o·me·chan·ics (âr′ō·mə·kăn′ĭks), n. the mechanics of air or gases. —**aer′o·me·chan′i·cal**, adj.

aer·om·e·ter (â·rŏm′ə·tər), n. an instrument for determining the weight, density, etc., of air or other gases.

aer·om·e·try (â·rŏm′ə·trĭ), n. pneumatics. —**aer·o·met·ric** (âr′ə·mĕt′rĭk), adj.

aeron., aeronautics.

aer·o·naut (âr′ə·nôt′), n. 1. the pilot of a balloon or other lighter-than-air craft. 2. a traveler in an airship. [back formation from AERONAUTICS. Cf. F aéronaute]

aer·o·nau·tic (âr′ə·nô′tĭk), adj. of aeronautics or aeronauts. Also, **aer′o·nau′ti·cal**. [t. NL: s. aeronautica, neut. pl. adj., pertaining to sailing in the air] —**aer′o·nau′ti·cal·ly**, adv.

aer·o·nau·tics (âr′ə·nô′tĭks), n. the science or art of flight in aircraft. [pl. of AERONAUTIC. See -ICS]

aer·o·pha·gi·a (âr′ə·fā′jĭ·ə), n. Psychiatry. morbid swallowing of air due to neurotic gastric disturbances.

aer·o·pho·bi·a (âr′ə·fō′bĭ·ə), n. Psychiatry. morbid fear of drafts of air, gases, and air-borne noxious influences.

aer·o·phore (âr′ə·fōr′), n. a portable device filled with compressed air and used in cases of asphyxia, etc.

aer·o·phyte (âr′ə·fīt′), n. Bot. epiphyte.

aer·o·plane (âr′ə·plān′), n. Chiefly Brit. airplane.

aer·o·scope (âr′ə·skōp′), n. an apparatus for collecting microscopic objects from the air. —**aer·o·scop·ic** (âr′ə·skŏp′ĭk), adj.

aer·o·sol (âr′ə·sōl′, -sŏl′), n. Phys. Chem. a system consisting of colloidal particles dispersed in a gas; a smoke or fog. [f. AERO- + SOL[5]]

aerosol bomb, a small metal container that sprays insecticide in a mist.

aer·o·stat (âr′ə·stăt′), n. 1. a balloon, airship, or any lighter-than-air craft. 2. an aviator. [f. AERO- + s. Gk. statós placed]

aer·o·stat·ic (âr′ə·stăt′ĭk), adj. 1. of aerostatics. 2. of, or capable of supporting, aerostats. Also, **aer′o·stat′i·cal**.

aer·o·stat·ics (âr′ə·stăt′ĭks), n. 1. the science of the equilibrium of air and other gases, and of the equilibrium of bodies sustained in them. 2. the science of lighter-than-air craft. [pl. of aerostatic. See AEROSTAT, -ICS]

aer·o·sta·tion (âr′ə·stā′shən), n. operation of aerostats. [t. F, der. aḗrostat AEROSTAT]

aer·o·ther·a·peu·tics (âr′ō·thĕr′ə·pū′tĭks), n. that branch of therapeutics which deals with the curative use of air or of artificially prepared atmospheres. Also, **aer·o·ther·a·py** (âr′ō·thĕr′ə·pĭ).

ae·ru·gi·nous (ĭ·rōō′jə·nəs), adj. bluish-green; like verdigris. [t. L: m. s. aerūginōsus].

aer·y[1] (âr′ĭ, ā′ə·rĭ), adj. Poetic. ethereal; lofty. [t. L: m. s. āerius airy]

aer·y[2] (âr′ĭ, ĭr′ĭ), n., pl. **aeries**. aerie.

aes-. For words with initial aes-, see also **es-**.

Aes·chi·nes (ĕs′kə·nēz′ or, esp. Brit., ēs′-), n. 389–314 B.C., Athenian orator: rival of Demosthenes.

Aes·chy·lus (ĕs′kə·ləs or, esp. Brit., ēs′-), n. 525–456 B.C., Greek tragic poet and dramatist. —**Aes·chy·le·an** (ĕs′kə·lē′ən or, esp. Brit., ēs′-), adj.

Aes·cu·la·pi·an (ĕs′kyə·lā′pĭ·ən or, esp. Brit., ēs′-), adj. 1. pertaining to Aesculapius. 2. medical. —n. 3. physician.

Aes·cu·la·pi·us (ĕs′kyə·lā′pĭ·əs or, esp. Brit., ēs′-), n. Rom. Myth. the god of medicine and healing.

Ae·sir (ā′sĭr, ē′-), n. pl. the gods of the Scandinavian mythology, dwelling in Asgard. [t. Icel., pl. of āss god]

---

b., blend of, blended; c., cognate with; d., dialect, dialectal: der., derived from: f., formed from; g., going back to; m., modification of; r., replacing; s., stem of; t., taken from; ?, perhaps. See the full key on inside cover.

Ae·sop (ē′səp, ē′sŏp), *n.* 620?–560? B.C., Greek writer of fables. —**Ae·so·pi·an** (ē sō′pǐ ən), *adj.*

aes·the·sia (ĕs thē′zhə), *n.* esthesia. Also, **aes·the·sis** (ĕs thē′sǐs). [t. Gk.: m. *aisthēsia*]

aes·thete (ĕs′thēt or, *esp. Brit.*, ēs′-), *n.* **1.** one who cultivates the sense of the beautiful; one very sensitive to the beauties of art or nature. **2.** one who affects great love of art, music, poetry, etc., and indifference to practical matters. Also, **esthete.** [t. Gk.: m.s. *aisthētēs* one who perceives]

aes·thet·ic (ĕs thĕt′ǐk or, *esp. Brit.*, ēs-), *adj.* **1.** pertaining to the sense of the beautiful or the science of aesthetics. **2.** having a sense of the beautiful; characterized by a love of beauty. Also, **esthetic.** [t. Gk.: m.s. *aisthētikós* perceptive]

aes·thet·i·cal (ĕs thĕt′ə kəl or, *esp. Brit.*, ēs-), *adj.* of or relating to aesthetics. Also, **esthetical.**

aes·thet·i·cal·ly (ĕs thĕt′ǐk lǐ or, *esp. Brit.*, ēs-), *adv.* **1.** according to aesthetics or its principles. **2.** in an aesthetic manner.

aes·the·ti·cian (ĕs′thə tǐsh′ən or, *esp. Brit.*, ēs′-), *n.* one versed in aesthetics. Also, **esthetician.**

aes·thet·i·cism (ĕs thĕt′ə sǐz′əm or, *esp. Brit.*, ēs-), *n.* **1.** the acceptance of artistic beauty and taste as a fundamental standard, ethical and other standards being secondary. **2.** an exaggerated devotion to art, music, or poetry, with indifference to practical matters. Also, **estheticism.**

aes·thet·ics (ĕs thĕt′ǐks or, *esp. Brit.*, ēs-), *n.* **1.** *Philos.* the science which deduces from nature and taste the rules and principles of art; the theory of the fine arts; the science of the beautiful, or that branch of philosophy which deals with its principles or effects; the doctrines of taste. **2.** *Psychol.* the study of the mind and emotions in relation to the sense of beauty. Also, **esthetics.** [pl. of AESTHETIC. See -ICS]

aes·ti·val (ĕs′tə vəl, ĕs tī′- or, *esp. Brit.*, ēs′-, ĕs-), *adj.* estival.

aes·ti·vate (ĕs′tə vāt′ or, *esp. Brit.*, ēs′-), *v.i.*, **-vated, -vating.** estivate. —**aes·ti·va′tion,** *n.*

aet-. For words with initial aet-, see also et-.

ae·ta·tis su·ae (ē tā′tǐs sōō′ē), *Latin.* in a certain year of one's age.

ae·ther (ē′thər), *n.* ether (defs. 2, 3, 4). —**ae·the·re·al** (ǐ thǐr′ǐ əl), *adj.*

ae·ti·ol·o·gy (ē′tǐ ŏl′ə jǐ), *n.* etiology. —**ae·ti·o·log·i·cal** (ē′tǐ ə lŏj′ə kəl), *adj.*

Aet·na (ĕt′nə), *n.* **Mount.** See **Etna, Mount.**

Ae·to·li·a (ē tō′lǐ ə), *n.* ancient district in W Greece.

af-, var. of **ad-** (by assimilation) before *f*, as in *affect.*

AF, Anglo-French. Also, **A.F.**

A.F., audio frequency. Also, **a.f.**

A.F.A.M., Ancient Free and Accepted Masons.

a·far (ə fär′), *adv.* **1.** from a distance (usually prec. by *from*): *he came from afar.* **2.** far away; at or to a distance (usually fol. by *off*): *he saw the place afar off.* [ME *a fer.* See A-¹, FAR]

a·feard (ə fǐrd′), *adj.* *Archaic or Dial.* afraid. Also, **a·feared.** [ME *afered,* OE *āfǣred*]

a·fe·brile (ā fē′brəl, ā fĕb′rəl), *adj.* without fever; feverless. [f. A-⁶ + FEBRILE]

aff (ăf), *prep., adv.* Scot. off.

af·fa·ble (ăf′ə bəl), *adj.* **1.** easy to talk to or to approach; polite; friendly: *an affable and courteous gentleman.* **2.** expressing affability; mild; benign: *an affable countenance.* [t. F, t. L: m.s. *affābilis* able to be spoken to] —**af·fa·bil·i·ty, af·fa·ble·ness,** *n.* —**af·fa·bly,** *adv.* —**Syn. 1.** courteous, urbane. See **civil.**

af·fair (ə fâr′), *n.* **1.** anything done or to be done; that which requires action or effort; business; concern: *an affair of great moment, the affairs of state.* **2.** (pl.) matters of interest or concern; particular doings or interests: *put your affairs in order.* **3.** an event or a performance; a particular action, operation, or proceeding: *when did this affair happen?* **4.** thing; matter (applied to anything made or existing, with a descriptive or qualifying term): *this machine is a complicated affair.* **5.** a private or personal concern; a special function, business, or duty: *attend to your own affairs.* **6.** a love affair. [t. F: m. *affaire,* g. *à faire* to do, f. *à* faire, t. OF: m. *afaire*]

af·faire d'a·mour (á fĕr′ dà mōōr′), *French.* a love affair.

af·faire de cœur (á fĕr′ də kœr′), *French.* an affair of the heart; a love affair.

af·faire d'hon·neur (á fĕr′ dô nœr′), *French.* a duel.

af·fect¹ (ə fĕkt′), *v.t.* **1.** to act on; produce an effect or a change in: *cold affects the body.* **2.** to impress; move (in mind or feelings): *the poetry affected me deeply.* **3.** (of pain, disease, etc.) to attack or lay hold of. —*n.* **4.** *Psychol.* feeling or emotion. **5.** *Obs.* affection; passion; sensation; inclination; inward disposition or feeling. [t. L: s. *affectus,* pp., influenced, attacked] —**Syn. 1.** AFFECT, EFFECT agree in the idea of exerting influence. To AFFECT is to concern, be of interest or importance to; to produce an effect in or upon something: *to affect one's conduct or health.* To EFFECT is to accomplish or bring about something: *to effect a reconciliation.* touch; move, stir.

af·fect² (ə fĕkt′), *v.t.* **1.** to make a show of; put on a pretense of; pretend; feign: *to affect ignorance.* **2.** to make a show of liking or imitating: *to affect a Southern accent.* **3.** to use or adopt by preference; choose; prefer: *the peculiar costume which he affected.* **4.** to assume the character or attitude of: *to affect the freethinker.* **5.** to

tend toward habitually or naturally: *a substance which affects colloidal form.* **6.** (of animals and plants) to inhabit; frequent: *moss affects the northern slopes.* **7.** *Archaic.* to take pleasure in; fancy; like. **8.** *Archaic.* to aim at; aspire to. —*v.i.* **9.** to profess; pretend: *he affected to be wearied.* [t. F: s. *affecter,* t. L: m. *affectāre*] —**af·fect′·er,** *n.* —**Syn. 1.** See **pretend.**

af·fec·ta·tion (ăf′ĭk tā′shən, -ĕk-), *n.* **1.** a striving for the appearance of (a quality not really or fully possessed); pretense of the possession or character; effort for the reputation (fol. by *of*): *an affectation of wit, affectation of great wealth.* **2.** artificiality of manner or conduct; effort to attract notice by pretense, assumption, or any assumed peculiarity: *his affectations are insufferable.* **3.** *Obs.* strenuous pursuit or desire (fol. by *of*). [t. L: s. *affectātio* a pursuit after] —**Syn. 2.** airs, mannerisms.

af·fect·ed¹ (ə fĕk′tǐd), *adj.* **1.** acted upon; influenced. **2.** influenced injuriously; impaired; attacked, as by climate or disease. **3.** moved; touched: *she was deeply affected.* [pp. of AFFECT¹]

af·fect·ed² (ə fĕk′tǐd), *adj.* **1.** assumed artificially: *affected airs, affected diction.* **2.** assuming or pretending to possess characteristics which are not natural: *an affected lady.* **3.** inclined or disposed: *well affected toward a project.* **4.** having to some extent: *affected with the national interest.* [pp. of AFFECT²] —**af·fect′ed·ly,** *adv.* —**af·fect′ed·ness,** *n.* —**Syn. 1.** pretended, feigned.

af·fect·ing (ə fĕk′tǐng), *adj.* having power to excite or move the feelings; tending to move the affections. —**af·fect′ing·ly,** *adv.* —**Syn.** touching, pathetic.

af·fec·tion¹ (ə fĕk′shən), *n.* **1.** a settled good will, love, or zealous attachment: *the affection of a parent for his child.* **2.** the state of having one's feelings affected; emotion or feeling: *over and above our reason and affections.* **3.** *Pathol.* a disease, or the condition of being diseased; a morbid or abnormal state of body or mind: *a gouty affection.* **4.** act of affecting; act of influencing or acting upon. **5.** state of being affected. **6.** *Philos.* a contingent, alterable, and accidental state or quality of being. **7.** *Psychol.* the affective aspect of a mental process. **8.** *Archaic.* a bodily state due to any influence. **9.** *Obs.* bent or disposition of mind. [t. L: s. *affectio* influence (active), state of mind, favorable disposition (passive)] —**Syn. 1.** devotion, fondness. See **love.** **3.** See **disease.** —**Ant. 1.** dislike.

af·fec·tion² (ə fĕk′shən), *n.* *Obs.* affectation. [f. AFFECT², v. + -ION]

af·fec·tion·al (ə fĕk′shən əl), *adj.* relating to or implying affection. [f. AFFECTION¹ + -AL¹]

af·fec·tion·ate (ə fĕk′shən ǐt), *adj.* **1.** characterized by or manifesting affection; possessing or indicating love; tender: *an affectionate embrace.* **2.** having great love or affection; warmly attached: *your affectionate brother.* **3.** *Obs.* strongly disposed or inclined. **4.** *Obs.* biased; partisan. —**af·fec′tion·ate·ly,** *adv.* —**af·fec′tion·ate·ness,** *n.* —**Syn. 1.** loving, fond. **2.** devoted.

af·fec·tive (ə fĕk′tǐv), *adj.* **1.** pertaining to the affections; emotional. **2.** exciting emotion; affecting. **3.** *Psychol.* pertaining to feeling or emotion, esp. to pleasurable or unpleasurable aspects of a mental process.

af·fer·ent (ăf′ər ənt), *adj.* *Physiol.* bringing to or leading toward a central organ or point (opposed to *efferent*): *afferent nerves or veins.* [t. L: s. *afferens,* ppr., bringing to]

af·fi·ance (ə fī′əns), *v.*, **-anced, -ancing,** *n.* —*v.t.* **1.** to bind by promise of marriage; betroth: *to affiance a daughter.* —*n.* **2.** the pledging of faith; esp. a marriage contract. **3.** trust; confidence; reliance. [ME, t. OF: m. *afiance,* der. *afier,* g. LL *affīdāre* pledge]

af·fi·anced (ə fī′ənst), *adj.* betrothed.

af·fi·ant (ə fī′ənt), *n.* *Law.* one who makes an affidavit.

af·fiche (á fēsh′), *n.* *French.* a posted notice; a poster.

af·fi·da·vit (ăf′ə dā′vǐt), *n.* *Law.* written declaration upon oath, esp. one made before an authorized official. [t. L: he has made oath]

af·fil·i·ate (*v.* ə fǐl′ǐ āt′; *n.* ə fǐl′ǐ ǐt, -āt′), *v.*, **-ated, -ating,** *n.* —*v.t.* **1.** to bring into association or close connection: *the two banks were affiliated by a common ownership of stock.* **2.** to attach or unite on terms of fellowship; associate (fol. by *with* in U. S. usage, by *to* in Brit. usage): *affiliated with the church.* **3.** to connect in the way of descent or derivation (fol. by *upon*). **4.** to adopt. **5.** *Law.* **a.** to fix the paternity of, as a bastard child: *the mother affiliated her child upon John Doe.* **b.** to refer to as being the child of or belonging to. —*v.i.* **6.** to associate oneself; be intimately united in action or interest. —*n.* **7.** *U.S.* a branch organization. **8.** one who is affiliated; associate; auxiliary. [t. LL: m. s. *affiliātus,* pp., adopted as a son]

af·fil·i·a·tion (ə fǐl′ǐ ā′shən), *n.* **1.** act of affiliating. **2.** state of being affiliated; association; relationship.

af·fined (ə fīnd′), *adj.* **1.** related; connected. **2.** *Obs.* bound. [f. s. F *affiné* related + -ED²]

af·fin·i·tive (ə fǐn′ə tǐv), *adj.* characterized by affinity; closely related.

af·fin·i·ty (ə fǐn′ə tǐ), *n., pl.* **-ties. 1.** a natural liking for, or attraction to, a person or thing. **2.** one for whom such a natural liking or attraction is felt. **3.** relationship by marriage or by ties other than those of blood (distinguished from *consanguinity*). **4.** inherent likeness or agreement as between things; close resemblance or connection. **5.** *Biol.* the phylogenetic relationship between two organisms or groups of organisms resulting in **a** resemblance in general plan or structure, or in the essential structural parts. **6.** *Chem.* that force by which the atoms of bodies of dissimilar nature unite in certain definite proportions to form a compound. [ME, t. F: m. *af(f)initē,* t. L: m. s. *affīnitas*]

af·firm (əfûrm′), *v.t.* **1.** to state or assert positively; maintain as true: *to affirm one's loyalty to one's country.* **2.** to establish, confirm, or ratify: *the appellate court affirmed the judgment of he lower court.* —*v.i.* **3.** to declare positively; assert solemnly. **4.** *Law.* to declare solemnly before a court or magistrate, but without oath (a practice allowed where the affirmant has scruples, usually religious, against taking an oath). [t. L: s. *af firmāre:* r. ME *aferme(n),* t. OF: m. *afermer*] —**af·firm′a·ble,** *adj.* —**af·firm′a·bly,** *adv.* —**af·firm′er,** *n.* —Syn. 1. See **declare.**

af·firm·ant (əfûr′mənt), *n.* one who affirms.

af·fir·ma·tion (ăf′ərmā′shən), *n.* **1.** the assertion that something is, or is true. **2.** that which is affirmed; a proposition that is declared to be true. **3.** establishment of something of prior origin; confirmation; ratification. **4.** *Law.* a solemn declaration accepted instead of a statement under oath. Also, **af·firm·ance** (əfûr′məns).

af·firm·a·tive (əfûr′mətĭv), *adj.* **1.** giving affirmation or assent; confirmatory; not negative: *an affirmative answer.* **2.** *Logic.* denoting a proposition in which a property is affirmed of a subject, as "all men are happy." —*n.* **3.** that which affirms or asserts; a positive proposition: *two negatives make an affirmative.* **4.** an affirmative word or phrase, as *yes* or *I do.* **5. the affirmative,** the agreeing or concurring side. [t. LL: m. s. *affirmātīvus;* r. ME *affirmatyf,* t. F] —**af·firm′a·tive·ly,** *adv.*

af·firm·a·to·ry (əfûr′mətōr′ĭ), *adj.* affirmative.

af·fix (*v.* əfĭks′; *n.* ăf′ĭks), *v.t.* **1.** to fix; fasten, join, or attach (fol. by *to*): *to affix stamps to a letter.* **2.** to impress (a seal or stamp). **3.** to attach (blame, reproach, ridicule, etc.). —*n.* **4.** that which is joined or attached. **5.** *Gram.* any meaningful element (prefix, infix, or suffix) added to a stem or base, as *-ed* added to *want* to form *wanted.* [t. ML: s. *affixare,* freq. of L *affigere* fasten to] —**af·fix′er,** *n.*

af·fix·ture (əfĭks′chər), *n.* act of affixing; attachment.

af·fla·ted (əflā′tĭd), *adj.* inspired.

af·fla·tus (əflā′təs), *n.* **1.** inspiration; an impelling mental force acting from within. **2.** divine communication of knowledge. [t. L: a blast]

af·flict (əflĭkt′), *v.t.* **1.** to distress with mental or bodily pain; trouble greatly or grievously: *to be afflicted with the gout.* **2.** *Obs.* to overthrow; rout. [t. L: s. *afflictus,* pp., thrown down] —**af·flict′er,** *n.* —Syn. 1. vex, harass, torment, plague.

af·flic·tion (əflĭk′shən), *n.* **1.** a state of pain, distress, or grief: *they sympathized with us in our affliction.* **2.** a cause of continued pain of body or mind, as sickness, loss, calamity, persecution, etc. [ME, t. L: s. *afflictio*] —Syn. 1. AFFLICTION, ADVERSITY, MISFORTUNE, TRIAL refer to an event or circumstance which is hard to bear. A MISFORTUNE is any seriously adverse or unfavorable occurrence: *he had the misfortune to break his leg.* AFFLICTION suggests not only a misfortune but the emotional effect of this: *blindness is one kind of affliction.* ADVERSITY suggests one of a succession of mishaps and afflictions: *Job remained patient under all his adversities.* TRIAL emphasizes the testing of one's character in undergoing misfortunes, trouble, etc.: *his son's conduct was a great trial to him.*

af·flic·tive (əflĭk′tĭv), *adj.* characterized by or causing pain; distressing. —**af·flic′tive·ly,** *adv.*

af·flu·ence (ăf′lŏŏəns), *n.* **1.** abundance of material goods; wealth: *to live in great affluence.* **2.** an abundant supply, as of thoughts, words, etc.; a profusion. **3.** a flowing to or toward; afflux. [t. F, t. L: m. s. *affluentia*]

af·flu·ent (ăf′lŏŏənt), *adj.* **1.** abounding in means; rich: *an affluent person.* **2.** abounding in anything; abundant. **3.** flowing freely: *an affluent fountain.* —*n.* **4.** a tributary stream. [ME, t. L: s. *affluens,* ppr., flowing to] —**af′flu·ent·ly,** *adv.* —Syn. 1. See **rich.**

af·flux (ăf′lŭks), *n.* **1.** that which flows to or toward **a** point: *an afflux of blood to the head.* **2.** act of flowing to; a flow or flowing to. [t. ML: s. *affluxus,* n., der. L *affluere* flow to]

af·ford (əfōrd′), *v.t.* **1.** to be able, or have the means (often prec. by *can* or *may* and fol. by an infinitive): *we can afford to sell cheap.* **2.** to be able to meet the expense of; spare the price of (often prec. by *can* or *may*): *he can't afford a car.* **3.** to be able to give or spare (often prec. by *can* or *may*): *I could not afford the loss of a single day.* **4.** to supply; furnish: *the transaction afforded him a good profit.* **5.** to be capable of yielding or providing: *the records afford no explanation.* **6.** to give or confer upon: *to afford one great pleasure, etc.* [ME *aforthen,* OE *geforthian* further, accomplish] —**af·ford′a·ble,** *adj.*

af·for·est (əfōr′ĭst, əfŏr′ĭst), *v.t.* to convert (bare or cultivated land) into forest, originally for the purpose of providing hunting grounds. [t. ML: s. *afforestāre.* See AD-, FOREST] —**af·for′est·a′tion,** *n.*

af·fran·chise (əfrăn′chīz), *v.t.,* **-chised, -chising.** to free from a state of dependence, servitude, or obligation. [t. F: m. (by assoc. with FRANCHISE, n.) *affranchiss-,* s. of *affranchir.* See A-⁵, FRANK¹]

af·fray (əfrā′), *n.* **1.** a public fight; a noisy quarrel; a brawl. **2.** *Law.* the fighting of two or more persons in a public place. —*v.t.* **3.** *Archaic.* to frighten. [ME *a(f)fray-*

(en), t. AF, var. of *effrayer,* OF *effreer,* g. LL *exfridāre,* f. *ex-* EX-¹ + *-fridāre,* der. *fridus* peace (of Gmc. orig.)]

af·fri·cate (ăf′rəkĭt), *n. Phonet.* a speech sound beginning with a stop and ending with a fricative, such as *ch* in *church* (which begins like *t* and ends like *sh*); or *ts* in *Betsy.* Also, **af·fric·a·tive** (ə frĭk′ə tĭv). [t. L: m.s. *africātus,* pp., rubbed on or against]

af·fright (əfrīt′), *Archaic.* —*v.t.* **1.** to frighten. —*n.* **2.** sudden fear or terror; fright. **3.** a source of terror. **4.** act of terrifying. [ME *afrighten,* OE *āfyrhtan,* f. *ā-* (intensive) + *fyrhtan* frighten]

af·front (əfrŭnt′), *n.* **1.** a personally offensive act or word; an intentional slight; an open manifestation of disrespect; an insult to the face: *an affront to the king.* **2.** an offense to one's dignity or self-respect. —*v.t.* **3.** to offend by an open manifestation of disrespect or insolence: *an affronting speech.* **4.** to put out of countenance; make ashamed or confused. **5.** to meet or encounter face to face; confront: *to affront death.* **6.** *Archaic.* to face. [ME *afront(en),* t. OF: m. *afronter,* g. LL *affrontāre*] —**af·front′er,** *n.* —**af·front′ing·ly,** *adv.* —Syn. 1. impertinence, contumely, indignity.

af·fron·tive (əfrŭn′tĭv), *adj. Archaic.* insulting.

af·fu·sion (əfū′zhən), *n.* the pouring on of water or other liquid. [f. s. L *affūsus,* pp., poured + -ION]

Afgh., Afghanistan.

Af·ghan (ăf′găn, -găn), *n.* **1.** a native of Afghanistan. **2.** Pushtu (language). **3.** (*l.c.*) a kind of woolen blanket, knitted, crocheted, or woven, usually in a geometric pattern. **4.** a breed of hound with a long narrow head and a long silky coat. —*adj.* 5. of Afghanistan or its people.

Af·ghan·i·stan (ăf găn′ə stăn′), *n.* a kingdom in S Asia, NW of India, E of Iran, and S of the Soviet Union. 7,000,000 pop. (est. 1942); 250,000 sq. mi. *Cap.:* Kabul.

a·field (əfēld′), *adv.* **1.** abroad; away from home. **2.** off the beaten path; far and wide: *to stray far afield in one's reading.* **3.** in or to the field or fields.

a·fire (əfīr′), *adv., adj.* on fire: *to set something afire.*

A.F.L., American Federation of Labor. Also, **A.F. of L.**

a·flame (əflām′), *adv., adj.* **1.** on fire; ablaze: *the house was all aflame.* **2.** glowing: *aflame with curiosity.*

a·float (əflōt′), *adv., adj.* **1.** borne on the water; in a floating condition: *the ship is afloat.* **2.** on board ship; at sea: *cargo afloat and ashore.* **3.** flooded: *the main deck was afloat.* **4.** moving without guide or control: *our affairs are all afloat.* **5.** passing from place to place; in circulation: *a rumor is afloat.*

a·flut·ter (əflŭt′ər), *adv., adj.* in a flutter.

a·foot (əfŏŏt′), *adv., adj.* **1.** on foot; walking: *I came afoot.* **2.** astir; in progress: *there is mischief afoot.*

a·fore (əfōr′), *adv., prep., conj. Archaic or Dial.* before. [ME *aforne,* OE *on foran.* See A-¹, FORE¹]

a·fore·men·tioned (əfōr′měn′shənd), *adj.* mentioned earlier or previously.

a·fore·said (əfōr′sĕd′), *adj.* said or mentioned previously.

a·fore·thought (əfōr′thôt′), *adj.* **1.** thought of beforehand; premeditated: *malice aforethought.* —*n.* **2.** premeditation; forethought.

a·fore·time (əfōr′tīm′), *adv.* **1.** in time past; in a former time; previously. —*adj.* **2.** former; previous.

a for·ti·o·ri (ā fōr′shĭ ōr′ī), *Latin.* for a still stronger reason; even more certain; all the more.

a·foul (əfoul′), *adv., adj.* **1.** *U.S.* in a state of collision or entanglement: *a ship with its shrouds afoul.* **2. run afoul of,** to become entangled with: *run afoul of the law.*

Afr., 1. Africa. 2. African.

a·fraid (əfrād′), *adj.* feeling fear; filled with apprehension: *afraid to go.* [ME *afraied,* orig. pp. of AFFRAY] —Syn. scared, fearful. AFRAID, ALARMED, FRIGHTENED, TERRIFIED all indicate a state of fear. AFRAID implies inner apprehensive disquiet: *afraid of (or in) the dark.* ALARMED implies that the feelings are aroused through realization of some imminent or unexpected danger to oneself or others: *alarmed by (or about) someone's illness.* FRIGHTENED means shocked with sudden, but usually short-lived, fear, esp. that arising from apprehension of physical harm: *frightened by (or about) an accident.* TERRIFIED suggests the emotional reaction when one is struck with a violent, overwhelming fear: *terrified by an earthquake.*

af·reet (ăf′rēt, əfrēt′), *n. Arabian Myth.* a powerful evil demon or monster. Also, **afrit.** [t. Ar.: m. *'ifrīt*]

a·fresh (əfrĕsh′), *adv.* anew; again: *to start afresh.*

Af·ric (ăf′rĭk), *adj.* African.

Af·ri·ca (ăf′rəkə), *n.* the second largest continent, S of Europe and between the Atlantic and Indian Oceans. 158,000,000 pop. (est. 1939); ab. 11,700,000 sq. mi.; ab. 4970 mi. long; ab. 4700 mi. wide.

Af·ri·can (ăf′rəkən), *adj.* **1.** of or from Africa; belonging to the black race of Africa; Negro. —*n.* **2.** a native of Africa; a member of the black race of Africa; a Negro.

African lily, agapanthus.

African sleeping sickness, *Pathol.* a disease, generally fatal, common in parts of Africa, usually marked by fever, wasting, and progressive lethargy, and

---

b., blend of, blended; c., cognate with; d., dialect, dialectal; der., derived from; f., formed from; g., going back to; m., modification of; r., replacing; s., stem of; t., taken from; ?, perhaps. See the full key on inside cover.

caused by a parasitic protozoan, *Trypanosoma gambiense*. The infection is carried by a tsetse fly, *Glossina palpalis*.

African violet, a plant, *Saintpaulia ionantha*, with violet, pink, or white flowers, popular in cultivation.

Af·ri·kaans (ăf'rə käns', -känz'), *n.* a language of South Africa which developed there out of the speech of the 17th century settlers from Holland and is still very like Dutch; South African Dutch. [t. S Afr. D, sp. var. of D *Afrikansch*]

Af·ri·kan·der (ăf'rə kän'dər), *n.* a native of Cape Colony or the neighboring regions of Africa born of white parents, esp. Dutch or Huguenot; a descendant of European settlers in southern Africa. [t. S Afr. D: m. *Afrikaander*, b. *Afrikaans* and *Hollander*]

Af·ri·kan·der·ism (ăf'rə kän'də rǐz/əm), *n.* a word, expression, usage, etc., peculiar to or originating among the Afrikanders.

af·rit (ăf'rēt, ə frēt'), *n.* afreet.

Afro-, a combining form meaning "African," "Negro." [t. L: m. s. *Afer* African]

Af·ro-A·mer·i·can (ăf'rō ə měr'ə kən), *U.S.* —*adj.* **1.** pertaining to Negroes of America. —*n.* **2.** an American Negro.

aft (ăft, äft), *adv. Naut.* at, in, or toward the stern. [OE *æftan* from behind (f. *æft*- behind + *-an*, suffix marking motion from), c. Goth. *aftana*]

Port
Fore or Bow
Aft or Stern
Starboard

af·ter (ăf'tər, äf'-), *prep.* **1.** behind in place; following behind: *men placed in a line one after another.* **2.** in pursuit of; in search of; with or in desire for: *run after him.* **3.** concerning: *to inquire after a person.* **4.** later in time than; in succession to; at the close of: *after supper, time after time I urged him to do it.* **5.** subsequent to and in consequence of: *after what has happened, I can never return.* **6.** below in rank or excellence; next to: *Milton is usually placed after Shakespeare among English poets.* **7.** in imitation of, or in imitation of the style of: *after Raphael, to make something after a model.* **8.** with the name of; for: *he was named after his uncle.* **9.** in proportion to; in accordance with: *after their intrinsic value.* **10.** according to the nature of; in agreement or unison with; in conformity to: *he swore after the manner of his faith, a man after my own heart.* —*adv.* **11.** behind; in the rear: *Jill came tumbling after.* **12.** later in time; afterward: *it was about three hours after, happy ever after.* —*adj.* **13.** later in time; next; subsequent; succeeding: *in after years.* **14.** *Naut.* farther aft, or toward the stern of the ship: *the after sail.* —*conj.* **15.** subsequent to the time that: *after the Portuguese had settled in East India.* [ME; OE *æfter* (f. *æf*- away from + *-ter*, comp. suffix)] —*Syn.* **1.** See **behind.**

af·ter·birth (ăf'tər bûrth', äf'-), *n.* the placenta and fetal membranes expelled from the uterus after parturition.

af·ter·brain (ăf'tər brān', äf'-), *n.* metencephalon.

af·ter·damp (ăf'tər dămp', äf'-), *n.* an irrespirable mixture of gases, consisting chiefly of carbon dioxide and nitrogen, left in a mine after an explosion or fire.

af·ter·deck (ăf'tər děk', äf'-), *n. Naut.* the weather deck abaft the midships house.

af·ter·din·ner (ăf'tər dǐn'ər, äf'-), *adj.* following dinner: *an after-dinner speech.*

af·ter·ef·fect (ăf'tər ə fěkt', äf'-), *n.* **1.** a delayed effect; effect that follows later. **2.** *Med.* a result appearing after the first effect due to an agent, usually a drug, has gone.

af·ter·glow (ăf'tər glō', äf'-), *n.* **1.** the glow frequently seen in the sky after sunset. **2.** a second or secondary glow, as in heated metal before it ceases to become incandescent.

af·ter·im·age (ăf'tər ĭm'ij, äf'-), *n. Psychol.* a visual image or other sense impression that persists after the withdrawal of the exciting stimulus.

af·ter·math (ăf'tər măth', äf'-), *n.* **1.** results, esp. of a catastrophe: *the aftermath of the storm.* **2.** a second mowing or crop of grass from land in the same season. [f. AFTER + *math* a mowing (OE *mæth*)]

af·ter·most (ăf'tər mōst', -məst, äf'-), *adj.* **1.** *Naut.* farthest aft. **2.** hindmost. [ME *aftermest*, OE *æftemest* last; the *-r-* owing to assoc. with *after.* See AFT, -MOST]

af·ter·noon (ăf'tər nōōn', äf'-), *n.* **1.** the time from noon until evening. **2.** the latter part: *the afternoon of life.* —*adj.* **3.** pertaining to the after part of the day: *afternoon shadows.*

afternoon tea, 1 light refreshments served late in the afternoon. **2.** an afternoon social gathering.

ai·ter·piece (ăf'tər pēs', äf'-), *n.* a short dramatic piece performed after a play.

af·ter·shaft (ăf'tər shăft', äf'tər shäft'), *n. Ornith.* **1.** a supplementary feather, usually small, arising from the under side of the base of the shafts of certain feathers in many birds. **2.** the shaft of such a feather.

af·ter·taste (ăf'tər tāst', äf'-), *n.* a taste remaining after the substance causing it is no longer in the mouth.

af·ter·thought (ăf'tər thôt', äf'-), *n.* **1.** reflection after an act; some explanation, answer, expedient, or the like, that occurs to one's mind too late, or afterward. **2.** a later or second thought.

af·ter·time (ăf'tər tīm', äf'-), *n.* future time.

af·ter·ward (ăf'tər wərd, äf'-), *adv.* in later or subsequent time; subsequently. Also, **af'ter·wards.** [OE *æfterweard*, var. of OE *æfteweard.* See AFT, -WARD; for *-r-*, see AFTERMOST]

af·ter·world (ăf'tər wûrld', äf'-), *n.* the future world.

ag-, var. of **ad-** (by assimilation) before *g*, as in *agglutinate.*

Ag, *Chem.* (L *argentum*) silver.

Ag., August.

A.G., **1.** Adjutant General. **2.** Attorney General.

a·ga (ä'gə), *n.* (in Turkey) **1.** a title of honor, usually implying respect for age. **2.** a general. Also, **agha.**

A·ga·dir (ä'gä dēr'), *n.* a seaport in SW Morocco: a center of international tension, 1911. 5626 (1936).

a·gain (ə gĕn' *or, esp. Brit.*, ə gān') *adv.* **1.** once more; in addition; another time; anew: *he did it all over again.* **2.** in an additional case or instance; moreover; besides; furthermore. **3.** on the other hand: *it might happen and again it might not.* **4.** back; in return; in reply: *to answer again.* **5.** in the opposite direction; to the same place or person: *to return again.* **6.** again and again, often; with frequent repetition. **7. as much again,** twice as much. [ME; OE *ongegn, adv.* and prep., opposite (to), toward, again, f. *on* in + *gegn* straight]

a·gainst (ə gĕnst' *or, esp. Brit.*, ə gānst'), *prep.* **1.** in an opposite direction to, so as to meet; toward; upon: *to ride against the wind, the rain beats against the window.* **2.** in contact with: *to lean against a wall.* **3.** in opposition to; adverse or hostile to: *twenty votes against ten, against reason.* **4.** in resistance to or defense from: *protection against burglars.* **5.** in preparation for; in provision for: *money saved against a rainy day.* **6.** having as background: *the pictures stand out against the dark wall.* **7.** in exchange for; in return for; as a balance to: *draw against merchandise shipped.* **8.** *Obs.* directly opposite; facing; in front of (now *over against*). —*conj.* **9.** *Archaic or Dial.* by the time that. [f. AGAIN + *-(e)s*, adv. gen. suff. + *-t* added later; for this *-t* see WHILST, etc.]

A·ga Khan III (ä'gə kän'), (*Aga Sultan Sir Mohammed Shah*) born 1872, leader, since 1885, of the Ismailian sect of Mohammedans in India.

ag·a·ma (ăg'ə mə), *n.* any lizard of the Old World family *Agamidae*, allied to the iguanas and including large and brilliantly colored species. [t. Carib]

Ag·a·mem·non (ăg'ə měm'nŏn, -nən), *n.* **1.** *Gk. Legend.* a king of Mycenae, son of Atreus and brother of Menelaus. He led the Greeks against Troy. Upon his return he was treacherously slain by his faithless wife, Clytemnestra. **2.** a tragedy by Aeschylus.

a·gam·ic (ə găm'ĭk), *adj.* **1.** *Biol.* **a.** asexual. **b.** occurring without sexual union; germinating without impregnation; not gamic. **2.** *Bot.* cryptogamic. Also, **ag·a·mous** (ăg'ə məs). [f. s. Gk. *ágamos* unwed + -IC] —**a·gam'i·cal·ly,** *adv.*

ag·a·mo·gen·e·sis (ăg'ə mō jěn'ə sĭs), *n. Biol.* asexual reproduction by buds, offshoots, cell division, etc. [f. Gk. *ágamo*(*s*) unmarried + GENESIS] —**ag·a·mo·ge·net·ic** (ăg'ə mō'jə nět'ĭk), *adj.*

A·ga·ña (ä gä'nyä), *n.* capital of Guam. 791 (1950).

ag·a·pan·thus (ăg'ə păn'thəs), *n.* any of several African liliaceous plants constituting the genus *Agapanthus* with umbels of blue or white flowers; African lily. [f. Gk.: s. *agápē* love + m. *ánthos* flower]

a·gape (ə gāp', ə găp'), *adv. adj.* with the mouth wide open; in an attitude of wonder or eagerness.

a·gar (ä'gär, ăg'ər), *n.* **1.** *Biol.* a culture medium with an agar-agar base: *a spore agar.* **2.** agar-agar.

a·gar-a·gar (ä'gär ä'gär, ăg'ər äg'ər), *n.* a gelatinlike product of certain seaweeds, used to solidify culture media and, in the Orient, for soups, etc. [t. Malay]

ag·a·ric (ăg'ə rĭk, ə gär'ĭk), *n.* an agaricaceous fungus. [t. L: s. *agaricum*, t. Gk.: m. *agarikón*; named after Agaria, a place in Sarmatia]

a·gar·i·ca·ceous (ə gär'ə kā'shəs), *adj.* belonging to the *Agaricaceae*, a family of fungi including mushrooms having blade-shaped gills on the underside of the cap.

Ag·as·siz (ăg'ə sĭ'; *for 2 also*, *Fr.* à gà sē'), *n.* **1.** Alexander, 1835–1910, U.S. zoölogist and geologist. **2.** his father, (**Jean**) **Louis** (**Rodolphe**) (zhäN lwē rô dôlf'), 1807–73, Swiss zoölogist and geologist, in the U. S.

ag·ate (ăg'ĭt), *n.* **1.** a variegated variety of quartz (chalcedony) showing colored bands or other markings (clouded, mosslike, etc.). **2.** a child's playing marble made of this substance, or of glass in imitation of it. **3.** a printing type (5½ point) of a size between pearl and nonpareil, known in England as *ruby.* [t. F: m. *agathe*, g. L *achatēs*, t. Gk.] —**ag'ate·like',** *adj.*

agate line, a measure of advertising space, $1/14$ of an inch deep and one column wide.

ag·ate·ware (ăg'ĭt wâr'), *n.* **1.** steel or iron household ware enameled in an agatelike pattern. **2.** pottery variegated to resemble agate.

A·gath·o·cles (ə găth'ə klēz'), *n.* 361–289 B.C., tyrant of Syracuse.

ag·at·ize (ăg'ə tīz'), *v.t.,* **-ized, -izing.** to change into, or make like, agate.

à gauche (à gōsh'), *French.* on or to the left-hand side.

a·ga·ve (ə gā′vĭ), *n.* any plant of the American (chiefly Mexican) amaryllidaceous genus *Agave*, species of which yield useful fibers, are used in making a fermented beverage, a distilled spirit, or a soap substitute, or are cultivated for ornament, as the century plant. [t. NL, t. Gk.: m. *Agauē*, proper n., fem. of *agauós* noble]

agcy., agency.

age (āj), *n., v.,* **aged, aging** or **ageing.** —*n.* **1.** the length of time during which a being or thing has existed; length of life or existence to the time spoken of or referred to: *his age is 20 years, a tree or building of unknown age.* **2.** the lifetime of an individual, or of the individuals of a class or species on an average: *the age of the horse is from 25 to 30 years.* **3.** a period of human life usually marked by a certain stage of physical or mental development, esp. a degree of development, measured by years from birth, which involves legal responsibility and capacity: *the age of discretion, the age of consent.* **4. of age,** *Law.* **a.** being any of several ages, usually 21 or 18, at which certain legal rights, as voting or marriage, are acquired. **b.** being 21 years old, in possession of full legal rights and responsibilities. **5.** the particular period of life at which one becomes naturally or conventionally qualified or disqualified for anything: *under age or over age for conscription.* **6.** one of the periods or stages of human life: *a person of middle age.* **7.** old age: *his eyes were dim with age.* **8.** a particular period of history, as distinguished from others; a historical epoch: *the age of Pericles, the Stone Age, the Middle Ages.* **9.** the people who live at a particular period. **10.** a generation or a succession of generations: *ages yet unborn.* **11.** *Colloq.* a great length of time: *I haven't seen you for an age or for ages.* **12.** *Cards.* edge (def. 11). **13.** *Psychol.* the comparative mental, emotional, etc. development, of a person, expressed by equating performance in various tests to the average age at which the same result is attained. **14.** *Geol.* a long or short part of earth history distinguished by special features: *the Ice Age.* **15.** any one of the stages in the history of mankind divided, according to the Greek poet Hesiod, into the golden, silver, bronze, heroic, and iron ages. The happiest and best was the first (or golden) age, and the worst the iron age. —*v.i.* **16.** to grow old: *he is aging rapidly.* —*v.t.* **17.** to make old; cause to grow or to seem old: *fear aged him overnight.* **18.** to bring to maturity or to a state fit for use: *to age wine.* [ME, t. OF: m. *aage*, earlier *e(d)age*, ult. f. m. L *aetas* + suffix *-āticum* -AGE] —**Syn. 8.** AGE, EPOCH, ERA, PERIOD all refer to an extent of time. AGE usually implies a considerable extent of time, esp. one associated with a dominant personality, influence, characteristic, or institution: *the age of chivalry.* EPOCH and ERA are often used interchangeably, but an ERA is an extent of time characterized by changed conditions and new undertakings: *an era of invention.* An EPOCH is properly the beginning of an era: *an epoch of armed aggression.* A PERIOD may be long or short, but usually has a marked condition or feature: *the glacial period, a period o expansion.*

-age, a noun suffix, frequent in words taken from French, as in *baggage, language, savage, voyage,* etc., now a common English formative, forming: **1.** collective nouns from names of things, as in *fru tage, leafage.* **2.** nouns denoting condition, rank, service, fee, etc., from personal terms, as in *bondage, parsonage.* **3.** nouns expressing various relations, from verbs, as in *breakage, cleavage, postage.* [t. OF, g. L *-āticum* neut. suffix]

a·ged (ā′jĭd *for 1, 2, 4;* ājd *for 3*), *adj.* **1.** having lived or existed long: *an aged man or tree.* **2.** pertaining to or characteristic of old age: *aged wrinkles.* **3.** of the age of: *a man aged 40 years.* **4.** *Phys. Geog.* old; approaching the state of a peneplain. —**a′ged·ly,** *adv.* —**a′ged·ness,** *n.* —**Syn. 1.** See **old.** —**Ant. 1.** See **young.**

a·gee (ə jē′), *adv., adj. Dial.* to one side; awry. Also, **ajee.** [f. A-¹ + GEE]

age·less (āj′lĭs), *adj.* never growing old.

age·long (āj′lông′, -lŏng′), *adj.* lasting for an age.

a·gen·cy (ā′jən sĭ), *n., pl.* **-cies. 1.** a commercial or other bureau furnishing some form of service for the public: *an advertising agency.* **2.** the place of business of an agent. **3.** *U.S.* an Indian agency. **4.** the office of agent; the business of an agent entrusted with the concerns of another. **5.** state of being in action or of exerting power; action; operation: *the agency of Providence.* **6.** a mode of exerting power; a means of producing effects; instrumentality: *by the agency of friends.*

a·gen·da (ə jĕn′də), *n.pl., sing.* **-dum** (-dəm). **1.** things to be done. **2.** matters to be brought before a committee, council, board, etc., as things to be done. [t. L, neut. pl. of gerundive of *agere* do]

a·gent (ā′jənt), *n.* **1.** a person acting on behalf of another, called his principal: *my agent has power to sign my name.* **2.** one who or that which acts or has the power to act: *a moral agent.* **3.** a natural force or object producing or used for obtaining specific results; instrumentality: *many insects are agents of fertilization.* **4.** an active cause; an efficient cause. **5.** an official: *an agent of the F.B.I.* **6.** *U.S.* an Indian agent. **7.** *Colloq.* a representative of a business firm, esp. a traveling salesman; a canvasser; solicitor. **8.** *Chem.* a substance which causes a reaction. **9.** *Brit.* a campaign manager; an election agent. —*adj.* **10.** acting (opposed to *patient* in the sense of sustaining action). [t. L: s. *agens*, ppr., driving, doing] —**Syn. 1.** representative, deputy.

a·gen·tial (ā jĕn′shəl), *adj.* **1.** pertaining to an agent or to an agency. **2.** *Gram.* agentive.

a·gen·ti·val (ā′jən tī′vəl), *adj.* agentive.

a·gen·tive (ā′jən tĭv), *Gram.* —*adj.* **1.** pertaining to, or productive of, a form which indicates agent or agency. —*n.* **2.** an agentive element or formation, as English *-er* in *painter.*

a·gent pro·vo·ca·teur (ä zhän′ prô vô kà tœr′), *pl.* **agents provocateurs** (à zhän′ prô vô kà tœr′). *French.* a secret agent hired to incite suspected persons to some illegal action, outbreak, etc., that will make them liable to punishment.

ag·er·a·tum (ăj′ərā′təm, ə jĕr′ə-), *n.* **1.** any plant of the asteraceous genus *Ageratum,* as A. *Houstonianum,* a garden annual with small, dense, blue or white flower heads. **2.** any of various other composite plants, bearing blue, or sometimes white, flowers. [t. L, t. Gk.: m. *agēraton* kind of plant, prop. neut. adj., not growing old]

Ag·ge·us (ə gē′əs), *n.* (in the Douay Bible) Haggai.

ag·glom·er·ate (*v.* ə glŏm′ə rāt′; *adj., n.* ə glŏm′ər ĭt, -ə rāt′), *v.,* **-ated, -ating,** *n.* —*v.t., v.i.* **1.** to collect or gather into a mass. —*adj.* **2.** gathered together into a ball or mass. **3.** *Bot.* crowded into a dense cluster, but not cohering. —*n.* **4.** a mass of things clustered together. **5.** a rock formation composed of rounded or angular volcanic fragments. [t. L: m. s. *agglomerātus,* pp., wound into a ball] —**ag·glom′er·a′tive,** *adj.*

ag·glom·er·a·tion (ə glŏm′ə rā′shən), *n.* **1.** an indiscriminately formed mass. **2.** act or process of agglomerating.

ag·glu·ti·nant (ə glōō′tə nənt), *adj.* **1.** uniting, as glue; causing adhesion. —*n.* **2.** an agglutinating agent.

ag·glu·ti·nate (*v.* ə glōō′tə nāt′; *adj.* ə glōō′tə nĭt, -nāt′), *v.,* **-nated, -nating,** *adj.* —*v.t., v.i.* **1.** to unite or cause to adhere, as with glue. **2.** *Gram.* to form by agglutination. —*adj.* **3.** united by or as by glue. **4.** *Gram.* agglutinative. [t. L: m.s. *agglūtinātus,* pp., pasted to]

agglutinating language, a language whose affixes are invariable and are juxtaposed instead of fused. Turkish and Hungarian are agglutinating languages. See **agglutination,** def. 5.

ag·glu·ti·na·tion (ə glōō′tə nā′shən), *n.* **1.** act or process of uniting by glue or other tenacious substance. **2.** state of being thus united; adhesion of parts. **3.** that which is united; a mass or group cemented together. **4.** *Immunol.* the clumping of bacteria, red blood corpuscles, or other cells, due to introduction of an antibody. **5.** *Gram.* a pattern or process of inflection and word formation in some languages, in which the constituent elements of words are relatively distinct and constant in form and meaning; esp. such a process involving the addition of several suffixes to a single root or stem. In Turkish *ev* means "house," *ev-ler* means "houses," *ev-den* means "from a house," and *ev-ler-den* means "from houses."

ag·glu·ti·na·tive (ə glōō′tə nā′tĭv), *adj.* **1.** tending or having power to agglutinate or unite: *an agglutinative substance.* **2.** *Gram.* (of a language or construction) characterized by agglutination.

ag·glu·ti·nin (ə glōō′tə nĭn), *n. Immunol.* an antibody which causes agglutination.

ag·glu·tin·o·gen (ăg′lŏŏ tĭn′ə jən), *n. Immunol.* an antigen present in a bacterial body which when injected into an animal causes the production of agglutinins.

ag·grade (ə grād′), *v.t.,* **-graded, -grading.** *Phys. Geog.* to raise the grade or level of (a river valley, a stream bed, etc.), as by depositing detritus. [f. AG- + GRADE, v.] —**ag·gra·da·tion** (ăg′rə dā′shən), *n.*

ag·gran·dize (ăg′rən dīz′, ə grăn′dīz), *v.t.,* **-dized, -dizing. 1.** to widen in scope; increase in size or intensity; enlarge; extend. **2.** to make great or greater in power, wealth, rank, or honor. **3.** to make (something) appear greater. [t. F: m. *agrandiss-,* s. *agrandir,* g. L *ad-* AD- + *grandīre* make great] —**ag·gran·dize·ment** (ə grăn′dĭz mənt), *n.* —**ag′gran·diz′er,** *n.*

ag·gra·vate (ăg′rə vāt′), *v.t.,* **-vated, -vating. 1.** to make worse or more severe; intensify, as anything evil, disorderly, or troublesome: *to aggravate guilt; grief aggravated her illness.* **2.** *Colloq.* to provoke; irritate; exasperate: *threats will only aggravate her.* [t. L: m. s. *aggravātus,* pp., added to the weight of] —**ag′gra·vat′ed,** *adj.* —**ag′gra·vat′ing,** *adj.* —**ag′gra·vat′ing·ly,** *adv.* —**ag′gra·va′tive,** *adj.* —**ag′gra·va′tor,** *n.* —**Syn. 1.** heighten. AGGRAVATE, INTENSIFY both mean to increase in degree. To AGGRAVATE is to make more serious or more grave: *to aggravate a danger, an offense, a wound.* To INTENSIFY is perceptibly to increase intensity, force, energy, vividness, etc.: *to intensify heat, color, rage.*

ag·gra·va·tion (ăg′rə vā′shən), *n.* **1.** increase of the intensity or severity of anything; act of making worse: *an aggravation of pain.* **2.** *Colloq.* something that irritates or exasperates.

ag·gre·gate (*adj., n.* ăg′rə gĭt, -gāt′; *v.* ăg′rə gāt′), *adj., n., v.,* **-gated, -gating.** —*adj.* **1.** formed by the conjunction or collection of particulars into a whole mass or sum; total; combined: *the aggregate amount of indebtedness.* **2.** *Bot.* **a.** (of a flower) formed of florets collected in a dense cluster but not cohering as in composite plants. **b.** (of a fruit) composed of a cluster of carpels belonging to the same flower, as the raspberry. —*n.* **3.** a sum, mass, or assemblage of particulars; a total or gross amount: *the aggregate of all past experience.* **4. in the aggregate,** taken together; considered as a whole; collectively. **5.** *Geol.* a mixture of different mineral substances separable by mechanical means, as granite. **6.** any hard material added to cement to make concrete. —*v.t.* **7.** to bring together; collect into one sum, mass, or body. **8.** to amount to (the number of): *the guns captured will aggregate five or six hundred.* —*v.i.* **9.** to combine and form a collection or mass. [t. L: m. s. *aggregātus*, pp., added to] —**ag′gre·gate·ly,** *adv.* —**ag·gre·ga·tive** (ăg′rə gā′tĭv), *adj.*

ag·gre·ga·tion (ăg′rə gā′shən), *n.* **1.** a combined whole; an aggregate: *an aggregation of isolated settlements.* **2.** act of collection into an unorganized whole. **3.** state of being so collected. **4.** *Ecol.* a group of organisms of the same or different species living closely together but less integrated than a society.

ag·gress (ə grĕs′), *v.i.* **1.** to commit the first act of hostility or offense; attack first. **2.** to begin a quarrel.

ag·gres·sion (ə grĕsh′ən), *n.* **1.** the action of a state in violating by force the rights of another state, particularly its territorial rights. **2.** any offensive action or procedure; an inroad or encroachment: *an aggression upon one's rights.* **3.** the practice of making assaults or attacks; offensive action in general. [t. L: s. *aggressio*]

ag·gres·sive (ə grĕs′ĭv), *adj.* **1.** characterized by aggression; tending to aggress; making the first attack: *an aggressive foreign policy.* **2.** energetic; vigorous. —**ag·gres′sive·ly,** *adv.* —**ag·gres′sive·ness,** *n.*

ag·gres·sor (ə grĕs′ər), *n.* a person who attacks first; one who begins hostilities; an assailant or invader. [t. L.]

ag·grieve (ə grēv′), *v.t.,* **-grieved, -grieving.** to oppress or wrong grievously; injure by injustice (used now chiefly in the passive). [ME *agreve(n)*, t. OF: m. *agrever*, g. L *aggravāre* exasperate]

ag·grieved (ə grēvd′), *adj.* **1.** injured; oppressed; wronged: *he felt himself aggrieved.* **2.** *Law.* deprived of legal rights or claims.

a·gha (ä′gə), *n.* aga.

a·ghast (ə gäst′, ə gäst′), *adj.* struck with amazement; filled with sudden fright or horror: *they stood aghast at this unforeseen disaster.* [ME *agast*, pp. of *agasten* terrify. Cf. OE *gæstan* in same sense]

ag·ile (ăj′əl or, *esp. Brit.,* ăj′īl), *adj.* **1.** quick and light in movement: *a robust and agile frame.* **2.** active; lively: *an agile mind.* [t. L: m.s. *agilis*] —**ag′ile·ly,** *adv.* —**Syn. 1.** nimble, sprightly.

a·gil·i·ty (ə jĭl′ə tĭ), *n.* the power of moving quickly and easily; nimbleness: *agility of the body or mind.* [late ME *agilite,* t. F, t. L: m.s. *agilitas*]

Ag·in·court (ăj′ĭn kōrt′; *Fr.* à zhän kōōr′), *n.* a village in N France, near Calais: site of a decisive victory of the English under Henry V over the French, 1415.

ag·i·o (ăj′ĭ ō′), *n., pl.* **-os. 1.** a premium on money in exchange. **2.** an allowance for the difference in value of two currencies. **3.** an allowance given or taken on bills of exchange from other countries, as to balance out exchange expenses. **4.** agiotage. [t. It: m. *aggio* exchange, premium = *aggio,* g. L *habeo* I have]

ag·i·o·tage (ăj′ĭ ə tĭj), *n.* **1.** the business of exchange. **2.** speculative dealing in securities. [t. F]

ag·i·tate (ăj′ə tāt′), *v.,* **-tated, -tating.** —*v.t.* **1.** to move or force into violent irregular action; shake or move briskly: *the wind agitates the sea.* **2.** to move to and fro; impart regular motion to: *to agitate a fan, etc.* **3.** to disturb, or excite into tumult; perturb: *the mind of man is agitated by various emotions.* **4.** to call attention to by speech or writing; discuss; debate: *to agitate the question.* **5.** to consider on all sides; revolve in the mind; plan. —*v.i.* **6.** to arouse or attempt to arouse public interest, as in some political or social question: *to agitate for the repeal of a tax.* [t. L: m. s. *agitātus,* pp., aroused, excited] —**ag·i·tat′ed·ly,** *adv.*

ag·i·ta·tion (ăj′ə tā′shən), *n.* **1.** act of agitating. **2.** state of being agitated: *she walked away in great agitation.* **3.** persistent urging of a political or social question before the public.

—**Syn. 2.** AGITATION, DISTURBANCE, EXCITEMENT, TURMOIL imply inner unrest and a nervous condition. AGITATION implies a shaken state of emotions, usually perceptible in the face or movements: *with evident agitation she opened the telegram.* DISTURBANCE implies an inner disquiet caused by worry, indecision, apprehension, and the like: *long-continued mental disturbance is a cause of illness.* EXCITEMENT implies a highly emotional state caused by either agreeable or distressing circumstances: *excitement over a proposed trip, unexpected good news, a fire.* TURMOIL suggests such a struggle or conflict of emotions that one is unable to think consecutively: *her thoughts were in a hopeless turmoil.*

a·gi·ta·to (ä′jē tä′tō), *adj. Music.* agitated; restless or hurried in movement or style. [It.]

ag·i·ta·tor (ăj′ə tā′tər), *n.* **1.** one who stirs up others, with the view of strengthening his own cause or that of his party, etc. **2.** a machine for agitating and mixing.

A·gla·ia (ə glā′ə), *n.* Gk. Myth. one of the Graces.

a·gleam (ə glēm′), *adv., adj.* gleaming.

ag·let (ăg′lĭt), *n.* **1.** a metal tag at the end of a lace. **2.** the points or ribbons generally used in the 16th and 17th centuries to fasten or tie dresses. **3.** aiguillette. Also, **aiglet.** [ME, t. F: m. *aiguillette* point, ult. der. L *acus* needle]

a·gley (ə glē′, ə glī′), *adv. Chiefly Scot. and N. Eng.* off the right line; awry; wrong. [f. A-¹ + Scot. *gley* squint]

a·glim·mer (ə glĭm′ər), *adv., adj.* glimmering.

a·glit·ter (ə glĭt′ər), *adv., adj.* glittering.

a·glow (ə glō′), *adv., adj.* glowing.

ag·mi·nate (ăg′mə nĭt. -nāt′), *adj.* aggregated or clustered together. Also, **ag′mi·nat′ed.** [f. s. L *agmen* troop + -ATE¹]

ag·nail (ăg′nāl′), *n.* **1.** hangnail. **2.** whitlow.

ag·nate (ăg′nāt), *n.* **1.** a kinsman whose connection is traceable exclusively through males. **2.** any male relation by the father's side. —*adj.* **3.** related or akin through males or on the father's side. **4.** allied or akin. [t. L: m. s. *agnātus,* pp., born to] —**ag·nat·ic** (ăg nāt′ĭk), *adj.* —**ag·na·tion** (ăg nā′shən), *n.*

Ag·ni (ŭg′nĭ), *n. Hindu Myth.* the god of fire, one of the three chief divinities of the Vedas. [t. Skt.]

ag·no·men (ăg nō′mən), *n., pl.* **-nomina** (-nŏm′ə nə). **1.** an additional (fourth) name given to a person by the ancient Romans in allusion to some achievement or other circumstance, as *Africanus* in *Publius Cornelius Scipio Africanus.* **2.** any nickname. [t. L: f. *ag-* AG- + *nōmen* name] —**ag·nom·i·nal** (ăg nŏm′ə nəl), *adj.*

ag·nos·tic (ăg nŏs′tĭk), *n.* **1.** one who holds that the ultimate cause (God) and the essential nature of things are unknown or unknowable or that human knowledge is limited to experience. —*adj.* **2.** pertaining to the agnostics or their doctrines. **3.** asserting the relativity and uncertainty of all knowledge. [f. s. Gk. *ágnōstos* unknown, unknowable + -IC] —**ag·nos′ti·cal·ly,** *adv.* —**Syn. 1.** See atheist.

ag·nos·ti·cism (ăg nŏs′tə sĭz′əm), *n.* **1.** the doctrine maintained by agnostics. **2.** an intellectual attitude or doctrine which asserts the relativity and therefore the uncertainty of all knowledge.

Ag·nus De·i (ăg′nəs dē′ī). **1.** *Eccles.* **a.** a figure of a lamb as emblematic of Christ. **b.** such a representation with the nimbus inscribed with the cross about its head, and supporting the banner of the cross. **2.** *Rom. Cath. Ch.* **a.** a wax medallion stamped with this figure and blessed by the Pope, or a fragment of such a medallion. **b.** a triple chant preceding the communion in the Mass. **c.** the music accompanying this prayer. **3.** *Anglican Ch.* **a.** an invocation beginning "O Lamb of God," said or sung in the communion service. **b.** a musical setting for this. [LL: Lamb of God. See John 1:29]

a·go (ə gō′), *adj.* **1.** gone; gone by; past (now follows noun): *some time ago.* —*adv.* **2.** in past time: *long ago.* [ME, var. of *agoon,* OE *āgān,* pp. of *āgān* go by, pass]

a·gog (ə gŏg′), *adj.* **1.** highly excited by eagerness or curiosity. —*adv.* **2.** in a state of eager desire; with excitement. [t. F; m. *en gogues* in a merry mood]

-agogue, a word element meaning "leading" or "guiding," found in a few agent nouns (often with pejorative value), as in *demagogue, pedagogue.* [t. Gk.: m.s. *agōgós* leading]

a·gon (ăg′ŏn, -ŏn), *n., pl.* **agones** (ə gō′nēz). Gk. Antiq. a contest for a prize, whether of athletes in the games or of poets, musicians, painters, and the like. [t. Gk.]

a·gone (ə gôn′, ə gŏn′), *adv., adj. Archaic.* ago.

a·gon·ic (ŭ gŏn′ĭk), *adj.* not forming an angle. [f. s. Gk. *ágōnos* without angles + -IC]

agonic line, a line on the earth's surface connecting points at which the declination of the earth's magnetic field is zero.

ag·o·nist (ăg′ə nĭst), *n. Physiol.* an actively contracting muscle considered in relation to its opposing muscle.

ag·o·nis·tic (ăg′ə nĭs′tĭk), *adj.* **1.** combative; striving to overcome in argument. **2.** aiming at effect; strained. **3.** pertaining to contests. Also, **ag′o·nis′ti·cal.** [t. Gk.: m.s. *agōnistikós*] —**ag′o·nis′ti·cal·ly,** *adv.*

ag·o·nize (ăg′ə nīz′), *v.,* **-nized, -nizing.** —*v.i.* **1.** to writhe with extreme pain; suffer violent anguish. **2.** to make great effort of any kind. —*v.t.* **3.** to distress with extreme pain; torture. [t. ML: m. s. *agōnizāre,* t. Gk.: m. *agōnizesthai* contend] —**ag′o·niz′ing·ly,** *adv.*

ag·o·ny (ăg′ə nĭ), *n., pl.* **-nies. 1.** extreme, and generally prolonged, pain; intense suffering. **2.** intense mental excitement of any kind. **3.** the struggle preceding natural death: *mortal agony.* **4.** *Rare.* a violent struggle. [ME *agonye,* t. LL: m. *agōnia,* t. Gk.: contest, anguish] —**Syn. 1.** throe, paroxysm, pang; ache. See **pain.** **2.** anguish, torment, torture.

ag·o·ra (ăg′ə rə), *n., pl.* **-rae** (-rē′). Anc. Greece. **1.** a popular political assembly. **2.** the place of such assembly, originally the market place. [t. Gk.]

ag·o·ra·pho·bi·a (ăg′ə rə fō′bĭ ə), *n. Psychiatry.* a morbid fear of being in an open space. [f. AGORA + -PHOBIA]

a·gou·ti (ə gōō′tĭ), *n., pl.* **-tis, -ties. 1.** any of several short-haired, short-eared, rabbitlike rodents of the genus *Dasyprocta,* of South and Central America and the West Indies, destructive to sugar cane. **2.** an irregularly barred pattern of the fur of certain rodents. **3.** an animal having fur of this pattern. [t.F, t. Sp.: m. *aguti,* native Guiana name]

Agouti, *Dasyprocta aguti*
(19 to 22 in. long)

a·gou·ty (ə gōō′tĭ), *n., pl.* **-ties.** agouti.

A·gra (ä′grə) n. **1.** a part of the United Provinces of Agra and Oudh in N India. 40,906,000 pop. (1941); 82,-176 sq. mi. **2.** a city in the United Provinces: site of the Taj Mahal. 284,149 (1941).

a·graffe (ə grăf′), n. **1.** a small cramp iron. **2.** a clasp for hooking together parts of clothing, etc. **3.** a device for checking vibration in a piano string. [t. F. var. of *agrafe* hook, f. *à* A-⁵ + *grafe* sharp-pointed tool (g. L *graphium*, t. Gk.: m. *graphion*); F meaning influenced by *agrappe* hook]

A·gram (ä′gräm), n. German name of **Zagreb.**

a·gran·u·lo·cy·to·sis (ə grăn′yŏŏ lō′sĭ tō′sĭs), n. *Pathol.* a serious, often fatal, blood disease, marked by a great reduction of the leucocytes.

a·graph·i·a (ā grăf′ĭ ə), n. *Pathol.* a cerebral disorder marked by total or partial inability to write. [t. NL, f. Gk.: a- A-⁶ + -*graphia* writing] —**a·graph′ic,** adj.

a·grar·i·an (ə grâr′ĭ ən), adj. **1.** relating to land, land tenure, or the division of landed property: *agrarian laws.* **2.** pertaining to the advancement of agricultural groups: *an agrarian experiment.* **3.** rural; agricultural. **4.** growing in fields; wild: *an agrarian plant.* —n. **5.** one who favors the equal division of land. [f. s. L *agrārius* pertaining to land + -AN] —**a·grar′i·an·ism,** n.

a·gree (ə grē′), v., **agreed, agreeing.** —v.i. **1.** to yield assent; consent (often fol. by *to,* esp. with reference to things and acts): *he agreed to accompany the ambassador, do you agree to the conditions?* **2.** to be of one mind; harmonize in opinion or feeling (often fol. by *with,* esp. with reference to persons): *I don't agree with you.* **3.** to live in concord or without contention; harmonize in action. **4.** to come to one opinion or mind; come to an arrangement or understanding; arrive at a settlement. **5.** to be consistent; harmonize (fol. by *with*): *this story agrees with others.* **6.** to be applicable or appropriate; resemble; be similar (fol. by *with*): *the picture does not agree with the original.* **7.** to be accommodated or adapted; suit (fol. by *with*): *the same food does not agree with every person.* **8.** *Gram.* to correspond in inflectional form, as in number, case, gender, or person (fol. by *with*). —v.t. **9.** to concede; grant (fol. by noun clause): *I agree that he is the ablest of us.* [MP *agre(en)*, t. OF: m. *agreer,* der. phrase *a gre* at pleasure]
—**Syn. 5.** AGREE, ACCORD, CORRESPOND imply comparing persons or things and finding that they harmonize. AGREE implies having or arriving at a condition in which no essential difference of opinion or detail is evident: *all the reports agree.* ACCORD emphasizes agreeing exactly, both in fact and in point of view: *this report accords with the other.* CORRESPOND suggests having an obvious similarity, though not agreeing in every detail: *part of this report corresponds with the facts.*

a·gree·a·ble (ə grē′ə bəl), adj. **1.** **1.** to one's liking; pleasing: *agreeable manners.* **2.** *Colloq.* willing or ready to agree or consent: *are you agreeable?* **3.** suitable; conformable (fol. by *to*). —**a·gree′a·bil′i·ty, a·gree′a·ble·ness,** n. —**a·gree′a·bly,** adv.

a·greed (ə grēd′), adj. arranged by common consent: *they met at the agreed time.*

a·gree·ment (ə grē′mənt), n. **1.** act of coming to a mutual arrangement. **2.** the arrangement itself. **3.** unanimity of opinion; harmony in feeling: *agreement among the members.* **4.** state of being in accord; concord; harmony; conformity: *agreement between observation and theory.* **5.** *Gram.* correspondence in number, case, gender, person, or some other formal category between syntactically connected words, esp. between one or more subordinate words and the word or words upon which they depend. For example: in *the boy runs, boy* is a singular noun and *runs* is a distinctively singular form of the verb. **6.** collective agreement. **7.** *Law.* **a.** an expression of assent by two or more parties to the same object. **b.** the phraseology, written or oral, of an exchange of promises.
—**Syn. 2.** AGREEMENT, BARGAIN, COMPACT, CONTRACT all suggest a binding arrangement between two or more parties. AGREEMENT ranges in meaning from mutual understanding to binding obligation. BARGAIN applies particularly to agreements about buying and selling. COMPACT applies to treaties or alliances between nations or to solemn personal pledges. CONTRACT is used especially in law and business for such agreements as are legally enforceable.

a·gré·ments (à grē mäN′), n.pl. *French.* agreeable qualities or circumstances. Also, **a·gré·mens′.**

a·gres·tic (ə grĕs′tĭk), adj. **1.** rural; rustic. **2.** unpolished. [f. s. L *agrestis* rural + -IC]

agric., **1.** agricultural. **2.** agriculture. Also, **agr.**

A·gric·o·la (ə grĭk′ə lə), n. **Gnaeus Julius** (nē′əs jōōl′-yəs), A.D. 37–93, Roman general: governor of Britain.

ag·ri·cul·ture (ăg′rə kŭl′chər), n. the cultivation of land, as in the raising of crops; husbandry; tillage; farming (in a broad sense, including horticulture, forestry, stock raising, etc.) [t. L: m.s. *agricultūra,* f. *agrī,* gen. of *ager* land + *cultūra* cultivation] —**ag′ri·cul′tur·al,** adj. —**ag′ri·cul′tur·al·ly,** adv.

ag·ri·cul·tur·ist (ăg′rə kŭl′chər ĭst), n. **1.** a farmer. **2.** an expert in agriculture. Also, *Now U.S.* **ag·ri·cul·tur·al·ist** (ăg′rə kŭl′chər əl ĭst).

A·gri·gen·to (ä′grē jĕn′tō), n. a city in S Sicily. 30,248 (1936). Formerly, **Girgenti.**

ag·ri·mo·ny (ăg′rə mō′nĭ), n., pl. **-nies. 1.** any plant of the rosaceous genus *Agrimonia,* esp. *A. Eupatoria,* a perennial herb with pinnate leaves and small yellow flowers. **2.** any of certain other plants, as hemp agri-

mony or bur marigold. [t. L: m. s. *agrimōnia,* var. of *argemōnia* a plant, t. Gk.: m. *argemōnē;* r. OE *agrimonia,* t. L, and ME *egrimoigne,* t. OF: m. *aigremoine*]

A·grip·pa (ə grĭp′ə), n. **Marcus Vipsanius** (mär′kəs vĭp sā′nĭ əs), 63–12 B.C., Roman statesman, general, engineer: victor over Antony and Cleopatra at Actium.

Ag·rip·pi·na II (ăg′rə pī′nə), A.D. 16?–59?, mother of the Roman emperor Nero.

agro-, a word element meaning "soil," "field," as in *agrology.* [t. Gk., comb. form of *agrós*]

ag·ro·bi·ol·o·gy (ăg′rō bī ŏl′ə jĭ), n. the quantitative science of plant life and plant nutrition. —**ag·ro·bi·o·log·ic** (ăg′rō bī′ə lŏj′ĭk), **ag′ro·bi′o·log′i·cal,** adj. —**ag′ro·bi′o·log′i·cal·ly,** adv. —**ag′ro·bi·ol′o·gist,** n.

ag·rol·o·gy (ə grŏl′ə jĭ), n. the applied phases of soil science. See pedology¹. —**ag·ro·log·ic** (ăg′rə lŏj′ĭk), **ag′ro·log′i·cal,** adj.

agron., agronomy.

ag·ro·nom·ics (ăg′rə nŏm′ĭks), n. the art and science of managing land and crops.

a·gron·o·my (ə grŏn′ə mĭ), n. **1.** the applied phases of both soil science and the several plant sciences, often limited to applied plant sciences dealing with crops. **2.** agriculture. —**ag·ro·nom·ic** (ăg′rə nŏm′ĭk), **ag′ro·nom′i·cal,** adj. —**a·gron′o·mist,** n.

ag·ros·tol·o·gy (ăg′rə stŏl′ə jĭ), n. the part of botany that treats of grasses. [f. s. Gk. *ágrōstis* kind of grass + -(o)LOGY]

a·ground (ə ground′), adv., adj. on the ground; stranded: *the ship ran aground.*

Agt., agent. Also, **agt.**

A·guas·ca·lien·tes (ä′gwäs kä lyĕn′tĕs), n. **1.** a state in central Mexico. 161,693 pop. (1940); 2499 sq. mi. **2.** the capital of this state. 82,234 (1940).

a·gue (ā′gū), n. **1.** *Pathol.* a malarial fever characterized by regularly returning paroxysms, marked by successive cold, hot, and sweating fits. **2.** a fit of shaking or shivering as if with cold; a chill. [ME, t. OF, t. Pr., t. L: m.s. *acūta (febris)* acute (fever)] —**a′gue·like′,** adj. —**a′gu·ish,** adj. —**a′gu·ish·ly,** adv.

a·gue·weed (ā′gū wēd′), n. *U.S.* **1.** the common boneset. **2.** a species of gentian, *Gentiana quinquefolia.*

A·gui·nal·do (ä′gē näl′dō), n. **Emilio** (ĕ mē′lyō), born 1870?, Filipino leader against Spain during the Spanish-American War and against the U. S. after the war.

A·gul·has (ə gŭl′əs; *Port.* ä gōō′lyäs), n. **Cape,** the southernmost point of Africa.

ah (ä), interj. an exclamation expressing pain, surprise, pity, complaint, dislike, joy, etc., according to the manner of utterance. [ME]

A.H., (L *anno Hejirae*) in the year of or from the Hejira (A.D. 622).

a.h., *Elect.* ampere-hour.

a·ha (ä hä′), interj. an exclamation expressing triumph, contempt, mockery, irony, surprise, etc., according to the manner of utterance. [ME]

A·hab (ā′hăb), n. *Bible.* king of Israel of the ninth century B.C., husband of Jezebel. I Kings 16–22.

A·has·u·e·rus (ə hăz′yŏŏ ĭr′əs, ə hăs′-, ə hăzh′ŏŏ-), n. *Bible.* king of Persia (known by the Greeks as Xerxes), husband of Esther. Book of Esther; Ezra 4:6.

a·head (ə hĕd′), adv. **1.** in or to the front; in advance; before. **2.** forward; onward. **3.** **be ahead,** *U.S.* to be to the good; be winning: *I was ahead $10 in the deal.* **4.** **get ahead of,** to surpass. [f. A-¹ + HEAD]

a·hem (ə hĕm′), interj. an utterance designed to attract attention, express doubt, etc.

Ah·med·a·bad (ä′məd ä bäd′), n. a city in W India, in Bombay province. 591,267 (1941). Also, **Ah′mad·a·bad′.**

Ah·med·na·gar (ä′məd nŭg′ər), n. a c ty in W India, in Bombay province. 54,193 (1941). Also, **Ah′mad·na′gar.**

a·hoy (ə hoi′), interj. *Naut.* a call used in hailing. [f. *a,* interj. + HOY]

Ah·ri·man (ä′rĭ mən), n. *Zoroastrianism.* the wicked Devil, supreme spirit of evil, antagonistic to Ormazd.

a·hun·gered (ə hŭng′gərd), adj. *Archaic.* hungry.

A·hu·ra Maz·da (ä′hŏŏ rə măz′də), Ormazd.

ai (ä′ĭ), n., pl. **ais** (ä′ĭz). a large three-toed sloth. *Bradypus tridactylus,* of Central and South America. [t. Brazilian: m. *(h)ai,* imit. of its cry]

ai·blins (ā′blĭnz), adv. ablins.

aid (ād), v.t. **1.** to afford support or relief to; help. **2.** to promote the course or accomplishment of; facilitate. —v.i. **3.** to give help or assistance. —n. **4.** help; support; assistance. **5.** one who or that which aids or yields assistance; a helper; an auxiliary. **6.** *U.S.* an aide-de-camp. **7.** a payment made by feudal vassals to their lord on special occasions. **8.** *Eng. Hist.* any of a variety of revenues received by the king in the Middle Ages after 1066 from his feudal vassals and from others of his subjects. [ME *aide(n),* t. OF: m. *aidier,* g. L *adjūtāre*] —**aid′er,** n. —**aid′less,** adj. —**Syn. 1.** See **help. 4.** succor; relief; subsidy; subvention. —**Ant. 2.** hinder.

A·i·da (ä ē′dä), n. an opera (1871) by Verdi.

aid-de-camp (ād′də kämp′), n., pl. **aids-de-camp.** *Chiefly U.S.* aide-de-camp.

aide (ād), n. an aide-de-camp. [t. F]

aide-de-camp (ād′də kämp′), n., pl. **aides-de-camp.** a subordinate military or naval officer acting as a confidential assistant to a superior. [t. F: camp assistant]

---

b., blend of, blended; c., cognate with; d., dialect, dialectal; der., derived from; f., formed from; g., going back to m., modification of; r., replacing; s., stem of; t., taken from; ?, perhaps. See the full key on inside cover.

aide-mé·moire (ĕd mĕ mwâr/), *n. French.* a memorandum of discussion, agreement, or action.

Ai·din (ī dēn/), *n.* Aydin.

ai·glet (ā/glĭt), *n.* aglet.

ai·grette (ā/grĕt, ā grĕt/), *n.* **1.** a plume or tuft of feathers arranged as a head ornament, esp. the back plumes of various herons. **2.** a copy in jewelry of such a plume. [t. F]

ai·guille (ā gwēl/, ā/gwēl), *n.* a needlelike rock mass or mountain peak. [t. F, in OF *aguille* needle, g. LL dim. of L *acus* needle]

ai·guil·lette (ā/gwĭ lĕt/), *n.* an ornamental tagged cord or braid on a uniform; aglet. [ʋ. F, dim. of *aiguille.* See AGLET]

Ai·ken (ā/kən), *n.* **Conrad Potter,** born 1889, U.S. poet.

ail (āl), *v.t.* **1.** to affect with pain or uneasiness; trouble. —*v.i.* **2.** to feel pain; be ill (usually in a slight degree); be unwell. [ME *ailen,* OE *eglan*]

ai·lan·thus (ā lăn/thəs), *n.* a simaroubaceous tree, *Ailanthus altissima,* with pinnate leaves and ill-scented greenish flowers, native in eastern Asia and planted in Europe and America as a shade tree. [t. NL, t. Amboinan: m. *aylanto* tree of heaven] —**ai·lan/thic,** *adj.*

ai·ler·on (ā/lə rŏn/), *n. Aeron.* a hinged, movable part of an airplane wing, usually part of the trailing edge, used primarily to maintain lateral balance or to bank, roll, etc. [t. F, dim. of *aile* wing. See AISLE]

ail·ing (ā/lĭng), *adj.* sickly. —**Syn.** See **sick.**

ail·ment (āl/mənt), *n.* a morbid affection of the body or mind; indisposition: *a slight ailment.*

aim (ām), *v.t.* **1.** to give a certain direction and elevation to (a gun, etc.), for the purpose of causing the projectile, when the weapon is discharged, to hit the object. **2.** to direct or point (something) at something: *to aim a satire at some vice.* —*v.i.* **3.** to strive; try (followed in the U.S. by *to* plus the infinitive, in England by *at* plus the gerund): *they aim to save something every month, they aim at saving something every month.* **4.** *U.S. and Dial.* to intend: *she aims to go tomorrow.* **5.** to direct efforts toward an object: *to aim high, at the highest.* **6.** *Obs.* to estimate; guess. —*n.* **7.** act of aiming or directing anything at or toward a particular point or object. **8.** the direction in which a missile is pointed; the line of sighting: *to take aim.* **9.** the point intended to be hit; thing or person aimed at. **10.** something intended or desired to be attained by one's efforts; purpose. **11.** *Obs.* conjecture; guess. [ME *ayme*(n), t. OF: m. (*a*)*esmer,* g. L (*ad*)*aestimāre estimate*] —**aim/er,** *n.* —**Syn. 10.** AIM, END, OBJECT all imply something which is the goal of one's efforts. AIM implies that toward which one makes a direct line, refusing to be diverted from it: *a nobleness of aim, one's aim in life.* END emphasizes the goal as a cause of effort: *the end for which one strives.* OBJECT emphasizes the goal as that toward which all efforts are directed: *the object of years of study.*

aim·less (ām/lĭs), *adj.* without aim; purposeless. —**aim/less·ly,** *adv.* —**aim/less·ness,** *n.*

ain (ān), *adj. Scot.* own.

aî·né (ĕ nā/), *adj. French.* of the greater age; elder; eldest. —**aî·née/,** *adj. fem.*

ain't (ānt), *Now Illiterate or Dial.* **1.** a contraction of *am not,* extended in use as contraction of *are not* and *is not.* **2.** a contraction (with loss of *h*) of *have not.*

Ain·tab (īn/täb/), *n.* Gaziantep.

Ai·nu (ī/nōō), *n.* **1.** a member of an aboriginal race of the northernmost islands of Japan, having Caucasian features, light skin, and hairy bodies. **2.** the language of the Ainus, of uncertain relationship.

air[1] (âr), *n.* **1.** a mixture of oxygen, nitrogen, and other gases, which surrounds the earth and forms its atmosphere. **2.** a movement of the atmosphere; a light breeze. **3.** *Obs.* breath. **4.** circulation; publication; publicity. **5.** the general character or complexion of anything; appearance. **6.** the peculiar look, appearance, and bearing of a person. **7.** (*pl.*) affected manner; manifestation of pride or vanity; assumed haughtiness: *to put on airs.* **8.** *Music.* **a.** a tune; a melody. **b.** the soprano or treble part. **c.** an aria. **d.** an Elizabethan art song. **9.** *Radio.* the atmosphere through which radio waves are sent. **10. in the air, a.** without foundation or actuality; visionary or uncertain. **b.** in circulation. **c.** undecided or unsettled (often prec. by *up*). **d.** angry; perturbed (often prec. by *up*). **11. on the air,** in the act of broadcasting; being broadcast. **12. take the air,** to go out of doors; walk or ride a little distance. **13. walk on air,** to feel very happy or elated. —*v.t.* **14.** to expose to the air; give access to the open air; ventilate. **15.** to expose ostentatiously; bring into public notice; display: *to air one's opinions or theories.* [ME *ayre, eir,* t. OF: m. *air,* g. L *āēr,* t. Gk.: air, mist] —**Syn. 2.** See **wind. 6.** demeanor; attitude. See **manner.**

air[2] (âr), *adv., adj. Scot.* **1.** before. **2.** early. [see ERE]

A·ïr (ä/ĭr), *n.* a native kingdom in E French West Africa, consisting of a plateau and oasis region in the Sahara. ab. 30,000 sq. mi. *Cap.:* Agades. Also, **Asben.**

air alert, 1. act of flying while waiting for combat orders or for enemy airplanes to appear. **2.** the signal to take stations for such action.

air base, an operations center for units of an air force.

air bladder, 1. a vesicle or sac containing air. **2.** *Ichthyol.* a symmetrical sac filled with air whose principal function is the regulation of the hydrostatic equilibrium of the body; a swim bladder. Also, **air cell.**

air-borne (âr/bôrn/), *adj. Mil.* (of ground forces) carried in airplanes or gliders: *air-borne infantry.*

air-bound (âr/bound/), *adj.* stopped up by air.

air brake, *U.S.* a brake, or system of brakes, operated by compressed air.

air brush, *Orig. U.S.* a kind of atomizer for spraying liquid paint upon a surface.

air castle, a daydream; a visionary scheme.

air chamber, 1. a chamber containing air, as in a pump or a lifeboat or in an organic body. **2.** a compartment of a hydraulic system containing air which by its elasticity equalizes the pressure and flow of liquid within the system.

air cock, *Mach.* a special type of valve for controlling the flow of air.

air-con·di·tion (âr/kən dĭsh/ən), *v.t. Orig. U.S.* **1.** to furnish with an air-conditioning system. **2.** to treat (air) with such a system. —**air/-con·di/tioned,** *adj.*

air conditioning, *Orig. U.S.* a system of treating air in buildings to assure temperature, humidity, dustlessness, and movement, at levels most conducive to personal comfort or manufacturing processes.

air-cool (âr/kōōl/), *v.t.* **1.** *Mach.* to remove the heat of combustion, friction, etc., from, as by air streams flowing over an engine jacket. **2.** to air-condition. —**air/-cooled/,** *adj.*

Air Corps, *U.S. Army.* former name (before May 1, 1942) of the **Army Air Forces.**

air·craft (âr/krăft/, -kräft/), *n., pl.* **-craft.** any machine supported for flight in the air by buoyancy (such as balloons and other lighter-than-air craft) or by dynamic action of air on its surfaces (such as airplanes, helicopters, gliders, and other heavier-than-air craft).

aircraft carrier, a warship, of varying size, equipped with a deck for the taking off and landing of aircraft, and storage space for the aircraft.

air·craft·man (âr/krăft/mən, -kräft/-), *n., pl.* **-men.** *Brit.* a private in the Royal Air Force.

air cushion, 1. an inflatable airtight cushion. **2.** air chamber (def. 2).

air cylinder, a cylinder containing air, esp. (with a piston) as a device for checking the recoil of a gun.

air drain, a space below a building to prevent dampness.

air·drome (âr/drōm/), *n.* a landing field for airplanes which has permanent or extensive buildings, equipment, shelters, etc. Also, *esp. Brit.,* **aerodrome.**

air·drop (âr/drŏp/), *n.* delivery of supplies, troops, etc., by parachute.

air-dry (âr/drī/), *v.,* **-dried, -drying,** *adj* —*t.* **1.** to remove moisture from by evaporation in free air. —*adj.* **2.** dry beyond further evaporation.

Aire·dale (âr/dāl/), *n.* a large, heavy kind of terrier with a rough brown or tan coat which is black or grizzled over the back. [from *Airedale* in Yorkshire, England]

air·field (âr/fēld/), *n.* a level area, usually equipped with hard-surfaced runways, on which airplanes take off and land.

Airedale
(23 in. high at the shoulder)

air·flow (âr/flō/), *n.* air currents caused by a moving aircraft, automobile, etc.

air·foil (âr/foil/), *n. Aeron.* any surface, such as a wing, aileron, or stabilizer, designed to help in lifting or controlling the aircraft by making use of the current of air through which it moves. [f. AIR + FOIL[2]]

Air Force, 1. *U.S.* the department consisting of practically all military and naval aviation forces, established July 26, 1947. **2.** (*l.c.*) *U.S.* (formerly) the largest unit in the Army Air Forces. **3.** *Brit.* Royal Air Force.

air·graph (âr/grăf/, -gräf/), *Brit.* —*n.* **1.** a letter photographed on film, sent by air, and then enlarged, similar to American V-Mail. —*v.t.* **2.** to send by airgraph.

air gun, a gun operated by compressed air.

air hole, 1. an opening to admit or discharge air. **2.** *U.S.* a natural opening in the frozen surface of a river or pond. **3.** *Aeron.* air pocket.

air·i·ly (âr/əlĭ), *adv.* **1.** in a gay manner; jauntily. **2.** lightly; delicately. —**air·i·ness** (âr/ĭ nĭs), *n.*

air·ing (âr/ĭng), *n.* **1.** an exposure to the air, or to a fire, as for drying. **2.** a walk, drive, etc., in the open air.

air jacket, 1. an envelope of enclosed air about part of a machine, as for checking the transmission of heat. **2.** *Brit.* a life belt.

air lane, a route regularly used by airplanes; airway.

air·less (âr/lĭs), *adj.* **1.** lacking air. **2.** without fresh air; stuffy. **3.** still.

air lift, 1. a system of transportation by aircraft, esp. that established in 1948 by the Western powers to supply Berlin during the Soviet blockade. **2.** the load carried by such a system. **3.** the act or process of transporting such a load. Also, **air/lift.**

air line, 1. *Aeron.* **a.** a system furnishing (usually) scheduled air transport between specified points. **b.** the airplanes, airports, navigational aids, etc., of such a system. **c.** a company that owns or operates such a system. **d.** a scheduled route followed by such a system. **2.** *Chiefly U.S.* a direct line; a line as direct as a beeline.

air-line (âr/lĭn/), *adj.* straight as a line in the air.

ăct, āble, dâre, ärt; ĕbb, ēqual; ĭf, īce; hŏt, ōver, ôrder, oil, bŏŏk, ōōze, out; ŭp, ūse, ûrge; ə = a in alone; ch, chief; g, give; ng, ring; sh, shoe; th, thin; ŧh, that; zh, vision. See the full key on inside cover.

air liner, a passenger aircraft operating over an air line.

air lock, *Civ. Eng.* an airtight transition compartment at the entrance of a pressure chamber in which men work, such as a submerged caisson.

air mail, *Orig. U.S.* 1. the system of transmitting mail by aircraft. 2. mail transmitted by aircraft.

air-mail (âr′māl′), *adj.* sent by or pertaining to air mail: *air-mail letter.*

air·man (âr′mən), *n.,* *pl.* **-men.** 1. an aviator. 2. an enlisted man in the U.S. or British Air Forces.

air mass, *Meteorol.* a body of air which approximates horizontal uniformity in its properties.

air-mind·ed (âr′mīn′dYd), *adj.* 1. interested in aviation or in the aviation aspects of problems. 2. favoring increased use of aircraft. **—air′-mind′ed·ness,** *n.*

Air Ministry, (in England) the government department dealing with civil and military aeronautics.

air·plane (âr′plān′), *n.* an aircraft, heavier than air, kept aloft by the upward thrust exerted by the passing air on its fixed wings, and driven by propellers, jet propulsion, etc. Also, *esp. Brit.,* **aeroplane.**

airplane carrier, aircraft carrier.

airplane cloth, 1. a cotton fabric of plain weave constructed to specification for parts of airplanes. 2. a similar fabric used for shirts and pajamas.

air plant, *Bot.* epiphyte.

air pocket, *Aeron.* a downward current of air, usually causing a sudden loss of altitude.

air·port (âr′pōrt′), *n.* a tract of land or water with facilities for aircraft landing, take-off, shelter, supply, and repair, often used regularly for receiving or discharging passengers and cargo.

air post, *Brit.* air mail.

air pressure, the pressure of the atmosphere.

air·proof (âr′prōōf′), *adj.* 1. impervious to air. **—v.t.** 2. to make impervious to air.

air pump, an apparatus for drawing in, compressing, and discharging air.

air raid, a raid or incursion by hostile aircraft, esp. for dropping bombs or other missiles. **—air′-raid′,** *adj.* **—air raider.**

air-raid shelter, a security area or place used as a refuge during an air attack.

air-raid warden, a person who has temporary police duties during an air-raid alert.

air rifle, an air gun with rifled bore.

air sac, *Orig. U.S.* 1. a sac containing air. 2. any of certain cavities and cells in a bird's body connected with the lungs. 3. a saclike dilatation of an insect trachea.

air·screw (âr′skrōō′), *n.* *Brit.* an airplane propeller.

air shaft, a ventilating shaft.

air·ship (âr′shYp′), *n.* a self-propelled, lighter-than-air craft with means of controlling the direction of flight, usually classed as rigid, semirigid, or nonrigid.

air·sick (âr′sYk′), *adj.* ill as the result of traveling in the air. **—air′sick′ness,** *n.*

air·slake (âr′slāk′), *v.t.,* **-slaked, -slaking.** to slake by moist air, as lime.

air speed, the forward speed of an aircraft relative to the air through which it moves.

air·spray (âr′sprā′), *adj.* pertaining to compressed-air spraying devices or to liquids used in them.

air·strip (âr′strYp′), *n.* *Aeron.* runway (def. 2).

air switch, *Elect.* a switch in which the interruption of the circuit occurs in air.

airt (ârt; *Scot.* ärt), *Scot.* **—n.** 1. a direction. **—v.t.** 2. to point out the way. Also, **airth** (ârth; *Scot.* ärth). [t. Gaelic: m. *aird* height]

air·tight (âr′tīt′), *adj.* 1. so tight or close as to be impermeable to air. 2. having no weak points or openings of which an opponent may take advantage.

air turbine. See turbine (def. 2).

air valve, a device for controlling the flow of air through a pipe.

air vesicle, *Bot.* a large air-filled pocket, present mainly in plants which float on water.

air·way (âr′wā′), *n.* 1. an air route fully equipped with emergency landing fields, beacon lights, radio beams, etc. 2. any passage in a mine used for purposes of ventilation; an air course.

air well, air shaft.

air·wom·an (âr′wŏŏm′ən), *n.,* *pl.* **-women.** a woman aviator.

air·wor·thy (âr′wûr′thY), *adj.* *Aeron.* meeting accepted standards for safe flight; equipped and maintained in condition to fly. **—air′wor′thi·ness,** *n.*

air·y (âr′Y), *adj.,* **airier, airiest.** 1. consisting of or having the character of air; immaterial: *airy phantoms.* 2. light in appearance; thin: *airy lace.* 3. light in manner; sprightly; gay; lively: *airy songs.* 4. light in movement; graceful; delicate: *an airy tread.* 5. light as air; unsubstantial; unreal; imaginary: *airy dreams.* 6. visionary; speculative. 7. performed in the air; aerial. 8. lofty; high in the air. 9. open to a free current of air; breezy: *airy rooms.*

A·i·sha (ä′ē·shä′), *n.* A.D. 613?–678, favorite wife of Mohammed and daughter of Abu-Bekr. Also, **Ayesha.**

aisle (īl), *n.* 1. a passageway between seats in a church, hall, etc. 2. *Archit.* a. a lateral division of a church or other building separated from the nave by piers or

columns. See diag. under **basilica.** b. a similar division at the side of the choir or a transept. c. any of the lateral divisions of a church or hall, as the nave. [var. of *isle,* trans. of late ML *insula* aisle (in L island); r. ME *ele,* t. OF, g. L *āla* shoulder, wing; *ai-* of current sp. from F *aile*] **—aisled** (īld), *adj.*

Aisne (ān; *Fr.* ĕn), *n.* a river in N France, flowing into the Oise river. 175 m. See map under **Compiègne.**

ait (āt), *n.* *Brit.* a small island. [ME *eyt,* OE *igeoth,* dim. of *īeg* island; history of forms not clear]

aitch (āch), *n.* the letter *H, h.*

aitch·bone (āch′bōn′), *n.* *Brit.* 1. the rump bone, as of beef. 2. the cut of beef which includes this bone. [ME *nache-bone; a nache-bone* became an *aitch-bone* by false division into words; *nache,* t. OF, ult. der. L *natis* buttock]

Ait·ken (āt′kən), *n.* 1. **Robert Grant,** 1864–1951, U.S. astronomer. 2. **William Maxwell,** (*Lord Beaverbrook*) born 1879, British newspaper publisher and statesman.

Aix (āks; *Fr.* ĕks), *n.* a city in SE France, N of Marseilles. 46,053 (1946).

Aix-la-Cha·pelle (āks′lä shä pĕl′; *Fr.* ĕks lä shà pĕl′), *n.* French name of **Aachen.**

A·jac·cio (ä yät′chō), *n.* a seaport in and the capital of Corsica: birthplace of Napoleon. 33,060 (1936).

a·jar[1] (ə jär′), *adj., adv.* neither quite open nor shut; partly opened: *leave the door ajar.* [ME *on char* on the turn; *char,* OE *cerr* turn. See A-[1], CHARWOMAN]

a·jar[2] (ə jär′), *adv., adj.* out of harmony; jarring: *ajar with the world.* [for *at jar* at discord. See JAR[3], n.]

A·jax (ā′jăks), *n.* *Gk. Legend.* 1. a mighty warrior of the Greeks before Troy. He killed himself in chagrin when Achilles' armor was awarded to Odysseus. 2. **the lesser Ajax,** a Locrian king, a hero in the Trojan War, second in swiftness only to Achilles. [t. L, t. Gk.: m. *Aías*]

a·jee (ə jē′), *adj.* *Dial.* agee.

Aj·mer (ŭj mʏr′), *n.* a city in NW India, within, though not part of, Rajputana. 147,258 (1941).

Ak·bar (ăk′bär), *n.* 1542–1605, Mogul emperor of India, 1556–1605.

a·kene (ā kēn′), *n.* achene.

a·kim·bo (ə kʏm′bō), *adj., adv.* with hand on hip and elbow bent outward: *to stand with arms akimbo.* [ME *in kene bowe,* appar., in keen bow, in a sharp bent; but cf. Icel. *kengboginn* bent double, crooked]

a·kin (ə kʏn′), *adj.* 1. of kin; related by blood. 2. allied by nature; partaking of the same properties. [contr. of phrase *of kin*] **—Syn.** 2. cognate; similar, analogous.

A·kins (ā′kʏnz), *n.* **Zoë** (zō′Y), born 1886, U.S. playwright.

A·ki·ta (ä′kē tä′), *n.* a seaport in N Japan, on Honshu island. 106,139 (1946).

Ak·kad (ăk′ăd, ä′käd), *n.* 1. Also, **Accad.** one of the four cities of Nimrod's kingdom. Gen. 10:10. In the cuneiform inscriptions it evidently includes most of N Babylonia. **—adj.** 2. Akkadian.

Ak·ka·di·an (ə kā′dYən, ə kä′-), *n.* 1. the eastern group of Semitic languages, all extinct, including Babylonian and Assyrian. 2. any member of this group. 3. one of the Akkadian people. **—adj.** 4. of or belonging to Akkad. 5. designating or pertaining to the primitive inhabitants of Babylonia or the non-Semitic language ascribed to them. 6. designating or pertaining to the (later) Semitic language of Babylonia.

Ak·ker·man (ăk′ər män′), *n.* a seaport in the SW Soviet Union, on the Black Sea at the mouth of the Dniester river. 34,000 (1930). Rumanian, **Cetatea Albă.**

Ak·kra (ăk′rə; *native* ə krä′), *n.* Accra.

Ak·ron (ăk′rən), *n.* a city in NE Ohio. 274,605 (1950).

Ak·sum (ăk′sōōm), *n.* the capital of an ancient Ethiopian kingdom. Also, **Axum.**

à l′, *French.* Form of **à la** used for either gender before a vowel or *h.*

al-, var. of ad- before *l,* as in *allure.*

-al[1], *adj.* a suffix meaning "of or pertaining to," "connected with," "of the nature of," "like," "befitting," etc., occurring in numerous adjectives and in many nouns of adjectival origin, as *annual, choral, equal, regal.* [t. L: s. *-ālis* (neut. *-āle*) pertaining to; often r. ME *-el,* t. F]

-al[2], a suffix forming nouns of action from verbs, as in *refusal, denial, recital, trial.* [t. L: m. *-āle* (pl. *ālia*), neut. of adj. suffix *-ālis;* often r. ME *-aille,* t. OF]

-al[3], *Chem.* a suffix indicating that a compound includes an alcohol or aldehyde group, as in *chloral.* [short for AL(COHOL) or AL(DEHYDE)]

AL, Anglo-Latin. Also, **AL., A.L.**

Al, *Chem.* aluminum.

a·la (ā′lə), *n., pl.* **alae** (ā′lē). 1. a wing. 2. a winglike part, process, or expansion, as of a bone, a shell, a seed, a stem, etc. 3. one of the two side petals of a papilionaceous flower. [t. L: wing]

à la (ä′lä, ä′lə; *Fr.* à là), 1. according to: *à la mode, à la Brooklyn.* 2. *Cookery.* with: **à la jardinière,** with various vegetables. Also, **a la.** [t. F: at, to, in + the fem. form used before a word beginning with a consonant]

Ala., Alabama.

A.L.A., American Library Association.

Al·a·ba·ma (ăl′ə băm′ə), *n.* 1. a State in the SE United States. 3,061,743 pop. (1950); 51,609 sq. mi. *Cap.:* Montgomery. *Abbr.:* Ala. 2. a river flowing from

central Alabama SW to the Mobile river. 315 mi.
—**Al·a·bam·i·an** (ăl/ə băm/Ÿ ən), **Al/a·bam/an,** adj., n.

al·a·bam·ine (ăl/ə băm/ēn, -Ÿn), n. Chem. a rare element of the halogen family claimed to have been found in monazite sands (1931) but not isolated. Symbol: Ab; at. no.: 85. [f. ALABAM(A) + -INE²]

al·a·bas·ter (ăl/ə băs/tər, -băs/-), n. 1. a finely granular variety of gypsum, often white and translucent, used for ornamental objects or work, such as lamp bases, figurines, etc. 2. a variety of calcite, often with a banded structure, used for similar purposes (**Oriental alabaster**). —adj. Also, **al·a·bas·trine** (ăl/ə băs/trŸn, -băs/-). 3. made of alabaster: an alabaster column. 4. resembling alabaster; smooth and white as alabaster: her alabaster throat. [ME, t. L, t. Gk.: m. alábastros, var. of alábastos an alabaster box]

à la bonne heure (à lă bô nœr/), French. 1. at the right moment. 2. just right; excellent; very well.

à la carte (ä/ lə kärt/; Fr. à lá kärt/), by the bill of fare: with a stated price for each dish: dinner à la carte. [t. F]

a·lack (ə lăk/), interj. Archaic. an exclamation expressive of sorrow, regret, or dismay. Also, **a·lack·a·day** (ə lăk/ə dā/).

a·lac·ri·ty (ə lăk/rə tŸ), n. 1. liveliness; briskness; sprightliness. 2. cheerful readiness or willingness. [t. L: m. s. alacritas] —**a·lac/ri·tous,** adj.

A·la Dagh (ä/lä däкн/), 1. a mountain range in S Turkey. Highest peak, ab. 11,000 ft. 2. a mountain range in E Turkey. Highest peak, ab. 11,500 ft.

A·lad·din (ə lăd/Ÿn), n. (in The Arabian Nights' Entertainments) the son of a poor widow in China. He becomes the possessor of a magic lamp and ring, with which he commands two jinns who gratify all his wishes.

A·la·göz (ä/lägœz/), n. a volcanic mountain in the SE Soviet Union in the Armenian Republic. 13,435 ft.

A·lai Mountains (ä lī/), a mountain range in the SW Soviet Union in Asia, in Kirghiz Republic: a part of the Tien Shan mountain system. Highest peaks, 16,000 to 18,000 ft.

à la king (ä/ lə kŸng/), (of a dish of diced cooked fowl, fish, etc.) creamed with pimiento or green pepper: chicken à la king.

Al·a·me·da (ăl/ə mē/də, -mā/-), n. a city in W California, SE of San Francisco. 64,430 (1950).

al·a·me·da (ăl/ə mā/də), n. Chiefly Southwestern U.S. a public walk shaded with poplar or other trees. [t. Sp., der. alamo poplar]

al·a·mo (ăl/ə mō/, ä/lə-), n., pl. **-mos.** Southwestern U.S. a cottonwood.

Al·a·mo (ăl/ə mō/), n. a mission building in San Antonio, Texas, which underwent a terrible siege by Mexicans in February, 1836, but was taken on March 6, and its entire garrison of American rebels killed.

al·a·mode (ăl/ə mōd/), n. a thin, glossy silk for hoods, scarfs, etc.

à la mode (ä/ lə mōd/, ăl/ə-; Fr. à lä mōd/), 1. in or according to the fashion. 2. Cookery. a. (of pie or other dessert) served with a portion of ice cream. b. (of beef) larded and braised or stewed with vegetables, herbs, etc., and served with a rich brown gravy. Also, **a la mode, a/la·mode/.** [t. F]

à la mort (à lä môr/), French. —adj. 1. half dead. 2. melancholy; dispirited. —adv. 3. mortally.

Å·land Islands (ä/lənd, ô/-; Swed. ō/län), a group of Finnish islands in the Baltic between Sweden and Finland. 27,676 pop. (1940); 572 sq. mi.

à la New·burg (ä/ lə/bûrg, nōō/-), cooked with a sauce of cream, egg yolk, butter, and usually wine.

al·a·nine (ăl/ə nēn/, -nŸn), n. an amino acid, CH₃·CH(NH₂)COOH, found in many proteins.

a·lar (ā/lər), adj. 1. pertaining to or having wings; alary. 2. winglike; winged. 3. Anat., Bot. **axillary.** [t. L: s. ālāris, der. āla wing]

Al·a·ric (ăl/ə rŸk), n. A.D. c370–410, king of the Visigoths: captured Rome, A.D. 410.

a·larm (ə lärm/), n. 1. a sudden fear or painful suspense excited by an apprehension of danger; apprehension; fright. 2. any sound, outcry, or information intended to give notice of approaching danger: a false alarm. 3. a self-acting contrivance of any kind used to call attention, rouse from sleep, warn of danger, etc. 4. a warning sound; signal for attention. 5. a call to arms. 6. Fencing. an appeal or a challenge made by a step or stamp on the ground with the advancing foot. —v.t. 7. to surprise with apprehension of danger; disturb with sudden fear. 8. to give notice of danger to; rouse to vigilance and exertions for safety. [ME alarme, t. OF, t. It.: m. allarme tumult, fright, der. all' arme to arms] —**a·larmed/,** adj. —**a·larm/ing·ly,** adv. —**Syn.** 1. consternation; terror, panic. See **fear.** 7. See **afraid.**

a·larm·ist (ə lär/mŸst), n. one given to raising alarms, esp. without sufficient reason, as by exaggerating dangers, prophesying calamities, etc. —**a·larm/ism,** n.

a·lar·um (ə lär/əm, ə lär/-), n. Archaic. alarm.

a·la·ry (ā/lə rŸ, ăl/ə-), adj. 1. of or pertaining to wings. 2. Biol. wing-shaped. [t. L: m. s. ālārius, der. āla wing]

a·las (ə lăs/, ə läs/), interj. an exclamation expressing sorrow, grief, pity, concern, or apprehension of evil. [ME allas, t. OF: m. a las. ha las, f. a, ha ah + las miserable, g. L lassus weary]

Alas., Alaska.

A·las·ka (ə lăs/kə), n. 1. a territory of the United States, in NW North America. 128,643 pop. (1950); 586,400 sq. mi. Cap.: Juneau. 2. Gulf of, a large gulf of the Pacific, on the S coast of Alaska. —**A·las/kan,** adj., n.

Alaska Highway, a highway extending from E British Columbia, Canada, to Fairbanks, Alaska: built as a U.S. military supply route, 1942. 1671 mi. Unofficially, **Alcan Highway.**

Alaska Peninsula, a long, narrow peninsula forming the SW extension of the mainland of Alaska. ab. 400 mi. long.

Alaska Range, a mountain range in S Alaska. Highest peak, Mt. McKinley, 20,300 ft.

a·late (ā/lāt), adj. 1. winged. 2. having membranous expansions like wings. Also, **a/lat·ed.** [t. L: m. s. ālātus winged]

alb (ălb), n. Eccles. a white linen robe with close sleeves, worn by an officiating priest. [ME and OE albe, t. L: m. alba (vestis) white (garment)]

Alb., 1. Also, **Alba.** Alberta (Canada). 2. Albania.

Al·ba (ăl/bə, äl/bä), n. **Duke of.** See **Alva.**

Al·ba·ce·te (äl/bä thě/tě, -sě/tě), n. a city in SE Spain. 64,222 (1940).

al·ba·core (ăl/bə kōr/), n., pl. **-cores,** (sometimes) **-core.** 1. the long-finned tunny, Germo alalunga, common in all warm or temperate seas, and highly valued for canning. 2. any of various fishes related to or resembling the tunny. [t. Pg.: m. albacor(a), t. Ar.: m. al-bakūra]

Al·ba Lon·ga (ăl/bə lông/gə, lŏng/-), a city of ancient Latium, SE of Rome: fabled birthplace of Romulus and Remus.

Al·ba·ni·a (ăl bā/nŸ ə, -băn/yə), n. 1. a republic in S Europe, in the Balkan Peninsula between Yugoslavia and Greece. 1,115,350 pop. (1945); 10,632 sq. mi. Cap.: Tirana. 2. Poetic and Rare. Scotland.

Al·ba·ni·an (ăl bā/nŸ ən, -băn/yən), adj. 1. pertaining to Albania (def. 1), its inhabitants, or their language. —n. 2. a native or inhabitant of Albania. 3. the language of Albania (def. 1), an Indo-European language.

Al·ba·ny (ôl/bə nŸ), n. 1. the capital of New York, in the E part, on the Hudson. 134,995 (1950). 2. a city in SW Georgia. 31,155 (1950). 3. a river in central Canada, flowing from W Ontario E to James Bay. 610 mi.

Alb worn by a priest

al·ba·ta (ăl bā/tə), n. German silver. [t. NL, prop. fem. of L albātus, pp., made white]

al·ba·tross (ăl/bə trôs/, -trŏs/), n. any of various large webfooted, tube-nosed sea birds related to the petrels, esp. of the genus Diomedea, of the Pacific and southern waters, noted for their powers of flight. [var. of algatross, t. Pg.: m. alcatraz seafowl, cormorant; change of -g- to -b- ? by association with L alba white (the bird's color)]

Wandering albatross, Diomedea exulans (42 in. long, wingspread 11 ft.)

Al·bay (äl bī/), n. former name of **Legaspi.**

al·be·do (ăl bē/dō), n. Astron. the ratio of the light reflected by a planet or satellite to that received by it. [t. L: whiteness]

al·be·it (ôl bē/Ÿt), conj. although; notwithstanding that: to choose a peaceful albeit inglorious retirement. [ME al be it although it be]

Al·be·marle Sound (ăl/bə märl/), a sound in NE North Carolina. ab. 60 mi. long.

Al·bé·niz (äl bě/nēth), n. **Isaac** (ē/sä äk/), 1860–1909, Spanish composer and pianist.

Al·ber·ich (äl/bər Ÿкн), n. Medieval Legend. king of the dwarfs and chief of the Nibelungs.

Al·bert (ăl/bərt), n. 1. **Prince,** (Francis Charles Augustus Albert Emanuel, Prince of Saxe-Coburg-Gotha) 1819–61, German prince, husband of Queen Victoria of Great Britain; known as Prince Consort. 2. **Lake,** a lake in central Africa between Uganda and the Belgian Congo: a source of the Nile. ab. 100 mi. long; ab. 1640 sq. mi.; ab. 2000 ft. high. Also, **Albert Ny·an·za** (nŸ ăn/zə, nyän/zä).

Albert I, 1875–1934, king of the Belgians, 1909–34.

Al·ber·ta (ăl bûr/tə), n. a province in W Canada. 796,169 pop. (1941); 255,285 sq. mi. Cap.: Edmonton.

Albert Edward, a mountain peak of the Owen Stanley range, in SE New Guinea. 13,030 ft.

Al·ber·tian (ăl bûr/shən), adj. pertaining to Prince Albert.

al·bert·ite (ăl/bər tīt/), n. an asphalt from the Albert mine in New Brunswick.

Albert Memorial, a monument to Prince Albert in Kensington Gardens, London.

Al·ber·tus Mag·nus (ăl bûr/təs măg/nəs), (Albert von Böllstadt) 1193?–1280, German scholastic philosopher; teacher of Thomas Aquinas; canonized in 1932.

al·bes·cent (ăl běs/ənt), adj. becoming white; whitish. [t. L: s. albescens, ppr.] —**al·bes/cence,** n.

ăct, āble, dâre, ärt; ĕbb, ēqual; Ÿf, īce; hŏt, ōver, ôrder, oil, bŏŏk, ōōze, out; ŭp, ūse, ûrge; ə = a in alone; ch, chief; g, give; ng, ring; sh, shoe; th, thin; ŧh, that; zh, vision. See the full key on inside cover.

Al·bi (ăl bē′), *n.* a city in S France: center of the Albigenses. 34,342 (1946).

Al·bi·gen·ses (ăl′bə jĕn′sēz), *n.pl.* the members of several sects in the south of France in the 12th and 13th centuries. [ML, der. *Albi* ALBI] —**Al·bi·gen·si·an** (ăl′bə jĕn′sĭ′ən, -shən), *adj., n.*

al·bi·nism (ăl′bə nĭz′əm), *n.* state or condition of being an albino. —**al·bi·nis·tic** (ăl′bə nĭs′tĭk), *adj.*

al·bi·no (ăl bī′nō *or, esp. Brit.,* -bē′-), *n., pl.* -**nos.** 1. a person with a pale, milky skin, light hair, and pink eyes. 2. an animal or plant with a marked deficiency in pigmentation. [t. Pg., der. *albo,* g. L *albus* white] —**al·bin·ic** (ăl bĭn′ĭk), *adj.*

Al·bi·on (ăl′bĭ ən), *n.* Poetic. Britain. [t. L, said to be der. *albus* white]

al·bite (ăl′bīt), *n.* a very common mineral of the plagioclase feldspar group, sodium aluminum silicate, NaAlSi₃O₈, usually white, occurring in many igneous rocks. [f. s. L *albus* white + -ITE¹]

Al·boin (ăl′boin, -bō ĭn), *n.* died A.D. 573?, king of the Langobards from A.D. 561? until his death.

al·bum (ăl′bəm), *n.* 1. a book consisting of blank leaves for the insertion or preservation of photographs, stamps, autographs, etc. 2. a visitor's register; visitor's book. [t. L: tablet, prop. neut. of *albus* white]

al·bu·men (ăl bū′mən), *n.* 1. the white of an egg. 2. *Bot.* the nutritive matter about the embryo in a seed. 3. *Chem.* albumin. [t. L (def. 1), der. *albus* white]

al·bu·men·ize (ăl bū′mə nīz′), *v.t.,* -**ized,** -**izing.** to treat with an albuminous solution.

al·bu·min (ăl bū′mən), *n.* Biochem. any of a class of water-soluble proteins composed of nitrogen, carbon, hydrogen, oxygen, and sulfur, occurring in animal and vegetable juices and tissues. [t. L: s. *albūmen* ALBUMEN]

al·bu·mi·nate (ăl bū′mə nāt′), *n.* Biochem. a compound resulting from the action of an alkali or an acid upon albumin.

al·bu·mi·noid (ăl bū′mə noid′), *n.* Biochem. 1. any of a class of simple proteins which are insoluble in all neutral solvents, as keratin, gelatin, collagen, etc. —*adj.* 2. resembling albumen or albumin. [f. s. L *albūmen* white of egg + -OID] —**al·bu/mi·noi′dal,** *adj.*

al·bu·mi·nous (ăl bū′mə nəs), *adj.* 1. of albumin. 2. containing albumin. 3. resembling albumin. Also, **al·bu·mi·nose** (ăl bū′mə nōs′).

al·bu·mi·nu·ri·a (ăl bū′mə nyŏŏr′ĭ ə, -nŏŏr′-), *n.* Pathol. the presence of albumin in the urine. [f. ALBUMIN + -URIA] —**al·bu/mi·nu/ric,** *adj.*

al·bu·mose (ăl′byə mōs′), *n.* Biochem. any of a class of compounds derived from albumins, etc. by the action of proteolytic enzymes. [f. ALBUM(IN) + -OSE²]

Al·bu·quer·que (ăl bə kûr′kĭ), *n.* a city in central New Mexico. 96,815 (1950).

al·bur·num (ăl bûr′nəm), *n.* Bot. the softer part of the wood between the inner bark and the heartwood; sapwood. [t. L, der. *albus* white]

Al·cae·us (ăl sē′əs), *n.* fl. c600 B.C., Greek lyric poet of Mytilene in Lesbos.

al·ca·hest (ăl′kə hĕst′), *n.* alkahest.

Al·ca·ic (ăl kā′ĭk), *adj.* 1. pertaining to Alcaeus or to certain meters or a form of strophe or stanza used by, or named after, him. —*n.* 2. (*pl.*) Alcaic verses or strophes.

al·caide (ăl kād′; *Sp.* äl kä′ēdē′), *n.* 1. a commander of a fortress. 2. a jailer; the warden of a prison. Also, **al·cayde′.** [t. Sp., t. Ar.: m. *al-qā′id* the commander]

al·cal·de (ăl käl′dĭ; *Sp.* äl käl′dē), *n.* (in Spain and Southwestern U.S.) a chief municipal officer with judicial powers. Also, *Southwestern U.S.* **al·cade** (ăl käd′). [t. Sp., t. Ar.: m. *al-qāḍī* the judge. See CADI]

Al·can Highway (ăl′kăn), unofficial name of **Alaska Highway.**

Al·ca·traz (ăl′kə trăz′), *n.* 1. an island in San Francisco Bay, in W California. 2. the U.S. federal penitentiary on this island.

Al·ca·zar (ăl′kə zär′, ăl käz′ər; *Sp.* äl kä′thär), *n.* 1. the palace of the Moorish kings (later, of Spanish royalty) at Seville. 2. (*l.c.*) a palace of the Spanish Moors. [t. Sp., t. Ar.: m. *al-qaṣr* the castle (*qaṣr,* t. L: m. s. *castrum* fortress)]

Al·ces·tis (ăl sĕs′tĭs), *n.* Gk. Legend. the wife of the Thessalian king Admetus, whose life she saved by dying in his place. She was brought back from Hades by Hercules.

al·che·mist (ăl′kə mĭst), *n.* one who practices or is versed in alchemy. —**al/che·mis/tic, al/che·mis/ti·cal,** *adj.*

al·che·mize (ăl′kə mīz′), *v.t.,* -**mized,** -**mizing.** to change by alchemy; transmute, as metals.

al·che·my (ăl′kə mĭ), *n.* 1. Medieval Chem. an art which sought in particular to transmute baser metals into gold, and to find a universal solvent and an elixir of life. 2. any magical power or process of transmuting. [ME *alkamye,* t. OF: m. *alkimie,* t. ML: m. s. *alchimia,* t. Ar.: m. *al-kīmīya′* (*kīmīyā′* ? t. LGk.: m. *chÿma* molten metal)] —**al·chem·ic** (ăl kĕm′ĭk), **al·chem/i·cal,** *adj.* —**al·chem/i·cal·ly,** *adv.*

Al·ci·bi·a·des (ăl′sə bī′ə dēz′), *n.* 450?–404 B.C., Athenian politician and general.

Al·ci·des (ăl sī′dēz), *n.* Hercules.

al·ci·dine (ăl′sə dīn′, -dĭn), *adj.* Ornith. pertaining to or resembling the *Alcidae,* the auk family.

Al·cin·o·üs (ăl sĭn′ō əs), *n.* Homeric Legend. the father of Nausicaä, a king of the Phaeacians, at whose court Ulysses related the story of his wanderings.

Alc·me·ne (ălk mē′nĭ), *n.* Gk. Legend. mother of Hercules by Zeus, who visited her in the guise of her husband.

al·co·hol (ăl′kə hôl′, -hŏl′), *n.* 1. a colorless, inflammable liquid (**ethyl alcohol,** C₂H₅OH), the intoxicating principle of fermented liquors, formed from certain sugars (esp. glucose) by fermentation, now usually prepared by treating grain with malt and adding yeast. 2. any intoxicating liquor containing this spirit. 3. *Chem.* any of a class of chemical compounds having the general formula ROH, where R represents an alkyl group; derived from the hydrocarbon by replacement of a hydrogen atom by the hydroxyl radical, OH. [t. ML: orig., fine powder; hence, essence or rectified spirits, t. Ar.: m. *al-kuḥl* the powdered antimony, kohl]

al·co·hol·ic (ăl′kə hôl′ĭk, -hŏl′ĭk), *adj.* 1. pertaining to or of the nature of alcohol. 2. containing or using alcohol. 3. caused by alcohol. 4. suffering from alcoholism. 5. preserved in alcohol. —*n.* 6. a person suffering from alcoholism. 7. one addicted to intoxicating drinks.

al·co·hol·ic·i·ty (ăl′kə hôl ĭs′ə tĭ′, -hŏ-), *n.* alcoholic quality or strength.

al·co·hol·ism (ăl′kə hôl ĭz′əm, -hŏl′-), *n.* a diseased condition due to the excessive use of alcoholic beverages.

al·co·hol·om·e·ter (ăl′kə hô lŏm′ə tər, -hŏ-), *n.* an instrument for finding the percentage of alcohol in a liquid. —**al/co·hol·om/e·try,** *n.*

Al·co·ran (ăl′kō rän′, -răn′), *n.* the Koran. [ME *alkaron,* ult. t Ar.: m. *al-qor′ān,* lit., the reading]

Al·cott (ôl′kət), *n.* 1. (Amos) Bronson, 1799–1888, U.S. transcendentalist philosopher, writer, and reformer. 2. his daughter, Louisa May, 1832-88, U.S. author.

al·cove (ăl′kōv), *n.* 1. a recess opening out of a room. 2. a recess in a room for a bed, for books in a library, or for other similar permanent furnishings. 3. any recessed space, as in a garden. [t. F, t. Sp.: m. *alcoba,* t. Ar.: m. *al-qubba* the vaulted space]

Al·cuin (ăl′kwĭn), *n.* A.D. 735–804, British churchman and scholar: teacher and friend of Charlemagne.

Al·cy·o·ne (ăl sī′ə nē′), *n.* a star of the third magnitude in the constellation Taurus: the brightest star in the group known as the Pleiades. [t. L, t. Gk.: m. *Alkyŏnē*]

Ald., Alderman. Also, **ald.**

Al·dan (äl dän′), *n.* a river flowing from the Yabloni Mountains in the SE Soviet Union in Asia NE to the Lena river. ab. 1300 mi.

Al·deb·a·ran (ăl dĕb′ə rən), *n.* one of the brightest stars in the sky, orange in color, in the constellation Taurus. [t. Ar.: the follower (i.e. of the Pleiades)]

al·de·hyde (ăl′də hīd′), *n.* one of a group of organic compounds with the general formula R–CHO which yield acids when oxidized and alcohols when reduced. [short for NL *al*(*cohol*) *dehyd*(*rogenātum*) alcohol deprived of hydrogen] —**al/de·hy/dic,** *adj.*

Al·den (ôl′dən), *n.* John, 1599?–1687, Pilgrim settler (1620) in Plymouth, Mass.

al·der (ôl′dər), *n.* 1. any shrub or tree of the betulaceous genus *Alnus* growing in moist places in northern temperate or colder regions. 2. any of various trees or shrubs resembling this genus. [ME; OE *alor, aler*]

al·der·man (ôl′dər mən), *n., pl.* -**men.** 1. U.S. one of a body of municipal officers with powers (executive, judicial, or legislative) varying according to locality, often representing a municipal ward. 2. *Eng.* one of the members, chosen by the elected councilors, in a borough or county council. 3. *Eng. Hist.* ealdorman. [ME; OE *aldormann, ealdormann,* f. *ealdor* chief, elder + *mann* man] —**al/der·man·cy, al/der·man·ship/,** *n.*

al·der·man·ic (ôl′dər măn′ĭk), *adj.* 1. of an alderman. 2. characteristic of aldermen.

al·der·man·ry (ôl′dər mən rĭ), *n., pl.* -**ries.** a district of a borough represented by an alderman.

Al·der·ney (ôl′dər nĭ), *n.* 1. one of the Channel Islands in the English Channel. 1521 pop. (1931); 3 sq. mi. 2. one of a breed of medium-sized dairy cattle, originating in Alderney.

Al·der·shot (ôl′dər shŏt′), *n.* 1. a city in S England, SW of London. 24,910 (est. 1946). 2. a large military training center there.

Al·dine (ôl′dīn, -dēn), *adj.* 1. of or from the press of Aldus Manutius and his family, of Venice (about 1490–1597), chiefly noted for compactly printed editions of the classics. —*n.* 2. Aldine and other early editions. 3. certain styles of printing types.

Al·ding·ton (ôl′dĭng tən), *n.* Richard, born 1892, British poet and novelist.

Aldm., Alderman.

al·dol (ăl′dôl), *n.* Chem. a colorless fluid, C₄H₈O₂, from an acetaldehyde condensation, used medicinally as a sedative and hypnotic. [f. ALD(EHYDE) + (ALCOH)OL]

al·dose (ăl′dōs), *n.* Chem. a sugar containing the aldehyde group or its hemiacetal equivalent.

Al·drich (ôl′drĭch), *n.* Thomas Bailey, 1836–1907, U. S. short-story writer, poet, and novelist

Al·dus Ma·nu·ti·us (ôl′dəs mə nū′shĭ əs, -nōō′-, ăl′dəs). See **Manutius.**

ale (āl), *n.* a malt beverage, darker, heavier, and more bitter than beer, containing about 6 per cent of alcohol by volume. [ME; OE *ealu*]

---

b., blend of, blended; c., cognate with; d., dialect, dialectal; der., derived from; f., formed from; g., going back to; m., modification of; r., replacing; s., stem of; t., taken from; ?, perhaps.   See the full key on inside cover.

a·le·a·to·ry (ā/lĭ̄ ə tōr/ĭ̄), *adj.* **1.** *Law.* depending on a contingent event: *an aleatory contract.* **2.** *Sociol.* having or pertaining to accidental causes and hence not predictable; felt as a matter of good or bad luck and thus easily attributed to benevolent or malevolent forces. [t. L: m. s. *āleātōrius*, der. *āleātor* dice player]

A·lec·to (ə lĕk/tō), *n. Gk. Myth.* one of the Furies.

a·lee (ə lē/), *adv., adj. Naut.* on or toward the lee side of a ship (opposed to *aweather*).

al·e·gar (ăl/ə gər, ā/lə-), *n.* ale vinegar; sour ale.

ale·house (āl/hous/), *n.* a house where ale is retailed.

A·lek·san·dro·pol (ä lĕ̆/ksän drô/pŏl), *n.* former name of Leninakan.

A·lek·san·drovsk (ä/lĕ ksän/drŏfsk), *n.* former name of Zaporozhe.

A·le·mán (ä/lĕ män/), *n.* **1. Mateo** (mä tě/ō), 1547?–1610, Spanish novelist. **2. Miguel** (mē gĕl/), born 1902, president of Mexico since 1946.

Al·e·man·nic (ăl/ə män/ĭk), *n.* the High German speech of Swabia, Württemberg, Switzerland, and Alsace.

A·lem·bert (dȧ län bĕr/), *n.* **Jean le Rond d'** (zhän lə rôn/), 1717?–83, French mathematician, philosopher, and writer: friend of Voltaire.

a·lem·bic (ə lĕm/bĭk), *n.* **1.** a vessel with a beaked cap or head, formerly used in distilling; an ancient retort. **2.** anything that transforms, purifies, or refines. [ME *alambic*, t. ML: s. *alambicus*, t. Ar.: m. *alanbīq* the still (*anbīq* t. Gk.: m. *ámbix* cup)]

A. Alembic; B. Lamp; C. Receiver

A·len·çon (à län sôn/), *n.* a city in NW France: lace. 19,715 (1946).

A·len·çon lace (ə lĕn/sən, -sŏn; *Fr.* à län sôn/), **1.** a delicate needle-point lace made in France. **2.** a machine reproduction of this lace, with a cordlike outline.

A·lep·po (ə lĕp/ō), *n.* a city in NW Syria. 257,300 (est. 1942). French, **A·lep** (à lĕp/).

Aleppo nutgall, the gall of *Quercus infectoria*, grown in Aleppo and rich in tannin.

a·lert (ə lûrt/), *adj.* **1.** vigilantly attentive: *an alert mind.* **2.** moving with celerity; nimble. —*n.* **3.** an attitude of vigilance or caution: *on the alert.* **4.** an air-raid alarm. **5.** the period during which an air-raid alarm is in effect. —*v.t.* **6.** to prepare (troops, etc.) for action. **7.** to warn of an impending raid or attack. [t. F: m. *alerte*, t. It.: m. *all' erta* on the lookout] —**a·lert/ed,** *adj.* —**a·lert/ly,** *adv.* —**a·lert/ness,** *n.*

—**Syn. 1.** ALERT, VIGILANT, WATCHFUL imply a wide-awake attitude, as of someone keenly aware of his surroundings. ALERT describes a ready and prompt attentiveness together with a quick intelligence: *the visitor to the city was alert and eager to see the points of interest.* VIGILANT suggests some immediate necessity for keen, active observation, and for continuing alertness: *knowing the danger, the scout was unceasingly vigilant.* WATCHFUL suggests carefulness and preparedness: *watchful waiting.* **2.** brisk, lively, quick, active.

-ales, *Bot.* a suffix of (Latin) names of order. [t. L, pl. of *-ālis*, adj. suffix. See *-AL¹*]

A·les·san·dri·a (ä/lĕs sän/drē ä/), *n.* a city in NW Italy, in Piedmont. 85,520 (est. 1946).

a·leu·rone (ə lōōr/ōn, ăl/yə rōn/), *n.* minute albuminoid granules (protein) found in connection with starch and oily matter, in the endosperm of ripe seeds, and in a special layer of cells in grains of wheat, etc. [t. Gk.: m. *áleuron* flour] —**a·leu·ron·ic** (ăl/yŏō rŏn/ĭk), *adj.*

Al·e·ut (ăl/ĭ̄ ōōt/), *n.* **1.** a native of the Aleutian Islands. **2.** the language spoken by the Aleutian Indians.

A·leu·tian (ə lōō/shən), *adj.* **1.** of or pertaining to the Aleutian Islands. —*n.* **2.** Aleut (def. 1).

Aleutian Islands, an archipelago extending W from the Alaska Peninsula for ab. 1200 mi.: a part of Alaska. 5521 (prelim. 1950). Also, **Aleutians.**

ale·wife¹ (āl/wīf/), *n., pl.* **-wives.** a North American fish, *Pomolobus pseudoharengus*, resembling a small shad but inferior as food. [orig. unexplained. Cf. obs. *allize*, t. F: m. *alose* shad]

ale·wife² (āl/wīf/), *n., pl.* **-wives.** a woman who keeps an alehouse. [f. ALE + WIFE]

Al·ex·an·der (ăl/ĭg zăn/dər, -zän/-), *n.* **Sir Harold** R.L.F., born 1891, British general: governor general of Canada, 1946–52.

Alexander I, **1.** (Russ.: *Aleksandr Pavlovich*) 1777–1825, czar of Russia, 1801–25. **2.** (Serb.: *Alexander Obrenovic*) 1876–1903, king of Serbia, 1889–1903. **3.** son of Peter I of Serbia, 1888–1934, king of Yugoslavia, 1921–34.

Alexander II, (Russ.: *Aleksandr Nikolaevich*) 1818–1881, czar of Russia, 1855–81.

Alexander III, (Russ.: *Aleksandr Aleksandrovich*) 1845–94, czar of Russia, 1881–94 (son of Alexander II).

Alexander VI, (*Roderigo Lanzol Borgia*) 1431?–1503, pope, 1492–1503.

Alexander Archipelago, numerous coastal islands in SE Alaska.

Alexander Nev·ski (nĕv/skĭ, nĕf/-), 1220?–63, Russian prince, warrior, and statesman.

Alexander Se·ve·rus (sə vĭr/əs), A.D. 208?–235, Roman emperor, A.D. 222–235.

Al·ex·an·der·son (ăl/ĭg zän/dər sən), *n.* **Ernst F. W.,** born 1878, U.S. engineer and inventor.

Alexander the Great, 356–323 B.C., king of Macedonia, 336–323 B.C.; conqueror of Greek city-states and Persian Empire from Asia Minor and Egypt to India.

Empire of Alexander the Great

Al·ex·an·dret·ta (ăl/ĭg zän drĕt/ə, -zän-), *n.* a seaport in S Turkey, on the Gulf of Alexandretta, an inlet of the Mediterranean. 11,859 (1940). Turkish, **Iskenderun.**

Al·ex·an·dri·a (ăl/ĭg zän/drĭ̄ ə, -zän/-), *n.* **1.** a seaport in N Egypt, on the Nile delta: founded by Alexander the Great, 332 B.C.; ancient center of learning. 729,900 (est. 1942). **2.** a city in NE Virginia, opposite the District of Columbia. 61,787 (1950). **3.** a city in central Louisiana, on the Red River. 34,913 (1950).

Al·ex·an·dri·an (ăl/ĭg zän/drĭ̄ ən, -zän/-), *adj.* **1.** of Alexandria, Egypt. **2.** pertaining to the schools of philosophy, literature, and science in ancient Alexandria. **3.** of Alexander the Great. **4.** Alexandrine.

Al·ex·an·drine (ăl/ĭg zän/drĭn, -drēn/, -zän/-), *Pros.* —*n.* **1.** a verse or line of poetry of six iambic feet. —*adj.* **2.** designating such verse or line. **3.** of or pertaining to Alexandria, Egypt. [t. F: m. *alexandrin*, from poems in this meter on *Alexander* the Great]

al·ex·an·drite (ăl/ĭg zän/drīt, -zän/-), *n.* a variety of chrysoberyl, green by daylight and red-violet by artificial light, used as a gem. [f. ALEXANDER II of Russia +-ITE¹]

A·le·xan·drou·po·lis (ä/lĕk sän drōō/pō lēs/), *n.* a seaport in NE Greece, in Western Thrace. 16,138 (1940). Formerly, **Dedeagach.**

a·lex·i·a (ə lĕk/sĭ̄ ə), *n. Psychiatry.* a cerebral disorder marked by inability to understand written speech. [f. A-⁶ + s. Gk. *léxis* a speaking + -IA]

a·lex·in (ə lĕk/sĭn), *n. Immunol.* **1.** any of certain substances in normal blood serum which destroy bacteria, etc. **2.** complement (def. 9). [f. s. Gk. *aléxein* ward off + -IN²] —**a·lex·in·ic** (ăl/ĕk sĭn/ĭk), *adj.*

a·lex·i·phar·mic (ə lĕk/sə fär/mĭk), *Med.* —*adj.* **1.** warding off poisoning or infection; antidotal; prophylactic. —*n.* **2.** an alexipharmic agent, esp. an internal antidote. [t. Gk.: m.s. *alexiphármakon* a remedy against poison; final syll., prop. -*ac*, conformed to the suffix -IC]

A·lex·i·us I (ə lĕk/sĭ̄ əs), (*Alexius Comnenus*) 1048–1118, emperor of the Byzantine Empire, 1081–1118.

al·fal·fa (ăl făl/fə), *n.* a European fabaceous forage plant, *Medicago sativa*, with bluish-purple flowers, now much cultivated in the U. S.; lucerne. [t. Sp., t. Ar.: m. *al-faṣfaṣa* the best sort of fodder]

Al·fie·ri (äl fyĕ/rē), *n.* **Count Vittorio** (vēt tô/ryō), 1749–1803, Italian dramatist and poet.

al·fil·a·ri·a (ăl fĭl/ə rē/ə), *n.* a low geraniaceous herb, *Erodium cicutarium*, with long-beaked fruit, native in Europe but widely naturalized elsewhere for forage. [t. Mex. Sp., der. Sp. *alfiler* pin, t. Ar.: m. *alkhilāl* a wooden pin; so called from the shape of the carpels]

al fi·ne (äl fē/nĕ), *Music.* to the end (a direction, as after a *da capo* or *dal segno*, to continue to *fine*, the indicated end). [It.]

Al·fon·so XII (äl fŏn/sō, -zō; *Sp.* äl fôn/sō), 1857–85, king of Spain, 1874–85.

Alfonso XIII, 1886–1941, king of Spain from 1886 until deposed in 1931.

al·for·ja (äl fôr/jə; *Sp.* äl fôr/hä), *n. Southwestern U.S.* **1.** a leather bag; saddlebag. **2.** a cheek pouch. [t. Sp., t. Ar.: m. *al-khorj* the double saddlebag]

Al·fred the Great (ăl/frĭd), A.D. 849–899, king of England, A.D. 871–899: defeated invading Danes and clinched the overlordship of the West Saxon royal house, built the first English fleet, encouraged education, and translated several Latin works into English, becoming the father of English prose literature.

al fres·co (äl frĕs/kō), in the open air; out of doors: *to dine al fresco.* [t. It.: see *fresco*]

al·fres·co (äl frĕs/kō), *adj.* open-air: *an alfresco café.*

alg., algebra.

al·ga (ăl/gə), *n., pl.* **-gae** (-jē). **1.** any chlorophyll-containing plant belonging to the phylum *Thallophyta*, comprising the seaweeds and various fresh-water forms and varying in form and size, from a single microscopic or sometimes large and branching cell, to forms with trunklike stems many feet in length. They constitute a subphylum, the *Algae*. **2.** a seaweed (def. 1). [t. L: seaweed] —**al/gal,** *adj.*

al·ga·ro·ba (ăl/gə rō/bə), *n.* **1.** any of certain mesquites, esp. *Prosopis juliflora* and its botanical variety *glandulosa.* **2.** its beanlike pod. **3.** the carob (tree). **4.** its beanlike fruit. [t. Sp., t. Ar.: m. *al-kharrūba.* See CAROB]

al·ge·bra (ăl/jə brə), *n.* **1.** the mathematical art of reasoning about (quantitative) relations by means of a systematized notation including letters and other symbols; the analysis of equations, combinatorial analysis, theory of fractions, etc. **2.** any special system of notation adapted to the study of a special system of relationship: *algebra of classes*. [t. ML, t. Ar.: m. *al-jebr, al-jabr* bone setting, hence algebraic reduction]

al·ge·bra·ic (ăl/jə brā/ĭk), *adj*. of or occurring in algebra. Also, **al/ge·bra/i·cal.** —**al/ge·bra/i·cal·ly,** *adv*.

al·ge·bra·ist (ăl/jə brā/ĭst), *n*. an expert in algebra.

Al·ge·ci·ras (ăl/jə sĭr/əs; *Sp*. äl/hĕ thē/räs, -sē/räs), *n*. a seaport in S Spain, on the Strait of Gibraltar. 26,114 (1940).

Al·ger (ăl/jər), *n*. **Horatio,** 1834–99, U.S. author of novels, esp. for boys.

Al·ge·ri·a (ăl jĭr/Ĭ ə), *n*. a French possession in N Africa, near the W end of the Mediterranean. 7,234,684 pop. (1936); 851,298 sq. mi. *Cap.*: Algiers. —**Al·ge/ri·an, Al·ge·rine** (ăl/jə rēn/), *adj*., *n*.

-algia, a noun suffix meaning "pain," as in *neuralgia*. [t. NL, t. Gk.]

al·gid (ăl/jĭd), *adj*. cold; chilly. [t. L: s. *algidus*] —**al·gid/i·ty,** *n*.

Al·giers (ăl jĭrz/), *n*. **1.** a seaport in and the capital of Algeria, in the N part. 264,232 (1936). **2.** one of the former Barbary States in N Africa, notorious for its pirates; modern Algeria.

al·gi·nate (ăl/jə nāt/), *n*. a gelatinous substance extracted from various kelps, esp. *Macrocystis pyrifera*, used in the manufacture of ice cream, in sizing cloth, and for various other industrial purposes. [f. *algin(ic)* (der. *algin*, substance obtained from algae) + -ATE[2]]

algo-, a word element meaning "pain," as in *algometer*. [comb. form repr. Gk. *álgos*]

al·goid (ăl/goid), *adj*. like algae. [f. ALG(A) + -OID]

Al·gol (ăl/gŏl), *n*. a star of the second magnitude in the constellation Perseus (def. 2). It is remarkable for its variability, which is due to periodic eclipse by a fainter stellar companion. [t. Ar.: the demon]

al·go·lag·ni·a (ăl/gə lăg/nĬ ə), *n. Psychiatry*. morbid enjoyment of sexually related pain, including both sadism and masochism. [f. ALGO- + m.s. Gk. *lagneía* lust]

al·gol·o·gy (ăl gŏl/ə jĬ), *n*. the branch of botany that deals with algae. —**al·go·log·i·cal** (ăl/gə lŏj/ə kəl), *adj*. —**al·gol/o·gist,** *n*.

al·gom·e·ter (ăl gŏm/ə tər), *n*. a device for determining sensitiveness to pain due to pressure. —**al·go·met·ric** (ăl/gə mĕt/rĬk), **al/go·met/ri·cal,** *adj*. —**al·gom/e·try,** *n*.

Al·gon·ki·an (ăl gŏng/kĬ ən), *adj*. **1.** *Stratig*. pertaining to a division of late pre-Cambrian rocks. **2.** Algonquian. —*n*. **3.** *Stratig*. a division of predominantly sedimentary rocks next older than Cambrian in parts of North America. **4.** Algonquian.

Al·gon·kin (ăl gŏng/kĬn), *n*. Algonquin.

Al·gon·qui·an (ăl gŏng/kĬ ən, -kwĬ ən), *n*. **1.** one of the principal linguistic stocks of North America, belonging to the Algonquian-Mosan phylum. and including languages spoken or formerly spoken from Labrador southward and westward through Canada and northern U.S. to the Rocky Mountains, including Micmac, Ojibwa, Penobscot, Delaware, Cree, Fox, Blackfoot, Cheyenne, Arapaho, etc., as well as Yurok in California. **2.** an Algonquian tribe member. —*adj*. **3.** belonging to or constituting this stock.

Algonquian-Mo·san (mō/sən), *n*. a great linguistic phylum of North America including Algonquian, Salishan, and Wakashan.

Al·gon·quin (ăl gŏng/kĬn, -kwĬn), *n*. **1.** a member of a group of North American Indian tribes formerly along the Ottawa river and the northern tributaries of the St. Lawrence, now living in the western U. S. **2.** their language, of Algonquian stock. **3.** any Algonquian Indian. Also, **Algonkin.**

al·go·pho·bi·a (ăl/gə fō/bĬ ə), *n. Psychiatry*. an abnormal dread of pain.

al·gor (ăl/gôr), *n. Pathol*. coldness or chill, esp. at the onset of fever. [t. L: cold]

al·go·rism (ăl/gə rĬz/əm), *n*. **1.** the Arabic system of arithmetical notation (with the figures 1, 2, 3, etc.). **2.** the art of computation with the Arabic figures, one to nine, plus the zero; arithmetic. [ME *algorisme*, t. OF, t. ML: m.s. *algorismus*, t. Ar.: m. *al-Khwārizmī* the native of *Khwārizm* Khiva (i.e., *Abū Ja/far Mohammed ibn Mūsā*, Arabian mathematician, author of a famous treatise on algebra translated into ML]

al·go·rithm (ăl/gə rĬth/əm), *n*. any peculiar method of computing, as the rule for finding the greatest common divisor. [var. of ALGORISM]

Al·ham·bra (ăl hăm/brə), *n*. **1.** the palace of the Moorish kings at Granada, Spain, completed in the 14th century. **2.** a city in SW California, near Los Angeles. 51,359 (1950). [t. Sp., t. Ar.: m. *al-hamrā'* the red (referring to the color of the soil)]

al·ham·bresque (ăl/hăm brĕsk/), *adj*. resembling the fanciful style of ornamentation of the Spanish Alhambra.

A·li (ä/lē, ä lē/), *n*. (*"the Lion of God"*) A.D. 600?–661, Arabian caliph, cousin and son-in-law of Mohammed. Also, **A·li ibn-a·bu-Ta·lib** (ä/lē Ĭb/ən ä bōō/tä lēb/).

a·li·as (ā/lĬ əs), *adv*., *n*., *pl*. **aliases.** —*adv*. **1.** at another time; in another place; in other circumstances; otherwise. Simpson *alias* Smith means a person calling himself at one time or one place Smith, at another Simpson. —*n*. **2.** an assumed name; another name. [t. L: at another time or palce]

A·li Ba·ba (ä/lē bä/bä, ăl/Ĭ băb/ə), the poor woodchopper, hero of a tale in *The Arabian Nights Entertainments*, who uses the magic words "open sesame" to open the door to the fabulous wealth in the cave of the Forty Thieves.

al·i·bi (ăl/ə bī/), *n*., *pl*. **-bis. 1.** *Law*. the defense by an accused person that he was elsewhere at the time the offense with which he is charged was committed. **2.** *U.S. Colloq*. an excuse. [t. L: elsewhere]

al·i·ble (ăl/ə bəl), *adj*. nutritive. [t. L: m.s. *alibilis*] —**al/i·bil/i·ty,** *n*.

Al·i·can·te (ăl/ə kăn/tĬ; *Sp*. ä/lē kän/tĕ), *n*. a seaport in SE Spain, on the Mediterranean. 96,729 (1940).

al·i·cy·clic (ăl/ə sĬ/klĬk, -sĬk/lĬk), *adj*. denoting organic compounds, essentially aliphatic in chemical behavior but differing structurally in that the essential carbon atoms are connected as in a ring instead of open chain.

al·i·dade (ăl/ə dād/), *n. Survey*. **1.** a telescope equipped with vertical circle and stadia cross hairs and mounted on a flat base, used to make measurements from a plane table. **2.** a similar instrument consisting of a brass rule with sighting holes at the ends. Also, **al·i·dad** (ăl/ə dăd/). [ME, t. ML: m. s. *alhidada*, t. Ar.: m. *al-'iḍāda* the revolving radius of a graduated circle]

al·ien (āl/yən, ā/lĬ ən), *n*. **1.** one born in or belonging to another country who has not acquired citizenship by naturalization and is not entitled to the privileges of a citizen. **2.** a foreigner. **3.** one who has been estranged or excluded. —*adj*. **4.** residing under another government or in another country than that of one's birth, and not having rights of citizenship in such place of residence. **5.** belonging or relating to aliens: *alien property*. **6.** foreign; strange; not belonging to one: *alien speech*. **7.** adverse; hostile; opposed (fol. by *to* or *from*): *ideas alien to our way of thinking*. [ME, t. L: s. *aliēnus* belonging to another] —**Syn. 2.** See **stranger.**

al·ien·a·ble (āl/yən ə bəl, ā/lĬ ən-), *adj*. capable of being sold or transferred. —**al/ien·a·bil/i·ty,** *n*.

al·ien·age (āl/yən Ĭj, ā/lĬ ən-), *n*. state of being an alien; the legal standing of an alien.

al·ien·ate (āl/yən āt/, ā/lĬ ə-), *v.t*., **-ated, -ating. 1.** to make indifferent or averse; estrange. **2.** to turn away: *to alienate the affections*. **3.** *Law*. to transfer or convey, as title, property, or other right, to another: *to alienate lands*. [t. L: m. s. *aliēnātus*, pp., estranged] —**al/ien·a/tor,** *n*.

al·ien·a·tion (āl/yən ā/shən, ā/lĬ ə-), *n*. **1.** a withdrawal or estrangement, as of feeling or the affections. **2.** *Law*. a transfer of the title to property by one person to another by conveyance (as distinguished from *inheritance*). **3.** *Psychiatry*. **a.** mental or psychiatric illness. **b.** legal insanity. [ME, t. L: s. *aliēnātio* a transferring, also insanity]

al·ien·ee (āl/yə nē/, ā/lĬ ə), *n*. one to whom property is alienated.

al·ien·ism (āl/yə nĬz/əm, ā/lĬ ə-), *n*. **1.** alienage. **2.** the study or treatment of mental diseases.

al·ien·ist (āl/yən Ĭst, ā/lĬ ən-), *n*. a psychiatrist who specializes in giving legal evidence. [t. F: m. *aliéniste*, f. s. L *aliēnus* insane + -*iste* -IST]

al·ien·or (āl/yən ər, ā/lĬ ən-, āl/yə nôr/, ā/lĬ ə), *n*. one who transfers property. Also, **a/lien·er.**

al·i·form (ăl/ə fôrm/, ā/lə-), *adj*. wing-shaped; winglike; alar. [f. s. L *āla* wing + -(I)FORM]

A·li·garh (ä/lē gûr/, ăl/ē-), *n*. a city in N India, in the United Provinces. 112,655 (1941).

a·light[1] (ə līt/), *v.i*., **alighted** or (*Rare*) **alit, alighting. 1.** to get down from a horse or out of a vehicle; dismount. **2.** to settle or stay after descending: *a bird alights on a tree*. **3.** to come accidentally, or without design (fol. by *on* or *upon*). [ME *alighte(n)*, OE *ālīhtan*, f. A-[1] + *līhtan* LIGHT[2], v.]

a·light[2] (ə līt/), *adv*., *adj*. provided with light; lighted up; burning. [Orig. pp. of *alight*, v., light up, but now regarded as f. A-[1] + LIGHT[1], n. Cf. AFIRE]

a·lign (ə līn/), *v.t*. **1.** to adjust to a line; lay out or regulate by line; form in line. **2.** to bring into line. —*v.i*. **3.** to fall or come into line; be in line. **4.** to join with others in a cause. Also, **aline.** [t. F: s. *aligner*, f. à A-[5] + *ligner* (g. L *līneāre* line)] —**a·lign/er,** *n*.

a·lign·ment (ə līn/mənt), *n*. **1.** an adjustment to a line; arrangement in a line. **2.** the line or lines formed. **3.** a ground plan of a railroad or highway. **4.** *Archaeol*. a line or an arrangement of parallel or converging lines of upright stones (menhirs). Also, **alinement.**

a·like (ə līk/), *adv*. **1.** in the same manner, form, or degree; in common; equally: *known to treat all customers alike*. —*adj*. **2.** having resemblance or similarity; having or exhibiting no marked or essential difference (used regularly of a plural substantive or idea, and only in the predicate): *he thinks all politicians are alike*. [ME, t. Scand.; cf. Icel. *ālīka* similar]

---

b., blend of, blended; c., cognate with; d., dialect, dialectal; der., derived from; f., formed from; g., going back to; m., modification of; r., replacing; s., stem of; t., taken from; ?, perhaps. See the full key on inside cover.

al·i·ment (n. ăl′ə mənt; v. -mĕnt′), n. **1.** that which nourishes; nutriment; food. **2.** that which sustains; support. —v.t. **3.** to sustain; support. [t. L: s. *alimentum* food] —**al′i·men′tal,** adj. —**al′i·men′tal·ly,** adv.

al·i·men·ta·ry (ăl′ə mĕn′tə rĭ), adj. **1.** concerned with the function of nutrition. **2.** pertaining to food; nutritious. **3.** providing sustenance or maintenance.

alimentary canal, the food passage in any animal from mouth to anus.

al·i·men·ta·tion (ăl′ə mĕn tā′shən), n. **1.** nourishment; nutrition. **2.** maintenance; support.

al·i·men·ta·tive (ăl′ə mĕn′tə tĭv), adj. nutritive.

al·i·mo·ny (ăl′ə mō′nĭ), n. **1.** *Law.* an allowance paid to a woman by her husband or former husband for her maintenance, granted by a court, upon a legal separation or a divorce, or while action is pending. In exceptional cases, in some States, a husband may receive alimony. **2.** maintenance. [t. L: m.s. *alimōnia* sustenance]

a·line (ə līn′), v.t., v.i., **alined, alining.** align. —**a·line′ment,** n. —**a·lin′er,** n.

A·li Pa·sha (ä′lē pä shä′), ("the Lion of Janina") 1741–1822, Turkish governor of Albania and part of Greece.

al·i·ped (ăl′ə pĕd′), adj. *Zool.* having the toes connected by a winglike membrane, as the bats. [t. L: s. *ālipēs* having winged feet]

al·i·phat·ic (ăl′ə făt′ĭk), adj. *Chem.* pertaining to or concerned with those organic compounds which are open chains, as the paraffins or olefins. [f. m.s. Gk. *áleiphar* oil, fat + -IC]

al·i·quant (ăl′ə kwənt), adj. *Math.* contained in a number or quantity, but not dividing it evenly: *5 is an aliquant part of 16.* [t. L: s. *aliquantus* some]

Al·i·quip·pa (ăl′ə kwĭp′ə), n. a borough in W Pennsylvania. 26,132 (1950).

al·i·quot (ăl′ə kwət), adj. *Math.* forming an exact proper divisor: *5 is an aliquot part of 15.* [t. L: some, several]

a·lis vo·lat pro·pri·is (ā′lĭs vō′lăt prō′prĭ ĭs), *Latin.* she flies with her own wings (motto of Oregon).

a·lit (ə lĭt′), v. *Rare.* pt. and pp. of **alight¹.**

a·li·un·de (ā′lĭ ŭn′dĭ), adv., adj. from another place: *evidence aliunde* (evidence outside the record). [L: from another place]

a·live (ə līv′), adj. (rarely used attributively). **1.** in life or existence; living. **2.** (by way of emphasis) of all living: *the proudest man alive.* **3.** in a state of action; in force or operation; unextinguished: *keep a memory alive.* **4.** full of life; lively: *alive with excitement.* **5. alive to,** attentive to; awake or sensitive to. **6.** filled as with living things; swarming; thronged. [ME *aliue,* OE *on līfe* in life] —**a·live′ness,** n. —**Ant. 1.** dead. **4.** lifeless.

a·liz·a·rin (ə lĭz′ə rĭn), n. one of the earliest known dyes, orig. obtained from madder but now made from anthraquinone. Also, **a·liz·a·rine** (ə lĭz′ə rĭn, -rēn′). [t. F: m. *alizarine,* der. *alizari,* t. Ar.: m. *al-'uṣāra* the extract]

alk., alkali.

al·ka·hest (ăl′kə hĕst′), n. the universal solvent sought by the alchemists. Also, **alcahest.** [t. NL, prob. coined by Paracelsus]

al·ka·les·cent (ăl′kə lĕs′ənt), adj. tending to become alkaline; slightly alkaline. —**al′ka·les′cence, al′ka·les′cen·cy,** n.

al·ka·li (ăl′kə lĭ′), n., pl. **-lis, -lies. 1.** *Chem.* **a.** any of various bases, the hydroxides of the alkali metals, and of ammonium, which neutralize acids to form salts and turn red litmus paper blue. **b.** any of various other more or less active bases, as calcium hydroxide. **c.** *Obsolesc.* any of various other compounds, as the carbonates of sodium and potassium. **2.** *Agric.* a soluble mineral salt, or a mixture of soluble salts, occurring in soils, etc., usually to the damage of crops. [ME *alkaly,* t. MF: m. *alcali,* t. Ar.: m. *al-qĭly,* later *al-qalī* the saltwort ashes]

alkali disease, *Vet. Sci.* botulism in wild ducks.

al·ka·li·fy (ăl′kə lə fī′), v., **-fied, -fying.** —v.t. **1.** to alkalize. —v.i. **2.** to become alkaline. —**al·ka·li·fi·a·ble** (ăl′kə lə fī′ə bəl, ăl kăl′ə-), adj.

alkali metal, *Chem.* a monovalent metal, one of the group including potassium, sodium, lithium, rubidium, and cesium, whose hydroxides are alkalis.

al·ka·lim·e·ter (ăl′kə lĭm′ə tər), n. an instrument for determining the quantity of carbon dioxide, usually in baking powder. —**al′ka·lim′e·try,** n.

al·ka·line (ăl′kə lĭn′, -lĭn), adj. of or like an alkali; having the properties of an alkali.

alkaline-earth metals, *Chem.* barium, strontium, calcium, and sometimes magnesium.

alkaline earths, *Chem.* the oxides of barium, strontium, calcium, and sometimes magnesium.

al·ka·lin·i·ty (ăl′kə lĭn′ə tĭ), n. alkaline condition; the quality which constitutes an alkali.

alkali soil, any of various soils in poorly drained or arid regions, containing a large amount of soluble mineral salts (chiefly of sodium) which in dry weather appear on the surface as a (usually white) crust or powder.

al·ka·lize (ăl′kə līz′), v.t., **-lized, -lizing.** to make alkaline; change into an alkali. [f. ALKAL(I) + -IZE] —**al′ka·li·za′tion,** n.

al·ka·loid (ăl′kə loid′), n. **1.** one of a class of basic nitrogenous organic compounds occurring in plants, such

as nicotine, atropine, morphine, or quinine. —adj. **2.** Also, **al′ka·loi′dal** resembling an alkali; alkaline.

al·ka·lo·sis (ăl′kə lō′sĭs), n. *Physiol.* excessively alkaline state of the body tissue and blood. [f. ALKAL(I) + -OSIS]

al·kanes (ăl′kānz), n.pl. *Chem.* methane series.

al·ka·net (ăl′kə nĕt′), n. **1.** a European boraginaceous plant, *Alkanna tinctoria,* whose root yields a red dye. **2.** the root. **3.** the dye. **4.** any of several similar plants, as the bugloss (*Anchusa officinalis*) and the puccoon (*Lithospermum*). [ME, t. Sp.: m. *alcaneta,* dim. of *alcana* henna]

al·kene (ăl′kēn), n. *Chem.* any of a group of unsaturated aliphatic hydrocarbons, with the general formula C_nH_{2n}, containing an unsaturated linkage or double bond, as ethylene, C_2H_4. [f. ALK(YL GROUP) + -ENE]

Alk·maar (älk mär′), n. a city in W Netherlands. 37,107 (est. 1946).

Al·ko·ran (ăl′kō rän′, -răn′), n. the Koran.

al·kyd resins, *Chem.* a group of sticky resins derived from dicarboxylic acids, as phthalic or maleic acids, in reaction with glycols or glycerol, and used as adhesives.

al·kyl·a·tion (ăl′kə lā′shən), n. *Chem.* the replacement of a hydrogen atom in an organic compound by an alkyl group.

al·kyl group, *Chem.* a univalent group or radical derived from an aliphatic hydrocarbon, by removal of a hydrogen atom, having the general formula C_nH_{2n+1}. Also, **alkyl radical.** [f. ALK(ALI) + -YL]

alkyl halide, *Chem.* an organic compound with the type formula RX, where R is a radical derived from a hydrocarbon of the methane series and X is a halogen, as methyl chloride, CH_3Cl.

al·kyne (ăl′kīn), n. *Chem.* an unsaturated, aliphatic hydrocarbon containing a triple bond; a member of the acetylene series. [f. ALK(YL) + -(I)NE²]

all (ôl), adj. **1.** the whole of (with reference to quantity, extent, duration, amount, or degree): *all Europe, all year.* **2.** the whole number of (with reference to individuals or particulars, taken collectively): *all men.* **3.** the greatest possible: *with all speed.* **4.** every (chiefly with *kinds, sorts, manner*). **5.** any; any whatever: *beyond all doubt.* —pron. **6.** the whole quantity or amount: *to eat all of something.* **7.** the whole number: *all of us.* **8.** everything: *is that all?* —n. **9.** a whole; a totality of things or qualities. **10.** one's whole interest, concern, or property: *to give, or lose, one's all.* **11.** Some special noun phrases are:
above all, before everything else.
after all, 1. after everything has been considered; notwithstanding. **2.** in spite of all that was done, said, etc.: *he lost the fight after all.*
all in all, everything together.
at all, 1. in any degree: *not bad at all.* **2.** for any reason. *I was surprised at his coming at all.* **3.** in any way: *no offense at all.*
for all (that), notwithstanding; in spite of.
in all, all included: *a hundred people in all.*
once and for all, for the final time.
—adv. **12.** wholly; entirely; quite: *all alone.* **13.** only; exclusively: *he spent his income all on pleasure.* **14.** each; apiece: *the score was one all.* **15.** *Poetic.* even; just. [ME; OE *all, eall,* c. G *all*]

all-, var. of **allo-** before vowels, as in *allonym.*

al·la bre·ve (ä′lə brĕv′ä; It. äl′lä brĕ′vĕ), *Music.* **1.** an expression denoting a species of time in which every measure contains a breve, or four minims. **2.** a time value of two minims or four crotchets to a measure, but taken at a rate twice as fast. [It.]

Al·lah (ăl′ə, ä′lə), n. the Mohammedan name of the Supreme Being. [t. Ar.: m. *Allāh,* contr. of *al-ilāh* the God]

Al·lah·a·bad (ăl′ə hə băd′, ä′lə hä bäd′), n. a city in N India, on the Ganges river. 260,630 (1941).

all-A·mer·i·can (ôl′ə mĕr′ə kən), adj. **1.** representing the entire U. S. **2.** composed exclusively of American members or elements. **3.** representing the best in any field of U.S. sport. —n. **4.** an all-American player.

Al·lan-a-Dale (ăl′ən ə dāl′), n. (in English balladry) the youth befriended by Robin Hood, who kept his sweetheart from wedding an aged knight and took her for his own bride.

al·lan·ite (ăl′ə nīt′), n. a mineral, a silicate of calcium, cerium, aluminum, and iron, chiefly occuring in brown to black masses or prismatic crystals. [named after Thomas *Allan,* 1777–1833, mineralogist. See -ITE¹]

al·lan·to·ic (ăl′ən tō′ĭk), adj. *Zool.* pertaining to the allantois.

al·lan·toid (ə lăn′toid), *Zool.* —adj. **1.** allantoic. —n. **2.** the allantois. —**al·lan·toi·dal** (ăl′ən toi′dəl), adj.

al·lan·to·is (ə lăn′tō ĭs), n. *Zool.* a fetal appendage of mammals, birds, and reptiles, typically developing as an extension of the urinary bladder. [t. NL, earlier *allantoīdes,* t. Gk.: m. *allantoeidēs* sausage-shaped]

al·lar·gan·do (äl′lär gän′dō), adj. *Music.* progressively slower and frequently increasing in power. [It.]

all-a·round (ôl′ə round′), adj. *U.S.* all-round.

al·lay (ə lā′), v.t., **-layed, -laying. 1.** to put at rest; quiet (tumult, fear, suspicion, etc.); appease (wrath). **2.** to mitigate; relieve or alleviate: *to allay pain.* [ME *aleyen,* OE *ālecgan* put down, suppress, f. *ā-* away +

lecgan lay; sp. *all-* by false identification of prefix *a-* with L *ad-*] —**al·lay′er**, *n.*
—**Syn. 1.** ALLAY, MODERATE, SOOTHE mean to reduce excitement or emotion. To ALLAY is to lay to rest or lull to a sense of security, possibly by making the emotion seem unjustified: *to allay suspicion, anxiety, fears.* To MODERATE is to tone down any excess and thus to restore calm: *to moderate the expression of one's grief.* To SOOTHE is to exert a pacifying or tranquilizing influence: *to soothe a terrified child.* **2.** lessen, diminish, reduce. —**Ant. 1.** excite.

all clear, a signal, etc., that an air raid is over.

al·le·ga·tion (ăl′ə gā′shən), *n.* **1.** act of alleging; affirmation. **2.** a statement offered as a plea, an excuse, or a justification. **3.** a mere assertion made without any proof. **4.** an assertion made by a party in a legal proceeding, which he undertakes to prove. [ME, t. L: s. *allēgātio*]

al·lege (ə lĕj′), *v.t.*, **-leged, -leging. 1.** to declare with positiveness; affirm; assert: *to allege a fact.* **2.** to declare before a court, or elsewhere as if upon oath. **3.** to assert without proof. **4.** to plead in support of; urge as a reason or excuse. **5.** *Archaic.* to cite or quote in confirmation. [ME *allegg(n)*, t. AF: m. *alegier* (g. L *ex-* EX¹- + *lītigāre* sue), with sense of L *allēgāre* adduce] —**al·lege′a·ble**, *adj.* —**al·leg′er**, *n.* —**Syn. 1.** state, asseverate, aver. —**Ant. 1.** deny.

al·leg·ed·ly (ə lĕj′ĭd lĭ), *adv.* according to allegation.

Al·le·ghe·ny (ăl′ə gā′nĭ), *n.* a river flowing from SW New York through W Pennsylvania into the Ohio river at Pittsburgh. 325 mi.

Allegheny Mountains, a mountain range in Pennsylvania, Maryland, West Virginia, and Virginia: a part of the Appalachian system. Also, **Alleghenies**.

al·le·giance (ə lē′jəns), *n.* **1.** the obligation of a subject or citizen to his sovereign or government; duty owed to a sovereign or state. **2.** observance of obligation; faithfulness to any person or thing. [ME *alegeaunce* (with *a-* of obscure orig.), t. OF: m. *ligeance.* See LIEGE] —**Syn. 1, 2.** See loyalty.

al·le·giant (ə lē′jənt), *adj.* loyal.

al·le·gor·i·cal (ăl′ə gôr′ə kəl, -gŏr′-), *adj.* consisting of or pertaining to allegory; of the nature of or containing allegory; figurative: *an allegorical poem, meaning, etc.* Also, **al′le·gor′ic.** —**al′le·gor′i·cal·ly**, *adv.*

al·le·go·rist (ăl′ə gôr′ĭst, ăl′ə gə rĭst), *n.* one who uses or writes allegory.

al·le·go·ris·tic (ăl′ə gə rĭs′tĭk), *adj.* relating in the form of allegory; interpreting with allegorical meaning.

al·le·go·rize (ăl′ə gə rīz′), *v.*, **-rized, -rizing.** —*v.t.* **1.** to turn into allegory; narrate in allegory. **2.** to understand in an allegorical sense; interpret allegorically. —*v.i.* **3.** to use allegory. —**al·le·go·ri·za·tion** (ăl′ə gôr′ə zā′shən, -gŏr′-), *n.* —**al′le·go·riz′er**, *n.*

al·le·go·ry (ăl′ə gôr′ĭ), *n., pl.* **-ries. 1.** figurative treatment of one subject under the guise of another; a presentation of an abstract or spiritual meaning under concrete or material forms. **2.** a symbolical narrative: *the political allegory of Piers Plowman.* **3.** an emblem. [ME *allegorie*, t. L: m. *allēgoria*, t. Gk.]

al·le·gret·to (ăl′ə grĕt′ō; *It.* äl′lĕ grĕt′tō), *adj., n., pl.* **-tos.** *Music.* —*adj.* **1.** more rapid than andante, but slower than allegro. —*n.* **2.** an allegretto movement, of a graceful character. [It., dim. of *allegro* ALLEGRO]

al·le·gro (ə lā′grō, ə lĕg′-; *It.* äl lĕ′grō), *adj., n., pl.* **-gros.** *Music.* —*adj.* **1.** brisk; rapid. —*n.* **2.** an allegro movement. [It., g. L *alacer* brisk]

al·lele (ə lēl′), *n. Biol.* shortened form of **allelomorph.** [t. Gk.: m.s. *allēlōn* (gen.) reciprocally] —**al·lel·ic** (ə lē′lĭk), *adj.*

al·le·lo·morph (ə lē′lə môrf′, ə lĕl′ə-), *n. Biol.* one of two or more alternative, hereditary units or genes at identical loci of homologous chromosomes, giving rise to contrasting Mendelian characters. [f. *allelo-* (comb. form of ALLELE) + -MORPH] —**al·le′lo·mor′phic**, *adj.* —**al·le′lo·mor′phism**, *n.*

al·le·lu·ia (ăl′ə lōō′yə), *interj.* **1.** praise ye the Lord; hallelujah. —*n.* **2.** a song of praise to God. [t. L t. Gk.: m. *allēloúia*, t. Heb.: m. *hallelūyāh* praise ye Jehovah]

al·le·mande (ăl′ə mănd′; *Fr.* ȧl mäNd′), *n.* **1.** either of two German dances. **2.** a piece of music based on their rhythms, often following the prelude in the classical suite. **3.** a figure in a quadrille. **4.** the dance itself. [F: lit., German]

Al·len (ăl′ən), *n.* **1. Ethan** (ē′thən), 1738–89, American soldier in the Revolutionary War: leader of "Green Mountain Boys" of Vermont. **2. Grant,** 1848–99, British novelist and writer on science. **3. (William) Hervey** (hûr′vĭ), 1889–1949, U.S. author.

Al·len·by (ăl′ən bĭ), *n.* **Edmund, 1st Viscount,** 1861–1936, British field marshal: commander of British forces in Palestine and Syria in World War I.

Al·len·town (ăl′ən toun′), *n.* a city in E Pennsylvania. 106,756 (1950).

al·ler·gen (ăl′ər jĕn′), *n. Immunol.* any substance which might induce an allergy. [f. ALLER(GY) + -GEN]

al·ler·gen·ic (ăl′ər jĕn′ĭk), *adj.* causing allergic sensitization.

al·ler·gic (ə lûr′jĭk), *adj.* **1.** of or pertaining to allergy. **2.** affected with allergy.

al·ler·gy (ăl′ər jĭ), *n., pl.* **-gies. 1.** a state of hypersensitiveness to certain things, as pollens, food, fruits, etc., to which an individual is abnormally sensitive in comparison with the majority of people who remain un-

affected. Hay fever, asthma, and hives are common allergies. **2.** altered susceptibility due to a first inoculation, treatment, or the like, as exhibited in reaction to a subsequent one of the same nature. See **anaphylaxis.** [t. NL: m. s. *allergia*, f. Gk.: s. *állos* other + *-ergia* work]

al·le·vi·ate (ə lē′vĭ āt′), *v.t.*, **-ated, -ating.** to make easier to be endured; lessen; mitigate: *to alleviate sorrow, pain, punishment, etc.* [t. LL: m. s. *alleviātus*, pp.] —**al·le′vi·a′tor**, *n.*

al·le·vi·a·tion (ə lē′vĭ ā′shən), *n.* **1.** act of alleviating. **2.** something that alleviates.

al·le·vi·a·tive (ə lē′vĭ ā′tĭv), *adj.* **1.** serving to alleviate. —*n.* **2.** something that alleviates.

al·le·vi·a·to·ry (ə lē′vĭ ə tôr′ĭ), *adj.* alleviative.

al·ley¹ (ăl′ĭ), *n., pl.* **-leys. 1.** a narrow, back street. **2.** a walk, enclosed with hedges or shrubbery, in a garden. **3.** a long narrow enclosure with a smooth wooden floor for bowling, etc. [ME *aley*, t. OF: m. *alee* a going, passage, der. *aler* go] —**Syn. 1.** See **street.**

al·ley² (ăl′ĭ), *n., pl.* **-leys.** a choice large playing marble. [dim. abbr. of ALABASTER]

al·ley·way (ăl′ĭ wā′), *n.* **1.** *U.S.* an alley or lane. **2.** a narrow passageway.

All Fools' Day, April Fools' Day.

all fours, 1. all four legs of an animal, or both arms and both legs of man (formerly *all four*): *to crawl on all fours.* **2. on all fours,** *Brit.* even (*with*); presenting exact comparison (*with*). **3.** *Cards.* seven-up.

all hail, *Archaic.* a salutation of greeting or welcome.

All·hal·low·mas (ôl′hăl′ō məs), *n.* the feast of Allhallows.

All·hal·lows (ôl′hăl′ōz), *n.* All Saints' Day.

All·hal·low·tide (ôl′hăl′ō tīd′), *n.* the time or season of Allhallows.

all·heal (ôl′hēl′), *n.* **1.** valerian (def. 1). **2.** selfheal.

al·li·a·ceous (ăl′ĭ ā′shəs), *adj.* **1.** *Bot.* belonging to the genus *Allium*, which includes the garlic, onion, leek, etc. **2.** having the odor or taste of garlic, onion, etc.

al·li·ance (ə lī′əns), *n.* **1.** state of being allied or connected; relation between parties allied or connected. **2.** marriage, or the relation or union brought about between families through marriage. **3.** formal agreement by two or more nations to coöperate for specific purposes. **4.** any joining of efforts or interests by persons, families, states, or organizations: *an alliance between church and state.* **5.** the persons or parties allied. **6.** relationship in qualities; affinity: *the alliance between logic and metaphysics.* [ME *aliaunce*, t. OF: m. *aliance*, g. L *alligantia*] —**Syn. 1.** association; coalition, combination; partnership. **3.** ALLIANCE, CONFEDERATION, LEAGUE, UNION all mean the joining of states for mutual benefit or to permit the joint exercise of functions. An ALLIANCE may apply to any connection entered into for mutual benefit. LEAGUE usually suggests closer combination or a more definite object or purpose. CONFEDERATION applies to a permanent combination for the exercise in common of certain governmental functions. UNION implies an alliance so close and permanent that the separate states or parties become essentially one.

Al·li·ance (ə lī′əns), *n.* a city in N E Ohio. 26,161 (1950).

al·lied (ə līd′, ăl′īd), *adj.* **1.** joined by treaty. **2.** related: *allied species.* **3.** (*cap.*) pertaining to the Allies.

Al·lier (ȧ lyĕ′), *n.* a river flowing from S France N to the Loire river. ab. 250 mi.

al·lies (ăl′īz, ə līz′), *n.* **1.** pl. of **ally. 2.** (*cap.*) (in World War I) the powers of the Triple Entente (Great Britain, France, and Russia), with the nations allied with them (Belgium, Serbia, Japan, Italy, etc., not including the United States), or, in loose use, with all the nations (including the United States) allied or associated with them as opposed to the Central Powers. **3.** (*cap.*) (in World War II) the United Nations.

al·li·ga·tor (ăl′ə gā′tər), *n.* **1.** the broad-snouted representative of the crocodile group found in the southeastern U. S. **2.** any crocodilian (usually but not always applied to broad-snouted species) in other parts of the world. **3.** *Metall.* a machine for bringing the balls of iron from a puddling furnace into compact form so that they can be handled. [t. Sp.: m. *el lagarto* the lizard, ult. g. L *lacertus* lizard]

alligator pear, avocado (def. 1).

all in, *U.S. Colloq.* exhausted.

all-in (ôl′ĭn′), *adj. Brit.* **1.** with extras included; inclusive: *at the all-in rate.* **2.** without restrictions: *all-in wrestling.*

al·lit·er·ate (ə lĭt′ə rāt′), *v.*, **-ated, -ating.** —*v.i.* **1.** to show alliteration (*with*): *the "h" in "harp" does not alliterate with the "h" in "honored."* **2.** to use alliteration: *Swinburne often alliterates.* —*v.t.* **3.** to compose or arrange with alliteration: *he alliterates the "w's" in that line.*

al·lit·er·a·tion (ə lĭt′ə rā′shən), *n.* **1.** the commencement of two or more stressed syllables of a word group: **a.** with the same consonant sound or sound group (**consonantal alliteration**), as in *from stem to stern.* **b.** with a vowel sound which may differ from syllable to syllable, (**vocalic alliteration**), as in *each to all.* **2.** the commencement of two or more words of a word group with the same letter, as in *apt alliteration's artful aid.* [f. AL- + s. L *lītera* letter + -ATION]

al·lit·er·a·tive (ə lĭt′ə rā′tĭv), *adj.* pertaining to or characterized by alliteration: *alliterative verse.* —**al·lit′er·a′tive·ly**, *adv.* —**al·lit′er·a′tive·ness**, *n.*

al·li·um (ăl′ĭ əm), *n. Bot.* a flower or plant of the liliaceous genus *Allium*, comprising bulbous plants with a

---

b., blend of, blended; c., cognate with; d., dialect, dialectal; der., derived from; f., formed from; g., going back to: m., modification of; r., replacing; s., stem of; t., taken from; ?., perhaps. See the full key on inside cover.

peculiar pungent odor, including the onion, leek, shallot, garlic, and chives. [t. L: garlic]

allo-, a word element indicating difference, alternation, or divergence, as in *allonym, allomerism*. Also, **all-**. [t. Gk., comb. form of *állos* other]

al·lo·cate (ăl′ə kāt′), *v.t.*, **-cated, -cating. 1.** to set apart for a particular purpose; assign or allot: *to allocate shares.* **2.** to fix the place of; locate. [t. ML: m. s. *allocātus*, pp. of *allocāre*, f. L: *al-* AL- + *locāre* place] —**Syn. 1.** See **assign.**

al·lo·ca·tion (ăl′ə kā′shən), *n.* **1.** act of allocating; apportionment. **2.** the share or proportion allocated. **3.** *Accounting.* a system of dividing expenses and incomes among the various branches, etc., of a business.

al·lo·cu·tion (ăl′ə kū′shən), *n.* an address, esp. a formal, authoritative one. [t. L: s. *allocūtiō*]

al·lo·di·al (ə lō′dĭ əl), *adj.* free from the tenurial rights of a feudal overlord. Also, **alodial.** [t. ML: s. *allōdiālis*]

al·lo·di·um (ə lō′dĭ əm), *n., pl.* **-dia** (-dĭ ə). land owned absolutely, not subject to any rent, service, or other tenurial right of an overlord. Also, **alodium.** [t. ML, t. OLG: m. *allōd* (f. *all* ALL + *ōd* property). See -IUM.]

al·log·a·my (ə lŏg′ə mĭ), *n.* cross-fertilization in plants. —**al·log′a·mous,** *adj.*

al·lom·er·ism (ə lŏm′ər ĭz′əm), *n.* variability in chemical constitution without change in crystalline form. [f. ALLO- + s. Gk. *méros* part + -ISM] —**al·lom′er·ous,** *adj.*

al·lo·mor·phism (ăl′ə môr′fĭz əm), *n.* allotropy.

al·lo·nym (ăl′ə nĭm), *n.* the name of someone else assumed by the author of a work. [f. ALL(O)- + m. Gk. *ónyma* name]

al·lo·path (ăl′ə păth′), *n.* one who practices or favors allopathy. Also, **al·lop·a·thist** (ə lŏp′ə thĭst).

al·lop·a·thy (ə lŏp′ə thĭ), *n.* the method of treating disease by the use of agents, producing effects different from those of the disease treated (opposed to *homeopathy*). —**al·lo·path·ic** (ăl′ə păth′ĭk), *adj.* —**al′lo·path′i·cal·ly,** *adv.*

al·lo·phane (ăl′ə fān′), *n.* a mineral, an amorphous hydrous silicate of aluminum, occurring in blue, green, or yellow masses, resinous to earthy. [t. Gk.: m. s. *allophanēs* appearing otherwise (with reference to its change of appearance under the blowpipe)]

al·lo·phone (ăl′ə fōn′), *n. Phonet.* one of several phones belonging to the same phoneme.

al·lo·plasm (ăl′ə plăz′əm), *n. Biol.* that part of protoplasm which is differentiated to perform a special function, as that of the flagellum.

al·lot (ə lŏt′), *v.t.,* **-lotted, -lotting. 1.** to divide or distribute as by lot; distribute or parcel out; apportion: *to allot shares.* **2.** to appropriate to a special purpose: *to allot money for a new park.* **3.** to assign as a portion (to); set apart; appoint. [t. OF: m. s. *aloter*, f. *a* to + *loter* divide by lot, der. *lot* lot, of Gmc. orig.] —**al·lot′ter,** *n.* —**Syn. 1.** See **assign.**

al·lot·ment (ə lŏt′mənt), *n.* **1.** distribution as by lot; apportionment, esp. in U.S. military use, the assignment of personnel to an organization for service or use. **2.** a portion or thing allotted; a share granted, esp. in U.S. military use, that portion of the pay of an officer or enlisted person that he authorizes to be paid directly to another person, such as a dependent, or an institution, such as an insurance company. **3.** *Brit.* one of a set of plots of ground separately let out for gardening.

al·lo·trope (ăl′ə trōp′), *n.* one of two or more existing forms of a chemical element: *charcoal, graphite, and diamond are allotropes of carbon.*

al·lo·trop·ic (ăl′ə trŏp′ĭk), *adj.* pertaining to or characterized by allotropy. Also, **al′lo·trop′i·cal.** —**al′lo·trop′i·cal·ly,** *adv.* —**al·lo·tro·pic·i·ty** (ăl′ə trə pĭs′ə tĭ′), *n.*

al·lot·ro·py (ə lŏt′rə pĭ), *n.* a property of certain chemical elements, as carbon, sulfur, and phosphorus, of existing in two or more distinct forms; allomorphism. Also, **al·lot′ro·pism.** [t. Gk.: m. s. *allotropía* variety. See ALLO-, -TROPY]

all′ ot·ta·va (ăl′lôt tä′vä), *Music.* a direction (8va), placed above or below the staff, to indicate that the passage covered is to be played one octave higher or lower respectively. [It.]

al·lot·tee (ə lŏt′ē′), *n.* one to whom something is allotted.

all-out (ôl′out′), *adj.* using all one's resources; complete: *an all-out effort.*

all·ov·er (*adj.* ôl′ō′vər; *n.* ôl′ō′vər), *adj.* **1.** extending or repeated all over, as a decorative pattern on embroidered or lace fabrics. **2.** having a pattern of this kind. —*n.* **3.** fabric with an allover pattern.

al·low (ə lou′), *v.t.* **1.** to grant permission to or for; permit: *to allow a student to be absent, no smoking allowed.* **2.** to let have; grant or give as one's share or suited to one's needs; assign as one's right: *to allow a person $100 for expenses, to allow someone so much a year.* **3.** to permit involuntarily, by neglect or oversight: *to allow a door to stand open.* **4.** to admit; acknowledge; concede: *to allow a claim.* **5.** to take into account; set apart; abate or deduct: *to allow an hour for changing trains.* **6.** *U.S. Dial.* to say; think. **7.** *Archaic.* to approve; sanction. —*v.i.* **8.** allow of; to permit; admit: *to allow of one's authority.* **9.** allow for, to make concession, allowance, or provision for: *to allow for breakage.* [ME *alowe(n)*, t. OF: m. *alower* praise (g. L *allaudāre*) confused with OF *alower* assign (g. LL *allocāre*)]

—**Syn. 1.** ALLOW, LET, PERMIT imply granting or conceding the right of someone to do something. ALLOW and PERMIT are often interchangeable, but PERMIT is the more positive. ALLOW implies complete absence of an attempt, or even an intent, to hinder. PERMIT suggests formal or implied assent or authorization. LET is the familiar, conversational term for both ALLOW and PERMIT. —**Ant. 1.** forbid.

al·low·a·ble (ə lou′ə bəl), *adj.* that may be allowed; legitimate; permissible. —**al·low′a·ble·ness,** *n.* —**al·low′a·bly,** *adv.*

al·low·ance (ə lou′əns), *n., v.,* **-anced, -ancing.** —*n.* **1.** a definite amount or share allotted. **2.** a definite sum of money allotted or granted to meet expenses or requirements: *an allowance of pocket money.* **3.** an addition on account of some extenuating or qualifying circumstance. **4.** a deduction: *the allowance for breakages.* **5.** acceptance; admission: *the allowance of a claim.* **6.** sanction; tolerance: *the allowance of slavery.* **7.** *Minting.* tolerance (def. 4). **8.** *Mach.* a prescribed variation in dimensions. Cf. **tolerance** (def. 3). —*v.t.* **9.** to put upon an allowance. **10.** to limit (supplies, etc.) to a fixed or regular amount. —**Syn. 4.** discount, rebate.

Al·lo·way (ăl′ə wā′), *n.* a hamlet in SW Scotland, near Ayr: birthplace of Robert Burns.

al·low·ed·ly (ə lou′ĭd lĭ), *adv.* admittedly; in a manner that is allowed.

al·loy (*n.* ăl′oi, ə loi′; *v.* ə loi′), *n.* **1.** a substance composed of two or more metals (or, sometimes, a metal and a nonmetal) which have been intimately mixed by fusion, electrolytic deposition, or the like. **2.** a less costly metal mixed with a more valuable one. **3.** standard; quality; fineness. **4.** admixture, as of good with evil; a deleterious element. [t. F: m. *aloi*, OF *alei*] —*v.t.* **5.** to mix (metals) so as to form an alloy. **6.** to reduce in value by an admixture of a less costly metal. **7.** to debase, impair, or reduce by admixture. [t. F: m. *aloyer*, in OF *aleier*, g. L *alligāre* combine]

all right, 1. safe and sound: *are you all right?* **2.** yes; okay. **3.** satisfactory (often ironically): *all right! you'll be sorry.* **4.** correctly; satisfactorily. **5.** without fail; certainly.

all-round (ôl′round′), *adj.* **1.** *U.S.* extending all about. **2.** able to do many things; having general use; not too specialized: *all-round education.* Also, *U.S.,* **all-around.**

All Saints' Day, a church festival celebrated Nov. 1 in honor of all the saints; Allhallows.

all·seed (ôl′sēd′), *n.* any of various many-seeded plants, as a goosefoot, *Chenopodium polyspermum,* and the knotgrass, *Polygonum aviculare.*

All Souls' Day, *Rom. Cath. Ch.* Nov. 2, a day of solemn prayer for mercy for all the souls in Purgatory.

all·spice (ôl′spīs′), *n.* **1.** the berry of a tropical American myrtaceous tree, *Pimenta officinalis.* **2.** a mildly sharp and fragrant spice made from it; pimento.

All·ston (ôl′stən), *n.* **Washington,** 1779–1843, U.S. artist and author.

All's Well That Ends Well, a comedy (extant form dated about 1602) by Shakespeare.

al·lude (ə lōōd′), *v.i.,* **-luded, -luding. 1.** to make an allusion: refer casually or indirectly (fol. by *to*): *he often alluded to his poverty.* **2.** to contain a casual or indirect reference (fol. by *to*): *the letter alludes to something now forgotten.* [t. L: m.s. *allūdere* play with]

al·lure (ə lōōr′), *v.,* **-lured, -luring,** *n.* —*v.t.* **1.** to attract by the offer of some real or apparent good; tempt by something flattering or acceptable. **2.** to fascinate; charm. —*n.* **3.** fascination; charm. [ME *alure(n),* t. OF: m. *alurer,* f. *a* to + *lurer* LURE] —**al·lur′er,** *n.*

al·lure·ment (ə lōōr′mənt), *n.* **1.** fascination; charm. **2.** the means of alluring. **3.** act or process of alluring.

al·lur·ing (ə lōōr′ĭng), *adj.* **1.** tempting; enticing; seductive. **2.** fascinating; charming. —**al·lur′ing·ly,** *adv.* —**al·lur′ing·ness,** *n.*

al·lu·sion (ə lōō′zhən), *n.* **1.** a passing or casual reference; an incidental mention of something, either directly or by implication: *a classical allusion.* **2.** *Obs.* a metaphor. [t. L: s. *allūsio* playing with]

al·lu·sive (ə lōō′sĭv), *adj.* **1.** having reference to something not fully expressed; containing, full of, or characterized by allusions. **2.** *Archaic.* metaphorical. —**al·lu′sive·ly,** *adv.* —**al·lu′sive·ness,** *n.*

al·lu·vi·al (ə lōō′vĭ əl), *adj.* **1.** of or pertaining to alluvium. —*n.* **2.** alluvial soil. **3.** *Australia.* gold-bearing alluvial soil. [f. s. L *alluvium* ALLUVIUM + -AL¹]

alluvial fan, *Phys. Geog.* a fan-shaped alluvial deposit formed by a stream where its velocity is abruptly decreased, as at the mouth of a ravine or at the foot of a mountain. Also, **alluvial cone.**

al·lu·vi·on (ə lōō′vĭ ən), *n.* **1.** alluvium. **2.** *Law.* gradual increase of land on a shore or a river bank by the recent action or recession of water, whether from natural or artificial causes. **3.** overflow; flood. [t. F, t. L: s. *alluvio* inundation]

al·lu·vi·um (ə lōō′vĭ əm), *n., pl.* **-viums, -via** (-vĭ ə). **1.** a deposit of sand, mud, etc., formed by flowing water. **2.** the sedimentary matter deposited thus within recent times, esp. in the valleys of large rivers. [t. L, neut. of *alluvius* alluvial, washed to]

al·ly (*v.* ə lī′; *n.* ăl′ī, ə lī′), *v.,* **-lied, -lying,** *n., pl.* **-lies.** —*v.t.* **1.** to unite by marriage, treaty, league, or confederacy; connect by formal agreement (fol. by *to* or *with*). **2.** to bind together; connect by some relation, as by resemblance or friendship; associate. —*v.i.* **3.** to enter into an alliance; join or unite. —*n.* **4.** one united or associated with another, esp. by treaty or league; an allied nation, sovereign, etc. **5.** one who helps another or coöperates with him; supporter; associate. [t. F: m. *allier*, g. L *alligāre* bind to; r. ME *alie*(*n*), t. OF: m. *alier*]

al·lyl alcohol (ăl′ĭl), a colorless liquid, C_3H_5OH, whose vapor is very irritating to the eyes.

allyl group or **radical**, *Chem.* a univalent aliphatic radical, C_3H_5, with a double bond. [f. L *all*(*ium*) garlic + -YL] —**al·lyl·ic** (ə lĭl′ĭk), *adj.*

allyl sulfide, *Chem.* a colorless or pale-yellow liquid, $(C_3H_5)_2S$, found in garlic and used medicinally.

Al·ma-A·ta (ăl′mä ä′tä), *n.* a city in the S Soviet Union in Asia: the capital of Kazak Republic. 230,528 (1939). Formerly, **Vyernyi.**

Al·ma·dén (ăl′mä děn′), *n.* a town in S Spain: mercury mines. 13,168 (1940).

Al·ma·gest (ăl′mə jĕst′), *n.* **1.** the famous Greek work on astronomy by Ptolemy. **2.** (*l.c.*) any of various medieval works of a like kind, as on astrology or alchemy. [ME *almageste*, t. OF, ult. t. Ar.: m. *al-majistī*, f. *al* the + m. Gk. *megistē* (*sýntaxis*) greatest (composition)]

al·mah (ăl′mə), *n.* (in Egypt) a professional dancing or singing girl. Also, **al′ma, alme, almeh.** [t. Ar.: m. *'ālima* (fem.) learned]

al·ma ma·ter (ăl′mə mä′tər, ăl′-, ăl′mə mā′tər), (*also cap.*) the school, college, or university in which one has been trained or is being trained. [t. L: fostering mother]

al·ma·nac (ôl′mə năk′), *n.* a calendar of the days of the year, in weeks and months, indicating the time of various events or phenomena during the period, as anniversaries, sunrise and sunset, changes of the moon and tides, etc., or giving other pertinent information. [ME *almenak*, t. ML: m. *almanac, almanach*, t. Sp., t. Ar.: m. *al-manākh* orig. the relative position of the sun and the planets throughout a given year, thence calendar]

al·man·dine (ăl′mən dēn′, -dĭn), *n.* a mineral, iron aluminum garnet, $Fe_3Al_2Si_3O_{12}$, used as a gem and abrasive. [f. ML *almand*(*ina*) (var. of *alabandīna*, der. L *Alabanda*, name of a city in Asia Minor) + -INE[2]]

al·man·dite (ăl′mən dīt′), *n.* almandine.

al-Man·sur (ăl′män sŏŏr′), *n.* (*Abu Djafar Abdallah*) A.D. 712?-775, Eastern calif, A.D. 754-775; founder of Bagdad.

Al·ma-Tad·e·ma (ăl′mə tăd′ə mə), *n.* **Sir Lawrence,** 1836–1912, British painter of Dutch descent.

al·me (ăl′mĕ), *n.* almah. Also, **al′meh.**

Al·me·rí·a (ăl′mĕ rē′ä), *n.* a seaport in S Spain, on the Mediterranean. 79,739 (1940).

al·might·y (ôl mī′tĭ), *adj.* **1.** possessing all power; omnipotent: *God Almighty.* **2.** having unlimited might; overpowering: *the almighty power of the press.* **3.** *U.S. Colloq.* great; extreme: *he's in an almighty fix.* —*n.* **4. the Almighty,** God. [ME; OE *ælmihtig, ealmihtig* all mighty] —**al·might′i·ly,** *adv.* —**al·might′i·ness,** *n.*

almighty dollar, *Colloq.* the power of money.

al·mond (ä′mənd, ăm′ənd), *n.* **1.** the stone (nut) or kernel (sweet or bitter) of the fruit of the almond tree, *Amygdalus Prunus*, which grows in warm temperate regions. **2.** the tree itself. **3.** a delicate, pale tan. **4.** anything shaped like an almond. [ME *almonde*, t. OF: m. *almande, alemande*, g. L *amygdala*, t. Gk.: m. *amygdálē*] —**al′mond·like,** *adj.*

al·mond-eyed (ä′mənd īd′, ăm′ənd-), *adj.* having eyes with a long or narrow oval shape, as some Chinese.

al·mon·er (ăl′mən ər, ä′mən-), *n.* a dispenser of alms or charity, esp. for a religious house, a princely household, etc. [ME *aumoner*, t. OF, g. LL *eleēmosynārius* of alms, der. LL *eleēmosyna* ALMS]

al·mon·ry (ăl′mən rĭ, ä′mən-), *n., pl.* **-ries.** the place where an almoner resides, or where alms are distributed.

al·most (ôl′mōst, ôl mōst′), *adv.* very nearly; all but. [ME; OE *eal mǣst*, var. of *æl mǣst* nearly]

—**Syn.** ALMOST (MOST), NEARLY, WELL-NIGH all mean within a small degree of or short space of. ALMOST implies very little short of: *almost exhausted, almost home.* MOST is colloquial for ALMOST. NEARLY implies a slightly greater distance or degree than ALMOST: *nearly well, nearly to the city.* WELL-NIGH, a more literary word, implies a barely appreciable distance or extent: *well-nigh forgotten, well-nigh home.*

alms (ämz), *n. sing.* or *pl.* that which is given to the poor or needy; anything given as charity. [ME *almes*, OE *ælmysse*, t. LL: m. s. *eleēmosyna*, t. Gk.: m. *eleēmosýnē* compassion, alms]

alms·house (ämz′hous′), *n.* *Brit.* a poorhouse (in U. S. use, only in historical or sentimental contexts).

alms·wom·an (ämz′wŏŏm′ən), *n., pl.* **-women.** a woman supported by alms.

al·muce (ăl′mūs), *n.* **1.** (formerly) a headdress shaped like a cowl. **2.** (later) a fur-lined tippet with a hood. [var. of AMICE[2]]

al·ni·co (ăl′nĭ kō′), *n.* an alloy of iron, nickel, aluminum, and cobalt, used for permanent magnets.

a·lo·di·um (ə lō′dĭ əm), *n., pl.* **-dia** (-dĭ ə). allodium. —**a·lo′di·al,** *adj.*

al·oe (ăl′ō), *n., pl.* **-oes. 1.** any plant of the liliaceous genus *Aloe*, chiefly African, various species of which yield a drug (aloes) and a fiber. **2.** (*often pl. construed as sing.*) a bitter purgative drug, the inspissated juice of several species of *Aloe*. **3.** *U.S.* the century plant (**American aloe**). **4.** (*pl. construed as sing.*) a fragrant resin of wood

(**aloes wood**) from an East Indian tree, *Aquilaria Agallocha*. [ME (usually pl.) *aloen*, OE *aluwan*, t. L: m. *aloē*, t. Gk.] —**al·o·et·ic** (ăl′ō ĕt′ĭk), *adj.*

a·loft (ə lôft′, ə lŏft′), *adv., adj.* **1.** high up; in or into the air; above the ground. **2.** *Naut.* at or toward the masthead; in the upper rigging. [ME, t. Scand.; cf. Icel. *ā lopti* in the air]

a·lo·ha (ə lō′ə, ä lō′hä), *n., interj. Hawaiian.* **1.** greetings. **2.** farewell.

al·o·in (ăl′ō ĭn), *n. Chem.* an intensely bitter, crystalline, purgative substance obtained from aloe.

a·lone (ə lōn′), *adj.* (*used in the pred. or following the noun*). **1.** apart from another or others: *to be alone.* **2.** to the exclusion of all others or all else: *man shall not live by bread alone.* **3. leave alone, a.** to allow (someone) to be by himself. **b.** *Colloq.* to refrain from bothering or interfering with. **4. let alone, a.** to refrain from bothering or interfering with. **b.** not to mention. **5.** *Obs.* unique. —*adv.* **6.** solitarily. **7.** only. [ME *al* one ALL (wholly) ONE] —**a·lone′ness,** *n.*

—**Syn. 1.** ALONE, LONE, LONELY, LONESOME all imply being without companionship or association. ALONE is colorless unless reinforced by *all*; it then suggests solitariness or desolation: *alone in the house, all alone on an island.* LONE is somewhat poetic or is intended humorously: *a lone sentinel, widow.* LONELY implies a sad or disquieting feeling of isolation. LONESOME connotes emotion, a longing for companionship.

a·long[1] (ə lông′, ə lŏng′), *prep.* **1.** implying motion or direction through or by the length of; from one end to the other of: *to walk along a highway.* —*adv.* **2.** by the length; lengthwise; parallel to or in a line with the length: *a row of primroses along by the hedge.* **3.** in a line, or with a progressive motion; onward. **4.** *U.S. Colloq.* (of time) some way on: *along towards evening.* **5.** in company; together (fol. by *with*): *I'll go along with you.* **6.** *U.S.* as a companion; with one: *he took his sister along.* **7. all along, a.** all the time. **b.** throughout. continuously. **c.** from end to end. **d.** at full length. **8. be along,** *Orig. U.S. Colloq.* to come to a place: *he will soon be along.* [ME; OE *andlang*]

a·long[2] (ə lông′, ə lŏng′), *adv. Dial.* owing to; on account of (fol. by *of*). [ME; OE *gelang*]

a·long·shore (ə lông′shôr′, ə lŏng′-), *adv.* by or along the shore or coast.

a·long·side (ə lông′sīd′, ə lŏng′-), *adv.* **1.** along or by the side; at or to the side of anything: *we brought the boat alongside.* —*prep.* **2.** beside; by the side of.

a·loof (ə lŏŏf′), *adv.* **1.** at a distance, but within view; withdrawn: *to stand aloof.* —*adj.* **2.** reserved; unsympathetic; disinterested. [f. A-[1] + *loof* LUFF, windward] —**a·loof′ly,** *adv.* —**a·loof′ness,** *n.* —**Ant. 1.** near.

al·o·pe·ci·a (ăl′ə pē′shĭ ə), *n. Pathol.* loss of hair; baldness. [t. L, t. Gk.: m. *alōpekía* mange of foxes]

A·lost (ä lôst′), *n.* a city in central Belgium, NW of Brussels. 41,451 (est. 1944). Flemish, **Aalst.**

a·loud (ə loud′), *adv.* **1.** with the natural tone of the voice as distinguished from whispering: *to read aloud.* **2.** with a loud voice; loudly: *to cry aloud.*

a·low (ə lō′), *adv. Archaic* or *Naut.* low down; below.

alp (ălp), *n.* **1.** a high mountain. **2. the Alps.** See **Alps.** [t. L: s. *Alpēs*, pl., the Alps; ? from Celtic]

al·pac·a (ăl păk′ə), *n.* **1.** a domesticated sheeplike South American ruminant of the genus *Lama* allied to the llama and the guanaco, having long, soft, silky hair or wool. **2.** the hair. **3.** a fabric made of it. **4.** a glossy, wiry, commonly black woolen fabric with cotton warp. **5.** a rayon and alpaca crepe, with a viscose and acetate rayon warp. [t. Sp., from *paco*, Peruv. animal name (to which the Ar. article, *al*, has been prefixed)]

Alpaca. *Lama pacos* (5 ft. high)

al·pen·glow (ăl′pən glō′), *n.* a reddish glow often seen on the summits of mountains before sunrise and after sunset. [trans. of G *alpenglühen*]

al·pen·horn (ăl′pən hôrn′), *n.* a long, powerful horn of wood or bark used in the Alps, as by cowherds. Also, **alphorn.** [t. G]

al·pen·stock (ăl′pən stŏk′), *n.* a strong staff pointed with iron, used by mountain climbers. [t. G]

al·pes·trine (ăl pĕs′trĭn), *adj.* **1.** alpine. **2.** *Bot.* subalpine (def. 2). [f. s. ML *alpestris* (der. L *Alpēs* Alps) + -INE[1]]

al·pha (ăl′fə), *n.* **1.** the first letter in the Greek alphabet (A, α), corresponding to A. **2.** the first; beginning. **3.** *Astron.* a star, usually the brightest of a constellation. **4.** *Chem.* (of a compound) one of the possible positions of substituted atoms or groups.

alpha and omega, beginning and end. Rev. 1:8.

al·pha·bet (ăl′fə bĕt′), *n.* **1.** the letters of a language in their customary order. **2.** any system of characters or signs for representing sounds or ideas. **3.** first elements: simplest rudiments: *the alphabet of radio.* [t. L: s. *alphabētum*, t. Gk.: m. *alphábētos*, f. *álpha* A + m. *bēta* B]

al·pha·bet·i·cal (ăl′fə bĕt′ə kəl), *adj.* **1.** in the order of the alphabet: *alphabetical arrangement.* **2.** pertaining to an alphabet; expressed in an alphabet: *alphabetical writing.* Also, **al′pha·bet′ic.** —**al′pha·bet′i·cal·ly,** *adv.*

---

b., blend of, blended; c., cognate with; d., dialect, dialectal; der., derived from; f., formed from; g., going back to; m., modification of; r., replacing; s., stem of; t., taken from; ?, perhaps. See the full key on inside cover.

al·pha·bet·ize (ăl′fə bə tīz′), *v.t.*, **-ized, -izing. 1.** to arrange in the order of the alphabet: *to alphabetize a list of names.* **2.** to express by an alphabet. —**al·pha·bet·i·za·tion** (ăl′fə bĕt′ə zā′shən), *n.* —**al′pha·bet·iz′er,** *n.*

alpha particle, *Physics.* a positively charged particle composed of two protons and two neutrons (and therefore equivalent to the nucleus of a helium atom) and spontaneously emitted by some radioactive material such as radium.

alpha ray, *Physics.* a stream of alpha particles.

alpha test, a psychological test measuring learning ability for those able to read and write, used by the U.S. Army in World War I.

Al·phe·us (ăl fē′əs), *n. Gk. Myth.* a river god, son of Oceanus and Tethys, who fell in love with the nymph Arethusa and, when she became a fountain to escape him, changed into a river and mingled with her.

alp·horn (ălp′hôrn′), *n.* alpenhorn.

al·pho·sis (ăl fō′sĭs), *n. Pathol.* lack of pigment in the skin, as in albinism. [f. s. Gk. *alphós* kind of leprosy + -OSIS]

Al·pine (ăl′pīn, -pĭn), *adj.* **1.** of or pertaining to any lofty mountain. **2.** very high; elevated. **3.** (*cap.*) of or pertaining to the Alps. **4.** *Bot.* growing on mountains, above the limit of tree growth. [t. L: m. s. *Alpīnus,* der. *Alpēs* the Alps]

alpine garden, a rock garden.

Al·pin·ism (ăl′pənĭz′əm), *n.* mountain climbing, esp. in the Alps. —**Al′pin·ist,** *n.*

Alps (ălps), *n.* a mountain system in S Europe, extending from France through Switzerland and Italy into Austria and Yugoslavia. Highest peak, Mt. Blanc, 15,781 ft. [see ALP]

al·read·y (ôl rĕd′ĭ), *adv.* by this (or that) time; previously to or at some specified time. [ME *al redy* all ready. See ALL, READY]

al·right (ôl rīt′), *adv.* all right (not generally regarded as good usage).

Al·sace (ăl sās′, ăl′săs; *Fr.* ál zás′), *n.* a region in NE France between the Vosges Mountains and the Rhine: a former province.

Al·sace-Lor·raine (ăl′săs lō-rān′, -săs; *Fr.* ál zás lô rĕn′), *n.* a region in NE France, including the former provinces of Alsace and Lorraine: a part of Germany, 1871–1919 and 1940–44. 1,915,-600 pop. (1936); 5607 sq. mi.

Al·sa·tia (ăl sā′shə), *n.* a district in central London, England, once a sanctuary for debtors and lawbreakers: formerly called Whitefriars. [t. ML. Latinization of G *Elsass,* lit., foreign settlement]

Al·sa·tian (ăl sā′shən), *adj.* **1.** of or pertaining to Alsace. **2.** of or pertaining to Alsatia. —*n.* **3.** a native or inhabitant of Alsace. **4.** an inhabitant of Alsatia (Whitefriars).

Al·sib (ăl′sĭb), *n.* the route for air travel between Montana and Moscow, which lies across Alaska and Siberia.

al·sike (ăl′sīk, -sĭk, ôl′-), *n.* a European clover, *Trifolium hybridum,* with whitish or pink flowers, much grown in the U.S. for forage. Also, **alsike clover.** [named after *Alsike,* in Sweden]

al·si·na·ceous (ăl′sə nā′shəs), *adj. Bot.* **1.** caryophyllaceous. **2.** relating to or resembling the chickweed. [f. Gk. *alsīn(ē)* + -ACEOUS]

Al Si·rat (ăl sĭ′rät′), *Mohammedanism.* **1.** the correct path of religion. **2.** the bridge, fine as a razor's edge, over which all who enter paradise must pass. [t. Ar.: m. *al-ṣirāṭ* the road, from L (*via*) *strata* paved (road). Cf. STREET]

al·so (ôl′sō), *adv.* in addition; too; further. [ME; OE *alswā, ealswā* all (wholly or quite) so] —**Syn.** likewise, besides, moreover.

alt (ălt), *adj. Music.* **1.** high. —*n.* **2. in alt,** in the first octave above the treble staff. [t. It.: s. *alto* high]

alt-, var. of **alto-** before vowels, as in *altazimuth.*

alt., 1. alternate. **2.** altitude. **3.** alto.

Alta., Alberta (Canada).

Al·ta·ic (ăl tā′ĭk), *n.* a group of languages made up of the Turkish, Manchurian, and Mongolian families.

Al·tai Mountains (ăl tī′, ăl-), a mountain system in central Asia, mostly in the Mongolian People's Republic and the S Soviet Union in Asia. Highest peak, Belukha, 14,890 ft.

Al·ta·ir (ăl tä′ĭr), *n.* a star of the first magnitude in the constellation Aquila. [t. Ar.: m. *al-ṭā′ir* the bird]

Al·ta·mi·ra (ăl′tä mē′rä), *n.* a cave in N Spain, near Santander: Old Stone Age color drawings of animals.

al·tar (ôl′tər), *n.* **1.** an elevated place or structure, on which sacrifices are offered or at which religious rites are performed. **2.** (in most Christian churches) the communion table. **3. lead to the altar,** to marry. [ME *alter,* OE *altar(e),* t. LL. Cf. L *altāria,* pl., high altar]

altar boy, acolyte (def. 2).

al·tar·piece (ôl′tər pēs′), *n.* a decorative screenlike piece behind and above an altar; a reredos.

alt·az·i·muth (ăl tăz′ə məth), *n.* a mounting of telescopes or transits which provides two axes, one horizontal and one vertical, so that the instrument may be turned in the plane of the horizon and in any vertical plane. Altazimuths are used to determine altitudes and azimuths of heavenly bodies. [f. ALT- + AZIMUTH]

Alt·dorf (ält′dôrf), *n.* a town in central Switzerland: the legendary home of William Tell. 4240 (1930).

al·ter (ôl′tər), *v.t.* **1.** to make different in some particular; modify. **2.** *Colloq.* to castrate or spay. —*v.i.* **3.** to become different in some respect. [t. F: s. *altérer,* ult. der. L *alter* other] —**Syn. 1.** See **adjust** and **change.**

alter., alteration.

al·ter·a·ble (ôl′tər ə bəl), *adj.* capable of being altered. —**al′ter·a·bil′i·ty, al′ter·a·ble·ness,** *n.* —**al′ter·a·bly,** *adv.*

al·ter·ant (ôl′tər ənt), *adj.* **1.** producing alteration. —*n.* **2.** something that causes alteration.

al·ter·a·tion (ôl′tə rā′shən), *n.* **1.** act of altering. **2.** condition of being altered. **3.** a change; modification.

al·ter·a·tive (ôl′tə rā′tĭv), *adj.* **1.** tending to alter. **2.** *Med.* gradually restoring healthy bodily functions. —*n.* **3.** *Med.* an alterative remedy.

al·ter·cate (ôl′tər kāt′, ăl′-), *v.i.,* **-cated, -cating.** to argue with zeal, heat, or anger; wrangle. [t. L: m. s. *altercātus,* pp., having wrangled]

al·ter·ca·tion (ôl′tər kā′shən, ăl′-), *n.* a heated or angry dispute; a noisy wrangle.

altered chord, *Music.* a chord in which at least one tone has been changed from its normal pitch in the key.

al·ter e·go (ăl′tər ē′gō, ĕg′ō), *Latin.* **1.** a second self. **2.** an inseparable friend. [L: lit., another I]

al·ter i·dem (ăl′tər ī′dĕm), *Latin.* another exactly similar.

al·ter·nant (ôl tûr′nənt, ăl-), *adj.* alternating. [t. L: s. *alternans,* ppr.]

al·ter·nate (*v.* ôl′tər nāt′, ăl′-; *adj., n.* ôl′tər nĭt, ăl′-), *v.,* **-nated, -nating,** *adj., n.* —*v.i.* **1.** to follow one another in time or place reciprocally (usually fol. by *with*): *day and night alternate with each other.* **2.** to change about by turns between points, states, actions, etc.: *he alternates between hope and despair.* **3.** *Elect.* to reverse direction or sign periodically. —*v.t.* **4.** to perform by turns, or one after another. **5.** to interchange successively: *to alternate hot and cold compresses.* —*adj.* **6.** being by turns; following each the other, recurringly; in succession: *alternate winter and summer.* **7.** reciprocal: *alternate acts of kindness.* **8.** every other one of a series: *read only the alternate lines.* **9.** *Bot.* **a.** (of leaves, etc.) placed singly at different heights on the axis, on each side alternately, or at definite angular distances from one another. **b.** opposite to the intervals between other organs: *petals alternate with sepals.* —*n.* **10.** *U.S.* a person authorized to take the place of and act for another in his absence; substitute. [t. L: m.s. *alternātus*] —**al′ter·nate·ness,** *n.* —**Ant. 6.** successive.

alternate angles, *Geom.* two nonadjacent angles made by the crossing of two lines by a third line, both angles being either interior or exterior, and being on opposite sides of the third line.

al·ter·nate·ly (ôl′tər nĭt lĭ, ăl′-), *adv.* **1.** in alternate order; by turns. **2.** in alternate position.

alternating current, *Elect.* a current that reverses direction in regular cycles.

al·ter·na·tion (ôl′tər nā′shən, ăl′-), *n.* alternate succession; appearance, occurrence, or change by turns.

alternation of generations, *Biol.* an alternating in a line of reproduction, between generations unlike and generations like a given progenitor, esp. the alternation of asexual with sexual reproduction.

al·ter·na·tive (ôl tûr′nə tĭv, ăl-), *n.* **1.** a possibility of one out of two (or, less strictly, more) things: *the alternative of remaining neutral or attacking.* **2.** one of the things thus possible: *they chose the alternative of attacking.* **3.** a remaining course or choice: *we had no alternative but to move.* —*adj.* **4.** affording a choice between two things, or a possibility of one thing out of two. **5.** (of two things) mutually exclusive, so that if one is chosen the other must be rejected: *alternative results of this or that course.* **6.** *Logic.* (of a proposition) asserting two or more alternatives, at least one of which is true. [t. ML: m. s. *alternātīvus*] —**al·ter′na·tive·ly,** *adv.* —**al·ter′na·tive·ness,** *n.* —**Syn. 1.** option, selection. See **choice.**

al·ter·na·tor (ôl′tər nā′tər, ăl′-), *n. Elect.* a generator of alternating current.

Alt·geld (ält′gĕld), *n.* **John Peter,** 1847–1902, governor of Illinois, 1892–96.

al·the·a (ăl thē′ə), *n.* **1.** any plant of of the genus *Althaea.* **2.** a malvaceous flowering garden shrub, *Hibiscus syriacus;* the rose of Sharon. **3.** (*cap.*) *Gk. Legend.* the mother of Meleager. Also, **al·thae′a.** [t. L, t. Gk.: m. *althaía* wild mallow]

alt·horn (ălt′hôrn′), *n.* a valved, brass-wind horn, a fourth or fifth below the ordinary cornet; a tenor saxhorn. Also, **alto horn.**

al·though (ôl thō′), *conj.* even though (practically equivalent to *though,* and preferred to it only for euphonic or metrical reasons). Also, **al·tho′**. [ME, f. *al* even + THOUGH. See ALL, adv.] —**Syn.** though, notwithstanding (that), even if.

al·tim·e·ter (ăl·tĭm′ə·tər, ăl′tə·mē′tər), *n.* **1.** a sensitive aneroid barometer used to measure altitudes, and graduated and calibrated accordingly, used in aircraft for finding distance above sea level, terrain, or some other reference point, by means of air pressure. **2.** any device used for the same purpose which operates by some other means, as by radio waves, etc. [f. ALTI- + METER]

al·tim·e·try (ăl·tĭm′ə·trĭ), *n.* the art of measuring altitudes, as with an altimeter.

al·tis·si·mo (ăl·tĭs′ə·mō′; *It.* äl·tēs′sē·mō′), *Music.* —*adj.* **1.** very high. —*n.* **2. in altissimo,** in the second octave above the treble staff. [It.]

al·ti·tude (ăl′tə·tūd′, -tōōd′), *n.* **1.** the height above sea level of any point on the earth's surface or in the atmosphere. **2.** extent or distance upward. **3.** *Astron.* the angular distance of a star, planet, etc., above the horizon. **4.** *Geom.* **a.** the perpendicular distance from the base of a figure to its highest point. **b.** the line through the highest point of a figure perpendicular to the base. **5.** a high point or region: *mountain altitudes.* **6.** high or exalted position, rank, etc. [ME, t. L: m. *altitūdo* height] —**Syn. 2.** See **height.** —**Ant. 2.** depth.

al·ti·tu·di·nal (ăl′tə·tū′də·nəl, -tōō′-), *adj.* relating to height.

al·to (ăl′tō), *n., pl.* **-tos,** *adj.* —*n. Music.* **1.** the lowest female voice; contralto. **2.** the highest male voice; countertenor. **3.** a singer with an alto voice. **4.** a musical part for an alto voice. **5.** the viola. **6.** an althorn. —*adj.* **7.** *Music.* of the alto; having the compass of the alto. **8.** high. [t. It., g. L *altus* high]

alto-, a word element meaning "high," as in *alto-stratus.* Also, **alt-, alti-.** [comb. form repr. L *altus*]

alto clef, *Music.* a sign locating middle C on the third line of the staff.

al·to·cu·mu·lus (ăl′tō·kū′myə·ləs), *n. Meteorol.* a cloud type consisting of globular masses or patches, more or less in a layer, somewhat darker underneath and larger than cirro-cumulus.

al·to·geth·er (ôl′tə·gĕ′th·ər), *adv.* **1.** wholly; entirely; completely; quite: *altogether bad.* **2.** in all: *the debt amounted altogether to twenty dollars.* **3.** on the whole: *altogether, I'm glad it's over.* —*n.* **4.** a whole. [var. of ME *altogeder*, f. *al* ALL, adj. + *togeder* TOGETHER]

alto horn, althorn.

Al·ton (ôl′tən), *n.* a city in SW Illinois. 32,550 (1950).

Al·to·na (äl′tō·nä), *n.* a city in N Germany, on the Elbe near Hamburg. 241,970 (1933).

Al·too·na (ăl·tōō′nə), *n.* a city in central Pennsylvania. 77,177 (1950).

al·to·re·lie·vo (ăl′tō·rĭ·lē′vō), *n., pl.* **-vos.** sculpture in high relief, in which at least one half the figures project from the background. [t. It.: m. *alto rilievo*]

al·to·ri·lie·vo (äl′tō·rē·lyĕ′vō), *n., pl.* **alti-rilievi** (äl′tē·rē·lyĕ′vē). Italian. alto-relievo.

al·to·stra·tus (ăl′tō·strā′təs), *n. Meteorol.* a moderately high, veillike or sheetlike cloud, without definite configurations, more or less gray or bluish.

al·tri·cial (ăl·trĭsh′əl), *adj. Ornith.* confined to the nesting place for a period after hatching. [t. NL: s. *altrīciālis*, der. L *altrix* nurse]

al·tru·ism (ăl′trŏŏ·Ĭz′əm), *n.* the principle or practice of seeking the welfare of others (opposed to *egoism*). [t. F: m. *altruisme*, der. It. *altrui* of or to others]

al·tru·ist (ăl′trŏŏ·Ĭst), *n.* a person devoted to the welfare of others (opposed to *egoist*).

al·tru·is·tic (ăl′trŏŏ·Ĭs′tĭk), *adj.* regardful of others; having regard to the well-being or best interests of others (opposed to *egoistic*). —**al′tru·is′ti·cal·ly,** *adv.*

al·u·la (ăl′yə·lə), *n., pl.* **-lae** (-lē′). *Ornith.* the group of 3 to 6 small, rather stiff, feathers growing on the first digit, pollex, or thumb of a bird's wing. [t. NL, dim. of L *āla* wing] —**al′u·lar,** *adj.*

al·um (ăl′əm), *n.* **1.** an astringent crystalline substance, a double sulfate of aluminum and potassium, $K_2SO_4·Al_2(SO_4)_3·24H_2O$, used in medicine, dyeing, and many technical processes. **2.** one of a class of double sulfates analogous to the potassium alum, having the general formula $R_2SO_4·X_2(SO_4)_3·24H_2O$, where R is a monovalent alkali metal or ammonium, and X one of a number of trivalent metals. **3.** *Obsolesc.* aluminum sulfate, $Al_2(SO_4)_3$. [ME, t. OF, g. L *alūmen*]

a·lu·mi·na (ə·lōō′mə·nə), *n.* **1.** *Mineral.* the oxide of aluminum, Al_2O_3, occurring widely in nature as corundum (in the ruby and sapphire, emery, etc.). **2.** *Obsolesc.* aluminum. [t. NL, der. L *alūmen* alum]

a·lu·mi·nate (ə·lōō′mə·nāt′), *n.* **1.** *Chem.* a salt of the acid form of aluminum hydroxide. **2.** *Mineral.* a metallic oxide combined with alumina.

a·lu·mi·nif·er·ous (ə·lōō′mə·nĭf′ər·əs), *adj.* containing or yielding aluminum.

al·u·min·i·um (ăl′yə·mĭn′Ĭ·əm), *n. Brit.* aluminum.

a·lu·mi·nize (ə·lōō′mə·nīz′), *v.t.,* **-nized, -nizing.** to treat with aluminum.

a·lu·mi·no·ther·my (ə·lōō′mə·nō·thûr′mĭ), *n. Metall.* a process of producing high temperatures by causing finely divided aluminum to react with the oxygen from another metallic oxide. Also, **a·lu′mi·no·ther′mics.** [f. *alumino*- (comb. form of ALUMINUM) + -THERMY]

a·lu·mi·nous (ə·lōō′mə·nəs), *adj.* of the nature of or containing alum or alumina. [t. L: m. s. *alūminōsus*]

a·lu·mi·num (ə·lōō′mə·nəm), *n.* Also, *Brit.,* **aluminium. 1.** a silver-white metallic element, light in weight, ductile, malleable, and not readily oxidized or tarnished, occurring combined in nature in igneous rocks, shales, clays, and most soils. It is much used in alloys and for lightweight utensils, castings, airplane parts, etc. *Symbol:* Al; *at. wt.:* 26.97; *at. no.:* 13; *sp. gr.:* 2.70 at 20°C. —*adj.* **2.** belonging to or containing aluminum. [t. NL, der. L *alūmen* alum]

a·lum·na (ə·lŭm′nə), *n., pl.* **-nae** (-nē). *Chiefly U.S.* fem. of **alumnus.**

a·lum·nus (ə·lŭm′nəs), *n., pl.* **-ni** (-nī). a graduate or former student of a school, college, university, etc. [t. L: foster child, pupil]

al·um·root (ăl′əm·rōōt′, -rŏŏt′), *n.* **1.** any of several plants of the saxifragaceous genus *Heuchera,* with astringent roots, esp. *H. americana.* **2.** the root.

a·lu·nite (ăl′yə·nīt′), *n.* a mineral, a hydrous sulfate of potassium and aluminum, $KAl_3(SO_4)_2(OH)_6$, commonly occurring in fine-grained masses. [f. F *alun* alum + -ITE¹]

Al·va (ăl′və; *Sp.* äl′vä), *n.* **Fernando Álvarez de Toledo** (fĕr·nän′dō äl′vä·rĕth′ dĕ tō·lě′dō), **Duke of,** 1508–82, Spanish general who ruthlessly suppressed a Protestant rebellion in the Netherlands in 1567. Also, **Alba.**

Al·va·ra·do (ăl′vä·rä′dō), *n.* **1. Alonso de** (ä·lôn′sō dě), died 1553?, Spanish soldier in conquests of Mexico and Peru. **2. Pedro de** (pě′drō dě), 1495?–1541, Spanish soldier: chief aide of Cortez in conquest of Mexico.

Ál·va·rez Quin·te·ro (ăl′vä·rĕth′ kēn·tě′rō), **Joaquín** (hwä·kēn′), 1873–1944, and his brother **Serafín** (sě·rä·fēn′), 1871–1938, Spanish dramatists.

al·ve·o·lar (ăl·vē′ə·lər), *adj.* **1.** *Anat., Zool.* pertaining to an alveolus or to alveoli. **2.** *Phonet.* with the tongue touching or near the alveolar ridge.

alveolar arch, that part of the upper jawbone in which the teeth are set.

alveolar ridge, the ridgelike inward projection of the gums between the hard palate and the upper front teeth.

al·ve·o·late (ăl·vē′ə·lĭt, -lāt′), *adj.* having alveoli; deeply pitted, as a honeycomb. Also, **al·ve′o·lat′ed.** —**al·ve′o·la′tion,** *n.*

al·ve·o·lus (ăl·vē′ə·ləs), *n., pl.* **-li** (-lī′). *Anat., Zool.* **1.** a little cavity, pit, or cell, as a cell of a honeycomb. **2.** an air cell of the lungs, formed by the terminal dilation of tiny air passageways. **3.** one of the terminal secretory units of a racemose gland. **4.** the socket which the jawbone in which the root or roots of a tooth are set. **5.** (*pl.*) alveolar ridge. [t. L, dim. of *alveus* a hollow]

al·vine (ăl′vĭn, -vīn), *adj. Med.* pertaining to the belly; intestinal. [t. L: m. s. *alvīnus,* der. *alvus* belly]

al·way (ôl′wā), *adv. Archaic or Poetic.* always. [ME; OE *ealneweg,* orig. *ealne weg.* See ALL, WAY]

al·ways (ôl′wāz, -wĭz), *adv.* **1.** all the time; uninterruptedly. **2.** every time; on every occasion (opposed to *sometimes* or *occasionally*): *he always works on Saturday.* [ME, f. ALWAY + adv. gen. suffix -(e)s] —**Syn. 1.** perpetually, everlastingly, forever, continually. Both ALWAYS and EVER refer to uniform or perpetual continuance. ALWAYS often expresses or implies repetition as producing the uniformity or continuance: *the sun always rises in the east.* EVER implies an unchanging sameness throughout: *natural law is ever to be reckoned with.*

a·lys·sum (ə·lĭs′əm), *n.* **1.** any of the herbs constituting the brassicaceous genus *Alyssum,* characterized by small yellow or white racemose flowers. **2.** sweet alyssum. [t. NL, t. Gk.: m. *álysson* name of a plant, lit., curing (canine) madness]

am (ăm; *unstressed* əm, m), *v.* 1st pers. sing. pres. indic. of *be.* [OE *am, eam,* var. of *eom,* c. Icel. *em,* Goth. *im.* Cf. Irish *am,* Gk. *eimí*]

Am, *Chem.* americium.

Am., **1.** America. **2.** American.

A.M., **1.** (L *ante meridiem*) before noon. **2.** the period from 12 midnight to 12 noon. Also, **a.m.**

A.M., amplitude modulation. Also, **AM**

A.M., (L *Artium Magister*) Master of Arts. Also, **M.A.**

A.M.A., American Medical Association.

am·a·da·vat (ăm′ə·də·văt′), *n.* a small finchlike East Indian bird, *Estrilda amandava,* exported as a cage bird. [East Indian]

am·a·dou (ăm′ə·dōō′), *n.* a spongy substance prepared from fungi (*Polyporus (Fomes) fomentarius* and allied species) growing on trees, used as tinder and in surgery. [t. F]

A·ma·ga·sa·ki (ä′mä·gä·sä′kē), *n.* a city in S Japan, on Honshu island, near Osaka. 172,567 (1946).

a·mah (ä′mə, ăm′ə), *n.* (used among Europeans in India and the Orient) **1.** a nurse, esp. a wet nurse. **2.** a maidservant. [Anglo-Indian, t. Pg.: m. *ama*]

a·main (ə·mān′), *adv. Archaic and Poetic.* **1.** with full force. **2.** at full speed. **3.** suddenly; hastily. **4.** exceedingly; greatly. [f. A-¹ + MAIN¹]

a·mal·gam (ə·măl′gəm), *n.* **1.** an alloy of mercury with another metal or metals. **2.** a rare mineral, an alloy of silver and mercury, occurring as silver-white crystals or grains. **3.** a mixture or combination. [ME, t. ML: s. *amalgama,* appar. m. L *malagma,* poultice, t. Gk.]

a·mal·gam·ate (ə măl′gə māt′), v., -ated, -ating. —v.t. 1. to mix so as to make a combination; blend; unite; combine: to amalgamate two companies. 2. Metall. to mix or alloy (a metal) with mercury. —v.i. 3. to combine, unite, or coalesce. 4. to blend with another metal, as mercury. —a·mal′gam·a·ble, adj. —a·mal′gam·a′tive, adj. —a·mal′gam·a′tor, n.

a·mal·gam·a·tion (ə măl′gə mā′shən), n. 1. act of amalgamating. 2. the resulting state. 3. Com. a consolidation of two or more corporations. 4. Ethnol. the biological fusion of diverse racial stocks. 5. Metall. the extraction of the precious metals from their ores by treatment with mercury.

Am·al·thae·a (ăm′əl thē′ə), n. Gk. Myth. 1. a nymph who nursed Zeus on a goat's milk. 2. the goat itself. Also, **Am′al·the′a.**

am·a·ni·ta (ăm′ə nī′tə), n. Bot. any fungus of the agaricaceous genus Amanita, comprised chiefly of poisonous species. [t. NL, t. Gk.: m. amanīta, pl., kind of fungi]

a·man·u·en·sis (ə măn′yŏŏ ĕn′sĭs), n., pl. -ses (-sēz). a person employed to write what another dictates or to copy what has been written by another; secretary. [t. L: secretary, orig. adj., f. (servus) ā manū secretary + -ensis belonging to]

am·a·ranth (ăm′ə rănth′), n. 1. Poetic. a flower that never fades. 2. any plant of the genus Amaranthus, which includes species cultivated for their showy flowers, as the love-lies-bleeding, or their colored foliage (green, purple, etc.). 3. a purplish-red azo dye used to color foods. [var. (by assoc. with Gk. ănthos flower) of amarant, t. L: s. amarantus, t. Gk.: m. amárantos unfading]

am·a·ran·tha·ceous (ăm′ə răn thā′shəs), adj. Bot. belonging to the family Amaranthaceae (or Amarantaceae), comprising mostly herbaceous or shrubby plants, as the cockscomb, the pigweed, the amaranth, etc.

am·a·ran·thine (ăm′ə răn′thĭn, -thīn), adj. 1. of or like the amaranth. 2. unfading; everlasting. 3. purplish.

am·a·relle (ăm′ə rĕl′), n. any variety of the sour cherry, Prunus Cerasus, with colorless juice.

Am·a·ril·lo (ăm′ə rĭl′ō), n. a city in NW Texas. 74,246 (1950).

am·a·ryl·li·da·ceous (ăm′ə rĭl′ə dā′shəs), adj. Bot. belonging to the Amaryllidaceae, or amaryllis family of plants, which includes the amaryllis, narcissus, snowdrop, agave, etc.

am·a·ryl·lis (ăm′ə rĭl′ĭs), n. 1. a bulbous plant, Amaryllis Belladonna, the belladonna lily, with large, lilylike, normally rose-colored flowers. 2. any of several related plants once referred to the genus Amaryllis. 3. (cap.) a shepherdess or country girl (in classical and later pastoral poetry). [t. L, t. Gk. (def. 3)]

Amaryllis, Amaryllis Belladonna

a·mass (ə măs′), v.t. 1. to gather for oneself; collect as one's own: to amass a fortune. 2. to collect into a mass or pile; bring together. [t. F: s. amasser, der. masse mass, g. L massa lump (of dough, etc.).] —a·mass′a·ble, adj. —a·mass′er, n. —a·mass′ment, n.

am·a·teur (ăm′ə chŏŏr′, -tyŏŏr′; ăm′ə tûr′), n. 1. one who cultivates any study or art or other activity for personal pleasure instead of professionally or for gain. 2. an athlete who has never competed for money. 3. a superficial or unskillful worker; dabbler. 4. one who admires. [t. F, t. L: m.s. amātor lover] —am′a·teur·ship′, n. —Syn. 3. dilettante, tyro, novice.

am·a·teur·ish (ăm′ə chŏŏr′ĭsh, -tyŏŏr′-, -tûr′-), adj. characteristic of an amateur; having the faults or deficiencies of an amateur. —am′a·teur′ish·ly, adv. —am′a·teur′ish·ness, n.

am·a·teur·ism (ăm′ə chŏŏ rĭz′əm, -tyŏŏ-, ăm′ə tûr′ĭz əm), n. the practice or character of an amateur.

A·ma·ti (ä mä′tē), n. 1. the name of a famous family of violinmakers of Cremona, Italy, who flourished in the 16th and 17th centuries. 2. a violin made by a member of this family. 3. **Nicolò** (nē′kô lô′), 1596–1684, Italian violinmaker: teacher of Antonio Stradivari.

am·a·tive (ăm′ə tĭv), adj. disposed to loving; amorous. [f. s. L amātus, pp., loved + -ive] —am′a·tive·ly, adv. —am′a·tive·ness, n.

am·a·tol (ăm′ə tŏl′, -tōl′), n. an explosive mixture of ammonium nitrate and TNT.

am·a·to·ry (ăm′ə tōr′ĭ), adj. pertaining to lovers or lovemaking; expressive of love: amatory poems, an amatory look. Also, **am′a·to′ri·al.** [t. L: m.s. amātōrius.]

am·au·ro·sis (ăm′ô rō′sĭs), n. partial or total loss of sight. [NL, t. Gk., der. amaurós dim] —am·au·rot·ic (ăm′ô rŏt′ĭk), adj.

a·maze (ə māz′), v., amazed, amazing, n. —v.t. 1. to overwhelm with surprise; astonish greatly. 2. Obs. to bewilder. —n. 3. Archaic. amazement. [OE āmasian. Cf. MAZE] —a·maz·ed·ly (ə mā′zĭd lĭ), adv. —a·maz′ed·ness, n. —Syn. 1. astound, dumfound. See surprise.

a·maze·ment (ə māz′mənt), n. 1. overwhelming surprise or astonishment. 2. Obs. stupefaction. 3. Obs. perplexity. 4. Obs. consternation.

a·maz·ing (ə mā′zĭng), adj. causing great surprise; wonderful. —a·maz′ing·ly, adv.

Am·a·zon (ăm′ə zŏn′, -zən), n. 1. a river in N South America, flowing from the Peruvian Andes E through N Brazil to the Atlantic: the largest river in the world.

ab. 3500 mi. 2. Gk. Legend. one of a race of female warriors said to dwell near the Black Sea. 3. one of a fabled tribe of female warriors in South America. 4. (often l.c.) a tall, powerful, aggressive woman. [ME, t. L, t. Gk.; orig. uncert.; the name of the river refers to female warriors seen in its vicinity]

Amazon ant, a species of red ant, Polyergus rufescens, that steals and enslaves the young of other species.

Am·a·zo·ni·an (ăm′ə zō′nĭ ən), adj. 1. characteristic of an Amazon; warlike; masculine. 2. pertaining to the Amazon river or the country adjacent to it.

am·a·zon·ite (ăm′ə zən īt′), n. Mineral. a green feldspar, a variety of microcline, used as an ornamental material. Also, **Amazon stone.** [f. Amazon river + -ITE[1]]

am·ba·ges (ăm bā′jēz), n.pl. winding or roundabout ways. [t. L: circuits]

am·ba·gious (ăm bā′jəs), adj. roundabout. —**am·ba′gious·ly,** adv. —**am·ba′gious·ness,** n.

Am·ba·la (əm bä′lə), n. a city in N India, in E Punjab. 62,419 (1941).

am·ba·ry (ăm bär′ĭ), n. 1. an East Indian plant, Hibiscus cannabinus, yielding a useful fiber. 2. the fiber itself. Also, **am·ba′ri.** [t. Hind.]

am·bas·sa·dor (ăm băs′ə dər), n. 1. a diplomatic agent of the highest rank, sent by one sovereign or state to another either as resident representative (**ambassador extraordinary and plenipotentiary**) or on temporary special service. 2. an authorized messenger or representative. Also, **embassador.** [ME ambassadour, t. F: m. ambassadeur, t. It.: m. ambasciatore; prob. of Celtic orig.] —**am·bas·sa·do·ri·al** (ăm băs′ə dōr′ĭ əl), adj. —**am·bas′sa·dor·ship′,** n.

am·bas·sa·dress (ăm băs′ə drĭs), n. 1. a female ambassador. 2. the wife of an ambassador.

am·ber (ăm′bər), n. 1. a pale-yellow, sometimes reddish or brownish, fossil resin of vegetable origin, translucent, brittle, and capable of gaining a negative electrical charge by friction. 2. the yellowish-brown color of resin. —adj. 3. of amber; like amber. [ME ambra, t. ML t. Ar.: m. 'anbar ambergris]

am·ber·gris (ăm′bər grēs′, -grĭs), n. an opaque, ashcolored substance, a morbid secretion of the sperm whale, fragrant when heated, usually found floating on the ocean or cast ashore, used chiefly in perfumery. [late ME imbergres, t. F: m. ambre gris gray amber]

am·ber·oid (ăm′bə roid′), n. synthetic amber made by compressing pieces of various resins, esp. amber, at a high temperature. Also, **ambroid.**

ambi-, a word element meaning "both," "around," "on both sides," as in ambidextrous. [comb. form repr. L ambi- around, or ambo both]

am·bi·dex·ter (ăm′bə dĕk′stər), n. 1. using both hands with equal facility. 2. double-dealing. —n. 3. a person who uses both hands equally well. 4. a double-dealer. [t. ML, f. ambi- AMBI- + dexter right] —**am′bi·dex′tral,** adj.

am·bi·dex·ter·i·ty (ăm′bə dĕk stĕr′ə tĭ), n. 1. ambidextrous facility. 2. unusual cleverness. 3. duplicity.

am·bi·dex·trous (ăm′bə dĕk′strəs), adj. 1. able to use both hands equally well. 2. unusually skillful; facile. 3. double-dealing; deceitful. —**am′bi·dex′trous·ly,** adv. —**am′bi·dex′trous·ness,** n.

am·bi·ent (ăm′bĭ ənt), adj. 1. completely surrounding: ambient air. 2. circulating. [t. L: s. ambiens, ppr., going around]

am·bi·gu·i·ty (ăm′bə gū′ə tĭ), n., pl. -ties. 1. doubtfulness or uncertainty of meaning: to speak without ambiguity. 2. an equivocal or ambiguous word or expression: the law is free of ambiguities. [ME ambiguite, t. L: m.s. ambiguitas.] —**Ant.** 1. explicitness.

am·big·u·ous (ăm bĭg′yŏŏ əs), adj. 1. open to various interpretations; having a double meaning; equivocal: an ambiguous answer. 2. of doubtful or uncertain nature; difficult to comprehend, distinguish, or classify: a rock of ambiguous character. 3. lacking clearness or definiteness; obscure; indistinct. [t. L: m. ambiguus doubtful] —**am·big′u·ous·ly,** adv. —**am·big′u·ous·ness,** n. —**Syn.** 1. AMBIGUOUS, EQUIVOCAL describe that which is not clear in meaning. That which is AMBIGUOUS leaves the intended sense doubtful; it need not be purposely deceptive. That which is EQUIVOCAL is equally capable of two or more interpretations, and is usually intended to be so for the purpose of mystifying. 3. puzzling, enigmatic.

am·bit (ăm′bĭt), n. 1. circumference. 2. boundary; limits. [ME, t. L: s. ambitus compass]

am·bi·tend·en·cy (ăm′bə tĕn′dən sĭ), n. Psychol. the coexistence of opposite tendencies.

am·bi·tion (ăm bĭsh′ən), n. 1. an eager desire for distinction, preferment, power, or fame. 2. the object desired or sought after: the crown was his ambition. 3. desire for work or activity; energy. —v.t. 4. to seek after eagerly; aspire to. [ME, t. L: s. ambitio striving for honors] —**am·bi′tion·less,** adj. —**Syn.** 1. aspiration.

am·bi·tious (ăm bĭsh′əs), adj. 1. having ambition; eagerly desirous of obtaining power, superiority, or distinction. 2. showing ambition: an ambitious attempt. 3. strongly desirous; eager: ambitious of power. 4. showy; pretentious: an ambitious style. [ME, t. L: m.s. ambitiōsus] —**am·bi′tious·ly,** adv. —**am·bi′tious·ness,** n. —**Syn.** 1. AMBITIOUS, ASPIRING, ENTERPRISING describe one who wishes to rise above his present position or condition. The AMBITIOUS man wishes to attain worldly success, and puts forth effort toward this end: ambitious for social position. The ENTERPRISING man, interested especially in wealth, is characterized by energy and daring in undertaking projects. The ASPIRING man wishes to rise (mentally or spiritually) to a higher level or plane, or to attain some end that he feels to be above his ordinary expectations.

am·biv·a·lence (ăm blv′ə ləns), *n. Psychol.* the co-existence of opposite and conflicting feelings about the same person or object. **—am·biv′a·lent**, *adj.*

am·bi·ver·sion (ăm′bə vûr′zhən, -shən), *n. Psychol.* state or condition intermediate between extrovert and introvert personality types.

am·bi·vert (ăm′bə vûrt′), *n. Psychol.* one who is intermediate between an introvert and an extrovert.

am·ble (ăm′bəl), *v.*, **-bled, -bling,** *—v.i.* 1. to move with the gait of a horse when it lifts first the two legs on one side and then the two on the other. 2. to go at an easy pace. *—n.* 3. an ambling gait. 4. an easy or gentle pace. [ME, t. OF: m. *ambler*, g. L *ambulāre* walk] **—am′bler,** *n.* **—am′bling·ly,** *adv.*

am·blyg·o·nite (ăm blĭg′ə nīt′), *n.* a mineral, a lithium aluminum fluophosphate, Li(AlF)PO₄. [t. G: m. *amblygonit*, f. s. Gk. *amblygónios* obtuse-angled + *-it* -ITE¹]

am·bly·o·pi·a (ăm′blĭ ō′pĭ ə), *n. Pathol.* dimness of sight, without apparent organic defect. [t. NL, t. Gk.] **—am·bly·op·ic** (ăm′blĭ ŏp′ĭk), *adj.*

am·bo (ăm′bō), *n.*, *pl.* **-bos.** (in early Christian churches) one of the two raised desks from which gospels and epistles were read or chanted. [t. ML, t. Gk.: m. *ámbōn*]

am·bo·cep·tor (ăm′bə sĕp′tər), *n. Immunol.* a substance which develops during infection in the blood and which according to Ehrlich has affinities for both the bacterial cell or red blood cells and the complement. [f. L *ambo* both + -CEPTOR]

Am·boi·na (ăm boi′nə), *n.* 1. an island in the U.S. of Indonesia, in the Moluccas. 66,821 pop. (1930); 314 sq. mi. 2. a seaport on this island. 17,334 (1930).

Amboina wood, Padouk wood. Also, **Am·boy′na wood.**

Am·boise (äN bwäz′), *n.* a historic town in central France, E of Tours: famous castle, long a royal residence. 3948 (1931).

am·broid (ăm′broid), *n.* amberoid.

Am·brose (ăm′brōz), *n.* **Saint,** A.D. 340?–397, bishop of Milan. **—Am·bro·si·an** (ăm brō′zĭ ən, -zhən), *adj.*

am·bro·sia (ăm brō′zhə), *n.* 1. the food of the gods of classical mythology, imparting immortality. 2. anything imparting the sense of divinity, as poetic inspiration, music, etc. 3. something especially delicious to taste or smell. 4. (*cap.*) *Bot.* the genus comprising the ragweeds. [t. L, t. Gk.: food of the gods, der. *ámbrotos* immortal]

am·bro·si·a·ceous (ăm brō′zĭ ā′shəs), *adj. Bot.* belonging to the *Ambrosiaceae*, or ragweed family of plants, which includes the ragweed, marsh elder, etc.

am·bro·sial (ăm brō′zhəl), *adj.* 1. exceptionally pleasing to taste or smell; especially delicious, fragrant, or sweet-smelling. 2. worthy of the gods; divine. Also, **am·bro′sian. —am·bro′sial·ly,** *adv.*

Ambrosian chant, a mode of singing or chanting introduced by St. Ambrose in Milan.

am·bro·type (ăm′brə tīp′), *n. Photog.* a picture or positive made from a glass negative by combining it with a dark background. [named after James *Ambrose* Cutting (1814–67), the inventor. See -TYPE]

am·bry (ăm′brĭ), *n.*, *pl.* **-bries.** 1. a storeroom; closet. 2. a pantry. [ME *almarie*, ult. t. L: m. *armārium* closet]

ambs·ace (āmz′ās′, ămz′-), *n.* 1. the double ace, the lowest throw at dice. 2. bad luck; misfortune. 3. the smallest amount or distance. Also, **amesace.** [ME *ambes as*, t. OF, g. L *ambās as* double ace]

am·bu·la·cral (ăm′byə lā′krəl), *adj. Zool.* denoting the radial areas of an echinoderm bearing the tubular protrusions by which locomotion is accomplished. [f. s. L *ambulācrum* walk, avenue + -AL¹]

am·bu·lance (ăm′byə ləns), *n.* a vehicle, boat, or aircraft, equipped for carrying the sick or wounded. [t. F, der. (*hôpital*) *ambulant* walking (hospital)]

ambulance chaser, *Slang.* a lawyer who incites persons to sue for damages because of accident.

am·bu·lant (ăm′byə lənt), *adj.* 1. moving from place to place; shifting. 2. *Med.* ambulatory (def. 4). [t. L: s. *ambulans*, ppr., walking]

am·bu·late (ăm′byə lāt′), *v.i.*, **-lated, -lating.** to walk or move about, or from place to place. [t. L: m. s. *ambulātus*, pp., walked] **—am′bu·la′tion,** *n.*

am·bu·la·to·ry (ăm′byə lə tōr′ĭ), *adj.*, *n.*, *pl.* **-ries.** *—adj.* 1. pertaining to or capable of walking. 2. adapted for walking, as the limbs of many animals. 3. moving about; not stationary. 4. *Med.* not confined to bed: *ambulatory patient.* 5. *Law.* not fixed; alterable or revocable: *ambulatory will.* *—n.* 6. *Archit.* a place for walking: a. the side aisle surrounding the choir or chance of a church. b. the arcaded walk around a cloister.

am·bus·cade (ăm′bəs kād′), *n.*, *v.*, **-caded, -cading.** *—n.* 1. an ambush. *—v.i.* 2. to lie in ambush. *—v.t.* 3. to attack from a concealed position. [t. F: m. *embuscade*, der. *embusquer*, b. It. *imboscata* and OF *embûcher*. See AMBUSH] **—am′bus·cad′er,** (*U.S.*) *n.*

am·bus·ca·do (ăm′bəs kā′dō), *n.*, *pl.* **-dos.** *Obs.* ambuscade.

am·bush (ăm′bŏŏsh), *n.* Also, **am′bush·ment.** 1. act of lying concealed so as to attack by surprise. 2. act of

attacking unexpectedly from a concealed position. 3. *Mil.* a secret or concealed station where troops lie in wait to attack unawares. *—v.t.* 4. to attack from ambush. [ME *enbusshe*, t. OF: m. *embusche*, ult. der. *bûche* bush, of Gmc. orig.] **—am′bush·er,** *n.* **—am′bush·like′,** *adj.*

A. M. D. G., (L *ad majorem Dei gloriam*) to the greater glory of God. Also, **AMDG**

a·me·ba (ə mē′bə), *n.*, *pl.* **-bas, -bae** (-bē). amoeba. **—a·me′bic,** *adj.* **—a·me·boid** (ə mē′boid), *adj.*

a·meer (ə mĭr′), *n.* amir.

a·mel·io·rate (ə mēl′yə rāt′), *v.t.*, *v.i.*, **-rated, -rating.** to make or become better; improve; meliorate. [f. s. F *améliorer* + -ATE¹; modeled on earlier MELIORATE] **—a·mel′io·ra·ble,** *adj.* **—a·mel′io·rant** (ə mēl′yə rənt). **—a·mel′io·ra′tive,** *adj.* **—a·mel′io·ra′tor,** *n.* **—Syn.** See **improve.**

a·mel·io·ra·tion (ə mēl′yə rā′shən), *n.* 1. act of ameliorating. 2. the resulting state. 3. something which is improved; an improvement.

a·men (ā′měn′, ä′-), *interj.* 1. it is so; so be it (used after a prayer, creed, or other formal statement). *—adv.* 2. verily; truly. *—n.* 3. an expression of concurrence or assent. [OE, t. LL, t. Gk., t. Heb.: certainty, truth]

A·men (ä′mən), *n.* a minor Theban god with the head of a ram, symbolizing fertility and life; later identified by the Egyptians with the sun god, Amen-Ra. their principal deity. Also, **Amon.** [t. Egypt., explained as "the one who hides his name"]

a·me·na·ble (ə mē′nə bəl, ə měn′ə-), *adj.* 1. disposed or ready to answer, yield, or submit; submissive; tractable. 2. liable to be called to account; answerable; legally responsible. 3. liable or exposed (to charge, claim, etc.): *amenable to criticism.* [f. s. F *amener* bring to (f. *à* to + *mener* bring, g. L *mināre* drive) + -ABLE] **—a·me′na·bil′i·ty, a·me′na·ble·ness,** *n.* **—a·me′na·bly,** *adv.*

amen corner, 1. *U.S.* a place in a church, usually at one side of the pulpit, once occupied by those worshipers who led the responsive amens during the service. 2. any special place in a church occupied by zealous worshipers.

a·mend (ə měnd′), *v.t.* 1. to alter (a motion, bill, constitution, etc.) by due formal procedure. 2. to change for the better; improve: *to amend one's ways.* 3. to remove or correct faults in; rectify: *an amended spelling.* *—v.i.* 4. to grow or become better by reforming oneself. [ME *amende(n)*, t. OF: m. *amender*, g. L *ēmendāre* correct] **—a·mend′a·ble,** *adj.* **—a·mend′er,** *n.*

a·mend·a·to·ry (ə měn′də tōr′ĭ), *adj.* *U.S.* serving to amend; corrective.

a·mend·ment (ə měnd′mənt), *n.* 1. act of amending; correction; improvement. 2. alteration of a motion, bill, constitution, etc. 3. a change so made, either by way of correction or addition.

a·mends (ə měndz′), *n. sing. or pl.* 1. reparation or compensation for a loss, damage, or injury of any kind; recompense. 2. *Obs.* recovery of health. [ME *amendes*, t. OF, pl. of *amende* reparation]

A·men·ho·tep III (ä′mən hō′těp, ăm′ən-), king of Egypt, 1411? B.C. -1375 B.C. Also, **Am·e·no·phis** (ăm′ə nō′fĭs).

Amenhotep IV, (*Ikhnaton*) died c1357 B.C., king of Egypt, c1375–c1357 B.C., the first ruler in history to declare his belief in one God. Also, **Amenophis.**

a·men·i·ty (ə měn′ə tĭ, -mē′nə-), *n.*, *pl.* **-ties.** 1. (*pl.*) agreeable features, circumstances, ways, etc.; civilities. 2. the quality of being pleasant or agreeable in situation, prospect, disposition, etc.; pleasantness: *the amenity of the climate.* [late ME, t. L: m.s. *amoenitas*]

a·men·or·rhe·a (ā měn′ə rē′ə), *n. Pathol.* absence of the menses. Also, **a·men′or·rhoe′a.** [f. A-⁶ + *meno-* (comb. form repr. Gk. *mēn* month) + -(R)RHEA]

A·men-Ra (ä′mən rä′), *n.* See **Amen** (god).

am·ent (ăm′ənt, ā′mənt), *n. Bot.* a spike of unisexual apetalous flowers with scaly bracts, usually deciduous; a catkin. [t. L: s. *amentum* strap, thong]

am·en·ta·ceous (ăm′ən tā′shəs), *adj.* 1. consisting of an ament. 2. bearing aments.

a·men·tia (ā měn′shə), *n. Psychiatry.* lack of intellectual development; imbecility; idiocy. [t. L: lack of reason]

am·en·tif·er·ous (ăm′ən tĭf′ər əs), *adj. Bot.* bearing aments or catkins.

a·men·ti·form (ə měn′tə fôrm′), *adj.* ament-shaped.

Amer., 1. America. 2. American.

a·merce (ə mûrs′), *v.t.*, **amerced, amercing.** 1. to punish by an arbitrary or discretionary fine, i.e., one not fixed by statute. 2. to punish by inflicting a discretionary penalty of any kind. [ME *amercy*, ult. der. OF phrase (*estre*) *a merci* (to be) at the mercy of] **—a·merce′a·ble,** *adj.* **—a·merce′ment,** *n.* **—a·merc′er,** *n.*

A·mer·i·ca (ə měr′ə kə), *n.* 1. the United States of America. 2. North America. 3. South America. 4. North America and South America. [named after *Americus* Vespucius. See VESPUCCI]

A·mer·i·can (ə měr′ə kən), *adj.* 1. of or pertaining to the United States of America: *an American citizen.* 2. of or pertaining to North or South America. 3. *Ethnol.*

Aments
A, Staminate;
B, Pistillate

noting or pertaining to the so-called "red" race, characterized by a reddish or brownish skin, dark eyes, black hair, and prominent cheekbones, and embracing the aborigines of North and South America (sometimes excluding the Eskimos), known as American Indians. —*n.* **4.** a citizen of the United States of America. **5.** a native or an inhabitant of the western hemisphere. **6.** an aborigine of the western hemisphere.

A·mer·i·ca·na (ə·mĕr′ə·kä′nə, -kăn′ə, -kä′nə), *n. pl.* books, papers, etc., relating to America, esp. to its history and geography. [t. NL. See -ANA]

American aloe, the century plant.

American Beauty, an American variety of rose, periodically bearing large crimson blossoms.

American cheese, a smooth white or yellow hard cheese with a slightly acid flavor; cheddar.

American eagle, the bald eagle, esp. as depicted on the coat of arms of the United States.

American Expeditionary Forces, troops sent into Europe by the U.S. Army during World War I.

American Federation of Labor, a federation of trade unions organized in 1886.

American Indian, Indian (def. 1).

A·mer·i·can·ism (ə·mĕr′ə·kə·nĭz′əm), *n.* **1.** devotion to or preference for the United States and its institutions. **2.** a custom, trait, or thing peculiar to the United States of America or its citizens. **3.** an English usage peculiar to the people of the United States.

A·mer·i·can·ize (ə·mĕr′ə·kə·nīz′), *v.t., v.i.,* **-ized,-izing.** to make or become American in character; assimilate to the customs and institutions of the United States. —**A·mer′i·can·i·za′tion,** *n.*

American Legion, a society, organized in 1919, now composed of veterans of the armed forces of the United States in World Wars I and II.

American party. See **know-nothing** (def. 3).

American plan, (in hotels) a system of paying a single fixed sum that includes both room and meals.

American Revolution, the war between Great Britain and her American colonies, 1775–83, by which the colonies won their independence. Also, *Brit.,* **War of American Independence.**

American Samoa, the islands of the Samoa group belonging to the U. S., including mainly Tutuila and the Manua islands. 18,937 pop. (1950); 76 sq. mi. *Cap.:* Pago Pago.

am·er·i·ci·um (ăm′ə·rĭsh′ĭ·əm), *n.* a radioactive element, one of the products of the bombardment of uranium and plutonium by very energetic helium ions. *Symbol:* Am; *at. no.:* 95. [f. AMERIC(A) + -IUM]

A·me·ri·go Ves·puc·ci (ä′mĕ·rō′gō vĕ·spoot′chē). See Vespucci.

Am·er·ind (ăm′ər·ĭnd), *n.* American Indian. [b. AMER(ICAN) and IND(IAN)] —**Am′er·in′di·an,** *adj., n.* —**Am′er·in′dic,** *adj.*

Ames (āmz), *n.* a city in central Iowa. 22,898 (1950).

ames·ace (āmz′ās′, āmz′-), *n.* ambsace.

am·e·thyst (ăm′ə·thĭst), *n.* **1.** *Mineral.* a coarsely crystallized purple or violet quartz used in jewelry. **2.** the violet sapphire (**oriental amethyst**). **3.** a purplish tint. [t. L: s. *amethystus,* t. Gk.: m. *amethystos* lit., remedy for drunkenness; r. ME *ametiste,* t. OF] —**am·e·thys·tine** (ăm′ə·thĭs′tĭn, -tīn), *adj.* —**am′e·thyst·like′,** *adj.*

am·e·tro·pi·a (ăm′ə·trō′pĭ·ə), *n. Pathol.* an abnormal condition of the eye causing faulty refraction of light rays, as in astigmatism, myopia, etc. [t. NL, f. Gk.: s. *ámetros* irregular + -*opia* -OPIA] —**am·e·trop·ic** (ăm′ə·trŏp′ĭk), *adj.*

Am·ha·ra (äm·hä′rə), *n.* a former kingdom in NW Ethiopia. *Cap.:* Gondar.

Am·har·ic (ăm·hăr′ĭk, äm·här′ĭk), *n.* **1.** the Semitic language which is official in Ethiopia. —*adj.* **2.** of or pertaining to Amhara.

Am·herst (ăm′ərst), *n.* **Jeffrey, Baron,** 1717–97, British field marshal.

a·mi (à·mē′), *n. masc., pl.* **amis** (à·mē′). *French.* a friend.

a·mi·a·ble (ā′mĭ·ə·bəl), *adj.* **1.** having or showing agreeable personal qualities, as sweetness of temper, kindheartedness, etc. **2.** friendly; kindly: *an amiable mood.* **3.** *Obs.* lovable; lovely. [ME *amyable,* t. OF: m. *amiable,* g. L *amīcābilis* friendly] —**a′mi·a·bil′i·ty, a′mi·a·ble·ness,** *n.* —**a′mi·a·bly,** *adv.* —**Syn. 1.** gracious.

am·i·an·thus (ăm′ĭ·ăn′thəs), *n. Mineral.* a fine variety of asbestos, with delicate, flexible filaments. [var. (with -*th* from *polyanthus*) of *amiantus,* t. L, t. Gk.: m. *amíantos* (*lithos*) undefiled (stone)]

am·ic (ăm′ĭk), *adj. Chem.* of an amide or amine.

am·i·ca·ble (ăm′ə·kə·bəl), *adj.* characterized by or exhibiting friendliness; friendly; peaceable: *an amicable settlement.* [t. L: m.s. *amīcābilis*] —**am′i·ca·bil′i·ty, am′i·ca·ble·ness.** —**am′i·ca·bly,** *adv.*

am·ice[1] (ăm′ĭs), *n. Eccles.* an oblong piece of linen worn about the neck and shoulders under the alb, or, formerly, on the head. [ME *amyse,* t. OF: m. *amis,* g. L *amictus* cloak]

am·ice[2] (ăm′ĭs), *n.* a furred hood or hooded cape, with long ends hanging down in front, formerly worn by the clergy. [late ME *amisse,* t. F: m. *aumusse,* t. Pr.: m. *almussa,* f. Ar. *al-* the + m. G *mützé* cap]

a·mi·cus cu·ri·ae (ə·mī′kəs kyŏor′ĭ·ē), *Law.* a per-

son not a party to the litigation who volunteers or is invited by the court to give advice to the court upon some matter pending before it. [L: a friend of the court]

a·mid (ə·mĭd′), *prep.* in the midst of or surrounded by; among; amidst. [ME *amidde,* OE *amiddan,* for *on middan* in the middle. See MID[1]] —**Syn.** See **among.**

am·ide (ăm′īd, -ĭd), *n. Chem.* **1.** a metallic derivative of ammonia in which the NH_2 grouping is retained, as *potassium amide,* KNH_2. **2.** an organic compound obtained by replacing the OH group in acids by the NH_2 radical. Also, **am·id** (ăm′ĭd). [f. AM(MONIA) + -IDE] —**a·mid·ic** (ə·mĭd′ĭk), *adj.*

am·i·din (ăm′ə·dĭn), *n.* the soluble matter of starch. [f. s. ML *amidum,* var. of L *amylum* (t. Gk.: m. *ámylon* fine meal) + -IN[2]]

amido-, *Chem.* **1.** a prefix denoting the replacement of a hydroxyl group by the NH_2 radical. **2.** (sometimes) amino-. [comb. form of AMIDE] —**a·mi·do** (ə·mē′do, ăm′ə·dō′), *adj.*

a·mi·do·gen (ə·mē′də·jən, ə·mĭd′ə-), *n. Chem.* the NH_2 radical. If attached to CO in a compound it is called an **amido group;** without CO, an **amino group.**

am·i·dol (ăm′ə·dŏl′, -dōl′), *n.* a colorless crystalline phenol derivative, $C_6H_8N_2O·2HCl$, used as a photographic developer.

a·mid·ships (ə·mĭd′shĭps), *adv. Naut.* **1.** in or toward the middle of a ship, or the part midway between stem and stern. **2.** lengthwise. Also, **a·mid′ship.**

a·midst (ə·mĭdst′), *prep.* amid. [ME *amiddes,* f. *amidde* amid + adv. gen. -*s*; for later -*t,* cf. AGAINST, etc.]

a·mie (à·mē′), *n., pl.* **amies** (à·mē′). *French.* fem. of **ami.**

Am·i·ens (ăm′ĭ·enz; *Fr.* à·myăN′), *n.* a city in N France, on the Somme river: cathedral; battles, 1914, 1918, 1944. 84,774 (1946).

am·i·gen (ăm′ə·jən), *n. Biochem.* **1.** a protein prepared by prodigesting hog pancreas and milk with various enzymes, and used in the treatment of malnutrition and widespread burns, and as an aid to surgical convalescence. **2.** (*cap.*) a trademark for this substance.

a·mi·go (ä·mē′gō; *Sp.* -gô), *n., pl.* **-gos** (-gōz; *Sp.* -gôs). **1.** a friend. **2.** a Spanish-speaking native friendly toward Americans. [Sp., g. L *amīcus*]

a·mine (ə·mēn′, ăm′ĭn), *n. Chem.* any of a class of compounds prepared from ammonia by replacing one, two, or all hydrogen atoms with organic radicals. Also, **am·in** (ăm′ĭn). [f. AM(MONIA) + -INE[2]]

amino-, *Chem.* a prefix denoting amino group. [comb. form of AMINE]

am·i·no acids (ăm′ə·nō, ə·mē′nō), *Chem.* a group of organic compounds derived from the acids, RCOOH, by replacement of hydrogen in the (R) group by the (NH_2) radical. They are the basic constituents of proteins.

amino group, the universal basic radical, NH_2. Also, **amino radical.**

a·mir (ə·mīr′), *n.* **1.** a Mohammedan prince, lord, or nobleman. **2.** a title of honor of the descendants of Mohammed. **3.** (*cap.*) the former title of the ruler of Afghanistan. **4.** a title of certain Turkish officials. Also, **ameer.** [t. Ar.: m. *amīr* commander. See EMIR]

Am·ish (ăm′ĭsh, ä′mĭsh), *U.S.* —*adj.* **1.** pertaining to Jakob Ammann, a Swiss Mennonite of the 17th century, or his followers. —*n. pl.* **2.** the Amish Mennonites.

a·miss (ə·mĭs′), *adv.* **1.** out of the proper course or order; in a faulty manner; wrongly: *to speak amiss.* **2. take amiss,** to be offended at; resent. —*adj.* **3.** improper; wrong; faulty (used only in the predicate). [ME *amis,* f. A-[1] + *mis* wrong. See MISS[1]]

am·i·to·sis (ăm′ə·tō′sĭs), *n. Biol.* the direct method of cell division characterized by simple cleavage of the nucleus, without the formation of chromosomes. [f. A-[6] + MITOSIS] —**am·i·tot·ic** (ăm′ə·tŏt′ĭk), *adj.*

am·i·ty (ăm′ə·tĭ), *n., pl.* **-ties.** friendship; harmony; good understanding, esp. between nations. [ME *amytie,* t. F: m. *amitié,* ult. der. L *amīcus* friend]

Am·man (äm′män), *n.* the capital of Trans-Jordan.

am·me·ter (ăm′mē′tər), *n. Elect.* an instrument for measuring the strength of electric currents in amperes. [f. AM(PERE) + -METER]

am·mi·a·ceous (ăm′ĭ·ā′shəs), *adj. Bot.* apiaceous.

am·mine (ăm′ēn, ə·mēn′), *n. Chem.* a compound containing one or more ammonia molecules in coördinate linkage. [f. AMM(ONIA) + -INE[2]]

am·mo (ăm′ō), *n. Colloq.* ammunition.

am·mo·cete (ăm′ə·sēt′), *n.* the larval stage of a lamprey, used as bait. It resembles the theoretical ancestor of the vertebrates. Also, **am′mo·coete′.** [f. AMMO(NIUM) + -CETE]

Am·mon (ăm′ən), *n.* classical name of the Egyptian divinity Amen, whom the Greeks identified with Zeus, the Romans with Jupiter. [t. L, t. Gk., t. Egypt.: m. *Amen*]

Am·mon (ăm′ən), *n.* a Biblical seminomadic Semitic people living east of the Jordan.

am·mo·nia (ə·mōn′yə, ə·mō′nĭ·ə), *n.* **1.** a colorless, pungent, suffocating gas, NH_3, a compound of nitrogen and hydrogen, very soluble in water. **2.** Also, **ammonia water** or **aqueous ammonia.** this gas dissolved in water, the common commercial form. [t. NL; so called as being obtained from sal *ammoniac.* See AMMONIAC]

am·mo·ni·ac (ə·mō′nĭ·ăk′), *n.* **1.** gum ammoniac. —*adj.* **2.** ammoniacal. [ME, t. L: s. *ammoniacum,* t. Gk.: m. *ammōniakón,* applied to a salt and a gum said to come from near the shrine of *Ammon* in Libya]

ăct, āble, dâre, ärt; ĕbb, ēqual; ĭf, īce; hŏt, ōver, ôrder, oil, bŏŏk, ōōze, out; ŭp, ūse, ûrge; ə = a in alone; ch, chief; g, give; ng, ring; sh, shoe; th, thin; ŧħ, that; zh, vision. See the full key on inside cover.

am·mo·ni·a·cal (ăm/ə·nī/ə·kəl), *adj.* **1.** consisting of, containing, or using ammonia. **2.** like ammonia.

am·mo·ni·ate (ə·mō/nĭ·āt/), *v.t.*, **-ated, -ating.** to treat or cause to unite with ammonia.

am·mon·ic (ə·mŏn/ĭk, ə·mō/nĭk), *adj.* of or pertaining to ammonia or ammonium.

am·mon·i·fi·ca·tion (ə·mŏn/ə·fə·kā/shən, ə·mō/nə-), *n.* **1.** act of impregnating with ammonia, as in fertilizer manufacture. **2.** state of being so impregnated. **3.** the formation of ammonia or its compounds, as in soil, etc., by soil organisms. [f. AMMONI(A) + -FICATION]

am·mon·i·fy (ə·mŏn/ə·fī/, ə·mō/nə-), *v.*, **-fied, -fying.** —*v.t.* **1.** to combine or impregnate with ammonia. **2.** to form into ammonia or ammonium compounds. —*v.i.* **3.** to become ammonified; produce ammonification.

am·mo·nite (ăm/ə·nīt/), *n.* one of the coiled, chambered fossil shells of the extinct cephalopod mollusks, suborder *Ammonoidea*. [t. NL: m. s. *Ammŏnītes*, der. ML *cornū Ammōnis* horn of Ammon]

am·mo·ni·um (ə·mō/nĭ·əm), *n.* *Chem.* a radical, NH₄, which plays the part of a metal in the compounds (**ammonium salts**) formed when ammonia reacts with acids. [f. AMMON(IA) + -IUM]

ammonium chloride, a white granular powder, NH₄Cl, used medicinally and industrially; sal ammoniac.

ammonium hydroxide, a basic compound, NH₄OH, made by dissolving ammonia in water and used extensively as a weak alkali.

ammonium nitrate, a white, soluble solid, the nitrate of ammonia, NH₄NO₃, used in explosives, freezing mixtures, and the preparation of nitrous oxide.

am·mu·ni·tion (ăm/yə·nĭsh/ən), *n.* **1.** all the material used in discharging all types of firearms or any weapon that throws projectiles; powder, shot, shrapnel, bullets, cartridges, and the means of igniting and exploding them, as primers and fuzes. Chemicals, bombs, grenades, mines, pyrotechnics are also ammunition. **2.** any material or means used in combat. **3.** *Obs.* military supplies. [t. F (obs.): m. *amunition* for *munition*, *la munition* being understood as *l'amunition*]

am·ne·sia (ăm·nē/zhə), *n.* *Psychiatry.* loss of a large block of interrelated memories. [t. NL, t. Gk.: forgetfulness] —**am·ne·sic** (ăm·nē/sĭk, -zĭk), **am·nes·tic** (ăm·nĕs/tĭk), *adj.*

am·nes·ty (ăm/nəs·tĭ), *n.*, *pl.* **-ties,** *v.,* **-tied, -tying.** —*n.* **1.** a general pardon for offenses against a government. **2.** the granting of immunity for past offenses against the laws of war. **3.** *Law.* protection against punishment granted a witness in order to compel him to testify to incriminating facts. **4.** a forgetting or overlooking of any offense. —*v.t.* **5.** to grant amnesty to; pardon. [t. L: m.s. *amnēstia*, t. Gk.: forgetfulness]

am·ni·on (ăm/nĭ·ən), *n.*, *pl.* **-nions, -nia** (-nĭ·ə). *Anat., Zool.* the innermost of the embryonic or fetal membranes of insects, reptiles, birds, and mammals; the sac containing the amniotic fluid and the embryo. [t. NL, t. Gk.] —**am·ni·on·ic** (ăm/nĭ·ŏn/ĭk), *adj.*

am·ni·ot·ic (ăm/nĭ·ŏt/ĭk), *adj.* *Anat., Zool.* of or pertaining to the amnion.

a·moe·ba (ə·mē/bə), *n.*, *pl.* **-bae** (-bē), **bas.** *Zool.* **1.** a microscopic, one-celled animal consisting of a naked mass of protoplasm constantly changing in shape as it moves and engulfs food. **2.** a protozoan of the genus *Amoeba*. Also, **ameba.** [t. NL, t. Gk.: m. s. *amoibē* change] —**a·moe/ba·like/,** *adj.*

am·oe·bae·an (ăm/ĭ·bē/ən), *adj.* *Pros.* alternately responsive, as verses in dialogue. Also, **am/oe·be/an.**

a·moe·bic (ə·mē/bĭk), *adj.* **1.** of, pertaining to, or resembling an amoeba. **2.** characterized by or due to the presence of, amoebae, as certain diseases. Also, **amebic.**

amoebic dysentery, a variety of dysentery whose causative agent is a protozoan, the *Endamoeba histolytica,* characterized esp. by intestinal ulceration.

a·moe·boid (ə·mē/boid), *adj.* *Biol.* resembling or related to amoebae. Also, **ameboid.** [f. AMOEB(A) + -OID]

a·mok (ə·mŭk/, ə·mŏk/), *n.* **1.** (among Malays) a psychic disturbance characterized by depression followed by overwhelming desire to murder. —*adv.* **2. run amok.** See **amuck.** [t. Malay: m. *amoq*]

a·mo·le (ə·mō/lā; *Sp.* ä·mō/lě), *n.* *Southwestern U.S.* **1.** the roots, etc., of various plants, as Mexican species of *Agave*, used as a substitute for soap. **2.** any such plant. [t. Mex. Sp., from Nahuatl]

A·mon (ä/mən), *n.* Amen (god).

a·mong (ə·mŭng/), *prep.* **1.** in or into the midst of; in association or connection with; surrounded by: *he fell among thieves.* **2.** to each of; by or for distribution to: *divide these among you.* **3.** in the number, class, or group of; of or out of: *that's among the things we must do.* **4.** with or by all or the whole of: *popular among the people.* **5.** by the joint or reciprocal action of: *settle it among yourselves.* **6.** each with the other; mutually: to *quarrel among themselves.* [OE *amang*, for *on* (*ge*)*mang* in the crowd, in the midst of]

—**Syn. 1.** AMONG, AMID, BETWEEN imply a position in the middle of. AMONG suggests a mingling with more than two objects: *he went among the crowd.* AMID, a more literary word, implies being in a middle place or surrounded by something: *to stand amid ruins.* BETWEEN refers to only two objects: *between two pillars.* In some special instances, in which each object is individually related to the rest, BETWEEN is used of more than two objects: *dealings between the states.*

a·mongst (ə·mŭngst/), *prep.* *Literary* or *Brit.* among.

[ME *amonges*, f. AMONG + adv. gen. *-es*; for later *-t* after the gen. *-s*, cf. AGAINST, etc.]

a·mon·til·la·do (ə·mŏn/tə·lä/dō; *Sp.* ä·môn/tē·lyä/dô), *n.* a pale-colored, quite dry, Spanish sherry. [t. Sp.]

a·mor·al (ā·mŏr/əl, ā·môr/-, ă-), *adj.* without moral quality; neither moral nor immoral. [f. A-⁶ + MORAL] —**a·mo·ral·i·ty** (ā/mə·răl/ə·tĭ, ăm/ə-), *n.* —**a·mor/-al·ly,** *adv.*

am·o·ret·to (ăm/ə·rĕt/ō; *It.* ä/mō·rĕt/tô), *n.*, *pl.* **-retti** (-rĕt/ĭ; *It.* -rĕt/tē). a little cupid. [t. It., dim. of *amore,* g. L *amor* love]

a·mo·ri·no (ä/mō·rē/nō), *n.*, *pl.* **-ni** (-nē). amoretto.

am·o·rist (ăm/ə·rĭst), *n.* **1.** a lover; a gallant. **2.** one who writes about love. [f. L *amor* love + -IST]

am·o·rous (ăm/ə·rəs), *adj.* **1.** inclined or disposed to love: *an amorous disposition.* **2.** in love; enamored. **3.** showing love: *amorous sigh.* **4.** pertaining to love: *amorous poetry.* [ME, t. OF, g. L *amōrōsus,* der. *amor* love] —**am/o·rous·ly,** *adv.* —**am/o·rous·ness,** *n.* —**Syn. 1.** loving; amatory. **3.** fond, tender.

a·mor pa·tri·ae (ā/môr pā/trĭ·ē/), *Latin.* love of country; patriotism.

a·mor·phism (ə·môr/fĭz·əm), *n.* **1.** state or quality of being amorphous. **2.** nihilism.

a·mor·phous (ə·môr/fəs), *adj.* **1.** lacking definite form; having no specific shape. **2.** of no particular kind or character; indeterminate; formless; unorganized: *an amorphous style.* **3.** *Geol.* occurring in a mass, as without stratification or crystalline structure. **4.** *Chem.* noncrystalline. [t. Gk.: m. *ámorphos*] —**a·mor/phous·ly,** *adv.* —**a·mor/phous·ness,** *n.*

am·or·ti·za·tion (ăm/ər·tə·zā/shən, ə·môr/-), *n.* **1.** act of amortizing a debt. **2.** the money devoted to this purpose. Also, **a·mor·tize·ment** (ə·môr/tĭz·mənt).

am·or·tize (ăm/ər·tīz/, ə·môr/tīz), *v.t.,* **-tized, -tizing. 1.** to liquidate or extinguish (an indebtedness or charge) usually by periodic payments (or by entries) made to a sinking fund, to a creditor, or to an account. **2.** *Old Eng. Law.* to convey to a corporation; alienate in mortmain. Also, *Brit.,* **am/or·tise/.** [ME *amortise*(*n*), t. OF: m. *amortiss-,* s. *amortir* deaden, buy out, der. *mort* death. Cf. ML *admortizāre*] —**am/or·tiz/a·ble,** *adj.*

A·mos (ā/məs), *n.* **1.** a Hebrew prophet of the eighth century B.C., author of the Old Testament book bearing his name. **2.** this book. [t. Heb.]

a·mount (ə·mount/), *n.* **1.** the sum total of two or more sums or quantities; the aggregate: *the amount of 7 and 9 is 16.* **2.** the sum of the principal and interest of a loan. **3.** quantity: *the amount of resistance.* **4.** the full effect, value, or import. —*v.i.* **5.** to reach, extend, or be equal in number, quantity, effect, etc. (fol. by *to*). [ME *amount*(*en*), t. OF: m. *amonter* mount up to, der. *amont* upward, orig. phrase *a mont* to the mountain]

a·mour (ə·mŏŏr/), *n.* **1.** a love affair. **2.** an illicit love affair. [t. F, prob. t. Pr.: m. *amor,* g. L *amor* love]

a·mour-pro·pre (å·mŏŏr prô/pr), *n.* *French.* self-esteem; self-respect.

A·moy (ä·moi/), *n.* a seaport in SE China, on an island in Formosa Strait. 234,000 (est. 1938).

amp., 1. amperage. **2.** ampere.

am·pe·lop·sis (ăm/pə·lŏp/sĭs), *n.* any plant of the vitaceous genus *Ampelopsis,* comprising climbing woody vines or shrubs. [t. NL, f. s. Gk. *ámpelos* vine + -*opsis* -OPSIS]

am·per·age (ăm·pĭr/ĭj, ăm/pər-), *n. Elect.* the strength of an electric current measured in amperes.

am·pere (ăm/pĭr, ăm·pĭr/), *n. Elect.* the usual unit of current strength; the current produced by an electromotive force of one volt acting through a resistance of one ohm. Also, **am·père** (äⁿ pěr/). [named after A. M. AMPERE.

Am·père (ăm·pĭr/; *Fr.* äⁿ·pěr/), *n.* **André Marie** (äⁿ-drě/ mä·rē/), 1775–1836, French physicist.

am·pere-hour (ăm/pĭr·our/), *n. Elect.* a unit equal to 3600 coulombs, the quantity of electricity transferred by a current of one ampere in one hour.

ampere turn, *Elect.* **1.** one complete turn or convolution of a conducting coil, through which one ampere of current passes. **2.** the magnetomotive force produced by one ampere passing through one complete turn or convolution of a coil multiplied by 10 /4π.

am·per·sand (ăm/pər·sănd/, ăm/pər·sănd/), *n.* the name of the character (&) meaning *and.* [contraction of *and per se — and,* & by itself (as a mere symbol given after the letters of the alphabet, and called *and*)]

am·phet·a·mine (ăm·fĕt/ə·mēn/, -mĭn), *n. Pharm.* a drug which, diluted with water, is used as a spray or inhaled to relieve nasal congestion and is taken internally to stimulate the central nervous system.

amphi-, a word element meaning "on both sides," "on all sides," "around," "round about," as in *Amphibia.* [t. Gk., repr. *amphi,* prep. and adv.]

am·phi·ar·thro·sis (ăm/fĭ·är·thrō/sĭs), *n.,* *pl.* **-ses** (-sēz). *Anat.* a form of articulation which permits slight motion, as that between the bodies of the vertebrae. [f. AMPHI- + Gk. *árthrōsis* articulation]

am·phi·as·ter (ăm/fĭ·ăs/tər), *n. Biol.* the achromatic spindle with two asters that forms during mitosis.

Am·phib·i·a (ăm·fĭb/ĭ·ə), *n. pl. Zool.* the class of vertebrates that comprises the frogs, salamanders, and caecilians (with various extinct types) representing the essential, basic characteristics of the ancestral stock of all and vertebrates. Typically they lay eggs that hatch in water, and the young go through a fishlike larval, or tadpole, stage, later metamorphosing into lung-breathing quadrupeds. [t. NL, neut. pl. of *amphibius*, t. Gk.: m. *amphíbios* living a double life]

am·phib·i·an (ăm fĭb′Ĭ ən), *n.* **1.** any animal of the class *Amphibia.* **2.** an amphibious plant. **3.** an airplane that can take off from and land on either land or water. —*adj.* **4.** belonging to the class *Amphibia.* **5.** capable of operating on land or water; amphibious.

am·phi·bi·ot·ic (ăm′fə bī ŏt′Ĭk), *adj. Zool.* living on land during an adult stage and in water during a larval stage. [f. AMPHI- + m. s. Gk. *biōtikós* pertaining to life]

am·phib·i·ous (ăm fĭb′Ĭ əs), *adj.* **1.** living both on land and in water; belonging to both land and water. **2.** capable of operating on both land and water; *amphibious plane.* **3.** of a twofold nature. [t. Gk.: m. *amphíbios* living a double life] —**am·phib′i·ous·ly,** *adv.* —**am·phib′i·ous·ness,** *n.*

am·phi·bole (ăm′fə bōl′), *n. Mineral.* any of a complex group of hydrous silicate minerals, containing chiefly calcium, magnesium, sodium, iron, and aluminum, and including hornblende, tremolite, asbestos, etc., and occurring as important constituents of many rocks. [t. F, t. Gk.: m.s. *amphíbolos* ambiguous]

am·phi·bol·ic[1] (ăm′fə bŏl′Ĭk), *adj.* of or pertaining to amphibole. [f. AMPHIBOL(E) + -IC]

am·phi·bol·ic[2] (ăm′fə bŏl′Ĭk), *adj.* equivocal; uncertain; changing; ambiguous. [f. AMPHIBOL(Y) + -IC]

am·phi·bo·lite (ăm fĭb′ə līt′), *n. Petrog.* a metamorphic rock composed basically of amphibole or hornblende. [f. AMPHIBOL(E) + -ITE[1]]

am·phi·bol·o·gy (ăm′fə bŏl′ə jĬ), *n.,* pl. **-gies.** ambiguity of speech, esp. from uncertainty of the grammatical construction rather than of the meaning of the words, as in *The Duke yet lives that Henry shall depose.* [t. LL: m. s. *amphibologia,* r. L *amphibolia* (see AMPHIBOLY), which was remodeled after *tautologia* and the like] —**am·phib·o·log·i·cal** (ăm fĭb′ə lŏj′ə kəl), *adj.*

am·phib·o·lous (ăm fĭb′ə ləs), *adj. Logic.* ambiguous; equivocal; susceptible of two meanings. [t. L: m. *amphibolus,* t. Gk.: m. *amphíbolos* thrown around]

am·phib·o·ly (ăm fĭb′ə lĬ), *n.,* pl. **-lies.** amphibology. [t. L: m. s. *amphibolia* ambiguity, t. Gk.]

am·phi·brach (ăm′fə brăk′), *n. Pros.* a trisyllabic foot in which the syllables come in the following order: short, long, short (quantitative meter), or unstressed, stressed, unstressed (accentual meter). Thus, *together* is an accentual amphibrach. [t. L: s. *amphibrachys,* t. Gk.: short on both sides]

am·phi·chro·ic (ăm′fə krō′Ĭk), *adj. Chem.* giving either of two colors, one with acids and one with alkalis. Also, **am·phi·chro·mat·ic** (ăm′fə krō măt′Ĭk). [f. AMPHI- + s. Gk. *chróa* color + -IC]

am·phi·coe·lous (ăm′fə sē′ləs), *adj. Anat., Zool.* concave on both sides, as the bodies of the vertebrae of fishes. [t. Gk.: m. *amphíkoilos* hollowed all around]

am·phic·ty·on (ăm fĭk′Ĭ ən), *n.* a deputy to the council of an amphictyony. [t. Gk.: m. s. *amphiktýones,* pl., dwellers around, neighbors]

am·phic·ty·on·ic (ăm fĭk′tĬ ŏn′Ĭk), *adj.* of or pertaining to an amphictyon or an amphictyony.

am·phic·ty·o·ny (ăm fĭk′tĬ ə nĬ), *n.,* pl. **-nies.** a religious league of ancient Greek states participating in the cult of a common deity. [t. Gk.: m. s. *amphiktyonía*]

am·phi·dip·loid (ăm′fə dĭp′loid), *n. Genetics.* a plant type possessing the sum of the chromosome numbers of two parental species, ordinarily arising from the doubling of the chromosomes of a hybrid of two species.

am·phi·go·ry (ăm′fə gôr′Ĭ), *n.,* pl. **-ries.** a meaningless rigmarole, as of nonsense verses or the like; a nonsensical parody. [t. F: m. *amphigouri,* orig. unknown] —**am·phi·gor·ic** (ăm′fə gôr′Ĭk, -gŏr′-), *adj.*

am·phi·gou·ri (ăm′fə gŏor′Ĭ), *n.,* pl. **-ris.** amphigory.

am·phim·a·cer (ăm fĭm′ə sər), *n. Pros.* a trisyllabic foot in which the syllables come in the following order: long, short, long (quantitative meter), or stressed, unstressed, stressed (accentual meter). Thus, *anodyne* is an accentual amphimacer. [t. L: m. s. *amphimacrus,* t. Gk.: m. *amphímakros* long on both sides]

am·phi·mix·is (ăm′fə mĭk′sĬs), *n.* **1.** *Biol.* the merging of the germ plasm of two organisms in sexual reproduction. **2.** *Embryol., Genetics.* the combining of paternal and maternal hereditary substances. [f. AMPHI- + Gk. *míxis* a mingling]

Am·phi·on (ăm fī′ən), *n. Gk. Myth.* the son of Antiope by Zeus, twin brother of Zethus, and husband of Niobe, who with his brother fortified Thebes with a wall, charming the stones into place by his lyre.

am·phi·ox·us (ăm′fĬ ŏk′səs), *n. Zool.* a small fishlike animal, the lancelet, showing vertebrate characteristics but lacking a vertebral column, important in discussions of vertebrate ancestry. [t. NL, f. Gk.: amphi- AMPHI- + m. *oxýs* sharp]

am·phi·pod (ăm′fə pŏd′), *n.* **1.** any of a type of small crustaceans, *Amphipoda,* including beach fleas, etc. —*adj.* **2.** of or pertaining to the amphipods.

am·phip·ro·style (ăm fĭp′rə stīl′, ăm′fə prō′stĬl), *adj. Archit.* having a prostyle porch in front and rear but no columns along the sides. [t. L: m. s. *amphiprostýlos,* t. Gk.]

am·phis·bae·na (ăm′fĬs bē′nə), *n.* **1.** a burrowing, blind, and limbless snakelike lizard of the family *Amphisbaenidae,* with obtuse head and tail, moving

forward or backward with equal ease. **2.** *Classical Myth.* a fabulous venomous serpent having a head at each end and able to move in either direction. [t. L, t. Gk.: m. *amphísbaina*] —**am·phis·bae′nic,** *adj.*

am·phi·the·a·ter (ăm′fə thē′ə tər), *n.* **1.** a level area of oval or circular shape surrounded by rising ground. **2.** any place for public contests or games; an arena. **3.** a building with tiers of seats around an arena or central area, as those used in ancient Rome for gladiatorial contests. **4.** a semicircular sloping gallery in a modern theater. Also, *esp. Brit.,* **am·phi·the·a·tre.** [t. L: m.s. *amphitheātrum,* t. Gk.: m. *amphitheātron*] —**am·phi·the·at·ric** (ăm′fə thĬ ăt′rĬk), **am·phi·the·at·ri·cal,** *adj.* —**am′phi·the·at′ri·cal·ly,** *adv.*

am·phi·the·ci·um (ăm′fə thē′shĬ əm), *n.,* pl. **-cia** (-shĬ ə). *Bot.* the layer or layers of cells in the capsule of a moss surrounding the spores. [t. NL, f. *amphi-* AMPHI- + *thēcium* (t. Gk.: m. *thēkíon,* dim. of *thēkē* case)]

am·phit·ri·cha (ăm fĭt′rə kə), *n.pl.* bacteria having the organs of locomotion on both poles. [f. AMPHI- + m. *trich-* (s. Gk. *thríx* hair)] —**am·phit′ri·chous,** *adj.*

Am·phi·tri·te (ăm′fə trī′tĬ), *n. Gk. Myth.* the goddess of the sea, daughter of Nereus and wife of Poseidon.

Am·phit·ry·on (ăm fĭt′rĬ ən), *n.* **1.** *Gk. Legend.* the husband of Alcmene. **2.** a host; an entertainer.

am·pho·ra (ăm′fə rə), *n., pl.* **-rae** (-rē′). a two-handled, narrow-necked vessel, commonly big-bellied and narrowed at the base, used by the ancient Greeks and Romans for holding wine, oil, etc. [t. L, t. Gk.: m. *amphoreús,* short for *amphiphoreús*] —**am′pho·ral,** *adj.*

am·pho·ter·ic (ăm′fə tĕr′Ĭk), *adj. Chem.* functioning as an acid or as a base. [f. s. Gk. *amphóteros* (comp. of *amphó* both) + -IC]

Amphorae

am·ple (ăm′pəl), *adj.,* **-pler, -plest.** **1.** of great extent, size, or amount; large; spacious. **2.** in full or abundant measure; copious; liberal. **3.** fully sufficient for the purpose or for needs; enough and to spare. [late ME, t.L: m.s. *amplus*] —**am′ple·ness,** *n.* —**Syn. 2.** AMPLE, COPIOUS, LIBERAL describe an abundant supply of something. AMPLE describes a plentiful amount: *to give ample praise.* COPIOUS implies an apparently inexhaustible and lavish abundance: *a copious flow of tears.* LIBERAL implies a generous supply (more than AMPLE but less than COPIOUS) together with a free and unrestricted dispensing of it: *liberal amounts of food were distributed to the needy.* —**Ant. 2.** scanty, meager.

am·plex·i·caul (ăm plĕk′sə kôl′), *adj. Bot.* clasping the stem, as some leaves do at their base. [t. NL: s. *amplexicaulis,* f. L: m. s. *amplexus* embracing + *caulis* stem]

am·pli·a·tion (ăm′plĬ ā′shən), *n. Now Rare or Obs.* enlargement; amplification. [t. L: s. *ampliātio*]

am·pli·fi·ca·tion (ăm′plə fə kā′shən), *n.* **1.** act of amplifying. **2.** expansion of a statement, narrative, etc., as for rhetorical purposes. **3.** a statement, narrative, etc., so expanded. **4.** an addition made in expanding. **5.** *Elect.* increase in the strength of current, voltage, or power. [t. L: s. *amplificātio*]

Amplexicaul leaves

am·pli·fi·ca·to·ry (ăm plĬf′ə kə tōr′Ĭ), *adj.* of the nature of enlargement or extension.

am·pli·fi·er (ăm′plə fī′ər), *n.* **1.** one who amplifies or enlarges. **2.** *Elect.* a device for increasing the amplitudes of electric waves or impulses by means of the control exercised by the input over the power supplied to the output from a local source of energy. Commonly it is a vacuum tube or a device employing vacuum tubes, but it may be an electric dynamo.

am·pli·fy (ăm′plə fī′), *v.,* **-fied, -fying.** —*v.t.* **1.** to make larger or greater; enlarge; extend. **2.** to expand in stating or describing, as by details, illustrations, etc. **3.** to exaggerate. **4.** *Elect.* to increase the amplitude of (impulses or waves). —*v.i.* **5.** to discourse at length; expatiate or dilate (usually fol. by *on*). [ME *amplify(en),* t. F: m. *amplifier,* t. L: m. s. *amplificāre* enlarge. See -FY] —**Ant. 1.** contract. **2.** condense.

am·pli·tude (ăm′plə tūd′, -tōod′), *n.* **1.** extension in space, esp. breadth or width; largeness; extent. **2.** large or full measure; abundance; copiousness. **3.** *Physics.* the distance or range from one extremity of an oscillation to the middle point or neutral value. **4.** *Elect.* the maximum strength of an alternating current during its cycle, as distinguished from the mean or effective strength. **5.** *Astron.* the arc of the horizon from the east or west point to a heavenly body at its rising or setting. [t. L: m. *amplitūdo*]

amplitude modulation, *Electronics.* a system of radio transmission in which the carrier wave is modulated by changing its amplitude (distinguished from *frequency modulation*).

am·ply (ăm′plĬ), *adv.* in an ample manner; sufficiently.

am·poule (ăm′pōol), *n. Med.* a sealed glass bulb used to hold hypodermic solutions. Also, **am·pule** (ăm′pūl). [t. F, g. L *ampulla* bottle]

am·pul·la (ăm pŭl′ə), *n., pl.* **-pullae** (-pŭl′ē). **1.** *Anat.* a dilated portion of a canal or duct, esp. of the semicircular canals of the ear. **2.** *Eccles.* **a.** a vessel for holding wine and water used at the altar. **b.** a vessel for holding consecrated oil. **3.** a two-handled bottle used by the ancient Romans for oil, etc. [t. L]

am·pul·la·ceous (ăm/pə lā/shəs), *adj.* like an ampulla; bottle-shaped. Also, **am·pul·lar** (ăm pŭl/ər).

am·pu·tate (ăm/pyŏŏ tāt/), *v.t.,* **-tated, -tating.** **1.** to cut off (a limb, arm, etc.) by a surgical operation. **2.** *Obs.* to prune, as branches of trees. [t. L: m. s. *amputātus,* pp.] **—am/pu·ta/tion,** *n.* **—am/pu·ta/tor,** *n.*

am·pu·tee (ăm/pyŏŏ tē/), *n.* one who has lost an arm, hand, leg, etc., by amputation.

am·ri·ta (əm rē/tə), *n. Hindu Myth.* **1.** the beverage of immortality. **2.** the immortality conferred by it. Also, **am·ree/ta.** [t. Skt.: m. *amrta* immortal; as n., the drink of immortality. Cf. Gk. *ăm(b)rotos* immortal]

Am·rit·sar (əm rĭt/sər), *n.* a city in NW India, in Punjab. 391,010 (1941).

Am·ster·dam (ăm/stər dăm/; *Du.* ăm/stər däm/), *n.* **1.** a seaport in and the parliamentary capital of the Netherlands, in the W part, on the Zuider Zee: ship canal. 780,070 (est. 1946). **2.** a city in E New York. 32,240 (1950).

amt., amount.

a·muck (ə mŭk/), *adv.* (*orig. adj.*) **1. run amuck, a.** to rush about in a murderous frenzy. **b.** to rush about wildly. **—n. 2.** amok. [var. of AMOK]

A·mu Dar·ya (ä mŏŏ/ där/yä), a river flowing from the Pamirs in central Asia NW to the Aral Sea. ab. 1400 mi. Also, **Oxus.**

am·u·let (ăm/yə lĭt), *n.* an object superstitiously worn to ward off (a literal), a protecting charm. [t. L: s. *amulētum*]

A·mund·sen (ä/mənd sən; *Nor.* ä/mŏŏn sən), *n.* **Roald** (rō/äl), 1872–1928, Norwegian explorer: discovered the South Pole in December, 1911.

A·mur (ä mŏŏr/), *n.* a river in E Asia, forming most of the boundary between N Manchuria and the SE Soviet Union, flowing into the Sea of Okhotsk. ab. 2700 mi.

a·muse (ə mūz/), *v.t.,* **amused, amusing. 1.** to hold the attention of agreeably; entertain; divert. **2.** to excite mirth in. **3.** to cause (time, leisure, etc.) to pass agreeably. **4.** *Archaic.* to keep in expectation by flattery, pretenses, etc. **5.** *Obs.* to engross. **6.** *Obs.* to puzzle. [t. OF: m. s. *amuser* occupy with trifles, divert, f. *a* to + *muser* stare. See MUSE[1]] **—a·mus/a·ble,** *adj.* **—a·mus/er,** *n.*

—Syn. 1. AMUSE, DIVERT, ENTERTAIN mean to occupy the attention with something pleasant. That which AMUSES dispels the tedium of idleness or pleases the fancy. DIVERT implies turning the attention from serious thoughts or pursuits to something light, amusing, or lively. That which ENTERTAINS usually does so because of a plan or program which engages and holds the attention by being pleasing and sometimes instructive.

a·mused (ə mūzd/), *adj.* **1.** filled with interest; pleasurably occupied. **2.** displaying amusement: *an amused expression.* **3.** aroused to mirth. **—a·mus·ed·ly** (ə mū/zĭd lĭ), *adv.*

a·muse·ment (ə mūz/mənt), *n.* **1.** state of being amused; enjoyment. **2.** that which amuses; pastime; entertainment. [t. F] **—Syn. 1.** recreation, frolic, pleasure, merriment. **2.** diversion, game.

a·mus·ing (ə mū/zĭng), *adj.* **1.** pleasantly entertaining or diverting. **2.** exciting moderate mirth; delighting the fancy. **—a·mus/ing·ly,** *adv.* **—a·mus/ing·ness,** *n.*

—Syn. 2. AMUSING, COMICAL, DROLL describe that which causes mirth. That which is AMUSING is quietly humorous or funny in a gentle, good-humored way: *the baby's attempts to talk were amusing.* That which is COMICAL causes laughter by being incongruous, witty, or ludicrous: *his huge shoes made the clown look comical.* DROLL adds to COMICAL the idea of strange or peculiar, and sometimes that of sly or waggish humor: *droll antics of a kitten, a droll imitation.*

a·mu·sive (ə mū/zĭv), *adj.* affording amusement or entertainment.

a·myg·da·la (ə mĭg/də lə), *n., pl.* **-lae** (-lē/). **1.** an almond. **2.** *Anat.* **a.** an almond-shaped part. **b.** a tonsil. [t. L, t. Gk.: m. *amygdálē* almond. Cf. OE *amygdal*]

a·myg·da·late (ə mĭg/də lĭt, -lāt/), *adj.* pertaining to, resembling, or made of almonds.

a·myg·da·lin (ə mĭg/də lĭn), *n.* a crystalline principle, $C_{20}H_{27}NO_{11} + 3H_2O$, existing in bitter almonds, and in the leaves, etc., of species of the genus *Prunus* and of some of its near allies.

a·myg·da·line (ə mĭg/də lĭn, -līn/), *adj.* of or pertaining to the amygdala.

a·myg·da·loid (ə mĭg/də loid/), *n.* **1.** *Petrog.* an igneous rock in which rounded cavities formed by the expansion of steam have later become filled with various minerals. **—adj.** Also, **a·myg·da·loi·dal.** **2.** (of rocks) containing amygdules. **3.** almond-shaped. [f. s. Gk. *amygdálē* almond + -OID]

a·myg·dule (ə mĭg/dūl, -dŏŏl), *n. Petrog.* one of the mineral nodules in amygdaloid.

am·yl (ăm/ĭl), *n. Chem.* a univalent radical, C_5H_{11}, derived from pentane. Its compounds are found in fusel oil, fruit extracts, etc. [t. L: s. *amylum* starch (t. Gk.: m. *ámylon*); the *-yl* was identified with -YL]

am·y·la·ceous (ăm/ə lā/shəs), *adj.* of the nature of starch; starchy. [f. AMYL(O)- + -ACEOUS]

amyl alcohol, *Chem.* a colorless liquid, $C_5H_{11}OH$, consisting of a mixture of two or more isomeric alcohols, derived from the pentanes and serving as a solvent and intermediate for organic syntheses.

am·yl·ase (ăm/ə lās/), *n. Biochem.* **1.** a starch-splitting enzyme in the blood and in certain plants, which hydrolyzes complex sugars to glucose. **2.** any of several

digestive enzymes, as amylopsin or ptyalin, which break down starches.

am·yl·ene (ăm/ə lēn/), *n. Chem.* any of certain unsaturated isomeric hydrocarbons with the formula C_5H_{10}; pentene.

amylo-, a combining form of **amyl** and **amylum.** Also, **amyl-.**

am·y·loid (ăm/ə loid/), *n. Pathol.* a hard, homogeneous, glossy substance deposited in tissues in certain kinds of degeneration. **—am/y·loi/dal,** *adj.*

am·y·lol·y·sis (ăm/ə lŏl/ə sĭs), *n. Biochem.* the conversion of starch into sugar. **—am·y·lo·lyt·ic** (ăm/ə lō lĭt/ĭk), *adj.*

am·y·lo·pec·tin (ăm/ə lō pĕk/tĭn), *n. Chem.* the gel component of starch. It turns red in iodine.

am·y·lop·sin (ăm/ə lŏp/sĭn), *n. Biochem.* an enzyme of the pancreatic juice, capable of converting starch into sugar. [b. AMYLO(LYSIS) and (PE)PSIN]

am·y·lose (ăm/ə lōs/), *n. Chem.* the sol component of starch. It turns intense blue in iodine.

am·y·lum (ăm/ə ləm), *n.* starch (def. 1). [t. L, t. Gk.: m. *ámylon* fine meal, starch]

am·y·tal (ăm/ə tôl/, -tăl/), *n. Pharm.* a colorless crystalline substance, $C_{11}H_{18}N_2O_3$, used esp. as a sedative.

an[1] (ăn; *unstressed* ən), the form of the indefinite article before an initial vowel sound. See **a**[1]. [ME; OE *ān.* See ONE]

an[2] (ăn; *unstressed* ən), *conj.* **1.** *Dial. and Colloq.* and. **2.** *Archaic and Dial.* if. Also, **an'.** [var. of AND]

an-[1], a prefix meaning "not," "without," "lacking," used before vowels and *h,* as in *anarchy.* Also, **a-**[6]. [t. Gk.]

an-[2], var. of **ad-,** before *n,* as in *announce.*

an-[3], var. of **ana-,** used before vowels, as in *anaerobe.*

-an, a suffix meaning: **1.** "belonging to," "pertaining or relating to," "adhering to," and commonly expressing connection with a place, person, leader, class, order, sect, system, doctrine, or the like, serving to form adjectives, many of which are also used as nouns, as *American, Christian, Elizabethan, republican,* and hence serving to form other nouns of the same type, as *historian, theologian.* **2.** *Zool.* relating to a certain class, as in *Mammalian.* [t. L: s. *-ānus;* r. ME *-ain, -en,* t. OF]

AN, Anglo-Norman. Also, **A.N.**

an., (L. *anno*) in the year.

a·na[1] (ā/nə, ä/nə), *n.* **1.** a collection of miscellaneous information about a particular subject. **2.** the information so collected. [independent use of -ANA]

an·a[2] (ăn/ə), *adv. Pharm.* in equal quantities; of each (used in medical prescriptions, with reference to ingredients, and often written āā). [ML, t. Gk. See ANA-]

ana-, a prefix meaning "up," "throughout," "again," "back," occurring originally in words from the Greek, but used also in modern words (English and other) formed after the Greek type, as in *anabatic.* [t. Gk., repr. *aná,* prep.]

-ana, a noun suffix denoting a collection of material pertaining to a given subject, as in *Shakespeariana, Americana.* [t. L, neut. pl. of *-ānus*]

an·a·bae·na (ăn/ə bē/nə), *n., pl.* **-nas.** *Bot.* any of the fresh-water algae constituting the genus *Anabaena,* commonly occurring in masses, and often contaminating drinking water, giving it a fishy odor and taste. [t. NL, der. Gk. *anabaínein* go up]

An·a·bap·tist (ăn/ə băp/tĭst), *n.* **1.** an adherent of a religious and social movement which arose in Europe shortly after 1520 and was distinguished by its strict requirements for church membership, insistence upon being baptized over again, rejection of infant baptism, and by its demands for social reforms. **2.** a member of a later sect or religious body holding the same doctrines. **3.** *Archaic.* Baptist (def. 1). **—An/a·bap/tism,** *n.*

an·a·bas (ăn/ə băs/), *n.* any fish of the genus *Anabas* of southern Asia, etc., as the climbing fish, *A. testudineus.* [t. NL, t. Gk., aorist participle of *anabaínein* go up]

a·nab·a·sis (ə năb/ə sĭs), *n., pl.* **-ses** (-sēz/). **1.** a march from the coast into the interior, as that of Cyrus the Younger against Artaxerxes II, described by Xenophon in his *Anabasis.* **2.** any military expedition. [t. Gk.]

an·a·bat·ic (ăn/ə băt/ĭk), *adj. Meteorol.* (of winds and air currents) moving upward or up a slope. [t. Gk.: m. s. *anabatikós* pertaining to climbing]

an·a·bi·o·sis (ăn/ə bī ō/sĭs), *n.* a bringing back to consciousness; reanimation (after apparent death). [t. NL, t. Gk.: revival] **—an·a·bi·ot·ic** (ăn/ə bī ŏt/ĭk), *adj.*

a·nab·o·lism (ə năb/ə lĭz/əm), *n. Biol.* constructive metabolism (opposed to *catabolism*). [f. s. Gk. *anabolē* a throwing up + -ISM] **—an·a·bol·ic** (ăn/ə bŏl/ĭk), *adj.*

an·a·branch (ăn/ə brănch/, -bränch/), *n. Phys. Geog.* a branch of a river which leaves the main stream and either enters it again, dries up, or sinks into the ground. [short for *anastomosing branch*]

an·a·car·di·a·ceous (ăn/ə kär/dĭ ā/shəs), *adj.* belonging to the *Anacardiaceae,* a family of trees and shrubs including the cashew, mango, pistachio, sumac, etc. [f. s. NL *Anacardiāceae* (f. *ana-* ANA- + s. Gk. *kardía* heart + -āceae -ACEAE) + -OUS]

a·nach·ro·nism (ə năk/rə nĭz/əm), *n.* **1.** a crediting of a person or thing to a time other, esp. earlier, than the actual period. **2.** something placed or occurring out of its proper time. [t. Gk.: s. *anachronismós*]

a·nach·ro·nis·tic (ə năk/rə nĭs/tĭk), *adj.* containing an anachronism. Also, **a·nach/ro·nis/ti·cal.**

---

b., blend of, blended; c., cognate with; d., dialect, dialectal; der., derived from; f., formed from; g., going back to; m., modification of; r., replacing; s., stem of; t., taken from; ?, perhaps. See the full key on inside cover.

a·nach·ro·nous (ə năk′rə nəs), *adj.* anachronistic. —**a·nach′ro·nous·ly,** *adv.*

an·a·cli·sis (ăn′ə klī′sĭs), *n. Psychoanal.* the choice of an object of libidinal attachment on the basis of a resemblance to early childhood protective and parental figures. [t. Gk.: m. *anáklisis* a leaning back]

an·a·clit·ic (ăn′ə klĭt′ĭk), *aaj. Psychoanal.* exhibiting or pertaining to anaclisis.

an·a·co·lu·thi·a (ăn′ə kə lōō′thĭ ə), *n.* lack of grammatical sequence or coherence, esp. in the same sentence. [t.L, t.Gk.: m. *anakolūthĭa*] —**an′a·co·lu′thic,** *adj.*

an·a·co·lu·thon (ăn′ə kə lōō′thŏn), *n., pl.* **-tha** (-thə). *Rhet.* a construction involving a break in grammatical sequence; a case of anacoluthia. [t. L, t. Gk.: m. *ana-kólouthon,* neut. adj., inconsequent]

an·a·con·da ((ăn′ə kŏn′də), *n.* **1.** a large South American snake, *Eunectes murinus,* of the boa family. **2.** any boa constrictor. [orig. unknown; ? t. Singhalese]

An·a·con·da (ăn′ə kŏn′də), *n.* a city in SW Montana: largest copper smelter in the world. 11,254 (1950).

A·nac·re·on (ə năk′rĭ ən), *n.* c563–c478 B.C., Greek lyric poet known for his love poems and drinking songs.

A·nac·re·on·tic (ə năk′rĭ ŏn′tĭk), *adj.* Also, **anacreontic. 1.** pertaining to or in the manner of Anacreon. **2.** pertaining to the praise of love and wine; convivial; amatory. —*n.* **3.** (*l.c.*) an Anacreontic poem.

an·a·cru·sis (ăn′ə krōō′sĭs), *n. Pros.* an unstressed syllable or syllable group which begins a line of verse but is not counted as part of the first foot, which properly begins with a stressed syllable. [t. L, t. Gk.: m. *aná-krousis,* der. *anakroúein* strike up]

an·a·dem (ăn′ə dĕm′), *n. Poetic.* a garland or wreath for the head. [t. L: m. *anadema,* t. Gk.: fillet]

an·a·di·plo·sis (ăn′ə də plō′sĭs), *n. Rhet.* repetition in the first part of one clause of a prominent word in the latter part of the preceding clause. [t. Gk.: repetition]

a·nad·ro·mous (ə năd′rə məs), *adj.* (of fishes) going from the sea up a river to spawn (contrasted with *catadromous*). [t. Gk.: m. *anádromos* running up]

a·nae·mi·a (ə nē′mĭ ə), *n.* anemia. —**a·nae′mic,** *adj.*

an·aer·obe (ăn âr′ōb), *n.* a bacterium or other microörganism which does not require free oxygen or is not destroyed by its absence (opposed to *aerobe*). [back formation from anaerobia, pl. of ANAEROBIUM]

an·aer·o·bic (ăn′â rō′bĭk), *adj.* **1.** *Biol., Physiol.* (of organisms or tissues) requiring the absence of free oxygen or not destroyed by its absence. **2.** pertaining to or caused by the absence of oxygen.

an·aer·o·bi·um (ăn′â rō′bĭ əm), *n., pl.* **-bia** (-bĭ ə). *Biol.* anaerobe. [NL, f. Gk.: an- AN-[1] + āero- AERO- + m. *bios* life]

an·aes·the·sia (ăn′əs thē′zhə), *n.* anesthesia. —**an·aes·thet·ic** (ăn′əs thĕt′ĭk), *adj., n.* —**an·aes·the·tist** (ə nĕs′thə tĭst), *n.* —**an·aes′the·tize′,** *v.t.* —**an·aes′-the·ti·za′tion,** *n.*

an·a·glyph (ăn′ə glĭf), *n.* something executed in low relief, as a cameo or an embossed ornament. [t. Gk.: s. *anáglyphos* wrought in low relief] —**an·a·glyph·ic** (ăn′-ə glĭf′ĭk), **an·a·glyp·tic** (ăn′ə glĭp′tĭk), *adj.*

an·a·go·ge (ăn′ə gō′jĭ), *n.* **1.** the spiritual interpretation or application of words, as of Scriptures. **2.** *Theol.* the application of the types and allegories of the Old to subjects of the New Testament. [t. LL, t. Gk.: a bringing up, elevation] —**an·a·gog·ic** (ăn′ə gŏj′ĭk), **an′-a·gog′i·cal,** *adj.* —**an′a·gog′i·cal·ly,** *adv.*

an·a·gram (ăn′ə grăm′), *n.* **1.** a transposition of the letters of a word or sentence to form a new word or sentence, as *Galenus* is an anagram of *angelus.* **2.** (*pl.* construed as *sing.*) a game in which the players build words by transposing or adding letters. [t. NL: m. *anagramma,* back formation from Gk. *anagrammatismós* transposition of letters] —**an·a·gram·mat·ic** (ăn′ə grə măt′ĭk), **an′-a·gram·mat′i·cal,** *adj.* —**an′a·gram·mat′i·cal·ly,** *adv.*

an·a·gram·ma·tize (ăn′ə grăm′ə tīz′), *v.t.,* **-tized, -tizing.** to transpose into an anagram.

a·nal (ā′nəl), *adj.* of, pertaining to, or near the anus.

anal., 1. analogous. **2.** analogy. **3.** analysis.

an·al·cite (ăn ăl′sīt, ăn′əl sīt′), *n.* a white or slightly colored zeolite mineral, generally found in crystalline form. Also, **an·al·cime** (ăn ăl′sĭm, -sīm). [f. m.s. Gk. *analkĕs* weak + -ITE[1]]

an·a·lects (ăn′ə lĕkts′), *n.pl.* selected passages from the writings of an author or of different authors. Also, **an·a·lec·ta** (ăn′ə lĕk′tə). [t. L: (m.) *analecta,* pl., t. Gk.: m. *análekta* things gathered]

an·a·lep·tic (ăn′ə lĕp′tĭk), *Med.* —*adj.* **1.** restoring; invigorating; giving strength after disease. **2.** awakening, esp. from drug stupor. —*n.* **3.** an analeptic remedy. [t. Gk.: m.s. *analēptikós* restorative]

anal fin, (in fishes) the median ventral unpaired fin (opposed to *dorsal fin*).

an·al·ge·si·a (ăn′əl jē′zĭ ə, -sĭ ə), *n. Med.* absence of sense of pain. [t. NL, t. Gk.]

an·al·ge·sic (ăn′əl jē′zĭk, -sĭk), *Med.* —*n.* **1.** a remedy that relieves or removes pain. —*adj.* **2.** pertaining to or causing analgesia.

an·a·log·i·cal (ăn′ə lŏj′ə kəl), *adj.* based on, involving, or expressing an analogy. Also, **an′a·log′ic.**

an·a·log·i·cal·ly (ăn′ə lŏj′ĭk lĭ), *adv.* by analogy.

a·nal·o·gist (ə năl′ə jĭst), *n.* **1.** one who employs or argues from analogy. **2.** one who looks for analogies.

a·nal·o·gize (ə năl′ə jīz′), *v.i.,* **-gized, -gizing. 1.** to make use of analogy in reasoning, argument, etc. **2.** to be analogous; exhibit analogy.

a·nal·o·gous (ə năl′ə gəs), *adj.* **1.** having analogy; corresponding in some particular. **2.** *Biol.* corresponding in function, but not evolved from corresponding organs, as the wings of a bee and those of a hummingbird. [t. L: m. *analogus,* t. Gk.: m. *análogos* proportionate] —**a·nal′o·gous·ly,** *adv.* —**a·nal′o·gous·ness,** *n.*

an·a·logue (ăn′ə lŏg′, -lŏg′), *n.* **1.** something having analogy to something else. **2.** *Biol.* an organ or part analogous to another. Also, **an′a·log′.** [t. F, t. Gk.: m. s. *análogon*]

a·nal·o·gy (ə năl′ə jĭ), *n., pl.* **-gies. 1.** an agreement, likeness, or correspondence between the relations of things to one another; a partial similarity in particular circumstances on which a comparison may be based: *the analogy between the heart and a pump.* **2.** agreement; similarity. **3.** *Biol.* an analogous relationship. **4.** (in linguistic change) the tendency of inflections and formations to follow existing models and regular patterns: *"adnoun" is formed on the analogy of "adverb."* **5.** *Logic.* a form of reasoning in which similarities are inferred from a similarity of two or more things in certain particulars. [t. L: m.s. *analogia,* t. Gk.: orig., equality of ratios, proportion]

a·nal·y·sis (ə năl′ə sĭs), *n., pl.* **-ses** (-sēz′). **1.** separation of a whole, whether a material substance or any matter of thought, into its constituent elements (opposed to *synthesis*). **2.** this process as a method of studying the nature of a thing or of determining its essential features: *the grammatical analysis of a sentence.* **3.** a brief presentation of essential features; an outline or summary, as of a book; a synopsis. **4.** *Math.* a. an investigation based on the properties of numbers. b. the discussion of a problem by algebra as opposed to geometry. **5.** *Chem.* a. intentionally produced decomposition or separation of a substance into its ingredients or elements, as to find their kind or quantity. b. the ascertainment of the kind or amount of one or more of the constituents of a substance, whether actually obtained in separate form or not. **6.** psychoanalysis. [t. ML, t. Gk.: a breaking up]

analysis of variance, *Statistics.* a procedure for resolving the total variance of a set of variates into component variances, which are associated with various factors affecting the variates.

an·a·lyst (ăn′ə lĭst), *n.* **1.** one who analyzes or who is skilled in analysis. **2.** a psychoanalyst.

an·a·lyt·ic (ăn′ə lĭt′ĭk), *adj.* **1.** pertaining to or proceeding by analysis (opposed to *synthetic*). **2.** (of languages) characterized by the use of separate words (**free forms**) rather than of inflectional adjuncts (**bound forms**) to show syntactic relationships (opposed to *synthetic*). **3.** *Logic.* (of a proposition) necessarily true because its denial involves a contradiction, as *all spinsters are unmarried.* Also, **an′a·lyt′i·cal.** [t. ML: s. *analyticus,* t. Gk.: m. *analytikós*] —**an′a·lyt′i·cal·ly,** *adv.*

analytic geometry, geometry treated by algebra, the position of any point being determined by numbers, and its coördinates with respect to a system of coördinates.

an·a·lyt·ics (ăn′ə lĭt′ĭks), *n.* mathematical or algebraic analysis. [n. use of ANALYTIC. See -ICS]

an·a·lyze (ăn′ə līz′), *v.t.,* **-lyzed, -lyzing. 1.** to resolve into elements or constituent parts; determine the elements or essential features of: *to analyze an argument.* **2.** to examine critically, so as to bring out the essential elements or give the essence of: *to analyze a poem.* **3.** to subject to mathematical, chemical, grammatical, etc., analysis. Also, *esp. Brit.,* **an′a·lyse′.** —**an′a·lyz′a·ble,** *adj.* —**an′a·lyz′er,** *n.*

A·nam (ə năm′), *n.* Annam.

an·am·ne·sis (ăn′ăm nē′sĭs), *n.* **1.** the recalling of things past; recollection. **2.** *Psychiatry.* a case history. [t. NL, t. Gk.: a recalling to mind]

an·a·mor·pho·scope (ăn′ə môr′fə skōp′), *n.* a curved mirror or other optical device for giving a correct image of a picture or the like distorted by anamorphosis.

an·a·mor·pho·sis (ăn′ə môr′fə sĭs, -môr fō′sĭs), *n., pl.* **-ses** (-sēz′, -sēz). **1.** a kind of drawing presenting a distorted image which appears in natural form under certain conditions, as when viewed at a raking angle or reflected from a curved mirror. **2.** the method of producing such drawings. [t. NL, t. Gk.: a forming anew]

an·an·drous (ă năn′drəs), *adj. Bot.* having no stamens. [t. Gk.: m. *ánandros* without a man]

An·a·ni·as (ăn′ə nī′əs), *n.* **1.** *Bible.* a character who was struck dead for lying. Acts 5:1–5. **2.** a liar.

an·an·thous (ă năn′thəs), *adj. Bot.* without flowers. [f. AN-[1] + s. Gk. *ánthos* flower + -OUS]

an·a·pest (ăn′ə pĕst′), *n. Pros.* a foot of three syllables, two short followed by one long (quantitative meter), or two unstressed followed by one stressed (accentual meter). Thus, *for the nonce* is an accentual anapest. Also, **an′a·paest′.** [t. L: m.s. *anapaestus,* t. Gk.: m. *anápaistos* struck back, reversed (as compared with a dactyl)] —**an′a·pes′tic,** *adj., n.*

an·a·phase (ăn′ə fāz′), *n. Biol.* the stage in mitotic cell division after cleavage of the chromosomes, in which the chromosomes move away from each other to opposite ends of the cell.

a·naph·o·ra (ə năf′ə rə), *n. Rhet.* repetition of the

same word or words at the beginning of two or more successive verses, clauses, or sentences. [t. L, t. Gk.: a bringing up]

an·aph·ro·dis·i·ac (ăn ăf'rə dĭz'ĭ ăk'), *Med.* —*adj.* 1. capable of diminishing sexual desire. —*n.* 2. an anaphrodisiac agent. [f. AN-¹ + APHRODISIAC]

an·a·phy·lax·is (ăn'ə fə lăk'sĭs), *n.* *Pathol.* increased susceptibility to a foreign protein resulting from previous exposure to it, as in serum treatment. [t. NL, f. Gk.: *ana-* ANA- + *phy̆laxis* a guarding] —**an·a·phy·lac'tic,** *adj.*

an·a·plas·mo·sis (ăn'ə plăz mō'sĭs), *n.* *Vet. Sci.* a disease of cattle caused by a blood-infecting protozoan parasite, transmitted by bloodsucking flies and ticks.

an·a·plas·tic (ăn'ə plăs'tĭk), *adj.* 1. *Surg.* replacing lost tissue or parts, or remedying natural defects, as by transplanting. 2. *Pathol.* **a.** (of cells) having reverted to a more primitive form. **b.** (of tumors) having a high degree of malignancy.

an·a·plas·ty (ăn'ə plăs'tĭ), *n.* anaplastic surgery. [f. s. Gk. *anáplastos* plastic + -Y³]

an·ap·tot·ic (ăn'ăp tŏt'ĭk), *adj.* (of languages) tending to become uninflected, in accordance with a theory that languages evolve from uninflected to inflected and back. [f. AN-³ + s. Gk. *áptōtos* indeclinable + -IC]

an·arch (ăn'ärk), *n.* an anarchist.

an·ar·chic (ănär'kĭk), *adj.* 1. of, like, or tending to anarchy. 2. advocating anarchy. 3. lawless. Also, **an·ar'chi·cal.** —**an·ar'chi·cal·ly,** *adv.*

an·ar·chism (ăn'ər kĭz'əm), *n.* 1. the doctrine (advocated under various forms) urging the abolition of government and governmenta, restraint as the indispensable condition of political and social liberty. 2. the methods or practices of anarchists. —**an·ar·chis·tic** (ăn'ər kĭs'tĭk), *adj.*

an·ar·chist (ăn'ər kĭst), *n.* 1. one who advocates anarchy as a political idea; a believer in an anarchic theory of society, esp. an adherent of the social theory of Proudhon, Bakunin, or Kropotkin. 2. one who seeks to overturn by violence all constituted forms and institutions of society and government, with no purpose of establishing any other system of order in the place of that destroyed. 3. any person who promotes disorder or excites revolt against an established rule, law, or custom. [f. s. Gk. *ánarchos* without a ruler + -IST]

an·ar·chy (ăn'ər kĭ), *n.* 1. a state of society without government or law. 2. political and social disorder due to absence of governmental control. 3. absence of government or governmental restraint. 4. a theory which regards the union of order with the absence of all direct or coercive government as the political ideal. 5. confusion in general; disorder. [t. Gk.: m.s. *anarchía* lack of a ruler]

an·ar·throus (ăn är'thrəs), *adj.* 1. *Zool.* without joints or articulated limbs. 2. (esp. in Greek grammar) used without the article. [t. Gk.: m. *ánarthros*]

an·a·sar·ca (ăn'ə sär'kə), *n.* *Pathol.* a pronounced generalized dropsy. [f. ANA- + Gk. *sárx* flesh] —**an'a·sar'cous,** *adj.*

an·as·tig·mat·ic (ăn'ə stĭg măt'ĭk, ă năs'tĭg-), *adj.* (of a lens) not astigmatic; forming point images of a point object located off the lens axis.

a·nas·to·mose (ə năs'tə mōz'), *v.t., v.i.,* **-mosed, -mosing.** *Physiol.* to communicate or connect by anastomosis.

a·nas·to·mo·sis (ə năs'tə mō'sĭs), *n., pl.* **-ses** (-sēz). 1. *Physiol.* communication between blood vessels by means of collateral channels. 2. *Biol.* connection between parts of any branching system. [t. NL, t. Gk.: opening] —**a·nas·to·mot·ic** (ə năs'tə mŏt'ĭk), *adj.*

a·nas·tro·phe (ə năs'trə fĭ), *n.* *Rhet.* inversion of the usual order of words. [t. L, t. Gk.: a turning back]

anat., 1. anatomical. 2. anatomy.

an·a·tase (ăn'ə tāz'), *n.* a black to brown mineral, titanium dioxide, TiO₂, occurring in octahedral crystals; octahedrite. [t. F, t. Gk.: m. *anátasis* extension]

a·nath·e·ma (ə năth'ə mə), *n., pl.* **-mas.** 1. a formal ecclesiastical curse involving excommunication. 2. any imprecation of divine punishment. 3. a curse; an execration. 4. a person or thing accursed or consigned to damnation or destruction. 5. a person or thing detested or loathed. [t. LL, t. Gk.: something devoted (to evil)]

a·nath·e·ma·tize (ə năth'ə ma tīz'), *v.,* **-tized, -tizing.** —*v.t.* 1. to pronounce an anathema against; denounce; curse. —*v.i.* 2. to pronounce anathemas; curse. —**a·nath'e·ma·ti·za'tion,** *n.*

an·a·tine (ăn'ə tĭn', -tĭn), *adj.* 1. of or pertaining to the *Anatidae,* the duck family. 2. resembling a duck; ducklike. [t. L: m.s. *anatīnus*]

An·a·to·li·a (ăn'ə tō'lĭ ə), *n.* a vast plateau between the Black and the Mediterranean seas: in ancient usage, synonymous with the peninsula of Asia Minor; in modern usage, applied to Turkey in Asia.

An·a·to·li·an (ăn'ə tō'lĭ ən), *adj.* 1. of or pertaining to Anatolia. 2. belonging to, or concerning, a group or family of languages that includes cuneiform Hittite and its nearest congeners.

an·a·tom·i·cal (ăn'ə tŏm'ə kəl), *adj.* pertaining to anatomy. Also, **an'a·tom'ic.** —**an'a·tom'i·cal·ly,** *adv.*

a·nat·o·mist (ə năt'ə mĭst), *n.* an expert in anatomy.

a·nat·o·mize (ə năt'ə mīz'), *v.t.,* **-mized, -mizing.** 1. to dissect, as a plant or an animal, to show the position, structure, and relation of the parts; display the

anatomy of. 2. to analyze or examine minutely. —**a·nat'o·mi·za'tion,** *n.*

a·nat·o·my (ə năt'ə mĭ), *n., pl.* **-mies.** 1. the structure of an animal or plant, or any of its parts. 2. the science of the structure of animals and plants 3. dissection of animals or plants, or their parts, for study of structure, position, etc. 4. an anatomical subject or model. 5. a skeleton. 6. any analysis or minute examination. [t. LL: m.s. *anatomia,* t. Gk., var. of *anatomē* dissection; r. ME *anothomia,* t. ML]

a·nat·ro·pous (ə năt'rə pəs), *adj.* *Bot.* (of an ovule) inverted at an early stage of growth, so that the micropyle is turned toward the funicle, the chalaza being situated at the opposite end. [t. NL: m. *anatropus* inverted. See ANA-, -TROPOUS]

a·nat·to (ə năt'ō, ä nä'tō), *n.* annatto.

An·ax·ag·o·ras (ăn'ăk săg'ə rəs), *n.* 500?–428 B.C., Greek philosopher.

A·nax·i·man·der (ə năk'sə măn'dər), *n.* 611?–547? B.C., Greek philosopher.

anc., ancient.

-ance, a suffix of nouns denoting action, state, or quality, or something exemplifying one of these, often corresponding to adjectives in *-ant,* as in *brilliance, distance,* or formed directly from verbs, as in *assistance, defiance.* [ME *-ance,* t. F, g. L *-antia, -entia,* orig. ppr. endings]

an·ces·tor (ăn'sĕs tər), *n.* 1. one from whom a person is descended, usually distantly; a forefather; a progenitor. 2. *Biol.* the actual or hypothetical form or stock of an earlier and presumably lower type, from which any organized being is known or inferred to have developed. 3. *Law.* one from whom an inheritance is derived (correlative of *heir*). [ME *ancestre,* t. OF, g. L *antecessor* predecessor] —**an·ces·tress** (ăn'sĕs trĭs), *n. fem.*

an·ces·tral (ăn sĕs'trəl), *adj.* pertaining to ancestors; descending or claimed from ancestors: *an ancestral home.* —**an·ces'tral·ly,** *adv.* —**Syn.** hereditary, inherited.

an·ces·try (ăn'sĕs trĭ), *n., pl.* **-tries.** 1. ancestral descent. 2. honorable descent. 3. a series of ancestors.

An·chi·ses (ăn kī'sēz), *n.* *Classical Legend.* a prince of Troy, father of Aeneas.

an·chor (ăng'kər), *n.* 1. a device for holding boats, vessels, floating bridges, etc., in place. 2. any similar device for holding fast or checking motion. 3. a metallic strap or belt built into masonry to hold facing or other materials. 4. a means of stability: *hope is his anchor.* 5. *Mil.* a key position in defense lines. 6. **at anchor,** anchored. 7. **cast anchor,** to put down or drop the anchor. 8. **weigh anchor,** to take up the anchor. —*v.t.* 9. to hold fast by an anchor. 10. to fix or fasten; affix firmly. —*v.i.* 11. to drop anchor; lie or ride at anchor. 12. to keep hold or be firmly fixed. [ME *anker, ancre,* OE *ancor,* t. L: s. *ancora,* t. Gk.: m. *ánkȳra*] —**an'chor·less,** *adj.* —**an'chor·like',** *adj.*

an·chor·age (ăng'kər ĭj), *n.* 1. a place for anchoring. 2. a charge for anchoring. 3. act of anchoring. 4. state of being anchored. 5. that to which anything is fastened. 6. a means of anchoring or making fast.

An·chor·age (ăng'kər ĭj), *n.* a seaport in S Alaska. 11,060 (prelim. 1950).

an·cho·ress (ăng'kə rĭs), *n.* a female anchorite.

an·cho·ret (ăng'kə rĭt, -rĕt'), *n.* anchorite. [t. LL: m. s. *anachōrēta* (t. Gk.: m. *anachōrētḗs* a recluse) by assoc. with obs. *anchor* hermit (OE *ancora*)] —**an·cho·ret·ic** (ăng'kə rĕt'ĭk) *adj.*

an·cho·rite (ăng'kə rīt'), *n.* one who has retired to a solitary place for a life of religious seclusion; a hermit. [ME *ancorite,* t. ML: m. s. *anachōrīta,* var. of LL *anachōrēta*] —**an·cho·rit·ic** (ăng'kə rĭt'ĭk), *adj.*

an·cho·vy (ăn'chō vĭ, -chə vĭ, ăn chō'vĭ), *n., pl.* **-vies.** 1. a small herringlike marine fish, *Engraulis encrasicholus,* abundant in South Europe, much used pickled and in the form of a salt paste. 2. any fish of the same family (*Engraulidae*). 3. *U.S.* any smelt. [t. Sp. and Pg.: m. *anchova,* prob. t. d. It. (Genoese): m. *anciova,* g. LL *apiuva,* t. Gk.: m. *aphy̆ē*]

anchovy pear, 1. the fruit of a West Indian tree, *Grias cauliflora,* often pickled, and somewhat resembling the mango. 2. the tree.

An·chu·sa (ăng kū'sə), *n.* a boraginaceous genus of rough hairy plants including the oxtongue. [t. L, t. Gk.: m. *ánchousa* alkanet]

an·chu·sin (ăng kū'sĭn), *n.* a red coloring matter obtained from the root of the alkanet, *Alkanna tinctoria.*

an·chy·lose (ăng'kə lōs'), *v.t., v.i.,* **-losed, -losing.** ankylose. —**an'chy·lo'sis,** *n.* —**an·chy·lot·ic** (ăng'kə lŏt'ĭk), *adj.*

an·cienne no·blesse (än syĕn' nô blĕs'), *French.* the ancient nobility, esp. of the ancien régime.

an·cien ré·gime (än syän' rĕ zhēm'), *French.* 1. the political and social system of France before the Revolution of 1789. 2. the old system of government.

an·cient¹ (ān'shənt), *adj.* 1. of or in time long past, esp. before the end of the Western Roman Empire, A.D. 476: *ancient history.* 2. dating from a remote period; of great age. 3. *Archaic.* very old (applied to persons). 4. *Archaic.* venerable. 5. *Law.* of 30 years' standing, or sometimes a lesser period, as 20 years: *in ancient matters the normal requirements of proof are relaxed.* —*n.* 6. a person who lived in ancient times, esp. one of the ancient Greeks, Romans, Egyptians, Hebrews, etc. 7. (*usually pl.*) one of the classical writers of antiquity. 8. *Archaic.* an old man. [ME *auncien,* t. OF: m. *ancien,*

g. LL *antiānus* former, old, der. L *ante* before] **—an′-cient·ness**, *n.*
—Syn. 2. ANCIENT, ANTIQUATED, ANTIQUE, OLD-FASHIONED refer to something dating from the past. ANCIENT implies existence or first occurrence in the past: *an ancient custom.* ANTIQUATED connotes something too old or no longer useful: *an antiquated building.* ANTIQUE suggests a curious or pleasing quality in something old: *antique furniture.* OLD-FASHIONED may disparage something as being out of date or may approve something old as being superior: *an old-fashioned hat, old-fashioned courtesy.* **—Ant. 2.** new.
an·cient² (ān′shənt), *n. Obs.* **1.** the bearer of a flag. **2.** a flag, banner, or standard; an ensign. [var. OF ENSIGN]
an·cient·ly (ān′shənt lĭ), *adv.* in ancient times; of old.
Ancient of Days, the eternal Supreme Being.
an·cient·ry (ān′shən trĭ), *n. Archaic.* **1.** ancient character or style. **2.** ancient times or lineage.
an·cil·lar·y (ān′sə lĕr′ĭ), *adj.* serving as an aid, adjunct, or accessory; auxiliary: *an ancillary science.* [t. L: m. *ancillāris* pertaining to a handmaid]
an·cip·i·tal (ān sĭp′ə təl), *adj. Bot., Zool.* two-edged: *ancipital stems.* [f. s. L *anceps* two-headed + -AL¹]
an·con (ăng′kŏn), *n., pl.* **ancones** (ăng kō′nēz). **1.** *Archit.* any projection, as a console, supporting a cornice or the like. **2.** *Anat.* the elbow. [t. L, t. Gk.: m. *ankōn* a bend, the elbow] **—an·co·ne·al** (ăng kō′nĭ əl,) *adj.*
An·co·na (ăn kō′nä), *n.* a seaport in E Italy, on the Adriatic. 94,687 (est. 1946).
-ancy, an equivalent of *-ance,* used chiefly in nouns denoting state or quality, as in *buoyancy.* [t. L: m.s. *-antia*]
an·cy·los·to·mi·a·sis (ān′sə lŏs′tə mī′ə sĭs), *n.* hookworm disease. Also, **ankylostomiasis.** [f. NL *Ancylostom(a)* genus of hookworms (f. Gk.: *ankylo(s)* bent, hooked + *stōma* mouth) + -IASIS]
and (ănd; *unstressed* ənd, ən), *conj.* **1.** with; along with; together with; besides; also; moreover (used to connect grammatically coördinate words, phrases, or clauses): *pens and pencils.* **2.** as well as: *nice and warm.* **3.** *Colloq.* to (used between verbs): *try and do it.* **4.** *Archaic or Literary.* also; then (used to introduce a sentence, implying continuation): *and he said unto Moses.* **5.** *Archaic or Dial.* if: *and you please.* [OE; akin to G *und*]
and., andante.
An·da·lu·sia (ān′də lōō′zhə, -shĭ ə), *n.* a region in S Spain, bordering on the Atlantic and the Mediterranean. 5,219,362 pop. (1940); 33,712 sq. mi. Spanish, **An·da·lu·cí·a** (ăn′dä lōō thē′ä). **—An′da·lu′sian,** *adj., n.*
an·da·lu·site (ān′də lōō′sīt), *n.* a mineral, aluminum silicate, Al₂SiO₅, found in schistose rocks. [named after ANDALUSIA. See -ITE¹]
An·da·man and Nic·o·bar Islands (ān′də mən; nĭk′ə bär′), two groups of islands in the Bay of Bengal, SW of Burma, forming a province of India. 33,768 pop. (1941); 3143 sq. mi. *Cap.:* Port Blair.
Andaman Islands, a group of islands in the E part of the Bay of Bengal. 21,316 pop. (1941); 2508 sq. mi.
an·dan·te (ān dän′tĭ; *It.* än dän′tĕ), *Music.* **—adj., adv. 1.** moderately slow and even. **—n. 2.** an andante movement or piece. [It.: lit., walking]
an·dan·ti·no (ān′dän tē′nō; *It.* än′dän tē′nô), *adj., adv., n., pl.* **-nos.** *Music.* **—adj., adv. 1.** slightly faster than andante. **—n. 2.** an andantino movement or piece. [It., dim. of *andante* ANDANTE]
An·de·an (ān dē′ən, ăn′dĭ-), *adj.* of or like the Andes.
An·der·lecht (ān′dər lĕкнт′), *n.* a city in central Belgium, near Brussels. 86,040 (est. 1941).
An·der·sen (ān′dər sən), *n.* **Hans Christian** (hänz krĭs′tyən), 1805–75, Danish author, esp. of fairy tales.
An·der·son (ān′dər sən), *n.* **1. Carl David,** born 1905, U.S. physicist. **2. Marian,** born 1908, U.S. contralto. **3. Maxwell,** born 1888, U.S. dramatist. **4. Sherwood,** 1876–1941, U.S. short-story writer, novelist, and newspaper editor. **5.** a city in central Indiana. 46,820 (1950).
An·der·son·ville (ān′dər sən vĭl′), *n.* a village in SW Georgia: site of a Confederate military prison.
An·des (ān′dēz), *n.pl.* a lofty mountain system in W South America, extending ab. 4500 mi. from N Colombia and Venezuela S to Cape Horn. Highest peak (of the western hemisphere), Aconcagua, 23,003 ft.
an·des·ine (ān′dĭ zĭn), *n.* a mineral of the plagioclase feldspar group. [f. ANDES + -INE²]
an·des·ite (ān′də zīt′), *n.* a volcanic rock composed essentially of plagioclase feldspar, resembling trachyte in appearance. [f. ANDES + -ITE¹]
and·i·ron (ănd′ī′ərn), *n.* one of a pair of metallic stands, usually of iron, used to support wood burned in an open fireplace. [ME *andyre,* t. OF: m. *andier,* ? t. Gallic: m. *andera* young cow (through use of cows' heads as decorations on andirons); *-iron* by assoc. with *iron*]
An·di·zhan (ān′dĭ zhän′), *n.* a city in the SW Soviet Union in Asia, in Uzbek Republic. 83,691 (1939).
and/or, and *or* or: *history and/or science* (meaning "history and science" or "history or science").
An·dor·ra (ān dôr′ə, -dôr′ä; *Sp.* än dôr′rä), *n.* a small republic in the E Pyrenees between France and Spain, under the joint suzerainty of France and the Spanish Bishop of Urgel. ab. 6000 pop. 191 sq. mi. *Cap.:* Andorra. French, **An·dorre** (äN dôr′).

andr-, var. of **andro-,** used before vowels, as in *androecium.*
an·dra·dite (ān′drə dīt′), *n.* a mineral, calcium-iron garnet, Ca₃Fe₂Si₃O₁₂, occurring in brown, green, or black crystals. [f. D'*Andrada* (Pg. mineralogist) + -ITE¹]
An·drás·sy (ăn dräs′ĭ; *Hung.* ŏn′drä shĭ), *n.* **1. Count Julius,** 1823–90, Hungarian statesman. **2.** his son, **Count Julius** (*Gyula*), 1860–1929, Hungarian statesman.
An·dré (ān′drā, än′drĭ), *n.* **Major John,** 1751–80, British officer hanged as spy in American Revolution.
An·dre·a del Sar·to (än drě′ä dĕl sär′tô). See **Sar·to.**
An·dre·a·nof Islands (ān′drě ä′nŏf), a group of islands in the W part of the Aleutian Islands. 1432 sq. mi.
An·dre·ev (än drě′yĕf), *n.* **Leonid Nikolaevich** (lĕ ŏ nēt′ nĭ kŏ lä′yĕ vĭch), 1871–1919, Russian short-story writer, dramatist, and novelist. Also, **An·dre′yev.**
An·drew (ān′drōō), *n. Bible.* one of the twelve apostles of Jesus. Mark 3:18; John 1:40–42.
An·drews (ān′drōōz), *n.* **Roy Chapman,** born 1884, U. S. naturalist, explorer, and author.
andro-, *Biol.* a word element meaning "man," "male," as contrasted with "female," as in *androsphinx.* Also, **andr-.** [t. Gk., comb. form of *anēr* man, male]
An·dro·cles (ān′drə klēz′), *n. Rom. Legend.* a slave spared in the arena by a lion from whose foot he had years before extracted a thorn. Also, **An·dro·clus** (ān′drə kləs).
an·dro·clin·i·um (ān′drə klĭn′ĭ əm), *n. Bot.* clinandrium.
an·droe·ci·um (ān drē′shĭ əm), *n., pl.* **-cia** (-shĭ ə). *Bot.* the stamens of a flower collectively. [t. NL, f. Gk.: *andr-* ANDR- + m. *oikíon* house] **—an·droe′cial,** *adj.*
an·dro·gen (ān′drə jən), *n. Biochem.* any substance, natural or synthetic, which promotes masculine characteristics. **—an·dro·gen·ic** (ān′drə jĕn′ĭk), *adj.*
an·drog·y·nous (ān drŏj′ə nəs), *adj.* **1.** *Bot.* having staminate and pistillate flowers in the same inflorescence. **2.** being both male and female; hermaphroditic. [t. L: m. *androgynus,* t. Gk.: m. *andrógynos* hermaphrodite] **—an·drog′y·ny,** *n.*
An·drom·a·che (ān drŏm′ə kē′), *n. Gk. Legend.* the wife of Hector and mother of Astyanax.
An·drom·e·da (ān drŏm′ə də), *n.* **1.** *Gk. Myth.* the daughter of Cassiopeia and wife of Perseus, who rescued her from a sea monster. **2.** *Astron.* a northern constellation containing within its borders the external stellar system known as the Great Nebula in Andromeda.
An·dros (ān′drəs), *n.* **Sir Edmund,** 1637–1714, British governor in the American Colonies.
An·dros·cog·gin (ān′drə skŏg′ĭn), *n.* a river flowing from NE New Hampshire through SW Maine into the Kennebec river. 171 mi.
an·dro·sphinx (ān′drə sfĭngks′), *n.* a sphinx with the head of a man.
an·dros·ter·one (ān drŏs′tə rōn′), *n. Biochem.* a sex hormone, C₁₉H₃₀O₂, usually present in male urine.
-androus, a word element meaning "male," as in *polyandrous.* [t. NL: m. *-androus,* t. Gk.: m. *-andros* of a man]
An·dva·ri (ān′dwä rē′), *n. Scand. Myth.* a dwarf who owned a great treasure (the hoard of the Nibelungs). It was taken from him by Loki.
-ane, **1.** a noun suffix used in chemical terms, esp. names of hydrocarbons of the methane or paraffin series, as *decane, pentane, propane.* **2.** an adjective suffix used when a similar form (with a different meaning) exists in **-an,** as *human, humane,* etc. [t. s. *-ānus,* adj. suffix]
a·near (ə nĭr′), *adv., prep. Poetic.* near.
an·ec·dot·age (ān′ĭk dō′tĭj), *n.* **1.** *Rare.* anecdotes collectively. **2.** *Colloq. or Humorous.* old age.
an·ec·do·tal (ān′ĭk dō′təl, ān′ĭk dō′təl), *adj.* pertaining to, marked by, or consisting of anecdotes.
an·ec·dote (ān′ĭk dōt′), *n.* a short narrative of a particular incident or occurrence of an interesting nature: *anecdotes of the president's childhood.* [t. ML: m. s. *anecdota,* t. Gk.: m. s. *anékdotos* unpublished]
an·ec·dot·ic (ān′ĭk dŏt′ĭk), *adj.* **1.** anecdotal. **2.** given to relating anecdotes. Also, **an′ec·dot′i·cal.**
an·ec·dot·ist (ān′ĭk dō′tĭst), *n.* a relater of anecdotes.
a·nele (ə nēl′), *v.t.,* **aneled, aneling.** *Archaic.* to administer extreme unction to. [ME *anelien,* f. *an-* on + *elien* to oil, der. OE *ele* oil, t. L: m. *oleum*]
a·ne·mi·a (ə nē′mĭ ə), *n. Pathol.* a quantitative deficiency of the hemoglobin, often accompanied by a reduced number of red blood cells, and causing pallor, weakness, and breathlessness. Also, **anaemia.** [NL, t. Gk.: m. *anaimía* want of blood]
a·ne·mic (ə nē′mĭk), *adj.* suffering from anemia. Also, **anaemic.**
anemo-, a word element meaning "wind," as in *anemometer.* [t. Gk., comb. form of *ánemos* wind]
a·nem·o·graph (ə nĕm′ə grăf′, -gräf′), *n. Meteorol.* an instrument for measuring and recording the velocity, force, or direction of the wind. **—a·nem′o·graph′ic,** *adj.*
an·e·mog·ra·phy (ăn′ə mŏg′rə fĭ), *n. Meteorol.* the art of measuring and recording the velocity and direction of the wind.
an·e·mom·e·ter (ān′ə mŏm′ə tər), *n. Meteorol.* an instrument for indicating wind velocity. **—an·e·mo·met·ric** (ān′ə mō mĕt′rĭk), **an′e·mo·met′ri·cal,** *adj.*
an·e·mom·e·try (ān′ə mŏm′ə trĭ), *n. Meteorol.* determination of the velocity of the wind by an anemometer.

ăct, āble, dâre, ärt; ĕbb, ēqual; ĭf, īce; hŏt, ōver, ôrder, oil, bŏŏk, ōōze, out; ŭp, ūse, ûrge; ə = a in alone; ch, chief; g, give; ng, ring; sh, shoe; th, thin; ᵺ, that; zh, vision. See the full key on inside cover.

a·nem·o·ne (ə něm′ə nē′), *n.* **1.** any plant of the ranunculaceous genus *Anemone*, esp. *A. quinquefolia*, a spring wild flower with slender stem and delicate whitish blossoms. **2.** a common marine animal of the phylum *Coelenterata*, of sedentary habits, with one or more circles of tentacles surrounding the mouth. [t. L, t. Gk.: wind flower]

an·e·moph·i·lous (ăn′ə mŏf′ə ləs), *adj. Bot.* (of seed plants) fertilized by wind-borne pollen. [f. ANEMO- + -PHILOUS; lit., wind-loving] —**an′e·moph′i·ly**, *n.*

a·nem·o·scope (ə něm′ə skōp′), *n. Meteorol.* any device showing the existence and direction of the wind.

a·nenst (ə něnst′), *prep.* anent [earlier *anent(i)st*, var. (with excrescent *-t*) of ME *anentes*, gen. of ANENT]

a·nent (ə něnt′), *prep.* **1.** *Archaic and Scot.* in regard to; concerning. **2.** *Brit. Dial.* in line with; beside. [var. (with excrescent *-t*) of ME *anen*, OE *on emn*, *on efen on even* (ground) with, beside]

an·er·gy (ăn′ər jǐ), *n.* **1.** *Pathol.* deficiency of energy. **2.** *Immunol.* lack of immunity to an antigen. [t. NL: m. s. *anergia*, f. Gk.: *an-* AN-[1] + *-ergia* work]

an·er·oid (ăn′ə roid′), *adj.* **1.** using no fluid. —*n.* **2.** an aneroid barometer. [f. A-[6] + s. Gk. *nērós* liquid + -OID]

aneroid barometer, an instrument for measuring atmospheric pressure and, indirectly, altitude, by registering the pressure exerted on the elastic top of a box or chamber exhausted of air.

an·es·the·sia (ăn′əs thē′zhə), *n.* **1.** *Med.* general or local insensibility, as to pain and other sensation, induced by certain drugs. **2.** *Pathol.* general loss of the senses of feeling, such as pain, heat, cold, touch, and other less common varieties of sensation. Also, **anaesthesia.** [t. NL, t. Gk.: m. *anaisthēsia* insensibility]

an·es·thet·ic (ăn′əs thět′Yk), *n.* **1.** a substance such as ether, chloroform, cocaine, etc., that produces anesthesia. —*adj.* **2.** pertaining to or causing physical insensibility. **3.** insensitive. Also, **anaesthetic.**

an·es·the·tist (ə něs′thə tǐst), *n.* a person who administers anesthetics, usually a specially trained doctor or nurse. Also, **anaesthetist.**

an·es·the·tize (ə něs′thə tīz′), *v.t.*, **-tized, -tizing.** to render physically insensible, as by an anesthetic. Also, **anaesthetize.** —**a·nes′the·ti·za′tion**, *n.*

an·e·thole (ăn′ə thōl′), *n. Chem.* a compound, $C_{10}H_{12}O$, found in anise and fennel oils, and used in perfumes and as an antiseptic and carminative, etc. [f. s. Gk. *ánēthon* anise (prop., dill) + -OLE]

A·ne·to (ä ně′tō), *n.* Spanish name of **Néthou, Pic de.**

an·eu·rysm (ăn′yə rǐz′əm), *n. Pathol.* a permanent cardiac or arterial dilatation usually caused by weakening of the vessel wall by diseases such as syphilis or arteriosclerosis. Also, **an′eu·rism.** [t. Gk.: m. *aneúrysma* dilation] —**an′eu·rys′mal, an′eu·ris′mal,** *adj.*

a·new (ə nǖ′, ə nōō′), *adv.* **1.** over again; once more: *to write a story anew.* **2.** in a new or different form or manner: *edited anew.* [ME *onew*, etc., OE *of-niowe*, r. OE *edniwe* once more]

an·frac·tu·os·i·ty (ăn frăk′chŏŏ ŏs′ə tǐ), *n.*, *pl.* **-ties. 1.** state or quality of being anfractuous. **2.** a channel, crevice, or passage full of windings and turnings.

an·frac·tu·ous (ăn frăk′chŏŏ əs), *adj.* characterized by windings and turnings; sinuous; circuitous: *an anfractuous path.* Also, **an·frac·tu·ose** (ăn frăk′chŏŏ ōs′). [t L: m. s. *anfractuōsus* winding]

An·ga·ra (än gä rä′), *n.* a river in the S Soviet Union in Asia, rising NE of Lake Baikal and flowing through it NW to the Yenisei river: called the Upper Tunguska in its lower course. ab. 1300 mi.

an·ga·ry (ăng′gə rǐ), *n. Internat. Law.* the right of a belligerent state to seize and use the property of neutrals for purposes of warfare, subject to payment of full compensation. [t. L: m. s. *angaria* forced service (to a lord), t. Gk.: m. *angareia* post service]

an·gel (ān′jəl), *n.* **1.** *Theol.* one of a class of spiritual beings, attendants of God (in medieval angelology divided, according to their rank, into nine orders, ranging from highest to lowest as follows: seraphim, cherubim, thrones, dominations or dominions, virtues, powers, principalities or princedoms, archangels, angels). **2.** a conventional representation of such a being, in human form, with wings. **3.** a messenger, esp. of God. **4.** a person, esp. a woman, who resembles an angel in beauty, kindliness, etc. **5.** an attendant or guardian spirit. **6.** *Colloq.* a financial backer of a play, campaign, actor, candidate, etc. **7.** an English gold coin, struck from 1470 to 1634, in value from 6s. 8d. to 10s., bearing a figure of the archangel Michael overcoming the dragon. [ME and OE, var. of *engel*, pre-E **angil*, t. L: m.s. *angelus*, t. Gk.: m. *ángelos*, orig., messenger]

an·gel·fish (ān′jəl fǐsh′), *n.*, *pl.* **-fishes**, (*esp. collectively*) **-fish. 1.** any shark of the genus *Squatina*, of Atlantic and Pacific waters, with a depressed flat body and large, winglike pectoral fins. **2.** any of several brightly colored marine fishes, as *Chaetodipterus faber*, and *Angelichthys ciliaris.* **3.** the scalare.

angel food cake, a delicate white cake made without shortening. Also, **angel cake.**

an·gel·ic (ăn jěl′ǐk), *adj.* **1.** of or belonging to angels. **2.** like or befitting an angel; saintly. Also, **an·gel′i·cal.** —**an·gel′i·cal·ly,** *adv.*

an·gel·i·ca (ăn jěl′ə kə), *n.* **1.** any plant of the genus *Angelica*, tall umbelliferous plants found in both hemi-

spheres, esp. *A. Archangelica* (*Archangelica officinalis*), cultivated in Europe for its aromatic odor and medicinal root, and for its stalks, which are candied; archangel. **2.** the candied stalks. **3.** (*cap.*) a sweet white California wine. [t. ML: angelic (herb)]

angelica tree, *U.S.* the Hercules-club (def. 2).

An·ge·li·co (än jě′lē kô′), *n.* **Fra** (frä), (*Giovanni da Fiesole*) 1387–1455, Italian painter.

An·gell (ăn′jəl), *n.* **1.** **James Burrill** (bûr′əl), 1829–1916, U. S. educator. **2.** his son, **James Rowland** (rō′lənd), 1869–1949, U. S. educator. **3.** **Sir Norman** (*Ralph Norman Angell Lane*), born 1874, British writer.

angelo-, a combining form of **angel.**

an·gel·ol·o·gy (ăn′jə lŏl′ə jǐ), *n.* doctrine concerning angels.

an·gel·shark (ăn′jəl shärk′), *n.* angelfish (def. 1).

An·ge·lus (ăn′jə ləs), *n. Rom. Cath. Ch.* **1.** a devotion in memory of the Annunciation. **2.** the bell (**Angelus bell**) tolled in the morning, at noon, and in the evening, to indicate the time when the Angelus is to be recited. [t. LL (the first word of the recitation). See ANGEL]

an·ger (ăng′gər), *n.* **1.** a revengeful passion or emotion directed against one who inflicts a real or supposed wrong; wrath; ire. **2.** *Obs. or Dial.* pain or smart, as of a sore. **3.** *Obs.* grief; trouble. —*v.t.* **4.** to excite to anger or wrath. **5.** *Obs. or Dial.* to cause to smart; inflame. [ME, t. Scand.; cf. Icel. *angr* grief, sorrow]
—**Syn.** **1.** displeasure; resentment, exasperation. ANGER, FURY, INDIGNATION, RAGE imply deep and strong feelings aroused by injury, injustice, wrong, etc. ANGER is a sudden violent displeasure accompanied by an impulse to retaliate: *a burst of anger.* INDIGNATION, a more formal word, implies deep and justified anger, often directed against something unworthy: *indignation at cruelty or against corruption.* RAGE is vehement anger: *rage at being frustrated.* FURY is rage so great that it resembles insanity: *the fury of a woman scorned.*

an·ger·ly (ăng′gər lǐ), *adv. Archaic.* angrily.

An·gers (ăn′jərz, ăng′gərz; Fr. äN zhě′), *n.* a city in W France. 94,408 (1946).

An·ge·vin (ăn′jə vǐn), *adj.* **1.** of or from Anjou. **2.** relating to the counts of Anjou or their descendants, esp. those who ruled in England, or to the period when they ruled. —*n.* **3.** an inhabitant of Anjou. **4.** a member of an Angevin royal house, esp. that of the Plantagenets in England. Also, **An·ge·vine** (ăn′jə vǐn, -vīn′). [t. F]

an·gi·na (ăn jī′nə; *in Med. often* ăn′jə-), *n. Pathol.* **1.** any inflammatory affection of the throat or fauces, as quinsy, croup, mumps, etc. **2.** angina pectoris. [t. L: quinsy, lit., strangling. Cf. Gk. *anchōnē*]

angina pec·to·ris (pěk′tə rǐs), *Pathol.* a syndrome characterized by paroxysmal, constricting pain below the sternum, most easily precipitated by exertion or excitement and caused by ischemia of the heart muscle, usually due to a coronary artery disease, such as arteriosclerosis. [NL: angina of the chest]

angio-, a word element meaning "vessel," or "container," as in *angiology.* [t. NL, t. Gk.: m. *angeio-*, comb. form of *angeion* vessel]

an·gi·ol·o·gy (ăn′jǐ ŏl′ə jǐ), *n.* the part of the science of anatomy that deals with blood vessels and lymphatics.

an·gi·o·ma (ăn′jǐ ō′mə), *n.*, *pl.* **-mas, -mata** (-mə tə). a tumor consisting chiefly of dilated or newly formed blood or lymph vessels. [f. ANGI(O)-+-OMA] —**an·gi·om·a·tous** (ăn′jǐ ŏm′ə təs, -ō′mə-), *adj.*

an·gi·o·sperm (ăn′jǐ ə spûrm′), *n.* a plant having its seeds enclosed in an ovary (opposed to *gymnosperm*). —**an′gi·o·sper′mous,** *adj.*

Ang·kor (ăng′kōr), *n.* a ruined city in SW French Indo-China, in NW Cambodia: the site of **Angkor Wat** (wät), an ancient Khmer temple.

an·gle[1] (ăng′gəl), *n.*, *v.*, **-gled, -gling.** —*n.* **1.** *Geom.* **a.** the space within two lines or three planes diverging from a common point, or within two planes diverging from a common line. **b.** the figure so formed. **c.** the amount of rotation needed to bring one line or plane into coincidence with another. **2.** an angular projection; a projecting corner: *the angles of a building.* **3.** a point of view; standpoint: *a new angle on the problem.* **4.** an aspect; side; phase: *to consider all angles of the question.* —*v.t.*, *v.i.* **5.** to move or bend in angles. [ME, t. F, g. L *angulus*]

Right Angle (90°) Acute Angle (60°) Acute Angle (30°)

Angles

an·gle[2] (ăng′gəl), *v.*, **-gled, -gling**, *n.* —*v.i.* **1.** to fish with hook and line. **2.** to try by artful means to get: *to angle for a compliment.* [v. use of n.] —*n.* **3.** *Archaic.* a fishhook or fishing tackle. [OE *angel*, *angul*; akin to ANGLE[1]]

an·gled (ăng′gəld), *adj.* having an angle or angles.

angle iron, 1. a bar of iron in the form of an angle. **2.** a rolled iron or steel bar with an L-shaped cross section, used mainly in iron constructions.

angle of attack, the acute angle between the chord of an aircraft wing or other airfoil and its direction of motion relative to the air.

ECD, Angle of incidence on surface AB; CD, Perpendicular; E'CD, Angle of reflection

b., blend of, blended; c., cognate with; d., dialect, dialectal; der., derived from; f., formed from; g., going back to; m., modification of; r., replacing; s., stem of; t., taken from; ?, perhaps. See the full key on inside cover.

angle of incidence, 1. the angle that a line, ray of light, etc., meeting a surface, makes with the perpendicular to that surface at the point of meeting. 2. the fixed angle between the plane of the wing chord and the axis of the fuselage. 3. *Brit.* angle of attack.

angle of reflection, the angle that a ray of light, or the like, reflected from a surface, makes with a perpendicular to that surface at the point of reflection.

an·gle·pod (ăng′gəl pŏd′), *n.* an asclepiadaceous plant, *Vincetoxicum* (or *Gonolobus*) *gonocarpos*, of the southern and central U.S.

an·gler (ăng′glər), *n.* 1. one who angles; one who fishes for pleasure. 2. a fish, *Lophius piscatorius* of the coasts of Europe or *L. americanus* of America, which attracts small fish, by the movement of a wormlike filament attached to its head just above the mouth. 3. any of various related fishes, with a modified free dorsal spine above the mouth, constituting the order *Pediculati*.

An·gles (ăng′gəlz), *n.* a West Germanic people that migrated from Sleswick to Britain in the fifth century A.D. and founded the kingdoms of East Anglia, Mercia, and Northumbria. As early as the 6th century their name was extended to all the Germanic inhabitants of Britain. [OE *Angle*, orig. the inhabitants of *Angel*, a district of what is now Sleswick, said to be named from its hooklike shape]

An·gle·sey (ăng′gəl sĭ), *n.* an island and county in NW Wales. 47,000 pop. (est. 1946); 276 sq. mi. *Co. seat:* Holyhead.

an·gle·site (ăng′glə sīt′), *n.* a mineral, lead sulfate, PbSO₄, found in massive forms or in colorless or variously tinted crystals: a minor ore of lead. [named after *Anglesey*, Wales. See -ITE¹]

an·gle·smith (ăng′gəl smĭth′), *n.* a blacksmith skilled in forging angle irons, beams, etc. into various forms used in shipbuilding.

an·gle·worm (ăng′gəl wûrm′), *n.* an earthworm used for bait in angling.

An·gli·a (ăng′glĭ ə), *n.* Latin name of **England.**

An·gli·an (ăng′glĭ ən), *adj.* 1. of or relating to the Angles or to East Anglia. —*n.* 2. an Angle. 3. the northern and eastern group of Old English dialects.

An·glic (ăng′glĭk), *n.* 1. a simplified form of English, devised by R. E. Zachrisson (1880–1937) and intended for use as an international auxiliary language. —*adj.* 2. Anglian.

An·gli·can (ăng′glə kən), *adj.* 1. of or pertaining to the Church of England. 2. related in origin to and in communion with the Church of England, as various episcopal churches in other parts of the world. 3. *Chiefly U.S.* English. —*n.* 4. a member of the Church of England or of a church in communion with it. 5. one who upholds the system or teachings of the Church of England. 6. one who emphasizes the authority of that church; a High Churchman. [t. ML: s. *Anglicānus*]

Anglican Church, the Church of England and the churches in other countries in full accord with it as to doctrine and church order, as the Church of Ireland, the Episcopal Church of Scotland, the Church of Wales, the Protestant Episcopal Church in the U.S., etc.

An·gli·can·ism (ăng′glə kə nĭz′əm), *n.* Anglican principles; the Anglican Church system.

An·gli·ce (ăng′glĭ sĭ), *adv.* in English; as the English would say it; according to the English way, as *Cōrdoba, Anglice Cordova.* [t. ML, der. *Anglicus* English]

An·gli·cism (ăng′glə sĭz′əm), *n.* 1. an English idiom. 2. *U.S.* a Briticism. 3. state of being English; characteristic English quality.

An·gli·cist (ăng′glə sĭst), *n.* an authority on English language and literature. [f. s. L *Anglicus* English +-IST]

An·gli·cize (ăng′glə sīz′), *v.t., v.i.,* **-cized, -cizing.** to make or become English in form or character: *to Anglicize the pronunciation of a Russian name.* Also, **anglicize.** —**An′gli·ci·za′tion,** *n.*

An·gli·fy (ăng′glə fī′), *v.t.,* **-fied, -fying.** to Anglicize.

an·gling (ăng′glĭng), *n.* act or art of fishing with a hook and line, usually attached to a rod.

An·glist (ăng′glĭst), *n.* an authority on England. [t. G]

Anglo-, a word element meaning "pertaining to England or the English," as in *Anglo-American.* [comb. form repr. ML *Anglus* Englishman, *Anglī* (pl.) the English]

An·glo-A·mer·i·can (ăng′glō ə mĕr′ə kən), *adj.* 1. belonging or relating to, or connected with, England and America, esp. the United States, or with the people of both: *Anglo-American commerce.* 2. pertaining to the English who have settled in America, esp. in the United States, or have become American citizens. —*n.* 3. a native or descendant of a native of England who has settled in America, esp. in the United States, or has become an American citizen.

An·glo-Cath·o·lic (ăng′glō kăth′ə lĭk), *n.* 1. one who emphasizes the Catholic character of the Anglican Church. 2. an Anglican Catholic, as opposed to a Roman or Greek Catholic. —*adj.* 3. of or pertaining to Anglo-Catholicism or Anglo-Catholics. —**An·glo-Cath·ol·i·cism** (ăng′glō kə thŏl′ə sĭz′əm), *n.*

An·glo-E·gyp·tian Sudan (ăng′glō ĭ jĭp′shən), a territory in NE Africa, S of Egypt: a condominium of Egypt and Great Britain. 5,945,600 pop. (est. 1936); ab. 1,008,100 sq. mi. *Cap.:* Khartoum.

An·glo-French (ăng′glō frĕnch′), *adj.* 1. English and French. 2. pertaining to Anglo-French (def. 3). —*n.*

3. that dialect of French current in England from the Norman Conquest to the end of the Middle Ages.

An·glo-In·di·an (ăng′glō ĭn′dĭ ən). *n.* 1. a person of British birth who has lived long in India. —*adj.* 2. of, pertaining to, or relating to England and India as politically associated.

An·glo·ma·ni·a (ăng′glō mā′nĭ ə), *n.* an excessive attachment to, respect for, or imitation of English institutions, manners, customs, etc. —**An′glo·ma′ni·ac,** *n.*

An·glo-Nor·man (ăng′glō nôr′mən), *adj.* 1. pertaining to that period, 1066–1154, when England was ruled by Normans. 2. pertaining to the Normans who settled in England, or their descendants, or their dialect of French. —*n.* 3. a Norman who settled in England after 1066, or one of his descendants. 4. Anglo-French.

An·glo·phile (ăng′glə fīl′, -fĭl), *n.* one who is friendly to or admires England or English customs, institutions, etc. Also, **An·glo·phil** (ăng′glə fĭl).

An·glo·phobe (ăng′glə fōb′), *n.* one who hates or fears England or the English.

An·glo·pho·bi·a (ăng′glə fō′bĭ ə), *n.* an intense hatred or fear of England, or of whatever is English.

An·glo-Sax·on (ăng′glō săk′sən), *n.* 1. one who belongs to the English-speaking world, irrespective of historical periods, political boundaries, geographical areas, or racial origins (the only medieval sense). 2. an Englishman of the period before the Norman conquest. 3. a person of English stock and traditions; in the U.S., usually a person of colonial descent and /or British origin. 4. Old English (def. 1). 5. the English language. 6. plain English. 7. pre-English (def. 1). —*adj.* 8. of, pertaining to, or characteristic of the Anglo-Saxons. 9. pertaining to Anglo-Saxon. [t. ML: s. *Anglo-Saxonēs* the English people; r. OE *Angulseaxan,* t. ML: m. *Anglī Saxonēs,* Latinizations of the OE folk names *Angle* and *Seaxan*]

An·go·la (ăng gō′lə), *n.* a Portuguese colony in SW Africa. 3,738,010 pop. (1940); 481,226 sq. mi. *Cap.:* Nova Lisbon. Also, **Portuguese West Africa.**

An·go·ra (ăng gôr′ə, ăn- *for 1;* ăng gōr′ə, ăng′gə rə *for 2*), *n.* 1. an Angora cat. 2. Ankara.

Angora cat, a long-haired variety of the domestic cat, orig. from Angora.

Angora goat, a variety of goat, orig. from Angora, reared for its long, silky hair which is called mohair.

an·gos·tu·ra bark (ăng′gəs tyŏŏr′ə, -tŏŏr′ə), *n.* the bitter aromatic bark of a South American rutaceous tree of the genus *Cusparia* (or *Galipea*), supposed to be valuable as a tonic. Also, **angostura.** [named after *Angostura,* town in Venezuela]

angostura bitters, 1. a bitter aromatic tonic prepared with barks, roots, herbs, etc., under a secret formula in Trinidad. 2. (*caps.*) a trademark for this tonic.

An·gra do He·ro·is·mo (ăng′grə dŏŏ ĕ′rŏŏ ēzh′mŏŏ), a seaport in the Azores, on Terceira island: former capital of the Azores. 12,115 (1940).

an·gry (ăng′grĭ), *adj.,* **-grier, -griest.** 1. feeling or showing anger or resentment (*with* or *at* a person, *at* or *about* a thing). 2. characterized by anger; wrathful: *angry words.* 3. *Med.* inflamed, as a sore; exhibiting inflammation. [ME; f. ANGER + -Y¹] —**an′gri·ly,** *adv.* —**an′gri·ness,** *n.* —**Syn.** 1. irate, incensed, enraged.

ang·strom unit (ăng′strəm), one tenth of a millimicron, i.e., a ten millionth of a millimeter; a unit used to express the length of very short waves. Also, **angstrom.** [named after A. J. *Angstrom* (1814–74), Swedish physicist]

an·guil·li·form (ăng gwĭl′ə fôrm′), *adj.* having the shape or form of an eel. [f. s. L *anguilla* eel + -(I)FORM]

an·guine (ăng′gwĭn), *adj.* pertaining to or resembling a snake. [t. L: m.s. *anguīnus*]

an·guish (ăng′gwĭsh), *n.* 1. excruciating or agonizing pain of either body or mind; acute suffering or distress: *the anguish of grief.* —*v.t., v.i.* 2. to affect with or suffer anguish. [ME, t. OF: m. *anguisse, angoisse,* g. L *angustia* straitness, pl. straits, distress] —**Syn.** 1. agony, torment, torture. See **pain.** —**Ant.** 1. delight.

an·gu·lar (ăng′gyə lər), *adj.* 1. having an angle or angles. 2. consisting of, situated at, or forming an angle. 3. of, pertaining to, or measured by an angle. 4. bony; gaunt. 5. acting or moving awkwardly. 6. stiff in manner; unbending. [t. L: s. *angulāris*] —**an′gu·lar·ly,** *adv.* —**an′gu·lar·ness,** *n.* —**Ant.** 1. round. 4. rotund.

an·gu·lar·i·ty (ăng gyə lăr′ə tĭ), *n., pl.* **-ties.** 1. angular quality. 2. (*pl.*) sharp corners; angular outlines.

an·gu·late (ăng′gyə lĭt, -lāt′), *adj.* of angular form; angled: *angulate stems.* Also, **an′gu·lat′ed.** [t. L: m. s. *angulātus,* pp., made angular] —**an′gu·late·ly,** *adv.*

an·gu·la·tion (ăng gyə lā′shən), *n.* angular formation.

An·gus (ăng′gəs), *n.* a county in E Scotland. 265,300 pop. (est. 1946); 873 sq. mi. *Co. seat:* Forfar.

An·halt (än′hält), *n.* a state in central Germany. 431,422 pop. (1939); 894 sq. mi. *Cap.:* Dessau.

an·hin·ga (än hĭng′gə), *n.* snakebird.

An·hwei (än′hwē′), *n.* a province in eastern China. 21,978,700 pop. (est. 1944); 54,319 sq. mi. *Cap.:* Anking. Also, **Nganhwei.**

an·hy·dride (än hī′drĭd, -drĭd), *n. Chem.* 1. a compound, formed by abstraction of water, an oxide of a nonmetal (**acid anhydride**) or a metal (**basic anhydride**) which forms an acid or a base, respectively, when united with water. 2. a compound from which water has been abstracted. Also, **an·hy·drid** (ăn hī′drĭd). [f. s. Gk. *ánydros* without water (with etymological *h* inserted) + -IDE]

an·hy·drite (ăn hī′drīt), *n.* a mineral, calcium sulfate, CaSO₄, usually in whitish or slightly colored masses.

an·hy·drous (ăn hī′drəs), *adj. Chem.* indicating loss of all water, esp. water of crystallization. [t. Gk.: m. *ánydros* without water (with *h* from *hydrous*)]

a·ni (ä′nē), *n., pl.* **anis.** either of two black cuckoolike birds of the genus *Crotophaga*, inhabiting the warmer parts of America. [native name]

an·il (ăn′ĭl), *n.* 1. a fabaceous shrub, *Indigofera suffruticosa*, one of the plants which yield indigo, native to the West Indies. 2. indigo; deep blue. [t. F, t. Pg., t. Ar.: m. *al-nīl*, f. al the + *nīl* (t. Skt.: m. *nīlī* indigo)]

an·ile (ăn′īl, ā′nīl), *adj.* of or like a weak old woman: *anile ideas.* [t. L: m. s. *anīlis*, der. *anus* old woman]

an·i·line (ăn′ə lĭn, -līn), *n.* 1. an oily liquid, C₆H₅-NH₂, obtained first from indigo but now prepared from benzene, and serving as the basis of many brilliant dyes, and in the manufacture of plastics, resins, etc. —*adj.* 2. pertaining to or derived from aniline: *aniline colors.* Also, **an·i·lin** (ăn′ə lĭn). [f. ANIL + -INE²]

aniline dye, any organic dye made from a coal-tar base (because the earliest ones were made from aniline).

a·nil·i·ty (ə nĭl′ə tĭ), *n., pl.* **-ties.** 1. anile state. 2. an anile notion or procedure.

an·i·mad·ver·sion (ăn′ə măd vûr′zhən, -shən), *n.* 1. a remark, usually implying censure; a criticism or comment: *to make animadversions on someone's conduct.* 2. act or fact of criticizing. [t. L: s. *animadversio*]

an·i·mad·vert (ăn′ə măd vûrt′), *v.i.* 1. to comment critically; make remarks by way of criticism or censure (fol. by *on* or *upon*). 2. *Obs.* to take cognizance or notice. [t. L: s. *animadvertere* regard, notice]

an·i·mal (ăn′ə məl), *n.* 1. any living thing that is not a plant, generally capable of voluntary motion, sensation, etc. 2. any animal other than man. 3. an inhuman person; brutish or beastlike person. —*adj.* 4. of, pertaining to, or derived from animals: *animal life, animal fats.* 5. pertaining to the physical or carnal nature of man, rather than his spiritual or intellectual nature: *animal needs.* [t. L: living being]
—**Syn.** 1, 3. ANIMAL, BEAST, BRUTE refer to sentient creatures as distinct from minerals and plants; fig., they usually connote qualities and characteristics below the human level. ANIMAL is the general word; fig., it applies merely to the body or to animallike characteristics: *an athlete is a magnificent animal.* BEAST refers to four-footed animals; fig., it suggests a base, sensual nature: *a glutton is a beast.* BRUTE implies absence of ability to reason; fig., it connotes savagery as well: *a drunken brute.*

an·i·mal·cule (ăn′ə măl′kūl), *n.* 1. a minute or microscopic animal, nearly or quite invisible to the naked eye, as an infusorian or rotifer. 2. *Rare.* a tiny animal, such as a mouse, fly, etc. [t. NL: m. s. *animalculum*, dim. of *L animal* living being] —**an·i·mal′cu·lar,** *adj.*

an·i·mal·cu·lum (ăn′ə măl′kyə ləm), *n., pl.* **-la** (-lə). animalcule.

animal husbandry, the science of breeding, feeding, and care of animals, esp. on a farm.

an·i·mal·ism (ăn′ə məl ĭz′əm), *n.* 1. animal state; state of being actuated by sensual appetites, and not by intellectual or moral forces; sensuality. 2. the doctrine that human beings are without a spiritual nature.

an·i·mal·ist (ăn′ə məl ĭst), *n.* one who believes in the doctrine of animalism. —**an′i·mal·is′tic,** *adj.*

an·i·mal·i·ty (ăn′ə măl′ə tĭ), *n.* 1. the animal nature in man. 2. animal life.

an·i·mal·ize (ăn′ə mə līz′), *v.t.,* **-ized, -izing.** to excite the animal passions of; brutalize; sensualize. —**an′i·mal·i·za′tion,** *n.*

animal kingdom, the animals of the world collectively (distinguished from *vegetable kingdom*).

an·i·mal·ly (ăn′ə məl ĭ), *adv.* physically.

animal magnetism, mesmerism.

animal spirits, exuberance of health and life; animation and good humor; buoyancy.

an·i·mate (*v.* ăn′ə māt′; *adj.* ăn′ə mĭt), *v.,* **-mated, -mating,** *adj.* —*v.t.* 1. to give life to; make alive. 2. to make lively, vivacious, or vigorous. 3. to encourage: *to animate weary troops.* 4. to move to action; actuate: *animated by religious zeal.* —*adj.* 5. alive; possessing life: *animate creatures.* 6. lively. [t. L: m. s. *animātus*] —**an′i·mat′er,** *n.* —**an′i·mat′ing·ly,** *adv.*
—**Syn.** 1. vivify, quicken, vitalize. 2. ANIMATE, INVIGORATE, STIMULATE mean to enliven. To ANIMATE is to create a liveliness: *health and energy animated his movements.* To INVIGORATE means to give physical vigor, to refresh, to exhilarate: *mountain air invigorates.* To STIMULATE is to arouse a latent liveliness on a particular occasion: *alcohol stimulates.*

an·i·mat·ed (ăn′ə mā′tĭd), *adj.* full of life, action, or spirit; lively; vigorous: *an animated debate.* —**an′i·mat′ed·ly,** *adv.*

animated cartoon, a motion picture consisting of a series of drawings, each slightly different from the ones before and after it, run through a projector.

an·i·ma·tion (ăn′ə mā′shən), *n.* 1. animated quality; liveliness; vivacity; spirit; life. 2. act of animating; act of enlivening. 3. the process of preparing animated cartoons. —**Syn.** 1. vigor, energy; enthusiasm, ardor.

an·i·ma·tism (ăn′ə mə tĭz′əm), *n.* the attribution of consciousness to inanimate objects.

a·ni·ma·to (ä′nē mä′tō), *adj. Music.* animated. [It.]

an·i·ma·tor (ăn′ə mā′tər), *n.* 1. one who or that which animates. 2. one who draws animated cartoons. [t. L]

an·i·mé (ăn′ə mā′, -mĭ), *n.* any of various resins or copals, esp. that from *Hymenaea Courbaril*, a tree of tropical America, used in making varnish, scenting pastilles, etc. [t. Sp., prob. t. native dialect]

an·i·mism (ăn′ə mĭz′əm), *n.* 1. the belief that all natural objects and the universe itself possess a soul. 2. the belief that natural objects have souls which may exist apart from their material bodies. 3. the doctrine that the soul is the principle of life and health. 4. belief in spiritual beings or agencies. [f. s. L *anima* soul + -ISM] —**an′i·mist,** *n., adj.* —**an′i·mis′tic,** *adj.*

a·ni·mis o·pi·bus·que pa·ra·ti (ăn′ə mĭs ō′pə bŭs′-kwē pə rā′tī), *Latin.* prepared in mind and resources (motto of South Carolina).

an·i·mos·i·ty (ăn′ə mŏs′ə tĭ), *n., pl.* **-ties.** a feeling of ill will or enmity animating the conduct, or tending to display itself in action (fol. by *between* or *against*). [late ME *animosite*, t. L: m. s. *animōsitas* courage]

an·i·mus (ăn′ə məs), *n.* 1. hostile spirit; animosity: *to feel an animus against someone.* 2. purpose; intention; animating spirit. [t. L: mind, feeling, will]

an·i·on (ăn′ī′ən), *n. Phys. Chem.* 1. a negatively charged ion which is attracted to the anode in electrolysis. 2. any negatively charged atom, radical, or molecule. [t. Gk.: going up (ppr. neut.)]

an·ise (ăn′ĭs), *n.* 1. an herbaceous plant, *Pimpinella Anisum*, of Mediterranean regions, yielding aniseed. 2. aniseed. [ME *anys*, t. OF: m. *anis*, t. L: *anīsum*, t. Gk.: m. *ánīson* dill, anise]

an·i·seed (ăn′ə sēd′, ăn′ĭs sēd′), *n.* the aromatic seed of the anise, used in medicine, in cookery, etc.

an·i·sette (ăn′ə zĕt′, -sĕt′), *n.* a cordial or liqueur flavored with aniseed. [t. F]

aniso-, a word element meaning "unlike" or "unequal." [comb. form repr. Gk. *ánisos* unequal]

an·i·so·car·pic (ăn ī′sə kär′pĭk, ăn′ī-), *adj. Bot.* (of a flower) having a lower number of carpels than of other floral parts.

an·i·so·dac·ty·lous (ăn ī′sə dăk′tə ləs, ăn′ī-), *adj. Zool.* unequal-toed; having the toes unlike.

an·i·sole (ăn′ə sōl′), *n.* a colorless fluid, C₇H₈O, used in the perfume industry and for killing lice. [f. s. L *anisum* ANISE + -OLE]

an·i·som·er·ous (ăn′ī sŏm′ər əs), *adj. Bot.* unsymmetrical (applied to flowers which do not have the same number of parts in each circle).

an·i·so·met·ric (ăn ī′sə mĕt′rĭk, ăn′ī-), *adj.* 1. not isometric; of unequal measurement. 2. (of crystals) having three dimensionally unequal axial directions.

an·i·so·me·tro·pi·a (ăn ī′sə me trō′pĭ ə, ăn′ī-), *n. Pathol.* inequality in the power of the two eyes to refract light. [t. NL: f. *aniso-* ANISO- + s. Gk. *mētron* measure + -opia -OPIA]

an·i·so·trop·ic (ăn ī′sə trŏp′ĭk, ăn′ī-), *adj.* 1. *Physics.* of different properties in different directions. 2. *Bot.* of different dimensions along different axes. —**an·i·sot·ro·py** (ăn′ī sŏt′rə pĭ), *n.*

An·jou (ăn′jōō; *Fr.* äɴ zhōō′), *n.* a region and former province in W France, in the Loire valley.

An·ka·ra (ăng′kä rä, -kə rə), *n.* the capital of Turkey, in the central part. 157,242 (1940). Also, **Angora.**

an·ker·ite (ăng′kə rīt′), *n.* a mineral related to dolomite but containing iron in place of part of the magnesium. [named after Prof. M. J. Anker, of Styria. See -ITE¹]

ankh (ängk), *n. Egyptian Art.* a tau cross with a loop at the top, used as a symbol of generation or enduring life. [t. Egypt.: life, soul]

An·king (än′kĭng′), *n.* a city in E China, on the Yangtze: capital of Anhwei province. 23,000 (est. 1938).

an·kle (ăng′kəl), *n.* 1. the aggregate joint connecting the foot with the leg. 2. the slender part of the leg above the foot. [ME *ankel*, t. Scand. (cf. Dan. *ankel*); r. OE *anclēow*(e)]

an·kle·bone (ăng′kəl bōn′), *n. Anat.* the astragalus.

an·klet (ăng′klĭt), *n.* 1. a sock which reaches just above the ankle. 2. an ornament for the ankle, corresponding to the bracelet for the wrist or forearm.

an·ky·lose (ăng′kə lōs′), *v.t., v.i.,* **-losed, -losing.** to grow together and consolidate, as two otherwise freely approximating similar or dissimilar hard tissues, like the bones of a joint or the root of a tooth and its surrounding bone. Also, **anchylose.**

an·ky·lo·sis (ăng′kə lō′sĭs), *n.* 1. *Pathol.* morbid adhesion of the bones of a joint. 2. *Anat.* union or consolidation of two similar or dissimilar hard tissues previously freely approximating, as the bones of a joint, or the root of a tooth and its surrounding bone. Also, **anchylosis.** [t. NL, t. Gk.: stiffening of the joints] —**an·ky·lot·ic** (ăng′kə lŏt′ĭk), *adj.*

an·ky·los·to·mi·a·sis (ăng′kə lŏs′tə mī′ə sĭs), *n.* ancylostomiasis.

[Illustration labeled: BULG. — Black Sea — Istanbul — ANKARA — TURKEY — SYRIA — MEDITERRANEAN SEA]

[Illustration labeled: Ankh]

an·lace (ăn′lĭs), *n.* a medieval dagger or short sword which was suspended from the girdle immediately in front of the person. [ME, t. OF: m. *ale(s)naz,* der. *alesne* awl, t. Gmc.: m. *alisna*]

An·la·ge (än′lä gə), *n., pl.* **-gen** (-gən). (*also l.c.*) Embryol. **1.** primordium. **2.** blastema. [G: setup, layout]

ann., 1. annual. **2.** annuity. **3.** (L *anni*) years.

an·na (än′ə), *n.* **1.** a money of account in India, the sixteenth part of a rupee. **2.** a coin of this value, equivalent to about 2 cents. [t. Hind.: m. *ānā*]

an·na·berg·ite (än′ə bûr′gīt), *n.* a mineral, hydrous nickel arsenate, Ni₃As₂O₈·8H₂O, occurring in apple-green masses. [named after *Annaberg,* town in Saxony. See -ITE¹]

an·nal (än′əl), *n.* a register or record of the events of a year. See **annals.**

an·nal·ist (än′əl ĭst), *n.* a chronicler of yearly events. —**an·nal·is′tic,** *adj.* —**an′nal·is′ti·cal·ly,** *adv.*

an·nals (än′əlz), *n.pl.* **1.** history or relation of events recorded year by year. **2.** historical records generally. **3.** a periodical publication containing formal reports of learned societies, etc. [t. L: m. *annālēs* (sc. *libri* books) a yearly record]

An·nam (ə năm′), *n.* a former kingdom and French protectorate along the E coast of French Indo-China: now part of Viet Nam. 5,656,000 pop. (1936); 56,988 sq. mi. *Cap.:* Hué. Also, **Anam.**

An·na·mese (än′ə mēz′, -mēs′), *adj., n., pl.* **-mese.** —*adj.* **1.** of or pertaining to Annam, its people, or their language. —*n.* **2.** a native of Annam. **3.** a literary language of Annam. **4.** the linguistic family to which this belongs, widespread in Tonkin and Annam, and of no certainly known relationships.

An·na·mite (än′ə mīt′), *n., adj.* Annamese.

An·nap·o·lis (ə năp′ə lĭs), *n.* the capital of Maryland, in the central part: a seaport on Chesapeake Bay; U. S. Naval Academy. 10,047 (1950).

Annapolis Royal, a town in W Nova Scotia, on an arm of the Bay of Fundy: the first settlement in Canada (1605). Formerly, **Port Royal.**

Ann Ar·bor (än är′bər), a city in SE Michigan. 48,251 (1950).

an·nates (än′āts, -ĭts), *n.pl. Eccles.* (formerly) the first year's revenue of a see or benefice, payable to the Pope. Also, **an·nats** (än′āts, -ĭts). [t. ML: m. *annāta* time, work, yield of a year, der. L *annus* year]

an·nat·to (ə nät′ō, ə nä′tō), *n.* **1.** a small tree, *Bixa orellana,* of tropical America. **2.** a yellowish-red dye obtained from the pulp enclosing its seeds, used for coloring fabrics, butter, varnish, etc. Also, **anatto.** [t. Carib]

Anne (än), *n.* 1665–1714, queen of England, 1702–14. (daughter of James II of England).

an·neal (ə nēl′), *v.t.* **1.** to heat (glass, earthenware, metals, etc.) to remove or prevent internal stress. **2.** to free from internal stress by heating and gradually cooling. **3.** to toughen or temper: *to anneal the mind.* [ME *anele(n),* OE *anǣlan,* f. *an* on + *ǣlan* burn]

Anne Bol·eyn (bŏŏl′ən). See **Boleyn.**

an·ne·lid (än′ə lĭd), *n. Zool.* a member of the *Annelida.* [t. F: m. *annélide,* f. m. s. L *ānellus* (dim. of *ānulus* ring) + -ide -ID²] —**an·nel·i·dan** (ə nĕl′ə dən), *adj., n.*

An·nel·i·da (ə nĕl′ə də), *n.pl. Zool.* a phylum of worms comprising earthworms, leeches, various marine worms, etc., characterized by their ringed or segmented bodies.

Anne of Austria, 1601–66, queen of Louis XIII of France: regent during minority of her son Louis XIV.

Anne of Bohemia, 1366–94, queen of Richard II of England.

Anne of Cleves (klēvz), 1515–57, the fourth wife of Henry VIII of England.

an·nex (*v.* ə nĕks′; *n.* än′ĕks), *v.t.* **1.** to attach, join, or add, esp. to something larger or more important; unite; append; subjoin. **2.** to attach as an attribute, concomitant, or consequence. —*n.* Also, *Brit.,* **an·nexe** (ə nĕks′). **3.** something annexed. **4.** a subsidiary building or an addition to a building. **5.** something added to a document; appendix; supplement: *an annex to a treaty.* [ME *a(n)nexe(n),* t. ML: m. *annexāre,* ult. der. L *annexus,* pp., joined] —**an·nex′a·ble,** *adj.*

an·nex·a·tion (än′ĭk sā′shən, -ĕk-), *n.* **1.** act of annexing, esp. new territory. **2.** fact of being annexed. **3.** something annexed. —**an′nex·a′tion·ist,** *n.*

an·ni·hi·la·ble (ə nī′ə lə bəl), *adj.* susceptible of annihilation. —**an·ni′hi·la·bil′i·ty,** *n.*

an·ni·hi·late (ə nī′ə lāt′), *v.t..* **-lated, -lating. 1.** to reduce to nothing; destroy utterly: *the bombing annihilated the city.* **2.** to destroy the form or collective existence of: *to annihilate an army.* **3.** to cancel the effect of; annul: *to annihilate a law.* **4.** *Rare.* to reduce to silence, helplessness, etc. [t. LL: m. s. *annihilātus,* pp.] —**an·ni′hi·la·tive,** *adj.* —**an·ni′hi·la·tor,** *n.*

an·ni·hi·la·tion (ə nī′ə lā′shən), *n.* **1.** act of annihilating. **2.** extinction; destruction. —**an·ni′hi·la′tion·ist,** *n.*

An·nis·ton (än′ĭs tən), *n.* a city in E Alabama. 31,066 (1950).

an·ni·ver·sa·ry (än′ə vûr′sə rĭ), *n., pl.* **-ries,** *adj.* —*n.* **1.** the yearly recurrence of the date of a past event. **2.** the celebration of such a date. —*adj.* **3.** returning or recurring each year. **4.** pertaining to an anniversary: *an anniversary gift.* [t. L: m. s. *anniversārius*]

an·no Dom·i·ni (än′ō dŏm′ə nī′), *Latin.* in the year of our Lord. *Abbr.:* A.D., as A.D. 597.

an·no·tate (än′ō tāt′), *v.,* **-tated, -tating.** —*v.t.* **1.** to supply with notes; remark upon in notes: *to annotate the works of Bacon.* —*v.i.* **2.** to make annotations or notes. [t. L: m. s. *annotātus,* pp.] —**an′no·ta′tor,** *n.*

an·no·ta·tion (än′ō tā′shən), *n.* **1.** act of annotating. **2.** a note commenting upon, explaining, or criticizing some passage of a book or other writing.

an·nounce (ə nouns′), *v.t.,* **-nounced, -nouncing. 1.** to make known publicly; give notice of. **2.** to state the approach or presence of: *to announce guests or dinner.* **3.** to make known to the mind or senses. [ME *anounce(n),* t. OF: m. *anoncier,* g. L *annuntiāre*] —**Syn. 1.** ANNOUNCE, PROCLAIM, PUBLISH mean to communicate something in a formal or public way. To ANNOUNCE is to give out news, often of something expected in the future: *to announce a lecture series.* To PROCLAIM is to make a widespread and general announcement of something of public interest: *to proclaim a holiday.* To PUBLISH is to make public in an official way, now esp. by printing: *to publish a book.*

an·nounce·ment (ə nouns′mənt), *n.* **1.** public or formal notice announcing something: *the announcement appeared in the newspapers.* **2.** act of announcing.

an·nounc·er (ə noun′sər), *n.* one who announces, esp. over the radio.

an·no ur·bis con·di·tae (än′ō ûr′bĭs kŏn′də tē′), *Latin.* in the year __ after the founding of the city (Rome, traditionally in 753 B.C.). *Abbr.:* A.U.C.

an·noy (ə noi′), *v.t.* **1.** to disturb (a person) in a way that displeases, troubles, or slightly irritates him. **2.** *Mil.* to molest; harm. —*v.i.* **3.** to be hateful or troublesome. —*n.* **4.** *Archaic or Poetic.* something annoying. [ME *anoye,* t. OF: m. *enui,* der. *en(n)uyer* displease, g. LL *inodiāre,* der. *in odiō* in hatred] —**an·noy′er,** *n.* —**Syn. 1.** harass, pester. See **bother, worry.**

an·noy·ance (ə noi′əns), *n.* **1.** that which annoys; a nuisance: *some visitors are an annoyance.* **2.** act of annoying. **3.** the feeling of being annoyed.

an·noy·ing (ə noi′ĭng), *adj.* causing annoyance: *annoying habits.* —**an·noy′ing·ly,** *adv.* —**an·noy′ing·ness,** *n.*

an·nu·al (än′yōō əl), *adj.* **1.** of, for, or pertaining to a year; yearly. **2.** occurring or returning once a year: *an annual celebration.* **3.** *Bot.* living but one growing season, as beans or maize. **4.** performed during a year: *the annual course of the sun.* —*n.* **5.** a plant living but one year or season. **6.** a literary production published annually. [t. LL: s. *annuālis;* r. ME *annuel,* t. OF] —**an′nu·al·ly,** *adv.*

annual parallax. See **parallax** (def. 3).

an·nu·i·tant (ə nū′ə tənt, ə nōō′-), *n.* one who receives an annuity.

an·nu·it coep·tis (än′yōō ĭt sĕp′tĭs), *Latin.* He (God) has favored our undertakings (adapted from Vergil, *Aeneid,* IX, 625; motto on reverse of the great seal of the United States).

an·nu·i·ty (ə nū′ə tĭ, ə nōō′-), *n., pl.* **-ties. 1.** a specified income payable at stated intervals for a fixed or a contingent period, often for the recipient's life, in consideration of a stipulated premium paid either in prior installment payments or in a single payment. **2.** the right to receive such an income, or the duty to make such a payment or payments. [ME *annuitee,* t. F: m. *annuité,* ult. der. L *annuus* yearly]

an·nul (ə nŭl′), *v.t.,* **-nulled, -nulling. 1.** to make void or null; abolish (used esp. of laws or other established rules, usages, and the like): *to annul a marriage.* **2.** to reduce to nothing; obliterate. [ME *anulle(n),* t. LL: m. *annullāre*] —**an·nul′la·ble,** *adj.*

an·nu·lar (än′yə lər), *adj.* having the form of a ring. [t. L: s. *annulāris*] —**an·nu·lar·i·ty** (än′yə lär′ə tĭ), *n.* —**an′nu·lar·ly,** *adv.*

annular eclipse, *Astron.* an eclipse of the sun in which a portion of its surface is visible as a ring surrounding the dark moon (opposed to *total eclipse*).

annular ligament, *Anat.* the general ligamentous envelope which surrounds the joints of the wrist or ankle.

An·nu·la·ta (än′yə lā′tə), *n.pl. Zool.* Annelida.

an·nu·late (än′yə lĭt, -lāt′), *adj.* **1.** formed of ringlike segments, as an annelid worm. **2.** having rings or ringlike bands. Also, **an′nu·lat′ed.**

an·nu·la·tion (än′yə lā′shən), *n.* **1.** formation with or into rings. **2.** a ringlike formation or part.

an·nu·let (än′yə lĭt), *n.* **1.** a little ring. **2.** *Archit.* an encircling band, molding, or fillet, as on a Doric capital. [f. s. L *annulus* ring + -ET]

an·nul·ment (ə nŭl′mənt), *n.* **1.** an invalidation, as of a marriage. **2.** act of annulling.

an·nu·lose (än′yə lōs′), *adj.* furnished with rings; composed of rings: *annulose animals.* [t. NL: m. s. *annulōsus,* der. L *annulus* ring]

an·nu·lus (än′yə ləs), *n., pl.* -li (-lī), **-luses.** a ring; a ringlike part, band, or space. [t. L, var. of *ānulus* ring]

an·nun·ci·ate (ə nŭn′shĭ āt′, -sĭ-), *v.t.,* **-ated, -ating.** to announce. [ME *annunciat,* ppl. adj., announced, t. ML: s. *annunciātus,* r. L. *annuntiātus,* pp.]

an·nun·ci·a·tion (ə nŭn′sĭ ā′shən, -shĭ-), *n.* **1.** (*often cap.*) the announcement by the angel Gabriel to the Virgin Mary of the incarnation of Christ. **2.** (*cap.*) the festival (March 25) instituted by the church in memory of this. **3.** *Rare.* act of announcing; proclamation.

an·nun·ci·a·tor (ənŭn/shĬ ā/tər, -sĬ-), *n.* 1. an announcer. 2. *U.S.* a signaling apparatus, generally used in conjunction with a buzzer, which displays a visual indication when energized by electric current.

An·nun·zi·o (dän nōōn/tsyō), *n.* **Gabriele d'** (gä/brē-ē/lĕ), 1863–1938, Italian poet, novelist, dramatist, army aviator, and soldier.

an·nus mi·ra·bi·lis (ăn/əs mə răb/ə lĬs), *Latin.* year of wonders; wonderful year.

a·no·ci·as·so·ci·a·tion (ə nō/sĬ ə sō/sĬ ā/shən, -shĬ ā/-shən), *n. Surg.* a method of treatment for preventing shock and other harmful effects resulting from an operation, consisting principally in giving general and local anesthesia and in avoiding all unnecessary trauma during the operation. Also, **a·no·ci·a·tion** (ə nō/sĬ ā/shən, -shĬ-). [f. A-⁶ + *noci-* (comb. form repr. L *nocēre* harm) + ASSOCIATION]

an·ode (ăn/ōd), *n.* 1. the electrode which gives off positive ions, or toward which negative ions or electrons move or collect, in a voltaic cell, electronic tube, or other device. 2. the positive pole of a battery or other source of current. 3. the plate of an electron tube. [t. Gk.: m. s. *ánodos* way up]

an·od·ic (ăn ŏd/Ĭk), *adj.* pertaining to an anode or the phenomena in its vicinity.

an·o·dyne (ăn/ə dīn/), *n.* 1. a medicine that relieves or removes pain. 2. anything relieving distress. —*adj.* 3. relieving pain. 4. soothing to the feelings. [t. L: m. s. *anōdynus*, t. Gk.: m. *anṓdynos* freeing from pain]

a·noint (ə noint/), *v.t.* 1. to put oil on; apply an unguent or oily liquid to. 2. to smear with any liquid. 3. to consecrate by applying oil. [ME *anoynte*(n), t. OF: m. *enoint*, pp. of *enoindre*, g. L *inunguere*] —**a·noint/er,** *n.* —**a·noint/ment,** *n.*

an·o·lyte (ăn/ə līt/), *n.* that part of an electrolyte which surrounds the anode in electrolysis. [b. ANODE and ELECTROLYTE]

a·nom·a·lism (ə nŏm/ə lĬz/əm), *n. Rare.* 1. anomalous quality. 2. an anomaly.

a·nom·a·lis·tic (ə nŏm/ə lĬs/tĬk), *adj.* of or pertaining to an anomaly.

anomalistic month, *Astron.* the average interval between consecutive passages of the moon through the perigee.

anomalistic year, *Astron.* the average interval between consecutive passages of the earth through the perihelion.

a·nom·a·lous (ə nŏm/ə ləs), *adj.* deviating from the common rule, type, or form; abnormal; irregular. [t. L: m. *anōmalus,* t. Gk.: m. *anōmalos* irregular] —**a·nom/-a·lous·ly,** *adv.* —**a·nom/a·lous·ness,** *n.*

a·nom·a·ly (ə nŏm/ə lĬ), *n., pl.* **-lies.** 1. deviation from the common rule or analogy. 2. something anomalous: *the anomalies of human nature.* 3. *Astron.* **a.** an angular quantity used in defining the position of a point in an orbit. **b. true anomaly,** the angular distance of a planet from the perihelion of its orbit, as observed from the sun. **c. mean anomaly,** a quantity increasing uniformly with the time and equal to the true anomaly at perihelion and aphelion. [t. L: m. s. *anōmalia,* t. Gk.]

a·nom·ic (ə nŏm/Ĭk), *n. Sociol.* a social vacuum marked by the absence of social norms or values, as in the case of a rooming-house area for single people in a large city. [f. s. Gk. *ánomos* lawless + -IC]

a·non (ə nŏn/), *adv. Archaic.* 1. in a short time; soon. 2. at another time. 3. at once; immediately. 4. **ever and anon,** now and then. [ME; OE *on ān* into one, *on āne* in one, immediately]

anon., anonymous.

an·o·nym (ăn/ə nĬm), *n.* 1. an assumed or false name. 2. an anonymous person or publication.

a·non·y·mous (ə nŏn/ə məs), *adj.* 1. without any name acknowledged, as that of author, contributor, or the like: *an anonymous pamphlet.* 2. of unknown name; whose name is withheld: *an anonymous author.* [t. Gk.: m. *anōnymos*] —**an·o·nym·i·ty** (ăn/ə nĬm/ə tĬ), **a·non/-y·mous·ness,** *n.* —**a·non/y·mous·ly,** *adv.*

a·noph·e·les (ə nŏf/ə lēz/), *n., pl.* **-les.** any mosquito of the genus *Anopheles,* which, when infested with the organisms causing malaria, may transmit the disease to human beings. [t. NL, t. Gk.: useless, hurtful]

a·no·rak (ä/nə räk/), *n.* a jacket with a hood, used in the polar regions. [t. Eskimo: m. *anoraq*]

an·or·thic (ăn ôr/thĬk), *adj. Crystall.* triclinic.

an·or·thite (ăn ôr/thīt), *n.* a mineral of the plagioclase feldspar group, calcium aluminum silicate, $CaAl_2Si_2O_8$, occurring in basic igneous rocks. [f. AN-¹ + s. Gk. *orthós* straight + -ITE¹] —**an·or·thit·ic** (ăn/ôr thĬt/Ĭk), *adj.*

an·or·tho·site (ăn ôr/thə sīt/), *n. Petrog.* a granular igneous rock composed largely of labradorite or a more calcic feldspar. [f. AN-¹ + Gk. *orthós* straight + -ITE¹. Cf. F *anorthose* a feldspar]

an·os·mi·a (ăn ŏz/mĬ ə, ăn ŏs/-), *n. Pathol.* loss of the sense of smell. [t. NL, f. Gk.: *an-* AN-¹ + s. *osmē* smell + -ia -IA] —**an·os/mic,** *adj.*

an·oth·er (ə nŭth/ər), *adj.* 1. a second; a further; an additional: *another piece of cake.* 2. a different; a distinct; of a different kind: *at another time, another man.* —*pron.* 3. one more; an additional one: *try another.* 4. a

different one; something different: *going from one house to another.* 5. one just like. 6. **one another,** one the other; each other: *love one another.* [ME; orig. *an other*]

an·oth·er-guess (ə nŭth/ər gĕs/), *adj. Archaic.* of another kind; of a different sort. [var. of *anothergets,* f. ANOTHER + *gets* (var. of *gates,* gen. of *gate* way)]

ans., answer.

an·sate (ăn/sāt), *adj.* having a handle or handlelike part: *ansate cross* (ankh). [t. L: m. s. *ansātus*]

An·schluss (än/shlŏŏs), *German.* joining or union, esp. the political union of Austria with Germany in 1938.

An·selm (ăn/sĕlm), *n.* **Saint,** 1033–1109, archbishop of Canterbury, scholastic theologian and philosopher.

an·ser·ine (ăn/sə rīn/, -sər Ĭn), *adj.* 1. *Ornith.* of or pertaining to the subfamily *Anserinae,* the goose family. 2. resembling a goose; gooselike. 3. stupid; foolish; silly. Also, **an/ser·ous.** [t. L: m.s. *anserīnus*]

An·son (ăn/sən), *n.* **George, Baron,** 1697–1762, British admiral and navigator.

an·swer (ăn/sər, än/-), *n.* 1. a spoken or written reply to a question, request, letter, etc. 2. a reply or response in act: *the answer was a volley of fire.* 3. a reply to a charge or an accusation. 4. *Law.* a pleading of facts by a defendant in opposition to those stated in the plaintiff's declaration. 5. a solution to a problem, esp. in mathematics. 6. *Music.* the entrance of a fugue subject, usually on the dominant, after its first presentation in the main key. —*v.i.* 7. to make answer; reply. 8. to respond by a word or act: *to answer with a nod.* 9. to act or suffer in consequence of (fol. by *for*): *to answer for one's sins.* 10. to be or declare oneself responsible or accountable (fol. by *for*): *I will answer for his safety.* 11. to be satisfactory or serve (fol. by *for*): *to answer for a purpose.* 12. to conform; correspond (fol. by *to*): *to answer to a description.* 13. **answer back,** to make a rude or impertinent reply. —*v.t.* 14. to make answer to; to reply or respond to: *to answer a person, or a question.* 15. to act in reply or response to: *to answer the bell.* 16. to serve or suit: *this will answer the purpose.* 17. to discharge (a responsibility, claim, debt, etc.). 18. to conform or correspond to; be similar or equivalent to: *to answer a description.* 19. to atone for; make amends for. [ME; OE *andswaru,* f. *and-* against + *-swaru,* akin to *swerian* swear] —**an/swer·er,** *n.* —**an/swer·less,** *adj.*

—**Syn.** 1. ANSWER, REPLY, RESPONSE, RETORT all mean words used to meet a question, remark, charge, etc. An ANSWER is a return remark: *an answer giving the desired information.* REPLY is somewhat more formal than ANSWER: *a reply to a letter.* A RESPONSE often suggests an answer to an appeal, exhortation, etc., or an expected or fixed reply: *a response to inquiry, a response in a church service.* A RETORT implies a keen, prompt answer, esp. one that turns a remark upon the person who made it: *a sharp retort.*

an·swer·a·ble (ăn/sər ə bəl, än/-), *adj.* 1. liable to be asked to give account; responsible (*to* a person, *for* an act, etc.): *he is answerable to me for all his acts.* 2. capable of being answered. 3. proportionate; correlative (fol. by *to*). 4. corresponding; suitable (fol. by *to*). —**an/swer·a·ble·ness,** *n.* —**an/swer·a·bly,** *adv.*

ant (ănt), *n.* 1. any of certain small hymenopterous insects constituting the family *Formicidae,* very widely distributed in thousands of species, all of which have some degree of social organization. 2. a termite. [ME *amte,* OE *ǣmete*] —**ant/like/,** *adj.*

an't (ănt, änt, änt), 1. contraction of *are not.* 2. *Chiefly Brit.* contraction of *am not.* 3. *Illiterate* or *Dial.* contraction of *is not, has not, or have not.*

ant-, var. of **anti-** esp. before a vowel or *h,* as in *antacid.*

-ant, 1. an adjective suffix, orig. participial, as in *ascendant, pleasant.* 2. a noun suffix used in words of participial origin, denoting agency or instrumentality, as in *servant, irritant.* [t. F, g. L *-ant-, -ent-,* nom. *-ans, -ens,* ppr. ending]

ant., antonym.

an·ta (ăn/tə), *n., pl.* **-tae** (-tē). *Archit.* a pier or pillar, formed by thickening a wall at its extremity, often having a base and a capital. [t. L (found only in pl.)]

ant·ac·id (ănt ăs/Ĭd), *adj.* 1. neutralizing acids; counteracting acidity, as of the stomach. —*n.* 2. an antacid agent or remedy. [f. ANT- + ACID]

An·tae·us (ăn tē/əs), *n. Gk. Myth.* an African giant who was invincible when in contact with the earth but was lifted into the air by Hercules and crushed. —**An·tae/an,** *adj.*

an·tag·o·nism (ăn tăg/ə nĬz/əm), *n.* 1. the activity or the relation of contending parties or conflicting forces; active opposition. 2. an opposing force, principle, or tendency. [t. Gk.: m.s. *antagṓnisma*]

an·tag·o·nist (ăn tăg/ə nĬst), *n.* 1. one who is opposed to or strives with another in any kind of contest; opponent; adversary. 2. *Physiol.* a muscle which acts in opposition to another (the agonist). [t. Gk.: s. *antagōnistḗs*] —**Syn.** 1. See **adversary.**

an·tag·o·nis·tic (ăn tăg/ə nĬs/tĬk), *adj.* acting in opposition; mutually opposing. —**an·tag/o·nis/ti·cal·ly,** *adv.*

an·tag·o·nize (ăn tăg/ə nīz/), *v.,* **-nized, -nizing.** —*v.t.* 1. to make hostile; make an antagonist of: *his speech antagonized half the voters.* 2. to act in opposition to; oppose. —*v.i.* 3. *Rare.* to act antagonistically.

An·ta·ki·ya (än/täk ē/yä), *n.* Arabic name of **Antioch.**

ant·al·ka·li (ănt ăl/kə lī/), *n., pl.* **-lis, -lies.** something that neutralizes alkalis or counteracts alkalinity. —**ant·al·ka·line** (ănt ăl/kə līn/, -lĬn), *adj., n.*

[caption:] **Anopheles,** *Anophele quadrimaculatus* (Line shows actual size)

An·ta·na·na·ri·vo (ăn'tə nä'/nə rē'vō, än'-), *n.* Tananarive.

ant·arc·tic (ănt ärk'tĭk, -är'-), *adj.* **1.** of, at, or near the South Pole. —*n.* **2.** **the Antarctic,** the Antarctic Ocean and Antarctica. [t. L: s. *antarcticus,* t. Gk.: m. *antarktikós* opposite the north; r. ME *antartik,* t. OF: m. *antartique*]

Ant·arc·ti·ca (ănt ärk'tə kə, -är'-), *n.* an uninhabited continent around the South Pole, almost wholly covered by a vast continental ice sheet. ab. 5,000,000 sq. mi. Also, **Antarctic Continent.**

Antarctic Circle, the northern boundary of the South Frigid Zone, 23° 28′ from the South Pole.

Antarctic Ocean, the ocean S of the Antarctic Circle.

Antarctic Zone, the South Frigid Zone, between the Antarctic Circle and the South Pole.

An·tar·es (ăn târ'ēz), *n.* a red giant star of the first magnitude in Scorpio. [t. Gk., f. *ant*(í) compared with + *Árēs* Mars; so called because its color resembles that of the planet]

ant bear, 1. a large terrestrial tropical American edentate, the great anteater, *Myrmecophaga jubata,* subsisting on termites, ants, and other insects, and having powerful front claws, a long, tapering snout and extensile tongue, and a shaggy gray coat marked with a conspicuous black band. **2.** the aardvark.

Ant bear (def. 1),
Myrmecophaga jubata
(23 in. high, overall length 7 ft., tail 2½ ft.)

an·te (ăn'tĭ), *n., v.* **-ted** or **-teed, -teing.** —*n.* **1.** *Poker.* a stake put into the pool by each player after seeing his hand but before drawing new cards, or sometimes, before seeing his hand. —*v.t., v.t.* **2.** *Poker.* to put (one's stake) into the pool. **3.** to pay (one's share) (usually fol. by *up*). [cf. L *ante* before]

ante-, a prefix meaning "before in space or time," as in *antedate, antediluvian, anteroom, antecedent.* [t. L]

ant·eat·er (ănt'ē'tər), *n.* **1.** any of three related edentates of tropical America, feeding chiefly on termites: **a.** the ant bear or **great anteater.** **b.** the tamandua or **lesser anteater. c.** silky or **two-toed anteater,** a yellowish, arboreal, prehensile-tailed species, *Cyclopes didactylus,* about the size of a rat. **2.** the aardvark. **3.** any of the pangolins or scaly anteaters of Africa and tropical Asia. **4.** any of the echidnas or spiny anteaters of Australia and New Guinea. **5. banded anteater,** an almost extinct insectivorous marsupial, *Myrmecobius fasciatus,* of South and West Australia.

an·te·bel·lum (ăn'tĭ bĕl'əm), *adj.* **1.** before the war. **2.** *U.S.* before the American Civil War. **3.** before World War I. [L: *ante bellum*]

an·te·cede (ăn'tə sēd'), *v.t.,* **-ceded, -ceding.** to go before, as in order; precede. [t. L: m. s. *antecēdere*]

an·te·ced·ence (ăn'tə sē'dəns), *n.* **1.** act of going before; precedence. **2.** *Astron.* (of a planet) apparent retrograde motion.

an·te·ced·en·cy (ăn'tə sē'dən sĭ), *n.* quality or condition of being antecedent.

an·te·ced·ent (ăn'tə sē'dənt), *adj.* **1.** going or being before; preceding; prior (often fol. by *to*): *an antecedent event.* —*n.* **2.** (*pl.*) **a.** ancestry. **b.** one's past history. **3.** a preceding circumstance, event, etc. **4.** *Gram.* the word or phrase, usually a noun or its equivalent, which is replaced by a pronoun or other substitute later (or rarely, earlier) in the sentence or in a subsequent sentence. In *Jack lost a hat and he can't find it, Jack* is the antecedent of *he,* and *hat* is the antecedent of *it.* **5.** *Math.* the first term of a ratio; the first or third term of a proportion. **6.** *Logic.* the first member of a conditional or hypothetical proposition. [t. L: s. *antecēdens,* ppr.] —**an'te·ced'ent·ly,** *adv.*

an·te·ces·sor (ăn'tə sĕs'ər), *n.* *Rare.* one who goes before; a predecessor.

an·te·cham·ber (ăn'tĭ chām'bər), *n.* a chamber or an apartment through which access is had to a principal apartment. [t. F: m. *antichambre,* t. It.: m. *anticamera,* f. *anti-* ANTE- + *camera* chamber (g. L *camera* vault)]

an·te·choir (ăn'tĭ kwīr'), *n.* an enclosed space in front of the choir of a church.

an·te·date (*v.* ăn'tĭ dāt', ăn'tĭ dāt'; *n.* ăn'tĭ dāt'), *v.,* **-dated, -dating,** *n.* —*v.t.* **1.** to be of older date than; precede in time: *the Peruvian empire antedates that of Mexico.* **2.** to date before the true time: *to antedate a check.* **3.** to assign to an earlier date: *to antedate a historical event.* **4.** to cause to return to an earlier time. **5.** to cause to happen sooner; accelerate. **6.** to take or have in advance; anticipate. —*n.* **7.** a prior date.

an·te·di·lu·vi·an (ăn'tĭ dĭ lōō'vĭ ən), *adj.* **1.** belonging to the period before the Flood. Gen. 7, 8. **2.** antiquated; primitive: *antediluvian ideas.* —*n.* **3.** one who lived before the Flood. **4.** one who is very old or old-fashioned. [f. ANTE- + s. L *dīluvium* de.uge + -AN]

an·te·fix (ăn'tə fĭks'), *n., pl.* **-fixes, -fixa.** *Archit.* **1.** an upright ornament at the eaves of a tiled roof, to conceal the foot of a row of convex tiles which cover the joints of the flat tiles. **2.** an ornament above the top molding of a cornice. [t. L: s. *antefixum,* prop. neut. of *antefixus* fixed before] —**an'te·fix'al,** *adj.*

an·te·flex·ion (ăn'tə flĕk'shən), *n.* *Pathol.* a bending forward, esp. of the body of the uterus.

an·te·lope (ăn'tə lōp'), *n., pl.* **-lope, -lopes. 1.** a slenderly built, hollow-horned ruminant allied to cattle, sheep, and goats, found chiefly in Africa and Asia. **2.** leather made from its hide. **3.** *U.S.* pronghorn. [ME. t. OF: m. *antelop,* t. ML: m.s. *antalopus,* t. LGk.: m. *anthólops*]

an·te me·rid·i·em (ăn'tĭ mə rĭd'ĭ ĕm', -əm), *Latin.* **1.** before noon. **2.** the time between 12 midnight and 12 noon. *Abbr.:* **A.M.** or **a.m.** —**an'te·me·rid'i·an,** *adj.*

an·te·mor·tem (ăn'tĭ môr'təm), *adj.* *Latin.* before death: *an ante-mortem confession.*

an·te·mun·dane (ăn'tĭ mŭn'dān), *adj.* before the creation of the world.

an·te·na·tal (ăn'tĭ nā'təl), *adj.* prenatal.

an·ten·na (ăn tĕn'ə), *n., pl.* **-tennas** for 1; **-tennae** (-tĕn'ē) for *2.* **1.** *Radio.* the conductor by which the electromagnetic waves are sent out or received, consisting commonly of a wire or set of wires; an aerial. **2.** *Zool.* one of the jointed appendages occurring in pairs on the heads of insects, crustaceans, etc., often called feelers. See diag. under **insect.** [t. L: a sailyard]

an·ten·nule (ăn tĕn'ūl), *n.* a small antenna, specif. one of the anterior pair in crustacea.

an·te·pen·di·um (ăn'tə pĕn'dĭ əm), *n., pl.* **-dia** (-dĭ ə). the decoration of the front of an altar, as a covering of silk, or a painted panel. [t. ML. See ANTE, PEND, -IUM]

an·te·pe·nult (ăn'tĭ pē'nŭlt, -pĭ nŭlt'), *n.* the last syllable but two in a word, as *syl-* in *monosyllable.* [t. L: short for *antepaenultima* (*syllaba*)] —**an·te·pe·nul·ti·mate** (ăn'tĭ pĭ nŭl'tə mĭt), *adj., n.*

an·te·ri·or (ăn tĭr'ĭ ər), *adj.* **1.** placed before; situated more to the front (opposed to *posterior*). **2.** going before in time; preceding; earlier: *an anterior age.* [t. L, compar. adj. der. *ante* before] —**an·te·ri·or·i·ty** (ăn tĭr'ĭ ŏr'ə tĭ, -ŏr'-), *n.* —**an·te'ri·or·ly,** *adv.*

an·te·room (ăn'tĭ rōōm', -rŏŏm'), *n.* **1.** a smaller room through which access is had to a chief apartment. **2.** a waiting room.

an·te·ver·sion (ăn'tĭ vûr'zhən, -shən), *n.* *Pathol.* a tipping forward of the uterus with its fundus directed toward the pubis. [t. L: s. *anteversio* a putting before]

an·te·vert (ăn'tĭ vûrt'), *v.t.* *Pathol.* to displace (the uterus) by tipping forward. [t. L: s. *antevertere* precede]

An·theil (ăn'tīl), *n.* **George,** born 1900, U.S. composer.

ant·he·li·on (ănt hē'lĭ ən, ăn thē'-), *n., pl.* **-lia** (-lĭ ə). a luminous ring seen around the shadow of the observer's head as thrown by the sun on a cloud, fog bank, or moist surface. [t. Gk., prop. neut. of *anthēlios* opposite to the sun]

an·thel·min·tic (ăn'thĕl mĭn'tĭk), *Med.* —*adj.* **1.** destroying or expelling intestinal worms. —*n.* **2.** an anthelmintic remedy. [f. ANT- + m. s. Gk. *hélmins* worm + -IC. See HELMINTHIC]

an·them (ăn'thəm), *n.* **1.** a hymn, as of praise, devotion, or patriotism. **2.** a piece of sacred vocal music, usually with words taken from the Scriptures. **3.** a hymn sung in alternate parts. —*v.t.* **4.** to celebrate with an anthem. [ME *antem,* OE *antemn*(e), *antefn*(e), t. VL: m. *antefna,* g. LL *antifona,* var. of *antiphōna,* t. Gk. See ANTIPHON]

an·the·mi·on (ăn thē'mĭ ən), *n., pl.* **-mia** (-mĭ ə). an ornament of floral forms in a flat radiating cluster, as in architectural decoration, vase painting, etc. [t. NL, t. Gk.: flower]

an·ther (ăn'thər), *n.* *Bot.* the pollen-bearing part of a stamen. See diag. under **flower.** [t. NL: s. *anthēra,* t. Gk., fem. of *anthēros* flowery]

an·ther·id·i·um (ăn'thə rĭd'ĭ əm), *n., pl.* **-theridia** (-thə rĭd'ĭ ə). *Bot.* a male sex organ containing motile male gametes. [t. NL, dim. of Gk. *anthērá* ANTHER] —**an'ther·id'i·al,** *adj.*

an·ther·o·zo·id (ăn'thər ə zō'ĭd, ăn'thər ə zoid'), *n.* *Bot.* the motile male gamete produced in an antheridium.

an·the·sis (ăn thē'sĭs), *n.* *Bot.* the period or act of expansion in flowers, esp. the maturing of the stamens. [t. NL, t. Gk.: full bloom]

ant hill, a mound of earth, leaves, etc., formed by a colony of ants in constructing their habitation.

antho-, a word element meaning "flower," as in *anthocyanin.* [t. Gk., comb. form of *ánthos*]

an·tho·cy·a·nin (ăn'thə sī'ə nĭn), *n.* any of a class of water-soluble pigments including most of those that give red and blue flowers these colors. Also, **an·tho·cy·an** (ăn'thə sī'ən).

an·tho·di·um (ăn thō'dĭ əm), *n., pl.* **-dia** (-dĭ ə). *Bot.* a flower head or capitulum, esp. the head (or so-called compound flower) of a composite plant. See illus. under **inflorescence.** [t. NL, f. s. Gk. *anthōdēs* flowerlike + -*ium* -IUM]

an·thol·o·gize (ăn thŏl'ə jīz'), *v.,* **-gized, -gizing.** —*v.i.* **1.** to make an anthology. —*v.t.* **2.** to include in an anthology.

an·thol·o·gy (ăn thŏl'ə jĭ), *n., pl.* **-gies. 1.** a collection of short, choice poems, especially epigrams, of varied authorship. **2.** any collection of literary pieces of varied authorship. [t. Gk.: m. s. *anthologia,* lit., a flower gathering] —**an·tho·log·i·cal** (ăn'thə lŏj'ə kəl), *adj.* —**an·thol'o·gist,** *n.*

An·tho·ny (ăn'tə nĭ, -thə- for 1; ăn'thə nĭ for 2), *n.* **1. Saint,** A.D. 251?–356?, Egyptian hermit; founder of Christian monasticism. **2. Susan Brownell** (brou'nĕl), 1820–1906, U. S. reformer and suffragist.

An·tho·ny of Padua (ăn'tə nǐ, -thə-), **Saint**, 1195–1231, Franciscan monk and preacher in Italy and France.

an·tho·phore (ăn'thə fōr'), *n.* *Bot.* a form of floral stipe, produced by the elongation of the internode between the calyx and the corolla, and bearing the corolla, stamens, and pistil. [t. Gk.: m.s. *anthophóros* flower-bearing]

an·tho·tax·y (ăn'thə tăk'sǐ), *n.* *Bot.* the arrangement of flowers on the axis of growth; inflorescence.

An·tho·zo·a (ăn'thə zō'ə), *n.pl.* *Zool.* a class of the phylum *Coelenterata*, comprising sessile marine animals of the polyp type, single or colonial, having a columnar body with the interior partitioned by septa and an oral disk with one to many circles of tentacles. It includes anemones, corals, sea pens, etc. **—an'-tho·zo'an**, *adj., n.*

Section of flower of wild pink. *Silene caroliniana*, showing A. anthophore within the calyx

an·thra·cene (ăn'thrə sēn'), *n.* a hydrocarbon, $C_{14}H_{10}$, found in coal tar, important commercially as a source of alizarin. [f. m.s. Gk. *ánthrax* coal + -ENE]

an·thra·cite (ăn'thrə sīt'), *n.* a mineral coal containing little of the volatile hydrocarbons and burning almost without flame; hard coal. [t. L: m. s. *anthracītes*, t. Gk.: m. *anthrakītēs* kind of precious stone (prop., coallike)] **—an·thra·cit·ic** (ăn'thrə sǐt'ǐk), *adj.*

an·thrac·nose (ăn thrăk'nōs), *n.* a necrotic plant disease with restricted lesions, as of bean and cotton plants. [f. Gk.: m.s. *ánthrax* carbuncle, coal + m. s. *nósos* disease]

an·thra·coid (ăn'thrə koid'), *adj.* resembling anthrax.

an·thra·qui·none (ăn'thrə kwə nōn', -kwǐn'ōn), *n.* *Chem.* a yellow crystalline substance, $C_{14}H_8O_2$, obtained from anthracene or phthalic anhydride, used in the preparation of alizarin. [f. ANTHRA(CENE) + QUINONE]

an·thrax (ăn'thrăks), *n., pl.* **-thraces** (-thrə sēz'). **1.** a malignant infectious disease of cattle, sheep, and other animals and of man, caused by *Bacillus anthracis*. **2.** a malignant carbuncle which is the diagnostic lesion of anthrax disease in man. [t. L, t. Gk.: carbuncle, coal]

anthrop-, **1.** anthropological. **2.** anthropology.

anthropo-, a word element meaning "man," "human being," as in *anthropocentric*. Also, **anthrop-**. [t. Gk., comb. form of *ánthropos*]

an·thro·po·cen·tric (ăn'thrə pō sĕn'trǐk), *adj.* **1.** regarding man as the central fact of the universe. **2.** assuming man to be the final aim and end of the universe. **3.** viewing and interpreting everything in terms of human experience and values.

an·thro·po·gen·e·sis (ăn'thrə pō jĕn'ə sǐs), *n.* the genesis or development of the human race, esp. as a subject of scientific study. Also, **an·thro·pog·e·ny** (ăn'-thrə pŏj'ə nǐ).

an·thro·pog·ra·phy (ăn'thrə pŏg'rə fǐ), *n.* the branch of anthropology that describes the varieties of mankind and their geographical distribution.

an·thro·poid (ăn'thrə poid'), *adj.* **1.** resembling man. **—n. 2.** an anthropoid ape. [t. Gk.: m. s. *anthrōpoeidḗs*]

anthropoid ape, any ape of the family *Pongidae* comprising the gorilla, chimpanzee, orangutan, and gibbon, without cheek pouches or developed tail.

anthropol., anthropology.

an·thro·pol·o·gist (ăn'thrə pŏl'ə jǐst), *n.* one who studies or is versed in anthropology.

an·thro·pol·o·gy (ăn'thrə pŏl'ə jǐ), *n.* **1.** the science that treats of the origin, development (physical, intellectual, moral, etc.), and varieties, and sometimes esp. the cultural development, customs, beliefs, etc., of mankind. **2.** the study of man's agreement with and divergence from other animals. **3.** the science of man and his works. **—an·thro·po·log·i·cal** (ăn'thrə pə lŏj'ə kəl), **an·thro·po·log·ic,** *adj.* **—an·thro·po·log·i·cal·ly,** *adv.*

an·thro·pom·e·try (ăn'thrə pŏm'ə trǐ), *n.* the measurement of the size and proportions of the human body. **—an·thro·po·met·ric** (ăn'thrə pō mĕt'rǐk), **an·thro·po·met'ri·cal,** *adj.*

an·thro·po·mor·phic (ăn'thrə pō môr'fǐk), *adj.* ascribing human form or attributes to beings or things not human, esp. to a deity.

an·thro·po·mor·phism (ăn'thrə pō môr'fǐz əm), *n.* anthropomorphic conception or representation, as of a deity. **—an'thro·po·mor'phist,** *n.*

an·thro·po·mor·phize (ăn'thrə pō môr'fīz), *v.t., v.i.,* **-phized, -phizing.** to ascribe human form or attributes (to).

an·thro·po·mor·pho·sis (ăn'thrə pō môr'fə sǐs), *n.* transformation into human form.

an·thro·po·mor·phous (ăn'thrə pō môr'fəs), *adj.* **1.** having or resembling the human form. **2.** anthropomorphic. [t. Gk.: m. *anthrōpómorphos*]

an·thro·pon·o·my (ăn'thrə pŏn'ə mǐ), *n.* the science that treats of the laws regulating the development of the human organism in relation to other organisms and to environment. Also, **an·thro·po·nom·ics** (ăn'thrə pō-nŏm'ǐks). **—an'thro·po·nom'i·cal,** *adj.*

an·thro·pop·a·thy (ăn'thrə pŏp'ə thǐ), *n.* ascription of human passions or feelings to beings not human, esp. to God. Also, **an'thro·pop'a·thism.** [t. Gk.: m. s. *anthrōpopátheia* humanity]

an·thro·poph·a·gi (ăn'thrə pŏf'ə jī'), *n. pl., sing.* **-agus** (-ə gəs). man-eaters; cannibals. [t. L, pl. of *anthrōpophagus,* t. Gk.: m. *anthrōpophágos*]

an·thro·poph·a·gite (ăn'thrə pŏf'ə jīt'), *n.* a man-eater; a cannibal.

an·thro·poph·a·gy (ăn'thrə pŏf'ə jǐ), *n.* the eating of human flesh; cannibalism. **—an·thro·po·phag·ic** (ăn'thrə pō făj'ǐk), **an·thro·po·phag·i·cal, an·thro·poph·a·gous** (ăn'thrə pŏf'ə gəs), *adj.*

an·ti (ăn'tī, ăn'tǐ), *n., pl.* **-tis.** *Colloq.* one who is opposed to a particular practice, party, policy, action, etc.

anti-, a prefix meaning "against," "opposed to," with the following particular meanings: **1.** opposed; in opposition: *anti-British, antislavery.* **2.** rival or spurious; pseudo-: *antibishop, anti-Messiah.* **3.** the opposite or reverse of: *antihero, anticlimax.* **4.** not; un-: *antilogical, antigrammatical.* **5.** placed opposite: *antipole, antichorus.* **6.** moving in a reverse or the opposite direction: *anticyclone.* **7.** *Med.* corrective; preventive; curative: *antifat, antipyretic; antistimulant.* Also, **ant-.** [t. Gk.]

an·ti-air·craft (ăn'tī âr'krăft', -kräft'), *adj.* designed for or used in defense against enemy aircraft.

anti-aircraft artillery, a type of artillery for firing on hostile aircraft, and with equipment for detecting the approach of hostile air units.

an·ti·ar (ăn'tǐ är'), *n.* **1.** the upas tree. **2.** an arrow poison prepared from its sap. [t. Javanese: m. *antjar*]

an·ti·bi·o·sis (ăn'tǐ bī ō'sǐs), *n.* *Biol.* an association between organisms which is injurious to one of them. [f. ANTI- + Gk. *bíōsis* act of living]

an·ti·bi·ot·ic (ăn'tǐ bī ŏt'ǐk), *n.* *Biochem.* a chemical agent produced by living organisms, possessing bacteriostatic or bactericidal properties, as penicillin.

an·ti·bod·y (ăn'tǐ bŏd'ǐ), *n., pl.* **-bodies.** any of various substances existing in the blood or developed in immunization which counteract bacterial poisons or destroy bacteria in the system.

an·tic (ăn'tǐk), *n., adj., v.,* **-ticked, -ticking. —n. 1.** (*often pl.*) a grotesque, fantastic, or ludicrous gesture or posture; fantastic trick. **2.** *Archaic.* a grotesque pageant; ridiculous interlude. **3.** *Archaic.* an actor using a mask. **4.** *Archaic.* a buffoon; clown. **—adj. 5.** *Archaic.* fantastic; odd; grotesque: *an antic disposition.* **—v.i. 6.** to perform antics; to caper. [t. It.: m. *antico* old (but used as if It. *grottesco* grotesque), g. L *antīquus*]

an·ti·cat·a·lyst (ăn'tǐ kăt'ə lǐst), *n.* *Chem.* a substance which prevents or slows a chemical reaction (opposed to *catalyst*).

an·ti·cath·ode (ăn'tǐ kăth'ōd), *n.* the plate, often of platinum, on which cathode rays impinge in an x-ray tube, thus producing x-rays.

an·ti·chlor (ăn'tǐ klōr'), *n.* *Chem.* any of various substances, esp. sodium thiosulfate, used for removing excess chlorine from paper pulp, textile, fiber, etc., after bleaching. [f. ANTI- + CHLOR(INE)] **—an·ti·chlo·ris·tic** (ăn'tǐ klō rǐs'tǐk), *adj.*

An·ti·christ (ăn'tǐ krīst'), *n.* *Theol.* **1.** a particular personage or power (variously identified or explained) conceived as appearing in the world as a mighty antagonist of Christ. **2.** (*sometimes l.c.*) an opponent of Christ; a person or power antagonistic to Christ. [t. Gk.: s. *antíchristos;* r. ME *antecrist,* t.OF] **—an·ti·chris·tian** (ăn'tǐ krǐs'chən), *adj., n.*

an·tic·i·pant (ăn tǐs'ə pənt), *adj.* **1.** anticipative (fol. by *of*). **—n. 2.** one who anticipates.

an·tic·i·pate (ăn tǐs'ə pāt'), *v.t.,* **-pated, -pating. 1.** to realize beforehand; foretaste or foresee: *to anticipate pleasure.* **2.** to expect: *to anticipate an acquittal.* **3.** to perform (an action) before another has had time to act. **4.** to be before (another) in doing something; forestall: *anticipated by his predecessors.* **5.** to consider or mention before the proper time: *to anticipate more difficult questions.* **6.** to cause to happen earlier; accelerate; precipitate: *to anticipate his arrival.* **7.** *Finance.* **a.** to expend (funds) before they are legitimately available for use. **b.** to discharge (an obligation) before it is due. [t. L: m.s. *anticipātus,* pp.] **—an·tic'i·pa'tor,** *n.* **—Syn. 1.** See **expect. 3.** preclude, obviate, prevent.

an·tic·i·pa·tion (ăn tǐs'ə pā'shən), *n.* **1.** act of anticipating. **2.** realization in advance; foretaste; expectation; hope. **3.** previous notion; slight previous impression; intuition. **4.** *Law.* a premature drawing from or assignment of money from a trust estate. **5.** *Music.* a tone introduced in advance of its harmony so that it sounds against the preceding chord.

A. Anticipation (def. 5)

an·tic·i·pa·tive (ăn tǐs'ə pā'tǐv), *adj.* anticipating or tending to anticipate; containing anticipation: *an anticipative action or look.* **—an·tic'i·pa'tive·ly,** *adv.*

an·tic·i·pa·to·ry (ăn tǐs'ə pə tōr'ǐ), *adj.* pertaining to, manifesting, or expressing anticipation. **—an·tic'i·pa·to'ri·ly,** *adv.*

an·ti·clas·tic (ăn'tǐ klăs'tǐk), *adj.* *Math.* (of a surface) having principal curvatures of opposite sign at a given point (opposed to *synclastic*).

an·ti·cler·i·cal (ăn'tǐ klĕr'ə kəl), *adj.* opposed to the influence and activities of the clergy in public affairs. **—an'ti·cler'i·cal·ism,** *n.*

an·ti·cli·max (ăn'tǐ klī'măks), *n.* **1.** a noticeable or ludicrous descent in discourse from lofty ideas or expressions to what is much less impressive. **2.** an abrupt descent in dignity; an inglorious conclusion. —**an·ti·cli·mac·tic** (ăn′tĭ klĭ măk′tĭk), *adj.*

an·ti·cli·nal (ăn′tĭ klī′nəl), *adj.* **1.** inclining in opposite directions from a central axis. **2.** *Geol.* **a.** inclining downward on both sides from a median line or axis, as an upward fold of rock strata. **b.** pertaining to such a fold. [f. ANTI- + CLIN(O)- + AL[1]]
an·ti·cline (ăn′tĭ klīn′), *n.* *Geol.* an anticlinal rock structure.
an·ti·cli·no·ri·um (ăn′tĭ-klī nōr′Ĭ əm), *n.*, *pl.* **-noria**

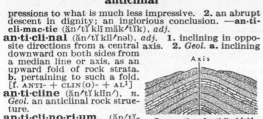

Cross section of anticlinal fold

(-nōr′Ĭ əm). *Geol.* a compound anticline, consisting of a series of subordinate anticlines and synclines, the whole having the general contour of an arch.
An·ti·cos·ti (ăn′tə kŏs′tĭ, -kŏs′-), *n.* an island in E Canada, in the estuary of the St. Lawrence: a part of Quebec. 424 pop. (1941); ab. 130 mi. long; 3043 sq. mi.
an·ti·cy·clone (ăn′tĭ sī′klōn), *n.* *Meteorol.* an extensive horizontal movement of the atmosphere spirally around and away from a gradually progressing central region of high barometric pressure, the spiral motion being clockwise in the Northern Hemisphere, counterclockwise in the Southern. —**an·ti·cy·clon·ic** (ăn′tĭ-sī klŏn′ĭk), *adj.*
an·ti·diph·the·rit·ic (ăn′tĭ dĭf′thə rĭt′ĭk), *Med.* —*adj.* **1.** curing or preventing diphtheria. —*n.* **2.** an antidiphtheritic remedy.
an·ti·dote (ăn′tĭ dōt′), *n.* **1.** a medicine or other remedy for counteracting the effects of poison, disease, etc. **2.** whatever prevents or counteracts injurious effects. [t. L: m. s. *antidotum,* t. Gk.: m. *antídotos* (verbal adj.) given against] —**an′ti·dot′al,** *adj.*
an·ti·drom·ic (ăn′tĭ drŏm′Ĭk), *adj.* *Physiol.* conducting nerve impulses in a direction opposite to the usual one. [ANTI- + s. Gk. *drómos* a running + -IC]
an·ti·en·er·gis·tic (ăn′tĭ en′ar jĭs′tĭk), *adj.* acting in a manner opposite to the energy applied.
An·tie·tam (ăn tē′təm), *n.* a creek flowing from S Pennsylvania through NW Maryland into the Potomac. One of the bloodiest battles of the Civil War was fought here (1862), after which McClellan allowed Lee to retreat across the Potomac.

an·ti·fe·brile (ăn′tĭ fē′brəl, -fĕb′rəl), *Med.* —*adj.* **1.** efficacious against fever; febrifuge; antipyretic. —*n.* **2.** an antifebrile agent.
An·ti·fed·er·al·ist (ăn′tĭ fĕd′ər əl Ĭst, -fĕd′rəl-), *n.* *U.S. Hist.* a member or supporter of the Antifederal Party. —**An′ti·fed′er·al·ism,** *n.*
An·ti·fed·er·al Party (ăn′tĭ fĕd′ər əl, -fĕd′rəl), *U.S. Hist.* the party which, before 1789, opposed the adoption of the proposed Constitution and after that favored its strict construction.
an·ti·fer·ment (ăn′tĭ fûr′mĕnt), *n.* any substance or agent that prevents or counteracts fermentation.
an·ti·freeze (ăn′tĭ frēz′), *n.* a liquid used in the radiator of an internal-combustion engine to lower the freezing point of the cooling medium.
an·ti·fric·tion (ăn′tĭ frĭk′shən), *n.* something that prevents or reduces friction; a lubricant.
an·ti·gen (ăn′tə jən), *n.* any substance which when injected into animal tissues will stimulate the production of antibodies. [f. ANTI(BODY) + -GEN] —**an·ti·gen·ic** (ăn′tə jĕn′Ĭk), *adj.*
An·tig·o·ne (ăn tĭg′ə nē′), *n.* *Gk. Legend.* a daughter of Oedipus by his mother, Jocasta. For performing funeral rites (forbidden by edict of Creon, King of Thebes) over her brother Polynices, she was condemned to be immured alive, and hanged herself.
An·tig·o·nus (ăn tĭg′ə nəs), *n.* ("Cyclops") 382?–301 B.C., Macedonian general under Alexander the Great; later, king of Asia.
An·ti·gua (ăn tē′gwə, -gə), *n.* one of the Leeward Islands, in the British West Indies. 40,122 pop. (est. 1942); 108 sq. mi. *cap.:* St. John.
an·ti·he·lix (ăn′tĭ hē′lĭks), *n.*, *pl.* **-helices** (-hĕl′ə sēz′), **-helixes.** *Anat.* the inner curved ridge of the pinna of the ear. See diag. under **ear.**
an·ti·his·ta·mine (ăn′tĭ hĭs′tə mēn′, -mĭn′), *n.* *Pharm.* any of certain medicines or drugs which neutralize or inhibit the effect of histamine in the body, used mainly in the treatment of allergic disorders and colds. —**an′ti·his′ta·mine′, an′ti·his′ta·min′ic,** *adj.*
an·ti·im·pe·ri·al·ist (ăn′tĭ Ĭm pĭr′Ĭ əl Ĭst), *n.* an opponent of imperialism. —**an′ti·im·pe′ri·al·is′tic,** *adj.*
an·ti·ke·to·gen·e·sis (ăn′tĭ kē′tə jĕn′ə sĭs), *n. Med.* prevention of the excessive formation of acetone bodies in the body, such as occurs in diabetes. [f. ANTI- + KETO(SIS) + -GENESIS] —**an′ti·ke′to·gen′ic,** *adj.*
an·ti·knock (ăn′tĭ nŏk′), *n.* a material, usually a lead compound, added to the fuel to eliminate or minimize detonation in an internal-combustion engine.
An·ti·Leb·a·non (ăn′tĭ lĕb′ə nən), *n.* a mountain range in SW Syria, E of the Lebanon Mountains.

An·til·les (ăn tĭl′ēz), *n.pl.* a chain of islands in the West Indies, divided into the **Greater Antilles** (Cuba, Hispaniola, Jamaica, and Puerto Rico), and the **Lesser Antilles** (a group of smaller islands to the SE). —**An·til·le·an** (ăn′tə lē′ən, ăn tĭl′Ĭ-), *adj.*
an·ti·log·a·rithm (ăn′tĭ lôg′ə rĭth′əm, -lŏg′ə-), *n.* *Math.* the number corresponding to a logarithm.
an·til·o·gy (ăn tĭl′ə jĭ), *n.*, *pl.* **-gies.** a contradiction in terms or ideas. [t. Gk.: m. s. *antilogía* contradiction]
an·ti·ma·cas·sar (ăn′tĭ mə kăs′ər), *n.* an ornamental covering for the backs and arms of chairs, sofas, etc., to keep them from being soiled by hair oil; a tidy. [f. ANTI- + *Macassar,* hair oil obtained from MACASSAR]
an·ti·ma·lar·i·al (ăn′tĭ mə lâr′Ĭ əl), *Med.* —*adj.* **1.** preventive of or efficacious against malaria. —*n.* **2.** an antimalarial agent.
an·ti·masque (ăn′tə măsk′, -mäsk′), *n.* a comic or grotesque interlude between the acts of a masque. Also, **an′ti·mask′.**
an·ti·mere (ăn′tə mĭr′), *n.* *Zool.* a segment or division of the body in the direction of one of the secondary or transverse axes, as either half of a bilaterally symmetrical animal or a radiating part of a radially symmetrical animal. —**an·ti·mer·ic** (ăn′tə mĕr′Ĭk), *adj.* —**an·tim·er·ism** (ăn tĭm′ər Ĭz′əm), *n.*
an·ti·mo·nic (ăn′tə mō′nĭk, -mŏn′Ĭk), *adj.* *Chem.* of or containing antimony, esp. in the pentavalent state (Sb+5).
an·ti·mo·nous (ăn′tə mō′nəs), *adj.* *Chem.* containing trivalent antimony (Sb+3). Also, **an·ti·mo·ni·ous** (ăn′tə-mō′nĬ əs).
an·ti·mon·soon (ăn′tĭ mŏn soon′), *n.* *Meteorol.* a current of air moving in a direction opposite to that of a given monsoon and lying above it.
an·ti·mo·ny (ăn′tə mō′nĬ), *n.* a brittle, lustrous, white metallic element occurring in nature free or combined, used chiefly in alloys and (in compounds) in medicine. *Symbol:* Sb; *at. no.:* 51; *at. wt.:* 121.76. [late ME, t. ML: m.s. *antimōnium*] —**an′ti·mo′ni·al,** *adj.*, *n.*
antimony glance, stibnite.
an·ti·mo·nyl (ăn′tə mə nĭl, ăn tĭm′ə-), *n.* *Chem.* a radical containing antimony and oxygen (SbO+1) which forms salts. [f. ANTIMON(Y) + -YL]
an·ti·neu·ral·gic (ăn′tĭ nyŏŏ răl′jĭk, -nŏŏ-), *Med.* —*adj.* **1.** preventing or relieving neuralgia or neuralgic pain. —*n.* **2.** an antineuralgic substance.
an·ti·node (ăn′tə nōd′), *n.* *Physics.* a point, line, or region in a vibrating medium at which the amplitude of variation of the disturbance is greatest, situated halfway between two adjacent nodes.
an·ti·no·mi·an (ăn′tə nō′mĬ ən), *n.* one who maintains that Christians are freed from the moral law by the dispensation of grace set forth in the gospel. —**an′ti·no′mi·an,** *adj.* —**an′ti·no′mi·an·ism,** *n.*
an·tin·o·my (ăn tĭn′ə mĭ), *n.*, *pl.* **-mies.** **1.** opposition between laws and principles. **2.** *Philos.* the mutual contradiction of two principles or correctly drawn inferences, each of which is supported by reason. [t. L: m. s. *antinomia,* t. Gk.]
An·ti·och (ăn′tĭ ŏk′), *n.* a city in S Turkey; capital of the ancient kingdom of Syria, 300–64 B.C. 26,939 (1940). Arabic, **Antakiya.** —**An·ti·o·chi·an** (ăn′tĭ ō′kĬ ən), *adj.*
An·ti·o·chus III (ăn tĭ′ə-kəs), ("*the Great*") 241?–187 B.C., king of Syria, 223–187 B.C.; fought against the Romans.

Antiochus IV, (*Antiochus Epiphanes*), died 164? B.C., king of Syria 175–164? B.C.
an·ti·ox·i·dant (ăn′tĭ ŏk′sə dənt), *n.* **1.** any substance which when added to rubber inhibits its deterioration. **2.** any substance inhibiting oxidation.
an·ti·pas·to (ăn′tē päs′tō), *n.* *Italian.* **1.** an appetizer course of relishes, smoked meat, fish, etc.; hors d'oeuvres. **2.** any food that heightens the appetite.
An·tip·a·ter (ăn tĭp′ə tər), *n.* 398?–319 B.C., general under Alexander the Great; regent of Macedonia.
an·ti·pa·thet·ic (ăn′tĭ pə thĕt′Ĭk, ăn′tĭ pə-), *adj.* having a natural antipathy, contrariety, or constitutional aversion (often fol. by *to*): *he was antipathetic to any kind of change.* Also, **an·tip′a·thet′i·cal.** —**an·tip′a·thet′i·cal·ly,** *adv.*
an·tip·a·thy (ăn tĭp′ə thĭ), *n.*, *pl.* **-thies.** **1.** a natural or settled dislike; repugnance; aversion. **2.** an instinctive contrariety or opposition in feeling: *their natural antipathy of temperament.* **3.** an object of natural aversion or settled dislike. [t. L: m. s. *antipathīa,* t. Gk.: m. *antipátheia,* der. *antipathḗs* having opposite feelings] —**Syn. 1.** See **aversion.** —**Ant. 1.** attraction.
an·ti·pe·ri·od·ic (ăn′tĭ pĭr′Ĭ ŏd′Ĭk), *adj.* **1.** efficacious against periodic diseases, as intermittent fever. —*n.* **2.** an antiperiodic agent.
an·ti·per·i·stal·sis (ăn′tĭ pĕr′ə stăl′sĭs), *n.* *Physiol.* inverted peristaltic action of the intestines, by which their contents are carried upward.
an·ti·per·son·nel (ăn′tĭ pûr′sə nĕl′), *adj.* *Mil.* used against individuals rather than against mechanized vehicles, materiel, etc.: *antipersonnel bombs.*
an·ti·phlo·gis·tic (ăn′tĭ flō jĭs′tĭk), *adj.* **1.** checking inflammation. —*n.* **2.** an antiphlogistic remedy.

an·ti·phon (ăn′tə fŏn′), *n.* **1.** a verse sung in response. **2.** *Eccles.* **a.** a psalm, hymn, or prayer sung in alternate parts. **b.** a verse or a series of verses sung as a prelude or conclusion to some part of the service. [t. ML: s. *antiphōna,* t. Gk.: (prop. neut. pl.) sounding in answer]

an·tiph·o·nal (ăn tĭf′ə nəl), *adj.* **1.** pertaining to antiphons or antiphony; responsive. —*n.* **2.** an antiphonary. —**an·tiph′o·nal·ly,** *adv.*

an·tiph·o·nar·y (ăn tĭf′ə nĕr′Y), *n., pl.* **-naries.** a book of antiphons.

an·tiph·o·ny (ăn tĭf′ə nY), *n., pl.* **-nies.** **1.** alternate or responsive singing by a choir in two divisions. **2.** a psalm, etc., so sung; an antiphon. **3.** a responsive musical utterance. —**an·ti·phon·ic** (ăn′tə fŏn′Yk), *adj.*

an·tiph·ra·sis (ăn tĭf′rə sĭs), *n. Rhet.* the use of words in a sense opposite to the proper meaning. [t. L, t. Gk.]

an·tip·o·dal (ăn tĭp′ə dəl), *adj.* **1.** *Geog.* on the opposite side of the globe; belonging to the antipodes. **2.** diametrically opposite: *antipodal characters.*

an·ti·pode (ăn′tə pōd′), *n.* a direct or exact opposite.

an·tip·o·des (ăn tĭp′ə dēz′), *n.pl.* **1.** places diametrically opposite to each other on the globe. **2.** those who dwell there. [t. L, t. Gk., pl. of *antipous* with feet opposite] —**an·tip·o·de·an** (ăn tĭp′ə dē′ən), *adj., n.*

An·tip·o·des (ăn tĭp′ə dēz′), *n.pl.* a group of small uninhabited islands, ab. 460 mi. SE of and belonging to New Zealand. ab. 20 sq. mi.

an·ti·pope (ăn′tĭ pōp′), *n.* one who is elected pope in opposition to another held to be canonically chosen.

an·ti·py·ret·ic (ăn′tĭ pī rĕt′Yk), *Med.* —*adj.* **1.** checking or preventing fever. —*n.* **2.** an antipyretic agent.

an·ti·py·rine (ăn′tĭ pī′rYn), *n. Pharm.* a white powder, $C_{11}H_{12}N_2O$, used as a sedative, antipyretic, antirheumatic, and antineuralgic.

antiq., antiquity.

an·ti·quar·i·an (ăn′tə kwâr′Y ən), *adj.* **1.** pertaining to the study of antiquities or to antiquaries. —*n.* **2.** antiquary. —**an′ti·quar′i·an·ism,** *n.*

an·ti·quar·y (ăn′tə kwĕr′Y), *n., pl.* **-quaries.** one versed in the knowledge of ancient things; a student or collector of antiquities. [t. L: m.s. *antiquārius* of antiquity]

an·ti·quate (ăn′tə kwāt′), *v.t.,* **-quated, -quating. 1.** to make old and useless by substituting something newer and better. **2.** to make antique. [t. L: m.s. *antīquātus,* pp., make old] —**an′ti·qua′tion,** *n.*

an·ti·quat·ed (ăn′tə kwā′tYd), *adj.* **1.** grown old; obsolete or obsolescent. **2.** ill-adapted to present use. **3.** aged. —**an′ti·quat′ed·ness,** *n.* —**Syn. 2.** See **ancient**[1].

an·tique (ăn tēk′), *adj., n., v.,* **-tiqued, -tiquing.** —*adj.* **1.** belonging to former times as contrasted with modern. **2.** dating from an early period: *antique furniture.* **3.** old-fashioned; antiquated: *an antique robe.* **4.** *Archaic.* aged; ancient. —*n.* **5.** an object of art or a furniture piece of a former period. **6.** the antique (usually Greek or Roman) style, esp. in art. **7.** *Print.* a style of type. —*v.t.* **8.** to make appear antique. [t. L: m. s. *antiquus* old] —**an·tique′ly,** *adv.* —**an·tique′ness,** *n.* —**Syn. 2.** See **ancient**[1].

an·tiq·ui·ty (ăn tĭk′wə tY), *n., pl.* **-ties. 1.** the quality of being ancient; great age: *a family of great antiquity.* **2.** ancient times; former ages: *the errors of dark antiquity.* **3.** the time before the Middle Ages. **4.** the ancients collectively; the people of ancient times. **5.** (*usually pl.*) something belonging to or remaining from ancient times.

an·ti·ra·chit·ic (ăn′tĭ rə kĭt′Yk), *adj.* pertaining to the prevention or cure of rickets.

an·ti·re·mon·strant (ăn′tĭ rĭ mŏn′strənt), *n.* **1.** one opposed to remonstrance or to those who remonstrate. **2.** (*cap.*) one of that party in the Dutch Calvinistic Church which opposed the Remonstrants or Arminians.

an·ti·rheu·mat·ic (ăn′tĭ rōō măt′Yk), *Med.* —*adj.* **1.** preventing or relieving rheumatism or rheumatic pain. —*n.* **2.** an antirheumatic substance.

an·tir·rhi·num (ăn′tə rī′nəm), *n.* any of the genus, *Antirrhinum,* of herbs, family *Scrophulariaceae,* natives of the Old World, introduced into North America; the snapdragon. [t. NL, t. Gk.: m. *antirrhīnon* calf's snout]

an·ti·scor·bu·tic (ăn′tĭ skôr bū′tYk), *Med.* —*adj.* **1.** efficacious against scurvy. —*n.* **2.** an antiscorbutic agent.

an·ti·Sem·ite (ăn′tĭ sĕm′īt, -sē′mīt), *n.* one hostile to the Jews. —**an·ti·Se·mit·ic** (ăn′tĭ sə mĭt′Yk), *adj.* —**an′ti·Se·mit′i·cal·ly,** *adv.* —**an·ti·Sem·i·tism** (ăn′tĭ sĕm′ə tYz′əm), *n.*

an·ti·sep·sis (ăn′tə sĕp′sYs), *n.* destruction of the microörganisms that produce sepsis or septic disease.

an·ti·sep·tic (ăn′tə sĕp′tYk), *adj.* **1.** pertaining to or affecting antisepsis. —*n.* **2.** an antiseptic agent.

an·ti·sep·ti·cal·ly (ăn′tə sĕp′tYk lY), *adv.* with the help of antiseptics.

an·ti·sep·ti·cize (ăn′tə sĕp′tə sīz′), *v.t.,* **-cized, -cizing.** to treat with antiseptics.

an·ti·se·rum (ăn′tĭ sYr′əm), *n., pl.* **-serums, -sera** (-sYr′ə). a fluid containing antibodies, as antitoxins or agglutinins obtained by inoculation of animals and used for injection into the blood stream of other animals to provide immunity to a specific disease.

an·ti·slav·er·y (ăn′tĭ slā′və rY), *adj.* opposed to slavery, esp. Negro slavery.

an·ti·so·cial (ăn′tĭ sō′shəl), *adj.* **1.** unwilling or unable to associate normally with one's fellows. **2.** opposed

to social order, or to the principles on which society is constituted. Also, **an′ti·so′cial·is′tic.**

an·ti·spas·mod·ic (ăn′tĭ spăz mŏd′Yk), *adj.* **1.** checking spasms, esp. of blood vessels or internal organs. —*n.* **2.** an antispasmodic agent.

An·tis·the·nes (ăn tĭs′thə nēz′), *n.* 444?–365? B.C., Greek philosopher, founder of the Cynic philosophy.

an·tis·tro·phe (ăn tĭs′trə fY), *n.* **1.** the part of an ancient Greek choral ode, answering to a previous strophe, sung by the chorus when returning from left to right. **2.** the second of two metrically corresponding systems in a poem. [t. L, t. Gk.: a turning about] —**an·ti·stroph·ic** (ăn′tĭ strŏf′Yk), *ad*

an·ti·tank (ăn′tĭ tăngk′), *adj. Mil.* designed for use against tanks or other armored vehicles: *antitank gun.*

an·tith·e·sis (ăn tĭth′ə sYs), *n., pl.* **-ses** (-sēz′). **1.** opposition; contrast: *the antithesis of theory and fact.* **2.** the direct opposite (fol. by *of* or *to*). **3.** *Rhet.* **a.** the setting of one clause or other member of a sentence against another to which it is opposed. **b.** a clause or member thus set in opposition, [t. LL, t. Gk.: opposition]

an·ti·thet·ic (ăn′tə thĕt′Yk), *adj.* **1.** of the nature of or involving antithesis. **2.** directly opposed or contrasted. Also, **an′ti·thet′i·cal.** —**an′ti·thet′i·cal·ly,** *adv.*

an·ti·tox·ic (ăn′tĭ tŏk′sYk), *adj.* **1.** counteracting toxic influences. **2.** of or serving as an antitoxin.

an·ti·tox·in (ăn′tĭ tŏk′sYn), *n.* **1.** a substance formed in the body, which counteracts a specific toxin. **2.** the antibody formed in immunization with a given toxin, used in treating certain infectious diseases or in immunizing against them. Also, **an·ti·tox·ine** (ăn′tĭ tŏk′sYn, -sēn).

an·ti·trade (ăn′tĭ trād′), *n.* **1.** any of the upper tropical winds moving counter to and above the trade winds, but descending beyond the trade wind limits, and becoming the westerly winds of middle latitudes. —*adj.* **2.** noting such a wind.

an·tit·ra·gus (ăn tĭt′rə gəs), *n., pl.* **-gi** (-jī′). *Anat.* a process of the external ear. See diag. under **ear.** [t. NL, t. Gk.: m. *antitragos*]

an·ti·trust (ăn′tĭ trŭst′), *adj.* opposed to trusts or large combinations of capital.

an·ti·type (ăn′tĭ tīp′), *n.* that which is foreshadowed by a type or symbol, as a New Testament event prefigured in the Old Testament. [t. Gk.: m. s. *antitypos* corresponding as a stamp to the die] —**an·ti·typ·ic** (ăn′tĭ tYp′Yk), **an·ti·typ′i·cal,** *adj.*

an·ti·un·ion (ăn′tĭ ūn′yən), *adj. U.S.* not recognizing or favoring trade unions or unionism.

an·ti·ven·in (ăn′tĭ vĕn′Yn), *n.* **1.** an antitoxin produced in the blood by repeated injections of venom, as of snakes. **2.** the antitoxic serum obtained from such blood.

ant·ler (ănt′lər), *n.* one of the solid deciduous horns, usually branched, of an animal of the deer family. [ME *auntelere,* t. OF: m. *antoillier* ult. der. L *ant(e)* before + *oculus* eye]

ant·lered (ănt′lərd), *adj.* **1.** having antlers. **2.** decorated with antlers.

ant lion, a larval neuropterous insect of the family *Myrmeleontidae,* the larva of which (doodlebug) digs a pit in sand, where it lies in wait for ants, etc.

Antler of a stag
A. Brow antler; B. Bay antler; C. Royal antler; D. Crown antler

An·to·fa·gas·ta (än′tô fä gäs′tä), *n.* a seaport in N Chile. 49,106 (1940).

An·toi·nette (ăn′twə nĕt′; *Fr.* ăn twä nĕt′), *n.* **Marie** (mə rē′; *Fr.* mà rē′), 1755–93, wife of Louis XVI: queen of France, 1774–93; executed during French Revolution.

An·to·ni·nus (ăn′tə nī′nəs), *n.* **Marcus Aurelius** (mâr′kəs ô rēl′yəs), A.D. 121–180, emperor of Rome, A.D. 161–180: Stoic philosopher and writer.

Antoninus Pi·us (pī′əs), A.D. 86–161, emperor of Rome, A.D. 138–161.

An·to·ni·us (ăn tō′nY əs), *n.* See **Antony, Mark.**

an·to·no·ma·sia (ăn′tə nō mā′zhə), *n. Rhet.* **1.** the identification of a person by an epithet or appellative not his name, as *his lordship.* **2.** the use of a personal name to denote a class of similar persons, as a *Shylock.* [t. L, t. Gk., der. *antonomázein* call instead]

An·to·ny (ăn′tə nY), *n.* **Mark,** (*Marcus Antonius*) 83?–30 B.C., Roman general: friend of Caesar; member of second triumvirate and rival of Octavian.

an·to·nym (ăn′tə nYm), *n.* a word opposed in meaning to another (opposed to **synonym**): "*good*" is the antonym of "*bad.*" [t. Gk.: m. *antónymia*]

an·tre (ăn′tər), *n. Chiefly Poetic.* a cavern; a cave. [t. F, t. L: m. s. *antrum,* t. Gk.: m. *ántron*]

An·trim (ăn′trYm), *n.* a county in NE Northern Ireland. 212,300 pop. (est. 1946); 1098 sq mi. *Co. seat:* Belfast.

an·trorse (ăn trôrs′), *adj. Bot., Zool.* bent or directed forward or upward. [t. NL: m.s. *antrorsus,* f. L *antero-* front- + *versus,* pp., turned] —**an·trorse′ly,** *adv.*

an·trum (ăn′trəm), *n., pl.* **-tra** (-trə). *Anat.* a cavity in a bone, esp. that in the maxilla. [t. L, t. Gk.: m. *ántron*]

An·tung (ăn′tŏŏng′; *Chin.* än′dŏŏng′), *n.* **1.** a province in NE China, in Manchuria. 3,334,000 pop. (1946); 24,487 sq. mi. *Cap.:* Tunghua. **2.** a seaport in this province, at the mouth of the Yalu river. 204,000 (est. 1938).

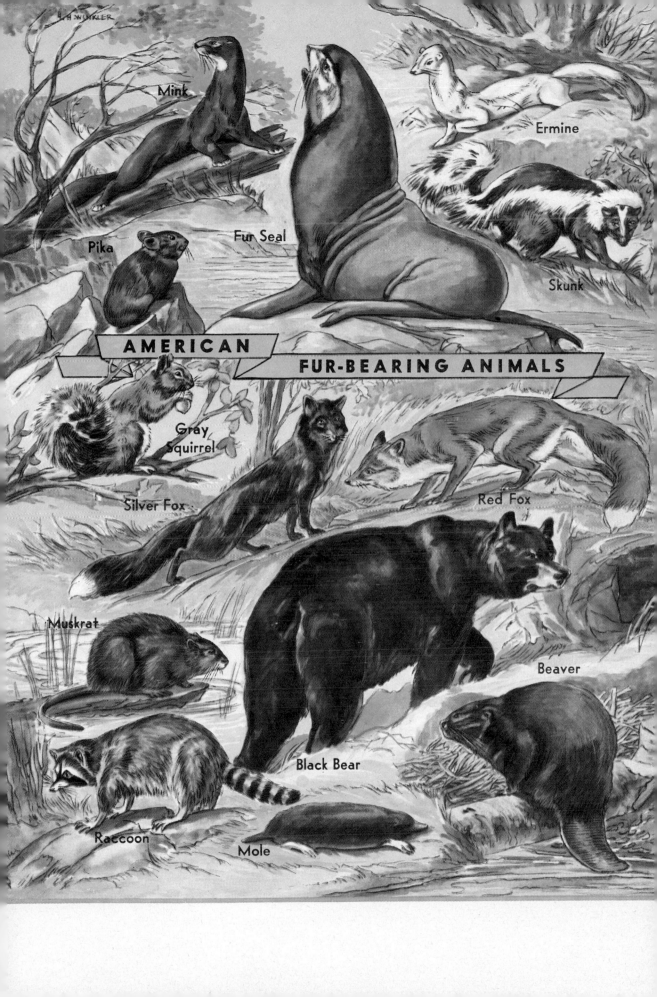

Mink

Ermine

Fur Seal

Skunk

Pika

AMERICAN FUR-BEARING ANIMALS

Gray Squirrel

Silver Fox

Red Fox

Muskrat

Beaver

Black Bear

Raccoon

Mole

Rocky Mountain Goat

Virginia Deer

Wapiti

Moose

Coyote

Rocky Mountain Sheep

Lynx

WILD ANIMALS OF NORTH AMERICA

Puma

Pronghorned Antelope

Bison

Grizzly Bear

Timber Wolf

Ant·werp (ănt′wərp), *n.* a seaport in N Belgium, on the Scheldt river. 257,897 (est. 1941). French, **An·vers** (än ver′). Flemish, **Ant·wer·pen** (änt′ver pən).

A·nu·bis (ə nū′bĭs, ə nōō′-), *n.* *Egyptian Myth.* a son of Osiris, identified by the Greeks with Hermes, and represented as having the head of a dog. [t. L, t. Gk.: m. *Anoubis*, t. Egypt.: m. *Anup* jackal]

A number 1, A one (def. 2).

an·u·ran (ə nyŏŏr′ən, ə nŏŏr′-), *adj., n. Zool.* salientian. [f. AN-[1] + m. s. Gk. *ourá* tail + -AN]

a·nus (ā′nəs), *n. Anat.* the opening at the lower end of the alimentary canal, through which the solid refuse of digestion is excreted. [t. L]

an·vil (ăn′vĭl), *n.* **1.** a heavy iron block with a smooth face, frequently of steel, on which metals, usually red- or white-hot, are hammered into de-sired shapes. **2.** anything on which blows are struck. **3.** the fixed jaw in certain measuring instruments. **4.** *Anat.* the incus. [ME *anvilt*, OE *anfilt*(*e*), c. MD *anvilte*]

Anvil (def. 1)

anx·i·e·ty (ăng zī′ə tĭ), *n., pl.* **-ties. 1.** distress or uneasiness of mind caused by apprehension of danger or misfortune. **2.** solicitous desire; eagerness. **3.** *Psychiatry.* a state of apprehension and psychic tension found in most forms of mental disorder. [t. L: m.s. *anxietas*] —**Syn. 1.** See **apprehension.**

anx·ious (ăngk′shəs, ăng′-), *adj.* **1.** full of anxiety or solicitude; greatly troubled or solicitous: *to be anxious about someone's safety.* **2.** earnestly desirous (fol. by infinitive or *for*): *anxious to please.* **3.** attended with or showing solicitude or uneasiness: *anxious forebodings.* [t. L: m. *anxius* troubled] —**anx′ious·ly,** *adv.* —**anx′ious·ness,** *n.* —**Syn. 1.** concerned, worried, disturbed.

anxious seat, *U.S.* a seat reserved at a revival meeting for those troubled by conscience and eager for spiritual assistance. Also, **anxious bench.**

an·y (ĕn′ĭ), *adj.* **1.** one, a, an, or (as *pl.*) some; whatever or whichever it may be: *if you have any witnesses, produce them.* **2.** in whatever quantity or number, great or small: *have you any butter?* **3.** every: *any schoolboy would know that.* **4.** (with a negative) none at all. **5. any one,** any single or individual (person or thing): *any one part of town.* —*pron.* **6.** (*sing.*) any person; anybody, or (as *pl.*) any persons: *he does better than any before him; unknown to any.* **7.** any single one or any ones; any thing or things; any quantity or number. —*adv.* **8.** in any degree; to any extent; at all: *do you feel any better?* [ME; OE ǣnig, der. ǟn one] —**Syn. 2.** See **some.**

an·y·bod·y (ĕn′ĭ bŏd′ĭ, -bə dĭ), *pron., n., pl.* **-bodies. 1.** any person. **2.** a person of some importance.

an·y·how (ĕn′ĭ hou′), *adv.* **1.** in any way whatever. **2.** in any case; at all events. **3.** in a careless manner.

an·y·one (ĕn′ĭ wŭn′, -wən), *pron.* any person; anybody. (Note: for **anyone** as two words, see **any,** def. 5.)

an·y·thing (ĕn′ĭ thĭng′), *pron.* **1.** any thing whatever; something, no matter what. —*n.* **2.** a thing of any kind. —*adv.* **3.** in any degree; to any extent.

an·y·way (ĕn′ĭ wā′), *adv.* **1.** in any way or manner. **2.** in any case; anyhow. **3.** carelessly; haphazard.

an·y·ways (ĕn′ĭ wāz′), *adv. Colloq.* in any way.

an·y·where (ĕn′ĭ hwâr′), *adv.* in, at, or to any place.

an·y·wise (ĕn′ĭ wīz′), *adv.* in any way or respect.

An·zac (ăn′zăk), *n.* **1.** a member of the Australian and New Zealand Army Corps during World War I. **2.** a soldier from Australia or New Zealand.

A·o·mo·ri (ä′ō mō′rē), *n.* a seaport in N Japan, at the N end of Honshu island. 67,234 (1946).

A one (ā′ wŭn′), *n.* **1.** (in shipping registers) a symbol indicating a ship of the highest grade, used for insurance, etc. **2.** *Colloq.* first-class; excellent; A number 1. Also, **A-1.**

A·o·ran·gi (ä′ō räng′gĭ), *n.* See **Cook, Mount.**

a·o·rist (ā′ə rĭst), *n. Gram.* **1.** a tense of the Greek verb expressing action (in the indicative, past action) without further limitation or implication. —*adj.* **2.** of or in the aorist. [t. Gk.: s. *aóristos* indefinite]

a·o·ris·tic (ā′ə rĭs′tĭk), *adj.* **1.** *Gram.* pertaining to the aorist. **2.** indefinite; indeterminate.

a·or·ta (ā ôr′tə), *n., pl.* **-tas, -tae** (-tē). *Anat.* the main trunk of the arterial system, conveying blood from the left ventricle of the heart to all of the body except the lungs. See diag. under **heart.** [t. NL, t. Gk.: m. *aortē*] —**a·or′tic, a·or′tal,** *adj.*

a·ou·dad (ä′ŏŏ dăd′), *n.* a wild sheep of northern Africa, *Ammotragus lervia.* [t. F, t. Berber: m. *audad*]

ap-, var. of **ad-,** before *p,* as in *appear.*

Ap., 1. Apostle. **2.** April.

A.P., Associated Press.

a·pace (ə pās′), *adv.* with speed; quickly; swiftly.

A·pach·e (ə păch′ĭ), *n., pl.* **Apaches, Apache. 1.** one of a group of Indian tribes of Athabascan speech stock in the southwestern U. S. **2.** any of several Athabascan languages of Arizona and the Rio Grande basin.

a·pache (ə päsh′, ə pãsh′; *Fr.* ȧ pȧsh′), *n.* a Parisian gangster or tough. [t. F, special use of **APACHE**]

Ap·a·lach·ee Bay (ăp′ə lăch′ĭ), a bay in N Florida.

Ap·a·lach·i·co·la (ăp′ə lăch′ə kō′lə), *n.* a navigable river flowing through NW Florida into the Gulf of Mexico. 90 mi.

ap·a·nage (ăp′ə nĭj), *n.* appanage.

a·pa·re·jo (ä′pä rĕ′hō), *n., pl.* **-jos** (-hōs). *Spanish.* a Mexican packsaddle formed of stuffed leather cushions.

A·par·ri (ä pär′rē), *n.* a seaport in the Philippine Islands, on N Luzon. 26,409 (1939).

a·part (ə pärt′), *adv.* **1.** in pieces, or to pieces: *to take a watch apart.* **2.** separately or aside in motion, place, or position. **3.** to or at one side, with respect to purpose or function: *to set something apart.* **4.** separately or individually in consideration. **5.** aside (used with a gerund or noun): *joking apart, what do you think?* **6. apart from,** aside from: *apart from other considerations.* —*adj.* **7.** separate; independent: *a class apart.* [ME, t. OF: m. *a part,* g. L *ad partem* to the side]

a·part·ment (ə pärt′mənt), *n. U.S.* **1.** a set of rooms, among other sets in one building, designed for use as a dwelling. **2.** a single room in a building. [t. F: m. *appartement,* t. It.: m. *appartemento,* der. *appartare* separate. See **APART**] —**Syn. 1.** APARTMENT, COMPARTMENT agree in denoting a space enclosed by partitions or walls. APARTMENT, however, emphasizes the idea of separateness or privacy: *one's own apartment.* COMPARTMENT suggests a section of a larger space: *compartments in a ship's hold, in an orange crate.*

apartment house, *U.S.* a building divided into apartments (def. 1). Also, **apartment building.**

ap·a·tet·ic (ăp′ə tĕt′ĭk), *adj. Zool.* assuming colors and forms which effect deceptive camouflage. [t. Gk.: m.s. *apatētikós* fallacious]

ap·a·thet·ic (ăp′ə thĕt′ĭk), *adj.* **1.** having or exhibiting little or no emotion. **2.** indifferent. Also, **ap′a·thet′i·cal.** —**ap′a·thet′i·cal·ly,** *adv.*

ap·a·thy (ăp′ə thĭ), *n., pl.* **-thies. 1.** lack of feeling; absence or suppression of passion, emotion, or excitement. **2.** lack of interest in things which others find moving or exciting. [t. L: m. s. *apathía,* t. Gk.: m. *apátheia* insensibility] —**Ant. 1.** ardor.

ap·a·tite (ăp′ə tīt′), *n.* a common mineral, calcium fluophosphate, $Ca_5FP_3O_{12}$, occurring crystallized and massive, and varying in color, used in the manufacture of phosphate fertilizers. [f. s. Gk. *apátē* deceit + -ITE[1]; so called because often mistaken for other minerals]

ape (āp), *n., v.,* **aped, aping.** —*n.* **1.** a tailless monkey or a monkey with a very short tail. **2.** an anthropoid ape. **3.** an imitator; a mimic. **4.** any monkey. —*v.t.* **5.** to imitate servilely; mimic. [ME; OE *apa;* c. G *affe*] —**ape′like′,** *adj.*

a·peak (ə pēk′), *adv. Naut.* in a vertical position or direction, or nearly so.

A·pel·doorn (ä′pəl dōrn′), *n.* a city in central Netherlands. 81,601 (est. 1946).

A·pel·les (ə pĕl′ēz), *n.* 360?–315? B.C., Greek painter.

Ap·en·nines (ăp′ə nīnz′), *n.pl.* a mountain range traversing Italy from NW to SW. Highest peak, Monte Corno. 9585 ft.

a·per·çu (ȧ pĕr sy′), *n., pl.* **-çus** (-sy′; *Fr.* -sy′). *French.* **1.** a hasty glance; a glimpse. **2.** an outline or summary. [F, prop. pp. of *apercevoir* perceive]

a·per·i·ent (ə pĭr′ĭ ənt), *Med.* —*adj.* **1.** purgative; laxative. —*n.* **2.** a medicine or an article of diet that acts as a mild laxative. [t. L. s. *aperiens,* ppr., opening]

a·pe·ri·od·ic (ā′pĭr ĭ ŏd′ĭk), *adj.* **1.** not periodic; irregular. **2.** *Physics.* deadbeat. [f. A-[6] + PERIODIC]

a·pé·ri·tif (ȧ pĕ rē tēf′), *n. French.* a small drink of alcoholic liquor taken to whet the appetite before a meal.

ap·er·ture (ăp′ər chər), *n.* **1.** a hole, slit, crack, gap, or other opening. **2.** *Optics.* an opening that limits the size of the bundle of rays that can traverse an optical instrument. [t. L: m. s. *apertūra*]

ap·er·y (ā′pər ĭ), *n., pl.* **-eries. 1.** apish behavior; mimicry. **2.** a silly trick. [APE + -RY]

a·pet·al·ous (ā pĕt′əl əs), *adj. Bot.* having no petals.

a·pex (ā′pĕks), *n., pl.* **apexes, apices** (ăp′ə sēz′, ā′pə-). **1.** the tip, point, or vertex of anything; the summit. **2.** climax; acme. [t. L: point, summit]

aph-, var. of **ap-, apo-** used before an aspirate, as in *aphelion.*

aph., aphetic.

a·phaer·e·sis (ə fĕr′ə sis), *n.* apheresis.

aph·a·nite (ăf′ə nīt′), *n. Petrog.* any fine-grained igneous rock having such compact texture that the constituent minerals cannot be detected with the naked eye. [f. s. Gk. *aphanḗs* obscure + -ITE[1]] —**aph·a·nit·ic** (ăf′ə nĭt′ĭk), *adj.*

a·pha·sia (ə fā′zhə), *n. Pathol.* impairment or loss of the faculty of using or understanding spoken or written language. [t. NL, t. Gk.: speechlessness]

a·pha·si·ac (ə fā′zĭ ăk′), *n. Pathol.* one affected with aphasia.

a·pha·sic (ə fā′zĭk, -sĭk), *Pathol.* —*adj.* **1.** pertaining to or affected with aphasia. —*n.* **2.** an aphasiac.

a·phe·li·on (ə fē′lĭ ən), *n., pl.* **-lia** (-lĭ ə). *Astron.* the point of a planet's or comet's orbit most distant from the sun (opposed to *perihelion*). [Hellenized form of NL *aphēlium.* See APH-, HELIO-]

Sun′ Aphelion
Perihelion

a·pher·e·sis (ə fĕr′ə sĭs), *n.* the omission of a letter, phoneme, or unstressed syllable at the beginning of a word, as in *squire* for *esquire.* Also, **aphaeresis.** [t. L, t. Gk.: m. *aphaíresis* removal] —**aph·e·ret·ic** (ăf′ə rĕt′ĭk), *adj.*

aph·e·sis (ăf'ə sĭs), *n.* (in historical linguistic process) the disappearance of an unstressed initial vowel or syllable. [t. Gk.: a letting go]

a·phet·ic (ə fĕt'ĭk), *adj.* pertaining to or due to aphesis.

a·phid (ā'fĭd, ăf'ĭd), *n.* any of the plant-sucking insects of the family *Aphididae*; a plant louse. [t. NL: s. *aphis*] —**a·phid·i·an** (ə fĭd'ĭ ən), *adj., n.*

Apple tree aphid.
Aphis mali (⅓ in. long)

a·phis (ā'fĭs, ăf'ĭs), *n., pl.* **aphides** (ăf'ə dēz'). an aphid.

a·pho·ni·a (ā fō'nĭ ə), *n. Pathol.* loss of voice, due to an organic or functional disturbance of the vocal organs. [t. Gk.: speechlessness]

a·phon·ic (ā fŏn'ĭk), *adj.* **1.** *Phonet.* **a.** unvoiced; without sound. **b.** voiceless (def. 5). **2.** *Pathol.* affected with aphonia. —*n.* **3.** *Pathol.* one affected with aphonia.

aph·o·rism (ăf'ər ĭz'əm), *n.* a terse saying embodying a general truth. [ML: s. *aphorismus*, t. Gk.: m. *aphorismós* definition, a short pithy sentence] —**aph'o·ris'·mic, aph·o·ris·mat·ic** (ăf'ə rĭz măt'ĭk), *adj.*

aph·o·rist (ăf'ər ĭst), *n.* a maker of aphorisms.

aph·o·ris·tic (ăf'ər ĭs'tĭk), *adj.* **1.** of, like, or containing aphorisms: *his sermons were always richly aphoristic.* **2.** given to making or quoting aphorisms. —**aph'o·ris'·ti·cal·ly,** *adv.*

aph·o·rize (ăf'ər īz'), *v.i.,* **-rized, -rizing.** to utter aphorisms; write or speak in aphorisms.

aph·ro·dis·i·ac (ăf'rə dĭz'ĭ ăk'), *Med.* —*adj.* **1.** arousing sexual desire. —*n.* **2.** a drug or food that arouses sexual desire. [t. Gk.: m. s. *aphrodisiakós* venereal]

Aph·ro·di·te (ăf'rə dī'tĭ), *n.* the Greek goddess of love and beauty, identified by the Romans with Venus.

a·phyl·lous (ā fĭl'əs), *adj. Bot.* naturally leafless. [t. Gk.: m. *áphyllos* leafless]

a·phyl·ly (ā fĭl'ĭ), *n. Bot.* leaflessness.

A·pi·a (ä pē'ä, ä'pē ä'), *n.* a seaport in and the capital of the Territory of Western Samoa, on Upolu island.

a·pi·a·ceous (ā'pĭ ā'shəs), *adj. Bot.* related to the umbelliferous genus *Apium,* including parsley, celery, etc. [f. s. L *apium* parsley + -ACEOUS]

a·pi·an (ā'pĭ ən), *adj.* of or pertaining to bees. [t. L: s. *apiānus*]

a·pi·ar·i·an (ā'pĭ âr'ĭ ən), *adj.* relating to bees or to the breeding and care of bees.

a·pi·a·rist (ā'pĭ ə rĭst), *n.* one who keeps an apiary.

a·pi·a·ry (ā'pĭ ĕr'ĭ), *n., pl.* **-aries.** a place in which bees are kept; a stand or shed for bees; a beehouse containing a number of beehives. [t. L: m.s. *apiārium*]

ap·i·cal (ăp'ə kəl, ā'pə-), *adj.* of, at, or forming the apex. [f. s. L *apex* summit + -AL¹] —**ap'i·cal·ly,** *adv.*

ap·i·ces (ăp'ə sēz', ā'pə-), *n.* pl. of **apex.**

a·pic·u·late (ə pĭk'yə lĭt, -lāt'), *adj. Bot.* tipped with a short, abrupt point, as a leaf.

a·pi·cul·ture (ā'pə kŭl'chər), *n.* the rearing of bees. [f. L: *api(s)* bee + CULTURE] —**a'pi·cul'tur·al,** *adj.* —**a'pi·cul'tur·ist,** *n.*

a·piece (ə pēs'), *adv.* for each piece, thing, or person; for each one; each: *an orange apiece, costing a dollar apiece.* [orig. two words, *a* to or for each + PIECE]

à pied (á pyĕ'), *French.* afoot; walking; on foot.

A·pis (ā'pĭs), *n.* the sacred bull of the ancient Egyptians, to which divine honors were paid. [t. L, t. Gk.: m. *Apis,* t. Egyptian: m. *ḥapi,* prob. the running (bull)]

ap·ish (ā'pĭsh), *adj.* **1.** having the qualities, appearance, or ways of an ape. **2.** slavishly imitative. **3.** foolishly affected. —**ap'ish·ly,** *adv.* —**ap'ish·ness,** *n.*

a·piv·o·rous (ā pĭv'ə rəs), *adj. Zool.* feeding on bees, as certain birds. [f. L *api(s)* bee + -VOROUS]

Apl., April.

a·pla·cen·tal (ā'plə sĕn'təl, ăp'lə-), *adj. Zool.* not placental; having no placenta, as the lowest mammals.

ap·la·nat·ic (ăp'lə năt'ĭk), *adj. Optics.* free from spherical aberration and coma. [f. m. s. Gk. *aplánētos* not wandering + -IC]

a·plas·tic anemia (ā plăs'tĭk), *Pathol.* a severe anemia due to destruction or depressed function of the bone marrow, with no regenerative hyperplasia.

ap·lite (ăp'līt), *n.* a fine-grained granite composed essentially of feldspar and quartz. [t. m.s. Gk. *haplóos* single, simple + -ITE¹] —**ap·lit·ic** (ăp lĭt'ĭk), *adj.*

a·plomb (ə plŏm'; *Fr.* á plôn'), *n.* **1.** imperturbable self-possession, poise, or assurance. **2.** the perpendicular position. [t. F: f. *à* according to + *plomb* plummet]

ap·ne·a (ăp nē'ə), *n. Pathol.* **1.** suspension of respiration. **2.** asphyxia. Also, **ap·noe·a.** [t. NL, t. Gk.: m. *ápnoia* lack of wind] —**ap·ne'al, ap·ne'ic,** *adj.*

A·po (ä'pō), *n.* a volcano in the Philippine Islands, on S Mindanao, near Davao: the highest peak in the Philippine Islands. 9610 ft.

apo-, a prefix meaning "from," "away," "off," "asunder," as in *apomorphine, apophyllite.* Also, **ap-, aph-.** [t. Gk. Cf. AB-]

Apoc., **1.** Apocalypse. **2.** Apocrypha. **3.** Apocryphal.

a·poc·a·lypse (ə pŏk'ə lĭps), *n.* **1.** (*cap.*) the Revelation of St. John the Divine. **2.** any of a class of writings, Jewish and Christian, which appeared from about 200 B.C. to A.D. 350, assuming to make revelation of the ultimate divine purpose. **3.** revelation; discovery; disclosure. [ME *apocalipse,* t. L: m.s. *apocalypsis,* t. Gk.: m. *apokálypsis*]

a·poc·a·lyp·tic (ə pŏk'ə lĭp'tĭk), *adj.* **1.** of or like an apocalypse; affording a revelation. **2.** pertaining to the Apocalypse, or book of Revelation. Also, **a·poc'a·lyp'·ti·cal.** —**a·poc'a·lyp'ti·cal·ly,** *adv.*

ap·o·carp (ăp'ə kärp'), *n. Bot.* a gynoecium with acarpous carpels.

ap·o·car·pous (ăp'ə kär'pəs), *adj. Bot.* having the carpels separate. [f. APO- + m. s. Gk. *karpós* fruit + -OUS]

ap·o·chro·mat·ic (ăp'ə krō măt'ĭk), *adj. Optics.* having a high degree of correction for chromatic and spherical aberration and for coma. [modeled on ACHROMATIC. See APO-]

Apocarpous fruit of rue anemone

a·poc·o·pate (ə pŏk'ə pāt'), *v.t.,* **-pated, -pating.** to shorten by apocope. —**a·poc'o·pa'tion,** *n.*

a·poc·o·pe (ə pŏk'ə pĭ), *n.* the cutting off of the last sound of a word. [t. L, t. Gk.: m. *apokopé* a cutting off]

A·poc·ry·pha (ə pŏk'rə fə), *n.pl.* **1.** (*cap.*) fourteen books, not considered canonical, included in the Septuagint and the Vulgate as an appendix to the Old Testament, but usually omitted from Protestant editions of the Bible. **2.** various religious writings of uncertain origin regarded by some as inspired, but rejected by most authorities. **3.** works of doubtful authorship or authenticity. [t. LL, neut. pl. of *apocryphus,* t. Gk.: m. *apókryphos* hidden]

a·poc·ry·phal (ə pŏk'rə fəl), *adj.* **1.** of doubtful authorship or authenticity. **2.** *Eccles.* **a.** (*cap.*) of or pertaining to the Apocrypha. **b.** of doubtful sanction; uncanonical. **3.** false; spurious. —**a·poc'ry·phal·ly,** *adv.* —**a·poc'ry·phal·ness,** *n.*

a·poc·y·na·ceous (ə pŏs'ə nā'shəs), *adj. Bot.* belonging to the *Apocynaceae,* or dogbane family, which includes the dogbane, periwinkle, oleander, and various other plants, mostly tropical, some having medicinal and industrial uses. [f. s. NL *Apocynum* the dogbane genus (t. Gk.: m. *apókynon* kind of plant) + -ACEOUS]

ap·o·dal (ăp'ə dəl), *adj. Zool.* **1.** having no distinct feet or footlike members. **2.** belonging to the *Apoda* or *Apodes* (various groups of apodal animals). Also, **ap·od** (ăp'ŏd). [f. s. Gk. *ápous* footless + -AL¹]

ap·o·dic·tic (ăp'ə dĭk'tĭk), *adj.* **1.** incontestable because demonstrated or demonstrable. **2.** *Logic.* denoting a proposition in which the relation of subject and predicate is asserted to be necessary. Also, **ap·o·deic·tic** (ăp'ə dīk'tĭk), **ap'o·dic'ti·cal.** [t. Gk.: m.s. *apodeiktikós* demonstrative] —**ap'o·dic'ti·cal·ly,** *adv.*

a·pod·o·sis (ə pŏd'ə sĭs), *n., pl.* **-ses** (-sēz'). (in a conditional sentence) the clause stating the consequence. [t. L, t. Gk.: return, answering clause]

a·pog·a·my (ə pŏg'ə mĭ), *n. Bot.* the development of a sporophyte from a cell or cells of the gametophyte other than the egg. [f. APO- + -GAMY] —**ap·o·gam·i·** (ăp'ə găm'ĭk), **a·pog'a·mous** *adj.*

ap·o·gee (ăp'ə jē'), *n.* **1.** *Astron.* the point in the orbit of a heavenly body (usually the moon) most distant from the earth (opposed to *perigee*). **2.** the highest or most distant point; climax. [t. F: m. *apogée,* t. L: m. *apogēum,* t. Gk.: m. *apógaion* (*diástēma*) (distance) from the earth] —**ap'o·ge'al, ap'o·ge'an,** *adj.*

Apogee   Earth   Perigee

ap·o·ge·ot·ro·pism (ăp'ə jĭ ŏt'rə pĭz'əm), *n. Bot.* growth or tendency away from the earth; negative geotropism. —**ap·o·ge·o·trop·ic** (ăp'ə jē ə trŏp'ĭk), *adj.*

A·pol·lo (ə pŏl'ō), *n., pl.* **-los.** **1.** a Greek (and Roman) deity, the god of light, healing, music, poetry, prophecy, youthful manly beauty, etc. **2.** a very beautiful young man. [t. L: m.s. *Apóllōn*]

ap·ol·lo·ni·an (ăp'ə lō'nĭ ən), *adj.* **1.** (*cap.*) pertaining to the cult of Apollo. **2.** serene; majestic; poised; having the properties of classic beauty.

A·pol·lyon (ə pŏl'yən), *n. Bible.* the destroyer; the angel of the bottomless pit. Rev. 9:11. [t. Gk.: prop. adj., destroying]

a·pol·o·get·ic (ə pŏl'ə jĕt'ĭk), *adj.* **1.** making apology or excuse for fault, failure, etc. **2.** defending by speech or writing. Also, **a·pol'o·get'i·cal.** [t. LL: s. *apologēticus,* t. Gk.: m. *apologētikós*] —**a·pol'o·get'i·cal·ly,** *adv.*

a·pol·o·get·ics (ə pŏl'ə jĕt'ĭks), *n.* the branch of theology concerned with the defense of Christianity.

ap·o·lo·gi·a (ăp'ə lō'jĭ'ə), *n.* an apology, as in defense or justification. [t. L, t. Gk.: a speech in defense]

a·pol·o·gist (ə pŏl'ə jĭst), *n.* **1.** one who makes an apology or defense in speech or writing. **2.** *Eccles.* **a.** a defender of Christianity. **b.** one of the authors of the early Christian apologies.

a·pol·o·gize (ə pŏl'ə jīz'), *v.i.,* **-gized, -gizing.** **1.** to offer excuses or regrets for some fault, insult, failure, or injury. **2.** to make a formal defense in speech or writing. —**a·pol'o·giz'er,** *n.*

ap·o·logue (ăp'ə lôg', -lŏg'), *n.* **1.** a didactic narrative; a moral fable. **2.** an allegory. [t. F, t. L: m. s. *apologus,* t. Gk.: m. *apólogos* a story, tale]

a·pol·o·gy (ə pŏl'ə jĭ), *n., pl.* **-gies.** **1.** an expression of regret offered for some fault, failure, insult, or injury. **2.** a formal defense in speech or writing, as of a cause or doctrine. **3.** a poor specimen or substitute; a makeshift: *a sad apology for a hat.* [see APOLOGIA] —**Syn. 1.** See **excuse. 2.** justification, vindication.

---

b., blend of, blended; c., cognate with; d., dialect, dialectal; der., derived from; f., formed from; g., going back to; m., modification of; r., replacing; s., stem of; t., taken from; ?, perhaps. See the full key on inside cover.

ap·o·mor·phine (ăp′ə môr′fēn, -fĭn), *n. Pharm.* an artificial crystalline alkaloid prepared from morphine: used in the form of the hydrochloride as an emetic and expectorant. Also, **ap·o·mor·phin** (ăp′ə môr′fĭn), **ap·o·mor·phi·a** (ăp′ə môr′fĭ ə).

ap·o·neu·ro·sis (ăp′ə nyŏŏ rō′sĭs, -nŏŏ-), *n., pl.* **-ses** (-sēz). *Anat.* a whitish fibrous membrane formed by the expansion of a tendon. [t. NL, t. Gk., der. *aponeuroústhai* become a tendon] **—ap·o·neu·rot·ic** (ăp′ə nyŏŏ rŏt′ĭk, -nŏŏ-), *adj.*

ap·o·pemp·tic (ăp′ə pĕmp′tĭk), *adj.* pertaining to sending away; valedictory. [t. Gk.: m.s. *apopemptikós*]

a·poph·a·sis (ə pŏf′ə sĭs), *n. Rhet.* denial of an intention to speak of something which is at the same time hinted or insinuated. [t. L, t. Gk.: denial]

ap·o·phthegm (ăp′ə thĕm′), *n.* apothegm. **—ap·o·phtheg·mat·ic** (ăp′ə thĕg măt′ĭk), **ap·o·phtheg·mat·i·cal**, *adj.*

a·poph·y·ge (ə pŏf′ə jē′), *n. Archit.* 1. the small, hollow outward spread at the bottom of the shaft of a column by which it joins the base. See diag. under **column**. 2. a similar but slighter spread at the top of the shaft. [t. Gk.: lit, an escape]

a·poph·yl·lite (ə pŏf′ə līt′, ăp′ə fĭl′īt), *n.* a mineral, a hydrous potassium and calcium, occurring in white crystals. [f. *apophýllon* leaf + -ITE¹; so named because of its tendency to exfoliate]

a·poph·y·sis (ə pŏf′ə sĭs), *n., pl.* **-ses** (-sēz′). *Anat. Bot., etc.* an outgrowth; a process; a projection or protuberance. [t. NL, t. Gk.: an offshoot]

ap·o·plec·tic (ăp′ə plĕk′tĭk), *adj.* Also, **ap′o·plec′ti·cal.** 1. of or pertaining to apoplexy. 2. having or inclined to apoplexy. **—n.** 3. a person having or predisposed to apoplexy. **—ap′o·plec′ti·cal·ly**, *adv.*

ap·o·plex·y (ăp′ə plĕk′sĭ), *n. Pathol.* 1. a sudden, usually marked, loss of bodily function due to rupture or occlusion of a blood vessel. 2. hemorrhage into the tissue of any organ. [ME *apoplexie*, t. L: m. *apoplēxia*, t. Gk., der. *apoplēssein* disable by a stroke]

a·port (ə pôrt′), *adv. Naut.* on or toward the port side.

ap·o·si·o·pe·sis (ăp′ə sī′ə pē′sĭs), *n. Rhet.* a sudden breaking off in the midst of a sentence, as if from unwillingness to proceed. [t. L, t. Gk., der. *aposiōpân* be silent] **—ap·o·si·o·pet·ic** (ăp′ə sī′ə pĕt′ĭk), *adj.*

a·pos·ta·sy (ə pŏs′tə sĭ), *n., pl.* **-sies.** a total desertion of, or departure from, one's principles, party, cause, etc. [ME *apostasie*, t. L: m. *apostasia*, t. Gk., var. of *apóstasis* defection, revolt]

a·pos·tate (ə pŏs′tāt, -tĭt), *n.* 1. one who forsakes his church, cause, party, etc. **—adj.** 2. guilty of apostasy.

a·pos·ta·tize (ə pŏs′tə tīz′), *v.i.,* **-tized, -tizing.** to commit apostasy.

a pos·te·ri·o·ri (ā pŏs tĭr′ī ôr′ī), from effect to cause; based upon actual observation or upon experimental data (opposed to *a priori*): *an a posteriori argument.* [t. L: from the subsequent or latter]

a·pos·til (ə pŏs′tĭl), *n.* a marginal annotation or note. Also, **a·pos′tille.** [t. F: (m.) *apostille*, der. *apostiller*, f. à to + *postille* marginal note, prob. t. ML: m. *postilla*, f. *post* after + *illa* those things]

a·pos·tle (ə pŏs′əl), *n.* 1. one of the twelve disciples sent forth by Christ to preach the gospel. 2. (among the Jews of the Christian epoch) a title borne by persons sent on foreign missions. 3. *Mormon Ch.* one of a council of twelve officials presiding over the Church and administering its ordinances. 4. a pioneer of any great moral reform. [ME *apostel*, OE *apostol*, t. L: s. *apostolus*, t. Gk.: m. *apóstolos* one sent away. Cf. ME *apostle*, t. OF] **—a·pos′tle·ship′**, *n.*

Apostles′ Creed, a creed of virtually universal acceptance in the Christian church, dating back to about A.D. 500 and traditionally ascribed to Christ's apostles. It begins "I believe in God the Father Almighty."

a·pos·to·late (ə pŏs′tə lĭt, -lāt′), *n.* 1. the dignity or office of an apostle. 2. *Rom. Cath. Ch.* the dignity or office of the Pope, the holder of the Apostolic See.

ap·os·tol·ic (ăp′ə stŏl′ĭk), *adj.* 1. pertaining to or characteristic of an apostle, esp. of the twelve apostles. 2. derived from the apostles in regular sequence. 3. of the Pope; papal. Also, **ap′os·tol′i·cal. —ap′os·tol′i·cal·ly**, *adv.* **—ap·os·tol·i·cism** (ăp′ə stŏl′ə sĭz′əm), *n.* **—a·pos·to·lic·i·ty** (ə pŏs′tə lĭs′ə tĭ), *n.*

Apostolic Fathers, 1. the fathers of the church whose lives overlapped those of any of the apostles. 2. works dating back to the second century, reputed to have been written by them.

Apostolic See, 1. the Church of Rome, traditionally founded by St. Peter. 2. (*l.c.*) any of the churches founded by apostles.

a·pos·tro·phe¹ (ə pŏs′trə fĭ), *n.* the sign (′) used to indicate: **a.** the omission of one or more letters in a word, as in *o'er* for *over.* **b.** the possessive case, as in *lion's.* **c.** certain plurals, as in *several M.D.'s.* [special use of APOSTROPHE², by confusion with F *apostrophe*, t. L: m. s. *apostrophus*, t. Gk.: m. *apóstrophos* turned away, elided] **—ap·os·troph·ic** (ăp′ə strŏf′ĭk), *adj.*

a·pos·tro·phe² (ə pŏs′trə fĭ), *n.* a digression from a discourse, esp. in the form of a personal address to someone not present. [t. L, t. Gk.: a turning away] **—ap·os·troph·ic** (ăp′ə strŏf′ĭk), *adj.*

a·pos·tro·phize (ə pŏs′trə fīz′), *v.,* **-phized, -phizing.** *Rhet.* **—v.t.** 1. to address by apostrophe. **—v.i.** 2. to utter an apostrophe.

apothecaries′ measure, a system of units used in compounding and dispensing liquid drugs. In the United States 60 minims (♏) = 1 fluid dram (f ℨ); 8 fluid drams = 1 fluid ounce (f ℨ); 16 fluid ounces = 1 pint (O.); 8 pints = 1 gallon (C.) (231 cubic inches). In Great Britain 20 minims = 1 fluid scruple; 3 fluid scruples = 1 fluid dram; 8 fluid drams = 1 fluid ounce; 20 fluid ounces = 1 pint; 8 pints = 1 imperial gallon (277.274 cubic inches).

apothecaries′ weight, a system of weights used in compounding and dispensing drugs: 20 grains = 1 scruple (℈); 3 scruples = 1 dram (ℨ); 8 drams = 1 ounce (ℨ); 12 ounces = 1 pound. The grain, ounce, and pound are the same as in troy weight, the grain alone being the same as in avoirdupois weight.

a·poth·e·car·y (ə pŏth′ə kĕr′ĭ), *n., pl.* **-caries.** 1. a druggist; a pharmacist. 2. (esp. in England and Ireland) a druggist licensed to prescribe medicine. [ME *apothecarie*, t. LL: m. *apothecārius* shopkeeper, der. L *apothēca*, t. Gk.; m. *apothēkē* storehouse; r. ME *apotecario*, t. OF: m. *apotecaire*. See -ARY¹]

ap·o·the·ci·um (ăp′ə thē′shĭ əm, -sĭ-), *n., pl.* **-cia** (-shĭ ə, -sĭ ə). *Bot.* the fruit of certain lichens, usually an open, saucer- or cup-shaped body, the inner surface of which is covered with a layer which bears asci. [t. NL, f. L: s. *apothēca* (t. Gk.: m. *apothēkē* storehouse) + dim. *-ium*] **—ap·o·the·cial** (ăp′ə thē′shəl), *adj.*

ap·o·thegm (ăp′ə thĕm′), *n.* a short, pithy, instructive saying; a terse remark or aphorism. Also, **apophthegm.** [t. Gk.: m. *apóphthegma*] **—ap·o·theg·mat·ic** (ăp′ə thĕg măt′ĭk), **ap·o·theg·mat·i·cal**, *adj.*

ap·o·them (ăp′ə thĕm′), *n. Geom.* a perpendicular from the center of a regular polygon to one of its sides. [f. APO- + m. Gk. *théma*; der. *tithénai* set]

AB, Apothem

a·poth·e·o·sis (ə pŏth′ĭ ō′sĭs, ăp′ə thē′ə sĭs), *n., pl.* **-ses** (-sēz, -sēz′). 1. exaltation to the rank of a god. 2. the glorification of any person. 3. a deified or glorified ideal. [t. L, t. Gk.: deification]

a·poth·e·o·size (ə pŏth′ĭ ə sīz′, ăp′ə thē′ə sīz′), *v.t.,* **-sized, -sizing.** to deify; glorify.

app., 1. apparent. 2. appendix. 3. appointed.

ap·pal (ə pôl′), *v.t.,* **-palled, -palling.** appall.

Ap·pa·lach·i·an Mountains (ăp′ə lăch′ĭ ən, -lā′chĭ ən, -chən), a mountain system of E North America, extending from Quebec province in Canada to N Alabama. Highest peak, Mt. Mitchell, 6711 ft. Also, **Appalachians.**

Appalachian tea, 1. the leaves of any of certain plants of the genus *Ilex,* of the eastern U.S., as the shrub or small tree, *I. vomitoria,* sometimes used as a tea. 2. a plant yielding such leaves. 3. a shrub, *Viburnum cassinoides,* of the eastern U.S.

ap·pall (ə pôl′), *v.t.* to overcome with fear; fill with consternation and horror. Also, **appal.** [ME *apalle*(n), t. OF: m. *apallir* become or make pale] **—Syn.** See **frighten.**

ap·pall·ing (ə pô′lĭng), *adj.* causing dismay or horror: *an appalling accident.* **—ap·pall′ing·ly**, *adv.*

ap·pa·nage (ăp′ə nĭj), *n.* 1. land or some other source of revenue assigned for the maintenance of a member of the family of a ruling house. 2. whatever belongs or falls to one's rank or station in life. 3. a natural or necessary accompaniment. Also, **apanage.** [t. F, der. OF *apuner*, t. ML: m. *apānāre* furnish with bread]

appar., 1. apparent. 2. apparently.

ap·pa·ra·tus (ăp′ə rā′təs, -răt′əs), *n., pl.* **-tus, -tuses.** 1. an assemblage of instruments, machinery, appliances, materials, etc., for a particular use. 2. any complex appliance for a particular purpose. 3. *Physiol.* a collection of organs, differing in structure, which all minister to the same function. 4. a subdivison of a political organization: *a communist espionage apparatus.* [t. L: preparation]

ap·par·el (ə păr′əl), *n., v.,* **-eled, -eling** or (*esp. Brit.*) **-elled, -elling. —n.** 1. a person's outer clothing; raiment. 2. aspect; guise. 3. *Naut.* the furnishings or equipment of a ship, as sails, anchors, guns, etc. **—v.t.** 4. to dress or clothe; adorn; ornament. [ME *aparaile*(n), t. OF: m. *apareiller* clothe, ult. der. L *ad-* AD- + dim. of *pār* equal] **—Syn.** 1. clothes, dress, attire, garb.

ap·par·ent (ə păr′ənt, ə pâr′-), *adj.* 1. capable of being clearly perceived or understood; plain or clear. 2. seeming; ostensible (as opposed to *actual* or *real*): *the apparent motion of the sun.* 3. exposed to the sight; open to view. 4. absolutely entitled to an inherited throne, title, or other estate, by right of birth (opposed to *presumptive*): *the heir apparent.* [t. L: s. *appārens*, appearing; r. ME *aparant*, t. OF] **—ap·par′ent·ly**, *adv.* **—ap·par′ent·ness**, *n.*
—Syn. 1. APPARENT, EVIDENT, OBVIOUS, PATENT all refer to something easily perceived. APPARENT applies to that which can readily be seen or perceived: *an apparent effort.* EVIDENT applies to that which facts or circumstances make plain: *his innocence was evident.* OBVIOUS applies to that which is unquestionable, because completely manifest or noticeable: *an obvious change of method.* PATENT, a more formal word, applies to that which is open to view or understanding by all: *a patent error.*

ap·pa·ri·tion (ăp′ə rĭsh′ən), *n.* 1. a ghostly appearance; a specter or phantom. 2. anything that appears, esp. something remarkable or phenomenal. 3. act of appearing. [t. LL: s. *appāritio*, in L service] —**ap′pa·ri′tion·al,** *adj.*

—**Syn. 1.** APPARITION, PHANTASM, PHANTOM are terms for a supernatural appearance. An APPARITION of a person or thing is an immaterial appearance which seems real, and is generally sudden or startling in its manifestation: *an apparition of a headless horseman.* Both PHANTOM and PHANTASM denote an illusory appearance, as in a dream; the former is usually pleasant and the latter frightening: *a phantom of a garden, a monstrous phantasm.*

ap·par·i·tor (ə păr′ə tər), *n.* a subordinate official of an ancient Roman magistrate or of a court. [t. L: (public) servant]

ap·pas·sio·na·to (ăp päs′syô nä′tô), *adj. Music.* impassioned; with passion or strong feeling. [It.]

ap·peal (ə pēl′), *n.* **1.** a call for aid, support, mercy, etc.; an earnest request or entreaty. **2.** application or reference to some person or authority for corroboration, vindication, decision, etc. **3.** *Law.* **a.** an application or proceeding for review by a higher tribunal. **b.** *Obs.* a formal charge or accusation. **4.** power to attract or to move the feelings: *the game has lost its appeal, sex appeal.* **5.** *Obs.* a summons or challenge. —*v.i.* **6.** to call for aid, mercy, sympathy, or the like; make an earnest entreaty. **7.** *Law.* to apply for review of a case or particular issue to a higher tribunal. **8.** to resort for proof, decision, or settlement: *to appeal to force.* **9.** to offer a peculiar attraction, interest, enjoyment, etc.: *this color appeals to me.* —*v.t.* **10.** *Law.* **a.** to apply for review of (a case) to a higher tribunal. **b.** *Obs.* to charge with a crime before a tribunal. [ME *apele(n)*, t. OF: m. *apeler*, g. L *appellāre* approach, address, summon] —**ap·peal′a·ble,** *adj.* —**ap·peal′er,** *n.* —**ap·peal′ing·ly,** *adv.*

—**Syn. 1.** prayer, supplication. **6.** APPEAL, ENTREAT, PETITION, SUPPLICATE mean to ask for something wished for or needed. APPEAL and PETITION may concern groups and formal or public requests. ENTREAT and SUPPLICATE are usually more personal and emotional. To APPEAL is to ask earnestly for help or support, on grounds of reason, justice, common humanity, etc.: *to appeal for contributions to a cause.* To PETITION is to ask by written request, by prayer, or the like, that something be granted: *to petition for more playgrounds.* ENTREAT suggests pleading: *the child entreated his father not to punish him.* To SUPPLICATE is to beg humbly, usually from a superior, powerful, or stern (official) person: *to supplicate that the lives of prisoners be spared.*

ap·pear (ə pĭr′), *v.i.* **1.** to come into sight; become visible: *a cloud appeared on the horizon.* **2.** to have an appearance; seem; look: *to appear wise.* **3.** to be obvious; be clear or made clear by evidence: *it appears to me that you are right.* **4.** to come or be placed before the public: *his biography appeared last year.* **5.** *Law.* to come formally before a tribunal, authority, etc., as defendant, plaintiff, or counsel. [ME *apere(n)*, t. OF: m. *aper-*, s. *apareir*, g. L *appārēre*] —**Syn. 2.** See **seem.**

ap·pear·ance (ə pĭr′əns), *n.* **1.** the act or fact of appearing, as to the eye, the mind, or the public. **2.** *Law.* the coming into court of a party to a suit. **3.** outward look or aspect; mien: *a man of noble appearance.* **4.** outward show or seeming; semblance: *to avoid the appearance of coveting an honor.* **5.** (*pl.*) indications or circumstances. **6.** an apparition. **7.** *Philos.* the sensory, or phenomenal, aspect of existence to an observer.

—**Syn. 3.** APPEARANCE, ASPECT, GUISE refer to the way in which something outwardly presents itself to view. APPEARANCE refers to the outward look: *the shabby appearance of his car.* ASPECT refers to the appearance at some particular time or in special circumstances; it often has emotional implications, either ascribed to the object itself or felt by the beholder: *in the dusk the forest had a terrifying aspect.* GUISE suggests a misleading appearance, assumed for an occasion or a purpose: *under the guise of friendship.*

ap·pease (ə pēz′), *v.t.*, **-peased, -peasing.** **1.** to bring to a state of peace, quiet, ease, or content: *to appease an angry king.* **2.** to satisfy: *to appease one's hunger.* **3.** to accede to the belligerent demands of (a country, government, etc.) by a sacrifice of justice. [ME *apese(n)*, t. OF: m. *apaisier*, der. *a* to + *pais* (g. L *pax*) peace] —**ap·peas′a·ble,** *adj.* —**ap·pease′ment,** *n.* —**appeas′er,** *n.*

—**Syn. 1.** pacify, calm, placate. **2.** allay, assuage. **3.** APPEASE, CONCILIATE, PROPITIATE imply trying to preserve or obtain peace. To APPEASE is to make anxious overtures and often undue concessions to satisfy the demands of someone with a greed for power, territory, etc.: *Chamberlain tried to appease Hitler at Munich.* To CONCILIATE is to win an enemy or opponent over by displaying a willingness to be just and fair: *when mutual grievances are recognized, conciliation is possible.* To PROPITIATE is to admit a fault, and, by trying to make amends, to allay hostile feeling: *to propitiate an offended neighbor.* —**Ant. 1.** enrage. **2.** sharpen. **3.** defy.

ap·pel (á pĕl′), *n. Fencing.* **1.** a tap or stamp of the foot, formerly serving as a warning of one's intent to attack. **2.** a smart stroke with the blade used for the purpose of procuring an opening. [t. F]

ap·pel·lant (ə pĕl′ənt), *n.* **1.** one who appeals. **2.** *Law.* one who appeals to a higher tribunal. —*adj.* **3.** appellate. [t. L: s. *appellans*, ppr., appealing]

ap·pel·late (ə pĕl′ĭt), *adj. Law.* **1.** pertaining to appeals. **2.** having power to review and decide appeals. [t. L: m. s. *appellātus*, pp., appealed]

ap·pel·la·tion (ăp′ə lā′shən), *n.* **1.** a name, title, or designation. **2.** act of naming. [t. L: s. *appellātio* name]

ap·pel·la·tive (ə pĕl′ə tĭv), *n.* **1.** a common noun as opposed to a proper name. **2.** a descriptive name; a designation, as *odd* in *Odd John.* —*adj.* **3.** pertaining to a common noun. **4.** designative; descriptive.

ap·pel·lee (ăp′ə lē′), *n. Law.* the defendant or respondent in an appellate proceeding. [t. F: m. *appelé*, pp. of *appeler* APPEAL]

ap·pend (ə pĕnd′), *v.t.* **1.** to add, as an accessory; subjoin; annex. **2.** to attach as a pendant. [t. L: s. *appendere* hang (something) on]

ap·pend·age (ə pĕn′dĭj), *n.* **1.** a subordinate attached part of anything. **2.** *Biol.* any member of the body diverging from the axial trunk. **3.** *Bot.* any subsidiary part superadded to another part.

ap·pend·ant (ə pĕn′dənt), *adj.* **1.** hanging to; annexed; attached. **2.** associated as an accompaniment or consequence: *the salary appendant to a position.* **3.** *Law.* pertaining to a legal appendant. —*n.* **4.** a person or thing attached or added. **5.** *Law.* an interest (usually in land) connected with or dependent on some other interest. Also, **ap·pend′ent.** —**ap·pend′ance, ap·pend′ence,** *n.*

ap·pen·dec·to·my (ăp′ən dĕk′tə mĭ), *n., pl.* **-mies.** *Surg.* excision of the vermiform appendix. [f. APPEND(IX) + -ECTOMY]

ap·pen·di·ci·tis (ə pĕn′də sī′tĭs), *n. Pathol.* inflammation of the vermiform appendix. [t. NL, f. s. L *appendix* APPENDIX + *-ītis* -ITIS]

ap·pen·di·cle (ə pĕn′də kəl), *n.* a small appendage. [t. L: m. s. *appendicula*, dim. of *appendix* APPENDIX] —**ap·pen·dic·u·lar** (ăp′ən dĭk′yə lər), *adj.*

ap·pen·dix (ə pĕn′dĭks), *n., pl.* **-dixes, -dices** (-də sēz′). **1.** matter which supplements the main text of a book, generally explanatory, statistical, or bibliographic material. **2.** *Anat.* **a.** a process or projection. **b.** the vermiform appendix. **3.** *Aeron.* the short tube at the bottom of a balloon bag, by which the intake and release of buoyant gas is controlled. [t. L: appendage, addition]

—**Syn. 1.** APPENDIX, SUPPLEMENT both mean material added after the end of a book. An APPENDIX gives useful additional information, without which, however, the rest of the book is complete: *in the appendix are forty detailed charts.* A SUPPLEMENT, bound in the book or published separately, is given for comparison, as an enhancement, to provide corrections, to present later information, and the like: *a yearly supplement is issued.*

ap·per·ceive (ăp′ər sēv′), *v.t.*, **-ceived, -ceiving.** *Psychol.* **1.** to be conscious of perceiving; comprehend. **2.** to comprehend by assimilating (a new idea) with the mass of concepts, etc., already in the mind. [der. APPERCEPTION, modeled on *perceive, perception*]

ap·per·cep·tion (ăp′ər sĕp′shən), *n. Psychol.* **1.** conscious perception. **2.** act of apperceiving. [t. F] —**ap′per·cep′tive,** *adj.*

ap·per·tain (ăp′ər tān′), *v.i.* to belong as a part, member, possession, attribute, etc.; pertain (fol. by *to*). [ME *aperteine(n)*, t. OF: m. *apartenir*, g. LL *appertinēre*]

ap·pe·tence (ăp′ə təns), *n.* **1.** strong natural craving; appetite; intense desire. **2.** instinctive inclination or natural tendency. **3.** material or chemical attraction or affinity. [t. L: m. s. *appetentia* seeking after]

ap·pe·ten·cy (ăp′ə tən sĭ), *n., pl.* **-cies.** appetence.

ap·pe·tite (ăp′ə tīt′), *n.* **1.** a desire for food or drink: *to work up an appetite.* **2.** a desire to supply any bodily want or craving: *the natural appetites.* **3.** an innate or acquired demand or propensity to satisfy a want: *an appetite for reading.* [ME *appetit*, t. OF, t. L: s. *appetītus* onset, desire for] —**Syn. 1-3.** longing, hunger.

ap·pe·ti·tive (ăp′ə tī′tĭv), *adj.* pertaining to appetite.

ap·pe·tiz·er (ăp′ə tī′zər), *n.* a food, or drink, that stimulates the desire for food.

ap·pe·tiz·ing (ăp′ə tī′zĭng), *adj.* exciting or appealing to the appetite. —**ap′pe·tiz′ing·ly,** *adv.*

Ap·pi·an Way (ăp′ĭ ən), a famous ancient Roman highway, extending from Rome to Brundisium: begun 312 B.C. by Appius Claudius Caecus. ab. 350 mi.

ap·plaud (ə plôd′), *v.i.* **1.** to express approval by clapping the hands, shouting, etc. **2.** to give praise; express approval. —*v.t.* **3.** to praise or show approval of by clapping the hands, shouting, etc.: *to applaud an actor.* **4.** to praise in any way; commend; approve: *to applaud one's conduct.* [t. L: s. *applaudere*] —**ap·plaud′er,** *n.*

ap·plause (ə plôz′), *n.* **1.** hand clapping, shouting, or other demonstrations of approval. **2.** any expression of approbation or approval. [t. L: m. s. *applausus*, pp.] —**ap·plau·sive** (ə plô′sĭv), *adj.* —**Syn. 2.** acclamation.

ap·ple (ăp′əl), *n.* **1.** the edible fruit, usually round and red, of a rosaceous tree, *Malus pumila* (*Pyrus Malus*). **2.** the tree, cultivated in most temperate regions. **3.** the fruit of any of certain other species of tree of the same genus. **4.** any of these trees. **5.** any of various other fruits, or fruitlike products or plants, usually specially designated, as the custard apple, love apple (tomato), May apple, oak apple. [ME; OE *æppel*, c. G *apfel*]

apple butter, a kind of thick, spiced applesauce.

apple green, a clear, light green.

ap·ple·jack (ăp′əl jăk′), *n. U.S.* **1.** a brandy distilled from fermented (i.e. hard) cider. **2.** See **cider.**

apple of discord, *Gk. Myth.* the golden apple inscribed "For the fairest," thrown by the goddess of discord among the Greek gods and awarded by Paris to Aphrodite, which led to the destruction of Troy.

apple of the eye, **1.** the pupil of the eye. **2.** something very precious or dear.

ap·ple·sauce (ăp′əl sôs′), *n.* **1.** apples stewed to a soft pulp. **2.** *U.S. Slang.* nonsense; bunk.

Ap·ple·ton (ăp′əl tən), *n.* a city in E Wisconsin. 34,010 (1950).

b., blend of, blended; c., cognate with; d., dialect, dialectal; der., derived from; f., formed from; g., going back to; m., modification of; r., replacing; s., stem of; t., taken from; ?, perhaps. See the full key on inside cover.

Appleton layers, the upper layers of the ionosphere, beyond the Heaviside layer, also important in the reflection of radio waves. [named after E. V. *Appleton*, British scientist (born 1892)]

ap·pli·ance (ə plī'əns), *n.* **1.** an instrument, apparatus, or device for a particular use: *electrical appliances.* **2.** act of applying; application. **3.** *Obs.* compliance. [f. m. APPLY + -ANCE]

ap·pli·ca·ble (ăp'lə kə bəl, ə plĭk'ə-), *adj.* capab'e of being applied; fit; suitable; relevant. —**ap'pli·ca·bil'·i·ty, ap'pli·ca·ble·ness,** *n.* —**ap'pli·ca·bly,** *adv.*

ap·pli·cant (ăp'lə kənt), *n.* one who applies; a candidate: *an applicant for a position.* [t. L: s. *applicans*, ppr.]

ap·pli·ca·tion (ăp'lə kā'shən), *n.* **1.** act of putting to a special use or purpose: *the application of common sense to a problem.* **2.** quality of being usable for a particular purpose or in a special way; relevance: *this has no application to the case.* **3.** act of applying: *the application of salve to a wound.* **4.** the thing or remedy applied. **5.** act of requesting. **6.** a written or spoken request or appeal. **7.** close attention; persistent effort: *application to one's studies.* [t. L: s. *applicātio* a joining to] —**Syn. 6.** solicitation, petition. **7.** See **effort.**

ap·pli·ca·tive (ăp'lə kā'tĭv), *adj.* applying or capable of being applied; applicatory; practical.

ap·pli·ca·tor (ăp'lə kā'tər), *n. Med.* a rodlike instrument for applying medication.

ap·pli·ca·to·ry (ăp'lə kə tōr'ĭ), *adj.* fitted for application or use; practical.

ap·plied (ə plīd'), *adj.* put to practical use, as a science when its laws are concrete phenomena (distinguished from *abstract, theoretical,* or *pure science*).

ap·pli·qué (ăp'lə kā'; *Fr.* ȧ plē kĕ'), *adj., n., v.,* -**quéd,** -**quéing.** —*adj.* **1.** formed with ornamentation of one material sewed or otherwise applied to another. —*n.* **2.** the ornamentation used to make an appliqué material. **3.** work so formed. —*v.t.* **4.** to apply or form as in appliqué work. [t. F, pp. of *appliquer* put on]

ap·ply (ə plī'), *v.,* -**plied,** -**plying.** —*v.t.* **1.** to lay on; bring into physical proximity or contact: *to apply a match to powder.* **2.** to bring to bear; put into practical operation, as a principle, law, rule, etc. **3.** to put to use; employ: *they know how to apply their labor.* **4.** to devote to some specific purpose: *to apply a sum of money to pay a debt.* **5.** to use (a word or statement) with reference to some person or thing as applicable or pertinent: *to apply the testimony to the case.* **6.** to give with earnestness or assiduity; employ with attention; set: *to apply one's mind to one's lessons.* —*v.i.* **7.** to have a bearing or reference; be pertinent: *the argument applies to the case.* **8.** to make application or request; ask: *to apply for a job.* [ME *aplie(n),* t. OF: m. *aplier,* g. L *applicāre* attach] —**ap·pli'er,** *n.* —**Syn. 4.** appropriate, allot, assign. **8.** petition.

ap·pog·gia·tu·ra (ə pŏj'·ə tyȯȯr'ə. -tȯȯr'ə; *It.* äp-pōd'jä tōō'rä), *n. Music.* a note of embellishment (short or long) preceding another note and taking a portion of its time. [It., der. *ap-poggiare,* prop., lean]

Written Played
A
B

Appoggiatura
A. short; B. long

ap·point (ə point'), *v.t.* **1.** to nominate or assign to a position, or to perform a function; set apart; designate: *to appoint a new secretary.* **2.** to constitute, ordain, or fix by decree, order, or decision; decree: *laws appointed by God.* **3.** to determine by authority or agreement; fix; settle: *a time appointed for the meeting.* **4.** *Law.* to designate (a person) to take the benefit of an estate created by a deed or will. **5.** to provide with what is requisite; equip. **6.** *Obs.* to point at by way of censure. —*v.i.* **7.** *Obs.* to ordain; resolve; determine. [ME *apoint(en),* t. OF: m. *apointer,* g. LL *appunctāre* repair, appoint] —**ap·point'er,** *n.* —**Syn. 2.** prescribe, establish. **5.** supply. See **furnish.**

ap·point·ee (ə poin tē', ăp'oin tē'), *n.* **1.** a person appointed. **2.** a beneficiary under a legal appointment.

ap·poin·tive (ə poin'tĭv), *adj.* pertaining to or dependent on appointment: *an appointive office.*

ap·point·ment (ə point'mənt), *n.* **1.** act of appointing, designating, or placing in office: *to fill a vacancy by appointment.* **2.** an office held by a person appointed. **3.** act of fixing by mutual agreement; engagement: *an appointment to meet at six o'clock.* **4.** (*usually pl.*) equipment, as for a ship, hotel, etc. **5.** decree; ordinance. —**Syn. 2.** APPOINTMENT, OFFICE, POST, STATION mean a place of duty or employment. APPOINTMENT refers to a position for which special qualifications are required. OFFICE often suggests a position of trust or authority. POST in the U.S. is usually restricted to military or other public positions; in England it may be used of any position. STATION means a sphere of duty or occupation; it emphasizes the location of work to be done. See **position.**

ap·poin·tor (ə poin'tər, ə poin tôr'), *n. Law.* one who exercises a power of appointment of property.

Ap·po·mat·tox (ăp'ə măt'əks), *n.* **1.** a town in central Virginia; Lee surrendered to Grant here, April 9, 1865. **2.** a river flowing from near this town E to the James river. ab. 150 mi.

ap·por·tion (ə pôr'shən), *v.t.* to divide and assign in just proportion or according to some rule; distribute or allocate proportionally: *to apportion expenses.* [t. F: m. s. *apportionner,* f. à to + portionner PORTION, v.]

ap·por·tion·ment (ə pôr'shən mənt), *n.* **1.** act of apportioning. **2.** *U.S.* the distribution of representation in the federal House of Representatives among the several States (or, in State legislatures, among the counties or other local areas).

ap·pose (ə pōz'), *v.t.,* -**posed,** -**posing. 1.** to put or apply (one thing) to or near to another. **2.** to place next, as one thing to another; place side by side, as two things. [t. F: m. s. *apposer,* f. à AD- + *poser* POSE[2], assoc. with derivatives of L *apponere.* See APPOSITE]

ap·po·site (ăp'ə zĭt), *adj.* suitable; well-adapted; pertinent: *an apposite answer.* [t. L: m. s. *appositus,* pp., put to] —**ap'po·site·ly,** *adj.* —**ap'po·site·ness,** *n.*

ap·po·si·tion (ăp'ə zĭsh'ən), *n.* **1.** act of adding to or together; a placing together; juxtaposition. **2.** *Gram.* a syntactic relation between expressions, usually consecutive, which have the same function and the same relation to other elements in the sentence, the second expression identifying or supplementing the first. For example: *Washington, our first President,* has *our first President* in apposition with *Washington.* —**ap'po·si'tion·al,** *adj.* —**ap'po·si'tion·al·ly,** *adv.*

ap·pos·i·tive (ə pŏz'ə tĭv), *n.* **1.** a word or phrase in apposition. —*adj.* **2.** *Gram.* placed in apposition. —**ap·pos'i·tive·ly,** *adv.*

ap·prais·al (ə prā'zəl), *n.* **1.** act of placing an estimated value on an asset or assets. **2.** valuation; an estimate of value, as for sale, assessment, or taxation. Also, **ap·praise'ment.**

ap·praise (ə prāz'), *v.t.,* -**praised,** -**praising. 1.** to estimate generally, as to quality, size, weight, etc. **2.** to value in current money; estimate the value of. Also, **ap·prize[1].** [b. APPRIZE[2] and PRAISE] —**ap·prais'a·ble,** *adj.* —**ap·prais'er,** *n.* —**ap·prais'ing·ly,** *adv.*

ap·pre·ci·a·ble (ə prē'shĭ ə bəl, -shə bəl), *adj.* capable of being perceived or estimated. —**ap·pre'ci·a·bly,** *adv.*

ap·pre·ci·ate (ə prē'shĭ āt'), *v.,* -**ated,** -**ating.** —*v.t.* **1.** to place a sufficiently high estimate on: *his great ability was not appreciated.* **2.** to be fully conscious of; be aware of; detect: *to appreciate the dangers of a situation.* **3.** to raise in value. —*v.i.* **4.** to increase in value. [t. L: m. s. *appretiātus,* pp., appraised] —**ap·pre'ci·a·tor,** *n.* —**Syn. 1.** APPRECIATE, ESTEEM, PRIZE, VALUE imply holding something in high regard. To APPRECIATE is to exercise wise judgment, delicate perception, and keen insight in realizing the worth of something. To ESTEEM is to feel respect combined with a warm, kindly feeling. To VALUE is to attach importance to a thing because of its worth (material or otherwise). To PRIZE is to value highly and cherish.

ap·pre·ci·a·tion (ə prē'shĭ ā'shən), *n.* **1.** act of estimating the qualities of things and giving them their due value. **2.** clear perception or recognition, esp. of aesthetic quality. **3.** increase in value of property. **4.** critical notice; critique.

ap·pre·ci·a·tive (ə prē'shĭ ā'tĭv, -shə tĭv), *adj.* capable of appreciating; feeling or manifesting appreciation. —**ap·pre'ci·a·tive·ly,** *adv.* —**ap·pre'ci·a'tive·ness,** *n.*

ap·pre·ci·a·to·ry (ə prē'shĭ ə tōr'ĭ, -shə-), *adj.* appreciative. —**ap·pre'ci·a·to'ri·ly,** *adv.*

ap·pre·hend (ăp'rĭ hĕnd'), *v.t.* **1.** to take into custody; arrest by legal warrant or authority. **2.** to grasp the meaning of; understand; conceive. **3.** to entertain suspicion or fear of; anticipate: *I apprehend no violence.* —*v.i.* **4.** to understand. **5.** to be apprehensive; fear. [t. L: s. *apprehendere* seize] —**ap'pre·hend'er,** *n.*

ap·pre·hen·si·ble (ăp'rĭ hĕn'sə bəl), *adj.* capable of being understood. —**ap'pre·hen'si·bil'i·ty,** *n.*

ap·pre·hen·sion (ăp'rĭ hĕn'shən), *n.* **1.** anticipation of adversity; dread or fear of coming evil. **2.** the faculty of apprehending; understanding. **3.** a view, opinion, or idea on any subject. **4.** act of arresting; seizure. [t. L: s. *apprehensio*] —**Syn. 1.** APPREHENSION, ANXIETY, MISGIVING imply an unsettled and uneasy state of mind. APPREHENSION is an active state of fear, usually of some danger or misfortune: *apprehension before opening a telegram.* ANXIETY is a somewhat prolonged state of apprehensive worry: *anxiety because of a reduced income.* MISGIVING implies a dubious uncertainty or suspicion, as well as uneasiness: *to have misgivings about the investment.*

ap·pre·hen·sive (ăp'rĭ hĕn'sĭv), *adj.* **1.** uneasy or fearful about something that may happen: *apprehensive of (or for) one's safety.* **2.** quick to learn or understand. **3.** perceptive (fol. by *of*). —**ap'pre·hen'sive·ly,** *adv.* —**ap'pre·hen'sive·ness,** *n.*

ap·pren·tice (ə prĕn'tĭs), *n., v.,* -**ticed,** -**ticing.** —*n.* **1.** one who works for another with obligations to learn a trade. **2.** a learner; a novice. —*v.t.* **3.** to bind to or put under the care of an employer for instruction in a trade. [ME *aprentys,* t. OF: m. *aprentis,* ult. der. L *appre(he)ndere* seize] —**ap·pren'tice·ship',** *n.*

ap·pressed (ə prĕst'), *adj.* pressed closely against or fitting closely to something.

ap·prise[1] (ə prīz'), *v.t.,* -**prised,** -**prising.** to give notice to; inform; advise (often fol. by *of*). Also, **apprize.** [t. F: m. *appris,* pp. of *apprendre* learn, teach. See APPRENTICE]

ap·prise[2] (ə prīz'), *v.t.,* -**prised,** -**prising.** appraise[1].

ap·prize[1] (ə prīz'). *v.t.,* -**prized,** -**prizing.** appraise. Also, **apprise.** [ME *aprise(n),* t. OF: m. *apriser,* der. phrase *à pris* for sale] —**ap·priz'er,** *n.*

ap·prize[2] (ə prīz'), *v.t.,* -**prized,** -**prizing.** apprise[1].

ap·proach (ə prōch'), *v.t.* **1.** to come nearer or near to: *to approach the city.* **2.** to come near to in quality, char-

acter, time, or condition: *approaching Homer as a poet.*
3. to bring near to something. **4.** to make advances or a
proposal to: *to approach the President with a suggestion.*
5. to begin work on; set about: *to approach a problem.*
—*v.i.* **6.** to come nearer; draw near: *the storm approaches.*
7. to come near in character, time, amount, etc.; approximate. —*n.* **8.** act of drawing near: *the approach of a
horseman.* **9.** nearness or close approximation: *a fair
approach to accuracy.* **10.** any means of access: *the approaches to a city.* **11.** the method used or steps taken
in setting about a task, problem, etc. **12.** (*sing. or pl.*)
advances made to a person. **13.** (*pl.*) *Mil.* works for
protecting forces in an advance against a fortified position. **14.** *Golf.* a stroke after teeing off, by which a
player endeavors to get his ball on the putting green.
[ME *aproche(n)*, t. OF: m. *aprochier*, g. LL *appropiāre*]
ap·proach·a·ble (ə prō′chə bəl), *adj.* **1.** capable of
being approached; accessible. **2.** (of a person) easy to
approach. —**ap·proach′a·bil′i·ty, ap·proach′a·ble-
ness,** *n.*
ap·pro·bate (ăp′rə bāt′), *v.t.,* **-bated, -bating.** *U.S.*
to approve officially. [t. L: m.s. *approbātus,* pp., favored]
ap·pro·ba·tion (ăp′rə bā′shən), *n.* **1.** approval; commendation. **2.** sanction. **3.** *Obs.* conclusive proof.
ap·pro·ba·tive (ăp′rə bā′tĭv), *adj.* approving; expressing approbation. Also, **ap·pro·ba·to·ry** (ə prō′bə-
tōr′ĭ). —**ap′pro·ba′tive·ness,** *n.*
ap·pro·pri·a·ble (ə prō′prĭ ə bəl), *adj.* capable of being appropriated.
ap·pro·pri·ate (*adj.* ə prō′prĭ ĭt; *v.* ə prō′prĭ āt′), *adj.,
v.,* **-ated, -ating.** —*adj.* **1.** suitable or fitting for a particular purpose, person, occasion, etc.: *an appropriate
example.* **2.** belonging or peculiar to one: *each played his
appropriate part.* —*v.t.* **3.** to set apart for some specific
purpose or use: *the legislature appropriated funds for the
university.* **4.** to take to or for oneself; take possession
of. [t. L: m. s. *appropriātus,* pp., made one's own] —**ap-
pro′pri·ate·ly,** *adv.* —**ap·pro′pri·ate·ness,** *n.* —**ap-
pro′pri·a′tive,** *adj.* —**ap·pro′pri·a′tor,** *n.* —Syn. **1.**
befitting, apt, meet, felicitous.
ap·pro·pri·a·tion (ə prō′prĭ ā′shən), *n.* **1.** anything
appropriated for a special purpose, as money. **2.** act of
appropriating. **3.** an act of a legislature authorizing
money to be paid from the treasury for a special use.
ap·prov·al (ə prōō′vəl), *n.* **1.** act of approving; approbation. **2.** sanction; official permission. **3. on approval,** for examination, without obligation to buy.
ap·prove (ə prōōv′), *v.,* **-proved, -proving.** —*v.t.* **1.** to
pronounce or consider good; speak or think favorably of:
to approve the policies of the administration. **2.** to confirm or sanction officially; ratify. **3.** *Obs.* to demonstrate
in practice; show. **4.** *Obs.* to make good; attest. **5.** *Obs.*
to prove by trial. **6.** *Obs.* to convict. —*v.i.* **7.** to speak
or think favorably (usually fol. by *of*): *to approve of him.*
[ME *aprove(n),* t. OF: m. *aprover,* g. L *approbāre*] —**ap-
prov′a·ble,** *adj.* —**ap·prov′er,** *n.* —**ap·prov′ing·ly,**
adv.
—Syn. **1.** APPROVE, COMMEND, PRAISE mean to have, and
usually to express, a favorable opinion. To APPROVE is to
have a very good opinion, expressed or not, of someone or
something: *he approved the new plan.* To COMMEND is to
speak or write approvingly, often formally and publicly, to
congratulate or honor for something done: *to commend a
fireman for a heroic act.* To PRAISE is to speak or write, often
in glowing and emotional terms, to or about one or more
persons: *to praise the Boy Scouts.* **2.** authorize, endorse.
approx., approximately.
ap·prox·i·mal (ə prŏk′sə məl), *adj.* *Anat.* near or adjacent, as surfaces of teeth.
ap·prox·i·mate (*adj.* ə prŏk′sə mĭt; *v.* ə prŏk′sə māt′),
adj., v., **-mated, -mating.** —*adj.* **1.** nearly exact, equal,
or perfect. **2.** near; close together. **3.** very similar.
—*v.t.* **4.** to come near to: approach closely to: *to approximate a solution to a problem.* **5.** to bring near. —*v.i.*
6. to come near in position, character, amount, etc. [t.
L: m. s. *approximātus,* pp.] —**ap·prox′i·mate·ly,** *adv.*
ap·prox·i·ma·tion (ə prŏk′sə mā′shən), *n.* **1.** a drawing, moving, or advancing near in space, position, degree,
or relation. **2.** *Math., Physics.* a result which is not
exact, but is sufficiently so for a given purpose.
ap·pur·te·nance (ə pûr′tə nəns), *n.* **1.** something accessory to another and more important thing; an adjunct. **2.** *Law.* a right, privilege, or improvement belonging to and passing with a principal property. **3.** (*pl.*)
apparatus; mechanism. [ME *appurtena(u)nce,* t. AF: m.
apurtenance, ult. der. L *appertinēre* belong to]
ap·pur·te·nant (ə pûr′tə nənt), *adj.* **1.** appertaining
or belonging; pertaining. —*n.* **2.** an appurtenance.
Apr., April.
a·près moi le dé·luge (à prĕ mwà′ lə dĕ′lyzh′),
French. after me the deluge (attributed to Louis XV).
a·pri·cot (ā′prə kŏt′, ăp′rə-), *n.* **1.** the downy yellow
fruit, somewhat resembling a small peach, of the tree,
Prunus armeniaca. **2.** the tree. **3.** a pinkish yellow or
yellowish pink. [var. of *apricock,* appar. b. L *praecoqua*
apricots (neut. pl. of *praecoquus* early ripe) and F
abricot apricot, t. Pg.: m. *albricoque,* t. Sp.: m. *albar(i)-
coque,* t. Ar.: m. *al-barqūq,* t. Gk.: m. *praikókion,* t. L (as
above)]
A·pril (ā′prəl), *n.* the fourth month of the year, containing 30 days. [t. L: s. *Aprīlis*]
April fool, a victim on April Fools' Day.
April Fools' Day, April 1; All Fools' Day; the day
observed by playing jokes on unsuspecting people.

a pri·o·ri (ā prī ōr′ī, ä prī ōr′ī), **1.** from cause to
effect; from a general law to a particular instance; valid
independently of observation (opposed to *a posteriori*).
2. claiming to report matters of fact but actually not
supported by factual study. [t. L: from something prior]
—**a·pri·or·i·ty** (ā′prī ōr′ə tĭ, -ŏr′-), *n.*
a·pron (ā′prən), *n.* **1.** a piece of apparel made in various ways for covering, and usually also protecting, the
front of the person more or less completely. **2.** a flat
continuous conveyor belt. **3.** *Mach.* that part of a lathe
carriage containing the clutches and gears that transmit
feeder or lead screw motion to the carriage. **4.** *Civ. Eng.*
a. any device for protecting a surface of earth, such as a
river bank, from the action of moving water. **b.** a platform to receive the water falling over a dam. **5.** a paved
or hard-packed area abutting on airfield buildings and
hangars. **6.** the part of the stage in front of the closed
curtain. **7.** *Geol.* a deposit of gravel and sand extending
forward from a moraine. —*v.t.* **8.** to put an apron on;
furnish with an apron. [ME *napron* (*a napron* being
later taken as *an apron*), t. OF: m. *naperon,* dim. of *nape,*
g. L *nappa* napkin, cloth] —**a′pron·like′,** *adj.*
ap·ro·pos (ăp′rə pō′), *adv.* **1.** to the purpose; opportunely. **2.** with reference or regard; in respect (fol. by
of): *apropos of nothing.* **3.** by the way. —*adj.* **4.** opportune; pertinent: *apropos remarks.* [t. F: m. *à propos*]
apse (ăps), *n.* **1.** *Archit.* a vaulted semicircular or
polygonal recess in a building, esp. at the end of the
choir of a church. See diag. under **basilica. 2.** *Astron.*
an apsis. [t. L: m. s. *apsis,* t. Gk.: m. *(h)apsís* loop, circle,
bow, arch, apse]
ap·si·dal (ăp′sə dəl), *adj.* **1.** *Archit.* pertaining to an
apse. **2.** *Astron.* pertaining to an apsis.
ap·sis (ăp′sĭs), *n., pl.* **-sides** (-sə dēz′). **1.** *Astron.* **a.** either of two points in an eccentric orbit, the one (**higher
apsis**) furthest from the center of attraction, and the
one (**lower apsis**) nearest to it. **b. line of apsides,** line
coinciding with the major axis of an orbit. **2.** *Archit.*
an apse. [t. L. See APSE]
apt (ăpt), *adj.* **1.** inclined; disposed; prone: *too apt to
slander others.* **2.** likely: *am I apt to find him at home?*
3. unusually intelligent; quick to learn: *an apt pupil.*
4. suited to the purpose or occasion: *an apt metaphor.*
5. *Archaic.* prepared; ready; willing. [ME, t. L: s. *aptus*
fastened, joined, fitted] —**apt′ly,** *adv.* —**apt′ness,** *n.*
—Syn. **2.** See **likely. 3.** clever, bright. **4.** APT, PERTINENT,
RELEVANT all refer to something suitable or fitting. APT means
to the point and particularly appropriate: *an apt comment.*
PERTINENT means pertaining to the matter in hand: *a pertinent remark.* RELEVANT means directly related to and important to the subject: *a relevant opinion.*
apt., *pl.* **apts.** apartment.
ap·ter·al (ăp′tər əl), *adj.* *Archit.* without columns or
a porch along the sides.
ap·ter·ous (ăp′tər əs), *adj.* **1.** *Zool.* wingless, as some
insects. **2.** *Bot.* without membranous expansions, as a
stem. [t. Gk.: m. *ápteros* without wings]
ap·ter·yg·i·al (ăp′tə rĭj′ĭ əl), *adj.* *Zool.* without
wings, fins, or limbs, as snakes and eels. [f. A-[6] + s. Gk.
pterýgion little wing + -AL[1]]
ap·ter·yx (ăp′tər ĭks), *n., pl.* **-teryxes**
(-tər ĭk sĭz). any of several flightless
ratite birds of New Zealand, constituting the genus *Apteryx,* allied to the
extinct moas; kiwi. [t. NL, f. Gk.: *a-
A-[6] + ptéryx* wing]
ap·ti·tude (ăp′tə tūd′, -tōōd′), *n.* **1.** a
natural tendency or acquired inclination; both capacity and propensity for
a certain course. **2.** readiness in learning; intelligence;
talent. **3.** state or quality of being apt; special fitness.
[t. ML: m. *aptitūdo,* der. L *aptus* fit]
aptitude test, a test for special fitness; a test given
to find out what sort of work a person has the ability to
learn, such as clerical work, mechanical work, etc.
Ap·u·le·ius (ăp′yə lē′əs), *n.* **Lucius** (lōō′shəs), born
A.D. 125?, Roman philosopher and satirist.
A·pu·lia (ə pū′lyə), *n.* a department in SE Italy.
2,887,000 pop. (est. 1943); 7442 sq. mi.
A·pu·re (ä pōō′rĕ), *n.* a river flowing from W Venezuela
E to the Orinoco. ab. 300 mi.
A·pu·rí·mac (ä′pōō rē′mäk), *n.* a river flowing from S
Peru NW to the Ucayli river. ab. 500 mi.
a·py·ret·ic (ā′pī rĕt′ĭk), *adj.* *Pathol.* free from fever.
[f. s. Gk. *apýretos* without fever + -IC]
AQ, achievement quotient.
Aq., (L *aqua*) water. Also, **aq.**
A·qa·ba (ä′kä bä′), *n.* a seaport in SW Trans-Jordan
at the N end of the Gulf of Aqaba, an arm of the Red Sea.
aq·ua (ăk′wə, ā′kwə), *n., pl.* **aquae** (ăk′wē, ā′kwē).
Chiefly Pharm. water; a liquid; a solution. [t. L: water]
aqua am·mo·ni·ae (ə mō′nĭ ē′), ammonia (def. 2).
Also, **aqua ammonia.** [NL]
aqua for·tis (fōr′tĭs), nitric acid. [NL: strong water]
aq·ua·ma·rine (ăk′wə mə rēn′), *n.* **1.** a transparent
light-blue or greenish-blue variety of beryl, used as a
gem. **2.** light blue-green or greenish blue. [t. L: m.
aqua marina sea water; r. *aigue marine,* t. F]
aq·ua·plane (ăk′wə plān′), *n., v.,* **-planed, -planing.**
—*n.* **1.** a board which skims over water when pulled at
high speed, used to carry a rider behind a towing speed-
boat. —*v.i.* **2.** to ride an aquaplane. [f. L *aqua* water
+ -PLANE[2]; modeled on AIRPLANE]

*Apteryx,
Apteryx australis
(27 in. long)*

aqua re·gi·a (rē′jī′ə), a mixture of one part of nitric acid and three parts of hydrochloric acid. [t. NL: royal water (with allusion to its power to dissolve gold)]

aq·ua·relle (ăk′wə rĕl′), *n.* a painting in transparent watercolors. [t. F, t. It.: m. *acquarello,* dim. of *acqua* water] —a′qua·rel′list, *n.*

a·quar·i·um (ə kwâr′ĭ əm), *n., pl.* **aquariums, aquaria** (ə kwâr′ĭ ə). a pond, tank, or establishment in which living aquatic animals or plants are kept, as for exhibition. [t. L, prop. neut. of *aquārius* pertaining to water]

A·quar·i·us (ə kwâr′ĭ əs), *n., gen.* **Aquarii** (ə kwâr′ĭ ī′). **1.** *Astron.* a zodiacal constellation; the water bearer. **2.** the eleventh sign of the zodiac. See diag. under **zodi·ac.** [t. L: water bearer, prop. adj., pertaining to water]

a·quat·ic (ə kwăt′ĭk, ə kwŏt′-), *adj.* **1.** of or pertaining to water. **2.** living or growing in water. **3.** practiced on or in water: *aquatic sports.* —*n.* **4.** *(pl.)* sports practiced on or in water. [t. L: s. *aquāticus* watery]

aq·ua·tint (ăk′wə tĭnt′), *n.* **1.** a process imitating the broad flat tints of ink or wash drawings by etching a microscopic crackle on the copperplate intended for printing. **2.** an etching made by this process. —*v.t., v.i.* **3.** to etch in aquatint. [t. F: m. *aquatinte,* t. It.: m. *acqua tinta,* g. L *aqua tincta* tinted water]

aqua vi·tae (vī′tē), **1.** alcohol. **2.** spirituous liquor, as brandy or whiskey. [t. ML: water of life]

aq·ue·duct (ăk′wə dŭkt′), *n.* **1.** *Civ. Eng.* **a.** a conduit or artificial channel for conducting water from a distance, the water usually flowing by gravity. **b.** a structure which carries a conduit or canal across a valley or over a river. **2.** *Anat.* a canal or passage through which liquids pass. [t. L: m. *aquae ductus* conveyance of water]

a·que·ous (ā′kwĭ əs, ăk′wĭ-), *adj.* **1.** of, like, or containing water; watery. **2.** (of rocks) formed of matter deposited in or by water.

aqueous ammonia, ammonia (def. 2).

aqueous humor, *Anat.* the limpid watery fluid which fills the space between the cornea and the crystalline lens in the eye.

aqueous rock. See **rock** (def. 2a).

Aq·ui·la (ăk′wə lə), *n., gen.* **-lae** (-lē′). *Astron.* a northern constellation lying south of Cygnus, and containing the bright star Altair. [t. L: eagle]

aq·ui·le·gi·a (ăk′wə lē′jĭ ə, ăk′wə-), *n. Bot.* any columbine. [t. ML, var. of *aquileja* columbine]

A·qui·le·ia (ă′kwē lē′yä), *n.* an ancient city at the N end of the Adriatic: important Roman center.

aq·ui·line (ăk′wə līn′, -lĭn), *adj.* **1.** of or like the eagle. **2.** (of the nose) curved like an eagle's beak; hooked. [t. L: m. s. *aquilīnus*]

A·qui·nas (ə kwī′nəs), *n.* **Thomas,** ("the Angelic Doctor") 1225? 1274, Italian scholastic philosopher and one of the great theologians of the Roman Catholic Church.

Aq·ui·taine (ăk′wə tān′), *n.* a lowland region in SW France: an ancient Roman province in Gaul; later a duchy. Latin, **Aq·ui·ta·ni·a** (ăk′wə tā′nĭ ə).

Duchy of Aquitaine, 1360

a quo (ā kwō′), *Latin.* from which; a point of departure (for something, an idea, etc.).

ar-, var. of **ad-** (by assimilation) before *r,* as in *arrear.*

-ar¹, **1.** an adjective suffix meaning "of or pertaining to," "of the nature of," "like," as in *linear, regular.* **2.** a suffix forming adjectives not directly related to nouns, as *similar, singular.* [t. L: s. *-āris;* r. ME *-er,* t. AF]

-ar², a noun suffix, as in *vicar, scholar, collar.* [repr. L *-ārius, -āris,* etc.]

-ar³, a noun suffix denoting an agent (replacing regular *-er¹*), as in *beggar, liar.* [special use of *-AR²*]

Ar, *Chem.* argon.

Ar., 1. Arabic. **2.** Aramaic. **3.** argentum.

ar., 1. arrival. **2.** arrive; arrives.

Ar·ab (ăr′əb), *n.* **1.** a native of Arabia, or a member of the Arabic race (now widely spread in Asia and Africa, and formerly in southern Europe); an Arabian. **2.** a horse of a graceful, intelligent breed, native to Arabia and adjacent countries. **3.** a street Arab. —*adj.* **4.** Arabian. [back formation from ARABY]

Arab., 1. Arabia. **2.** Arabic.

ar·a·besque (ăr′ə bĕsk′), *n.* **1.** a kind of ornament in which flowers, foliage, fruits, vases, animals, and figures (in strict Mohammedan use, no animate objects) are represented in a fancifully combined pattern. **2.** a pose in ballet in which the dancer stands on one leg with one arm extended in front, and the other leg and arm behind. —*adj.* **3.** in the Arabian style, esp. of ornamentation. [t. F: Arabian, t. It.: m. *arabesco,* der. *Arabo* Arab]

A·ra·bi·a (ə rā′bĭ ə), *n.* a peninsula in SW Asia, including Saudi Arabia, Yemen, Oman, Aden, and other political divisions: divided in ancient times into **Arabia De·ser·ta** (dĭ zûr′tə), the N part, **Arabia Fe·lix** (fē′lĭks), the S part (sometimes restricted to Yemen), and **Arabia Pe·trae·a** (pə trē′ə), the NW part. 7,000,000 pop. (est. 1942); ab. 1,000,000 sq. mi.

A·ra·bi·an (ə rā′bĭ ən), *adj.* **1.** pertaining to Arabia or the Arabs. —*n.* **2.** an Arab (def. 1).

Arabian camel. See **camel** (def. 1a).

Arabian Desert, a large desert in Egypt between the Nile valley and the Red Sea.

Arabian Nights' Entertainments, The, a collection of Eastern folk tales derived in part from Indian and Persian sources and dating from the 10th century A.D. Also known as **The Thousand and One Nights.**

Arabian Sea, the NW part of the Indian Ocean, between India and Arabia.

Ar·a·bic (ăr′ə bĭk), *adj.* **1.** belonging to or derived from Arabia or the Arabians. **2.** *(l.c.)* designating certain species of acacia growing in Arabia and other eastern countries. —*n.* **3.** any of the languages that developed out of the language of the Arabians of the time of Mohammed, now spoken in North Africa, Egypt, Arabia, Palestine, Syria, and Iraq. **4.** the standard literary and classical language as established by the Koran. [t. L: s. *Arabicus*]

Arabic numerals, the characters 0, 1, 2, 3, 4, 5, 6, 7, 8, 9 introduced into general European use since the 12th century. Also, **Arabic figures.**

a·rab·i·nose (ə răb′ə nōs′, ăr′ə bə-), *n.* the pentose sugar, $C_5H_{10}O_5$ derived from plant gums or made synthetically from glucose. [f. ARAB(IC) + -IN² + -OSE²]

Ar·ab·ist (ăr′əb ĭst), *n.* an authority on Arabia and the Arabs or on the Arabic language and literature.

ar·a·ble (ăr′ə bəl), *adj.* **1.** capable, without much modification, of producing crops by means of tillage. —*n.* **2.** arable land. [t. L: m. s. *arābilis* that can be plowed; r. *earable* (f. *ear,* v., plow + -ABLE)] —ar′a·bil′i·ty, *n.*

Arab League, a limited confederation constituted March 22, 1945, by Egypt, Iraq, Lebanon, Saudi Arabia, Syria, Trans-Jordan, and Yemen, with Arab Palestine as a special member.

Ar·a·by (ăr′ə bĭ), *n. Poetic.* Arabia. [ME *Arabye,* t. F]

a·ra·ceous (ə rā′shəs), *adj. Bot.* belonging to the *Araceae,* or arum family of plants, which includes the arums, skunk cabbage, sweet flag, calla lily, taro, etc. [f. AR(UM) + -ACEOUS]

A·rach·ne (ə răk′nĭ), *n. Gk. Myth.* a Lydian maiden who challenged Athene to a contest in weaving, and was turned into a spider. [t. L, t. Gk.: lit., spider]

a·rach·nid (ə răk′nĭd), *n.* any arthropod of the class *Arachnida,* which includes the spiders, scorpions, mites, etc. [f. s. Gk. *aráchnē* spider, spider's web + -ID²] —a·rach·ni·dan (ə răk′nə dən), *adj., n.*

a·rach·noid (ə răk′noid), *adj.* **1.** resembling a spider's web. **2.** of or belonging to the arachnids. **3.** *Anat.* pertaining to the serous membrane (between the dura mater and the pia mater) enveloping the brain and spinal cord. **4.** *Bot.* formed of or covered with long, delicate hairs or fibers. —*n.* **5.** an arachnid. **6.** the arachnoid membrane. [t. Gk.: m. s. *arach-noeídēs* like a cobweb]

Kingdom of Aragon, 1212-1492

A·rad (ä räd′), *n.* a city in W Rumania, on the Mureş river. 85,043 (est. 1943).

A·ra·fu·ra Sea (ä′rə fŏor′ə), a sea between N Australia and SW New Guinea.

Ar·a·gon (ăr′ə gŏn′; *Sp.* ä′rä gôn′), *n.* a region in NE Spain: formerly a kingdom; later a province. 1,058,806 pop. (1940); 18,181 sq. mi.

A·ra·gon (ä rä gôn′), *n.* **Louis** (lwē), born 1891, French novelist, poet, and journalist.

a·rag·o·nite (ə răg′ə nīt′, ăr′ə gə-), *n.* a mineral, calcium carbonate, $CaCO_3$, chemically identical with calcite but differing in crystallization, and in having a higher specific gravity, less marked cleavage, etc. [f. ARAGON + -ITE¹]

A·ra·gua·ya (ä′rä gwī′yä), *n.* a river in central Brazil, flowing N to the Tocantins river. ab. 1000 mi.

a·ra·li·a·ceous (ə rā′lĭ ā′shəs), *adj. Bot.* belonging to the *Araliaceae,* a large family of plants including American spikenard, ginseng, etc.

Ar·al Sea (ăr′əl), an inland sea in the SW Soviet Union in Asia, E of the Caspian Sea. 26,166 sq. mi. Also, **Lake Aral.**

A·ram (ā′răm, âr′əm), *n.* Hebrew name of ancient Syria.

Aram., Aramaic.

Ar·a·ma·ic (ăr′ə mā′ĭk), *n.* **1.** any of a group of Semitic languages which became the speech of Syria, Palestine, and Mesopotamia after circa 300 B.C., including Syriac and the language of Christ. —*adj.* **2.** pertaining to Aram, or to the languages spoken there. [m. ARAMEAN, modeled on *Hebraic*]

Ar·a·me·an (ăr′ə mē′ən), *n.* **1.** a Semite of the division associated with Aram. **2.** the Aramaic language. Also, **Ar′a·mae′an.** [f. s. L *Aramaeus* (t. Gk.: m. *Aramaîos*) pertaining to Aram or Syria + -AN]

A·rap·a·ho (ə răp′ə hō′), *n.*, *pl.* **-ho.** **1.** (*pl.*) a tribe of North American Indians, of Algonquian speech stock, once dwelling in the Colorado plains, and now in Oklahoma and Wyoming. **2.** a member of this tribe. Also, **A·rap′a·hoe′.**

ar·a·pai·ma (ar′ə pī′mə), *n.* a large fresh-water fish, *Arapaima gigas*, of Brazil and Guiana, said to attain a length of 15 feet and a weight of 400 pounds. [S Amer. native name]

Ar·a·rat (ăr′ə răt′), *n.* a volcanic mountain with two peaks in E Turkey, near the boundary with Iran and the Soviet Union: mentioned in Gen. 8:4. 16,696 ft.

A·ras (ä räs′), *n.* a river flowing from E Turkey along a portion of the border between NW Iran and the SW Soviet Union into the Kura river. Ancient, **A·rax·es** (ə răk′sēz).

Ar·au·ca·ni·a (är′ô kā′nĭ ə; *Sp.* ä′rou kä′nyä), *n.* a former region in central Chile.

Ar·au·ca·ni·an (är′ô kā′nĭ ən), *n.* **1.** one of a tribe of Indians in central Chile. **2.** a linguistic stock of Chile and northern Argentina.

ar·au·car·i·a (är′ô kâr′ĭ ə), *n.* any tree of the pinaceous genus *Araucaria* of South America, Australia, and Polynesia. [t. NL: f. *Arauco*, province of S Chile + *-āria* -ARIA]

A·ra·wak (ä′rä wäk′), *n.* one of a numerous and widely scattered Indian language stock of northern and northeastern South America, and the West Indies. —**A′ra·wa′kan**, *adj.*

ar·ba·lest (är′bə lĭst), *n.* a powerful medieval crossbow. Also, **ar′ba·list.** [t. OF: m. *arbaleste* kind of catapult, g. L *arcuballista*. See ARC, BALLISTA] —**ar′ba·lest·er**, *n.*

Ar·be·la (är bē′lə), *n.* an ancient city of Assyria, E of Nineveh: Alexander defeated Darius near here, 331 B.C.

ar·bi·ter (är′bə tər), *n.* **1.** a person empowered to decide points at issue. **2.** one who has the sole or absolute power of judging or determining. [t. L: witness, judge]

ar·bi·tra·ble (är′bə trə bəl), *adj.* capable of arbitration; subject to the decision of an arbiter or arbitrator.

ar·bi·trage (är′bə trĭj, är′bə träzh′ *for 1*; är′bə trĭj *for 2*), *n.* **1.** *Finance.* the simultaneous purchase and sale of the same securities, commodities, or moneys in different markets to profit from unequal prices. **2.** *Rare.* arbitration. [t. F, der. *arbitrer* arbitrate]

ar·bi·tral (är′bə trəl), *adj.* pertaining to an arbiter or to arbitration. [t. LL: s. *arbitrālis*, der. L *arbiter* judge]

ar·bit·ra·ment (är bĭt′rə mənt), *n.* **1.** arbitration. **2.** the decision or sentence pronounced by an arbiter. **3.** the power of absolute and final decision. [t. ML: s. *arbitrāmentum*, r. ME *arbitrement*, t. OF]

ar·bi·trar·y (är′bə trĕr′ĭ), *adj.* **1.** subject to individual will or judgment; discretionary. **2.** capricious; uncertain; unreasonable: *an arbitrary interpretation.* **3.** uncontrolled by law; using or abusing unlimited power; despotic; tyrannical: *an arbitrary government.* [t. L: m. s. *arbitrārius* of arbitration, uncertain] —**ar′bi·trar′i·ly**, *adv.* —**ar′bi·trar′i·ness**, *n.*

ar·bi·trate (är′bə trāt′), *v.*, **-trated, -trating.** —*v.t.* **1.** to decide as arbiter or arbitrator; determine. **2.** to submit to arbitration; settle by arbitration: *to arbitrate a dispute regarding wages.* —*v.i.* **3.** to act as arbiter; decide between opposing parties or sides. **4.** to submit a matter to arbitration. [t. L: m. s. *arbitrātus*, pp.] —**ar′bi·tra′tive**, *adj.*

ar·bi·tra·tion (är′bə trā′shən), *n.* **1.** *Law.* the hearing and determining of a dispute between parties by a person or persons chosen or agreed to by them. **2.** *Internat. Law.* the application of judicial methods to the settlement of international disputes. —**ar′bi·tra′tion·al**, *adj.*

ar·bi·tra·tor (är′bə trā′tər), *n.* a person chosen to decide a dispute, esp. one empowered to examine the facts and to decide a point at issue. Also, *Obs.*, **ar·bi·trer** (är′bə trər).

ar·bi·tress (är′bə trĭs), *n.* a female arbiter.

Ar·blay (där′blā; *Fr.* där blĕ′), *n.* **Madame d′,** (*Frances* or *Fanny Burney*) 1752–1840, British novelist.

ar·bor[1] (är′bər), *n.* **1.** a bower formed by trees, shrubs, or vines, often on a latticework. **2.** *Obs.* a grass plot; lawn; garden; orchard. Also, *esp. Brit.*, **arbour.** [ME (*h*)*erber*, t. AF, var. of OF (*h*)*erbier*, g. L *herbārium*, der. *herba* plant; influenced by L *arbor* tree]

ar·bor[2] (är′bər), *n.* **1.** *Mach.* **a.** a beam, shaft, axis, or spindle. **b.** a bar or shaft used to support either the work or the cutting tools during a machining process. **2.** *Foundry.* a reinforcing member of a core or mold. [Latinized var. of earlier *arber*, t. F: m. *arbre*]

ar·bor[3] (är′bər), *n.*, *pl.* **arbores** (är′bə rēz′). a tree (used chiefly in botanical names). [t. L]

Arbor Day, a day, varying in date, observed in individual States of the U.S. for the planting of trees.

ar·bo·re·al (är bōr′ĭ əl), *adj.* **1.** pertaining to trees; treelike. **2.** living in or among trees. **3.** *Zool.* adapted for living and moving about in trees, as the limbs and skeleton of opossums, squirrels, monkeys, and apes.

ar·bo·re·ous (är bōr′ĭ əs), *adj.* **1.** abounding in trees; wooded. **2.** arboreal. **3.** arborescent. [t. L: m. *arboreus* pertaining to trees]

ar·bo·res·cent (är′bə rĕs′ənt), *adj.* treelike in size and form. [t. L: s. *arborescens*, ppr., becoming a tree] —**ar′bo·res′cence**, *n.*

ar·bo·re·tum (är′bə rē′təm), *n.*, *pl.* **-tums, -ta** (-tə). a plot of land where different trees or shrubs are grown for study or popular interest. [t. L: a plantation of trees]

ar·bo·ri·cul·ture (är′bə rĭ kŭl′chər), *n.* the cultivation of trees and shrubs. [f. *arbori-* (comb. form repr. L *arbor* tree) + CULTURE]

ar·bor·i·za·tion (är′bər ə zā′shən), *n.* a treelike appearance, as in certain minerals or fossils.

ar·bor·ous (är′bər əs), *adj.* of or pertaining to trees.

ar·bor vi·tae (är′bər vī′tē), **1.** an evergreen tree of the coniferous genus *Thuja*, esp. *T. occidentalis*, planted for hedges, etc. See **red cedar** (def. 2). **2.** *Anat.* a treelike appearance in a vertical section of the cerebellum, due to the arrangement of the white and gray nerve tissues. Also, **ar′bor·vi′tae.** [L: tree of life]

ar·bour (är′bər), *n.* *Chiefly Brit.* arbor[1].

Ar·buth·not (är bŭth′nət, är′bəth nŏt′), *n.* **John,** 1667–1735, British satirist and physician: friend of Swift.

ar·bu·tus (är bū′təs), *n.* **1.** any of the evergreen shrubs or trees of the ericaceous genus *Arbutus*, esp. *A. unedo*, of southern Europe, with scarlet berries, cultivated for ornament and food. **2.** a creeping ericaceous plant, *Epigaea repens*, of the U.S., with fragrant white and pink flowers (**trailing arbutus**). [t. L: strawberry tree]

arc (ärk), *n.*, *v.*, **arced** (ärkt), **arcing** (är′kĭng) or **arcked, arcking.** —*n.* **1.** *Geom.* any part of a circle or other curved line. **2.** *Elect.* the luminous bridge formed by the passage of a current across a gap between two conductors or terminals, due to the incandescence of the conducting vapors. **3.** *Astron.* the part of a circle representing the apparent course of a heavenly body. **4.** anything bow-shaped. —*v.i.* **5.** to form an electric arc. [ME *ark*, t. L: m. s. *arcus* bow]

Arc (därk), *n.* **Jeanne d′** (zhän), Joan of Arc.

ARC, American Red Cross. Also, **A.R.C.**

Arcs of circles

ar·cade (är kād′), *n.*, *v.*, **-caded, -cading.** —*n.* **1.** *Archit.* **a.** series of arches supported on piers or columns. **b.** an arched, roofed-in gallery. **2.** an arched or covered passageway, usually with shops on either side. —*v.t.* **3.** to provide with or form as an arcade or arcades. [t. F, t. It.: m. *arcata* arch, der. *arco* bow, arch, g. L *arcus*]

Ar·ca·di·a (är kā′dĭ ə), *n.* a mountainous district in ancient Greece, proverbial for the contented pastoral simplicity of its people. [t. L, t. Gk.: m. *Arkadīa*]

Ar·ca·di·an (är kā′dĭ ən), *adj.* **1.** of or pertaining to Arcadia. **2.** pastoral; rustic; simple; innocent. —*n.* **3.** a native or an inhabitant of Arcadia.

Ar·ca·dy (är′kə dĭ), *n.* *Poetic.* Arcadia.

ar·ca·num (är kā′nəm), *n.*, *pl.* **-na** (-nə). **1.** (*often pl.*) a secret; a mystery. **2.** a supposed great secret of nature which the alchemists sought to discover. **3.** a secret and powerful remedy. [t. L, neut. of *arcānus* secret, hidden]

ar·ca·ture (är′kə chər), *n.* *Archit.* **1.** an arcade of small dimensions. **2.** a blind arcade, used merely to decorate. [f. s. ML *arcāta* arch + -URE]

arc-bou·tant (är bōō tän′), *n.*, *pl.* **arcs-boutants** (är bōō tän′), *French.* a flying buttress.

arch[1] (ärch), *n.* **1.** a curved structure resting on supports at both extremities, used to sustain weight, to bridge or roof an open space, etc. **2.** something bowed or curved; any bow-like part: *the arch of the foot.* **3.** any curvature in the form of an arch: *the arch of the heavens.* —*v.t.* **4.** to cover with a vault, or span with an arch. **5.** to throw or make into the shape of an arch or vault; curve: *a horse arches its neck.* —*v.i.* **6.** to form an arch. [ME, t. OF: m. *arche,* a fem. var. of *arc* (g. L *arcus* bow), due to confusion with *arche* ark (g. L *arca* coffer)]

arch[2] (ärch), *adj.* **1.** chief; most important; principal: *the arch rebel.* **2.** cunning; sly; roguish: *an arch smile.* —*n.* **3.** *Obs.* a chief. [separate use of ARCH-] —**arch′ly**, *adv.* —**arch′ness**, *n.*

arch-, a prefix meaning "first," "chief," as in *archbishop, archpriest.* [ME *arch-*, OE *arce-*, *erce-*, t. L: m. *arch-, arche-, archi-*, t. Gk., comb. forms of *archós* chief]

Arch., Archbishop.

arch., **1.** archaic. **2.** archaism. **3.** archery. **4.** archipelago. **5.** architect. **6.** architectural. **7.** architecture.

Ar·chae·an (är kē′ən), *adj., n.* Archean.

archaeo-, a word element meaning "primeval," "primitive," "ancient," as in *archaeology, archaeopteryx.* [t. Gk.: m. *archaio-*, comb. form of *archaios*]

archaeol., **1.** archaeological. **2.** archaeology.

ar·chae·o·log·i·cal (är′kĭ ə lŏj′ə kəl), *adj.* of or pertaining to archaeology. Also, **archeological, ar′chae·o·log′ic.** —**ar′chae·o·log′i·cal·ly,** *adv.*

Arch
A, Abutment; S, Springer; V, Voussoir; In, Intrados; Ex, Extrados; K, Keystone; I, Impost; P, Pier

ar·chae·ol·o·gy (är′kĭ ŏl′ə jĭ), *n.* **1.** the scientific study of any prehistoric culture by excavation and description of its remains. **2.** *Now Rare.* ancient history; the study of antiquity. Also, **archeology.** [t. Gk.: m. s. *archaiologia* antiquarian lore] —**ar′chae·ol′o·gist,** *n.*

ar·chae·op·ter·yx (är′kĭ ŏp′tər ĭks), *n.* a fossil bird, the oldest known avian type, with teeth and a long, feathered, vertebrate tail, found in the later Jurassic. [t. NL, f. *archaeo-* ARCHAEO- + Gk. *ptéryx* wing, bird]

Ar·chae·o·zo·ic (är′kĭ ə zō′ĭk), *adj., n.* Archeozoic.

ar·cha·ic (är kā′ĭk), *adj.* **1.** marked by the characteristics of an earlier period; antiquated. **2.** no longer used in ordinary speech or writing; borrowed from older usage. [t. Gk.: m.s. *archaïkós* antique] —**ar·cha′i·cal·ly,** *adv.*

ar·cha·ism (är′kĭ ĭz′əm, -kā-), *n.* **1.** something archaic, as a word or expression. **2.** the use of what is archaic, as in literature. **3.** archaic quality or style. [t. Gk.: s. *archaïsmós*] —**ar′cha·ist,** *n.* —**ar′cha·is′tic,** *adj.*

ar·cha·ize (är′kĭ īz′, -kā-), *v.,* **-ized, -izing.** —*v.t.* **1.** to give an archaic appearance or quality to. —*v.i.* **2.** to use archaisms. —**ar′cha·iz′er,** *n.*

arch·an·gel (ärk′ān′jəl), *n.* **1.** a chief or principal angel; one of a particular order of angels. **2.** *Bot.* angelica (def. 1). [ME, t. L: s. *archangelus,* t. Gk.: m. *archángelos* chief angel] —**arch·an·gel·ic** (ärk′ən jĕl′ĭk), *adj.*

Arch·an·gel (ärk′ān′jəl), *n.* a seaport in the NW Soviet Union, on the **Gulf of Archangel** (Dvina Bay), an arm of the White Sea. 281,091 (1939). Russian, **Arkhangelsk.**

arch·bish·op (ärch′bĭsh′əp), *n.* a bishop of the highest rank. [OE *arcebiscop* (r. *hēahbiscop* high bishop), repr. L *archiepiscopus,* t. Gk.: m. *archiepískopos.* See ARCH-, BISHOP]

arch·bish·op·ric (ärch′bĭsh′əp rĭk), *n.* the see, diocese, or office of an archbishop.

archd., **1.** archdeacon. **2.** archduke.

arch·dea·con (ärch′dē′kən), *n.* **1.** an ecclesiastic who has charge of the temporal and external administration of a diocese, with jurisdiction delegated from the bishop. **2.** *Rom. Cath. Ch.* (generally) a title of honor conferred only on a member of a cathedral chapter. [OE *arcediacon,* t. L: m. s. *archidiāconus,* t. Gk.: m. *archidiákonos*] —**arch·dea·con·ate** (ärch′dē′kən ĭt), **arch′dea′con·ship′,** *n.*

arch·dea·con·ry (ärch′dē′kən rĭ), *n., pl.* **-ries.** the jurisdiction, residence, or office of an archdeacon.

arch·di·o·cese (ärch′dī′ə sēs′, -sĭs), *n.* the diocese of an archbishop.

arch·du·cal (ärch′dū′kəl, -dōō′-), *adj.* pertaining to an archduke or an archduchy.

arch·duch·ess (ärch′dŭch′ĭs), *n.* **1.** the wife of an archduke. **2.** a princess of the Austrian imperial family.

arch·duch·y (ärch′dŭch′ĭ), *n., pl.* **-duchies.** the territory of an archduke or an archduchess.

arch·duke (ärch′dūk′, -dōōk′), *n.* a title of the sovereign princes of the former ruling house of Austria.

arche-[1], var. of **archi-,** as in *archegonium.*

arche-[2], var. of **archeo-** before vowels.

Ar·che·an (är kē′ən), *adj.* **1.** pertaining to the oldest known rocks. —*n.* **2.** a division of early pre-Cambrian rocks, predominantly igneous and metamorphic. Also, **Archaean.** [f. ARCHE(O)- + -AN]

arched (ärcht), *adj.* **1.** made, covered, or spanned with an arch. **2.** having the form of an arch.

ar·che·go·ni·um (är′kə gō′nĭ əm), *n., pl.* **-nia** (-nĭ ə). *Bot.* the female reproductive organ in ferns, mosses, etc. [t. NL, f. s. Gk. *archégonos* first of a race + *-ium* -IUM] —**ar′che·go′ni·al,** *adj.* —**ar·che·go·ni·ate** (är′kə gō′nĭ ĭt, -āt′), *adj.*

arch·en·e·my (ärch′ĕn′ə mĭ), *n., pl.* **-mies. 1.** a chief enemy. **2.** Satan; the Devil.

ar·chen·ter·on (är kĕn′tə rŏn′), *n.* *Embryol.* the primitive enteron or digestive cavity of a gastrula. [f. ARCH- + Gk. *énteron* intestine] —**ar·chen·ter·ic** (är′kĕn tĕr′ĭk), *adj.*

archeo-, var. of **archaeo-,** as in *Archeozoic.*

ar·che·ol·o·gy (är′kĭ ŏl′ə jĭ), *n.* archaeology. —**ar·che·o·log·i·cal** (är′kĭ ə lŏj′ə kəl), —**ar′che·o·log′ic,** *adj.* —**ar′che·o·log′i·cal·ly,** *adv.* —**ar′che·ol′o·gist,** *n.*

Ar·che·o·zo·ic (är′kĭ ə zō′ĭk), *adj.* pertaining to the oldest part of earth history during which earliest forms of life presumably appeared. —*n.* **2.** the Archeozoic era or series of rocks. Also, **Archaeozoic.** [f. ARCHEO- + s. Gk. *zōḗ* life + -IC]

arch·er (är′chər), *n.* **1.** one who shoots with a bow and arrow; a bowman. **2.** (*cap.*) *Astron.* **a.** the zodiacal constellation Sagittarius. **b.** the sign named from it. [ME, t. AF, var. of OF *archier,* g. L *arcārius,* der. *arcus* bow]

arch·er·y (är′chər ĭ), *n.* **1.** the practice, art, or skill of an archer. **2.** archers collectively. **3.** an archer's bows, arrows, and other weapons.

ar·che·spore (är′kə spōr′), *n.* *Bot.* the primitive cell, or group of cells, which give rise to the cells from which spores are derived. Also, **ar·che·spo·ri·um** (är′kə spōr′ĭ əm). —**ar′che·spo′ri·al,** *adj.*

ar·che·type (är′kə tĭp′), *n.* a model or first form; the original pattern or model after which a thing is made. [t. L: m. s. *archetypum,* t. Gk.: m. *archétypon,* neut. of *archétypos* first-molded, original] —**ar·che·typ·al** (är′kə tī′pəl), **ar·che·typ·i·cal** (är′kə tĭp′ə kəl), *adj.*

arch·fiend (ärch′fēnd′), *n.* **1.** a chief fiend. **2.** Satan.

archi-, a prefix: **1.** var. of **arch-. 2.** *Biol.* "original" or "primitive," as in *archiplasm.* [t. L, t. Gk. See ARCH-]

ar·chi·carp (är′kə kärp′), *n.* *Bot.* the female sex organ in various ascomycetous fungi, commonly a pluricellular coiled hypha differentiated into a terminal trichogyne and the ascogonium.

ar·chi·di·a·co·nal (är′kĭ dī ăk′ə nəl), *adj.* of or pertaining to an archdeacon or his office. —**ar·chi·di·ac·o·nate** (är′kĭ dī ăk′ə nĭt), *n.*

ar·chi·e·pis·co·pal (är′kĭ ĭ pĭs′kə pəl), *adj.* of or pertaining to an archbishop or his office. —**ar·chi·e·pis·co·pate** (är′kĭ ĭ pĭs′kə pĭt, -pāt′), *n.*

ar·chi·man·drite (är′kə măn′drĭt), *n.* *Gk. Ch.* **1.** the head of a monastery; an abbot. **2.** a superior abbot, having charge of several monasteries. **3.** a title given to distinguished celibate priests. [t. ML: m. *archimandrīta,* t. LGk.: m. s. *archimandrītēs*]

Archimedean screw, a device consisting essentially of a spiral passage within an inclined cylinder for raising water to a height when rotated.

Ar·chi·me·des (är′kə mē′dēz), *n.* 287?–212 B.C., a Greek mathematician, physicist, and inventor: discovered principles of specific gravity and of the lever. —**Ar·chi·me·de·an** (är′kə mē′dĭ ən, -mə dē′ən), *adj.*

ar·chine (är shēn′), *n.* a Russian unit of length equal to 28 inches.

arch·ing (är′chĭng), *n.* arched work or formation.

ar·chi·pel·a·go (är′kə pĕl′ə gō′), *n., pl.* **-gos, -goes. 1.** any large body of water with many islands. **2.** the island groups in such a body of water. **3. the Archipelago,** the Aegean Sea, with its many islands. [t. It.: m. *arcipelago,* lit., chief sea, f. *arci-* ARCHI- + m. Gk. *pélagos* sea] —**ar·chi·pe·lag·ic** (är′kə pə lăj′ĭk), *adj.*

ar·chi·plasm (är′kə plăz′əm), *n.* **1.** the most basic or primitive living substance; protoplasm. **2.** *Cytology.* (in cell division) the substance surrounding the centrosome. Also, **archoplasm.**

archit., architecture.

ar·chi·tect (är′kə tĕkt′), *n.* **1.** one whose profession it is to design buildings and superintend their construction. **2.** the deviser, maker, or creator of anything. [t. L: s. *architectus,* t. Gk.: m. *architéktōn* chief builder]

ar·chi·tec·ton·ic (är′kə tĕk tŏn′ĭk), *adj.* **1.** pertaining to architecture. **2.** pertaining to construction or design of any kind. **3.** resembling architecture in manner or technique of structure. **4.** (of a science or structure) giving the principle of organization of a system. [t. L: s. *architectonicus,* t. Gk.: m. *architektonikós*]

ar·chi·tec·tur·al (är′kə tĕk′chər əl), *adj.* **1.** of or pertaining to architecture. **2.** conforming to the basic principles of architecture. **3.** having the qualities of architecture. —**ar′chi·tec′tur·al·ly,** *adv.*

ar·chi·tec·ture (är′kə tĕk′chər), *n.* **1.** the art or science of building, including plan, design, construction, and decorative treatment. **2.** the character or style of building: *the architecture of Paris.* **3.** the action or process of building; construction. **4.** a building. **5.** buildings collectively. [t. L: m. s. *architectūra*]

ar·chi·trave (är′kə trāv′), *n.* *Archit.* **1.** the lowest division of an entablature, resting immediately on the columns. See diag. under **column. 2.** a band of moldings or other ornamentation about a rectangular door or other opening or a panel. **3.** a decorative band about openings or panels of any shape. [t. It.: f. *archi-* ARCHI- + *trave* (g. L *trabs* beam)]

ar·chi·val (är kī′vəl), *adj.* pertaining to archives or valuable records; contained in such archives or records.

ar·chives (är′kīvz), *n.pl.* **1.** a place where public records or other historical documents are kept. **2.** documents or records relating to the activities, rights, claims, treaties, constitutions, etc., of a family, corporation, community, or nation. [t. F, t. L: m. *archīvum,* t. Gk.: m. *archeîon* public building, pl., records]

ar·chi·vist (är′kə vĭst), *n.* a custodian of archives.

ar·chi·volt (är′kə vōlt′), *n.* *Archit.* a band of moldings or other ornamentation about an arched opening. [t. It.: s. *archivolto,* f. *archi-* arch + *volto* turned]

ar·chon (är′kŏn), *n.* **1.** a higher magistrate in ancient Athens. **2.** any ruler. [t. Gk.: m. *árchōn* ruler, prop. ppr. of *árchein* be first, rule] —**ar′chon·ship′,** *n.*

ar·cho·plasm (är′kə plăz′əm), *n.* archiplasm.

arch·priest (ärch′prēst′), *n.* **1.** a priest holding first rank, as among the members of a cathedral chapter or among the clergy of a district outside the episcopal city. **2.** *Rom. Cath. Ch.* a priest acting as superior of the Roman Catholic secular clergy in England, first appointed in 1598 and superseded by a vicar apostolic in 1623. —**arch′priest′hood,** *n.*

arch·way (ärch′wā′), *n.* *Archit.* **1.** an entrance or passage under an arch. **2.** a covering or enclosing arch.

-archy, a word element meaning "rule," "government," as in *monarchy.* [t. Gk.: m. *-archia*]

arc light, 1. Also, **arc lamp.** a lamp in which the light source of high intensity is an electric arc, usually between carbon rods. **2.** the light produced.

arc·o·graph (är′kə gräf′), *n.* *Geom., etc.* an instrument for drawing arcs, having a flexible arc-shaped part adjusted by an extensible straight bar connecting its sides; cyclograph.

arc sine, tangent, etc. *Trig.* the angle, measured in radians, whose sine, tangent, etc., is a given number.

arc·tic (ärk′tĭk or, esp. for 4, är′tĭk), adj. **1.** of, at, or near the North Pole; frigid. **2.** Astron. of, near, or lying under the Great and the Little Bear. —n. **3.** the arctic regions. **4.** (pl.) warm waterproof overshoes. [t. L: s. arcticus, t. Gk.: m. arktikós of the Bear (constellation), northern; r. ME artik, t. OF: m. artique]

Arctic Circle, the southern boundary of the North Frigid Zone, 23°28′ from the North Pole.

Arctic Ocean, an ocean N of North America, Asia, and the Arctic Circle. ab. 5,400,000 sq. mi.

Arctic Zone, the section of the earth's surface lying between the Arctic Circle and the North Pole.

Arc·tu·rus (ärk tyōōr′əs, -tōōr′-), n. Astron. a bright star of the first magnitude in the constellation Boötes. [t. L, t. Gk.: m. Arktoûros, lit., guard of the Bear, f. árktos a bear, the Great Bear + oûros guardian]

ar·cu·ate (är′kyōō ĭt, -āt′), adj. bent or curved like a bow. Also, **ar′cu·at′ed.** [t. L: m. s. arcuātus, pp.]

-ard, a noun suffix, orig. intensive but now often depreciative or without special force, as in coward, drunkard, wizard. Also, **-art.** [t. OF: -ard, -art, t. G: m. -hart, -hard hardy, c. HARD]

ar·deb (är′dĕb), n. a unit of capacity used for dry measure in Egypt and neighboring countries, officially equivalent in Egypt to 5.62 U. S. bushels, but varying greatly in different localities. [t. Ar.: m. ardabb, t. Gk.: m. artábē, t. O Pers.: m. artaba]

Ar·den (är′dən), n. Forest of, a forest district formerly in central and E England, now restricted to N Warwickshire: scene of Shakespeare's As You Like It.

ar·den·cy (är′dən sĭ), n. warmth of feeling; ardor.

Ar·dennes (är dĕn′), n. Forest of, a wooded plateau along the Meuse river, in NE France, SE Belgium, and Luxemburg: German counteroffensive, Dec. 1944–Jan., 1945.

ar·dent (är′dənt), adj. **1.** glowing with feeling, earnestness, or zeal; passionate; fervent: ardent vows, an ardent patriot. **2.** glowing; flashing. **3.** burning, fiery, or hot. [t. L: s. ardens, ppr., burning; r. ME ardaunt, t. OF: m. ardant] —**ar′dent·ly,** adv. —Syn. **1.** fervid, eager, enthusiastic; vehement.

Forest of Ardennes

ardent spirits, strong alcoholic liquors made by distillation, as brandy, whiskey, or gin.

ar·dor (är′dər), n. **1.** warmth of feeling; fervor; eagerness; zeal. **2.** burning heat. Also, esp. Brit., **ar′dour.** [ME, t. OF, g. L] —Syn. **1.** fervency, passion.

ar·du·ous (är′jōō əs), adj. **1.** requiring great exertion; laborious; difficult: an arduous enterprise. **2.** energetic; strenuous: making an arduous effort. **3.** hard to climb; steep: an arduous path. **4.** hard to endure; severe; full of hardships: an arduous winter. [t. L: m. arduus] —**ar′du·ous·ly,** adv. —**ar′du·ous·ness,** n. —Syn. **1.** toilsome, onerous, wearisome, exhausting.

are[1] (är; unstressed ər), v. pres. indic. pl. of the verb be. [d. OE (Northumbrian) aron]

are[2] (âr, är), n. Metric System. a surface measure equal to 100 square meters, or 119.6 square yards; a hundredth of a hectare. [t. F, t. L: m. s. ārea AREA]

ar·e·a (âr′ĭ ə), n., pl. areas, (in Biol., often) areae (âr′ĭ ē′). **1.** any particular extent of surface; region; tract: the settled area. **2.** extent, range, or scope: the whole area of science. **3.** a piece of unoccupied ground; an open space. **4.** the space or site on which a building stands; the yard attached to or surrounding a house. **5.** Brit. areaway (def. 1). **6.** Math. amount of surface (plane or curved); two-dimensional extent. **7.** Anat., Physiol. a zone of the cerebral cortex with a specific function. [t. L: piece of level ground, open space] —**ar′e·al,** adj.

ar·e·a·way (âr′ĭ ə wā′), n. **1.** a sunken area leading to a cellar or basement entrance, or in front of basement or cellar windows. **2.** U.S. a passageway.

ar·e·ca (är′ə kə, ə rē′-), n. **1.** any palm of the genus Areca, of tropical Asia and the Malay Archipelago, esp. A. Catechu, the betel palm, which bears a nut (the **areca nut**). **2.** the nut itself. **3.** any of various palms formerly referred to the genus Areca. Also, **areca palm** for 1, 3. [t. Pg., t. Malayalam: m. ādekka, ult. t. Tamil]

A·re·ci·bo (ä′rĕ sē′bô), n. a seaport in N Puerto Rico. 28,500 (prelim. 1950).

a·re·na (ə rē′nə), n. **1.** the oval space in a Roman amphitheater for combats or other performances. **2.** the scene of any contest. **3.** a field of conflict or endeavor: the arena of politics. [t. L: sand, sandy place]

ar·e·na·ceous (är′ə nā′shəs), adj. sandlike; sandy. [t. L: m. arēnāceus sandy]

ar·e·nic·o·lous (är′ə nĭk′ə ləs), adj. inhabiting sand. [f. s. L arēna sand + -(I)COLOUS]

aren't (ärnt for 1, änt for 2), **1.** contraction of are not. **2.** Chiefly Brit. am not (def. 2).

ar·e·o·cen·tric (âr′ĭ ō sĕn′trĭk), adj. Astron. having the planet Mars as center. [f. areo- (comb. form of ARES) + CENTRIC]

a·re·o·la (ə rē′ə lə), n., pl. **-lae** (-lē′), **-las.** Biol. **1.** a ring of color, as around a pustule or the human nipple.

2. a small interstice, as between the fibers of connective tissue. [t. L, dim. of ārea AREA] —**a·re·o·lar,** adj. —**a·re·o·late** (ə rē′ə lĭt, -lāt′), adj. —**ar·e·o·la·tion** (âr′ĭ ə lā′shən), n.

ar·e·ole (âr′ĭ ōl′), n. Biol. an areola. [t. F, t. L: m. areola, dim. of ārea open space]

Ar·e·op·a·gite (âr′ĭ ŏp′ə jĭt′, -gīt′), n. Gk. Hist. a member of the council of the Areopagus. —**Ar·e·op·a·git·ic** (âr′ĭ ŏp′ə jĭt′ĭk), adj.

Ar·e·op·a·git·i·ca (âr′ĭ ŏp′ə jĭt′ə kə), n. a pamphlet (1644) by Milton, advocating freedom of the press.

Ar·e·op·a·gus (âr′ĭ ŏp′ə gəs), n. **1.** a hill in Athens, Greece, to the west of the Acropolis. **2.** Gk. Hist. the council which met on this hill, originally having wide public functions but later a purely judicial body. **3.** any high tribunal. [t. L, t. Gk.: m. Areiópagos hill of Ares (Mars.) Cf. Acts, 17, 19, 22]

A·re·qui·pa (ä′rĕ kē′pä), n. a city in S Peru. 79,185 (1940).

Ar·es (âr′ēz), n. the Greek god of war, identified by the Romans with Mars. [t. L, t. Gk.]

a·rête (ə rāt′), n. Phys. Geog. a sharp ridge of a mountain; the divide between two glaciated valleys. [t. F, g. L arista awn, spine]

ar·e·thu·sa (är′ə thōō′zə), n. **1.** any plant of the North American genus Arethusa, consisting of one species, A. bulbosa, a small bog orchid with a pink, or occasionally white, flower. **2.** (cap.) Gk. Myth. a nymph metamorphosed into a spring on the island of Ortygia (near Syracuse, Sicily) to save her from the pursuing river god, Alpheus.

A·re·ti·no (ä′rĕ tē′nō), n. Pietro (pyĕ′trō), 1492–1556, Italian satirist and dramatist.

A·rez·zo (ä rĕt′tsō), n. a city in central Italy. 64,937 (est. 1946).

Arg., Argentina.

arg., argentum.

ar·gal[1] (är′gəl), n. argol.

ar·gal[2] (är′gəl), n. argali.

ar·ga·li (är′gə lĭ), n., pl. **-li.** a wild sheep of Asia, Ovis ammon, with long, thick, spirally curved horns. Also, **argal.** [t. Mongolian]

Siberian argali. Ovis ammon (4 ft. high at the shoulder, spread of horns 3 ft.)

ar·gent (är′jənt), n. **1.** Archaic or Poetic. silver. **2.** something resembling it. **3.** Obs. money. —adj. **4.** like silver; silvery-white. [t. F, g. L argentum silver]

ar·gen·tal (är jĕn′təl), adj. of, pertaining to, containing, or resembling silver.

ar·gen·te·ous (är jĕn′tĭ əs), adj. silvery. [t. L: m. argenteus]

Ar·gen·teuil (ȧr zhän tœ′ĭ), n. a city in N France, on the Seine near Paris. 53,543 (1946).

ar·gen·tic (är jĕn′tĭk), adj. Chem. of or containing silver, with a valence greater than the corresponding argentous compound.

ar·gen·tif·er·ous (är′jən tĭf′ər əs), adj. silver-bearing. [f. s. L argentum silver + -(I)FEROUS]

Ar·gen·ti·na (är′jən tē′nə; Sp. är′hĕn tē′nä), n. a republic in S South America. 15,909,950 pop. (est. 1943); 1,073,698 sq. mi. Cap.: Buenos Aires.

Ar·gen·tine (är′jən tēn′, -tīn′), n. **1.** a native or inhabitant of Argentina. —adj. **2.** of or pertaining to Argentina. Also, **Ar·gen·tin·e·an** (är′jən tĭn′ĭ ən).

ar·gen·tine (är′jən tīn′, -tēn′), adj. **1.** pertaining to or resembling silver. [f. s. L argentum silver + -INE[1]] —n. **2.** a silvery substance obtained from fish scales, used in making imitation pearls. [f. s. L argentum silver + -INE[2]]

ar·gen·tite (är′jən tīt′), n. a mineral, silver sulfide, Ag[2]S, a dark lead-gray sectile mineral occurring in crystals and massive: an important ore of silver. [f. s. L argentum silver + -ITE[1]]

ar·gen·tous (är jĕn′təs), adj. Chem. containing monovalent silver (Ag+[1]), as argentous chloride, AgCl.

ar·gen·tum (är jĕn′təm), n. Chem. silver. [t. L]

ar·gil (är′jĭl), n. clay, esp. potter's clay. [var. of argil(l)e, t. L: m. argilla, t. Gk.: white clay]

ar·gil·la·ceous (är′jə lā′shəs), adj. **1.** of the nature of or resembling clay; clayey. **2.** containing a considerable amount of clayey matter.

ar·gil·lite (är′jə līt′), n. any compact sedimentary rock composed mainly of clay minerals. [f. s. L argilla white clay + -ITE[1]]

ar·gi·nine (är′jə nīn′), n. one of the essential amino acids, $C_6H_{14}N_4$, which make up plant and animal proteins, present in the sperm of salmon and herring.

Ar·give (är′jīv, -gĭv), adj. **1.** of or pertaining to Argos. **2.** Greek. —n. **3.** a native of Argos. **4.** any Greek.

Ar·go (är′gō), n. **1.** Astron. a very large southern constellation, now divided into four, lying largely south of Canis Major. **2.** Gk. Legend. the ship in which Jason sailed in quest of the golden fleece.

ar·gol (är′gəl), n. crude tartar. Also, **argal.** [ME argoile, t. AF: m. argoil]

Ar·go·lis (är′gə lĭs), n. **1.** an ancient district in SE Greece. **2.** Gulf of, a gulf of the Aegean, in SE Greece.

ar·gon (är′gŏn), n. a colorless, odorless, chemically inactive, monatomic, gaseous element. Symbol: A; at. no.: 18; at. wt.: 39.94. [t. NL, t. Gk., prop. neut. of argós idle]

Ar·go·naut (är′gə nôt′), *n.* **1.** *Gk. Legend.* a member of the band that sailed to Colchis with Jason in the ship Argo in search of the golden fleece. **2.** a person who emigrated to California in 1848 at the time of the discovery of gold there. **3.** (*l.c.*) the paper nautilus. [t. L: s. *Argonauta*, t. Gk.: m. *Argonautēs* (f. *Argō* Argo + *nautēs* sailor)] —**Ar′go·nau′tic,** *adj.*

Ar·gonne Forest (är′gŏn; *Fr.* är gōn′), a wooded region in NE France: battles, 1918, 1944.

Ar·gos (är′gŏs, -gəs), *n.* an ancient city in SE Greece, the center of Argolis: a powerful rival of Sparta, Athens, and Corinth.

ar·go·sy (är′gə sǐ), *n.*, *pl.* **-sies.** **1.** a large merchant ship, esp. one with a rich cargo. **2.** a fleet of such ships. [t. It.: m. *Ragusea* a vessel of Ragusa, Dalmatian port]

ar·got (är′gō, -gət), *n.* the peculiar language or jargon of any class or group; originally, that of thieves and vagabonds, devised for purposes of disguise and concealment. [t. F; orig. unknown] —**ar·got·ic** (är gŏt′ĭk), *adj.*

ar·gue (är′gū), *v.*, **-gued, -guing.** —*v.i.* **1.** to present reasons for or against a thing: *to argue for or against a proposed law.* **2.** to contend in argument; dispute: *to argue with someone.* —*v.t.* **3.** to state the reasons for or against: *the counsel argued the cause.* **4.** to maintain in reasoning: *to argue that something must be so.* **5.** to persuade, drive, etc., by reasoning: *to argue one out of a plan.* **6.** to show; prove; imply: *his clothes argue poverty.* [ME *argue(n)*, t. OF: m. *arguer*, g. L *argūtāre*, freq. of *arguere* show] —**ar′gu·a·ble,** *adj.* —**ar′gu·er,** *n.* —**Syn. 1.** ARGUE, DEBATE, DISCUSS imply using reasons or proofs to support or refute an assertion, proposition, or principle. ARGUE implies reasoning or trying to understand; it does not necessarily imply opposition: *to argue with oneself.* To DISCUSS is to present varied opinions and views: *to discuss ways and means.* To DEBATE is to interchange formal (usually opposing) arguments, esp. on public questions: *to debate a proposed amendment.*

ar·gu·fy (är′gyə fī), *v.t.*, *v.i.*, **-fied, -fying.** *Colloq.* or *Dial.* to argue or wrangle. [f. ARGU(E) + -FY]

ar·gu·ment (är′gyə mənt), *n.* **1.** an argumentation; debate. **2.** a process of reasoning; series of reasons. **3.** a statement or fact tending to improve a point. **4.** an address or composition intended to convince others of the truth of something. **5.** an abstract or summary of the chief points in a book or sections of a book. **6.** *Math.* (of a function) an independent variable. **7.** *Obs.* evidence or proof. **8.** *Obs.* a matter of contention. [ME, t. L: s. *argūmentum* proof] —**Syn. 1.** ARGUMENT, CONTROVERSY, DISPUTE imply the expression of opinions for and against some idea. An ARGUMENT usually arises from a disagreement between two persons, each of whom advances facts supporting his own point of view. A CONTROVERSY or a DISPUTE may involve two or more persons. A DISPUTE is an oral contention, usually brief, and often of a heated, angry, or undignified character: *a violent dispute over a purchase.* A CONTROVERSY is an oral or written expression of contrary opinions, and may be dignified and of some duration: *a political controversy.*

ar·gu·men·ta·tion (är′gyə mən tā′shən), *n.* **1.** reasoning; discussion. **2.** a discussion dealing with a controversial point. **3.** the setting forth of reasons together with the conclusion drawn from them. **4.** the premises and conclusion so set forth.

ar·gu·men·ta·tive (är′gyə měn′tə tǐv), *adj.* **1.** addicted to argument; disputatious. **2.** controversial. —**ar′gu·men·ta·tive·ly,** *adv.* —**ar′gu·men·ta·tive·ness,** *n.*

ar·gu·men·tum (är′gyə měn′təm), *n.* *Latin.* argument, as **argumentum ad hominem,** argument using the opponent's own words or acts as evidence for one's views.

Ar·gus (är′gəs), *n.* **1.** *Gk. Legend.* a giant with a hundred eyes, set to guard the heifer Io. His eyes were transferred, after his death, to the peacock's tail. **2.** any observant or vigilant person. **3.** (*l.c.*) any pheasant of the Malayan genera *Argusianus* and *Rheinardia,* marked with eyelike spots.

Ar·gus-eyed (är′gəs īd′), *adj.* keen-eyed; vigilant.

Ar·gyle (är′gīl), *n.* **1.** (*also l.c.*) a diamond-shaped pattern of two or more colors, used in knitting socks, sweaters, etc. —*adj.* **2.** (*also l.c.*) having such a pattern. [var. ARGYLL; arbitrary designation]

Ar·gyll (är gǐl′), *n.* a county in W Scotland. 62,800 pop. (est. 1946); 3110 sq. mi. Also, **Ar·gyll·shire** (är gǐl′shǐr, -shər).

ar·gy·rol (är′jər ōl′, -rŏl′), *n.* *Pharm.* **1.** a compound of silver and a protein, applied to mucous membranes as a mild antiseptic. **2.** (*cap.*) a trademark for this substance. [f. s. Gk. *árgyros* silver + *-ol* (unexplained)]

a·rhyth·mi·a (ə rĭth′mǐ ə), *n.* *Pathol.* arrhythmia.

a·ri·a (ä′rǐ ə, âr′Yə), *n.* **1.** an air or melody. **2.** an elaborate melody for a single voice, with accompaniment, in an opera, oratorio, etc., esp. one consisting of a principal and a subordinate section, and a repetition of the first with or without alterations. [t. It., g. L *āēr* air]

-aria, *Bot., Zool.* a suffix used in names of genera and groups. [t. L, neut. pl. n. and adj. termination]

A·ri·ad·ne (är′ǐ ăd′nǐ), *n.* *Gk. Legend.* a daughter of Minos and Pasiphaë. She gave Theseus the thread whereby he escaped from the labyrinth.

Ar·i·an (âr′Yən), *adj.* **1.** pertaining to Arius. —*n.* **2.** an adherent of the Arian doctrine. See **Arius.** [t. L: s. *Ariānus,* der. *Arius*] —**Ar′i·an·ism,** *n.*

Ar·i·an (âr′Yən), *adj.*, *n.* Aryan.

-arian, a compound suffix of adjectives and nouns, often referring to pursuits, doctrines, etc., or to age, as in *antiquarian, humanitarian, octogenarian.* [f. -ARY¹ + -AN]

A·ri·ca (ä rē′kä), *n.* **1.** a seaport in N Chile. 14,064. (1940). **2.** See **Tacna-Arica.**

ar·id (är′ǐd), *adj.* **1.** dry; without moisture; parched with heat. **2.** uninteresting; dull; lifeless. [t. L: s. *āridus* dry] —**a·rid·i·ty** (ə rǐd′ə tǐ), **ar′id·ness,** *n.* —**ar′id·ly,** *adv.* —**Syn. 1.** See **dry.** —**Ant. 1.** humid.

Ar·i·el (âr′Yəl), *n.* **1.** (in Shakespeare's *Tempest*) a spirit of the air who is required to use his magic to help Prospero. **2.** *Astron.* the innermost of the four satellites of Uranus. [t. LL, t. Gk., t. Heb: m. *arī′ēl*]

ar·i·el (âr′Yəl), *n.* an Arabian gazelle, *Gazella arabica.* Also, **ariel gazelle.** [t. Ar.: m. *aryal* stag or ibex]

Ar·ies (âr′ēz, -Yēz′), *n.*, *gen.* **Arietis** (ə rī′ə tǐs). **1.** the Ram, a zodiacal constellation between Pisces and Taurus. **2.** the first sign of the zodiac (♈), which the sun enters about March 21. See **zodiac.** [t. L: a ram]

ar·i·et·ta (är′Yět′ə; *It.* ä′rē ět′tä), *n.* *Music.* a short aria. Also, **ar·i·ette** (är′Yět′). [It. dim. of *aria.* See ARIA]

a·right (ə rīt′), *adv.* rightly; correctly; properly.

ar·il (är′ĭl), *n.* *Bot.* an accessory covering or appendage of certain seeds, esp. one arising from the placenta, funicle or hilum. [t. NL: m. s. *arillus,* der. ML *arillī* dried grapes, t. Sp.: m. *arillos*]

ar·il·late (är′ə lāt′), *adj. Bot.* having an aril.

ar·il·lode (är′ə lōd′), *n. Bot.* a false aril; an aril which originates from the micropyle instead of at or below the hilum, as in the nutmeg. [see ARIL, -ODE¹]

Ar·i·ma·thae·a (är′ə mə thē′ə), *n.* a town in ancient Palestine. Matt. 27:57. Also, **Ar′i·ma·the′a.**

ar·i·ose (är′Yōs′, är′Yōs′), *adj.* characterized by melody; songlike. [Anglicization of ARIOSO]

a·ri·o·so (ä ryō′sō), *adj., adv. Music.* in the manner of an air or melody. [It., der. *aria* ARIA]

A·ri·os·to (ä′rē ŏs′tō), *n.* **Ludovico** (loō′dō vē′kō), 1474–1533, Italian poet, author of *Orlando Furioso.*

-arious, an adjective suffix meaning "connected with," "having to do with," as in *gregarious.* [t. L: m. *-ārius*]

a·rise (ə rīz′), *v.i.*, **arose, arisen, arising. 1.** to come into being or action; originate; appear: *new questions arise, a cry arose.* **2.** to result or proceed (fol. by *from*): *accidents arise from carelessness.* **3.** to move upward. **4.** to get up from sitting, lying, or kneeling. [ME *arise(n),* OE *ārīsan,* f. *ā-* up + *rīsan* rise]

a·ris·ta (ə rǐs′tə), *n.*, *pl.* **-tae** (-tē). **1.** *Bot.* a bristlelike appendage of grain, etc.; an awn. **2.** *Entomol.* a prominent bristle on the antenna of some dipterous insects. [t. L. See ARETE]

a·ris·tate (ə rǐs′tāt), *adj.* **1.** *Bot.* having aristae; awned. **2.** *Zool.* tipped with a thin spine. [t. LL: m. s. *aristātus,* der. L *arista* awn]

Ar·is·ti·des (är′ə stī′dēz), *n.* ("the Just") 530?–468? B.C., Athenian statesman and general.

Ar·is·tip·pus (är′ə stǐp′əs), *n.* 435?–356? B.C., Greek philosopher, who founded a school at Cyrene.

aristo-, a word element meaning "best," "superior," as in *aristocratic.* [t. Gk., comb. form of *áristos* best]

ar·is·toc·ra·cy (är′ə stŏk′rə sǐ), *n.*, *pl.* **-cies. 1.** a government or a state characterized by the rule of a nobility, elite, or privileged upper class. **2.** a body of persons holding exceptional prescriptive rank or privileges; a class of hereditary nobility. **3.** government by the best men in the state. **4.** a governing body composed of the best men in the state. **5.** any class ranking as socially or otherwise superior. [t. L: m.s. *aristocratia,* t. Gk.: m. *aristokratía* rule of the best. See ARISTO-, -CRACY]

a·ris·to·crat (ə rǐs′tə krăt′, är′Ystə-), *n.* **1.** one who has the tastes, manners, etc., of the members of a superior group or class. **2.** a member of an aristocracy. **3.** an advocate of an aristocratic form of government.

a·ris·to·crat·ic (ə rǐs′tə krăt′Yk, är′Ys-), *adj.* **1.** befitting an aristocrat; stylish, grand, or exclusive. **2.** belonging to or favoring the aristocracy. **3.** of or pertaining to government by an aristocracy. Also, **a·ris′to·crat′i·cal.** —**a·ris′to·crat′i·cal·ly,** *adv.*

a·ris·to·lo·chi·a·ceous (ə rǐs′tə lō′kǐ ā′shəs), *adj. Bot.* belonging to the *Aristolochiaceae,* a family of plants including birthwort, Dutchman's-pipe, etc. [f. s. L *Aristolochia* birthwort genus (t. Gk.: m. s. *aristolócheia*) + -ACEOUS]

Ar·is·toph·a·nes (är′ə stŏf′ə nēz′), *n.* 448?–385? B.C., Athenian poet and writer of comedy.

Ar·is·to·te·lian (är′Ys tə tēl′yən, -tē′lǐ ən), *adj.* **1.** of or pertaining to Aristotle or to his doctrines. —*n.* **2.** a follower of Aristotle. **3.** one who thinks in particulars and scientific deductions as distinct from the metaphysical speculation of Platonism. —**Ar′is·to·te′lian·ism,** *n.*

Aristotelian logic, 1. the logic of Aristotle, esp. in the modified form taught in the Middle Ages. **2.** formal logic, dealing with the logical form, rather than the content, of propositions, and based on the four propositional forms: all S is P; no S is P; some S is P; some S is not P.

Ar·is·tot·le (är′ə stŏt′əl), *n.* 384–322 B.C., Greek philosopher: pupil of Plato; tutor of Alexander the Great.

a·ris·to·type (ə rǐs′tə tīp′), *n.* **1.** a process of photographic printing in which paper coated with silver chloride in gelatin is used. **2.** a print made by this process.

arith., 1. arithmetic. 2. arithmetical.

a·rith·me·tic (n. ə·rĭth′mə·tĭk; adj. är′ĭth·mĕt′ĭk), n. 1. the art of computation with figures (the most elementary branch of mathematics). 2. Also, **theoretical arithmetic.** the theory of numbers; the study of the divisibility of whole numbers, the remainders after division, etc. 3. a book on this subject. —adj. 4. Also, **ar·ith·met′i·cal.** of or pertaining to arithmetic. [t. L: s. arithmētica, t. Gk: m. arithmētikḗ, prop. fem. of arithmētikós of or for reckoning; r. ME arsmetik, t. OF: m. arismetique] —**ar′ith·met′i·cal·ly,** adv.

a·rith·me·ti·cian (ə·rĭth′mə·tĭsh′ən, är′ĭth-), n. an expert in arithmetic.

arithmetic mean, Math. the mean obtained by adding several quantities together and dividing the sum by the number of quantities. For example: the arithmetic mean of 1, 5, 2, 8 is 4.

arithmetic progression, a sequence in which each term is obtained by the addition of a constant number to the preceding term. For example: 1, 4, 7, 10, 13, and 6, 1, −4, −9, −14 are arithmetic progressions. Also, **arithmetic series.**

A·ri·us (ə·rī′əs, âr′ĭ-), n. died A.D. 336, Christian priest at Alexandria, who held that Christ the Son was not consubstantial with God the Father.

Ariz., Arizona.

Ar·i·zo·na (âr′ə·zō′nə), n. a State in the SW United States. 749,587 pop. (1950); 113,909 sq. mi. Cap.: Phoenix. Abbr.: Ariz. —**Ar′i·zo′nan, Ar·i·zo·ni·an** (âr′ə·zō′nĭ·ən), adj., n.

Ar·ju·na (är′jŏŏ·nə), n. Hindu Myth. the chief hero of the great epic of India, the Mahabharata.

ark (ärk), n. 1. the vessel built by Noah for safety during the Flood. Gen. 6–9. 2. Also, **ark of the covenant.** a chest or box of great sanctity representing the presence of the Deity, borne by the Israelites in their desert wandering (Num. 10:35), the most sacred object of the tabernacle and of the temple in Jerusalem, where it was kept in the holy of holies. 3. Now Dial. a chest; box. [ME; OE arc, earc, t. L: m. s. arca a chest, coffer]

Ark., Arkansas.

Ar·kan·sas (är′kən·sô′; also for 2 är·kăn′zəs), n. 1. a State in the S central United States. 1,909,511 pop. (1950); 53,103 sq. mi. Cap.: Little Rock. Abbr.: Ark. 2. a river flowing from the Rocky Mountains in central Colorado into the Mississippi in SE Arkansas. 1450 mi. —**Ar·kan·san** (är·kăn′zən), n.

Ar·khan·gelsk (är·hän′gĕlsk), n. Russian name of Archangel.

Ark·wright (ärk′rīt), n. **Sir Richard,** 1732–92, British inventor of the spinning jenny.

Arl·berg (ärl′bĕrĸн), n. 1. a mountain pass in W Austria. ab. 5900 ft. high. 2. a tunnel beneath this pass.

arles (ärlz), n. pl. or sing. Scot. and N. Eng. money paid in advance as a pledge. [ME erles, appar. through OF, der. L arrha earnest money]

Arles (ärlz; Fr. ärl), n. a city in SE France, on the Rhône river: Roman ruins. 35,017 (1946).

Ar·ling·ton (är′lĭng·tən), n. 1. a county in NE Virginia, opposite Washington, D.C.: site of a national cemetery; Tomb of the Unknown Soldier. 135,449 (1950). 2. a town in E Massachusetts. 44,353 (1950).

arm¹ (ärm), n. 1. the upper limb of the human body from the shoulder to the hand. 2. this limb, exclusive of the hand. 3. the fore limb of any vertebrate. 4. some part of an organism like or likened to an arm. 5. any armlike part, as of a lever or of the yard (**yardarm**) of a ship. 6. a projecting support for the forearm at the side of a chair, sofa, etc. 7. an inlet or cove: an arm of the sea. 8. power; might; strength; authority: the arm of the government. 9. **at arm's length,** at a distance, yet almost in reach. 10. **with open arms,** cordially. [OE arm, earm, c. G arm, L armus shoulder, Gk. harmós joint] —**arm′less,** adj. —**arm′like′,** adj.

arm² (ärm), n. 1. (usually pl.) an offensive or defensive implement for use in war; a weapon. 2. Mil. a combat branch of the military service, as the infantry, cavalry, field artillery, air corps, etc. [rarely used sing. of ARMS] —v.i. 3. to enter into a state of hostility or of readiness for war. —v.t. 4. to equip with arms. 5. to activate (a fuze) so that it will explode the charge at the time desired. 6. to cover or provide with whatever will add strength, force, or security. 7. to fit or prepare (a thing) for any specific purpose or effective use. [ME arme(n), t. F: m. armer, g. L armāre]

Ar·ma·da (är·mä′də, -mā′-), n. 1. Also, the **Spanish or Invincible Armada,** a fleet sent by Spain against England in 1588, but shattered and dispersed by storms. 2. (l.c.) any fleet of warships. [t. Sp., g. L armāta armed forces (prop. pp. neut. pl. of armāre ARM², v.). See ARMY]

ar·ma·dil·lo (är′mə·dĭl′ō), n., pl. **-los.** any of a great variety of burrowing mammals, having a jointed, protective covering of bony plates. They constitute a suborder, Cingulata, of the edentates, distributed in many species throughout South America and north to Texas, and widely used for food. They are omnivo-

Texas armadillo, Dasypus novemcinctus
(2½ ft. long)

rous and mostly nocturnal. The **Texas armadillo,** Dasypus novemcinctus, is unique for always producing quadruplets of identical sex. [t. Sp., dim. of armado armed, g. L armātus, pp.]

Ar·ma·ged·don (är′mə·gĕd′ən), n. 1. Bible. the place where the final battle will be fought between the forces of good and evil (probably named in reference to Megiddo). Rev. 16:16. 2. any great crucial armed conflict.

Ar·magh (är·mä′), n. a county in Northern Ireland. 111,100 pop. (est. 1946); 489 sq. mi. Co. seat: Armagh.

ar·ma·ment (är′mə·mənt), n. 1. the weapons with which a military unit, esp. a combat airplane, armored vehicle, or warship, is equipped. 2. a land, sea, or air force equipped for war. 3. the process of equipping or arming for war. [t. L: s. armāmenta, pl., implements, equipment, ship's tackle]

ar·ma·ture (är′mə·chər), n. 1. armor. 2. Biol. the protective covering of an animal or plant, or any part serving for defense or offense. 3. Elect. **a.** the iron or steel applied across the poles of a permanent magnet to close it, or to the poles of an electromagnet to communicate mechanical force. See illus. under **electromagnet.** **b.** the part of an electrical machine which includes the main current-carrying winding (distinguished from the field). **c.** a pivoted part of an electrical device, as a buzzer or relay, activated by a magnetic field. 4. Sculpture. a framework built as a support for clay figures during construction. [t. L: m.s. armātūra armor]

arm·chair (ärm′châr′), n. a chair with arms to support the forearms or elbows.

armed (ärmd), adj. 1. bearing arms. 2. supported or maintained by arms: armed peace.

armed forces, all of the principal naval or military forces, including the army, navy, marines, air forces, coast guard, etc. Also, **armed services.**

Ar·me·ni·a (är·mē′nĭ·ə, -mēn′yə), n. 1. an ancient country in W Asia: now a region in the SW Soviet Union, E Turkey, and NW Iran. 2. Official name, **Armenian Soviet Socialist Republic.** a constituent republic of the Soviet Union, in S Caucasia. 1,281,599 pop. (1939); ab. 11,500 sq. mi. Cap.: Erivan.

Armenia (def 2)

Ar·me·ni·an (är·mē′nĭ·ən, -mēn′yən), adj. 1. pertaining to Armenia or to its inhabitants. —n. 2. a native of Armenia. 3. the language of the Armenians, an Indo-European language.

Ar·men·tières (är·män·tyĕr′), n. a city in extreme N France: battles, 1914, 1918. 22,667 (1946).

ar·met (är′mĭt), n. Armor. a helmet with movable front plates to cover the face. [t. F, dim. of arme ARM²]

arm·ful (ärm′fŏŏl′), n., pl. **-fuls.** as much as the arm, or both arms, can hold.

arm·hole (ärm′hōl′), n. a hole in a garment for the arm.

ar·mi·ger (är′mə·jər), n. 1. one entitled to armorial bearings. 2. an armorbearer to a knight; a squire. [t. ML: squire, L armor bearer]

ar·mil·lar·y (är′mə·lĕr′ĭ, är·mĭl′ə·rĭ), adj. consisting of hoops or rings. [f. s. L armilla armlet, ring + -ARY¹]

armillary sphere, Astron. an arrangement of rings, all circles of a single sphere, showing the relative positions of the principal circles of the celestial sphere.

arm·ing (är′mĭng), n. Naut. a piece of tallow placed in a cavity at the lower end of a sounding lead to bring up a sample of the sand, mud, etc., of the sea bottom.

Ar·min·i·an (är·mĭn′ĭ·ən), adj. 1. of or pertaining to Jacobus Arminius or his doctrines. —n. 2. an adherent of the Arminian doctrines. —**Ar·min′i·an·ism,** n.

Ar·min·i·us (är·mĭn′ĭ·əs), n. 1. (Hermann) 17? B.C.–A.D. 21, Germanic hero: defeated Roman army, A.D. 9. 2. **Jacobus** (jə·kō′bəs), (Jacob Harmensen) 1560–1609, Dutch Protestant theologian, who modified certain Calvinistic doctrines, esp. that of predestination.

ar·mip·o·tent (är·mĭp′ə·tənt), adj. mighty in arms or war. [ME, t. L: s. armipotens powerful in arms]

ar·mi·stice (är′mə·stĭs), n. a temporary suspension of hostilities by agreement of the parties, as to discuss peace; a truce. [t. NL: m. s. armistitium, f. L: armi- (comb. form of arma arms) + -stitium (der. sistere stop)]

Armistice Day, November 11, the anniversary of the cessation of hostilities of World War I in 1918.

arm·let (ärm′lĭt), n. 1. Chiefly Brit. an ornamental band worn on the arm. 2. a little arm: an armlet of the sea.

ar·moire (är·mwär′), n. a large wardrobe or movable cupboard, with doors and shelves. [t. F. See AMBRY]

ar·mor (är′mər), n. 1. defensive equipment; any covering worn as a protection against offensive weapons. 2. a metallic sheathing or protective covering, esp. metal plates,

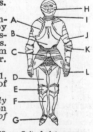

Suit of plate armor,
15th century
A. Palette; B. Breastplate; C. Tasset;
D. Cuisse; E. Kneepiece;
F. Jambeau; G. Solleret;
H. Helmet; I. Gorget;
J. Brassard; K. Elbow
piece; L. Gauntlet

used on warships, armored vehicles, airplanes, and fortifications. **3.** any protective covering, as the scales of a fish. **4.** that which serves as a protection or safeguard. **5.** the outer wrapping of metal, usually fine, braided steel wires, on a cable, primarily for the purpose of mechanical protection. —*v.t.* **6.** to cover with armor or armor plate. Also, *esp. Brit.,* **armour.** [ME *armure,* t. OF: m. *armeüre,* g. L *armātūra*]

armor., arms and armor.

ar·mor·bear·er (är′mər bâr′ər), *n.* a retainer bearing the armor or arms of a warrior.

ar·mored (är′mərd), *adj.* **1.** protected by armor or armor plate. **2.** consisting of troops using armored vehicles: *armored engineers.* Also, *esp. Brit.,* **armoured.**

armored car, a military combat vehicle with wheels, light armor, and, usually, machine guns.

armored forces, military forces composed of tank units and armored infantry, artillery, and other supporting troops. Also, *Brit.,* **armoured troops.**

ar·mor·er (är′mər ər), *n.* **1.** a maker or repairer of armor. **2.** a manufacturer of arms. **3.** an enlisted man in charge of the upkeep of small arms, machine guns, bicycles, etc. Also, *esp. Brit.,* **ar′mour·er.**

ar·mo·ri·al (är mōr′ĭ əl), *adj.* **1.** belonging to heraldry or to heraldic bearing. —*n.* **2.** a book containing heraldic bearings and devices.

armorial bearings, a coat of arms.

Ar·mor·ic (är mōr′ĭk, -mŏr′-), *adj.* **1.** pertaining to Armorica. —*n.* **2.** a native of Armorica. **3.** the Breton language. Also, **Ar·mor′i·can.**

Ar·mor·i·ca (är mōr′ə kə. -mŏr′-), *n.* an ancient region in NW France, corresponding generally to Brittany.

armor plate, a plate or plating of specially hardened steel used to cover warships, tanks, aircraft, fortifications, etc., to protect them from enemy fire. —**ar′mor-plat′ed,** *adj.* —**armor plating.**

ar·mor·y (är′mər ĭ), *n., pl.* **-mories. 1.** a storage place for weapons and other war equipment. **2.** *U.S. Army.* a building which is the headquarters and drill center of a National Guard unit. **3.** *U.S.* a place where arms and armor are made; an armorer's shop; an arsenal. **4.** (formerly) arms or armor collectively. **5.** *Archaic.* heraldic bearings or arms. **6.** the art of blazoning arms. **7.** heraldry. Also, *esp. Brit.,* **ar′mour·y.** [ME *armurie.* See ARMOR, -Y³]

ar·mour (är′mər), *n., v.t.* Chiefly Brit. armor.

arm·pit (ärm′pĭt′), *n.* Anat. the hollow under the arm at the shoulder; the axilla.

arms (ärmz), *n.pl.* **1.** arm² (def. 1). **2.** Mil. **small arms,** all weapons of small caliber operated or carried by hand, as rifles, pistols, submachine guns, and machine guns. **3.** heraldic bearings. [ME *armes,* t. OF, g. L *arma*]

ar·mure (är′myʊr), *n.* a woolen or silk fabric woven with ridges in a small pattern. [t. F. See ARMOR]

ar·my (är′mĭ), *n., pl.* **-mies. 1.** (*cap. or l.c.*) the military forces of a nation, exclusive of the naval and, in some countries, the air forces. **2.** (in large military land forces) the second largest unit, consisting of two or more corps. **3.** a large body of men trained and armed for war. **4.** any body of persons organized for any cause: *the Salvation Army.* **5.** a host; a great multitude. [ME *armee,* t. OF, g. L *armāta* armed forces]

Army Air Forces, *U.S. Army.* a unit comprising almost all aviation, with its personnel, equipment, etc. It became part of the **Air Force** on July 26, 1947.

army ant, any of the driver ants of the American tropics, genus *Eciton.*

army of occupation, an army established in conquered territory to maintain order and to ensure the carrying out of peace or armistice terms.

Army of the United States, the temporary military organization of the U.S. in time of war or emergency, including the Regular Army, the National Guard, selective service personnel, etc. Cf. **United States Army.**

army worm, 1. a kind of caterpillar, the larva of a noctuid moth, *Leucania unipuncta,* which often travels in hosts over a region, destroying grass, grain, etc. **2.** some similarly destructive larva.

Arn·hem (ärn′hĕm), *n.* a city in central Netherlands, on the Rhine: battle, 1944. 91,828 (est. 1946).

ar·ni·ca (är′nə kə), *n.* **1.** any plant of the asteraceous genus *Arnica.* esp. *A. montana,* of Europe. **2.** a tincture of the flowers of *A. montana* and other species of *Arnica* much used as an external application in sprains and bruises. [t. NL; orig. unknown]

Ar·no (är′nō), *n.* a river flowing from the Apennines in central Italy W to the Ligurian Sea near Pisa. ab. 140 mi.

Ar·nold (är′nəld), *n.* **1.** Benedict, 1741–1801, American general in the Revolutionary War who turned traitor. **2.** Sir Edwin, 1832–1904, British poet and journalist. **3.** Henry H., ("*Hap*") 1886–1950, U. S. general. **4.** Matthew, 1822–88, British essayist, poet, and literary critic. **5.** Thomas, 1795–1842, British clergyman: headmaster of Rugby (father of Matthew). **6.** Thurman Wesley, born 1891, U. S. lawyer and writer.

Ar·nold von Win·kel·ried (är′nōlt fən vĭng′kəl rēt′), died 1386?, Swiss hero in the battle of Sempach (1386), fought against the Austrians.

ar·oid (ăr′oid, âr′-), *Bot.* —*adj.* **1.** araceous. —*n.* **2.** any araceous plant. [f. AR(UM) + -OID]

a·roint thee! (ə roint′), *Archaic.* avaunt! begone!

a·ro·ma (ə rō′mə), *n.* **1.** an odor arising from spices, plants, etc., esp. an agreeable odor; fragrance. **2.** (of wines and spirits) the odor or bouquet. **3.** a characteristic, subtle quality. [t. L, t. Gk.: spice, sweet herb] —**Syn. 1.** See **perfume.**

ar·o·mat·ic (ăr′ə măt′ĭk), *adj.* **1.** having an aroma; fragrant; sweet-scented; spicy. **2.** *Chem.* of or pertaining to aromatic compounds. —*n.* **3.** a plant, drug, or medicine which yields a fragrant smell, as sage, certain spices and oils, etc. —**ar′o·mat′i·cal·ly,** *adv.*

aromatic compounds, *Chem.* a class of organic compounds including benzene, naphthalene, anthracene, and their derivatives, which contain an unsaturated ring of carbon atoms. Many have an agreeable odor.

a·ro·ma·ti·za·tion (ə rō′mə tə zā′shən), *n. Chem.* the catalytic conversion of aliphatic hydrocarbons to aromatic hydrocarbons.

a·ro·ma·tize (ə rō′mə tīz′), *v.t.,* **-tized, -tizing.** to make aromatic or fragrant.

A·roos·took (ə rōōs′tʊʊk, -tĭk), *n.* a river flowing from N Maine NE to the St. John river. ab. 140 mi.

a·rose (ə rōz′), *v.* pt. of **arise.**

a·round (ə round′), *adv.* **1.** in a circle or sphere; round about; on every side. **2.** *U.S.* here and there; about: *to travel around.* **3.** *U.S. Colloq.* somewhere about or near: *to wait around for a person.* —*prep.* **4.** about; on all sides; encircling; encompassing: *a halo around his head.* **5.** *U.S. Colloq.* here and there in: *to roam around the country.* **6.** *U.S. Colloq.* somewhere in or near: *to stay around the house.* **7.** *U.S. Colloq.* approximately; near in time, amount, etc.: *around ten o'clock, around a million.*

a·rouse (ə rouz′), *v.,* **aroused, arousing.** —*v.t.* **1.** to excite into action; stir or put in motion or exertion; awaken: *arouse attention, arouse one from sleep.* —*v.i.* **2.** to become aroused. [der. ROUSE¹, modeled on ARISE] —**a·rous·al** (ə rou′zəl), *n.* —**a·rous′er,** *n.* —**Syn. 1.** animate, inspirit; incite; stimulate.

ar·peg·gi·o (är pĕj′ĭ ō′, -pĕj′ō), *n., pl.* **-gios.** Music. **1.** the sounding of the notes of a chord in rapid succession instead of simultaneously. **2.** a chord thus sounded. [t. It., der. *arpeggiare* play on the harp]

Written   Played
Arpeggio

ar·pent (är′pənt; *Fr.* är päṅ′), *n.* an old French unit of length equal to about 63¼ yards. It is still used in the province of Quebec and in parts of Louisiana.

ar·que·bus (är′kwə bəs), *n.* harquebus.

arr., 1. arranged. **2.** arrival. **3.** arrive; arrived.

ar·rack (ăr′ək), *n.* any of various spirituous liquors distilled in the East Indies and elsewhere in the East from toddy (def. 2), molasses, or other materials. [ult. t. Ar: m. *'araq* (fermented) juice]

ar·raign (ə rān′), *v.t.* **1.** *Law.* to call or bring before a court to answer to a charge or accusation. **2.** to accuse or charge in general. —*n.* **3.** arraignment. [ME *araine(n),* t. AF: m. *arainer,* uit. g. L *arratiōnāre* call to account] —**ar·raign′er,** *n.*

ar·raign·ment (ə rān′mənt), *n.* **1.** *Law.* act of arraigning. **2.** a calling in question for faults; accusation.

Ar·ran (ăr′ən), *n.* an island in SW Scotland, in the Firth of Clyde. 4500 pop. (1931); 166 sq. mi.

ar·range (ə rānj′), *v.,* **-ranged, -ranging.** —*v.t.* **1.** to place in proper, desired, or convenient order; adjust properly: *to arrange books on a shelf.* **2.** to come to an agreement or understanding regarding: *to arrange a bargain.* **3.** to prepare or plan: *to arrange the details of a meeting.* **4.** *Music.* to adapt (a composition) for a particular mode of rendering (by voices or instruments). —*v.i.* **5.** to make a settlement; come to an agreement. **6.** to make preparations. [ME *araynge(n),* t. OF: m.s. *arangier,* f. a- A-⁵ + *rangier* RANGE, v.] —**ar·rang′er,** *n.* —**Syn. 1.** array; group, sort. **2.** settle, determine.

ar·range·ment (ə rānj′mənt), *n.* **1.** act of arranging. **2.** state of being arranged. **3.** the manner in which things are arranged. **4.** a final settlement; adjustment by agreement. **5.** (*usually pl.*) preparatory measure; previous plan; preparation. **6.** something arranged in a particular way: *a floral arrangement.* **7.** *Music.* **a.** the adaptation of a composition to voices or instruments, or to a new purpose. **b.** a piece so adapted. [t. F]

ar·rant (ăr′ənt), *adj.* **1.** downright; thorough: *an arrant fool.* **2.** notorious. **3.** *Obs.* wandering. [var. of ERRANT] —**ar′rant·ly,** *adv.*

ar·ras (ăr′əs), *n.* **1.** rich tapestry. **2.** a tapestry weave. **3.** a wall hanging. [named after ARRAS]

Ar·ras (ăr′əs; *Fr.* ä räs′), *n.* a city in N France: battles in World War I. 33,345 (1946).

ar·ray (ə rā′), *v.t.* **1.** to place in proper or desired order, as troops for battle. **2.** to clothe with garments, esp. of an ornamental kind; deck. [ME *araye(n),* t. AF: m. *arayer,* var. of OF *areyer,* der. *arei,* n., array] —*n.* **3.** order, as of troops drawn up for battle. **4.** an impressive group of things on exhibition, as a window display. **5.** regular order or arrangement. **6.** attire; dress. [ME, t. AF: m. *arai,* var. of OF *arei,* f. *a* to + *rei* order, of Gmc. origin] —**Syn. 1.** arrange, range, marshal.

ar·ray·al (ə rā′əl), *n.* **1.** act of arraying; muster; array. **2.** whatever is arrayed.

ar·rear (ə rĭr′), *n.* **1.** state of being behind or behindhand. **2.** (*usually pl.*) that which is behind in payment; a debt which remains unpaid, though due. **3.** **in arrear** or **in arrears,** behind in payments. **4.** *Archaic.* the rear. [ME *arere,* t. OF, g. L *ad-* AD- + *retrō* backward]

ar·rear·age (ərĭr′ĭj), *n.* **1.** state or condition of being behind in payments due or in arrears. **2.** arrears; amount or amounts overdue. **3.** a thing or part kept in reserve. [ME *arerage*, t. OF. See ARREAR, -AGE]

ar·rest (ərĕst′), *v.t.* **1.** to seize (a person) by legal authority or warrant. **2.** to capture; seize. **3.** to catch and fix: *to arrest the attention.* **4.** to bring to a standstill; stop; check: *to arrest the current of a river.* **5.** *Med.* to stop the active growth of: *arrested cancer.* —*n.* **6.** taking a person into custody in connection with a legal proceeding. **7.** any seizure or taking by force. **8.** act of stopping. **9.** state of being stopped. **10.** *Mach.* any device for arresting motion in a mechanism. [ME *arest(e)*, t. OF: (m.) *areste* stoppage, der. *arester*, g. LL *adrestāre* (f. L: *ad-* AD- + *restāre* stop)] —**ar·rest′er**, *n.* —**ar·rest′ment**, *n.* —**Syn. 4.** See **stop. 6.** apprehension, imprisonment. **8.** stoppage, halt.

ar·rest·ing (ərĕs′tĭng), *adj.* catching the attention; striking: *an arresting painting.*

Ar·rhe·ni·us (ärrā′nēŏŏs), *n.* **Svante August** (svän′tĕou′gŏŏst), 1859-1927, Swedish physicist and chemist.

ar·rhyth·mi·a (ərĭth′mĭə), *n.* *Pathol.* any disturbance in the rhythm of the heart beat. Also, **arhythmia.** [t. Gk.: want of rhythm] —**ar·rhyth·mic** (ərĭth′-mĭk, ərĭth′-), *adj.*

ar·ride (ərīd′), *v.t.*, **-rided, -riding.** *Archaic.* to be agreeable or pleasing to. [t. L: m.s. *arrīdēre* smile at]

ar·ri·ère-ban (är′ĭ är′băn′; *Fr.* àryĕrbäɴ′), *n.* **1.** a group of vassals who owed military service, esp. to French kings. **2.** the message calling on this group for duty. [t. F, f. Gmc.: *hari, heri* army + *ban* proclamation]

ar·rière-pen·sée (àryĕrpäɴsĕ′), *n.* *French.* a mental reservation; hidden motive.

ar·ris (är′ĭs), *n.* *Archit.* **1.** a sharp ridge, as between adjoining channels of a Doric column. **2.** the line, edge, or hip in which the two straight or curved surfaces of a body, forming an exterior angle, meet. [t. F: m. *areste*, g. L *arista* ear of grain, bone of a fish]

ar·riv·al (ərī′vəl), *n.* **1.** act of arriving: *the time of arrival.* **2.** the reaching or attainment of any object or condition: *arrival at a decision.* **3.** the person or thing that arrives, or has arrived. —**Syn. 1.** advent, coming.

ar·rive (ərīv′), *v.*, **-rived, -riving.** —*v.i.* **1.** to come to a certain point in the course of travel; reach one's destination. **2.** to reach in any course or process; attain (fol. by *at*): *to arrive at a conclusion.* **3.** to come: *the time has arrived.* **4.** to attain a position of success in the world. **5.** *Obs.* to come to shore. —*v.t.* **6.** *Obs.* to reach; come to. **7.** *Obs.* to happen to. [ME *a(r)rive(n)*, t. OF: m. *a(r)river*, g. LL *arrīpāre* come to shore] —**Syn. 1.** ARRIVE, COME both mean to reach a stopping place. ARRIVE directs the attention to the final point of an activity or state: *the train arrived at noon.* COME rarely refers to the actual moment of arrival but refers instead to the progress toward it. —**Ant. 1.** depart.

ar·ro·ba (ärrô′bä), *n.* **1.** a Spanish and Portuguese unit of weight of varying value, in Mexico, etc., equal to 25.37 pounds avoirdupois, and in Brazil to 32.38 pounds avoirdupois. **2.** a unit of liquid measure of varying value, used in Spain, etc., and commonly equal (when used for wine) to 4.26 U.S. gallons. [t. Sp., t. Ar.: m. *al-rub‘* the quarter]

ar·ro·gance (är′əgəns), *n.* quality of being arrogant; offensive exhibition of assumed or real superiority; overbearing pride. Also, **ar′ro·gan·cy.** [ME, t. F, t. L: m.s. *arrogantia*] —**Syn.** haughtiness, insolence, disdain.

ar·ro·gant (är′əgənt), *adj.* **1.** making unwarrantable claims or pretensions to superior importance or rights; overbearingly assuming; insolently proud. **2.** characterized by or proceeding from arrogance: *arrogant claims.* [ME, t. L: s. *arrogans*, ppr., assuming] —**ar′ro·gant·ly,** *adv.* —**Syn. 1.** presumptuous, haughty, imperious, supercilious. See **proud.** —**Ant. 1.** meek. **2.** modest.

ar·ro·gate (är′əgāt′), *v.t.*, **-gated, -gating. 1.** to claim unwarrantably or presumptuously; assume or appropriate to oneself without right. **2.** to attribute or assign to another without just reason. [t. L: m. s. *arrogātus*, pp., assumed, asked of] —**ar′ro·ga′tion,** *n.*

ar·ron·disse·ment (àrôɴdēsmäɴ′), *n., pl.* **-ments** (-mäɴ′). *French.* **1.** the largest administrative division of a French department. Each arrondissement is divided into cantons. **2.** a borough of Paris.

ar·row (är′ō), *n.* **1.** a slender, straight, generally pointed, missile weapon made to be shot from a bow. The shaft is nearly always made of light wood, fitted with feathers at the nock end to help guide it. **2.** anything resembling an arrow in form. **3.** a figure used in maps, architectural drawings, etc., to indicate direction, as of winds, currents, rivers. **4.** (*cap.*) *Astron.* Sagitta. **5.** See **broad arrow.** [ME and OE *arwe*, c. Icel. *ör*] —**ar′row·less,** *adj.* —**ar′row·like′,** *adj.*

ar·row·head (är′ōhĕd′), *n.* **1.** the head of an arrow, usually wedge-shaped or barbed. **2.** any plant of the genus *Sagittaria*, usually aquatic, species of which have arrowheaded leaves. **3.** *Art.* the dart in an egg-and-dart ornament. See illus. under **egg-and-dart.**

ar·row·root (är′ōrōōt′, -rŏŏt′), *n.* **1.** a tropical American plant, *Maranta arundinacea*, or related species, whose rhizomes yield a nutritious starch. **2.** the starch itself. **3.** a similar starch from other plants, used in light puddings, cookies, etc.

ar·row·wood (är′ōwŏŏd′), *n.* any of several shrubs and small trees, as the wahoo and certain viburnums, with tough, straight shoots, once used for arrows.

ar·row·worm (är′ōwûrm′), *n.* a small transparent pelagic animal of elongate form with fins, comprising the class or phylum *Chaetognatha.*

ar·row·y (är′ō ĭ), *adj.* **1.** like an arrow in shape, speed, effect, etc.; swift or piercing. **2.** consisting of arrows.

ar·roy·o (əroi′ō), *n., pl.* **-os** (-ōz) (chiefly in southwest U.S. and parts of Spanish America) a small, steep-sided watercourse or gulch, usually dry except after heavy rains, and with a nearly flat floor and U-shaped cross section. [t. Sp., ult. g. L *arrūgia* shaft, pit]

ar·se·nal (är′sənəl), *n.* **1.** a repository or magazine of arms and military stores of all kinds for land or naval service. **2.** a building having that incidental purpose but used mainly for the training of troops. **3.** a public establishment where military equipment or munitions are manufactured. [t. It.: m. *arsenale* dock (d. Venetian *arzanà*), t. Ar.: m. *dar ṣinā′a* workshop]

ar·se·nate (är′sənāt′, -nĭt), *n.* *Chem.* salt of arsenic acid.

ar·se·nic (*n.* är′sənĭk, ärs′nĭk; *adj.* ärsĕn′ĭk), *n.* **1.** a grayish-white element having a metallic luster, volatilizing when heated, and forming poisonous compounds. *Symbol:* As; *at. wt.:* 74.91; *at. no.:* 33. **2.** arsenic trioxide, As_2O_3, which is used in medicine and the arts, and in poisons for vermin. **3.** a mineral, the native element, occurring in white or gray masses. —*adj.* **4.** of or containing arsenic, esp. in the pentavalent state (As^{+5}). [ME *arsenik*, t. L: m. s. *arsenicum*, t. Gk.: m. *arsenikón* orpiment]

arsenic acid, *Chem.* a water-soluble crystalline compound, H_3AsO_4, used in the manufacture of arsenates.

ar·sen·i·cal (ärsĕn′əkəl), *adj.* **1.** containing or relating to arsenic. —*n.* **2.** (*pl.*) a group of insecticides, drugs, etc., containing arsenic.

ar·se·nide (är′sənīd′, -nĭd), *n.* *Chem.* a compound containing two elements, of which arsenic is the negative one, as *silver arsenide*, AgₐAs.

ar·se·nite (är′sənīt′), *n.* *Chem.* **1.** a salt of any of the hypothetical arsenous acids. **2.** arsenic (def. 2).

ar·se·niu·rct (ärsō′nyorĕt′, sĕn′yə-), *n.* *Chem.* arsenide. [f. ARSENI(C) + -URET]

ar·se·niu·ret·ed (ärsē′nyərĕt′ĭd, -sĕn′yə-), *adj. Chem.* combined with arsenic so as to form an arsenide.

ar·se·no·py·rite (är′sənōpī′rĭt, ärsĕn′ə-), *n.* a common mineral, iron arsenic sulfide, FeAsS, occurring in silver-white to steel-gray crystals or masses, an important ore of arsenic. [f. *arseno-* (comb. form of ARSENIC) + PYRITE]

ar·se·nous (är′sənəs), *adj.* *Chem.* containing trivalent arsenic (As^{+3}), as *arsenous chloride*, $AsCl_3$.

ar·sine (ärsēn′, är′sĕn), *n.* *Chem.* **1.** arseniuretted hydrogen, AsH_3, a colorless, inflammable, highly poisonous gas, with a fetid garliclike odor, used in chemical warfare. **2.** any derivative of this compound, in which one or more hydrogen atoms are replaced by organic radicals. [f. ARS(ENIC) + -INE²]

ar·sis (är′sĭs), *n., pl.* **-ses** (-sēz). **1.** *Pros.* **a.** (originally) the unaccented syllable of a foot in verse. **b.** (in later use) the unstressed part of a rhythmical unit (opposed to *thesis*). **2.** *Music.* the anacrusis, or upbeat (opposed to *thesis*). [t. L, t. Gk.: a raising (appar. of hand or voice)]

ar·son (är′sən), *n.* *Law.* the malicious burning of a house or outbuilding belonging to another, or (as fixed by statute) the burning of any building (including one's own). [t. AF, g. LL *arsio* a burning]

ars·phen·a·mine (ärs′fĕn ə mēn′, -fĕn ăm′ĭn), *n.* *Pharm.* a yellow crystalline powder subject to rapid oxidation, $C_{12}H_{12}N_2O_2As_2.2HCl + 2H_2O$, used to treat diseases caused by spirochete organisms, esp. syphilis and trench mouth; first known as "606." [f. ARS(ENIC) + PHEN(YL) + AMINE]

ars po·e·ti·ca (ärz′ pōĕt′ə kə), *Latin.* the art of poetry or poetics.

art¹ (ärt), *n.* **1.** the production or expression of what is beautiful, appealing, or of more than ordinary significance. **2.** *Journ.* any illustration in a newspaper or magazine. **3.** a department of skilled performance: *industrial art.* **4.** (*pl.*) a branch of learning or university study. **5.** (*pl.*) liberal arts. **6.** skilled workmanship, execution, or agency (often opposed to *nature*). **7.** craft; cunning: *glib and oily art.* **8.** studied action; artificiality in behavior. **9.** (*usually pl.*) an artifice or artful device: *the innumerable arts and wiles of politics.* **10.** *Archaic.* learning or science. [ME, t. OF, g. s. L *ars* skill, art]

art² (ärt), *v. Archaic* or *Poetic.* 2nd pers. sing. pres. indic. of **be.** [ME; OE *eart*]

-art, var. of **-ard,** as in *braggart.*

art, *pl.* **arts. 1.** article. **2.** artificial.

ar·tal (är′täl), *n.* pl. of **rotl.**

Ar·ta·xerx·es (är′tə zûrk′sēz), died 359? B.C., king of Persia, 404?-359? B.C.

ar·te·fact (är′təfäkt′), *n.* artifact.

ar·tel (ärtĕl′; *Russ.* -tĕl′y), *n.* (in the Soviet Union) a peasants' or workers' coöperative enterprise. [Russ.]

Ar·te·mis (är′tə mĭs), *n.* *Gk. Myth.* a goddess, sister of Apollo, represented as a virgin huntress and associated with the moon: identified by the Romans with Diana. [t. L, t. Gk.]

ar·te·mis·i·a (är′tə mĭz′ĭ ə, -mĭsh′-), *n.* **1.** any of a very large genus of plants, *Artemisia*, of the family *Compositae*, abundant in dry regions, and mostly of the northern hemisphere. **2.** a North American species, A.

tridentata, the sagebrush of the western plains. [t. L, t. Gk.: herb like wormwood]

ar·te·ri·al (är tĭr´ĭ əl), *adj.* **1.** *Physiol.* pertaining to the blood in the arteries which has been charged with oxygen during its passage through the lungs, and, in the higher animals, is usually bright red. **2.** *Anat.* of, pertaining to, or resembling the arteries. **3.** having a main channel and many branches: *arterial drainage.*

ar·te·ri·al·ize (är tĭr´ĭ ə līz), *v.t.*, **-ized, -izing.** *Physiol.* to convert (venous blood) into arterial blood by the action of oxygen in lungs. —**ar·te´ri·al·i·za´tion,** *n.*

ar·te·ri·o·scle·ro·sis (är tĭr´ĭ ō skla rō´sĭs), *n. Pathol.* an arterial disease occurring esp. in the elderly, characterized by inelasticity and thickening of the vessel walls, with lessened blood flow. [t. NL, f. Gk.: *arterio-* (comb. form of *artērĭa* artery) + m. *sklērōsis* hardening] —**ar·te·ri·o·scle·rot·ic** (är tĭr´ĭ ō skla rŏt´ĭk), *adj.*

ar·ter·y (är´tər ĭ), *n., pl.* **-teries. 1.** *Anat.* a blood vessel which conveys blood from the heart to any part of the body. **2.** a main channel in any ramifying system of communication, or transportation, as in drainage or highways. [ME *arterie*, t. L: m. *artērĭa*, t. Gk.]

ar·te·sian well (är tē´zhən), a well whose shaft penetrates through an impervious layer into a water-bearing stratum from which the water rises under pressure. [t. F: m. *artēsien* pertaining to Ar-Tois]

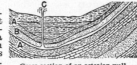

Cross section of an artesian well
A. Impermeable strata;
B. Permeable strata;
C, Artesian boring and well

Ar·te·veld (är´tə vĕlt´), *n.* **1.** Jacob van (yä´kŏp vän), 1290?-1345, statesman of Flanders. **2.** his son, **Philip van** (fē´lĭp vän), 1340?-82, popular leader of Flanders. Also, **Ar·te·vel·de** (är´tə vĕl´də).

art·ful (ärt´fəl), *adj.* **1.** crafty; cunning; tricky: *artful schemes.* **2.** skillful in adapting means to ends; ingenious. **3.** done with or characterized by art or skill. **4.** *Rare.* artificial. —**art´ful·ly,** *adv.* —**art´ful·ness,** *n.*

ar·thral·gia (är thrăl´jə), *n. Pathol.* pain in a joint. —**ar·thral´gic,** *adj.*

ar·thri·tis (är thrī´tĭs), *n. Pathol.* inflammation of a joint, as in gout or rheumatism. [t. L, t. Gk.: joint disease] —**ar·thrit·ic** (är thrĭt´ĭk), *adj.*

arthro-, *Anat.* a word element meaning "joint," as in *arthropathy.* Also, **arthr-.** [t. Gk., comb. form of * árthron*]

ar·thro·mere (är´thrə mĭr´), *n. Zool.* one of the segments or parts into which the body of articulate animals is divided.

ar·thro·pod (är´thrə pŏd´), *n.* any of the *Arthropoda*, the phylum of segmented invertebrates, having jointed legs, as the insects, arachnids, crustaceans, and myriapods. —**ar·throp·o·dous** (är thrŏp´ə dəs), *adj.*

ar·thro·spore (är´thrə spor´), *n.* **1.** *Bacteriol.* an isolated vegetative cell which has passed into a resting state, occurring in bacteria, and not regarded as a true spore. **2.** *Bot.* one of a number of spores of various low fungi and algae, united in the form of a string of beads, formed by fission.

Ar·thur (är´thər), *n.* **1.** legendary king in ancient Britain: leader of Knights of the Round Table. **2.** Chester Alan, 1830-86, 21st president of the U.S., 1881-85

Ar·thu·ri·an (är thōor´ĭ ən), *adj.* of or pertaining to Arthur, who, with his knights, formed the subject of a great body of medieval romantic literature.

ar·ti·choke (är´tə chōk´), *n.* **1.** a herbaceous, thistlelike plant, *Cynara Scolymus*, with an edible flowerhead. **2.** the edible portion, used as a table vegetable. **3.** Jerusalem artichoke. [t. d. It.: m. *articiocco*, t. Pr.: m. *arquichaut*, t. Ar.: m. *al-kharshūf*]

Artichoke,
Cynara Scolymus

ar·ti·cle (är´tə kəl), *n., v.,* **-cled, -cling.** —*n.* **1.** a literary composition on a specific topic, forming an independent part of a book or literary publication, esp. of a newspaper, magazine, review, or other periodical. **2.** an individual piece or thing of a class; an item or particular: *an article of food or dress.* **3.** a thing, indefinitely: *what is that article?* **4.** (in English and in some other languages) either of the two words *a* or *an* (**indefinite article**) and *the* (**definite article**), whose main function is to precede nouns of a certain class (**common nouns**), esp. when these are not preceded by other limiting modifiers. **5.** a clause, item, point, or particular in a contract, treaty, or other formal agreement; a condition or stipulation in a contract or bargain. **6.** a separate clause or provision of a statute. **7.** a matter or subject. **8.** *Archaic.* juncture or moment. —*v.t.* **9.** to set forth in articles; charge or accuse specifically. **10.** to bind by articles of covenant or stipulation: *to article an apprentice.* **11.** to bind by articles of agreement. —*v.i.* **12.** to make specific charges. **13.** *Law.* to object in writing to the credibility of depositions. **14.** *Obs.* to agree by articles; stipulate. [ME, t. F, t. L: m. *articulus*, dim. of *artus* joint]

Articles of Confederation, the first constitution of the thirteen American colonies, adopted in 1781 by the Continental Congress and lasting till 1788.

ar·tic·u·lar (är tĭk´yə lər), *adj.* of or pertaining to the joints. [t. L: s. *articulāris*]

ar·tic·u·late (*adj.,* n. är tĭk´yə lĭt; *v.* är tĭk´yə lāt), *adj., v.,* **-lated, -lating,** *n.* —*adj.* **1.** clear; distinct. **2.** uttered clearly in distinct syllables. **3.** capable of speech; not speechless. **4.** having joints or articulations; composed of segments. —*v.t.* **5.** to utter articulately. **6.** *Phonet.* to make the movements and adjustments of the speech organs necessary to utter (a speech sound). **7.** to unite by a joint or joints. —*v.i.* **8.** to utter distinct syllables or words: *to articulate distinctly.* **9.** *Phonet.* to articulate a speech sound. **10.** to form a joint. **11.** *Obs.* to make terms of agreement. —*n.* **12.** a segmented invertebrate. [t. L: m. s. *articulātus*, pp.] —**ar·tic´u·late·ly,** *adv.* —**ar·tic´u·late·ness,** *n.* —**ar·tic´u·la·tive,** *adj.* —**ar·tic´u·la´tor,** *n.*

ar·tic·u·la·tion (är tĭk´yə lā´shən), *n.* **1.** *Phonet.* **a.** act or process of articulating speech. **b.** the adjustments and movements of speech organs involved in pronouncing a particular sound, taken as a whole. **c.** any of these adjustments and movements. **d.** any speech sound, esp. a consonant. **2.** act of jointing. **3.** a jointed state or formation; a joint. **4.** *Bot.* **a.** a joint or place between two parts where separation may take place spontaneously, as at the point of attachment of a leaf. **b.** a node in a stem, or the space between two nodes. **5.** *Anat., Zool.* a joint, as the joining or juncture of bones or of the movable segments of an arthropod.

ar·ti·fact (är´tə făkt´), *n.* **1.** any object made by man with a view to subsequent use. **2.** *Biol.* a substance, structure, or the like, not naturally present in tissue but formed by reagents, death, etc. Also, **artefact.** [f. L: *arti-* (comb. form of *ars* art) + s. *factus*, pp., made]

ar·ti·fice (är´tə fĭs), *n.* **1.** a crafty device or expedient; a clever trick or stratagem. **2.** craft; trickery **3.** skillful or apt contrivance. **4.** *Obs.* workmanship. [t. F, t. L: m. s. *artificium*] —**Syn. 1.** ruse, subterfuge, wile. **2.** guile, deception, deceit. See **cunning.**

ar·tif·i·cer (är tĭf´ə sər), *n.* **1.** a skillful or artistic worker; craftsman. **2.** one who is skillful in devising ways of making things; an inventor. **3.** *Mil.* a soldier mechanic who does repairs.

ar·ti·fi·cial (är´tə fĭsh´əl), *adj.* **1.** made by human skill and labor (opposed to *natural*). **2.** made in imitation of or as a substitute; not genuine. **3.** feigned; fictitious; assumed. **4.** full of affectation; affected. **5.** *Biol.* based on arbitrary rather than organic criteria. **6.** *Obs.* artful; crafty. [ME t. L: s. *artificiālis*] —**ar´ti·fi´cial·ly,** *adv.* —**ar´ti·fi´cial·ness,** *n.*

artificial horizon, **1.** a level reflector, as a surface of mercury, used in determining the altitudes of stars, etc. **2.** the bubble in a sextant or octant for aerial use.

ar·ti·fi·ci·al·i·ty (är´tə fĭsh´ĭ ăl´ə tĭ), *n., pl.* **-ties. 1.** artificial quality. **2.** an artificial thing or trait.

artificial selection. See **selection** (def. 3)

ar·til·ler·y (är tĭl´ər ĭ), *n.* **1.** mounted guns, movable or stationary, light or heavy, as distinguished from small arms. **2.** the troops, or the branch of an army, concerned with the service of such guns. **3.** the science which treats of the use of such guns. [ME *artilrie*, t. OF: m. *artillerie* implements of war]

ar·til·ler·y·man (är tĭl´ər ĭ mən), *n., pl.* **-men.** one who serves a piece of artillery. Also, **ar·til´ler·ist.**

ar·ti·o·dac·tyl (är´tĭ ō dăk´tĭl), *adj.* **1.** *Zool.* having an even number of toes or digits on each foot. —*n.* **2.** any animal of the mammalian order *Artiodactyla*, which comprises the even-toed quadrupeds, as the swine, the hippopotami, and the ruminants: cattle, sheep, goats, deer, camels, etc., sometimes classified as a suborder of ungulates. [f. Gk.: *ártio(s)* even + m.s. *dáktylos* finger or toe] —**ar´ti·o·dac´ty·lous,** *adj.*

ar·ti·san (är´tə zən), *n.* **1.** one skilled in an industrial art. **2.** *Obs.* an artist. [t. F, t. It.: m. *artigiano*, der. *arte* guild] —**Syn. 1.** See **artist.**

art·ist (är´tĭst), *n.* **1.** a person who practices one of the fine arts, esp. a painter or a sculptor. **2.** a member of one of the histrionic professions, as an actor or singer. **3.** one who exhibits art in his work, or makes an art of his employment. **4.** a trickster. **5.** *Obs.* an artisan. [t. F: m. *artiste*, t. It.: m. *artista*, g. LL. See ART¹, -IST] —**Syn 1.** ARTIST, ARTISAN are persons having superior skill or ability, or capable of a superior kind o fworkmanship. An ARTIST is a person engaged in some type of fine art. An ARTISAN is engaged in a commercial or manual enterprise.

ar·tiste (är tēst´; *Fr.* ȧr tēst´), *n. French.* an artist, esp. an actor, singer, dancer, or other public performer.

ar·tis·tic (är tĭs´tĭk), *adj.* **1.** conformable to the standards of art; aesthetically excellent or admirable. **2.** of, like, or befitting an artist. Also, **ar·tis´ti·cal.** —**ar·tis´ti·cal·ly,** *adv.*

art·ist·ry (är´tĭs trĭ), *n., pl.* **-ries. 1.** artistic workmanship, effect, or quality. **2.** artistic pursuits.

art·less (ärt´lĭs), *adj.* **1.** free from deceit, cunning, or craftiness; ingenuous: *an artless mind.* **2.** natural; simple: *artless beauty.* **3.** lacking art, knowledge, or skill. —**art´less·ly,** *adv.* —**art´less·ness,** *n.*

Ar·tois (är twä´), *n.* a former province in N France: artesian wells. See map under **Agincourt.**

art·y (är´tĭ), *adj.* **artier, artiest.** *Colloq.* ostentatious in display of artistic interest. —**art´i·ness,** *n.*

A·ru·ba (ä rōō´bä), *n.* an island in the Dutch West Indies, off the NW coast of Venezuela. 39,300 pop. (est. 1944); 69 sq. mi.

A·ru Islands (ä′rōō), an island group in the Dutch East Indies, SW of New Guinea. 18,176 pop. (1930); 3306 sq. mi.

ar·um (âr′əm), n. 1. any plant of the genus *Arum*, having an inflorescence consisting of a spadix enclosed in a large spathe, as the cuckoopint. 2. any of various allied plants in cultivation, as the calla lily. [t. L, t. Gk.: m. *áron* the wake-robin] —**ar′um·like′**, adj.

Ar·un·del (âr′ən·del; *local* ärn′dəl), n. a town in S England, in Sussex: famous old castle; 3103 (1939).

a·run·di·na·ceous (ə·rŭn′də·nā′shəs), adj. *Bot.* pertaining to or like a reed or cane; reedlike; reedy. [t. L: m. *arundināceus*]

A.R.V., American Revised Version (of the Bible).

-ary¹, 1. an adjective suffix meaning pertaining to, attached chiefly to nouns (*honorary*) and to stems appearing in other words (*voluntary*). 2. a suffix forming nouns from other nouns or adjectives indicating location or repository (*dictionary*, *granary*, *apiary*), officers (*functionary*, *secretary*), or other relations (*adversary*). 3. a suffix forming collective numeral nouns, esp. in time units (*centenary*). [t. L: m. -*ārius*, neut. -*ārium*]

-ary², var. of **-ar¹,** as in *exemplary*, *military*.

Ar·y·an (âr′Yən, -yən, âr′-; är′yon), n. 1. *Ethnol.* a member or descendant of the prehistoric people who spoke Indo-European. 2. (in Nazi doctrine) a gentile of Indo-European stock. —adj. 3. of or pertaining to an Aryan or the Aryans. Also, **Arian.** [f. Skt. *Arya*, name by which the Sanskrit-speaking immigrants into India called themselves + -AN] —**Ar′y·an,** adj.

Ar·y·an·ize (âr′Yə·nīz′, -yə-, âr′-), v.t., -ized, -izing. (in Nazi doctrine) to remove all non-Aryan persons from (office, business, etc.).

ar·yl (âr′Yl), adj. *Chem.* of or pertaining to any of the organic radicals obtained from the aromatic hydrocarbons by removing a hydrogen atom, as phenyl (C_6H_5) from benzene (C_6H_6). [f. AR(OMATIC) + -YL]

ar·yl·a·mines (âr′Yl·ə·mēnz′, -ăm′Ynz), n. pl. *Chem.* a group of amines in which one or more of the hydrogen atoms of ammonia are replaced with aromatic radicals.

ar·y·te·noid (âr′ə·tē′noid, ə·rĭt′ə·noid′), *Anat.* —adj. 1. ladle- or cup-shaped (applied to two small cartilages at the top of the larynx, and to some of the muscles connected with them). —n. 2. an arytenoid cartilage. [t. Gk.: m. s. *arytainoeidēs* ladle-shaped] —**ar·y·te·noi·dal** (âr′ə·tə·noi′dəl, ə·rĭt′ə-), adj.

as¹ (ăz; *unstressed* əz), adv. 1. to such a degree or extent: *as good as gold.* 2. **as well as,** as much or as truly as; just as; as also: *good as well as beautiful.* 3. **as well,** equally; also; too: *beautiful, and good as well.* —conj. 4. the consequent in the correlations *as . . . as, same . . . as,* etc., noting degree, extent, manner, etc. (*as good as gold, in the same way as before*), or in the correlations *so as, such as,* noting purpose or result (fol. by infinitive): *to listen so as to hear.* 5. (without antecedent) in the degree, manner, etc., of or that: *to be good as gold, do as we do.* 6. when or while. 7. since; because. 8. for instance. 9. even or just (now chiefly in the phrase, *as yet*). 10. *Colloq.* (in independent clauses) that: *I don't know as I do.* 11. *Eng. Dial.* than. 12. **as for, as to,** with respect to. 13. **as if, as though,** as it would be if. 14. **as it were,** in some sort; so to speak. —rel. pron. 15. that; who; which (esp. after *such* and *the same*): *I had the same troubles as you had.* —prep. 16. in the role, function, or status of: *to appear as Othello.* [ME, *as, als, alse, also,* OE *alswā, ealswā* all so, quite so, quite as. Cf. ALSO] —Syn. 7. See **because.**

as² (ăs), n., pl. **asses** (ăs′Yz). 1. a copper coin, the unit of the early monetary system of Rome, first nominally of the weight of a pound (12 ounces). About 80 B.C., having fallen to half an ounce, it ceased to be issued. 2. a unit of weight. 12 ounces; the pound, equal to 327.4 grams, or 5,053 grains. [t. L]

as-, var. of **ad-,** before *s,* as in *assert.*

As, *Chem.* arsenic.

AS., Anglo-Saxon. Also, **A.-S., A.S.**

as·a·fet·i·da (ăs′ə·fĕt′ə·də), n. a gum resin having an alliaceous odor, obtained from the roots of several species of the umbelliferous genus *Ferula* and used in medicine. Also, **as′a·foet′i·da, assafetida, assafoetida.** [t. ML: f. *asa* (t. Pers.: m. *azā* mastic) + L *fētida, foetida* fetid]

As·ben (ăs′bĕn′), n. Aïr (French West Africa).

as·bes·tos (ăs·bĕs′təs, ăz-), n. 1. *Mineral.* a. a fibrous amphibole, used for making incombustible or fireproof articles. b. the mineral chrysotile, similarly used. 2. a fabric woven from asbestos fibers, used for theater curtains, firemen's gloves, etc. 3. *Theat.* a fireproof curtain. Also, **as·bes′tus.** [t. L, t. Gk.: unquenchable; r. ME *asbeston,* t. OF] —**as·bes·tine** (ăs·bĕs′tĭn, ăz-), adj.

As·bur·y (ăz′bər̆Y), n. Francis, 1745–1816, first bishop of the Methodist Episcopal Church in America.

As·bur·y Park (ăz′bĕr′Y, -bər̆Y), a city in E New Jersey: seacoast resort. 17,094 (1950).

as·ca·rid (ăs′kə·rĭd), n. *Zool.* any of the *Ascaridae,* a family of nematode worms including the roundworm and pinworm. [t. NL: s. *ascaridae.* t. Gk.: m. *askarídes* (pl.) threadworms]

as·cend (ə·sĕnd′), v.i. 1. to climb or go upward; mount; rise. 2. to rise to a higher point or degree; proceed from an inferior to a superior degree or level. 3. to go toward the source or beginning; go back in time. 4. *Music.* to rise in pitch; pass from any tone to a higher one. —v.t. 5. to go or move upward upon or along;

climb; mount: *to ascend a hill or ladder.* [ME *ascende(n),* t. L: m. *ascendere* climb up] —**as·cend′a·ble, as·cend′i·ble,** adj. —Syn. 1. soar. 2. tower. 5. See **climb.**

as·cend·an·cy (ə·sĕn′dən·sĭ), n. state of being in the ascendant; governing or controlling influence; domination. Also, **as·cend′en·cy, as·cend′ance, as·cend′ence.**

as·cend·ant (ə·sĕn′dənt), n. 1. the position of dominance or controlling influence; superiority; predominance. 2. an ancestor (opposed to *descendant*). 3. *Astrol.* a. the point of the ecliptic or the sign of the zodiac rising above the horizon at the time of a birth, etc. b. the horoscope. —adj. 4. superior; predominant. 5. *Bot.* directed or curved upward. Also, **as·cend′ent.**

as·cend·er (ə·sĕn′dər), n. 1. one who or that which ascends. 2. *Print.* the part of such letters as *b, h, d,* and *f* that rises above the body of most lower-case letters.

as·cend·ing (ə·sĕn′dĭng), adj. *Bot.* growing or directed upward, esp. obliquely or in a curve from the base.

as·cen·sion (ə·sĕn′shən), n. 1. act of ascending; ascent. 2. (*often cap.*) *Eccles.* the bodily passing of Christ from earth to heaven. Acts 1:9. 3. (*cap.*) Ascension Day. [ME, t. L: s. *ascensio*]

As·cen·sion (ə·sĕn′shən), n. a British island in the S Atlantic. 159 (est. 1938); 34 sq. mi.

Ascension Day, the fortieth day after Easter, commemorating the ascension of Christ; Holy Thursday.

as·cen·sive (ə·sĕn′sĭv), adj. ascending; rising.

as·cent (ə·sĕnt′), n. 1. act of ascending; upward movement; rise. 2. a rising from a lower to a higher state, degree, or grade; advancement. 3. act of climbing or traveling up. 4. the way or means of ascending; upward slope. 5. a procedure toward a source or beginning. 6. gradient. [der. ASCEND, modeled on DESCENT]

as·cer·tain (ăs′ər·tān′), v.t. 1. to find out by trial, examination, or experiment, so as to know as certain; determine. 2. *Archaic.* to make certain, clear, or definitely known. [ME *acertain,* t. OF: s. *acertener* make certain, der. a- A-⁵ + *certain* CERTAIN] —**as′cer·tain′a·ble,** adj. —**as′cer·tain′a·ble·ness,** n. —**as′cer·tain′a·bly,** adv. —**as′cer·tain′ment,** n. —**Syn.** 1. See **learn.**

as·cet·ic (ə·sĕt′Yk), n. 1. a person who leads an abstemious life. 2. one who practices religious austerities. 3. (in the early Christian Church) a monk; hermit. —adj. 4. pertaining to asceticism or ascetics. 5. rigorously abstinent; austere. 6. unduly strict in religious exercises or mortifications. [t. Gk.: m. s. *askētikós* pertaining to a monk or hermit, der. *askētēs* monk, hermit (orig. athlete)]

as·cet·i·cal (ə·sĕt′ə·kəl), adj. pertaining to ascetic discipline or practice. —**as·cet′i·cal·ly,** adv.

as·cet·i·cism (ə·sĕt′ə·sĭz′əm), n. 1. the life or practice of an ascetic; the principles and historic course of the ascetics. 2. *Theol.* the theory or systematic exposition of the means (whether negative, as self-denial and abstinence, or positive, as the exercise of natural and Christian virtues) by which a complete conformity with the divine will may be attained. 3. rigorous self-discipline.

Asch (ăsh), n. Sholom (shō′ləm), born 1880, U.S. author, born in Poland.

As·cham (ăs′kəm), n. Roger, 1515–68, British scholar and writer: tutor of Queen Elizabeth.

as·ci (ăs′ī), n. pl. of **ascus.**

As·cid·i·a (ə·sĭd′Yə), n.pl. *Zool.* the Tunicata.

as·cid·i·an (ə·sĭd′Yən), *Zool.* —n. 1. a tunicate or sea squirt. See **Tunicata.** —adj. 2. of or belonging to the *Ascidia* or *Tunicata.* [f. ASCIDI(UM) + -AN]

as·cid·i·um (ə·sĭd′Yəm), n., pl. -cidia (-sĭd′Yə), *Bot.* a baglike or pitcherlike part. See illus. under **pitcher plant.** [t. NL, t. Gk.: m. *askídion,* dim. of *askós* bag]

as·ci·tes (ə·sī′tēz), n. *Pathol.* dropsy of the belly or peritoneum. [t. L, t. Gk.: m. *askītēs* (sc. *nósos* disease) a kind of dropsy, der. *askós* bag, belly] —**as·cit·ic** (ə·sĭt′Yk), adj.

as·cle·pi·a·da·ceous (ăs·klē′pĭ′ə·dā′shəs), adj. *Bot.* belonging to the *Asclepiadaceae,* or milkweed family of plants. [f. s. NL *Asclēpias* the milkweed genus (t. Gk.: m. *asklēpiás* kind of plant, named after *Asklēpiós* Asclepius) + -ACEOUS]

As·cle·pi·a·de·an (ăs·klē′pĭ′ə·dē′ən), *Class. Pros.* —adj. 1. noting or pertaining to a kind of verse consisting of a spondee, two (or three) choriambi, and an iamb. —n. 2. an Asclepiadean verse. [so called after the Greek poet Asclepiades]

As·cle·pi·us (ăs·klē′pĭ′əs), n. Gk. Myth. the god of medicine and a son of Apollo. Aesculapius is his Roman counterpart.

asco-, a word element meaning "bag." [t. Gk.: m. *asko-,* comb. form of *askós*]

as·co·carp (ăs′kə·kärp′), n. *Bot.* (in ascomycetous fungi) the fructification bearing the asci, a general term embracing apothecium, perithecium, etc.

as·co·go·ni·um (ăs′kə·gō′nĭ′əm), n., pl. **-nia** (-nĭ′ə). *Bot.* (in certain ascomycetous fungi) 1. the female sexual organ. 2. the portion of the archicarp which receives the antheridial nuclei and puts out the hyphae bearing the asci. —**as′co·go′ni·al,** adj.

as·co·my·cete (ăs′kə·mī·sēt′), n. *Bot.* a fungus of the class *Ascomycetes,* including the yeasts, mildews, truffles, etc., characterized by bearing the sexual spores in a sac.

as·co·my·ce·tous (ăs′kə·mī·sē′təs), adj. *Bot.* belonging or pertaining to the *Ascomycetes.*

a·scor·bic acid (ăskôr′bĭk), *Biochem.* the antiscorbutic vitamin, or Vitamin C, $C_6H_8O_6$, found in citrus fruits, tomatoes, paprika, and green vegetables, and also made industrially.

as·co·spore (ăs′kə spôr′), *n. Bot.* a spore formed within an ascus. —**as·cos·po·rous** (ăs kŏs′pə rəs, ăs′kə spôr′əs), **as·co·spor·ic** (ăs′kə spôr′ĭk, -spôr′-), *adj.*

Ascot

as·cot (ăs′kət), *n.* 1. a kind of scarf or necktie with broad ends, tied and arranged so that the ends are laid flat, one across the other. —*adj.* 2. (*cap.*) noting or pertaining to the celebrated race course at Ascot, in Berkshire, England, or the horse races held there.

as·cribe (ə skrīb′), *v.t.*, **-cribed, -crib·ing.** 1. to attribute, impute, or refer, as to a cause or source; assign: *the alphabet is usually ascribed to the Phoenicians.* 2. to consider or allege to belong. [t. L: m.s. *ascribere* add to a writing; r. ME *ascrive*(n), t. OF: m. *ascriv-*, s. *ascrire*] —**as·crib′a·ble**, *adj.* —Syn. 1. See **attribute.**

as·crip·tion (ə skrĭp′shən), *n.* 1. act of ascribing. 2. a statement ascribing something, specif., praise to the Deity. Also, **adscription.**

as·cus (ăs′kəs), *n., pl.* **asci** (ăs′ī). *Bot.* the sac in ascomycetes in which the sexual spores are formed. [t. NL, t. Gk.: m. *askós* bag, wineskin, bladder]

-ase, *Chem.* a noun suffix used in names of enzymes, as in *glucase, lactase, pectase.* [from (DIAST)ASE]

a·sep·sis (ə sĕp′sĭs, ā-), *n.* 1. absence of the microörganisms that produce sepsis or septic disease. 2. *Med.* methods or treatment, as by surgical operation, characterized by the use of instruments, dressings, etc., that are free from such microörganisms. [f. A-⁶ + SEPSIS]

a·sep·tic (ə sĕp′tĭk, ā-), *adj.* free from the living germs of disease, fermentation, or putrefaction. —**a·sep′ti·cal·ly**, *adv.*

a·sex·u·al (ā sĕk′shŏŏ əl), *adj. Biol.* 1. not sexual. 2. having no sex or no sexual organs. 3. independent of sexual processes. —**a·sex·u·al·i·ty** (ā sĕk′shŏŏ ăl′ə tĭ), *n.* —**a·sex′u·al·ly**, *adv.*

As·gard (ăs′gärd, äs′-), *n. Scand. Myth.* the heavenly abode of the gods, connected with the earth by a rainbow bridge (Bifrost). Also, **As·garth** (ăs′gärth), **As·gar·dhr** (äs′gär′thər). [t. Icel.: m.s. *āsgardhr*, f. *āss* god + *gardhr* yard]

ash¹ (ăsh), *n.* 1. the powdery residue of matter that remains after burning: *the ashes are still hot;* (used as sing. chiefly in scientific and commercial language as in *soda ash*). 2. *Geol.* finely pulverized lava thrown out by a volcano in eruption. See **ashes.** [ME; OE *asce, æsce*]

ash² (ăsh), *n.* 1. any tree of the oleaceous genus *Fraxinus,* esp. *F. excelsior* of Europe and Asia or *F. americana* of North America (**white ash**). 2. the wood, tough, straight-grained, and elastic, and valued as timber. [ME *asch*, OE *æsc*, c. G *esche*]

a·shamed (ə shāmd′), *adj.* 1. feeling shame; abashed by guilt. 2. unwilling or restrained through fear of shame. —**a·sham·ed·ly** (ə shā′mĭd lĭ), *adv.* —**a·sham′ed·ness**, *n.*
—Syn. 1. ASHAMED, HUMILIATED, MORTIFIED refer to a condition of discomfort and embarrassment. ASHAMED describes a feeling of guilt combined with regret: *ashamed of a fault.* HUMILIATED describes a feeling of being humbled or disgraced: *humiliated by public ridicule.* MORTIFIED describes a feeling of deep chagrin, embarrassment, and confusion: *mortified by her clumsiness.* —Ant. 1. proud.

A·shan·ti (ə shăn′tĭ), *n.* 1. a British colony in W Africa: a part of the Gold Coast; a former native kingdom. 579,000 pop. (1931); 24,379 sq. mi. *Cap.:* Kumasi. 2. a native or an inhabitant of Ashanti.

Ash·bur·ton (ăsh′bûr′tən, -bərtən), *n.* **Alexander Baring, 1st Baron,** 1774–1848, British statesman.

ash can, 1. a can or metal receptacle for ashes. 2. *Colloq.* a depth bomb.

ash·en¹ (ăsh′ən), *adj.* 1. ash-colored; gray. 2. consisting of ashes. [f. ASH¹ + -EN²]

ash·en² (ăsh′ən), *adj.* 1. pertaining to the ash tree or its timber. 2. made of wood from the ash tree. [f. ASH² + -EN²]

ash·es (ăsh′ĭz), *n. pl.* 1. ruins, as from destruction by burning: *the ashes of an ancient empire.* 2. the remains of the human body after cremation. 3. a dead body or corpse; mortal remains. See also **ash¹.**

Ashe·ville (ăsh′vĭl), *n.* a city in W North Carolina. 53,000 (1950).

ash gray, pale gray of ashes. Also, **ash color.**

Ash·ke·naz·im (ăsh′kə năz′ĭm), *n.pl.* German, Polish, and Russian Jews (as distinguished from the *Sephardim* or Spanish-Portuguese Jews). [Heb., pl. of *Ashk′naz,* a descendant of Japheth (Gen. 10:3); also, in medieval use, Germany] —**Ash′ke·naz′ic,** *adj.*

Ash·kha·bad (ăsh′kä bäd′), *n.* the capital of the Turkmen republic of the U.S.S.R., in the S central part. 126,580 (1939). Formerly, **Poltoratsk.**

Ash·land (ăsh′lənd), *n.* a city in NE Kentucky, on the Ohio river. 31,131 (1950).

ash·lar (ăsh′lər), *n. Bldg. Trades.* 1. a squared block of building stone, finished or rough. 2. such stones collectively. 3. masonry made of them. Also, **ash′ler.** [ME *asheler,* t. OF: m. *aisselier,* ult. der. L *axis* board]

a·shore (ə shôr′), *adv., adj. Naut.* 1. to shore; on or to the land. 2. on land (opposed to *aboard* or *afloat*).

Ash·ta·bu·la (ăsh′tə bū′lə), *n.* a city in NE Ohio: a port on Lake Erie. 23,696 (1950).

Ash·ton-un·der-Lyne (ăsh′tən ŭn′dər lĭn′), *n.* a city in W England, near Manchester. 47,050 (est. 1946).

Ash·to·reth (ăsh′tə rĕth′), *n.* an ancient Semitic goddess. See **Astarte.** [t. Heb.]

A·shur (ä′shŏŏr), *n.* Assur.

A·shur·ba·ni·pal (ä′shŏŏr bä′nĭ päl′), *n.* died 626? B.C., king of Assyria, 668?–626? B.C.

Ash Wednesday, the first day of Lent.

ash·y (ăsh′ĭ), *adj.,* **ashier, ashiest.** 1. ash-colored; pale as ashes. 2. consisting of ashes. 3. sprinkled or covered with ashes.

A·sia (ā′zhə, ā′shə), *n.* the largest continent, bounded by Europe and the Pacific, Arctic, and Indian Oceans. ab. 1,250,000,000 pop.; ab. 16,000,000 sq. mi.

Asia Minor, a peninsula in W Asia between the Black and the Mediterranean Seas, including most of Asiatic Turkey. See **Anatolia.**

A·si·at·ic (ā′zhĭ ăt′ĭk, ā′shĭ-), *adj.* 1. of, belonging to, or characteristic of Asia or its inhabitants. —*n.* 2. a native of Asia. Also, **A·sian** (ā′zhən, ā′shən).

Asiatic beetle, a scarabaeid beetle, *Anomala orientalis,* that destroys crops, introduced into the U.S. from the Orient.

Asiatic cholera, *Pathol.* an infectious epidemic disease, originally from Asia, which is often fatal. See **cholera** (def. 1b).

a·side (ə sīd′), *adv.* 1. on or to one side; to or at a short distance; apart; away from some position or direction: *to turn aside.* 2. away from one's thoughts or consideration: *to put one's cares aside.* 3. aside from, U.S. a. apart from; excluding. b. except for. —*n.* 4. *Theat.* a part of an actor's lines not supposed to be heard by others on the stage and intended only for the audience.

as·i·nine (ăs′ə nīn′), *adj.* stupid; obstinate. [t. L; m.s. *asininus,* der. *asinus* ass] —**as′i·nine′ly,** *adv.* —**as·i·nin·i·ty** (ăs′ə nĭn′ə tĭ), *n.*

A·sir (ä sēr′), *n.* a district in SW Saudi Arabia.

-asis, a word element forming names of diseases. [t. L, t. Gk.]

ask (ăsk, äsk), *v.t.* 1. to put a question to: *ask him.* 2. to seek to be informed about: *to ask the way;* (or, with a double object) *to ask him the way.* 3. to seek by words to obtain; request: *to ask advice or a favor.* 4. to solicit from; request of (with a personal object, and with or without *for* before the thing desired): *I ask you a great favor, ask him for advice.* 5. to demand; expect: *to ask a price for something.* 6. to call for; require: *the job asks time.* 7. to invite: *to ask guests.* 8. to publish (banns); publish the banns of (persons). —*v.i.* 9. to make inquiry; inquire: *she asked after or about him.* 10. to request or petition (fol. by *for*): *ask for bread.* [ME *asken,* OE *āscian,* also *ācsian,* c. OHG *eiscōn*] —**ask′er,** *n.* —Syn. 9. See **inquire.**

a·skance (ə skăns′), *adv.* 1. with suspicion, mistrust, or disapproval: *he looked askance at both business offers.* 2. with a side glance; sidewise. Also, **a·skant** (ə skănt′). [orig. uncert.]

a·skew (ə skū′), *adv.* 1. to one side; out of line; obliquely; awry. —*adj.* 2. oblique. [f. A-¹ + SKEW]

Ask·ja (äsk′yü), *n.* a volcano in Iceland. 3376 ft.

a·slant (ə slănt′, ə slänt′), *adv.* 1. at a slant; slantingly; obliquely. —*adj.* 2. slanting; oblique. —*prep.* 3. slantingly across; athwart. [ME *on slont, on slent* on slope. Cf. Sw. *slänt* slope]

a·sleep (ə slēp′), *adv.* 1. in or into a state of sleep. —*adj.* 2. sleeping. 3. dormant; inactive. 4. (of the foot, hand, leg, etc.) numb. 5. dead.

a·slope (ə slōp′), *adv.* 1. at a slope. —*adj.* 2. sloping.

As·ma·ra (äs mä′rə), *n.* the capital of Eritrea. ab. 85,000 pop.; ab. 7700 ft. high.

As·mo·de·us (ăz′mə dē′əs, äs′-), *n.* (in Jewish demonology) an evil spirit. [t. L: m. *Asmodaeus,* t. Gk.: m. *Asmodatos,* t. Heb.: m. *Ashmadai*]

As·nières (ä nyĕr′), *n.* a city in N France, near Paris. 72,273 (1946).

a·so·cial (ā sō′shəl), *adj.* 1. *Psychol., Sociol., etc.* avoiding or withdrawn from the environment; not social. 2. inconsiderate of the interests or needs of others; selfish; not scrupulous.

A·so·ka (ə sō′kə), *n.* died 226? B.C., Buddhist king in India, 264?–226? B.C.

A·so·san (ä′sō sän′), *n.* a volcano in SW Japan, on Kyushu island. 5630 ft. high; crater, 12 mi. across.

asp¹ (ăsp), *n.* 1. any of several poisonous snakes, esp. the Egyptian cobra, *Naje haje,* said to have caused Cleopatra's death, and much used by snake charmers. 2. the common European viper or adder. 3. *Archaeol.* the uraeus. [t. L: m. *aspis,* t. Gk.]

asp² (ăsp), *n., adj.* aspen. [OE *æspe* (see ASPEN)]

as·par·a·gus (ə spăr′ə gəs), *n.* 1. any plant of the liliaceous genus *Asparagus,* esp. *A. officinalis,* cultivated for its edible shoots. 2. the shoots, used as a table vegetable. [t. L, t. Gk.: m. *aspáragos*]

as·par·tic acid (ə spär′tĭk), *Biochem.* an amino acid, $HOOCCH(NH_2)CH_2COOH$, occurring in proteins.

As·pa·sia (ăs pā′shə, -zhə), *n.* fl. c445 B.C., Athenian courtesan, mistress of Pericles.

as·pect (ăs′pĕkt), n. **1.** appearance to the eye or mind; look: *the physical aspect of the country*. **2.** countenance; facial expression. **3.** a way in which a thing may be viewed or regarded: *both aspects of a question*. **4.** view commanded; exposure: *the house has a southern aspect*. **5.** the side or surface facing a given direction: *the dorsal aspect of a fish*. **6.** *Gram.* **a.** (in some languages) a category of verb inflection denoting various relations of the action or state of the verb to the passage of time, as duration, repetition, or completion. Examples: *he ate* (completed action); *he was eating* (incompleted action); *he ate and ate* (durative action). **b.** (in other languages) one of several contrasting constructions with similar meanings: *the durative aspect*. **c.** a set of such categories or constructions in a particular language. **d.** the meaning of, or typical of, such a category or construction. **e.** such categories or constructions, or their meanings collectively. **7.** *Astrol.* the relative position of planets as determining their influence. **8.** *Archaic.* a look; glance. [ME, t. L: s. *aspectus*, der. *aspicere* look at] —**Syn. 1.** See **appearance. 4.** prospect, outlook.

aspect ratio, *Aeron.* the ratio of the span of an airfoil to its mean chord.

as·pec·tu·al (ăs·pĕk′chŏŏ·əl), *adj. Gram.* **1.** of, pertaining to, or producing a particular aspect or aspects. **2.** used as or like a form inflected for a particular aspect.

as·pen (ăs′pən), n. **1.** any of various species of poplar, as *Populus tremula* of Europe, and *P. tremuloides* (**quaking aspen**) or *P. alba* (**white aspen**) in America, with leaves that tremble in the slightest breeze. —*adj.* **2.** of or pertaining to the aspen. Also, **asp.** [ME *aspen*, adj., f. *asp* white poplar (OE *æspe*) + -EN²]

as·per (ăs′pər), n. an old Egyptian and Turkish silver coin, now only a money of account equal to ¹/₁₂₀ of a piaster. [t. F: m. *aspre* (or t. It.: m. *aspero*), t. MGk.: m. *áspron*, t. L: m. *asper* (*nummus*) rough (coin)]

As·per·ges (ə·spûr′jēz), n. *Rom. Cath. Ch.* **1.** the rite of sprinkling the altar, clergy, and people with holy water before high mass on Sundays. **2.** the anthem beginning "Asperges," sung while the priest performs this rite. [L: thou shalt sprinkle]

as·per·gil·lo·sis (ăs·pûr·ji·lō′sĭs), n., pl. **-ses** (-sēz) *Vet. Sci.* disease in an animal caused by aspergilli.

as·per·gil·lum (ăs·pər·jĭl′əm), n., pl. **-gilla** (-jĭl′ə), **-gillums.** *Rom. Cath. Ch.* a brush or instrument for sprinkling holy water; aspersorium. [f. L: s. *aspergere* sprinkle + *-illum,* dim. suffix]

as·per·gil·lus (ăs·pər·jĭl′əs), n., pl. **-gilli** (-jĭl′ī). *Bot.* any fungus of the genus *Aspergillus,* family *Aspergillaceae,* whose sporophores are distinguished by a bristly, knoblike top. [see ASPERGILLUM]

as·per·i·ty (ăs·pĕr′ə·tĭ), n., pl. **-ties. 1.** roughness or sharpness of temper; severity; acrimony. **2.** hardship; difficulty; rigor. **3.** roughness of surface; unevenness. **4.** something rough or harsh. [t. L: m. s. *asperitas* roughness; r. ME *asprete*, t. OF]

as·perse (ə·spûrs′), v.t., **-persed, -persing. 1.** to assail with damaging charges or insinuations; cast reproach upon; slander. **2.** to sprinkle; bespatter. [t. L: m. s. *aspersus,* pp., sprinkled] —**as·pers′er,** n.

as·per·sion (ə·spûr′zhən, -shən), n. **1.** a damaging imputation; a derogatory criticism: *to cast aspersions on one's character.* **2.** act of aspersing: *to baptize by aspersion.* **3.** a shower or spray.

as·per·so·ri·um (ăs·pər·sōr′ĭ·əm), n., pl. **-soria** (-sōr′-ĭ·ə), **-soriums.** *Rom. Cath. Ch.* **1.** a vessel for holding holy water. See illus. under **stoup.** [t. ML. See ASPERSE, -ORIUM]

as·phalt (ăs′fôlt, -fălt), n. **1.** any of various dark-colored, solid bituminous substances, composed mostly of mixtures of hydrocarbons, occurring native in various parts of the earth. **2.** a similar artificial substance, the by-product of petroleum-cracking operations. **3.** a mixture of such a substance with crushed rock, etc., used for pavements, etc. —*v.t.* **4.** to cover or pave with asphalt. [t. LL: s. *asphaltum*, t. Gk.: m. *ásphalton*] —**as·phal′tic,** adj. —**as′phalt·like,** adj.

as·phal·tum (ăs·făl′təm), n. asphalt.

as·pho·del (ăs′fə·dĕl′), n. **1.** any of various liliaceous plants of the genera *Asphodelus* and *Asphodeline,* native in southern Europe, with white, pink, or yellow flowers. **2.** any of various other plants, as the daffodil. [t. L: s. *asphodelus,* t. Gk.: m. *asphódelos*]

as·phyx·i·a (ăs·fĭk′sĭ·ə), n. *Pathol.* the extreme condition caused by lack of oxygen and excess of carbon dioxide in the blood, caused by sufficient interference with respiration, as in choking. [t. Gk.: stopping of the pulse]

as·phyx·i·ant (ăs·fĭk′sĭ·ənt), *adj.* **1.** asphyxiating or tending to asphyxiate. —*n.* **2.** an asphyxiating agent or substance. **3.** an asphyxiating condition.

as·phyx·i·ate (ăs·fĭk′sĭ·āt′), v., **-ated, -ating.** —*v.t.* **1.** to produce asphyxia in. —*v.i.* **2.** to become asphyxiated. —**as·phyx′i·a′tion,** n. —**as·phyx′i·a′tor,** n.

as·pic¹ (ăs′pĭk), n. an appetizing jelly used as a garnish or as a base for meat, vegetables, etc. [t. F; orig. uncert.]

as·pic² (ăs′pĭk), n. *Poetic.* an asp¹. [t. F, g. L *aspis*]

as·pic³ (ăs′pĭk), n. the great lavender, *Lavandula latifolia,* yielding an oil used in perfumery. [t. F, t. ML: m. (*lavendula*) *spica* (lavender) spike]

as·pi·dis·tra (ăs·pə·dĭs′trə), n. a smooth, stemless Asiatic herb, *Aspidistra elatior,* family Liliaceae, bearing

large evergreen leaves often striped with white, widely grown as a house plant. [t. NL, der. Gk. *aspís* shield]

as·pir·ant (ə·spīr′ənt, ăs′pə·rənt), n. **1.** a person who aspires; one who seeks advancement, honors, a high position, etc. —*adj.* **2.** aspiring.

as·pi·rate (*v.* ăs′pə·rāt′; *n., adj.* ăs′pə·rĭt), v., **-rated, -rating,** n., adj. —*v.t.* **1.** *Phonet.* **a.** to release (a stop) in such a way that the breath escapes with audible friction, as in *title* where the first *t* is aspirated, the second is not. **b.** to begin (a word or syllable) with an *h* sound, as in *when* (pronounced *hwen*), *howl,* opposed to *wen, owl.* **2.** *Med.* to remove (fluids) from body cavities by use of an aspirator. **3.** to draw or remove by suction. —*n.* **4.** *Phonet.* a puff of unvoiced air before or after another sound, represented in many languages by *h,* and in Greek by the "sign of rough breathing" (‛). —*adj.* **5.** *Phonet.* aspirated. [t. L: m. s. *aspīrātus,* pp., breathed on]

as·pi·ra·tion (ăs·pə·rā′shən), n. **1.** act of aspiring; lofty or ambitious desire. **2.** act of aspirating; a breath. **3.** *Phonet.* **a.** the fricative unstopping or release of a stop consonant, as in *too,* where the breath escapes with audible friction as the *t* is brought to an end by the withdrawal of the tongue from contact with the gums. **b.** the use of an aspirate in pronunciation. **4.** *Med.* act of removing a fluid, as pus or serum, from a cavity of the body, by a hollow needle or trocar connected with a suction syringe.

as·pi·ra·tor (ăs′pə·rā′tər), n. **1.** an apparatus or device employing suction. **2.** a jet pump used in laboratories to produce a partial vacuum. **3.** *Med.* an instrument for removing fluids from the body by suction.

as·pir·a·to·ry (ə·spīr′ə·tōr′ĭ), *adj.* pertaining to or suited for aspiration.

as·pire (ə·spīr′), v.i., **-pired, -piring. 1.** to long, aim, or seek ambitiously; be eagerly desirous, esp. for something great or lofty (fol. by *to, after,* or an infinitive): *to aspire after immortality, to aspire to be a leader among men.* **2.** *Archaic or Poetic.* to rise up; soar; mount; tower. [ME *aspyre,* t. L: m. s. *aspīrāre* breathe on] —**as·pir′er,** n. —**as·pir′ing,** adj. —**Syn. 1.** See **ambitious.**

as·pi·rin (ăs′pə·rĭn), n. *Pharm.* a white crystalline derivative of salicylic acid, C₉H₈O₄, used to relieve the pain of headache, rheumatism, gout, neuralgia, etc. [f. A(CETYL) + SPIR(AEIC) acid (old name for salicylic acid) + -IN²; G coinage, orig. used as trademark]

a·squint (ə·skwĭnt′), *adv., adj.* with an oblique glance. [f. A-¹ + *squint* (of obscure orig.; cf. D *schuinte* slope]

As·quith (ăs′kwĭth), n. **Herbert Henry,** (*1st Earl of Oxford and Asquith*) 1852–1928, British statesman: prime minister of Great Britain, 1908–16.

ass (ăs), n. **1.** a long-eared, usually ash-colored mammal, *Equus asinus,* related to the horse, serving as a slow, patient, sure-footed beast of burden; the donkey. **2.** any allied wild species, as the Mongolian wild ass, *E. hemionus.* See illus. under **onager. 3.** a fool; a blockhead. [ME; OE *assa,* t. OWelsh: m. *asyn* ass, t. L: m. s. *asinus*]

as·sa·fet·i·da (ăs′ə·fĕt′ə·də), n. asafetida. Also, **as·sa·foet′i·da.**

as·sa·gai (ăs′ə·gī′), n., pl. **-gais,** v.t., **-gaied, -gaiing.** assegai.

as·sa·i¹ (äs·sä′ē), *adv. Music.* very: *allegro assai* (very quick). [It.]

as·sa·i² (ə·sä′ē), n. **1.** any of several slender Brazilian palms of the genus *Euterpe,* esp. *E. edulis,* a species bearing a purple fruit from which a beverage is made by infusion. **2.** the beverage itself. [t. Pg.: m. *assahy,* t. Brazilian]

Ass, *Equus asinus* (Ab. 3 ft. high at the shoulder)

as·sail (ə·sāl′), v.t. **1.** to set upon with violence; assault. **2.** to set upon vigorously with arguments, entreaties, abuse, etc. **3.** to undertake with the purpose of mastering. [ME *asaile(n),* t. OF: m. *asalir,* g. VL *adsalīre,* f. L: *ad-* AD- + *salīre* leap] —**as·sail′a·ble,** adj. —**as·sail′er,** n. —**as·sail′ment,** n. —**Syn. 1.** See **attack.**

as·sail·ant (ə·sā′lənt), n. **1.** one who assails. —*adj.* **2.** assailing; attacking.

As·sam (ăs·săm′), n. a province in NE India. 10,205,000 (1941); 54,951 sq. mi. *Cap.:* Shillong. —**As·sa·mese** (ăs′ə·mēz′, -mēs′), adj., n.

as·sas·sin (ə·săs′ĭn), n. **1.** one who undertakes to murder, esp. from fanaticism or for a reward. **2.** (*cap.*) one of an order of Mohammedan fanatics, active in Persia and Syria from about 1090 to 1272, whose chief object was to assassinate Crusaders. [t. F, t. ML: s. *assassīnus,* t. Ar.: m. *hashshāshīn,* pl., hashish eaters]

as·sas·si·nate (ə·săs′ə·nāt′), v.t., **-nated, -nating. 1.** to kill by sudden or secret, premeditated assault. **2.** to blight or destroy treacherously: *to assassinate a person's character.* [t. ML: m. s. *assassīnātus,* pp.] —**as·sas′si·na′tion,** n. —**as·sas′si·na′tor,** n. —**Syn. 1.** murder.

assassin bug, any insect of the heteropterous family *Reduviidae.* All are predaceous and some are bloodsucking parasites of warm-blooded animals.

as·sault (ə·sôlt′), n. **1.** act of assailing; an attack; onslaught. **2.** *Mil.* the stage of close combat in an attack. **3.** *Law.* an unlawful physical attack upon another; an attempt or offer to do violence to another, with or without a battery, as by holding a stone or club in a threatening manner. **4.** rape[1]. —*v.t.* **5.** to make an assault upon; attack; assail. [ME *assaut,* t. OF, der. *asalir* ASSAIL] —**as·sault′er,** *n.* —**Syn. 1.** onset, charge. **5.** See **attack.**

assault and battery, *Law.* an assault with an actual touching or other violence upon another.

as·say (*v.* ə sā′; *n.* ə sā′, ăs′ā), *v.t.* **1.** to examine by trial; put to test or trial: *to assay one's strength.* **2.** *Metall.* to analyze (an ore, alloy, etc.) in order to determine the quantity of gold, silver, or other metal in it. **3.** *Pharm., etc.* to subject (a drug, etc.) to an analysis for the determination of its potency. **4.** to try in combat. **5.** to attempt; endeavor; essay. **6.** to judge the quality of; evaluate. —*v.i.* **7.** *U.S.* to contain, as shown by analysis, a certain proportion of (usually precious) metal. —*n.* **8.** *Metall.* determination of the amount of metal, esp. gold or silver, in an ore, alloy, etc. **9.** *Pharm., etc.* determination of the strength, purity, etc., of a pharmaceutical substance or ingredient. **10.** a substance undergoing analysis or trial. **11.** a listing of the findings in assaying a substance. **12.** *Obs.* examination; trial; attempt; essay. [ME, t. OF, g. LL *exagium* a weighing. Cf. ESSAY, n.] —**as·say′er,** *n.*

as·se·gai (ăs′ə gī′), *n., pl.* **-gais,** *v.,* **-gaied, -gaing.** —*n.* **1.** the slender throwing spear of the Kaffirs. **2.** a South African cornaceous tree, *Curtisia faginea,* from whose wood such spears are made. —*v.t.* **3.** to pierce with an assegai. Also, **assagai.** [t. Sp.: m. *azagaya,* t. Ar.: f. *al* the + (Berber) *zaghāyah* spear]

as·sem·blage (ə sĕm′blĭj), *n.* **1.** a number of persons or things assembled; an assembly. **2.** act of assembling. **3.** state of being assembled. [t. F]

as·sem·ble (ə sĕm′bəl), *v.,* **-bled, -bling.** —*v.t.* **1.** to bring together; gather into one place, company, body, or whole. **2.** to put or fit (parts) together; put together the parts of (a mechanism, etc.). —*v.i.* **3.** to come together; gather; meet. [ME *as(s)emble(n),* t. OF: m. *as(s)embler,* g. L *assimulāre* compare, imitate] —**as·sem′bler,** *n.* —**Syn. 1.** See **gather. 2.** See **manufacture. 3.** congregate.

as·sem·bly (ə sĕm′blĭ), *n., pl.* **-blies. 1.** a company of persons gathered together, usually for the same purpose, whether religious, political, educational, or social. **2.** (*cap.*) *Govt.* a legislative body, sometimes esp. a lower house of a legislature. **3.** *French Hist.* the first of the Revolutionary assemblies, in session 1789–91. **4.** act of assembling. **5.** state of being assembled. **6.** *Mil.* **a.** a signal, as by drum or bugle, for troops to fall into ranks or otherwise assemble. **b.** the movement of forces, tanks, soldiers, etc., scattered by battle or battle drill, toward and into a small area. **7.** the putting together of complex machinery, as airplanes, from interchangeable parts of standard dimensions. **8.** such parts, before or after assembling. [ME *as(s)emblee,* t. OF] —**Syn. 1.** assemblage, gathering. See **convention.**

assembly line, an arrangement of machines, tools, and workers in which each worker performs a special operation on an incomplete unit, which usually passes down a line of workers until it is finished.

as·sem·bly·man (ə sĕm′blĭ mən), *n., pl.* **-men.** *U.S.* a member of a legislative assembly, esp. of a lower house.

as·sent (ə sĕnt′), *v.i.* **1.** to agree by expressing acquiescence or admitting truth; express agreement or concurrence (often fol. by *to*): *to assent to a statement.* —*n.* **2.** agreement, as to a proposal; acquiescence; concurrence. [ME *as(s)ente(n),* t. OF: m. *as(s)enter,* g. L *assentīrī,* freq. of *assentīrī*] —**Syn. 1.** acquiesce, accede, concur. See **consent.**

as·sen·ta·tion (ăs′ĕn tā′shən), *n.* the practice of assenting, esp. obsequiously.

as·sen·tor (ə sĕn′tər), *n.* **1.** Also, **as·sent′er.** one who assents. **2.** *Brit. Govt.* one of the eight voters who endorse the nomination, by a proposer and seconder, of a candidate for election to Parliament, as required by law.

as·sert (ə sûrt′), *v.t.* **1.** to state as true; affirm; declare: *to assert that one is innocent.* **2.** to maintain or defend (claims, rights, etc.). **3.** to put (oneself) forward boldly and insistently. [t. L: s. *assertus,* pp., joined to] —**as·sert′er, as·ser′tor,** *n.* —**Syn. 1.** See **declare.** —**Ant. 1.** deny.

as·ser·tion (ə sûr′shən), *n.* **1.** a positive statement; an unsupported declaration. **2.** act of asserting. —**Syn. 1.** allegation.

as·ser·tive (ə sûr′tĭv), *adj.* given to asserting; positive; dogmatic. —**as·ser′tive·ly,** *adv.* —**as·ser′tive·ness,** *n.*

as·ser·to·ry (ə sûr′tər ĭ), *adj.* affirming; assertive.

asses′ bridge, *Geom.* pons asinorum (Euclid, I 5).

as·sess (ə sĕs′), *v.t.* **1.** to estimate officially the value of (property, income, etc.) as a basis for taxation. **2.** to fix or determine the amount of (damages, a tax, a fine, etc.). **3.** to impose a tax or other charge on. [ME *as-sesse(n),* t. OF: m. *assesser,* g. LL *assessāre* fix a tax, freq. of L *assidēre* sit at] —**as·sess′a·ble,** *adj.*

as·sess·ment (ə sĕs′mənt), *n.* **1.** act of assessing. **2.** an amount assessed as payable; an official valuation of taxable property, etc., or the value assigned.

as·ses·sor (ə sĕs′ər), *n.* **1.** one who makes assessments for purposes of taxation. **2.** an advisory associate or assistant. **3.** a judge or magistrate. **4.** one who shares another's position, rank, or dignity. [t. L: s. *assessor,* ML *assessor* of taxes; r. ME *assessour,* t. OF] —**as·ses·so·ri·al** (ăs′ə sōr′ĭ əl), *adj.*

as·set (ăs′ĕt), *n.* **1.** a useful thing or quality: *neatness is an asset.* **2.** a single item of property.

as·sets (ăs′ĕts), *n.pl.* **1.** *Com.* resources of a person or business consisting of such items as real property, machinery, inventories, notes, securities, cash, etc. **2.** property or effects (opposed to *liabilities*). **3.** *Accounting.* the detailed listing of property owned by a firm and money owing to it. **4.** *Law.* **a.** property in the hands of an executor or administrator sufficient to pay the debts or legacies of the testator or intestate. **b.** any property available for paying debts, etc. [orig. sing., t. OF: what is assigned, der. *asseter* place, ult. der. VL *adsidēre* seat at]

as·sev·er·ate (ə sĕv′ə rāt′), *v.t.,* **-ated, -ating.** to declare earnestly or solemnly; affirm positively. [t. L: m. s. *assevērātus,* pp.,]

as·sev·er·a·tion (ə sĕv′ə rā′shən), *n.* **1.** act of asseverating. **2.** an emphatic assertion.

As·shur (ä′shòòr), *n.* Assur.

as·si·du·i·ty (ăs′ə dū′ə tĭ, -dōō′-), *n., pl.* **-ties. 1.** constant or close application; diligence. **2.** (*pl.*) devoted or solicitous attentions.

as·sid·u·ous (ə sĭj′ŏŏ əs), *adj.* **1.** constant; unremitting: *assiduous reading.* **2.** constant in application; attentive; devoted. [t. L: m. *assiduus* sitting down to] —**as·sid′u·ous·ly,** *adv.* —**as·sid′u·ous·ness,** *n.*

as·sign (ə sīn′), *v.t.* **1.** to make over or give, as in distribution; allot: *to assign rooms at a hotel.* **2.** to appoint, as to a post or duty: *assign to stand guard.* **3.** to designate; specify: *to assign a day.* **4.** to ascribe; attribute; refer: *to assign a reason.* **5.** *Law.* to transfer: *to assign a contract.* **6.** *Mil.* to place permanently on duty with a unit or under a commander. —*v.i.* **7.** *Law.* to transfer property, esp. in trust for the benefit of creditors. —*n.* **8.** (*usually pl.*) *Law.* a person to whom the property or interest of another is or may be transferred: *my heirs and assigns.* [ME *assigne(n),* t. OF: m. *as(s)igner,* g. L *assignāre*] —**as·sign′er,** *Chiefly Law* **as·sign·or** (ə sī nôr′, ăs′ə nôr′), *n.* —**Syn. 1.** ASSIGN, ALLOCATE, ALLOT mean to apportion or measure out. To ASSIGN is to distribute available things, designating them to be given to or reserved for specific persons or purposes: *to assign duties.* To ALLOCATE is to earmark or set aside parts of things available or expected in the future, each for a specific purpose: *to allocate income to various types of expenses.* To ALLOT implies making restrictions as to amount, size, purpose, etc., and then apportioning or assigning: *to allot spaces for parking.*

as·sign·a·ble (ə sī′nə bəl), *adj.* **1.** capable of being specified. **2.** capable of being attributed. **3.** *Law.* capable of being assigned. —**as·sign′a·bil′i·ty,** *n.* —**as·sign′a·bly,** *adv.*

as·sig·nat (ăs′ĭg năt′; *Fr.* ȧ sē nyȧ′), *n.* *French Hist.* one of the notes (paper currency) issued from 1789 to 1796 by the revolutionary government on the security of confiscated lands. [t. F, t. L: s. *assignātus,* pp. See ASSIGN, v.]

as·sig·na·tion (ăs′ĭg nā′shən), *n.* **1.** an appointment for a meeting, now esp. an illicit love meeting. **2.** act of assigning; assignment.

as·sign·ee (ə sī nē′, ăs′ə nē′), *n.* *Law.* one to whom some right or interest is transferred, either for his own enjoyment or in trust.

as·sign·ment (ə sīn′mənt), *n.* **1.** something assigned, as a particular task or duty. **2.** act of assigning. **3.** *Law.* **a.** the transference of a right, interest, or title, or the instrument of transfer. **b.** a transference of property to assignees for the benefit of creditors.

as·sim·i·la·ble (ə sĭm′ə lə bəl), *adj.* capable of being assimilated. —**as·sim′i·la·bil′i·ty,** *n.*

as·sim·i·late (ə sĭm′ə lāt′), *v.,* **-lated, -lating.** —*v.t.* **1.** to take in and incorporate as one's own; absorb (fol. by *to* or *with*). **2.** *Physiol.* to convert (food, etc.) into a substance suitable for absorption into the system. **3.** to make like; cause to resemble (fol. by *to* or *with*). **4.** to compare; liken (fol. by *to* or *with*). **5.** *Phonet.* to articulate more like another sound in the same utterance, as *ant* for earlier *amt.* —*v.i.* **6.** to be or become absorbed. **7.** *Physiol.* (of food, etc.) to be converted into the substance of the body; be absorbed into the system. **8.** to become or be like; resemble (fol. by *to* or *with*). [t. L: m. s. *assimilātus,* pp., likened]

as·sim·i·la·tion (ə sĭm′ə lā′shən), *n.* **1.** act or process of assimilating. **2.** state or condition of being assimilated. **3.** *Physiol.* the conversion of absorbed food into the substance of the body. **4.** *Bot.* the total process of plant nutrition, including absorption of external foods and photosynthesis. **5.** *Sociol.* the merging of cultural traits from previously distinct cultural groups, not involving biological amalgamation.

as·sim·i·la·tive (ə sĭm′ə lā′tĭv), *adj.* characterized by assimilation; assimilating. Also, **as·sim·i·la·to·ry** (ə sĭm′ə lə tōr′ĭ).

As·sin·i·boin (ə sĭn′ə boin′), *n.* a Siouan language.

As·sin·i·boine (ə sĭn′ə boin′), *n.* a river in S Canada, flowing from SE Saskatchewan into the Red River in S Manitoba. ab. 450 mi.

As·si·si (äs sē′zē), *n.* a town in central Italy, SE of Perugia: birthplace of St. Francis. 9034 (1936).

as·sist (ə sĭst′), *v.t.* **1.** to give support, help, or aid to in some undertaking or effort, or in time of distress. **2.** to be associated with as an assistant. —*v.i.* **3.** to give aid or help. **4.** to be present, as at a meeting, ceremony, etc. —*n.* **5.** *Baseball.* a play which helps to put a

---

ăct, āble, dâre, ärt; ĕbb, ēqual; ĭf, īce; hŏt, ōver, ôrder, oil, bŏŏk, ōōze, out; ŭp, ūse, ûrge; ə = a in alone; ch, chief; g, give; ng, ring; sh, shoe; th, thin; ŧh, that; zh, vision. See the full key on inside cover.

runner out, officially scored and credited as such. **6.** a helpful act. [t. F: s. *assister*, t. L: m. *assistere* stand by] —**as·sist′er**, (*Law.*) **as·sis′tor**, *n.* —**Syn. 1.** sustain, befriend; back. See **help.** —**Ant. 1.** block, frustrate.

as·sist·ance (ə sĭs′təns), *n.* act of assisting; help; aid. [t. F; r. ME *assystence*, t. ML: m. s. *assistentia*]

as·sist·ant (ə sĭs′tənt), *n.* **1.** one who assists a superior in some office or work; helper. —*adj.* **2.** assis.ing; helpful. **3.** associated with a superior in some office or work: *assistant manager.* —**Syn. 1.** aide, adjutant.

As·siut (ä sŭt′), *n.* Asyut

as·size (ə sīz′), *n.* **1.** a sitting or session of a legislative or administrative agency. **2.** an edict, ordinance, or enactment made at such a session or sitting, or issued by such an agency. **3.** (*usually pl.*) a trial session, civil or criminal, held periodically in specific locations in England, usually by a judge of a superior court or circuit. **4.** judgment: *the last or great assize.* [ME, t. OF: m. *as(s)ise* session, der. *aseeir*, g. L *assidēre* sit by]

assn., association. Also, **Assn.**

assoc., **1.** associate. **2.** associated. **3.** association.

as·so·ci·a·ble (ə sō′shĭ ə bəl, -shə bəl), *adj.* capable of being associated. [t. F] —**as·so′ci·a·bil′i·ty,** *n.*

as·so·ci·ate (*v.* ə sō′shĭ āt′; *n., adj.* ə sō′shĭ ĭt, -āt′), *v.,* -**ated,** -**ating,** *n., adj.* —*v.t.* **1.** to connect by some relation, as in thought. **2.** to join as a companion, partner, or ally. **3.** to unite; combine: *coal associated with shale.* —*v.i.* **4.** to enter into a league or union; unite. **5.** to keep company, as a comrade or .ntimate: *to associate only with wealthy people.* —*n.* **6.** a partner in interest, as in business or in an enterprise or action. **7.** a companion or comrade: *my most intimate associates.* **8.** a confederate; an accomplice; an ally. **9.** anything usually accompanying or associated with another; an accompaniment or concomitant. **10.** one who is admitted to a subordinate degree of membersh.p in an association or insti.ution: *an associate of the Royal Academy.* —*adj.* **11.** associated, esp. as a companion or colleague: *an associate partner.* **12.** having subordinate membership; without full rights and privileges. **13.** allied; concomitant. [orig. adj., ME *associat*, t. L: s. *associātus*, pp. joined to] —**Syn. 6.** See **acquaintance.**

Associated Press, a business organization of newspapers throughout the U.S. together with correspondents abroad for the reporting and distribution of news.

as·so·ci·a·tion (ə sō′sĭ ā′shən, -shĭ-), *n.* **1.** an organization of people with a common purpose and having a formal structure. **2.** act of associating. **3.** state of being associated. **4.** companionship or intimacy. **5.** connection or combination. **6.** the connection of ideas in thought, or an idea connected with or suggested by a subject of thought. **7.** *Ecol.* a group of plants of one or more species living together under uniform environmental conditions and having a uniform and distinctive aspect. **8.** *Brit.* association football. —**as·so′ci·a′tion·al,** *adj.* —**Syn. 1.** alliance, union. **4.** fellowship.

association football, *Chiefly Brit.* soccer.

association of ideas, *Psychol.* the tendency of a sensation, perception, thought, etc. to recall others previously coexisting in consciousness with it or with states similar to it.

as·so·ci·a·tive (ə sō′shĭ ā′tĭv), *adj.* **1.** pertaining to or resulting from association. **2.** tending to associate or unite. —**as·so′ci·a′tive·ly,** *adv.*

as·soil (ə soil′), *v.t. Archaic.* **1.** to absolve; acquit; pardon. **2.** to atone for. [ME, t. OF, pres. indic. of *a(s)soldre*, g. L *absolvere* loosen]

as·so·nance (ăs′ə nəns), *n.* **1.** resemblance of sounds. **2.** *Pros.* a substitute for rhyme, in which the same vowel sounds, though with different consonants, are used in the terminal words of lines, as *penitent* and *reticence.* **3.** partial agreement or correspondence. [t. F, der. *assonant*, t. L: s. *assonans*, ppr., sounding to] —**as′so·nant,** *adj., n.*

as·sort (ə sôrt′), *v.t.* **1.** to distribute according to sort or kind; classify. **2.** to furnish with a suitable assortment or variety of goods; make up of articles likely to suit a demand. **3.** to group or classify (*with*). —*v.i.* **4.** to agree in sort or kind; be matched or suited. **5.** to associate; consort. [late M E t. MF: s. *assorter* distribute, join, der. *a-* A-[5] + *sorte* kind, b. with *sort* lot, fate]

as·sort·ed (ə sôr′tĭd), *adj.* **1.** consisting of selected kinds; arranged in sorts or varieties. **2.** consisting of various kinds; miscellaneous. **3.** matched; suited.

as·sort·ment (ə sôrt′mənt), *n.* **1.** act of assorting; distribution; classification. **2.** an assorted collection.

ASSR, Autonomous Soviet Socialist Republic. Also, **A.S.S.R.**

asst., assistant.

as·suage (ə swāj′), *v.t.,* -**suaged,** -**suaging. 1.** to make milder or less severe; mitigate; ease: *to assuage grief or wrath.* **2.** to appease; satisfy: *to assuage appetite, thirst, craving, etc.* **3.** to molli;y; paci y: *to assuag. God with sacrifice.* [ME *assuage(n),* t. OF: m. *a(s)suagier,* ult. .. L: ad- AD- + deriv. of *suāvis* sweet] —**as·suage′ment,** *n.* —**as·suag′er,** *n.*

As·suan (ăs wän′), *n.* Aswan. Also, **As·souan′.**

as·sua·sive (ə swā′sĭv), *adj.* soothing; alleviative.

as·sume (ə soom′), *v.t.,* -**sumed,** -**suming. 1.** to take for granted or without proof; suppose as a fact: *assume a principle in reasoning.* **2.** to take upon oneself; undertake: *to assume office, an obligation,* etc. **3.** to take

on or put on oneself: *to assume new habits of life.* **4.** to pretend to have or be; feign: *to assume a false humility.* **5.** to appropriate or arrogate: .o *assume a right to oneself.* **6.** *Archaic.* to take into relation or association; adopt. [late M E t L: m.s. *assūmere* take up] —**as·sum′a·ble,** *adj.* —**as·sum′er,** *n.* —**Syn. 1.** presuppose. **4.** See **pretend.**

as·sumed (ə soomd′), *adj.* **1.** pretended. **2.** taken for granted. **3.** usurped.

as·sum·ing (ə soo′mĭng), *adj.* arrogant; presuming.

as·sump·sit (ə sŭmp′sĭt), *n. Law.* **1.** a legal action for breach of a simple contract (a promise not under seal). **2.** an actionable promise. [t. L: he undertook]

as·sump·tion (ə sŭmp′shən), *n.* **1.** act of taking for granted or supposing. **2.** something taken for granted; a supposition. **3.** act of taking to or upon oneself. **4.** arrogance; presumption. **5.** *Eccles.* **a.** (*often cap.*) the bodily taking up into heaven of the Virgin Mary after her death. **b.** (*cap.*) a feast commemorating it, celebrated on August 15. —**Syn. 2.** conjecture, hypothesis, theory, postulate. **4.** effrontery, forwardness.

as·sump·tive (ə sŭmp′tĭv), *adj.* **1.** taken for granted. **2.** characterized by assumption. **3.** presumptuous.

As·sur (ăs′ər), *n.* the supreme national god of Assyria. Also, **Ashur, Asshur, Asur.**

as·sur·ance (ə shoor′əns), *n.* **1.** a positive declaration intended to give confidence. **2.** pledge; guaranty; surety. **3.** full confidence or trust; freedom from doubt; certainty. **4.** freedom from timidity; self-reliance; courage. **5.** presumptuous boldness; impudence. **6.** *Brit.* insurance. —**Syn. 3.** See **trust. 4, 5.** See **confidence.**

as·sure (ə shoor′), *v.t.,* -**sured,** -**suring. 1.** to declare earnestly to; inform or tell positively. **2.** to make (one) sure or certain; convince, as by a promise or declaration. **3.** to make (a future event) sure; ensure: *this assures the success of our work.* **4.** to secure or confirm; render safe or stable: *to assure a person's position.* **5.** to give confidence to; encourage. **6.** to insure, as against loss. [ME *assure(n),* t. OF: m. *aseūrer,* g. LL *assecūrāre*]

as·sured (ə shoord′), *adj.* **1.** made sure; sure; certain. **2.** bold; confident. **3.** boldly presumptuous. —*n.* **4.** *Insurance.* **a.** the beneficiary under a policy. **b.** the person whose life or property is covered by a policy. —**as·sur·ed·ly** (ə shoor′ĭd lĭ), *adv.* —**as·sur′ed·ness,** *n.*

as·sur·er (ə shoor′ər), *n.* **1.** one who assures. **2.** *Brit.* one who grants a policy of insurance.

as·sur·gent (ə sûr′jənt), *adj. Bot.* curving upward, as leaves; ascending. [t. L: s. *assurgens,* ppr., rising up] —**as·sur′gen·cy,** *n.*

As·syr·i·a (ə sĭr′ĭ ə), *n.* an ancient empire in SW Asia: greatest extent from ab. 750–612 B.C. *Cap.:* Nineveh.

As·syr·i·an (ə sĭr′ĭ ən), *adj.* **1.** pertaining to Assyria, the Assyrians, or their language. —*n.* **2.** a native or an inhabitant of Assyria. **3.** a Semitic language of the Akkadian group, spoken in northern Mesopotamia.

As·syr·i·ol·o·gy (ə sĭr′ĭ ŏl′ə jĭ), *n.* the science of Assyrian antiquities. —**As·syr′i·ol′o·gist,** *n.*

As·tar·te (ăs tär′tĭ), *n.* an ancient Semitic deity, goddess of fertility and reproduction worshiped by the Phoenicians, corresponding to the Hebrew Ashtoreth and the Babylonian and Assyrian Ishtar, and regarded as a moon goddess by the Greeks and Romans. [t. L, t. Gk., t. Phoenician: m. *Ashtareth*]

a·stat·ic (ā stăt′ĭk), *adj.* **1.** unstable; unsteady. **2.** *Physics.* having no tendency .o take a definite position. [f. s. Gk. *ástatos* unstable + -IC] —**a·stat′i·cal·ly,** *adv.* —**a·stat·i·cism** (ā stăt′ə sĭz′əm), *n.*

as·ter (ăs′tər), *n.* **1.** *Bot.* any plant of the large composite genus *Aster,* having rays varying from white or pink to blue around a yellow disk. **2.** a plant of some allied genus, as *Callistephus chinensis* (China aster). **3.** *Biol.* either of two star-shaped structures formed in a cell during mitosis. [t. L, t. Gk.: star]

-aster[1], a suffix used to form nouns denoting something that imperfectly resembles or merely ape the true thing, or an inferior or petty instance of someth ng, as *critic-aster, poetaster, oleaster.* [t. L]

-aster[2], *Chiefly Biol.* a suffix meaning "star." [repr. Gk. *astḗr*]

as·ter·a·ceous (ăs′tə rā′shəs), *adj. Bot.* belonging to the *Asteraceae* or *Carduaceae,* the aster family of plants usually included in the *Compositae.*

as·ter·i·at·ed (ăs tĭr′ĭ ā′tĭd), *adj. Crystall.* exhibiting asterism, as a star sapphire. [f. s. Gk. *astérios* starry + -ATE[1] + -ED[2]]

as·ter·isk (ăs′tər ĭsk), *n.* **1.** the figure of a star (*), used in wr.ting and printing as a reference mark or to indicate omission, doubtful matter, etc. **2.** something in the shape of a star or asterisk. [t. LL: m.s. *asteriscus,* t. Gk.: m. *asterískos,* dim. of *astḗr* star]

as·ter·ism (ăs′tə rĭz′əm), *n.* **1.** *Astron.* **a.** a group of stars. **b.** a constellation. **2.** *Crystal.* a property of some crystallized minerals of showing a stari..e lum.nous figure in transmitted light or, in a cabochon-cut stone, by reflected light. **3.** three asterisks (*.* or *.*.) placed before a passage to direct attention to it. [t. Gk.: s. *asterismós,* der. *asterízein* mark with stars]

a·stern (ə stûrn′), *adv., adj. Naut.* **1.** to the rear (of);

behind; in a backward direction. **2.** in the rear; in a position behind.

a·ster·nal (ā stûr′nəl), *adj. Anat., Zool.* not reaching to or connected with the sternum. [f. A-⁶ + STERNAL]

as·ter·oid (ăs′tə roid′), *n.* **1.** *Zool.* any of the *Asteroidea*; a starfish. **2.** *Astron.* one of several hundred planetoids with orbits lying mostly between those of Mars and Jupiter. —*adj.* **3.** starlike. [t. Gk.: m. s. *asteroeidēs* starlike] —**as′ter·oi′dal**, *adj.*

As·ter·oi·de·a (ăs′tə roi′dĭ′ə), *n.pl. Zool.* a class of echinoderms characterized by a starlike body with radiating arms or rays, as the starfishes. —**as′ter·oi′de·an**, *n., adj.*

as·the·ni·a (ăs thē′nĭ′ə, ăs′thə nĭ′ə), *n. Pathol.* lack or loss of strength; debility. [NL, t. Gk.: m. *asthéneia*] —**as·then′ic** (ăs thĕn′ĭk), *adj.*

asth·ma (ăz′mə, ăs′-), *n.* a paroxysmal disorder of respiration, with labored breathing, a feeling of constriction in the chest, and coughing. [t. Gk.: panting; r. ME *asma*, t. ML]

asth·mat·ic (ăz măt′ĭk, ăs-), *adj.* **1.** suffering from asthma. **2.** pertaining to asthma. —*n.* **3.** one suffering from asthma. —**asth·mat′i·cal·ly**, *adv.*

As·ti (ăs′tē), *n.* a city in NW Italy, in Piedmont. 52,126 (est. 1946).

as·tig·mat·ic (ăs′tĭg măt′ĭk), *adj.* pertaining to, exhibiting, or correcting astigmatism.

a·stig·ma·tism (ə stĭg′mə tĭz′əm), *n.* a defect of the eye or of a lens whereby rays of light from an external point converge unequally in different meridians, thus causing imperfect vision or images. [f. A-⁶ + s. Gk. *stígma* point + -ISM]

a·stir (ə stûr′), *adj., adv.* **1.** in a stir; in motion or activity. **2.** up and about; out of bed.

As·to·lat (ăs′tō lăt′), *n.* a place in the Arthurian romances, possibly in Surrey.

a·stom·a·tous (ā stŏm′ə təs, ā stō′mə-), *adj. Zool., Bot.* having no mouth, stoma, or stomata. [f. A-⁶ + s. Gk. *stóma* mouth + -OUS]

as·ton·ied (ə stŏn′ĭd), *adj. Archaic.* dazed; bewildered.

as·ton·ish (ə stŏn′ĭsh), *v.t.* to strike with sudden and overpowering wonder; surprise greatly; amaze. [ear′ier *astony*, ? OE *āstunian*, intensive of *stunian* resound. Cf. ASTOUND, STUN] —**as·ton′ish·er**, *n.* —**Syn.** astound, startle, shock. See **surprise**.

as·ton·ish·ing (ə stŏn′ĭsh ĭng), *adj.* causing astonishment; amazing. —**as·ton′ish·ing·ly**, *adv.*

as·ton·ish·ment (ə stŏn′ĭsh mənt), *n.* **1.** overpowering wonder or surprise; amazement. **2.** an object or cause of amazement.

As·tor (ăs′tər), *n.* **John Jacob,** 1763–1848, U.S. capitalist and fur merchant.

As·to·ri·a (ăs tōr′ĭ′ə), *n.* a seaport in NW Oregon, near the mouth of the Columbia river. 12,331 (1950).

as·tound (ə stound′), *v.t.* **1.** to overwhelm with amazement; astonish greatly. —*adj.* **2.** *Archaic.* astonished. [pp. of obs. *astone, astun.* See ASTONISH, STUN] —**as·tound′ing·ly**, *adv.* —**Syn.** 1. See **surprise**.

astr., **1.** astronomer. **2.** astronomical. **3.** astronomy.

as·tra·chan (ăs′trə kən), *n.* **1.** astrakhan. **2.** (*cap.*) a tart variety of apple, usually red or yellow.

a·strad·dle (ə străd′əl), *adv., adj.* with one leg on each side; in a straddling position; astride.

As·trae·a (ăs trē′ə), *n. Gk. Myth.* the goddess of justice, daughter of Zeus and Themis, the last of the immortals to leave mankind.

as·tra·gal (ăs′trə gəl), *n. Archit.* **1.** a small convex molding cut into the form of a string of beads. **2.** a plain convex molding. See diag. under **column.** [t. L: s. *astragalus*. See ASTRAGALUS]

as·trag·a·lus (ăs trăg′ə ləs), *n., pl.* **-li** (-lī′). *Anat.* the uppermost bone of the tarsus; anklebone; talus. [t. L, t. Gk.: m. *astrágalos*] —**as·trag′a·lar**, *adj.*

as·tra·khan (ăs′trə kən), *n.* **1.** a kind of fur of young lambs, with lustrous closely curled wool, from Astrakhan. **2.** Also, **astrakhan cloth.** a fabric with curled pile resembling it. Also, **astrachan.**

As·tra·khan (ăs′trə kăn′; *Russ.* ä′strä hän′y), *n.* a city at the mouth of the Volga, in the SE Soviet Union in Europe. 253,655 (1939).

as·tral (ăs′trəl), *adj.* **1.** pertaining to or proceeding from the stars; consisting of or resembling stars; starry; stellar. **2.** *Biol.* relating to or resembling an aster; star-shaped. **3.** *Theosophy.* pertaining to a supersensible substance supposed to pervade all space and form the substance of a second body belonging to each individual. [t. L: s. *astrālis*, der. *astrum* star, t. Gk.: m. *ástron*]

astral lamp, an oil lamp designed to avoid the shadow cast upon the table by ordinary lamps.

a·stray (ə strā′), *adv., adj.* out of the right way or away from the right; straying; wandering.

as·trict (ə strĭkt′), *v.t.* **1.** to bind fast; confine; constrain or restrict. **2.** to bind morally or legally. [t. L: s. *astrictus*, pp., drawn close] —**as·tric′tion**, *n.*

a·stride (ə strīd′), *adv., adj.* **1.** in the posture of striding or of straddling. —*prep.* **2.** with one leg on each side of.

as·tringe (ə strĭnj′), *v.t.,* **-tringed, -tringing.** to compress; bind together; constrict. [t. L: m. s. *astringere*]

as·trin·gent (ə strĭn′jənt), *adj.* **1.** *Med.* contracting; constrictive; styptic. **2.** stern or severe; austere. —*n.* **3.** *Med.* a substance which contracts the tissues or canals

of the body, thereby diminishing discharges, as of blood. [t. L: s. *astringens*, ppr.] —**as·trin′gen·cy,** *n.* —**as·trin′gent·ly,** *adv.* —**Syn.** 2. See **acid.**

astro-, a word element meaning "star," as in *astrology.* [t. Gk., comb. form of *ástron*]

astrol., 1. astrologer. **2.** astrological. **3.** astrology.

as·tro·labe (ăs′trə lāb′), *n.* an astronomical instrument of different forms, used for taking the altitude of the sun or stars, and for the solution of various other problems in astronomy and in navigation. [t. ML: m. s. *astrolabium*, t. Gk.: m. *astrolábon* (*órganon*) armillary sphere; r. ME *astrelabe*, t. OF]

as·trol·o·gy (ə strŏl′ə jĭ), *n.* **1.** a study or science which assumes, and professes to interpret, the influence of the heavenly bodies on human affairs. **2.** (formerly) practical astronomy, the earliest form of the science. [ME, t. L: m. s. *astrologia*, t. Gk. See ASTRO-, -LOGY] —**as·trol′o·ger**, *n.* —**as·tro·log·i·cal** (ăs′trə lŏj′ə kəl), **as′tro·log′ic**, *adj.* —**as′tro·log′i·cal·ly**, *adv.*

as·trom·e·try (ə strŏm′ə trĭ), *n.* measurement of the positions, motions, and distances of the celestial bodies.

astron., 1. astronomer. **2.** astronomical. **3.** astronomy.

as·tron·o·mer (ə strŏn′ə mər), *n.* an expert in astronomy; a scientific observer of the celestial bodies.

as·tro·nom·i·cal (ăs′trə nŏm′ə kəl), *adj.* **1.** of, pertaining to, or connected with astronomy. **2.** very large, like the numbers used in astronomical calculations. Also, **as′tro·nom′ic.** —**as′tro·nom′i·cal·ly**, *adv.*

astronomical year. See **year** (def. 5).

as·tron·o·my (ə strŏn′ə mĭ), *n.* the science of the celestial bodies, their motions, positions, distances, magnitudes, etc. [ME *astronomie*, t. L: m. *astronomia*, t. Gk. See ASTRO-, -NOMY]

as·tro·pho·tog·ra·phy (ăs′trō fə tŏg′rə fĭ), *n.* the photography of stars and other celestial objects. —**as·tro·pho·to·graph·ic** (ăs′trō fō′tə grăf′ĭk), *adj.*

as·tro·phys·ics (ăs′trō fĭz′ĭks), *n.* astronomical physics, treating of the physical properties and phenomena of the celestial bodies. —**as′tro·phys′i·cal**, *adj.* —**as·tro·phys·i·cist** (ăs′trō fĭz′ə sĭst), *n.*

as·tro·sphere (ăs′trə sfĭr′), *n. Biol.* **1.** the central portion of an aster, in which the centrosome lies. **2.** the whole aster exclusive of the centrosome.

as·tu·cious (ăs tū′shəs, -tōō′-), *adj.* astute. [t. F: m. *astucieux*]

As·tu·ri·as (ăs tŏŏr′ĭ′əs; *Sp.* äs tōŏr′yäs), *n.* a former kingdom and province in NW Spain.

as·tute (ə stūt′, ə stōōt′), *adj.* of keen penetration or discernment; sagacious; shrewd; cunning. [t. L: m. s. *astūtus*, der. *astus* adroitness, cunning] —**as·tute′ly**, *adv.* —**as·tute′ness**, *n.* —**Syn.** artful, crafty, wily, sly.

As·ty·a·nax (ăs tī′ə năks′), *n. Gk. Legend.* the young son of Hector and Andromache, thrown from the walls of Troy by the victorious Greeks.

a·sty·lar (ā stĭl′ər), *adj. Archit.* without columns. [f. s. Gk. *ástylos* without columns + -AR¹]

A·sun·ción (ä′sōōn syōn′, -thyōn′), *n.* the capital of Paraguay, on the Paraguay river. 177,001 (est. 1941).

a·sun·der (ə sŭn′dər), *adv., adj.* **1.** into separate parts; in or into pieces: *to tear asunder.* **2.** apart or widely separated: *as wide asunder as the poles.* [ME *asunder*, o(n)*sunder*, OE *on sundran* apart. See A-¹, SUNDER]

A·sur (ü′sōōr), *n.* Assur.

As·wan (ăs wän′), *n.* **1.** a city in SE Egypt, on the Nile. 22,600 (est. 1938). **2.** a large dam across the Nile nearby. 6400 ft. long. Also, **As·wân′, Assuan, Assouan.**

a·syl·lab·ic (ā′sĭ lăb′ĭk), *adj.* not syllabic.

a·sy·lum (ə sī′ləm), *n.* **1.** an institution for the maintenance and care of the blind, the insane, orphans, etc. **2.** an inviolable refuge, as formerly for criminals and debtors; a sanctuary. **3.** *Internat. Law.* a temporary refuge granted political offenders, esp. in a foreign legation. **4.** any secure retreat. [t. L, t. Gk.: m. *ásylon*, neut. of *ásylos* inviolable] —**Syn.** 1. See **hospital.**

a·sym·met·ric (ā′sə mĕt′rĭk, ăs′ə-), *adj.* **1.** not symmetrical; without symmetry. **2.** *Logic.* denoting relations which, if they hold between one term and a second, do not hold between the second and the first: *the relation "being an ancestor of" is asymmetric.* Also, **a′sym·met′ri·cal.** —**a′sym·met′ri·cal·ly**, *adv.*

a·sym·me·try (ā sĭm′ə trĭ), *n.* lack of symmetry or proportion. [t. Gk.: m.s. *asymmetría*]

as·ymp·tote (ăs′ĭm tōt′), *n. Math.* a straight line that is the limit of a tangent to a curve as the point of contact moves off to infinity. [t. Gk.: m.s. *asýmptōtos* not close] —**as·ymp·tot·ic** (ăs′ĭm tŏt′ĭk), **as′ymp·tot′i·cal**, *adj.* —**as′ymp·tot′i·cal·ly**, *adv.*

a·syn·chro·nism (ā sĭng′krə nĭz′əm, ā sĭn′-), *n.* want of synchronism, or coincidence in time. —**a·syn′chro·nous**, *adj.*

a·syn·de·ton (ə sĭn/də tŏn/, -tən), *n. Rhet.* the omission of conjunctions. [t. L, t. Gk., neut. of *asýndetos* unjoined] —**as·yn·det·ic** (ăs/ən dĕt/ĭk), *adj.* —**as/yn·det/i·cal·ly,** *adv.*

A·syut (ä sūt/), *n.* a city in central Egypt, on the Nile. 62,800 (est. 1942). Also, **As·yût/, Assiut.**

at (ăt; *unstressed* ət, ĭt), *prep.* a particle specifying a point occupied, attained, sought, or otherwise concerned, as in place, time, order, experience, etc., and hence used in many idiomatic phrases expressing circumstantial or relative position, degree or rate, action, manner: *to stand at the door, to aim at a mark, to clutch at a straw, at home, at hand, at noon, at zero, at work, at ease, at length, at a risk, at cost, at one's best.* [ME; OE *æt;* c. Icel. *at,* L *ad* AD-]

at-, var. of ad- before *t,* as in *attend.*

at·a·bal (ăt/ə bäl/), *n.* a kind of drum used by the Moors. Also, **attabal.** [t. Sp., t. Ar.: m. *aṭ-ṭabl* the drum]

at·a·brine (ăt/ə brĭn, -brēn/), *n. Pharm.* **1.** Also, **atebrin.** an antimalarial substance, $C_{23}H_{30}N_3OCl$, with properties similar to plasmochin. **2.** (*cap.*) a trademark for this substance.

at·a·ghan (ăt/ə găn/), *n.* yataghan.

A·ta·hual·pa (ä/tä wäl/pä), *n.* died 1533, last Inca king of Peru.

At·a·lan·ta (ăt/ə lăn/tə), *n. Gk. Myth.* a virgin huntress who helped to kill the Calydonian boar (see **Meleager**). All suitors whom she could outrun were put to death, but she was vanquished by one who dropped three golden apples given him by Aphrodite, which Atalanta stopped to pick up.

at·a·man (ăt/ə mən), *n., pl.* **-mans.** a chief of Cossacks, elected by the whole group, serving as a chairman in peace, a leader in war; a hetman. [t. Russ.]

at·a·mas·co (ăt/ə măs/kō), *n.* **1.** an amaryllidaceous plant, *Zephyranthes atamasco,* of the southeastern U.S., bearing a single white lilylike flower. **2.** any species of this genus. Also, **atamasco lily.** [t. N Amer. Ind.]

a·tav·ic (ə tăv/ĭk), *adj.* **1.** of or pertaining to remote ancestors. **2.** atavistic.

at·a·vism (ăt/ə vĭz/əm), *n.* **1.** *Biol.* the reappearance in an individual of characteristics of some more or less remote ancestor that have been absent in intervening generations. **2.** reversion to an earlier type. [f. s. L *atavus* ancestor + -ISM] —**at/a·vist,** *n.* —**at/a·vis/tic,** *adj.*

a·tax·i·a (ə tăk/sĭ ə), *n. Pathol.* **1.** loss of coördination of the muscles, esp. of the extremities. **2.** locomotor ataxia. [t. NL, t. Gk.: disorder] —**a·tax/ic,** *adj.*

At·ba·ra (ăt/bä rä/), *n.* a river flowing from NW Ethiopia NW to the Nile in the Anglo-Egyptian Sudan. ab. 500 mi.

Atch·i·son (ăch/ə sən), *n.* a city in NE Kansas, on the Missouri river. 12,792 (1950).

ate (āt; *Brit.* ĕt), *v.* pt. of *eat.*

A·te (ā/tĭ), *n. Gk. Myth.* a goddess personifying the fatal blindness or recklessness which produces crime, and the divine punishment which follows it. [t. Gk.]

-ate¹, a suffix forming: **1.** adjectives equivalent to -ed (in participial and other adjectives), as in *accumulate, separate.* **2.** nouns denoting esp. persons charged with some duty or function, or invested with some dignity, right, or special character, as in *advocate, candidate, curate, legate, prelate.* **3.** nouns denoting some product or result of action, as in *mandate* (lit., a thing commanded). **4.** verbs, orig. taken from Latin past participles but now formed from any Latin or other stem, as in *actuate, agitate, calibrate.* [t. L: m. *-ātus, -āta, -ātum*]

-ate², *Chem.* a suffix forming nouns denoting a salt formed by action of an acid on a base, added to the stem of the name of the acid, as in *acetate.* [t. L: m. *-ātum,* neut. of *-ātus* -ATE¹]

-ate³, a suffix forming nouns denoting condition, estate, office, officials, or an official, etc., as in *consulate, episcopate, magistrate, senate* [t. L: m. *-ātus,* suffix making nouns of 4th declension]

at·e·brin (ăt/ə brĭn), *n. Pharm.* atabrine (def. 1).

at·el·ier (ăt/əl yā/; *Fr.* ȧ tə lyĕ/), *n.* the workshop or studio of an artist. [t. F: workplace, orig. pile of chips, der. OF *astele* chip, g. LL *astella,* r. L *astula*]

a tem·po (ä tĕm/pō), *Music.* resuming the speed which obtained preceding *rit.* or *accel.* [It.]

Ath·a·bas·can (ăth/ə băs/kən), *n.* an American Indian linguistic stock of the Na-Dene phylum, including languages of northwest Canada and Alaska (e.g., Chippewa), of the Pacific coast, esp. Oregon and California (e.g., Hupa), and of Arizona and the Rio Grande basin (notably Navaho and Apache). Also, **Athapascan.**

Ath·a·bas·ka (ăth/ə băs/kə), *n.* **1. Lake,** a lake in W Canada, in NW Saskatchewan and NE Alberta. ab. 200 mi. long; ab. 3000 sq. mi. **2.** a river flowing from W Alberta NE to Lake Athabaska. 765 mi.

ath·a·na·sia (ăth/ə nā/zhə), *n.* deathlessness; immortality. Also, **a·than·a·sy** (ə thăn/ə sĭ). [t. Gk.]

Ath·a·na·sian (ăth/ə nā/zhən), *adj.* **1.** of or pertaining to Athanasius. —*n.* **2.** *Theol.* a follower of Athanasius or a believer in his creed.

Athanasian Creed, *Theol.* a (probably) post-Augustinian creed or formulary of Christian faith, of unknown authorship, formerly ascribed to Athanasius.

Ath·a·na·sius (ăth/ə nā/shəs), *n.* **Saint,** A.D. 296?-373, bishop of Alexandria: opponent of Arianism.

Ath·a·pas·can (ăth/ə păs/kən), *n.* Athabascan.

A·thar·va-Ve·da (ə tär/və vā/də, -vē/də), *n.* See Veda.

a·the·ism (ā/thĭ ĭz/əm), *n.* **1.** the doctrine that there is no God. **2.** disbelief in the existence of a God (or of gods). **3.** godlessness. [f. s. Gk. *átheos* without a god + -ISM]

a·the·ist (ā/thĭ ĭst), *n.* one who denies or disbelieves the existence of God or gods. —**Syn.** ATHEIST, AGNOSTIC, INFIDEL, SKEPTIC refer to persons not inclined toward religious belief. An ATHEIST is one who denies the existence of a Deity or divine beings. An AGNOSTIC is one who believes it impossible to know anything about God or about the creation of the universe. INFIDEL means an unbeliever, especially a nonbeliever in Mohammedanism or Christianity. A SKEPTIC doubts and is critical of all accepted doctrines and creeds.

a·the·is·tic (ā/thĭ ĭs/tĭk), *adj.* pertaining to or characteristic of atheists; involving, containing, or tending to atheism: *atheistic doctrines.* Also, **a·the·is/ti·cal.** —**a/the·is/ti·cal·ly,** *adv.*

ath·el·ing (ăth/əl ĭng, ăth/-), *n. Early English Hist.* a man of royal blood; a prince. [ME; OE *ætheling,* f. *æthelu* noble family + *-ing,* suffix of appurtenance]

Ath·el·stan (ăth/əl stăn/), *n.* A.D. 895?-940, king of England, A.D. 925-940.

A·the·na (ə nē/nə), *n.* the Greek goddess of wisdom, arts, industries, and prudent warfare, identified by the Romans with Minerva. Also, **A·the·ne** (ə thē/nĭ). [t. Gk.: m. *Athénē*]

ath·e·nae·um (ăth/ə nē/əm), *n.* **1.** an institution for the promotion of literary or scientific learning. **2.** a library or reading room. **3.** (*cap.*) a sanctuary of Athena at Athens, built by the Roman emperor Hadrian, and frequented by poets and men of learning. Also, **ath/e·ne/um.** [t. L, t. Gk.: m. *Athēnaion* temple of Athena]

A·the·ni·an (ə thē/nĭ ən), *adj.* **1.** pertaining to Athens, Greece. —*n.* **2.** a native or citizen of Athens, Greece.

Ath·ens (ăth/ĭnz), *n.* **1.** the capital of Greece, in the SE part. 481,225 (est. 1945). Greek, **A·the·nai** (ä thē/nĕ). **2.** a city in N Georgia. 28,180 (1950).

a·ther·man·cy (ə thûr/mən sĭ), *n. Physics.* the power of stopping radiant heat.

a·ther·ma·nous (ə thûr/mə nəs), *adj. Physics.* impermeable to or able to stop radiant heat. [f. A-⁶ + s. Gk. *thermaínein* heat + -OUS]

Ath·er·ton (ăth/ər tən), *n.* **Gertrude Franklin** (*Gertrude Franklin Horn*), 1857-1948, U.S. novelist.

a·thirst (ə thûrst/), *adj.* **1.** having a keen desire; eager (often fol. by *for*). **2.** *Archaic or Poetic.* thirsty.

ath·lete (ăth/lēt), *n.* **1.** any one trained to exercises of physical agility and strength. **2.** *Brit.* one trained for track and field events only. [t. L: m.s. *āthlēta,* t. Gk.: m. *athlētēs* contestant in games]

athlete's foot, a contagious disease, a ringworm of the feet, caused by a fungus that thrives on moist surfaces.

ath·let·ic (ăth lĕt/ĭk), *adj.* **1.** physically active and strong. **2.** of, like, or befitting an athlete. **3.** of or pertaining to athletics. —**ath·let/i·cal·ly,** *adv.* —**ath·let·i·cism** (ăth lĕt/ə sĭz/əm), *n.*

ath·let·ics (ăth lĕt/ĭks), *n.* **1.** (*usually construed as pl.*) athletic sports, as running, rowing, boxing, etc. **2.** *Brit.* track and field events only. **3.** (*usually construed as sing.*) the practice of athletic exercises; the principles of athletic training.

at-home (ət hōm/), *n.* a reception of visitors at certain hours during which a host or hostess has announced he or she will be "at home."

Ath·os (ăth/ŏs, ā/thŏs; *Gk.* ä/thôs), *n.* **Mount, 1.** the easternmost of three prongs of the peninsula of Chalcidice, in NE Greece: site of an independent republic of 20 monasteries. 4860 pop. (1928); 121 sq. mi.; ab. 35 mi. long. **2.** a headland there. 6350 ft.

a·thwart (ə thwôrt/), *adv.* **1.** from side to side; crosswise. **2.** perversely; awry; wrongly. **3.** *Naut.* at right angles to a ship's keel. —*prep.* **4.** from side to side of; across. **5.** in opposition to; contrary to. **6.** *Naut.* across the line or course of. [f. A-¹ + THWART, adv.]

a·tilt (ə tĭlt/), *adj., adv.* **1.** at a tilt or inclination; tilted. **2.** in a tilting encounter.

-ation, a suffix forming nouns denoting action or process, state or condition, a product or result, or something producing a result, often accompanying verbs or adjectives of Latin origin ending in *-ate,* as in *agitation, decoration, elation, migration, separation,* but also formed in English from any stem, as in *botheration, flirtation, starvation.* Also, **-ion, -tion.** [t. L: s. *-ātio* = -ATE¹ + -ION; identical with G *-ation,* F *-ation,* etc., all from L]

-ative, an adjective suffix expressing tendency, disposition, function, bearing, connection, etc., as in *affirmative, demonstrative, talkative.* See **-ive.** [t. L: m. s. *-ātīvus* = -ATE¹ + -IVE; repr. also F *-atif* (masc.), *-ative* (fem.)]

At·kins (ăt/kĭnz), *n.* **Tommy.** See **Tommy Atkins.**

Atl., Atlantic.

At·lan·ta (ăt lăn/tə), *n.* the capital of Georgia, in the N part. 331,314 (1950).

At·lan·te·an (ăt/lăn tē/ən), *adj.* **1.** pertaining to the demigod Atlas. **2.** having the strength of Atlas. **3.** pertaining to Atlantis. [f. s. L *Atlantēus* pertaining to Atlas + -AN. See ATLAS]

at·lan·tes (ăt lăn/tēz), *n.pl., sing.* **atlas.** *Archit.* figures of men used as supporting or decorative columns. [t. L, t. Gk. See ATLAS (def. 4).]

---

b., blend of, blended; c., cognate with; d., dialect, dialectal; der., derived from; f., formed from; g., going back to; m., modification of; r., replacing; s., stem of; t., taken from; ?, perhaps. See the full key on inside cover.

At·lan·tic (ăt·lăn'tĭk), n. **1.** the Atlantic Ocean. —adj. **2.** of or pertaining to the Atlantic Ocean. **3.** pertaining to the demigod Atlas. [t. L: s. *Atlanticus*, t. Gk.: m. *Atlantikós* pertaining to Atlas]

Atlantic Charter, the joint declaration of Roosevelt and Churchill (August 14, 1941) resulting from a meeting at sea, and setting forth a program of peace purposes and principles to which each power admitted to the United Nations subsequently subscribed.

Atlantic City, a city in SE New Jersey: seashore resort. 61,657 (1950).

Atlantic Ocean, an ocean bordered by North and South America in the Western Hemisphere, and Europe and Africa in the Eastern Hemisphere: divided by the equator into the **North Atlantic** and the **South Atlantic.** ab. 31,530,000 sq. mi.; with connecting seas, ab. 41,-000,000 sq. mi.; greatest known depth, 27,360 ft.

Atlantic Pact, a treaty (1948) providing for collective defense, signed by the U. S., Canada, Great Britain, France, Belgium, The Netherlands, Luxembourg, Norway, Denmark, Iceland, Italy, and Portugal.

At·lan·tis (ăt·lăn'tĭs), n. a mythical island in the Atlantic Ocean, first mentioned by Plato, supposedly west of Gibraltar, said to have finally sunk into the sea.

at·las (ăt'ləs), n. **1.** a bound collection of maps. **2.** a volume of plates or tables illustrating any subject. **3.** *Anat.* the first cervical vertebra, which supports the head. **4.** (*cap.*) a demigod in classical mythology, condemned to support the sky on his shoulders, and identified with the Atlas Mountains. **5.** (*cap.*) one who supports a heavy burden; a mainstay. **6.** sing. of **atlantes.** [t. L, t. Gk.; def. 1–3, 5, 6 are special uses of 4]

atlas folio, *Bibliog.* largest book-size folio, with leaves 16 x 25 inches.

Atlas Mountains, a mountain range in NW Africa, extending for ab. 1500 mi. through Morocco, Algeria, and Tunisia. Highest peak, Mt. Tizi, 14,764 ft.

At·li (ăt'lĭ), n. *Scand. Legend.* the king of the Huns who married Gudrun, widow of Sigurd, for her inheritance, slew her brothers, and was killed by her in turn. [Icel. var. of ATTILA]

at·man (ăt'mən), n. *Hinduism.* **1.** the breath. **2.** the principle of life. **3.** the individual soul. **4.** (*cap.*) the World Soul, from which all individual souls derive, and to which they return as the supreme goal of existence. **5.** (*cap.*) Brahma, the Supreme Being. [Skt.]

at·mos·phere (ăt'məs·fĭr'), n. **1.** the gaseous fluid surrounding the earth; the air. **2.** this medium at a given place. **3.** *Astron.* the gaseous envelope surrounding any of the heavenly bodies. **4.** *Chem.* any gaseous envelope or medium. **5.** a conventional unit of pressure, the normal pressure of the air at sea level, about 15 pounds per square inch. **6.** environing or pervading influence: *an atmosphere of freedom.* **7.** the quality in a work of art which produces a predominant mood or impression. [t. NL: m. s. *atmosphaera*, f. Gk.: *atmó(s)* vapor + m. *sphaîra* SPHERE]

at·mos·pher·ic (ăt'məs·fĕr'ĭk), adj. Also, **at'mos·pher'i·cal. 1.** pertaining to, existing in, or consisting of the atmosphere: *atmospheric vapors.* **2.** caused, produced, or operated on by the atmosphere: *atmospheric pressure.* —n. **3.** (*pl.*) *Radio.* extraneous noises, crackling, etc., caused by stray electrical currents from storms or other atmospheric disturbance being picked up by the receiver; static. —**at'mos·pher'i·cal·ly,** adv.

at. no., atomic number.

at·oll (ăt'ŏl, ə·tŏl'), n. a ringlike coral island enclosing a lagoon. [? t. Malayalam: m. *aḍal* uniting]

at·om (ăt'əm), n. **1.** *Physics, Chem.* the smallest unitary constituent of a chemical element, composed of a more or less complex aggregate of protons, neutrons, and electrons, whose number and arrangement determine the element. **2.** a hypothetical particle of matter so minute as to admit of no division. **3.** anything extremely small; a minute quantity. [t. L: s. *atomus*, t. Gk.: m. *átomos* indivisible] —**Syn. 3.** iota.

a·tom·ic (ə·tŏm'ĭk), adj. **1.** pertaining to atoms. **2.** propelled or driven by atomic energy. **3.** *Chem.* existing as free uncombined atoms. **4.** extremely minute. Also, **a·tom'i·cal.** —**a·tom'i·cal·ly,** adv.

atomic age, the period in history initiated by the first use of the atomic bomb and characterized by atomic energy as a military, political, and industrial factor.

atomic bomb, 1. a bomb whose potency is derived from nuclear fission of atoms of fissionable material, with consequent conversion of part of their mass into energy. **2.** a bomb whose explosive force comes from a chain reaction based on nuclear fission in U-235 or in plutonium. It was first used militarily on Hiroshima, Japan (August 6, 1945). The explosion of such a bomb is extremely violent and is attended by great heat, a brilliant light, and strong gamma-ray radiation. Also, **atom bomb, A-bomb.**

atomic energy, energy obtained from changes within the atomic nucleus, chiefly from nuclear fission.

Atomic Energy Commission, *U.S.* a board formed in 1946, consisting of 5 civilian members, for the domestic control of atomic energy.

at·o·mic·i·ty (ăt'ə·mĭs'ə·tĭ), n. *Chem.* **1.** the number of atoms in the molecule of a gas. **2.** valence.

atomic number, *Chem., Physics.* the number of positive charges on the nucleus of an atom of a given element, and therefore also the number of electrons normally surrounding the nucleus, or the number of protons within the nucleus.

a·tom·ics (ə·tŏm'ĭks), n. the branch of nuclear physics dealing with atomic energy, nuclear fission, etc.

atomic structure, *Physics.* the theoretically derived concept of an atom composed of a positively charged nucleus surrounded and electrically neutralized by negatively charged electrons, revolving in orbits at varying distances from the nucleus, the constitution of the nucleus and the arrangement of the electrons differing with the different chemical elements.

atomic theory, 1. *Physics, Chem.* the modern theory of the atom as having a complex internal structure and electrical properties. **2.** *Physics.* the mathematical and geometrical description of the motions of the electrons in the atom about the nucleus. **3.** *Philos.* atomism (def. 2). Also, **atomic hypothesis.**

atomic warfare, warfare by atomic bombs, etc.

atomic weight, *Chem.* the average weight of an atom of an element measured in units each of which corresponds to one sixteenth of the average weight of the oxygen atom. *Abbr.:* at. wt.

at·om·ism (ăt'ə·mĭz'əm), n. **1.** the atomic theory. **2.** *Philos.* the theory that minute discrete, finite, and indivisible elements are the ultimate constituents of all matter. —**at'om·ist,** n. —**at'om·is'tic,** adj.

at·om·ize (ăt'ə·mīz'), v.t., **-ized, -izing. 1.** to reduce to atoms. **2.** to reduce to fine particles or spray. —**at'·om·i·za'tion,** n.

at·om·iz·er (ăt'ə·mī'zər), n. an apparatus for reducing liquids to a fine spray, as for medicinal application.

at·o·my¹ (ăt'ə·mĭ), n., pl. **-mies.** *Archaic.* **1.** an atom; a mote. **2.** a pygmy. [t. L: m. *atomī* atoms]

at·o·my² (ăt'ə·mĭ), n., pl. **-mies.** *Obs.* a skeleton. [der. ANATOMY, taken as *an atomy*]

a·ton·al (ā·tō'nəl), adj. *Music.* having no key. [f. A-⁶ + TONAL] —**a·ton'al·ism,** n. —**a·ton'al·is'tic,** adj. —**a·ton'al·ly,** adv.

a·to·nal·i·ty (ā'tō·năl'ə·tĭ), n. *Music.* **1.** the absence of key or tonal center. **2.** an atonal principle or style of composition.

a·tone (ə·tōn'), v., **atoned, atoning.** —v.i. **1.** to make amends or reparation, as for an offense or a crime, or for an offender (fol. by *for*). **2.** to make up, as for errors or deficiencies (fol. by *for*). **3.** *Obs.* to agree. —v.t. **4.** to make amends for; expiate. **5.** to harmonize; make harmonious. **6.** *Rare.* to bring into unity. [back formation from ATONEMENT] —**a·ton'er,** n.

a·tone·ment (ə·tōn'mənt), n. **1.** satisfaction or reparation for a wrong or injury; amends. **2.** *Theol.* the reconciliation of God and man by means of the life, sufferings, and death of Christ. **3.** *Archaic.* reconciliation; agreement. [f. phrase *at one* in accord + -MENT]

a·ton·ic (ə·tŏn'ĭk), adj. **1.** *Phonet.* **a.** unaccented. **b.** *Obs.* voiceless (def. 5). **2.** *Pathol.* characterized by atony. —n. **3.** *Gram.* an unaccented word, syllable, or sound.

at·o·ny (ăt'ə·nĭ), n. *Pathol.* lack of tone or energy; muscular weakness, esp. in a contractile organ. [t. ML: m. s. *atonia*, t. Gk.: languor]

a·top (ə·tŏp'), adj., adv. **1.** on or at the top. —prep. **2.** on the top of: *atop the house.*

at·ra·bil·ious (ăt'rə·bĭl'yəs), adj. melancholic or hypochondriac; splenetic. Also, **at'ra·bil'iar.** [f. L *ātra bīli(s)* black bile + -OUS] —**at'ra·bil'ious·ness,** n.

a·trem·ble (ə·trĕm'bəl), adv. in a trembling state.

A·treus (ā'trōōs, ā'trĭ·əs), n. *Gk. Legend.* a king of Mycenae, and a son of Pelops. His evil deeds and those of his house gave many themes to the Greek dramatists.

a·trip (ə·trĭp'), adj. *Naut.* (of an anchor) raised just enough to clear the bottom.

a·tri·um (ā'trĭ·əm), n., pl. **atria** (ā'trĭ·ə). **1.** *Archit.* **a.** the central main room of an ancient Roman private house. **b.** a courtyard, mostly surrounded by colonnades, in front of early Christian or medieval churches. **2.** *Anat.* an auricle of the heart. [(def. 1) t. L; (def. 2) t. NL, special use of L *atrium*]

a·tro·cious (ə·trō'shəs), adj. **1.** extremely or shockingly wicked or cruel; heinous: *an atrocious criminal.* **2.** shockingly bad or lacking in taste; execrable: *an atrocious pun.* [f. ATROCI(TY) + -OUS] —**a·tro'cious·ly,** adv. —**a·tro'cious·ness,** n.

a·troc·i·ty (ə·trŏs'ə·tĭ), n., pl. **-ties. 1.** quality of being atrocious. **2.** an atrocious deed or thing. [t. L: m.s. *atrōcitas*]

at·ro·phied (ăt'rə·fĭd), adj. exhibiting or affected with atrophy; wasted.

at·ro·phy (ăt'rə·fĭ), n., v., **-phied, -phying.** —n. **1.** *Pathol.* a wasting away of the body or of an organ or part, as from defective nutrition or other cause. **2.** degeneration. —v.t., v.i. **3.** to affect with or undergo atrophy. [earlier *atrophie*, t. L: m. *atrophia*, t. Gk.: lack of nourishment] —**a·troph·ic** (ə·trŏf'ĭk), adj.

at·ro·pine (ăt'rə·pēn', -pĭn), n. a poisonous crystalline alkaloid, $C_{17}H_{23}NO_3$, obtained from belladonna and other solanaceous plants, which prevents the response of various body structures to certain types of nerve stimulation. Also, **at·ro·pin** (ăt′rə pĭn). [f. s. NL *Atropa*, the belladonna genus (t. Gk.: m. *átropos*. See ATROPOS) + -INE²]

at·ro·pism (ăt′rə pĭz′əm), *n.* *Pathol.* the morbid state induced by atropine.

At·ro·pos (ăt′rə pŏs′), *n.* *Gk. Myth.* one of the Fates. She cut off the thread of life. [t. Gk.: lit., inflexible]

att., attorney.

at·ta·bal (ăt′ə băl′), *n.* atabal.

at·tach (ə tăch′), *v.t.* **1.** to fasten to; affix; join; connect: *to attach a cable.* **2.** to join in action or function. **3.** *Mil.* to place on duty with or in assistance to a military unit temporarily. **4.** to connect as an adjunct; associate: *a curse is attached to this treasure.* **5.** to assign or attribute: *to attach significance to a gesture.* **6.** to bind by ties of affection or regard. **7.** *Law.* to take (persons or property) by legal authority. **8.** *Obs.* to lay hold of; seize. —*v.i.* **9.** to adhere; pertain; belong (fol. by *to* or *upon*): *no blame attaches to him.* [ME *attache*(n), t. OF: m. *atachier*, f. a- AD- + word akin to TACK¹] —**at·tach′a·ble**, *adj.* —**Syn. 1.** subjoin.

at·ta·ché (ăt′ə shā′ or, *esp. Brit.,* ə tăsh′ā; *Fr.* à tà shě′), *n.* one attached to an official staff, esp. that of an embassy or legation. [F, prop. pp. of *attacher* ATTACH]

at·tach·ment (ə tăch′mənt), *n.* **1.** act of attaching. **2.** state of being attached. **3.** affection that binds one to another person or to a thing; regard. **4.** that which attaches; a fastening or tie: *the attachments of a pair of skis or of a harness.* **5.** an adjunct or supplementary device: *attachments to a reaping machine.* **6.** *Law.* seizure of property or person by legal authority; esp., seizure of a defendant's property before obtaining judgment against him. —**Syn. 3.** love, devotedness, devotion. **4.** junction, connection. **5.** See addition.

at·tack (ə tăk′), *v.t.* **1.** to set upon with force or weapons; begin hostilities against: *attack the enemy.* **2.** to direct unfavorable criticism, argument, etc., against; blame or abuse violently. **3.** to set about (a task) or go to work on (a thing) vigorously. **4.** (of disease, destructive agencies, etc.) to begin to affect. —*v.i.* **5.** to make an attack; begin hostilities. —*n.* **6.** the act of attacking; onslaught; assault. **7.** an offensive military operation with the aim of overcoming the enemy and destroying his armed forces and will to resist. **8.** *Pathol.* seizure by disease. **9.** the initial movement in a performance or contest; onset. [t. F: m. *attaquer*, t. It.: m. *attaccare* attack, ATTACH] —**at·tack′er**, *n.* —**Syn. 1.** ATTACK, ASSAIL, ASSAULT, MOLEST all mean to set upon someone forcibly, with hostile or inimical intent AT- TACK is the most general word and applies to a beginning of hostilities, esp. those definitely planned: *to attack from ambush.* ASSAIL implies vehement, sudden, and sometimes repeated attack: *to assail with weapons, with gossip* ASSAULT almost always implies bodily violence: *to assault with intent to kill.* To MOLEST is to interfere with, to threaten, or to assault: *he was safe, and where no one could molest him.* **2.** criticize, censure; impugn. —**Ant. 1.** defend.

at·tain (ə tān′), *v.t.* **1.** to reach, achieve, or accomplish by continued effort: *to attain one's ends.* **2.** to come to or arrive at in due course: *to attain the opposite shore.* —*v.i.* **3.** attain to; to arrive at; succeed in reaching or obtaining. [ME *attaine*(n), t. OF: m. *ataindre*, g. L *attingere* touch upon] —**Syn. 1.** secure. See gain¹.

at·tain·a·ble (ə tā′nə bəl), *adj.* capable of being attained. —**at·tain′a·bil′i·ty, at·tain′a·ble·ness,** *n.*

at·tain·der (ə tān′dər), *n.* **1.** the legal consequence of judgment of death or outlawry for treason or felony, involving the loss of all civil rights. **2.** *Obs.* dishonor. [ME, t. OF: m. *ataindre* ATTAIN; later assoc. with F *taindre* stain, g. L *tingere*. See ATTAINT]

at·tain·ment (ə tān′mənt), *n.* **1.** act of attaining. **2.** something attained; a personal acquirement.

at·taint (ə tānt′), *v.t.* **1.** *Law.* to condemn by a sentence or a bill or act of attainder. **2.** to disgrace. **3.** *Archaic.* to accuse. **4.** *Obs.* to prove the guilt of. —*n.* **5.** attainder. **6.** a stain, disgrace; taint. **7.** *Obs.* a touch or hit, esp. in tilting. [ME *ataint*(n), t. OF: m. *ataint*, pp. of *ataindre* ATTAIN; in part confused with TAINT]

at·tain·ture (ə tān′chər), *n.* **1.** attainder. **2.** imputation.

at·tar (ăt′ər), *n.* a perfume or essential oil obtained from flowers or petals, esp. of damask roses. [t. Pers.: m. ′*aṭar*, t. Ar.: m. ′*iṭr*]

at·tem·per (ə tĕm′pər), *v.t.* **1.** to qualify, modify, or moderate by mixing or blending (with something different or opposite). **2.** to regulate or modify the temperature of. **3.** to soothe; mollify; mitigate. **4.** to accommodate; adapt (fol. by *to*). [t. L: s. *attemperāre* fit; r. ME *atempre*(n), t. OF: m. *atemprer*]

at·tempt (ə tĕmpt′), *v.t.* **1.** to make an effort at; try; undertake; seek: *to attempt a conversation, to attempt to study.* **2.** to attack; make an effort against: *to attempt a person's life.* **3.** *Archaic.* to tempt. —*n.* **4.** effort put forth to accomplish something; a trial or essay. **5.** an attack or assault: *an attempt upon one's life.* [t. L: s. *attemptāre* try] —**at·tempt′a·bil′i·ty,** *n.* —**at·tempt′a·ble,** *adj.* —**at·tempt′er,** *n.* —**Syn. 1.** See try. **4.** undertaking, endeavor.

at·tend (ə tĕnd′), *v.t.* **1.** to be present at: *to attend school or a meeting.* **2.** to go with as a concomitant or result; accompany: *a cold attended with fever.* **3.** to minister to; devote one's services to. **4.** to wait upon or accompany as a servant. **5.** to take charge of; tend. **6.** to give heed to; listen to. **7.** *Archaic.* to wait for; expect. —*v.i.* **8.** to be present. **9.** to give attention; pay re- gard or heed. **10.** to apply oneself: *to attend to one's work.* **11.** to take care or charge of: *to attend to a task.* **12.** to be consequent (*on*). **13.** to wait (*on*) with service. **14.** *Obs.* to wait. [ME *atende*(n), t. OF: m. *atendre*, g. L *attendere* stretch toward] —**Syn. 4.** See accompany.

at·tend·ance (ə tĕn′dəns), *n.* **1.** act of attending. **2.** the persons present. **3.** *Obs.* attendants collectively.

at·tend·ant (ə tĕn′dənt), *n.* **1.** one who attends another, as for service or company. **2.** *Chiefly Brit.* an usher or clerk. **3.** one who is present, as at a meeting. **4.** that which goes along with or follows as a natural consequence. —*adj.* **5.** being present or in attendance; accompanying. **6.** concomitant; consequent: *attendant evils.* —**Syn. 1.** escort; retainer, servant.

at·ten·tion (ə tĕn′shən), *n.* **1.** act or faculty of attending. **2.** *Psychol.* concentration of the mind upon an object; maximal integration of the higher mental processes. **3.** observant care; consideration; notice: *your letter will receive early attention.* **4.** civility or courtesy: *attention to a stranger.* **5.** (*pl.*) acts of courtesy indicating regard, as in courtship. **6.** *Mil.* **a.** a command to take an erect position, with eyes to the front, arms hanging to the sides, heels together, and toes turned outward at an angle of 45 degrees. **b.** state of so standing: *at attention.* [ME *attencioun*, t. L: m. s. *attentio*] —**Syn. 4.** homage, deference; respect.

at·ten·tive (ə tĕn′tĭv), *adj.* **1.** characterized by or giving attention; observant. **2.** assiduous in service or courtesy; polite; courteous. —**at·ten′tive·ly,** *adv.* —**at·ten′tive·ness,** *n.* —**Syn. 1.** regardful, mindful.

at·ten·u·ant (ə tĕn′yŏŏ ənt), *adj.* **1.** diluting, as a liquid. —*n.* **2.** *Med.* a medicine or agent that thins the blood, etc. [t. L: s. *attenuans,* ppr.]

at·ten·u·ate (*v.* ə tĕn′yŏŏ āt′; *adj.* ə tĕn′yŏŏ ĭt, -āt′), *v.,* -ated, -ating, *adj.* —*v.t.* **1.** to make thin; make slender or fine. **2.** to weaken or reduce in force, intensity, effect, quantity, or value. —*v.i.* **3.** to become thin or fine; lessen. —*adj.* **4.** attenuated; thin. **5.** *Bot.* tapering gradually to a narrow extremity. [t. L: m. s. *attonuātus,* pp., made thin]

at·ten·u·a·tion (ə tĕn′yŏŏ ā′shən), *n.* **1.** act of attenuating. **2.** the resulting state.

at·test (ə tĕst′), *v.t.* **1.** to bear witness to; certify; declare to be correct, true, or genuine; declare the truth of, in words or writing; esp., affirm in an official capacity: *to attest the truth of a statement.* **2.** to give proof or evidence of; manifest: *his works attest his industry.* —*v.i.* **3.** to certify to the genuineness of a document by signing as witness. —*n.* **4.** *Archaic.* witness; testimony; attestation. [t. L: s. *attestārī* bear witness] —**at·test′er, at·tes′tor,** *n.*

at·tes·ta·tion (ăt′ĕs tā′shən), *n.* **1.** act of attesting. **2.** an attesting declaration; testimony; evidence.

at·tic (ăt′ĭk), *n.* **1.** (*often pl. in Brit.*) that part of a building, esp. a house, directly under a roof; a garret. **2.** a room or rooms in that part. **3.** a low story or decorative wall above an entablature or the main cornice of a building. [t. F: m. *attique,* t. L: m.s. *Atticus* Attic]

At·tic (ăt′ĭk), *adj.* **1.** pertaining to Attica. **2.** (*often l.c.*) displaying simple elegance, incisive intelligence, and delicate wit. —*n.* **3.** a native or an inhabitant of Attica; an Athenian. **4.** the Ionic dialect of ancient Athens which became the standard of Greek literature (from the 5th century B.C.). [t. L: s. *Atticus,* t. Gk.: m. *Attikós*]

At·ti·ca (ăt′ĭ kə), *n.* the region about ancient Athens, in SE Greece.

Attica, 431 B. C.

Attic faith, inviolable faith.

At·ti·cism (ăt′ə sĭz′əm), *n.* **1.** peculiarity of style or idiom belonging to Attic Greek. **2.** Attic elegance of diction. **3.** concise and elegant expression. Also, **at/ti·cism.**

At·ti·cize (ăt′ə sīz′), *v.,* -cized, -cizing. —*v.i.* **1.** to affect Attic style, usages, etc.; intermingle with Attic elements. **2.** to favor or side with the Athenians. —*v.t.* **3.** to make conformable to Attic usage. Also, **atticize.** [t. Gk.: m.s. *Attikízein* (def. 2)]

Attic salt, dry, delicate wit. Also, **Attic wit.**

At·ti·la (ăt′ə lə), *n.* ("*Scourge of God*") died A.D. 453, king of Huns who invaded Europe: defeated at Châlons- sur-Marne, A.D. 451, by the Romans and Visigoths.

at·tire (ə tīr′), *v.,* -tired, -tiring, *n.* —*v.t.* **1.** to dress, array, or adorn, esp. for special occasions, ceremonials, etc. —*n.* **2.** clothes or apparel, esp. rich or splendid garments. **3.** the horns of a deer. [ME *atire*(n), t. OF: m. *atirer* put in order, der. a- AD- + *tire* row]

at·tire·ment (ə tīr′mənt), *n.* *Obs.* dress; attire.

at·ti·tude (ăt′ə tūd′, -tōōd′), *n.* **1.** position, disposition, or manner with regard to a person or thing: *a menacing attitude.* **2.** position of the body appropriate to an action, emotion, etc. **3.** *Aeron.* the inclination of the three principal axes of an aircraft relative to the wind, to the ground, etc. **4.** a pose in ballet in which the dancer stands on one leg, the other bent behind. [t. F, t. It.: m. *attitudine* aptness, t. ML: m.s. *aptitūdo* APTITUDE] —**Syn. 2.** See position.

at·ti·tu·di·nize (ăt′ə tū′də nīz′, -tōō′-), *v.i.,* -nized, -nizing. to assume attitudes; pose for effect. —**at/ti·tu/di·niz/er,** *n.*

At·tle·bor·o (ăt/əl bŭr/ō), *n.* a city in SE Massachusetts. 23,809 (1950).

Att·lee (ăt/lĭ), *n.* **Clement Richard,** born 1883, British statesman: prime minister, 1945–1951.

at·torn (ə tûrn/), *Law.* —*v.i.* **1.** to acknowledge the relation of tenant to a new landlord. —*v.t.* **2.** to turn over to another; transfer. [t. ML: s. *attornāre,* t. OF: m. *atorner* transfer, f. *a-* AD- + *torner* turn] —**at·torn/ment,** *n.*

at·tor·ney (ə tûr/nĭ), *n., pl.* **-neys. 1.** a lawyer; attorney at law. **2.** one duly appointed or empowered by another to transact any business for him (**attorney in fact**). [ME *atorne,* t. OF, pp. of *atorner* assign] —**at·tor/ney·ship/,** *n.*

attorney at law, *Law.* an officer of the court authorized to appear before it as representative of a party to a legal controversy.

attorney general, *pl.* **attorneys general, attorney generals.** the chief law officer of the state or nation and head of its legal department.

at·tract (ə trăkt/), *v.t.* **1.** to act upon by a physical force causing or tending to cause approach or union (opposed to *repel*). **2.** to draw by other than physical influence; invite or allure; win: *to attract attention or admirers.* —*v.i.* **3.** to possess or exert the power of attraction. [t. L: s. *attractus,* pp., drawn to] —**at·tract/a·ble,** *adj.* **at·trac·tor, at·tract/er,** *n.*

at·trac·tion (ə trăk/shən), *n.* **1.** act, power, or property of attracting. **2.** allurement; enticement. **3.** that which allures or entices; a charm. **4.** *Physics.* a situation in which, under the influence of forces, bodies tend to draw together and particles of matter tend to unite or cohere. **5.** *Theat.* an entertainment offered to the public: *coming attractions.*

at·trac·tive (ə trăk/tĭv), *adj.* **1.** appealing to one's liking or admiration; engaging; alluring; pleasing. **2.** having the quality of attracting. —**at·trac/tive·ly,** *adv.* —**at·trac/tive·ness,** *n.*

at·tra·hent (ăt/rə hənt), *adj.* drawing; attracting. [t. L: s. *attrahens,* ppr., drawing to]

attrib., 1. attribute. **2.** attributive. **3.** attributively.

at·trib·ute (*v.* ə trĭb/ūt; *n.* ăt/rə būt/), *v.,* **-uted, -uting,** *n.* —*v.t.* **1.** to consider as belonging; regard as owing, as an effect to a cause (often fol. by *to*). —*n.* **2.** something attributed as belonging; a quality, character, characteristic, or property: *wisdom is one of his attributes.* **3.** *Gram.* **a.** a word or phrase grammatically subordinate to another, serving to limit (identify, particularize, describe, or supplement) the meaning of the form to which it is attached. For example: in *the red house, red* limits the meaning of *house;* it is an attribute of *house.* **b.** an attributive word; adjunct. **4.** *Fine Arts.* a symbol of office, character, or personality: *the eagle is the attribute of Jupiter.* **5.** *Logic.* that which is predicated or affirmed of a subject. **6.** *Obs.* reputation; honor. [ME (as adj.), t. L: m. s. *attribūtus,* pp., assigned] —**at·trib/ut·a·ble,** *adj.* —**at·trib/ut·er, at·trib/u·tor,** *n.*
—**Syn. 1.** ATTRIBUTE, ASCRIBE, IMPUTE imply regarding something as having had a definite origin. ATTRIBUTE and ASCRIBE are often used interchangeably, to imply something's having originated with a definite person or from a definite cause. ASCRIBE is, however, neutral as to implications; whereas, possibly because of an association with *tribute,* ATTRIBUTE is coming to have a complimentary connotation: *to ascribe one's health to outdoor life, an accident to carelessness; to attribute one's success to a friend's encouragement.* IMPUTE has gained uncomplimentary connotations, and usually means to accuse or blame someone or something as a cause or origin: *to impute dishonesty to him.* **2.** See **quality.**

at·tri·bu·tion (ăt/rə bū/shən), *n.* **1.** act of attributing; ascription. **2.** that which is ascribed; an attribute. **3.** authority or function assigned.

at·trib·u·tive (ə trĭb/yə tĭv), *adj.* **1.** pertaining to or having the character of attribution or an attribute. **2.** *Gram.* expressing an attribute; in English, applied esp. to adjectives and adverbs preceding the words which they modify (distinguished from *predicate* and *appositive*), as *first* in *the first day.* —*n.* **3.** a word expressing an attribute; attributive word, phrase, or clause. —**at·trib/u·tive·ly,** *adv.* —**at·trib/u·tive·ness,** *n.*

at·trite (ə trīt/), *adj.* worn by rubbing or attrition. Also, **at·trit/ed.** [t. L: m.s. *attritus,* pp.]

at·tri·tion (ə trĭsh/ən), *n.* **1.** a rubbing against; friction. **2.** a wearing down or away by friction; abrasion.

At·tu (ăt/tōō/), *n.* the westernmost of the Aleutian Islands: taken by U.S. forces after bitter fighting, May-June, 1943.

at·tune (ə tūn/, ə tōōn/), *v.t.,* **-tuned, -tuning.** to adjust to tune or harmony; bring into accord, or sympathetic relationship. [f. AT- + TUNE]

atty., attorney.

a·twain (ə twān/), *adv. Archaic.* in twain; in two; asunder. [ME; f. A-1 + TWAIN]

at·weel (ăt wēl/), *adv. Scot.* in truth; surely.

a·tween (ə twēn/), *prep., adv. Archaic.* between.

at. wt., atomic weight.

a·typ·i·cal (ā tĭp/ə kəl), *adj.* not typical; not conforming to the type; irregular; abnormal. Also, **a·typ/ic.** [f. A-6 + TYPICAL] —**a·typ/i·cal·ly,** *adv.*

au (ō), *French.* to the; at the; with the. See **à la.**

Au, *Chem.* (L *aurum*) gold.

A.U., angstrom unit. Also, **a.u., A.U., Au., a.u., A.u.**

au·bade (ō bäd/), *n. French.* a morning serenade.

Au·ber (ō bĕr/), *n.* **Daniel François Esprit** (dà nyĕl/ frän swà/ zĕs prē/), 1782–1871, French composer.

au·berge (ō bĕrzh/), *n. French.* an inn; tavern.

Au·ber·vil·liers (ō bĕr vē lyĕ/), *n.* a city in N France, near Paris. 53,010 (1946).

au·burn (ô/bərn), *n.* **1.** a reddish-brown or golden-brown color. —*adj.* **2.** having auburn color: *auburn hair.* [ME *auburne,* t. OF: m. *auborne,* g. L *alburnus* whitish, der. *albus* white]

Au·burn (ô/bərn), *n.* **1.** a city in central New York: State prison. 36,722 (1950). **2.** a city in SW Maine, on the Androscoggin river. 23,134 (1950).

Au·bus·son rug (ō bY sôn/), a fine French rug, handmade, with a flat tapestry weave.

A.U.C., 1. ab urbe condita. **2.** anno urbis conditae.

Auck·land (ôk/lənd), *n.* the principal seaport of New Zealand, on N North Island. 106,800; with suburbs, 223,700 (est. 1941).

au con·traire (ō kôn trĕr/), *French.* **1.** on the contrary. **2.** on the opposite or adverse side.

au cou·rant (ō kōō rän/), *French.* up to date.

auc·tion (ôk/shən), *n.* **1.** a public sale at which property or goods are sold to the highest bidder. **2.** *Cards.* **a.** auction bridge. **b.** (in bridge or certain other games) the competitive bidding to fix a contract that a player or players undertake to fulfill. —*v.t.* **3.** to sell by auction (fol. by *off*): *he auctioned off his furniture.* [t. L: s. *auctio* an increasing]

auction bridge, a variety of bridge in which the players bid to declare the trump or no-trump.

auc·tion·eer (ôk/shə nỹr/), *n.* **1.** one who conducts sales by auction. —*v.t.* **2.** to auction.

auction pitch, *Cards.* a form of seven-up with bidding to determine the trump or "pitch."

au·da·cious (ô dā/shəs), *adj.* **1.** bold or daring; spirited; adventurous: *audacious warrior.* **2.** reckless or bold in wrongdoing; impudent and presumptuous. [f. AUDACI(TY) + -OUS] —**au·da/cious·ly,** *adv.* —**au·da/cious·ness,** *n.* —**Syn. 2.** unabashed, shameless.

au·dac·i·ty (ô dăs/ə tĭ), *n.* **1.** boldness or daring, esp. reckless boldness. **2.** effrontery or insolence. [f. s. L *audācia* daring + -TY²]

Au·den (ô/dən), *n.* **Wystan Hugh** (wĭs/tən), born 1907, British poet in U.S.

au·di·ble (ô/də bəl), *adj.* capable of being heard; actually heard; loud enough to be heard. [t. ML: m. s. *audībilis,* der. L *audīre* hear] —**au/di·bil/i·ty, au/di·ble·ness,** *n.* —**au/di·bly,** *adv.*

au·di·ence (ô/dĭ əns), *n.* **1.** an assembly of hearers or spectators: *the audience at a movie.* **2.** the persons reached by a book, radio broadcast, etc.; public. **3.** liberty or opportunity of being heard or of speaking with or before a person or group. **4.** *Govt.* admission of a diplomatic representative to a sovereign or high officer of government; formal interview. **5.** act of hearing or attending to words or sounds. [ME, t. OF. g. L *audientia* attention, hearing]

au·di·ent (ô/dĭ ənt), *adj.* hearing; listening. [t. L: s. *audiens,* ppr.]

au·dile (ô/dĭl), *n. Psychol.* one in whose mind auditory images are especially distinct. [f. AUD(IO)- + -ILE]

au·di·o (ô/dĭ ō/), *adj. Electronics.* designating electronic apparatus using audio frequencies: *audio amplifier.*

audio-, a word element meaning "hear," "of or for hearing," as in *audiometer.* [comb. form repr. L *audīre* hear]

audio frequency, *Physics, Electronics.* a frequency of the order of audible frequencies of sound waves; a frequency between 15 and 20,000 cycles per second.

au·di·om·e·ter (ô/dĭ ŏm/ə tər), *n. Med.* an instrument for gauging and recording the power of hearing.

au·di·o-vis·u·al aids (ô/dĭ ō vĭzh/ōō əl), films, recordings, photographs, and other nontextual materials, used in classroom instruction and library collections.

au·di·phone (ô/də fōn/), *n. Med.* a kind of diaphragm held against the upper teeth to assist hearing by transmitting sound vibrations to the auditory nerve.

au·dit (ô/dĭt), *n.* **1.** an official examination and verification of accounts and records, esp. of financial accounts. **2.** an account or a statement of account. **3.** *Archaic.* a judicial hearing. **4.** *Rare.* audience; hearing. —*v.t.* **5.** to make audit of; examine (accounts, etc.) officially. **6.** *U.S.* to attend (classes, lectures, etc.) as an auditor. —*v.i.* **7.** to examine and verify an account or accounts by reference to vouchers. [late ME *audite,* t. L: m.s. *audītus* a hearing]

au·di·tion (ô dĭsh/ən), *n.* **1.** act, sense, or power of hearing. **2.** a hearing given to a musician, speaker, etc. to test voice qualities, performance, etc. **3.** what is heard. —*v.t., v.i.* **4.** to give an audition (to). [t. L: s. *audītio* a hearing]

au·di·tive (ô/də tĭv), *adj.* auditory.

au·di·tor (ô/də tər), *n.* **1.** a hearer; listener. **2.** a person appointed and authorized to examine accounts and accounting records, compare the charges with the vouchers, verify balance sheet and income items, and state the result. **3.** *U.S.* a university student who is registered as taking a given course but not for credit and without obligation to do the work of the course. —**au·di·tress** (ô/də trĭs), *n. fem.*

au·di·to·ri·um (ô/də tôr/Y əm), *n., pl.* **-toriums, -toria** (-tôr/Y ə). **1.** the space for the audience in a church, theater, school, or other building. **2.** a building for public gatherings; a hall. [t. L]

au·di·to·ry (ô′dә tōr′Ĭ), *adj., n., pl.* **-ries.** —*adj.* **1.** *Anat., Physiol.* pertaining to hearing or to the sense of hearing, or to the organs of hearing: *the auditory nerve.* —*n.* **2.** an assembly of hearers; an audience. **3.** an auditorium, specif. the nave in a church. [t. L: m.s. *audītōrius* (-ōrium, neut.)]

Au·du·bon (ô′dә bŏn′), *n.* **John James,** 1785?–1851, U. S. naturalist, who painted and wrote about the birds of North America.

Au·er (ou′ әr), *n.* **Leopold** (lā′ô pōlt′), 1845–1930, Hungarian violinist.

au fait (ō fā′; *Fr.* ō fĕ′), *French.* having experience or practical knowledge of a thing; expert; versed.

Auf·klä·rung (ouf′klĕ′rŏŏng), *n. German.* **1.** enlightenment. **2.** *Europ. Hist.* Enlightenment (def. 3). [G.: lit., clearing up]

au fond (ō fôn′), *French.* at bottom or to the bottom; thoroughly; in reality; fundamentally.

auf Wie·der·seh·en (ouf vē′dәr zā′әn), *German.* until we meet again; good-by for the present.

Aug., August.

aug., augmentative.

Au·ge·an sta·bles (ô jē′әn), *Gk. Legend.* the stables in which a king (**Augeas**) kept 3000 oxen and which had not been cleaned for thirty years. Hercules accomplished the task in a single day by turning the river Alpheus through the stable.

au·ger (ô′gәr), *n.* **1.** a carpenter's tool larger than a gimlet, with a spiral groove for boring holes in wood. **2.** a large tool for boring holes deep in the ground. [ME, var. of *nauger* (*a nauger* being taken as *an auger*), OE *nafogār*]

aught[1] (ôt), *n.* **1.** anything whatever; any part: *for aught I know.* —*adv.* **2.** in any degree; at all; in any respect. Also, **ought.** [ME *aught, ought,* OE *āwiht, ōwiht* at all, anything, f. *ā, ō* ever + *wiht* thing.]

Augers (def. 1)

aught[2] (ôt), *n.* a cipher (0). [appar. alter. of NAUGHT; *a naught* being taken as *an aught*]

Au·gier (ō zhyĕ′), *n.* **Guillaume Victor Émile** (gē yōm′ vēk tōr′ ĕ mēl′), 1820–89, French dramatist.

au·gite (ô′jīt), *n.* a mineral, a silicate, chiefly of calcium, magnesium, iron, and aluminum, a dark-green to black variety of pyroxene, characteristic of basic eruptive rocks like basalt. [t. L: m. *augītēs* precious stone, t. Gk.] —**au·git·ic** (ô jĭt′Ĭk), *adj.*

aug·ment (*v.* ôg mĕnt′; *n.* ôg′mĕnt), *v.t.* **1.** to make larger; enlarge in size or extent; increase. **2.** *Gram.* to add an augment to. —*v.i.* **3.** to become larger. —*n.* **4.** *Gram.* (in Greek, Sanskrit, etc.) a prefixed vowel or a lengthened initial vowel, which characterizes certain forms in the inflection of verbs. [ME *augment*(en), t. L: m. *augmentāre* increase] —**aug·ment′a·ble,** *adj.* —**aug·ment′er,** *n.* —**Syn. 1.** See **increase.**

aug·men·ta·tion (ôg′mĕn tā′shәn), *n.* **1.** act of augmenting. **2.** augmented state. **3.** that by which anything is augmented. **4.** *Music.* modification of a theme by increasing the time value of all its notes.

aug·ment·a·tive (ôg mĕn′tә tĬv), *adj.* **1.** serving to augment. **2.** *Gram.* pertaining to or productive of a form denoting increased size or intensity. In Spanish, *-ôn* added to a word indicates increased size, (*silla,* "chair"; *sillôn,* "armchair"); hence it is an augmentative suffix. —*n.* **3.** *Gram.* an augmentative element or formation.

aug·ment·ed (ôg mĕn′tĬd), *adj. Music.* (of an interval) greater by a half step than the corresponding perfect or major interval.

au gra·tin (ō grä′tәn; *Fr.* ō grå tăn′), *French.* cooked or baked covered with either browned crumbs or cheese, or with both.

Augs·burg (ôgz′bûrg; *Ger.* ouks′bŏŏrкн), *n.* a city in S Germany, in Bavaria. 185,374 (1934).

au·gur (ô′gәr), *n.* **1.** one of a body of ancient Roman officials charged with observing and interpreting omens, for guidance in public affairs. **2.** any soothsayer; prophet. —*v.t.* **3.** to divine or predict, as from omens; prognosticate. **4.** to afford an omen of. —*v.i.* **5.** to conjecture from signs or omens; presage. **6.** to be a sign; bode (*well* or *ill*). [t. L]

au·gu·ry (ô′gyә rĬ), *n., pl.* **-ries.** **1.** the art or practice of an augur; divination. **2.** a rite or observation of an augur. **3.** an omen, token, or indication. [ME, t. L: m. s. *augurium*]

Au·gust (ô′gәst), *n.* the eighth month of the year, containing 31 days. [named after AUGUSTUS]

au·gust (ô gŭst′), *adj.* **1.** inspiring reverence or admiration; of supreme dignity or grandeur; majestic: *an august spectacle.* **2.** venerable: *your august father.* [t. L: s. *augustus*] —**au·gust′ly,** *adv.* —**au·gust′ness,** *n.*

Au·gus·ta (ô gŭs′tә), *n.* **1.** a city in E Georgia, on the Savannah river. 71,508 (1950). **2.** the capital of Maine, in the SW part, on the Kennebec river. 20,913 (1950).

Au·gus·tan (ô gŭs′tәn), *adj.* **1.** pertaining to Augustus Caesar, the first Roman emperor, or to his reign (the **Augustan Age**), which marked the golden age of Latin literature. **2.** pertaining to the Augustan age in Roman literature or to the highest point in the literature of any

country. **3.** having some of the characteristics of Augustan literature, as classicism, correctness, brilliance, nobility. —*n.* **4.** an author in an Augustan age.

Au·gus·tine (ô′gә stēn′, ō gŭs′tĬn), *n.* **1. Saint,** (*Austin*) A.D. 354–430, leader of the early Christian Church: author of *City of God* and *Confessions;* bishop of Hippo in N Africa. **2. Saint,** died A.D. 604, Roman monk: headed group of missionaries that landed in England A.D. 597 and began the conversion of the English to Christianity; first archbishop of Canterbury.

Au·gus·tin·i·an (ô′gә stĬn′Ĭ әn), *adj.* **1.** pertaining to St. Augustine (A.D. 354–430), to his doctrines, or to any religious order following his rule. —*n.* **2.** a member of any of several religious orders deriving their name and rule from St. Augustine, esp. a member of the order of mendicant friars (**Hermits of St. Augustine** or **Austin Friars**). **3.** one who adopts the views or doctrines of St. Augustine. —**Au′gus·tin′i·an·ism, Au·gus·tin·ism** (ô gŭs′tә nĬz′әm), *n.*

Au·gus·tus (ô gŭs′tәs), *n.* (*Gaius Julius Caesar Octavianus, Augustus Caesar*) 63 B.C.–A.D. 14, first Roman emperor, 27 B.C. to A.D. 14: reformer, patron of arts and literature; heir and successor to Julius Caesar. Before 27 B.C., called **Octavian.**

au jus (ō zhy′), *French.* (meat) served in its own gravy.

auk (ôk), *n.* any of certain short-winged, three-toed diving birds of the family *Alcidae* of northern seas, esp. certain species of this family, as the **razor-billed auk,** *Alca torda,* and the extinct, flightless **great auk,** *Pinguinis impennis.* [t. Scand.; cf. Dan. *alke*]

auk·let (ôk′lĬt), *n.* any of various small members of the auk family found in north Pacific waters, as the **crested auklet,** *Aethia cristatella,* and its allies.

au lait (ō lā′; *Fr.* ō lĕ′). *French.* prepared or served with milk.

auld (ôld), *adj. Scot.* old.

auld lang syne (ôld′ lăng sĬn′), *Scot.* **1.** old times; old days: times fondly remembered. **2.** old or long friendship.

Razor-billed auk.
Alca torda
(17 in. long)

au·lic (ô′lĬk), *adj.* pertaining to a royal court. [t. L: s. *aulicus,* t. Gk.: m. *aulikôs* of the court]

Aulic Council, a personal council of the Holy Roman Emperor exercising chiefly judicial powers.

au na·tu·rel (ō nå ty rĕl′), *French.* **1.** in the natural state; naked. **2.** cooked plainly. **3.** uncooked.

aunt (ănt, änt), *n.* **1.** the sister of one's father or mother. **2.** the wife of one's uncle. **3.** *Chiefly Brit.* a benevolent elderly lady. [ME, t. OF: m. *ante,* g. L *amita*]

aunt·ie (ăn′tĬ, än′-), *n.* a familiar or diminutive form of **aunt.** Also, **aunt′y.**

au·ra (ôr′ә), *n., pl.* **auras, aurae** (ôr′ē). **1.** a distinctive air, atmosphere, character, etc.: *an aura of culture.* **2.** a subtle emanation proceeding from a body and surrounding it as an atmosphere. **3.** *Elect.* the motion of the air at an electrified point. **4.** *Pathol.* a sensation, as of a current of cold air, or other sensory experience, preceding an attack of epilepsy, hysteria, etc. [t. L, t. Gk.: air]

au·ral[1] (ôr′әl), *adj.* of or pertaining to an aura. [f. AUR(A) + -AL[1]]

au·ral[2] (ôr′әl), *adj.* of, or perceived by, the organs of hearing. [f. s. L *auris* ear + -AL[1]] —**au′ral·ly,** *adv.*

Au·rang·zeb (ôr′әng zĕb′), *n.* 1618–1707, Mogul emperor of Hindustan, 1658–1707. Also, **Au′rung·zeb′.**

au·re·ate (ôr′Ĭ Ĭt, -āt′), *adj.* **1.** golden. **2.** brilliant; splendid. [ME *aureat,* t. L: s. *aureātus* adorned with gold]

Au·re·li·an (ô rē′lĬ әn, -rēl′yәn), *n.* (*Lucius Domitius Aurelianus*) A.D. 212?–275, Roman emperor, 270–275.

Au·re·li·us (ô rē′lĬ әs, ô rēl′yәs), *n.* See **Antoninus.**

au·re·ole (ôr′Ĭ ōl′), *n.* **1.** a radiance surrounding the head or the whole figure in the representation of a sacred personage. **2.** any encircling ring of light or color; a halo. **3.** *Astron.* corona (defs. 1, 2). Also, **au·re·o·la** (ô rē′ә lә). [t. L: m. *aureola,* fem. of *aureolus* golden]

au·re·o·my·cin (ô′rĬ ō mī′sĬn), *n.* a recently developed antibiotic that is effective against certain diseases caused by viruses or Rickettsia, such as Rocky Mountain spotted fever.

au re·voir (ō rә vwär′), *French.* until we see each other again; good-by for the present.

au·ric (ôr′Ĭk), *adj. Chem.* of or containing gold, esp. in the trivalent state (Au^{+3}). [f. s. L *aurum* gold + -IC]

au·ri·cle (ôr′ә kәl), *n.* **1.** *Anat.* **a.** the projecting outer portion of the ear; the pinna. **b.** one of two chambers of the heart through which blood from the veins passes into the ventricles. See diag. under **heart. 2.** *Bot., Zool.* a part like or likened to an ear. [t. L: m.s. *auricula,* dim. of *auris* ear] —**au′ri·cled,** *adj.*

au·ric·u·la (ô rĬk′yә lә), *n., pl.* **-lae** (-lē′), **-las.** a yellow primrose, *Primula Auricula,* native in the Alps; bear's-ear. [t. L: the external ear. See AURICLE]

au·ric·u·lar (ô rĬk′yә lәr), *adj.* **1.** of or pertaining to the organs of hearing. **2.** perceived by or addressed to the ear: *auricular confession.* **3.** dependent on hearing; aural. **4.** shaped like an ear; auriculate. **5.** *Anat.* pertaining to an auricle of the heart. **6.** *Ornith.* noting certain feathers, usually of peculiar structure, which overlie and defend the outer opening of a bird's ear. —*n.* **7.** (*usually pl.*) *Ornith.* an auricular feather.

au·ric·u·late (ô rĬk′yә lĬt, -lāt′), *adj.* **1.** having auricles, or earlike parts. **2.** shaped like an ear.

---

b., blend of, blended; **c.,** cognate with; **d.,** dialect, dialectal; **der.,** derived from; **f.,** formed from; **g.,** going back to. **m.,** modification of; **r.,** replacing; **s.,** stem of; **t.,** taken from; **?,** perhaps. See the full key on inside cover;

au·rif·er·ous (ô rĭf′ər əs), *adj.* yielding or containing gold. [f. L *aurifer* gold-bearing + -OUS]

Au·ri·ga (ô rī′gə), *n.* a northern constellation containing Capella. [t. L: charioteer]

au·rist (ôr′ĭst), *n.* a physician expert in treating diseases of the ear; an otologist. [f. s. L *auris* ear + -IST]

au·rochs (ôr′ŏks), *n., pl.*
-rochs. a European wild ox,
Bos primigenius, now extinct. [t. G, var. of *auerochs,*
MHG *ūr-ochse,* f. *ūr* (c. OE
ūr wild ox) + *ochse* ox]

Aurochs, *Bos primigenius*
(Ab. 6 ft. high at the shoulder)

Au·ro·ra (ô rôr′ə), *n.* **1.**
Class. Myth. dawn, often personified, by the Romans and others, as a goddess (Eos). **2.** (*l.c.*) the rise or dawn of something. **3.** (*l.c.*) *Meteorol.* an electrical atmospheric phenomenon, consisting of streamers, bands, curtains, arcs, etc., of light, ordinarily confined to high altitudes; the polar lights (aurora borealis or aurora australis). **4.** a city in NE Illinois. 50,576 (1950). [t. L]

aurora aus·tra·lis (ô strā′lĭs). *Meteorol.* the aurora of the Southern Hemisphere, a phenomenon similar to the aurora borealis. [NL]

aurora bo·re·al·is (bôr′ĭ ăl′ĭs, -ā′lĭs), *Meteorol.* the aurora of the Northern Hemisphere, a luminous meteoric phenomenon appearing at night. [NL]

au·ro·ral (ô rôr′əl), *adj.* **1.** of or like the dawn. **2.** pertaining to a polar aurora. **—au·ro′ral·ly,** *adv.*

au·ro·re·an (ô rôr′ĭ ən), *adj. Poetic.* belonging to the dawn; auroral.

au·rous (ôr′əs), *adj.* **1.** *Chem.* containing monovalent gold (Au+1). **2.** of or containing gold. [f. AUR(UM) + -OUS]

au·rum (ôr′əm), *n. Chem.* gold. *Symbol:* Au. [t. L]

Au·sa·ble (ô sā′bəl), *n.* a river in NE New York, flowing through **Ausable Chasm,** a scenic gorge 2 mi. long, into Lake Champlain.

aus·cul·tate (ô′skəl tāt′), *v.t., v.i.,* **-tated, -tating.**
Med. to examine by auscultation. **—aus·cul·ta·tive**
(ô′skəl tā′tĭv, ô skŭl′tə-), **aus·cul·ta·to·ry** (ô skŭl′tə tōr′ĭ), *adj.* **—aus′cul·ta′tor,** *n.*

aus·cul·ta·tion (ô′skəl tā′shən), *n.* **1.** *Med.* the act of listening, either directly or through a stethoscope or other instrument, to sounds within the body, as a method of diagnosis, etc. **2.** act of listening. [t. L: s. *auscultātio* a listening]

Aus·gleich (ous′glīкн), *n., pl.* **-gleiche** (-glī′кнə). *German.* **1.** an arrangement or compromise between parties. **2.** the agreement made between Austria and Hungary in 1867, regulating the relations between the countries and setting up the Dual Monarchy.

aus·pex (ô′spĕks), *n., pl.* **auspices** (ô′spə sēz′). an augur (def. 1). [t. L]

aus·pi·cate (ô′spə kāt′), *v.,* **-cated, -cating.** *Obs. or Rare.* **—v.t.** **1.** to initiate with ceremonies calculated to ensure good luck; inaugurate. **—v.i.** **2.** to augur. [t. L: m.s. *auspicātus,* pp.]

aus·pice (ô′spĭs), *n., pl.* **auspices** (ô′spə sĭz). **1.** (*usually pl.*) favoring influence; patronage: *under the auspices of the State Department.* **2.** a propitious circumstance. **3.** a divination or prognostication, originally from birds. [t. F, t. L: m.s. *auspicium*]

aus·pi·cial (ô spĭsh′əl), *adj.* **1.** of or pertaining to auspices: *auspicial rites.* **2.** auspicious.

aus·pi·cious (ô spĭsh′əs), *adj.* **1.** of good omen; betokening success; favorable: *an auspicious moment.* **2.** favored by fortune; prosperous; fortunate. [f. s. L *auspicium* divination + -OUS] **—aus·pi′cious·ly,** *adv.* **—aus·pi′cious·ness,** *n.*

Aus·ten (ô′stən), *n.* **Jane,** 1775–1817, British novelist.

Aus·ter (ô′stər), *n. Poetic.* the south wind personified. [t. L]

aus·tere (ô stĭr′), *adj.* **1.** harsh in manner; stern in appearance; forbidding. **2.** severe in disciplining or restraining oneself; morally strict. **3.** grave; sober; serious. **4.** severely simple; without ornament: *austere writing.* **5.** rough to the taste; sour or harsh in flavor. [ME, t. L: m.s. *austērus,* t. Gk.: m. *austērós*] **—aus·tere′ly,** *adv.* **—aus·tere′ness,** *n.*

aus·ter·i·ty (ô stĕr′ə tĭ), *n., pl.* **-ties. 1.** austere quality; severity of manner, life, etc. **2.** (*usually pl.*) a severe or ascetic practice. **—Syn. 2.** See **hardship.**

Aus·ter·litz (ô′stər lĭts; *Ger.* ous′tər-), *n.* a town in central Czechoslovakia, in Moravia: Napoleon defeated the combined Russian and Austrian armies here, 1805.

Aus·tin (ô′stən), *n.* **1.** the capital of Texas, in the central part, on the Colorado river. 132,459 (1950). **2.** a city in SE Minnesota. 23,100 (1950). **3. Alfred,** 1835–1913, British poet. **4. John,** 1790–1859, British writer on law. **5. Warren Robinson,** born 1877, U.S. diplomat. **6.** Saint Augustine (def. 1).

Austin friar, Augustinian (def. 2).

aus·tral (ô′strəl), *adj.* **1.** southern. **2.** (*cap.*) Australian. [t. L: s. *austrālis* (def. 2)]

Austral·, **1.** Australasia. **2.** Australia.

Aus·tral·a·sia (ô′strə lā′zhə, -shə), *n.* Australia, New Zealand, and neighboring islands of the S Pacific Ocean. **—Aus′tral·a′sian,** *adj., n.*

Aus·tral·ia (ô strāl′yə), *n.* **1.** the continent SE of Asia. 7,197,538 pop. (1946); 2,948,366 sq. mi. **2. Commonwealth of,** a dominion of the British Commonwealth of Nations, consisting of the federated states and territories of Australia and Tasmania. 7,448,601 pop. (1946); 2,974,581 sq. mi. *Cap.:* Canberra.

Aus·tral·ian (ô strāl′yən), *adj.* **1.** of or pertaining to Australia. **—n. 2.** a native or inhabitant of Australia. **3.** an Australian aborigine. **4.** any of the languages of the Australian aborigines.

Australian Alps, a mountain range in SE Australia. Highest peak, Mt. Kosciusko, 7328 ft.

Australian ballot, *Govt.* a ballot which ensures secrecy in voting, originally used in South Australia.

Australian Capital Territory, a federal territory in SE Australia, within New South Wales: Canberra, the capital, is located there. 14,981 pop. (1946). 939 sq. mi. Formerly, **Federal Capital Territory.**

Aus·tra·sia (ô strā′zhə, -shə), *n.* the E part of the kingdom of the Franks comprising parts of what is now NE France, W. Germany, and Belgium. *Cap.:* Metz. **—Aus·tra′sian,** *adj., n.*

Austrasia, A.D. 481–814

Aus·tri·a (ô′strĭ ə), *n.* a country in central Europe. 7,000,000 pop. (est. 1946); 32,381 sq. mi. *Cap.:* Vienna. German, **Osterreich.** **—Aus′tri·an,** *adj., n.*

Aus·tri·a-Hun·ga·ry (ô′strĭ ə hŭng′gə rĭ), *n.* a former monarchy in central Europe, including the empire of Austria, kingdom of Hungary, and various crownlands: dissolved, 1918. **—Aus·tro-Hun·gar·i·an** (ô′strō hŭng gâr′ĭ ən), *adj.*

Austro-, a word element meaning "Austria," "Austrian."

Aus·tro·ne·sia (ô′strō nē′zhə, -shə), *n.* islands of the central and south Pacific. [f. *austro-* (repr. AUSTER) + s. Gk. *nêsos* island + -IA]

Aus·tro·ne·sian (ô′strō nē′zhən, -shən), *adj.* **1.** of or pertaining to Austronesia. **—n. 2.** a family of languages spoken in the Pacific, consisting of four divisions, Indonesian, Melanesian, Micronesian, and Polynesian; Malayo-Polynesian.

Austria-Hungary, 1871–1914

aut-, var. of auto¹ before most vowels, as in **autacoid.**

au·ta·coid (ô′tə koid′), *n. Physiol.* a substance secreted by one organ into the blood stream or lymph, and controlling organic processes elsewhere in the body; a hormone. [f. AUT- + m.s. Gk. *ákos* remedy + -OID]

au·tar·chy (ô′tär kĭ), *n., pl.* **-chies. 1.** absolute sovereignty. **2.** self-government. **3.** autarky. [t. Gk.: m.s. *autarchía* self-rule] **—au·tar′chic,** *adj.*

au·tar·ky (ô′tär kĭ), *n., pl.* **-kies. 1.** the condition of self-sufficiency, esp. economic, as applied to a state. **2.** a national policy of economic independence. Also, **autarchy.** [t. Gk.: m.s. *autárkeia*] **—au·tar′ki·cal,** *adj.* **—au′tar·kist,** *n., adj.*

au·te·cism (ô tē′sĭz əm), *n.* autoecism. **—au·te·cious** (ô tē′shəs), *adj.*

au·te·col·o·gy (ô′tə kŏl′ə jĭ), *n.* that branch of ecology which deals with the individual organism and its environment. Cf. **synecology.**

auth., 1. author. **2.** authorized.

au·then·tic (ô thĕn′tĭk), *adj.* **1.** entitled to acceptance or belief; reliable; trustworthy: *an authentic story.* **2.** of the authorship or origin reputed; of genuine origin: *authentic documents.* **3.** *Law.* executed with all due formalities: *an authentic deed.* **4.** *Obs.* authoritative. Also, **au·then′ti·cal.** [t. LL: s. *authenticus,* t. Gk.: m. *authentikós* warranted] **—au·then′ti·cal·ly,** *adv.*

au·then·ti·cate (ô thĕn′tə kāt′), *v.t.,* **-cated, -cating. 1.** to make authoritative or valid. **2.** to establish as genuine. **—au·then′ti·ca′tion,** *n.* **—au·then′ti·ca′tor,** *n.*

au·then·tic·i·ty (ô′thən tĭs′ə tĭ, -thĕn-), *n.* quality of being authentic; reliability; genuineness.

au·thor (ô′thər), *n.* **1.** a person who writes a novel, poem, essay, etc.; the composer of a literary work, as distinguished from a compiler, translator, editor, or copyist. **2.** the originator, beginner, or creator of anything. **3.** the literary production(s) of a writer: *to find a passage in an author.* [ME *autor,* t. OF, t. L: m. *auctor* originator] **—au·thor·ess** (ô′thər ĭs), *n. fem.* **—au·tho·ri·al** (ô thôr′ĭ əl), *adj.* **—au′thor·less,** *adj.*

au·thor·i·tar·i·an (ə thôr′ə târ′ĭ ən, ə thŏr′-), *adj.* **1.** favoring the principle of subjection to authority as opposed to that of individual freedom. **—n. 2.** one who favors authoritarian principles. [f. AUTHORIT(Y) + -ARIAN] **—au·thor′i·tar′i·an·ism,** *n.*

au·thor·i·ta·tive (ə thŏr'ə tā'tĭv, ə thŏr'-), *adj.* **1.** having due authority; having the sanction or weight of authority: *an authoritative opinion.* **2.** having an air of authority; positive; peremptory; dictatorial. **—au·thor'-i·ta·tive·ly,** *adv.* **—au·thor'i·ta'tive·ness,** *n.* **—Syn. 1.** conclusive, unquestioned. **2.** impressive, dogmatic.

au·thor·i·ty (ə thŏr'ə tĭ, ə thŏr'-), *n., pl.* **-ties. 1.** the right to determine, adjudicate, or otherwise settle issues or disputes; the right to control, command, or determine. **2.** a person or body with such rights. **3.** an accepted source of information, advice, etc. **4.** a standard author or his writing; an expert on a subject. **5.** a statute, court rule, or judicial decision which establishes a rule or principle of law; a ruling. **6.** title to respect or acceptance; commanding influence. **7.** a warrant for action; justification. **8.** testimony; witness. [t. F: m. *authorité*; r. ME *auctorite*, t. L: m.s. *auctōritas*] **—Syn. 1.** AUTHORITY, CONTROL, INFLUENCE denote a power or right to direct the actions or thoughts of others. AUTHORITY is a power or right, usually because of rank or office, to issue commands and to punish for violations: *to have authority over subordinates.* CONTROL is either authority or influence applied to the complete and successful direction or manipulation of persons or things: *to be in control of a project.* INFLUENCE is a personal and unofficial power derived from deference of others to one's character, ability, or station; it may be exerted unconsciously or may operate through persuasion: *to have influence over one's friends.*

au·thor·i·za·tion (ô'thər ə zā'shən), *n.* act of authorizing; permission from or establishment by an authority.

au·thor·ize (ô'thə rīz'), *v.t.*, **-ized, -izing. 1.** to give authority or legal power to; empower (to do something): *to authorize a sheriff.* **2.** to give authority for; formally sanction (an act or proceeding). **3.** to establish by authority or usage: *authorized by custom.* **4.** to afford a ground for; warrant; justify. **—au'thor·iz'er,** *n.*

au·thor·ized (ô'thə rīzd'), *adj.* **1.** authoritative; endowed with authority. **2.** legally or duly sanctioned.

Authorized Version, 1. an English revision of the Bible prepared in England under James I and published in 1611. **2.** any translation of the Bible endorsed by church authority for use in public worship.

au·thor·ship (ô'thər shĭp'), *n.* **1.** the occupation or career of writing books, articles, etc. **2.** origin as to author, composer, or compiler: *the authorship of a book.*

Auth. Ver., Authorized Version (of the Bible).

au·tism (ô'tĭz əm), *n.* **1.** *Psychol.* fantasy; introverted thought; daydreaming; marked subjectivity of interpretation. **2.** *Psychiatry.* such a state, with introversive behavior, noted in several psychopathological conditions. [f. AUT- + -ISM] **—au·tis·tic** (ô tĭs'tĭk), *adj.*

au·to (ô'tō), *n., pl.* **-tos.** automobile. [shortened form]

auto-¹, a word element meaning "self," "same" as in *autograph.* Also, **aut-.** [t. Gk., comb. form of *autós*]

auto-², a combining form of **automobile,** as in *auto-park.*

auto., automobile.

Au·to·bahn (ou'tō bän'), *n., pl.* **-bahnen** (-bä'nən). (in Germany) a superhighway having no speed limit.

au·to·bi·o·graph·ic (ô'tə bī'ə grăf'ĭk), *adj.* dealing with one's life history. Also, **au'to·bi'o·graph'i·cal.** **—au'to·bi'o·graph'i·cal·ly,** *adv.*

au·to·bi·og·ra·phy (ô'tə bī ŏg'rə fĭ, -bĭ-), *n., pl.* **-phies.** an account of a person's life written by himself. **—au'to·bi·og'ra·pher,** *n.*

au·to·cade (ô'tə kād'), *n.* a procession or train of motor vehicles. [f. AUTO-² + (CAVAL)CADE]

au·toch·thon (ô tŏk'thən), *n., pl.* **-thons, -thones** (-thə nēz'). **1.** an aboriginal inhabitant. **2.** *Ecol.* one of the indigenous animals or plants of a region. [t. Gk.: lit., sprung from the land itself]

au·toch·tho·nous (ô tŏk'thə nəs), *adj.* pertaining to autochthons; aboriginal; indigenous. Also, **au·toch'-tho·nal, au·toch·thon·ic** (ô'tŏk thŏn'ĭk). **—au·toch'-tho·nism, au·toch'tho·ny,** *n.* **—au·toch'tho·nous·ly,** *adv.*

au·to·clave (ô'tə klāv'), *n.* **1.** a heavy vessel in which chemical reactions take place under high pressure. **2.** a pressure cooker. **3.** *Med.* a strong closed vessel in which steam under pressure effects sterilization. [t. F: self-regulation, f. *auto-* AUTO-¹ + m.s. L *clāvis* key]

au·toc·ra·cy (ô tŏk'rə sĭ), *n., pl.* **-cies. 1.** uncontrolled or unlimited authority over others, invested in a single person; the government or power of an absolute monarch. **2.** independent or self-derived power. [t. Gk.: m.s. *autokráteia* absolute power]

au·to·crat (ô'tə krăt'), *n.* **1.** an absolute ruler; a monarch who holds and exercises the powers of government as by inherent right, not subject to restrictions. **2.** a person invested with, or claiming to exercise, absolute authority. [t. Gk.: m. s. *autokratēs* ruling by oneself]

au·to·crat·ic (ô'tə krăt'ĭk), *adj.* pertaining to or of the nature of autocracy; absolute; holding independent and unlimited powers of government. Also, **au'to·crat'-i·cal.** **—au'to·crat'i·cal·ly,** *adv.*

au·to·da·fé (ô'tō dä fā'), *n., pl.* **autos-da-fé.** the public declaration of the judgment passed on persons tried in the courts of the Spanish Inquisition, followed by execution of the sentences imposed, including the burning (by civil authorities) of heretics at the stake. Also, *Spanish,* **au·to de fé** (ou'tō dĕ fĕ'). [t. Pg.: act of (the) faith]

au·toe·cism (ô tē'sĭz əm), *n. Bot.* the development of the entire life cycle of a parasitic fungus on a single host

or group of hosts. Also, **autecism.** Cf. **heteroecism.** [f. AUT- + m.s. Gk. *oîkos* house + ISM] **—au·toe·cious,** (ô tē'shəs), *adj.*

au·to·e·rot·ic (ô'tō ĭ rŏt'ĭk), *adj. Psychoanal.* producing sexual emotion without association with another person.

au·to·er·o·tism (ô'tō ĕr'ə tĭz'əm), *n. Psychoanal.* the arousal and satisfaction of sexual emotion within or by oneself, usually by masturbation. Also, **au·to·e·rot·i·cism** (ô'tō ĭ rŏt'ə sĭz'əm).

au·tog·a·my (ô tŏg'ə mĭ), *n. Bot.* fecundation of the ovules of a flower by its own pollen; self-fertilization (opposed to *allogamy*). **—au·tog'a·mous,** *adj.*

au·to·gen·e·sis (ô'tō jĕn'ə sĭs), *n. Biol.* abiogenesis. Also, **au·tog·e·ny** (ô tŏj'ə nĭ).

au·to·ge·net·ic (ô'tō jə nĕt'ĭk), *adj.* **1.** self-generated. **2.** *Biol.* pertaining to autogenesis. **—au'to·ge·net'i·cal·ly,** *adv.*

au·tog·e·nous (ô tŏj'ə nəs), *adj.* **1.** self-produced; self-generated. **2.** *Physiol.* pertaining to substances generated in the body. [f. s. Gk. *autogenēs* self-produced + -OUS] **—au·tog'e·nous·ly,** *adv.*

au·to·gi·ro (ô'tə jī'rō), *n., pl.* **-ros. 1.** an aircraft with horizontal revolving wings on a shaft above the fuselage which sustain the machine or allow it to descend slowly and steeply, forward propulsion being secured by a conventional propeller. **2.** (*cap.*) a trademark for this aircraft. Also, **au'to·gy'ro.** [t. Sp. See AUTO-¹, GYRO-]

au·to·graph (ô'tə grăf', -gräf'), *n.* **1.** a person's own signature. **2.** a person's own handwriting. **3.** a manuscript in the author's handwriting. *—adj.* **4.** written by a person's own hand: *an autograph letter.* **5.** containing autographs: *an autograph album.* *—v.t.* **6.** to write one's name on or in: *to autograph a book.* **7.** to write with one's own hand. [t. L: s. *autographum,* t. Gk.: m. *autógraphon.* See AUTO-¹, -GRAPH] **—au'to·graph'ic, au'to·graph'i·cal,** *adj.* **—au'to·graph'i·cal·ly,** *adv*

au·tog·ra·phy (ô tŏg'rə fĭ), *n.* autograph writing.

au·to·harp (ô'tō härp'), *n.* a zither played with the fingers or a plectrum, which is capable of playing chords by arrangements of dampers and is easily learned.

au·to·hyp·no·sis (ô'tō hĭp nō'sĭs), *n.* self-induced hypnosis or hynotic state. **—au·to·hyp·not·ic** (ô'tō hĭp nŏt'ĭk), *adj.*

au·toi·cous (ô toi'kəs), *adj. Bot.* having antheridia and archegonia on the same plant: synoicous, paroicous, or otherwise. [f. AUT(o)- + m. s. Gk. *oîkos* house + -OUS]

au·to·in·fec·tion (ô'tō ĭn fĕk'shən), *n. Pathol.* infection from within the body.

au·to·in·oc·u·la·tion (ô'tō ĭn ŏk'yə lā'shən), *n.* inoculation of a healthy part with an infective agent from a diseased part of the same body.

au·to·in·tox·i·ca·tion (ô'tō ĭn tŏk'sə kā'shən), *n. Pathol.* poisoning with toxic substances formed within the body, as during intestinal digestion.

au·to·ki·net·ic (ô'tō kĭ nĕt'ĭk, -kī-), *adj.* self-moving; automatic. Also, **au·to·ki·net'i·cal.** [f. s. Gk. *autoknētos* self-moved + -IC]

au·to·ly·sin (ô'tə lī'sĭn, ô tŏl'ə-), *n.* an agent effecting autolysis.

au·tol·y·sis (ô tŏl'ə sĭs), *n. Biochem.* the breakdown of plant or animal tissue by the action of enzymes contained in the tissue affected; self-digestion. [f. AUTO-¹ + -LYSIS] **—au·to·lyt·ic** (ô'tə lĭt'ĭk), *adj.*

au·to·mat (ô'tə măt'), *n.* a restaurant using automatic apparatus for serving articles of food to customers upon the dropping of the proper coins or tokens into a slot. [t. Gk.: s. *autómaton.* See AUTOMATON]

au·tom·a·ta (ô tŏm'ə tə), *n.* pl. of **automaton.**

au·to·mat·ic (ô'tə măt'ĭk), *adj.* **1.** having the power of self-motion; self-moving or self-acting; mechanical. **2.** *Physiol.* occurring independently of volition, as certain muscular actions. **3.** (of a firearm, pistol, etc.) utilizing the recoil, or part of the force of the explosive, to eject the spent cartridge shell, introduce a new cartridge, cock the arm, and fire it repeatedly. **4.** done unconsciously or from force of habit; mechanical (opposed to *voluntary*). *—n.* **5.** a machine which operates automatically. **6.** automatic pistol. **7.** automatic rifle. [f. s. Gk. *autómatos* self-acting + -IC] **—au'to·mat'i·cal·ly,** *adv.* **—Syn. 2.** AUTOMATIC, INVOLUNTARY both mean not under the control of the will. That which is AUTOMATIC, however, is an invariable reaction to a fixed type of stimulus: *the patella reflex is automatic.* That which is INVOLUNTARY is an unexpected response which varies according to the occasion, circumstances, mood, etc: *an involuntary cry of pain.*

automatic pilot, *Aeron.* an automatic steering device in an aircraft.

automatic pistol, a pistol that has a mechanism that throws out the empty shell, puts in a new one, and prepares the pistol to be fired again.

automatic rifle, a type of light machine gun which can be fired by single shots or automatically.

au·tom·a·tism (ô tŏm'ə tĭz'əm), *n.* **1.** action or condition of being automatic; mechanical or involuntary action. **2.** *Philos.* the doctrine that all activities of animals, including men, are controlled only by physiological causes, consciousness being considered a noncausal by-product; epiphenomenonalism. **3.** *Physiol.* the involuntary functioning of an organic process, esp. muscular, without neural stimulation. **4.** *Psychol.* an act performed by an individual without his awareness or will, as sleepwalking. **5.** *Surrealism.* relaxing or evading of conscious thought to bring unconscious and repressed ideas and feelings to artistic expression. —au·tom′a·tist, n.

au·tom·a·ton (ô·tŏm′ə·tŏn′, -tən), n., pl. **-tons, -ta** (-tə). **1.** a mechanical figure or contrivance constructed to act as if spontaneously through concealed motive power. **2.** a person who acts in a monotonous routine manner, without active intelligence. **3.** something capable of acting spontaneously or without external impulse. [t. Gk., prop. neut. of automatos self-acting]

au·to·mo·bile (n. ô′tə·mə·bēl′, ô′tə·mō′bēl, -mə·bēl′; adj. ô′tə·mō′bĭl, -bēl), n. **1.** Chiefly U.S. a vehicle, esp. one for passengers, carrying its own power-generating and propelling mechanism, for travel on ordinary roads. —adj. **2.** automotive. [f. F. See AUTO-¹, MOBILE] —au·to·mo·bil·ist (ô′tə·mə·bēl′ĭst, -mō′bĭl′ĭst), n.

au·to·mo·tive (ô′tə·mō′tĭv), adj. **1.** pertaining to the design, operation, manufacture, and sale of automobiles. **2.** propelled by a self-contained power plant.

au·to·nom·ic (ô′tə·nŏm′ĭk), adj. **1.** autonomous, **2.** Physiol. pertaining to or designating a system of nerves and ganglia (the **autonomic, involuntary,** or **vegetative nervous system**) leading from the spinal cord and brain to glands, blood vessels, the viscera, and the heart and smooth muscles, constituting their efferent innervation and controlling their involuntary functions (opposed to cerebrospinal). **3.** Bot. produced by internal forces or causes; spontaneous. —au′to·nom′i·cal·ly, adv.

au·ton·o·mous (ô·tŏn′ə·məs), adj. **1.** Govt. **a.** self-governing; independent; subject to its own laws only. **b.** pertaining to an autonomy. **2.** Biol. existing as an independent organism and not as a mere form or state of development of an organism. **3.** Bot. autonomic. [t. Gk.: m. autónomos (def. 1)] —au·ton′o·mous·ly, adv.

au·ton·o·my (ô·tŏn′ə·mĭ), n., pl. **-mies.** Govt. **1.** the condition of being autonomous; self-government, or the right of self-government; independence. **2.** a self-governing community. [t. Gk.: m. s. autonomía] —au·ton′o·mist, n.

au·to·plas·ty (ô′tə·plăs′tĭ), n. Surg. the repair of defects with tissue from another part of the patient. [f. s. Gk. autóplastos self-formed + -Y³] —au′to·plas′tic, adj.

au·top·sy (ô′tŏp·sĭ, ô′təp-), n., pl. **-sies. 1.** inspection and dissection of a body after death, as for determination of the cause of death; a post-mortem examination. **2.** personal observation. [t. Gk.: m. s. autopsía seeing with one's own eyes]

au·to·some (ô′tə·sōm′), n. Genetics. any chromosome other than the sex chromosome in species having both types of chromosomes.

au·to·sug·ges·tion (ô′tō·səg·jĕs′chən), n. Psychol. suggestion arising from within a person (as opposed to one from an outside source, esp. another person).

au·tot·o·my (ô·tŏt′ə·mĭ), n. Zool. self-crippling by casting off damaged or trapped appendages such as tails by lizards, legs by spiders, crabs, etc.

au·to·tox·e·mi·a (ô′tō·tŏk·sē′mĭ·ə), n. auto-intoxication. Also, **au′to·tox·ae′mi·a.**

au·to·tox·in (ô′tə·tŏk′sĭn), n. Pathol. a toxin or poisonous principle formed within the body and acting against it. —au′to·tox′ic, adj.

au·to·troph·ic (ô′tə·trŏf′ĭk), adj. Bot. (of plants) building their own nutritive substances, esp. by photosynthesis or chemosynthesis.

au·to·truck (ô′tō·trŭk′), n. an automobile truck.

au·to·type (ô′tə·tīp′), n. **1.** facsimile. **2.** a photographic process for producing permanent prints in a carbon pigment. **3.** a picture so produced. —au·to·typ·ic (ô′tə·tĭp′ĭk), adj. —au·to·typ·y (ô′tə·tī′pĭ), n.

au·tox·i·da·tion (ô·tŏk′sə·dā′shən), n. Chem. **1.** the oxidation of a compound by its exposure to air. **2.** an oxidation reaction in which another substance must be included for the reaction to be completed.

au·tumn (ô′təm), n. **1.** the third season of the year, between summer and winter; fall. (In U.S. it is formal or poetic; in England it is the usual word.) **2.** a period of maturity passing into decline. [t. L.: s. autumnus; r. ME automne, t. OF]

au·tum·nal (ô·tŭm′nəl), adj. **1.** belonging to or suggestive of autumn; produced or gathered in autumn. **2.** past maturity or middle life. —au·tum′nal·ly, adv.

autumnal equinox. See **equinox.** Also, **autumnal point.**

au·tun·ite (ô′tə·nīt′), n. a yellow mineral, a hydrous calcium uranium phosphate, $CaU_2P_2O_{12}.8H_2O$, occurring in crystals as nearly square tablets: a minor ore of uranium. [named after Autun, city in eastern France. See -ITE²]

Au·vergne (ō·vârn′, ō·vûrn′; Fr. ō·vĕrn′y), n. a former province in central France.

aux (ō), French. to the; at the; with the. See **à la.**

aux., auxiliary. Also, **auxil.**

Aux Cayes (ō kā′), a seaport on the SW coast of Haiti. ab. 15,000.

aux·il·ia·ry (ôg·zĭl′yər·ĭ, -zĭl′ə-), adj., n., pl. **-ries** —adj. **1.** giving support; helping; aiding; assisting. **2.** subsidiary; additional: auxiliary troops. **3.** used as a reserve: an auxiliary engine. —n. **4.** person or thing that gives aid of any kind; helper. **5.** auxiliary verb. **6.** (pl.) foreign troops in the service of a nation at war. **7.** Naval. a naval vessel designed for other than combat purposes, as a tug, supply ship, transport, etc. **8.** a sailing vessel

carrying auxiliary power. [t. L: m.s. auxiliārius, der. auxilium aid] —Syn. **2.** subordinate, ancillary. **4.** ally.

auxiliary verb, a verb customarily preceding certain forms of other verbs, used to express distinctions of time, aspect, mood, etc., as do, am, etc., in I do think; I am going; we have spoken; may we go?; can they see?; we shall walk.

aux·in (ôk′sĭn), n. Bot., Chem. a class of substances which in minute amounts regulate or modify the growth of plants, esp. root formation, bud growth, fruit and leaf drop, etc. [? var. of auxein, f. Gk. aúxē increase + -IN²]

aux·o·chrome (ôk′sə·krōm′), n. Chem. any group of atoms which make a chromogen acidic or basic, giving it the ability to adhere to wool and silk. [f. auxo- (repr. Gk. auxánein increase) + CHROME]

av., **1.** avenue. **2.** average. **3.** avoirdupois.

A/V, ad valorem. Also, **a.v.**

A.V., Authorized Version (of the Bible).

a·vail (ə·vāl′), v.i. **1.** to have force or efficacy; be of use; serve. **2.** to be of value or profit. —v.t. **3.** to be of use or value to; profit; advantage. **4.** avail oneself of, to give oneself the advantage of. —n. **5.** efficacy for a purpose; advantage to an object or end: of little or no avail. **6.** (pl.) profits or proceeds. [ME, f. OF: a- A-⁵ + vail, 1st person sing. pres. indic. of valoir, g. L valēre be strong, have effect] —a·vail′ing·ly, adv.

a·vail·a·bil·i·ty (ə·vā′lə·bĭl′ə·tĭ), n., pl. **-ties. 1.** state of being available: the availability of a candidate. **2.** that which or one who is available.

a·vail·a·ble (ə·vā′lə·bəl), adj. **1.** suitable or ready for use; at hand; of use or service: available resources. **2.** having sufficient power or efficacy; valid. **3.** Archaic. profitable; advantageous. —a·vail′a·ble·ness, n. —a·vail′a·bly, adv. —Syn. **1.** accessible, usable.

av·a·lanche (ăv′ə·lănch′, -länch′), n., v. **-lanched, -lanching.** —n. **1.** a large mass of snow, ice, etc., detached from a mountain slope and sliding or falling suddenly downward. **2.** anything like an avalanche in suddenness and destructiveness: an avalanche of misfortunes. —v.i. **3.** to come down in, or like, an avalanche. [b. d. F avalanche (der. OF avaler go down, der. L ad- AD- + vallis valley) and d. F (Swiss) lavenche of pre-Latin orig.]

Av·a·lon (ăv′ə·lŏn′; Fr. à·và·lôn′), n. Celtic Legend. an island represented as an earthly paradise in the western seas, to which King Arthur and other heroes were carried at death. Also, **Av′al·lon′.** [t. ML: s. (insula island) Avallōnis (Geoffrey of Monmouth)]

a·vant-garde (à·vän·gàrd′), n. French. the vanguard.

av·a·rice (ăv′ə·rĭs), n. insatiable greed for riches; inordinate, miserly desire to gain and hoard wealth. [ME, t. OF, t. L: m.s. avāritia greed] —Syn. cupidity.

av·a·ri·cious (ăv′ə·rĭsh′əs), adj. characterized by avarice; greedy of wealth; covetous. —av′a·ri′cious·ly, adv. —av′a·ri′cious·ness, n.

a·vast (ə·văst′, ə·väst′), interj. Naut. stop! hold! cease! stay! [prob. t. D: m. houd vast hold fast]

av·a·tar (ăv′ə·tär′), n. **1.** Hindu Myth. the descent of a deity to the earth in an incarnate form or some manifest shape; the incarnation of a god. **2.** a concrete manifestation; embodiment. [t. Skt.: m. avatāra descent]

a·vaunt (ə·vônt′, ə·vänt′), adv. Archaic. away! go! [ME, t. F: m. avant forward, g. L abante from before]

A.V.C., American Veterans' Committee, an organization of veterans of World War II.

avdp., avoirdupois.

a·ve (ä′vĭ, ä′vā), interj. **1.** hail! welcome! **2.** farewell! good-by! —n. **3.** the salutation "ave." **4.** (cap.) Ave Maria. **5.** (cap.) the time for the recitation of the Angelus, so called because the Ave Maria is thrice repeated in it. [t. L, impv. of avēre to be or fare well]

Ave., avenue. Also, **ave.**

Ave·bur·y (āv′bər·ĭ), n. See **Lubbock,** Sir John.

a·vec plai·sir (à·vĕk′ plě·zēr′), French. with pleasure.

A·vel·la·ne·da (à·vě′yä·ně′dä), n. a city in E Argentina, near Buenos Aires. 399,021 (est. 1944).

A·ve Ma·ri·a (ä′vĭ mə·rē′ə, ä′vä), **1.** the "Hail, Mary," a prayer in the Roman Catholic Church, based on the salutation of the angel Gabriel to the Virgin Mary and the words of Elizabeth to her. Luke 1:28, 42. **2.** the hour for saying the prayer. **3.** a recitation of this prayer. **4.** the bead or beads on a rosary used to count off each prayer as spoken. Also, **A·ve Mar·y** (ä′vĭ mâr′ĭ). [L: hail, Mary]

av·e·na·ceous (ăv′ə·nā′shəs), adj. Bot. of or like oats; of the oat kind. [t. L: m. avēnāceus, der. avēna oats]

a·venge (ə·vĕnj′), v., **avenged, avenging.** —v.t. **1.** to take vengeance or exact satisfaction for: to avenge a death. **2.** to take vengeance on behalf of: avenge your brother. —v.i. **3.** to take vengeance. [ME avenge(n), t. OF: m. avengier, f. a- A-⁵ + vengier revenge, g. L vindicāre punish] —a·veng′er, n. —a·veng′ing·ly, adv. —Syn. **1, 2.** AVENGE, REVENGE both mean to inflict pain or harm in return for pain or harm inflicted on oneself or those persons or causes to which one feels loyalty. The two words were formerly interchangeable, but have been differentiated until they now convey widely diverse ideas. AVENGE is now restricted to inflicting punishment as an act of retributive justice or as a vindication of the right: to avenge a murder by bringing the criminal to trial. REVENGE implies inflicting pain or harm to retaliate for real or fancied wrongs; a reflexive pronoun is now always used with this verb: Iago wished to revenge himself upon Othello.

ăct, āble, dâre, ärt; ĕbb, ēqual; ĭf, īce; hŏt, ōver, ôrder, oil, bŏŏk, ōoze, out; ŭp, ūse, ûrge; ə = a in alone; ch, chief; g, give; ng, ring; sh, shoe; th, thin; ŧh, that; zh, vision. See the full key on inside cover.

av·ens (ăv′ĭnz), *n.* any of the perennial rosaceous herbs constituting the genus *Geum*. [ME, t. OF: m. *avence*, t. ML: m.s. *avencia* kind of clover]

Av·en·tine (ăv′ən tīn′, -tĭn), *n.* one of the seven hills on which Rome was built. [t. L: m.s. *Aventīnus*]

a·ven·tu·rine (ə vĕn′chə rĭn), *n.* **1.** an opaque, brown glass containing fine, gold-colored particles. **2.** any of several varieties of minerals, esp. quartz or feldspar, spangled with bright particles of mica, hematite, or other minerals. Also, **a·ven′tu·rin.** [t. F, t. It.: m. *avventurina*, der. *avventura* chance (the mineral being rare and found only by chance)]

av·e·nue (ăv′ə nū′, -nōō′), *n.* **1.** a wide street. **2.** the main way of approach, usually lined with trees, through grounds to a country house or monumental building (in England, limited to one bordered by trees). **3.** a way or an opening for entrance into a place: *the avenue to India.* **4.** means of access or attainment: *avenue of escape, avenues of success.* [t. F, orig. pp. fem. of *avenir*, g. L *advenīre* come to] **—Syn. 1.** See **street.**

a·ver (ə vûr′), *v.t.,* **averred, averring. 1.** to affirm with confidence; declare in a positive or peremptory manner. **2.** *Law.* to allege as a fact. [ME *aver(en)*, t. OF: s. *averer*, ult. der. L *ad-* **AD-** + *vērus* true]

av·er·age (ăv′ər ĭj, ăv′rĭj), *n., adj., v.,* **-aged, -aging.** **—n. 1.** an arithmetical mean. **2.** *Math.* a quantity intermediate to a set of quantities. **3.** the ordinary, normal, or typical amount, rate, quality, kind, etc.; the common run. **4.** *Com.* **a.** a small charge paid by the master on account of the ship and cargo, such as pilotage, towage, etc. **b.** an expense, partial loss, or damage to ship or cargo. **c.** the incidence of such an expense or loss on the owners or their insurers. **d.** an equitable apportionment among all the interested parties of such an expense or loss. **—adj. 5.** of or pertaining to an average; estimated by average; forming an average. **6.** intermediate, medial, or typical in amount, rate, quality, etc. **—v.t. 7.** to find an average value for; reduce to a mean. **8.** to result in, as an arithmetical mean; amount to, as a mean quantity: *wheat averages 56 pounds to a bushel.* **—v.i. 9.** *U.S.* to have or show an average: *to average as expected.* **10. average down,** to purchase more of a security or commodity at a lower price to reduce the average cost of one's holdings. **11. average up,** to purchase more of a security or commodity at a higher price to take advantage of a contemplated further rise in prices. [cf. F *avarie* customs duty, etc. t. It. *avaria*, t. Ar.: m. ʿ*awārīya* damages. See **-AGE**] **—av′er·age·ly,** *adv.*

a·ver·ment (ə vûr′mənt), *n.* **1.** act of averring. **2.** a positive statement.

A·ver·nus (ə vûr′nəs), *n.* **1.** a lake near Naples, Italy, looked upon by the ancients as an entrance to hell, from whose waters vile-smelling vapors arose, supposedly killing birds over it. **2.** hell. [t. L] **—A·ver′nal,** *adj.*

A·ver·ro·ës (ə vĕr′ō ēz′), *n.* 1126?–1198, Arabian philosopher in Spain: influence on Christian and Jewish thought. Arabic, **ibn-Rushd.** Also, **A·ver′rho·ës′.**

Av·er·ro·ism (ăv′ə rō′ĭz əm), *n.* the philosophy of Averroës, consisting chiefly of a pantheistic interpretation of the doctrines of Aristotle. Also, **Av′er·rho·ism.** **—Av′er·ro′ist,** *n.* **—Av′er·ro·is′tic,** *adj.*

a·verse (ə vûrs′), *adj.* **1.** disinclined, reluctant, or opposed: *averse to* (formerly *from*) *flattery.* **2.** *Bot.* turned away from the central axis (opposed to *adverse*). [t.L: m.s. *āversus,* pp., turned away] **—a·verse′ly,** *adv.* **—a·verse′ness,** *n.* **—Syn. 1.** unwilling, loath. See **reluctant.**

a·ver·sion (ə vûr′zhən, -shən), *n.* **1.** an averted state of the mind or feelings; repugnance, antipathy, or rooted dislike (usually fol. by *to*). **2.** a cause of dislike; an object of repugnance. **3.** *Obs.* a turning away. **—Syn. 1.** distaste, abhorrence. AVERSION, ANTIPATHY, LOATHING connote strong dislike or detestation. AVERSION is an unreasoning desire to avoid that which displeases,annoys, or offends: *an aversion to* (or *toward*) *cats.* ANTIPATHY is a distaste, dislike, or disgust toward something: *an antipathy toward* (or *for*) *braggarts.* LOATHING connotes a combination of hatred and disgust, or detestation: *a loathing for* (or *toward*) *venison, a criminal.*

a·vert (ə vûrt′), *v.t.* **1.** to turn away or aside: *to avert one's eyes.* **2.** to ward off; prevent: *to avert evil.* [ME, t. OF: s. *avertir,* g. L *āvertere* turn away] **—a·vert′er,** *n.* **—a·vert′i·ble, a·vert′a·ble,** *adj.*

a·ver·tin (ə vûr′tĭn), *n.* **1.** tribromoethanol. **2.** (*cap.*) a trademark for it.

A·ves (ā′vēz), *n.pl. Zool.* the class of vertebrates comprising the birds, distinguished from all other animals by their feathers, and from their closest relatives, the *Reptilia,* by their warm-bloodedness, the hard shell of their eggs, and significant anatomical features. [t. L, pl. of *avis* bird]

A·ves·ta (ə vĕs′tə), *n.* the Books of Wisdom, or sacred scriptures, of Zoroastrianism.

A·ves·tan (ə vĕs′tən), *n.* **1.** the language of the Avesta, closely related to Old Persian. **—adj. 2.** of or pertaining to the Avesta or its language. [f. AVESTA + -AN]

avi-, a word element meaning "bird". [t. L, comb. form of *avis* bird]

a·vi·an (ā′vĭ ən), *adj. Zool.* of or pertaining to birds.

a·vi·ar·y (ā′vĭ ĕr′ĭ), *n., pl.* **-aries.** a large cage or a house or enclosure in which birds are kept. [t. L: m. s. *aviārium,* der. *avis* bird]

a·vi·ate (ā′vĭ āt′, ăv′ĭ-), *v.i.,* **-ated, -ating.** to fly in an aircraft. [back formation from AVIATION]

a·vi·a·tion (ā′vĭ ā′shən, ăv′ĭ-), *n.* **1.** act, art, or science of flying by mechanical means, esp. with heavier-than-air craft. **2.** the aircraft (with its equipment) of an air force. [t. F. See AVI-, -ATION]

a·vi·a·tor (ā′vĭ ā′tər, ăv′ĭ-), *n.* a pilot of an airplane or other heavier-than-air craft. **—a·vi·a·trix** (ā′vĭ ā′trĭks, ăv′ĭ-), **a·vi·a·tress** (ā′vĭ ā′trĭs, ăv′ĭ-), *n. fem.*

Av·i·cen·na (ăv′ə sĕn′ə), *n.* A.D. 980–1037, Arabic physician and philosopher. Arabic, **ibn-Sina.**

a·vi·cul·ture (ā′vĭ kŭl′chər), *n.* the rearing or keeping of birds. **—a′vi·cul′tur·ist,** *n.*

av·id (ăv′ĭd), *adj.* **1.** keenly desirous; eager; greedy (often fol. by *of* or *for*): *avid of pleasure or power.* **2.** keen: *avid hunger.* [t. L: s. *avidus* eager] **—av′id·ly** *adv.*

av·i·din (ăv′ə dĭn, ə vĭd′ĭn), *n. Biochem.* a substance found in the white of egg which prevents the action of biotin and thus injures the egg white.

a·vid·i·ty (ə vĭd′ə tĭ), *n.* eagerness; greediness.

a·vi·fau·na (ā′və fô′nə), *n.* the birds of a given region; avian fauna. **—a′vi·fau′nal,** *adj.*

av·i·ga·tion (ăv′ə gā′shən), *n.* aerial navigation. [b. AVIATION and NAVIGATION]

A·vi·gnon (á vē nyôN′), *n.* a city in SE France, on the Rhone river: papal residence, 1309–77. 59,982 (1946).

Á·vi·la Ca·ma·cho (ä′vēlä′ kä mä′chō), **Manuel** (mä nwĕl′), born 1897, president of Mexico, 1940–46.

a·vion (á vyôN′), *n. French.* airplane.

a·vir·u·lent (ā vĭr′yə lənt, ā vĭr′ə-), *adj.* (of organisms) having no virulence, as a result of age, heat, etc.

a·vi·so (ə vī′zō), *n., pl.* **-sos. 1.** dispatch. **2.** a boat used esp. for carrying dispatches. [t. Sp.]

a·vi·ta·min·o·sis (ā vī′tə mə nō′sĭs, ā′və tăm′ə nō′sĭs), *n. Pathol.* a disease caused by a lack of vitamins. [f. A-[6] + VITAMIN + -OSIS]

Av·lo·na (ăv lô′nä), *n.* Valona.

av·o·ca·do (ăv′ə kä′dō, ä′və-), *n., pl.* **-dos. 1.** a tropical American fruit, green to black in color and commonly pearshaped, borne by the lauraceous tree, *Persea americana,* and its variety *drymifolia,* eaten raw, esp. as a salad fruit; alligator pear. **2.** the tree. [t. d. Sp. (prop. lawyer), alter. of *aguacate,* t. Mex.: m. *ahuacatl*]

Avocado,
Persea americana

av·o·ca·tion (ăv′ə kā′shən), *n.* **1.** a minor or occasional occupation; a hobby. **2.** *Colloq.* one's regular occupation, calling, or vocation. **3.** *Archaic.* diversion or distraction. **4.** *Obs.* a calling away. [t. L: s. *āvocātio* a calling off]

a·voc·a·to·ry (ə vŏk′ə tōr′ĭ), *adj.* calling away, off, or back.

av·o·cet (ăv′ə sĕt′), *n.* any of several long-legged, web-footed shore birds constituting the genus *Recurvirostra,* of both New World and Old, having a long, slender beak curving upward toward the end. Also, **avoset.** [t. F: m. *avocette,* t. It.: m. *avocetta*]

A·vo·ga·dro (ä′vô gä′drō), *n.* **Count Amadeo** (ä′mä dĕ′ô), 1776–1856, Italian physicist and chemist.

a·void (ə void′), *v.t.* **1.** to keep away from; keep clear of; shun; evade: *to avoid a person or a danger.* **2.** *Law.* to make void or of no effect; invalidate. **3.** *Obs.* to empty; eject or expel. [ME *avoide(n),* v. AF: m. *avoider,* var. of OF *esvuidier* empty out. f. *es-* EX-[1] + *vuidier* (g. L *viduāre*) empty. See VOID, adj.] **—a·void′a·ble,** *adj.* **—a·void′-a·bly,** *adv.* **—a·void′er,** *n.*

—Syn. 1. AVOID, ESCAPE mean to come through peril, actual or potential, without suffering serious consequences. To AVOID is to succeed in keeping away from something harmful or undesirable: *to avoid meeting an enemy.* ESCAPE suggests encountering peril but coming through it safely: *to escape drowning.*

a·void·ance (ə voi′dəns), *n.* **1.** act of keeping away from: *avoidance of scandal.* **2.** *Law.* a making void.

avoir., avoirdupois.

av·oir·du·pois (ăv′ər də poiz′), *n.* **1.** avoirdupois weight. **2.** *U.S. Colloq.* weight. [ME *avoir de pois,* t. OF: goods sold by weight, lit., to have weight]

avoirdupois weight, the system of weights in British and U. S. use for goods other than gems, precious metals, and drugs: $27^{11}/_{32}$ grains = 1 dram; 16 drams = 1 ounce; 16 ounces = 1 pound; 112 pounds (Brit.) or 100 pounds (U. S.) = 1 hundredweight; 20 hundredweight = 1 ton. The pound contains 7000 grains.

A·von (ā′vən, ăv′ən), *n.* **1.** a river in central England, flowing SE past Stratford (Shakespeare's birthplace) to the Severn. 80 mi. **2.** a river in S England, flowing W to the mouth of the Severn. 75 mi. **3.** a river in S England, flowing S to the English Channel. ab. 60 mi.

av·o·set (ăv′ə sĕt′), *n.* avocet.

à vo·tre san·té (á vô′tr säN tā′), *French.* to your health.

a·vouch (ə vouch′), *v.t.* **1.** to make frank acknowledgment or affirmation of; declare or assert with positiveness. **2.** to assume responsibility for; guarantee. **3.** to admit; confess. [ME *avouche(n),* t. OF: m. *avochier,* t. L: m. *advocāre* summon] **—a·vouch′ment,** *n.*

a·vow (ə vou′), *v.t.* to declare frankly or openly; own; acknowledge; confess: *to avow one's principles.* [ME *avowe(n),* t. OF: m. *avoer,* g. L *advocāre* summon] **—a·vow′a·ble,** *adj.* **—a·vow′er,** *n.*

a·vow·al (ə vou′əl), *n.* an open statement of affirmation; frank acknowledgment or admission.

a·vowed (ə voud′), *adj.* acknowledged; declared: *an avowed enemy.* —**a·vow·ed·ly** (ə vou′ĭd lĭ), *adv.* —**a·vow′ed·ness,** *n.*

a·vul·sed (ə vŭl′sĭd), *adj. Surg.* (of a wound) having the tissue torn away.

a·vul·sion (ə vŭl′shən), *n.* **1.** a tearing away. **2.** *Law.* the sudden removal of soil by change in a river's course or by a flood, from the land of one owner to that of another. **3.** a part torn off. [t. L: s. *āvulsiō*]

a·vun·cu·lar (ə vŭng′kyə lər), *adj.* **1.** of or pertaining to an uncle: *avuncular affection.* **2.** *Humorous.* of or pertaining to a pawnbroker. [f. s. L *avunculus* uncle (dim. of *avus* grandfather) + -AR¹]

a·wa (ə wô′, ə wä′), *adv. Scot.* away.

a·wait (ə wāt′), *v.t.* **1.** to wait for; look for or expect. **2.** to be in store for; be ready for. **3.** *Obs.* to lie in wait for. —*v.i.* **4.** to wait as in expectation. [ME *awaite(n),* t. ONF: m. *awaitier,* f. a- A⁵ + *waitier* watch. See WAIT] —**Syn. 1.** See **expect.**

a·wake (ə wāk′), *v.,* **awoke** or **awaked, awaking,** *adj.* —*v.t., v.i.* **1.** to wake up; rouse from sleep. **2.** to come or bring to a realization of the truth; to rouse to action, attention, etc.: *he awoke to the realities of life.* —*adj.* **3.** waking; not sleeping. **4.** vigilant; alert: *awake to a danger.* [ME; OE weak v. *awacian* and (for pret. and pp.) OE strong v. *onwæcnan,* later *awæcnan* (pret. *onwōc, awōc,* pp. *onwacen, awacen*)]

a·wak·en (ə wā′kən), *v.t., v.i.* to awake; waken. [ME *awak(e)ne(n),* OE *onwæcnan,* later *awæcnian*] —**a·wak′en·er,** *n.*

a·wak·en·ing (ə wā′kən ĭng), *adj.* **1.** rousing; alarming. —*n.* **2.** act of awaking from sleep. **3.** a revival of interest or attention.

a·ward (ə wôrd′), *v.t.* **1.** to adjudge to be due or merited; assign or bestow: *to award prizes.* **2.** to bestow by judicial decree; assign or appoint by deliberate judgment, as in arbitration. —*n.* **3.** something awarded, as a payment or medal. **4.** *Law.* a. a decision after consideration; a judicial sentence. **b.** the decision of arbitrators on points submitted to them. [ME *awarde(n),* t. AF: m. *awarder,* var. of *esguarder* observe, decide, f.: *ex* EX¹- + *guardāre* watch, guard, of Gmc. orig.] —**a·ward′a·ble,** *adj.* —**a·ward′er,** *n.*

a·ware (ə wâr′), *adj.* cognizant or conscious (*of*); informed: *aware of the danger.* [ME; OE *gewær* watchful. See WARE², WARY] —**a·ware′ness,** *n.* —**Syn.** See **conscious.**

a·wash (ə wŏsh′, ə wôsh′), *adv., adj.* **1.** *Naut.* just level with the surface of the water, so that the waves break over. **2.** covered with water. **3.** washing about; tossed about by the waves.

a·way (ə wā′), *adv.* **1.** from this or that place; off: *to go away.* **2.** far; apart: *away back, away from the subject.* **3.** aside: *turn your eyes away.* **4.** out of possession, notice, use, or existence: *to give money away.* **5.** continuously; on: *to blaze away.* **6.** without hesitation: *fire away.* **7. away with,** take away: *away with this man.* **8. do** or **make away with,** to put out of existence; get rid of; kill. —*adj.* **9.** absent: *away from home.* **10.** distant: *six miles away.* [ME; OE *aweg,* earlier *on weg* on way]

awe (ô), *n., v.,* **awed, awing.** —*n.* **1.** respectful or reverential fear, inspired by what is grand or sublime: *in awe of God.* **2.** *Archaic.* power to inspire fear or reverence. **3.** *Obs.* fear or dread. —*v.t.* **4.** to inspire with awe. **5.** to influence or restrain by awe. [ME, t. Scand.; cf. Icel. *agi* fear]

a·weather (ə wĕth′ər), *adv., adj. Naut.* on or to the weather side; toward the wind.

a·weigh (ə wā′), *adj. Naut.* (of an anchor) raised just enough to be clear of the bottom.

awe·less (ô′lĭs), *adj.* awless.

awe·some (ô′səm), *adj.* **1.** inspiring awe. **2.** characterized by awe. —**awe′some·ly,** *adv.* —**awe′some·ness,** *n.*

awe-struck (ô′strŭk′), *adj.* filled with awe. Also, **awe-strick·en** (ô′strĭk′ən).

aw·ful (ô′fəl), *adj.* **1.** inspiring fear; dreadful; terrible. **2.** *Colloq.* extremely bad; unpleasant; ugly. **3.** *Colloq.* very; very great. **4.** full of awe; reverential. **5.** inspiring reverential awe; solemnly impressive. [ME; f. AWE + -FUL, r. OE *egeful* dreadful] —**aw′ful·ly,** *adv.* —**aw′ful·ness,** *n.*

a·while (ə hwīl′), *adv.* for a short time or period.

awk·ward (ôk′wərd), *adj.* **1.** lacking dexterity or skill; clumsy; bungling. **2.** ungraceful; ungainly; uncouth: *awkward gestures.* **3.** ill-adapted for use or handling; unhandy: *an awkward method.* **4.** requiring caution; somewhat hazardous: *there's an awkward step there.* **5.** difficult to handle; dangerous: *an awkward customer.* **6.** embarrassing or trying: *an awkward predicament.* **7.** *Obs.* untoward; perverse. [f. *auk* backhanded (t. Scand.; cf. Icel. *öfugr* turned the wrong way) + -WARD] —**awk′ward·ly,** *adv.* —**awk′ward·ness,** *n.* —**Syn. 1.** unskillful, unhandy, inexpert; inept.

awl (ôl), *n. Carp., etc.* a pointed instrument for piercing small holes in leather, wood, etc. [ME *al,* OE *æl,* c. G *ahle*]

aw·less (ô′lĭs), *adj.* without awe; fearless; not to be awed. Also, **awe·less.**

Awls
A. Bradawl; B. Sewing awl

awl·wort (ôl′wûrt′), *n.* a small, stemless, aquatic cruciferous plant, *Subularia aquatica,* with slender, sharp-pointed leaves.

awn (ôn), *n. Bot.* **1.** a bristlelike appendage of a plant, esp. on the glumes of grasses. **2.** such appendages collectively, as those forming the beard of wheat, barley, etc. **3.** any similar bristle. [ME, t. Scand.; cf. Sw. *agn,* Icel. *ögn* husk] —**awned,** *adj.* —**awn′less,** *adj.*

awn·ing (ô′nĭng) *n.* **1.** a rooflike shelter of canvas, etc., before a window or door, over a deck, etc., as for protection from the sun. **2.** a shelter. [orig. unknown]

a·woke (ə wōk′), *v.* pt. and pp. of **awake.**

A.W.O.L. (*pronounced as initials or, in Mil. slang,* ā′wôl), *Mil.* absent without leave.

a·wry (ə rī′), *adv., adj.* **1.** with a turn or twist to one side; askew: *to glance or look awry.* **2.** away from reason or the truth. **3.** amiss; wrong: *our plans went awry.* [ME *on wry.* See A-¹, WRY]

ax (ăks), *n., pl.* **axes,** *v.,* **axed, axing.** —*n.* **1.** an instrument with a bladed head on a handle or helve, used for hewing, cleaving, chopping, etc. **2. have an ax to grind,** *Orig. U.S.* to have a private purpose or selfish end to attain. —*v.t.* **3.** to shape or trim with an ax. Also, **axe.** [ME; OE *æx,* akin to G *axt,* L *ascia,* Gk. *axīnē*] —**ax′like′,** *adj.*

ax., axiom.

ax·es¹ (ăk′sēz), *n.* pl. of **axis.**

ax·es² (ăk′sĭz), *n.* pl. of **ax.**

ax·i·al (ăk′sĭ əl), *adj.* **1.** of, pertaining to, or forming an axis. **2.** situated in an axis or on the axis. Also, **ax·ile** (ăk′sĭl, -sīl).

ax·i·al·ly (ăk′sĭ ə lĭ), *adv.* in the line of the axis.

ax·il (ăk′sĭl), *n. Bot.* the angle between the upper side of a leaf or stem and the supporting stem or branch. [t. L: m.s. *axilla* armpit]

ax·il·la (ăk sĭl′ə), *n., pl.* **axil·lae** (ăk sĭl′ē). **1.** *Anat.* the armpit. **2.** *Ornith.* the corresponding region on a bird. **3.** *Bot.* an axil. [t. L]

ax·il·lar (ăk′sə lər), *n. Ornith.* (usually *pl.*) a feather growing from the axilla (def. 2).

A. Axil

ax·il·lar·y (ăk′sə lĕr′ĭ), *adj., n., pl.* **-laries.** —*adj.* **1.** pertaining to the axilla. **2.** *Bot.* pertaining to or growing from the axil (of plants). —*n.* **3.** *Ornith.* axillar.

ax·i·ol·o·gy (ăk′sĭ ŏl′ə jĭ), *n. Philos.* the science of values in general, including ethics, aesthetics, religion, etc. [f. Gk. *ăxio(s)* worthy + -LOGY] —**ax·i·o·log·i·cal** (ăk′sĭ ə lŏj′ə kəl), *adj.*

ax·i·om (ăk′sĭ əm), *n.* **1.** a recognized truth. **2.** an established and universally accepted principle or rule. **3.** *Logic, Math., etc.* a proposition which is assumed without proof for the sake of studying the consequences that follow from it. [t. L: m. *axiōma,* t. Gk.: a requisite]

ax·i·o·mat·ic (ăk′sĭ ə măt′ĭk), *adj.* **1.** pertaining to or of the nature of an axiom; self-evident. **2.** aphoristic. Also, **ax′i·o·mat′i·cal.** —**ax′i·o·mat′i·cal·ly,** *adv.*

ax·is¹ (ăk′sĭs), *n., pl.* **axes** (ăk′sēz). **1.** the line about which a rotating body, such as the earth, turns. **2.** the central line of any symmetrical, or nearly symmetrical, body: *the axis of a cylinder, of the eye, etc.* **3.** *Anat.* **a.** a central or principal structure, about which something turns or is arranged: *the skeletal axis.* **b.** the second cervical vertebra. **4.** *Bot.* the longitudinal support on which organs or parts are arranged; the stem, root; the central line of any body. **5.** *Aeron.* any one of three lines defining the attitude of an airplane, one being generally determined by the direction of forward motion and the other two at right angles to it. **6.** *Fine Arts.* one or more theoretical central lines around which an artistic form is organized or composed. **7.** an alliance of two or more nations to coördinate their foreign and military policies, and to draw in with them a group of dependent or supporting powers. **8. the Axis,** the alliance of Germany, Italy, and Japan prior to and during World War II, beginning with the Rome-Berlin Axis (1936). [t. L: axle, axis, board. Cf. AXLE]

ax·is² (ăk′sĭs), *n.* any of several species of East Asiatic deer, as *Axis axis* and related forms, with white spots. Also, **axis deer.** [t. L]

ax·le (ăk′səl), *n.* **1.** *Mach.* the pin, bar, shaft, or the like, on which or with which a wheel or pair of wheels rotate. **2.** either end (spindle) of an axletree or the like. **3.** the whole (fixed) axletree, or a similar bar connecting and turning with two opposite wheels of a vehicle. [OE *earl(e)* shoulder, crossbeam (in *eaxle-gespann* crossbeam attachment place). Cf. Icel. *öxl* shoulder, axle]

ax·le·tree (ăk′səl trē′), *n.* a bar fixed crosswise under an animal-drawn vehicle, with a rounded spindle at each end upon which a wheel rotates. [ME, f. AXLE + TREE]

ax·man (ăks′mən), *n., pl.* **-men.** one who wields an ax.

Ax·min·ster carpet (ăks′mĭn′stər), a kind of carpet having a stiff jute back and a cut pile of wool.

ax·o·lotl (ăk′sə lŏt′əl), *n., pl.* **axolotyles. 1.** any of several Mexican salamanders that breed in the larval stage, in Mexico prized as food. **2.** the larva of any salamander (esp. of the genus *Ambystoma*

Axolotl, *Ambystoma mexicanus* (6 to 12 in. long)

that mature sexually in the larval stage. [t. Mex.]

ax·on (ăk′sŏn), *n. Anat.* the appendage of the neuron which transmits impulses away from the cell. Also, **ax·one** (ăk′sōn). [t. Gk.: axis]

ax·seed (ăks′sēd′), *n.* an Old World fabaceous plant, *Cornilla varia*, with pink flowers, naturalized in the U. S.

Ax·um (äk′sŏom), *n.* Aksum.

ay[1] (ā), *adv. Poetic or Dial.* ever; always. Also, **aye**. [ME *ei*, *ai*, t. Scand.; cf. Icel. *ei*, c. OE *ā* ever]

ay[2] (ā), *interj. Archaic or Dial.* Ah! Oh! [ME *ey*, m. phrase *ay me*, t. F: m. *ahi*, *aï*. Cf. It. *ahime*, Sp. *ay de mi*]

ay[3] (ī), *adv., n.* aye.[1]

A·ya·cu·cho (ä′yäkōō′chō), *n.* a city in SW Peru; victory of the revolutionists near here ended Spain's domination in the New World, 1824. 16,642 (1940).

a·yah (ä′yə), *n.* (in India) a native maid or nurse. [t. Hind.: m. *āya*, t. Pg.: m. *aia*, fem. of *aio* tutor]

Ay·din (ī·dēn′), *n.* a city in W Turkey, SE of Smyrna: ancient ruins. 17,732 (1940). Also, **Aidin.**

aye[1] (ī), *adv.* **1.** yes. —*n.* **2.** an affirmative vote or voter, esp. in British Parliament, corresponding to *yea* in Congress. Also, **ay.** [earlier *I*, ? var. of ME *yie*, OE *gī* YEA (with loss of *y* as in if)]

aye[2] (ā), *adv.* ay.[1]

aye-aye (ī′ī′), *n.* a nocturnal lemur, *Daubentonia madagascariensis*, of Madagascar, about the size of a cat and with rodentlike front teeth. [t. F, t. Malagasy: m. *aiay*; prob. imit. of its cry]

A·ye·sha (ä′Ishä′), *n.* Aisha.

Ay·ma·ra (ī′märä′), *n.* an important Indian nationality and speech group in Bolivia and Peru, still existing about Lake Titicaca. —**Ay′ma·ran′**, *adj.*

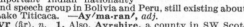

Aye-aye
Daubentonia madagascariensis
(Total length 3 ft., 8 in. high)

Ayr (âr), *n.* **1.** Also, **Ayrshire.** a county in SW Scotland. 309,200 pop. (est. 1946); 1132 sq. mi. **2.** its county seat: a: eaport. 42,500 (est. 1946).

Ayr·shire (âr′shĭr, -shər), *n.* **1.** one of a hardy breed of dairy cattle, well-muscled, of medium size, brown and white in color, originating in the shire of Ayr. **2.** Ayr (def. 1).

A·yu·thi·a (ä ū′thē ä; *Thai* -tē ä), *n.* a city in central Siam, on the Menam: former capital of Siam. ab. 50,000.

az-, var. of **azo-** used before vowels, as in *azole.*

a·za·le·a (ə zāl′yə), *n.* any plant of a particular group (*Azalea*) of the ericaceous genus *Rhododendron*, comprising species with handsome, variously colored flowers, some of which are familiar in cultivation. *Azalea* was once a botanical genus but is now a nursery or horticultural classification. [t. NL, t. Gk.: (fem. adj.) dry; so named as growing in dry soil]

a·zan (ä zän′), *n.* (in Mohammedan countries) the call to prayer, proclaimed by the crier (muezzin) from the minaret of a mosque five times daily. [t. Ar.: m. *adhān* invitation. See MUEZZIN]

A·za·ña y Dí·ez (ä thä′nyä ē dē′ĕth), **Manuel** (mä-nwĕl′), 1880–1940, Spanish statesman: prime minister, 1931–33, 1936; president, 1936–39.

A·za·zel (ə zä′zəl, ăz′ə zĕl′), *n.* **1.** the leader of the rebellious sons of God who entered into sexual relations with the daughters of men. Gen. 6:1–4. **2.** (in Arabic writers) one of the jinns taken prisoners by the angels for their transgressions. [t. Heb.: m. *‘azā′ zĕl*]

a·zed·a·rach (ə zĕd′ə räk′), *n.* the chinaberry tree (def. 1).

a·ze·o·trope (ə zē′ə trōp′), *n. Phys. Chem.* any solution having constant minimum and maximum boiling points. [f. A-[6] + *zeo-* (comb. form repr. Gk. *zein* boil) + -TROPE]

Az·er·bai·jan (ăz′ər bī jän′; *Russ.* ä′zĕr bī-jän′), *n.* **1.** Official name, **Azerbaijan Soviet Socialist Republic.** one of the constituent republics of the Soviet Union, in Caucasia. 3,209,727 pop. (1939); ab. 33,000 sq. mi.

Cap.: Baku. **2.** a province in NW Iran. ab. 1,500,000 pop.; ab. 35,000 sq. mi. *Cap.:* Tabriz.

A·zer·bai·ja·ni·an (ä′zər bī jä′nĬ ən), *n.* a Turkic language.

az·i·muth (ăz′ə məth), *n.* **1.** *Astron., Navig.* the arc of the horizon from the celestial meridian to the foot of the great circle passing through the zenith, the nadir, and the point of the celestial sphere in question (in astronomy commonly reckoned from the south point of the horizon toward the west point: in navigation reckoned from the north point of the horizon toward the east point). **2.** *Survey., Gunnery, etc.* an angle measured clockwise from the south or north. [ME *azimut*, t. OF, t. Ar.: m. *assumūt*, s. (=al) the + *sumūt*, pl. of. *samt* way] —**az·i·muth·al** (ăz′ə mŭth′əl), *adj.* —**az′·i·muth′al·ly**, *adv.*

az·ine (ăz′ēn, -Ĭn), *n. Chem.* any of a group of organic compounds having six atoms, one or more of them nitrogen, arranged in a ring, the number of nitrogen atoms being indicated by a prefix, as in *diazine*, *triazine*, *tetrazine*. Also, **az·in** (ăz′Ĭn). [f. AZ- + -INE[2]]

azo-, *Chem.* a word element meaning nitrogen. [t. Gk.: s. *ázōos* lifeless] —**az·o** (ăz′ō, ā′zō), *adj.*

az·o·ben·zene (ăz′ō bĕn′zēn, -bĕn zēn′, ā′zō-), *n. Chem.* an orange-red crystalline substance, $C_6H_5N = NC_6H_5$, obtained from nitrobenzene in an alkaline solution.

azo dyes, *Chem.* a large group of synthetic coloring substances which contain the **azo group**, -N=N-.

a·zo·ic (ə zō′Ĭk), *adj. Geol.* pertaining to geologic time before life appeared. [f. s. Gk. *ázōos* lifeless + -IC]

az·ole (ăz′ōl, ə zōl′), *n. Chem.* any of a group of organic compounds having five atoms, one or more of them nitrogen, arranged in a ring. The number of nitrogen atoms is indicated by a prefix, as in *diazole*. [f. AZ- + -OLE]

az·on bomb (ăz′ŏn), a half-ton aerial bomb fitted with radio equipment and a special tail assembly which enables the bombardier to change the direction of its fall (to a certain extent) by remote control.

a·zon·ic (ā zŏn′Ĭk), *adj.* not confined to any particular zone or region; not local.

A·zores (ə zōrz′, ā′zōrz), *n.* a group of islands in the N Atlantic, W of and belonging to Portugal. 287,091 pop. (1940); 890 sq. mi.

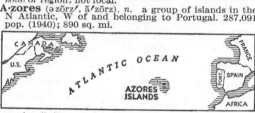

az·ote (ăz′ōt, ə zōt′), *n. Obs.* nitrogen. [t. F, t. Gk.: m.s. *ázōtos*, prop., ungirt (mistakenly thought to mean lifeless, the gas being unfit to support life in respiration)] —**az·ot·ed** (ăz′ō tĬd, ə zō′tĬd), *adj.*

az·oth (ăz′ŏth), *n. Alchemy.* **1.** mercury, as the assumed first principle of all metals. **2.** the universal remedy of Paracelsus. [t. F, var. of *azoch*, t. Ar.: m. *az-zāwūg* the mercury]

a·zot·ic (ə zŏt′Ĭk), *adj.* of or pertaining to azote; nitric.

az·o·tize (ăz′ə tīz′), *v.t.*, **-tized, -tizing.** to nitrogenize.

A·zov (ä zôf′), *n.* **Sea of,** a sea NE of the Black Sea and connected with it by Kerch Strait. ab. 14,500 sq. mi. Also, **A·zof′.** See map under **Black Sea.**

Az·ra·el (ăz′rĬ əl), *n.* (in Jewish and Mohammedan angelology) the angel who separates the soul from the body at the moment of death. [t. Heb.]

Az·tec (ăz′tĕk), *n.* **1.** a member of an Indian people dominant in Central Mexico at the time of the Spanish invasion (1519). **2.** a Uto-Aztecan language of the Nahuatl subgroup, still extensively spoken in Mexico; Nahuatl. —**Az′tec·an**, *adj.*

az·ure (ăzh′ər, ā′zhər), *adj.* **1.** of a sky-blue color. —*n.* **2.** blue of unclouded sky. **3.** a blue pigment, now esp. cobalt blue. **4.** the sky. [ME, t. OF: m. *azur*, t. Ar.: m. *lāzward*, t. Pers.: m. *lajward* lapis lazuli]

az·u·rite (ăzh′ə rīt′), *n.* **1.** a blue mineral, a hydrous copper carbonate $[Cu_3(CO_3)_2(OH)_2]$, an ore of copper. **2.** a gem of moderate value, ground from this mineral.

az·y·gous (ăz′ə gəs), *adj. Zool., Bot.* not being one of a pair; single. [t. Gk.: m. *ázygos*]

B

B, b (bē), *n., pl.* **B's** or **Bs, b's** or **bs.** **1.** the second letter of the English alphabet. **2.** the second in any series: *schedule B.* **3.** *U.S.* the second highest mark for school or college work. **4.** *Music.* **a.** the seventh tone in the scale of C major or the second tone in the relative minor scale of A minor. **b.** a string, key, or pipe tuned

b., blend of, blended; c., cognate with; d., dialect, dialectal; der., derived from; f., formed from; g., going back to; m., modification of; r., replacing; s., stem of; t., taken from; ?, perhaps. See the full key on inside cover.

to this note. **c.** a written or printed note representing this tone. **d.** (in solmization) the seventh tone of the scale of C.

B, *Chem.* boron.

B., **1.** bay. **2.** Bible. **3.** British. **4.** Brotherhood.

b., **1.** *Baseball.* base; baseman. **2.** bass. **3.** basso. **4.** book. **5.** born. **6.** breadth. **7.** brother. **8.** blend of; blended.

Ba, *Chem.* barium.

B.A., **1.** (L *Baccalaureus Artium*) Bachelor of Arts. **2.** British America.

baa (bä, bä), *v.,* **baaed, baaing,** *n.* —*v.i.* **1.** to cry as a sheep; bleat. —*n.* **2.** the bleating of a sheep. [imit.]

Ba·al (bā′əl, bäl), *n., pl.* **Baalim** (bā′əl Ym). **1.** any of numerous local deities among the ancient Semitic peoples, typifying the productive forces of nature and worshiped with much sensuality. **2.** a solar deity, the chief god of the Phoenicians. **3.** any false god. [t. Heb.: m. *ba′al* lord] —**Ba′al·ism,** *n.* —**Ba′al·ist, Ba·al·ite** (bā′ə līt′), *n.*

Baal·bek (bäl′běk), *n.* a ruined city in E Lebanon: Temple of the Sun. Ancient Greek name, **Heliopolis.**

ba·ba (bä′bə; *Fr.* bȧ bȧ′), *n.* a yeast-raised cake of brioche dough, flavored with rum, etc., and baked.

bab·bitt (băb′Yt), *n. Metall.* **1.** Babbitt metal. **2.** a bearing or lining of Babbitt metal. —*v.t.* **3.** to line, face, or furnish with Babbitt metal.

Bab·bitt (băb′Yt), *n.* **1.** a self-satisfied person who conforms readily to middle-class ideas and ideals, esp. of business success. Cf. **Babbittry. 2.** Irving, 1865–1933, U.S. educator and critic.

Babbitt metal, *Metall.* **1.** an antifriction metal, an alloy of tin, antimony, lead, and copper, used for bearings, etc. **2.** any of various similar alloys. [named after Isaac *Babbitt* (1799–1862), U. S. inventor]

Bab·bitt·ry (băb′Yt rY), *n.* (*often l.c.*) the attitude of the self-satisfied middle class, having social conformity and business success as its ideals, as typified by the title character of Sinclair Lewis' novel *Babbitt* (1923).

bab·ble (băb′əl), *v.,* **-bled, -bling,** *n.* —*v.i.* **1.** to utter words imperfectly or indistinctly. **2.** to talk idly, irrationally, or foolishly; chatter. **3.** to make a continuous murmuring sound: *a babbling stream.* —*v.t.* **4.** to utter incoherently or foolishly. **5.** to reveal foolishly or thoughtlessly: *to babble a secret.* —*n.* **6.** inarticulate speech. **7.** senseless or foolish prattle. **8.** a murmuring sound. [ME *babele*(n); cf. imit. orig. Cf. Icel. *babla*] —**bab′ble·ment,** *n.* —**bab′bler,** *n.*

babe (bāb), *n.* **1.** baby. **2.** an innocent or inexperienced person. **3.** *Slang.* girl. [ME]

Ba·bel (bā′bəl), *n.* **1.** *Bible.* an ancient city (Babylon) where the building of a tower intended to reach heaven was begun and a confounding of the language of the people took place. Gen. 11:4–9. **2.** (*usually l.c.*) a confused mixture of sounds. **3.** (*usually l.c.*) a scene of noise and confusion. [t. Heb.: m. *Bābel* Babylon]

Bab el Man·deb (băb′ ĕl män′dĕb), a strait between E Africa and SW Arabia, connecting the Red Sea and the Gulf of Aden. 20 mi. wide.

Ba·ber (bä′bər), *n.* (*Zahir ed-Din Mohammed*) 1483–1530, founder of Mogul Empire. Also, **Ba′bar.**

ba·bies′-breath (bā′bYz brĕth′), *n.* **1.** a tall herb, *Gypsophila paniculata,* of the pink family, bearing numerous small, fragrant, white or pink flowers. **2.** any of certain other plants, as the grape hyacinth, *Muscari.* Also, **baby's-breath.**

bab·i·ru·sa (băb′ə rōō′sə, bä′bə-) *n.* an East Indian swine, *Babirussa babyrussa.* The male has peculiar curved tusks growing upward, one pair from each jaw. Also, **bab′i·rous′sa, bab′i·rus′sa.** [t. Malay: m. *bābi rūsa* hog deer]

Babirusa, *Babirussa babyrussa*
(2 ft. or more high
at the shoulder)

Bab·ism (bä′bYzəm), *n.* the doctrine of a pantheistic Persian sect, founded about 1844, inculcating a high morality, recognizing the equality of the sexes, and forbidding polygamy. —**Bab′ist,** *n., adj.*

ba·boo (bä′bōō), *n., pl.* **-boos. 1.** a Hindu gentleman. **2.** a native clerk who writes English. **3.** any native having a smattering of English culture, esp. with a ludicrous effect. Also, **ba′bu.** [t. Hind.: m. *bābū*] —**ba·boo·ism,** *n.*

ba·boon (bă bōōn′), *n.* any of various large, terrestrial monkeys, with a doglike muzzle, large cheek pouches, and a short tail, which constitute the genus *Papio* of Africa and Arabia. [ME *babewyne,* t. OF: m. *babouin* stupid person] —**ba·boon′ish,** *adj.*

ba·boon·er·y (bă bōō′nər Y), *n.* baboonish condition or behavior.

ba·bul (bä bōōl′, bä′bōōl), *n.* **1.** any of several trees of the mimosaceous genus *Acacia,* which yield a gum, esp. *A. arabica* of India. **2.** the gum, pods, or bark of such a tree. [t. Hind.]

ba·bush·ka (bə bōōsh′kə), *n.* a woman's scarf, often triangular, used as a hood with the ends tied under the chin. [t. Russ.: lit., grandmother]

ba·by (bā′bY), *n., pl.* **-bies,** *adj., v.,* **-bied, -bying.** —*n.* **1.** an infant; young child of either sex. **2.** the youngest member of a family, group, etc. **3.** a childish person.

4. *Slang.* an invention or creation of which one is particularly proud. **5.** *Slang.* girl. —*adj.* **6.** of, like, or suitable for a baby; *baby carriage.* **7.** infantile; babyish: *baby face.* **8.** *Colloq.* small; comparatively little: *a baby grand* (piano). —*v.t.* **9.** to treat like a young child; pamper. [ME *babi, babee,* dim. of *babe*] —**ba′by·hood′,** *n.* —**ba′by·ish,** *adj.* —**ba′by·ish·ly,** *adv.* —**ba′by·ish·ness,** *n.* —**ba′by·like′,** *adj.*

ba·by-blue-eyes (bā′bY blōō′Yz′), *n.* **1.** a plant, *Nemophila insignis,* of the Pacific coast of the U.S., with spotted blue blossoms. **2.** a similar plant, *Nemophila phacelioides,* common in Oklahoma. **3.** a plant, *N. menziesi atomaria,* occurring in Northwestern U.S.

Bab·y·lon (băb′ə lən, -lŏn′), *n.* **1.** an ancient city of SW Asia, on the Euphrates river, famed for its magnificence and culture: the capital of Babylonia and later of the Chaldean Empire. **2.** any great, rich, and luxurious or wicked city. [t. L, t. Gk., t. Akkadian: m. *Bāb Ilu* the gate of the god *Il*]

Bab·y·lo·ni·a (băb′ə lō′nY ə), *n.* an ancient empire in SW Asia, in the lower Euphrates valley: period of greatness, 2800 B.C.–1750 B.C.

Bab·y·lo·ni·an (băb′ə lō′nY ən), *adj.* **1.** pertaining to Babylon or Babylonia. **2.** sinful. —*n.* **3.** an inhabitant of ancient Babylonia. **4.** a language of Babylonia, esp. the Semitic language of the Akkadian group.

ba·by's-breath (bā′bYz brĕth′), *n.* babies′-breath.

baby sitter, a person hired (usually for an evening) to take charge of a child while the parents are away.

bac·ca·lau·re·ate (băk′ə lôr′Y Yt), *n.* **1.** the bachelor's degree. **2.** a religious service usually associated with commencement ceremonies. **3.** *Chiefly U.S.* a baccalaureate sermon. [t. ML: m.s. *baccalaureātus,* der. *baccalaureus* (as if f. L *bacca* berry + *laureus* of laurel), var. of *baccalarius* BACHELOR]

baccalaureate sermon, (in some U.S. colleges and schools) a farewell sermon to a graduating class.

bac·ca·rat (băk′ə rä′, băk′ə rä′; *Fr.* bȧ kȧ rȧ′), *n.* a gambling game at cards played by a banker and two or more punters. Also, **bac′ca·ra′.** [t. F; orig. unknown]

bac·cate (băk′āt), *adj. Bot.* **1.** berrylike. **2.** bearing berries. [t. L: m. s. *baccātus* berried]

Bac·chae (băk′ē), *n.pl. Class. Myth.* **1.** the female attendants of Bacchus. **2.** the priestesses of Bacchus. **3.** the women who took part in the Bacchanalia.

bac·cha·nal (băk′ə nəl), *n.* **1.** a follower of Bacchus. **2.** a drunken reveler. **3.** an occasion of drunken revelry; an orgy. —*adj.* **4.** pertaining to Bacchus; bacchanalian. [t. L: s. *bacchānālis*]

Bac·cha·na·li·a (băk′ə nā′lY ə, -nāl′yə), *n.pl.* **1.** a Roman festival in honor of Bacchus. **2.** (*l.c.*) drunken orgies. [L. neut. pl. of *bacchānālis* BACCHANAL, *adj.*] —**bac′cha′na·li·an,** *adj.* —**bac′cha·na/li·an·ism,** *n.*

bac·chant (băk′ənt), *n., pl.* **bacchants, bacchantes** (bə kăn′tēz). **1.** a priest, priestess, or votary of Bacchus; a bacchanal. **2.** a drunken reveler. [t. L: s. *bacchans,* ppr., celebrating the festival of Bacchus] —**bac·chan·tic** (bə kăn′tYk), *adj.*

bac·chan·te (bə kăn′tē, bə kănt′, băk′ənt), *n.* a female bacchant. [t. F, t. L: m. s. *bacchans* BACCHANT]

Bac·chic (băk′Yk), *adj.* **1.** relating to or in honor of Bacchus; connected with bacchanalian rites or revelries. **2.** (*l.c.*) jovial; riotously or jovially intoxicated; drunken.

Bac·chus (băk′əs), *n. Rom. Myth.* the god of wine. See **Dionysus.** [t. L, t. Gk.: m. *Bākchos*]

bacci-, *Bot.* a word element meaning "berry," as in *bacciform.* [t. L, comb. form of *bacca*]

bac·cif·er·ous (băk sYf′ər əs), *adj. Bot.* bearing or producing berries. [f. L *baccifer* + -ous]

bac·ci·form (băk′sə fôrm′), *adj. Bot.* berry-shaped.

bac·civ·o·rous (băk sYv′ə rəs), *adj. Zool.* feeding on berries.

bach (băch), *v.i. U.S. Slang.* to keep house alone. [der. BACHELOR]

Bach (bäкн), *n.* **1. Johann Sebastian** (yō′hän sä bäs′tYän′), 1685–1750, German organist and composer. **2.** his son, **Karl Philipp Emanuel** (kärl fē′lYp ā mä′nōō əl′), 1714–88, German composer.

bach·e·lor (băch′ə lər, băch′lər), *n.* **1.** an unmarried man of any age. **2.** a person who has taken the first or lowest degree at a college or university: *bachelor of arts.* **3.** a young knight who followed the banner of another. **4.** a young male fur seal kept from the breeding grounds by the older males. [ME *bacheler,* t. OF, t. ML: m.s. *baccalāris, baccalārius,* appar. orig. small farmholder, ? akin to L *baculum* staff] —**bach·e·lor·dom** (băch′ə lər dəm, băch′lər-), *n.* —**bach′e·lor·hood′,** *n.* —**bach′e·lor·ship′,** *n.*

bach·e·lor-at-arms (băch′ə lər ət ärmz′, băch′lər-), *n., pl.* **bachelors-at-arms.** bachelor (def. 3).

bach·e·lor's-but·ton (băch′ə lərz bŭt′ən, băch′lərz-), *n.* any of various plants with round flower heads, esp. the cornflower, or double-flowered varieties of ranunculus.

bac·il·lar·y (băs′ə lĕr′Y), *adj.* **1.** Also, **ba·cil·li·form** (bə sYl′ə fôrm′), of or like a bacillus; rod-shaped. **2.** *Bac-*

teriol. characterized by bacilli. Also, **ba·cil·lar** (bə·sĭl′ər, băs′ələr). [f. s. L *bacillus* little rod + -ARY²]

ba·cil·lus (bə·sĭl′əs), *n., pl.* **-cilli** (-sĭl′ī). *Bacteriol.* **1.** any of the group of rod-shaped bacteria which produce spores in the presence of free oxygen. See illus. under **bacteria.** **2.** (formerly) any of the rod-shaped or cylindrical bacteria. **3.** any bacterium. [t. LL, dim. of *baculus* rod].

back¹ (băk), *n.* **1.** the hinder part of the human body, extending from the neck to the end of the spine. **2.** the part of the body of animals corresponding to the human back. **3.** the rear portion of any part or organ of the body: *the back of the head.* **4.** the whole body, with reference to clothing: *the clothes on his back.* **5.** the part opposite to or farthest from the face or front; the hinder side; the rear part: *the back of a hall.* **6.** the part covering the back, as of clothing. **7.** the spine: *to break one's back.* **8.** any rear part of an object serving to support, protect, etc.: *the back of a book.* **9.** the strength to carry a burden. **10.** *Football, etc.* **a.** a player behind the forward line. **b.** the position occupied by this player. **11. behind one's back,** in secret; when one is absent. **12. turn one's back on,** to forsake or neglect. . —*v.t.* **13.** to support, as with authority, influence, or money (often fol. by *up*). **14.** to cause to move backward; reverse the action of (often fol. by *up*): *to back a car.* **15.** to bet in favor of: *to back a horse in the race.* **16.** to get upon the back of; mount. **17.** to furnish with a back: *to back a book.* **18.** to lie at the back of; form a back or background for: *a beach backed by hills.* **19.** to write or print on the back of; endorse. —*v.i.* **20.** to go backward (often fol. by *up*). **21.** *Naut.* (of wind) to change direction counterclockwise. **22.** Some special verb phrases are: **back and fill, 1.** *Naut.* to trim the sails so that the wind strikes them first on the forward and then on the after side (done against the wind in a narrow channel to maneuver a ship from bank to bank without making headway but floating with the current). **2.** *U.S. Colloq.* to vacillate. **back down,** to retreat from or abandon an argument, opinion, claim, etc. **back off,** to recede from contact. **back out** or **out of,** to withdraw from or abandon (an engagement, promise, etc.). **back water, 1.** *Naut.* to reverse the direction of a vessel. **2.** *U.S. Colloq.* to retreat from an opinion, etc. —*adj.* **23.** lying or being behind: *a back door.* **24. (in) back of,** *U.S. Colloq.* behind. **25.** away from the front position or rank; remote: *back settlements.* **26.** belonging to the past: *back files.* **27.** overdue: *back pay.* **28.** coming or going back; backward: *back current.* **29.** *Phonet.* pronounced with the tongue drawn back in the mouth, as, in most varieties of English, the vowels of *bought, boat,* and *boot.* [ME *bak,* OE *bæc,* c. Icel. *bak*]
—**Syn. 23.** BACK, HIND, POSTERIOR, REAR refer to something situated behind something else. BACK means the opposite of front: *back window.* HIND, and the more formal word POSTERIOR, suggest the rearmost of two or more, often similar, objects: *hind legs, posterior lobe.* REAR is used of buildings, conveyances, etc., and in military language it is the opposite of fore: *rear end of a truck, rear echelon.*

back² (băk), *adv.* **1.** at, to, or toward the rear; backward: *to step back.* **2.** toward the past: *to look back on one's youth.* **3.** toward the original starting point, place, or condition: *to go back to the old home.* **4.** in reply; in return: *to pay back a loan.* **5.** in reversal of the usual course: *to take back a gift.* [aphetic var. of ABACK]

back³ (băk), *n.* a tub or vat. [t. D: m. *bak,* t. F: m. *bac* tub, trough, ferryboat]

back·ache (băk′āk′), *n.* an ache in one's back.

Back Bay, a fashionable residential section of Boston.

back·bite (băk′bīt′), *v.,* **-bit, -bitten** or (*Colloq.*) **-bit, biting.** —*v.t.* **1.** to attack the character or reputation of secretly. —*v.i.* **2.** to speak evil of the absent. —**back′-bit′er,** *n.* —**back′bit′ing,** *n.*

back·board (băk′bōrd′), *n.* **1.** a board placed at or forming the back of anything. **2.** *Med.* a board worn to support or straighten the back. **3.** *Basketball.* the vertical surface to which the basket is attached. —*v.t.* **4.** *Med.* to subject to the wearing of a backboard.

back·bone (băk′bōn′), *n.* **1.** *Anat.* the spinal or vertebral column; the spine. **2.** something resembling a backbone in appearance, position, or function. **3.** strength of character; resolution. **4.** *Bibliog.* the back or bound edge of a book; spine. —**back′boned′,** *adj.*

back·break·ing (băk′brā′kĭng), *adj.* physically exhausting.

back·cross (băk′krôs′, -krŏs′), *Genetics.* —*v.t.* **1.** to cross a hybrid (of the first generation) with either of its parents. —*n.* **2.** an instance of such crossing.

back·door (băk′dōr′), *adj.* secret; clandestine.

back·drop (băk′drŏp′), *n.* *Theat.* the rear curtain of a stage setting.

backed (băkt), *adj.* having a back: *a high-backed chair.*

back·er (băk′ər), *n.* anything, esp. a person, that supports or gives aid in an enterprise.

back·fall (băk′fôl′), *n.* **1.** that which falls back. **2.** a fall in which a wrestler is thrown upon his back.

back·field (băk′fēld′), *n.* *Football.* those players who are in back of the front line, consisting of the quarterback, the two halfbacks, and the fullback.

back·fire (băk′fīr′), *v.,* **-fired, -firing,** *n.* —*v.i.* **1.** (of an internal-combustion engine) to have a premature explosion in the cylinder or in the admission or exhaust passages. **2.** to check a forest or prairie fire by burning off an area in advance of it. **3.** to bring results opposite to those planned: *the plot backfired.* —*n.* **4.** (in an internal-combustion engine) premature ignition of the fuel, resulting in loss of power and loud explosive sound in the manifold. **5.** an explosion coming out of the breech of a firearm. **6.** a fire purposely started in advance of a fire in order to fight it.

back formation, *Gram.* **1.** the formation of a word from one that looks like its derivative, as *typewrite* from *typewriter, donate* from *donation.* **2.** a word so formed.

back·gam·mon (băk′găm′ən, băk′găm′ən), *n.* **1.** a game played by two persons on a board having two tables or parts, with pieces or men moved in accordance with throws of dice. **2.** a victory at this game, esp. one resulting in a tripled score. —*v.t.* **3.** to defeat at backgammon; esp. to win a triple score over. [f. BACK¹, adj. + GAMMON; game so called because the pieces often must go back and reënter]

back·ground (băk′ground′), *n.* **1.** the ground or parts situated in the rear. **2.** the surface or ground against which the parts of a picture are relieved, or the portions of a picture represented as more distant (opposed to *foreground*). **3.** the social, historical, and other antecedents which explain an event or condition: *the background of the war.* **4.** a person's origin, education, etc. in relation to present character, status, etc. **5. in the background,** out of sight or notice; in obscurity.

back·hand (băk′hănd′), *n.* **1.** the hand turned backward in making a stroke, as in tennis. **2.** a stroke, as in tennis, by a right-handed player from the left of the body (or the reverse for a left-handed player). **3.** writing which slopes backward or to the left. —*adj.* **4.** backhanded. —**Ant. 1.** forehand.

back·hand·ed (băk′hăn′dĭd), *adj.* **1.** performed with the hand turned backward, crosswise, or in any oblique direction, or with the back of the hand in the direction of the stroke. **2.** sloping to the left: *backhanded writing.* **3.** oblique or opposite in meaning; insincere; indirect: *a backhanded compliment.* **4.** (of a rope) twisted in the opposite way from the usual or right-handed method. —**back′hand′ed·ly,** *adv.* —**back′hand′ed·ness,** *n.*

back·house (băk′hous′), *n.* **1.** an outhouse at the back of a main building. **2.** a privy.

back·ing (băk′ĭng), *n.* **1.** aid or support of any kind. **2.** supporters or backers collectively. **3.** that which forms the back or is placed at or attached to the back of anything to support or strengthen it.

back·lash (băk′lăsh′), *n.* **1.** *Mach.* the jarring reaction, or the play, between loosely fitting or worn parts of a machine or mechanical device. **2.** *Angling.* a tangled line on a reel, caused by a faulty cast.

back·log (băk′lôg′, -lŏg′), *n.* *U.S.* **1.** a large log at the back of the hearth to keep up the fire. **2.** something serving as a reserve, or support.

back number, *Orig. U.S.* **1.** an out-of-date issue of a serial publication. **2.** anything out-of-date.

back·set (băk′sĕt′), *n.* **1.** a setback; a reverse. **2.** an eddy or countercurrent.

back·sheesh (băk′shēsh), *n., v.t., v.i.* baksheesh. Also, **back′shish.**

back·side (băk′sīd′), *n.* **1.** the back part. **2.** the rump.

back·sight (băk′sīt′), *n.* *Survey.* **1.** a sight on a previously occupied instrument station. **2.** (in leveling) the reading on a rod that is held on a point of known elevation, and which is to be used in computing the height of the instrument.

back·slide (băk′slīd′), *v.i.,* **-slid, -slidden** or **-slid, -sliding.** to relapse into error or sin. —**back′slid′er,** *n.*

back·spin (băk′spĭn′), *n.* reverse spinning of a ball causing it to bounce backwards, as in tennis.

back·stage (băk′stāj′), *adv.* **1.** behind the curtain in a theater; on the stage, or in the wings or dressing rooms. **2.** toward the rear of the stage; upstage. —*adj.* **3.** located, occurring, etc., backstage.

back·stairs (băk′stârz′), *adj.* indirect; underhand. Also, **back′stair′.**

back·stay (băk′stā′), *n.* **1.** *Mach.* a supporting or checking piece in a mechanism. **2.** *Naut.* a stay or supporting rope leading from a masthead backward to the ship's side or stern.

back·stitch (băk′stĭch′), *n.* **1.** stitching or a stitch in which the thread doubles back each time on the preceding stitch. —*v.t., v.i.* **2.** to sew by backstitch.

back·stop (băk′stŏp′), *n.* *U.S. Sports.* a wall, wire screen, player, etc., to prevent a ball from going too far.

back·stroke (băk′strōk′), *n.* **1.** a backhanded stroke. **2.** a blow or stroke in return; recoil. **3.** *Swimming.* a stroke made while on one's back.

back·sword (băk′sōrd′), *n.* **1.** a sword with only one sharp edge; a broadsword. **2.** a cudgel with a basket hilt, used like a foil in fencing. **3.** a backswordman.

back·sword·man (băk′sōrd′mən), *n., pl.* **-men.** one who uses a backsword. Also, **back′swords′man.**

back talk, impertinent talk; answering back.

back·track (băk′trăk′), *v.i.* *U.S.* **1.** to return over the same course or route. **2.** to withdraw from an undertaking, position, etc.; pursue a reverse policy.

back·ward (băk′wərd), *adv.* Also, **back′wards. 1.** toward the back or rear **2.** with the back foremost.

3. in the reverse of the usual or right way; retrogressively: *to read or spell backward.* 4. toward the past. 5. in time past. —*adj.* 6. directed toward the back or past. 7. reversed; returning: *a backward movement or journey.* 8. behind in time or progress; late; slow: *a backward learner or country.* 9. reluctant; hesitating; bashful: *a backward child.* [ME *bakward,* f. *bak* BACK[1] + -WARD] —back′ward·ly, *adv.* —back′ward·ness, *n.* —Syn. 6. retrograde, retrogressive. 8. tardy; behindhand. 9. disinclined; timid, retiring. —Ant. 1. forward.

back·wash (băk′wŏsh′, -wôsh′), *n.* 1. *Naut.* the water thrown back by oars, paddle wheels, or the like. 2. a condition lasting after the event which caused it.

back·wa·ter (băk′wô′tər, -wŏt′ər), *n.* 1. water held or forced back, as by a dam, flood, tide, etc. 2. a place or state of stagnant backwardness.

back·woods (băk′wo͝odz′), *n.pl. Orig. U.S.* 1. wooded or partially uncleared and unsettled districts. —*adj.* Also, **back′wood′.** 2. of or pertaining to the backwoods. 3. unsophisticated; uncouth.

back·woods·man (băk′wo͝odz′mən), *n., pl.* **-men.** 1. one living in the backwoods. 2. an uncouth person.

ba·con (bā′kən), *n.* the back and sides of the hog, salted and dried or smoked. [ME, t. OF, t. Gmc.; cf. OHG *bahho,* MHG *bache* buttock, ham]

Ba·con (bā′kən), *n.* 1. **Francis,** (*Baron Verulam, Viscount St. Albans*) 1561–1626, British essayist, philosopher, and statesman. 2. **Nathaniel,** 1642?–76, American colonist, born in England: leader of a rebellion in 1676, demanding greater suffrage and lower taxes. 3. **Roger,** (*Friar Bacon* or "*the Admirable Doctor*") 1214?–1294?, British philosopher and scientist.

Ba·co·ni·an (bā kō′n′ən), *adj.* 1. of or pertaining to Francis Bacon or his doctrines. —*n.* 2. an adherent of the Baconian philosophy.

Baconian theory, the theory attributing the authorship of Shakespeare's plays to Francis Bacon.

bac·te·re·mi·a (băk′tə rē′mĭ ə), *n. Pathol.* the presence (for transient periods) of bacteria in the blood.

bacteri-, a word element meaning "bacteria" or "bacterial." Also, **bacter-, bacterio-, bactero-.** [comb. form of BACTERIUM]

bac·te·ri·a (băk tĭr′ĭ ə), *n., pl.* of **bacterium.** the morphologically simplest group of nongreen vegetable organisms, various species of which are concerned in fermentation and putrefaction, the production of disease, the fixing of atmospheric nitrogen, etc.; a schizomycete. [t. NL. See BACTERIUM] —bac·te′ri·al, *adj.* —bac·te′ri·al·ly, *adv.*

Bacteria (greatly magnified)

A. Cocci (spherical): 1, *Staphylococcus pyogenes aureus.* 2, *Streptococcus pyogenes.* B. Bacilli (rod): 3, *Bacillus sporogenes.* 4, *Bacillus proteus.* 5, *Bacillus subtilis.* 6, *Bacillus typhosus.* C, Spirilla (spiral): 7, *Vibrio cholerae asiaticae.* 8, *Spirillum undulum.* 9, *Theospirillum.* 10, *Spirochaeta*

bac·te·ri·cide (băk tĭr′ə sīd′), *n.* an agent capable of destroying bacteria. —bac·te′ri·cid′al, *adj.*

bac·te·rin (băk′tə rĭn), *n. Immunol.* a vaccine prepared from bacteria. [f. BACTER- + -IN²]

bacteriol., bacteriology.

bac·te·ri·ol·o·gy (băk tĭr′ĭ ŏl′ə jĭ), *n.* the science that deals with bacteria. —bac·te·ri·o·log·i·cal (băk tĭr′ĭ ə lŏj′ə kəl), *adj.* —bac·te′ri·o·log′i·cal·ly, *adv.* —bac·te′ri·ol′o·gist, *n.*

bac·te·ri·ol·y·sis (băk tĭr′ĭ ŏl′ə sĭs), *n.* disintegration or dissolution of bacteria. —bac·te·ri·o·lyt·ic (băk tĭr′ĭ ə lĭt′ĭk), *n., adj.*

bac·te·ri·o·phage (băk tĭr′ĭ ə fāj′), *n. Bacteriol.* an ultramicroscopic agent which causes the dissolution of certain bacteria (regarded by some as a living agent, by others as an enzyme).

bac·te·ri·o·sta·sis (băk tĭr′ĭ ə stā′sĭs), *n. Bacteriol.* the prevention of the development of bacteria. —bac·te·ri·o·stat·ic (băk tĭr′ĭ ə stăt′ĭk), *adj.*

bac·te·ri·um (băk tĭr′ĭ əm), *n. Bacteriol.* 1. sing. of **bacteria.** 2. a group of nonsporeforming bacteria (in distinction to the bacillus and clostridium groups). [t. NL, t. Gk.: m. *baktērion,* dim. of *báktron* stick]

bac·ter·ize (băk′tə rīz′), *v.t.,* **-ized, -izing.** to change in composition by means of bacteria. —bac′ter·i·za′tion, *n.*

bactero-, var. of bacteri-.

bac·ter·oid (băk′tə roid′), *n. Bacteriol.* one of the minute rodlike or branched organisms (regarded as forms of bacteria) found in the root nodules of nitrogen-fixing plants, as the legumes. —bac′te·roi′dal, *adj.*

Bactrian camel, *Camelus bactrianus* (Ab. 9 ft. long, ab. 7½ ft. high at the humps)

Bac·tri·a (băk′trĭ ə), *n.* an ancient country in W Asia

between the Oxus river and the Hindu Kush Mountains. —Bac′tri·an, *adj., n.*

Bactrian camel, the two-humped camel, *Camelus bactrianus.* See illus. in preceding column.

ba·cu·li·form (bə kū′lə fôrm′, băk′yə-), *adj. Biol.* rod-shaped. [f. s. L *baculum* rod + -(I)FORM]

bac·u·line (băk′yə lĭn, -lĭn′), *adj.* pertaining to the rod or to its use in punishing. [f. s. L *baculum* rod + -INE¹]

bad¹ (băd), *adj.* **worse, worst,** *n., adv.* —*adj.* 1. not good: *bad conduct, a bad life.* 2. defective; worthless: *a bad coin, a bad debt.* 3. not sufficient for use; inadequate: *bad heating.* 4. incorrect; faulty: *a bad shot.* 5. not valid; not sound: *a bad claim.* 6. having an injurious or unfavorable tendency or effect: *bad air or food.* 7. in ill health; sick: *to feel bad.* 8. regretful; contrite; sorry; upset: *to feel bad about an error.* 9. unfavorable; unfortunate: *bad news.* 10. offensive; disagreeable; painful: *a bad temper.* 11. severe: *a bad sprain.* 12. rotten; decayed. —*n.* 13. that which is bad. 14. a bad condition, character, or quality. —*adv.* 15. badly. [ME *badde;* ? back formation from OE *bæddel* effeminate person] —bad′ness, *n.*
—Syn. 1. depraved, corrupt, base, sinful, criminal, villainous, atrocious. BAD, EVIL, ILL, WICKED are closest in meaning, in reference to that which is lacking in moral qualities or is actually vicious and reprehensible. BAD is the broadest and simplest term: *a bad man, bad habits.* EVIL applies to that which violates or leads to the violation of moral law: *evil practices.* ILL now appears mainly in certain fixed expressions, with a milder implication than that in evil: *ill will, ill-natured.* WICKED implies willful and determined doing of what is very wrong: *a wicked plan.* 3. inferior, poor, deficient. 6. disadvantageous. 9. adverse.

bad² (băd), *v.* pt. of **bid.**

Ba·da·józ (bä′dä hôth′), *n.* a city in SW Spain. 55,869 (1940).

bad blood, hate; long-standing enmity; dislike.

bade (băd), *v.* pt. of **bid.**

Ba·den (bä′dən), *n.* 1. a state in SW Germany. 2,502,442 pop. (1939); 5818 sq. mi. *Cap.:* Karlsruhe. 2. Also, **Ba′den-Ba′den.** a city in this state. 33,165 (1939).

Ba·den-Pow·ell (bā′dən pō′əl), *n.* **Robert Stephenson Smyth, 1st Baron,** 1857–1941, British general who founded the Boy Scouts in 1908.

bad form, *Chiefly Brit.* a breach of good manners.

badge (băj), *n., v.,* **badged, badging.** —*n.* 1. a mark, token, or device worn as a sign of allegiance, membership, authority, achievement, etc. 2. any emblem, token, or distinctive mark. —*v.t.* 3. to furnish or mark with a badge. [ME *bage, bagge;* orig. unknown]

badg·er (băj′ər), *n.* 1. any of the various burrowing carnivorous mammals of the *Mustelidae,* as *Meles meles,* a European species about two feet long, and *Taxidea taxus,* a similar American species. 2. the fur of this mammal. 3. (in Australia) **a.** a wombat. **b.** a bandicoot (def. 2). —*v.t.* 4. to harass; torment. [earlier *bageard.* ? f. BADGE (with allusion to white mark on head) + -ARD]

American badger, *Taxidea taxus* (28 in. long, tail ab. 5½ in.)

bad·i·nage (băd′ə näzh′, băd′ə nĭj), *n., v.,* **-naged, -naging.** —*n.* 1. light playful banter or raillery. —*v.t.* 2. to drive or force by badinage. [t. F, der. *badiner* jest, der. *badin* fool, t. Pr., der. *badar* gape, g. LL *badāre*]

bad·lands (băd′lăndz′), *n.pl.* a barren area in which soft rock strata are eroded into varied, fantastic forms.

Bad Lands, a barren, badly eroded region in SW South Dakota and NW Nebraska.

bad·ly (băd′lĭ), *adv.* 1. in a bad manner; ill. 2. very much: *to need or want badly.*

bad·min·ton (băd′mĭn tən), *n.* a game, similar to lawn tennis, but played with a high net and shuttlecock. [named after *Badminton,* in Gloucestershire, England]

Ba·do·glio (bä dō′lyō), *n.* **Pietro** (pyĕ′trô), born 1871, Italian general.

bad-tem·pered (băd′tĕm′pərd), *adj.* having a bad temper; cross.

Bae·da (bē′də), *n.* Bede.

Bae·de·ker (bā′də kər), *n.* any of the series of guidebooks for travelers issued by the German publisher Karl Baedeker, 1801–59, and his successors.

Baeke·land (bāk′lănd′; *Flem.* bä′kə länt′), *n.* **Leo Hendrik** (lē′ō hĕn′drĭk; *Flem.* lā′ō), 1863–1944, Belgian-American chemist. Cf. **Bakelite.**

baff (băf), *Golf.* —*v.i.* 1. to strike the ground with the club in making a stroke. —*n.* 2. a baffling stroke, unduly lofting the ball. [? imit.]

Baf·fin (băf′ĭn), *n.* **William,** 1584?–1622, British navigator who explored arctic North America.

Baffin Bay, a part of the Arctic Ocean between Greenland and the Canadian arctic islands.

Baffin Island, a large Canadian island between Greenland and Hudson Bay. ab. 1000 mi. long.

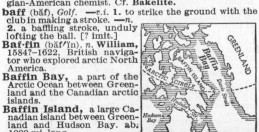

baf·fle (băf/əl), v., **-fled, -fling,** n. —v.t. **1.** to thwart or frustrate disconcertingly; balk; confuse. **2.** Naut. (of the wind, current, etc.) to beat about; force to take a variable course. **3.** Obs. to hoodwink; cheat. —v.i. **4.** to struggle ineffectually, as a ship in a gale. —n. **5.** a balk or check; perplexity. **6.** an artificial obstruction for checking or deflecting the flow of gases (as in a boiler), sounds (as in a radio), etc. [orig. uncert.] —**baf/fle·ment,** n. —**baf/fler,** n. —**baf/fling,** adj. —**baf/fling·ly,** adv.

baff·y (băf/ĭ), n., pl. **baffies.** Golf. a short wooden club with a deeply pitched face, for lofting the ball.

bag (băg), n., v., **bagged, bagging.** —n. **1.** a receptacle of leather, cloth, paper, etc., capable of being closed at the mouth; a pouch. **2.** Chiefly Brit. a suitcase or other portable receptacle for carrying articles as in traveling. **3.** a purse or moneybag. **4.** the contents of a bag. **5.** Hunting. a sportsman's take of game, etc. **6.** any of various measures of capacity. **7.** something resembling or suggesting a bag. **8.** a sac, as in an animal body. **9.** an udder. **10.** a baggy part. **11.** Baseball. **a.** a base (def. 7). **b.** a bag of sand used to mark a base. **12. hold the bag,** U.S. Colloq. to be left with the blame, responsibility, etc. —v.i. **13.** to swell or bulge. **14.** to hang loosely like an empty bag. —v.t. **15.** to cause to swell or bulge; distend. **16.** to put into a bag. **17.** to kill or catch, as in hunting. [ME bagge, t. Scand.; cf. Icel. baggi pack, bundle]
—**Syn. 1.** BAG, SACK, referring to a pouchlike object, are often used interchangeably, esp. in the Middle West. A BAG, though it may be of any size, is usually small, and made o such materials as paper, leather, etc. A SACK is usually large, oblong, and made of coarse material.

B. Ag. (L Baccalaureus Agriculturae) Bachelor of Agriculture. Also, **B. Agr.**

ba·gasse (bəgăs/; Fr. bȧgȧs/), n. crushed sugar cane or beet refuse from sugar making. [t. F, t. Pr.: m. bagasso]

bag·a·telle (băg/ətĕl/), n. **1.** a trifle. **2.** a game played on a board having at one end holes into which balls are to be struck with a cue. **3.** pinball. **4.** a short and light musical composition, usually for the piano. [t. F, t. It.: m. bagatella, dim. of baga, baca berry]

Bag·dad (băg/dăd), n. the capital of Iraq, in the central part, on the Tigris river. 449,881 (est. 1941). Also, **Bagh·dad** (băg dăd/, băg/dăd).

Bage·hot (băj/ət), n. **Walter,** 1826–77, British economist, political journalist, and critic.

bag·gage (băg/ĭj), n. **1.** trunks, suitcases, etc., used in traveling; luggage. **2.** Brit. the portable equipment of an army. [ME, t. OF: m. bagage, der. bagues, pl., bundles, or der. baguer tie up]

bag·ging (băg/ĭng), n. woven material, as of hemp or jute, for bags.

bag·gy (băg/ĭ), adj., **-gier, -giest.** baglike; hanging loosely. —**bag/gi·ly,** adv. —**bag/gi·ness,** n.

bag·man (băg/mən), n., pl. **-men.** Brit., Now Rare or Obs. a traveling salesman.

bagn·io (băn/yō, băn/-), n., pl. **bagnios. 1.** a prison for slaves, as in the Orient. **2.** a brothel. **3.** a bath or bathing house. [t. It.: m. bagno, g. L balneum bath]

bag·pipe (băg/pīp/), n. (often pl.) a reed instrument consisting of a melody pipe and one or more accompanying drone pipes protruding from a windbag into which the air is blown by the mouth or a bellows. —**bag/pip/er,** n.

ba·guette (băgĕt/), n. **1.** a gem cut in a long, rectangular shape. **2.** this shape. **3.** Archit. a small, convex, semicircular molding. Also, **ba·guet/.** [t. F: wand, rod, t. It.: m. bacchetta, dim. of bacchio, g. L baculum]

Scottish bagpipe

Ba·gui·o (băg/ĭyō/; Sp. bȧ/gyô), n. a city in the Philippine Islands, on Luzon: summer capital. 24,117 pop. (1939); 4961 ft. high.

bag·worm (băg/wûrm/), n. the caterpillar of any moth of the family Psychidae. It constructs a bag of silk, leaves, etc., in which it lives.

bah (bä, bȧ), interj. an exclamation of contempt.

ba·ha·dur (bəhô/dŏor, -hä/-), n. a title of respect commonly affixed to the names of European officers in Indian documents, or used in ceremonious mention by natives: Jonas Sahib Bahadur. [t. Hind.: brave, hero]

Ba·hai (bəhä/ē), n., pl. **-hais,** adj. —n. **1.** an adherent of Bahaism. —adj. **2.** of or pertaining to Bahaism or a Bahai. [t. Pers.: m. Bahā (u'llāh) splendor (of God), title of the leader]

Ba·ha·ism (bəhä/ĭzəm), n. Relig. Babism as accepted by the followers of Mirza Husayn Ali, who in 1863 proclaimed himself leader of the Babists under the name Baha-ullah. —**Ba·ha/ist** n., adj.

Ba·ha·ma Islands (bəhä/mə; esp. Brit. and locally bəhä/mə), a group of islands in the British West Indies, SE of Florida and NE of Cuba: a British colony. 73,000 pop. (est. 1942); 4375 sq. mi. Cap.: Nassau. Also, **Bahamas.**

Ba·ha·wal·pur (bəhä/wəl pŏor, bä/wəl-), n. a state in Pakistan, in the Punjab. 1,341,200 pop. (1941). 16,430 sq. mi.

Ba·hi·a (bäē/ə, bəē/ə), n. São Salvador.

Ba·hi·a Blan·ca (bäē/ä bläng/kä), a seaport in E Argentina. 121,055 (est. 1944).

Bah·rein Islands (bärān/), a group of islands in the W Persian Gulf: a British protectorate. 120,000 pop. (est. 1942); 232 sq. mi. Cap.: Manama.

baht (bät), n., pl. **bahts, baht.** the Siamese monetary unit in silver, with a U.S. gold equivalent of $.4424. [t. Siamese]

Ba·iae (bā/yē), n. an ancient resort city in SW Italy: villas of Julius Caesar, Nero, and Pompey.

Bai·kal (bīkäl/), n. **Lake,** a lake in the S Soviet Union in Asia: the deepest lake in the world. ab. 13,000 sq. mi.; ab. 5000 ft. deep.

bail¹ (bāl), Law. —n. **1.** property given as surety that a person released from custody will return at an appointed time. **2.** the person or persons giving it. **3.** the position or the privilege of being bailed. **4.** release from prison on bond. **5.** the court granting such a release. —v.t. **6.** to grant or to obtain the liberty of (a person under arrest) on security given for his appearance when required, as in court for trial. **7.** to deliver possession of (goods, etc.) for storage, hire, or other special purpose, without transfer of ownership. [ME bayle, t. OF: m. bail control, baillier deliver, g. L bājulāre carry]

bail² (bāl), n. **1.** the semicircular handle of a kettle or pail. **2.** a hooplike support, as for a wagon cover. [ME beyl, prob. t. Scand.; cf. Icel. beyglast become bent]

bail³ (bāl), v.t. **1.** to dip out of a boat, as with a bucket: to bail water out of a boat. **2.** to clear of water by dipping (usually fol. by out): to bail out a boat. —v.i. **3.** to bail water. **4.** to make a parachute jump (fol. by out). —n. **5.** a bucket or other vessel for bailing. [ME bayle, t. OF: m. baille bucket, g. VL bajula vessel] —**bail/er,** n.

bail⁴ (bāl), n. **1.** Cricket. either of the two small bars or sticks laid across the tops of the stumps which form the wicket. **2.** a bar for separating horses in a stable. **3.** (pl.) Obs. the wall of an outer court of a feudal castle. [ME baile, t. OF: barrier; of obscure origin]

bail·a·ble (bā/ləbəl), adj. Law. **1.** capable of being set free on bail. **2.** admitting of bail: a bailable offense.

bail·ee (bā/lē/), n. Law. one to whom goods are delivered in bailment.

bai·ley (bā/lĭ), n., pl. **-leys.** the wall of defense about the outer court of a feudal castle, or the outer court itself (still used in some proper names, as in Old Bailey, London). [ME baily; var. of BAIL⁴]

Bai·ley (bā/lĭ), n. **Liberty Hyde,** born 1858, U.S. botanist, horticulturist, and writer.

bail·ie (bā/lĭ), n. (in Scotland) a municipal officer or magistrate, corresponding to an English alderman. [ME bailli, t. OF, var. of baillif BAILIFF]

bail·iff (bā/lĭf), n. **1.** an officer similar to a sheriff or his deputy, employed to execute writs and processes, make arrests, keep order in the court, etc. **2.** (in England) a person charged with local administrative authority, or the chief magistrate in certain towns. **3.** (esp. in England) an overseer of a landed estate. [ME baillif, t. OF, der. baillir govern. See BAIL⁴]

bail·i·wick (bā/ləwĭk), n. **1.** the district within which a bailie or bailiff has jurisdiction. **2.** a person's area of skill, work, etc. [f. BAILIE + wick office (ME wike, OE wīce)]

bail·ment (bāl/mənt), n. Law. **1.** act of bailing a prisoner or accused person. **2.** act of bailing goods, etc.

bail·or (bāl/mənt, bā/lôr/), n. Law. one who delivers goods, etc., in bailment.

bails·man (bālz/mən), n., pl. **-men.** Law. one who gives bail or security.

bain-ma·rie (băn̄ mȧ rē/), n., pl. **bains-marie** (băn̄-mȧ rē/) Chiefly Brit. a vessel containing hot water, in which another vessel is placed to heat its contents. [F: bath of Miriam (sister of Moses), in the Middle Ages considered an alchemist]

Bai·ram (bī răm/, bĭ/räm), n. either of two Mohammedan festivals, one (lesser Bairam) immediately after Ramadan, the other (greater Bairam) 70 days after it. [t. Turk.: m. bai ram]

Baird Mountains (bârd), a mountain range in NW Alaska, forming the W end of the Brooks Range.

bairn (bârn; Scot. bärn), n. Scot. and N. Eng. a child; a son or daughter. [Scot. var. of obs. E barn(e) child, OE bearn]

bait (bāt), n. **1.** food, or some substitute, used as a lure in angling, trapping, etc. **2.** an allurement; enticement. **3.** a halt for refreshment or rest during a journey. —v.t. **4.** to prepare (a hook or trap) with bait. **5.** to lure as with bait; captivate. **6.** to set dogs upon (an animal) for sport. **7.** to worry; torment. **8.** to give food and drink to (horses, etc.), esp. during a journey. —v.i. **9.** Now Chiefly Brit. to stop for food or refreshment during a journey. **10.** to take food; feed. [ME, t. Scand.; cf. Icel. beita] —**bait/er,** n.

baize (bāz), n. **1.** a soft, usually green, woolen fabric resembling felt, used chiefly for the tops of billiard tables. **2.** an article of this fabric. [earlier bays, t. F: m. baies, pl., der. bai bay-colored, g. L badius]

Ba·ja Ca·li·for·nia (bä′hä kä′lē fôr′nyä), Spanish name of Lower California.

bake (bāk), v., **baked, baking,** n. —v.t. **1.** to cook by dry heat in an oven, under coals, or on heated metals or stones. **2.** to harden by heat. —v.i. **3.** to bake bread etc. **4.** to become baked. —n. **5.** U.S. a social occasion, at which the chief food is baked. **6.** Scot. a cracker. [ME bake(n), OE bacan, c. G backen]

bake·house (bāk′hous′), n. a building or room to bake in; a bakery.

Ba·ke·lite (bā′kə līt′), n. a trademark for a thermo-setting plastic derived by heating phenol or cresol with formaldehyde and ammonia under pressure, used for radio cabinets, telephone receivers, electric insulators, and molded plastic ware. [named after L. H. Baekeland]

bak·er (bā′kər), n. **1.** one who bakes; one who makes and sells bread, cake, etc. **2.** a small portable oven.

Bak·er (bā′kər), n. **1.** Mount, a mountain in NW Washington, in the Cascade Range. 10,750 ft. **2.** George Pierce, 1866–1935, U.S. critic, author, and professor of drama. **3.** Newton Diehl (dēl), 1871–1937, U.S. lawyer: Secretary of War, 1916–21. **4.** Ray Stannard, ("David Grayson") 1870–1946, U.S. author.

Baker Island, a small island in the Pacific, near the equator, belonging to the U.S. 1 sq. mi.

baker's dozen, thirteen, reckoned as a dozen.

Bak·ers·field (bā′kərz fēld′), n. a city in S California, N of Los Angeles. 34,784 pop. (1950).

bak·er·y (bā′kə rĭ), n., pl. **-eries.** a baker's shop; place where baked goods are made or sold.

bak·ing (bā′kĭng), n. **1.** act of one who or that which bakes. **2.** the quantity baked at one time; a batch.

baking powder, any of various powders used as a substitute for yeast in baking, composed of sodium bi-carbonate mixed with an acid substance capable of set-ting carbon dioxide free when the mixture is moistened.

baking soda, sodium bicarbonate, NaHCO₃.

bak·sheesh (băk′shēsh), (used in India, Turkey, etc.) —n. **1.** a tip, present, or gratuity. —v.t., v.i. **2.** to give a tip (to). Also, **bak′shish, backsheesh, backshish.** [t. Pers.: m. bakhshīsh, der. bakhshīdan give]

Bakst (bäkst), n. Léon Nikolaevich (lē ôn′ nĭ kô lä′-yə vĭch), 1866–1924, Russian painter and designer.

Ba·ku (bä kōō′), n. a seaport in the Soviet Union on the Caspian Sea: capital of Azerbaijan. 809,347 (1939).

Ba·ku·nin (bä kōō′nĭn), n. Mikhail Aleksandrovich (mĭ hä ēl′ ä′lĕ ksän′drô vĭch), 1814–76, Russian an-archist and writer.

bal., balance.

Ba·laam (bā′ləm), n. a Mesopotamian diviner, who, when commanded to curse the Israelites, blessed them and uttered favorable prophecies, after having been re-buked by the ass he rode. Num. 22–23.

Bal·a·kla·va (băl′ə klä′və; Russ. bä′lä klä′vä), n. a seaport in the SW Soviet Union, on the Black Sea: scene of the "Charge of the Light Brigade" in the Crimean War, 1854. 2323 (1926).

bal·a·lai·ka (băl′ə lī′kə), n. a Russian mu-sical instrument with a triangular body and a guitar neck. [t. Russ.]

bal·ance (băl′əns), n., v. **-anced, -ancing.** —n. **1.** an instrument for weighing, typically a bar poised or swaying on a central support according to the weights borne in scales (pans) suspended at the ends. **2.** power to decide as by a balance; authoritative control: his fate hung in the balance. **3.** state of equilibrium or equipoise; equal distribution of weight, amount, etc. **4.** mental steadiness; habit of calm behavior, judgment, etc. **5.** harmonious arrange-ment or adjustment, esp. in the arts of design. **6.** something used to produce equilibrium; a counterpoise. **7.** act of balancing; comparison as to weight, amount, importance, etc.; estimate. **8.** U.S. the remainder or rest. **9.** Com. **a.** equality between the totals of the two sides of an account. **b.** difference between the debit total and the credit total of an account. **c.** unpaid difference represented by the excess of debits over credits. **10.** an adjustment of accounts. **11.** Dancing. a balancing movement. **12.** Horol. a wheel which oscillates against the tension of a hairspring for regulat-ing the beats of a watch or clock. **13.** (cap.) Astron. the zodiacal constellation Libra or the sign named for it. —v.t. **14.** to weigh in a balance. **15.** to estimate the relative weight or importance of; compare: balance probabilities; offset. **17.** to bring to or hold in equilibrium; poise: to balance a book on one's head. **18.** to arrange, adjust, or proportion the parts of symmetrically. **19.** to be equal or proportionate to. **20.** Com. **a.** to add up the two sides of (an account) and determine the difference. **b.** to make the necessary entries in (an account) so that the sums of the two sides will be equal. **c.** to settle by paying what remains due on an account; equalize or adjust. **21.** Dancing. to move in rhythm to and from: to balance one's partner. —v.i. **22.** to have an equality or equivalence in weight, parts, etc.; be in equilibrium: the account doesn't balance, do these scales balance? **23.** Com. to reckon or adjust ac-counts. **24.** to waver, hesitate. **25.** Dancing. to move forward and backward, or in opposite directions. [ME, t. OF, g. LL bilanx having two scales]

—Syn. **4.** poise, composure. **8.** See **remainder.**

Balalaika

balance of power, a distribution and an opposition of forces among nations such that no single nation will be strong enough to dominate all the others.

balance of trade, the difference between the ex-ports and imports of a country, said to be favorable or unfavorable as exports are greater or less than imports.

bal·anc·er (băl′ən sər), n. **1.** one who or that which balances. **2.** Entomol. halter². **3.** an acrobat.

balance sheet, Com. **1.** a tabular statement of both sides of a set of accounts, in which the debit and credit balances add up as equal. **2.** a statement of the financial position of a business on a specified date.

balance wheel, Horol. balance (def. 12).

Ba·la·ra·ma (bŭl′ə rä′mə), n. Hindu Myth. the elder brother of Krishna and an incarnation of Vishnu.

bal·as (băl′əs, bā′ləs), n. Mineral. a rose-red variety of spinel. Also, **balas ruby.** [ME, t. OF: m. balais, t. Ar.: m. balakksh kind of ruby, t. Pers.: m. Badakhshan, a province where found]

bal·a·ta (băl′ə tə), n. **1.** the dried juice or gum (**balata gum**) obtained from the bully tree, Manikara bidentata, used as a substitute for gutta-percha and in making chewing gum. **2.** the bully tree. [t. Amer. Sp.]

Ba·la·ton (bŏ′lô tôn′), n. a lake in W Hungary: the largest lake in central and western Europe. ab. 50 mi. long. German, **Platten See.**

Bal·bo (băl′bô), n. Italo (ē′tä lô′), 1896–1940, Italian aviator, general, and statesman.

Bal·bo·a (băl bô′ə; Sp. bäl bô′ä), n. **1.** Vasco Núñez de (väs′kô nōō′nyĕth dĕ), 1475?–1517, Spanish adven-turer and explorer who discovered the Pacific Ocean in 1513. **2.** a seaport in the Canal Zone at the Pacific terminus of the Panama Canal. 4117 (prelim. 1950). **3.** (l.c.) a silver coin of Panama, valued at one dollar.

bal·brig·gan (băl brĭg′ən), n. a kind of unbleached cotton, originally made at Balbriggan, in Ireland, used esp. in hosiery and underwear.

bal·co·ny (băl′kə nĭ), n., pl. **-nies. 1.** a balustraded or raised and railed platform projecting from the wall of a building. **2.** a gallery in a theater. [t. It.: m. balcone, der. balco scaffold, t. OHG. See BALK] —**bal′co·nied,** adj.

bald (bôld), adj. **1.** lacking hair on some part of the scalp: a bald head or person. **2.** destitute of some natural growth or covering: a bald mountain. **3.** bare; plain; unadorned: a bald prose style. **4.** open; undisguised: a bald lie. **5.** Zool. having white on the head: bald eagle. [ME balled, f. obs. ball white spot (cf. Welsh bali white-ness) + -ED³] —**bald′ly,** adv. —**bald′ness,** n.

bal·da·chin (băl′də kĭn, bôl′-), n. **1.** Archit. a fixed canopy, of metal, wood, or stone, above the isolated high altar of a church or above a tomb. **2.** a portable canopy carried in religious processions. Also, **bal′da·quin.** [t. F: m. baldaquin, t. It.: m. baldacchino, orig., silk from Bagdad, der. Bal-dacco Bagdad]

bald cypress, a tree, Taxodium distichum, of the Southern swamp-lands of the U.S.

bald eagle, a large eagle, Hali-aeetus leucocephalus, of the U. S. and Canada, having a fully feath-ered head and, when adult, a white head and tail.

Bal·der (bôl′dər), n. Scand. Myth. son of Odin, and one of the chief deities, god of the summer sun, and called "the Good." Also, **Bal·dr** (băl′dər).

Bald eagle.
Haliaeetus leucocephalus
(Ab. 3 ft. high,
wingspread 7 ft.)

bal·der·dash (bôl′dər dăsh′), n. **1.** a senseless jumble of words; nonsense. **2.** Obs. mix-ture of liquors.

bald·head (bôld′hĕd′), n. **1.** one who has a bald head. **2.** a breed of domestic pigeons. —**bald′head′ed,** adj.

bald·pate (bôld′pāt′), n. **1.** one who has a bald head. **2.** the American widgeon. —**bald′pat′ed,** adj.

bal·dric (bôl′drĭk), n. a belt, sometimes richly orna-mented, worn diagonally from shoulder to hip, support-ing a sword, horn, etc. [ME bawdrik, orig. and history obscure; akin to MHG balderich girdle; r. ME baudry, t. OF, t. MHG (as above)]

Bald·win (bôld′wĭn), n. **1.** James Mark, 1861–1934, U.S. psychologist. **2.** Stanley (Earl Baldwin of Bewd-ley), 1867–1947, British statesman: prime minister, 1923–1924, 1924–29, 1935–37. **3.** a variety of red, or red-and-yellow, winter apple, grown esp. in the northeast U.S.

Baldwin I, 1058–1118, crusader and first king of Jerusalem, 1100–18.

bale¹ (bāl), n., v., **baled, baling.** —n. **1.** a large bundle or package prepared for storage or transportation, esp. one closely compressed and secured by cords, wires, hoops, or the like, sometimes with a wrapping: a bale of hay. —v.t. **2.** to make into bales. [ME, t. Flem., t. OF: m. balle, t. OHG: m. balla BALL¹] —**bal′er,** n.

bale² (bāl), n. Archaic. **1.** evil; harm; misfortune. **2.** woe; misery; sorrow. [ME; OE balu, bealo]

Bâle (bäl), n. French name of **Basel.**

Bal·e·ar·ic Islands (băl′ĭ ăr′ĭk), a group of islands in the W Mediterranean: a province of Spain. 407,497 pop. (1940); 1936 sq. mi. Cap.: Palma. Spanish, **Ba·le·a·res** (bä′lĕ ä′rĕs).

ba·leen (bə lēn′), n. Zool. whalebone (def. 1). [ME balene, t. OF: m. baleine, g. L balaena whale]

bale·fire (bāl′fīr′), n. 1. a large fire in the open air; bonfire. 2. a beacon or signal fire. 3. the fire of a funeral pile. [ME balefyre, OE bǣlfȳr]

bale·ful (bāl′fəl), adj. 1. full of menacing or malign influences; pernicious. 2. Obs. wretched; miserable. [ME; OE bealofull] —bale′ful·ly, adv. —bale′fulness, n.

Bal·four (băl′fŏŏr), n. Arthur James (1st Earl of Balfour), 1848–1930, British statesman and writer: prime minister, 1902–05.

Balfour Declaration, a statement (Nov. 2, 1917) that the British government "view with favour the establishment in Palestine of a National Home for the Jewish people," but that "nothing shall be done which may prejudice the civil and religious rights of existing non-Jewish communities in Palestine."

Ba·li (bä′lē), n. an island in the U. S. of Indonesia, E of Java. 1,101,393 pop. (1930); 2147 sq. mi. Cap.: Singaraja.

Ba·li·nese (bä′lə nēz′, -nēs′), adj., n., pl. **-nese**. —adj. 1. of or pertaining to Bali, its people, or their language. —n. 2. a native or inhabitant of Bali. 3. the language of Bali, an Indonesian language.

Bal·iol (bāl′yəl, bā′lĬ əl), n. John de, 1249–1315, king of Scotland, 1292–96.

balk (bôk), v.i. 1. to stop, as at an obstacle: he balked a making the speech. 2. (of horses) to stop short and stubbornly refuse to go on. —v.t. 3. to place a balk in the way of; hinder; thwart: balked in one's hopes. 4. to let slip; fail to use: to balk an opportunity. —n. 5. a check or hindrance; a defeat or disappointment. 6. a miss, slip, or failure: to make a balk. 7. a strip of land left unplowed. 8. a crossbeam in the roof of a house which unites and supports the rafters; tie beam. 9. Civ. Eng. one of the stringers of a military bridge. 10. Baseball. an illegal deceptive motion of a pitcher as if to pitch when a runner or runners are on base. 11. Billiards. a. any of the eight panels or compartments lying between the cushions of the table and the balk lines. b. in balk, inside any of these spaces. Also, baulk. [ME; OE balca ridge, c. OHG balco beam] —balk′er, n.

Bal·kan (bôl′kən), adj. 1. pertaining to the Balkan States or their inhabitants. 2. pertaining to the Balkan Peninsula. 3. pertaining to the Balkan Mountains. —n. 4. the Balkans, the Balkan States.

Bal·kan·ize (bôl′kə nīz′), v.t., -ized, -izing. to divide into small states hostile to one another. —Bal′kan·i·za′tion, n.

Balkan Mountains, a mountain range extending from W Bulgaria to the Black Sea. Highest peak, ab. 7800 ft.

Balkan Peninsula, a peninsula in S Europe, lying S of the Danube and bordered by the Adriatic, Ionian, Aegean, and Black Seas.

Balkan States, the countries in the Balkan Peninsula: Yugoslavia, Rumania, Bulgaria, Albania, Greece, and the European part of Turkey.

Bal·khash (bäl′häsh), n. a salt lake in the SW Soviet Union in Asia, in Kazak Republic. 7115 sq. mi.

balk line (bôk), 1. Sports. (in track events) the starting line. 2. Billiards. a. a straight line drawn across the table, behind which the cue balls are placed in beginning a game. b. any of four lines, each near to and parallel with one side of the cushion, which divide the table into a large central panel or compartment and eight smaller compartments (**balks**) lying between this. c. balk (def. 11a).

balk·y (bô′kĬ), adj., **balkier, balkiest**. U.S. given to balking: a balky horse.

ball[1] (bôl), n. 1. a spherical or approximately spherical body; a sphere. 2. a round or roundish body, of different materials and sizes, hollow or solid, for use in various games, as baseball, football, tennis, or golf. 3. a game played with a ball, esp. baseball. 4. Baseball. a. a ball in play or action, as tossed, thrown, struck, etc.: a low or high ball, a curved ball. b. a ball pitched too high or low or not over the plate, and not struck at by the batter. 5. Mil. a. a solid projectile for a cannon, rifle, pistol, etc. (as distinguished from a shell), usually spherical. b. projectiles, esp. bullets, collectively. 6. any part of a thing, esp. of the human body, that is rounded or protuberant: the ball of the thumb. 7. Astron. a planetary or celestial body, esp. the earth. 8. **play ball, a.** (in games) to put the ball in motion. b. to start any action. c. U.S. Colloq. to work together; coöperate. —v.t. 9. to make into a ball. 10. to wind into balls: to ball cotton. 11. U.S. Slang. to bring to a state of hopeless confusion or difficulty (fol. by up). —v.i. 12. to form or gather into a ball. [ME bal, t. Scand.; cf. Icel. böllr]
—Syn. 1. BALL, GLOBE, SPHERE, ORB agree in referring to a round or rounded object. BALL may be applied to any round or roundish object or part: a rubber ball. GLOBE and SPHERE denote something thought of as either exactly or approximately round: in the form of a globe, a perfect sphere. ORB is now found only in elevated or scientific use; it is applied esp. to the eye and to the heavenly bodies: the orb of the full moon.

ball[2] (bôl), n. a social assembly for dancing. [t. F: m. bal, der. OF baler dance, g. LL ballāre]

Ball (bôl), n. **John,** died 1381, British priest: one of the leaders of Wat Tyler's peasants' revolt in 1381.

bal·lad (băl′əd), n. 1. a simple, often crude, narrative poem, of popular origin, composed in short stanzas, esp. one of romantic character and adapted for singing. 2. any poem written in similar style. 3. any light, simple song, esp. one of sentimental or romantic character, having two or more stanzas, all sung to the same melody. 4. the musical setting for a folk or literary ballad. [ME balade, t. OF, t. Pr.: m. balada dancing song, dance, der. balar dance, g. LL ballāre]

bal·lade (bə läd′, bă-; Fr. bả lảd′), n. 1. a poem consisting commonly of 3 stanzas having an identical rhyme scheme, followed by an envoy. The same last line is used for each of the stanzas and the envoy. 2. Music. a composition in free style and romantic mood, often for solo piano or for orchestra. [t. F. See BALLAD]

bal·lad·mon·ger (băl′əd mŭng′gər), n. 1. a seller of ballads. 2. a bad poet.

bal·lad·ry (băl′ə drĬ), n. ballad poetry.

ballad stanza, the metrical form for ballad verse, ordinarily consisting of four lines.

ball and chain, 1. a heavy iron ball fastened by a chain to a prisoner's leg. 2. any restraint.

ball-and-sock·et joint (bôl′ən sŏk′Ĭt), a joint formed by a ball or knob in a socket, admitting a degree of rotary movement in every direction.

Bal·la·rat (băl′ə răt′, băl′ə răt′), n. a city in SE Australia, in Victoria. 39,470 (est. 1943).

bal·last (băl′əst), n. 1. any heavy material carried by a ship or boat for insuring proper stability, so as to avoid capsizing and to secure the greatest effectiveness of the propelling power. 2. something heavy, as bags of sand, placed in the car of a balloon for control of altitude or, less frequently, of attitude. 3. anything that gives mental, moral, or political stability or steadiness. 4. gravel, broken stone, slag, etc., placed between and under the ties of a railroad to give stability, provide drainage, and distribute the load. —v.t. 5. to furnish with ballast: to ballast a ship. 6. to give steadiness to; keep steady. [t. ODan.: m. barlast (f. bar mere + last load), or t. MLG: f. bal bad + last load]

ball bearing, Mach. 1. a bearing in which the shaft or journal turns upon a number of steel balls running in an annular track. 2. any of the steel balls so used. —ball′-bear′ing, adj.

ball cock, a device for regulating the supply of water in a tank, cistern, or the like, consisting essentially of a valve connected with a hollow floating ball which by its rise or fall shuts or opens the valve.

bal·le·ri·na (băl′ə rē′nə; It. băl′lē rē′nä), n., pl. **-nas**, (It.) **-ne** (-nĕ). 1. the principal female dancer in a ballet company. 2. any female ballet dancer. [t. It.]

bal·let (băl′ā, bă lā′; Fr. bả lĕ′), n. 1. a spectacular entertainment, often designed to tell a story, and rendered by a company of professional dancers. 2. a dance interlude in an operatic performance. 3. the style of dancing used in such a performance, using intricate steps and expressive gestures. 4. the company of dancers. [t. F, t. It.: m. balletto, dim. of ballo dance]

bal·let·o·mane (bă lĕt′ə mān′), n. a ballet enthusiast.

ball·flow·er (bôl′flou′ər), n. Archit. a medieval ornament resembling a ball placed in a circular flower, the three (or four) petals of which form a cup around it.

Bal·liol (băl′yəl, bā′lĬ əl), n. a college of Oxford University founded before 1268.

bal·lis·ta (bə lĬs′tə), n., pl. **-tae** (-tē). an ancient military engine for throwing stones or other missiles. [t. L, der. Gk. bállein throw]

bal·lis·tics (bə lĬs′tĬks), n. the science or study of the motion of projectiles, such as bullets, shells, bombs, etc. **Interior ballistics** is the study of the motion of projectiles within the bore of a gun; **exterior ballistics** is the study of the motion of projectiles after they leave the muzzle of a gun. —bal·lis′tic, adj. —bal·lis·ti·cian (băl′Ĭs tĬsh′ən), n

Ballista

bal·lo·net (băl′ə nĕt′), n. an air or gasbag compartment in a balloon or airship, used to control buoyancy and maintain shape. [t. F: m. ballonnet, dim. of ballon balloon]

bal·loon (bə lōōn′), n. 1. a bag made of some material impermeable to gas and filled with some gas lighter than ordinary air, designed to rise and float in the atmosphere, and in the large forms having a car or compartment attached for passengers. 2. an inflatable rubber bag, usually brightly colored, used as a children's toy. 3. Chem. a round-bottomed flask. 4. (in drawings, etc.) a balloon-shaped figure enclosing words represented as issuing from the mouth of the speaker. —v.i. 5. to go up or ride in a balloon. 6. to swell or puff out like a balloon. —v.t. 7. to fill with air; inflate or distend (something) like a balloon. —adj. 8. puffed out like a balloon: balloon sleeves. [t. It.: m. ballone, aug. of balla ball] —bal·loon′ist, n.

balloon jib, Naut. a large triangular sail of light canvas used by yachts in light winds, instead of the jib.

balloon tire, Auto., etc. a low-pressure pneumatic tire with a broad tread for reducing the shock of bumps.

balloon vine, a sapindaceous tropical climbing plant, *Cardiospermum Halicacabum*, with big bladderlike pods.

bal·lot (băl′ət), *n., v.,* **-loted, -loting.** —*n.* **1.** a ticket, paper, etc., used in voting. **2.** the whole number of votes cast or recorded: *there was a large ballot.* **3.** the method of secret voting by means of printed or written ballots, or by means of voting machines. **4.** voting in general, or a round of voting. **5.** (formerly) a little ball used in voting. —*v.i.* **6.** to vote by ballot. **7.** to draw lots: *to ballot for places.* —*v.t.* **8.** to vote on by ballot. [t. It.: m. *ballotta,* bullet lot, dim. of *balla* ball] —**bal′-lot·er,** *n.*

bal·lotte·ment (bə lŏt′mənt), *n. Med.* **1.** an unreliable method of diagnosing pregnancy by the rebound of a fetal part displaced from its position by a sudden push with the examining finger. **2.** a similar method employed in testing for floating kidney, movable abdominal tumors, etc. [t. F: a tossing, der. *ballotter* toss as a ball]

ball·play·er (bôl′plā′ər), *n.* **1.** a baseball player. **2.** one who plays ball.

ball point pen, a fountain pen in which the point is a fine ball bearing, depositing an extremely thin film of ink. It will write for a longer period with a single reservoir of ink than a conventional pen.

ball·room (bôl′rōōm′, -rŏŏm′), *n.* a large room with a polished floor for balls or dancing.

ball valve, *Mach.* a valve controlled by a ball which is lifted by the upward pressure of the fluid and descends by gravity.

bal·ly (băl′ĭ), *Eng. Slang.* —*adj.* **1.** confounded (used humorously or for emphasis). —*adv.* **2.** very.

bal·ly·hoo (n. băl′ĭ hōō′; v. băl′ĭ hōō′, băl′ĭ hōō′), *n., pl.* **-hoos,** *v.,* **-hooed, -hooing.** *U.S. Slang.* —*n.* **1.** a clamorous attempt to win customers or advance any cause; blatant advertising or publicity. **2.** clamor or outcry. —*v.t., v.i.* **3.** to advertise or push by ballyhoo. [orig. obscure]

bal·ly·rag (băl′ĭ răg′), *v.t.* bullyrag.

balm (bäm), *n.* **1.** any of various oily, fragrant, resinous substances, often of medicinal value, exuding from certain plants, esp. tropical trees of the burseraceous genus *Commiphora.* **2.** a plant or tree yielding such a substance. **3.** any aromatic or fragrant ointment. **4.** aromatic fragrance; sweet odor. **5.** any of various aromatic menthaceous plants, esp. of the genus *Melissa,* as *M. officinalis,* a lemon-scented perennial herb. **6.** anything which heals, soothes, or mitigates pain. [ME *basme,* t. OF, g. L *balsamum* BALSAM]

bal·ma·caan (băl′mə kän′), *n.* a man's short, full-skirted overcoat of rough woolen cloth, with raglan shoulders. [named after *Balmacaan,* in Scotland]

balm of Gilead, 1. any of several species of the genus *Commiphora* (esp. *C. opobalsamum* and *C. meccanensis*), which yield a fragrant oleoresin. **2.** the resin itself. **3.** a North American poplar, *Populus candicans.*

Bal·mor·al (băl mŏr′əl, -môr′əl), *n.* **1.** a colored woolen petticoat formerly worn under a looped-up skirt. **2.** (*also l.c.*) a kind of laced shoe. **3.** a kind of brimless Scotch cap with a flat top projecting all around the head. [named after *Balmoral* Castle in Scotland]

Bal·mung (bäl′mŏŏng), *n.* (in the *Nibelungenlied*) the sword of Siegfried.

balm·y (bä′mĭ), *adj.,* **balmier, balmiest. 1.** mild and refreshing; soft; soothing: *balmy weather.* **2.** having the qualities of balm; aromatic; fragrant: *balmy leaves.* **3.** producing balm. **4.** *Eng. Slang.* weak-minded; silly. —**balm′i·ly,** *adv.* —**balm′i·ness,** *n.* —**Syn. 1.** fair, gentle, temperate, clement.

bal·ne·al (băl′nĭ əl), *adj.* of or pertaining to baths or bathing. [f. s. L *balneum* bath + -AL¹]

bal·ne·ol·o·gy (băl′nĭ ŏl′ə jĭ), *n. Med.* the science of using baths and bathing in therapeutics. [f. s. L *balneum* bath + -(o)LOGY]

ba·lo·ney (bə lō′nĭ), *n.* **1.** *Slang.* nonsense; foolishness. **2.** *Colloq.* bologna sausage. Also, **boloney.**

bal·sa (bôl′sə, bäl′-), *n.* **1.** a bombacaceous tree, *Ochroma lagopus,* of tropical America, with an exceedingly light wood used for life preservers, rafts, etc. **2.** a raft made of balsa wood. **3.** any life raft. [t. Sp.]

bal·sam (bôl′səm), *n.* **1.** any of various fragrant exudations from certain trees, esp. of the burseraceous genus *Commiphora* (see **balm** def. 1), as the balm of Gilead (**balsam of Mecca**). **2.** the similar products (**balsam of Peru** and **balsam of Tolu**) yielded by the leguminaceous trees, *Myroxylon Pereirae* and *M. Balsamum* of Central and South America. **3.** oleoresin (def. 1). **4.** any of certain transparent turpentines, as Canada balsam. **5.** a plant or tree yielding a balsam. **6.** the balsam fir. **7.** any of various plants of the balsaminaceous genus *Impatiens,* as *I. Balsamina,* a common garden annual. **8.** any aromatic ointment, whether for ceremonial or medicinal use. **9.** any healing or soothing agent or agency. [OE, t. L: s. *bálsamum,* m. Gk.: m. *bálsamon*] —**bal·sa·ma·ceous** (bôl′sə mā′shəs, băl′-), *adj.*

balsam fir, 1. a North American species of fir, *Abies balsamea,* which yields Canada balsam. **2.** the wood of this tree. **3.** any of certain other firs.

bal·sam·ic (bôl săm′ĭk, băl′-), *adj.* of, like, or containing balsam. —**bal·sam′i·cal·ly,** *adv.*

bal·sam·if·er·ous (bôl′səm ĭf′ər əs, băl′-), *adj.* yielding balsam. [f. BALSAM + -(I)FEROUS]

bal·sa·mi·na·ceous (bôl′sə mə nā′shəs, băl′-), *adj. Bot.* belonging to the Balsaminaceae, a family of plants

with odd-shaped flowers, including many tropical species and also the balsams of the genus *Impatiens.* [f. s. Gk. *balsaminē* balsam plant + -ACEOUS]

balsam poplar, a poplar, *Populus Tacamahaca,* with broad heart-shaped leaves, cultivated as a shade tree.

balsam spruce, an evergreen conifer of genus *Abies.*

Balt., Baltic.

Bal·tic (bôl′tĭk), *adj.* **1.** of, near, or on the Baltic Sea. **2.** of or pertaining to the Baltic States. —*n.* **3.** a group of Indo-European languages, including Lettish, Lithuanian, and the extinct Old Prussian. [t. ML: s. *Balticum,* ? der. L *balteus* belt]

Baltic Sea, a sea in N Europe, bounded by Sweden, Finland, the Soviet Union, Poland, Germany, and Denmark. ab. 160,000 sq. mi.

Baltic States, the formerly independent republics of Estonia, Latvia, and Lithuania, sometimes including Finland.

Bal·ti·more (bôl′tə môr′), *n.* **1.** a seaport in N Maryland, on an estuary near Chesapeake Bay. 949,708 pop.; with suburbs, 1,161,852 (1950). **2. Lord.** See **Calvert,** Sir George.

Baltic Sea

Baltimore oriole, an American oriole, *Icterus galbula.* [so named because the black and orange of the male were the colors of Lord Baltimore's livery]

Bal·to-Sla·vic (bôl′tō slä′vĭk, -slăv′ĭk), *n.* a grouping of Indo-European languages comprising the Baltic and Slavic groups.

Ba·lu·chi·stan (bə lōō′chə stän′, -stăn′), *n.* a province in W Pakistan, bordering the Arabian Sea: formerly subdivided into British territory and three native states. 857,800 pop. (1941); 134,002 sq. mi. *Cap.:* Quetta.

bal·us·ter (băl′ə stər), *n. Archit.* **1.** one of a series of short, pillarlike supports for a railing, as of a staircase. **2.** (*pl.*) balustrade. [t. F: m. *baluslre,* t. It.: m. *balaust(r)o,* t. L: m. *balaustium,* t. Gk.: m. *balaustion* pomegranate flower]

bal·us·trade (băl′ə strād′), *n. Archit.* a series of balusters supporting a railing. [t. F, t. It.: m. *balaustrata*]

Baluster and balustrade

Bal·zac (băl′zăk, bôl′-; *Fr.* bál-zák′), *n.* **Honoré de** (ô nô rā′ də), 1799–1850, French novelist.

Bam·berg (băm′bûrg; *Ger.* bäm′bĕrкн), *n.* a city in central Germany, in Bavaria. 59,466 (1939).

bam·bi·no (băm bē′nō; *It.* bäm bē′nō), *n., pl.* **-ni** (-nē). **1.** a child or baby. **2.** an image of the infant Jesus. [t. It., dim. of *bambo* simple]

bam·boo (băm bōō′), *n., pl.* **-boos. 1.** any of the woody or treelike tropical and semitropical grasses of the genus *Bambura* (or *Bambos*) and allied genera. **2.** the hollow woody stem of such a plant, used for building purposes and for making furniture, poles, etc. [earlier *bambus,* t. D: m. *bamboes.* Cf. Malay *bambu*]

bam·boo·zle (băm bōō′zəl), *v.,* **-zled, -zling.** —*v.t.* **1.** to deceive by trickery; impose upon. **2.** to perplex; mystify. —*v.i.* **3.** to practice imposition or trickery. —**bam·boo′zle·ment,** *n.* —**bam·boo′zler,** *n.*

ban¹ (băn), *v.,* **banned, banning,** *n.* —*v.t.* **1.** to prohibit; interdict: *to ban a meeting or book.* **2.** *Archaic.* to pronounce an ecclesiastical curse upon. **3.** *Archaic.* to curse; execrate. —*n.* **4.** an authoritative interdiction. **5.** informal denunciation or prohibition, as by public opinion. **6.** *Law.* a sentence of outlawry. **7.** *Eccles.* a formal ecclesiastical denunciation; excommunication. **8.** a malediction; curse. [ME, t. Scand.; cf. Icel. *banna* forbid, curse, c. OE *bannan* summon] —**Syn. 1.** forbid, taboo. **4.** prohibition, proscription.

ban² (băn), *n.* **1.** a public proclamation or edict. **2.** (*pl.*) banns. **3.** (in feudal times) the summons of the sovereign's vassals for military service, or the whole body liable to the summons. [OE *gebann*]

ban³ (băn), *n.* **1.** the governor of Croatia and Slavonia. **2.** *Hist.* one of the wardens of the southern marches of Hungary. [t. Hung., t. Pers.: lord]

ban⁴ (băn), *n., pl.* **bani** (bä′nĭ). a Rumanian coin worth one-hundredth part of a leu. [Rum.]

ba·nal (bā′nəl, bə năl′, -näl′, băn′əl), *adj.* hackneyed; trite. [t. F, der. OF *ban,* t. Gmc.: proclamation, c. BAN²] —**ba·nal·i·ty** (bə năl′ə tĭ, bā-), *n.* —**ba′nal·ly,** *adv.* —**Syn.** See **commonplace.**

ba·nan·a (bə năn′ə), *n.* **1.** a plant of the tropical genus *Musa,* of which various species are cultivated for their nutritious fruit. **2.** the fruit, esp. that of *M. sapientum,* with yellow or red rind. [t. Pg., Sp., from native name]

banana oil, *Chem.* amyl acetate, $CH_3CO_2C_5H_{11}$, a sweet-smelling, colorless, liquid ester, used as a solvent and in artificial fruit flavors.

Ba·nat (bä nät′), *n.* an agricultural region in SW Rumania and NE Yugoslavia.

Ban·bur·y (băn′bĕr′ĭ, -bə rĭ, băm′-), *n.* a historic town in Oxfordshire, S England, esp. important in 16th and 17th centuries. ab. 14,000.

ăct, āble, dâre, ärt; ĕbb, ēqual; ĭf, īce; hŏt, ōver, ôrder, oil, bŏŏk, ōōze, out; ŭp, ūse, ûrge; ə = a in alone; ch, chief; g, give; ng, ring; sh, shoe; th, thin; ŧh, that; zh, vision. See the full key on inside cover.

Ban·croft (băn′krôft, -krŏft), *n.* George, 1800–91, U. S. historian and statesman.

band[1] (bănd), *n.* **1.** a company of persons (rarely animals) joined or acting together; a company, party, or troop. **2.** a company of musicians playing instruments usually for marching or open-air performance, namely, brass wind, wood wind, and percussion. **3.** an orchestra playing popular music, esp. for dancing. **4.** a division of a nomadic tribe; a group of individuals who move and camp together. —*v.t.* **5.** to unite in a troop, company, or confederacy. —*v.i.* **6.** to unite; confederate. [t. F: m. *bande*, ult. from Gmc., but sense devel. purely Rom.] —**Syn. 1.** See **company.**

band[2] (bănd), *n.* **1.** a thin, flat strip of some material for binding, confining, trimming, or some other purpose: *hat band, rubber band.* **2.** a fillet, belt, or strap. **3.** a stripe, as of color or decorative work. **4.** the form of falling or flat collar commonly worn by men and women in the seventeenth century in western Europe. **5.** a linen or cambric collar with two pendent strips in front, sometimes worn by clergymen (Geneva bands). **6.** one of the pendent strips. **7.** *Radio.* a group of frequencies which can be tuned in closely together, as by means of a particular set of condensers. —*v.t.* **8.** to mark with bands; stripe. [ME *bande*, t. F, ult. c. BAND[3]]

band[3] (bănd), *n.* **1.** (*usually pl.*) anything which binds the person or the limbs; a shackle, manacle, or fetter. **2.** an obligation; bond: *the nuptial bands.* [ME, t. Scand.; cf. Icel. *band*]

band·age (băn′dǐj), *n.*, *v.*, **-aged, -aging.** —*n.* **1.** a strip of cloth or other material used to bind up a wound, etc. **2.** anything used as a band or ligature. —*v.t.* **3.** to bind or cover with a bandage. [t. F, der. *bande* band] —**band′ag·er,** *n.*

ban·dan·na (băn·dăn′ə), *n.* **1.** a large colored handkerchief with spots or figures, usually white on a red or blue background. **2.** any large handkerchief. Also, **ban·dan′a.** [appar. der. Hind. *bandhnu*, mode of dyeing in which the cloth is tied so as to prevent parts from receiving the dye]

Ban·da Sea (băn′dä), a sea between Celebes and New Guinea, S of the Moluccas and N of Timor.

band·box (bănd′bŏks′), *n.* a light box of pasteboard, thin wood, etc., for holding a hat, collars, etc.

ban·deau (băn·dō′, băn′dō), *n.*, *pl.* **-deaux** (-dōz′, -dōz). a band worn about or on the head; a headband; a fillet. [t. F, dim. of *bande* BAND[2]]

ban·de·role (băn′də·rōl′), *n.* **1.** a small flag or streamer borne on a lance, at a masthead, etc. **2.** a narrow scroll usually bearing an inscription. **3.** a sculptured band adapted to receive an inscription. **4.** a square banner borne at the funeral of a great man and placed over the tomb. Also, **ban′de·rol′, bannerol.** [t. F, t. It.: m. *banderola* small banner, der. *bandiera* banner]

ban·di·coot (băn′də·kōōt′), *n.* **1.** any of the very large East Indian rats constituting the genus *Nesokia*, as *N. bandicota*. **2.** any of various long-clawed, insectivorous marsupials of the family *Peramelidae* of Australia, etc. [t. Telugu: m. *pandikokku* pig rat]

ban·dit (băn′dǐt), *n.*, *pl.* **-dits, banditti** (băn·dǐt′ǐ). **1.** a robber, esp. one who robs by violence. **2.** an outlaw. [t. It.: m. *bandito*, prop. pp. of *bandire* proscribe]

ban·dit·ry (băn′dǐt·rǐ), *n.* **1.** the work or practice of bandits. **2.** bandits collectively; banditti.

Ban·djer·ma·sin (băn′jər·mä′sǐn), *n.* Dutch name of **Banjermasin.**

band·mas·ter (bănd′măs′tər, -mäs′-tər), *n.* the conductor of a band.

Ban·doeng (băn′dōōng), *n.* Dutch name of **Bandung.**

ban·dog (băn′dŏg′, -dôg′), *n.* **1.** any dog kept tied or chained. **2.** a mastiff or bloodhound. [ME *band-dogge*; f. BAND[1] + DOG]

ban·do·leer (băn′də·lǐr′), *n.* a broad belt worn over the shoulder by soldiers, and having a number of small loops or pockets each containing a cartridge or cartridges. Also, **ban′do·lier′.** [t. F: m. *bandoulière*, t. Sp.: m. *bandolera*, der. *banda* band, sash, t. It., of Gmc. orig.]

ban·do·line (băn′də·lēn′, -lǐn), *n.* a mucilaginous preparation used for keeping the hair smooth or in curls, waves, etc. [t. F, b. *bandeau* band and L *linere* smear]

ban·dore (băn·dōr′, băn′dōr), *n.* an old musical string instrument resembling the lute or the guitar. Also, **pandora, pandore.** [t. Sp.: m. *bandurria*, var. of *pandora*, t. LL: m. *pandūra*, t. Gk.: m. *pandoūra* musical instrument with three strings]

band saw, *Mach.* a saw consisting of an endless toothed steel band passing over two wheels.

band shell, an open, elliptical or spherical, acoustically resonant structure in which music is played.

bands·man (băndz′mən), *n.*, *pl.* **-men.** a musician who plays in a band.

band·stand (bănd′stănd′), *n.* a platform, often roofed, for outdoor band performances.

Ban·dung (băn′dōōng), *n.* a city in the U. S. of Indonesia, in W Java. 166,815 (1930). Dutch, **Bandoeng.**

band wagon, **1.** a wagon carrying a band of music, as at the head of a procession or parade. **2.** **climb aboard the band wagon,** *U.S. Colloq.* to shift one's vote or aid to an apparently successful candidate or cause.

ban·dy (băn′dǐ), *v.*, **-died, -dying,** *adj.*, *n.*, *pl.* **-dies.** —*v.t.* **1.** to throw or strike to and fro, or from side to side, as a ball in tennis. **2.** to pass from one to another, or back and forth; give and take: *to bandy blows or words.* —*adj.* **3.** (of legs) having a bend or crook outward. —*n. Obs.* **4.** an old method of playing tennis. **5.** *Chiefly Brit.* hockey or shinny. **6.** a hockey or shinny club. [orig. obscure. Cf. F *bander* bandy, *se bander* band together, ? der. *bande* side]

ban·dy-leg·ged (băn′dǐ lĕg′ǐd, -lĕgd′), *adj.* having crooked legs; bowlegged.

bane (bān), *n.* **1.** that which causes death or destroys life. **2.** a deadly poison. **3.** a thing that ruins or spoils. **4.** ruin; destruction; death. [ME; OE *bana* slayer]

bane·ber·ry (bān′bĕr′ǐ), *n.*, *pl.* **-ries.** **1.** any plant of the ranunculaceous genus *Actaea*, comprising herbs which bear nauseous poisonous berries. **2.** the berry.

bane·ful (bān′fəl), *adj.* destructive; pernicious; poisonous: *a baneful superstition, baneful herbs.* —**bane′-ful·ly,** *adv.* —**bane′ful·ness,** *n.*

Banff (bămf), *n.* **1.** Also, **Banff-shire** (bămf′shǐr, -shər). a county in NE Scotland. 51, 000 pop. (est. 1946); 630 sq. mi. **2.** its county seat: a seaport. 3433 (1939). **3.** a resort town in **Banff National Park,** a scenic park (2585 sq. mi.) in the Rocky Mountains in SW Alberta, Canada. 2187 pop. (1941).

bang[1] (băng), *n.* **1.** a loud, sudden, explosive noise, as the discharge of a gun. **2.** a resounding stroke or blow. **3.** *Colloq.* a sudden, impetuous movement: *he started off with a bang.* **4.** energy; spirit. **5.** *U.S. Slang.* thrill, excitement. —*v.t.* **6.** to strike or beat resoundingly; slam: *to bang a door.* —*v.i.* **7.** to strike violently or noisily: *to bang on the door.* **8.** to make a loud noise as of violent blows: *the guns banged away.* —*adv.* **9.** with a bang; suddenly and loudly; abruptly. [cf. Icel. *banga* to hammer, *bang* hammering, bungling]

bang[2] (băng), *n.* **1.** (*often pl.*) a fringe of banged hair. —*v.t.* **2.** to cut (the hair) so as to form a fringe over the forehead. **3.** to dock (the tail of a horse, etc.). [short for *bangtail* docked (horse's) tail, f. *bang* (nasal var. of *bag* cut) + TAIL[1]]

bang[3] (băng), *n.* bhang.

Ban·ga·lore (băng′gə·lōr′), *n.* a city in S India: the capital of Mysore state. 248,334 (1941).

Bang·ka (băng′kə; *Du.* bäng′kä), *n.* an island in the U. S. of Indonesia, E of Sumatra: tin mines. 205,363 (1930); 4611 sq. mi. *Cap.:* Muntok. Also, **Banka.**

Bang·kok (băng′kŏk), *n.* **1.** the capital of Siam, on the Menam river: the principal port of Siam. 685,000 (1937). **2.** (*l.c.*) a kind of Siamese straw. **3.** (*l.c.*) a hat woven of thin strands of this straw.

ban·gle (băng′gəl), *n.* **1.** a bracelet in the form of a ring, without a clasp. **2.** an ornamental anklet. [t. Hind.: m. *bangrī* bracelet of glass]

Ban·gor (băng′gôr, -gər), *n.* a city in S Maine: a port on the Penobscot river. 31,558 (1950).

Bang's disease (băngz). *Vet. Sci.* an infectious disease of cattle caused by a bacterium, *Brucella abortus*, which infects the genital organs and frequently causes abortions. This organism is one of several which causes undulant fever or brucellosis of man.

bang-up (băng′ŭp′), *adj. Slang.* first-rate.

Bang·we·u·lu (băng′wǐ·ōō′lōō), *n.* a shallow lake and swamp in NE Northern Rhodesia. ab. 150 mi. long.

ba·ni (bä′nǐ), *n.* pl. of **ban**[4].

ban·ian (băn′yən), *n.* **1.** a loose shirt, jacket, or gown worn in India. **2.** a Hindu trader or merchant of a particular caste which abstains from eating flesh. **3.** banyan. [t. Pg., prob. t. Ar.: m. *banyān*, t. Gujerati: m. *vāniyo* merchant, t. Skt.: m. *vanij*]

ban·ish (băn′ǐsh), *v.t.* **1.** to condemn to exile; expel from or relegate to a country or place by authoritative decree. **2.** to compel to depart; send, drive, or put away: *to banish sorrow.* [ME *banysshe(n)*, t. OF: m. *baniss-*, s. *banir*, g. LL *bannīre* ban; of Gmc. orig. and akin to BAN[1], v.] —**ban′ish·er,** *n.* —**ban′ish·ment,** *n.* —**Syn. 1.** exile, expatriate, outlaw.

ban·is·ter (băn′ǐs·tər), *n.* **1.** baluster. **2.** (*pl.*) the balustrade of a staircase. Also, **bannister.** [var. of BALUSTER]

Ban·jer·ma·sin (băn′jər·mä′sǐn), *n.* a seaport on the S coast of Borneo. 65,698 (1930). Dutch, **Bandjermasin.**

ban·jo (băn′jō), *n.*, *pl.* **-jos.** a musical instrument of the guitar family, having a circular body covered in front with tightly stretched parchment, and played with the fingers or a plectrum. [var. of BANDORE] —**ban′jo·ist,** *n.*

bank[1] (băngk), *n.* **1.** a long pile or heap: *a bank of earth, snow, or cloud.* **2.** a slope or acclivity. **3.** *Phys. Geol.* the slope immediately bordering a stream course along which the water normally runs. **4.** *Oceanog.* a broad submarine elevation on the continental shelf lying some distance off the coast, over which the water is relatively shallow. **5.** *Coal Mining.* the surface around the mouth of a shaft. **6.** *Aeron.* the lateral inclination of an airplane, esp. during a curve. **7.** *Billiards, Pool.* the cushion of the table. —*v.t.* **8.** to border with or like a bank; embank. **9.** to form into a bank or heap (fol. by *up*): *to bank up the snow.* **10.** *Aeron.* to tip or incline (an airplane) laterally. **11.** *Billiards, Pool.* **a.** to drive (a ball) to the cushion.

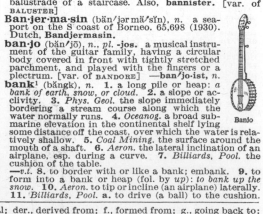

Bandicoot.
Macrotis lagotis
(Total length 2 ft., tail 8 in.)

Banjo

b. to pocket (the object ball) by driving it against the bank. **12.** to cover up (a fire) with ashes or fuel and close the dampers, to make it burn long and slowly. —*v.i.* **13.** to rise in or form banks, as clouds or snow. **14.** *Aeron.* to tip or incline an airplane laterally. [ME *banke*, prob. t. Scand.] —**Syn. 1.** embankment, mound, ridge. **3.** See **shore¹**.

bank² (băngk), *n.* **1.** an institution for receiving and lending money (in some cases, issuing notes or holding demand deposits that serve as money) or transacting other financial business. **2.** the office or quarters of such an institution. **3.** (in games) **a.** the stock or fund of pieces from which the players draw. **b.** the fund of the manager or the dealer. **4.** any storage place. **5.** any store or reserve: *a blood bank.* **6.** *Obs.* a sum of money, esp. as a fund for use in business. **7.** *Obs.* a money changer's table, counter, or shop. —*v.i.* **8.** to exercise the functions of a bank or banker. **9.** to keep money in, or have an account with, a bank. **10.** (in games) to hold the bank. **11.** *Colloq.* to rely or count (fol. by *on* or *upon*). —*v.t.* **12.** to deposit in a bank. [ME *banke*, t. F: m. *banque*, t. It.: m. *banca*, orig. bench, table; of Gmc. orig. See **BANK¹, BENCH**]

bank³ (băngk), *n.* **1.** an arrangement of objects in line. **2.** *Music.* a row of keys in an organ. **3.** a bench for rowers in a galley. **4.** a row or tier of oars. **5.** the rowers on one bench or to one oar. —*v.t.* **6.** to arrange in a bank. [ME *banck*, t. OF: m. *banc* bench, t. LL: s. *bancus*; from the Gmc. source of **BENCH**]

Ban·ka (băng'kə), *n.* Bangka.

bank·a·ble (băngk'ə bəl), *adj.* receivable by a bank.

bank acceptance, a draft endorsed or otherwise formally acknowledged by a bank on which it is drawn.

bank account, 1. an account with a bank. **2.** balance standing to the credit of a depositor at a bank.

bank bill, a draft drawn by one bank on another, payable on demand or at a specified future date.

bank·book (băngk'bŏŏk'), *n.* a book held by a depositor in which a bank enters a record of his account.

bank clerk, *Brit.* a teller (def. 2).

bank discount, interest on a loan, deducted in advance from the face value of the note.

bank·er¹ (băngk'ər), *n.* **1.** one who manages or works for a bank, usually a bank officer. **2.** (in games) the keeper or holder of the bank. [f. **BANK²** + **-ER²**]

bank·er² (băngk'ər), *n.* a vessel employed in the cod fishery on the banks off Newfoundland. [f. **BANK¹** + **-ER²**]

bank·er³ (băngk'ər), *n.* *Bldg. Trades.* the bench or table upon which bricklayers and stone masons prepare and shape their material. [f. **BANK³** + **-ER²**. Cf. It. *banco*]

banker's acceptance, bank acceptance.

banker's bill, bank bill.

bank holiday, 1. a weekday on which banks are closed by law; legal holiday. **2.** *Brit.* a secular day on which banks are closed and the law therefore exempts the parties to negotiable paper from their obligations.

bank·ing (băngk'ĭng), *n.* the business of a bank or banker.

banking account, *Brit.* bank account.

bank note, a promissory note, payable on demand, issued by a bank and intended to circulate as money.

bank paper, 1. drafts, bills, and acceptances payable by banks. **2.** commercial paper which may be discounted in a bank.

bank rate, 1. the rate of discount fixed by a bank or banks. **2.** the discount charge set by a central bank, as by the Federal Reserve Bank.

bank·rupt (băngk'rŭpt, -rəpt), *n.* **1.** *Law.* a person who upon his own petition or that of his creditors is adjudged insolvent by a court, and whose property is administered for and divided among his creditors, under a bankruptcy law. **2.** any insolvent debtor; one unable to satisfy any just claims made upon him. —*adj.* **3.** *Law.* subject to, or under, legal process because of insolvency; insolvent. **4.** at the end of one's resources; lacking (fol. by *in*): *to be bankrupt in thanks.* **5.** pertaining to bankrupts. —*v.t.* **6.** to make bankrupt. [t. F: m. (after L *ruptus* broken) *banqueroute*, t. It.: m. *bancarotta* bankruptcy, f. *banca* bank + *rotta*, pp. fem. of *rompere* break, g. L *rumpere*]

bank·rupt·cy (băngk'rŭpt sĭ, -rəp sĭ), *n.,* pl. **-cies. 1.** state of being or becoming bankrupt. **2.** utter ruin.

Banks (băngks), *n.* **Sir Joseph,** 1743–1820, British naturalist.

bank·si·a (băngk'sĭ ə), *n.* any plant of the Australian genus *Banksia,* comprising shrubs and trees with leathery leaves and dense cylindrical heads of flowers. [t. NL, named after Sir Joseph **BANKS**]

Bank·side (băngk'sīd'), *n.* a former theatrical district in London, England, along the south bank of the Thames, the site of Shakespeare's Globe Theater.

ban·ner (băn'ər), *n.* **1.** the flag of a country, army, troop, etc. **2.** an ensign or the like bearing some device or motto, as one borne in processions. **3.** a piece of cloth, attached by one side to a pole or staff, formerly used as the standard of a sovereign, lord, or knight. **4.** anything displayed as a profession of principles: *the banner of freedom.* **5.** *Her.* a square flag bearing heraldic devices. **6.** *Journalism.* the headline which extends across the width of the newspaper, usually at the top of the first page. —*adj.* **7.** leading or foremost: *a banner year for crops.* [ME *banere,* t. OF, der. LL *bandum* standard; of Gmc. orig. (cf. Goth. *bandwo* sign)]

ban·ner·et¹ (băn'ər ĭt, -ərĕt'), *n.* **1.** *Hist.* a knight who could bring a company of followers into the field under his own banner. **2.** a rank of knighthood; knight banneret. [ME *baneret,* t. OF, der. *baniere* **BANNER**]

ban·ner·et² (băn'ərĕt'), *n.* a small banner. Also, **ban·ner·ette'.** [t. OF, dim. of *baniere* **BANNER**]

ban·ner·ol (băn'ərŏl'), *n.* banderole.

ban·nis·ter (băn'ĭs tər), *n.* banister.

ban·nock (băn'ək), *n.* *Scot. and Brit. Dial.* a flat cake made of oatmeal, barley meal, etc., commonly baked on a griddle. [OE *bannuc* bit, small piece, t. OBrit. Cf. OCornish *banna* drop]

Ban·nock·burn (băn'ək bûrn', băn'ək bûrn'), *n.* a village in central Scotland, in Stirling county: site of the victory of the Scots (1314) under Robert Bruce over the English, which assured the independence of Scotland.

banns (bănz), *n.pl. Eccles.* notice of an intended marriage, given three times in the parish church of each of the espoused. Also, **bans.** [var. of *bans,* pl. of **BAN²,** n.]

ban·quet (băng'kwĭt), *n., v.,* **-queted, -queting.** —*n.* **1.** a feast. **2.** a ceremonious public dinner. —*v.t., v.i.* **3.** to entertain (another) or regale (oneself) at a banquet. [t. F, t. It.: m. *banchetto,* dim. of *banco* bench] —**ban·quet·er,** *n.* —**Syn. 1.** See feast.

ban·quette (băng kĕt'), *n.* **1.** *Fort.* a platform or step along the inside of a parapet, for soldiers to stand on when firing. **2.** a bench for passengers on top of a stage-coach. **3.** *Southern U.S.* a sidewalk. **4.** a ledge running across the back of a buffet. [t. F]

Ban·quo (băng'kwō, -kō), *n.* (in Shakespeare's *Macbeth*) a murdered thane whose ghost appears to Macbeth.

ban·shee (băn'shē, băn shē'), *n. Irish and Scot.* a supernatural being supposed to give warning by its wails of an approaching death in the family. Also, **ban'shie.** [t. Irish: m. *bean sidhe* woman of the fairies]

ban·tam (băn'təm), *n.* **1.** (*often cap.*) a domestic fowl of any of certain varieties or breeds characterized by very small size. **2.** a small, quarrelsome person. —*adj.* **3.** diminutive; tiny. [prob. named after **BANTAM**]

Ban·tam (băn'təm; *Du.* bän täm'), *n.* a village in W Java: first Dutch settlement in the East Indies.

ban·tam·weight (băn'təm wāt'), *n.* a boxer of very light weight (not more than 118 pounds).

ban·ter (băn'tər), *n.* **1.** playfully teasing language; good-humored raillery. —*v.t.* **2.** to address with banter; chaff. —*v.i.* **3.** to use banter. [orig. unknown] —**ban·ter·er,** *n.* —**ban·ter·ing·ly,** *adv.* —**Syn. 1.** badinage, joking, jesting. **2.** tease.

Ban·ting (băn'tĭng), *n.* **Sir Frederick Grant,** 1891–1941, Canadian physician: discoverer of insulin treatment of diabetes.

Ban·ting·ism (băn'tĭng ĭz'əm), *n. Med.* a method of reducing one's weight, based upon a high protein and low fat and carbohydrate diet. [named after William *Banting,* 1797–1878, British dietitian]

bant·ling (bănt'lĭng), *n. Contemptuous.* a young child; brat. [f. var. of obs. *bandle* swaddling band + -**ING¹**]

Ban·tu (băn'tŏō), *n., pl.* **-tu, -tus,** *adj.* —*n.* **1.** (*pl.*) a large family of Negro tribes inhabiting central and southern Africa. **2.** a member of any of these tribes. **3.** a principal linguistic family of Africa, its languages being prevalent from the Equator to South Africa, including Swahili, Kaffir, and Zulu. —*adj.* **4.** of or pertaining to the Bantu tribes or languages.

Ban·ville (băn vēl'), *n.* **Théodore Faullain de** (tē ô-dôr' fô län' də), 1823–91, French poet and dramatist.

ban·yan (băn'yən), *n.* an East Indian fig tree, *Ficus benghalensis,* whose branches send out adventitious roots to the ground, sometimes causing the tree to spread over a wide area. Also, **banian.** [orig. a particular tree under which Banian traders had built a pagoda]

ban·zai (bän'zä'ē, -zī'), *interj.* **1.** a Japanese complimentary salutation or patriotic shout, as in honor of the emperor, meaning: **a.** long life. **b.** forward; attack. —*adj.* **2.** reckless; suicidal. [t. Jap.: ten thousand years]

Banyan, *Ficus benghalensis* (70 to 100 ft. high)

ba·o·bab (bā'ō băb', bä'-), *n.* a large, exceedingly thick-trunked bombacaceous tree of the genus *Adansonia,* esp. *A. digitata,* native to tropical Africa, bearing a gourdlike fruit. [t. native African]

Bap., Baptist. Also, **Bapt.**

bap·tism (băp'tĭz əm), *n.* **1.** *Eccles.* a ceremonial immersion in water, or application of water, as an initiatory rite or sacrament of the Christian church. **2.** any similar ceremony or action of initiation, dedication, etc. —**bap·tis·mal** (băp tĭz'məl), *adj.* —**bap·tis·mal·ly,** *adv.*

baptism of fire, 1. the first battle a soldier experiences. **2.** any severe ordeal; crucial test.

Bap·tist (băp'tĭst), *n.* **1.** *Relig.* a member of a Christian denomination which maintains that baptism (usually implying immersion) should follow only upon a personal profession of Christian faith. **2.** one who baptizes. **3. the Baptist,** John, the forerunner of Christ.

bap·tis·ter·y (băp'tĭs tər ĭ, -tĭs trĭ), *n., pl.* **-teries. 1.** a building, or a part of a church, in which baptism is administered. 2. (in Baptist churches) a tank containing water for baptism by immersion. [t. L: m.s. *baptistērium*, t. Gk.: m. *baptistērion*]

bap·tist·ry (băp'tĭs trĭ), *n.*, *pl.* **-ries.** baptistery.

bap·tize (băp tīz', băp'tīz), *v.*, **-tized**, **-tizing.** —*v.t.* 1. to immerse in water, or sprinkle or pour water on, in the Christian rite of baptism. 2. to cleanse spiritually; initiate or dedicate by purifying. 3. to christen. —*v.i.* 4. to administer baptism. [ME *baptise(n)*, t. OF: m. *baptiser*, t. LL: m. s. *baptizāre*, t. Gk.: m. *baptizein* immerse] —**bap·tiz'er**, *n.*

bar¹ (bär), *n.*, *v.*, **barred**, **barring**, *prep.* —*n.* 1. a relatively long and evenly shaped piece of some solid substance, esp. one of wood or metal used as a guard or obstruction, or for some mechanical purpose: *the bars of a fence or gate.* 2. crowbar. 3. an oblong piece of any solid material: *a bar of soap or candy.* 4. the amount of material in a bar. 5. *Com.* an ingot, lump, or wedge of gold or silver. 6. a band or stripe: *a bar of light.* 7. *Oceanog.* a long ridge of sand or gravel in coastal waters, near or slightly above the surface, and extending across the mouth of a bay or parallel to the shore. 8. anything which obstructs, hinders, or impedes; an obstacle; a barrier: *a bar to vice.* 9. *Music.* **a.** the line marking the division between two measures of music. **b.** See **double bar. c.** the unit of music contained between two bar lines; measure. 10. a counter or a place where liquors, etc., are served to customers. 11. the legal profession. 12. the practicing members of the legal profession in a given community. 13. a railing in a courtroom separating the general public from the part of the room occupied by the judges, jury, attorneys, etc. 14. the place in court where prisoners are stationed: *a prisoner at the bar.* 15. *Law.* **a.** an objection which nullifies an action or claim. **b.** a stoppage or defeat of an alleged right of action. 16. any tribunal: *the bar of public opinion.* 17. *Physics.* a unit of pressure equal to 1,000,000 dynes per square centimeter. 18. a space, between the molar and canine teeth of a horse, in which the bit is fitted. 19. *U.S.* (in a bridle) the mouthpiece connecting the checks. 20. (in lace) bride² (def. 1). 21. *Her.* a band, properly horizontal, crossing the field. —*v.t.* 22. to provide or fasten with a bar or bars: *to bar the door.* 23. to shut in or out by or as by bars. 24. to block (a way, etc.) as with a barrier; prevent or hinder, as access. 25. to debar, as a person or action; exclude; except. 26. to mark with bars, stripes, or bands. —*prep.* 27. except; omitting; but: *bar none.* [ME *barre*, t. OF, g. Gallo-Rom. *barra*, collective of Gallic *barros* thick end of bushes] —**Syn.** 8. BAR, BARRIER, BARRICADE mean something put in the way of advance. BAR has the general meaning of hindrance or obstruction: *a bar across the doorway.* BARRIER suggests an impediment to progress, literal or figurative, or a defensive obstruction against attack: *a river barrier.* A BARRICADE is esp. a pile of articles hastily gathered or a rude earthwork for protection in street fighting: *a barricade of wooden boxes.*

A B
Bar (def. 9)
A, single; B, double

bar² (bär), *n.* *U.S.* a mosquito net.

bar., 1. barometer. 2. barrel. 3. barrister.

B. Ar., Bachelor of Architecture.

Bar·ab·bas (bə răb'əs), *n.* *Bible.* a condemned robber or insurrectionist whose release was demanded of Pilate by the mob when they had an opportunity to free Jesus. Mark 15:6–11; John 18:40.

barb¹ (bärb), *n.* 1. a point or pointed part projecting backward from a main point, as of a fishhook, an arrowhead, or a fence wire. 2. *Bot.*, *Zool.* a beardlike growth or part. 3. *Ornith.* one of the processes attached to the rachis of a feather. 4. a breed of domestic pigeons similar to the carriers or homers, having a short, broad bill. 5. any of a large number of small, Old World cyprinid fishes of the genera *Barbus* or *Puntius*, widely cultivated for use in home aquariums. 6. (*usually pl.*) *Vet. Sci.* a small protuberance under the tongue in horses and cattle, esp. when inflamed and swollen. 7. a linen covering for the throat and breast, formerly worn by women mourners, and now by nuns. 8. a band or small scarf of lace, worn by women. 9. *Obs.* a beard. —*v.t.* 10. to furnish with a barb or barbs: *to barb a hook.* [ME *barbe*, t. OF, t. L: m. *barba* beard] —**barbed**, *adj.*

barb² (bärb), *n.* a horse of a breed brought from Barbary to Spain by the Moors. [t. F: m. *barbe*]

Bar·ba·dos (bär bā'dōz, bär'bə dōz'), *n.* an island in the West Indies: a British colony. 202,588 pop. (est. 1943); 166 sq. mi. *Cap.*: Bridgetown.

bar·bar·i·an (bär bâr'ĭ ən), *n.* 1. a man in a rude, savage state; an uncivilized person. 2. an uncultured person; a philistine. 3. a foreigner (orig. a non-Greek). —*adj.* 4. uncivilized. 5. foreign. [t. F: m. *barbarien*, der. L *barbaria* foreign country] —**bar·bar'i·an·ism**, *n.* —**Syn.** 4. rude, savage, primitive, wild. BARBARIAN, BARBARIC, BARBAROUS pertain to uncivilized people. BARBARIAN is the general word for anything uncivilized: *a barbarian tribe.* BARBARIC has both unfavorable and mildly favorable connotations, implying crudeness of taste or practice, or conveying an idea of rude magnificence and splendor: *barbaric noise.* BARBAROUS emphasizes the inhumanity and cruelty of barbarian life: *barbarous customs.*

bar·bar·ic (bär băr'ĭk), *adj.* 1. uncivilized: *barbaric invaders.* 2. of, like, or befitting barbarians: *a barbaric*

empire. 3. crudely rich or splendid: *barbaric decorations.* [ME *barbarik*, t. L: m. s. *barbaricus* t. Gk.: m. *barbarikōs* foreign, barbaric] —**bar·bar'i·cal·ly,** *adv.* —**Syn.** 1. See **barbarian.**

bar·ba·rism (bär'bə rĭz'əm), *n.* 1. barbarous or uncivilized condition. 2. something belonging or proper to a barbarous condition; a barbarous act. 3. the use in a language of forms or constructions felt by some to be undesirably alien to the established mode or custom of the language. 4. such a form or construction, as *complected, all the farther.*

bar·bar·i·ty (bär băr'ə tĭ), *n.*, *pl.* **-ties.** 1. brutal or inhuman conduct; cruelty. 2. act of cruelty or inhumanity. 3. crudity of style, taste, etc.

bar·ba·rize (bär'bə rīz'), *v.i.*, *v.t.*, **-rized**, **-rizing.** to make or become barbarous. —**bar'ba·ri·za'tion,** *n.*

Bar·ba·ros·sa (bär'bə rŏs'ə), *n.* surname of Emperor Frederick I of Germany, meaning "red beard."

bar·ba·rous (bär'bə rəs), *adj.* 1. uncivilized: *barbarous countries.* 2. excessively harsh: *barbarous treatment.* 3. harsh-sounding: *wild and barbarous music.* 4. not conforming or conformed to classical standards or accepted usage, as language. 5. foreign (orig. non-Greek). [t. L: m. *barbarus*, t. Gk.: m. *bárbaros*, orig., babbling] —**bar'ba·rous·ly,** *adv.* —**bar'ba·rous·ness,** *n.* —**Syn.** 1. See **barbarian.** 2. cruel, ferocious, inhuman, brutal.

Bar·ba·ry (bär'bə rĭ), *n.* a region in N Africa, extending from W of Egypt to the Atlantic, and including the former Barbary States.

Barbary ape, an ape, *Macaca sylvana*, of northern Africa and Gibraltar.

Barbary Coast, the Mediterranean coastline of the former Barbary States: infested with pirates who harassed Mediterranean trade.

Barbary Coast (Ca. 1800)

Barbary States, Morocco, Algiers, Tunis, and Tripoli.

bar·bate (bär'bāt), *adj. Zool., Bot.* bearded; tufted or furnished with hairs. [t. L: m. s. *barbātus* bearded]

bar·be·cue (bär'bə kū), *n.*, *v.*, **-cued, -cuing.** —*n.* 1. *U.S.* a large social or political entertainment, usually in the open air, at which animals are roasted whole. 2. a dressed ox or other animal roasted whole. 3. a framework on which animals are broiled or roasted whole or in large pieces. —*v.t.* 4. to broil or roast whole or in large pieces before an open fire, on a spit or gridiron, often seasoning with vinegar, spices, salt, and pepper. 5. to cook (sliced or diced meat or fish) in a highly seasoned sauce. [t. Sp.: m. *barbacoa*, t. Haitian: m. *barboka*]

barbed wire, iron wire to which barbs are attached at short intervals, used largely for fencing in livestock, protecting a defensive military position, etc.

bar·bel (bär'bəl), *n.* 1. a slender cylindrical tactile process appended to the mouth of certain fishes. 2. any of various cyprinoid fishes of the genus *Barbus*, esp. *B. barbus*, of Europe. [ME *barbelle*, t. OF: m. *barbel*, g. LL *barbellus*, dim. of *barbus*]

bar·bel·late (bär'bə lāt', bär bĕl'ĭt, -āt), *adj. Bot.*, *Zool.* having short, stiff hairs. [f. s. NL *barbella* (dim. of L *barbula* little beard) + -ATE¹]

bar·ber (bär'bər), *n.* 1. one whose occupation it is to shave or trim the beard and to cut and dress the hair of customers. —*v.t.* 2. to trim or dress the beard and hair of. [ME *barbour*, t. AF, ult. der. L *barba* beard]

bar·ber·ry (bär'bĕr'ĭ), *n.*, *pl.* **-ries.** 1. a shrub of the genus *Berberis*, esp. *B. vulgaris.* 2. its red, elongated, acid fruit. [ME *barbere*, t. ML: m.s. *barbaris*, *berberis*]

Bar·ber·ton (bär'bər tən), *n.* a city in NE Ohio, near Akron. 27,820 (1950).

bar·bet (bär'bĭt), *n.* 1. a dog with long curly hair; poodle. 2. any of numerous tropical nonpasseriform birds of the family *Capitonidae*, most of which are brightly colored and large-headed, and have bristles at the base of the bill. [t. F, masc. dim. of *barbe* beard]

bar·bette (bär bĕt'), *n.* 1. a platform or mound of earth within a fortification, from which guns may be fired over the parapet instead of through embrasures. 2. *Naval.* an armored cylinder to protect a turret on a warship. [t. F, fem. dim. of *barbe* beard]

bar·bi·can (bär'bə kən), *n.* 1. an outwork of a castle or fortified place. 2. an outpost of any nature, as a bridge tower, or a defense outside of the moat protecting the approach to the drawbridge. [ME, t. OF: m. *barbacane*, t. ML: m. *barbicana*; ult. orig. obscure, ? t. Ar.-Pers.: m. *bāb khāne* gate house, or Pers.: m. *bālā khāne* high house]

bar·bi·cel (bär'bə sĕl'), *n. Ornith.* one of the minute processes fringing the barbules of certain feathers. [t. NL: m. s. *barbicella*, dim. of L *barba* beard]

Bar·bi·rol·li (bär'bə rŏl'ĭ, -rō'lĭ), *n.* **John,** born 1899, British conductor, formerly in the U.S.

bar·bi·tal (bär'bə tăl', -tôl'), *n. Pharm.* a drug, diethyl-barbituric acid, sold as sleeping pills; veronal. [f. BARBIT(URIC) + -AL³]

barbital sodium, *Pharm.* a sleeping powder, $C_8H_{11}N_2O_3Na$, the sodium salt of barbital.

bar·bi·tu·rate (bär·bĭch′ə·rāt′, -rĭt; bär′bə·tyŏŏr′āt, -ĭt), *n. Chem.* a derivative of barbituric acid.

bar·bi·tu·ric acid (bär′bə·tyŏŏr′ĭk, -tŏŏr′-), *Chem.* an acid, $C_4H_4N_2O_3$, a crystalline powder from which several hypnotic and sedative drugs are derived. [*barbituric*, f. s. Gk. *bárbiton* lyre + URIC]

Bar·bi·zon School (bär′bə·zŏn′, *Fr.* bȧr·bē·zôn′), a group of French landscape painters of the third quarter of the 19th century, including **Théodore** Rousseau and Daubigny, who worked chiefly at Barbizon, a village in N France.

Bar·bu·da (bär·bōō′də), *n.* one of the Leeward Islands, in the British West Indies: a dependency of Antigua. 903 pop. (1921); 62 sq. mi.

bar·bule (bär′būl), *n.* **1.** a little barb. **2.** one of the small processes fringing the barbs of a feather. [t. L: m. s. *barbula*, dim. of *barba* beard]

Bar·busse (bär·bӱs′), *n.* **Henri** (än ₫ē′), 1873?-1935, French journalist and author.

Bar·ca (bär′kə), *n.* **1.** a politically influential family of ancient Carthage. Hamilcar, Hasdrubal, and Hannibal belonged to it. **2.** Cyrenaica.

bar·ca·role (bär′kə·rōl′), *n.* **1.** a boating song of the Venetian gondoliers. **2.** a piece of music composed in the style of such songs. Also, **bar′ca·rolle′.** [t. F: m. *barcarolle* t. It.: m. *barcar(u)ola* boatman's song, der. *barcar(u)olo* a boatman, der. *barca* BARK³]

Bar·ce·lo·na (bär′sə·lō′nə; *Sp.* bär′thě·lô′nä), *n.* a seaport in NE Spain, on the Mediterranean. 1,109,000 (est. 1945).

B. Arch., Bachelor of Architecture.

Bar·clay de Tol·ly (bär·klī′ də tô′lĭ), **Prince Mikhail** (mĭ′hä·ēl′), 1761-1818, Russian field marshal: commander in chief against Napoleon in war of 1812.

bard¹ (bärd), *n.* **1.** one of an ancient Celtic order of poets. **2.** a poet. [ME, t. Celtic (cf. Irish *bard*, Welsh *bardd*), whence also L *bardus*, Gk. *bárdos*] **—bard′ic,** *adj.*

ard² (bärd), *Armor.* **—n. 1.** any of various pieces of defensive armor for a horse. **—v.t. 2.** to caparison with bards. Also, **barde.** [t. F, t. Ar.: m. *bardha'ah* packsaddle]

bare¹ (bâr), *adj.,* **barer, barest,** *v.,* **bared, baring. —adj. 1.** without covering or clothing; naked or nude: *bare knees.* **2.** with the head uncovered. **3.** without the usual furnishings, contents, etc.: *bare walls.* **4.** open to view; unconcealed; undisguised. **5.** unadorned; bald; plain: *the bare facts.* **6.** napless or threadbare. **7.** scarcely or just sufficient; mere: *bare necessaries.* **—v.t. 8.** to make bare. [ME; OE *bær*, c. G *bar*] **—bare′ness,** *n.* **—Syn. 7.** See **mere¹. 8.** uncover, strip; unmask.

bare² (bâr), *v. Archaic.* pt. of **bear.**

bare·back (bâr′bǎk′), *adv., adj.* with the back (of a horse, etc.) bare; without saddle. **—bare′backed′,** *adj.*

bare·faced (bâr′fāst′), *adj.* **1.** with the face uncovered. **2.** undisguised; boldly open. **3.** shameless; impudent; audacious: *a barefaced lie.* **—bare·fac·ed·ly** (bâr′fā′sĭd·lĭ, fāst′lĭ), *adv.* **bare·fac′ed·ness,** *n.*

bare·foot (bâr′fŏŏt′), *adj., adv.* with the feet bare.

bare·foot·ed (bâr′fŏŏt′ĭd), *adj.* having the foot bare.

bare·hand·ed (bâr′hăn′dĭd), *adj.* **1.** with hands uncovered. **2.** with empty hands; without means.

bare·head·ed (bâr′hĕd′ĭd), *adj., adv.* with the head uncovered.

Ba·reil·ly (bə·rā′lĭ), *n.* a city in N India, in the United Provinces. 192,688 (1941). Also, **Ba·re′li.**

bare·leg·ged (bâr′lĕg′ĭd, -lĕgd′), *adj.* with bare legs.

bare·ly (bâr′lĭ), *adv.* **1.** only; just; no more than: *she is barely sixteen.* **2.** without disguise or concealment; openly: *a question barely put.* **3.** nakedly. **4.** *Archaic.* merely; only. **—Syn. 1.** See **hardly.**

Bar·ents Sea (bär′ĕnts; *Russ.* bä·rĕnts′), a part of the Arctic Ocean between NE Europe and the islands of Spitzbergen, Franz Josef Land, and Novaya Zemlya.

bare·sark (bâr′särk), *n.* **1.** *Scand. Legend.* a berserker. **—adv. 2.** without armor. [translation var. of *berserk*, taken as *bare* + *serk* sark, shirt]

bar·gain (bär′gĭn), *n.* **1.** an agreement between parties settling what each shall give and take, or perform and receive, in a transaction. **2.** such an agreement as affecting one of the parties: *a losing bargain.* **3.** that which is acquired by bargaining. **4.** an advantageous purchase. **5. into the bargain,** over and above what is stipulated; moreover; besides. **6. strike a bargain,** to make a bargain; come to terms. **—v.i. 7.** *Colloq.* to discuss the terms of a bargain; haggle over terms. **8.** to come to an agreement; make a bargain. **—v.t. 9.** to arrange by bargain; stipulate. [ME, t. OF: m. *bargaigne*] **—bar′gain·er,** *n.* **—Syn. 1.** See **agreement. 7.** See **trade.**

barge (bärj), *n., v.,* **barged, barging. —n. 1.** an unpowered vessel used for transporting freight; a lighter. **2.** a vessel of state used in pageants. **3.** a ship's boat used in visits of courtesy. **4.** *Naval.* a boat reserved for a flag officer. **5.** (in New England) a large two-seated, four-wheel coach. **—v.t. 6.** to carry or transport by barge. **—v.i. 7.** to move in the slow, heavy manner of a barge. **8.** *Colloq.* to force oneself rudely (fol. by *into*). **9.** *Colloq.* to bump; collide. [ME, t. OF, g. der. of L *bāris*, t. Gk.: (Egyptian) boat, barge]

barge·board (bärj′bōrd′), *n.* an overhanging board along the projecting sloping edge of a gable roof.

barge couple, one of the pair of rafters in a gable carrying the overhanging portion of the roof.

barge course, the part of a gable roof that projects beyond the end wall.

barge·man (bärj′mən), *n., pl.* **-men. 1.** one of the crew of a barge. **2.** one who has charge of a barge. Also, *esp. Brit.,* **bar·gee** (bär·jē′).

Bar Harbor, a town on Mount Desert island, in S Maine: summer resort. 2572 (1950).

Ba·ri (bä′rĭ), *n.* a seaport in SE Italy, on the Adriatic. 244,522 (est. 1946). Italian, **Ba·ri del·le Pu·glie** (bä′rē dĕl′lĕ pŏŏ′lyĕ).

bar·ic¹ (băr′ĭk), *adj. Chem.* of or containing barium. [f. BAR(IUM) + -IC]

bar·ic² (băr′ĭk), *adj.* of or pertaining to weight, esp. that of the atmosphere. [f. s. Gk. *báros* weight + -IC]

ba·ril·la (bə·rĭl′ə), *n.* **1.** either of two European saltworts, *Salsola Kali* and esp. *S. Soda*, whose ashes yield an impure carbonate of soda. **2.** the alkali obtained from the ashes of these and certain other maritime plants. [t. Sp.: m. *barrilla*]

Bar·ing (bâr′ĭng), *n.* **Alexander.** See **Ashburton.**

barit., *Music.* baritone.

bar·ite (bâr′īt, băr′-), *n.* a common mineral, barium sulfate, $BaSO_4$, occurring in tabular crystals: the principal ore of barium. Also, **barytes.** [f. BAR(IUM) + -ITE¹]

bar·i·tone (băr′ə·tōn′), *Music.* **—n. 1.** a male voice or voice part intermediate between tenor and bass. **2.** a singer with such a voice. **3.** a large, valved brass instrument, slightly smaller in bore than a euphonium, used chiefly in military bands. **—adj. 4.** of or pertaining to the baritone; having the compass of the baritone. Also, **barytone.** [t. Gk.: m. *barytonos* deep-sounding]

bar·i·um (bâr′ĭ·əm, băr′-), *n. Chem.* a whitish malleable, active, divalent, metallic element occurring in combination chiefly as barito or as withcrite. *Symbol:* Ba; *at. wt.:* 137.36; *at. no.:* 56; *sp. gr.:* 3.5 at 20°C. [t. NL; f. BAR(YTES) + -IUM]

bark¹ (bärk), *n.* **1.** the abrupt, explosive cry of a dog. **2.** a similar sound made by another animal or by a person. **3.** *Colloq.* **—v.i. 4.** to utter an abrupt, explosive cry or a series of such cries, as a dog. **5.** to make a similar sound: *the big guns barked.* **6.** to speak or cry out sharply or gruffly. **7.** *Slang.* to advertise a cheap show at its entrance. **8.** *U.S. Colloq.* to cough. **9. bark up the wrong tree,** *U.S.* to mistake one's object: assail or pursue the wrong person or purpose. **—v.t. 10.** to utter or give forth with a bark: *to bark out an order.* [ME *berke(n)*, OE *beorcan*]

bark² (bärk), *n.* **1.** *Bot.* the external covering of the woody stems, branches, and roots of plants, as distinct and separable from the wood itself. **2.** *Tanning.* a mixture of oak and hemlock barks. **—v.t. 3.** to strip off the bark of; peel. **4.** to remove a circle of bark from. **5.** to cover or enclose with bark. **6.** to treat with a bark infusion; tan. **7.** to rub off the skin of: *to bark one's shins.* [ME, t. Scand.; cf. Dan. *bark*] **—bark′er,** *n.*

bark³ (bärk), *n. Naut.* **a.** a three-masted vessel, fore-and-aft-rigged on the mizzenmast, and square-rigged on the two other masts. **b.** a sailing vessel of small size. **2.** *Poetic.* a boat or sailing vessel. Also, **barque.** [t. F: m. *barque*, t. It.: m. *barca*, g. LL]

bark beetle, any beetle of the family *Scolytidae*, the adults and larvae of which do great damage to living trees, esp. to conifers.

bark·keep·er (bär′kē′pər), *n.* **1.** one who owns or manages a bar where liquors are served to customers. **2.** a bartender. Also, *U.S.,* **bar′keep′.**

bark·en·tine (bär′kən·tēn′), *n. Naut.* a three-masted vessel with the foremast square-rigged and the mainmast and mizzenmast fore-and-aft-rigged. Also, **bark′an·tine′, barquentine.** [extension of BARK³ after *brigantine*]

bark·er (bär′kər), *n.* **1.** an animal or person that barks. **2.** *Colloq.* one who stands before a store, theater, etc., calling passers-by to enter. [f. BARK¹ + -ER¹]

Bark·ley (bärk′lĭ), *n.* **Alben William,** born 1877, vice-president of the U.S. since 1949.

bark·y (bär′kĭ), *adj.,* **barkier, barkiest.** consisting of or containing bark; covered with or resembling bark.

bar·ley (bär′lĭ), *n.* a widely distributed cereal plant of the genus *Hordeum*, whose awned flowers grow in tightly bunched spikes, with three small additional spikes at each node. It is used as food, and in the making of beer, ale, and whiskey. [ME *barly*, OE *bærlīc*]

bar·ley·corn (bär′lĭ·kôrn′), *n.* **1.** barley, or a grain of barley. **2.** a measure equal to one third of an inch.

Bar·ley·corn (bär′lĭ·kôrn′), *n.* **John,** a humorous personification of barley as used in malt liquor, or malt liquor itself.

barley sugar, sugar boiled, formerly in a decoction of barley, until it has become brittle and transparent.

Bar·low (bär′lō), *n.* **Joel,** 1754-1812, U.S. poet and diplomat.

barm (bärm), *n.* yeast formed on malt liquors while fermenting. [ME *berme*, OE *beorma*, c. G. *bärme*]

bar·maid (bär′mād′), *n. Brit.* a woman or girl who serves customers in a bar.

Bar·me·cide (bär′mə·sĭd′), *n.* a member of a noble Persian family of Bagdad who, according to a tale in *The Arabian Nights' Entertainments*, gave a beggar a pretended feast with empty dishes.

Bar·men (bär′mən), *n.* See **Wuppertal.**

bar miz·vah (bär mĭts′və), *Jewish Relig.* **1.** a boy of thirteen, the age at which he acquires religious obligations. **2.** *U.S. Colloq.* the ceremony and feast marking this. Also, **bar mitz′vah.** [t. Heb.]

barm·y (bär′mĭ), *adj.*, **barmier, barmiest. 1.** containing or resembling barm; frothy. **2.** *Brit. Slang.* flighty; silly; weak-minded.

barn (bärn), *n.* a building for storing hay, grain, etc., and often for stabling live stock. [ME *bern*, OE *berern*, f. *bere* barley + *ærn* place, house]

Bar·na·bas (bär′nə bəs), *n.* the surname of the Cyprian Levite Joseph, an apostle and companion of Paul. Acts 4:36, 37.

bar·na·cle[1] (bär′nə kəl), *n.* **1.** any of certain crustaceans of the group *Cirripedia*, as the **goose barnacles**, the stalked species which cling to ship bottoms and floating timber, and the **rock barnacles**, the species which attach themselves to marine rocks. **2.** a thing or person that clings tenaciously. [late ME *bernacle*, of obscure orig. (cf. ML *bernacula*, F *bernicle*, *barnacle*); r. ME *bernekke*, *bernake* (cf. ML *bernaca*, OF *bernaque*)] **—bar′na·cled,** *adj.*

Goose barnacle, *Lepas fascicularis*

bar·na·cle[2] (bär′nə kəl), *n.* **1.** (*usually pl.*) an instrument with two hinged branches for pinching the nose of an unruly horse. **2.** (*pl.*) *Colloq.* spectacles. [ME *bernacle*, t. OF: m. *bernac*]

Bar·nard (bär′nərd), *n.* **George Gray,** 1863–1938, U.S. sculptor.

Bar·na·ul (bär′nä ōōl′), *n.* a city in the S Soviet Union in Asia, on the Ob river. 148,129 (1939).

Bar·ne·veldt (bär′nə vĕlt′), *n.* **Jan van Olden** (yän vän ōl′dən), 1547–1619, Dutch statesman and patriot.

barn owl, a widely distributed owl, *Tyto alba*, commonly frequenting barns, where it destroys mice.

Barns·ley (bärnz′lĭ), *n.* a city in central England, N of Sheffield. 73,100. (est. 1946)

barn·storm (bärn′stôrm), *v.i.* *U.S. Colloq.* **1.** to conduct a campaign or speaking tour in rural areas. **2.** *Theat.* to act in plays in small country towns where there are no theaters. [back formation from *barnstormer*, lit., one who storms the barn] **—barn′storm·er,** *n.* **—barn′storm·ing,** *n.*, *adj.*

barn swallow. See **swallow**[2] (def. 1).

Bar·num (bär′nəm), *n.* **Phineas Taylor** (fĭn′ỹəs), 1810–91, U.S. showman: established circus (1871).

barn·yard (bärn′yärd′), *n.* a yard next to a barn.

baro-, a word element meaning "weight," "pressure," as in *barogram*. [comb. form repr. Gk. *báros* weight]

Ba·roc·chio (bä rōk′kyō), *n.* See **Vignola.**

Ba·ro·da (bə rō′də), *n.* **1.** a native state in W India. 2,855,000 (1941); 8236 sq. mi. **2.** the capital of this state. 153,301 (1941).

bar·o·gram (bär′ə grăm′), *n.* *Meteorol.* a record traced by a barograph or similar instrument.

bar·o·graph (bär′ə grăf′, -gräf′), *n.* *Meteorol.* an automatic recording barometer. **—bar′o·graph′ic,** *adj.*

Ba·ro·ja (bä rō′hä), *n.* **Pío** (pē′ō), born 1872, Spanish novelist.

ba·rom·e·ter (bə rŏm′ə tər), *n.* **1.** an instrument for measuring atmospheric pressure, thus determining height, weather changes, etc. **2.** anything that indicates changes. **—bar·o·met·ric** (bär′ə mĕt′rĭk), **bar′o·met′ri·cal,** *adj.* **—bar′o·met′ri·cal·ly,** *adv.*

bar·on (bär′ən), *n.* **1.** a member of the lowest grade of nobility. **2.** *Brit.* **a.** a feudal vassal holding his lands directly from the king; a member of the House of Lords. **b.** a member of a borough holding directly from the crown. **3.** *U.S.* a powerful industrialist or financier. [ME, t. OF, g. L *bāro* hulking fellow]

bar·on·age (bär′ən ĭj), *n.* **1.** the whole body of British barons. **2.** the dignity or rank of a baron.

bar·on·ess (bär′ən ĭs), *n.* **1.** the wife of a baron. **2.** a lady holding a baronial title in her own right.

bar·on·et (bär′ən ĭt, -ə nĕt′), *n.* a member of a British hereditary order of honor, ranking below the barons and made up of commoners, designated by *Sir* before the name, and *Baronet*, usually abbreviated *Bart.*, after: *Sir John Smith, Bart.*

bar·on·et·age (bär′ən ĭt ĭj, -ə nĕt′-), *n.* **1.** the dignity or rank of a baronet. **2.** the order of baronets; baronets collectively.

bar·on·et·cy (bär′ən ĭt sĭ, -ə nĕt′-), *n.*, *pl.* **-cies.** the rank or patent of a baronet.

ba·rong (bärông′, -rŏng′), *n.* a large, broad-bladed knife or cleaver used by the Moros. [native name]

ba·ro·ni·al (bə rō′nĭ əl), *adj.* **1.** pertaining to a baron, a barony, or to the order of barons. **2.** befitting a baron.

bar·o·ny (bär′ə nĭ), *n.*, *pl.* **-nies. 1.** the rank or dignity of a baron. **2.** the domain of a baron. [ME *baronie*, t. OF, der. *baron* BARON]

ba·roque (bə rōk′; *Fr.* bȧ rôk′), *n.* **1.** *Art.* **a.** a style developed in Italy in the 16th century characterized by heavy and contorted forms and exaggeration of ornamental and pictorial effects. **b.** work of this style and period. **2.** anything so extravagantly ornamented as to be in bad taste. **—***adj.* **3.** pertaining to the baroque. **4.** irregular in shape. [t. F, t. Pg.: m. *barroco* irregular]

Barouche

bar·o·scope (bär′ə skōp′), *n.* an instrument showing roughly the variations in atmospheric pressure. **—bar·o·scop·ic** (bär′ə skŏp′ĭk), **bar′o·scop′i·cal,** *adj.*

ba·rouche (bə rōōsh′), *n.* a four-wheeled carriage with a seat outside for the driver, and seats inside for two couples facing each other, and with a calash top over the back seat. [t. d. G: m. *barutsche*, t. It.: m. *biroccio*, g. L *birotus* two-wheeled]

bar pin, a long, slender, decorative pin or brooch.

barque (bärk), *n.* bark[3].

bar·quen·tine (bär′kən tēn′), *n.* barkentine.

bar·rack[1] (bär′ək), *n.* (*usually pl.*) **1.** a building or range of buildings for lodging soldiers, esp. in garrison. **2.** any large, plain building in which many people are lodged. **—***v.t.*, *v.i.* **3.** to lodge in barracks. [t. F: m. *baraque*, t. It.: m. *baracca*; orig. uncert.]

bar·rack[2] (bär′ək), *Austral. and Brit.* **—***v.i.* **1.** to shout boisterously for or against a player or team; to root. **—***v.t.* **2.** to shout for or against. [back formation from *barracking* banter, var. of *barrakin*, *barrikin* gibberish (Cockney slang)] **—bar′rack·er,** *n.*

bar·ra·cu·da (bär′ə kōō′də), *n.*, *pl.* **-da, -das.** any of several species of elongate, predaceous, tropical and subtropical marine fishes of the genus *Sphyraena*, some of which are extensively used for food. [t. Sp., t. W. Ind.]

bar·rage (bə räzh′; *esp. Brit.* bär′äzh for 1, 2, 4; bär′ĭj for 3), *n.*, *v.*, **-raged, -raging. —***n.* **1.** *Mil.* a barrier of artillery fire used to prevent the enemy from advancing, to enable troops behind it to operate with a minimum of casualties, or to cut off the enemy's retreat in one or more directions. **2.** any overwhelming quantity: *a barrage of questions.* **3.** *Civ. Eng.* an artificial obstruction in a watercourse to increase the depth of the water, facilitate irrigation, etc. **—***v.t.* **4.** to cut off by or subject to a barrage. [t. F, der. *barrer*, v. Cf. F phrase *tir de barrage* barrage fire]

bar·ra·mun·da (bär′ə mŭn′də), *n.*, *pl.* **-da, -das.** a lungfish, *Neoceratodus forsteri*, of the rivers of Australia. Also, **bar·ra·mun·di** (bär′ə mŭn′dĭ). [native Australian]

bar·ran·ca (bə räng′kə; *Sp.* bär räng′kä), *n.* a steep-walled ravine or gorge. [t. Sp.]

Bar·ran·quil·la (bär′rän kē′yä), *n.* a port in N Colombia, on the Magdalena river. 197,830 (est. 1944).

bar·ra·tor (bär′ə tər), *n.* *Law.* one who commits barratry. Also, **bar′ra·ter.** [ME *baratour*, t. OF: m. *barateor* fraudulent dealer, der. *barater* exchange, cheat]

bar·ra·try (bär′ə trĭ), *n.* *Law.* **1.** fraud by a master or crew at the expense of the owners of the ship or its cargo. **2.** the offense of frequently exciting and stirring up suits and quarrels. **3.** the purchase or sale of ecclesiastical preferments or of offices of state. [ME *barratrie*, t. OF: m. *baraterie*. See BARRATOR] **—bar′ra·trous,** *adj.* **—bar′ra·trous·ly** *adv.*

barred (bärd), *adj.* **1.** provided with one or more bars: *a barred gate.* **2.** striped; streaked: *barred fabrics.*

barred owl, a large owl, *Strix varia*, of eastern North America, with dark brown eyes and with no feather "horns" on the head.

bar·rel (bär′əl), *n.*, *v.*, **-reled, -reling** or (*esp. Brit.*) **-relled, -relling. —***n.* **1.** a wooden cylindrical vessel, with slightly bulging sides made of staves hooped together and with flat, parallel ends. **2.** the quantity which such a vessel of some standard size can hold (as 31½ U.S. gallons of liquid, 105 U.S. dry quarts of fruits and vegetables). **3.** any vessel, case, or part similar in form. **4.** *Ordn.* the tube of a gun. **5.** *Mach.* the chamber of a pump, in which the piston works. **6.** *Horol.* the cylindrical case in a watch or clock within which the mainspring is coiled. **7.** *Ornith.* the hard, horny, hollow part of the stem at the base of a feather; the calamus or quill. **8.** *Naut.* the main portion of a capstan, about which the rope winds, between the drumhead at the top and the pawl rim at the bottom. See illus. under **capstan.** **—***v.t.* **9.** to put or pack in a barrel or barrels. [ME *barel.* t. OF: m. *baril*, prob. der. *barre* bar, stave]

bar·rel-house (bär′əl hous′), *adj.* *Jazz.* in a rough and crude style, as in low-class night clubs where (usually) only blues are played and sung. [orig. a cheap drinking establishment with a row of barrels in evidence]

barrel organ, a musical instrument in which air from a bellows is admitted to a set of pipes by means of pins inserted into a revolving barrel; hand organ.

barrel roll, *Aeron.* a complete rotation of an airplane on its main or longitudinal axis.

bar·ren (bär′ən), *adj.* **1.** incapable of producing, or not producing, offspring; sterile: *a barren woman.* **2.** unproductive; unfruitful: *barren land.* **3.** destitute of interest or attraction. **4.** mentally unproductive; dull; stupid. **5.** not producing results; fruitless: *a barren pen.* **—***n.* **6.** (*usually pl.*) level or slightly rolling land, usually with a sandy soil and few trees, relatively infertile. [ME *barein*, t. OF: m. *baraine*, of pre-L orig.] **—bar′ren·ly,** *adv.* **—bar′ren·ness,** *n.*

Barren Grounds, a region of windswept, almost uninhabited tundras in N Canada, esp. around Hudson Bay. Also, **Barren Lands.**

Bar·rès (bá·rĕs'), *n.* **Maurice** (mō·rēs'), 1862–1923, French novelist, writer on politics, and politician.

bar·ret (băr'ĭt), *n.* a kind of small cap, esp. a biretta. [t. F: m. *barrette* cap, t. It.: m. *berretta*. See BIRETTA]

bar·rette (bə·rĕt'), *n.* a clasp for holding a woman's hair. [t. F, dim. of *barre* bar]

bar·ri·cade (băr'ə·kād', băr'ə·kād'), *n., v., -caded, -cading.* —*n.* **1.** a defensive barrier hastily constructed, as in a street, to stop an enemy. **2.** any barrier or obstruction to passage: *a barricade of rubbish.* —*v.t.* **3.** to obstruct or block with a barricade. **4.** to shut in and defend with or as with a barricade. [t. F, prob. t. Pr.: m. *barricada* a barricade, orig. made of casks filled with earth, der. *barrica* cask] —**bar'ri·cad'er,** *n.* —Syn. 1. See bar[1].

Bar·rie (băr'ĭ), *n.* **Sir James Matthew,** 1860–1937, Scottish novelist, short-story writer, and playwright.

bar·ri·er (băr'ĭ·ər), *n.* **1.** anything built or serving to bar passage, as a stockade or fortress, or a railing. **2.** any natural bar or obstacle: *a mountain barrier.* **3.** anything that restrains or obstructs progress, access, etc.: *a trade barrier.* **4.** a limit or boundary of any kind: *the barriers of caste.* **5.** *(often cap.) Phys. Geog.* the portion of the polar icecap of Antarctica extending miles out beyond land, and resting in places on the ocean bottom. **6.** *Oceanog.* a bar built off shore by waves and currents, separated from the mainland by lagoons or marshes. **7.** *(pl.)* the palisades or railing surrounding the ground where tourneys and jousts were carried on. [ME *barrere*, t. AF, der. *barre* bar] —Syn. 1. See bar[1].

barrier reef, *Oceanog.* a long narrow ridge of coral close to or above the surface of the sea off the coast of a continent or island: *the Great Barrier Reef.*

bar·ring (băr'ĭng), *prep.* excepting; except for: *barring accidents, I'll be there.*

bar·ri·o (băr'rō̄'), *n., pl. -os.* (in Spain and countries colonized by Spain) one of the divisions into which a town or city, together with the contiguous rural territory, is divided. [t. Sp.]

bar·ris·ter (băr'ĭs·tər), *n.* **1.** *Eng.* a counselor admitted to plead at the bar in any court. **2.** *Colloq.* a lawyer. [f. *barri-* (comb. form of BAR[1]) + -STER]

bar·room (băr'rōōm', -rŏŏm'), *n. U.S.* a room containing a bar for the sale of liquors.

Bar·ros (băr'rōŏsh), *n.* **Joao de** (zhwoun' də), ("the Portuguese Livy") 1496–1570, Portuguese historian.

bar·row[1] (băr'ō), *n.* **1.** a flat rectangular frame used for carrying a load, esp. such a frame with projecting shafts at each end for handles. **2.** a wheelbarrow. **3.** *Brit.* a pushcart used by costermongers. [ME *barewe*, OE *bearwe*; prob. akin to OE *beran* BEAR[1], v.]

bar·row[2] (băr'ō), *n.* **1.** *Anthropol.* a burial mound of the prehistoric inhabitants of Great Britain. **2.** a hill (now chiefly in place names). [ME *barowe,* OE *beorg* hill, mound, c. G *berg* hill, mountain]

bar·row[3] (băr'ō), *n.* a castrated male swine. [ME *barow,* OE *bearg*]

Bar·row (băr'ō), *n.* **1.** Also, **Barrow-in-Furness** (băr'ō-ĭn-fûr'nĕs). a seaport in NW England, in Lancashire, 67,240 (est. 1946). **2. Point,** the N tip of Alaska.

Bar·ry (băr'ĭ; Fr. bá·rē'), *n.* **Du.** See Du Barry.

Bar·ry·more (băr'ə·mōr'), *n. U.S.* family of actors: **Maurice,** (Herbert Blythe) 1847–1905, father of **Ethel,** born 1879, **John,** 1882–1942, and **Lionel,** born 1878.

bar sinister, 1. *Her.* (erroneously) a baton or a bend sinister. See illus. under bend sinister. **2.** the implication or proof of bastard birth.

Bart., Baronet.

bar·tend·er (băr'tĕn'dər), *n. U.S.* a man who mixes and serves drinks in a bar.

bar·ter (băr'tər), *v.i.* **1.** to trade by exchange of commodities rather than by the use of money. —*v.t.* **2.** to exchange in trade, as one commodity for another; trade. **3.** to bargain away unwisely or dishonorably (fol. by *away*). —*n.* **4.** act of bartering. **5.** the thing bartered. [ME *bartre,* freq. of obs. *barrat.* v., t. OF: m. *barater* exchange, cheat. Cf. BARRATOR] —**bar'ter·er,** *n.* —Syn. 1, 2. See trade.

Bar·thol·di (băr·thŏl'dĭ; Fr. bár·tōl·dē'), *n.* **Frédéric Auguste** (frē·dē·rēk' ō·gyst') 1834–1904, French sculptor who executed the Statue of Liberty.

Bar·thol·o·mew (băr·thŏl'ə·mū'), *n. Bible.* one of the twelve apostles. Mark 3:18.

bar·ti·zan (băr'tə·zən, băr'tə·zăn'), *n. Archit.* a small overhanging turret on a wall or tower. [alter. of BRATTICING] —**bar·ti·zaned** (băr'tə·zənd, băr'tə·zănd'), *adj.*

Bartizan
A. Merlon; B. Embrasure; C
Loophole; D. Machicolation

Bart·lett (bärt'lĭt), *n.* **1.** Also, **Bartlett pear.** *Hort.* a large, yellow, juicy variety of pear. **2. John,** 1820–1905, U. S. publisher and compiler.

Bar·tók (bŏr'tōk), *n.* **Béla** (bā'lŏ), 1881–1945, Hungarian composer.

Bar·to·lom·me·o (băr'tô·lôm mě'ō), **Fra** (frä), (Baccio della Porta) 1475–1517, Italian painter.

Bar·ton (băr'tən), *n.* **Clara,** 1821–1912, U.S. woman who organized the American Red Cross in 1881.

Bar·uch (băr'ək), *n. Bible.* the amanuensis and friend of Jeremiah and nominal author of the Book of Baruch in the Apocrypha. Jer. 32:13.

Ba·ruch (bə·rōōk'), *n.* **Bernard Mannes** (măn'əs), born 1870, U. S. statesman and financier.

ba·ry·ta (bə·rī'tə), *n. Chem.* **1.** barium oxide, BaO. **2.** barium (in phrases): *carbonate of baryta.* [see BARYTES] —**ba·ryt·ic** (bə·rĭt'ĭk), *adj.*

ba·ry·tes (bə·rī'tēz), *n.* barite. [t. Gk.: weight]

bar·y·tone[1] (băr'ə·tōn'), *adj., n. Music.* baritone.

bar·y·tone[2] (băr'ə·tōn'), *adj.* **1.** (in Greek) pronounced with the (theoretical) grave accent on the last syllable. —*n.* **2.** a barytone word. [t. Gk.: m. s. *barȳtonos* with grave accent]

bas·al (bā'səl), *adj.* **1.** of, at, or forming the base. **2.** fundamental: *basal characteristics.* **3.** *Physiol.* a. indicating a standard low level of activity of an organism as present during total rest. **b.** of an amount required to maintain this level. —**bas'al·ly,** *adv.*

basal metabolic rate, *Physiol.* the rate of oxygen intake and heat discharge in an organism in a basal state.

basal metabolism, *Physiol.* the energy turnover of the body at a standard low level of activity.

ba·salt (bə·sôlt', băs'ôlt), *n.* the dark, dense igneous rock of a lava flow or minor intrusion, composed essentially of labradorite and pyroxene, and often displaying a columnar structure. [t. L: s. *basaltes* a dark, hard marble in Ethiopia] —**ba·sal'tic,** *adj.*

ba·salt·ware (bə·sôlt'wâr', băs'ôlt-), *n.* unglazed stoneware developed by Josiah Wedgwood, usually black, with a dull gloss.

bas bleu (bä blœ'), bluestocking. [F word trans. into F]

bas·cule (băs'kūl), *n. Civ. Eng.* a device operating like a balance or seesaw, esp. an arrangement of a movable bridge (**bascule bridge**) by which the rising floor or section is counterbalanced by a weight. [t. F: a seesaw, r. *bacule,* appar. f. *ba(ttre)* strike and *cul* the posteriors]

base[1] (bās), *n., adj., v., based, basing.* —*n.* **1.** the bottom of anything, considered as its support; that on which a thing stands or rests. **2.** a fundamental principle or groundwork; foundation; basis: *the base of needed reforms.* **3.** *Archit.* **a.** that part of a column on which the shaft rests. See diag. under **column. b.** the lowest member of a wall, monument, or the like. **c.** the lower elements of a complete structure. **4.** *Bot., Zool.* **a.** the part of an organ nearest its point of attachment. **b.** the point of attachment. **5.** the principal element or ingredient of anything, considered as its fundamental part. **6.** that from which a commencement, as of action or reckoning, is made. **7.** *Baseball.* one of the four corners of the diamond. **8.** a starting point for racers, etc. **9.** the goal in hockey and in certain other games. **10.** *Mil.* **a.** a fortified or more or less protected area or place from which the operations of an army or an air force proceed. **b.** a supply installation for a large military force. **11.** *Geom.* the line or surface forming that part of a figure on which it is supposed to stand. **12.** *Math.* the number which serves as a starting point for a logarithmic or other numerical system. **13.** *Survey.* an accurately measured line forming one side of a triangle or system of triangles from which all other sides are computed. **14.** *Chem.* **a.** a compound which reacts with an acid to form a salt, as ammonia, calcium hydroxide, certain nitrogen-containing organic compounds (as the amines and alkaloids) etc. **b.** the hydroxide of a metal or of an electropositive element or radical. **c.** a radical or molecule which takes up or accepts protons. **15.** *Gram.* the form to which affixes are added in the construction of a complex word, sometimes equivalent to *stem* or *theme.* For example: *want* is the base in *unwanted.* **16.** *Her.* the lower part of a shield. —*adj.* **17.** serving as a base. —*v.t.* **18.** to make or form a base or foundation for. **19.** to establish, as a fact or conclusion (fol. by *on* or *upon*). **20.** to place or establish on a base or basis; ground; found; establish. [ME, t. OF, t. L: m.s. *basis,* t. Gk.: a stepping, a step, pedestal, base] —Syn. 1. BASE, BASIS, FOUNDATION refer to anything upon which a structure is built and upon which it rests. BASE usually refers to a literal supporting structure: *the base of a statue.* BASIS more often refers to a figurative support: *the basis of a report.* FOUNDATION implies a solid, secure understructure: *the foundation of a skyscraper or a rumor.*

base[2] (bās), *adj., baser, basest, n.* —*adj.* **1.** morally low; without dignity of sentiment; mean-spirited; selfish; cowardly. **2.** characteristic of an inferior person or thing. **3.** of little value: *the base metals.* **4.** debased or counterfeit: *base coin.* **5.** of illegitimate birth. **6.** *Old Eng. Law.* **a.** not held or holding by honorable tenure. **b. base estate,** an estate held by services not honorable, or by villeinage. **c. base tenant,** the tenant of such an estate. **7.** deep or grave in sound; bass: *the base tones of a piano.* **8.** not classical or refined: *base language.* **9.** *Archaic.* of humble origin or station. **10.** *Archaic.* of small height. **11.** *Archaic.* low in place, position, or degree. —*n.* **12.** *Music. Obs.* bass[1]. [ME, t. OF: m. *bas,* g. LL *bassus* low] —**base'ly,** *adv.* —**base'ness,** *n.* —Syn. 1. despicable, contemptible. See mean[2]. **2.** servile, ignoble.

base·ball (bās'bôl'), *n.* **1.** a game of ball played by two sides of nine players each, on a diamond enclosed by lines connecting four bases, a complete circuit of which must be made by a player after batting, in order to score a run. 2. the ball used in playing this game.

base·board (bās′bōrd′), *n.* 1. a line of boarding around the interior walls of a room, next to the floor. 2. a board forming the base of anything.

base·born (bās′bōrn′), *adj.* 1. of humble birth. 2. born out of wedlock. 3. base-natured; mean.

base-burn·er (bās′bûr′nər), *n. U.S.* a stove or furnace with a self-acting fuel hopper over the fire chamber.

base hit, *Baseball.* a hit on which a batter runs to first base or beyond unless a fielder has made an error or another runner is forced out by the batter's advance.

Ba·sel (bä′zəl), *n.* a city in NW Switzerland, on the Rhine. 167,000 (est. 1944). French, **Basle, Bâle.**

base·less (bās′lĭs), *adj.* having no base; without foundation; groundless: *a baseless claim.*

base level, *Phys. Geog.* the lowest level to which running water can theoretically erode the land.

base·man (bās′mən), *n., pl.* **-men.** *Baseball.* a player stationed at first, second, or third base.

base·ment (bās′mənt), *n.* 1. a story of a building partly or wholly underground. 2. the portion of a structure which supports those portions which come above it. 3. the substructure of a columnar or arched construction.

ba·ses[1] (bā′sēz), *n.* pl. of **basis**[1].

bas·es[2] (bā′sĭz), *n.* pl. of **base**[1].

bash (băsh), *Dial. or Slang.* —*v.t.* 1. to strike with a crushing or smashing blow. —*n.* 2. a crushing blow. [b. BAT[1] and MASH]

Ba·shan (bā′shən), *n.* a fertile region E of the Jordan in ancient Palestine: famous for its cattle and sheep.

ba·shaw (bə shô′), *n.* 1. pasha. 2. *Colloq.* an important personage; a bigwig. [t. Turk.: m. *bāsha,* var. of *pāsha* PASHA]

bash·ful (băsh′fəl), *adj.* 1. uncomfortably diffident or shy; timid and easily embarrassed. 2. indicative of, accompanied with, or proceeding from bashfulness. [f. obs. *bash,* v. (apheltic var. of ABASH) + -FUL] —**bash′ful·ly,** *adv.* —**bash′ful·ness,** *n.* —Syn. 1. See **shy**[1].

bash·i·ba·zouk (băsh′ĭ bə zōōk′), *n.* one of a class of irregular mounted troops in the Turkish military service. [t. Turk.: m. *bashi-bozuq* irregular soldier]

Bash·kir (băsh kĭr′) *n.* an autonomous republic in the E Soviet Union in Europe. 3,144,713 pop. (1939); ab. 54,200 sq. mi. *Cap.:* Ufa. Official name, **Bashkir Autonomous Soviet Socialist Republic.**

bas·ic (bā′sĭk), *adj.* 1. of, pertaining to, or forming a base; fundamental: *a basic principle, ingredient, etc.* 2. *Chem.* **a.** pertaining to, of the nature of, or containing a base. **b.** not having all of the hydroxyls of the base replaced by the acid radical, or having the metal or its equivalent united partly to the acid radical and partly to oxygen. **c.** alkaline. 3. *Metall.* noting, pertaining to, or made by a steelmaking process in which the furnace is lined with a basic or nonsiliceous material, principally burned magnesite and a small amount of ground basic slag, to aid in sintering. 4. *Geol.* (of rocks) having relatively little silica.

bas·i·cal·ly (bā′sĭk lĭ), *adv.* fundamentally.

Basic English, a simplified English with a restricted vocabulary, intended as an international auxiliary language and for use in teaching English.

ba·sic·i·ty (bā sĭs′ə tĭ), *n. Chem.* 1. state of being a base. 2. the power of an acid to react with bases, dependent on the number of replaceable hydrogen atoms of the acid.

basic slag, the slag in a basic lined furnace used to remove impurities from metal, as in steelmaking, and as a fertilizer.

ba·sid·i·o·my·cete (bə sĭd′ĭ ō mī sēt′), *n. Bot.* a basidiomycetous organism. [t. NL: m. *Basidiomycetes.* See BASIDIUM, -MYCETES]

ba·sid·i·o·my·ce·tous (bə sĭd′ĭ ō mī sē′təs), *adj. Bot.* belonging or pertaining to the *Basidiomycetes,* a large group of fungi which bear the spores on a basidium, including the smuts, rusts, mushrooms, puffballs, etc.

ba·sid·i·um (bə sĭd′ĭ əm), *n., pl.* **-sidia** (-sĭd′ĭ ə). *Bot.* a special form of sporophore, characteristic of basidiomycetous fungi, on which the sexual spores are borne, usually at the tips of slender projections. [f. BAS(IS) + -IDIUM] —**ba·sid′i·al,** *adj.*

bas·il (băz′əl). *n.* a plant of the mint family *Labiatae,* genus *Ocimum,* as *O. Basilicum* (sweet basil). [ME *basile,* t. OF, t. L: short for *basilicum,* t. Gk.: m. *basilikón* (neut.), lit., royal]

Bas·il (băz′əl), *n.* Saint, ("*the Great*") A.D. 329?–379, bishop of Caesarea, in Asia Minor. Also, **Basilius.**

Basidia

bas·i·lar (băs′ə lər), *adj.* 1. pertaining to or situated at the base, esp. the base of the skull. 2. basal. Also, **bas·i·lar·y** (băs′ə lĕr′ĭ).

ba·sil·ic (bə sĭl′ĭk), *adj.* 1. kingly; royal. 2. of or pertaining to a basilica. Also, **ba·sil·i·can** (bə sĭl′ə kən). [t. F: m. *basilique,* t. L: m. s. *basilicus,* t. Gk.: m. *basilikós* kingly]

ba·sil·i·ca (bə sĭl′ə kə), *n.* 1. (*cap.*) (in ancient Rome) a large oblong building near the forum, used as a hall of justice and public meeting place. 2. *Archit.* an oblong building, esp. a church with a nave higher than its aisles. 3. one of the seven main churches of Rome or another Roman Catholic church accorded the same religious privileges. See illus. in preceding column. [t. L, t. Gk.: m. *basilikḗ,* fem. of *basilikós* royal]

basilic vein, *Anat.* a large vein on the inner side of the arm.

bas·i·lisk (băs′ə lĭsk, băz′-), *n.* 1. *Class. Legend.* a fabulous creature (serpent, lizard, or dragon) said by the ancients to kill by its breath or look. 2. a tropical American lizard of the genus *Basiliscus,* of the family *Iguanidae,* with a crest on the back of the head and along the back and tail. [t. L: m.s. *basiliscus,* t. Gk.: m. *basiliskos,* prop. dim. of *basileús* king]

Ba·sil·i·us (bə sĭl′ĭ əs, -zĭl′-), *n.* Basil (saint).

ba·sin (bā′sən), *n.* 1. a circular container of greater width than depth, contracting toward the bottom, used chiefly to hold water or other liquid, esp. for washing. 2. any container of similar shape, as the pan of a balance. 3. the quantity held by such a container. 4. a natural or artificial hollow place containing water. 5. *Geol.* an area in which the strata dip from the margins toward a common center. 6. *Phys. Geog.* **a.** a hollow or depression in the earth's surface, wholly or partly surrounded by higher land: *ocean basin, lake basin, river basin.* **b.** the tract of country drained by a river and its tributaries. [ME, t. OF: m. *bacin,* g. LL *bachīnus,* der. *bacca* water vessel] —**ba′sined,** *adj.* —**ba′sin·like′,** *adj.*

Hooded basilisk, *Basiliscus mitratus* (2½ to 3 ft. long)

bas·i·net (băs′ə nĭt, -nĕt′), *n.* Armor. a steel cap of somewhat globular form. [ME, t. OF: m. *bacinet,* dim. of *bacin* BASIN]

ba·si·on (bā′sĭ ŏn′), *n. Craniom.* a point on the anterior margin of the foramen magnum, in the midsagittal plane of the skull. [t. NL, der. Gk. *básis* base]

ba·sip·e·tal (bā sĭp′ə təl), *adj. Bot.* (of a plant structure) developing toward the base during growth.

ba·sis (bā′sĭs), *n., pl.* **-ses** (-sēz). 1. the bottom or base of anything, or that on which it stands or rests. 2. a groundwork or fundamental principle. 3. the principal constituent; principal ingredient. [t. L, t. Gk. See BASE[1]] —Syn. 1, 2. See **base**[1].

bask (băsk, bäsk), *v.i.* 1. to lie in or be exposed to a pleasant warmth: *to bask in the sunshine.* 2. to enjoy a pleasant situation: *he basked in royal favor.* —*v.t.* 3. to expose to warmth, heat, etc. [ME *baske(n),* t. Scand.; cf. Icel. *badhask,* refl. of *badha* bathe]

Bas·ker·ville (băs′kər vĭl), *n.* a style of type.

bas·ket (băs′kĭt, bäs′-), *n.* 1. a receptacle made of twigs, rushes, thin strips of wood, or other flexible material, woven together. 2. a container made of pieces of thin veneer, used for packing berries, vegetables, etc. 3. the contents of a basket. 4. anything like a basket in shape or use. 5. *Basketball.* **a.** a short open net suspended before the backboard through which the ball must pass to score points. **b.** a score, counting one point on a free throw and two for a field goal. [ME; orig. unknown] —**bas′ket·less,** *adj.* —**bas′ket·like′,** *adj.*

bas·ket·ball (băs′kĭt bôl′, bäs′-), *n.* 1. a game played, usually indoors, by two teams of five (six, if women) players each. Points are scored by throwing the ball through the baskets placed at either end of the oblong court. 2. the round leather ball used in this game.

basket hilt, a basketlike hilt of a sword, etc., serving to cover and protect the hand. —**bas′ket-hilt′ed,** *adj.*

bas·ket·ry (băs′kĭt rĭ, bäs′-), *n.* 1. basketwork; baskets. 2. the art or process of making baskets.

basket weave, a plain weave with two or more yarns woven together, resembling that of a basket.

bas·ket·work (băs′kĭt wûrk′, bäs′-), *n.* work of the basket kind or weave; wickerwork; interwoven work.

bask·ing shark (băs′kĭng, bäs′-), a very large shark, *Cetorhinus maximus,* which frequently comes to the surface to bask in the sun.

Basle (bäl), *n.* French name of **Basel.**

ba·so·phile (bā′sə fīl, -fĭl), *n. Biol.* a cell or cell constituent with an affinity for basic dyes. [f. *baso-* (repr. BASIC) + -PHILE] —**ba·so·phil·ic** (bā′sə fĭl′ĭk), *adj.*

Basque (băsk), *n.* 1. one of a people of unknown origin inhabiting the western Pyrenees regions in France and Spain. 2. their language, historically connected only with Iberian. 3. (*l.c.*) a woman's bodice extending over the hips. 4. (*l.c.*) a short skirt or piece hanging from the waistline of a woman's (formerly a man's) garment. —*adj.* 5. of or pertaining to the Basques or their language. [t. F, t. L: m. s. *Vasco* inhabitant of *Vasconia*]

Basque Provinces, a region in N Spain, bordering on the Bay of Biscay, populated mostly by Basques.

Bas·ra (bŭs′rȧ, bäs′rä), *n.* a port in SE Iraq, near the head of the Persian Gulf. 99,450 (est. 1941). Also, **Busra, Busrah.**

bas-re·lief (bä′rĭ lēf′, bȧs′-; bä′rĭ lēf′, bȧs′-), *n.* sculpture in low relief, in which the figures' project only slightly from the background. [t. F, t. It.: m. *basso-rilievo* low relief]

bass[1] (bās), *adj. Music.* **1.** low in pitch; of the lowest pitch or range: *a bass voice, part, singer, or instrument.* **2.** of or pertaining to the lowest part in the harmonized music. —*n.* **3.** the bass part. **4.** a bass voice, singer, or instrument. [var. of BASE[2] (see def. 12)]

bass[2] (băs), *n., pl.* **basses,** (*esp. collectively*) **bass. 1.** any of various spiny-finned fishes, as: **a.** any fish of the family *Serranidae.* **b.** any of certain fishes of the family *Centrarchidae.* **c.** any of several similar fishes of other families. **2.** (*orig.*) the European perch, *Perca fluviatilis.* [var. of d. E *barse*, OE *bærs*]

bass[3] (băs), *n.* **1.** the basswood or linden. **2.** *Bot.* bast. [alter. of BAST]

bass clef (bās), *Music.* the symbol placed on the fourth line of a staff to indicate that the notes are pitched below middle C; F clef. See illus. under **clef.**

bass drum (bās), *Music.* a musical instrument, the largest of the drum family, having a cylindrical body and two membranes.

bas·set[1] (băs′ĭt), *n.* a long-bodied, short-legged dog resembling a dachshund but larger and heavier. Also, **bas·set hound.** [t. F, orig. dim. of *bas* low]

Basset
(11 to 15 in. high at the shoulder)

bas·set[2] (băs′ĭt), *n., v.,* **-seted, -seting.** *Geol., Min-ing.* —*n.* **1.** an outcrop, as of the edges of strata. —*v.i.* **2.** to crop out. [? t. F: something low. See BASSET[1]]

Basse·terre (bȧs târ′), *n.* a seaport in the British West Indies: the capital of St. Kitts. 8000 (1937).

Basse-Terre (bȧs târ′; *Fr.* bȧs tĕr′), *n.* a seaport in and the capital of Guadeloupe, in the French West Indies. 17,992 (1944).

basset horn, *Music.* an alto clarinet with a soft tone. [trans. of F *cor de basset,* trans. of It. *corno di bassetto* (dim. of *basso* low)]

bass horn (bās), *Music.* **1.** a tuba. **2.** *Obsolesc.* a wind instrument related to the serpent.

bas·si·net (băs′ȧ nĕt′, băs′ȧ nĕt′), *n.* **1.** a basket with a hood over one end, for use as a baby's cradle. **2.** a form of perambulator. [t. F, dim. of *bassin* BASIN]

bas·so (băs′ō, bäs′ō; *It.* bäs′sô), *n., pl.* **-sos, -si** (-sē). *Music.* one who sings bass; a bass. [t. It., g. LL *bassus* low]

bas·soon (bă sōōn′, bȧ-), *n. Music.* a woodwind instrument of the oboe class in baritone range, having a doubled wooden tube or body and a long, curved metallic crook to receive the reed. [t. F: m. *basson,* t. It.: m. *bassone,* aug. of *basso* low]

Man playing a bassoon

basso pro·fun·do (prō fŭn′dō; *It.* prô fōōn′dô). *Music.* the lowest bass voice or singer. [t. It.: deep bass]

bas·so-re·lie·vo (băs′ō rĭ lē′vō), *n., pl.* **-vos.** bas-relief. [t. It.]

bas·so-ri·lie·vo (băs′ō rĭ lyĕ′vō), *n., pl.* **bassi-rilievi** (băs′sē rē lyĕ′vē). basso-relievo. [It.]

Bass Strait (băs), a strait between Australia and Tasmania. 80–150 mi. wide.

bass viol (bās), *Music.* viola da gamba (def. 1).

bass·wood (băs′wŏŏd′), *n.* **1.** a linden, esp. *Tilia americana.* **2.** its wood.

bast (băst), *n.* **1.** *Bot.* phloem. **2.** the inner bark of the linden and other trees, used in making matting, etc. [ME; OE *bæst,* c. G *bast*]

bas·tard (băs′tȧrd), *n.* **1.** an illegitimate child. **2.** something irregular, inferior, spurious, or unusual. —*adj.* **3.** illegitimate in birth. **4.** spurious; not genuine; false. **5.** of abnormal or irregular shape or size; of unusual make or proportions. **6.** having the appearance of; resembling in some degree. [ME, t. OF: prob. f. *bast* packsaddle + *-ard* -ARD, through meaning of mule; for semantic development, cf. MULATTO]

bas·tard·ize (băs′tȧr dīz′), *v.,* **-ized, -izing.** —*v.t.* **1.** to declare or prove to be a bastard. **2.** to debase. —*v.i.* **3.** to become debased. —**bas′tard·i·za′tion,** *n.*

bas·tard·ly (băs′tȧrd lĭ), *adj.* **1.** bastard; baseborn. **2.** spurious; counterfeit.

bastard wing, *Ornith.* alula.

bas·tar·dy (băs′tȧr dĭ), *n., pl.* **-dies. 1.** condition of a bastard; illegitimacy. **2.** act of begetting a bastard.

baste[1] (bāst), *v.t.,* **basted, basting.** to sew slightly; sew with temporary stitches, as a garment in the first stages of making; tack. [ME, t. OF: m. *bastir,* t. OG; cf. OHG *bestan* sew with bast, der. *bast* BAST]

baste[2] (bāst), *v.t.,* **basted, basting.** to moisten (meat, etc.) while cooking, with drippings, butter, etc. [? t. F; cf. OF *basser* soak, moisten]

baste[3] (bāst), *v.t.,* **basted, basting. 1.** to beat with a

stick; thrash; cudgel. **2.** to denounce or scold vigorously. [t. Scand.; cf. Icel. *beysta* beat, thresh]

Bas·ti·a (bä stē′ä), *n.* a seaport on the NE coast of Corsica: the former capital of Corsica. 49,327 (1946).

bas·tille (băs tēl′; *Fr.* bȧs tē′y), *n.* **1. the Bastille,** a famous fortress in Paris, used as a prison, built in the 14th century and destroyed July 14, 1789. **2.** any prison, esp. one conducted in a tyrannical way. **3.** a tower, as of a castle; a small fortress. Also, **bas·tile′.** [ME, t. F, g. LL *bastīlia* (pl.), der. *bastire* build]

Bastille Day, July 14, a national holiday of the French republic, commemorating the fall of the Bastille.

bas·ti·na·do (băs′tȧ nā′dō), *n., pl.* **-does,** *v.,* **-doed, -doing.** —*n.* **1.** a blow or a beating with a stick, etc. **2.** an Oriental mode of punishment consisting in blows with a stick on the soles of the feet, or on the buttocks. **3.** a stick or cudgel. —*v.t.* **4.** to beat with a stick, etc., esp. on the soles of the feet or on the buttocks. Also, *Archaic,* **bas·ti·nade** (băs′tȧ nād′). [t. Sp.: m. *bastonada,* der. *baston* stick]

bast·ing (bās′tĭng), *n.* **1.** sewing with slight or temporary stitches. **2.** (*pl.*) the stitches taken, or the threads used. [f. BASTE[1] + -ING[1]]

bas·tion (băs′chȧn, -tĭ̇ȧn). *n.* **1.** *Fort.* a projecting portion of a rampart or fortification, forming an irregular pentagon attached at the base to the main work. **2.** a fortified place. [t. F, t. It.: m. *bastione,* der. *bastire* build] —**bas′tioned,** *adj.*

Bas·togne (băs tōn′; *Fr.* bȧs tôn′y), *n.* a town in SE Belgium: U. S. forces were besieged here during the German counteroffensive, Dec., 1944. 4005 (1930).

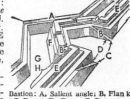
Bastion: A, Salient angle; B, Flank; C, Ramp; D, Gorge; E, Parapet; F, Face; G, Moat; H, Curtain

Ba·su·to·land (bȧ sōō′tō lănd′), *n.* a British protectorate in, but not an administrative part of, the Union of South Africa. 562,311 pop. (1936); 11,716 sq. mi. *Cap.*: Maseru.

bat[1] (băt), *n., v.,* **batted, batting.** —*n.* **1.** *Sports.* **a.** the club used in certain games, as baseball and cricket, to strike the ball. **b.** a racket, esp. one used in ping-pong and tennis. **c.** act of batting in a game. **d.** the right or turn to bat. **e. at bat,** in the position of the batter. **2.** a heavy stick, club, or cudgel. **3.** *Colloq.* a blow as with a bat. **4.** any fragment of brick or hardened clay. **5.** *Brit. Dial.* or *Colloq.* rate of motion, or speed. **6.** *Slang.* a spree; binge: *to go on a bat.* **7.** batt. —*v.t.* **8.** to strike or hit with or as with a bat or club. —*n.t.* **9.** *Baseball, etc.* **a.** to strike at the ball with the bat. **b.** to take one's turn as a batter. **10.** *Slang.* to rush. [ME *batte,* OE *batt* cudgel]

bat[2] (băt), *n.* **1.** any of the nocturnal or crepuscular flying mammals constituting the order *Chiroptera,* characterized by modified forelimbs which serve as wings and are covered with a membranous skin extending to the hind limbs. **2. blind as a bat,** blind. [var. of ME *bakke,* t. Scand.; cf. Dan. *-bakke*] —**bat′like′,** *adj.*

Silver-haired bat.
Lasionycteris noctivagans
(4 in. long)

bat[3] (băt), *v.t.,* **batted, batting.** *Colloq.* to wink. [var. of *bate* flutter, t. OF: m. *batre,* g. L *batere* beat]

Ba·taán (bȧ tän′; *local* bä′tä-än′), *n.* a peninsula on W Luzon, in the Philippine Islands: U. S. troops surrendered to the Japanese, April 9, 1942.

Ba·tan·gas (bä täng′gäs), *n.* a seaport in the Philippines, on SW Luzon. 49,164 (1939).

Ba·ta·vi·a (bȧ tā′vĭ̇ȧ), *n.* a seaport in and the capital of the U. S. of Indonesia, on the NW coast of Java. 533,015 (1930). Official name, **Jakarta.**

batch (băch), *n.* **1.** the quantity of bread made at one baking. **2.** a quantity or number coming at one time or taken together: *a batch of prisoners.* **3.** the quantity of material prepared or required for one operation. [ME *batche,* OE *gebæc* baking, der. *bacan* bake]

bate (bāt), *v.t.,* **bated, bating. 1.** to moderate or restrain (the breath): *to wait with bated breath.* **2.** to lessen; abate. [aphetic var. of ABATE]

ba·teau (bä tō′; *Fr.* bȧ tô′), *n., pl.* **-teaux** (-tōz′; *Fr.* -tô′). **1.** a light boat, esp. one having a flat bottom and tapering ends. **2.** a pontoon of a floating bridge. [t. F, in OF *batel.* Cf. ML *batellus,* dim. of *bat(t)us* boat, prob. t. OE: m. *bāt*]

bat·fish (băt′fĭsh′), *n.* **1.** any of the flat-bodied marine fishes of the family *Ogcocephalidae,* as *Ogcocephalus vespertilio,* common along the southern Atlantic coast of the U.S. **2.** a California sting ray, *Aetobatis cali-fornicus.* [f. BAT[2] + FISH, n.]

bat·fowl (băt′foul′), *v.i.* to catch birds at night by dazzling them with a light, then taking them in a net. [prob. f. BAT[1] + FOWL, v.] —**bat′fowl′er,** *n.*

bath[1] (băth, bàth), *n.*, *pl.* **baths** (bãthz, bàthz), *v.* —*n.*
1. a washing of the body in, or an exposure of it to the action of, water or other liquid, or vapor, etc., as for cleansing, refreshment, medical treatment, etc. **2.** water or other agent used for this purpose. **3.** a vessel for containing this, as a bathtub. **4.** a room equipped for bathing; bathroom. **5.** a building containing apartments for bathing, or fitted up for bathing. **6.** (*often pl.*) one of the elaborate bathing establishments of the ancients. **7.** (*usually pl.*) a town or place resorted to for medical treatment by bathing, etc. **8.** a preparation, as an acid solution, in which something is immersed. **9.** the vessel containing such a preparation. **10.** a device for heating or cooling apparatus by means of a surrounding medium such as sand, water, or oil. **11.** state of being covered by a liquid. —*v.t.* **12.** to put or wash in a bath. [ME; OE *bæth*, c. G *bad*] —**bath'less**, *adj.*

bath[2] (băth), *n.* either of two Hebrew units of liquid measure, equivalent to about 10 and 10¾ U.S. gallons respectively.

Bath (båth, bàth), *n.* **1.** a city in SW England: mineral springs. 76,150 (est. 1946). **2.** a seaport in SW Maine. 10,644 (1950).

Bath brick, a compacted mass of fine siliceous sand, used for scouring metal. [named after *Bath*, England]

Bath chair, an invalid's wheeled chair. Also, **bath chair.**

bathe (bãth), *v.*, **bathed**, **bathing**, *n.* —*v.t.* **1.** to immerse in water or other liquid for cleansing, refreshment, etc. **2.** to wet; wash. **3.** to moisten or suffuse with any liquid. **4.** to apply water or other liquid to, with a sponge, cloth, etc. **5.** to cover or surround with anything like water. —*v.i.* **6.** to take a bath. **7.** to swim for pleasure. **8.** to be covered or surrounded as if with water. —*n.* **9.** *Brit.* act of bathing, as in the sea. [ME *bathien*, OE *bathian*, der. *bæth* bath] —**bath'er**, *n.*

bath-house (băth'hous', bàth'-), *n.* **1.** a house or building for bathing. **2.** a structure, as at the seaside, containing dressing rooms for bathers.

batho-, a word element meaning "deep," as in *batholith.* [comb. form repr. Gk. *báthos* depth]

bath-o-lith (băth'əlĭth), *n.* *Geol.* a large body of igneous rock, bounded by irregular, cross-cutting surfaces or fault planes, and believed to have crystallized at a considerable depth below the earth's surface. Also, **bath-o-lite** (băth'əlĭt'). —**bath'o-lith'ic, bath-o-lit-ic** (băth'əlĭt'ĭk), *adj.*

ba-thom-e-ter (bəthŏm'ətər), *n.* *Oceanog.* a device for ascertaining the depth of water.

ba-thos (bā'thŏs), *n.* **1.** a ludicrous descent from the elevated to the commonplace; anticlimax. **2.** triteness or triviality in style. **3.** insincere pathos; sentimentality. [t. Gk.: depth] —**ba-thet-ic** (bəthĕt'ĭk), *adj.*

bath-robe (băth'rōb', bàth'-), *n.* a long, loose garment for wear in going to and from a bath.

bath-room (băth'rōōm', -rŏŏm', bàth'-), *n.* **1.** a room fitted up for taking a bath. **2.** toilet.

Bath-she-ba (băth shē'bə, băth'shĭ-), *n.* *Bible.* wife of Uriah the Hittite, loved by David; later, David's wife and mother of Solomon. II Sam. 11, 12.

bath-tub (băth'tŭb', bàth'-), *n.* a tub to bathe in, esp. one forming a permanent fixture in a bathroom.

Bath-urst (băth'ərst), *n.* **1.** a seaport in and the capital of Gambia colony, in British West Africa. 12,153 (1931). **2.** a town in SE Australia, in New South Wales. 11,210 (est. 1940).

bath-y-sphere (băth'əsfïr'), *n.* *Oceanog.* a spherical diving apparatus from which to study deep-sea life. [f. Gk. *bathy*(s) deep + -SPHERE]

ba-tik (bətēk', băt'ĭk), *n.* **1.** a method of printing cloth using a wax deposit in the desired pattern. **2.** the fabric so decorated. Also, **battik.** [t. Malay (Javanese)]

ba-tiste (bətēst'), *n.* a fine, delicate cotton fabric of plain weave. [t. F: m. *Baptiste*, name of the alleged first maker]

bat-man (băt'mən), *n.*, *pl.* **-men.** a British army officer's assigned soldier servant.

ba-ton (bă tŏn', băt'ən; *Fr.* bà tôn'), *n.* **1.** a staff, club, or truncheon, esp. as a mark of office or authority. **2.** *Music.* the wand used by a conductor. **3.** *Her.* a sinisterwise ordinary cut off at each end, borne in England as a mark of bastardy. [t. F, r. obs. *baston*, t. OF, der. LL *bastum*; orig. uncert.]

Bat-on Rouge (băt'ən rōōzh'), the capital of Louisiana, in SE part: a port on the Mississippi. 125,629 (1950).

ba-tra-chi-an (bətrā'kĭ ən), *Zool.* —*adj.* **1.** of or pertaining to the *Batrachia*, a term formerly applied to the *Amphibia*, though sometimes restricted to the salientians. —*n.* **2.** an amphibian, sometimes more esp. a salientian. [f. s. Gk. *bátrachos* frog + -IAN]

bats-man (băts'mən), *n.*, *pl.* **-men.** *Brit.* a batter[3].

batt (băt), *n.* a sheet of matted cotton wool. Also, **bat.**

batt., **1.** battalion. **2.** battery.

bat-tal-ion (bətăl'yən), *n.* **1.** *Mil.* a ground force unit composed of three or more companies or similar units. **2.** an army in battle array. **3.** (*often pl.*) a large number; force. [t. F: m. *battaillon*, t. It.: m. *battaglione*]

bat-ten[1] (băt'ən), *v.i.* **1.** to thrive as by feeding; grow fat. **2.** to feed gluttonously; live in luxury at the expense of others. —*v.t.* **3.** to cause to thrive as by feeding; fatten. [t. Scand.; cf. Icel. *batna* improve, der. *bati* change for the better. Cf. OE *bet* better]

bat-ten[2] (băt'ən), *n.* **1.** a light strip of wood usually

having an oblong cross section and used to fasten main members of a structure together. **2.** *Naut.* **a.** a thin strip of wood inserted in a sail to keep it flat. **b.** a strip of wood, as one used to secure the edges of a tarpaulin over a hatchway. —*v.t.* **3.** to furnish with battens. **4.** *Naut.* to fasten (as hatches) with battens and tarpaulins (usually fol. by *down*). [var. of BATON]

bat-ter[1] (băt'ər), *v.t.* **1.** to beat persistently or hard; pound. **2.** to damage by beating or hard usage. —*v.i.* **3.** to deal heavy, repeated blows; pound. —*n.* **4.** *Print.* **a.** a damaged spot on the face of type or plate. **b.** the resulting defect in print. [ME *batere*(n); freq. of BAT[1]]

bat-ter[2] (băt'ər), *n.* a mixture of flour, milk or water, eggs, etc., beaten together for use in cookery. [ME *bater*, *batour.* Cf. OF *bature* beating]

bat-ter[3] (băt'ər), *n.* *U.S.* one who wields a bat or whose turn it is to bat, as in baseball, cricket, etc. [f. BAT[1] + -ER[1]]

bat-ter[4] (băt'ər), *Archit.* —*v.i.* **1.** (of walls, etc.) to slope backward from the base. —*n.* **2.** the receding slope, usually decreasing in thickness. [orig. uncert.]

battering ram, an ancient military engine with a heavy horizontal beam for battering down walls, etc.

Bat-ter-sea (băt'ərsĭ), *n.* a SW borough of London, England, on the Thames. 111,790 (est. 1946).

bat-ter-y (băt'ərĭ), *n.*, *pl.* **-teries. 1.** *Elect.* a combination of two or more galvanic cells electrically connected to work together to produce electric energy. **2.** a set or series of similar machines, parts, or the like, as a group of boilers. **3.** *Mil.* **a.** a parapet or fortification equipped with artillery. **b.** two or more pieces of artillery used for combined action. **c.** a tactical unit of artillery, usually consisting of four guns together with the artillerymen, equipment, etc. **d.** the personnel or complement of officers and men attached to it. **e. in battery**, (of an artillery piece) in firing position, having recuperated from recoil. **4.** *Naval.* a group of guns on, or the whole armament of, a vessel of war. **5.** *Baseball.* the pitcher and catcher together. **6.** act of beating or battering. **7.** *Law.* an unlawful attack upon another by beating or wounding, or even by touching in an offensive manner. **8.** the instrument used in battering. [t. F: m. *batterie*, der. *battre* beat]

Bat-ter-y (băt'ərĭ), *n.* a park in New York City at the S tip of Manhattan, on upper New York Bay.

bat-tik (băt'ĭk), *n.* batik.

bat-ting (băt'ĭng), *n.* **1.** act or manner of using a bat in a game of ball. **2.** cotton or wool in batts or sheets, used as filling for quilts or bedcovers.

bat-tle[1] (băt'əl), *n.*, *v.*, **-tled, -tling.** —*n.* **1.** a hostile encounter or engagement between opposing forces. **2.** participation in such hostile engagements: *wounds received in battle.* **3.** a fight between two persons or animals. **4.** *Archaic.* a battalion. —*v.i.* **5.** to engage in battle. **6.** to struggle; strive: *to battle for freedom.* —*v.t.* **7.** to fight. [ME *batayle*, t. OF: m. *bataille*, g. LL *battālia*, der. L *battuere* beat] —**bat'tler**, *n.*

—**Syn. 1.** BATTLE, ACTION, SKIRMISH mean a conflict between organized armed forces. A BATTLE is a prolonged and general conflict pursued to a definite decision: *the Battle of the Bulge in World War II.* An ACTION is part of a spirited military operation, offensive or defensive: *the army was involved in a number of brilliant actions during the battle.* A SKIRMISH is a slight engagement, often preparatory to larger movements: *attempted reconnaissance led to several minor skirmishes.* **2.** warfare, combat.

bat-tle[2] (băt'əl), *v.t.* *Archaic.* to furnish with battlements. [see BATTLEMENT]

bat-tle-ax (băt'əlăks'), *n.* **1.** an ax for use as a weapon of war. **2.** *Slang.* a cantankerous old woman. Also, **bat'tle-axe'.**

Battle Creek, a city in S Michigan. 48,666 (1950).

battle cruiser, a warship of maximum speed and firepower, but with lighter armor than a battleship.

battle cry, **1.** a cry or shout of troops in battle. **2.** the phrase or slogan in any contest or campaign.

bat-tle-dore (băt'əldōr'), *n.*, *v.*, **-dored, -doring.** —*n.* **1.** an instrument shaped like a tennis racket, but smaller, used in striking a shuttlecock in play. **2.** Also, **battledore and shuttlecock.** the game played with this racket and a shuttlecock. —*v.t.* **3.** to toss to and fro. [ME *batyldore*, ? f. *bater* BATTER[1] + *dore* beetle, with dissimilation]

battle fatigue, *Psychiatry.* a type of psychoneurosis occurring among soldiers engaged in active warfare, and often making continued service in danger zones impossible; combat fatigue.

bat-tle-field (băt'əl fēld'), *n.* the field or ground on which a battle is fought. Also, **bat-tle-ground** (băt'əlground').

bat-tle-ment (băt'əl mənt), *n.* (*often pl.*) *Archit.* an indented parapet, having a series of openings, orig. for shooting through; a crenelated upper wall. [ME *batelment*, ? ult. der. OF *bastiller* fortify] —**bat-tle-ment-ed** (băt'əl mĕn'tĭd), *adj.*

bat-tle-plane (băt'əl plān'), *n.* an airplane designed for combat use.

battle royal, **1.** a fight in which more than two combatants are engaged. **2.** a hard fight or a heated argument; a fight to the finish.

Battlement: A. Merlon; B. Crenel; C. Loophole; D. Machicolation

---

b., blend of, blended; c., cognate with; d., dialect, dialectal; der., derived from; f., formed from; g., going back to; m., modification of; r., replacing; s., stem of; t., taken from; ?. perhaps. See the full key on inside cover.

bat·tle-scarred (băt′əl skärd′), *adj.* bearing scars or damages received in battle.

bat·tle·ship (băt′əl shĭp′), *n.* one of a class of warships which are the most heavily armored and equipped with the most powerful batteries.

battle wagon, *Slang.* a battleship.

bat·tue (bă tōō′, -tū′; *Fr.* bȧ tÿ′), *n. Chiefly Brit.* 1. *Hunting.* **a.** the beating or driving of game from cover, to be killed by sportsmen. **b.** a hunt of this kind. 2. undiscriminating slaughter of defenseless or unresisting crowds. [t. F, prop. fem. pp. of *battre* beat]

bat·ty (băt′ĭ), *adj.,* **-tier, -tiest.** 1. *U.S. Slang.* crazy; silly. 2. of or like a bat.

Ba·tum (bä tōōm′), *n.* a seaport in the SW Soviet Union, on the SE coast of the Black Sea. 70,807 (1939).

bau·ble (bô′bəl), *n.* 1. a cheap piece of ornament; trinket; gewgaw. 2. a jester's staff. [ME *babel,* t. OF: toy, prob. der. *bel,* g. L *bellus* pretty]

Bau·cis and Phi·le·mon (bô′sĭs; fə lē′mən), a poor and aged Phrygian couple who offered hospitality to Zeus and Hermes in disguise, and were rewarded.

Bau·de·laire (bōd lĕr′), *n.* **Pierre Charles** (pyĕr shärl), 1821–67, French poet and critic.

Bau·douin I (bō dwăn′), *n.* born 1930, king of Belgium since 1951.

bau·drons (bô′drənz), *n. Scot.* a cat.

Bau·haus (bou′hous′), *n. German.* a school established in Weimar in 1918 by Walter Gropius (born 1883) to create a functional experimental architecture, utilizing all the resources of art, science, and technology.

baulk (bôk), *v.i., v.t., n.* balk.

Bau·tzen (bout′sən), *n.* a city in E Germany, on the Spree river: Napoleon's victory over the Prussians and Russians, 1813. 41,877 (1939).

baux·ite (bôk′sīt, bō′zīt), *n.* a rock, consisting chiefly of aluminum oxide or hydroxide with various impurities: the principal ore of aluminum. [f. Les *Baux,* in southern France + -ITE¹]

Ba·var·i·a (bə vâr′ĭə), *n.* a state in S Germany: formerly a kingdom. 8,222,982 pop. (1939); 29,378 sq. mi. *Cap.:* Munich. German, **Bayern.**

Ba·var·i·an (bə vâr′ĭən), *adj.* 1. of or pertaining to Bavaria, its inhabitants, or their dialect. —*n.* 2. a native or an inhabitant of Bavaria. 3. the High German speech of most of Bavaria and Austria, and of the Sudeten Germans.

baw·bee (bô bē′, bô′bē), *n. Scot.* 1. an old Scotch bullion coin, originally worth about 3 halfpence of English coin, later 6d. 2. *Colloq.* a halfpenny. [named after a mintmaster, the laird of Sille*bawby*]

baw·cock (bô′kŏk′), *n. Archaic or Dial.* (used familiarly) a fine fellow. [t. F: m. *beau coq* fine cock]

bawd (bôd), *n.* a procuress or procurer. [ME *bawde,* ? t. F: m. *baud* gay, t. WGmc.; cf. OE *bald* bold]

bawd·y (bô′dĭ), *adj.,* **bawdier, bawdiest.** obscene; indecent. —**bawd′i·ly,** *adv.* —**bawd′i·ness,** *n.*

bawl (bôl), *v.t.* 1. to utter or proclaim by outcry; shout out. 2. to cry for sale, as a hawker. 3. *U.S. Colloq.* to scold (fol. by *out*). —*v.i.* 4. to cry or wail lustily. —*n.* 5. a loud shout; an outcry. [ME *bawl(en),* prob. t. ML: m. *baulāre* bark as a dog; but cf. Icel. *baula* low as a cow] —**bawl′er,** *n.*

Bax·ter (băk′stər), *n.* **Richard,** 1615–91, British Puritan preacher, scholar, and writer.

bay¹ (bā), *n. Phys. Geog.* 1. a recess or inlet in the shore of a sea or lake between two capes or headlands, not as large as a gulf but larger than a cove. 2. a recess of land, partly surrounded by hills. 3. *U.S.* an arm of a prairie, extending into woods and partly surrounded by them. [ME *baye,* t. OF: m. *baie,* g. LL *baia,* of doubtful orig.]

bay² (bā), *n.* 1. *Archit.* **a.** the part of a window included between two mullions. **b.** a recessed space projecting outward from the line of a wall, as to contain a window. **c.** a bay window. **d.** *Chiefly Brit.* a space or division of a wall, building, etc., between two vertical architectural features or members. 2. *Aeron.* **a.** any portion of an airplane set off by two successive bulkheads or other bracing members. **b.** a compartment in an aircraft: *a bomb bay, an engine bay.* 3. a compartment, as in a barn for storing hay. 4. *Naut.* the forward part of a ship between decks on either side, formerly often used as a hospital. [ME, t. OF: m. *baee* an opening, ult. der. LL *badāre* gape]

bay³ (bā), *n.* 1. a deep, prolonged bark, as of a hound in hunting. 2. a stand made by a hunted animal to face or repel pursuers, or of a person forced to face a foe or difficulty: *to stand at bay, be brought to bay.* 3. the position of the pursuers or foe thus kept off. —*v.i.* 4. to bark, esp. with a deep prolonged sound, as a hound in hunting. —*v.t.* 5. to beset with deep prolonged barking. 6. to express by barking. 7. to bring to or hold at bay. [ME *baye(n),* t. OF: m. *baier;* ? g. LL *badāre* gape]

Architectural bays
F. Window bay;
C. Triforium
bay; A. Arch
of aisle

bay⁴ (bā), *n.* 1. the European laurel, *Laurus nobilis;* sweet bay. 2. a West Indian tree, *Pimenta acris,* whose leaves are used in making bay rum. 3. any of various laurellike trees. 4. *U.S.* any of several magnolias. 5. an honorary garland or crown bestowed for victory or excellence. 6. (*pl.*) fame; renown. [ME, t. OF: m. *baie,* g. L *bāca,* bacca berry]

bay⁵ (bā), *n.* 1. reddish-brown; chestnut. 2. a bay horse. —*adj.* 3. (of horses, etc.) of the color bay. [ME, t. OF: m. *bai,* g. L *badius*]

Ba·yard (bā yärd′), *n.* 1. **Pierre Terrail, Seigneur de** (pyĕr ter rä′y, sĕn yœr′ də), c1473–1524, the heroic French knight "without fear and without reproach." 2. any man of heroic courage and unstained honor.

Bay·ard (bā′ərd), *n.* 1. a magical legendary horse in medieval chivalric romances. 2. a mock-heroic name for any horse. 3. (*l.c.*) *Archaic.* a bay horse. [ME, t. OF: f. *bai* BAY⁵ + -*ard* -ARD]

bay·ber·ry (bā′bĕr′ĭ), *n., pl.* **-ries.** 1. any of certain shrubs or trees of the genus *Myrica,* as *M. carolinensis,* a shrub common on seacoasts, and *M. cerifera* (wax myrtle). 2. the berry of such a plant. 3. a West Indian tree, *Pimenta acris,* whose leaves are used in making bay rum. [f. BAY⁴ + BERRY]

Bay City, a city in E Michigan: a port near the mouth of the Saginaw river. 52,523 (1950).

Bay·ern (bī′ərn), *n.* German name of **Bavaria.**

Ba·yeux tapestry (bä yōō′, bä-; *Fr.* bȧ yœ′), a strip of linen 231 feet long and 20 inches wide, preserved in Bayeux, a town in NW France. Its colored embroidery pictures events leading to the Norman conquest of England, and it probably dates from the 12th century.

Bayle (bĕl), *n.* **Pierre** (pyĕr), 1647–1706, French philosopher and critic.

bay·o·net (bā′ə nĭt), *n., v.,* **-neted, -neting.** —*n.* 1. a stabbing or slashing instrument of steel, made to be attached to or at the muzzle of a rifle. —*v.t.* 2. to kill or wound with the bayonet. [t. F: m. *baïonette,* der. *Ba-yonne,* in France, where first made]

Ba·yonne (bā yōn′ *for 1;* bä yôn′ *for 2*), *n.* 1. a city in NE New Jersey. 77,203 (1950). 2. a seaport in SW France, near the Bay of Biscay. 32,620 (1946).

bay·ou (bī′ōō), *n., pl.* **-ous.** *Southern U.S.* an arm or outlet of a lake, river, etc. [t. Louisiana F, t. Choctaw (Muskhogean): m. *bayuk* small stream]

Bay·reuth (bī′roit′), *n.* a city in central Germany, in N Bavaria: music festivals founded by Richard Wagner. 45,028 (1939).

bay rum, a fragrant liquid used as a cosmetic, etc., esp. after shaving, prepared by distilling the leaves of the bayberry, *Pimenta acris,* with rum, or by mixing oil from them with alcohol, water, and other oils.

Bay State, Massachusetts.

bay tree, the European laurel, *Laurus nobilis.*

bay window, 1. a window forming an extension in a room and projecting outward from the wall of the building, esp. one rising from the ground or basement. 2. *Humorous.* a fat man's protuberance in front.

bay·wood (bā′wŏŏd′), *n.* a kind of mahogany, esp. found near the Gulf of Campeche, in Mexico.

ba·zaar (bə zär′), *n.* 1. a market place or quarter containing shops. 2. any place or establishment for the sale of miscellaneous goods. 3. a sale of miscellaneous articles for some charitable or other special object. Also, **ba·zar′.** [t. F: m. *bazar,* t. Ar., t. Pers.]

Ba·zaine (bä zĕn′), *n.* **François Achille** (frän swä′ ȧ shēl′), 1811–88, French general and marshal.

Ba·zin (bä zăn′), *n.* **Réné François Nicolas Marie** (rə nĕ′ frän swä′ nē kô lä′ mȧ rē′), 1853–1932, French novelist.

ba·zoo·ka (bə zōō′kə), *n. Mil.* a cylindrical rocket launcher, an individual infantry weapon penetrating several inches of armor plate, used to destroy tanks and other armored military vehicles.

B.B.A., Bachelor of Business Administration.

bbl., *pl.* **bbls.** barrel.

B.C., 1. before Christ. From 20 B.C. to A.D. 50 is 70 years. 2. Bachelor of Chemistry. 3. British Columbia.

B.C.E., 1. Bachelor of Chemical Engineering. 2. Bachelor of Civil Engineering.

bd., *pl.* **bds.** 1. board. 2. bond. 3. bound. 4. bundle.

B.D., Bachelor of Divinity.

B/D, bank draft.

bdel·li·um (dĕl′ĭəm, -yəm), *n.* 1. a fragrant gum resin obtained from certain burseraceous plants, as *Commiphora.* 2. a plant yielding it. 3. a substance mentioned in the Bible (Gen. 2:12 and Num. 11:7), variously interpreted to mean gum resin, carbuncle, crystal, or pearl. [ME *bdelyum* (Wyclif), t. L (Vulgate): m. *bdellium* (Gen. 2:12 and Num. 11:7), t. Gk.: m. *bdéllion,* translating Heb. *b'dōlakh*]

bd. ft., 1. board feet. 2. board foot.

bdl., *pl.* **bdls.** bundle.

B.D.S., Bachelor of Dental Surgery.

be (bē; *unstressed* bĭ), *v., pres. indic. sing.* 1 **am;** 2 **are** or (*Archaic*) **art;** 3 **is;** *pl.* **are;** *pt. indic.* 1 **was;** 2 **were** or (*Archaic*) **wast** or **wert;** 3 **was;** *pl.* **were;** *pres. subj.* **be;** *pt. subj.* 1 **were;** 2 **were** or (*Archaic*) **wert;** 3 **were;** *pl.* **were;** *pp.* **been;** *ppr.* **being.** —*substantive.* 1. to exist; have reality; live; take place; occur; remain as before: *he is no more, it was not to be, think what might have been, the wedding was last week.* —*copula.* 2. a link connecting a subject with predicate or qualifying words in assertive, interrogative, and imperative sentences, or serving to form infinitive and participial phrases: *you are late, he is much to blame, is he here? try to be just, the art of being agreeable.* —*auxiliary.* **3.** used with the present participle of a principal verb to form the progressive tense (*I am waiting*), or with a past participle in passive forms, regularly of transitive verbs (*the date was fixed, it must be done*) and formerly, as still to some extent, of intransitives (*I am done, he is come*). [ME *been*, OE *beon*, g. IE base *bheu-* become; now used to make inf., pres. and past participles, and pres. subj.; for pres. ind., see AM, IS, ARE (g. IE base *es-* exist); for pret., see WAS, WERE (g. IE base *wes-* remain)]

be-, a prefix of W Germanic origin, meaning "about," "around," "all over," and hence having an intensive and often disparaging force, much used as an English ormative of verbs (and their derivatives), as in *besiege, becloud, bedaub, beplaster, bepraise,* and often serving to form transitive verbs from intransitives or from nouns or adjectives, as in *begrudge, belabor, befriend, belittle.* [OE, unstressed form of *bī* by]

Be, *Chem.* beryllium.

B.E., **1.** Bachelor of Education. **2.** Bachelor of Engineering. **3.** bill of exchange.

B/E, bill of exchange. Also, **b.e.**

beach (bēch), *n.* **1.** the sand or loose waterworn pebbles of the seashore. **2.** that part of the shore of the sea, or of a large river or lake, washed by the tide or waves. —*v.t., v.i.* **3.** *Naut.* to run or haul up (a ship or boat) on the beach. [cf. OE *bece* brook] —**beach'less,** *adj.* —Syn. **2.** coast, seashore, strand. See **shore**[1].

beach-comb·er (bēch'kō'mər), *n.* **1.** one who lives by gathering articles along the beaches, as from wreckage; a vagrant of the beach or coast, esp. a white man in South Pacific regions. **2.** a long wave rolling in from the ocean.

beach flea, any of various small hopping amphipods (family *Orchestidae*) found on beaches; a sand hopper.

Beach flea,
Orchestia agilis
(enlarged)

beach·head (bēch'hed'), *n.* the area of lodgment which is the first objective of a military force landing on an enemy shore.

beach-la-Mar (bēch'lə mär'), *n.* a pidgin language based on English, spoken in the Southwest Pacific.

beach wagon, *U.S.* station wagon.

beach·y (bē'chĭ), *adj. Obs. or Rare.* covered with pebbles or sand.

bea·con (bē'kən), *n.* **1.** a guiding or warning signal, such as a fire, esp. one on a pole, tower, hill, etc. **2.** a tower or hill used for such purposes. **3.** a lighthouse, signal buoy, etc., on a coast or over dangerous spots at sea to warn and guide vessels. **4.** a radio beacon. **5.** any person, thing, or act that warns or guides. —*v.t.* **6.** to serve as a beacon to; guide. **7.** to furnish or mark with beacons. —*v.i.* **8.** to serve or shine as a beacon. [ME *beken*, OE *bēac(e)n*] —**bea'con·less,** *adj.*

Bea·cons·field (bē'kənz fēld'), *n.* See **Disraeli.**

bead (bēd), *n.* **1.** a small ball of glass, pearl, wood, etc., with a hole through it, strung with others like it, and used as an ornament or in a rosary. **2.** (*pl.*) a necklace. **3.** (*pl.*) a rosary. **4.** say, tell, or count one's beads, to say prayers and count them off by means of the beads on the rosary. **5.** any small globular or cylindrical body. **6.** a bubble rising through effervescent liquid. **7.** a mass of such bubbles on the surface of a liquid. **8.** a drop of liquid: *beads of sweat, etc.* **9.** the front sight of a gun. **10.** aim. **11.** *Archit., etc.* **a.** a narrow convex molding, usually more or less semicircular in section. **b.** any of various pieces similar in some sections to this type of molding. **12.** *Chem.* a globule of borax or some other flux, supported on a platinum wire, in which a small amount of some substance is heated in a flame as a test for its constituents, etc. **13.** *Metall.* the rounded mass of refined metal obtained by cupellation. —*v.t.* **14.** to ornament with beads. —*v.i.* **15.** to form beads; form in beads or drops. [ME *bede* prayer, rosary bead, aphetic var. of *ibed,* OE *gebed* prayer] —**bead'ed,** *adj.* —**bead'-like',** *adj.*

bead·house (bēd'hous'), *n.* an almshouse whose beneficiaries were required to pray for the founder. Also, **bedehouse.**

bead·ing (bē'dĭng), *n.* **1.** material composed of or adorned with beads. **2.** narrow lacelike trimming. **3.** narrow openwork trimming through which ribbon may be run. **4.** *Archit.* **a.** a bead. **b.** beads collectively.

bea·dle (bē'dəl), *n.* **1.** an official in British universities who, bearing a mace, supervises and leads processions. **2.** *Eccles.* a parish officer having various subordinate duties, as keeping order during services, waiting on the clergyman, etc. Also, *Archaic,* **bedel, bedell.** [southeastern ME *bedel,* OE *bydel* apparitor, herald]

bea·dle·dom (bē'dəl dəm), *n.* a stupid show or exercise of authority, as by subordinate officials.

bead·roll (bēd'rōl'), *n.* **1.** *Rom. Cath. Ch.* a list of persons to be prayed for. **2.** any list or catalogue.

bead-ru·by (bēd'rōō'bĭ), *n., pl.* **-bies.** the false lily of the valley, *Maianthemum canadense,* a low herb with small white flowers and red bead-shaped berries.

beads·man (bēdz'mən), *n., pl.* **-men.** **1.** one who prays for another, as a duty, and esp. when paid for it. **2.** an inmate of a poorhouse. Also, **bedesman.** —**beads·wom·an** (bēdz'wŏom'ən), *n., fem.*

bead·work (bēd'wûrk'), *n.* **1.** ornamental work made of or with beads. **2.** beading.

bead·y (bē'dĭ), *adj.,* **beadier, beadiest. 1.** beadlike; small, globular, and glittering: *beady eyes.* **2.** covered with or full of beads.

bea·gle (bē'gəl), *n.* one of a breed of small hounds with short legs and drooping ears, used esp. in hunting. [ME *begle;* orig. uncert.]

Beagle,
(15 in. high at the shoulder

beak[1] (bēk), *n.* **1.** the horny bill of a bird; the neb. **2.** a horny head part in animals, as in turtle, duckbill, etc., similar to a bird's beak. **3.** *Slang.* a person's nose. **4.** anything beaklike or ending in a point, as the lip of a pitcher or a beaker. **5.** *Bot.* a narrowed or prolonged tip. **6.** *Naut.* a powerful construction of metal, or of timber sheathed with metal, forming a part of the bow of many older type warships, for ramming an enemy's ship. **7.** *Archit.* a little pendent fillet with a channel behind it forming a drip and preventing water from trickling down the faces of lower architectural members. [ME *beke,* t. OF: m. *bec,* g. LL *beccus,* of Celtic orig.] —**beaked** (bēkt, bē'kĭd), *adj.* —**beak'less,** *adj.* —**beak'like',** *adj.*

beak[2] (bēk), *n. Brit. Colloq.* **1.** magistrate; judge. **2.** *Brit. Slang.* schoolmaster. [orig. unknown]

beak·er (bē'kər), *n.* **1.** a large drinking vessel with a wide mouth. **2.** contents of a beaker. **3.** a flat-bottomed cylindrical vessel, usually with a pouring lip. [var. (influenced by BEAK[1]) of d. E *bicker,* ME *biker,* t. Scand.; cf. Icel. *bikarr* (? ult. t. L: m. *bicārium*)]

beam (bēm), *n.* **1.** a thick and relatively long piece of timber, shaped for use. **2.** a similar piece of metal, stone, etc. **3.** *Bldg. Trades.* one of the principal horizontal supporting members in a building or the like, as for supporting a roof or floor. **4.** *Shipbuilding.* one of the strong transverse pieces of timber or metal stretching across a ship to support the deck, hold the sides in place, etc. **5.** *Naut.* **a.** the side of a vessel, or the direction at right angles to the keel, with reference to the wind, sea, etc. **b.** the greatest breadth of a ship. **6.** the widest part. **7.** *Mach.* **a.** an oscillating lever of a steam engine, transferring the motion from piston rod to crankshaft. **b.** a roller or cylinder in a loom, on which the warp is wound before weaving. **c.** a similar cylinder on which cloth is wound as it is woven. **8.** the transverse bar of a balance from the ends of which the scales or pans are suspended. **9.** a ray, or bundle of parallel rays, of light or other radiation. **10.** the angle at which a microphone or loud-speaker functions best. **11.** the cone-shaped range of effective use of a microphone or loud-speaker. **12.** a gleam; suggestion: *a beam of hope.* **13.** *Radio, Aeron.* a signal transmitted along a narrow course, used to guide pilots through darkness, bad weather, etc. **14.** on the beam, **a.** on the course indicated by a radio beam. **b.** *Naut.* at right angles with the keel. **c.** *Slang.* just right; exact; correct. **15.** off the beam, **a.** not on the course indicated by a radio beam. **b.** *Slang.* wrong; incorrect. **16.** fly the beam, *Radio, Aeron.* to be guided by a beam. —*v.t.* **17.** to emit in or as in beams or rays. **18.** *Radio.* to transmit (a signal) on a narrow beam. —*v.i.* **19.** to emit beams, as of light. **20.** to look or smile radiantly. [ME *beem,* OE *bēam* tree, piece of wood, ray of light, c. G *baum* tree] —**beamed,** *adj.* —**beam'less,** *adj.* —**beam'like',** *adj.* —Syn. **19.** See **shine.**

Beaker
(def. 3)

beam-ends (bēm'endz'), *n.pl. Naut.* **1.** the ends of a ship's beams. **2.** on her beam-ends, so far inclined on one side that the deck beams are practically vertical.

beam·ing (bē'mĭng), *adj.* radiant; bright; cheerful. —**beam'ing·ly,** *adv.*

beam-pow·er tube (bēm'pou'ər), *Radio.* a vacuum tube in which the stream of electrons flowing to the plate is focused by the action of a set of auxiliary, charged elements, giving an increase in output power.

beam·y (bē'mĭ), *adj.,* **beamier, beamiest. 1.** emitting beams, as of light; radiant. **2.** broad in the beam, as a ship. **3.** *Zool.* having antlers, as a stag.

bean (bēn), *n.* **1.** the edible nutritious seed of various species of leguminous plants, esp. of the genus *Phaseolus.* **2.** a plant producing such seeds, used as a snap bean, as a shell bean, or as dry beans. **3.** any of various other beanlike seeds or plants, as the coffee bean. **4.** *Slang.* head. —*v.t.* **5.** *Slang.* to hit on the head, esp. with a baseball. [ME *bene,* OE *bēan,* c. G *bohne*] —**bean'like',** *adj.*

bean-bag (bēn'băg'), *n.* a small cloth bag filled with beans, used as a toy.

bean caper, a small tree, *Zygophyllum Fabago,* of the eastern Mediterranean regions, whose flower buds are used as a substitute for capers.

bean·ie (bē'nĭ), *n.* a small brimless hat.

bean·o (bē'nō), *n.* bingo.

bean-pole (bēn'pōl'), *n.* **1.** a tall pole for a bean plant to climb on. **2.** *Slang.* a tall, lanky person.

bean-stalk (bēn'stôk'), *n.* the stem of a bean plant.

bean tree, any of several trees bearing pods resembling those of a bean, as the catalpa and the carob tree.

---

b., blend of, blended; c., cognate with; d., dialect, dialectal; der., derived from; f., formed from; g., going back to; m., modification of; r., replacing; s., stem of; t., taken from; ?, perhaps. See the full key on inside cover.

bear[1] (bâr), v., bore or (Archaic) bare, borne or born, bearing. —v.t. 1. to hold up; support: to bear the weight of the roof. 2. to carry: to bear gifts. 3. to conduct; guide; take: they bore him in his quarters. 4. to press or push against: the crowd was borne back by the police. 5. to render; afford; give: to bear testimony. 6. to transmit or spread (gossip, tales, etc.). 7. to sustain without yielding or suffering injury (usually negative unless qualified): I can't bear your scolding. 8. to undergo: to bear the blame. 9. to accept or have as an obligation: to bear responsibility, cost, etc. 10. to hold up under; be capable of: his claim doesn't bear close examination. 11. to be fit for or worthy of: the story doesn't bear repeating. 12. to have and be entitled to: to bear title. 13. to possess as a quality, characteristic, etc.; have in or on: bear traces, an inscription, etc. 14. to stand in (a relation or ratio): the relation that price bears to profit. 15. to carry in the mind: to bear love, a grudge, etc. 16. to exhibit; show. 17. to have and use; exercise: to bear sway. 18. to manage (oneself, one's body, head, etc.): to bear oneself erectly. 19. to conduct (oneself). 20. to give birth to: to bear quintuplets. 21. to produce by natural growth: plants bear leaves. 22. to confirm; prove (fol. by out): the facts will bear me out. —v.i. 23. to hold, or remain firm, as under pressure (often fol. by up). 24. to be patient (fol. by with). 25. to press (fol. by on, against, down, etc.). 26. to have an effect, reference, or bearing (fol. by on): time bears heavily on him. 27. to tend in course or direction; move; go. 28. to be situated: the ship bears due west. 29. to bring forth young, fruit, etc. [ME bere(n), OE beran; akin to G gebären bring forth, L ferre bear, Gk. phērein, Skt. bhar-] —Syn. 4. thrust, drive, force. 7. tolerate, brook, abide. 8. BEAR, STAND, ENDURE refer to supporting the burden of something distressing, irksome, or painful. BEAR is the general word and STAND its colloquial equivalent, but with an implication of stout spirit: to bear a disappointment well, to stand a loss. ENDURE implies continued resistance and patience in bearing through a long time: to endure torture. 15. entertain, harbor, cherish.

bear[2] (bâr), n., v., beared, bearing, —n. 1. any of the plantigrade, carnivorous or omnivorous mammals of the family Ursidae, having massive bodies, coarse heavy fur, relatively short limbs, and almost rudimentary tails. 2. any of various animals resembling the bear, as the ant bear. 3. a gruff, clumsy, or rude person. 4. (in general business) one who believes that conditions are or will be unfavorable. 5. Stock Exchange. one who sells short with the expectation of covering at a lower price (opposed to a bull). 6. Astron. either of two constellations in the northern hemisphere, the **Great Bear** (Ursa Major) and the **Little Bear** (Ursa Minor). 7. **the Bear**, Russia. —adj. 8. of, having to do with, or caused by declining prices in stocks, etc.: bear market. —v.t. 9. Stock Exchange, etc. to attempt to lower the price of; operate in for a decline in price. [ME bere, OE bera, c. G bär]

American black bear,
Euarctos americanus (5 ft. long)

bear·a·ble (bâr′ə bəl), adj. capable of being borne; endurable. —**bear′a·ble·ness**, n. —**bear′a·bly**, adv.

bear·bait·ing (bâr′bā′tǐng), n. the sport of setting dogs to fight a captive bear.

bear·ber·ry (bâr′bĕr′ĭ), n., pl. -ries. 1. a trailing evergreen ericaceous shrub, Arctostaphylos Uva-ursi, bearing small bright-red berries and tonic, astringent leaves. 2. a related species, A. alpina, bearing black berries (**alpine bearberry** or **black bearberry**). 3. any of certain other plants, as Ilex decidua, a holly of the southern U.S. 4. the American, or large, cranberry, Oxycoccus macrocarpus.

beard (bĭrd), n. 1. the growth of hair on the face of an adult man, sometimes exclusive of the mustache. 2. Zool. a tuft, growth, or part resembling or suggesting a human beard, as the tuft of long hairs on the lower jaw of a goat, or a cluster of fine, hairlike feathers at the base of the beak of certain birds. 3. Bot. a tuft or growth of awns or the like, as in wheat, barley, etc. 4. a barb or catch on an arrow, fishhook, knitting needle, crochet needle, etc. 5. Print. the part of a type which connects the face with the shoulder of the body; the neck. See diag. under **type**. —v.t. 6. to seize, pluck, or pull the beard of. 7. to oppose boldly; defy. 8. to supply with a beard. [ME berd, OE beard, c. G bart] —**beard′ed**, adj. —**beard′less**, adj. —**beard′less·ness**, n. —**beard′like′**, adj.

Beard (bĭrd), n. 1. **Charles Austin**, 1874–1948, and his wife, **Mary**, born 1876, U.S. historians. 2. **Daniel Carter**, 1850–1941, one of the founders of the Boy Scouts of America.

Beards·ley (bĭrdz′lĭ), n. **Aubrey Vincent** (ô′brĭ), 1872–98, British illustrator.

beard·tongue (bĭrd′tŭng′), n. any plant of the scrophulariaceous genus Pentstemon.

bear·er (bâr′ər), n. 1. a person or thing that carries, upholds, or brings. 2. one who presents an order for money or goods. 3. a tree or plant that yields fruit or flowers. 4. the holder of rank or office. 5. pallbearer.

bear garden, 1. a place for keeping or exhibiting bears, as for bearbaiting. 2. any place of tumult.

bear grass, 1. any of several American plants of the liliaceous genus Yucca, having grasslike foliage. 2. any of certain similar liliaceous plants, as the camass.

bear·ing (bâr′ĭng), n. 1. the manner in which a person bears or carries himself, including posture, gestures, etc.: a man of dignified bearing. 2. act, capability, or period of producing or bringing forth: a tree past bearing. 3. that which is produced; a crop. 4. act of enduring or capacity to endure. 5. reference or relation (fol. by on): some bearing on the problem. 6. Archit. a. a supporting part, as in a structure. b. the contact area between a load-carrying member and its support. 7. Mach. a part in which a journal, pivot, or the like, turns or moves. 8. (often pl.) direction or relative position: the pilot lost his bearings. 9. Geog. a horizontal angle measured from 0 to 90° fixing the direction of a line with respect to either the north or south direction. True bearings are referred to the true north direction, **magnetic bearings** to magnetic north (or south). 10. Her. any single device on a coat of arms; a charge. —Syn. 1. See **manner**.

bearing rein, a checkrein (def. 1).

bear·ish (bâr′ĭsh), adj. 1. like a bear; rough; burly; morose; rude. 2. Stock Exchange, etc. unfavorable and tending to cause a decline in price. —**bear′ish·ly**, adv. —**bear′ish·ness**, n.

bear leader, a tutor or traveling companion of a wealthy or aristocratic youth.

Bear River, a river in Utah, Wyoming, and Idaho, flowing into Great Salt Lake. ab. 450 mi.

bear's-breech (bârz′brěch′), n. one of the acanthus plants, Acanthus mollis.

bear's-ear (bârz′ĭr′), n. a primrose, the auricula.

bear's-foot (bârz′fŏŏt′), n. any of various species of hellebore, esp. Helleborus foetidus.

bear·skin (bâr′skĭn′), n. 1. the skin or pelt of a bear. 2. a tall black fur cap worn esp. by soldiers. 3. a coarse, shaggy woolen cloth for overcoats.

bear·wood (bâr′wŏŏd′), n. a buckthorn, Rhamnus purshiana.

beast (bēst), n. 1. any animal except man, but esp. a large four-footed one. 2. the animal nature common to man and nonhumans. 3. a coarse, filthy, or otherwise beastlike human. [ME beste, t. OF, g. LL besta, var. of L bestia] —**beast′like′**, adj. —Syn. 1. See **animal**.

beast·ly (bēst′lĭ), adj., -lier, -liest. 1. of or like a beast; bestial. 2. Brit. Colloq. nasty; disagreeable. —adv. 3. Brit. Colloq. exceedingly. —**beast′li·ness**, n.

beast of burden, an animal used to carrying loads.

beat (bēt), v., beat, beaten or beat, beating, n. —v.t. 1. to strike repeatedly, as in chastising, threshing, metalworking, making a batter, etc. 2. to dash against: rain beating the trees. 3. to flutter, flap, or rotate in. 4. to sound as on a drum. 5. to break, forge, or make by blows. 6. to produce or destroy (an idea, habit, etc.) by repeated efforts. 7. to make (a path) by repeated treading. 8. Music. to mark (time) by strokes, as with the hand or a metronome. 9. Hunting. to scour (the forest, grass, or brush) for game. 10. to overcome in a contest; defeat. 11. to be superior to. 12. to be too difficult for; baffle. 13. U.S. Slang. to swindle; get ahead of: he beat him. 14. **beat a retreat**, to withdraw hurriedly. —v.i. 15. to strike repeated blows; pound. 16. to throb or pulsate. 17. to dash (against, on, etc.). 18. to resound under blows, as a drum. 19. to win in a contest. 20. to play, as on a drum. 21. to scour cover for game. 22. Physics. to make a beat or beats. 23. to permit beating. 24. Naut. to make progress to windward by sailing full and by, first on one tack and then on the other. 25. **beat about the bush**, to approach a matter in a roundabout way; avoid coming to the point. —n. 26. a stroke or blow. 27. the sound made by it. 28. a throb or pulsation. 29. Horol. the stroke made by the action of the escapement of a watch or clock. 30. one's beaten path or habitual round. 31. Music. a. the audible, visual, or mental marking of the metrical divisions of music. b. a stroke of the hand, baton, etc., marking time division or accent for music during performance. 32. Pros. the accent stress, or ictus, in a foot or rhythmical unit of poetry. 33. Physics. a periodic pulsation caused by simultaneous occurrence of two waves, currents, or sounds of slightly different frequency. 34. U.S. Journalism. the publishing of some piece of news in advance of, or to the exclusion of, its rivals. 35. a subdivision of a county, as in Mississippi. —adj. 36. U.S. Colloq. exhausted; worn out. [ME bete(n), OE bēatan, c. Icel. bauta] —Syn. 1. BEAT, HIT, POUND, STRIKE, THRASH refer to the giving of a blow or blows. BEAT implies the giving of repeated blows: to beat a rug. To HIT is usually to give a single blow, definitely directed: to hit a ball. To POUND is to give heavy and repeated blows, often with the fist: to pound a nail, the table. To STRIKE is to give one or more forceful blows suddenly or swiftly: to strike a gong. To THRASH implies inflicting repeated blows as punishment, to show superior strength, and the like: to thrash a child. 16. See **pulsate**.

beat·en (bē′tən), adj. 1. having undergone blows; hammered. 2. much trodden; commonly used: the beaten path. 3. defeated. 4. exhausted.

beat·er (bē′tər), n. 1. a person or thing that beats. 2. an implement or device for beating something: an egg beater. 3. Hunting. one who rouses or beats up game.

be·a·tif·ic (bē′ə tĭf′ĭk), *adj.* **1.** rendering blessed. **2.** blissful: *a beatific vision or smile.* [t. LL: s. *beātificus*] —**be′a·tif′i·cal·ly,** *adv.*

be·at·i·fi·ca·tion (bĭ ăt′ə fə kā′shən), *n.* **1.** act of beatifying. **2.** state of being beatified. **3.** *Rom. Cath. Ch.* the official act of the Pope whereby a deceased person is declared to be enjoying the happiness of heaven, and therefore a proper subject of religious honor and public cult in certain places.

be·at·i·fy (bĭ ăt′ə fī′), *v.t.,* **-fied, -fy·ing. 1.** to make blissfully happy. **2.** *Rom. Cath. Ch.* to declare (a deceased person) to be among the blessed, and thus entitled to specific religious honor. [t. F: m.s. *beatifier,* t. L: m. *beātificāre* make happy]

beat·ing (bē′tĭng), *n.* **1.** act of a person or thing that beats. **2.** the same act administered as punishment; whipping. **3.** a defeat. **4.** a pulsation or throb.

be·at·i·tude (bĭ ăt′ə tūd′, -tōōd′), *n.* **1.** supreme blessedness; exalted happiness. **2.** (*often cap.*) *Theol.* any one of the declarations of blessedness pronounced by Christ in the Sermon on the Mount, as "Blessed are the poor, etc." Matt. 5:3-11. [t. L: m. *beātitūdo*]

Be·a·trice (bē′ə trĭs; *It.* bĕ′ä trē′chĕ), *n.* (in Dante's *Vita Nuova* and *Commedia Divina*) a symbolic figure developed from the lady of Dante's love on earth.

Beat·ty (bē′tĭ), *n.* **David,** (*1st Earl of the North Sea and of Brooksby*) 1871-1936, British admiral.

beau (bō), *n., pl.* **beaus, beaux** (bōz; *Fr.* bō). **1.** a lover; swain. **2.** an escort. **3.** a dandy; fop. [ME, t. OF, n. use of *beau* (earlier *bel*) handsome, g. L *bellus.* See BELLE], *adj.*

Beau Brum·mell (brŭm′əl), **1.** (*George Bryan Brummell*) 1778-1840, a man who set the fashion in men's clothes in England. **2.** a fop; dandy.

Beau·fort scale (bō′fərt), *Meteorol.* a numerical scale for indicating the force or velocity of the wind, ranging from 0 for calm to 12 for hurricane, or velocities above 75 miles per hour. [named after Sir Francis *Beaufort,* 1774-1857, British admiral who devised it]

beau geste (bō zhĕst′), *pl.* **beaux gestes** (bō zhĕst′). *French.* a fine gesture, often only for effect.

Beau·har·nais (bō är nĕ′), *n.* **1. Eugénie Hortense de,** (œ zhē nē′ ôr tä̃s′ də), 1783-1837, queen of Holland: wife of Louis Bonaparte. **2. Joséphine de,** (jō′zə fēn′; *Fr.* zhō zĕ fēn′), 1763-1814, first wife of Napoleon: empress of France, 1804-09.

beau i·de·al (ī dē′əl, ī dēl′), **1.** a conception of perfect beauty. **2.** a model of excellence. [t. F]

Beau·mar·chais (bō mär shĕ′), *n.* **Pierre Augustin Caron de** (pyĕr ōgÿs tăn′ kå rôn′ də), 1732-99, French dramatist.

beau monde (bō′ mônd′; *Fr.* bō mônd′), *French.* the fashionable world.

Beau·mont (bō′mŏnt), *n.* **1.** a city in SE Texas. 94,014 (1950). **2. Francis,** 1584-1616, British dramatist: collaborated with John Fletcher.

Beau·re·gard (bō′rə gärd′; *Fr.* bōr går′), *n.* **Pierre Gustave Toutant de** (pyĕr gÿs tȧv′ tōō tän′ də), 1818-93, Confederate general in the U.S. Civil War.

beau·te·ous (bū′tĭ əs), *adj. Chiefly Poetic.* beautiful. —**beau′te·ous·ly,** *adv.* —**beau′te·ous·ness,** *n.*

beau·ti·cian (bū tĭsh′ən), *n.* a person who operates or works in a beauty parlor.

beau·ti·ful (bū′tə fəl), *adj.* having beauty; delighting the eye; admirable to the taste or the mind. —**beau′ti·ful·ly,** *adv.* —**beau′ti·ful·ness,** *n.* —**Syn.** BEAUTIFUL, HANDSOME, LOVELY, PRETTY refer to a pleasing appearance. That is BEAUTIFUL which has perfection of form, color, etc., or noble and spiritual qualities: *a beautiful landscape, girl* (not *man*). HANDSOME often implies stateliness or pleasing proportion and symmetry: *a handsome man.* That which is LOVELY is beautiful but in a warm and endearing way: *a lovely smile.* PRETTY implies a moderate but noticeable beauty, esp. in that which is small or of minor importance: *a pretty child.* —**Ant.** ugly.

beau·ti·fy (bū′tə fī′), *v.t., v.i.,* **-fied, -fy·ing** to make or become beautiful. [f. BEAUTY + -FY] —**beau·ti·fi·ca·tion** (bū′tə fə kā′shən), *n.* —**beau′ti·fi′er,** *n.*

beau·ty (bū′tĭ), *n., pl.* **-ties. 1.** that quality of any object of sense or thought whereby it excites an admiring pleasure; qualification of a high order for delighting the eye or the aesthetic, intellectual, or moral sense. **2.** something beautiful, esp. a woman. **3.** a grace, charm, or pleasing excellence. [ME *beute,* t. OF: m. *beaute, der. beau.* See BEAU] —**Syn. 1.** loveliness, pulchritude.

beauty parlor, *U.S.* an establishment for the hairdressing, manicuring, etc., of women. Also, **beauty shop.**

beauty spot, 1. a patch worn on the face or elsewhere to set off the fairness of the skin. **2.** a mole or other trifling mark on the skin. **3.** any spot, place, or feature of especial beauty.

beaux (bōz; *Fr.* bō), *n.* a pl. of beau.

beaux-arts (bō zàr′), *n.pl. French.* the fine arts, as painting, sculpture, etc.

beaux-es·prits (bō zĕs prē′), *French.* pl. of bel-esprit.

bea·ver[1] (bē′vər), *n.* **1.** an amphibious rodent of the genus *Castor,* valued for its fur and formerly for castor, and noted for its ingenuity in damming

Beaver, *Castor canadensis*
(43 in. long, including tail)

streams with trees, branches, stones, mud, etc. **2.** its fur. **3.** a flat, round hat made of beaver fur or a similar fabric. **4.** a man's high silk hat. **5.** a heavy woolen cloth. [ME *bever,* OE *beofor,* akin to G *biber*] —**bea′ver·like′,** *adj.*

bea·ver[2] (bē′vər), *n.* *Armor.* **1.** a piece of armor protecting the lower part of the face. **2.** a visor (def. 1). [ME, t. OF: m. *baviere,* orig., bib, der. *bave* saliva]

bea·ver·board (bē′vər bôrd′), *n.* **1.** a light, stiff sheeting made of wood fiber and used in building, esp. for partitions, temporary structures, etc. **2.** (*cap.*) a trademark for this substance.

B. Beaver

Bea·ver·brook (bē′vər brŏŏk′), *n.* **William Maxwell Aitken** (āt′kĭn), **1st Baron,** born 1879, British newspaper publisher, born in Canada.

be·bee·rine (bə bĭr′ēn, -ĭn), *n.* *Pharm.* an alkaloid resembling quinine, obtained from the bark of the greenheart and other plants.

be·bee·ru (bə bĭr′ōō), *n.* greenheart (def. 1). [native name in Guiana]

Be·bel (bā′bəl), *n.* **Ferdinand August** (fĕr′dĭ nänt′ ou′gōost), 1840-1913, German socialist and writer.

be·bop (bē′bŏp), *n.* *Jazz.* a style of composition and performance characterized by dissonant harmony, complex rhythmic devices, and experimental, often bizarre, instrumental effects. [fanciful coinage] —**be′bop·per,** *n.*

be·calm (bĭ käm′), *v.t.* **1.** (*usually in pp.*) to halt (a ship, etc.) by a lack of wind. **2.** to calm.

be·came (bĭ kām′), *v.* pt. of become.

be·cause (bĭ kôz′, -kŏz′), *conj.* **1.** for the reason that; due to the fact that: *the game was called because it rained.* —*adv.* **2.** by reason; on account (fol. by *of*): *the game was called because of rain.* [ME *bi cause* by cause] —**Syn. 1.** BECAUSE, AS, SINCE, FOR, INASMUCH AS agree in implying a reason for an occurrence or action. BECAUSE introduces a direct reason: *I was sleeping because I was tired.* As and SINCE are so casual as to imply merely circumstances attendant on the main statement. *as* (*or since*) *I was tired, I was sleeping.* The reason, proof, or justification introduced by FOR is like an afterthought or a parenthetical statement: *I was sleeping, for I was tired.* INASMUCH AS implies concession; the main statement is true in view of the circumstances introduced by this conjunction: *inasmuch as I was tired, it had seemed best to sleep.*

bec·ca·fi·co (bĕk′ə fē′kō), *n., pl.* **-cos.** any of several small European birds, esp. the garden warbler, *Sylvia hortensis,* esteemed as a delicacy in Italy. [t. It.: f. *becca(re)* peck + *fico* fig]

bé·cha·mel sauce (bě shà měl′), a white sauce flavored with carrots, onions, seasoning, etc. [t. F, named after the inventor, Louis de *Béchamel*]

be·chance (bĭ chăns′, -chäns′), *v.i., v.t.,* **-chanced, -chancing.** to befall.

be·charm (bĭ chärm′), *v.t.* to charm; captivate.

bêche-de-mer (běsh də měr′), *n.* **1.** a trepang. **2.** Beach-la-Mar. [F: sea spade]

Bech·u·a·na (běch′ŏŏ ä′nə, běk′yŏŏ-), *n., pl.* **-ana, -anas.** a Bantu living in the region of S Africa between the Orange and Zambesi rivers.

Bech·u·a·na·land (běch′ŏŏ ä′nə lănd′, běk′yŏŏ-), *n.* a British protectorate in S Africa. 265,800 pop. (1936); ab. 275,000 sq. mi. *Cap.:* Mafeking.

beck[1] (běk), *n.* **1.** a beckoning gesture. **2.** *Scot.* a bow or curtsy of respect. **3. at one's beck and call,** ready to obey one immediately; subject to one's slightest wish. —*v.t., v.i.* **4.** to beckon. [short for BECKON]

beck[2] (běk), *n.* *Chiefly Brit. Dial.* a brook. [ME, t. Scand.; cf. Icel. *bekkr,* akin to OE *bece*]

beck·et (běk′ĭt), *n.* *Naut.* any of various contrivances for holding spars, etc., in position, as a short rope with a knot at one end which can be secured in a loop at the other end. **2.** a loop or ring of rope forming a handle, or the like. [orig. unknown]

Beck·et (běk′ĭt), *n.* **Saint Thomas à,** 1118?-70, archbishop of Canterbury: murdered because of his opposition to Henry II's policies toward the church.

becket bend, *Naut.* sheet bend.

Beck·ford (běk′fərd), *n.* **William,** 1759-1844, British writer.

beck·on (běk′ən), *v.t., v.i.* **1.** to signal, summon, or direct by a gesture of the head or hand. **2.** to lure; entice. —*n.* **3.** a beckoning. [ME *beknen,* OE *bēcnan,* der. *bēacen* sign. Cf. BEACON] —**beck′on·er,** *n.*

be·cloud (bĭ kloud′), *v.t.* **1.** to darken or obscure with clouds. **2.** to make confused: *becloud the argument.*

be·come (bĭ kŭm′), *v.,* **became, become, becoming.** —*v.i.* **1.** to come into being; come or grow to be (as stated): *he became tired.* **2.** to be the fate (*of*): *what will become of him?* —*v.t.* **3.** to befit in appearance; suit: *that dress becomes you.* [ME *becume(n),* OE *becuman* come about, happen]

be·com·ing (bĭ kŭm′ĭng), *adj.* **1.** attractive: *a becoming dress.* **2.** suitable; proper: *a becoming sentiment.* —*n.* **3.** any process of change. **4.** *Aristotelian Metaphys.* any change involving realization of potentialities, as a movement from the lower level of potentiality to the higher level of actuality. —**be·com′ing·ly,** *adv.* —**be·com′ing·ness,** *n.* —**Syn. 2.** fitting, meet, appropriate.

Bec·que·rel (běk rěl′), *n.* **1. Alexandre Edmond** (à lěk sän′dr ěd môn′), 1820-91, French physicist (son of Antoine César and father of Antoine Henri). **2. Antoine**

César (än twän′ sĕ zär′), 1788–1878, French physicist. **3. Antoine Henri** (än twän′ än rē′), 1852–1908, French physicist.

Bec·que·rel rays, *Obsolesc.* rays emitted by radioactive substances, [named after A. H. *Becquerel*]

bed (bĕd), *n., v.,* **bedded, bedding.** —*n.* **1.** a piece of furniture upon which or within which a person sleeps. **2.** the mattress and bedclothes together with the bedstead. **3.** the bedstead alone. **4.** the use of a bed for the night; lodging. **5.** matrimonial rights and duties. **6.** any resting place. **7.** something resembling a bed in form or position. **8.** a piece of ground (in a garden) in which plants are grown. **9.** the bottom of a body of water. **10.** a piece or part forming a foundation or base. **11.** a rock layer or stratum. **12.** a foundation surface of earth or rock supporting a track or pavement; *a road bed.* **13.** the under surface of a brick, shingle, slate, or tile in position. **14.** either of the horizontal surfaces of a stone in position. **15.** the flat surface in a printing press on which the form of type is laid. **16.** *Zool.* flesh enveloping the base of a claw. —*v.t.* **17.** to provide with a bed. **18.** to put to bed. **19.** to make a bed for (a horse, cattle, etc.) (fol. by *down*). **20.** *Hort.* to plant in or as in a bed. **21.** to lay flat, or in a bed or layer. **22.** to embed, as in a substance. **23.** *Archaic.* to go to bed with. —*v.i.* **24.** to go to bed. **25.** *Geol.* to form a compact layer or stratum. [ME; OE *bedd*, c. D *bed*, G *bett*] **—bed′less,** *adj.* **—bed′like′,** *adj.*

be·daub (bĭ dôb′), *v.t.* **1.** to daub all over; besmear; soil. **2.** to ornament gaudily or excessively.

be·daz·zle (bĭ dăz′əl), *v.t.,* **-zled, -zling.** to blind or confuse by dazzling.

bed·bug (bĕd′bŭg′), *n.* a small flat, wingless, hemipterous, bloodsucking insect, *Cimex lectularius,* that infests houses and esp. beds; cimex.

Bedbug. *Cimex lectularius* (⅓ in. long)

bed·cham·ber (bĕd′chăm′bər), *n.* bedroom.

bed·clothes (bĕd′klōz′, -klōᵺz′), *n.pl.* coverings for a bed; sheets, blankets, etc.

bed·ding (bĕd′ĭng), *n.* **1.** blankets, sheets, for a bed; bedclothes. **2.** litter; straw, etc., as a bed for animals. **3.** *Bldg. Trades.* foundation or bottom layer of any kind. **4.** *Geol.* arrangement of rocks in strata.

Bed·does (bĕd′ōz), *n.* **Thomas Lovell** (lŭv′əl), 1803–1849, British dramatist and poet.

Bede (bēd), *n.* **Saint,** ("the Venerable Bede") A.D. 673?–735, British monk, historian, and theologian; wrote earliest history of England. Also, **Baeda.**

be·deck (bĭ dĕk′), *v.t.* to deck out; showily adorn.

bede·house (bēd′hous′), *n.* beadhouse.

be·del (bē′dəl), *n. Archaic.* beadle. Also, **be′dell.**

bedes·man (bēdz′mən), *n., pl.* **-men.** beadsman. **—bedes·wom·an** (bēdz′wŏŏm′ən), *n. fem.*

be·dev·il (bĭ dĕv′əl), *v.t.,* **-iled, -iling** or (*Brit.*) **-illed, -illing. 1.** to treat diabolically; torment maliciously. **2.** to possess as with a devil; bewitch. **3.** to confound; muddle; spoil. **—be·dev′il·ment,** *n.*

be·dew (bĭ dū′, -dōō′), *v.t.* to wet with or as with dew.

bed·fast (bĕd′făst′, -fäst′), *adj.* confined to bed.

bed·fel·low (bĕd′fĕl′ō), *n.* **1.** a sharer of one's bed. **2.** close companion: *politics makes strange bedfellows.*

Bed·ford (bĕd′fərd), *n.* **1. John Plantagenet, Duke of,** 1389–1435, British regent of France. **2.** a city in central England. 51,890 (est. 1946). **3.** Bedfordshire.

Bedford cord, cotton, worsted, rayon, or silk, distinctively woven with a lengthwise, corded effect.

Bed·ford·shire (bĕd′fərd shĭr′, -shər), *n.* a county in central England. 285,000 pop. (est. 1946); 473 sq. mi. *Co. seat:* Bedford. Also, **Bedford, Beds.**

be·dight (bĭ dīt′), *v.t.,* **-dight, -dight** or **-dighted, -dighting.** *Archaic.* to deck out; array.

be·dim (bĭ dĭm′), *v.t.,* **-dimmed, -dimming.** to make dim. **—Ant.** illuminate, illumine.

Bed·i·vere (bĕd′ə vĭr′), *n.* **Sir,** *Arthurian Legend.* the knight who brought the dying King Arthur to the barge in which the three queens bore him to the Isle of Avalon.

be·di·zen (bĭ dī′zən, -dĭz′ən), *v.t.* to dress or adorn gaudily. [be- + DIZEN] **—be·di′zen·ment,** *n.*

bed·lam (bĕd′ləm), *n.* **1.** a scene of wild uproar and confusion. **2.** (*cap.*) an insane asylum in SE London, Hospital of St. Mary of Bethlehem. **3.** any lunatic asylum; a madhouse. [ME *bedlem,* alter. of *Bethlehem*]

bed·lam·ite (bĕd′lə mīt′), *n.* a lunatic.

bed linen, sheets and pillowcases.

Bed·loe Island (bĕd′lō), a small island in upper New York Bay: site of the Statue of Liberty.

bed molding, *Archit.* **1.** the molding, or series of moldings, between the corona and the frieze of an entablature. **2.** any molding under a projection.

Bed·ou·in (bĕd′ōŏ ĭn), *n.* **1.** an Arab of the desert, in Asia or Africa; nomadic Arab. **2.** a nomad; wanderer. [t. F, t. Ar.: m. *badawiyin,* pl. of *badawī* desert dweller]

bed·pan (bĕd′păn′), *n.* **1.** a shallow toilet pan for use by persons confined to bed. **2.** a warming pan.

bed·plate (bĕd′plāt′), *n.* a plate, platform, or frame supporting the lighter parts of a machine.

bed·post (bĕd′pōst′), *n.* one of the upright supports of a bedstead.

be·drag·gle (bĭ drăg′əl), *v.t.,* **-gled, -gling.** to make limp and soiled as with wet or dirt.

bed·rail (bĕd′rāl′), *n.* the board between the head and foot boards at the side of a bed.

bed·rid (bĕd′rĭd′), *adj.* **1.** bedridden. **2.** worn out. [ME *bedrede,* OE *bedreda, -rida,* lit., bed rider]

bed·rid·den (bĕd′rĭd′ən), *adj.* confined to bed. [var. (by confusion with pp.) of BEDRID]

bed·rock (bĕd′rŏk′), *n.* **1.** *Geol.* unbroken solid rock, overlaid in most places by soil or rock fragments. **2.** bottom layer; lowest stratum. **3.** any firm foundation.

bed·room (bĕd′rōōm′, -rŏŏm′), *n.* a sleeping room.

Beds (bĕdz), *n.* Bedfordshire.

bed·side (bĕd′sīd′), *n.* **1.** the side of a bed, esp. as the place of one in attendance on the sick. —*adj.* **2.** attending a sick person: *a good bedside manner.* **3.** at or for a bedside: *a bedside table.*

bed·sore (bĕd′sōr′), *n.* a sore due to prolonged contact with a bed, as in a long illness.

bed·spread (bĕd′sprĕd′), *n.* an outer covering, usually decorative, for a bed.

bed·spring (bĕd′sprĭng′), *n.* a set of springs supporting a mattress.

bed·stead (bĕd′stĕd′, -stĭd), *n.* the framework of a bed supporting the springs and a mattress.

bed·straw (bĕd′strô′), *n.* a rubiaceous plant, *Galium verum* (**our Lady's bedstraw**) or some allied species: formerly used like straw for beds.

bed·time (bĕd′tīm′), *n.* time to go to bed.

bed·ward (bĕd′wərd), *adv.* to bed. Also, **bed′wards.**

bee¹ (bē), *n.* **1.** any of various hymenopterous insects of the superfamily *Apoidea,* which includes many social and solitary bees of several families, as the bumblebees, honeybees, etc. **2.** the common honeybee, *Apis mellifera.* **3. bee in one's bonnet or head, a.** an obsession. **b.** a slightly crazy idea, attitude, fad, etc. **4.** *U.S.* a local gathering for work, entertainment, contests, etc.: *husking bee, spelling bee.* [ME; OE *bēo*] **—bee′-like′,** *adj.*

Common honeybee. *Apis mellifera*
A, Queen; B, Worker; C, Drone

bee² (bē), *n. Naut.* a piece of hard wood, bolted to the side of the bowsprit, through which to reeve stays. [OE *bēag, bēah* ring]

bee balm, a perennial garden flower of the genus *Monarda,* esp. the Oswego tea, *Monarda didyma.*

Bee·be (bē′bĭ), *n.* **Charles William,** born 1877, U.S. naturalist, explorer, and writer.

bee beetle, a European beetle, *Trichodes apiarius,* which sometimes infests beehives.

bee·bread (bē′brĕd′), *n.* a protein food mixture, containing pollen, manufactured and stored up by bees for their young.

beech (bēch), *n.* **1.** any tree of the genus *Fagus,* of temperate regions, having a smooth gray bark, and bearing small edible triangular nuts. **2.** the wood of such a tree. [ME *beche,* OE *bēce*] **—beech′en,** *adj.*

Bee·cham (bē′chəm), *n.* **Sir Thomas,** born 1879, British orchestral conductor and impressario.

beech·drops (bēch′drŏps′), *n.* **1.** a low annual plant, *Leptamnium virginianum,* without green foliage, parasitic upon the roots of the beech. **2.** the squawroot.

Bee·cher (bē′chər), *n.* **1. Henry Ward,** 1813–87, U.S. preacher and writer. **2.** his father, **Lyman** (lī′mən), 1775–1863, U.S. preacher and theologian.

beech mast, the edible nuts of the beech, esp. when lying on the ground.

beech·nut (bēch′nŭt′), *n.* the small, triangular, edible nut of the beech.

bee eater, any of the family *Meropidae,* comprising Old World insectivorous birds with a long, slender bill, and brilliant plumage.

beef (bēf), *n., pl.* **beeves** (bēvz) for 1; **beefs** for 5, *v.* —*n.* **1.** a bull, cow, or steer of the genus *Bos,* esp. if intended for meat. **2.** the flesh of such an animal, used for food. **3.** *Colloq.* brawn; muscular strength. **4.** *Colloq.* weight, as of human flesh. **5.** *U.S. Slang.* a complaint. —*v.i.* **6.** *U.S. Slang.* to complain; grumble. [ME, t. OF: m. *boef,* g. L *bōs* ox] **—beef′less,** *adj.*

beef cattle, cattle raised for beef, such as Hereford.

beef·eat·er (bēf′ē′tər), *n.* **1.** one who eats beef. **2.** a well-fed person. **3.** a yeoman of the English royal guard or a warder of the Tower of London.

bee fly, any fly of the dipterous family *Bombyliidae,* members of which more or less resemble bees.

beef·steak (bēf′stāk′), *n.* a slice of beef for broiling, etc.

beef tea, an extract of beef made by heating chopped beef in water and straining it.

beef·wit·ted (bēf′wĭt′ĭd), *adj.* thick-witted; stupid.

beef·y (bē′fĭ), *adj.* **beefier, beefiest.** fleshy; brawny; solid; heavy. **—beef′i·ness,** *n.*

bee gum, *South and West U.S.* **1.** a gum tree, hollowed as by decay, in which bees live or from which hives are made. **2.** a beehive.

bee·hive (bē′hīv′), *n.* **1.** a hive or receptacle, conventionally dome-shaped, serving as a habitation for bees. **2.** a crowded, busy place.

bee·keep·er (bē′kē′pər), *n.* one who raises bees.

bee killer, a robber fly (family *Asilidae*).

bee-line (bē′lĭn′), *n.* a direct line, like the course of bees returning to a hive.

Be-el-ze-bub (bē′ĕl′zə bŭb′), *n.* **1.** Bible. "the prince of the devils" (Matt. 12:24); the devil. **2.** a devil. **3.** (in Milton's *Paradise Lost*) one of the fallen angels, second only to Satan himself. [ult. t. Heb.: m. *Ba′al-zebub* Philistine god, II Kings 1:2 (? meaning "lord of flies")]

bee martin, the kingbird, *Tyrannus tyrannus*.

been (bĭn), *v.* pp. of **be**.

bee plant, any plant much used by bees for food materials, esp. the cleome (*Cleome surrelata*) or figwort.

beer (bĭr), *n.* **1.** an alcoholic beverage made by brewing and fermentation from cereals, usually malted barley, and flavored with hops, etc., to give a bitter taste. **2.** any of various beverages, whether alcoholic or not made from roots, molasses or sugar, yeast, etc.: *root beer, ginger beer.* [ME *bere*, OE *bēor*, c. G *bier*]

Beer (bĭr), *n.* **Thomas,** 1889–1940, U.S. author.

beer and skittles, Brit. drinks and pleasure.

Beer-bohm (bĭr′bōm), *n.* **Sir Max,** born 1872, British author and caricaturist.

Beer-she-ba (bĭr shē′bə, bĭr′shĭ-), *n.* Bible. a town near the southern extremity of Biblical Palestine. See **Dan** (def. 2).

beer-y (bĭr′ĭ), *adj.,* **beerier, beeriest. 1.** of, like, or abounding in beer. **2.** affected by or suggestive of beer. —**beer′i-ness,** *n.*

beest-ings (bēs′tĭngz), *n.pl.* colostrum, the first milk of a mammal, esp. a cow, after giving birth. Also, **biest-ings.** [OE var. of *bȳsting*, der. *bēost* beestings, c. G *biest*]

bees-wax (bēz′wăks′), *n.* **1.** the wax secreted by bees, of which they construct their honeycomb; wax (def. 1). —*v.t.* **2.** to rub, polish, or treat with beeswax.

bees-wing (bēz′wĭng′), *n.* a thin film formed in port and some other wines after long keeping.

beet (bēt), *n.* **1.** any of various biennial plants of the chenopodiaceous genus *Beta*, whose varieties include the **red beet,** which has a fleshy edible root, and the **sugar beet,** which yields sugar. **2.** the root of such a plant. **3.** the leaves served as a salad or cooked vegetable. [OE *bēte*, t. L: m. *bēta*] —**beet′like′,** *adj.*

Bee-tho-ven (bā′tō vən; *Ger.* bāt′hō-fən), *n.* **Ludwig van** (lōōd′vĭkн fän), 1770–1827, German composer.

bee-tle¹ (bē′təl), *n.* **1.** any insect of the order *Coleoptera*, characterized by having forewings modified as hard, horny structures, useless in flight. **2.** any of various insects resembling beetles, as the common cockroach. [ME *bētylle, bityl,* OE *bitula,* lit., *biter*]

Ground beetle, *Calosoma scrutator* (1¼ in. long)

bee-tle² (bē′təl), *n., v.,* **-tled, -tling.** —*n.* **1.** a heavy hammering or ramming instrument, usually of wood, used to drive wedges, force down paving stones, consolidate earth, etc. **2.** any of various wooden instruments for beating linen, mashing potatoes, etc. —*v.t.* **3.** to use a beetle on; drive, ram, beat, or crush with a beetle. **4.** to finish (cloth) by means of a beetling machine. [ME and d. OE *bētel,* r. OE *bīetl,* der. *bēatan* beat]

bee-tle³ (bē′təl), *adj., v.,* **-tled, -tling.** —*adj.* **1.** projecting, overhanging: *beetle brows.* —*v.i.* **2.** to project; jut out; overhang. [back formation from BEETLE-BROWED] —**bee′tling,** *adj.*

bee-tle-browed (bē′təl broud′), *adj.* **1.** having heavy projecting eyebrows. **2.** scowling; sullen. [ME *bitel-browed,* f. *bitel* biting + BROW + -ED³. See BEETLE¹]

bee-tle-head (bē′təl hĕd′), *n.* a stupid person; blockhead. [see BEETLE²] —**bee′tle-head′ed,** *adj.*

bee tree, a hollow tree used by wild bees as a hive, esp. the basswood or American linden.

beet sugar, sugar from the roots of the sugar beet.

beeves (bēvz), *n.* pl. of **beef** (def. 1).

bef., before.

B.E.F., British Expeditionary Forces.

be-fall (bĭ fôl′), *v.,* **-fell, -fallen, -falling.** —*v.i.* **1.** to happen or occur. **2.** Archaic. to come (*to*) as by right. —*v.t.* **3.** to happen to. [ME *befallen,* OE *befeallan*]

be-fit (bĭ fĭt′), *v.t.,* **-fitted, -fitting.** to be fitting or appropriate for; be suited to: *his clothes befit the occasion.*

be-fit-ting (bĭ fĭt′ĭng), *adj.* fitting; proper. —**be-fit′ting-ly,** *adv.* —**Syn.** appropriate, suitable, seemly.

be-fog (bĭ fŏg′, -fôg′), *v.t.,* **-fogged, -fogging.** to involve in fog or obscurity; confuse.

be-fool (bĭ fōōl′), *v.t.* **1.** to fool; deceive; dupe. **2.** to treat as a fool.

be-fore (bĭ fōr′), *adv.* **1.** in front; in advance; ahead. **2.** in time preceding; previously. **3.** earlier or sooner: *begin at noon, not before.* —*prep.* **4.** in front of; ahead of; in advance of: *before the house.* **5.** previously to; earlier than: *before the war.* **6.** ahead of; in the future of; awaiting: *the golden age is before us.* **7.** in preference to; rather than: *they would die before yielding.* **8.** in precedence of, as in order or rank: *we put freedom before fame.* **9.** in the presence or sight of: *before an audience.* **10.** under the jurisdiction or consideration of: *before a magistrate.* —*conj.* **11.** previously to the time when: *before we go.* **12.** sooner than; rather than: *I will die before I submit.* [ME *before(n),* OE *beforan,* f. *be* by + *foran* before] —**Ant. 1.** behind. **2.** afterward. **3.** later.

be-fore-hand (bĭ fōr′hănd′), *adv., adj.* in anticipation; in advance; ahead of time.

be-fore-time (bĭ fōr′tĭm′), *adv.* Archaic. formerly.

be-foul (bĭ foul′), *v.t.* to make foul; defile; sully.

be-friend (bĭ frĕnd′), *v.t.* to act as a friend to; aid.

be-fud-dle (bĭ fŭd′əl), *v.t.,* **-dled, -dling. 1.** to make stupidly drunk. **2.** to confuse, as with glib argument.

beg (bĕg), *v.,* **begged, begging.** —*v.t.* **1.** to ask for in charity; ask as alms. **2.** to ask for, or of, with humility or earnestness, or as a favor: *to beg forgiveness, to beg him to forgive me.* **3.** to take for granted without warrant: *to beg the point.* **4. beg the question,** to assume the very point raised in a question. —*v.i.* **5.** to ask alms or charity; live by asking alms. **6.** to ask humbly or earnestly: *begging for help.* [ME *beggen,* OE *bedecian*] —**Syn. 2.** entreat, pray, crave, implore, beseech, petition. BEG and REQUEST are used in certain conventional formulas, in the sense of *ask.* BEG, once a part of many formal expressions used in letter writing, debate, etc., is now used chiefly in courteous formulas like *I beg your pardon, the Committee begs to report,* etc. REQUEST, more impersonal and now more formal, is used in giving courteous orders (*you are requested to report*) and in commercial formulas like *to request payment.*

be-gan (bĭ găn′), *v.* pt. of **begin.**

be-gat (bĭ găt′), *v.* Archaic. pt. of **beget.**

be-get (bĭ gĕt′), *v.t.,* **begot, begotten** or **begot, begetting. 1.** to procreate or generate (used chiefly of the male parent). **2.** to cause; produce as an effect. [ME *begete(n),* f. BE- + GET, r. OE *begitan*] —**be-get′ter,** *n.*

beg-gar (bĕg′ər), *n.* **1.** one who begs alms, or lives by begging. **2.** a penniless person. **3.** (in playful use) a wretch or rogue: *a cute little beggar.* —*v.t.* **4.** to reduce to beggary; impoverish. **5.** to exhaust the resources of: *to beggar description.* [ME *begger,* f. BEG + -ER¹. See -AR³] —**beg-gar-dom** (bĕg′ər dəm), *beg′gar-hood′,* *n.*

beg-gar-ly (bĕg′ər lĭ), *adj.* like or befitting a beggar; wretchedly poor; mean. —**beg′gar-li-ness,** *n.*

beg-gar's-lice (bĕg′ərz lĭs′), *n.* **1.** (construed as *pl.*) seeds or fruits which stick to clothing. **2.** (*sing.* or *pl.*) any plant producing them. Also, **beg′gar-lice′.**

beg-gar's-tick (bĕg′ərs tĭk′), *n.* **1.** one of the prickly awns of *Bidens frondosa* or similar plants. **2.** (*pl.*) the plant itself.

beg-gar-tick (bĕg′ər tĭk′), *n.* **1.** beggar's-tick. **2.** beggar's-lice.

beg-gar-y (bĕg′ər ĭ), *n.* **1.** the condition of utter poverty. **2.** beggar's collectively.

Beg-hard (bĕg′ärd, bĭ gärd′), *n.* a member of one of certain former religious communities of men which arose in Flanders in the 13th century, living after the manner of the Beguines. [t. ML: s. *Beghardus*]

be-gin (bĭ gĭn′), *v.,* **began, begun, beginning.** —*v.i.* **1.** to enter upon an action; take the first step; commence; start. **2.** to come into existence; arise; originate. —*v.t.* **3.** to take the first step in; set about; start; commence. **4.** to originate; be the originator of. [ME *beginne(n),* OE *beginnan*] —**be-gin′ner,** *n.* —**Syn. 3.** BEGIN, COMMENCE, INITIATE, START (when followed by noun or gerund) refer to setting into motion or progress something which continues for some time. BEGIN is the common term: *to begin knitting a sweater.* COMMENCE is a more formal word, often suggesting a more prolonged or elaborate beginning: *to commence proceedings in court.* INITIATE implies an active and often ingenious first act in a new field: *to initiate a new procedure.* START means to make a first move or to set out on a course of action: *to start paving a street.* **4.** institute, inaugurate, initiate. —**Ant. 1.** end.

be-gin-ning (bĭ gĭn′ĭng), *n.* **1.** act or fact of entering upon an action or state. **2.** the point of time or space at which anything begins: *the beginning of the Christian era.* **3.** the first part or initial stage of anything: *the beginnings of science.* **4.** origin; source; first cause: *humility is the beginning of wisdom.* —**Syn. 1.** initiation, inauguration, inception. **2.** start. —**Ant. 1.** ending. **2.** end.

be-gird (bĭ gûrd′), *v.t.,* **-girt** or **-girded, -girding.** to gird about; encompass; surround. [ME *begirden,* OE *begyrdan.* See BE-, GIRD¹]

be-gone (bĭ gôn′ -gŏn′), *v.i.* to go away; depart (usually as an imperative).

be-gon-ia (bĭ gōn′yə, -gō′nĭ ə), *n.* any plant of the tropical genus *Begonia,* including species much cultivated for their handsome, succulent, often varicolored leaves and waxy flowers. [named after Michel *Bégon* (1638–1710), French patron of science]

be-got (bĭ gŏt′), *v.* pt. and pp. of **beget.**

be-got-ten (bĭ gŏt′ən), *v.* pp. of **beget.**

be-grime (bĭ grīm′), *v.t.,* **-grimed, -griming.** to make grimy.

be-grudge (bĭ grŭj′), *v.t.,* **-grudged, -grudging. 1.** to be discontented at seeing (a person) have (something): *to begrudge a man his good fortune.* **2.** to be reluctant to give, grant, or allow: *to begrudge him the money he earned.* —**Syn. 1.** See envy.

be-guile (bĭ gīl′), *v.t.,* **-guiled, -guiling. 1.** to influence by guile; mislead; delude. **2.** to take away from by artful tactics (fol. by *of*). **3.** to charm or divert. **4.** to while away (time) pleasantly. —**be-guile′ment,** *n.* —**be-guil′er,** *n.* —**Syn. 1.** deceive, cheat.

Be-guin (bĕg′ĭn; *Fr.* bĕ găN′), *n.* a Beghard.

be-guine (bĭ gēn′), *n.* **1.** a South American dance in bolero rhythm. **2.** a modern social dance based on the beguine. **3.** music for either of these dances.

Beg·uine (bĕg′ēn; Fr. bĕ gēn′), n. a member of one of certain communities of Roman Catholic women who devote themselves to a religious life but retain private property and may leave at any time. The first of these communities was founded at Liège in the 12th century. [ME begyne, t. MFlem., t. OF: m. beguine, der. beg- in begarde, t. MD: m. begaert mendicant (friar)]

be·gum (bē′gəm), n. India. 1. a Mohammedan woman ruler. 2. a high-ranking Mohammedan lady, often a widow. [t. Hind.: m. begam]

be·gun (bĭ gŭn′), v. pp. of **begin**.

be·half (bĭ hăf′, -häf′), n. 1. side or part (prec. by on): on behalf of his country. 2. interest, favor, or aid (prec. by in): to plead in behalf of a cause. [ME behalve beside, in OE a phrase, be healfe (him) by (his) side; later used as n. by confusion with ME on his halve on his side. See HALF]

be·have (bĭ hāv′), v., -haved, -having. —v.i. 1. to conduct oneself or itself; act: the ship behaves well. 2. to act properly: did the child behave? —v.t. 3. **behave one-self, a.** to conduct oneself in a specified way. b. to conduct oneself properly. [late ME, appar. f. BE- + HAVE hold oneself a certain way]

be·hav·ior (bĭ hāv′yər), n. 1. manner of behaving or acting. 2. Psychol. the actions or activities of the individual as matters of psychological study. 3. the action of any material: the behavior of tin under heat. Also, Brit., **be·hav′iour.**
—Syn. 1. demeanor, manners. BEHAVIOR, CONDUCT, DE-PORTMENT refer to one's mode of acting. BEHAVIOR refers to one's actions before or toward others, esp. on a particular occasion: his behavior at the party was childish. CONDUCT refers to actions v ewed collectively, esp. as measured by an ideal standard of behavior: conduct is judged according to principles of ethics. DEPORTMENT is behavior as related to a code or to an arbitrary standard: deportment is guided by rules of etiquette.

be·hav·ior·ism (bĭ hāv′yə rĭz′əm), n. Psychol. a theory or method that regards objective and accessible facts of behavior or activity of man and animals, as the only proper subject for psychological study. —**be·hav′-ior·ist,** n., adj. —**be·hav′ior·is/tic,** adj.

behavior pattern, Sociol. a recurrent way of acting by an individual or group toward a given object or in a given situation.

be·head (bĭ hĕd′), v.t. to cut off the head of; kill or execute by decapitation.

be·held (bĭ hĕld′), v. pt. and pp. of **behold**.

be·he·moth (bĭ hē′məth, bē′ə-), n. 1. Bible. an animal, perhaps the hippopotamus, mentioned in Job 40:15. 2. U.S. Colloq. a huge and powerful man, beast, etc. [t. Heb.: m. bəhēmōth, pl. of bahēmah beast]

be·hest (bĭ hĕst′), n. bidding or injunction; mandate or command. [ME; OE behǣs promise]

be·hind (bĭ hīnd′), prep. 1. at the back of; in the rear of: behind the house. 2. after; later than: behind schedule. 3. less advanced than; inferior to: behind his class in mathematics. 4. on the farther side of; beyond: behind the mountain. 5. supporting; promoting: he is behind the play. 6. hidden or unrevealed by: malice lay behind her smile. —adv. 7. at or toward the back; in the rear. 8. in a place, state, or stage already passed. 9. remaining; in reserve: greater support is behind. 10. in arrears; behindhand: behind in his rent. 11. slow, as a watch or clock. [ME behinden, OE behindan. See BE-, HIND¹]
—Syn. 1, 2. BEHIND, AFTER both refer to a position following something else. BEHIND applies primarily to position in space, and suggests that one person or thing is at the back of another; it may also refer to a (fixed) time: he stood behind the train, the train is behind schedule. AFTER applies primarily to time; when it denotes position in space, it is not used with precision, and refers usually to bodies in motion: rest after a hard day's work; they entered the room, one after another.

be·hind·hand (bĭ hīnd′hănd′), adv., adj. 1. behind time; late. 2. behind others in progress; backward. 3. in arrears; in debt.

Be·his·tun (bā′hĭs tōōn′), n. a ruined town in W Iran: site of a cliff containing an account carved in Persian, Elamite, and Babylonian cuneiform, which provided the key to cuneiform. Also, **Bisutun.**

be·hold (bĭ hōld′), v., beheld, beholding. —v.t. 1. to observe; look at; see. —inter. 2. look! see! [ME beholde(n), OE behaldan keep] —**be·hold′er,** n.

be·hold·en (bĭ hōl′dən), adj. held or bound by obligation; owing; obliged.

be·hoof (bĭ hōōf′), n. use; advantage; benefit. [OE behōf profit, need, c. G behuf]

be·hoove (bĭ hōōv′), v., -hooved, -hooving. —v.t. 1. to be needful or proper for or incumbent on (chiefly in impersonal use): it behooves me to see him. —v.i. 2. Archaic. to be needful, proper, or due (chiefly in impersonal use). Also, esp. Brit., **be·hove** (bĭ hōv′). [ME behove(n), OE behōfian need. See BEHOOF]

Beh·ring (bā′rĭng), n. 1. Emil von (ā′mēl fən), 1854–1917. German physician and bacteriologist. 2. Vitus (vē′tōōs). See **Bering,** Vitus.

Behr·man (bâr′mən), n. S(amuel) N(athaniel), born 1893, U. S. dramatist.

beige (bāzh), n. very light brown, as of undyed wool; light gray with brownish tinge. [t. F]

Bei·lan Pass (bā län′), a mountain pass NW of Aleppo: the ancient gateway from Asia Minor to Syria.

be·ing (bē′ĭng), n. 1. existence, as opposed to non-existence. 2. conscious existence; life: the aim of our being. 3. mortal existence; lifetime. 4. substance or nature: of such a being as to arouse fear. 5. something that exists: inanimate beings. 6. a living thing. 7. a human being; person. 8. (cap.) God. 9. Philos. a. that which has actuality either materially or in idea. b. absolute existence in a complete or perfect state, lacking no essential characteristic; essence.

Bei·ra (bā′rə), n. a seaport in Mozambique. 24,742 (1940).

Bei·rut (bā′rōōt, bā rōōt′), n. a seaport in and the capital of Lebanon. 233,700 (est. 1942). Also, **Beyrouth.**

be·jew·el (bĭ jōō′əl), v.t., -eled, -eling or (esp. Brit.) -elled, -elling. to adorn with or as with jewels.

bel (bĕl), n. Physics. the unit which measures power ratios equal to the logarithm to the base 10 of the ratio of any two powers. [named after A. G. BELL]

Bel (bāl), n. a deity of the Babylonians and Assyrians, god of the earth. [L: s. Bēlus, t. Gk.: m. Bēlos BAAL]

be·la·bor (bĭ lā′bər), v.t. 1. to beat vigorously; ply with heavy blows. 2. to assail persistently, as with ridicule. 3. Obs. to labor at. Also, Brit., **be·la′bour.**

Be·las·co (bĭ lăs′kō), n. David, 1854–1931, U.S. play-wright and theatrical manager.

be·lat·ed (bĭ lā′tĭd), adj. coming or being late or too late. —**be·lat′ed·ly,** adv. —**be·lat′ed·ness,** n.

be·lay (bĭ lā′), v.t., v.i., -layed, -laying. 1. Naut. to fasten (a rope) by winding around a pin or short rod inserted in a holder so that both ends of the rod are clear. 2. to stop (used chiefly in the imperative). [ME belegge(n), OE beleċ-gan cover. See BE-, LAY¹]

belaying pin, Naut. a pin for use in securing the ends of ropes.

bel can·to (bĕl kän′tō), Music. a smooth, cantabile style of singing. [It.]

Belaying pins, with ropes belayed on them

belch (bĕlch), v.i. 1. to eject wind spasmodically and noisily from the stomach through the mouth; eructate. 2. to emit contents violently, as a gun, geyser, or volcano. 3. to issue spasmodically; gush forth. —v.t. 4. to eject spasmodically or violently; give forth. —n. 5. a belching; eructation. 6. a burst of flame, smoke, gas, etc. [ME belche(n). Cf. OE belcettan] —**belch′er,** n.

bel·dam (bĕl′dəm), n. 1. an old woman, esp. an ugly one; hag. 2. Obs. grandmother. Also, **bel·dame** (bĕl′dəm, -dām′). [ME, grandmother, f. bel- (t. OF: bel-, belle fair) used like GRAND (def. 9) + dam DAME]

be·lea·guer (bĭ lē′gər), v.t. 1. to surround with an army. 2. to surround; beleaguered with annoyances. [t. D: m.s. belegeren, f. be- about + leger camp] —**be·lea′-guered,** adj. —**be·lea′guer·er,** n.

Be·lém (bē lĕn′), n. a seaport in N Brazil, on the Pará river. 227,460 (est. 1944). Also, **Pará.**

bel·em·nite (bĕl′əm nīt′), n. Puleontol. a conical fos-sil, several inches long, consisting of the internal cal-careous rod of an extinct animal allied to the cuttlefish; a thunderstone. [f. s. Gk. bélemnon dart + -ITE¹]

bel·es·prit (bĕl ĕs prē′), n., pl. **beaux-esprits** (bō-zĕs prē′). French. a person of great wit or intellect.

Bel·fast (bĕl′făst, -făst; bĕl făst′, -fäst′), n. a seaport in and the capital of Northern Ireland. 441,700 (est. 1946).

Bel·fort (bĕl fôr′), n. a fortress city in E France, strate-gically located on a pass between the Vosges and Jura Mountains: siege 1870–71; battle, 1944. 37,387 (1946).

bel·fry (bĕl′frĭ), n., pl. -fries. 1. a bell tower, either attached to a church or other building or standing apart. 2. that part of a steeple or other structure in which a bell is hung. 3. a frame of timberwork which sustains a bell. [ME belfray, dissimilated var. of berfrey, t. OF: m. berfrei, t. Gmc.; cf. MHG bercfrit defense shelter] —**bel·fried** (bĕl′frĭd), adj.

Belg., 1. Belgian. 2. Belgium.

bel·ga (bĕl′gə), n. the Belgian currency unit in foreign exchange, introduced 1926, worth five Belgian francs.

Bel·gian (bĕl′jən, -jĭ ən), n. 1. a native or an inhabit-ant of Belgium. —adj. 2. of or pertaining to Belgium.

Belgian Congo, a Belgian colony in central Africa. 10,600,000 pop. (est. 1942); 902,274 sq. mi. Cap.: Leopoldville. Formerly, **Congo Free State.** See map under Victoria, Lake.

Belgian hare, one of a breed of domestic rabbits notable for large size.

Bel·gic (bĕl′jĭk), adj. 1. of or pertaining to the Belgae, an ancient warlike people of northern Gaul. 2. Belgian. [t. L: s. Belgicus, der. Belgae]

Bel·gium (bĕl′jəm, -jĭ əm), n. a kingdom in W Europe, on the North Sea, N of France. 8,344,534 pop. (est. 1945); 11,779 sq. mi. Cap.: Brussels. French, **Bel·gique** (bĕl zhēk′).

Bel·grade (bĕl grād′, bĕl′grād), n. the capital of Yu-goslavia, in the E part, on the Danube. 238,775 (1931). Serbian, **Beograd.**

Bel·gra·vi·a (bĕl grā′vĭ ə), n. a fashionable district in London, England, adjoining Hyde Park.

Bel·gra·vi·an (bĕl grā′vĭ ən), adj. 1. of Belgravia. 2. aristocratic; fashionable.

Be·li·al (bē′lĭ əl, bēl′yəl), n. 1. Theol. the spirit of evil personified; the devil; Satan. 2. (in Milton's Paradise Lost) one of the fallen angels. 3. (in the Bible and rabbinical commentary) worthlessness, wickedness, or destruction. [t. Heb.: m. bəlī-ya′al worthlessness]

be·lie (bǐ lī′), *v.t.*, **-lied, -lying.** **1.** to misrepresent: *his face belied his thoughts.* **2.** to show to be false: *his trembling belied his words.* **3.** to prove false to; fail to justify: *to belie one's faith.* **4.** to lie about; slander. [ME *belye*(n), OE *beleogan*, f. *be-* BE- + *leogan* LIE¹] —**be·li′er,** *n.*

be·lief (bǐ lēf′), *n.* **1.** that which is believed; an accepted opinion. **2.** conviction of the truth or reality of a thing, based upon grounds insufficient to afford positive knowledge: *statements unworthy of belief.* **3.** confidence; faith; trust: *a child's belief in his parents.* **4.** a religious tenet or tenets: *the Christian belief.* [ME *bileve* (with *-ē-* from v.), r. early ME *bileafe*, r. OE *geleafa*, c. G *glaube*] —**Syn. 2.** BELIEF, CERTAINTY, CONVICTION refer to acceptance of, or confidence in, an alleged fact or body of facts as true or right without positive knowledge or proof. BELIEF is such acceptance in general: *belief in astrology.* CERTAINTY indicates unquestioning belief and positiveness in one's own mind that something is true: *I know this for a certainty.* CONVICTION is settled, profound, or earnest belief that something is right: *a conviction that a decision is just.*

be·lieve (bǐ lēv′), *v.*, **-lieved, -lieving.** —*v.i.* **1.** to have confidence (*in*); trust; rely through faith (*on*). **2.** to be persuaded of the truth of anything; accept a doctrine, principle, system, etc. (fol. by *in*): *to believe in public schools.* —*v.t.* **3.** to have belief in; credit; accept as true: *to believe a person or a story.* **4.** to think: *I believe he has left the city.* [ME *bileve*(n), f. *bi-* + *lēven*, d. OE *lēfan*; r. OE (*ge*)*lēfan*, c. G *glauben*] —**be·liev′a·ble,** *adj.* —**be·liev′er,** *n.* —**be·liev′ing·ly,** *adv.*

be·like (bǐ līk′), *adv.* *Archaic.* or *Dial.* very likely, perhaps; probably. [f. BE- + LIKE¹]

Bel·i·sar·i·us (bĕl′ǝ sâr′ĭ ǝs), *n.* A.D. 505?–565, general of the Eastern Roman Empire.

Be·li·tong (bĕ lē′tŏng), *n.* Billiton.

be·lit·tle (bǐ lǐt′ǝl), *v.t.*, **-littled, -littling.** to make little or less important; depreciate; disparage.

be·live (bǐ līv′), *adv. Scot.* before long; soon.

Be·lize (bĕ lēz′), *n.* a seaport in and the capital of British Honduras. 17,289 (1941).

bell¹ (bĕl), *n.* **1.** a metallic sounding instrument, typically cup-shaped with flaring mouth, rung by the strokes of a tongue or clapper or a hammer. **2.** the stroke or sound of such an instrument (used on shipboard to indicate time): *rise at the bell.* **3.** anything of the form of a bell. **4.** the large end of a funnel, or the end of a pipe, tube, or any musical wind instrument, when its edge is turned out and enlarged. **5.** *Zool.* umbrella (def. 2). —*v.t.* **6.** to put a bell on. **7.** to cause to swell (*out*) like a bell. —*v.i.* **8.** to take or have the form of a bell. **9.** to produce bells; be in bell (said of hops when the seed vessels are forming). [ME and OE *belle.* See BELL², BELLOW] —**bell′-like′,** *adj.*

bell² (bĕl), *v.i.*, *v.t.* **1.** to bellow like a deer in rutting time. **2.** *Obs.* to bellow; roar. —*n.* **3.** the cry of a rutting deer. [ME *belle*(n), OE *bellan* roar, c. G *bellen* bark]

Bell (bĕl), *n.* **Alexander Graham,** 1847–1922, U.S. scientist, born in Scotland: invented the telephone.

bel·la·don·na (bĕl′ǝ dŏn′ǝ), *n.* **1.** a poisonous solanaceous plant, *Atropa Belladonna*; deadly nightshade. **2.** a poisonous drug from this plant. [t. It.: lit., fair lady]

belladonna lily, the amaryllis (def. 1).

Bel·la·my (bĕl′ǝ mǐ), *n.* **Edward,** 1850–98, U.S. author.

bell·bird (bĕl′bûrd′), *n.* any of various birds of the southern hemisphere whose notes resemble the sound of a bell, as the honey eater.

bell·boy (bĕl′boi′), *n.* *U.S.* an employee in a hotel who attends to the wants of guests in their rooms.

bell buoy, *Naut.* a buoy having a bell hung on it to ring from the action of the waves. See illus. under **buoy.**

belle (bĕl), *n.* a woman or girl admired for her beauty; a reigning beauty. [t. F, fem. of *beau* BEAU]

Bel·leau Wood (bĕl′ō; *Fr.* bĕ lō′), a forest in N France, NW of Château-Thierry: now a memorial to the U. S. Marines who won a battle there, 1918.

Bel·leek (bǝ lēk′), *n.* a fragile, ornamental porcelain with a bright luster. Also, **Belleek ware.** [named after *Belleek*, Northern Ireland]

Belle Isle, Strait of, the strait between Labrador and Newfoundland. 10–15 mi. wide.

Bel·ler·o·phon (bǝ lĕr′ǝ fŏn′), *n.* *Gk. Legend.* a hero of Corinth who, on the winged horse Pegasus, slew the monster Chimera.

belles-let·tres (bĕl lĕt′r), *n.pl.* the finer or higher forms of literature; literature regarded as a fine art. [F] —**bel·let·rist** (bĕl lĕt′rĭst), *n.* —**bel·le·tris·tic** (bĕl′lĕ trĭs′tĭk), *adj.* —**Syn.** See **literature.**

Belle·ville (bĕl′vĭl), *n.* **1.** a city in SW Illinois. 32,721 (1950). **2.** a city in NE New Jersey. 32,019 (1950).

bell·flow·er (bĕl′flou′ǝr), *n.* a campanula.

bell glass, bell jar.

bell·hop (bĕl′hŏp′), *n.* *U.S. Colloq.* bellboy.

bel·li·cose (bĕl′ǝ kōs′), *adj.* inclined to war; warlike; pugnacious. [t. L: m. s. *bellicōsus*, der. *bellum* war] —**bel′li·cose′ly,** *adv.* —**bel·li·cos·i·ty** (bĕl′ǝ kŏs′ǝ tǐ), *n.*

bel·lig·er·ence (bǝ lǐj′ǝr ǝns), *n.* **1.** warlike nature. **2.** act of carrying on war; warfare.

bel·lig·er·en·cy (bǝ lǐj′ǝr ǝn sǐ), *n.* position or status as a belligerent; state of being actually engaged in war.

bel·lig·er·ent (bǝ lǐj′ǝr ǝnt), *adj.* **1.** warlike; given to waging war. **2.** of warlike character: *a belligerent tone.* **3.** waging war; engaged in war: *the belligerent powers.* **4.** pertaining to war, or to those engaged in war: *belligerent rights, etc.* —*n.* **5.** a state or nation at war, or a member of the military forces of such a state. [t. L: m. s. *belligerans*, ppr.] —**bel·lig′er·ent·ly,** *adv.*

Bel·ling·ham (bĕl′ĭng hăm′), *n.* a seaport in NW Washington. 34,112 (1950).

Bel·li·ni (bĕl lē′nē), *n.* **1. Gentile** (jĕn tē′lĕ), 1427?–1507, Venetian painter (son of Jacopo). **2. Giovanni** (jō vän′nē), 1430?–1516, Venetian painter (son of Jacopo). **3. Jacopo** (yä′kōpō′), 1400?–70, Venetian painter. **4. Vincenzo** (vēn chĕn′tsō), 1801?–35, Italian composer of opera.

bell jar, a bell-shaped glass vessel or cover, as for protecting delicate instruments, bric-a-brac, etc., or for holding gases in chemical operations. Also, **bell glass.**

bell·man (bĕl′mǝn), *n.*, *pl.* **-men.** a man who carries or rings a bell, esp. a town crier or watchman.

bell metal, a hard alloy of copper and tin of low damping capacity, used for bells.

bell-mouthed (bĕl′mouthd′, -moutht′), *adj.* having a flaring mouth like that of a bell.

Bel·loc (bĕl′ǝk, -ŏk), *n.* **Hilaire** (hǐ lâr′), born 1870, British essayist, poet, and satirist, born in France.

Be·lo Ho·ri·zon·te (bĕ′lō rē zôn′tǝ), a city in SE Brazil. 230,668 (est. 1944). Also, **Belo Horizonte.**

Bel·lo·na (bǝ lō′nǝ), *n.* *Rom. Myth.* goddess of war (sister or wife of Mars). [t. L]

bel·low (bĕl′ō), *v.i.* **1.** to make a hollow, loud, animal cry, as a bull or cow. **2.** to roar; bawl: *bellowing with rage.* —*v.t.* **3.** to utter in a loud deep voice: *to bellow forth an answer.* —*n.* **4.** act or sound of bellowing. [ME *belwe*(n), appar. b. OE *bellan* BELL² and *bylgan* bellow] —**bel′low·er,** *n.* —**Syn. 2.** See **cry.**

bel·lows (bĕl′ōz, -ǝs), *n. sing. and pl.* **1.** an instrument or machine for producing a strong current of air, as for a draft for a fire or sounding a musical instrument, consisting essentially of an air chamber which can be expanded to draw in air through a valve and contracted to expel the air through a tube or tubes. **2.** anything resembling or suggesting a bellows, as the collapsible part of a camera or enlarger. **3.** the lungs. [ME *belwes*, pl., OE *belg* short for *blǣst-belg* blast-bag. See BELLY]

Bel·lows (bĕl′ōz), *n.* **George,** 1882–1925, U.S. artist.

bell·weth·er (bĕl′wĕth′ǝr), *n.* **1.** a wether or other male sheep which leads the flock, usually bearing a bell. **2.** a person whom others follow blindly.

bell·wort (bĕl′wûrt′), *n.* **1.** any campanulaceous plant. **2.** a plant of the liliaceous genus *Uvularia*, bearing a delicate, slenderly bell-shaped, yellow flower.

bel·ly (bĕl′ǐ), *n.*, *pl.* **-lies,** *v.*, **-lied, -lying.** —*n.* **1.** the front or under part of a vertebrate body from the breastbone to the pelvis, containing the abdominal viscera; the abdomen. **2.** the stomach with its adjuncts. **3.** appetite for food; gluttony. **4.** the womb. **5.** the inside or interior of anything: *the belly of a ship.* **6.** a protuberant or bulging surface of anything: *the belly of a flask.* **7.** *Anat.* the fleshy part of a muscle. **8.** the front, inner, or under surface or part (opposed to *back*). **9.** *Music.* the front surface of a violin or similar instrument. —*v.t.*, *v.i.* **10.** to swell out. [ME *bely*, OE *belig* bag, skin, var. of *belg* (whence *bellow*(s))]

bel·ly·band (bĕl′ĭ bănd′), *n.* a band worn about the belly, as of a harnessed horse. See illus. under **harness.**

Bel·mont (bĕl′mŏnt), *n.* a town in E Massachusetts, near Boston. 27,381 (1950).

Be·lo Ho·ri·zon·te (bĕ′lō rē zôn′tǝ), Bello Horizonte.

Be·loit (bǝ loit′), *n.* a city in S Wisconsin. 29,590 (1950).

be·long (bǐ lông′, -lŏng′), *v.i.* **1.** to have one's rightful place; to bear relation as a member, adherent, inhabitant, etc. (fol. by *to*): *he belongs to the Grange.* **2. belong to,** **a.** to be the property of: *the book belongs to him.* **b.** to be an appurtenance, adjunct, or part of: *that cover belongs to this jar.* **c.** to be a property, function, or concern of: *attributes which belong to nature.* **3.** to have the proper social qualifications: *he doesn't belong.* **4.** to be proper or due. [ME *belonge*(n), f. BE- + *longe* belong, der. *long*, adj., aphetic var. of d. *along*, OE *gelang* belonging to]

be·long·ing (bǐ lông′ĭng, -lŏng′-), *n.* **1.** something that belongs. **2.** (*pl.*) possessions; goods; personal effects.

be·lov·ed (bǐ lŭv′ĭd, -lŭvd′), *adj.* **1.** greatly loved; dear to the heart. —*n.* **2.** one who is greatly loved.

be·low (bǐ lō′), *adv.* **1.** in or to a lower place; lower down; beneath. **2.** on or to a lower floor; downstairs. **3.** on earth. **4.** in hell or the infernal regions. **5.** at a later point on a page or in writing: *see the statistics below.* **6.** in a lower rank or grade: *he was demoted to the class below.* —*prep.* **7.** lower down than: *below the knee.* **8.** lower in rank, degree, amount, rate, etc., than: *below cost, below freezing.* **9.** too low or base to be worthy of. [ME *bilooghe* by low. See BE-, LOW¹] —**Syn. 7.** BELOW, UNDER, BENEATH indicate position in some way lower than something else. BELOW implies being in a lower plane: *below the horizon, the water line.* UNDER implies being lower in a perpendicular line: *the plaything is under a chair.* BENEATH may have a meaning similar to BELOW, but more usually denotes being under so as to be covered, overhung, or overtopped: *the pool beneath the falls.*

Bel·shaz·zar (bĕl shăz′ǝr), *n.* son of Nebuchadnezzar, and king of Babylonia. Dan. 5. [t. Heb.]

---

b., blend of, blended; c., cognate with; d., dialect, dialectal; der., derived from; f., formed from; g., going back to; m., modification of; r., replacing; s., stem of; t., taken from; ?, perhaps. See the full key on inside cover.

belt (bĕlt), *n.* **1.** a band of flexible material for encircling the waist. **2.** any encircling or transverse band, strip, or stripe. **3.** *Ecol.* a region having distinctive properties or characteristics: *the cotton belt.* **4.** *Mach.* **a.** a flexible band or cord connecting and passing about each of two or more wheels, pulleys, or the like, to transmit or change the direction of motion. See illus. under **shafting. b. belt conveyor,** a similar belt used to transport objects from one place to another in an industrial plant. **5.** *Naval.* a series of armor plates around a ship. **6.** *Mil.* **a.** a cloth strip with loops, or a series of metal links with grips, for holding cartridges which are fed into an automatic gun. **b.** a band of leather or webbing, worn around the waist and used as a support for weapons, ammunition, etc. —*v.t.* **7.** to gird or furnish with a belt. **8.** to surround or mark as if with a belt. **9.** to fasten on (a sword, etc.) by means of a belt. **10.** to beat with a belt, strap, etc. **11.** *Colloq.* to give a thwack or blow to. [OE, prob. ult. t. L: m.s. *balteus*] —**belt′less,** *adj.*
—**Syn. 3.** BELT and ZONE agree in their original meaning of a girdle or band. BELT is more used in popular or journalistic writing: *the corn or wheat belt.* ZONE tends to be used in technical language: *the Torrid Zone, a parcel-post zone.*

Bel·tane (bĕl′tān), *n.* an ancient Celtic festival observed on May Day in Scotland and Ireland. [ME (Scot.), t. Gaelic: m. *bealltainn*; of obscure orig.]

belt·ing (bĕl′tĭng), *n.* **1.** material for belts. **2.** belts collectively. **3.** a belt.

belt line, a transportation system partially or wholly surrounding a city, terminal, district, or port.

be·lu·ga (bəloō′gə), *n.* a cetacean, *Delphinapterus leucas,* chiefly Arctic, having a rounded head, and white in color. [t. Russ.: m. *bielukha,* der. *bielo-* white]

bel·ve·dere (bĕl′vədîr′; *It.* bĕl′vĕdĕ′rĕ), *n.* **1.** an upper story or any structure or building designed to afford a fine view. **2.** (*cap.*) the Vatican art gallery in Rome. [t. It.: beautiful view]

be·ma (bē′mə), *n., pl.* **-mata** (-mətə). *Gk. Orth. Ch.* the enclosed space surrounding the altar; the sanctuary or chancel. [t. Gk.: step, platform]

be·maul (bĭ môl′), *v.t.* to maul severely.

be·mean (bĭ mēn′), *v.t.* to make mean; debase (oneself).

be·mire (bĭ mīr′), *v.t.,* **-mired, -miring. 1.** to soil with mire. **2.** to sink in mire.

be·moan (bĭ mōn′), *v.t.* **1.** to moan over; bewail; lament. **2.** to express pity for. —*v.i.* **3.** to lament; mourn. [f. BE- + MOAN; r. ME *bemene*(n), OE *bemǣnan*]

be·mused (bĭ mūzd′), *adj.* **1.** confused; muddled; stupefied. **2.** lost in thought; preoccupied.

ben[1] (bĕn), *n. Scot.* the inner room (parlor) of a cottage. [ME, var. of *binne,* OE *binnan* within, c. G *binnen*]

ben[2] (bĕn), *n.* **1.** a tree, *Moringa oleifera,* of Arabia, India, and elsewhere, bearing a winged seed (nut) which yields an oil (**oil of ben**), used in extracting flower perfumes, lubricating delicate machinery, etc. **2.** the seed of such a tree. [t. Ar.: m. *bān*]

ben·a·dryl (bĕn′ədrĭl), *n. Pharm.* **1.** a synthetic drug used esp. to relieve hay fever and hives. **2.** (*cap.*) a trademark for this drug.

be·name (bĭ nām′), *v.t.,* **-named; -named, -nempt,** or **-nempted; -naming.** *Archaic.* to name; denominate.

Be·na·res (bə nä′rĭz), *n.* a city in N India, on the Ganges: holy city of Hinduism. 263,100 (1941).

Ben·bow (bĕn′bō), *n.* **John,** 1653–1702, British admiral.

bench (bĕnch), *n.* **1.** a long seat for several people. **2.** the seat on which judges sit in court. **3.** the position or office of a judge: *elected to the bench.* **4.** the body of persons sitting as judges. **5.** a seat occupied by persons in their official capacity. **6.** the office or dignity of those occupying it. **7.** the persons themselves. **8.** the strong work table of a carpenter or other mechanic. **9.** a platform on which animals are placed for exhibition, esp. at a dog show. **10.** a dog show. **11.** *Phys. Geog.* a flat, terracelike tract of land on a valley slope, above the stream bed, or along a coast, above the level of sea or lake. **12.** *Mining.* a step or working elevation in a mine. **13. on the bench,** *Sports.* not participating. —*v.t.* **14.** to furnish with benches. **15.** to seat on a bench. **16.** to place in exhibition: *to bench a dog.* **17.** *Sports.* to remove from a game: *the player was benched for too many fouls.* [ME; OE *benc.* See BANK[2], BANK[3]] —**bench′less,** *adj.*

bench dog, a dog on exhibition, as at a dog show.

bench·er (bĕn′chər), *n.* **1.** (in England) a senior member of an Inn of Court. **2.** one who handles an oar.

bench mark, *Survey.* a point of known elevation, usually a mark cut into some durable material, as stone or a concrete post with a bronze plate to serve as a reference point in running a line of levels for the determination of elevations.

bench warrant, *Law.* a warrant issued or ordered by a judge or court for the apprehension of an offender.

bend[1] (bĕnd), *v.,* **bent** or (*Archaic*) **bended, bending,** *n.* —*v.t.* **1.** to bring (a bow, etc.) into a state of tension by curving it. **2.** to force into a different or particular, esp. curved, shape, as by pressure. **3.** to cause to submit: *to bend someone to one's will.* **4.** to turn in a particular direction. **5.** to incline mentally (fol. by *to* or *towards*). **6.** *Naut.* to fasten. **7.** *Archaic.* to strain or brace tensely (fol. by *up*). —*v.i.* **8.** to become curved, crooked, or bent. **9.** to assume a bent posture; stoop. **10.** to bow in submission or reverence; yield; submit. **11.** to turn or incline in a particular direction; be directed. **12.** to direct one's energies. —*n.* **13.** act of bending. **14.** state of being bent. **15.** a bent part; curve; crook. **16. the bends,** *U.S. Colloq.* **a.** caisson disease. **b.** aero-embolism. **17.** *Naut.* **a.** (*pl.*) the wales of a ship. **b.** a knot by which a rope is fastened to another rope or to something else. [ME *bende*(*n*), OE *bendan* bind, bend (a bow)] —**bend′a·ble,** *adj.*
—**Syn. 2.** curve, crook, flex. **9.** BEND, BOW, STOOP imply taking a bent posture. BEND and BOW are used of the head and upper body; STOOP is used of the body only.

bend[2] (bĕnd), *n. Her.* a diagonal band extending from the dexter chief to the sinister base. [OE *bend* band; in ME identified with OF *bende* band]

Ben Da·vis (bĕn dā′vĭs), a variety of red winter apple.

bend·ed (bĕn′dĭd), *adj.* **1.** *Archaic.* bent. —*v.* **2.** *Archaic.* pt. and pp. of **bend**[1].

bend·er (bĕn′dər), *n.* **1.** one who or that which bends, as a pair of pliers. **2.** *U.S. Slang.* a drinking spree. **3.** *Baseball.* a curve (def. 5). **4.** *Brit. Slang.* a sixpence.

Ben·di·go (bĕn′dəgō′), *n.* a city in SE Australia, in Victoria: gold mining. 30,800 (est. 1938).

bend sinister, *Her.* a diagonal band extending from the sinister chief to the dexter base (a mark of bastardy).

Bend sinister

bene-, a word element meaning "well", as in *benediction.* [t. L, comb. form of *bene,* adv.]

be·neath (bĭ nēth′, -nēth′), *adv.* **1.** below; in a lower place, position, state, etc. **2.** underneath: *the heaven above and the earth beneath.* —*prep.* **3.** below; under: *beneath the same roof.* **4.** farther down than; underneath; lower in place than. **5.** lower down on a slope than: *beneath the crest of a hill.* **6.** inferior in position, power, etc. to: *a captain is beneath a major.* **7.** unworthy of; below the level or dignity of: *beneath contempt.* [ME *benethe,* OE *beneothan,* f. *be* by + *neothan* below] —**Syn. 3.** See below. —**Ant. 1.** above.

Ben·e·dic·i·te (bĕn′ə dĭs′ə tĭ), *n.* **1.** *Eccles.* the canticle beginning in Latin "Benedicite, omnia opera Domini," and in English "O all ye works of the Lord." **2.** a musical setting for it. **3.** (*l.c.*) an invocation for a blessing. —*interj.* **4.** (*l.c.*) bless you! [t. L, 2d pers. pl. impv. of *benedicere* bless]

Ben·e·dick (bĕn′ə dĭk), *n.* **1.** (in Shakespeare's *Much Ado About Nothing*) the confident bachelor who courts and finally marries Beatrice. **2.** (*l.c.*) benedict.

ben·e·dict (bĕn′ə dĭkt), *n.* **1.** a newly married man, esp. one who has been long a bachelor. **2.** a married man. [var. of BENEDICK]

Ben·e·dict (bĕn′ə dĭkt), *n.* **Saint,** A.D. 480?–543?, Italian monk: founded Benedictine order.

Benedict, *n.* the name adopted by 15 popes, esp.: **1. XIV,** 1675–1758, Italian pope, 1704–58: patron of art, archaeology, and learning. **2. XV,** 1854–1922, Italian pope, 1914–22.

Ben·e·dic·tine (bĕn′ə dĭk′tĭn, -tēn, -tīn *for 1;* bĕn′ə dĭk′tēn *for 2*), *n. Rom. Cath. Ch.* a member of an order of monks founded at Monte Cassino, between Rome and Naples, by St. Benedict about A.D. 530 or of various congregations of nuns following his rule. The rules of the order (**Benedictine rule**) enjoined silence and useful employment when not in divine service. **2.** (*usually l.c.*) a French liqueur orig. made by Benedictine monks. —*adj.* **3.** pertaining to St. Benedict or to an order following his rule. [t. F: m. *bénédictin*]

ben·e·dic·tion (bĕn′ə dĭk′shən), *n. Eccles.* **1.** act of uttering a blessing. **2.** the form of blessing pronounced by an officiating minister, as at the close of divine service, etc. **3.** a ceremony by which things are set aside for sacred uses, as a church, vestments, bells, etc. **4.** the advantage conferred by blessing; a mercy or benefit. [ME, t. L: s. *benedictio*] —**ben′e·dic′tion·al,** *adj.* —**ben·e·dic·to·ry** (bĕn′ə dĭk′tə rĭ), *adj.*

Ben·e·dic·tus (bĕn′ə dĭk′təs), *n. Eccles.* **1.** the short canticle or hymn beginning in Latin "Benedictus qui venit in nomine Domini," and in English "Blessed is He that cometh in the name of the Lord." **2.** the canticle or hymn beginning in Latin "Benedictus Dominus Deus Israel," and in English "Blessed be the Lord God of Israel." **3.** a musical setting of either of these canticles. [t. L: pp., blessed]

ben·e·fac·tion (bĕn′ə făk′shən), *n.* **1.** act of conferring a benefit; doing of good. **2.** the benefit conferred; charitable donation. [t. LL: s. *benefactio*]

ben·e·fac·tor (bĕn′ə făk′tər, bĕn′ə făk′-), *n.* **1.** one who confers a benefit; kindly helper. **2.** one who makes a bequest or endowment. [t. L] —**ben·e·fac·tress** (bĕn′ə făk′trĭs, bĕn′ə făk′-), *n. fem.*

be·nef·ic (bə nĕf′ĭk), *adj.* beneficent. [t. L: s. *beneficus*]

ben·e·fice (bĕn′ə fĭs), *n., v.,* **-ficed, -ficing.** —*n.* **1.** an ecclesiastical living. **2.** the revenue itself. —*v.t.* **3.** to invest with a benefice or ecclesiastical living. [ME, t. OF, t. L: m.s. *beneficium* benefit, favor]

be·nef·i·cence (bə nĕf′ə səns), *n.* **1.** the doing of good; active goodness or kindness; charity. **2.** beneficent act or gift; benefaction. [t. L: m. s. *beneficentia*]

be·nef·i·cent (bə nĕf′ə sənt), *adj.* doing good or causing good to be done; conferring benefits; kindly in action or purpose. —**be·nef′i·cent·ly,** *adv.*

ben·e·fi·cial (bĕn′ə fĭsh′əl), *adj.* **1.** conferring benefit; advantageous; helpful. **2.** *Law.* **a.** helpful in the meeting of needs: *a beneficial association.* **b.** involving the personal enjoyment of proceeds: *a beneficial owner.* —**ben′e·fi′cial·ly,** *adv.* —**ben′e·fi′cial·ness,** *n.* —**Syn. 1.** salutary, wholesome, serviceable. —**Ant. 1.** harmful.

ben·e·fi·ci·ar·y (bĕn′ə fĭsh′ĭ ĕr′ĭ, -fĭsh′ər ĭ), *n., pl.* **-aries. 1.** one who receives benefits, profits, or advantages. **2.** *Law.* a person designated as the recipient of funds or other property under a trust, insurance policy, etc. **3.** *Eccles.* the holder of a benefice.

ben·e·fit (bĕn′ə fĭt), *n., v.,* **-fited, -fiting.** —*n.* **1.** act of kindness. **2.** anything that is for the good of a person or thing. **3.** a theatrical performance or other public entertainment to raise money for a worthy purpose. **4.** a payment or other assistance given by an insurance company, mutual benefit society, or public agency. —*v.t.* **5.** to do good to; be of service to. —*v.i.* **6.** to gain advantage; make improvement. [partial Latinization of ME *benfet,* t. AF, g. L *benefactum,* f. *bene-* BENE- + *factum* thing done. See FACT and cf. FEAT] —**ben′e·fit·er,** *n.* —**Syn. 1.** favor, service. **2.** See **advantage.**

benefit of clergy, 1. church rites, as of marriage. **2.** an early right of church authorities to try and to punish, in an ecclesiastical court, any clergyman accused of serious crime (abolished in U.S. in 1790 and in England in 1827).

benefit society, *Insurance.* an association of persons to create a fund (as by dues or assessments) for the assistance of members and their families in sickness, death, etc. Also, **benefit association.**

Ben·e·lux (bĕn′ə lŭks), *n.* a customs union (since Jan. 1, 1948) of Belgium, the Netherlands, and Luxemburg.

be·nempt (bĭ nĕmpt′), *v. Archaic.* a pp. of **bename**

Be·neš (bĕn′ĕsh), *n.* **Eduard** (ĕ′dŏŏ ärt′), 1884–1948, Czechoslovakian patriot and statesman: president of Czechoslovakia, 1935–1938 and 1945–1948.

Be·nét (bĭ nā′), *n.* **1. Stephen Vincent,** 1898–1943, U.S. poet. **2.** his brother, **William Rose,** 1886–1950, U.S. writer.

Be·ne·ven·to (bĕ′nĕ vĕn′tô), *n.* a city in S Italy: location of the Arch of Trajan. 26,692 (1936).

be·nev·o·lence (bə nĕv′ə ləns), *n.* **1.** desire to do good for others; good will; charitableness. **2.** an act of kindness; charitable gift. **3.** *Eng. Hist.* a forced contribution to the sovereign. —**Ant. 1.** malevolence.

be·nev·o·lent (bə nĕv′ə lənt), *adj.* **1.** desiring to do good for others. **2.** intended for benefits rather than profit: *a benevolent institution.* [t. L: s. *benevolens* well-wishing; r. ME *benyvolent,* t. OF: m. *benivolent*] —**be·nev′o·lent·ly,** *adv.*

Ben·gal (bĕn gôl′, bĕng-), *n.* **1.** a former province in NE India: now divided into **East Bengal** (in Pakistan) and **West Bengal** (in India). 60,307,000 pop. (1941); 77,442 sq. mi. *Cap.:* Calcutta. **2. Bay of,** a part of the Indian Ocean between India and Burma.

Ben·ga·lese (bĕn′gə lēz′, -lēs′, bĕng′-), *adj., n., pl.* **-lese.** —*adj.* **1.** of or pertaining to Bengal. —*n.* **2.** a native or inhabitant of Bengal.

Ben·ga·li (bĕn gô′lĭ, bĕng-), *n.* **1.** a native or an inhabitant of Bengal. **2.** the language of Bengal, an Indic language. —*adj.* **3.** of or pertaining to Bengal, its inhabitants, or their language; Bengalese.

ben·ga·line (bĕng′gə lēn′, bĕng′gə lēn′), *n.* a corded fabric resembling poplin but with heavier cords. It may be silk or rayon with worsted cord. [t. F]

Bengal light (bĕn′gôl, bĕng′-), a vivid, sustained, blue light used in signaling, fireworks, etc.

Ben·ga·si (bĕn gä′zĭ), *n.* a seaport in N Libya. 58,381 (1936). Also, **Ben·gha′zi.**

Be·ni (bĕ′nē), *n.* a river flowing from W Bolivia NE to the Madeira river. ab. 600 mi.

be·night·ed (bĭ nī′tĭd), *adj.* **1.** intellectually or morally ignorant; unenlightened: *a benighted heathen.* **2.** overtaken by darkness or night. [pp. of *benight,* v., f. BE- + NIGHT]

be·nign (bĭ nīn′), *adj.* **1.** of a kind disposition; kind. **2.** showing or caused by gentleness or kindness: *a benign smile.* **3.** favorable; propitious: *benign planets.* **4.** (of weather) salubrious. **5.** *Pathol.* not malignant: *a benign tumor.* [ME *benigne,* t. OF, t. L: m.s. *benignus* kind] —**be·nign′ly,** *adv.* —**Ant. 2.** sinister. **3.** malign.

be·nig·nant (bĭ nĭg′nənt), *adj.* **1.** kind, esp. to inferiors; gracious: *benignant sovereign.* **2.** exerting a good influence; beneficial. **3.** *Pathol.* benign. [b. BEN(IGN) and (MAL)IGNANT] —**be·nig·nan·cy** (bĭ nĭg′nən sĭ), *n.* —**be·nig′nant·ly,** *adv.*

be·nig·ni·ty (bĭ nĭg′nə tĭ), *n., pl.* **-ties. 1.** state or quality of being benign; kindness; graciousness. **2.** a good deed; gracious favor.

Be·ni Ha·san (bĕ′nĭ hä′săn), a village in central Egypt, on the Nile, N of Asyut: ancient cliff tombs.

Be·nin (bĕ nēn′), *n.* **1.** a former nat ve kingdom in W Africa: now a district in Nigeria. 493,200 pop. (1931); 8627 sq. mi. **2.** a river in S Nigeria flowing into the **Bight of Benin,** a wide bay in the Gulf of Guinea.

ben·i·son (bĕn′ə zən, -sən), *n. Archaic.* benediction. [ME *benisoun,* t. OF: m. *beneison,* g. s. L *benedictio*]

ben·ja·min (bĕn′jə mən), *n.* benzoin (def. 1). [var. (by assimilation to *Benjamin*) of *benjoin* BENZOIN]

Ben·ja·min (bĕn′jə mən), *n.* **1.** *Bible.* **a.** the youngest son of Jacob by Rachel, and brother of Joseph. **b.** a tribe of Israel said to have Benjamin as its ancestor. **2. Judah Philip,** 1811–84, Confederate statesman.

Ben·ja·min-Con·stant (bän zhȧ män′ kôns tän′), *n.* See **Constant,** Jean Joseph Benjamin.

Ben Lo·mond (bĕn lō′mənd), *n.* a mountain in W Scotland, E of Loch Lomond, 3192 ft.

ben·ne (bĕn′ĭ), *n.* the sesame, *Sesamum indicum,* from the seeds of which a fixed oil (**oil of benne** or **benne oil**) is expressed. [t. Malay]

ben·net (bĕn′ĭt), *n. Bot.* **1.** the American avens, esp. the species *Geum virginianum* and *G. canadense.* **2.** herb bennet. [ME *beneit* in *herbe beneit,* prob. t. OF: m. *herbe beneite,* trans. of ML *herba benedicta* blessed herb]

Ben·nett (bĕn′ĭt), *n.* **1.** (**Enoch**) **Arnold,** 1867–1931, British novelist. **2. James Gordon,** 1795–1872, U.S. journalist. **3. Richard Bedford,** 1870–1947, Canadian statesman.

Ben Ne·vis (bĕn nĕ′vĭs, nĕv′ĭs), a peak in W Scotland in Inverness county: the highest point in the British Isles. 4406 ft.

Ben·ning·ton (bĕn′ĭng tən), *n.* a village in SW Vermont: the British were defeated near here by the "Green Mountain Boys," 1777. 8002 (1950).

Be·no·ni (bĕ nō′nĭ), *n.* a city in the Union of South Africa, near Johannesburg: gold mines. With suburbs, 74,123 (1946).

bent[1] (bĕnt), *adj.* **1.** curved; crooked: *a bent stick, bow, etc.* **2.** determined; set; resolved (fol. by *on*). —*n.* **3.** bent state or form. **4.** direction taken (usually figurative); inclination; leaning; bias: *a bent for painting.* **5.** capacity of endurance. **6.** *Civ. Eng.* a transverse frame of a bridge or a building, designed to support either vertical or horizontal loads. [pp. of BEND[1]] —**Syn. 4.** tendency, propensity, proclivity, predilection.

bent[2] (bĕnt), *n.* **1.** bent grass. **2.** a stalk of such grass. **3.** (formerly) any stiff grass or sedge. **4.** *Scot. and N. Eng.* a grassy tract, a moor, or a hillside. [ME; OE *beonet,* c. G *binse* rush]

bent grass, any of the species of the graminaceous genus *Agrostis,* esp. the redtop.

Ben·tham (bĕn′thəm, -təm), *n.* **Jeremy** (jĕr′ə mĭ). 1748–1832, British jurist and utilitarian philosopher.

Ben·tham·ism (bĕn′thə mĭz′əm, bĕn′tə-), *n.* the variety of utilitarianism put forth by Jeremy Bentham, characterized esp. by moral and ethical evaluation of actions in terms of their power to produce pleasure (the only good) or pain (the only evil). —**Ben·tham·ite** (bĕn′thə mīt′, bĕn′tə-), *n.*

ben·thos (bĕn′thŏs), *n. Ecol.* the animals and plants that are fixed to or crawl upon the sea bottom. [t. Gk.: depth (of the sea)] —**ben′thic, ben·thon·ic** (bĕn thŏn′ĭk), *adj.*

Bent·ley (bĕnt′lĭ), *n.* **Richard,** 1662–1742, British scholar and critic.

Ben·ton (bĕn′tən), *n.* **Thomas Hart,** born 1889, U.S. painter.

Be·nu·e (bā′nŏŏ ä′), *n.* a river in W Africa, flowing from the Cameroons W to the Niger river in Nigeria. ab. 800 mi.

be·numb (bĭ nŭm′), *v.t.* **1.** to make numb; deprive of sensation: *benumbed by cold.* **2.** to render inactive; stupefy. [ME *benome(n),* OE *benumen,* pp. of *beniman* deprive]

benz-, var. of **benzo-,** used before vowels.

benz·al·de·hyde (bĕn zăl′də hīd′), *n. Chem.* an aldehyde, C_6H_5CHO, obtained from natural oil of bitter almonds or other oils, or produced artificially, used in dyes, as a flavoring agent, etc.

Ben·ze·drine (bĕn′zə drēn′, -drĭn), *n. Pharm.* a trademark for amphetamine.

ben·zene (bĕn′zēn, bĕn zēn′), *n. Chem.* a colorless, volatile, inflammable, liquid aromatic hydrocarbon, C_6H_6, obtained chiefly from coal tar, and used as a solvent for resins, fats, etc., and in the manufacture of dyes, etc.

benzene ring, *Chem.* the graphic representation of the structure of benzene as a hexagon with a carbon atom at each of its points. Each carbon atom is united with an atom of hydrogen, one or more of which may be replaced to form benzene derivatives. Also, **benzene nucleus.**

ben·zi·dine (bĕn′zə dēn′, -dĭn), *n. Chem.* a basic compound, $C_6H_4C_6H_4NH_2$, occurring as grayish scales or a crystalline powder, used in the manufacture of certain dyes, as Congo red. [f. BENZ- + -IDINE[2]]

ben·zine (bĕn′zēn, bĕn zēn′), *n.* a colorless, volatile, inflammable liquid, a mixture of various hydrocarbons, obtained in the distillation of petroleum, and used in cleaning, dyeing, etc.

benzo-, *Chem.* a combining form meaning "pertaining to or derived from benzoin" or designating the presence of benzoic acid. Also, **benz-.**

ben·zo·ate (bĕn′zō āt′, -ĭt), *n. Chem.* a salt or ester of benzoic acid.

ben·zo·ic acid (bĕn zō′ĭk), *Chem., Pharm., etc.* a white, crystalline acid, C_6H_5COOH, obtained from benzoin and other balsams or from toluene, used in medicine, aniline dye manufacture, as a food preservative, etc.

---

b., blend of, blended; c., cognate with; d., dialect, dialectal; der., derived from; f., formed from; g., going back to; m., modification of; r., replacing; s., stem of; t., taken from; ?, perhaps. See the full key on inside cover.

ben·zoin (bĕn′zoin, -zō′ĭn, bĕn zō′ĭn). *n.* **1.** a balsamic resin obtained from species of *Styrax*, esp. *S. Benzoin*, a tree of Java, Sumatra, etc., and used in perfumery, medicine, etc. **2.** any plant of the lauraceous genus *Lindera* (also known as *Benzoin*) which includes the spicebush and other aromatic plants. [earlier *benjoin*, t. F, through Sp. or Pg. t. Ar. : m. *lubān jāwi* incense of Java (*lu-* appar. taken as 'the')]

ben·zol (bĕn′zŏl, -zōl), *n.* crude industrial benzene.

ben·zo·phe·none (bĕn′zō fĭ nōn′), *n.* *Chem.* a water-insoluble crystalline ketone, $C_6H_5COC_6H_5$, used in organic synthesis. [f. BENZO- + PHEN- + -ONE]

ben·zo·yl (bĕn′zō ĭl, -ēl′), *n.* *Chem.* a univalent radical, C_6H_5CO, present in benzoic acid and allied compounds.

ben·zyl (bĕn′zĭl, -zēl), *n.* *Chem.* a univalent organic radical, $C_6H_5CH_2$, from toluene.

Be·o·grad (bĕ ō′gräd), *n.* Serbian name of **Belgrade**.

Be·o·wulf (bā′ə wŏolf′), *n.* **1.** an English alliterative epic poem of the early 8th century. **2.** its hero.

be·queath (bǐ kwēth′, -kwēth′), *v.t.* **1.** *Law.* to dispose by last will of (personal property, esp. money). **2.** to hand down; pass on. **3.** *Obs.* to commit; entrust. [ME *bequethe(n)*, OE *becwethan*, f. BE- + *cwethan* say] —**be·queath·al** (bǐ kwē′thəl), *n.*

be·quest (bǐ kwĕst′), *n.* **1.** *Law.* a disposition in a will concerning personal property, esp. money. **2.** a legacy. [ME *biqueste*, f. OE BE- + *cwis(s)* saying]

Bé·ran·ger (bĕ rän zhĕ′), *n.* **Pierre Jean de** (pyĕr zhän də), 1780–1857, French poet.

be·rate (bǐ rāt′), *v.t.*, **-rated, -rating.** to scold.

Ber·ber (bûr′bər), *n.* **1.** a member of a group of North African tribes living in Barbary and the Sahara. **2.** the Hamitic languages of the Berbers, spoken from Tunisia west to the Atlantic and in the Sahara, including Kabyle, Tuareg, and other languages. —*adj.* **3.** of or pertaining to the Berbers or their language.

Ber·ber·a (bûr′bər ə), *n.* a seaport and the capital of British Somaliland, on the Gulf of Aden. ab. 30,000.

ber·be·ri·da·ceous (bûr′bə rǐ dā′shəs), *adj.* belonging to the *Berberidaceae*, a family of plants including the barberry, May apple, blue cohosh, etc.

ber·ber·ine (bûr′bər ēn′), *n.* *Chem.* a widely distributed alkaloid, $C_{20}H_{19}NO_5$, found in the barberry and a considerable number of plants whose extracts have a yellow color and a bitter taste.

ber·ceuse (bĕr sœz′), *n.*, *pl.* **-ceuses** (-sœz′). *Music.* a cradlesong; lullaby.

Berch·tes·ga·den (bĕrкн′təs gä′dən), *n.* a town in SE Germany, in Bavaria: site of the fortified mountain chalet of Adolf Hitler. 4491 (1939).

Ber·di·chev (bĕr dē′chĕf), *n.* a city in the SW Soviet Union, in the Ukrainian Republic. 66,306 (1939).

be·reave (bǐ rēv′), *v.t.*, **-reaved** *or* **-reft, -reaving.** **1.** to deprive (*of*) ruthlessly, esp. of hope, joy, etc. : *bereft of all their lands.* **2.** to make desolate through loss (*of*), esp. by death: *bereaved of their mother.* **3.** *Obs.* to take away by violence. [ME *bereve(n)*, OE *bereafian*, f. BE- + *reafian* rob] —**be·reave′ment**, *n.*

Ber·e·ni·ce's Hair (bĕr′ə nī′sēz), *Astron.* the constellation Coma Berenices.

be·ret (bə rā′, bĕr′ā; *Fr.* bě rě′), *n.* a soft, round, visorless cap that fits closely. [t. F, t. Bearnese: m. *berret*, g. Gallo Rom. *birretum* cap, der. LL *birrum* cloak]

Be·re·zi·na (*Pol.* bŏ′rĕ zē′nä; *Russ.* -zĭ′nä), *n.* a river in the W Soviet Union, flowing SE to the Dnieper river: crossed with heavy losses by Napoleon's army during the retreat of 1812. ab. 350 mi.

berg (bûrg), *n.* *Oceanog.* iceberg. [short for ICEBERG]

Ber·ga·mo (bĕr′gä mō′), *n.* a city in N Italy, in Lombardy. 101,184 (est. 1946).

ber·ga·mot (bûr′gə mŏt′), *n.* **1.** a small tree of the citrus family, *Citrus Bergamia*, the rind of whose fruit yields a fragrant essential oil (**essence of bergamot**). **2.** the oil or essence itself. **3.** any of various plants of the mint family, as *Monarda fistulosa*, yielding an oil resembling essence of bergamot. **4.** *Hort.* one of a group of globular oblate, evenly and regularly shaped pears. [t. F: m. *bergamote*, t. It.: m. *bergamotta*, appar. t. Turk.: m. *begarmūdi* prince's pear]

Ber·gen (bûr′gən; *Nor.* bĕr′gən), *n.* a seaport in SW Norway, on the Atlantic. 106,662 (est. 1939).

Ber·ge·rac (bĕr zhĕ′răk′), *n.* **Savinien Cyrano de** (sà vē nyăn′ sē rà nō′ də), 1619–55, French soldier, duelist, and romantic writer: hero of play by Rostand.

Berg·son (bûrg′sən, bĕrg′-; *Fr.* bĕrg sŏn′), *n.* **Henri** (än rē′), 1859–1941, French philosopher and writer. —**Berg·so·ni·an** (bûrg sō′nĭ ən, bĕrg′-), *adj.*, *n.*

Berg·son·ism (bûrg′sə nĭz′əm, bĕrg′-), *n.* *Philos.* Henri Bergson's doctrine of creative evolution, emphasizing duration as the central fact of experience and an *élan vital* (vital drive) as an original life force essentially governing all organic processes.

be·rhyme (bǐ rīm′), *v.t.*, **-rhymed, -rhyming.** to celebrate in verse. Also, **be·rime′.**

be·rib·boned (bǐ rǐb′ənd), *adj.* adorned with ribbons.

ber·i·ber·i (bĕr′ē bĕr′ē), *n.* *Pathol.* a disease of the peripheral nerves caused by deficiency in vitamin B_1, and marked by pain in and paralysis of the extremities, and severe emaciation or swelling of the body. It is common in China, Japan, and the Philippines. [t. Singhalese, redupl. of *beri* weakness]

Ber·ing (bĭr′ĭng, bâr′-; *Dan.* bā′rĭng), *n.* **Vi·tus** (vē′-tōos), 1680–1741, Danish navigator and explorer of the N Pacific for Russia. Also, **Behring.**

Ber·ing Sea (bĭr′ĭng, bâr′-), a part of the N Pacific N of the Aleutian Islands. ab. 878,000 sq. mi.

Bering Strait, the strait between Alaska and the Soviet Union in Asia, connecting the Bering Sea and the Arctic Ocean. 36 mi. wide.

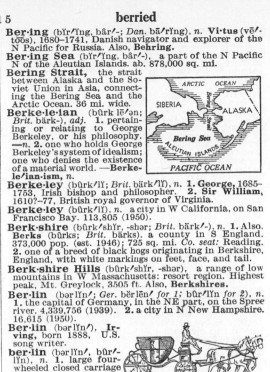

Berke·le·ian (bûrk lē′ən; *Brit.* bärk-), *adj.* **1.** pertaining or relating to George Berkeley, or his philosophy. —*n.* **2.** one who holds George Berkeley's system of idealism; one who denies the existence of a material world. —**Berke·le′ian·ism,** *n.*

Berke·ley (bûrk′lĭ; *Brit.* bärk′lĭ), *n.* **1. George,** 1685–1753, Irish bishop and philosopher. **2. Sir William,** 1610?–77, British royal governor of Virginia.

Berke·ley (bûrk′lĭ), *n.* a city in W California, on San Francisco Bay. 113,805 (1950).

Berk·shire (bûrk′shĭr, -shər; *Brit.* bärk′-), *n.* **1.** Also, **Berks** (bûrks; *Brit.* bärks), a county in S England. 373,000 pop. (est. 1946); 725 sq. mi. *Co. seat:* Reading. **2.** one of a breed of black hogs originating in Berkshire, England, with white markings on feet, face, and tail.

Berk·shire Hills (bûrk′shĭr, -shər), a range of low mountains in W Massachusetts: resort region. Highest peak, Mt. Greylock, 3505 ft. Also, **Berkshires.**

Ber·lin (bər lĭn′; *Ger.* bĕr lēn′ *for* 1; bûr′lĭn *for* 2), *n.* **1.** the capital of Germany, in the NE part, on the Spree river. 4,339,756 (1939). **2.** a city in N New Hampshire. 16,615 (1950).

Ber·lin (bər lĭn′), **Ir·ving,** born 1888, U.S. song writer.

ber·lin (bər lĭn′, bûr′lĭn), *n.* **1.** large four-wheeled closed carriage hung between two perches, and having two interior seats. **2.** *Auto.* berline. **3.** Berlin wool. [named after *Berlin*, capital of Prussia]

Berlin

ber·line (bər lĭn′; *Fr.* bĕr lēn′), *n.* **1.** *Auto.* a limousine with a movable glass partition behind the driver's seat. **2.** berlin (def. 1).

Berlin wool, a soft woolen yarn for knitting, etc.

Ber·li·oz (bĕr′lĭ ōz′; *Fr.* bĕr lyōz′), *n.* **Louis Hector** (lwē ĕk tôr′), 1803–69, French composer.

berm (bûrm), *n.* *Fort.* a narrow terrace between the rampart and moat. Also, **berme.** [t. F: (m.) *berme*, t. MD]

Ber·me·jo (bĕr mĕ′hō), *n.* a river in N Argentina, flowing SE to the Paraguay river. ab. 550 mi.

Ber·mu·da (bər mū′də), *n.* a group of islands in the Atlantic, 580 miles E of North Carolina: a British colony; resort. 33,925 pop. (est. 1944); 19 sq. mi. *Cap.*: Hamilton. Also, **Bermudas. —Ber·mu·di·an** (bər mū′dǐ ən), *adj.*

Bermuda onion, *Hort.* any of several mild flat varieties of onion grown on a large scale in Texas and, to some extent, in other parts of the U.S. and in Bermuda.

Bern (bûrn; *Fr.* bĕrn), *n.* **1.** the capital of Switzerland, in the W part. 133,700 (est. 1944). **2.** a canton in W Switzerland. 745,200 pop. (est. 1944); 2658 sq. mi. *Cap.*: Bern. Also, **Berne.** (bûr nĕz′, -nēs′), *n.*, *adj.*

Ber·na·dotte (bûr′nə dŏt′; *Fr.* bĕr nà dôt′), *n.* **Jean Baptiste Jules** (zhän bà tēst′ zhyl), 1764–1844, French marshal under Napoleon: king of Sweden and Norway, 1818–44, as Charles XIV.

Ber·nard (bûr′nərd, bər närd′), *n.* **1. Saint.** A.D. 923–1008 (*Bernard of Menthon*), French monk. **2. Saint,** (*Bernard of Cluny*) fl. 1140, French monk. **3. Saint,** (*Bernard of Clairvaux*, "the *Mellifluous Doctor*") 1090?–1153, French monk, preacher, and mystical writer.

Ber·nard·ine (bûr′nər dĭn, -dēn′), *adj.* **1.** of or pertaining to St. Bernard of Clairvaux. **2.** of or pertaining to the Cistercians. —*n.* **3.** a Cistercian.

Ber·nese Alps (bûr′nēz′, -nēs′), a range of the Alps in SW Switzerland. Highest peak, Finsteraarhorn, 14,026 ft.

Bern·har·di (bĕrn här′dĭ), *n.* **Friedrich A. J. von** (frē′drǐкн fən), 1849–1930, German general.

Bern·hardt (bûrn′härt; *Fr.* bĕr när′), *n.* **Sarah,** (*Rosine Bernard*) 1845–1923, French actress.

Ber·ni·na (bĕr nē′nä), *n.* a mountain peak (13,295 ft.) in SE Switzerland, in the Rhaetian Alps, traversed by Bernina Pass (7640 ft. high), leading into N Italy.

ber·ret·ta (bə rĕt′ə), *n.* *Eccles.* biretta.

ber·ried (bĕr′ĭd), *adj.* **1.** covered or laden with berries. **2.** of the form or nature of a berry; baccate. **3.** (of lobsters, etc.) having eggs.

ber·ry (bĕr′ĭ), n., pl. -ries, v. -ried, -rying. —n. 1. any small, (usually) stoneless, juicy fruit, irrespective of botanical structure, as the gooseberry, strawberry, hackberry, etc. 2. the hip of the rose. 3. a dry seed or kernel, as of wheat. 4. Bot. a simple fruit having a pulpy pericarp in which the seeds are embedded, as the grape, gooseberry, currant, tomato, etc. 5. one of the eggs of the lobster. —v.i. 6. to bear or produce berries. 7. to gather berries. [ME and OE berie, c. G beere] —ber′ry·less, adj. —ber′ry·like′, adj.

Ber·ry (bĕr′ĭ; Fr. bĕ·rē′), n. a former province in central France. Also, **Ber·ri**′.

ber·sa·glie·re (bĕr′sä lyĕ′rĕ), n. one of a class of riflemen or sharpshooters in the Italian army.

ber·serk (bûr′sûrk), adj. 1. violently and destructively frenzied. —n. 2. berserker.

ber·serk·er (bûr′sûr kər), n. Scand. Legend. one of ancient Norse warriors of great strength and courage, reputed to have fought with frenzied fury in battle; baresark. [t. Icel.: m. berserkr wild warrior; orig. uncert.]

berth (bûrth), n. 1. Railroads. a shelflike space allotted to a passenger in a vessel or in a railroad sleeping car as a sleeping space. 2. Naut. a. an apartment in a ship where a number of officers or men mess and reside. b. a sailor's bunk on board ship. c. a place for a hammock, or a repository for chests. d. a space allowed for safety or convenience between a vessel and other vessels, rocks, etc. e. room for a vessel to moor at a dock or to ride at anchor. 3. Brit. job; position. —v.t. 4. Naut. to assign or allot anchoring ground to; give space to lie in, as a ship in a dock. —v.i. 5. Naut. to come to a dock, anchorage, or moorage. [orig. uncert.; prob. der. BEAR¹]

ber·tha (bûr′thə), n. a kind of collar or trimming, as of lace, worn about the shoulders by women, as on a low-necked waist. [t. F: m. berthe, der. Berthe Bertha, Charlemagne's mother, noted for her modesty]

Ber·til·lon system (bûr′tə lŏn′; Fr. bĕr tē yôN′), a system of identifying persons, esp. criminals, by a record of individual physical measurements and peculiarities. [named after the inventor, A. Bertillon]

Ber·wick (bĕr′ĭk), n. a county in SE Scotland. 25,000 pop. (est. 1946); 457 sq. mi. Co. seat: Duns. Also, **Ber·wick·shire** (bĕr′ĭk shĭr′, -shər).

Ber·wyn (bûr′wĭn), n. a city in NE Illinois, near Chicago. 51,280 (1950).

ber·yl (bĕr′əl), n. 1. a mineral, beryllium aluminum silicate, $Be_1Al_2Si_6O_{18}$, usually green (but also blue, rose, white, and golden) and both opaque and transparent, the latter variety including the gems emerald and aquamarine: the principal ore of beryllium. 2. pale bluish green; sea green. [ME, t. L: m.s. beryllus, t. Gk.: m. bēryllos] —ber·yl·ine (bĕr′ə lĭn, -līn′), adj.

be·ryl·li·um (bĭ rĭl′ĭ əm), n. Chem. a steel-gray, divalent, hard, light, metallic element, the salts of which are said to have a sweetish taste (hence it is called glucinum by the French). Its chief use is in copper alloys not subject to fatigue, used for springs and contacts. Symbol: Be; at. wt.: 9.02; at. no.: 4; sp. gr.: 1.8 at 20°C. [f. BERYL + -IUM]

Ber·ze·li·us (bər zē′lĭ əs; Swed. bĕr sā′lĭ ŏŏs), n. **Jöns Jakob** (yœns yä′kŏp), **Baron**, 1779–1848, Swedish chemist.

Bes (bĕs), n. Egypt. Relig. a beneficent god of pleasure, and protector against sorcery. [t. Egypt.: m. Bĕs, Bĕses]

Be·san·çon (bə zän sôN′), n. a city in E France, on the Doubs river: Roman ruins. 63,507 (1946).

Bes·ant (bĕz′ənt for 1; bə zănt′; older bĕz′ənt for 2), n. 1. **Annie** (**Wood**), 1847–1933, British theosophist. 2. **Sir Walter**, 1836–1901, British novelist.

be·seech (bĭ sēch′), v.t., -sought, -seeching. 1. to implore urgently. 2. to beg eagerly for; solicit. [ME biseche(n), f. BE- + sechen, OE sēcan seek] —be·seech′er, n. —be·seech′ing, adj. —be·seech′ing·ly, adv. —be·seech′ing·ness, n. —Syn. 1. entreat, pray.

be·seem (bĭ sēm′), v.t. 1. to be fit for or worthy of. —v.i. 2. to be seemly or fitting.

be·set (bĭ sĕt′), v.t., -set, -setting. 1. to attack on all sides; assail; harass: beset by enemies, difficulties, etc. 2. to surround; hem in. 3. to set or place upon; bestud: beset with jewels. [ME besette(n), OE besettan, f. BE- + settan SET] —be·set′ment, n.

be·set·ting (bĭ sĕt′ĭng), adj. constantly attacking, tempting, etc.: our besetting sins.

be·shrew (bĭ shrōō′), v.t. Archaic. to curse; invoke evil upon: beshrew me. [ME beshrewen, f. BE- + SHREW¹]

be·side (bĭ sīd′), prep. 1. by or at the side of; near: sit down beside me. 2. compared with. 3. over and above; in addition to. 4. apart from; not connected with: beside the point or question. 5. beside oneself, out of one's senses through strong emotion. —adv. 6. in addition; besides. [ME; OE be sīdan by side]
—Syn. 1. BESIDE, BESIDES may both be used as prepositions, though with different meanings. BESIDE is almost exclusively used as a preposition meaning "by the side of": beside the house, the stream. BESIDES is used as a preposition meaning "in addition to" or "over and above": besides these honors he receiʌed a sum of money.

be·sides (bĭ sīdz′), adv. 1. moreover. 2. in addition. 3. otherwise; else. —prep. 4. over and above; in addition to. 5. other than; except. [f. BESIDE + adv. -s]
—Syn. 1. BESIDES, MOREOVER both indicate som thing additional to what has already been stated. BESIDES often

suggests that the addition is in the nature of an afterthought: the bill cannot be paid as yet; besides the work is not completed. MOREOVER is more formal and implies that the addition is something particular, emphatic, or important: I did not like the house; moreover, it was too high-priced. 4. See **beside**.

be·siege (bĭ sēj′), v.t., -sieged, -sieging. 1. to lay siege to. 2. to crowd around. 3. to assail or ply, as with requests, etc. —be·siege′ment, n. —be·sieg′er, n.

be·smear (bĭ smĭr′), v.t. 1. to smear over. 2. to befoul; sully; soil. [ME bismeren, OE besmerian. See BE-, SMEAR]

be·smirch (bĭ smûrch′), v.t. 1. to soil; discolor. 2. to detract from the honor of: to besmirch one's name.

be·som (bē′zəm), n. 1. brush or twigs bound together as a broom. 2. a broom of any kind. [ME besum broom, rod, OE besema, c. G besen]

be·sot (bĭ sŏt′), v.t., -sotted, -sotting. 1. to stupefy with drink; make a drunkard of. 2. to make stupid or foolish. 3. to infatuate.

be·sought (bĭ sôt′), v. pt. and pp. of beseech.

be·spake (bĭ spāk′), v. Archaic. pt. of bespeak.

be·span·gle (bĭ spăng′gəl), v.t., -gled, -gling. to adorn with, or as with, spangles.

be·spat·ter (bĭ spăt′ər), v.t. 1. to soil by spattering; sprinkle with dirt, water, etc. 2. to slander.

be·speak (bĭ spēk′), v.t., -spoke or (Archaic) -spake, -spoken or -spoke, -speaking. 1. to ask for in advance: to bespeak a calm hearing or the reader's patience. 2. Brit. to reserve beforehand; engage in advance; make arrangements for: to bespeak a seat in a theater. 3. Poetic. to speak to; address. 4. to show; indicate: this bespeaks a kindly heart. 5. Obs. to foretell; forebode. [ME bespeken, OE besprecan speak against, speak of, f. be- BE- + sprecan (for loss of -r- see SPEAK)]

be·spec·ta·cled (bĭ spĕk′tə kəld), adj. wearing eyeglasses.

be·spread (bĭ sprĕd′), v.t., -spread, -spreading. to spread over; cover with.

be·sprent (bĭ sprĕnt′), adj. Poetic. besprinkled; bestrewed. [pp. of bespreng (obs.), OE besprengan]

be·sprin·kle (bĭ sprĭng′kəl), v.t., -kled, -kling. to sprinkle over with something; bespatter.

Bes·sa·ra·bi·a (bĕs′ə rā′bĭ ə), n. a territory in the SW Soviet Union: formerly a province of Rumania. 2,815,240 pop. (est. 1943); 17,151 sq. mi. —**Bes′sa·ra′bi·an**, adj., n.

Bes·se·mer (bĕs′ə mər), n. 1. **Sir Henry**, 1813–98, British engineer: inventor of Bessemer process. 2. a city in central Alabama. 28,445 (1950).

Bessemer converter, Metall. a huge pear-shaped metal container used in the Bessemer process.

Bessemer process, Metall. a process of producing steel, in which impurities are removed by forcing a blast of air through molten iron.

best (bĕst), adj. (superlative of good). 1. of the highest quality, excellence, or standing: the best judgment. 2. most advantageous, suitable, or desirable: the best way. 3. largest; most: the best part of a day. —adv. (superlative of well). 4. most excellently or suitably; with most advantage or success. 5. in or to the highest degree; most fully. 6. had best, would be wiser, safer, etc., to. 7. the best thing, state, or part. 8. one's finest clothing. 9. utmost or best quality: at one's best. 10. at best, under the best circumstances. 11. get or have the best of, to defeat. 12. make the best of, to manage as well as one can (under unfavorable or adverse circumstances). —v.t. 13. to defeat; beat. 14. to outdo; surpass. [ME beste, OE betst, c. Goth batist-]

be·stead (bĭ stĕd′), v., -steaded, -steaded or -stead, -steading, adj. —v.t. 1. to help; assist; serve; avail. —adj. 2. Archaic. placed; situated. [ME, f. BE- + stead, v., help, be of use to, der. stead, n., profit, support]

bes·tial (bĕs′chəl, bĕst′yəl), adj. 1. of or belonging to a beast. 2. brutal; inhuman; irrational. 3. depravedly sensual; carnal. [ME, t. L: s. bestiālis] —bes′tial·ly, adv.

bes·ti·al·i·ty (bĕs′chĭ ăl′ə tĭ, -tĭ ăl′-), n. 1. bestial character or conduct; beastliness. 2. excessive appetites or indulgence. 3. unnatural sexual relations with an animal; sodomy.

bes·tial·ize (bĕs′chə līz′, bĕst′yə-), v.t., -ized, -izing. to make bestial.

bes·ti·ar·y (bĕs′tĭ ĕr′ĭ), n., pl. -aries. a collection of moralized fables about natural history objects, mostly animals, attributed to an Alexandrian Greek of the 4th century after Christ. It was universally known in the Middle Ages. [t. ML: m. s. bestiārium, prop. neut. of L bestiārius pertaining to beasts]

be·stir (bĭ stûr′), v.t., -stirred, -stirring. to stir up; rouse to action. [ME bestyrie(n), OE bestyrian heap up]

best man, the chief attendant of the bridegroom at a wedding.

be·stow (bĭ stō′), v.t. 1. to present as a gift; give; confer. 2. to dispose of; apply to some use. 3. Colloq. to provide quarters for. 4. to put; stow; deposit; store. —be·stow′al, n. —be·stow′ment, n.

be·strad·dle (bĭ străd′əl), v.t., -dled, -dling. to bestride.

be·strew (bǐ·strōō′), *v.t.*, **-strewed**, **-strewed** or **-strewn**, **-strewing**. **1.** to strew or cover (a surface). **2.** to strew or scatter about. **3.** to lie scattered over. [ME *bistrewe(n)*, OE *bestrēowian*]

be·stride (bǐ·strīd′), *v.t.*, **-strode** or **-strid**, **-stridden** or **-strid**, **-striding**. **1.** to get or be astride of; spread the legs on both sides of. **2.** to step over or across. [ME *bestride(n)*, OE *bestrīdan*, f. BE- + *strīdan* stride]

best seller, **1.** a book that has a very large sale during a given period. **2.** the author of such a book.

be·stud (bǐ·stŭd′), *v.t.*, **-studded**, **-studding**. to set with studs distributed over a surface; dot.

bet (bĕt), *v.*, **bet** or **betted**, **betting**, *n.* —*v.t.* **1.** to pledge as a forfeit to another who makes a similar pledge in return, in support of an opinion; stake; wager. —*v.i.* **2.** to lay a wager. —*n.* **3.** a pledge of something to be forfeited, in case one is wrong, to another who has the opposite opinion. **4.** that which is pledged. [orig. uncert.] —**bet′ter**, **bet′tor**, *n*

bet., between.

be·ta (bā′tə, bē′-), *n.* the 2nd letter of the Greek alphabet (B, β), often used to designate the second in a series, esp. in scientific classification, as: **a.** *Astron.* (of a constellation) the second brightest star: *Rigel is β (or Beta) Orionis.* **b.** *Chem.* (of a compound) one of the possible positions of substituted atoms or groups: *β eucaine* or *betaeucaine*.

be·ta·eu·caine (bā′tə·ū′kān, bē′tə-), *n.* eucaine (def. 2).

be·ta·ine (bē′tə·ēn′, -ǐn; bǐ·tā′ēn, -ǐn), *n. Chem.* a nonpoisonous crystalline substance, $C_5H_{11}O_2N(H_2O)$, a sweetish-tasting alkaloid, found in sugar beets, cottonseed, the sprouts of wheat and barley; related chemically to glycine. Also, **be·ta·in** (bē′tə·ǐn, bǐ·tā′-). [f. L *bēta* beet + -INE[2]]

be·take (bǐ·tāk′), *v.t.*, **-took**, **-taken**, **-taking**. —**betake oneself**, **1.** to go: *she betook herself to the market.* **2.** to resort to; undertake: *he betook himself to flight.*

be·ta·naph·thol (bā′tə·nǎf′thōl, -thŏl, -nǎp′-, bē′tə-), *n. Chem.* a crystalline antiseptic, $C_{10}H_7CH$.

beta particle, *Physics.* an electron in a beta ray.

beta ray, *Physics.* a ray emitted by radium and other radioactive substances, resembling the cathode ray and consisting of electrons.

beta test, *Psychol.* an intelligence test requiring no use of written or spoken language, used by the U. S. Army in World War I.

be·ta·tron (bā′tə·trŏn′, bē′-), *n. Physics.* a device based on the principle of the transformer, which accelerates electrons to high energy by a magnetic field varying with time.

be·tel (bē′təl), *n.* an East Indian pepper plant, *Piper Betle.* Cf. **betel nut.** [t. Pg.: m. *betele*, earlier *vitele*, t. Malay: m. *vettila*, Tamil *vettilei*]

Be·tel·geuse (bē′təl·jōōz′, bĕt′əl·jœz′), *n. Astron.* a giant reddish star of the first magnitude in the constellation Orion. Also, **Be′tel·geux′.** [t. F, ? t. Ar.: m. *bīt-al-jāuza* the giant's shoulder]

betel nut, the areca nut, chewed extensively by East Indian natives.

betel palm, a tall, graceful, Asiatic palm, *Areca Catechu*, that bears the areca nut or betel nut, so named from its association in native usage with the betel plant.

bête noire (bāt′ nwär′; *Fr.* bĕt nwär′), *French.* something that one especially dislikes or dreads, either a person, task, or object; bugbear. [F: black beast]

Beth·a·ny (bĕth′ə·nǐ), *n.* a village in Arab Palestine, near Jerusalem, at the foot of the Mount of Olives.

beth·el (bĕth′əl), *n.* **1.** a hallowed spot. Gen. 28:19. **2.** a church or chapel for seamen, often afloat in a harbor. **3.** *Brit.* a dissenters' chapel or meeting house. [t. Heb.: m. *bēth-ēl* house of God]

Beth·el (bĕth′əl), *n.* ancient town in Arab Palestine.

Be·thes·da (bə·thĕz′də), *n.* **1.** *Bible.* a pool with healing powers in Jerusalem. John 5:2–4. **2.** a chapel.

be·think (bǐ·thǐngk′), *v.*, **-thought**, **-thinking**. —*v.t.* (generally reflexive) **1.** to think; consider. **2.** to remember; recall. **3.** to determine; resolve. **4.** *Obs.* to bear in mind; remember. —*v.i.* **5.** *Archaic.* to consider; meditate. [ME *bethenken*, OE *bethencan*, f. BE- + *thencan* consider]

Beth·le·hem (bĕth′lǐ·əm, -hĕm′), *n.* **1.** a town in central Arab Palestine, near Jerusalem; birthplace of Jesus and of David. 8820. (est. 1944). **2.** a city in E Pennsylvania. 66,340 (1950).

Beth·mann-Holl·weg (bāt′män hôl′vāKH), *n.* **Theobald von** (tā′ō bält′ fən), 1856–1921, German statesman: chancellor of Germany, 1909–17.

Beth·nal Green (bĕth′nəl), a NE industrial borough of London, England. 59,210 (est. 1946).

be·thought (bǐ·thôt′), *v.* pt. and pp. of **bethink.**

Beth·sa·i·da (bĕth·sā′ə·də), *n.* an ancient town in N Israel, near the N shore of the Sea of Galilee.

be·tide (bǐ·tīd′), *v.*, **-tided**, **-tiding**. —*v.t.* **1.** to happen;

befall; come to: woe betide the villain! —*v.i.* **2.** to come to pass. [ME *betide(n)*, f. BE- + *tiden*, OE *tīdan* betide]

be·times (bǐ·tīmz′), *adv.* **1.** before it is too late; early. **2.** soon. [ME *betymes*, f. *betime* by time + adv. -s]

bê·tise (bě·tēz′), *n.* **1.** stupidity. **2.** a stupid or foolish act or remark. **3.** an absurdity; trifle. [F, der. *bête* beast]

be·to·ken (bǐ·tō′kən), *v.t.* **1.** to give evidence of; indicate. **2.** to be or give a token of; portend.

bé·ton (bě·tŏn′), *n.* a kind of concrete composed of a mixture of cement, sand, and gravel.

bet·o·ny (bĕt′ə·nǐ), *n.* **1.** a plant, *Stachys* (formerly *Betonica*) *officinalis*, of the mint family, formerly used in medicine and dyeing. **2.** any of various similar plants. [t. LL: m. *betoni(ca)*; r. ME *beteine*, t. OF; r. OE *betonice*, t. LL (as above)]

be·took (bǐ·tŏŏk′), *v.* pt. of **betake.**

be·tray (bǐ·trā′), *v.t.* **1.** to deliver or expose to an enemy by treachery or disloyalty. **2.** to be unfaithful in keeping or upholding: *to betray a trust.* **3.** to be disloyal to; disappoint the hopes or expectations of. **4.** to reveal or disclose in violation of confidence: *to betray a secret.* **5.** to reveal unconsciously (something one would preferably conceal). **6.** to show; exhibit: *no one betrayed any wish to quarrel.* **7. betray oneself**, to reveal one's real character, plans, etc. **8.** to deceive; mislead. **9.** to seduce and abandon. [ME *bitraien*, f. bi- + *traien*, t. OF: m. *traïr*, ult. g. L *trādere* give over] —**be·tray′al**, *n.* —**be·tray′er**, *n.*

be·troth (bǐ·trōth′, -trŏth′), *v.t.* **1.** to promise to marry. **2.** to arrange for the marriage of; affiance. [ME *betrouthen*, var. of *betreuthien*, der. BE- + *treuthe*, OE *trēowth* pledge. See TROTH, TRUTH]

be·troth·al (bǐ·trō′thəl, -trŏ′thəl), *n.* act or ceremony of betrothing; engagement. Also, **be·troth′ment.**

be·trothed (bǐ·trōthd′, -trŏtht′), *adj.*, **1.** engaged to be married. —*n.* **2.** an engaged person.

bet·ter (bĕt′ər), *adj.* (*comparative of* good). **1.** of superior quality or excellence: *a better position.* **2.** of superior value, use, fitness, desirability, acceptableness, etc.: *a better time for action.* **3.** larger; greater: *the better part of a lifetime.* **4.** improved in health; healthier. —*adv.* (*comparative of* well). **5.** in a more excellent way or manner: *to behave better.* **6.** in a superior degree: *to know a man better.* **7.** more: *better than a mile to town.* **8. had better**, would be wiser, safer, etc., to. **9. better off**, in better circumstances. **10. think better of**, to reconsider and decide more favorably or wisely. —*v.t.* **11.** to make better; improve; increase the good qualities of. **12. better oneself**, to improve one's social standing, education, etc. **13.** to improve upon; surpass; exceed: *they bettered working conditions.* —*n.* **14.** that which has superior excellence, etc.: *the better of two choices.* **15.** (*usually pl.*) one's superior in wisdom, wealth, etc. **16.** superiority; mastery: *to get the better of someone.* [ME *bettre*, OE *betera*, c. Goth. *batiza*] —**Syn. 11.** See **improve.** —**Ant. 1.** worse. **11.** worsen.

bet·ter·ment (bĕt′ər·mənt), *n.* **1.** improvement. **2.** (*usually pl.*) *Law.* an improvement of real property, other than mere repairs.

Bet·ter·ton (bĕt′ər·tən), *n.* **Thomas,** 1635?–1710, British actor.

bet·u·la·ceous (bĕch′ŏŏ·lā′shəs), *adj. Bot.* belonging to the *Betulaceae*, a family of trees and shrubs including the birch, alder, etc. [f. s. L *betula* birch + -ACEOUS]

be·tween (bǐ·twēn′), *prep.* **1.** in the space separating (two points, objects, etc.). **2.** intermediate to, in time, quantity, or degree: *between 12 and 1 o'clock, between pink and red.* **3.** connecting: *a link between parts.* **4.** involving; concerning: *war between nations, choice between things.* **5.** by joint action or possession of: *to own land between them.* —*adv.* **6.** in the intervening space or time; in an intermediate position or relation: *visits far between.* [ME *betwene*, OE *betwēonan, betwēonum*, f. *be* by + *-twēonan, twēonum*, der. *twā* two] —**Syn. 1.** See **among.**

be·twixt (bǐ·twǐkst′), *prep., adv.* **1.** *Archaic and Poetic* between. **2. betwixt and between**, neither the one nor the other; in a middle position. [ME *betwix*, OE *betweox, betweon*, for final *-t*, cf. *against*, etc.]

Beu·lah (bū′lə), *n. Bible.* the land of Israel. Isa. 62:4. [t. Heb.: m. *bě'ulāh* married]

Beu·then (boi′tən), *n.* German name of **Bytom.**

bev·a·tron (bĕv′ə·trŏn′), *n. Physics.* a type of electro-nuclear machine.

bev·el (bĕv′əl), *n., v.*, **-eled**, **-eling** or (*esp. Brit.*) **-elled**, **-elling**, *adj.* —*n.* **1.** the inclination that one line or surface makes with another when not at right angles. **2.** an adjustable instrument for drawing angles or adjusting the surface of work to a particular inclination. —*v.t., v.i.* **3.** to cut or slant at a bevel. —*adj.* **4.** oblique; sloping; slanted. [orig. obscure]

bevel gear, *Mach.* a gear in which the axis or shaft of the driver forms an angle with the axis or shaft of the wheel driven. See illus. under **gear.**

bevel square, an adjustable tool used by woodworkers for laying out angles and for testing the accuracy of surfaces worked to a slope.

bev·er·age (bĕv′ər·ǐj, bĕv′rǐj), *n.* a drink of any kind: *intoxicating beverages.* [ME, t. OF: m. *bevrage*, der. *beure*, g. L *bibere* drink]

Bevel square

Bev·er·idge (bĕv′ər·ǐj, bĕv′rǐj), *n.* **Sir William Henry**, born 1879, British economist.

Bev·er·ly (bĕv/ər lĭ), *n.* a city in NE Massachusetts. 28,884 (1950).

Beverly Hills, a city in SW California, near Los Angeles. 29,032 (1950).

Bev·in (bĕv/ĭn), *n.* **Ernest,** 1881–1951, British labor leader: foreign minister, 1945–1951.

bev·y (bĕv/ĭ), *n., pl.* **bevies.** 1. a flock of birds, esp. larks or quails. 2. a group, esp. of girls or women. [ME *bevey;* orig. uncert.]

be·wail (bĭ wāl/), *v.t.* 1. to express deep sorrow for; lament. —*v.i.* 2. to express grief.

be·ware (bĭ wâr/), *v.i., v.t.,* **-wared, -waring.** to be wary, cautious, or careful (of). [prop. two words, BE + WARE², adj.]

be·wil·der (bĭ wĭl/dər), *v.t.* to confuse or puzzle completely; perplex. [f. BE- + WILDER] —**be·wil/dered,** *adj.* —**be·wil/dered·ly,** *adv.* —**be·wil/der·ing,** *adj.* —**be·wil/der·ing·ly,** *adv.* —**Syn.** mystify, nonplus, confound, daze. See **puzzle.**

be·wil·der·ment (bĭ wĭl/dər mənt), *n.* 1. bewildered state. 2. a confusing maze or tangle.

be·witch (bĭ wĭch/), *v.t.* 1. to affect by witchcraft or magic; throw a spell over. 2. to enchant. —**be·witch/er,** *n.* —**be·witch/er·y,** *n.* —**be·witch/ing,** *adj.* —**be·witch/ing·ly,** *adv.* —**be·witch/ment,** *n.* —**Syn.** 2. fascinate, captivate.

be·wray (bĭ rā/), *v.t. Obs.* 1. to reveal; disclose. 2. to betray; expose. [ME *bewreien,* f. BE- + *wreien,* OE *wrēgan* accuse]

bey (bā), *n., pl.* **beys.** 1. the governor of a minor Turkish province. 2. a Turkish title of respect for important persons (placed after the proper name). 3. the title of the native head of Tunis. [t. Turk.: m. *beg*]

Beyle (bĕl), *n.* **Marie Henri** (må rē/ än rē/), real name of Stendhal.

be·yond (bĭ yŏnd/), *prep.* 1. on or to the farther side of: *beyond the house.* 2. farther on than; more distant than: *beyond the horizon.* 3. later than: *they stayed beyond the time limit.* 4. outside the understanding, limits, or reach of; past: *beyond human comprehension.* 5. superior to; surpassing; above: *wise beyond all others.* 6. more than; in excess of; over and above. —*adv.* 7. farther on or away: *as far as the house and beyond.* —*n.* 8. the life after the present one. [ME *beyonde,* OE *begeondan,* f. *be* by + *geondan* beyond]

Bey·routh (bā/rōōt, bā rōōt/), *n.* Beirut.

bez·ant (bĕz/ənt, bə zănt/), *n.* 1. the solidus, a gold coin, of the Byzantine emperors, widely circulated in Europe during the middle ages. 2. *Archit.* an ornament in the form of a flat disk. [ME, t. OF: m. *besant,* g. L *Bȳzantius* Byzantine]

bez·el (bĕz/əl), *n.* 1. a sloping face or edge of a chisel or other cutting tool. 2. the upper oblique faces of a brilliant-cut gem. 3. the grooved ring or rim holding a gem or watch crystal in its setting. [prob. t. F, der. *biais* slant. See BIAS]

Bé·ziers (bē zyē/), *n.* a city in S France. 64,561 (1946).

be·zique (bə zēk/), *n. Cards.* a game, resembling pinochle, played with 64 cards. [t. F: m. *bésigue*]

be·zoar (bē/zōr), *n.* 1. a calculus or concretion found in the stomach or intestines of certain animals, esp. ruminants, formerly reputed to be efficacious against poison. 2. *Obs.* a counterpoison or antidote. [t. Ar.: m. *bāzahr,* t. Pers.: m. *pādzahr* counterpoison]

be·zo·ni·an (bĭ zō/nĭ ən), *n. Archaic.* an indigent rascal; scoundrel. [der. obs. *besonio,* t. It.: m. *bisogno* need, needy fellow]

b.f., *Printing.* boldface. Also, **bf.**

B.F.A., Bachelor of Fine Arts.

Bha·ga·vad-Gi·ta (bŭg/ə vəd gē/tä), *n. Hinduism.* a famous episode of eighteen chapters, in the *Mahabharata,* wherein the divine incarnation Krishna expounds the duties of the caste system along with devotion to Deity. [t. Skt.: the Song of the Blessed One]

bhang (băng), *n.* 1. the Indian hemp plant. 2. a preparation of its leaves and tops used in India as an intoxicant and narcotic. Also, **bang.** [t. Hind.: m. *bhāng,* g. Skt. *bhangā* hemp]

Bhau·na·gar (bou nŭg/ər), *n.* a seaport in W India. 102,851 (1941). Also, **Bhav·na·gar** (bäv nŭg/ər).

bhees·ty (bēs/tĭ), *n. India.* water carrier. Also, **bhees/tie.** [t. Hind.: m. *bhīstī,* t. Pers.: m. *bihishtī* water carrier, deriv. (presumably jocular) of *bihisht* paradise]

Bho·pal (bō päl/), *n.* 1. an independent state in the central part of the peninsula of India. 785,300 pop. (1941); 6921 sq. mi. 2. its capital. 75,228 (1941).

Bhu·tan (bōō tän/), *n.* a principality in the Himalayas NE of India: partly controlled by Great Britain. 250,000 pop. (est. 1942); ab. 19,300 sq. mi. *Cap.:* Punaka.

bi-, a prefix meaning: 1. twice, doubly, two, as in *bilateral, binocular, biweekly.* 2. (in science) denoting in general two, as in *bicarbonate.* Also, **bin-.** [t. L, comb. form of *bis* twice, doubly, der. L *duo* two]

Bi, *Chem.* bismuth.

B.I., British India.

Bi·a·fra (bē ä/frə), *n.* **Bight of,** a wide bay in the E part of the Gulf of Guinea, off the W coast of Africa.

Bia·lys·tok (byä lĭ/stŏk), *n.* a city in E Poland. 55,659 (1946). Russian, **Byelostok.**

bi·an·gu·lar (bī ăng/gyə lər), *adj.* having two angles or corners.

bi·an·nu·al (bī ăn/yōō əl), *adj.* occurring twice a year. —**bi·an/nu·al·ly,** *adv.*

bi·an·nu·late (bī ăn/yōō lĭt, -lāt/), *adj. Zool.* having two rings or ringlike bands, as of color.

Bi·ar·ritz (bē/ə rĭts/; *Fr.* byà rēts/), a city in SW France, on the Bay of Biscay: resort. 22,022 (1946).

bi·as (bī/əs), *n., adj., adv., v.,* **biased, biasing** or (*esp. Brit.*) **biassed, biassing.** —*n.* 1. an oblique or diagonal line of direction, esp. across a woven fabric: *to cut cloth on the bias.* 2. a particular tendency or inclination, esp. one which prevents unprejudiced consideration of a question. 3. *Bowling.* a. a bulge or a greater weight on one side of the bowl, causing it to swerve. b. the swerved course of a bowl, due to shape or weighting. 4. *Radio.* the direct voltage placed on the grid of an electronic tube. —*adj.* 5. cut, set, folded, etc., diagonally. —*adv.* 6. slantingly; obliquely. —*v.t.* 7. to influence, usually unfairly; prejudice; warp. [t. F: m. *biais* slant, prob. g. L **biaxius* having two axes]

—**Syn.** 2. BIAS, PREJUDICE mean a strong inclination of the mind or a preconceived opinion about something or someone. A BIAS may be favorable or unfavorable: *bias in favor of or against an idea.* PREJUDICE implies a preformed judgment even more unreasoning than BIAS, and usually implies an unfavorable opinion: *prejudice against a race.* —**Ant.** 2. impartiality. 5. straight.

bi·au·ric·u·lar (bī/ô rĭk/yə lər), *adj. Anat.* 1. having two auricles. 2. pertaining to the two ears.

bi·au·ric·u·late (bī/ô rĭk/yə lĭt, -lāt/), *adj. Biol.* having two auricles or earlike parts.

bi·ax·i·al (bī ăk/sĭ əl), *adj.* 1. having two axes. 2. (of a crystal) having two directions in which no double refraction occurs. —**bi·ax/i·al·ly,** *adv.*

bib (bĭb), *n., v.,* **bibbed, bibbing.** —*n.* 1. article of clothing, worn under the chin by a child, esp. while eating, to protect the dress. 2. the upper part of an apron. —*v.t.* 3. *Obs.* to tipple. [ME *bibben;* orig. uncert., ? t. L: m. *bibere* drink] —**bib/like/,** *adj.*

Bib., 1. Bible. 2. Biblical.

bib and tucker, *Colloq.* clothes.

bi·bas·ic (bī bā/sĭk), *adj. Chem.* dibasic.

bib·ber (bĭb/ər), *n.* a steady drinker; tippler.

bib·cock (bĭb/kŏk/), *n. Plumbing.* a faucet having a nozzle bent downward.

bi·be·lot (bĭb/lō; *Fr.* bē blō/), *n.* small object of curiosity, beauty, or rarity. [t. F]

bi·bi·va·lent (bī/bī vā/lənt, bī bĭv/ə-), *adj. Chem.* denoting an electrolytic compound which splits into two ions, each with a valence of two.

Bibl., 1. biblical. 2. bibliographical. Also, **bibl.**

Bi·ble (bī/bəl), *n.* 1. the collection of sacred writings of the Christian religion, comprising the Old and the New Testament. 2. the Old Testament only. 3. (*often l.c.*) the sacred writings of any religion. 4. (*l.c.*) any book accepted as authoritative. [ME *bibul,* t. ML: m. s. *biblia,* t. Gk., pl. of *biblíon,* dim. of *bíblos* book]

Bib·li·cal (bĭb/lə kəl), *adj.* 1. of or in the Bible. 2. in accord with the Bible. —**Bib/li·cal·ly,** *adv.*

Biblical Latin, the form of Latin used in the translation of the Bible, which became current in Western Europe at the beginning of the Middle Ages.

Bib·li·cist (bĭb/lə sĭst), *n.* 1. an adherent of the letter of the Bible; a fundamentalist. 2. a Biblical scholar.

biblio-, a word element meaning: 1. book, as in *bibliophile.* 2. Bible, as in *bibliolatry.* [t. Gk., comb. form of *biblíon* book]

bib·li·o·film (bĭb/lĭ ə fĭlm/), *n.* a microfilm used esp. in libraries for reproducing valuable or much-used books.

bibliog., 1. bibliographer. 2. bibliography.

bib·li·og·ra·pher (bĭb/lĭ ŏg/rə fər), *n.* an expert in bibliography. Also, **bib·li·o·graph** (bĭb/lĭ ə grăf/, -gräf/). [f. s. Gk. *bibliográphos* written + -ER²]

bib·li·og·ra·phy (bĭb/lĭ ŏg/rə fĭ), *n., pl.* **-phies.** 1. a compilation of a complete or a selective literature on a particular subject; a list of works by a given author. 2. the art of describing books authoritatively with respect to authorship, format, imprint, etc.; the study of variations in editions, issues, etc. —**bib·li·o·graph·ic** (bĭb/lĭ ə grăf/ĭk), **bib/li·o·graph/i·cal,** *adj.*

bib·li·ol·a·try (bĭb/lĭ ŏl/ə trĭ), *n.* excessive reverence for the Bible. —**bib/li·ol/a·ter,** *n.* —**bib/li·ol/a·trous,** *adj.*

bib·li·o·man·cy (bĭb/lĭ ō măn/sĭ), *n.* divination by means of a book, as the Bible, opened at random to some verse taken as significant.

bib·li·o·ma·ni·a (bĭb/lĭ ō mā/nĭ ə), *n.* an enthusiasm for collecting books. —**bib·li·o·ma·ni·ac** (bĭb/lĭ ō mā/nĭ ăk/), *adj., n.* —**bib·li·o·ma·ni·a·cal** (bĭb/lĭ ō mə nī/ə kəl), *adj.*

bib·li·op·e·gy (bĭb/lĭ ŏp/ə jĭ), *n.* art of binding books. [f. BIBLIO- + m. s. Gk. -*pēgia,* der. *pēgnýnai* fasten]

bib·li·o·phile (bĭb/lĭ ə fīl/, -fĭl), *n.* a lover of books. Also, **bib·li·o·phil** (bĭb/lĭ ə fĭl), **bib·li·oph·i·list** (bĭb/lĭ ŏf/ə lĭst). [t. F. See BIBLIO-, -PHILE] —**bib/li·oph/i·lism,** *n.* —**bib/li·oph/i·lis/tic,** *adj.*

bib·li·o·pole (bĭb/lĭ ə pōl/), *n.* a bookseller, esp. a dealer in books unique for their rarity, artistic format, etc. Also, **bib·li·o·p·list** (bĭb/lĭ ŏp/ə lĭst). [t. L: m. *bibliopōla,* t. Gk.: m. *bibliopṓlēs*] —**bib·li·o·pol·ic** (bĭb/lĭ ə pŏl/ĭk), **bib/li·o·pol/i·cal,** *adj.* —**bib·li·o·pol·ism** (bĭb/lĭ ŏp/ə lĭz/əm), **bib/li·op/o·ly,** *n.*

Bib·list (bĭb/lĭst, bī/blĭst), *n.* 1. one who regards the Bible as the only rule of faith. 2. a Biblicist.

bib·u·lous (bĭb′yə ləs), *adj.* **1.** addicted to alcoholic drinking. **2.** absorbent; spongy. [t. L: m. *bibulus* freely drinking] —**bib′u·lous·ly,** *adv.* —**bib′u·lous·ness,** *n.*

bi·cam·er·al (bī kăm′ər əl), *adj. Govt.* having two branches, chambers, or houses, as a legislative body.

bicarb., sodium bicarbonate.

bi·car·bo·nate (bī kär′bə nĭt, -nāt′), *n. Chem.* a salt of carbonic acid, containing the HCO_3^{-1} radical; an acid carbonate, as *sodium bicarbonate*, $NaHCO_3$.

bice (bīs), *n.* blue or green as of carbonates of copper. [ME *bis*, t. OF: dark-colored, brownish-gray]

bi·cen·te·nar·y (bī sĕn′tə nĕr′ĭ, bī′sĕn tĕn′ə rĭ), *adj., n., pl.* **-naries.** *Chiefly Brit.* bicentennial.

bi·cen·ten·ni·al (bī′sĕn tĕn′ĭ əl), *adj.* **1.** consisting of or lasting 200 years: *a bicentennial period.* **2.** occurring every 200 years. —*n.* **3.** a 200th anniversary. **4.** its celebration. Also, *esp. Brit.*, **bicentenary.**

bi·ceph·a·lous (bī sĕf′ə ləs), *adj. Bot., Zool.* having two heads. [f. BI- + m. s. Gk. *kephalē* head + -OUS]

bi·ceps (bī′sĕps), *n. Anat.* a muscle having two heads of origin, esp. in *Anat.* **a. biceps brachii,** the muscle on the front of the upper arm, which bends the forearm. **b. biceps femoris,** the hamstring muscle on the back of the thigh. [L: two-headed]

bi·chlo·ride (bī klōr′īd, -ĭd), *n. Chem.* **1.** a compound in which two atoms of chlorine are combined with another element or radical. **2.** bichloride of mercury.

bichloride of mercury, *Chem.* corrosive sublimate.

bi·chro·mate (bī krō′māt), *n. Chem.* **1.** dichromate. **2.** chromate of potassium, $K_2Cr_2O_7$.

bi·cip·i·tal (bī sĭp′ə təl), *adj.* **1.** having two heads. **2.** *Anat.* pertaining to the biceps. [f. s. L *biceps* two-headed + -AL¹]

bick·er (bĭk′ər), *v.i.* **1.** to engage in petulant argument; wrangle. **2.** to run rapidly; move quickly; rush; hurry. **3.** to quiver; flicker; glitter. —*n.* **4.** an angry dispute; squabble. [ME *biker*(en). Cf. MLG *bicken* prick, thrust] —**bick′er·er,** *n.*

Bi·col (bē kol′), *n.* Bikol.

bi·col·lat·er·al (bī′kə lăt′ər əl), *adj. Bot.* (of a bundle) having the xylem lined with phloem on both its inner and outer faces.

bi·col·or (bī′kŭl′ər), *adj.* of two colors: *a bicolor flower.* Also, **bi′col′ored.**

bi·con·cave (bī kŏn′kāv, bī′kŏn kāv′), *adj.* concave on both sides, as a lens. See illus. under **lens.**

bi·con·vex (bī kŏn′vĕks, bī′kŏn vĕks′), *adj.* convex on both sides, as a lens. See illus. under **lens.**

bi·corn (bī′kôrn), *adj. Bot., Zool.* having two horns or hornlike parts. Also, **bi·cor·nu·ate** (bī kôr′nyōō ĭt, -āt′). [t. L: s. *bicornis* two-horned]

bi·cor·po·ral (bī kôr′pə rəl), *adj.* having two bodies. Also, **bi·cor·po·re·al** (bī′kôr pōr′ĭ əl).

bi·cron (bī′krŏn, bĭk′rŏn), *n. Physics.* one billionth of a meter.

bi·cus·pid (bī kŭs′pĭd), *adj.* Also, **bi·cus·pi·date** (bī kŭs′pĭ dāt′). **1.** having two cusps or points, as certain teeth. —*n.* **2.** *Anat.* one of eight such teeth in man, four on each jaw between the cuspid and the first molar teeth. [f. BI- + s. L *cuspis* point]

bi·cy·cle (bī′sə kəl, -sĭk′əl), *n., v.,* **-cled, -cling.** —*n.* **1.** a vehicle with two wheels, one in front of the other, and having a saddlelike seat for the rider. It is steered by turning a handlebar and driven by pedals or a motor. —*v.i.* **2.** to ride a bicycle. [t. F: f. *bi-* BI- + m.s. Gk. *kýklos* circle, wheel] —**bi′cy·cler, bi′cy·clist,** *n.*

bi·cy·clic (bī sī′klĭk, -sĭk′lĭk), *adj.* **1.** consisting of or having two circles. **2.** *Bot.* in two whorls, as the stamens of a flower. Also, **bi·cy′cli·cal.**

bid (bĭd), *v.,* **bade** or **bad** (for 1, 2) or **bid** (for 3-8), **bidden** or **bid, bidding,** *n.* —*v.t.* **1.** to command; order; direct: *bid them depart.* **2.** to say as a greeting or benediction: *to bid farewell.* **3.** *Com.* to offer, as a price at an auction or as terms in a competition to secure a contract. **4.** *Com.* **a.** to overbid all offers for (property) at an auction in order to retain ownership (fol. by *in*). **b.** to increase (the market price) by increasing bids (fol. by *up*). **5.** *Cards.* to enter a bid of a given quantity or suit: *to bid two no-trump, bid spades.* —*v.i.* **6.** to make an offer to purchase at a price. **7. bid fair,** to seem likely. —*n.* **8.** act of one who bids. **9.** *Cards.* **a.** the number of points or tricks a player offers to make. **b.** the turn of a person to bid. **10.** *Colloq.* an invitation. **11.** an attempt to attain some goal or purpose: *a bid for election.* [ME *bidde*(n), OE (*ge*)*biddan* beg, ask, pray; sense devel. influenced by ME *bede*(n), OE *bēodan* offer, proclaim, command] —**bid′der,** *n.* —**Syn. 1.** charge.

bi·dar·ka (bī där′kə), *n.* the sealskin boat of the Alaskan Eskimo. Also, **bi·dar·kee** (bī där′kē). [t. Russ., dim. of *baidara* coracle]

bid·da·ble (bĭd′ə bəl), *adj.* **1.** willing to do what is asked; obedient; docile. **2.** *Cards.* adequate to bid upon: *a biddable hand at bridge.*

Bid·de·ford (bĭd′ə fərd), *n.* a city in SW Maine. 20,836 (1950).

bid·den (bĭd′ən), *v.* pp. of **bid.**

bid·ding (bĭd′ĭng), *n.* **1.** invitation; command; order. **2.** a bid. **3.** bids collectively.

Bid·dle (bĭd′əl), *n.* **1. John,** 1615-62, British theologian: founder of Unitarianism in England. **2. Nicholas,** 1786-1844, U.S. financier.

bid·dy (bĭd′ĭ), *n., pl.* **-dies.** chicken. [orig. uncert.]

bide (bīd), *v.,* **bided** (for 1, 2) or **bode** (for 3), **biding.** —*v.t.* **1. bide one's time,** to wait for a favorable opportunity. **2.** *Archaic.* to encounter. **3.** *Archaic.* to endure; bear. —*v.i.* **4.** *Archaic.* to dwell; abide; wait; remain; continue. [ME *biden*, OE *bīdan*]

bield (bēld), *n. Scot.* shelter.

Bie·le·feld (bē′lə fĕlt′), *n.* a city in NW Germany. 129,466 (1939).

bien en·ten·du (byăn năn tän dy′), *French.* naturally; of course.

Bienne (byĕn). *n.* **Lake of,** a lake in NW Switzerland: traces of prehistoric lake dwellings. 16 sq. mi. Also, **Bie·ler·see** (bē′lər zā′).

bi·en·ni·al (bī ĕn′ĭ əl), *adj.* **1.** happening every two years: *biennial games.* **2.** *Bot.* completing its normal term of life in two years, flowering and fruiting the second year, as beet, winter wheat. —*n.* **3.** any event occurring once in two years. **4.** *Bot.* a biennial plant [f. s. L *biennium* two-year period + -AL¹] —**bi·en′ni·al·ly,** *adv.*

bien·ve·nu (byăn və ny′), *adj. French.* welcome —**bien·ve·nue′,** *adj., fem.*

Bien·ville (byăn vēl′), *n.* **Jean Baptiste Le Moyne, Sieur de** (zhän bà tēst′ lə mwän′, syœr də), 1680-1768, French governor of Louisiana: founder of New Orleans.

bier (bĭr), *n.* a frame or stand on which a corpse, or the coffin containing it, is laid before burial. [ME *bere*, OE *bēr, bær,* c. G *bahre*]

Bierce (bĭrs), *n.* **Ambrose Gwinett** (gwĭ nĕt′), 1842-1914?, U.S. journalist and short-story writer.

biest·ings (bēs′tĭngz), *n. pl.* beestings.

bi·fa·cial (bī fā′shəl), *adj.* **1.** having two faces or fronts. **2.** having the opposite surfaces alike. **3.** *Bot.* having the opposite surfaces unlike, as a leaf.

bi·far·i·ous (bī fâr′ĭ əs), *adj. Bot.* in two vertical rows. [t. L. m. *bifarius* twofold] —**bi·far′i·ous·ly,** *adv.*

biff (bĭf), *n. U.S. Slang.* **1.** a blow; punch. —*v.t.* **2.** to hit; punch.

bif·fin (bĭf′ĭn), *n. Brit.* a red variety of winter cooking apple. [var. of *beefing*, f. BEEF (from the color) + -ING¹]

bi·fid (bī′fĭd), *adj.* cleft into two parts or lobes. [t. L: s. *bifidus*] —**bi·fid′i·ty,** *n.* —**bi·fid′ly,** *adv.*

bi·fi·lar (bī fī′lər), *adj.* furnished or fitted with two filaments or threads. —**bi·fi′lar·ly,** *adv.*

bi·flag·el·late (bī flăj′ə lāt′, -lĭt), *adj. Zool.* having two whiplike appendages or flagella.

bi·flex (bī′flĕks), *adj.* bent at two places.

bi·fo·cal (bī fō′kəl), *adj.* **1.** (esp. in *Optics*) having two foci. **2.** (of spectacle or eyeglass lenses) having two portions, one for near and one for far vision. —*n.* **3.** (*pl.*) eyeglasses with bifocal lenses.

bi·fo·li·ate (bī fō′lĭ ĭt, -āt), *adj.* having two leaves.

bi·forked (bī′fôrkt′), *adj.* bifurcate.

bi·form (bī′fôrm), *adj.* having or combining two forms, as a centaur, mermaid, etc. Also, **bi′formed′.** [t. L: s. *biformis*]

Bif·rost (bĭv′rŏst), *n. Scand. Myth.* the rainbow bridge of the gods from heaven to earth. [t. Icel.: m. *Bifröst*]

bi·fur·cate (*v.* bī′fər kāt′, bī fûr′kāt; *adj. also* -kĭt), *v.,* **-cated, cating,** *adj.* —*v.t., v.i.* **1.** to divide or fork into two branches. —*adj.* **2.** divided into two branches. [t. ML: m.s. *bifurcātus*, der. L *bi-* BI- + *furca* fork] —**bi·fur·ca′tion,** *n.*

big (bĭg), *adj.,* **bigger, biggest,** *adv.* —*adj.* **1.** large in size, height, width, amount, etc. **2.** pregnant: *big with child.* **3.** filled; teeming: *eyes big with tears.* **4.** important in influence, standing, wealth, etc.: *the big man of his town.* **5.** haughty; pompous; boastful: *a big talker.* **6.** generous; kindly: *a big person forgives others.* **7.** loud: *a big voice.* **8.** *Obs.* very strong; powerful. —*adv.* **9.** *Colloq.* boastfully: *to talk big.* [ME; orig. uncert.] —**big′gish,** *adj.* —**big′ly,** *adv.* —**big′ness,** *n.* —**Syn. 1.** large, huge, immense; bulky, massive; capacious, voluminous; extensive. See **great. 4.** important, consequential. **5.** inflated, arrogant. —**Ant. 1.** little, small.

big·a·mist (bĭg′ə mĭst), *n.* a person guilty of bigamy.

big·a·mous (bĭg′ə məs), *adj.* **1.** having two wives or husbands at the same time; guilty of bigamy. **2.** involving bigamy. [t. ML: m. *bigamus*, f. *bi-* BI- + *-gamus* (t. Gk.: m. *-gamos* married)] —**big′a·mous·ly,** *adv.*

big·a·my (bĭg′ə mĭ), *n. Law.* the crime of marrying while one has a wife or husband still living, from whom no valid divorce has been effected. [ME *bigamie*, t. OF, der. *bigame* BIGAMOUS]

big·ar·reau (bĭg′ə rō′, bĭg′ə rō′), *n. Hort.* a kind of large, sweet, heart-shaped cherry with firm flesh. [t. F]

Big Ben, the bell in the clock tower of the Houses of Parliament in London, England.

Big Bertha, *Colloq.* a German gun or cannon, esp. one of large size, as used during World War I.

Big Dipper, *Astron.* the Dipper (def. 3a).

Big Five, 1. the United States, Great Britain, France, Italy, and Japan in World War I and at the Paris Peace Conference, 1919. **2.** the United States, Great Britain, Russia, China, and France, in the United Nations.

big game, 1. large animals, esp. when hunted for sport. **2.** an important prize or objective.

big·gin (bĭg′ĭn), *n.* **1.** a cap, esp. a child's. **2.** *Brit. Dial.* a nightcap. [t. F: m. *béguin* cap worn by Beguines]

big·ging (bĭg′ĭn), *n. Scot. and N. Eng.* a building; home. [der. *big* build (ME *biggen*, t. Scand.)]

big·head (bĭg′hĕd′), n. 1. Vet. Sci. an inflammatory swelling of the tissues of the head of sheep. 2. Colloq. conceit. —**big′-head′ed**, adj.

big-heart·ed (bĭg′här′tĭd). adj. generous; kind.

big·horn (bĭg′hôrn′), n., pl. **-horn, -horns**. a wild sheep, Ovis canadensis, of the Rocky Mountains, with large, curving horns.

Big Horn, a river flowing from central Wyoming to the Yellowstone river in S Montana. 336 mi.

Big Horn Mountains, a mountain range in N Wyoming, in the Rocky Mountains. Highest peak, Cloud Peak, 13,165 ft. Also, **Big Horns**.

Bighorn. Ovis canadensis
(3½ ft. high at the shoulder,
5 ft. 10 in. long)

bight (bīt), n. 1. the part of a rope between the ends. 2. the loop or bent part of a rope, as distinguished from the ends. 3. a bend or curve in the shore of a sea or a river. 4. a body of water bounded by such a bend; a bay. —v.t. 5. to fasten with a bight of rope. [OE byht a bend]

big·no·ni·a (bĭg·nō′nĭ·ə), n. any plant of the genus Bignonia, which comprises climbing shrubs, American and mostly tropical, much cultivated for their showy trumpet-shaped flowers, [t. NL; named after Bignon, librarian to Louis XV]

big·no·ni·a·ceous (bĭg·nō′nĭ·ā′shəs), adj. Bot. belonging or pertaining to the Bignoniaceae, a family of plants including trumpet creeper, catalpa, etc.

big·ot (bĭg′ət), n. a person who is intolerantly convinced of a particular creed, opinion, practice, etc. [t. F; orig. uncert.]

big·ot·ed (bĭg′ə·tĭd), adj. intolerantly convinced of a particular creed, practice, etc. —**big′ot·ed·ly**, adv.

big·ot·ry (bĭg′ə·trĭ), n., pl. **-ries**. 1. intolerant attachment to a particular creed, opinion, practice, etc. 2. actions or beliefs of a bigot.

big tree, an extremely large coniferous tree of California, Sequoiadendron giganteum (formerly Sequoia gigantea). Cf. sequoia.

big·wig (bĭg′wĭg′), n. Colloq. a very important person.

Bi·har (bē·här′), n. 1. a province in NE India. 36,340,-000 (1941); 69,745 sq. mi. Cap.: Patna. 2. a city in this province. 54,551 (1941).

Bihar and O·ris·sa (ərĭs′ə), a former province in NE India: now divided into the two provinces of Bihar and Orissa.

bi·hour·ly (bī·our′lĭ), adj. occurring every two hours.

bi·jou (bē′zhōō, bē·zhōō′), n., pl. **-joux** (-zhōōz, -zhōōz′). 1. a jewel. 2. something small and choice. [t. F]

bi·jou·te·rie (bē·zhōō′tə·rĭ), n. jewelry. [t. F]

bi·ju·gate (bī′jŏŏ·gāt, bĭ·jŏŏ′gāt), adj. Bot. (of leaves) having two pairs of leaflets or pinnae. Also, **bi·ju·gous** (bĭ′jŏŏ·gəs). [f. BI- + JUGATE]

Bi·ka·ner (bē′kə·nĭr′), n. 1. a native state in NW India, in Rajputana. 1,292,900 pop. (1941); 23,181 sq. mi. 2. the capital of this state. 127,226 (1941).

bike (bīk), n., v., biked, biking. Colloq. bicycle. [alter. of BICYCLE]

Bi·ki·ni (bē·kē′nē), n. an atoll in the N Pacific, in the Marshall Islands: atomic bomb tests, 1946. 3 sq. mi.

Bi·kol (bē·kôl′), n. a member of a Malayan tribe in SE Luzon and nearby Philippine islands, converted to Christianity early in the Spanish conquest. Also, **Bicol**.

bi·la·bi·al (bī·lā′bĭ·əl), Phonet. —adj. 1. pronounced with the two lips brought close together or touching. In the English bilabial consonants p, b, and m, the lips touch; in the bilabial w, they do not. —n. 2. a bilabial speech sound.

bi·la·bi·ate (bī·lā′bĭ·āt′, -ĭt), adj. Bot. two-lipped, as a corolla.

bil·an·der (bĭl′ən·dər, bĭ′lən-), n. Naut. a small merchant vessel with two masts, used on canals and along the coast in Holland, etc. [t. D: m. bijlander, f. bij by + land land + -er -ER]

bi·lat·er·al (bī·lăt′ər·əl), adj. 1. Bot., Zool. pertaining to both sides: bilateral symmetry. 2. pertaining to or affecting two or both sides. 3. disposed on opposite sides of an axis; two-sided; often, symmetrical. 4. Law, etc. (of a contract) binding the parties to reciprocal obligations. —**bi·lat′er·al·ism, bi·lat′er·al·ness**, n. —**bi·lat′er·al·ly**, adv.

Bilabiate calyx and corolla of sage. Salvia

Bil·ba·o (bĕl·bä′ō), n. a seaport in N Spain, near the Bay of Biscay. 208,000 (est. 1945).

bil·ber·ry (bĭl′bĕr′ĭ), n., pl. **-ries**. the fruit of the shrub of several species of Vaccinium. [f. bil (t. Scand.; cf. Dan. bølle bilberry) + BERRY]

bil·bo¹ (bĭl′bō), n., pl. **-boes**. (usually pl.) a long iron bar or bolt with sliding shackles and a lock, formerly used to confine the feet of prisoners. [orig. uncert.]

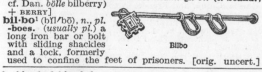

Bilbo

bil·bo² (bĭl′bō), n., pl. **-boes**. Archaic. a sword. [short for Bilbo sword of Bilbao (Spain)]

bile (bīl), n. 1. Physiol. a bitter yellow or greenish liquid secreted by the liver and aiding in digestion, principally by emulsifying fats. 2. ill nature; peevishness. [t. F, t. L: m. s. bilis]

bi·lec·tion (bĭ·lĕk′shən), n. Archit. bolection.

bile·stone (bīl′stōn′), n. Pathol. a gallstone.

bilge (bĭlj), n., v., bilged, bilging. —n. 1. Naut. a. the approximately flat under portion of a ship's hull. b. the lowest portion of a ship's interior. c. Also, **bilge water**. foul water that collects in a ship's bilge. 2. Slang. foolishness. 3. the wider part or belly of a cask. —v.i. 4. Naut. a. to spring a leak in the bilge. b. to bulge or swell out. —v.t. 6. to break in the bilge of. [orig. unknown]

bilge keel, Naut. either of two keellike projections extending lengthwise along a ship's bilge, one on each side, to retard rolling. Also, **bilge piece**.

bilg·y (bĭl′jĭ), adj. Naut. smelling like bilge water.

bil·i·ar·y (bĭl′ĭ·ĕr′ĭ), adj. 1. Physiol. a. of bile. b. conveying bile: a biliary duct. 2. Pathol. bilious: biliary colic. [t. NL: m. biliāris, der. L bīlis bile]

bi·lin·e·ar (bī·lĭn′ĭ·ər), adj. Math. of, pertaining to, or having reference to two lines: bilinear coördinates.

bi·lin·gual (bī·lĭng′gwəl), adj. 1. able to speak one's native language and another with approximately equal facility. 2. expressed or contained in two different languages. —n. 3. a bilingual person. [f. s. L bilinguis speaking two languages + -AL¹] —**bi·lin′gual·ly**, adv.

bi·lin·gual·ism (bī·lĭng′gwəl·ĭz′əm), n. 1. habitual use of two languages. 2. ability in being bilingual.

bil·ious (bĭl′yəs), adj. 1. Physiol., Pathol. pertaining to bile or to an excess secretion of bile. 2. Pathol. suffering from, caused by, or attended by trouble with the bile or liver. 3. peevish; testy; cross. [t. L: m. s. bīliōsus full of bile] —**bil′ious·ly**, adv. —**bil′ious·ness**, n.

-bility, a suffix forming nouns from adjectives in -ble, as in nobility. [ME -bilite, t. F, t. L: m. s. -bilitas]

bilk (bĭlk), v.t. 1. to evade payment of (a debt); defraud; cheat. 2. to frustrate. 3. to escape from; elude. —n. 4. a trick; a fraud. 5. a cheater; a swindler. [orig. unknown]

bill¹ (bĭl), n. 1. an account of money owed for goods or services supplied. 2. a bill of exchange. 3. U.S. a piece of paper money (usually with its amount): a dollar bill. 4. Govt. a form or draft of a proposed statute presented to a legislature, but not yet enacted or passed and made law. 5. a written or printed public notice or advertisement: post no bills. 6. any written paper containing a statement of particulars: a bill of charges or expenditures. 7. Law. a written statement, usually of complaint, presented to a court. 8. a printed theater program or the like. 9. program; entertainment: good bill at the theater. 10. Obs. an acknowledgment of debt; a promissory note. —v.t. 11. to enter in a bill; make a bill or list of: to bill goods. 12. to charge for by bill; send a bill to: the store will bill me. 13. to announce by bill or public notice: a new actor was billed for this week. 14. to schedule on a program. [ME bille, t. Anglo-L: m. billa, var. of ML bulla seal (see BULLA)] —Syn. 5. bulletin.

bill² (bĭl), n. 1. that part of the jaws of a bird covered with a horny sheath; a beak. —v.i. 2. to join bills or beaks, as doves. [ME; OE bile beak]

bill³ (bĭl), n. 1. a medieval shafted weapon with a broad hook-shaped blade and a spike at the back. 2. a sharp, hooked instrument used for pruning, etc.; billhook. 3. Naut. the point or extremity of the fluke of an anchor. [OE bill sword, c. G bille pickax]

bill⁴ (bĭl), n. the cry of the bittern. [cf. OE bylgan bellow, c. Icel. bylga roar]

bil·la·bong (bĭl′ə·bông′), n. Australia. 1. a branch of a river flowing away from the main stream, in some cases returning to it lower down. 2. a stagnant backwater. [native Australian]

bill·board¹ (bĭl′bôrd′), n. U.S. a board on which notices or advertisements are posted. [f. BILL¹ (def. 6) + BOARD]

bill·board² (bĭl′bôrd′), n. Naut. a projection placed abaft the cathead, for the bill or fluke of an anchor to rest on. [f. BILL³ (def. 3) + BOARD]

bil·let¹ (bĭl′ĭt), n., v., -leted, -leting. —n. 1. lodging for a soldier, esp. lodging in private or nonmilitary public buildings. 2. Mil. an official order, written or verbal, directing the person to whom it is addressed to provide such lodging. 3. a place assigned, as to each of the crew of a man-of-war for slinging his hammock. 4. job; appointment. 5. a small paper or note in writing. —v.t. 6. Mil. to direct (a soldier) by ticket, note, or verbal order, where to lodge. 7. to provide lodging for; quarter. [ME billette, t. OF, b. bille a writing and bulette certificate, der. bulle BULL²]

bil·let² (bĭl′ĭt), n. 1. a small thick stick of wood, esp. one cut for fuel. 2. Metall. a bar or slab of iron or steel, esp. when obtained from an ingot by forging, etc. 3. Archit. one of a series of short rods forming part of a molding. 4. a short strap used for connecting various straps and portions of a harness. 5. a pocket or loop into which the end of a strap is inserted after passing through a buckle. [ME billette, t. OF: m. billete, dim. of bille log]

Bill³

billboard² (def. 2

Architectural billets

b., blend of, blended; c., cognate with; d., dialect, dialectal; der., derived from; f., formed from; g., going back to; m., modification of; r., replacing; s., stem of; t., taken from; ?, perhaps. See the full key on inside cover.

House Wren

Robin

Golden-crowned Kinglet

Redstart

Chickadee

Cedar Waxwing

Brown Thrasher

Wood Thrush

Cardinal

Goldfinch

Yellow Warbler

Baltimore Oriole

Scarlet Tanager

Ruby-throated Hummingbird

Blue Jay

Red-winged Blackbird

Redheaded Woodpecker

Bluebird

SONG and PERCHING BIRDS

A.H.WINKLER

Wood Duck

Ring-necked Pheasant

Blue-winged Teal

Canvasback

Gadwall

Mallard

Wilson's Snipe

Ruffed Grouse

GAME BIRDS

AMERICAN

Quail

White-fronted Goose

Canada Goose

Valley Quail

Mountain Quail

Wild Turkey

Woodcock

Prairie Chicken

A.H.WINZER

bil·let-doux (bĭl′ĭ dōō′, bĭl′ā-; *Fr.* bē yĕ dōō′), *n.*, *pl.* **billets-doux** (bĭl′ĭ dōōz′, bĭl′ā-; *Fr.* bē yĕ dōō). a love letter. [t. F: lit., sweet note]

bill·fish (bĭl′fĭsh′), *n.*, *pl.* **-fishes**, (*esp. collectively*) **-fish**. one of various fishes with a long beak or snout, as the gar, needlefish, or spearfish.

bill·fold (bĭl′fōld′), *n.* *U.S.* a folding leather case for carrying banknotes, personal cards, etc.

bill·head (bĭl′hĕd′), *n.* **1.** a printed heading on paper for making out bills. **2.** a sheet of paper with such a heading. **3.** a printed form for itemized statements.

bill·hook (bĭl′hŏŏk′), *n.* bill[3] (def. 2).

bil·liard (bĭl′yərd), *adj.* **1.** of or used in billiards. —*n.* **2.** *U.S. Colloq.* carom (def. 1).

bil·liards (bĭl′yərdz), *n.* a game played by two or more persons on a rectangular table enclosed by an elastic ledge or cushion, with balls (**billiard balls**) of ivory or other hard material, driven by means of cues. [t. F: m. *billard*, der. *bille* log. Cf. BILLET[2]] —**bil·liard·ist**, *n.*

bill·ing (bĭl′ĭng), *n.* the relative position in which a performer or act is listed on handbills, posters, and programs: *a star gets top billing.*

Bil·lings (bĭl′ĭngz), *n.* **1.** a city in S Montana, on the Yellowstone river. 31,834 (1950). **2. Josh,** pen name of H. W. Shaw.

bil·lings·gate (bĭl′ĭngz gāt′; *esp. Brit.* -gĭt), *n.* coarse language or abuse. [orig., the kind of language heard at *Billingsgate*, a gate and fish market in London]

bil·lion (bĭl′yən), *n.* **1.** *U.S.* a thousand millions. **2.** *Brit.* a million millions. [t. F: f. *bi-* + (*mi*)*llion*, i.e., the second power of one million (def. 2 agrees with earlier, def. 1 with later F usage)] —**bil′lionth**, *adj., n.*

bil·lion·aire (bĭl′yə nâr′), *n.* the owner of a billion dollars, francs, pounds, etc.

Bil·li·ton (bēl′lē tŏn′, bĭ′lē tŏn′), *n.* an island in the U. S. of Indonesia, SW of Borneo. 73,429 pop. (1930); 1866 sq. mi. Also, **Belitong.**

bill of attainder, a legal act depriving a person of his property if found guilty of treason or felony.

bill of exchange, a written authorization or order to pay a specified sum of money to a specified person.

bill of fare, a list of foods that are to be served, or that may be ordered.

bill of health, a certificate as to the health of a ship's company at the time of her clearing any port.

bill of lading, a written receipt given by a carrier for goods accepted for transportation.

bill of rights, 1. a formal statement of the fundamental rights of the people of a nation. **2.** (*cap.*) such a statement incorporated in the Constitution of the United States as Amendments 1–10, and in all State constitutions. **3.** (*caps.*) an English statute of 1689 confirming, with minor changes, the Declaration of Rights, declaring the rights and liberties of the subjects and settling the succession in William III and Mary II.

bill of sale, a document transferring title in personal property from seller to buyer.

bil·lon (bĭl′ən), *n.* **1.** an alloy used in coinage, consisting of gold or silver with a preponderating admixture of some base metal. **2.** an alloy of silver with copper or the like in very large proportion, used for coins of small denomination. **3.** any coin struck from such an alloy. [t. F, der. *bille* log]

bil·low (bĭl′ō), *n.* **1.** a great wave or surge of the sea. **2.** any surging mass: *billows of smoke.* —*v.i.* **3.** to rise or roll in or like billows; surge. [t. Scand.; cf. Icel. *bylgja*]

bil·low·y (bĭl′ō ĭ), *adj.*, **-lower, -lowiest.** full of billows; surging: *billowy flames.* —**bil′low·i·ness,** *n.*

bill-post·er (bĭl′pōs′tər), *n.* one who posts bills and advertisements. Also, **bill-stick·er** (bĭl′stĭk′ər).

bil·ly (bĭl′ĭ), *n.*, *pl.* **-lies. 1.** *Colloq.* a policeman's club. **2.** a small cudgel. **3.** Also, **bil·ly·can** (bĭl′ĭ kăn′). *Australia.* tin kettle or pot, used by bushmen in making tea. [special use of *Billy*, pet var. of *William*, man's name]

bil·ly·cock (bĭl′ĭ kŏk′), *n.* **1.** *Brit.* a round, low-crowned, soft felt hat. **2.** a derby hat. [var. of *bullycocked* (*hat*), i.e. hat cocked in the style of a bully]

billy goat, a male goat.

bi·lo·bate (bī lō′bāt), *adj.* having or divided into two lobes: *a bilobate leaf.* Also, **bi·lo′bat·ed, bi·lobed** (bī′-lōbd′).

bi·loc·u·lar (bī lŏk′yə lər), *adj.* divided into two chambers or cells, or containing two cells internally. Also, **bi·loc′u·late** (bī lŏk′yə lĭt, -lāt′).

Bi·lox·i (bĭ lŏk′sĭ), *n.* a city in SE Mississippi, on the Gulf of Mexico. 37,425 (1950).

bil·sted (bĭl′stĕd), *n.* the liquidambar tree.

bil·tong (bĭl′tŏng′), *n.* (in South Africa) strips of lean meat dried in the open air. [t. S Afr. D]

bim·a·nous (bĭm′ə nəs, bī mā′-), *adj.* *Zool.* two-handed. [f. s. NL *bimana* (*animālia*) two-handed (animals) + -ous]

bi·man·u·al (bī măn′yŏŏ əl), *adj.* involving the use of both hands. —**bi·man′u·al·ly,** *adv.*

bi·men·sal (bī mĕn′səl), *adj.* occurring once in two months; bimonthly.

bi·mes·tri·al (bī mĕs′trĭ əl), *adj.* **1.** occurring every two months; bimonthly. **2.** lasting two months. [f. L *bimestri*(*s*) of two months' duration + -AL[1]]

bi·me·tal·lic (bī′mə tăl′ĭk), *adj.* **1.** of or pertaining to two metals. **2.** pertaining to bimetallism. [t. F: m. *bimétallique*]

bi·met·al·lism (bī mĕt′ə lĭz′əm), *n.* **1.** the use of two metals, ordinarily gold and silver, at a fixed relative value, as the monetary standard. **2.** the doctrine or policies supporting such a standard. —**bi·met′al·list,** *n.*

bi·month·ly (bī mŭnth′lĭ), *adj., n., pl.* **-lies,** *adv.* —*adj.* **1.** occurring every two months. **2.** occurring twice a month; semimonthly. —*n.* **3.** a bimonthly publication. —*adv.* **4.** every two months. **5.** twice a month; semimonthly.

bi·mo·tored (bī mō′tərd), *adj.* *Aeron.* having two separate engines.

bin (bĭn), *n., v.,* **binned, binning.** —*n.* **1.** a box or enclosed place used for storing grain, coal, and the like. —*v.t.* **2.** to store in a bin. [ME *binne,* OE *binn*(*e*) crib]

bin-, a form of **bi-,** sometimes used before a vowel, as in *binoxide.* [prob. t. L: m. *bīnī* two apiece]

bi·nal (bī′nəl), *adj.* **1.** double; twofold. **2.** *Phonet.* (of a syllable) having two pitch beats. [t. NL: s. *bīnālis,* der. L *bīnī* two apiece. Cf. G *zweigipfelig*]

bi·na·ry (bī′nə rĭ), *adj., n., pl.* **-ries.** —*adj.* **1.** consisting of, indicating, or involving two. —*n.* **2.** a whole composed of two. **3.** *Astron.* a binary star. [t. L; m. s. *bīnārius* consisting of two things]

binary compound, *Chem.* a compound containing only two elements or radicals.

binary star, *Astron.* a system of two stars which revolve round their common center of gravity.

bi·nate (bī′nāt), *adj.* double; produced or borne in pairs. [t. NL: m. s. *bīnātus,* der. L *bīnī* two at a time] —**bi′nate·ly,** *adv.*

bin·au·ral (bĭn ôr′əl), *adj.* **1.** of, with, or for both ears: *binaural hearing, a binaural stethoscope.* **2.** having two ears.

Binate leaf

bind (bīnd), *v.,* **bound, binding,** *n.* —*v.t.* **1.** to make fast with a band or bond. **2.** to encircle with a band or ligature: *bind one's hair up.* **3.** to swathe or bandage (often fol. by *up*). **4.** to fasten around; fix in place by girding. **5.** to cause to cohere. **6.** to unite by any legal or moral tie: *bound by duty, debt, etc.* **7.** to hold to a particular state, place, employment, etc. **8.** to place under obligation or compulsion (usually passive): *all are bound to obey the laws.* **9.** *Law.* to put under legal obligation (often with *over*): *to bind a man over to keep the peace.* **10.** to make compulsory or obligatory: *to bind the order with a deposit.* **11.** to indenture as an apprentice (often fol. by *out*). **12.** *Pathol.* to hinder or restrain (the bowels) from their natural operations; constipate. **13.** to fasten or secure within a cover, as a book. **14.** to cover the edge of, as for protection or ornament. —*v.i.* **15.** to become compact or solid; cohere. **16.** to be obligatory: *an obligation that binds.* **17.** to tie up anything, esp. sheaves of grain. —*n.* **18.** something that binds. **19.** *Music.* a tie, slur or brace. [ME *binden,* OE *bindan,* c. G *binden*] —**Syn. 1.** gird, fasten, attach, tie. **8.** oblige, obligate, constrain. —**Ant. 1.** free, loose. **2.** loosen.

bind·er (bīn′dər), *n.* **1.** person or thing that binds. **2.** a detachable cover for loose papers. **3.** one who binds books; a bookbinder. **4.** *Agric.* **a.** an attachment to a harvester or reaper for binding the cut grain. **b.** a machine that both cuts and binds grain. **5.** *Law.* an informal contract, operative pending the execution of a more formal document. **6.** *Metall.* a substance used: **a.** to hold crushed ore dust together before and during sintering or refining. **b.** to hold metallic powders (mixed sometimes with nonmetals) together after compacting and before sintering in powder metallurgy. **c.** to hold the sand of a core or mold together in founding.

bind·er·y (bīn′də rĭ), *n., pl.* **-eries.** an establishment for binding books.

bind·ing (bīn′dĭng), *n.* **1.** act of fastening or uniting. **2.** anything that binds. **3.** the covering within which the leaves of a book are bound. **4.** a strip that protects or adorns the edge of cloth, etc. —*adj.* **5.** having power to bind or oblige; obligatory: *a binding engagement.* —**bind′ing·ly,** *adv.* —**bind′ing·ness,** *n.*

bind·weed (bīnd′wēd′), *n.* any of various twining or vinelike plants, esp. certain species of *Convolvulus.*

bine (bīn), *n.* **1.** a twining plant stem, as of the hop. **2.** any bindweed. **3.** woodbine (defs. 1, 2). [var. of BIND]

Bi·net (bĭ nā′; *Fr.* bē nĕ′), *n.* **Alfred** (ál frĕd′), 1857–1911, French psychologist: deviser of Binet test.

Bi·net test (bĭ nā′; *Fr.* bē nĕ′), *Psychol.* a test for determining the relative development of the intelligence of children and others, consisting of a series of questions and tasks graded with reference to the ability of the normal child to deal with them at successive age levels. Also, **Binet-Si·mon test** (-sī′mən; *Fr.* -sē môN′).

Bing·en (bĭng′ən), *n.* a town in W Germany, on the Rhine: whirlpool; tourist center. 16,547 (1939).

Bing·ham·ton (bĭng′əm tən), *n.* a city in S New York, on the Susquehanna river. 80,674 (1950).

bin·go (bĭng′gō), *n.* a game similar to lotto; beano.

Binh·Dinh (bĭn′y dĭn′y, bĭn′dĭn′), *n.* a city in E French Indo-China, in Viet Nam. ab. 147,000.

bin·na·cle (bĭn′ə kəl), *n.* *Naut.* a special stand of nonmagnetic material built in the hull for housing the compass and fitted with lights by which the compass can be read at night. [earlier *bittacle,* t. Pg.: m. *bitacola,* or t. Sp.: m. *bitácula,* ult. t. L: m. *habitāculum* dwelling place]

bin·o·cle (bĭn′ə kəl), *n.* binocular. [t. F, t. NL: m. s. *bīnoclus,* f. L: *bīn*(ī) two at a time + m. *oculus* eye]

bin·oc·u·lar (bə nŏk′yə lər, bī-), *adj.* **1.** involving two eyes: *binocular vision.* —*n.* **2.** (*often pl.*) a double telescope, microscope, or field glass used by both eyes at once. —**bin·oc′u·lar′i·ty,** *n.* —**bin·oc′u·lar·ly,** *adv.*

bi·no·mi·al (bī nō′mÿ əl), *n.* **1.** *Alg.* an expression which is a sum or difference of two terms, as 3x+2y and x²–4x. **2.** *Zool., Bot.* a name of two terms, denoting respectively genus and species, as *Felis leo,* the lion. —*adj.* **3.** *Alg.* consisting of or pertaining to two terms or a binomial. **4.** *Zool., Bot.* consisting of or characterized by binomials. [f. s. LL *binōmius* having two names + -AL¹] —**bi·no′mi·al·ly,** *adv.*

binomial distribution, *Statistics.* a distribution giving the probability of obtaining a specified number of successes in a set of trials where each trial can end in either a success or a failure.

bi·nu·cle·ate (bī nū′klÿ āt′, -nōō′-), *adj.* having two nuclei, as some cells. Also, **bi·nu′cle·ar, bi·nu′cle·at′ed.**

Bin·yon (bÿn′yən), *n.* **Lawrence,** 1869–1943, British poet, translator, and art historian.

bio-, a word element meaning "life," "living things," as in *biology.* [t. Gk., comb. form of *bíos* life]

Bí·o-Bí·o (bē′ō bē′ō), *n.* a river in central Chile from the Andes NW to the Pacific at Concepción. ab. 250 mi.

bi·o·cat·a·lyst (bī′ō kăt′ə lÿst), *n.* *Biochem.* a substance, as an enzyme, vitamin, or hormone, which acts as a biochemical catalyst.

bi·o·cel·late (bī ŏs′ə lāt′, bī′ō sĕl′ÿt), *adj.* *Zool., Bot.* marked with two ocelli or eyelike parts.

bi·o·chem·is·try (bī′ō kĕm′Ÿs trÿ), *n.* the chemistry of living matter. *Abbrev.:* **biochem.** —**bi·o·chem·i·cal** (bī′ō kĕm′ə kəl), **bi·o·chem′ic,** *adj.* —**bi·o·chem′i·cal·ly,** *adv.* —**bi·o·chem′ist,** *n.*

bi·o·dy·nam·ics (bī′ō dī năm′Ÿks, -dÿ-), *n.* the branch of biology that treats of energy, or of the activity of living organisms (opposed to *biostatics*). —**bi·o·dy·nam′-ic, bi·o·dy·nam′i·cal,** *adj.*

biog., **1.** biographical. **2.** biography.

bi·o·gen (bī′ə jən), *n.* *Biol., Biochem.* a hypothetical protein molecule, large and unstable, assumed to be basic to fundamental biological processes, as assimilation and disassimilation.

bi·o·gen·e·sis (bī′ō jĕn′ə sÿs), *n.* *Biol.* the doctrine that living organisms come from other living organisms (opposed to *abiogenesis*). Also, **bi·og·e·ny** (bī ŏj′ə nÿ). —**bi·o·ge·net·ic** (bī′ō jə nĕt′ÿk), *adj.* —**bi·o·ge·net′-i·cal·ly,** *adv.*

bi·o·ge·og·ra·phy (bī′ō jÿ ŏg′rə fÿ), *n.* *Ecol.* the study of the geographical distribution of living things.

bi·og·ra·pher (bī ŏg′rə fər, bÿ-), *n.* a writer of biography.

bi·o·graph·i·cal (bī′ə grăf′ə kəl), *adj.* **1.** of or pertaining to a person's life. **2.** pertaining to biography. Also, **bi·o·graph′ic.** —**bi·o·graph′i·cal·ly,** *adv.*

bi·og·ra·phy (bī ŏg′rə fÿ, bÿ-), *n., pl.* **-phies. 1.** a written account of a person's life. **2.** such writings collectively. [t. Gk.: m. s. *biographía*]

biol., **1.** biological. **2.** biology.

bi·o·log·i·cal (bī′ə lŏj′ə kəl), *adj.* Also, **bi·o·log′ic. 1.** pertaining to biology. **2.** of or pertaining to the products and operations of applied biology: *a biological preparation or test.* —*n.* **3.** *Biol., Pharm.* any biochemical product, esp. serums, vaccines, etc., produced from microörganisms. —**bi·o·log′i·cal·ly,** *adv.*

biological factor, *Sociol.* any biological and noncultural element that affects the way men live together.

bi·ol·o·gy (bī ŏl′ə jÿ), *n.* the science of life or living matter in all its forms and phenomena, often esp. with reference to origin, growth, reproduction, structure, etc. —**bi·ol′o·gist,** *n.*

bi·o·lu·mi·nes·cence (bī′ō lōō′mə nĕs′əns), *n.* the production of light by living organisms. —**bi·o·lu′mi·nes′cent,** *adj.*

bi·ol·y·sis (bī ŏl′ə sÿs), *n.* *Biol.* dissolution of a living being; death; the destruction of the phenomena of life. —**bi·o·lyt·ic** (bī′ə lÿt′ÿk), *adj.*

bi·o·met·rics (bī′ō mĕt′rÿks), *n.* **1.** *Biol.* the application of mathematical-statistical theory to biology. **2.** biometry. —**bi·o·met′ric, bi·o·met′ri·cal,** *adj.* —**bi·o·met′ri·cal·ly,** *adv.*

bi·om·e·try (bī ŏm′ə trÿ), *n.* the calculation of the probable duration of human life.

Bi·on (bī′ŏn), *n.* fl. c100 B.C., Greek pastoral poet.

bi·o·nom·ics (bī′ō nŏm′ÿks), *n.* ecology (def. 1). [f. BIO- + *-nomics,* as in ECONOMICS] —**bi′o·nom′ic, bi·o·nom′i·cal,** *adj.* —**bi·o·nom′i·cal·ly,** *adv.* —**bi·on·o·mist** (bī ŏn′ə mÿst), *n.*

bi·o·phys·ics (bī′ō fÿz′ÿks), *n.* that brand of biology which deals with biological structures and processes in terms of physics. —**bi·o·phys′i·cal,** *adj.*

bi·op·sy (bī′ŏp sÿ), *n.* *Med.* the excision and diagnostic study of a piece of tissue from a living body.

bi·o·scope (bī′ō skōp′), *n.* an early form of motion picture projector (about 1900).

bi·os·co·py (bīs′ŏkə pÿ), *n.* *Med.* examination of the body to discover whether or not it is alive.

-biosis, a word element meaning "way of life," as in *symbiosis.* [comb. form repr. Gk. *bíosis*]

bi·o·stat·ics (bī′ō stăt′ÿks), *n.* the branch of biology that treats of the structure of organisms in relation to their functions (opposed to *biodynamics*). —**bi·o·stat′-ic, bi·o·stat′i·cal,** *adj.*

bi·o·ta (bī ō′tə), *n.* *Ecol.* the animal and plant life of a region or period. [t. NL, t. Gk.: m. *biotē* life]

bi·ot·ic (bī ŏt′Ÿk), *adj.* pertaining to life. Also, **bi·ot′-i·cal.**

bi·o·tin (bī′ə tÿn), *n.* *Biochem.* a crystalline acid, C₁₀H₁₆N₂O₃S, one of the vitamin B complex factors; vitamin H. It will prevent the death of animals that have been fed large quantities of raw white of eggs. Cf. **airdin.**

bi·o·tite (bī′ə tīt′), *n.* a very common mineral of the mica group, occurring in dark-black, brown, or green sheets and scales, an important constituent of igneous rocks. [named after J. B. Biot (1774–1862), French physicist. See -ITE¹] —**bi·o·tit·ic** (bī′ə tÿt′Ÿk), *adj.*

bi·o·type (bī′ə tīp′), *n.* *Biol.* a group of organisms with the same hereditary characteristics; genotype. —**bi·o·typ·ic** (bī′ə tÿp′Ÿk), *adj.*

bi·pa·ri·e·tal (bī′pə rī′ə təl), *adj.* *Anat.* pertaining to both parietal bones.

bip·a·rous (bÿp′ərəs), *adj.* **1.** *Zool.* bringing forth offspring in pairs. **2.** *Bot.* bearing two branches or axes.

bi·par·ti·san (bī pär′tə zən), *adj.* representing or characterized by two parties. —**bi·par′ti·san·ship′,** *n.*

bi·par·tite (bī pär′tīt), *adj.* **1.** *Law.* being in two corresponding parts: *a bipartite contract.* **2.** *Bot.* divided into two parts nearly to the base, as a leaf. [t. L: m. s. *bipartītus,* pp., divided into two parts] —**bi·par′tite·ly,** *adv.* —**bi·par·ti·tion** (bī′pär tÿsh′ən), *n.*

bi·ped (bī′pĕd), *Zool.* —*n.* **1.** a two-footed animal. —*adj.* **2.** having two feet. [t. L: s. *bipēs* two-footed]

bi·pe·dal (bī′pə dəl, bÿp′ə-), *adj.* biped.

bi·pet·al·ous (bī pĕt′ə ləs), *adj.* *Bot.* having two petals.

bi·phen·yl (bī fĕn′əl, -fē′nəl), *n.* *Chem.* a colorless crystalline compound, C₆H₅C₅H₅, composed of two phenyl groups. The benzidine dyes are derivatives of biphenyl.

bi·pin·nate (bī pÿn′āt), *adj.* *Bot.* pinnate, as a leaf, with the divisions also pinnate.

bi·plane (bī′plān′), *n.* an airplane with two wings, one above and usually slightly forward of the other.

bi·pod (bī′pŏd), *n.* a two-legged support, as for an automatic rifle. [f. BI- + -POD. Cf. TRIPOD.]

bi·po·lar (bī pō′lər), *adj.* **1.** having two poles. **2.** pertaining to or found at both poles. —**bi·po·lar·i·ty** (bī′pōlăr′ə tÿ), *n.*

bi·quad·rate (bī kwŏd′rāt, -rÿt), *n.* *Math.* the fourth power.

bi·quad·rat·ic (bī′kwŏd răt′Ÿk), *adj.* *Math.* involving the fourth, but no higher, power of the unknown or variable.

bi·ra·di·al symmetry (bī rā′dÿ əl), *Biol.* symmetry manifested both bilaterally and radially in the same creature, as in ctenophores.

birch (bûrch), *n.* **1.** any tree or shrub of the genus *Betula,* comprising species with a smooth, laminated outer bark and close-grained wood. **2.** the wood itself. **3.** a birch rod, or a bundle of birch twigs, used as a whip. —*adj.* **4.** birchen. —*v.t.* **5.** to beat or punish with a birch. [ME *birche,* OE *bierce,* c. G *birke*]

birch·en (bûr′chən), *adj.* **1.** of or pertaining to birch. **2.** consisting or made of birch.

bird (bûrd), *n.* **1.** any of the *Aves,* a class of warmblooded vertebrates having a body more or less completely covered with feathers, and the forelimbs so modified as to form wings by means of which most species fly. **2.** *Sports.* **a.** a game bird. **b.** a clay pigeon. **3.** *Slang.* a person, esp. one having some peculiarity. **4.** *Slang.* a sound of derision: *to get the bird.* **5.** *Archaic.* the young of any fowl. —*v.i.* **6.** to catch or shoot birds. [ME *byrd, bryd,* OE *brid(d)* young bird, chick] —**bird′-less,** *adj.* —**bird′like,** *adj.*

bird call, **1.** a sound made by a bird. **2.** a sound imitating that of a bird. **3.** a device used to imitate the sound of a bird.

bird dog, a dog trained to help hunt birds, usually a pointer or setter, sometimes a spaniel.

bird-foot (bûrd′fŏŏt′), *n.* bird's-foot.

bird grass, **1.** a grass, *Poa trivialis,* grown in temperate climates of North America largely for lawns and turf. **2.** knotgrass, *Polygonum aviculare.*

bird·ie (bûr′dÿ), *n.* **1.** bird; small bird. **2.** *Golf.* a score of one stroke under par on a hole.

bird·lime (bûrd′līm′), *n., v.,* **-limed, -liming.** —*n.* **1.** a sticky material, prepared from holly, mistletoe or other plants and smeared on twigs to catch small birds that light on it. —*v.t.* **2.** to smear or catch with or as with birdlime.

bird·man (bûrd′măn′, -mən), *n., pl.* **-men** (-mĕn′, -mən). **1.** fowler. **2.** ornithologist. **3.** *Colloq.* aviator.

bird of paradise, any bird of the family *Paradiseidae,* of New Guinea, etc., noted for magnificent plumage, as *Paradisea apoda.*

bird of passage, a bird that migrates seasonally.

bird of peace, dove.

bird of prey, *Ornith.* any of numerous predaceous, flesh-eating birds such as the eagles, hawks, kites, vultures, owls, etc., most of which have strong beaks and claws for catching, killing and tearing to pieces the animals on which they feed.

Bipinnate leaf

---

b., blend of, blended; c., cognate with; d., dialect, dialectal; der., derived from; f., formed from; g., going back to; m., modification of; r., replacing; s., stem of; t., taken from; ?, perhaps. See the full key on inside cover.

bird pepper, a variety of extremely strong pepper, *Capsicum frutescens*, with small, elongated berries.

bird·seed (bûrd/sēd/), *n.* small seed, esp. that of a grass, *Phalaris canariensis*, used as food for birds.

bird's-eye (bûrdz/ī/), *adj.* **1.** seen from above: *a bird's-eye view of a city.* **2.** general; not detailed: *a bird's-eye view of history.* **3.** having spots or markings resembling birds' eyes: *bird's-eye maple.* —*n.* **4.** any of various plants with small, round, bright-colored flowers, as a primrose, *Primula farinosa*, or the germander speedwell, *Veronica chamaedrys.* **5.** a type of weave with small, eyelike figures. **6.** a fabric, either cotton or linen, with this weave, used for diapers or toweling.

bird's-foot (bûrdz/fŏŏt/), *n.* **1.** any of various plants whose leaves, flowers, or pods resemble or suggest the foot or claw of a bird, esp. plants of the leguminous genus *Ornithopus*, which have clawlike pods. **2.** any similar plant, esp. bird's-foot trefoil or fenugreek. Also, **bird-foot.**

bird's-foot fern, 1. a fern, *Adiantopsis radiata*, of tropical America. **2.** a fern, *Pellea mucronata*, growing in hilly parts of the U. S. Pacific seaboard.

bird's-foot trefoil, 1. a fabaceous plant, *Lotus corniculatus*, the legumes of which spread like a crow's foot. **2.** any similar plant of the same genus.

bird's-foot violet, *Bot.* a handsome violet, *Viola pedata*, cultivated for its large light-blue or whitish flowers with yellow eyes (the State flower of Wisconsin).

bird·wom·an (bûrd/wŏŏm/ən), *n., pl.* **-women.** *Colloq.* a female aviator.

bi·reme (bī/rēm), *n.* a galley having two banks or tiers of oars. [t. L: m.s. *birēmis*, lit., two-oared]

bi·ret·ta (ba rĕt/ə), *n.* a stiff, square cap with three (or four) upright projecting pieces extending from the center of the top to the edge, worn by Roman Catholic ecclesiastics. Also, **berretta.** [t. It.: m. *berretta*, der. L *birrus* cap]

Bir·ken·head (bûr/kən hĕd/, bûr/kən hĕd/), *n.* **1.** a seaport in W England, on the Mersey opposite Liverpool. 131,900 (est. 1946). **2.** Frederick Edwin Smith, 1st Earl of, 1872–1930, British lawyer, statesman, and writer.

birl (bûrl), *v.t., v.i.* *Lumbering.* to cause (a floating log) to rotate rapidly by treading upon it.

Bir·ming·ham (bûr/mĭng əm *for 1*; -hăm/ *for 2*), *n.* **1.** a city in central England. 1,063,000 (est. 1946). **2.** a city in central Alabama. 326,037 (1950).

birth (bûrth), *n.* **1.** fact of being born: *the day of his birth.* **2.** act of bearing or bringing forth; parturition. **3.** lineage; extraction; descent: *of Grecian birth.* **4.** high or noble lineage. **5.** supposedly natural heritage: *a musician by birth.* **6.** that which is born. **7.** any coming into existence; origin: *the birth of Protestantism.* [ME *byrth(e)*, t. Scand.; cf. Icel. *byrdh*] —Syn. **3.** parentage, race, family.

birth control, the regulation of birth through the deliberate control or prevention of conception.

birth·day (bûrth/dā/), *n.* **1.** (of persons) the day of one's birth. **2.** (of things) origin or beginning. **3.** the anniversary of one's birth or the origin of something.

birth·mark (bûrth/märk/), *n.* a congenital mark on the body.

birth·night (bûrth/nīt/), *n.* the night of one's birth.

birth·place (bûrth/plās/), *n.* place of birth or origin.

birth rate, the proportion of the number of births in a place in a given time to the total population.

birth·right (bûrth/rīt/), *n.* any right or privilege to which a person is entitled by birth.

birth·root (bûrth/rŏŏt/, -rŏŏt/), *n.* **1.** a species of trillium, *Trillium erectum*, the roots of which are used in medicine. **2.** any of certain other species of trillium.

birth·stone (bûrth/stōn/), *n.* a stone which has been selected as appropriate for wear by persons born within a designated period, superstitiously endowed with mystic powers for good or ill fortune.

birth·wort (bûrth/wûrt/), *n.* **1.** a plant, *Aristolochia Clematitis*, a native of Europe, reputed to facilitate childbirth. **2.** any of certain other species of the same genus. **3.** the birthroot.

bis (bĭs), *adv.* **1.** twice. **2.** a second time: used (esp. in music) to direct a repetition. [t. L. See BI-]

Bi·sa·yan (bē sä/yən), *n.* Visayan.

Bi·sa·yas (bē sä/yäs), *n.* Spanish name of the Visayan Islands.

Bis·cay (bĭs/kā, -kĭ), *n.* Bay of, a large bay of the Atlantic between W France and N Spain.

bis·cuit (bĭs/kĭt), *n.* **1.** *U.S.* a kind of bread in small, soft cakes, raised with baking powder or soda, sometimes with yeast. **2.** *Brit.* a dry and crisp or hard bread in thin, flat cakes, made without yeast or other raising agent; a cracker. **3.** a pale-brown color. **4.** pottery after the first baking and before glazing. [ME *besquite*, t. OF: m. *bescuit*, f. *bes* (g. L *bis*) twice + *cuit*, pp. of *cuire* cook (g. L *coquere*)] —**bis/cuit·like/,** *adj.*

bise (bēz), *n.* a dry, cold north or northeast wind in southeastern France, Switzerland, and adjoining regions. [t. F, t. Gmc.; cf. OHG *bisa*]

bi·sect (bī sĕkt/), *v.t.* **1.** to cut or divide into two parts. **2.** *Geom.* to cut or divide into two equal parts. —*v.i.* **3.** to split into two, as a road; fork. —**bi·sec/tion,** *n.* —**bi·sec/tion·al,** *adj.* —**bi·sec/tion·al·ly,** *adv.*

bi·sec·tor (bī sĕk/tər), *n.* *Geom.* a line or plane bisecting an angle or line segment.

bi·sec·trix (bī sĕk/trĭks), *n., pl.* **bisectrices** (bī/sĕk trī/sēz). **1.** *Crystall.* either of the two directions which bisect the acute (**acute bisectrix**) or obtuse (**obtuse bisectrix**) angles of the optic axes in a biaxial crystal. **2.** *Geom.* a bisector.

bi·ser·rate (bī sĕr/āt, -ĭt), *adj.* *Bot.* doubly serrate; notched like a saw, with the teeth also notched.

bi·sex·u·al (bī sĕk/shŏŏ əl), *adj.* *Biol.* **1.** of both sexes. **2.** combining male and female organs in one individual; hermaphroditic. —*n.* **3.** *Biol.* one who has the reproductive organs of both sexes. **4.** *Psychiatry.* a person sexually attracted by either sex. —**bi·sex/u·al·ism,** *n.* —**bi·sex/u·al·ly,** *adv.*

bish·op (bĭsh/əp), *n., v.,* **-oped, -oping.** —*n.* **1.** an overseer over a number of local churches or a diocese, being in the Greek, Roman Catholic, Anglican, and other churches a member of the highest order in the ministry. **2.** a spiritual overseer. **3.** *Chess.* a piece which moves obliquely on squares of the same color. **4.** a hot drink made of port wine, oranges, cloves, etc. —*v.t.* **5.** to appoint to the office of bishop. —*v.i.* **6.** to function as bishop. [ME; OE *bisc(e)op*, t. VL: (m.) s. (e)*biscopus*, var. of L *episcopus*, t. Gk.: m. *epískopos* overseer] —**bish/op·less,** *adj.*

bish·op·ric (bĭsh/əp rĭk), *n.* the see, diocese, or office of a bishop. [ME *bisshoprike*, OE *bisceoprīce*, f. *bisceop* bishop + *rīce* dominion]

bish·op's-cap (bĭsh/əps kăp/), *n.* miterwort (def. 1).

Bis·kra (bĭs/krä), *n.* a town and oasis in NE Algeria, in the Sahara. 20,625 (1936).

Bis·marck (bĭz/märk; *Ger.* bĭs/-), *n.* **1.** Otto von (ō/tō fən), (*Prince Otto Eduard Leopold von Bismarck Schönhausen*) 1815–98, German statesman: first chancellor of modern German Empire, 1871–1890. **2.** the capital of North Dakota, in the central part. 18,640 (1950).

Bismarck Archipelago, a group of islands in the SE Pacific NE of New Guinea, including the Admiralty Islands, New Britain, New Ireland, and adjacent islands: under Australian administration. ab. 19,200 sq. mi.

bis·muth (bĭz/məth), *n.* *Chem.* a brittle, metallic element, having compounds used in medicine. *Symbol:* Bi; *at. no.:* 83; *at. wt.:* 209.00; *sp. gr.:* 9.8 at 20° C. [t. G, var. of *wismut*; orig. uncert.] —**bis/muth·al,** *adj.*

bis·mu·thic (bĭz mū/thĭk, -mŭth/ĭk), *adj.* *Chem.* of or containing bismuth, esp. in the pentavalent state, Bi⁵.

bis·muth·in·ite (bĭz mŭth/ə nīt/), *n.* a mineral, bismuth sulfide, Bi₂S₃, occurring in lead-gray masses, an ore of bismuth.

bis·muth·ous (bĭz/məth əs), *adj.* *Chem.* containing trivalent bismuth, Bi³.

bi·son (bī/sən, -zən), *n., pl.* **-son.** *Zool.* a large North American bovine ruminant, *Bison bison* (**American bison,** or buffalo), with high, well-haired shoulders. [t. L, t. Gmc.; cf. G *wisent*]

American bison, *Bison bison* (10 to 12 ft. long, ab. 6 ft. high at the shoulder)

bisque[1] (bĭsk), *n.* **1.** any smooth, creamy soup. **2.** a thick soup made of shellfish or game stewed long and slowly. **3.** ice cream made with powdered macaroons or nuts. [t. F]

bisque[2] (bĭsk), *n.* a point, extra turn, or the like, allowed to a player as odds in tennis and other games. [t. F; orig. unknown]

bis·sex·tile (bĭ sĕks/tĭl), *adj.* **1.** containing or noting the extra day of leap year. —*n.* **2.** leap year. [t. LL: m. s. *bissextīlis* (*annus*) leap year]

bis·ter (bĭs/tər), *n.* **1.** a brown pigment extracted from the soot of wood, much used in pen and wash drawings. **2.** a dark-brown color. Also, **bis/tre.** [t. F: m. *bistre;* orig. unknown, ? akin to F *bis* dark gray]

bis·tort (bĭs/tôrt), *n.* **1.** a European perennial herb, *Polygonum Bistorta*, with a twisted root, which is sometimes used as an astringent; snakeweed. **2.** a plant of other allied species, as **Virginia bistort,** *P. virginianum*, and **Alpine bistort,** *P. viviparum.* [f. L: *bis* twice + s. *torta*, pp. fem., twisted]

bis·tou·ry (bĭs/tə rĭ), *n., pl.* **-ries.** *Surg.* a small, narrow surgical knife. [t. F: m. *bistouri*, der. *bistourner* turn out of shape, castrate, t. Pr.: m. *bistornar* (r. OF *bestorner*)]

bis·tro (bĭs/trō; *Fr.* bē strō/), *n.* *Colloq.* **1.** a small, unpretentious tavern or café. **2.** a bartender.

bi·sul·fate (bī sŭl/fāt), *n.* *Chem.* a salt of sulfuric acid, containing the radical HSO₄⁻¹. Also, **bi·sul/phate.**

bi·sul·fide (bī sŭl/fīd, -fĭd), *n.* *Chem.* a disulfide. Also, **bi·sul/phide.**

bi·sul·fite (bī sŭl/fīt), *n.* *Chem.* a salt of sulfurous acid, containing the radical HSO₃⁻¹. Also, **bi·sul/phite.**

bi·sym·met·ri·cal (bī/sĭ mĕt/rə kəl), *adj.* *Bot.* having two planes of symmetry at right angles to each other. Also, **bi/sym·met/ric.** —**bi/sym·met/ri·cal·ly,** *adv.* —**bi·sym·me·try** (bī sĭm/ə trĭ), *n.*

bit[1] (bĭt), *n.*, *v.*, **bitted, bitting.** —*n.* **1.** the metallic mouthpiece of a bridle, with the adjacent parts to which the reins are fastened. See illus. under **harness. 2.** anything that curbs or restrains. **3.** *Mach.* the cutting, or penetrating part of various tools: **a.** the cutting portion of an ax or hatchet or the removable cutter in the plane, bitstock, etc. **b.** the movable boring or drilling part (in many forms) used in a carpenter's brace, a drilling machine, or the like. **4.** the part of a key which enters the lock and acts on the bolt and tumblers. —*v.t.* **5.** to put a bit in the mouth of. **6.** to curb; restrain. **7.** to grind a bit on. [ME *byt*, OE *bite* action of biting] —**bit′less,** *adj.*

Spiral bits (def. 3b)

bit[2] (bĭt), *n.* **1.** a small piece or quantity of anything: *a bit of string, a bit of one's mind.* **2.** a short time: *wait a bit.* **3.** *U.S. Colloq.* twelve and a half cents: *two bits* (25 cents). **4.** any small coin: *a three-penny bit.* **5.** a Spanish or Mexican silver real worth twelve and a half cents, formerly current in parts of the U. S. [ME *bite*, OE *bita* bit, morsel] —**Syn. 1.** particle, speck, grain, mite; whit, iota, jot; scrap, fragment.

bi·tar·trate (bī tär′trāt), *n. Chem.* a tartrate in which only one of the acid hydrogens of tartaric acid is replaced by a metal or a positive radical; an acid tartrate.

bitch (bĭch), *n.* **1.** a female dog. **2.** a female of canines generally. **3.** *Vulgar.* a woman, esp. a disagreeable or lewd one. **4.** *Slang.* a complaint. —*v.i.* **5.** *Slang.* to complain. —*v.t.* **6.** *Slang.* to spoil; bungle. [ME *biche*, OE *bicce*, c. Icel. *bikkja*]

bite (bīt), *v.*, **bit, bitten or bit, biting.** —*v.t.* **1.** to cut into or wound, or cut (*off*, *out*, etc.) with the teeth. **2.** to grip with the teeth. **3.** to cut or pierce. **4.** to sting, as an insect. **5.** to cause to smart or sting. **6.** to eat into or corrode, as an acid does. **7.** *Etching.* to use acid for eating into such parts of a copper or other surface as are left bare of a protective coating. **8.** to make a great impression on. **9.** to close the teeth tightly on. **10.** to take firm hold or act effectively on. **11.** to cheat; deceive. —*v.i.* **12.** to press the teeth (*into*, *on*, etc.); snap. **13.** *Angling.* (of fish) to take the bait. **14.** to accept a deceptive offer or suggestion. **15.** to act effectively; grip; hold. —*n.* **16.** act of biting. **17.** a wound made by biting. **18.** a cutting, stinging, or nipping effect. **19.** a piece bitten off. **20.** food: *not a bite to eat.* **21.** a small meal. **22.** *Mach.* **a.** the catch or hold that one object or one part of a mechanical apparatus has on another. **b.** a surface brought into contact to obtain a hold or grip, as in a lathe, chuck, or similar device. **23.** (in a file) the roughness or power of abrasion. [ME *biten*, OE *bītan*, c. G *beissen*] —**bit′er**, *n.*

Bi·thyn·i·a (bĭ thĭn′ĭ ə), *n.* an ancient country in NW Asia Minor.

bit·ing (bī′tĭng), *adj.* **1.** nipping; keen: *biting cold.* **2.** cutting; sarcastic: *a biting remark.* —**bit′ing·ly,** *adv.* —**bit′ing·ness,** *n.*

Bi·tolj (bē′tôl′y), *n.* a city in S Yugoslavia. 33,024 (1931). Turkish, **Monastir.**

bit·stock (bĭt′stŏk′), *n. Mach.* the stock or handle by which a boring bit is held and rotated; a brace.

bitt (bĭt), *Naut.* —*n.* **1.** a strong post of wood or iron projecting (usually in pairs) above the deck of a ship, and used for securing cables, lines for towing, etc. —*v.t.* **2.** to put (a cable, etc.) round the bitts. [var. of BIT[1]]

bit·ten (bĭt′ən), *v.* pp. of bite.

bit·ter (bĭt′ər), *adj.* **1.** having a harsh, disagreeable taste, like that of quinine. **2.** hard to admit or receive: *a bitter lesson.* **3.** hard to bear; grievous; distressful: *a bitter sorrow.* **4.** causing pain; piercing; stinging: *bitter cold.* **5.** characterized by intense animosity: *bitter hatred.* **6.** harsh; sarcastic; cutting: *bitter words.* —*n.* **7.** that which is bitter; bitterness. —*v.t.* **8.** to make bitter. [OE *biter*; akin to BITE] —**bit′ter·ish,** *adj.* —**bit′ter·ly,** *adv.* —**bit′ter·ness,** *n.* —**Syn. 6.** acrimonious, caustic. —**Ant. 1.** sweet. **2.** pleasant.

bitter end, *Naut.* the extreme tail end of a cable or rope. The bitter end of an anchor cable is secured to the ship inside the chain locker. [f. *bitter* (f. BITT + -ER[1]) + END[1]]

Bitter Lakes, two lakes that form part of the Suez Canal, in NE Egypt.

bit·tern[1] (bĭt′ərn), *n.* any of several herons, as *Botaurus lentiginosus* of North America, and the common bittern, *Botaurus stellaris*, of Europe. [ME *bitter, botor,* t. OF: m. *butor*; orig. uncert. Cf. L *būtio* bittern]

bit·tern[2] (bĭt′ərn), *n.* a bitter, oily liquid remaining in saltmaking after the salt has crystallized out of sea water or brine, used as a source of bromine, etc. [d. var. of *bittering*, f. BITTER + -ING[1]]

American bittern, *Botaurus lentiginosus* (27 in. l ong)

bitter principle, *Chem.* any of several hundred natural compounds, usually of vegetable origin, having a bitter taste, and not admitting of any chemical classification.

bit·ter·root (bĭt′ər rōōt′, -rŏot′), *n.* a portulacaceous plant, *Lewisia rediviva*, having fleshy roots and hand-

some pink flowers, growing in the mountains of Idaho, Montana, etc. (the State flower of Montana).

Bitterroot Range, a range of the Rocky Mountains, on the boundary between Idaho and Montana. Highest peak, ab. 10,000 ft. Also, **Bitter Root Range.**

bit·ters (bĭt′ərz), *n.pl.* **1.** a liquor (generally a spirituous liquor) in which bitter herbs or roots are steeped. **2.** *Pharm.* **a.** a liquid, usually alcoholic, impregnated with a bitter medicine, as gentian, quassia, etc., used as a stomachic, tonic, or the like. **b.** bitter medicinal substances in general, as quinine, gentian, etc.

bit·ter·sweet (*n.* bĭt′ər swēt′; *adj.* bĭt′ər swēt′), *n.* **1.** the woody nightshade, *Solanum Dulcamara*, a climbing or trailing solanaceous plant with scarlet berries. **2.** any climbing plant of the genus *Celastrus*, with orange capsules opening to expose red-coated seeds, esp. *Celastrus scandens.* —*adj.* **3.** both bitter and sweet to the taste. **4.** both pleasant and painful.

bit·ter·weed (bĭt′ər wēd′), *n.* **1.** any of various plants containing a bitter principle, as the ragweed and the horseweed. **2.** any sneezeweed of genus *Helenium*, esp. *H. tenuifolium.*

bi·tu·men (bĭ tū′mən, -tōō′-, bĭ′chủ ŏō-), *n.* **1.** any of various natural substances, as asphalt, maltha, gilsonite, etc., consisting mainly of hydrocarbons. **2.** a brown tar or asphaltlike substance used in painting. [t. L] —**bi·tu·mi·noid** (bĭ tū′mə noid′, -tōō′-), *adj.*

bi·tu·mi·nize (bĭ tū′mə nīz′, -tōō′-), *v.t.*, **-nized, -nizing.** to convert into or treat with bitumen. —**bi·tu′mi·ni·za′tion,** *n.*

bi·tu·mi·nous (bĭ tū′mə nəs, -tōō′-), *adj.* of, like, or containing bitumen: *bituminous shale.*

bituminous coal, soft coal, a mineral coal which contains volatile hydrocarbons and tarry matter, and burns with a yellow, smoky flame.

bi·va·lent (bī vā′lənt, bĭv′ə-), *adj.* **1.** *Chem.* **a.** having a valence of two. **b.** having two valences, as mercury, with valences 1 and 2. **2.** *Biol.* pertaining to composites of two similar or identical chromosomes, or chromosome sets. —*n.* **3.** *Biol.* a bivalent pair or set of chromosomes. —**bi·va·lence** (bī vā′ləns, bĭv′ə ləns), **bi·va′len·cy,** *n.*

bi·valve (bī′vălv′), *n. Zool.* **1.** a mollusk having two shells hinged together, as the oyster, clam, mussel; a lamellibranch. —*adj.* **2.** *Bot.* having two valves, as a seedcase. **3.** *Zool.* having two shells, usually united by a hinge. —**bi·val·vu·lar** (bī văl′vyə lər), *adj.*

biv·ou·ac (bĭv′ŏō ăk′, bĭv′wăk), *n.*, *v.*, **-acked, -acking.** —*n.* **1.** an area in the field where troops rest or assemble, usually having no shelter or protection from enemy fire, or only tents, or shelter made from anything available. —*v.i.* **2.** to rest or assemble in such an area. [t. F, prob. t. d. G: m. *biwache*. Cf. G *beiwacht* patrol]

bi·week·ly (bī wēk′lĭ), *adj.*, *n.*, *pl.* **-lies,** *adv.* —*adj.* **1.** occurring every two weeks. **2.** occurring twice a week; semiweekly. —*n.* **3.** a periodical issued every other week. —*adv.* **4.** every two weeks. **5.** twice a week.

bi·year·ly (bī yîr′lĭ), *adj.*, *adv.* **1.** biennial. **2.** twice yearly.

bi·zarre (bĭ zär′), *adj.* singular in appearance, style, or general character; whimsically strange; odd. [t. F: odd, prob. t. Sp.: m. *bizarro* brave, ? t. Basque: m. *bizar* beard] —**bi·zarre′ly,** *adv.* —**bi·zarre′ness,** *n.*

Bi·zer·te (bĭ zûr′tə; *Fr.* bē zěrt′). *n.* a seaport in N Tunisia. 28,468 (1936). Also, **Bi·zer·ta** (bē zěr′tä). Ancient, **Hippo Zarytus.**

Bi·zet (bē zā′; *Fr.* bē zě′), *n.* **Georges** (zhôrzh), (*Alexandre César Léopold Bizet*) 1838–75, French composer.

Bi·zo·ni·a (bī zō′nĭ ə, bĭ-), *n.* the combined U.S. and British zones of occupation in Germany after World War II.

Björn·son (byœrn′sŏn), *n.* **Björnstjerne** (byœrn′styěr′nə), 1832–1910, Norwegian poet, novelist, and dramatist.

bk., 1. bank. **2.** book.

bkg., banking.

bl., 1. bale; bales. **2.** barrel; barrels.

B.L., Bachelor of Laws.

b.l., 1. *Com.* bill of lading. **2.** *Ordn.* breech loading.

blab (blăb), *v.*, **blabbed, blabbing,** *n.* —*v.t.* **1.** to reveal indiscreetly and thoughtlessly. —*v.i.* **2.** to talk or chatter indiscreetly and thoughtlessly. —*n.* **3.** idle, indiscreet chattering. **4.** a person who blabs. —**blab′ber,** *n.*

black (blăk), *adj.* **1.** without brightness or color. **2.** wearing black or dark clothing, armor, etc.: *the black prince.* **3.** *Anthrop.* **a.** pertaining or belonging to an ethnic group characterized by dark skin pigmentation. **b.** pertaining specif. to the "black races" of Africa, Oceania, and Australia, the Negroes, Negritos, Papuans, Melanesians, and Australian aborigines. **4.** soiled or stained with dirt. **5.** characterized by absence of light; involved or enveloped in darkness: *a black night.* **6.** gloomy; dismal: *a black outlook.* **7.** boding ill; sullen; forbidding: *black words, black looks.* **8.** without any moral light or goodness; evil; wicked. **9.** caused or marked by ruin or desolation. **10.** indicating censure, disgrace, or liability to punishment: *a black mark on one's record.* **11.** (of coffee) without milk or cream. —*n.* **12.** a member of a dark-skinned people; a Negro. **13.** a black speck, flake, or spot, as of soot. **14.** black clothing, esp. as a sign of mourning: *to be in black.* **15.** *Chess, Checkers.* the dark-colored men or pieces. **16.** black pigment: *lamp black.* **17. in the black,** financially solvent. —*v.t.* **18.** to make black; put black on. **19.** to clean and polish (shoes) with blacking.

b., blend of, blended; **c.,** cognate with; **d.,** dialect, dialectal; **der.,** derived from; **f.,** formed from; **g.,** going back to; **m.,** modification of; **r.,** replacing; **s.,** stem of; **t.,** taken from; **?,** perhaps. See the full key on inside cover.

20. *Mil.* to obscure by concealing all light in defense against air raids (fol. by *out*). —*v.i.* **21.** to become black; take on a black color. **22.** to lose consciousness (fol. by *out*). [ME *blak*, OE *blæc*, c. OHG *blah–*, *blach–*] —**black′ish,** *adj.* —**black′ish·ly,** *adv.* —**black′ness,** *n.* —**Syn. 1.** sable, ebon; swart, swarthy; dark, dusky; sooty, inky. —**Ant. 1.** colorful. **4.** clean. **6.** hopeful. **7.** friendly.

Black (blăk), *n.* Hugo Lafayette, born 1886, U.S. political official: associate justice of U.S. Supreme Court since 1937.

black·a·moor (blăk′ə·mŏŏr′), *n.* **1.** a Negro. **2.** any dark-skinned person. [var. of *black Moor*]

black-and-blue (blăk′ən·blōō′), *adj.* discolored, as by bruising.

Black and Tan, 1. an armed force of about 6,000 men sent by the British government to Ireland in June, 1920, to suppress revolutionary activity; so called from the color of their uniforms. **2.** a member of this force.

black and white, 1. print or writing. **2.** a drawing or picture done in black and white only.

black art, witchcraft; magic.

black·ball (blăk′bôl′), *n.* **1.** an adverse vote. **2.** a black ball placed in a ballot box signifying a negative vote. —*v.t.* **3.** to vote against. **4.** to ostracize. **5.** to reject (a candidate) by placing a black ball in the ballot box. —**black′ball′er,** *n.*

black bass, an American fresh-water fish of the genus *Micropterus*, which comprises five species of which the best-known are the **large-mouthed bass,** *M. salmoides*, the **small-mouthed bass,** *M. dolomieu*, and the **spotted bass,** *M. punctulatus*.

black bear, a species of American bear, *Euarctos americanus*, with a pale face and dense black fur.

black belt, *U.S.* **1.** a preponderantly Negro area in a city or State. **2.** a narrow belt of dark-colored, calcareous soils in central Alabama and Mississippi highly adapted to agriculture, esp. cotton growing.

black·ber·ry (blăk′bĕr′ĭ), *n.*, *pl.* **-ries. 1.** the fruit, black or very dark purple when ripe, of certain species of the genus *Rubus*. **2.** the plant. [ME *blakeberie*, OE *blacu berie*] —**black′ber′ry·like′,** *adj.*

blackberry lily, a perennial iridaceous plant, *Belamcanda chinensis*, with red-spotted, orange, lilylike flowers and globose seeds resembling blackberries.

black bindweed, 1. a twining Old World vine, *Tamus communis*, with red berries. **2.** a climbing European herb, *Polygonum Convolvulus*, found widely in America as a tenacious weed.

black·bird (blăk′bûrd′), *n.* **1.** one of various birds of the American family *Icteridae*, as the **crow blackbird**, *Quiscalus quiscula*, the **rusty blackbird**, *Euphagus carolinus*, and the **red-winged blackbird**, *Agelaius phoeniceus*. **2.** any of various unrelated birds having black plumage in the male.

black·board (blăk′bōrd′), *n.* a smooth dark board, used in schools, etc., for writing or drawing with chalk.

black book, 1. a book of names of people liable to censure or punishment. **2. be in one's black books,** to be in disfavor.

black·boy (blăk′boi′), *n.* the grass tree.

black buck, a common Indian antelope, *Antilope cervicapra*, of medium size and blackish-brown color.

Black·burn (blăk′bərn), *n.* **1.** a city in NW England, in Lancashire. 107,840 (est. 1946). **2. Mount,** a peak in SE Alaska, in the Wrangell Mountains. 16,140 ft.

Black Canyon, a canyon of the Colorado river between Arizona and Nevada: site of Boulder Dam.

black·cap (blăk′kăp′), *n.* **1.** any of several birds having the top of the head black, as the chickadee and certain warblers, esp. the Old World blackcap, *Sylvia atricapilla*. **2.** *U.S.* a popular name of the plant and fruit of the black raspberry, *Rubus occidentalis*.

black·cock (blăk′kŏk′), *n.* the male of the European black grouse, *Lyrurus tetrix*.

Black Country, a midlands district around Birmingham, England, begrimed by numerous factories, etc.

black·damp (blăk′dămp′), *n.* *Mining.* chokedamp.

Black Death, bubonic plague, which spread over Europe in the 14th century.

black diamond, 1. a carbonado (def. 2). **2.** (*pl.*) coal.

black disease, *Vet. Sci.* an acute, highly fatal disease of sheep caused by general intoxication from *Clostridium novyi*, an anaerobic organism which multiplies in the liver in areas damaged by the common liver fluke.

black dog, *Colloq.* melancholy; the blues.

black·en (blăk′ən), *v.*, **-ened, -ening.** —*v.t.* **1.** to make black; darken. **2.** to speak evil of; defame. —*v.i.* **3.** to grow or become black. —**black′en·er,** *n.*

black eye, 1. discoloration of the skin around the eye, resulting from a blow, etc. **2.** *Colloq.* a cause of shame, dishonor, etc.

black-eyed Su·san (blăk′īd′ sōō′zən), any of a number of plants having flowers with a dark center against a lighter, usually yellow, background, such as the composite herb, *Rudbeckia hirta*, and the acanthaceous vine, *Thunbergia alata* (the state flower of Maryland).

black·face (blăk′fās′), *n.* **1.** *Theat.* **a.** an entertainer playing a Negro. **b.** the make-up for the role of a Negro. **2.** *Print.* a heavy-faced type.

black·fel·low (blăk′fĕl′ō), *n.* an aboriginal of Australia.

black·fish (blăk′fĭsh′), *n.*, *pl.* **-fishes,** (*esp. collectively*) **-fish. 1.** the black whale. **2.** any of various dark-colored fishes, as the tautog, *Tautoga onitis*, or the sea bass, *Centropristes striatus*, or a small fresh-water food fish, *Dallia pectoralis*, of Alaska and Siberia, notable for its ability to revive after having been long frozen.

black flag, the pirate flag, usually of black cloth with the white skull and crossbones on it.

black fly, any of the minute, black-bodied gnats of the dipterous family *Simuliidae*; the larvae are aquatic.

Black·foot (blăk′fŏŏt′), *n.*, *pl.* **-feet** (-fēt′), **-foot. 1.** a member of a North American tribe of Indians (the Blackfeet) of Algonquian stock. **2.** an Algonquian language of Saskatchewan, Alberta, and Montana. —*adj.* **3.** of or pertaining to the Blackfeet.

Black Forest, a forest-covered mountainous region in SW Germany. Highest peak. Feldberg, ab. 4900 ft. German, **Schwarzwald.**

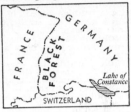

Black Friar, 1. a Dominican friar (from the distinctive black mantle). **2.** a Benedictine monk.

black grouse, a large grouse, *Lyrurus tetrix*, found in the northern parts of Europe and western Asia. The male is black, the female mottled gray and brown.

black·guard (blăg′ärd, -ərd), *n.* **1.** a coarse, despicable person; a scoundrel. —*v.t.* **2.** to revile in scurrilous language. —*v.i.* **3.** to behave like a blackguard. [f. BLACK + GUARD] —**black′guard·ism,** *n.*

black·guard·ly (blăg′ərd·lĭ), *adj.* **1.** of, like, or befitting a blackguard. —*adv.* **2.** in the manner of a blackguard.

black gum, a tree of the family *Nyssaceae*, as *Nyssa sylvatica* and *N. biflora*. See **tupelo.**

Black Hand, 1. an anarchistic society in Spain, repressed in 1883. **2.** *U.S.* a criminal secret society, esp. of Italians, organized for blackmail and deeds of violence about the last decade of the 19th century. **3.** *U.S.* any similar group. [trans. of Sp. *mano negra*]

black haw, 1. a North American shrub or small tree of the honeysuckle family, *Viburnum prunifolium*, bearing white flowers and black drupes. **2.** the sheepberry.

Black Hawk, 1767–1838, American Indian chief of the Sac and Fox tribes.

black·head (blăk′hĕd′), *n.* **1.** a small wormlike, black-tipped, fatty mass in a follicle of the face. **2.** any of several birds having a black head, as the scaup duck, *Aythya marila*. **3.** *Vet. Sci.* a malignant, infectious, protozoan disease of turkeys, chickens, and many wild birds, attacking esp. the intestines and liver.

black·heart (blăk′härt′), *n.* **1.** plant disease, as of potatoes and various trees, in which internal plant tissues blacken. **2.** a kind of cherry bearing a large, sweet, somewhat heart-shaped fruit with a nearly black skin.

black-heart·ed (blăk′här′tĭd), *adj.* evil.

Black Hills, a group of mountains in W South Dakota and NE Wyoming. Highest peak, Harney Peak, 7242 ft.

Black Hole, 1. a small prison cell in Fort William, Calcutta, into which, in 1756, 146 Europeans were thrust for a night, only 23 of whom were alive in the morning. **2.** (*l.c.*) a military cell or lockup.

black horehound, a fetid European weed, *Ballota nigra*, with purple flowers, prevalent in waste land.

black·ing (blăk′ĭng), *n.* any preparation for producing a black coating or finish, as on shoes, stoves, etc.

black·jack (blăk′jăk′), *n.* **1.** a short club, usually leather-covered, consisting of a heavy head on an elastic shaft. **2.** a large drinking cup or jug for beer, ale, etc., orig. one made of leather coated externally with tar. **3.** the black flag of a pirate. **4.** a small oak, *Quercus marilandica*, of the eastern U. S., with a nearly black bark and a wood of little value except for fuel. **5.** *Mineral.* a dark, iron-rich variety of sphalerite. **6.** caramel or burnt sugar for coloring spirits, vinegar, coffee, etc. **7.** *Cards.* twenty-one. —*v.t.* **8.** to strike or beat with a blackjack. **9.** to compel by threat.

Leather blackjacks

black knot, a fungus plant disease appearing as black knotlike masses on the branches, esp. on plums and cherries.

black lead, graphite; plumbago.

black·leg (blăk′lĕg′), *n.* **1.** *Vet. Sci.* an infectious, generally fatal disease of cattle and sheep characterized by painful, gaseous swellings in the muscles, usually of the upper parts of the legs. **2.** a plant disease, as of cabbage and potato, in which the lower stems turn black and decay. **3.** a swindler, esp. in racing or gambling. **4.** *Brit. Colloq.* a strikebreaker; scab.

black letter, *Print.* a heavy-faced type in gothic style like that in early English printed books. —**black′·let′ter,** *adj.*

black-letter day, an unlucky day.

black list, a list of persons under suspicion, disfavor, censure, etc.

black-list (blăk′lĭst′), *v.t.* to put on a black list.
black·ly (blăk′lĭ), *adv.* with a black or dark appearance; darkly; gloomily; wickedly.
black magic, magic used for evil purposes.
black·mail (blăk′māl′), *n.* **1.** *Law.* **a.** any payment extorted by intimidation, as by threats of injurious revelations or accusations. **b.** the extortion of such payment. **2.** a tribute formerly exacted in the north of England and in Scotland by freebooting chiefs for protection from pillage. —*v.t.* **3.** to extort blackmail from. [f. BLACK + *mail* coin, rent (ME *maille*, t. OF)] —**black′mail′er,** *n.*
Black Ma·ri·a (mə·rī′ə), *Colloq.* a closed vehicle used for conveying prisoners to and from jail.
black mark, a mark of failure or censure.
black market, an illegal market violating price controls, rationing, etc.
black measles, *Pathol.* a malignant form of measles.
Black·more (blăk′mōr), *n.* **Richard Doddridge** (dŏd′-rĭj), 1825–1900, British novelist.
Black Mountains, a mountain range in W North Carolina: a part of the Appalachian system. Highest peak, Mt. Mitchell, 6711 ft.
black nightshade, a common weed, *Solanum nigrum*, with white flowers and black edible berries.
black·out (blăk′out′), *n.* **1.** *Mil.* the extinguishing of all visible lights in a city, etc., as a war protection. **2.** *Theat.* the extinguishing of all stage lights. **3.** unconsciousness, esp. in aviation. **4.** loss of memory.
black pepper, a hot, sharp condiment prepared from the dried berries of a tropical vine, *Piper nigrum*.
black·poll (blăk′pōl′), *n.* a North American warbler, *Dendroica striata*, the adult male of which has the top of the head black.
Black·pool (blăk′pōol′), *n.* a seaport in NW England, in Lancashire: resort. 150,340 (est. 1946).
Black Prince, 1330–76, Edward, Prince of Wales (the son of Edward III of England).
Black Rod, 1. (in England) an usher (**gentleman usher of the black rod**) of the King's chamber, the Order of the Garter, and the House of Lords (so called from the rod he carries). **2.** a similar official in British colonial legislatures.
Black Sea, a sea S of E Europe, bounded by the Soviet Union, Turkey, Rumania, and Bulgaria. ab. 164,000 sq. mi.; greatest depth, ab. 7200 ft. Also, **Euxine Sea.** Ancient, **Pontus Euxinus.**
black sheep, a person worthless despite good background.
Black Shirt, *Europ. Hist.* a member of a fascist organization in Europe, such as the Italian fascist militia, or Hitler's Schutzstaffel.
black·smith (blăk′smĭth′), *n.* **1.** a person who makes horseshoes and shoes horses. **2.** an artisan who works in iron. [f. BLACK (in ref. to iron or black metal) + SMITH¹. Cf. WHITESMITH]
black·snake (blăk′snāk′), *n.* **1.** a nonvenomous snake, *Coluber constrictor*, of the U. S., attaining a length of 5 to 6 ft., and notably agile and strong. **2.** any of various other snakes of a black or very dark color. **3.** *U.S.* a heavy, tapering, flexible whip of braided cowhide or the like. Also, **black snake.**
black spruce, 1. a conifer of North America, *Picea mariana*, noted for its extremely dark green needles. **2.** an easily worked light wood from this tree.
Black·stone (blăk′stōn, -stən), *n.* **Sir William,** 1723–80, British judge and writer on law.
black·tail (blăk′tāl′), *n.* the mule deer.
black tea, a tea which has been allowed to wither and ferment in the air for some time, before being subjected to a heating process.
black·thorn (blăk′thôrn′), *n.* **1.** a much-branched, thorny shrub of the Old World *Prunus spinosa*, bearing white flowers and small plumlike fruits; sloe. **2.** a species of the genus *Crataegus*, as *C. tomentosa*.
Black Volta. See **Volta** (def. 2).
black vomit, *Pathol.* **1.** a dark-colored substance, consisting chiefly of altered blood, vomited in some cases of yellow fever, usually presaging a fatal issue of the disease. **2.** act of throwing up this matter. **3.** the disease itself.
Black·wall hitch (blăk′wôl′), a hitch made with a rope over a hook so that it holds fast when pulled but is loose otherwise. See illus. under **knot.**
black walnut, 1. a tree, *Juglans nigra*, of North America, which yields a valuable timber. **2.** the nut thereof. **3.** the wood of this tree.
black·wa·ter fever (blăk′wô′tər, -wŏt′ər), *Pathol.* a severe form of malaria found chiefly in the tropics but occasionally in the southern U. S.
black·weed (blăk′wēd′), *n.* the common ragweed.
Black·wells Island (blăk′wĕlz, -wəlz), former name of Welfare Island.
black whale, a dolphinlike cetacean of the genus *Globicephalus*; a blackfish.
black widow, a poisonous female spider, *Latrodectus mactans*, common in the U. S., that eats its mate.

blad·der (blăd′ər), *n.* **1.** *Anat., Zool.* **a.** a distensible pelvic sac with membranous and muscular walls, for storage and expulsion of urine secreted by the kidneys. **b.** any similar sac or receptacle. **2.** *Pathol.* a vesicle, blister, cyst, etc., filled with fluid or air. **3.** *Bot.* a sac or the like containing air, as in certain seaweeds. **4.** anything inflated, empty, or unsound. [ME; OE *blǣdre* bladder, blister, akin to BLOW², v., BLAST] —**blad′der·less,** *adj.* —**blad′der·like′,** *adj.* —**blad′der·y,** *adj.*
bladder campion, a plant, *Silene latifolia* (*Silene inflata*), so called from its inflated calyx.
bladder ket·mi·a (kĕt′mĭ·ə), a cultivated annual plant, *Hibiscus Trionum*, with a bladdery calyx.
blad·der·nose (blăd′ər·nōz′), *n.* a large seal, *Cystophora cristata*, of the northern Atlantic, the male of which has a large, distensible, hoodlike sac upon the head; the hooded seal.
blad·der·nut (blăd′ər·nŭt′), *n.* **1.** the bladderlike fruit capsule of any shrub or small tree of the genus *Staphylea*, as *S. trifolia* of the eastern U. S. **2.** the shrub itself.
bladder worm, *Zool.* the bladderlike encysted larva of a tapeworm; a cysticercus, coenurus, or hydatid.
blad·der·wort (blăd′ər·wûrt′), *n.* any of various herbs of the large genus *Utricularia*, including aquatic, terrestrial, and epiphytic forms throughout the world.
blade (blād), *n.* **1.** the flat cutting part of sword, knife, etc. **2.** a sword. **3.** the leaf of a plant, esp. of a grass or cereal. **4.** *Bot.* the broad part of a leaf, as distinguished from the stalk or petiole. See illus. under **leaf.** **5.** a thin, flat part of something, as of an oar or a bone. **6.** a dashing, swaggering, or rakish young fellow. **7.** *Anat.* the scapula or shoulder blade. **8.** *Phonet.* the upper surface and edges of the tongue for a short distance back from the tip. [ME; OE *blǣd*, c. G *blatt*] —**blad′ed,** *adj.* —**blade′less,** *adj.* —**blade′like′,** *adj.*
Bla·go·vesh·chensk (blä′gŏ·vĕsh′chĕnsk), *n.* a city in the SE Soviet Union in Asia, on the Amur river. 58,761 (1939).
blah (blä), *n.* *U.S. Slang.* nonsense; rubbish.
blain (blān), *n.* *Pathol.* an inflammatory swelling or sore. [ME *bleine*, OE *blegen*]
Blaine (blān), *n.* **James Gillespie** (gĭ·lĕs′pĭ), 1830–1893, U. S. statesman.
Blake (blāk), *n.* **1. Robert,** 1599–1657, British admiral. **2. William,** 1757–1827, British poet and artist.
blam·a·ble (blā′mə·bəl), *adj.* deserving blame; censurable. —**blam′a·ble·ness,** *n.* —**blam′a·bly,** *adv.*
blame (blām), *v.,* **blamed, blaming,** *n.* —*v.t.* **1.** to lay the responsibility of (a fault, error, etc.) on a person: *I blame the accident on him.* **2.** to find fault with; censure: *I don't blame you for doing that.* **3.** *U.S. Slang* and *Dial.* to blast (as a humorous imperative or optative): *Blame my hide if I go.* —*n.* **4.** imputation of fault; censure. **5.** responsibility for censure. [ME *blamen*, t. OF: m. *blasmer*, g. LL *blasphēmāre* BLASPHEME]
—**Syn. 1, 2.** reproach, reprove, reprehend. BLAME, CENSURE, CONDEMN imply finding fault with someone (or something). To BLAME is to hold accountable for, and disapprove because of, some error, mistake, omission, neglect, or the like: *who is to blame for the disaster?* The verb CENSURE differs from the noun in connoting scolding or rebuking even more than adverse criticism: *to censure one for extravagance.* To CONDEMN is to express an adverse (esp. legal) judgment, without recourse: *to condemn conduct, a building, a man to death.* **4.** reprehension, condemnation, stricture. **5.** guilt, culpability, fault. —**Ant. 2.** praise.
blamed (blāmd), *U.S. Slang and Dial.* —*adj.* **1.** confounded. —*adv.* **2.** confoundedly; excessively.
blame·ful (blām′fəl), *adj.* deserving blame. —**blame′-ful·ly,** *adv.* —**blame′ful·ness,** *n.*
blame·less (blām′lĭs), *adj.* free from blame; guiltless. —**blame′less·ly,** *adv.* —**blame′less·ness,** *n.* —**Syn.** irreproachable, inculpable. See **innocent.** —**Ant.** guilty.
blame·wor·thy (blām′wûr′thĭ), *adj.* deserving blame. —**blame′wor′thi·ness,** *n.*
Blanc (blän), *n.* **1. Jean Joseph Charles Louis** (zhän zhô·zĕf′ shàrl lwē), 1811–82, French socialist and historian. **2. Mont** (môN), a mountain on the French-Italian border: the highest peak of the Alps. 15,781 ft.
Blan·ca Peak (blăng′kə), a mountain in S Colorado; the highest peak in the Sangre de Cristo range. 14,390 ft.
blanch (blănch, blänch), *v.t.* **1.** to whiten by removing color. **2.** *Hort.* to whiten or prevent from becoming green by excluding the light (a process applied to the stems or leaves of plants, such as celery, lettuce, etc.). **3.** to remove the skin from (nuts, fruits, etc.) by immersion in boiling water, then in cold. **4.** to separate (the grains or strands of rice, macaroni, etc.) by immersing in boiling water, then in cold. **5.** to scald (meat, etc.). **6.** *Metall.* to give a white luster to (metals), as by means of acids. **7.** to make pale, as with sickness or fear. —*v.i.* **8.** to become white; turn pale. [ME *blaunche(n)*, t. OF: m. *blanchir*, der. *blanc* white. See BLANK] —**blanch′er,** *n.* —**Syn. 1.** See **whiten.**
blanc·mange (blə·mänzh′, -mäNzh′), *n.* a jellylike preparation of milk thickened with cornstarch, gelatin, or the like, and flavored. [ME *blanmanger*, t. OF: m. *blanc-manger*, lit., white food]
bland (blănd), *adj.* **1.** gentle or agreeable, as of persons. **2.** soothing or balmy, as air. **3.** nonirritating, as food or medicines. **4.** nonstimulating, as medicines. [t. L: s. *blandus*] —**bland′ly,** *adv.* —**bland′ness,** *n.* —**Syn. 1.** suave, urbane. **3.** soft, mild.

blan·dish (blăn′dĭsh), *v.t.* to treat flatteringly; coax; cajole. [ME *blaundysh(en)*, t. OF: m. *blandiss*-, s. *blandir*, g. L *blandīre* flatter] —**blan′dish·er**, *n.*

blan·dish·ment (blăn′dĭsh mənt), *n.* **1.** flattering action or speech. **2.** something that pleases or allures.

blank (blăngk), *adj.* **1.** (of paper, etc.) free from marks; not written or printed on. **2.** not filled out: *a blank check.* **3.** unrelieved or unbroken by ornament or opening: *a blank wall.* **4.** lacking some usual or completing feature. **5.** void of interest, results, etc. **6.** showing no attention, interest, or emotion: *a blank face.* **7.** disconcerted; nonplussed: *a blank look.* **8.** complete, utter, or unmitigated: *blank stupidity.* **9.** white or pale. —*n.* **10.** a place where something is lacking: *a blank in one's memory.* **11.** a space in a printed form to be filled in. **12.** a printed form containing such spaces. **13.** a dash put in place of an omitted letter or word, esp. profanity or obscenity. **14.** *Mach.* a piece of metal prepared to be stamped or cut into a finished object, such as a coin or key. **15.** *Archery.* the white mark in the center of a butt or target at which an arrow is aimed. **16.** the object toward which anything is directed; aim; target. —*v.t.* **17.** to make blank or void: *to blank out an entry.* **18.** *Colloq.* to keep (an opponent) from scoring in a game. **19.** *Mach.* to stamp or punch out of flat stock as with a die. [ME, t. OF: m. *blanc* white, t. Gmc.; cf. G *blank* bright, shining] —**blank′ness**, *n.* —**Syn. 1-4.** See **empty.**

blank cartridge, *Ordn.* a cartridge containing powder only, without a bullet.

blank check, 1. a check bearing a signature but no stated amount. **2.** a free hand; carte blanche.

blank endorsement, *Com.* an endorsement on a check or note naming no payee, and payable to bearer.

blan·ket (blăng′kĭt), *n.* **1.** a large rectangular piece of soft, loosely woven fabric, usually wool, used esp. as a bedcovering. **2.** a covering for a horse, etc. **3.** *U.S. and Canada.* the chief garment worn by some Indians. **4.** any thin, extended covering: *a blanket of snow.* —*v.t.* **5.** to cover with or as with a blanket. **6.** to obscure by increasing prominence of the background (often fol. by *out*). **7.** to toss in a blanket, as for punishment. **8.** *Naut.* to take the wind out of the sails of (a vessel) by passing to windward of it. —*adj.* **9.** covering or intended to cover a group or class of things conditions, etc.: *a blanket indictment.* [ME, t. OF: m. *blankete*, dim. of *blanc* white] —**blan′ket·less**, *adj.*

blan·ket·ing (blăng′kĭt ĭng), *n. Radio.* the effect of a signal from a powerful transmitter which interferes with or prevents the reception of other signals.

blank·ly (blăngk′lĭ), *adv.* **1.** without expression or understanding. **2.** totally; fully; in every respect.

blank verse, 1. unrhymed verse. **2.** the unrhymed iambic pentameter verse most frequently used in English dramatic, epic, and reflective poems.

blare (blâr), *v.*, blared, blaring, *n.* —*v.i.* **1.** to emit a loud raucous sound. —*v.t.* **2.** to sound loudly; proclaim noisily. —*n.* **3.** a loud raucous noise. **4.** glaring intensity of color. [ME *blaren*, t. MD]

blar·ney (blär′nĭ), *n.*, *v.*, -neyed, -neying. —*n.* **1.** flattering or wheedling talk; cajolery. —*v.t.*, *v.i.* **2.** to ply or beguile with blarney; use blarney; wheedle. [see **Blarney stone**]

Blarney stone, a stone in Blarney Castle near Cork, Ireland, said to confer skill in flattery to anyone who kisses it.

Blas·co I·bá·ñez (bläs′kō ē bä′nyŏth), **Vicente** (vē thĕn′tĕ), 1867–1928, Spanish novelist.

bla·sé (blä zā′, blä′zā; *Fr.* blȧ zĕ′), *adj.* indifferent to and bored by pleasures or life. [t. F, pp. of *blaser* exhaust, satiate, ? t. D: m. *blasen* blow]

blas·pheme (blăs fēm′), *v.*, -phemed, -pheming. —*v.t.* **1.** to speak impiously or irreverently of (God or sacred things). **2.** to speak evil of; abuse. —*v.i.* **3.** to utter impious words. [t. LL: m. s. *blasphēmāre*, t. Gk.: m. *blasphēmeīn* speak ill; r. ME *blasfeme(n)*, t. OF: m. *blasfemer*] —**blas·phem′er**, *n.* —**Syn. 1.** See **curse.**

blas·phe·mous (blăs′fə məs), *adj.* uttering, containing, or exhibiting blasphemy. —**blas′phe·mous·ly**, *adv.* —**blas′phe·mous·ness**, *n.*

blas·phe·my (blăs′fə mĭ), *n.*, *pl.* -mies. **1.** impious utterance or action concerning God or sacred things. **2.** *Jewish Relig.* **a.** (in Talmudic law) cursing and reviling the "ineffable name" of the Lord. **b.** (in later Hebrew history) the violation of religious law by pronouncing one of the four-letter symbols for God rather than using one of the substitute words. **3.** *Theol.* the crime of assuming to oneself the rights or qualities of God. **4.** irreverent behavior toward anything held sacred. [t. LL: m. s. *blasphēmia*, t. Gk.: slander; r. ME *blasfemie*, t. OF] —**Syn. 1.** profanity, cursing, swearing.

blast (blăst, bläst), *n.* **1.** a sudden blowing or gust of wind. **2.** the blowing of a trumpet, whistle, etc. **3.** the sound produced by this. **4.** a forcible stream of air from the mouth, from bellows, or the like. **5.** *Metall.* air under pressure directed into a blast furnace, cupola, etc. to support combustion. **6.** a jet of exhaust steam directed into a smokestack to augment the draft, as in a locomotive. **7.** a draft thus increased. **8.** *Mining, Civ. Eng.*, etc. the charge of dynamite or other explosive used at one firing in blasting operations. **9.** the act of exploding; explosion. **10.** any pernicious or destructive influence, esp. on animals or plants; a blight. —*v.t.*

11. to blow (a trumpet, etc.). **12.** to cause to shrivel or wither; blight. **13.** to affect with any pernicious influence; ruin; destroy: *to blast one's hope.* **14.** to tear (rock, etc.) to pieces with an explosive. —*v.i.* **15.** to wither; be blighted. [ME; OE *blǣst*] —**blast′er**, *n.* —**Syn. 1.** See **wind**[1].

-blast, *Biol.* a combining form meaning "embryo," "sprout," "germ," as in *ectoblast.* [t. Gk.: s. *blastós*]

blast·ed (blăs′tĭd, bläs′tĭd), *adj.* **1.** withered; shriveled; blighted. **2.** damned (a euphemism).

blas·te·ma (blăs tē′mə), *n.*, *pl.* -mata (-mə tə). *Embryol.* an aggregation of embryonic cells, capable of differentiation into primordia and organs. [t. NL, t. Gk.: sprout] —**blas·tem·ic** (blăs tĕm′ĭk, -tē′mĭk), *adj.*

blast furnace, *Metall.* a vertical, steel, cylindrical furnace using a forced blast to produce molten iron which may be converted into steel or formed into pig iron.

blas·tie (blăs′tĭ, bläs′-), *n. Scot.* a dwarf.

blast·ment (blăst′mənt, bläst′-), *n.* a blasting; a blast or blight.

blasto-, *Biol.* a word element meaning "embryo" or "germ," as in *blastocyst.* Also, before vowels, **blast-.** [t. Gk., comb. form of *blastós*]

blas·to·coele (blăs′tə sēl′), *n. Embryol.* the cavity of a blastula, arising in the course of cleavage. Also, **blas′to·coel′.**

blas·to·cyst (blăs′tə sĭst), *n. Embryol.* **1.** the germinal vesicle. **2.** the vesicular stage in early mammalian development, following cleavage.

blas·to·derm (blăs′tə dûrm′), *n. Embryol.* **1.** the primitive membrane or layer of cells which results from the segmentation of the ovum. **2.** the membrane forming the wall of the blastula, and in most vertebrates enclosing a cavity or a yolk mass. —**blas′to·der′mic**, *adj.*

blas·to·disc (blăs′tə dĭsk). *n. Embryol.* the small disk of protoplasm, containing the egg nucleus, which appears on the surface of the yolk mass in the very heavily yolked eggs, as in birds and reptiles. Also, **blas′to·disk.**

blas·to·gen·e·sis (blăs′tə jĕn′ə sĭs), *n. Biol.* **1.** reproduction by gemmation or budding. **2.** the theory of the transmission of hereditary characters by germ plasm.

blas·to·mere (blăs′tə mĭr′), *n. Embryol.* any cell produced during cleavage. —**blas·to·mer·ic** (blăs′tə mĕr′ĭk), *adj.*

blas·to·pore (blăs′tə pōr′), *n. Embryol.* the orifice of an archenteron. —**blas·to·por·ic** (blăs′tə pôr′ĭk, -pŏr′-) *adj.*

blas·to·sphere (blăs′tə sfĭr′), *n. Embryol.* **1.** a blastula. **2.** a blastocyst (def. 2).

blas·tu·la (blăs′chŏŏ lə), *n.*, *pl.* -lae (-lē′). *Embryol.* an early developmental stage of a metazoan, consisting in typical cases of a hollow sphere formed by a single layer of cells. [t. NL, dim. of Gk. *blastós* sprout, germ] —**blas′tu·lar**, *adj.*

Blastula
After numerous cleavages: A, Exterior view; B, Cross section

blat (blăt), *v.*, blatted, blatting. —*v.i.* **1.** to cry out, as a calf or sheep. —*v.t.* **2.** *Colloq.* to utter loudly and indiscreetly; blurt. [imit. Cf. **bleat**]

bla·tant (blā′tənt), *adj.* **1.** loud-mouthed; offensively noisy; in coarse taste. **2.** obtrusive: *a blatant error.* **3.** bleating: *blatant herds.* [coined by Spenser. Cf. L *blatīre* babble] —**bla′tan·cy**, *n.* —**bla′tant·ly**, *adv.*

blath·er (blăth′ər), *n.* **1.** foolish talk. —*v.i.*, *v.t.* **2.** to talk or utter foolishly. Also, **blether.** [ME, t. Scand.; cf. Icel. *bladhra* talk nonsense]

blath·er·skite (blăth′ər skĭt′), *n.* one given to voluble, empty talk. [f. **blather** + *skite* **skate**[3]]

blau·bok (blou′bŏk′), *n.*, *pl.* -bok, -boks. a bluish South African antelope, *Hippotragus leucophaeus*, extinct since 1800, with backward-curving horns. [t. S Afr. D: m. *blauwbok* blue buck]

Bla·vat·sky (blȧ vät′skĭ), *n.* **Madame**, (*Elena Petrovna Blavatskaya, nee Hahn*) 1831–91, Russian theosophist.

blaw (blô), *v.t.*, *v.i. Scot. and Brit. Dial.* to blow.

blaze[1] (blāz), *n.*, *v.*, blazed, blazing. —*n.* **1.** a bright flame or fire. **2.** a bright, hot gleam or glow: *the blaze of day.* **3.** a sparkling brightness: *a blaze of jewels.* **4.** a sudden, intense outburst, as of fire, passion, fury. **5.** (*pl.*) *Slang.* hell. —*v.i.* **6.** to burn brightly. **7.** to shine like flame. **8.** *Poetic.* to be meritoriously conspicuous. —*v.t.* **9.** to exhibit vividly. [ME and OE *blase* torch, flame] —**Syn. 1.** See **flame.**

blaze[2] (blāz), *n.*, *v.*, blazed, blazing. —*n.* **1.** a spot or mark made on a tree, as by removing a piece of the bark, to indicate a boundary or a path in a forest. **2.** a white spot on the face of a horse, cow, etc. —*v.t.* **3.** to mark with blazes: *to blaze a trail.* [t. LG: m. *blǣse* white mark on head of horse or steer, c. Icel. *blesa*]

blaze[3] (blāz), *v.t.*, blazed, blazing. **1.** to make known; proclaim; publish. **2.** *Obs.* to blow, as from a trumpet. [ME *blase(n)*, t. MD, c. Icel. *blāsa* blow]

blaz·er (blā′zər), *n.* **1.** *Colloq.* anything intensely bright or hot. **2.** a bright-colored jacket worn by tennis players and others. **3.** a dish under which there is a receptacle for coals to keep it hot.

blazing star, 1. a person whose rare qualities attract universal attention. 2. any of certain plants with showy flower clusters, as the liliaceous herb *Aletris farinosa* or the composite perennial *Liatris squarrosa*.

bla·zon (blā'zən), *v.t.* 1. to describe in heraldic terminology. 2. to depict (heraldic arms, etc.) in proper form and color. 3. to set forth conspicuously or publicly; display; proclaim. —*n.* 4. a heraldic shield; armorial bearings. 5. the heraldic description of armorial bearings. 6. pompous display. [ME *blason*, t. OF: shield, later armorial bearings] —**bla'zon·er,** *n.* —**bla'zon·ment,** *n.*

bla·zon·ry (blā'zən rĭ), *n.* 1. brilliant decoration or display. 2. *Her.* **a.** armorial bearings. **b.** a description of heraldic devices.

bldg., building.

-ble, var. of **-able,** as in *noble;* occurring first in words of Latin orig. which came into English through French, later in words taken directly from Latin. Also, after consonant stems, **-ible.** [t. OF, g. L *-bilis,* suffix forming verbal adjectives]

bleach (blēch), *v.t., v.i.* 1. to make or become white, pale, or colorless. —*n.* 2. a bleaching agent. 3. degree of paleness achieved in bleaching. 4. act of bleaching. [ME *blechen,* OE *blǣcean*] —**Syn.** 1. See **whiten.**

bleach·er (blē'chər), *n.* 1. one who or that which bleaches. 2. a vessel used in bleaching. 3. (*usual'y pl.*) an uncovered seat or stand for spectators at games.

bleach·er·y (blē'chə rĭ), *n., pl.* **-eries.** a place or establishment where bleaching is carried on.

bleaching powder, a powder used for bleaching, esp. chloride of lime.

bleak (blēk), *adj.* 1. bare, desolate, and windswept: *a bleak plain.* 2. cold and piercing: *a bleak wind.* 3. dreary: *a bleak prospect.* [ME *bleke* pale, b. *bleche* (OE *blǣc*) and *blake* (OE *blāc*), c. G *bleich*] —**bleak'ly,** *adv.* —**bleak'ness,** *n.*

blear (blĭr), *v.t.* 1. to make (the eyes or sight) dim, as with tears or inflammation. —*adj.* 2. (of the eyes) dim from a watery discharge. 3. *Rare.* dim; indistinct. —*n.* 4. a blur; a bleared state. [ME *blere(n);* orig. uncert.]

blear-eyed (blĭr'īd'), *adj.* 1. having blear eyes. 2. dull of perception.

blear·y (blĭr'ĭ), *adj.,* **blearier, bleariest.** bleared. —**blear'i·ness,** *n.*

bleat (blēt), *v.i.* 1. to cry as a sheep, goat, or calf. —*v.t.* 2. to give forth with a bleat. 3. to babble; prate. —*n.* 4. the cry of a sheep, goat, or calf. 5. any similar sound. [ME *blete(n),* OE *blǣtan*] —**bleat'er,** *n.*

bleb (blĕb), *n. Rare.* 1. a blister or pustule. 2. a bubble. —**bleb'by,** *adj.*

bleed (blēd), *v.,* **bled** (blĕd), **bleeding,** *adj.* —*v.i.* 1. to lose blood, from the body or internally from the vascular system. 2. to be severely wounded or die, as in battle: *bled for the cause.* 3. to cause blood to flow, esp. surgically. 4. (of blood, etc.) to flow out. 5. to exude sap, juice, etc. 6. (of color in dyeing) to run. 7. to feel pity, sorrow, or anguish: *a nation bleeds for its dead heroes.* 8. *Slang.* to pay money as when overcharged or threatened with extortion. 9. *Print.* to run off the edges of a printed page, either by design or through mutilation caused by too close trimming. —*v.t.* 10. to cause to lose blood, esp. surgically. 11. to lose or emit (blood or sap). 12. to drain, draw sap, liquid, etc., from. 13. *Colloq.* to obtain, as in excessive amount, or extort money from. 14. *Print.* **a.** to permit (printed illustrations or ornamentation) to run off the page or sheet. **b.** to trim the margin of (a book or sheet) so closely as to mutilate the text or illustration. —*n.* 15. *Print.* a sheet or page margin trimmed in this way. 16. a part thus trimmed off. —*adj.* 17. characterized by bleeding: *a bleed page.* [ME *blede(n),* OE *blēdan,* der. *blōd* blood]

bleed·er (blē'dər), *n.* a person predisposed to bleeding; hemophiliac.

bleeding heart, any of various plants of the genus *Dicentra,* esp. *D. spectabilis,* a common garden plant with racemes of red heart-shaped flowers.

blem·ish (blĕm'ĭsh), *v.t.* 1. to destroy the perfection of. —*n.* 2. a defect; a disfigurement; stain. [ME *blemissh(en),* t. OF: m. *blemiss-,* s. *ble(s)mir* make livid] —**blem'ish·er,** *n.* —**Syn.** 1. injure, mar, damage, impair, deface. 2. See **defect.**

blench¹ (blĕnch), *v.i.* to shrink; flinch; quail. [ME *blenchen,* g. OE *blencan* deceive] —**blench'er,** *n.*

blench² (blĕnch), *v.i., v.t.* to make or become pale or white; blanch. [var. of BLANCH]

blend (blĕnd), *v.,* **blended** or **blent, blending,** *n.* —*v.t.* 1. to mix smoothly and inseparably together. 2. to mix (various sorts or grades) in order to obtain a particular kind or quality. 3. to prepare by such mixture. —*v.i.* 4. to mix or intermingle smoothly and harmoniously. 5. to have no perceptible separation: *sea and sky seemed to blend.* —*n.* 6. act or manner of blending: *tea of our own blend.* 7. a mixture or kind produced by blending. 8. *Linguistics.* a word made by putting together parts of other words, as *dandle,* a blend of *dance* and *handle.* [ME *blenden,* OE *blendan, blandan,* c. Icel. *blanda*] —**Syn.** 1. mingle, combine, coalesce. See **mix.**

blende (blĕnd), *n.* 1. sphalerite; zinc sulfide. 2. any of certain other sulfides. [t. G, der. *blenden* blind, deceive]

blend·ed (blĕn'dĭd), *adj.* (of a whiskey) consisting of either two or more straight whiskeys, or of whiskey or whiskeys and neutral spirits.

Blen·heim (blĕn'əm), *n.* a village in SW Germany, on the Danube: famous victory of the Duke of Marlborough over the French, 1704. German, **Blindheim.**

Blenheim spaniel, one of a breed of small spaniels with short head and very long ears, kept as pets. [from *Blenheim* Palace, in Oxfordshire, England]

blen·ni·oid (blĕn'ĭ oid'), *adj. Ichthyol.* 1. resembling a blenny. 2. pertaining to the blennies.

blen·ny (blĕn'ĭ), *n., pl.* **-nies.** any of various fishes of the genus *Blennius* and allied genera, with an elongated tapering body and small pelvic fins inserted farther forward than the pectoral fins. [t. L: m. s. *blennius,* t. Gk.: m. *blénnos* blenny, orig. slime]

blent (blĕnt), *v.* pt. and pp. of **blend.**

bleph·a·ri·tis (blĕf'ə rī'tĭs), *n. Pathol.* inflammation of the eyelids. [f. s. Gk. *blépharon* eyelid + -ITIS]

Blé·riot (blē ryō'), *n.* **Louis** (lwē), 1872–1936, French airplane inventor and aviator.

bles·bok (blĕs'bŏk'), *n.* a large South African antelope, *Damaliscus albifrons,* having a blaze on the face. Also, **bles-buck** (blĕs'bŭk'). [t. S Afr. D: blaze buck]

bless (blĕs), *v.t.,* **blessed** or **blest, blessing.** 1. to consecrate by a religious rite; make or pronounce holy. 2. to request of God the bestowal of divine favor on. 3. to bestow good of any kind upon: *a nation blessed with peace.* 4. to extol as holy; glorify. 5. to protect or guard from evil. 6. *Eccles.* to make the sign of the cross over. [ME *blessen,* OE *blētsian, blēdsian* consecrate, orig. with blood, der. *blōd* blood]

bless·ed (blĕs'ĭd, blĕst), *adj.* 1. consecrated; sacred; holy. 2. divinely or supremely favored; fortunate; happy. 3. beatified. 4. bringing happiness; pleasurable. 5. damned (euphemism). 6. (used for emphasis): *every blessed cent.* —**bless'ed·ly,** *adv.* —**bless'ed·ness,** *n.*

Blessed Sacrament. See **sacrament** (def. 3).

Blessed Trinity, trinity (def. 1).

Blessed Virgin, the Virgin Mary.

bless·ing (blĕs'ĭng), *n.* 1. act or words of one who blesses. 2. a special favor, mercy, or benefit. 3. a favor or gift bestowed by God, thereby bringing happiness. 4. the invoking of God's favor upon a person. 5. praise; devotion; worship. 6. a cursing (euphemism).

blest (blĕst), *v.* 1. pt. and pp. of **bless.** —*adj.* 2. blessed.

bleth·er (blĕth'ər), *v.i., v.t., n.* blather.

blew (blōō), *v.* pt. of **blow.**

Bli·da (blē'dä), *n.* a city in N Algeria. 25,871 (1936).

blight (blīt), *n.* 1. a widespread and destructive plant disease, such as chestnut blight, potato late blight, and apple fire blight. 2. any cause of destruction, ruin, or frustration. —*v.t.* 3. to cause to wither or decay; blast. 4. to destroy; ruin; frustrate. —*v.i.* 5. to suffer blight. [orig. unknown]

blimp (blĭmp), *n.* 1. a small, nonrigid airship or dirigible, used chiefly for observation. 2. *Colloq.* any dirigible. [orig. uncert.]

blind (blīnd), *adj.* 1. lacking the sense of sight. 2. unwilling, or unable to try, to understand: *blind to all arguments.* 3. not controlled by reason: *blind tenacity.* 4. not possessing or proceeding from intelligence. 5. lacking all awareness: *a blind stupor.* 6. drunk. 7. hard to see or understand: *blind reasoning.* 8. hidden from view: *a blind corner.* 9. having no outlets. 10. closed at one end: *a blind street.* 11. done without seeing: *blind flying.* 12. made without knowledge in advance: *a blind bargain.* 13. of or pertaining to blind persons. —*v.t.* 14. to make blind, as by injuring, dazzling, or bandaging the eyes. 15. to make obscure or dark. 16. to deprive of discernment or judgment. 17. to outshine; eclipse. —*n.* 18. something that obstructs vision or keeps out light, as a window shade or a blinker for a horse. See illus. under **harness.** 19. a lightly built structure of brush or other growths, esp. one in which hunters conceal themselves while hunting. 20. a cover for masking action or purpose; decoy. 21. the blind, sightless people. [OE, c. G *blind*] —**blind'ing,** *adj.* —**blind'ing·ly,** *adv.* —**blind'ly,** *adv.* —**blind'ness,** *n.* —**Syn.** 1. BLIND, STONE-BLIND, PURBLIND mean lacking in vision. BLIND means unable to see with the physical eyes. STONE-BLIND emphasizes complete blindness. PURBLIND refers to weakened vision, literally or figuratively. 3. irrational, uncritical. 18. See **curtain.** 19. hiding place; ambush.

blind·age (blīn'dĭj), *n. Mil.* a screen or other structure as for protecting men in a trench. [t. F, der. *blinder* to armor, t. G: m. *blinden* blind]

blind alley, 1. a road, street, etc., closed at one end. 2. a position or situation offering no hope of progress or improvement.

blind·er (blīn'dər), *n.* 1. person or thing that blinds. 2. *U.S.* a blinker for a horse.

blind·fish (blīnd'fĭsh'), *n.* any of several small fishes with rudimentary, functionless eyes, found in subterranean streams, as *Amblyopsis spelaeus,* best known from the Mammoth Cave, in Kentucky.

blind·fold (blīnd'fōld'), *v.t.* 1. to prevent sight by covering (the eyes); cover the eyes of. 2. to impair the clear thinking of. —*n.* 3. a bandage over the eyes. —*adj.* 4. with eyes covered: *a blindfold test.* 5. rash; unthinking. [f. BLIND + FOLD¹ wrap up, r. *blindfell,* lit., a blind-fall. Cf. OE *(ge)blindfellian* make blind]

Blind·heim (blĭnt'hīm), *n.* German name of **Blenheim.**

blind·man's buff (blīnd′mănz bŭf′), a game in which a blindfolded player tries to catch and identify one of the others. [see BUFF²]

blind spot, 1. *Anat.* a small area on the retina, insensitive to light, at which the optic nerve leaves the eye. See diag. under **eye. 2.** a matter about which one is ignorant or unintelligent, despite knowledge of related things. **3.** *Radio.* an area in which signals are weak and their reception poor.

blind staggers, *Vet. Sci.* stagger (def. 13).

blind·sto·ry (blīnd′stōr′ĭ), n., pl. **-ries.** *Archit.* a story without windows or windowlike openings. See illus. under **clerestory.**

blind tiger, *Obs. U.S. Slang.* an illegal liquor saloon. Also, **blind pig.**

blind-worm (blīnd′wûrm′), n. a European species of limbless lizard, *Anguis fragilis,* related to the glass snakes, *Ophisaurus.*

blink (blĭngk), v.i. **1.** to wink, esp. rapidly and repeatedly. **2.** to look with winking or half-shut eyes. **3.** to cast a glance; take a peep. **4.** to look evasively or with indifference; ignore (often fol. by *at*). **5.** to shine unsteadily or dimly; twinkle. —v.t. **6.** to cause to blink. **7.** to see dimly. **8.** to shut the eyes to; evade; shirk. —n. **9.** a blinking. **10.** a glance or glimpse. **11.** a gleam; glimmer. **12.** *Meteorol.* iceblink. [ME *blinken,* var. of *blenken* blench. Cf. G *blinken*] —**Syn. 1.** See **wink.**

blink·ard (blĭngk′ərd), n. **1.** one who blinks habitually or who sees imperfectly. **2.** one who lacks intellectual perception.

blink·er (blĭngk′ər), n. **1.** a device for flashing light signals. **2.** either of two flaps on a bridle, to prevent a horse from seeing sidewise or backward; a blinder. **3.** (*pl.*) goggles.

bliss (blĭs), n. **1.** lightness of heart; blitheness; gladness. **2.** supreme happiness or delight. **3.** *Theol.* the joy of heaven. **4.** a cause of great joy or happiness. [ME *blisse,* OE *bliss, blīths,* der. *blīthe* BLITHE] —**Syn. 2.** See **happiness.** —**Ant. 2.** despair.

bliss·ful (blĭs′fəl), adj. full of, abounding in, enjoying, or conferring bliss; supremely joyful. —**bliss′ful·ly,** adv. —**bliss′ful·ness,** n.

blis·ter (blĭs′tər), n. **1.** a thin vesicle on the skin, containing watery matter or serum, as from a burn or other injury. **2.** any similar swelling, as an air bubble in a casting or a paint blister. **3.** *Mil.* a transparent bulge on the fuselage of an airplane, usually for mounting a gun. —v.t. **4.** to raise a blister or blisters on. **5.** to subject to burning shame or disgrace. —v.i. **6.** to rise in blisters; become blistered. [ME *blister, blester,* ? t. OF: m. *blestre* clod, lump (prob. of Gmc. orig.)] —**blis′ter·y,** adj.

blister beetle, any of various beetles of the family *Meloidae,* many of which produce a secretion capable of blistering the skin, as the Spanish fly.

blister gas, *Chem. Warfare.* a poison gas that burns or blisters the tissues of the body.

blister rust, *Bot.* a disease esp. of white pine trees, manifested by cankers and in the spring by blisters, raised by fungi of the genus *Cronartium.*

B. Lit., Bachelor of Literature.

blithe (blīth, blĭth), adj. joyous, merry, or gay in disposition; glad; cheerful. [ME; OE *blīthe* kind, pleasant, joyous] —**blithe′ly,** adv. —**Syn.** mirthful, sprightly, lighthearted, buoyant. —**Ant.** solemn.

blithe·some (blīth′səm, blĭth′-), adj. light-hearted; merry; cheerful: *a blithesome nature.* —**blithe′some·ly,** adv. —**blithe′some·ness,** n.

B. Litt., Bachelor of Letters.

blitz (blĭts), n. **1.** *Mil.* war waged by surprise, swiftly and violently, as by the use of aircraft, tanks, etc. **2.** any swift, vigorous attack or onset. —v.t. **3.** to attack with a blitz. Also, **blitz·krieg** (blĭts′krēg′). [t. G: lightning war]

bliz·zard (blĭz′ərd), n. *Meteorol.* **1.** a violent windstorm with dry, driving snow and intense cold. **2.** a widespread and heavy snowstorm. [var. of d. *blizzer* blaze, flash, blinding flash of lightning; sense widened from lightning to storm. Cf. OE *blysa, blyse* torch, and *blysian* burn. Appar. first used in present sense in Iowa in 1870]

B. LL., Bachelor of Laws.

bloat (blōt), v.t. **1.** to make distended, as with air, water, etc.; cause to swell. **2.** to puff up; make vain or conceited. **3.** to cure (fishes) as bloaters. —v.i. **4.** to become swollen; be puffed out or dilated. —n. **5.** *Vet. Sci.* (in cattle, sheep, and horses) a distention of the rumen or paunch or of the large colon by gases of fermentation, caused by eating ravenously of green forage, esp. legumes. [der. *bloat,* adj., ME *blout* puffy, t. Scand.; cf. Icel. *blautr* soft]

bloat·er (blō′tər), n. **1.** a herring cured by being salted and briefly smoked and dried. **2.** a mackerel similarly cured. **3.** a deep-water cisco, of the whitefish family, *Leucichthys* species, of the Great Lakes.

blob (blŏb), n. **1.** a small globe of liquid; a bubble. **2.** a small lump, drop, splotch, or daub. [? imit.]

bloc (blŏk), n. **1.** *Europ. Pol.* a coalition of factions or parties for a particular measure or purpose. **2.** *U.S. Pol.* a group of legislators, usually of both parties, who vote together for some particular interest: *the Farm bloc in Congress.* [t. F. See BLOCK]

block (blŏk), n. **1.** a solid mass of wood, stone, etc., usually with one or more plane or approximately plane faces. **2.** a blockhead. **3.** a mold or piece on which something is shaped or kept in shape, as a hat block. **4.** a piece of wood prepared for cutting, or as cut, for wood engraving. **5.** *Print.* the base on which a plate is mounted to make it type-high. **6.** a platform on which a person is beheaded. **7.** a platform from which an auctioneer sells. **8.** *Mach.* a device consisting of one or more grooved pulleys mounted in a casing or shell, to which a hook or the like is attached, used for transmitting power, changing the direction of motion, etc.

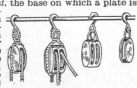

Single and double blocks (def. 8)

9. an obstacle or hindrance. **10.** a blocking or obstructing, or blocked or obstructed state or condition. **11.** *Pathol.* an obstruction, as of a nerve. **12.** *Sports.* a hindering of an opponent's actions. **13.** a quantity, portion, or section taken as a unit or dealt with at one time: *block of tickets.* **14.** *U.S.* a portion of a city, town, etc. enclosed by (usually four) neighboring and intersecting streets. **15.** *U.S.* the length of one side of this. **16.** *Chiefly Brit.* a large building divided into separate houses, shops, etc. **17.** a large number of shares taken together, as on the stock exchange. **18.** one of the short divisions into which a railroad is divided for signaling purposes. **19.** *Philately.* a group of four or more unseparated stamps, not in a strip. —v.t. **20.** to fit with blocks; mount on a block. **21.** to shape or prepare on or with a block. **22.** to sketch or outline roughly or in a general plan, without details (often fol. by *out*). **23.** to obstruct (a space, progress); check (a person) by placing obstacles in the way; stop up. **24.** *Pathol., Physiol.* to stop the passage of impulses in (a nerve, etc.). **25.** *Football.* to bump (an opponent) out of the play. —v.i. **26.** to act so as to obstruct an opponent, as in football, boxing, and baseball. [ME *blok,* appar. t. OF: m. *bloc* block, mass, t. Gmc. (cf. G *block*)] —**block′er,** n.

block·ade (blŏ kād′), n., v., **-aded, -ading.** —n. **1.** *Naval, Mil.* the shutting up of a place, esp. a port, harbor, or part of a coast by hostile ships or troops to prevent entrance or exit. **2.** any obstruction of passage or progress. —v.t. **3.** to subject to a blockade. —**block-ad′er,** n.

block·age (blŏk′ĭj), n. an obstruction.

block and tackle, the pulley blocks and ropes used for hoisting.

block·bust·er (blŏk′bŭs′tər), n. *Colloq.* an aerial bomb containing high explosives and weighing from 4 to 8 tons, used as a large scale demolition bomb.

block·head (blŏk′hĕd′), n. a stupid fellow; a dolt.

block·house (blŏk′hous′), n. **1.** *Mil.* a fortified structure with ports or loopholes for gunfire, used against bombs, artillery, and small arms fire. **2.** (formerly) a building, usually of hewn timber and with a projecting upper story, having loopholes for musketry. **3.** a house built of squared logs.

block·ish (blŏk′ĭsh), adj. like a block; dull; stupid. —**block′ish·ly,** adv. —**block′ish·ness,** n.

Block Island, an island in the Atlantic, S of Rhode Island: a part of that State.

block lava, *Geol.* lava flows composed of rough angular blocks.

block letter, *Print.* a type face or letter designed without serifs.

block line, *Mach.* a rope, wire, chain, etc., running through a series of pulleys.

block plane, a small plane used for cutting across the grain of the wood.

block print, *Fine Arts.* a design printed by means of blocks of wood or metal.

block signal, a fixed railway signal governing the movements of trains entering and using a block.

block system, 1. a series of consecutive railroad blocks. **2.** a method of controlling train movements by means of blocks and block signals.

block·y (blŏk′ĭ), adj., **blockier, blockiest. 1.** heavily built; stocky. **2.** marked by blocks or patches of unequally distributed light and shade, as in a photograph.

Bloem·fon·tein (bloom′fŏn tān′), n. a city in the central part of the Union of South Africa: the capital of the Orange Free State. With suburbs, 82,322 (1946).

Blois (blwä), n. a city in central France, on the Loire river: historic castle. 26,774 (1946).

bloke (blōk), n. *Chiefly Brit. Slang.* man; fellow; guy.

blond (blŏnd), adj. **1.** (of hair, skin, etc.) light-colored. **2.** (of a person) having light-colored hair and skin. —n. **3.** a blond person. **4.** lace or net of silk, orig. unbleached, manufactured in France, now, esp., black silk lace. [t. F, t. ML: s. *blondus* yellow. Cf. OE *blondenfeax* grayhaired] —**blonde,** adj., n. fem. —**blond′ness,** n.

blood (blŭd), n. **1.** the fluid that circulates in the arteries and veins or principal vascular system of animals, in man being of a red color and consisting of a pale-yellow plasma containing semisolid corpuscles. **2.** body fluids spilling or spilled out; gore. **3.** the vital principle; life. **4.** bloodshed; slaughter; murder. **5.** the juice or sap of plants. **6.** temper or state of mind: *a person of hot blood.* **7.** man's fleshly nature: *the frailty of men's blood.* **8.** *Chiefly Brit.* a man of fire or spirit. **9.** a rake. **10.** physical and cultural extraction. **11.** royal extraction. **12.** descent from a common ancestor: *related by blood.* **13.** *Stock Breeding.* recorded and respected ancestry; purebred breeding. **14. in cold blood,** calmly, coolly, and deliberately. —*v.t.* **15.** *Hunting.* to give (hounds, etc.) a first taste or sight of blood. **16.** *Obs.* to stain with blood. [ME; OE *blōd,* c. G *blut*] —**blood'-like',** *adj.*

blood bank, 1. a place where blood plasma is stored. **2.** such a supply of blood.

blood count, the count of the number of red or white blood cells in a specific volume of blood.

blood·cur·dling (blŭd'kûr'dlYng), *adj.* frightening; terrifyingly horrible.

blood·ed (blŭd'Yd), *adj.* **1.** having blood: *warm-blooded animals.* **2.** (of horses, etc.) derived from ancestors of good blood; having a good pedigree. **3.** having been through battle: *blooded troops.*

blood group, blood type.

blood·guilt·y (blŭd'gYl'tY), *adj.* guilty of murder or bloodshed. —**blood'guilt'i·ness,** *n.*

blood heat, the normal temperature (about 98.6°F.) of human blood.

blood·hound (blŭd'hound'), *n.* one of a breed of large, powerful dogs with a very acute sense of smell, used for tracking game, human fugitives, etc.

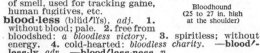

Bloodhound
(25 to 27 in. high
at the shoulder)

blood·less (blŭd'lYs), *adj.* **1.** without blood; pale. **2.** free from bloodshed: *a bloodless victory.* **3.** spiritless; without energy. **4.** cold-hearted: *bloodless charity.* —**blood'-less·ly,** *adv.* —**blood'less·ness,** *n.*

blood·let·ting (blŭd'lĕt'Yng), *n.* act of letting blood by opening a vein.

blood·mo·bile (blŭd'mə bēl'), *n.* a small truck with medical equipment for receiving blood donations.

blood money, 1. a fee paid to a hired murderer. **2.** compensation paid to the survivors of a slain man.

blood plasma, the liquid part of human blood, often stored in hospitals, etc., for transfusions.

blood poisoning, *Pathol.* a morbid condition of the blood due to the presence of toxic matter or microörganisms; toxemia; septicemia; pyemia.

blood pressure, *Physiol.* the pressure of the blood against the inner walls of the blood vessels, varying in different parts of the body, during different phases of contraction of the heart, and under different conditions of health, exertion, etc.

blood-red (blŭd'rĕd'), *adj.* **1.** of the deep red color of blood. **2.** red with blood.

blood relation, one related by birth. Also, **blood relative.**

blood·root (blŭd'rōōt', -rŏŏt'), *n.* **1.** a North American papaveraceous plant, *Sanguinaria canadensis,* with red root and root sap. **2.** an Old World rosaceous plant, *Potentilla tormentilla,* with a reddish root.

blood serum, serum (def. 1).

blood·shed (blŭd'shĕd'), *n.* destruction of life; slaughter. Also, **blood'shed'ding.**

blood·shot (blŭd'shŏt'), *adj.* (of the eyes) red from dilated blood vessels. [var. of *blood-shotten,* f. BLOOD + *shot*(ten), pp. of SHOOT]

blood·stain (blŭd'stān'), *n.* a spot or trace of blood.

blood·stained (blŭd'stānd'), *adj.* **1.** stained with blood. **2.** guilty of bloodshed.

blood·stone (blŭd'stōn'), *n.* *Jewelry.* a greenish variety of chalcedony with small bloodlike spots of red jasper scattered through it; heliotrope.

blood stream, the blood flowing through a circulatory system.

blood·suck·er (blŭd'sŭk'ər), *n.* **1.** any animal that sucks blood, esp. a leech. **2.** an extortioner. **3.** sponger (def. 2).

blood test, a test of a sample of blood to determine blood type, presence of infection, parentage, etc.

blood·thirst·y (blŭd'thûrs'tY), *adj.* eager to shed blood; murderous. —**blood'thirst'i·ly,** *adv.* —**blood'-thirst'i·ness,** *n.*

blood transfusion, the injection of blood from one person or animal into the blood stream of another.

blood type, one of several classifications into which the blood may be grouped with reference to its agglutinogens. Also, **blood group.**

blood vessel, any of the vessels (arteries, veins, capillaries) through which the blood circulates.

blood·wort (blŭd'wûrt'), *n.* **1.** any of the plants, with red roots, constituting the family *Haemodoraceae,* esp. the red root, *Gyrotheca tinctoria,* of North America. **2.** any of various other plants with red roots, leaves, etc., as the dock or the rattlesnake weed. **3.** bloodroot.

blood·y (blŭd'Y), *adj.,* **blood·i·er, blood·i·est,** *v.,* **blood·ied, blood·y·ing,** *adv.* —*adj.* **1.** stained with blood. **2.** attended with bloodshed: *a bloody battle.* **3.** inclined to bloodshed. **4.** of, of the nature of, or pertaining to blood; containing or composed of blood. **5.** *Brit. Slang.* damned. —*v.t.* **6.** to stain with blood. —*adv.* **7.** *Brit.*

Slang. very. [ME *blody,* OE *blōdig*] —**blood'i·ly,** *adv.* —**blood'i·ness,** *n.* —**Syn. 3.** bloodthirsty, murderous.

bloom[1] (blōōm), *n.* **1.** the flower of a plant. **2.** flowers collectively. **3.** state of having the buds opened. **4.** a flourishing, healthy condition: *the bloom of youth.* **5.** a glow or flush on the cheek indicative of youth and health. **6.** *Bot.* a whitish powdery deposit or coating, as on the surface of certain fruits and leaves. **7.** any similar surface coating or appearance. **8.** any of certain minerals occurring as a pulverulent incrustation. —*v.i.* **9.** to produce or yield blossoms. **10.** to flourish. **11.** to be in a state of healthful beauty and vigor. **12.** to glow with a warm color. —*v.t.* **13.** to cause to yield blossoms. **14.** to cause to flourish. **15.** to invest with luster or beauty. **16.** to cause a cloudy area on (something shiny). [ME *blom*(e), t. Scand.; cf. Icel. *blōm* flower, *blōmi* prosperity] —**bloom'less,** *adj.* —**Syn. 4.** freshness, glow, flush.

bloom[2] (blōōm), *n.* a semifinished steel ingot rolled to reduced size. [OE *blōma* lump of metal]

bloom·er (blōō'mər), *n.* **1.** (*pl.*) loose trousers gathered at the knee, worn by women as part of gymnasium, riding, or other like dress. **2.** (*pl.*) a woman's undergarment so designed. **3.** a costume for women, advocated about 1850 by Mrs. Amelia Bloomer of New York, consisting of a short skirt and loose trousers buttoned around the ankle. [named after Mrs. *Bloomer.* See def. 3]

Bloom·field (blōōm'fēld'), *n.* a city in NE New Jersey. 49,307 (1950).

bloom·ing (blōō'mYng), *adj.* **1.** in bloom; blossoming; in flower. **2.** glowing as with youthful freshness and vigor. **3.** flourishing; prospering. —**bloom'ing·ly,** *adv.*

Bloom·ing·ton (blōō'mYng tən), *n.* **1.** a city in central Illinois. 34,163 (1950). **2.** a city in S Indiana. 28,163 (1950).

bloom·y (blōō'mY), *adj.* **1.** covered with blossoms; in full flower. **2.** having a bloom (def. 6), as fruit.

blos·som (blŏs'əm), *n. Bot.* **1.** the flower of a plant, esp. of one producing an edible fruit. **2.** the state of flowering: *the apple tree is in blossom.* —*v.i.* **3.** *Bot.* to produce or yield blossoms. **4.** to flourish; develop (often fol. by *out*). [ME *blosme, blossem,* OE *blōs*(t)m(a) flower] —**blos'som·less,** *adj.* —**blos'som·y,** *adj.*

blot[1] (blŏt), *n., v.,* **blot·ted, blot·ting.** —*n.* **1.** a spot or stain, esp. of ink on paper. **2.** a blemish or reproach on character or reputation. **3.** an erasure or obliteration, as in a writing. —*v.t.* **4.** to spot, stain, or bespatter. **5.** to darken; make dim; obscure or eclipse. **6.** to make indistinguishable (fol. by *out*): *blot out a memory.* **7.** to dry with absorbent paper or the like. **8.** to destroy; wipe out completely (fol. by *out*). **9.** to paint coarsely; daub. —*v.i.* **10.** (of ink, etc.) to spread in a stain. **11.** to become blotted or stained: *this paper blots easily.* [ME; orig. uncert.] —**blot'less,** *adj.* —**Syn. 1.** blotch, splotch. **8.** obliterate, erase, efface.

blot[2] (blŏt), *n.* **1.** *Backgammon.* an exposed piece liable to be taken or forfeited. **2.** an exposed or weak point, as in an argument or course of action. [cf. Dan. *blot* bare]

blotch (blŏch), *n.* **1.** a large irregular spot or blot. —*v.t.* **2.** to mark with blotches; blot, spot, or blur. [b. BLOT[1] and BOTCH[2]] —**blotch'y,** *adj.*

blot·ter (blŏt'ər), *n.* **1.** a piece of blotting paper used to absorb excess ink, to protect a desk, etc. **2.** a book in which transactions or occurrences, as sales, arrests, etc., are recorded as they take place.

blotting paper, a soft, absorbent, unsized paper.

blouse (blous, blouz), *n.* **1.** a loosely fitting waist worn by women or children, sometimes worn outside the skirt and belted. **2.** a single-breasted, semifitting jacket worn with the service uniform of the U. S. Army. **3.** a loose upper garment, reaching about to the knees, worn esp. by peasants in France, Russia, etc. [t. F, ? t. Pr.: m. (*lano*) *blouso* short (wool)] —**blouse'like',** *adj.*

blow[1] (blō), *n.* **1.** a sudden stroke with hand, fist, or weapon. **2.** a sudden shock, or a calamity or reverse. **3.** a sudden attack or drastic action. **4. at one blow,** with a single act. **5. come to blows,** to start to fight. [northern ME *blaw*; orig. uncert.] —**Syn. 1.** buffet, thump, thwack, rap, slap, cuff, box. BLOW, STROKE both refer to a sudden and forceful impact, but differ both literally and figuratively, in that the first emphasizes the violence of the impact: *a blow from a hammer, a blow to one's hopes.* STROKE indicates precision and finality, often together with the idea of unexpectedness: *the stroke of a piston, a forehand stroke, a stroke of lightning.*

blow[2] (blō), *v.,* **blew, blown, blowing,** *n.* —*v.i.* **1.** (of the wind or air) to be in motion. **2.** to move along, carried by or as by the wind: *the dust was blowing.* **3.** to produce or emit a current of air, as with the mouth, a bellows, etc.: *blow on your hands.* **4.** *Music.* (of horn, trumpet, etc.) to give out sound. **5.** to make a blowing sound; whistle. **6.** to breathe hard or quickly; pant. **7.** *Colloq.* to boast; brag. **8.** *Zool.* (of a whale) to spout. **9.** (of a fuse, light bulb, vacuum tube, tire, etc.) to go bad; become unusable (often fol. by *out*). **10. blow over, a.** to cease; subside. **b.** to be forgotten. **11. blow up, a.** to come into being: *a storm blew up.* **b.** to explode: *the ship blew up.* **c.** *Colloq.* to lose one's temper. **d.** *Colloq.* to scold; abuse. —*v.t.* **12.** to drive by means of a current of air. **13.** to spread by report. **14.** to drive a current of air upon. **15.** to clear or empty by forcing air through. **16.** to shape (glass, etc.) with a current of air. **17.** to cause to sound, esp. by a current of air. **18.** to cause to explode (fol. by *up, to bits,* etc.). **19.** *Photog.* to reproduce by enlargement (fol. by *up*). **20.** to expel

---

noisily (fol. by *off*). **21.** to put (a horse) out of breath by fatigue. **22.** (pp. **blowed**) *Slang.* to damn (a euphemism). **23.** *U.S. Slang.* to spend money on. **24.** *U.S. Slang.* to squander; spend quickly. —*n.* **25.** a blast of air or wind. **26.** act of producing a blast of air, as in playing a wind instrument. **27.** *Colloq.* boasting or brag. **28.** *Metall.* **a.** the blast of air used in making steel in a converter. **b.** the time during which, or that part of a process in which, it is used. [ME *blowe(n)*, OE *blāwan*]
blow³ (blō), *v.,* **blew, blown, blowing,** *n.* —*v.i., v.t.* **1.** to blossom; bloom; flower. —*n.* **2.** a yield or display of blossoms. **3.** state of blossoming. [ME *blowen,* OE *blōwan*]
blow·er (blō'ər), *n.* **1.** a person or thing that blows. **2.** a machine for forcing air through a furnace, building, mine, etc. **3.** *Colloq.* a boaster.
blow·fish (blō'fĭsh'), *n.* puffer (def. 2).
blow·fly (blō'flī'), *n., pl.* **-flies.** any of various true flies, *Diptera,* which deposit their eggs or larvae on carcasses or meat, or in sores, wounds, etc.
blow·gun (blō'gŭn'), *n.* a pipe or tube through which missiles are blown by the breath.
blow·hole (blō'hōl'), *n.* **1.** an air or gas vent. **2.** either of two nostrils or spiracles, or a single one, at the top of the head in whales and other cetaceans, through which they breathe. **3.** a hole in the ice to which whales or seals come to breathe. **4.** *Metall.* a defect in a casting caused by trapped steam or gas.
blow·ing (blō'ĭng), *n.* **1.** the sound of any vapor or gas issuing from a vent under pressure. **2.** *Metall.* a disturbance caused by gas or steam blowing through molten metal.
blown¹ (blōn), *adj.* **1.** inflated; distended. **2.** out of breath; fatigued; exhausted. **3.** flyblown. **4.** formed by blowing: *blown glass.* [see BLOW²]
blown² (blōn), *adj. Hort.* fully expanded or opened, as a flower. [see BLOW³]
blow·off (blō'ôf', -ŏf'), *n.* **1.** a current of escaping surplus steam, water, etc. **2.** a device which permits and channels such a current. **3.** *Slang.* one who brags.
blow·out (blō'out'), *n.* **1.** a rupture of an automobile tire. **2.** a sudden or violent escape of air, steam, or the like. **3.** *Colloq.* a big entertainment or spree.
blow·pipe (blō'pīp'), *n.* **1.** a tube through which a stream of air or gas is forced into a flame to concentrate and increase its heating action. **2.** *Glass Blowing.* a long iron pipe used to gather and blow the viscous glass into hollow ware. **3.** blowgun. **4.** *Med.* an instrument used to observe or clean a cavity.
blow·torch (blō'tôrch'), *n.* a small portable apparatus which gives an extremely hot gasoline flame intensified by a blast, used in plumbing, etc.
blow·tube (blō'tūb', -tōōb'), *n.* **1.** blowgun. **2.** blowpipe (def. 2).
blow·up (blō'ŭp'), *n.* **1.** an explosion or other drastic trouble. **2.** a violent outburst of temper or scolding. **3.** *Photog.* an enlargement.
blow·y (blō'ĭ), *adj.* windy.
blowz·y (blou'zĭ), *adj.,* **blowzier, blowziest. 1.** disheveled; unkempt: *blowzy hair.* **2.** red-faced. Also, **blowzed** (blouzd). [der. *blowse* wench; ult. orig. unknown]
B.L.S., Bachelor of Library Science.
blub·ber (blŭb'ər), *n.* **1.** *Zool.* the fat found between the skin and muscle of whales and other cetaceans, from which oil is made. **2.** act of blubbering. —*v.i.* **3.** to weep, usually noisily and with contorted face. —*v.t.* **4.** to say while weeping. **5.** to disfigure with weeping. —*adj.* **6.** disfigured with blubbering. [ME *bluber,* n., *blubren,* v.; appar. imit.] —**blub'ber·er,** *n.* —**blub'ber·ing·ly,** *adv.*
blub·ber·y (blŭb'ər ĭ), *adj.* **1.** abounding in or resembling blubber. **2.** (of a cetacean) fat. **3.** blubbered; disfigured; swollen.
blu·cher (blōō'kər, -chər), *n.* **1.** a kind of strong leather half boot. **2.** a shoe with the vamp continued up beneath the top, which laps over it from the sides. [named after Field Marshal von *Blücher*]
Blü·cher (blōō'kər, -chər; *Ger.* blY'Khər), *n.* Gebhart Leberecht von (gĕp'härt lā'bə rĕKHt' fən), 1742–1819, Prussian field marshal.
bludg·eon (blŭj'ən), *n.* **1.** a short, heavy club with one end loaded, or thicker and heavier than the other. —*v.t.* **2.** to strike or fell with a bludgeon. **3.** to force (someone) into something; bully. [orig. unknown] —**bludg'eon·er, bludg'eon·eer** (blŭj'ə nĭr'), *n.*
blue (blōō), *n., adj., bluer, bluest, v., blued, bluing** or **blueing.** —*n.* **1.** the pure hue of clear sky; deep azure (between green and violet in the spectrum). **2.** the **blue,** *Poetic.* **a.** the sky. **b.** the sea. **3.** bluing. **4.** a blue thing. **5.** a person who wears blue, or is a member of a group characterized by some blue symbol. **6.** bluestocking. **7.** (*pl.*) See **blues. 8. out of the blue,** unexpectedly; from an unforeseen or unknown source. —*adj.* **9.** (of the skin) discolored by cold, contusion, or fear, or vascular collapse. **10.** depressed in spirits. **11.** dismal or unpromising: *a blue outlook.* **12.** characterized by or stemming from rigid morals or religion: *blue laws.* **13.** marked by blasphemy: *the air was blue with oaths.* **14. once in a blue moon,** rarely and exceptionally. —*v.t.* **15.** to make blue; dye a blue color. **16.** to tinge with bluing. [ME *blew,* t. OF: m. *bleu,* t. Gmc. (cf. G *blau*)] —**blue'ly,** *adv.* —**blue'ness,** *n.* —Syn. **10.** despondent, dejected, downhearted.

blue baby, an infant with congenital cyanosis.
Blue·beard (blōō'bĭrd'), *n.* **1.** (in folklore) a nickname of the Chevalier Raoul, whose seventh wife found in a forbidden room the bodies of the other six. **2.** any person alleged to have murdered a number of his wives or other women.
blue·bell (blōō'bĕl'), *n.* **1.** any of various plants with blue bell-shaped flowers, as the harebell (**bluebell of Scotland**), or a liliaceous plant, *Scilla nonscripta,* of the Old World. **2.** (*usually pl.*) the lungwort, *Mertensia virginica,* of the U.S.
blue·ber·ry (blōō'bĕr'ĭ), *n., pl.* **-ries. 1.** the edible berry, usually bluish, of any of various shrubs of the ericaceous genus *Vaccinium.* **2.** any of these shrubs.
blue·bill (blōō'bĭl'), *n.* scaup duck.
blue·bird (blōō'bûrd'), *n.* **1.** any bird of the genus *Sialia,* comprising small North American passerine songbirds whose prevailing color is blue; esp. the well-known eastern bluebird, *S. sialis,* which appears early in the spring. **2.** any of various other birds of which the predominant color is blue.
blue blood, 1. the alleged hereditary exclusiveness or trait of aristocratic families. **2.** *Colloq.* an aristocrat. —**blue'-blood'ed,** *adj.*
blue·bon·net (blōō'bŏn'ĭt), *n.* **1.** the cornflower, *Centaurea Cyanus.* **2.** *Bot.* a blue-flowering lupine, esp. one, *Lupinus subcarnosus,* adopted as the State flower of Texas. **3.** a broad, flat bonnet of blue wool, formerly much worn in Scotland. **4.** a Scottish soldier who wore such a bonnet. **5.** any Scot. Also, **blue bonnet, blue cap** (blōō'kăp').
blue book, 1. *U.S. Colloq.* a directory of socially prominent persons. **2.** *U.S.* a blank book used in taking college examinations, usually with a blue cover. **3.** a British parliamentary or other official publication, bound in a blue cover. Also, **blue'book'.**
blue·bot·tle (blōō'bŏt'əl), *n.* **1.** the cornflower (def. 1). **2.** any of various other plants with blue flowers, esp. of the genera *Campanula* and *Scilla.* **3.** bluebottle fly.
bluebottle fly, any of several large, metallic blue-and-green flies of the dipterous family *Calliphoridae.* The larvae of some are parasites of domestic animals.
blue cheese, an American type of Roquefort cheese.
blue·coat (blōō'kōt'), *n.* **1.** a person who wears a blue coat or uniform. **2.** a policeman. **3.** a soldier in the U.S. Army in earlier times. —**blue'-coat'ed,** *adj.*
blue-curls (blōō'kûrlz'), *n.* **1.** any plant of the labiate genus *Trichostema,* comprising herbs with blue to pink or (rarely) white flowers and long, curved filaments. **2.** the selfheal (def. 1). Also, **blue curls.**
blue devils, 1. low spirits. **2.** delirium tremens.
blue-eyed grass (blōō'īd'), any of numerous plants of the iridaceous genus *Sisyrinchium,* having grasslike leaves and small, usually blue, flowers.
Blue·fields (blōō'fēldz'), *n.* a seaport in E Nicaragua. 10,099 (est. 1941).
blue·fish (blōō'fĭsh'), *n., pl.* **-fishes,** (*esp. collectively*) **-fish. 1.** a predaceous marine food fish, *Pomatomus saltatrix,* bluish or greenish in color, of the Atlantic coast of the Americas. **2.** any of many diverse kinds of fishes, usually of a bluish color.
blue flag, any North American plant of the genus *Iris,* esp. *I. versicolor* (**larger blue flag**), and *I. prismatica* (**slender blue flag**), the former being the State flower of Tennessee.
blue fox, 1. a variety of the small Arctic fox, *Alopex lagopus,* having a year-round bluish pelt. **2.** any fox of this species while having a bluish fur in the summer season. **3.** the blue fur. **4.** any white fox fur dyed blue.
blue·gill (blōō'gĭl'), *n.* a fresh-water sunfish, *Lepomis macrochirus,* of the Mississippi valley, much used for food and important among the smaller game fishes.
blue grama. See **grama grass.**
blue·grass (blōō'grăs', -gräs'), *n.* **1.** any of the grasses in the genus *Poa,* as the Kentucky bluegrass, *P. pratensis,* etc. **2. the Bluegrass,** the Bluegrass Region.
Bluegrass Region, a region in central Kentucky, famous for its luxuriant crops of bluegrass.
blue-green (blōō'grēn'), *n.* a color about midway between blue and green in the spectrum.
blue-green algae, *Bot.* unicellular or filamentous, asexual algae belonging to the class *Myxophyceae* (*Cyanophyceae*), usually bluish-green as the result of blue pigments added to their chlorophyll.
blue grouse, a local name for any grouse of the North American genus *Dendragapus,* as the dusky grouse (*D. obscurus*) of the Rocky Mountain region.
blue gum, eucalyptus.
blue-hearts (blōō'härts'), *n.* a perennial North American scrophulariaceous herb, *Buchnera americana,* with deep-purple flowers.
blue·ing (blōō'ĭng), *n.* bluing.
blue·ish (blōō'ĭsh), *adj.* bluish.
blue·jack (blōō'jăk'), *n.* a small oak, *Quercus cinerea* (or *brevifolia*), of the southern U.S.
blue·jack·et (blōō'jăk'ĭt), *n.* a sailor.
blue·jay (blōō'jā'), *n.* a well-known crested jay, *Cyanocitta cristata,* of the Eastern U.S. and Canada.
blue laws, *U.S.* severe or puritanical laws (from an alleged code said to have been adopted in the colonies of Connecticut and New Haven).

ăct, āble, dâre, ärt; ĕbb, ēqual; ĭf, īce; hŏt, ōver, ôrder, oil, bŏŏk, ōōze, out; ŭp, ūse, ûrge; ə = a in alone; ch, chief; g, give; ng, ring; sh, shoe; th, thin; ŧh, that; zh, vision. See the full key on inside cover.

blue mass, *Pharm.* a preparation of metallic mercury with other ingredients, used for making blue pills.

Blue Mountains, a low range of mountains in NE Oregon and SE Washington.

Blue Nile. See Nile, Blue.

blue-pen·cil (blōō/pĕn/səl), *v.t.,* **-ciled, -ciling** or (*esp. Brit.*) **-cilled, -cilling.** to alter, abridge, or cancel with, or as with, a pencil that makes a blue mark, as in editing a manuscript.

blue peter, *Naut.* a blue flag with a white square in the center, hoisted as a signal for immediate sailing, to recall boats, etc. [f. BLUE + *peter,* orig. REPEATER]

blue pill, *Pharm.* a pill of blue mass, used as an alterative, cathartic, etc.

blue-point (blōō/point/), *n.* a small oyster suitable for serving raw.

Blue peter

blue-print (blōō/prĭnt/), *n.* **1.** a process of photographic printing, based on ferric salts, in which the prints are white on a blue ground: used chiefly in making copies of tracings. **2.** a detailed outline or plan. —*v.t.* **3.** to make a blueprint of.

blue racer, a variety of black snake, occurring in central U.S.

blue ribbon, 1. first prize; highest award. **2.** a badge indicating a pledge of abstinence from alcohol. **3.** a blue ribbon worn as a badge of honor, esp. by members of the Order of the British knighthood.

Blue Ridge, a mountain range extending from N Virginia SW to N Georgia: a part of the Appalachians.

blues (blōōz), *n. pl.* **1.** despondency; melancholy. **2.** *Jazz.* a type of song, of American Negro origin, predominantly melancholy in character and usually performed in slow tempo. [short for BLUE DEVILS]

blue-sky law (blōō/skī/), a law designed to prevent the sale of fraudulent securities.

blue-stock·ing (blōō/stŏk/ĭng), *n.* **1.** a woman who affects literary or intellectual tastes. **2.** a member of a mid-eighteenth century London literary circle. [so called because members of this group (def. 2) did not wear formal dress] —**blue/stock/ing·ism,** *n.*

blue·stone (blōō/stōn/), *n.* a bluish argillaceous sandstone used for building purposes, flagging, etc.

blue streak, *Colloq.* something moving very fast.

blu·et (blōō/ĭt), *n.* **1.** any of various plants with blue flowers, as the cornflower. **2.** (*often pl.*) any of various species of *Houstonia,* esp. *Houstonia caerulea.* [ME *blewet,* t. F: m. *bluet,* dim. of *bleu* blue]

blue vitriol, sulfate of copper, $CuSO_4 \cdot 5H_2O$, a compound occurring in large, transparent, deep-blue triclinic crystals, used in calico printing, medicine, etc.

blue·weed (blōō/wēd/), *n.* a bristly, boraginaceous weed, *Echium vulgare,* with showy blue flowers, a native of Europe naturalized in the U.S.

blue-winged teal (blōō/wĭngd/), a small pond and river duck, *Anas discors,* of North America, with grayish-blue patches on the wings.

blue·wood (blōō/wŏŏd/), *n.* a rhamnaceous shrub or small tree, *Condalia obovata,* of western Texas and northern Mexico, often forming dense chaparral.

bluff¹ (blŭf), *adj.* **1.** somewhat abrupt and unconventional in manner; hearty; frank. **2.** presenting a bold and nearly perpendicular front, as a coastline. **3.** *Naut.* (of a ship) presenting a broad, flattened front. —*n.* **4.** a cliff, headland, or hill with a broad, steep face. [prob. t. LG: m. *blaf* flat] —**bluff/ly,** *adv.* —**bluff/ness,** *n.* —**Syn. 1.** See blunt. **2.** steep, precipitous.

bluff² (blŭf), *v.t.* **1.** to mislead by presenting a bold front. **2.** to gain by bluffing: *he bluffed his way.* **3.** *Poker.* to deceive by a show of confidence in the strength of one's cards. —*v.i.* **4.** to mislead someone by presenting a bold front. —*n.* **5.** act of bluffing. **6.** one who bluffs; a bluffer. [orig. uncert.] —**bluff/er,** *n.*

blu·ing (blōō/ĭng), *n.* a substance, as indigo, used to whiten clothes, or give them a slight bluish tinge. Also, **blueing.**

blu·ish (blōō/ĭsh), *adj.* somewhat blue. Also, **blueish.** —**blu/ish·ness,** *n.*

Blum (blōōm), *n.* Léon (lĕ ôN/), 1872–1950, French statesman.

blun·der (blŭn/dər), *n.* **1.** a gross or stupid mistake. —*v.i.* **2.** to move or act blindly, stupidly, or without direction or steady guidance. **3.** to make a gross or stupid mistake, esp. through mental confusion. —*v.t.* **4.** to bungle; botch. **5.** to utter thoughtlessly; blurt out. [ME *blondren;* orig. uncert.] —**blun/der·er,** *n.* —**blun/der·ing·ly,** *adv.* —**Syn.** 1. error. See mistake.

blun·der·buss (blŭn/dər bŭs/), *n.* **1.** a short musket of wide bore with expanded muzzle to scatter shot, bullets, or slugs at close range. **2.** a stupid, blundering person. [alter. of D *donderbus,* f. *donder* thunder + *buss* gun, orig. box]

blunge (blŭnj), *v.t.,* **blunged, blunging.** to mix (clay or the like) with water, forming a liquid suspension. [b. BLEND and PLUNGE]

Blunderbuss

blung·er (blŭn/jər), *n.* a large vessel containing rotating arms for mechanical mixing.

blunt (blŭnt), *adj.* **1.** having an obtuse, thick, or dull edge or point; rounded; not sharp. **2.** abrupt in address or manner. **3.** slow in perception or understanding; dull. —*v.t.* **4.** to make blunt. **5.** to weaken or impair the force, keenness, or susceptibility of. [ME; orig. unknown] —**blunt/ly,** *adv.* —**blunt/ness,** *n.* —**Syn. 1.** See dull. **2.** BLUNT, BLUFF, BRUSQUE, CURT characterize manners and speech. BLUNT suggests lack of polish and of regard for the feelings of others: *blunt and tact ess.* BLUFF implies an unintentional roughness together with so much good-natured heartiness that others rarely take offense: *a bluff sea captain.* BRUSQUE connotes sharpness and abruptness of speech or manner: *a brusque denial.* CURT applies esp. to disconcertingly concise language: *a curt reply.*

blur (blûr), *v.,* **blurred, blurring,** *n.* —*v.t.* **1.** to obscure or sully as by smearing with ink, etc.; stain. **2.** to obscure by making confused in form or outline; make indistinct. **3.** to dim the perception or susceptibility of; make dull or insensible. —*v.i.* **4.** to become indistinct: *the vision blurred.* **5.** to make blurs. —*n.* **6.** a smudge or smear which obscures. **7.** a blurred condition; indistinctness. [? akin to BLEAR] —**blur/ry,** *adj.*

blurb (blûrb), *n.* an announcement or advertisement, esp. an effusively laudatory one. [a word coined by Gelett BURGESS]

blurt (blûrt), *v.t.* **1.** to utter suddenly or inadvertently; divulge unadvisedly (usually fol. by *out*). —*n.* **2.** an abrupt utterance. [appar. imit.]

blush (blŭsh), *v.i.* **1.** to redden as from embarrassment or shame. **2.** to feel shame (*at, for,* etc.). **3.** (of the sky, flowers, etc.) to become rosy. —*v.t.* **4.** to make red; flush. **5.** to make known by a blush. —*n.* **6.** a reddening, as of the face. **7.** rosy or pinkish tinge. [ME *blusche(n),* OE *blyscan* redden] —**blush/er,** *n.,* —**blush/ful,** *adj.* —**blush/ing·ly,** *adv.*

blus·ter (blŭs/tər), *v.i.* **1.** to roar and be tumultuous, as wind. **2.** to be loud, noisy, or swaggering; utter loud empty menaces or protests. —*v.t.* **3.** to force or accomplish by blustering. —*n.* **4.** boisterous noise and violence. **5.** noisy, empty menaces or protests; inflated talk. [cf. Icel. *blāstr* blowing] —**blus/ter·er,** *n.* —**blus/ter·ing·ly,** *adv.* —**blus/ter·y, blus/ter·ous,** *adj.*

blvd., boulevard.

B.M., 1. Bachelor of Medicine. **2.** British Museum.

B.M.E., 1. Bachelor of Mechanical Engineering. **2.** Bachelor of Mining Engineering.

B. Met., Bachelor of Metallurgy.

B. Mus., Bachelor of Music.

bn., battalion.

B'nai B'rith (bə nā/ bə rēth/, brĭth/), a fraternal organization of Jewish men. [t. Heb.: m. *bĕnē bĕrīth* sons of the covenant]

bo·a (bō/ə), *n., pl.* **boas. 1.** any of various nonvenomous snakes of the family *Boidae,* notable for their vestiges of hind limbs, as the **boa constrictor** of the American tropics. **2.** a long, snake-shaped wrap of silk, feather, or other material, worn about the neck by women. [t. L]

Bo·ab·dil (bō/äb dĭl; *Sp.* bô/äb dēl/), *n.* (*abu-Abdallah,* "*El Chico*") died 1492?, last Moorish king of Granada, 1482–92.

boa constrictor, 1. a boa, *Constrictor constrictor,* of Central and South America, noted for its size and crushing power. **2.** any large python or other snake of the boa family.

Bo·ad·i·ce·a (bō/ăd ə sē/ə), *n.* Boudicca.

Bo·a·ner·ges (bō/ə nûr/jēz), *n.* **1.** (*construed as pl.*) *Bible.* surname given by Christ to James and John, explained as meaning "sons of thunder." Mark, 3:17. **2.** (*construed as sing.*) a vociferous preacher or orator. [t, LL, t. Gk., from the Aram. surname equiv. to Heb. *bĕnē regesh* "sons of thunder"]

boar (bōr), *n.* **1.** the uncastrated male of swine. **2.** the wild boar. [ME *boor,* OE *bār*]

board (bōrd), *n.* **1.** a piece of timber sawed thin, and of considerable length and breadth compared with the thickness. **2.** (*pl.*) *Theat.* the stage. **3.** a flat slab of wood for some specific purpose: *an ironing board.* **4.** a sheet of wood, paper, etc., with or without markings, for some special use: *a chessboard.* **5.** stiff cardboard covered with paper, cloth, or the like, to form the binding for a book. **6.** a table, esp. to serve food on. **7.** daily meals, esp. as provided for pay. **8.** an official body of persons who direct or supervise some activity: *a board of directors, of trade, of health.* **9.** the border or edge of anything, as in *seaboard.* **10.** *Naut.* **a.** the side of a ship. **b.** one leg, or tack, of the course of a ship beating to windward. **11. by the board,** over the ship's side. **12. go by the board,** to be destroyed, neglected, or forgotten. **13. on board,** on or in a ship, plane, or vehicle. —*v.t.* **14.** to cover or close with boards. **15.** to furnish with food, or with food and lodging, esp. for pay. **16.** to arrange for the furnishing of meals to. **17.** to go on board of or enter (a ship, train, etc.). **18.** to come up alongside of (a ship), as to attack or to go on board. **19.** *Obs.* to approach; accost. —*v.i.* **20.** to take one's meals, or be supplied with food and lodging at a fixed price: *several of us board at the same rooming house.* [OE *bord* board, table, shield]

board·er (bōr/dər), *n.* **1.** one who is supplied with meals. **2.** a person chosen to board an enemy ship.

board foot, a unit of measure equal to the cubic contents of a piece of lumber one foot square and one inch thick, used in measuring logs and lumber.

board·ing (bôr/dĭng), *n.* **1.** wooden boards collectively. **2.** a structure of boards, as in a fence or a floor.

boarding house, a place, usually a home, at which board is furnished, often with lodging.

boarding school, a school at which board and lodging are furnished for the pupils.

board measure, *Bldg. Trades.* a system of cubic measure in which the unit is the board foot.

board of health, a government department concerned with public health.

board of trade, **1.** a businessmen's association. **2.** (*cap.*) (in England) the national ministry that supervises and encourages commerce and industry.

board rule, a measuring device having scales for finding the cubic contents of a board without calculation.

board·walk (bôrd/wôk/), *n.* **1.** *U.S.* a promenade made of wooden boards, usually along a beach. **2.** any walk made of boards or planks.

boar·fish (bôr/fĭsh/), *n.* any of various fishes of different genera which have a projecting snout, esp. a small spiny-rayed European fish, *Capros aper.*

boar·hound (bôr/hound/), *n.* any of various large dogs used orig. for hunting wild boars, esp. a dog of a German breed (**German boarhound**) or a Great Dane.

boar·ish (bôr/ĭsh), *adj.* swinish; sensual; cruel.

Bo·as (bō/ăz), *n.* **Franz** (fränts), 1858–1942, U. S. anthropologist, born in Germany.

boast[1] (bōst), *v.i.* **1.** to speak exaggeratedly and objectionably, esp. about oneself. **2.** to speak with pride (fol. by *of*). —*v.t.* **3.** to speak of with excessive pride, vanity, or exultation. **4.** to be proud in the possession of: *the town boasts a new school.* —*n.* **5.** a thing boasted of. **6.** exaggerated or objectionable speech; bragging. [ME *bosten;* orig. unknown] —**boast/er,** *n.* —**boast/ing·ly,** *adv.*
—**Syn. 1, 2.** Boast, brag imply vocal self-praise or claims to superiority over others. Boast usually refers to a particular ability, possession, etc., which may be one of such kind as to justify a good deal of pride: *he boasts of his ability as a singer.* Brag, a more colloquial term, usually suggests a more ostentatious and exaggerated boasting but less well-founded: *he loudly brags of his marksmanship.*

boast[2] (bōst), *v.t.* to dress or shape (stone, etc.) roughly. [orig. uncert.]

boast·ful (bōst/fəl), *adj.* given to or characterized by boasting. —**boast/ful·ly,** *adv.* —**boast/ful·ness,** *n.*

boat (bōt), *n.* **1.** a vessel for transport by water, constructed to provide buoyancy by excluding water and shaped to give stability and permit propulsion. **2.** a small ship, generally for specialized use. **3.** a small vessel carried for use by a large one. **4.** *Colloq.* a ship. **5.** an open dish resembling a boat: *a gravy boat.* **6. in the same boat,** faced with the same, esp. unfortunate, circumstances. —*v.i.* **7.** to go in a boat. —*v.t.* **8.** to transport in a boat. [ME *boot,* OE *bāt*]

boat·bill (bōt/bĭl/), *n.* a bird of the genus *Cochlearius,* of the heron family, containing the single species *C. cochlearius,* a tropical American.

boat hook, a metal hook fixed to a pole, for pulling or pushing a boat.

boat·house (bōt/hous/), *n.* a house or shed for sheltering boats.

boat·ing (bō/tĭng), *n.* the use of boats, esp. for pleasure.

boat·load (bōt/lōd/), *n.* **1.** the cargo that a vessel carries. **2.** the cargo that a vessel is capable of carrying.

boat·man (bōt/mən), *n., pl.* -men. a person skilled in the use of small craft. —**boat/man·ship/,** *n.*

boat·swain (bō/sən; *rarely* bōt/swān/), *n.* a warrant officer on a warship, or a petty officer on a merchant vessel, in charge of rigging, anchors, cables, etc. Also, **bo's'n, bosun.**

Bo·az (bō/ăz), *n. Bible.* husband of Ruth. Ruth 2–4. [t. Heb.: m. *Bo'az*]

bob[1] (bŏb), *n., v.,* **bobbed, bobbing.** —*n.* **1.** a short jerky motion: *a bob of the head.* —*v.t.* **2.** to move quickly down and up: *to bob the head.* **3.** to indicate with such a motion: *to bob a greeting.* —*v.i.* **4.** to make a jerky motion with head or body. **5.** to move about with jerky motions. [ME; orig. uncert.]

bob[2] (bŏb), *n., v.,* **bobbed, bobbing.** —*n.* **1.** a style of short haircut for women and children. **2.** a horse's tail cut short. **3.** a small dangling or terminal object, as the weight on a pendulum or a plumb line. **4.** *Angling.* **a.** a knot of worms, rags, etc., on a string. **b.** a float for a fishing line. **5.** *Colloq.* a bunch; a cluster. **6.** a bobsled or bob skate. —*v.t.* **7.** to cut short; dock. —*v.i.* **8.** *Angling.* to fish with a bob. [ME *bobbe* bunch, cluster, knob; orig. obscure]

bob[3] (bŏb), *n., v.,* **bobbed, bobbing.** —*n.* **1.** a tap; light blow. —*v.t.* **2.** to tap; strike lightly. [ME *bobben;* ? imit.]

bob[4] (bŏb), *n. Brit. Colloq.* a shilling. [orig. uncert.]

Bo·ba·dil·la (frän thēs/kō dē), *n.* **Francisco de** (frän thēs/kō dē), died 1502, Spanish colonial governor in the West Indies: sent Columbus back to Spain in chains.

bob·ber (bŏb/ər), *n.* **1.** one who or that which bobs. **2.** a fishing bob.

bob·ber·y (bŏb/ər ĭ), *n., pl.* -beries. *Colloq.* a disturbance. [Anglo-Ind., t. Hindu: m. *bāp re* O father!]

bob·bin (bŏb/ĭn), *n.* a reel, cylinder, or spool upon which yarn or thread is wound, as used in spinning, machine sewing, etc. [t. F: m. *bobine,* der. *bobiner* to wind up, der. OF *baube* stammering, g. L *balbus*]

Bobbin and Joan (jōn), the European arum, *Arum maculatum.*

bob·bi·net (bŏb/ə nĕt/), *n.* lacelike fabric of hexagonal mesh, made on a lace machine. [var. of *bobbin-net,* f. BOBBIN + NET[1]]

bobbin lace, lace made by hand with bobbins of thread, the threads being twisted around pins stuck into a pattern placed on a pillow.

bob·by (bŏb/ĭ), *n., pl.* -bies. *Brit. Colloq.* a policeman. [special use of *Bobby,* for Sir *Robert* Peel (1788–1850), who improved the police system of London]

bobby pin, a metal hairpin with close prongs.

bob·by·socks (bŏb/ĭ sŏks/), *n.pl. Colloq.* anklets (def. 1), esp. as worn by young girls.

bob·by·sox·er (bŏb/ĭ sŏks/ər), *n. Colloq.* a girl or young woman who enthusiastically follows adolescent fashions and fads. Also, **bob/by sox/er.**

bob·cat (bŏb/kăt/), *n.* an American wildcat, esp. the species *Lynx rufus,* which is widespread in the U.S.

Bobolink.
Dolichonyx oryzivorus
(7 to 7½ in. long)

bob·o·link (bŏb/ə lĭngk/), *n.* a common North American passerine songbird, *Dolichonyx oryzivorus,* which winters in South America. [short for *Bob o' Lincoln,* supposed to be the bird's call]

bob skate, a type of skate with two parallel runners.

bob·sled (bŏb/slĕd/), *n., v.,* -sledded, -sledding. *U.S.* —*n.* **1.** (formerly) a sled formed of two short sleds coupled one behind the other. The modern bobsled couples the runners only, the seat portion being continuous. **2.** either of the short sleds. —*v.i.* **3.** to ride on a bobsled. Also, **bob·sleigh** (bŏb/slā/). [f. BOB[2] + SLED]

bob·stay (bŏb/stā/), *n. Naut.* a rope, chain, or rod from the outer end of the bowsprit to the cutwater, holding the bowsprit in. See illus. under **bowsprit.**

bob·tail (bŏb/tāl/), *n.* **1.** a short or docked tail. **2.** a bobtailed animal. —*adj.* **3.** bobtailed; cut short. —*v.t.* **4.** to cut short the tail of; dock.

bob·white (bŏb/hwīt/), *n.* a common North American quail, *Colinus virginianus,* known locally as the partridge. [imit. of its call]

bo·cac·cio (bō kä/chō), *n.* a brown or reddish species of rock cod of the California coast. [t. It.: m. *boccaccio* one having a large mouth]

Boc·cac·ci·o (bō kä/chYō/; *It.* bôk kät/chō), *n.* **Giovanni** (jō vän/nē), 1313–75, Italian writer and poet.

Boche (bŏsh, bōsh), *n. Slang.* (in World War I) a German. Also, **boche.** [t. F, ? alter. of F *caboche* head, pate, noodle, der. d. stem *cab-,* g. L *caput* head]

Bo·chum (bō/кЙŌŌm), *n.* a city in W Germany, in the Ruhr. 305,485 (1939).

bock beer (bŏk), a strong, dark beer, commonly brewed in the spring. Also, **bock.** [t. G: m. *bockbier,* for *Eimbocker bier* beer of Eimbock, or Einbeck, in Prussia]

bode[1] (bōd), *v.,* boded, boding. —*v.t.* **1.** to be an omen of; portend. **2.** *Archaic.* to announce beforehand; predict. —*v.i.* **3.** to portend. [ME *boden,* OE *bodian* announce, foretell, der. *boda* messenger] —**bode/ment,** *n.*

bode[2] (bōd), *v.* pt. and pp. of **bide** (def. 3).

bo·de·ga (bō dē/gə; *Sp.* bō dĕ/gä), *n.* a wineshop. [Sp., g. L *apothēca,* t. Gk.: m. *apothḗkē* storehouse]

Bo·den See (bō/dən zā/), German name of the **Lake of Constance.**

bod·ice (bŏd/ĭs), *n.* **1.** a woman's laced outer garment covering the waist and bust, common in peasant dress. **2.** *Chiefly Brit.* a woman's fitted waist or dress body. **3.** *Obs.* stays or a corset. [var. of *bodies,* pl. of BODY]

Bodice

bod·i·less (bŏd/ĭlĭs), *adj.* having no body or material form; incorporeal.

bod·i·ly (bŏd/əlĭ), *adj.* **1.** of or pertaining to the body. **2.** corporeal or material, in contrast with spiritual or mental. —*adv.* **3.** as a whole; without taking apart. —**Syn. 2.** See **physical.**

bod·ing (bō/dĭng), *n.* **1.** a foreboding; omen. —*adj.* **2.** foreboding; ominous. —**bod/ing·ly,** *adv.*

bod·kin (bŏd/kĭn), *n.* **1.** a small pointed instrument for making holes in cloth, etc. **2.** a long pin-shaped instrument used by women to fasten up the hair. **3.** a blunt needlelike instrument for drawing tape, cord, etc., through a loop, hem, or the like. **4.** *Obs.* a small dagger; a stiletto. [ME *boydekin* dagger; orig. unknown]

Bod·lei·an (bŏd lē/ən, bŏd/lĭ-), *n.* the library of Oxford University reëstablished by Sir Thomas Bodley, 1545–1613, British diplomat and scholar.

Bo·do·ni (bə dō/nĭ *for 1;* bō dō/nē *for 2*), *n.* **1.** *Print.* a style of type. **2.** **Giambattista** (jäm/bät tēs/tä), 1740–1813, Italian printer.

bod·y (bŏd/ĭ), *n., pl.* bodies, *v.,* bodied, bodying, *adj.* —*n.* **1.** the physical structure of an animal (and sometimes, in *Biol.,* of a plant) living or dead. **2.** a corpse; carcass. **3.** the trunk or main mass of a thing. **4.** *Zool.* the physical structure of an animal minus limbs and head. **5.** *Archit.* the central structure of a building, esp. the nave of a church; the major mass of a building. **6.** a vehicle minus wheels and other appendages. **7.** *Naut.* the hull of a ship. **8.** *Aeron.* the fuselage of a plane. **9.**

Print. the shank of a type, supporting the face. **10.** *Geom.* a figure having the three dimensions, length, breadth, and thickness; a solid. **11.** *Physics.* anything having inertia; a mass. **12.** the major portion of an army, population, etc. **13.** the central part of a speech or document, minus introduction, conclusion, indexes, etc. **14.** *Colloq. and Dial.* a person. **15.** *Law.* the physical person of an individual. **16.** a collective group, or an artificial person: *body politic, body corporate.* **17.** a number of things or people taken together. **18.** consistency or density; substance; strength as opposed to thinness: *wine of a good body.* **19.** that part of a dress which covers the trunk, or the trunk above the waist. —*v.t.* **20.** to invest with or as with a body. **21.** to represent in bodily form (usually fol. by *forth*). —*adj.* **22.** *Print.* (of type) used mainly for the text, generally less than 14 pts. (as distinguished from *display type*). —**bod′ied,** *adj.* [ME; OE *bodig*]
—Syn. 1, 2. BODY, CARCASS, CORPSE agree in referring to a physical organism. BODY refers to the material organism of an individual man or animal, either living or dead: *the muscles in a horse's body, the body of a victim (man or animal)*. CARCASS refers only to the dead body of an animal, unless applied humorously or contemptuously to the human body: *a sheep's carcass, save your carcass.* CORPSE refers only to the dead body of man: *preparing a corpse for burial.*

body cavity, *Zool., Anat., etc.* the general or common cavity of the body, as distinguished from special cavities or those of particular organs.

body corporate, *Law.* a person, association, or group of persons legally incorporated; a corporation.

bod·y·guard (bŏd′ĭ gärd′), *n.* **1.** a personal or private guard, as for a high official. **2.** a retinue; escort.

body politic, *Pol. Sci.* a people as forming a political body under an organized government.

body snatching, act of robbing a grave to obtain a subject for dissection. —**body snatcher.**

Boe·o·tia (bē ō′sha), *n.* a district and republic in ancient Greece, NW of Athens. *Cap.:* Thebes.

Boe·o·tian (bē ō′shən), *adj.* **1.** of or pertaining to Boeotia or the Boeotians. **2.** dull; stupid. —*n.* **3.** a native or inhabitant of Boeotia. **4.** a dull, stupid person.

Boer (bōr; *Du.* bōor), *n.* **1.** a South African of Dutch extraction. —*adj.* **2.** of or pertaining to the Boers. [t. D: peasant, countryman. See BOOR]

Boer War, 1. a war in which Great Britain fought against the Transvaal and Orange Free State, 1899–1902. **2.** a war between Great Britain and the Transvaal, 1880–81.

Bo·e·thi·us (bō ē′thĭ əs), *n.* **Anicius Manlius Severinus** (ə nĭsh′ĭ əs măn′lĭ əs sĕv′ə rī′nəs), A.D. 475?–525? Roman philosopher and statesman. Also, **Bo·ece** (bō ēs′), **Bo·e·tius** (bō ē′shəs).

bog (bŏg, bôg), *n., v.,* **bogged, bogging.** —*n.* **1.** wet, spongy ground, with soil composed mainly of decayed vegetable matter. **2.** an area or stretch of such ground. —*v.t., v.i.* **3.** to sink in or as in a bog. [t. Irish or Gaelic: soft] —**bog′gish,** *adj.* —**bog′gy,** *adj.*

bog asphodel, either of two liliaceous plants, *Nathecium ossifragum* of Europe, and *N. americanum* of the U.S., growing in boggy places.

bo·gey (bō′gĭ), *n., pl.* **-geys. 1.** a bogy. **2.** *Golf.* **a.** par (def. 4). **b.** one stroke above par on a hole. [var. of BOGY]

bog·gle¹ (bŏg′əl), *v.,* **-gled, -gling,** *n.* —*v.i.* **1.** to take alarm; start with fright. **2.** to hesitate, as if afraid to proceed; waver; shrink. **3.** to dissemble; equivocate. **4.** to be awkward; bungle. —*n.* **5.** act of shying or taking alarm. **6.** *Colloq.* bungle; botch. [? special use of BOGGLE²] —**bog′gler,** *n.*

bog·gle² (bŏg′əl), *n.* bogle.

bo·gie (bō′gĭ), *n.* bogy.

bo·gle (bō′gəl, bŏg′əl), *n.* a bogy; a specter. Also, **boggle.** [der. obs. *bog,* var. of BUG bugbear]

bog oak, oak (or other wood) preserved in peat bogs.

Bo·go·tá (bō′gō tä′), *n.* the capital of Colombia, in the central part. 416,107 (est. 1943).

bog·trot·ter (bŏg′trŏt′ər, bôg′-), *n.* **1.** one who lives among bogs. **2.** *Contemptuous.* a rural Irishman.

bo·gus (bō′gəs), *adj.* *U.S.* counterfeit; spurious; sham.

bo·gy (bō′gĭ), *n., pl.* **-gies. 1.** a hobgoblin; evil spirit. **2.** anything that haunts and annoys one. **3.** *Mil. Slang.* an unidentified or unrecognized aircraft. Also, **bogey, bogie.** [der. obs. *bog.* See BOGLE]

Bo·he·mi·a (bō hē′mǐ ə, -hēm′yə), *n.* **1.** Czech, **Čechy.** a province in W Czechoslovakia: formerly in Austria; a part of Bohemia-Moravia, 1939–45. 6,754,000 pop. (est. 1946); 20,101 sq. mi. *Cap.:* Prague. **2.** a district inhabited by Bohemians (def. 3). **3.** the social circles in which a Bohemian atmosphere is prevalent.

Bo·he·mi·a-Mo·ra·vi·a (bō hē′mǐ ə mō rä′vǐ ə, bō-hēm′yə-), *n.* a former German protectorate including Bohemia and Moravia (1939–1945).

Bo·he·mi·an (bō hē′mǐ ən, -hēm′yən), *n.* **1.** a native or inhabitant of Bohemia. **2.** the Czech language. **3.** (*often l.c.*) a person with artistic or intellectual tendencies who lives and acts with disregard for conventional rules of behavior. **4.** a Gypsy. —*adj.* **5.** pertaining to Bohemia, its people, or their language. **6.** pertaining to or characteristic of Bohemians (def. 3). —**Bo·he′mi·an·ism,** *n.*

Bohemian Forest, a low forest-covered mountain range on the boundary between SW Czechoslovakia and SE Germany. Highest peak, Mt. Arber, 4780 ft. German, **Böh·mer Wald** (bœ′mər vält′).

Bo·hol (bō hŏl′), *n.* one of the Philippine Islands, in the central part. 499,549 pop. (1939); 1492 sq. mi.

Bohr (bōr), *n.* **Niels** (nēls), born 1885, Danish physicist.

Bohr theory, *Physics.* a theory of atomic structure in which the electrons are described as revolving in individual orbits about a central part.

bo·hunk (bō′hŭngk′), *n.* *U.S. Slang.* (in contemptuous use) an unskilled or semiskilled foreign-born laborer, specif., a Bohemian, Magyar, Slovak, or Croatian. Cf. **hunky².**

Bo·iar·do (bō yär′dō), *n.* **Matteo Maria** (mät tě′ō mä-rē′ä), 1434–94, Italian poet.

boil¹ (boil), *v.i.* **1.** to change from liquid to gaseous state, producing bubbles of gas that rise to the surface of the liquid, agitating it as they rise. **2.** to be in a similarly agitated state: *the sea was boiling.* **3.** to be agitated by angry feeling. **4.** to contain, or be contained in, a liquid that boils: *the pot is boiling, the meat is boiling.* **5. boil over, a.** to overflow while boiling. **b.** to be unable to repress excitement, anger, etc. —*v.t.* **6.** to cause to boil. **7.** to separate (sugar, salt, etc.) from something containing it by heat. **8. boil down, a.** to reduce by boiling. **b.** to shorten; abridge. —*n.* **9.** act of boiling. **10.** state or condition of boiling. [ME *boile(n),* t. OF: m. *boillir,* g. L *bullīre*]
—Syn. 3. BOIL, SEETHE, SIMMER, STEW are used figuratively to refer to agitated states of emotion. To BOIL suggests the state of being very hot with anger or rage: *rage made his blood boil.* To SEETHE is to be deeply stirred, violently agitated, or greatly excited: *a mind seethes with conflicting ideas.* To SIMMER means to be on the point of bursting out or boiling over: *to simmer with curiosity, with anger.* To STEW is colloquial for to worry, to be in a restless state of anxiety and excitement: *to stew about (or over) one's troubles.*

boil² (boil), *n.* *Pathol.* a painful suppurating inflammatory sore forming a central core, caused by microbic infection; a furuncle. [ME *bile,* OE *bȳle*]

Boi·leau-Des·pré·aux (bwà lō′ dě prē ō′), *n.* **Nicolas** (nē kō lä′), 1636–1711, French critic and poet.

boiled shirt, *U.S.* a white or dress shirt.

boil·er (boi′lər), *n.* **1.** a closed vessel together with its furnace, in which steam or other vapor is generated for heating or for driving engines. **2.** a vessel for boiling or heating. **3.** *Brit.* a stove for heating water. **4.** a tank for storing hot water.

boiling point, the temperature at which a liquid vaporizes, equal for water to 212°F or 100°C at sea level.

Boi·se (boi′zĭ, -sĭ), *n.* the capital of Idaho, in the SW part, built on the site of **Fort Boise,** a post on the Oregon trail. 34,393 (1950).

Bois-le-Duc (bwà lə dүk′), *n.* French name of **'s Hertogenbosch.**

bois·ter·ous (boi′stər əs), *adj.* **1.** rough and noisy; clamorous; unrestrained. **2.** (of waves, weather, wind, etc.) rough and stormy. **3.** *Obs.* rough and massive. [ME *boistrous,* earlier *boistous;* orig. unknown] —**bois′-ter·ous·ly,** *adv.* —**bois′ter·ous·ness,** *n.* —Syn. 1. uproarious, obstreperous, roistering. —Ant. 1. sedate.

Bo·jar·do (bō yär′dō), *n.* See **Boiardo.**

Boj·er (boi′ər), *n.* **Johan** (yō hän′), born 1872, Norwegian novelist and playwright.

Bok (bŏk), *n.* **Edward William,** 1863–1930, U.S. editor and writer, born in the Netherlands.

Bo·kha·ra (bō kä′rə; *Russ.* bŏŏ hä′rä), *n.* **1.** a former state in W Asia: now a region in the Uzbek Republic of the Soviet Union. **2.** the chief city of this region. 50,382 (1939). Also, **Bukhara.**

Bol., Bolivia.

bo·la (bō′lə; *Sp.* bō′lä), *n.* a weapon used by the Indians and Gauchos of southern South America, consisting of two or more heavy balls secured to the ends of one or more strong cords, which entangle the victim at which it is thrown. Also, **bo·las** (bō′ləs; *Sp.* bō′läs). [t. Sp.: a ball, g. L *bulla* bubble, round object]

Bo·lan Pass (bō län′), a pass in NE Baluchistan. ab. 54 mi. long.

bo·lar (bō′lər), *adj.* of or pertaining to bole or clay.

bold (bōld), *adj.* **1.** not hesitating in the face of actual or possible danger or rebuff. **2.** not hesitating to breach the rules of propriety; forward. **3.** calling for daring, unhesitating action. **4.** overstepping usual bounds or conventions. **5.** conspicuous to the eye: *bold handwriting.* **6.** steep; abrupt: *a bold promontory.* **7.** *Obs.* trusting; assured. **8. make bold to,** to venture to. [ME; OE *bald, beald*] —**bold′ly,** *adv.* —**bold′ness,** *n.*
—Syn. 1. fearless, courageous, brave, intrepid, daring. **2.** BOLD, BRAZEN, FORWARD, PRESUMPTUOUS may refer to manners in a derogatory sense. BOLD suggests impudence, shamelessness, and immodesty (esp. in women): *a bold stare.* BRAZEN suggests the same, together with a defiant manner: *a brazen hussy.* FORWARD implies making oneself unduly prominent or bringing oneself to notice with too much assurance. PRESUMPTUOUS implies overconfidence, effrontery, taking too much for granted. —Ant. 2. modest.

b., blend of, blended; c., cognate with; d., dialect, dialectal; der., derived from; f., formed from; g., going back to; m., modification of; r., replacing; s., stem of; t., taken from; ?, perhaps. See the full key on inside cover.

bold·face (bōld′fās′), *n. Print.* type that has thick, heavy lines, used for emphasis, etc.

bold-faced (bōld′fāst′), *adj.* **1.** impudent; brazen. **2.** *Print.* (of type) having thick lines.

bole¹ (bōl), *n. Bot.* the stem or trunk of a tree. [ME, t. Scand.; cf. Icel. *bolr*]

bole² (bōl), *n.* any one of a class of soft, brittle, unctuous clays varying in color and affording pigments. [t. LL: m.s. *bolus*, t. Gk.: m. *bōlos* clod, lump]

bo·lec·tion (bō·lĕk′shən), *n. Archit.* a molding which projects beyond the surface of the work it decorates. Also, **bilection.** [orig. uncert.]

bo·le·ro (bō·lâr′ō; *Sp.* bô·lĕ′rō), *n., pl.* **-ros. 1.** a lively Spanish dance in three-four time. **2.** the music for it. **3.** a short jacket ending above or at the waistline. [t. Sp.]

bo·le·tus (bō·lē′təs), *n.* any species of the genus *Boletus,* a group of umbrella-shaped mushrooms in which the stratum of tubes on the underside of the cap is easily separable. [t. L, t. Gk.: m. *bōlĭtēs* kind of mushroom]

Bol·eyn (bŏŏl′ĭn), *n.* **Anne,** 1507–36, second wife of Henry VIII of England: mother of Queen Elizabeth.

bo·lide (bō′līd, -lĭd), *n. Astron.* a large, brilliant meteor, esp. one that explodes. [t. F, t. L: m. s. *bolis* large meteor, t. Gk.: missile]

Bol·ing·broke (bŏl′ĭng·brŏŏk′; *older* bŏŏl′-), *n.* **Henry St. John** (sĭn′jən), **1st Viscount,** 1678–1751, British statesman and writer.

Bol·i·var (bŏl′ə·vər; *Sp.* bô·lē′vär), *n.* **Simón** (sĭ′mən; *Sp.* sē·môn′), 1783–1830, Venezuelan statesman: leader of revolt of South American colonies from Spanish rule.

bol·i·var (bŏl′ə·vər; *Sp.* bô·lē′vär), *n., pl.* **bolivars,** *Sp.* **bolivares** (bô·lē·vä′rĕs). the silver coin of Venezuela and its monetary unit, equal to 30 cents. [named after Simon BOLIVAR]

Bo·liv·i·a (bō·lĭv′ĭ·ə, bə-; *Sp.* bô·lē′vyä), *n.* a republic in W South America. 3,533,900 pop. (est. 1942); 416,040 sq. mi. *Capitals:* La Paz and Sucre. —**Bo·liv′i·an,** *adj., n.*

bo·li·via·no (bō·lē′vyä′nō), *n., pl.* **-nos** (-nōs). the monetary unit of Bolivia; equal to 2.3 cents. [t. Bolivian Sp.]

boll (bōl), *n. Bot.* a rounded seed vessel or pod of a plant, as of flax or cotton. [var. of BOWL¹]

bol·lard (bŏl′ərd), *n. Naut.* a vertical post on which hawsers are made fast. [? f. BOLE¹ + -ARD]

boll weevil (bōl), a snout beetle, *Anthonomus grandis,* that attacks the bolls of cotton.

boll·worm (bōl′wûrm′), *n.* **1.** the larva, **pink bollworm,** of the moth *Platyedra gossypiella,* one of the worst pests of cotton. **2.** corn earworm.

Cotton boll weevil, *Anthonomus grandis* A, Larva; B, Adult; C, Pupa (line = actual total length of adult; lower section of line = length of body)

bo·lo (bō′lō), *n., pl.* **-los** (-lōz). large, heavy single-edged knife for hacking used in the Philippine Islands and in the U.S. Army. [t. Sp.; t. native d.]

Bo·lo·gna (bə·lōn′yə; *It.* bô·lô′nyä), *n.* a city in N Italy. 320,787 (est. 1946). —**Bo·lo·gnese** (bō′lə·nēz′, -nēs′), *adj., n. sing. and pl.*

bologna sausage, a large-sized variety of sausage containing a mixture of meats. Also, **bo·lo·gna** (bə·lō′nə, -lōn′yə, -lō′nĭ).

bo·lo·graph (bō′lə·grăf′, -gräf′), *n. Physics.* a record made by a bolometer. [f. s. Gk. *bolḗ* ray + -(o)GRAPH] —**bo/lo·graph′ic,** *adj.*

bo·lom·e·ter (bō·lŏm′ə·tər), *n. Physics.* an electrical resistance element for measuring minute amounts of radiant energy. [f. s. Gk. *bolḗ* ray + -(o)METER] —**bo·lo·met′ric** (bō′lə·mĕt′rĭk), *adj.*

bo·lo·ney (bə·lō′nĭ), *n. U.S.* baloney.

Bol·she·vik (bŏl′shə·vĭk, bōl′-), *n., pl.* **Bolsheviki** (-vē′kē; *Russ.* bŏl′shĕ·vĭ·kē′), **-viks. 1.** (in Russia) **a.** (1903–1917) a member of the more radical majority of the Social Democratic Party, advocating abrupt and forceful seizure of power by the proletariat. **b.** (since 1918) a member of the Russian Communist Party. **2.** (in any country) a member of the Communist Party. **3.** (in derisive use) any radical or progressive. Also, **bolshevik.** [t. Russ., der. *bolshe* greater, more, with allusion to the majority (Russ. *bolshinstvo*) of the party]

Bol·she·vism (bŏl′shə·vĭz′əm, bōl′-), *n.* the doctrines, methods, or procedure of the Bolsheviki. **2.** (*sometimes l.c.*) the principles or practices of ultraradical socialists or political ultraradicals generally.

Bol·she·vist (bŏl′shə·vĭst, bōl′-), *n.* **1.** a follower or advocate of the doctrines or methods of the Bolsheviki. **2.** (*sometimes l.c.*) an ultraradical socialist; any political ultraradical. —*adj.* **3.** Bolshevistic.

Bol·she·vis·tic (bŏl′shə·vĭs′tĭk, bōl′-), *adj.* pertaining to or characteristic or suggestive of Bolshevists or Bolshevism. Also, **bolshevistic.**

Bol·she·vize (bŏl′shə·vīz′, bōl′-), *v.,* **-vized, -vizing.** —*v.t.* **1.** to bring under the influence or domination of Bolshevists; render Bolshevik or Bolshevistic. —*v.i.* **2.** to become Bolshevik or Bolshevistic; act like a Bolshevik. Also, **bolshevize.** —**Bol′she·vi·za′tion,** *n.*

bol·són (bŏl·sŏn′; *Sp.* bôl·sôn′), *n. Phys. Geog.* a broad and nearly flat mountain-rimmed desert basin with interior drainage. [t. Sp.: large purse. See BURSE]

bol·ster (bōl′stər), *n.* **1.** a long underpillow for a bed. **2.** something suggesting or resembling this in form or use. **3.** a pillow, cushion, or pad. —*v.t.* **4.** to support with or as with a pillow. **5.** to prop, support, or uphold (something weak, unworthy, etc.) (often fol. by *up*). [ME *bolstre,* OE *bolster,* c. G *polster*] —**bol/ster·er,** *n.*

bolt¹ (bōlt), *n.* **1.** a movable bar which when slid into a socket fastens a door, gate, etc. **2.** the part of a lock which is protruded from and drawn back into the case, as by the action of the key. **3.** a strong metal pin, often with a head at one end and with a screw thread at the other to receive a nut. See illus. under **nut. 4.** a sudden swift motion or escape. **5.** sudden desertion of a meeting, political party, program, etc. **6.** a woven length of cloth. **7.** a roll of wall paper. **8.** a sudden dash, run, flight, etc. **9.** a jet of water, molten glass, etc. **10.** an arrow, esp. one for a crossbow. **11.** a shaft of lightning; a thunderbolt. —*v.t.* **12.** to fasten with or as with bolts. **13.** *U.S. Pol.* to break away from; refuse to support. **14.** to shoot; discharge (a missile). **15.** to blurt; utter hastily. **16.** to swallow (one's food) hurriedly or without chewing. **17.** to make (cloth, wall paper, etc.) into bolts. —*v.i.* **18.** to make a sudden, swift movement; spring away suddenly. **19.** *U.S. Pol.* to break away, as from a party; refuse to support one's party. **20.** to eat hurriedly or without chewing. —*adv.* **21.** suddenly; with sudden meeting or collision. **22. bolt upright,** stiffly upright. [ME and OE, c. G *bolz*] —**bolt′er,** *n.* —**bolt′less,** *adj.* —**bolt′like′,** *adj.*

bolt² (bōlt), *v.t.* **1.** to sift through a cloth or sieve. **2.** to examine or search into, as if by sifting. [ME *bult(en),* t. OF: m. *bulter* sift, t. MD: m. *buitelen*] —**bolt′er,** *n.*

bolt·head (bōlt′hĕd′), *n.* **1.** the head of a bolt. **2.** *Chem.* (formerly) a matrass.

Bol·ton (bōl′tən), *n.* a city in W England, in Lancashire. 161,830 (est. 1946).

bol·to·ni·a (bŏl·tō′nĭ·ə), *n.* a tall asteraceous perennial, genus *Boltonia,* of the U.S., sometimes cultivated. [t. NL; named after James *Bolton* (d. 1795), British botanist]

bolt·rope (bōlt′rōp′), *n.* **1.** *Naut.* a rope or the cordage sewed on the edges of a sail or the like to strengthen it. **2.** a superior grade of rope.

bo·lus (bō′ləs), *n.* a round mass of medicine, larger than an ordinary pill, forming a dose. [t. LL, t. Gk.: m. *bōlos* lump]

bomb (bŏm), *n.* **1.** *Mil.* a hollow (usually spherical) projectile filled with a bursting charge, and exploded by means of a fuse, by impact, or otherwise. **2.** any similar missile or device: *a dynamite bomb, an aerial bomb.* **3.** *Geol.* a rough spherical or ellipsoidal mass of lava ejected from a volcano. —*v.t.* **4.** to hurl bombs at; drop bombs upon, as from an airplane; bombard. —*v.i.* **5.** to hurl or drop bombs. **6.** to explode a bomb or bombs. [t. F: m. *bombe,* t. It.: m. *bomba,* g. L *bombus* a booming sound, t. Gk.: m. *bómbos*]

bom·ba·ca·ceous (bŏm′bə·kā′shəs), *adj. Bot.* belonging to the *Bombacaceae,* a family of woody plants including the silk-cotton trees and the baobab. [f. s. LL *bombax* (for L *bombyx,* t. Gk.: silkworm, silk) + -ACEOUS]

bom·bard (*v.* bŏm·bärd′; *n.* bŏm′bärd), —*v.t.* **1.** to attack or batter with artillery. **2.** to attack with bombs. **3.** to assail vigorously: *bombard someone with questions.* —*n.* **4.** the earliest kind of cannon, orig. throwing stone balls. [ME *bumbarde,* t. OF: cannon, der. L *bombus* loud noise. See BOMB] —**bom·bard′er,** *n.* —**bom·bard′ment,** *n.*

bom·bar·dier (bŏm′bər·dĭr′), *n.* **1.** *Mil.* member of bombing plane crew who operates the bomb release mechanism. **2.** *Hist.* artilleryman. [t. F]

bom·bar·don (bŏm′bər·dən, bŏm·bär′dən), *n. Music.* **1.** a bass reed stop of the organ. **2.** a large, deep-toned, valved brass-wind instrument not unlike a tuba. [t. It.: m. *bombardone;* akin to BOMBARD]

bom·bast (bŏm′băst), *n.* **1.** high-sounding words; speech too high-flown for the occasion. **2.** *Obs.* cotton or other material used to stuff garments; padding. —*adj.* **3.** *Obs.* bombastic. [earlier *bombace,* t. F, g. LL *bombax* cotton, for L *bombyx* silkworm, silk, t. Gk.]

bom·bas·tic (bŏm·băs′tĭk), *adj.* (of speech, etc.) high-sounding; high-flown; inflated; turgid. Also, **bom·bas′ti·cal.** —**bom·bas′ti·cal·ly,** *adv.*

Bom·bay (bŏm·bā′), *n.* **1.** a province in W India: formerly a presidency. 20,850,000 pop. (1941); 76,443 sq. mi. **2.** the capital of this province: a seaport on the Arabian Sea. 1,489,883 (1941).

bom·ba·zine (bŏm′bə·zēn′, bŏm′bə·zēn′), *n.* a fine-twilled fabric with a silk warp and worsted weft, formerly much used (in black) for mourning. Also, **bom′ba·sine′.** [t. F: m. *bombasin,* t. LL: s. *bombasinum,* der. *bombax.* See BOMBAST]

bomb bay, *Aeron., Mil.* the compartment from which bombs are dropped.

bombe (bôṇb), *n. French.* a melon or circular mold containing one or more flavors of ice cream or ice.

bomb·er (bŏm′ər), *n. Mil.* an airplane employed to drop bombs.

bomb·proof (bŏm′prŏŏf′), *adj.* **1.** strong enough to resist the impact and explosive force of bombs or shells striking on the outside. —*n.* **2.** a structure of such design and strength as to resist the penetration and the shattering force of shells, usually, at least in part, beneath the level of the ground.

ăct, āble, dâre, ärt; ĕbb, ēqual; ĭf, īce; hŏt, ōver, ôrder, oil, bŏŏk, ōōze, out; ŭp, ūse, ûrge; ə = a in alone; ch, chief; g, give; ng, ring; sh, shoe; th, thin; ŧħ, that; zh, vision. See the full key on inside cover.

bomb rack, a device for carrying bombs in an aircraft.

bomb·shell (bŏm'shĕl'), *n.* **1.** a bomb. **2.** like a **bombshell,** with sudden or devastating effect: *his resignation came like a bombshell.*

bomb·sight (bŏm'sīt'), *n. Mil.* an aiming instrument used to tell when to drop a bomb from an aircraft so that it will hit a specified target.

bom·by·cid (bŏm'bə sĭd), *n.* any of the *Bombycidae,* the family of moths that includes the silkworm moths. [f. s. L *bombyx* silkworm (t. Gk.) + -ID²]

Bon (bŏn), *n.* **Cape,** a cape on the NE coast of Tunisia: surrender of the German Afrika Korps, May 12, 1943.

bo·na fi·de (bō'nə fī'dĭ), in good faith; in all sincerity; without fraud. [t. L] —**bo·na-fide** (bō'nə-fīd', bŏn'ə-), *adj.*

bon a·mi (bôn nå mē'), *French.* **1.** a good friend. **2.** a lover.

bo·nan·za (bō năn'zə), *n. U.S.* **1.** a rich mass of ore, as found in mining. **2.** a mine of wealth; good luck: *to strike a bonanza.* [t. Sp.: fair weather, prosperity, der. L *bonus* good]

Bo·na·parte (bō'nə pärt'; *Fr.* bô nå pårt'), *n.* **1. Jérôme** (jə rōm'; *Fr.* zhĕ rōm'), 1784–1860, king of Westphalia (brother of Napoleon I). **2. Joseph** (jō'zəf; *Fr.* zhō zĕf'), 1768–1844, king of Naples and Spain (brother of Napoleon I). **3. Louis** (*Fr.* lwē; *Du.* lōō ē'), 1778–1846, king of Holland (brother of Napoleon I). **4. Louis Napoléon,** 1808–73, president of France, 1848–52; as Napoleon III, emperor of France, 1852–70 (son of Louis Bonaparte). **5. Lucien** (lōō'shən; *Fr.* lу syăn'), 1775–1840, Prince of Cannino (brother of Napoleon I). **6. Napoléon** (nə pō'lĭ ən; *Fr.* nå pô lĕ ôn'), 1769–1821, Corsican-born French general: emperor of France as Napoleon I, 1804–1815. **7. Napoléon,** (*Duke of Reichstadt*) 1811–32, called Napoleon II, but never ruled France (son of Napoleon I). Also, *Italian,* **Buonaparte.**

Bo·na·part·ist (bō'nə pär'tĭst), *n.* an adherent of the Bonapartes or their policies. —**Bo'na·part·ism,** *n.*

Bo·na·ven·ture (bŏn'ə vĕn'chər), *n.* **Saint,** ("*the Seraphic Doctor*") 1221–74, Italian scholastic theologian. Also, *Italian,* **Bo·na·ven·tu·ra** (bô'nä vĕn tōō'-rä).

bon·bon (bŏn'bŏn'; *Fr.* bôn bôn'), *n.* **1.** a fondant, fruit, or nut center dipped in fondant or chocolate. **2.** a piece of confectionery. [t. F, der. *bon* good]

bon·bon·niere (bôn bôn nyĕr'), *n. French.* a box for candies.

bond (bŏnd), *n.* **1.** something that binds, fastens, confines, or holds together. **2.** a cord; rope; band; ligament. **3.** something that unites individual people into a group. **4.** something that constrains a person to a certain line of behavior. **5.** a bondsman or security. **6.** a sealed instrument under which a person or corporation guarantees to pay a stated sum of money on or before a specified day. **7.** any written obligation under seal. **8.** *Law.* the written promise of a surety, originally expressed as a promise to pay a sum of money to be void in case no default occurs by the person whose conduct or performance is guaranteed. **9.** *Govt.* the state of dutiable goods on which the duties are unpaid, when stored, under a bond, in charge of the government (esp. in phrase *in bond*). **10.** *Finance.* a certificate of ownership of a specified portion of a debt due by government, a railroad, or other corporation to individual holders, and usually bearing a fixed rate of interest. **11.** *Insurance.* **a.** a surety agreement. **b.** the money deposited, or the promissory arrangement entered into, under any such agreement. **12.** a substance that causes particles to adhere; a binder. **13.** *Chem.* a unit of combining power equivalent to that of one hydrogen atom. **14.** bond paper. **15.** *Masonry.* the connection of the stones or bricks in a wall, etc., made by overlapping them in order to bind the whole into a compact mass. —*v.t.* **16.** to put (goods, an employee, official, etc.) on or under bond. **17.** *Finance.* to place a bonded debt on; mortgage. **18.** *Masonry.* to cause (bricks or other building materials) to hold together firmly by laying them in some overlapping pattern. —*v.i.* **19.** to hold together from being bonded, as bricks in a wall. [ME, var. of BAND³] —**bond'er,** *n.*

—**Syn. 3.** BOND, LINK, TIE agree in referring to a force or influence which unites people. BOND and TIE are sometimes used interchangeably. BOND, however, usually emphasizes the strong and enduring quality of affection; whereas TIE may refer more especially to duty, obligation, or responsibility: *bonds of memory, blessed be the tie that binds, family ties.* A LINK is a definite connection, though a slighter one; it may indicate affection or merely some traceable influence or desultory communication: *a close link between friends, a perceptible link, a tenuous link.*

bond·age (bŏn'dĭj), *n.* **1.** slavery or involuntary servitude; serfdom. **2.** state of being bound by or subjected to external control. **3.** *Early Eng. Law.* tenure of land by villeinage. —**Syn. 1.** See **slavery.**

bond·ed (bŏn'dĭd), *adj.* **1.** secured by or consisting of bonds: *bonded debt.* **2.** placed in bond: *bonded goods.*

bonded warehouse, a warehouse for holding goods in bond. See **bond,** def. 9.

bond·hold·er (bŏnd'hōl'dər), *n.* a holder of a bond or bonds issued by a government or corporation. —**bond'hold'ing,** *adj., n.*

bond·maid (bŏnd'mād'), *n.* **1.** a female slave. **2.** a female bound to service without wages.

bond·man (bŏnd'mən), *n., pl.* **-men. 1.** a male slave.

2. a man bound to service without wages. **3.** *Old Eng. Law.* a villein or other unfree tenant.

bond paper, a superior variety of white paper.

bond servant, one who serves in bondage; a slave.

bonds·man (bŏndz'mən), *n., pl.* **-men.** *Law.* one who is bound or who by bond becomes surety for another.

bond·wom·an (bŏnd'wŏom'ən), *n., pl.* **-women.** a female slave.

bone (bōn), *n., v.,* **boned, boning.** —*n.* **1.** *Anat., Zool.* **a.** any of the discrete pieces of which the skeleton of a vertebrate is composed. **b.** the hard tissue which composes skeleton. **2.** a bone or piece of a bone with the meat adhering to it, as an article of food. **3.** (*pl.*) the skeleton. **4.** (*pl.*) a body. **5.** any of various similar substances, such as ivory, whalebone, etc. **6.** something made of bone, or of a substance resembling bone. **7.** (*pl.*) *U.S. Slang.* the dice in the game of craps. **8.** (*pl.*) *Theat.* **a.** noisemakers of bone or wood used by a minstrel endman. **b.** an endman in a minstrel troupe. **9.** a strip of whalebone used to stiffen corsets, etc. **10.** feel in one's bones, *U.S.* to feel intuitively. **11.** make no bones of or about, to be quite direct in dealing with. —*v.t.* **12.** to take out the bones of: *to bone a turkey.* **13.** to put whalebone into (clothing). **14.** *Agric.* to put ground bone into, as fertilizer. —*v.i.* **15.** *Slang.* to study hard and fast; cram (often fol. by *up*). [ME *boon,* OE *bān,* c. G *bein* leg] —**bone'less,** *adj.* —**bone'-like',** *adj.*

Bône (bōn), *n.* a seaport in NE Algeria. 83,275 (1936). Also, **Bo·na** (bō'nä). See **Hippo Regius.**

bone ash, the remains of bones calcined in the air.

bone·black (bōn'blăk'), *n.* a black carbonaceous substance obtained by calcining bones in closed vessels. Also, **bone black.**

bone china, a kind of china in which bone ash is used.

bone-dry (bōn'drī'), *adj. Colloq.* dry as a bone (applied esp. to the effect of rigidly enforced prohibition laws).

bone·head (bōn'hĕd'), *n.* a stupid, obstinate person; a blockhead. —**bone'head'ed,** *adj.*

bone meal, *Agric.* bones ground to a coarse powder, used as a fertilizer or animal feed.

bone oil, a fetid, tarry liquid obtained in the dry distillation of bone.

bon·er (bō'nər), *n. Colloq.* a foolish blunder.

bone·set (bōn'sĕt'), *n.* the plant, *Eupatorium perfoliatum;* thoroughwort.

bon·fire (bŏn'fīr'), *n.* **1.** a large fire in an open place, for entertainment, celebration, or as a signal. **2.** any fire built in the open. [earlier *bonefire;* heaps of wood and bones were burned at certain old festivals]

bon·go (bŏng'gō), *n., pl.* **-gos.** a large forest-dwelling antelope, *Taurotragus eurycerus,* of tropical Africa, of a chestnut color striped with white, with spiraling horns.

Bon·heur (bô nœr'), *n.* **Rosa** (rō zä'), (*Marie Rosalie Bonheur*) 1822–99, French painter of animals.

bon·ho·mie (bŏn'ə mē'; *Fr.* bô nô mē'), *n.* frank and simple good-heartedness; a good-natured manner. Also, **bon'hom·mie'.** [t. F, der. *bonhomme* good man]

Bon·i·face (bŏn'ə fās'), *n.* **1.** name given to 9 popes, esp. **Boniface VIII** (*Benedetto Gaetani*), c1235–1303, Italian ecclesiastic: pope 1294–1303. **2. Saint,** (*Wynfrith*) A.D. 680?–755?, English monk who became a missionary in Germany. **3.** a jovial innkeeper in *The Beaux' Stratagem* (1707) by George Farquhar. **4.** (*l.c.*) any landlord or innkeeper.

Bo·nin Islands (bō'nĭn), a group of islands in the N Pacific, SE of and belonging to Japan. 7361 pop. (1940); 40 sq. mi. Japanese, **Ogasawa Jima.**

bo·ni·to (bə nē'tō), *n., pl.* **-tos, -toes. 1.** any of the mackerellike fishes of the genus *Sarda,* as *S. sarda* of the Atlantic. **2.** any of several related species, as the **oceanic bonito** or skipjack, *Katsuwonus pelamis.* [t. Sp].

bon jour (bôn zhōōr'), *French.* good day; hello.

bon mot (bôn mō'), *pl.* **bons mots** (bôn mōz'; *Fr.* mō'), an especially fitting word or expression; a clever saying; witticism. [F: lit., good word]

Bonn (bŏn; *Ger.* bôn), *n.* a city in W Germany, on the Rhine: capital of Federal Republic of Germany; Beethoven's birthplace. 100,788 (1939).

bonne (bôn, bŭn), *n. French.* **1.** a maidservant. **2.** a child's nurse. [F, fem. of *bon* good. See BOON²]

bonne a·mi (bôn å mē'), *French.* fem. of **bon ami.**

bonne bouche (bôn bōōsh'), *French.* a tidbit.

bonne foi (bôn fwå'), *French.* good faith; sincerity.

bon·net (bŏn'ĭt), *n.* **1.** a woman's or child's outdoor head covering, commonly fitting down over the hair, and often tied on with strings. **2.** *Chiefly Scot.* a man's or boy's cap. **3.** a bonnetlike headdress. **4.** any of various hoods, covers, or protective devices. **5.** a cowl or wind cap for a chimney to stabilize the draft. **6.** *Brit.* an automobile hood. **7.** *Naut.* an additional piece of canvas laced to the foot (formerly the top) of a jib or other sail. —*v.t.* **8.** to put a bonnet on. [ME *bonet,* t. OF: cap (orig. its material); ? of Gmc. orig.] —**bon'net·like',** *adj.*

bon·net rouge (bô nĕ rōōzh'), *pl.* **bonnets rouges** (bô nĕ rōōzh'). *French.* **1.** a red liberty cap, worn by extremists at the time of the French Revolution. **2.** an extremist or radical. [F: red cap]

bon·ny (bŏn'ĭ), *adj.,* **-nier, -niest. 1.** pleasing to the eye; handsome; pretty. **2.** *Brit. Dial.* plump and

---

b., blend of, blended; *c.,* cognate with; *d.,* dialect, dialectal; *der.,* derived from; *f.,* formed from; *g.,* going back to; *m.,* modification of; *r.,* replacing; *s.,* stem of; *t.,* taken from; *?,* perhaps. See the full key on inside cover.

healthy. **3.** *Scot. and N. Eng.* fine (often used ironically). Also, **bon′nie.** [ME *bonie*. See BOON[2]] **—bon′ni·ly,** *adv.* **—bon′ni·ness,** *n.*

bon·ny·clab·ber (bŏn′Ĭ klăb′ər), *n.* sour, thick milk. [t. Irish: m. *bainne clabair*, lit., milk of the clabber (i.e.? the churn dasher)]

bon soir (bôn swȧr′), *French.* good evening; good night.

bon·spiel (bŏn′spēl, -spəl), *n. Scot.* a curling match between two clubs, parishes, etc. [orig. obscure]

bon·te·bok (bŏn′tĬ bŏk′), *n.* a large, red, South African antelope, *Damaliscus pygargus*, with a blaze on the face, now almost extinct. [t. S Afr. D: pied buck]

bon ton (bôn tôn′), good or elegant form or style; good breeding; fashionable society. [F: good tone]

bo·nus (bō′nəs), *n.* **1.** something given or paid over and above what is due. **2.** a sum of money paid to an employee, an agent of a company, a returned soldier, etc., over and above his regular pay. **3.** something free added in a corporate sale of securities. **4.** *Insurance.* dividend. **5.** a premium paid for a loan, contract, etc. **6.** something extra. [t. L: (adj.) good]

—Syn. 2. BONUS, BOUNTY, PREMIUM refer to something extra beyond a stipulated payment. A BONUS is a gift to reward performance, paid either by a private employer or by a government: *a bonus based on salary, the soldiers' bonus.* A BOUNTY is a public aid or reward offered to stimulate interest in a specific purpose or undertaking and to encourage performance: *a bounty for killing wolves.* A PREMIUM is usually something additional given as an inducement to buy, produce, or the like: *a premium with a magazine subscription.*

bon vi·vant (bôn vē vänʹ), *pl.* **bons vivants** (bôn vē vänʹ). *French.* **1.** a person who lives luxuriously, self-indulgently, etc. **2.** a jovial companion.

bon vo·yage (bôn vwȧ yazhʹ), *French.* pleasant trip.

bon·y (bō′nĬ), *adj.,* **bonier, boniest. 1.** of or like bone. **2.** full of bones. **3.** having prominent bones; big-boned. **—bon′i·ness,** *n.*

bonze (bŏnz), *n.* a Buddhist monk, esp. of Japan or China. [t. F, t. Pg.: m. *bonzo,* t. Jap.: m. *bonzō,* t. Chinese: m. *fan sung* ordinary (member) of the assembly]

boo (boo), *interj., n., pl.* **boos,** *v.,* **booed, booing. —interj. 1.** an exclamation used to express contempt, disapprobation, etc., or to frighten. **—n. 2.** this exclamation. **—v.i. 3.** to cry "boo." **—v.t. 4.** to cry "boo" at; show disapproval of by booing.

boob (boob), *n. U.S. Slang.* a fool; a dunce. [see BOOBY]

boo·by (boo′bĬ), *n., pl.* **-bies. 1.** a stupid person; a dunce. **2.** the worst student, player, etc., of a group. **3.** Also, **booby gannet.** any of various gannets, as the white-bellied booby (*Sula leucogaster*) of the Bahama Islands, etc. [prob. t. Sp.: m. *bobo* fool, also the bird booby, g. L *balbus* stammering] **—boo′by·ish,** *adj.*

booby hatch, 1. *Naut.* a wooden hood over a hatch. **2.** *U.S. Colloq.* insane asylum. **3.** *U.S. Slang.* jail.

booby prize, a prize given in good-natured ridicule to the worst player in a game or contest.

booby trap, a hidden bomb or mine so placed that it will be set off by an unsuspecting person through such means as moving an apparently harmless object.

boo·dle (boo′dəl), *n., v.,* **-dled, -dling,** *U.S. Slang.* **—n. 1.** (often in contemptuous use) the lot, pack, or crowd: *the whole boodle.* **2.** a bribe or other illicit gain in politics. **—v.i. 3.** to obtain money dishonestly, as by corrupt bargains. [t. D: m. *boedel, boel* stock, lot] **—boo′dler,** *n.*

boog·ie-woog·ie (bŏog′Ĭ wŏog′Ĭ), *Jazz.* a form of instrumental blues using melodic variations over a constantly repeated bass figure.

boo·hoo (boo′hoo′), *v.,* **-hooed, -hooing,** *n., pl.* **-hoos. —v.i. 1.** to weep noisily; blubber. **—n. 2.** the sound of noisy weeping. [imit.]

book (bŏok), *n.* **1.** a written or printed work of some length, as a treatise or other literary composition, esp. on consecutive sheets fastened or bound together. **2.** a number of sheets of writing paper bound together and used for making entries, as of commercial transactions. **3.** a division of a literary work, esp. one of the larger divisions. **4. the Book,** the Bible. **5.** *Music.* the text of an opera, operetta, etc. **6.** *Theat.* a play script. **7.** a record of bets, as on a horserace. **8.** *Cards.* the number of tricks or cards which must be taken before any trick counts in the score. In bridge it is six tricks. **9.** a set of tickets, checks, stamps, etc., bound together like a book. **10.** a pile or package of leaves, as of tobacco. **11.** anything that serves for the recording of facts or events: *the book of Nature.* **12. bring to book,** to bring to account. **13. by (the) book,** a. formally. b. authoritatively; correctly. **14. in one's books,** in one's favor. **15. on the books,** entered on the list of members. **16. without book,** a. by memory. b. without authority. **—v.t. 17.** to enter in a book or list; record; register. **18.** to engage (a place, passage, etc.) beforehand. **19.** to put down for a place, passage, etc. **20.** to engage (a person or company) for a performance or performances. **—v.i. 21.** to register one's name. **22.** to engage a place, services, etc. [ME; OE *bōc,* c. G *buch*] **—book′less,** *adj.*

book·bind·er (bŏok′bīn′dər), *n.* one whose business or work is the binding of books.

book·bind·er·y (bŏok′bīn′də rĬ), *n., pl.* **-eries.** an establishment for binding books.

book·bind·ing (bŏok′bīn′dĬng), *n.* the process or art of binding books.

book·case (bŏok′kās′), *n.* a set of shelves for books.

book club, 1. a club which lends or sells (usually at a discount) books to its members. **2.** a club organized for the discussion and reviewing of books.

book end, a support placed at the end of a row of books to hold them upright.

book·ie (bŏok′Ĭ), *n. Colloq.* bookmaker (def. 2).

book·ing (bŏok′Ĭng), *n.* an engagement to perform.

book·ish (bŏok′Ĭsh), *adj.* **1.** given to reading or study. **2.** more acquainted with books than with real life. **3.** of or pertaining to books; literary. **4.** stilted; pedantic. **—book′ish·ly,** *adv.* **—book′ish·ness,** *n.*

book jacket, a detachable paper cover, usually attractively illustrated, protecting the binding of a book.

book·keep·er (bŏok′kē′pər), *n.* one who keeps account books, as for a business house.

book·keep·ing (bŏok′kē′pĬng), *n.* the work or art of keeping account books or systematic records of money transactions.

book learning, knowledge gained by reading books, in distinction to that obtained through observation and experience. Also, **book knowledge, book·lore** (bŏok′lōr′). **—book-learn·ed** (bŏok′lûr′nĬd), *adj.*

book·let (bŏok′lĬt), *n.* a little book, esp. one with paper covers; pamphlet.

book louse, any insect of the order *Corrodentia,* which damages books by eating away the glue, and is injurious to other products in houses, granaries, etc.

book·mak·er (bŏok′mā′kər), *n.* **1.** a maker of books. **2.** a professional betting man who accepts the bets of others, as on horses in racing.

book·man (bŏok′mən), *n., pl.* **-men. 1.** a studious or learned man; a scholar. **2.** *Colloq.* a person whose occupation is selling or publishing books.

book·mark (bŏok′märk′), *n.* **1.** a ribbon or the like placed between the pages of a book to mark a place. **2.** a bookplate.

book·mo·bile (bŏok′mə bēl′), *n. U.S.* an automobile or small truck constructed to carry books, serving as a traveling library as for small communities in which libraries are not accessible.

book of account, *Com.* **1.** (*pl.*) the original records and books used in recording business transactions. **2.** an original entry or other account book.

Book of Common Prayer, the service book of the Church of England, essentially adopted but changed in details by other churches of the Anglican communion.

Book of Mormon. See MORMON (def. 2).

book·plate (bŏok′plāt′), *n.* a label, bearing the owner's name, a design, etc., for pasting in a book.

book·rack (bŏok′răk′), *n.* **1.** a rack for supporting an open book. **2.** a rack for holding books.

book review, critical discussion of a book, esp. of a newly published book. **—book reviewer. —book reviewing.**

book scorpion, any of the minute arachnids, superficially resembling a tailess scorpion, which constitute the order *Chelonethi* (*Pseudoscorpionida*), as *Chelifer cancroides,* found in old books, etc.

book·sell·er (bŏok′sĕl′ər), *n.* a person whose occupation or business is selling books.

book·stack (bŏok′stăk′), *n.* a set of bookshelves one above another, as in a library; a stack.

book·stall (bŏok′stôl′), *n.* **1.** a stall at which books (usually secondhand) are sold. **2.** *Brit.* a newsstand.

book·stand (bŏok′stănd′), *n.* **1.** bookrack. **2.** bookstall.

book·store (bŏok′stōr′), *n. U.S.* a store where books are sold. Also, *orig. Brit.,* **book·shop** (bŏok′shŏp′).

book·worm (bŏok′wûrm′), *n.* **1.** any of various insects that feed on books. **2.** a person closely addicted to reading or study.

boom[1] (boom), *v.i.* **1.** to make a deep, prolonged, resonant sound; make a rumbling, humming, or dr ning noise. **2.** to move with a resounding rush or great impetus. **3.** to progress or flourish vigorously, as a business, a city, etc. **—v.t. 4.** to give forth with a booming sound (usually fol. by *out*): *the clock boomed out twelve.* **5.** to push (a cause, a new product, etc.) vigorously. **—n. 6.** a deep, hollow, continued sound. **7.** a roaring, rumbling, or reverberation, as of waves or distant guns. **8.** the cry of the bittern. **9.** a buzzing, humming, or droning, as of a bee or beetle. **10.** a rapid increase in price, development, numbers, etc. **11.** a rise in popularity, as of a political candidate, or efforts to bring it about. **—adj. 12.** *U.S.* caused by a boom: *boom prices.* [imit. Cf. ZOOM]

boom[2] (boom), *n.* **1.** *Naut.* a long pole or spar used to extend the foot of certain sails. **2.** a chain or cable or a series of connected floating timbers, etc., serving to obstruct navigation, to confine floating timber, etc. **3.** the area thus shut off. **4.** *Mach.* a spar or beam projecting from the mast of a derrick, supporting or guiding the weights to be lifted. [t. D: tree, beam. See BEAM]

B, Boom; G, Gaff

boom-and-bust (boom′ən bŭst′), *n. Colloq.* a period of abnormal economic prosperity followed by a severe depression.

boom·er·ang (bōō/mə răng/), *n.* **1.** a bent or curved piece of hard wood used as a missile by the native Australians, one form of which can be so thrown as to return to the thrower. **2.** a scheme, plan, argument, etc., which recoils upon the user. —*v.i.* **3.** (of a scheme, etc.) to cause unexpected harm to the originator. [t. native d.]

Boomerangs

Boom·er State (bōō/mər), Oklahoma.

boon[1] (bōōn), *n.* **1.** a benefit enjoyed; a thing to be thankful for; a blessing. **2.** *Archaic.* that which is asked; a favor sought. [ME, t. Scand.; cf. Icel. *bōn* request, petition]

boon[2] (bōōn), *adj.* **1.** jolly; jovial; convivial: *boon companion.* **2.** *Poetic.* kindly; gracious; bounteous. [ME, t. OF: m. *bon,* g. L *bonus* good]

boon·dog·gle (bōōn/dŏg/əl), *n., v.,* **-gled, -gling.** *U.S.* —*n.* **1.** a belt, knife sheath, ax handle, or other product of simple manual skill. **2.** a cord of plaited leather worn round the neck by Boy Scouts. **3.** *Slang.* work of little or no practical value. —*v.i.* **4.** *Slang.* to do work of little or no practical value. —**boon/dog/gler,** *n.* —**boon/-dog/gling,** *n.*

Boone (bōōn), *n.* **Daniel,** 1735–1820, American pioneer, esp. in Kentucky.

boor (bōōr), *n.* **1.** a clownish, rude, or unmannerly person. **2.** a peasant; a rustic. **3.** an illiterate or clownish peasant. **4.** a Dutch or German peasant. **5.** any foreign peasant. **6.** (*cap.*) a Dutch colonist. [t. D: m. *boer* peasant, or t. LG: m. *būr* peasant]

boor·ish (bōōr/ĭsh), *adj.* of or like a boor; rustic; rude. —**boor/ish·ly,** *adv.* —**boor/ish·ness,** *n.*

boost (bōōst), *U.S.* —*v.t.* **1.** to lift or raise by pushing from behind or below. **2.** to advance or aid by speaking well of. **3.** to increase; push up: *to boost prices.* —*n.* **4.** an upward shove or push. **5.** an aid that helps one to rise in the world. [b. BOOM and HOIST]

boost·er (bōō/stər), *n. U.S.* **1.** one that boosts. **2.** *Elect.* a device connected in series with a current for increasing or decreasing the nominal circuit voltage.

boot[1] (bōōt), *n.* **1.** a covering, usually of leather, for the foot and leg, reaching at least to the middle of the calf, and often to the knee or higher. **2.** *Brit.* any shoe or outer foot covering reaching above the ankle. **3.** an instrument of torture for the leg. **4.** any sheathlike protective covering: *a boot for a weak automobile tire.* **5.** a protective covering for the foot and part of the leg of a horse. **6.** a protecting apron or cover for the driver's seat of a vehicle. **7.** *Chiefly Brit.* a receptacle or place for baggage at either end of a vehicle. **8.** *Music.* the box in the reed pipe of an organ which holds the reed. **9.** a kick. **10.** *Slang.* a dismissal; discharge. **11. lick the boots of,** to be subservient to; flatter. —*v.t.* **12.** to put boots on. **13.** to torture with the boot. **14.** *Slang.* to kick; drive or compel by kicking. **15.** *Football.* to kick; punt. **16.** *Slang.* to dismiss; discharge. **17.** *Sports.* to fumble (the ball). [ME *bote,* t. OF; of Gmc. orig. See SABOT]

boot[2] (bōōt), *n.* **1. to boot,** into the bargain; in addition. **2.** *Archaic* or *Dial.* something given into the bargain; an additional consideration. **3.** *Obs.* profit; advantage. **4.** *Obs.* relief; remedy. —*v.i.* **5.** *Obs.* or *Poetic.* to be of profit, advantage, or avail: *it boots not to complain.* —*v.t.* **6.** *Obs.* to enrich; benefit. [ME *bote,* OE *bōt* advantage]

boot[3] (bōōt), *n. Archaic.* booty; spoil; plunder. [special use of BOOT[2] by assoc. with BOOTY]

boot·black (bōōt/blăk/), *n.* a person whose occupation it is to shine shoes, boots, etc.

boot·ed (bōō/tĭd), *adj.* **1.** equipped with boots. **2.** *Ornith.* (of the tarsus of certain birds) covered with a continuous horny, bootlike sheath.

boot·ee (bōō tē/; or esp. for 1 bōō/tĭ), *n.* **1.** a baby's knitted shoe. **2.** a kind of half boot for women.

Bo·ö·tes (bō ō/tēz), *n.* a northern constellation containing the first magnitude star Arcturus. [t. L, t. Gk.: oxdriver]

booth (bōōth, bōō̵th), *n., pl.* **booths** (bōō̵thz). **1.** a temporary structure of boughs, canvas, boards, etc., as for shelter. **2.** a stall or light structure for the sale of goods or for display purposes, as at a market or fair. **3.** a small compartment for a telephone, motion picture projector, etc. **4.** a small temporary structure used by voters at elections. [ME *bōthe,* t. Scand.; cf. Dan. *bod*]

Booth (bōōth; *Brit.* bōō̵th), *n.* **1. Ballington,** 1859–1940, founder of the Volunteers of America (son of William). **2. Edwin Thomas,** 1833–93, U. S. actor (brother of John Wilkes). **3. Evangeline Cory,** 1865?–1950, general of the Salvation Army, 1934–39 (daughter of William). **4. John Wilkes,** 1838–65, U.S. actor: assassin of Abraham Lincoln (brother of Edwin T.). **5. Junius Brutus,** 1796–1852, British actor in England and America (father of Edwin and John). **6. William,** 1829–1912, British preacher: founder of the Salvation Army. **7. William Bramwell,** 1856–1929, general of the Salvation Army (son of William).

Boo·thi·a (bōō/thĭ ə), *n.* **1.** an arctic peninsula in N Canada: the northernmost part of the mainland of North America; location of the north magnetic pole. **2. Gulf of,** a gulf between this peninsula and Baffin Island.

boot·jack (bōōt/jăk/), *n.* a device used to hold a boot while the foot is drawn out of it.

Boo·tle (bōō/təl), *n.* a seaport in W England, on the Mersey estuary near Liverpool. 65,590 (est. 1946).

boot·leg (bōōt/lĕg/), *n., v.,* **-legged, -legging,** *adj. U.S.* —*n.* **1.** alcoholic liquor secretly and unlawfully made, sold, or transported. **2.** that part of a boot which covers the leg. —*v.t.* **3.** to deal in (liquor or other goods) illicitly. —*v.i.* **4.** to carry goods, as liquor, about secretly for illicit sale. —*adj.* **5.** made, sold, or transported unlawfully. **6.** unlawful; clandestine. **7.** of or pertaining to bootlegging. [def. 2 orig. meaning; others arose from the practice of concealing illegal liquor in the bootleg] —**boot/leg/ger,** *n.*

boot·less (bōōt/lĭs), *adj.* without advantage; unavailing; useless. [OE *bōtlēas* unpardonable, f. *bōt* BOOT[2] + *-lēas* -LESS] —**boot/less·ly,** *adv.* —**boot/less·ness,** *n.*

boot·lick (bōōt/lĭk/), *U.S. Slang.* —*v.t.* **1.** to curry favor with; toady to (a person). —*v.i.* **2.** to be a toady. —**boot/lick/er,** *n.* —**boot/lick/ing,** *n., adj.*

boots (bōōts), *n., pl.* **boots.** *Brit.* a servant, as at a hotel, who blacks or polishes shoes, etc.

boots and saddles, *U.S. Army.* a cavalry bugle call for mounted formation.

boot tree, an instrument inserted into a boot or shoe to stretch it or preserve its shape.

boo·ty (bōō/tĭ), *n., pl.* **-ties.** **1.** spoil taken from an enemy in war; plunder; pillage. **2.** that which is seized by violence and robbery. **3.** a prize or gain, without reference to use of force. [late ME *boyte;* cf. G *beute*]

booze (bōōz), *n., v.,* **boozed, boozing.** *Colloq.* —*n.* **1.** alcoholic liquor. **2.** a drinking bout; spree. —*v.i., v.t.* **3.** to drink immoderately. [var. of BOUSE[2]] —**booz/er,** *n.*

booz·y (bōō/zĭ), *adj.,* **boozier, booziest.** *Colloq.* **1.** drunken. **2.** addicted to liquor. —**booz/i·ness,** *n.*

bop (bŏp), *n.* bebop.

bor., **1.** borough. **2.** boron.

bo·ra (bōr/ə), *n. Meteorol.* a violent, dry, cold wind on the coasts of the Adriatic, blowing from the north or northeast. [t. d. It., g. L *boreas* north wind]

bo·rac·ic (bə răs/ĭk, bō-), *adj. Chem.* boric.

bo·ra·cite (bōr/ə sīt/), *n.* a mineral, a borate and chloride of magnesium, $Mg_6Cl_2B_{14}O_{26}$, occurring in white or colorless crystals or fine-grained masses, strongly pyroelectric.

bor·age (bûr/ĭj, bôr/-, bŏr/-), *n.* **1.** a plant, *Borago officinalis,* native of southern Europe, with hairy leaves and stems, used in salads and medicinally. **2.** any of various allied or similar plants. [ME, t. AF: m. *burage,* var. of OF *bourrace,* der. *bourrer* stuff, ult. der. ML *burra* wool]

bo·rag·i·na·ceous (bə răj/ə nā/shəs, bō-), *adj.* belonging to the *Boraginaceae,* or borage family of plants, including borage, bugloss, heliotrope, forget-me-not, etc.

Bo·rah (bōr/ə), *n.* **William Edgar,** 1865–1940, U. S. senator from Idaho, 1906–40.

bo·rate (*n.* bōr/āt, -ĭt; *v.* bōr/āt), *n., v.,* **-rated, -rating.** *Chem.* —*n.* **1.** a salt of orthoboric acid. **2.** (loosely) a salt of any boric acid. —*v.t.* **3.** to treat with borate, boric acid, or borax.

bo·rax (bōr/əks, -ăks), *n.* a white, crystalline sodium borate, $Na_2B_4O_7.10H_2O$, occurring native or prepared artificially and used as a flux, cleansing agent, in the manufacture of glass, etc. [t. ML, t. Ar.: m. *buwraq,* t. Pers.: m. *bōrah* (OPers. *bōrak*); r. ME *boras,* t. OF]

Bor·deaux (bôr dō/), *n.* **1.** a seaport in SW France, on the Garonne river. 253,751 (1946). **2.** wine produced in the region surrounding Bordeaux. Red Bordeaux wines are called *clarets.* White Bordeaux wines include *sauternes* (sweet) and *graves* (dry). **3.** Bordeaux mixture.

Bordeaux mixture, *Hort.* a fungicide consisting of a mixture of copper sulfate, lime, and water.

bor·der (bôr/dər), *n.* **1.** a side, edge, or margin. **2.** the line that separates one country, state, or province from another; frontier line. **3.** the district or region that lies along the boundary line of a country. **4.** *U.S.* the frontier of civilization. **5. the Border,** the region along the boundary between England and Scotland. **6.** brink; verge. **7.** an ornamental strip or design around the edge of a printed page, a drawing, etc. **8.** a piece of ornamental trimming around the edge of a garment, cap, etc. **9.** *Hort.* a narrow strip of ground in a garden, enclosing a portion of it. —*v.t.* **10.** to make a border about; adorn with a border. **11.** to form a border or boundary to. **12.** to lie on the border of; adjoin. —*v.i.* **13. border on** or **upon, a.** to touch or abut at the border. **b.** to approach closely in character; verge. [ME *bordure,* t. OF, der. *bord* side, edge; of Gmc. orig. See BOARD] —**bor/dered,** *adj.* —**bor/der·less,** *adj.* —**Syn. 1.** See **edge.** **12.** See **adjoining.**

bor·der·er (bôr/dər ər), *n.* **1.** one who dwells on or near the border of a country, region, etc. **2.** one who makes borders.

bor·der·land (bôr/dər lănd/), *n.* **1.** land forming a border or frontier. **2.** an uncertain intermediate district, space, or condition.

border line, boundary line; frontier.

bor·der·line (bôr/dər līn/), *adj.* **1.** on or near a border or boundary. **2.** uncertain; indeterminate; debatable.

Border States, 1. *U.S. Hist.* the slave States inclined to compromise instead of seceding: Delaware, Maryland, Virginia, Kentucky, Missouri; sometimes extended to include North Carolina, Tennessee, and Arkansas. **2.** *U.S.* the States touching the Canadian border.

3. certain of the countries of central and northern Europe, bordering on the Soviet Union and formerly belonging to the Russian Empire: Finland, Poland (prior to 1940), Estonia, Latvia and Lithuania.

bor·dure (bôr′jər), *n.* *Her.* the outer fifth of the shield. [ME, t. OF. See BORDER]

bore[1] (bôr), *v.*, **bored**, **boring**, *n.* —*v.t.* **1.** *Mach.* to pierce (a solid substance) or make (a round hole, etc.) with an auger, drill, or other rotated instrument. **2.** to force by persistent forward thrusting. —*v.i.* **3.** *Mach.* to make a hole, as with an auger or drill. **4.** to admit of being pierced with an auger or the like, as a substance. —*n. Mach.* **5.** a hole made by boring, or as if by boring. **6.** the inside diameter of a hollow cylindrical object or device, such as a bushing or bearing, or the barrel of a gun. [ME *boren*, OE *borian*, c. G *bohren*; akin to L *forāre* pierce] —Syn. 1. perforate.

bore[2] (bôr), *v.*, **bored**, **boring**, *n.* —*v.t.* **1.** to weary by tedious repetition, by dullness, by unwelcome attentions, etc. —*n.* **2.** a dull, tiresome, or uncongenial person. **3.** a cause of ennui or annoyance. [orig. unknown]

bore[3] (bôr), *n.* *Oceanog.* an abrupt rise of the tide which breaks in an estuary, rushing violently up the channel. [ME, t. Scand.; cf. Icel. *bāra* wave]

bore[4] (bôr), *v.* pt. of **bear**[1].

bo·re·al (bôr′ēəl), *adj.* **1.** pertaining to the north wind. **2.** northern. **3.** pertaining to Boreas. [t. L: s. *boreālis*, der. *Boreas* north wind]

Bo·re·as (bôr′ēəs), *n.* the north wind, as personified or deified by the Greeks.

bore·dom (bôr′dəm), *n.* bored state; tedium; ennui.

bor·er (bôr′ər), *n.* **1.** one that bores or pierces. **2.** *Mach.* a tool used for boring; an auger. **3.** *Entomol.* any insect that burrows in trees, fruits. etc., esp. any beetle of certain groups. **4.** *Zool.* any of various mollusks, etc., that bore into wood, etc. **5.** a marsipobranch fish, as a hagfish, that bores into other fish to feed on their flesh.

bore·some (bôr′səm), *adj.* tedious and uninteresting; dull; boring.

Bor·ger·hout (bôr′кнərhout′), *n.* a city in N Belgium, near Antwerp. 52,320 (est. 1941).

Bor·ghe·se (bôrgĕ′sĕ), *n.* a noble Italian family, orig. from the republic of Siena, important in Italian society and politics from the 16th to the early 19th century.

Bor·gia (bôr′jä), *n.* **1.** **Cesare** (chĕ′zärĕ), 1476–1507, Italian cardinal, military leader, and politician. **2.** **Lucrezia** (lŏŏ krĕ′tsyä), 1480–1519, sister and the political tool of Cesare; patroness of culture; Duchess of Ferrara. **3.** **Rodrigo Lanzol** (rô drē′gō län zôl′), 1431–1503, Italian cardinal: became Pope Alexander VI (father of Cesare and Lucrezia Borgia).

Bor·glum (bôr′gləm), *n.* **(John) Gutzon** (gŭt′sən), 1867–1941, U. S. sculptor and painter.

bo·ric (bôr′ĭk), *adj.* *Chem.* of or containing boron; boracic.

boric acid, **1.** *Chem.*, *Pharm.* a white crystalline acid, H_3BO_3, occurring in nature or prepared from borax, used in aqueous solution as a mild antiseptic. **2.** *Chem.* any of a group of acids containing boron.

bo·ride (bôr′īd), *n.* *Chem.* a compound usually containing two elements only, of which boron is the more electropositive one.

bor·ing (bôr′ĭng), *n.* *Mach.* **1.** act or process of piercing or perforating. **2.** the hole so made. **3.** (*pl.*) the chips, fragments, or dust produced in boring.

Bo·ris III (bôr′ĭs), 1894–1943, king of Bulgaria, 1918–1943.

born (bôrn), *adj.* **1.** brought forth by birth. **2.** possessing from birth the quality or character stated: *a born fool.* [prop. pp. of BEAR[1]; ME and OE *boren*]

borne (bôrn), *v.* **1.** pp. of **bear** in all meanings except in the sense "brought forth" where *born* is now used, except after *have* or when followed by *by: the child was born, she has borne a child.* **2.** p.a. of **bear**.

Bor·ne·o (bôr′nĭ ō′), *n.* an island in the Malay Archipelago, including the British controlled territories of British North Borneo, Brunei, and Sarawak, and (formerly) Dutch Borneo. ab. 3,000,000 pop. ab. 290,000 sq. mi.

bor·ne·ol (bôr′nĭ ōl′, -ōl′), *n.* *Chem. Bot.* terpene alcohol, $C_{10}H_{17}OH$, closely resembling common camphor, found in concrete masses in the trunk of *Dryobalanops aromatica*, a large tree of Borneo, Sumatra, etc. [f. BORNEO + -OL[1]]

Born·holm (bôrn′hōlm), *n.* a Danish island in the Baltic, S of Sweden. 46,416 pop. (1940); 227 sq. mi.

born·ite (bôr′nīt), *n.* a common mineral, copper iron sulfide, Cu_5FeS_4, occurring in masses of brownish color on fresh surfaces: an important ore of copper. [named after I. von *Born* (1742–91), Austrian mineralogist. See -ITE[1]]

Bor·nu (bôr nōō′), *n.* a former sultanate in W Africa, S and W of Lake Chad: now largely a province in Nigeria. ab. 50,000 sq. mi.

Bo·ro·din (bŏ′rŏ dēn′), *n.* **Aleksandr Porfirevich** (ă′lĕ ksän′dər pŏr fĭr′yĕ′vĭch), 1834–87, Russian composer.

Bo·ro·di·no (bŏ′rŏ dĭ′nô′), *n.* a village in the W Soviet Union, 70 mi. W of Moscow: Napoleon's victory here made possible the capture of Moscow, 1812.

bo·ron (bôr′ŏn), *n.* *Chem.* a nonmetallic element present in borax, etc., and obtained in either an amorphous or a crystalline form when reduced from its compounds. *Symbol:* B; *at. wt.:* 10.82; *at. no.:* 5. [b. BORAX and CARBON]

bo·ro·sil·i·cate (bôr′ō sĭl′ə kĭt, -kāt′), *n.* *Chem.* a salt of boric and silicic acids.

bo·ro·si·lic·ic acids (bôr′ō sə lĭs′ĭk), *Chem.* hypothetical acids yielding borosilicate.

bor·ough (bûr′ō), *n.* **1.** (in certain States of the U.S.) an incorporated municipality smaller than a city. **2.** one of the five administrative divisions of Greater New York. **3.** *Brit.* **a.** an urban community incorporated by royal charter, equivalent in general to *city* in U. S. **b.** an urban election constituency, usually subdivided. **c.** (formerly) a fortified town, or a town possessing municipal organization. [ME *burgh* town, OE *burg* stronghold, c. G *burg*]

bor·ough-Eng·lish (bûr′ō ĭng′glĭsh), *n.* *Law.* a customary system of inheritance in parts of England which gave the entire estate to the youngest son.

bor·row (bŏr′ō, bôr′ō), *v.t.* **1.** to take or obtain (a thing) on the promise to return it or its equivalent; obtain the temporary use of. **2.** to get from another or from a foreign source; appropriate or adopt: *borrowed words.* **3.** *Arith.* (in subtraction) to take from one denomination to add to the next lower. —*v.i.* **4.** to borrow something. [ME *borowe(n)*, OE *borgian*, der. *borg* a pledge] —**bor′row·er**, *n.*

Bor·row (bŏr′ō, bôr′ō), *n.* **George**, 1803–81, British traveler, writer, and student of languages, esp. Romany.

Bors (bôrs), *n.* **Sir,** *Arthurian Legend.* **1.** Also, **Sir Bors de Ganis.** a knight of the Round Table, nephew of Lancelot. **2.** a natural son of King Arthur.

borsch (bôrsh), *n.* a Russian stock soup containing beets, served hot or chilled. Also, **borscht** (bôrsht).

bort (bôrt), *n.* flawed, low quality diamonds, and diamond fragments, valuable only for crushing to diamond dust. [cf. OF *bort* bastard] —**bort′y**, *adj.*

bor·zoi (bôr′zoi), *n.*, *pl.* **-zois.** a Russian wolfhound.

Bo·san·quet (bō′zən kĕt′, -kĭt′), *n.* **Bernard,** 1848–1923, British philosopher and writer.

bos·cage (bŏs′kĭj), *n.* a mass of growing trees or shrubs; woods, groves, or thickets. Also, **bos′kage.** [ME, t. OF, der. *bosc*, t. Gmc. See BOSK]

bosch·bok (bŏsh′bŏk′), *n.* bushbuck. [t. S Afr. D: f. *bosch* wood + *bok* buck]

bosch·vark (bŏsh′värk′), *n.* bush pig. [t. S Afr. D: wood pig]

Bose (bōs), *n.* **Sir Jagadis Chandra** (jə gə dēs′ chŭn′dra), 1858–1937, Indian physicist and plant physiologist.

bosh[1] (bŏsh), *n.* *Colloq.* complete nonsense; absurd or foolish talk or opinions. [t. Turk.: empty, vain]

bosh[2] (bŏsh), *n.* the lower portion of a blast furnace, extending from the widest part to the hearth. [cf. G *böschung* slope]

bosk (bŏsk), *n.* *Archaic or Poetic.* a thicket; a small wood, esp. of bushes. [ME, var. of *busk*, var. of BUSH[1]]

bos·ket (bŏs′kĭt), *n.* a grove; a thicket. Also, **bosquet.** [t. F: m. *bosquet*, t. It.: m. *boschetto*, dim. of *bosco* wood. See BUSH[1]]

bosk·y (bŏs′kĭ), *adj.* **1.** woody; covered with bushes. **2.** shady. —**bosk′i·ness**, *n.*

bo's'n (bō′sən), *n.* *Naut.* boatswain.

Bos·ni·a (bŏz′nĭ ə), *n.* a former Turkish province in S Europe: a part of Austria, 1878–1918; now a part of Bosnia and Herzegovina. See map under **Austria-Hungary.** —**Bos′ni·an**, *adj.*, *n.*

Bosnia and Her·ze·go·vi·na (hĕr′tsə gō vē′nə), a constituent republic of Yugoslavia, in the W part. 2,324,000 pop. (1931); 19,909 sq. mi. *Cap.:* Sarajevo.

bos·om (bŏŏz′əm, bōō′zəm), *n.* **1.** the breast of a human being. **2.** that part of a garment which covers the breast. **3.** the breast, conceived of as the seat of thought or emotion. **4.** the enclosure formed by the breast and the arms; affectionate embrace. **5.** something likened to the human bosom: *the bosom of the earth.* —*adj.* **6.** of or pertaining to the bosom. **7.** intimate or confidential: *a bosom friend.* —*v.t.* **8.** to take to the bosom; embrace; cherish. **9.** to hide from view; conceal. [ME; OE *bōsm*, c. G *busen*]

Bos·po·rus (bŏs′pərəs), *n.* a strait connecting the Black Sea and the Sea of Marmara. 18 mi. long.

bos·quet (bŏs′kĭt), *n.* bosket.

boss[1] (bôs, bŏs), *n.* **1.** *Chiefly U.S. Colloq.* one who employs or superintends workmen; a foreman or manager. **2.** *U.S.* a politician who controls his party organization, as in a particular district. —*v.t.* **3.** to be master of or over; manage; direct; control. —*v.i.* **4.** to be boss. **5.** to be too domineering and authoritative. —*adj.* **6.** chief; master. **7.** *Slang.* first-rate. [t. D: m. *baas* master]

boss[2] (bôs, bŏs), *n.* **1.** *Bot.*, *Zool.* a protuberance or roundish excrescence on the body or on some organ of an animal or plant. **2.** *Geol.* a knoblike mass of rock, esp. such an outcrop of eruptive rock. **3.** an ornamental protuberance of metal, ivory, etc. **4.** *Archit.* a knoblike projection of ornamental character, as at the intersection of ribs or groins. **5.** *Mach.* the enlarged part of a

ăct, āble, dâre, ärt; ĕbb, ēqual; ĭf, īce; hŏt, ōver, ôrder, oil, bŏŏk, ōōze, out; ŭp, ūse, ûrge; ə = a in alone; ch, **chief**; g, give; ng, ring; sh, shoe; th, thin; ŧh, that; zh, vision. See the full key on inside cover.

shaft. —*v.t.* **6.** to ornament with bosses. **7.** to emboss[1]. [ME *bos*, t. OF: m. *boce*. See BOTCH[2]]

boss[3] (bôs, bŏs), *n.* *U.S.* a name for a cow. [cf. L *bŏs* ox]

boss·ism (bôs′Yz əm, bŏs′Yz-), *n.* *U.S.* control by bosses, esp. political bosses.

Bos·suet (bô swĕ′), *n.* **Jacques Bénigne** (zhăk bĕ-nēn′y), 1627–1704, French bishop and writer.

boss·y[1] (bôs′Y, bŏs′Y), *adj.*, **bossier, bossiest.** *Colloq.* given to acting like a boss; domineering. [f. BOSS[1] + -Y[1]]

boss·y[2] (bôs′Y, bŏs′Y), *adj.* studded with bosses; projecting as decorative work. [f. BOSS[2] + -Y[1]]

boss·y[3] (bôs′Y, bŏs′Y), *n.*, *pl.* **-sies.** *U.S.* a familiar name for a cow or calf. [f. BOSS[3] + -Y[2]]

Bos·ton (bôs′tən, bŏs′tən), *n.* **1.** the capital of Massachusetts, in the E part: the largest city and seaport in New England. 801,444; with suburbs, 2,354,507 (1950). **2.** (*l.c.*) a game of cards, played by four persons with two packs of cards. **3.** (*l.c.*) a social dance, a modification of the waltz. —**Bos·to·ni·an** (bôs tō′nY ən, bŏs tō′-), *adj.*, *n.*

Boston brown bread, a dark-brown steamed bread made of corn meal and rye meal (or Graham or wheat flour), sweetened with molasses.

Boston ivy, *Hort.* Japanese ivy.

Boston Massacre, *U.S. Hist.* a riot on March 5, 1770, arising from the resentment of Boston citizens against British troops quartered in the city.

Boston rocker, a wooden American rocking chair having curved seat, spindle back, and headpiece usually stenciled with gilt design.

Boston Tea Party, *U.S. Hist.* a raid on British ships in Boston Harbor on Dec. 16, 1773, in which colonists of Boston, disguised as Indians, threw tea into the harbor as a protest against British taxes on the commodity.

Boston terrier, any of a breed of small, smooth-coated dogs with short hair and brindle or dark-brown coat with white markings, originated in the U. S. by crossing the English bulldog and the bull terrier. Also, **Boston bull.**

bo·sun (bō′sən), *n.* *Naut.* boatswain.

Bos·well (bŏz′wĕl, -wəl), *n.* **1. James,** 1740–95, Scottish author: biographer of Samuel Johnson. **2.** any devoted biographer.

Boston terrier (12 to 16 in. high)

Bos·worth Field (bŏz′wûrth, -wərth), a battlefield in central England, near Leicester, where Richard III was defeated and slain by the future Henry VII (the first Tudor ruler of England) in 1485.

bot (bŏt), *n.* an insect larva infesting the skin, sinuses, nose, eye, stomach, or other parts of animals or man. Also, **bott.** See **botfly.** [orig. uncert.]

bot., **1.** botanical. **2.** botanist. **3.** botany

bo·tan·i·cal (bə tăn′ə kəl), *adj.* Also, **bo·tan·ic. 1.** pertaining to plants: *botanical survey, botanical drugs.* —*n.* **2.** *Pharm.* a drug made from part of a plant, as from roots, leaves, bark, etc. [f. ML *botanicus* (t. Gk.: m. *botanikós*) + -AL[1]] —**bo·tan′i·cal·ly,** *adv.*

bot·a·nist (bŏt′ə nYst), *n.* one who is skilled in botany.

bot·a·nize (bŏt′ə nīz′), *v.*, **-nized, -nizing.** —*v.i.* **1.** to study plants botanically. **2.** to collect plants for botanical study. —*v.t.* **3.** to explore botanically. —**bot′a·niz′er,** *n.*

bot·a·ny (bŏt′ə nY), *n.*, *pl.* **-nies. 1.** the science of plants; branch of biology that deals with plant life. **2.** the plant life of a region: *the botany of Cuba.* **3.** the biology of a plant or plant group: *the botany of deciduous trees.* [f. *botan(ic)* (see BOTANICAL) + -Y[3]]

Botany Bay, 1. a bay on the SE coast of Australia, near Sydney: former British penal colony. **2.** any place of detention or punishment.

botch[1] (bŏch), *v.t.* **1.** to spoil by poor work; bungle. **2.** to do or say in a bungling manner. **3.** to mend or patch in a clumsy manner. —*n.* **4.** a clumsy, poor piece of work; a bungle: *his baking was a complete botch.* **5.** a clumsily added part or patch. [ME *bocchen*; orig. uncert.] —**botch′er,** *n.* —**botch′er·y,** *n.*

botch[2] (bŏch), *n.* *Archaic or Dial.* a swelling on the skin; a boil; an eruptive disease. [ME *boche*, t. ONF, var. of *boce* ulcer]

botch·y (bŏch′Y), *adj.*, **botchier, botchiest,** poorly made or done; bungled.

bot·fly (bŏt′flī′), *n.*, *pl.* **-flies.** *Parasitol.* any of various dipterous insects of the families *Oestridae* and *Gastrophilidae,* the larvae of which are parasitic in the skin or other parts of animals or man. [see BOT]

both (bōth), *adj.*, *pron.* **1.** the one and the other; the two together: *give both dates, both had been there.* —*conj.* **2.** alike; equally: *both men and women, he is both ready and willing.* [ME *bothe, bathe,* t Scand.; cf. Icel. *bāaïir,* c. G *beide*]

Bo·tha (bō′tə), *n.* **Louis** (lŏō ē′), 1863–1919, South African general and statesman.

both·er (bŏth′ər), *v.t.* **1.** to give trouble to; annoy; pester; worry. **2.** to bewilder; confuse. —*v.i.* **3.** to trouble oneself. **4.** to cause annoyance or trouble. —*n.* **5.** something bothersome. **6.** an annoying disturbance. **7.** worried or perplexed state. **8.** someone who bothers. —*interj.* **9.** *Chiefly Brit.* a mild exclamation. [orig. unknown]

—**Syn. 1.** BOTHER, ANNOY, PLAGUE, TEASE imply persistent interference with one's comfort or peace of mind. BOTHER

suggests causing trouble or weariness or repeatedly interrupting in the midst of pressing duties. To ANNOY is to vex or irritate by bothering. PLAGUE is a strong word, connoting unremitting annoyance and harassment. To TEASE is to pester, as by long-continued whining and begging.

both·er·a·tion (bŏth′ə rā′shən), *interj.* **1.** an exclamation indicating vexation or annoyance. —*n.* **2.** act of bothering. **3.** state of being bothered.

both·er·some (bŏth′ər səm), *adj.* troublesome.

Both·ni·a (bŏth′nY ə), *n.* **Gulf of,** an arm of the Baltic, extending N between Sweden and Finland. ab. 400 mi. long.

Both·well (bŏth′wĕl, -wəl, bŏth′-), *n.* **James Hepburn, Earl of,** 1536?–78, third husband of Mary, Queen of Scots.

both·y (bŏth′Y, bŏth′Y), *n.*, *pl.* **bothies.** *Scot.* a hut or small cottage, esp. for lodging farm hands or workmen. [? der. BOOTH]

bo tree (bō), the pipal or sacred fig tree, *Ficus religiosa,* of India, under which the founder of Buddhism is reputed to have attained the enlightenment which constituted him the Buddha. [*bo,* t. Sinhalese, t. Pali: m. *bodhi-(taru)* perfect knowledge (tree)]

bot·ry·oi·dal (bŏt′rY oi′dəl), *adj.* having the form of a bunch of grapes. Also, **bot′ry·oid′.** [f. m. s. Gk. *botryoeidēs* + -AL[1]] —**bot′ry·oi′dal·ly,** *adv.*

bot·ry·o·my·co·sis (bŏt′rY ō mī kō′sYs), *n.* a disease of horses, usually following castration, in which there is tumefaction of the stump of the spermatic cord.

bot·ry·ose (bŏt′rY ōs′), *adj.* **1.** botryoidal. **2.** racemose.

bots (bŏts), *n. pl.* a disease caused by the attachment of the larvae of botflies to the stomach of a horse.

Bot·sa·res (bŏt′sä rēs′), *n.* **Markos** (mär′kôs). See **Bozzaris,** Marco.

bott (bŏt), *n.* *Parasitol.* bot.

Bot·ti·cel·li (bŏt′ə chĕl′Y; *It.* bôt′tē chĕl′lē), *n.* **Sandro** (sän′drō), (*Alessandro di Mariano dei Filipepi*) 1447–1510, Italian painter.

bot·tle[1] (bŏt′əl), *n.*, *v.*, **-tled, -tling.** —*n.* **1.** a portable vessel with a neck or mouth, now commonly made of glass, used for holding liquids. **2.** the contents of a bottle; as much as a bottle contains: *a bottle of wine.* **3. the bottle,** intoxicating liquor. **4.** bottled milk for babies: *raised on the bottle.* —*v.t.* **5.** to put into or seal in a bottle; esp. in England, to can or put up fruit or vegetables. **6. bottle up,** to shut in or restrain closely: *to bottle up one's feelings.* [ME *botel,* t. OF: m. *botele,* g. LL *butticula,* dim. of *buttis* BUTT[4]] —**bot′tle·like′,** *adj.* —**bot′tler,** *n.*

bot·tle[2] (bŏt′əl), *n.* *Brit. Dial.* a bundle, esp. of hay. [ME *botel,* t. OF, dim. of *botte* bundle]

bottle green, a deep green.

bot·tle·neck (bŏt′əl nĕk′), *n.* **1.** a narrow entrance or passageway. **2.** a place, or stage in a process, where progress is retarded.

bot·tle·nose (bŏt′əl nōz′), *n.* *Zool.* any of various cetaceans, as *Hyperoodon ampullatus.*

bottle tree, any of several trees, species of the genus *Sterculia* (*Firmiana*), native to warmer regions, as *S. rupestris* (**narrow-leaved bottle tree**) and *S. trichosiphon* (**broad-leaved bottle tree**).

bot·tom (bŏt′əm), *n.* **1.** the lowest or deepest part of anything, as distinguished from the top: *the bottom of a hill, of a page, etc.* **2.** the under side: *the bottom of a flatiron.* **3.** the ground under any body of water: *the bottom of the sea.* **4.** (*usually pl.*) *Phys. Geog.* low-lying alluvial land adjacent to a river. **5.** *Naut.* the part of a ship below the wales. **6.** a ship. **7.** the seat of a chair. **8.** the buttocks. **9.** the fundamental part; basic aspect: *from the bottom of my heart.* **10.** *Brit.* the inmost part or inner end of a recess, bay, lane, etc. **11. at bottom,** in reality; fundamentally. —*v.t.* **12.** to furnish with a bottom. **13.** to base or found (fol. by *on* or *upon*). **14.** to get to the bottom of; fathom. —*v.i.* **15.** to be based; rest. **16.** to strike against the bottom or end; reach the bottom. —*adj.* **17.** lowest; undermost: *bottom prices.* **18.** fundamental: *the bottom cause.* [ME; OE *botm,* c. G *boden*] —**Syn. 1.** base, foot.

bottom land, *Phys. Geog.* bottom (def. 4).

bot·tom·less (bŏt′əm lYs), *adj.* **1.** without a bottom. **2.** immeasurably deep. **3. the bottomless pit,** hell.

bot·tom·ry (bŏt′əm rY), *n.*, *pl.* **-ries.** *Marine Law.* a contract, of the nature of a mortgage, by which the owner of a ship borrows money to make a voyage, pledging the ship as security. [modeled on D *bodemerij*]

bot·u·lin (bŏch′ə lYn), *n.* the toxin causing botulism.

bot·u·li·nus (bŏch′ə lī′nəs), *n.* the bacterium *Clostridium botulinum,* which forms botulin.

bot·u·lism (bŏch′ə lYz əm), *n.* a disease of the nervous system caused by botulin developed in spoiling foods eaten by animals and man. [f. s. L *botulus* sausage + -ISM]

Bou·cher (bōō shĕ′), *n.* **François** (frän swä′), 1703–70, French painter.

Bou·ci·cault (bōō′sY kôlt′, -kō′), *n.* **Dion** (dī′ŏn, -ən). 1822–90, Irish dramatist and actor.

bou·clé (bōō klā′; *Fr.* bōō klĕ′), *n.* yarn with loops. which produces a woven or knitted fabric with rough appearance. [t. F]

Bou·dic·ca (bōō dYk′ə), *n.* died A.D. 62, British queen who led an unsuccessful revolt against the Roman government of Britain. Also, **Boadicea.**

---

b., blend of, blended; c., cognate with; d., dialect, dialectal; der., derived from; f., formed from; g., going back to; m.. modification of; r.. replacing; s., stem of; t.. taken from; ?. perhaps. See the full key on inside cover.

bou·doir (bōō′dwär, -dwôr), *n.* a lady's bedroom or private sitting room. [t. F, der. *bouder* pout, sulk]

bouf·fant (bōō fän′), *adj. French.* puffed out; full, as sleeves or draperies. **—bouf·fante** (bōō fänt′), *adj. fem.*

bou·gain·vil·lae·a (bōō′gən vïl′ÿ ə). *n.* any plant of the nyctaginaceous South American genus *Bougainvillaea*, comprising shrubs with small flowers, species of which are cultivated for ornament.

Bou·gain·ville (bōō gän′vĕl′ *for 1*; bōō′gən vïl′, *Fr.* bōō găn vēl′ *for 2*), *n.* **1. Louis Antoine de** (lwē än twän′ də) 1729–1811, French navigator. **2.** the largest of the Solomon Islands, in the S Pacific. 39,309 pop. (1940). 3880 sq. mi.

bough (bou), *n.* **1.** a branch of a tree, esp. one of the larger of main branches. **2.** *Archaic.* the gallows. [ME; OE bōg, bōh shoulder, bough, c. D boeg, LG bug, Icel. bōgr shoulder, bow of a ship] **—bough′less**, *adj.* **—Syn. 1.** See **branch.**

bought (bôt), *v.* pt. and pp. of **buy.**

bought·en (bôt′ən), *adj. Dial.* bought or purchased, esp. as opposed to homemade.

bou·gie (bōō′jĭ, bōō′zhĭ; *Fr.* bōō zhē′), *n.* **1.** *Med.* **a.** a slender flexible instrument for introduction into passages of the body for dilating or opening, etc. **b.** a suppository. **2.** a wax candle. [t. F, prop., name of an Algerian town, center of wax trade]

Bou·gue·reau (bōō grō′), *n.* **Adolphe William** (ä dôlf′ wĕl yäm′), 1825–1905, French painter.

bouil·la·baisse (bōōl′yə bäs′; *Fr.* bōō yä bĕs′), *n.* a kind of stew or chowder made of fish and vegetables. [t. F, t. Pr.: m. *bouiabaisso*, f. *boui* boil + *abaisso* (go) down]

bouil·lon (bōōl′yŏn, -yən; *Fr.* bōō yôn′), *n.* a clear, thin soup made by boiling meat, etc. [t. F, der. *bouillir* boil]

Bou·lan·ger (bōō län zhē′), *n.* **Georges Ernest Jean Marie** (zhôrzh ĕr nĕst′ zhän må rē′), 1837–91, French general and politician.

boul·der (bōl′dər), *n.* a detached and rounded or worn rock, esp. one of some size. Also, **bowlder.** [short for *boulder stone*, ME *bulder-*, t. Scand.; cf. d. Sw. *buldersten* big stone (in a stream)]

Boul·der (bōl′dər), *n.* a city in N Colorado. 19,999 (1950).

Boulder Canyon, the canyon of the Colorado river above Boulder Dam, between Arizona and Nevada.

Boulder Dam, a large dam on the Colorado river, in SE Nevada and NW Arizona: the highest dam in the world. 727 ft. high; 1180 ft. long. Official name, Hoover Dam.

Bou·le (bōō′lē), *n.* **1.** the legislative assembly of modern Greece. **2.** (*sometimes l.c.*) a legislative, advisory, or administrative council in ancient Greek states. [t. Gk.]

boul·e·vard (bōōl′ə värd′, bōō′lə-), *n.* a broad avenue of a city, often having trees and used as a promenade. [t. F, t. MLG: m. *boleverk.* See **BULWARK**] **—Syn.** See **street.**

bou·le·ver·se·ment (bōōl vĕrs mäN′), *n. French.* an overturning; upsetting; confusion; turmoil.

Bou·logne (bōō lōn′, -loin′, bə-; *Fr.* bōō lôN′y), *n.* a seaport in N France. 34,898 (1946). Also, **Bou·logne-sur-Mer** (bōō lôN′y sэr sĕn′).

Bou·logne Bil·lan·court (bōō lôN′y bē yäN kōōr′), a city in N France, near Paris. 79,410 (1946). Also, **Bou·logne-sur-Seine** (bōō lôN′y sэr sĕn′).

boul·ter (bōl′tər), *n.* a long, stout fishing line with several hooks attached.

bounce (bouns), *v.*, **bounced, bouncing,** *n., adv.* **—***v.i.* **1.** to move with a bound, and rebound, as a ball: *a ball bounces back from the wall.* **2.** to burst noisily or angrily (*into* or *out of*): *to bounce into and out of a room.* **—***v.t.* **3.** to cause to bound or rebound: *to bounce a ball, to bounce a child up and down.* **4.** *Slang.* to eject or discharge summarily. **5.** *Brit.* to persuade (someone) by bluff. **—***n.* **6.** a rebound or bound: *catch the ball on the first bounce.* **7.** a sudden spring or leap. **8.** *Brit.* impudence; bluster, swagger. **9.** ability to bounce; resilience. **10.** *Slang.* expulsion; discharge; dismissal. **—***adv.* **11.** with a bounce; suddenly. [ME *bunsen* thump, t. LG, der. *bums!* thump! Cf. D *bonzen* thwack, etc.]

bounc·er (boun′sər), *n.* **1.** one who or that which bounces. **2.** *U.S. Slang.* one employed in a place of public resort to eject disorderly persons. **3.** something large of its kind. **4.** *Brit.* an impudent, pert person.

bounc·ing (boun′sĭng), *adj.* **1.** stout, strong, or vigorous: *a bouncing baby.* **2.** exaggerated; big; hearty; noisy: *a bouncing lie.*

bouncing Bet (bĕt), the common soapwort. Also, **bouncing Bess** (bĕs).

bound¹ (bound), *adj.* **1.** tied; in bonds: *a bound prisoner.* **2.** made fast as by a band or bond: *bound by one's word.* **3.** secured within a cover, as a book. **4.** under obligation, legally or morally: *in duty bound to help.* **5.** destined or sure: *it is bound to happen.* **6.** determined or resolved: *he is bound to go.* **7.** *Pathol.* constipated; costive. **8. bound up in** or **with, a.** inseparably connected with. **b.** having the affections centered in: *his life is bound up in his children.* [pp. of **BIND**]

bound² (bound), *v.i.* **1.** to move by leaps; leap; jump; spring. **2.** to rebound, as a ball. **—***v.t.* **3.** to cause to bound. **—***n.* **4.** a leap onward or upward; a jump. **5.** a rebound. [t. F: m. s. *bondir* leap, orig., resound, ? g. L *bombitāre* hum] **—Syn. 1.** See **skip¹.**

bound³ (bound), *n.* **1.** (*usually pl.*) a limiting line, or boundary: *the bounds of space and time.* **2.** that which limits, confines, or restrains. **3.** (*pl.*) territory on or near a boundary. **4.** (*pl.*) an area included within boundary lines: *within the bounds of his estate, within the bounds of reason.* **—***v.t.* **5.** to limit as by bounds. **6.** to form the boundary or limit of. **7.** to name the boundaries of. **—***v.i.* **8.** to have its boundaries (*on*); abut. [ME *bounde, boune*, t. OF: m. *bodne*, g. LL *butina*] **—Syn. 1.** border, frontier. **5.** demarcate, circumscribe.

bound⁴ (bound), *adj.* **1.** going or intending to go; on the way (*to*); destined (*for*): *the train is bound for Denver.* **2.** *Archaic.* prepared; ready. [ME *boun*, t. Scand.; cf. Icel. *būinn*, pp. of *būa* get ready]

bound·a·ry (boun′də rĭ, -drĭ), *n., pl.* **-ries.** something that indicates bounds or limits; a limiting or bounding line. [f. **BOUND³,** n. + **-ARY¹**]

bound·en (boun′dən), *adj.* **1.** obliged; under obligation. **2.** obligatory: *one's bounden duty.* [var. of **BOUND¹**]

bound·er (boun′dər), *n. Chiefly Brit. Colloq.* an obtrusive, ill-bred person; a vulgar upstart.

bound form, a linguistic form which never occurs by itself but always as part of some larger construction, as *-ed* in *seated.*

bound·less (bound′lĭs), *adj.* without bounds; unlimited: *his boundless energy amazed them.* **—bound′less·ly,** *adv.* **—bound′less·ness,** *n.*

boun·te·ous (boun′tĭ əs), *adj.* **1.** giving or disposed to give freely; generously liberal. **2.** freely bestowed; plentiful; abundant. [f. *bounte* (earlier var. of **BOUNTY**) + -ous; r. ME *bontyvous*, der. OF *bontif* benevolent] **—boun′te·ous·ly,** *adv.* **—boun′te·ous·ness,** *n.*

boun·ti·ful (boun′tə fəl), *adj.* **1.** liberal in bestowing gifts, favors, or bounties; munificent; generous. **2.** abundant; ample: *a bountiful supply.* **—boun′ti·ful·ly,** *adv.* **—boun′ti·ful·ness,** *n.*

boun·ty (boun′tĭ), *n., pl.* **-ties. 1.** generosity in giving. **2.** whatever is given bounteously; a benevolent, generous gift. **3.** a premium or reward, esp. one offered by a government. [ME *bounte*, t. OF: m. *bonte(t)*, g. L *bonitas* goodness] **—Syn. 1.** munificence, liberality, charity. **3.** See **bonus.**

bou·quet (bō kā′, bōō-, *for 1*; bōō kā′ *for 2*; *Fr.* bōō kĕ′), *n.* **1.** a bunch of flowers; a nosegay. **2.** the characteristic aroma of wines, liqueurs, etc. [t. F: bunch, clump of trees, d. var. of OF *bosquet* little wood, dim. of *bosc* wood. See **BUSH¹**]

Bour·bon (bōōr′bən, *Fr.* bōōr bôN′ *for 1–3*; bûr′bən *for 4, occas. for 3*), *n.* **1.** a member of the last house of the royal family of France, or of any of its branches, as the former royal family of Spain. **2. Charles** (shärl), 1490–1527, French general. **3.** (in derogatory use) an extreme conservative, or one devoted to ideas suited only to past conditions. **4.** (*l.c.*) Also, **bourbon whiskey.** a straight whiskey distilled from a mash containing 51% or more corn, orig. the corn whiskey produced in Bourbon county, Ky.

Bour·bon·ism (bōōr′bə nïz′əm; *occas.* bûr′-) *n.* **1.** adherence to the system of government and the ideas for which the Bourbons stood. **2.** extreme conservatism, as in politics. **—Bour′bon·ist,** *n.*

bour·don (bōōr′dən, bôr′dən), *n. Music.* **1.** the drone of a bagpipe, or a monotonous and repetitious ground melody. **2.** a low-pitched tone; a bass. [t. F]

bourg (bōōrg; *Fr.* bōōr), *n.* **1.** a town. **2.** a French market town. [t. F, g. LL *burgus*, t. Gmc. See **BOROUGH**]

bour·geois¹ (bōōr zhwä′, bōōr′zhwä; *Fr.* bōōr zhwä′), *n., pl.* **-geois.** **—***n.* **1.** a member of the middle class. **2.** any person owning property. **—***adj.* **3.** belonging to or consisting of the middle class. **4.** lacking in refinement or elegance. [t. F] **—bour·geoise** (bōōr zhwäz′; *Fr.* bōōr zhwäz′), *n., adj. fem.*

bour·geois² (bər jois′), *n.* a printing type (9 point) of a size between brevier and long primer. [? proper name]

bour·geoi·sie (bōōr′zhwä zē′; *Fr.* bōōr zhwä zē′), *n.* **1.** the bourgeois class. **2.** (in Marxist ideology) the antithesis of the proletariat or wage-earning class. [t. F]

bour·geon (bûr′jən), *n., v.* burgeon.

Bourges (bōōrzh), *n.* a city in central France. 51,040 (1946).

Bour·get (bōōr zhĕ′), *n.* **Paul** (pōl), 1852–1935, French novelist and critic.

Bour·gogne (bōōr gôN′y), *n.* French name of **Burgundy.**

bourn¹ (bôrn), *n.* burn². Also, **bourne.**

bourn² (bôrn, bōōrn), *n.* **1.** a bound; limit. **2.** destination; goal. **3.** realm; domain. Also, **bourne.** [t. F: m. *borne*]

Bourne·mouth (bôrn′məth, bōrn′-), *n.* a city in S England: seaside resort. 135,270 (est. 1946).

bour·rée (bōō rē′), *n.* **1.** an old French and Spanish dance, somewhat like a gavotte. **2.** the music for it.

Bourse (bōōrs), *n.* a stock exchange, esp. that of Paris. [t. F: orig. purse, g. LL *bursa*, t. Gk.: m. *bÿrsa* hide]

bouse¹ (bous, bouz), *v.t.*, **boused, bousing.** *Naut.* to haul with tackle. Also, **bowse.** [orig. unknown]

bouse[2] (bōōz, bouz), *n.*, *v.*, **boused**, **bousing.** —*n.*
1. liquor or drink. 2. a drinking bout; a carouse. —*v.i.*,
v.i. 3. to drink, esp. to excess. [ME *bous* drinking vessel,
t. MD: m. *buse*]

bou·stro·phe·don (bōō/strə fē/dən, bou/-), *n.* an ancient method of writing in which the lines run alternately from right to left and from left to right. [t. Gk.:
adv., with turning like that of oxen in plowing]

bous·y (bōō/zĭ, bou/-), *adj.* intoxicated; boozy.

bout (bout), *n.* 1. a contest; a trial of strength. 2. a
turn at work or any action. 3. period; spell: *a bout of
illness.* [var. of obs. *bought* bend, turn, der. BOW[1]]

bou·ton·niere (bōō/tə nyär/), *n.* a buttonhole bouquet or flower. Also, *French.* **bou·ton·nière** (bōō tō-
nyēr/). [t. F: buttonhole]

bo·vid (bō/vĭd), *adj.* *Zool.* of or pertaining to the *Bovidae*, or ox family, comprising the hollow-horned ruminants, as oxen, sheep, and goats.

bo·vine (bō/vīn, -vĭn), *adj.* 1. of the ox family
(*Bovidae*). 2. oxlike. 3. stolid; dull. —*n.* 4. a bovine
animal. [t. LL: m. s. *bovīnus*, der. L *bōs* ox]

bow[1] (bou), *v.i.* 1. to bend or curve downward; stoop:
the pines bowed low. 2. to yield; submit: *to bow to the
inevitable.* 3. to bend the body or head in worship,
reverence, respect, or submission. 4. to incline the head
or body, or both, in salutation. —*v.t.* 5. to bend or
incline in worship, submission, respect, civility, or agreement: *to bow one's head.* 6. to cause to submit; subdue;
crush. 7. to cause to stoop: *age had bowed his head.* 8. to
express by a bow, or by bowing: *to bow one's thanks.*
9. to usher (*in, out,* etc.) with a bow. 10. *Archaic and
Dial.* to cause to bend; make curved or crooked. —*n.*
11. an inclination of the head or body in salutation,
assent, thanks, reverence, respect, or submission. [ME
bowe(n), OE *būgan*, c. G *biegen* bend] —**Syn. 1.** See **bend**[1].

bow[2] (bō), *n.* 1. a strip of elastic wood or other material
bent by a string stretched between its ends, used for
shooting arrows. 2. a bend or curve. 3. a looped knot,
as of ribbon, composed of one or two loops and two ends;
a bowknot. 4. *Music.* **a.** an implement, orig. curved but
now almost always straight, with horsehairs stretched
upon it, for playing any member of the violin family of
instruments. **b.** a single stroke of such an implement.
5. something curved or arc-shaped. 6. *U. S.* one of the
supports for a pair of spectacles, reaching to the ears.
7. a U-shaped piece under an animal's neck to hold a
yoke. 8. a rainbow. —*adj.* 9. curved; bent like a bow:
bow legs. —*v.t.*, *v.i.* 10. to bend into the form of a bow;
curve. 11. *Music.* to perform by means of a bow upon a
stringed instrument. [ME *bowe*, OE *boga*, c. G *bogen*]
—**bow/less**, *adj.* —**bow/like/**, *adj.*

bow[3] (bou), *n.* 1. the front or forward end of a ship,
boat, airship, etc. See illus. under **aft.** 2. the foremost
oar used in rowing a boat. 3. the person who pulls that
oar; the bow oar; bowman. [? t. Dan.: m. *bov*, c. BOUGH]

bow compass (bō), *Geom.* any of various compasses,
as one having the legs joined by a bow-shaped piece.

bowd·ler·ize (boud/lə rīz/), *v.t.*, **-ized**, **-izing.** to expurgate prudishly. [from Thomas *Bowdler*, who in 1818
published an expurgated edition of Shakespeare]
—**bowd/ler·ism**, *n.* —**bowd/ler·i·za/tion**, *n.*

bow·el (bou/əl, boul), *n.*, *v.*, **-eled**, **-eling** or (*esp. Brit.*)
-elled, **-elling.** —*n.* 1. *Anat.* **a.** an intestine. **b.** (*usually
pl.*) the parts of the alimentary canal below the stomach;
the intestines or entrails. 2. the inward or interior parts.
3. (*pl.*) *Archaic.* feelings of pity or compassion. —*v.t.*
4. to disembowel. [ME *bouel*, t. OF: m. *boel*, g. L
botellus, dim. of *botulus* sausage]

bow·er[1] (bou/ər), *n.* 1. a leafy shelter or recess; an
arbor. 2. *Now Only Poetic.* a rustic dwelling; a cottage.
3. *Poetic.* a chamber; a boudoir. —*v.t.* 4. to enclose in
or as in a bower; embower. [ME *bour*, OE *būr* a dwelling,
cottage, akin to *būan* dwell] —**bow/er·like/**, *adj.*

bow·er[2] (bou/ər), *n.* an anchor carried at a ship's bow.
Also, **bower anchor.** [f. BOW[3] + -ER[2]]

bow·er[3] (bou/ər), *n.* (in euchre and other card games)
the knave of trumps (**right bower**) or the other knave
of the same color (**left bower**); the highest cards in the
game, unless the joker (often called the **best bower**) is
used. [t. G: m. *bauer* peasant, jack (in cards)]

bow·er[4] (bou/ər), *n.* one who or that which bows or
bends. [f. BOW[1] + -ER[1]]

bow·er[5] (bō/ər), *n.* *Music.* a player with the bow on a
violin or other stringed instrument. [f. BOW[2] + -ER[1]]

bow·er·bird (bou/ər bûrd/), *n.* any of various Australian and Papuan oscine birds, related to birds of
paradise, as *Ptilonorhynchus violaceus*, which build
bowerlike structures, used, not as nests, but as places of
resort to attract the females.

Bow·ers (bou/ərz), *n.* **Claude Gernade** (zhər näd/)
born 1878, U.S. diplomat and historian.

bow·er·y[1] (bou/ər ĭ), *adj.* bowerlike; containing bow-
ers; shady: *a bowery maze.* [f. BOWER[1] + -Y[1]]

bow·er·y[2] (bou/ər ĭ, bou/rĭ), *n.*, *pl.* **-eries.** 1. (among
the Dutch settlers of New York) a farm or country seat.
2. **the Bowery,** a long, wide street in New York City,
notorious for its saloons, run-down hotels, etc. [t. D:
m. *bouwerij* (def. 1), der. *bouwer* farmer]

bow·fin (bō/fĭn/), *n.* a North American fresh-water
ganoid fish, *Amia calva*, not highly regarded as food.

bow hand (bō), 1. *Archery.* the hand that holds the
bow, usually the left hand. 2. *Music.* the hand that
draws the bow, usually the right hand.

bow·head (bō/hĕd/), *n.* the whale, *Balaena mysticetus*,
of arctic seas.

bow·ie knife (bō/ĭ, bōō/ĭ),
a heavy sheath knife having a
long, single-edged blade.
[named after James *Bowie*
(1796–1836), U.S. pioneer]

Bowie State, Arkansas.

bow·knot (bō/nŏt/), *n.* bow[2]
(def. 3).

Bowie knife and sheath

bowl[1] (bōl), *n.* 1. a rather deep, round dish or basin,
used chiefly for holding liquids, food, etc. 2. the contents of a bowl. 3. a rounded, hollow part: *the bowl of a
pipe.* 4. a large drinking cup; a goblet. 5. festive
drinking; conviviality. 6. any bowl-shaped depression
or formation. 7. an edifice with a bowllike interior,
as for athletic contests, etc. [ME *bolle*, OE *bolla*, c.
Icel. *bolli.* See BOLL] —**bowl/like/**, *adj.*

bowl[2] (bōl), *n.* 1. one of the balls, having little or no
bias, used in playing ninepins or tenpins. 2. one of the
biased or weighted balls used in the game of bowls. 3. a
cast or delivery of the ball in bowling. 4. *Mach.* a
rotating cylindrical part in a machine, as one to reduce
friction. —*v.i.* 5. to play with bowls, or at bowling.
6. to roll a bowl, as in the game of bowls. 7. to move
along smoothly and rapidly. 8. *Cricket.* to deliver the
ball to be played by the batsman. —*v.t.* 9. to roll or
trundle, as a ball, hoop, etc. 10. to knock or strike, as
by the ball in bowling (fol. by *over* or *down*). 11. to disconcert; upset (fol. by *over*). 12. to carry or convey as
in a wheeled vehicle. 13. *Cricket.* to eliminate (a batsman) by bowling (fol. by *out*). [ME *boule*, t. OF: ball, g.
L *bulla* bubble] —**bowl/er**, *n.*

bowl·der (bōl/dər), *n.* boulder.

bow·leg (bō/lĕg/), *n.* *Pathol.* 1. outward curvature of
the legs causing a separation of the knees when the
ankles are close or in contact. 2. a leg so curved. —**bow-
leg·ged** (bō/lĕg/ĭd, bō/lĕgd/), *adj.*

bowl·er (bō/lər), *n. Brit.* derby (cf. 4). [f. BOWL[1] + -ER[2]]

Bowles (bōlz), *n.* **Samuel**, 1826–78, U.S. journalist.

bow·line (bō/lĭn, -lĭn/), *n.* 1. Also, **bowline knot**, a
knot which forms a nonslipping loop. 2.
Naut. **a.** a rope leading forward and
fastened to the leech of a square sail, used
to steady the weather leech of the sail and
keep it forward. **b. on a bowline,** sailing
close to the wind.

Bowline (def. 1)

bowl·ing (bō/lĭng), *n.* 1. act of playing with or at
bowls. 2. the game of bowls. 3. *U.S., Canada.* tenpins.

bowling alley, 1. a long enclosure for playing at
bowls, etc. 2. a covered place with a long, narrow
planked enclosure, for playing at tenpins.

bowling green, *Chiefly Brit.* a level plot of turf for
bowling.

Bowling Green, 1. a city in S Kentucky. 18,347 (1950).
2. a small open space in New York City, at the foot of
Broadway.

bowls (bōlz), *n.* 1. a game, common in Great Britain
and parts of the U. S. and Canada, in which the players
roll biased or weighted balls along the sward in an effort
to bring them as near as possible to a stationary ball
called the *jack.* 2. skittles, ninepins or (*U.S.*) tenpins.

bow·man[1] (bō/mən), *n.*, *pl.* **-men.** 1. an archer. 2. (in
medieval warfare) a soldier armed with a bow. [f. BOW[2]
+ MAN]

bow·man[2] (bou/mən), *n.*,
pl. **-men.** *Naut.* bow[3] (def.
3). [f. BOW[3] + MAN]

bow oar (bou), bow[3] (def.
3).

bow pen (bō), *Geom.* a
bow compass with a pen at
the end of one leg.

bowse (bous, bouz), *v.t.*,
bowsed, **bowsing.** bouse[1].

bow·shot (bō/shŏt/), *n.*
the distance a bow sends an
arrow.

bow·sprit (bou/sprĭt,
bō/-), *n.* *Naut.* a large spar
projecting forward from the
stem of a ship or other vessel. [ME *bouspret*, f. *bou* bow
of a ship + *spret* (OE *sprēot* pole)]

A, Bowsprit; B, Jib boom; C, Bobstay

Bow Street, a street in London, England, on
which is the principal metropolitan police court.

bow·string (bō/strĭng/), *n.*, *v.*, **-stringed** or **-strung**,
-stringing. —*n.* 1. the string of a bow. 2. a string
used, as by the Turks, for strangling offenders. —*v.t.*
3. to strangle with a bowstring or any string or band.

bowstring hemp, any of various fibrous plants
(genus *Sansevieria*) of Asia and Africa, cultivated in
the U.S. for ornament.

bow tie (bō), a small bow-shaped necktie.

bow window (bō), a rounded bay window.

bow·wow (bou/wou/), *n.* 1. the bark of a dog. 2. an
imitation of this. 3. (in childish use) a dog.

bow·yer (bō/yər), *n.* a maker or seller of bows.

box[1] (bŏks), *n.* 1. a case or receptacle, usually rectangular, of wood, metal, cardboard, etc., with a lid or
removable cover. 2. the quantity contained in a box.
3. a package or case containing presents. 4. the present

or gift itself. **5.** a compartment or place shut or railed off for the accommodation of a small number of people in a public place, esp. in theaters, opera houses, ballrooms, etc. **6.** a small shelter: *a sentry's box.* **7.** *Brit.* a small house, as for use while following some sport: *a shooting box.* **8.** a box stall. **9.** the driver's seat on a coach. **10.** the section of a wagon in which passengers or parcels are carried. **11.** part of a page of a periodical set off by lines, border, or white space. **12.** *Mach.* an enclosing, protecting, or hollow part; a casing; a chamber; a bush; a socket. **13.** *Baseball.* the space where the batter stands (or, less often, the pitcher or coaches). **14.** *Agric.* a bowl or pit cut in the side of a tree for collecting sap. —*v.t.* **15.** to put into a box. **16.** to enclose or confine as in a box (often fol. by *up*). **17.** to furnish with a box. **18.** to form into a box or the shape of a box. **19.** *Naut.* to boxhaul (often fol. by *off*). **20.** to make a hole or cut in (a tree) for the sap to collect. **21. box the compass,** *Naut.* to name the points of the compass in their order. [special use of BOX³] —**box'like'**, *adj.*

box² (bŏks), *n.* **1.** a blow as with the hand or fist. —*v.t.* **2.** to strike with the hand or fist, esp. on the ear. **3.** to fight in a boxing match. —*v.i.* **4.** to fight with the fists; spar. [ME; orig. unknown]

box³ (bŏks), *n.* **1.** an evergreen shrub or small tree of the genus *Buxus,* esp. *B. sempervirens,* much used for ornamental borders, hedges, etc., and yielding a hard, durable wood. **2.** the wood itself. See **boxwood. 3.** any of various other shrubs or trees, esp. species of eucalyptus. [OE, t. L: m.s. *buxus,* t. Gk.: m. *pýxos*]

box bed, 1. a bed completely enclosed so as to resemble a box. **2.** a bed that folds up in the form of a box.

box·ber·ry (bŏks'bĕr'ĭ), *n., pl.* **-ries. 1.** the checkerberry. **2.** the partridgeberry.

box calf, a chrome-tanned calfskin with square markings produced by graining.

box camera, a boxlike camera, without bellows.

box·car (bŏks'kär'), *n.* **1.** *Railroads.* an enclosed and covered freight car. **2.** (*pl.*) a pair of sixes on the first throw in the game of craps.

box coat, 1. an outer coat with a straight, unfitted back. **2.** a heavy overcoat worn by coachmen.

box elder, a fast-growing North American maple, *Acer negundo,* cultivated for shade.

box·er (bŏk'sər), *n.* **1.** one who boxes; a pugilist. **2.** a handsome, smooth-coated, brown dog of medium size, related to the bulldog and terrier.

Box·er (bŏk'sər), *n.* a member of a Chinese secret society, which practiced ritualistically the traditional Chinese posture boxing, supposed to make them immune to bullets and swords. The Boxers originally preached the overthrow of the Manchu Empire, but in 1900 they attacked foreigners and native Christians and besieged the legations at Peking until an international expeditionary force raised the siege.

box·haul (bŏks'hôl'), *v.t. Naut.* to veer (a ship) round on her heel by bracing the head yards aback, etc.

box·ing¹ (bŏk'sĭng), *n.* **1.** the material used to make boxes or casings. **2.** a boxlike enclosure; a casing. **3.** act of putting into or furnishing with a box. [f. BOX¹ + -ING¹]

box·ing² (bŏk'sĭng), *n.* act or art of fighting with the fists, with or without boxing gloves. [f. BOX² + -ING¹]

Boxing Day, *Brit.* the first weekday after Christmas, when Christmas gifts are given to employees, etc.

boxing glove, a padded glove worn in boxing.

box iron, a smoothing iron which is heated by placing a hot iron in its boxlike holder.

box kite, a kite consisting of a light box-shaped frame, covered except on the ends and a space along the middle.

box office, *Theat.* **1.** the office in which tickets are sold. **2.** receipts from a play or other entertainment. **3.** the ability of an entertainment or performer to draw an audience: *this show will be good box office.*

box pleat, a double pleat, with the material folded under at each side. Also, **box plait.**

box seat, a seat in a theater box, etc.

box stall, a large and usually square stall for a horse or other large animal.

box·thorn (bŏks'thôrn'), *n.* matrimony vine.

box·wood (bŏks'wŏŏd'), *n.* **1.** the hard, fine-grained, compact wood of the box (genus *Buxus*), much used for wood engravers' blocks, musical and mathematical instruments, etc. **2.** the tree or shrub itself. Cf. **box³** (def. 1).

boy (boi), *n.* **1.** a male child, from birth to full growth, but esp. to the beginning of youth. **2.** a young man who lacks maturity, vigor, judgment, etc. **3.** a grown man. **4.** a young servant; a page. **5.** (in India, China, Japan, etc.) a native male servant, working as a butler, waiter, house boy, etc. [ME *boy, boi*; orig. uncert.]

bo·yar (bō'yär', boi'är), *n.* **1.** *Russian Hist.* a member of the old nobility of Russia, before Peter the Great made rank depend on state service. **2.** one of a privileged class in Rumania. Also, **bo·yard** (bō'yärd', boi'ərd). [t. Russ.: m. *boyarin* lord]

boy·cott (boi'kŏt), *v.t.* **1.** to combine in abstaining from, or preventing dealings with, as a means of intimidation or coercion: *to boycott a person, business house, etc.* **2.** to abstain from buying or using: *to boycott a commercial product.* —*n.* **3.** the practice of boycotting. **4.** an instance of boycotting. [from Captain *Boycott,* the first victim (1880), agent of an Irish landlord]

boy·hood (boi'hŏŏd), *n.* **1.** state or period of being a boy. **2.** boys collectively.

boy·ish (boi'ĭsh), *adj.* of, like, or befitting a boy. —**boy'ish·ly,** *adv.* —**boy'ish·ness,** *n.*

Boyle (boil), *n.* **Robert,** 1627–91, British chemist and physicist.

Boyne (boin), *n.* a river in E Eire, near which William III defeated James II (1690). 70 mi.

boy scout, 1. a member of an organization of boys (the **Boy Scouts**), founded in England in 1908 by Lieut. Gen. Sir Robert S. S. Baden-Powell, to develop in its members manly character, self-reliance, and usefulness to others. **2.** a member of any similar society elsewhere.

boy·sen·ber·ry (boi'zən bĕr'ĭ), *n., pl.* **-ries.** a blackberrylike fruit with a flavor similar to that of raspberries, developed by crossing various species of *Rubus.*

Boz·zar·is (bō zăr'ĭs, -zär'-; Gk. bôt'sä rēs'), *n.* **Marco** (mär'kō), 1788?–1823, Greek patriot.

bp., 1. baptized. 2. birthplace. 3. bishop.

b.p., 1. Also, B/P. Com. bills payable. 2. *Physics, Chem.* boiling point.

B.P.E., Bachelor of Physical Education.

B.P.H., Bachelor of Public Health.

B.Ph., Bachelor of Philosophy. Also, **B.Phil.**

B.P.O.E., Benevolent and Protective Order of Elks.

Br, *Chem.* bromine.

Br., 1. Britain. 2. British.

br., 1. branch. 2. brig. 3. bronze. 4. brother.

b.r., *Com.* bills receivable. Also, **B/R.**

bra (brä), *n. Colloq.* brassière.

Bra·bant (brə bănt', brä'bənt; *Du.* brä'bänt; *Fr.* brä·bäN'), *n.* **1.** a former duchy in W Europe: now divided into three provinces, two in Belgium and one in the Netherlands. See map under **Agincourt. 2.** a province in central Belgium. 1,773,635 pop. (est. 1945); 1208 sq. mi. *Cap.:* Brussels.

brace (brās), *n., v.,* **braced, bracing.** —*n.* **1.** something that holds parts together or in place, as a clasp or clamp. **2.** anything that imparts rigidity or steadiness. **3.** *Mach.* a device for holding and turning tools for boring or drilling; a bitstock. See illus. under **brace and bit. 4.** *Bldg. Trades.* a piece of timber, metal, etc., used to support or position another piece or portion of a framework. **5.** *Naut.* (on a square-rigged ship) a rope by which a yard is swung about and secured horizontally. **6.** *Music.* leather loops sliding upon the tightening cords of a drum to change their tension and therewith the pitch. **7.** (*often pl.*) *Dentistry.* a round or flat metal wire placed against surfaces of the teeth, and used to straighten irregularly arranged teeth. **8.** *Med.* an appliance for supporting a weak joint or joints. **9.** (*pl.*) *Chiefly Brit.* suspenders. **10.** a pair; a couple. **11.** one of two characters { or } for connecting written or printed lines. **12.** *Music.* connected staves. **13.** a defense or protection for the arm, specif. one used in archery. [ME *brase,* t. OF (see BRACE, v.)] —*v.t.* **14.** to furnish, fasten, or strengthen with or as with a brace. **15.** to fix firmly; make steady. **16.** to make tight; increase the tension of. **17.** to act as a stimulant to. **18.** *Naut.* to swing or turn around (the yards of a ship) by means of the braces. —*v.i.* **19. brace up,** *Colloq.* to rouse one's strength or vigor. [ME *brase*(n), t. OF: m. *bracier* embrace, der. *brace* the two arms (cf. def. 10), g. L *brāchia*] —Syn. 10. See **pair.**

brace and bit, *Mach.* a boring tool consisting of a bit and a handle for rotating it.

brace·let (brās'lĭt), *n.* **1.** an ornamental band or circlet for the wrist or arm. **2.** *Humorous.* a handcuff. [ME, t. OF, dim. of *bracel,* ult. der. L *brāc(c)hium* arm]

brac·er¹ (brā'sər), *n.* **1.** one who or that which braces, binds, or makes firm. **2.** *U.S. Colloq.* a stimulating drink; tonic. [f. BRACE + -ER¹]

brac·er² (brā'sər), *n. Archery.* a guard for the left wrist and lower arm worn as a protection against the friction or the catching of the bowstring. [ME *braser,* t. OF: m. *brasseüre,* der. *bras* arm, g. L *brāchium*]

brach (brăch, brăk), *n. Obs.* a bitch of the hound kind. Also, **brach·et** (brăch'ĭt). [ME *braches,* pl., t. OF, pl. of *brachet,* dim of *brac,* t. OHG: m. *bracco* a hound hunting by scent]

bra·chi·al (brā'kĭ əl, brăk'ĭ-), *adj. Zool.* **1.** belonging to the arm, foreleg, wing, pectoral fin, or other forelimb of a vertebrate. **2.** belonging to the upper part of such member, from the shoulder to the elbow. **3.** armlike, as an appendage. [t. L: s. *brāchiālis*]

bra·chi·al·gi·a (brā'kĭ ăl'jĭ ə, brăk'ĭ-), *n. Pathol.* pain in the nerves of the upper arm.

bra·chi·ate (brā'kĭ ĭt, -āt', brăk'ĭ-), *adj. Bot.* having widely spreading branches in alternate pairs.

brachio-, a word element meaning "arm," as in *brachiopod.* Also, before vowels, **brachi-.** [t. NL, comb. form repr. L *brāchium,* or its source, Gk. *brachīon*]

bra·chi·o·pod (brā'kĭ ə pŏd', brăk'ĭ-), *n. Zool.* any of the *Brachiopoda.*

Bra·chi·op·o·da (brā'kĭ ŏp'ə də, brăk'ĭ-), *n.pl. Zool.* a phylum of mollusklike animals, the lamp shells, having dorsal and ventral shells. Most members are now extinct.

Brace and bit

bra·chi·um (brā′kĭ əm, brăk′ĭ-), *n., pl.* **brachia** (brā′-kĭ ə, brăk′ĭ ə). *Anat., Zool.* **1.** the upper arm, from the shoulder to the elbow. **2.** the part of any limb, as in the wing of a bird, corresponding to it. **3.** an armlike part or process. [t. L: arm]

brachy-, a word element meaning "short," as in *brachycephalic.* [t. Gk., comb. form of *brachȳs*]

brach·y·ce·phal·ic (brăk′ĭ sə făl′ĭk), *adj. Cephalom.* short-headed; having a breadth of head at least four fifths as great as the length from front to back. Also, **brach·y·ceph·a·lous** (brăk′ĭ sĕf′ə ləs).—**brach′y·ceph′-a·ly,** *n.*

brach·y·cra·nic (brăk′ĭ krā′nĭk), *adj. Craniom.* short-headed; having a breadth of skull at least four fifths as great as the length from front to back.

bra·chyl·o·gy (brə kĭl′ə jĭ), *n., pl.* **-gies.** brevity of diction; a concise or abridged form of expression. [t. Gk.: m.s. *brachylogía.* See BRACHY-, -LOGY]

bra·chyp·ter·ous (brə kĭp′tər əs), *adj. Ornith.* short-winged. [f. BRACHY- + -PTEROUS]

brach·y·u·ran (brăk′ĭ yŏŏr′ən), *adj.* **1.** belonging or pertaining to the *Brachyura,* a group of stalk-eyed decapod crustaceans with short tails, the common crabs. —*n.* **2.** a brachyuran crustacean.

brach·y·u·rous (brăk′ĭ yŏŏr′əs), *adj. Zool.* short-tailed, as the crabs (opposed to *macrurous*).

brac·ing (brā′sĭng), *adj.* **1.** strengthening; invigorating. —*n.* **2.** a brace. **3.** braces collectively. —**brac′-ing·ly,** *adv.*

brack·en (brăk′ən), *n. Brit.* **1.** a large fern or brake, esp. *Pteridium aquilinum.* **2.** a clump of brakes. [ME *braken,* t. Scand.; cf. Sw. *bräken* fern]

brack·et (brăk′ĭt), *n.* **1.** a wooden, metal, etc., support of triangular outline placed under a shelf or the like. **2.** a shelf or shelves supported by a bracket. **3.** *Archit.* an ornamental projection from the face of a wall, intended to support a statue, pier, etc.; a corbel. See illus. under **corbel.** **4.** a projecting fixture for gas or electricity. **5.** one of two marks, [ ], used in writing or printing to enclose parenthetical matter, interpolations, etc. **6.** *Math.* **a.** (*pl.*) parentheses of various forms indicating that the enclosed quantity is to be treated as a unit. **b.** (loosely) vinculum (def. 2). **7.** a grouping of taxpayers based on the amount of their income: *low income bracket.* **8.** *Gunnery.* range or elevation producing both shorts and overs on a target. —*v.t.* **9.** to furnish with or support by a bracket or brackets. **10.** to place within brackets; couple with a brace. **11.** to associate or mention together. **12.** *Gunnery.* to place (shots) both over and short of a target. [earlier *bragget,* t. F: m. *braguette,* t. Pr., or Sp., dim. of *braga,* g. L *brācae,* pl., breeches; of Celtic orig.]

brack·et·ing (brăk′ĭt ĭng), *n. Archit.* the series of wooden supports, often of fanciful jigsaw form, nailed to the ceiling, joists, and battening to support cornices.

brack·ish (brăk′ĭsh), *adj.* **1.** slightly salt; having a saltish or briny flavor. **2.** distasteful. [f. *brack* brackish (t. D: m. *brak*) + -ISH¹]—**brack′ish·ness,** *n.*

bract (brăkt), *n. Bot.* a specialized leaf or leaflike part, usually situated at the base of a flower or inflorescence. [t. L: m. s. *bractea* thin plate of metal]—**brac-te·al** (brăk′tĭ əl), *adj.*—**bract′less,** *adj.*

brac·te·ate (brăk′tĭ ĭt, -āt′), *adj. Bot.* having bracts.

brac·te·o·late (brăk′tĭ ə lĭt, -lāt′), *adj.* having bracteoles.

brac·te·ole (brăk′tĭ ōl′), *n. Bot.* a small or secondary bract, as on a pedicel. Also, **bract·let** (brăkt′lĭt).

Bracts of marigold
A. of pedicel;
B. of flower

brad (brăd), *n.* **1.** a small wire nail with a head like a finishing nail. —*v.t.* **2.** to turn down (the end of a nail which projects a short way through the work). **3.** to upset or enlarge (the end of a rivet) by hammering. [ME *brad,* var. of *brod,* t. Scand.; cf. Icel. *broddr* spike]

brad·awl (brăd′ôl′), *n. Carp.* an awl for making small holes in wood for brads, etc. See illus. under **awl.**

Brad·dock (brăd′ək), *n.* **1. Edward,** 1695–1755, British general in America. **2.** a city in SW Pennsylvania, near Pittsburgh: the site of General Braddock's defeat by the French and Indians, 1755. 16,488 (1950).

Brad·ford (brăd′fərd), *n.* **1. Gamaliel,** 1863–1932, U. S. writer of biographical essays. **2. William,** 1590–1657, second governor of the English colony at Plymouth, Massachusetts. **3.** a city in N England, in Yorkshire, 280,160 (est. 1946). **4.** a city in N Pennsylvania. 17,354 (1950).

Brad·ley (brăd′lĭ), *n.* **1. Henry,** 1845–1923, British philologist and lexicographer. **2. Omar Nelson,** born 1893, U.S. general: Chief of Staff 1948–49; chairman, Joint Chiefs of Staff since 1949.

Brad·street (brăd′strēt′), *n.* **1. Anne,** 1612?–72, American poet. **2.** her husband, **Simon,** 1603–97, governor of the Massachusetts colony.

Bra·dy (brā′dĭ), *n.* **Mathew B.,** 1823?–1896, U.S. photographer, esp. of the Civil War.

brae (brā, brē), *n. Scot.* and *N. Eng.* a slope; a declivity; a hillside. [ME *bra,* t. Scand.; cf. Icel. *brā* eyelash, c. OE *brēaw* eyebrow, eyelid, G *braue* eyebrow]

brag (brăg), *v.,* **bragged, bragging,** *n., adj.* —*v.i.* **1.** to use boastful language; boast: *he likes to brag.* —*v.t.* **2.** to

boast of. —*n.* **3.** a boast or vaunt; bragging. **4.** a thing to boast of. **5.** a boaster. —*adj.* **6.** unusually fine; first rate. [t. Scand.; cf. Icel. *bragga sig* take heart, *braggast* thrive]—**brag′ger,** *n.* —**Syn. 1.** See **boast¹.**

Bra·ga (brä′gə), *n.* **Teófilo** (tĕ ô′fē lŏŏ), 1843–1924, Portuguese author and statesman.

Bragg (brăg), *n.* **1. Braxton,** 1817–76, Confederate general in the U.S. Civil War. **2. Sir William Henry,** 1862–1942, British physicist who with his son **William Lawrence,** born 1890, won the Nobel Prize in 1915.

brag·ga·do·ci·o (brăg′ə dō′shĭ ō′), *n., pl.* **-os. 1.** empty boasting; brag. **2.** a boasting person; a braggart. [from *Braggadochio,* name of a boastful character in Spenser's "Faerie Queen"]

brag·gart (brăg′ərt), *n.* **1.** one given to bragging. —*adj.* **2.** bragging; boastful. [t. F (obs.): m. *bragard* boastful]—**brag′gart·ism,** *n.*

Bra·gi (brä′gĭ), *n. Scand. Myth.* son of Odin, and god of poetry; Odin's principal skald in Valhalla. His wife is Ithunn. Also, **Bra·ge** (brä′gə).

Brahe (brä; *Dan.* brä′ĕ), *n.* **Tycho** (tȳ′kō), 1546–1601, Danish astronomer.

Brah·ma (brä′mə), *n.* **1.** (in philosophic Hinduism) the impersonal Supreme Being, the primal Source and the ultimate Goal of all being; Atman, the World Soul. **2.** (in later Hinduism) a trinity of the personal Creator along with Vishnu the Preserver and Siva the Destroyer. [t. Skt.: m. *brāhma,* neut., worship, prayer, the impersonal divinity (see def. 1); m. *brahmā,* masc., worshiper, priest, the divinity as personified (see def. 2)]

brah·ma (brä′mə, brā′-), *n.* a breed of large domestic fowls, of Asiatic origin, with feathered legs and small wings and tail. [named after and short for BRAHMAPUTRA]

Brah·man (brä′mən), *n., pl.* **-mans.** a member of the highest, or priestly, caste among the Hindus. Also, **Brahmin.** [t. Skt.: m. *brāhmana*]—**Brah·man·ic** (brä măn′-ĭk), **Brah·man·i·cal,** *adj.*

Brah·man (brä′mən), *n. U.S.* an animal of one of the breeds of cattle of the species *Bos indicus,* originating in India.

Brah·man·ism (brä′mə nĭz′əm), *n.* the religious and social system of the Brahmans and orthodox Hindus, characterized by the caste system and diversified pantheism. —**Brah′man·ist,** *n.*

Brah·ma·pu·tra (brä′mə pŏŏ′trə), *n.* a river flowing from SW Tibet through NE India, joining the Ganges in E Pakistan to flow into the Bay of Bengal. ab. 1800 mi.

Brah·min (brä′mĭn), *n., pl.* **Brahmin. 1.** Brahman. **2.** a person of great culture and intellect. **3.** a snobbish or aloof intellectual.

Brahms (brämz; *Ger.* bräms), *n.* **Johannes** (yō hän′-əs), 1833–97, German composer.

braid (brād), *v.t.* **1.** to weave together strips or strands of; plait. **2.** to form by such weaving. **3.** to bind or confine (the hair) with a band, ribbon, etc. **4.** to trim (garments) with braid. —*n.* **5.** a braided length, or plait, of hair, etc. **6.** a narrow band or tape, formed by plaiting or weaving together several strands of silk, cotton wool, or other material, used as trimming for garments, etc. **7.** a band, ribbon, etc., for binding or confining the hair. [ME *braide(n),* OE *bregdan* move quickly, move to and fro, weave, c. Icel. *bregdha*]—**braid′er,** *n.*

braid·ing (brā′dĭng), *n.* **1.** braids collectively. **2.** braided work.

brail (brāl), *n.* **1.** *Naut.* one of certain ropes fastened fast to the after leech of a sail, to assist in taking in the sail. —*v.t.* **2.** to gather or haul in (a sail) by means of brails (usually fol. by *up*). [ME *brayle,* t. OF: m. *braiel* cincture, g. L *brācāle* belt, der. *brācae* breeches]

Brǎ·i·la (brə ē′lä), *n.* a city in E Rumania: a port on the Danube. 75,249 (est. 1943).

Braille (brāl), *n.* a system of writing or printing for the blind, in which combinations of tangible dots or points are used to represent letters, etc. Also, **braille.** [after Louis *Braille* (1809–52)]

Braille on saff
A. Peak brail; B. Throat
brail; C. Lower brail

brain (brān), *n.* **1.** (*sometimes pl.*) the soft convoluted mass of grayish and whitish nerve substance which fills the cranium of man and other vertebrates. **2.** *Zool.* (in many invertebrates) a part of the nervous system more or less corresponding to the brain of vertebrates. **3.** (*usually pl.*) understanding; intellectual power; intelligence. —*v.t.* **4.** to dash out the brains of. [ME; OE *brægen,* c. MLG *bregen*]—**Syn. 3.** See **mind¹.**

brain cell, *Anat.* a neuron in the brain.

brain fever, *Pathol.* cerebrospinal meningitis.

brain·less (brān′lĭs), *adj.* mentally weak; witless; stupid. —**brain′less·ness,** *n.*

brain·pan (brān′păn′), *n.* the skull or cranium.

brain·sick (brān′sĭk′), *adj.* crazy; mad. —**brain′-sick·ly,** *adv.* —**brain′sick·ness,** *n.*

brain storm, 1. a sudden, violent attack of mental disturbance. **2.** *Colloq.* sudden inspiration, idea, etc.

brain trust, a group of experts who give counsel, help shape policy, etc. —**brain truster.**

brain wave, 1. (*pl.*) *Med.* electroencephalogram. **2.** *Colloq.* a sudden idea or inspiration.

---

b., blend of, blended; c., cognate with; d., dialect, dialectal; der., derived from; f., formed from; g., going back to; m., modification of; r., replacing; s., stem of; t., taken from; ?, perhaps. See the full key on inside cover.

brain·y (brā′nĭ), *adj.*, **brainier, brainiest.** having brains; intelligent; clever. **—brain′i·ness,** *n.*

braise (brāz), *v.t.*, **braised, braising.** to cook (meat or vegetables) by sautéing in fat and then cooking slowly in very little moisture. [t. F: m. *braiser,* der. *braise* hot charcoal, live coals; of Gmc. orig.]

brake¹ (brāk), *n.*, *v.*, **braked, braking.** **—n. 1.** any mechanical device for arresting the motion of a wheel or a vehicle by means of friction. **2.** (*pl.*) the drums, shoes, tubes, levers, etc., making up the brake system. **3.** a tool or machine for breaking up flax or hemp, to separate the fiber. **4.** Also, **break.** *Brit.* a large, high-set, four-wheeled vehicle, with crosswise seats, a seat in front for the driver, and another behind for footmen, now little used. **5.** *Obs.* an old instrument of torture. **—v.t. 6.** to slow or stop the motion of (a wheel, automobile, etc.) as by a brake. **7.** to furnish with brakes. **8.** to process (flax or hemp) by crushing it in a brake. **—v.i. 9.** to use or run a brake. **10.** to run a hoisting machine. [ME, t. MLG and/or MD] **—brake′less,** *adj.*

brake² (brāk), *n.* a place overgrown with bushes, shrubs, brambles, or cane; a thicket. [cf. MLG *brake*]

brake³ (brāk), *n.* any large or coarse fern, esp. *Pteridium aquilina* or some allied species. [ME, var. of BRACKEN]

brake⁴ (brāk), *v.* *Obs.* or *Archaic.* pt. of **break.**

brake·age (brā′kĭj), *n.* **1.** the action of a brake or set of brakes, as in stopping a vehicle. **2.** brakes collectively.

brake band, a part of brake mechanism consisting of a flexible band which grips a drum when tightened.

brake drum, the steel or cast-iron part attached to the wheel hub or transmission shaft to which a brake lining is applied.

brake horsepower, the amount of horsepower delivered to the transmission by the engine.

brake lining, the material, usually asbestos combined with other materials, used as the friction-producing element of a brake.

brake·man (brāk′mən), *n.*, *pl.* **-men.** *Railroads.* a member of a train crew, assisting the conductor in the operation of a train; trainman. Also, *Brit.,* **brakes′man.**

Bra·man·te (brä män′tĕ), *n.* **Donato d'Agnolo** (dō nä′tō dä′nyō lō), 1444?–1514, Italian architect and painter.

bram·ble (brăm′bəl), *n.*, *v.*, **-bled, -bling. —n. 1.** any plant of the rosaceous genus *Rubus.* **2.** *Scot.* the common blackberry, *R. fruticosus.* **3.** any rough prickly shrub, as the dog rose. **—v.i. 4.** *Brit.* to gather blackberries. [OE *bræmbel, brembel,* var. of *bræmel, bremel,* der. *brōm* broom] **—bram′bly,** *adj.*

bram·bling (brăm′blĭng), *n.* an Old World finch, *Fringilla montifringilla,* closely related to the chaffinch.

bran (brăn), *n.* **1.** the ground husk of wheat or other grain, separated from flour or meal by bolting. **2.** by-products of grain processing used as feed. [ME, t. OF]

Bran (brăn), *n.* a Brython deity, and early mythical king of Britain.

branch (brănch, bränch), *n.* **1.** *Bot.* a division or subdivision of the stem or axis of a tree, shrub, or other plant (the ultimate or smaller ramifications being called branchlets, twigs, or shoots). **2.** a limb, offshoot, or ramification: *the branches of a deer's horns.* **3.** any member or part of a body or system; a section or subdivision: *the various branches of learning.* **4.** a local operating division of a business house, a library, or the like. **5.** a line of family descent, in distinction from some other line or lines from the same stock. **6.** (in the classification of languages) a subdivision of a family; a group. **7.** *Geog.* **a.** a tributary stream. **b.** any stream that is not a large river or a bayou. **—v.i. 8.** to put forth branches; spread in branches. **9.** to divide into separate parts or subdivisions; diverge. **—v.t. 10.** to divide as into branches. **11.** to adorn with needlework; decorate with embroidery, as in textile fabrics. [ME, t. OF: m. *branche,* g. LL *branca* paw, claw] **—branch′less,** *adj.* **—branch′like′,** *adj.*
—Syn. 1. BRANCH, BOUGH, LIMB refer to divisions of a tree. BRANCH is general, meaning either a large or a small division. BOUGH refers only to the larger branches: *a bough loaded with apples.* A LIMB is a large primary division of a tree trunk or of a bough: *to climb out on a limb.*

bran·chi·a (brăng′kĭ ə), *n. pl.* *Ichthyol.* branchiae. [t. L (sing.), t. Gk.: m. *bránchia* (neut. pl.) gills] **—bran′-chi·al,** *adj.*

bran·chi·ae (brăng′kĭ ē′), *n. pl.* *Ichthyol.* the respiratory organs or gills of fishes, etc.

bran·chi·ate (brăng′kĭ ĭt, -āt′), *adj.* *Ichthyol.* having branchiae.

bran·chi·o·pod (brăng′kĭ ə pŏd′), *n.* *Zool.* any of the *Branchiopoda,* a group of crustaceans having branchiae or gills on the feet. [f. s. Gk. *bránchia* gills + -(o)POD]

brand (brănd), *n.* **1.** a trademark or trade name to identify a product, as that of a distributor, or a manufacturer or other producer. **2.** kind, grade, or make, as indicated by a brand, stamp, trademark, or the like. **3.** a mark made by burning or otherwise, to indicate kind, grade, make, ownership, etc. **4.** a mark formerly put upon criminals with a hot iron. **5.** any mark of infamy; a stigma. **6.** an iron for branding. **7.** a burning or partly burned piece of wood. **8.** *Archaic* or *Poetic.* a sword. **—v.t. 9.** to mark with a brand. **10.** to mark with infamy; stigmatize. [OE; akin to BURN¹] **—brand′-er,** *n.*

Bran·deis (brăn′dīs), *n.* **Louis Dembitz** (dĕm′bĭts), 1856–1941, U.S. lawyer and writer: associate justice of the U.S. Supreme Court, 1916–39.

Bran·den·burg (brăn′dən bûrg′; *Ger.* brän′dən bŏŏrκн), *n.* **1.** a province in NE Germany. 2,333,000 pop. (1946); 10,412 sq. mi. (1946). **2.** the capital of this province. 83,726 (1939).

Bran·des (brän′dĕs), *n.* **Georg Morris Cohen** (gĭ′ōrg mō′rĭs kō′ən), 1842–1927, Danish critic and scholar.

bran·died (brăn′dĭd), *adj.* flavored or treated with brandy.

bran·dish (brăn′dĭsh), *v.t.* **1.** to shake or wave, as a weapon; flourish. **—n. 2.** a wave or flourish, as of a weapon. [ME *braundish(en),* t. OF: m. *brandiss-,* s. *brandir,* der. *brand* sword; of Gmc. orig. See BRAND] **—bran′dish·er,** *n.*

brand·ling (brănd′lĭng), *n.* a small, reddish-brown earthworm, *Helodrilus foetidus,* with yellow markings, found chiefly in manure piles.

brand-new (brănd′nū′, -nōō′), *adj.* quite new. Also, **bran-new** (brăn′nū′, -nōō′).

bran·dy (brăn′dĭ), *n.*, *pl.* **-dies,** *v.*, **-died, -dying. —n. 1.** the spirit distilled from the fermented juice of grapes or, sometimes, of apples, peaches, plums, etc. **—v.t. 2.** to mix, flavor, or preserve with brandy. [short for *brandy-wine,* t. D: m. *brandewijn* burnt (i.e. distilled) wine]

Bran·dy·wine (brăn′dĭ wīn′), *n.* a creek in SE Pennsylvania and N Delaware: American defeat by the British, 1777.

branks (brăngks), *n. pl.* a bridle formerly used to punish a scold. [orig. uncert.]

bran·ny (brăn′ĭ), *adj.* of, containing, or like bran.

brant (brănt), *n.*, *pl.* **brants,** (*esp. collectively*) **brant.** any of several species of small, dark-colored geese of the genus *Branta,* esp. *B. bernicla,* breeding in high northern latitudes and migrating south in the autumn. Also, **brent.** [cf. Icel. *brandgás*]

Brant (brănt), *n.* **Joseph** (native name, *Thayenda-negea*), 1742–1807, Mohawk Indian chief who fought with the British in the American Revolution.

Brant·ford (brănt′fərd), *n.* a city in SE Canada, in Ontario, near Hamilton. 24,253 (1941).

brash (brăsh), *adj.* **1.** headlong; hasty; rash. **2.** impertinent; impudent. **3.** *U.S. Local.* (used esp. of timber) brittle. **—n. 4.** loose fragments of rock. **5.** *Naut.* small fragments of crushed ice collected by winds or currents near the shore. **6.** *Dial.* an attack of illness. **7.** *Dial.* a shower. [orig. obscure] **—brash′y,** *adj.*

bra·sier (brā′zhər), *n.* brazier.

Bra·sil (brə sēl′), *n.* Portuguese and Spanish name of Brazil.

bras·i·lin (brăz′ə lĭn), *n.* *Chem.* brazilin.

Bra·șov (brä shŏv′), *n.* a city in central Rumania. 85,506 (est. 1943). German, **Kronstadt.** Hungarian, **Brassó.**

brass (brăs, bräs), *n.* **1.** a durable, malleable, and ductile yellow alloy, consisting essentially of copper and zinc. **2.** a utensil, ornament, or other article made of brass. **3.** *Mach.* a bearing, bush, or the like. **4.** *Music.* **a.** a musical instrument of the trumpet or horn families. **b.** such instruments collectively in a band or orchestra. **5.** *Brit.* a memorial tablet incised with an effigy, coat of arms or the like. **6.** metallic yellow; lemon, amber, or reddish yellow. **7.** *U.S. Slang.* high-ranking officials, esp. high-ranking officers of the army and navy. **8.** *Colloq.* excessive assurance; impudence; effrontery. **9.** *Brit. Slang.* money. **—adj. 10.** made of brass. **11.** using musical instruments made of brass. [ME *bras,* OE *bræs*] **—brass′like′,** *adj.*

brass·age (brăs′ĭj, bräs′ĭj), *n.* a charge to cover costs of coining money. [t. F, der. *brasser* stir (welded metal), ult. der. L *brace* white corn, of Celtic orig.]

bras·sard (brăs′ärd), *n.* **1.** a badge worn around the upper arm. **2.** Also, **bras·sart** (brăs′ərt). a piece of armor for the arm. See illus. under **armor.** [t. F, der. *bras* arm]

brass hat, *Slang.* a high-ranking army or navy officer.

bras·si·ca·ceous (brăs′ĭ kā′shəs), *adj.* *Bot.* belonging to the family *Brassicaceae* (often called *Cruciferae*) of herbaceous plants, including the common cabbage, watercress, etc. [f. s. L *brassica* cabbage + -ACEOUS]

brass·ie (brăs′ĭ, bräs′ĭ), *n.* a long-shafted golf club with a wooden head soled with a brass plate. Also, **brassy.**

bras·sière (brə zĭr′), *n.* a woman's undergarment which supports the breasts. [t. F: little camisole, der. *bras* arm]

brass knuckles, piece of metal fitted across the knuckles, used in fighting.

Bras·só (brŏsh′shō), *n.* Hungarian name of Brasov.

brass tacks, *Colloq.* basic facts; realities.

brass·ware (brăs′wâr′, bräs′-), *n.* articles made of brass.

brass winds, *Music.* brass (def. 4b).

brass·y¹ (brăs′ĭ, bräs′ĭ), *adj.*, **brassier, brassiest. 1.** made of or covered with brass. **2.** resembling brass. **3.** harsh and metallic: *brassy tones.* **4.** *Colloq.* brazen. [f. BRASS + -Y¹] **—brass′i·ly,** *adv.* **—brass′i·ness,** *n.*

brass·y² (brăs′ĭ, bräs′ĭ), *n.*, *pl.* **-ies.** *Golf.* brassie.

brat (brăt), *n.* a child, used usually in contempt or irritation. [cf. d. *brat* rag, trash, OE *bratt* cloak]

Bra·ti·sla·va (brä′tĭ′slä′və), *n.* a city in S Czecho-slovakia, on the Danube: a former capital of Hungary. 123,844 (1930). German, **Pressburg.** Hungarian, **Po-zsony.**

brat·tice (brăt′ĭs), *n., v.,* **-ticed, -ticing.** —*n.* 1. a par-tition or lining, as of planks or cloth, forming an air passage in a mine. —*v.t.* 2. to provide with a brattice; line with planks or cloth. [ME *bretage,* t. OF: m. *bretesche* parapet, ? t. OE: m. *brittisc* British, i.e., foreign (fortification)]

brat·tle (brăt′əl), *n., v.,* **-tled, -tling.** —*n.* 1. a clatter-ing noise. —*v.i.* 2. to scamper noisily.

braun·ite (brou′nīt), *n.* a mineral, manganese oxide and silicate, $Mn_7^"SiO_{12}$, an ore of manganese.

Braun·schweig (broun′shvīкн), *n.* German name of **Brunswick.**

bra·va·do (brə vä′dō), *n., pl.* **-does, -dos.** boasting; swaggering; pretense. [t. Sp.: m. *bravada.* See BRAVE] —**Syn.** See **courage.**

brave (brāv), *adj.,* **braver, bravest,** *n., v.,* **braved,** **braving.** —*adj.* 1. possessing or exhibiting courage or courageous endurance. 2. making a fine appearance. 3. *Archaic.* excellent; fine; admirable. —*n.* 4. a brave person. 5. a North American Indian or other savage warrior. 6. *Obs.* a bully. 7. *Obs.* a boast; a challenge; a defiance. —*v.t.* 8. to meet or face courageously: *to brave misfortunes.* 9. to defy; challenge; dare. 10. *Obs.* to make splendid. —*v.i.* 11. *Obs.* to boast; brag. [t. F, t. It.: m. *bravo* brave, bold, fine, t. Sp.: vicious (first applied to bulls). g. L *prāvus*] —**brave′ly,** *adv.* —**brave′ness,** *n.*
—**Syn.** 1. BRAVE, COURAGEOUS, FEARLESS, GALLANT refer to confident bearing in the face of difficulties or dangers. BRAVE is the most comprehensive; it is especially used of that confident fortitude or daring that actively faces and endures anything threatening. COURAGEOUS implies a higher or nobler kind of bravery, esp. as resulting from an inborn quality of mind or spirit which faces or endures perils or difficulties without fear and even with enthusiasm. FEARLESS implies unflinching spirit and coolness in the face of danger. GALLANT implies chivalrous, impetuous, dashing, or showy bravery.

brav·er·y (brā′vər ĭ), *n., pl.* **-eries.** 1. brave spirit or conduct; courage; valor. 2. showiness; splendor; magnif-icence. —**Syn.** 1. intrepidity, fearlessness, boldness, daring, prowess, heroism, pluck. See **courage.**

bra·vo[1] (brä′vō), *interj., n., pl.* **-vos.** —*interj.* 1. well done! good! —*n.* 2. a shout of "bravo!" [t. It., prop. adj. See BRAVE]

bra·vo[2] (brä′vō, brä′-), *n., pl.* **-voes, -vos.** a daring bandit or assassin or murderer. [t. It. See BRAVE]

bra·vu·ra (brə vyŏŏr′ə; *It.* brä vōō′rä), *n.* 1. *Music.* a florid passage or piece, requiring great skill and spirit in the performer. 2. a display of daring; brilliant performance. —*adj.* 3. *Music.* spirited; florid; brilliant (chiefly applied to vocal compositions, but occasionally to instrumental). [t. It.: bravery, spirit]

braw (brô, brä), *adj. Scot. and N. Eng.* fine or fine-looking; excellent. [var. of BRAVE]

brawl[1] (brôl), *n.* 1. a noisy quarrel; a squabble. 2. a bubbling or roaring noise; a clamor. —*v.i.* 3. to quarrel angrily, noisily; wrangle. 4. to make a bubbling or roaring noise, as water flowing over a rocky bed. [ME *brall(en),* der. *brawl* brawler, var. of *broll* brat, contr. of *brothel* good-for-nothing, der. OE *brēothan* go to ruin] —**brawl′er,** *n.* —**Syn.** 1. See **disorder.**

brawl[2] (brôl), *n.* an old folk dance of French origin. [orig. unknown]

brawn (brôn), *n.* 1. well-developed muscles. 2. mus-cular strength. 3. a boar's or swine's flesh, esp. when boiled and pickled. [ME *brawne,* t. OF: m. *braon,* t. Gmc.; cf. G *braten* roast]

brawn·y (brô′nĭ), *adj.,* **brawnier, brawniest.** mus-cular; strong. —**brawn′i·ness,** *n.*

brax·y (brăk′sĭ), *Vet. Sci.* —*n.* 1. an acute bacterial disease of sheep involving inflammation of the bowels. usually fatal. —*adj.* 2. affected with braxy. [prob. n. use of adj., OE *bræcsēoc* ill with falling sickness, f. *bræc* rheum + *sēoc* sick]

bray[1] (brā), *n.* 1. a harsh, breathy cry, as of the don-key. 2. any similar loud, harsh sound. —*v.i.* 3. to utter a loud and harsh cry as the donkey. 4. to make a loud, harsh, disagreeable sound, as a trumpet. —*v.t.* 5. to utter with a loud, harsh sound, like the donkey. [ME *braye(n),* t. OF: m. *braire*] —**bray′er,** *n.*

bray[2] (brā), *v.t.* to pound or crush fine, as in a mortar. [ME *braye(n),* t. OF: m. *breier*]

bray·er (brā′ər), *n. Print.* a small roller for inking type or plates by hand (usually for making a proof). [f. BRAY[2] + -ER[1]]

Braz., 1. Brazil. 2. Brazilian.

bra·za (brä′thä, -sä), *n.* a unit of length in Spanish-speaking countries, representing the reach of outspread arms, officially 5.48 U.S. ft. in Spain, and 5.68 U.S. ft. in Argentina. [t. Sp., der. *brazo* arm, g. L *brāchium*]

braze[1] (brāz), *v.t.,* **brazed, brazing.** 1. to make of brass. 2. to cover or ornament with brass, or as if with brass. 3. to make brasslike. [OE *brasian,* der. *bræs* brass]

braze[2] (brāz), *v.t.,* **brazed, brazing.** *Metall.* to unite (pieces of brass, steel, etc.) by intensely heating the parts to be joined and applying any one of a number of high melting solders which range in melting point from alloys rich in silver to pure copper. [? t. F: m. *braser,* der. *braise* live coals. See BRAISE]

bra·zen (brā′zən), *adj.* 1. made of brass. 2. like brass, as in sound, color, strength, etc. 3. shameless or impu-dent: *brazen effrontery.* —*v.t.* 4. to face with boldness and effrontery (fol. by *out*). 5. to make brazen or bold. [ME *brasen,* OE *bræsen,* der. *bræs* brass] —**bra′zen·ly,** *adv.* —**bra′zen·ness,** *n.* —**Syn.** 3. See **bold.**

bra·zen-faced (brā′zən fāst′), *adj.* openly shameless; impudent.

bra·zier[1] (brā′zhər), *n.* a person who works in brass. Also, **brasier.** [ME *brasiere;* f. BRAZE[2], v. + -IER]

bra·zier[2] (brā′zhər), *n.* a metal receptacle for holding burning charcoal or other fuel, as for heating a room. Also, **brasier.** [t. F: m. *brasier,* der. *braise* live coals.]

Bra·zil (brə zĭl′), a republic in South America. 45,300,-000 pop. (est. 1941); 3,286,170 sq. mi. *Cap.:* Rio de Ja-neiro. Official name, **United States of Brazil.** Por-tuguese and Spanish, **Brasil.** —**Bra·zil·ian** (brə-zĭl′yən), *adj., n.*

bra·zil (brə zĭl′), *n.* 1. a dyewood from various tropical American trees of the genus *Caesalpinia* (esp. *C. echinata*) and allied genera, yielding reds and purples. 2. the red dyestuff extracted from it. 3. (orig.) a hard East Indian dyewood yielding a red color, from the tree *Caesalpinia sappan.* [ME *brasile,* t. Sp. or Pg.: m. *brasil,* t. OF: m. *brēsil* reddish-tinted wood, der. *brēze,* *braise* glowing coals; Brazil was named after the tree]

braz·i·lin (brăz′ə lĭn), *n. Chem.* a yellow substance, $C_{16}H_{14}O_5$, from brazil, used as a dye and indicator. Also, **brasilin.**

Brazil nut, the triangular edible seed (nut) of the tree *Bertholletia excelsa* and related species, of Brazil, etc.

bra·zil·wood (brə zĭl′wŏŏd′), *n.* brazil.

Bra·zos (brä′zōs; *locally* brăz′əs, brä′zəs), *n.* a river flowing from N Texas SE to the Gulf of Mexico. 870 mi.

Braz·za·ville (brá zá vēl′), *n.* the capital of Middle Congo and of French Equatorial Africa: a port on the Congo river. ab. 40,000.

breach (brēch), *n.* 1. act or result of breaking; a break or rupture. 2. a gap made in a wall, dike, fortification, etc.; rift; fissure. 3. an infraction or violation, as of law, trust, faith, promise, etc. 4. a severance of friendly relations. 5. the springing of a whale from the water. 6. *Archaic.* the breaking of waves; the dashing of surf. 7. *Obs.* wound. —*v.t.* 8. to make a breach or opening in. [ME *breche,* OE *brǣce*] —**Syn.** 4. alienation, quarrel.

breach of promise, *Law.* a violation of one's promise, esp. of a promise to marry.

breach of the peace, *Law.* a violation of the pub-lic peace, by a riot, disturbance, etc.

breach of trust, 1. *Law.* a violation of duty by a trustee. 2. *Colloq.* a violation of duty by any fiduciary.

bread (brĕd), *n.* 1. a kind of food made of flour or meal, milk or water, etc., made into a dough or batter, with or without yeast or the like, and baked. 2. food or sustenance; livelihood: *to earn one's bread.* 3. *Eccles.* the wafer or bread used in the Eucharist. 4. **break bread, a.** to partake of or share food. **b.** *Eccles.* to ad-minister or join in Communion. —*v.t.* 5. *Cookery.* to cover or dress with bread crumbs or meal. [ME *breed,* OE *brēad,* c. G *brot*] —**bread′less,** *adj.*

bread and butter, 1. bread spread with butter. 2. *Colloq.* means of living; livelihood.

bread-and-but·ter (brĕd′ən bŭt′ər), *adj.* 1. seeking the means of living; mercenary. 2. *Colloq.* belonging to or in the stage of adolescence. 3. *Colloq.* matter-of-fact. 4. expressing thanks for hospitality, as a letter.

bread·fruit (brĕd′frōōt′), *n.* 1. a large, round, starchy fruit yielded by a moraceous tree, *Artocarpus communis* (*A. altilis*), of the Pacific islands, etc., much used, baked or roasted, for food. 2. the tree bearing this fruit.

bread line, a line of needy persons assembled to re-ceive food given as charity.

bread mold, a black fungus, *Rhizopus nigricans,* often seen on bread.

bread·root (brĕd′rōōt′, -rŏŏt′), *n.* the edible farina-ceous root of *Psoralea esculenta,* a fabaceous plant of central North America.

bread·stuff (brĕd′stŭf′), *n.* 1. grain, flour, or meal for making bread. 2. bread.

breadth (brĕdth, brĕtth), *n.* 1. *Math.* the measure of the second principal diameter of a surface or solid, the first being length, and the third (in the case of a solid) thickness; width. 2. an extent or piece of something as measured by its width, or of definite or full width: *a breadth of cloth.* 3. freedom from narrowness or restraint; liberality: *breadth of view.* 4. size in general; extent. 5. *Art.* broad or general effect due to subordination of details or nonessentials. [f. earlier *breade* (OE *brǣdu*) + -TH[1]; modeled on LENGTH]

breadth·ways (brĕdth′wāz′, brĕtth′-), *adv.* in the direction of the breadth. Also, **breadth·wise** (brĕdth′-wīz′, brĕtth′-).

bread·win·ner (brĕd′wĭn′ər), *n.* one who earns a livelihood for himself and those dependent upon him.

break (brāk), *v.,* **broke** or (*Archaic*) **brake; broken,** or (*Archaic*) **broke; breaking;** *n.* —*v.t.* 1. to divide into parts violently; reduce to pieces or fragments. 2. to violate: *to break a law or promise.* 3. to dissolve or annul (often fol. by *off*). 4. to fracture a bone of. 5. to lacerate; wound: *break the skin.* 6. to discontinue abruptly; interrupt; suspend: *to break the silence.* 7. to destroy the regularity of. 8. to put an end to; overcome.

9. to interrupt the uniformity or sameness of: *to break the monotony.* **10.** to destroy the unity, continuity, or arrangement of. **11.** to exchange for a smaller amount or smaller units. **12.** to make one's way through; penetrate. **13.** *Law.* **a.** to open or force one's way into (a dwelling, store, etc.). **b.** to contest (a will) successfully by judicial action. **14.** to make one's way out of: *to break jail.* **15.** to exceed; outdo: *to break a record.* **16.** to disclose or divulge, with caution or delicacy. **17.** to disable or destroy by or as by shattering or crushing. **18.** (pp. **broke**) to ruin financially, or make bankrupt. **19.** to reduce in rank. **20.** to impair or weaken in strength, spirit, force, or effect. **21.** to train to obedience; tame (often fol. by *in*). **22.** to train away from a habit or practice (fol. by *of*). **23.** *Elect.* to render (a circuit) incomplete; stop the flow of (a current). —*v.i.* **24.** to become broken; separate into parts or fragments, esp. suddenly and violently. **25.** to become suddenly discontinuous or interrupted; leave off abruptly. **26.** to become detached (fol. by *off*, etc.). **27.** to dissolve and separate (fol. by *up*). **28.** to sever relations (fol. by *with*). **29.** to change suddenly, as in sound, movement, or direction. **30.** to free oneself or escape suddenly, as from restraint (often fol. by *away*). **31.** to force a way (fol. by *in*, *through*, etc.). **32.** to burst (fol. by *in*, *forth*, *from*, etc.). **33.** to come suddenly, as into notice. **34.** to dawn, as the day. **35.** (of a fish) to come to the surface. **36.** to give way or fail as under strain (often fol. by *down*). **37.** (of the heart) to be crushed or overwhelmed. **38.** (of stock exchange prices) to drop quickly and considerably. **39.** *Music.* **a.** to change or go from one register to another, as a musical instrument or the voice. **b.** to change or be interrupted unmusically, as a voice or tone. **40.** *Ling.* to undergo breaking. **41.** *Pool.* to make a break (def. 59). **42.** Some special verb phrases are:
break away, (in racing) to start prematurely.
break camp, to pack up tents and equipment and resume a march.
break down, 1. to take down or destroy by breaking. **2.** to overcome. **3.** to analyze.
break off, 1. to sever by breaking. **2.** to put a sudden stop to; discontinue.
break out, 1. to issue forth; arise. **2.** *Pathol.* (of certain diseases) to appear in eruptions. **3.** to have a sudden appearance of various eruptions on the skin.
break step, *Mil.* to cease marching in cadence.
break up, 1. to separate; disband. **2.** to put an end to; discontinue. **3.** to cut up (fowl, etc.).
—*n.* **43.** a forcible disruption or separation of parts; a breaking; a fracture, rupture, or shattering. **44.** an opening made by breaking; a gap. **45.** a rush away from a place; an attempt to escape: *a break for freedom.* **46.** an interruption of continuity; suspension; stoppage. **47.** an abrupt or marked change, as in sound or direction. **48.** *Colloq.* an opportunity; chance. **49.** *Colloq.* a social error or slip; an unfortunate remark. **50.** a small amount; portion. **51.** a brief rest, as from work. **52.** *Pros.* a pause or caesura. **53.** *Jazz.* a solo passage, usually of about two bars, during which the band accompaniment breaks off, or rests. **54.** *Music.* the point in the scale where the quality of voice of one register changes to that of another, as from chest to head. **55.** (on the stock exchange) a sudden drop in prices. **56.** *Elect.* an opening or discontinuity in a circuit. **57.** *Print.* **a.** one or more blank lines between two paragraphs. **b.** (*pl.*) dots (. . .) to show where something has been omitted in printed material. **58.** *Billiards.* run (def. 99). **59.** *Pool.* **a.** the shot that breaks or scatters the balls as piled together at the beginning of the game. **b.** the right to the first play. **60.** *Baseball, Cricket, etc.* change in direction of a ball, usually caused by spinning it when thrown. **61.** *Bowling.* a failure to knock down all ten pins after bowling twice. **62.** brake (def. 4). [ME *breke(n)*, OE *brecan,* c. G *brechen*] —**break′a·ble,** *adj.*
—**Syn. 1.** BREAK, CRUSH, SHATTER, SMASH mean to reduce to parts, violently or by force. BREAK means to divide by means of a blow, a collision, a pull, or the like: *to break a chair, a leg, a strap.* To CRUSH is to subject to (usually heavy or violent) pressure so as to press out of shape or reduce to shapelessness or to small particles: *to crush a beetle.* To SHATTER is to break in a way to cause the pieces to fly in many directions: *to shatter a light globe.* To SMASH is to break noisily and suddenly into many pieces: *to smash a glass.* **2.** transgress, disobey, contravene.
break·age (brā′kĭj), *n.* **1.** act of breaking; a break. **2.** the amount or quantity of things broken. **3.** *Com.* an allowance or compensation for loss or damage of articles broken in transit or in use.
break·bone fever (brāk′bōn′), *Pathol.* dengue.
break·down (brāk′doun′), *n.* **1.** a breaking down, as of a machine, of physical or mental health, etc.; a collapse. **2.** *Chem.* **a.** decomposition. **b.** analysis. **3.** *U.S.* a noisy, lively folk dance.
break·er[1] (brā′kər), *n.* **1.** one who or that which breaks. **2.** a wave that breaks or dashes into foam. [f. BREAK + -ER[1]] —**Syn. 2.** See **wave.**
break·er[2] (brā′kər), *n. Naut.* a small water cask for use in a boat. [t. Sp.: alter. of *barrica* cask]
break·fast (brĕk′fəst), *n.* **1.** the first meal of the day; a morning meal. **2.** the food eaten at the first meal. **3.** a meal or food in general. —*v.i.* **4.** to take breakfast. —*v.t.* **5.** to supply with breakfast. [ME *brekfast,* f. *brek* break + *fast* FAST[2]] —**break′fast·er,** *n.*

breakfast food, a cold or hot cereal generally eaten for breakfast.
break·ing (brā′kĭng), *n.* (in the history of English and of some other languages) the change of a vowel to diphthong under the influence of a following consonant or combination of consonants; e.g., in Old English, the change of *-a-* to *-ea-* and of *-e-* to *-eo-* before preconsonantal *-r-* or *-l-* and before *-h-,* as in *earm* (arm) developed from *arm* and *eorthe* (earth) from *erthe.*
break·neck (brāk′nĕk′), *adj.* dangerous; hazardous.
break of day, dawn; daybreak.
break·through (brāk′thrōō′), *n. Mil.* a movement or advance all the way through and beyond a defensive system into the unorganized areas in the rear.
break·up (brāk′ŭp′), *n.* disintegration; disruption; dispersal.
break·wa·ter (brāk′wô′tər, -wŏt′ər), *n.* a barrier which breaks the force of waves, as before a harbor.
bream[1] (brēm), *n.,* *pl.* **breams,** (*esp. collectively*) **bream.** **1.** any of various fresh-water cyprinoid fishes of the genus *Abramis,* as *A. brama* of Europe, with a compressed, deep body. **2.** any of various related and similar species, as the **white bream,** *Blicca bjoerkna.* **3.** a sea bream. **4.** Also, *Southern U.S.,* **brim.** any of various fresh-water sunfishes of the genus *Lepomis.* [ME *breme,* t. F, t. OG; cf. OS *bressemo*]
bream[2] (brēm), *v.t. Naut.* to clean (a ship's bottom) by applying burning furze, reeds, etc., to soften the pitch and loosen adherent matter. [cf. MD *brem(e)* furze]
breast (brĕst), *n.* **1.** *Anat., Zool.* the outer front part of the thorax, or the front part of the body from neck to belly; the chest. **2.** *Zool.* the corresponding part in lower animals. **3.** *Anat., Zool.* the mammary or milk gland, esp. of a woman, or of female animals whose milk glands are similarly formed. **4.** that part of a garment which covers the chest. **5.** the bosom regarded as the seat of thoughts and feelings. **6.** thoughts; feelings; mind. **7.** any surface or part resembling or likened to the human breast. **8.** *Mining.* the face or heading at which the working is going on. —*v.t.* **9.** to meet or oppose with the breast. **10.** to meet boldly or advance against; face. [ME *brest,* OE *brēost,* akin to G *brust*]
breast·bone (brĕst′bōn′), *n. Anat., Zool.* sternum.
Breas·ted (brĕs′tĭd), *n.* **James Henry,** 1865–1935, U. S. archaeologist, and historian of ancient Egypt.
breast·pin (brĕst′pĭn′), *n.* a pin worn on the breast or at the throat; a brooch.
breast·plate (brĕst′plāt′), *n.* **1.** armor for the front of the torso. **2.** part of the harness that runs across a saddle horse's breast. **3.** a square ornament worn on the breast by the Jewish high priest.

Breastplate. (def. 1) 16th century

breast stroke, *Swimming.* a stroke made in the prone position in which both hands move simultaneously forward, outward and rearward from in front of the chest.
breast·work (brĕst′wûrk′), *n. Fort.* a defensive work usually breast high, hastily thrown up.
breath (brĕth), *n.* **1.** *Physiol.* the air inhaled and exhaled in respiration. **2.** respiration, esp. as necessary to life. **3.** ability to breathe, esp. freely: *out of breath.* **4.** time to breathe; pause or respite. **5.** a single respiration. **6.** the brief time required for it; an instant. **7.** an utterance; whisper. **8.** a light current of air. **9.** *Phonet.* voiceless expiration of air, used in the production of many speech sounds, such as *p* or *f.* **10.** moisture emitted in respiration, esp. when condensed and visible. **11.** a trivial circumstance; a trifle. **12.** an odorous exhalation, or the air impregnated by it. **13.** *Obs.* odor; vapor. **14. below** or **under one's breath,** in a low voice or whisper. [ME *breeth,* OE *brǣth* odor, exhalation; akin to G *brodem* exhalation, vapor]
breathe (brēth), *v.,* **breathed** (brēthd), **breathing.** —*v.i.* **1.** to inhale and exhale air; respire. **2.** (in speech) to control the outgoing breath in producing voice and speech sounds. **3.** to pause, as for breath; take rest (only in infinitive): *give me a chance to breathe.* **4.** to blow lightly, as air. **5.** to live; exist. **6.** to exhale an odor. **7.** to be redolent (*of*). —*v.t.* **8.** to inhale and exhale in respiration. **9.** to allow to rest or recover breath. **10.** to put out of breath; tire or exhaust. **11.** to give utterance to; whisper. **12.** to express; manifest. **13.** to exhale: *dragons breathing fire.* **14.** to inject by breathing; infuse. **15.** to exercise briskly. —**breath′a·ble,** *adj.*
breathed (brĕtht, brēthd *for 1*; brĕtht *for 2*), *adj.* **1.** *Phonet.* without use of the vocal chords; voiceless. **2.** having a breath, as in *sweet-breathed.*
breath·er (brē′thər), *n.* **1.** a pause, as for breath. **2.** *Colloq.* something, as exercise, that stimulates or exhausts the breath. **3.** one who or that which breathes.
breath·ing (brē′thing), *n.* **1.** act of one that breathes; respiration. **2.** a single breath. **3.** the short time required for it. **4.** a pause, as for breath. **5.** utterance or words. **6.** aspiration or longing. **7.** gentle blowing, as of wind. **8.** *Gram.* **a.** aspiration; pronunciation with reference to the use or omission of an *h*-sound. **b.** a sign to indicate this, as in Greek.

breathing space, opportunity to breathe easily; time to rest.

breath·less (brĕth′lĭs), *adj.* **1.** out of breath: *the blow left him breathless.* **2.** with the breath held, as in suspense: *breathless listeners.* **3.** that takes away the breath: *a breathless ride.* **4.** dead. **5.** motionless, as the air. **—breath′less·ly,** *adv.* **—breath′less·ness,** *n.*

breath-tak·ing (brĕth′tā′kĭng), *adj.* causing extreme excitement: *a breath-taking performance.*

breath·y (brĕth′ĭ), *adj.* (of the voice) characterized by excessive emission of breath.

brec·ci·a (brĕch′ə, brĕsh′-; *It.* brĕt′chä), *n.* rock composed of angular fragments of older rocks cemented together. [t. It.]

Breck·in·ridge (brĕk′ĭn rĭj), *n.* **John Cabell** (kăb′əl), 1821–75, vice-president of the U. S., 1857–61: Confederate general in the U.S. Civil War.

Breck·noch·shire (brĕk′nək shĭr′), *n.* a county in S Wales. 52,000 pop. (est. 1946); 733 sq. mi. *Co. seat:* Brecon. Also, **Brech′noch, Brec·on** (brĕk′ən).

bred (brĕd), *v.* pt. and pp. of **breed.**

Bre·da (brā dä′), *n.* a city in S Netherlands. 82,668 (est. 1946).

brede (brēd), *n. Archaic.* a braid or plait; anything interwoven; embroidery. [var. of BRAID]

bree (brē), *n. Scot.* broth; juice. [OE *briw* pottage]

breech (*n.* brēch; *v.* brēch, brĭch), *n.* **1.** the lower part of the trunk of the body behind; the posteriors or buttocks. **2.** the hinder or lower part of anything. **3.** *Ordn.* the mass of metal behind the bore of a cannon, or the part of a small arm back of the barrel. **4.** *Mach.* the lowest part of a pulley. **—v.t. 5.** *Ordn.* to fit or furnish (a gun) with a breech. **6.** to clothe with breeches. [ME *breeche,* OE *brēc,* pl., c. Icel. *brækr,* pl. of *brōk.* Cf. L *brācae,* pl., breeches, of Celtic orig.]

breech·block (brēch′blŏk′), *n. Ordn.* a movable piece of metal which closes the breech end of the barrel in certain firearms.

breech·cloth (brēch′klôth′, -klŏth′), *n.* a cloth worn about the breech. Also, **breech·clout** (brēch′klout′).

breech·es (brĭch′ĭz), *n.pl.* **1.** a garment worn by men (and by women for riding, etc.), covering the hips and thighs. **2.** trousers. [f. BREECH + *-es* (pl. ending)]

breeches buoy, *Naut.* a lifesaving apparatus, like a short pair of breeches, moving on a rope stretched from a wreck to the shore or another ship.

breech·ing (brĭch′ĭng, brē′chĭng), *n.* **1.** the part of a harness which passes around a horse's breech. See illus. under **harness. 2.** a smoke pipe connecting one or more boilers with a chimney. **3.** *Naval.* a strong rope fastened to a ship's side, to check the recoil of a gun or to secure it.

breech·load·er (brēch′lō′dər), *n. Ordn.* a firearm, as a rifle, loaded at the breech.

breech·load·ing (brēch′lō′dĭng), *adj. Ordn.* loaded at the breech.

Breeches buoy

breed (brēd), *v.,* **bred, breeding,** *n.* **—v.t. 1.** to produce (offspring). **2.** to procure by the mating of parents; propagate. **3.** *Hort.* **a.** to cause to reproduce by controlled pollination. **b.** to improve by controlled pollination and selection. **4.** to raise (livestock, etc.). **5.** to procreate; engender. **6.** to cause; occasion; produce: *dirt breeds disease.* **7.** to be the native place or the source of: *stagnant water breeds mosquitoes.* **8.** to produce by training. **—v.i. 9.** to produce offspring. **10.** to be engendered or produced; grow; develop. **11.** to procure the birth of young, as in raising stock. **—n. 12.** *Genetics.* a relatively homogenous group of animals within a species, developed and maintained by man. **13.** race; lineage; strain. **14.** sort; kind. [ME *brede(n),* OE *brēdan* nourish, der. *brōd* brood] **—breed′er,** *n.*

breed·ing (brē′dĭng), *n.* **1.** act of one who or that which breeds. **2.** the rearing of livestock to improve their quality or merit. **3.** *Hort.* the production of new forms by selection, crossing, and hybridizing. **4.** nurture; training. **5.** the results of training as shown in behavior and manners; manners; esp. good manners.

Breed's Hill (brēdz). See **Bunker Hill.**

breeks (brēks, brĭks), *n.pl. Scot.* and *N. Eng.* breeches.

breeze[1] (brēz), *n.* **1.** a wind or current of air, esp. a light or moderate one. **2.** *Meteorol.* any wind of Beaufort scale numbers 2 to 6 inclusive, comprising velocities from 4 to 31 miles per hour. **3.** *Chiefly Brit. Colloq.* a disturbance or quarrel. [t. Sp. (and Pg.): m. *briza*] **—Syn. 1.** See **wind**[1].

breeze[2] (brēz), *n.* a gadfly. [ME *brese,* OE *breosa*]

breeze[3] (brēz), *n. Brit.* cinders; dust of charcoal, coke, or coal. [prob. t. F: m. *braise* live coals, cinders]

breez·y (brē′zĭ), *adj.,* **breezier, breeziest. 1.** abounding in breezes; windy. **2.** fresh; sprightly. **—breez′i·ly,** *adv.* **—breez′i·ness,** *n.*

Bre·genz (brā′gĕnts), *n.* a city in W Austria: a port on the Lake of Constance. 18,332 (1939).

breg·ma (brĕg′mə), *n., pl.* **-mata** (-mə tə). *Craniom.* the point of junction of the sagittal and coronal sutures of the skull. [t. Gk.: front of the head] **—breg·mat·ic** (brĕg măt′ĭk), *adj.*

bre·loque (brĕ lôk′), *n.* a trinket or small object worn suspended from a chain, ribbon, etc. [t. F]

Brem·en (brĕm′ən; *Ger.* brā′mən), *n.* **1.** a small state in NW Germany. 450,084 pop. (1939); 99 sq. mi. **2.** the capital of this state: a port on the Weser river; a member of the Hanseatic League. 424,137 (1939).

Brem·er·ha·ven (brĕm′ər hä′vən; *Ger.* brā′mər hä′fən), *n.* a seaport in NW Germany at the mouth of the Weser river. 25,779. (1933).

Brem·er·ton (brĕm′ər tən), *n.* a city in W Washington, on Puget Sound: navy yard; largest drydocks in the U.S. 27,678 (1940).

Bren gun (brĕn), *Brit.* a kind of machine gun. [f. *Br*(no), in Czechoslovakia, where they were first manufactured + *En*(field), where construction was perfected]

Bren·ner Pass (brĕn′ər), a pass in the Alps on the Italian-Austrian border. 4470 ft. high.

brent (brĕnt), *n.* brant.

br′er (brŭr, brĕr), *n. Southern U.S. Dial.* brother.

Bre·scia (brĕ′shä), *n.* a city in N Italy, in Lombardy. 143,591 (est. 1946).

Bres·lau (brĕz′lou; *Ger.* brĕs′-), *n.* a city in SW Poland, on the Oder river: formerly in Germany. 168,000 (1946). Polish, **Wroclaw.**

Brest (brĕst), *n.* a seaport in NW France: surrendered by German forces, Sept., 1944. 74,991 (1946).

Brest Li·tovsk (brĕst′ lĭ tôfsk′), a city in the W Soviet Union, on the Bug river: formerly in Poland; German-Russian peace treaty, 1918. 50,700 (1931). Polish, **Brzesc nad Bugiem.**

Bre·tagne (brĕ tän′y), *n.* French name of **Brittany.**

breth·ren (brĕth′rĭn), *n.* **1.** pl. of **brother. 2.** fellow members. **—Syn. 1, 2.** See **brother.**

Bret·on (brĕt′ən; *Fr.* brə tôn′), *n.* **1.** a native of Brittany. **2.** the Celtic language of Brittany. **—adj. 3.** pertaining to Brittany, the Bretons, or their language. [t. F. See BRITON]

Bre·ton (brə tôn′), *n.* **André** (äṅ drĕ′), born 1896, French poet, essayist, and critic.

Bret·ton Woods Conference (brĕt′ən), an international conference called at Bretton Woods, N.H., in July, 1944, to deal with international monetary and financial problems.

Breu·ghel (brœ′gəl), *n.* Brueghel.

breve (brēv), *n.* **1.** a mark (˘) placed over a vowel to show that it is short, as in ŭ. **2.** *Law.* **a.** an initial writ. **b.** a writ, as one issued by a court of law. **3.** *Music.* the longest modern note, equivalent to two semibreves or whole notes. See illus. under **note.** [t. It., g. L *brevis* short]

bre·vet (brə vĕt′ *or,* esp. *Brit.,* brĕv′ĭt), *n., v.,* **-vetted, -vetting** *or* **-veted, -veting. —n. 1.** a commission promoting a military officer to a higher rank without increase of pay and with limited exercise of the higher rank. **—v.t. 2.** to appoint or promote by brevet. [ME t. F, dim. of *bref* letter. See BRIEF]

brevi-, a word element meaning "short," as in *brevifoliate.* [t. L, comb. form of *brevis*]

bre·vi·ar·y (brē′vĭ ĕr′ĭ, brĕv′ĭ-), *n., pl.* **-aries. 1.** *Rom. Cath. Ch.* a book of daily prayers and readings to be read by those in major orders. **2.** *Eccles.* a similar book in some other churches. [t. L: m.s. *breviarium* abridgment, prop. neut. of *breviārius* abridged]

bre·vier (brə vĭr′), *n.* a printing type (8 point) of a size between minion and bourgeois. [so called from use in printing breviaries; said to be t. G: breviary, t. F: m. *bréviaire,* g. L *breviārium*]

brev·i·ros·trate (brĕv′ə rŏs′trāt), *adj. Ornith.* having a short beak or bill.

brev·i·ty (brĕv′ə tĭ), *n., pl.* **-ties. 1.** shortness of time or duration; briefness: *the brevity of human life.* **2.** condensation in speech; conciseness. [t. L: m. s. *brevitas,* der. *brevis* short]

—Syn. 2. BREVITY, CONCISENESS refer to the use of few words in speaking. BREVITY emphasizes the short duration of speech: *reduced to extreme brevity.* CONCISENESS emphasizes compactness of expression: *clear in spite of great conciseness.*

brew (brōō), *v.t.* **1.** to make (beer, ale, etc.) from malt, etc., by steeping, boiling, and fermentation. **2.** to prepare (a beverage) by or as by brewing. **3.** to concoct or contrive; bring about: *to brew mischief.* **—v.i. 4.** to brew beer, ale, etc. **5. be brewing,** to be in preparation; be forming or gathering: *trouble was brewing.* **—n. 6.** a quantity brewed in a single process. **7.** a particular brewing or variety of malt liquor. [ME *brewen,* OE *brēowan.* Cf. BROTH] **—brew′er,** *n.*

brew·age (brōō′ĭj), *n.* a fermented liquor brewed from malt.

brew·er·y (brōō′ər ĭ, brōōr′ĭ), *n., pl.* **-eries.** an establishment for brewing malt liquors.

brew·ing (brōō′ĭng), *n.* **1.** act of one who brews. **2.** a quantity brewed at once.

brew·is (brōō′ĭs), *n. Now Dial.* **1.** broth. **2.** bread soaked in broth, gravy, etc. [ME *browes,* t. OF: m. *broez,* ult. t. OHG: m. *brod* BROTH]

Brew·ster (brōō′stər), *n.* **William,** 1560?–1644, English colonist: leader of the Pilgrims at Plymouth.

Bri·and (brē äṅ′), *n.* **Aristide** (á rēs tēd′), 1862–1932, French statesman: minister of France 11 times.

bri·ar (brī′ər), *n.* brier. **—bri′ar·y,** *adj.*

---

b., blend of, blended; c., cognate with; d., dialect, dialectal; der., derived from; f., formed from; g., going back to; m., modification of; r., replacing; s., stem of; t., taken from; ?, perhaps. See the full key on inside cover.

Bri·ar·e·us (brī âr′ĭ əs), *n.* *Gk.* *Myth.* a hundred-armed, fifty-headed giant who helped Zeus against the Titans. —**Bri·ar′e·an**, *adj.*

bri·ar·root (brī′ər rōōt′, -rŏŏt′), *n.* brierroot.

bri·ar·wood (brī′ər wŏŏd′), *n.* brierwood.

bribe (brīb), *n., v.,* **bribed, bribing.** —*n.* **1.** any valuable consideration given or promised for corrupt behavior in the performance of official or public duty. **2.** anything given or serving to persuade or induce. —*v.t.* **3.** to give or promise a bribe to. **4.** to influence or corrupt by a bribe. —*v.i.* **5.** to give bribes; practice bribery. [ME; cf. OF *bribe* piece of bread given to a beggar, *briber* beg, c. Sp. *bribar*] —**brib′a·ble,** *adj.* —**brib′a·bil′i·ty,** *n.* —**brib′er,** *n.*

brib·er·y (brī′bə rĭ), *n., pl.* **-eries.** act or practice of giving or accepting bribes.

bric-a-brac (brĭk′ə brăk′), *n.* miscellaneous ornamental articles of antiquarian, decorative, or other interest. [t. F]

brick (brĭk), *n.* **1.** a block of clay, usually rectangular, hardened by drying in the sun or burning in a kiln, and used for building, paving, etc. **2.** such blocks collectively. **3.** the material. **4.** any similar block. **5.** *Colloq.* a good fellow. —*v.t.* **6.** to lay, line, wall, or build with brick. [ME *bryke,* t. F: m. *brique,* t. MD: m. *bricke,* akin to BREAK] —**brick′like′,** *adj.*

brick·bat (brĭk′băt′), *n.* **1.** a piece of broken brick, esp. one used as a missile. **2.** any rocklike missile. **3.** *Colloq.* an unkind remark; caustic criticism.

brick·kiln (brĭk′kĭl′, -kĭln′), *n.* a kiln or furnace in which bricks are baked or burned.

brick·lay·ing (brĭk′lā′ĭng), *n.* the art or occupation of laying bricks in construction. —**brick′lay′er,** *n.*

brick red, yellowish or brownish red.

brick·work (brĭk′wûrk′), *n.* brick construction (as contrasted with that of other materials).

brick·y (brĭk′ĭ), *adj.* consisting or made of bricks.

brick·yard (brĭk′yärd′), *n.* a place where bricks are made.

bri·cole (brĭ′kōl′, brĭk′əl), *n.* **1.** *Billiards.* a shot in which the cue ball strikes the cushion first. **2.** an indirect action or unexpected stroke. [t. F, t. Pr.: m. *bricola* catapult]

brid·al (brī′dəl), *adj.* **1.** of or pertaining to a bride or a wedding. —*n.* **2.** a wedding. **3.** *Archaic.* a wedding feast. [ME *bridale,* OE *brȳdealo* bride ale, f. *brȳd* bride + *ealo* ale, feast, assoc. with adj. suffix -AL[1]]

Bridal Veil, a waterfall in Yosemite National Park, California. 620 ft. high.

bridal wreath, any of several shrubs of the rosaceous genus *Spiraea,* bearing sprays of small white flowers, esp. *S. prunifolia.*

bride[1] (brīd), *n.* a woman newly married, or about to be married. [ME; OE *brȳd,* c. G *braut*]

bride[2] (brīd), *n.* **1.** (in needlework, lacemaking, etc.) a bar, link, or tie. **2.** an ornamental bonnet string. [t. F: bridle, string, tie, t. Gmc. See BRIDLE]

Bride (brīd), *n.* Saint. See Brigid, Saint.

bride·groom (brīd′grōōm′, -grŏŏm′), *n.* a man newly married, or about to be married. [var. of ME *bride-gome,* OE *brydguma,* f. *brȳd* bride + *guma* man (c. L *homo*)]

brides·maid (brīdz′mād′), *n.* a young unmarried woman who attends the bride at a wedding.

bride·well (brīd′wĕl, -wəl), *n.* **1.** *Brit.* a house of correction for the confinement of vagrants and disorderly persons (so called from a former prison in London at St. Bride's well). **2.** *Colloq.* any prison or house of correction.

bridge[1] (brĭj), *n., v.,* **bridged, bridging.** —*n.* **1.** a structure spanning a river, chasm, road, or the like, and affording passage. **2.** *Naut.* a raised platform from side to side of a ship above the rail, for the officer in charge. **3.** *Anat.* the ridge or upper line of the nose. **4.** *Dentistry.* an artificial replacement of a missing tooth or teeth, supported by natural teeth adjacent to the space. A bridge may be fixed or removable. **5.** *Music.* a piece raising the strings of a musical instrument above the sounding board. **6.** (on eyeglasses) the part which joins the two lenses and rests on the bridge or side of the nose. **7.** *Elect.* an instrument for measuring electrical impedance. **8.** *Railroads.* an overhead structure above railroad tracks on which signals are placed. **9.** *Metall.* a ridge or wall-like projection of fire brick or the like, at either end of the hearth in a metallurgical furnace. **10.** *Billiards.* a notched piece of wood with a long handle, sometimes used to support a cue when the distance is otherwise too great to reach; rest. —*v.t.* **11.** to make a bridge over; span. **12.** to make (a way) by a bridge. [ME *brigge,* OE *brycg,* c. G *brücke*] —**bridge′a·ble,** *adj.*

bridge[2] (brĭj), *n.* *Cards.* a game derived from whist in which one partnership plays to fulfill a certain declaration against opponents acting as defenders. See **contract** (def. 6) and **auction bridge.** [orig. uncert.]

bridge·board (brĭj′bōrd′), *n.* a notched board at the side of a wooden stair, supporting the treads and risers.

bridge·head (brĭj′hĕd′), *n.* **1.** a position held on the enemy side of a river of defile, to cover the crossing of friendly troops. **2.** a defensive work covering or protecting the end of a bridge toward the enemy.

Bridge of Sighs, a bridge in Venice through which prisoners were led for trial in the ducal palace.

Bridge·port (brĭj′pōrt′), *n.* a seaport in SW Connecticut, on Long Island Sound. 158,709 (1950).

Bridg·es (brĭj′ĭz), *n.* Robert, 1844-1930, British poet laureate, 1913-30.

Bridges Creek, an estate in E Virginia, on the Potomac: birthplace of George Washington; restored as a national monument, 1932. Now called **Wakefield.**

Bridg·et (brĭj′ĭt), *n.* Saint. See Brigid, Saint.

Bridge·town (brĭj′toun′), *n.* a seaport in and the capital of Barbados, in the British West Indies. ab. 13,000.

bridge·work (brĭj′wûrk′), *n.* **1.** *Dentistry.* **a.** dental bridges collectively. **b.** any of several different types of dental bridges. **2.** the building of bridges.

bridg·ing (brĭj′ĭng), *n.* *Bldg. Trades.* a piece or an arrangement of pieces fixed between floor or roof joists to keep them in place.

bri·dle (brī′dəl), *n., v.,* **-dled, -dling.** —*n.* **1.** the part of the harness of a horse, etc., about the head, consisting usually of headstall, bit, and reins, and used to restrain and guide the animal. **2.** anything that restrains or curbs. **3.** *Mach.* a link, flange, or other attachment for limiting the movement of any part of a machine. **4.** *Naut.* a short chain or rope span both ends of which are made fast. **5.** a bridling, or drawing up the head, as in disdain. —*v.t.* **6.** to put a bridle on. **7.** to control as with a bridle; restrain; curb. —*v.i.* **8.** to draw up the head and draw in the chin, as in disdain or resentment. [ME; OE *brīdel,* earlier *brigdils*] —**bri′dler,** *n.*

bridle path, a path used by horseback riders.

bri·doon (brĭ dōōn′), *n.* a light snaffle or bit without crossbars, and on a rein, used in certain military bridles in addition to the principal bit and its rein. [t. F: m. *bridon,* der. *bride* bridle]

Brie cheese (brē), a kind of salted, white, soft cheese, ripened with bacterial action, waxy to semiliquid, originating in Brie, France.

brief (brēf), *adj.* **1.** of little duration. **2.** using few words; concise; succinct. **3.** abrupt or curt. —*n.* **4.** a short and concise writing or statement. **5.** an outline, the form of which is determined by set rules, of all the possible arguments and information on one side of a controversy: *a debater's brief.* **6.** *Law.* **a.** a writ summoning one to answer to any action. **b.** a memorandum of points of fact or of law for use in conducting a case. **7.** briefing. **8.** *Rom. Cath. Ch.* a papal letter less formal than a bull, sealed with the Pope's signet ring or stamped with the device borne on this ring. **9.** *Obs.* a letter. **10. in brief,** in few words; in short. —*v.t.* **11.** to make an abstract or summary of. **12.** to instruct by a brief or briefing. **13.** *Law.* to retain as advocate in a suit. [t. F, g. L *brevis*] —**brief′ly,** *adv.* —**brief′ness,** *n.* —**Syn. 1.** short-lived, fleeting, transitory, ephemeral. See **short.** **2.** terse, compact. **4.** See **summary.**

brief case, a flat, rectangular leather case used for carrying documents, books, manuscripts, etc.

brief·ing (brē′fĭng), *n.* a short, accurate summary of the details of a flight mission, given to the crew of a combat plane just before it takes off on a mission.

brief·less (brēf′lĭs), *adj.* having no brief, as a lawyer without clients.

brief of title, an abstract of the legal documents concerning the conferring and transferring of ownership of a given piece of property.

bri·er[1] (brī′ər), *n.* **1.** a prickly plant or shrub, esp. the sweetbrier, or the greenbriers. **2.** a tangled mass of prickly plants. **3.** a thorny stem or twig. Also, **briar.** [ME *brere,* OE *brēr*] —**bri′er·y,** *adj.*

bri·er[2] (brī′ər), *n.* **1.** the white heath, *Arica arborea,* of France and Corsica, whose woody root is used for making tobacco pipes. **2.** a pipe made of this woody root. Also, **briar.** [t. F: m. *bruyère* heath, g. a LL deriv. of Gallic *brūcus* heather]

bri·er·root (brī′ər rōōt′, -rŏŏt′), *n.* **1.** the root wood of the brier. **2.** certain other woods from which tobacco pipes are made. **3.** a pipe made of brierroot. Also, **briarroot.**

bri·er·wood (brī′ər wŏŏd′), *n.* brierroot. Also, **briarwood.**

Bri·eux (brē œ′), *n.* Eugène (œ zhĕn′), 1858-1932, French dramatist.

brig[1] (brĭg), *n.* *Naut.* **1.** a two-masted vessel square-rigged on both masts. **2.** the compartment of a ship where prisoners are confined. [short for BRIGANTINE]

brig[2] (brĭg), *n., v.* *Scot. and N. Eng.* bridge.

Brig., *Mil.* **1.** Brigade. **2.** Brigadier.

bri·gade (brĭ gād′), *n., v.,* **-gaded, -gading.** —*n.* **1.** a unit consisting of several regiments, squadrons, groups, or battalions. **2.** a large body of troops. **3.** a body of individuals organized for a special purpose: *a fire brigade.* —*v.t.* **4.** to form into a brigade. **5.** to group together. [t. F, t. It.: m. *brigata* troop, der. *brigare* strive, contend]

brig·a·dier (brĭg′ə dĭr′), *n.* **1.** *Brit. Army.* a rank between colonel and major general. **2.** *Colloq. U.S. Army.* a brigadier general. **3.** (formerly) a noncommissioned rank in the Napoleonic armies. [t. F, der. *brigade* BRIGADE]

brigadier general, *pl.* **brigadier generals.** *U.S. Army.* an officer between colonel and major general.

brig·and (brĭg′ənd), *n.* a bandit; one of a gang of robbers in mountain or forest regions. [ME *brigant*, t. OF, t. It.: m. *brigante*, der. *brigare*. See BRIGADE] —**brig′-and·ish**, *adj.*

brig·and·age (brĭg′ən dĭj), *n.* the practice of brigands; plundering. Also, **brig′and·ism.**

brig·an·dine (brĭg′ən dēn′, -dĭn′), *n. Armor.* a flexible body armor of overlapping steel plates riveted to the exterior covering of linen, velvet, leather, etc. [late ME *brigandyne*, t. OF: m. *brigandine*]

brig·an·tine (brĭg′ən tēn′, -tĭn′), *n. Naut.* a two-masted vessel in which the foremast is square-rigged and the mainmast bears a fore-and-aft mainsail and square topsails. [t. F: m. *brigantin*, t. It.: m. *brigantino*, der. *brigante* BRIGAND]

bright (brīt), *adj.* **1.** radiating or reflecting light; luminous; shining. **2.** filled with light. **3.** vivid or brilliant, as color. **4.** clear or translucent, as liquids. **5.** radiant or splendid. **6.** illustrious or glorious, as a period. **7.** quick-witted or intelligent. **8.** clever or witty, as a remark. **9.** animated; lively; cheerful, as a person. **10.** characterized by happiness or gladness. **11.** favorable or auspicious: *bright prospects.* —*n.* **12.** *Archaic.* brightness; splendor. —*adv.* **13.** in a bright manner; brightly. [ME; OE *bryht, beorht,* c. OHG *beraht,* Icel. *bjartr,* Goth. *bairhts*] —**bright′ly,** *adv.* —**Syn. 1.** refulgent, effulgent, lustrous, lucent, beaming, lambent. BRIGHT, BRILLIANT, RADIANT, SHINING refer to that which gives forth, is filled with, or reflects light. BRIGHT suggests the general idea: *bright flare, stars, mirror.* BRILLIANT implies a strong, unusual, or sparkling brightness, often changeful or varied and too strong to be agreeable: *brilliant sunlight.* RADIANT implies the pouring forth of steady rays of light, esp. such as is agreeable to the eyes: *a radiant face.* SHINING implies giving forth or reflecting a strong or steady light: *shining eyes.* —**Ant. 1.** dull, dim.

Bright (brīt), *n.* **John,** 1811–89, British orator and statesman.

bright·en (brī′tən), *v.i., v.t.* to become or make bright or brighter.

bright·ness (brīt′nĭs), *n.* **1.** bright quality. **2.** luminosity apart from hue; value. Pure white is of maximum brightness and pure black is of zero brightness.

Brigh·ton (brī′tən), *n.* **1.** a city in SE England, on the English channel: seaside resort. 146,190 (est. 1946). **2.** a city in SE Australia, near Melbourne. 29,706 (1933).

Bright's disease, *Pathol.* a disease characterized by albuminuria and heightened blood pressure. [named after R. *Bright,* British physician, who described it]

Brig·id (brĭj′ĭd, brē′ĭd), *n.* **Saint,** A.D. 453–523, Irish abbess: a patron saint of Ireland. Also, **Bride, Bridget, Brig·it** (brĭj′ĭt, brē′ĭt).

brill (brĭl), *n., pl.* **brill** or **brills.** a European flatfish, *Scophthalmus rhombus,* closely allied to the turbot.

Brill (brĭl), *n.* **Abraham Arden,** 1874–1948, U.S. psychoanalyst and author, born in Austria.

bril·liance (brĭl′yəns), *n.* **1.** great brightness; splendor; luster. **2.** remarkable excellence or distinction; conspicuous mental ability. **3.** *Color.* brightness (def. 2). Also, **bril′lian·cy.** —**Syn. 1.** radiance, effulgence.

bril·liant (brĭl′yənt), *adj.* **1.** shining brightly; sparkling; glittering; lustrous. **2.** distinguished; illustrious: *a brilliant achievement.* **3.** having or showing great intelligence or keenness. —*n.* **4.** a diamond (or other gem) of a particular cut, typically round in outline and shaped like two pyramids united at their bases, the top one cut off near the base and the bottom one close to the apex, with many facets on the slopes. **5.** this form. **6.** a printing type (about 3½ point). [t. F: m. *brillant,* ppr. of *briller,* corresponding to It. *brillare* shine, sparkle, ? g. LL *brillāre,* der. L *bēryllus* BERYL] —**bril′liant·ly,** *adv.* —**bril′liant·ness,** *n.* —**Syn. 1.** See **bright.**

bril·lian·tine (brĭl′yən tēn′), *n.* **1.** a toilet preparation for the hair. **2.** a dress fabric resembling alpaca. [t. F]

brim¹ (brĭm), *n., v.,* **brimmed, brimming.** —*n.* **1.** the upper edge of anything hollow; rim: *the brim of a cup.* **2.** a projecting edge: *the brim of a hat.* **3.** *Archaic.* edge or margin. —*v.i.* **4.** to be full to the brim: *a brimming glass.* —*v.t.* **5.** to fill to the brim. [ME *brimme* shore, OE *brim* sea. Cf. Icel. *brim* surf]

brim² (brĭm), *n. Southern U.S.* bream (def. 4). [var. of BREAM¹]

brim·ful (brĭm′fŏŏl′), *adj.* full to the brim; all full.

brim·mer (brĭm′ər), *n.* a cup or bowl full to the brim.

brim·stone (brĭm′stōn′), *n.* **1.** sulfur. **2.** virago. [ME *brinston,* etc., f. *brinn(en)* burn + *ston* stone] —**brim′ston′y,** *adj.*

Brin·di·si (brēn′dē zē′), *n.* a seaport in SE Italy: an important Roman city and naval station. 38,451 (1936). Ancient, **Brundisium.**

brin·dle (brĭn′dəl), *n.* **1.** a brindled coloring. **2.** brindled animal. [back formation from BRINDLED]

brin·dled (brĭn′dəld), *adj.* gray or tawny with darker streaks or spots. Also, **brin·ded** (brĭn′dĭd). [cf. Icel. *bröndóttr;* ? akin to BRAND]

brine (brīn), *n., v.,* **brined, brining.** —*n.* **1.** water saturated or strongly impregnated with salt. **2.** water strongly salted for pickling. **3.** the sea or ocean. **4.** the water of the sea. —*v.t.* **5.** to treat with or steep in brine. [ME; OE *brȳne*] —**brin′ish,** *adj.*

Bri·nell machine (brĭ nĕl′), *Metall.* an instrument for calculating the hardness (**Brinell hardness**) of metal, esp. heat-treated steels, by forcing a hard steel or tungsten carbide ball of standard dimensions into the material being tested, under a fixed pressure. [named after J. A. *Brinell* (1849–1925), Swedish engineer]

Brinell number, *Metall.* a numerical expression of Brinell hardness, found by determining the diameter of a dent made by the Brinell machine.

bring (brĭng), *v.t.,* **brought, bringing. 1.** to cause to come with oneself; take along to the place or person sought; conduct or convey. **2.** to cause to come, as to a recipient or possessor to the mind or knowledge, into a particular position or state, to a particular opinion or decision, or into existence, view, action, or effect. **3.** to lead or induce: *he couldn't bring himself to do it.* **4.** *Law.* to put forward before a tribunal; declare in or as if in court. **5.** Some special verb phrases are:

bring about, to cause; accomplish.

bring around or **round, 1.** to convince of an opinion. **2.** to restore to consciousness, as after a faint.

bring forth, 1. to produce. **2.** to give rise to; cause.

bring forward, 1. to produce to view. **2.** to adduce.

bring out, 1. to expose; show; reveal. **2.** to publish.

bring to, 1. to bring back to consciousness. **2.** *Naut.* to head a ship close to or into the wind and kill her headway by manipulating helm and sails.

bring up, 1. to care for during childhood; rear. **2.** to introduce to notice or consideration. **3.** to cause to advance, as troops.

[ME *bringen,* OE *bringan,* c. G *bringen*] —**bring′er,** *n.* —**Syn. 1.** transport. BRING, FETCH imply conveying or conducting to or towards the place where the speaker is. To BRING is simply so to convey or conduct: *bring it to me, I'm permitted to bring my dog here with me.* (It is the opposite of TAKE, which means to convey or conduct away from the place where the speaker is: *bring it back here, take it back there.*) FETCH is chiefly British and means to go, get, and bring back: *fetch it here tomorrow.* —**Ant. 1.** take.

bring·ing-up (brĭng′ĭng ŭp′), *n.* childhood training or care.

brink (brĭngk), *n.* **1.** the edge or margin of a steep place or of land bordering water. **2.** any extreme edge; verge. [ME, t. Scand.; cf. Dan. *brink*] —**Syn.** See **edge.**

brin·y (brī′nĭ), *adj.,* **brinier, briniest.** of or like brine; salty: *a briny taste.* —**brin′i·ness,** *n.*

bri·oche (brē′ōsh, -ŏsh; *Fr.* brē ôsh′), *n.* a kind of light, sweet bun or roll, raised with eggs and yeast. [t. F, der. *brier,* d. form of *broyer* knead]

bri·o·lette (brē′ə lĕt′; *Fr.* brē ô-), *n.* a pear-shaped gem having its entire surface cut with triangular facets. [t. F]

bri·quette (brĭ kĕt′), *n.* a molded block of compacted coal dust for fuel. Also, **bri·quet′.** [t. F]

bri·sance (brē zäns′), *n.* the shattering power of high explosives.

Bris·bane (brĭz′bān, -bən), *n.* a seaport in E Australia: the capital of Queensland. 344,200 (est. 1941).

Bri·se·is (brī sē′ĭs), *n.* (in the *Iliad*) a beautiful maiden captured by Achilles: the cause of his quarrel with Agamemnon.

brisk (brĭsk), *adj.* **1.** quick and active; lively: *a brisk breeze, a brisk walk.* **2.** sharp and stimulating: *brisk weather.* **3.** (of liquors) effervescing vigorously: *brisk cider.* —*v.t., v.i.* **4.** to make or become brisk; liven (*up*). [? akin to BRUSQUE] —**brisk′ly,** *adv.* —**brisk′ness,** *n.* —**Syn. 1.** spry, energetic. —**Ant. 1.** languid.

bris·ket (brĭs′kĭt), *n.* the breast of an animal, or the part of the breast lying next to the ribs. [ME *brusket,* appar. t. OF: m. *bruschet,* t. Gmc.; cf. LG *bröske,* Icel. *brjósk* cartilage]

bris·ling (brĭs′lĭng), *n.* the sprat.

bris·tle (brĭs′əl), *n., v.,* **-tled, -tling.** —*n.* **1.** one of the short, stiff, coarse hairs of certain animals, esp. hogs, used extensively in making brushes, etc. **2.** any short, stiff hair or hairlike appendage (often used facetiously of human hair). —*v.i.* **3.** to stand or rise stiffly, like bristles. **4.** to erect the bristles, as an irritated animal (often fol. by *up*): *the hog bristled up.* **5.** to be thickly set with something suggestive of bristles: *the plain bristled with bayonets, the enterprise bristled with difficulties.* **6.** to be visibly roused or stirred (usually fol. by *up*). —*v.t.* **7.** to erect like bristles: *the rooster bristled up his crest.* **8.** to furnish with a bristle or bristles. **9.** to make bristly. [ME *bristel,* f. *brist* (OE *byrst*) + *-el,* dim. suffix] —**bris′tly,** *adj.*

bris·tle·tail (brĭs′əl tāl′), *n.* any of various wingless insects of the order *Thysanura,* having long bristlelike caudal appendages.

Bris·tol (brĭs′təl), *n.* **1.** a seaport in SW England, on the Avon river near its confluence with the Severn estuary. 444,000 (est. 1946). **2.** a city in central Connecticut. 35,961 (1950).

Bristol board, a fine, smooth kind of pasteboard, sometimes glazed.

Bristol Channel, an arm of the Atlantic between Wales and SW England.

brit (brĭt), *n.* **1.** small animals forming the food of whalebone whales. **2.** the young of herring and sprat.

Brit., 1. Britain. **2.** British.

Brit·ain (brĭt′ən), *n.* **1.** Great Britain. **2.** Britannia (def. 1a).

Bri·tan·ni·a (brĭ tăn′ĭ ə, -tăn′yə), *n.* **1.** Roman name for: **a.** the largest island of the British Isles. **b.** the Roman province in that island. **2.** British Empire. **3.** Great Britain. **4.** *Chiefly Poetic.* England, Scotland,

and Ireland. **5.** the feminine personification of Great Britain or the British Empire. **6.** Britannia metal. [t. L]

Britannia metal, a white alloy of tin, copper, and antimony, usually with small amounts of zinc, etc., used for tableware.

Bri·tan·nic (brĭ tăn′ĭk), *adj.* **1.** British: *His Britannic Majesty.* **2.** Brythonic. [t. L: s. *Britannicus*]

Brit·i·cism (brĭt′ə sĭz′əm), *n.* an English usage peculiar to British people. The use of *lift* (cf. *U.S. elevator*) is a typical Briticism.

Brit·ish (brĭt′ĭsh), *adj.* **1.** of or pertaining to Great Britain, the British Empire, or its inhabitants. **2.** of or pertaining to the ancient Britons. —*n.* **3.** the British people, taken collectively. **4.** the language spoken in southern England (now regarded as the English standard). **5.** the language of the ancient Britons and the languages which have developed from it, namely Welsh, Cornish (no longer spoken), and Breton. [ME *Brytysshe,* OE *Bryttisc,* der. *Bryttas, Brettas* Britons, from Celtic]

British America, British North America.

British Columbia, a province in W Canada, on the Pacific coast. 817,861 pop. (1941); 366,255 sq. mi. *Cap.:* Victoria.

British Commonwealth of Nations, the United Kingdom of Great Britain and Northern Ireland, the Dominions (Canada, Australia, New Zealand, Union of South Africa, Pakistan, Ceylon), India, and Eire.

British East Africa, a comprehensive term for Kenya, Tanganyika Territory, Uganda, and Zanzibar.

British Empire, the territories under the leadership or control of the British crown, including those in the British Commonwealth of Nations together with their colonies, protectorates, dependencies, and mandates. 481,100,000 pop. (1931); ab. 11,460,000 sq. mi.

Brit·ish·er (brĭt′ĭsh ər), *n.* a native or inhabitant of Britain.

British Guiana, a British crown colony on the NE coast of South America. 364,000 pop. (est. 1943); 89,480 sq. mi. *Cap.:* Georgetown. See map under **Guiana.**

British Honduras, a British crown colony in N Central America. 62,000 pop. (est. 1942); 8598 sq. mi. *Cap.:* Belize.

British India, (formerly) that part (17 provinces) of India subject to British law; now divided between the dominions of India and Pakistan. 295,809,000 pop. (1941); 865,446 sq. mi. *Cap.:* New Delhi.

British Isles, a group of islands in W Europe: Great Britain, Ireland, the Isle of Man, and adjacent islands. 50,231,000 pop. (est. 1937); 120,592 sq. mi.

British Malaya, a comprehensive term for that part of the Malay peninsula under British influence: the Federation of Malaya and the colony of Singapore.

British North America, **1.** Canada and Newfoundland. **2.** all parts of the British Empire in or near North America.

British North Borneo, a British crown colony in NE Borneo. 304,443 pop. (est. 1939); 29,347 sq. mi. *Cap.:* Sandakan. Also, **North Borneo.**

British Somaliland, a British protectorate in E Africa, on the Gulf of Aden. 347,390 pop. (est. 1937); ab. 68,000 sq. mi. *Cap.:* Berbera. See map under **Aden.**

British thermal unit, the amount of heat required to raise the temperature of one pound of water one degree Fahrenheit.

British West Africa, a comprehensive term for Nigeria, the Gold Coast, Sierra Leone, and Gambia.

British West Indies, the British islands in the West Indies, including the Bahama Islands, Jamaica, Barbados, Trinidad, Tobago, and islands of the Leeward and Windward groups. 2,230,200 pop. (est. 1937); ab. 12,500 sq. mi.

British Zone. See **Germany.**

Brit·on (brĭt′ən), *n.* **1.** a native or inhabitant of Great Britain, or (sometimes) of the British Empire. **2.** one of the Celtic people who in early times occupied the southern part of the island of Britain. [t. ML: s. *Brito;* r. ME *Breton,* t. OF, g. L *Bretto*]

brits·ka (brĭts′kə), *n.* an open carriage with a calash top and space for reclining. Also, **britzka, britzska.** [t. Pol.: m. *bryczka,* dim. of *bryka* freight wagon]

Brit·ta·ny (brĭt′ə nĭ), *n.* a peninsula in NW France between the English Channel and the Bay of Biscay: a former duchy and province. French, **Bretagne.**

brit·tle (brĭt′əl), *adj.* **1.** breaking readily with a comparatively smooth fracture, as glass. —*n.* **2.** a confection of melted sugar, usually with nuts, brittle when cooled: *peanut brittle.* [ME *britel,* der. OE *brēotan* break] —**brit′tle·ness,** *n.* —**Syn. 1.** breakable, frangible, fragile. See **frail**[1].

Brit·ton (brĭt′ən), *n.* **Nathaniel Lord** (nə thăn′yəl), 1859–1934, U.S. botanist.

britz·ka (brĭts′kə), *n.* britska. Also, **britz′ska.**

Br·no (bûr′nô), *n.* a city in central Czechoslovakia: the capital of Moravia. 295,400 (est. 1940). German, **Brünn.**

bro., *pl.* **bros.** brother. Also, **Bro.**

broach (brōch), *n.* **1.** *Mach.* an elongated and tapered tool with serrations which enlarges a given hole as the tool is pulled through the hole, which may be round, square, etc. See illus. under **reamer.** **2.** a spit for roasting meat. **3.** a gimlet for tapping casks. —*v.t.* **4.** to enlarge and finish with a broach. **5.** to tap or pierce. **6.** to draw as by tapping: *to broach liquor.* **7.** to mention or suggest for the first time: *to broach a subject.* —*v.i.* **8.** *Naut.* (of a ship) to veer to windward, esp. so as to be broadside to the wind (fol. by *to*). [ME *broche,* t. OF, g. L *brocc(h)us* projecting] —**broach′er,** *n.*

broad (brôd), *adj.* **1.** of great breadth: *a broad river or street.* **2.** of great extent; large; *the broad expanse of ocean.* **3.** widely diffused; open; full: *broad daylight.* **4.** not limited or narrow; liberal: *broad experience.* **5.** of extensive range or scope: *broad sympathies.* **6.** main or general: *the broad outlines of a subject.* **7.** plain or clear: *a broad hint.* **8.** bold; plain-spoken. **9.** indelicate; indecent: *a broad joke.* **10.** (of conversation) rough; coarse; countrified. **11.** unconfined; free; unrestrained: *broad mirth.* **12.** (of pronunciation) strongly dialectal: *broad Scots.* **13. broad a,** the *a* (ä) sound in *father,* esp. in a word customarily pronounced, in standard American usage, with the *a* (a) of *glad,* as in *half* or *can't* or *laughable.* —*adv.* **14.** fully: *broad awake.* —*n.* **15.** the broad part of anything. [ME *brood,* OE *brād,* c. G *breit*] —**broad′ish,** *adj.* —**broad′ly,** *adv.* —**Syn. 1.** See **wide.** **2.** extensive, ample, vast. —**Ant. 1.** narrow.

broad arrow, **1.** a mark of the shape of a broad arrowhead, placed upon British governmental stores. **2.** *Archery.* an arrow having an expanded head.

broad·ax (brôd′ăks′), *n.* **1.** an ax for hewing timber. **2.** a battleax. Also, **broad′axe′.**

broad bean, a variety of edible bean, *Vicia faba.*

broad·bill (brôd′bĭl′), *n.* **1.** any of various birds with a broad bill, as the scaup duck, shoveler, and spoonbill. **2.** a swordfish.

broad·brim (brôd′brĭm′), *n.* **1.** a hat with a broad brim, as that worn by Quakers. **2.** (*cap.*) *U.S. Colloq.* a Friend or Quaker.

broad·cast (brôd′kăst′, -käst′), *v.,* -**cast** or -**casted** -**casting,** *n., adj., adv.* —*v.t.* **1.** to send (messages, speeches, music, etc.) by radio. **2.** to cast or scatter abroad over an area, as seed in sowing. **3.** to spread or disseminate widely: *to broadcast gossip.* —*v.i.* **4.** to send radio messages, speeches, etc. **5.** to scatter or disseminate something widely. —*n.* **6.** that which is broadcasted. **7.** *Radio.* **a.** the broadcasting of radio messages, speeches, etc. **b.** a radio program. **c.** a single period of broadcasting. **8.** the method of sowing by scattering seed. —*adj.* **9.** sent out by broadcasting, as radio messages, speeches, music, etc. **10.** of or pertaining to broadcasting. **11.** cast abroad or all over an area, as seed sown thus. **12.** widely spread or disseminated: *broadcast discontent.* —*adv.* **13.** so as to reach an indefinite number of radio receiving stations or instruments in various directions. **14.** so as to be cast abroad over an area: *seed sown broadcast.* —**broad′cast′er,** *n.*

Broad Church, *Eccles.* a designation of those members of the Anglican communion who favor a liberal interpretation of doctrine and ritual, and such conditions of membership as will promote wide Christian inclusiveness. —**Broad′-Church′,** *adj.* —**Broad′-Church′man,** *n.*

broad·cloth (brôd′klôth′, -klŏth′), *n.* **1.** cotton broadcloth, cotton shirting or dress material, usually mercerized, resembling fine poplin. **2.** rayon broadcloth, spun rayon fabric similar to cotton broadcloth. **3.** woolen broadcloth, woolen dress goods with nap laid parallel with selvage.

broad·en (brô′dən), *v.i., v.t.* to become or make broad; widen.

broad gauge. See **gauge** (def. 10). Also, **broad′-gage′, broad′-gauged′, broad′-gaged′.**

broad jump, *Sports.* **1.** a jump horizontally, either from rest (**standing broad jump**) or with a running start (**running broad jump**). **2.** an athletic contest for the longest such jump.

broad·leaf (brôd′lēf′), *n.* any of several cigar tobaccos which have broad leaves.

broad·loom carpet (brôd′lōōm′), any kind of carpet, from 54 inches to 18 feet wide, woven on a broad loom to avoid the need for seams.

broad·mind·ed (brôd′mīn′dĭd), *adj.* free from prejudice or bigotry; liberal; tolerant. —**broad′-mind′ed·ly,** *adv.* —**broad′-mind′ed·ness,** *n.*

broad seal, the official seal of a country or state.

broad·side (brôd′sīd′), *n.* **1.** *Naut.* the whole side of a ship above the waterline, from the bow to the quarter. **2.** *Naval.* **a.** all the guns that can be fired to one side of a ship. **b.** a simultaneous discharge of all the guns on one side of a vessel of war. **3.** any comprehensive attack, as of criticism. **4.** Also, **broad·sheet** (brôd′shēt′). a sheet of paper, esp. of large size, printed on one side only, as for distribution or posting. **5.** any broad surface or side, as of a house.

broad·sword (brôd′sōrd′), *n.* a straight, broad, flat, sword, usually with a basket hilt.

Broad·way (brôd′wā′), *n.* a street in New York City, famous for its theaters.

Brob·ding·nag (brŏb′dĭng·năg′), *n.* the region in Swift's *Gulliver's Travels*, where everything was of enormous size. —**Brob′ding·nag′i·an**, *adj.*, *n.*

bro·cade (brō·kād′), *n.*, *v.*, **-caded**, **-cading**. —*n.* 1. fabric woven with an elaborate design from any yarn. The right side has a raised effect. —*v.t.* 2. to weave with a design or figure. [t. Sp.: m. *brocado*, c. It. *broccato* der. *broccare* interweave with gold or silver, der. L *brocc(h)us*. See BROACH] —**bro·cad′ed**, *adj.*

broc·a·tel (brŏk′ə·tĕl′), *n.* 1. a kind of brocade, in which the design is in high relief. 2. an ornamental marble with variegated coloring esp. from Italy and Spain. Also, **broc′a·telle′**. [t. F.: m. *brocatelle*, t. It.: m. *broccatello*]

broc·co·li (brŏk′ə·lĭ), *n.* 1. a plant of the mustard family, *Brassica oleracea* var. *botrytis*, resembling the cauliflower. 2. a form of this plant which does not produce a head, the green saps and the stalk of which are a common vegetable. Also, **broccoli sprouts.** [t. It., pl. of *broccolo* sprout, der. L *broccus* projecting]

bro·ché (brō·shā′; *Fr.* brô·shě′), *adj.* woven with a pattern; brocaded. [t. F, pp. of *brocher* BROCADE, v.]

bro·chette (brō·shĕt′; *Fr.* brô-), *n.* 1. a skewer, for use in cookery. 2. **en brochette** (ĕn; *Fr.* ăn), on a small spit. [t. F, dim. of *broché* spit. See BROACH]

bro·chure (brō·shŏŏr′; *Fr.* brô·shyr′), *n.* a pamphlet. [t. F, der. *brocher* stitch]

Brock·en (brŏk′ən), *n.* a mountain in central Germany: the highest peak in the Harz Mountains; prominent in German folklore. 3745 ft.

brock·et (brŏk′ĭt), *n.* 1. a small swamp deer, genus *Mazama*, of tropical America. 2. the male red deer in the second year, with the first growth of straight horns.

Brock·ton (brŏk′tən), *n.* a city in E Massachusetts. 62,860 (1950).

bro·gan (brō′gən), *n.* a coarse, stout shoe. [t. Irish]

Bro·glie (brō·glē′), *n.* **Achille Charles Léonce Victor de** (à·shěl′ shàrl lě·ôns′ vēk·tôr′ də), 1785–1870, French statesman.

brogue[1] (brōg), *n.* an Irish accent in the pronunciation of English. [appar. special use of BROGUE[2]]

brogue[2] (brōg), *n.* a strongly made, comfortable type of ordinary shoe, often with decorative perforations on the vamp and foxing. [t. Irish, Gaelic: m. *brôg* shoe]

broi·der (broi′dər), *v.t.* *Archaic.* to embroider. [ME *broudre(n)*, t. OF: m. *bro(u)der*, *brosder*, of Gmc. orig.] —**broi′der·y**, *n.*

broil[1] (broil), *v.t.* 1. to cook by direct heat, as on a gridiron or in an oven broiler; grill. 2. to scorch; make very hot. —*v.i.* 3. to be subjected to great heat. 4. to burn with impatience, etc. —*n.* 5. a broiling. 6. something broiled. [ME *brule(n)*, ? t. OF: m. *bruiller* burn, g. LL verb, prob. b. Gmc. *brand* a burning and L *ustulāre* burn a little (der. *ūrere* burn)]

broil[2] (broil), *n.* 1. an angry quarrel or struggle; a disturbance; a tumult. —*v.i.* 2. to quarrel; brawl. [ME, t. OF: m. *brouiller* disorder, prob. der. *bro(u)* broth, t. OHG: m. *brod*. Cf. BREWIS]

broil·er (broi′lər), *n.* 1. any device for broiling meats or fish; a grate or pan for broiling. 2. a young chicken suitable for broiling.

bro·kage (brō′kĭj), *n.* brokerage.

broke (brōk), *v.* 1. pt. of **break.** 2. *Archaic and still often Colloq.* pp. of **break.** —*adj.* 3. *Slang.* out of money; bankrupt.

bro·ken (brō′kən), *v.* 1. pp. of **break.** —*adj.* 2. reduced to fragments. 3. ruptured; torn; fractured. 4. changing direction abruptly: *a broken line.* 5. fragmentary or incomplete: *a broken set.* 6. infringed or violated. 7. interrupted or disconnected: *broken sleep.* 8. weakened in strength, spirit, etc. 9. reduced to submission; tamed: *the horse was not yet broken to the saddle.* 10. imperfectly spoken, as language. 11. ruined; bankrupt: *the broken fortunes of his family.* —**bro′ken·ly**, *adv.* —**bro′ken·ness**, *n.*

bro·ken-down (brō′kən·doun′), *adj.* shattered or collapsed; having given way.

bro·ken-heart·ed (brō′kən·här′tĭd), *adj.* crushed by grief.

Broken Hill, a city in SE Australia, in New South Wales: the center of a rich mining district. 26,291 (1933).

broken wind, heaves. —**bro′ken-wind′ed**, *adj.*

bro·ker (brō′kər), *n.* 1. an agent who buys or sells for a principal on a commission basis without having title to the property. 2. a middleman or agent. [ME *brocor*, t. AF: m. *brocour*, orig., broacher (of casks), tapster (hence retailer); akin to BROACH]

bro·ker·age (brō′kər·ĭj), *n.* 1. the business of a broker. 2. the commission of a broker.

bro·mal (brō′măl), *n.* *Chem.*, *Pharm.* a colorless, oily liquid, CBr₃CHO, used in medicine as an anodyne and hypnotic. [f. BROM(INE) + AL(COHOL)]

bro·mate (brō′māt), *n.*, *v.*, **-mated**, **-mating**. —*n.* 1. *Chem.* a salt of bromic acid. —*v.t.* 2. to combine with bromine.

Brom·berg (brŏm′bûrg; *Ger.* brôm′bĕrᴋн), *n.* German name of **Bydgoszcz.**

brome grass (brōm), any grass of the genus *Bromus*, widely distributed in about 40 species, esp. *B. inermis*, a perennial used for hay and pasture. Also, **brome.** [brome, t. L: m. s. *bromus*, t. Gk.: m. *brómos* kind of oats]

bro·me·li·a·ceous (brō·mē′lĭ·ā′shəs), *adj.* *Bot.* belonging to the *Bromeliaceae*, a large family of herbaceous plants, mostly of tropical Americas, and including the pineapple, and Spanish moss, and many ornamentals. [f. s. NL *Bromelia* (named after Olaf *Bromel* (1639–1705), Swedish botanist) + -ACEOUS]

Brom·field (brŏm′fēld′), *n.* **Louis,** born 1896, U.S. novelist.

bro·mic (brō′mĭk), *adj.* *Chem.* containing pentavalent bromine (Br+⁵).

bromic acid, *Chem.* an acid, HBrO₃, containing bromine and oxygen, used as an oxidizing agent.

bro·mide (brō′mīd, -mĭd), *n.* 1. Also, **bro·mid** (brō′mĭd). *Chem.* a compound usually containing two elements only, one of which is bromine. 2. *Slang.* a person who is platitudinous and boring. 3. *Slang.* a tiresome platitude. [def. 2 and 3 from the use of certain bromides as sedatives]

bro·mid·ic (brō·mĭd′ĭk), *adj.* *Colloq.* pertaining or proper to a bromide; being a bromide; trite.

bro·mi·nate (brō′mə·nāt′), *v.t.*, **-nated**, **-nating.** *Chem.* to treat or combine with bromine. —**bro′mi·na′tion**, *n.*

bro·mine (brō′mēn, -mĭn), *n.* *Chem.* an element, a dark-reddish fuming liquid, resembling chlorine and iodine in chemical properties. Symbol: Br; *at. wt.*: 79.92; *at. no.*: 35; *sp. gr.* (liquid): 3.119 at 20°C. Also, **bro·min** (brō′mĭn). [f. s. Gk. *brômos* stench + -INE²]

bro·mism (brō′mĭzəm), *n.* *Pathol.* a morbid skin condition due to excessive use of bromides.

bron·chi (brŏng′kī), *n.* *Anat.* pl. of **bronchus.**

bron·chi·a (brŏng′kĭ·ə), *n. pl. Anat.* the ramifications of the bronchi or tubes. [t. LL, t. Gk., der. *brônchos* windpipe]

bron·chi·al (brŏng′kĭ·əl), *adj. Anat.* pertaining to the bronchia or bronchi.

bronchial tube, *Anat.* the bronchi, or the bronchi and their ramifications. See diag. under **lung.**

bron·chi·tis (brŏng·kī′tĭs), *n. Pathol.* inflammation of the membrane lining of the windpipe and bronchial tubes. [NL; f. BRONCH(O)- + -ITIS] —**bron·chit·ic** (brŏng·kĭt′ĭk), *adj.*

bron·cho (brŏng′kō), *n.*, *pl.* **-chos.** *bronco.*

broncho-, a word element meaning "bronchial." Also, **bronch-.** [t. Gk., comb. form of *brônchos* windpipe]

bron·cho·bust·er (brŏng′kō·bŭs′tər), *n.* broncobuster.

bron·cho·pneu·mo·nia (brŏng′kō·nyŏŏ·mō′nyə, -nŏŏ-), *n. Pathol.* inflammation of the bronchia and lungs; a form of pneumonia.

bron·chor·rha·gi·a (brŏng′kə·rā′jĭ·ə), *n. Obs. Pathol.* hemorrhage from the bronchial tubes.

bron·cho·scope (brŏng′kə·skōp′), *n. Med.* a tubular instrument for examining bronchi and for the removal of foreign bodies therefrom.

bron·chus (brŏng′kəs), *n.*, *pl.* **-chi** (-kī). *Anat.* either of the two main branches of the trachea. See diag. under **lung.** [t. NL, t. Gk.: m. *brônchos* windpipe]

bron·co (brŏng′kō), *n.*, *pl.* **-cos.** a pony or mustang of the western U.S., esp. one that is not broken, or is only imperfectly broken. Also, **broncho.** [t. Sp.: rough, rude]

bron·co·bust·er (brŏng′kō·bŭs′tər), *n. Western U.S.* one who breaks broncos to the saddle. Also, **broncho·buster.**

Bron·të (brŏn′tĭ), *n.* 1. **Anne,** (*Acton Bell*) 1820–49, British novelist. 2. her sister, **Charlotte,** (*Currer Bell*) 1816–55, British novelist. 3. her sister, **Emily Jane,** (*Ellis Bell*) 1818 -48, British novelist.

bron·to·sau·rus (brŏn′tə·sôr′əs), *n. Paleontol.* a large amphibious herbivorous dinosaur of the American Jurassic, 60 feet or more in length. [f. *bronto-*, comb. form of Gk. *brontē* thunder + -SAURUS]

Brontosaurus, *Apatosaurus excelsus* (66 ft. long, 12 ft. high)

Bronx (brŏngks), *n.* **The,** a N borough of New York City. 1,451,277 (1950); 54 sq. mi.

bronze (brŏnz), *n.*, *v.*, **bronzed**, **bronzing.** —*n.* 1. *Metall.* a. a durable brown alloy, consisting essentially of copper and tin. b. any of various other copper base alloys, such as **aluminum bronze, manganese bronze, silicon bronze,** etc. The term implies a product superior in some way to brass. 2. a metallic brownish color. 3. a work of art, as a statue, statuette, bust, or medal, composed of bronze, whether cast or wrought. —*v.t.* 4. to give the appearance or color of bronze to. 5. to make brown, as by exposure to the sun. [t. F, t. It.: m. *bronzo*] —**bronz′y**, *adj.*

Bronze Age, 1. *Archaeol.* the age in the history of Old World mankind (between the Stone and Iron Ages) marked by the use of bronze implements. 2. (*l.c.*) *Gk. Myth.* the third period of the history of man, marked by war and violence, following the gold and silver ages.

brooch (brōch, brŏŏch), *n.* a clasp or ornament for the dress, having a pin at the back for passing through the clothing and a catch for securing the point of the pin. [var. of BROACH]

brood (brŏŏd), *n.* 1. a number of young creatures produced or hatched at one time; a family of offspring or

young. **2.** breed or kind. —*v.t.* **3.** to sit as a bird over (eggs or young); incubate. **4.** to dwell persistently or moodily in thought on; ponder. —*v.i.* **5.** to sit as a bird over eggs to be hatched. **6.** to rest fixedly. **7.** to meditate with morbid persistence. —*adj.* **8.** kept for breeding purposes: *a brood mare.* [ME; OE *brōd*, c. G *brut*. Cf. BREED]
—**Syn. 1.** BROOD, LITTER refer to young creatures. BROOD is esp. applied to the young of fowls and birds hatched from eggs at one time and raised under their mother's care: *a brood of young turkeys.* LITTER is applied to a group of young animals brought forth at a birth: *a litter of kittens or pups.*

brood·er (brōō′dər), *n.* **1.** a device or structure for the artificial rearing of young chickens or other birds. **2.** one who or that which broods.

brood·y (brōō′dĭ), *adj.*, **broodier, broodiest. 1.** moody. **2.** inclined to brood or sit on eggs: *a broody hen.*

brook[1] (brŏŏk), *n.* a small, natural stream of fresh water, flowing through a glen or through woods, meadows, etc. [ME; OE *brōc* stream, c. G *bruch* marsh; akin to BREAK] —**Syn.** rivulet, run, burn, branch.

brook[2] (brŏŏk), *v.t.* to bear; suffer; tolerate (usually in a negative sentence). [ME *brouke(n)*, OE *brūcan*, c. G *brauchen* use; akin to L *fruī* enjoy]

Brooke (brŏŏk), *n.* **1.** Sir James, (1803–68). British soldier and adventurer: rajah of Sarawak. **2.** Rupert, 1887–1915, British poet.

Brook Farm, the scene of a famous, but unsuccessful, communistic experiment at West Roxbury, Mass., 1841–47, participated in by George Ripley, C. A. Dana, Nathaniel Hawthorne, and others.

brook·let (brŏŏk′lĭt), *n.* a little brook.

Brook·line (brŏŏk′lĭn), *n.* a town in E Massachusetts, near Boston. 57,589 (1950).

Brook·lyn (brŏŏk′lĭn), *n.* a borough of New York City, on W Long Island. 2,738,175 (1950); 89 sq. mi.

Brooklyn Bridge, a large suspension bridge over the East River, in New York City, uniting the boroughs of Manhattan and Brooklyn: built 1867–84. 5989 ft. long.

Brooks (brŏŏks), *n.* **1.** Phillips, 1835–93, U.S. Protestant Episcopal bishop and pulpit orator. **2.** Van Wyck, born 1886, U.S. author and critic.

Brooks Range, a mountain range in N Alaska, forming a watershed between the Yukon river and the Arctic Ocean. Highest peak, ab. 5000 ft.

brook trout, 1. the common speckled trout of eastern North America, *Salvelinus fontinalis.* **2.** the common stream trout of northern Europe, *Salmo trutta fario;* brown trout.

brook·weed (brŏŏk′wēd′), *n.* either of two primulaceous plants, *Samolus valerandi,* of the Old World, and *S. floribundus,* of North America, both bearing small white flowers.

broom (brōōm, brŏŏm), *n.* **1.** a sweeping implement consisting of a brush of twigs or plant stems on a handle. **2.** any of the shrubby fabaceous plants of the genus *Cytisus,* esp. *C. scoparius,* common in western Europe, which grows on uncultivated ground and has long, slender branches bearing yellow flowers. —*v.t.* **3.** to sweep. [ME *brōme,* OE *brōm,* c. OHG *brāmo.* Cf. BRAMBLE] —**broom′y,** *adj.*

broom·corn (brōōm′kôrn′, brŏŏm′-), *n.* a variety of sorghum with long, stiff panicles, used in brooms.

broom·rape (brōōm′rāp′, brŏŏm′-), *n.* any of various parasitic plants, esp. of the genus *Orobanche,* living on the roots of broom and other plants.

broom·stick (brōōm′stĭk′, brŏŏm′-), *n.* the long stick forming the handle of a broom.

bros., brothers. Also, **Bros.**

brose (brōz), *n. Scot.* a dish made by stirring boiling liquid into oatmeal or other meal. [Scot. var. of BREWIS]

broth (brŏth, brôth), *n.* **1.** thin soup of concentrated meat or fish stock. **2.** water in which meat or fish has been boiled, sometimes with vegetables or barley. [ME and OE, c. OHG *brod.* Cf. BREW, BREWIS]

broth·el (brŏth′əl, brôth′-), *n.* a house of prostitution. [ME; orig. worthless person, later whore, der. OE *brothen* ruined, degenerate, pp. of *brēothan* decay; in mod. use, short for *brothel house* whore house]

broth·er (brŭth′ər), *n., pl.* **brothers, brethren,** *v.* —*n.* **1.** a male child of the same parents (**whole brother**). **2.** a male child of only one of one's parents (**half brother**). **3.** a male member of the same kinship group, nationality, profession, etc.; an associate; a fellow countryman, fellow man, etc. **4.** *Eccles.* **a.** a male lay member of a religious organization which has a priesthood. **b.** a man who devotes himself to the duties of a religious order without taking holy orders, or while preparing for holy orders. **5.** (*pl.*) all members of a particular race, or of the human race in general. —*v.t.* **6.** to treat or address as a brother. [ME; OE *brōther,* c. G *bruder*]
—**Syn. 1.** BROTHERS, BRETHREN are plurals of BROTHER. BROTHERS are kinsmen, sons of the same parents: *my mother lives with my brothers.* BRETHREN, now archaic in the foregoing sense, is used of male members of a congregation or of a fraternal organization: *the brethren will meet at the church.*

broth·er·hood (brŭth′ərhŏŏd′), *n.* **1.** condition or quality of being a brother or brothers. **2.** quality of being brotherly. **3.** a fraternal or trade organization. **4.** all those engaged in a particular trade or profession.

broth·er-in-law (brŭth′ər ĭn lô′), *n., pl.* **brothers-in-law. 1.** one's husband's or wife's brother. **2.** one's sister's husband. **3.** the husband of one's wife's or husband's sister.

Brother Jon·a·than (jŏn′əthən), **1.** the government of the United States of America. **2.** a typical American.

broth·er·ly (brŭth′ərlĭ), *adj.* **1.** of, like, or befitting a brother; fraternal. —*adv.* **2.** as a brother; fraternally. —**broth′er·li·ness,** *n.*

brough·am (brōō′əm, brōōm, brō′əm). *n.* **1.** a four-wheeled, boxlike, closed carriage for two or four persons, with the driver's perch outside. **2.** *Auto.* **a.** a limousine having an open driver's compartment. **b.** an early type of automobile resembling a coupé, often with electric power. [named after Lord *Brougham* (1778–1868), British statesman]

brought (brôt), *v.* pt. and pp. of **bring.**

Broun (brōōn). *n.* (**Matthew**) **Heywood Campbell,** 1888–1939, U. S. journalist.

brow (brou), *n.* **1.** *Anat.* the ridge over the eye. **2.** the hair growing on that ridge; eyebrow. **3.** (*sing. or pl.*) the forehead: *to knit one's brows.* **4.** the countenance. **5.** the edge of a steep place. [ME *browe,* OE *brū*]

brow·beat (brou′bēt′), *v.t.,* **-beat, -beaten, -beating.** to intimidate by overbearing looks or words; bully.

brown (broun), *n.* **1.** a dark shade with yellowish or reddish hue. —*adj.* **2.** of the color brown. **3.** having skin of that color. **4.** sunburned or tanned. **5.** pertaining to the Malay race. —*v.t., v.i.* **6.** to make or become brown. [ME; OE *brūn,* c. G *braun*] —**brown′, ish,** *adj.* —**brown′ness,** *n.*

Brown (broun), *n.* **1.** Charles Brockden, 1771–1810, U.S. novelist. **2.** John ("*of Osawatomie*"), 1800–1859, U.S. abolitionist who incited the slaves to a rebellion but was captured at Harpers Ferry, tried, and hanged. **3.** Robert, 1773–1858, British botanist.

brown algae, *Bot.* algae belonging to the class *Phaeophyceae,* usually brown as a result of brown pigments added to their chlorophyll.

brown bear, 1. a variety of the common black bear, *Ursus americanus,* having a brownish coat. **2.** a variety of the black bear of Europe and America, *Ursus arctos,* inhabiting northern regions.

brown betty, a baked pudding made of apples, or other fruit, bread crumbs, sugar, butter, spice, etc.

brown bread, 1. any bread made of flour darker in color than the bolted wheat flour, esp., graham or whole wheat bread. **2.** Boston brown bread.

brown coal, lignite.

Browne (broun), *n.* **1.** Charles Farrar (fär′ər). ("*Artemus Ward*") 1834–67, U.S. humorist. **2.** Sir Thomas, 1605–82, British physician and author.

Brown·i·an movement (brou′nĭ ən), *Physics.* a rapid oscillatory motion often observed in very minute particles suspended in water or other liquid: first noticed (in 1827) by Robert Brown. Also, **Brownian motion.**

brown·ie (brou′nĭ), *n.* **1.** (in folklore) a little brown goblin, esp. one who helps secretly in household work. **2.** *U.S.* a small, highly shortened chocolate cake, often containing nuts. **3.** (*cap.*) a trademark for a type of inexpensive box camera. **4.** any inexpensive box camera. **5.** (*cap.*) a member of the junior division (ages 8–11) of the Girl Scouts or (*Brit.*) the Girl Guides. —**Syn. 1.** See **fairy.**

Brown·ing (brou′nĭng), *n.* **1.** Elizabeth Barrett (bär′ĭt), 1806–61, British poetess. **2.** her husband, Robert, 1812–89, British poet.

brown rice, rice from which the bran layers and germs have not been removed by polishing.

brown rot, *Plant Pathol.* a disease, esp. of apples, peaches, plums, and cherries, caused by fungi of the genus *Sclerotinia.*

Brown Shirt, 1. a member of Hitler's storm troopers (Sturmabteilungen). **2.** (loosely) any Nazi.

brown·stone (broun′stōn′), *n.* **1.** a reddish-brown sandstone, extensively used as a building material. —*adj.* **2.** belonging or pertaining to the well-to-do class.

brown study, deep, serious absorption in thought.

brown sugar, unrefined or partially refined sugar.

Browns·ville (brounz′vĭl), *n.* a seaport in S Texas, near the mouth of the Rio Grande. 36,066 (1950).

Brown Swiss, one of a breed of large-boned and well-muscled dairy cattle. giving large quantities of milk.

brown-tail moth (broun′tāl′), a tussock moth, *Euproctis chrysorrhoea,* having white wings, in the larval stage very destructive to trees.

brown thrasher, a well-known songbird, *Toxostoma rufum,* of the eastern U.S. Also, **brown thrush.**

brown trout, brook trout (def. 2).

browse (brouz), *v.,* **browsed, browsing,** *n.* —*v.t.* **1.** (of cattle, deer, etc.) to nibble at; eat from. **2.** (of cattle, deer, etc.) to feed on; pasture on; graze. —*v.i.* **3.** (of cattle, etc.) to graze. **4.** to glance at random through a book or books. —*n.* **5.** tender shoots or twigs of shrubs and trees as food for cattle, deer, etc. [appar. t. MF: m. *broust* young sprout, t. Gmc.; cf. OS *brustian* to sprout] —**brows′er,** *n.*

Bruce (brōōs), *n.* **1. Robert the,** (*Robert I, Robert Bruce*) 1274–1329, king of Scotland, 1306–29; preserved the independence of Scotland by victory over the English at Bannockburn in 1314. **2. Stanley Melbourne,** born 1883, prime minister of Australia, 1923–29.

bru·cel·lo·sis (brōō′sə lō′sĭs), *n. Vet. Sci., Pathol.* infection with bacteria of the *Brucella* group, frequently causing abortions in animals and undulant fever in man.

bruc·ine (brōō′sēn, -sĭn), *n. Pharm., Chem.* a bitter, poisonous alkaloid, $C_{23}H_{26}N_2O_4$, obtained from the nux vomica tree, *Strychnos nux vomica*, and from other species of the same genus, resembling strychnine in action but less powerful. Also, **bruc·in** (brōō′sĭn). [f. James Bruce (1730–94), Scottish explorer of Africa + -INE[2]]

Brue·ghel (brœ′gəl), *n.* a Flemish family of genre and landscape painters: **Pieter,** 1525?–1569, the father of **Pieter,** 1564–1637, and **Jan,** 1568–1625. Also, **Brue·gel, Breu′ghel,**

Bru·ges (brōō′jĭz, brōōzh; *Fr.* bryzh), *n.* a city in NW Belgium: connected by canal with its seaport, Zeebrugge. 51,780 (est. 1941). Flemish, **Brug·ge** (brœkн′ə).

bru·in (brōō′ĭn), *n.* a bear. [t. MD: lit., brown, the name of the bear in *Reynard the Fox*]

bruise (brōōz), *v.,* **bruised, bruising,** *n.* —*v.t.* 1. to injure by striking or pressing, without breaking the skin or drawing blood. 2. to injure or hurt superficially: *to bruise a person's feelings.* 3. to crush (drugs or food) by beating or pounding. —*v.i.* 4. to develop a discolored spot on the skin as the result of a blow, fall, etc. 5. to be injured superficially: *his feelings bruise easily.* —*n.* 6. an injury due to bruising; a contusion. [ME *bruse(n), brise(n),* coalescence of OE *brȳsan* crush, bruise and OF *br(u)isier* break, ult. der. Gallic *bris-, brus-* beat]

bruis·er (brōō′zər), *n.* 1. a boxer. 2. *Colloq.* a tough fellow; bully.

bruit (brōōt), *v.t.* 1. to noise abroad; rumor (mainly in the passive): *the report was bruited about.* —*n.* 2. *Archaic.* rumor. 3. *Archaic.* a din. [ME, t. OF, der. *bruire* make a noise]

Bru·maire (bry mĕr′), *n.* the second month, October 22 to November 20, in the calendar adopted (1793) by the first French republic. [t. F, der. *brume* BRUME]

bru·mal (brōō′məl), *adj.* wintry. [t. L: s. *brūmālis*]

brume (brōōm), *n.* mist; fog. [t. F: fog, t. Pr.: m. *bruma,* g. L *brūma* winter, winter solstice, lit., shortest day] —**bru·mous** (brōō′məs), *adj.*

brum·ma·gem (brŭm′ə jəm), *adj.* 1. showy but inferior and worthless. —*n.* 2. a showy but inferior and worthless thing. [alter. of *Birmingham,* in England]

Brum·mell (brŭm′əl), *n.* See **Beau Brummell.**

brunch (brŭnch), *n.* a mid-morning meal that serves both as breakfast and lunch. [b. BREAKFAST and LUNCH]

Brun·dis·i·um (brŭn dĭz′ĭ əm), *n.* ancient name of **Brindisi.**

Bru·nei (brōō nī′), *n.* 1. a British protectorate in NW Borneo. 39,000 pop. (est. 1939); ab. 2220 sq. mi. 2. the capital of this protectorate: a seaport. ab. 10,000.

Bru·nel·les·chi (brōō′něl lĕs′kē), *n.* **Filippo** (fē lēp′pô), 1377?–1446, Florentine architect.

bru·net (brōō nĕt′), *adj.* 1. (of skin, eyes, or hair) dark; brown. 2. (of a person) having dark or brown hair, eyes, or skin. —*n.* 3. a man or boy with dark hair, skin, and eyes. [t. F, dim. of *brun,* fem. *brune* brown; of Gmc. orig. Cf. BROWN]

bru·nette (brōō nĕt′), *adj.* 1. brunet. —*n.* 2. a woman or girl with dark hair, skin, and eyes.

Brün·hild (brȳn′hĭld; *Ger.* brōōn′hĭlt), *n.* 1. (in the *Nibelungenlied*) a legendary queen of Iceland, wife of King Gunther, for whom she is won by Siegfried. 2. (in the corresponding Scandinavian legend) a Valkyrie, won by Sigurd for Gunnar. Also, **Brynhild.** [t. G. Cf. Icel. *Brynhildr*]

Brünn (bryn), *n.* German name of **Brno.**

Brün·ne·hil·de (brȳn′ə hĭl′də), *n.* the heroine of Wagner's *Ring of the Nibelungs.* Cf. **Siegfried.**

Bru·no (brōō′nô), *n.* 1. **Giordano** (jôr dä′nô), 1548?–1600, Italian philosopher. 2. **Saint,** c1030–1101, monk: born at Cologne; founder of Carthusian order.

Bruns·wick (brŭnz′wĭk), *n.* 1. a state in central Germany. 802,873 pop. (1939); 1418 sq. mi. 2. the capital of this state. 196,068 (1939). German, **Braunschweig.**

brunt (brŭnt), *n.* 1. the shock or force of an attack, etc.; the main stress, force, or violence: *to bear the brunt of their criticism.* 2. *Rare or Archaic.* a violent attack.

Bru·sa (brōō′sä), *n.* Bursa.

brush[1] (brŭsh), *n.* 1. an instrument consisting of bristles, hair, or the like, set in or attached to a handle, used for painting, cleaning, polishing, rubbing, etc. 2. act of brushing; an application of a brush. 3. the bushy tail of an animal, esp. of a fox. 4. the art or skill of a painter of pictures. 5. a brief encounter. 6. a quick ride across country. 7. *Elect.* a. a conductor serving to maintain electric contact between stationary and moving parts of a machine or other apparatus. b. a brush discharge. —*v.t.* 8. to sweep, rub, clean, polish, etc. with a brush. 9. to touch lightly in passing; pass lightly over. 10. to remove by brushing or by lightly passing over. —*v.i.* 11. to move or skim with a slight contact. 12. to move quickly or in haste; rush. [ME *brusshe,* t. OF: m. *broisse,* t. Gmc.; cf. MHG *bürste* brush] —**brush′y,** *adj.* —Syn. 5. See **struggle.**

brush[2] (brŭsh), *n.* 1. a dense growth of bushes, shrubs, etc.; scrub; a thicket. 2. *U.S.* lopped or broken branches; brushwood. 3. *U.S.* backwoods; a sparsely settled wooded region. [ME *brusche,* t. OF: m. *broche,* ? of Gallic orig.] —**brush′y,** *adj.*

brush discharge, *Elect.* corona (def. 6).

brush-off (brŭsh′ôf′, -ŏf′), *n. U.S. Slang.* an abrupt or final dismissal or refusal.

brush·wood (brŭsh′wŏŏd′), *n.* 1. branches of trees

cut or broken off. 2. densely growing small trees and shrubs. [f. BRUSH[2] + WOOD[1]]

brusque (brŭsk; *esp. Brit.* brŏŏsk; *Fr.* brysk), *adj.* abrupt in manner; blunt; rough: *a brusque welcome.* Also, **brusk.** [t. F, t. It.: m. *brusco* rude, sharp, g. L *bruscum,* b. L *ruscum* butcher's-broom and *brūcum* broom] —**brusque′ly,** *adv.* —**brusque′ness,** *n.* —Syn. See **blunt.**

brus·que·rie (bryskə rē′), *n.* brusqueness. [F]

Brus·sels (brŭs′əlz), *n.* the capital of Belgium, in the central part. 185,514 (est. 1941); with suburbs, 898,352 (est. 1944). French, **Bruxelles.**

Brussels carpet, a kind of worsted carpet woven on a Jacquard loom, in which uncut loops form a heavy pile.

Brussels lace, handmade lace from Brussels.

Brussels sprouts, 1. plants of *Brassica oleracea,* var. *gemmifera,* having small edible heads or sprouts along the stalk, which resemble miniature cabbage heads. 2. the heads or sprouts themselves.

brut (bryt), *adj.* (of wines, usually champagne) very dry. [t. F: raw]

bru·tal (brōō′təl), *adj.* 1. savage; cruel; inhuman. 2. crude; coarse; harsh. 3. irrational; unreasoning. 4. of or pertaining to lower animals. —**bru′tal·ly,** *adv.* —Syn. 1. See **cruel.**

Brussels sprouts

bru·tal·i·ty (brōō tăl′ə tĭ), *n., pl.* **-ties.** 1. quality of being brutal. 2. a brutal act.

bru·tal·ize (brōō′tə līz′), *v.t., v.i.,* **-ized, -izing.** to make or become brutal. —**bru′tal·i·za′tion,** *n.*

brute (brōōt), *n.* 1. a nonhuman animal; beast. 2. a brutal person. 3. the animal qualities, desires, etc., of man. —*adj.* 4. wanting reason; animal; not human. 5. not characterized by intelligence; irrational. 6. characteristic of animals; of brutal character or quality. 7. savage; cruel. 8. sensual; carnal. [t. F: m. *brut,* t. L: s. *brūtus* dull] —Syn. 1. See **animal.**

bru·ti·fy (brōō′tə fī′), *v.t., v.i.,* **-fied, -fying.** to brutalize.

brut·ish (brōō′tĭsh), *adj.* 1. brutal. 2. gross; carnal; bestial. 3. lacking civilized sensibilities; like an animal. —**brut′ish·ly,** *adv.* —**brut′ish·ness,** *n.* —Syn. 2. See **beastly.**

Bru·tus (brōō′təs), *n.* **Marcus Junius** (mär′kəs jŏŏ′nĭ əs), 85?–42 B.C., Roman provincial administrator; one of the assassins of Julius Caesar.

Brux·elles (bryk sĕl′; *local* bryk sĕl′), *n.* French name of **Brussels.**

Bry·an (brī′ən), *n.* **William Jennings,** 1860–1925, U.S. political leader.

Bry·ansk (brĭ änsk′; *Russ.* bryänsk′), *n.* a city in the W Soviet Union. 87,473 (1939).

Bry·ant (brī′ənt), *n.* **William Cullen,** 1794–1878, U.S. poet.

Bryce (brīs), *n.* **James, Viscount,** 1838–1922, British historical and political writer, and diplomat.

Bryce Canyon National Park, a national park in SW Utah: fantastically eroded pinnacles. 55 sq. mi.

Bryn·hild (brĭn′hĭld; *Icelandic* brȳn′-), *n.* Brunhild.

bry·ol·o·gy (brī ŏl′ə jĭ), *n.* the part of botany that treats of bryophytes. [f. Gk. *brȳo(n)* moss + -LOGY] —**bry·o·log·i·cal** (brī′ə lŏj′ə kəl), *adj.* —**bry·ol′o·gist,** *n.*

bry·o·ny (brī′ə nĭ), *n., pl.* **-nies.** any plant of the Old World cucurbitaceous genus *Bryonia,* comprising vines or climbers with acrid juice and emetic and purgative properties. [t. L: m. *bryōnia,* t. Gk.]

bry·o·phyte (brī′ə fīt′), *n. Bot.* any of the *Bryophyta,* a primary division or group of plants comprising the true mosses and liverworts. [t. NL: m. *Bryophyta,* pl., f. Gk. *brȳo(n)* moss + -phyta (see -PHYTE)] —**bry·o·phyt·ic** (brī′ə fĭt′ĭk), *adj.*

Bry·o·zo·a (brī′ə zō′ə), *n. pl. Zool.* a phylum of marine and fresh-water animals, of sessile habits, forming branching, encrusting, or gelatinous colonies of many small polyps, each having a circular or horseshoe-shaped ridge bearing ciliated tentacles. Branching marine types are termed sea moss and are used as ornaments.

Bry·o·zo·an (brī′ə zō′ən), *Zool.* —*adj.* 1. of or pertaining to the *Bryozoa.* —*n.* 2. any of the *Bryozoa.* [f. Gk. *brȳo(n)* moss + zo- + -AN]

Bryth·on (brĭth′ən), *n.* 1. a Celt in Britain using the Brythonic form of the Celtic language, which was confined mainly to the western part of southern Britain after the English conquest. 2. a Briton. [t. Welsh]

Bry·thon·ic (brĭ thŏn′ĭk), *adj.* 1. pertaining to the Celtic dialects used in northwestern and southwestern England, Wales, and Brittany. —*n.* 2. the British subgroup of Celtic.

Brześć nad Bu·giem (bzhĕshch′ näd bōŏ′gyĕm), *n.* Polish name of **Brest Litovsk.**

B.S., 1. Bachelor of Science. 2. Bachelor of Surgery.

b.s., *Com.* 1. balance sheet. 2. bill of sale.

B.S.A., 1. Bachelor of Scientific Agriculture. 2. Boy Scouts of America.

B.Sc., (L *Baccalaureus Scientiae*) Bachelor of Science.

Bt., Baronet.

B.T., (L *Baccalaureus Theologia*) Bachelor of Theology. Also, **B.Th.**

---

b., blend of, blended; c., cognate with; d., dialect, dialectal; der., derived from; f., formed from; g., going back to; m., modification of; r., replacing; s., stem of; t., taken from; ?, perhaps. See the full key on inside cover.

B.T.U. *Physics.* British thermal unit, or units. Also, **B.t.u., B.th.u., Btu.**

bu., bushel; bushels.

bu·bal (bū′bəl), *n.* a large antelope, one of the hartebeests, *Alcelaphus boselaphus,* of northern Africa. Also, **bu·ba·lis** (bū′bə lĭs). [t. L: s. *būbalus* an oxlike antelope, t. Gk.: m. *boúbalos*]

bu·ba·line (bū′bəlīn′, -lĭn), *adj.* **1.** (of antelopes) resembling or like the bubal, as the hartebeests, blesbok, etc. **2.** pertaining to or resembling the true buffaloes.

bub·ble (bŭb′əl), *n., v.,* **-bled, -bling. —n. 1.** a small globule of gas in or rising through a liquid. **2.** a small globule of gas in a thin liquid envelope. **3.** a globule of air or gas, or a globular vacuum, in a solid substance. **4.** anything that lacks firmness, substance, or permanence; a delusion; a worthless, deceptive matter. **5.** an inflated speculation, esp. if fraudulent. **6.** act or sound of bubbling. **—v.i. 7.** to send up bubbles; effervesce. **8.** to flow or run with a gurging noise; gurgle. **—v.t. 9.** to cause to bubble; make (bubbles). **10.** *Archaic.* to cheat; deceive; swindle. [ME *bobel,* c. D *bobbelen,* Sw. *bubla.* Cf. BURBLE] **—bub′bly,** *adj.*

bub·bler (bŭb′lər), *n.* a drinking fountain from which one drinks without a cup.

bu·bo (bū′bō), *n., pl.* **-boes.** *Pathol.* an inflammatory swelling of a lymphatic gland, esp. in the groin or armpit. [t. LL, t. Gk.: m. *boubōn,* lit., groin]

bu·bon·ic (bū bŏn′ĭk), *adj. Pathol.* **1.** of or pertaining to a bubo. **2.** accompanied by or affected with buboes.

bubonic plague, *Pathol.* a contagious epidemic disease in which the victims suffer chills, fevers, and buboes and are prostrate, and which often has rat fleas as its carrier.

bu·bon·o·cele (bū bŏn′ə sēl′), *n. Pathol.* an inguinal hernia, esp. one in which the protrusion of the intestine is limited to the region of the groin.

Bu·ca·ra·man·ga (bōō kä′rä mäng′gä), *n.* a city in N Colombia. 62,678 (est. 1943).

buc·cal (bŭk′əl), *adj. Anat.* **1.** of or pertaining to the cheek. **2.** pertaining to the sides of the mouth or to the mouth; oral. **3.** pertaining to the mouth as a whole. [f. s. L *bucca* cheek, mouth + -AL[1]]

buc·ca·neer (bŭk′ə nĭr′), *n.* **1.** a pirate. **2.** one of the piratical adventurers who raided Spanish colonies and shipping in America. [t. F: m. *boucanier,* der. *boucan* frame for curing meat, of Carib orig.]

buc·ci·na·tor (bŭk′sə nā′tər), *n. Anat.* a thin, flat muscle lining the cheek, assisting in mastication, blowing wind instruments, etc. [t. L: trumpeter, der. *buccināre* blow a trumpet]

bu·cen·taur[1] (bū sĕn′tôr), *n.* the state barge of Venice, from which the doge and other officials on Ascension Day performed the ceremonial marriage of the state with the Adriatic, by dropping a ring into the sea. [t. It.: m. *bucentoro,* orig. unknown]

bu·cen·taur[2] (bū sĕn′tôr), *n.* a mythical monster, half man and half bull; a centaur with the body of a bull instead of a horse. [f. Gk.: m. *boûs* ox + m.s. *kéntauros* centaur]

Bu·ceph·a·lus (bū sĕf′ə ləs), *n.* the war horse of Alexander the Great.

Buch·an (bŭk′ən; *Scot.* bŭкн′ən), *n.* **John,** (*Baron Tweedsmuir*) 1875–1940, Scottish novelist and historian: governor general of Canada, 1935–40.

Bu·chan·an (bū kăn′ən, bə-), *n.* **James,** 1791–1868, 15th president of the U.S., 1857–61.

Buch·en·wald (bōōk′ən wôld′; *Ger.* bōōкн′ən vält′), *n.* a Nazi concentration camp in central Germany, near Weimar, infamous for atrocities perpetrated there.

Buch·man·ism (bōōk′mə nĭz′əm), *n.* a religious movement emphasizing Christian fellowship or "sharing" in small groups, public confession of sins, divine guidance, absolute honesty, purity, love, and unselfishness; the Oxford Group. [named after Frank *Buchman* (born 1878) who founded it] **—Buch·man·ite** (bōōk′mə nīt), *n.*

buck[1] (bŭk), *n.* **1.** the male of the deer, antelope, rabbit, hare, sheep, or goat. **2.** male of certain other animals: *buck shad.* **3.** a fop; a dandy. **4.** *U.S. Colloq.* a male Indian or Negro. **5.** *U.S. Slang.* a dollar. **—adj. 6.** *Mil. Slang.* of the lowest of several ranks involving the same principal designation: *buck private, buck sergeant.* [ME *bukke,* coalescence of OE *bucca* he-goat and *bucc* male deer, c. G *bock*]

buck[2] (bŭk), *v.i.* **1.** (of a saddle or pack animal) to leap with arched back and come down with head low and forelegs stiff, in order to dislodge rider or pack. **2.** *U.S. Colloq.* to resist obstinately; object strongly: *to buck at improvements.* **3.** *U.S. Colloq.* (of a vehicle) to jerk and bounce. **4.** *Colloq.* to become more cheerful, vigorous, etc. (fol. by *up*). **5.** *Brit.* to boast. **—v.t. 6.** to throw or attempt to throw (a rider) by bucking. **7.** *U.S.* to strike with the head; butt. **8.** *U.S. Colloq.* to resist obstinately; object strongly to. **9.** *Colloq.* to make more cheerful, vigorous, etc. (fol. by *up*). **10.** *Football.* to charge into (the line of opponents) with the ball. **—n. 11.** act of bucking. [special use of BUCK[1]; in def. 7, alter. of BUTT[3]]

buck[3] (bŭk), *n.* **1.** a sawhorse. **2.** *Gymnastics.* a leather-covered cylindrical block, adjustable in height, used for leaping or diving over, etc. [t. D: m. *zaagbok*]

buck[4] (bŭk), *n.* **1.** *Poker.* any object in the pot which reminds the winner that he has some privilege or duty when his turn to deal next comes. **2. pass the buck,** *U.S. Colloq.* to shift the responsibility or blame to another person. [orig. uncert.]

Buck (bŭk), *n.* **Pearl,** born 1892, U.S. novelist.

buck·a·roo (bŭk′ə rōō′, bŭk′ə rōō′), *n., pl.* **-roos.** *Western U.S.* a cowboy. Also, **buck·ay·ro** (bə kâr′ō). [alter. of Sp. *vaquero,* der. *vaca* cow, g. L *vacca*]

buck bean, a plant, *Menyanthes trifoliata,* with white or pink flowers, growing in bogs.

buck·board (bŭk′bôrd′), *n.* a light four-wheeled carriage in which a long elastic board or lattice frame is used in place of body and springs.

Buckboard

buck·een (bŭk ēn′), *n. Ireland.* a young man of the middle class or lower aristocracy who copies the habits of wealthier people.

buck·er (bŭk′ər), *n.* a horse that bucks.

buck·et (bŭk′ĭt), *n., v.,* **-eted, -eting. —n. 1.** a vessel, usually round with flat bottom and a semicircular handle, for carrying water, sand, etc. **2.** anything resembling or suggesting this. **3.** one of the scoops attached to or forming the endless chain in certain types of conveyers or elevators. **4.** a cupped vane of a water wheel, turbine, etc. **5.** a bucketful. **—v.t. 6.** to lift, carry, or handle in a bucket (often fol. by *up* or *out*). **7.** to ride (a horse) fast and without care about its fatigue. **8.** to handle (orders, etc.) as in a bucket shop. **—v.i. 9.** *Colloq.* to move or ride fast. [ME *bocket,* appar. t. OF: m. *buket* pail, tub, prob. der. some cognate of OE *būc* pitcher] **—buck·et·ful** (bŭk′ĭt fŏŏl′), *n.*

bucket seat, a folding seat for one person in racing cars, and in some airplanes.

bucket shop, *Finance.* a fraudulent establishment operating ostensibly for the transaction of a legitimate stock exchange or similar business, but actually speculating on its own account against its customers' purchases and sales by failing to execute some so that customers' gains are the establishment's loss and vice versa. [orig. a place where liquor was obtained and carried away in buckets brought by the customers]

buck·eye (bŭk′ī′), *n.* **1.** any of various trees or shrubs, genus *Aesculus,* allied to the true horse chestnut, as *A. glabra* (**Ohio buckeye**), a large tree with an ill-smelling bark. **2.** (*cap.*) *Colloq.* an inhabitant of Ohio, the Buckeye State. [f. BUCK[1] stag + EYE, in allusion to the appearance of the seed]

buck fever, *U.S. Colloq.* nervous excitement of an inexperienced hunter upon the approach of game.

buck·hound (bŭk′hound′), *n.* a hound for hunting bucks, etc., similar to the staghound, but smaller.

Buck·ing·ham (bŭk′ĭng əm), *n.* **1. George Villiers** (vĭl′ərz, -yərz), **1st Duke of,** 1592–1628, British courtier, politician, and military leader: lord high admiral, 1617. **2.** his son, **George Villiers, 2nd Duke of,** 1628–1687, British courtier and writer. **3.** Buckinghamshire.

Buckingham Palace, the London residence of the British sovereign, at the west end of St. James's Park.

Buck·ing·ham·shire (bŭk′ĭng əm shĭr′, -shər), *n.* a county in S England. 353,000 pop. (est. 1946); 749 sq. mi. *Co. seat:* Aylesbury. Also, **Buckingham, Bucks.**

buck·ish (bŭk′ĭsh), *adj.* dapperish; foppish. **—buck′ish·ly,** *adv.* **—buck′ish·ness,** *n.*

buck·le (bŭk′əl), *n., v.,* **-led, -ling. —n. 1.** a clasp consisting of a rectangular or curved rim with one or more movable tongues, used for fastening together two loose ends, as of a belt or strap; any similar contrivance used for such a purpose. **2.** an ornament of metal, beads, etc., of similar appearance. **3.** a bend, bulge, or kink, as in a saw blade. **—v.t. 4.** to fasten with a buckle or buckles. **5.** to shrivel, by applying heat or pressure; bend; curl. **6.** to prepare (oneself) for action; apply (oneself) vigorously to something. **—v.i. 7.** to set to work with vigor (fol. by *down to*). **8.** to bend, warp, or give way suddenly, as with heat or pressure. **9.** to grapple; contend. [ME *bocle,* t. F: m. *boucle* buckle, boss of a shield, g. L *buccula,* dim. of *bucca* cheek, mouth]

Buck·le (bŭk′əl), *n.* **Henry Thomas,** 1821–62, British historian.

buck·ler (bŭk′lər), *n.* **1.** a round shield, with grip for holding, and sometimes with straps through which the arm is passed. **2.** any means of defense; a protection. **—v.t. 3.** to be a buckler or shield to; support; defend. [ME *bokeler,* t. OF: m. *boucler* shield, orig., one with a boss, der. *boucle* boss. See BUCKLE, *n.*]

buck·o (bŭk′ō), *n., pl.* **-oes.** a bully.

buck·ra (bŭk′rə), *n.* a white man (used among the Negroes of the African coast, the West Indies, and the southern U.S.). [? t. West African (Calabar): m. *mbākara* demon, powerful being, white man]

buck·ram (bŭk′rəm), *n., v.,* **-ramed, -raming. —n. 1.** stiff cotton fabric for interlining, binding books, etc. **2.** stiffness of manner; extreme preciseness or formality. **—v.t. 3.** to strengthen with buckram. **4.** to give (a person, etc.) a false appearance of importance or strength. [ME *bokeram.* Cf. OF *boquerant,* It. *bucherame.* ? ult. der. *Bukhāra,* name of town and region in Central Asia whence cloth was exported]

Bucks (bŭks), *n.* Buckinghamshire.
buck·saw (bŭk'sô'), *n.* a saw consisting of a blade set across an upright frame or bow, used with both hands in cutting wood on a sawbuck or saw-horse.

buck·shot (bŭk'shŏt'), *n.* a large size of lead shot used on big game.

buck·skin (bŭk'skĭn'), *n.* **1.** the skin of a buck or deer. **2.** a strong, soft, yellowish or grayish leather, orig. prepared from deerskins, now usually from sheepskins. **3.** (*pl.*) breeches made of buckskin. **4.** (*cap.*) a buckskin-clad American soldier of the Revolutionary War. **5.** *U.S.* a horse of the color of buckskin.

Bucksaw

buck·thorn (bŭk'thôrn'), *n.* **1.** any of several trees or shrubs (sometimes thorny) belonging to the genus *Rhamnus*, as *R. cathartica*, a shrub whose berries were formerly much used in medicine as a purgative, and *R. frangula*, yielding the **buckthorn bark** used in medicine. **2.** a tree or shrub of the sapotaceous genus *Bumelia*, esp. *B. lycioides*, a tree common in the southern and part of the central U.S.

buck·tooth (bŭk'tōōth'), *n.*, *pl.* **-teeth** (-tēth'). a projecting tooth.

buck·wheat (bŭk'hwēt'), *n.* **1.** a herbaceous plant, *Fagopyrum sagittatum*, cultivated for its triangular seeds, which are used as a food for animals, and made into a flour for pancakes, etc. **2.** the seeds. **3.** the flour. [f. *buck* (OE *bōc* beech) + WHEAT. Cf. obs. *buckmast* beech mast, D *boekweit*, G *buchweizen* buckwheat, lit., beech wheat, from its beechnut-shaped seed]

bu·col·ic (būkŏl'ĭk), *adj.* Also, **bu·col'i·cal.** **1.** of or pertaining to shepherds; pastoral. **2.** rustic; rural; agricultural: *bucolic isolation.* —*n.* **3.** Humorous. a farmer; a shepherd; a rustic. **4.** a pastoral poem. [t. L: s. *būcolicus*, t. Gk.: m. *boukolikόs* rustic] —**bu·col'i·cal·ly**, *adv.*

Bu·co·vi·na (bōō'kə vē'nə; *Rum.* bŏō kô vē'nä), *n.* **1.** a province in N Rumania. 338,895 pop. (est. 1943); 1912 sq. mi. (1946). **2.** Northern, a region in the SW Soviet Union, in the Ukrainian Republic: formerly a part of Rumania. ab. 460,000 pop.; 2119 sq. mi. Also, **Bukovina.**

Bu·cu·reş·ti (bōō kōō rĕsht'), *n.* Rumanian name of **Bucharest.**

bud[1] (bŭd), *n.*, *v.*, **budded, budding.** —*n.* **1.** *Bot.* **a.** a small axillary or terminal protuberance on a plant, containing rudimentary foliage (**leaf bud**), the rudimentary inflorescence (**flower bud**), or both (**mixed bud**). **b.** an undeveloped or rudimentary stem or branch of a plant. **2.** *Zool.* (in certain animals of low organization) a prominence which develops into a new individual, sometimes permanently attached to the parent and sometimes becoming detached; a gemma. **3.** *Anat.* any small rounded part, as a tactile bud or a gustatory bud. **4.** an immature or undeveloped person or thing. **5.** nip in the **bud,** to stop (something) before it really gets started. —*v.i.* **6.** to put forth or produce buds, as a plant. **7.** to begin to grow and develop. **8.** to be in an early stage of development. —*v.t.* **9.** to cause to bud. **10.** *Hort.* to graft by inserting a single bud into the stock. [ME *budde*; orig. uncert.]

Leaf buds of the elm (def. 1a)

bud[2] (bŭd), *n.* Familiar. **1.** brother. **2.** man or boy (as a term of address). [alter. of BROTHER]

Bu·da·pest (bōō'də pĕst', bōō'də pĕst'; *Hung.* bŏó'dŏ-pĕsht'), *n.* the capital of Hungary, on the Danube: formed by the union of the cities of Buda and Pest (1872). 1,035,000 pop. (est. 1946).

Bud·dha (bŏōd'ə), *n.* "The Enlightened One," a title applied esp. to the great religious teacher, variously known as Siddhartha and Gautama (or Gotama), or Sakyamuni, who flourished in India about the 6th century B.C., regarded by his followers as the latest of a series of teachers (Buddhas) possessing perfect enlightenment and wisdom. [t. Skt.: wise, enlightened]

Bud·dhism (bŏōd'ĭz əm), *n.* the cult, founded by Buddha, which teaches that life is intrinsically full of suffering, and that the supreme felicity (Nirvana) is to be striven for by psychological and ethical self-culture. —**Bud'dhist,** *n.*, *adj.* —**Bud·dhis'tic,** *adj.*

bud·dle·ia (bŭd lē'ə, bŭd'lĭ ə), *n.* any of the genus *Budleja*, mainly tropical ornamental perennials of the family *Loganiaceae*, having a two-celled many-seeded fruit. [NL; named after Adam *Buddle* (d. 1715), botanist]

bud·dy (bŭd'ĭ), *n.*, *pl.* **-dies.** *U.S. Colloq.* a comrade or mate. [see BUD[2]]

Bu·dën·ny (bōō dĕn'ĭ; *Russ.* bōō dyôn'nĭ), *n.* Semën Mikhailovich (sĕ myôn' mĭ hī'lŏ vĭch), born 1883, Russian general in 1917 Revolution and World War II: marshal of Soviet Union since 1935.

budge (bŭj), *v.*, **budged, budging.** —*v.i.* **1.** to move slightly; give way (usually with negative). —*v.t.* **2.** to cause to budge (usually with negative). [t. F: m. s. *bouger*, ult. der. L *bullīre* BOIL[1]]

budg·et (bŭj'ĭt), *n.*, *v.*, **-eted, -eting.** —*n.* **1.** an estimate, often itemized, of expected income and expense, or operating results, for a given period in the future. **2.** a plan of operations based on such an estimate. **3.** an itemized allotment of funds for a given period.

4. a stock; a collection. **5.** *Obs.* a small bag; a pouch. —*v.t.* **6.** to plan allotment of (funds, time, etc.). **7.** to deal with (specific funds) in a budget. [late ME *bougette*, t. F, dim. of *bouge* bag, g. L *bulga*] —**budg·et·ar·y** (bŭj'ə tĕr'ĭ), *adj.*

Bud·weis (bŏōt'vīs), *n.* a city in W Czechoslovakia, on the Moldau river. 43,134 (1930). Czech, **České Budějovice.**

Bu·ell (bū'əl), *n.* **Don Carlos** (dŏn kär'lōs), 1818–98, Union general in the U.S. Civil War.

Bue·na Vis·ta (bwĕ'nä vēs'tä), a battlefield in N Mexico, near Saltillo: the American forces withstood a severe attack here in the Mexican War, 1847.

Bue·nos Ai·res (bwā'nəs ī'rĭz, bō'nəs âr'ēz; *Sp.* bwĕ'nōs ī'rĕs), a seaport in the eastern part of Argentina, in the E part, on the Río de la Plata. 2,567,763 (est. 1944).

buff[1] (bŭf), *n.* **1.** a kind of thick leather, orig. and properly made of buffalo skin but later also of other skins, light-yellow with napped surface, used for making belts, pouches, etc. **2.** a thick coat of buff leather, worn esp. by soldiers. **3.** yellowish-brown; medium or dark tan. **4.** *Colloq.* the bare skin. —*adj.* **5.** made of buff (leather). **6.** having the color of buff. —*v.t.* **7.** to polish (metal) or to give a grainless finish of high luster to (plated surfaces). **8.** to dye or stain in a buff color. [appar. for earlier *buffle*, t. F: buffalo, t. It.: m. *buffalo*. See BUFFALO]

buff[2] (bŭf), *v.t.* **1.** to reduce or deaden the force of, as a buffer. —*n.* **2.** *Obs.* a blow; a slap; a buffet; surviving in *blindman's buff.* [late ME *buffe*, ? t. OF; or back formation from BUFFET[1]. But cf. LG *buff* blow]

buf·fa·lo (bŭf'ə lō'), *n.*, *pl.* **-loes, -los,** (*esp. collectively*) **-lo,** *v.*, **-loed, -loing.** —*n.* **1.** any of several mammals of the ox kind, as *Bos bubalus* or *Bubalus buffelus*, an Old World species, orig. from India, valued as a draft animal, and *Bos caffer* or *Bubalus caffer* (**Cape buffalo**), a South African species, and *Bison bison* (the **American buffalo** or **bison**). **2.** buffalo robe. **3.** buffalo fish. —*v.t.* *U.S. Slang.* **4.** to baffle; confound; mystify. **5.** to impress or intimidate by a display of power, importance, etc. [t. It.: m. *bufalo*, g. d. L *būfalus*, var. of *būbalus* BUBAL]

Buf·fa·lo (bŭf'ə lō'), *n.* a city in W New York: a port on Lake Erie. 580,132 (1950).

buffalo berry, 1. the edible scarlet berry of *Shepherdia argentea* of the oleaster family of the U.S. and Canada. **2.** the shrub itself.

Buffalo Bill, sobriquet of **William Frederick Cody.**

buffalo bug, carpet beetle. Also, **buffalo moth.**

buffalo fish, any of several large carplike North American fresh-water fishes of the subfamily *Ictiobinae* of the sucker family (*Catostomidae*), comprising the genera *Ictiobus* and *Megastomatobus*.

buffalo grass, 1. a short grass, *Buchloe dactyloides*, very prevalent on the dry plains east of the Rocky Mountains. **2.** any of many species of short grasses.

Buffalo Indian, Plains Indian.

buffalo robe, the skin of an American bison, prepared with the hair on, used as a lap robe.

buff·er[1] (bŭf'ər), *n.* **1.** an apparatus, such as the one at the end of a railroad car, for deadening the concussion between a moving body and the one against which it strikes. **2.** anything serving to neutralize the shock of opposing forces. [f. BUFF[2], v. + -ER[1]]

buff·er[2] (bŭf'ər), *n.* **1.** a device for polishing; buffing wheel; buff stick. **2.** a worker who uses such a device. [f. BUFF[1] + -ER[1]]

buffer state, a smaller state lying between potentially hostile larger states.

buf·fet[1] (bŭf'ĭt), *n.*, *v.*, **-feted, -feting.** —*n.* **1.** a blow, as with the hand or fist. **2.** a violent shock or concussion. —*v.t.* **3.** to strike, as with the hand or fist. **4.** to contend against; battle. —*v.i.* **5.** to struggle with blows of hand or fist. **6.** to force one's way by a fight, struggle, etc. [ME, t. OF, dim. of *buffe* a blow] —**buf'fet·er,** *n.*

buf·fet[2] (bə fā', bŏō-; *Brit.* bŭf'ĭt; *Fr.* by fĕ'), *n.* **1.** a sideboard or cabinet for holding china, plate, etc. **2.** a counter, bar, or the like, for lunch or refreshments. **3.** a restaurant or lunchroom containing such a counter or bar. —*adj.* **4.** (of a meal) spread on tables or buffets from which the guests serve themselves. [t. F: orig., chair, table]

buff·ing wheel (bŭf'ĭng), buff wheel.

buf·fle·head (bŭf'əl hĕd'), *n.* a small North American duck, *Glaucionetta albeola*, the male of which has fluffy head plumage; butterball. [f. *buffle* buffalo + HEAD]

buf·fo (bōō'fō; *It.* bōōf'fô), *n.*, *pl.* **-fi** (-fē). *Music.* (in opera) a comedy part, usually bass. [t. It.: ridiculous, der. *buffare* blow with puffed cheeks]

Buf·fon (byfôn'), *n.* **Georges Louis Leclerc** (zhôrzh lwĕ lə klĕr'), **Comte de,** 1707–88, French naturalist.

buf·foon (bə fōōn'), *n.* **1.** one who amuses others by tricks, odd gestures and postures, jokes, etc. **2.** one given to coarse or undignified joking. [t. F: m. *bouffon*, t. It.: m. *buffone* jester, der. *buffa* a jest] —**buf·foon·er·y** (bə fōō'nə rĭ), *n.* —**buf·foon'ish,** *adj.*

buff stick, a small stick covered with leather or the like, used in polishing.

buff wheel, a wheel for polishing metal, etc., commonly covered with leather bearing a polishing powder.

bug (bŭg), *n.* **1.** any insect of the suborder *Heteroptera* (order *Hemiptera*), characterized by having the forewings thickened at base and membranous at tip, and the hindwings membranous. Sucking mouth parts enable the majority to suck plant juices and others to feed on animals, including man. **2.** (in popular usage) almost any insect. **3.** *Chiefly Brit.* a bedbug. **4.** (*often pl.*) *U.S. Colloq.* defect or difficulty: *eliminating the bugs in television.* **5.** *Lit.* or *Dial.* a bogy; hobgoblin. [ME *bugge.* Cf. Welsh *bug* bogy, ghost]

Bug (*Pol.* bŏŏg, bŏŏk; *Russ.* bōōg), *n.* **1.** a river forming part of the boundary between E Poland and the W Soviet Union, flowing NW to the Vistula. 450 mi. **2.** a river in the SW Soviet Union, flowing SE to the estuary of the Dnieper. 470 mi.

bug·a·boo (bŭg′ə bōō′), *n.*, *pl.* **-boos.** some imaginary thing that causes fear or worry; a bugbear; a bogy. [f. BUG bogy + BOO (def. 1); for the -a-, cf. BLACKAMOOR]

bug·bane (bŭg′bān′), *n.* any of various tall erect herbs of the ranunculaceous genus *Cimicifuga,* as *C. americana* of the eastern U.S., bearing clusters of white flowers supposed to repel insects.

bug·bear (bŭg′bâr′), *n.* **1.** any source, real or imaginary, of needless fright or fear. **2.** *Obs.* a goblin that eats up naughty children. [f. BUG (def. 5) + BEAR²]

bug·ger (bŭg′ər), *n.* **1.** one guilty of bestiality or sodomy. **2.** a foul, contemptible person. **3.** *U.S. Low Slang.* fellow; person; child. [t. F: m. *bougre,* t. ML: m. s. *Bulgarus* a Bulgarian, a heretic; certain Bulgarian heretics being charged with this crime] —**bug′·ger·y,** *n.*

bug·gy¹ (bŭg′ĭ), *n.*, *pl.* **-gies.** *U.S.* a light four-wheeled carriage with a single seat and a transverse spring. [orig. uncert.]

bug·gy² (bŭg′ĭ), *adj.* **-gier, -giest.** infested with bugs. [f. BUG + -Y¹]

Buggy

bu·gle¹ (bū′gəl), *n.*, *v.*, **-gled, -gling.** —*n.* **1.** a cornet-like military wind instrument, usually metal, used for sounding signals and sometimes furnished with keys or valves. —*v.i.* **2.** to sound a bugle. —*v.t.* **3.** to call by bugle. [ME, t. OF, g. L *būculus,* dim. of *bōs* ox] —**bu′gler,** *n.*

Bugle

bu·gle² (bū′gəl), *n.* any plant of the menthaceous genus *Ajuga,* esp. *A. reptans,* a low, blue-flowered herb. [t. F, g. LL *bugula* kind of plant]

bu·gle³ (bū′gəl), *n.* a tubular glass bead, usually black, used for ornamenting women's apparel. [orig. uncert.]

bu·gle·weed (bū′gəl wēd′), *n.* **1.** a plant of the menthaceous genus *Lycopus,* esp. *L. virginicus,* an herb with reputedly medicinal properties. **2.** the wild indigo. **3.** the bugle³.

bu·gloss (bū′glŏs, -glôs), *n.* any of various boraginaceous plants, as *Anchusa officinalis,* an Old World medicinal herb with rough leaves, and *Lycopsis arvensis,* a bristly, blue-flowered herb. [t. F: m. *buglosse,* t. L: m. *būglossa,* t. Gk.: m. *bouglōssos* oxtongue]

bug·seed (bŭg′sēd′), *n.* an annual chenopodiaceous herb, *Corispermum hyssopifolium,* of northern temperate regions (so called from the flat, oval shape of its seeds).

buhl (bōōl), *n.* elaborate inlaid work of woods, metals, tortoise shell, ivory, etc. Also, **buhl·work** (bōōl′wûrk′). [appar. Germanized sp. of F *boulle* or *boule,* named after A.C. *Boulle* or *Boule* (1642–1732), French cabinetmaker]

buhr (bûr), *n.* burr¹ (def. 2). **2.** burr⁴.

buhr·stone (bûr′stōn′), *n.* burstone.

build (bĭld), *v.,* **built** or (*Archaic*) **builded, building,** *n.* —*v.t.* **1.** to construct (something relatively complex) by assembling and combining parts: *build a house or an empire.* **2.** to establish, increase, and strengthen (often fol. by *up*): *build up a business.* **3.** to base; form; construct: *to build one's hopes on promises.* **4.** to fill in with houses (fol. by *up*). **5.** *Games.* **a.** to make (words) from letters. **b.** to add (cards) to each other according to number, suit, etc. —*v.i.* **6.** to engage in the art or business of building. **7.** to form or construct a plan, system of thought, etc. (fol. by *on* or *upon*). —*n.* **8.** manner or form of construction: *a person's build.* [ME *bilden, bulde*(n), OE *byldan,* der. *bold* dwelling, house]

build·er (bĭl′dər), *n.* **1.** a person who builds. **2.** a person who contracts for the construction of buildings and supervises the workmen who build them. **3.** a substance, as an abrasive or filler, used with soap or another cleaning compound.

build·ing (bĭl′dĭng), *n.* **1.** anything built or constructed. **2.** the act, business, or art of constructing houses, etc.

—**Syn. 1.** BUILDING, EDIFICE, STRUCTURE refer to something built. BUILDING and STRUCTURE may apply to either a finished or an unfinished product of construction, and carry no implications as to size or condition. EDIFICE is not only a more formal word, but narrower in application, referring to a completed structure, and usually a large and imposing one. BUILDING generally connotes a useful purpose (houses, schools, business offices, etc.); STRUCTURE suggests the planning and constructive process.

building and loan association, *Finance.* an organization featuring a savings plan for members who intend to purchase or build a home.

built (bĭlt), *v.* pt. and pp. of **build.**

built-in (bĭlt′ĭn′), *adj.* built so as to be an integral, permanent part of a larger unit, as a wing of a house, or a bookcase in a room.

Bui·ten·zorg (boi′tən zôrкн′, bœĭ′-), *n.* a city in the U.S. of Indonesia, in W Java. 65,431 (1930).

Bu·kha·ra (bŏŏ hä′rä), *n.* Bokhara.

Bu·kha·rin (bŏŏ hä′rĭn), *n.* **Nikolai Ivanovich** (nĭ-kŏ lī′ Ĭ vä′nŏ vĭch), 1888–1938, Russian editor, writer, and communist leader.

Bu·ko·vi·na (bŏŏ′kə vē′nə; *Rum.* bŏŏ kô vē′nä), *n.* Bucovina.

Bu·la·wa·yo (bŏŏ′lə wä′yō), *n.* a city in SW Southern Rhodesia: mining center. 39,817 (1941).

bulb (bŭlb), *n.* **1.** *Bot.* **a.** a bud, having fleshy leaves and usually subterranean, in which the stem is reduced to a flat disk, rooting from the under side, as in the onion, lily, etc. **b.** a plant growing from a bulb. **2.** any round, enlarged part, esp. one at the end of a long, slender body: *the bulb of a thermometer.* **3.** *Elect.* **a.** the glass housing, in which partial vacuum has been established, which contains the filament of an incandescent electric lamp. **b.** an incandescent electric lamp. **4.** an electron tube. **5.** *Anat.* **a. bulb of the spinal cord** or **brain,** the medulla oblongata. **b. bulb of the urethra,** the rounded mass of erectile tissue that surrounds the urethra at the posterior end of the penis, just in front of the anus. [t. L: s. *bulbus,* t. Gk.: m. *bolbós*] —**bulb·ar** (bŭl′bər), *adj.*

bulb·if·er·ous (bŭl bĭf′ər əs), *adj.* producing bulbs.

bul·bil (bŭl′bĭl), *n.* *Bot.* **1.** a little bulb. **2.** a small aerial bulb growing in the axils of leaves, as in the tiger lily, or replacing flower buds, as in the common onion. [t. NL: m.s. *bulbillus,* dim. of L *bulbus* BULB]

bulb·ous (bŭl′bəs), *adj.* **1.** bulb-shaped; bulging. **2.** having, or growing from, bulbs. Also, **bul·ba·ceous** (bŭl bā′shəs).

bul·bul (bŏŏl′bŏŏl), *n.* any bird of the tropical Old World family *Pycnonotidae,* much referred to in Persian poetry, and famed as songsters. [t. Pers.]

Bul·finch (bŏŏl′fĭnch), *n.* **1. Charles,** 1763–1844, U.S. architect. **2.** his son, **Thomas,** 1796–1867, author and compiler of myths.

Bulg., **1.** Bulgaria. **2.** Bulgarian.

Bul·gar (bŭl′gər, bōŏl′-), *n.* Bulgarian.

Bul·gar·i·a (bŭl gâr′ĭ ə, bŏŏl-), *n.* a republic in SE Europe. 7,022,206 pop. (1946); 42,800 sq. mi. (1946). *Cap.:* Sofia.

Bul·gar·i·an (bŭl gâr′ĭ ən, bŏŏl-), *n.* **1.** a native or inhabitant of Bulgaria. **2.** a Slavic language, the language of Bulgaria. —*adj.* **3.** of or pertaining to Bulgaria, its people, or their language.

bulge (bŭlj), *n.,* *v.,* **bulged, bulging.** —*n.* **1.** a rounded projecting or outswelling part; protuberance; hump. **2.** *Naut.* the bilge, or bottom of a ship's hull. —*v.i.* **3.** to swell out; be protuberant. —*v.t.* **4.** to make protuberant. [ME, t. OF: m. *boulge,* g. L *bulga* bag, of Celtic orig.] —**bulg′y,** *adj.*

Bulge (bŭlj), **Battle of the,** the final German counteroffensive of World War II, begun Dec. 16, 1944, and thrusting deep into Allied territory in N and E Belgium: repulsed, Jan., 1945.

bulg·er (bŭl′jər), *n.* *Golf.* a club with a convex face.

bu·lim·i·a (bū lĭm′ĭ ə), *n.* *Pathol.* morbidly voracious appetite; a disease marked by constant and insatiable hunger. [t. NL, t. Gk.: m. *boulimia* great hunger] —**bu·lim′ic,** *adj.*

bulk¹ (bŭlk), *n.* **1.** magnitude in three dimensions: *a ship of great bulk.* **2.** the greater part; the main mass or body: *the bulk of a debt.* **3.** goods or cargo not in packages, boxes, bags, etc. **4. in bulk, a.** unpackaged. **b.** in large quantites. **5.** *Rare.* the body of a living creature. —*v.i.* **6.** to be of bulk, size, weight, or importance. **7.** to increase in bulk; size; swell. —*v.t.* **8.** to cause to swell or grow large. [ME *bolke* heap, t. Scand.; cf. Icel. *bŭlki* heap, cargo] —**Syn. 1.** See **size.**

bulk² (bŭlk), *n.* *Bldg. Trades.* a structure, as a stall, projecting from the front of a building. [orig. uncert. Cf. BALK (def. 8)]

bulk·head (bŭlk′hĕd′), *n.* **1.** *Naut.* one of the upright partitions dividing a ship into compartments. **2.** *Civ. Eng.* a partition built in a subterranean passage to prevent the passage of air, water, or mud. **3.** *Bldg. Trades.* **a.** a horizontal or inclined outside door over a stairway leading to the cellar. **b.** a boxlike structure on a roof, etc., covering the head of a staircase or other opening.

bulk·y (bŭl′kĭ), *adj.,* **bulkier, bulkiest.** of great and usually cumbersome bulk or size. —**bulk′i·ly,** *adv.* —**bulk′i·ness,** *n.* —**Syn.** massive, ponderous, unwieldy.

bull¹ (bŏŏl), *n.* **1.** the male of a bovine animal, esp. of the genus *Bos,* with sexual organs intact and capable of reproduction. **2.** the male of certain other animals: *a bull elephant.* **3.** a bull-like person. **4.** (in general business) one who believes that conditions are or will be favorable. **5.** (in stock exchange slang) one who buys in the hope of profit from a rise in prices (opposed to *bear*). **6.** (*cap.*) *Astron.* **a.** the zodiacal constellation Taurus. **b.** the sign named for it. **7.** bulldog. —*adj.* **8.** male. **9.** bull-like; large. **10.** (in the stock exchange, etc.) pertaining to the bulls; marked by a rise in price. —*v.t.* **11.** (in the stock exchange, etc.) to endeavor to raise the price of (stocks, etc.). **12.** to operate in, for a rise in price. [ME *bule,* OE *bula;* also ME *bulle,* OE *bull-* in *bulluc* bull calf. Cf. Icel. *boli*]

bull[2] (bŏŏl), *n.* **1.** a bulla or seal. **2.** *Rom. Cath. Ch.* a formal papal document having a bulla attached. [ME *bulle*, t. L: m. *bulla*, ML seal, document, L bubble, knob]

Bull (bŏŏl), *n.* **Ole Bornemann** (ō′lə bŏr′nə män′), 1810–80, Norwegian violinist and composer.

bul·la (bŏŏl′ə, bŭl′ə), *n., pl.* **bullae** (bŏŏl′ē, bŭl′ē). **1.** a seal attached to an official document, as a papal bull. **2.** *Pathol.* a large vesicle. **b.** a blisterlike or bubble-like part of a bone. [t. L. See BULL[2]]

bul·late (bŏŏl′āt, -ĭt, bŭl′-), *adj.* **1.** *Bot., Zool.* having the surface covered with irregular and slight elevations, giving a blistered appearance. **2.** *Anat.* inflated; vaulted. [t. L: m. s. *bullātus* having bubbles]

bull·bat (bŏŏl′băt′), *n.* the nighthawk (def. 1).

bull brier, a smilacaceous North American plant, *Smilax Pseudochina*, with tuberous rootstocks.

bull·dog (bŏŏl′dôg′, -dŏg′), *n.* **1.** a large-headed, short-haired, heavily built variety of dog, of comparatively small size but very muscular and courageous. **2.** a short-barreled revolver of large caliber. **3.** the servant or assistant who accompanies the proctor at Oxford and Cambridge Universities when on duty. —*adj.* **4.** like or characteristic of a bulldog: *bulldog tenacity*. —*v.t.* **5.** to attack in the manner of a bulldog. **6.** *Western U.S.* to throw (a calf, etc.) by seizing it by the horns.

English bulldog
(13 in. or more high
at the shoulder)

bull·doze (bŏŏl′dōz′), *v.t.,* **-dozed, -dozing.** *U.S. Slang.* to coerce or intimidate by violence or threats.

bull·doz·er (bŏŏl′dō′zər), *n. U.S. Slang.* **1.** a person who intimidates. **2.** a powerful caterpillar tractor having a vertical blade at the front end for moving earth, tree stumps, rocks, etc.

Bul·ler (bŏŏl′ər), *n.* **Sir Redvers Henry** (rĕd′vərz), 1839–1908, British general.

bul·let (bŏŏl′ĭt), *n.* **1.** a small metal projectile, part of a cartridge, for firing from small arms. See diag. under **cartridge. 2.** a small ball. [t. F: m. *boulet(te)*, dim. of *boule* ball]

bul·let·head (bŏŏl′ĭt hĕd′), *n.* **1.** a round head. **2.** a person having such a head. **3.** an obstinate or stupid person. —**bul′let·head′ed,** *adj.*

bul·le·tin (bŏŏl′ə tən, -tĭn), *n.* **1.** a brief account or statement, as of news or events, issued for the information of the public. **2.** a periodical publication, as of a learned society. —*v.t.* **3.** to make known by a bulletin. [t. F, t. It.: m. *bullettino*, dim. of *bulletta*, dim. of *bulla* edict. See BULL[2], BULLA]

bulletin board, a board for the posting of bulletins, notices, announcements, etc.

bul·let·proof (bŏŏl′ĭt prŏŏf′), *adj.* capable of resisting the impact of a bullet.

bull·fight (bŏŏl′fīt′), *n.* a combat between men and a bull or bulls in an enclosed arena. —**bull′fight′er,** *n.* —**bull′fight′ing,** *n.*

bull·finch[1] (bŏŏl′fĭnch′), *n.* **1.** a rosy-breasted European fringilline bird, *Pyrrhula pyrrhula*, with a short, stout bill, valued as a cage bird. **2.** any of various allied or similar birds. [f. BULL[1] + FINCH]

bull·finch[2] (bŏŏl′fĭnch′), *n.* a hedge high enough to impede hunters. [orig. uncert.]

bull·frog (bŏŏl′frŏg′, -frôg′), *n.* a large frog, as the American *Rana catesbeiana*, which has an exceptionally deep bass voice.

bull·head (bŏŏl′hĕd′), *n.* **1.** (in America) any species of *Ameiurus*; horned pout. See **catfish** (def. 1). **2.** any of various other fishes with a large or broad head, esp. those with a spine on each side of the head. **3.** any cottoid fish, esp. those of fresh water (*Cottus*). **4.** an obstinate or stupid person.

bull·head·ed (bŏŏl′hĕd′ĭd), *adj.* obstinate; blunderingly stubborn; stupid. —**bull′head′ed·ness,** *n.*

bul·lion (bŏŏl′yən), *n.* **1.** gold or silver in the mass. **2.** gold or silver in the form of bars or ingots. **3.** a cordlike trimming made of twisted gold or silver wire, or a trimming of cord covered with gold or silver thread (**bullion fringe**), used to ornament uniforms, etc. [ME *bullioun*, t. AF: m. *bullion* mint, der. *bouillir* boil, g. L *bullīre*; in part confused with OF *billon* debased metal]

bull·ish (bŏŏl′ĭsh), *adj.* **1.** like a bull. **2.** obstinate or stupid. **3.** (in the stock exchange, etc.) tending to cause a rise in price. **4.** optimistic.

Bull Moose, a member of the Progressive Party (def. 1).

bull-necked (bŏŏl′nĕkt′), *adj.* thick-necked.

bull nose, *Vet. Sci.* a disease of swine caused by bacterial infection of the tissues of the snout which causes gross malformation of the part and frequently serious blocking of the nasal passages.

bull·ock (bŏŏl′ək), *n.* a castrated male of a bovine animal, not having been used for reproduction; ox; steer. [ME *bullok*, OE *bulluc*. See BULL[1], -OCK]

bull pen, *U.S.* **1.** a pen for a bull or bulls. **2.** *Colloq.* a place for the temporary confinement of prisoners or suspects. **3.** *Colloq.* other places of temporary or crowded stay, as sleeping quarters in a lumber camp. **4.** *Base-*

ball. a place where emergency or relief pitchers warm up during a game.

bull·pout (bŏŏl′pout′), *n.* horned pout.

bull ring, an arena for a bullfight.

bull·roar·er (bŏŏl′rōr′ər), *n.* a long, thin, narrow piece of wood attached to a string, by which it is whirled in the air, making a roaring sound: used for religious rites by certain primitive tribes, as of Australian aborigines, American Indians, etc., and as a children's toy; thunder stick.

Bull Run, a small river in NE Virginia: two important battles of the Civil War were fought near here, both resulting in defeat for the Union forces, 1861, 1862. See map under **Antietam.**

bull's-eye (bŏŏlz′ī′), *n.* **1.** the central spot, usually black, of a target. **2.** a shot that strikes the bull's-eye. **3.** a small circular opening or window. **4.** a thick disk or lenslike piece of glass inserted in a deck or the like to admit light. **5.** *Naut.* an oval or circular wooden block having a groove around it and a hole in the center through which to reeve a rope. **6.** *Chiefly Brit.* a round, hard lump of candy.

bull snake, the gopher snake. See **gopher** (def. 4).

bull terrier, one of a breed of dogs produced by crossing the bulldog and the terrier.

bull tongue, a simple form of plow, so called from its shape.

bull-tongue (bŏŏl′tŭng′), *v.t., v.i.* to plow with a bull tongue.

Bull terrier, white variety
(18 in. high at the shoulder)

bul·ly[1] (bŏŏl′ĭ), *n., pl.* **-lies,** *v.,* **-lied, -lying,** *adj., interj.* —*n.* **1.** a blustering, quarrelsome, overbearing person who browbeats smaller or weaker people. **2.** *Archaic.* a man hired to do violence. **3.** *Obs.* a pimp; procurer. **4.** *Obs.* good friend; good fellow. **5.** *Obs.* sweetheart; darling. —*v.t.* **6.** to act the bully toward. —*v.i.* **7.** to be loudly arrogant and overbearing. —*adj.* **8.** *Colloq.* fine; excellent; very good. **9.** dashing; jovial; highspirited. —*interj.* **10.** *Colloq.* good! well done! [orig. uncert.]

bul·ly[2] (bŏŏl′ĭ), *n.* bully beef. [? t. F: m. *bouilli* boiled beef, prop. pp. of *bouillir* boil]

bully beef, canned or pickled beef.

bul·ly·rag (bŏŏl′ĭ răg′), *v.t.,* **-ragged, -ragging.** to bully; badger; abuse; tease. Also, **ballyrag.**

bully tree, any of various sapotaceous trees of tropical America, as *Manilkara bidentata* of Guiana, which yields the gum balata. [said to be f. m. *balata* + TREE]

Bü·low (by′lō), *n.* **Prince Bernhard von** (bĕrn′härt fən), 1849–1929, chancellor of Germany, 1900–09.

bul·rush (bŏŏl′rŭsh′), *n.* **1.** (in Biblical use) the papyrus, *Cyperus papyrus*. **2.** any of various large rushes or rushlike plants, as *Scirpus lacustris*, a tall perennial from which mats, bottoms of chairs, etc., are made. **3.** any of various rushes of the genus *Scirpus*. [f. *bull* large (cf. *bull trout*) + RUSH[2]]

bul·wark (bŏŏl′wərk), *n.* **1.** *Fort.* a defensive mound of earth or other material carried round a place; a rampart. **2.** any protection against annoyance or injury from outside. **3.** (usually pl.) *Naut.* a solid part of a ship's side extending like a fence above the level of the deck. —*v.t.* **4.** to fortify with a bulwark or rampart; secure by a fortification; protect. [ME *bulwerk*. Cf. G *bollwerk*, appar. orig. bole (tree trunk) work. Cf. BOULEVARD]

Bul·wer (bŏŏl′wər), *n.* **William Henry Lytton Earle** (lĭt′ən), (*Baron Dalling and Bulwer*) 1801–72, British diplomat and author, known as Sir Henry Bulwer.

Bul·wer-Lyt·ton (bŏŏl′wər lĭt′ən), *n.* See **Lytton.**

bum (bŭm), *n., v.,* **bummed, bumming.** *U.S. Colloq.* —*n.* **1.** a shiftless or dissolute person. **2.** an habitual loafer and tramp. **3.** a drunken orgy; a debauch. —*v.t.* **4.** to get for nothing; borrow without expectation of returning. —*v.i.* **5.** to sponge on others for a living; lead an idle or dissolute life. —*adj.* **6.** of poor, wretched, or miserable quality; bad. [orig. meaning "rump"; akin to BUMP] —**bum′mer,** *n.*

bum·bail·iff (bŭm′bā′lĭf), *n. Brit. Contemptuous.* a bailiff or underbailiff employed in serving writs, making arrests, etc.

bum·ble·bee (bŭm′bəl bē′), *n.* any of various large, hairy social bees of the family *Bombidae*. [f. *bumble* buzz + BEE[1]]

Bumblebee (queen),
Bombus americanorum
(Ab. ¾ in. long)

bum·boat (bŭm′bōt′), *n. Naut.* a boat used in peddling provisions and small wares among vessels lying in port or off shore. —**bum·boat·man** (bŭm′bōt′mən), *n.*

bum·kin (bŭm′kĭn), *n. Naut.* a bumpkin[2].

bump (bŭmp), *v.t.* **1.** to come more or less violently in contact with; strike; collide with. **2.** to cause to strike or collide: *to bump one's head against the wall.* —*v.i.* **3.** to come in contact with; collide (often fol. by *against, into*). —*n.* **4.** act of bumping; a blow. **5.** the shock of a blow or collision. **6.** a swelling or contusion from a blow. **7.** a small area raised above the level of the surrounding surface, as on the skull or on a road. **8.** *Aeron.* a rapidly rising current of air which gives an airplane a dangerous jolt or upward thrust. [imit.]

bump·er (bŭm′pər), n. 1. a person or thing that bumps. 2. *Auto.* a horizontal bar affixed to the front or rear of a car to give protection in collisions. 3. a cup or glass filled to the brim, esp. when drunk as a toast. 4. *Colloq.* something unusually large. —*adj.* 5. unusually abundant: *bumper crops.* —*v.t.* 6. to fill to the brim. 7. to drink a bumper as a toast to. —*v.i.* 8. to drink toasts.

bump·kin[1] (bŭmp′kĭn), n. an awkward, clumsy yokel. [t. MD: m. *bommekyn* little barrel]

bump·kin[2] (bŭmp′kĭn), n. *Naut.* a beam or spar projecting outward from the bow, side, or stern of a ship to extend a sail, secure blocks, or the like. Also, **bumkin.** [t. MD: m. *boomken* little tree]

bump·tious (bŭmp′shəs), adj. offensively self-assertive: *he's a bumptious young upstart.* [f. BUMP + -tious, modeled on FRACTIOUS, etc.] —**bump′tious·ly,** adv. —**bump′tious·ness,** n.

bump·y (bŭm′pĭ), adj., **bumpier, bumpiest.** 1. of uneven surface: *a bumpy road.* 2. full of jolts: *a bumpy ride.* 3. giving rise to jolts: *bumpy air.* —**bump′i·ly,** adv. —**bump′i·ness,** n.

bun (bŭn), n. 1. a kind of bread roll, variously shaped, usually only slightly sweetened, and sometimes containing spice, dried currants, citron, etc. 2. hair arranged in a bun shape. [ME *bunne;* orig. uncert.]

bu·na (bōo′nə, bŭ′-), n. *Chem.* 1. any synthetic rubber made by copolymerizing butadiene with other material. 2. (orig.) a synthetic rubber made by polymerizing butadiene by means of styrene. [f. BU(TADIENE) + NA (the symbol for sodium)]

bunch (bŭnch), n. 1. a connected group; cluster: *a bunch of bananas.* 2. a group of things; lot: *a bunch of papers.* 3. *Colloq.* a group of human beings: *a fine bunch of boys.* 4. a knob; lump; protuberance. —*v.t.* 5. to group together; make a bunch of. —*v.i.* 6. to gather into a cluster or protuberance; gather together. [ME *bunche;* orig. uncert.] —**Syn. 1, 2.** See **bundle.**

bunch·ber·ry (bŭnch′bĕr′ĭ), n., pl. **-ries.** a dwarf species of cornel, *Cornus canadensis,* bearing dense clusters of bright-red berries.

Bunche (bŭnch), n. **Ralph,** born 1904, U. S. diplomat.

buncher resonator. See **klystron.**

bunch·flow·er (bŭnch′flou′ər), n. 1. a liliaceous plant, *Melanthium virginicum,* of the U.S., bearing grasslike leaves and a panicle of small greenish flowers. 2. any other plant of the same genus.

bunch grass, any of various grasses in different regions of the U.S. growing in distinct clumps.

bunch·y (bŭn′chĭ), adj., **bunchier, bunchiest.** 1. having bunches. 2. bulging or protuberant.

bun·co (bŭng′kō), n., pl. **-cos,** v., **-coed, -coing.** *U.S. Colloq.* —n. 1. a swindle in which a person is lured to some place and there fleeced at a game or otherwise victimized; a confidence game. 2. any swindle or misrepresentation. —*v.t.* 3. to victimize by a bunco. Also, **bunko.** [short for BUNCOMBE]

bun·combe (bŭng′kəm), n. 1. insincere speechmaking intended merely to please political constituents. 2. insincere talk; claptrap; humbug. Also, **bunkum.** [from a Congressional representative's phrase, "talking for *Buncombe*" (county of North Carolina)]

bunco steerer, *U.S. Colloq.* a swindler.

Bund (bŏond; *Ger.* bŏont), n., pl. **Bünde** (bn′də). 1. a short form of "German-American Volksbund," a Nazi-inspired and directed organization in the U.S. 2. an alliance or league. [t. G]

bund (bŭnd), n. (in India, China, Japan, etc.) an embankment; an embanked quay. [t. Hind.: m. *band*]

Bun·del·khand (bŭn′dəl·kŭnd′, -kʜŭnd′), n. a group of native states in central India: a part of the Central India Agency.

Bun·des·rat (bŏon′dəs·rät′), n. 1. (formerly) a federal legislative council of representatives from the 26 states of the German Empire. 2. the federal council of Switzerland. Also, **Bun·des·rath** (bŏon′dəs·rät′). [G]

bun·dle (bŭn′dəl), n., v., **-dled, -dling.** —n. 1. a group bound together: *a bundle of hay.* 2. something wrapped for carrying; package. 3. a number of things considered together. 4. *Bot.* an aggregation of strands of specialized conductive and mechanical tissue. —*v.t.* 5. to tie or wrap in a bundle. 6. to dress snugly (fol. by *up*). 7. to send away hurriedly or unceremoniously (fol. by *off,* etc.). —*v.i.* 8. to leave hurriedly or unceremoniously (fol. by *off, out,* etc.). 9. to dress warmly (fol. by *up*). 10. to sleep or lie in the same bed without undressing, esp. of sweethearts, as in early New England. [ME *bundel.* t. MD, c. G *bündel;* akin to OE *byndele* binding together] —**bun′dler,** n. —**Syn. 1.** BUNDLE, BUNCH refer to a number of things or an amount of something fastened or bound together. BUNDLE implies a close binding or grouping together, and often refers to a wrapped package: *a bundle of laundry, of dry-goods.* A BUNCH is a number of things, usually all of the same kind, fastened together either tightly or loosely: *a bunch of roses or of keys.*

bung (bŭng), n. 1. a stopper for the hole of a cask. 2. a bunghole. —*v.t.* 3. to close with or as a bung (often fol. by *up*). 4. to beat; bruise; maul (often fol. by *up*). [ME *bunge.* t. MD: m. *bonghe*]

bun·ga·low (bŭng′gə·lō′), n. 1. a cottage, commonly of one story or a story and a half, esp. for country or seaside residence. 2. (in India) a one-storied thatched or tiled house, usually surrounded by a veranda. [t. Hind.: m. *banglā,* lit., of Bengal]

bung·hole (bŭng′hōl′), n. a hole or orifice in a cask through which it is filled.

bun·gle (bŭng′gəl), v., **-gled, -gling,** n. —*v.i.* 1. to do something awkwardly and clumsily. —*v.t.* 2. to do clumsily and awkwardly; botch. —n. 3. a bungling performance. 4. a bungled job. [? imit.] —**bun′gler,** n. —**bun′gling·ly,** adv.

Bu·nin (bōo′nĭn), n. **Ivan Alekseevich** (ĭ vän′ ä′lĕk-sē′yə vĭch), born 1870, Russian poet and novelist.

bun·ion (bŭn′yən), n. *Pathol.* a swelling on the foot caused by the inflammation of a synovial bursa, esp. of the great toe. [orig. obscure]

bunk[1] (bŭngk), n. 1. a built-in platform bed, as on a ship. 2. *Colloq.* any bed. —*v.i.* 3. *Colloq.* to occupy a bunk; sleep, esp. in rough quarters. [orig. unknown]

bunk[2] (bŭngk), n. *U.S. Slang.* humbug; nonsense. [short for BUNCOMBE]

bunk·er (bŭng′kər), n. 1. a fixed chest or box; a large bin or receptacle: *a coal bunker.* 2. *Golf.* **a.** an obstruction or obstacle on a course. **b.** a sandy hollow or other rough place on the course. **c.** an obstacle, usually a small ridge, generally preceded by a sand trap. —*v.t.* 3. *Golf.* to drive (a ball) into a bunker. [orig. uncert.]

Bunker Hill, a hill in Charlestown, Massachusetts: the first major battle of the American Revolution was fought on adjoining Breed's Hill, June 17, 1775.

bun·ko (bŭng′kō), n., pl. **-kos,** v., **-koed, -koing.** bunco.

bun·kum (bŭng′kəm), n. buncombe.

bun·ny (bŭn′ĭ), n., pl. **-nies.** *Colloq.* 1. a rabbit. 2. *U.S.* a squirrel.

Bun·sen (bŭn′sən; *Ger.* bŏon′zən), n. **Robert Wilhelm** (rō′bĕrt vĭl′hĕlm), 1811–99, German chemist.

Bunsen burner, a type of gas burner with which a very hot, practically nonluminous flame is obtained by allowing air to enter at the base and mix with the gas.

bunt[1] (bŭnt), *v.t.* 1. (of a goat or calf) to push with the horns or head. 2. *Baseball.* to bounce (the ball) from the loosely held bat so that it goes only a short distance. —*v.i.* 3. to push (something) with the horns or head. 4. *Baseball.* to bunt a ball. —n. 5. a push with the head, or horns; butt. 6. *Baseball.* **a.** act of bunting. **b.** a bunted ball. [nasalized var. of BUTT[2]]

bunt[2] (bŭnt), n. 1. *Naut.* the middle part of a square sail. 2. the bagging part of a fishing net or the like. [orig. unknown]

bunt[3] (bŭnt), n. *Plant Pathol.* a disease of wheat in which the kernels are replaced by black fungus spores. [orig. unknown]

bun·ting[1] (bŭn′tĭng), n. 1. coarse open fabric of worsted or cotton used for flags, signals, etc. 2. flags, esp. a vessel's flags, collectively. [orig. uncert.]

bun·ting[2] (bŭn′tĭng), n. any of numerous small fringilline birds of the genera *Emberiza, Passerina,* and *Plectrophenax* as, respectively, the **reed bunting** (*E. shoeniclus*) of Europe, the **indigo bunting** (*P. cyanea*) of U.S. and Canada, and the **snow bunting** (*P. nivalia*) of arctic regions. [ME *bountyng;* orig. uncert.]

bunt·line (bŭnt′lĭn, -lĭn′), n. *Naut.* one of the ropes attached to the foot of a square sail to haul it up to the yard for furling. [f. BUNT[2] + LINE[1]]

Bun·yan (bŭn′yən), n. 1. **John,** 1628–88, British preacher: author of *Pilgrim's Progress.* 2. **Paul,** hero of American lumberjack tall tales.

Buo·na·par·te (bwô′nä·pär′tĕ), n. Italian spelling of **Bonaparte.**

Buo·nar·ro·ti (bwô′närrô′tē), n. See **Michelangelo.**

buoy (boi, bōō′ĭ), n. *Naut.* 1. a distinctively marked and shaped anchored float, sometimes carrying a light, whistle, or bell, marking a channel or obstruction. 2. a life buoy. —*v.t.* 3. to support by or as by a buoy; keep afloat in a fluid. 4. *Naut.* to furnish or mark with a buoy or buoys: *to buoy or buoy off a channel.* 5. to bear up or sustain, as hope or courage does. —*v.i.* 6. to float; rise by reason of lightness. [ME *boye.* t. MD: m. *boeie* buoy, ult. t. L: m. *boia* fetter]

A. Bell buoy; B. Spar buoy; C. Light buoy; D. Whistle buoy
Buoys (def. 1)

buoy·age (boi′ĭj, bōō′ĭj), n. *Naut.* 1. a system of buoys. 2. buoys collectively. 3. the providing of buoys.

buoy·an·cy (boi′ən·sĭ, bōō′yən·sĭ), n. 1. the power to float or rise in a fluid; relative lightness. 2. the power of supporting a body so that it floats; upward pressure exerted by the fluid in which a body is immersed. 3. elasticity of spirit; cheerfulness.

buoy·ant (boi′ənt, bōō′yənt), adj. 1. tending to float or rise in a fluid. 2. capable of keeping a body afloat, as a liquid. 3. not easily depressed; cheerful. 4. cheering or invigorating. —**buoy′ant·ly,** adv.

bu·pres·tid (bū prĕs′tĭd), n. any beetle of the family *Buprestidae,* comprising the metallic wood borers, noted for their brilliant coloration. [f. s. L *būprestis,* t. Gk.: m. *boúprestis,* lit., ox-burner + -ID[2]]

bur (bûr), n., v., **burred, burring.** —n. 1. *Bot.* the rough, prickly case around the seeds of certain plants, as of the chestnut and burdock. 2. any bur-bearing plant. 3. something that adheres like a bur. 4. *Mach.* burr[1] (defs. 1, 2, 3). —*v.t.* 5. to extract or remove burs from. Also, **burr.** [ME *burre,* t. Scand.; cf. Dan. *borre*]

ăct, āble, dâre, ärt; ĕbb, ēqual; ĭf, īce; hŏt, ōver, ôrder, oil, bŏŏk, ōōze, out; ŭp, ūse, ûrge; ə = a in alone; ch, chief; g, give; ng, ring; sh, shoe; th, thin; ᵗh, that; zh, vision. See the full key on inside cover.

bu·ran (bōō rän′), *n.* a violent storm of wind on the steppes of Russia and Siberia, esp. one accompanied by driving snow and intense cold. [t. Turk.]

Bur·bage (bûr′bĭj), *n.* **Richard**, 1567?–1619, British actor: associate of Shakespeare.

Bur·bank (bûr′băngk), *n.* **1. Luther**, 1849–1926, U.S. horticulturist who produced a number of new varieties. **2.** a city in SW California. 78,577 (1950).

bur·ble (bûr′bəl), *v.*, **-bled, -bling,** *n.* —*v.i.* **1.** to make a bubbling sound; bubble. **2.** to speak with a burble. —*n.* **3.** a bubbling or gentle gush. **4.** a bubbling flow of speech. **5.** *Aeron.* the breakdown of smooth airflow around a wing at a high angle of attack. [prob. imit.]

bur·bot (bûr′bət), *n.*, *pl.* **-bots,** (*esp. collectively*) **-bot.** a fresh-water fish of the cod family, *Lota lota*, of Europe, Asia, and North America, with an elongated body and a barbel on the chin. [ME *borbot*, t. F: m. *borbote* (appar. der. L *barba* beard, b. with *borbe* slime)]

burd (bûrd), *n.* *Obs. except Poetic.* a lady; a maiden.

bur·den[1] (bûr′dən), *n.* **1.** that which is carried; a load. **2.** that which is borne with difficulty: *burden of responsibilities.* **3.** *Naut.* a. the weight of a ship's cargo. **b.** the carrying capacity of a ship: *a ship of a hundred tons burden.* —*v.t.* **4.** to load heavily. **5.** to load oppressively; oppress. Also, *Archaic,* **burthen.** [var. of *burthen,* OE *byrthen;* akin to BEAR[1]] —**Syn. 1.** See **load.**

bur·den[2] (bûr′dən), *n.* **1.** something often repeated or much dwelt upon; the principal idea. **2.** *Music.* the refrain or recurring chorus of a song. [ME *burdoun,* t. OF: m. *bourdon* a humming, the drone of a bagpipe, der. L *burda* pipe; later assoc. with BURDEN[1]]

burden of proof, *Chiefly Law.* **1.** the obligation to offer evidence which the court or jury could reasonably believe, in support of a contention, failing which the party will lose its case. **2.** the obligation to establish an alleged fact by convincing the tribunal of its probable truth (**the burden of persuasion**).

bur·den·some (bûr′dən səm), *adj.* oppressively heavy. Also, *Archaic,* **burthensome.** —**bur′den·some·ly,** *adv.* —**bur′den·some·ness,** *n.*

bur·dock (bûr′dŏk), *n.* a plant of the composite genus *Arctium,* esp. *A. lappa,* a coarse, broad-leaved weed with prickly heads or burs which stick to the clothing. [f. BUR + DOCK[1]]

bu·reau (byŏŏr′ō), *n.*, *pl.* **-eaus, -eaux** (-ōz). **1.** a chest of drawers for holding clothing, etc., often provided with a mirror. **2.** *Brit.* a desk or writing table with drawers for papers. **3.** a division of a government department or independent administrative unit. **4.** an office for giving out information, etc.: *travel bureau.* [t. F: desk, office, OF *burel* cloth-covered table, kind of woolen cloth, ult. der. L *būra,* var. of *burra* long-haired woolen cloth]

bu·reauc·ra·cy (byŏŏ rŏk′rə sĭ), *n.*, *pl.* **-cies.** *Govt.* **1.** government by bureaus. **2.** the body of officials administering bureaus. **3.** excessive multiplication of, and concentration of power in, administrative bureaus. **4.** excessive governmental red tape and routine. [t. F: m. *bureaucratie.* See BUREAU, -CRACY]

bu·reau·crat (byŏŏr′ə krăt′), *n.* *Govt.* **1.** an official of a bureaucracy. **2.** an official who works by fixed routine without exercising intelligent judgment. —**bu′reau·crat′ic,** *adj.* —**bu′reau·crat′i·cal·ly,** *adv.*

bu·rette (byŏŏ rĕt′), *n.* *Chem.* a graduated glass tube, commonly having a stopcock at the bottom, used for accurately measuring, or measuring out, small quantities of liquid. Also, **bu·ret′.** [t. F: cruet, dim. of *buire* vessel for wine, etc. Cf. BUCKET]

burg (bûrg), *n.* **1.** *Colloq.* a city or town. **2.** *Hist.* a fortified town. [var. of BURGH]

-burg, (in compound names) city or town, as in *Parkersburg.* [var. of BOROUGH]

burg·age (bûr′gĭj), *n.* *Law.* **1.** (in England) a tenure whereby burgesses or townsmen hold their lands or tenements of the king or other lord, usually for a fixed money rent. **2.** (in Scotland) that tenure by which the property in royal burghs is held under the crown, proprietors being liable to the (nominal) service of watching and warding. [t. ML: m. *burgāgium,* der. *burgus,* Latinized form of BURG(H), BOROUGH]

Bur·gas (bŏŏr gäs′), *n.* a seaport in E Bulgaria, on the Gulf of Burgas (inlet of Black Sea). 36,230 (1934).

bur·gee (bûr′jē), *n.* *Naut.* a swallow-tailed flag or pendant, in the merchant service generally bearing the ship's name. [orig. uncert.; ? der. *burge* burgeon]

bur·geon (bûr′jən), *n.* **1.** a bud; a sprout. —*v.i.* **2.** to begin to grow, as a bud; to put forth buds, shoots, as a plant (often fol. by *out, forth*). —*v.t.* **3.** to put forth as buds. Also, **bourgeon.** [ME *burjon,* t. OF, ? t. Gmc.]

bur·gess (bûr′jĭs), *n.* **1.** an inhabitant, esp. a citizen or freeman, of an English borough. **2.** *Hist.* a representative of a borough, corporate town, or university in the British Parliament. **3.** *U.S. Hist.* a representative in the popular branch of the colonial legislature of Virginia or Maryland. [ME *burgeis,* t. OF, g. LL *burgēnsis* a citizen. Cf. BOURGEOIS]

Bur·gess (bûr′jĭs), *n.* **(Frank) Gelett** (jə lĕt′), 1866–1951, U.S. illustrator and humorist.

burgh (bûrg; *Scot.* bûr′ō, -ə), *n.* a borough (applied to chartered towns in Scotland). [var. of BOROUGH] —**burgh′al** (bûr′gəl), *adj.*

burgh·er (bûr′gər), *n.* an inhabitant of a borough; a citizen.

Burgh·ley (bûr′lĭ), *n.* **William Cecil,** 1520–98, British statesman: adviser to Elizabeth. Also, **Burleigh.**

bur·glar (bûr′glər), *n.* one who commits burglary. [cf. Anglo-L *burglātor,* var. of *burgātor,* Latinization of AF *burgur* burglar, der. *burgier* pillage]

bur·glar·i·ous (bərglâr′Ĭəs), *adj.* pertaining to or involving burglary. —**bur·glar′i·ous·ly,** *adv.*

bur·glar·ize (bûr′glərīz′), *v.t.* **-ized, -izing.** *Colloq.* to commit burglary upon.

bur·gla·ry (bûr′glərĭ), *n.*, *pl.* **-ries.** *Criminal Law.* the felony of breaking into and entering the house of another at night with intent to commit a felony therein, extended by statute to cover the breaking and entering of any of various buildings, by night or day.

bur·gle (bûr′gəl), *v.t.*, *v.i.*, **-gled, -gling.** *Colloq.* to commit burglary; burglarize.

bur·go·mas·ter (bûr′gə măs′tər, -mäs′tər), *n.* the chief magistrate of a municipal town of Holland, Flanders, Germany, or Austria. [t. D: m. *burgemeester,* lit. town master]

bur·go·net (bûr′gə nĕt′), *n.* *Armor.* an open helmet usually with pivoted peak and hinged cheek pieces. [t. F: m. *bourguignotte,* der. *Bourgogne* Burgundy]

bur·goo (bûr′gōō, bûr gōō′), *n.*, *pl.* **-goos. 1.** a thick oatmeal gruel, esp. as used by seamen. **2.** *U.S. Dial.* a kind of thick, highly seasoned soup. **3.** *U.S. Dial.* a picnic at which such soup is served. [orig. uncert.]

Bur·gos (bŏŏr′gŏs), *n.* a city in N Spain: famous cathedral. 60,425 (1940).

Bur·goyne (bər goin′), *n.* **John,** 1722–92, British general in American Revolutionary War.

bur·grave (bûr′grāv), *n.* *Ger. Hist.* **1.** the appointed head of a fortress. **2.** hereditary governor of a castle or town. [t. G: m. *burggraf,* f. *burg* castle +*graf* count]

Bur·gun·di·an (bər gŭn′dĬ ən), *adj.* **1.** of or pertaining to Burgundy or its people. —*n.* **2.** a native or an inhabitant of Burgundy.

Bur·gun·dy (bûr′gən dĭ), *n.*, *pl.* **-dies. 1.** French, **Bourgogne.** a region in SE France: a former kingdom, duchy, and province. See map under **Brittany. 2.** (*often l.c.*) wine, of many varieties, red and white, mostly still, full, and dry, produced in the Burgundy region. **3.** (*often l.c.*) some similar wine made elsewhere.

bur·i·al (bĕr′Ĭ əl), *n.* act of burying. [f. BURY + -AL[2] (cf. *funeral*); r. ME *buriel,* OE *byrgels* burying place, g. pre-E **burgh-* + *-ils* (var. of *-isl*) suffix; for dropping of *-s* (mistaken for plural sign), cf. RIDDLE, CHERRY]

burial ground, a tract of land for the burial of deceased persons.

bur·i·er (bĕr′Ĭər), *n.* one who or that which buries.

bu·rin (byŏŏr′Ĭn), *n.* **1.** a tempered steel rod, with a lozenge-shaped point and a rounded handle, used for engraving furrows in metal. **2.** a similar tool used by marble workers. [t. F, prob. of Gmc. orig.; cf. OHG *bora* gimlet. See BORE[1]]

burke (bûrk), *v.t.*, **burked, burking. 1.** to murder, as by suffocation, so as to leave no or few marks of violence. **2.** to get rid of by some indirect maneuver. [from W. *Burke,* hanged at Edinburgh in 1829 for murders of this kind]

Burke (bûrk), *n.* **Edmund,** 1729–97, British statesman, orator, and writer.

burl (bûrl), *n.* **1.** a small knot or lump in wool, thread, or cloth. **2.** a dome-shaped growth on the trunk of a tree; a wartlike structure sometimes two feet across and a foot or more in height, sliced to make a veneer known as **burlwood veneer.** —*v.t.* **3.** to remove burls from (cloth) in finishing. [ME *burle,* t. OF: m. *bourle,* ult. der. LL *burra* flock of wool] —**burled,** *adj.*

bur·lap (bûr′lăp), *n.* coarse fabric made of jute, hemp, or the like; gunny.

Bur·leigh (bûr′lĭ), *n.* Burghley.

bur·lesque (bər lĕsk′), *n.*, *adj.*, *v.*, **-lesqued, -lesquing.** —*n.* **1.** an artistic composition, esp. literary or dramatic, which, for the sake of laughter, vulgarizes lofty material or treats ordinary material with mock dignity. **2.** any ludicrous take-off or debasing caricature. **3.** *U.S.* a theatrical entertainment featuring coarse, crude, often vulgar comedy and dancing. —*adj.* **4.** involving ludicrous or debasing treatment of a solemn subject. **5.** of or pertaining to risqué burlesque. —*v.t.* **6.** to make ridiculous by mocking representation. —*v.i.* **7.** to use caricature. [t. F, t. It.: m. *burlesco,* der. *burla* jest, mockery] —**bur·les′quer,** *n.*

bur·ley (bûr′lĭ), *n.*, *pl.* **-leys.** (*often cap.*) an American tobacco grown esp. in Kentucky and southern Ohio.

Bur·lin·game (bûr′lĬn gām′, -lĬng gām′), *n.* **Anson** (ăn′sən), 1820–70, U.S. diplomat.

Bur·ling·ton (bûr′lĬng tən), *n.* **1.** a city in NW Vermont, on Lake Champlain. 33,155 (1950). **2.** a city in SE Iowa, on the Mississippi. 30,613 (1950). **3.** a city in N North Carolina. 26,560 (1950).

bur·ly (bûr′lĬ), *adj.*, **-lier, -liest. 1.** great in bodily size; stout; sturdy. **2.** bluff; brusque. [ME *borli, burlich, burli;* orig. uncert.] —**bur′li·ly,** *adv.* —**bur′li·ness,** *n.*

Bur·ma (bûr′mə), *n.* an independent republic in SE Asia, until 1948 a British dependency: historically subdivided into **Lower Burma** (coastal region W of Siam), **Upper Burma** (inland districts), and the Shan States. 14,667,000 pop. (1931); 233,492 sq. mi. *Cap.:* Rangoon.

Bur·man (bûr′mən), *adj.*, *n.* Burmese.

bur marigold, any of various herbs of the composite genus *Bidens*, esp. those with conspicuous yellow flowers.

Burma Road, a strategic highway extending from Lashio, Burma, through mountainous regions to Kunming, China, (in 1938) and later to Chungking: used during World War II for supplying Allied military forces in China.

Bur·mese (bər·mēz′, -mēs′) *n.*, *pl.* **-mese**, *adj.* **1.** a native or inhabitant of Burma. **2.** the principal language of Burma, a Sino-Tibetan language. —*adj.* **3.** of or pertaining to Burma, its people, or their language.

burn[1] (bûrn), *v.*, **burned** or **burnt, burning,** *n.* —*v.i.* **1.** to be on fire: *the fuel burns.* **2.** (of a furnace, etc.) to contain fire. **3.** to feel heat or a physiologically identical sensation: *his face burned in the wind.* **4.** to give light: *the lights in the house burned all night.* **5.** to glow like fire. **6.** (in games) to be extremely close to finding a concealed object or guessing an answer. **7.** to feel strong passion: *he was burning with anger.* **8.** *Chem.* to undergo combustion; oxidize. **9.** to become discolored, tanned, or charred through heat. —*v.t.* **10.** to consume, partly or wholly, with fire. **11.** to cause to feel the sensation of heat. **12.** to injure, discolor, char, or treat with heat. **13.** to produce with fire: *to burn charcoal.* **14.** *Chem.* to cause to undergo combustion; oxidize. —*n.* **15.** a burned place. **16.** *Pathol.* an injury, produced by heat, or by abnormal cold, chemicals, poison gas, electricity, or lightning. A **first-degree burn** is characterized by reddening; a **second-degree burn** by blistering; a **third-degree burn** by charring. **17.** the operation of burning or baking, as in brickmaking. [coalescence in later ME of OE *beornan*, v.i. (c. Goth. *brinnan*) and OE *bærnan*, v.t. (c. Goth. *brannjan*) with (weak) inflexion of *bærnan* and phonetic form of *beornan*]
—**Syn. 10.** BURN, SCORCH, SEAR, SINGE refer to the effect of fire or heat. To BURN is to consume, wholly or in part, by contact with fire or excessive heat: *to burn leaves.* SCORCH implies superficial or slight burning on the surface, resulting in a change of color or in injury to the texture because of shriveling or curling: *to scorch a dress while ironing.* SEAR refers esp to the drying or hardening caused by heat: *to sear a roast of meat.* SINGE esp. applies to a superficial burning that takes off the ends or projections of something: *to singe hair.*

burn[2] (bûrn), *n.* *Scot. and N. Eng.* a brook or rivulet. Also, **bourn, bourne,** [ME *burne, hourne,* OE *burna, hurne,* akin to G *born, brunnen* spring]

Burne-Jones (bûrn′jōnz′), **Sir Edward,** 1833–98, British painter and designer.

burn·er (bûr′nər), *n.* **1.** one who or that which burns. **2.** that part of a gas fixture, lamp, etc., from which flame issues or in which it is produced.

bur·net (bûr′nĭt), *n.* a plant of the rosaceous genus *Sanguisorba*, esp. *S. minor*, an erect herb whose leaves are used for salad. [ME, t. OF: m. *brunette*, dim. of *brun* brown]

Bur·nett (bər·nĕt′), *n.* **Frances Hodgson** (hŏj′sən), 1849–1924, U.S. novelist.

Bur·ney (bûr′nĭ), *n.* **Frances** (or **Fanny**), (*Madame D'Arblay*) 1752–1840, British novelist and diarist.

burn·ing (bûr′nĭng), *adj.* **1.** intense; serious; much discussed: *a burning question.* —*n.* **2.** the final heat treatment used to develop hardness and other properties in ceramic products. —**burn′ing·ly,** *adv.*

burn·ing-bush (bûr′nĭng bŏosh′), *n.* any of various plants, esp. the wahoo, *Euonymus atropurpureus.*

burning glass, a lens used to produce heat or ignite substances by focusing the sun's rays.

bur·nish (bûr′nĭsh), *v.t.* **1.** to polish (a surface) by friction. **2.** to make smooth and bright. —*n.* **3.** gloss; brightness; luster. [ME *burnish(en)*, t. OF: m. *burniss-*, s. *burnir* make brown, polish, der. *brun* brown, t. Gmc.; see BROWN]

bur·nish·er (bûr′nĭsh ər), *n.* a tool, usually with a smooth, slightly convex head, used for polishing, as in porcelain painting, dentistry, etc.

Burn·ley (bûrn′lĭ), *n.* a city in NW England, in Lancashire. 83,720 (est. 1946).

bur·noose (bər·nōōs′, bûr′nōōs), *n.* a hooded mantle or cloak, such as that worn by Arabs, etc. See illus. just above. Also, **bur·nous** (bər·nōōs′, bûr′nōōs). [t. F: (m.) *burnous,* t. Ar.: m. *burnus*]

Burns (bûrnz), *n.* **Robert,** 1759–96, Scottish poet.

Burn·side (bûrn′sīd′), *n.* **Ambrose Everett,** 1824–81, Union general in the U.S. Civil War.

burn·sides (bûrn′sīdz′), *n.pl.* a style of beard consisting of side whiskers and a mustache, the chin being clean-shaven. [named after Gen. A. E. BURNSIDE]

burnt (bûrnt), *v.* pt. and pp. of **burn.**

Burnoose

Burnsides

burnt offering, *Relig.* an offering burnt upon an altar in sacrifice to a deity.

burnt umber, 1. reddish brown. **2.** See **umber** (def. 1).

bur oak, an oak tree of eastern North America, *Quercus macrocarpa*, having a hard, tough, and durable wood.

burr[1] (bûr), *n.* **1.** any of various tools and appliances for cutting or drilling. **2.** Also, **buhr.** a rough protuberance, ridge, or area left on metal after cutting, drilling, ploughing with an engraver's tool, etc. **3.** a rough or irregular protuberance on any object, as on a tree. **4.** burr. —*v.t.* **5.** to form a rough point or edge on. [var. of BUR]

burr[2] (bûr), *n.* **1.** a washer placed at the head of a rivet. **2.** the blank punched out of a piece of sheet metal. [earlier *burre*, ME *burrowe, burwhe* circle]

burr[3] (bûr), *n.* **1.** a guttural pronunciation of the letter *r* (as in certain Northern English dialects). **2.** any rough or dialectal pronunciation. **3.** a whirring noise or sound. —*v.i.* **4.** to speak with a burr. **5.** to speak roughly, indistinctly, or inarticulately. **6.** to make a whirring noise or sound. —*v.t.* **7.** to pronounce with a burr. [appar. imit.; ? assoc. with idea of roughness in BUR]

burr[4] (bûr), *n.* **1.** burstone. **2.** a mass of harder siliceous rock in soft rock. Also, **buhr.** [orig. uncert.; ? akin to BUR]

Burr (bûr), *n.* **Aaron,** 1756–1836, vice-president of the U.S., 1801–05.

bur reed, any plant of the genus *Sparganium*, whose species have ribbonlike leaves and burlike heads of fruit.

bur·ro (bûr′ō, bŏor′ō), *n.*, *pl.* **-ros.** *Southwestern U.S.* **1.** a pack donkey. **2.** any donkey. [t. Sp., der. *burrico* small horse, g. L *burricus*]

Bur·roughs (bûr′ōz), *n.* **John,** 1837–1921, U. S. naturalist and writer.

bur·row (bûr′ō), *n.* **1.** a hole in the ground made by a rabbit, fox, or similar small animal, for refuge and habitation. **2.** a similar place of retreat, shelter, or refuge. —*v.i.* **3.** to make a hole or passage (in, into, or under something). **4.** to lodge in a burrow. **5.** to hide. —*v.t.* **6.** to put a burrow or burrows into (a hill, etc.). **7.** to hide (oneself), as in a burrow. [ME *borow*. Cf. OE *beorg* burial place, *gebeorg* refuge, *burgen* grave] —**bur′row·er,** *n.*

burrowing owl, a long-legged, terrestrial owl, *Speotyto cunicularia*, of North and South America, which digs its nesting burrow in open prairie land; ground owl.

burr·stone (bûr′stōn′), *n.* burstone.

bur·ry (bûr′ĭ), *adj.* full of burs; burlike; prickly: *burry wool.*

bur·sa (bûr′sə), *n.*, *pl.* **-sae** (-sē), **-sas.** *Anat., Zool.* a pouch, sac, or vesicle, esp. a sac containing synovia, to facilitate motion, as between a tendon and a bone. [t. ML: bag, purse, t. Gk.: m. *bŷrsa* hide] —**bur′sal,** *adj.*

Bur·sa (bōōr′sä), *n.* a city in NW Turkey: one-time capital of the Ottoman Empire. 77,598 (1940). Also, **Brusa.**

bur·sar (bûr′sər), *n.* a treasurer or business officer, esp. of a college. [t. ML: m. *bursarius*, der. *bursa* purse]

bur·sar·i·al (bər·sâr′ĭ əl), *adj.* of, pertaining to, or paid to or by a bursar, or a bursary.

bur·sa·ry (bûr′sə rĭ), *n.*, *pl.* **-ries.** **1.** *Eccles.* the treasury of a monastery. **2.** (in Scotland) a scholarship granted by a college. [t. ML: m.s. *bursaria*]

Bur·schen·schaft (bŏor′shən shäft′), *n.*, *pl.* **-schaften** (-shäf′tən). *German.* any of certain associations of students at German universities, formed to promote patriotism, Christian conduct, and liberal ideas, but now purely social fraternities. [G, der. *bursch* student]

burse (bûrs), *n.* **1.** a pouch or case for some special purpose. **2.** (in Scotland) **a.** a fund to provide allowances for students. **b.** an allowance so provided. **3.** *Eccles.* a case or receptacle for the corporal. [t. F: m *bourse* wallet, g. L *bursa*, t. Gk.:m. *bŷrsa* hide]

bur·seed (bûr′sēd′), *n.* a species of stickseed, *Lappula echinata*, introduced into the U. S. from Europe.

bur·ser·a·ceous (bûr′sə rā′shəs), *adj.* *Bot.* belonging to the family Burseraceae, of shrubs or trees of warm, often arid, countries, with compound leaves.

bur·si·form (bûr′sə fôrm′), *adj.* *Anat., Zool.* pouch-shaped; saccate. [f. s. ML *bursa* bag, purse + -(I)FORM]

bur·si·tis (bər·sī′tĭs), *n.* *Pathol.* inflammation of a bursa. [t. NL. See BURSA, -ITIS]

burst (bûrst), *v.*, **burst, bursting,** *n.* —*v.i.* **1.** to fly apart or break open with sudden violence. **2.** to issue forth suddenly and forcibly from or as from confinement. **3.** to break or give way from violent pain or emotion: *to burst into speech or tears.* **4.** to be extremely full, as if ready to break open. **5.** to become visible, audible, evident, etc. suddenly and clearly. —*v.t.* **6.** to cause to burst; break suddenly and violently. **7.** to cause or suffer the rupture of. —*n.* **8.** act of bursting. **9.** a sudden display of activity or energy: *a burst of applause or speed.* **10.** a sudden expression or manifestation of emotion, etc. **11.** a sudden and violent issuing forth. **12.** *Mil.* **a.** the explosion of a projectile, esp. in a specified place: *an air burst.* **b.** series of shots fired by one pressure on the trigger of an automatic weapon. **13.** the result of bursting: *a burst in the dike.* **14.** a sudden opening to sight or view. [ME *berst(en)*, *burst(en)*, etc., OE *berstan*; form *burst* orig. past only; c. G *bersten*, Icel. *bresta*] —**burst′er,** *n.* —**Syn. 1.** crack, explode. **6.** rend, tear.

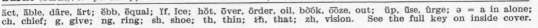

bur·stone (bûr'stōn'), n. 1. Geol. any of various siliceous rocks used for millstones. 2. a millstone of such material. Also, **buhr, buhrstone, burrstone.** [f. BURR⁴ + STONE]

bur·then (bûr'thən), n., v.t. Archaic. burden¹. —**bur·then·some,** adj.

bur·ton (bûr'tən). n. Naut. 1. any of various kinds of tackle used for setting up rigging, raising sails, etc. 2. any of various small tackles, esp. one having a two-sheave and a one-sheave block.

Bur·ton (bûr'tən), n. 1. **Harold Hitz,** born 1888, associate justice of U.S. Supreme Court since 1945. 2. **Sir Richard Francis,** 1821–90, British traveler and author. 3. **Robert,** 1577–1640, British clergyman, scholar, and author.

Bur·ton-on-Trent (bûr'tən ŏn trĕnt'), a city in central England, in Staffordshire. 48,470 (est. 1946).

bur·weed (bûr'wēd'), n. any of various plants having a burlike fruit, as the cocklebur, burdock, etc.

bur·y (bĕr'ĭ), v.t., **buried, burying.** 1. to put in the ground and cover with earth. 2. to put (a corpse) in the ground or a vault, or into the sea, often with ceremony. 3. to cause to sink in: to bury a dagger in one's heart. 4. to cover in order to conceal from sight. 5. to withdraw (oneself): he buried himself in his work. 6. to put out of one's mind: to bury an injury. [ME berien, buryen, OE byrgan, akin to OE beorg burial place, burgen, byrgen grave] —**bur/i·er,** n. —**Syn.** 2. inter, entomb, inhume.

burying ground, a burial ground.

Bur·y St. Ed·munds (bĕr'ĭ sănt ĕd'məndz), a city in E England: famous medieval shrine. 17,515 (1939).

bus (bŭs), n., pl. **buses, busses.** 1. a motor vehicle with a long body equipped with seats or benches for passengers, usually operating as part of a scheduled service line; an omnibus. 2. a similar horse-drawn vehicle. 3. Colloq. a passenger automobile or airplane. [short for OMNIBUS]

bus., 1. business. 2. bushel; bushels.

bus boy, a waiter's helper in a restaurant or other public dining room, doing the more menial tasks.

bus·by (bŭz'bĭ), n., pl. **-bies.** a tall fur hat with a bag hanging from the top over the right side, worn by hussars, etc., in the British Army.

bush¹ (bŏŏsh), n. 1. a plant, esp. a low one with many branches, which usually arise from or near the ground. 2. Bot. a small cluster of shrubs appearing as a single plant. 3. something resembling or suggesting this, as a thick, shaggy head of hair. 4. a fox's tail. 5. Geog. a stretch of land covered with bushy vegetation or trees. 6. a tree branch hung as a sign before a tavern or vintner's shop. 7. any tavern sign. 8. a wineshop. —v.i. 9. to be or become bushy; branch or spread as or like a bush. —v.t. 10. to cover with bushes; protect with bushes set round about; support with bushes. [ME; unexplained var. of busk, t. Scand.; cf. Dan. busk]

Busby

bush² (bŏŏsh), Mach. —n. 1. a lining of metal or the like let into an orifice to guard against wearing by friction, erosion, etc. 2. a metal lining, usually detachable, used as a bearing. —v.t. 3. to furnish with a bush; line with metal. [t. MD; m. busse, n.]

bush., bushel; bushels.

bush·buck (bŏŏsh'bŭk'), n. a rather small African antelope, Tragelaphus scriptus, frequenting forests and bushy regions. Also, **boschbok.**

bush cranberry, cranberry tree.

bush·el¹ (bŏŏsh'əl), n. 1. a unit of dry measure containing 4 pecks, equivalent in the U. S. (and formerly in England) to 2,150.42 cubic inches (**Winchester bushel**), and in Great Britain to 2,219.36 cubic inches (**Imperial bushel**). 2. a container of this capacity. 3. a unit of weight equal to the weight of a bushel of a given commodity. [ME boyschel, t. OF: m. boissiel, dim. of boisse, ult. der. Gallic word meaning hollow of the hand]

bush·el² (bŏŏsh'əl), v.t., **-eled, -eling** or (esp. Brit.) **-elled, -elling.** U.S. to alter or repair (a garment). [orig. uncert.] —**bush'el·er;** esp. Brit., **bush'el·ler,** n. —**bush·el·man,** (bŏŏsh'əl mən), n.

bush·ham·mer (bŏŏsh'hăm'ər), n. a hammer having a face studded with pyramidal points or the like for dressing stone.

Bu·shi·do (bōō'shē dô'), n. 1. a code of behavior attributed to the warriors of feudal Japan, actually a growth of the end of the feudal period, tinged with Confucian influences. 2. (in modern usage) fanatical disregard of life in the service of the emperor. Also, **bushido.** [Jap.: lit. the way of the warrior]

bush·i·ness (bŏŏsh'ĭ nĭs), n. bushy state or form.

bush·ing (bŏŏsh'ĭng), n. Elect. a lining for a hole, intended to insulate and/or protect from abrasion one or more conductors which pass through it. [f. BUSH² + -ING¹]

Bu·shire (bōō shēr'), n. a seaport in SW Iran, on the Persian Gulf. ab. 25,000.

bush league, Baseball, Colloq. a minor league.

bush·man (bŏŏsh'mən), n., pl. **-men.** 1. a woodsman. 2. Australia. a pioneer; dweller in the bush. 3. (cap.) a member of a South African Negroid race. 4. (cap.) the language of the Bushmen.

bush·mas·ter (bŏŏsh'măs'tər, -mäs'tər), n. a large venomous serpent, Lachesis mutus, of tropical America.

bush pig, a wild swine, Potamochaerus porcus, of South and East Africa, with white face markings; boschvark.

bush·rang·er (bŏŏsh'rān'jər), n. 1. a person who ranges or dwells in bush or woods. 2. Australia. a criminal who hides in bush and leads a predatory life.

bush tit, any of several small chickadeelike birds of the genus Psaltiparus, known for their beautiful pendant nests.

bush·whack·er (bŏŏsh'hwăk'ər), n. U.S. 1. one accustomed to range in the woods. 2. U.S. Hist. a Confederate guerrilla. 3. any guerrilla.

bush·whack·ing (bŏŏsh'hwăk'ĭng), n. U.S. 1. travel through bushy country, on foot or in a boat. 2. guerrilla tactics.

bush·y (bŏŏsh'ĭ), adj., **bushier, bushiest.** 1. resembling a bush. 2. full of or overgrown with bushes.

bus·i·ly (bĭz'əlĭ), adv. in a busy manner; actively.

busi·ness (bĭz'nĭs), n. 1. one's occupation, profession, or trade. 2. Econ. the purchase and sale of goods in an attempt to make a profit. 3. Com. a person, partnership, or corporation engaged in this; an established or going enterprise or concern. 4. volume of trade; patronage. 5. one's place of work. 6. that with which one is principally and seriously concerned. 7. that with which one is rightfully concerned. 8. affair; matter. 9. Theat. any movement or gesture by an actor used for dramatic expression (generally not applied to actions like exits, etc.). [ME busines, OE (North) bisignes. See BUSY, -NESS] —**Syn.** 1. See **occupation.**

business college, U.S. a school that gives training in the clerical side of business and commerce.

busi·ness·like (bĭz'nĭs līk'), adj. conforming to the methods of business or trade; methodical; systematic.

busi·ness·man (bĭz'nĭs măn'), n., pl. **-men** (-mĕn'). a man who engages in business or commerce. —**busi·ness·wom·an** (bĭz'nĭs wŏŏm'ən), n. fem.

busk¹ (bŭsk), v.t. Scot. and Dial. to prepare. [ME buske(n), t. Scand.; cf. Icel. būask, refl. of būa make ready]

busk² (bŭsk), n. 1. a strip of wood, steel, whalebone, or other stiffening material placed in the front of a corset to keep it in form. 2. Dial. the whole corset. [t. F: m. busc, t. It.: m. busco stick]

bus·kin (bŭs'kĭn), n. 1. a half boot, or outer covering for the foot and leg reaching to the calf or higher. 2. the high shoe or cothurnus of ancient Greek and Roman tragic actors. 3. tragedy; tragic drama. [orig. uncert. Cf. F brousequin, D broosken, Sp. borceguí, It. borzacchino]

Ancient buskins

bus·kined (bŭs'kĭnd), adj. 1. wearing buskins. 2. pertaining to tragedy.

bus·man's hol·iday (bŭs'mənz), a holiday on which, by choice, one does one's regular work.

Bus·ra (bŭs'rə), n. Basra. Also, **Bus'rah.**

buss (bŭs), n., v.t., v.i. Colloq. kiss. [cf. d. G buss]

bus·ses (bŭs'ĭz), n. pl. of **bus.**

bust¹ (bŭst), n. 1. the head and shoulders of a person done in sculpture, either in the round or in relief. 2. the chest or breast; the bosom. [t. F: m. buste, t. It.: m. busto, g. L bustum bust, funeral monument, funeral]

bust² (bŭst), v.i. Colloq. or Slang. 1. to burst. 2. to go bankrupt (often fol. by up). —v.t. 3. to burst. 4. to bankrupt; ruin (often fol. by up). 5. (in the Army) to reduce in rank or grade, usually to the rank of private. 6. to subdue (a bronco, etc.). 7. to hit. —n. 8. a complete failure; bankruptcy. 9. a drunken party; brawl. [d. or vulgar var. of BURST]

bus·tard (bŭs'tərd), n. any of several large Old World birds of the family Otididae allied to both the cranes and the plovers, inhabiting open country of Europe and Africa. [ME, t. OF, b. bistarde (t. lt.: m. bistarda) and oustarde, both g. L avis tarda slow bird]

bust·er (bŭs'tər), n. 1. a person or thing that busts: trustbuster. 2. Slang. something very big or unusual for its kind. 3. Slang. a roisterer. 4. Slang. a frolic; a spree. 5. U.S. Colloq. a small boy. 6. Australia. a violent, cold, southerly wind.

bus·tle¹ (bŭs'əl), v., **-tled, -tling,** n. —v.i. 1. to move or act with a great show of energy (often fol. by about). —v.t. 2. to cause to bustle. —n. 3. activity with great show of energy; stir; commotion. [? var. of obs. buskle, freq. of BUSK¹] —**bus'tling·ly,** adv.

bus·tle² (bŭs'əl), n. 1. fullness outside the skirt, as exaggerated fullness at the back of a peplum, large bows, etc. 2. (formerly) a pad, cushion, or wire framework worn by women on the back part of the body below the waist, to expand and support the skirt. [? der. BUSTLE¹]

bus·y (bĭz'ĭ), adj., **busier, busiest,** v., **busied, busying.** —adj. 1. actively and attentively engaged: busy with his work. 2. not at leisure; otherwise engaged. 3. full of or characterized by activity: a busy life. 4. officious; meddlesome; prying. [ME busi, bisi, OE bysig, c. D bezig, LG besig] —v.t. 5. to keep occupied; make or keep busy; to busy oneself keeping the lawn in order. [ME bisien, OE bysgian, der. bysig BUSY, adj.] —**bus'y·ness,** n. —**Syn.** 1. BUSY, DILIGENT, INDUSTRIOUS imply active or earnest effort to accomplish something, or a habitual atti-

---

b., blend of, blended; c., cognate with; d., dialect, dialectal; der., derived from; f., formed from; g., going back to; m., modification of; r., replacing; s., stem of; t., taken from; ?, perhaps. See the full key on inside cover.

tude of such earnestness. BUSY means actively employed, temporarily or habitually: *a busy official.* DILIGENT suggests earnest and constant effort or application, and usually connotes fondness for, or enjoyment of, what one is doing: *a diligent student.* INDUSTRIOUS often implies a habitual characteristic of steady and zealous application, often with a definite goal: *an industrious clerk working for promotion.*

bus·y·bod·y (bĭz′ĭ bŏd′ĭ), *n., pl.* **-bodies.** a person who pries into and meddles in the affairs of others.

but[1] (bŭt; *unstressed* bət), *conj.* **1.** on the contrary; yet: *they all went but I didn't.* **2.** excepting, except, or save: *anywhere but here.* **3.** except that (followed by a clause, often with *that* expressed): *nothing would do but, or but that, I should come in.* **4.** without the circumstance that, or that not: *it never rains but it pours.* **5.** otherwise than: *I can do nothing but go.* **6.** that (esp. after *doubt, deny,* etc., with a negative): *I don't doubt but he will do it.* **7.** that not (after a negative or question): *the children never played but that a quarrel followed.* **8.** who or which not: *no leader worthy of the name ever existed but he was an optimist* (who was not an optimist). —*prep.* **9.** with the exception of; except; save: *no one replied but me.* —*adv.* **10.** only; just: *there is but one God.* **11.** all but, almost: *all but dead.* —*n.* **12.** a restriction or objection: *no buts about it.* [ME; OE *b(e)ūta(n)* on the outside, without, f. *be-* by + *ūt* out + *-an* adv. suffix]
—**Syn. 1.** BUT, HOWEVER, NEVERTHELESS, STILL, YET are words implying opposition (with a possible concession). BUT marks an opposition or contrast, though in a casual way: *we are going, but we shall return.* HOWEVER indicates a less marked opposition, but displays a second consideration to be compared with the first: *we are going; however* (notice this also) *we shall return.* NEVERTHELESS implies a concession, something which should not be forgotten in making a summing up: *we are going; nevertheless (do not forget that) we shall return.* STILL implies that in spite of a preceding concession, something must be considered as possible or even inevitable: *we have to go on foot; still (it is probable and possible that) we'll get there.* YET implies that in spite of a preceding concession, there is still a chance for a different outcome: *we are going; yet (in spite of all, some day) we shall return.* **2.** See except[1].
but[2] (bŭt), *n. Scot.* the outer room of a house consisting of two rooms; the kitchen, the other room being the ben. [n. use of BUT[1], adv. (etymological sense)]

bu·ta·di·ene (bū′tə dī′ēn, -dī ēn′), *n. Chem.* an inflammable, colorless, hydrocarbon gas, C₄H₆, used in making synthetic rubber. [f. BUTA(NE) + DI- + -ENE]

bu·tane (bū′tān, bū tān′), *n. Chem.* a saturated aliphatic hydrocarbon, C₄H₁₀, existing in two isomeric forms and used as a fuel and a chemical intermediate. [f. BUT(YL) + -ANE]

bu·ta·none (bū′tə nōn′), *n. Chem.* an inflammable ketone, C₄H₈O, used as a solvent and in making plastics.

butch·er (bŏch′ər), *n.* **1.** a retail dealer in meat. **2.** one who slaughters certain domesticated animals, or dresses their flesh, for food or for market. **3.** a person guilty of cruel or indiscriminate slaughter. **4.** *U.S.* a person who sells candy, etc. on a train. —*v.t.* **5.** to kill or slaughter for food or for market. **6.** to murder indiscriminately or brutally. **7.** to bungle; botch: *to butcher a job.* [ME *bocher,* t. OF, der. *boc* he-goat, t. Gmc. See BUCK[1]] —**butch′er·er,** *n.* —**Syn. 5.** See **slaughter.**

butch·er·bird (bŏch′ər bûrd′), *n.* any of various shrikes of the genus *Lanius,* which impale their prey upon thorns.

butch·er·ly (bŏch′ər lĭ), *adj.* like, or characteristic of, a butcher.

butch·er's-broom (bŏch′ərz brōōm′, -brŏŏm′), *n.* a shrubby liliaceous evergreen, *Ruscus aculeatus,* of England, used for making brooms.

butch·er·y (bŏch′ər ĭ), *n., pl.* **-eries. 1.** a slaughterhouse. **2.** the trade or business of a butcher. **3.** brutal slaughter of human beings; carnage.

Bute (būt), *n.* **1.** Also, **Bute·shire** (būt′shĭr, -shər). a county in SW Scotland, composed of islands. 18,900 pop. (est. 1946); 218 sq. mi. *Co. seat:* Rothesay. **2.** an island in the Firth of Clyde: a part of this county. 12,112 pop. (1931); ab. 50 sq. mi.

bu·tene (bū′tēn), *n. Chem.* one of three isomeric butylenes, C₄H₈.

but·ler (bŭt′lər), *n.* **1.** the head male servant of a household. **2.** the male servant having charge of the wines and liquors, etc. [ME *buteler,* t. AF: m. *butuiller,* der. *bouteille* bottle] —**but′ler·ship′,** *n.*

But·ler (bŭt′lər), *n.* **1. Benjamin Franklin,** 1818–93, U. S. politician and Union general in the Civil War. **2. Joseph,** 1692–1752, British bishop, theologian, and author. **3. Nicholas Murray,** 1862–1947, U. S. educator: president, Columbia University, 1902–45. **4. Samuel,** 1612–80, British poet. **5. Samuel,** 1835–1902, British writer. **6.** a city in W Pennsylvania. 23,482 (1950).

butler's pantry, a room between the kitchen and the dining room arranged for the storage of china and silverware and containing a sink.

but·ler·y (bŭt′lər ĭ), *n., pl.* **-leries.** a butler's room or pantry; a buttery. [f. BUTLER + -Y³; r. ME *botelerye,* t. OF: m. *bouteillerie* storeroom for wine]

butt[1] (bŭt), *n.* **1.** the end or extremity of anything, esp. the thicker, larger, or blunt end, as of a musket, fishing rod, whip handle, arrow, log, etc. **2.** an end which is not used up: *a cigarette butt.* **3.** buttock. [ME *bott* buttock; appar. short for BUTTOCK]

butt[2] (bŭt), *n.* **1.** a person or thing that is an object

of wit, ridicule, sarcasm, etc., or contempt. **2.** (in rifle practice) **a.** a wall of earth behind the targets of a target range, which prevents bullets from scattering over a large area. **b.** (*pl.*) a wall in front of the targets of a target range, behind which men can safely lower, score, and raise targets during firing. **3.** a hinge for a door or the like, secured to the butting surfaces or ends instead of the adjacent sides. **4.** *Obs.* a goal; limit. —*v.i.* **5.** to have an end or projection (*on*); be adjacent (*to*). —*v.t.* **6.** to join an end of (something); join the ends of (two things) together. [late ME, t. OF: m. *bout* end, extremity, of Gmc. orig.]

butt[3] (bŭt), *v.t.* **1.** to strike with the head or horns. —*v.i.* **2.** to strike something or at something with the head or horns. **3.** to project. **4.** *Colloq.* to interrupt; interfere; intrude (fol. by *in*). —*n.* **5.** a push with head or horns. [ME *butt(en),* t. OF: m. *bouter* strike, thrust, abut, touch, der. *bout* end, of Gmc. orig.]

butt[4] (bŭt), *n.* **1.** a large cask for wine, beer, or ale. **2.** any cask or barrel. **3.** a unit of capacity, equal to two hogsheads. [late ME; cf. OF *botte, bote,* c. It. *botte,* g. LL *butta, buttis* vessel, cask]

butte (būt), *n. Western U. S. and Canada.* an isolated hill or mountain rising abruptly above the surrounding land. [t. F: hill, prop., mound for target]

Butte (būt), *n.* a city in SW Montana: important mining center. 33,251 (1950).

but·ter (bŭt′ər), *n.* **1.** the fatty portion of milk, separating as a soft whitish or yellowish solid when milk or cream is agitated or churned. **2.** this substance, processed for cooking and table use. **3.** any of various other soft spreads for breads: *apple butter, peanut butter.* **4.** any of various substances of butterlike consistency, as various metallic chlorides, and certain vegetable oils solid at ordinary temperatures. —*v.t.* **5.** to put butter on or in. **6.** *Colloq.* to flatter grossly (often fol. by *up*). [ME; OE *butere,* t. L: m. s. *būtyrum,* t. Gk.: m. *boútyron*] —**but′ter·like′,** *adj.*

but·ter-and-eggs (bŭt′ər ən ĕgz′), *n.* any of certain plants whose flowers are of two shades of yellow, as the toadflax.

but·ter·ball (bŭt′ər bôl′), *n.* **1.** the bufflehead. **2.** *Colloq.* a fat, round person.

butter bean, a variety of small-seeded lima beans, *Phaseolus lunatus,* grown in the South.

but·ter·bur (bŭt′ər bûr′), *n.* an Old World perennial herb composite, *Petasites vulgaris,* bearing large woolly leaves said to have been used to wrap butter.

but·ter·cup (bŭt′ər kŭp′), *n.* a plant of the genus *Ranunculus,* esp. *R. acris* or *R. bulbosus,* with yellow cup-shaped flowers.

but·ter·fat (bŭt′ər făt′), *n.* butter; milk fat; a mixture of glycerides, mainly butyrin, olein, and palmitin.

but·ter·fin·gers (bŭt′ər fĭng′gərz), *n.* a person who drops things easily.

but·ter·fish (bŭt′ər fĭsh′), *n., pl.* **-fishes,** (*esp. collectively*) **-fish. 1.** a small, flattened, marine food fish, *Poronotus triacanthus,* of the Atlantic coast of the U. S., having very small scales and smooth skin. **2.** an elongated blenny, *Pholis gunnellus,* of both coasts of the North Atlantic.

but·ter·fly (bŭt′ər flī′), *n., pl.* **-flies. 1.** any of a group of lepidopterous insects characterized by clubbed antennae, large, broad wings, often conspicuously colored and marked, and diurnal habits. **2.** a person who flits aimlessly from one thing to another. [OE *buttorflēoge,* f. *buttor-* (comb. form of *butere*) + *flēoge* fly, c. G *butterfliege;* ? orig. used of a butter-colored (yellow) species]

butterfly fish, any of the tropical marine fishes of the family *Chaetodontidae,* as *Chaetodon copistratus,* which are suggestive of the butterfly.

butterfly table, a small, occasional table with drop leaves having butterfly-shaped supports.

butterfly weed, 1. either of two closely related North American milkweeds, *Asclepias tuberosa* and *A. decumbens,* bearing orange-colored flowers. **2.** an erect North American herb, *Gaura coccinea,* related to the evening primrose, with wandlike spikes of red flowers.

but·ter·ine (bŭt′ə rēn′, -rĭn), *n.* an artificial butter; oleomargarine.

but·ter·milk (bŭt′ər mĭlk′), *n.* the more or less acidulous liquid remaining after the butter has been separated from milk or cream.

but·ter·nut (bŭt′ər nŭt′), *n.* **1.** the edible oily nut of an American tree, *Juglans cinerea,* of the walnut family. **2.** the tree itself. **3.** the souari nut. **4.** dark brown. **5.** *U.S. Civil War.* **a.** a member of the copperhead branch of the Democratic Party in the North. **b.** a Confederate soldier.

but·ter·scotch (bŭt′ər skŏch′), *n.* **1.** a kind of taffy made with butter. **2.** a flavor produced in puddings, frostings, ice cream, etc., by a combination of brown sugar, vanilla extract, and butter, with other ingredients.

but·ter·weed (bŭt′ər wēd′), *n.* **1.** any wild plant having conspicuously yellow flowers or leaves. **2.** the horseweed. **3.** a ragwort or groundsel, *Senecio glabellus.*

but·ter·wort (bŭt′ər wûrt′), *n.* any plant of the genus *Pinguicula,* small herbs whose leaves secrete a viscid substance in which small insects are caught.

but·ter·y[1] (bŭt′ər ĭ), *adj.* **1.** like, containing, or spread with, butter. **2.** *Colloq.* grossly flattering. [f. BUTTER + -Y¹]

but·ter·y² (bŭt'ər'ĭ, bŭt'rĭ), *n.*, *pl.* **-teries.** 1. a room or apartment in which the wines, liquors, and provisions of a household are kept; a pantry. 2. a room in colleges at Oxford and Cambridge Universities from which certain articles of food and drink are supplied to the students. [ME *boterie*, t. OF, der. *bot(t)e* cask]

butt joint, *Bldg. Trades.* a joint formed by two pieces of wood or metal united end to end without overlapping.

but·tock (bŭt'ək), *n.* 1. *Anat.* **a.** either of the two protuberances which form the rump. **b.** (*pl.*) the rump. 2. (*sing. or pl.*) *Naut.* the convex aftermost portion of a ship's body above the water line. [ME *buttok*, OE *buttuc*]

but·ton (bŭt'ən), *n.* 1. a disk or knob on a piece of cloth which, when passed through a slit or loop in the same piece or another, serves as a fastening. 2. anything resembling a button. 3. *Bot.* a bud or other protuberant part of a plant. 4. a young or undeveloped mushroom. 5. a disk pressed to close an electric circuit, as in ringing a bell. 6. (*pl.*) *Brit. Colloq.* a bellboy or page. 7. *Assaying, etc.* a globule or mass of metal lying at the bottom of a crucible after fusion. 8. *Fencing.* the protective knob fixed to the point of a foil. 9. *Western U.S.* the hard bonelike structure at the end of the rattles of a rattlesnake. 10. *U.S.* a guessing game. —*v.t.* 11. to fasten with a button or buttons. 12. to provide with a button or buttons. 13. *Fencing.* to touch with the button of the foil. —*v.i.* 14. to be capable of being buttoned. [ME *boton*, t. OF, der. *bouter* thrust. See BUTT²] —**but/ton·er,** *n.* —**but/ton·like/,** *adj.*

but·ton·ball (bŭt'ən bôl/), *n.* the buttonwood (def. 1).

but·ton·bush (bŭt'ən boŏsh/), *n.* a name given to *Cephalanthus occidentalis,* a North American shrub, on account of its globular flower heads.

but·ton·hole (bŭt'ən hōl/), *n.*, *v.*, **-holed, -holing.** —*n.* 1. the hole, slit, or loop through which a button is passed. —*v.t.* 2. to sew with buttonhole stitch. 3. to make buttonholes in. 4. to seize by or as by the buttonhole and detain in conversation. —**but/ton·hol/er,** *n.*

buttonhole stitch, *Sewing.* a looped stitch used to strengthen the edge of material, as in a buttonhole.

but·ton·hook (bŭt'ən hŏŏk/), *n.* a small metal or other stiff hook used for buttoning shoes, gloves, etc.

but·ton·mold (bŭt'ən mōld/), *n.* a disk of bone, wood, or metal, to be covered with fabric to form a button.

button snakeroot, any of a composite genus, *Liatris,* of perennial herbs with racemose or spicate heads of handsome rose-purple flowers.

button tree, 1. a tropical tree or shrub, *Conocarpus erecta,* with heavy, hard, compact wood and buttonlike fruits. 2. the buttonwood.

but·ton·wood (bŭt'ən woŏd/), *n.* 1. a tall, North American plane tree, *Platanus occidentalis,* yielding a useful timber (so called from its small pendulous fruit). 2. the button tree.

but·ton·y (bŭt'ən ĭ), *adj.* 1. like a button. 2. having many buttons.

but·tress (bŭt'rĭs), *n.* 1. *Archit.* a structure built against a wall or building for the purpose of giving it stability. 2. any prop or support. 3. a thing shaped like a buttress. —*v.t.* 4. *Archit.* to support by a buttress. 5. to prop up; support. [ME *boterace*, t. OF: m. *bouterez*, pl., der. *bouter* thrust, abut]

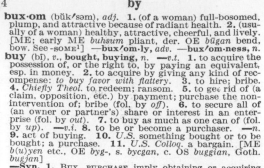

A, Buttress;
B, Flying buttress

butt shaft, a blunt or barbless arrow.

butt weld, *Bldg. Trades.* a weld formed by joining the flattened ends of two pieces of iron at a white heat.

bu·tyl (bū'tĭl), *n. Chem.* a univalent radical, C_4H_9, from butane. [f. BUT(YRIC) + -YL]

butyl alcohols, *Chem.* a group of three isomeric alcohols of the formula C_4H_9OH.

bu·tyl·ene (bū'tə lēn/), *n. Chem.* any of three isomeric gaseous hydrocarbons of the formula C_4H_8, belonging to the ethylene series. [f. BUTYL + -ENE]

butyl rubber, *Chem.* 1. a synthetic rubber, prepared by polymerization of butylene containing a little butadiene, particularly useful for inner tubes of automobile tires because of its leakproof qualities. 2. (*cap.*) a trademark for this substance.

bu·tyn (bū'tĭn), *n. Chem.* 1. a colorless para-aminobenzoic ester, $H_2NC_6H_4COO(CH_2)_3N(C_4H_9)_2.H_2SO_4$, used in dentistry as a local anesthetic. 2. (*cap.*) a trademark for this substance.

bu·tyr·a·ceous (bū/tə rā/shəs), *adj.* of the nature of, resembling, or containing butter. [f. s. L *būtyrum* butter + -ACEOUS]

bu·tyr·ate (bū/tə rāt/), *n. Chem.* a salt or ester of butyric acid.

bu·tyr·ic (bū tĭr'ĭk), *adj. Chem.* pertaining to or derived from butyric acid. [f. s. L *būtyrum* butter + -IC]

butyric acid, *Chem.* either of two isomeric acids, C_3H_7COOH, esp. the one, a rancid liquid, present in spoiled butter, etc., as an ester and sometimes free.

bu·tyr·in (bū/tər ĭn), *n. Chem.* a colorless liquid fat or ester present in butter, and formed from glycerin and butyric acid. [f. s. L *būtyrum* butter + -IN²]

bux·om (bŭk'səm), *adj.* 1. (of a woman) full-bosomed, plump, and attractive because of radiant health. 2. (usually of a woman) healthy, attractive, cheerful, and lively. [ME; early ME *buhsum* pliant, der. OE *būgan* bend, bow. See -SOME¹] —**bux/om·ly,** *adv.* —**bux/om·ness,** *n.*

buy (bī), *v.*, **bought, buying,** *n.* —*v.t.* 1. to acquire the possession of, or the right to, by paying an equivalent, esp. in money. 2. to acquire by giving any kind of recompense: *to buy favor with flattery.* 3. to hire; bribe. 4. *Chiefly Theol.* to redeem; ransom. 5. to get rid of (a claim, opposition, etc.) by payment; purchase the nonintervention of; bribe (fol. by *off*). 6. to secure all of (an owner or partner's) share or interest in an enterprise (fol. by *out*). 7. to buy as much as one can of (fol. by *up*). —*v.i.* 8. to be or become a purchaser. —*n.* 9. act of buying. 10. *U.S.* something bought or to be bought; a purchase. 11. *U.S. Colloq.* a bargain. [ME *b(u)yen* etc., OE *byg-*, s. *bycgan*, c. OS *buggian*, Goth. *bugjan*]

—**Syn.** 1. BUY, PURCHASE imply obtaining or acquiring property or goods for a price. BUY is the common and informal word, applying to any such transaction: *to buy a house, vegetables at the market.* PURCHASE is more formal and may connote buying on a larger scale, in a finer store, and the like: *to purchase a year's supplies.* —**Ant.** 1. sell.

buy·er (bī'ər), *n.* 1. one who buys; a purchaser. 2. a purchasing agent, as for a department or chain store.

buyers' strike, an attempt on the part of consumers to lower price levels by boycotting retailers or certain types of goods.

buzz (bŭz), *n.* 1. a low, vibrating, humming sound, as of bees. 2. a rumor or report. 3. *Colloq.* a phone call. —*v.i.* 4. to make a low, vibrating, humming sound. 5. to speak or whisper with such a sound. 6. to move busily from place to place. 7. *Brit. Colloq.* to go; leave (usually fol. by *off* or *along*). —*v.t.* 8. to make a buzzing sound with: *the fly buzzed its wings.* 9. to spread (a rumor) secretively. 10. to communicate with buzzes, as in signaling. 11. *Colloq.* to make a phone call to. 12. *Aeron.* **a.** to fly a plane very low over: *to buzz a field.* **b.** to signal or greet (someone) by flying a plane low and slowing the motor spasmodically. [imit.]

buz·zard (bŭz'ərd), *n.* 1. any of various more or less heavily built hawks of the genus *Buteo* and allied genera, as *B. vulgaris,* a rather sluggish European species. 2. any of various carrion-eating birds, as the turkey buzzard or turkey vulture, *Cathartes aura.* —*adj.* 3. *Obs.* senseless; stupid. [ME *busard,* t. OF, der. *buse* buzzard, g. L *būteo* kind of hawk]

Turkey buzzard,
Cathartes aura
(Ab. 2½ ft. long)

Buzzards Bay, an inlet of the Atlantic, in SE Massachusetts. ab. 30 mi. long.

buzz bomb, *Mil.* a type of self-steering aerial bomb, launched from large land-based rocket platforms, and used by the Germans in World War II, esp. over England.

buzz·er (bŭz'ər), *n.* 1. one who or that which buzzes. 2. a signaling apparatus similar to an electric bell, but without hammer or gong, and serving to produce sound by the vibration of an armature.

buzz saw, a small circular saw, so named because of the noise it makes.

buzz·wig (bŭz'wĭg/), *n.* 1. a large, bushy wig. 2. a person wearing such a wig. 3. a person of consequence.

B.V., 1. (L *Beata Virgo*) Blessed Virgin. 2. (L *bene vale*) farewell.

B.V.M., (L *Beata Virgo Maria*) Blessed Virgin Mary.

bvt., 1. brevet. 2. brevetted.

B.W.I., British West Indies.

bx., *pl.* **bxs.** box.

by (bī), *prep.* 1. near to: *a house by the river.* 2. using as a route: *he came by the highway.* 3. through or on as a means of conveyance: *he journeyed by water.* 4. to and past a point near: *he went by the church.* 5. within the compass or period of: *by day, by night.* 6. not later than: *by two o'clock.* 7. to the extent of: *larger by a half.* 8. by evidence or authority of: *by his own account.* 9. with the participation of: *regretted by all.* 10. before; in the presence of: *to swear by all that is sacred.* 11. through the agency or efficacy of: *founded by Napoleon, done by force.* 12. after; in serial order: *piece by piece.* 13. combined with in multiplication or relative dimension: *five feet by six feet.* 14. involving as unit of measure: *beef by the pound.* —*adv.* 15. near to something: *it's near by.* 16. to and past a point near something: *the car drove by.* 17. aside: *put it by for the moment.* 18. over; past: *in times gone by.* 19. **by and by,** at some time in the future; before long; presently. 20. **by and large,** in general; on the whole. —*adj.* 21. situated to one side. 22. secondary, incidental. —*n.* 23. bye. [ME; OE *bī,* stressed form answering to unstressed *be-,* c. G *bei* by, near]

—**Syn.** 11. BY, THROUGH, WITH indicate agency or means of getting something done or accomplished. BY is regularly used to denote the agent (person or force) in passive constructions: *it is done by many, destroyed by fire.* It also indicates means: *send it by airmail* WITH denotes the instrument (usually consciously) employed by an agent: *he cut it with the scissors* THROUGH designates particularly immediate agency or instrumentality or reason or motive: *through outside aid, to yield through fear, wounded through carelessness.*

---

b., blend of, blended; c., cognate with; d., dialect, dialectal; der., derived from; f., formed from; g., going back to; m., modification of; r., replacing; s., stem of; t., taken from; ?, perhaps. See the full key on inside cover.

by-, a prefix meaning: **1.** secondary; incidental, as in *by-product*. **2.** out of the way; removed, as in *byway*. **3.** near, as in *bystander*. Also, **bye-**.

by-and-by (bī′ən bī′), *n.* the (near) future.

by·bid·der (bī′bĭd′ər), *n.* a person employed to bid at an auction in order to raise the prices.

Byd·goszcz (bĭd′gŏshch), *n.* a city in NW Poland. 134,000 (1946). German, **Bromberg**.

bye (bī), *n.* Also, **by.** **1.** *Sports.* state of having no competitor in a contest where several competitors are engaged in pairs. **2.** *Golf.* the holes of a stipulated course still unplayed after the match is finished. **3.** *Cricket.* a run made on a ball not struck by the batsman. **4.** something subsidiary, secondary, or out of the way. **5. by the bye,** incidentally; by the way. —*adj.* **6.** by. [var. spelling of BY, prep., in noun use]

bye-, var. of **by-**, as in *bye-election*.

bye-bye (bī′bī′), *interj. Childish or Colloq.* good-by.

by·e·lec·tion (bī′ĭ lĕk′shən), *n. Brit.* a special election not held at the time of a general election, to fill a vacancy in Parliament. Also, **bye′-e·lec′tion.**

Bye·lo·rus·sian Soviet Socialist Republic (bĕl′ō rŭsh′ən), White Russian Soviet Socialist Republic.

Bye·lo·stok (bĕ′lō stôk′), *n.* Russian name of **Bialystok.**

by·gone (bī′gôn′, -gŏn′), *adj.* **1.** past; gone by; out of date: *bygone days.* —*n.* **2.** that which is past.

by·law (bī′lô′), *n.* **1.** a standing rule, as of a corporation or society, not in its constitution. **2.** a subsidiary law. **3.** *Brit.* an ordinance of a municipality or community. [f. BY- + LAW; r. ME *bilawe*, f. *by* town (t. Scand; cf. Dan. *by*) + *lawe* law]

by·line (bī′līn′), *n. U.S.* a line under the heading of a newspaper or magazine article giving the writer's name.

by·name (bī′nām′), *n.* **1.** a secondary name; cognomen; surname. **2.** a nickname.

Byng (bĭng), *n.* **Julian Hedworth George,** (*Viscount Byng of Vimy*) 1862–1935, British general: governor general of Canada, 1921–26.

by-pass (bī′pás′, -päs′), *n.* **1.** a road enabling motorists to avoid towns and other heavy traffic points or any obstruction to easy travel on a main highway. **2.** a secondary pipe or other channel connected with a main passage as for conducting a liquid or gas around a fixture, pipe, or appliance. **3.** *Elect.* a shunt (def. 8). —*v.t.* **4.** to avoid (obstructions, etc.) by following a by-pass. **5.** to cause (fluid, etc.) to follow such a channel. **6.** to go over the head of (one's immediate supervisor, etc.).

by-past (bī′pást′, -päst′), *adj.* bygone; past.

by-path (bī′páth′, -päth′), *n.* a private path; an indirect course or means; byway.

by-play (bī′plā′), *n.* action or speech carried on aside while the main action proceeds, esp. on the stage.

by-prod·uct (bī′prŏd′əkt), *n.* a secondary or incidental product, as in a process of manufacture.

Byrd (bûrd), *n.* **Richard Evelyn,** born 1888, rear admiral in U. S. Navy: polar explorer.

byre (bīr), *n. Brit.* a cow barn or shed. [OE *bȳre*. der. OE *būr* hut. Cf. BOWER¹]

Byrne (bûrn), *n.* **Donn** (dŏn), pen name of **Brian Oswald Donn-Byrne.**

Byrnes (bûrnz), *n.* **James Francis,** born 1879, U.S. statesman and jurist: secretary of state, 1945–47.

byr·nie (bûr′nĭ), *n.* a shirt of mail; a hauberk. [var. of ME *brynie*, t. Scand.; cf. Icel. *brynja*, c. OE *byrne* coat of mail]

by-road (bī′rōd′), *n.* a side road.

By·ron (bī′rən), *n.* **George Gordon, Lord** (*6th Baron Byron*) 1788–1824, British poet.

By·ron·ic (bī rŏn′ĭk), *adj.* **1.** of or pertaining to Lord Byron. **2.** possessing the characteristics of Byron or his poetry, esp. melancholy, melodramatic energy, etc. —**By·ron′i·cal·ly,** *adv.*

bys·sus (bĭs′əs), *n., pl.* **byssuses, byssi** (bĭs′ī). **1.** *Zool.* a collection of silky filaments by which certain mollusks attach themselves to rocks. **2.** (among the ancients) **a.** (orig.) a fine yellowish flax, or the linen made from it, as the Egyptian mummy cloth. **b.** (later) cotton or silk. [t. L, t. Gk.: m. *býssos* of Oriental orig.]

by·stand·er (bī′stăn′dər), *n.* a person present but not involved; a chance looker-on.

by-street (bī′strēt′), *n.* a separate, private, or obscure street; a side street; a byway.

By·tom (bī′tŏm), *n.* a city in S Poland: formerly in Germany. 93,000 (1946). German, **Beuthen.**

by·way (bī′wā′), *n.* **1.** a secluded, private, or obscure road. **2.** a subsidiary or obscure field of research, endeavor, etc.

by·word (bī′wûrd′), *n.* **1.** a word or phrase the frequent use of which characterizes some person or group. **2.** a word or phrase used proverbially; a common saying; a proverb. **3.** an object of general reproach, derision, scorn, etc. **4.** an epithet, often of scorn. [OE *bīword*]

by-work (bī′wûrk′), *n.* work done in addition to one's regular work, as in intervals of leisure.

Byz·an·tine (bĭz′ən tēn′, -tīn′, bĭ zăn′tĭn), *adj.* **1.** of or pertaining to Byzantium. **2.** of or pertaining to the Byzantine Empire. **3.** of or pertaining to, or resembling Byzantine architecture. —*n* **4.** a native or inhabitant of Byzantium. [t. L: m. *Byzantīnus*]

Byzantine architecture, a style of architecture developed in Byzantium and its provinces during the 5th and 6th centuries A.D., characterized by centralized plans, vaulting, and rich use of light, shade, colorful mosaics, paintings, and decoration.

Byzantine Empire, the Eastern Empire after the fall of the Western Roman Empire in A.D. 476, having Constantinople as its capital. See map just below.

Byzantine Empire, A. D. 814

By·zan·ti·um (bĭ zăn′shĭ əm, -tĭ əm), *n.* an ancient Greek city on the Bosporus, commanding the entrance to the Black Sea: Constantine built the city of Constantinople on this site, A.D. 330.

Bz., benzene.

C

C, c (sē), *n., pl.* **C's** or **Cs, c's** or **cs.** **1.** the third letter of the English alphabet. **2.** *Music.* **a.** the first, or keynote, of the C major scale, the third note of the scale of the A minor. **b.** a written or printed note representing this tone. **c.** a string, key, or pipe tuned to this note. **d.** (in solmization) the first tone of the scale of C, called *do.* **3.** (as a mark at school or college) fair; satisfactory.

C, 1. Chem. carbon. **2.** U.S. Slang. a hundred-dollar bill. **3.** (L *centum*) 100. See **Roman numerals.**

C., 1. Cape. **2.** Catholic. **3.** Celsius (=Centigrade). **4.** Celtic. **5.** Centigrade. **6.** Conservative.

c., 1. (L *circa, circiter, circum*) about. **2.** *Elect.* capacity. **3.** *Baseball.* catcher. **4.** cent; cents. **5.** *Football.* center. **6.** centigrade. **7.** centime. **8.** centimeter. **9.** century. **10.** chapter. **11.** copyright. **12.** cubic. **13.** cognate with.

ca′ (kä, kô), *v.t., v.i. Scot.* to call, esp. in the sense "to drive." [var. of CALL]

Ca, *Chem.* calcium.

ca., 1. (L *circa*) about: *ca.* A.D. 476. **2.** centiare.

C.A., 1. Central America. **2.** Chartered Accountant. **3.** Coast Artillery.

CAA, Civil Aeronautics Administration.

Caa·ba (kä′bə), *n.* Kaaba.

cab¹ (kăb), *n.* **1.** taxicab. **2.** any of various one-horse vehicles for public hire, as the hansom or the brougham. **3.** the covered part of a locomotive or truck, where the engineer or driver sits. [short for CABRIOLET]

cab² (kăb), *n.* a Hebrew measure equal to about two quarts. Also, **kab.** [t. Heb.: m. *qab* vessel]

CAB, Civil Aeronautics Board.

ca·bal (kə băl′), *n., v.,* **-balled, -balling.** —*n.* **1.** the secret schemes of a small group of plotters; an intrigue. **2.** a small group of secret plotters. —*v.i.* **3.** to form a cabal; intrigue; conspire; plot. [var. of *cabbal,* t. ML: s. *cabbāla.* See CABALA]

cab·a·la (kăb′ə lə, kə bä′-), *n.* **1.** (among certain Jewish rabbis and medieval Christians) a system of esoteric theosophy, based on a mystical interpretation of the Scriptures. **2.** any occult or secret doctrine or science. Also, **cabbala, kabala, kabbala.** [t. ML: m. *cabbāla,* t. Heb.: m. *qabbālāh* tradition] —**cab′a·lism,** *n.* —**cab′a·list,** *n.*

cab·a·lis·tic (kăb/ə lĭs/tĭk), *adj.* **1.** pertaining to the cabala. **2.** mystic; occult. Also, **cab/a·lis/ti·cal.**

ca·bal·le·ro (kăb/əl yâr/ō; *Sp.* kä/bä lyĕ/rô), *n., pl.* **-ros. 1.** a Spanish gentleman. **2.** *Southwestern U.S.* **a.** a horseman. **b.** an escort; admirer. [t. Sp., g. L *caballārius* horseman. See CAVALIER]

ca·ba·ña (kä bä/nyä), *n.* **1.** a cabin; cottage; hut. **2.** a bathhouse near water's edge. [t. Sp.]

ca·bane (kə bän/), *n. Aeron.* a mastlike structure on some early airplanes, for anchoring bracing wires. [t. F. See CABIN]

cab·a·ret (kăb/ə rā/ for 1, 2; kăb/ə rĕt/ for 3), *n.* **1.** a restaurant that provides musical or other entertainment and space for dancing by patrons. **2.** *Brit.* the entertainment; floor show. **3.** a small table, stand, or tray with a set of dishes and utensils for serving tea, coffee, etc. [t. F (prob. Gascon): cellar, der. L *cavus* hollow]

cab·bage¹ (kăb/ĭj), *n., v.,* **-baged, -baging.** *—n.* **1.** any of various cultivated varieties of the cruciferous plant *Brassica oleracea,* var. *capitata,* with short stem and leaves formed into a compact, edible head. **2.** the head of the ordinary cabbage. *—v.i.* **3.** to form a head like a cabbage. [ME *caboche,* t. F, prob. t. Pr.: m. *caboso,* der. *cap* head, g. L *caput*]

cab·bage² (kăb/ĭj), *n., v.,* **-baged, -baging.** *—n.* **1.** something stolen, esp. pieces of cloth by a tailor when making garments. *—v.t., v.i.* **2.** to steal; pilfer: *cabbaging whole yards of cloth.* [orig. uncert.]

cabbage palm, any of several palm trees with large terminal leaf buds which are eaten like cabbage, as *Sabal palmetto* of the southeastern U.S., *Roystonea oleracea* of the West Indies. Also, **cabbage tree.**

cabbage palmetto, a cabbage palm, *Sabal palmetto.*

cab·ba·la (kăb/ə lə, kə bä/-), *n.* cabala. Also, **kabbala.** **—cab/ba·lism,** *n.,* **—cab/ba·list,** *n.*

cab·by (kăb/ĭ), *n., pl.* **-bies.** *Colloq.* a cab driver.

Cab·ell (kăb/əl), *n.* **James Branch,** born 1879, U.S. novelist, essayist, and critic.

ca·ber (kā/bər), *n. Scot.* a pole or beam, esp. one thrown as a trial of strength in the Highland game of tossing the caber. [t. Gaelic: m. *cabar* pole]

Ca·be·za de Va·ca (kä bĕ/thä dĕ vä/kä), **Álvar Núñez** (äl/vär nōō/nyĕth), c1490–c1557, Spanish explorer in North and South America.

cab·e·zon (kăb/ə zŏn/; *Sp.* kä/bĕ sôn/), *n.* a large Pacific fish, *Scorpaenichthys marmoratus,* of the sculpin family.

cab·in (kăb/ĭn), *n.* **1.** a small house; hut. **2.** an apartment or room in a ship, as for passengers. **3.** (in a passenger ship) a section comprising staterooms, etc., allotted to the use of the higher fare passengers. **4.** (in a warship) the apartment used by the commanding officer or flag officer. **5.** *Aeron.* the enclosed place for the pilot, passengers, or cargo. *—v.i.* **6.** to live in a cabin. *—v.t* **7.** to confine; enclose tightly; cramp. [ME *cabane,* t. F, t. Pr.: m. *cabana,* g. LL *capanna,* of uncert. orig.] **—Syn. 1.** cot, shanty, shack. See **cottage.**

cabin boy, a boy employed to wait on the officers and passengers of a ship.

cab·i·net (kăb/ə nĭt), *n.* **1.** (*also cap.*) a council advising a sovereign or executive; the group of ministers who help to manage the government of a nation. **2.** a piece of furniture with shelves, drawers, etc., for holding or displaying valuable objects, dishes, etc. **3.** a case with compartments for precious objects, etc. **4.** a private room. **5.** *Archaic.* a small room. **6.** *Obs.* a small cabin. *—adj.* **7.** pertaining to a political cabinet: *a cabinet meeting.* **8.** pertaining to a private room. **9.** private; confidential; secret. **10.** of suitable value, beauty, or size for a private room, small case, etc.: *a cabinet edition of Milton.* [t. F., t. It.: m. *gabinetto,* ? der. *gabbia* cage, g. L *cavea;* in some senses, dim. of CABIN]

cab·i·net·mak·er (kăb/ə nĭt mā/kər), *n.* a workman who uses tools, woodworking machines, and lumber to build items for storage and household equipment.

cab·i·net·work (kăb/ə nĭt wûrk/), *n.* **1.** the making of fine furniture, etc. **2.** the product made.

ca·ble (kā/bəl), *n., v.,* **-bled, -bling.** *—n.* **1.** a thick, strong rope, often one of several wires twisted together. **2.** *Naut.* **a.** the rope or chain used to hold a vessel at anchor. **b.** cable's length. **3.** *Elect.* a stranded conductor, or a combination of conductors insulated from one another. **4.** cablegram. *—v.t.* **5.** to send (a message) by submarine cable. **6.** to send a cablegram to. **7.** to fasten with a cable. **8.** to furnish with a cable or cables. *—v.i.* **9.** to send a message by submarine cable. [ME *cable, cabel,* c. D, MLG, MHG, g *kabel,* all t. Rom.; cf. F *cable* (t. Pr.), Sp. *cable,* all g. LL *capulum* halter]

Ca·ble (kā/bəl), *n.* **George Washington,** 1844–1925, U. S. novelist and writer about Southern life.

ca·ble·gram (kā/bəl grăm/), *n.* a telegram sent by a submarine cable.

ca·ble·laid (kā/bəl lād/), *adj.* (of a rope) made by laying three plain-laid ropes together with a left-handed twist.

cable railway, a railway on which the cars (**cable cars**) are pulled by a moving cable under the roadway.

cable's length, *Naut.* a unit of length (720 ft. in the U. S. Navy; 608 ft. in the British Navy).

ca·blet (kā/blĭt), *n.* a small cable, esp. a cable-laid rope under 10 inches in circumference. [f. CABLE + -ET]

cab·man (kăb/mən), *n., pl.* **-men.** a cab driver.

cab·bob (kə bŏb/), *n.* kabob.

cab·o·chon (kăb/ə shŏn/; *Fr.* kȧ bô shôN/), *n.* a precious stone of convex hemispherical form, which has been polished but not cut into facets. [t. F, der. *caboche* head]

ca·boo·dle (kə bōō/dəl), *n. Colloq.* the (whole) lot, pack, or crowd.

ca·boose (kə bōōs/), *n.* **1.** *U.S.* a car (usually the last) on a freight train, used by the train crew. **2.** *Brit.* a kitchen on the deck of a ship; galley. [t. LG: m. *kabuus*]

Cab·ot (kăb/ət), *n.* **1. John,** c1450–1498?, Italian navigator who explored for England: discovered continent of North America in 1497. **2.** his son, **Sebastian,** 1474?–1557, British navigator and explorer.

ca·bril·ia (kə brĭl/ə), *n.* any of various serranoid fishes, as the grouper, *Epinephelus guttatus,* of the West Indies, etc. [t. Sp.: a prawn, dim. of *cabra* goat]

cab·ri·ole (kăb/rĭ ōl/), *n. Furnit.* a curved, tapering leg, often ending in the form of an animal's paw, used esp. by Chippendale. [t. F. See CAPRIOLE]

Cabrioles
A. 17th century;
B. 18th century

cab·ri·o·let (kăb/rĭ ə lā/), *n.* **1.** a type of automobile resembling a coupé, with a folding top; a convertible coupé. **2.** a light, hooded one-horse carriage with two seats. [t. F, der. *cabriole* a leap. See CAPRIOLE]

cac-, var. of **caco-.**

ca'·can·ny (kä kän/ĭ, kô-), *Orig. Scot. Slang, now Brit.* deliberate slowdown of production on the part of workers. [lit., drive gently. See CA' (CALL), v., CANNY]

Cabriolet, 19th century

ca·ca·o (kə kā/ō, -kā/ō), *n., pl.* **-caos. 1.** a small evergreen sterculiaceous tree, *Theobroma cacao,* a native of tropical America, cultivated for its seeds, the source of cocoa, chocolate, etc. **2.** the fruit and seeds of this tree. [t. Sp., t. Mex. (Aztec): m. *caca-uatl*]

cacao bean, the seed of the cacao tree.

cacao butter, a fatty substance obtained from the seeds of the cacao, used in making soaps, cosmetics, etc. Also, **cocoa butter.**

cach·a·lot (kăsh/ə lŏt/, -lō/), *n.* the sperm whale. [t. F, t. Pg.: m. *cacholote,* ult. der. L *caccabus* pot]

cache (kăsh), *n., v.,* **cached, caching.** *—n.* **1.** a hiding place, esp. one in the ground, for provisions, treasure, etc. **2.** the store of provisions, etc., so hidden. *—v.t.* **3.** to put in a cache; conceal; hide. [t. F, der. *cacher* hide]

ca·chet (kă shā/, kăsh/ā; *Fr.* kȧ shĕ/), *n.* **1.** a seal as on a letter. **2.** a distinguishing mark or character. **3.** *Pharm.* a hollow wafer for enclosing an ill-tasting medicine. **4.** *Philately.* a slogan, design, etc., stamped or printed on mail. [t. F, der. *cacher* hide]

ca·chex·i·a (kə kĕk/sĭ ə), *n. Pathol.* general ill health, with emaciation, due to a chronic disease, as cancer. Also, **ca·chex·y** (kə kĕk/sĭ). [t. NL, t. Gk.: bad condition] **—ca·chec·tic** (kə kĕk/tĭk), *adj.*

cach·in·nate (kăk/ə nāt/), *v.i.,* **-nated, -nating.** to laugh loudly or immoderately. [t. L: m. s. *cachinnātus,* pp.] **—cach/in·na/tion,** *n.*

ca·chou (kə shōō/, kä-), *n.* **1.** catechu. **2.** a pill or pastille for sweetening the breath. [t. F, t. Pg.: m. *cachu,* t. Malay: m. *kāchu* CATECHU]

ca·chu·cha (kä chōō/chä), *n. Spanish.* **1.** a lively dance. **2.** the music for it.

ca·cique (kə sēk/), *n.* **1.** a chief of an Indian clan or tribe in Mexico and the West Indies. **2.** any of a genus of American oscine passerine birds of the family *Icteridae,* including numerous species of Mexico and Central and South America, typical forms having a large bill somewhat swollen at the base. [t. Sp., t. Arawak]

cack·le (kăk/əl), *v.,* **-led, -ling,** *n.* *—v.i.* **1.** to utter a shrill, broken sound or cry, as a hen after laying an egg. **2.** to laugh brokenly. **3.** to chatter noisily. *—v.t.* **4.** to utter with cackles; express by cackling. *—n.* **5.** act or sound of cackling. **6.** idle talk. [ME *cakelen;* imit. Cf. D *kakelen,* LG *kākelen,* Swed. *kackla*] **—cack/ler,** *n.*

caco-, a word element meaning "bad," "deformed," or "unpleasant," used esp. in forming medical terms. Also, **cac-.** [t. Gk.: m. *kako-,* comb. form of *kakós* bad]

cac·o·de·mon (kăk/ə dē/mən), *n.* an evil spirit; a devil. Also, **cac·o·dae/mon.** [t. Gk.: m. *kakodaímon*]

cac·o·dyl (kăk/ə dĭl), *n. Chem.* **1.** any compound containing the $CH_3)_2As$ radical. **2.** a poisonous, ill-smelling liquid, $As_2(CH_3)_4$. [f. m.s. Gk. *kakṓdēs* ill-smelling + -YL] **—cac/o·dyl/ic,** *adj.*

cac·o·ë·thes (kăk/ō ē/thēz), *n.* an irresistible urge; mania. [t. L, t. Gk.: m. *kakóēthes* bad habit (prop. neut. of *kakóēthēs* malignant)]

cac·o·gen·ics (kăk/ə jĕn/ĭks), *n. Sociol.* dysgenics. [f. CACO- + (EU)GENICS] **—cac/o·gen/ic,** *adj.*

ca·cog·ra·phy (kə kŏg/rə fĭ), *n.* **1.** bad handwriting (opposed to *calligraphy*). **2.** incorrect spelling (opposed to *orthography*). [t. CACO- + -GRAPHY] **—ca·cog/ra·pher,** *n.* **—cac·o·graph·ic** (kăk/ə grăf/ĭk), **cac/o·graph/i·cal,** *adj.*

cac·o·mis·tle (kăk′ə mĭs′əl), n. a carnivorous animal, *Bassariscus astutus*, of Mexico and the southwestern U.S., related to the raccoon but smaller, with a sharper snout and longer tail. Also, **cac·o·mix·le** (kăk′ə mĭks′əl, -mĭk′səl). [t. Sp.: m. *cacomixtle*, t. Aztec, f. *claco* middle-sized + *miztli* lion]

Cacomistle,
Bassariscus astutus
(Total length 32 in., tail 17 in.)

ca·coph·o·nous (kə kŏf′ə nəs), adj. having a harsh sound; discordant.

ca·coph·o·ny (kə kŏf′ə nĭ), n., pl. **-nies. 1.** the quality of having a harsh sound; dissonance. **2.** *Music.* frequent use of discords of a harshness and relationship difficult to understand. [t. NL: m.s. *cacophonia*, t. Gk.: m. *kakophōnía*]

cac·ta·ceous (kăk tā′shəs), adj. *Bot.* belonging to the *Cactaceae*, or cactus family.

cac·tus (kăk′təs), n., pl. **-tuses, -ti** (-tī). any of various fleshy-stemmed plants of the family *Cactaceae*, usually leafless and spiny, often producing showy flowers, chiefly natives of the hot, dry regions of America. [t. L, t. Gk.: m. *káktos* kind of prickly plant]

ca·cu·mi·nal (kə kū′mə nəl), *Phonet.* **—adj. 1.** pronounced with the tip of the tongue curled back so as to touch the roof of the mouth above the gums; cerebral. **—n. 2.** a cacuminal consonant. [f. s. L *cacūmen* top + -AL¹]

cad (kăd), n. **1.** a contemptible, ill-bred person; one who does not behave like a gentleman. **2.** *Brit.* (*Oxford Univ. Slang*) townsman (defs. 1, 2). [short for CADDIE (def. 2)]

ca·das·tral map (kə dăs′trəl), *Survey.* a map showing boundaries and ownership of land. [cadastral, t. F, der. *cadastre* register of property, g. LL *capitāstrum*, der. L *caput* head]

cadastral survey, *Survey.* a survey relating to boundaries and subdivision of land.

ca·dav·er (kə dăv′ər, -dā′vər), n. a dead body, esp. of a human being; a corpse. [t. L] **—ca·dav′er·ic,** adj.

ca·dav·er·ine (kə dăv′ərēn), n. *Biochem.* a colorless ptomaine, $C_5H_{14}N_2$, produced by protein hydrolysis and by the putrefaction of animal tissues.

ca·dav·er·ous (kə dăv′ərəs), adj. **1.** of or like a corpse. **2.** pale; wan; ghastly. **3.** haggard and thin. **—ca·dav′er·ous·ly,** adv. **—ca·dav′er·ous·ness,** n.

cad·die (kăd′ĭ), n., v., **-died, -dying. —n. 1.** *Golf.* an attendant, hired to carry the player's clubs, find the ball, etc. **2.** a person who runs errands, does odd jobs, etc. **—v.i. 3.** to work as a caddie. Also, **caddy.** [t. F: m. *cadet* CADET]

cad·dis (kăd′ĭs), n. a kind of woolen yarn or braid.

cad·dis fly (kăd′ĭs), any of various adult insects of the order *Trichoptera*, characterized by four membranous, more or less hairy wings. Also, **cad′dice fly.** [orig. uncert.]

cad·dish (kăd′ĭsh), adj. *Chiefly Brit.* ill-bred; ungentlemanly: *caddish behavior.* **—cad′dish·ly,** adv. **—cad′dish·ness,** n.

caddis worm, the larva of the caddis fly, used as fish bait. Also, **caddis, cad·dice** (kăd′ĭs).

Cad·do·an (kăd′ōən), n. a family of North American Indian languages spoken in the upper Missouri valley in N Dakota, in the Platte valley in Nebraska (Pawnee), and in SW Arkansas and neighboring parts of Oklahoma, Texas, and Louisiana.

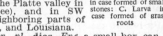
Caddis fly and worms
A, Caddis fly; B, Larva in case formed of small stones; C, Larva in case formed of grass roots

cad·dy¹ (kăd′ĭ), n., pl. **-dies,** *Eng.* a small box, can or chest, esp. one for holding tea. [var. of CATTY²]

cad·dy² (kăd′ĭ), n., pl. **-dies,** v.i., **-died, dying.** cad-die.

cade¹ (kād), n. a species of juniper, *Juniperus oxycedrus*, of the Mediterranean area, whose wood on destructive distillation yields an oily liquid (**oil of cade**) used in treating skin affections. [t. F, t. Pr.]

cade² (kād), adj. (of the young of animals) left by the mother and raised by hand: *a cade lamb.* [orig. uncert.]

ca·delle (kə děl′), n. a small blackish beetle, *Tenebrioides mauritanicus*, all stages of which are commonly destructive to cereals. [t. F, t. Pr.: m. *cadello*, g. L *catellus*, fem. *catella* little animal]

ca·dence (kā′dəns), n. **1.** rhythmic flow, as of verses; rhythm. **2.** the beat of any rhythmical movement. **3.** a fall of the voice, as in speaking. **4.** the general modulation of the voice. **5.** *Music.* a sequence of notes or chords which indicates the momentary or complete end of a composition, section, phrase, etc. **6.** *Mil.* the rate of stepping in marching: *a cadence of 120 steps per minute.* Also, **ca′den·cy.** [ME, t. F, t. It.: m. *cadenza*, g. LL *cadentia*, der. s. L *cadens*, ppr., falling] **—ca′denced,** adj.

ca·dent (kā′dənt), adj. **1.** having cadence. **2.** *Archaic.* falling. [t. L: s. *cadens*, ppr., falling]

ca·den·za (kə děn′zə), n. *Music.* an elaborate flourish or showy passage introduced near the end of an aria or in a movement of a concerto. [t. It. See CADENCE]

ca·det (kə dĕt′), n. **1.** a student training for service as an officer in the U.S. Army. (Students in the Naval Academy training for service as officers in the U.S. Navy are called **midshipmen**). **2.** a gentleman, usually a younger son, who entered the army to prepare for a subsequent commission. **3.** a younger son or brother. **4.** the youngest son. **5.** *Colloq.* a pander. [t. F, t. Gascon: m. *capdet* chief, der. *cap* head, g. L *caput*] **—ca·det′-ship, ca·det·cy** (kə dĕt′sĭ), n.

cadge (kăj), v., cadged, cadging. *Brit.* **—v.i. 1.** to sponge. **2.** to peddle or beg. **—v.t. 3.** to get by peddling or begging. **—cadg′er,** n.

cadg·y (kăj′ĭ), adj. *Scot.* **1.** cheerful. **2.** wanton.

ca·di (kä′dĭ, kā′-), n., pl. **-dis.** a judge in a Moslem community, whose decisions are based on Mohammedan religious law. Also, **kadi.** [t. Ar.: m. *qāḍī* judge]

Cad·il·lac (kăd′ə lăk′; Fr. kȧ dē yȧk′), n. **Antoine de la Mothe** (än twän′ də lȧ mōt′), 1657?–1730, French colonial governor in North America: founder of Detroit.

Cá·diz (kā′dĭz, kə dĭz′; Sp. kä′dēth, -dēs), n. a seaport in SW Spain, on the Gulf of Cádiz, a bay of the Atlantic. 87,767 (1940).

Cad·me·an (kăd mē′ən), adj. pertaining to Cadmus.

Cadmean victory, a victory in which the victor suffers as much as the vanquished.

cad·mi·um (kăd′mĭəm), n. *Chem.* a white, ductile divalent metallic element like tin in appearance: used in plating and in making certain alloys. *Symbol:* Cd; *at. wt.:* 112.41; *at. no.:* 48; *sp. gr.:* 8.6 at 20°C. [t. NL, der. L *cadmia*, t. Gk.: m. *kadmeía* (gē) Cadmean (earth), i.e. calamine (with which cadmium is usually associated)] **—cad′mic,** adj.

cadmium orange, a yellow color approaching orange.

cadmium yellow, a bright, or lemon, yellow color.

Cad·mus (kăd′məs), n. *Gk. Legend.* a Phoenician prince who planted the teeth of a dragon he had slain, from which many warriors suddenly sprang up who fought each other until only five survived. These five, led by Cadmus, founded Thebes. He is said by several accounts to have brought an alphabet from Phoenicia (or Egypt) to Greece.

Ca·dor·na (kä dôr′nä), n. **Count Luigi** (lŌŌ ē′jē), 1850–1928, Italian general: chief of staff, 1914–17.

ca·dre (kä′dər; Mil. usually kăd′rĭ), n. **1.** *Mil.* the key group of officers and enlisted men necessary to establish and train a new military unit. **2.** a framework. [t. F: frame, t. It.: m. *quadro*, g. L *quadrum* a square]

ca·du·ce·us (kə dū′sĭ əs, -dŌŌ′-), n., pl. **-cei** (-sĭ ī). **1.** the staff carried by Hermes, or Mercury, as herald or messenger of the gods. **2.** a similar staff used as an emblem of the medical profession and as the insignia of the U. S. Army Medical Corps. [t. L, t. d. Gk.: m. *kārýkeion* herald's staff] **—ca·du′ce·an,** adj.

ca·du·ci·ty (kə dū′sə tĭ, -dŌŌ′-), n. **1.** the infirmity of old age; senility. **2.** frailty; transitoriness. [t. F: m. *caducité.* See CADUCOUS]

ca·du·cous (kə dū′kəs, -dŌŌ′-), adj. **1.** *Bot.* **a.** tending to fall. **b.** deciduous; dropping off very early, as leaves. **2.** *Zool.* subject to shedding. **3.** transitory. [t. L: m. *cadūcus* falling]

cae·cil·i·an (sē sĭl′ĭ ən), n. any of the limbless and elongate burrowing amphibians of the order *Apoda.* [f. s. L *caecilia* lizard + -AN]

caeco-, a word element meaning "the caecum." Also, before vowels, **caec-.**

cae·cum (sē′kəm), n., pl. **-ca** (-kə). *Anat., Zool.* a cul-de-sac, esp., the one at the beginning of the human large intestine, bearing the vermiform appendix. See diag. under **intestine.** [t. L, neut. of *caecus* blind] **—cae′cal,** adj.

Cæd·mon (kăd′mən), n. fl. A.D. 670, English poet, the first to compose religious verse in the vernacular.

Cae·li·an (sē′lĭ ən), n. the southeastern hill of the seven hills of ancient Rome.

Caen (kän; Fr. kän), n. a seaport in N France, near the English channel. 51,471 (1946).

caeno-, var. of ceno-¹.

cae·o·ma (sē ō′mə), n. *Bot.* (in fungi) an aecium in which the spores are formed in chains and not enclosed in a peridium. [f. m.s. Gk. *kaíein* smelt + -OMA]

Caer·le·on (kärlē′ən), n. a town in SW England, in Monmouthshire: site of an ancient Roman fortress; supposed seat of King Arthur's court. 3625 (1939).

Caer·nar·von·shire (kärnär′vən shîr′, -shər), n. a county in NW Wales. 123,000 pop. (est. 1946); 569 sq. mi. *Co. seat:* Caernarvon. Also, **Caer·nar′von, Car·narvon.**

caes·al·pin·i·a·ceous (sĕz′ăl pĭn′ĭ ā′shəs, sĕs′-), adj. *Bot.* belonging to the *Caesalpiniaceae,* a family of leguminous plants including the honey locust, royal poinciana, Kentucky coffee tree, and numerous tropical genera. [f. s. NL *Caesalpinia,* the typical genus (named after Andrea *Cesalpini* (1519–1603), Italian botanist) + -ACEOUS]

Cae·sar (sē′zər), n. **1. Gaius Julius** (gā′əs jŌŌl′yəs), 102 or 100–44 B.C., Roman general, statesman, and historian: conqueror of Gaul, Britain, etc. **2.** a title of the Roman emperors from Augustus to Hadrian, and later of the heir presumptive. **3.** any emperor. **4.** a tyrant; dictator. [cf. CZAR, KAISER]

Caduceus

Caes·a·re·a (sĕs/ə rē/ə, sĕz/-), *n.* **1.** an ancient seaport in NW Israel: the Roman capital of Palestine. **2.** ancient name of **Kayseri.**

Cae·sar·e·an (sĭ zâr/ĭ ən), *n.* **1.** a Caesarean operaation or section. —*adj.* **2.** pertaining to Caesar or the Caesars: *a Caesarean conquest.* Also, **Cae·sar/i·an, Cesarean, Cesarian.**

Caesarean operation, *Surg.* the operation by which a fetus is taken from the uterus by cutting through the walls of the abdomen and uterus (supposedly performed at the birth of Caesar). Also, **Caesarean section.**

Cae·sar·ism (sē/zə rĭz/əm), *n.* absolute government; imperialism. —**Cae/sar·ist,** *n.*

cae·si·um (sē/zĭ əm), *n. Chem.* cesium.

caes·pi·tose (sĕs/pə tōs/), *adj.* cespitose.

cae·su·ra (sĭ zhŏŏr/ə, -zyŏŏr/ə), *n., pl.* **-suras, -surae** (-zhŏŏr/ē, -zyŏŏr/ē). **1.** *Eng. Pros.* a break, esp. a sense pause, usually near the middle of a verse, and marked in scansion by a double vertical line, as in *know then thyself ‖ presume not God to scan.* **2.** *Greek and Latin Pros.* a division made by the ending of a word within a foot (or sometimes at the end of a foot), esp. in certain recognized places near the middle of a verse. Also, **cesura.** [t. L: a cutting] —**cae·su/ral,** *adj.*

ca·fé (kă fā/, kə-; *Fr.* kȧ fĕ/), *n.* **1.** a restaurant. **2.** a barroom. **3.** coffee. [t. F. See COFFEE]

ca·fé au lait (kȧ fā/ ō lā/, kăf/ĭ-; *Fr.* kȧ fĕ/ ō lĕ/), *French.* **1.** hot coffee with scalded milk. **2.** a light brown.

ca·fé noir (kă fā/ nwär/; *Fr.* kȧ fĕ/ nwär/), *French.* black coffee.

caf·e·te·ri·a (kăf/ə tĭr/ĭ ə), *n.* a restaurant in which the patrons wait on themselves, carrying the food, as served out to them, to tables where it is eaten. [t. Mex. Sp.: coffee shop]

caf·feine (kăf/ēn, kăf/ĭ ĭn), *n.* a bitter crystalline alkaloid, $C_8H_{10}N_4O_2$, obtained from coffee, tea, etc., used in medicine as a stimulant, diuretic, etc. Also, **caf/fein.** [t. F: m. *caféine,* der. *café* coffee]

caf·tan (kăf/tən, kăf tän/), *n.* a long garment having long sleeves and tied at the waist by a girdle, worn under a coat in the Near East. Also, **kaftan.** [t. Turk., Pers.: m. *qaftān*] —**caf/taned,** *adj.*

cage (kāj), *n., v.,* **caged, caging.** —*n.* **1.** a boxlike receptacle or enclosure for confining birds or other animals, made with openwork of wires, bars, etc. **2.** anything that confines or imprisons; prison. **3.** something like a cage in structure or purpose. **4.** the car or enclosed platform of an elevator. **5.** any skeleton framework. **6.** *Ordn.* a steel framework upon which guns are supported. **7.** *Baseball.* **a.** a metal backstop used mainly in batting practice. **b.** a catcher's mask. **8.** *Hockey.* the structure forming the goal. —*v.t.* **9.** to put or confine in or as in a cage. [ME, t. OF, g. L *cavea* enclosure]

cage·ling (kāj/lĭng), *n.* a caged bird.

cage·y (kā/jĭ), *adj.,* **cagier, cagiest.** *Colloq.* cautious; shrewd. Also, **cag/y.** —**cag/i·ly,** *adv.* —**cag/i·ness,** *n.*

Ca·glia·ri (kä/lyä rē/), *n.* **1.** a seaport in S Sardinia. 128,933 (est. 1946). **2. Paolo** (pä/ō lō/), 1528–88, (*real name of Paul Veronese*) Venetian painter.

Ca·glios·tro (kä lyôs/trō), *n.* **Count Alessandro di** (ä/lĕs sän/drō dē), (*Giuseppe Balsamo*) 1743–95, unscrupulous Italian adventurer and supposed magician.

ca·hier (kä yā/; *Fr.* kȧ yĕ/), *n.* **1.** a number of sheets of paper or leaves of a book placed together, as for binding. **2.** a report of the proceedings of any body. [t. F, g. LL word meaning fourth, group of four sheets. See QUIRE[1]]

ca·hoot (kə hōōt/), *n. U.S. Slang.* **1. in cahoot** or **cahoots,** in partnership; in league. **2. go cahoots,** to become partners. [? t. F: m. *cahute* hut, cabin]

Cai·a·phas (kā/ə fəs, kī/-), *n.* a high priest of the Jews from sometime before A.D. 37: presided at the Council of Sadducees which condemned Jesus to death.

Cai·cos Islands (kī/kōs). See **Turks and Caicos Islands.**

cai·man (kā/mən), *n.* cayman.

Cain (kān), *n.* **1.** the first son of Adam and Eve, who murdered his brother Abel. Gen. 4. **2.** a murderer.

Caine (kān), *n.* (**Sir Thomas Henry**) **Hall,** 1853–1931, British novelist.

caino-, var. of ceno-[1].

Cai·no·zo·ic (kī/nə zō/ĭk, kā/-), *adj., n.* Cenozoic.

ca·ïque (kä ēk/), *n.* a long, narrow skiff or rowboat used on the Bosporus. [t. F, t. It.: m. *caicco,* t. Turk.]

Ça i·ra (sȧ/ ē rȧ/), *French.* it will go on (refrain of a song of the French Revolution).

caird (kârd), *n. Scot.* a traveling tinker; a tramp or vagrant. [t. Gaelic: m. *ceard* tinker]

Caird (kârd), *n.* **Edward,** 1835–1908, British philosopher and theologian.

cairn (kârn), *n.* a heap of stones set up as a landmark, monument, tombstone, etc. [Scot., t. Gaelic: m. *carn* pile of stones] —**cairned** (kârnd), *adj.*

Cai·ro (kī/rō *for 1;* kâr/ō *for 2*), *n.* **1.** the capital of Egypt, in the N part, on the E bank of the Nile: wartime conference of Roosevelt, Churchill, and Chiang Kai-shek, Nov., 1943. 1,396,500 (est. 1942) **2.** a city in S Illinois at the confluence of the Mississippi and Ohio rivers. 12,123 (1950).

cais·son (kā/sən, -sŏn), *n.* **1.** a structure in which men can work on river bottoms, etc., consisting essentially of an airtight box or chamber with an open bottom, the water being kept out by the high air pressure maintained within. **2.** a boatlike structure used as a gate for a dock or the like. **3.** pontoon (def. 3). **4.** a wooden chest containing bombs or explosives, used as a mine; an ammunition chest. **5.** an ammunition wagon. [t. F: b. *caisse* chest and earlier *casson* (t. It.: m. *cassone,* aug. of *cassa,* g. L *capsa* box). See CASE[2]]

caisson disease, *Pathol.* a disease marked by paralysis and other nervous symptoms, developed in coming from an atmosphere of high pressure, as in a caisson, to air of ordinary pressure; bends.

Caith·ness (kāth/nĕs, kāth nĕs/), *n.* a county in NE Scotland. 23,200 pop. (est. 1946); 686 sq. mi. *Co. seat:* Wick.

cai·tiff (kā/tĭf), *Archaic and Poetic.* —*n.* **1.** a base, despicable person. —*adj.* **2.** base; despicable. [ME *caitif,* t. ONF, g. LL *cactīvus,* b. L *captīvus* (see CAPTIVE) and Gallic word meaning captured]

ca·jole (kə jōl/), *v.t., v.i.,* **-joled, -joling.** to persuade by flattery or promises; wheedle; coax. [t. F: m.s. *cajoler,* ? b. *caresser* caress and *enjôler* capture] —**ca·jole/ment,** *n.* —**ca·jol/er,** *n.*

ca·jol·er·y (kə jō/lə rĭ), *n., pl.* **-eries.** persuasion by flattery or promises; wheedling; coaxing.

Ca·jun (kā/jən), *n. Louisiana.* a descendant of the exiles from Acadia; Acadian. Also, **Caijan.** [var. of ACADIAN. Cf. *Injun* for *Indian*]

caj·u·put (kăj/ə pət), *n.* **1.** a small myrtaceous tree or shrub of the Moluccas and neighboring islands, *Melaleuca cajuputi* or *minor,* a variety of *M. leucadendron.* **2.** a green, odorous oil distilled from the leaves of this tree, used as a stimulant, antispasmodic, and diaphoretic. **3.** a lauraceous tree, *Umbellularia californica,* whose aromatic leaves are used medicinally. Also, **caj/e·put.** [t. Malay, f. *kāyu* wood + *pūtih* white]

cake (kāk), *n., v.,* **caked, caking.** —*n.* **1.** a sweet baked food in loaf or layer form, made with or without shortening, usually with flour, sugar, eggs, flavoring, usually with baking powder or soda, and a liquid. **2.** a flat, thin mass of bread, esp. unleavened bread. **3.** pancake; griddlecake. **4.** a shaped or molded mass of other food: *a fish cake,* **5.** a shaped or compressed mass: *a cake of soap, ice, etc.* **6. take the cake, a.** to win the prize. **b.** to surpass all others; excel. —*v.t.* **7.** to form into a cake or compact mass. —*v.i.* **8.** to become formed into a cake or compact mass: *mud caked on his shoes.* [ME, t. Scand.; cf. Icel. *kaka;* akin to D *koek,* G *kuchen*]

cakes and ale, good things and enjoyments of life.

cake·walk (kāk/wôk/), *n.* **1.** a promenade or march, of American Negro origin, in which the couples with the most intricate or eccentric steps receive cakes as prizes. **2.** a dance based on this promenade. **3.** music for this dance. —*v.i.* **4.** to walk or dance in or as in a cakewalk. —**cake/walk/er,** *n.*

Cal., **1.** California. **2.** *Physics.* large calorie.

cal., **1.** *Physics.* small calorie. **2.** caliber.

Ca·la·bar (kăl/ə bär/, kăl/ə bär/), *n.* **1.** a river and estuary in SE Nigeria. **2.** a seaport near the mouth of this river. 16,653 (1931).

Calabar bean, the violently poisonous seed of a fabaceous African climbing plant, *Physostigma venenosum,* the active principle of which is physostigmine.

cal·a·bash (kăl/ə băsh/), *n.* **1.** any of various gourds, esp. the fruit of the bottle gourd, *Lagenaria siceraria.* **2.** any of the plants bearing them. **3.** the fruit of a bignoniaceous tree, *Crescentia cujete,* of tropical America. **4.** Also, **calabash tree.** the tree itself. **5.** the dried hollow shell of the calabash (either def. 1 or 3) used as a vessel or otherwise. **6.** a bottle, kettle, tobacco-pipe bowl, etc., made from it. **7.** *U.S.* a gourd used as a rattle, drum, etc., esp. by Indians. [t. F: m. *calebasse,* t. Sp.: m. *calabaza* gourd, ? t. Pers.: m. *kharbuz* melon]

cal·a·boose (kăl/ə bōōs/, kăl/ə bōōs/), *n. U.S. Colloq.* lockup; jail. [t. Sp.: m. *calabozo* dungeon, orig. uncert.]

Ca·la·bri·a (kə lā/brĭ ə; *It.* kä lä/bryä), *n.* **1.** a department in SW Italy. 1,900,500 pop. (est. 1942); 5828 sq. mi. **2.** an ancient district at the SE extremity of Italy.

ca·la·di·um (kə lā/dĭ əm), *n.* a plant of the araceous genus *Caladium,* mostly herbs of the American tropics, cultivated for their variegated, colorful leaves. [NL, t. Malay: m. *kelādy*]

Cal·ais (kăl/ā, -ĭs; *Fr.* kȧ lĕ/), *n.* a seaport in N France, on the Strait of Dover: the nearest French port to England; taken by Canadian forces, Sept., 1944. 50,048 (1946).

cal·a·man·co (kăl/ə măng/kō), *n., pl.* **-cos.** a glossy woolen fabric checkered or brocaded in the warp so that the pattern shows on one side only, much used in the 18th century.

cal·a·man·der (kăl/ə măn/dər), *n.* the hard wood of a tree, *Diospyros quaesita,* of Ceylon and India, used for cabinet work. [orig. uncert.]

cal·a·mine (kăl/ə mīn/, -mĭn), *n.* **1.** a mineral, hydrous zinc silicate, $ZnSiO_3(OH)_2$, an ore of zinc; hemimorphite. **2.** *Chiefly Brit.* smithsonite (def. 1). [t. F, t. ML: m. *calamina,* appar. alter. of L *cadmia.* See CADMIUM]

cal·a·mint (kăl/ə mĭnt), *n.* any plant of the labiate genus *Satureja,* esp. *S. calaminthe* and *S. nepeta.* [t. L: m. s. *calaminthē,* t. Gk.: m. *kalaminthē;* r. ME *calament,* t. F, t. ML: s. *calamentum*]

cal·a·mite (kăl/ə mīt/), *n.* a Paleozoic fossil plant. [t. NL: m. *Calamītes,* t. Gk.: m. *kalamītēs* reedlike]

---

b., blend of, blended; c., cognate with; d., dialect, dialectal; der., derived from; f., formed from; g., going back to; m., modification of; r., replacing; s., stem of; t., taken from; ?, perhaps. See the full key on inside cover.

ca·lam·i·tous (kə lăm'ə təs), *adj.* causing or involving calamity; disastrous: *a calamitous defeat.* [t. L: m. s. *calamitōsus*] —**ca·lam'i·tous·ly,** *adv.* —**ca·lam'i·tous·ness,** *n.*

ca·lam·i·ty (kə lăm'ə tĭ), *n., pl.* **-ties. 1.** grievous affliction; adversity; misery. **2.** a great misfortune; a disaster. [late ME *calamyte,* t. L: m.s. *calamitas*] —**Syn. 2.** reverse, blow, catastrophe, cataclysm. See **disaster.**

cal·a·mus (kăl'ə məs), *n., pl.* **-mi** (-mī'). **1.** the sweet flag, *Acorus calamus.* **2.** its aromatic root. **3.** any palm of the genus *Calamus,* yielding rattan, canes, etc. **4.** the hollow base of a feather; a quill. [t. L, t. Gk.: m. *kálamos* reed]

ca·lash (kə lăsh'), *n.* **1.** a light, low-wheeled carriage, either with or without a folding top. **2.** the folding top (**calash top**) of such a vehicle. **3.** a kind of hood formerly worn by women. [t. F: m. *calèche,* t. G: m. *kalesche,* t. Slavic; cf. Bohemian *kolésa*]

Calash

cal·a·ver·ite (kăl'ə vâr'īt), *n.* a silver-white mineral, gold telluride, AuTe₂, containing a little silver: an ore of gold. [f. *Calaver(as)* (county in California where first found) + -ITE¹]

cal·ca·ne·um (kăl kā'nĭ əm), *n., pl.* **-nea** (-nĭ ə). calcaneus.

cal·ca·ne·us (kăl kā'nĭ əs), *n., pl.* **-nei** (-nĭ ī'). **1.** (in man) the largest tarsal bone, forming the prominence of the heel. **2.** the corresponding bone in other vertebrates. Also, **calcaneum.** [L: heel]

cal·car (kăl'kär), *n., pl.* **calcaria** (kăl kâr'ĭ ə). *Biol.* a spur, or spurlike process. [t. L: a spur]

cal·ca·rate (kăl'kə rāt'), *adj. Biol.* furnished with a calcar or calcaria; spurred. Also, **cal'ca·rat'ed.**

cal·car·e·ous (kăl kâr'ĭ əs), *adj.* of, containing, or like calcium carbonate; chalky: *calcareous earth.* [var. of *calcarious,* t. L: m. *calcārius* pertaining to lime]

cal·ca·rif·er·ous (kăl'kə rĭf'ər əs), *adj. Biol.* bearing a spur or spurs. [f. CALCAR + -(I)-FEROUS]

cal·ce·i·form (kăl'sĭ ə fôrm', kăl sē'-), *adj. Bot.* calceolate. [f. s. L *calceus* a shoe + -(I)-FORM]

cal·ce·o·lar·i·a (kăl'sĭ ə lâr'ĭ ə), *n.* any plant of the genus *Calceolaria,* often cultivated for its slipperlike flowers. [NL, f. s. L *calceolus* slipper dim. of *calceus* shoe) | -*āria* -ARIA]

cal·ce·o·late (kăl'sĭ ə lāt'), *adj. Bot.* having the form of a shoe or slipper, as the labellum of certain orchids.

cal·ces (kăl'sēz), *n.* pl. of **calx.**

Cal·chas (kăl'kəs), *n. Gk. Legend.* a priest of Apollo who aided the Greeks in the Trojan war.

cal·cic (kăl'sĭk), *adj.* pertaining to or containing lime or calcium. [f. s. L *calx* lime + -IC]

cal·cif·er·ol (kăl sĭf'ə rōl', -rŏl'), *n. Biochem.* vitamin D₂; a fat-soluble, crystalline alcohol, C₂₈H₄₃OH, found in milk and fish-liver oils and produced by the activation of ergosterol by ultraviolet irradiation.

cal·cif·er·ous (kăl sĭf'ər əs), *adj.* **1.** *Chem.* forming salts of calcium, esp. calcium carbonate. **2.** containing calcium carbonate. [f. s. L *calx* lime + -(I)FEROUS]

cal·cif·ic (kăl sĭf'ĭk), *adj. Zool., Anat.* making or converting into salt of lime or chalk.

cal·ci·fi·ca·tion (kăl'sə fə kā'shən), *n.* **1.** a changing into lime. **2.** *Physiol.* the deposition of lime or insoluble salts of calcium and magnesium, as in a tissue. **3.** *Anat., Geol.* a calcified formation. **4.** a soil process in which the surface soil is supplied with calcium in such a way that the soil colloids are always close to saturation.

cal·ci·fy (kăl'sə fī'), *v.t., v.i.,* **-fied, -fying.** *Physiol.* to make or become calcareous or bony; harden by the deposit of calcium salts. [f. s. L *calx* lime + -(I)FY]

cal·ci·mine (kăl'sə mīn', -mĭn), *n., v.,* **-mined, -mining.** —*n.* **1.** a white or tinted wash for walls, ceilings, etc. —*v.t.* **2.** to wash or cover with calcimine. Also, **kalsomine.** [m. KALSOMINE by assoc. with CALCIUM]

cal·cine (kăl'sĭn, -sīn), *v.t., v.i.,* **-cined, -cining. 1.** to convert or be converted into calx by heat. **2.** to burn to a friable substance; roast. **3.** to oxidize by heat. **4.** to frit. [t. F: m.s. *calciner,* ult. der. L *calx* lime] —**cal·ci·na·tion** (kăl'sə nā'shən), *n.* —**cal·cin·a·to·ry** (kăl'sĭn ə tôr'ĭ, kăl'sĭn-), *adj., n.*

cal·cite (kăl'sīt), *n.* one of the commonest minerals, calcium carbonate, CaCO₃, occurring in a great variety of crystalline forms. Limestone, marble, and chalk consist largely of calcite. [f. s. L *calx* lime + -ITE¹]

cal·ci·um (kăl'sĭ əm), *n. Chem.* a silver-white divalent metal, occurring combined in limestone, chalk, gypsum, etc. *Symbol:* Ca; *at. wt.:* 40.08; *at. no.:* 20; *sp. gr.:* 1.52 at 20°C. [t. NL, f. s. L *calx* lime + -IUM]

calcium carbide, *Chem.* a crystalline compound of calcium and carbon, CaC₂, which reacts with water to form acetylene.

calcium carbonate, *Chem.* a crystalline compound, CaCO₃, occurring in nature as calcite, etc.

calcium chloride, *Chem.* a white, deliquescent powder, CaCl₂, used as a drying agent, preservative, dust preventer, etc.

calcium hydroxide, *Chem.* slaked lime, Ca(OH)₂.

calcium light, a brilliant white light produced by heating lime to incandescence in an oxyhydrogen or other hot flame.

calcium phosphate, *Chem.* any of several phosphates of calcium occurring naturally in some rocks and in animal bones, and used in medicine, industry, etc.

calc-sin·ter (kălk'sĭn'tər), *n. Mineral.* travertine. [t. G: m. *kalksinter* lime slag]

calc-tu·fa (kălk'tōō'fə), *n. Geol.* calcareous tufa. Also, **calc-tuff** (kălk'tŭf'). See **tufa** (def. 1).

cal·cu·la·ble (kăl'kyə lə bəl), *adj.* **1.** that can be calculated. **2.** that can be counted on; reliable; dependable.

cal·cu·late (kăl'kyə lāt'), *v.,* **-lated, -lating.** —*v.t.* **1.** to ascertain by mathematical methods; compute: *to calculate the velocity of light.* **2.** to make suitable, adapt, or fit for a purpose: *calculated to inspire confidence.* **3.** *U.S. Colloq. or Dial.* to intend; plan. **4.** *U.S. Colloq. or Dial.* to think; guess. —*v.i.* **5.** to make a computation; form an estimate. **6.** to count or rely (fol. by *on* or *upon).* [t. L: m.s. *calculātus,* pp., counted. See CALCULUS] —**Syn. 1.** count, figure, cast, estimate, weigh.

cal·cu·lat·ing (kăl'kyə lā'tĭng), *adj.* **1.** that performs calculations: *a calculating machine.* **2.** shrewd; cautious. **3.** selfishly scheming.

cal·cu·la·tion (kăl'kyə lā'shən), *n.* **1.** act or process of calculating; computation. **2.** result or product of calculating. **3.** an estimate based on the various facts in a case; a forecast. **4.** forethought; prior or careful planning. —**cal'cu·la'tive,** *adj.* —**Syn. 4.** circumspection, caution, wariness. See **prudence.**

cal·cu·la·tor (kăl'kyə lā'tər), *n.* **1.** one who calculates or computes. **2.** a machine that performs mathematical operations mechanically. **3.** a set of tables that facilitates calculation. [t. L]

cal·cu·lous (kăl'kyə ləs), *adj. Pathol.* characterized by the presence of calculus or stone.

cal·cu·lus (kăl'kyə ləs), *n., pl.* **-li** (-lī'), **-luses. 1.** *Math.* a method of calculation, esp. a highly systematic method of treating problems by a special system of algebraic notation. See **differential, infinitesimal,** and **integral calculus. 2.** *Pathol.* a stone or concretion found in the gall bladder, kidneys, or other parts of the body. [t. L: stone used in counting, dim. of *calx* small stone, lime]

Cal·cut·ta (kăl kŭt'ə), *n.* a seaport in NE India, in W Bengal, on the Hooghly river: capital of British India, 1772–1912. 2,108,891 (1941).

cal·dar·i·um (kăl där'ĭ əm), *n., pl.* **-daria** (-dâr'ĭ ə). (in Roman baths) a room with hot water. [t. L]

Cal·de·cott award (kŏl'də kət), an annual award for an outstanding illustrated juvenile book. [named after Randolph *Caldecott,* 1846–86, British illustrator]

Cal·de·rón de la Bar·ca (kŏl'də rōn' də lä bär'kə; *Sp.* käl'dā rôn' dā lä bär'kä), **Pedro** (pě'drō), 1600–81, Spanish dramatist and poet.

cal·dron (kôl'drən), *n.* a large kettle or boiler. Also, **cauldron.** [ME *cauderon,* t. ONF: m. *caudron,* g. deriv. of L *caldāria,* der. *cal(i)dus* hot]

Cald·well (kôld'wěl, -wəl), *n.* **Erskine** (ûr'skĭn), born 1903, U.S. author.

Ca·leb (kā'ləb), *n.* a Hebrew leader, sent as a spy into the land of Canaan. Num. 13:6, etc.

Cal·e·do·ni·a (kăl'ə dō'nĭ ə), *n. Chiefly Poetic.* Scotland. —**Cal'e·do'ni·an,** *adj., n.*

Caledonian Canal, a ship canal traversing N Scotland, extending from the Atlantic NE to the North sea. 60½ mi.

cal·e·fa·cient (kăl'ə fā'shənt), *n.* **1.** *Med.* a substance which produces a sensation of heat when applied to the body, as mustard. —*adj.* **2.** heating; warming. [t. L: s. *calefaciens,* ppr., making hot]

cal·e·fac·tion (kăl'ə făk'shən), *n.* **1.** act of heating. **2.** a heated state. [t. L: s. *calefactio*] —**cal'e·fac'tive,** *adj.*

cal·e·fac·to·ry (kăl'ə făk'tər ĭ), *adj. pl.* **-ries.** —*adj.* **1.** serving to heat. —*n.* **2.** a heated sitting room in a monastery. [t. L: m.s. *calefactōrius* having heating power]

cal·en·dar (kăl'ən dər), *n.* **1.** any of various systems of reckoning time, esp. with reference to the beginning, length, and divisions of the year: *the Gregorian calendar.* **2.** a tabular arrangement of the days of each month and week in a year. **3.** a list or register, esp. one arranged chronologically, as a list of the cases to be tried in a court. **4.** *Obs.* a guide or example. —*v.t.* **5.** to enter in a calendar; register. [t. L: m. s. *calendārium* account book, der. *calendae* calends; r. ME *calender,* t. AF]

calendar day, the period from one midnight to the following one.

calendar month. See **month** (def. 1).

calendar year. See **year** (def. 1).

cal·en·der (kăl'ən dər), *n.* **1.** a machine in which cloth, paper, or the like is smoothed, glazed, etc., by pressing between revolving cylinders. —*v.t.* **2.** to press in a calender. [t. F: m. *calandre,* prob. t. Pr.: m. *calandra,* ult. g. L *cylindrus* CYLINDER] —**cal'en·der·er,** *n.*

Cal·en·der (kăl'ən dər), *n. (often l.c.)* (in Mohammedan countries) one of an order of mendicant dervishes founded in the 14th century. [t. Pers.: m. *qalandar*]

ăct, āble, dâre, ärt; ĕbb, ēqual; ĭf, īce; hŏt, ōver, ôrder, oil, bŏŏk, ōōze, out; ŭp, ūse, ûrge; ə = a in alone; ch, chief; g, give; ng, ring; sh, shoe; th, thin; ŧh, that; zh, vision. See the full key on inside cover.

cal·ends (kăl/əndz), *n.pl.* (in the Roman calendar) the first day of the month. Also, **kalends**. [ME *kalendes* (rarely sing.), OE *cālend* (beginning of) a month, t. L: s. *calendae* (usually *kalendae*)]

ca·len·du·la (kəlĕn/jələ), *n.* **1.** any plant of the asteraceous genus *Calendula*, esp. *C. officinalis*, a common marigold. **2.** the dried florets of this plant, used in medicine as a vulnerary, etc. [NL, dim. of L *calendae* CALENDS; so called as flowering almost every month of the year.]

cal·en·ture (kăl/ənchər, -chŏor/), *n.* a violent fever with delirium, affecting persons in the tropics, esp. on shipboard. [t. F, t. Sp.: m. *calentura* heat, der. L *calēre* be hot]

ca·le·sa (kälĕ/sä), *n.* (in the Philippines) a calash.

ca·les·cent (kəlĕs/ənt), *adj.* growing warm; increasing in heat. [t. L: s. *calescens*, ppr., growing hot] —**ca·les/-cence,** *n.*

calf[1] (kăf, käf), *n., pl.* **calves. 1.** the young of the cow or of other bovine mammals (in cattle usually under one year of age). **2.** the young of certain other animals, as the elephant, seal, and whale. **3.** calfskin leather. **4.** *Colloq.* an awkward, silly boy or man. **5.** a mass of ice detached from a glacier, iceberg, or floe. **6. kill the fatted calf,** to prepare an elaborate welcome. [d. OE, r. OE *cealf*, c. G *kalb*]

calf[2] (kăf, käf), *n., pl.* **calves.** the fleshy part of the back of the human leg below the knee. [ME, t. Scand.; cf. Icel. *kálfi*]

calf love, temporary infatuation of a boy or girl for a person of the opposite sex.

calf·skin (kăf/skĭn/, käf/-), *n.* **1.** the skin or hide of a calf. **2.** leather made from it.

Cal·ga·ry (kăl/gərĭ), *n.* a city in SW Canada, in Alberta. 88,904 (1941).

Cal·houn (kălhōōn/, kə-), *n.* **John Caldwell,** 1782-1850, vice-president of the U.S., 1825-32.

Ca·li (kä/lē), *n.* a city in SW Colombia. 127,471 (est. 1943).

Cal·i·ban (kăl/əbăn/), *n.* **1.** the ugly, beastlike slave of Prospero in Shakespeare's *The Tempest.* **2.** a man who has a degraded, bestial nature.

cal·i·ber (kăl/əbər), *n.* **1.** the diameter of something of circular section, as a bullet, or esp. that of the inside of a tube, as the bore of a gun. **2.** *Ordn.* the diameter of the bore of a gun taken as a unit in stating its length: *a fifty caliber 1¼-inch gun.* **3.** degree of capacity or ability; personal character. **4.** degree of merit, or importance; quality. Also, *esp. Brit.,* **cal/i·bre.** [t. F: m. *calibre*, t. It.: m. *calibro*, t. Ar.: m. *qālib* mold]

cal·i·brate (kăl/əbrāt/), *v.t.,* **-brated, -brating.** to determine, check, or rectify the graduation of (any instrument giving quantitative measurements). —**cal/-i·bra/tion,** *n.* —**cal/i·bra/tor,** *n.*

cal·i·ces (kăl/əsēz/), *n.* pl. of **calix.**

ca·li·che (kälē/chĕ), *n. Geol.* **1.** a surface deposit consisting of sand or clay impregnated with crystalline salts, such as sodium nitrate or sodium chloride. **2.** a horizon of calcium or mixed carbonates in soils of semiarid regions. [Amer. Sp., der. *cal* lime, g. L *calx*]

cal·i·cle (kăl/ə kəl), *n.* a cuplike depression or formation, as in corals. [t. L: m. s. *caliculus,* dim. of *calix* cup]

cal·i·co (kăl/əkō/), *n., pl.* **-coes, -cos,** *adj.* —*n.* **1.** *U.S.* a printed cotton cloth, superior to percale. **2.** *Brit.* white cotton cloth. **3.** (*orig.*) cotton cloth imported from India. —*adj.* **4.** made of calico. **5.** resembling printed calico; spotted; piebald. [named after CALICUT]

cal·i·co·back (kăl/əkōbăk/), *n.* a brilliantly marked red-and-black bug, *Murgantia histrionica,* destructive to cabbages; the harlequin cabbage bug.

calico bass, a fresh-water food fish, *Pomoxys sparoides,* of the eastern and central U.S.

calico bush, the mountain laurel, *Kalmia latifolia.* Also, **calico flower, calico tree.**

Cal·i·cut (kăl/əkŭt/), *n.* a seaport in SW India, in Madras province. 126,352 (1941).

ca·lif (kā/lĭf, kăl/ĭf), *n.* caliph.

Calif., official abbreviation for California.

cal·if·ate (kăl/əfāt/,-fĭt), *n.* caliphate.

Cal·i·for·nia (kăl/əfôr/nyə, -fôr/nĭə), *n.* **1.** a State in the W United States, on the Pacific coast. 10,586,223 pop. (1950); 158,693 sq. mi. *Cap.:* Sacramento. *Abbr.:* Calif. **2.** Gulf of, an arm of the Pacific, extending NW between the W coast of Mexico and the peninsula of Lower California. ab. 750 mi. long. —**Cal/i·for/nian,** *adj., n.*

California condor, a very rare bird of prey, *Gymnogyps californianus,* inhabiting a restricted part of California. It is the largest land bird of North America.

California fuchsia. See fuchsia (def. 2).

California poppy, a papaveraceous pale-green herb with showy yellow flowers, *Eschscholtzia californica;* the State flower of California.

ca·lig·i·nous (kəlĭj/ənəs), *adj. Rare.* misty; dim; dark. [t. L: m.s. *cālīginōsus* misty] —**ca·lig·i·nos·i·ty** (kəlĭj/ənŏs/ə tĭ), *n.*

Ca·lig·u·la (kəlĭg/yələ), *n.* **Gaius Caesar** (gā/əs sē/zər), A.D. 12-41, Roman emperor, A.D. 37-41.

cal·i·pash (kăl/əpăsh/, kăl/əpăsh/), *n.* that part of a turtle next to the upper shield, a greenish gelatinous substance. Also, **callipash.** [orig. uncert.]

cal·i·pee (kăl/əpē/, kăl/əpē/), *n.* that part of a turtle next to the lower shield, consisting of a yellowish gelatinous substance. [cf. CALIPASH]

cal·i·per (kăl/əpər), *n.* **1.** (*usually pl.*) a tool, in its simplest form having two legs and resembling a draftsman's compass, used for obtaining inside and outside measurements. —*v.t.* **2.** to measure with calipers. Also, **calliper.** [var. of CALIBER]

A B C
Calipers
A. Outside calipers; B. Inside calipers; C. Spring adjusting calipers

caliper rule, a caliper with one jaw fixed to, or integral with, a graduated straight bar on which the other jaw slides.

ca·liph (kā/lĭf, kăl/ĭf), *n.* successor (usually of Mohammed): a title for the head of the Moslem state. Also, **calif, kaliph, khalif, khalifa.** [ME *califfe,* t. OF: m. *calife,* t. ML: m. *calīpha,* t. Ar.: m. *khalīfa* successor, vicar]

cal·iph·ate (kăl/əfāt/, -fĭt), *n.* the rank, jurisdiction or government of a caliph. Also, **califate.**

cal·i·sa·ya (kăl/əsā/yə), *n.* the medicinal bark of the tree *Cinchona calisaya.* [t. S. Amer. Sp., prob. t. Kechua]

cal·is·then·ics (kăl/əsthĕn/ĭks), *n.* **1.** (*construed as sing.*) the practice or art of calisthenic exercises; exercising the muscles for the purpose of gaining health, strength, and grace of form and movement. **2.** (*construed as pl.*) light gymnastic exercises designed to develop grace as well as organic vigor and health. Also, **callisthenics.** [f. *cali-* (var. of CALLI-) + s. Gk. *sthénos* strength + -ICS] —**cal/is·then/ic,** *adj.*

ca·lix (kā/lĭks, kăl/ĭks), *n., pl.* **calices** (kăl/əsēz/). *Rom. Cath. Ch.* a chalice (def. 2). [t. L: cup]

calk[1] (kôk), *v.t.* **1.** to fill or close (a seam, joint, etc.), as in a boat. **2.** to make (a vessel) watertight by filling the seams between its planks with oakum or other material driven snug. **3.** to drive the edges of (plating) together to prevent leakage. **4.** to fill or close the seams or crevices of (a tank, window, boiler, etc.) in order to make watertight, airtight, steamtight, etc. Also, **caulk.** [ME *caulke(n),* t. ONF: m. *cauquer,* g. L *calcāre* tread, press]

calk[2] (kôk), *n.* **1.** a projection on a horseshoe to prevent slipping. **2.** *U.S.* a similar device on the heel or sole of a shoe. —*v.t.* **3.** to provide with calks. **4.** to injure with a calk. [ult. t. L: m. s. *calx* heel, or m. *calcāneum* heel, or m. *calcar* spur]

calk·er (kô/kər), *n.* **1.** one who calks ships, etc. **2.** a calking tool or device. Also, **caulker.** [f. CALK[1] + -ER[1]]

call (kôl), *v.t.* **1.** to cry out in a loud voice. **2.** (of a bird or animal) to utter its characteristic cry. **3.** to announce; proclaim: *call a halt.* **4.** to read over (a roll or list) in a loud tone. **5.** to attract the attention of by loudly uttering something. **6.** to rouse from sleep as by a call: *call me at 8 o'clock.* **7.** to command or request to come; summon: *the boy was called by his mother, call a cab, call a witness.* **8.** to summon to an office, duty, etc.: *call someone to the ministry.* **9.** to convoke or convene, as a meeting or assembly: *call Congress into session.* **10.** to bring under consideration or discussion: *call a case.* **11.** to telephone to. **12.** to attract or lure (wild birds, etc.) by a particular cry or sound. **13.** *Baseball.* **a.** to terminate (a game) because of darkness, rain, etc. **b.** to indicate (a pitched ball) as a strike. **14.** to demand payment or fulfillment of (a loan, etc.). **15.** to demand (bonds, etc.) for payment. **16.** to give a name to; name: *his parents named him James but the boys call him Jim.* **17.** to designate as something specified: *he called me a liar.* **18.** to reckon; consider; estimate: *to call a thing a success, I call that mean.* **19.** *Billiards.* to request (the player) to state his intended shot. **20.** *Poker.* to require (a player) to show his hand, after equaling his bet.

—*v.i.* **21.** to speak loudly, as to attract attention; shout; cry: *who calls so loudly?* **22.** to make a short visit; stop at a place on some errand or business: *to call at a house or place for a person or thing, or upon a person.* **23.** to telephone a person. **24.** *Poker.* to demand a showing of hands. **25.** Special verb phrases are: **call away,** to order off; divert: *necessity called him.* **call back, 1.** to recall; summon or bring back. **2.** to revoke; retract: *call back an oath.* **call down, 1.** to invoke from above; cause to descend. **2.** to reprimand; scold. **call for, 1.** to go and get. **2.** to require; demand; need: *the occasion calls for a cool head.* **call forth,** to bring or summon into action. **call in, 1.** to collect: *call in debts.* **2.** to withdraw from circulation: *call in gold notes.* **3.** to invite: *call in neighbors.* **call into being,** to create. **call on, 1.** to appeal to: *call on a person for a song.* **2.** to make a short visit to: *to call on friends.* **call out, 1.** to utter in a loud voice. **2.** to summon into service: *call out the militia.* **3.** to bring into play; elicit: *call out new abilities.* **call up, 1.** to bring into action, discussion, etc. **2.** to require payment of. **3.** to communicate (with) by telephone. **4.** to recollect: *call up my sorrows afresh.* —*n.* **26.** a cry or shout. **27.** the cry of a bird or other animal. **28.** an instrument for imitating this cry and attracting or luring the animal. **29.** a summons or

---

b., blend of, blended; c., cognate with; d., dialect, dialectal; der., derived from; f., formed from; g., going back to; m., modification of; r., replacing; s., stem of; t., taken from; ?, perhaps. See the full key on inside cover.

signal sounded by a bugle, bell, etc. **30.** a note blown on a horn to encourage the hounds. **31.** a short visit: *to make a call on someone.* **32.** a summons; invitation; bidding. **33.** *Theat.* a notice of rehearsal posted by the stage manager. **34.** a mystic experience of divine appointment to a vocation or service. **35.** a request or invitation to become pastor of a church, a professor in a university, etc. **36.** a need or occasion: *he had no call to say such things.* **37.** a demand or claim: *to make a call on a person's time.* **38.** a roll call. **39.** *Poker.* a demand for the showing of hands. **40.** a contract which permits its purchaser to buy a certain amount of stock, etc., at a specified price for a limited period of time. **41.** a demand for payment of an obligation, esp. where payment is at the option of the creditor. **42. call for margin,** a demand for payment upon the balance owed a stock or commodity broker because of the shrinking value of the security. **43. on call,** payable or subject to return without advance notice.
[ME *calle*(n), (cf. OE *calla* herald), r. OE *ceallian*, c. Icel. *kalla*]
—**Syn. 7.** CALL, INVITE, SUMMON imply requesting the presence or attendance of someone at a particular place. CALL is the general word: *to call a meeting.* To INVITE is to ask someone courteously to come as a guest, a participant, etc., leaving him free to refuse: *to invite guests to a concert, invite them to contribute to a fund.* SUMMON implies sending for someone, using authority or formality in requesting his presence, and (theoretically) not leaving him free to refuse: *to summon a witness, members of a committee.*

cal·la (kăl'ə), *n.* **1.** a plant of the genus *Zantedeschia* (or *Richardia*), native in Africa, esp. *Z. aethiopicum,* (**calla lily**), which has a large white spathe enclosing a yellow spadix, and is familiar in cultivation. **2.** an araceous plant, *Calla palustris,* of cold marshes of Europe and North America, with heart-shaped leaves. [t. NL, ? special use of L *calla* plant name]

call·a·ble (kôl'ə bəl), *adj.* **1.** that may be called. **2.** subject to redemption upon notice, as a bond. **3.** subject to payment on demand, as money loaned.

cal·lant (kă'lənt), *n. Scot. and N. Eng.* a lad; a boy. Also, **cal·lan** (kă'lən). [t. D or LG: m. *kalant*, t. F: m. *chaland* customer]

Cal·la·o (kä yä'ô), *n.* a seaport in W Peru, near Lima. 84,438 (1940).

call·board (kôl'bôrd'), *n.* a bulletin board, as in a theater for notices of rehearsal periods, etc.

call·boy (kôl'boi'), *n.* **1.** a boy who summons actors just before they go on the stage. **2.** a bellboy.

call·er[1] (kô'lər), *n.* **1.** one that calls. **2.** one who makes a short visit. [f. CALL + -ER[1]] —**Syn. 2.** See **visitor.**

cal·ler[2] (kăl'ər, kä'lər), *adj.* **1.** *Scot. and N. Eng.* fresh, as fish, vegetables, etc. **2.** fresh and cool. [? d. var. of *calver* fresh]

Cal·les (kä'yĕs), *n.* **Plutarco Elías** (plōō tär'kō ĕ lē'-äs), 1877–1945, Mexican general and statesman: president of Mexico, 1924–28.

calli-, a word element meaning "beauty." [t. Gk.: m. *kalli-*, comb form. of *kállos*]

cal·lig·ra·phy (kə lĭg'rə fĭ), *n.* **1.** beautiful handwriting. **2.** handwriting; penmanship. [t. Gk.: m. s. *kalligraphía*] —**cal·lig'ra·pher, cal·lig'ra·phist,** *n.* —**cal·li·graph·ic** (kăl'ə grăf'ĭk), *adj.*

call·ing (kô'lĭng), *n.* **1.** act of one that calls. **2.** vocation, profession, or trade. **3.** summons. **4.** invitation. **5.** convocation.

calling card, a small card bearing one's name, used on various social or business occasions.

cal·li·o·pe (kə lī'ə pē'; for 1, also kăl'ĭ ōp'), *n.* **1.** a harsh musical instrument consisting of a set of steam whistles, played from a keyboard. **2.** (*cap.*) *Gk. Myth.* the Muse of heroic poetry. [t. L, t. Gk.: m. *kalliópē*, lit. beautiful-voiced]

cal·li·op·sis (kăl'ĭ ŏp'sĭs), *n.* a coreopsis.

cal·li·pash (kăl'ə păsh', kăl'ə păsh'), *n.* calipash.

cal·li·per (kăl'ə pər), *n., v.t.* caliper.

cal·lis·then·ics (kăl'əs thĕn'ĭks), *n.* calisthenics. —**cal'lis·then'ic,** *adj.*

Cal·lis·to (kə lĭs'tō), *n. Gk. Myth.* a nymph attendant on Artemis, punished for an amour with Zeus by being changed into a bear, and slain by Artemis.

call loan, a loan repayable on demand.

call market, the market for lending call money.

call money, funds available or loaned on call.

cal·los·i·ty (kə lŏs'ə tĭ), *n., pl.* -ties. **1.** a callous condition. **2.** *Bot.* a. a hardened or thickened part of a plant. **3.** callus (def. 1a).

cal·lous (kăl'əs), *adj.* **1.** hardened. **2.** hardened in mind, feelings, etc. **3.** having a callus; indurated, as parts of the skin exposed to friction. —*v.i., v.t.* **4.** to become or make hard or callous. [t. L: m. s. *callōsus* hard-skinned] —**cal'lous·ly,** *adv.* —**cal'lous·ness,** *n.* —**Syn. 1.** See **hard.**

cal·low (kăl'ō), *adj.* **1.** immature or inexperienced: *a callow youth.* **2.** (of a young bird) featherless; unfledged. [OE *calu, calw-,* c. G *kahl*] —**cal'low·ness,** *n.*

call rate, interest charge on call loans.

call slip, a printed form used by a library patron to request the use of a particular book.

call to quarters, *U.S. Army.* a bugle call fifteen minutes before taps which warns soldiers to go to quarters.

cal·lus (kăl'əs), *n., pl.* -luses, *v.* —*n.* **1.** *Pathol., Physiol.* a. a hardened or thickened part of the skin; a callosity. b. a new growth of osseous matter at the ends of a fractured bone, serving to unite them. **2.** *Bot.* a. the tissue which forms over the wounds of plants, protecting the inner tissues and causing healing. b. a deposit on the perforated area of a sieve tube. —*v.i.* **3.** to make a callus. [t. L: hardened skin]

calm (käm), *adj.* **1.** without motion; still; *a calm sea.* **2.** not windy. **3.** free from excitement or passion; tranquil: *a calm face, voice, manner, etc.* —*n.* **4.** freedom from motion or disturbance; stillness. **5.** absence of wind. **6.** freedom from agitation, excitement, or passion; tranquillity; serenity. —*v.t.* **7.** to make calm: *calm fears, calm an excited dog, etc.* —*v.i.* **8.** to become calm (usually fol. by *down*). [ME *calme,* t. OF, t. It.: m. *calma* (as if orig., heat of the day, hence, time for resting, quiet), g. LL b. Gk. *kaûma* burning heat and L *calēre* be hot] —**calm'ly,** *adv.* —**calm'ness,** *n.*
—**Syn. 1.** quiet, motionless. **3.** placid, peaceful, serene, self-possessed. CALM, COLLECTED, COMPOSED, COOL imply the absence of agitation. CALM implies an unruffled state, esp. under disturbing conditions: *calm in a crisis.* COLLECTED implies complete command of oneself, usually as the result of an effort: *he remained collected in spite of the excitement.* One who is COMPOSED has or has gained dignified self-possession: *pale but composed.* COOL implies the apparent absence of strong feeling or excitement, esp. in circumstances of danger or strain: *so cool that he seemed calm.* **7.** still, quiet, tranquilize. —**Ant. 3.** agitated, excited.

cal·ma·tive (kăl'mə tĭv, kä'mə-), *adj., n. Med.* sedative.

calm·y (kä'mĭ), *adj. Poetic.* calm. [f. CALM, n. + -Y[1]]

cal·o·mel (kăl'ə mĕl', -məl), *n. Pharm.* mercurous chloride, Hg_2Cl_2, a white, tasteless solid, used in medicine as a mercurial, a purgative, etc. [t. F, short for *calomélas,* f. Gk.: m. s. *kalós* beautiful + *mélās* black]

ca·lor·ic (kə lôr'ĭk), *n.* **1.** heat. **2.** *Old Physics.* a hypothetical imponderable fluid whose presence in matter determined its thermal state. —*adj.* **3.** pertaining or relating to heat. **4.** (of engines) driven by heated air. [t. F: m. *calorique,* der. L *calor* heat. Cf. CALORIE] —**ca·lor·ic·i·ty** (kăl'ə rĭs'ə tĭ), *n.*

cal·o·rie (kăl'ə rĭ), *n.* **1.** *Physics.* a. gram calorie or small calorie, the quantity of heat required to raise the temperature of one gram of water one degree centigrade, usually specified as determined at, or close to, 16°C. b. kilogram calorie or large calorie, a quantity of heat, equal to 1000 gram calories. **2.** *Physiol.* a. a unit equal to the large calorie, used to express the heat output of an organism and the fuel or energy value of food. b. a quantity of food capable of producing such a unit of energy. Also, **calory.** [t. F, der. L *calor* heat]

cal·o·rif·ic (kăl'ə rĭf'ĭk), *adj.* pertaining to conversion into heat. [t. L: s. *calorificus* heat-producing]

cal·o·rim·e·ter (kăl'ə rĭm'ə tər), *n. Physics, etc.* an apparatus for measuring quantities of heat. [f. L *calor* heat + -(I)METER]

cal·o·rim·e·try (kăl'ə rĭm'ə trĭ), *n. Physics.* the measurement of heat. —**cal·o·ri·met·ric** (kăl'ə rə mĕt'rĭk, kə lôr'-, -lŏr'-), **cal·o·ri·met'ri·cal,** *adj.* —**cal·o·ri·met'ri·cal·ly,** *adv.*

cal·o·ry (kăl'ə rĭ), *n., pl.* -ries. calorie.

ca·lotte (kə lŏt'), *n.* a plain skullcap, as that worn by Catholic ecclesiastics. [t. F, dim. of *cale* cap. Cf. CAUL]

cal·o·yer (kăl'ə yər, kə loi'ər), *n.* a monk of the Greek Orthodox Church. [t. F, t. It.: m. *caloiero,* t. LGk.: m. *kalógēros* venerable, monk]

cal·pac (kăl'păk), *n.* a large black cap of sheepskin or other heavy material, worn by Armenians, Turks, etc. Also, **cal'pack.** [t. Turk.: m. *qālpāq*]

cal·trop (kăl'trəp), *n.* **1.** *Bot.* a. any of various plants having spiny heads or fruit, esp. of the genera *Tribulus* and *Kallstroemia.* b. the star thistle. c. an Old World plant, *Tribulus terrestris.* d. the water chestnut. **2.** *Mil.* an iron ball with four projecting spikes so disposed that when the ball is on the ground one of them always points upward, used to obstruct the passage of cavalry, etc. Also, **cal'trap, cal'trop.** [ME *cal·ketrappe,* OE *col(te)træppe, calcatrippe* spiny plant, appar. f. m. s. L *calx* heel + m. ML *trappa* trap]

Caltrop (def. 2)

cal·u·met (kăl'yə mĕt', kăl'yə mĕt'), *n.* a long, ornamented tobacco pipe used by North American Indians on ceremonial occasions, esp. in token of peace. [t. d. F, g. dim. of L *calamus* reed]

ca·lum·ni·ate (kə lŭm'nĭ āt'), *v.t.,* -ated, -ating. to make false and malicious statements about; slander. [t. L: m.s. *calumniātus,* pp.] —**ca·lum'ni·a'tor,** *n.*

ca·lum·ni·a·tion (kə lŭm'nĭ ā'shən), *n.* **1.** act of calumniating; slander. **2.** a calumny.

ca·lum·ni·ous (kə lŭm'nĭ əs), *adj.* of, involving, or using calumny; slanderous; defamatory. Also, **ca·lum·ni·a·to·ry** (kə lŭm'nĭ ə tôr'ĭ). —**ca·lum'ni·ous·ly,** *adv.*

cal·um·ny (kăl'əm nĭ), *n., pl.* -nies. **1.** a false and malicious statement designed to injure someone's reputation. **2.** slander. [t. L: m.s. *calumnia*]

cal·var·i·a (kăl vâr'ĭ ə), *n.* the dome of the skull. [t. L. See CALVARY]

Cal·va·ry (kăl'və rĭ), *n., pl. for 2* -ries. **1.** Golgotha, the place where Jesus was crucified. Luke 23:33. **2.** (*l.c.*) a sculptured representation of the Crucifixion, usually erected in the open air. [t. L: m. s. *calvāria* skull, used to render the Aramaic name. See GOLGOTHA]

calve (kăv, käv), v., **calved, calving.** —*v.i.* **1.** to give birth to a calf. **2.** (of a glacier, iceberg, etc.) to give off a detached piece. —*v.t.* **3.** to give birth to (a calf). **4.** to give off (a detached piece). [ME *calve(n)*, der. *calf* calf; r. OE *cealfian*, der. *cealf* calf]

Cal·vé (kál vě´), n. **Emma** (ěm´ə; *Fr.* ěm mà´), (*Emma de Roquer Gaspari*), 1863?–1942, French operatic soprano.

Cal·vert (kăl´vərt), n. **1. Sir George**, (*1st Baron Baltimore*) c1580–1632, British statesman: projector of colony of Maryland. **2.** his son, **Leonard**, 1606–47, first governor of the British colony of Maryland.

calves (kăvz, kävz), n. pl. of **calf.**

Cal·vin (kăl´vĭn), n. **John**, 1509–64, religious reformer and theologian, born in France: leader of the Protestant Reformation in Geneva, Switzerland.

Cal·vin·ism (kăl´və nĭz´əm), n. **1.** *Theol.* **a.** the doctrines and church practices taught by John Calvin, who emphasized the sovereignty of God, predestination, the authority of Scriptures, presbyterian polity, and strict church discipline. **b.** the doctrines of later theologians who accepted Calvin's teachings with various modifications. **2.** adherence to these doctrines. —**Cal´vin·ist**, n., adj. —**Cal´vin·is´tic, Cal´vin·is´ti·cal**, adj.

cal·vi·ti·es (kăl vĭsh´ĭ ēz´), n. baldness. [t. L]

calx (kălks), n., pl. **calxes, calces** (kăl´sēz). **1.** the oxide or ashy substance which remains after metals, minerals, etc., have been thoroughly roasted or burned. **2.** lime. [t. L: small stone, lime]

cal·y·ces (kăl´ə sēz´, kā´lə-), n. pl. of **calyx.**

cal·y·cine (kăl´ə sĭn, -sīn´), adj. pertaining to or resembling a calyx. Also, **ca·lyc·i·nal** (kə lĭs´ə nəl).

cal·y·cle (kăl´ə kəl), n. *Bot.* a set of bracts resembling an outer calyx. [t. L: m. s. *calyculus*, dim. of *calyx* calyx]

Cal·y·don (kăl´ə dŏn´), n. an ancient city in W Greece, in Aetolia. —**Cal·y·do·ni·an** (kăl´ə dō´nĭ ən), adj.

Calydonian hunt, *Gk. Legend.* the pursuit, by Meleager and a band of heroes, of a savage boar (**Calydonian boar**) sent by Artemis to ravage Calydon.

Ca·lyp·so (kə lĭp´sō), n., pl. **-sos. 1.** *Gk. Legend.* a sea nymph who for seven years detained Odysseus on the island of Ogygia. **2.** (*l.c.*) a terrestrial orchid of the genus *Calypso* (*Cytherea*), widespread in the Northern Hemisphere, having a single variegated purple, yellow, and white flower. —*adj.* **3.** (*l.c.*) pertaining to a musical style of West Indian Negro origin, influenced by jazz, usually having a flexible accent in its topical, often improvised, lyrics.

ca·lyp·tra (kə lĭp´trə), n. *Bot.* **1.** the hood which covers the lid of the capsule in mosses. **2.** a hoodlike part connected with the organs of fructification in flowering plants. **3.** a root cap. [t. NL, t. Gk.: m. *kalýptra* veil]

ca·lyp·tro·gen (kə lĭp´trə jən), n. *Bot.* the histogen layer which develops into the root cap.

ca·lyx (kā´lĭks, kăl´ĭks), n., pl. **calyxes, calyces** (kăl´ə sēz´, kā´lə-). **1.** *Bot.* the outermost group of floral parts, usually green; the sepals. **2.** *Anat., Zool.* a cuplike part. [t. L, t. Gk.: m. *kályx* covering, husk, calyx]

Floral calyxes
A. Trisepalous calyx; B. Gamosepalous (united) calyx; C. Bilabiate calyx

cam (kăm), n. *Mach.* a device for converting regular rotary motion into irregular rotary or reciprocating motion, etc., commonly consisting of an oval-, needle-, or heart-shaped, or other specially shaped flat piece, an eccentric wheel, or the like, fastened on and revolving with a shaft, and engaging with other mechanism. [t. D or LG: m. *kam, kamm* cog. See COMB]

Cams
A. Elliptical cam; B. Cant wheel; C. Heart cam

Ca·ma·cho (kä mä´chô), n. **Manuel Avila.** See **Ávila Camacho.**

Ca·ma·güey (kä´mä gwā´), n. a city in central Cuba. 78,458 (1943).

ca·ma·ra·de·rie (kä´mə rä´də rĭ), n. comradeship; close friendship. [t. F]

cam·a·ril·la (kăm´ə rĭl´ə; *Sp.* kä´mä rē´lyä), n. a group of private advisers; a cabal; a clique. [t. Sp., dim. of *cámara* CHAMBER]

cam·ass (kăm´ăs), n. **1.** any of various plants of the lily family (genus *Camassia*), esp. *C. quamash*, a species in western North America, with sweet, edible bulbs. **2.** death camass. Also, **cam´as.** [t. N Amer. Ind., from Chinook jargon, der. *chamas* sweet (Nootka)]

cam·ber (kăm´bər), v.t., v.i. **1.** to arch slightly; bend or curve upward in the middle. —n. **2.** a slight arching or convexity above, as of a ship's deck. **3.** a slightly arching piece of timber. **4.** *Aeron.* the rise of the curve of an airfoil, usually expressed as the ratio of the rise to the length of the chord of the airfoil. [t. d. F: m. *cambre*, adj., bent, g. L *camur*]

Cam·ber·well (kăm´bər wĕl´, -wəl), n. a residential borough of S London, England. 169,470 (est. 1946).

cam·bist (kăm´bĭst), n. **1.** a dealer in bills of exchange. **2.** an expert in the science of monetary exchange. **3.** a manual giving the moneys, weights, and measures of different countries, with their equivalents. [t. F: m. *cambiste*, t. It.: m. *cambista*, der. *cambiare* CHANGE]

cam·bi·um (kăm´bĭ əm), n. *Bot.* a layer of soft cellular tissue (or meristem) between the bark and wood (or phloem and xylem) in plants, from which new bark and new wood originate. [t. LL: exchange]

Cam·bo·di·a (kăm bō´dĭ ə), n. a state in SW French Indo-China. 3,046,000 pop. (1936); 69,884 sq. mi. (1940). *Cap.:* Pnom-Penh. French, **Cam·bodge** (kän bôj´).

cam·bo·gi·a (kăm bō´jĭ ə), n. *Pharm.* gamboge (def. 1).

Cam·bon (kän bôn´), n. **1. Jules Martin** (zhül mártăn´), 1845–1935, French diplomat and administrator. **2. Pierre Paul** (pyěr pōl) 1843–1924, French diplomat.

Cam·brai (kän brě´), n. a city in N France: battles, 1917, 1918. 26,129 (1946).

Cam·bri·a (kăm´brĭ ə), n. medieval name of Wales.

Cam·bri·an (kăm´brĭ ən), adj. **1.** *Stratig.* pertaining to the oldest geological period or a system of rocks characterized by presence of numerous well-preserved fossils. **2.** pertaining to Cambria (Wales). —n. **3.** *Stratig.* the period or system comprising the first main division of the Paleozoic era or rocks. **4.** a Welshman.

cam·bric (kăm´brĭk), n. a cotton or linen fabric of fine close weave, usually white. [t. Flem.: m. *Kameryk* CAMBRAI]

cambric tea, a mixture of hot water and milk, with sugar and, sometimes, a little tea.

Cam·bridge (kām´brĭj), n. **1.** a city in E England. 78,370 (est. 1946). **2.** the university located there. **3.** a city in E Massachusetts, near Boston. 120,740 (1950). **4.** Cambridgeshire.

Cam·bridge·shire (kām´brĭj shĭr´, -shər), n. a county in E England. 154,000 pop. (est. 1946); 492 sq. mi. *Co. seat:* Cambridge. Also, **Cambridge.**

Cam·by·ses (kăm bī´sēz), died 522 B.C., son of Cyrus the Great and father of Persia, 529–522 B.C.

Cam·den (kăm´dən), n. a city in SW New Jersey: a port on the Delaware. 124,555 (1950).

came [1] (kām), v. pt. of **come.**

came [2] (kām), n. a slender grooved bar of lead for holding together the pieces of glass in windows of latticework or stained glass. [appar. var. of *calm* mold for casting metallic objects]

cam·el (kăm´əl), n. **1.** either of two large Old World ruminant quadrupeds of the genus *Camelus*, used as beasts of burden: **a.** the **arabian camel**, or dromedary, with one hump (*C. dromedarius*). **b.** the **Bactrian camel**, with two humps (*C. bactrianus*). **2.** *Civ. Eng. Naut.* a pontoon (def. 2). [OE, t. L: s. *camēlus*, t. Gk.: m. *kámēlos*; of Semitic orig.]

cam·el·eer (kăm´ə lĭr´), n. **1.** a camel driver. **2.** a soldier on a camel.

cam·el·hair (kăm´əl hâr´), n. **1.** camel's hair. —adj. **2.** camel's-hair.

ca·mel·ia (kə mēl´yə, -mē´lĭ ə), n. a plant, *Camellia* (or *Thea*) *japonica*, native in Asia, with glossy evergreen leaves and white, pink, red, or variegated waxy roselike flowers, familiar in cultivation. [named after G. J. Kamel, Moravian Jesuit missionary]

Ca·mel·o·pard (kə mĕl´ə pärd´), n. **1.** Also, **Ca·mel·o·par·da·lis** (kə mĕl´ə pär´də lĭs). *Astron.* a northern constellation. **2.** (*l.c.*) *Obsolesc.* a giraffe. [t. LL: s. *camēlopardus*, L *camēlopardālis*, t. Gk.: m. *kamēlopárdalis* giraffe]

Cam·e·lot (kăm´ə lŏt´), n. the legendary site of King Arthur's palace and court, probably near Exeter, England.

camel's hair, 1. the hair of the camel, used for cloth, painters' brushes, certain oriental rugs, etc. **2.** cloth made of this hair, or of a substitute, usually tan in color.

camel's-hair (kăm´əlz hâr´), adj. **1.** made of camel's hair. **2.** (of a painter's brush) made from the tail hairs of squirrels.

Cam·em·bert (kăm´əm bâr´; *Fr.* kà mäN bĕr´), n. a rich, yellowish variety of soft cheese.

Ca·me·nae (kə mē´nē), n.pl. (in early Roman religion) prophetic nymphs of the springs and fountains, later identified with the Greek Muses.

cam·e·o (kăm´ĭ ō´), n., pl. **cameos. 1.** an engraving in relief upon a gem, stone, etc., with differently colored layers of the stone often utilized to produce a background of one hue and a design of another. **2.** a gem, stone, etc., so engraved. [t. It.: m. *cammeo*; prob. of Oriental orig.]

cam·er·a (kăm´ərə, kăm´rə), n., pl. **-eras** for *1–2*, **-erae** (-ərē´) for *3*. **1.** a photographic apparatus in which sensitive plates or film are exposed, the image being formed by means of a lens. **2.** (in a television transmitting apparatus) the device in which the picture to be televised is formed before it is changed into electrical impulses. **3.** a judge's private room. **4. in camera, a.** *Law.* in the privacy of a judge's chambers. **b.** privately. [t. L: arch, vault, ML *chamber*, treasury. Cf. CHAMBER]

cam·er·al (kăm/ər əl), *adj.* pertaining to a camera (esp. defs. 3, 4).

camera lu·ci·da (lōō/sə də), *Optics.* an optical instrument by which the image of an external object is projected on a sheet of paper, etc., upon which it may be traced. [t. LL: light chamber]

cam·er·a·man (kăm/ər ə măn/, kăm/rə-), *n.*, *pl.* **-men.** a man who operates a camera, esp. a motion picture camera.

camera ob·scu·ra (ŏb skyōōr/ə), a darkened boxlike device in which images of external objects, received through an aperture, as with a convex lens, are exhibited in their natural colors on a surface arranged to receive them: used for sketching, exhibition purposes, etc. [t. LL: dark chamber]

Cam·e·roon (kăm/ə rōōn/), *n.* an active volcano in S Cameroons: the highest peak on the W coast of Africa. 13,370 ft.

Cam·e·roons (kăm/ə rōōnz/), *n.* **1.** German, **Kamerun.** a region in W Africa: a former German protectorated; divided into two mandates (now trusteeships) of Cameroons (to Gt. Britain) and Cameroun (to France), 1919. **2.** a British trusteeship in the NW part of this region: administered as a part of Nigeria. 886,000 pop. (est. 1941). 34,081 sq. mi.

Ca·me·roun (kăm rōōn/), *n.* a territory in W Africa, under the trusteeship of France. 2,341,000 pop. (1936); 162,900 sq. mi. *Cap.:* Yaoundé.

cam·i·on (kăm/Ĭ ən; *Fr.* kȧ myôN/), *n.* **1.** a strongly built cart or wagon for transporting heavy loads. **2.** a truck, as for military supplies. [t. F; orig. uncert.]

cam·i·sole (kăm/ə sōl/), *n.* **1.** *Chiefly Brit.* an ornamental underbodice, worn under a thin outer bodice. **2.** a woman's dressing jacket. **3.** a sleeved jacket or jersey once worn by men. **4.** a type of strait jacket. [t. F, t. Sp.: m. *camisola*, dim. of *camisa* shirt]

cam·let (kăm/lĭt), *n.* **1.** a durable waterproof cloth used for cloaks, etc. **2.** apparel made of this material. **3.** a rich fabric, apparently orig. made of camel's or goat's hair, formerly in use. [var. of *camelot*, t. F; r. late ME *chamelot*, t. OF, prob. t. Ar.: m. *khamla*, der. *khaml* nap]

Cam·maerts (kä/märts), *n.* **Émile** (ĕ mēl/), born 1878, Belgian poet.

Cam·o·ëns (kăm/ō ĕns/), *n.* **Luis Vaz de** (lōō ēsh/ väzh də), 1524?–80, Portuguese poet. Portuguese, **Ca·mões** (kə mô Ĭnsh/).

cam·o·mile (kăm/ə mīl/), *n.* **1.** any plant of the asteraceous genus *Anthemis,* esp. *A. nobilis* (the common camomile of Europe and of gardens elsewhere), an herb with strongly scented foliage and flowers which are used medicinally. **2.** any of various allied plants, as *Matricaria Chamomilla* (**German camomile**). Also, **chamomile.** [ME *camemille,* t. L: m. *chamomilla,* var. of *chamaemēlon,* t. Gk.: m. *chamaímēlon* earth apple]

Ca·mor·ra (kə môr/ə, -môr/o; *It.* kä môr/rä), *n.* **1.** a Neapolitan secret society, first publicly known about 1820, which developed into a powerful political organization, and has been associated with blackmail, robbery, etc. **2.** (*l.c.*) some similar society or group. [t. It., t. Sp.: dispute, quarrel] —**Ca·mor/rism,** *n.* —**Ca·mor/rist,** *n.*

cam·ou·flage (kăm/ə fläzh/), *n., v.,* **-flaged, -flaging.** —*n.* **1.** *Mil.* act, art, means, or result of disguising things to deceive the enemy, as by painting or screening objects so that they are lost to view in the background, or by making up objects which, from a distance, have the appearance of fortifications, guns, roads, etc. **2.** disguise; deception; false pretense. —*v.t.* **3.** to disguise, hide, or deceive by means of camouflage: *camouflaged ships.* [t. F, der. *camoufler* disguise]

cam·ou·fleur (kăm/ə flûr/; *Fr.* kȧ mōō flœr/), *n. Mil.* one who conceals military objects by camouflage.

camp (kămp), *n.* **1.** a place where an army or other body of persons is lodged in tents or other temporary means of shelter. **2.** the tents, etc., collectively. **3.** the persons sheltered. **4.** an encamping, or camping out. **5.** a body of troops, etc., camping and moving together. **6.** army life. **7.** a group of people favoring the same ideals, doctrines, etc. **8.** any position in which ideals, doctrines, etc., are strongly entrenched. —*v.i.* **9.** to establish or pitch a camp. **10.** to live temporarily in a tent (often fol. by *out*). **11.** to take a position stubbornly: *camped in front of the office of the president.* —*v.t.* **12.** to put or station (troops, etc.) in a camp; shelter. [t. F, t. It.: m. *campo* field, g. L *campus*] —**camp/er,** *n.*

Cam·pa·gna (käm pän/yə; *It.* käm pä/nyä), *n.* **1.** a low plain surrounding the city of Rome, Italy. **2.** (*l.c.*) any flat open plain; champaign. [t. It., g. L *campānia* level plain]

cam·paign (kăm pān/), *n.* **1.** the military operations of an army in the field during one season or enterprise. **2.** any course of aggressive activities for some special purpose: *a sales campaign.* **3.** the competition by rival political candidates and organizations for public office. —*v.i.* **4.** to serve in, or go on, a campaign. [t. F: m. *campagne,* ult. der. L *campus* plain] —**cam·paign/er,** *n.*

Cam·pa·ni·a (käm pä/nyə; *It.* käm pä/nyä), *n.* a department in SW Italy. 3,698,695 pop. (1936); 5214 sq. mi.

cam·pa·ni·le (kăm/pə nē/lĬ; *It.* käm/pä nē/lĕ), *n., pl.* **-niles, -nili** (-nē/lē). a bell tower (often a detached structure). [t. It., der. *campana* bell, g. L]

cam·pa·nol·o·gy (kăm/pə nŏl/ə jĬ), *n.* **1.** the study of bells. **2.** the principles of bell founding, bell ringing, etc. [t. NL: m.s. *campanologia,* f. s. LL *campāna* bell + -(o)*logia* -(o)LOGY] —**cam/pa·nol/o·gist, cam/pa·nol/o·ger,** *n.*

cam·pan·u·la (kăm păn/yə lə), *n.* any plant of the genus *Campanula,* as the harebell or the Canterbury bell; a bellflower. [t. NL, dim. of LL *campāna* bell]

cam·pan·u·la·ceous (kăm păn/yə lā/shəs), *adj. Bot.* belonging to the *Campanulaceae,* or campanula family of plants.

cam·pan·u·late (kăm păn/yə lĬt, -lāt/), *adj.* bell-shaped, as a corolla.

Camp·bell (kăm/bəl, kăm/əl), *n.* **1. Colin** (kŏl/Ĭn), (*Baron Clyde*) 1792–1863, British general. **2. Thomas,** 1777–1844, British poet and editor.

Camp·bell-Ban·ner·man (kăm/bəl băn/ər mən, kăm/əl-), *n.* **Sir Henry,** 1836–1908, prime minister of Great Britain, 1905–08.

Camp·bell·ite (kăm/bə lĬt/, kăm/ə-), *n.* a member of the body of Christians known as Disciples of Christ. [f. *Campbell* + -ITE[1]; named after the Rev. Alexander Campbell, founder]

camp chair, a light folding chair.

camp·craft (kămp/kräft/, -kräft/), *n.* the art of outdoor camping.

Cam·pe·che (käm pĕ/chĕ), *n.* **1.** a state in SE Mexico, on the peninsula of Yucatán. 90,460 pop. (1940); 19,672 sq. mi. **2.** the capital of this state: a seaport. 23,277 (1940). **3. Gulf of,** the SW part of the Gulf of Mexico.

camp·fire (kămp/fĬr/), *n.* **1.** a fire in a camp for warmth or cooking. **2.** a reunion of soldiers, scouts, etc.

campfire girl, a member of an organization for girls from 12 to 20 (**Campfire Girls of America**), building good character, citizenship, and health.

camp follower, a person who follows a camp or an army without official connection, as a washerwoman, prostitute, etc.

camp·ground (kămp/ground/), *n.* a place for a camp or a camp meeting.

cam·phene (kăm/fēn, kăm fēn/), *n. Chem.* a hydrocarbon, $C_{10}H_{16}$, present in certain essential oils.

cam·phol (kăm/fŏl, -fōl), *n. Chem.* borneol.

cam·phor (kăm/fər), *n.* **1.** a whitish, translucent, crystalline, pleasant-odored terpene ketone, $C_{10}H_{16}O$, obtained chiefly from the camphor tree and used in medicine, the manufacture of celluloid, etc. **2.** any of various similar substances. [t. ML: s. *camphora,* t. Ar.: m. *kāfūr,* t. Malay: m. *kāpūr*; r. ME *caumfre,* t. AF] —**cam·phor·ic** (kăm fôr/Ĭk, -fŏr/-), *adj.*

cam·phor·ate (kăm/fə rāt/), *v.t.,* **-ated, -ating.** to impregnate with camphor.

camphor ball, a moth ball, usually consisting of naphthalene, and sometimes of camphor, etc.

camphor tree, **1.** a lauraceous tree. *Cinnamomum camphora,* of Japan, Formosa, China, etc., yielding camphor. **2.** any of various similar trees, as *Dryobalanops aromatica* of Borneo, etc., which yields borneol.

Cam·pi·nas (kəm pē/nəs, käm-), *n.* a city in S Brazil. 78,914 (1940).

cam·pi·on (kăm/pĬ ən), *n.* any of certain plants of the pink family, of the genera *Silene* or *Lychnis,* as the **rose campion,** *L coronaria.* [prob. ult. der. L *campus* field]

Cam·pi·on (kăm/pĬ ən), *n.* **Thomas,** 1567–1620, British song writer and poet.

camp meeting, a religious gathering, usually lasting for some days, held in a tent, in the open air, or in an open pavilion.

cam·po (käm/pō, käm/-), *n., pl.* **-pos.** (in South America) an extensive, nearly level, grassy plain with some scattered herbaceous growth and occasional stunted trees. [t. Pg., Sp., g. L *campus* field, plain]

Cam·po·bel·lo (käm/pō bĕl/ō), *n.* a Canadian island in the Bay of Fundy: a part of New Brunswick.

Cam·po For·mio (käm/pō fôr/myô), a village in NE Italy: treaty between France and Austria, 1797. Modern, **Cam·po·for·mi·do** (käm/pō fôr/mē dô/).

cam·po san·to (käm/pō sän/tô), *Italian.* a cemetery. [It.: sacred field]

camp·stool (kămp/stōōl/), *n.* a light folding seat.

cam·pus (kăm/pəs), *n. U.S.* the grounds of a college or other school. [t. L: field]

cam·shaft (kăm/shăft/, -shäft/), *n. Mach.* a shaft with cams.

can[1] (kăn; *unstressed* kən), *v., pres. sing.* 1. **can;** 2. **can** or (*Archaic*) **canst;** 3. **can;** *pt.* **could.** —*aux.* **1.** to know how to; be able to; have the ability, power, right, qualifications, or means to: *you can lift the box.* **2.** *Colloq.* may; have permission: *Can I speak to you a moment?* —*v.t., v.i.* **3.** *Obs.* to know. [ME and OE *cann, can,* 1st and 3d pers. sing. pres. ind. (pret. *cūthe*) of *cunnan,* c. G *können.* Cf. KEN and KNOW]

—**Syn. 1.** CAN denotes power or ability to do something: *the child can talk.* MAY refers to probability, possibility, or permission: *our son may* (possibility or probability) *play football Saturday if the doctor says he may* (permission). The two words are often confused in asking or granting permission; MAY is the better usage, though CANNOT is often used informally in denying permission: *May I go? Yes, you may go* (or, *you may not or cannot go*). CANNOT may also be used to express either extreme negation of ability or negation of probability: *I cannot work such long hours, I cannot* (possibly) *be mistaken.* **2.** CAN BUT, CANNOT BUT are formal expressions suggesting that there is no possible alternative to doing a certain thing. CAN BUT is equivalent to informal CAN ONLY: *we can but do our best* (1. and *must* make the attempt; or 2. and no more than that should be expected of us). CANNOT BUT (do) is equivalent to informal CAN'T HELP (doing): *we cannot but protest against injustice,* (we are under moral obligation to do so). CANNOT HELP BUT is common in familiar use, but is not otherwise considered good usage.

can² (kăn), *n., v.,* **canned, canning.** —*n.* **1.** a container for food, milk, etc., usually of sheet iron coated with tin or other metal. **2.** a receptacle for garbage, ashes, etc. **3.** *Chiefly Brit.* a container for holding or carrying liquids. **4.** a drinking cup; tankard. **5.** *U.S. Colloq.* a depth bomb. —*v.t.* **6.** to put in a can or jar, esp. a sealed one. **7.** *U.S. Slang.* to dismiss; fire. [ME and OE *canne,* c. G *kanne* can, pot, mug]

Can., 1. Canada. 2. Canadian.

Ca·na (kā'nə), *n.* an ancient town in N Israel, in the province of Galilee: the scene of Christ's first miracle. John 2:1, 11.

Ca·naan (kā'nən), *n.* **1.** the ancient region, included in modern Palestine, lying between the Jordan, the Dead Sea, and the Mediterranean: the land promised by God to Abraham. Gen. 12. **2.** Palestine. **3.** any land of promise. **4.** *Bible.* the descendant of Ham, the son of Noah. Gen. 10. [t. Heb.: m. *kana'an*]

Canaan, c1450 B. C.

Ca·naan·ite (kā'nənīt'), *n.* **1.** a member of the Semitic people inhabiting Palestine at the time of the Hebrew conquest. **2.** a group of Semitic languages, including Hebrew and Phoenician, spoken chiefly in ancient Palestine and Syria. —**Ca'naan·it'ish, Ca·naan·it·ic** (kā'nə nĭt'ĭk), *adj.*

Can·a·da (kăn'ədə), *n.* a dominion of the British Commonwealth of Nations, in N North America. 11,506,655 pop. (1941); 3,690,410 sq. mi. *Cap.:* Ottawa.

Canada balsam, a transparent turpentine obtained from the balsam fir, *Abies balsamea,* used for mounting objects for the microscope.

Canada goose, the common wild goose, *Branta canadensis,* of North America.

Canada jay, a plain grayish bird, *Perisoreus canadensis.*

Canada lily, a lily, *Lilium canadense,* with several nodding flowers and recurved sepals, common in NE U.S.

Canada thistle, an Old World herb, *Cirsium arvense,* with small purple or white flower heads, now a troublesome weed in North America.

Ca·na·di·an (kə nā'dĭ ən), *adj.* **1.** of Canada or its people. —*n.* **2.** a native or inhabitant of Canada.

Canadian River, a river flowing from the Rocky Mountains in NE New Mexico E to the Arkansas river in E Oklahoma. 906 mi.

ca·naille (kə nāl'; *Fr.* kå nä'y), *n.* riffraff; the rabble. [t. F, t. It.: m. *canaglia,* der. *cane* dog, g. L *canis*]

ca·nal (kə năl'), *n., v.,* **-nalled, -nalling** or **-naled, -naling.** —*n.* **1.** an artificial waterway for navigation, irrigation, etc. **2.** a long, narrow arm of the sea penetrating far inland. **3.** a tubular passage or cavity, esp. in an animal or plant, for food, air, etc.; a duct. **4.** *Astron.* one of the long, narrow, dark lines on the surface of the planet Mars. **5.** *Obs.* a channel or watercourse. —*v.t.* **6.** to make a canal through. **7.** to furnish with canals. [late ME, t. L: s. *canālis* canal, groove, channel]

canal boat, a craft built to fit canal locks.

can·a·lic·u·lus (kăn'ə lĭk'yə ləs), *n., pl.* **-li** (-lī'). *Anat., Zool.* a small canal or tubular passage, as in bone. [t. L, dim. of *canālis* channel. See CANAL] —**can·a·lic'u·lar, can·a·lic·u·late** (kăn'ə lĭk'yə lĭt, -yə lāt'), **can·a·lic'u·lat'ed,** *adj.*

ca·nal·ize (kə năl'īz, kăn'ə līz'), *v.t.* **-ized, -izing. 1.** to make a canal or canals through. **2.** to convert into a canal. **3.** to divert into certain channels; give a certain direction to or provide a certain outlet for. —**ca·nal·i·za·tion** (kə năl'ə zā'shən, kăn'ə lə-), *n.*

canal rays, *Physics.* the rays (consisting of positively charged ions) which pass through a hole in the cathode, in a direction away from the anode, when an electric discharge takes place in a vacuum tube.

Canal Zone, a strip of territory 10 mi. wide across the Isthmus of Panama, on both sides of the Panama Canal, excluding the cities of Panama and Colón: perpetually leased to and governed by the U.S. 52,822 pop. (1950); 553 sq. mi.

can·a·pé (kăn'ə pĭ, -pā'; *Fr.* kå nå pĕ'), *n.* a thin piece of bread, toast, etc., spread or topped with cheese, caviar, anchovies, or other appetizing foods. [t. F. See CANOPY]

ca·nard (kə närd'; *Fr.* kå när'), *n.* **1.** a false story, report, or rumor; a hoax. **2.** *Aeron.* a very early kind of airplane, having a pusher engine with the rudder and elevator assembly in front of the wings. [t. F: lit., duck]

Ca·na·rese (kă'nə rēz', -rēs'), *n., adj.* Kanarese.

ca·nar·y (kə när'ĭ), *n., pl.* **-naries. 1.** Also, **canary bird,** a well-known cage bird, a kind of finch, *Serinus canarius,* native of the Canary Islands, and orig. of a brownish or greenish color, but through modification in the domesticated state now usually a light, clear yellow. **2.** Also, **canary yellow,** a light, clear yellow

color. **3.** a sweet white wine of the Canary Islands, resembling sherry. **4.** *Obs.* a lively French and English dance, similar to the jig. [named after the islands]

canary grass, any of various grasses of the genus *Phalaris,* as *P. canariensis,* native in the Canary Islands, which yields a seed used as food for cage birds, or *P. arundinacea* (**reed canary grass**), a species widely used throughout the Northern Hemisphere as fodder.

Canary Islands, a group of mountainous islands in the Atlantic, near the NW coast of Africa, forming two provinces of Spain. 680,294 pop. (1940); 2894 sq. mi. Also, **Canaries.** [t. F: m. *Canarie* (the principal island), t. Sp.: m. *Canaria,* in L *canāria insula* isle of dogs]

canary seed, birdseed.

ca·nas·ta (kə năs'tə), *n.* a card game of the rummy family in which the main object is to meld sets of seven or more cards. [t. Sp.: ? m. *canastra* kind of basket. Cf. CANISTER]

Can·ber·ra (kăn'běrə, -bərə) *n.* the capital of Australia, in the SE part, in the Australian Capital Territory. 7325 (1933).

Can·by (kăn'bĭ), *n.* Henry Seidel (sī'del), born 1878, U.S. author and critic.

can·can (kăn'kăn; *Fr.* kän kän'), *n.* a disorderly form of quadrille marked by extravagant leaping and kicking, which came into vogue about 1830 at the public balls of Paris. [t. F]

can·cel (kăn'səl), *v.,* **-celed, -celing** or (*esp. Brit.*) **-celled, -celling,** *n.* —*v.t.* **1.** to cross out (writing, etc.) by drawing a line or lines over. **2.** to make void; annul. **3.** to mark or perforate (a postage stamp, streetcar transfer, etc.) to render it invalid for re-use. **4.** to neutralize; counterbalance; compensate for. **5.** *Math.* to eliminate by striking out (a factor common to both terms of a fraction, equivalent quantities on opposite sides of an equation, etc.). **6.** *Print.* to omit. —*n.* **7.** act of canceling. **8.** *Print.* omission. **9.** *Print., Bookbinding.* an omitted part, or the replacement for it. [late ME, t. L: m.s. *cancellāre* to make like a lattice, to strike out a writing] —**can'cel·er,** *esp. Brit.,* **can'cel·ler,** *n.*

—**Syn. 1, 3.** CANCEL, DELETE, ERASE, OBLITERATE refer to indicating that something is no longer to be considered usable or in force. To CANCEL is to cross something out by stamping a mark over it, drawing lines through it, and the like: *to cancel a stamp, a word.* To DELETE is to omit something from written matter or from matter to be printed, often in accordance with a printer's symbol indicating this is to be done: *to delete part of a line.* To ERASE is to remove by scraping or rubbing: *to erase a capital letter.* To OBLITERATE is to blot out entirely, so as to remove all sign or trace of: *to obliterate a record, an inscription.* **2.** countermand, revoke, rescind.

can·cel·late (kăn'sə lāt'), *adj. Anat.* of spongy or porous structure, as bone. Also, **can'cel·lous.** [t. L: m.s. *cancellātus,* pp., latticed. See CANCEL]

can·cel·la·tion (kăn'sə lā'shən), *n.* **1.** act of canceling. **2.** the marks or perforations made in canceling. **3.** something canceled.

can·cer (kăn'sər), *n.* **1.** *Pathol.* a malignant and invasive growth or tumor, esp. one originating in epithelium, tending to recur after excision and to metastasize to other sites. **2.** any evil condition or thing that spreads destructively. **3.** (*cap.*) *Astron.* a constellation and a sign of the zodiac, represented by the form of a crab. See illus. under **zodiac.** [t. L: crab, tumor] —**can'cer·ous,** *adj.*

Cancellate bone structure

Can·cer (kăn'sər), *n.* **Tropic of.** See **tropic** (1a, 3a).

can·croid (kăng'kroid), *adj.* **1.** *Pathol.* resembling a cancer, as certain tumors. **2.** *Zool.* resembling a crab. —*n.* **3.** *Pathol.* a form of cancer of the skin.

can·de·la·bra (kăn'də lä'brə, -lä'-), *n.* **1.** pl. of **candelabrum. 2.** (*properly pl. but taken as sing. with pl.* **-bras**) candelabrum.

can·de·la·brum (kăn'də lä'brəm, -lä'-), *n., pl.* **-bra** (-brə), **-brums.** an ornamental branched candlestick. [t. L, der. *candēla* candle]

can·dent (kăn'dənt), *adj.* glowing with heat; at a white heat. [t. L: s. *candens,* ppr., shining]

can·des·cent (kăn dĕs'ənt), *adj.* glowing; incandescent. [t. L: s. *candescens,* ppr., beginning to glow] —**can·des'cence,** *n.* —**can·des'cent·ly,** *adv.*

Can·di·a (kăn'dĭə), *n.* **1.** Greek, **Herakleion.** a seaport in N Crete. 42,557 (1940). **2.** Crete.

can·did (kăn'dĭd), *adj.* **1.** frank; outspoken; open and sincere: *candid account.* **2.** honest; impartial: *candid mind.* **3.** white. **4.** clear; pure. [t. L: s. *candidus* white, sincere] —**can'did·ly,** *adv.* —**can'did·ness,** *n.* —**Syn. 1.** See **frank.**

can·di·date (kăn'də dāt', -dĭt), *n.* **1.** one who seeks an office, an honor, etc. **2.** one who is selected by others as a contestant for an office, etc. [t. L: m.s. *candidātus* clad in white, as a Roman candidate for office] —**can·di·da·cy** (kăn'də də sĭ); *Brit.,* **can·di·da·ture** (kăn'də də chər); **can'di·date·ship',** *n.*

candid camera, a small handy camera, esp. one having a fast lens for unposed or informal pictures.

can·died (kăn′dĭd), *adj.* **1.** impregnated or incrusted with or as with sugar. **2.** crystallized, as sugar. **3.** honeyed or sweet; flattering.

Can·di·ot (kăn′dĭ ŏt′), *adj.* **1.** Cretan. —*n.* **2.** a native or inhabitant of Crete. Also, **Can·di·ote** (kăn′dĭ ōt′).

can·dle (kăn′dəl), *n.*, *v.*, **-dled, -dling.** —*n.* **1.** a long, usually slender, piece of tallow, wax, etc., with an embedded wick, burned to give light. **2.** something like this in appearance or use. **3.** *Photom.* **a.** the luminous intensity of a standard candle. **b. standard candle,** a candle of specified size, composition, character of wick, and rate of burning, whose flame is taken as a unit of luminous intensity. **c. international candle,** a unit of luminous intensity established by international agreement, based on the standard candle but defined in terms of specially constructed electric lamps. —*v.t.* **4.** to examine (esp. eggs for freshness) by holding between the eye and a light. [OE *candel,* t. L: s. *candēla*] —**can′dler,** *n.*

can·dle·ber·ry (kăn′dəl bĕr′ĭ), *n., pl.* **-ries. 1.** the wax myrtle (genus *Myrica*). **2.** its berry. **3.** the candlenut.

can·dle·fish (kăn′dəl fĭsh′), *n.* a small edible fish, *Thaleichthys pacificus,* of the northwestern coast of America, of the smelt family, with flesh so oily that when the fish is dried it may be used as a candle.

can·dle·foot (kăn′dəl fŏŏt′), *n.* a foot-candle.

can·dle·hold·er (kăn′dəl hōl′dər), *n.* candlestick.

can·dle·light (kăn′dəl līt′), *n.* **1.** the light of a candle. **2.** artificial light. **3.** twilight; dusk.

Can·dle·mas (kăn′dəl məs), *n.* an ecclesiastical festival, Feb. 2, in honor of the presentation of the infant Jesus in the Temple and the purification of the Virgin Mary. Candles are blessed on this day. [ME *candel-masse,* OE *candelmæsse.* See CANDLE, -MAS]

can·dle·nut (kăn′dəl nŭt′), *n.* **1.** the oily fruit or nut of a euphorbiaceous tree, *Aleurites moluccana,* of the South Sea Islands, etc., the kernels of which, when strung together, are used as candles by the natives. **2.** the tree itself.

can·dle·pin (kăn′dəl pĭn′), *n. Tenpins.* **1.** a slender, candle-shaped pin. **2.** (*pl.*) a game using such pins.

candle power, *Photom.* **1.** the illuminating capacity or luminous intensity of a standard candle. **2.** luminous intensity (of a light) or illuminating capacity (of a lamp or other device), measured in candles.

can·dle·stick (kăn′dəl stĭk′), *n.* a holder for a candle.

can·dle·wick (kăn′dəl wĭk′), *n.* **1.** the wick of a candle. —*adj.* **2.** of a fabric, usually unbleached muslin, into which small, short bunches of wicking have been hooked to form a design, used for bedspreads, etc.

can·dle·wood (kăn′dəl wŏŏd′), *n.* **1.** any resinous wood used for torches or as a substitute for candles. **2.** any of various trees or shrubs yielding such wood.

can·dor (kăn′dər), *n.* **1.** frankness, as of speech; sincerity; honesty. **2.** freedom from bias; fairness; impartiality. **3.** *Obs.* kindliness. **4.** *Obs.* purity. Also, *Brit.,* **can′dour.** [t. L: brightness, purity, candor]

can·dy (kăn′dĭ), *n., pl.* **-dies,** *v.,* **-died, -dying.** —*n.* **1.** any of a variety of confections made with sugar, syrup, etc., combined with other ingredients. **2.** a single piece of such a confection. —*v.t.* **3.** to cook in sugar or syrup, as sweet potatoes or carrots. **4.** to cook in heavy syrup until transparent, as fruit, fruit peel, or ginger. **5.** to reduce (sugar, etc.) to a crystalline form, usually by boiling down. **6.** to cover with sugarlike crystals, as of ice. **7.** to make sweet, palatable, or agreeable. —*v.i.* **8.** to become covered with sugar. **9.** to crystallize. [short for *sugar candy,* t. F: m. *sucre candi* candied sugar (*candi* der. Ar. *qand* sugar, t. Pers., appar. c. Skt. *khanda* piece)]

candy pull, a social gathering of young people, for the purpose of making taffy or molasses candy.

can·dy·tuft (kăn′dĭ tŭft′), *n.* a plant of the brassicaceous genus *Iberis,* esp. *I. umbellata,* a cultivated annual with tufted flowers, orig. from the island of Candia, and *I. amara.* [f. *Candy* (for CANDIA) + TUFT]

cane (kān), *n., v.,* **caned, caning.** —*n.* **1.** a walking stick. **2.** a long, hollow or pithy, jointed woody stem, as that of bamboo, rattan, sugar cane, certain palms, etc. **3.** a plant having such a stem. **4.** such stems as a material. **5.** any of various tall, woody, bamboolike grasses, esp. of the genus *Arundinaria,* as *A. macrosperma* (**large cane**) and *A. tecta* (**small cane**), of the southern U.S. **6.** the stem of raspberries or blackberries. **7.** sugar cane. **8.** the stem of a bamboo, etc., used as a rod for flogging. **9.** a slender piece of sealing wax, etc. —*v.t.* **10.** to beat with a cane. **11.** to furnish or make with cane: *to cane chairs.* [ME, t. OF, t. Pr. or It., g. L *canna,* t. Gk.: m. *kánna* reed. Cf. Heb. *qāneh*] —**can′er,** *n.*

Ca·ne·a (kä nē′ä; *Gk.* hän yä′), *n.* a seaport in and the capital of Crete. 28,213 (1940). Greek, **Khania.**

cane·brake (kān′brāk′), *n.* a thicket of canes.

ca·nel·la (kə nĕl′ə), *n.* the cinnamonlike bark of a West Indian tree, *Canella winterana,* used as a condiment and in medicine. [t. ML: cinnamon, dim. of L *canna* CANE]

ca·neph·o·ra (kə nĕf′ə rə), *n., pl.* **-rae** (-rē′). **1.** (in ancient Greece) one of the maidens who bore upon their heads baskets containing the materials for sacrifice in certain religious festivals. **2.** a caryatid having a basketlike cushion upon the head. [t. L, t. Gk.: m. *kanēphóros* basket bearer]

cane sugar, sugar obtained from sugar cane, identical with that obtained from the sugar beet; sucrose.

can·field (kăn′fēld), *n. Cards.* a game of solitaire often adapted to gambling purposes.

cangue (kăng), *n.* (in China) a kind of portable pillory worn about the neck by criminals. [t. F, prob. t. Pg.: m. *canga* yoke, t. Annamite: m. *gong*]

Ca·nic·u·la (kə nĭk′yə lə), *n. Astron.* Sirius; the Dog Star. [t. L, dim. of *canis* dog]

ca·nic·u·lar (kə nĭk′yə lər), *adj. Astron.,* etc. pertaining to the Dog Star or its rising.

ca·nine (kā′nīn, kə nīn′), *adj.* **1.** of or like a dog; pertaining to or characteristic of dogs. **2.** *Anat., Zool.* of or pertaining to the four pointed teeth, esp. prominent in dogs, situated one on each side of each jaw, next to the incisors. —*n.* **3.** *Zool.* any animal of the dog family, the Canidae, including the wolves, jackals, hyenas, coyotes, and foxes. **4.** a dog. **5.** a canine tooth. [t. L: m.s. *canīnus* pertaining to a dog]

Ca·nis (kā′nĭs), *n. Zool.* the canine genus that includes the domestic dog, *Canis familiaris,* the wild dogs, the wolves, and the jackals, all having 42 teeth. [t. L: dog]

Ca·nis Ma·jor (kā′nĭs mā′jər), *gen.* **Canis Majoris** (mə jôr′ĭs). *Astron.* the Great Dog, a southern constellation containing Sirius, the Dog Star, the brightest of the stars. [t. L: greater dog]

Ca·nis Mi·nor (kā′nĭs mī′nər), *gen.* **Canis Minoris** (mī nôr′ĭs). *Astron.* the Little, or Lesser, Dog, a small ancient constellation following Orion and south of Gemini. It contains the star Procyon. [t. L: lesser dog]

can·is·ter (kăn′ĭs tər), *n.* **1.** a small box, usually of metal, for holding tea, coffee, etc. **2.** case shot (**canister shot**). [t. L: m.s. *canistrum,* t. Gk.: m. *kánastron* wicker basket]

can·ker (kăng′kər), *n.* **1.** *Pathol.* a gangrenous or ulcerous sore, esp. in the mouth. **2.** *Vet. Sci.* a disease affecting horses' feet, usually the sole, characterized by a foul-smelling exudate. **3.** *Plant Pathol.* a stem disease in which a dead area is surrounded by living tissue. **4.** anything that corrodes, corrupts, destroys, or irritates. **5.** *Obs.* or *Dial.* dog rose. —*v.t.* **6.** to infect with canker. **7.** to corrupt; destroy slowly. —*v.i.* **8.** to become infected with or as with canker. [ME; OE *cancer,* t. L: m. *cancr-,* s. *cancer* gangrene]

can·ker·ous (kăng′kər əs), *adj.* **1.** of the nature of or resembling canker. **2.** causing canker.

can·ker·worm (kăng′kər wûrm′), *n.* a striped green caterpillar injurious to fruit trees and other plants. It is the larva of any of several geometrid moths.

can·na (kăn′ə), *n.* any plant of the tropical genus *Canna* (family *Cannaceae*), various species of which are cultivated for their large, handsome leaves and showy flowers. [t. L: reed. See CANE]

can·na·bin (kăn′ə bĭn), *n.* a poisonous resin extracted from Indian hemp. [f. CANNAB(IS) + -IN²]

can·na·bis (kăn′ə bĭs), *n.* hashish; the dried pistillate parts of Indian hemp. [t. L: hemp]

Can·nae (kăn′ē), *n.* an ancient town in SE Italy: Romans defeated by Hannibal, 216 B.C.

canned (kănd), *adj.* **1.** preserved in a can or jar. **2.** *Slang.* recorded: *canned music.* **3.** *Slang.* prepared in advance.

can·nel coal (kăn′əl), a compact coal burning readily and brightly. Also, **cannel.** [appar. for *candle coal*]

can·ner (kăn′ər), *n.* one who cans meat, fruit, etc., for preservation.

can·ner·y (kăn′ər ĭ), *n., pl.* **-neries.** a place where meat, fish, fruit, etc. are canned.

Cannes (kăn, kănz; *Fr.* kän), *n.* a city in SW France, on the Mediterranean: coastal resort. 45,548 (1946).

can·ni·bal (kăn′ə bəl), *n.* **1.** a human being, esp. a savage, that eats human flesh. **2.** any animal that eats its own kind. —*adj.* **3.** pertaining to or characteristic of cannibals. **4.** given to cannibalism. [t. Sp.: m. *Caníbal,* for *Caríbal,* der. *Caribe* Carib]

can·ni·bal·ism (kăn′ə bə lĭz′əm), *n.* **1.** the practice of eating one's own kind. **2.** savage cruelty; barbarism. —**can′ni·bal·is′tic,** *adj.* —**can′ni·bal·is′ti·cal·ly,** *adv.*

can·ni·bal·ize (kăn′ə bə līz′), *v.t.,* **-ized, -izing.** *U.S. Army.* to repair (damaged motor vehicles, airplanes, tanks, etc.) by the use of parts of other assembled vehicles, etc., instead of using spare parts. —**can′ni·bal·i·za′tion,** *n.*

can·ni·kin (kăn′ə kĭn), *n.* a little can; a cup. [t. M Flem. or D: m. *cannekin* little can]

can·ning (kăn′ĭng), *n.* act, process, or business of preserving meat, fruits, etc., in sealed cans or jars.

Can·ning (kăn′ĭng), *n.* **1.** Charles John, (*Earl Canning*) 1812–62, governor general and 1st viceroy of India. **2.** his father, **George,** 1770–1827, British prime minister, 1827.

can·non (kăn′ən), *n., pl.* **-nons,** (*esp. collectively*) **-non,** *v.* —*n.* **1.** a mounted gun for firing heavy projectiles, a gun, howitzer, or mortar. **2.** *Mach.* a hollow cylinder fitted over a shaft and capable of revolving independently. **3.** a smooth round bit. **4.** the part of a bit that is in the horse's mouth. **5.** the metal loop of a bell by which it is hung. **6.** *Zool.* **a.** the cannon bone. **b.** the part of the leg in which it is situated, instep. **7.** *Brit.* a carom in billiards. —*v.i.* **8.** to discharge cannon. **9.** *Brit.* to make a carom in billiards. [t. F: m. *canon,* t. It.: m. *cannone,* aug. of *canna* tube, g. L *canna.* See CANE]

Can·non (kăn′ən), *n.* **Joseph Gurney** (gûr′nĭ), ("*Uncle Joe*"), 1836–1926, U.S. politician and legislator.

can·non·ade (kăn′ə nād′), *n.*, *v.*, **-aded, -ading.** —*n.* **1.** a continued discharge of cannon, esp. during an attack. —*v.t.*, *v.i.* **2.** to attack with or discharge cannon. [t. F: m. *canonnade*]

cannon ball, a missile, usually round and made of iron or steel, designed to be fired from a cannon.

cannon bone, *Zool.* the greatly developed middle metacarpal or metatarsal bone of hoofed quadrupeds, extending from wrist or ankle to the first joint of the digit. See illus. under **horse.** [f. CANNON (as being tube-shaped) + BONE]

can·non·eer (kăn′ə nĭr′), *n.* an artilleryman. [t. F: m. *canonnier*]

cannon fodder, soldiers (as the material used up in war).

can·non·ry (kăn′ənrĭ), *n.*, *pl.* **-ries. 1.** a discharge of artillery. **2.** artillery (def. 1).

cannon shot, 1. a ball or shot for a cannon. **2.** the shooting of a cannon. **3.** the range of a cannon.

can·not (kăn′ŏt, kă nŏt′, kə-), *v.* a form of can not. —**Syn.** See can[1].

can·nu·la (kăn′yə lə), *n.* *Surg.* a metal tube for insertion into the body, used to draw off fluid or to introduce medication. [t. L, dim. of *canna.* See CANE]

can·nu·lar (kăn′yə lər), *adj.* tubular. Also, **can·nu·late** (kăn′yə lāt′, -lĭt).

can·ny (kăn′ĭ), *adj.*, **-nier, -niest,** *adv.* *Scot.* —*adj.* **1.** careful; cautious; wary. **2.** knowing; sagacious; shrewd; astute. **3.** frugal; thrifty. **4.** skilled; expert. **5.** (chiefly with a negative) safe to deal or meddle with. **6.** quiet; gentle. **7.** snug; cozy. **8.** pretty; attractive. **9.** *Archaic.* having supernatural powers. —*adv.* **10.** in a canny manner. [appar. der. CAN[1]] —**can′ni·ly,** *adv.* —**can′ni·ness,** *n.*

ca·noe (kə nōō′), *n.*, *v.*, **-noed, -noeing.** —*n.* **1.** any light and narrow boat, often canvas-covered, that is propelled by paddles in place of oars. **2.** any native boat of very light construction, as the Algonquian birch bark canoe. —*v.i.* **3.** to paddle a canoe. **4.** to go in a canoe. —*v.t.* **5.** to transport by canoe. [t. F, t. Sp.: m. *canoa,* t. Carib: m. *kanoa*] —**ca·noe′ing,** *n.* —**ca·noe′ist,** *n.*

ca·noe·wood (kə nōō′wŏŏd′), *n.* the tulip tree.

can·on[1] (kăn′ən), *n.* **1.** *Chiefly Brit.* an ecclesiastical rule or law enacted by a council or other competent authority, and (in the Rom. Cath. Ch.) approved by the Pope. **2.** the body of ecclesiastical law. **3.** any rule or law. **4.** a fundamental principle. **5.** a standard; criterion. **6.** the books of the Bible recognized by the Christian Church as genuine and inspired. **7.** any officially recognized set of sacred books. **8.** a catalogue or list, as of the saints acknowledged by the church. **9.** *Liturgy.* that part of the mass between the Sanctus and the Communion. **10.** *Music.* a kind of composition in which the same melody is played or sung through by two or more voice parts at the same or at a different pitch. **11.** a large size of printing type (48 point). [OE, t. L: rule, canon, t. Gk.: m. *kanōn* straight rod, rule, standard] —**Syn. 4.** See **principle.**

can·on[2] (kăn′ən), *n.* **1.** *Chiefly Brit.* one of a body of dignitaries or prebendaries attached to a cathedral or a collegiate church; a member of the chapter of a cathedral or a collegiate church. **2.** *Rom. Cath. Ch.* one of the members (**canons regular**) of certain religious orders. [ME *canoun,* t. ONF: m. *canon,* t. ML. See CANNON]

ca·ñon (kăn′yən; *Sp.* kä nyōn′), *n.* canyon.

canon bit, cannon (def. 4).

can·on·ess (kăn′ən ĭs), *n.* one of a community of women living under a rule, but not under a vow.

ca·non·i·cal (kə nŏn′ə kəl), *adj.* **1.** pertaining to, established by, or conforming to a canon or canons. **2.** included in the canon of the Bible. **3.** authorized; recognized; accepted: *canonical criticism.* —*n.* **4.** (*pl.*) the dress prescribed by canon for the clergy when officiating. [t. ML: s. *canonicālis,* der. L *canonicus,* t. Gk.: m. *kanonikós.* See CANON[1]] —**ca·non′i·cal·ly,** *adv.*

canonical hour, 1. *Eccles.* any of certain periods of the day set apart for prayer and devotion, namely, matins (with lauds), prime, tierce, sext, nones, vespers, and complin. **2.** *Brit.* any hour between 8 A.M. and 3 P.M. during which marriage may be legally performed in parish churches.

ca·non·i·cate (kə nŏn′ə kāt′, -kĭt), *n.* the office or dignity of a canon; a canonry.

can·on·ic·i·ty (kăn′ə nĭs′ə tĭ), *n.* canonical character.

can·on·ist (kăn′ən ĭst), *n.* one versed in canon law.

can·on·ize (kăn′ə nīz′), *v.t.*, **-ized, -izing. 1.** *Eccles.* to place in the canon of saints. **2.** to glorify. **3.** to make canonical: *canonized books.* —**can′on·i·za′tion,** *n.*

canon law, the body of ecclesiastical law.

can·on·ry (kăn′ənrĭ), *n.*, *pl.* **-ries. 1.** the office or benefice of a canon. **2.** the body or group of canons.

can·on·ship (kăn′ən shĭp′), *n.* the position or office of canon; canonry.

can opener, a device for opening cans.

Ca·no·pic (kə nō′pĭk), *adj.* **1.** *Archaeol.* of or from Canopus, as a kind of vase used to hold the entrails of embalmed bodies. **2.** denoting a vase used elsewhere to hold the ashes of the dead. [t. L: s. *Canōpicus,* der. *Canōpus* CANOPUS (def. 2)]

Ca·no·pus (kə nō′pəs), *n.* **1.** *Astron.* a star of the first magnitude in the constellation Carina: the second in order of brightness of the stars; Alpha Carinae. **2.** an ancient seacoast city in Lower Egypt, 15 miles east of Alexandria.

can·o·py (kăn′ə pĭ), *n.*, *pl.* **-pies,** *v.*, **-pied, -pying.** —*n.* **1.** a covering suspended or supported over a throne, bed, etc., or held over a person, sacred object, etc. **2.** an overhanging protection or shelter. **3.** *Archit.* an ornamental rooflike projection or covering. **4.** the sky. —*v.t.* **5.** to cover with or as with a canopy: *clouds canopy the sky.* [ME *canape,* t. ML: s. *canapēum,* alter. of L *cōnōpēum* net curtains, t. Gk.: m. *kōnōpeīon* mosquito net]

ca·no·rous (kə nôr′əs), *adj.* melodious; musical. [t. L: m. *canōrus*] —**ca·no′rous·ly,** *adv.*

Ca·nos·sa (kə nôs′ə; *It.* kä nôs′sä), *n.* a ruined castle in N Italy: scene of the penance of Emperor Henry IV of the Holy Roman Empire before Pope Gregory VII in 1077.

Ca·no·va (kä nō′vä), *n.* **Antonio** (än tô′nyô), 1757–1822, Italian sculptor.

Can·ro·bert (kän rō bĕr′), *n.* **François Certain** (frän swä′ sĕr tăn′), 1809–95, marshal of France.

Can·so (kăn′sō), *n.* **Cape,** the NE extremity of the mainland of Nova Scotia.

canst (kănst), *v.* *Archaic* or *Poetic.* 2nd pers. sing. pres. of can.

cant[1] (kănt), *n.* **1.** insincere statements, esp. conventional pretense of enthusiasm for high ideals; insincere expressions of goodness or piety. **2.** the special language or jargon spoken by thieves, gypsies, etc. **3.** the words, phrases, etc., peculiar to a particular class, party, profession, etc. **4.** whining or singsong speech, esp. of beggars. —*v.i.* **5.** to make religious remarks insincerely or hypocritically; pretend goodness or piety. **6.** to speak in the whining or singsong tone of a beggar; beg. [cf. OE *cantere* singer, t. L: m. *cantor*] —**cant′er,** *n.*

cant[2] (kănt), *n.* **1.** a salient angle. **2.** a sudden movement that tilts or overturns a thing. **3.** a slanting or tilted position. **4.** an oblique line or surface, as one formed by cutting off the corner of a square or cube. **5.** an oblique or slanting face of anything. **6.** a sudden pitch or toss. —*v.t.* **7.** *Mech.* to bevel. **8.** to put in an oblique position; tilt; tip. **9.** to throw with a sudden jerk. —*v.i.* **10.** to take or have an inclined position; tilt; turn. [t. MD, or MLG: m. *kant,* both prob. t. ONF: m. *cant,* g. L *canthus* corner, side]

cant[3] (kănt), *adj.* *Brit. Dial.* hearty; merry. [t. LG]

can't (kănt, känt), contraction of *cannot.*

Cant., 1. Canterbury. **2.** Canticles.

Cantab., (L *Cantabrigiensis*) of Cambridge.

can·ta·bi·le (kän tä′bē lĕ), *Music.* —*adj.* **1.** songlike and flowing in style. —*n.* **2.** a cantabile style, passage, or piece. [It., t. LL: m.s. *cantābilis* that may be sung]

Can·ta·brig·i·an (kăn′tə brĭj′ĭ ən), *adj.* **1.** of Cambridge (England) or Cambridge University. —*n.* **2.** a native or inhabitant of Cambridge. **3.** a student or graduate of Cambridge University. [f. *Cantabrigia* Latin form of the name Cambridge + -(A)N]

can·ta·lev·er (kăn′tə lĕv′ər), *n.* cantilever. Also, **can·ta·li·ver** (kăn′tə lē′vər).

can·ta·loupe (kăn′tə lōp′), *n.* a variety of melons, *Cucumis melo,* var. *cantalupensis,* with hard, scaly, or warty rinds, esp. a small, ribbed, delicately flavored muskmelon. Also, **can′ta·loup′.** [t. F: m. *cantaloup,* t. It.: m. *Cantalupo,* a former estate of the Pope near Rome, where it was first grown in Europe]

can·tan·ker·ous (kăn tăng′kər əs), *adj.* ill-natured; quarrelsome; perverse or contrary, as in disposition: *a cantankerous old maid.* [? der. ME *contek* contention] —**can·tan′ker·ous·ly,** *adv.* —**can·tan′ker·ous·ness,** *n.*

can·ta·ta (kən tä′tə), *n.* *Music.* **1.** a choral composition, either sacred and resembling a short oratorio, or secular, as a lyric drama set to music but not to be acted. **2.** (*orig.*) a metrical narrative set to recitative, or alternate recitative and air, usually for a single voice, accompanied by one or more instruments. [t. It., der. *cantare* sing, g. L]

can·ta·tri·ce (*It.* kän′tä trē′chĕ; *Fr.* kän tà trēs′), *n.*, *pl. It.* **-trici** (-trē′chē), *Fr.* **-trices** (-trēs′). a female singer. [F and It., t. L: m.s. *cantātrix*]

can·teen (kăn tēn′), *n.* **1.** *U.S.* a small container used by soldiers and others for carrying water or other liquids. **2.** a place in a military camp, reservation, etc., for the sale of personal necessities and supplies to members of the army. **3.** *U.S. Army* (formerly) Post Exchange. **4.** a place where free entertainment is provided for enlisted men, usually in a town or city near an army camp or post or naval shore station. **5.** a box or chest containing table utensils, etc., used by army officers and others. [t. F: m. *cantine,* t. It.: m. *cantina* cellar, wine cellar, der. *canto* side, g. L *canthus*]

can·ter (kăn′tər), *n.* **1.** an easy gallop. —*v.i.*, *v.t.* **2.** to go or ride at a canter. [abbr. of *Canterbury gallop* (as of pilgrims to Canterbury, England)]

Can·ter·bur·y (kăn′tər bĕr′ĭ; *Brit.* -brĭ), *n.* **1.** a city in SE England, in Kent: famous cathedral; medieval pilgrimages to the tomb of Saint Thomas à Becket. 23,780 (est. 1946). **2.** a city in SE Australia, near Sydney. 79,058 (1933).

Canterbury bell, a plant, *Campanula medium,* cultivated for its showy violet-blue, pink, or white flowers.

---

b., blend of, blended; c., cognate with; d., dialect, dialectal; der., derived from; f., formed from; g., going back to; m., modification of; r., replacing; s., stem of; t., taken from; ?, perhaps. See the full key on inside cover.

Canterbury Tales, The, an uncompleted sequence of tales by Chaucer, for the most part written after 1387.

can·thar·i·des (kăn thăr′ə dēz′), *n.pl.,* *sing.* **cantharis** (kăn′thər ĭs). **1.** a preparation of powdered blister beetles, esp. the Spanish fly, *Lytta vesicatoria,* used medicinally as a skin irritant, diuretic, and aphrodisiac. **2.** (*sing.*) the beetle itself. [t. L, t. Gk.: pl., blister flies]

Cant hook

cant hook, a wooden lever with a movable iron hook near the lower end, used for grasping and canting or turning over logs, etc.

can·thus (kăn′thəs), *n., pl.* **-thi** (-thī). *Anat.* the angle or corner on each side of the eye, formed by the junction of the upper and lower lids. [t. NL, t. Gk.: m. *kanthôs* corner of the eye]

can·ti·cle (kăn′tə kəl), *n.* **1.** one of the nonmetrical hymns or chants, chiefly from the Bible, used in church services. **2.** a little song; a song. **3.** (*cap.,* pl.) a book of the Old Testament, also known as the *Song of Solomon.* [ME, t. L: m.s. *canticulum,* dim. of *canticum* song]

A, Inner canthus;
B, Outer canthus

Can·ti·gny (kän tē nyē′), *n.* a village in N France, S of Amiens: first major battle of U. S. forces in World War I, May, 1918.

can·ti·lev·er (kăn′tə lĕv′ər, -lē′vər), *n.* **1.** *Mach.* a free part of any horizontal member projecting beyond a support. **2.** *Civ. Eng.* either of two bracketlike arms projecting toward each other from opposite banks or piers, serving to form the span of a bridge (**cantilever bridge**) when united. **3.** *Aeron.* a form of wing construction in which no external bracing is employed (**cantilever wing**). **4.** *Archit.* an extended bracket for supporting a balcony, cornice, or the like. Also, **cantalever, cantaliver.** [orig. uncert.]

can·ti·na (kăn tē′nə; *Sp.* kän tē′nä), *n.* Southwestern *U.S.* a saloon. [t. Sp.]

can·tle (kăn′təl), *n.* **1.** the hind part of a saddle, usually curved upward. See illus. under **saddle. 2.** a corner; piece; portion. [ME *cantel,* t. ONF, dim. of *cant* corner, CANT²]

can·to (kăn′tō), *n., pl.* **-tos.** one of the main or larger divisions of a long poem, as in Scott's *Marmion.* [t. It., g. L *cantus* song]

can·ton (kăn′tən, -tŏn, kăn tŏn′ *for 1-6;* kăn tŏn′, -tŏn′, *esp. Brit.* -tōōn′ *for 7*), *n.* **1.** a small territorial district, esp. one of the states of the Swiss confederation. **2.** a subdivision of a French arrondissement. **3.** *Her.* a square division in the upper dexter corner of an escutcheon, etc. **4.** a division, part, or portion of anything. —*v.t.* **5.** to divide into parts or portions. **6.** to divide into cantons or territorial districts. **7.** to allot quarters to (soldiers, etc.). [t. F: corner, ult. der. L *can·thus* corner, CANT²] —**can·ton·al** (kăn′tən əl), *adj.*

Can·ton (kăn tŏn′ *for 1;* kăn′tən *for 2*), *n.* **1.** Chinese, **Kwangchow.** a seaport in SE China, on the Chu-Kiang: the capital of Kwangtung province. 852,000 (est. 1938). **2.** a city in NE Ohio. 116,912 (1950).

Can·ton crepe (kăn′tŏn), a thin, light silk or rayon crepe with a finely wrinkled surface, heavier in texture than crepe de chine. [named after *Canton,* China]

Can·ton·ese (kăn′tə nēz′, -nēs′), *n., pl.* **-ese,** *adj.* —*n.* **1.** a Chinese language of southern China. **2.** a native or inhabitant of Canton. —*adj.* **3.** pertaining to Canton, its inhabitants, or their language.

Can·ton flannel (kăn′tən), a cotton twill fabric, napped on one side.

can·ton·ment (kăn tŏn′mənt, -tŏn′-; *esp. Brit.* -tōōn′-), *n.* **1.** a camp (usually of large size) where men are trained for military service. **2.** military quarters. **3.** the winter quarters of an army. [t. F: m. *cantonnement*]

Can·ton River (kăn tŏn′), Chu-Kiang.

can·tor (kăn′tər, -tôr), *n. Eccles.* **1.** an officer whose duty is to lead the singing in a cathedral or in a collegiate or parish church; a precentor. **2.** the Jewish religious official singing the liturgy. [t. L: singer]

can·trip (kăn′trĭp), *n. Orig. and Chiefly Scot.* **1.** a charm; a spell. **2.** a trick.

can·tus (kăn′təs), *n., pl.* **-tus. 1.** a song; melody. **2.** an ecclesiastical style of music. [t. L. See CHANT.]

can·tus fir·mus (kăn′təs fûr′məs), **1.** *Eccles.* the ancient traditional vocal music of the Christian Church, having its form settled and its use prescribed by ecclesiastical authority. **2.** *Music.* a fixed melody to which other melodic parts are added. [ML]

cant·y (kăn′tĭ, kän′-), *adj. Scot. and N. Eng.* **1.** cheerful. **2.** lively; brisk. [t. LG: m. *kantig* cheerful]

Ca·nuck (kə nŭk′), *n. Colloq. or Slang.* a Canadian, esp. a French Canadian.

Ca·nute (kə nōōt′, -nūt′), *n.* A.D. 994?–1035, Danish king of England, 1017–35; of Denmark, 1018–35; and of Norway, 1028–35. Also, **Cnut, Knut.**

can·vas (kăn′vəs), *n.* **1.** a closely woven, heavy cloth of hemp, flax, or cotton, used for tents, sails, etc. **2.** a piece of this material on which an oil painting is made. **3.** an oil painting on canvas. **4.** a tent, or tents collectively. **5.** sailcloth. **6.** sails collectively. **7.** any fabric, of linen, cotton, etc., of a coarse loose weave,

used as a foundation for embroidery stitches, for interlining, etc. [ME *canevas,* t. ONF, ult. der. L *cannabis* hemp]

can·vas·back (kăn′vəs băk′), *n.* a North American wild duck, *Aythya valisineria,* with a whitish back, prized for the delicacy of its flesh.

can·vass (kăn′vəs), *v.t.* **1.** to examine carefully; investigate by inquiry; discuss; debate. **2.** to solicit votes, subscriptions, opinions, etc., from (a district, group of people, etc.). **3.** *Brit.* to engage in a political campaign. **4.** *Obs.* to criticize severely. —*v.i.* **5.** to solicit votes, opinions, etc. **6.** to review election returns. **7.** to engage in discussion or debate. —*n.* **8.** examination; close inspection; scrutiny. **9.** a soliciting of votes, orders, etc. **10.** a campaign for election to government office. [var. of CANVAS, *n.;* orig. meaning to toss (someone) in a canvas sheet (cf. def. 4)] —**can′vass·er,** *n.*

can·yon (kăn′yən), *n. U.S.* a deep valley with steep sides, often with a stream flowing through it. Also, **cañon.** [t. Sp.: m. *cañón* tube, der. *caña,* g. L *canna* reed]

can·zo·ne (kän tsō′nĕ), *n., pl.* **-zoni** (-tsō′nē). **1.** a variety of lyric poetry in the Italian style, of Provençal origin, which closely resembled the madrigal. **2.** any ballad or song. [It., g. L *cantio* song.]

can·zo·net (kăn′zə nĕt′), *n.* a short song, esp. a light and gay one.

caou·tchouc (kōō′chŏŏk, kōō chŏŏk′; *esp. Brit.* kōō′-chŏŏk), *n.* **1.** the gummy coagulated juice of certain tropical plants; India rubber. **2.** pure rubber. [t. F, t. Sp.: m. *cauchú,* of S Amer. orig.]

cap (kăp), *n., v.,* **capped, capping.** —*n.* **1.** a covering for the head, esp. one fitting closely and made of softer material than a hat, and having little or no brim. **2.** a covering of lace, etc., for a woman's head, usually worn indoors. **3.** a special headdress denoting rank, occupation, etc.: *a cardinal's cap, nurse's cap.* **4.** a mortarboard. **5.** anything resembling or suggestive of a covering for the head in shape, use, or position. **6.** the acme. **7.** *Bot.* the pileus of a mushroom. **8.** a percussion cap. **9.** a noise-making device for toy pistols, made of a small quantity of explosive wrapped in paper or other thin material. **10.** capital; capital letter. **11.** a name given (with distinctive qualifications, as in *foolscap*) to several large sizes of writing paper. —*v.t.* **12.** to provide or cover with or as with a cap. **13.** to complete. **14.** to surpass; follow up with something as good or better. **15.** to serve as a cap, covering, or top to; overlie. [ME *cappe,* OE *cæppe,* t. LL: m.s. *cappa, cāpa* cap, hooded cloak, cape, appar. der. *caput* head]

cap., **1.** capital. **2.** capitalize. **3.** capitalized. **4.** (*pl.* **caps.**) capital letter. **5.** (L *capitulum, caput*) chapter.

ca·pa·bil·i·ty (kā′pə bĭl′ə tĭ), *n., pl.* **-ties. 1.** quality of being capable; capacity; ability. **2.** quality of admitting of certain treatment. **3.** (*usually pl.*) a quality, ability, etc., that can be developed or used.

ca·pa·ble (kā′pə bəl), *adj.* **1.** having much intelligence or ability; competent; efficient; able: *a capable instructor.* **2.** capable of, **a.** having the ability, strength, etc., to; qualified or fitted for: *a man capable of judging art.* **b.** susceptible to; open to the influence or effect of: *a situation capable of improvement.* **c.** wicked enough for: *capable of murder.* [t. LL: m. *capābilis*] —**ca′pa·ble·ness,** *n.* —**ca′pa·bly,** *adv.* —**Syn. 1.** See **able.**

ca·pa·cious (kə pā′shəs), *adj.* capable of holding much. [f. CAPACI(TY) + -OUS] —**ca·pa′cious·ly,** *adv.* —**ca·pa′cious·ness,** *n.* —**Syn.** spacious, roomy.

ca·pac·i·tance (kə păs′ə təns), *n. Elect.* **1.** the ratio of a change in quantity of electricity (in a conductor) to the corresponding change in potential. **2.** the property of being able to collect a charge of electricity. **3.** a condenser. [f. CAPACIT(Y) + -ANCE]

ca·pac·i·tate (kə păs′ə tāt′), *v.t.,* **-tated, -tating. 1.** to make capable; enable. **2.** to furnish with legal powers. —**ca·pac′i·ta′tion,** *n.*

ca·pac·i·tive (kə păs′ə tĭv), *adj. Elect.* pertaining to capacity.

ca·pac·i·tor (kə păs′ə tər), *n. Elect.* a condenser.

ca·pac·i·ty (kə păs′ə tĭ), *n., pl.* **-ties. 1.** the power of receiving or containing. **2.** cubic contents; volume. **3.** power of receiving impressions, knowledge, etc.; mental ability: *the capacity of a scholar.* **4.** power, ability, or possibility of doing something (fol. by *of, for,* or infinitive): *capacity for self-protection.* **5.** quality of being susceptible to certain treatment. **6.** position; function; relation: *in the capacity of legal adviser.* **7.** legal qualification. **8.** *Elect.* **a.** capacitance. **b.** a measure of output performance. [late ME *capacyte,* t. L: m.s. *capācitas*] **Syn. 4.** competency.

Cap·a·neus (kăp′ə nĕs′, -nōōs′, kə pā′nĭ əs), *n. Gk. Legend.* one of the Seven against Thebes, destroyed by Zeus for blasphemy. See **Seven against Thebes.**

cap-a-pie (kăp′ə pē′), *adv.* from head to foot. Also, **cap′-à-pie′.** [t. F (obs.)]

ca·par·i·son (kə păr′ə sən), *n.* **1.** a covering, usually ornamented, laid over the saddle or harness of a horse, etc. **2.** dress; equipment; outfit. —*v.t.* **3.** to cover with a caparison. **4.** to dress finely; deck. [t. F: m. *caparasson,* t. Sp.: m. *caparazón,* t. Pr.: m. *caparaso,* der. *capa* CAPE¹]

cape¹ (kāp), *n.* a sleeveless garment fastened round the neck and falling loosely over the shoulders, worn separately or attached to a coat, etc. [t. F, t. Sp.: m. *capa,* g. LL *cāpa.* See CAP.]

cape[2] (kāp), *n.* **1.** a piece of land jutting into the sea or some other body of water. **2. the Cape**, the Cape of Good Hope. [ME, t. F: m. *cap*, t. Pr., g. L *caput* head]

Cape Bret·on (brĭt'ən, brĕt'ən), an island forming the NE part of Nova Scotia. 110,703 pop. (1941); 3970 sq. mi.

Cape buffalo. See buffalo (def. 1).

Cape Colony, former name of **Cape of Good Hope** (def. 2).

Cape Dutch, South African Dutch.

Cape Gi·rar·deau (jē'rär dō'), a city in SE Missouri, on the Mississippi. 21,578 (1950).

Ča·pek (chä'pĕk), *n.* Karel (kä'rĕl), 1890–1938, Czech dramatist, novelist, and producer.

cap·e·lin (kăp'ə lĭn), *n.* either of two small fishes of the smelt family, of the coasts of the North Atlantic (*Mallotus villosus*) and North Pacific (*M. catervarius*). [t. F: m. *caplan, capelan*, prob. t. Pr. See CHAPLAIN]

Ca·pel·la (kə pĕl'ə), *n. Astron.* a brilliant star of the first magnitude in the constellation Auriga. [t. L: lit., she-goat]

Cape of Good Hope, 1. a cape near the S extremity of Africa. **2.** Also, **Cape Province.** Formerly, **Cape Colony.** a province in the Union of South Africa. 4,016,-801 pop. (1946). 277,169 sq. mi. *Cap.*: Cape Town.

ca·per[1] (kā'pər), *v.i.* **1.** to leap or skip about in a sprightly manner; prance. *—n.* **2.** a playful leap or skip. **3.** a prank; capricious action; hare-brained escapade. [fig. use of L *caper* he-goat] *—ca'per·er, n.*

ca·per[2] (kā'pər), *n.* **1.** a shrub, *Capparis spinosa,* of Mediterranean regions. **2.** its flower bud, which is pickled and used for garnish or seasoning. [ME *caperis,* t. L: m. *capparis,* t. Gk.: m. *kápparis*]

cap·er·cail·lie (kăp'ər kāl'yĭ), *n.* the wood grouse, *Tetrao urogallus,* a very large gallinaceous bird of northern Europe. Also, **cap·er·cail·zie** (kăp'ər kāl'yĭ, -kāl'zĭ). [t. Gaelic: m. *capullcoille,* lit., horse-wood, with *r* for *l* by dissimilation]

Ca·per·na·um (kə pûr'nā əm, -nĭ-), *n.* an ancient town in N Israel, on the Sea of Galilee: the center of Jesus' ministry in Galilee.

Ca·pet (kā'pĭt, kăp'ĭt; *Fr.* kà pĕ'), *n.* **Hugh** or *Fr.* **Hugues** (yg), A.D. 938?–996, king of France, A.D. 987–996.

Ca·pe·tian (kə pē'shən), *adj.* **1.** pertaining or relating to the French dynasty (987–1328) founded by Hugh Capet. *—n.* **2.** a member of this dynasty.

Cape Town, a seaport in the Union of South Africa, near the Cape of Good Hope: seat of the Parliament. With suburbs, 454,052 (1946). Also, **Cape'town'.**

Cape Verde Islands (vûrd), a group of Portuguese islands in the Atlantic, W of French West Africa. 158,000 pop. (est. 1943); 1557 sq. mi. *Cap.*: Praia.

Cape York Peninsula, a large peninsula in NE Australia between the Gulf of Carpentaria and the Coral Sea.

cap·ful (kăp'fŏŏl'), *n., pl.* **-fuls.** as much as a cap will hold.

Cap-Ha·i·tien (kàp à ē syäN', -tyäN'), *n.* a seaport in N Haiti. 12,000 (est. 1931).

ca·pi·as (kā'pĭ əs, kăp'ĭ-), *n. Law.* a writ commanding an officer to take a person specified into custody. [t. L: take thou]

cap·i·ba·ra (kăp'ə bä'rə), *n.* capybara.

cap·il·la·ceous (kăp'ə lā'shəs), *adj.* hairlike; capillary. [t. L: m. *capillāceus* hairy]

cap·il·lar·i·ty (kăp'ə lăr'ə tĭ), *n.* **1.** state of being capillary. **2.** *Physics.* capillary action.

cap·il·lar·y (kăp'ə lĕr'ĭ), *adj., n., pl.* **-laries.** *—adj.* **1.** pertaining to or occurring in or as in a tube of fine bore. **2.** *Physics.* **a.** pertaining to the property of surface tension. **b. capillary action,** the elevation or depression of the surface of liquids in fine tubes, etc., due to surface tension and the forces of cohesion and adhesion. **c. capillary attraction** or **repulsion,** the apparent attraction or repulsion between a liquid and a tube, etc., observed in such phenomena. **3.** *Bot.* resembling hair in the manner of growth or in shape. **4.** *Anat.* pertaining to a capillary or capillaries. *—n.* **5.** *Anat.* one of the minute blood vessels between the terminations of the arteries and the beginnings of the veins. **6.** Also, **capillary tube.** a tube with a small bore. [t. L: m. *capillāris* pertaining to the hair]

ca·pi·ta (kăp'ə tə), *n.* pl. of **caput.**

cap·i·tal[1] (kăp'ə təl), *n.* **1.** the city or town which is the official seat of government in a county, state, etc. **2.** a capital letter. **3.** the wealth, whether in money or property, owned or employed in business by an individual, firm, corporation, etc. **4.** an accumulated stock of such wealth. **5.** any form of wealth employed or capable of being employed in the production of more wealth. **6.** *Accounting.* **a.** assets remaining after deduction of liabilities; the net worth of a business. **b.** the ownership interest in a business. **7.** any source of profit, advantage, power, etc. **8.** capitalists as a group or class. **9.** resources. *—adj.* **10.** pertaining to capital: *capital stock.* **11.** principal; highly important. **12.** chief,

esp. as being the official seat of government of a country, state, etc. **13.** excellent or first-rate. **14.** (of letters) of the large size used at the beginning of a sentence or as the first letter of a proper name. **15.** involving the loss of the head or life, usually as punishment; punishable by death. **16.** fatal; serious: *a capital error.* **17.** of the largest, most heavily armed, etc., type: *a capital ship.* [ME, t. L: s. *capitālis* pertaining to the head or to life, chief (ML *capitāle,* n., wealth)]
—Syn. 11. The adjectives CAPITAL, CHIEF, MAJOR, PRINCIPAL apply to a main or leading representative of a kind. CAPITAL may mean larger or more prominent, or it may suggest preëminence and excellence of quality: *capital letter, city, investment.* CHIEF means leading, highest in office or power: *the chief clerk.* MAJOR may refer to greatness of importance, number, or quantity: *a major operation, the major part of a population.* PRINCIPAL refers to most distinguished, influential, or foremost: *principal officer, export.*
—Ant. 11. minor, lesser.

cap·i·tal[2] (kăp'ə təl), *n. Archit.* the head, or uppermost part, of a column, pillar, etc. [ME *capital(e),* t. L: m.s. *capitellum,* dim. of *caput* head; influenced by CAPITAL[1], adj.]

Capitals
A. Doric; B. Ionic; C. Corinthian

capital account, 1. a business account stating the owner's or shareholder's interest in the assets. **2.** (*pl.*) *Accounting.* accounts showing the net worth, as in a business enterprise, as assets minus liabilities.

capital expenditure, *Accounting.* an addition to the value of a fixed asset, as by the purchase of a new building.

capital gain, profit from the sale of assets, such as bonds, real estate, etc.

capital goods, *Econ.* goods used in the production of other goods.

cap·i·tal·ism (kăp'ə tə lĭz'əm; *Brit. also* kə pĭt'ə-), *n.* **1.** a system under which the means of production, distribution, and exchange are in large measure privately owned and directed. **2.** the concentration of capital in the hands of a few, or the resulting power or influence. **3.** a system favoring such concentration of wealth.

cap·i·tal·ist (kăp'ə tə lĭst; *Brit. also* kə pĭt'əl-), *n.* one who has capital, esp. extensive capital employed in business enterprises.

cap·i·tal·is·tic (kăp'ə tə lĭs'tĭk; *Brit. also* kə pĭt'ə-), *adj.* pertaining to capital or capitalists; founded on or believing in capitalism: *capitalistic production.* **—cap'-i·tal·is'ti·cal·ly,** *adv.*

cap·i·tal·i·za·tion (kăp'ə təl ə zā'shən; *Brit. also* kə pĭt'əl-), *n.* **1.** act of capitalizing. **2.** the authorized or outstanding stocks and bonds of a corporation. **3.** *Accounting.* **a.** the total investment of the owner or owners in a business enterprise. **b.** the total corporate liability. **c.** the total arrived at after addition of liabilities. **4.** conversion into stocks or bonds. **5.** act of computing the present value of future periodical payments.

cap·i·tal·ize (kăp'ə tə līz'; *Brit. also* kə pĭt'ə līz'), *v.t.,* **-ized, -izing. 1.** to write or print in capital letters, or with an initial capital. **2.** to authorize a certain amount of stocks and bonds in the corporate charter: *to capitalize a corporation.* **3.** to convert (floating debt) into stock or shares. **4.** *Accounting.* to set up (expenditures) as business assets in the books of account instead of treating as expense. **5.** to supply with capital. **6.** to estimate the value of (a stock or an enterprise). **7.** to take advantage of; turn to one's advantage (often fol. by *on*): *capitalize on one's opportunities.*

capital levy, a tax based on total assets.

cap·i·tal·ly (kăp'ə tə lĭ), *adv.* in a capital manner; excellently; very well.

capital ship, one of a class of the largest warships; a battleship, battle cruiser, or aircraft carrier.

capital stock, 1. the total shares issued by a corporation. **2.** the book value of all the shares of a corporation, including unissued shares and those not completely paid in.

capital surplus, the surplus of a business, exclusive of its earned surplus.

cap·i·tate (kăp'ə tāt'), *adj. Bot.* having a globular head; collected in a head. [t. L: m. s. *capitātus* having a head]

cap·i·ta·tion (kăp'ə tā'shən), *n.* **1.** a numbering or assessing by the head. **2.** a poll tax. **3.** a fee or payment of a uniform amount for each person. [t. LL: s. *capitātio* poll tax]

Cap·i·tol (kăp'ə təl), *n.* **1.** the building at Washington, D.C., used by the Congress of the U. S. for its sessions. **2.** (*often l.c.*) a building occupied by a State legislature; Statehouse. **3.** the ancient temple of Jupiter at Rome, on the Capitoline. [ME *capitole,* t. L: m.s. *Capitōlium* (cf. def. 3, 4), der. *caput* head]

Cap·i·to·line (kăp'ə tə lĭn'), *adj.* **1.** of or pertaining to the Capitol at Rome, the hill on which it stood, or the god Jupiter (who was worshiped there). *—n.* **2.** one of the seven hills of ancient Rome.

ca·pit·u·lar (kə pĭch'ə lər), *n.* **1.** a member of an ecclesiastical chapter. **2.** (*pl.*) the laws or statutes of a chapter or of an ecclesiastical council. *—adj.* **3.** *Bot.* capitate. **4.** pertaining to an ecclesiastical or other chapter: *a capitular cathedral.* [t. ML: s. *capitulāris,* der. L *capitulum* CAPITULUM]

ca·pit·u·lar·y (kə·pĭch′ə·lĕr′ĭ), *adj.*, *n.*, *pl.* **-laries.** —*adj.* **1.** pertaining to a chapter, esp. an ecclesiastic one. —*n.* **2.** a member of a chapter, esp. an ecclesiastic one. **3.** (*pl.*) the ordinances or laws of a Frankish sovereign.

ca·pit·u·late (kə·pĭch′ə·lāt′), *v.i.*, **-lated, -lating.** to surrender unconditionally or on stipulated terms. [t. ML: m. s. *capitulātus*, pp. of *capitulāre* arrange in chapters, der. L *capitulum* CAPITULUM]

ca·pit·u·la·tion (kə·pĭch′ə·lā′shən), *n.* **1.** a surrender unconditionally or upon certain terms. **2.** the instrument containing a surrender. **3.** a statement of the heads of a subject; a summary or enumeration. **4.** (*pl.*) any of the treaties of the sultans of Turkey which granted to foreigners residing there rights of personality of law, extraterritoriality, etc. **5.** a treaty by which Christian states obtained the right to establish courts for their nationals in non-Christian states.

ca·pit·u·lum (kə·pĭch′ə·ləm), *n.*, *pl.* **-la** (-lə). **1.** *Bot.* a close head of sessile flowers; a flower head. **2.** *Anat.* the head of a bone. [t. L: small head, capital of column, chapter, dim. of *caput* head]

Cap′n (kăp′ən), *n.* Captain.

ca·pon (kā′pŏn, -pən), *n.* a rooster castrated to improve the flesh for use as food. [OE *capun*, t. L: m. s. *cāpo*]

cap·o·ral (kăp′ə·răl′), *n.* a kind of tobacco. [t. F, t. It.: m. *caporale* superior]

Cap·o·ret·to (kăp′ə·rĕt′ō; It. kä′pô·rĕt′tô), *n.* a village in NE Italy: scene of a disastrous Italian defeat by the Austrians and Germans, 1917.

ca·pote (kə·pōt′; Fr. kȧ·pôt′), *n.* **1.** a long cloak with a hood. **2.** a close, caplike bonnet worn by women and children. **3.** the hood or top of a vehicle. [t. F, dim. of *cape* hood]

Cap·pa·do·cia (kăp′ə·dō′shə), *n.* an ancient country in E Asia Minor: later a Roman province.

cap·pa·ri·da·ceous (kăp′ə·rĭ·dā′shəs), *adj.* *Bot.* belonging to the *Capparidaceae*, or caper family of plants. [f. *capparid* (f. s. L *capparis* + -ID^2) the caper plant + -ACEOUS]

capped hock, *Vet. Sci.* any swelling, inflammatory or otherwise, on the point of the hock of horses.

cap·per (kăp′ər), *n.* **1.** one who or that which caps. **2.** *U.S. Slang.* an informer, esp. for gamblers. **3.** *U.S. Slang.* a by-bidder at an auction.

cap·re·o·late (kăp′rĭ·ə·lāt′, kə·prē′-), *adj.* **1.** *Bot.* having tendrils. **2.** *Anat.* resembling tendrils. [f. s. L *capreolus* tendril + -ATE^1]

Ca·pri (kä′prē), *n.* a rocky island in the Bay of Naples, in W Italy: famous for its scenery and grottoes. 7984 pop. (1936); 5⅓ sq. mi.

ca·pric·ci·o (kə·prē′chĭ·ō′; It. kä·prēt′chō), *n.*, *pl.* **-cios,** It. **ci** (-chē). **1.** a caper; a prank. **2.** a caprice. **3.** *Music.* a composition in a free, irregular style. [t. It., der. *capro* goat, g. L *caper*]

ca·pric·ci·o·so (kə·prē′chĭ·ō′sō; It. kä′prēt·chô′sō), *adj.* *Music.* capricious; fantastic in style.

ca·price (kə·prēs′), *n.* **1.** a sudden change of mind without apparent or adequate motive; whim. **2.** a tendency to change one's mind without apparent or adequate motive; whimsicality; capriciousness. **3.** *Music.* capriccio (def. 3). [t. F, t. It.: m. *capriccio* CAPRICCIO]

ca·pri·cious (kə·prĭsh′əs), *adj.* **1.** subject to, led by, or indicative of caprice or whim. **2.** *Obs.* fanciful or witty. —**ca·pri′cious·ly,** *adv.* —**ca·pri′cious·ness,** *n.* —Ant. **1.** stable, constant.

Cap·ri·corn (kăp′rə·kôrn′), *n.* *Astron.* **1.** a zodiacal constellation between Sagittarius and Aquarius. **2.** the tenth sign of the zodiac. See diag. under **zodiac.** Also, **Cap·ri·cor·nus** (kăp′rə·kôr′nəs). [t. L: s. *Capricornus*, lit., goat-horned]

cap·ri·fo·li·a·ceous (kăp′rə·fō′lĭ·ā′shəs), *adj.* *Bot.* belonging to the *Caprifoliaceae*, a family of plants including the honeysuckle, elder, viburnum, snowberry, etc. [f. s. ML *caprifolium* honeysuckle + -ACEOUS]

cap·ri·ole (kăp′rĭ·ōl′), *n.*, *v.*, **-oled, -oling.** —*n.* **1.** a caper or leap. **2.** an upward spring made by a horse with all four feet and without advancing. —*v.i.* **3.** to execute a capriole. [t. F, t. It.: m. *capriola* caper, der. *capro* goat, g. L *caper*]

ca·pro·ic acid (kə·prō′ĭk), an organic acid, CH₃-(CH₂)₄COOH, found in fatty animal tissue and in coconut oil, used to make artificial flavoring agents. [f. *capro-* (comb. form repr. L *caper* goat) + -IC; so called from its smell]

caps. capital letters.

cap·sa·i·cin (kăp·sā′ə·sĭn), *n.* *Chem.* a bitter irritant principle from paprika; colorless crystalline amide, C₁₈H₂₇NO₃, related to guaiacol. [f. L *capsa* box + -IC + -IN²]

cap screw, a screw bolt with a long thread and a square or hexagonal head, used to secure covers of steam cylinders, etc. See illus. under **screw.**

cap·si·cum (kăp′sĭ·kəm), *n.* **1.** any plant of the solanaceous genus *Capsicum*, as *C. frutescens*, the common pepper of the garden, in many varieties, with mild to hot, pungent seeds enclosed in a podded or bell-shaped pericarp which also ranges from mild to extremely hot. **2.** the fruit of these plants, or some preparation of it, used as a condiment and once widely used internally and externally as a local irritant. [t. NL: f. s. L *capsa* box + -*icum*, neut. of -*icus* -IC]

cap·size (kăp·sīz′), *v.*, **-sized, -sizing.** —*v.i.* **1.** to overturn: *the boat capsized.* —*v.t.* **2.** to upset: *they capsized the boat.* [orig. unknown] —Syn. See **upset.**

cap·stan (kăp′stən), *n.* a device resembling a windlass but with a vertical axis, commonly turned by a bar or lever, and winding a cable, for raising weights (as an anchor). [ME, t. Pr.: m. *cabestan*, earlier *cabestran*, der. *cabestre*, g. L *capistrum* halter]

Capstan
A. Capstan head; B. Barrel; C. Toothed rim and pawls; D. Capstan bar

capstan bar, one of the levers, generally of wood, by which a capstan is turned.

cap·stone (kăp′stōn′), *n.* a finishing stone of a structure.

cap·su·lar (kăp′sə·lər), *adj.* of, in, or like a capsule.

cap·su·late (kăp′sə·lāt′), *adj.* enclosed in or formed into a capsule. Also, **cap′su·lat′ed.**

cap·sule (kăp′səl), *n.* **1.** a gelatinous case enclosing a dose of medicine. **2.** *Bot.* **a.** a dry dehiscent fruit, composed of two or more carpels. **b.** the spore case of various cryptogamic plants. **3.** *Anat., Zool.* **a.** a membranous sac or integument. **b.** either of two strata of white matter in the cerebrum. **4.** a small case, envelope, or covering. **5.** a thin metal covering for the mouth of a corked bottle. [earlier *capsul*, t. L: s. *capsula*, dim. of *capsa* box]

Capsules (def. 2a), after dehiscence
A. Asphodel; B. Prickly poppy; C. Violet

Capt., Captain.

cap·tain (kăp′tən, -tĭn), *n.* **1.** one who is at the head of or in authority over others; a chief; leader. **2.** an officer in most armies, ranking above a first lieutenant and below a major. **3.** a military leader. **4.** the commander or master of a merchant ship or other vessel. **5.** an officer in the navy ranking above a commander and below a rear admiral, usually in command of a warship. **6.** the leader of a baseball team, racing crew, etc. —*v.t.* **7.** to lead or command as a captain. [ME *capitain*, t. OF, t. LL: m.s. *capitāneus* chief, der. L *caput* head] —**cap′tain·cy,** *n.* —**cap′tain·ship,** *n.*

cap·tion (kăp′shən), *n.* **1.** a heading or title, as of a chapter, article, or page. **2.** *Print.* a legend for a picture or illustration. **3.** *Motion Pictures.* the title of a scene, the text of a speech, etc., shown on the screen. **4.** *Law.* that part of a legal document which states time, place, etc., of execution or performance. [t. L: s. *captio*]

cap·tious (kăp′shəs), *adj.* **1.** apt to notice and make much of trivial faults or defects; faultfinding; difficult to please. **2.** proceeding from a faultfinding or caviling disposition: *captious remarks.* **3.** apt or designed to ensnare or perplex, esp. in argument: *captious questions.* [t. L: m. s. *captiōsus* fallacious, sophistical] —**cap′tious·ly,** *adv.* —**cap′tious·ness,** *n.*

cap·ti·vate (kăp′tə·vāt′), *v.t.*, **-vated, -vating.** **1.** to enthrall by beauty or excellence; enchant; charm. **2.** *Obs.* to capture; subjugate. [t. LL: m.s. *captivātus*, pp., taken captive] —**cap′ti·va′tion,** *n.* —**cap′ti·va′tor,** *n.* —Syn. **1.** See **charm.**

cap·tive (kăp′tĭv), *n.* **1.** a prisoner. **2.** one who is enslaved by love, beauty, etc. —*adj.* **3.** made or held prisoner, esp. in war. **4.** kept in confinement or restraint. **5.** enslaved by love, beauty, etc.; captivated. **6.** of or pertaining to a captive. [t. L: m.s. *captivus*]

captive balloon, a balloon held in a particular place by means of a rope or cable, as for observation purposes.

cap·tiv·i·ty (kăp·tĭv′ə·tĭ), *n.*, *pl.* **-ties.** state or period of being captive. —Syn. bondage, servitude, slavery.

cap·tor (kăp′tər), *n.* a person who captures.

cap·ture (kăp′chər), *v.*, **-tured, -turing,** *n.* —*v.t.* **1.** to take by force or stratagem; take prisoner; seize: *the chief was captured.* [v. use of n.] —*n.* **2.** act of capturing. **3.** the thing or person captured. [t. F, t. L: m. *captūra*] —**cap′tur·er,** *n.* —Syn. **1.** catch, apprehend, arrest, snare, grab, nab. **2.** seizure, arrest, apprehension. —Ant. **1.** liberate.

Cap·u·a (kăp′yŏŏ·ə; It. kä′pwä), *n.* a town in SW Italy, near Naples. 10,128 (1936).

ca·puche (kə·pōōsh′, -pōōch′), *n.* a hood or cowl; esp. the long, pointed cowl of the Capuchins.

cap·u·chin (kăp′yŏŏ·chĭn, -shĭn), *n.* **1.** a prehensile-tailed, Central and South American monkey, *Cebus capucinus*, whose head hair presents a cowllike appearance. **2.** any monkey of the genus *Cebus*. **3.** a hooded cloak for women. **4.** (*cap.*) *Rom. Cath. Ch.* one of an order of Franciscan friars, a reformed branch of the Observants, wearing a long cowl. [t. F, t. It.: m. *cappuccino*, der. *cappuccio* hood]

Capuchin monkey, *Cebus capucinus* (Total length 3 ft., tail 15 in.)

Cap·u·let (kăp′yə lĕt′, -lĭt), n. the family name of Juliet in Shakespeare's *Romeo and Juliet*.

ca·put (kā′pət, kăp′ət), n., pl. **capita** (kăp′ə tə). *Anat.* any head or headlike expansion on a structure, as on a bone. [L: the head]

cap·y·ba·ra (kăp′ĭ bä′rə), n. the largest living rodent, *Hydrochaerus hydrochaeris*, 3 or 4 feet long, living along the banks of South American rivers, sand-colored and virtually tailless. Also, **capibara**. [t. Pg.: m. *capibara*, t. Tupi: m. *kapigwara* grass eater]

Capybara, *Hydrochaerus hydrochaeris* (3 to 4 ft. long, ab 2 ft. high)

car (kär), n. 1. an automobile. 2. a vehicle running on rails, as a streetcar. 3. *Brit.* a wheeled vehicle in many varieties often one with two wheels. 4. the part of a balloon, elevator, etc., for carrying the passengers, etc. 5. *Poetic.* a chariot, as of war or triumph. 6. a perforated box floated in water, used to preserve live fish, etc. [ME *carre*, t. ONF, g. LL *carrus*, of Celtic orig.]

ca·ra·ba·o (kä′rə bä′ō), n., pl. **-baos.** (in the Philippine Islands) the water buffalo. [t. Philippine Sp., t. Malay: m. *karbau*]

car·a·bin (kär′ə bĭn), n. carbine. Also, **car·a·bine** (kär′ə bĭn′).

car·a·bi·neer (kär′ə bə nĭr′), n. a carbineer. Also, **car′a·bi·nier′.**

Car·a·cal·la (kär′ə kăl′ə), n. (*Marcus Aurelius Antoninus Bassianus*), A.D. 188–217, Roman emperor, A.D. 211–217.

ca·ra·ca·ra (kär′ə kär′ə), n. any of certain vulturelike birds of the subfamily *Polyborinae* of the warmer parts of America, as Audubon's caracara (*Polyborus cheriway*). [t. Sp., Pg., t. Tupi; imit. of its cry]

Ca·ra·cas (kə rä′kəs; Sp. kärä′käs), n. the capital of Venezuela, in the N part. 269,030 (1941).

car·a·col (kär′ə kŏl′), n., v.i. **-colled, -colling.** caracole.

car·a·cole (kär′ə kōl′), n., v., **-coled, -coling.** —n. 1. a half turn executed by a horseman in riding. —v.i. 2. to execute caracoles; wheel. [t. F, t. Sp.: m. *caracol* snail, wheeling movement, ult. der. L *scarabaeus* scarab]

Ca·rac·ta·cus (kə răk′tə kəs), n. fl. A.D. c50, British chieftain who opposed the Romans. Also, **Ca·rad·oc** (kə răd′ək).

car·a·cul (kär′ə kəl), n. 1. the skin of the very young of certain Asiatic or Russian sheep, karakul, dressed as a fur, resembling astrakhan, but with flatter, looser curl. 2. karakul (sheep). Also, **karakul**.

ca·rafe (kə răf′, -räf′), n. a glass water bottle. [t. F, t. It.: m. *caraffa*, prob. t. Sp.: m. *garrafa*, t. Ar.: m. *gharrâf* drinking vessel]

car·a·mel (kär′ə məl, -mĕl′; *Midwest often* kär′məl), n. 1. burnt sugar, used for coloring and flavoring food, etc. 2. a kind of candy, commonly in small blocks, made from sugar, butter, milk, etc. [t. F, t. Sp.]

car·a·mel·ize (kär′ə mə līz′), v.t., v.i., **-ized, -izing.** to convert or be converted into caramel.

ca·ran·goid (kə răng′goid), adj. 1. belonging to or resembling the *Carangidae*, a family of spiny-rayed fishes including the cavally, pompano, pilot fish, etc. —n. 2. a carangoid fish. [t. NL *Caranx*, the typical genus (cf. Sp. *carangue* a West Indian flatfish) + -OID]

car·a·pace (kär′ə pās′), n. a shield, test, or shell covering some or all of the dorsal part of an animal. [t. F, t. Sp.: m. *carapacho*]

car·at (kär′ət), n. 1. a unit of weight in gem stones, 200 mg. (about 3 grains of troy or avoirdupois weight). 2. karat. [t. F, t. It.: m. *carato*, t. Ar.: m. *qīraṭ* light weight, t. Gk.: m. *kerátion* carob bean, carat, dim. of *kéras* horn]

car·a·van (kär′ə văn′), n. 1. a group of merchants or others traveling together, as for safety, esp. over deserts, etc., in Asia or Africa. 2. a large covered vehicle for passengers or goods. 3. a van. 4. *Brit.* a house on wheels; a trailer. [t. F: m. *caravane*, t. Pers.: m. *kārwān*]

car·a·van·sa·ry (kär′ə văn′sə rĭ), n., pl. **-ries.** 1. (in the Near East) a kind of inn for the accommodation of caravans. 2. any large inn or hotel. Also, **car·a·van·se·rai** (kär′ə văn′sə rī′, -rā′). [ult. t. Pers.: m. *kārwānsarāī*, f. *kārwān* caravan + *sarāī* inn]

car·a·vel (kär′ə vĕl′), n. a kind of small ship formerly used esp. by the Spaniards and Portuguese. Also, **carvel**. [t. F: m. *caravelle*, t. It.: m. *caravella*. Cf. LL *carabus*, Gk. *kárabos* kind of light ship]

car·a·way (kär′ə wā′), n. 1. an umbelliferous condimental herb, *Carum Carvi*, bearing aromatic seedlike fruit (**caraway seeds**) used in cookery and medicine. 2. the fruit or seeds. [late ME, t. ML: m. *carui*, t. Ar.: m. *karawyā*. Cf. L *careum*, Gk. *káron*]

carb-, var. of carbo- before vowels, as in *carbazole*.

car·bam·ic acid (kär băm′ĭk), a hypothetical compound, NH₂COOH, known only in the form of its salts and esters. [f. CARB- + AM(IDE) + -IC]

car·ba·zole (kär′bə zōl′), n. a weakly acidic, crystalline compound, C₁₂H₉N, found with anthracene in coal tar. Many dyes are derived from it. [f. CARB- + AZ- + -OLE]

car·bide (kär′bīd, -bĭd), n. *Chem.* a compound of carbon with a more electropositive element or radical. [f. CARB- + -IDE]

car·bine (kär′bīn, -bēn), n. a short rifle (or, formerly, musket) carried by combat soldiers and noncommissioned officers who are not equipped with rifles. Also, **carabin, carabine**. [t. F: m. *carabine*, orig. a small harquebus, der. *carabin* a mounted soldier armed with this weapon, prob. alter. of ONF *escarrabin* corpsebearer, ult. der. L *scarabaeus* SCARAB]

car·bi·neer (kär′bə nĭr′), n. (formerly) a soldier armed with a carbine. Also, **carabineer, carabinier**.

car·bi·nol (kär′bə nōl′), n. 1. methyl alcohol. 2. an alcohol derived from it. [f. m. CARBON + -OL¹]

carbo-, a word element meaning "carbon," as in *carborundum*. Also, **carb-**. [comb. form of CARBON]

car·bo·cy·clic compounds (kär′bō sī′klĭk, -sĭk′lĭk), *Chem.* a group of organic compounds in which all the atoms composing the ring are carbon atoms, as naphthalene.

car·bo·hy·drate (kär′bō hī′drāt), n. any of a class of organic compounds which are polyhydroxy aldehydes or polyhydroxy ketones, or change to such substances on simple chemical transformations, such as hydrolysis, oxidation, or reduction. They form the supporting tissues of plants and are important food for animals.

car·bo·lat·ed (kär′bə lā′tĭd), adj. containing carbolic acid.

car·bol·ic acid (kär bŏl′ĭk), phenol (def. 1). [f. CARB- + -OL² + -IC]

car·bo·lize (kär′bə līz′), v.t., **-lized, -lizing.** to treat with carbolic acid.

car·bon (kär′bən), n. 1. *Chem.* a widely distributed element which forms organic compounds in combination with hydrogen, oxygen, etc., and which occurs in a pure state as the diamond and as graphite, and in an impure state as charcoal. *Symbol:* C; *at. wt.:* 12.010; *at. no.:* 6; *sp. gr.:* (of diamond) 3.51 at 20°C.; (of graphite) 2.26 at 20°C. 2. *Elect.* **a.** the carbon rod through which current is conducted between the electrode holder and the arc in carbon arc lighting or welding. **b.** the rod or plate, composed in part of carbon, used in batteries. 3. a sheet of carbon paper. 4. a duplicate copy made by using carbon paper: *a carbon of a letter*. [t. F; m. *carbone*, t. L: m.s. *carbo* coal, charcoal]

car·bo·na·ceous (kär′bə nā′shəs), adj. of, like, or containing carbon.

car·bo·na·do (kär′bə nā′dō), n., pl. **-does, -dos,** v.. **-doed, -doing.** —n. 1. a piece of meat, fish, etc., scored and broiled. 2. an opaque, dark-colored, massive form of diamond, found chiefly in Brazil, and used for drills; black diamond. —v.t. 3. to score and broil. 4. to slash; hack. [t. Sp.: m. *carbonada*, der. *carbón*, g. L *carbo* coal]

Car·bo·na·ri (kär′bō nä′rē), n.pl., sing. **-ro** (-rō) the members of a 19th century secret political society, of revolutionary aims, in Italy, France, and Spain. [It. pl., of *carbonaro* charcoal burner] —**Car′bo·na′rism,** n.

car·bon·a·ta·tion (kär′bən ə tā′shən), n. *Chem.* saturation or reaction with carbon dioxide.

car·bon·ate (n. kär′bə nāt′, -nĭt; v. kär′bə nāt′), n., v., **-ated, -ating.** —n. 1. *Chem.* a salt of carbonic acid, as *calcium carbonate*, CaCO₃. —v.t. 2. to form into a carbonate. 3. to charge or impregnate with carbon dioxide. [t. NL: m. *carbonātum* (something) carbonated]

car·bon·a·tion (kär′bə nā′shən), n. 1. saturation with carbon dioxide, as in making soda water. In *Chem.*, the preferred form is **carbonatation**. 2. reaction with carbon dioxide to remove lime, as in sugar refining. 3. carbonization.

carbon cycle, *Astrophysics.* a cycle of nuclear transformations, with the release of atomic energy, in the interiors of the stars, by means of which hydrogen is gradually converted into helium.

carbon dioxide, a colorless, odorless, incombustible gas, CO₂, used extensively in industry as dry ice, in carbonated beverages, fire extinguishers, etc. It is present in the atmosphere and formed during respiration.

carbon dioxide snow, *Chem.* carbon dioxide, CO₂, solidified under great pressure; dry ice. It is used as a refrigerant because it passes directly from a solid to a gas absorbing a great amount of heat.

car·bon·ic (kär bŏn′ĭk), adj. *Chem.* containing tetravalent carbon, as *carbonic acid*, H₂CO₃.

carbonic acid, the acid, H₂CO₃, formed when carbon dioxide dissolves in water, known in the form of its salts and esters, the carbonates.

carbonic-acid gas, carbon dioxide.

Car·bon·if·er·ous (kär′bə nĭf′ər əs), *Stratig.* —adj. 1. pertaining to a geological period or a system of rocks preceding the Permian and corresponding to combined Mississippian and Pennsylvanian of North American usage. 2. (*l.c.*) producing coal. —n. 3. a late Paleozoic period or system next following the Devonian. [f. CARBON + -(I)FEROUS]

car·bon·i·za·tion (kär′bən ə zā′shən), n. 1. formation of carbon from organic matter. 2. coal distillation, as in coke ovens.

car·bon·ize (kär′bə nīz′), v.t., **-ized, -izing.** 1. to char, forming carbon. 2. to coat or enrich with carbon.

carbon monoxide, a colorless, odorless, poisonous gas, CO, burning with a pale-blue flame, formed when carbon burns with an insufficient supply of air.

carbon paper, 1. paper faced with a preparation of carbon or other material, used between two sheets of plain paper in order to reproduce upon the lower sheet that which is written or typed on the upper. **2.** a paper for making photographs by the carbon process.

car·bon process, a method of making photographic prints by the use of a pigment, such as carbon, contained in sensitized gelatin.

carbon tetrachloride, a noninflammable, colorless liquid, CCl₄, used as in medicine, and as a fire extinguisher, cleaning fluid, solvent, etc.

car·bon·yl (kär′bən ĭl), *n. Chem.* **1.** the divalent radical >CO occurring in acids, ketones, aldehydes, and their derivatives. **2.** a compound containing metal combined with carbon monoxide, as *nickel carbonyl,* Ni(CO)₄. [f. CARBON + -YL] **—car′bon·yl′ic,** *adj.*

car·bo·run·dum (kär′bə rŭn′dəm), *n.* **1.** silicon carbide, SiC, an important abrasive produced in the electric furnace. **2.** (*cap.*) a trademark for this substance. [f. CARBO-+ (CO)RUNDUM]

car·box·yl group (kär bŏk′sĭl), *Chem.* a univalent radical, COOH, present in and characteristic of the formulas of all organic acids. Also, **carboxyl radical.** [f. CARB- + OXY(GEN) + -YL]

car·boy (kär′boi), *n.* a large glass bottle, esp. one protected by basketwork or a wooden box, as for containing acids. [t. Pers.: m. *qarābah* large flagon]

car·bun·cle (kär′bŭng kəl), *n.* **1.** a painful circumscribed inflammation of the subcutaneous tissue, resulting in suppuration and sloughing, and having a tendency to spread (somewhat like a boil, but more serious in its effects). **2.** a garnet cut in a convex rounded form without facets. **3.** (formerly) a rounded red gem, as a ruby or garnet. **4.** deep red. **5.** brownish red. [ME, t. ONF, g. L *carbunculus,* dim. of *carbo* (live) coal] **—car′bun·cled,** *adj.* **—car·bun·cu·lar** (kär bŭng′kyə lər), *adj.*

car·bu·ret (kär′bə rāt′, -byə rĕt′), *v.t.* **-reted, -reting** or (*esp. Brit.*) **-retted, -retting.** to combine or mix with carbon or hydrocarbons. [f. CARB- + -URET]

car·bu·re·tion (kär′bə rā′shon, kär′byə rĕsh′ən), *n.* (of internal-combustion engines) the process of metering air and fuel to an engine intake system in the proper proportions for combustion.

car·bu·re·tor (kär′bə rā′tər, -byə rĕt′ər), *n.* an apparatus for adding hydrocarbons to nonluminous or poor gases, or to air for the purpose of producing an illuminating or explosive gas. Also, *esp. Brit.,* **car·bu·ret·tor** (kär′byə rĕt′ər).

car·bu·rize (kär′bə rīz′, -byə-), *v.t.,* **-rized, -rizing. 1.** to cause to unite with carbon. **2.** to carburet. **—car′bu·ri·za′tion,** *n.* **—car′bu·riz′er,** *n.*

car·byl·a·mine (kär′bĭl ə mēn′, -ăm′ĭn), *n.* an organic compound containing the group -NC.

car·ca·jou (kär′kə jōō′, -zhōō′), *n.* the American glutton, *Gulo luscus;* wolverine. [t. Canadian F, t. Amer. Ind. (Algonquin); cf. Montagnais *kurkuẓu,* Ojibwa *gwing-waage,* Cree *kikkwahakes*]

car·ca·net (kär′kə nĕt′, -nĭt), *n.* **1.** *Archaic.* an ornamental collar or necklace. **2.** *Obs.* or *Hist.* an ornamental band for the head. [f. F *carcan* (of Gmc. orig.) + -ET]

car·cass (kär′kəs), *n.* **1.** the dead body of an animal or (now *only* in contempt) of a human being. **2.** (now chiefly in contempt or humor). a living body. **3.** the body of a slaughtered animal after removal of the offal, etc. **4.** anything from which life and power are gone.**5.** an unfinished framework or skeleton, as of a house or ship. Also, **car′case.** [f. m. *carcasse,* t. It.: m. *carcassa;* r. ME *carkeis,* t. AF] **—Syn. 1.** See **body.**

Car·cas·sonne (kár kȧ sôn′), *n.* a city in S France. 38,139 (1946).

car·cin·o·gen (kär sĭn′ə jən), *n. Pathol.* any substance which tends to produce a cancer in a body.

car·ci·no·ma (kär′sə nō′mə), *n., pl.* **-mata** (-mə tə), **-mas.** *Pathol.* a malignant and invasive epithelial tumor that spreads by metastasis and often recurs after excision; a cancer. [t. L, t. Gk.: m. *karkīnōma* a cancer]

car·ci·no·ma·to·sis (kär′sə nō mə tō′sĭs), *n. Pathol.* a condition marked by the production of an overwhelming number of carcinomata throughout the body. **—car·ci·nom·a·tous** (kär′sə nŏm′ə təs, -nō′mə-), *adj.*

card¹ (kärd), *n.* **1.** a piece of stiff paper or thin pasteboard, usually rectangular, for various uses: *a postal card, a union card* (showing membership in a trade union). **2.** one of a set of small cardboards with spots, figures, etc., used in playing various games. **3.** (*pl.*) a game or games played with such a set. **4.** a piece of cardboard with more or less elaborate ornamentation, bearing complimentary greeting: *a Christmas card.* **5.** a program of the events at races, etc. **6.** the circular piece of paper, etc., on which the 32 points indicating direction are marked in a compass. **7.** *Colloq.* a person of some indicated characteristic: *a queer card.* **8.** *Colloq.* an amusing or facetious person. **—v.t. 9.** to provide with a card. **10.** to fasten on a card. **11.** to write, list, etc., on cards. [ME, t. F: m. *carte,* t. L: m. *charta* (see CHART)]

card² (kärd), *n.* **1.** an implement used in disentangling and combing out fibers of wool, flax, etc., preparatory to spinning. **2.** a similar implement for raising the nap on cloth. **—v.t. 3.** to dress (wool, etc.) with a card. [ME *carde,* t. F: teasel, wool card, t. Pr.: m. *carda,* ult. der. *carere* card; prob. influenced by L *carduus* thistle] **—card′er,** *n.*

Card., Cardinal.

car·da·mom (kär′də məm), *n.* **1.** the aromatic seed capsule of various zingiberaceous plants of the genera *Amomum* and *Elettaria,* native in tropical Asia, used as

a spice or condiment and in medicine. **2.** any of the plants. Also, **car·da·mon** (kär′də mən), **car′da·mum.** [t. L: s. *cardamōmum,* t. Gk.: m. *kardámōmon*]

card·board (kärd′bōrd′), *n.* a thin, stiff pasteboard, used for signs, boxes, etc.

card case, a small pocket case for visiting cards, etc.

card catalogue, a definite arrangement of cards of uniform size (**catalogue cards**) in drawers, each card usually identifying a single publication in a library.

Cár·de·nas (kär′dē näs′), *n.* **1.** Lázaro (lä′sä rô′), born 1895, president of Mexico, 1934–40. **2.** a seaport in N W Cuba. 37,144 (1943).

cardi-, var. of **cardio-** before vowels, as in *cardialgia.*

car·di·ac (kär′dĭ ăk′), *adj.* **1.** pertaining to the heart. **2.** pertaining to the esophageal portion of the stomach. **—n. 3.** *Med.* a cardiac remedy. [t. L: s. *cardiacus* of the heart, t. Gk.: m. *kardiakós*]

cardiac glucoside, *Pharm.* one of a group of drugs used to stimulate the heart in cases of heart failure, obtained from a number of plants, as the foxglove, squill, or yellow oleander.

car·di·al·gi·a (kär′dĭ ăl′jĭ ə), *n. Pathol.* heartburn (def. 1). [f. CARDI- + -ALGIA]

Car·diff (kär′dĭf), *n.* a seaport in SE Wales. 232,450 (est. 1946).

car·di·gan (kär′də gən), *n.* a close-fitting knitted woolen jacket. Also, **cardigan jacket, cardigan sweater.** [named after seventh Earl of *Cardigan* (1797–1868)]

Car·di·gan (kär′də gən), *n.* **1.** a variety of the Welsh Corgi breed of dogs. See **Welsh Corgi. 2.** Cardiganshire.

Car·di·gan·shire (kär′dĭ gən shïr′, -shər), *n.* a county in W Wales. 52,000 pop. (est. 1946); 692 sq. mi. *Co. seat:* Cardigan. Also, **Cardigan.**

car·di·nal (kär′də nəl), *adj.* **1.** of prime importance; chief; principal; fundamental: *of cardinal significance.* **2.** deep rich red. **—n. 3.** one of the seventy members of the Sacred College of the Roman Catholic Church, ranking next to the Pope. **4.** Also, **cardinal bird, cardinal grosbeak.** a crested North American finch, *Richmondina cardinalis.* The male is brilliant red, the female brown, and both sexes sing. **5.** any of various similar birds. **6.** a deep rich red. **7.** a cardinal number. [ME, t. L: s. *cardinālis* pertaining to a hinge, chief] **—car′di·nal·ly,** *adv.* **—car′di·nal·ship′,** *n.*

car·di·nal·ate (kär′də nəl āt′), *n. Rom. Cath. Ch.* **1.** the body of cardinals. **2.** the office, rank, dignity, or incumbency of a cardinal.

cardinal flower, a North American plant, *Lobelia cardinalis,* with showy red flowers.

cardinal number, any of the numbers *one, two, three,* etc. (in distinction from *first, second, third,* etc. which are *ordinal* numbers). Also, **cardinal numeral.**

cardinal points, the four chief directions of the compass; the north, south, east, and west points.

cardinal virtues, 1. the most important elements of good character. **2.** *Ancient Philos.* justice, prudence, temperance, and fortitude.

card·ing (kär′dĭng). *n.* the process of preparing fibers as wool, cotton, etc. for spinning

cardio-, a word element meaning "heart." Also, **cardi-.** [t. Gk.: m. *kardio-,* comb. form of *kardía*]

car·di·o·gram (kär′dĭ ə grăm′), *n.* a tracing made by the cardiograph.

car·di·o·graph (kär′dĭ ə grăf′, -gräf′), *n.* an instrument for recording by a line graph the movements of the heart. [f. CARDIO- + GRAPH] **—car′di·o·graph′ic,** *adj.* **—car·di·og·ra·phy** (kär′dĭ ŏg′rə fĭ), *n.*

car·di·oid (kär′dĭ oid′), *n. Math.* a somewhat heart-shaped curve, being the path of a point on a circle which rolls externally, without slipping on another equal circle. [t. Gk.: m.s. *kardioeidēs* heart-shaped. See CARDIO-,-OID]

car·di·ol·o·gy (kär′dĭ ŏl′ə jĭ), *n.* the study of the heart and its functions.

Cardioid

car·di·tis (kär dī′tĭs), *n. Pathol.* inflammation of the pericardium, myocardium, or endocardium, separately or in combination. [f. CARD(IO)- + -ITIS]

car·doon (kär dōōn′), *n.* a perennial edible plant, *Cynara Cardunculus,* native in Mediterranean regions, related to the artichoke. [t. F: m. *cardon,* t. Pr., der. L *carduus* thistle]

Car·do·zo (kär dō′zə), *n.* **Benjamin Nathan,** 1870–1938, associate justice, U. S. Supreme Court, 1932–38.

card·sharp (kärd′shärp′), *n.* a person, esp. a professional gambler, who cheats at card games. Also, **card′sharp′er. —card′sharp′ing,** *n.*

car·du·a·ceous (kär′jōō ā′shəs), *adj. Bot.* belonging to the family Carduaceae, regarded as part of the *Compositae* by most botanists, and including goldenrods, asters, boltonias, fleabanes, and many other genera throughout the world. [f. s. NL *Carduāceae* (der. L *carduus* thistle)+ -OUS]

Car·duc·ci (kär dōōt′chē), *n.* **Giosuè** (jô swě′), 1835–1907, Italian poet.

care (kâr), *n., v.,* **cared, caring. —n. 1.** worry; anxiety; concern: *care had aged him.* **2.** a cause of worry, anxiety, distress, etc.: *to be free from care.* **3.** serious attention; solicitude; heed; caution: *devote great care to work.* **4.** protection; charge: *under the care of a doctor.* **5.** an object of concern or attention. **6.** *Obs.* grief;

mental distress. —*v.i.* **7.** to be concerned or solicitous: have thought or regard. **8.** to be unconcerned or to have no special preference (with a negative): *I don't care if I do.* **9.** to make provision or look out (fol. by *for*): *I'll care for his education.* **10.** to have an inclination, liking, fondness, or affection (fol. by *for*). **11.** to be inclined (fol. by *to*): *I don't care to do it today.* [ME; OE *caru* (*cearu*), c. Goth. *kara*]
—**Syn. 1.** See **concern.3.** To take CARE, PAINS, TROUBLE (to do something) implies watchful, conscientious effort to do something exactly right. To take CARE implies the performance of one particular detail: *she took care to close the cover before striking the match.* To take PAINS suggests a sustained carefulness, an effort to see that nothing is overlooked but that every small detail receives attention: *to take pains with fine embroidery.* To take TROUBLE implies an effort which requires a considerable amount of activity and exertion: *to take the trouble to prepare suitable arrangements.*

ca·reen (kərēn′), *v.t.* **1.** to cause (a ship) to lie wholly or partly on its side, as for repairing or the like. **2.** to clean or repair (a ship in such a position). **3.** to cause (a ship) to heel over. —*v.i.* **4.** to lean, sway, or tip to one side, as a ship. **5.** to careen a ship. —*n.* **6.** a careening. **7.** the position of a careened ship. [t. F: m. *carine*, t. L: m. *carina* keel] —**ca·reen′er,** *n.*

ca·reer (kərîr′), *n.* **1.** general course of action or progress of a person through life, as in some profession, in some moral or intellectual action, etc. **2.** an occupation, profession, etc. followed as one's lifework: *a career in law.* **3.** success in a profession, occupation, etc. **4.** a course, esp. a swift one. **5.** speed; full speed. **6.** *Obs.* a charge at full speed. —*v.i.* **7.** to run or move rapidly along. [t. F: m. *carrière,* t. It.: m. *carriera,* der. *carro,* g. L *carrus.* See CAR] —**ca·reer′ist,** *n.*

care·free (kâr′frē′), *adj.* without anxiety or worry.

care·ful (kâr′fəl), *adj.* **1.** cautious in one's actions. **2.** taking pains in one's work; exact; thorough. **3.** (of things) done or performed with accuracy or caution. **4.** solicitously mindful (fol. by *of, about, in*): *careful of the rights of others, about your person, in speech.* **5.** *Archaic.* troubled. **6.** *Archaic.* attended with anxiety. —**care′ful·ly,** *adv.* —**care′ful·ness,** *n.*
—**Syn. 1.** watchful, guarded, chary, circumspect. CARE-FUL, CAUTIOUS, DISCREET, WARY imply a watchful guarding against something. CAREFUL implies guarding against mistakes, by paying strict and close attention to details, and, often, trying to use good judgment: *he was careful to distinguish between them.* CAUTIOUS implies a fear of some unfavorable situation, and investigation before coming to conclusions: *cautious about investments.* DISCREET implies being prudent in speech and action, and being trustworthy as a confidant: *discreet in manner, in keeping secrets.* WARY implies a vigilant lookout for a danger suspected or feared: *wary of polite strangers.* **2.** painstaking, meticulous. **4.** solicitous, attentive, heedful, regardful.

care·less (kâr′lĭs), *adj.* **1.** not paying enough attention to what one does. **2.** not exact or thorough: *careless work.* **3.** done or said heedlessly or negligently; unconsidered: *a careless remark.* **4.** not caring or troubling; having no care or concern; unconcerned (fol. by *of, about, in*): *careless of his health, about his person, in speech.* **5.** artless. **6.** *Archaic.* free from anxiety. —**care′less·ly,** *adv.* —**care′less·ness,** *n.* —**Syn. 1.** incautious, unwary, indiscreet, reckless. **2.** inaccurate, negligent.

ca·ress (kərĕs′), *n.* **1.** an act or gesture expressing affection, as an embrace, pat, kiss, etc. —*v.t.* **2.** to touch or pat gently to show affection. **3.** to touch, etc., as if in affection. **4.** to treat with favor, kindness, etc. [t. F: m. *caresse,* t. It.: m. *carezza,* der. L *cārus* dear] —**ca·ress′er,** *n.* —**ca·ress′ing·ly,** *adv.*

car·et (kăr′ət), *n.* a mark (∧) made in written or printed matter to show the place where something is to be inserted. [t. L: there is lacking]

care·tak·er (kâr′tā′kər), *n.* a person who takes care of a thing, place, or person.

Ca·rew (kərōō′; *sometimes* kâr′ōō), *n.* **Thomas,** c1595–c1645, British poet.

care·worn (kâr′wôrn′), *adj.* showing signs of care; tired and troubled with worries: *a careworn mother.*

car·fare (kär′fâr′), *n.* the amount charged for a ride on a streetcar, bus, etc.

car·go (kär′gō), *n., pl.* **-goes, -gos. 1.** the lading or freight of a ship. **2.** load. [t. Sp., der. *cargar* load] —**Syn. 1.** See **freight.**

Car·ib (kăr′ĭb), *n.* **1.** a member of an Indian people of NE South America, formerly dominant through the Lesser Antilles. **2.** an extensive linguistic stock of the West Indies and of NE South America. [t. Sp.: m. *Caribe.* See CANNIBAL] —**Car′ib·an,** *adj.*

Car·ib·be·an (kăr′ə bē′ən, kə rĭb′ē-), *adj.* **1.** pertaining to the Caribs, the Lesser Antilles, or the Caribbean Sea. —*n.* **2.** a Carib. **3.** Also, **Caribbean Sea.** a sea between Central America, the West Indies, and South America. ab. 750,000 sq. mi.; greatest known depth, 20,568 ft.

car·i·bou (kăr′ə bōō′), *n., pl.* **-bous,** (*esp. collectively*) **bou.** any of several North American species or varieties of reindeer, esp. *Rangifer caribou* (and *R. tarandus*). See illus. in next col. [t. Canadian F, t. Algonquian (Micmac): m. *xalibu* pawer, scratcher]

car·i·ca·ture (kăr′ĭ kə chər, -chŏŏr′), *n., v., -tured, -turing. —n.* **1.** a picture, description, etc., ludicrously exaggerating the peculiarities or defects of persons or things. **2.** the art or process of making such pictures, etc. **3.** any imitation or copy so inferior as to be ludicrous. —*v.t.* **4.** to make a caricature of; represent in caricature. [t. F, t. It.: m. *caricatura,* der. *caricare* (over)load, exaggerate. See CHARGE, v.] —**car′i·ca·tur·ist,** *n.*

car·ies (kâr′ēz, -ĭ ēz′), *n.* decay, as of bone or teeth, or of plant tissue. [t. L]

Caribou.
Rangifer caribou
(Total length 6 ft., ab. 4 ft. high at the shoulder)

car·il·lon (kăr′ə lŏn′, -lən, kə rĭl′yən), *n., v., -lonned, -lonning. —n.* **1.** a set of stationary bells hung in a tower and sounded by manual or pedal action, or by machinery. **2.** a melody played on such bells. **3.** an organ stop which imitates the peal of bells. **4.** a set of horizontal metal plates, struck by hammers, used in the modern orchestra. —*v.i.* **5.** to play a carillon. [t. F: chime of (orig. four) bells, alter. of OF *carignon,* ult. der. L *quattuor* four]

car·il·lon·neur (kăr′ə lə nûr′; *Fr.* ká rē yô nœr′), *n.* one who plays a carillon. [F]

ca·ri·na (kə rī′nə), *n., pl.* **-nae** (-nē). *Bot., Zool.* a keel-like part or ridge. [t. L: keel] —**ca·ri′nal,** *adj.*

Ca·ri·na (kə rī′nə), *n. gen.* **-nae** (-nē). *Astron.* a southern constellation, containing the bright star, Canopus: one of the subordinate constellations into which Argo is divided.

car·i·nate (kăr′ə nāt′), *adj. Bot., Zool.* formed with a carina; keellike. Also, **car′i·nat′ed.** [t. L: m. s. *carīnātus,* pp., keel-shaped]

Ca·rin·thi·a (kə rĭn′thĭ ə), *n.* a province in S Austria. 405,129 pop. (1934); 3681 sq. mi. *Cap.:* Klagenfurt.

Ca·ri·o·ca (kăr′ĭ ō′kə; *Port.* kä′rē ô′kə), *n.* a native of Rio de Janeiro.

car·i·ole (kăr′ĭ ōl′), *n.* **1.** a small, open, two-wheeled vehicle. **2.** a covered cart. Also, **carriole.** [t. F: m. *carriole,* t. It.: m. *carriuola,* ult. der. L *carrus.* Cf. CARRYALL]

car·i·ous (kâr′ĭ əs), *adj.* having caries, as teeth; decayed. [t. L: m. s. *cariōsus*] —**car·i·os·i·ty** (kâr′ĭ ŏs′ə tĭ), **car′i·ous·ness,** *n.*

cark·ing (kär′kĭng), *adj.* anxious; troubled.

carl (kärl), *n.* **1.** *Scot.* a robust fellow. **2.** *Archaic.* a churl. **3.** *Archaic.* a farmer. **4.** *Obs.* a bondman. Also, **carle.** [OE, t. Scand.; cf. Icel. *karl* man, c. *Charles* proper name. Cf. CHURL]

car·line (kär′lĭn, kěr′-), *n. Chiefly Scot.* **1.** an old woman. **2.** a hag; witch. [northern ME *kerling,* t. Scand.; cf. Icel. *kerling* old woman. See CARL]

car·ling (kär′lĭng), *n.* one of the fore-and-aft timbers in a ship which form part of the deck framework.

Car·lisle (kär līl′), *n.* a city in NW England, in Cumberland county. 63,830 (est. 1946).

Car·list (kär′lĭst), *n.* **1.** a supporter of the claims of Don Carlos of Spain, or of his successors, to the Spanish throne. **2.** a partizan of Charles X of France, and of the elder branch of the Bourbons. —**Car′lism,** *n.*

car·load (kär′lōd′), *n. Chiefly U.S.* **1.** the amount carried by a car, esp. a freight car. **2.** the legal minimum weight entitling a shipper to a rate (**carload rate**) lower than that charged for less than this weight.

carload lot, *U.S.* a standard carload shipment of freight which measures up to the legal minimum amount.

Car·los (kär′lŏs; *Sp.* -lōs), *n.* **Don** (*Sp.* dôn), (*Count of Molina*) 1788–1855, a Spanish prince and pretender (second son of Charles IV).

Car·lo·ta (kär lō′tä), 1840–1927, wife of Maximilian, Archduke of Austria: Empress of Mexico, 1864–67.

Car·lo·vin·gi·an (kär′lə vĭn′jĭ ən), *adj.* Carolingian.

Carls·bad (kärlz′băd; *Ger.* kärls′bät), *n.* a city in W Czechoslovakia: mineral springs; Carlsbad decrees, 1819. 53,311 (1939). German, **Karlsbad.** Czech, **Karlovy Vary.**

Carlsbad Caverns, a series of enormous limestone caverns in SE New Mexico.

Carl·son (kärl′sən), *n.* **1. Anton Julius** (än′tōn), born 1875, U.S. physiologist, born in Sweden. **2. Evans Fordyce** (fôr′dīs), 1896–1947, U.S. Marine Corps general in World War II.

Car·lyle (kär līl′), *n.* **Thomas,** 1795–1881, Scottish essayist and historian.

car·ma·gnole (kär′mən yōl′; *Fr.* kár má nyôl′), *n.* a dance and song popular during the French Revolution. [t. F, ?from *Carmagnola,* town in NW Italy]

car·man (kär′mən), *n., pl.* **-men. 1.** one of the crew of a streetcar or the like. **2.** one who drives a car or cart.

Car·man (kär′mən), *n.* (**William**) **Bliss,** 1861–1929, Canadian poet who spent most of his life in the U.S.

Car·ma·ni·a (kär mā′nĭ ə), *n.* a province of the ancient Persian Empire, on the Gulf of Oman.

Car·mar·then·shire (kär mär′tħən shīr′, -shər), *n.* a county in S Wales. 166,000 pop. (est. 1946); 919 sq. mi. *Co. seat.:* Carmarthen. Also, **Car·mar′then.**

Car·mel (kär′məl), *n.* **Mount,** a ridge in NW Israel. near the Mediterranean coast. ab. 14 mi. long; highest point, ab. 1800 ft.

Car·mel·ite (kär′məlīt′), *n.* **1.** a mendicant friar belonging to a religious order founded at Mt. Carmel, Palestine, in the 12th century; a white friar. **2.** a nun belonging to this order. [t. LL: m. *Carmēlītēs,* t. Gk.: m. *Karmēlītēs* inhabitant of Mt. Carmel]

car·min·a·tive (kär mĭn′ə tĭv, kär′mə nā′tĭv), *n.* **1.** a drug causing expulsion of gas from the stomach or bowel. —*adj.* **2.** expelling gas from the body; relieving flatulence. [f. s. L *carminātus,* pp., carded + -IVE]

car·mine (kär′mĭn, -mīn), *n.* **1.** a crimson or purplish-red color. **2.** a crimson pigment obtained from cochineal. —*adj.* **3.** crimson or purplish-red. [t. ML: m.s. *carmīnus,* contr. of *carmesīnus,* der. Sp. *carmesí* CRIMSON]

car·nage (kär′nĭj), *n.* **1.** the slaughter of a great number, as in battle; butchery; massacre. **2.** *Archaic.* dead bodies, as of men slain in battle. [t. F, t. It: m. *carnaggio,* der. *carne* meat, g. s. L *caro* flesh]

car·nal (kär′nəl), *adj.* **1.** not spiritual; merely human; temporal; worldly. **2.** pertaining to the flesh or the body, its passions and appetites; sensual. **3.** sexual. [ME, t. L: s. *carnālis,* der. L *caro* flesh] —**car·nal′i·ty,** *n.* —**car′nal·ly,** *adv.* —**Syn. 2.** fleshly, bodily, animal. **3.** lustful, impure, gross, worldly.

car·nall·ite (kär′nəlīt′), *n.* a mineral, a hydrous potassium magnesium chloride, $KMgCl_3.6H_2O$: a valuable source of potassium. [named after R. von *Carnall* (1804–1874), Prussian mining official. See -ITE[1]]

Car·nar·von (kär när′vən), *n.* Caernarvonshire.

car·nas·si·al (kär năs′ĭ əl), *Zool.* —*adj.* **1.** (of teeth) adapted for shearing flesh, as certain of the upper and lower cheek teeth of cats, civets, dogs, etc. —*n.* **2.** a carnassial tooth, esp. the last upper premolar or the first lower molar tooth of certain carnivores. [f. m. F *carnassier* flesh-eating (t. Pr.: m. *carnasier,* der. L *caro* flesh) + -AL[1]]

Car·nat·ic (kär năt′ĭk), *n.* a historically important region on the SE coast of India: now in Madras province.

car·na·tion (kär nā′shən), *n.* **1.** any of numerous cultivated varieties of clove pink, *Dianthus Caryophyllus,* with fragrant flowers of various colors: the State flower of Ohio. **2.** pink; light red. **3.** the colors of flesh as represented in painting. [t. F, t. It.: m. *carnagiōne* flesh-color, der. *carne* meat, g. s. L *caro* flesh]

car·nau·ba (kär nou′bə), *n.* **1.** the Brazilian wax palm, *Copernicia cerifera.* **2.** a yellowish or greenish wax derived from the young leaves of this tree, used as a polish, and in phonograph records. [t. Brazilian Pg.]

Car·ne·gie (kär nā′gĭ), *n.* **Andrew,** 1835–1919, U. S. steel manufacturer and philanthropist; born in Scotland.

car·nel·ian (kär nēl′yən), *n.* a red or reddish variety of chalcedony, used in jewelry, etc. Also, **cornelian.** [alter. (due to ɑɑɑoc. with L *caro* flesh) of ME *corneline,* t. OF, of uncert. orig. Cf. ML *corneltus*]

car·ni·fy (kär′nə fī′), *v.i., v.t.,* **-fied, -fying.** to turn into or form flesh; make or become fleshlike. [t. L: m. *carnificāre.* See -FY]

Car·ni·o·la (kär nyō′lä), *n.* a former duchy and crownland of Austria: now in NW Yugoslavia.

car·ni·val (kär′nə vəl), *n.* **1.** an amusement show, usually traveling from place to place, having side shows, a Ferris wheel, merry-go-rounds, etc. **2.** any merrymaking, usually noisy and riotous; revelry. **3.** the season immediately preceding Lent, often observed with merrymaking. [t. It.: m. *carnevale,* alter. of *carnesciale,* der. *carnescialare, carnelasciare* leave off (eating) meat]

Car·niv·o·ra (kär nĭv′ə rə), *n.pl. Zool.* See **carnivore** (def. 1).

car·ni·vore (kär′nə vôr′), *n.* **1.** *Zool.* one of the *Carnivora,* the order of mammals, chiefly flesh-eating, that includes the cats, dogs, bears, seals, etc. **2.** *Bot.* a flesh-eating plant. [see CARNIVOROUS]

car·niv·o·rous (kär nĭv′ə rəs), *adj.* flesh-eating. [t. L: m. *carnivorus*] —**car·niv′o·rous·ly,** *adv.* —**car·niv′o·rous·ness,** *n.*

Car·not cycle (kär nō′), a cycle of engine operations giving the maximum thermal efficiency obtainable by an engine working between any two temperatures.

car·no·tite (kär′nə tīt′), *n.* a mineral, a yellow, earthy, hydrous potassium uranium vanadate: an ore of uranium. [named after A. *Carnot,* French inspector general of mines. See -ITE[1]]

car·ob (kär′əb), *n.* **1.** the fruit of a caesalpinaceous tree, *Ceratonia Siliqua,* of the Mediterranean regions, a long, dry pod containing hard seeds in a sweet pulp, used for feeding animals and sometimes eaten by man. **2.** the tree. [t. F: m. *carobe,* t. Ar.: m. *kharrūba*]

ca·roche (kə rōch′, -rōsh′), *n.* an old form of stately coach or carriage. [t. F (obs.): m. *carroche,* t. It.: m. *carroccio,* aug. of *carro* chariot, g. L *carrus;* akin to CAR]

car·ol (kär′əl), *n., v.,* **-oled, -oling** or (*esp. Brit.*) **-olled, -olling. 1.** a song, esp. of joy. **2.** a Christmas song or hymn. **3.** *Obs.* a kind of circular dance. —*v.i.* **4.** to sing, esp. in a lively, joyous manner; warble. —*v.t.* **5.** to sing joyously. **6.** to praise or celebrate in song. [ME, t. OF: m. *carole;* prob. from Celtic root *cor-* circle, b. with L *choraula* minstrel, chorus leader, t. Gk.: m. *choraũlēs*] —**car′ol·er;** *esp. Brit.,* **car′ol·ler,** *n.*

Car·ol II (kär′əl; *Rum.* kä′rôl), born 1893, king of Rumania; 1930–40.

Car·o·le·an (kär′ə lē′ən), *adj. Brit.* characteristic of the time of Charles I and II: *a Carolean costume.*

Car·o·li·na (kär′ə lī′nə), *n.* **1.** a former English colony on the Atlantic coast of North America: officially divided into North Carolina and South Carolina, 1729. **2.** the **Carolinas,** North Carolina and South Carolina.

Car·o·line (kär′ə lĭn′, -lĭn), *adj.* of or pertaining to some person named Charles, as Charles I or Charles II of England, or the period in which he flourished.

Caroline Islands, a group of over 500 islands in the Pacific, E of the Philippine Islands: formerly a Japanese mandate; now under U.S. administration. 54,900 pop. (est. 1937); 525 sq. mi.

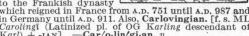

Car·o·lin·gi·an (kär′ə lĭn′jĭ ən), *adj.* belonging to the Frankish dynasty which reigned in France from A.D. 751 until A.D. 987 and in Germany until A.D. 911. Also, **Carlovingian.** [f. s. ML *Carolingī* (Latinized pl. of OG *Karling* descendant of *Karl*) + -IAN] —**Car′o·lin·gi·an,** *n.*

Car·o·lin·i·an (kär′ə lĭn′ĭ ən), *adj.* **1.** of or pertaining to North and South Carolina or to either one of them. **2.** Carolingian. **3.** Caroline. —*n.* **4.** a native or inhabitant of North or South Carolina.

car·o·lus (kär′ə ləs), *n., pl.* **-luses, -li** (-lī′). any of various coins issued under monarchs named Charles, esp. an English gold coin struck in the reign of Charles I, orig. worth 20 and later 23 shillings. [t. ML: Charles]

car·om (kär′əm), *n.* **1.** *Billiards.* a shot in which the ball struck with the cue is made to hit two balls in succession. **2.** any strike and rebound, as a ball striking a wall and glancing off. —*v.i.* **3.** to make a carom. **4.** to strike and rebound. Also, **carrom.** [earlier *carambole,* t. F, t. Sp.: m. *carambola;* ? identical with *carambola,* name of fruit, t. Malay: m. *carambil*]

car·o·tene (kär′ə tēn′), *n. Chem.* any of three isomeric red hydrocarbons, $C_{40}H_{56}$, found in many plants, esp. carrots, and transformed to vitamin A in the liver. Also, **car·o·tin** (kär′ə tĭn). [f. s. L *carota* CARROT + -ENE]

ca·rot·e·noid (kə rŏt′ə noid′), *Chem.* —*n.* **1.** any of a group of red and yellow pigments, chemically similar to carotene, contained in animal fat and some plants. —*adj.* **2.** similar to carotene. **3.** pertaining to carotenoids. Also, **ca·rot′i·noid.** [f. CAROTENE + -OID]

ca·rot·id (kə rŏt′ĭd), *Anat.* —*n.* **1.** either of the two great arteries, one on each side of the neck, which carry blood to the head. —*adj.* **2.** pertaining to the carotids. [t. Gk.: s. *karōtídes,* pl., der. *kāros* stupor (thought to be caused by compression of these arteries)] —**ca·rot′id·al,** *adj.*

ca·rous·al (kə rou′zəl), *n.* **1.** a noisy or drunken feast or other social gathering; jovial revelry. **2.** carrousel (def. 2). [f. CAROUSE, v. + -AL[2]]

ca·rouse (kə rouz′), *n., v.,* **-roused, -rousing.** —*n.* **1.** a noisy or drunken feast; jovial revelry. —*v.i.* **2.** to engage in a carouse; drink deeply. [n. and v. uses of obs. adv., t. G: m. *gar aus* wholly out]

car·ou·sel (kär′ə zěl′, -sěl′), *n.* carrousel.

carp[1] (kärp), *v.i.* to find fault; cavil; complain unreasonably: *to carp at minor errors.* [ME *carpe(n),* t. Scand.; cf. Icel. *karpa* wrangle, dispute] —**carp′er,** *n.* —**carp′ing·ly,** *adv.*

carp[2] (kärp), *n., pl.* **carps,** (*esp. collectively*) **carp. 1.** a large, coarse fresh-water food fish, *Cyprinus carpio* (family *Cyprinidae*), commonly bred in ponds. **2.** any of various other fishes of the same family, also known as minnows. [ME *carpe,* t. OF, t. Pr.: m. *carpa,* g. LL *carpa;* of Gmc. orig.]

-carp, a noun termination meaning "fruit," used in botanical terms, as *endocarp.* [comb. form repr. Gk. *karpós*]

carp., carpentry.

car·pal (kär′pəl), *Anat.* —*adj.* **1.** pertaining to the carpus: *the carpal joint.* —*n.* **2.** a carpale. [t. NL: s. *carpālis,* der. L *carpus* wrist]

car·pa·le (kär pā′lĭ), *n., pl.* **-lia** (-lĭ′ə). *Anat.* any of the bones of the wrist. Also, **carpal.** [t. NL, neut. of *carpālis* CARPAL]

Car·pa·thi·an Mountains (kär pā′thĭ ən), a mountain system in central Europe, extending ab. 800 mi. from N Czechoslovakia to central Rumania. Highest peak, Gerlachovka, 8737 ft. Also, **Carpathians.**

Car·pa·tho-U·kraine (kär pā′thō ū krān′), *n.* a region in the SW Soviet Union, in the Ukrainian Republic: ceded by Czechoslovakia, 1945. 725,357 pop. (1930); 4871 sq. mi. Formerly, **Ruthenia** or **Carpathian Ruthenia.**

car·pe di·em (kär′pĭ dī′ĕm), enjoy the present day, trusting as little as possible to the future. [L]

car·pel (kär′pəl), *n. Bot.* a simple pistil, or a single member of a compound pistil: regarded as a modified leaf. [t. NL: m. s. *carpellum,* der. Gk. *karpós* fruit] —**car·pel·lar·y** (kär′pə lěr′ĭ), *adj.*

car·pel·late (kär′pə lāt′), *adj. Bot.* having carpels.

Car·pen·tar·i·a (kär′pən tãr′ĭ ə), *n.* **Gulf of,** a large gulf on the N coast of Australia. ab. 420 mi. wide; ab. 480 mi. long.

Carpels
A. Flower with simple pistils;
B. Tricarpellary fruit

---

car·pen·ter (kär/pən tər), *n.* **1.** a workman who uses tools and lumber in the building of houses and other wooden structures. —*v.i.* **2.** to do carpenter's work. —*v.t.* **3.** to make by carpentry. [ME, t. ONF: m. *carpentier*, g. LL *carpentārius* wagon maker, der. L *carpentum* wagon] —**car/pen·ter·ing,** **car/pen·try,** *n.*

Car·pen·ter (kär/pən tər), *n.* **John Alden,** born 1876, U.S. composer.

carpenter bee, any of various solitary bees of the family *Xylocopidae* that make their nests in wood, boring tunnels in which to deposit their eggs.

car·pet (kär/pĭt), *n.* **1.** a heavy fabric, commonly of wool, for covering floors. **2.** a covering of this material. **3.** any covering like a carpet: *they walked on the grassy carpet.* **4. on the carpet, a.** under consideration or discussion. **b.** before an authority for a reprimand. —*v.t.* **5.** to cover or furnish with, or as with, a carpet. **6.** to reprimand. [ME *carpete*, t. ML: m. *carpeta*, ult. der. L *carpere* card (wool)]

car·pet·bag (kär/pĭt băg/), *n.* a bag for traveling, esp. one made of carpeting.

car·pet·bag·ger (kär/pĭt băg/ər), *n.* **1.** a person who takes up residence in a place, with no more property than he brings in a carpetbag, to seek special advantages for himself. **2.** (in U. S. history) **a.** *Contemptuous.* a Northerner who went to the South after the Civil War to seek political or other advantages made possible by the disorganized condition of political affairs. **b.** a wildcat banker in the western U. S. who had no office and could not be found when wanted.

carpet beetle, a small beetle, *Anthrenus scrophulariae,* whose larvae are destructive to carpets and other woolen fabrics; buffalo bug. Also, **carpet bug.**

car·pet·ing (kär/pĭt ĭng), *n.* **1.** material for carpets. **2.** carpets in general.

car·pet·weed (kär/pĭt wēd/), *n.* a North American prostrate weed, *Mollugo verticillata.*

car·pi (kär/pī), *n.* pl. of **carpus.**

-carpic, a word element related to **-carp,** as in *endocarpic.* [f. -CARP + -IC]

carpo-, a word element meaning "fruit" as in *carpology.* [t. Gk.: m. *karpo-,* comb. form of *karpós*]

car·po·go·ni·um (kär/pə gō/nĭ əm), *n.,* pl. **-nia** (-nĭ ə). *Bot.* the one-celled female sex organ of the red algae (*Rhodophyceae*) which, when fertilized, gives rise to the carpospores. [NL; see CARPO-, -GONIUM] —**car/po·go/ni·al,** *adj.*

car·pol·o·gy (kär pŏl/ə jĭ), *n.* the branch of botany that relates to fruits. —**car·po·log·i·cal** (kär/pə lŏj/ə kəl), *adj.* —**car·pol/o·gist,** *n.*

car·poph·a·gous (kär pŏf/ə gəs), *adj.* fruit-eating.

car·po·phore (kär/pə fôr/), *n.* *Bot.* **1.** a slender prolongation of the floral axis, bearing the carpels of some compound fruits, as in the geranium and in many umbelliferous plants. **2.** the fruit body of the higher fungi.

car·port (kär/pôrt), *n.* a roofed, wall-less shed projecting from the side of a building, used as a shelter for a motor vehicle.

car·po·spore (kär/pə spôr/), *n.* *Bot.* a nonmotile spore of the red algae.

-carpous, a combining form related to **-carp,** as in *apocarpous.* [f. -CARP + -OUS]

car·pus (kär/pəs), *n.,* pl. **-pi** (-pī). *Anat.* **1.** the part of the upper extremity between the hand and the forearm; the wrist. **2.** the wrist bones collectively; the group of bones between the bones of the hand and the radius. See diag. under **shoulder.** [t. NL; t. Gk.: m. *karpós* wrist]

Carpophore (def. 1), with carpels

car·rack (kär/ək), *n.* *Archaic.* a galleon. [ME *caracke,* t. OF: m. *carraque,* t. Sp., Pg.: m. *carraca,* t. Ar.: m. *qarāqīr,* pl. of *qurqūr* merchant vessel; or m. *harraqa* boat]

car·ra·geen (kär/ə gēn/), *n.* Irish moss (def. 1). Also, **car/ra·gheen/.** [named after *Carragheen,* in S Eire]

Car·ran·za (kə rän/zə; *Sp.* kär rän/sä), *n.* **Venustiano** (vĕ/nōō styä/nō), 1859–1920, president of Mexico, 1915–20.

Car·ra·ra (kär rä/rä), *n.* a city in NW Italy: famous for its marble. 59,328 (est. 1946).

car·rel (kär/əl), *n.* (in a library) a small area or cubicle near the stacks used by faculty members and certain students for individual study.

Car·rel (kə rĕl/, kär/əl; *Fr.* kå rĕl/), *n.* **Alexis** (ə lĕk/sĭs; *Fr.* å lĕk sē/), 1873–1944, U.S. surgeon and biologist, born in France.

car·riage (kär/ĭj; *also for 7* kăr/ĭj), *n.* **1.** a wheeled vehicle for conveying persons, usually drawn by horses, esp. one designed for comfort and elegance. **2.** *Brit.* a railway car. **3.** a wheeled support, as for a cannon. **4.** a part, as of a machine, designed for carrying something. **5.** manner of carrying the head and body; bearing: *the carriage of a soldier.* **6.** act of transporting; conveyance: *the expenses of carriage.* **7.** the price or cost of transportation. **8.** management. [ME *cariage,* t. ONF, der. *carier.* See CARRY] —**Syn. 5.** deportment.

car·rick bend (kär/ĭk), *Naut.* a kind of knot for joining cables or hawsers. See illus. under **knot.**

carrick bitt, *Naut.* one of the bitts which support the windlass.

car·ri·er (kär/ĭ ər), *n.* **1.** a person or thing that carries. **2.** a person, company, etc. that undertakes to convey goods or persons for hire. **3.** *Mach.* a mechanism

by which something is carried or moved. **4.** *Immunol.* an individual harboring specific organisms, who, though often immune to the agent harbored, may transmit the disease to others. **5.** *Chem.* a catalytic agent which brings about a transfer of an element or group of atoms from one compound to another. **6.** Also, **carrier wave.** *Radio.* the wave whose amplitude, frequency or phase is to be varied or modulated to transmit a signal. **7.** carrier pigeon.

carrier pigeon, 1. a pigeon trained to fly home from great distances and thus transport written messages; a homing pigeon. **2.** one of a breed of domestic pigeons characterized by a huge wattle at the base of the beak.

car·ri·ole (kär/ĭ ōl/), *n.* cariole.

car·ri·on (kär/ĭ ən), *n.* **1.** dead and putrefying flesh. **2.** rottenness; anything vile. —*adj.* **3.** feeding on carrion. **4.** of or like carrion. [ME *caroine,* t. ONF, var. of central OF *charoigne,* ult. der. L *caro* flesh]

carrion crow, 1. any of various crows, as the common European crow, *Corvus corone.* **2.** a black vulture, *Coragyps atratus,* of the southern U. S., etc.

Car·roll (kär/əl), *n.* **1. Charles,** 1737–1832, American patriot and legislator. **2. Lewis,** (*Charles Lutwidge Dodgson*) 1832–98, British mathematician and writer.

car·rom (kär/əm), *n., v.i.* carom.

car·ro·ma·ta (kär/rō mä/tä), *n.* (in the Philippines) a light, two-wheeled covered vehicle, usually drawn by one horse. [t. Sp.: m. *carromato,* der. carro cart, g. L *carrus*]

car·ron·ade (kär/ə nād/), *n.* a short piece of muzzle-loading ordnance, formerly in use, esp. in ships. [der. *Carron* (Scotland), site of a cannon foundry]

car·ron oil (kär/ən), *Pharm.* a liniment containing limewater and oil, used esp. for burns.

car·rot (kär/ət), *n.* **1.** a plant of the umbelliferous genus *Daucus,* esp. *D. Carota,* in its wild form a widespread, familiar weed, and in cultivation valued for its yellowish edible root. **2.** the root. [t. F: m. *carotte,* t. L: m. s. *carōta,* t. Gk.: m. *karōtón*]

car·rot·y (kär/ət ĭ), *adj.* **1.** like a carrot root in color; yellowish-red. **2.** having red hair.

car·rou·sel (kär/ə zĕl/, -sĕl/), *n.* **1.** a merry-go-round (def. 1). **2.** a tournament in which horsemen executed various formations. Also, **carousel.** [t. F, t. It.: m. *carosello,* der. carro, g. L *carrus* cart]

car·ry (kär/ĭ), *v.,* **-ried, -rying,** *n.,* pl. **-ries.** —*v.t.* **1.** to convey from one place to another in a car, ship, pocket, hand, etc. **2.** to transmit or transfer in any manner; take or bring: *the wind carries sounds, he carries his audience with him.* **3.** to bear the weight, burden, etc., of; sustain. **4.** *U.S.* to take a (leading or guiding part) in singing; bear or sustain (a part or melody). **5.** to hold (the body, head, etc.) in a certain manner. **6.** to behave or comport (oneself). **7.** to take, esp. by force; capture; win. **8.** to secure the election of (a candidate) or the adoption of (a motion or bill). **9.** to extend or continue in a given direction or to a certain point: *to carry the war into enemy territory.* **10.** to impel or drive. **11.** *Southern U.S.* to lead, escort, or conduct: *to carry a girl to a dance, a mule to the barn.* **12.** to lead or impel; conduct. **13.** to have as an attribute, property, consequence, etc.: *his opinion carries great weight.* **14.** to support or give validity to (a related claim, etc.): *one decision carries another.* **15.** *Com.* **a.** to keep on hand or in stock. **b.** to keep on one's account books, etc. **16.** to bear as a crop. **17.** to support (cattle): *our grain supply will carry the cattle through the winter.* **18.** *Golf.* to advance beyond or go by (an object or expanse) with one stroke. **19.** *Hunting.* to retain and pursue (a scent). —*v.i.* **20.** to act as a bearer or conductor. **21.** to have or exert propelling force: *the rifle carries almost a mile.* **22.** to be transmitted, propelled, or sustained: *my voice carries farther than his.* **23.** to bear the head in a particular manner, as a horse. **24.** Some special verb phrases: **carry away,** to influence greatly or beyond reason.

carry forward, 1. to make progress with. **2.** *Bookkeeping.* to transfer (an amount, etc.) to the next column, page, etc.

carry off, 1. to win (the prize, honor, etc.) **2.** to face consequences boldly: *he carried it off well.* **3.** to cause the death of.

carry on, 1. to manage; conduct. **2.** *U.S.* to behave in an excited, foolish, or improper manner. **3.** *Chiefly Brit.* to continue; keep up without stopping.

carry out, to accomplish or complete (a plan, scheme, etc.): *to carry out the details of his plan.*

carry over, to postpone; hold off until later.

carry through, 1. to accomplish; complete. **2.** to support or help (in a difficult situation, etc.). —*n.* **25.** range, as of a gun. **26.** *Golf.* the distance traversed by a ball before it alights. **27.** *U.S.* land separating navigable waters, over which a canoe or boat must be carried; a portage. **28.** a carrying. [ME *carie(n),* t. ONF: m. *carier,* g. LL *carricāre* convey by wagon, der. L *carrus.* See CAR] —**Syn. 1.** CARRY, CONVEY, TRANSPORT, TRANSMIT, imply taking or sending something from one place to another. CARRY means to take by means of the hands, of a vehicle, etc.: *to carry a book.* CONVEY is a more formal word, suggesting a means of taking, but not any particular method of taking; it is also used figuratively: *to convey wheat to market, a message of sympathy.* TRANSPORT means to carry or convey goods, now usually by vehicle or vessel: *to transport milk to customers.* TRANSMIT implies chiefly sending or transferring messages, hereditary tendencies, etc.: *to transmit a telegram.*

car·ry·all (kăr′ȳôl′), *n.* **1.** a light, covered, one-horse family carriage, with two seats. **2.** a closed motorcar having two passenger benches extending the length of the body. [f. CARRY + ALL; r. CARRIOLE by pop. etym.]

car·ry·o·ver (kăr′ȳō′vər), *n.* **1.** the part left over to a later period, account, etc. **2.** *Bookkeeping.* the total of one page of an account carried forward to the next.

car·sick (kär′sĭk′), *adj.* nauseated by the motion of a train, automobile, etc.

Car·son (kär′sən), *n.* **1.** **Christopher,** ("*Kit*") 1809–68, U.S. frontiersman and scout. **2.** **Sir Edward Henry,** (*Baron Carson*) 1854–1935, Irish politician and public official in England.

Carson City, the capital of Nevada, in the W part. 3082 (1950).

cart (kärt), *n.* **1.** a heavy two-wheeled vehicle, commonly without springs, for the conveyance of heavy goods. **2.** a light two-wheeled vehicle with springs, used for business or pleasure. **3.** any small vehicle moved by hand. **4.** *Obs.* a chariot. —*v.t.* **5.** to convey in or as in a cart. —*v.i.* **6.** to drive a cart. [metathetic var. of OE *cræt*, c. Icel. *kartr*] —**cart′er,** *n.*

cart·age (kär′tĭj), *n.* the act or cost of carting.

Car·ta·ge·na (kär′tə jē′ne; *Sp.* kär′tä hĕ′nä), *n.* **1.** a seaport in SE Spain. 98,960 (est. 1944). **2.** a seaport in N Colombia. 73,190 (1938).

carte[1] (kärt; *Fr.* kȧrt), *n.* *Fencing.* quarte. [t. F: m. *quarte,* t. It.: m. *quarta* fourth]

carte[2] (kärt; *Fr.* kȧrt), *n.* **1.** menu. Cf. **à la carte.** **2.** *Now Rare or Obs.* a playing card. **3.** *Obs.* a map or chart. [t. F. See CARD[1]]

Carte (kärt). *n.* **Richard D'Oyly** (doi′lĭ′), 1844–1901, British theatrical producer.

carte blanche (kärt′ blänsh′; *Fr.* kȧrt blänsh′), *pl.* **cartes blanches** (kärts′ blänsh′; *Fr.* kȧrt blänsh′). *French.* **1.** a signed paper left blank for the person to whom it is given to fill in his own conditions. **2.** unconditional authority; full power.

car·tel (kär′tĕl′, kär′təl), *n.* **1.** an international syndicate, combine or trust generally formed to regulate prices and output in some field of business. **2.** a written agreement between belligerents, esp. for the exchange of prisoners. **3.** (*often cap.*) (in French or Belgian politics) a group acting as a unit toward a common goal. **4.** a challenge to single combat. [t. F, t. It.: m. *cartello,* dim. of *carta,* g. L *charta* paper. See CHART]

car·te·lize (kär′tə līz), *v.i.,* *v.t.,* **-lized, -lizing.** to organize into cartels or a cartel (def. 1). —**car′te·li·za′tion,** *n.*

Car·ter (kär′tər), *n.* **Howard,** 1873–1939, British archaeologist in Egypt.

Car·ter·et (kär′tər ĭt), *n.* **John** (*Earl Granville*), 1690–1763, British statesman.

Car·te·sian (kär tē′zhən), *adj.* **1.** pertaining to Descartes, to his mathematical methods, or to his dualistic philosophy which began with the famous phrase *Cogito, ergo sum* (I think, therefore I am), saw physical nature mechanistically, and in science emphasized rationalism and logic. —*n.* **2.** a believer in the philosophy of Descartes. [t. NL: s. *Cartesiānus,* der. *Cartesius,* Latinized form of the name of René Descartes] —**Car·te′sian·ism,** *n.*

Car·thage (kär′thĭj), *n.* an ancient city-state in N Africa, near modern Tunis: destroyed by the Romans, 146 B.C. —**Car·tha·gin·i·an** (kär′thə jĭn′ɪ̯ən), *adj., n.*

Car·thu·sian (kär thōo′zhən), *Rom. Cath. Ch.* —*n.* **1.** a member of an austere monastic order founded by St. Bruno in 1086 near Grenoble, France. —*adj.* **2.** belonging to this order. [t. ML: m.s. *Cartusiānus,* der. *Chatrousse,* name of a village in Dauphine near which the first monastery of the order was built]

Carthage, c133 B.C.

Car·tier (kȧr tyĕ′), *n.* **Jacques** (zhȧk), 1491?–c1557, French navigator: discoverer of the St. Lawrence river.

car·ti·lage (kär′tə lĭj, kärt′lĭj), *n.* *Anat., Zool.* **1.** a firm, elastic, flexible substance of a translucent whitish or yellowish color, consisting of connective tissue; gristle. **2.** a part or structure composed of cartilage. [t. F, t. L: m. *cartilāgo* gristle]

cartilage bone, a bone that is developed from cartilage (distinguished from *membrane bone*).

car·ti·lag·i·nous (kär′tə lăj′ɪ̯ nəs), *adj.* **1.** of or resembling cartilage. **2.** *Zool.* having the skeleton composed mostly of cartilage, as sharks and rays.

cart·load (kärt′lōd′), *n.* the amount a cart can hold.

car·to·gram (kär′tə grăm′), *n.* a diagrammatic presentation in highly abstracted or simplified form, commonly of statistical data, on a map base or distorted map base. [t. F: m. *cartogramme.* See CARD[1], -GRAM]

car·tog·ra·phy (kär tŏg′rə fĭ), *n.* the production of maps, including construction of projections, design, compilation, drafting, and reproduction. Also, **chartography.** [f. *carto-* (comb. form of ML *carta* chart, map) + -GRAPHY] —**car·tog′ra·pher,** *n.* —**car·to·graph·ic** (kär′tə grăf′ĭk), **car·to·graph·i·cal,** *adj.* —**car′to·graph′i·cal·ly,** *adv.*

car·ton (kär′tən), *n.* a cardboard box. [t. F. See CARTOON]

car·toon (kär tōon′), *n.* **1.** a sketch or drawing as in a newspaper or periodical, symbolizing or caricaturing some subject or persons of current interest, in an exaggerated way. **2.** *Fine Arts.* a drawing, of the same size as a proposed decoration or pattern in fresco, mosaic, tapestry, etc., for which it serves as a model to be transferred or copied. **3.** a comic strip. **4.** an animated cartoon. —*v.t.* **5.** to represent by a cartoon. [t. F: m. *carton,* t. It.: m. *cartone* pasteboard, cartoon, aug. of *carta,* g. L *charta* paper. See CHART] —**car·toon′ist,** *n.*

car·touche (kär tōosh′), *n.* **1.** *Archit.* a French Renaissance motif, usually an oval tablet with ornamental scrollwork. **2.** an oval or oblong figure, as on ancient Egyptian monuments, enclosing characters which express royal names. **3.** the case containing the inflammable materials in certain fireworks. **4.** cartridge (def. 1). **5.** a box for cartridges. Also, **car·touch′.** [t. F, t. It. *cartoccio,* aug. of *carta,* g. L *charta* paper. See CHART]

car·tridge (kär′trĭj), *n.* **1.** a cylindrical case of pasteboard, metal, or the like, for holding a complete charge of powder, and often also the bullet or the shot, for a rifle, machine gun, or other small arm. **2.** a case containing any explosive charge, as for blasting. **3.** *Photog.* **a.** a case or holder for a roll of camera film, used in daylight loading. **b.** such a case loaded with film. [m. CARTOUCHE]

Cartridge: A, Metallic case of copper or brass; B, Bullet; R, Primer; F, Fulminate; P, Powder

cartridge belt, a belt (def. 6b) for ammunition with loops for cartridges or pockets for clips of cartridges.

cartridge clip, a metal frame or container holding cartridges for a magazine rifle or automatic pistol; clip.

car·tu·lar·y (kär′chŏŏ lĕr′ĭ), *n., pl.* **-laries.** chartulary.

cart·wheel (kärt′hwēl′), *n.* **1.** a somersault performed sidewise. **2.** *Slang.* any large coin, esp. the silver dollar.

Cart·wright (kärt′rīt′), *n.* **Edmund,** 1743–1823, British clergyman: inventor of the power-driven loom.

car·un·cle (kär′ŭng kəl, kərŭng′-), *n.* **1.** *Bot.* a protuberance at or surrounding the hilum of a seed. **2.** *Zool.* a fleshy excrescence, as on the head of a bird; a fowl's comb. [t. L: m. s. *caruncula,* dim. of *caro* flesh] —**ca·run·cu·lar** (kə rŭng′kyə lər), **ca·run′cu·lous,** *adj.*

ca·run·cu·late (kə rŭng′kyə lĭt, -lāt′), *adj.* having a caruncle. Also, **ca·run′cu·lat′ed.**

Ca·ru·so (kə rōō′sō; *It.* kä rōō′zō), *n.* **Enrico** (ĕn rē′kô), 1873–1921, Italian operatic tenor.

carve (kärv), *v.,* **carved, carving.** —*v.t.* **1.** to fashion by cutting: *to carve a block of stone into a statue.* **2.** to produce by cutting: *to carve a design in wood.* —*v.i.* **3.** to decorate by cutting figures, designs, etc. **4.** to cut meat. [ME *kerve(n),* OE *ceorfan* cut, c. G *kerben* notch; akin to Gk. *gráphein* mark. write] —**carv′er,** *n.*

car·vel (kär′vəl), *n.* caravel.

car·vel-built (kär′vəl bĭlt′), *adj.* (of a ship) built with the planks flush, not overlapping. Cf. **clinker-built.**

carv·en (kär′vən), *adj. Poetic.* carved.

Car·ver (kär′vər), *n.* **1.** **George Washington,** c1864–1943, U.S. botanist and chemist. **2.** **John,** 1575?–1621, Pilgrim leader: first governor of Plymouth Colony.

carv·ing (kär′vĭng), *n.* **1.** act of fashioning or producing by cutting. **2.** carved work; a carved design.

Car·y (kâr′ĭ), *n.* **1.** **Alice,** 1820–71, U.S. poet (sister of Phoebe Cary). **2.** **Henry Francis,** 1772–1844, British writer and translator. **3.** **Phoebe,** 1824–71, U.S. poet (sister of Alice Cary).

car·y·at·id (kăr′ĭ ăt′ĭd), *n., pl.* **-ids, -ides** (-ə dēz′). *Archit.* a figure of a woman used like a supporting column. [t. L: s. *Caryātides,* pl., t. Gk.: m. *Karyátides,* lit., women of Caryae] —**car′y·at′i·dal,** *adj.*

car·y·o·phyl·la·ceous (kăr′ĭ ō fə lā′shəs), *adj. Bot.* **1.** belonging to the *Caryophyllaceae* (sometimes called *Silenaceae*) or pink family of plants. **2.** resembling the pink. [f. m.s. Gk. *karyóphyllon* clove tree + -ACEOUS]

Caryatids

car·y·op·sis (kăr′ĭ ŏp′sĭs), *n., pl.* **-opses** (-ŏp′sēz), **-opsides** (-ŏp′sə dēz′). *Bot.* a small, one-celled, one-seeded, dry indehiscent fruit with the pericarp adherent to the seed coat as in wheat. [f. m.s. Gk. *káryon* nut + -OPSIS]

ca·sa·ba (kə sä′bə), *n.* a kind of winter muskmelon, having a yellow rind and sweet, juicy flesh. Also, **casaba melon, cassaba.** [named after *Kassaba,* town near Smyrna, Asia Minor]

Ca·sa·bian·ca (kä zä byäɴkä′), *n.* **Louis de** (lwē də), c1752–98, French naval officer whose son died trying to save him from his burning ship.

Ca·sa·blan·ca (kä′sä bläng′kä, kăs′ə bläng′kə), *n.* a seaport in NW Morocco: wartime conference of Roosevelt and Churchill, Jan., 1943. 257,430 (1936).

Ca·sa Gran·de (kä′sä grän′dā, -dĭ), a national monument in S Arizona, near the Gila river: remarkable ruins of a prehistoric culture.

Cas·a·no·va (käz′ə nō′və, käs′-; *It.* kä′sä nô′vä), **Giovanni Jacopo** (jō vän′nē yä′kō pô), 1725–98, Italian adventurer and writer.

Ca·sau·bon (kə sô′bən; *Fr.* kå zō bôN′), *n.* **Isaac** (ē′zäk′), 1559–1614, French classical scholar.

Cas·bah (käz′bä), *n.* Kasbah.

cas·cade (käs kād′), *n. v.,* **-caded, -cading.** —*n.* **1.** a waterfall over steep rocks, or a series of small waterfalls. **2.** an arrangement of lace, etc., in folds falling one over another in a zigzag fashion. **3.** a type of firework resembling a waterfall in effect. **4.** *Chem.* a series of vessels, from each of which a liquid successively overflows to the next, thus presenting a large absorbing surface, as to a gas. **5.** *Elect.* an arrangement of component devices, each of which feeds into the next in succession. —*v.i.* **6.** to fall in or like a cascade. [t. F, t. It.: m. *cascata,* der. *cascare,* der. L *cadere* fall]

Cascade Range, a mountain range extending from N California to British Columbia: a part of the Coast Range. Highest peak, Mt. Rainier, 14,408 ft.

cas·car·a (käs kär′ə), *n.* a species of buckthorn, *Rhamnus Purshiana,* of the Pacific coast of the U.S., yielding cascara sagrada. Also, **cascara buckthorn.** [t. Sp.: bark, der. *casca* bark, skin]

cas·ca·ra sa·gra·da (sə grä′də), the bark of the cascara, used as a cathartic or laxative. [t. Sp.: sacred bark]

cas·ca·ril·la (käs′kə rĭl′ə), *n.* **1.** Also, **cascarilla bark.** the bitter aromatic bark of a West Indian euphorbiaceous shrub, *Croton Eluteria,* used as a tonic. **2.** the shrub itself. [t. Sp., dim. of *cáscara* bark]

Cas·co Bay (käs′kō), a bay in SW Maine.

case[1] (käs), *n.* **1.** an instance of the occurrence, existence, etc. of something. **2.** the actual state of things: *that is not the case.* **3.** a question or problem of moral conduct: *a case of conscience.* **4.** situation; condition; plight. **5.** a state of things involving a question for discussion or decision. **6.** a statement of facts, reasons, etc.: *a strong case for the proposed law.* **7.** an instance of disease, etc., requiring medical or surgical treatment or attention. **8.** a medical or surgical patient. **9.** *Law.* **a.** a suit or action at law; a cause. **b.** a set of facts giving rise to a legal claim, or to a defense to a legal claim. **10.** *Gram.* **a.** a category in the inflection of nouns, pronouns, and adjectives, denoting the syntactic relation of these words to other words in the sentence, indicated by the form or the position of the words. **b.** a set of such categories in a particular language. **c.** the meaning of, or typical of, such a category. **d.** such categories or their meanings collectively. **11.** *Colloq.* a peculiar or unusual person: *he's a case.* **12. in any case,** under any circumstances; anyhow. **13. in case,** if; if it should happen that. **14. in case of,** in the event of. [ME, t. OF: m. *cas,* g. L *cāsus* a falling, occurrence]

—**Syn. 1.** CASE, INSTANCE, EXAMPLE, ILLUSTRATION suggest the existence or occurrence of a particular thing representative of its type. CASE and INSTANCE are closely allied in meaning, as are EXAMPLE and ILLUSTRATION. CASE is a general word, meaning a fact, occurrence, or situation typical of a class: *a case of assault and battery.* An INSTANCE is a concrete factual case which is adduced to explain a general idea: *an instance of a brawl in which an assault occurred.* An EXAMPLE is one typical case, from many similar ones, used to make clear or explain the working of a principle (what may be expected of any others of the group): *this boy is an example of the effect of strict discipline.* An ILLUSTRATION exemplifies a theory or principle similarly, except that the choice may be purely hypothetical: *the work of Seeing Eye dogs is an illustration of what is thought to be intelligence in animals.*

case[2] (käs), *n. v.,* **cased, casing.** —*n.* **1.** a thing for containing or enclosing something; a receptacle. **2.** a sheath or outer covering: a knife case. **3.** a box with its contents. **4.** the amount contained in a box or other container. **5.** a frame or framework, as of a door. **6.** *Bookbinding.* a completed book cover ready to be fitted to form the binding of a book. **7.** *Print.* a tray, of wood or metal, divided into compartments for holding types for the use of a compositor and usually arranged in a set of two, the **upper case** for capitals, etc., and the **lower case** for small letters, etc. —*v.t.* **8.** to put or enclose in a case; cover with a case. [ME *casse,* t. ONF, g. L *capsa* box, receptacle.]

ca·se·ase (kā′sĭ ās′), *n. Biochem.* a bacterial enzyme which dissolves casein. [f. CASE(IN) + -ASE]

ca·se·ate (kā′sĭ āt′), *v.i.,* **-ated, -ating.** *Pathol.* to undergo caseous degeneration; become like cheese in consistency and appearance. [f. s. L *cāseus* cheese + -ATE[1]]

ca·se·a·tion (kā′sĭ ā′shən), *n. Pathol.* transformation into a soft cheeselike mass, as in tuberculosis.

case·hard·en (käs′här′dən), *v.t.* **1.** *Metall.* to make the outside surface of (alloys having an iron base) hard leaving the interior tough and ductile by carburizing and heat treatment. **2.** to harden in spirit so as to render insensible to external impressions or influences.

case history, all the relevant information or material gathered about an individual, family, group, etc., and ordered so as to give it significance (usually genetic) to the student or the like: used esp. in social work, sociology, psychiatry, and medicine. Also, **case record.**

ca·se·in (kā′sĭ ĭn, -sēn), *n. Biochem.* a protein precipitated from milk, as by rennet, and forming the basis of cheese and certain plastics. [f. s. L *cāseus* cheese + -IN[2]]

ca·se·in·o·gen (kā′sĭ ĭn′ə jən, -sē′nə-), *n. Biochem.* the principal protein of milk, which in the presence of rennet is converted into casein.

case knife, 1. a knife carried or kept in a case. **2.** a table knife.

case law, law established by judicial decisions in particular cases, instead of by legislative action.

case·mate (käs′māt′), *n.* **1.** an armored enclosure for guns in a warship. **2.** a vault or chamber, esp. in a rampart, with embrasures for artillery. [t. F, t. It.: m. *casamatta,* ult. t. Gk.: m. *chásmata* opening (as military term)] —**case′mat·ed,** *adj.*

case·ment (käs′mənt), *n.* **1.** a window sash opening on hinges, which are generally attached to the upright side of its frame. **2.** a window with such sashes. **3.** *Poetic.* any window. **4.** a casing or covering. [f. CASE[2] + -MENT] —**case′ment·ed,** *adj.*

Case·ment (käs′mənt), *n.* **(Sir) Roger (David),** 1864–1916, Irish patriot: hanged by the British for treason.

ca·se·ose (kā′sĭ ōs′), *n. Biochem.* any of various soluble products formed in the gastric and pancreatic digestion of casein and caseinogen. [f. CASE(IN) + -OSE[2]]

ca·se·ous (kā′sĭ əs), *adj.* of or like cheese. [f. s. L *cāseus* cheese + -OUS]

ca·sern (kə zûrn′), *n.* (formerly) a lodging for soldiers in a garrison town; a barrack. Also, **ca·serne′.** [t. F: m. *caserne,* orig., small room for soldiers, t. Pr.: m. *cazerna,* g. LL var. of *quaterna* group of four]

case shot, a collection of small projectiles in a case, to be fired from a cannon.

case system, an inductive method of teaching based upon the study of reported cases rather than of textbooks and commentaries.

case·worm (käs′wûrm′), *n.* a caddis worm or other caterpillar that constructs a case around its body.

cash[1] (käsh), *n.* **1.** money, esp. money on hand. **2.** money, or an equivalent (as a check), paid at the time of making a purchase. —*v.t.* **3.** to give or obtain cash for (a check, etc.). **4.** *U.S. Colloq.* (in poker, etc.) **cash in one's chips,** to hand in and get cash for. **5. cash in on,** *U.S. Colloq.* **a.** to gain a return from. **b.** to turn to one's advantage. —*v.i.* **6.** *U.S. Colloq.* to die (fol by *in*). [t. F: m. *caisse,* t. Pr.: m. *caissa,* g. L *capsa* box]

cash[2] (käsh), *n., pl.* **cash.** any of several low-denomination coins of China, India, and East Indies, esp. a Chinese copper coin. [t. Pg.: m. *caixa,* t. Tamil: m. *kāsu*]

ca·shaw (kə shô′), *n.* cushaw.

cash·book (käsh′bŏŏk′), *n.* a book in which to record money received and paid out.

cash discount, 1. a term of sale by which the purchaser deducts a percentage from the bill if he pays within a stipulated period. **2.** the amount deducted.

cash·ew (käsh′ōō, kə shōō′), *n.* **1.** an anacardiaceous tree, *Anacardium occidentale,* native in tropical America, whose bark yields a medicinal gum. **2.** its fruit, a small, edible, kidney-shaped nut (**cashew nut**). [t. F: alter. of *acajou,* t. Brazilian Pg.: m. *acajú,* t. Tupi]

cash·ier[1] (kă shĭr′), *n.* one who has charge of cash or money, esp. one who superintends monetary transactions, as in a bank; in England, a teller. [t. F: m. *caissier,* der. *caisse* cash box. See CASH[1]]

cash·ier[2] (kă shĭr′), *v.t.* **1.** to dismiss from a position of command or trust, esp. with disgrace. **2.** to discard; reject. [t. D: m. *casseren,* t. F: m. *casser* break, discharge, annul, g. L *quassāre* shake, break, and LL *cassāre* annul]

cashier's check, a check drawn by a bank upon its own funds and signed by its cashier.

cash·mere (käsh′mĭr), *n.* **1.** the fine downy wool at the roots of the hair of Kashmir goats of India. **2.** a shawl made of this hair. **3.** a wool fabric of twill weave. Also, **kashmir.**

Cash·mere (käsh mĭr′), *n.* Kashmir.

ca·shoo (kə shōō′), *n.* catechu.

cash register, a cash box with a mechanism for indicating amounts of sales, etc.

cas·i·mire (käs′ə mĭr′), *n.* cassimere.

cas·ing (kā′sĭng), *n.* **1.** a case or covering. **2.** material for a case or covering. **3.** the framework around a door or window. **4.** *U.S.* the outermost covering of an automobile tire. **5.** any frame or framework. **6.** an iron pipe or tubing, esp. as used in oil and gas wells.

ca·si·no (kə sē′nō), *n., pl.* **-nos. 1.** a building or large room for meetings, amusements, etc.; a clubhouse, in England and Europe, usually understood to be devoted to gambling. **2.** a small country house or lodge. **3.** cassino. [t. It., dim. of *casa* house, g. L *casa* cottage]

cask (käsk, käsk), *n.* **1.** a barrellike container made of staves, and of varying size, for holding liquids, etc., often one larger and stronger than an ordinary barrel. **2.** the quantity such a container holds. [appar. t. Sp.: m. *casco* skull, helmet, cask (for wine, etc.), der. *cascar* break, g. LL *quassicāre,* der. *quassāre* break, shake] ⫽

cas·ket (käs′kĭt, käs′-), *n.* **1.** *Chiefly U.S.* a coffin. **2.** a small chest or box, as for jewels. —*v.t.* **3.** to put or enclose in a casket. [orig. uncert.]

Cas·lon (käz′lən), *n.* **1. William,** 1692–1766, British type founder. **2.** *Print.* an old-style type modeled after the types designed by William Caslon.

Cas·par·i·an strip (käs pâr′ĭ ən), *Bot.* a thickened strip in the radial walls of some endodermal cells.

---

b., blend of, blended; c., cognate with; d., dialect, dialectal; der., derived from; f., formed from; g., going back to; m., modification of; r., replacing; s., stem of; t., taken from; ?, perhaps. See the full key on inside cover.

Cas·per (kăs′pər), *n.* a city in central Wyoming. 23,673 (1950).

Cas·pi·an Sea (kăs′pĭ ən), a salt lake between SE Europe and Asia: the largest inland body of water in the world. ab. 169,000 sq. mi.; 85 ft. below sea level.

Caspian Sea

casque (kăsk), *n.* *Chiefly Poetic.* a helmet (def. 1, esp. 1b). [t. F, t. Sp.: m. *casco* helmet. See CASK] —**casqued** (kăskt), *adj.*

Cass (kăs), *n.* Lewis, 1782–1866, U. S. statesman.

cas·sa·ba (kə sä′bə), *n.* casaba.

Cas·san·dra (kə săn′drə), *n.* 1. *Class. Legend.* a prophetess daughter of Priam and Hecuba of ancient Troy, who was fated never to be believed. 2. any woman who warns in vain of coming evil.

cas·sa·reep (kăs′ə rēp), *n.* the inspissated juice of the root of the bitter cassava, used in cookery.

cas·sa·tion (kă sā′shən), *n.* annulment; cancellation; reversal. [t. LL: s. *cassātio*, der. *cassāre* annul]

Cas·satt (kə săt′), *n.* Mary, 1845?–1926, U. S. painter.

cas·sa·va (kə să′və), *n.* 1. any of several tropical euphorbiaceous plants of the genus *Manihot*, as *M. esculenta* (**bitter cassava**) and *M. dulcus* (**sweet cassava**), cultivated for their tuberous roots, which yield important food products. 2. a nutritious starch from the roots, the source of tapioca. [earlier *casavi*, t. Sp.: m. *cazabe*, t. Haitian (Taino): m. *cacábi, cazábbi*]

Cas·se·grain·i·an telescope (kăs′ə grā′nĭ ən), a reflecting telescope in which the primary mirror is perforated so that the light may pass through it to the eyepiece or photographic plate.

Cas·sel (kăs′əl; *Ger.* käs′əl), *n.* Kassel.

cas·se·role (kăs′ə rōl′), *n.* 1. a baking dish of glass, pottery, etc., usually with a cover. 2. any food, usually a mixture, cooked in such a dish. 3. a small dish with a handle, used in chemical laboratories. 4. *Chiefly Brit.* a stewpan. 5. **en casserole** (än käs rôl′), *French.* served or cooked in a casserole. [t. F, ult. der. *casse* pan, g. L *cattia*, t. Gk.: m. *kyáthion* little cup, dim. of *kyáthos*]

cas·sia (kăsh′ə, kăs′ĭə), *n.* 1. a variety of cinnamon from the tree *Cinnamomum Cassia*, of southern China (**cassia bark**). 2. the tree itself. 3. any of the caesalpiniaceous herbs, shrubs, and trees constituting the genus *Cassia*, as *C. Fistula*, an ornamental tropical tree with long pods (**cassia pods**) whose pulp (**cassia pulp**) is a mild laxative, and *C. acutifolia* and *C. angustifolia*, which yield senna. 4. cassia pods. 5. cassia pulp. [OE, t. L, t. Gk.: m. *kasía*, t. Heb.: m. *qǝtsī'āh*]

cas·si·mere (kăs′ə mĭr′), *n.* a plain or twilled woolen cloth. Also, **casimire.** [var. of CASHMERE]

cas·si·no (kə sē′nō), *n.* a game in which faced cards on the table are taken with eligible cards in the hand. Also, **casino.** [var. of CASINO]

Cas·si·no (kə sē′nō; *It.* käs sē′nō), *n.* a city in central Italy, ab. 45 mi. NW of Naples: site of Monte Cassino, a famous Benedictine abbey; scene of bitter fighting between the Allied and German armies, Jan.-May, 1944.

Cas·si·o·pe·ia (kăs′ĭ ə pē′ə), *n.* 1. a northern circumpolar constellation east of Cepheus, on the opposite side of Polaris from the Dipper. 2. *Gk. Myth.* the wife of Cepheus and mother of Andromeda.

Cassiopeia's Chair, the most conspicuous group of stars in the constellation Cassiopeia, supposed to resemble a chair in outline.

cas·sit·er·ite (kə sĭt′ə rīt′), *n.* a common mineral, tin dioxide, SnO₂: the principal ore of tin. [f. m.s. Gk. *kassíteros* tin + -ITE¹]

Cas·si·us Lon·gi·nus (kăsh′əs lŏn jī′nəs), Gaius (gā′əs), d. 42 B.C., Roman politician and general, who led a conspiracy against Julius Caesar.

cas·sock (kăs′ək), *n.* 1. a long, close-fitting garment worn by ecclesiastics and others engaged in church functions. 2. a shorter, light, double-breasted coat or jacket, usually of black silk, worn under the Geneva gown. 3. a clergyman. [t. F: m. *casaque*, t. It.: m. *casacca*, root *cas-* (cf. F *chasuble*), ? identical with L *casa* house, hut]

cas·so·war·y (kăs′ə wĕr′ĭ), *n., pl.* **-waries.** any of several large, three-toed, flightless, ratite birds constituting the genus *Casuarius*, of Australasian regions, superficially resembling the ostrich but smaller. [t. Malay: m. *kasuāri*]

Cassowary. *Casuarius casuarius* (Total length 5 ft.)

cast (kăst), *v.*, **cast, cast·ing,** *n.* —*v.t.* 1. to throw; fling; hurl (often fol. by *away, off, out*, etc.). 2. to throw off or away. 3. to direct (the eye, a glance, etc.). 4. to cause (light, etc.) to fall upon something or in a certain direction. 5. to throw out (a fishline, anchor, etc.). 6. to throw down; throw (an animal) on its back or side; throw to the ground, as in wrestling. 7. to part with; lose. 8. to shed or drop (hair, fruit, etc.), esp. prematurely. 9. to bring forth (young), esp. abortively. 10. to send off (a swarm), as bees do. 11. to throw or set aside; discard or reject; dismiss or disband. 12. to throw forth, as from within; emit or eject; vomit. 13. to throw up (earth, etc.), as with a shovel. 14. to put or place, esp. hastily or forcibly. 15. to deposit (a ballot, vote, etc.). 16. to bestow; confer. 17. to arrange; plan out. 18. *Theat.* to allot parts, or parts of, (a play) to actors; select (actors) for a play. 19. *Metall.* to form (molten metal, etc.) into a particular shape by pouring into a mold; to produce (an object or article) by such a process. 20. to compute or calculate; add, as a column of figures. 21. to compute or calculate astrologically, as a horoscope; forecast. 22. to ponder or consider; contrive, devise, or plan. 23. to turn or twist; warp. 24. *Naut.* to bring (a boat) round. 25. to let go or let loose, as a vessel from a mooring (fol. by *loose, off*, etc.). —*v.i.* 26. to throw. 27. to receive form in a mold. 28. to calculate or add. 29. to conjecture; forecast. 30. to consider; plan or scheme. 31. to search this way and that, as for the scent in hunting (often fol. by *about*). 32. to warp, as timber. 33. *Naut.* to turn, esp. to get the boat's head away from the wind; tack. 34. Some special verb phrases are:

cast about, (fol. by *for* or an infinitive). 1. to look about one mentally, as for an excuse. 2. scheme.

cast away, 1. to reject. 2. to shipwreck.

cast back, 1. to refer to something past. 2. to show resemblance to a remote ancestor.

cast down, to depress; discourage.

cast off, 1. to discard or reject. 2. to let go.

cast up, 1. to compute; calculate. 2. to eject; vomit. 3. to turn up.

—*n.* 35. act of casting or throwing. 36. that which is cast. 37. the distance to which a thing may be cast or thrown. 38. *Games.* **a.** a throw of dice. **b.** the number rolled. 39. *Angling.* **a.** act of throwing the line or net on the water. **b.** *Brit.* a line so thrown. **c.** the leader with flies attached, used in angling. 40. *Hunting.* a dispersal of the dogs in all directions to recapture a scent. 41. a stroke of fortune; fortune or lot. 42. a ride offered on one's way. 43. the form in which something is made or written; arrangement. 44. *Theat.* the actors to whom the parts in a play are assigned. 45. *Metall.* **a.** act of casting or founding. **b.** the quantity of metal cast at one time. 46. something shaped in a mold while in a fluid or plastic state; a casting. 47. any impression or mold made from a thing. 48. *Med.* rigid surgical dressing usually made of plaster of paris bandage. 49. a reproduction or copy, as a plaster model, made in a mold. 50. outward form; appearance. 51. sort; kind; style. 52. tendency; inclination. 53. a permanent twist or turn: *to have a cast in one's eye.* 54. a warp. 55. a slight tinge of some color; hue; shade. 56. a dash or trace; a small amount. 57. computation; calculation; addition. 58. a conjecture; forecast. 59. *Zool.* one of the wormlike coils of sand passed by the lugworm or other worms. 60. *Ornith.* a mass of feathers, fur, bones, or other indigestible matters ejected from the stomach by a hawk or other bird. 61. *Pathol.* effused plastic matter produced in the hollow parts of various diseased organs. —*adj.* 62. *Theat.* (of a production) having all actors selected. [ME *casten*, t. Scand.; cf. Icel. *kasta* throw] —**Syn.** 1. See **throw.** 52. See **turn.**

Cas·ta·li·a (kăs tā′lĭ ə), *n.* 1. a spring on Mount Parnassus in Greece, sacred to Apollo and the Muses and regarded as a source of inspiration. 2. any source of inspiration. —**Cas·ta·li·an,** *adj.*

cas·ta·net (kăs′tə nĕt′), *n.* a pair or one of a pair, of shells of ivory or hard wood held in the palm of the hand and struck together as an accompaniment to music and dancing. [t. Sp.: m. *castañeta*, dim. of *castaña*, g. L *castanea* chestnut]

cast·a·way (kăst′ə wā′, käst′-), *n.* 1. a shipwrecked person. 2. an outcast. —*adj.* 3. cast adrift. 4. thrown away.

caste (kăst, käst), *n.* 1. *Sociol.* an endogamous and hereditary social group limited to persons in a given occupation or trade, having mores distinguishing it from other such groups. 2. *Hinduism.* **a.** one of the artificial divisions or social classes into which the Hindus are rigidly separated and of which the privileges or disabilities are transmitted by inheritance. **b.** the system or basis of this division. 3. any rigid system of social distinctions. 4. the position or rank conferred by the Hindu social system or any similar system: *to lose caste.* [t. Sp., Pg.: m. *casta* breed, race, t. L: m. *castus* pure, CHASTE]

Castanets

cas·tel·lan (kăs′tə lən), *n.* the governor of a castle. [t. L: s. *castellānus* (der. *castellum*; see CASTLE); r. ME *castelain*, t. ONF]

cas·tel·la·ny (kăs′tə lā′nĭ), *n., pl.* **-nies.** 1. the office of a castellan. 2. the land belonging to a castle.

cas·tel·lat·ed (kăs′tə lā′tĭd), *adj.* 1. *Archit.* built like a castle, esp. with turrets and battlements. 2. having very many castles. —**cas·tel·la′tion,** *n.*

cast·er (kăs′tər, käs′-), *n.* 1. one who or that which casts. 2. a small wheel on a swivel, set under a piece of furniture, etc., to facilitate moving it. 3. a bottle or cruet for holding a condiment. 4. a stand containing a set of such bottles. Also, **castor** for 2, 3, and 4.

cas·ti·gate (kăs′tə gāt′), *v.t.*, **-gated, -gating.** to punish in order to correct; criticize severely. [t. L: m.s. *castīgātus*, pp.] —**cas′ti·ga′tion,** *n.* —**cas′ti·ga′tor,** *n.*

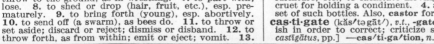

Ca·sti·glio·ne (käs/tēlyō′nĕ), *n.* **Baldassare** (bäl/-dässä/rĕ), 1478–1529, Italian diplomat and author.

Cas·tile (kăstēl/), *n.* a former kingdom comprising most of Spain. Spanish, **Cas·til·la** (käs-tē/lyä).

Cas·tile (kăs/tēl), *adj.* (of soap, etc.) **1.** (*often l.c.*) made with olive oil and soda. **2.** (*often l.c.*) made with similar ingredients. —*n.* **3.** Castile soap.

Cas·til·ian (kăstĭl/yən), *n.* **1.** the accepted standard form of the Spanish language as spoken in Spain. **2.** the dialect of Castile. **3.** a native or inhabitant of Castile. —*adj.* **4.** of or pertaining to Castile.

cast·ing (kăs/tĭng, käs/-), *n.* **1.** act or process of one that casts. **2.** that which is cast; any article which has been cast in a mold.

casting vote, the deciding vote of the presiding officer when the votes are equally divided.

cast iron, an alloy of iron, carbon, and other elements, cast as a soft and strong, or as a hard and brittle iron, depending on the mixture and methods of molding.

cast-i·ron (kăst/ī/ərn, käst/-), *adj.* **1.** made of cast iron. **2.** inflexible; rigid; unyielding. **3.** strong; hardy.

cas·tle (kăs/əl, käs/əl), *n.*, *v.*, **-tled**, **-tling**. —*n.* **1.** a fortified residence, as of a prince or noble in feudal times. **2.** the chief and strongest part of the fortifications of a medieval city. **3.** a strongly fortified, permanently garrisoned stronghold. **4.** a large and stately residence, esp. one which imitates the forms of a medieval castle. **5.** *Chess.* the rook. —*v.t.* **6.** to place or enclose in or as in a castle. **7.** *Chess.* to move (the king) in castling. —*v.i.* **8.** *Chess.* **a.** to move the king two squares and bring the castle to the first square the king has passed over. **b.** (of the king) to be moved in this manner. [ME *castel*, t. ONF, g. L *castellum* fortress, dim. of *castrum* fortified place; r. OE *castel* village, t. L (Vulgate): m.s. *castellum*] —**cas/tled**, *adj.* —**Syn.** 4. palace, chateau, mansion.

castle in the air, a visionary project; a daydream. Also, **castle in Spain**.

Cas·tle·reagh (kăs/əlrā′, käs/əl-), *n.* **Robert Stewart, Viscount**, (*2nd Marquess of Londonderry*) 1769–1822, British statesman.

cast-off (kăst/ôf′, -ŏf′, käst/-), *adj.* **1.** thrown away; rejected; discarded: *castoff clothing.* —*n.* **2.** a person or thing that has been cast off.

cas·tor[1] (kăs/tər, käs/-), *n.* **1.** a brownish unctuous substance with a strong, penetrating odor, secreted by certain glands in the groin of the beaver, used in medicine and perfumery. **2.** a beaver (hat). **3.** some similar hat. **4.** a beaver. [t. L, t. Gk.: m. *kástōr* beaver]

cas·tor[2] (kăs/tər, käs/-), *n.* caster (defs. 2, 3, and 4).

Cas·tor (kăs/tər, käs/-), *n.* *Astron.* Alpha Geminorum; the more northerly of the two bright stars in Gemini.

Castor and Pollux, *Gk. Myth.* twin sons of Leda and brothers of Helen (called the Dioscuri or sons of Zeus), famous for protection of sailors, and for brotherly affection. Pollux, who was immortal, spent alternate days with the gods and with his mortal brother in Hades.

castor bean, *U.S.* **1.** the seed of the castor-oil plant. **2.** the castor-oil plant.

castor oil, a viscid oil obtained from the castor bean, used as a cathartic, etc.

cas·tor-oil plant (kăs/tər oil′, käs/-), a tall euphorbiaceous plant, *Ricinus communis*, native to India but widely naturalized, yielding the castor bean.

cas·tra·me·ta·tion (kăs/trə mə tā/shən), *n.* the laying out of camps. [t. F, f. L: *castra* camp + s. *mētātio* measurement]

cas·trate (kăs/trāt), *v.t.*, **-trated**, **-trating**. **1.** to deprive of the testicles; emasculate. **2.** to deprive of the ovaries. **3.** to mutilate (a book, etc.) by removing parts; expurgate. [t. L: m. s. *castrātus*, pp.] —**cas·tra/tion**, *n.*

cast steel, *Metall.* steel rendered homogeneous by being melted in crucibles or pots.

cas·u·al (kăzh/ōŏ əl), *adj.* **1.** happening by chance: *a casual meeting.* **2.** unpremeditated; offhand; without any definite intention: *a casual remark, etc.* **3.** careless; tending to leave things to chance; negligent; unconcerned: *a casual air.* **4.** irregular; occasional: *a casual observer.* **5.** accidental: *a casual fire.* **6.** *Brit.* pertaining to persons receiving charity or work from a district in which they do not permanently live. **7.** *Obs.* uncertain. —*n.* **8.** a worker employed only irregularly. **9.** *Brit.* one who receives occasional relief at a workhouse, etc. **10.** a soldier temporarily at a station or other place of duty, and usually en route to another station. [t. LL: s. *cāsuālis* by chance; r. ME *casuel*, t. OF] —**cas/u·al·ly**, *adv.* —**cas/u·al·ness**, *n.* —**Syn.** 1. unexpected, fortuitous, unforeseen. See **accidental**. —**Ant.** 1. planned. 2. deliberate. 3. formal.

cas·u·al·ty (kăzh/ōŏ əl tĭ′), *n.*, *pl.* **-ties**. **1.** an unfortunate accident, esp. one involving bodily injury or death; a mishap. **2.** *Mil.* **a.** a soldier who is missing in action, or who has been killed, wounded, or captured as a result of enemy action. **b.** (*pl.*) loss in numerical strength through any cause, as death, wounds, sickness,

capture, or desertion. **3.** one who is injured or killed in an accident. **4.** any person injured accidentally.

cas·u·ist (kăzh/ōŏ ĭst), *n.* **1.** one who studies and resolves cases of conscience or conduct. **2.** an oversubtle or disingenuous reasoner upon such matters. [t. F: m. *casuiste*, der. L *cāsus* CASE[1]]

cas·u·is·tic (kăzh/ōŏ ĭs/tĭk), *adj.* **1.** pertaining to casuists or casuistry. **2.** oversubtle; intellectually dishonest; sophistical: *casuistic distinctions.* Also, **cas/·u·is/ti·cal.** —**cas/u·is/ti·cal·ly**, *adv.*

cas·u·ist·ry (kăzh/ōŏ Ys trĭ), *n.*, *pl.* **-ries**. the application, or, from an outside point of view, misapplication, of general ethical principles to particular cases of conscience or conduct.

ca·sus bel·li (kā/səs bĕl/ī), *Latin.* an event or political occurrence which brings about a declaration of war.

cat (kăt), *n.*, *v.*, **catted**, **catting**. —*n.* **1.** a domesticated carnivore, *Felis domestica* (or *F. catus*), widely distributed in a number of breeds. **2.** any digitate carnivore of the family *Felidae*, as the lion, tiger, leopard, jaguar, etc., of the genus *Felis*, and the short-tailed species that constitute the genus *Lynx*, and esp. any of the smaller species of either genus. **3.** a spiteful and gossipy woman. **4.** cat-o′-nine-tails. **5.** *Games.* **a.** *Chiefly Brit.* the tapering piece of wood used in the game of tipcat. **b.** *Chiefly Brit.* the game itself. **c.** *Chiefly Brit.* the bat used in this game. **d.** a boy's game of ball. **6.** a catboat. **7.** a catfish. **8.** *Naut.* a tackle used in hoisting an anchor to the cathead. —*v.t.* **9.** to flog with a cat-o′-nine-tails. **10.** to hoist (an anchor) to the cathead. [ME; OE *catt, catte*, c. G *katze*, F *chat*; ult. orig. unknown] —**cat/like′**, *adj.*

cat., **1.** catalogue. **2.** catechism.

cata-, a prefix meaning "down," "against," "back," occurring orig. in words from the Greek, but used also in modern words (English and other) formed after the Greek type, as in *catabolism, catalogue, catalysis, catastrophe.* Also, before a vowel, *cat-*; before an aspirate, **cath-**. [t. Gk.: m. *kata-*, also (before a vowel) *kat-*, (before an aspirate) *kath-*, repr. *katá*, prep., down, through, against, according to]

ca·tab·o·lism (kə tăb/ə lĭz/əm), *n.* *Physiol., Biol.* a breaking down process; destructive metabolism (opposed to *anabolism*). Also, **katabolism**. [f. m.s. Gk. *katabolē* a throwing down + -ISM] —**cat·a·bol·ic** (kăt/ə bŏl/ĭk), *adj.* —**cat/a·bol/i·cal·ly**, *adv.*

ca·tab·o·lite (kə tăb/ə līt′), *n.* *Physiol., Biol.* a product of catabolic action.

cat·a·caus·tic (kăt/ə kôs/tĭk), *adj.* *Math., Optics.* denoting a caustic surface or curve formed by a reflection of light. See **diacaustic**.

cat·a·chre·sis (kăt/ə krē/sĭs), *n.*, *pl.* **-ses** (-sēz). **1.** misuse or strained use of words. **2.** *Philol.* the employment of a word under a false form through misapprehension in regard to its origin: *causeway* and *crayfish* or *crayfish* have their forms by catachresis. [t. L, t. Gk.: m. *katáchrēsis* misuse] —**cat·a·chres·tic** (kăt/ə krĕs/tĭk), **cat·a·chres/ti·cal**, *adj.* —**cat/a·chres/ti·cal·ly**, *adv.*

cat·a·cli·nal (kăt/ə klī/nəl), *adj.* *Phys. Geog.* descending with the dip, as a valley. [f. CATA- + CLIN- + -AL[1]]

cat·a·clysm (kăt/ə klĭz′əm), *n.* **1.** any violent upheaval, esp. one of a social or political nature. **2.** *Phys. Geog.* a sudden and violent physical action producing changes in the earth's surface. **3.** an extensive flood. [t. L: s. *cataclysmos*, t. Gk.: m. *kataklysmós* deluge]

cat·a·clys·mic (kăt/ə klĭz/mĭk), *adj.* **1.** of, pertaining to, or resulting from a cataclysm. **2.** of the nature of, or having the effect of, a cataclysm: *cataclysmic changes.* Also, **cat/a·clys/mal.**

cat·a·comb (kăt/ə kōm′), *n.* (*usually pl.*) an underground cemetery, esp. one consisting of tunnels and rooms with recesses dug out for coffins and tombs. [ME *catacombe*, OE *catacumbe*, t. LL: m. *catacumbas*]

ca·tad·ro·mous (kə tăd/rə məs), *adj.* (of fishes) going down a river to the sea to spawn.

cat·a·falque (kăt/ə fălk′), *n.* a raised structure on which the body of a deceased personage lies or is carried in state. [t. F, t. It.: m. *catafalco*, g. LL word f. *cata-* CATA- + s. *fala* tower + *-icum* -IC); akin to SCAFFOLD]

Cat·a·lan (kăt/ə lăn′, -lən), *adj.* **1.** pertaining to Catalonia, its inhabitants, or their language. —*n.* **2.** a native or inhabitant of Catalonia. **3.** a Romance language spoken in Catalonia, closely related to Provençal. [t. Sp.]

cat·a·lase (kăt/ə lās′), *n.* *Chem.* an oxidizing enzyme which decomposes peroxides into water and oxygen. [f. CATAL(YSIS) + -ASE]

cat·a·lec·tic (kăt/ə lĕk/tĭk), *adj.* (of a line of poetry) lacking part of the last foot. Thus the italicized second line is catalectic:

> One more unfortunate,
> *Weary of breath.*

[t. LL: s. *catalēcticus*, t. Gk.: m. *katalēktikós* incomplete]

cat·a·lep·sy (kăt/ə lĕp/sĭ), *n.* *Pathol., Psychiatry.* a morbid bodily condition marked by suspension of sensation, muscular rigidity, fixity of posture, and often by loss of contact with environment. [t. LL: m. *catalēpsis*, t. Gk.: m. *katálēpsis* seizure] —**cat/a·lep/tic**, *adj.*, *n.*

cat·a·lin (kăt/ə lĭn), *n.* **1.** a synthetic resin used in costume jewelry, etc. **2.** (*cap.*) a trademark for it.

Cat·a·li·na Island (kăt/ə lē/nə), Santa Catalina.

cat·a·lo (kăt/ə lō′), *n.*, *pl.* **-loes**, **-los**. a hybrid resulting from crossing the American bison (buffalo) with cattle of the domestic breeds. Also, **cattalo**. [b. CAT(TLE) and (BUFF)ALO]

cat·a·log (kăt′əlôg′, -lŏg′), *n.*, *v.t.* catalogue. —**cat′a·log·er, cat·a·log′ist,** *n.*

cat·a·logue (kăt′əlôg′, -lŏg′), *n.*, *v.*, **-logued, -loguing.** —*n.* **1.** a list, usually in alphabetical order, with brief notes on the names, articles, etc., listed. **2.** a record of the books and other resources of a library or a collection, indicated on cards, or, occasionally, in book form. **3.** any list or register. —*v.t.* **4.** to make a catalogue of; enter in a catalogue. **5.** *Library Science.* to describe the bibliographical and technical features of (a publication and the subject matter it treats). [t. F, t. LL: m.s. *catalogus*, t. Gk.: m. *katálogos* a list] —**cat′a·logu′er, cat′a·logu′ist,** *n.* —**Syn. 1.** See **list**[1].

Cat·a·lo·ni·a (kăt′əlō′nĭə), *n.* a region in NE Spain. 2,890,974 pop. (1940); 12,289 sq. mi. Spanish, **Ca·ta·lu·ña** (kä′tälōō′nyä).

ca·tal·pa (kətăl′pə), *n.* any tree of the bignoniaceous genus *Catalpa*, of America and Asia, as *C. speciosa*, of the U. S., having large cordate leaves and bell-shaped white flowers. [t. NL, t. N Amer. Ind. (prob. Creek): m. *kutuhlpa* winged head]

ca·tal·y·sis (kətăl′əsĭs), *n.*, *pl.* **-ses** (-sēz′). *Chem.* the causing or accelerating of a chemical change by the addition of a substance (**catalyst**) which is not permanently affected by the reaction. [t. NL, t. Gk.: m. *katálysis* dissolution] —**cat·a·lyt·ic** (kăt′ə lĭt′ĭk), *adj.*, *n.* —**cat′a·lyt′i·cal·ly,** *adv.*

cat·a·lyst (kăt′əlĭst), *n. Chem.* a substance that causes catalysis.

cat·a·lyze (kăt′əlīz′), *v.t.*, **-lyzed, -lyzing.** *Chem.* to act upon by catalysis. —**cat′a·lyz′er,** *n.*

cat·a·ma·ran (kăt′əmərăn′), *n.* **1.** *Naut.* **a.** a float or raft, usually of several logs or pieces of wood lashed together. **b.** any craft with twin parallel hulls. **2.** *Colloq.* a quarrelsome person, esp. a woman. [t. Tamil: m. *katta-maram* tied tree or wood]

Catamaran

cat·a·me·ni·a (kăt′əmē′nĭə), *n.pl. Physiol.* menses. [t. NL, t. Gk.: m. *kataménia*, neut. pl. of *kataménios* monthly] —**cat′a·me′ni·al,** *adj.*

cat·a·mount (kăt′əmount′), *n.* **1.** a wild animal of the cat family. **2.** (in America) **a.** the cougar. **b.** the lynx. **3.** catamountain. [var. of CATAMOUNTAIN cat of mountain]

cat·a·moun·tain (kăt′əmoun′tən, -tĭn), *n.* a wild animal of the cat family, as the European wild cat, or the leopard or panther. Also, **cat-o′-mountain.**

Ca·ta·nia (kätä′nyä), *n.* a seaport in E Sicily. 269,102 (est. 1946).

cat·a·pho·re·sis (kăt′əfərē′sĭs), *n.* **1.** *Med.* the causing of medicinal substances to pass through or into living tissues in the direction of flow of a positive electric current. **2.** *Phys. Chem.* electrophoresis. [t. NL, f. Gk.: m. *kata-* CATA- + *phórēsis* a carrying] —**cat·a·pho·ret·ic** (kăt′ə fə rĕt′ĭk), *adj.*

cat·a·phyll (kăt′əfĭl), *n. Bot.* a simplified leaf form, as a bud scale or a scale on a cotyledon or rhizome.

cat·a·pult (kăt′əpŭlt′), *n.* **1.** an ancient military engine for throwing darts, stones, etc. **2.** a device for launching an airplane from the deck of a ship, esp. a ship not equipped with a flight deck. **3.** *Brit.* a slingshot. —*v.t.* **4.** to hurl as from a catapult. **5.** *Brit.* to hit (an object) by means of a slingshot. [t. L: s. *catapulta*, t. Gk.: m. *katapéltēs*]

Catapult (def. 1)

cat·a·ract (kăt′ərăkt′), *n.* **1.** a descent of water over a steep surface; a waterfall, esp. one of considerable size. **2.** any furious rush or downpour of water; deluge. **3.** an abnormality of the eye, characterized by opacity of the lens. [ME *cataracte*, t. L: m. *cataracta* waterfall, t. Gk.: m. *kataráktēs* down rushing]

ca·tarrh (kətär′), *n.* inflammation of a mucous membrane, esp. of the respiratory tract, accompanied by excessive secretions. [t. F: m. *catarrhe*, t. L: m. *catarrhus*, t. Gk.: m. *katárrhous* running down] —**ca·tarrh′al,** *adj.*

ca·tas·ta·sis (kətăs′təsĭs), *n.*, *pl.* **-ses** (-sēz′). the part of a drama, preceding the catastrophe, in which the action is at its height. [t. NL, t. Gk.: m. *katástasis* appointment, settlement, condition]

ca·tas·tro·phe (kətăs′trəfĭ), *n.* **1.** a sudden and widespread disaster. **2.** a final event or conclusion, usually an unfortunate one; a disastrous end. **3.** (in a drama) the point at which the circumstances overcome the central motive, introducing the close or conclusion; the dénouement. **4.** a sudden, violent disturbance, esp. of the earth's surface; a cataclysm. [t. Gk.: m. *katastrophē* overturning] —**cat·a·stroph·ic** (kăt′ə strŏf′ĭk), *adj.* —**Syn. 2.** See **disaster**.

ca·tas·tro·phism (kətăs′trəfĭz′əm), *n. Geol.* the doctrine that certain vast geological changes in the earth's history were caused by catastrophes rather than gradual evolutionary processes. —**ca·tas′tro·phist,** *n.*

cat·a·to·ni·a (kăt′ətō′nĭə), *n. Psychiatry.* a syndrome seen most frequently in schizophrenia, with muscular rigidity and mental stupor, sometimes alternating with great excitement and confusion. [f. CATA- + Gk. *-tonía,* der. *tónos* tension] —**cat·a·ton·ic** (kăt′ə tŏn′ĭk), *adj.*, *n.*

Ca·taw·ba (kətô′bə), *n.* **1.** *Hort.* a reddish grape of the eastern U. S. **2.** a light, dry, white wine made from this grape. **3.** a Siouan language of Virginia and the Carolinas. **4.** name of that part of the Wateree river which is in North Carolina.

cat·bird (kăt′bûrd′), *n.* **1.** a slate-colored North American songbird, *Dumetella carolinensis,* allied to the mockingbird, having a call resembling the mewing of a cat. **2.** *Australia.* any of several common birds which produce catlike cries.

cat·boat (kăt′bōt′), *n.* a boat with one mast, which is set well forward, and a single sail extended by gaff and boom.

cat brier, any of various species of *Smilax,* as the greenbrier, *Smilax rotundifolia.*

cat·call (kăt′kôl′), *n.* **1.** a cry like that of a cat, or an instrument for producing a similar sound, used to express disapproval, at a theater, meeting, etc. —*v.i.* **2.** to sound catcalls. —*v.t.* **3.** to express disapproval of by catcalls.

catch (kăch), *v.*, **caught, catching,** *n.*, *adj.* —*v.t.* **1.** to capture, esp. after pursuit; take captive. **2.** to ensnare, entrap, or deceive. **3.** to be in time to reach (a train, boat, etc.). **4.** to come upon suddenly; surprise or detect, as in some action: *I caught him doing it.* **5.** to strike; hit: *the blow caught him on the head.* **6.** to intercept and seize (a ball, etc.). **7.** to check (one's breath, etc.). **8.** to get, receive, incur, or contract (often used figuratively): *to catch a cold, I caught the spirit of the occasion.* **9.** to lay hold of; grasp, seize, or snatch; grip or entangle: *a nail caught his sleeve.* **10.** to allow to be caught; be entangled with: *to catch one's finger in a door, catch one's coat on a nail.* **11.** to fasten with or as with a catch. **12.** to get by attraction or impression: *to catch the eye, the attention, etc.* **13.** to captivate; charm. **14.** to understand by the senses or intellect: *to catch a speaker's words.* **15. catch it,** to get a scolding or beating. —*v.i.* **16.** to become fastened or entangled: *the kite caught in the trees.* **17.** to take hold: *the door lock catches.* **18. catch at, a.** to grasp or snatch. **b.** to be glad to get: *he caught at the chance.* **19.** to overtake something moving (fol. by *up, up with,* or *up to*). **20.** to play as catcher in a baseball game. **21.** to become lighted, take fire, ignite: *the kindling caught instantly.* **22.** to spread or be communicated, as a disease. **23. catch on,** *Colloq.* **a.** to become popular. **b.** to grasp mentally; understand. —*n.* **24.** act of catching. **25.** anything that catches, esp. a device for checking motion. **26.** that which is caught, as a quantity of fish. **27.** anything worth getting. **28.** *Colloq.* a person of either sex regarded as a desirable matrimonial prospect. **29.** a fragment: *catches of a song.* **30.** *Music.* a round, esp. one in which the words are so arranged as to produce ludicrous effects. **31.** *Baseball, etc.* the catching and holding of a batted or thrown ball before it touches the ground. —*adj.* **32.** catchy (defs. 1, 2). [ME *cache*(n), *cacche*(n), t. ONF: m. *cachier,* g. LL. *captiāre,* der. L *capere* take] —**Syn. 9.** CATCH, CLUTCH, GRASP, SEIZE imply taking hold suddenly of something. To CATCH may be to reach after and get: *he caught my hand.* To CLUTCH is to take firm hold of (often out of fear or nervousness), and retain: *the child clutched his mother's hand.* To GRASP also suggests both getting and keeping hold of, with a connotation of eagerness and alertness, rather than fear (lit. or fig.): *to grasp one's hand in welcome, to grasp an idea.* To SEIZE implies the use of force or energy in taking hold of suddenly (lit. or fig.): *to seize a criminal, seize an opportunity.*

catch-all (kăch′ôl′), *n.* a bag, basket, or other receptacle for odds and ends.

catch basin, a receptacle at an opening into a sewer to retain matter that would not pass readily through the sewer.

catch·er (kăch′ər), *n.* **1.** one who or that which catches. **2.** *Baseball.* the player who stands behind the bat or home base to catch the pitched ball.

catcher resonator. See **klystron**.

catch·fly (kăch′flī′), *n.* any of various plants, esp. of the genus *Silene,* having a viscid secretion on stem and calyx in which small insects are sometimes caught.

catch·ing (kăch′ĭng), *adj.* **1.** infectious. **2.** attractive; fascinating; captivating; alluring.

catch·ment basin (kăch′mənt), *Phys. Geog.* a drainage area, esp. of a reservoir or river. Also, **catchment area.**

catch·pen·ny (kăch′pĕn′ĭ), *adj.*, *n.*, *pl.* **-nies.** —*adj.* **1.** made to sell readily at a low price, regardless of value or use. —*n.* **2.** anything of little value or use, made merely for quick sale.

catch phrase, a phrase that attracts attention.

catch·pole (kăch′pōl′), *n. Archaic or Hist.* a petty officer of justice, esp. one who makes arrests for debt. Also, **catch′poll′.** [ME *cachepol,* OE *kæcepol,* t. ML: m.s. *cacepollus* chase-fowl. See CATCH, PULLET]

catch·up (kăch′əp, kĕch′-), *n. some U.S.* any of several sauces or condiments for meat, fish, as *tomato* or *mushroom catchup.* Also, **catsup, ketchup.** [var. of KETCHUP]

catch·weight (kăch/wāt/), *n. Sports.* the chance or optional weight of a contestant, as contrasted with a weight fixed by agreement, etc.

catch·word (kăch/wûrd/), *n.* **1.** a word or phrase caught up and repeated for effect as by a political party. **2.** a word printed at the top of a page in a dictionary or other reference book to indicate the first or last article on that page. **3.** a device, used esp. in old books, to assist the reader by inserting at the foot of one page the first word of the following page. **4.** an actor's cue.

catch·y (kăch/ĭ), *adj.,* **catchier, catchiest. 1.** pleasing and easily remembered: *a catchy tune.* **2.** tricky; deceptive: *a catchy question.* **3.** occurring in snatches; fitful: *a catchy wind.*

cate (kāt), *n. (usually pl.) Archaic.* a choice food; a delicacy; a dainty. [aphetic var. of ME *acate,* t. ONF: m. *acat,* der. *acater* buy, g. LL *accaptāre* acquire]

cat·e·che·sis (kăt/ə̄kē/sĭs), *n., pl.* **-ses** (-sēz). oral religious instruction, formerly esp. before baptism or confirmation. [t. L, t. Gk.: m. *katēchēsis* oral instruction]

cat·e·chet·i·cal (kăt/ə̄kĕt/ĭkəl), *adj.* pertaining to teaching by question and answer. Also, **cat/e·chet/ic.**

cat·e·chin (kăt/ə̄chĭn, -kĭn), *n.* an amorphous, yellow compound, $C_{15}H_{14}O_6$, used in tanning and dyeing.

cat·e·chism (kăt/ə̄kĭz/əm), *n.* **1.** *Eccles.* **a.** an elementary book containing a summary of the principles of the Christian religion, esp. as maintained by a particular church, in the form of questions and answers. **b.** the contents of such a book. **2.** a similar book of instruction in other subjects. **3.** *Pol.* a series of formal questions put to political candidates, etc., to bring out their views. **4.** *Obs.* catechetical instruction. [t. LL: s. *catēchismus,* der. Gk. *katēchizein.* See CATECHIZE]

cat·e·chist (kăt/ə̄kĭst), *n.* **1.** one who catechizes. **2.** *Eccles.* one appointed to instruct catechumens in the principles of religion as a preparation for baptism. —**cat/e·chis/tic, cat/e·chis/ti·cal,** *adj.*

cat·e·chize (kăt/ə̄kīz/), *v.t.,* **-chized, -chizing. 1.** to instruct orally by means of questions and answers, esp. in Christian doctrine. **2.** to question with reference to belief. **3.** to question closely or excessively. Also, **cat/e·chise/.** [t. LL: m. s. *catēchizāre,* t. Gk.: m. *katēchizein,* teach orally] —**cat/e·chi·za/tion,** t. —**cat/e·chiz/er,** *n.*

cat·e·chol (kăt/ə̄chŏl, -kōl), *n. Chem., etc.* a white crystalline benzene derivative, $C_6H_6O_2$, used in photography; pyrocatechol. [f. CATECH(U) + -OL²]

cat·e·chu (kăt/ə̄chōō, -kū/), *n.* any of several astringent substances obtained from various tropical plants, esp. from the wood of two East Indian species of acacia, *Acacia Catechu* and *A. Suma,* used in medicine, dyeing, tanning, etc.; cutch. Also, **cashoo.** [t. NL, t. Malay: m. (unexplained) *kachu*]

cat·e·chu·men (kăt/ə̄kū/mən), *n.* **1.** *Eccles.* one under instruction in the rudiments of Christianity, as in the early church; a neophyte. **2.** a person being taught the elementary facts, principles, etc. of any subject. [t. LL: s. *catēchūmenus,* t. Gk.: m. *katēchoúmenos,* ppr. pass. of *katēcheîn.* See CATECHIZE] —**cat/e·chu/me·nal,** *adj.*

cat·e·gor·i·cal (kăt/ə̄gôr/ĭkəl, -gŏr/-), *adj.* **1.** not involving a condition, qualification, etc.; explicit; direct: *a categorical answer.* **2.** *Logic.* (of a proposition) analyzable into a subject and an attribute related by a copula, as in *all men are mortal.* **3.** of, pertaining to, or in a category. —**cat/e·gor/i·cal·ly,** *adv.* —**cat/e·gor/i·cal·ness,** *n.*

categorical imperative, 1. *Ethics.* the rule of Immanuel Kant that one must do only what he can will that all others should do under similar circumstances. **2.** the unconditional command of conscience.

cat·e·go·ry (kăt/ə̄gôr/ĭ), *n., pl.* **-ries. 1.** a classificatory division in any field of knowledge, as a phylum or any of its subdivisions in biology. **2.** any general or comprehensive division; a class. **3.** *Logic, Metaphys.* **a.** a basic mode or phase of existence, as space, quantity, quality. **b.** a basic form or organizing principle of reason as the principle of causality. [t. L: m. s. *catēgoria,* t. Gk.: m. *katēgoría* assertion]

ca·te·na (kə̄tē/nə), *n., pl.* **-nae** (-nē). a chain or connected series, esp. of extracts from the writings of the fathers of the church. [t. L: chain]

cat·e·nar·y (kăt/ə̄nĕr/ĭ; *esp. Brit.* kə̄tē/nərĭ), *n., pl.* **-naries,** *adj. Math.* —*n.* **1.** the curve assumed approximately by a heavy uniform cord or chain hanging freely from two points not in the same vertical line. —*adj.* **2.** Also, **cat·e·nar·i·an** (kăt/ə̄nâr/ĭən). pertaining to a catenary. [t. L: m.s. *catēnārius* relating to a chain]

cat·e·nate (kăt/ə̄nāt/), *v.t.,* **-nated, -nating.** to link together; form into a connected series: *catenated cells.* —**cat/e·na/tion,** *n.*

ca·ter (kā/tər), *v.i.* **1.** to provide food, service, etc.: *to cater for a banquet.* **2.** to provide means of amusement, pleasure, etc.: *to cater to popular taste.* [v. use of obs. *cater,* ME *catour,* aphetic var. of *acatour* buyer of provisions, t. OF: m. *acateor* buyer. See CATE]

cat·er·an (kăt/ərən), *n.* a freebooter or marauder of the Scottish Highlands. [t. ML: s. *caterānus,* Latinization of ME (Scot.) *catherein,* etc., t. Gaelic: m. *ceathairne* peasantry. See KERN¹]

cat·er-cor·nered (kăt/ə̄kôr/nərd, kăt/ər-), *adj.* **1.** diagonal. —*adv.* **2.** diagonally. [f. *cater,* adv., diagonally (t. F: m. *quatre* four) + *cornered*]

ca·ter-cous·in (kā/tər kŭz/ən), *n.* **1.** one related by or as by cousinship. **2.** an intimate friend.

ca·ter·er (kā/tərər), *n.* **1.** a purveyor of food or provisions, as for entertainments, etc. **2.** one who caters. —**ca·ter·ess** (kā/tər ĭs), *n. fem.*

cat·er·pil·lar (kăt/ə̄pĭl/ər, kăt/ər-), *n.* **1.** the moth-like larva of a butterfly or a moth. **2.** Also, **caterpillar tractor.** a tractor having the driving wheels moving inside endless tracks on either side, thus being capable of hauling heavy loads over rough or soft ground. **3.** (*cap.*) a trademark for this tractor. **4.** any device, as a tank or steam shovel, moving on endless belt (caterpillar) treads. **5.** one who preys on others; extortioner. [late ME *catyrpel(er),* of uncert. orig. Cf. OF *chatepelose,* lit., hairy cat]

cat·er·waul (kăt/ər wôl/), *v.i.* **1.** to cry as cats in rutting time. **2.** to utter a similar sound; howl or screech. **3.** to quarrel like cats. —*n.* Also, **cat/er·waul/ing. 4.** the cry of a cat in rutting time. **5.** any similar sound. [ME *caterw(r)awen,* f. *cater* (cf. G *kater* tomcat) + *wrawen* howl]

cat·fall (kăt/fôl/), *n. Naut.* the rope or tackle for hoisting an anchor to the cathead.

cat·fish (kăt/fĭsh/), *n., pl.* **-fishes,** (*esp. collectively*) **-fish. 1.** any of numerous fishes having some fancied resemblance to a cat, such as one of the fishes characterized by long barbels, of the North American fresh-water family *Ameiuridae,* many of which are used for food. **2.** any fish of the order *Nematognathi,* as a bullhead.

cat·gut (kăt/gŭt/), *n.* **1.** the intestines of sheep or other animals, dried and twisted, used as strings for musical instruments, etc. **2.** a violin. **3.** stringed instruments collectively.

cath-, var. of **cata-,** before an aspirate, as in *cathode.*

Cath., Catholic.

ca·thar·sis (kə̄thär/sĭs), *n.* **1.** *Aesthetics.* the effect of art in purifying the emotions (applied by Aristotle to the relief or purgation of the emotions of the audience or performers effected through pity and terror by tragedy and certain kinds of music). **2.** *Psychoanal.* an effective discharge with symptomatic relief but not necessarily a cure of the underlying pathology. **3.** *Psychiatry.* psychotherapy which encourages and permits discharge of pent-up and socially unacceptable effects. **4.** *Med.* purgation. [t. NL, t. Gk.: m. *kátharsis* a cleansing]

ca·thar·tic (kə̄thär/tĭk), *adj.* **1.** Also, **ca·thar/ti·cal.** evacuating the bowels; purgative. —*n.* **2.** a purgative. [t. L: s. *catharticus,* t. Gk.: m. *kathartikós* fit for cleansing, purgative]

Ca·thay (kă thā/), *n. Archaic or Poetic.* China. [t. ML: s. *Cat(h)aya;* cf. Russ. *Kitai,* said to be of Tatar orig.]

cat·head (kăt/hĕd/), *n. Naut.* a projecting timber or beam near the bow, to which the anchor is hoisted.

ca·the·dra (kə̄thē/drə, kăth/ə̄-), *n., pl.* **-drae** (-drē, -drē/). **1.** the seat or throne of a bishop in the principal church of his diocese. **2.** an official chair, as of a professor in a university. [t. L, t. Gk.: m. *kathédra* chair]

ca·the·dral (kə̄thē/drəl), *n.* **1.** the principal church of a diocese, containing the bishop's throne. **2.** (in non-episcopal denominations) any of various important churches. —*adj.* **3.** pertaining to or containing a bishop's throne. **4.** pertaining to or emanating from a chair of office or authority.

Cath·er (kăth/ər), *n.* **Willa Sibert** (wĭl/ə̄ sē/bərt), 1876–1947, U. S. novelist.

Cath·er·ine (kăth/rĭn, -ərĭn), *n.* **Saint,** died A.D. 307, Christian martyr of Alexandria who was beheaded.

Catherine I, c 1683–1727, consort of Peter the Great, and empress of Russia, 1725–27.

Catherine II, ("*the Great*") 1729–96, consort of Czar Peter, and empress of Russia, 1762–96.

Catherine of Ar·a·gon (ăr/ə̄gən, -gŏn/), 1485–1536, first wife of Henry VIII of England and mother of Mary I of England.

Catherine of Sie·na (syĕ/nä), **Saint,** 1347–80, Italian ascetic and mystic (Dominican tertiary).

cath·e·ter (kăth/ə̄tər), *n. Med.* a flexible or rigid hollow tube employed to drain fluids from body cavities or to distend body passages, esp. one for passing into the bladder through the urethra to draw off urine. [t. LL, t. Gk.: m. *kathetḗr,* der. *kathiénai* let down]

cath·e·ter·ize (kăth/ə̄tərīz/), *v.t.,* **-ized, -izing.** to introduce a catheter into.

ca·thex·is (kə̄thĕk/sĭs), *n. Psychoanal.* **1.** the investment of emotional significance in an activity, object, or idea. **2.** the charge of psychic energy so invested. [t. Gk.: m. *káthexis* holding, retention; rendering G *besetzung* (Freud)]

cath·ode (kăth/ōd), *n.* **1.** the electrode which emits electrons or gives off negative ions and toward which positive ions move or collect, in a voltaic cell, electronic or x-ray tube, or other device. **2.** the negative pole of a battery or other source of electric current (opposed to *anode*). Also, **kathode.** [t. Gk.: m. s. *káthodos* way down] —**ca·thod·ic** (kă thŏd/ĭk), *adj.*

cathode ray, a stream of electrons generated at the cathode during an electric discharge in a vacuum tube; used to generate x-rays.

cathode ray tube, *Electronics.* a vacuum tube that generates a focused beam of electrons which can be deflected by electric and/or magnetic fields. The terminus of the beam is visible as a spot or line of luminescence caused by its impinging on a sensitized screen at one end

---

b., blend of, blended; c., cognate with; d., dialect, dialectal; der., derived from; f., formed from; g., going back to; m., modification of; r., replacing; s., stem of; t., taken from; ?, perhaps. See the full key on inside cover.

of the tube. Cathode ray tubes are used to study the shapes of electric waves, to reproduce pictures in television receivers, as an indicator in radar sets, etc.

cath·o·lic (kăth/ə lĭk, kăth/lĭk), *adj.* **1.** pertaining to the whole Christian body or church. **2.** universal in extent; involving all; of interest to all. **3.** having sympathies with all; broad-minded; liberal: *to be catholic in one's tastes, interests, etc.*

Cath·o·lic (kăth/ə lĭk, kăth/lĭk), *adj.* **1.** *Theol.* **a.** (among Roman Catholics) claiming to possess exclusively the notes or characteristics of the one, only, true, and universal church—unity, visibility, indefectibility, apostolic succession, universality, and sanctity (used in this sense, with these qualifications, only by the Church of Rome, as applicable only to itself and its adherents, and to their faith and organization; often qualified, especially by those not acknowledging these claims, by prefixing the word *Roman*). **b.** (among Anglicans) noting or pertaining to the conception of the Church as the body representing the ancient undivided Christian witness, comprising all the orthodox churches which have kept the apostolic succession of bishops, and including the Anglican Church, the Roman Catholic Church, the Eastern Orthodox Church, Church of Sweden, the Old Catholic Church (in the Netherlands and elsewhere), etc. **2.** pertaining to the Western Church. —*n.* **3.** a member of a catholic church, esp. of the Church of Rome. [t. L: s. *catholicus*, t. Gk.: m. *katholikós* (def. 2)] —**ca·thol·i·cal·ly** (kə thŏl/ĭk lĭ), *adv.*

Catholic Church, *Rom. Cath. Ch.* a visible society of baptized, professing the same faith under the authority of the invisible Head (Christ) and the authority of the visible head (the pope and the bishops in communion with him).

Ca·thol·i·cism (kə thŏl/ə sĭz/əm), *n.* **1.** the faith, system, and practice of the Catholic Church, esp. the Roman Catholic Church. **2.** (*l.c.*) catholicity (def. 1).

cath·o·lic·i·ty (kăth/ə lĭs/ə tĭ), *n.* **1.** the quality of being catholic; universality; broad-mindedness. **2.** (*cap.*) the Roman Catholic Church or its doctrines and usages.

ca·thol·i·cize (kə thŏl/ə sīz/), *v.t., v.i.,* **-cized, -cizing.** to make or become catholic or (*cap.*) Catholic.

ca·thol·i·con (kə thŏl/ə kən), *n.* a universal remedy; a panacea. [t. Gk.: m. *katholikón*]

Cat·i·line (kăt/ə lĭn/), *n.* **1.** (*Lucius Sergius Catilina*) 108?–62 B.C. Roman politician and conspirator. **2.** any base political conspirator.

cat·i·on (kăt/ī/ən), *n. Phys. Chem.* **1.** a positively charged ion which is attracted to the cathode in electrolysis. **2.** any positively charged ion, radical, or molecule. Also, **kation.** [t. Gk.: m. *kation*, ppr. neut., going down]

cat·kin (kăt/kĭn), *n. Bot.* an ament, as of the willow or birch. [t. D: m. *katteken* little cat]

cat·ling (kăt/lĭng), *n. Now Rare.* **1.** a little cat; a kitten. **2.** catgut; a catgut string. **3.** a surgical knife. [f. CAT + -LING[1]]

cat nap, *U.S.* a short, light nap or doze.

cat·nip (kăt/nĭp), *n.* a plant, *Nepeta Cataria,* of the mint family, with strongly scented leaves of which cats are fond. Also, *Brit.,* **cat·mint** (kăt/mĭnt/). [f. CAT + *nip,* var. of *nep* catnip, var. of *nept,* t. ML: s. *nepta,* L *nepeta*]

Ca·to (kā/tō), *n.* **1. Marcus Porcius** (mär/kəs pôr/shĭ əs), ("*the Elder*" or "*the Censor*") 234–149 B.C., Roman statesman, soldier, and writer. **2.** his greatgrandson **Marcus Porcius,** ("*the Younger*") 95–46 B.C., Roman statesman, soldier, and Stoic philosopher.

Catkins of birch
A, Male;
B, Female

cat-o'-moun·tain (kăt/ə moun/tən, -tĭn), *n.* catamountain.

cat-o'-nine-tails (kăt/ə nīn/tālz/), *n., pl.* **-tails.** a whip, usually having nine knotted lines or cords fastened to a handle, used to flog offenders.

ca·top·trics (kə tŏp/trĭks), *n.* that branch of optics dealing with the formation of images by mirrors. [t. Gk.: m.s. *katoptrikós* of or in a mirror. See -ICS] —**ca·top/tric, ca·top/tri·cal,** *adj.*

cat·rigged (kăt/rĭgd/), *adj.* rigged like a catboat.

cat's cradle, a child's game in which two players alternately stretch a looped string over their fingers in such a way as to produce different designs.

cat's-eye (kăts/ī/), *n.* any of certain gems exhibiting a chatoyant luster, but esp. a variety of chrysoberyl (the **oriental** or **precious cat's-eye**).

Cats·kill Mountains (kăts/kĭl), a range of low mountains in E New York. Highest peak, Slide Mountain, 4204 ft. Also, **Catskills.**

cat's-paw (kăts/pô/), *n.* **1.** a person used by another to serve his purposes; a tool. **2.** *Naut.* **a.** a kind of hitch in the bight of a rope, made to hook a tackle on. **b.** a light breeze which ruffles the surface of the water over a comparatively small area. Also, **cats/paw/.**

cat·stick (kăt/stĭk/), *n.* a stick used in certain games.

cat·sup (kăt/səp, kĕch/əp), *n.* catchup.

Catt (kăt), *n.* **Carrie Chapman** (kăr/ĭ chăp/mən), 1859–1947, U.S. leader in women's suffrage movements.

cat·tail (kăt/tāl/), *n.* **1.** a tall reedlike marsh plant, *Typha latifolia,* with flowers in long, dense cylindrical

spikes; reed mace. **2.** any of several other plants of the same genus. **3.** *Bot.* an ament or catkin.

cat·ta·lo (kăt/ə lō/), *n., pl.* **-loes, -los.** catalo.

Cat·te·gat (kăt/ə găt/), *n.* Kattegat.

cat·tish (kăt/ĭsh), *adj.* **1.** catlike; feline; **2.** spiteful. —**cat/tish·ly,** *adv.* —**cat/tish·ness,** *n.*

cat·tle (kăt/əl), *n.* **1.** *U.S.* ruminants of the bovine kind, of any age, breed, or sex. **2.** (formerly, and still in England) such animals together with horses and other domesticated animals. **3.** insects, vermin, or other. animals considered contemptuously or in a mass. **4.** *Contemptuous.* human beings. [ME *catel,* t. ONF, g. L *capitāle* wealth, stock. See CAPITAL[1], n.]

cat·tle·man (kăt/əl mən), *n., pl.* **-men. 1.** a person employed in tending or rearing cattle. **2.** *U.S.* one who rears cattle on a large scale; the owner of a cattle ranch.

cat·ty[1] (kăt/ĭ), *adj.,* **-tier, -tiest. 1.** catlike. **2.** quietly or slyly malicious; spiteful: *a catty gossip.* [f. CAT + -Y[1]] —**cat/ti·ly,** *adv.* —**cat/ti·ness,** *n.*

cat·ty[2] (kăt/ĭ), *n., pl.* **-ties.** (in China and elsewhere in the East) a weight equal to about 1⅓ pounds avoirdupois. [t. Malay: m. *katī*]

Ca·tul·lus (kə tŭl/əs), *n.* **Gaius Valerius** (gā/əs və lĭr/ĭ əs), 84?–54? B.C., Roman lyric poet.

cat·walk (kăt/wôk/), *n.* any narrow walking space on a bridge, or in an aircraft.

cat whisker, *Radio.* the wire forming one contact of the crystal in a crystal detector.

Cau·ca·sia (kô kā/zhə, -shə), *n.* a region in the Soviet Union between the Black and Caspian seas: divided by the Caucasus Mountains into Ciscaucasia (in Europe) and Transcaucasia (in Asia). Also, **Caucasus.**

Cau·ca·sian (kô kā/zhən, -shən, -kăzh/ən, -kăsh/ən), *adj.* **1.** pertaining to the so-called "white race," embracing the chief peoples of Europe, southwestern Asia, and northern Africa, so named because the native peoples of the Caucasus were considered typical. **2.** of or pertaining to the Caucasus mountain range. Also, **Cau·cas·ic** (kô kăs/ĭk). —*n.* **3.** a member of the Caucasian race. **4.** a native of the Caucasus.

Cau·ca·sus (kô/kə səs), *n.* **1.** a mountain range in the S Soviet Union in Europe, in Caucasia. Highest peak, Mt. Elbrus (highest in Europe), 18,465 ft. **2.** Caucasia.

cau·cus (kô/kəs), *n.* **1.** *U.S.* a meeting of the local members of a political party to nominate candidates, elect delegates to a convention, etc., or of the members of a legislative body who belong to the same party to determine upon action in that body. **2.** (in England) a local committee of a political party exercising a certain control over its affairs or actions. —*v.i.* **3.** to hold or meet in a caucus. [orig. unknown; ? alter. of *caulkers'* (*meeting*), from the fact that such meetings were orig. held where ship business was carried on, or ? of Amer. Ind. orig.]

cau·dad (kô/dăd), *adv. Anat., Zool.* toward the tail or posterior end of the body (opposed to *cephalad*). [f. L: s. *cauda* tail + *ad* to]

cau·dal (kô/dəl), *adj. Zool.* **1.** of, at, or near the tail. **2.** taillike: *caudal appendages.* [t. NL: s. *caudālis,* der. L *cauda* tail] —**cau/dal·ly,** *adv.*

cau·date (kô/dāt), *adj. Zool.* having a tail or taillike appendage. Also, **cau/dat·ed.** [t. NL: m. s. *caudātus,* der. L *cauda* tail]

cau·dex (kô/dĕks), *n., pl.* **-dices** (-də sēz/), **-dexes.** *Bot.* **1.** the axis of a plant, including both stem and root. **2.** a stem bearing the remains or scars of petioles. **3.** the woody or thickened persistent base of a herbaceous perennial. [t. L: tree trunk. See CODEX]

cau·dil·lo (kô dēl/yō, -dĭl/yō; *Sp.* kou dē/lyō, -yō), *n., pl.* **-los** (-yoz; *Sp.* -lyōs, -yōs). (in Spanish-speaking countries) the head of the state; leader.

Cau·dine Forks (kô/dĭn), two narrow mountain passes in S Italy, near Benevento: site of a Roman defeat by the Samnites, 321 B.C.

cau·dle (kô/dəl), *n.* a warm drink for the sick, as of wine or ale mixed with eggs, bread, sugar, spices, etc. [ME *caudel,* t. ONF, dim. of *caud,* g. L *calidus* warm]

caught (kôt), *v.* pt. and pp. of **catch.**

caul (kôl), *n.* a part of the amnion sometimes covering the head of a child at birth, superstitiously supposed to bring good luck and to be an infallible preservative against drowning. [ME *calle,* t. F: m. *cale* kind of cap]

cauld (kôld, kăld, kôd), *adj., n. Scot.* cold.

caul·dron (kôl/drən), *n.* caldron.

cau·les·cent (kô lĕs/ənt), *adj. Bot.* having an obvious stem rising above the ground. [f. s. L *caulis* stalk + -ESCENT]

cau·li·cle (kô/lə kəl), *n. Bot.* a small or rudimentary stem. [t. L: m. s. *cauliculus,* dim. of *caulis* stalk]

cau·li·flow·er (kô/lə flou/ər; *Colloq. often* kŏl/ĭ-), *n.* **1.** a cultivated cruciferous plant, *Brassica oleracea* var., *botrytis,* whose inflorescence forms a compact, fleshy head. **2.** the head, used as a vegetable. [half adoption, half trans. of NL *cauliflora,* lit., cabbage-flower]

cauliflower ear, an ear that has been misshaped by battering blows.

cau·line (kô/lĭn, -līn), *adj. Bot.* of or pertaining to a stem, esp. pertaining to or arising from the upper part of a stem. [f. s. L *caulis* stalk + -INE[1]]

cau·lis (kô/lĭs), *n., pl.* **-les** (-lēz). *Bot.* the main stalk or stem of a plant, esp. of a herbaceous plant. [t. L]

caulk (kôk), *v.t.* calk[1]. —**caulk/er,** *n.*

ăct, āble, dâre, ärt; ĕbb, ēqual; ĭf, īce; hŏt, ōver, ôrder, oil, bŏŏk, ōōze, out; ŭp, ūse, ûrge; ə = a in alone; ch, chief; g, give; ng, ring; sh, shoe; th, thin; ŧh, that; zh, vision. See the full key on inside cover.

caus·al (kô′zəl), *adj.* **1.** of, constituting, or implying a cause. **2.** *Gram.* expressing a cause, as a conjunction. —**caus′al·ly,** *adv.*

cau·sal·gi·a (kô zăl′jĭ ə), *n.* a neuralgia distinguished by a burning pain along certain nerves, usually of the upper extremities. [f. m.s. Gk. *kaûsos* burning heat + -ALGIA]

cau·sal·i·ty (kô zăl′ə tĭ), *n., pl.* -ties. **1.** the relation of cause and effect. **2.** causal quality or agency.

cau·sa si·ne qua non (kô′zə sī′nĭ kwā nŏn′), *Latin.* a requisite or indispensable condition.

cau·sa·tion (kô zā′shən), *n.* **1.** the action of causing or producing. **2.** the relation of cause to effect. **3.** anything that produces an effect; a cause.

caus·a·tive (kô′zə tĭv), *n.* **1.** *Gram.* a word (usually a verb) denoting causation, as *made* in *he made me eat the apple.* —*adj.* **2.** *Gram.* **a.** pertaining to an affix or other form by which causatives are derived from an underlying word. For example: Gothic *jan* is a causative affix in *fulljan* (cause to be full, fill). **b.** pertaining to a word or words so derived, esp. one formed from an underlying word that lacks this meaning: *"to fell" is the causative of "to fall."* **3.** acting as a cause; productive (fol. by *of*). —**caus′a·tive·ly,** *adv.* —**caus′a·tive·ness,** *n.*

cause (kôz), *n., v.,* **caused, causing.** —*n.* **1.** that which produces an effect; the thing, person, etc. from which something results. **2.** the ground of any action or result; reason; motive. **3.** good or sufficient reason: *to complain without cause.* **4.** *Law.* **a.** a ground of legal action; the matter over which a person goes to law. **b.** a case for judicial decision. **5.** any subject of discussion or debate. **6.** that side of a question which a person or party supports; the aim, purpose, etc. of a group. **7.** *Philos.* the end or purpose for which a thing is done or produced (now only in *final causes*). —*v.t.* **8.** to be the cause of; bring about. [ME, t. L: m. *causa*] —**caus′a·ble,** *adj.* —**cause′less,** *adj.* —**caus′er,** *n.*
—**Syn. 1.** CAUSE, OCCASION refer to the starting of effects into motion. A CAUSE is an agency, perhaps acting through a long time, or a long standing situation, which produces an effect: *the cause of the quarrel between the two men was jealousy.* An OCCASION is an event which provides an opportunity for the effect to become evident, or perhaps promotes its becoming evident: *the occasion was the fact that one man's wages were increased.* **3.** See **reason. 8.** effect, make, create, produce.

cause cé·lè·bre (kōz sĕ lĕb′r), *French.* a celebrated legal case.

cau·se·rie (kō′zə rē′; *Fr.* kōz rē′), *n.* **1.** a talk or chat. **2.** a short, informal essay, article, etc. [t. F, der. *causer* talk, t. L: m. *causārī* plead]

cause·way (kôz′wā′), *n.* **1.** a raised road or path, as across low or wet ground. **2.** a highway or paved way. —*v.t.* **3.** to pave, as a road or street, with cobbles or pebbles. **4.** to provide with a causeway. [var. of *causey way.* See CAUSEY]

cau·sey (kô′zĭ), *n., pl.* -seys. *Brit. Dial.* causeway. [ME *cauce,* t. ONF: m. *caucie,* earlier *cauciee* (cf. F *chaussée*), g. LL *calciāta* paved road]

caus·tic (kôs′tĭk), *adj.* **1.** capable of burning, corroding, or destroying living tissue: *caustic soda.* **2.** severely critical or sarcastic: *a caustic remark.* **3.** *Math., Optics.* **a.** denoting a surface to which all the light rays emanating from a single point and reflected by a curved surface (as a concave mirror) are tangent. **b.** denoting a curve formed by a plane section of such a surface. **c.** denoting an analogous surface or curve resulting from refraction. —*n.* **4.** a caustic substance: *lunar caustic.* **5.** *Math., Optics.* a caustic surface or curve. [t. L: s. *causticus,* t. Gk.: m. *kaustikós* capable of burning] —**caus′ti·cal·ly,** *adv.* —**caus·tic·i·ty** (kôs tĭs′ə tĭ), *n.*

caustic potash, potassium hydroxide, KOH, used in the manufacture of soap, and glass.

caustic soda, sodium hydroxide, NaOH, used in metallurgy and photography.

cau·ter·ize (kô′tə rīz′), *v.t.,* -ized, -izing. to burn with a hot iron, or with fire or a caustic, esp. for curative purposes; treat with a cautery. —**cau′ter·i·za′tion,** *n.*

cau·ter·y (kô′tə rĭ), *n., pl.* -teries. **1.** an escharotic substance or a hot iron used to destroy tissue. **2.** the process of destroying tissue with a cautery. [t. L: m.s. *cautērium,* t. Gk.: m. *kautērion,* dim. of *kautḗr* branding iron]

cau·tion (kô′shən), *n.* **1.** prudence in regard to danger or evil; carefulness; wariness: *proceed with caution.* **2.** a warning against danger or evil; anything serving as a warning. **3.** *Colloq.* a person or thing that is unusual, odd, amazing, etc. —*v.t.* **4.** to give warning to; advise or urge to take heed. [ME, t. *cautio;* r. ME *caucion* security, t. OF] —**Syn. 1.** circumspectness, watchfulness, heed, care. **2.** admonition, advice. **4.** See **warn.** —**Ant. 1.** recklessness.

cau·tion·ar·y (kô′shə nĕr′ĭ), *adj.* of the nature of or containing a warning: *cautionary advice.*

cau·tious (kô′shəs), *adj.* having or showing caution or prudence to avoid danger or evil; very careful. —**cau′tious·ly,** *adv.* —**cau′tious·ness,** *n.* —**Syn.** prudent, discreet, guarded, wary, circumspect. See **careful.** —**Ant.** rash, heedless.

Cau·ver·y (kô′və rĭ), *n.* a river in S India, flowing from the Western Ghats SE to the Bay of Bengal: sacred to the Hindus. ab. 400 mi. Also, **Kaveri.**

Cav., Cavalry.

cav·al·cade (kăv′əl kăd′, kăv′əl kād′), *n.* **1.** a procession of persons on horseback or in horse-drawn carriages. **2.** any procession. [t. F, t. It.: m. *cavalcata,* der. *cavalcare,* g. LL *caballicāre* ride on horseback]

cav·a·lier (kăv′ə lĭr′), *n.* **1.** a horseman, esp. a mounted soldier; a knight. **2.** one having the spirit or bearing of a knight; a courtly gentleman; a gallant. **3.** a man escorting a woman or acting as her partner in dancing. **4.** (*cap.*) an adherent of Charles I of England in his contest with Parliament. —*adj.* **5.** haughty, disdainful, or supercilious. **6.** offhand or unceremonious. **7.** (*cap.*) of or pertaining to the Cavaliers. —*v.i.* **8.** to play the cavalier. **9.** to be haughty or domineering. [t. F, t. It.: m. *cavalliere,* der. *cavallo* horse, g. L *caballus*]

cav·a·lier·ly (kăv′ə lĭr′lĭ), *adv.* **1.** in a cavalier manner. —*adj.* **2.** characteristic of a cavalier; arrogant.

Cavalier poets, a group of English poets (Herrick, Carew, Lovelace, Suckling, etc.), mainly at the court of Charles I, who produced a body of graceful lyrical poetry.

ca·val·la (kə văl′ə), *n., pl.* -la, -las. cavally.

ca·val·ly (kə văl′ĭ), *n., pl.* -lies. **1.** any of various carangoid fishes of the genus *Caranx,* esp. *C. hippos,* a food fish of both coasts of tropical America. **2.** the cero. [t. Pg.: m. *cavalla,* or t. Sp.: m. *caballa* horse mackerel, g. L *caballa mare*]

cav·al·ry (kăv′əl rĭ), *n., pl.* -ries. **1.** *Mil.* **a.** that part of a military force composed of troops that serve on horseback. **b.** mounted soldiers collectively. **c.** (in armored forces) an element having reconnaissance in force as its principal mission. **2.** horsemen, horses, etc., collectively. **3.** *Obs.* horsemanship, esp. of a knight. [t. F: m. *cavalerie,* t. It.: m. *cavalleria* knighthood, der. *cavalliere.* See CAVALIER¹] —**cav·al·ry·man** (kăv′əl rĭ mən), *n.*

cav·a·ti·na (kăv′ə tē′nə; *It.* kä′vä tē′nä), *n., pl.* -ne (-nĕ). *Music.* a simple song or melody, properly one without a second part and a repeat; an air. [t. It.]

cave (kāv), *n., v.,* **caved, caving.** —*n.* **1.** a hollow in the earth, esp. one opening more or less horizontally into a hill, mountain, etc. **2.** *Eng. Pol.* a secession, or a group of seceders, from a political party on some special question. —*v.t.* **3.** to hollow out. **4.** to cause to fall (fol. by *in*). —*v.i.* **5.** to fall or sink, as ground (fol. by *in*). **6.** *Colloq.* to give, yield, or submit (fol. by *in*). [ME, t. OF, t. L: m. *cava* hollow (places), neut. pl.]

ca·ve·at (kā′vĭ ăt′), *n.* **1.** *Law.* a legal notice to a court or public officer to suspend a certain proceeding until the notifier is given a hearing: *a caveat filed against the probate of a will.* **2.** any warning or caution. [t. L: let him beware]

ca·ve·at emp·tor (kā′vĕ ăt′, ĕmp′tôr), *Latin.* let the buyer beware (since he buys without recourse).

ca·ve·a·tor (kā′vĭ ā′tər), *n.* one who enters a caveat.

cave-in (kāv′ĭn′), *n.* a collapse, as of a mine, etc.

Cav·ell (kăv′əl), *n.* Edith Louisa, 1865–1915, British nurse, executed by the Germans in World War I.

cave man, **1.** a cave dweller; a man of the Old Stone Age. **2.** *Colloq.* a man who behaves in a rough, primitive manner, esp. toward women.

cav·en·dish (kăv′ən dĭsh), *n.* tobacco softened, sweetened, and pressed into cakes. [named after the maker]

Cav·en·dish (kăv′ən dĭsh), *n.* Henry, 1731?–1810, British physicist and chemist.

cav·ern (kăv′ərn), *n.* a cave, esp. a large cave. [ME *caverne,* t. F, t. L: m. *caverna* cave]

cav·ern·ous (kăv′ər nəs), *adj.* **1.** containing caverns. **2.** deep-set: *cavernous eyes.* **3.** hollow and deep-sounding: *a cavernous voice.* **4.** full of small cavities; porous. **5.** of a cavern: *cavernous darkness.* —**cav′ern·ous·ly,** *adv.*

ca·vet·to (kə vĕt′ō; *It.* kä vĕt′tō), *n., pl.* -ti (-tĭ; *It.* -tē). -tos. *Archit.* a concave molding, as in a cornice, with the curve usually a quarter circle. See diag. under **column.** [t. It., dim. of *cavo,* g. L *cavum* hollow (place)]

cav·i·ar (kăv′ĭ är′, kăv′ĭ-, kăv′ĭ är′), *n.* **1.** the roe of sturgeon and other large fish, pressed and salted as a relish. **2.** caviar to the general, something beyond appeal to the popular taste. Also, **cav′i·are.** [t. F, t. It.: m. *caviaro,* t. Turk.: m. *khāviār;* r. *cavialy,* t. It.: m. *caviale,* var. of *caviaro;* ult. orig. unknown]

cav·i·corn (kăv′ə kôrn′), *adj.* *Zool.* hollow-horned, as the ruminants with true horns, as distinguished from bony antlers. [f. L: *cavi-* (comb. form of *cavus* hollow) + s. *-cornis* horned]

cav·il (kăv′əl), *v.,* -iled, -iling or (*esp. Brit.*) -illed, -illing, *n.* —*v.* **1.** to raise irritating and trivial objections; find fault unnecessarily. —*n.* **2.** a trivial and annoying objection. **3.** the raising of such objections. [t. F: m. s. *caviller,* t. L: m. *cavillārī,* der. *cavilla* a jeering] —**cav′il·er,** *esp. Brit.,* **cav′il·ler,** *n.*

cav·i·ta·tion (kăv′ə tā′shən), *n.* the rapid formation and collapse of vapor pockets in a flowing liquid in regions of very low pressure, a frequent cause of serious structural damage to propellers, pumps, etc.

Ca·vi·te (kä vē′tĕ, kə-), *n.* a seaport in the Philippine Islands, on Manila Bay: naval base. 38,254 (1939).

cav·i·ty (kăv′ə tĭ), *n., pl.* -ties. **1.** any hollow place; a hollow: *a cavity in the earth.* **2.** *Anat.* a hollow space within the body, an organ, a bone, etc. **3.** *Dentistry.* the loss of tooth structure, most commonly produced by caries. A cavity may be artificially made to support dental restorations. [t. F: m. *cavitē,* t. LL: m.s. *cavitas* hollowness] —**Syn. 1.** See **hole.**

---

b., blend of, blended; c., cognate with; d., dialect, dialectal; der., derived from; f., formed from; g., going back to; m., modification of; r., replacing; s., stem of; t., taken from; ?, perhaps. See the full key on inside cover.

ca·vort (kə vôrt′), *v.i.* *U.S. Colloq.* to prance or caper about. [orig. unknown]

Ca·vour (kä voor′), *n.* **Camillo Benso di** (kä mēl′lō bĕn′sô dē), 1810–61, Italian statesman who was a leader in the unification of Italy.

ca·vy (kā′vĭ), *n.*, *pl.* **-vies.** any of various short-tailed South American rodents, esp. those of the genus *Cavia* (including the domesticated guinea pig) or the family *Caviidae*. [t. NL: m.s. *Cavia*, t. Galibi: m. *cabiai*]

caw (kô), *n.* **1.** the cry of the crow, raven, etc. —*v.i.* **2.** to utter this cry or a similar sound. [imit.]

Cawn·pore (kôn′pōr′), *n.* a city in N India, on the Ganges. 487,324 (1941). Also, **Cawn·pur** (kôn′poor′).

Cax·ton (kăk′stən), *n.* **1. William**, 1422?–91, first British printer: translator and author. **2.** *Bibliog.* any book printed by Caxton, all of which are in black letter. **3.** *Print.* a kind of type imitating Caxton's black letter.

cay (kā, kē), *n.* a small island; key.

cay·enne (kī ĕn′, kā-), *n.* a hot, biting condiment composed of the ground pods and seeds of *Capsicum frutescens* var. *longum*; red pepper. Also, **cayenne pepper.** [named after *Cayenne*, in French Guiana]

Cay·enne (kī ĕn′, kā-), *n.* a seaport in and the capital of French Guiana. 11,700 (1936).

cay·man (kā′mən), *n.*, *pl.* **-mans.** any of several tropical American crocodilians having overlapping scutes, constituting the genus *Caiman* and related types. Also, **caiman.** [t. Sp., Pg.: m. *caiman*, t. Car b]

Cay·man Islands (kī mǎn′), three islands NW of and belonging to Jamaica, in the British West Indies. 7000 pop. (est. 1939); 104 sq. mi.

Ca·yu·ga (kā ū′gə, kī-), *n.*, *p.* **-ga, -gas.** a member of a tribe of North American Indians, the smallest tribe of the Iroquois Confederacy. [t. d. Amer. Ind.: m. *kweñio/gwen* the place where locusts were taken out]

Cayuga Lake, a lake in central New York: one of the Finger Lakes. ab. 40 mi. long.

cay·use (kī ūs′), *n.* *Western U.S.* an Indian pony. [named after the *Cayuse* Indians, now living in Oregon]

Cb, *Chem.* columbium.

C.B., 1. (L *Chirurgiae Baccalaureus*) Bachelor of Surgery. **2.** *Brit.* Companion of the Bath.

C.B.E., Commander of the Order of the British Empire.

cc., cubic centimeter or centimeters. Also, **c.c.**

C clef, *Music.* a sign locating the position of middle C on the staff.

Cd, *Chem.* cadmium.

cd., cord; cords.

Ce, *Chem.* cerium.

C.E., Civil Engineer.

Ce·a·rá (sě′ä rä′), *n.* Fortaleza.

cease (sēs), *v.*, **ceased, ceasing,** *n.* —*v.i.* **1.** to stop (moving, speaking, etc.): *she ceased to cry.* **2.** to come to an end. **3.** *Obs.* to pass away. —*v.t.* **4.** to put a stop or end to; discontinue: *to cease work.* —*n.* **5.** cessation, obs. except in **without cease,** endlessly. [ME *cess(en)*, t. OF: m. *cesser*, g. L *cessare*, freq. of *cedere* go, yield] —Syn. 1. See **stop.** —Ant. 1. begin.

cease-fire (sēs′fīr′), *n.* truce.

cease·less (sēs′lĭs), *adj.* without **stop or pause; un**ending; incessant. —**cease′less·ly,** *adv.*

Ce·bú (sě boo′), *n.* **1.** one of the Philippine Islands, in the central part of the group. 947,309 pop. (1939); 1703 sq. mi. **2.** a seaport on this island. 146,817 (1939).

Čech·y (chě′hĭ), *n.* Czech name of **Bohemia.**

Cec·il (sĕs′əl), *n.* **1. Edgar Algernon Robert** (ăl′jər-nən), (*1st Viscount Cecil of Chelwood*) born 1864, British statesman. **2. William.** See **Burghley.**

Ce·cil·ia (sĭ sēl′yə), *n.* **Saint,** died A.D. 230?, Roman martyr: patron saint of music.

Ce·cro·pi·a moth (sĭ krō′pĭ ə), a large North American silk-producing moth, *Samia cecropia*.

Ce·crops (sē′krŏps), *n.* *Gk. Legend.* the founder and first king of Attica: represented as half dragon.

ce·dant ar·ma to·gae (sē′dănt är′mə tō′jē), *Latin.* let military power be subject to civil authority (motto of Wyoming. Cicero, *De Officiis* 1:22,41.

ce·dar (sē′dər), *n.* **1.** any of the Old World coniferous trees constituting the genus *Cedrus*, as *C. libani* (**cedar of Lebanon**), a stately tree native in Asia Minor, etc. **2.** any of various junip rs, as *Juniperus virginiana* (**red cedar**), an American tree with a fragrant reddish wood used for making lead pencils, etc. **3.** any of various other coniferous trees, as *Chamaecyparis thyoides*, a species of the swamps of the eastern U. S., *Thuja occidentalis*, the arbor vitae (both called **white cedar**), and *Libocedrus decurrens*, the **incense cedar** of California. **4.** any of various nonpinaceous tropical trees, a *Cedrela odorata* (**Spanish cedar**), a timber tree whose wood is used for cigar boxes. **5.** the wood of any of these trees. [ME *cedir*, etc., OE *ceder*, t. L: m.s. *ce rus*, t. Gk.: m. *kĕdros*; r. ME *cedre*, t. OF]

cedar bird, *Ornith.* a waxwing, *Bombycilla cedrorum*, of North America. Also, **cedar waxwing.**

ce·darn (sē′dərn), *adj.* *Poetic.* **1.** of cedar trees. **2.** made of cedar wood.

Cedar Rapids, a city in E Iowa. 72,296 (1950).

cede (sēd), *v.t.*, **ceded, ceding.** to yield or formally resign and surrender to another; make over, as by treaty: *to cede territory*. [t. L: m.s. *cēdere* go, withdraw, yield, grant] —**Syn.** grant, transfer. —**Ant.** retain.

ce·dil·la (sĭ dĭl′ə), *n.* a mark placed under *c* before *a*, *o*, or *u*, as in *façade*, to show that it has the sound of *s*. [t. Sp.: *cedilla*, now *zedilla*, the mark (orig. a *z* written after **c**), **g.** dim. of L *zēta*, t. Gk.: name of letter *z*]

ced·u·la (sĕj′ə lə; *Sp.* thě′doo lä′), *n.* **1.** (in Spanish-speaking countries) any of various orders, certificates, or the like. **2.** any of certain securities issued by South and Central American governments. **3.** (in the Philippine Islands) **a.** a personal registration tax certificate. **b.** the tax itself. [t. Sp. See **schedule**]

ce·i·ba (sě′ē bä, thě′-; *also for 2* sī′bə), *n.* **1.** the silk-cotton tree. **2.** silk-cotton; kapok. [t. Sp., t. Carib]

ceil (sēl), *v.t.* **1.** to overlay (the interior upper surface of a building or room) with wood, plaster, etc. **2.** to provide with a ceiling. [late ME. Cf. F *ciel* sky, heaven, canopy, g. L *caelum* sky, heaven]

ceil·ing (sē′lĭng), *n.* **1.** the overhead interior lining of a room; the surface of a room opposite the floor. **2.** a lining applied for structural reasons to a structural framework, esp. in the interior surfaces of a ship. **3.** top limit: *price ceilings on rent.* **4.** *Aeron.* **a.** the maximum altitude from which the earth can be seen on a particular day, usually equal to the distance between the earth and the base of the lowest cloud bank. **b.** the maximum altitude to which a particular aircraft can rise under specified conditions. **5.** act of one who ceils. [der. **ceil**]

cel·an·dine (sĕl′ən dīn′), *n.* **1.** a papaveraceous plant, *Chelidonium majus* (**greater celandine**), with yellow flowers. **2.** a ranunculaceous plant, *Ranunculus Ficaria* (**lesser celandine**), with yellow flowers. [ME *celidoine*, t. OF, g. L *chelidonia*, t. Gk.: m. *chelidónion*, der. *chelidōn* swallow]

cel·a·nese (sĕl′ə nēz′), *n.* **1.** an acetate rayon yarn or fabric. **2.** (*cap.*) a trademark for this yarn or fabric.

-cele¹, a word element meaning "tumor," as in *varicocele*. [comb. form repr. Gk. *kēlē*]

-cele², var. of **-coele.**

Cel·e·bes (sĕl′ə bēz′; *Du.* sě lä′bĕs), *n.* an island in the U.S. of Indonesia, separated from the Philippine Islands by the **Celebes Sea**. With adjacent islands, 4,231,900 pop. (1930); 72,986 sq. mi.

cel·e·brant (sĕl′ə brənt), *n.* **1.** the officiating priest in the celebration of the Eucharist. **2.** a participant in a public religious rite. **3.** a participant in any celebration.

cel·e·brate (sĕl′ə brāt′), *v.*, **-brated, -brating.** —*v.t.* **1.** to observe (a day) or commemorate (an event) with ceremonies or festivities. **2.** to make known publicly; proclaim. **3.** to sound the praises of; extol. **4.** to perform with appropriate rites and ceremonies; solemnize. —*v.i.* **5.** to observe a day or commemorate an event with ceremonies or festivities. **6.** to perform a religious ceremony, esp. Mass. [t. L: m.s. *celebrātus*, pp.] —**cel′e·bra′tor,** *n.* —**Syn.** 3. laud, glorify, honor.

cel·e·brat·ed (sĕl′ə brā′tĭd), *adj.* famous; renowned; well-known. —**Syn.** See **famous.**

cel·e·bra·tion (sĕl′ə brā′shən), *n.* **1.** act of celebrating. **2.** that which is done to celebrate anything.

ce·leb·ri·ty (sə lĕb′rə tĭ), *n.*, *pl.* **-ties.** **1.** a famous or well-known person. **2.** state of being famous or well-known; fame; renown.

ce·ler·i·ty (sə lĕr′ə tĭ), *n.* swiftness; speed. [ME *celerite*, t. L: m.s. *celeritas*]

cel·er·y (sĕl′ər ĭ), *n.* a plant, *Apium graveolens*, of the parsley family, whose blanched leafstalks are used raw for salad, and cooked as a vegetable. [t. F: m. *céleri*, t. d. It.: m. *sellari* (pl.), g. LL *selinon*, t. Gk.: parsley]

ce·les·ta (sə lĕs′tə), *n.* a musical instrument consisting essentially of steel plates struck by hammer , and having a keyboard. [t. F, t. L: m. *caelestis* heavenly]

ce·les·tial (sə lĕs′chəl), *adj.* **1.** pertaining to the spiritual or invisible heaven; heavenly; divine: *celestial bliss.* **2.** pertaining to the sky or visible heaven. **3.** (*cap.*) of or pertaining to the former Chinese Empire or the Chinese people. —*n.* **4.** an inhabitant of heaven **5.** (*cap.*) *Humorous.* a nat ve o :China; a Chinese. [ME, t OF, f. *celesti*- (m.s. L *caelestis* heavenly) + -*al*-AL¹] —**ce·les′-tial·ly,** *adv.* —**Ant.** 1. terrestrial. 2. earthly.

Celestial City, the goal of the journey in Bunyan's *Pilgrim's Progress*; the heavenly Jerusalem. Rev. 21.

Celestial Empire, the Chinese Empire.

celestial equator, *Astron.*, *Navig.* a great circle of the celestial sphere, the plane of which is perpendicular to the axis of the earth.

celestial globe, a model of the celestial sphere, on which the relative positions of the stars may be indicated without distortion.

celestial latitude. See **latitude** (def. 3).

celestial longitude. See **longitude** (def. 2).

celestial sphere, the imaginary spherical shell formed by the sky, usually represented as an infinite sphere of which the observer's position is the center.

Cel·es·tine V (sĕl′əs tīn′, sə lĕs′tĭn, -tīn), **Saint,** c1215–96, Italian hermit: pope in 1294.

cel·es·tite (sĕl′əs tīt′), *n.* a white to delicate-blue mineral, strontium sulfate, $SrSO_4$, occurring in tabular crystals, the principal ore of strontium. Also, **cel·es·tine** (sĕl′əs tĭn, -ə stīn′). [f. m.s. L *caelestis* heavenly (in allusion to the delicate blue of some specimens) + -ITE¹]

ăct, āble, dâre, ärt; ĕbb, ēqual; ĭf, īce; hŏt, ōver, ôrder, oil, bŏŏk, ōoze, out; ŭp, ūse, ûrge; ə = a in alone; ch, chief; g, give; ng, ring; sh, shoe; th, thin; ŧħ, that; zh, vision. See the full key on inside cover.

ce·li·ac (sē/lǐ ăk/), *adj. Anat.* pertaining to the cavity of the abdomen. Also, **coeliac.** [t. L: (m.) s. *coeliacus,* t. Gk.: m. *koiliakós* of the belly]

cel·i·ba·cy (sĕl/ə bə sǐ/; *esp. Brit.* sə lǐb/ə sǐ/), *n., pl.* **-cies.** **1.** the unmarried state. **2.** abstention by vow from marriage: *the celibacy of priests.*

cel·i·bate (sĕl/ə bǐt, -bāt/), *n.* **1.** one who remains unmarried, esp. for religious reasons. —*adj.* **2.** unmarried. [t. L: m. s. *caelibātus,* der. *caelebs* unmarried]

cell (sĕl), *n.* **1.** a small room in a convent, prison, etc. **2.** any small compartment, bounded area, receptacle, case, etc. **3.** a small group acting as a unit within a larger organization. **4.** *Biol.* **a.** a plant or animal structure, usually microscopic, containing nuclear and cytoplasmic material, enclosed by a semipermeable membrane (animal) or cell wall (plant); the structural unit of plant and animal life. **b.** a minute cavity or interstice, as in animal or plant tissue. **5.** *Entomol.* one of the areas into which an insect's wing is divided by the veins. **6.** *Embryol.* an internal cavity of an ovary. **7.** *Bot.* the pollen sac of an anther. **8.** *Elect.* a device which generates ·electricity and which forms the whole, or a part of, a voltaic battery. consisting in one of its simplest forms of two plates, each of a different metal, placed in a jar containing a dilute acid or other electrolyte (**voltaic cell**). **9.** *Phys. Chem.* a device for producing electrolysis, consisting essentially of the electrolyte, its container, and the electrodes (**electrolytic cell**). **10.** *Aeron.* **a.** the part of the wing structure of a biplane on either side of the fuselage. **b.** the gas container of a balloon. **11.** *Eccles.* a monastery or nunnery, usually small, dependent on a larger religious house. [ME *celle,* OE *cell,* t. L: s. *cella* room]

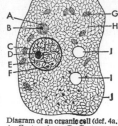

Diagram of an organic cell (def. 4a.) A, Centrosphere; B, Centrosome; C, Nucleus; D, Nucleolus; E, Chromatin network; F, Karyosome; G, Plastid; H, Cytoplasm; I, Vacuole; J, Cell wall

cel·la (sĕl/ə), *n., pl.* **cellae** (sĕl/ē). *Archit.* (in ancient Greek or Roman temples) an enclosed inner room, the sanctuary containing the statue of the divinity. [t. L]

cel·lar (sĕl/ər), *n.* **1.** a room or set of rooms for the storage of foodstuffs, etc., now always either wholly or partly underground, and usually beneath a building. **2.** an underground room or story. **3.** a wine cellar. **4.** a supply or stock of wines. **5. the cellar,** *Sports.* the lowest position in a ranked series: *my team is in the cellar this week.* —*v.t.* **6.** to place or store in a cellar. [t. L: m. s. *cellārium* pantry; r. ME *celer,* t. AF, var. of OF *celier,* g. L *cellārium*]

cel·lar·age (sĕl/ər ǐj), *n.* **1.** cellar space. **2.** charges for storage in a cellar.

cel·lar·er (sĕl/ər ər), *n.* the steward of a monastery.

cel·lar·et (sĕl/ə rĕt/), *n.* a cabinet for wine bottles, etc.

cell division, *Biol.* the division of a cell in reproduction or growth.

Cel·li·ni (chə lē/nǐ; *It.* chĕl lē/nē), *n.* **Benvenuto** (bĕn/vĕ nōō/tô), 1500–71, Italian sculptor, artist in metal, and autobiographer.

cel·list (chĕl/ǐst), *n.* a player on the cello. Also, **'cel/list, violoncellist.**

cel·lo (chĕl/ō), *n., pl.* **-los.** the baritone of the violin family, which is rested vertically on the floor between the player's knees. Also, **'cel/lo, violoncello.** [short form of VIOLONCELLO]

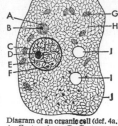

Man playing a cello

cel·loi·din (sə loi/dǐn), *n. Microscopy.* a concentrated form of pyroxylin used to embed tissues for cutting and microscopic examination.

cel·lo·phane (sĕl/ə fān/), *n.* **1.** a transparent, paperlike product of viscose, impervious to moisture, germs, etc., used to wrap candy, tobacco, etc. **2.** (*cap.*) a trademark for this product. [f. CELL(UL)O(SE) + -PHANE]

cel·lu·lar (sĕl/yə lər), *adj.* pertaining to or characterized by cellules or cells, esp. minute compartments or cavities. [t. NL: s. *cellulāris,* der. L *cellula* little room]

cel·lule (sĕl/ūl), *n.* a little cell. [t. L: m. *cellula*]

cel·lu·li·tis (sĕl/yə lī/tǐs), *n. Pathol.* inflammation of cellular tissue. [t. NL, f. s. L *cellula* little cell + *-ītis* -ITIS]

cel·lu·loid (sĕl/yə loid/), *n.* **1.** a substance consisting essentially of soluble guncotton and camphor, usually highly inflammable, variously used as a substitute for ivory, vulcanite, etc. **2.** (*cap.*) a trademark for this substance. [f. CELLUL(OSE) + -OID]

cel·lu·lose (sĕl/yə lōs/), *n. Chem.* an inert substance, a carbohydrate, the chief constituent of the cell walls of plants, and forming an essential part of wood, cotton, hemp, paper, etc. [f. s. L *cellula* little cell + -OSE²]

cellulose acetate, *Chem.* an acetic ester of cellulose used to make textiles, artificial leathers, yarns, etc.

cellulose nitrate, *Chem.* a nitric ester of cellulose used in the manufacture of lacquers and explosives.

cel·lu·lous (sĕl/yə ləs), *adj.* full of or consisting of cells.

cell wall, *Biol.* the definite boundary or wall which is usually part of the structure of a biological cell, esp. a plant cell. See **cell** (def. 4a.).

ce·lom (sē/ləm), *n. Zool.* coelom.

Cels., Celsius.

Cel·si·us thermometer (sĕl/sǐ əs), **1.** centigrade thermometer. **2.** Also, **Celsius scale.** a centigrade scale or thermometer, from which the modern thermometer was developed (1743) by inverting the freezing point (orig. 100°) and boiling point (orig. 0°) of water.

Celt (sĕlt; *esp. Brit.* kĕlt), *n.* a member of an Indo-European people now represented chiefly by the Irish, Gaels, Welsh, and Bretons. Also, **Kelt.** [t. L: s. *Celtae,* pl., t. Gk.: m. *Keltoí*]

celt (sĕlt), *n. Archaeol.* an ax of stone or metal without perforation or groove for hafting. [t. LL: s. *celtis* chisel]

Celt., Celtic.

Celt·ic (sĕl/tǐk; *esp. Brit.* kĕl/tǐk), *n.* **1.** a group of Indo-European languages including Irish, Scotch, Gaelic, Welsh, Breton, etc., surviving now in Ireland, the Scottish Highlands, Wales, and Brittany. —*adj.* **2.** of the Celts or their language. Also, **Keltic.**

Celto-, a word element meaning "Celtic."

ce·ment (sǐ mĕnt/), *n.* **1.** any of various substances which are soft when first prepared but later become hard or stonelike, used for joining stones, making floors, etc. **2.** a material of this kind (the ordinary variety, often called **hydraulic cement**) commonly made by burning a mixture of clay and limestone, used for making concrete for foundations or the like, covering floors, etc. **3.** *Petrog.* the compact groundmass surrounding and binding together the fragments of clastic rocks. **4.** anything that binds or unites. **5.** *Dentistry.* an adhesive plastic substance used to fill teeth or to pack fillings or inlays into teeth. **6.** *Metall.* the powder utilized during cementation. —*v.t.* **7.** to unite by, or as by, cement: *a friendship cemented by time.* **8.** to coat or cover with cement. —*v.i.* **9.** to become cemented; join together or unite; cohere. [t. L: m.s. *caementum* rough stone; r. ME *siment,* t. OF] —**ce·ment/er,** *n.*

ce·men·ta·tion (sē/mən tā/shən, sĕm/ən-), *n.* **1.** act, process, or result of cementing. **2.** *Metall.* the heating of two substances in contact in order to effect some change in one of them; esp., the formation of steel by heating iron in powdered charcoal.

ce·ment·ite (sǐ mĕn/tīt), *n. Metall.* a carbide of iron, Fe₃C, used in steel to add strength and hardness.

ce·men·tum (sǐ mĕn/təm), *n. Dentistry.* a hard tissue which forms the outer surfaces of the root of a tooth. See diag. under **tooth.**

cem·e·ter·y (sĕm/ə tĕr/ǐ), *n., pl.* **-teries.** a burial ground, esp. one not attached to a church; graveyard. [late ME *cymytery,* t. LL: m.s. *coemētērium,* t. Gk.: m. *koimētērion*]

-cene, a word element meaning "recent," "new," as in *pleistocene.* [comb. form repr. Gk. *kainós*]

ce·nes·the·sia (sē/nəs thē/zhə), *n.* coenesthesia. Also, **ce·nes·the·sis** (sē/nəs thē/sǐs).

Ce·nis (sə nē/), *n.* **Mont** (môN), **1.** a pass in the Alps between France and Italy. 6835 ft. high. **2.** a railway tunnel to the W of this pass. ab. 8 mi. long.

ceno-¹, a word element meaning "new," "recent," as in *Cenozoic.* Also, **caeno-, caino-.** [see -CENE]

ceno-², a word element meaning "common." Also, **coeno-.** [t. Gk.: m. *koino-,* comb. form of *koinós*]

ce·no·bite (sē/nə bīt/, sĕn/ə-), *n.* one of a religious order living in a convent or community. Also, **coenobite.** [t. LL: m. s. *coenobita,* der. *coenobium,* t. Gk.: m. *koinóbion* convent, neut. of *koinóbios* living in community] —**ce·no·bit·ic** (sē/nə bǐt/ǐk, sĕn/ə-), **ce/no·bit/i·cal,** *adj.* —**ce·no·bit·ism** (sē/nə bǐt/ǐz əm, sĕn/ə-), *n.*

ce·no·gen·e·sis (sē/nə jĕn/ə sǐs, sĕn/ə-), *n. Biol.* development of an individual which does not repeat the phylogeny of its race, stock, or group (opposed to *palingenesis*). Also, **kenogenesis.** [f. CENO-¹ + GENESIS] —**ce·no·ge·net·ic** (sē/nə jə nĕt/ǐk, sĕn/ə-), *adj.*

cen·o·taph (sĕn/ə tăf/, -täf/), *n.* a sepulchral monument erected in memory of a deceased person whose body is elsewhere. [t. L: m. s. *cenotaphium,* t. Gk.: m. *kenotáphion* an empty tomb] —**cen/o·taph/ic,** *adj.*

Ce·no·zo·ic (sē/nə zō/ǐk, sĕn/ə-), *Stratig.* —*adj.* **1.** pertaining to the geological era or rocks of most recent age, extending to the present. —*n.* **2.** the era or rocks representing the most recent major division of earth history. Also, **Cainozoic.** [f. CENO-¹ + ZO(O)- + -IC]

cense (sĕns), *v.t.,* **censed, censing.** to burn incense near or in front of; perfume with incense. [aphetic var. of INCENSE¹]

cen·ser (sĕn/sər), *n.* a container in which incense is burned. [ME *censere,* t. OF: m. *encensier.* See INCENSE¹]

cen·sor (sĕn/sər), *n.* **1.** an official who examines books, plays, news reports, motion pictures, radio programs, etc., for the purpose of suppressing parts deemed objectionable on moral, political, military, or other grounds. **2.** any person who supervises the manners or morality of others. **3.** an adverse critic; a faultfinder. **4.** a member of the board of two officials of republican Rome who kept the register or census of the citizens, let public contracts, and supervised manners and morals. **5.** *Psychoanal.* censorship. —*v.t.* **6.** to examine and act upon as a censor does. [t. L] —**cen·so·ri·al** (sĕn sōr/ǐ əl), *adj.*

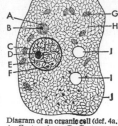

Acolyte with censer

cen·so·ri·ous (sĕn sōr′ĭ əs), *adj.* severely critical; faultfinding; carping. —**cen·so′ri·ous·ly,** *adv.* —**cen·so′ri·ous·ness,** *n.*

cen·sor·ship (sĕn′sər shĭp′), *n.* **1.** act of censoring. **2.** the office or power of a censor. **3.** the time during which a censor holds office. **4.** *Psychoanal.* (in dream theory) Freud's first term for the psychological force which represses ideas, impulses, and feelings, and prevents them from entering consciousness in their original form.

cen·sur·a·ble (sĕn′shər ə bəl), *adj.* deserving censure. —**cen′sur·a·ble·ness, cen′sur·a·bil′i·ty,** *n.* —**cen′sur·a·bly,** *adv.*

cen·sure (sĕn′shər), *n., v.,* **-sured, -suring.** —*n.* **1.** an expression of disapproval adverse or hostile criticism; blaming. —*v.t.* **2.** to criticize adversely; disapprove; find fault with; condemn. —*v.i.* **3.** to give censure, adverse criticism, or blame. [ME, t. L: m. *censūra* censorship, judgment. Cf. CENSOR] —**cen′sur·er,** *n.* —**Syn. 1.** condemnation, reproof. See **abuse. 3.** reprove, rebuke, reprimand. See **blame. —Ant.** praise.

cen·sus (sĕn′səs), *n.* **1.** an official enumeration of inhabitants, with details as to age, sex, pursuits, etc. **2.** (in ancient Rome) the registration of citizens and their property, for purposes of taxation. [t. L]

census tract, a standard area in certain large American cities used by the U. S. Census Bureau for purposes of population enumeration.

cent (sĕnt), *n.* **1.** the hundredth part of the U.S. dollar. **2.** a bronze coin of this value. **3.** the hundredth part of monetary units elsewhere. [? t. L: short for *centēsimus* hundredth]

cent-, var. of **centi-,** as in *centare.*

cent., **1.** centigrade. **2.** central. **3.** centum (in *per cent.*) **4.** century.

cen·tal (sĕn′təl), *n.* *Rare.* a hundredweight. [f. s. L *centum* hundred + AL¹]

cen·tare (sĕn′târ; *Fr.* sän târ′), *n.* centiare.

cen·taur (sĕn′tôr), *n.* **1.** *Gk. Legend.* one of a race of monsters having the head, trunk, and arms of a man, and the body and legs of a horse. **2.** (*cap.*) *Astron.* Centaurus. [ME, t. L: s. *Centaurus,* t. Gk.: m. *Kēntauros*]

Cen·tau·rus (sĕn tôr′əs), *n., gen.* **Centauri** (sĕn tôr′ī). *Astron.* a southern constellation containing the first magnitude stars Alpha Centauri (the star nearest to the solar system) and Beta Centauri. [see CENTAUR]

cen·tau·ry (sĕn′tôrĭ), *n., pl.* **-ries. 1.** either of two gentianaceous Old World herbs, *Chlora perfoliata* and *Centaurium umbellatum* (*Erythraea centaurium*), with medicinal properties. **2.** any plant of the genus *Centaurium* (*Erythraea*). **3.** any of certain other plants, as those of the gentianaceous genus *Sabatia* (American centaury). [ME *centaurie,* t. ML: m. *centauria,* r. L *centaurēum,* t. Gk. m. *kentaúreion,* der. *Kēntauros* centaur (here the centaur Chiron, reputed discoverer of the plant's medicinal virtues)]

cen·ta·vo (sĕn tä′vō; *Sp.* -vō), *n., pl.* **-vos** (-vōz; *Sp.* -vōs). a small coin or minor monetary unit equal to the hundredth part of a particular monetary unit, esp. **a.** one hundredth of a peso, as in Mexico, the Philippine Islands, Cuba, etc. **b.** one hundredth of an escudo, in Portugal. [t. Amer. Sp. See CENT]

cen·te·nar·i·an (sĕn′tə nâr′ĭ ən), *adj.* **1.** pertaining to or having lived 100 years. —*n.* **2.** one who has reached the age of a hundred.

cen·te·nar·y (sĕn′tə nĕr′ĭ; *esp. Brit.* sĕn tēn′ərĭ, -tē′- nərĭ), *adj., n., pl.* **-naries.** —*adj.* **1.** pertaining to a period of 100 years. **2.** recurring once in every 100 years. —*n.* **3.** a 100th anniversary. **4.** a period of 100 years; a century. [t. L: m.s. *centēnārius* of or containing 100]

cen·ten·ni·al (sĕn tĕn′ĭ əl), *adj.* **1.** pertaining to, or marking the completion of 100 years. **2.** pertaining to a 100th anniversary. **3.** lasting 100 years. **4.** 100 years old. —*n.* **5.** a 100th anniversary. **6.** its celebration. [f. s. L *centennium* 100 years + -AL¹; modeled on BIENNIAL] —**cen·ten′ni·al·ly,** *adv.*

cen·ter (sĕn′tər), *n.* **1.** *Geom.* the middle point, as the point within a circle or sphere equally distant from all points of the circumference or surface, or the point within a regular polygon equally distant from the vertices. **2.** a point, pivot, axis, etc., round which anything rotates or revolves. **3.** a principal point, place, or object: *a shipping center.* **4.** a person, thing, group, etc., occupying the middle position. esp. troops. **5.** (*usually cap.*) (in continental Europe). **a.** that part of a legislative assembly which sits in the center of the chamber, a position customarily assigned to representatives holding views intermediate between those of the conservatives or Right and the liberals or Left. **b.** a party holding such views. **6.** *Football, etc.* the middle player in the forward line. **7.** *Basketball.* **a.** the place in the center of the court from which a game is started. **b.** a player, usually very tall, who attempts to tap the ball to a teammate when a jump ball is thrown by a referee at the beginning of play. **8.** *Physiol.* a cluster of nerve cells governing a specific organic process: *the vasomotor center.* **9.** *Math.* the mean position of a figure or system. **10.** *Mach.* **a.** a tapered rod mounted in the headstock spindle (**live center**) or the tailstock spindle (**dead center**) of a lathe, upon which the work to be turned is placed. **b.** one of two similar points on some other machine, as a planing machine, enabling an object to be turned on its axis. **c.** a tapered indentation in a piece

to be turned on a lathe into which the center is fitted. —*v.t.* **11.** to place in or on a center. **12.** to collect at a center. **13.** to determine or mark the center of. **14.** to adjust, shape, or modify (an object, part, etc.) so that its axis or the like is in a central or normal position. —*v.i.* **15.** to be at or come to a center. Also, *esp. Brit.,* **centre.** [ME *centre,* t. OF, t. L: m. *centrum,* t. Gk.: m. *kéntron* sharp point, center] —**Syn. 1.** See **middle.**

center bit, a carpenter's bit with a sharp, projecting center point, used for boring holes.

cen·ter·board (sĕn′tər bôrd′), *n.* *Naut.* a movable fin keel that can be drawn up in shoal water into a housing or well. Also, *Brit.,* **centreboard.**

cen·ter·ing (sĕn′tər ĭng), *n.* a temporary framing, for supporting permanent framework during construction. Also, *Brit.,* **centring.**

center of gravity, *Mech.* that point of a body (or system of bodies) from which it could be suspended or on which it could be supported and be in equilibrium in any position in a uniform gravitational field.

center of mass, *Mech.* that point of a body (or system of bodies) at which its entire mass could be concentrated without changing its linear inertia in any direction. For ordinary bodies near the earth, it is identical with the center of gravity.

cen·ter·piece (sĕn′tər pēs′), *n.* an ornamental piece of silver, glass, or the like, or of embroidery, lace, or like material, for the center of a table, etc. Also, *Brit.,* **centrepiece.**

cen·tes·i·mal (sĕn tĕs′ə məl), *adj.* hundredth; pertaining to division into 100ths. [f. s. L *centēsimus* hundredth + -AL¹] —**cen·tes′i·mal·ly,** *adv.*

cen·tes·i·mo (sĕn tĕs′ə mō′; *It., Sp.* -tĕ′sē mō′), *n., pl. It.* **-mi** (-mē′), **-mos** (-moz′; *Sp.* -mōs′). **1.** an Italian copper coin and monetary unit, the hundredth part of a lira. **2.** (in Panama and Uruguay) the hundredth part of a peso. [t. It., g. L *centēsimus* hundredth]

centi-, a word element meaning "hundred," applied in the metric system to the division of the unit by 100, as in centigram. Also, **cent-.** [t. L, comb. form of *centum*]

cen·ti·are (sĕn′tĭ âr′; *Fr.* säntyâr′), *n.* a square meter. Also, **centare.** [t. F. See CENTI-, ARE²]

cen·ti·grade (sĕn′tə grād′), *adj.* **1.** divided into 100 degrees, as a scale. **2.** pertaining to the centigrade thermometer. [t. F. See CENTI-, -GRADE]

centigrade thermometer, a thermometer based on a scale of equal degrees between zero (fixed at the melting point of ice) and 100° (fixed at the boiling point of water) at a pressure of 760 mm. of mercury; Celsius thermometer. See illus. under **thermometer.**

cen·ti·gram (sĕn′tə grăm′), *n.* one hundredth of a gram, equivalent to 0.1543 grain. Also, *esp. Brit.,* **cen′ti·gramme′.** [t. F: m. *centigramme.* See CENTI-, GRAM, *n.*]

cen·ti·li·ter (sĕn′tə lē′tər), *n.* one one-hundredth of a liter, equivalent to 0.0102 cubic inch, or 0.338 U.S. fluid ounce. Also, *esp. Brit.,* **cen′ti·li′tre.** [t. F: m. *centilitre.* See CENTI-, LITER]

cen·time (sän′tēm; *Fr.* säntēm′), *n.* the hundredth part of a franc. [t. F: f. *cent* hundred + suffix -*ime*]

cen·ti·me·ter (sĕn′tə mē′tər), *n.* one hundredth of a meter, equivalent to .3937 in. Also, *esp. Brit.,* **cen′ti·me′tre.** [t. F: m. *centimètre.* See CENTI-, -METER]

cen·ti·me·ter-gram-sec·ond (sĕn′tə mē′tər grăm′- sĕk′ənd), *adj.* a system of units employed in science, based on the centimeter, gram, and second as the primary units of length, mass, and time. Also, *Brit.,* **centimetre-gramme-second.**

cen·ti·mo (sĕn′tə mō′; *Sp.* -tē mō′), *n., pl.* **-mos** (-mōz′; *Sp.* -mōs′). the hundredth part of a bolivar, colon, or peseta. [t. Sp., t. F: m. *centime*]

cen·ti·pede (sĕn′tə pēd′), *n.* any member of the class *Chilopoda,* active, predaceous, and mostly nocturnal arthropods having an elongated flattened body of numerous segments each with a single pair of legs, the first pair of which is modified into poison fangs. Few are dangerous to man. [t. L: m. s. *centipeda* hundred-footed insect]

cent·ner (sĕnt′nər), *n.* **1.** (in several European countries) a unit of weight of 50 kilograms, equivalent to 110.23 pounds avoirdupois. **2.** *Rare.* a unit of 100 kilograms. [t. Flem.: m. *centener,* t. L: m. s. *centēnārius* of a hundred]

centr-, var. of **centro-** before vowels.

cen·tra (sĕn′trə), *n.* pl. of **centrum.**

cen·tral (sĕn′trəl), *adj.* **1.** of or forming the center. **2.** in, at, or near the center. **3.** constituting that from which other related things proceed or upon which they depend. **4.** principal; chief; dominant: *the central idea, the central character in a novel.* **5.** *Anat., Physiol.* **a.** pertaining to the brain and spinal cord of the nervous system (as distinguished from *peripheral*). **b.** of or relating to the centrum or body of a vertebra. **6.** *Phonet.* pronounced with the tongue in a neutral position, as for example, the final vowel in *sofa* or *idea.* —*n.* **7.** the central office of a telephone system, in which connections are made between different lines. **8.** an operator at such an office. [t. L: s. *centrālis.* See CENTER] —**cen′- tral·ly,** *adv.*

Central America, continental North America S of Mexico, comprising the six republics of Guatemala, Honduras, El Salvador, Nicaragua, Costa Rica, Panama, and the colony British Honduras. 8,796,427 pop.; 227,933 sq. mi. —**Central American.**

central cylinder, *Bot.* stele (def. 4).

Central Falls, a city in NE Rhode Island. 23,550 (1950).

Central India, a group of states in central India, which formerly constituted the **Central India Agency.** 7,506,400 pop. (1941); 52,047 sq. mi.

cen·tral·ism (sĕn′trə lĭz′əm), *n.* **1.** centralization, or a centralizing system. **2.** the principle of centralization, esp. in government. —**cen′tral·ist,** *n., adj.*

cen·tral·i·ty (sĕn trăl′ə tĭ), *n.* central position or state.

cen·tral·i·za·tion (sĕn′trəl ə zā′shən), *n.* **1.** act of centralizing. **2.** fact of being centralized. **3.** the concentration of administrative power in a central government. **4.** *Sociol.* a process whereby social groups and institutions become increasingly dependent on a central group or institution.

cen·tral·ize (sĕn′trə līz′), *v.t.,* **-ized, -izing. 1.** to draw to or toward a center. **2.** to bring under one control, esp. in government. —*v.i.* **3.** to come together at a center. —**cen′tral·iz′er,** *n.*

Central Powers, (in World War I) Germany and Austria-Hungary, often with their allies Turkey and Bulgaria, as opposed to the Allies.

Central Provinces and Be·rar (bā rär′), a province in central India. 16,814,000 pop. (1941); 98,575 sq. mi. *Cap.:* Nagpur.

Central time. See **standard time.**

cen·tre (sĕn′tər), *n., v.,* **-tred, -tring.** *Chiefly Brit.* center.

centri-, var. of **centro-,** as in *centrifugal.*

cen·tric (sĕn′trĭk), *adj.* **1.** pertaining to or situated at the center; central. **2.** *Physiol.* pertaining to or originating at a nerve center. Also, **cen′tri·cal.** —**cen′tri·cal·ly,** *adv.* —**cen·tric·i·ty** (sĕn trĭs′ə tĭ), *n.*

cen·trif·u·gal (sĕn trĭf′yə gəl), *adj.* **1.** moving or directed outward from the center. **2.** pertaining to or operated by centrifugal force: *a centrifugal pump.* **3.** *Physiol.* efferent. —*n.* **4.** a solid or perforated cylinder rotated rapidly to separate solids from liquids. [f. CENTRI- + s. L *fugere* flee + -AL¹] —**cen·trif′u·gal·ly,** *adv.* —**Ant. 1.** centripetal.

centrifugal force, the force outward exerted by a body moving in a curved path; the reaction of centripetal force. Also, **centrifugal action.**

cen·tri·fuge (sĕn′trə fūj′), *n.* a machine consisting of a rotating container in which substances of different densities may be separated by the centrifugal force. [t. F: centrifugal]

cen·tring (sĕn′trĭng), *n.* *Brit.* centering.

cen·trip·e·tal (sĕn trĭp′ə təl), *adj.* **1.** proceeding or directed toward the center. **2.** operating by centripetal force. **3.** *Physiol.* afferent. [f. s. NL *centripetus* centerseeking + -AL¹] —**cen·trip′e·tal·ly,** *adv.*

centripetal force, a force acting on a body, which is directed toward the center of a circle or curve, which causes it to move in the circle or curve. Also, **centripetal action.**

cen·trist (sĕn′trĭst), *n.* (in continental Europe) a member of a political party of the Center. See **center** (def. 5a). [t. F: m. *centriste,* der. *centre* center]

centro-, a word element meaning "center." Also, **centr-, centri-.** [comb. form repr. L *centrum* and Gk. *kéntron*]

cen·tro·bar·ic (sĕn′trə băr′ĭk), *adj.* pertaining to the center of gravity. [f. CENTRO- + s. Gk. *báros* weight + -IC]

cen·troid (sĕn′troid), *n.* *Mech.* the point in an area common to all lines whose moment of area is zero.

cen·tro·some (sĕn′trə sōm′), *n.* *Biol.* a minute protoplasmic body regarded by some as the active center of cell division in mitosis. See diag. under **cell.** [f. CENTRO- + -SOME³] —**cen·tro·som·ic** (sĕn′trə sŏm′ĭk), *adj.*

cen·tro·sphere (sĕn′trə sfĭr′), *n.* **1.** *Biol.* the protoplasm around a centrosome; the central portion of an aster, containing the centrosome. See diag. under **cell.** **2.** *Geol.* the central or interior portion of the earth.

cen·trum (sĕn′trəm), *n., pl.* **-trums, -tra** (-trə). **1.** a center. **2.** *Zool.* the body of a vertebra. [t. L. See CENTER]

cen·tu·ple (sĕn′tyə pəl, -tə-), *adj., v.,* **-pled, -pling.** —*adj.* **1.** a hundred times as great; hundredfold. —*v.t.* **2.** to increase 100 times. [t. F, t. LL: m.s. *centuplus* hundredfold]

cen·tu·pli·cate (*v.* sĕn tū′plə kāt′, -tōō′-; *adj., n.* sĕn tū′plə kĭt, -kāt′,-tōō′-), *v.,* **-cated, -cating,** *adj., n.* —*v.t.* **1.** to increase 100 times; centuple. —*adj.* **2.** hundredfold. —*n.* **3.** a number or quantity increased a hundredfold. —**cen·tu′pli·ca′tion,** *n.*

cen·tu·ri·al (sĕn tyŏŏr′ĭ əl, -tōŏr′-), *adj.* pertaining to a century. [t. L: s. *centuriālis*]

cen·tu·ri·on (sĕn tyŏŏr′ĭ ən, -tōŏr′-), *n.* (in the ancient Roman Army) the commander of a century. [ME, t. L: s. *centurio,* der. *centuria.* See CENTURY]

cen·tu·ry (sĕn′chə rĭ), *n., pl.* **-ries. 1.** a period of one hundred years. **2.** one of the successive periods of 100 years reckoned forward or backward from a recognized chronological epoch, esp. from the assumed date of the birth of Jesus. **3.** any group or collection of 100. **4.** (in the ancient Roman army) a company, consisting of approximately one hundred men. **5.** one of the voting divisions of the ancient Roman people, each division having one vote. **6.** (*cap.*) *Print.* a style of type. [t. L: m. s. *centuria* a division of a hundred things]

century plant, a Mexican species of agave, *Agave americana,* cultivated for ornament: popularly supposed not to blossom until a century old.

ceorl (chĕŏrl). *n.* (in Old English times) a freeman of the lowest rank, neither a noble nor a slave. [OE. See CHURL] —**ceorl′ish,** *adj.*

cephal-, var. of **cephalo-,** before vowels, as in *cephalad.*

ceph·al·ad (sĕf′ə lăd′), *adv.* *Anat., Zool.* toward the head (opposed to *caudad*). [f. CEPHAL- + L *ad* to]

ce·phal·ic (sə făl′ĭk), *adj.* **1.** of or pertaining to the head. **2.** situated or directed toward the head. **3.** of the nature of a head. [t. L: s. *cephalicus,* t. Gk.: m. *kephalikós* of the head]

-cephalic, a word element meaning "head," as in *brachycephalic* (related to **cephalo-**).

cephalic index, *Cephalom.* the ratio of the greatest breadth of head to its greatest length from front to back, multiplied by 100.

ceph·a·li·za·tion (sĕf′ə lə zā′shən), *n.* *Zool.* a tendency in the development of animals to localization of important organs or parts in or near the head.

cephalo-, a word element denoting the "head," as in *cephalopod.* Also, **cephal-.** [t. Gk.: m. *kephalo-,* comb. form of *kephalé*]

Ceph·a·lo·chor·da·ta (sĕf′ə lō kôr dā′tə), *n.* a chordate subphylum including the lancelets, having fishlike characters but lacking a vertebral column.

ceph·a·lo·chor·date (sĕf′ə lō kôr′dāt), *adj.* **1.** denoting or pertaining to the *Cephalochordata.* —*n.* **2.** a member of the *Cephalochordata.* [f. CEPHALO- + CHORD + -ATE¹]

cephalom., cephalometry.

ceph·a·lom·e·ter (sĕf′ə lŏm′ə tər), *n.* an instrument for measuring the head or skull; a craniometer.

ceph·a·lom·e·try (sĕf′ə lŏm′ə trĭ), *n.* the science of the measurement of heads. [f. CEPHALO- + -METRY]

Ceph·a·lo·ni·a (sĕf′ə lō′nĭ ə, -lōn′yə), *n.* the largest of the Ionian Islands, off the W coast of Greece. 59,323 pop. (1940); 287 sq. mi. Greek, **Kephallenia.**

ceph·a·lo·pod (sĕf′ə lə pŏd′), *n.* a member of the class *Cephalopoda.* [f. CEPHALO- + -POD]

Ceph·a·lop·o·da (sĕf′ə lŏp′ə də), *n.pl.* the most highly organized class of mollusks, including the cuttlefish, squid, octopus, etc., the members of which have tentacles attached to the head. —**ceph′a·lop′o·dan,** *adj., n.*

ceph·a·lo·tho·rax (sĕf′ə lō thōr′ăks), *n.* *Zool.* the anterior part of the body in certain arachnids and crustaceans, consisting of the coalesced head and thorax.

ceph·a·lous (sĕf′ə ləs), *adj.* having a head. [f. CEPHAL- + -OUS]

-cephalous, a word element related to **cephalo-.** [f. CEPHAL- + -OUS]

Ceph·e·id variable (sĕf′ĭ ĭd), *Astron.* a variable star in which changes in brightness are due to bodily pulsations.

Ce·pheus (sē′fūs, -fĭəs), *n.* **1.** *Astron.* a northern circumpolar constellation between Cassiopeia and Draco. **2.** *Gk. Legend.* the Ethiopian king who was the husband of Cassiopeia and the father of Andromeda.

-ceptor, a word element meaning "taker," "receiver." [t. L]

cer-, var. of **cero-,** used before vowels, as in *ceraceous.*

ce·ra·ceous (sə rā′shəs), *adj.* waxy.

Ce·ram (sē räm′; *Port.* sĕ räN′; *Du.* sā′räm), *n.* an island of the Moluccas in the U.S. of Indonesia, W of New Guinea. 100,000 pop. (1930); 7191 sq. mi.

ce·ram·ic (sə răm′ĭk), *adj.* pertaining to products made from clay and similar materials, such as pottery, brick, etc., or to their manufacture: *ceramic art.* Also, **keramic.** [t. Gk.: m. s. *keramikós* of or for potters' clay, pottery]

ce·ram·ics (sə răm′ĭks), *n.* **1.** (*construed as sing.*) the art and technology of making clay products and similar ware. **2.** (*construed as pl.*) articles of earthenware, porcelain, etc. [pl. of CERAMIC. See -ICS] —**cer·a·mist** (sĕr′ə mĭst), *n.*

ce·rar·gy·rite (sə rär′jə rīt′), *n.* a mineral, silver chloride: an important silver ore in some places. [f. m. Gk. *kér(as)* horn + s. Gk. *árgyros* silver + -*ītēs* -ITE¹]

ce·rate (sĭr′āt), *n.* *Pharm.* an unctuous (often medicated) preparation for external application, consisting of lard or oil mixed with wax, rosin, or the like, esp. one which has a firmer consistence than a typical ointment and does not melt when in contact with the skin. [t. L: m. s. *cerātum,* neut. pp., covered with wax]

cer·a·tin (sĕr′ə tĭn), *n.* *Zool.* keratin. [f. CERAT- + -IN²]

cerato-, a word element meaning: **1.** *Zool.* horn, horny, or hornlike. **2.** *Anat.* the cornea. Also, before vowels, **cerat-.** [t. Gk.: m. *kerāto-,* comb. form of *kéras* horn]

ce·rat·o·dus (sə răt′ə dəs, sĕr′ə tō′dəs), *n.* a fish of the extinct lungfish genus *Ceratodus,* or of the closely related existent genus *Neoceratodus,* as *N. forsteri,* the barramunda of Australia, so called from the horn like ridges of the teeth. [NL, f. *cerat-* CERAT- + m. Gk. *odoús* tooth]

cer·a·toid (sĕr′ə toid′), *adj.* hornlike; horny. [t. Gk.: m. s. *keratoeidēs* hornlike]

Cer·ber·us (sûr′bər əs), *n.* **1.** *Class. Myth.* a dog, usually represented as having three heads, which guarded the entrance of the infernal regions. **2.** a watchful and formidable or surly keeper or guard. —**Cer·be·re·an** (sər bĭr′ĭ ən), *adj.*

---

b., blend of, blended; c., cognate with; d., dialect, dialectal; der., derived from; f., formed from; g., going back to; m., modification of; r., replacing; s., stem of; t., taken from; ?, perhaps. See the full key on inside cover.

cer·car·i·a (sərkâr′ĭə), n., pl. **-cariae** (-kâr′ĭē′), Zool. a larval stage of flukes, Trematoda, characterized by a body usually bearing a taillike appendage, but sometimes enclosed in the tail. [NL, f. cerc- (comb. form repr. Gk. kếrkos tail) + -āria -ARIA] —**cer·car′i·al**, adj. —**cer·car′i·an**, adj., n.

cere[1] (sĭr), n., Ornith. a membrane of waxy appearance at the base of the upper mandible of certain birds, esp. birds of prey and parrots, in which the nostrils open. [late ME sere, t. ML: m. cēra, in L wax, c. Gk. kếrós]

cere[2] (sĭr), v.t., **cered, cering. 1.** Obs. to wax. **2.** Poetic. to wrap in or as in a cerecloth, esp. a corpse. [ME, t. L: m.s. cērāre, to wax]

ce·re·al (sĭr′ĭəl), n. **1.** any gramineous plant yielding an edible farinaceous grain, as wheat, rye, oats, rice, maize, etc. **2.** the grain itself. **3.** some edible preparation of it, esp. (U.S.) a breakfast food made from some cereal. —adj. **4.** of or pertaining to grain or the plants producing it. [t. L: s. Cereālis pertaining to Ceres.]

cer·e·bel·lum (sĕr′əbĕl′əm), n., pl. **-bellums, -bella** (-bĕl′ə). Anat., Zool. a large expansion of the hindbrain, concerned with the coördination of voluntary movements, posture, and equilibration. In man it lies at the back of and below the cerebrum and consists of two lateral lobes and a central lobe. [t. L, dim. of cerebrum brain] —**cer·e·bel′lar**, adj.

cer·e·bral (sĕr′əbrəl; for 1, 2, also sərē′brəl), adj. **1.** Anat., Zool. of or pertaining to the cerebrum or the brain. **2.** thoughtful; intellectual. **3.** Phonetics. cacuminal. —n. **4.** Phonetics. a cerebral consonant. [t. NL: s. cerebrālis, der. L cerebrum brain]

cer·e·brate (sĕr′əbrāt′), v., **-brated, -brating.** —v.i. **1.** to use the cerebrum or brain; experience brain action. **2.** to think. —v.t. **3.** to perform by brain action.

cer·e·bra·tion (sĕr′əbrā′shən), n. **1.** the action (conscious or unconscious) of the cerebrum or brain. **2.** thinking; thought.

cer·e·bric (sĕr′əbrĭk, sərĕb′rĭk, -rē′brĭk), adj. pertaining to or derived from the brain.

cerebro-, a word element meaning "cerebrum." Also, before vowels, **cerebr-**.

cer·e·bro·spi·nal (sĕr′ə brō spī′nəl), adj. Anat., Physiol. **1.** pertaining to or affecting both the brain and the spinal cord. **2.** pertaining to the brain and the spinal cord together with their cranial and spinal nerves (distinguished from autonomic).

cerebrospinal meningitis, Pathol. an acute inflammation of the meninges of the brain and spinal cord caused by a specific organism, and accompanied by fever and occasionally red spots on the skin; brain fever.

cer·e·brum (sĕr′əbrəm), n., pl. **-brums, -bra** (-brə). Anat., Zool. **1.** the anterior and upper part of the brain, consisting of two hemispheres, partially separated by a deep fissure but connected by a broad band of fibers, and concerned with voluntary and conscious processes. **2.** these two hemispheres together with other adjacent parts; the prosencephalon, thalamencephalon, and mesencephalon together. [t. L: brain]

cere·cloth (sĭr′klôth′, -klŏth′), n. waxed cloth, or a waxed cloth, used esp. for wrapping the dead. [earlier cered cloth. See CERE, v.]

cere·ment (sĭr′mənt), n. (usually pl.) **1.** cerecloth. **2.** any graveclothes. [f. CERE, v. + -MENT. Cf. F cirement]

cer·e·mo·ni·al (sĕr′ə mō′nĭ əl), adj. **1.** pertaining to, marked by, or of the nature of ceremonies or ceremony; ritual; formal. —n. **2.** a system of ceremonies, rites, or formalities prescribed for or observed on any particular occasion; a rite or ceremony. **3.** Rom. Cath. Ch. **a.** the order for rites and ceremonies. **b.** a book containing it. **4.** a formality, esp. of etiquette; the observance of ceremony. —**cer′e·mo′ni·al·ism**, n. —**cer′e·mo′ni·al·ist**, n., —**cer′e·mo′ni·al·ly**, adv.

cer·e·mo·ni·ous (sĕr′ə mō′nĭ əs), adj. **1.** carefully observant of ceremony; formally or elaborately polite. **2.** pertaining to, marked by, or consisting of ceremony; formal: a ceremonious reception. —**cer′e·mo′ni·ous·ly**, adv. —**cer′e·mo′ni·ous·ness**, n.

cer·e·mo·ny (sĕr′ə mō′nĭ), n., pl. **-nies. 1.** the formalities observed on some solemn or important public or state occasion. **2.** a formal religious or sacred observance; a solemn rite. **3.** any formal act or observance, esp. a meaningless one. **4.** a gesture or act of politeness or civility. **5.** formal observances or gestures collectively; ceremonial observances. **6.** strict adherence to conventional forms; formality: to leave a room without ceremony. **7. stand on ceremony,** to be excessively formal or polite. [t. ML: m.s. cēremōnia, L caerimōnia sacred rite; r. ME serimonie, t. OF]
—Syn. 1, 2. CEREMONY, RITE. RITUAL refer to set observances and acts traditional in religious services or on public occasions. CEREMONY applies to more or less formal dignified acts on religious or public occasions: a marriage ceremony, an inaugural ceremony. A RITE is an established, prescribed, or customary form of religious or other solemn practice: the rite of baptism. RITUAL refers to the form of conducting worship or to a code of ceremonies in general: Masonic rituals.

Ce·res (sĭr′ēz), n. an ancient Italian goddess of agriculture, under whose name the Romans adopted the worship of the Greek goddess Demeter. [t. L]

ce·re·us (sĭr′ĭəs), n. any plant of the cactaceous genus Cereus, of tropical America, as C. Jamacaru, of northern Brazil, which grows to about 40 feet. [t. L: wax candle]

ce·ri·a (sĭr′ĭə), n. Chem. cerium oxide, CeO₂, used in small percentages in incandescent mantles for gas.

ce·ric (sĭr′ĭk, sĕr′-), adj. Chem. containing cerium, esp. in the tetravalent state, Ce^{+4}.

Ce·ri·go (chě′rē gô′), n. one of the Ionian Islands, off the S coast of Greece. 9560 pop. (1940); 108 sq. mi. Greek, Kythera. See Cythera.

ce·rise (sə rēz′, -rēs′), n., adj. bright red; cherry. [t. F: cherry]

ce·ri·um (sĭr′ĭəm), n. Chem. a steel-gray, ductile metallic element of the rare-earth group found only in combination. Symbol: Ce; at. wt.: 140.13; at no.: 58. [t. NL, named after the asteroid Ceres]

cerium metals, Chem. See **rare-earth elements.**

Cer·nă·u·ti (chĕr′nə ŏŏts′), n. a city in the SW Soviet Union: formerly in Rumania. 109,821 (1939). Polish, Czernowitz. Russian, Chernovitsy.

cer·nu·ous (sûr′nyŏŏ əs, -nŏŏ-), adj. Bot. drooping or bowing downward, as a flower or bud. [t. L: m. cernuus stooping]

ce·ro (sĭr′ō), n., pl. **ceros. 1.** a large tropical Atlantic mackerellike fish, Scomberomorus regalis, of importance for food and game. **2.** any related species.

cero-, a word element meaning "wax," as in cerotype. Also, **cer-.** [t. Gk.: m. kēro-, comb. form of kếrós]

ce·ro·plas·tic (sĭr′ə plăs′tĭk, sĕr′ə-), adj. **1.** pertaining to modeling in wax. **2.** modeled in wax.

ce·rot·ic acid (sĭ rŏt′ĭk), Chem. the monobasic fatty acid, $C_{26}H_{53}COOH$, of beeswax. [f. m.s. Gk. kērôton waxed + -IC]

ce·ro·type (sĭr′ə tīp′, sĕr′-), n. a process of engraving in which the design or the like is cut on a wax-coated metal plate, from which a printing surface is subsequently produced by stereotyping or by electrotyping.

ce·rous (sĭr′əs), adj. Chem. containing trivalent cerium, (Ce+³). [f. CER(IUM) + -OUS]

Cer·ro de Pas·co (sĕr′rô dĕ päs′kô), a town in central Peru: famous silver mining district. 17,882 pop. (1941); 14,280 ft. high.

Cer·ro Gor·do (sĕr′rô gôr′dô), a mountain pass in E Mexico between Veracruz and Jalapa: battle, 1847.

cert., 1. certificate. **2.** certify. **3.** certified.

cer·tain (sûr′tən), adj. **1.** having no doubt; confident; assured (often fol. by of before a noun, gerund, or pronoun): I am certain of being able to finish it by tomorrow. **2.** sure; inevitable; bound to come (fol. by an infinitive): it is certain to happen. **3.** established as true or sure; unquestionable; indisputable: it is certain that he tried. **4.** fixed; agreed upon: on a certain day. **5.** definite or particular, but not named or specified: certain persons. **6.** that may be depended on; trustworthy; unfailing; reliable: his aim was certain. **7.** some though not much: a certain reluctance. **8.** Obs. steadfast. —n. **9. for certain,** without any doubt; surely. [ME, t. OF, der. L certus fixed, certain, orig. pp.] —Syn. **1.** positive; convinced, satisfied. **2.** See **sure. 3.** incontrovertible irrefutable, incontestable. **4.** prescribed, specified.

cer·tain·ly (sûr′tən lĭ), adv. **1.** with certainty; without doubt; assuredly. —interj. **2.** yes! of course!

cer·tain·ty (sûr′tən tĭ), n., pl. **-ties. 1.** state of being certain. **2.** something certain; an assured fact. [ME certeinte, t. AF] —Syn. **2.** See **belief.**

cer·tes (sûr′tēz), adv. Archaic. certainly; verily. [ME, t. OF, g. LL certas, adv., der. L certus CERTAIN]

certif., 1. certificate. **2.** certificated.

cer·ti·fi·a·ble (sûr′tə fī′ə bəl), adj. **1.** capable of being certified. **2.** Brit. liable to be committed to a mental institution.

cer·tif·i·cate (n. sər tĭf′ə kĭt; v. sər tĭf′ə kāt′), n., v., **-cated, -cating.** —n. **1.** a writing on paper certifying to the truth of something, or to status, qualifications, privileges, etc. **2.** a document issued to a person completing an educational course, issued either by an institution not authorized to grant diplomas, or to a student not qualifying for a diploma. **3.** Law. a statement, written and signed, which is by law made evidence of the truth of the facts stated, for all or for certain purposes. **4.** a certificate issued by the U.S. government and circulating as money, bearing a statement that gold (**gold certificate**) or silver (**silver certificate**) to a specified amount has been deposited in the Treasury for its redemption. —v.t. **5.** to attest by a certificate. **6.** to furnish with or authorize by a certificate. [late ME, t. ML: m.s. certificātum, neut. pp. of certificāre. See CERTIFY]

certificate of deposit, a written acknowledgment of a bank that it has received from the person named a specified sum of money as a deposit.

certificate of incorporation, a statement filed with a state official in forming a corporation, stating its name, purposes, the nature and distribution of the stock to be issued, and other matters required by an incorporation law.

certificate of indebtedness, a short-term, negotiable, interest-bearing note representing indebtedness.

certificate of origin, a shipping document having consular certification that names a boat's origin and type of goods aboard, often required before importation.

cer·ti·fi·ca·tion (sûr′tə fə kā′shən, sər tĭf′ə-), n. **1.** act of certifying. **2.** state of being certified. **3.** a certified statement. **4.** the writing on the face of a check by which it is certified. **5.** Law. a certificate attesting the truth of some statement or event.

cer·ti·fied (sûr′tə fīd′), *adj.* 1. having, or proved by, a certificate. 2. guaranteed; reliably endorsed. 3. *Brit.* committed to a mental institution.

certified milk, *U.S.* milk from dairies conforming with official standards on sanitation, etc., and therefore requiring no pasteurization.

certified public accountant, *U.S.* one having an official accountant certificate after fulfilling all legal requisites. *Abbr.:* C.P.A.

cer·ti·fy (sûr′tə fī′), *v.t.,* **-fied, -fy·ing.** 1. to guarantee as certain; give reliable information of. 2. to testify to or vouch for in writing. 3. to assure or inform with certainty. 4. to guarantee; endorse reliably. 5. (of a bank, or one of its officials) to acknowledge in writing upon (a check) that the bank on which it is drawn has funds of the drawer sufficient to pay it. —*v.i.* 6. to give assurance; testify (fol. by *to*); vouch (fol. by *for*). [ME *certifie(n)*, t. F: m. *certifier*, t. ML: m. *certificāre*] —**cer′ti·fi′er,** *n.*

cer·ti·o·ra·ri (sûr′shĭ ə râr′ī), *n. Law.* a writ issuing from a superior court calling up the record of a proceeding in an inferior court for review. [t. L: to be informed (lit., made more certain)]

cer·ti·tude (sûr′tə tūd′, -tōōd′), *n.* certainty. [late ME, t. LL: m. *certitūdo*]

ce·ru·le·an (sə rōō′lĭ ən), *adj., n.* deep blue; sky blue; azure. [f. m.s. L *caeruleus* dark blue + -AN]

ce·ru·men (sə rōō′mən), *n. Anat.* a yellowish waxlike secretion from certain glands in the external auditory canal, acting as a lubricant and arresting the entrance of dust, insects, etc.; earwax. [t. NL, der. L *cēra* wax]

ce·ruse (sĭr′ōōs, sĭ rōōs′), *n.* white lead; a mixture or compound of hydrate and carbonate of lead, much used in painting. [ME, t. L: m. *cērussa*]

ce·rus·site (sĭr′ə sīt′), *n.* a mineral, lead carbonate, $PbCO_3$, in white crystals or massive: an important ore of lead. [f. s. L *cērussa* white lead + -ITE[1]]

Cer·van·tes Sa·a·ve·dra (sər văn′tēz; *Sp.* thěr vän′tĕs sä′ä vě′drä), **Miguel de** (mē gěl′ dě), 1547–1616, Spanish novelist.

Cer·ve·ra y To·pe·te (thěr vě′rä ē tô pě′tě), **Pas·cual** (päs kwäl′), 1839–1909, Spanish admiral.

cervic-, a combining form of **cervical.** Also, **cervico-.**

cer·vi·cal (sûr′və kəl), *adj. Anat.* pertaining to the cervix or neck. [f. s. L *cervix* neck + -AL[1]]

cer·vi·ci·tis (sûr′və sī′təs), *n.* inflammation of the cervix (of the uterus).

cervico-, a combining form of **cervic-,** used before vowels.

Cer·vin (sěr văn′), *n.* **Mont** (môN), French name of the **Matterhorn.**

cer·vine (sûr′vīn, -vĭn), *adj.* 1. deerlike. 2. of deer or the deer family, the *Cervidae.* 3. of a deep tawny color. [t. L: m. s. *cervinus* pertaining to deer]

cer·vix (sûr′vĭks), *n., pl.* **cervixes, cervices** (sər vī′sēz). 1. the neck. 2. the neck of the uterus, which dilates just before parturition. 3. any necklike part. [t. L]

Ce·sar·e·an (sĭ zâr′ĭ ən), *adj., n.* Caesarean. Also, **Ce·sar′i·an.**

ce·si·um (sē′zĭ əm), *n. Chem.* a rare extremely active, soft, monovalent metallic element showing blue lines in the spectrum. *Symbol:* Cs; *at. wt.:* 132.91; *at. no.:* 55; *sp. gr.:* 1.9 at 20° C. melts at 28.5° C. Also, **caesium.** [NL, special use of L *caesium* (neut.) bluish-gray]

Čes·ké Bu·de·jo·vi·ce (chěs′kě bōō′dyě yŏ′vĭ tsě), Czech name of **Budweis.**

ces·pi·tose (sěs′pə tōs′), *adj. Bot.* matted together; growing in dense tufts. Also, **caespitose.** [f. m.s. L *caespes* turf + -OSE[1]] —**ces′pi·tose′ly,** *adv.*

ces·sa·tion (sě sā′shən), *n.* a ceasing; discontinuance; pause: *a cessation of hostilities.* [t. L: s. *cessātiō*]

ces·sion (sěsh′ən), *n.* 1. act of ceding, as by treaty. 2. something, as territory, ceded. [t. L: s. *cessio*]

ces·sion·ar·y (sěsh′ə něr′ĭ), *n., pl.* **-aries.** 1. a transferee. 2. assignee. 3. grantee.

cess·pool (sěs′pōōl′), *n.* 1. a cistern, well, or pit for retaining the sediment of a drain or for receiving the filth of a water closet, etc. 2. any filthy receptacle or place: *a cesspool of iniquity.* [orig. uncert.]

c'est-à-dire (sě tà dēr′), *French.* that is to say.

c'est la guerre (sě lä gěr′), *French.* it is war.

Ces·to·da (sěs tō′də), *n.pl. Zool.* tapeworms, a class of internally parasitic platyhelminths or flatworms, characterized by the long tapelike body divided into joints.

ces·tode (sěs′tōd), *n.* a tapeworm. [f. m.s. Gk. *kestós* girdle + -ODE[1]]

ces·toid (sěs′toid), *adj. Zool.* (of worms) ribbonlike.

ces·tus[1] (sěs′təs), *n.* 1. a belt or girdle. 2. *Class. Myth.* the girdle of Aphrodite or Venus, which was said to be decorated with everything that could awaken love. [t. L, t. Gk.: m. *kestós* girdle, lit., stitched]

ces·tus[2] (sěs′təs), *n. Rom. Antiq.* a hand covering made of leather strips often loaded with metal, worn by boxers. [t. L: m. *caestus,* prob. var. sp. of *cestus* CESTUS[1]]

ce·su·ra (sə zhŏŏr′ə, -zyŏŏr′ə), *n.* caesura. —**ce·su′ral,** *adj.*

cet-, a word element meaning "whale." [comb. form repr. L *cētus* and Gk. *kētos* whale]

ce·ta·cean (sə tā′shən), *adj.* 1. belonging to the *Cetacea,* an order of aquatic, chiefly marine, mammals, including the whales, dolphins, porpoises, etc. —*n.* 2. a cetacean mammal. [f. s. NL *Cetācea,* pl. (see CET-, -ACEA) + -AN] —**ce·ta′ceous,** *adj.*

ce·tane number (sē′tān), *Chem., etc.* a measure of the ignition quality of Diesel engine fuels. The fuel is compared with mixtures of the alpha form of methylnaphthalene (value = 0) and a hydrocarbon, $C_{16}H_{34}$ of the methane series (**cetane**) (value = 100).

Ce·ta·tea Al·bă (chě tä′tyä äl′bə), Rumanian name of **Akkerman.**

ce·te·ra de·sunt (sět′ə rə dē′sənt), *Latin.* the remaining (parts) are missing.

ce·te·ris pa·ri·bus (sět′ə rĭs păr′ə bəs), *Latin.* the others (other things) being equal.

Ce·tin·je (tsě′tĭ nyě), *n.* a city in SW Yugoslavia: the capital of Montenegro. 8982 (1931).

cet. par., ceteris paribus.

Ce·tus (sē′təs), *n., gen.* **Ceti** (sē′tī). *Astron.* a constellation lying across the equator and containing an important variable star. [t. L, t. Gk. See CET-]

Ceu·ta (sū′tə; *Sp.* thě ōō′tä, sě-), *n.* a seaport in Spanish Morocco, on the Strait of Gibraltar. 59,600 (1930).

Cé·vennes (sě věn′), *n.* a mountain range in S France. Highest peak, Mt. Mézenc, 5753 ft.

Cey·lon (sĭ lŏn′), *n.* an island in the Indian Ocean, S of Idnia: a British dominion (since 1948). 6,197,000 pop. (est. 1943). 25,232 sq. mi. *Cap.:* Colombo. —**Cey·lo·nese** (sē′lə nēz′, -nēs′), *adj., n.*

Ceylon moss, a seaweed, *Gracilaria lichenoides,* of Ceylon and the East Indies, and one of the algae from which agar-agar is obtained.

Cé·zanne (sě zän′; *Fr.* sě zàn′), *n.* **Paul** (pōl), 1839–1906, French painter.

cf., 1. *Bookbinding.* calf. 2. *Baseball.* center fielder. 3. (L *confer*) compare.

C.F.I., cost, freight, and insurance. Also, **c.f.i.**

cg., centigram; centigrams.

C.G., 1. Coast Guard. 2. Commanding General.

cgs, centimeter-gram-second (system). Also, **c.g.s.**

Ch., 1. chapter. 2. *Chess.* check. 3. church. Also, **ch.**

chab·a·zite (kăb′ə zīt′), *n.* a zeolite mineral, essentially a hydrated sodium calcium aluminum silicate, occurring commonly in red to colorless crystals that are nearly cubes. [earlier *chabazie,* t. F, misspelling of Gk. *chalázie* (voc.), der. *chálaza* hailstone. See -ITE[1]]

Cha·blis (shăb′lĭ; *Fr.* shà blē′), *n.* a very dry white table wine from the Burgundy wine region in France. [named after *Chablis,* town in N central France]

cha·bouk (chä′bōōk), *n.* a horsewhip, often used in the Orient for inflicting corporal punishment. Also, **cha′buk.** [t. Pers. and Hind.: m. *chābuk*]

cha·cha·la·ca (chä′chä lä′kä), *n.* a loud-voiced guan, *Ortalis vetula,* inhabiting brushlands of southern Texas, Mexico, and Central America. The name is onomatopoeic.

chac·ma (chăk′mə), *n.* a large South African baboon, *Papio comatus,* about the size of a mastiff. [t. Hottentot]

Cha·co (chä′kô), *n.* 1. a part of the Gran Chaco region in central South America, formerly in dispute between Bolivia and Paraguay: boundary fixed by arbitration, 1938. ab. 100,000 sq. mi. 2. See **Gran Chaco.**

Chacma
Papio comatus
(Total length 4½ ft.
tail 21 in.)

cha·conne (shà kôn′), *n.* 1. an old-time dance, probably of Spanish origin. 2. music for it. [t. F, t. Sp.: m. *chacona,* t. Basque: m. *chacun* pretty]

cha·cun à son goût (shà kœn nà sôn gōō′). *French.* everyone to his own taste.

Chad (chăd), *n.* 1. **Lake,** a lake in N Africa at the junction of French Equatorial Africa, French West Africa, and Nigeria. 10,000 to 20,000 sq. mi. (seasonal variation). 2. a French colony E of this lake: a part of French Equatorial Africa. 1,432,000 pop. (1936); 454,826 sq. mi. *Cap.:* Fort-Lamy.

Chad·wick (chăd′wĭk), *n.* **James,** born 1891, British physicist.

Chaer·o·ne·a (kěr′ə nē′ə), *n.* an ancient city in E Greece, in Boeotia: victory of Philip of Macedon over the Athenians, 338 B.C.

chae·ta (kē′tə), *n., pl.* **-tae** (-tē). *Zool.* a bristle or seta, esp. of a chaetopod. [NL, t. Gk.: m. *chaitē* hair]

chaeto-, a word element meaning "hair," as in *chaetopod.* Also, before vowels, **chaet-.** [comb. form repr. Gk. *chaitē*]

chae·toph·o·rous (kĭ tŏf′ə rəs), *adj. Zool.* bearing bristles; setigerous or setiferous.

chae·to·pod (kē′tə pŏd′), *n. Zool.* any of the *Chaetopoda,* a class or group of annelids having the body made up of more or less similar segments provided with muscular processes bearing setae.

chafe (chāf), *v.,* **chafed, chafing,** *n.* —*v.t.* 1. to warm by rubbing. 2. to wear or abrade by rubbing. 3. to make sore by rubbing. 4. to irritate; annoy. 5. to heat; make warm. —*v.i.* 6. to rub; press with friction. 7. to become worn or sore by rubbing. 8. to be irritated or annoyed. —*n.* **9.** irritation; annoyance. **10.** heat, wear, or soreness caused by rubbing. [ME *chaufe(n)*, t. OF: m. *chaufer*, g. LL contr. of L *calefacere* make hot]

chaf·er (chā′fər), *n.* *Chiefly Brit.* any scarabaeid beetle. Cf. **U.S. June bug.** [ME *cheaffer*, *chaver*, OE *ceafor.* Cf. G *käfer*]

chaff[1] (chăf, chäf), *n.* **1.** the husks of grains and grasses separated from the seed. **2.** straw cut small for fodder. **3.** worthless matter; refuse; rubbish. [ME *chaf*, OE *ceaf*, c. D *kaf*] —**chaff′y,** *adj.*

chaff[2] (chăf, chäf), *v.t., v.i.* **1.** to ridicule or tease good-naturedly; banter. —*n.* **2.** good-natured ridicule or teasing; raillery. [? special use of CHAFF[1]] —**chaff′er,** *n.*

chaf·fer (chăf′ər), *n.* **1.** bargaining; haggling. —*v.i.* **2.** to bargain; haggle. **3.** to bandy words. —*v.t.* **4.** to trade or deal in; barter. **5.** to bandy (words). [ME *chaffare*, earlier *chapfare* trading journey, f. OE *cēap* trade + *faru* a going] —**chaf′fer·er,** *n.*

chaf·finch (chăf′ĭnch), *n.* a common European finch, *Fringilla coelebs*, with a pleasant short song, often kept as a cage bird. [OE *ceaffinc.* See CHAFF[1], FINCH]

chaf·ing dish (chā′fĭng), **1.** an apparatus consisting of a metal dish with a lamp or heating appliance beneath it, for cooking food or keeping it hot. **2.** a vessel to hold charcoal, etc., for heating anything set over it.

Cha·gall (shä gäll′), *n.* **Marc**, born 1887, Russian painter in U.S.

Cha·gres (chä′grĕs), *n.* a river in Panama, flowing through Gatun Lake to the Caribbean.

cha·grin (shə grĭn′), *n.* **1.** a feeling of vexation and disappointment or humiliation. —*v.t.* **2.** to vex by disappointment or humiliation. [t. F. See SHAGREEN]

Cha·har (chä′här′), *n.* a province in Inner Mongolia, in NE China. 2,035,000 pop. (est. 1944); 107,698 sq. mi.

chain (chān). *n.* **1.** a connected series of metal or other links for connecting, drawing, confining, restraining, etc., or for ornament. **2.** something that binds or restrains. **3.** (*pl.*) bonds or fetters. **4.** (*pl.*) bondage. **5.** a series of things connected or following in succession. **6.** a range of mountains. **7.** a number of similar establishments, as banks, theaters, hotels, etc. under one ownership and management. **8.** *Chem.* a linkage of atoms of the same element, as carbon to carbon. **9.** *Survey.* **a.** a measuring instrument consisting of 100 wire rods or links, each 7.92 inches long (**surveyor's** or **Gunter's chain**), or one foot long (**engineer's chain**). **b.** the length of a surveyor's chain (66 feet) or engineer's chain (100 feet). —*v.t.* **10.** to fasten or secure with a chain. **11.** to fetter; confine or restrain: *chained to his desk.* [ME *chayne*, t. OF: m. *chaeine*, g. L *catēna*] —**chain′less,** *adj.*

chain gang, *Chiefly U.S.* a group of prisoners usually chained together when in camp, in transit, etc.

chain lightning, *U.S.* lightning visible in wavy, zigzag, or broken lines.

chain mail, flexible body armor made of metal links.

chain·man (chān′mən), *n., pl.* **-men.** a man who holds the chain in making surveying measurements.

chain-re·act·ing (chān′rĭ ăk′tĭng), *adj.* *Physics.* (of a substance) undergoing or capable of undergoing a chain reaction.

chain reaction, *Physics.* a molecular or atomic process which, once started, automatically continues and spreads.

chain shot, a shot consisting of two balls or half balls connected by a short chain.

chain stitch, a kind of ornamental stitching in which each stitch forms a loop through the forward end of which the next stitch is taken.

chain store, 1. a group of retail stores under the same ownership and management and merchandised from a common point or points. **2.** one such store.

chain·work (chān′wûrk′), *n.* decorative work esp. when looped or woven together as in the links of a chain.

chair (châr), *n.* **1.** a seat with a back and legs or other support, often with arms, usually for one person. **2.** a seat of office or authority. **3.** the position of a judge, chairman, presiding officer, etc. **4.** the person occupying the seat or office, esp. the chairman of a meeting. **5. take the chair, a.** to assume the chairmanship of a meeting; begin or open a meeting. **b.** to preside at a meeting. **6. electric chair. 7. sedan chair. 8.** *Railroads.* a metal block to support and secure a rail. —*v.t.* **9.** to place or seat in a chair. **10.** to install in office or authority. **11.** *Brit.* to place in a chair and carry aloft, esp. in triumph. [ME *chaiere*, t. OF, g. L *cathedra* seat, t. Gk.: m. *kathédra*]

chair car, *U.S. Railroads.* **1.** a parlor car. **2.** a car with two adjustable seats on each side of the aisle.

chair·man (châr′mən), *n., pl.* **-men. 1.** the presiding officer of a meeting, committee, board, etc. **2.** someone employed to carry or wheel a person in a chair.

chair·wom·an (châr′wŏŏm′en), *n., pl.* **-women.** a female chairman (def. 1).

chaise (shāz), *n.* **1.** Also, *Colloq.* **shay.** a light, open carriage, usually with a hood, esp. a one-horse, two-wheeled carriage for two persons. **2.** a post chaise. [t. F: chair, chaise, var. of *chaire.* See CHAIR]

Chaise, 18th and 19th centuries

chaise longue (shāz′ lông′; *Fr.* shĕz lôNG′), a kind of couch or reclining chair with seat prolonged to form a full-length leg rest. [t. F: long chair]

cha·la·za (kə lā′zə), *n., pl.* **-zas, -zae** (-zē). **1.** *Zool.* one of the two albuminous twisted cords which fasten an egg yolk to the shell membrane. **2.** *Bot.* the point of an ovule or seed where the integuments are united to the nucellus. [t. NL, t. Gk.: hail, lump] —**cha·la′zal,** *adj.*

chal·can·thite (kăl kăn′thĭt), *n.* blue vitriol.

Chal·ce·don (kăl′sĭ dŏn′, kăl sē′dən), *n.* an ancient city in NW Asia Minor, on the Bosporus, opposite Byzantium.

chal·ced·o·ny (kăl sĕd′ə nĭ, kăl′sə dō′nĭ), *n., pl.* **-nies.** a microcrystalline translucent variety of quartz, often milky or grayish. [ME, t. L (Vulgate): m. s. *chalcedonius*, t. Gk.: m. *chalkēdōn* in Rev. 21: 19]

chal·cid fly (kăl′sĭd), any of the *Chalcididae*, a family of small hymenopterous insects, often of bright metallic colors, whose larvae are mostly parasitic on various stages of other insects. Also, **chalcid.** [*chalcid*, f. s. Gk. *chalkós* copper (with allusion to the metallic coloration) + -ID[2]]

Chal·cid·i·ce (kăl sĭd′ə sĭ), *n.* a peninsula in NE Greece. Greek, **Khalkidike.**

chalco-, a word element meaning "copper" or "brass." Also, before vowels, **chalc-.** [t. Gk.: m. *chalko-*, comb. form of *chalkós*]

chal·co·cite (kăl′kə sīt), *n.* a common mineral, cuprous sulfide, Cu_2S, an important ore of copper.

chal·cog·ra·phy (kăl kŏg′rə fĭ), *n.* the art of engraving on copper or brass. —**chal·cog′ra·pher,** *n.* —**chal·co·graph·ic** (kăl′kə grăf′ĭk), **chal·co·graph′i·cal,** *adj.*

chal·co·py·rite (kăl′kə pī′rīt, -pŷr′īt), *n.* a very common mineral, copper iron sulfide, $CuFeS_2$, occurring in brass-yellow crystals or masses: the most important ore of copper; copper pyrites.

Chal·de·a (kăl dē′ə), an ancient region in S Babylonia.

Chal·de·an (kăl dē′ən), *n.* **1.** one of an ancient Semitic people that formed the dominant element in Babylonia. **2.** an astrologer, soothsayer, or enchanter. Dan. 1:4; 2:2. **3.** Biblical Aramaic. —*adj.* **4.** of or belonging to ancient Chaldea. **5.** pertaining to astrology, occult learning, etc. Also, **Chal·dee** (kăl dē′, kăl′dē), *Obsolesc.*, **Chal·da·ic** ((kăl dā′ĭk)). [f. m.s. L *Chaldaeus* (t. Gk.: m. *Chaldaios*) + -AN]

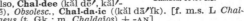
Chaldea, c1450 B.C.

chal·dron (chôl′dron), *n.* an English dry measure for coal, coke, lime, etc., equal to 32 or 36 or more bushels in different commodities and localities. [t. F: m. *chaudron* kettle; var. of CALDRON]

cha·let (shă lā′, shăl′ā; *Fr.* shä lĕ′), *n.* **1.** a herdsman's hut in the Swiss mountains. **2.** a kind of cottage, low and with wide eaves, common in Alpine regions. **3.** any cottage or villa built in this style. [t. F (Swiss)]

Cha·lia·pin (shä lyä′pĭn), *n.* **Fëdor Ivanovich** (fyô′dōr Y vä′nō vYch), 1873–1938, Russian operatic bass singer.

chal·ice (chăl′ĭs), *n.* **1.** *Poet.* a drinking cup. **2.** *Eccles.* **a.** a cup for the wine of the eucharist or mass. **b.** the wine contained in it. **3.** a cuplike blossom. [ME, t. OF, g. L *calix* cup; r. ME *caliz*, *calc*, OE *calic*, t. L: m. *calix*] —**chal·iced** (chăl′ĭst), *adj.*

chalk (chôk), *n.* **1.** a soft powdery limestone consisting chiefly of fossil shells of foraminifers. **2.** a prepared piece of chalk or chalklike substance for marking; a blackboard crayon. **3.** a mark made with chalk. **4.** a score, or record of credit given, as at a tavern, etc. —*v.t.* **5.** to mark or write with chalk. **6.** to rub over or whiten with chalk. **7.** to treat or mix with chalk. **8.** to make pale; blanch. **9. chalk up,** to score or earn: *they chalked up two runs in the first inning.* [ME *chalke*, OE *cealc*, t. L: m. s. *calx* lime] —**chalk′like′,** *adj.* —**chalk′y,** *adj.* —**chalk′i·ness,** *n.*

chalk·stone (chôk′stōn′), *n.* *Pathol.* a chalklike concretion in the tissues or small joints of one with gout.

chal·lenge (chăl′ĭnj), *n., v.,* **-lenged, -lenging.** —*n.* **1.** a call to engage in a contest of skill, strength, etc. **2.** a call to fight, as a battle, a duel, etc. **3.** a demand to explain. **4.** *Mil.* the demand of a sentry for identification or the countersign. **5.** *Law.* a formal objection to the qualifications of a juror or to the legality of an entire jury. **6.** *U.S.* the assertion that a vote is invalid or that a voter is not legally qualified. —*v.t.* **7.** to summon to a contest of skill, strength, etc. **8.** to demand defiantly. **9.** to take exception to; call in question: *to challenge the wisdom of a procedure.* **10.** *Mil.* to halt and demand identification or countersign from. **11.** *Law.* to take formal exception to (a juror or jury). **12.** to have a claim to because of qualities or character: *a matter which challenges attention.* **13.** *Archaic.* to lay claim to. **14.** *U.S.* to assert that (a vote) is invalid or (a voter) is not qualified to vote. —*v.i.* **15.** to make or issue a challenge. **16.** *Hunting.* (of hounds) to cry or give tongue on picking up the scent. [ME *chalange*, t. OF: m. *chalenge*, g. L *calumnia* CALUMNY] —**chal′lenge·a·ble,** *adj.* —**chal′leng·er,** *n.*

chal·lis (shăl′ĭ), *n.* a printed fabric of plain weave in wool, cotton, or rayon. Also, **chal′lie.** [orig. uncert.]

chal·one (kăl'ōn), *n. Physiol.* an endocrine secretion which reduces physiological activity. [t. Gk.: m. *chaloûn*, ppr., slackening]

Châ·lons (shà·lôn'), *n.* **1.** Also, **Châ·lons-sur-Marne** (shà·lôn'syr märn'). a city in NE France: defeat of Attila, A.D. 451. 30,329 (1946). **2.** Also, **Châ·lons-sur-Saône** (shà·lôn'syr sōn'). a city in E France. 32,683 (1946).

Chalons (def. 1)

chal·u·meau (shăl'yə mō'; *Fr.* shà ly mō'), *n. Music.* the low register of the clarinet. [t. F, in OF *chalemel* a musical instrument, g. L *calamellus*, dim. of *calamus* reed]

chal·yb·e·ate (kə lĭb'ĭ·āt'), *adj.* **1.** containing or impregnated with salts of iron, as a mineral spring, medicine, etc. —*n.* **2.** a chalybeate water, medicine, or the like. [appar. t. NL: m. s. *chalybēātus*, der. L *chalybēius* of steel, der. *chalybs*, t. Gk.: m. *chályps* iron]

cham (kăm), *n. Archaic.* khan[1].

cham·ber (chām'bər), *n.* **1.** a room or apartment, usually a private room, and esp. a bedroom. **2.** (*pl.*) *Brit.* rooms for residence in the house or building of another; apartments. **3.** a room in a palace or official residence. **4.** the meeting hall of a legislative or other assembly. **5.** (*pl.*) a place where a judge hears matters not requiring action in court. **6.** (*pl.*) (in England) quarters of lawyers and others, esp. in the Inns of Court. **7.** the place where the moneys due a government, etc., are received and kept; a treasury or chamberlain's office. **8.** a legislative, judicial, or other like body: *the upper or the lower chamber of a legislature.* **9.** a compartment or enclosed space; a cavity. **10.** a receptacle for one or more cartridges in a firearm, or for a shell in a gun or other cannon. **11.** that part of the barrel of a gun which receives the charge. —*v.t.* **12.** to put or enclose in, or as in, a chamber. **13.** to provide with a chamber. [ME, t. OF: m. *chambre*, g. L *camera*] —**cham'bered**, *adj.*

chamber concert, a concert of chamber music.

cham·ber·lain (chām'bər lĭn), *n.* **1.** an official charged with the management of a sovereign's or nobleman's living quarters. **2.** an official who receives rents and revenues, as of a municipal corporation; a treasurer. **3.** the high steward or factor of a nobleman. **4.** a high official of a royal court. [ME *chamberleyn*, t. OF: m. *chamberlenc*, t. Gmc.; cf. OHG *chamarlinc*]

Cham·ber·lain (chām'bər lĭn), *n.* **1.** (**Arthur**) **Nev·ille** (nĕv'ĭl), 1869–1940, British prime minister, 1937–40. **2. Joseph,** 1836–1914, British statesman (father of Sir Austen and Neville Chamberlain). **3. Sir** (**Joseph**) **Austen,** 1863–1937, British statesman.

cham·ber·maid (chām'bər mād'), *n.* a female servant who takes care of bedrooms.

chamber music, music suited for performance in a room or a small concert hall, esp. for two or more (but usually less than ten) solo instruments.

chamber of commerce, an association, primarily of businessmen, to protect and promote the business activities of a city, etc.

cham·bray (shăm'brā), *n.* a fine variety of gingham, commonly plain, but with the warp and weft of different colors. [var. of CAMBRIC]

cha·me·le·on (kə mē'lĭ ən, -mēl'yən), *n.* **1.** any of a group of lizards, *Chamaeleontidae*, esp. of the genus *Chamaeleon*, characterized by the greatly developed power of changing the color of the skin, very slow locomotion, and a projectile tongue. **2.** an inconstant person. [ME *camelion*, t. L: m. *chamaeleon*, t. Gk.: m. *chamailéōn*, lit., ground lion] —**cha·me·le·on·ic** (kə mē'lĭ ŏn'ĭk). *adj.*

African chameleon, *Chamaeleon chamaeleon* (8 in. long)

cham·fer (chăm'fər), *n.* an oblique surface cut on the edge or corner of a solid, usually a board, made by removing the arris and usually sloping at 45°. [appar. t. F: m. *chamfrain*, der. *chanfraindre*, f. *chant* side + *fraindre* (g. L *frangere* break)]

cham·fron (chăm'frən), *n. Armor.* chanfron. Also, **cham·frain** (chăm'frĭn).

cham·ois (shăm'ĭ; *Fr.* shà mwä'), *n., pl.* **-ois. 1.** an agile goatlike antelope, *Rupicapra rupicapra*, of high mountains of Europe and southwestern Russia. **2.** Also, **cham'my.** a soft, pliable leather made from various skins dressed with oil (esp. fish oil), orig. prepared from the skin of the chamois; shammy. [t. F, g. LL *camox*]

cham·o·mile (kăm'ə mīl'), *n.* camomile.

Cha·mo·nix (shà'mō nē'), *n.* a mountain valley in E France, N of Mont Blanc.

Cha·mor·ro (chä môr'rō), *n.* an inhabitant of Guam, the Marianas, etc.

Chamois, *Rupicapra rupicapra* (Total length 3½ ft., 2 ft. 4 in. high at the shoulder)

champ[1] (chămp), *v.t.* **1.** to bite upon, esp. impatiently: *horses champing the bit.* **2.** to crush with the teeth and chew vigorously or noisily; munch. **3.** *Scot.* to mash; crush. —*v.i.* **4.** to make vigorous chewing or biting movements with the jaws and teeth. —*n.* **5.** act of champing. [? nasalized var. (cf. BUNT) of *chop* bite at, der. *chap, chop* jaw]

champ[2] (chămp), *n. Slang.* a champion.

cham·pac (chăm'păk, chŭm'pŭk), *n.* an East Indian tree, *Michelia Champaca*, of the magnolia family, with fragrant golden flowers and a handsome wood used for making images, furniture, etc. Also, **cham'pak.** [t. Hind.]

cham·pagne (shăm pān'), *n.* **1.** a sparkling white wine produced in the wine region of Champagne, France, or elsewhere. **2.** the nonsparkling (still) dry white table wine produced in the region of Champagne. **3.** a very pale yellow or greenish-yellow color. —*adj.* **4.** having the color of champagne.

Cham·pagne (shăm pān'; *Fr.* shän pàn'y), *n.* a region in NE France: formerly a province.

cham·paign (shăm pān'), *n.* **1.** level, open country; plain. —*adj.* **2.** level and open. [ME *champaigne*, t. OF, g. L *campānia.* See CAMPAIGN]

Cham·paign (shăm pān'), *n.* a city in E Illinois. 39,563 (1950).

cham·per·ty (chăm'pər tĭ), *n. Law.* a sharing in the proceeds of litigation by one who promotes it. [ME *champartie*, t. OF: m. *champart* share of the produce of land, g. L *campī pars* part of the field] —**cham'per·tous,** *adj.*

cham·pi·gnon (shăm pĭn'yən; *esp. Brit.* chăm-; *Fr.* shän pe nyôn'), *n.* a mushroom (defs. 2, 3). [t. F, ult. der. L *campānia* flat land, der. *campus* field]

cham·pi·on (chăm'pĭ ən), *n.* **1.** one who holds first place in any sport, etc., having defeated all opponents. **2.** anything that takes first place in competition. **3.** one who fights for or defends any person or cause: *a champion of the oppressed.* **4.** a fighter or warrior. —*v.t.* **5.** to act as champion of; defend; support. **6.** *Obs.* to defy. —*adj.* **7.** first among all contestants or competitors. **8.** *Colloq.* first-rate. [ME, t. OF, g. LL *campio*, der. L *campus* field (of battle)] —**cham·pi·on·ess** (chăm'pĭ ŏn ĭs), *n. fem.* —**cham'pi·on·less,** *adj.* —**Syn. 3.** defender, protector, vindicator. **5.** maintain, fight for, advocate.

cham·pi·on·ship (chăm'pĭ ən shĭp'), *n.* **1.** the position of being a champion. **2.** the honor of being a champion in competition. **3.** advocacy or defense.

Cham·plain (shăm plān'; *also for 2, Fr.* shän plăn'), *n.* **1. Lake,** a lake between New York and Vermont. 125 mi. long; ab. 600 sq. mi. **2. Samuel de** (sà my ĕl' də), 1567–1635, French explorer who founded Quebec: the first French governor of Canada.

Cham·pol·lion (shän pô lyôn'), *n.* **Jean François** (zhän fränswà'), 1790–1832, French Egyptologist.

Champs É·ly·sées (shän zĕ lē zē'), *French.* a famous avenue and the gardens surrounding it, in Paris, France. [F: lit., Elysian Fields]

chance (chăns, chäns), *n., v.,* **chanced, chanc·ing,** *adj.* —*n.* **1.** the absence of any known reason why an event should turn out one way rather than another, spoken of as if it were a real agency: *chance governs all.* **2.** fortune; fate; luck. **3.** a possibility or probability of anything happening: *the chances are two to one against us.* **4.** an opportunity: *now is your chance.* **5.** *Baseball.* an opportunity, in fielding, for a put-out or an assist. **6.** a risk or hazard: *take a chance.* **7.** *Archaic.* an unfortunate event; a mishap. **8.** *U.S. Colloq.* a quantity or number (usually followed by *of*). **9. by chance,** accidentally. —*v.i.* **10.** to happen or occur by chance. **11.** to come by chance (fol. by *on* or *upon*). —*v.t.* **12.** *Colloq.* to take the chances or risks of; risk (usually fol. by impersonal *it*). —*adj.* **13.** due to chance: *a chance occurrence.* [ME *chea(u)nce*, t. OF: m. *cheance*, g. LL *cadentia* a falling out, der. *cadens* ppr., falling] —**Syn. 10.** See **happen. 13.** casual, accidental, fortuitous.

chan·cel (chăn'səl, chän'-), *n.* the space about the altar of a church, usually enclosed, for the clergy and other officials. [ME, t. OF, g. LL *cancellus*, L *cancellī* bars, lattice (which enclosed the chancel)]

chan·cel·ler·y (chăn'sə lə rĭ, -slə rĭ, chän'-), *n., pl.* **-leries. 1.** the position of a chancellor. **2.** the office or department of a chancellor. **3.** the office attached to an embassy, etc. **4.** the building or room occupied by a chancellor's department. [ME *chancelerie*, t. OF, der. *chancelier* CHANCELLOR]

chan·cel·lor (chăn'sə lər, -slər, chän'-), *n.* **1.** the title of various important judges and other high officials. **2.** *U.S.* the presiding judge of a court of equity or chancery. **3.** (formerly) the chief minister of state in Germany or Austria. **4.** a secretary, as of a king, nobleman, or embassy. **5.** the chief administrative officer in certain American universities. **6.** an honorary official in British universities. [ME *chanceler*, t. AF, var. of OF *chancelier*, g. L *cancellārius*, orig. officer stationed at a tribunal. See CHANCEL] —**chan'cel·lor·ship'**, *n.*

Chancellor of the Exchequer, the minister of finance in the British Government.

Chan·cel·lors·ville (chăn'sə lərz vĭl', chăn'-), *n.* a village in NE Virginia: site of a Confederate victory, 1863.

chance-med·ley (chăns'měd'lĭ, chäns'-), *n. Law.* a sudden quarrel with violence, in the course of which one party kills or wounds another in self-defense or in the heat of passion. [t. AF: m. *chance medlée* mixed chance]

chan·cer·y (chăn′sər ĭ, chän′-), *n., pl.* **-ceries. 1.** the office or department of a chancellor. **2.** a chancellery. **3.** an office of public records, esp., in England, of the Lord Chancellor. **4.** *Eng.* the Lord Chancellor's court, now a division of the High Court of Justice. **5.** *Law.* **a.** Also, **court of chancery.** court having jurisdiction in equity; court of equity. **b.** equity (defs. 3a, b). **6. in chancery, a.** *Law.* in litigation in a court of chancery. **b.** *Boxing.* (of a contestant's head) held under his opponent's arm. **c.** in a helpless or embarrassing position. [ME, var. of CHANCELLERY]

chan·cre (shăng′kər), *n.* the initial lesion of syphilis, commonly a more or less distinct ulcer or sore with a hard base. [t. F, g. L *cancer* crab, cancer]

chanc·y (chăn′sĭ, chän′-), *adj.,* **chancier, chanciest.** *Colloq. or Dial.* uncertain.

chan·de·lier (shăn′də lĭr′), *n.* a branched support for a number of lights, esp. one suspended from a ceiling. [t. F: f. *chandel* candle + suffix *-ier*]

chan·delle (shăn děl′; *Fr.* shän-), *n. Aeron.* an abrupt climbing turn approximately to a stall, in which momentum is used to obtain a higher rate of climb. [t. F]

Chan·der·na·gor (chŭn′dər nəgôr′), *n.* a French dependency in NE India, near Calcutta: a port on the Hooghly river. 38,284 pop. (1941); 3½ sq. mi. Also, **Chan·dar·na·gar** (chŭn′dər nŭg′ər).

chan·dler (chăn′dlər, chän′-), *n.* **1.** a dealer or trader: *a ship chandler.* **2.** one who makes or sells candles. **3.** a retailer of groceries, etc. [ME *cha(u)ndeler*, t. AF, var. of OF *chandelier* candle-seller, der. OF *chandeile* CANDLE]

chan·dler·y (chăn′dlər ĭ, chän′-), *n., pl.* **-dleries. 1.** a storeroom for candles. **2.** the warehouse, wares, or business of a chandler.

Chan·dra·gup·ta (chŭn′drə gŏŏp′tə), *n.* fl. c300 B.C., king of northern India, c315–c296 or c291 B.C. Greek, **Sandrocottus.**

chan·fron (chăn′frən), *n.* armor for a horse's head. Also, **chamfron, chamfrain.** [ME *shamfron*, t. OF: m. *chanfrain;* orig. uncert.]

Chang·chow·fu (chăng′chou′fŏŏ′; *Chin.* chäng′jō′-fōō′), *n.* a city in SE China, in Fukien province. ab. 500,000. Also, **Lungki.**

Chang·chun (chäng′chŏŏn′), *n.* a city in NE China: the capital of Manchuria. 395,900 (est. 1939). Also, **Hsinking.**

change (chānj), *v.,* **changed, changing.** *n.* —*v.t.* **1.** to make different; alter in condition, appearance, etc.; turn (often fol. by *into*): *change one's habits.* **2.** to substitute another or others for; exchange for something else: *to change trains.* **3.** to give or get smaller money in exchange for: *to change a five-dollar bill.* **4.** to give or get different money in exchange for: *to change dollars into francs.* **5.** to give and take reciprocally; interchange: *to change places with someone.* **6.** to remove and replace the covering or coverings of: *to change a bed.* **7.** change front, *Mil.* to shift a military force in another direction. **8.** **change hands,** to pass from one hand or possessor to another. —*v.i.* **9.** to become different; alter (fol. by *to* or *into*). **10.** to make a change or an exchange. **11.** to change trains or other conveyances. **12.** to change one's clothes. —*n.* **13.** variation; alteration; modification; deviation; transformation. **14.** the substitution of one thing for another. **15.** variety or novelty. **16.** the passing from one place, state, form, or phase to another: *change of the moon.* **17.** the supplanting of one thing by another. **18.** that which is or may be substituted for another. **19.** a fresh set of clothing. **20.** money given in exchange for an equivalent of higher denomination. **21.** a balance of money that is returned when the sum tendered in payment is larger than the sum due. **22.** coins of low denomination. **23.** Also, **'change.** *Com.* an exchange (def. 10). **24.** any of the various sequences in which a peal of bells may be rung. **25.** *Obs.* changefulness; caprice. [ME *change(n),* t. OF: m. *changier,* g. LL *cambiāre,* L *cambīre*] —**chang′er,** *n.*

—**Syn. 1.** transmute, transform. CHANGE, ALTER both mean to make a difference in the state or condition of a thing or to substitute another state or condition. To CHANGE is to make a material difference so that the thing is distinctly other than it was: *to change one's opinion, one's shoes.* To ALTER is to make some partial change, as in appearance, but usually to preserve the identity: *to alter a dress (to change a dress* would mean to put on a different one).

change·a·ble (chān′jə bəl), *adj.* **1.** liable to change or to be changed; variable. **2.** of changing color or appearance: *changeable silk.* —**change′a·bil′i·ty, change′a·ble·ness,** *n.* —**change′a·bly,** *adv.* —**Syn. 1.** alterable; vacillating, inconstant, fickle.

change·ful (chānj′fəl), *adj.* changing; variable; inconstant. —**change′ful·ly,** *adv.* —**change′ful·ness,** *n.*

change·less (chānj′lĭs), *adj.* unchanging. —**change′less·ly,** *adv.* —**change′less·ness,** *n.*

change·ling (chānj′lĭng), *n.* **1.** a child supposed to have been secretly substituted for another, esp. by fairies. **2.** *Archaic.* an inconstant person. **3.** *Archaic or Dial.* an idiot.

change of life, menopause.

change of venue, *Law.* the removal of trial to another jurisdiction.

change ringing, act of ringing the changes on a peal of bells.

Chang·sha (chäng′shä′), *n.* a city in SE China: the capital of Hunan province. 149,000 (est. 1939).

Chang·teh (chäng′dŭ′), *n.* a city in S China, in Hunan province. ab. 300,000.

Chang Tso·lin (jäng′ tsō′lĭn′), 1873–1928, Chinese general: military ruler of Manchuria, 1918–28.

chan·nel[1] (chăn′əl), *n., v.,* **-neled, -neling** or (*esp. Brit.*) **-nelled, -nelling.** —*n.* **1.** the bed of a stream or waterway. **2.** the deeper part of a waterway. **3.** a wide strait, as between a continent and an island. **4.** *Naut.* a navigable route between two bodies of water. **5.** a means of access. **6.** a course into which something may be directed. **7.** a route through which anything passes or progresses: *channels of trade.* **8.** a frequency band wide enough for one-way communication, the exact width of a channel depending upon the type of transmission involved (as telegraph, telephone, radio, television, etc.). **9.** a tubular passage for liquids or fluids. **10.** a groove or furrow. —*v.t.* **11.** to convey through a channel. **12.** to direct toward or into some particular course: *to channel one's interests.* **13.** to excavate as a channel: *a river channeling its course through the rocks.* **14.** to form a channel in; groove. [ME *chanel,* t. OF, g. L *canālis* CANAL]

chan·nel[2] (chăn′əl), *n.* one of the horizontal planks or ledges attached outside of a ship to give more spread to the lower shrouds. [var. of *chain-wale* (see WALE[1])]

channel iron, a rolled iron bar whose section is shaped like three sides of a rectangle.

Channel Islands, a British island group in the English Channel, near the coast of France, consisting of Alderney, Guernsey, Jersey, and smaller islands. 93,205 pop. (1931); 75 sq. mi.

Chan·ning (chăn′ĭng), *n.* **William Ellery** (ĕl′ər ĭ), 1780–1842, U.S. Unitarian clergyman and writer.

chan·son (shăn′sən; *Fr.* shäN sôN′), *n.* a song. [t. F, g. L *cantio*]

chan·son de geste (shäN sôN′ də zhĕst′), *French.* one of a class of old French epic poems.

chant (chănt, chänt), *n.* **1.** a song; singing. **2.** a short, simple melody, specif. one characterized by single notes to which an indefinite number of syllables are intoned, used in singing the psalms, canticles, etc., in the church service. **3.** a psalm, canticle, or the like, chanted or for chanting. **4.** the singing or intoning of all or portions of a liturgical service. **5.** any monotonous song. **6.** a monotonous intonation of the voice in speaking —*v.t.* **7.** to sing. **8.** to celebrate in song. **9.** to sing to a chant, or in the manner of a chant, esp. in the church service. —*v.i.* **10.** to sing. **11.** to sing a chant. [ME *chaunte(n),* t. OF: m. *chanter,* g. L *cantāre,* der. *canere* sing]

chan·tage (chän′tĭj, chän′-; *Fr.* shäN täzh′), *n. French.* blackmailing. [cf. F *faire chanter* to make (one) sing, to extort something]

chant·er (chăn′tər, chän′-), *n.* **1.** one who chants; a singer. **2.** a chorister; a precentor. **3.** the chief singer or priest of a chantry. **4.** the pipe of a bagpipe, provided with finger holes for playing the melody.

chan·te·relle (shăn′tə rĕl′, chăn′-), *n.* the mushroom, *Cantharellus cibarius,* a favorite edible species in France. [t. F, t. NL: m. *cantharella,* dim. of L *cantharus* drinking vessel, t. Gk.: m. *kántharos*]

chan·teuse (shän tœz′), *n. French.* a woman singer.

chant·ey (shăn′tĭ, chän′-), *n., pl.* **-eys.** a sailors' song, esp. one sung in rhythm to work. Also, **chanty, shanty.** [alter. of F *chanter* sing. See CHANT]

chan·ti·cleer (chăn′tə klĭr′), *n.* a name for the rooster, orig. in the medieval epic *Reynard the Fox.* [ME *chauntecler,* t. OF: m. *Chantecler,* lit., clear singer, f. *chante* (impv. of *chanter* sing) + *cler* clear]

Chan·til·ly (shăn tĭl′ĭ; *Fr.* shäN tē yē′), *n.* a town in N France, N of Paris: noted for its lace. 4986 (1936).

chant·ress (chăn′trĭs, chän′-), *n.* a female chanter or singer. [ME *chaunteresse,* t. OF: m. *chanteresse*]

chan·try (chăn′trĭ, chän′-), *n., pl.* **-tries.** *Eccles.* **1.** an endowment for the singing or saying of mass for the souls of the founders or of persons named by them. **2.** a chapel or the like so endowed. **3.** the priests of a chantry endowment. **4.** a chapel attached to a church, used for minor services. [ME *chanterie,* t. F: singing]

chant·y (shăn′tĭ, chän′tĭ), *n., pl.* **chanties.** chantey.

Chao·an (chou′än′), *n.* a city in SE China, in Kwangtung province. 920,900 (est. 1939). Also, **Chao·chow·fu** (chou′jō′fōō′).

cha·os (kā′ŏs), *n.* **1.** utter confusion or disorder wholly without organization or order; a confused mixture. **2.** the infinity of space or formless matter supposed to have preceded the existence of the ordered universe. **3.** *Obs.* a chasm or abyss. [t. L, t. Gk.]

cha·ot·ic (kā ŏt′ĭk), *adj.* in utter confusion or disorder. —**cha·ot′i·cal·ly,** *adv.* —**Ant.** orderly, systematic.

chap[1] (chăp), *v.,* **chapped, chapping,** *n.* —*v.t.* **1.** (of cold or exposure) to crack, roughen, and redden (the skin). **2.** to cause (the earth, wood, etc.) to split, crack, open in clefts. —*v.i.* **3.** to become chapped. —*n.* **4.** a fissure or crack, esp. in the skin. **5.** *Scot.* a blow; a knock. [ME *chapp(en);* orig. uncert.]

chap[2] (chăp), *n.* **1.** *Colloq.* a fellow; man or boy. **2.** *Obs. or Dial.* a customer. [short for CHAPMAN]

chap[3] (chŏp, chăp), *n.* chop[3]. [? special use of CHAP[1]]

chap., **1.** Chaplain. **2.** chapter. Also, **Chap.**

cha·pa·re·jos (chä′pä rä′hōs), *n.pl.* chaps. Also, **cha·pa·re·jos** (chä′pä rĕ′hōs). [Mex. Sp. var. of *chaparreras,* der. *chaparro* bramble bush]

chaparral 202 charge

chap·ar·ral (chăp/ə răl/), *n.* *Southwestern U.S.* **1.** a close growth of low evergreen oaks. **2.** any dense thicket. [t. Sp., der. *chaparro* evergreen oak, ? t. Basque]

chaparral cock, a terrestrial cuckoo of the SW United States, *Geococcyx californianus;* the road runner.

chaparral pea, a spiny leguminous bush, *Pickeringia montana*, sometimes forming dense thickets in the Pacific coast regions of the U. S.

chap·book (chăp/bŏŏk/), *n.* one of a type of small books or pamphlets of popular tales, ballads, etc., such as were formerly hawked about by chapmen.

chape (chāp), *n.* the metal mounting or trimming of a scabbard, esp. at the point. [ME, t. F. See CAP]

cha·peau (shā pō/; *Fr.* shá-), *n., pl.* **-peaux, -peaus** (-pōz/; *Fr.* -pō/). a hat. [t. F, g. L *capellus,* dim. of *capa, cappa.* See CAP]

chapeau bras (brä/), *French.* a small three-cornered hat, formerly in use, which could be folded flat and carried under the arm. [F, f. *chapeau* hat + *bras* arm]

chap·el (chăp/əl), *n.* **1.** a private or subordinate place of prayer or worship; an oratory. **2.** a separately dedicated part of a church, or a small independent churchlike edifice, devoted to special services. **3.** a room or building for worship in a college, royal court, etc. **4.** (in England) a place of worship of a religious body outside of the Established Church. **5.** a separate place of public worship dependent on the church of a parish. **6.** a religious service in a chapel. **7.** a choir or orchestra of a chapel, court, etc. **8.** a print shop or printing house. **9.** the body of printers belonging to a printing house. [ME *chapele,* t. OF, g. LL *cappella* sanctuary for relics (such as the cape of St. Martin), dim. of *capa, cappa.* See CAP]

chap·er·on (shăp/ə rōn/), *n.* **1.** an older person, usually a matron, who, for propriety, attends a young unmarried woman in public or accompanies a party of young unmarried men and women. —*v.t.* **2.** to attend or accompany as chaperon. [t. F: hood, der. *chape* CAPE[1]] —**chap·er·on·age** (shăp/ə rō/nĭj), *n.*

chap·er·one (shăp/ə rōn/), *n., v.,* **-oned, -oning.** chaperon.

chap·fall·en (chŏp/fô/lən, chăp/-), *adj.* dispirited; chagrined; dejected. Also, **chopfallen.**

chap·i·ter (chăp/ə tər), *n.* *Archit.* a capital[2]. [t.F. See CHAPTER]

chap·lain (chăp/lĭn), *n.* **1.** an ecclesiastic attached to the chapel of a royal court, college, etc., or to a military unit. **2.** one who says the prayer, invocation, etc., for an organization or at an assembly or gathering. [ME *chapelayn,* t. OF: m. *chapelain,* g. LL *capellānus,* der. *capella* CHAPEL; r. OE *capellān,* t. LL (as above)] —**chap/lain·cy, chap/lain·ship/,** *n.*

chap·let (chăp/lĭt), *n.* **1.** a wreath or garland for the head. **2.** a string of beads. **3.** *Rom. Cath. Ch.* **a.** a string of beads for counting prayers, one third of the length of a rosary. **b.** the prayers so counted thereon. **4.** *Archit.* a small molding carved in the shape of beads or the like. [ME *chapelet,* t. OF, dim. of *chapel* headdress. See CHAPEAU] —**chap/let·ed,** *adj.*

Chap·lin (chăp/lən), *n.* **Charles Spencer,** born 1889, U.S. screen actor, born in England.

chap·man (chăp/mən), *n., pl.* **-men. 1.** *Brit.* a hawker or peddler. **2.** *Archaic.* a merchant. [ME; OE *cēapman,* f. *cēap* trade + *man* man]

Chap·man (chăp/mən), *n.* **George,** 1559?-1634, British poet, dramatist, and translator.

chaps (chăps, shăps), *n.pl.* *Western U.S.* strong leather riding breeches or overalls, having no seat, worn esp. by cowboys. Also, **chaparajos, chaparejos.** [short for CHAPARAJOS]

chap·ter (chăp/tər), *n.* **1.** a main division, usually numbered, of a book, treatise, or the like. **2.** a branch, usually localized, of a society or fraternity. **3.** *Eccles.* **a.** an assembly of the monks in a monastery, or of those in a province, or of the entire order. **b.** a general assembly of the canons of a church. **c.** a meeting of the elected representatives of the provinces or houses of a religious community. **d.** the body of such canons or representatives collectively. **4.** any general assembly. **5.** *Liturgy.* a short Scriptural quotation read at various parts of the office, as after the last psalm in the service of lauds, prime, tierce, etc. —*v.t.* **6.** to divide into or arrange in chapters. [ME *chapitre,* t. OF, var. of *chapitle,* g. L *capitulum* small head, capital of column, chapter, dim. of *caput* head]

chapter house, 1. *Eccles.* a building, attached to a cathedral or monastery, in which the chapter meets. **2.** the building of a chapter of a society, etc.

Cha·pul·te·pec (chə pul/tə pĕk/; *Sp.* chä pōōl/tĕ pĕk/), *n.* a fortress near Mexico City: famous for resistance to the U.S. forces in the Mexican War, 1847.

cha·que·ta (chäkĕ/tä), *n.* *Spanish.* a heavy jacket, esp. a leather one worn by cowboys. [Sp., t. F: m. *jaquette* jacket, der. *jaque* short garment, of obscure orig.]

char[1] (chär), *v.,* **charred, charring.** —*v.t.* **1.** to burn or reduce to charcoal. **2.** to burn slightly; scorch. —*v.i.* **3.** to become charred. —*n.* **4.** a charred substance. **5.** charcoal. [? short for CHARCOAL] —**char/ry,** *adj.*

char[2] (chär), *n., pl.* **chars,** (*esp. collectively*) **char.** any trout of the genus *Salvelinus,* esp. *S. alpinus* (the common char of Europe). Also, **charr.** [cf. Gaelic *ceara* red]

char[3] (chär), *n., v.,* **charred, charring.** *Chiefly Brit.* —*n.* **1.** a charwoman. **2.** a turn or single piece of work,

esp. household work; an odd job; a chore. —*v.i.* **3.** to do small jobs. **4.** to do housework by the day. —*v.t.* **5.** to do (odd jobs). Also, **chare.** [ME *cherre,* OE *cerr,* *cyrr* turn, time, occasion, affair]

char-à-banc (shăr/ə băng/, -băngk/; *Fr.* shá rá bän/), *n., pl.* **-bancs** (-băngz/, -băngks/; *Fr.* -bän/). *Brit.* a long motor bus with transverse seats, much used in sightseeing. Also, **char/a·banc/.** [t. F: m. *char à bancs* car with benches]

char·a·cin (kăr/ə sĭn), *n.* a fish of the family *Characinidae,* native to Africa or South America, and commonly kept in home aquariums.

char·ac·ter (kăr/ĭk tər), *n.* **1.** the aggregate of qualities that distinguishes one person or thing from others. **2.** one such quality or feature; a characteristic. **3.** moral constitution, as of a person or people. **4.** good moral constitution or status. **5.** reputation. **6.** good repute. **7.** an account of the qualities or peculiarities of a person or thing. **8.** a formal statement from an employer concerning the qualities and habits of a former servant or employee. **9.** status or capacity. **10.** a person: *a good or strange character.* **11.** *Colloq.* an odd person. **12.** a person represented in a drama, story, etc. **13.** *Theat.* a part or role. **14.** *Genetics.* any trait, function, structure, or substance of an organism resulting from the development of a gene interacting with the environment and the remainder of the gene complex; a hereditary characteristic. **15.** a significant visual mark or symbol. **16.** a symbol as used in a writing system, as a letter of the alphabet. **17.** the symbols of a writing system collectively. **18.** a style of writing or printing. **19.** *Obs.* a cipher or cipher message. —*v.t.* **20.** to portray; describe. **21.** *Archaic.* to engrave or inscribe. [t. L, t. Gk.: m. *charaktēr* instrument for marking, mark; r. ME *caractere,* t. F] —**char/ac·ter·less,** *adj.*
—**Syn. 1.** CHARACTER, INDIVIDUALITY, PERSONALITY refer to the sum of the characteristics possessed by a person. CHARACTER refers esp. to moral qualities, ethical standards, principles, and the like: *a man of sterling character.* INDIVIDUALITY refers to the distinctive qualities which make one recognizable as a person differentiated from others: *a man of strong individuality.* PERSONALITY refers particularly to the combination of outer and inner characteristics that determine the impression which one makes upon others: *a man of vivid or pleasing personality.* **5.** See **reputation.**

char·ac·ter·is·tic (kăr/ĭk tə rĭs/tĭk), *adj.* **1.** pertaining to, constituting, or indicating the character or peculiar quality; typical; distinctive. —*n.* **2.** a distinguishing feature or quality. **3.** *Math.* the integral part of a logarithm. —**Syn. 2.** attribute, property, trait, peculiarity. See **feature.**

char·ac·ter·is·ti·cal·ly (kăr/ĭk tə rĭs/tĭk lĭ), *adv.* in a characteristic manner; typically.

char·ac·ter·i·za·tion (kăr/ĭk tə rə zā/shən, -trə zā/-), *n.* **1.** portrayal; description. **2.** act of characterizing. **3.** the creation of fictitious characters.

char·ac·ter·ize (kăr/ĭk tə rīz/), *v.t.,* **-ized, -izing. 1.** to mark or distinguish as a characteristic; be a characteristic of. **2.** to describe the character or peculiar quality of. **3.** to give character to. —**char/ac·ter·iz/er,** *n.*

char·ac·ter·y (kăr/ĭk tə rĭ, -trĭ), *n., pl.* **-teries. 1.** the use of characters or symbols for the expression of meaning. **2.** characters or symbols collectively.

cha·rade (shə rād/; *esp. Brit.* shə räd/), *n.* a parlor game in which a player or players act out in pantomime a word or phrase which the others try to guess. [t. F, t. Pr.: m. *charrado* entertainment, der. *charra* chat]

char·coal (chär/kōl/), *n.* **1.** the carbonaceous material obtained by the imperfect combustion of wood or other organic substances. **2.** a pencil of charcoal for drawing. **3.** a drawing made with such a pencil. —*v.t.* **4.** to blacken, write, or draw with charcoal. [ME *charcole;* orig. uncert.]

charcoal burner, a stove, etc., burning charcoal.

Char·cot (shăr kō/), *n.* **Jean Martin** (zhän mär tăn/), 1825-93, French specialist in nervous diseases.

chard (chärd), *n.* a variety of beet, *Beta vulgaris,* var. *Cicla,* having large leafstalks and midribs which are used as a vegetable (**Swiss chard**). [t. F: m. *charde,* g. L *carduus* thistle, artichoke]

chare (chär), *n., v.,* **chared, charing.** *Chiefly Brit.* char[3].

charge (chärj), *v.,* **charged, charging,** *n.* —*v.t.* **1.** to put a load or burden on or in. **2.** to fill or furnish (a thing) with the quantity, as of powder or fuel, that it is fitted to receive. **3.** to supply with a quantity of electricity or electrical energy: *to charge a storage battery.* **4.** to fill (air, water, etc.) with other matter in a state of diffusion or solution. **5.** to load or burden (the mind, heart, etc.). **6.** to lay a command or injunction upon. **7.** to instruct authoritatively, as a judge does a jury. **8.** to impute as a fault: *charge him with carelessness.* **9.** to lay blame upon; blame; accuse (usually fol. by *with*): *to charge someone with negligence.* **10.** to hold liable for payment; enter a debit against. **11.** to list or record as a debt or obligation; enter as a debit. **12.** to impose or ask as a price: *charge $5 for it.* **13.** to attack by rushing violently against. **14.** *Her.* to place a bearing on (a shield, etc.).
—*v.i.* **15.** to make an onset; rush, as to an attack. **16.** to place the price of a thing to one's debit. **17.** to ask payment. **18.** to make a debit, as in an account. **19.** (of dogs) to lie down at command.
—*n.* **20.** a load or burden. **21.** the quantity of anything

---
b., blend of, blended; c., cognate with; d., dialect, dialectal; der., derived from; f., formed from; g., going back to; m., modification of; r., replacing; s., stem of; t., taken from; ?, perhaps. See the full key on inside cover.

which an apparatus is fitted to hold, or holds, at one time. **22.** a quantity of explosive to be set off at one time. **23.** a duty or responsibility laid upon or entrusted to one. **24.** care, custody, or superintendence: *to have charge of a thing.* **25.** anything or anybody committed to one's care or management. **26.** *Eccles.* a parish or congregation committed to the spiritual care of a pastor. **27.** a command or injunction; exhortation. **28.** an accusation. **29.** *Law.* an address by a judge to a jury at the close of a trial, instructing them as to the legal points, the weight of evidence, etc., affecting their verdict in the case. **30.** expense or cost: *improvements made at a tenant's own charge.* **31.** a sum or price charged: *a charge of 50 cents for admission.* **32.** a pecuniary burden, encumbrance, tax, or lien; cost; expense; liability to pay. **33.** an entry in an account of something due. **34.** an impetuous onset or attack, as of soldiers. **35.** a signal by bugle, drum, etc., for a military charge. **36.** the accumulation of electricity or electrical energy in or upon a piece of equipment. **37.** *Her.* bearing (def. 10). **38.** in charge, a. in command; having supervision. **b.** *Brit.* under arrest by the police. **39. in charge of, a.** having the care or supervision of: *in charge of the class.* **b.** under the care or supervision of: *in charge of the teacher.* [ME *charge(n),* t. OF: m. *charg(i)er,* g. LL *carricāre* load. See CAR]
—**Syn. 6.** enjoin, exhort. **9.** indict, arraign. **28.** indictment, imputation, allegation. **31.** See **price.** **34.** onslaught, assault. —**Ant. 9.** acquit, absolve.

charge·a·ble (chär′jə bəl), *adj.* **1.** that may or should be charged. **2.** liable to be accused or held responsible; indictable. **3.** liable to become a charge on the public.

char·gé d'af·faires (shär zhā′ də fār′; *Fr.* shär-zhě′ dŭ fěr′), *n., pl.* **chargés d'affaires** (shär zhāz′ də-fār′; *Fr.* shär zhě′ dā fěr′). *Govt.* **1.** (in full: **chargé d'affaires ad interim**) an official placed in charge of diplomatic business during the temporary absence of the ambassador or minister. **2.** an envoy to a state to which a diplomat of higher grade is not sent. Also, **char·gé′.** [t. F: lit., entrusted with affairs.]

charg·er[1] (chär′jər), *n.* **1.** one who or that which charges. **2.** a horse intended, or suitable, to be ridden in battle. **3.** *Elect.* an apparatus which charges storage batteries. [f. CHARGE, v. + -ER[1]]

charg·er[2] (chär′jər), *n.* **1.** a platter. **2.** a large, shallow dish for liquids. [ME *chargeour;* akin to CHARGE]

char·i·ly (châr′ə lĭ), *adv.* **1.** carefully; warily. **2.** sparingly. —**Ant. 1.** boldly. **2.** liberally.

char·i·ness (châr′ĭ nĭs), *n.* **1.** chary quality; caution; sparingness. **2.** *Obs.* scrupulous integrity.

Char·ing Cross (chăr′ĭng), a district in central London, England.

char·i·ot (chăr′ĭ ət), *n.* **1.** a two-wheeled vehicle used by the ancients in war, racing, processions, etc. **2.** a light four-wheeled pleasure carriage. **3.** any more or less stately carriage. —*v.t.* **4.** to convey in a chariot. —*v.i.* **5.** to drive a chariot; ride in a chariot. [ME, t. OF, aug. of *chār.* See CAR]

char·i·ot·eer (chăr′ĭ ə tēr′), *n.* **1.** a chariot driver. **2.** (*cap.*) *Astron.* the northern constellation Auriga.

char·i·ta·ble (chăr′ə tə bəl), *adj.* **1.** generous in gifts to relieve the needs of others. **2.** kindly or lenient in judging others. **3.** pertaining to or concerned with charity: *a charitable institution.* [ME, t. OF, der. *charite* CHARITY] —**char′i·ta·ble·ness,** *n.* —**char′i·ta·bly,** *adv.*
—**Syn. 1.** beneficent, liberal, bountiful. **2.** broadminded. —**Ant. 1.** selfish. **2.** severe, intolerant.

char·i·ty (chăr′ə tĭ), *n., pl.* **-ties. 1.** almsgiving; the private or public relief of unfortunate or needy persons; benevolence. **2.** something given to a person or persons in need; alms. **3.** a charitable act or work. **4.** a charitable fund, foundation, or institution. **5.** benevolent feeling, esp. toward those in need. **6.** Christian love. I Cor. 13. [ME *charite,* t. OF, g. s. L *cāritas* dearness]

cha·riv·a·ri (shə rĭv′ə rē′, shĭv′ə rē′, shä′rĭ vä′rĭ), *n., pl.* **-ris.** a mock serenade of discordant noises made with pans, horns, etc. after a wedding. [t. F]

chark (chärk), *n.* **1.** charcoal (def. 1). —*v.t.* **2.** to char; convert into coke. [back formation from CHARCOAL]

char·kha (chär′kə), *n.* (in India and the East Indies) a cotton gin or spinning wheel. Also, **char′ka.** [t. Hind.]

char·la·dy (chär′lā′dĭ), *n., pl.* **-dies.** *Brit.* a charwoman.

char·la·tan (shär′lə tən), *n.* one who pretends to more knowledge or skill than he possesses; a quack. [t. F, t. It.: m. *ciarlatano* der. *ciarlare* chatter] —**char·la·tan·ic** (shär′lə tăn′ĭk), *adj.*

char·la·tan·ism (shär′lə-tə nĭz′əm), *n.* the practices of a charlatan. Also, **char·la·tan·ry** (shär′lə tən rĭ).

Char·le·magne (shär′lə-mān′; *Fr.* shär lə mán′y), *n.* ("*Charles the Great*") A.D. 742–814, king of the Franks, A.D. 768–814: as Charles I, emperor of the Holy Roman Empire, A.D. 800–814.

Char·le·roi (shär lə rwá′), *n.* a city in S Belgium. 28,175 (est. 1944). Also, **Char′le·roy′.**

Charles (chärlz), *n.* **1.** Cape, a cape in E Virginia at

the N side of the entrance to Chesapeake Bay. **2.** a river in E Massachusetts, flowing between Boston and Cambridge to the Atlantic. 47 mi. **3.** (*Prince of Edinburgh*), born 1948, son of Elizabeth II, heir presumptive to the throne of Great Britain.

Charles I (chärlz; *Fr.* shärl), **1.** Charlemagne. **2.** ("*the Bald*") A.D. 823–877, king of France, A.D. 840–877: as Charles II, emperor of the Holy Roman Empire, A.D. 875–877. **3.** 1600–49, king of Great Britain and Ireland from 1625 until executed in 1649 (son of James I). **4.** 1500–58, king of Spain, 1516–66: as Charles V, emperor of the Holy Roman Empire, 1519–1556. **5.** 1887–1922, emperor of Austria: as Charles IV, king of Hungary, 1916–18.

Charles II, 1. See **Charles I** (def. 2). **2.** 1630–85, king of Great Britain and Ireland, 1660–85 (son of Charles I, 1600–49).

Charles IV, 1. ("*Charles the Fair*") 1294–1328, king of France, 1322–28. **2.** See **Charles I** (def. 5).

Charles V, 1. ("*Charles the Wise*") 1337–80, king of France, 1364–80. **2.** See **Charles I** (def. 4).

Charles VI, ("*the Mad*" or "*the Well-Beloved*") 1368–1422, king of France, 1380–1422.

Charles VII, ("*Charles the Victorious*") 1403–61, king of France, 1422–61 (son of Charles VI of France).

Charles IX, 1550–74, king of France, 1560–74.

Charles X, 1757–1836, king of France, 1824–30.

Charles XII, 1682–1718, king of Sweden, 1697–1718.

Charles XIV, John, 1763–1844, king of Sweden and Norway, 1818–44. See **Bernadotte.**

Charles Edward Stuart, ("*the Young Pretender*" or "*Bonnie Prince Charlie*") 1720–88, grandson of James II of Great Britain and Ireland.

Charles Louis, (Ger. *Karl Ludwig Johann*) 1771–1847, archduke of Austria.

Charles Mar·tel (mär tĕl′; *Fr.* mår-), A.D. 690?–741, ruler of the Franks, A.D. 714–741: grandfather of Charlemagne; checked Moorish invasion, A.D. 732.

Charles's Wain (chärl′zĭz wān′), *Brit.* the Big Dipper. See **dipper** (def. 3a). [OE *Carles wægn* Carl's wagon (Carl = Charlemagne)]

Charles the Great, Charlemagne.

Charles·ton (chärlz′tən), *n.* **1.** the capital of West Virginia, in the W part. 73,501 (1950). **2.** a seaport in SE South Carolina. 70,174 (1950). **3.** a kind of fox trot, of Southern Negro origin, popular in the 1920's.

Charles·town (chärlz′toun′), *n.* a former city in E Massachusetts: since 1874 a part of Boston; navy yard; battle of Bunker Hill, June 17, 1775.

char·ley horse (chär′lĭ), *U.S. Colloq.* stiffness of the leg or arm due to excessive muscular use, or injury.

char·lock (chär′lək), *n.* the wild mustard, *Brassica arvensis,* often troublesome as a weed in grainfields. [ME *carlok,* OE *cerlic*]

char·lotte (shär′lət), *n.* a sweet dish (hot or cold) of many varieties, commonly made by lining a mold with cake or bread and filling with fruit or a cream, custard, or gelatin. [t. F, orig., woman's name]

Char·lotte (shär′lət), *n.* a city in S North Carolina. 134,042 (1950).

Char·lot·te A·ma·li·e (shär lŏt′ə ä mä′lĭ ə), a seaport in and the capital of the Virgin Islands (U.S.), on St. Thomas island. 11,463 (prelim. 1950). Formerly, **St. Thomas.**

Char·lot·ten·burg (shär lŏt′ən bûrg′; *Ger.* shär lŏt′ən-bōōrkн′), *n.* a part of Berlin, Germany. 299,955 (1939).

char·lotte russe (shär′lət rōōs′), a mold of sponge cake filled with whipped cream or a similar preparation. [t. F: Russian charlotte]

Char·lottes·ville (shär′ləts vĭl′), *n.* a city in central Virginia. 25,969 (1950).

Char·lotte·town (shär′lət toun′), *n.* the capital of Prince Edward Island, Canada: a seaport. 14,821 (1941).

charm[1] (chärm), *n.* **1.** an irresistible power to please and attract; fascination. **2.** some quality or feature exerting a fascinating influence: *feminine charms.* **3.** something which possesses this power. **4.** a trinket to be worn on a chain, bracelet, etc. **5.** something worn for its supposed magical effect; an amulet. **6.** any action supposed to have magical power. **7.** the chanting or recitation of a magic verse or formula. **8.** a verse or formula credited with magical power. —*v.t.* **9.** to attract powerfully by beauty, etc.; please greatly. **10.** to act upon with or as with a charm; enchant. **11.** to endow with or protect by supernatural powers. —*v.i.* **12.** to be fascinating or pleasing. **13.** to use charms. **14.** to act as a charm. [ME *charme,* t. OF, g. L *carmen* song, incantation] —**charm′er,** *n.* —**Syn. 1.** attractiveness, allurement. **10.** fascinate, captivate, entrance; enrapture, transport, ravish, delight; allure.

charm[2] (chärm), *n.* *Obs.* or *Dial.* blended singing of birds, children, etc. [ME *cherm(e),* OE *cerm, ceorm,* var. of *cierm* outcry. Cf. CHIRM]

char·meuse (shär mœz′), *n.* a soft, flexible variety of satin. [t. F: lit., charmer (fem.)]

charm·ing (chär′mĭng), *adj.* **1.** pleasing; delightful. **2.** exercising magic power. —**charm′ing·ly,** *adv.*

char·nel (chär′nəl), *n.* a repository for dead bodies. [ME, t. OF, g. LL *carnāle,* prop. neut. adj. See CARNAL]

charnel house, a house or place in which the bodies or bones of the dead are deposited.

ăct, āble, dâre, ärt; ĕbb, ēqual; Yf, īce; hŏt, ōver, ôrder, oil, bŏŏk, ōōze, out; ŭp, ūse, ûrge; ə = a in alone; ch, chief; g, give; ng, ring; sh, shoe; th, thin; ŧh, that; zh, vision. See the full key on inside cover.

Char·on (kâr′ən, kăr′-), *n.* **1.** *Class. Myth.* the ferryman who conveyed souls of the dead across the Styx. **2.** (in humorous use) any ferryman.

Char·pen·tier (shár pän tyē′), *n.* **Gustave** (gȳs tȧv′), born 1860, French composer.

char·poy (chär′poi′), *n.* the common light bedstead of India. [t. Hind.: m. *chārpāī*, lit., four-footed, t. Pers.: m. *chahār-pāī*]

char·qui (chär′kY), *n.* jerked meat, esp. beef. [t. Sp., t. Kechua (Peruvian): m. *echarqui*]

charr (chär), *n.*, *pl.* **charrs,** (*esp. collectively*) **charr.** [char².]

chart (chärt), *n.* **1.** a sheet exhibiting information in tabulated or methodical form. **2.** a graphic representation, as by curves, of a dependent variable such as temperature, price, etc. **3.** a map, esp. a hydrographic or marine map. **4.** an outline map showing special conditions or facts: *a weather chart.* —*v.t.* **5.** to make a chart of. **6.** to plan: *to chart a course of action.* [t. F: m. *charte,* g. L *c(h)arta* paper, t. Gk.: m. *chártēs* leaf of paper] —**chart′less,** *adj.* —**Syn. 3.** See **map.**

char·ter (chär′tər), *n.* **1.** the articles or certificate of incorporation taken in connection with the law under which a corporation is organized. **2.** authorization from a central or parent organization to establish a new branch, chapter, etc. **3.** a grant by a sovereign power creating a corporation, as the royal charters granted to British colonies in America. **4.** Also, **charter party.** a contract by which part or all of a ship is leased for a voyage or a stated time. **5.** special privilege or immunity. —*v.t.* **6.** to establish by charter: *to charter a bank.* **7.** to lease or hire by charter. **8.** to hire (a car, etc.). —*adj.* **9.** done or held in accordance with a charter. [ME *chartre,* t. OF, g. L *chartula,* dim. of *charta.* See **chart**] —**char′ter·er,** *n.* —**Syn. 8.** See **hire.**

char·tered accountant (chär′tərd), *n.* (in the British Empire) a member of the institute of accountants granted a royal charter. *Abbr.:* C.A.

charter member, one of the original members of an organization.

Chart·ism (chär′tYz əm), *n.* the principles or movement of a party of political reformers, chiefly workingmen, active in England from 1838 to 1848 (so called from the **People's Charter,** the document which contained their principles and demands). [f. s. L *charta* charter + -ism; pronunciation influenced by *charter*] —**Chart′ist,** *n., adj.*

char·tog·ra·phy (kär tŏg′rə fY), *n.* cartography.

Char·tres (shär′trə; *Fr.* shär′tr), *n.* a city in N France: famous cathedral. 26,422 (1946).

char·treuse (shár trœz′), *n.* **1.** an aromatic liqueur made by the Carthusian monks, at Grenoble, France, and Tarragona, Spain. **2.** (*cap.*) a trademark for this liqueur. **3.** a clear, light green with a yellowish tinge. **4.** a Carthusian monastery. [t. F]

char·tu·lar·y (kär′chŏŏ lĕr′Y), *n., pl.* -**laries.** a register of charters, title deeds, etc. Also, **cartulary.** [t. ML: m. s. *c(h)artulārium,* der. L *c(h)artula.* See **charter**]

char·wom·an (chär′wŏŏm′ən), *n., pl.* -**women.** a woman hired to do chars, or odd jobs of household work, or to do such work by the day. [f. char³ + woman]

char·y (chär′Y), *adj.,* **charier, chariest.** **1.** careful; wary. **2.** shy. **3.** fastidious; choosy. **4.** sparing (often fol. by *of*): *chary of his praise.* [ME *chari,* OE *cearig* sorrowful, der. *caru* care] —**Ant. 1.** trustful. **2.** confident. **3.** uncritical. **4.** lavish.

Cha·ryb·dis (kə rYb′dYs), *n.* *Gk. Legend.* See **Scylla.** —**Cha·ryb′di·an,** *adj.*

chase¹ (chās), *v.,* **chased, chasing.** —*v.t.* **1.** to pursue in order to seize, overtake, etc. **2.** to pursue with intent to capture or kill, as game; hunt. **3.** to drive by pursuing. **4.** to put to flight. —*v.i.* **5.** to follow in pursuit: *to chase after someone.* **6.** *Colloq.* to run or hasten. —*n.* **7.** act of chasing; pursuit. **8.** an object of pursuit; a thing chased. **9.** the occupation or sport of hunting. **10.** *Brit.* an unenclosed tract of privately owned land reserved for animals to be hunted. **11.** *Brit.* the right of keeping game or of hunting on the land of others. **12.** a steeplechase. [ME *chace(n),* t. OF: m. *chacier,* g. L *captiāre* seize. See **catch**]

chase² (chās), *n., v.,* **chased, chasing.** —*n.* **1.** a rectangular iron frame in which composed type, etc., is secured or locked, for printing or plate-making. **2.** a groove, furrow, or trench; a lengthened hollow. **3.** *Ordn.* **a.** the part of a gun in front of the trunnions. **b.** the part containing the bore. —*v.t.* **4.** to groove or indent, so as to make into a screw. **5.** to cut in making a screw head. [t. F: m. *châsse,* g. L *capsa* box]

chase³ (chās), *v.t.,* **chased, chasing.** to ornament (metal) by engraving or embossing. [apheptic var. of **enchase**]

Chase (chās), *n.* **1. Salmon Portland** (săl′mən), 1808–1873, chief justice of the U.S. Supreme Court, 1864–73. **2. Stuart,** born 1888, U.S. economist and writer.

chas·er¹ (chā′sər), *n.* **1.** one who or that which chases or pursues. **2.** *U.S. Colloq.* a drink of water, beer, or other mild beverage taken after a drink of liquor. **3.** Also, **chase gun.** a gun on a vessel esp. for use when in chase or being chased. **4.** a hunter. [f. chase¹ + -er¹]

chas·er² (chā′sər), *n.* a multiple-toothed tool used in cutting screw threads. [f. chase² + -er¹]

chas·er³ (chā′sər), *n.* a person who engraves metal. [f. chase³ + -er¹]

chasm (kăz′əm), *n.* **1.** a yawning fissure or deep cleft in the earth's surface; a gorge. **2.** a breach or wide fissure in a wall or other structure. **3.** a marked interruption of continuity; gap. **4.** a sundering breach in relations: *the chasm of death.* [t. L: m. *chasma,* t. Gk.] —**chas·mal** (kăz′məl), *adj.*

chas·sé (shä sā′; *Colloq.* sä shā′), *n., v.,* **chasséd, chasséing.** *Dancing.* —*n.* **1.** a kind of gliding step in which one foot is kept in advance of the other. —*v.i.* **2.** to execute a chassé. [t. F: lit., chase]

chasse·pot (shäs pō′), *n.* a breechloading rifle, closed with a sliding bolt, introduced into the French army after the war between Austria and Prussia in 1866. [named after A. A. *Chassepot* (1833–1905), the (French) inventor]

chas·seur (shä sûr′; *Fr.* shȧ sœr′), *n.* **1.** (in the French army) one of a body of troops (cavalry or infantry) equipped and trained for rapid movement. **2.** a uniformed footman or attendant; a liveried servant. **3.** a huntsman. [t. F: lit., chaser]

chas·sis (shăs′Y, -Ys, chăs′Y), *n., pl.* **chassis** (shăs′Yz, chăs′-). **1.** *Auto.* the frame, wheels, and machinery of a motor vehicle, on which the body is supported. **2.** *Ordn.* the frame or railway on which a gun carriage moves backward and forward. **3.** the main landing gear of an aircraft; that portion of the landing gear that supports an aircraft. **4.** *Radio.* **a.** the foundation on which the sections of a radio set are mounted. **b.** the collection of various sections of a receiving set mounted on a foundation. [t. F. See **chase²**]

chaste (chāst), *adj.* **1.** pure with respect to unlawful sexual intercourse; virtuous. **2.** free from obscenity; decent. **3.** undefiled or stainless. **4.** pure in style; subdued; simple. **5.** *Obs.* unmarried [ME, t. OF, g. L *castus* pure] —**chaste′ly,** *adv.* —**chaste′ness,** *n.* —**Ant. 1.** immoral. **2.** coarse. **3.** debased. **4.** ornate.

chas·ten (chā′sən), *v.t.* **1.** to inflict suffering upon for purposes of moral improvement; chastise. **2.** to restrain; subdue. **3.** to make chaste in style. [f. obs. *chaste,* v., chasten (t. OF: m. *chastier,* g. L *castigāre*) + -en¹] —**chas′ten·er,** *n.*

chas·tise (chăs tīz′), *v.t.,* **-tised, -tising. 1.** to inflict corporal punishment upon. **2.** *Archaic.* to restrain; chasten. **3.** *Archaic.* to refine; purify. [ME; f. obs. *chaste* chasten + -ise] —**chas·tise·ment** (chăs′tYz mənt, chăs tīz′-), *n.* —**chas·tis′er,** *n.*

chas·ti·ty (chăs′tə tY), *n.* quality of being chaste. [ME *chastete,* t. OF, f. *chaste* chaste + -te -ty²]

chas·u·ble (chăz′yə bəl, chăs′-), *n.* *Eccles.* a sleeveless outer vestment worn by the celebrant at mass. [t. F (r. ME *chesible,* t. OF), g. LL *casubula,* for L *casula* cloak, dim. of *casa* house]

chat (chăt), *v.,* **chatted, chatting,** *n.* —*v.i.* **1.** to converse in a familiar or informal manner. —*n.* **2.** informal conversation. **3.** any of several passerine birds, as the yellow-breasted chat (*Icteria virens*) of the U. S., known for their chattering cries. [short for **chatter**]

cha·teau (shä tō′; *Fr.* shä-), *n., pl.* -**teaux** (-tōz′; *Fr.* -tō′). **1.** a French castle. **2.** a stately residence imitating a French castle. **3.** a country estate, esp. a fine one. [t. F, g. L *castellum*]

Cha·teau·bri·and (shä tō brē äN′), *n.* **François René** (fräN swä′ rə nē′), **Vicomte de,** 1768–1848, French author and statesman.

Châ·teau-Thier·ry (shä tō′ tē′ə rY; *Fr.* shȧ tō tyē rē′), a town in N France, on the Marne river: the scene of heavy fighting, 1918. 7413 (1936).

Château wine, the wine produced from grapes grown at a given vineyard or chateau in the Bordeaux wine region of France.

chat·e·laine (shăt′ə lān′; *Fr.* shät lĕn′), *n.* **1.** the mistress of a castle. **2.** the mistress of an elegant or fashionable household. **3.** a device for suspending keys, trinkets, etc., worn at the waist by women. **4.** a woman's lapel ornament. [t. F. See **castellan**]

Chat·ham (chăt′əm), *n.* **1. 1st Earl of.** See **Pitt, William. 2.** a city in SE England. 40,160 (est. 1946).

Chatham Islands, an island group in the S Pacific, ab. 500 mi. E of and belonging to New Zealand. 372 sq. mi.

cha·toy·ant (shə toi′ənt), *adj.* **1.** changing in luster or color. **2.** *Jewelry.* reflecting a single streak of light when cut in a cabochon. [t. F, ppr. of *chatoyer* change luster like a cat's eye, der. *chat* cat]

Chat·ta·hoo·chee (chăt′ə hōō′chY), *n.* a river flowing from N Georgia S along a part of the boundary between Alabama and Georgia into the Apalachicola river. ab. 500 mi.

Chat·ta·noo·ga (chăt′ə nōō′gə), *n.* a city in SE Tennessee on the Tennessee river: two battles of the Civil War were fought near here, 1863. 131,041 (1950).

chat·tel (chăt′əl), *n.* **1.** a movable article of property. **2.** any article of tangible property other than land, buildings, and other things annexed to land. **3.** a slave. [ME *chatel,* t. OF. See **cattle**] —**Syn. 1.** See **property.**

chattel mortgage, *U.S.* a mortgage on household, movable, or other personal property.

chat·ter (chăt′ər), *v.i.* **1.** to utter a succession of quick, inarticulate, speechlike sounds: *a chattering monkey.* **2.**

[Illustration at right margin]
A, Chasuble;
B, Chalice;
C, Maniple

to talk rapidly and to little purpose; jabber.　3. to make a rapid clicking noise by striking together, as the teeth from cold.　4. *Mach.* to vibrate in cutting, so as to form a series of nicks or notches.　—*v.t.* 5. to utter rapidly or idly.　6. to cause to chatter.　—*n.* 7. idle or foolish talk.　8. act or sound of chattering. [ME; imit.]

chat·ter·box (chăt/ər bŏks/), *n.* a very talkative person.

chat·ter·er (chăt/ər ər), *n.*　1. one who chatters.　2. any member of the tropical American bird family *Cotingidae*, fruit-eating birds of diverse coloration.

chatter mark,　1. a mark left by a tool that has been chattering.　2. one of a series of irregular gouges made on rock surfaces by the slipping of rock fragments held in the lower portion of a glacier.

Chat·ter·ton (chăt/ər ton), *n.* **Thomas,** 1752–70, British poet.

chat·ty (chăt/Y), *adj.,* -**ti·er,** -**ti·est.** given to or full of chat or familiar talk; conversational: *a chatty letter or person.* —**chat/ti·ly,** *adv.* —**chat/ti·ness,** *n.*

Chau·cer (chô/sər), *n.* **Geoffrey** (jĕf/rĭ), 1340?–1400, British poet.

Chau·ce·ri·an (chô sĭr/Y ən), *adj.* 1. of, pertaining to, or characteristic of Chaucer's writings.　—*n.* 2. a scholar devoted to Chaucer.

chauf·fer (chô/fər), *n.* a small, portable stove. [t. F: m. *chauffoir* heater]

chauf·feur (shō/fər, shō fûr/), *n.* the paid and licensed operator of a private motor car. [t. F: stoker, der. *chauffer* heat. See CHAFE]

chaul·moo·gra (chôl mōō/grə), *n.* an East Indian tree of the genus *Taraktogenos* (or *Hydnocarpus*) the seeds of which yield a fixed oil used in the treatment of leprosy and skin diseases. [t. E Ind. (Bengali)]

chaunt (chônt, chänt), *n., v.t., v.i.　Obs.* chant.

chausses (shōs), *n.pl.* medieval armor of mail for the legs and feet. [t. F, der. L *calceus* shoe]

chaus·sure (shō syr/), *n.　French.* a foot covering. [F, der. *chausser* to shoe, g. L *calceāre*]

Chau·tau·qua (shə tô/kwə), *n.*　1. a village in SW New York, on Chautauqua Lake: a summer educational center.　2. the annual Chautauqua assembly.　3. (*often l.c.*) any similar assembly esp. one of a number meeting in a circuit of communities.　—*adj.* 4. pertaining to an institution, or a system of popular education, employing summer schools assembling annually at Chautauqua, N.Y., with courses of home reading and study.　5. (*often l.c.*) pertaining to a chautauqua: *a chautauqua program.*

chau·vin·ism (shō/və nYz/əm), *n.* blind enthusiasm for military glory; zealous and belligerent patriotism or devotion to any cause. [t. F: m. *chauvinisme;* from Nicholas *Chauvin,* an old soldier and overenthusiastic admirer of Napoleon I] —**chau/vin·ist,** *n., adj.* —**chau/vin·is/tic,** *adj.* —**chau/vin·is/ti·cal·ly,** *adv.*

Cha·vannes (shá ván/), *n.* **Puvis de** (py vē/ də). See Puvis de Chavannes.

chaw (chô), *v.t., v.i., n.　Dial.* chew.

chaz·zan (KHä zän/, KHä/zən), *n.* a Jewish cantor. Also, **hazzan.** [t. Heb.: lit., governor, prefect]

Ch.B., (L *Chirurgiae Baccalaureus*) Bachelor of Surgery·

Ch.E., Chemical Engineer. Also, **Che.E.**

cheap (chēp), *adj.*　1. of a relatively low price; at a bargain.　2. costing little labor or trouble.　3. charging low prices: *a very cheap store.*　4. of little account; of small value; mean: *cheap conduct.*　5. embarrassed; sheepish: *feeling cheap about his mistake.*　6. obtainable at a low rate of interest: *when money is cheap.*　7. of decreased value or purchasing power, as currency depreciated due to inflation.　—*adv.* 8. at a low price; at small cost. [ME *cheep* (in phrases, as *greet cheep* cheap, lit., great bargain) OE *cēap,* c. G *kauf* bargain] —**cheap/ly,** *adv.* —**cheap/ness,** *n.*
—**Syn.** 1. CHEAP, INEXPENSIVE agree in their suggestion of low cost. CHEAP now usually suggests shoddiness, inferiority, showy imitation, complete unworthiness, and the like: *a cheap kind of fur.* INEXPENSIVE emphasizes lowness of price and suggests that the value is fully equal to the cost: *an inexpensive dress.* —**Ant.** 1. expensive, dear.

cheap·en (chē/pən), *v.t.*　1. to make cheap or cheaper.　2. to belittle; bring into contempt.　3. *Archaic.* to bargain for.　—*v.i.* 4. to become cheap or cheaper. —**cheap/en·er,** *n.*

Cheap·side (chēp/sīd/), *n.* the central east-and-west thoroughfare of London, England.

cheat (chēt), *n.*　1. a fraud; swindle; deception.　2. a person who cheats or defrauds.　3. *Law.* the fraudulent obtaining of another's property by a false pretense or trick.　4. an impostor.　5. an annual, weedy grass, *Bromus secalinus;* chess.　—*v.t.* 6. to defraud; swindle.　7. to deceive; impose upon.　8. to beguile; elude.　—*v.i.* 9. to practice fraud. [ME *chet(e),* aphetic form of *achet,* var. of ESCHEAT] —**cheat/er,** *n.* —**cheat/ing·ly,** *adv.*
—**Syn.** 1. imposture, artifice, trick, hoax.　2. swindler, trickster, sharper.　6. CHEAT, DECEIVE, TRICK, VICTIMIZE refer to the use of fraud or artifice deliberately to hoodwink someone or to obtain an unfair advantage over him. CHEAT implies conducting matters fraudulently esp. for profit to oneself: *cheat him at cards.* DECEIVE suggests deliberately misleading or deluding, to produce misunderstanding or to prevent someone from knowing the truth: *to deceive one's parents.* To TRICK is to deceive by a stratagem, often of a petty, crafty, or dishonorable kind: *to trick someone into signing a note.* To VICTIMIZE is to make a victim of; the

emotional connotation makes the cheating, deception, or trickery seem particularly dastardly: *to victimize a blind man.*

che·bec (chĭ bĕk/), *n.* the least flycatcher.

check (chĕk), *v.t.*　1. to stop or arrest the motion of suddenly or forcibly.　2. to restrain; hold in restraint or control.　3. to investigate or verify as to correctness.　4. to note (an item, etc.) with a mark, as to indicate examination or correctness (often fol. by *off*).　5. to leave in temporary custody: *check your umbrellas at the door.*　6. to accept for temporary custody: *small parcels checked here.*　7. *U.S.* to send to a destination under the privilege of a passage ticket: *we checked two trunks through to Portland.*　8. *U.S.* to accept for conveyance, and to convey, under the privilege of a passage ticket: *check this trunk to Portland.*　9. to mark in a pattern of checks or squares: *a checked dress.*　10. *Agric.* to plant in check-rows.　11. *Chess.* to place an opponent's king under direct attack.　12. to draw out (money) by checks (fol. by *out*).
—*v.i.* 13. to prove to be right; to correspond accurately: *the reprint checks with the original item for item.*　14. *U.S.* to make an inquiry or investigation for verification, etc. (usually fol. by *up* or *on*): *I'll check up on the matter.*　15. to make a stop; pause.　16. *Chess.* to make a move that puts the opponent's king in check.　17. to crack or split, usually in small checks.　18. *Hunting.* (of dogs) to stop on losing the scent or to verify it.　19. *Falconry.* (of a hawk) to forsake the proper prey and follow baser game (fol. by *at*).　20. *U.S.* to leave and pay for one's quarters at a hotel (fol. by *out*).
—*n.* 21. a person or thing that checks or restrains.　22. in check, under restraint.　23. a sudden arrest or stoppage; repulse; rebuff.　24. control with a view to ascertaining performance or preventing error.　25. a controlled and carefully observed operation or test procedure to determine actual or potential performance.　26. a means or standard to insure against error, fraud, etc.　27. a mark put against an item or the like to indicate that it has been examined or verified.　28. Also, *Brit.,* **cheque.** *Banking.* a written order, usually on a standard printed form, directing a bank to pay money.　29. a slip or ticket showing amount owed for food or beverages consumed, or goods purchased.　30. a token given as a means of identification: *a hat check.*　31. a pattern formed of squares, as on a checkerboard.　32. one of the squares.　33. a fabric having a check pattern.　34. *Chess.* the exposure of the king to direct attack.　35. a counter used in card games; the chip in poker.　36. a small crack.　37. *Masonry.* a rabbet-shaped cutting on the edge of a stone, by which it is fitted to another stone.　—*adj.* 38. serving to check, control, verify, etc.　39. ornamented with a checkered pattern; checkered.
—*interj.* 40. *Chess.* an optional call to warn one's opponent that his king is exposed to direct attack.
[ME *chek,* t. OF: m. *eschec,* b. OF *eschac* check (ult. t. Pers.; see CHECKMATE) and OF *eschiec* booty (t. Gmc.; cf. OHG *scāh*)] —**check/a·ble,** *adj.* —**check/er,** *n.*
—**Syn.** 1. See **stop.**　2. CHECK, CURB, REPRESS, RESTRAIN refer to putting a control on movement, progress, action, etc. CHECK implies arresting suddenly, halting or causing to halt: *to check a movement toward reform.* CURB implies the use of a means such as a chain, strap, frame, wall, etc., to guide or control or to force to stay within definite limits: *to curb a horse.* REPRESS, formerly meaning to suppress, now implies preventing the action or development which might naturally be expected: *to repress evidences of excitement.* RESTRAIN implies the use of force to put under control, or chiefly, to hold back: *to restrain a person from violent acts.*　21. obstacle, obstruction, hindrance, restriction, restraint, curb, damper.　30. ticket, coupon, tag.

check·book (chĕk/bŏŏk/), *n.* a book containing blank checks or orders on a bank.

checked (chĕkt), *adj.*　1. having a pattern of squares; checkered.　2. *Phonet.* situated in a closed syllable.

check·er (chĕk/ər), *n.*　1. one of the pieces used in checkers.　2. a checkered pattern　3. one of the squares of a checkered pattern.　4. the checker tree.　5. its fruit.　—*v.t.* 6. to mark like a checkerboard.　7. to diversify in color; variegate.　8. to diversify in character; subject to alternations. Also, *Brit.,* **chequer.** [ME *cheker,* t. AF: m. *escheker* chessboard, der. *eschec* CHECK]

check·er·ber·ry (chĕk/ər bĕr/Y), *n., pl.* -**ries.**　1. the red fruit of the American wintergreen, *Gaultheria procumbens.*　2. the plant itself.　3. the partridgeberry.

check·er·board (chĕk/ər bôrd/), *n.* a board marked off into sixty-four squares of two alternating colors, on which checkers and chess are played. Also, *Brit.,* **chequerboard.**

check·ered (chĕk/ərd), *adj.*　1. marked by wide or frequent alternations; diversified: *a checkered career.*　2. marked with squares.　3. diversified in color. Also, *Brit.,* **chequered.**

check·ers (chĕk/ərz), *n.* a game played by two persons, each with twelve pieces, on a checkerboard; draughts. Also, *Brit.,* **chequers.**

checker tree, either of the European service trees, *Sorbus domestica* and *S. torminalis.*

check·hook (chĕk/hŏŏk/), *n.* (in a harness) a hook on the saddle for holding the end of the checkrein.

checking account, a bank deposit which is subject to withdrawal by check at any time by the depositor.

check line, = checkrein.

check list, *U.S.* items listed together for convenience of comparison or other checking purposes.

ăct, āble, dâre, ärt; ĕbb, ēqual; Yf, īce; hŏt, ōver, ôrder, oil, bŏŏk, ōōze, out; ŭp, ūse, ûrge; ə ɔ a in alone; ch, chief; g, give; ng, ring; sh, shoe; th, thin; ᵺ, that; zh, vision.　See the full key on inside cover.

check·mate (chĕk′māt′), *n.*, *v.*, **-mated, -mating,** *interj.* —*n.* **1.** *Chess.* **a.** act of putting the opponent's king into an inextricable check, thus bringing the game to a close. **b.** the position of the pieces when a king is checkmated. **2.** defeat; overthrow. —*v.t.* **3.** *Chess.* to put (an opponent's king) into inextricable check. **4.** to check completely; defeat. —*interj.* **5.** *Chess.* the announcing by a player that he has put his opponent's king into inextricable check. [ME *chek mat*, ult. t. Ar.: m. *shāh māt* the king is dead]

check·off (chĕk′ôf′, -ŏf′), *n.* collection of union dues by deduction from each worker's wages, as indicated on the employer's payroll.

check·rein (chĕk′rān′), *n.* **1.** a short rein attached to the saddle of a harness to prevent a horse from lowering its head. See illus. under **harness. 2.** a short rein joining the bit of one of a span of horses to the driving rein of the other.

check·room (chĕk′rōōm′, -rŏŏm′), *n.* a place where hats, coats, parcels, etc. can be left in temporary custody.

check·row (chĕk′rō′), *Agric.* —*n.* **1.** one of a number of rows of trees or plants, esp. corn, in which the distance between adjacent trees or plants is equal to that between adjacent rows. —*v.t.* **2.** to plant in checkrows.

check·up (chĕk′ŭp′), *n.* **1.** an examination or close scrutiny for purposes of verification as to accuracy, comparison, etc. **2.** a comprehensive physical examination.

Ched·dar cheese (chĕd′ər), American cheese. Also, **ched′dar.**

chedd·ite (chĕd′īt, shĕd′īt), *n.* an explosive used for blasting made up of a chlorate or perchlorate mixture with a fatty substance, such as castor oil. [t. F: f. *Chedde* place name (of Savoy) + -*ite* -ITE¹]

cheek (chēk), *n.* **1.** either side of the face below eye level. **2.** the side wall of the mouth between the upper and lower jaws. **3.** something resembling the human cheek in form or position, as either of two parts forming corresponding sides of a thing. **4.** *Colloq.* impudence or effrontery. —*v.t.* **5.** *Brit. Colloq.* to address or confront with impudence or effrontery. [ME *cheke*, OE *cēce*, c. D *kaak*]

cheek·bone (chēk′bōn′), *n.* the bone or bony prominence below the outer angle of the eye.

cheek by jowl, side by side; in close intimacy.

cheek pouch, a bag in the cheek of certain animals, as squirrels, for carrying food.

cheek·y (chē′kĭ), *adj.*, **cheekier, cheekiest.** *Colloq.* impudent; insolent: *a cheeky fellow, cheeky behavior.* —**cheek′i·ly,** *adv.* —**cheek′i·ness,** *n.*

cheep (chēp), *n.* **1.** to chirp; peep. —*v.t.* **2.** to express by cheeps. —*n.* **3.** a chirp. [imit.] —**cheep′er,** *n.*

cheer (chĭr), *n.* **1.** a shout of encouragement, approval, congratulation, etc. **2.** that which gives joy or gladness; encouragement; comfort. **3.** state of feeling or spirits: *what cheer?* **4.** gladness, gaiety, or animation: *to make cheer.* **5.** food; provisions. **6.** *Archaic.* expression of countenance. —*v.t.* **7.** to salute with shouts of approval, congratulation, etc. **8.** to inspire with cheer; gladden (often fol. by *up*). **9.** to encourage or incite. —*v.i.* **10.** to utter cheers of approval, etc. **11.** to become cheerful (often fol. by *up*). **12.** *Obs.* to be in a particular state of spirits. [ME *chere*, t. OF: face, g. LL *cara*] —**cheer′er,** *n.* —**cheer′ing·ly,** *adv.*
—**Syn. 8.** CHEER, GLADDEN, ENLIVEN mean to make happy or lively. To CHEER is to comfort, to restore hope and cheerfulness to (now often CHEER UP, when thoroughness, a definite time, or a particular point in the action is referred to): (Cf. *eat up, drink up, hurry up*): *to cheer a sick person; soon cheered him up.* To GLADDEN does not imply a state of sadness to begin with, but suggests bringing pleasure or happiness to someone: *to gladden some one's heart with good news.* ENLIVEN suggests bringing vivacity and liveliness: *to enliven a dull evening, a party.* **9.** exhilarate, animate. **10.** shout, applaud, acclaim. —**Ant. 8.** depress. **9.** discourage.

cheer·ful (chĭr′fəl), *adj.* **1.** full of cheer; in good spirits: *a cheerful person.* **2.** promoting cheer; pleasant; bright: *cheerful surroundings.* **3.** arising from good spirits or cheerfulness: *cheerful song.* **4.** hearty or ungrudging: *cheerful giving.* —**cheer′ful·ly,** *adv.* —**cheer′ful·ness,** *n.* —**Syn. 1.** cheery, gay, blithe.

cheer·i·o (chĭr′ĭō′), *interj.*, *n.*, *pl.* **-os.** *Chiefly Brit. Colloq.* **1.** hello. **2.** good-by.

cheer·less (chĭr′lĭs), *adj.* without cheer; joyless; gloomy. —**cheer′less·ly,** *adv.* —**cheer′less·ness,** *n.*

cheer·ly (chĭr′lĭ), *adv.* cheerfully.

cheer·y (chĭr′ĭ), *adj.*, **cheerier, cheeriest. 1.** in good spirits; blithe; gay. **2.** promoting cheer; enlivening. —**cheer′i·ly,** *adv.* —**cheer′i·ness,** *n.*

cheese¹ (chēz), *n.* **1.** the curd of milk separated from the whey and prepared in many ways as a food. **2.** a cake or definite mass of this substance. **3.** something of similar shape or consistence, as a mass of pomace in cider making. **4.** a low curtsy. [ME *chese*, OE *cēse*, c. G *käse*, ult. t. L: m. *cāseus*]

cheese² (chēz), *v.t.*, **cheesed, cheesing.** *Slang.* to stop; leave off, esp. in the exclamation **cheese it!**, look out! run away! [alter. of CEASE]

cheese³ (chēz), *n.* *Slang.* the correct or proper thing. [prob. t. Pers., Hind.: m. *chīz* thing]

cheese cake, a kind of cake or open pie filled with a custardlike preparation containing cheese.

cheese·cloth (chēz′klôth′, -klŏth′), *n.* a coarse cotton fabric of open texture, orig. used for wrapping cheese.

cheese·par·ing (chēz′pâr′ĭng), *adj.* **1.** meanly economical; parsimonious. —*n.* **2.** something of little or no value. **3.** niggardly economy.

chees·y (chē′zĭ), *adj.*, **cheesier, cheesiest. 1.** like cheese: *cheesy taste or consistency.* **2.** *U.S. Slang.* of poor quality. —**chees′i·ness,** *n.*

chee·tah (chē′tə), *n.* an animal of the cat family, *Acinonyx jubatus*, of southwestern Asia and Africa, resembling the leopard but having certain doglike characteristics, often trained for hunting deer, etc. Also, **chetah.** [t. Hind.: m. *chītā*]

Cheetah, *Acinonyx jubatus*
(Total length ab. 7 ft., tail 2½ ft., 2½ ft. high at the shoulder)

chef (shĕf), *n.* a cook, esp. a head cook. [t. F. See CHIEF]

chef-d'oeu·vre (shĕ dœ′vr), *n.*, *pl.* **chefs-d'oeuvre** (shĕ dœ′vr). *French.* a masterpiece, esp. of an author, painter, etc.

Che·foo (chē′fōō′), *n.* a seaport in NE China, in Shantung province. 131,659 (est. 1931).

cheiro-, var. of chiro-.

Che·ka (chĕ′kä), *n.* (formerly) the special commission in the Soviet Union for protection against counterrevolution; a secret police. The name later was changed to OGPU. [t. Russ.: f. *che* + *ka*, names of the initials of the *chrezvychainaya komissiya* extraordinary commission]

Che·khov (chĕk′ôf, -ŏf; *Russ.* chĕ′hôf), *n.* **Anton Pavlovich** (än tôn′ pä vlô′vĭch), 1860–1904, Russian short-story writer and dramatist. Also, **Tchekhoff.**

Che·kiang (chĕ′kyäng′; *Chin.* jŭ′jyäng′), *n.* a province in E China. 21,762,200 pop. (est. 1944); 39,474 sq. mi.

che·la¹ (kē′lə), *n.*, *pl.* **-lae** (-lē). the nipperlike organ or claw terminating certain limbs of crustaceans and arachnids. [t. NL, t. Gk.: m. *chēlē* claw]

che·la² (chā′lä), *n.* (in India) a disciple of a religious teacher. [t. Hind.: m. *chēlā*, disciple]

Chela of lobster

che·late (kē′lāt), *adj.* *Zool.* having a chela.

che·lif·er·ous (kĭ lĭf′ər əs), *adj.* bearing chelae.

che·li·form (kē′lə fôrm′), *adj.* nipperlike.

che·loid (kē′loid), *n.* *Pathol.* keloid.

che·lo·ni·an (kĭ lō′nĭ ən), *adj.* **1.** of or belonging to the *Chelonia*, an order or group of reptiles comprising the turtles. —*n.* **2.** a turtle. [f. s. NL *Chelonia*, pl. (cf. Gk. *chelōnē* tortoise) + -AN]

Chel·sea (chĕl′sĭ), *n.* **1.** a borough in SW London, England: artists' and writers' section. 47,450 (est. 1946). **2.** a city in E Massachusetts, near Boston. 38,912 (1950).

Chel·ten·ham (chĕlt′nəm), *n.* **1.** a city in W England. 61,320 (est. 1946). **2.** *Print.* a style of type.

Chel·ya·binsk (chĕl yä′bĭnsk), *n.* a city in the W Soviet Union in Asia, in the Ural area. 273,127 (1939).

Chel·yus·kin (chĕl yŏŏs′kĭn), *n.* **Cape,** a cape in the N Soviet Union in Asia, on Taimyr Peninsula: the northernmost point of Asia.

chem-, var. of chemo-, used before vowels, as in *chemism.*

chem., **1.** chemical. **2.** chemist. **3.** chemistry.

chem·ic (kĕm′ĭk), *adj.* **1.** alchemic. **2.** chemical. [short for ALCHEMIC]

chem·i·cal (kĕm′ə kəl), *adj.* **1.** of or concerned with the science or the operations or processes of chemistry. —*n.* **2.** a substance produced by or used in a chemical process. —**chem′i·cal·ly,** *adv.*

chemical engineering, the science or profession of chemistry applied to industrial processes.

chemical warfare, warfare with asphyxiating, poisonous, and corrosive gases, oil flames, etc.

chem·i·lum·i·nes·cence (kĕm′ə lŏŏ′mə nĕs′əns), *n.* (in chemical reactions) the production of light at low temperatures.

che·min de fer (shə măn′ də fĕr′), *French.* **1.** a railroad. **2.** a variation of baccarat.

che·mise (shə mēz′), *n.* a woman's loose-fitting shirtlike undergarment. [t. F, g. LL *camisia* shirt (prob. t. Celtic); r. ME *kemes*, OE *cemes*, t. LL: m. *camisia*]

chem·i·sette (shĕm′ə zĕt′), *n.* a woman's garment of linen, lace, etc., worn with a low-cut or open bodice to cover the neck and breast. [t. F, dim. of *chemise*]

chem·ism (kĕm′ĭz əm), *n.* chemical action.

chem·ist (kĕm′ĭst), *n.* **1.** one versed in chemistry or professionally engaged in chemical operations. **2.** *Brit.* druggist. **3.** *Obs.* alchemist. [var. of ALCHEMIST]

chem·is·try (kĕm′ĭs trĭ), *n.*, *pl.* **-tries. 1.** the science that treats of or investigates the composition of substances and various elementary forms of matter (**chemical elements**). **2.** chemical properties, reactions, etc.: *the chemistry of carbon.* [f. CHEMIST + -RY]

Chem·nitz (kĕm′nĭts), *n.* a city in E Germany, in Saxony. 337,657 (1939).

chemo-, a word element representing chemic or chemical. Also, **chem-.**

chem·o·syn·the·sis (kĕm′ō sĭn′thə sĭs), *n.* *Bot.* production by plants of nutritive substances from carbon dioxide and water with energy derived from other chemical reactions.

---

chem·o·tax·is (kĕm/ō tăk/sĭs), *n. Biol.* the property in a cell or organism of exhibiting attraction or repulsion to chemical substances.

chem·o·ther·a·peu·tics (kĕm/ō thĕr/ə pū/tĭks), *n. Med.* chemotherapy. —**chem/o·ther/a·peu/tic,** *adj.*

chem·o·ther·a·py (kĕm/ō thĕr/ə pĭ), *n. Med.* the treatment of disease by means of chemicals which have a specific toxic effect upon the disease-producing micro-organisms. —**chem/o·ther/a·pist,** *n.*

che·mot·ro·pism (kĭ mŏt/rə pĭz/əm), *n. Bot., Zool.* the property in plant and other organisms of turning or bending (toward or away), as by unequal growth, in response to the presence of chemical substances.

Che·mul·po (chĕ/mŏŏl pō/), *n.* a seaport in W Korea. 117,098 (est. 1939). Japanese, **Jinsen.**

chem·ur·gy (kĕm/ûr jĭ), *n.* a division of applied chemistry concerned with the industrial use of organic substances, esp. from farm produce, as soybeans, peanuts, etc. —**chem·ur/gic, chem·ur/gi·cal,** *adj.*

Che·nab (chĭ năb/), *n.* a river flowing through S Kashmir and SW through Pakistan to the Sutlej river in W Punjab.

Cheng·teh (chŭng/dŭ/), *n.* a city in NE China: the capital of Jehol province; the former summer residence of the Manchu emperors. 162,195 (est. 1931). Also, **Jehol.**

Cheng·tu (chŭng/dōō/), *n.* a walled city in central China, the capital of Szechwan. 315,000 (est. 1939).

che·nille (shə nēl/), *n.* **1.** a velvety cord of silk or worsted, used in embroidery, fringe, etc. **2.** fabric made with a fringed silken thread used as the weft in combination with wool or cotton. [t. F: caterpillar, g. L *canicula* little dog]

che·no·pod (kē/nə pŏd/, kĕn/ə-), *n.* any plant of the genus *Chenopodium* or the family *Chenopodiaceae.* [f. *cheno-* (comb. form repr. Gk. *chēn* goose) + -POD]

che·no·po·di·a·ceous (kē/nə pō/dĭ ā/shəs, kĕn/ə-), *adj. Bot.* belonging to the *Chenopodiaceae,* or goosefoot family of plants, which includes the beet and mangel-wurzel, spinach, and orach, also many species peculiar to saline, alkaline, or desert regions. [f. s. NL *Chenopodium* (see CHENOPOD) + -ACEOUS]

Che·ops (kē/ŏps), *n.* fl. c3900 or c3700 or c2700 B.C., king of Egypt, of 4th dynasty: builder of great pyramid at Elgiza. Also, **Khufu.**

cheque (chĕk), *n. Brit.* check (def. 28).

cheq·uer (chĕk/ər), *n. Brit.* checker.

cheq·uer·board (chĕk/ər bôrd/), *n. Brit.* checkerboard.

cheq·uered (chĕk/ərd), *adj. Brit.* checkered.

cheq·uers (chĕk/ərz), *n. Brit.* checkers.

Cher (shĕr), *n.* a river in central France, flowing NW to the Loire river. ab. 220 mi.

Cher·bourg (shâr/bŏŏrg; *Fr.* shĕr bōōr/), *n.* a fortified seaport in NW France: taken by U.S. forces, June, 1944. 39,760 (1946).

cher·chez la femme (shĕr shĕ/ là fàm/), *French* search for the woman.

cher·ish (chĕr/ĭsh), *v.t.* **1.** to hold or treat as dear. **2.** to care for tenderly; nurture. **3.** to cling fondly to (ideas, etc.): *cherishing no resentment.* [ME *cherische(n),* t. F: m. *chĕriss-,* s. *chĕrir,* der. *cher* dear, g. L *cārus*] —**cher/ish·er,** *n.* **cher/ish·ing·ly,** *adv.*
—**Syn. 1.** CHERISH, FOSTER, HARBOR imply giving affection, care, or shelter to something. CHERISH suggests regarding or treating something as an object of affection or as valuable: *to cherish a memory or a friendship.* FOSTER implies sustaining and nourishing something with care, esp. in order to promote, increase, or strengthen it: *to foster a hope, enmity, crime.* HARBOR suggests giving shelter to or entertaining something undesirable, esp. evil thoughts or intentions: *to harbor malice or a grudge.* —**Ant. 2.** neglect. **3.** relinquish.

Cher·no·vi·tsy (chĕr/nō vĭ tsĭ), *n.* Russian name of Cernăuti.

cher·no·zem (chĕr/nō zĕm/), *n.* the normal soil of subhumid grasslands, having a deep, rich, black topsoil and a lower layer of lime accumulation. [t. Russ.]

Cher·o·kee (chĕr/ə kē/, chĕr/ə kē/), *n., pl.* **-kee, -kees.** **1.** a member of an important tribe of North American Indians of Iroquoian family whose first known center was in the southern Alleghenies, and whose present center is Oklahoma. **2.** an Iroquoian language.

Cherokee rose, a smooth-stemmed white rose, *Rosa laevigata,* of Chinese origin, cultivated in the southern U. S.

che·root (shə rōōt/), *n.* a cigar having open, unpointed ends. [t. F: m. *chĕroute,* t. Tamil: m. *shuruttu* a roll]

cher·ry (chĕr/ĭ), *n., pl.* **-ries,** *adj.* —*n.* **1.** the fruit of any of various trees of the genus *Prunus,* consisting of a pulpy, globular drupe enclosing a one-seeded smooth stone. **2.** the tree itself. **3.** its wood. **4.** any of various fruits or plants resembling the cherry. **5.** bright red; cerise. —*adj.* **6.** bright-red; cerise. **7.** made of the wood of the cherry tree. [ME *chery, chiri,* back formation from OE *ciris* (the *-s* being taken for plural sign), t. VL: m. **ceresia,* der. L *cerasus* cherry tree, t. Gk.: m. *kerasós.* Cf. F *cerise,* ONF *cherise,* etc., g. VL (as above)]

cherry stone, the clam, *Venus mercenaria,* when larger than a littleneck.

cher·so·nese (kûr/sə nēz/, -nēs/), *n.* **1.** a peninsula. **2. the Chersonese,** Gallipoli Peninsula. [t. L: m.s. *chersonēsus,* t. Gk.: m. *chersónēsos*]

chert (chûrt), *n.* a compact rock consisting essentially of cryptocrystalline quartz. —**chert/y,** *adj.*

cher·ub (chĕr/əb), *n., pl.* **cherubs** for 3, 4; **cherubim** (chĕr/ə bĭm, -yŏō bĭm) for 1, 2. **1.** *Bible.* a kind of celestial being. Gen. 3:24; Ezek. 1 and 10. **2.** *Theol.* a member of the second order of angels, distinguished by knowledge, often represented as a beautiful winged child or as a winged head of a child. **3.** a beautiful or innocent person, esp. a child. **4.** a person with a chubby, innocent face. [ME and OE *cherubin,* pl., ult. t. Heb.: m. *kerūb* sing., *karubĭm,* pl.] —**che·ru·bic** (chə rōō/bĭk), *adj.* —**che·ru/bi·cal·ly,** *adv.*

Che·ru·bi·ni (kĕ/rōō bē/nē), *n.* **Maria Luigi Carlo Zenobio Salvatore** (mä rē/ā lōō ē/jē kär/lō dze nō/byō säl/vä tō/rĕ), 1760–1842, Italian composer in France.

cher·vil (chûr/vĭl), *n.* **1.** a herbaceous plant, *Anthriscus Cerefolium,* of the parsley family, with aromatic leaves used to flavor soups, salads, etc. **2.** any of various plants of the same genus or allied genera. [ME *chervelle,* OE *cerfille,* t. L: m. s. *caerephylla,* pl. of *caerephyllum,* t. Gk.: m. *chairéphyllon*]

cher·vo·nets (chĕr vô/nĭts, -nĕts), *n., pl.* **-vontsi** (-vônt/sĭ). the gold unit of the U.S.S.R. monetary system, equal to ten rubles, or about $8.72. [t. Russ.]

Ches·a·peake Bay (chĕs/ə pēk/), a large inlet of the Atlantic, in Maryland and Virginia. ab. 200 mi. long; 4-40 mi. wide.

Chesh·ire (chĕsh/ər, -ĭr), *n.* a county in W England. 1,182,000 pop. (est. 1946); 1015 sq. mi. *Co. seat:* Chester. Also, **Chester.**

Cheshire cat, a constantly grinning cat, in *Alice in Wonderland,* named from the old simile "to grin like a Cheshire cat."

chess¹ (chĕs), *n.* a game played by two persons, each with sixteen pieces, on a checkerboard. [ME, t. OF: aphetic m. *esches, eschecs,* pl. See CHECK]

chess² (chĕs), *n., pl.* **chess, chesses.** one of the planks forming the roadway of a floating bridge. [orig. uncert.]

chess³ (chĕs), *n.* cheat (def. 5). [orig. uncert.]

chess·board (chĕs/bôrd/), *n.* the board, identical with a checkerboard, used for playing chess.

chess·man (chĕs/măn/, -mən), *n., pl.* **-men** (-mĕn/, -mən). one of the pieces used in the game of chess.

chest (chĕst), *n.* **1.** the trunk of the body from the neck to the belly; the thorax. **2.** a box, usually a large, strong one, for the safekeeping of valuables. **3.** the place where the funds of a public institution, etc., are kept. **4.** the funds themselves. **5.** a box in which certain goods, as tea, are packed for transit. **6.** the quantity contained in such a box. **7.** chest of drawers. [ME; OE *cest, cist,* t. L: s. *cista,* t. Gk.: m. *kĭstē* box]

Ches·ter (chĕs/tər), *n.* **1.** a city in SE Pennsylvania. 66,039 (1950). **2.** a walled city in W England. 47,130 (est. 1946). **3.** Cheshire.

Ches·ter·field (chĕs/tər fēld/), *n.* **1.** Philip Dormer Stanhope (dôr/mər stăn/ŏp), 4th Earl of, 1694–1773, British statesman and author. **2.** (*l.c.*) an overcoat, usually single-breasted, with concealed buttons. **3.** (*l.c.*) a sofa or divan with a back and arms.

Ches·ter·field·i·an (chĕs/tər fēl/dĭ ən), *adj.* like the Earl of Chesterfield; lordly; elegant; cold; suave.

Ches·ter·ton (chĕs/tər tən), *n.* Gilbert Keith, 1874–1936, British essayist, critic, and novelist.

Chester White, one of an early-maturing white breed of hog which originated in Chester county, Pennsylvania.

chest·nut (chĕs/nŭt/, -nət), *n.* **1.** the edible nut of trees of the genus *Castanea,* of the beech family. **2.** any of the trees, as *C. sativa* (**European chestnut**), *C. dentata* (**American chestnut**), or *C. crenata* (**Japanese chestnut**). **3.** the wood. **4.** any of various fruits or trees resembling the chestnut, as the horse chestnut. **5.** reddish brown. **6.** *Colloq.* an old or stale joke, anecdote, etc. **7.** the callosity on the inner side of a horse's leg. —*adj.* **8.** reddish-brown. **9.** (in England, of horses) sorrel. [f. obs. *chesten* chestnut (ME; OE *cisten-,* var. of **cesten,* g. WGmc. **kastinia,* t. L: m. *castanea,* t. Gk.: m. *kastanĕa*) + NUT; r. ME *chasteine,* t. OF]

chest of drawers, *Chiefly Brit.* a piece of furniture consisting of a set of drawers fitted into a frame, used for clothing, linen, etc. Cf. U.S. **bureau or dresser.**

chest-on-chest (chĕst/ŏn chĕst/), *n.* a chest of drawers placed upon a slightly wider chest of drawers, usually having feet.

chest·y (chĕs/tĭ), *adj.,* **chestier, chestiest.** *Slang.* proud; conceited.

che·tah (chē/tə), *n.* cheetah.

che·val-de-frise (shə văl/ də frēz/), *n., pl.* **chevaux-de-frise** (shə vō/ də frēz/). (*usually pl.*) an obstacle of projecting spikes or barbed wire used to close a gap to the enemy. [t. F: lit., horse of Friesland]

che·val glass (shə văl/), a full-length mirror mounted so as to swing in a frame. [*cheval,* t. F: support, horse]

chev·a·lier (shĕv/ə lĭr/), *n.* **1.** a member of certain orders of honor or merit: *a chevalier of the Legion of Honor.* **2.** a knight. **3.** *French Hist.* **a.** the lowest title of rank in the old nobility. **b.** a cadet of the old nobility. **4.** a chivalrous man. [ME *chevalere,* t. OF: m. *chevalier,* der. *cheval* horse, g. L *caballus.* See CAVALIER]

Chev·i·ot (chĕv/ĭ ət, chē/vĭ-; commonly shĕv/ĭ ət for 2), *n.* **1.** a breed of sheep valued for their thick wool (so called from the Cheviot Hills). **2.** (*l.c.*) a worsted fabric in a coarse twill weave, used for coats, suits, etc.

Cheviot Hills, a range of hills on the boundary between England and Scotland. Highest point, 2676 ft.

chev·ron (shĕv′rən), *n.* **1.** a badge consisting of stripes meeting at an angle, worn on the sleeve (by noncommissioned officers, policemen, etc.) as an indication of rank, of service, wounds in war, etc. **2.** *Her.* the lower half of a bend and a bend sinister meeting at the center of the shield, like an inverted V. **3.** a similar decoration, as in an architectural molding. [t. F: rafter, chevron, der. F *chèvre* goat, g. L *caper*]

Chevrons, U.S. Army A. Sergeant; B. Master Sergeant; C. Private, first class

chev·ro·tain (shĕv′rətān′, -tĭn), *n.* any of the very small deerlike ruminants, family *Tragulidae*, of the genera *Tragulus*, of Asia, and *Hyemoschus*, of Africa. [t. F, dim. of OF *chevrot* kid, dim. of *chèvre* she-goat]

chev·y (chĕv′ĭ), *v.t., v.i.,* **chevied, chevying,** *n., pl.* **chevies.** *Brit.* chivvy.

Chevy Chase. See Otterburn.

chew (cho͞o), *v.t.* **1.** to crush or grind with the teeth; masticate. **2.** to meditate on; consider deliberately. —*v.i.* **3.** to perform the act of crushing or grinding with the teeth. **4.** *Colloq.* to use tobacco for chewing. **5.** to meditate. —*n.* **6.** act of chewing. **7.** that which is chewed; a portion, as of tobacco, for chewing. [ME *chewen,* OE *cēowan,* akin to G *kauen*] —**chew′er,** *n.*

chew·ing gum (cho͞o′ĭng), a preparation for chewing, usually made of sweetened and flavored chicle.

che·wink (chĭ·wĭngk′), *n.* a bird, *Pipilo erythrophthalmus,* of the finch family, common in eastern North America; towhee. [imit. of its note]

Chey·enne (shĭ·ĕn′), *n.* the capital of Wyoming, in the SE part. 31,935 (1950).

Chey·enne (shĭ·ĕn′), *n., pl.* **-enne, -ennes. 1.** a Plains tribe of the Algonquian linguistic family, formerly in central Minnesota, later in North and South Dakota; now divided between Montana (Northern Cheyenne) and Oklahoma (Southern Cheyenne). **2.** a member of this tribe. [t. Dakota Sioux: m. *shahi′yena, shai-ena,* or t. Teton Sioux: m. *shai·ela* people of alien speech, der. *sha′ia* speak a strange tongue]

Cheyenne River, a river flowing from E Wyoming NE to the Missouri in central South Dakota. ab. 360 mi.

Chey·ne (chā′nĭ, chān), *n.* **Thomas Kelly,** 1841–1915, British clergyman and Biblical scholar.

chg., *pl.* **chgs.** charge.

chi (kī), *n.* the twenty-second letter (X, χ, = English *ch* or *kh*) of the Greek alphabet.

Chi·an (kī′ən), *adj.* **1.** of or pertaining to Chios. —*n.* **2.** a native or inhabitant of Chios.

Chiang Kai-shek (chyäng′ kī′shĕk′), born 1886, commander in chief of the Chinese armed services: president of China, 1943–1949 and since March, 1950.

Chi·an·ti (kǐ·än′tǐ; *It.* kē·än′tē), *n.* a dry, red, full-bodied Italian table wine, usually bottled in a colorful straw-covered bottle. [named after the *Chianti* Mountains in Tuscany]

Chi·a·pas (chē·ä′päs), *n.* a state in S Mexico. 679,885 pop. (1940); 28,732 sq. mi. *Cap.:* Tuxtla Gutiérrez.

chi·a·ro·scu·ro (kǐ·är′ə·skyo͝or′ō), *n., pl.* **-ros. 1.** the treatment or general distribution of light and shade in a picture. **2.** pictorial art employing only light and shade. **3.** a sketch in light and shade. Also, **chi·a·ro·o·scu·ro** (kǐ·är′ə·ō·skyo͝or′ō). [t. It.: clear-dark] —**chi·a′ro·scu′rist,** *n.*

chi·asm (kī′ăzəm), *n. Anat.* a crossing or decussation, esp. that of the optic nerves at the base of the brain.

chi·as·ma (kǐ·ăz′mə), *n., pl.* **-mata** (-mətə). *Biol.* a crossing point in conjugating chromosomes. [t. NL, t. Gk.: arrangement in the form of the Greek letter *chi* (X)] —**chi·as′mal, chi·as′mic,** *adj.*

chi·as·ma·typ·y (kǐ·ăz′mə·tī′pǐ), *n. Biol., Genetics.* the crossing over of segments of allelomorphic chromosomes during synapsis, with possible interchange of factors. —**chi·as′ma·type′,** *adj., n.*

Chi·ba (chē′bä′), *n.* a city in central Japan, on Honshu island, near Tokyo. 106,420 (1946).

Chib·cha (chĭb′chə), *n.* **1.** an extinct tribe of civilized South American Indians, formerly living in a high plateau of Bogotá, Colombia. **2.** a member of this tribe.

Chib·chan (chĭb′chən), *n.* a South American Indian speech family including the Chibcha and other tribes of Colombia.

chi·bouk (chǐ·bo͞ok′, -bo͝ok′), *n.* a Turkish tobacco pipe with a long, stiff stem (sometimes 4 or 5 feet long). Also, **chi·bouque′.** [t. Turk.: m. *chībūq*]

chic (shēk, shǐk), *adj.* **1.** cleverly attractive in style; stylish. —*n.* **2.** style; cleverly attractive style, esp. in dress. [t. F, ? der. *chicane* CHICANE]

Chi·ca·go (shǐ·kô′gō, -kä′-), *n.* a city in NE Illinois; a port on Lake Michigan; the second largest city in the U.S. 3,620,962; with suburbs, 5,475,535 (1950). —**Chi·ca′go·an,** *n.*

Chicago Heights, a city in NE Illinois, S of Chicago. 24,551 (1950).

chi·ca·lo·te (chē′kä·lō′tĕ), *n.* any of several prickly papaveraceous plants of arid tropical and subtropical America, as *Argemone mexicana* and *A. platyceras.* [Mex. Sp., t. Nahuatl: m. *chicalotl*]

chi·cane (shǐ·kān′), *n., v., -caned, -caning.* —*n.* **1.** chicanery. **2.** *Bridge.* a hand without trumps. —*v.i.*

3. to use chicanery. —*v.t.* **4.** to trick by chicanery. **5.** to quibble over; cavil at. [t. F, der. *chicaner* quibble, ? t. MLG: m. *schikken* arrange] —**chi·can′er,** *n.*

chi·can·er·y (shǐ·kā′nər·ǐ), *n., pl.* **-eries. 1.** trickery, quibbling, or sophistry. **2.** a quibble or subterfuge.

chic·co·ry (chǐk′ə·rǐ), *n., pl.* **-ries.** chicory.

Chi·chen It·zá (chē·chĕn′ ēt·sä′), the ruins of an ancient Mayan city, in central Yucatán state, Mexico.

chi·chi (shē′shē′), *adj.* pretentiously elegant, sophisticated, or stylish.

chick (chǐk), *n.* **1.** a young chicken or other bird. **2.** a child. **3.** *U.S. Slang.* a young girl.

chick·a·dee (chǐk′ə·dē′), *n.* any of several North American birds of the family *Paridae,* esp. the black-capped titmouse, *Parus atricapillus.* [imit. of cry]

Chick·a·mau·ga (chǐk′ə·mô′gə), *n.* a creek in NW Georgia: scene of a Confederate victory, 1863.

chick·a·ree (chǐk′ə·rē′), *n.* the red squirrel, *Sciurus hudsonius,* of North America. [imit. of cry]

Chick·a·saw (chǐk′ə·sô′), *n., pl.* **-saw, -saws. 1.** a warlike Muskhogean tribe of North American Indians, formerly in northern Mississippi, now in Oklahoma. **2.** a member of this tribe.

chick·en (chǐk′ən, -ĭn), *n.* **1.** the young of the domestic fowl (or of certain other birds). **2.** a domestic fowl of any age, or its flesh. **3.** any of certain other birds as **Mother Carey's chicken** (the stormy petrel) or the **prairie chicken** (the prairie hen). **4.** *Colloq.* a young person, esp. a young girl. [ME *chiken,* OE *cicen, ciken.* Cf. D *kieken*]

chicken breast, *Pathol.* a malformation of the chest in which there is abnormal projection of the sternum and the sternal region, often associated with rickets.

chicken feed, *U.S. Slang.* **1.** small change (pennies, nickels, etc.). **2.** meager wages or other recompense.

chicken hawk, any of various hawks that prey on poultry, esp. *Buteo borealis,* the red-tailed hawk common in the U. S.

chick·en-heart·ed (chǐk′ən·här′tĭd, chǐk′ǐn-), *adj.* timid; cowardly.

chicken pox, a mild, contagious eruptive disease, commonly of children; varicella.

chick·pea (chǐk′pē′), *n.* **1.** a leguminous plant. *Cicer arietinum,* bearing edible pealike seeds, much used for food in southern Europe. **2.** its seed. [earlier *chich* (*pease*), t. F: m. (*pois*) *chiche,* g. L *cicer* vetch]

chick·weed (chǐk′wēd′), *n.* **1.** any of various plants of the caryophyllaceous genus *Stellaria,* as *S. media,* a common Old World weed whose leaves and seeds are relished by birds. **2.** any of various allied plants.

chic·le (chǐk′əl), *n.* a gumlike substance obtained from certain tropical American trees, as the sapodilla, used in the manufacture of chewing gum, etc. Also, **chicle gum.** [t. Amer. Sp., t. Mex.: m. *žiktli*]

chi·co (chē′kō), *n., pl.* **-cos.** greasewood (def. 1). [t. S. Amer.]

Chic·o·pee (chǐk′ə·pē′), *n.* a city in S Massachusetts, on the Connecticut river. 49,211 (1950).

chic·o·ry (chǐk′ə·rǐ), *n., pl.* **-ries. 1.** a perennial plant, *Cichorium intybus,* with bright-blue flowers, cultivated as a salad plant and for its root, which is used roasted and ground as a substitute for or adulterant for coffee. **2.** the root. **3.** *Brit.* endive. Also, **chiccory.** [t. F: m. *chicorée,* t. L: m. s. *cichorēum,* t. Gk.: m. *kichōreion*]

chide (chīd), *v.,* **chided** or **chid; chided, chid** or **chidden; chiding.** —*v.i.* **1.** to scold; find fault. —*v.t.* **2.** to drive, impel, etc., by chiding. **3.** to express disapproval of. [ME *chiden,* OE *cīdan*] —**chid′er,** *n.* —**chid′ing·ly,** *adv.* —**Syn. 3.** reprove, rebuke, censure.

chief (chēf), *n.* **1.** the head or leader of a body of men; the person highest in authority. **2.** the head or ruler of a clan or a tribe. **3.** *U.S. Army.* a title of certain advisors to the Chief of Staff who do not, in most instances, command the troop units of their arms or services: *Chief of Engineers, Chief Signal Officer, etc.* **4.** *Slang.* boss. **5.** *Her.* the upper third of an escutcheon. —*adj.* **6.** highest in rank or authority. **7.** most important: *his chief merit, the chief difficulty.* **8.** standing at the head. —*adv.* **9.** *Archaic.* chiefly; principally. [ME, t. OF, g. L *caput* head] —**Syn. 7.** foremost, essential, leading, principal. See **capital**[1]. —**Ant. 6.** subordinate.

chief constable, *Brit.* chief of police.

chief justice, 1. *Law.* the presiding judge of a court having several members. **2.** (*caps.*) the presiding judge of the U. S. Supreme Court (in full, **Chief Justice of the United States**).

chief·ly (chēf′lǐ), *adv.* **1.** principally; above all. **2.** mainly; mostly. —**Syn.** See **especially.**

Chief of Staff, *U.S. Army.* **1.** the senior officer of the Army, responsible to the President and the Secretary of War for the readiness and use of the Army. **2.** (*l.c.*) the senior staff officer in a division or higher unit.

chief·tain (chēf′tən, -tǐn), *n.* **1.** a leader of a group, band, etc. **2.** the chief of a clan or a tribe. [ME *chieftayne,* var. of *chevetaine,* t. OF, g. LL *capitānus.* See CAPTAIN] —**chief′tain·cy, chief′tain·ship,** *n.*

chield (chēld), *n. Scot.* a young man; a fellow. Also, **chiel** (chēl). [var. of CHILD]

chiff·chaff (chĭf'chăf', -chäf'), *n.* a common, plain-colored Old World warbler, *Phylloscopus collybita.*

chif·fon (shĭ fŏn', shĭf'ŏn), *n.* **1.** sheer fabric of silk or rayon in plain weave. **2.** any bit of feminine finery, as of ribbon or lace. [t. F, der. *chiffe* rag]

chif·fo·nier (shĭf'ə nĭr'), *n.* a high chest of drawers or bureau, often having a mirror. Also, **chif·fon·nier'.** [t. F: m. *chiffonnier*, der. *chiffon* rag]

chig·ger (chĭg'ər), *n.* **1.** the parasitic larva of certain kinds of mites, which causes severe itching when attached to the skin; redbug. **2.** chigoe. [alter.of CHIGOE]

chi·gnon (shēn'yŏn; *Fr.* shē nyôn'), *n.* a large rolled arrangement of the hair, worn at the back of the head by women. [t. F, ult. der. L *catēna* chain]

chig·oe (chĭg'ō), *n.* a flea, *Tunga Penetrans,* of the West Indies, South America, Africa, etc., the female of which buries itself in the skin of men and animals. [t. W Ind. Cf. F *chique*]

Chih·li (chē'lē'; *Chin.* jŭ'lē'), *n.* **1.** former name of **Hopeh. 2.** Gulf of, former name of **Pohai.**

Chi·hua·hua (chĭ wä'wä), *n.* **1.** a state in N Mexico. 623,944 pop. (1940); 94,831 sq. mi. **2.** the capital of this state. 56,805 (1940). **3.** the smallest type of dog, originating in Mexico.

chil-, var. of chilo-, used before vowels.

chil·blain (chĭl'blān'), *n.* (*usually pl.*) *Pathol.* an inflammation on the hands and feet caused by exposure to cold and moisture. [f. CHIL(L) + BLAIN] —**chil'-blained',** *adj.*

child (chīld), *n., pl.* **children. 1.** a baby or infant. **2.** a boy or girl. **3.** a childish person. **4.** a son or daughter. **5.** any descendant. **6.** any person or thing regarded as the product or result of particular agencies, influences, etc.: *children of light.* **7.** *Brit. Dial.* a female infant. **8.** *Archaic.* childe. **9. with child,** pregnant. [ME *child,* pl. *childre*(n), OE *cild,* pl. *cild*(ru)] —**child'less,** *adj.* —**child'less·ness,** *n.*

child·bear·ing (chīld'bâr'ĭng), *n.* producing or bringing forth children.

child·bed (chīld'bĕd'), *n.* the condition of a woman giving birth to a child; parturition.

childbed fever, puerperal fever.

child·birth (chīld'bûrth'), *n.* parturition.

childe (chīld), *n. Archaic.* a youth of noble birth. Also, **child.**

Chil·der·mas (chĭl'dər məs), *n. Obs.* Holy Innocents' Day.

child·hood (chīld'hŏŏd), *n.* state or time of being a child.

child·ing (chīl'dĭng), *adj.* bearing children; pregnant.

child·ish (chīl'dĭsh), *adj.* **1.** of, like, or befitting a child. **2.** puerile; weak; silly. [ME *childisch,* OE *cīldisc*] —**child'ish·ly,** *adv.* —**child'ish·ness,** *n.*

—**Syn. 1, 2.** CHILDISH, INFANTILE, CHILDLIKE refer to characteristics or qualities of childhood. The ending *-ish* has unfavorable connotations; CHILDISH therefore refers to characteristics which are undesirable and unpleasant: *childish selfishness, outbursts of temper.* INFANTILE, originally a general word, now often carries an even stronger idea of disapproval or scorn than does CHILDISH: *infantile reasoning, behavior.* The ending *-like* has pleasing connotations; CHILDLIKE therefore refers to the characteristics which are desirable and admirable: *childlike innocence, trust.*

child labor, the employment in gainful occupations of children below a minimum age determined by law or custom. The minimum legal age for full-time employment is 16 years in the U.S., according to federal law; standards regulating intra-state employment vary in different states.

child·like (chīld'līk'), *adj.* like or befitting a child, as in innocence, frankness, etc. —**child'like'ness,** *n.* —**Syn.** See childish.

child·ly (chīld'lĭ), *adj.* childlike; childish.

chil·dren (chĭl'drən, -drĭn), *n.* pl. of child.

children of Israel, the Hebrews; Jews.

child's play, something very easy or simple.

Chil·e (chĭl'ĭ; *Sp.* chē'lĕ), *n.* a republic in SW South America, on the Pacific coast. 5,237,432 pop. (est. 1943); 286,396 sq. mi. *Cap.:* Santiago. —**Chil'e·an,** *adj., n.*

chil·e con car·ne (chĭl'ĭ kŏn kär'nĭ; *Sp.* chē'lĕ kŏn kär'nĕ), a popular Mexican dish made from meat and finely chopped red pepper, served with beans. Also, **chil'i con car'ne.** [t. Sp.: chili with meat]

Chile saltpeter, sodium nitrate, NaNO3, a crystalline compound used as a fertilizer.

chil·i (chĭl'ĭ), *n., pl.* **chilies.** the pod of species of capsicum, esp. *Capsicum frutescens.* Also, **chil'e, chilli, chili pepper.** [t. Sp.: m. *chile,* t. Mex. (Nahuatl): m. *chilli*]

chil·i·ad (kĭl'ĭ ăd'), *n.* **1.** a thousand. **2.** a thousand years. [t. Gk.: s. *chīliás,* der. *chīlioi* thousand]

chil·i·arch (kĭl'ĭ ärk'), *n.* the commander of a thousand men. [t. Gk.: s. *chīliárchēs*]

chil·i·asm (kĭl'ĭ ăz'əm), *n. Theol.* the doctrine of the reign of Christ on earth for a thousand years. [t. Gk.: s. *chīliasmós,* der. *chīliás.* See CHILIAD] —**chil·i·ast** (kĭl'ĭ ăst'), *n.* —**chil'i·as'tic,** *adj.*

chili sauce, a highly flavored sauce made of tomatoes cooked with chili, spices, and other seasonings.

Chil·koot Pass (chĭl'kōot), a mountain pass through the Coast Range in SE Alaska, ab. 20 mi. north of Skagway, leading to the upper Yukon valley. ab. 3500 ft. high.

chill (chĭl), *n.* **1.** coldness, esp. a moderate but penetrating coldness. **2.** a sensation of cold, usually with shivering. **3.** the cold stage of ague, etc. **4.** a depressing influence or sensation. **5.** a metal mold for making chilled castings. —*adj.* **6.** cold; tending to cause shivering. **7.** shivering with cold. **8.** depressing or discouraging. **9.** not warm or hearty: *a chill reception.* —*v.i.* **10.** to become cold. **11.** to be seized with a chill. **12.** *Metall.* to become hard, esp. on the surface, by sudden cooling, as a metal mold. —*v.t.* **13.** to affect with cold; make chilly. **14.** to make cool or freeze: *to chill wines.* **15.** to depress; discourage: *chill his hopes.* **16.** *Metall.* to harden (cast iron or steel) on the surface by casting in a metal mold. [ME *chile,* OE *ciele, cile* coolness; akin to COOL, COLD] —**chill'er,** *n.* —**chill'ing·ly,** *adv.* —**chill'ness,** *n.* —**Syn. 6, 13.** See cold.

chil·li (chĭl'ĭ), *n., pl.* **-lies.** chili.

Chil·li·coth·e (chĭl'ə kŏth'ĭ), *n.* a city in S Ohio. 20,133 (1950).

Chil·lon (shə lŏn', shĭl'ən; *Fr.* shē yôn'), *n.* an ancient castle in W Switzerland, at the E end of Lake Geneva.

chil·ly (chĭl'ĭ), *adj.,* **-lier, -liest,** *adv.* —*adj.* **1.** producing a sensation of cold; causing shivering. **2.** feeling cold; sensitive to cold. **3.** without warmth of feeling: *a chilly reception.* —*adv.* **4.** in a chill manner. —**chil'li·ly,** *adv.* —**chil'li·ness,** *n.* —**Syn. 1.** See cold.

chilo-, a word element meaning "lip," "labial." [t. Gk.: m. *cheilo-,* comb. form of *cheîlos* lip]

chi·lo·plas·ty (kī'lə plăs'tĭ), *n.* plastic surgery of the lip.

chi·lo·pod (kī'lə pŏd'), *n.* a centipede.

Chil·tern hundreds (chĭl'tərn), *Brit.* an office held under the crown, for which members of Parliament apply, by a legal fiction, when they wish to resign.

chi·mae·ra (kī mĭr'ə, ki-), *n.* **1.** any of the fishes of the family *Chimaeridae.* The male has a spiny clasping organ over the mouth. **2.** any similar fish of the group *Holocephali,* which includes this family. **3.** chimera. [t. L. See CHIMERA]

chim·ar (chĭm'ər), *n.* chimere.

chimb (chĭm), *n.* chime².

Chim·bo·ra·zo (chĭm'bə rä'zō, -rä'-; *Sp.* chēm'bô rä'-sō), *n.* a volcanic mountain in central Ecuador, in the Andes. 20,702 ft.

chime¹ (chīm), *n., v.,* **chimed, chiming.** —*n.* **1.** an arrangement for striking a bell or bells so as to produce a musical sound: *a door chime.* **2.** a set of vertical metal tubes struck with a hammer, as used in the modern orchestra. **3.** carillon (def. 1, 3). **4.** (*often pl.*) carillon (def. 2). **5.** harmonious sound in general; music; melody. **6.** harmonious relation; accord. —*v.i.* **7.** to sound harmoniously or in chimes, as a set of bells. **8.** to produce a musical sound by striking a bell, etc.; ring chimes. **9.** to speak in cadence or singsong. **10.** to harmonize; agree. **11. chime in, a.** to break suddenly into a conversation, esp. to express agreement. **b.** to join in harmoniously (in music). —*v.t.* **12.** to give forth (music, etc.), as a bell or bells. **13.** to strike a(bell, etc.) so as to produce musical sound. **14.** to put, bring, indicate, etc., by chiming. **15.** to utter or repeat in cadence or singsong. [ME *chimbe,* appar. back formation from OE *cimbal,* t. L: m.s. *cymbalum* cymbal] —**chim'er,** *n.*

chime² (chĭm), *n.* the edge or brim of a cask or the like, formed by the ends of the staves beyond the head or bottom. Also, **chimb, chine.** [ME *chimb*(*e*), OE *cimb* (in compounds and derivatives), c. G *kimme* edge]

chi·me·ra (kī mĭr'ə, ki-), *n., pl.* **-ras. 1.** (*often cap.*) a mythological fire-breathing monster, commonly represented with a lion's head, a goat's body, and a serpent's tail. **2.** a grotesque monster, as in decorative art. **3.** a horrible or unreal creature of the imagination; a vain or idle fancy. **4.** *Genetics.* an organism composed of two or more genetically distinct tissues, as **a.** an organism which is partly male and partly female. **b.** an artificially produced individual having tissues of several species. Also, **chimaera.** [t. L: m. *Chimaera,* t. Gk.: m. *Chimaira* lit., she-goat; r. ME *chimere,* t. F]

chi·mere (chĭ mĭr', shĭ-), *n.* a loose upper robe, esp. of a bishop, to which the lawn sleeves are usually attached. Also, **chim·ar, chim·er** (chĭm'ər, shĭm'-). [ME *chemer,* ? t. Anglo-L: m.s. *chimēra.* See SIMAR]

chi·mer·i·cal (kī mĕr'ə kəl, -mĭr'-, ki-), *adj.* **1.** unreal; imaginary; visionary. **2.** wildly fanciful. Also, **chi·mer'ic.** —**chi·mer'i·cal·ly,** *adv.*

chim·ney (chĭm'nĭ), *n., pl.* **-neys. 1.** a structure, usually vertical, containing a passage or flue by which the smoke, gases, etc., of a fire or furnace are carried off and by means of which a draft is created. **2.** that part of such a structure which rises above a roof. **3.** *Chiefly Brit.* the smokestack or funnel of a locomotive, steamship, etc. **4.** a tube, commonly of glass, surrounding the flame of a lamp to promote combustion and keep the flame steady. **5.** anything resembling a chimney, such as the vent of a volcano. **6.** *Now Dial.* fireplace. [ME *chimenee,* t. OF, g. LL *camīnāta,* der. L *camīnus* furnace, t. Gk.: m. *kámīnos*] —**chim'ney·less,** *adj.*

chimney corner, 1. the corner or side of a fireplace. **2.** a place near the fire. **3.** fireside.

chimney piece, 1. *Chiefly Brit.* mantelpiece. **2.** *Obs.* a decoration over a fireplace.

chimney pot, *Brit.* a cylindrical or other pipe, as of earthenware or sheet metal, fitted on the top of a chimney to increase the draft and prevent smoking.

chimney swallow, 1. *Brit.* barn swallow. **2.** *U.S.* See **swallow** (def. 2).

chimney sweep, one whose business it is to clean out chimneys. Also, **chimney sweeper.**

chimney swift, an American swift, *Chaetura pelagica*, which often builds its nest in a disused chimney.

chim·pan·zee (chĭm′păn zē′, chĭm păn′zĭ), *n.* a highly intelligent anthropoid ape, *Pan troglodytes*, of equatorial Africa, smaller, with larger ears, and more arboreal than the gorilla. [t. native language in Angola, W. Afr.]

chin (chĭn), *n., v.,* **chinned, chinning.** —*n.* **1.** the lower extremity of the face, below the mouth. **2.** the point of the under jaw. —*v.t.* **3.** to bring one's chin up to (a horizontal bar, from which one is hanging), by bending the elbows; bring (oneself) to this position. **4.** *Colloq.* to talk to. **5.** *Colloq.* to bring up to the chin, as a violin. **6.** to chin oneself. —*v.i.* **7.** *Colloq.* to talk. [ME; OE *cin,* c. G *kinn*]

Chimpanzee, *Pan troglodytes* (4 ft. long)

Chin., Chinese.

chi·na (chī′nə), *n.* **1.** a vitreous, translucent ceramic ware, orig. produced in China. **2.** any porcelain ware. —*adj.* **3.** indicating the 20th event of a series, as a wedding anniversary.

Chi·na (chī′nə), *n.* a republic in E Asia. ab. 457,835,000 pop.; ab. 4,475,000 sq. mi. *Cap.:* Nanking; provisional capital, 1937–46, Chungking.

China aster, any variety of a species of asterlike plant, *Callistephus chinensis*.

chi·na bark (kī′nə, kē′nə), cinchona (def. 2). [t. Peruvian, var. of *kina, quina* bark. See QUININE]

chi·na·ber·ry (chī′nə bĕr′ĭ), *n., pl.* **-ries.** chinaberry tree.

chinaberry tree, 1. a tree, *Melia Azedarach*, native to Asia but widely planted elsewhere for its ornamental yellow fruits. **2.** a soapberry, *Sapindus marginatus*, of Mexico, the West Indies, and the southern U.S. Also, *U.S.,* **chi·na tree** (chī′nə).

Chi·na·man (chī′nə mən), *n., pl.* **-men.** *Offensive.* a native or inhabitant of China; a Chinese.

China Sea, a W part of the Pacific, divided by Formosa Strait into the South and East China Seas.

Chi·na·town (chī′nə toun′), *n.* the Chinese quarter of a city.

chi·na·ware (chī′nə wâr′), *n.* dishes, etc., of china.

chin·ca·pin (chĭng′kə pĭn), *n.* chinquapin.

chinch (chĭnch), *n.* **1.** the bedbug. **2.** chinch bug. [t. Sp.: m. *chinche,* g. L *cīmex* bug]

chinch bug, a small American hemipterous insect of the genus *Blissus*, destructive to wheat, etc., esp. *B. leucopterus*.

chin·chil·la (chĭn chĭl′ə), *n.* **1.** a small South American rodent of the genus *Chinchilla*, whose valuable skin is dressed as a fur. **2.** a thick, napped, woolen fabric for coats, esp. children's coats. [t. Sp., dim. of *chinche* bug]

Chinchilla, *Chinchilla chinchilla* (Total length 17 in., tail 6 in.)

chin·cough (chĭn′kôf′, -kŏf′), *n.* whooping cough.

Chin·dwin (chĭn′dwĭn′), *n.* river in Burma. ab. 550 mi.

chine[1] (chīn), *n. Local, Eng.* a ravine formed in rock by the action of running water. [ME, n. use of *chine,* v., crack, akin to OE *cīnan, cine* chink, fissure]

chine[2] (chīn), *n.* **1.** the backbone or spine. **2.** the whole or a piece of the backbone of an animal with adjoining parts, cut for cooking. **3.** a ridge or crest, as of land. [ME *chyne,* t. OF: m. *eschine,* t. Gmc. See SHIN]

chine[3] (chīn), *n.* chime[2].

Chi·nese (chī nēz′, -nēs′), *n., pl.* **-nese,** *adj.* —*n.* **1.** the standard language of China, based on the speech of Peking; Mandarin. **2.** a group of languages of the Sino-Tibetan family including standard Chinese and most of the other languages of China. **3.** any of the Chinese languages, which vary among themselves to the point of mutual unintelligibility. **4.** a native of China. —*adj.* **5.** of or pertaining to China, its inhabitants, or their language.

Chinese Empire, China under the rule of various imperial dynasties: replaced by a republic, Jan., 1912.

Chinese lantern, a collapsible lantern of thin, colored paper, often used for decorative lighting.

Chinese puzzle, 1. a very complicated puzzle. **2.** anything very complicated.

Chinese red, scarlet; orange-red; red chrome.

Chinese Wall. See Great Wall of China.

Chinese white, a pigment made from barium sulfate, largely used in water colors alone and for giving opacity to other colors.

Chinese windlass, *Mach.* a differential windlass.

Chinese wood oil, tung oil.

Ch'ing (chǐng), *n.* the last imperial dynasty in China, 1644–1911, founded by the Manchus.

Ching·hai (jǐng′hī′), *n.* a province in W China. ab. 1,533,900 pop. (est. 1944); 269,187 sq. mi. *Cap.:* Sining. Also, **Koko Nor.**

Chin Hills (chĭn), a mountainous region in W Upper Burma.

chink[1] (chĭngk), *n.* **1.** a crack, cleft, fissure. **2.** a narrow opening. —*v.t.* **3.** to fill up chinks in. [appar. f. OE *cinu, cine* crack, fissure + -k, suffix. See -OCK]

chink[2] (chĭngk), *v.t., v.i.* **1.** to make, or cause to make, a short, sharp, ringing sound, as of coins or glasses striking together. —*n.* **2.** a chinking sound. **3.** *Slang.* coin or ready cash. [imit.]

Chink (chĭngk), *n. U.S.* (in contemptuous use) a Chinaman.

chin·ka·pin (chĭng′kə pĭn), *n.* chinquapin.

Chin·kiang (chĭn′kyäng′), *n.* a city in E China: a port on the Yangtze. 217,000 (est. 1937).

Chino-, a combining form meaning "Chinese."

Chi·nook (chĭ nŏŏk′, -nŏŏk′), *n., pl.* **-nook, -nooks. 1. Lower Chinook,** a North American Indian tribe living on the north side of the Columbia river from its mouth 15 miles upstream. **2. Upper Chinook,** several extinct tribes (Cascades, Multnomah, Wasco, Wishram, Clackamas) speaking mutually intelligible dialects, on lower Columbia river, east of Lower Chinook. **3.** a member of any of these groups. **4.** a North American Indian linguistic family comprising two languages, Lower and Upper Chinook, and assigned by some linguists to the larger Penutian linguistic family. **5.** (*l.c.*) a warm, dry wind which blows at intervals down the eastern slopes of the Rocky Mountains. **6.** (*l.c.*) a warm, moist southwest wind on the coast of Washington and Oregon (**wet chinook**). **7.** chinook salmon. [m. *Tsinúk* (Chehalis name)]

Chi·nook·an (chĭ nŏŏ′kən, -nŏŏk′ən), *n.* a family of American Indian languages, of the Penutian linguistic phylum, including Chinook.

Chinook jargon, a lingua franca composed of words from Chinook and other Indian languages and from English and French. It was formerly widely used among traders and Indians in the Columbia river country.

chinook salmon, a variety of salmon, *Oncorhynchus tshawytscha*, largest of the Pacific salmon, and valued as a food fish; king salmon; quinnat salmon.

chin·qua·pin (chĭng′kə pĭn), *n.* **1.** the dwarf chestnut, *Castanea pumila*, a shrub or small tree of the U. S., bearing a small, edible nut, solitary in the bur. **2.** a fagaceous tree of the Pacific coast, *Castanopsis chrysophylla*. **3.** the nut of either of these trees. Also, **chincapin, chinkapin.** [t. N Amer. Ind. (Algonquian); cf. Delaware *činkwa* large, *min* fruit, seed]

chintz (chĭnts), *n.* **1.** a printed cotton fabric glazed or unglazed, used esp. for draperies. **2.** (orig.) painted or stained calico from India. [var. of *chints,* pl. of *chint,* t. Hind.: m. *chīnt*]

Chi·os (kī′ŏs; *Gk.* hē′ŏs), *n.* **1.** a Greek island in the Aegean, near the W coast of Turkey. 83,202 pop. (1940); 322 sq. mi. **2.** the capital of this island: a seaport. 27,798 (1940). Greek, **Khios.**

chip[1] (chĭp), *n., v.,* **chipped, chipping.** —*n.* **1.** a small piece, as of wood, separated by chopping, cutting, or breaking. **2.** a very thin slice or piece of food, candy. etc.: *potato chips, chocolate chips.* **3.** (*pl.*) *Brit.* French fried potatoes. **4.** a mark made by chipping. **5.** *Games.* a counter, as of ivory or bone, used in certain card games, etc. **6.** *Colloq.* a small (cut) piece of diamond, etc. **7.** anything trivial or worthless, or dried up or without flavor. **8.** a piece of dried dung. **9.** wood, straw, etc., in thin strips for weaving into hats, baskets, etc. **10.** *Golf.* chip shot. [cf. OE *cipp* log]
—*v.t.* **11.** to hew or cut with an ax, chisel, etc. **12.** to cut or break off (bits or fragments). **13.** to disfigure by breaking off fragments. **14.** to shape or produce by cutting away pieces. **15.** *Colloq.* to contribute, as to a fund (often fol. by *in*). **16.** *Games.* to bet by means of chips, as in poker. **17.** *Obs.* to pare (bread) by cutting away the crust. —*v.i.* **18.** to break off in small pieces. **19. chip in, a.** to contribute money, help, etc. **b.** to interrupt. **20.** *Games.* to bet a chip or chips, as in poker. **21.** *Golf.* to make a chip shot. [ME *chippen,* OE *cippian.* Cf. MLG, MD *kippen* chip eggs, hatch]

chip[2] (chĭp), *v.,* **chipped, chipping,** *n.* —*v. i.* **1.** to utter a short chirping or squeaking sound. —*n.* **2.** a short chirping or squeaking cry. [imit.]

chip[3] (chĭp), *n. Wrestling.* a tricky or special method by which an opponent can be thrown. [der. *chip,* v., trip. Cf. Icel. *kippa* scratch, pull]

chip log, *Naut.* See **log** (def. 2b).

chip·munk (chĭp′mŭngk), *n.* any of various small striped terrestrial squirrels of the American genus *Tamias*, and the European and American genus *Eutamias*, esp. *T. striatus* of eastern North America. [t. N Amer. Ind. (Ojibwa): m. *ačitamo* squirrel]

chipped beef, *U.S.* very thin slices of smoked beef.

Chip·pen·dale (chĭp′ən dāl′), *n.* **1. Thomas,** 1718?–79, British cabinet maker and furniture designer. —*adj.* **2.** pertaining to, or in the style of, Thomas Chippendale.

chip·per[1] (chĭp′ər), *adj. U.S. Colloq.* lively; cheerful. [cf. Northern E *kipper* frisky]

Chipmunk, *Tamias striatus* (Total length 9 to 10 in.)

chip·per[2] (chĭp′ər), v.i. 1. to chirp or twitter. 2. to chatter or babble. [f. CHIP[2] + -ER[5]]

chip·per[3] (chĭp′ər), n. one who or that which chips or cuts. [f. CHIP[1] + -ER[1]]

Chip·pe·wa (chĭp′ə wä′, -wā′, -wə), n. 1. an Ojibwa Indian. 2. the Ojibwa language.

Chip·pe·way (chĭp′ə wā′), n. Chippewa. —**Chip·pe·way′an**, n.

chip·ping sparrow, any of several small North American sparrows of the genus *Spizella*, as *S. passerina*, commonly found about houses.

chip·py (chĭp′ĭ), n., pl. **-pies**. the chipping sparrow.

chip shot, *Golf*. a short shot made in approaching the green using a wrist motion.

chirk (chûrk), *U.S. Colloq.* —v.i., v.t. 1. to cheer (fol. by *up*). —adj. 2. cheerful. [ME *chirken*, OE *circian* roar]

chirm (chûrm), v.i. 1. to chirp, as a bird; sing; warble. —n. 2. the chirping of birds. [ME; OE *cierm*]

chiro-, a word element meaning "hand," as in *chiropractic*. [t. Gk.: m. *cheiro-*, comb. form of *cheir*]

chi·rog·ra·phy (kī rŏg′rə fĭ), n. handwriting. —**chi·rog′ra·pher**, n. —**chi·ro·graph·ic** (kī′rə grăf′ĭk), **chi′ro·graph′i·cal**, adj.

chi·ro·man·cy (kī′rə măn′sĭ), n. the art of telling one's fortune by the appearance of the hand; palmistry. —**chi′ro·man′cer**, n.

Chi·ron (kī′rŏn), n. *Gk. Myth.* a wise and beneficent centaur, teacher of Achilles, Asclepius, and others.

chi·rop·o·dy (kī rŏp′ə dĭ, kĭ-), n. the treatment of minor foot ailments, such as corns, bunions, etc. [f. CHIRO- + m.s. Gk. *-podia*, der. *poús* foot] —**chi·rop′o·dist**, n.

chi·ro·prac·tic (kī′rə prăk′tĭk), n. 1. a therapeutic system based upon the theory that disease is caused by interference with nerve function, the method being to restore normal condition by adjusting body structures, esp. the spinal column. 2. a chiropractor. [f. CHIRO- + m.s. Gk. *praktikós* practical]

chi·ro·prac·tor (kī′rə prăk′tər), n. one who practices chiropractic.

chi·rop·ter (kī rŏp′tər), n. any of the *Chiroptera*, the order of mammals that comprises the bats. [t. NL: s. *chiroptera*, pl., f. *chiro-* CHIRO- + Gk. *pterá* wings]

chi·rop·ter·an (kī rŏp′tər ən), n. chiropter. —**chi·rop′ter·an**, adj.

chirp (chûrp), v.i. 1. to make a short, sharp sound, as small birds and certain insects. 2. to make any similar sound. —v.t. 3. to sound or utter in a chirping manner. —n. 4. a chirping sound. [? var. of CHIRK] —**chirp′er**, n.

chirp·y (chûr′pĭ). adj. *Colloq.* cheerful; lively; gay.

chirr (chûr), v.i. 1. to make a shrill trilling sound, as a grasshopper. 2. to make a similar sound. —n. 3. the sound of chirring. Also, **chirre**, **churr**. [appar. back formation from CHIRRUP]

chir·rup (chĭr′əp, chûr′-), v., **-ruped**, **-ruping**, n. —v.i. 1. to chirp. 2. to make a chirping sound, as to a cage bird or a horse. —v.t. 3. to utter with chirps. 4. to make a chirping sound to. 5. act or sound of chirruping. [var. of CHIRP] —**chir′rup·er**, n.

chir·rup·y (chĭr′əp ĭ, chûr′-), adj. chirpy.

chi·rur·geon (kī rûr′jən), n. *Archaic*. a surgeon. [b. L *chirurgus* surgeon (t. Gk.: m. *cheirourgós*) and SURGEON; r. ME *cirurgien*, t. OF]

chi·rur·ger·y (kī rûr′jə rĭ), n. *Archaic*. surgery. —**chi·rur′gic**, **chi·rur′gi·cal**, adj.

chis·el (chĭz′əl), n., v., **-eled**, **-eling** or (*esp. Brit.*) **-elled**, **-elling**. —n. 1. a tool, as of steel, with a cutting edge at the extremity, usually transverse to the axis, for cutting or shaping wood, stone, etc. —v.t. 2. to cut, shape, etc. with a chisel. 3. *Now U.S. Slang.* **a.** to cheat; swindle. **b.** to get by cheating or trickery. —v.i. 4. to work with a chisel. 5. *U.S. Slang.* to use trickery; take unfair advantage: *to chisel on an examination*. [ME, t. ONF, ult. der. L *caesus*, pp., cut] —**chis′el·er** (*esp. Brit.*, **chis′el·ler**, n.

chis·eled (chĭz′əld), adj. 1. cut, shaped, etc., with a chisel. 2. clear-cut. Also, *esp. Brit.*, **chis′elled**.

Chi·shi·ma (chē′shē mä′), n. Japanese name of the **Kurile Islands**.

Chi·şi·nă·u (kē′shē nŭ′ о̄о̄), n. Rumanian name of **Kishinev**.

chi-square test (kī′skwâr′), *Statistics*. a test devised by Karl Pearson for testing the mathematical goodness of fit of a frequency curve to an observed frequency distribution. It has a wide variety of applications.

chit[1] (chĭt), n. 1. a voucher of money owed for food, drink, etc. 2. *Chiefly Brit.* a note; a short memorandum. [short for *chitty*, t. Hind.: m. *chitthī*]

chit[2] (chĭt), n. a young person, esp. a pert girl. [? akin to KITTEN; assoc. with obs. *chit* sprout]

Chi·ta (chĭ′tä′), n. a city in the SE Soviet Union in Asia, E of Lake Baikal. 102,555 (1939).

chit·chat (chĭt′chăt′), n. 1. light conversation on one subject or another; small talk. 2. matters about which people are gossiping; gossip. [varied redupl. of CHAT]

chi·tin (kī′tĭn), n. a characteristic horny organic component of the cuticula of arthropods. [t. F: m. *chitine*, der. Gk. *chitōn* tunic] —**chi′tin·ous**, adj.

chi·ton (kī′tŏn, -tŏn), n. 1. *Gk. Antiq.* a garment for both sexes, usually worn next to the skin. 2. any of a group of sluggish, limpetlike mollusks which adhere to rocks. [t. Gk.]

Chit·ta·gong (chĭt′ə gŏng′), n. a seaport in the E division of Pakistan, near the Bay of Bengal. 92,301 (1941).

chit·ter·ling (chĭt′ər lĭng), n. 1. (*usually pl.*) a part of the small intestine of swine, etc., esp. as cooked for food. 2. *Obs.* a frill or ruff. [cf. G *kütteln* entrails]

chiv·al·ric (shĭv′əl rĭk, shĭ văl′rĭk), adj. 1. pertaining to chivalry. 2. chivalrous.

chiv·al·rous (shĭv′əl rəs), adj. 1. having the high qualities characteristic of chivalry, such as courage, courtesy, generosity, loyalty, etc. 2. chivalric. [ME, t. OF: m. *chevalereus*, der. *chevalier* CHEVALIER] —**chiv′al·rous·ly**, adv. —**chiv′al·rous·ness**, n.

chiv·al·ry (shĭv′əl rĭ), n. 1. the ideal qualifications of a knight, such as courtesy, generosity, valor, dexterity in arms, etc. 2. the rules and customs of medieval knighthood. 3. the medieval system or institution of knighthood. 4. a group of knights. 5. gallant warriors or gentlemen. 6. *Obs.* the position or rank of a knight. [ME, t. OF: m. *chevalerie*, der. *chevalier* CHEVALIER]

chive (chīv), n. a small bulbous plant, *Allium Schoenoprasum*, related to the leek and onion, with long, slender leaves which are used as a seasoning in cookery. Also, **chive garlic**. [ME, t. ONF, g. L *caepa* onion]

chiv·vy (chĭv′ĭ), v., **-vied**, **-vying**, n., pl. **-vies**. *Brit.* —v.t. 1. to chase; run after. 2. to harass; nag; torment. —v.i. 3. to race; scamper. —n. 4. a hunting cry. 5. a hunt, chase, or pursuit. 6. the game of prisoners' base. Also, **chevy**, **chiv′y**. [? short for *chevy chase*]

Ch.J., Chief Justice.

Chka·lov (chkä′lôf), n. Orenburg.

chlam·y·date (klăm′ə dāt′). adj. *Zool.* having a mantle or pallium, as a mollusk. [f. s. Gk. *chlamýs* mantle + -ATE[1]]

chla·myd·e·ous (klə mĭd′ĭ əs), adj. *Bot.* pertaining to or having a floral envelope. [f. s. NL *chlamydeae*, pl., (der. Gk. *chlamýs* mantle) + -OUS]

chla·mys (klā′mĭs, klăm′ĭs), n., pl. **chlamyses** (klā′mĭs ĭz, klăm′ĭs-), **chlamydes** (klăm′ə dēz′). *Gk. Antiq.* a short mantle or cloak worn by men. [t. L, t. Gk.]

Chlod·wig (klŏt′vĭкн), n. German name for **Clovis I**.

Chlo·e (klō′ĭ), n. (in pastoral and other literature) a name for a maiden, esp. one beloved. Also, **Chlo′ë**.

chlor-[1], a word element meaning "green," as in *chlorine*. Also, **chloro-**[1]. [t. Gk., comb. form of *chlōrós*]

chlor-[2], a combining form denoting "chlorine," as in *chloral*. Also, **chloro-**[2].

chlo·ral (klōr′əl), n. *Chem., Pharm.* 1. a colorless, mobile liquid, CCl$_3$CHO, first prepared from chlorine and alcohol and used as a hypnotic. 2. a white, crystalline substance CCl$_3$CH(OH)$_2$ (**chloral hydrate**) formed by combining liquid chloral with water, and used as a hypnotic. [f. CHLOR-[2] + AL(COHOL)]

chlo·ra·mine (klōr′ə mēn′), n. *Chem.* an unstable, colorless liquid, NH$_2$Cl, with a pungent odor, derived from ammonia.

chlo·rate (klōr′āt, -ĭt), n. *Chem.* a salt of chloric acid.

chlo·ren·chy·ma (klə rĕng′kə mə), n. *Bot.* parenchyma tissue containing chlorophyll.

chlo·ric (klōr′ĭk), adj. *Chem.* of or containing chlorine in the pentavalent state.

chloric acid, *Chem.* an acid, HClO$_3$, which exists only in solution and as salts. [f. CHLOR-[2] + -IC]

chlo·ride (klōr′īd, -ĭd), n. 1. a compound usually of two elements only, one of which is chlorine. 2. a salt of hydrochloric acid.

chloride of lime, *Chem., etc.* a white powder used in bleaching and disinfecting, made by treating slaked lime with chlorine, and regarded (when dry) as calcium oxychloride, CaOCl$_2$.

chlo·rin·ate (klōr′ə nāt′), v.t., **-ated**, **-ating**. 1. *Chem.* to combine or treat with chlorine. 2. to disinfect (water) by means of chlorine. 3. *Metall.* to treat (a gold ore) with chlorine gas in order that the gold may be removed as a soluble chloride. —**chlo′rin·a′tion**, n. —**chlo′rin·a′tor**, n.

chlo·rine (klōr′ēn, -ĭn), n. *Chem.* a greenish-yellow gaseous element (occurring combined in common salt, etc.), incombustible, and highly irritating to the organs of respiration. It is used as a powerful bleaching agent and in various industrial processes. *Symbol:* Cl; *at. wt.:* 35.46; *at. no.:* 17. Also, **chlo·rin** (klōr′ĭn). [f. CHLOR-[1] + -INE[2]]

chlo·rite[1] (klōr′īt), n. a group of minerals, hydrous silicates of aluminum, ferrous iron, and magnesium, occurring in green platelike crystals or scales. [t. Gk.: m.s. *chlōrîtis* kind of green stone]

chlo·rite[2] (klōr′īt), n. *Chem.* a salt of chlorous acid, as *potassium chlorite*, KClO. [f. CHLOR-[2] + -ITE[1]]

chloro-[1], var. of chlor-[1], used before consonants, as in *chlorophyll*.

chloro-[2], var. of chlor-[2], used before consonants, as in *chloroform*.

chlo·ro·a·ce·tic acid (klōr′ō ə sē′tĭk, -ə sĕt′ĭk), *Chem., Pharm., etc.* a colorless, crystalline, deliquescent compound, CH$_2$ClCOOH, used as a corn and wart remover and in the manufacture of dyes.

chlo·ro·form (klōr′ə fôrm′), n. 1. *Chem., Pharm., etc.* a colorless volatile liquid, CHCl$_3$, used as an anesthetic and solvent. —v.t. 2. to administer chloroform to. 3. to put chloroform on (a cloth, etc.). [f. CHLORO-[2] + FORM(YL)]

---

chlo·ro·hy·drin (klōr/ə hī/drĭn), *n. Chem.* any of a class of organic compounds containing a chlorine atom and a hydroxyl group, usually on adjacent carbon atoms.

chlo·ro·my·ce·tin (klōr/ə mī sē/tən), *n.* a recently developed antibiotic, the first to be synthesized, similar to penicillin, especially effective in the treatment of virus and rickettsial diseases such as Rocky Mountain spotted fever, undulant fever, typhoid fever, and typhus.

chlo·ro·phyll (klōr/ə fĭl), *n. Bot., Biochem.* the green coloring substance of leaves and plants, having two forms: bluish-black **chlorophyll a**, $C_{55}H_{72}MgN_4O_5$, and yellowish-green **chlorophyll b**, $C_{55}H_{70}MgN_4O_6$. It is associated with the production of carbohydrates by photosynthesis in plants and is used as a dye for cosmetics and oils. Also, **chlo·ro·phyl.** [f. CHLORO-¹ + -PHYLL]

chlo·ro·phyl·lous (klōr/ə fĭl/əs), *adj.* of or containing chlorophyll. Also, **chlo·ro·phyl·lose** (klōr/ə fĭl/ōs).

chlo·ro·pic·rin (klōr/ō pĭk/rĭn, -pĭ/krĭn), *n. Chem., etc.* a colorless liquid, CCl_3NO_2, used as an insecticide and as a chemical agent in warfare. Also, **chlorpicrin.** [f. CHLORO-¹ + PICR(IC) + -IN²]

chlo·ro·plast (klōr/ə plăst/), *n. Bot.* a plastic containing chlorophyll. [f. CHLORO-¹ + -PLAST]

chlo·ro·prene (klōr/ə prēn/), *n.* a colorless fluid, CH_2-CClCH-CH_2, produced from acetylene and hydrogen chloride, which polymerizes readily to neoprene.

chlo·ro·sis (klōrō/sĭs), *n.* 1. abnormal yellow color of a plant, even from lack of iron in the soil. 2. a benign type of iron-deficiency anemia in adolescent girls, marked by a pale yellow-green complexion. [t. NL; see CHLOR-¹, -OSIS]

chlo·rous (klōr/əs), *adj.* containing trivalent chlorine, as *chlorous acid*, $HClO_2$, which occurs only in solution or as its salts, the chlorites. [f. CHLOR² + -OUS]

chlor·pic·rin (klōr pĭk/rĭn, -pĭ/krĭn), *n.* chloropicrin.

chm. chairman. Also, **chmn.**

Choate (chōt), *n.* 1. **Joseph Hodges,** 1832–1917, U.S. lawyer and diplomat. 2. **Rufus,** 1799–1859, U.S. lawyer, orator, and statesman.

chock (chŏk), *n.* 1. a block or wedge of wood, etc., for filling in a space, esp. for preventing movement, as of a wheel or a cask. 2. *Naut.* **a.** a metal or wooden fitting through which a mooring line, anchor cable, towline or similar rope passes, usually on or in the rail. **b.** a shaped standard on which a boat, barrel, or other object rests. —*v.t.* 3. to furnish with or secure by a chock or chocks. 4. *Naut.* to place (a boat) upon chocks. —*adv.* 5. as close or tight as possible; quite: *chock against the edge.* [prob. t. ONF: m. *choque* log or block of wood. Cf. It. *ciocco* burning log]

chock-a-block (chŏk/ə blŏk/), *adv.* 1. *Naut.* with the blocks drawn close together, as when a tackle is hauled to the utmost. 2. in a jammed or crowded condition.

chock-full (chŏk/fŏŏl/), *adj.* full to the utmost; crammed. Also, **chuck-full, choke-full.**

choc·o·late (chŏk/ə lĭt, chŏk/-, chôk/lĭt, chŏk/lĭt, chŏk/-), *n.* 1. a preparation of the seeds of cacao, roasted, husked, and ground (without removing any of the fat), often sweetened and flavored, as with vanilla. 2. a beverage or a candy made from this. 3. dark brown. —*adj.* 4. made or flavored with chocolate. 5. having the color of chocolate. [t. Sp., t. Mex.: m. *chocolatl* bitter water]

Choc·taw (chŏk/tô), *n., pl.* **-taw, -taws.** 1. a large Muskhogean tribe of North American Indians, formerly living chiefly in southern Mississippi, now in Oklahoma. 2. a member of this tribe.

choice (chois), *n., adj.,* **choicer, choicest.** —*n.* 1. act of choosing; selection. 2. power of choosing; option. 3. the person or thing chosen: *this book is my choice.* 4. an abundance and variety from which to choose: *a wide choice of candidates.* 5. that which is preferred or preferable to others; the best part of anything. 6. an alternative. 7. a well-chosen variety. —*adj.* 8. worthy of being chosen; excellent; superior. 9. carefully selected: *delivered in choice words.* [ME *chois,* t. OF, der. *choisir* choose, of Gmc. orig. and akin to CHOOSE] —**choice/ly,** *adv.* —**choice/ness,** *n.*
—**Syn. 2.** CHOICE, ALTERNATIVE, OPTION, PREFERENCE all suggest the power of choosing between (two) things. CHOICE implies the opportunity to choose: *a choice of evils.* ALTERNATIVE suggests that one has a choice between only two possibilities. It is often used with a negative to mean that there is no second possibility: *to have no alternative.* OPTION emphasizes free right or privilege of choosing: *to exercise one's option.* PREFERENCE applies to a choice based on liking or partiality: *to state a preference.* See **fine¹.**

choir (kwīr), *n.* 1. a company of singers. esp. an organized group employed in church service. 2. any company or band, or a division of one: *a choir of dancers, string choir.* 3. *Archit.* **a.** that part of a church used by the singers. **b.** (in a medieval cruciform church) the body of the church which extends from the crossing to the east, or altar, end. **c.** (in cathedrals, etc.) the area between the nave and the main altar. 4. *Theol.* any of the nine orders of the celestial hierarchy. —*v.i., v.t.* 5. to sing in chorus. [ME *quer,* t. OF: m. *cuer,* g. L *chorus.* See CHORUS]

choir·boy (kwīr/boi/), *n.* a boy who sings in a choir.

choir loft, a gallery in which the choir is stationed.

choir·mas·ter (kwīr/măs/tər, -mäs/tər), *n.* the leader or director of a choir.

Choi·seul (shwä zœl/), *n.* one of the British Solomon Islands, E of New Guinea. 4051 pop. (1931); 981 sq. mi.

choke (chōk), *v.,* **choked, choking,** *n.* —*v.t.* 1. to stop the breath of, by squeezing or obstructing the windpipe; strangle; stifle; suffocate. 2. to stop, as the breath or utterance, by or as by strangling or stifling. 3. to check the growth, progress, or action of: *to choke off discussion.* 4. to stop by filling; obstruct; clog; congest. 5. to suppress, as a feeling or emotion. 6. to fill chock-full. 7. (in internal combustion engines) to enrich the fuel mixture by diminishing the air supply to the carburetor, as when starting a motor. —*v.i.* 8. to suffer strangling or suffocation. 9. to be obstructed or clogged. —*n.* 10. act or sound of choking. 11. (in internal-combustion engines) the mechanism by which the air supply to a carburetor is diminished or stopped. 12. *Mach.* any such mechanism which, by blocking a passage, regulates the flow of air, etc. 13. *Elect.* a choke coil. 14. a narrowed part, as in a chokebore. [ME *choke*(n), *cheke*(n), aphetic variants of ME *achoke*(n), *acheke*(n), OE *acēocian*]

choke·ber·ry (chōk/bĕr/Y), *n., pl.* **-ries.** 1. the astringent berrylike fruit of shrubs of the North American rosaceous genus *Aronia,* esp. *A. arbutifolia.* 2. the plant bearing it.

choke·bore (chōk/bōr/), *n.* 1. (in a shotgun) a bore which narrows toward the muzzle to prevent shot from scattering too widely. 2. a shotgun with such a bore.

choke-cher·ry (chōk/chĕr/Y), *n., pl.* **-ries.** 1. any of several species of cherry, esp. *Prunus virginiana* of North America, which bears an astringent fruit. 2. the fruit.

choke coil, *Elect.* a coil of large inductance which allows steady currents to pass freely but chokes off or greatly weakens all rapid fluctuations, esp. such a coil as is used in electronic apparatus.

choke·damp (chōk/dămp/), *n. Mining.* mine atmosphere so low in oxygen and high in carbon dioxide as to cause choking; blackdamp.

choke-full (chōk/fŏŏl/), *adj.* chock-full.

chok·er (chō/kər), *n.* 1. one who or that which chokes. 2. *Colloq.* a necklace worn tightly around the neck. 3. *Colloq.* a neckcloth or a high collar.

chok·ing (chō/kYng), *adj.* 1. so full of emotion that one almost chokes: *to speak in a choking voice.* 2. that chokes; that makes one feel as if he is being choked: *a choking sensation.* —**chok/ing·ly,** *adv.*

chok·y (chō/kY), *adj.,* **chokier, chokiest.** tending to choke or suffocate one. Also, **chok/ey.**

chol-, a word element meaning "gall" or "bile." Also, **chole-, cholo-.** [t. Gk., comb. form of *cholē* bile]

chol·e·cys·tec·to·my (kŏl/ə sĭs tĕk/tə mY), *n., pl.* **-mies.** *Surg.* removal of the gall bladder.

chol·e·cys·tos·to·my (kŏl/ə sĭs tŏs/tə mY), *n., pl.* **-mies.** *Surg.* a draining of the gall bladder with the organ left in place, usually done to remove stones.

chol·er (kŏl/ər), *n.* 1. irascibility; anger; wrath, irritability. 2. *Old Physiol.* bile (that one of the four humors supposed when predominant to cause irascibility and anger). 3. *Obs.* biliousness. [t. LL: s. *cholera* bile, t. Gk.: name of the disease; r. ME *colere,* t. OF]

chol·er·a (kŏl/ərə), *n.* 1. *Pathol.* **a.** an acute disorder of the digestive tract, marked by diarrhea, vomiting, cramps, etc. (**sporadic cholera, bilious cholera,** or **cholera morbus**). **b.** an acute, infectious disease, due to a specific microörganism, endemic in India, etc., and epidemic generally, marked by profuse diarrhea, vomiting, cramps, etc., and often fatal (**Asiatic cholera**). 2. *Vet. Sci.* any disease characterized by violent diarrhea. See **hog cholera** and **fowl cholera.** [t. L, t. Gk.] —**chol·e·ra·ic** (kŏl/ə rā/Yk), *adj.*

cholera in·fan·tum (Yn făn/təm), *Pathol.* sporadic cholera in infants. [L: cholera of infants]

cholera mor·bus (môr/bəs), *Pathol.* sporadic cholera. Also, **cholera nos·tras** (nŏs/trăs). [L: cholera disease]

chol·er·ic (kŏl/ər Yk), *adj.* 1. irascible; angry. 2. *Obs.* bilious. 3. *Obs.* causing biliousness.

cho·les·ter·ol (kə lĕs/tə rōl/, -rŏl/), *n. Biochem.* a fatlike substance, $C_{27}H_{45}OH$, found in bile and gallstones, and in the blood and brain, the yolk of eggs, etc. Also, **cho·les·ter·in** (kə lĕs/tər Yn). [f. CHOLE- + Gk. *ster*(*eós*) solid + -OL²]

cho·lic acid (kō/lYk, kŏl/Yk), *Biochem.* a white crystalline hydroxy acid, $C_{24}H_{40}O_5$, derived from bile acids and related to the sex hormones and cholesterol (**cholic t.** Gk.: m.s. *cholikós* of bile]

cho·line (kō/lēn, kŏl/ēn, -Yn), *n. Biochem.* a viscous ptomaine, $C_5H_{15}NO_2$, found in the lecithin of many plants and animals.

chol·la (chōl/yä; *Sp.* chô/yä), *n.* any of several spiny treelike cacti of the genus *Opuntia.* esp. *O. fulgida,* of the southwestern U.S. and Mexico.

cholo-, var. of **chol-** before consonants.

Cho·lon (shôlôn/; *Indo.* chə lŭn/), *n.* a city in S French Indo-China, near Saigon. 145,000 (1936).

Cho·lu·la (chô lŏŏ/lä), *n.* a town in S central Mexico, near Puebla: ancient Aztec ruins.

chon·dri·o·somes (kŏn/drY ə sōmz/), *n. Biol.* minute structures occurring in the cytoplasm of cells. [f. Gk. *chondrío*(n), dim. of *chóndros* cartilage + -SOME(s)³]

chon·dro·ma (kŏn drō/mə), *n., pl.* **-mas, -mata** (mə tə). *Pathol.* a cartilaginous tumor or growth. [f. s. Gk. *chóndros* cartilage + -OMA]

choose (chōōz), *v.,* **chose, chosen** or (*Obs.*) **chose, choosing.** —*v.t.* 1. to select from a number, or in preference to another or other things or persons. 2. to prefer and decide (to do something): *he chose to run for*

b., blend of, blended; c., cognate with; d., dialect, dialectal; der., derived from; f., formed from; g., going back to; m., modification of; r., replacing; s., stem of; t., taken from; ?, perhaps. See the full key on inside cover.

election. **3.** to want; desire. —*v.i.* **4.** to make a choice. **5. cannot choose but,** cannot do otherwise than: *he cannot choose but hear.* [ME *chose(n),* OE *ceōsan;* var. of ME *chēse(n),* OE *cēosan;* c. G *kiesan,* Goth. *kiusan;* akin to L *gustāre* taste] —**choos'er,** *n.*

—**Syn. 1.** CHOOSE, SELECT, PICK, ELECT, PREFER indicate a decision that one or more possibilities are to be regarded more highly than others. CHOOSE suggests a decision on one of a number of possibilities because of its apparent superiority: *to choose a course of action.* SELECT suggests a choice made for fitness: *to select the proper golf club.* PICK, an informal word, suggests a selection on personal grounds: *to pick a winner.* The formal word ELECT suggests a kind of official action: *to elect a chairman, a member of a scientific society.* PREFER, also formal, emphasizes the desire or liking for one thing more than for another or others: *to prefer coffee to tea.* —**Ant. 1.** reject.

chop¹ (chŏp), *v.,* **chopped, chopping,** *n.* —*v.t.* **1.** to cut with a quick, heavy blow or series of blows, using an ax, etc. **2.** to make by so cutting. **3.** to cut in pieces; mince. **4.** *Tennis, Cricket, etc.* to hit (a ball) with a chop stroke. —*v.i.* **5.** to make a quick, heavy stroke or a series of strokes, as with an ax. **6.** to go, come, or move suddenly or violently. —*n.* **7.** act of chopping. **8.** a cutting blow. **9.** *Boxing.* a short, downward cutting blow. **10.** a piece chopped off. **11.** a slice of mutton, lamb, veal, pork, etc., usually one containing a rib. **12.** a short, irregular, broken motion of waves. **13.** *Obs.* a chap; crack; cleft. [var. of CHAP¹] —**Syn. 1.** See cut.

chop² (chŏp), *v.,* **chopped, chopping.** —*v.i.* **1.** to turn, shift, or change suddenly, as the wind. **2.** *Obs.* to barter. **3.** *Obs.* to bandy words; argue. —*v.t.* **4.** chop logic, to reason or dispute argumentatively; argue. **5.** *Now Brit. Dial.* to barter; exchange. [var. of obs. *chap* barter, ME *chapien,* OE *cēapian.* Cf. CHEAP]

chop³ (chŏp), *n.* **1.** *(usually pl.)* a jaw. **2.** *(pl.)* the oral cavity. Also, **chap.** [? special use of CHOP¹]

chop⁴ (chŏp), *n.* **1.** (in India, China, etc.) **a.** an official stamp or seal, or a permit or clearance. **b.** a design, corresponding to a brand or trademark, stamped on goods to indicate their special identity. **2.** *Anglo-Indian Colloq.* quality. [t. Hind.: m. *chhāp* impression, stamp]

chop chop! (chŏp′chŏp′), (common in fiction about China). "bring it quickly" [Pidgin English *chop* quick]

chop·fall·en (chŏp′fô′lən), *adj.* chapfallen.

chop·house¹ (chŏp′hous′), *n.* an eating house making a specialty of chops, steaks, etc. [f. CHOP¹ + HOUSE]

chop·house² (chŏp′hous′), *n.* (in China) a custom house. [f. CHOP⁴ + HOUSE]

Cho·pin (shō′păn; *Fr.* shô pĂN′), *n.* Frédéric François (frĕ dĕ rēk′ frän swä′), 1810?–49, Polish-French pianist and composer.

cho·pine (chō pēn′, chŏp′ĭn), *n.* a kind of shoe with a very thick sole of cork or the like, sometimes suggesting a short stilt, formerly worn esp. by women. Also, **chop·in** (chŏp′ĭn). [t. Sp., der. *chapa* bit of leather, t. F: m. *chape* CHAPE]

chop·per (chŏp′ər), *n.* **1.** one who or that which chops. **2.** a short ax with a large blade used for cutting up meat, etc.; a butcher's cleaver.

chop·ping¹ (chŏp′ĭng), *adj.* choppy (def. 1).

chop·ping² (chŏp′ĭng), *adj. Brit. Colloq.* large and strong; bouncing: *a chopping baby boy.*

chop·py (chŏp′ĭ), *adj.,* **-pier, -piest. 1.** (of the sea, etc.) forming short, irregular, broken waves. **2.** (of the wind) shifting or changing suddenly or irregularly; variable. [f. CHOP² + -Y¹]

chop·stick (chŏp′stĭk′), *n.* one of the small sticks, as of wood or ivory, used in pairs by the Chinese, etc., to raise food to the mouth. [f. Pidgin English *chop* quick + STICK¹]

chop stroke, *Tennis, Cricket, etc.* a downward stroke made with the racket at an angle.

chop su·ey (chŏp′ sōō′ĭ), *U.S.* a mixed dish served in Chinese restaurants, consisting of small pieces of meat, chicken, etc., cooked together with onions, bean sprouts, green peppers, mushrooms, or other vegetables and seasoning, in a gravy or sauce, eaten commonly with soy sauce and rice. Also, **chop′ soo′y.** [t. Chinese: mixed bits]

cho·ra·gus (kə rā′gəs, kō-), *n., pl.* **-gi** (-jī). **1.** the leader and sponsor of an ancient Greek chorus. **2.** any conductor of an entertainment or festival. [t. L, t. Gk.: m. *chorāgós, chorēgós* leader of the chorus] —**cho·rag·ic** (kə răj′ĭk, -rā′jĭk), *adj.*

cho·ral (*adj.* kōr′əl; *n.* kə rāl′, kō-, kōr′əl), *adj.* **1.** of a chorus or a choir. **2.** sung by or adapted for a chorus or a choir. —*n.* **3.** a choral composition. **4.** a hymn tune. **5.** a simple sacred tune, esp. of the German Protestant church, having a plain melody, a strong harmony, and a stately rhythm. [t. ML: s. *chorālis,* der. L *chorus.* See CHORUS] —**cho′ral·ly,** *adv.*

cho·rale (kə răl′, -räl′, kō-, kōr′əl), *n.* choral.

chord¹ (kôrd), *n.* **1.** a string of a musical instrument. **2.** a feeling or emotion. **3.** *Geom.* that part of a straight line between two of its intersections with a curve. **4.** *Civ. Eng.* one of the main members which lie along the top or bottom edge of a truss framework. **5.** *Aeron.*

Geometrical chords AB, AC chords subtending arcs ACB and AC

a straight line joining the trailing and leading edges of an airfoil section. **6.** *Anat.* a cord (def. 4). [t. L′s. *chorda* cord, string, t. Gk.: m. *chordē* gut, string of a musical instrument. Cf. CORD] —**chord′al,** *adj.*

chord² (kôrd), *n. Music.* a combination of three or more tones in harmonic relation, sounded simultaneously. [var. spelling (influenced by CHORD¹) of *cord,* aphetic var. of ACCORD, n.]

chor·date (kôr′dāt), *Zool.* —*adj.* **1.** belonging or pertaining to the *Chordata,* the phylum that includes the true vertebrates and those animals *(protochordates)* that have a notochord, such as the lancelets and the tunicates. —*n.* **2.** a chordate animal. [t. NL: m. s. *chordātus* having a chord. See CHORD¹]

chore (chōr), *n. U.S.* **1.** a small or odd job; a piece of minor domestic work. **2.** *(pl.)* routine work around a house or farm. **3.** a hard or unpleasant task. [ME *churre,* OE *cyrr,* var. of *cierr, cerr.* See CHARE]

cho·re·a (kə rē′ə, kō-), *n.* **1.** *Pathol.* an acute disease of children characterized by irregular, involuntary, and uncontrollable movements in the face or extremities; St. Vitus's dance. **2.** *Vet. Sci.* a disease of the nervous system characterized by degenerations which cause irregular, jerky, involuntary muscular movements. It is frequent in dogs, usually as an aftereffect of canine distemper. [t. NL, t. Gk.: m. *choreia* dance]

cho·re·og·ra·pher (kōr′ĭ ŏg′rə fər), *n.* a person who creates dance compositions; a dance director.

cho·re·og·ra·phy (kōr′ĭ ŏg′rə fĭ), *n.* **1.** the art of composing ballets, etc., and arranging separate dances. **2.** the art of representing the various movements in dancing by a system of notation. **3.** the art of dancing. Also, *esp. Brit.,* **cho·reg·ra·phy** (kə rĕg′rə fĭ, kō-). [f. *choreo-* (comb. form repr. Gk. *choreia* dance) + -GRAPHY] —**cho·re·o·graph·ic** (kōr′ĭ ə grăf′ĭk), *adj.*

cho·ri·amb (kōr′ĭ ămb′, kōr′-), *n. Pros.* a foot of four syllables, two short between two long.

cho·ri·am·bus (kōr′ĭ ăm′bəs, kōr′-), *n., pl.* **-bi** (-bī), **-buses.** choriamb. [t. L, t. Gk.: m. *choriambos*]

cho·ric (kōr′ĭk, kŏr′-), *adj.* of or for a chorus.

cho·ri·oid (kōr′ĭ oid′), *adj., n. Anat.* choroid.

cho·ri·on (kōr′ĭ ŏn′), *n. Embryol.* the outermost of the extra embryonic membranes of land vertebrates, contributing to the placenta in the placental mammals and next to the shell (or the shell membrane) in egg-laying types. [t. NL, t. Gk.] —**cho′ri·on′ic,** *adj.*

chor·is·ter (kōr′ĭs tər, kŏr′-), *n.* **1.** a singer in a choir. **2.** a male singer in a church choir; a choirboy. **3.** a choir leader. [f. s. ML *chorista* chorister + -ER¹; r. ME *queristre,* t. AF, der. *quer* CHOIR]

cho·rog·ra·phy (kə rŏg′rə fĭ, kō-), *n. Geog.* the systematic description and analysis of regions or of a region. [t. L: m.s. *chorographia,* t. Gk.] —**cho·rog′ra·pher,** *n.* —**cho·ro·graph·ic** (kōr′ə grăf′ĭk), **cho·ro·graph′i·cal,** *adj.* —**cho′ro·graph′i·cal·ly,** *adv.*

cho·roid (kōr′oid), *Anat.* —*adj.* **1.** like the chorion; membranous (applied esp. to a delicate, highly vascular membrane or coat of the eyeball between the sclerotic coat and the retina). —*n.* **2.** the choroid coat of the eye. Also, **chorioid.** See diag. under eye. [t. Gk.: m.s. *choroeidēs,* prop. *chorīoeidēs* like a membrane]

chor·tle (chōr′təl), *v.,* **-tled, -tling,** *n.* —*v.t., v.i.* **1.** to chuckle or utter with glee. —*n.* **2.** a gleeful chuckle. [b. CHUCKLE and SNORT; coined by Lewis Carroll in *Through the Looking-Glass* (1871)] —**chor′tler,** *n.*

cho·rus (kōr′əs), *n., pl.* **-ruses,** *v.,* **-rused, -rusing** —*n.* **1.** *Music.* **a.** a group of persons singing in concert. **b.** (in an opera, oratorio, etc.) such a company singing in connection with soloists or individual singers. **c.** a piece of music for singing in concert. **d.** a part of a song in which others join the principal singer or singers. **e.** any recurring refrain. **2.** simultaneous utterance in singing, speaking, etc. **3.** the sounds uttered. **4.** (in musical shows) **a.** the company of dancers and singers. **b.** the singing or song of such a company. **5.** (in ancient Greek use) **a.** a dance performed by a company of persons and accompanied with song or narration, orig. as a religious rite. **b.** a company of singers, dancers, or narrators supplementing the performance of the main actors. **6.** (in later use) **a.** a company of persons, or a single person, having a similar function in a play, esp. in the Elizabethan drama. **b.** a part of a drama rendered by such a company or person. —*v.t.* **7.** to sing or utter in chorus. —*v.i.* **8.** to sing or speak in chorus. [t. L, t. Gk.: m. *chorós* dance, band of dancers, chorus]

chorus girl, *Theat.* a female member of the chorus (of a musical comedy or the like). —**chorus boy.**

Chor·zów (hō′zhōof), *n.* Królewska Huta.

chose¹ (chōz), *v.* pt. and obs. pp. of **choose.**

chose² (shōz), *n. Law.* **1.** a thing; an article of personal property. **2. chose in action,** an intangible property right, as a right to collect a debt or damages. [t. F: thing, g. L *causa* CAUSE]

cho·sen (chō′zən), *v.* **1.** pp. of **choose.** —*adj.* **2.** selected from a number; preferred. **3.** *Theol.* elect.

Cho·sen (chō′sĕn′), *n.* Japanese name of **Korea.**

cho·sen people (chō′zən), the Israelites; the Jews. Ex. 19, etc.

Chou (jō), *n.* a Chinese dynasty, beginning in legendary times and continuing into historical times. The traditional date for its foundation, 1122 B.C., cannot be verified; it ended c249 B.C.

Chou En-lai (jō′ ĕn′lī′), born 1898, Chinese communist leader.

chough (chŭf), *n.* a European crow, *Pyrrhocorax pyrrhocorax*, of a glossy black color, with red feet and beak. [ME *choghe*. Cf. OE *cēo*]

chouse (chous), *v.*, **choused, chousing,** *n.* *Archaic.* —*v.t.* **1.** to swindle; cheat; dupe (often fol. by *of* or *out of*). —*n.* **2.** a swindle. **3.** a swindler. **4.** a dupe. [var. of *chiaus*, ? t. Turk.: m. *chāush* official messenger (esp. a Turkish envoy who in 1609 perpetrated a swindle)]

chow (chou), *n.* **1.** one of a Chinese breed of dogs of medium size, with a thick, even coat of brown or black hair and a black tongue. **2.** *U.S. Slang.* food. [short for CHOW-CHOW]

chow-chow (chou′chou′), *n.* **1.** a Chinese mixed fruit preserve. **2.** *China, India, etc.* any mixed food, or food in general, or a meal. **3.** a mixed pickle in mustard (orig. East Indian). **4.** chow (def. 2). [Pidgin English]

Chow
(20 in. high at the shoulder)

chow·der (chou′dər), *n.* *U.S.* a kind of soup or stew made of clams, fish, or vegetables, with potatoes, onions, and various other ingredients and seasoning. [prob. t. F: m. *chaudière* caldron, g. LL *caldāria*, der. *caldus, calidus* hot]

chow mein (chou′ mān′), a stew of mushrooms, celery, onions, and various Chinese vegetables, topped with shredded chicken, shrimp, etc., and served with fried noodles. [t. Chinese: fried flour]

Chr., Christian.

Chres·tien de Troyes (krĕ tyăn′ də trwä′), c1140-c1191, French poet. Also, **Chré·tien′ de Troyes.**

chres·tom·a·thy (krĕs tŏm′ə thĭ), *n.*, *pl.* **-thies.** a collection of selected passages, esp. from a foreign language. [t. Gk.: m. s. *chrēstomátheia*, lit., useful learning]

chrism (krĭz′əm), *n.* *Eccles.* **1.** a consecrated oil used by certain churches in the rites of baptism, confirmation, etc. **2.** consecrated oil generally. **3.** a sacramental anointing; the rite of confirmation, esp. in the Greek Church. Also, **chrisom.** [learned respelling of ME *crisme*, OE *crisma*, t. L: m. *chrīsma*, t. Gk.: unguent, unction] —**chris′mal,** *adj.*

chris·ma·to·ry (krĭz′mə tōr′ĭ), *n.*, *pl.* **-ries.** *Eccles.* a receptacle for the chrism. [t. ML: m. s. *chrīsmatōrium*]

chris·om (krĭz′əm), *n.* *Eccles.* **1.** chrism. **2.** *Obs.* a white cloth or robe formerly put on a child at baptism, and also at burial if the child died soon after baptism. [var. of CHRISM]

Christ (krīst), *n.* *Bible.* **1.** the Anointed; the Messiah expected by the Jews. **2.** Jesus of Nazareth, as fulfilling this expectation. [learned respelling of ME and OE *Crist*, t. L: m. s. *Christus*, t. Gk.: m. *Christōs* anointed, trans. of Heb. *māshīaḥ* anointed, messiah]

Christ·church (krīst′chûrch′), *n.* a seaport in New Zealand, on the E coast of South Island. 101,200; with suburbs, 135,500 (est. 1941).

christ·cross (krĭs′krôs′, -krŏs′), *n.* the figure or mark of a cross. [lit., Christ's cross]

christ·cross-row (krĭs′krôs′rō′, -krŏs′-), *n.* *Archaic* or *Dial.* the alphabet. Also, **crisscross-row.**

chris·ten (krĭs′ən), *v.t.* **1.** to receive into the Christian church by baptism; baptize. **2.** to give a name to at baptism. **3.** to name and dedicate; give a name to; name. **4.** *Colloq.* to make use of for the first time. [ME *cristene(n)*, OE *cristnian* make Christian (by baptism), der. *cristen* Christian, t. L: m. s. *Christiānus*]

Chris·ten·dom (krĭs′ən dəm), *n.* **1.** Christians collectively. **2.** the Christian world. **3.** *Obs.* Christianity. [ME and OE *cristendōm*, f. *cristen* Christian + -DOM]

chris·ten·ing (krĭs′ən ĭng, krĭs′nĭng), *n.* the ceremony of baptism, esp. as accompanied by the giving of the name to the infant baptized.

Christ·hood (krīst′hŏŏd), *n.* the condition of being the Christ.

Chris·tian (krĭs′chən), *adj.* **1.** pertaining to or derived from Jesus Christ or his teachings. **2.** believing in or belonging to the religion of Jesus Christ. **3.** pertaining to Christianity or Christians. **4.** exhibiting a spirit proper to a follower of Jesus Christ; Christlike. **5.** *Colloq.* decent or respectable. **6.** *Colloq.* human, or not brutal. —*n.* **7.** one who believes in Jesus Christ; an adherent of Christianity. **8.** one who exemplifies in his life the teachings of Christ. **9.** *Colloq.* a decent or presentable person. **10.** *Colloq., Dial.* a human being as distinguished from an animal. **11.** the hero of Bunyan's *Pilgrim's Progress*. **12.** *U.S.* a Campbellite. [t. L: s. *Christiānus*]

Christian X, 1870–1947, king of Denmark, 1912–47.

Christian Brothers, a Roman Catholic religious order of laymen, founded in 1684 for the education of the poor (in full, **Brothers of the Christian Schools**).

Christian Era, the period extending from the assumed date of the birth of Jesus, adopted in Christian countries.

Chris·tia·ni·a (krĭs tyä′nĭ ä; *also for 2* krĭs′chĭ ăn′ĭ ə, -tĭ-), *n.* **1.** former name of **Oslo.** **2.** Also, **Christiania turn** or **Christy.** *Skiing.* a type of turn originating in Norway in which the body is swung around from a

crouching position, in order to turn the skis into a new direction or to stop quickly.

Chris·ti·an·i·ty (krĭs′chĭ ăn′ə tĭ), *n.*, *pl.* **-ties. 1.** the Christian religion. **2.** Christian beliefs or practices; Christian quality or character. **3.** a particular Christian religious system. **4.** state of being a Christian.

Chris·tian·ize (krĭs′chə nīz′), *v.*, **-ized, -izing.** —*v.t.* **1.** to make Christian. **2.** to imbue with Christian principles. —*v.i.* **3.** to become Christian; profess Christianity. —**Chris′tian·i·za′tion,** *n.* —**Chris′tian·iz′·er,** *n.*

Chris·tian·like (krĭs′chən līk′), *adj.* like or befitting a Christian.

Chris·tian·ly (krĭs′chən lĭ), *adj.* **1.** Christianlike. —*adv.* **2.** in a Christian manner.

Christian name, the name given one at baptism, as distinguished from the family name; the given name.

Christian Science, a system of religious teaching, based on the Scriptures, the most notable application of which is the treatment of disease by mental and spiritual means, founded about 1866 by Mrs. Mary Baker Glover Eddy of Concord, N. H. —**Christian Scientist.**

Chris·ti·na (krĭs tē′nə), *n.* 1626–89, queen of Sweden, 1632–89 (daughter of Gustavus Adolphus).

Christ·less (krīst′lĭs), *adj.* **1.** without Christ or the spirit of Christ. **2.** unchristian. —**Christ′less·ness,** *n.*

Christ·like (krīst′līk′), *adj.* like Christ; showing the spirit of Christ. —**Christ′like′ness,** *n.*

Christ·ly (krīst′lĭ), *adj.* **1.** of or like Christ. **2.** Christlike. —**Christ′li·ness,** *n.*

Christ·mas (krĭs′məs), *n.* **1.** the annual festival of the Christian church commemorating the birth of Jesus: celebrated on December 25. **2.** Dec. 25 (**Christmas Day**), now generally observed as an occasion for gifts, greetings, etc. [ME *cristmasse*, OE *Cristes mæsse* mass of Christ. See -MAS]

Christmas Carol, a story (1843) by Dickens.

Christmas Eve, the evening preceding Christmas.

Christmas Island, 1. a British island in the Indian ocean, ab. 190 mi. S of Java. 1237 pop. (est. 1936); 60 sq. mi. **2.** one of the Gilbert and Ellice Islands, in the central Pacific: the largest atoll in the Pacific. 30 mi. across.

Christmas pudding, *Brit.* plum pudding.

Christ·mas·tide (krĭs′məs tīd′), *n.* the season of Christmas. [f. CHRISTMAS + TIDE[1] time]

Christmas tree, an evergreen, white, or artificial tree hung with decorations at Christmas.

Chris·to et ec·cle·si·ae (krĭs′tō ĕt ĕklē′zĭ ē′), *Latin.* for Christ and the church, or the Christian congregation.

Chris·tophe (krēs tôf′), *n.* **Henri** (än rē′), 1767–1820, Negro general and king of Haiti, 1811–20.

Chris·to·pher (krĭs′tə fər), *n.* **Saint,** died A.D. 250?, Christian martyr: protector of travelers.

Christ's-thorn (krīsts′thôrn′), *n.* any of certain Old World thorny shrubs or small trees supposed to have been used for Christ's crown of thorns, as the rhamnaceous plants *Zizyphus Spina-Christi* and *Paliurus.*

Chris·ty (krĭs′tĭ), *n.* Christiania (def. 2).

Chris·ty (krĭs′tĭ), *n.* **Howard Chandler,** born 1873, U.S. illustrator and painter.

-chroic, adjectival word element indicating color (of skin, plants, etc.). Cf. **-chrous.** [t. Gk.: m.s. *chrōikós* colored]

chrom-, 1. a word element referring to color as in *chromic, chromite.* **2.** *Chem.* **a.** a word element referring to chromium, as in *chromic, bichromate.* **b.** a combining form in chemistry used to distinguish a colored compound from its colorless form. Also, **chromo-.** [def. 1, see -CHROME; def. 2, see CHROMIUM]

-chrom-, a word element synonymous with **chrom-,** as in *polychromatic.*

chro·ma (krō′mə), *n.* **1.** purity of a color, or of its freedom from white or gray. **2.** intensity of distinctive hue; saturation of a color. [t. Gk.: color]

chromat-, var. of **chromato-** before vowels.

chro·mate (krō′māt), *n.* *Chem.* a salt of chromic acid which contains the radical CrO_4^{-2}.

chro·mat·ic (krō măt′ĭk), *adj.* **1.** pertaining to color or colors. **2.** *Music.* **a.** involving a modification of the normal scale by the use of accidentals. **b.** progressing by semitone to a tone having the same letter name, as in C to C-sharp. [t. L: s. *chrōmaticus*, t. Gk.: m. *chrōmatikós* relating to color (chiefly in musical sense)] —**chro·mat′i·cal·ly,** *adv.*

chromatic aberration, *Optics.* (of a lens system) the variation of either the focal length or the magnification, with different wave lengths of light, characterized by prismatic coloring at the edges of, and color distortion within, the optical image.

chro·mat·ics (krō măt′ĭks), *n.* the science of colors. Also, **chro·ma·tol·o·gy** (krō′mə tŏl′ə jĭ). —**chro·ma·tist** (krō′mə tĭst), *n.*

chromatic scale, *Music.* a scale progressing entirely by semitones. See illus. under **scale.**

chro·ma·tid (krō′mə tĭd), *n.* *Biol.* one of two identical chromosomal strands into which a chromosome splits longitudinally preparatory to cell division.

chro·ma·tin (krō′mə tĭn), *n.* *Biol.* that portion of the animal or plant cell nucleus which readily takes on stains. See diag. under **cell.** [f. CHROMAT- + -IN[2]]

chromato-, 1. a word element referring to color. 2. a word element meaning "chromatin." [t. Gk., comb. form of *chrōma* color]

chro·ma·tol·y·sis (krō/mətŏl/əsĭs), *n. Biol., Pathol.* the dissolution and disintegration of chromatin.

chro·ma·to·phore (krō/mətəfōr/), *n.* 1. *Zool.* **a.** a pigmented body or cell, as one of those which through contraction and expansion produce a temporary color in cuttlefishes, etc. **b.** a colored mass of protoplasm. 2. *Bot.* one of the plastids in plant cells. —**chro·ma·to·phor·ic** (krō/mə tə fōr/ĭk, -fŏr/ĭk), *adj.*

chrome (krōm), *n., v.,* **chromed, chroming.** —*n.* 1. chromium, esp. as a source of various pigments, as chrome yellow and chrome green. 2. *Dyeing.* the dichromate of potassium or sodium. —*v.t.* 3. *Dyeing.* to subject to a bath of dichromate of potassium or sodium. [t. F, t. Gk.: m. *chrōma* color]

-chrome, a word element meaning "color," as in *polychrome.* [t. Gk.: m. *chrōma*]

chrome alum, *Chem.* 1. ammonium chromic sulphate, $Cr_2(SO_4)_3(NH_4)_2SO_4 \cdot 24H_2O$, a water-soluble, green crystalline compound. 2. a dark-violet double sulfate of chromium and potassium, $KCr(SO_4)_2 \cdot 12H_2O$, crystallizing like common alum, and used in dyeing.

chrome green, the permanent green color made from chromic oxide, or any similar pigment made largely from chromic oxide, employed in printing textiles, etc.

chrome red, a bright-red pigment consisting of the basic chromate of lead.

chrome steel, steel of great hardness and strength, containing chromium, carbon, and other elements. Also, **chromium steel.**

chrome yellow, any of several yellow pigments in shades from lemon to deep orange, composed of chromates of lead, barium, or zinc, esp. the first.

chro·mic (krō/mĭk), *adj. Chem.* of or containing chromium, esp. in the trivalent state (Cr^{+3}).

chromic acid, *Chem.* a hypothetical acid, H_2CrO_4, which exists only in solution and forms chromates.

chro·mite (krō/mīt), *n.* 1. *Chem.* a salt of chromous acid. 2. a common mineral, iron magnesium chromite, $(Fe, Mg)Cr_2O_4$: the principal ore of chromium.

chro·mi·um (krō/mĭ əm), *n. Chem.* a lustrous, hard, brittle metallic element occurring in compounds, which are used for making pigments in photography to harden gelatin, as a mordant, etc. *Symbol:* Cr; *at. wt.:* 52.01; *at. no.:* 24; *sp. gr.:* 7.1. [f. Gk. *chrōm(a)* color + -IUM]

chromium steel, chrome steel.

chro·mo (krō/mō), *n., pl.* **-mos.** chromolithograph.

chromo-, var. of chrom-, used before consonants, as in **chromogen.**

chro·mo·gen (krō/mə jən), *n.* 1. *Chem.* any substance found in organic fluids which forms colored compounds when oxidized. 2. *Dyeing.* a colored compound which, though not a dye itself, can be converted into a dye.

chro·mo·gen·ic (krō/mə jĕn/ĭk), *adj.* 1. producing color. 2. pertaining to chromogen or a chromogen. 3. (of bacteria) forming some characteristic color or pigment, usually valuable in identification.

chro·mo·lith·o·graph (krō/mōlĭth/ə grăf/, -gräf/), *n.* a picture produced by chromolithography.

chro·mo·li·thog·ra·phy (krō/mōlĭ thŏg/rə fĭ), *n.* the process of lithographing in colors. —**chro·mo·li·thog·ra·pher** (krō/mōlĭ thŏg/rə fər), *n.* —**chro·mo·lith·o·graph/ic,** *adj.*

chro·mo·mere (krō/mə mĭr/), *n. Biol.* one of the chromatin granules or a chromosome.

chro·mo·phore (krō/mə fōr/), *n. Chem.* 1. any chemical group which produces color in a compound, as the azo group -N=N-. 2. the structural layout of atoms which is found in many colored organic compounds.

chro·mo·pho·to·graph (krō/mōfō/tə grăf/, -gräf/), *n.* a picture produced by chromophotography.

chro·mo·pho·tog·ra·phy (krō/mōfə tŏg/rə fĭ), *n.* photography in colors. —**chro/mo·pho/to·graph/ic,** *adj.*

chro·mo·plasm (krō/mə plăz/əm), *n. Biol.* chromatin.

chro·mo·plast (krō/mə plăst/), *n. Bot.* a plastid, or specialized mass of protoplasm, containing coloring matter other than chlorophyll.

chro·mo·some (krō/mə sōm/), *n. Biol.* each of several threadlike, rodlike, or beadlike bodies which contain the chromatin during the meiotic and the mitotic processes. [f. CHROMO- + -SOME[3]] —**chro/mo·so/mal,** *adj.*

chromosome number, *Biol.* the characteristic number of chromosomes for each biological species. In sex cells this number is haploid (1n); in fertilized eggs it is diploid (2n), one half coming from the egg, one half from the sperm; more numerous numbers may be triploid (3n), tetraploid (4n), polyploid (5+n).

chro·mo·sphere (krō/mə sfĭr/), *n. Astron.* 1. a scarlet, gaseous envelope surrounding the sun outside the photosphere, from which enormous masses of hydrogen, and other gases are erupted. 2. a gaseous envelope surrounding a star. —**chro·mo·spher·ic** (krō/məsfĕr/ĭk), *adj.*

chro·mous (krō/məs), *adj. Chem.* containing divalent chromium (Cr^{+2}).

chro·myl (krō/məl, -mēl), *adj. Chem.* containing the radical CrO_2^{-2}.

chron-, a word element meaning "time," as in *chronaxie.* Also, **chrono-.** [t. Gk., comb. form of *chrónos*]

Chron., *Bible.* Chronicles.

chron., 1. chronological. 2. chronology.

chro·nax·ie (krō/năk sĭ), *n. Physiol.* the minimum time that a current of twice the threshold strength (that value below which no excitation occurs) must flow in order to excite a tissue. Also, **chro/nax·y.** [f. CHRON- + m. Gk. *axía* value]

chron·ic (krŏn/ĭk), *adj.* 1. inveterate; constant: *a chronic smoker.* 2. continuing a long time: *chronic civil war.* 3. having long had a disease, habit, or the like: *a chronic invalid.* 4. (of disease) long continued (opposed to *acute*). Also, **chron/i·cal.** [t. L: s. *chronicus,* t. Gk.: m. *chronikós* concerning time] —**chron/i·cal·ly,** *adv.* —**Syn.** 1. habitual, confirmed, hardened.

chron·i·cle (krŏn/ə kəl), *n., v.,* **-icled, -icling.** —*n.* 1. a record of events in the order of time; a history. —*v.t.* 2. to record in or as in a chronicle. [ME, t. AF, var. of OF *cronique,* t. ML: m. *chronica,* t. Gk.: m. *chronikā* annals, neut. pl.] —**chron/i·cler,** *n.*

Chron·i·cles (krŏn/ə kəlz), *n.* two historical books of the Old Testament, following Kings.

chrono-, var. of chron-, used before consonants, as in *chronogram.*

chron·o·gram (krŏn/ə grăm/), *n.* 1. an inscription or the like in which certain letters, usually distinguished from the others, express by their values as Roman numerals a date or epoch. 2. a record made by a chronograph. —**chron·o·gram·mat·ic** (krŏn/ō grə măt/ĭk), *adj.*

chron·o·graph (krŏn/ə grăf/, -gräf/), *n.* a clock-driven instrument for recording the exact instant of occurrences, or for measuring small intervals of time. —**chron/o·graph/ic,** *adj.*

chron·o·log·i·cal (krŏn/ə lŏj/ə kəl), *adj.* 1. arranged in the order of time: *chronological tables.* 2. pertaining to or in accordance with chronology: *chronological character.* Also, **chron/o·log/ic.** —**chron/o·log/i·cal·ly,** *adv.*

chro·nol·o·gist (krə nŏl/ə jĭst), *n.* one versed in chronology. Also, **chro·nol/o·ger.**

chro·nol·o·gy (krə nŏl/ə jĭ), *n., pl.* **-gies.** 1. a particular statement of the supposed or accepted order of past events. 2. the science of arranging time in periods and ascertaining the dates and historical order of past events.

chro·nom·e·ter (krə nŏm/ə tər), *n.* a timekeeper with special mechanism for ensuring accuracy, for use in determining longitude at sea or for any purpose where very exact measurement of time is required. —**chron·o·met·ric** (krŏn/ə mĕt/rĭk), **chron/o·met/ri·cal,** *adj.* —**chron/o·met/ri·cal·ly,** *adv.*

chro·nom·e·try (krə nŏm/ə trĭ), *n.* 1. the art of measuring time accurately. 2. the measuring of time by periods or divisions.

chron·o·scope (krŏn/ə skōp/), *n.* an instrument for measuring accurately very small intervals of time, as in determining the velocity of projectiles.

-chroous, -chroic. [suffix f. s. Gk. *chróa* surface, color + -ous]

chrys·a·lid (krĭs/əlĭd), *Entomol.* —*n.* 1. a chrysalis. —*adj.* 2. pertaining to a chrysalis.

chrys·a·lis (krĭs/əlĭs), *n., pl.* **chrysalises, chrysalides** (krĭ săl/ə dēz/), the hard-shelled pupa of a moth or butterfly; an obtected pupa. [t. L: m. *chrysallis,* t. Gk.: gold-colored sheath of butterflies]

Chrysalis of swallowtail butterfly (Lateral view)

chry·san·the·mum (krĭ săn/thə məm), *n.* 1. any of the perennial asteraceous plants constituting the genus Chrysanthemum, as *C. Leucanthemum,* the oxeye daisy. 2. any of many cultivated varieties of *C. mortifolium,* a native of China, and of other species of Chrysanthemum, notable for the diversity of color and size of their autumnal flowers. 3. the flower. [t. L, t. Gk.: m. *chrȳsán·themon,* lit., golden flower]

Chry·se·is (krī sē/ĭs), *n. Gk. Legend* (in the Iliad) the beautiful daughter of Chryses, a priest of Apollo. She was captured and given to Agamemnon.

chrys·el·e·phan·tine (krĭs/ĕl ə făn/tĭn, -tĭn), *adj.* overlaid with gold and ivory (used in describing objects of ancient Greece). [t. Gk.: m. s. *chrȳselephántinos*]

chrys·o·ber·yl (krĭs/ə bĕr/əl), *n.* a mineral, beryllium aluminate, $BeAl_2O_4$, occurring in green or yellow crystals, sometimes used as a gem. [t. L: m.s. *chrȳsobēryllus,* t. Gk.: m. *chrȳsobēryllos*]

chrys·o·lite (krĭs/ə līt/), *n.* olivine. [ME *crisolite,* t. ML: m. *crīsolitus,* t. Gk.: m. *chrȳsolithos,* t. Gk.: a bright yellow stone (prob. topaz)]

chrys·o·prase (krĭs/ə prāz/), *n.* a nickel-stained, apple-green chalcedony, much used in jewelry. [t. L: m. s. *chrȳsoprasus,* t. Gk.: m. *chrȳsóprasos,* lit., gold leek; r. ME *crisopace,* t. OF]

Chrys·os·tom (krĭs/əs təm, krĭ sŏs/təm), *n.* **Saint John,** A.D. 347?–407, archbishop of Constantinople.

chrys·o·tile (krĭs/ə tĭl), *n. Mineral.* a fibrous variety of serpentine.

chtho·ni·an (thō/nĭ ən), *adj. Chiefly Gk. Myth.* dwelling in the earth; pertaining to the deities or spirits of the underworld. [f. s. Gk. *chthónios* in the earth + -AN]

chub (chŭb), *n., pl.* **chubs,** (*esp. collectively*) **chub.** 1. a common fresh-water fish, *Leuciscus cephalus,* of Europe, with a thick fusiform body. 2. any of several allied fishes, as the *Semotilus atromaculatus* of America. 3. any of several unrelated American fishes, esp. the tautog of the Atlantic and the deep-water whitefishes (*Coregonidae*) of the Great Lakes. [ME *chubbe*]

chub·by (chŭb′ĭ), *adj.*, **-bier, -biest.** round and plump: *a chubby face, chubby cheeks.*

chuck[1] (chŭk), *v.t.* **1.** to pat or tap lightly, as under the chin. **2.** *Brit.* to throw with a quick motion, usually a short distance. **3.** *Brit. Slang.* to eject (fol. by *out*): *they chucked him out of the cabaret.* **4.** *Brit. Slang.* to resign from: *he's chucked his job.* **5. chuck it,** *Brit. Slang.* stop it. **—***n.* **6.** a light pat or tap, as under the chin. **7.** *Brit.* a toss; a short throw. [prob. imit., but cf. F *choquer* knock]

chuck[2] (chŭk), *n.* **1.** the cut of beef between the neck and the shoulderblade. **2.** a block or log used as a chock. **3.** *Mach.* a mechanical device for holding tools or work in a machine: *lathe chuck,* etc. [var. of CHOCK]

Simple chuck[2] (def. 3)

chuck[3] (chŭk), *v.i., v.t.* **1.** to cluck. **—***n.* **2.** a clucking sound. **3.** *Archaic.* a term of endearment. [imit.]

chuck-full (chŭk′fōōl′), *adj.* chock-full.

chuck·le (chŭk′əl), *v.,* **chuckled, chuckling,** *n.* **—***v.i.* **1.** to laugh in a soft, amused manner, usually with satisfaction. **2.** to laugh to oneself. **3.** to cluck, as a fowl. **—***n.* **4.** a soft, amused laugh, usually with satisfaction. **5.** *Obs.* the call of a hen to her young; a cluck. [freq. of CHUCK[3]] **—chuck′ler,** *n.* **—Syn.** 4. See **laugh.**

chuck·ie·head (chŭk′əl hĕd′), *n. Colloq.* a blockhead. **—chuck′le·head′ed,** *adj.* **—chuck′le·head′ed·ness,** *n.*

chuck-luck (chŭk′lŭk′), *n. U.S.* a dice game in which the players bet on the possible combinations formed by three dice thrown from an hourglass-shaped metal container. Also, **chuck′-a-luck′.**

chuck wagon, *Western U.S.* a wagon carrying provisions, stoves, etc., for cowboys, harvest hands, etc.

chuck-will's-wid·ow (chŭk′wĭlz wĭd′ō), *n.* a goat-sucker, *Caprimulgus corolinensis,* of the southern U.S., resembling the whippoorwill but larger.

chud·dar (chŭd′ər), *n.* a kind of fine, plain-colored woolen shawl made in India. Also, **chud·dah** (chŭd′ə), **chud′der.** [t. Hind.: m. *chadar* square piece of cloth]

Chud·sko·e (chōōd skō′yĕ), *n.* Russian name of Peipus.

chuff[1] (chŭf), *n.* **1.** a rustic. **2.** a boor; a churl. **3.** a miserly fellow. [orig. unknown] **—chuff′y,** *adj.* **—chuff′i·ly,** *adv.* **—chuff′i·ness,** *n.*

chuff[2] (chŭf, chōōf), *adj. Eng. Dial.* fat-cheeked; chubby. [adj. use of obs. *chuff,* n., muzzle]

chug (chŭg), *n., v.,* **chugged, chugging.** **—***n.* **1.** a short, dull explosive sound: *the steady chug of an engine.* **—***v.i.* **2.** to make this sound. **3.** to move while making this sound: *the train chugged along.* [imit.]

Chu-Kiang (chōō′jyäng′), *n.* a river in SE China, forming a large estuary below Canton. ab. 100 mi. Also, **Canton River** or **Pearl River.**

chuk·ker (chŭk′ər), *n. Polo.* one of the periods of play. Also, **chuk′kar.** [t. Hind.: m. *chakar*]

chum (chŭm), *n., v.,* **chummed, chumming.** **—***n.* **1.** an intimate friend or companion: *boyhood chums.* **2.** a roommate, as at college. **—***v.i.* **3.** to associate intimately. **4.** to share the same room or rooms with another. [orig. uncert.]

chum·my (chŭm′ĭ), *adj.,* **-mier, -miest.** intimate; sociable. **—chum′mi·ly,** *adv.*

chump (chŭmp), *n.* **1.** *Colloq.* a blockhead or dolt. **2.** a short, thick piece of wood. **3.** the thick, blunt end of anything. **4.** *Slang.* the head. **—chump′ish,** *adj.*

Chung·king (chŏŏng′kĭng′; *Chin.* jōŏng′chĭng′), *n.* a city in central China, on the Yangtze: provisional capital of China, 1937–46. 535,000 (est. 1939).

chunk (chŭngk), *n.* **1.** a thick mass or lump of anything: *a chunk of bread.* **2.** *Colloq.* a thickset and strong person. **3.** a strong and stoutly built horse or other animal. **4.** a substantial amount (of something). [nasalized var. of CHUCK[2], n.]

chunk·y (chŭngk′ĭ), *adj.,* **chunkier, chunkiest.** **1.** thick or stout; thickset; stocky. **2.** in a chunk or chunks. **—chunk′i·ness,** *n.*

church (chûrch), *n.* **1.** an edifice for public Christian worship. **2.** public worship of God in a church; church service. **3.** the whole body of Christian believers. **4.** any division of this body professing the same creed and acknowledging the same ecclesiastical authority; a Christian denomination: *the Methodist Church.* **5.** that part of the whole Christian body, or of a particular denomination, belonging to the same city, country, nation, etc. **6.** a body of Christians worshiping in a particular building or constituting one congregation. **7.** the ecclesiastical organization or power as distinguished from the state. **8.** the clerical profession. **9.** a place of public worship of a non-Christian religion. **10.** any non-Christian religious society, organization, or congregation: *the Jewish church.* **—***v.t.* **11.** to conduct or bring to church, esp. for special services. **12.** to subject to church discipline. **13.** to perform a church service of thanksgiving for (a woman after childbirth). [ME *churche, chirche,* OE *cir(i)ce, cyrice* (c. G *kirche*), ult. t. Gk.: m. *kȳriakón* (*dōma*) Lord's (house)]

church·go·er (chûrch′gō′ər), *n.* **1.** one who goes to church, esp. habitually. **2.** *Chiefly Brit.* a member of the Established Church, in contrast to a Nonconformist. **—church′go′ing,** *n., adj.*

Church·ill (chûrch′ĭl, -əl), *n.* **1. John.** See **Marlborough,** Duke of. **2. Lord Randolph,** 1849–95, British statesman (father of Winston L. S. Churchill). **3. Winston,** 1871–1947, U. S. novelist. **4. Winston Leonard Spencer,** born 1874, British statesman and writer: prime minister, 1940–45 and since 1951. **5.** a river in Canada, flowing from E Saskatchewan NE through Manitoba to Hudson Bay. ab. 1000 mi. **6.** a seaport and railway terminus on Hudson Bay at the mouth of this river.

church·less (chûrch′lĭs), *adj.* **1.** without a church. **2.** not belonging to or attending any church.

church·like (chûrch′līk′), *adj.* resembling, or appropriate to, a church: *churchlike silence.*

church·ly (chûrch′lĭ), *adj.* **1.** of or appropriate for the church or a church; ecclesiastical. [OE *ciriclīc;* f. CHURCH + -LY] **—church′li·ness,** *n.*

church·man (chûrch′mən), *n., pl.* **-men. 1.** an ecclesiastic; a clergyman. **2.** an adherent or active supporter of a church. **3.** *Brit.* a member of the Established Church. **—church′man·ly,** *adj.* **—church′man·ship′,** *n.*

Church of Christ, Scientist, (official name) Christian Science.

Church of England, the national Church continuous with English history, Catholic in faith and order, but incorporating many emphases of the Protestant Reformation and establishing independence from the papacy.

Church of Jesus Christ of Latter-day Saints, (official name) the Mormon Church.

Church of Rome, Roman Catholic Church.

church text, *Print.* Old English (def. 2).

church·ward (chûrch′wərd), *adv.* **1.** Also, **church′wards.** toward the church. **—***adj.* **2.** directed toward the church: *churchward summons.*

church·ward·en (chûrch′wôr′dən), *n.* **1.** *Anglican Ch.* a lay officer who looks after the secular affairs of the church, and who, in England, is the legal representative of the parish. **2.** *Prot. Episc. Ch.* a lay church officer who, with other members of the vestry, is in charge of the temporal management of the parish. **3.** *Colloq.* a clay tobacco pipe with a very long stem.

church·wom·an (chûrch′wŏŏm′ən), *n., pl.* **-women.** a female member of a church, esp. of an Anglican church.

church·yard (chûrch′yärd′), *n.* the yard or ground adjoining a church, often used as a graveyard.

churl (chûrl), *n.* **1.** a peasant; a rustic. **2.** a rude, boorish, or surly person. **3.** a niggard; miser. **4.** *Eng. Hist.* a freeman of the lowest rank. [ME; OE *ceorl* freeman of the lowest rank, c. G *kerl.* Cf. CARL]

churl·ish (chûr′lĭsh), *adj.* **1.** of a churl or churls. **2.** like a churl; boorish; rude; surly. **3.** niggardly; sordid. **4.** difficult to work or deal with, as soil. **—churl′ish·ly,** *adv.* **—churl′ish·ness,** *n.*

churn (chûrn), *n.* **1.** a vessel or machine in which cream or milk is agitated to make butter. **2.** any of various similar vessels or machines. **3.** *Brit.* a milk can. **—***v.t.* **4.** to stir or agitate in order to make into butter: *to churn cream.* **5.** to make by the agitation of cream: *to churn butter.* **6.** to shake or agitate with violence or continued motion. **—***v.i.* **7.** to operate a churn. **8.** to move in agitation, as a liquid or any loose matter: *leaves churning.* [ME *chyrne,* OE *cyrin,* c. Icel. *kirna* tub, pail] **—churn′er,** *n.*

churn·ing (chûr′nĭng), *n.* **1.** act of one that churns. **2.** the butter made at one time.

churr (chûr), *v.i.,* chirr. [? var. of CHIRR]

chute[1] (shōōt), *n.* **1.** a channel, trough, tube, shaft, etc., for conveying water, grain, coal, etc., to a lower level; a shoot. **2.** a waterfall; a steep descent, as in a river; a rapid. **3.** parachute. [b. F *chute* a fall (b. OF *cheue* and OF *cheoite,* both der. OF *cheoir* fall, g. L *cadere*) and E SHOOT]

chute[2] (shōōt), *n.* a steep slope, as for tobogganing [Frenchified spelling of d. E. *shoot, shute,* ME *show* steep slope, akin to SHOOT v.]

Chu Teh (jōō′ dŭ′), born 1886, leader of Chinese communist army.

chut·ney (chŭt′nĭ), *n., pl.* **-neys.** a sauce or relish of East Indian origin compounded of both sweet and sour ingredients (fruits, herbs, etc.) with spices and other seasoning. Also, **chut′nee.** [t. Hind.: m. *chatnī*]

chy·la·ceous (kīlā′shəs), *adj.* of or resembling chyle.

chyle (kīl), *n.* a milky fluid containing emulsified fat and other products of digestion, formed from the chyme in the small intestine and conveyed by the lacteals and the thoracic duct to the veins. [t. NL: m.s. *chȳlus,* t. Gk.: m. *chȳlós* juice, chyle] **—chy′lous,** *adj.*

chyme (kīm), *n.* the pulpy matter into which food is converted by gastric digestion. [t. L: m.s. *chȳmus,* t. Gk.: m. *chȳmós* juice] **—chy′mous,** *adj.*

chym·is·try (kĭm′ĭs trĭ), *n. Archaic.* chemistry. **—chym′ist,** *n.* **—chym′ist,** *n.*

Cia., (Sp. *Compañía*) Company.

Cib·ber (sĭb′ər), *n.* **Colley** (kŏl′ĭ), 1671–1757, British actor and dramatist.

ci·bo·ri·um (sĭ bōr′ĭ əm), *n., pl.* **-boria** (-bōr′ĭ ə). **1.** a permanent canopy placed over an altar. **2.** any vessel designed to contain the consecrated bread or sacred wafers for the eucharist. [t. ML: canopy, in L drinking cup, t. Gk.: m. *kibōrion* cup, seed vessel of the Egyptian bean]

Ciborium (def. 2)

ci·ca·da (sĭ kā′də, -kä′-), *n.*, *pl.* **-das, -dae** (-dē). any insect of the family *Cicadidae*, which comprises large homopterous insects noted for the shrill sound produced by the male by means of vibrating membranes or drums on the under side of the abdomen.

ci·ca·la (sĭ kä′lə; *It.* sē kä′lä), *n.*, *pl.* **-las,** *It.* **-le** (-lĕ). cicada. [t. It. or L]

Imago of cicada. Cicada septendecim

cic·a·tric·le (sĭk′ə trĭk′əl), *n.* *Embryol.* the small blastodisc on the yolk of an unincubated bird's egg. [t. L: m.s. *cicatrīcula* a small scar]

cic·a·trix (sĭk′ə trĭks, sĭ kā′trĭks), *n.*, *pl.* **cicatrices** (sĭk′ə trī′sēz). 1. the new tissue which forms over a wound or the like, and later contracts into the scar. 2. *Bot.* the scar left by a fallen leaf, seed, etc. Also, **cic·a·trice** (sĭk′ə trĭs). [t. L] —**cic·a·tri·cial** (sĭk′ə trĭsh′əl), *adj.* —**cic·at·ri·cose** (sĭ kăt′rə kōs′, sĭk′ə-trĭ-), *adj.*

cic·a·trize (sĭk′ə trīz′), *v.*, **-trized, -trizing.** —*v.t.* 1. to heal by inducing the formation of a cicatrix. —*v.i.* 2. to become healed by the formation of a cicatrix. —**cic′a·tri·za′tion,** *n.* —**cic′a·triz′er,** *n.*

cic·e·ly (sĭs′ə lĭ), *n.*, *pl.* **-lies.** a plant of the parsley family, *Myrrhis odorata* (the **sweet cicely** of England), grown for its pleasing odor and sometimes used as a pot-herb. [? t. L: m.s. *seselis,* t. Gk.: kind of plant]

Cic·e·ro (sĭs′ə rō), *n.* 1. **Marcus Tullius,** (mär′kəs tŭl′ĭ əs), 106–43 B.C., Roman statesman, orator, and writer. 2. a city in NE Illinois, near Chicago. 67,544 (1950). —**Cic·e·ro·ni·an** (sĭs′ə rō′nĭ ən), *adj.*

cic·e·ro·ne (sĭs′ə rō′nĭ, chĭch′ə-; *It.* chē′chĕ rō′nĕ), *n.,* *pl.* **-nes** (-nĭz), *It.* **-ni** (-nē). a guide who shows and explains the antiquities, curiosities, etc., of a place. [t. It., t. L: abl. sing. of *Cicero* CICERO (def. 1)]

cich·lid (sĭk′lĭd), *n.* any of the *Cichlidae,* a family of spiny-rayed, fresh-water fishes of South America, Africa and southern Asia, superficially resembling the American sunfishes: often kept in home aquariums. [t. NL: s. *Cichlidae,* pl., der. Gk. *kíchlē* kind of sea fish] —**cich-loid** (sĭk′loid), *n.,* *adj.*

ci·cho·ri·a·ceous (sĭ kōr′ĭ ā′shəs), *adj.* belonging to the *Cichoriaceae,* or chicory family (a composite family) of plants, as the dandelion, endive, lettuce, salsify, etc. [f. s. L *cichorium* chicory + -ACEOUS]

ci·cis·be·o (sĭ sĭs′bĭ ō′; *It.* chē′chēz bĕ′ō), *n.,* *pl.* **-bei** (-bĭ ē′; *It.* chē′bĕ′ē). a professed gallant of a married woman. [t. It.]

Cid (sĭd; *Sp.* thēd), *n.* ("*El Cid Campeador*"; *Ruy Díaz de Bivar*) 1040?–99, Spanish soldier and hero of the wars against the Moors. [t. Sp., t. Ar.: m. *sayyid* lord]

-cidal, adjective form of *-cide²*. [f. - CIDE² + -AL¹]

-cide¹, a word element meaning "killer," as in **matri-cide¹.** [t. L: m. *-cida,* der. *caedere* kill]

-cide², a word element meaning "act of killing," as in **matricide².** [t. L: m. *-cidium,* der. *caedere* kill]

ci·der (sī′dər), *n.* the expressed juice of apples (or formerly of some other fruit), used for drinking, either before fermentation (**sweet cider**) or after fermentation (**hard cider**), or for making applejack, vinegar, etc. Also, *Brit.,* **cyder.** [ME *sidre,* t. OF, g. LL *sicera,* t. Gk.: m. *síkera,* repr. Heb. *shēkār* strong drink]

cider press, a press for crushing apples for cider.

ci·de·vant (sē də vän′), *adj.* French. former; late: *a ci-devant official.* [F: heretofore]

Cie., (F *Compagnie*) Company. Also, **cie.**

Cien·fue·gos (syĕn fwĕ′gōs), *n.* a seaport in S Cuba. 49,452 (1943).

C.I.F., cost, insurance, and freight (included in the price quoted). Also, **c.i.f.**

ci·gar (sĭ gär′), *n.* a small, shaped roll of tobacco leaves prepared for smoking. [t. Sp.: m. *cigarro,* ? der. *cigarra* grasshopper, g. L *cicāla,* var. of *cicāda* CICADA]

cig·a·rette (sĭg′ə rĕt′, sĭg′ə rĕt′), *n.* a roll of finely cut tobacco for smoking, usually enclosed in thin paper. Also, **cig′a·ret′.** [t. F, dim. of *cigare* CIGAR]

cil·i·a (sĭl′ĭ ə), *n.pl.,* *sing.* **cilium** (sĭl′ĭ əm). 1. the eyelashes. 2. *Zool.* short hairs on the surface of protozoans or of metazoan cells accomplishing locomotion or producing a current. 3. *Bot.* minute, hairlike processes. [t. L, pl. of *cilium* eyelid, eyelash]

Flower with cilia

cil·i·ar·y (sĭl′ĭ ĕr′ĭ), *adj.* 1. noting or pertaining to a delicate ring of tissue in the eye from which the lens is suspended by means of fine ligaments. See diag. under eye. 2. pertaining to cilia.

Cil·i·a·ta (sĭl′ĭ ā′tə), *n. pl. Zool.* a class of protozoans distinguished by the cilia on part or all of the body, among the most common of microscopic animals.

cil·i·ate (sĭl′ĭ ĭt, -āt), *n.* one of the *Ciliata.* —**cil′i·at′ed,** *adj.*

cil·ice (sĭl′ĭs), *n.* 1. a garment of haircloth; a hair shirt. 2. haircloth. [t. F, t. L: m.s. *cilicium,* t. Gk.: m. *kilíkion* coarse cloth made of (orig. Cilician) goat's hair; r. OE *cilic,* t. L (as above)]

Ci·li·cia (sĭ lĭsh′ə), *n.* an ancient country and Roman province in SE Asia Minor.

Ci·li·cian Gates (sĭ lĭsh′ən), a narrow mountain pass

in SE Asia Minor, leading from ancient Cappadocia into Cilicia.

cil·i·o·late (sĭl′ĭ ə lĭt, -lāt′), *adj.* furnished with minute cilia.

Ci·ma·bu·e (chē′mä bōō′ĕ), *n.* **Giovanni** (jô vän′nē), 1240?–1302? Florentine painter: teacher of Giotto.

Cim·ar·ron (sĭm′ə rŏn′, sĭm′ə rōn′, -rŏn′), *n.* a river flowing from NE New Mexico E to the Arkansas river in Oklahoma. ab. 600 mi.

ci·mex (sī′mĕks), *n.,* *pl.* **cimices** (sĭm′ə sēz′). the bed-bug (of the genus *Cimex*). [t. L: bug]

Cim·me·ri·an (sĭ mĭr′ĭ ən), *adj.* 1. pertaining to or suggestive of a mythical western people said by Homer to dwell in perpetual darkness. 2. very dark; gloomy.

Ci·mon (sī′mən), *n.* 507?–449 B.C., Athenian military and naval commander, and statesman: son of Miltiades.

cinch¹ (sĭnch), *U.S.* —*n.* 1. a strong girth for a saddle or pack. 2. *Colloq.* a firm hold or tight grip. 3. *Slang.* something sure or easy. —*v.t.* 4. to gird with a cinch; gird or bind firmly. 5. *Slang.* to seize on or make sure of. [t. Sp.: m. *cincha,* g. L *cincta* girdle, der. L *cingere* gird]

cinch² (sĭnch), *n.* *Cards.* a variety of seven-up. [? t. Sp.: m. *cinco* five]

cin·cho·na (sĭn kō′nə), *n.* 1. any of the rubiaceous trees or shrubs constituting the genus *Cinchona,* as *C. calisaya,* native in the Andes, and cultivated there in Java and India for their bark, which yields quinine and other alkaloids. 2. the medicinal bark of such trees or shrubs; Peruvian bark. [t. NL, named after the Countess of *Chinchón* (1576–1639), wife of a Spanish viceroy of Peru] —**cin·chon·ic** (sĭn kŏn′ĭk), *adj.*

cin·cho·nine (sĭn′kə nēn′, -nĭn), *n.* a colorless, crystalline alkaloid, $C_{19}H_{22}ON_2$, obtained from various species of the cinchona bark, used as an antiperiodic and quinine substitute.

cin·cho·nism (sĭn′kə nĭz′əm), *n.* an abnormal condition due to the excessive use of cinchona or quinine, characterized by buzzing in the ears, giddiness, etc.

cin·cho·nize (sĭn′kə nīz′), *v.t.,* **-nized, -nizing.** to treat with cinchona or quinine.

Cin·cin·nat·i (sĭn′sə năt′ĭ, -năt′ə), *n.* a city in SW Ohio, on the Ohio river. 503,998 (1950).

Cin·cin·na·tus (sĭn′sə nā′təs), *n.* **Lucius Quinctius** (lōō′shəs kwĭngk′tĭ əs), 519?–439? B.C., Roman patriot. He was called from his farm to be dictator in 458 and 439 B.C. Each time he resigned his dictatorship and returned to his farm when the enemy was defeated.

cinc·ture (sĭngk′chər), *n.,v.,* **-tured, -turing.** —*n.* 1. a belt or girdle. 2. something surrounding or encompassing like a girdle; a surrounding border. 3. act of girding or encompassing. —*v.t.* 4. to gird with or as with a cincture; encircle; encompass. [t. L: m.s. *cinctūra* girdle]

cin·der (sĭn′dər), *n.* 1. a burned-out or partially burned piece of coal, wood, etc. 2. (*pl.*) any residue of combustion; ashes. 3. (*pl.*) *Geol.* coarse scoriae thrown out of volcanoes. —*v.t.* 4. to reduce to cinders: *cindering flame.* [ME *cyndir, sindir,* OE *sinder* cinder, slag. c. G *sinter*] —**cin′der·y,** *adj.*

Cin·der·el·la (sĭn′də rĕl′ə), *n.* 1. heroine of a well-known fairy tale. 2. any girl, esp. one of unrecognized beauty, who is forced to be a household drudge, or who, for the time being, is despised and oppressed.

cinder track, a path covered with small cinders, used in running races.

cin·e·ma (sĭn′ə mə), *n.* 1. a motion picture. 2. **the cinema,** motion pictures collectively. 3. a motion picture theater. [short for CINEMATOGRAPH] —**cin·e·mat·ic** (sĭn′ə măt′ĭk), *adj.* —**cin′e·mat′i·cal·ly,** *adv.*

cin·e·ma·tize (sĭn′ə mə tīz′), *v.t., v.i.,* **-tized, -tizing.** *Brit.* cinematograph (def. 3).

cin·e·mat·o·graph (sĭn′ə măt′ə grăf′, -gräf′), *Brit.* —*n.* 1. a motion-picture projector. 2. a motion-picture camera. —*v.t., v.i.* 3. to take motion pictures (of). Also, **kinematograph.** [f. *cinemato-* (comb. form repr. Gk. *kínēma* motion) + -GRAPH] —**cin·e·ma·tog·ra·pher** (sĭn′ə mə tŏg′rə fər), *n.* —**cin·e·mat′o·graph′ic,** *adj.* —**cin′e·mat′o·graph′i·cal·ly,** *adv.* —**cin′e·ma·tog′ra·phy,** *n.*

cin·e·ole (sĭn′ĭ ōl′), *n.* *Chem.* a colorless liquid, $C_{10}H_{18}O$, a terpene ether found in eucalyptus and other essential oils and used in medicine; eucalyptol. Also, **cin·e·ol** (sĭn′ĭ ōl′, -ŏl′). [t. NL: m. *oleum cinae* (reversed), oil of wormwood]

cin·e·rar·i·a (sĭn′ə râr′ĭ ə), *n.* any of various horticultural varieties of the asteraceous plant *Senecio cruentus* (or *Cineraria cruenta*), a native of the Canary Islands, with heart-shaped leaves and clusters of flowers with white, blue, purple, red, or variegated rays. [t. NL, prop. fem. of L *cinerārius* pertaining to ashes (with reference to the soft white down on the leaves)]

cin·e·rar·i·um (sĭn′ə râr′ĭ əm), *n.,* *pl.* **-raria** (-râr′ĭ ə), a place for depositing the ashes of the dead after cremation. [t. L] —**cin·e·rar·y** (sĭn′ə rĕr′ĭ), *adj.*

cin·e·ra·tor (sĭn′ə rā′tər), *n.* an incinerator.

cin·e·re·ous (sə nĭr′ĭ əs), *adj.* 1. in the state of ashes: *cinereous bodies.* 2. resembling ashes. 3. ashen; ash-colored; grayish: *cinereous crow.* Also, **cin·e·ri·tious** (sĭn′ə rĭsh′əs). [t. L: m. *cinereus* ash-colored]

cin·gu·lum (sĭng′gyə ləm), *n.,pl.* **-la** (-lə). *Anat., Zool.* a belt, zone, or girdlelike part. [t. L: girdle] —**cin·gu-late** (sĭng′gyə lĭt, -lāt′), **cin′gu·lat′ed,** *adj.*

cin·na·bar (sĭn′ə bär′), n. 1. a mineral, mercuric sulfide, occurring in red crystals or masses: the principal ore of mercury. It is very heavy (*sp. gr.*: 8.1). 2. red mercuric sulfide, used as a pigment. 3. bright red; vermilion. [t. L: m. *cinnabaris*, t. Gk.: m. *kinnábari*; of Oriental orig.; r. ME *cynoper*, t. ML]

cin·nam·ic (sĭ năm′ĭk, sĭn′ə mĭk), adj. of or obtained from cinnamon.

cinnamic acid, an unsaturated acid, $C_6H_5CH\cdot CH\cdot CO_2H$, derived from cinnamon, balsams, etc.

cin·na·mon (sĭn′ə mən), n. 1. the aromatic inner bark of any of several lauraceous trees of the genus *Cinnamomum* of the East Indies, etc., esp. **Ceylon Cinnamon,** *C. zeylanicum*, much used as a spice, and **Saigon cinnamon,** *C. loureirii*, used in medicine as a cordial and carminative. 2. a tree yielding cinnamon. 3. any of various allied or similar trees. 4. cassia bark. 5. yellowish or reddish brown. [t. LL, t. Gk.: m. *kinnamon*; r. ME *cynamome*, t. F: m. *cinnamome*. Ult. of Semitic orig.; cf. Heb. *qinnāmōn*]

cinnamon bear, the cinnamon-colored variety of the black bear of North America, *Euarctos americanus.*

cinnamon stone, a light, brown grossularite garnet.

cinque (sĭngk), n. the five at dice, cards, etc. [t. F; r. ME *cink*, t. OF; g. L *quinque* five]

cin·que·cen·tist (chĭng′kwə chĕn′tĭst), n. an Italian writer or an artist of the 16th century.

cin·que·cen·to (chĭng′kwə chĕn′tō), n. the 16th century, with reference to Italy, esp. to the Italian art or literature of that period. [t. It.: five hundred, short for *mille cinquecento* one thousand five hundred]

cinque·foil (sĭngk′foil′), n. 1. any species of the rosaceous genus *Potentilla*, as the **creeping cinquefoil** (*P. reptans*) of the Old World and the **silvery cinquefoil** (*P. argentea*) of North America. 2. a decorative design or feature resembling the leaf of cinquefoil, as an architectural ornament or opening of a generally circular or rounded form divided into five lobes by cusps. 3. *Her.* a five-leafed clover, used as a bearing. [ME *synkefoile*, through OF (of unrecorded), g. L *quinquefolium*, f. *quinque* five + *folium* leaf]

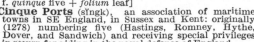

Cinquefoil (def. 2)

Cinque Ports (sĭngk), an association of maritime towns in SE England, in Sussex and Kent: originally (1278) numbering five (Hastings, Romney, Hythe, Dover, and Sandwich) and receiving special privileges in return for aiding in the naval defense of England.

C I O, Congress of Industrial Organizations. Also, **C.I.O.**

ci·on (sī′ən), n. scion (def. 2). (Cion is the usual spelling of scion in U. S. horticulture and nursery practice).

-cion, a suffix having the same function as **-tion,** as in *suspicion.* [t. L: s. *-cio*, f. *-c*, final vowel in verb stem, + *-io*, n. suffix. Cf. -SION, -TION]

Ci·pan·go (sĭ păng′gō), n. *Poetic.* Japan.

ci·pher (sī′fər), n. 1. an arithmetical symbol (0) which denotes naught, or no quantity or magnitude. 2. any of the Arabic numerals or figures. 3. Arabic numerical notation collectively. 4. something of no value or importance. 5. a person of no influence; a nonentity. 6. a secret method of writing, as by a specially formed code of symbols. 7. writing done by such a method. 8. the key to a secret method of writing. 9. a combination of letters, as the initials of a name, in one design; a monogram. —v.i. 10. to use figures or numerals arithmetically. —v.t. 11. to calculate numerically; figure. 12. to write in, or as in, cipher. Also, **cypher.** [ME *siphre*, t. ML: m. *ciphra*, t. Ar.: m. *ṣifr*, lit., empty. Cf. ZERO]

cip·o·lin (sĭp′ə lĭn), n. a variety of marble with alternate white and greenish zones and a laminated structure. [t. F, t. It.: m. *cipollino* (so called from its layered structure), dim. of *cipolla* onion, g. L *cēpa*]

cir., (L *circa, circiter, circum*) about. Also, **circ.**

cir·ca (sûr′kə), *prep., adv.* about (used esp. in approximate dates). *Abbr.:* ca., c. *or* c: *born ca. 1550.* [t. L]

Cir·cas·sia (sər kăsh′ə, -ĭə), n. a region NW of the Caucasus Mountains in the S Soviet Union in Europe, bordering on the Black Sea.

Cir·cas·sian (sər kăsh′ən, -ĭən), n. 1. a native or inhabitant of Circassia. 2. a North Caucasic language.

Cir·ce (sûr′sĭ), n. 1. *Gk. Legend.* the enchantress represented by Homer as turning the companions of Odysseus into swine by a magic drink. 2. a dangerously or irresistibly fascinating woman. —**Cir·ce·an** (sər sē′ən), adj.

cir·ci·nate (sûr′sə nāt′), adj. 1. made round; ring-shaped. 2. *Bot.* rolled up on the axis at the apex, as a leaf, etc. [t. L: m. s. *circinātus*, pp.] —**cir′ci·nate′ly,** adv.

cir·cle (sûr′kəl), n., v., **-cled, -cling.** —n. 1. a closed plane curve consisting of all points equally distant from a point within it, called the center. 2. the portion of a plane bounded by such a curve. 3. any circular object, formation, or arrangement. 4. a ring; a circlet; crown. 5. the ring of a circus. 6. a section of seats in a theater: *dress circle.* 7. the area within

Circinate fronds of a young fern

which something acts, exerts influence, etc. 8. a series ending where it began, and perpetually repeated: *the circle of the year.* 9. *Logic.* an inconclusive form of reasoning in which unproved statements, or their equivalents, are used to prove each other; vicious circle. 10. a complete series forming a connected whole; cycle: *the circle of the sciences.* 11. a number of persons bound by a common tie; a coterie. 12. an administrative division, esp. of a province. 13. *Geog.* a parallel of latitude. 14. *Astron.* a. the orbit of a heavenly body. b. its period of revolution. c. an instrument for observing the transit of stars across the meridian of the observer. 15. a sphere or orb. 16. a ring of light in the sky; halo. —v.t. 17. to enclose in a circle; surround: *the enemy circled the hill.* 18. to move in a circle or circuit round: *he circled the house cautiously.* —v.i. 19. to move in a circle. [t. L: m.s. *circulus*, dim. of *circus* circle, ring; r. ME *cercle*, t. OF] —**cir′cler,** n.

—**Syn.** 11. CIRCLE, CLUB, COTERIE, SET, SOCIETY are terms applied to more or less restricted social groups. A CIRCLE may be a pleasant little group meeting chiefly for conversation; in the plural it often suggests a whole section of society interested in one mode of life, occupation, etc.: *a sewing circle, a language circle, in theatrical circles.* CLUB implies an association with definite requirements for membership, fixed dues, and often a stated time of meeting: *an athletic club.* COTERIE suggests a little group closely and intimately associated because of great congeniality: *a literary coterie.* SET refers to a number of persons of similar background, upbringing, interests, etc., somewhat like a CLIQUE (SEE RING) but without disapproving connotations; it often implies wealth or interest in social activities: *the country club set.* A SOCIETY is a group associated to further common interests of a cultural or practical kind: *a Humane Society.*

cir·clet (sûr′klĭt), n. 1. a small circle. 2. a ring. 3. a ring-shaped ornament, esp. for the head.

circling disease, a fatal infectious bacterial disease of cattle and sheep which damages the nervous system and often causes the afflicted animal to walk in circles.

cir·cuit (sûr′kĭt), n. 1. act of going or moving around. 2. a circular journey; a round. 3. a roundabout journey or course. 4. a periodical journey from place to place, to perform certain duties, as of judges to hold court or ministers to preach. 5. the persons making such a journey. 6. the route followed, places visited, or district covered by such a journey. 7. the line going around or bounding any area or object; the distance about an area or object. 8. the space within a bounding line. 9. a number of theaters controlled by one manager or visited in turn by the same actors, etc. 10. *Elect.* a. the complete path of an electric current, including the generating apparatus or other source, or a distinct segment of the complete path. b. a more or less elaborately contrived arrangement of conductors, wave guides, electronic tubes, and other devices, for the investigation or utilization of electrical phenomena. c. the diagram of the connections of such apparatus. —v.t. 11. to go or move around; make the circuit of. —v.i. 12. to go or move in a circuit. [ME, t. L: s. *circuitus*]

circuit breaker, a device for interrupting an electric circuit between separable contacts under normal or abnormal conditions.

circuit court, 1. a court holding sessions at various intervals in different sections of a judicial district. 2. the court of general jurisdiction found in a number of the states.

circuit court of appeal, the federal intermediate court which sits in each of the federal circuits and reviews judgments of the federal district courts and whose judgments are in turn reviewed by the Supreme Court of the U.S.

cir·cu·i·tous (sər kū′ə təs), adj. roundabout; not direct. —**cir·cu′i·tous·ly,** adv. —**cir·cu′i·tous·ness,** n.

circuit rider, a Methodist minister who rides from place to place to preach along a circuit.

cir·cu·i·ty (sər kū′ə tĭ), n. circuitous quality; roundabout character: *circuity of language or of a path.*

cir·cu·lar (sûr′kyə lər), adj. 1. of or pertaining to a circle. 2. having the form of a circle; round. 3. moving in or forming a circle or a circuit. 4. moving or occurring in a cycle or round. 5. circuitous; roundabout; indirect. 6. pertaining to a circle or set of persons. 7. (of a letter, etc.) addressed to a number of persons or intended for general circulation. —n. 8. a circular letter, notice, or statement for circulation among the general public for business or other purposes. [t. L: s. *circulāris*, der. L *circulus* circle; r. ME *circuler*, t. AF] —**cir·cu·lar·i·ty** (sûr′kyə lăr′ə tĭ), n. —**cir′cu·lar·ly,** adv.

cir·cu·lar·ize (sûr′kyə lə rīz′), v.t., **-ized, -izing.** 1. to send circulars to. 2. to make into a circular letter, etc. 3. to make circular. —**cir′cu·lar·i·za′tion,** n. —**cir′cu·lar·iz′er,** n.

circular measure, a measurement system for circles.

1 circle	= 360 degrees (4 quadrants)
1 quadrant	= 90 degrees
1 degree	= 60 minutes
1 minute	= 60 seconds

circular mil, a unit used principally for measuring the cross-sectional area of wires, being the area of a circle having the diameter of one mil.

circular saw, a saw consisting of a circular plate or disk with a toothed edge, which is rotated at high speed in machines for sawing logs, cutting lumber.

circular triangle, a triangle in which the sides are arcs of circles.

cir·cu·late (sûr/kyə lāt/), v., -lated, -lating. —v.i. 1. to move in a circle or circuit; move or pass through a circuit back to the starting point, as the blood in the body. 2. to pass from place to place, from person to person, etc.; be disseminated or distributed. —v.t. 3. to cause to pass from place to place, person to person, etc.: to circulate a rumor. [t. L: m.s. circulātus, pp., made circular, gathered into a circle] —cir/cu·la/tive, adj. —cir/cu·la/tor, n. —cir·cu·la·to·ry (sûr/kyə lə tōr/ĭ), adj.

circulating decimal, a decimal in which a series of digits is repeated ad infinitum, as 0.147232323 . . .

circulating library, a library whose books circulate among the members or subscribers.

circulating medium, 1. any coin or note passing, without endorsement, as a medium of exchange. 2. such coins or notes collectively.

cir·cu·la·tion (sûr/kyə lā/shən), n. 1. act of circulating, or moving in a circle or circuit. 2. the recurrent movement of the blood through the various vessels of the body. 3. any similar circuit or passage, as of the sap in plants. 4. the transmission or passage of anything from place to place, person to person, etc. 5. the distribution of copies of a publication among readers. 6. the number of copies of each issue of a newspaper, magazine, etc., distributed. 7. coin, notes, bills, etc., in use as currency; currency.

circum-, a prefix referring to movement around, motion on all sides, as in circumvent, circumnavigate, circumference. [t. L, prefix use of circum, adv. and prep., orig. acc. of circus circle, ring. See CIRCUS]

cir·cum·am·bi·ent (sûr/kəm ăm/bĭ ənt), adj. surrounding; encompassing: circumambient gloom. —cir/cum·am/bi·ence, cir/cum·am/bi·en·cy, n.

cir·cum·am·bu·late (sûr/kəm ăm/byə lāt/), v.t., v.i., -lated, -lating. to walk or go about. —cir/cum·am/·bu·la/tion, n.

cir·cum·bend·i·bus (sûr/kəm běn/də bəs), n. (in humorous use) a roundabout way; a circumlocution.

cir·cum·cise (sûr/kəm sīz/), v.t., -cised, -cising. 1. to remove the foreskin of (males), esp. as a religious rite. 2. to perform an analogous operation on (females). 3. to purify spiritually. [ME circumcise(n), t. L: m. s. circumcīsus, pp., cut around] —cir/cum·cis/er, n.

cir·cum·ci·sion (sûr/kəm sĭzh/ən), n. 1. act or rite of circumcising. 2. spiritual purification. 3. the circumcision, a. the Jews, as the circumcised people of the Bible. b. those spiritually purified. 4. (cap.) a church festival in honor of the circumcision of Jesus, observed on Jan. 1. [ME circumcisi(o)um, t. L: m.s. circumcisio]

cir·cum·fer·ence (sər kŭm/fər əns), n. 1. the outer boundary, esp. of a circular area. 2. the length of such a boundary. 3. the space within a bounding line. [t. L: m.s. circumferentia] —cir·cum·fer·en·tial (sər kŭm/fə rěn/shəl), adj.

cir·cum·flex (sûr/kəm flěks/), adj. 1. noting, or having a particular accent (^, ~, ˜), indicating orig. a combination of rising and falling pitch (as in ancient Greek), later a long vowel (as in the French bête, earlier beste), quality of sound (as in phonetic notation), etc. 2. bending or winding around. —n. 3. the circumflex accent. —v.t. 4. to bend around. [t. L: s. circumflexus, pp., bent round] —cir·cum·flex·ion (sûr/kəm flěk/shən), n.

cir·cum·flu·ent (sər kŭm/flōō ənt), adj. flowing around; encompassing: two circumfluent rivers.

cir·cum·flu·ous (sər kŭm/flōō əs), adj. 1. flowing around; encompassing: circumfluous tides. 2. surrounded by water. [t. L: m. circumfluus flowing around]

cir·cum·fuse (sûr/kəm fūz/), v.t., -fused, -fusing. 1. to pour around; diffuse. 2. to surround as with a fluid; suffuse. [t. L: m.s. circumfūsus, pp., poured around] —cir·cum·fu·sion (sûr/kəm fū/zhən), n.

cir·cum·ja·cent (sûr/kəm jā/sənt), adj. lying around; surrounding: the circumjacent parishes.

cir·cum·lo·cu·tion (sûr/kəm lō kū/shən), n. 1. a roundabout way of speaking; the use of too many words. 2. a roundabout expression. [t. L: s. circumlocūtio] —cir·cum·loc·u·to·ry (sûr/kəm lŏk/yə tōr/ĭ), adj.

cir·cum·nav·i·gate (sûr/kəm năv/ə gāt/), v.t., -gated, -gating. to sail around; make the circuit of by navigation. —cir/cum·nav/i·ga/tion, n. —cir/cum·nav/i·ga/tor, n.

cir·cum·nu·tate (sûr/kəm nū/tāt, -nōō/-), v.i., -tated, -tating. (of the apex of a stem or other growing part of a plant) to bend or move around in an irregular circular or elliptical path. —cir/cum·nu·ta/tion, n.

cir·cum·po·lar (sûr/kəm pō/lər), adj. around one of the poles of the earth or of the heavens.

cir·cum·ro·tate (sûr/kəm rō/tāt), v.i., -tated, -tating. to rotate like a wheel.

cir·cum·scis·sile (sûr/kəm sĭs/ĭl), adj. Bot. opening along a transverse circular line, as a seed vessel.

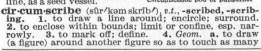

Circumscissile pod of pimpernel

cir·cum·scribe (sûr/kəm skrīb/), v.t., -scribed, -scribing. 1. to draw a line around; encircle; surround. 2. to enclose within bounds; limit or confine, esp. narrowly. 3. to mark off; define. 4. Geom. a. to draw (a figure) around another figure so as to touch as many

points as possible. b. (of a figure) to enclose (another figure) in this manner. [t. L: m.s. circumscrībere draw a line around, limit] —cir/cum·scrib/er, n.

cir·cum·scrip·tion (sûr/kəm skrĭp/shən), n. 1. act of circumscribing. 2. circumscribed state; limitation. 3. anything that circumscribes, surrounds, or encloses. 4. periphery; outline. 5. a circumscribed space. 6. a circular inscription on a coin, seal, etc. 7. Archaic. limitation of a meaning; definition. —cir/cum·scrip/-tive, adj.

cir·cum·so·lar (sûr/kəm sō/lər), adj. around the sun: circumsolar course.

cir·cum·spect (sûr/kəm spěkt/), adj. 1. watchful on all sides; cautious; prudent: circumspect in behavior. 2. well-considered: circumspect ambition. [late ME, t. L: s. circumspectus, pp., considerate, wary] —cir/cum·spect/ly, adv. —cir/cum·spect/ness, n.

cir·cum·spec·tion (sûr/kəm spěk/shən), n. circumspect observation or action; caution; prudence.

cir·cum·spec·tive (sûr/kəm spěk/tĭv), adj. given to or marked by circumspection; watchful; cautious: a circumspective approach.

cir·cum·stance (sûr/kəm stăns/), n., v., -stanced, -stancing. —n. 1. a condition, with respect to time, place, manner, agent, etc., which accompanies, determines, or modifies a fact or event. 2. (usually pl.) the existing condition or state of affairs surrounding and affecting an agent: forced by circumstances to do a thing. 3. an unessential accompaniment of any fact or event; a secondary or accessory matter; a minor detail. 4. (pl.) the condition or state of a person with respect to material welfare: a family in reduced circumstances. 5. an incident or occurrence: his arrival was a fortunate circumstance. 6. detailed or circuitous narration; specification of particulars. 7. Archaic. ceremonious accompaniment or display: pomp and circumstance. 8. under no circumstances, never; regardless of events. 9. under the circumstances, because of the conditions; such being the case. —v.t. 10. to place in particular circumstances or relations. 11. Obs. to furnish with details. 12. Obs. to control or guide by circumstances. [ME, t. L: m.s. circumstantia surrounding condition] —cir/cum·stanced/, adj.

cir·cum·stan·tial (sûr/kəm stăn/shəl), adj. 1. of, pertaining to, or derived from circumstances: circumstantial evidence. 2. of the nature of a circumstance or unessential accompaniment; secondary; incidental. 3. dealing with or giving circumstances or details; detailed; particular. 4. pertaining to conditions of material welfare: circumstantial prosperity. —cir/cum·stan/tial·ly, adv.

circumstantial evidence, proof of facts offered as evidence from which other facts are to be inferred (contrasted with direct evidence).

cir·cum·stan·ti·al·i·ty (sûr/kəm stăn/shĭ ăl/ə tĭ), n., pl. -ties. 1. the quality of being circumstantial; minuteness; fullness of detail. 2. a circumstance; a particular detail.

cir·cum·stan·ti·ate (sûr/kəm stăn/shĭ āt/), v.t., -ated -ating. 1. to set forth or support with circumstances or particulars. 2. to describe fully or minutely. —cir/cum·stan/ti·a/tion, n.

cir·cum·val·late (sûr/kəm văl/āt), adj., v., -lated, -lating. —adj. 1. surrounded by, or as by, a rampart, etc. —v.t. 2. to surround with, or as with, a rampart, etc. [t. L: m.s. circumvallātus, pp., surrounded with a rampart] —cir/cum·val·la/tion, n.

cir·cum·vent (sûr/kəm věnt/), v.t. 1. to surround or encompass as by stratagem; entrap. 2. to gain advantage over by artfulness or deception; outwit; overreach. 3. to go around: circumvent the bridge. [t. L: s. circumventus, pp., surrounded] —cir/cum·vent/er, cir/cum·ven/tor, n. —cir/cum·ven/tion, n. —cir/cum·ven/tive, adj.

cir·cum·vo·lu·tion (sûr/kəm və lōō/shən), n. 1. the act of rolling or turning around. 2. a single complete turn. 3. a winding or folding about something. 4. a fold so wound. 5. a winding in a sinuous course; a sinuosity. 6. roundabout course or procedure.

cir·cum·volve (sûr/kəm vŏlv/), v.t., v.i., -volved, -volving. to revolve. [t. L: m.s. circumvolvere roll around]

cir·cus (sûr/kəs), n. 1. a company of performers, animals, etc., esp. a traveling company. 2. the performance itself. 3. a circular arena surrounded by tiers of seats, for the exhibition of wild animals, acrobatic feats, etc. 4. (in ancient Rome) a large, usually oblong, or oval, roofless enclosure, surrounded by tiers of seats rising one above another, for chariot races, public games, etc. 5. anything like the Roman circus, as a natural amphitheater, a circular range of houses, etc. 6. flying circus. 7. Brit. a place, originally circular, where several streets come together: Piccadilly Circus. 8. uproar; a display of rowdy sport. 9. an exhibition. 10. Obs. a circlet or ring. [t. L, t. Gk.: m. kírkos ring]

Circus Max·i·mus (măk/sə məs), the great Roman circus in the hollow between the Palatine and the Aventine.

cirque (sûrk), n. 1. a circular space, esp. a natural amphitheater, as in mountains. 2. Poetic. a circle or ring of any kind. 3. a circus. [t. F, t. L: m. s. circus]

cir·rate (sĭr/āt), adj. having cirri. [t. L: m. s. cirrātus curled, der. cirrus curl]

cir·rho·sis (sĭ rō'sĭs), *n.* *Pathol.* a disease of the liver characterized by increase of connective tissue and alteration in gross and microscopic make-up. [t. NL, f. m.s. Gk. *kirrhós* tawny + *-osis* -OSIS] —**cir·rhot·ic** (sĭ rŏt'ĭk), *adj.*

cir·ri·ped (sĭr'ə pĕd'), *n.* **1.** any of the *Cirripedia*, an order or group of crustaceans, typically having slender legs bearing bristles used in gathering food. —*adj.* **2.** having legs like cirri. **3.** pertaining to the *Cirripedia*. [t. NL: m. s. *Cirripedia*, pl.; f. cirri- CIRRO- + *-pedia* footed]

cirro-, a combining form of **cirrus.**

cir·ro·cu·mu·lus (sĭr'ō kū'myə ləs), *n.* *Meteorol.* a cloud of high altitude, consisting of small fleecy balls or flakes, often in rows or ripples.

cir·rose (sĭr'ōs, sĭ rōs'), *adj.* **1.** having a cirrus or cirri. **2.** resembling cirri. **3.** *Meteorol.* of the nature of cirrus clouds. Also, **cir·rous** (sĭr'əs).

cir·ro·stra·tus (sĭr'ō strā'təs), *n.* *Meteorol.* a high veillike cloud or sheet of haze, often giving rise to halos around the sun and moon, sometimes very thin and only slightly whitening the blue of the sky. —**cir'ro·stra'·tive,** *adj.*

cir·rus (sĭr'əs), *n.*, *pl.* **cirri** (sĭr'ī). **1.** *Bot.* a tendril. **2.** *Zool.* a filament or slender appendage serving as a barbel, tentacle, foot, arm, etc. **3.** *Meteorol.* a variety of cloud having a thin, fleecy or filamentous appearance, normally occurring at great altitudes and consisting of minute ice crystals. [t. L: curl, tuft, fringe]

cir·soid (sûr'soid), *adj.* varixlike; varicose. [t. Gk.: m.s. *kirsoeidḗs*]

cis-, a prefix denoting relative nearness (this side of) applied to time as well as space, as in *cisalpine.* Cf. **citra-**. [t. L, prefix use of *cis*, prep.]

cis·al·pine (sĭs ăl'pĭn, -pīn), *adj.* on this (the Roman or south) side of the Alps.

cis·at·lan·tic (sĭs'ət lăn'tĭk), *adj.* on this (the speaker's or writer's) side of the Atlantic.

Cis·cau·ca·sia (sĭs'kô kā'zhə, -shə), *n.* that part of Caucasia north of the Caucasus Mountains.

cis·co (sĭs'kō), *n.*, *pl.* **-coes, -cos.** *U.S.* any of several species of whitefish of the genus *Leucichthys*, esp. *L. artedi*, the lake herring of the Great Lakes. [t. N Amer. Ind.]

cis·mon·tane (sĭs mŏn'tān), *adj.* on this (esp. the north) side of the mountains.

cis·pa·dane (sĭs'pə dān', sĭs pā'dān), *adj.* on this (the Roman or south) side of the river Po. [f. cis- + m.s. L *Padānus* of the Po river]

cis·soid (sĭs'oid), *Geom.* —*n.* **1.** a curve having a cusp at the origin and a point of inflection at infinity. —*adj.* **2.** included between the concave sides of two intersecting curves (opposed to *sistroid*): *a cissoid angle*. [t. Gk.: m.s. *kissoeidḗs* ivy-like]

cist[1] (sĭst), *n.* *Class. Antiq.* a box or chest, esp. for sacred utensils. [t. L: s. *cista*; t. Gk.: m.s. *kístē* CHEST]

cist[2] (sĭst, kĭst), *n.* a prehistoric sepulchral tomb or casket. [t. Welsh, t. L: s. *cista*. See CIST[1]]

cis·ta·ceous (sĭs tā'shəs), *adj.* belonging to the *Cistaceae*, or rockrose family of plants. [f. s. Gk. *kístos* rockrose + -ACEOUS]

Cis·ter·cian (sĭs tûr'shən), *n.* **1.** a member of an order of monks and nuns founded in 1098 at Citeaux, near Dijon, France, under the rule of St. Benedict. —*adj.* **2.** belonging to this order.

Cistercian Rule, an adaptation of the Benedictine Rule stressing contemplation and extreme asceticism.

cis·tern (sĭs'tərn), *n.* **1.** a reservoir, tank, or vessel for holding water or other liquid. **2.** *Anat.* a reservoir or receptacle of some natural fluid of the body. [ME, t. L: s. *cisterna*, der. *cista* box]

cit., **1.** citation. **2.** cited. **3.** citizen.

cit·a·del (sĭt'ə dəl, -dĕl'), *n.* **1.** a fortress in or near a city, intended to keep the inhabitants in subjection, or, in a siege, to form a final point of defense. **2.** any strongly fortified place; a stronghold. **3.** a heavily armored structure on a warship. [t. F: m. *citadelle*, t. It.: m. *cittadella*, der. *città* CITY]

ci·ta·tion (sī tā'shən), *n.* **1.** act of citing or quoting. **2.** the quoting of a passage, book, author, etc.; a reference to an authority or a precedent. **3.** a passage cited; a quotation. **4.** mention or enumeration. **5.** call or summons, esp. to appear in court. **6.** a document containing such a summons. **7.** *Mil.* mention of a soldier or unit, in orders, usually for gallantry: *Presidential citation.* [ME *citacion*, t. L: m.s. *citātio*] —**ci·ta·to·ry** (sī'tə tōr'ī), *adj.*

cite (sīt), *v.t.*, **cited, citing. 1.** to quote (a passage, book, author, etc.), esp. as an authority. **2.** to mention in support, proof, or confirmation; refer to as an example. **3.** to summon officially or authoritatively to appear in court. **4.** to summon or call; rouse to action: *cited to the field of battle.* **5.** to call to mind; mention: *citing my own praise.* **6.** *Mil.* to mention (a soldier, unit, etc.) in orders, as for gallantry. [late ME, t. L: m. *citāre*, freq. of *ciēre*, *cīre*, move, excite, call] —**cit'a·ble, cite'a·ble,** *adj.*

cith·a·ra (sĭth'ə rə), *n.* kithara. [L form of KITHARA]

cith·er (sĭth'ər), *n.* cittern. Also, **cith·ern** (sĭth'ərn). [t. L: m.s. *cithara* CITHARA]

cit·ied (sĭt'ĭd), *adj.* **1.** occupied by a city or cities. **2.** formed into or like a city.

cit·i·fied (sĭt'ĭ fīd'), *adj.* having city habits, fashions, etc.

cit·i·zen (sĭt'ə zən, -sən), *n.* **1.** a member, native or naturalized, of a state or nation (as distinguished from *alien*). **2.** a person owing allegiance to a government and entitled to its protection. **3.** an inhabitant of a city or town, esp. one entitled to its privileges or franchises. **4.** an inhabitant or denizen. **5.** a civilian (as distinguished from a soldier, police officer, etc.). [ME *citisein*, t. AF, var. of OF *citeain*, der. *cite* CITY] —**cit·i·zen·ess** (sĭt'ə zən ĭs, -sən ĭs), *n. fem.*

citizen of the world, a person who is concerned about all nations, not just his own.

cit·i·zen·ry (sĭt'ə zən rī, -sən-), *n.*, *pl.* **-ries.** citizens collectively.

cit·i·zen·ship (sĭt'ə zən shĭp', -sən-), *n.* the status of a citizen, with its rights and duties.

cit·ole (sĭt'ōl, sĭ tōl'), *n.* cittern.

citra-, a prefix synonymous with **cis-**. [t. L, repr. *citrā*, adv. and prep., akin to *cis*. See CIS-]

cit·ral (sĭt'rəl), *n.* a liquid aldehyde, $C_9H_{15}CHO$, with a strong lemonlike odor, obtained from the oils of lemon, orange, etc., used in perfumery. [f. CITR(US) + AL(DEHYDE)]

cit·rate (sĭt'rāt, sī'trāt), *n.* *Chem.* a salt or ester of citric acid.

cit·re·ous (sĭt'rī əs), *adj.* lemon-yellow; greenish-yellow. [t. L: m. *citreus* of the citron tree]

cit·ric acid (sĭt'rĭk), *Chem.* an acid, $C_6H_8O_7 \cdot H_2O$, contained in many fruits, especially in limes and lemons. [f. s. L *citrus* citron tree + -IC]

cit·rin (sĭt'rĭn), *n.* *Biochem.* vitamin P.

cit·rine (sĭt'rĭn), *adj.* **1.** pale-yellow; lemon-colored. —*n.* **2.** a pellucid yellow variety of quartz. [ME, t. F: m. *citrin*, der. L *citrus* citron tree]

cit·ron (sĭt'rən), *n.* **1.** a pale-yellow fruit resembling the lemon but larger and with thicker rind, borne by a small tree or large bush, *Citrus medica*, allied to the lemon and lime. **2.** the tree itself. **3.** the rind of the fruit, candied or preserved. [t. F, t. It.: m. *citrone*, der. L *citrus* citron tree]

cit·ron·el·la (sĭt'rə nĕl'ə), *n.* a fragrant grass, *Andropogon nardus*, of southern Asia, cultivated as the source of an oil (**citronella oil**) used in making liniment, perfume, and soap. [t. NL; named from its citronlike odor]

cit·ron·el·ial (sĭt'rə nĕl'əl), *n.* a colorless, liquid aldehyde, $C_9H_{17}CHO$, found in essential oils, and used as a flavoring agent and in the perfume industry.

citron melon, *U.S.* a round, hard-fleshed watermelon, *Citrulluo vulgaris*, var. *citroides*, used for preserving.

citron wood, 1. the wood of the citron. **2.** the wood of the sandarac.

cit·rus (sĭt'rəs), *n.* **1.** any tree or shrub of the rutaceous genus *Citrus*, which includes the citron, lemon, lime, orange, grapefruit, etc. —*adj.* **2.** Also, **cit'rous.** of or pertaining to such trees or shrubs: *citrus fruit.* [t. L]

cit·tern (sĭt'ərn), *n.* an old musical instrument, related to the guitar, having a flat pear-shaped soundbox and wire strings. Also, **cither, cithern, gittern, zittern.** [b. L *cithara* CITHARA and GITTERN]

cit·y (sĭt'ī), *n.*, *pl.* **cities. 1.** a large or important town. **2.** *U.S.* an incorporated municipality, usually governed by a mayor and a board of aldermen or councilmen. **3.** *Canada.* a municipality of high rank, usually based on population. **4.** *Brit.* a borough, usually the seat of a bishop, upon which the dignity of the title has been conferred by the Crown. **5.** **the City,** the part of London, England, in which the commercial and financial interests are chiefly centered. **6.** city-state. **7.** the inhabitants of a city collectively. [ME *cite*, t. OF, g. L *cīvitas* citizenship, the state, a city] —**Syn. 1.** See **community.**

Woman playing a cittern

city editor, 1. *U.S.* the editor in charge of local news. **2.** *Brit.* the editor in charge of the financial and commercial news.

city father, one of the officials and prominent citizens of a city.

city hall, the administration building of a city government.

city man *Brit.* a financier; a person employed in the banking establishments of the City (def. 5). Also, **City man.**

city manager, a person not publicly elected but appointed by a city council to manage a city.

City of God, heaven.

City of Seven Hills, Rome.

city planning, public control of the physical development of a city, by means of a plan regulating street layout, locations of buildings, etc.

cit·y-state (sĭt'ī stāt'), *n.* a sovereign state consisting of an autonomous city with its dependencies.

Ciu·dad Bo·lí·var (sū däd' bō lē'vär), a city in E Venezuela: a port on the Orinoco. 19,764 (1941).

Ciu·dad Juá·rez (sū däd' hwä'rĕs), a city in N Mexico, across the Rio Grande from El Paso, Texas. 48,881 (1940).

---

b., blend of, blended; c., cognate with; d., dialect, dialectal; der., derived from; f., formed from; g., going back to; m., modification of; r., replacing; s., stem of; t., taken from; ?, perhaps. See the full key on inside cover.

Ciu·dad Tru·jil·lo (sū dãd′ trōō hē′yô), the capital of the Dominican Republic, on the S coast: the first European settlement in America (1496). 131,271 (est. 1946). Formerly, **Santo Domingo.**

civ., 1. civil. 2. civilian.

civ·et (sĭv′ĭt), n. 1. a yellowish unctuous substance with a strong musklike odor, obtained from a pouch in the genital region of civets and used in perfumery. 2. any of the catlike carnivorous mammals of southern Asia and Africa (subfamily *Viverrinae*) having glands in the genital region that secrete civet. 3. any of certain allied or similar animals, as the **palm civet.** Also, **civet cat** (for defs. 2, 3). [t. F: m. *civette*, t. It.: m. *zibetto*, t. Ar.: m. *zabād*]

African civet, *Civettictis civetta* (Total length 4 to 4½ ft., ab. 1 ft high)

civ·ic (sĭv′ĭk), adj. 1. of or pertaining to a city; municipal: *civic problems.* 2. of or pertaining to citizenship; civil: *civic duties.* 3. of citizens: *civic pride.* [t. L: s. *cīvicus*, der. *cīvis* citizen]

civ·ics (sĭv′ĭks), n. the science of civic affairs.

civ·ies (sĭv′ĭz), n.pl. *U.S. Colloq.* civilian clothes (as disting. from military). Also, *Brit. Colloq.*, **civvies.**

civ·il (sĭv′əl), adj. 1. of or consisting of citizens: *civil life, civil society.* 2. of the commonwealth or state: *civil affairs.* 3. of citizens in their ordinary capacity, or the ordinary life and affairs of citizens (distinguished from *military, ecclesiastical, etc.*). 4. of the citizen as an individual: *civil liberty.* 5. befitting a citizen: *a civil duty.* 6. of, or in a condition of, social order or organized government; civilized. 7. polite; courteous. 8. not rude or discourteous. 9. (of divisions of time) legally recognized in the ordinary affairs of life: *the civil year.* 10. *Law.* **a.** of or in agreement with Roman civil law. **b.** of the civil law, as the medieval and modern law derived from the Roman system. **c.** pertaining to the private rights of individuals and to legal proceedings connected with these (distinguished from *criminal, military, or political*). [ME *civile*, t. L: m.s. *cīvīlis* pertaining to citizens] —**Syn.** 7, 8. respectful, deferential, gracious, complaisant, suave, affable, urbane, courtly. CIVIL, AFFABLE, COURTEOUS, POLITE all imply avoidance of rudeness toward others. CIVIL suggests a minimum observance of social requirements. AFFABLE suggests ease of approach, often with a touch of condescension. COURTEOUS implies positive dignified, sincere, and thoughtful consideration for others. POLITE implies habitual courtesy, arising from a consciousness of one's training and the demands of "good manners." —**Ant.** 7, 8. boorish, churlish.

civil engineer, one versed in the design, construction, and maintenance of public works, such as roads, bridges, dams, canals, aqueducts, harbors, etc.

civil engineering, action, work, or profession of a civil engineer.

ci·vil·ian (sĭ vĭl′yən), n. 1. one engaged in civil pursuits (distinguished from a soldier, etc.). 2. one versed in or studying the Roman or civil law.

ci·vil·i·ty (sĭ vĭl′ə tĭ), n., pl. **-ties.** 1. courtesy; politeness. 2. a polite attention or expression. 3. *Archaic.* civilization; culture; good breeding.

civ·i·li·za·tion (sĭv′ə lə zā′shən), n. 1. an advanced state of human society, in which a high level of art, science, religion, and government has been reached. 2. those people or nations that have reached such a state. 3. the type of culture, society, etc. of a specific group: *Irish civilization.* 4. act or process of civilizing.

civ·i·lize (sĭv′ə līz′), v.t. **-lized, -lizing.** to make civil; bring out of a savage state; elevate in social and individual life; enlighten; refine. [t. ML: m.s. *cīvīlizāre.* See CIVIL, -IZE] —**civ′i·liz′a·ble,** adj. —**civ′i·liz′er,** n.

civ·i·lized (sĭv′ə līzd′), adj. 1. having an advanced culture, society, etc. 2. polite; well-bred; refined. 3. of or pertaining to civilized people.

civil law, 1. the laws of a state or nation regulating ordinary private matters (distinguished from criminal, military, or political matters). 2. the body of law proper to the city or state of Rome, as distinct from that common to all nations. 3. the systems of law derived from Roman law (distinguished from *common law, canon law*).

civil liberty, complete liberty of opinion, etc., restrained only as much as necessary for the public good.

civil list, *Brit.* the provision of money by Parliament for the king and his household.

civ·il·ly (sĭv′ə lĭ), adv. 1. in accordance with civil law. 2. politely; considerately; gently.

civil marriage, a marriage performed by a government official rather than a clergyman.

civil rights, *U.S.* rights to personal liberty established by the 13th and 14th Amendments to the Constitution and other Congressional Acts.

civil servant, *Chiefly Brit.* a civil service employee.

civil service, the public service concerned with all affairs not military, naval, legislative, or judicial.

civil war, 1. a war between parties, regions, etc. within their own country. 2. (*cap.*) **a.** the American war between the North and South (1861–65). **b.** the war in England between the Parliamentarians and Royalists (1642–52).

civ·ism (sĭv′ĭz əm), n. good citizenship.

civ·vies (sĭv′ĭz), n.pl. *Brit. Colloq.* civies.

Cl, *Chem.* chlorine.

cl., 1. carload. 2. centiliter. 3. class. 4. classification. 5. clause.

clab·ber (klăb′ər), n. 1. bonnyclabber. —v.i. 2. (of milk) to become thick in souring. [t. Irish: m. *clabar*, short for *bainne clabair* bonnyclabber, curds]

clach·an (klähK′ən), n. *Gaelic.* a small village or hamlet. [t. Gaelic, der. *clach* stone]

clack (klăk), v.i. 1. to make a quick, sharp sound, or a succession of such sounds, as by striking or cracking. 2. to talk rapidly and continually, or with sharpness and abruptness; chatter. 3. to cluck or cackle. —v.t. 4. to utter by clacking. 5. to cause to clack. —n. 6. a clacking sound. 7. something that clacks, as a rattle. 8. rapid, continual talk; chatter. 9. *Slang.* the tongue. [ME *clacke;* imit.] —**clack′er,** n.

Clack·man·nan (klăk măn′ən), n. a county in central Scotland. 34,500 pop. (est. 1946); 55 sq. mi. *Co. seat:* Clackmannan. Also, **Clack·man·nan·shire** (klăk măn′nən shĭr,′ -shər).

clad (klăd), v. pt. and pp. of **clothe.**

clado-, a word element meaning "sprout," "branch." Also, before vowels, **clad-.** [comb. form repr. Gk. *klădos* sprout]

clad·o·phyll (klăd′e fĭl), n. *Bot.* a leaflike flattened branch. Also, **clad·ode** (klăd′ōd).

Cladophyll

claim (klām), v.t. 1. to demand by or as by virtue of a right; demand as a right or as due. 2. to assert, and demand the recognition of (a right, title, possession, etc.); assert one's right to. 3. to assert or maintain as a fact. 4. to require as due or fitting. —n. 5. a demand for something as due; an assertion of a right or alleged right. 6. an assertion of something as a fact. 7. a right to claim or demand; a just title to something. 8. that which is claimed; a piece of public land to which formal claim is made for mining or other purposes. 9. a payment demanded in accordance with an insurance policy, a workmen's compensation law, etc. [ME *claime(n),* t. OF: m. *claimer, clamer,* g. L *clāmāre* call] —**claim′a·ble,** adj. —**claim′er,** n. —**Syn.** 1. See demand. —**Ant.** 3. deny.

claim·ant (klā′mənt), n. one who makes a claim.

claiming race, a race in which horses are "claimed" for a fixed amount prior to the running of the race.

clair·voy·ance (klâr voi′əns), n. 1. power of seeing objects or actions beyond the natural range of vision. 2. quick intuitive knowledge of things; sagacity. [t. F]

clair·voy·ant (klâr voi′ənt), adj. 1. having the power of seeing objects or actions beyond the natural range of vision. —n. 2. a clairvoyant person. [t. F, f. *clair* clear + *voyant,* ppr. of *voir* see, g. L *vidēre*]

clam[1] (klăm), n., v., **clammed, clamming.** —n. 1. any of various bivalve mollusks, esp. certain edible species, as *Venus mercenaria* (the **hard clam** or **round clam**) or *Mya arenaria* (the **soft clam** or **long clam**) of the Atlantic coast of North America. 2. *U.S. Colloq.* a secretive or silent person. —v.i. 3. to gather or dig clams. [special use of CLAM[2], with reference to the shell]

clam[2] (klăm), n. 1. a clamp (def. 1). 2. (*pl.*) pincers (def. 1). [ME; OE *clamm* band, bond]

cla·mant (klā′mənt), adj. 1. clamorous. 2. urgent. [t. L: s. *clāmans,* ppr., crying out]

clam·a·to·ri·al (klăm′ə tōr′ĭ əl), adj. of or pertaining to the *Clamatores,* a large group of passerine birds with relatively simple vocal organs and little power of song, as the flycatchers. [f. s. NL *Clāmātores* (pl. of L *clāmātor* one who cries out) + -IAL]

clam·bake (klăm′bāk′), n. *U.S.* 1. a picnic at the seashore at which the baking of clams (usually on hot stones under seaweed) is a main feature. 2. *Humorous.* any social gathering, esp. a very gay one. 3. *U.S. Slang.* a bungled rehearsal, esp. of a radio program.

clam·ber (klăm′bər), v.i., v.t. 1. to climb, using both feet and hands; climb with effort or difficulty. —n. 2. a clambering. [ME *clambren, clameren,* ? freq. of OE *clæmman* press; semantic devel. infl. by assoc. with CLIMB] —**clam′ber·er,** n.

clam·my (klăm′ĭ), adj., **-mier, -miest.** covered with a cold, sticky moisture; cold and damp. [? t. Flem.: m. *klammig* sticky, etc.] —**clam′mi·ness,** n.

clam·or (klăm′ər), n. 1. a loud outcry. 2. a vehement expression of desire or dissatisfaction. 3. popular outcry. 4. any loud and continued noise. —v.i. 5. to make a clamor; raise an outcry. —v.t. 6. to drive, force, put, etc., by clamoring. 7. to utter noisily. 8. *Obs.* to disturb with clamor. Also, *Brit.*, **clam′our.** [ME, t. OF, g. L *clāmor* a cry, shout] —**clam′or·er,** n. —**Syn.** 1. shouting, uproar. 2. vociferation. 4. See noise.

clam·or·ous (klăm′ər əs), adj. 1. full of, marked by, or of the nature of clamor; vociferous; noisy. 2. vigorous in demands or complaints. —**clam′or·ous·ly,** adv.

clamp[1] (klămp), n. 1. a device, usually of some rigid material, for strengthening or supporting objects or fastening them together. 2. an appliance with opposite sides or parts that may be screwed or otherwise brought together to hold or compress something. 3. one of a pair of movable pieces, made of lead or other soft material, for covering the jaws of a vise and enabling it to grasp without

Clamp (def. 2)

bruising. —*v.t.* **4.** to fasten with or fix in a clamp. —*v.i.* **5. clamp down,** *Colloq.* **a.** to press down. **b.** to become more strict. [t. MD: m. *klampe* clamp, cleat]

clamp² (klămp), *v.i.* to tread heavily; clump. [imit.]

clamp·er (klăm′pər, klăm′-), *n.* **1.** a clamp; pincer. **2.** an iron frame with sharp prongs, fastened to the sole of the shoe to prevent slipping on ice.

clam·shell (klăm′shĕl′), *n.* **1.** the shell of a clam. **2.** a dredging bucket made of two similar pieces hinged together at one end.

clan (klăn), *n.* **1.** a group of families or households, as among the Scottish Highlanders, the heads of which claim descent from a common ancestor. **2.** a group of people of common descent. **3.** a clique, set, society, or party. **4.** a social unit in a tribe in which descent is reckoned in the maternal line; a group of people supposed to be descended from a common ancestor, descent being reckoned in the female line. [t. Gaelic: m. *clann* family, stock]

clan·des·tine (klăn dĕs′tĭn), *adj.* secret; private; concealed (generally implying craft or deception): *a clandestine marriage.* [t. L: m. s. *clandestīnus*] —**clan·des′tine·ly,** *adv.* —**clan·des′tine·ness,** *n.*

clang (klăng), *v.i.* **1.** to give out a loud, resonant sound, as metal when struck; ring loudly or harshly. —*v.t.* **2.** to cause to resound or ring loudly. —*n.* **3.** a clanging sound. [imit. Cf. L *clangere*]

clan·gor (klăng′gər, klăng′ər), *n.* **1.** loud, resonant sound, as of pieces of metal struck together or of a trumpet; a clang. **2.** clamorous noise. —*v.i.* **3.** to make a clangor; clang. Also, *Brit.*, **clan′gour.** [t. L] —**clan′gor·ous,** *adj.* —**clan′gor·ous·ly,** *adv.*

clank (klăngk), *n.* **1.** sharp, hard, metallic sound: *the clank of chains.* —*v.i.* **2.** to make such a sound. **3.** to move with such sounds. —*v.t.* **4.** to cause to resound sharply, as metal in collision. [t. D: m. *klank*]

clan·nish (klăn′ĭsh), *adj.* **1.** of, pertaining to, or characteristic of a clan. **2.** disposed to adhere closely, as the members of a clan. **3.** imbued with or influenced by the sentiments, prejudices, etc., peculiar to clans. —**clan′nish·ly,** *adv.* —**clan′nish·ness,** *n.*

clans·man (klănz′mən), *n.*, *pl.* **-men.** a member of a clan. —**clans·wom·an** (klănz′wŏŏm′ən), *n. fem.*

clap (klăp), *v.,* **clapped, clapping,** *n.* —*v.t.* **1.** to strike with a quick, smart blow, producing an abrupt, sharp sound; slap; pat. **2.** to strike together resoundingly, as the hands to express applause. **3.** to applaud in this manner. **4.** to flap (the wings). **5.** to put, place, apply, etc., promptly and effectively. **6.** *Colloq.* to make or arrange hastily (often fol. by *up* or *together*). —*v.i.* **7.** to make an abrupt, sharp sound as of bodies in collision. **8.** to move or strike with such sound. **9.** to clap the hands, as in applause. —*n.* **10.** act or sound of clapping. **11.** a resounding blow; a slap. **12.** a loud and abrupt or explosive noise, as of thunder. **13.** a sudden stroke, blow, or act. **14.** an applauding; applause. **15.** a clapper. **16.** *Obs.* a sudden mishap. [ME *clappen,* OE *clæppan,* c. D and LG *klappen*]

clap·board (klăb′ərd, klăp′bōrd′), *n.* **1.** *U.S.* a long, thin board, thicker along one edge than along the other, used in covering the outer walls of buildings being laid horizontally, the thick edge of each board overlapping the thin edge of the board below it. **2.** *Brit.* a size of oak board used for making barrel staves and for wainscoting. —*adj.* **3.** of or pertaining to clapboard: *a clapboard roof.* —*v.t.* **4.** to cover with clapboards. [t. MD: m. *klapholt,* with BOARD for -*holt* wood]

clap·per (klăp′ər), *n.* **1.** one who or that which claps. **2.** the tongue of a bell. **3.** *Slang.* the tongue. **4.** any clapping contrivance, as either of a pair of bones.

clap·per·claw (klăp′ər klô′), *v.t.* *Archaic or Dial.* **1.** to claw or scratch with the hand and nails. **2.** to revile.

clap·trap (klăp′trăp′), *n.* **1.** any artifice or expedient for winning applause or impressing the public. **2.** pretentious but insincere or empty language.

claque (klăk), *n.* **1.** a set of hired applauders in a theater. **2.** any group of persons ready to applaud from interested motives. [t. F, der. *claquer* clap]

clar·a·bel·la (klăr′ə bĕl′ə), *n.* an organ stop which gives soft, sweet tones. [f. L *clāra* (fem. of *clārus* clear) + *bella* (fem. of *bellus* beautiful)]

Clare (klâr), *n.* a county in W Eire, in Munster. 86,192 pop. (est. 1943); 1231 sq. mi. *Co. seat:* Ennis.

clar·ence (klăr′əns), *n.* a closed four-wheeled carriage with a curved glass front and inside seats for four persons. [named after the Duke of *Clarence,* 1765–1837, (afterwards William IV of England)]

Clar·en·don (klăr′ən dən), *n.* **1. Edward Hyde, 1st Earl of,** 1609–74, British statesman and historian. **2. The Council of,** a council (1164) occasioned by the opposition of Thomas à Becket to Henry II. **3.** (*l.c.*) a condensed form of printing type, like roman in outline but with thicker lines.

clar·et (klăr′ət), *n.* **1.** the red (orig. the light-red or yellowish) table wine of Bordeaux, France. **2.** a similar wine made elsewhere, as **California claret.** **3.** Also, **claret red.** deep purplish red. **4.** *Slang.* blood. —*adj.* **5.** deep purplish red. [ME, t. OF: somewhat clear, light-colored, dim. of *cler,* g. L *clārus* clear]

claret cup, an iced beverage made of claret and carbonated water with lemon juice, brandy (or other spirits), fruits, sugar, etc.

clar·i·fy (klăr′ə fī′), *v.t., v.i.,* **-fied, -fying.** to make or become clear, pure, or intelligible. [ME *clarifie*(*n*), t. OF: m. *clarifier,* t. LL: m. *clārificāre*] —**clar′i·fi·ca′tion,** *n.* —**clar′i·fi′er,** *n.*

clar·i·net (klăr′ə nĕt′), *n.* a wind instrument in the form of a cylindrical tube with a single reed attached to its mouthpiece. Also, **clar·i·o·net** (klăr′Y ə nĕt′), t. F: m. *clarinette,* dim. of *clarine* clarion] —**clar′i·net′ist, clar′i·net′tist,** *n.*

clar·i·on (klăr′Y ən), *adj.* **1.** clear and shrill. —*n.* **2.** an old kind of trumpet, having a curved shape. **3.** *Poetic.* the sound of this instrument. **4.** any similar sound [ME, t. ML: s. *clārio,* der. L *clārus* clear]

clar·i·ty (klăr′ə tY), *n.* clearness: *clarity of thinking.* [t. L: m. s. *clāritas;* r. ME *clarte,* t. OF]

Clark (klärk), *n.* **1. George Rogers,** 1752–1818, U. S. soldier and frontiersman. **2.** his brother, **William,** 1770–1838, U. S. soldier and explorer: joint commander of Lewis and Clark expedition, 1804–06, to Oregon.

Clarks·burg (klärks′bûrg), *n.* a city in N West Virginia, on the Monongahela river. 32,014 (1950).

cla·ro (klä′rō), *adj., n., pl.* **-ros.** —*adj.* **1.** (of cigars) light-colored and, usually, mild. —*n.* **2.** such a cigar. [t. Sp., g. L *clārus* clear]

clart (klärt), *v.t. Scot. and N. Eng.* to smear or spot with something sticky or dirty.

clar·y (klăr′Y), *n., pl.* **claries.** any of several ornamental garden plants of the *Salvia* family, esp. *S. sclarea.* [late ME; ? aphetic var. of *esclary,* r. OE *slarie.* Cf. OF *sclaree,* ML *sclarea*]

clash (klăsh), *v.i.* **1.** to make a loud, harsh noise. **2.** to collide, esp. noisily. **3.** to conflict; disagree. —*v.t.* **4.** to strike with a resounding or violent collision. **5.** to produce (sound, etc.) by, or as by, collision. —*n.* **6.** the noise of, or as of, a collision. **7.** a collision, esp. a noisy one. **8.** a conflict; opposition, esp. of views or interests. [b. CLAP and DASH] —**Syn. 8.** See **struggle.**

clasp (klăsp, klȧsp), *n.* **1.** a device, usually of metal, for fastening things or parts together; any fastening or connection; anything that clasps. **2.** a grasp; an embrace. **3.** a military decoration consisting of a small design of metal fixed on the ribbon which represents a medal that the bearer has been awarded, the clasp usually indicating an additional award. —*v.t.* **4.** to fasten with, or as with, a clasp. **5.** to furnish with a clasp. **6.** to take hold of with an enfolding grasp: *clasping hands.* [ME *claspe*(*n*), *clapse*(*n*); orig. uncert.] —**clasp′er,** *n.* —**Syn. 6.** grasp, clutch, hug.

clasp knife, a knife with a blade (or blades) folding into the handle.

class (klȧs, klăs), *n.* **1.** a number of persons or things, regarded as forming one group through the possession of similar qualities; a kind; sort. **2.** any division of persons or things according to rank or grade. **3.** *Brit. Univ.* a division of candidates for honors degrees into groups, according to merit. **4.** *Sociol.* a social stratum sharing essential economic, political, or cultural characteristics, and having the same social position. **5.** the system of dividing society; caste. **6.** social rank, esp. high rank. **7.** the assembly of such a group. **8. the classes,** the higher ranks of society, as distinguished from the masses. **9.** *Chiefly U.S. Slang.* excellence; merit. **10.** *U.S.* a number of pupils in a school, or of students in a college, pursuing the same studies, ranked together, or graduated in the same year. **11.** a type of accommodation in railroad carriages and on steamers: *shall we get a ticket for first class?* **12.** drafted or conscripted soldiers, or men available for draft or conscription, all of whom were born in the same year. **13.** *Zool., Bot.* the usual major subdivision of a phylum or subphylum, commonly comprising a plurality of orders, as the *gastropods,* the *mammals,* the *angiosperms.* **14.** *Gram.* a form class. **15.** *Eccles.* class. **16.** (in early Methodism) one of several small companies, each composed of about twelve members under a leader, into which each society or congregation was divided. —*v.t.* **17.** to arrange, place, or rate as to class: *to class justice with wisdom.* —*v.i.* **18.** to take or have a place in a particular class: *those who class as believers.* [earlier *classe,* t. F, t. L: m. s. *classis* class (of people, etc.), army, fleet] —**class′a·ble,** *adj.* —**class′er,** *n.*

class., **1.** classic. **2.** classical. **3.** classification. **4.** classified.

class·book (klȧs′bŏŏk′, klăs′-), *n.* *U.S.* **1.** a book in which a record of student attendance, grades, etc. is kept. **2.** a souvenir book issued by a graduating class, containing pictures, reports, etc.

class consciousness, awareness of one's social or economic rank in society. —**class-con·scious** (klȧs′-kŏn′shəs, klăs′-), *adj.*

class day, (in American colleges and schools) a day during the commencement season on which the members of the graduating class celebrate the completion of their course with special ceremonies.

clas·sic (klăs′Yk), *adj.* **1.** of the first or highest class or rank. **2.** serving as a standard, model, or guide. **3.** of or characteristic of Greek and Roman antiquity, esp. with reference to literature and art. **4.** in the style of the ancient Greek and Roman literature or art;

---

b., blend of, blended; c., cognate with; d., dialect, dialectal; der., derived from; f., formed from; g., going back to; m., modification of; r., replacing; s., stem of; t., taken from; ?, perhaps. See the full key on inside cover.

classical. **5.** of, or adhering to, an established set of artistic or scientific standards and methods. **6.** of literary or historical renown. —*n.* **7.** an author or a literary production of the first rank, esp. in Greek or Latin. **8.** (*pl.*) the literature of ancient Greece and Rome. **9.** an artist or an artistic production of the highest class. **10.** one versed in the classics. **11.** one who adheres to classical rules and models. [t. L: s. *classicus* pertaining to a class, of the first or highest class]

clas·si·cal (klăs′ə kəl), *adj.* **1.** classic. **2.** in accordance with ancient Greek and Roman models in literature or art, or with later systems of principles modeled upon them. **3.** pertaining to or versed in the ancient classics. **4.** marked by classicism. **5.** conforming to established taste or critical standards; adhering to traditional forms. **6.** teaching, or relating to, academic branches of knowledge (the humanities, general sciences, etc.), distinguished from technical subjects. **7.** accepted as being standard in a given field of knowledge, as distinguished from novel or unusual theories: *classical physics.* **8.** *Eccles.* pertaining to a classis. —**clas′si·cal′i·ty,** *n.* —**clas′si·cal·ly,** *adv.*

classical architecture, 1. any architectural style distinguished by clarity and balance of design and plan, expressive of poise and dignity, and as a rule by the use of a Greek or Roman vocabulary. **2.** the architecture of Greek and Roman antiquity. **3.** the architectural style popular from 1770–1840, esp. in the Anglo-Saxon countries, France, and central Europe, which intended to revive Greek and Roman architecture.

classical economics, a system of thought developed by Adam Smith and Ricardo, according to whom the wealth of nations is promoted by free competition with a minimum of government intervention and by division of labor being the source of wealth.

clas·si·cism (klăs′ə sĭz′əm), *n.* **1.** the principles of classic literature or art, or adherence to them. **2.** the classical style in literature or art, characterized esp. by attention to form with the general effect of regularity, simplicity, balance, proportion, and controlled emotion (contrasted with *romanticism*). **3.** a classical idiom or form. **4.** classical scholarship or learning. Also, **clas·si·cal·ism** (klăs′ə kə lĭz′əm).

clas·si·cist (klăs′ə sĭst), *n.* **1.** one who advocates the study of the ancient classics. **2.** an adherent of classicism in literature or art. **3.** an authority on Greek and Roman studies. Also, **clas·si·cal·ist** (klăs′ə kal·ist).

clas·si·cize (klăs′ə sīz′), *v.,* **-cized, -cizing.** —*v.t.* **1.** to make classic. —*v.i.* **2.** to conform to the classic style.

clas·si·fi·ca·tion (klăs′ə fə kā′shən), *n.* **1.** act or the result of classifying. **2.** *Zool., Bot.* the assignment of plants and animals to groups within a system of categories distinguished by structure, origin, etc. The usual series of categories is phylum (in zoölogy) or division (in botany), class, order, family, genus, species, and variety. **3.** one of the several degrees (restricted, confidential, secret, top secret, etc.) of security protection for government documents, papers, etc. **4.** *Library Science.* a system for arranging publications according to broad fields of knowledge and specific subjects within each field. —**clas·si·fi·ca·to·ry** (klăs′ə fə kā′tə rĭ, klə sĭf′ə kə tôr′ĭ), *adj.*

classified ad, want ad.

clas·si·fi·er (klăs′ə fī′ər), *n.* **1.** one who or that which classifies. **2.** *Chem.* a device for separating solids of different characteristics by controlled rates of settling.

clas·si·fy (klăs′ə fī′), *v.t.,* **-fied, -fying. 1.** to arrange or distribute in classes; place according to class. **2.** *Mil.* to mark or otherwise declare (a document, paper, etc.) of value to the enemy and limit and safeguard its handling and use. [f. L *classi(s)* CLASS + -FY] —**clas′si·fi′a·ble,** *adj.*

class inclusion, *Logic.* the relation between one class and a second when every object that belongs to the first class also belongs to the second. For example: the class of *men* is included in the class of *animals.*

clas·sis (klăs′ĭs), *n., pl.* **classes** (klăs′ēz). *Eccles.* (in certain Reformed churches) **1.** the organization of pastors and elders which governs a group of local churchs; a presbytery. **2.** the group of churches governed by such an organization. [t. L. See CLASS]

class·mate (klăs′māt′, kläs′-), *n.* a member of the same class, as at school or college.

class meaning, *Gram.* **1.** the meaning of a grammatical category or a form class, common to all forms showing the category or to all members of the form class, as in the meaning of possession common to all English nouns in the possessive case. **2.** that part of the meaning of a linguistic form which it has by virtue of membership in a particular form class, as the past tense meaning of *ate* (opposed to *lexical meaning*).

class number, *Library Science.* the classification number of a book in a library to indicate its subject class and location on the library shelves, usually a Dewey decimal or a Library of Congress classification symbol.

class·room (klăs′rōōm′, -rōōm′, kläs′-), *n.* a room in a school or college in which classes meet.

class struggle, 1. conflict between different classes in the community. **2.** (in Marxist thought) the struggle for political and economic power carried on between capitalists and workers.

class·y (klăs′ĭ), *adj. Slang.* of high class, rank, or grade; stylish; fine.

clas·tic (klăs′tĭk), *adj.* **1.** *Biol.* breaking up into fragments or separate portions; dividing into parts; causing or undergoing disruption or dissolution: *clastic action, the clastic pole of an ovum, a clastic cell.* **2.** pertaining to an anatomical model made up of detachable pieces. **3.** *Geol.* noting or pertaining to rock or rocks composed of fragments or particles of older rocks or previously existing solid matter; fragmental [f. m.s. Gk. *klastós* broken + -IC]

clath·rate (klăth′rāt), *adj.* resembling a lattice; divided or marked like latticework.

clat·ter (klăt′ər), *v.i.* **1.** to make a rattling sound, as of hard bodies striking rapidly together. **2.** to move rapidly with such a sound. **3.** to talk fast and noisily; chatter. —*v.t.* **4.** to cause to clatter. —*n.* **5.** a clattering noise; disturbance. **6.** noisy talk; din of voices. **7.** idle talk; gossip. [ME *clatren,* OE *clatrian*; of imit. orig. Cf. D *klateren* rattle] —**clat′ter·er,** *n.*

Clau·del (klō děl′), *n.* **Paul Louis Charles** (pōl lwē shärl), born 1868, French diplomat, poet, and dramatist.

clau·di·ca·tion (klô dĭ kā′shən), *n.* a limp.

Clau·di·us I (klô′dĭ əs), 10 B.C.–A.D. 54, Roman emperor, A.D. 41–54.

Claudius II, (*"Gothicus"*) A.D. 214–70, Roman emperor, A.D. 268–70.

clause (klôz), *n.* **1.** *Gram.* a group of words containing a subject and a predicate, forming part of a compound or complex sentence, or coextensive with a simple sentence. **2.** part of a written composition containing complete sense in itself, as a sentence or paragraph (in modern use commonly limited to such parts of legal documents, as of statutes, contracts, wills, etc.). [ME *claus,* t. ML: s. *clausa* in sense of L *clausula* clause] —**claus′al,** *adj.*

Clau·se·witz (klou′zə vĭts), *n.* **Karl von** (kärl fən), 1780–1831, German military officer and author of books on military science.

claus·tral (klôs′trəl), *adj.* cloistral; cloisterlike. [t. LL: s. *claustrālis,* der. *claustrum* enclosure, CLOISTER]

claus·tro·pho·bi·a (klôs′trə fō′bĭ ə), *n. Psychiatry.* a morbid dread of closed or narrow places. [t. NL, f. *claustro-* (comb. form repr. L *claustrum* enclosure) + *-phobia* -PHOBIA]

cla·vate (klā′vāt), *adj.* club-shaped. [t. L: m. s. *clāvātus,* pp., studded with nails; sense influenced by assoc. with L *clāva* club]

clave (klāv), *v. Archaic.* pt. of **cleave**

cla·ver (klā′vər, klăv′-), *Scot.* —*n.* **1.** idle talk. —*v.i.* **2.** to talk idly; gossip.

clav·i·chord (klăv′ə kôrd′), *n.* an ancient keyboard instrument, in which the strings were softly struck with metal blades vertically projecting from the rear ends of the keys. [t. ML: m. s. *clāvicordium,* f. L: *clāvi(s)* key + m.s. *chorda* string (see CHORD¹) + *-ium* -IUM]

clav·i·cle (klăv′ə kəl), *n. Anat. Zool.* **1.** a bone of the pectoral arch. **2.** (in man) either of two slender bones each articulating with the sternum and a scapula and forming the anterior part of a shoulder; the collarbone. See diag. under **shoulder.** [t. L: m.s. *clāvicula,* dim. of *clāvis* key] —**cla·vic·u·lar** (klə vĭk′yə lər), *adj.*

clav·i·corn (klăv′ə kôrn′), *adj.* **1.** having club-shaped antennae, as many beetles of the group *Clavicornia.* **2.** belonging to this group. —*n.* **3.** a clavicorn beetle. [t. NL: s. *clāvicornis,* f. *clavi-* (comb. form repr. *clāva* club) + *-cornis* horned] —**clav·i·cor·nate** (klăv′ə kôr′nāt), *adj.*

clav·i·er¹ (klăv′ĭ ər, klə vĭr′), *n.* the keyboard of a musical instrument. [t. F, der. L *clāvis* key]

cla·vier² (klə vĭr′), *n.* any musical instrument with a keyboard, as a harpsichord, clavichord, piano, or organ. [t. G, t. F: keyboard]

clav·i·form (klăv′ə fôrm′), *adj.* club-shaped; clavate.

claw (klô), *n.* **1.** a sharp, usually curved, nail on the foot of an animal. **2.** *Obs.* the foot of an animal armed with such nails. **3.** any part or thing resembling a claw, as the cleft end of the head of a hammer. —*v.t.* **4.** to tear, scratch, seize, pull, etc., with or as with claws. **5.** to scratch gently, as to relieve itching. **6.** to make, bring, etc., by clawing: *claw a hole.* [ME *clawen,* OE *clawian,* der. *clawu,* n., c. G *klaue*]

claw hammer, 1. a hammer having a head with one end curved and cleft for drawing nails. **2.** *U.S. Colloq.* a dress coat.

clay (klā), *n.* **1.** a natural earthy material which is plastic when wet, consisting essentially of hydrated silicates of aluminum, and used for making bricks, pottery, etc. **2.** earth; mud. **3.** earth as the material from which the human body was originally formed. **4.** the human body. [ME; OE *clǣg,* c. D and G *klei*] —**clay·ey** (klā′ĭ), *adj.* —**clay·ish,** *adj.*

Clay (klā), *n.* **Henry,** 1777–1852, U.S. statesman and orator.

clay·bank (klā′băngk′), *n.* a yellow shade; dun; brownish yellow.

clay·more (klā′môr′), *n.* **1.** a heavy two-edged sword formerly used by the Scottish Highlanders. **2.** a basket-hilted broadsword, often single-edged, used by Highlanders. [t. Gaelic: m. *claidheamh mòr* great sword]

clay pigeon, *Trapshooting.* a disc of baked clay or other material hurled into the air as a target.

clay stone, 1. a deeply decomposed igneous rock. **2.** argillite.

clay·to·ni·a (klā tō′nĬ ə), *n.* any of the low, succulent portulacaceous herbs constituting the genus *Claytonia.* [named after Dr. J. *Clayton* (1685?–1773), American botanist]

-cle, var. of **-cule.** [t. L: m. *-culus, -cula, -culum;* in some words, t. F]

clean (klēn), *adj.* **1.** free from dirt or filth; unsoiled; unstained. **2.** free from foreign or extraneous matter. **3.** free from defect or blemish. **4.** unadulterated; pure. **5.** entirely (or almost so) without corrections; easily readable: *clean printer's proofs.* **6.** free from encumbrances or obstructions: *a clean harbor.* **7.** (of a ship) **a.** having its bottom free of marine growth, etc. **b.** empty; having nothing in its cargo spaces. **8.** free from any form of defilement; morally pure; innocent; upright; honorable. **9.** free from dirty habits, as an animal. **10.** (among the Jews) **a.** (of persons) free from ceremonial defilement. **b.** (of animals, fowl, and fish) permissible to eat. **11.** neatly or evenly made or proportioned; shapely; trim. **12.** free from awkwardness; not bungling; dextrous; adroit: *a clean boxer, a clean leap.* **13.** complete; perfect: *a clean sweep.* —*adv.* **14.** in a clean manner; cleanly. **15.** wholly; completely; quite. —*v.t.* **16.** to make clean. **17. clean out, a.** to rid of dirt, etc. **b.** to use up; exhaust. **c.** *U.S. Slang.* to drive out by force. **d.** *U.S. Colloq.* to empty or rid (a place) of occupants, contents, etc.: *clean out the larder.* **18. clean up, a.** to rid of dirt, etc. **b.** to put in order; tidy up. **c.** to finish up; reach the end of. **d.** *U.S. Colloq.* to make a large profit. —*v.i.* **19.** to perform or to undergo a process of cleaning. **20.** to get rid of dirt, etc. (fol. by *up*): *to clean up for dinner.* [ME *clene,* OE *clæne* pure, clear, c. D and G *klein* small] —**clean′a·ble,** *adj.* —**clean′ness,** *n.*
—**Syn. 1.** CLEAN, CLEAR, PURE refer to freedom from soiling, flaw, stain, or mixture. CLEAN refers esp. to freedom from soiling: *a clean dress.* CLEAR refers particularly to freedom from flaw or blemish: *a clear pane of glass.* PURE refers esp. to freedom from mixture or stain: *a pure metal, not diluted but pure and full strength.* **8.** unsullied, chaste, virtuous. **16.** scour, scrub, sweep, brush, wipe, mop, dust, wash, rinse, lave. CLEAN, CLEANSE refer to removing dirt or impurities. To CLEAN is the general word with no implication of method or means: *to clean windows, a kitchen, streets.* CLEANSE is esp. used of thorough cleaning by chemical or other technical process; figuratively applies to moral or spiritual purification: *to cleanse parts of machinery, one's soul of guilt.* —**Ant. 1.** soiled. **8.** impure. **16.** soil.

clean-cut (klēn′kŭt′), *adj.* **1.** sharply or distinctly outlined. **2.** well-shaped. **3.** definite. **4.** neat and wholesome: *a clean-cut boy.*

clean·er (klē′nər), *n.* **1.** one who or that which cleans. **2.** an apparatus or preparation for cleaning.

clean·ly (*adj.* klĕn′lĬ; *adv.* klēn′lĬ), *adj., -lier, -liest, adv.* —*adj.* **1.** personally neat; careful to keep or make clean. **2.** habitually clean. **3.** *Obs.* cleansing; making clean. —*adv.* **4.** in a clean manner. —**clean·li·ly** (klĕn′-lə lĬ), *adv.* —**clean·li·ness** (klĕn′lĬ nĬs), *n.*

cleanse (klĕnz), *v.t.,* **cleansed, cleansing. 1.** to make clean. **2.** to remove by, or as by, cleaning: *his leprosy was cleansed.* [ME *clense(n),* OE *clǽnsian,* der. *clǽne* clean] —**cleans′er,** *n.* —**Syn. 1.** See **clean.**

clean-shav·en (klēn′shā′vən), *adj.* having all the hairs shaved off.

Cle·an·thes (klĬ ăn′thēz), *n.* c300–c232 B.C., Greek Stoic philosopher.

clean·up (klēn′ŭp′), *n.* **1.** act or process of cleaning up, esp. of gambling, vice, graft, etc. **2.** *Slang.* a very large profit.

clear (klĬr), *adj.* **1.** free from darkness, obscurity, or cloudiness; light. **2.** bright; shining. **3.** transparent; pellucid: *good, clear wine.* **4.** of a pure, even color: *a clear complexion.* **5.** distinctly perceptible to the eye, ear, or mind; easily seen, heard, or understood. **6.** distinct; evident; plain. **7.** free from confusion, uncertainty, or doubt. **8.** perceiving or discerning distinctly: *a clear head.* **9.** convinced; certain. **10.** free from guilt or blame; innocent. **11.** serene; calm; untroubled. **12.** free from obstructions or obstacles; open: *a clear space.* **13.** unentangled or disengaged; free; quit or rid (fol. by *of*). **14.** having no parts that protrude, are rough, etc. **15.** freed or emptied of contents, cargo, etc. **16.** without limitation or qualification: *the clear contrary.* **17.** without obligation or liability; free from debt. **18.** without deduction or diminution: *a clear $1000.* **19.** *Phonet.* (of e sounds) light, palatal, ē-like. **20.** *Obs.* illustrious. —*adv.* **21.** in a clear manner; clearly, distinctly; entirely. —*v.t.* **22.** to make clear; free from darkness, cloudiness, muddiness, indistinctness, confusion, uncertainty, obstruction, contents, entanglement, obligation, liability, etc. **23.** to free from imputation, esp. of guilt; prove or declare to be innocent. **24.** to pass or get over without entanglement or collision. **25.** to pay (a debt) in full. **26.** to pass (checks, etc.) through a clearing house. **27.** to obtain the money required for. **28.** to gain as clear profit: *to clear $1000 in a transaction.* **29.** to free (a ship, cargo, etc.) from legal detention at a port by satisfying the customs and other required conditions. **30.** *U.S.* to try or otherwise dispose of (the cases awaiting court action): *to clear the docket.* —*v.i.* **31.** to become clear. **32.** to exchange checks and bills, and settle balances, as in a clearing house. **33.** (of a ship) **a.** to comply with the customs and other

conditions legally imposed upon leaving or entering a port. **b.** to leave port after having complied with such conditions. **34.** Some special verb phrases are: **clear away, off,** etc.. **1.** to remove so as to leave something clear. **2.** to disappear; vanish. **clear out,** *Colloq.* to go away. **clear up, 1.** to make clear. **2.** to solve; explain. **3.** to put in order; tidy up. **4.** to become brighter, lighter, etc. —*n.* **35.** a clear or unobstructed space. **36. in the clear, a.** between the bounding parts. **b.** free. [ME *cler,* t. OF, g. L *clārus*] —**clear′a·ble,** *adj.* —**clear′er,** *n.* —**Syn. 1.** See **clean. 3.** translucent, limpid, crystalline, diaphanous. **5.** intelligible, comprehensible. **6.** obvious, manifest, apparent. **7.** unmistakable, unambiguous.

clear·ance (klĬr′əns), *n.* **1.** act of clearing. **2.** a clear space; a clearing. **3.** an intervening space, as between machine parts for free play. **4.** *Banking.* an exchange of checks and other commercial paper drawn on members of a clearinghouse, usually effected at a daily meeting of the members. **5.** the clearing of a ship at a port. **6.** the official certificate or papers (**clearance papers**) indicating this.

Cle·ar·chus (klĬ är′kəs), *n.* died 401 B.C., Spartan general.

clear-cut (klĬr′kŭt′), *adj.* cut or formed with clearly defined outlines; distinctly defined.

clear-eyed (klĬr′īd′), *adj.* **1.** having clear, bright eyes; clear-sighted. **2.** mentally acute or discerning.

clear-head·ed (klĬr′hĕd′Ĭd), *adj.* having or showing a clear head or understanding. —**clear′-head′ed·ness,** *n.*

clear·ing (klĬr′Ĭng), *n.* **1.** act of one who or that which clears. **2.** a tract of cleared land, as in a forest. **3.** the mutual exchange between banks of checks and drafts, and the settlement of the differences. **4.** (*pl.*) the total of claims settled at a clearing house.

clearing house, a place or institution where mutual claims and accounts are settled, as between banks.

clear·ly (klĬr′lĬ), *adv.* in a clear manner. —**Syn.** CLEARLY, DEFINITELY, DISTINCTLY, EVIDENTLY imply the way in which something is plainly understood or understandable. CLEARLY suggests without doubt or obscurity: *expressed clearly.* DEFINITELY means explicitly, with precision: *definitely phrased.* DISTINCTLY means without blurring or confusion: *distinctly enunciated.* EVIDENTLY means patently, unquestionably: *evidently an error.*

clear·ness (klĬr′nĬs), *n.* state or quality of being clear; distinctness; plainness.

clear-sight·ed (klĬr′sī′tĬd), *adj.* having clear sight; having keen mental perception; discerning; perspicacious: *clear-sighted businessman, reason, etc.* —**clear′-sight′ed·ly,** *adv.* —**clear′-sight′ed·ness,** *n.*

clear-starch (klĬr′stärch′), *v.t., v.i.* to stiffen and dress (linen, etc.) with clear or transparent (boiled) starch. —**clear′starch′er,** *n.*

clear-sto·ry (klĬr′stōr′Ĭ), *n., pl.* **-ries.** clerestory.

clear·wing (klĬr′wĭng′), *n.* a moth with wings for the most part destitute of scales and transparent, esp. any of the family *Aegeriidae,* many species of which are injurious to plants.

cleat (klēt), *n.* **1.** a small wedge-shaped block, as one fastened to a spar or the like as a support, check, etc. **2.** *Naut.* **a.** a piece of wood nailed down to secure something from slipping. **b.** a piece of wood or iron consisting of a bar with arms, to which ropes are belayed. **3.** a piece of wood or iron fastened across anything for support, security, etc. **4.** a piece of iron fastened under a shoe to preserve the sole. **5.** *Coal Mining.* the cleavage (plane) in coal to which it breaks, as **face cleat** (prominent), **butt cleat** (poor). —*v.t.* **6.** to supply or strengthen with cleats; fasten to or with a cleat. [ME *clete* wedge, c. D *kloot* ball. Cf. CLOT]

Cleats (def. 2b), one of which is lashed to a stay

cleav·a·ble (klē′və bəl), *adj.* that may be cleft or split.

cleav·age (klē′vĬj), *n.* **1.** act of cleaving. **2.** state of being cleft or split; division. **3.** *Biol.* the total or partial division of the egg into smaller cells or blastomeres. **4.** *Crystall.* the tendency to break in certain definite directions, yielding more or less smooth surfaces. **5.** *Chem.* the breaking down of a molecule or compound into simpler molecules or compounds.

cleave[1] (klēv), *v.i.,* **cleaved** or (*Archaic*) **clave, cleaved, cleaving. 1.** to stick or adhere; cling or hold fast (fol. by *to*). **2.** to be attached or faithful (fol. by *to*). [ME *cleve(n),* OE *cleofian,* c. G *kleben*]

cleave[2] (klēv), *v.,* **cleft** or **cleaved** or **clove, cleft** or **cleaved** or **cloven, cleaving.** —*v.t.* **1.** to part by, or as by, a cutting blow, esp. along the grain or any other natural line of division. **2.** to split; rend apart; rive. **3.** to penetrate or pass through (air, water, etc.). **4.** to make by or as by cutting: *to cleave a path through the wilderness.* **5.** to separate or sever by, or as by, splitting. —*v.i.* **6.** to part or split, esp. along a natural line of division. **7.** to penetrate or pass (fol. by *through*). [ME *cleven,* OE *cleofan,* c. G *klieben.* Cf. Gk. *glýphein* carve]

cleav·er (klē′vər), *n.* **1.** one who or that which cleaves. **2.** a heavy knife or long-bladed hatchet used by butchers for cutting up carcasses.

cleav·ers (klē′vərz), *n. sing. and pl.* **1.** a rubiaceous plant, *Galium aparine,* with short hooked bristles by means of which it adheres to clothing, etc. **2.** any of certain related species. [ME *clivre* (der. CLEAVE[1]), r. OE *clife*]

cleek (klēk), *n.* *Golf.* a club having an iron head with a long, narrow face. [akin to CLUTCH[1]]

clef (klĕf), *n.* *Music.* a symbol placed upon a staff to indicate the name and pitch of the notes corresponding to its lines and spaces. The **G clef** (or **treble clef**) indicates that the second line of the staff corresponds to the G next above middle C. The **F clef** (or **bass clef**) indicates that the fourth line of the staff corresponds to the F next below middle C. [t. F, g. L *clāvis* key]

G Clef F Clef

cleft[1] (klĕft), *n.* **1.** a space or opening made by cleavage; a split. **2.** a division formed by cleaving. **3.** (in horses) a crack on the bend of the pastern. [ME *clift*, OE *geclyft* split, crack, fissure] —Syn. **1.** fissure, crevice, crack.

cleft[2] (klĕft), *v.* **1.** pt. and pp. of **cleave**[2]. —*adj.* **2.** cloven; split; divided. **3.** (of a leaf) having divisions formed by incisions or narrow sinuses which extend halfway, or more than halfway, to the midrib or the base.

cleft palate, a congenital defect of the palate in which a longitudinal fissure exists in the roof of the mouth.

clei·do·ic (klī′dō′ĭk), *adj.* *Embryol.* closed-up. Cleidoic eggs, as those of birds and insects, have little more than gaseous exchange with the environment. [f. m. Gk. *kleidó(ein)* lock up + -IC]

Cleis·the·nes (klīs′thə nēz′), *n.* fl. 508 B.C., Athenian statesman.

cleis·tog·a·my (klī stŏg′ə mĭ), *n.* *Bot.* the condition of having (usually in addition to the ordinary, fully developed flowers) small, inconspicuous flowers which do not open, but are pollinated from their own anthers, as in the case of the pansy. [f. m. Gk. *kleistó(s)* closed + -GAMY] —**cleis·tog′a·mous, cleis·to·gam·ic** (klī′stə găm′ĭk), *adj.*

clem·a·tis (klĕm′ə tĭs), *n.* **1.** any of the flowering vines or erect shrubs constituting the ranunculaceous genus *Clematis*, as *C. virginiana*, the virgin's-bower of the U.S. **2.** any plant of the allied genus *Atragene*. [t. L, t. Gk.: m. *klēmatis*, dim. of *klēma* vine branch]

Cle·men·ceau (klĕm′ən sō′; *Fr.* klĕ′mäN sō′), *n.* **Georges Eugène Benjamin** (zhôrzh œ zhĕn′ băN zhä măN′), 1841–1929, French statesman, journalist, editor, author, and physician: premier of France, 1906–09 and 1917–20.

clem·en·cy (klĕm′ən sĭ), *n., pl.* -**cies.** **1.** the quality of being clement; mildness of temper, as shown by a superior to an inferior, or by an aggrieved person to the offender; disposition to spare or forgive; mercy; leniency; forbearance. **2.** an act or deed showing mercy or leniency. **3.** mildness: *the clemency of the weather.* [t. L: m. s. *clēmentia*] —Ant. **1.** harshness. **3.** severity.

Clem·ens (klĕm′ənz), *n.* **Samuel Langhorne** (lăng′hôrn, -ərn), ("Mark Twain"), 1835–1910, U. S. author and humorist.

clem·ent (klĕm′ənt), *adj.* **1.** mild or merciful in disposition; lenient; compassionate. **2.** (of the weather, etc.) mild or pleasant. [late ME, t. L: s. *clēmens*] —**clem′ent·ly,** *adv.*

Clem·ent VII (klĕm′ənt), (*Giulio de′Medici*) 1478?–1534, Italian ecclesiastic: pope, 1523–34 (nephew of Lorenzo de′ Medici).

Clement of Alexandria, A.D. c150–c215, Greek Christian theologian and writer.

clench (klĕnch), *v.t.* **1.** to close (the hands, teeth, etc.) tightly. **2.** to grasp firmly; grip. **3.** to settle decisively; clinch. **4.** *Naut.* to clinch. —*n.* **5.** act of clenching. **6.** a tight hold; grip. **7.** that which holds fast or clenches. **8.** *Naut.* a clinch. [ME *clench(en)*, OE -*clencan* (in *beclencan* hold fast)]

cle·o·me (klĭ ō′mĭ), *n.* any of the numerous herbaceous or shrubby plants constituting the caparidaceous genus *Cleome*, mostly natives of tropical regions, and often bearing showy flowers.

Cle·om·e·nes III (klĭ ŏm′ə nēz′), died 220? B.C., king of Sparta, 235?–220? B.C.

Cle·on (klē′ŏn), *n.* died 422 B.C., Athenian general and political opponent of Pericles.

Cle·o·pa·tra (klē′ə pā′trə, -păt′rə, -pā′trə), *n.* 69?–30 B.C., queen of Egypt, 47–30 B.C. She saved her kingdom by winning the love of Julius Caesar and Marcus Antonius, but was defeated by Octavian. After her death by suicide, Egypt became a Roman province.

clepe (klēp), *v.t.,* **cleped** or **clept** (also **ycleped** or **yclept**), **cleping.** *Archaic.* to call; name (now chiefly in the pp. as *ycleped* or *yclept*). [ME *clepien*, OE *cleopian*]

clep·sy·dra (klĕp′sə drə), *n., pl.* -**dras, -drae** (-drē′) a device for measuring time by the regulated flow of water or mercury through a small aperture. [t. L, t. Gk.: m. *klepsŷdra*]

clep·to·ma·ni·a (klĕp′tə mā′nĭə), *n.* kleptomania. —**clep′to·ma′ni·ac,** *n.*

clere·sto·ry (klĭr′stôr′ĭ), *n., pl.* -**ries.** **1.** the upper part of the nave, transepts, and choir of a building, esp. a church, perforated with a series of windows above the aisle roofs, and forming the chief source of light for the building. See illus. in next col. **2.** any similar raised construction, as that for ventilating a railroad car. Also, **clearstory.**

See illus. in next col.

cler·gy (klûr′jĭ), *n., pl.* -**gies.** the body of men ordained for ministration in the Christian church, in distinction from the laity. [ME *clergie*, t. OF, ult. der. LL *clēricus* CLERIC]

cler·gy·man (klûr′jĭ mən), *n., pl.* -**men.** **1.** a member of the clergy. **2.** an ordained Christian minister.

cler·ic (klĕr′ĭk), *n.* **1.** a member of the clergy. **2.** a member of a clerical party. —*adj.* **3.** pertaining to the clergy; clerical. [t. LL: s. *clēricus*, t. Gk.: m. *klērikós*, der. *klēros* clergy, orig., lot, allotment]

A, Clerestory; B, Blindstory or triforium

cler·i·cal (klĕr′ĭ kəl), *adj.* **1.** pertaining to a clerk or copyist, or to clerks: *a clerical error.* **2.** of, pertaining to, or characteristic of the clergy or a clergyman. **3.** upholding the power or influence of the clergy in politics. —*n.* **4.** a cleric. **5.** (*pl.*) *Colloq.* clerical garments. **6.** a person or a party trying to extend the power of the church in government. [t. LL: s. *clēricālis*, der. *clēricus* clergyman] —**cler′i·cal·ly,** *adv.*

cler·i·cal·ism (klĕr′ə kəl ĭz′əm), *n.* **1.** clerical principles. **2.** clerical power or influence in politics. **3.** support of such power or influence. —**cler′i·cal·ist,** *n.*

cler·i·sy (klĕr′ə sĭ), *n.* learned men as a whole; the literati. [t. ML: m.s. *clēricia*]

clerk (klûrk; *Brit.* klärk), *n.* **1.** one employed in an office, shop, etc., to keep records or accounts, attend to correspondence, etc. **2.** *U.S.* an assistant in business, esp. a retail salesman or saleswoman. **3.** one who keeps the records and performs the routine business of a court, legislature, board, etc. **4.** *Chiefly Legal.* a clergyman; ecclesiastic. **5.** a layman charged with various minor ecclesiastical duties. **6.** *Archaic.* a person able to read, or to read and write. **7.** *Archaic.* a scholar. —*v.i.* **8.** to act or serve as a clerk. [ME; OE *clerc, cleric,* t. LL: s. *clēricus* CLERIC] —**clerk′ship,** *n.*

clerk·ly (klûrk′lĭ; *Brit.* klärk′-), *adj.,* -**lier, -liest,** *adv.* —*adj.* **1.** of a clerk or clerks. **2.** *Archaic.* scholarly. —*adv.* **3.** in the manner of a clerk. —**clerk′li·ness,** *n.*

Clerk-Max·well (klärk′măks′wəl, -wĕl), *n.* **James,** 1831–79, British physicist.

Cler·mont-Fer·rand (klĕr môN′fĕ räN′), *n.* a city in central France. 109,119 (1946).

cleve·ite (klēv′īt), *n.* a crystallized variety of uraninite. [named after P. T. *Cleve* (born 1840), Swedish chemist]

Cleve·land (klēv′lənd), *n.* **1.** (**Stephen) Grover** (grō′vər), 1837–1908, 22nd and 24th president of the U.S., 1885–89, 1893–97. **2.** a city in NE Ohio: a port on Lake Erie. 914,808; with suburbs, 1,453,556 (1950).

Cleveland Heights, a city in NE Ohio, near Cleveland. 59,141 (1950).

clev·er (klĕv′ər), *adj.* **1.** bright mentally; having quick intelligence; able. **2.** dexterous or nimble with the hands or body. **3.** showing adroitness or ingenuity: *a clever remark, a clever device.* **4.** *Colloq. or Dial.* suitable; convenient; satisfactory. **5.** *U.S. Colloq.* good-natured. **6.** *Dial.* handsome. **7.** *Dial.* in good health. [ME *cliver;* orig. uncert.] —**clev′er·ish,** *adj.* —**clev′er·ly,** *adv.* —**clev′er·ness,** *n.* —Syn. **1.** ingenious, talented, quick-witted. **2.** skillful, adroit. —Ant. **1.** stupid. **2.** clumsy.

clev·is (klĕv′ĭs), *n.* a piece of metal, usually U-shaped, with a pin or bolt passing through holes at the two ends, as for attaching an implement to a drawbar for pulling. [akin to CLEAVE[2]]

C, Clevis

clew (klōō), *n.* **1.** a ball or skein of thread, yarn, etc. **2.** *Legend.* a ball of thread unwound to serve as a guide through a labyrinth. **3.** (*often spelled* **clue**) anything that serves to guide or direct in the solution of a problem, mystery, etc. **4.** (*pl. or sing.*) the rigging for a hammock. **5.** *Naut.* either lower corner of a square sail or the after lower corner of a fore-and-aft sail. —*v.t.* **6.** to coil into a ball. **7.** to direct or point out by a clew. **8.** *Naut.* to haul (the lower corners of a sail) up to the yard by means of the clew lines (fol. by *up*). [ME *clewe,* OE *cleowen,* c. D *kluwen*]

clew iron, a ring in the corner of a sail bearing thimbles to which the clew lines are secured.

clew line, a rope by which a clew of a square sail is hauled to the yard.

cli·ché (klē shā′; *Fr.* -shĕ′), *n., pl.* -**chés** (-shăz′; *Fr.* -shĕ′). **1.** a trite, stereotyped expression, idea, practice, etc., as *sadder but wiser, strong as an ox.* **2.** *Print.* **a.** a stereotype or electrotype plate. **b.** a reproduction made in a like manner. [t. F, pp. of *clicher* to stereotype. Cf. G *klitsch* doughy mass]

Cli·chy (klē shē′), *n.* a city in N France, on the Seine near Paris. 53,029 (1946).

click (klĭk), *n.* **1.** a slight, sharp sound: *the click of a latch.* **2.** some clicking mechanism, as a detent or a pawl. **3.** *Phonet.* a speech sound produced by allowing air to flow suddenly into a partial vacuum in the mouth or in part of the mouth. —*v.i.* **4.** to emit or make a slight, sharp sound, or series of such sounds, as by the cocking of a pistol. **5.** *Slang.* to make a success; make a hit. —*v.t.* **6.** to cause to click; strike with a click. [imit. Cf. D *klikken*] —**click′er,** *n.*

click beetle, an elaterid beetle that makes a clicking sound in springing up, as after having been laid on its back; snapping beetle.

cli·ent (klī/ənt), *n.* **1.** one who applies to a lawyer for advice or commits his cause or legal interests to a lawyer's management. **2.** a customer. **3.** (in ancient Rome) **a.** (orig.) a hereditary dependent of one of the nobility. **b.** a plebeian who lived under the patronage of a patrician. **4.** anyone under the patronage of another; a dependent. [ME, t. L: s. *cliens* retainer] —**cli·en·tal** (klī ĕn/təl, klī/ən təl), *adj.*

cli·en·tele (klī/ən tĕl/), *n.* **1.** the customers, patients, etc. (of a lawyer, doctor, businessman, etc.) as a whole. **2.** dependents or followers. Also, **cli·ent·age** (klī/ən tĭj). [t. L: m. *clientēla* a body of retainers]

cliff (klĭf), *n.* the high, steep face of a rocky mass; precipice. Also, *Archaic or Dial.,* **clift** (klĭft). [ME and OE *clif,* c. Icel. *klif*]

cliff dweller, 1. one who dwells on a cliff. **2.** (*usually cap.*) one of a prehistoric people of the southwestern U. S., ancestors of the Pueblo Indians, who built houses in caves or on ledges of the cliffs. —**cliff dwelling.**

cliff swallow, a colonial North American bird, *Petrochelidon pyrrhonota,* so called because it attaches its bottle-shaped nests of mud to cliffs and walls.

cliff·y (klĭf/ĭ), *adj.* having, or formed by, cliffs; craggy.

Clif·ton (klĭf/tən), *n.* a city in NE New Jersey. 64,511 (1950).

cli·mac·ter·ic (klī măk/tər ĭk, klī/măk tĕr/ĭk), *adj.* **1.** pertaining to a critical period; crucial. —*n.* **2.** a year in which important changes in health, fortune, etc. occur: *the grand climacteric (the sixty-third year).* **3.** *Physiol.* a period of decrease of reproductive activity in men and women, culminating, in women, in the menopause. **4.** any critical period. Also, **cli·mac·ter·i·cal** (klī/măk tĕr/ə kəl). [t. L: s. *clīmactēricus,* t. Gk.: m. *klīmaktērikós* of the nature of a critical period]

cli·mac·tic (klī măk/tĭk), *adj.* pertaining to or forming a climax: *climactic arrangement.* Also, **cli·mac/ti·cal.**

cli·mate (klī/mĭt), *n.* **1.** the composite or generalization of weather conditions of a region, as temperature, pressure, humidity, precipitation, sunshine, cloudiness, and winds, throughout the year, averaged over a series of years. **2.** an area of a particular kind of climate. [ME *climat,* t. L: s. *clima,* t. Gk.: m. *klīma* clime, zone, lit., slope (of the earth from equator to pole)] —**cli·mat·ic** (klī măt/ĭk), *adj.* —**cli·mat/i·cal·ly,** *adv.*

cli·ma·tol·o·gy (klī/mə tŏl/ə jĭ), *n.* the science that deals with climates or climatic conditions. —**cli·ma·to·logic** (klī/mə tə lŏj/ĭk), **cli/ma·to·log/i·cal,** *adj.* —**cli/ma·tol/o·gist,** *n.*

cli·max (klī/măks), *n.* **1.** the highest point of anything; the culmination. **2.** that point in the drama in which it is clear that the central motive will or will not be successful. **3.** *Rhet.* **a.** a figure consisting in a series of related ideas so arranged that each surpasses the preceding in force or intensity. **b.** (popularly) the last term or member of this figure. **4.** *Ecol.* that stage in the ecological succession or evolution of a plant-animal community, which is stable and self-perpetuating. —*v.i., v.t.* **5.** to reach, or bring to, the climax. [t. L, t. Gk.: m. *klīmax* ladder, staircase, climax]

climb (klīm), *v.,* **climbed** or (*Archaic*) **clomb, climbed** or (*Archaic*) **clomb, climbing,** *n.* —*v.i.* **1.** to mount or ascend, esp. by using both hands and feet. **2.** to rise slowly by, or as by, continued effort. **3.** to slope upward. **4.** to ascend by twining or by means of tendrils, adhesive tissues, etc., as a plant. **5. climb down,** **a.** to descend, esp. by using both hands and feet. **b.** *Colloq.* to withdraw from an untenable position. —*v.t.* **6.** to ascend, go up, or get to the top of, esp. by the use of hands and feet. **7.** to descend (a ladder, pole, etc.), esp. by using both hands and feet (fol. by *down*). —*n.* **8.** a climbing; an ascent by climbing. **9.** a place to be climbed. [ME *climben,* OE *climban,* c. D and G *klimmen*] —**climb/a·ble,** *adj.*

—**Syn. 1.** CLIMB, ASCEND, MOUNT, SCALE imply a moving upward. To CLIMB is to make one's way upward with effort: *to climb a mountain.* ASCEND, in its literal meaning (*to go up*). is general: but it now usually suggests a gradual or stately movement, with or without effort, often to a considerable degree of altitude: *to ascend stairs, to ascend the Hudson River.* MOUNT may be interchangeable with ascend, but also suggests climbing on top of or astride of: *to mount a platform, a horse.* SCALE, a more literary word, implies difficult or hazardous climbing up or over something: *to scale a summit.* —**Ant. 1, 6.** descend.

climb·er (klī/mər), *n.* **1.** one who or that which climbs. **2.** a person who strives to associate with social superiors. **3.** a climbing plant. **4.** a spike attached to a shoe to assist in climbing poles, etc.

climb indicator, *Aeron.* an instrument to show the rate of ascent or descent, operating on a differential pressure principle.

climbing fish, a small East Indian fish, *Anabas testudineus,* which is reputed to climb trees.

climbing irons, iron frames with spikes attached, worn on the feet or legs to help in climbing trees, etc.

clime (klīm), *n.* *Poetic.* **1.** a tract or region of the earth. **2.** climate. [t. L: m. *clima* CLIMATE]

cli·nan·dri·um (klī năn/drĭ əm), *n., pl.* **-dria** (-drĭ ə). a cavity in the apex of the column in orchids, in which the anthers rest; the androclinium. [t. NL, f. s. Gk. *klīnē* bed + s. Gk. *anēr* man + *-ium* -IUM]

clinch (klĭnch), *v.t.* **1.** to secure (a driven nail, etc.) by beating down the point. **2.** to fasten (work) together thus. **3.** to settle (a matter) decisively. **4.** *Naut.* to fasten by a clinch. —*v.i.* **5.** *Boxing, etc.* to grasp tightly; grapple. **6.** to beat down the point of a nail, etc. in order to fasten something. —*n.* **7.** act of clinching. **8.** *Boxing, etc.* a grasp; grapple. **9.** a clinched nail or fastening. **10.** the clinched part of a nail, etc. **11.** *Naut.* a kind of hitch in which the end of the rope is fastened back by seizing. **12.** *Obs.* a pun. [later var. of CLENCH]

clinch·er (klĭnch/ər), *n.* **1.** one who or that which clinches. **2.** a nail, etc. for clinching. **3.** something decisive.

cling (klĭng), *v.,* **clung, clinging,** *n.* —*v.i.* **1.** to adhere closely; stick. **2.** to hold fast, as by grasping or embracing; cleave. **3.** to be or remain close. **4.** to remain attached (to an idea, hope, memory, etc.). **5.** *Obs.* to cohere. —*n.* **6.** the act of clinging; adherence; attachment. [ME *clingen,* OE *clingan* stick or draw together, shrivel] —**cling/er,** *n.* —**cling/ing·ly,** *adv.*

cling·fish (klĭng/fĭsh/), *n., pl.* **-fishes,** (*esp. collectively*) **fish.** any fish of the family *Gobiesocidae,* all of which have a ventral sucking disc constructed from the pectoral as well as the pelvic fins. They use this disc to adhere tightly to rocks.

Cling·mans Dome (klĭng/mənz), a mountain on the border between North Carolina and Tennessee: the highest peak in the Great Smoky Mountains. 6642 ft.

cling·stone (klĭng/stōn/), *adj.* **1.** having a stone to which the pulp adheres closely, as certain peaches. —*n.* **2.** a clingstone peach.

cling·y (klĭng/ĭ), *adj.* apt to cling; adhesive or tenacious: *dirt of a wet and clingy nature.*

clin·ic (klĭn/ĭk), *n.* **1.** a place, as in connection with a medical school or a hospital, for the treatment of non-resident patients. **2.** the instruction of medical students by examining or treating patients in their presence. **3.** a class of students assembled for such instruction. **4.** the place for such instruction. —*adj.* **5.** clinical. [t. LL: s. *clīnicus* pertaining to a bed, t. Gk.: m. *klīnikós*]

clin·i·cal (klĭn/ə kəl), *adj.* **1.** pertaining to a clinic. **2.** pertaining to or used in a sickroom. **3.** concerned with observation and treatment of disease in the patient (as distinguished from an artificial experiment). **4.** administered on a sickbed or deathbed: *clinical conversion or baptism.* —**clin/i·cal·ly,** *adv.*

clinical thermometer, an instrument used to determine the body temperature.

cli·ni·cian (klĭ nĭsh/ən), *n.* a physician who studies diseases at the bedside, or is skilled in clinical methods.

clink[1] (klĭngk), *v.i., v.t.* **1.** to make, or cause to make, a light, sharp, ringing sound. **2.** to rhyme or jingle. —*n.* **3.** a clinking sound. **4.** a rhyme; jingle. **5.** the rather piercing cry of some birds, as the stonechat. [ME *clynk(e).* Cf. D *klinken*]

clink[2] (klĭngk), *n.* *Colloq.* a prison; jail; lockup. [appar. from *Clink* prison on Clink Street, London]

clink·er[1] (klĭng/kər), *n.* **1.** a hard brick, used for paving, etc. **2.** a partially vitrified mass of brick. **3.** the scale of oxide formed on iron during forging. **4.** a mass of incombustible matter fused together, as in the burning of coal. —*v.i.* **5.** to form clinkers in burning, as coal. [t. D: m. *klinker* kind of brick]

clink·er[2] (klĭng/kər), *n.* one who or that which clinks. [f. CLINK[1] + -ER[1]]

clink·er-built (klĭng/kər bĭlt/), *adj.* made of pieces, as boards or plates of metal, which overlap one another.

clink·stone (klĭngk/stōn/), *n.* *Petrog.* any of several varieties of phonolite which give out a ringing sound when struck.

cli·nom·e·ter (klī nŏm/ə tər, klĭ-), *n.* an instrument used to determine inclination or slope. [f. *clino-* (comb. form repr. L -*clīnāre* incline) + -METER]

cli·no·met·ric (klī/nə mĕt/rĭk), *adj.* **1.** (of crystals) having oblique angles between one or all axes. **2.** pertaining to or determined by a clinometer. Also, **cli/no·met/ri·cal.**

clin·quant (klĭng/kənt), *adj.* **1.** glittering, esp. with tinsel; decked with garish finery. —*n.* **2.** imitation gold leaf; tinsel. **3.** *Obs.* tinsel; false glitter. [t. F, ppr. of obs. *clinquer* clink, tinkle, glitter, t. D: m. *klinken*]

Clin·ton (klĭn/tən), *n.* **1. De Witt** (də wĭt/), 1769–1828, U.S. political leader: governor of New York State; sponsor of the Erie Canal. **2. George,** 1739–1812, governor of New York State: vice-president of the U.S., 1805–12. **3. James,** 1733–1812, American general in Revolutionary War. **4. Sir Henry,** 1738?–95, commander in chief of the British forces in the American Revolutionary War. **5.** a city in E Iowa, on the Mississippi. 30,379 (1950).

clin·to·ni·a (klĭn tō/nĭ ə), *n.* any plant of the liliaceous genus *Clintonia,* comprising stemless perennial herbs with a few broad, ribbed, basal leaves, and white or greenish-yellow flowers on a short peduncle. [t. NL; named after De Witt *Clinton*]

Cli·o (klī/ō), *n.* *Class. Myth.* the Muse of history.

clip[1] (klĭp), *v.,* **clipped, clipping,** *n.* —*v.t.* **1.** to cut, or cut off or out, as with shears; trim by cutting. **2.** to cut or trim the hair or fleece of; shear. **3.** to pare the edge of (a coin). **4.** to cut short; curtail. **5.** to omit sounds of (a word) in pronouncing. **6.** *Colloq.* to hit with a quick, sharp blow. —*v.i.* **7.** to clip or cut something. **8.** to cut articles or pictures from a newspaper, magazine, etc. **9.** to move swiftly. **10.** *Archaic.* to fly rapidly. —*n.* **11.** act of clipping. **12.** anything clipped off, esp. the wool shorn at a single shearing of sheep. **13.** the amount of wool shorn in one season. **14.** (*pl.*) shears. **15.** *Colloq.* a quick, sharp blow or punch. [ME *clippen*, t. Scand.; cf. Icel. *klippa*]

clip² (klĭp), *n., v.,* **clipped, clipping.** —*n.* **1.** a device for gripping and holding tightly; a metal clasp, esp. one for papers, letters, etc. **2.** a flange on the upper surface of a horseshoe. **3.** cartridge clip. **4.** *Archaic or Dial.* an embrace. —*v.t., v.i.* **5.** to grip tightly; hold together by pressure. **6.** to encircle; encompass. **7.** *Football.* to stop (a player who does not have the ball) by illegally hurling the body across his legs from behind. **8.** *Archaic or Dial.* to embrace or hug. [ME *clippe(n)*, OE *clyppan* embrace]

clip-fed (klĭp′fĕd′), *adj.* (of a rifle) loading from a cartridge clip into the magazine.

clip·per (klĭp′ər), *n.* **1.** one who or that which clips or cuts. **2.** (*often pl.*) a cutting tool, esp. shears. **3.** (*often pl.*) a tool with rotating or reciprocating knives for cutting hair. **4.** one that clips, or moves swiftly, as a horse. **5.** a sailing vessel built and rigged for speed. **6.** an airliner, esp. a flying boat, designed for long flights over a sea or ocean. **7.** *Slang.* a first-rate person or thing.

clip·per-built (klĭp′ər·bĭlt′), *adj. Naut.* built on sharp, rakish lines conducive to fast sailing.

clip·ping (klĭp′ĭng), *n.* **1.** act of one who or that which clips. **2.** a piece clipped off or out, as from a newspaper. —*adj.* **3.** that clips. **4.** *Colloq.* swift: *a clipping pace.* **5.** *Slang.* first-rate or excellent.

clique (klēk, klĭk), *n., v.,* **cliqued, cliquing.** —*n.* **1.** a small set or coterie, esp. one that is snobbishly exclusive. —*v.i.* **2.** *Colloq.* to form, or associate in, a clique. [t. F, der. OF *cliquer* make a sharp sound. Cf. CLAQUE] —**Syn. 1.** See **ring¹**.

cli·quish (klē′kĭsh, klĭk′ĭsh), *adj.* of, pertaining to, or savoring of a clique: *a cliquish fashion.* —**cli′quish·ly,** *adv.* —**cli′quish·ness,** *n.*

cli·to·ris (klī′tə·rĭs, klĭt′ə·rĭs), *n. Anat.* the erectile organ of the vulva, homologous to the penis of the male. [t. NL, t. Gk.: m. *kleitoris,* der. *kleiein* shut]

Clive (klīv), *n.* **Robert,** (*Baron Clive of Plassey*) 1725–1774, British general and statesman in India. His victory in the Battle of Plassey in 1757 was important in giving Great Britain control of India.

clk., clerk.

clo·a·ca (klō·ā′kə), *n., pl.* **-cae** (-sē). **1.** a sewer. **2.** a privy. **3.** a place or receptacle of moral filth. **4.** *Zool.* **a.** the common cavity into which the intestinal, urinary, and generative canals open in birds, reptiles, amphibians, many fishes, and certain mammals (*monotremes*). **b.** a similar cavity in invertebrates. [t. L, prob. der. *cluere* cleanse] —**clo·a′cal,** *adj.*

cloak (klōk), *n.* **1.** a loose outer garment. **2.** that which covers or conceals; disguise; pretext. —*v.t.* **3.** to cover with, or as with, a cloak. **4.** to hide; conceal. [ME *cloke,* t. OF, g. LL *cloca* cloak, orig. bell; ? of Celtic orig. See CLOCK¹]

cloak·room (klōk′rōōm′, -rŏŏm′), *n.* **1.** a room where cloaks, overcoats, etc., may be left temporarily. **2.** *Brit.* a toilet or rest room.

cloche (klōsh), *n.* **1.** a bell-shaped cover used in cooking or in greenhouses. **2.** a bell-shaped, close-fitting woman's hat. [t. F: lit., bell. See CLOCK¹]

clock¹ (klŏk), *n.* **1.** an instrument for measuring and indicating time, having pointers which move round on a dial to mark the hour, etc. **2.** such a timepiece not carried on the person (distinguished from a *watch*). —*v.t.* **3.** to time, test, or ascertain by the clock. [ME *clokke,* t. MD: m. *clocke* instrument for measuring time; cf. OE *clugge* bell, ONF *cloke* bell]

clock² (klŏk), *n.* **1.** an embroidered or woven ornament on each side of a stocking, extending from the ankle upward. —*v.t.* **2.** to embroider with such an ornament. [orig. uncert.] —**clocked,** *adj.*

clock·mak·er (klŏk′mā′kər), *n.* a person who makes or repairs clocks.

clock·wise (klŏk′wīz′), *adv., adj.* in the direction of rotation of the hands of a clock.

clock·work (klŏk′wûrk′), *n.* **1.** the mechanism of a clock. **2.** any mechanism similar to that of a clock. **3.** like clockwork, with perfect regularity or precision.

clod (klŏd), *n.* **1.** a lump or mass, esp. of earth or clay. **2.** earth; soil. **3.** anything earthy or base, as the body in comparison with the soul: *this corporeal clod.* **4.** a stupid person; blockhead; dolt. **5.** a part of the shoulder of beef. [ME *clodde,* OE *clodd* (in *clodhamer* fieldfare). Cf. CLOUD] —**clod′dish,** *adj.* —**clod′dish·ness,** *n.* —**clod′dy,** *adj.*

clod·hop·per (klŏd′hŏp′ər), *n.* **1.** a clumsy boor; rustic; bumpkin. **2.** (*pl.*) strong, heavy shoes.

clod·hop·ping (klŏd′hŏp′ĭng), *adj.* loutish; boorish.

clod·poll (klŏd′pōl′), *n.* a blockhead; a stupid person. Also, **clod′pole′, clod·pate** (klŏd′pāt′).

clog (klŏg, klôg), *v.,* **clogged, clogging,** *n.* —*v.t.* **1.** to encumber; hamper; hinder. **2.** to hinder or obstruct, esp. by sticky matter; choke up. —*v.i.* **3.** to become clogged, encumbered, or choked up. **4.** to stick; stick together. **5.** to do a clog dance. —*n.* **6.** anything that impedes motion or action; an encumbrance; a hindrance. **7.** a heavy block, as of wood, fastened to a man or beast to impede movement. **8.** a kind of shoe with a

thick sole usually of wood. **9.** a similar but lighter shoe worn in the clog dance. **10.** a clog dance. **11.** *Now Chiefly Eng.* a thick piece of wood. [ME *clog, clogge*; orig. uncert.] —**clog′gy,** *adj.*

clog almanac, an early form of almanac, made by cutting notches, etc. on a clog or block, usually of wood.

clog dance, a dance performed with clogs to beat time to the music. —**clog dancer.** —**clog dancing.**

cloi·son·né (kloi′zə·nā′; *Fr.* klwả·zô·nĕ′), *n.* enamelwork in which color areas are separated by thin, metal bands fixed edgewise to the ground. [t. F, der. *cloison* partition] —**cloi′son·né′,** *adj.*

clois·ter (klois′tər), *n.* **1.** a covered walk, esp. one adjoining a building, as a church, commonly running round an open court (garth) and opening onto it with an open arcade or colonnade. **2.** a place of religious seclusion; a monastery or nunnery; a convent. **3.** any quiet, secluded place. **4.** life in a monastery or nunnery. —*v.t.* **5.** to confine in a cloister or convent. **6.** to confine in retirement; seclude. **7.** to furnish with a cloister or covered walk. **8.** to convert into a cloister or convent. [ME *cloistre,* t. OF, b. *cloison* partition (cf. CLOISONNÉ) and L *claustrum* enclosed place] —**clois′ter·like′,** *adj.* —**Syn. 2.** See **convent**.

clois·tered (klois′tərd), *adj.* solitary; retired from the world: *cloistered seclusion, cloistered virtue.*

cloister garth. See **garth** (def. 1).

clois·tral (klois′trəl), *adj.* **1.** of, pertaining to, or living in a cloister. **2.** cloisterlike: *a cloistral house.*

cloke (klōk), *n., v. Obs.* cloak.

clomb (klōm), *v. Archaic and Dial.* pt. and pp. of **climb.**

clone (klōn), *n. Hort.* a group of plants originating as parts of the same individual, from buds or cuttings. Also, **clon** (klŏn). [t. Gk.: m. *klōn* slip, twig]

clo·nus (klō′nəs), *n. Pathol.* a rapid succession of flexion and extension of a group of muscles, usually signifying an affection of the brain or spinal cord. [t. NL, t. Gk.: m. *klōnos* commotion, turmoil] —**clon·ic** (klŏn′ĭk), *adj.* —**clo·nic·i·ty** (klō·nĭs′ə·tĭ), *n.*

Cloots (klōts), *n.* **Jean Baptiste du Val-de-Grâce** (zhän bả·tēst′ dʏ vȧl·də·gräs′), **Baron de,** ("*Anacharsis Clootz*") 1755–94, Prussian leader in French Revolution.

close (*v.* klōz; *adj., adv.* klōs; *n.* klōz *for 44–47,* klōs *for 48–50*), *v.,* **closed, closing,** *adj.,* **closer, closest,** *adv., n.* —*v.t.* **1.** to stop or obstruct (a gap, entrance, aperture, etc.). **2.** to stop or obstruct the entrances, apertures, or gaps in. **3.** to shut in or surround on all sides; enclose; cover in. **4.** to bring together the parts of; join; unite: *to close the ranks of troops.* **5.** to bring to an end: *to close a debate, bargain, etc.* **6.** *Naut.* to come close to. **7.** *U.S.* to get rid of, usually at a reduced price (fol. by *out*): *close out a stock of shoes.* —*v.i.* **8.** to become closed; shut. **9.** to come together; unite. **10.** to come close. **11.** to grapple; engage in close encounter (fol. by *with*). **12.** to come to terms (fol. by *with*). **13.** to agree (fol. by *on, upon*). **14.** to come to an end; terminate. **15.** *Stock Exch.* to be worth at the end of a trading period. [ME *close(n),* t. OF: m. *clos-,* s. *clore,* g. L *claudere* shut; r. OE *clȳsan*] —*adj.* **16.** shut; shut tight; not open. **17.** shut in; enclosed. **18.** completely enclosing. **19.** without opening; with all openings covered or closed. **20.** confined; narrow: *close quarters.* **21.** lacking fresh or freely circulating air: *a close room.* **22.** heavy; oppressive: *a spell of close weather.* **23.** narrowly confined, as a prisoner **24.** practicing secrecy; secretive; reticent. **25.** parsimonious; stingy. **26.** scarce, as money. **27.** not open to public or general admission, competition, etc. **28.** under prohibition as to hunting or fishing: *a close season.* **29.** having the parts near together: *a close texture.* **30.** compact; condensed. **31.** near, or near together, in space, time, or relation: *in close contact.* **32.** intimate; confidential: *close friendship.* **33.** based upon a strong uniting feeling of love, honor, etc.: *a close union of nations.* **34.** fitting tightly, as a cap. **35.** short; near the surface. **36.** not deviating from the subject under consideration: *close attention.* **37.** strict; searching; minute: *close investigation.* **38.** not deviating from a model or original: *a close translation.* **39.** nearly even or equal: *a close contest.* **40.** strictly logical: *close reasoning.* **41.** *Phonet.* pronounced with a relatively small opening above the tongue. *Beet* and *boot* have the closest English vowels. **42.** *Rare.* viscous; not volatile. —*adv.* **43.** in a close manner; closely. [ME *clos,* t. F, g. L *clausus,* pp., shut] —*n.* **44.** act of closing. **45.** the end or conclusion. **46.** a junction; union. **47.** a close encounter; a grapple. **48.** an enclosed place; an enclosure; any piece of land held as private property. **49.** an enclosure about or beside a building, cathedral, etc. **50.** *Scot. and Brit. Dial.* a narrow entry or alley, or a court to which it leads.[(defs. 44–47) n. use of v.; (defs. 48–50) ME *clos,* t. F, g. L *clausum* enclosed place] —**close·ly** (klōs′lĭ), *adv.* —**close·ness** (klōs′nĭs), *n.* —**clos·er** (klō′zər), *n.* —**Syn. 1.** CLOSE, SHUT mean to cause something not to be open. CLOSE suggests blocking an opening or vacant place: *to close a breach in a wall.* It also connotes force and more refinement than SHUT. The informal word SHUT refers esp. to blocking or barring openings intended for literal or figurative ingress and egress: *to shut a door, mouth, gate, etc.* **5.** end, conclude, terminate, finish, complete. **21.** unventilated, muggy. **25.** penurious, miserly. **45.** See **end¹**.

close call (klōs), *U.S. Colloq.* a narrow escape.

closed (klōzd), *adj.* *Phonet.* (of syllables) ending with a consonant.

closed chain, *Chem.* a linking of atoms in an organic molecule which may be represented by a structural formula which forms a ring or cycle.

closed corporation, an incorporated business the stock of which is owned by a small group.

closed gentian, a gentian, *Gentian* (or *Dasytephana*) *Andrewsii*, of the eastern and central U.S.

closed primary, a direct primary in which only persons meeting tests of party membership may vote.

closed shop, a shop in which union membership is a condition of hiring as well as employment, or one in which the employer must call on the union to furnish employees.

close-fist·ed (klōs′fĭs′tĭd), *adj.* stingy; miserly.

close-grained (klōs′grānd′), *adj.* (of wood) having the grain close or fine in texture.

close-hauled (klōs′hôld′), *adj.* *Naut.* sailing as close to the wind as a vessel will sail, with sails trimmed as flat as possible.

close-lipped (klōs′lĭpt′), *adj.* not talking or telling much.

close-mouthed (klōs′mouᵺd′, -moutht′), *adj.* reticent; uncommunicative.

close-or·der drill (klōs′ôr′dər), *U.S. Army.* practice in formation marching and other movements, the carrying of arms during formal marching, and the formal handling of arms for ceremonies and guard.

close position (klōs), *Music.* arrangement of a chord so that the parts are as close together as possible.

close quarters. 1. a small, cramped place or position. 2. direct and close contact in a fight.

close shave, *Colloq.* a narrow escape.

clos·et (klŏz′ĭt), *n.* 1. a small room, enclosed recess, or cabinet for clothing, food, utensils, etc. 2. a small private room, esp. one for prayer, thought, etc. 3. a water closet; toilet. —*adj.* 4. pertaining to a closet; private; secluded. 5. suited for use or enjoyment in privacy: *a closet drama* (one to be read rather than acted). 6. engaged in private study or speculation; speculative; unpractical. —*v.t.* 7. to shut up in a private room for a conference, interview, etc. [ME, t. OF, dim. of *clos*, g. L *clausum* enclosed place]

close-up (klōs′ŭp′), *n.* 1. *Motion Pictures.* a picture taken at close range or with a long focal length lens, on a relatively large scale. 2. an intimate view or presentation of anything.

clos·trid·i·um (klŏs trĭd′Ῑəm), *n.* any of the group of spore-forming, anaerobic bacteria.

clo·sure (klō′zhər), *n.*, *v.*, **-sured, -suring.** —*n.* 1. act of closing or shutting. 2. state of being closed. 3. a bringing to an end; conclusion. 4. that which closes or shuts. 5. *Obs.* that which encloses or shuts in; enclosure. 6. *Phonet.* an articulation which keeps the breath from moving outward by closing the passage at some point. 7. *Parl. Proc.* a method of closing a debate and causing an immediate vote to be taken on the question under discussion, as by moving the previous question, corresponding to U.S. *cloture*. —*v.t.*, *v.i.* 8. *Parl. Proc.* to end (a debate, etc.) by closure. [ME, t. OF, g. LL *clausūra*, der. L *clausus*, pp., shut]

clot (klŏt), *n.*, *v.*, **clotted, clotting.** —*n.* 1. a mass or lump. 2. a semisolid mass, as of coagulated blood. —*v.i.* 3. to form into clots; coagulate. —*v.t.* 4. to cause to clot; cover with clots. [ME; OE *clott* lump, c. G *klotz* block, log]

cloth (klôth, klŏth), *n.*, *pl.* **cloths** (klôᵺz, klôᵺz; klŏᵺz, klŏᵺz). 1. a fabric formed by weaving, felting, etc., from wool, hair, silk, flax, cotton, or other fiber, used for garments, upholstery, and many other purposes. 2. a piece of such a fabric for a particular purpose: *a table-cloth.* 3. a particular profession, esp. that of a clergyman. 4. **the cloth,** the clergy. 5. sails collectively. 6. a sail. 7. *Obs.* a garment; clothing. 8. *Obs.* a livery or customary garb, as of a trade or profession. [ME; OE *clāth*, c. G *kleid* garment]

clothe (klōᵺ), *v.t.*, **clothed** or **clad, clothing.** 1. to dress; attire. 2. to provide with clothing. 3. to cover with, or as with, clothing. [ME *clothen*, OE *clāthian*]

clothes (klōz, klōᵺz), *n. pl.* 1. garments for the body; articles of dress; wearing apparel. 2. bedclothes. [orig., pl. of CLOTH] —**Syn.** 1. clothing, attire, raiment, vesture, costume, garb; vestments, habiliments.

clothes·horse (klōz′hôrs′, klōᵺz′-), *n.* a frame on which to hang clothes, etc., esp. for drying.

clothes·line (klōz′līn′, klōᵺz′-), *n.* a rope on which to hang clothes, etc., to dry after being washed.

clothes moth, any of certain small moths whose larvae feed on wool, fur, etc.

clothes·pin (klōz′pĭn′, klōᵺz′-), *n.* a forked piece of wood or other device for fastening articles on a clothesline.

clothes pole, a pole that holds up a clothesline.

clothes·press (klōz′prĕs′, klōᵺz′-), *n.* a receptacle for clothes, as a chest, wardrobe, or closet.

clothes tree, an upright pole with hooks near the top for hanging coats, hats, etc.

cloth·ier (klōᵺ′yər, -Ῑər), *n.* a maker or seller of woolen cloth or of clothes.

cloth·ing (klōᵺ′ĭng), *n.* 1. garments collectively; clothes; raiment; apparel. 2. a covering.

Clo·tho (klō′thō), *n.* *Gk. Myth.* one of the three Fates. [t. L, t. Gk.: m. *Klōthō*, lit., the spinner]

cloth yard, 36 inches; 3 feet.

clot·ty (klŏt′Ῑ), *adj.* 1. full of clots; clotted. 2. tending to clot.

clo·ture (klō′chər), *n.* *U.S. Parl. Proc.* closure of a debate. [t. F, g. L *claustūra*, var. of *clausūra* CLOSURE]

cloud (kloud), *n.* 1. a visible collection of particles of water or ice suspended in the air, usually at an elevation above the earth's surface. 2. any similar mass, esp. of smoke or dust. 3. a dim or obscure area in something otherwise clear or transparent. 4. a patch or spot differing in color from the surrounding surface. 5. anything that obscures, darkens, or causes gloom, trouble, suspicion, disgrace, etc. 6. a great number of insects, birds, etc., flying together: *a cloud of locusts.* 7. **in the clouds, a.** imaginary; unreal. **b.** impractical. —*v.t.* 8. to overspread or cover with, or as with, a cloud or clouds. 9. to overshadow; obscure; darken. 10. to make gloomy. 11. to place under suspicion, disgrace, etc. 12. to variegate with patches of another color. —*v.i.* 13. to grow cloudy; become clouded. [ME *cloud(e)* rock, clod, cloud, OE *clūd* rock, hill]

—**Syn.** 7. CLOUD, FOG, HAZE, MIST differ somewhat in their figurative uses. CLOUD connotes esp. daydreaming: *his mind is in the clouds.* FOG and HAZE connote esp. bewilderment or confusion: *to go around in a fog (haze).* MIST has an emotional connotation and suggests tears: *a mist in one's eyes.*

cloud·ber·ry (kloud′bĕr′Ῑ), *n.*, *pl.* **-ries.** 1. the orange-yellow edible fruit of *Rubus chamaemorus*, a small raspberry of the northern hemisphere. 2. the plant.

cloud·burst (kloud′bûrst′), *n.* a sudden and very heavy rainfall.

cloud chamber, *Physics.* a closed chamber containing saturated water vapor which indicates the presence of moving particles by the trails of water condensation which they produce.

cloud·land (kloud′lănd′), *n.* a region of unreality, imagination, etc.; dreamland.

cloud·less (kloud′lĭs), *adj.* without clouds; clear. —**cloud′less·ly,** *adv.* —**cloud′less·ness,** *n.*

cloud·let (kloud′lĭt), *n.* a little cloud.

cloud rack, a group of drifting clouds.

cloud·y (klou′dĭ), *adj.*, **cloudier, cloudiest.** 1. full of or overcast with clouds: *a cloudy sky.* 2. of or like a cloud or clouds; pertaining to clouds. 3. having cloudlike markings: *cloudy marble.* 4. not clear or transparent: *a cloudy liquid.* 5. obscure; indistinct: *cloudy notions.* 6. darkened by gloom, trouble, etc.: *cloudy looks.* 7. under suspicion, disgrace, etc.: *a cloudy reputation.* —**cloud′i·ly,** *adv.* —**cloud′i·ness,** *n.* —**Syn.** 1. overclouded, lowering.

clough (klŭf, klou), *n.* *Prov. Eng.* a narrow valley; a ravine; a glen. [ME, c. OHG *klāh*]

Clough (klŭf), *n.* **Arthur Hugh,** 1819–61, British poet.

clout (klout), *n.* 1. *Colloq. or Dial.* a blow, esp. with the hand; a cuff. 2. *Baseball Slang.* a powerful blow with the bat. 3. the mark shot at in archery. 4. a shot that hits the mark. 5. *Archaic or Dial.* a patch, or piece of cloth or other material used to mend something. 6. *Archaic or Dial.* any worthless piece of cloth; a rag. —*v.t.* 7. *Colloq. or Dial.* to strike, esp. with the hand; cuff. 8. *Archaic or Dial.* to bandage. 9. *Archaic or Dial.* to patch; mend. [ME; OE *clūt* piece of cloth or metal. Cf. CLOT]

clove¹ (klōv), *n.* 1. the dried flower bud of a tropical myrtaceous tree, *Eugenia aromatica*, used whole or ground as a spice. 2. the tree. [ME *clowe*, t. OF: m. *clou* (g. L *clāvus* nail), in *clou de girofle* nail of clove (see GILLYFLOWER), so called from the shape]

clove² (klōv), *n.* *Bot.* one of the small bulbs formed in the axils of the scales of a mother bulb, as in garlic. [OE *clufu* clove, bulb, tuber]

clove³ (klōv), *v.* pt. of **cleave²**.

clove hitch, *Naut.* a form of hitch for fastening a rope about a spar, etc., in which two rounds of rope are crossed about the spar, with the ends of the rope issuing in opposite directions between the crossed parts. See illus. under **knot.**

clo·ven (klō′vən), *v.* 1. pp. of **cleave²**. —*adj.* 2. cleft; split; divided: *cloven feet or hoofs.* 3. cleaved.

clo·ven-foot·ed (klō′vən fo͝ot′Ῑd), *adj.* 1. having cloven feet. 2. devilish; Satanic.

cloven hoof, the figurative indication of Satan or evil temptation. Also, **cloven foot.**

clo·ven-hoofed (klō′vən ho͝oft′, -ho͞oft′), *adj.* 1. having split hoofs, once assumed to represent the halves of a single undivided hoof, as in cattle. 2. devilish; Satanic.

clove pink, a pink, *Dianthus caryophyllus*, with a spicy scent like that of cloves; a carnation.

clo·ver (klō′vər), *n.* 1. any of various herbs of the fabaceous genus *Trifolium*, with trifoliolate leaves and dense flower heads, many species of which, as *T. pratense* (the common red clover), are cultivated as forage plants. 2. any of various plants of allied genera, as melilot (sweet clover). 3. **in clover,** in comfort or luxury. [ME *clovere*, OE *clāfre*, c. D *klaver*]

clo·ver·leaf (klō′vər lēf′), *n.*, *pl.* **-leaves.** *U.S.* a system of routing traffic between two intersecting superhighways, wherein one highway passes over the other and the feeder roads connecting them are usually arranged in the pattern of a four-leaf clover.

Clo·vis I (klō′vĭs; *Fr.* klô vēs′), (Ger. *Chlodwig*) A.D:

b., blend of, blended; c., cognate with; d., dialect, dialectal; der., derived from; f., formed from; g., going back to; m., modification of; r., replacing; s., stem of; t., taken from; ?, perhaps. See the full key on inside cover.

465?–511, king of the Franks, A.D. 481–511: first of the Merovingian dynasty of Frankish kings.

clown (kloun), *n.* **1.** a jester or buffoon in a circus, pantomime, etc. **2.** a peasant; a rustic. **3.** a coarse, ill-bred person; a boor. —*v.i.* **4.** to act like a clown. [orig. uncert. Cf. Icel. *klunni* clumsy fellow] —**clown'-ish,** *adj.* —**clown'ish·ly,** *adv.* —**clown'ish·ness,** *n.*

clown·er·y (kloun'ər'ĭ), *n., pl.* **-eries.** clownish behavior.

cloy (kloi), *v.t.* **1.** to weary by an excess of food, sweetness, pleasure, etc.; surfeit; satiate. —*v.i.* **2.** to cause to feel satiated or surfeited: *cloyed palate of the epicure, cloying with particulars.* [aphetic var. of obs. *acloy* to stop up, drive in a nail, ? t. MF: m. *encloyer,* der. *clou,* g. L *clāvus* nail] —**cloy'ing·ly,** *adv.* —**cloy'ing·ness,** *n.*

club (klŭb), *n., v.,* **clubbed, clubbing.** —*n.* **1.** a heavy stick, usually thicker at one end than at the other, suitable for a weapon; a cudgel. **2.** a stick or bat used to drive a ball, etc., in various games. **3.** a stick with a crooked head used in golf, hockey, etc. **4.** Indian club. **5.** a group of persons organized for a social, literary, athletic, political, or other purpose. **6.** the building or rooms occupied by such a group. **7.** a black trefoil-shaped figure on a playing card. **8.** a card bearing such figures. **9.** (*pl.*) the suit so marked. —*v.t.* **10.** to beat with, or as with, a club. **11.** to gather or form into a clublike mass. **12.** to unite; combine; join together. **13.** to contribute as one's share toward a joint expense; make up by joint contribution (often fol. by *up* or *together*). **14.** to defray by proportional shares: *to club the expense.* **15.** to invert (a rifle, etc.) so as to use as a club. —*v.i.* **16.** to combine or join together as for a common purpose. **17.** to gather into a mass. **18.** to contribute to a common fund. [ME *clubbe,* t. Scand.; cf. Icel. *klubba;* akin to CLUMP] —**Syn. 5.** society, association. See **circle.**

club·ba·ble (klŭb'ə·bəl), *adj.* fit to be a member of a social club; sociable. Also, **club'a·ble.**

club car, a railroad passenger car equipped with easy chairs, card tables, buffet, etc.

club·foot (klŭb'fŏŏt'), *n.* **1.** a deformed or distorted foot. **2.** the condition of such a foot; talipes. —**club'-foot'ed,** *adj.*

club·hand (klŭb'hănd'), *n.* **1.** a deformed or distorted hand, similar in nature and causation to a clubfoot. **2.** the condition of such a hand.

club·haul (klŭb'hôl'), *v.t. Naut.* to cause (a ship), in an emergency, to go on the other tack by letting go the lee anchor, and pulling on a hawser leading from the anchor to the lee quarter, the hawser being cut when the ship gathers way on the new tack.

club·house (klŭb'hous'), *n.* a building occupied by a club.

club·man (klŭb'mən), *n., pl.* **-men.** a member of a fashionable club. —**club'wom'an,** *n. fem.*

club moss, any plant of the genus *Lycopodium.*

club·room (klŭb'rŏŏm'), *n.* a room belonging to or used by a club.

club sandwich, a sandwich of toast (usually three slices) with a filling of cold chicken, turkey, bacon, or ham, lettuce with tomato, mayonnaise dressing, etc.

club steak, a loin steak.

cluck (klŭk), *v.i.* **1.** to utter the cry of a hen brooding or calling her chicks. **2.** to make a similar sound. —*v.t.* **3.** to call or utter by clucking: *clucking her sympathy.* —*n.* **4.** the sound uttered by a hen when brooding, or in calling her chicks. **5.** any clucking sound. [var. of *clock* (now Scot. and d.), OE *cloccian*]

clue (klŏŏ), *n., v.,* **clued, cluing.** —*n.* **1.** anything that serves to guide or direct in the solution of a problem, mystery, etc. **2.** clew. —*v.t.* **3.** to clew. [var. of CLEW]

Cluj (klŏŏzh), *n.* a city in NW Rumania. 110,956 (1941). German, **Klausenburg.** Hungarian, **Kolozsvár.**

clum·ber (klŭm'bər), *n.* one of a breed of spaniels with short legs and long, heavy body, valued as retrievers. Also, **clumber spaniel.** [named after *Clumber,* estate of the Duke of Newcastle, in Nottinghamshire, England]

clump (klŭmp), *n.* **1.** a cluster, esp. of trees, or other plants. **2.** *Bacteriol.* a cluster of agglutinated bacteria. **3.** a lump or mass. **4.** a clumping tread, sound, etc. **5.** a thick extra sole on a shoe. —*v.i.* **6.** to walk heavily and clumsily. **7.** *Bacteriol.* to gather or be gathered into clumps. —*v.t.* **8.** to gather into or form a clump; mass. **9.** *Bacteriol.* to gather or form in clumps. [back formation from *clumper* lump, OE *clympre*] —**clump'y, clump'ish,** *adj.*

Clumber
(1½ ft. high)

clum·sy (klŭm'zĭ), *adj.,* **-sier, -siest. 1.** awkward in movement or action; without skill or grace: *a clumsy workman.* **2.** awkwardly done or made; unwieldy; ill-contrived: *a clumsy apology.* [der. obs. v. *clumse* be benumbed with cold, t. Scand.; cf. Swed. *klummsen* be-numbed] —**clum'si·ly,** *adv.* —**clum'si·ness,** *n.* —**Syn. 1.** ungraceful, ungainly, lumbering, lubberly. **2.** unhandy, unskillful, maladroit, inexpert, bungling.

clung (klŭng), *v.* pt. and pp. of **cling.**

Clu·ny (klŏŏ·nē'), *n.* a town in E France: ruins of a famous Benedictine abbey. 3678 (1936).

Clu·ny lace (klŏŏ'nĭ), **1.** a lace made by hand with bobbins, originally in France. **2.** a machine lace copied from it.

clu·pe·id (klŏŏ'pĭ·ĭd), *n.* **1.** any of the *Clupeidae,* a family of (chiefly) marine, teleostean fishes, including the herrings, sardines, menhaden, and shad. —*adj.* **2.** relating to the family *Clupeidae.* [t. NL: s. *Clupeidae,* pl., f. s. *Clupea* the herring genus (L *clupea* kind of small river-fish) + *-idae* (see -ID²)]

clu·pe·oid (klŏŏ'pĭ·oid'), *adj.* **1.** herringlike. —*n.* **2.** any member of the *Isospondyli,* an order of fishes including the clupeids, salmon, smelts, etc.

clus·ter (klŭs'tər), *n.* **1.** a number of things of the same kind, growing or held together; a bunch: *a cluster of grapes.* **2.** a group of things or persons near together. **3.** *U.S. Army.* a small metal design placed on the ribbon representing an awarded medal, which indicates that the same medal has been awarded again: *oak-leaf cluster.* —*v.t.* **4.** to gather into a cluster. **5.** to furnish or cover with clusters. —*v.i.* **6.** to form a cluster or clusters. [OE, var. of *clyster* bunch] —**clus'ter·y,** *adj.*

clutch¹ (klŭch), *v.t.* **1.** to seize with, or as with, the hands or claws; snatch. **2.** to grip or hold tightly or firmly. —*v.i.* **3.** to try to seize or grasp (fol. by *at*). —*n.* **4.** the hand, claw, paw, etc., when grasping. **5.** (*chiefly pl.*) power of disposal or control; mastery: *in the clutches of an enemy.* **6.** act of clutching; a snatch; a grasp. **7.** a tight grip or hold. **8.** a device for gripping something. **9.** a coupling or appliance by which working parts of machinery (as a pulley and a shaft) may be made to engage or disengage at will. [ME *clucche(n),* var. of *clycche(n),* OE *clyccan* crook or bend, close (the hand), clench] —**Syn. 1.** See **catch.**

clutch² (klŭch), *n.* **1.** a hatch of eggs; the number of eggs produced or incubated at one time. **2.** a brood of chickens. —*v.t.* **3.** to hatch (chickens). [var. of d. *cletch,* akin to *cleck* hatch, t. Scand.; cf. Sw. *kläcka*]

clut·ter (klŭt'ər), *v.t.* **1.** to heap, litter, or strew in a disorderly manner. —*v.i.* **2.** to run in disorder; move with bustle and confusion. **3.** to make a clatter. **4.** to speak so rapidly and inexactly that distortions of sound and phrasing result. —*n.* **5.** a disorderly heap or assemblage; litter. **6.** confusion; disorder. **7.** confused noise; clatter. [var. of *clotter,* der. CLOT; associated with CLUSTER]

Clyde (klīd), *n.* **1.** a river in S Scotland, flowing into the Firth of Clyde: shipbuilding. 106 mi. **2. Firth of,** an inlet of the Atlantic, in SW Scotland. 64 mi. long.

Clyde·bank (klīd'băngk'), *n.* a city in SW Scotland, on the Clyde. 44,108 (1939).

Clydes·dale (klīdz'dāl'), *n.* one of a breed of active, strong, and hardy draft horses originally raised in Clydesdale, Scotland.

Clydesdale terrier, a variety of Skye terrier bred for smallness.

clyp·e·ate (klĭp'ĭ·āt'), *adj.* shaped like a round shield or buckler. [t. L: m. s. *clypeātus,* pp., furnished with a shield]

clyp·e·us (klĭp'ĭ·əs), *n., pl.* **clypei** (klĭp'ĭ·ī'). the area of the facial wall of an insect's head between the labrum and the front, usually separated from the latter by a groove. [t. L: prop., *clipeus* round shield] —**clyp'e·al,** *adj.*

clys·ter (klĭs'tər), *n. Med.* an enema. [ME *clister,* t. L: m. *clyster,* t. Gk.: m. *klystēr* syringe]

Cly·tem·nes·tra (klī'təm·nĕs'trə), *n. Gk. Legend.* the daughter of Tyndareus and Leda, wife of Agamemnon. See **Agamemnon, Aegisthus, Orestes.** Also, **Cly'taem·nes'tra.**

cm., centimeter; centimeters.

cml., commercial.

Cni·dus (nī'dəs), *n.* ancient city of Caria, in SW Asia Minor: Athenian naval victory over the Spartans, 394 B.C.

Cnos·sus (nŏs'əs), *n.* Knossos.

Cnut (kə·nōōt', kə·nūt'), *n.* Canute.

co-, **1.** a prefix signifying association and accompanying action, occurring before vowels and before *h* and *gn,* as in *coadjutor, cohabit, cognate.* Also used in variants of words of Latin origin in place of the regular *com-, con-,* etc. as in *co-centric,* for *concentric, co-mingle,* for *commingle,* etc. Cf. **com-.** **2.** *Math., Astron.* a prefix meaning "complement of," as in *cosine, codeclination.* [t. L, var. of *com-* COM-]

Co, *Chem.* cobalt.

Co., **1.** Company. **2.** County. Also, **co.**

C.O., **1.** Commanding Officer. **2.** conscientious objector.

c.o., **1.** care of. **2.** carried over. Also, **c/o**

coach (kōch), *n.* **1.** a large, closed, four-wheeled carriage. **2.** an enclosed automobile, usually having two doors. **3.** a public passenger bus. **4.** a railroad passenger car, esp. as distinguished from a parlor car, etc. **5.** a person who trains athletes for a contest, etc. **6.** *Baseball.* a person stationed near first or third base to advise the players of his team while they run the bases. **7.** a private tutor who prepares a student for an examination. —*v.t.* **8.** to give instruction or advice to in the capacity of a coach. —*v.i.* **9.** to act as a coach. **10.** to study with or be instructed by a coach. [earlier *cochee,* t. Hung.: m. *kocsi*]

coach-and-four (kōch'ən·fôr'), *n.* a coach drawn by four horses.

ăct, āble, dâre, ärt; ĕbb, ēqual; ĭf, īce; hŏt, ōver, ôrder, oil, bŏŏk, ōōze, out; ŭp, ūse, ûrge; ə = a in alone; ch, chief; g, give; ng, ring; sh, shoe; th, thin; ŧh, that; zh, vision. See the full key on inside cover.

coach dog, Dalmatian (def. 3).

coach·er (kō'chər), *n.* **1.** one who coaches; a coach. **2.** coach horse.

coach horse, a horse used or fitted to draw a coach.

coach·man (kōch'mən), *n., pl.* **-men.** **1.** a man employed to drive a coach or carriage. **2.** a certain kind of artificial fly for angling. **—coach'man·ship',** *n.*

co·ac·tion (kō ăk'shən), *n.* force or compulsion, either in restraining or in impelling. [t. F, t. L: s. coactio]

co·ac·tive (kō ăk'tĭv), *adj.* compulsory; coercive. **—co·ac'tive·ly,** *adv.*

co·ad·ju·tor (kō ăj'ə tər, kō'ə jōō'tər), *n.* **1.** an assistant. **2.** an assistant to a bishop or other ecclesiastic. **3.** a bishop who assists another bishop, with the right of succession. [t. LL: f. co- co- + adjūtor helper; r. ME coadiutoure, t. OF]

co·ad·ju·tress (kō ăj'ə trĭs), *n.* a female coadjutor or assistant.

co·ad·ju·trix (kō ăj'ə trĭks), *n., pl.* **coadjutrices** (kō-ăj'ə trī'sēz). coadjutress.

co·ad·u·nate (kō ăj'ə nĭt, -nāt'), *adj.* Zool., Bot. united by growth. [t. L: m.s. coadūnātus, pp., joined together] **—co·ad·u·na'tion,** *n.*

co·ad·ven·ture (kō'əd vĕn'chər), *v.,* **-tured, -turing,** *n.* **—v.i.** **1.** to share in an adventure. **—n.** **2.** adventure in which two or more share. **—co'ad·ven'tur·er,** *n.*

co·ag·u·la·ble (kō ăg'yə lə bəl), *adj.* capable of being coagulated: *this substance is highly coagulable.* **—co·ag'u·la·bil'i·ty,** *n.*

co·ag·u·lant (kō ăg'yə lənt), *n.* a substance that produces coagulation. [t. L: s. coāgulans, ppr., curdling]

co·ag·u·late (v. kō ăg'yə lāt'; adj. kō ăg'yə lĭt, -lāt'), *v.,* **-lated, -lating,** *adj.* **—v.t., v.i.** **1.** to change from a fluid into a thickened mass; curdle; congeal. **—adj.** **2.** *Obs.* coagulated. [t. L: m. s. coāgulātus, pp., curdled] **—co·ag'u·la'tion,** *n.* **—co·ag'u·la'tive,** *adj.* **—co·ag'u·la'tor,** *n.*

co·ag·u·lum (kō ăg'yə ləm), *n., pl.* **-la** (-lə). Physiol. etc. a clump, clot, curd, precipitate, or gel. [t. L: rennet]

Co·a·hui·la (kō'ä wē'lä), *n.* a state in N Mexico. 550,717 pop. (1940); 58,067 sq. mi. *Cap.:* Saltillo.

coal (kōl), *n.* **1.** a black or dark-brown combustible mineral substance consisting of carbonized vegetable matter, used as a fuel: **hard coal** (anthracite), **soft coal** (bituminous coal), **brown coal** (lignite). **2.** a piece of wood or other combustible substance either glowing, charred, or burned out. **3.** charcoal. **4. take, call, rake,** etc., **over the coals,** to scold; to reprimand. **—v.t.** **5.** to burn to coal or charcoal. **6.** to provide with coal. **—v.i.** **7.** to take in coal for fuel. [ME cole, OE col live coal, c. G kohle]

coal car, *U.S.* **1.** a railway car designed to carry coal. **2.** a car used in hauling coal in or from a mine.

coal·er (kō'lər), *n.* a railroad, ship, etc., used mainly to haul or supply coal.

co·a·lesce (kō'ə lĕs'), *v.i.,* **-lesced, -lescing.** **1.** to grow together or into one mass, community, etc. **2.** to unite so as to form one mass, community, etc. [t. L: m. s. coalescere] **—co'a·les'cence,** *n.* **—co'a·les'cent,** *adj.*

coal field, an area containing coal deposits.

coal·fish (kōl'fĭsh'), *n.* **1.** the sablefish. **2.** a North Atlantic gadoid food fish, *Pollachius virens,* a species of pollack. [named from the color of its back]

coal gas, **1.** the gas formed by burning coal. **2.** a gas used for illuminating and heating, produced by distilling bituminous coal, consisting chiefly of hydrogen, methane and carbon monoxide.

coal heaver, one who carries or shovels coal.

coal hod, *U.S. and Dial.* a small pail for carrying coal.

coal·ing station (kō'lĭng), a place at which coal is supplied to ships, locomotives, etc.

co·a·li·tion (kō'ə lĭsh'ən), *n.* **1.** union into one body or mass; fusion. **2.** a combination or alliance, esp., a temporary one between persons, factions, states, etc. [t. ML: s. coalitio, der. L coalescere coalesce] **—co'-a·li'tion·ist,** *n.*

coal measures, Geol. **1.** coal-bearing strata. **2.** (caps.) a portion of the Carboniferous system, characterized by coal deposits.

coal mine, a mine or pit from which coal is obtained. **—coal miner. —coal mining.**

coal oil, kerosene.

coal pit, **1.** a pit where coal is dug. **2.** *U.S.* a place where charcoal is made.

coal·sack (kōl'săk'), *n.* **1. southern coalsack,** a large dark space near the southern constellation Crux. **2. northern coalsack,** a dark space in the Milky Way in the northern constellation Cygnus. Also, **Coalsack.**

coal tar, a thick, black, viscid liquid formed during the distillation of coal (as in the manufacture of illuminating gas), and which upon further distillation yields benzene, anthracene, phenol, etc. (from which are derived a large number of dyes and synthetic compounds), and a final residuum (**coal-tar pitch**) which is used in making pavements, etc.

coal-tar creosote, impure phenol or carbolic acid, distinct from the creosote of wood tar.

coal·y (kō'lĭ), *adj.* of, like, or containing coal.

coam·ing (kō'mĭng), *n.* **1.** a raised border around an opening in a deck, roof, or floor, designed to prevent water from running below. **2.** *Naut.* one of the pieces, esp. of the fore-and-aft pieces, of such a border.

co·arc·tate (kō ärk'tāt), *adj.* *Entomol.* denoting an insect pupa enclosed in the hardened cuticula (puparium) of a preceding larval instar. [t. L: m. s. coarctātus, pp., pressed together; r. ME coartate, t. L: m. s. coartātus, var. of coarctātus]

Coarctate pupa. A. Lateral view; B. Dorsal view (Vertical line shows actual size)

coarse (kōrs), *adj.,* **coarser, coarsest.** **1.** of inferior or faulty quality; not pure or choice; common; base: *coarse manners, coarse lad.* **2.** composed of relatively large parts or particles: *coarse sand.* **3.** lacking in fineness or delicacy of texture, structure, etc. **4.** harsh. **5.** lacking delicacy of feeling, manner, etc.; not refined. **6.** (of metals) unrefined. [adjectival var. of COURSE, n., with the sense of ordinary] **—coarse'ly,** *adv.* **—coarse'ness,** *n.* **—Syn. 5.** vulgar, gross, crass, indelicate, ribald.

coarse-grained (kōrs'grānd'), *adj.* **1.** having a coarse texture or grain. **2.** indelicate; crude; gross.

coars·en (kōr'sən), *v.t., v.i.* to make or become coarse.

coast (kōst), *n.* **1.** the land next to the sea; the seashore. **2.** the region adjoining it. **3. the Coast,** (in the U. S.) the region bordering on the Pacific Ocean. **4.** *Archaic.* the boundary or border of a country. **5.** a hill or slope down which one may slide on a sled. **6.** a slide or ride down a hill, etc. **7. the coast is clear,** the danger is gone. **—v.i.** **8.** *U.S.* to slide on a sled down a snowy or icy hillside or incline. **9.** *U.S.* to descend a hill, etc., as on a bicycle, without using pedals. **10.** to proceed or sail along, or sail from port to port of, a coast. **11.** to move along after effort has ceased; to keep going on acquired momentum. **12.** *Obs.* to proceed in a roundabout way. **13.** *Obs.* to go or pass (along, etc.). **—v.t.** **14.** to proceed along the coast of. **15.** to go along or near to (a coast). **16.** to keep alongside of (a person moving). **17.** *Obs.* to go or pass by the side or border of. [ME coste, t. OF, g. L costa rib, side] **—Syn. 1.** See shore[1].

coast·al (kōs'təl), *adj.* of or at a coast: *coastal defense.*

Coast Artillery Corps, a branch and combat arm of the U. S. Army, troops of which man the coastal defenses and the anti-aircraft units of the army.

coast·er (kōs'tər), *n.* **1.** one who or that which coasts. **2.** a vessel engaged in coastwise trade. **3.** a sled for coasting. **4.** an amusement railway with deep dips and sharp curves. **5.** a tray, sometimes on wheels, for holding a decanter to be passed around a dining table. **6.** a small dish or tray placed under glasses, etc., to protect a table from moisture or heat.

coaster brake, a brake on freewheel bicycles, operated by back pressure on the pedals.

coast guard, **1.** (caps.) *U.S.* the government organization employed in the coastal lifesaving service, antismuggling patrol, etc. **2.** any organization for the prevention of smuggling, etc. **3.** a member of any such organization.

coast·ing trade (kōs'tĭng), trade between ports along the same coast.

coast·line (kōst'līn'), *n.* the outline or contour of a coast.

Coast Range, a series of mountain ranges along the Pacific coast of North America, extending from Lower California to SE Alaska. Highest peak, San Gorgonio, 11,485 ft. Also, **Coast Mountains** in British Columbia.

coast·ward (kōst'wərd), *adv.* **1.** Also, **coast'wards.** toward the coast. **—adj.** **2.** directed toward the coast: *coastward movement.*

coast·wise (kōst'wīz'), *adv.* **1.** Also, **coast·ways** (kōst'wāz'). along the coast. **—adj.** **2.** following the coast: *coastwise drift.*

coat (kōt), *n.* **1.** an outer garment with sleeves, covering the upper part of the body. **2.** a natural integument or covering, as the hair, fur, or wool of an animal, the bark of a tree, or the skin of a fruit. **3.** anything that covers or conceals: *a coat of paint.* **4.** *Obs.* a garment indicating profession, class, etc. **5.** *Obs.* profession, class, etc., so indicated. **6.** *Obs. or Dial.* a petticoat or skirt. **—v.t.** **7.** to cover or provide with a coat. **8.** to cover with a layer or coating; cover as a layer or coating does. [ME cote, t. OF, t. Gmc.; cf. OS cott woolen coat, ML cotta kind of tunic] **—coat'less,** *adj.*

coat and skirt, *Brit.* a tailored suit for women.

coat card, Cards. face card.

coat·ed (kō'tĭd), *adj.* **1.** (of paper) having a highly polished coating applied to provide a smooth surface for printing. **2.** (of a fabric) having a plastic, paint, or pyroxylin coating, making it impervious to moisture. **3.** having a coat.

coat·ee (kō tē'), *n.* a short coat.

co·a·ti (kō ä'tĭ), *n., pl.* **-tis.** any of the tropical American plantigrade carnivores constituting the genus *Nasua,* closely related to the raccoon, and having an elongated body, a long ringed tail, and an attenuated, flexible snout. Also, **co·a·ti-mon·di, co·a·ti-mun·di** (kō-ä'tĭ mŭn'dĭ). [t. Brazilian]

Coati, *Nasua narica* (3½ ft. long, tail 18 in.)

coat·ing (kō'tĭng), *n.* **1.** a layer of any substance spread over a surface. **2.** material for coats.

---

coat of arms, **1.** a surcoat or tabard embroidered with heraldic devices, worn by medieval knights over their armor. **2.** the heraldic bearings of a person; a hatchment; an escutcheon. [trans. of F *cotte d'armes*]

coat of mail, *pl.* **coats of mail.** a hauberk; a defensive garment made of interlinked metal rings, overlapping metal plates, etc.

co·au·thor (kō·ô′thər), *n.* a joint author.

Coat of arms (def. 2)

coax (kōks), *v.t.* **1.** to influence by gentle persuasion, flattery, etc. **2.** to get or win by coaxing. **3.** *Obs.* to fondle. **4.** *Obs.* to befool. —*v.i.* **5.** to use gentle persuasion, etc. [der. obs. *cokes*, n., fool; of doubtful orig. Cf. COCKNEY] —**coax′er,** *n.* —**coax′ing·ly,** *adv.* —**Syn. 1.** wheedle, cajole, beguile, inveigle, persuade.

co·ax·i·al (kō·ăk′sĭ əl), *adj.* **1.** having a common axis or coincident axes. **2.** (of a cable) composed of an insulated central conductor with tubular stranded conductors laid over it concentrically and separated by layers of insulation. Also, **co·ax·al** (kō ăk′səl).

cob¹ (kŏb), *n.* **1.** *U.S.* a corncob. **2.** a male swan. **3.** a short-legged, thick-set horse. **4.** *U.S.* a horse with an unnaturally high gait. **5.** *Brit. Dial.* a man of importance; leader. **6.** *Brit. Dial.* a roundish mass, lump, or heap. **7.** *Brit.* a mixture of clay and straw, used as a building material. [ME; orig. obscure]

cob² (kŏb), *n.* a gull, esp. the great black-backed gull, *Larus marinus.* Also, **cobb.** [orig. unknown. Cf. D *kob*]

co·balt (kō′bôlt), *n.* **1.** *Chem.* a silver-white metallic element with a faint pinkish tinge, occurring in compounds the silicates of which afford important blue coloring substances for ceramics. *Symbol:* Co; *at. wt.:* 58.94; *at. no.:* 27; *sp. gr.:* 8.9 at 20°C. **2.** a blue pigment containing cobalt. [t. G: m. *kobalt*, var. of *kobold* goblin]

cobalt bloom, the mineral erythrite, hydrous cobalt arsenate, $Co_3As_2O_8 \cdot 8H_2O$, usually of a peach-red color, and often occurring as a pulverulent incrustation.

cobalt blue, any of a number of pigments containing an oxide of cobalt.

co·bal·tic (kō bôl′tĭk), *adj.* *Chem.* of or containing cobalt, esp. in the trivalent state (Co^{+3}).

co·bal·tite (kō bôl′tīt), *n.* a mineral, cobalt arsenic sulfide, CoAsS, silver-white with a reddish tinge: an ore of cobalt. Also, **co·balt·ine** (kō′bôl tēn′, -tĭn).

co·bal·tous (kō bôl′təs), *adj.* *Chem.* containing divalent cobalt (Co^{+2}).

Cobb (kŏb), *n.* **Irvin Shrewsbury,** 1876–1944, U.S. humorist and writer.

Cob·bett (kŏb′ĭt), *n.* **William,** 1763–1835, British journalist and politician, in America and England.

cob·bing (kŏb′ĭng), *n.* *Metall.* old refractory material removed from furnaces.

cob·ble (kŏb′əl), *n., v.,* **-bled, -bling.** —*n.* **1.** a cobble stone. **2.** (*pl.*) cob coal. —*v.t.* **3.** to pave with cobblestones. **4.** to mend (shoes, etc.); patch **5.** to put together roughly or clumsily. [? der. from COB¹, def. 6]

cob·bler (kŏb′lər), *n.* **1.** one who mends shoes. **2.** a clumsy workman. **3.** an iced drink made of wine, fruits, sugar, etc. **4.** *U.S.* a deep-dish fruit pie with a rich biscuit crust, usually only on top.

cob·ble·stone (kŏb′əl stōn′), *n.* a natural rounded stone, large enough for use in paving.

cob coal, a large round lump of coal.

Cob·den (kŏb′dən), *n.* **Richard,** 1804–65, British manufacturer, merchant, economist, and statesman.

co·bel·lig·er·ent (kō′bə lĭj′ər ənt), *n.* a nation, state, or individual that coöperates with, but is not bound by a formal alliance to, another in carrying on war.

Cóbh (kōv), *n.* a seaport in S Eire. 5816 (1941). Formerly, **Queenstown.**

Cob·ham (kŏb′əm), *n.* **John Oldcastle** (ōld′kăs′əl, -käs′əl), **Lord,** died 1417, British martyr: leader of a Lollard conspiracy.

co·ble (kō′bəl, kŏb′əl), *n.* *Scot. and Eng.* a kind of flat-bottomed rowboat or fishing boat. [ME; cf. OE *cuopl*, Welsh *ceubal*, ML *caupulus*]

Co·blenz (kō′blĕnts), *n.* a city in W Germany at the junction of the Rhine and Moselle rivers. 91,098 (1939). German, **Koblenz.**

cob·nut (kŏb′nŭt′), *n.* **1.** the nut of certain cultivated varieties of hazel, *Corylus Avellana grandis.* **2.** a tree bearing such nuts.

co·bra (kō′brə), *n.* any snake of the genus *Naja*, exceedingly venomous and characterized by the ability to dilate its neck so that it assumes a hoodlike form. [short for Pg. *cobra* (g. L *colubra* serpent) *de capello* hood snake]

co·bra de ca·pel·lo (kō′brə dē kə pĕl′ō), *pl.* **cobras de capello.** a cobra, *Naja tripudians*, common in India.

Co·burg (kō′bûrg; *Ger.* kō′bŏŏrk), *n.* a city in central Germany, in N Bavaria. 32,552 (1939).

cob·web (kŏb′wĕb′), *n.* **1.** a web or net spun by a spider to catch its prey. **2.** a single thread spun by a spider. **3.** anything finespun, flimsy, or unsubstantial. **4.** a network of plot or intrigue; an insidious snare. [ME *coppeweb*, f. *coppe* spider (OE *-coppe* in *ātorcoppe* spider) + WEB] —**cob′webbed′,** *adj.* —**cob′web·by,** *adj.*

co·ca (kō′kə), *n.* **1.** either of two shrubs, *Erythroxylon coca* and *Erythroxylon truxillense*, native in the Andes and cultivated in Java and elsewhere. **2.** their dried leaves, which are chewed for their stimulant properties and which yield cocaine and other alkaloids. [t. Peruvian: m. *cuca*]

co·caine (kō kān′, kō′kān; *tech. often* kō′kə ēn′), *n.* a bitter crystalline alkaloid, $C_{17}H_{21}NO_4$, obtained from coca leaves, used as a local anesthetic. Also, **co·cain′.** [f. COCA + -INE²]

co·cain·ism (kō kā′nĭz əm, kō′kə nĭz′əm), *n.* a morbid condition due to excessive or habitual use of cocaine.

co·cain·ize (kō kā′nīz, kō′kə nīz′), *v.t.,* **-ized, -izing.** to treat with or affect by cocaine. —**co·cain′i·za′tion,** *n.*

coc·cid (kŏk′sĭd), *n.* any insect of the homopterous superfamily *Coccoidea*, including the scale insects, etc.

coc·cid·i·oi·dal gran·u·lo·ma (kŏk sĭd′Ĭ oi′dəl grăn′yŏŏ lō′mə), a fungus disease of the lymph nodes of sheep, cattle, dogs, and man, somewhat like tuberculosis.

coc·cid·i·o·sis (kŏk sĭd′Ĭ ō′sĭs), *n.* any one of a series of specific infectious diseases caused by epithelial protozoan parasites, which usually affect the intestines. The disease is known in birds, cattle, swine, sheep, and dogs; it rarely occurs in man.

coc·cus (kŏk′əs), *n., pl.* **-ci** (-sī). **1.** *Bacteriol.* a spherical organism when free, slightly flattened when two or more form in apposition, as in the *Neisseria gonorrhoeae* or *N. meningitidis.* **2.** *Bot.* one of the carpels of a schizocarp. **3.** *Pharm.* cochineal. [t. NL, t. Gk.: m. *kókkos* grain, seed] —**coc·coid** (kŏk′oid), *adj.*

Cocci (def. 2)
A, Fruit composed of ten cocci;
B, Fruit composed of four cocci

coc·cyx (kŏk′sĭks), *n., pl.* **coccyges** (kŏk sī′jēz). **1.** a small triangular bone forming the lower extremity of the spinal column in man, consisting of four ankylosed rudimentary vertebrae. See diag. under **spinal column. 2.** a corresponding part in certain other animals. [t. L, t. Gk.: m. *kókkyx* coccyx, orig., cuckoo] —**coc·cyg·e·al** (kŏk sĭj′Ĭ əl), *adj.*

Co·cha·bam·ba (kō′chä bäm′bä), *n.* a city in central Bolivia. 60,000 (est. 1942); 8394 ft. high.

co·chin (kō′chĭn, kŏch′Ĭn), *n.* a breed of large domestic fowls, of Asiatic origin, resembling the brahma but slightly smaller. Also, **Cochin.** [named after COCHIN-CHINA]

Co·chin (kō′chĭn), *n.* a seaport near the SW extremity of India: the first European fort in India was built here by the Portuguese, 1503. 26,320 (1941).

Co·chin-Chi·na (kō′chĭn chī′nə, kŏch′Ĭn), *n.* a former state in S French Indo-China: now part of Viet Nam. 4,616,000 pop. (1936); 24,980 sq. mi. *Cap.:* Saïgon. French, **Co·chin·chine** (kō shăn shēn′).

coch·i·neal (kŏch′ə nēl′, kŏch′ə nēl′), *n.* a red dye prepared from the dried bodies of the females of a scale insect, *Dactylopius coccus*, which lives on cactuses of Mexico, Central America, and other warm regions. [t. F: m. *cochenille*, t. Sp.: m. *cochinilla*, orig. wood louse, der. *cochino* pig]

coch·le·a (kŏk′lĬ ə), *n., pl.* **-leae** (-lĬ ē′). a division, spiral in form, of the internal ear, in man and most other mammals. See diag. under **ear.** [t. L, t. Gk.: m. *kochlĭās* snail, something spiral] —**coch′le·ar,** *adj.*

coch·le·ate (kŏk′lĬ āt′), *adj.* shaped like a snail shell; spiral. Also, **coch′le·at·ed.** [t. L: m.s. *cochleātus*]

cock¹ (kŏk), *n.* **1.** a rooster. **2.** the male of any bird, esp. of the gallinaceous kind. **3.** the crowing of the cock. **4.** *Archaic.* the time of its crowing, in the early morning. **5.** a weathercock. **6.** a leader; chief person; ruling spirit. **7.** a device for permitting or arresting the flow of a liquid or gas from a receptacle or through a pipe; a faucet, tap, or stop valve. **8.** (in a firearm) **a.** that part of the lock which by its fall or action causes the discharge; the hammer. **b.** the position into which the cock or hammer is brought by being drawn partly or completely back, preparatory to firing. **9.** *Curling.* the mark aimed at. —*v.t.* **10.** to pull back and set the cock or hammer of (a firearm) preparatory to firing. —*v.i.* **11.** to cock the firing mechanism of a gun. [ME *cok*, OE *cocc*]

cock² (kŏk) *v.t.* **1.** to set or turn up or to one side, often in an assertive, jaunty, or significant manner. —*v.i.* **2.** to stand or stick up conspicuously. **3.** *Dial.* to strut; swagger; put on airs of importance. —*n.* **4.** act of turning the head, a hat, etc. up or to one side in a jaunty or significant way. **5.** the position of anything thus placed. [prob. special use of COCK¹]

cock³ (kŏk), *n.* **1.** a conical pile of hay, etc. —*v.t.* **2.** to pile (hay, etc.) in such piles. [ME. Cf. Norw. *kok* heap]

cock·ade (kŏ kād′), *n.* a knot of ribbon, rosette, etc., worn on the hat as a badge or a part of a uniform. [alter. of *cockard*, t. F: m. *cocarde*, der. *coq* cock] —**cock·ad′ed,** *adj.*

cock-a-hoop (kŏk′ə hōōp′, -hŏŏp′), *adj.* in a state of unrestrained joy or exultation.

Cock·aigne (kŏ kān′), *n.* a fabulous land of luxury and idleness. [ME *cokaigne*, t. OF, ? t. MLG: m. *kokenje* sugar cakes given children at fairs]

cock·a·lo·rum (kŏk′ə lôr′əm), *n.* *Colloq.* a self-important little man.

cock-and-bull story (kŏk′ən bŏŏl′), an absurd improbable story told as true.

cock·a·teel (kŏk′ə tēl′), n. a small, crested, long-tailed Australian parrot, *Leptolopus hollandicus*, common as a cage bird. Also, **cock′a·tiel′**. [t. D: m. *kaketielje*. Cf. COCKATOO]

cock·a·too (kŏk′ə tōō′), n. any of the crested parrots constituting the genera *Kakatoë*, *Callocephalon*, or *Calyptorhynchus*, forming the subfamily *Kakatuinae*, of the East Indies, Australia, etc., often white, or white and yellow, pink, or red. [t. D: m. *kaketoe*, t. Malay: m. *kakatūa*]

cock·a·trice (kŏk′ə trĭs), n. 1. a fabulous serpent with deadly glance, reputed to be hatched by a serpent from a cock's egg, and commonly represented with the head, legs, and wings of a cock and the body and tail of a serpent. 2. *Bible.* an unidentified species of venomous serpent. [ME *cocatris*, t. OF, der. L *calcāre* tread; used to render Gk. *ichneūmōn* ICHNEUMON; assoc. with COCK¹]

Crested cockatoo, *Kakatoë sulphurea* (13 in. long)

cock bead, *Joinery.* a bead which is not flush with the general surface, but raised above it.

cock·boat (kŏk′bōt′), n. a small boat, esp. one used as a tender.

cock·chaf·er (kŏk′chā′fər), n. any of certain scarabaeid beetles, esp. the European species, *Melolontha melolontha*, which is very destructive to forest trees. [f. COCK¹ (def. 6, with reference to size) + CHAFER]

cock·crow (kŏk′krō′), n. the time at which cocks crow; dawn. Also, **cock′crow′ing**.

cocked hat (kŏkt), 1. a hat having the brim turned up on two or three sides. 2. **knock into a cocked hat,** to damage or destroy completely.

cock·er¹ (kŏk′ər), n. 1. a cocker spaniel. 2. one who promotes or patronizes cockfighting. [f. COCK¹, v. + -ER¹]

cock·er² (kŏk′ər), v.t. to pamper. [? freq. of obs. *cock*, v. ; ? orig. meaning make a cock of]

cock·er·el (kŏk′ər əl, kŏk′rəl), n. a young domestic cock. [dim. of COCK¹]

cocker spaniel, one of a breed of small spaniels trained for use in hunting or kept as pets.

cock·eye (kŏk′ī′), n. an eye that squints, or is affected with strabismus. [f. COCK², v. + EYE]

Cocker spaniel (11 in. high)

cock·eyed (kŏk′īd′), adj. 1. having a squinting eye; cross-eyed. 2. *Slang.* twisted or slanted to one side. 3. *Slang.* foolish; absurd.

cock·fight (kŏk′fīt′), n. a fight between gamecocks usually armed with spurs. —**cock′fight′ing,** n., adj.

cock·horse (kŏk′hôrs′), n. a child's rocking horse or hobbyhorse.

cock·ish (kŏk′ĭsh), adj., *Colloq.* cocklike; cocky. —**cock′ish·ly,** adv. —**cock′ish·ness,** n.

cock·le¹ (kŏk′əl), n., v., **-led, -ling. —**n. 1. any of the bivalve mollusks with somewhat heart-shaped, radially ribbed valves which constitute the genus *Cardium*, esp. *C. edule*, the common edible species of Europe. 2. any of various allied or similar mollusks. 3. cockleshell. 4. a wrinkle; pucker. 5. **cockles of the heart,** the inmost parts or depths of the heart. 6. a small shallow or light boat. 7. *U.S.* a small crisp candy of sugar and flour, bearing a motto. —*v.i.* 8. to contract into wrinkles; pucker. 9. to rise into short, irregular waves. —*v.t.* 10. to cause to wrinkle or pucker: *a book cockled by water.* [ME *cockille*, t. F: m. *coquille*, b. F *coque* shell and L *conchylium*, t. Gk.: m. *konchýlion*, dim. of *kónchē* mussel or cockle, CONCH]

cock·le² (kŏk′əl), n. a weed generally, as the darnel, *Lolium temulentum*, or rye grass, *L. perenne.* [ME; OE *coccel*]

cock·le·boat (kŏk′əl bōt′), n. a cockboat.

cock·le·bur (kŏk′əl bûr′), n. 1. any plant of the composite genus *Xanthium*, comprising coarse weeds with spiny burs. 2. the burdock, *Arctium Lappa.*

cock·le·shell (kŏk′əl shĕl′), n. 1. a shell of the cockle. 2. a shell of some other mollusk, as the scallop. 3. a small, light boat.

cock·loft (kŏk′lôft′, -lŏft′), n. a small upper loft; a small garret.

cock·ney (kŏk′nĭ), n., pl. **-neys,** adj. —n. (*often cap.*) 1. a native or resident of London, especially of the East End (often with reference to those who have marked peculiarities of pronunciation and dialect). 2. their pronunciation or dialect. 3. *Obs.* a pampered child. 4. *Obs.* a squeamish, affected, or effeminate person. —*adj.* 5. of cockneys or their dialect. [ME *cokeney* cock's egg (i.e., malformed egg), f. *coken,* gen. pl. of *cok* cock + *ey,* OE *æg* egg] —**cock′ney·ish,** adj.

cock·ney·dom (kŏk′nĭ dəm), n. 1. the region of cockneys. 2. cockneys collectively.

cock·ney·ese (kŏk′nĭ ēz′, -ēs′), n. cockney dialect.

cock·ney·fy (kŏk′nĭ fī′), v.t., **-fied, -fying.** to give a cockney character to.

cock·ney·ism (kŏk′nĭ ĭz′əm), n. 1. cockney quality or usage. 2. a cockney peculiarity, as of speech.

cock-of-the-rock (kŏk′əv thə rŏk′), n. a brilliant orange-red bird of the genus *Rupicola* with the bill hidden by the frontal plumes, found in northern South America.

cock of the woods, the pileated woodpecker, *Ceophloeus pileatus*, of North America.

cock·pit (kŏk′pĭt′), n. 1. (in some airplanes) an enclosed space containing seats for the pilot and copilot. 2. a recess aft, in the deck of a yacht or other boat, which provides a small amount of deck space at a lower level. 3. (in the old type of warship) an apartment below the water line, used as quarters for certain officers and as a dressing station for the wounded. 4. a pit or enclosed place for cockfights. 5. a place where a contest is fought, or which has been the scene of many contests or battles: *Belgium, the cockpit of Europe.*

cock·roach (kŏk′rōch′), n. any of various orthopterous insects of the family *Blattidae*, usually nocturnal, and having a flattened body, as the following important cosmopolitan species: the pale, yellowish-brown common cockroach (Croton bug, *Blattela germanica*) introduced from Europe, and the dark-brown or black oriental roach (black beetle, *Blatta orientalis*) spread by commerce. These and other species are important household pests. [f. COCK¹ + ROACH, popular analysis of Sp. *cucaracha*. Cf. popular *sparrow grass* for *asparagus,* etc.]

cocks·comb (kŏks′kōm′), n. 1. the comb or caruncle of a cock. 2. the cap of a professional fool, resembling a cock's comb. 3. an amaranthaceous garden plant, *Celosia cristata,* with flowers, commonly crimson or purple, in a broad spike somewhat resembling the comb of a cock. 4. some other species of *Celosia.* 5. a coxcomb.

cocks·head (kŏks′hĕd′), n. an herb of the genus *Onobrychis,* esp. *O. Caputgalli* and *O. sativa.*

cock·shut (kŏk′shŭt′), n. *Obs. or Brit. Dial.* the close of the day; evening; twilight.

cock·shy (kŏk′shī′), n., pl. **-shies.** *Brit.* 1. act or sport of throwing missiles at a target. 2. an object of attack.

cock·spur (kŏk′spûr′), n. a North American species of thorn, *Crataegus Crusgalli,* frequently cultivated as a small ornamental tree.

cock·sure (kŏk′shŏŏr′), adj. 1. perfectly sure or certain; completely confident in one's own mind. 2. too certain; overconfident. 3. *Obs.* perfectly secure or safe. —**cock′sure′ness,** n. —**Ant.** 1. doubtful. 2. cautious.

cock·swain (kŏk′sən, -swān′), n. coxswain.

cock·tail (kŏk′tāl′), n. 1. any of various short mixed drinks, consisting typically of gin, whiskey, or brandy, with different admixtures, such as vermouth, fruit juices, etc., usually chilled and frequently sweetened. 2. a portion of oysters, clams, crabmeat, etc., served in a small glass with a sauce. 3. a mixture of fruits served in a glass. 4. a horse with a docked tail. 5. a horse which is not thoroughbred. 6. an ill-bred person passing as a gentleman. [orig. unknown]

cock·y (kŏk′ĭ), adj., **cockier, cockiest.** *Colloq.* arrogantly smart; pertly self-assertive; conceited: *a cocky fellow, air, answer.* —**cock′i·ly,** adv. —**cock′i·ness,** n.

cock·y·ol·ly bird (kŏk′ĭ ŏl′ĭ), a pet name for any small bird. Also, **cock′y·ol′y.**

co·co (kō′kō), n., pl. **-cos.** 1. a tall, slender tropical palm, *Cocos nucifera,* which produces the coconut; coconut palm. 2. the coconut fruit or seed. Also, **cocoa.** [t. Sp., Pg.: grinning face]

co·coa¹ (kō′kō), n. 1. the roasted, husked, and ground seeds of the cacao, *Theobroma cacao,* from which much of the fat has been removed. 2. a beverage made from cocoa powder. 3. brown; yellowish brown; reddish brown. —*adj.* 4. of or pertaining to cocoa. 5. of the color of cocoa. [var. of CACAO]

co·coa² (kō′kō), n. misspelling of **coco.**

cocoa butter, cacao butter.

co·con·scious·ness (kō kŏn′shəs nĭs), n. *Psychol.* mental processes dissociated from the main stream of thought or from the dominant personality integration. —**co·con′scious,** adj. —**co·con′scious·ly,** adv.

co·co·nut (kō′kə nŭt′, -nət), n. the seed of the coconut palm, large, hard-shelled, lined with a white edible meat, and containing a milky liquid. Also, **co′coa·nut′.**

coconut palm, coco (def. 1). Also, **coconut tree.**

co·coon (kə kōōn′), n. 1. the silky envelope spun by the larva of many insects, as silkworms, serving as a covering while they are in the chrysalis or pupal state. 2. any of various similar protective coverings, as the silky case in which certain spiders enclose their eggs. [t. F: m. *cocon,* der. *coque* shell]

Co·cos Islands (kō′kŏs), a British group of 20 coral islands in the Indian Ocean, SW of Java. 1142 pop. (1931); 1½ sq. mi. Also, **Keeling Islands.**

co·cotte (kō kŏt′, kə-; *Fr.* kô kôt′), n. a courtesan; immoral woman. [t. F: hen, der. *coq* rooster]

Coc·teau (kŏk tō′), **Jean** (zhän), born 1891, French poet, novelist, dramatist, critic, and artist.

Co·cy·tus (kō sī′təs), n. *Class. Myth.* a river of Hades, connected with the Acheron.

cod¹ (kŏd), n., pl. **cods,** (*esp. collectively*) **cod.** 1. one of the most important North Atlantic food fishes, *Gadus callarias.* 2. any of several other gadoid fishes, as the Pacific cod, *Gadus macrocephalus.* 3. any of various unrelated fishes, as the rockfish (def. 3). [ME; orig. uncert.]

---

b., blend of, blended; c., cognate with; d., dialect, dialectal; der., derived from; f., formed from; g., going back to; m., modification of; r., replacing; s., stem of; t., taken from; ?, perhaps. See the full key on inside cover.

cod² (kŏd), *n.* **1.** a bag or sack. **2.** *Dial.* a pod. [ME; OE *codd*]

Cod (kŏd), *n.* **Cape,** a sandy peninsula in SE Massachusetts between **Cape Cod Bay** and the Atlantic: traversed near its base by the **Cape Cod Canal** (8 mi. long).

C.O.D., **1.** *U.S.* collect on delivery. **2.** *Brit.* cash on delivery. Also, **c.o.d.**

co·da (kō′də), *n.* *Music.* a more or less independent passage, at the end of a composition, introduced to bring it to a satisfactory close. [t. It., g. L *cauda* tail]

cod·dle (kŏd′əl), *v.t.,* **-dled, -dling.** **1.** to boil gently; stew (fruit, etc.). **2.** to treat tenderly; nurse or tend indulgently; pamper. [var. of and v. use of *caudle* kind of gruel, t. ONF: m. *caudel,* g. ML *caldellum,* dim. of *cal(i)dum* hot drink, neut. of L *calidus* hot]

code (kōd), *n., v.,* **coded, coding.** —*n.* **1.** any systematic collection or digest of the existing laws of a country, or of those relating to a particular subject: *the Civil Code of France.* **2.** any system or collection of rules and regulations. **3.** a system of signals for communication by telegraph, heliograph, etc. **4.** a system of arbitrarily chosen words, etc., used for brevity or secrecy. —*v.t.* **5.** to arrange in a code; enter in a code. **6.** to translate into a code. [ME, t. F, t. L: m. s. *cōdex.* See CODEX]

co·dec·li·na·tion (kō′dĕk lə nā′shən), *n.* *Astron.* the complement of the declination.

co·de·fend·ant (kō′dĭ fĕn′dənt), *n.* a joint defendant.

co·deine (kō′dēn), *n.* a white, crystalline, slightly bitter alkaloid, $C_{18}H_{21}NO_3H_2O$, obtained from opium, used in medicine as an analgesic, sedative, and hypnotic. Also, **co·de·in** (kō′dĭ ĭn), **co·de·ia** (kō dē′ə). [f. m.s. Gk. *kṓdeia* head, poppy head + -INE²]

Code Na·po·lé·on (kōd nȧ pō lē ôn′), the body of French private law, the Civil Code, promulgated between 1804–07.

co·det·ta (kō dĕt′tä), *n.* *Italian.* a short coda.

co·dex (kō′dĕks), *n., pl.* **codices** (kō′də sēz′, kŏd′ə-). a manuscript volume of an ancient classic, the Scriptures, etc. [t. L, earlier *caudex* tree trunk, book]

Co·dex Ju·ris Ca·no·ni·ci (kō′dĕks jōōr′ĭs kə nŏn′ə sī′), *Rom. Cath. Ch.* an official collection of general church law made effective in 1918. [L]

cod·fish (kŏd′fĭsh′), *n., pl.* **-fishes,** (*esp. collectively*) **-fish.** cod¹.

codg·er (kŏj′ər), *n.* **1.** *Colloq.* an odd or peculiar (old) person: *a lovable old codger.* **2.** *Brit. Dial.* a mean, miserly person.

co·di·ces (kō′də sēz′ kŏd′ə-), *n.* pl. of **codex.**

cod·i·cil (kŏd′ə səl), *n.* **1.** a supplement to a will, containing an addition, explanation, modification, etc., of something in the will. **2.** some similar supplement. [t. L: m. s. *cōdicillus,* dim. of *codex.* See CODEX]

cod·i·cil·la·ry (kŏd′ə sĭl′ə rĭ), *adj.* of the nature of a codicil.

cod·i·fi·ca·tion (kŏd′ə fə kā′shən, kō′də-), *n.* **1.** the act, process, or result of arranging in a code. **2.** *Law.* the reducing of unwritten customs or case law to statutory form.

cod·i·fy (kŏd′ə fī′, kō′də-), *v.t.,* **-fied, -fying.** **1.** to reduce (laws, etc.) to a code. **2.** to digest; arrange in a systematic collection. [f. COD(E) + -(I)FY. Cf. F *codifier*] —**cod′i·fi′er,** *n.*

cod·ling¹ (kŏd′lĭng), *n.* **1.** *Brit.* any of several varieties of elongated apples, used for cooking purposes. **2.** an unripe, half-grown apple. Also, **cod·lin** (kŏd′lĭn). [ME *querdling,* f. *querd* (orig. unknown) + -LING¹]

cod·ling² (kŏd′lĭng), *n.* the young of the cod. [ME; f. COD¹ + -LING¹]

codling moth, a small moth, *Carpocapsa pomonella,* whose caterpillar (larva) feeds on the pulp around the core of apples and other fruits. Also, **codlin moth.**

cod-liv·er oil (kŏd′lĭv′ər), a fixed oil, extracted from the liver of the common cod or of allied species, extensively used in medicine as a source of vitamins A and D.

cod·piece (kŏd′pēs′), *n.* (in 15th and 16th century male costume) a bagged appendage to the front of tight-fitting hose or breeches. [f. COD² + PIECE]

Co·dy (kō′dĭ), *n.* **William Frederick,** ("*Buffalo Bill*") 1846–1917, U. S. Army scout and showman.

co·ed (kō′ĕd′), *n.* *U.S. Colloq.* a female student in a coeducational institution, esp. in a college or university. Also, **co′-ed′.** [short for COEDUCATIONAL (student)]

co·ed·u·ca·tion (kō′ĕj ə kā′shən), *n.* joint education, esp. of both sexes in the same institution and classes. —**co′ed·u·ca′tion·al,** *adj.*

co·ef·fi·cient (kō′ə fĭsh′ənt), *n.* **1.** *Math.* a number or quantity placed (generally) before and multiplying another quantity: *3 is the coefficient of x in 3x.* **2.** *Physics.* a quantity, constant for a given substance, body, or process under certain specified conditions, that serves as a measure of some one of its properties: *coefficient of friction.* —*adj.* **3.** coöperating.

coe·horn (kō′hôrn), *n.* a small mortar for throwing grenades, used in the 18th century.

-coele, a word element referring to some small cavity of the body. Also, **-cele.** [comb. form repr. Gk. *ko îla* belly and *ko îlos* hollow]

Coe·len·ter·a·ta (sĭ lĕn′tə rā′tə), *n.* *Zool.* a phylum of invertebrate animals that includes the hydras, jelly-fishes, sea anemones, corals, etc., and is characterized by a single internal cavity serving for digestion, excretion, and other functions, and the tentacles on the oral end.

coe·len·ter·ate (sĭ lĕn′tə rāt′, -tər ĭt), *Zool.* —*n.* **1.** a member of the phylum *Coelenterata.* —*adj.* **2.** belonging to the *Coelenterata.* [f. COELENTER(ON) + -ATE¹]

coe·len·ter·on (sĭ lĕn′tə rŏn′), *n., pl.* **-tera** (-tər ə). *Zool.* the body cavity of a coelenterate. [f. *coel-* (comb. form repr. Gk. *koîlos* hollow) + Gk. *énteron* intestine]

coe·li·ac (sē′lĭ ăk′), *adj.* *Anat.* celiac.

coe·lom (sē′ləm), *n.* *Zool.* the body cavity of a metazoan, as distinguished from the intestinal cavity. Also, **coe·lome** (sē′lōm), **celom.** [t. Gk.: m. *koîlōma* a hollow]

coe·nes·the·sia (sē′nəs thē′zhə, -zhĭ ə, sĕn′əs-), *n.* *Psychol.* the general sense of life, the bodily consciousness, or the total impression from all contemporaneous organic sensations, as distinct from special and well-defined sensations, such as those of touch or sight. Also, **cenesthesia, coe·nes·the·sis** (sē′nəs thē′sĭs, sĕn′əs-), **cenesthesis.**

coeno-, var. of **ceno-².** Also, before vowels, **coen-.**

coe·no·bite (sē′nə bīt′, sĕn′ə-), *n.* cenobite.

coe·no·cyte (sē′nə sīt′, sĕn′ə-), *n.* *Biol.* an organism made up of many protoplasmic units enclosed by one cell wall, as in some algae and fungi.

coe·nu·rus (sĭ nyŏŏr′əs, -nŏŏr′-), *n.* the larva of a tapeworm of the genus *Multiceps,* in which a number of heads (**scolices**) form in the bladder. One species causes a disease called *gid* in sheep. [t. NL, f. *coen-* COEN- + m. Gk. *ourá* tail]

co·en·zyme (kō ĕn′zīm), *n.* *Biochem.* a biocatalyst required by certain enzymes to produce their reactions.

co·e·qual (kō ē′kwəl), *adj.* **1.** equal in rank, ability, etc. —*n.* **2.** a person or thing coequal with another. —**co·e·qual·i·ty** (kō′ĭ kwŏl′ə tĭ), *n.* —**co·e′qual·ly,** *adv.*

co·erce (kō ûrs′), *v.t.,* **-erced, -ercing.** **1.** to restrain or constrain by force, law, or authority; force or compel, as to do something. **2.** to compel by forcible action: *coerce obedience.* [t. L: m.s. *coercēre* hold together] —**co·er′cer,** *n.* —**co·er′ci·ble,** *adj.*

co·er·cion (kō ûr′shən), *n.* **1.** act or power of coercing; forcible constraint. **2.** government by force.

co·er·cive (kō ûr′sĭv), *adj.* serving or tending to coerce. —**co·er′cive·ly,** *adv.* —**co·er′cive·ness,** *n.*

co·es·sen·tial (kō′ĭ sĕn′shəl), *adj.* united in essence; having the same essence or nature. —**co·es·sen·ti·al·i·ty** (kō′ĭ sĕn′shĭ ăl′ə tĭ), **co′es·sen′tial·ness,** *n.* —**co′es·sen′tial·ly,** *adv.*

co·e·ta·ne·ous (kō′ĭ tā′nĭ əs), *adj.* of the same age or duration; coeval; contemporary. [t. LL: m. *coae-tāneus* of the same age]

co·e·ter·nal (kō′ĭ tûr′nəl), *adj.* equally eternal; existing with another eternally. —**co′e·ter′nal·ly,** *adv.*

co·e·ter·ni·ty (kō′ĭ tûr′nə tĭ), *n.* coexistence from eternity with another eternal being.

Coeur-d'A·lène (kûr′də lān′), *n.* a Salishan language.

co·e·val (kō ē′vəl), *adj.* **1.** of the same age, date, or duration; equally old. **2.** contemporary; coincident. —*n.* **3.** a contemporary. **4.** one of the same age. [f. m.s. L *coaevus* of the same age + -AL¹] —**co·e′val·ly,** *adv.*

co·ex·ec·u·tor (kō′ĭg zĕk′yə tər), *n.* a joint executor.

co·ex·ec·u·trix (kō′ĭg zĕk′yə trĭks), *n., pl.* **-executrices** (-ĭg zĕk′yə trī′sēz), a female coexecutor.

co·ex·ist (kō′ĭg zĭst′), *v.i.* to exist together or at the same time. —**co′ex·ist′ence,** *n.* —**co′ex·ist′ent,** *adj.*

co·ex·tend (kō′ĭk stĕnd′), *v.t., v.i.* to extend equally through the same space or duration. —**co·ex·ten·sion** (kō′ĭk stĕn′shən), *n.*

co·ex·ten·sive (kō′ĭk stĕn′sĭv), *adj.* having equal or coincident extension. —**co′ex·ten′sive·ly,** *adv.*

cof·fee (kôf′ĭ, kŏf′ĭ), *n.* **1.** a beverage, consisting of a decoction or infusion of the roasted and ground or crushed seeds (**coffee beans**) of the two-seeded fruit (**coffee berry**) of *Coffea arabica* and other species of *Coffea,* rubiaceous trees and shrubs of tropical regions. **2.** the berry or seed of such plants. **3.** the tree or shrub itself. **4.** the color of coffee (the beverage), esp. with cream added; dark brown. [t. Turk.: m. *qahveh,* t. Ar.: m. *qahwa*]

coffee house, a public room where coffee and other refreshments are supplied. British coffee houses formerly held a position similar to modern club houses.

coffee nut, **1.** the fruit of the Kentucky coffee tree. **2.** the tree.

coffee shop, a public room, as in a hotel, where coffee and food are served. Also, **coffee room.**

coffee tree, **1.** any tree, as *Coffea arabica,* yielding coffee beans. **2.** the Kentucky coffee tree.

cof·fer (kôf′ər, kŏf′ər), *n.* **1.** a box or chest, esp. one for valuables. **2.** (*pl.*) a treasury; funds. **3.** any of various boxlike enclosures, as a cofferdam. **4.** an ornamental sunken panel in a ceiling or soffit. —*v.t.* **5.** to deposit or lay up in or as in a coffer or chest. **6.** to ornament with coffers or sunken panels: *a coffered ceiling.* [ME *cofre,* t. OF: chest, g. L *cophinus* basket. See COFFIN]

cof·fer·dam (kôf′ər dăm′, kŏf′ər-), *n.* a watertight enclosure constructed in rivers, etc., and then pumped dry so that bridge foundations, etc., may be constructed in the open.

Coffers of a ceiling (def. 4)

cof·fin (kôf′ĭn, kŏf′ĭn), n. 1. the box or case in which a corpse is placed for burial. 2. the part of a horse's foot containing the coffin bone. —v.t. 3. to put or enclose in or as in a coffin. [ME *cofin*, t. OF: small basket, coffin, t. L: m. s. *cophinus*, t. Gk.: m. *kóphinos* basket]

Cof·fin (kôf′ĭn, kŏf′ĭn), n. Robert P(eter) Tristram (trĭs′trəm), born 1892, U.S. author.

coffin bone, the terminal phalanx in the foot of the horse and allied animals, enclosed in the hoof.

cof·fle (kôf′əl), n. a train of men or beasts, esp. of slaves, fastened together. [t. Ar.: m. *qāfila* caravan]

C. of S., Chief of Staff.

cog[1] (kŏg), n. 1. a tooth or projection (usually one of a series) on a wheel, etc., for transmitting motion to, or receiving motion from, a corresponding tooth or part with which it engages. 2. a cogwheel. [ME *cogge*, akin to CUDGEL]

cog[2] (kŏg), v., cogged, cogging. —v.t. 1. to manipulate or load (dice) unfairly. —v.i. 2. to cheat, esp. at dice. [orig. obscure]

cog., cognate.

co·gen·cy (kō′jən sĭ), n. power of proving or producing belief; convincing force.

co·gent (kō′jənt), adj. compelling assent or belief; convincing; forcible: *a cogent reason*. [t. L: s. *cōgens*, ppr., forcing, collecting] —**co′gent·ly**, adv.

cog·i·tate (kŏj′ə tāt′), v., -tated, -tating. —v.i. 1. to think hard; ponder; meditate. —v.t. 2. to think about; devise. [t. L: m.s. *cōgitātus*, pp.] —**cog′i·ta′tor**, n.

cog·i·ta·tion (kŏj′ə tā′shən), n. 1. meditation. 2. the faculty of thinking. 3. a thought; a design or plan.

cog·i·ta·tive (kŏj′ə tā′tĭv), adj. 1. meditating. 2. given to meditation; thoughtful: *cogitative pause*. —**cog′i·ta′tive·ly**, adv.

co·gi·to, er·go sum (kŏj′ə tō′, ûr′gō sŭm′), *Latin.* I think, therefore I exist (the philosophical principle of Descartes).

co·gnac (kōn′yăk, kŏn′-; *Fr.* kô nyàk′), n. 1. (*often cap.*) the brandy distilled in and shipped from the legally delimited area surrounding the town of Cognac, France. 2. French brandy in general. 3. any good brandy.

cog·nate (kŏg′nāt), adj. 1. related by birth; of the same parentage, descent, etc. 2. related in origin: *cognate languages, words, etc.* 3. allied in nature or quality. —n. 4. a person or thing cognate with another. [t. L: m. s. *cognātus*]

cog·na·tion (kŏg nā′shən), n. cognate relationship.

cog·ni·tion (kŏg nĭsh′ən), n. 1. act or process of knowing; perception. 2. the product of such a process; thing thus known, perceived, etc. 3. *Obs.* knowledge. [ME, t. L: s. *cognitio* a getting to know] —**cog·ni·tive** (kŏg′nə tĭv), adj.

cog·ni·za·ble (kŏg′nə zə bəl, kŏn′ə-; kŏg nī′-), adj. 1. capable of being perceived or known. 2. within the jurisdiction of a court. —**cog′ni·za·bly**, adv.

cog·ni·zance (kŏg′nə zəns, kŏn′ə-), n. 1. knowledge; notice; perception: *to have or take cognizance of a fact, remark, etc.* 2. *Law.* **a.** judicial notice as taken by a court in dealing with a cause. **b.** the right of taking judicial notice, as possessed by a court. **c.** acknowledgment; admission, as a plea admitting the fact alleged in the declaration. 3. the range or scope of knowledge, observation, etc. [ME *conisance*, t. OF: m. *conoissance*, der. *conoistre*, g. L *cognoscere* come to know]

cog·ni·zant (kŏg′nə zənt, kŏn′ə-), adj. 1. having cognizance; aware (fol. by *of*). 2. competent to take judicial notice, as of causes.

cog·nize (kŏg′nīz), v.t., -nized, -nizing. to perceive; become conscious of; know.

cog·no·men (kŏg nō′mən), n., pl. -nomens, -nomina (-nŏm′ə nə), 1. a surname. 2. any name, esp. a nickname. 3. the third and commonly the last name (in order) of a Roman citizen, indicating his house or family, as in "Caius Julius *Caesar*." [t. L] —**cog·nom·i·nal** (kŏg nŏm′ə nəl, -nō′mə-), adj.

cog·no·scen·te (kŏ′nyō shĕn′tĕ), n., pl. -ti (-tē). a connoisseur. Also, **conoscente.** [It., var. of *conoscente*, ppr. of *conoscere*, g. L *cognoscere* know]

cog·nos·ci·ble (kŏg nŏs′ə bəl), adj. capable of being known. —**cog·nos′ci·bil′i·ty**, n.

cog·no·vit (kŏg nō′vĭt), n. *Law.* an acknowledgment or confession by a defendant that the plaintiff's cause, or a part of it, is just, wherefore the defendant, to save expense, suffers judgment to be entered without trial. [t. L: he acknowledged]

co·gon (kō gōn′), n. a tall, coarse grass, *Imperata cylindrica*, of the tropics and subtropics furnishing an excellent material for thatching. [t. Sp., t. Tagalog]

cog railway, a railway having locomotives with a cogged center drive wheel engaging with a cogged rail, to provide sufficient traction for climbing steeper grades than is possible with ordinary wheels.

cog·wheel (kŏg′hwēl′), n. a wheel with cogs, for transmitting or receiving motion. [late ME]

Cogwheels

co·hab·it (kō hăb′ĭt), v.i. 1. to live together as husband and wife. 2. *Archaic.* to dwell or reside in company or in the same place. [t. LL: s. *cohabitāre* dwell with] —**co·hab′it·ant, co·hab′it·er**, n. —**co·hab′i·ta′tion**, n.

Co·han (kō hăn′), n. George Michael, 1878–1942, U.S. actor, playwright, and producer.

co·heir (kō âr′), n. a joint heir. —**co·heir′ess**, n. *fem.*

Co·hen (kō′ən), n. Octavus Roy, born 1891, U.S. short-story writer and novelist.

co·here (kō hĭr′), v.i., -hered, -hering. 1. to stick together; be united; hold fast, as parts of the same mass. 2. to be naturally or logically connected. 3. to agree; be congruous. [t. L: m. s. *cohaerēre* stick together] —Syn. 1. See stick[2].

co·her·ence (kō hĭr′əns), n. 1. act or state of cohering; cohesion. 2. natural or logical connection. 3. congruity; consistency. Also, **co·her′en·cy.** —Syn. 1, 2. COHERENCE, COHESION imply a sticking together. COHERENCE is more often applied figuratively, relating to the order and consistency of thought or of statements: *the coherence of an argument, of a report.* COHESION usually applies to the literal sticking together of material things: *the cohesion of wood and glue in plywood.*

co·her·ent (kō hĭr′ənt), adj. 1. cohering; sticking together. 2. having a natural or due agreement of parts; connected. 3. consistent; logical. —**co·her′ent·ly**, adv.

co·her·er (kō hĭr′ər), n. *Radio.* a device, usually a tube filled with a conducting substance in granular form, whose electrical resistance decreases when struck by radio waves: used in detecting radio waves.

co·he·sion (kō hē′zhən), n. 1. act or state of cohering, uniting, or sticking together. 2. *Physics.* the state or process by which the particles of a body or substance are bound together. 3. *Bot.* the congenital union of one part with another. —Syn. 1. See coherence.

co·he·sive (kō hē′sĭv), adj. 1. characterized by or causing cohesion. 2. cohering; tending to cohere. —**co·he′sive·ly**, adv. —**co·he′sive·ness**, n.

co·ho·bate (kō′hō bāt′), v.t., -bated, -bating. *Pharm.* to distill again from the same or a similar substance, as a distilled liquid poured back upon the matter remaining in the vessel, or upon another mass of similar matter. [t. ML: m.s. *cohobātus*, pp. of *cohobāre*; der. obs. med. term *cohob* of uncert. orig.]

Co·hoes (kō hōz′), n. a city in E New York, on the Hudson. 21,272 (1950).

co·hort (kō′hôrt), n. 1. one of the ten divisions in an ancient Roman legion, numbering from 300 to 600 men. 2. any group of warriors. 3. any group or company. [t. L: s. *cohors* (orig. enclosure; see COURT)]

co·hosh (kō′hŏsh, kō hŏsh′), n. either of two perennial herbs of the Eastern U. S., the ranunculaceous *Cimicifuga racemosa* (**black cohosh**), or the berberidaceous *Caulophyllum thalictroides* (**blue cohosh**), both used medicinally. [t. N Amer. Ind. (Mass.): m. *kuški* rough]

co·hune (kō hōōn′), n. a pinnate-leaved palm, *Orbignya Cohune*, native of Central America, bearing large nuts whose meat yields an oil resembling that of the coconut. Also, **cohune palm.**

coif (koif), n. 1. a hood-shaped cap worn under a veil, as by nuns. 2. a close-fitting cap of various kinds, as one worn by European peasant women. 3. a cap like the skullcap, retained until the common introduction of the wig, esp. as the headdress of barristers. 4. the rank or position of a sergeant at law. —v.t. 5. to cover or dress with, or as with, a coif. [ME, t. OF: m. *coife*, g. LL *cofea* cap; appar. of Gmc. orig. (cf. MHG *kupfe* cap)]

coif·feur (kwä fœr′), n. a hairdresser. [t. F, der *coiffer.* See COIFFURE]

coif·fure (kwä fyŏŏr′, *Fr.* kwà fyr′), n. 1. a style of arranging or combing the hair. 2. a head covering; headdress. [t. F, der. *coiffer*, lit., furnish with a coif]

coign (koin), n. 1. a projecting corner. 2. a wedge. Also, **coigne.** [var. of COIN (def. 4)]

coign of vantage, a good position or place for observation or action.

coil[1] (koil), v.t. 1. to wind into rings one above another, twist or wind spirally: *to coil a rope.* —v.i. 2. to form rings, spirals, etc.; wind. 3. to move in winding course. —n. 4. a connected series of spirals or rings into which a rope or the like is wound. 5. a single such ring. 6. an arrangement of pipes, coiled or in a series, as in a radiator. 7. a continuous pipe having inlet and outlet, or flow and return ends. 8. *Elect.* **a.** a conductor, as a copper wire, wound up in a spiral or other form. **b.** a device composed essentially of such a conductor. 9. *Philately.* a stamp issued in a roll, usually of 500 stamps, and usually perforated vertically or horizontally only. **b.** a roll of such stamps. [cf. F *cueillir* gather, g. a LL form r. L *colligere*. See COLLECT]

coil[2] (koil), n. 1. disturbance; tumult; bustle. 2. trouble. [orig. unknown]

Co·im·ba·tore (kō ĭm′bä tōr′), n. a city in SW India, in Madras province. 130,348 (1941).

coin (koin), n. 1. a piece of metal stamped and issued by the authority of the government for use as money. 2. such pieces collectively. 3. **pay (someone) in his own coin**, to treat (someone) as he has treated others. 4. *Archit.* **a.** a corner or an angle. **b.** a cornerstone. **c.** a wedge-shaped stone of an arch. —v.t. 5. to make (money) by stamping metal. 6. to convert (metal) into money. 7. *Colloq.* to make or gain (money) rapidly. 8. to make; invent; fabricate: *to coin words.* —v.i. 9. *Brit. Colloq.* to counterfeit money, etc. [ME, t. F: wedge, corner, die, g. L *cuneus* wedge] —**coin′a·ble**, adj. —**coin′er**, n.

b., blend of, blended; c., cognate with; d., dialect, dialectal; der., derived from; f., formed from; g., going back to; m., modification of; r., replacing; s., stem of; t., taken from; ?, perhaps. See the full key on inside cover.

coin·age (koi'nĭj), *n.* **1.** act, process, or right of making coins. **2.** that which is coined. **3.** coins collectively; the currency. **4.** anything made, invented, or fabricated.

co·in·cide (kō'ĭn sīd'), *v.i.,* **-cided, -ciding. 1.** to occupy the same place in space, the same point or period in time, or the same relative position. **2.** to correspond exactly (in nature, character, etc.). **3.** to agree or concur (in opinion, etc.). [t. ML: m.s. *coincidere*, f. L: *co- + incidere* fall on]

co·in·ci·dence (kō'ĭn sə dəns), *n.* **1.** condition or fact of coinciding. **2.** a striking occurrence of two or more events at one time apparently by mere chance.

co·in·ci·dent (kō'ĭn'sə dənt), *adj.* **1.** coinciding; occupying the same place or position. **2.** happening at the same time. **3.** exactly corresponding. **4.** in exact agreement (fol. by *with*): *duty coincident with interest.* —co·in'ci·dent·ly, *adv.*

co·in·ci·den·tal (kō'ĭn'sə děn'təl), *adj.* showing or involving coincidence. —co·in·ci·den'tal·ly, *adv.*

co·in·her·it·ance (kō'ĭn hĕr'ə təns), *n.* joint inheritance. —co'in·her'i·tor, *n.*

co·in·sur·ance (kō'ĭn shŏŏr'əns), *n.* **1.** insurance jointly with another or others. **2.** a form of fire and various other forms of property insurance in which a person taking out insurance on property for less than its full value is regarded as a joint insurer and becomes jointly and proportionately responsible for losses.

co·in·sure (kō'ĭn shŏŏr'), *v.t., v.i.,* **-sured, -suring.** to insure jointly with another or others; insure on the basis of coinsurance.

coir (koir), *n.* the prepared fiber of the husk of the coconut fruit, used in making rope, matting, etc. [t. Malayalam: m. *kāyar* cord]

co·i·tal ex·an·the·ma (kō'ə təl ĕk'sən thē'mə), a virus disease affecting horses and cattle characterized by the appearance of vesicles which later become pustules on the mucous membranes of the genital organs and neighboring skin. It is transmitted by copulation.

co·i·tion (kō'ĭsh'ən), *n.* sexual intercourse. Also, **co·i·tus** (kō'ĭ təs). [t. L: s. *coitio*, der. *coīre* go together]

coke[1] (kōk), *n., v.,* **coked, coking.** —*n.* **1.** the solid product resulting from the distillation of coal in an oven or closed chamber, or by imperfect combustion: used as a fuel in metallurgy, etc. It consists almost wholly of carbon. —*v.t., v.i.* **2.** to convert into or become coke. [? var. of *colk* core]

coke[2] (kōk), *n. Slang.* cocaine. [short for COCAINE]

cok·er (kō'kər), *n.* (*usually pl.*) *U.S.* an inhabitant of the mountains of West Virginia and Pennsylvania.

col (kŏl; *Fr.* kôl), *n.* **1.** *Phys. Geog.* a saddle or pass between two higher-standing parts of a mountain range or ridge. **2.** *Meteorol.* the region of relatively low pressure between two anticyclones. [t. F, g. L *collum* neck]

col-[1], variant of **com-**, by assimilation before *l*, as in *collateral.*

col-[2], variant of **colo-** before vowels, as in *colectomy.*

Col., **1.** Colorado. **2.** Colossians. **3.** Colonel.

col., column.

co·la[1] (kō'lə), *n.* kola. [Latinization of *Kola, Kolla, Goora,* in Negro languages of W Africa]

co·la[2] (kō'lə), *n.* pl. of **colon.**

col·an·der (kŭl'ən dər, kŏl'-), *n.* a strainer for draining off liquids, esp. in cookery. Also, **cullender.** [cf. ML *cōlātōrium,* der. *cōlāre* strain]

cola nut, kola nut.

co·lat·i·tude (kō lǎt'ə tūd', -tōōd'), *n. Astron., Navig.* the complement of the latitude; the difference between a given latitude and 90°.

Col·bert (kōl bĕr'), *n.* **Jean Baptiste** (zhän bå tēst'), 1619–83, French statesman and financier.

col·can·non (kəl kǎn'ən, kŏl'kǎn-), *n.* an Irish dish made of cabbage (or greens) and potatoes boiled and mashed together. [f. COLE + -*cannon* (of uncert. orig. and meaning)]

Col·ches·ter (kōl'chěs'tər; *Brit.* kōl'chĭs tər), *n.* a city in E England, in Essex. 48,780 (est. 1946).

col·chi·cine (kōl'chə sēn', -sĭn, kŏl'kə-), *n. Pharm.* the active principle of colchicum (def. 3).

col·chi·cum (kōl'chə kəm, kŏl'kĭ-), *n.* **1.** any plant of the Old World liliaceous genus *Colchicum,* sep. *C. autumnale,* a crocuslike plant. **2.** the dried seeds or corms of this plant. **3.** a medicine or drug prepared from them, used esp. for gout. [t. L, t. Gk.: m. *kolchikón;* appar. named after COLCHIS]

Col·chis (kōl'kĭs), *n.* the legendary land of Medea and the Golden Fleece.

col·co·thar (kōl'kə thər), *n.* the brownish-red oxide of iron which remains after the heating of ferrous sulphate, used as a polishing agent, etc. [t. ML, t. Ar.: m. *qolqotār*]

cold (kōld), *adj.* **1.** having a temperature lower than the normal temperature of the body: *cold hands.* **2.** having a relatively low temperature; having little or no warmth: *cold water, a cold day.* **3.** producing or feeling, esp. in a high degree, a lack of warmth: *I am cold.* **4.** dead. **5.** *U.S.* unconscious because of a severe blow, shock, etc. **6.** deficient in passion, emotion, enthusiasm, ardor, etc.: *cold reason.* **7.** not affectionate, cordial, or friendly: unresponsive: *a cold reply.* **8.** lacking sensual desire; frigid. **9.** failing to excite feeling or interest. **10.** imperturbable. **11.** depressing; dispiriting: *cold news.* **12.** faint; weak: *a cold scent.* **13.** distant from the object of search. **14.** *Art.* blue in effect, or inclined

toward blue in tone: *a picture cold in tone.* **15.** slow to absorb heat, as a soil containing a large amount of clay and hence retentive of moisture. **16. cold feet,** *Slang.* loss of courage or confidence for carrying out some undertaking. **17. in cold blood,** calmly; coolly and deliberately. —*n.* **18.** the relative absence of heat. **19.** the sensation produced by loss of heat from the body, as by contact with anything having a lower temperature than that of the body. **20.** an indisposition caused by exposure to cold, characterized by catarrh, hoarseness, coughing, etc. **21. catch** or **take cold,** to suffer from such a cold. **22.** cold weather. **23. in the cold,** neglected; ignored. [ME; d. OE *cald,* r. OE *ceald,* c. G *kalt.* Cf. L *gelidus* icy] —**cold'ish,** *adj.* —**cold'ly,** *adv.* —**cold'ness,** *n.*

—**Syn. 2.** COLD, CHILL, CHILLING, CHILLY, COOL refer to various degrees of absence of heat. COLD refers to temperature possibly so low as to cause suffering: *cold water.* CHILL, now chiefly poetical, suggests a raw cold which causes shivering and numbness: *how bitter chill it was.* CHILLING carries a connotation of (killing) frost: *a chilling wind.* CHILLY is a weaker word, though it also connotes shivering and discomfort: *a chilly room.* COOL means merely somewhat cold, not warm: *cool and comfortable.* All have figurative uses. **6.** indifferent —**Ant. 2.** hot. **6.** emotional.

cold-blood·ed (kōld'blŭd'ĭd), *adj.* **1.** without feeling; unsympathetic; cruel: *a cold-blooded murder.* **2.** sensitive to cold. **3.** designating or pertaining to animals, as fishes and reptiles, whose blood temperature ranges from the freezing point upward, in accordance with the temperature of the surrounding medium. —**cold'-blood'ed·ly,** *adv.* —**cold'-blood'ed·ness,** *n.*

cold chisel, a strong steel chisel used on cold metal.

cold cream, a cooling unguent for the skin.

cold·frame (kōld'frām'), *n.* a small glass-covered structure, and the bed of earth which it covers, used to protect plants.

cold front, *Meteorol.* **1.** the contact surface between two air masses where the cooler mass is advancing against and under the warmer mass. **2.** the line of intersection of this surface with the surface of the earth.

Cold Harbor, a locality NE of Richmond, Virginia: the scene of Civil War battles, 1862, 1864.

cold-heart·ed (kōld'här'tĭd), *adj.* lacking sympathy or feeling; indifferent; unkind.

cold pack, a cold towel, ice bag, etc., applied to the body to reduce swelling. relieve pain, etc.

cold shoulder, an open show of indifference or disregard: *to give one the cold shoulder.*

cold-shut (kōld'shŭt'), *n. Metall.* an imperfectly fused junction of two streams of metal in a mold.

cold snap, a sudden period of cold weather.

cold sore, a vesicular eruption on the face often accompanying a cold or a febrile condition; herpes simplex.

cold steel, a sword, bayonet, etc.

cold storage, the storage of food, furs, etc. in an artificially cooled place.

cold sweat, perspiration and coldness caused by fear, nervousness, etc.

cold war, intense economic and political rivalry just short of military conflict.

cold wave, *Meteorol.* a rapid and considerable fall in temperature, usually affecting a large area.

cole (kōl), *n.* any of various plants of the genus *Brassica,* esp. rape, *Brassica napus.* [ME *col(e),* OE *cāl,* var. of *cāw(e)l,* t. L: m.s. *caulis* stalk, cabbage]

co·lec·to·my (kə lĕk'tə mĭ), *n., pl.* **-mies.** *Surg.* the removal of all or part of the colon or large intestine.

cole·man·ite (kōl'mə nīt'), *n.* a mineral, hydrous calcium borate, $Ca_2B_6O_{11}5H_2O$, occurring in colorless to milky-white crystals. [named after W. T. *Coleman,* of San Francisco]

co·le·op·ter·on (kō'lĭ ŏp'tə rŏn', kŏl'ĭ-), *n.* a coleopterous insect; a beetle. Also, **co'le·op'ter·an.** [t. NL, t. Gk.: m. *koleópteron,* adj. (neut.), sheath-winged]

co·le·op·ter·ous (kō'lĭ ŏp'tər əs, kŏl'ĭ-), *adj.* belonging or pertaining to the order *Coleoptera,* the beetles. [t. Gk.: m. *koleópteros* sheath-winged]

Coleopteron. *Cicindela campestris* A. Head; B. Prothorax; C. Abdomen; D. Elytra; E. Wings; F. Antennae

co·le·op·tile (kō'lĭ ŏp'tĭl, kŏl'ĭ-), *n. Bot.* (in grasses) the first leaf above the ground, forming a sheath around the stem tip.

co·le·or·hi·za (kō'lĭ ə rī'zə, kŏl'ĭ-), *n., pl.* **-zae** (-zē). *Bot.* the sheath which envelops the radicle in certain plants, and which is penetrated by the root in germination. [t. NL, f. Gk.: m. *koleó(s)* sheath + *rhíza* root]

Cole·ridge (kōl'rĭj), *n.* **Samuel Taylor,** 1772–1834, British poet, critic, and philosopher.

cole·slaw (kōl'slô'), *n. U.S.* a salad of finely sliced cabbage. [t. D: m. *koolsla,* f. *kool* cabbage + *sla,* m. *salade* salad]

Col·et (kŏl'ĭt), *n.* **John,** 1467?–1519, British educator and clergyman: a leader of humanism in England.

co·le·us (kō'lĭ əs), *n.* any plant of the menthaceous genus *Coleus,* of tropical Asia and Africa, species of which are cultivated for their showy, colored foliage. [NL, t. Gk.: m. *koleós* sheath (so called from the union of the filaments about the style)]

ǎct, āble, dâre, ärt; ĕbb, ēqual; ĭf, īce; hŏt, ōver, ôrder, oil, bŏŏk, ōōze, out; ŭp, ūse, ûrge; ə = a in alone; **ch,** chief; g, give; ng, ring; sh, shoe; th, thin; t̲h̲, that; zh, vision.   See the full key on inside cover.

cole·wort (kōl/wûrt/), *n.* any plant of the genus *Brassica*, esp. kale and rape.

Col·fax (kōl/făks), *n.* Schuyler (skī/lər), 1823–85, U.S. political leader: vice-president of the U.S., 1869–73.

col·ic (kōl/ĭk), *Pathol., Vet. Sci.* —*n.* 1. paroxysmal pain in the abdomen or bowels. —*adj.* 2. pertaining to or affecting the colon or the bowels. [ME *colyke*, t. L: m.s. *cōlicus*, t. Gk.: m. *kōlikós* pertaining to the colon] —**col·ick·y** (kōl/ĭk ĭ), *adj.*

col·ic·root (kōl/ĭk rōōt/, -rŏŏt/), *n.* 1. either of two North American liliaceous herbs, *Aletris farinosa* and *A. aurea*, having small yellow or white flowers in a spikelike raceme, and a root reputed to relieve colic. 2. any of certain other plants reputed to cure colic,

col·ic·weed (kōl/ĭk wēd/), *n.* *U.S.* 1. the squirrel corn. 2. the Dutchman's-breeches. 3. any of species of *Corydalis* (*Capnoides*), esp. the pale corydalis, *C. flavula* of the eastern U.S.

Co·li·gny (kō lē nyē/), *n.* Gaspard de (gás pàr/ də), 1519–72, French admiral and Huguenot leader. Also, **Co·li·gni/.**

Co·li·ma (kō lē/mä), *n.* 1. a state in SW Mexico, on the Pacific coast. 78,806 pop. (1940); 2010 sq. mi. 2. the capital of this state. 22,601 (1940). 3. a volcano NW of this city, in Jalisco state. 14,220 ft.

-coline, -colous. [f. s. L *colere* inhabit +-INE[1]]

col·i·se·um (kōl/ə sē/əm), *n.* 1. an amphitheater, stadium, large theater, etc., for public meeting and entertainment. 2. (*cap.*) Colosseum. [t. ML: COLOSSEUM]

co·li·tis (kō lī/tĭs, kə-), *n.* *Pathol.* inflammation of the mucous membrane of the colon. [t. NL; see COL(ON), -ITIS]

coll., 1. college. 2. collegiate. 3. collective. 4. colloquial.

col·lab·o·rate (kə lăb/ə rāt/), *v.i.*, '-rated, -rating. 1. to work, one with another; coöperate, as in literary work. 2. to coöperate treacherously: *collaborating with the Nazis.* [t. LL: m.s. *collabōrātus*, pp.] —**col·lab/o·ra/tion,** *n.* —**col·lab/o·ra/tor,** **col·lab/o·ra/tion·ist,** *n.*

col·lage (kə läzh/, kō-; *Fr.* kô läzh/), *n.* *Surrealism.* an abstract composition employing various materials, such as newspaper clippings, fragments of advertisements, etc., with lines and colors supplied by the artist. [F]

col·la·gen (kōl/ə jən), *n.* *Biochem.* the protein contained in connective tissue and bones which yields gelatin on boiling. [t. F: m. *collagène*, f. m. Gk. *kólla* glue + -*gène* -GEN]

col·lapse (kə lăps/), *v.*, -lapsed, -lapsing. *n.* —*v.i.* 1. to fall or cave in; crumble suddenly: *the roof collapsed.* 2. to be made so that parts can be folded, placed, etc., together: *this bridge table collapses.* 3. to break down; come to nothing; fail: *the project collapsed.* 4. to lose strength, courage, etc., suddenly. 5. *Pathol.* **a.** to sink into extreme weakness. **b.** (of lungs) to come into an airless state. —*v.t.* 6. to cause to collapse. —*n.* 7. a falling in or together. 8. a sudden, complete failure; a breakdown. [t. L: m.s. *collapsus*, pp., fallen together] —**col·laps/i·ble, col·laps/a·ble,** *adj.* —**col·laps/i·bil/i·ty,** *n.*

col·lar (kōl/ər), *n.* 1. anything worn or placed around the neck. 2. the part of a shirt, blouse, coat, etc., around the neck, usually folded over. 3. a leather or metal band put around an animal's neck to restrain or identify it. 4. part of a harness around the horse's neck that bears some of the weight of the load drawn. See illus. under **harness.** 5. an ornamental necklace worn as insignia of an order of knighthood. 6. *Zool.* any of various markings, or structures, about the neck, suggesting a collar; a torques. 7. *Mach.* an enlargement encircling a rod or shaft, and serving usually as a holding or bearing piece. —*v.t.* 8. to put a collar on; furnish with a collar. 9. to seize by the collar or neck. 10. *Slang.* to lay hold of, seize, or take. 11. to roll up and bind (meat, fish, etc.) for cooking. [t. L: m. *collāre,* der. *collum* neck; r. ME *coler,* t. AF] —**col/lar·less,** *adj.*

col·lar·bone (kōl/ər bōn/), *n.* clavicle.

col·lard (kōl/ərd), *n.* a kind of edible kale, *Brassica oleracea,* var. *acephala,* grown in southern U.S. [var. of COLEWORT, with second element assimilated to -ARD]

col·lar·et (kōl/ə rĕt/), *n.* a woman's small collar or neckpiece of lace, embroidery, chiffon, fur, or other material. Also, **col/lar·ette/.** [f. COLLAR + -ET, r. *colleret,* t. F: m. *collerette,* dim. of *collier* collar]

col·late (kō lāt/, kə-, kōl/āt), *v.t.,* -lated, -lating. 1. to compare (texts, statements, etc.) in order to note points of agreement or disagreement. 2. *Bookbinding.* to verify the arrangement of, as the sheets of a book after they have been gathered, usually by inspecting the signature at the foot of the first page of each sheet. 3. *Bibliog.* to verify the number and order of the sheets of (a volume) as a means of determining its completeness. 4. *Eccles.* to present by collation, as to a benefice. [t. L: m.s. *collātus,* pp., brought together] —**col·la·tor** (kō lā/tər, kə-, kōl/ā tər), *n.*

col·lat·er·al (kə lăt/ər əl), *adj.* 1. situated at the side. 2. running side by side. 3. *Bot.* standing side by side. 4. accompanying; attendant; auxiliary. 5. additional; confirming: *collateral security.* 6. secured by collateral: *a collateral loan.* 7. aside from the main subject, course, etc.; secondary; indirect. 8. descended from the same stock, but in a different line; not lineal. 9. pertaining to those so descended. —*n.* 10. security pledged for the payment of a loan. 11. a collateral kinsman. [ME, t.

ML: s. *collaterālis.* See COL-, LATERAL] —**col·lat/er·al·ly,** *adv.*

col·la·tion (kǒ lā/shən, kə-), *n.* 1. act of collating. 2. description of the technical features of a book; volumes, size, pages, illustrations, etc. 3. the presentation of a clergyman to a benefice, esp. by a bishop who is himself the patron or has acquired the patron's rights. 4. a light meal which may be permitted on days of general fast. 5. a light meal. 6. act of reading and conversing on the lives of the saints, or the Scriptures (a practice instituted in monasteries by St. Benedict). [ME *collacion,* t. L: m.s. *collātio* a bringing together]

col·la·tive (kǒ lā/tĭv, kōl/ā-), *adj.* 1. collating. 2. *Eccles.* presented by collation: *collative benefices.*

col·league (kōl/ēg), *n.* an associate in office, professional work, etc. [t. F: m. *collègue* t. L: m. *collēga* one chosen with another] —**col/league·ship/,** *n.*

col·lect[1] (kə lĕkt/), *v.t.* 1. to gather together; assemble. 2. to accumulate; make a collection of. 3. to receive or compel payment of: *to collect a bill.* 4. to regain control of (one's thoughts, faculties, etc., or oneself). 5. to infer. —*v.i.* 6. to gather together; assemble. 7. to accumulate: *rain water collecting in the drainpipe.* 8. to gather or bring together books, stamps, coins, etc., usually as a hobby. —*adj., adv.* 9. to be paid for on delivery: *to send a telegram collect.* [t. L: s. *collectus,* pp., gathered together] —**col·lect/a·ble, col·lect/i·ble,** *adj.* —**Syn.** 1. See **gather.**

col·lect[2] (kōl/ĕkt), *n.* any of certain brief prayers used in Western churches as before the epistle in the communion service, and, in Anglican churches, also in morning and evening prayers. [ME *collecte,* t. ML: m. *collecta* short prayer, orig., a gathering together. See COLLECT[1]]

col·lec·ta·ne·a (kōl/ĕk tā/nĭ ə), *n. pl.* collected passages; a miscellany; anthology. [t. L, neut. pl. of *collectāneus* collected]

col·lect·ed (kə lĕk/tĭd), *adj.* having control of one's faculties; self-possessed. —**col·lect/ed·ly,** *adv.* —**col·lect/ed·ness,** *n.* —**Syn.** See **calm.**

col·lec·tion (kə lĕk/shən), *n.* 1. act of collecting. 2. that which is collected; a set of objects, specimens, writings, etc., gathered together. 3. a sum of money collected, esp. for charity or church use. —**Syn.** 2. accumulation, aggregation. [ME, t. L: s. *collectio*]

col·lec·tive (kə lĕk/tĭv), *adj.* 1. formed by collection. 2. forming a collection or aggregate; aggregate; combined. 3. pertaining to a group of individuals taken together. 4. (of a fruit) formed by the coalescence of the pistils of several flowers, as the mulberry or the pineapple. —*n.* 5. a collective noun. 6. a collective body; aggregate. 7. *Govt.* a unit of organization or the organization in a collectivist system. —**col·lec/tive·ly,** *adv.*

collective agreement, 1. the contract, written or oral, made between an employer or employers and a union in behalf of all the employees represented by the union. 2. the schedule of wages, rules, and working conditions agreed upon.

collective bargaining, the process by which wages, hours, rules, and working conditions are negotiated and agreed upon by a union with an employer for all the employees collectively whom it represents.

collective behavior, *Sociol.* the concerted behavior of individuals acting under the influence of each other.

collective noun, *Gram.* a noun that under the singular form expresses a grouping of individual objects or persons, as *herd, jury,* and *clergy.* The singular verb is used when the noun is thought of as naming a single unit, acting as one, as *family* in *my family is related to Washington.* The plural verb is used when the noun is thought of as composed of individuals who retain their separateness, as *My family are all at home.*

collective security, a policy or principle in international relations, designed to preserve world peace, according to which all countries collectively guarantee the security of individual countries, as by sanctions or multilateral alliances against an aggressor.

col·lec·tiv·ism (kə lĕk/tə vĭz/əm), *n.* the socialistic principle of control by the people collectively, or the state, of all means of production or economic activities. —**col·lec/tiv·ist,** *n.,* *adj.* —**col·lec/tiv·is/tic,** *adj.*

col·lec·tiv·i·ty (kōl/ĕk tĭv/ə tĭ), *n., pl.* -ties. 1. collective character. 2. a collective whole. 3. the people collectively.

col·lec·ti·vize (kə lĕk/tə vīz), *v.t.,* -vized, -vizing. to organize (a people, industry, economy, etc.) according to the principles of collectivism. —**col·lec/ti·vi·za/-tion,** *n.*

col·lec·tor (kə lĕk/tər), *n.* 1. one who or that which collects. 2. a person employed to collect debts, duties, taxes, etc. 3. one who collects books, paintings, stamps, shells, etc., esp. as a hobby. 4. *Elect.* any device for collecting current from contact conductors. [ME, t. LL] —**col·lec/tor·ship/,** *n.*

collector resonator. See **klystron.**

col·leen (kōl/ēn, kə lēn/), *n.* *Irish.* girl. [t. Irish: m. *cailín*]

col·lege (kōl/ĭj), *n.* 1. an institution of higher learning, esp. one not divided (like a university) into distinct schools and faculties, and affording a general or liberal education rather than technical or professional training. 2. a constituent unit of a university, furnishing courses of instruction in the liberal arts and sciences, usually leading to the degree of bachelor. 3. an institution for special or professional instruction, as in medicine, pharmacy, agriculture, or music, often set up as a part of a university. **4.** an endowed, self-governing association of scholars incorporated within a university as at the universities of Oxford and Cambridge in England. **5.** a similar corporation outside a university. **6.** the building or buildings occupied by an institution of higher education. **7.** (in French use) an institution for secondary education. **8.** an organized association of persons having certain powers and rights, and performing certain duties or engaged in a particular pursuit: *an electoral college.* **9.** a company; assemblage. **10.** a body of clergy living together on a foundation for religious service, etc. **11.** *Brit. Slang.* a prison. [ME, t. OF, t. L: m.s. *collēgium* association, a society]

College of Cardinals, *Rom. Cath. Ch.* the Sacred College which comprises all the cardinals and which elects and advises the Pope. Official name, **Sacred College of Cardinals.**

College of Propaganda. See **propaganda** (def. 3).

col·leg·er (kŏl′ĭjər), *n.* (at Eton College, England) a student who is supported on a foundation provided by the college.

college widow, *U.S. Colloq.* an unmarried woman living in a college town who has received the attentions of students of several successive classes.

col·le·gian (kəlē′jən, -jĭ ən), *n.* **1.** a student in, or a graduate of, a college. **2.** a member of a college.

col·le·giate (kəlē′jĭt, -jĭ ĭt), *adj.* **1.** of or pertaining to a college. **2.** of, for, or like college students: *collegiate life, collegiate dictionaries.* **3.** of the nature of or constituted as a college. Also, **col·le·gi·al** (kəlē′jĭ əl).

collegiate church, 1. a church which is endowed for a chapter of canons (usually with a dean), but which has no bishop's see. **2.** (loosely) a chapel connected with a college. **3.** *U.S.* a church or group of churches under the general management of one consistory or session. **4.** a consolidation of formerly distinct churches under one or more pastors. **5.** (in Scotland) a church or congregation the active pastor of which is the colleague and successor of the emeritus pastor.

col·len·chy·ma (kəlĕng′kə mə), *n.* *Bot.* a layer of modified parenchyma consisting of cells which are thickened at the angles and commonly elongated. [NL, f. Gk.: m.s. *kólla* glue + *énchyma* infusion]

col·let (kŏl′ĭt), *n., v., -leted, -leting.* —*n.* **1.** a collar or enclosing band. **2.** the enclosing rim within which a jewel is set. **3.** *Horol.* the tiny collar which supports the inner terminal of the hairspring. —*v.t.* **4.** to set in a collet: *colleted in gold.* [t. F, dim. of *col* neck, g. L *collum*]

col·lide (kəlīd′), *v.i., -lided, -liding.* **1.** to come together with force; come into violent contact; crash: *the two cars collided.* **2.** to clash; conflict. [t. L: m.s. *collīdere*]

col·lie (kŏl′ĭ), *n.* a dog of any of certain intelligent varieties much used for tending sheep, esp. one of Scotch breed, usually with a heavy coat of long hair and a bushy tail.

Collie
(2 ft. high at the shoulder)

col·lier (kŏl′yər), *n.* *Chiefly Brit.* **1.** a ship for carrying coal. **2.** a coal miner. **3.** *Obs.* one who carries or sells coal.

Col·lier (kŏl′yər), *n.* **Jeremy,** 1650–1726, British clergyman and author.

col·lier·y (kŏl′yə rĭ), *n., pl. -lieries.* a coal mine, including all buildings and equipment.

col·li·gate (kŏl′ə gāt′), *v.t., -gated, -gating.* **1.** to bind or fasten together. **2.** *Logic.* to bind (facts) together by a general description or by a hypothesis which applies to them all. [t. L: m.s. *colligātus*, pp., bound together] —**col·li·ga′tion,** *n.*

col·li·mate (kŏl′ə māt′), *v.t., -mated, -mating.* **1.** to bring into line; make parallel. **2.** to adjust accurately the line of sight of (a telescope). [t. L: m.s. *collīmātus*, pp., var. (by false reading) of *collīneātus*, pp., brought into line with] —**col′li·ma′tion,** *n.*

col·li·ma·tor (kŏl′ə mā′tər), *n.* *Optics.* **1.** a fixed telescope for use in collimating other instruments. **2.** the receiving lens or telescope of a spectroscope.

col·lin·e·ar (kə lĭn′ĭ ər), *adj.* lying in the same straight line. [f. COL-¹ + LINEAR] —**col·lin′e·ar·ly,** *adv.*

Col·ling·wood (kŏl′ĭng wŏŏd′), *n.* a city in SE Australia, near Melbourne. 30,661 (1933).

Col·lins (kŏl′ĭnz), *n.* **1. Michael,** 1890–1922, Irish revolutionist and patriot. **2. William,** 1721–59, British poet. **3. (William) Wilkie,** 1824–89, British novelist.

col·lin·si·a (kə lĭn′sĭ ə, -zĭ ə), *n.* any of the scrophulariaceous herbs constituting the genus *Collinsia*, bearing whorled, (usually) parti-colored flowers. [t. NL, named after Z. *Collins* (1764–1831), American botanist]

col·li·sion (kə lĭzh′ən), *n.* **1.** act of colliding; a coming violently into contact; crash. **2.** a clash; conflict. [late ME, t. L: m.s. *collīsio*, der. L *collīdere* COLLIDE]

col·lo·cate (kŏl′ō kāt′), *v.t., -cated, -cating.* **1.** to set or place together. **2.** to arrange in proper order: *collocated events.* [t. L: m.s. *collocātus*, pp., set in a place]

col·lo·ca·tion (kŏl′ō kā′shən), *n.* **1.** act of collocating. **2.** state or manner of being collocated. **3.** arrangement, esp. of words in a sentence.

col·lo·di·on (kə lō′dĭ ən), *n.* soluble guncotton dissolved in a mixture of ether and alcohol, used to form a coating or film on wounds, photographic plates, etc. [f. Gk.: m.s. *kollôdēs* gluelike + *-ion,* suffix]

col·logue (kə lōg′), *v.i., -logued, -loguing.* *Dial.* to confer secretly; plot mischief; conspire.

col·loid (kŏl′oid), *n.* **1.** *Phys. Chem.* a gelatinous or other substance which when dissolved in a liquid will not diffuse readily through vegetable or animal membranes (*contrasted with crystalloid*). Colloidal particles are about 10^{-7} to 5×10^{-5} cm. in diameter, larger than most inorganic molecules, and remain suspended indefinitely. They are large molecules, as proteins, or groups of molecules, with many properties depending upon their large specific surface. **2.** *Med.* a homogeneous gelatinous substance occurring in some diseased states. [f. m.s. Gk. *kólla* glue + -OID]

col·loi·dal (kə loi′dəl), *adj.* *Phys. Chem.* pertaining to, or of the nature of, a colloid: *colloidal gold, silver, etc.*

col·lop (kŏl′əp), *n.* *Brit. Dial.* **1.** a small slice of bacon or other meat. **2.** a small slice or piece of anything. **3.** a fold or roll of flesh on the body. [ME *colope, colloppe.* Cf. Sw. *kollops,* now *kalops*]

colloq., 1. colloquial. **2.** colloquialism. **3.** colloquially.

col·lo·qui·al (kə lō′kwĭ əl), *adj.* **1.** characteristic of or appropriate to ordinary or familiar conversation rather than formal speech or writing. In standard American English, *he hasn't got any* is colloquial, while *he has none* is formal. **2.** conversational. —**col·lo′qui·al·ly,** *adv.* **3.** colloquial. —**Syn. 1, 2.** COLLOQUIAL, CONVERSATIONAL, INFORMAL refer to types of speech or to usages not on a formal level. COLLOQUIAL is often mistakenly used with a connotation of disapproval, as if it meant vulgar or "bad" or "incorrect" usage, whereas it is merely a familiar style used in speaking rather than in writing. CONVERSATIONAL refers to a style used in the oral exchange of ideas, opinions, etc.: *an easy conversational style.* INFORMAL means without formality, without strict attention to set forms, unceremonious: *an informal manner of speaking.* —**Ant. 1, 2.** formal.

col·lo·qui·al·ism (kə lō′kwĭ ə lĭz′əm), *n.* **1.** a colloquial expression. **2.** colloquial style or usage.

col·lo·quy (kŏl′ə kwĭ), *n., pl. -quies.* **1.** a speaking together; a conversation. **2.** a conference. **3.** (in certain Reformed churches) a governing body corresponding to a presbytery. [t. L: m.s. *colloquium* conversation] —**col′lo·quist,** *n.*

col·lo·type (kŏl′ə tīp′), *n.* **1.** a photomechanical process of printing in ink from a gelatin plate. **2.** the plate. **3.** a print made from it. [f. *collo-* (comb. form repr. Gk. *kólla* glue) + -TYPE]

col·lude (kə lōōd′), *v.i., -luded, -luding.* **1.** to act together through a secret understanding. **2.** to conspire in a fraud. [t. L: m.s. *collūdere* play with] —**col·lud′er,** *n.*

col·lu·nar·i·um (kŏl′yə når′ĭ əm), *n.* *Med.* a solution for application to the nose; nose drops.

col·lu·sion (kə lōō′zhən), *n.* **1.** secret agreement for a fraudulent purpose; conspiracy. **2.** *Law.* a secret understanding between two or more persons prejudicial to another, or a secret understanding to appear as adversaries though in agreement: *collusion of husband and wife to obtain a divorce.* [ME, t. L: s. *collūsio* a playing together]

col·lu·sive (kə lōō′sĭv), *adj.* involving collusion; fraudulently concerted: *a collusive treaty.* —**col·lu′sive·ly,** *adv.* —**col·lu′sive·ness,** *n.*

col·ly (kŏl′ĭ), *v., -lied, -lying, n.* *Archaic or Dial.* —*v.t.* **1.** to blacken as with coal dust; begrime. —*n.* **2.** grime; soot. [var. of *collow,* ME *colwen,* der. *col* COAL]

col·lyr·i·um (kə lĭr′ĭ əm), *n., pl. -lyria* (-lĭr′ĭ ə), -**liriums.** *Med.* a solution for application to the eye; an eyewash. [t. L, t. Gk.: m. *kollýrion* poultice, eye salve]

Col·mar (Fr. kôl mår′; Ger. kôl′măr), *n.* a city in NE France. 46,124 (1946).

Cöln (kœln), *n.* German name of **Cologne.**

colo-, a combining form of **colon²**.

Colo., Colorado.

col·o·cynth (kŏl′ə sĭnth), *n.* **1.** a cucurbitaceous plant, *Citrullus colocynthis,* of the warmer parts of Asia, the Mediterranean region, etc., bearing a fruit with a bitter pulp which yields a purgative drug. **2.** the fruit. **3.** the drug. [t. L: m. *colocynthis,* t. Gk.: m. *kolokynthís*]

co·logne (kə lōn′), *n.* a perfumed toilet water; eau de Cologne. Also, **Cologne water.** [for *Cologne water* (made at Cologne, Germany, since 1709)]

Co·logne (kə lōn′; Fr. kô lôn′y), *n.* a city in W Germany. 772,221 (1939). German, **Köln, Cöln.**

Co·lombes (kô lônb′), *n.* city in France. 61,047 (1946).

Co·lom·bi·a (kə lŭm′bĭ ə; Sp. kô lôm′byä), *n.* a republic in NW South America. 9,807,432 pop. (est. 1943); 439,828 sq. mi. *Cap.:* Bogotá. —**Co·lom′bi·an,** *adj., n.*

Co·lom·bo (kə lŏm′bō), *n.* a seaport in and the capital of Ceylon, on the W coast. 284,155 (est. 1938).

co·lon¹ (kō′lən), *n., pl. -lons* for 1, -**la** (-lə) *for 2.* **1.** a point of punctuation (:) marking off a main portion of a sentence (intermediate in force between the semicolon and the period). **2.** *Anc. Pros.* one of the members or sections of a rhythmical period, consisting of a sequence of from two to six feet under a principal ictus or beat. [t. L, t. Gk.: m. *kôlon* limb, member, clause]

co·lon² (kō′lən), *n., pl. -lons, -la** (-lə). *Anat.* that portion of the large intestine which extends from the caecum to the rectum. See diag. under **intestine.** [ME, t. L, t. Gk.: m. *kôlon* food, colon]

co·lon³ (kō lōn'; *Sp.* kô lô n'), *n., pl.* **colons**, *Sp.* **colo·nes** (kô lô'nĕs). the unit in the Costa Rican monetary system (= 25c in U.S.) and the El Salvador monetary system (= 50c in U.S.). [t. Amer. Sp.: lit., Columbus]

Co·lón (kō lôn'; *Sp.* kô lôn'), *n.* a seaport in Panama at the Atlantic end of the Panama Canal. 44,393 (1940).

colo·nel (kûr'nəl), *n.* an officer ranking in most armies between lieutenant colonel and brigadier general. In England it is an honorary rank. [earlier *coronel* (whence the pronunc.), t. F: m. *coronnel*, var. of *colonnel*, t. It.: m. *colonnello*, dim. of *colonna* COLUMN] —**colo'-nel·cy, colo'nel·ship'**, *n.*

co·lo·ni·al (kə lō'nĭ əl), *adj.* **1.** of or pertaining to a colony or colonies. **2.** pertaining to the thirteen British colonies which became the United States of America, or to their period. **3.** *Ecol.* forming a colony. **4.** (*cap.*) *Archit.* of the American colonies; largely derived from contemporaneous English styles, as Queen Anne, often translated into new building materials (brick, wood) and simpler forms. —*n.* **5.** an inhabitant of a colony. —**co·lo'ni·al·ly**, *adv.*

co·lo·ni·al·ism (kə lō'nĭ ə lĭz'əm), *n.* the policy of a nation seeking to extend or retain its authority over other peoples or territories.

co·lon·ic (kə lŏn'ĭk), *adj.* of or affecting the colon.

col·o·nist (kŏl'ə nĭst), *n.* **1.** an inhabitant of a colony. **2.** a member of a colonizing expedition.

col·o·nize (kŏl'ə nīz'), *v.,* **-nized, -nizing.** —*v.t.* **1.** to plant or establish a colony in; settle: *England colonized Australia.* **2.** to form a colony of: *to colonize laborers in a mining region.* —*v.i.* **3.** to form a colony. **4.** to settle in a colony. —**col'o·ni·za'tion**, *n.* —**col'o·niz'er**, *n.*

col·on·nade (kŏl'ə nād'), *n.* **1.** *Archit.* a series of columns set at regular intervals, and usually supporting an entablature, a roof, or a series of arches. **2.** a long row of trees. [t. F. t. It.: m. *colonnato*, der. *colonna*, g. L *columna* COLUMN] —**col'on·nad'ed**, *adj.*

col·o·ny (kŏl'ə nĭ), *n., pl.* **-nies. 1.** a group of people who leave their native country to form in a new land a settlement subject to, or connected with, the parent state. **2.** the country or district settled or colonized. **3.** any people or territory separated from but subject to a ruling power. **4. the Colonies**, those British colonies that formed the original thirteen States of America: New Hampshire, Massachusetts, Rhode Island, Connecticut, New York, New Jersey, Pennsylvania, Delaware, Maryland, Virginia, North Carolina, South Carolina, and Georgia. **5.** a number of foreigners from a particular country living in a city or country, esp. in one locality: *the American colony in Paris.* **6.** any group of individuals of similar occupation, etc., usually living in a community of their own: *a colony of artists.* **7.** the district or quarter inhabited by any such number or group. **8.** an aggregation of bacteria growing together as the descendants of a single cell. **9.** *Ecol.* a group of animals or plants of the same kind living or growing together in close association. [ME *colonie*, t. L: m. *colōnia*]

col·o·phon (kŏl'ə fŏn', -fən), *n.* an inscription at the close of a book, used esp. in the 15th and 16th centuries, indicating the title, author, and information about the publication and printing of the book. [t. LL, t. Gk.: m. *kolophōn* summit, finishing touch]

col·o·pho·ny (kŏl'ə fō'nĭ, kə lŏf'ə nĭ), *n.* common rosin, the hard amorphous substance derived from the oleoresin of the pine. [t. L: m. s. *Colophōnia* (*rēsīna*) (resin) of Colophon (Ionian city in Asia Minor)]

col·or (kŭl'ər), *n.* **1.** the evaluation by the visual sense of that quality of light (reflected or transmitted by a substance) which is basically determined by its spectral composition; that quality of a visual sensation distinct from form. Any color may be expressed in terms of three factors: hue, chroma (purity or saturation), and brightness (or value). Generally the most obvious or striking feature of a color is its hue, which gives it its name. The color is qualified if necessary as pale, dark, dull, light, etc. **2.** complexion. **3.** a ruddy complexion. **4.** racial complexion other than white, esp. Negro. **5.** a blush. **6.** vivid or distinctive quality, as of literary work. **7.** details in description, customs, speech, habits, etc., of a place or period, included for the sake of realism: *a novel about the Pilgrims with much local color.* **8.** that which is used for coloring; pigment; paint; dye. **9.** *Painting.* the general effect of all the hues entering into the composition of a picture. **10.** *Print.* the amount and quality of ink used. **11.** any distinctive color, symbol, badge, etc., of identification: *the colors of a school, jockey, etc.* **12.** (*pl.*) **a.** a flag, ensign, etc., as of a military body or a ship. **b.** *U.S. Navy.* the ceremony of hoisting the national flag at 8 A.M. and of lowering it at sunset. **13.** outward appearance or aspect; guise or show. **14.** a pretext. **15.** kind; sort; variety; general character. **16.** timbre of sound. **17.** an apparent or prima-facie right or ground (esp. in legal use): *to hold possession under color of title.* **18.** *U.S.* a trace or particle of valuable mineral, esp. gold, as shown by washing auriferous gravel, etc. **19.** *Her.* heraldic tincture. **20. change color**, to turn pale or red. **21. give or lend color**, to make probable or realistic. **22. lose color**, to turn pale. **23. show one's colors**, to show one's true nature, opinions, etc. [ME, t. OF, g. L] —*v.t.* **24.** to give or apply color to; tinge; paint; dye. **25.** to cause to appear different from the reality. **26.** to give a special character or distinguishing quality to: *an account colored by personal feelings.* —*v.i.* **27.** to take on or change color. **28.** to flush; blush. Also, *Brit.*, **colour.**

[ME *coloure*(n), t. OF: m. *colo*(u)*rer*, g. L *cōlōrāre*] —**col'or·er**, *n.*

col·or·a·ble (kŭl'ər ə bəl), *adj.* **1.** capable of being colored. **2.** specious; plausible. **3.** pretended; deceptive. Also, *Brit.*, **colourable.** —**col'or·a·bil'i·ty, col'-or·a·ble·ness**, *n.* —**col'or·a·bly**, *adv.*

Col·o·rad·o (kŏl'ə răd'ō, -rä'dō), *n.* **1.** a State in the W United States. 1,325,089 pop. (1950); 104,247 sq. mi. *Cap.:* Denver. *Abbr.:* Colo. **2.** a river flowing from N Colorado through Utah and Arizona into the Gulf of California: Grand Canyon; Boulder Dam. 1360 mi. **3.** a river flowing from W Texas SE to the Gulf of Mexico. 840 mi. —**Col'o·rad'an**, *adj., n.*

col·o·rad·o (kŏl'ə răd'ō, -rä'dō), *adj.* (of cigars) of medium color and strength. [t. Sp.: colored, red]

Colorado Desert, an arid region in SE California, including the Salton Sink. ab. 2000 sq. mi.

Colorado Springs, a city in central Colorado: resort. 45,472 (1950).

col·or·a·tion (kŭl'ə rā'shən), *n.* coloring; appearance as to color. Also, *Brit.*, **colouration.**

col·o·ra·tu·ra (kŭl'ə rə tyŏŏr'ə, -tŏŏr'ə), *n.* **1.** runs, trills, and other florid decorations in vocal music. **2.** music marked by this. **3.** a lyric soprano of high range who specializes in such music. Also, **col·or·a·ture** (kŭl'ə rə chŏŏr'). [t. It., der. *colorare* to color, g. L *colōrāre*]

col·or·bear·er (kŭl'ər bâr'ər), *n.* one who carries the colors or standard, esp. of a military body.

color blindness, defective color perception, independent of the capacity for distinguishing light and shade, and form. —**col'or-blind'**, *adj.*

col·ored (kŭl'ərd), *adj.* **1.** having color. **2.** belonging wholly or in part to some other race than the white, esp. to the Negro race. **3.** pertaining to the Negro race. **4.** specious; deceptive: *a colored statement.* **5.** influenced or biased. **6.** *Bot.* of some hue other than green. Also, *Brit.*, **coloured.**

col·or·ful (kŭl'ər fəl), *adj.* **1.** abounding in color. **2.** richly picturesque: *a colorful historical period.* **3.** presenting or suggesting vivid or striking scenes: *a colorful narrative.* Also, *Brit.*, **col'our·ful.** —**col'or·ful·ly**, *adv.* —**col'or·ful·ness**, *n.*

color guard, a guard having charge of the colors, as of a regiment.

col·or·if·ic (kŭl'ə rĭf'ĭk), *adj.* **1.** producing or imparting color. **2.** pertaining to color. [f. COLOR + -(I)FIC]

col·or·im·e·ter (kŭl'ə rĭm'ə tər), *n.* an instrument for analyzing colors into their components, as by measuring a given color in terms of a standard color, of a scale of colors, or of certain primary colors. [f. COLOR + -(I)-METER] —**col·or·i·met·ric** (kŭl'ər ə mĕt'rĭk), **col'or·i·met'ri·cal**, *adj.* —**col'or·im'e·try**, *n.*

col·or·ing (kŭl'ər ĭng), *n.* **1.** act or method of applying color. **2.** appearance as to color. **3.** characteristic aspect or tone. **4.** specious appearance; show. **5.** a substance used to color something. Also, *Brit.*, **colouring.**

col·or·ist (kŭl'ər ĭst), *n.* **1.** a user of color, as in painting. **2.** a painter who devotes himself specially to effects of color. Also, *Brit.*, **colourist.** —**col'or·is'tic**, *adj.*

col·or·less (kŭl'ər lĭs), *adj.* **1.** without color. **2.** pallid; dull in color. **3.** without vividness or distinctive character. **4.** unbiased; neutral. Also, *Brit.*, **colourless.** —**col'or·less·ly**, *adv.* —**col'or·less·ness**, *n.*

color line, the line of social or political distinction between the white and colored races.

color sergeant, a sergeant who has charge of battalion or regimental colors.

co·los·sal (kə lŏs'əl), *adj.* **1.** gigantic; huge; vast. **2.** like a colossus. —**co·los'sal·ly**, *adv.* —**Syn. 1.** See **gigantic.**

Col·os·se·um (kŏl'ə sē'əm), *n.* **1.** an amphitheater in Rome, the greatest in antiquity, begun by the emperor Vespasian and inaugurated (A.D. 80) by Titus. **2.** (*l.c.*) coliseum. [t. L, prop. neut. of *colossēus* colossal. Cf. COLOSSUS]

Co·los·sian (kə lŏsh'ən), *n.* **1.** a native or an inhabitant of Colossae, an ancient city of Phrygia, in Asia Minor. **2.** one of the Christians of Colossae, to whom Paul addressed one of his epistles. **3.** (*pl.*) the book of the New Testament called *The Epistle of Paul the Apostle to the Colossians.* —**Co·los'sian**, *adj.*

co·los·sus (kə lŏs'əs), *n., pl.* **-lossi** (-lŏs'ī), **-lossuses. 1.** (*cap.*) the legendary bronze statue of Apollo at Rhodes. See **Seven Wonders of the World. 2.** any statue of gigantic size. **3.** anything colossal or gigantic. [ME, t. L, t. Gk.: m. *kolossŏs*]

co·los·to·my (kə lŏs'tə mĭ), *n., pl.* **-mies.** *Surg.* the incision of an artificial opening into the colon for drainage.

co·los·trum (kə lŏs'trəm), *n.* the milk secreted before and for a few days after parturition. [t. L]

col·our (kŭl'ər), *n., v.t., v.i. Brit.* color. —**col'our·a'-tion**, *n.* —**col'oured**, *adj.* —**col'our·er**, *n.* —**col'-our·ful**, *adj.* —**col'our·ing**, *n.* —**col'our·ist**, *n.* —**col'our·less**, *adj.*

col·our·a·ble (kŭl'ər ə bəl), *adj. Brit.* colorable. —**col'-our·a·bil'i·ty, col'our·a·ble·ness**, *n.*

-colous, a word element indicating habitat. [f. s. L *colere* inhabit + -OUS]

col·pi·tis (kŏl pī'tĭs), *n. Pathol.* vaginitis. [f. m. s. Gk. *kŏlpos* bosom, womb + -ITIS]

col·por·tage (kŏl'pōr'tĭj; *Fr.* kôl pôr tàzh'), *n.* the work of a colporteur. [t. F, der. *colporter* hawk, lit., carry on the neck, f. *col* neck + *porter* carry]

col·por·teur (kŏl'pōr'tər; *Fr.* kôl pôr tœr'), *n.* 1. a hawker of books, etc. 2. one employed to travel about distributing Bibles, religious tracts, etc., gratuitously or at a low price. [t. F. See COLPORTAGE.]

colt (kōlt), *n.* 1. a young horse or animal of the horse kind, esp. a young male. 2. a young or inexperienced person. 3. *Naut.* a rope's end in chastising. [ME and OE] —**colt'ish**, *adj.* —**colt'ish·ly**, *adv.* —**colt'ish·ness**, *n.*

Colt (kōlt), *n. Trademark.* a type of revolver. [named after Samuel *Colt*, the inventor]

col·ter (kōl'tər), *n.* a sharp blade or wheel attached to the beam of a plow, used to cut the ground in advance of the plowshare. Also, **coulter**. [ME and OE *culter*, t. L: knife]

colts·foot (kōlts'fŏŏt'), *n., pl.* -**foots**. a composite perennial, *Tussilago Farfara*, native to the Old World but widespread as a weed, formerly used in medicine.

col·u·brine (kŏl'yə brīn', -brĭn), *adj.* 1. of or resembling a snake; snakelike. 2. of or pertaining to the snake family *Colubridae* (or the subfamily *Colubrinae*). In older definitions, this family included various venomous snakes as well as the great majority of nonvenomous snakes of the world. [t. L: m. s. *colubrīnus* like a serpent]

co·lu·go (kə lōō'gō), *n., pl.* -**gos**. the flying lemur.

Col·um (kŏl'əm), *n.* **Padraic** (pô'drĭk), born 1881, Irish poet.

Co·lum·ba (kə lŭm'bə), *n.* **Saint**, A.D. 521–97, Irish missionary to Scotland.

col·um·bar·i·um (kŏl'əm bâr'Yom), *n., pl.* -**baria** (-bâr'Y ə). 1. a sepulchral vault or other structure with recesses in the walls to receive the ashes of the dead. 2. one of the recesses. [t. L, orig., dovecote, der. *columba* dove]

Co·lum·bi·a (kə lŭm'bY ə), *n.* 1. the capital of South Carolina, in the central part. 86,914 (1950). 2. a city in central Missouri. 31,974 (1950). 3. a river flowing from SE British Columbia through Washington and along the boundary between Washington and Oregon into the Pacific. 1214 mi. 4. America, or the United States, esp. as a feminine personification. 5. a white-faced breed of sheep developed from a foundation of crossbred sheep. It is noted for its rapid growing lambs, heavy fleeces of medium wool, good size, and vigor.

Co·lum·bi·an (kə lŭm'bY ən), *adj.* 1. pertaining to America or the United States. 2. pertaining to Columbus. —*n.* 3. a printing type (16 point) of a size between English and great primer. [f. s. NL *Columbia* poetic name for America + -AN]

co·lum·bic (kə lŭm'bĭk), *adj. Chem.* containing pentavalent columbium (Cb⁺⁵), as *columbic acid*, $HCbO_3$.

col·um·bine[1] (kŏl'əm bīn'), *n.* any plant of the ranunculaceous genus *Aquilegia*, comprising erect branching herbs with handsome flowers, as *A. canadensis* (the common wild columbine of North America), and various other species, with blue, purple, white, pink, or yellow flowers. [ME, t. LL: m. *columbīna*, prop. fem. of L *columbīnus* dovelike; from the resemblance of the inverted flower to a group of doves]

col·um·bine[2] (kŏl'əm bīn', -bĭn), *adj.* 1. of a dove. 2. dovelike; dove-colored. [ME *columbyn*, t. L: m.s. *columbīnus*]

Col·um·bine (kŏl'əm bīn'), *n.* a female character in comedy (orig. the early Italian) and pantomime, the sweetheart of Harlequin. [t. It.: m. *Colombina*, der. *colomba* dove, g. L *columba*]

co·lum·bite (kə lŭm'bīt), *n.* a black crystalline mineral, iron columbite, $FeCb_2O_6$, often containing manganese and tantalum. It is the principal ore of columbium. [f. COLUMB(IUM) + -ITE[1]]

co·lum·bi·um (kə lŭm'bY əm), *n. Chem.* a steel-gray metallic element resembling tantalum in its chemical properties; niobium. *Symbol:* Cb (or Nb); *at. wt.:* 92.91; *at. no.:* 41; *sp. gr.:* 8.4 at 20°C. [t. NL, named after *Columbia* the United States.]

co·lum·bous (kə lŭm'bəs), *adj. Chem.* containing trivalent columbium (Cb⁺³), as *columbous chloride*, $CbCl_3$.

Co·lum·bus (kə lŭm'bəs), *n.* 1. **Christopher**, (Sp. *Cristóbal Colón*; It. *Cristoforo Colombo*) 1446?–1506, Italian navigator in Spanish service: discoverer of America, 1492. 2. the capital of Ohio, in the central part. 375,901 (1950). 3. a city in W Georgia. 79,611 (1950).

Columbus Day, a day, Oct. 12, publicly appointed or observed as a holiday in various individual States of the U.S. in honor of the discovery of America by Columbus on Oct. 12, 1492.

col·u·mel·la (kŏl'yə mĕl'ə), *n., pl.* -**mellae** (-mĕl'ē). *Anat., Zool., Bot.* a small columnlike part; an axis. [t. L, dim. of *columna* COLUMN] —**col'u·mel'lar**, *adj.*

co·lu·mel·li·form (kŏl'yə mĕl'ə fôrm'), *adj.* like a columella.

col·umn (kŏl'əm), *n.* 1. *Archit.* **a.** an upright shaft or body of greater length than thickness, usually serving as a support; a pillar. **b.** a vertical architectural member consisting typically of an approximately cylindrical shaft with a base and a capital. See diag. in next col. 2. any columnlike object, mass, or formation: *a column of smoke*. 3. one of the two or more vertical rows of lines of type or printed matter of a page. 4. a regular contri-

bution to a newspaper, usually signed, and consisting of comment, news, or feature material. 5. a journalistic department devoted to short articles, poems, etc., of a humorous, entertaining, or esp. readable kind, furnished by a particular editor or writer without or with the aid of contributors. 6. a line of ships following one after another. 7. a formation of troops, narrow laterally and extended from front to rear. [t. L: s. *columna* pillar, post; r. ME *colompne*. t. OF] —**col·umned** (kŏl'əmd), *adj.* —**Syn.** 1. COLUMN, PILLAR refer to upright supports in architectural structures. PILLAR is the general word: *the pillars supporting the roof.* A COLUMN is a particular kind of pillar, esp. one with three identifiable parts: shaft, base, and capital: *columns of the Corinthian style.*

co·lum·nar (kə lŭm'nər), *adj.* 1. shaped like a column. 2. printed, arranged, etc., in columns.

co·lum·ni·a·tion (kə lŭm'nY ā'shən), *n.* 1. the use of columns in a structure. 2. the columns used.

col·umn·ist (kŏl'əm Yst, -əm nĭst), *n.* the editor or conductor of a special column in a newspaper.

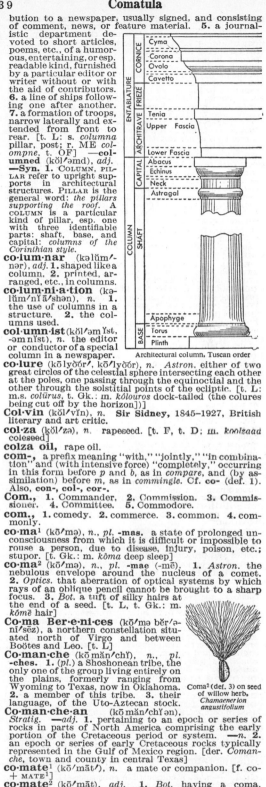

Architectural column. Tuscan order

(labels top to bottom:) ENTABLATURE — CORNICE: Cyma, Corona, Ovolo, Cavetto; FRIEZE; ARCHITRAVE: Tenia, Upper Fascia, Lower Fascia; CAPITAL: Abacus, Echinus, Neck, Astragal; COLUMN — SHAFT; Apophyge; BASE: Torus, Plinth

co·lure (kō lyŏŏr', kō'lyŏŏr), *n. Astron.* either of two great circles of the celestial sphere intersecting each other at the poles, one passing through the equinoctial and the other through the solstitial points of the ecliptic. [t. L: m.s. *colūrus*, t. Gk.: m. *kólouros* dock-tailed (the colures being cut off by the horizon)]]

Col·vin (kŏl'vĭn), *n.* **Sir Sidney**, 1845–1927, British literary and art critic.

col·za (kŏl'zə), *n.* rapeseed. [t. F, t. D; m. *koolzaad* coleseed]

colza oil, rape oil.

com-, a prefix meaning "with," "jointly," "in combination" and (with intensive force) "completely," occurring in this form before *p* and *b*, as in *compare*, and (by assimilation) before *m*, as in *commingle*. Cf. co- (def. 1). Also, **con-, col-, cor-**.

Com., 1. Commander. 2. Commission. 3. Commissioner. 4. Committee. 5. Commodore.

com., 1. comedy. 2. commerce. 3. common. 4. commonly.

co·ma[1] (kō'mə), *n., pl.* -**mas**. a state of prolonged unconsciousness from which it is difficult or impossible to rouse a person, due to disease, injury, poison, etc.; stupor. [t. Gk.: m. *kōma* deep sleep]

co·ma[2] (kō'mə), *n., pl.* -**mae** (-mē). 1. *Astron.* the nebulous envelope around the nucleus of a comet. 2. *Optics.* that aberration of optical systems by which rays of an oblique pencil cannot be brought to a sharp focus. 3. *Bot.* a tuft of silky hairs at the end of a seed. [t. L, t. Gk.: m. *kómē* hair]

Co·ma Ber·e·ni·ces (kō'mə bĕr'ə nī'sēz), a northern constellation situated north of Virgo and between Boötes and Leo. [t. L]

Co·man·che (kō măn'chY), *n., pl.* -**ches**. 1. (*pl.*) a Shoshonean tribe, the only one of the group living entirely on the plains, formerly ranging from Wyoming to Texas, now in Oklahoma. 2. a member of this tribe. 3. their language, of the Uto-Aztecan stock.

Coma[2] (def. 3) on seed of willow herb, *Chamaenerion angustifolium*

Co·man·che·an (kō măn'chY ən), *Stratig.* —*adj.* 1. pertaining to an epoch or series of rocks in parts of North America comprising the early portion of the Cretaceous period or system. —*n.* 2. an epoch or series of early Cretaceous rocks typically represented in the Gulf of Mexico region. [der. *Comanche*, town and county in central Texas]

co·mate[1] (kō'māt'), *n.* a mate or companion. [f. co- + MATE[1]]

co·mate[2] (kō'māt), *adj.* 1. *Bot.* having a coma. 2. hairy; tufted. [t. L: m. s. *comātus* having long hair]

com·a·tose (kŏm'ə tōs', kō'mə-), *adj.* affected with coma; lethargic; unconscious. [f. *comat-* (comb. form repr. Gk. *kōma* COMA[1]) + -OSE[1]] —**com'a·tose'ly**, *adv.*

Co·mat·u·la (kə măch'ə lə), *n., pl.* -**lae** (-lē'). *Zool.* a genus of crinoids or feather stars, characterized by lack of a stalk, hence able to move about. [t. NL, prop. fem. of L *comātulus*, dim. of *comātus* COMATE[2]]

co·mat·u·lid (kə măch′ə lĭd), *n.* an extant free-swimming crinoid, as *Comatula* and related forms. [t. NL: s. *Comatulidae*, the family containing the *Comatula*]

comb[1] (kōm), *n.* **1.** a toothed piece of bone, metal, etc., for arranging or cleaning the hair, or for keeping it in place. **2.** a currycomb. **3.** any comblike instrument, object, or formation. **4.** a card for dressing wool, etc. **5.** the fleshy, more or less serrated excrescence or growth on the head of the domestic fowl. **6.** something resembling or suggesting this, as the crest of a wave. **7.** a honeycomb, or any similar group of cells. —*v.t.* **8.** to dress (the hair, etc.) with, or as with, a comb. **9.** to card (wool). **10.** to scrape as with a comb. **11.** to search everywhere in: *she combed the files for the missing letter.* —*v.i.* **12.** to roll over or break at the crest, as a wave. [OE *comb*, var. of *camb*, c. G *kamm*]

comb[2] (kōōm, kōm), *n.* combe.

comb., combining.

com·bat (*v., n.* kŏm′băt, kŭm′-; *v. also* kəm băt′), *v.*, **-bated, -bating** or (*esp. Brit.*) **-batted, -batting**, *n.* —*v.t.* **1.** to fight or contend against; oppose vigorously. —*v.i.* **2.** to fight; battle; contend (fol. by *with* or *against*). —*n.* **3.** a fight between two men, armies, etc. [t. F, der. *combattre*, v., g. L *com*- COM- + *batt*(*u*)*ere* beat] —**com·bat·a·ble** (kŏm′băt ə bəl, kŭm′-, kəm băt′-), *adj.* —**com′bat·er,** *n.* —**Syn. 3.** struggle, conflict. See **fight.**

com·bat·ant (kŏm′bə tənt, kŭm′-, kəm băt′ənt), *n.* **1.** a person or group that fights. —*adj.* **2.** combating; fighting. **3.** disposed to combat.

combat fatigue, *Psychiatry.* battle fatigue.

combat infantryman's badge, *U.S.* the badge awarded to every infantryman of World War II who proved himself in battle.

com·ba·tive (kŏm′bə tĭv, kŭm′-, kəm băt′ĭv), *adj.* ready or inclined to fight; pugnacious. —**com′ba·tive·ly,** *adv.* —**com′bat·ive·ness,** *n.*

combe (kōōm, kōm), *n. Eng.* a narrow valley or deep hollow, esp. one enclosed on all sides but one. Also, **comb, coomb,** [OE *cumb*]

combed yarn (kōmd), cotton or worsted yarn made of fibers laid parallel.

comb·er (kō′mər), *n.* **1.** one who or that which combs. **2.** a long, curling wave.

com·bi·na·tion (kŏm′bə nā′shən), *n.* **1.** act of combining. **2.** state of being combined. **3.** a number of things combined. **4.** something formed by combining. **5.** an alliance of persons or parties. **6.** the set or series of numbers or letters used in setting the mechanism of a certain type of lock (**combination lock**) used on safes, etc. **7.** the parts of the mechanism operated by this. **8.** a suit of underwear in one piece. **9.** *Math.* **a.** the arrangement of a number of individuals into various groups, as *a*, *b*, and *c* into *ab*, *ac*, and *bc*. **b.** a group thus formed. [t. LL: s. *combīnātiō*] —**com′bi·na′tion·al,** *adj.* —**Syn. 3.** COMBINATION, COMPOSITE, COMPOUND all mean a union of individual parts. COMBINATION implies a grouping which is close but which may be easily dissolved. A COMPOSITE is a stronger union, in which the parts have become subordinate to a unity. COMPOUND implies a more or less complete merging of individual parts into an organic whole.

com·bi·na·tive (kŏm′bə nā′tĭv, kəm bī′nə-), *adj.* **1.** tending or serving to combine. **2.** pertaining to combination.

com·bin·a·to·ri·al analysis (kəm bī′nə tōr′ĭ əl), *Math.* the branch of mathematics which studies permutations, and combinations, etc., esp. used in statistics and probability.

com·bine (*v.* kəm bīn′; *n.* kŏm′bīn, kəm bīn′ for 6, 7, kŏm′bīn for 8), *v.*, **-bined, -bining.** —*v.t.* **1.** to bring or join into a close union or whole; unite; associate; coalesce. **2.** to possess or exhibit in union: *a plan which combines the best features of several other plans.* —*v.i.* **3.** to unite; coalesce. **4.** to unite for a common purpose; join forces. **5.** to enter into chemical union. —*n.* **6.** a combination. **7.** *U.S. Colloq.* a combination of persons or groups for the furtherance of their political, commercial or other interests. **8.** *U.S.* a machine for cutting and threshing ripe standing grain and seed such as wheat, soybeans, and clover. [late ME *combyne*(*n*), t. LL: m. *combīnāre* together] —**com·bin′a·ble,** *adj.* —**com·bin′er,** *n.* —**Syn. 1.** See **mix.**

combined operations, war operations carried out by coöperation of land, sea, and air forces.

comb·ings (kō′mĭngz), *n.pl.* hairs removed with a comb.

combining form, *Gram.* a special form of a word used in compounds: *England* and *English*, but *Anglo-* in *Anglophile* and *Anglo-French.*

comb jelly, ctenophore.

com·bust (kəm bŭst′), *adj. Astrol.* so near the sun as to be obscured by it. [ME, t. L: s. *combustus*, pp., burned up]

com·bus·ti·ble (kəm bŭs′tə bəl), *adj.* **1.** capable of catching fire and burning; inflammable. **2.** easily excited. —*n.* **3.** a combustible substance. [t. LL: m. s. *combūstibilis,* der. L *combūstus,* pp. See COMBUST] —**com·bus′ti·bil′i·ty, com·bus′ti·ble·ness,** *n.* —**com·bus′ti·bly,** *adv.*

com·bus·tion (kəm bŭs′chən), *n.* **1.** act or process of burning. **2.** *Chem.* **a.** rapid oxidation accompanied by heat and usually light. **b.** chemical combination attended by heat and light. **c.** slow oxidation not accompanied by high temperature and light. **3.** violent excitement; tumult. —**com·bus′tive,** *adj.*

combustion tube, a tube of hard glass in which a substance may be burned in a current of air or oxygen (usually used in a furnace).

comdg., commanding.

Comdr., commander. Also, **comdr.**

Comdt., commandant. Also, **comdt.**

come (kŭm), *v.,* **came, come, coming.** —*v.i.* **1.** to move toward the speaker or toward a particular place; approach. **2.** to arrive by movement or in course of progress; approach or arrive in time, succession, etc.: *when Christmas comes.* **3.** to move into view; appear: *the light comes and goes.* **4.** to extend; reach: *the dress comes to her knees.* **5.** to take place; occur; happen. **6.** to occur at a certain point, position, etc. **7.** to be available, produced, offered, etc.: *toothpaste comes in a tube.* **8.** to occur to the mind. **9.** to befall a person. **10.** to issue; emanate; be derived. **11.** to arrive or appear as a result: *this comes of carelessness.* **12.** to enter or be brought into a specified state or condition: *to come into use.* **13.** to enter into being or existence; be born. **14.** to become: *to come untied.* **15.** to turn out to be: *his dream came true.* **16.** (in the imperative, used to call attention, express remonstrance, etc.): *Come, that will do!* **17.** to germinate, as grain. **18.** Some special verb phrases are:

come about, 1. to arrive in due course; come to pass. **2.** *Naut.* to tack.
come across, 1. to meet with, esp. by chance. **2.** *Colloq.* to pay or give.
come at, 1. to reach. **2.** to get. **3.** to rush at; attack.
come back, 1. to return, esp. in memory. **2.** *Colloq.* to return to a former position or state.
come by, to obtain; acquire.
come down, 1. to lose wealth, rank, etc. **2.** to be handed down by tradition or inheritance.
come forward, to offer one's services, etc.; volunteer.
come in, 1. to enter. **2.** to arrive. **3.** to become useful, fashionable, etc.
come into, 1. to get. **2.** to inherit.
come off, 1. to happen; occur. **2.** to end. **3.** to reach the end; acquit oneself: *to come off with honors.*
come on, 1. to meet unexpectedly. **2.** to make progress; develop. **3.** to appear on stage.
come out, 1. to appear; be published. **2.** to be revealed; show itself. **3.** to make a debut in society, on the stage, etc. **4.** to emerge; reach the end.
come out with, 1. to tell; say. **2.** to bring out; publish.
come over, to happen to: *what's come over him?*
come round, 1. to relent. **2.** to recover; revive. **3.** to change (an opinion, direction, etc.).
come through, *U.S.* **1.** to succeed; reach an end. **2.** to experience religious conversion. **3.** to do as expected or hoped.
come to, 1. to recover consciousness. **2.** to amount to; equal. **3.** *Naut.* to take the way off a vessel, as by bringing her head into the wind, anchoring, etc.
come up, 1. to arise; present itself. **2.** *Brit.* to come into residence at a school or university.
—*v.t.* **19.** *Slang.* to do; perform. **20.** *Colloq.* or *Slang.* to play the part of. [ME *comen,* OE *cuman,* c. G *kommen*] —**Syn. 2.** See **arrive.** —**Ant. 2.** leave, depart.

come-at-a·ble (kŭm ăt′ə bəl), *adj. Colloq.* accessible.

come·back (kŭm′băk′), *n.* **1.** *Colloq.* a return to a former position, prosperity, etc. **2.** *Slang.* a retort; repartee. **3.** *U.S. Slang.* a ground for complaint.

co·me·di·an (kə mē′dĭ ən), *n.* **1.** an actor in comedy. **2.** a writer of comedy. **3.** a very amusing person. [f. m. COMEDY + -AN. Cf. F *comédien*]

co·me·di·enne (kə mē′dĭ ĕn′; *Fr.* kô mě dyĕn′), *n.* an actress in comedy. [t. F, fem. of *comédien* comedian]

com·e·do (kŏm′ə dō′), *n., pl.* **comedos, comedones** (kŏm′ə dō′nēz). a blackhead (def. 1). [t. L: glutton]

come·down (kŭm′doun′), *n. Colloq.* an unexpected or humiliating descent from dignity, importance, or prosperity.

com·e·dy (kŏm′ə dĭ), *n., pl.* **-dies. 1.** a play, movie, etc., of light and humorous character, typically with a happy or cheerful ending; a drama in which the central motive of the play triumphs over circumstances and is therefore successful. **2.** that branch of the drama which concerns itself with this form of composition. **3.** the comic element of drama, of literature generally, or of life. **4.** any literary composition dealing with a theme suitable for comedy, or employing the methods of comedy. **5.** any comic or humorous incident or series of incidents. [ME *comedye,* t. ML: m. *cōmēdia,* L *cōmoedia,* t. Gk.: m. *kōmōidia,* der. *kōmōidós* comedian, f. s. *kōmos* mirth + *ōidós* singer]

Comedy of Errors, an early comedy (first acted, 1594) by Shakespeare.

come·ly (kŭm′lĭ), *adj.,* **-lier, -liest. 1.** pleasing in appearance; fair. **2.** proper; seemly; becoming. [ME; OE *cȳmlic,* f. *cȳme* comely + *līc.* See -LY, LIKE] —**come′li·ness,** *n.* —**Syn. 1.** pretty, handsome, beautiful, good-looking, personable. —**Ant. 1.** unattractive.

Co·me·ni·us (kə mē′nĭ əs), *n.* **John Amos,** (*Jan Amos Komensky*) 1592–1670, Moravian educational reformer and bishop.

come-on (kŭm′ŏn′, -ôn′), *n. U.S. Slang.* inducement; lure.

com·er (kŭm′ər), *n.* **1.** one who or that which comes, or has lately come. **2.** *Colloq.* one who or something that is coming on or promising well.

co·mes·ti·ble (kə měs′tə bəl), *adj.* **1.** edible; eatable. —*n.* **2.** something edible; an article of food. [late ME, t. LL: m.s. *comestibilis*, der. L *comestus*, var. of *comēsus*, pp., eaten up]

com·et (kŏm′ĭt), *n.* a celestial body moving about the sun in an elongated orbit, usually consisting of a central mass (the *nucleus*) surrounded by a misty envelope (the *coma*) which extends into a stream (the *tail*) in the direction away from the sun. [ME, t. L: s. *comēta*, t. Gk.: m. *komētēs*, lit., long-haired] —**com·et·ar·y** (kŏm′ə těr′ĭ), *adj.* —**co·met·ic** (kə mět′ĭk), *adj.*

comet seeker, a telescope of low power but with a wide field, used to search for comets. Also, **comet finder.**

com·fit (kŭm′fĭt, kŏm′-), *n.* a dry sweetmeat; a bonbon. [ME, t. OF, g. L *confectus*, pp., prepared]

com·fort (kŭm′fərt), *v.t.* **1.** to soothe when in grief; console; cheer. **2.** to make physically comfortable. **3.** *Obs.* to aid; encourage. —*n.* **4.** relief in affliction; consolation; solace. **5.** the feeling of relief or consolation. **6.** a person or thing that affords consolation. **7.** a cause or matter of relief or satisfaction. **8.** a state of ease, with freedom from pain and anxiety, and satisfaction of bodily wants. **9.** that which promotes such a state. **10.** *U.S.* a comforter; bedcover. **11.** *Obs.* strengthening aid; assistance. [ME *conforte*(n), t. OF: m. *conforter*, g. L *confortāre* strengthen] —**com′fort·ing·ly,** *adv.* —**com′fort·less,** *adj.* —**com′fort·less·ly,** *adv.* —**com′fort·less·ness,** *n.*
—**Syn. 1.** COMFORT, CONSOLE, RELIEVE, SOOTHE imply assuaging sorrow, worry, discomfort, or pain. To COMFORT is to lessen the sadness or sorrow of someone, and to strengthen by inspiring with hope and restoring a cheerful outlook: *to comfort a despairing person.* CONSOLE, a more formal word, means to make grief or distress seem lighter, by means of kindness and thoughtful attentions: *to console a bereaved parent.* RELIEVE means to lighten, lessen, or remove pain, trouble, discomfort, or hardship: *to relieve a needy person.* SOOTHE means to pacify or calm: *to soothe a child.* **8. See ease.**

com·fort·a·ble (kŭmf′tə bəl, kŭm′fər tə bəl), *adj.* **1.** giving comfort, support, or consolation. **2.** producing or attended with comfort or ease of mind or body. **3.** being in a state of comfort or ease; easy and undisturbed. **4.** adequate. **5.** *Obs.* cheerful. —*n.* **6.** *U.S.* a quilted bedcover. —**com′fort·a·ble·ness,** *n.* —**com′fort·a·bly,** *adv.*

com·fort·er (kŭm′fər tər), *n.* **1.** one who or that which comforts. **2.** (*cap.*) the Holy Spirit. **3.** *Chiefly Brit.* a woolen scarf for wrapping round the neck in cold weather. **4.** *U.S.* a quilted bedcover.

com·frey (kŭm′frĭ), *n., pl.* **-freys.** any plant of the boraginaceous genus *Symphytum,* of Europe and Asia, as *S. officinale,* formerly used as a vulnerary. [ME *cumfirie,* t. ML: m. *cumfiria,* appar. var. of L *conferva*]

com·ic (kŏm′ĭk), *adj.* **1.** of, pertaining to, or of the nature of comedy, as distinct from tragedy. **2.** acting in or composing comedy. **3.** provoking laughter; humorous; funny; laughable. —*n.* **4.** a comic actor. **5.** *Colloq.* a comic periodical. **6.** (*pl.*) *Colloq.* the comic strips. **7.** the amusing element in art, life, etc. [t. L: s. *cōmicus,* t. Gk.: m. *kōmikos*]

com·i·cal (kŏm′ə kəl), *adj.* **1.** provoking laughter, or amusing; funny. **2.** *Obs.* pertaining to or of the nature of comedy. —**com′i·cal′i·ty,** *n.* —**com′i·cal·ly,** *adv.* —**com′i·cal·ness,** *n.* —**Syn. 1.** See **amusing.**

comic opera, a diverting opera with spoken dialogue and a happy ending.

comic strip, a series of several drawings, either in color or black and white, relating a comic incident, an adventure or mystery story, etc.

Com. in Chf., Commander in Chief.

Co·mines (kô mēn′), *n.* Philippe de (fē lēp′ də), 1445?–1511?, French historian and diplomat. Also, **Commines.**

Com·in·form (kŏm′ĭn fôrm′), *n.* an organization established in late 1947 by the Communist parties of nine European countries for mutual advice and coördinating activity.

com·ing (kŭm′ĭng), *n.* **1.** approach; arrival; advent. —*adj.* **2.** that comes; approaching. **3.** on the way to fame or success.

Com·in·tern (kŏm′ĭn tûrn′, kŏm′ĭn tûrn′), *n.* the Third Communist International, dissolved, 1943, the organization of the Russian Communist Party, headed by its Politburo, for extending world revolution. Also, **Komintern.** [t. Russ.; short for *Communist International*]

co·mi·ti·a (kə mĭsh′ĭ ə), *n. Rom. Antiq.* an assembly of the people convened to pass on laws, nominate magistrates, etc. [t. L, pl. of *comitium* place of assembly] —**co·mi′tial** (kə mĭsh′əl), *adj.*

com·i·ty (kŏm′ə tĭ), *n., pl.* **-ties.** **1.** courtesy; civility. **2.** *Internat. Law.* courtesy between nations, as in respect shown by one country for the laws, judicial decisions, and institutions of another. [t. L: m.s. *cōmitas* courtesy]

Comm., **1.** commander. **2.** commerce. **3.** commission. **4.** committee. **5.** commonwealth. Also, **comm.**

com·ma (kŏm′ə), *n.* **1.** a mark of punctuation (,) used to indicate the smallest interruptions in continuity of thought or grammatical construction. **2.** *Anc. Pros.* **a.** a fragment or smaller section of a colon. **b.** the part of dactylic hexameter ending with, or that beginning with, the caesura. **c.** the caesura itself. [t. L, t. Gk.: m. *kômma* short clause]

comma bacillus, a slightly curved bacterium, *Vibrio Cholerae,* which causes Asiatic cholera. It is contracted by eating or drinking contaminated food, and causes a violent form of dysentery.

com·mand (kə mănd′, -mänd′), *v.t.* **1.** to order or direct with authority. **2.** to require with authority; demand: *he commanded silence.* **3.** to have or exercise authority over; be in control over; be master of; have at one's bidding or disposal. **4.** to dominate by reason of location; overlook: *a hill commanding the sea.* **5.** to deserve and get (respect, sympathy, etc.). **6.** to have charge of and authority over (a military or naval unit or station). —*v.i.* **7.** to issue commands. **8.** to occupy a dominating position; look down upon or over a region, etc. —*n.* **9.** act of commanding or ordering. **10.** an order given by a commander. **11.** *Mil.* **a.** an order in prescribed words, usually given in a loud voice to troops at close-order drill. **b.** the second part of any two-part, close-order drill command. **c.** an administrative and tactical unit of the Army Air Forces, usually made up of three or more wings. **d.** a body of troops, etc. or an area, station, etc., under a commander. **12.** the possession or exercise of controlling authority. **13.** control; mastery; disposal. **14.** *Brit.* a royal invitation. **15.** power of dominating a region by reason of location; extent of view or outlook. [ME *comande*(n), t. OF: m. *comander,* g. LL *commandāre,* f. L com- COM- + *mandāre* enjoin] —**com·mand′ing·ly,** *adv.* —**Syn. 1.** bid, enjoin, charge, instruct. See **direct. 3.** govern, control, manage. See **rule. 5.** exact, compel, secure. **10.** direction, bidding, injunction, charge.

com·man·dant (kŏm′ən dănt′, -dänt′), *n.* **1.** the commanding officer of a place, group, etc.: *the commandant of a navy yard.* **2.** the title of the senior officer and head of the U.S. Marine Corps. **3.** *U.S. Army.* a title generally given to the heads of military schools. **4.** a commander. [t. F, orig. ppr. of *commander* COMMAND]

com·man·deer (kŏm′ən dĭr′), *v.t.* **1.** to order or force into active military service. **2.** to seize (private property) for military or other public use. **3.** *Colloq.* to seize arbitrarily. [t. S. Afr. D: s. *commandeeren,* t. F: m. *commander* command]

com·mand·er (kə măn′dər, -män′-), *n.* **1.** one who commands. **2.** one who exercises authority; a leader; a chief officer. **3.** the chief commissioned officer (irrespective of rank) of a military unit. **4.** *U.S. Navy.* an officer ranking below a captain and above a lieutenant commander. **5.** the chief officer of a commandery in the medieval orders of Knights Hospitalers, Templars, etc. **6.** a member of a higher class in a modern fraternal order of knighthood. —**com·mand′er·ship′,** *n.*

commander in chief, *pl.* **commanders in chief. 1.** (*sometimes caps.*) the supreme commander of the armed forces of the nation: *the President is the Commander in Chief of the army and navy.* **2.** an officer in command of a particular portion of an army or navy.

com·mand·er·y (kə măn′də rĭ, -män′-), *n., pl.* **-eries. 1.** the office or district of a commander. **2.** (among certain medieval orders of knights) a district controlled by a commander. **3.** a local branch or lodge in certain secret orders.

commanding officer, *U.S. Army.* a commander of any rank from second lieutenant to colonel.

com·mand·ment (kə mănd′mənt, -mänd′-), *n.* **1.** a command or mandate. **2.** any one of the precepts (the **Ten Commandments**) spoken by God to Israel (Exodus 20: Deut. 10) or delivered to Moses (Exodus 24:12 and 34) on Mount Sinai. **3.** act, fact, or power of commanding.

com·man·do (kə măn′dō, -män′-), *n., pl.* **-dos, -does. 1.** (in World War II) **a.** a special type of allied military unit used for organized raids against Axis forces. **b.** *Chiefly U.S.* a member of this unit. **2.** *South Africa.* an armed force raised for service against marauders. [t. S Afr. D, t. Pg.]

command performance, a performance of a play, etc., before a ruler, etc., usually at his request.

command post, *U.S. Army.* the field headquarters of the commander of a military unit.

com·meas·ur·a·ble (kə mĕzh′ər ə bəl), *adj.* having the same measure; commensurate.

com·meas·ure (kə mĕzh′ər), *v.t.,* **-ured, -uring.** to equal in measure; be coextensive with.

comme il faut (kô mēl fō′), *French.* as it should be; proper; properly.

com·mem·o·rate (kə mĕm′ə rāt′), *v.t.,* **-rated, -rating. 1.** to serve as a memento of. **2.** to honor the memory of by some solemnity or celebration. **3.** to make honorable mention of. [t. L: m.s. *commemorātus,* pp., brought to remembrance] —**com·mem′o·ra′tor,** *n.*

com·mem·o·ra·tion (kə mĕm′ə rā′shən), *n.* **1.** act of commemorating. **2.** a service, celebration, etc., in memory of some person or event. **3.** a memorial. —**com·mem′o·ra′tion·al,** *adj.*

com·mem·o·ra·tive (kə mĕm′ə rā′tĭv, -rə tĭv), *adj.* **1.** serving to commemorate. **2.** (of stamps) issued to celebrate a particular historical event, in honor of a famous personage, etc. —*n.* **3.** anything that commemorates. —**com·mem′o·ra′tive·ly,** *adv.*

com·mem·o·ra·to·ry (kə mĕm′ə rə tō′rĭ), *adj.* commemorative (def. 1).

com·mence (kə mĕns′), *v.i., v.t.,* **-menced, -mencing.** to begin; start. [ME *comence*(n), t. OF: m. *comencer,* g. LL *cominitiāre,* f. com- COM- + *initiāre* begin] —**com·menc′er,** *n.* —**Syn.** See **begin.** —**Ant.** finish, end.

com·mence·ment (kə mĕns′mənt), *n.* **1.** act or fact of commencing; beginning. **2.** (in universities, colleges, etc.) the ceremony of conferring degrees or granting diplomas at the end of the academic year. **3.** the day on which this takes place.

com·mend (kə mĕnd′), *v.t.* **1.** to present or mention as worthy of confidence, notice, kindness, etc.; recommend. **2.** to entrust; give in charge; deliver with confidence: *into Thy hands I commend my spirit.* **3.** *Archaic.* to recommend (a person) to the kind remembrance of another. [ME *commend(en)*, t. L: m. *commendāre* commit. Cf. COMMAND] —**com·mend′a·ble**, *adj.* —**com·mend′a·ble·ness**, *n.* —**com·mend′a·bly**, *adv.* —**Syn. 1.** praise, laud, extol. See **approve.**

com·men·dam (kə mĕn′dăm), *n. Eccles.* **1.** the tenure of a benefice to be held until the appointment of a regular incumbent, the benefice being said to be held *in commendam.* **2.** a benefice so held. [t. ML, acc. sing. of *commenda,* as in *dare in commendam* give in trust]

com·men·da·tion (kŏm′ən dā′shən), *n.* **1.** act of commending; recommendation; praise. **2.** something that commends. **3.** (*pl.*) *Archaic or Obs.* complimentary greeting. —**Syn. 2.** eulogy, encomium.

com·mend·a·to·ry (kə mĕn′də tôr′Y), *adj.* **1.** serving to commend; approving; praising. **2.** holding a benefice in commendam. **3.** held in commendam.

com·men·sal (kə mĕn′səl), *adj.* **1.** eating together at the same table. **2.** (of an animal or plant) living with, on, or in another, but neither one at the expense of the other (distinguished from *parasite*). —*n.* **3.** a companion at table. **4.** a commensal animal or plant. [t. ML: s. *commensālis,* f. L: *com-* com- + *mensālis* belonging to the table] —**com·men′sal·ism**, *n.* —**com·men·sal·i·ty** (kŏm′ĕn săl′ə tY), *n.* —**com·men′sal·ly**, *adv.*

com·men·su·ra·ble (kə mĕn′shə rə bəl, -sə rə-), *adj.* **1.** having a common measure or divisor. **2.** suitable in measure; proportionate. [t. LL: m.s. *commensūrābilis* having a common measure] —**com·men′su·ra·bil′i·ty**, *n.* —**com·men′su·ra·bly**, *adv.*

com·men·su·rate (kə mĕn′shə rYt, -sə-), *adj.* **1.** having the same measure; of equal extent or duration. **2.** corresponding in amount, magnitude, or degree. **3.** proportionate; adequate. **4.** having a common measure; commensurable. [t. LL: m.s. *commensūrātus,* f. L: *com-* com- + *mensūrātus,* pp., measured] —**com·men′su·rate·ly**, *adv.* —**com·men·su·ra·tion** (kə mĕn′shə rā′shən, -sə-), *n.*

com·ment (kŏm′ĕnt), *n.* **1.** a note in explanation, expansion, or criticism of a passage in a writing, book, etc.; an annotation. **2.** explanatory or critical matter added to a text. **3.** a remark, observation, or criticism. —*v.i.* **4.** to write explanatory or critical notes upon a text. **5.** to make remarks. —*v.t.* **6.** to make comments or remarks on; furnish with comments. [ME, t. LL: s. *commentum* exposition, L contrivance, invention, prop. pp. neut.] —**com′ment·er,** *n.* —**Syn. 3.** See **remark.**

com·men·tar·y (kŏm′ən tĕr′Y), *n., pl.* **-taries. 1.** a series of comments or annotations. **2.** an explanatory essay or treatise: *a commentary on the Bible.* **3.** anything serving to illustrate a point; comment. **4.** (*usually pl.*) a record of facts or events: *the Commentaries of Caesar.* —**com·men·tar·i·al** (kŏm′ən târ′Y əl), *adj.*

com·men·ta·tor (kŏm′ən tā′tər), *n.* a person who makes critical or explanatory remarks about news events, etc. [t. L]

com·merce (kŏm′ərs), *n.* **1.** interchange of goods or commodities, esp. on a large scale between different countries (**foreign commerce**) or between different parts of the same country (**domestic** or **internal commerce**); trade; business. **2.** social relations. **3.** sexual intercourse. **4.** intellectual interchange. [t. F, t. L: m.s. *commercium* trade] —**Syn. 1.** See **trade.**

com·mer·cial (kə mûr′shəl), *adj.* **1.** of, or of the nature of, commerce. **2.** engaged in commerce. **3.** prepared merely for sale. **4.** not entirely or chemically pure: *commercial soda, etc.* —*n.* **5.** *Radio.* a commercial announcement or program. **6.** *Brit. Colloq.* a traveling salesman. —**com·mer·ci·al·i·ty** (kə mûr′shY ăl′ə tY), *n.* —**com·mer′cial·ly**, *adv.* —**Syn. 1.** COMMERCIAL, MERCANTILE refer to the activities of business, industry, and trade. COMMERCIAL is the broader term, covering all the activities and relationships of industry and trade. In a derogatory sense it may mean such a preoccupation with the affairs of commerce as results in indifference to considerations other than wealth: *commercial treaties, relations, law, a merely commercial viewpoint.* MERCANTILE applies to the actual purchase and sale of goods, or to the transactions of business: *a mercantile house or class.*

commercial agency, a concern which investigates for the benefit of its subscribers the financial standing, reputation, and credit rating of individuals, firms, corporations, and others engaged in business.

commercial college, *U.S.* a school that trains people for careers in business.

com·mer·cial·ism (kə mûr′shə lĭz′əm), *n.* **1.** the principles, methods, and practices of commerce. **2.** commercial spirit. **3.** a commercial custom or expression. —**com·mer′cial·ist**, *n.* —**com·mer′cial·is′tic**, *adj.*

com·mer·cial·ize (kə mûr′shə lĭz′), *v.t.,* **-ized, -izing.** to make commercial in character, methods, or spirit; make a matter of profit. —**com·mer′cial·i·za′tion**, *n.*

commercial paper, negotiable paper, as drafts, bills of exchange, etc., given in the course of business.

commercial traveler, a traveling agent, esp. for a wholesale business house, who solicits orders for goods.

Com·mie (kŏm′Y), *n.* (*also l.c.*) *Colloq.* Communist.

com·mi·na·tion (kŏm′ə nā′shən), *n.* **1.** a threat of punishment or vengeance. **2.** a denunciation. **3.** (in the liturgy of the Church of England) a penitential office proclaiming God's anger and judgments against sinners. [late ME, t. L: s. *comminātio* a threatening] —**com·min·a·to·ry** (kə mĭn′ə tôr′Y, kŏm′Yn-), *adj.*

Com·mines (kô mēn′), *n.* Comines.

com·min·gle (kə mĭng′gəl), *v.t., v.i.,* **-gled, -gling.** to mingle together; blend.

com·mi·nute (kŏm′ə nūt′, -nōōt′), *v.t.,* **-nuted, -nuting.** to pulverize; triturate. [t. L: m.s. *comminūtus,* pp., made smaller] —**com′mi·nu′tion**, *n.*

com·mis·er·ate (kə mĭz′ə rāt′), *v.t.,* **-ated, -ating.** to feel or express sorrow or sympathy for; pity. [t. L: m.s. *commiserātus,* pp.] —**com·mis′er·a′tion**, *n.* —**com·mis′er·a′tive,** *adj.* —**com·mis′er·a′tive·ly**, *adv.*

com·mis·sar (kŏm′ə sär′), *n.* head of a government department (commissariat) in any republic of the U.S.S.R. [t. Russ: m. *kommisar,* t. F: m. *commissaire*]

com·mis·sar·i·at (kŏm′ə sâr′Y ət), *n.* **1.** the department of an army charged with supplying provisions, etc. **2.** the organized method or manner by which food, equipment, transport, etc., is delivered to the armies. **3.** any of the governmental divisions of the U.S.S.R. [t. F, der. *commissaire.* See COMMISSARY]

com·mis·sar·y (kŏm′ə sĕr′Y), *n., pl.* **-saries. 1.** a store that supplies food and equipment, esp. in an army, mining camp, or lumber camp. **2.** *Mil.* an officer of the commissariat. **3.** one to whom some charge is committed by a superior power; a deputy. **4.** *Eccles.* an officer who, by delegation from the bishop, exercises spiritual jurisdiction in remote parts of a diocese, or is entrusted with the performance of duties of the bishop in his absence. **5.** (in the Soviet Union) a commissar. **6.** (in France) a police official, usually just below the police chief and mayor. [ME, t. ML: m.s. *commissārius,* der. L *commissus,* pp., committed] —**com·mis·sar·i·al** (kŏm′ə sâr′Y əl), *adj.* —**com·mis·sar′y·ship′**, *n.*

com·mis·sion (kə mĭsh′ən), *n.* **1.** act of committing or giving in charge. **2.** an authoritative order, charge, or direction. **3.** authority granted for a particular action or function. **4.** a document or warrant granting authority to act in a given capacity or conferring a particular rank. **5.** a body of persons authoritatively charged with particular functions. **6.** the condition of being placed under special authoritative charge. **7.** the condition of anything in active service or use: *to be in or out of commission.* **8.** a task or matter committed to one's charge. **9.** authority to act as agent for another or others in commercial transactions. **10.** the committing or perpetrating of a crime, error, etc. **11.** that which is committed. **12.** a sum or percentage allowed to an agent for his services. **13.** the position or rank of an officer in the army or navy: *to hold or resign a commission.* **14.** the document conferring authority issued by the President to officers in the army and navy, and others, and by state governments to justices of the peace and others. **15.** the power thus granted. **16.** *Naval.* **a.** the condition of a ship ordered to active service, and supplied with a captain and crew. **b. put in** or **into commission,** to transfer (a ship) to active service. —*v.t.* **17.** to give a commission to. **18.** to authorize; send on a mission. **19.** to put (a ship, etc.) in commission. **20.** to give a commission or order for. [ME, t. L: s. *commissio* a committing]

com·mis·sion·aire (kə mĭsh′ə nâr′), *n. Brit.* a person who does miscellaneous small errands for the public; messenger; porter. [t. F: m. *commissionnaire*]

commissioned officer, an army or naval officer holding rank by commission, including in the U.S. second lieutenants, ensigns, and all above them.

com·mis·sion·er (kə mĭsh′ə nər), *n.* **1.** one commissioned to act officially; a member of a commission. **2.** a government official in charge of a department: *police commissioner.* **3.** *Slang.* a betting broker. —**com·mis′sion·er·ship′**, *n.*

commission merchant, an agent who receives goods for sale on a commission basis, or who buys on this basis and has the goods delivered to a principal.

commission plan, a system of municipal government in which all the powers of the city are concentrated in the hands of a commission.

com·mis·sure (kŏm′ə shŏŏr′), *n.* **1.** a joint; seam; suture. **2.** *Bot.* the joint or face by which one carpel coheres with another. **3.** *Anat., Zool.* a connecting band of nerve tissue, etc. [late ME, t. L: m.s. *commissūra* joining] —**com·mis·su·ral** (kə mĭsh′ə rəl, kŏm′ə sŏŏr′əl), *adj.*

Botanical commissure
AB, line of the commissural faces of the two carpels

com·mit (kə mĭt′), *v.t.,* **-mitted, -mitting. 1.** to give in trust or charge; entrust; consign. **2.** to consign for preservation: *to commit to writing, memory, etc.* **3.** to consign to custody: *to commit a person to jail.* **4.** to consign, esp. for safekeeping; commend: *to commit one's soul to God.* **5.** to hand over for treatment, disposal, etc.: *to commit a manuscript to the flames.* **6.** *Parl.*

---

b., blend of, blended; *c.,* cognate with; *d.,* dialect, dialectal; *der.,* derived from; *f.,* formed from; *g.,* going back to; *m.,* modification of; *r.,* replacing; *s.,* stem of; *t.,* taken from; *?,* perhaps.   See the full key on inside cover.

Proc. to refer (a bill, etc.) to a committee for consideration. **7.** to do; perform; perpetrate: *to commit murder, an error, etc.* **8.** to bind by pledge or assurance; pledge. [ME *committe(n)*, t. L: m. *committere* bring together, join, entrust] **—com·mit′ta·ble,** *adj.*

com·mit·ment (kə·mĭt′mənt), *n.* **1.** act of committing. **2.** state of being committed. **3.** *Parl. Proc.* the act of referring or entrusting to a committee for consideration. **4.** consignment, as to prison. **5.** *Law.* a written order of a court directing that someone be confined in prison (formerly more often termed a *mittimus*). **6.** perpetration or commission, as of a crime. **7.** act of committing, pledging, or engaging oneself. **8.** *Stock Exchange.* an agreement to sell or purchase; a sale or purchase. Also, **com·mit′tal** for defs. 1, 3, 4, 6, 7.

com·mit·tee (kə·mĭt′ē), *n.* **1.** a person or a group of persons elected or appointed to investigate, report, or act in special cases. **2. standing committee,** a permanent committee, as of a legislature, society, etc., intended to consider all matters pertaining to a designated subject. **3.** *Law.* one to whom the care of a person (as a lunatic) or an estate is committed. [t. AF, orig. pp., committed]

com·mit·tee·man (kə·mĭt′ē·mən, -măn′), *n., pl.* **-men** (-mən, -měn′). a member of a committee. **—com·mit·tee·wom·an** (kə·mĭt′ē·wŏŏm′ən), *n. fem.*

committee of correspondence, (during the American Revolutionary period) a committee appointed by a town or colony to communicate or coördinate the measures variously taken toward redress of grievances.

committee of the whole, a legislative body consisting of all the members present, sitting in a deliberative rather than a legislative capacity, for informal debate and preliminary consideration of matters awaiting legislative action.

Committee of Ways and Means, a committee (usually in a legislative body) to whom financial matters are referred.

com·mix (kə·mĭks′), *v.t., v.i.* to mix together; blend.

com·mix·ture (kə·mĭks′chər), *n.* a mixing together; the product of mixing; mixture. [t. L: m.s. *commixtūra*]

com·mode (kə·mōd′), *n.* **1.** a piece of furniture containing drawers or shelves. **2.** a stand or cupboard containing a chamber pot or washbasin. **3.** a large, high headdress worn by women about 1700. [t. F, t. L: m.s. *commodus* fit, convenient, useful]

com·mo·di·ous (kə·mō′dĭ·əs), *adj.* **1.** convenient and roomy; spacious: *a commodious harbor.* **2.** convenient or satisfactory for the purpose. [late ME, t. ML: m.s. *commodiōsus.* See COMMODE] **—com·mo′di·ous·ly,** *adv.* **—com·mo′di·ous·ness,** *n.*

com·mod·i·ty (kə·mŏd′ə·tĭ), *n., pl.* **-ties.** **1.** a thing that is of use or advantage. **2.** an article of trade or commerce. **3.** *Obs.* a quantity of goods.

commodity dollar, *U.S.* a proposed currency unit whose gold content would vary with fluctuations in an official index of commodity prices.

commodity money, *U.S.* a proposed form of currency using commodity dollars as units.

com·mo·dore (kŏm′ə·dōr′), *n.* **1.** *U.S. Navy.* an officer of a rank next below that of rear admiral. **2.** *British Navy.* an officer in temporary command of a squadron, sometimes having a captain under him on the same ship. **3.** *Naval.* the senior captain when three or more ships of war are cruising in company. **4.** (in the U. S. Navy or Merchant Marine) the officer in command of a convoy. **5.** the senior captain of a line of merchant vessels. **6.** the president or head of a yacht club or boat club. [earlier *commodore,* possibly t. D: m. *kommandeur,* t. F: m. *commandeur,* der. *commander* command]

Com·mo·dus (kŏm′ə·dəs), *n.* **Lucius Aelius Aurelius** (lōō′shəs ē′lĭ·əs ô·rē′lĭ·əs), A.D. 161–192, Roman emperor, A.D. 180–192 (son and successor of Marcus Aurelius).

com·mon (kŏm′ən), *adj.* **1.** belonging equally to, or shared alike by, two or more or all in question: *common property.* **2.** joint; united: *to make common cause against the enemy.* **3.** pertaining or belonging to the whole community; public: *common council.* **4.** generally or publicly known; notorious: *a common scold.* **5.** widespread; general; ordinary: *common knowledge.* **6.** of frequent occurrence; familiar; usual: *a common event, common salt.* **7.** hackneyed; trite. **8.** of mediocre or inferior quality; mean; low. **9.** coarse; vulgar: *common manners.* **10.** ordinary; having no rank, etc.: *common soldier, the common people.* **11.** *Anat.* denoting a trunk from which two or more arteries, veins, or nerves are given off: *the common carotid arteries.* **12.** *Pros.* (of a syllable) either long or short. **—n. 13.** a tract of land owned or used in common, esp. by all the members of a community; now usually a park in the midst of the town. **14. in common,** in joint possession, use, etc.; jointly. **15.** *Law.* the power, shared with other persons to enter on the land or waters of another, and to remove something therefrom, as by pasturing cattle, catching fish, etc. **16.** (*sometimes cap.*) *Eccles.* an office or form of service used on a festival of a particular kind. **17.** *Obs.* the community or public. **18.** *Obs.* the common people. [ME, *comun,* t. OF, g. L *commūnis* common, general] **—com′mon·ness,** *n.*

—Syn. 5. universal, prevalent, popular. See **general. 10.** COMMON, VULGAR, ORDINARY refer to the usual or most often experienced; often with derogatory connotations of cheapness or inferiority. COMMON means the accustomed or

usually experienced; or the inferior, and the opposite of exclusive or aristocratic: *she is a common person.* VULGAR properly means belonging to the people, or characteristic of common people; it connotes low taste, coarseness or ill breeding: *the vulgar view of things, vulgar in manners and speech.* ORDINARY means what is to be expected in the usual order of things; or only average, or below average: *the quality is just ordinary.* **—Ant. 1.** individual. **6.** unusual.

com·mon·a·ble (kŏm′ən·ə·bəl), *adj.* **1.** held in common, or subject to general use, as lands. **2.** that may be pastured on common land.

com·mon·age (kŏm′ən·ĭj), *n.* **1.** the use of anything in common, esp. of a pasture. **2.** the right to such use. **3.** state of being held in common. **4.** that which is so held, as land. **5.** the commonalty.

com·mon·al·ty (kŏm′ən·əl·tĭ), *n., pl.* **-ties.** **1.** the common people as distinguished from the nobility, etc. **2.** the members of an incorporated body.

common carrier, an individual or company, such as a railroad or steamship line, which transports the public or goods for hire.

common council, *Now Rare.* **1.** the local legislative body of a city. **2.** its lower branch.

common denominator, *Math.* a number, usually the least, divisible by the denominators of a set of fractions.

common divisor, *Math.* a number which is an exact divisor of two or more given numbers. Also, **common factor.**

com·mon·er (kŏm′ən·ər), *n.* **1.** one of the common people; a member of the commonalty. **2.** (at Oxford University, etc.) a student who pays for his commons, etc., and is not supported by any foundation. **3.** one who has a joint right in common land.

common fraction, *Math.* a fraction having the numerator above and the denominator below a horizontal or diagonal line (as opposed to a *decimal fraction*).

common gender, *Gram.* (in a language having masculine and feminine gender classes) a class of nouns which change gender according to meaning.

common law, 1. the system of law originating in England, as distinct from the civil or Roman law and the canon or ecclesiastical law. **2.** the unwritten law, esp. of England, based on custom or court decision, as distinct from statute law. **3.** the law administered through the system of writs, as distinct from equity, admiralty, etc. **—com′mon-law′,** *adj.*

common-law marriage, a marriage without a marriage ceremony, civil or ecclesiastical, generally resulting from living together as man and wife.

common logarithm, *Math.* a logarithm using 10 as the base.

com·mon·ly (kŏm′ən·lĭ), *adv.* **1.** in a common manner. **2.** usually; generally; ordinarily. **—Ant. 2.** rarely.

common measure, *Music.* duple and quadruple rhythm. Also, **common time.**

common multiple, *Math.* a number divisible by two or more given numbers. The least (or lowest) common multiple is the smallest common multiple of a set of numbers.

common name. See **name** (def. 9).

common noun, *Gram.* (in English and some other languages) a noun that can be preceded by an article or other limiting modifier, in meaning applicable to any one or all of the members of a class, as *man, men, city, cities,* in contrast to *Lincoln, New York.* Cf. **proper noun.**

com·mon·place (kŏm′ən·plās′), *adj.* **1.** ordinary; uninteresting; without individuality: *a commonplace person.* **2.** trite; hackneyed: *a commonplace remark.* **—n. 3.** a well-known, customary, or obvious remark; a trite or uninteresting saying. **4.** anything common, ordinary, or uninteresting. **5.** a place or passage in a book or writing noted as important for reference or quotation. [trans. of L *locus commūnis,* Gk. (*koinós*) *topós* a stereotyped topic, argument, or passage in literature] **—com′mon·place′ness,** *n.*

—Syn. 2. COMMONPLACE, BANAL, HACKNEYED, STEREOTYPED, TRITE describe words, remarks, and styles of expression which are lifeless and uninteresting. COMMONPLACE characterizes thought which is dull, ordinary, and platitudinous: *commonplace and boring.* That is BANAL which seems inane, insipid, and pointless: *a heavy and banal affirmat on of the obvious.* HACKNEYED characterizes that which seems stale and worn out through over use: *a hackneyed comparison.* STEREOTYPED emphasizes the fact that situations felt to be similar invariably call for the same thought in exactly the same form and the same words: *so stereotyped as to seem automatic.* TRITE describes that which was originally striking and apt, but which has become so well known and been so commonly used that all interest has been worn out of it: *true but trite.*

commonplace book, a book in which noteworthy passages, poems, comments, etc. are written.

common pleas, 1. *U.S.* any of various courts of civil jurisdiction in several States. **2.** *England.* (historically) the chief common-law court of civil jurisdiction, now merged in the King's Bench Division of the High Court.

common prayer, 1. the liturgy or public form of prayer prescribed by the Church of England to be used in all churches and chapels in public worship. **2.** (*cap.*) the Book of Common Prayer.

common room, (in schools and colleges) a clubroom, latterly extended to factories, sanitariums, etc.

com·mons (kŏm′ənz), *n. pl.* **1.** the common people as distinguished from their rulers or a ruling class; the

commonalty. 2. the body of people not of noble birth or ennobled, as represented in England by the House of Commons. **3.** (*cap.*) the representatives of this body. **4.** (*cap.*) the elective house of the Parliament of Great Britain and Northern Ireland, Canada, and some of the other Dominions. **5.** *Brit.* food provided at a common table, as in colleges. **6.** food or provisions in general. **7.** a large dining room, esp. at a university.

common school, *U.S.* a public school below the grade of a high school.

common sense, sound practical sense; normal intelligence. —**com'mon-sense',** *adj.*

Common Sense, an influential pamphlet (1776) by Thomas Paine, advocating American independence.

common stock, stock which ordinarily has no preference in the matter of dividends or assets and represents the residual ownership of a corporate business.

common time, common measure.

com·mon·weal (kŏm'ən wēl'), *n.* **1.** the common welfare; the public good. **2.** *Archaic.* the body politic; a commonwealth. Also, **common weal.**

com·mon·wealth (kŏm'ən wĕlth'), *n.* **1.** the whole body of people of a nation or state; the body politic: *British Commonwealth of Nations.* **2.** a state in which the supreme power is held by the people; a republican or democratic state. **3.** (*cap.*) the English government from the abolition of the monarchy in 1649 until the establishment of the Protectorate in 1653. **4.** any body of persons united by some common interest. **5.** *Obs.* the public welfare. [f. COMMON + WEALTH]

com·mo·tion (kə mō'shən), *n.* **1.** violent or tumultuous motion; agitation. **2.** political or social disturbance; sedition; insurrection. —**Syn. 1.** disturbance, disorder, turmoil, tumult, riot, turbulence. See **ado.**

com·move (kə mōōv'), *v.t.,* **-moved, -moving.** to move violently; ag.tate; excite. [t. L: m.s. *commovēre*; r. ME *commoeve(n),* t. F: m. *commouvoir*]

com·mu·nal (kŏm'yə nəl, kə mū'nəl), *adj.* **1.** pertaining to a commune or a community. **2.** of or belonging to the people of a community: *communal land.* —**com'mu·nal·ly** (kŏm'yə nə lĭ, kə mū'-), *adv.*

com·mu·nal·ism (kŏm'yə nə lĭz'əm, kə mū'-), *n.* a theory or system of government according to which each commune is virtually an independent state, and the nation merely a federation of such states. —**com'mu·nal·ist,** *n.* —**com'mu·nal·is'tic,** *adj.*

com·mu·nal·ize (kŏm'yə nə līz', kə mū'-), *v.t.,* **-ized, -izing.** to make communal; convert into municipal property. —**com'mu·nal·i·za'tion,** *n.* —**com'mu·nal·iz'er,** *n.*

Com·mu·nard (kŏm'yə närd'), *n.* (*often l.c*) a member or supporter of the Paris Commune of 1871. [t. F]

com·mune[1] (*v.* kə mūn'; *n.* kŏm'ūn), *v.,* **-muned, -muning,** *n.* —*v.i.* **1.** to converse; talk together; interchange thoughts or feelings. —*n.* **2.** interchange of ideas or sentiments; friendly conversation. [ME *com-(m)une(n),* t. OF: m. *comuner* hare, der. *comun* common]

com·mune[2] (kə mūn'), *v.i.,* **-muned, -muning.** to partake of the Eucharist. [ME *comunen,* t. OF: m. *communier,* g. L *commūnicāre* COMMUNICATE]

com·mune[3] (kŏm'ūn), *n.* **1.** the smallest administrative division in France, Italy, Switzerland, etc., governed by a mayor assisted by a municipal council. **2.** a similar division in some other country. **3.** any community organized for the protection and promotion of local interests, and subordinate to the state. **4.** the government or citizens of a commune. **5.** *Ethnol.* a representative group in primitive society. **6. the Commune, a.** a revolutionary committee which took the place of the municipality of Paris in the French Revolution of 1789, and soon usurped the supreme authority in the state. It was suppressed by the Convention in 1794. **b.** a socialistic government of Paris from March 18 to May 27, 1871. [t. F, fem. of *commun* common]

com·mu·ni·ca·ble (kə mū'nə kə bəl), *adj.* **1.** capable of being communicated. **2.** communicative. [t. ML: m.s. *commūnicābilis*] —**com·mu'ni·ca·bil'i·ty, com·mu'ni·ca·ble·ness,** *n.* —**com·mu'ni·ca·bly,** *adv.*

com·mu·ni·cant (kə mū'nə kənt), *n.* **1.** one who partakes, or is entitled to partake, of the Eucharist; a member of a church. **2.** one who communicates. —*adj.* **3.** communicating; imparting.

com·mu·ni·cate (kə mū'nə kāt'), *v.,* **-cated, -cating.** —*v.t.* **1.** to give to another as a partaker; impart; transmit. **2.** to impart knowledge of; make known. **3.** to adm.nister the Eucharist to. **4.** *Archaic.* to share in or partake of. —*v.i.* **5.** to have interchange of thoughts. **6.** to have or form a connecting passage. **7.** to partake of the Eucharist. **8.** *Obs.* to take part or participate. [t. L: m.s. *commūni ātus,* pp., shared] —**com·mu'ni·ca'tor,** *n.*

—**Syn. 1.** COMMUNICATE, IMPART d note giving to a person or thing a part or share o something, now usually something immaterial, as knowledge, thou.hts, hopes, qualities, or properties. COMMUNICATE the more common word, implies often an indirect or gradual transmission: *to communicate by means of letters, telegrams, etc.; to communicate one's wishes to someone else.* IMPART usually implies directness of action: *to impart information.* —**Ant. 1.** withhold. **2.** conceal.

com·mu·ni·ca·tion (kə mū'nə kā'shən), *n.* **1.** act or fact of communicating; transmission. **2.** the imparting or interchange of thoughts, opinions, or information by speech, writing, or signs. **3.** that which is communicated

or imparted. **4.** a document or message imparting views, information, etc. **5.** passage, opportunity of passage, or a means of passage between places. **6.** (*pl.*) **a.** the means of sending military messages, orders, etc., as by telephone, telegraph, radio, couriers. **b.** routes and transportation for moving troops and supplies overseas, or in a theater of operations.

com·mu·ni·ca·tive (kə mū'nə kā'tĭv), *adj.* **1.** inclined to communicate or impart. **2.** talkative: not reserved. **3.** of or pertaining to communication. —**com·mu'ni·ca'tive·ly,** *adv.* —**com·mu'ni·ca'tive·ness,** *n.*

com·mu·ni·ca·to·ry (kə mū'nĭ kə tō'rĭ), *adj.* of or pertaining to communication.

com·mun·ion (kə mūn'yən), *n.* **1.** act of sharing, or holding in common; participation. **2.** state of things so held. **3.** association; fellowship. **4.** interchange of thoughts or interests; communication; intimate talk. **5.** *Eccles.* **a.** a body of persons having one common religious faith; a religious denomination. **b.** reception of the Eucharist. **c.** the celebration of the Lord's Supper; the Eucharist. [ME, t. L: s. *commūnio* fellowship]

com·mun·ion·ist (kə mūn'yən ĭst), *n. Eccles.* **1.** a person with a particular view or interpretation of communion. **2.** a communicant.

com·mu·ni·qué (kə mū'nə kā', kə mū'nə kā'), *n.* an official bulletin or communication, usually to the press or public. [t. F]

com·mu·nism (kŏm'yə nĭz'əm), *n.* **1.** a theory or system of social organization based on the holding of all property in common, actual ownership being ascribed to the community as a whole or to the state. **2.** a system of social organization in which all economic activity is conducted by a totalitarian state dominated by a single and self-perpetuating political party. **3.** communalism. [t. F: m. *communisme,* der. *commun.* See COMMON]

com·mu·nist (kŏm'yə nĭst), *n.* **1.** an advocate of communism. **2.** (*often cap.*) a person who belongs to the Communist Party, esp. the party in the Soviet Union. **3.** (*usually cap.*) a Communard. —*adj.* **4.** pertaining to communists or communism. —**com'mu·nis'tic, com'mu·nis'ti·cal,** *adj.* —**com'mu·nis'ti·cal·ly,** *adv.*

Communist Manifesto, a pamphlet (1848) by Karl Marx and Friedrich Engels: first statement of the principles of modern communism.

Communist Party, a political party professing the principles of communism.

com·mu·ni·tar·i·an (kə mū'nə tăr'ĭən), *n.* **1.** a member of a communistic community. **2.** an advocate of such a community.

com·mu·ni·ty (kə mū'nə tĭ), *n., pl.* **-ties. 1.** a social group of any size whose members reside in a specific locality, share government, and have a cultural and historical heritage. **2. the community,** the public. **3.** *Eccles.* a group of men or women leading a common life according to a rule. **4.** *Ecol.* a group of organisms, both plant and animal, living together in an ecologically related fashion in a definite region: *an oak forest community.* **5.** joint possession, enjoyment, liability, etc.: *community of property.* **6.** similar character; agreement; identity: *community of interests.* [t. L: m.s. *commūnitas;* r. ME *comunete,* t. OF]

—**Syn. 1.** COMMUNITY, HAMLET, VILLAGE, TOWN, CITY are terms for groups of people living in somewhat close association, and usually under common rules. COMMUNITY is a general term, and TOWN is often loosely applied. A commonly accepted set of connotations envisages HAMLET as a small group, VILLAGE as a somewhat larger one, TOWN still larger, and CITY as very large Size is, however, not the true basis of differentiation, but properly sets off only HAMLET. Incorporation, or the absence of it, and the type of government determine the classification of the others.

community center, *U.S.* a building in which members of a community meet for social or other purposes.

community chest, *U.S. and Canada.* a fund for local welfare activities, built by voluntary contributions.

com·mu·nize (kŏm'yə nīz'), *v.t.,* **-nized, -nizing. 1.** to make the property of the community. **2.** to make communistic. —**com'mu·ni·za'tion,** *n.*

com·mut·a·ble (kə mū'tə bəl), *adj.* that may be commuted; exchangeable. —**com·mut'a·bil'i·ty,** *n.*

com·mu·tate (kŏm'yə tāt'), *v.t.,* **-tated, -tating.** *Elect.* **1.** to reverse the direction of (a current or currents), as by a commutator. **2.** to convert (alternating current) into direct current by use of a commutator.

com·mu·ta·tion (kŏm'yə tā'shən), *n.* **1.** act of substituting one thing for another; substitution; exchange. **2.** the substitution of one kind of payment for another. **3.** *U.S.* regular travel between home (usually distant) and work, generally using a commutation ticket. **4.** the changing of a penalty, etc. for another less severe.

commutation ticket, *U.S.* a ticket issued at a reduced rate, as by a railroad company, entitling the holder to be carried over a given route a certain number of times or during a certain period.

com·mu·ta·tive (kə mū'tə tĭv, kŏm'yə tā'tĭv), *adj.* of or pertaining to commutation, exchange, substitution, or interchange.

commutative law, *Logic.* a law asserting that the order in which certain logical operations are performed is indifferent. For example: *Smith is ill or out of town* is equipollent with *Smith is out of town or ill.*

com·mu·ta·tor (kŏm'yə tā'tər), *n. Elect.* **1.** a device for reversing the direction of a current. **2.** (in a dynamo)

b., blend of, blended; **c.,** cognate with; **d.,** dialect, dialectal; **der.,** derived from; **f.,** formed from; **g.,** going back to; **m.,** modification of; **r.,** replacing; **s.,** stem of; **t.,** taken from; **?,** perhaps. See the full key on inside **cover.**

a cylindrical ring or disk assembly of conducting members, individually insulated in a supporting structure with an exposed surface for contact with current-collecting brushes, and mounted on the armature shaft.

com·mute (kə mūt′), *v.*, **-muted**, **-muting**. —*v.t.* **1.** to exchange for another or something else; give and take reciprocally; interchange. **2.** to change (one kind of payment) into or for another, as by substitution. **3.** to change (a penalty, etc.) for one less burdensome or severe. —*v.i.* **4.** to make substitution. **5.** to serve as a substitute. **6.** to make a collective payment, esp. of a reduced amount, as an equivalent for a number of payments. **7.** *U.S.* to travel regularly between home (usually distant) and work, generally using a commutation ticket. [t. L: m.s. *commūtāre* change wholly] —**com·mut′er**, *n.*

Com·ne·nus (kŏm nē′nəs), *n.* a dynasty of Byzantine emperors that ruled at Constantinople, 1057?–1185, and at Trebizond in Asia Minor, 1204–1461?

Co·mo (kō′mō), *n.* **1.** Lake, a lake in N Italy, in Lombardy. 35 mi. long; 56 sq. mi. **2.** a city on this lake. 74,138 (est. 1946).

Com·o·rin (kŏm′ə rĭn), *n.* Cape, a cape at the S tip of India.

Com·o·ro Islands (kŏm′ə rō′), a group of French islands in Mozambique Channel between N Madagascar and E Africa. 129,000 pop. (1936); 849 sq. mi.

co·mose (kō′mōs), *adj.* hairy; comate. [t. L: m.s. *cōmōsus* covered with hair]

comp., **1.** comparative. **2.** compare. **3.** compilation. **4.** compiled. **5.** composition. **6.** compound.

com·pact[1] (*adj., v.* kəm pǎkt′; *n.* kŏm′pǎkt), *adj.* **1.** joined or packed together; closely and firmly united; dense; solid. **2.** arranged within a relatively small space. **3.** expressed concisely; pithy; terse; not diffuse. **4.** composed or made (fol. by *of*). —*v.t.* **5.** to join or pack closely together; consolidate; condense. **6.** to make firm or stable. **7.** to form or make by close union or conjunction; make up or compose. **8.** *Metall.* to press (metallic and other powders) in a die. —*n.* **9.** a small case containing a mirror, face powder, a puff, and (sometimes) rouge. **10.** *Metall.* the molded shape obtained after pressing metallic and other powders in a die. [t. L: s. *compactus*, pp., joined together] —**com·pact′ly**, *adv.* —**com·pact′ness**, *n.*

com·pact[2] (kŏm′pǎkt), *n.* an agreement between parties; a covenant; a contract. [t. L: s. *compactum*, prop. pp. ncut., having agreed with] —**Syn.** treaty, pact. See **agreement.**

com·pan·ion[1] (kəm pǎn′yən), *n.* **1.** one who accompanies or associates with another. **2.** a person, usually a woman, employed to accompany or assist another. **3.** a mate or match for a thing. **4.** a handbook; guide: *Woman's Home Companion.* **5.** a member of the lowest rank in an order of knighthood, or of a grade in an order. **6.** *Obs.* a fellow (used in contempt). —*v.t.* **7.** to be a companion to; accompany. [t. LL: s. *compānio* messmate, der. L *pānis* bread; r. ME *compainoun*, t. OF: m. *compaignon*] —**com·pan′ion·less**, *adj.* —**Syn.** 1. mate, comrade, associate, partner. See **acquaintance.**

com·pan·ion[2] (kəm pǎn′yən), *n.* **1.** a covering or hood over the top of a companionway. **2.** a companionway. [t. D: m. *kampanje* quarterdeck. Cf. It. *camera della campagna* storeroom]

com·pan·ion·a·ble (kəm pǎn′yən ə bəl), *adj.* fitted to be a companion; sociable. —**com·pan′ion·a·ble·ness**, *n.* —**com·pan′ion·a·bly**, *adv.*

com·pan·ion·ate (kəm pǎn′yən ĭt), *adj.* of, by, or like companions.

companionate marriage, a suggested form of marriage without the traditional rights and obligations of the spouses and with a simplified divorce completely terminating the relationship of childless couples.

companion cell, *Bot.* a cell associated with a sieve tube and, collectively, forming one of the elements of phloem.

com·pan·ion·ship (kəm pǎn′yən shĭp′), *n.* association as companions; fellowship.

com·pan·ion·way (kəm pǎn′yən wā′), *n.* *Naut.* **1.** the space or shaft occupied by the steps leading down from the deck to a cabin. **2.** the steps themselves.

com·pa·ny (kŭm′pə nĭ), *n., pl.* **-nies**, *v.*, **-nied**, **-nying.** —*n.* **1.** a number of individuals assembled or associated together; group of people. **2.** an assemblage of persons for social purposes. **3.** companionship; fellowship; association. **4.** a guest or guests. **5.** society collectively. **6.** a number of persons united or incorporated for joint action, esp. for business: *a publishing company.* **7.** the member or members of a firm not specifically named in the firm's title: *John Jones and Company.* **8.** a medieval trade guild. **9.** *Mil.* **a.** a subdivision of a regiment or battalion. **b.** any relatively small group of soldiers. **10.** *Naut.* a ship's crew, including the officers. **11.** bear or keep company, to associate or go with. **12.** part company, to cease association or friendship with. —*v.i.* **13.** to associate. —*v.t.* **14.** *Archaic,* to accompany. [ME *compainie*, t. OF. See COMPANION[1]]
—**Syn. 1.** COMPANY, BAND, PARTY, TROOP refer to a group of people formally or informally associated. COMPANY i the general word and means any group of people: *a company of travelers.* BAND used esp. of a band of musicians, suggests a relatively small group pursuing the same purpose or sharing a common fate: *concert by a band, a band of survivors.* PARTY,

except when used of a political group, usually implies an indefinite and temporary assemblage as for some common pursuit: *an exploring party.* TROOP, used specifically of a body of cavalry, usually implies a number of individuals organized as a unit: *a troop of cavalry.* **2.** assembly, gathering concourse, crowd. **6.** firm, house, corporation, syndicate.

company union, *U.S.* **1.** a union dominated by the employer of its members. **2.** a union confined to employees of one business or corporation.

compar., comparative.

com·pa·ra·ble (kŏm′pə rə bəl), *adj.* **1.** capable of being compared. **2.** worthy of comparison. —**com′·pa·ra·ble·ness**, *n.* —**com′pa·ra·bly**, *adv.*

com·par·a·tive (kəm pǎr′ə tĭv), *adj.* **1.** of or pertaining to comparison. **2.** proceeding by or founded on comparison: *comparative anatomy.* **3.** estimated by comparison; not positive or absolute; relative. **4.** *Gram.* **a.** denoting the intermediate degree of the comparison of adjectives and adverbs. **b.** denoting the form of an adjective or adverb inflected to show this degree. **c.** having or pertaining to the function or meaning of this degree of comparison. —*n.* **5.** *Gram.* **a.** the comparative degree. **b.** a form in it, as English *lower* in contrast to *low* and *lowest, more gracious* in contrast to *gracious* and *most gracious.* —**com·par·a·tive·ly**, *adv.*

com·pa·ra·tor (kŏm′pə rā′tər), *n.* any of various instruments for making comparisons, as of lengths or distances, tints of colors, etc.

com·pare (kəm pâr′), *v.*, **-pared, -paring**, *n.* —*v.t.* **1.** to represent as similar or analogous; liken (fol. by *to*). **2.** to note the similarities and differences of (fol. by *with*). **3.** to bring together for the purpose of noting points of likeness and difference: *to compare two pieces of cloth.* **4.** **compare notes,** to exchange views, ideas, impressions, etc. **5.** *Gram.* to form or display the degrees of comparison of (an adjective or adverb). —*v.i.* **6.** to bear comparison; be held equal. **7.** to vie. —*n.* **8.** comparison: *joy beyond compare.* [ME, t. F: m.s. *comparer*, g. L *comparāre*, lit., bring together] —**com·par′er**, *n.* —**Syn. 1, 2.** COMPARE, CONTRAST agree in placing together two or more things and examining them to discover characteristics, qualities, etc. To COMPARE means to examine in order to discover like or unlike characteristics. We compare things of the same class *with* each other; one of unlike classes *to* the other: *to compare one story with another, a man to a mountain.* To CONTRAST is to examine with an eye to differences; or to place together so that the differences are striking. We contrast one thing *with* another: *to contrast living conditions in peace and in war.*

com·par·i·son (kəm pǎr′ə sən), *n.* **1.** act of comparing. **2.** state of being compared. **3.** a likening; an illustration by similitude; a comparative estimate or statement. **4.** *Rhet.* the considering of two things with regard to some characteristic which is common to both, as the likening of a hero to a lion in courage. **5.** capability of being compared or likened. **6.** *Gram.* **a.** that function of an adverb or adjective used to indicate degrees of superiority or inferiority in quality, quantity, or intensity. **b.** the patterns of formation involved therein. **c.** the degrees of a particular word, displayed in a fixed order, as *mild, milder, mildest, less mild, least mild.* [ME, t. OF: m. *comparaison*, g. L *comparātio*, der. *comparāre.* See COMPARE]

com·part·ment (kəm pärt′mənt), *n.* **1.** a part or space marked or partitioned off. **2.** a separate room, section, etc.: *a compartment on a train, a watertight compartment in a ship.* **3.** *Archit., Art.* an ornamental division of a larger design. —*v.t.* **4.** to divide into compartments. [t. F: m. *compartiment*, t. It.: m. *compartimento*, der. LL *compartīrī* divide] —**Syn. 2.** See **apartment.**

com·pass (kŭm′pəs), *n.* **1.** an instrument for determining directions, consisting essentially of a freely moving needle indicating magnetic north and south. **2.** the enclosing line or limits of any area; measurement round. **3.** space within limits; area; extent; range; scope. **4.** the total range of tones of a voice or of a musical instrument. **5.** due or proper limits; moderate bounds. **6.** a passing round; a circuit; a detour. **7.** (*usually pl.*) an instrument for describing circles, measuring distances, etc., consisting generally of two movable legs hinged at one end. **8.** *Obs.* a circle. —*v.t.* **9.** to go or move round; make the circuit of. **10.** to extend or stretch around; hem in; encircle. **11.** to attain or achieve; accomplish; obtain. **12.** to contrive; scheme. **13.** to make curved or circular. **14.** to grasp with the mind. [ME *compas*, t. OF, der. *compasser* divide exactly, ult. der. L *compassus* equal step] —**com′pass·a·ble**, *adj.* —**Syn. 3.** See **range.**

compass card, a circular card attached to the needle of a mariners' compass, on which the degrees or points indicating direction are marked.

com·pas·sion (kəm pǎsh′ən), *n.* **1.** a feeling of sorrow or pity for the sufferings or misfortunes of another; sympathy. —*v.t.* **2.** to compassionate.

Compass card

[ME, t. LL: s. *compassio* sympathy] —**Syn. 1.** ruth, commiseration, mercy.

com·pas·sion·ate (*adj.* kəm păsh'ən ĭt; *v.* kəm păsh'-ə nāt'), *adj.*, *v.*, **-ated, -ating.** —*adj.* **1.** having or showing compassion. **2.** *Obs.* pitiable. —*v.t.* **3.** to have compassion for; pity. —**com·pas'sion·ate·ly,** *adv.* —**com·pas'sion·ate·ness,** *n.* —**Syn. 1.** pitying, sympathizing, sympathetic, tender, kind, merciful.

compass plant, any of various plants whose leaves tend to lie in a plane at right angles to the strongest light, hence usually north and south, esp. *Silphium laciniatum*, or *Lactuca* (wild lettuce).

com·pat·i·ble (kəm păt'ə bəl), *adj.* capable of existing together in harmony; such as to agree; consistent; congruous (usually fol. by *with*). [t. ML: m.s. *compatibilis*, der. LL *compatī* suffer with] —**com·pat'i·bil'i·ty, com·pat'i·ble·ness,** *n.* —**com·pat'i·bly,** *adv.*

com·pa·tri·ot (kəm pā'trĭ ət *or*, *esp. Brit.*, -păt'rĭ ət), *n.* **1.** a fellow countryman or fellow countrywoman. —*adj.* **2.** of the same country. [t. L: s. *compatriōta*] —**com·pa'tri·ot·ism,** *n.*

com·peer (kəm pĭr', kŏm'pĭr), *n.* **1.** an equal or peer; a comrade; an associate. —*v.t.* **2.** *Archaic.* to be the equal of; match. [ME *comper*, t. OF. See com-, peer]

com·pel (kəm pĕl'), *v.t.*, **-pelled, -pelling. 1.** to force or drive, esp. to a course of action. **2.** to secure or bring about by force. **3.** to force to submit; subdue. **4.** to overpower. **5.** to drive together; unite by force; herd. [ME *compelle(n)*, t. L: m. *compellere*] —**com·pel'la·ble,** *adj.* —**com·pel'ler,** *n.*
—**Syn. 1.** constrain, oblige, coerce. Compel, impel agree in the idea of using (physical or other) force to cause something to be done. Compel means to constrain someone, in some way, to yield or to do what one wishes: *to compel a recalcitrant debtor to pay, fate compels men to face danger and trouble*. Impel may mean literally to push forward; but is usually applied figuratively, meaning to provide a strong motive or incentive toward a certain end: *wind impels a ship, curiosity impels me to speak*.

com·pel·la·tion (kŏm'pə lā'shən), *n.* **1.** act or manner of addressing a person. **2.** form of address or designation; appellation. [t. L: s. *compellātio*]

com·pen·di·ous (kəm pĕn'dĭ əs), *adj.* containing the substance of a subject in a brief form; concise. [t. L: m.s. *compendiōsus* abridged] —**com·pen·di·ous·ly,** *adv.* —**com·pen·di·ous·ness,** *n.*

com·pen·di·um (kəm pĕn'dĭ əm), *n.*, *pl.* **-diums, -dia** (-dĭ ə). a comprehensive summary of a subject; a concise treatise; an epitome. Also, **com·pend** (kŏm'pĕnd). [t. L: a saving, a short way]

com·pen·sate (kŏm'pən sāt'), *v.*, **-sated, -sating.** —*v.t.* **1.** to counterbalance; offset; make up for. **2.** to make up for something to; recompense. **3.** *Mech.* to counterbalance (a force or the like); adjust or construct so as to offset or counterbalance variations or produce equilibrium. **4.** to change the gold content (of the monetary unit) to counterbalance price fluctuations and thereby stabilize its purchasing power. —*v.i.* **5.** to provide or be an equivalent; make up; make amends (fol. by *for*). [t. L: m. s. *compensātus*, pp., counterbalanced] —**com·pen·sa·tor,** *n.* —**Syn. 2.** remunerate, reward, pay.

compensating gear, *Mach.* differential gear.

com·pen·sa·tion (kŏm'pən sā'shən), *n.* **1.** act of compensating. **2.** something given or received as an equivalent for services, debt, loss, suffering, etc.; indemnity. **3.** *Biol.* the improvement of any defect by the excessive development or action of another structure or organ of the same structure. **4.** *Psychol.* behavior which compensates for some personal trait, as a weakness or inferiority. —**com'pen·sa'tion·al,** *adj.* —**Syn. 2.** recompense, remuneration, payment, amends, reparation.

com·pen·sa·to·ry (kŏm'pĕn'/sə tōr'ĭ), *adj.* serving to compensate. Also, **com·pen·sa·tive** (kŏm'pən sā'tĭv, kəm pĕn'/sə tĭv).

com·pete (kəm pēt'), *v.i.*, **-peted, -peting.** to contend with another for a prize, profit, etc.; engage in a contest; vie: *to compete in a race, in business, etc.* [t. L: m. s. *competere* contend for, (earlier) come together]
—**Syn.** Compete, contend, contest mean to strive to outdo or excel: they may apply to individuals or groups. Compete implies having a sense of rivalry and of striving to do one's best as well as to outdo another: *to compete for a prize*. Contend suggests opposition or disputing as well as rivalry: *to contend with an opponent, against obstacles.* Contest suggests struggling to gain or hold something, as well as contending or disputing: *to contest a position or ground (in battle), to contest a decision.*

com·pe·tence (kŏm'pə təns), *n.* **1.** quality of being competent; adequacy; due qualification or capacity. **2.** sufficiency; a sufficient quantity. **3.** an income sufficient to furnish the necessities of life, without great luxuries. **4.** *Law.* quality or position of being legally competent; legal capacity or qualification (which presupposes the meeting of certain minimum requirements of age, soundness of mind, citizenship, or the like). **5.** *Embryol.* the sum total of possible reactions of any group of blastemic cells under varied external conditions.

com·pe·ten·cy (kŏm'pə tən sĭ), *n.* **1.** competence (defs. 1–4). **2.** *Law.* (of a witness) eligibility to be sworn and testify (presupposing the meeting of minimum requirements of ability to observe, remember, and recount).

com·pe·tent (kŏm'pə tənt), *adj.* **1.** fitting, suitable, or

sufficient for the purpose; adequate; properly qualified. **2.** rightfully belonging; permissible (fol. by *to*). **3.** *Law.* (of a witness, a party to a contract, etc.) having legal capacity or qualification. [t. L: s. *competens*, ppr., being fit] —**com'pe·tent·ly,** *adv.* —**Syn. 1.** fit, qualified, capable, proficient. See able.

com·pe·ti·tion (kŏm'pə tĭsh'ən), *n.* **1.** act of competing; rivalry. **2.** a contest for some prize or advantage. **3.** the rivalry between two or more business enterprises to secure the patronage of prospective buyers. **4.** *Sociol.* rivalry for the purpose of obtaining some advantage over some other person or group, but not involving the destruction of such person or group. **5.** *Ecol.* the struggle among organisms, both of the same and of different species, for food, space, and other factors of existence. [t. L: s. *competitio*]

com·pet·i·tive (kəm pĕt'ə tĭv), *adj.* of, pertaining to, involving, or decided by competition: *a competitive examination*. Also, **com·pet·i·to·ry** (kəm pĕt'ə tōr'ĭ). —**com·pet'i·tive·ly,** *adv.* —**com·pet'i·tive·ness,** *n.*

com·pet·i·tor (kəm pĕt'ə tər), *n.* one who competes; a rival. —**com·pet·i·tress** (kəm pĕt'ə trĭs), *n. fem.* —**Syn.** See opponent.

Com·piègne (kôṅ pyeṅ'ⁿ), *n.* a city in N France, on the Oise river: nearby were signed the armistices between the Allies and Germany, 1918, and between Germany and France, 1940. 18,218 (1946).

com·pi·la·tion (kŏm'pə lā'shən), *n.* **1.** act of compiling: *the compilation of an index to a book.* **2.** something compiled, as a book.

com·pile (kəm pīl'), *v.t.*, **-piled, -piling. 1.** to put together (literary materials) in one book or work. **2.** to make (a book, etc.) of materials from various sources. [ME *compile(n)*, t. OF: m. *compiler*, g. L *compīlāre* snatch together and carry off] —**com·pil'er,** *n.*

com·pla·cen·cy (kəm plā'sən sĭ), *n.*, *pl.* **-cies. 1.** a feeling of quiet pleasure; satisfaction; gratification; self-satisfaction. **2.** that which gives satisfaction; a cause of pleasure or joy; a comfort. **3.** friendly civility; a civil act. Also, **com·pla'cence.**

com·pla·cent (kəm plā'sənt), *adj.* **1.** pleased, esp. with oneself or one's own merits, advantages, etc.; self-satisfied. **2.** pleasant; complaisant. [t. L: s. *complacens*, ppr., pleasing] —**com·pla'cent·ly,** *adv.*

com·plain (kəm plān'), *v.i.* **1.** to express grief, pain, uneasiness, censure, resentment, or dissatisfaction; find fault. **2.** to tell of one's pains, ailments, etc. **3.** to state a grievance; make a formal accusation. [ME *complayn(en)*, t. OF: m. *complaindre*, g. LL *complangere* lament] —**com·plain'er,** *n.* —**com·plain'ing·ly,** *adv.*
—**Syn. 1.** Complain, grumble, growl, murmur, whine are terms for expressing dissatisfaction or discomfort. To complain is to protest against or lament a condition or cause of wrong, etc.: *to complain about high prices.* To grumble is to utter surly, ill-natured complaints half to oneself: *to grumble about the service.* To growl may express more anger than grumble: *to growl ungraciously in reply to a question.* To murmur is to complain in low or suppressed tones, and may indicate greater dissatisfaction than grumble: *to murmur against a government.* To whine is to complain or beg in a mean-spirited, objectionable way, using a nasal tone; whining often connotes also persistence in begging or complaining: *to whine like a coward, like a spoiled child.* —**Ant. 1.** rejoice.

com·plain·ant (kəm plā'nənt), *n.* one who makes a complaint, as in a legal action.

com·plaint (kəm plānt'), *n.* **1.** an expression of grief, regret, pain, censure, resentment, or discontent; lament; faultfinding. **2.** a cause of grief, discontent, lamentation, etc. **3.** a cause of bodily pain or ailment; a malady. **4.** *U.S. Law.* the first pleading of the plaintiff in a civil action, stating his cause of action. [ME, t. OF: m. *complainte*, der. *complaindre.* See complain]

com·plai·sance (kəm plā'zəns, kŏm'plə zăns'), *n.* **1.** quality of being complaisant. **2.** a complaisant act. [t. F]

com·plai·sant (kəm plā'zənt, kŏm'plə zănt'), *adj.* disposed to please; obliging; agreeable; gracious; compliant. [t. F, ppr. of *complaire* please, g. L *complacēre*] —**com·plai'sant·ly,** *adv.*

com·plect·ed (kəm plĕk'tĭd), *adj.* *U.S. Dial. or Colloq.* complexioned, as in *dark-complected*.

com·ple·ment (*n.* kŏm'plə mənt; *v.* kŏm'plə mĕnt'), *n.* **1.** that which completes or makes perfect. **2.** the quantity or amount that completes anything. **3.** either of two parts or things needed to complete each other. **4.** full quantity or amount; complete allowance. **5.** the full number of officers and crew required to man a ship. **6.** a word or words used to complete a grammatical construction, esp. in the predicate, as an object (*man* in *he saw the man*), predicate adjective (*tall* in *the tree is tall*), or predicate noun (*John* in *his name is John*). **7.** *Geom.* the angular amount needed to bring a given angle to a right angle. **8.** *Music.* the interval which added to a given interval completes an octave. **9.** *Immunol.* a thermolabile substance which is normally present in all sera. —*v.t.* **10.** to complete; form a complement to. [ME, t. L: s. *complēmentum* that which fills up, (later) fulfillment]
—**Syn. 10.** Complement, supplement both mean to make an addition or additions to something. To complement is to

provide something felt to be lacking or needed; it is often applied to putting together two things, each of which supplies what is lacking in the other, to make a complete whole: *two discussions from different points of view may complement each other.* To SUPPLEMENT is merely to add to; no lack or deficiency is implied nor is there an idea of a definite relationship between parts: *some additional remarks may supplement either discussion or both.*

com·pie·men·tal (kŏm′plə mĕn′təl), *adj.* complementary. —**com′ple·men′tal·ly**, *adv.*

com·ple·men·ta·ry (kŏm′plə mĕn′-tə rĭ, -trĭ), *adj.* 1. forming a complement; completing. 2. complementing each other.

complementary angle, the complement of the given angle.

complementary cells, *Bot.* cells fitting closely together in the lenticel.

complementary colors, pairs of colors which when mixed in equal proportions produce white or gray, as yellow and blue.

Complementary angles Angle BCD, complement of angle ACB; Arc BD, complement of arc AB

com·plete (kəm plēt′), *adj., v.,* **-plet·ed, -plet·ing.** —*adj.* 1. having all its parts or elements; whole; entire; full. 2. finished; ended; concluded. 3. thorough; consummate; perfect in kind or quality. 4. *Archaic.* (of persons) accomplished; skilled; expert. —*v.t.* 5. to make complete; make whole or entire. 6. to make perfect. 7. to bring to an end; finish; fulfill. [ME *compleet*, t. L: m.s. *complētus*, pp., filled up, completed] —**com·plete′ly**, *adv.* —**com·plete′ness**, *n.* —**com·plet′er**, *n.* —**com·ple′tive**, *adj.*

—**Syn. 1-3.** COMPLETE, ENTIRE, INTACT, PERFECT imply that there is no lack or defect, nor has any part been removed. COMPLETE implies that a certain unit has all its parts, fully developed or perfected; and may apply to a process or purpose carried to fulfillment: *a complete explanation.* ENTIRE means whole, having unbroken unity: *an entire book.* INTACT implies retaining completeness and original condition: *a package delivered intact.* PERFECT emphasizes not only completeness but also high quality and absence of defects or blemishes: *a perfect diamond.* 7. consummate, accomplish, flower. —**Ant. 1.** partial. **3.** defective

com·ple·tion (kəm plē′shən), *n.* 1. act of completing. 2. state of being completed. 3. conclusion; fulfillment.

com·plex (*adj.* kəm plĕks′, kŏm′plĕks; *n.* kŏm′plĕks), *adj.* 1. composed of interconnected parts; compound; composite. 2. characterized by an involved combination of parts. 3. complicated; intricate. 4. *Gram.* (of a word) consisting of two parts, at least one of which is a bound form, as *boyish* (consisting of the word *boy* and the bound form *-ish*). —*n.* 5. a complex whole or system; a complicated assemblage of particulars. 6. *Psychol.* a group of related ideas, feelings, memories, and impulses which operate together and may be repressed or inhibited together. 7. *Colloq.* a fixed idea; an obsessing notion. [t. L: s. *complexus*, pp., having embraced] —**com·plex′ly**, *adv.* —**com·plex′ness**, *n.* —**Syn. 2, 3.** involved, perplexing. —**Ant. 2, 3.** simple.

complex fraction, *Math.* a fraction expressing a ratio between fractions or mixed numbers, or between a fraction or mixed number and a whole number.

com·plex·ion (kəm plĕk′shən), *n.* 1. the natural color and appearance of the skin, esp. of the face. 2. appearance; aspect; character. 3. *Old Physiol.* constitution or nature of body and mind, regarded as the result of certain combined qualities. 4. *Obs.* nature; disposition; temperament. [ME, t. LL: s. *complexio* constitution, in L combination] —**com·plex′ion·al,** *adj.*

com·plex·i·ty (kəm plĕk′sə tĭ), *n., pl.* **-ties.** 1. state or quality of being complex; intricacy. 2. something complex: *the automobile was a complexity far beyond her mechanical skill.*

complex sentence, a sentence containing one or more dependent clauses in addition to the main clause. For example: *When the clock strikes* (dependent clause), *it will be three o'clock* (main clause).

com·pli·a·ble (kəm plī′ə bəl), *adj.* compliant. —**com·pli′a·ble·ness,** *n.* —**com·pli′a·bly,** *adv.*

com·pli·ance (kəm plī′əns), *n.* 1. act of complying; an acquiescing or yielding. 2. a disposition to yield to others. 3. base subservience. 4. **in compliance with,** in keeping or accordance with. Also, **com·pli′an·cy** for 1-3.

com·pli·ant (kəm plī′ənt), *adj.* complying; yielding; obliging: *they were uncomfortably compliant.* [f. m. COM-PLY + -ANT] —**com·pli′ant·ly,** *adv.*

com·pli·ca·cy (kŏm′plə kə sĭ), *n., pl.* **-cies.** 1. complicated state. 2. a complication.

com·pli·cate (*v.* kŏm′plə kāt′; *adj.* kŏm′plə kĭt), *v.,* **-cat·ed, -cat·ing,** *adj.* —*v.t.* 1. to make complex, intricate, or involved. 2. to fold or twine together; combine intricately (fol. by *with*). —*adj.* 3. complex; involved. 4. *Bot.* folded upon itself: *a complicate embryo.* 5. *Zool.* (of insects' wings) folded longitudinally one or more times. [t. L: m. s. *complicātus*, pp., folded together]

com·pli·cat·ed (kŏm′plə kā′tĭd), *adj.* 1. composed of interconnected parts; not simple; complex. 2. consisting of many parts not easily separable; difficult to analyze, understand, explain, etc. —**com·pli·cat′ed·ly,** *adv.* —**com·pli·cat′ed·ness,** *n.*

com·pli·ca·tion (kŏm′plə kā′shən), *n.* 1. act of complicating. 2. a complicated or involved state or condition. 3. a complex combination of elements or things.

4. a complicating element. 5. *Pathol.* a concurrent disease or a fortuitous condition which aggravates the original disease.

com·plic·i·ty (kəm plĭs′ə tĭ), *n., pl.* **-ties.** 1. state of being an accomplice; partnership in wrongdoing. 2. complexity.

com·pli·er (kəm plī′ər), *n.* one who complies.

com·pli·ment (*n.* kŏm′plə mənt; *v.* kŏm′plə mĕnt′), *n.* 1. an expression of praise, commendation, or admiration: *he paid you a high compliment.* 2. a formal act or expression of civility, respect, or regard: *the compliments of the season.* 3. polite, esp. insincere, praise or commendation; flattery. 4. a present; gift. —*v.t.* 5. to pay a compliment to: *to compliment a woman on her new hat.* 6. to show kindness or regard for by a gift or other favor: *he complimented us with tickets for the exhibition.* 7. to congratulate; felicitate: *to compliment a prince on the birth of a son.* [t. F, t. It.: m. *complimento*, t. Sp.: m. *cumplimiento*, der. *cumplir* fulfill, ult. g. L *complēre*] —**Syn. 1.** praise, tribute. —**Ant. 1.** disparagement.

com·pli·men·ta·ry (kŏm′plə mĕn′tə rĭ, -trĭ), *adj.* 1. of the nature of, conveying, or addressing a compliment. 2. politely flattering. 3. *U.S.* free: *a complimentary ticket.* —**com′pli·men′ta·ri·ly,** *adv.*

com·plin (kŏm′plĭn), *n. Eccles.* the last of the seven canonical hours, or the service for it, orig. occurring after the evening meal, but now usually following immediately upon vespers. Also, **com·pline** (kŏm′plĭn, -plĭn). [ME *compelin,* var. of *cumplie,* t. OF, g. L *complēta* (*hōra*) completed (hour)]

com·plot (*n.* kŏm′plŏt; *v.* kəm plŏt′), *n., v.,* **-plot·ted, -plot·ting.** —*n.* 1. a joint plot; a conspiracy. —*v.t., v.i.* 2. to plot together. [t. F: plot, OF concerted plan, also crowd, struggle; orig. uncert.] —**com·plot′ter,** *n.*

com·ply (kəm plī′), *v.i.,* **-plied, -ply·ing.** 1. to act in accordance with wishes, requests, commands, requirements, conditions, etc. (fol. by *with*). 2. *Obs.* to be courteous or conciliatory. [appar. t. It.: m. *complire* fulfill, complete, t. Sp.: m. *cumplir,* ult. g. L *complēre* COM-PLETE; in part appar. affected by PLY] —**Syn. 1.** acquiesce, yield, conform, obey. —**Ant. 1.** refuse, resist.

com·po (kŏm′pō), *n., pl.* **-pos.** shortened form of *composition,* esp. as the name of various composite substances in industrial use.

com·po·nent (kəm pō′nənt), *adj.* 1. composing; constituent. —*n.* 2. a constituent part. 3. *Mech.* one of the parts of a force, velocity, or the like, out of which the whole may be compounded or into which it may be resolved. [t. L: s. *compōnens,* ppr., composing] —**Syn. 2.** See **element.**

com·po·ny (kəm pō′nĭ), *adj. Her.* composed of a single row of squares, metal and color alternating. Also, **com·po·né** (kəm pō′nā; *Fr.* kôN pô nĕ′).

com·port (kəm pōrt′), *v.t.* 1. to bear or conduct (oneself); behave. —*v.i.* 2. to agree or accord; suit (fol. by *with*). [t. F: s. *comporter* bear, behave, g. L *comportāre* carry together]

com·port·ment (kəm pōrt′mənt), *n.* bearing; demeanor; behavior.

com·pose (kəm pōz′), *v.,* **-posed, -pos·ing.** —*v.t.* 1. to make or form by uniting parts or elements. 2. to be the parts or elements of. 3. to make up; constitute: *currency composed of silver.* 4. to put or dispose in proper form or order. 5. to arrange the parts or elements of (a picture, etc.). 6. to devise and make (a literary or musical production). 7. to arrange or settle, as a quarrel, etc. 8. to bring (the body or mind) to a condition of repose, calmness, etc.; calm; quiet. 9. *Print.* a. to set (type). b. to set the types for (an article, etc.). —*v.i.* 10. to practice composition. 11. to enter into composition. [late ME *compose(n),* t. OF: m. *composer* (see COM-POSE[2]), but assoc. with derivatives of L *compōnere.* See COMPOSITE]

com·posed (kəm pōzd′), *adj.* calm; tranquil; serene. —**com·pos·ed·ly** (kəm pō′zĭd lĭ), *adv.* —**com·pos′ed·ness,** *n.* —**Syn.** See **calm.** —**Ant.** agitated, perturbed.

com·pos·er (kəm pō′zər), *n.* 1. one who or that which composes. 2. a writer of music. 3. an author.

composing room, the room in which compositors work in a printing establishment.

composing stick, *Print.* a small (usually) metal tray of adjustable width, in which type is set.

com·pos·ite (kəm pŏz′ĭt), *adj.* 1. made up of various parts or elements; compound. 2. *Bot.* belonging to the Compositae, a family of plants, including the daisy, dandelion, aster, etc., in which the florets are borne in a close head surrounded by a common involucre of bracts. The *Compositae* are sometimes divided into several families: *Ambrosiaceae, Carduaceae* or *Asteraceae,* and *Cichoriaceae.* 3. (*cap.*) *Archit.* noting or pertaining to a classical order in which capital and entablature combine features of the Corinthian and Ionic orders. —*n.* 4. something composite; a compound. 5. *Bot.* a composite plant. [t. L: m.s. *compositus,* pp. of *compōnere* put together, compound, compose] —**com·pos′ite·ly,** *adv.* —**com·pos′ite·ness,** *n.* —**Syn. 4.** See **combination.**

composite number, *Math.* a number exactly divisible by some number other than itself and unity.

composite photograph, a photograph obtained by combining two or more separate photographs.

com·po·si·tion (kŏm′pə zĭsh′ən), *n.* 1. act of combining parts or elements to form a whole. 2. manner in which such parts are combined. 3. resulting state or product. **4.** make-up; constitution. **5.** a compound or composite substance. **6.** *Fine Arts.* organization or grouping of the different parts of a work of art so as to achieve a unified whole. **7.** the art of putting words and sentences together in accordance with the rules of grammar and rhetoric: *Greek prose composition.* **8.** act of producing a literary work. **9.** the art of composing music. **10.** the resulting production or work. **11.** a short essay written as a school exercise. **12.** *Gram.* the formation of compounds: *the composition of "bootblack" from "boot" and "black."* **13.** a settlement by mutual agreement. **14.** an agreement or compromise, esp. one by which a creditor (or group of creditors) accepts partial payment from a debtor. **15.** a sum of money so paid. **16.** the setting up of type for printing.

com·po·si·tion of forces, *Mech.* the union or combination of two or more forces, velocities, or the like (called *components*) acting in the same or in different directions, into a single equivalent force, velocity, or the like (called the *resultant*).

com·pos·i·tor (kəm pŏz′ə tər), *n.* *Print.* typesetter.

com·pos men·tis (kŏm′pəs měn′tĭs), *Latin.* sane.

com·post (kŏm′pōst), *n.* **1.** a composition; compound. **2.** a mixture of various substances, as dung, dead leaves, etc., undergoing decay, used for fertilizing land. [ME, t. OF, g. L *compositus,* pp., compounded]

com·po·sure (kəm pō′zhər), *n.* serene state of mind; calmness; tranquillity. **—Syn.** equability, calmness.

com·po·ta·tion (kŏm′pə tā′shən), *n.* a drinking or tippling together. [t. L: s. *compōtātio* drinking together]

com·po·ta·tor (kŏm′pə tā′tər), *n.* one who drinks or tipples with another. [t. LL]

com·pote (kŏm′pōt; *Fr.* kôn pôt′), *n.* a preparation or dish of fruit stewed in a syrup. [t. F, in OF *compote,* g. L *compos(i)ta,* fem. of *compositus.* See COMPOSITE]

com·po·tier (kŏm′pə tyē′; *Fr.* kôn pô tyē′), *n.* a dish, usually of glass, china, or silver and having a supporting stem, used for holding compotes, fruit, etc. [t. F]

com·pound[1] (*adj.* kŏm′pound, kŏm pound′; *n.* kŏm′-pound; *t.* kəm pound′), *adj.* **1.** composed of two or more parts, elements, or ingredients, or involving two or more actions, functions, etc.; composite. **2.** *Gram.* (of a word) consisting of two or more parts which are also words, but distinguished from a phrase by special phonetic features, in English often consisting of reduction of stress on one constituent, as in *housetop, blackberry,* historically also *cupboard, breakfast.* **3.** *Zool.* (of an animal) composed of a number of distinct individuals which are connected to form a united whole or colony. **—n. 4.** something formed by compounding or combining parts, elements, etc. **5.** *Chem.* a pure substance composed of two or more elements whose composition is constant. **6.** *Gram.* a compound word. **—v.t. 7.** to put together into a whole; combine. **8.** to make or form by combining parts, elements, etc.; construct. **9.** to make up or constitute. **10.** to settle or adjust by agreement, esp. for a reduced amount, as a debt. **11.** *Law.* to agree, for a consideration, not to prosecute or punish a wrongdoer for: *to compound a crime or felony.* **12.** to pay (interest) on the accrued interest as well as the principal. **13.** *Elect.* to connect a portion of the field turns of (a direct-current dynamo) in series with the armature circuit. **—v.i. 14.** to make a bargain; come to terms; compromise. **15.** to settle a debt, etc., by compromise. [ME *compoune(n),* t. OF: m. *compondre,* g. L *compōnere* put together] **—com·pound′a·ble,** *adj.* **—com·pound′-er,** *n.* **—Syn. 4.** See **combination.**

com·pound[2] (kŏm′pound), *n.* an enclosure containing a residence or other establishment of Europeans. [cf. Malay *kampong* enclosure]

Compound E, cortisone.

compound eye, an arthropod eye subdivided into many individual light-receptive elements, each including a lens, a transmitting apparatus, and retinal cells.

compound flower, the flower head of a composite plant.

compound fraction, *Math.* a complex fraction or a fraction of a fraction.

compound fracture, a break in a bone such that the fracture line communicates with an open wound.

compound interest, interest paid, not only on the principal, but on the interest after it has periodically come due and, remaining unpaid, been added to the principal.

compound leaf, a leaf composed of a number of leaflets on a common stalk. It may be either digitately or pinnately compound, and the leaflets may be themselves compound.

compound number, a quantity expressed in more than one denomination or unit, as the length 1 foot 6 inches.

Pinnately compound leaf

compound sentence, a sentence having two or more coördinate independent clauses, usually joined by one or more conjunctions. For example: *the lightning flashed* (independent clause) *and* (conjunction) *the rain fell* (independent clause).

com·pra·dor (kŏm′prə dôr′), *n.* (in China, etc.) a native agent or factotum, as of a foreign business house. Also, **com′pra·dore′.** [t. Pg.: a buyer, purveyor]

com·pre·hend (kŏm′prĭ hĕnd′), *v.t.* **1.** to understand the meaning or nature of; conceive; know. **2.** to take in or embrace; include; comprise. [ME, t. L: s. *comprehendere* seize] **—com′pre·hend′i·ble,** *adj.* **—com′pre·hend′-ing·ly,** *adv.* **—Syn. 1.** See **know. 2.** See **include.**

com·pre·hen·si·ble (kŏm′prĭ hĕn′sə bəl), *adj.* capable of being comprehended; intelligible. **—com′pre·hen′si·bil′i·ty, com′pre·hen′si·ble·ness,** *n.* **—com′pre·hen′si·bly,** *adv.*

com·pre·hen·sion (kŏm′prĭ hĕn′shən), *n.* **1.** act or fact of comprehending. **2.** inclusion; comprehensiveness; perception or understanding. **3.** capacity of the mind to understand; power to grasp ideas; ability to know. **4.** *Logic.* the sum of all those attributes which make up the content of a given conception (distinguished from *extension* or *extent*). For example: *rational, sensible, moral,* etc., form the comprehension of the conception *man.*

com·pre·hen·sive (kŏm′prĭ hĕn′sĭv), *adj.* **1.** comprehending; inclusive; comprehending much; of large scope. **2.** comprehending mentally; having a wide mental grasp. **—com′pre·hen′sive·ly,** *adv.* **—com′-pre·hen′sive·ness,** *n.* **—Syn. 1.** broad, wide, extensive, full.

com·press (*v.* kəm prĕs′; *n.* kŏm′prĕs), *v.t.* **1.** to press together; force into less space. [ME *compresse(n),* t. L: m. *compressāre*] **—n. 2.** *Med.* a soft pad of lint, linen, or the like, held in place by a bandage, used as a means of pressure or to supply moisture, cold, heat, or medication. **3.** an apparatus or establishment for compressing cotton bales, etc. [t. L: s. *compressa,* prop. fem. pp., pressed together] **—com·press′i·ble,** *adj.* **—com·press′i·bil′i·ty,** *n.* **—Syn. 1.** condense, squeeze, constrict. See **contract.**

com·pressed (kəm prĕst′), *adj.* **1.** pressed into less space; condensed. **2.** pressed together. **3.** flattened. **4.** *Bot.* flattened laterally or along the length. **5.** *Zool.* narrow from side to side, and therefore of greater height than width. **—Ant. 1.** expanded.

compressed air, mechanically compressed air the expansive force of which is used to operate drills, brakes, etc.

com·pres·sion (kəm prĕsh′ən), *n.* **1.** act of compressing. **2.** compressed state. **3.** (in internal-combustion engines) the reduction in volume and increase of pressure of the air or combustible mixture in the cylinder prior to ignition, produced by the motion of the piston toward the cylinder head after intake. Also, **com·pres·sure** (kəm prĕsh′ər) for 1, 2.

com·pres·sive (kəm prĕs′ĭv), *adj.* compressing; tending to compress. **—com·pres′sive·ly,** *adv.*

com·pres·sor (kəm prĕs′ər), *n.* **1.** one who or that which compresses. **2.** *Anat.* a muscle that compresses some part of the body. **3.** *Surg.* an instrument for compressing a part of the body. **4.** a machine, usually driven by electric or steam power, by which a gas is compressed so that its expansion may be utilized as a source of power. In refrigeration the compressor is used to compress the gas so that it can be condensed with water or air at prevailing temperatures. [t. L]

com·prise (kəm prīz′), *v.t.* **-prised, -prising. 1.** to comprehend; include; contain. **2.** to consist of; be composed of. Also, **com·prize′.** [ME *comprise(n),* t. F: m. *compris,* pp. of *comprendre,* g. L *compre(he)ndere* seize] **—com·pris′a·ble,** *adj.* **—com·pris′al,** *n.* **—Syn. 1.** See **include.**

com·pro·mise (kŏm′prə mīz′), *n., v.,* **-mised, -mising. —n. 1.** a settlement of differences by mutual concessions; an adjustment of conflicting claims, principles, etc., by yielding a part of each; arbitration. **2.** anything resulting from compromise. **3.** something intermediate between different things. **4.** an endangering, esp. of reputation; exposure to danger, suspicion, etc. **—v.t. 5.** to settle by a compromise. **6.** to make liable to danger, suspicion, scandal, etc.; endanger the reputation of. **7.** to involve unfavorably; commit. **8.** *Obs.* to bind by bargain or agreement. **9.** *Obs.* to bring to terms. **—v.i. 10.** to make a compromise. [ME, t. F: m. *compromis,* g. L *comprōmissum* a mutual promise to abide by a decision, prop. pp. neut.] **—com′pro·mis′er,** *n.*

comp·tom·e·ter (kŏmp tŏm′ə tər), *n.* **1.** a high-speed adding and calculating machine. **2.** (*cap.*) a trademark for this machine.

Comp·ton (kŏmp′tən), *n.* **1. Arthur Holly,** born 1892, U.S. physicist. **2. Karl Taylor,** born 1887, U.S. physicist. **3.** a city in SW California. 47,990 (1950).

comp·trol·ler (kən trō′lər), *n.* controller (def. 1). [var. sp. of CONTROLLER] **—comp·trol′ler·ship,** *n.*

com·pul·sion (kəm pŭl′shən), *n.* **1.** act of compelling; constraint; coercion. **2.** state of being compelled. **3.** *Psychol.* **a.** a strong irrational impulse to carry out a given act. **b.** the act. [late ME, t. LL: s. *compulsio*]

com·pul·sive (kəm pŭl′sĭv), *adj.* **1.** compulsory. **2.** (esp. in *Psychol.*) pertaining to compulsion. **—com·pul′sive·ly,** *adv.*

com·pul·so·ry (kəm pŭl′sə rĭ), *adj.* **1.** using compulsion; compelling; constraining: *compulsory measures.* **2.** compelled; forced; obligatory. **—com·pul′so·ri·ly,** *adv.* **—com·pul′so·ri·ness,** *n.* **—Ant. 1, 2.** voluntary.

com·punc·tion (kəm pŭngk′shən), *n.* uneasiness of conscience or feelings; regret for wrongdoing or giving pain to another; contrition; remorse. [ME, t. LL: s. *com-punctio* remorse]

---

com·punc·tious (kəm pŭngk′shəs), *adj.* causing compunction; causing misgiving, regret, or remorse.

com·pur·ga·tion (kŏm′pər gā′shən), *n.* an early common-law method of trial in which the defendant is acquitted if a specified number of friends or neighbors would swear to his innocence or veracity. [t. LL: s. *compurgātio,* der. L *compurgāre* purify completely]

com·pur·ga·tor (kŏm′pər gā′tər), *n.* one who testifies to another's innocence or veracity.

com·pu·ta·tion (kŏm′pyə tā′shən), *n.* 1. act, process, or method of computing; calculation. 2. a result of computing; the amount computed.

com·pute (kəm pūt′), *v.,* **-puted, -puting.** —*v.t.* 1. to determine by calculation; reckon; calculate: *to compute the distance of the moon from the earth.* —*v.i.* 2. to reckon; calculate. —*n.* 3. computation; reckoning. [t. L: m.s. *computāre* reckon. Cf. COUNT[1]] —**com·put′a·bil/i·ty,** *n.* —**com·put′er,** *n.* —Syn. 1. estimate, count, enumerate, figure.

com·rade (kŏm′rād *or, esp. Brit.,* -rĭd, kŭm′rĭd), *n.* 1. an associate in occupation or friendship; a close companion; a fellow; a mate. 2. fellow member of a political party; fraternal organization, etc. [t. F: m. *camarade,* t. Sp.: m. *camarada,* lit., group living in one room, der. *cámara* room, g. L *camera* CHAMBER] —**com′rade·ship′,** *n.*

Com·stock (kŭm′stŏk, kŏm′-), *n.* **Anthony,** 1844–1915, U.S. crusader against vice.

com·stock·er·y (kŭm′stŏk′ər ĭ, kŏm′-), *n.* overzealous censorship of the fine arts and literature, often mistaking outspokenly honest works for salacious productions.

Comte (kônt; *Fr.* kôNt), *n.* **Auguste** (ō gyst′), 1798–1857, French philosopher, founder of positivism. —**Com·ti·an** (kŏm′tĭ ən, kôN′-), *adj.* —**Comt·ism** (kŏm′tĭz əm, kôN′-), *n.* —**Comt′ist,** *n., adj.*

Co·mus (kō′məs), *n. Later Class. Myth.* a young god of revelry, represented by Milton as the son of Bacchus and Circe. [t. L, t. Gk.: m. *kômos* revel]

con[1] (kŏn), *adv.* 1. against a proposition, opinion, etc.; not pro (for). —*n.* 2. the argument, arguer, or voter against (something). [short for L *contrā,* adv., in opposition, as prep., against]

con[2] (kŏn), *v.t.,* **conned, conning.** to learn; study; commit to memory; peruse or examine carefully. [var. of CAN, OE *can, con,* a finite form of *cunnan* know]

con[3] (kŏn), *v.,* **conned, conning,** *n. Naut.* —*v.t.* 1. to direct the steering of (a ship). —*n.* 2. the position taken by the person who cons. 3. act of conning. [var. of obs. *cond,* short for *condue,* t. OF: m. *conduire* CONDUCT]

con[4] (kŏn), *adj., v.,* **conned, conning.** *U.S. Slang.* —*adj.* 1. confidence: *con game, con man.* —*v.t.* 2. to swindle; defraud. [short for CONFIDENCE (GAME or MAN)]

con-, var. of **com-,** before consonants except *b, h, l, m, p, r, w,* as in *convene, condone,* and, by assimilation, before *n,* as in *connection.* Cf. **co-** (def. 1).

con., 1. conclusion. 2. consolidated. 3. (L *contra*) against.

Co·na·kry (kō nä krē′), *n.* a seaport in and the capital of French Guinea. 18,600 (1936). Also, **Konakri.**

con a·mo·re (kôn ä mô′rĕ), *Italian.* 1. with love, tender enthusiasm, or zeal. 2. *Music.* (as a direction) tenderly and lovingly.

Co·nant (kō′nənt), *n.* **James Bryant,** born 1893, U.S. chemist and educator: president of Harvard since 1933.

co·na·tion (kō nā′shən), *n. Psychol.* that portion of mental life having to do with striving, embracing desire and volition. [t. L: s. *cōnātio* an endeavoring, effort]

con·a·tive (kŏn′ə tĭv, kō′nə-), *adj.* 1. *Psychol.* pertaining to or of the nature of conation. 2. *Gram.* expressing endeavor or effort: *a conative verb.*

co·na·tus (kō nā′təs), *n., pl.* **-tus.** 1. an effort or striving. 2. a force or tendency simulating a human effort. [t. L: effort, endeavor]

con bri·o (kôn brē′ō), *Music.* with vigor; vivaciously. [It.]

con·cat·e·nate (kŏn kăt′ə nāt′), *v.,* **-nated, -nating,** *adj.* —*v.t.* 1. to link together; unite in a series or chain. —*adj.* 2. linked together as in a chain. [t. L: m.s. *catēnātus,* pp.]

con·cat·e·na·tion (kŏn kăt′ə nā′shən), *n.* 1. act of concatenating. 2. state of being concatenated; connection, as in a chain. 3. a series of interconnected or interdependent things or events.

con·cave (*adj., v.* kŏn kāv′, kŏn′kāv′; *n.* kŏn kāv′), *adj., n., v.,* **-caved, -caving.** —*adj.* 1. curved like the interior of a circle or hollow sphere; hollow and curved. 2. *Obs.* hollow. —*n.* 3. a concave surface, part, line, etc. —*v.t.* 4. to make concave. [t. L: m.s. *concavus*] —**con·cave′ly,** *adv.* —**con·cave′ness,** *n.* —Ant. 1. convex.

A, Concave or plano-concave lens; B, Concavo-concave lens; C, Concavo-convex lens

con·cav·i·ty (kŏn kăv′ə tĭ), *n., pl.* **-ties.** 1. state of being concave. 2. a concave surface or thing; a hollow; cavity.

con·ca·vo-con·cave (kŏn kā′vō kŏn kāv′), *adj.* concave on both sides.

con·ca·vo-con·vex (kŏn kā′vō kŏn vĕks′), *adj.* 1. concave on one side and convex on the other. 2. denoting or pertaining to a lens in which the concave face has

a greater degree of curvature than the convex face, the lens being thinnest in the middle.

con·ceal (kən sēl′), *v.t.* 1. to hide; withdraw or remove from observation; cover or keep from sight. 2. to keep secret; forbear to disclose or divulge. [ME *concele(n),* t. OF: m. *conceler,* g. L *concēlāre* hide] —**con·ceal/a·ble,** *adj.* —**con·ceal/er,** *n.* —Syn. 1. See hide.

con·ceal·ment (kən sēl′mənt), *n.* 1. act of concealing. 2. state of being concealed. 3. a means or place of hiding.

con·cede (kən sēd′), *v.,* **-ceded, -ceding.** —*v.t.* 1. to admit as true, just, or proper; admit. 2. to grant as a right or privilege; yield. —*v.i.* 3. to make concession; yield; admit. [t. L: m.s. *concēdere*] —**con·ced′ed·ly,** *adv.* —**con·ced′er,** *n.* —Ant. 1. deny. 2. refuse.

con·ceit (kən sēt′), *n.* 1. an exaggerated estimate of one's own ability, importance, wit, etc. 2. favorable opinion; esteem. 3. personal opinion or estimation. 4. the faculty of conceiving; apprehension. 5. that which is conceived in the mind; a thought; an idea. 6. imagination; fancy. 7. a fancy; whim; a fanciful notion. 8. a fanciful thought, idea, or expression, esp. of strained or far-fetched nature. 9. the use of such thoughts, ideas, etc., as a literary characteristic. 10. *Obs.* a fancy article. —*v.t.* 11. to flatter (esp. oneself). 12. to conceive mentally; apprehend. 13. to imagine. 14. *Archaic or Dial.* to take a fancy to; have a good opinion of. [ME *conceyte;* der. CONCEIVE, modeled on DECEIT] —Syn. 1. self-esteem, vanity, egotism, complacency. See pride. —Ant. 1. humility.

con·ceit·ed (kən sē′tĭd), *adj.* 1. having an exaggerated opinion of one's abilities, importance, etc. 2. *Dial.* having an opinion. 3. *Obs.* intelligent; clever. 4. *Dial.* fanciful; whimsical. —**con·ceit′ed·ly,** *adv.* —**con·ceit′ed·ness,** *n.* —Syn. 1. vain, proud, egotistical, self-satisfied, priggish.

con·ceiv·a·ble (kən sē′və bəl), *adj.* capable of being conceived; imaginable. —**con·ceiv′a·bil/i·ty, con·ceiv′a·ble·ness,** *n.* —**con·ceiv′a·bly,** *adv.*

con·ceive (kən sēv′), *v.,* **-ceived, -ceiving.** —*v.t.* 1. to form (a notion, opinion, purpose, etc.). 2. to form a notion or idea of; imagine. 3. to apprehend in the mind; understand. 4. to hold as an opinion; think; believe. 5. to experience or entertain (a feeling). 6. to express, as in words. 7. to become pregnant with. —*v.i.* 8. to form an idea; think (fol. by *of*). 9. to become pregnant. [ME *conceive(n),* t. OF: m. *conceveir,* g. L *concipere* take in] —**con·ceiv′er,** *n.* —Syn. 2, 8. See imagine.

con·cent (kən sĕnt′), *n.* concord of sounds, voices, etc. [t. L: s. *concentus* a singing together]

con·cen·ter (kŏn sĕn′tər), *v.t., v.i.* to bring or converge to a common center; concentrate. Also, *esp. Brit.,* **concentre.**

con·cen·trate (kŏn′sən trāt′), *v.,* **-trated, -trating,** *n.* —*v.t.* 1. to bring or draw to a common center or point of union; cause to come close together; bring to bear on one point; direct toward one object; focus. 2. to intensify the action of; make more intense, stronger, or purer by removing or reducing the proportion of what is foreign or inessential. 3. *Mining.* to separate (metal or ore) from rock, sand, etc., so as to improve the quality of the valuable portion. —*v.i.* 4. to converge to a center. 5. to become more intense, stronger, or purer. —*n.* 6. a concentrated form of something; a product of concentration. [f. CON- + s. L *centrum* center + -ATE[1]] —**con·cen·tra·tive** (kŏn′sən trā′tĭv, kən sĕn′trə-), *adj.* —**con′cen·tra·tive·ness,** *n.* —**con′cen·tra/tor,** *n.* —Syn. 1. See contract. 4. radiate. 4. diverge.

con·cen·tra·tion (kŏn′sən trā′shən), *n.* 1. act of concentrating. 2. concentrated state. 3. exclusive attention to one object; close mental application. 4. *Mil.* a. the assembling of military or naval forces in a particular area in preparation for further operations. b. a specified intensity and duration of artillery fire placed on a small area. 5. something concentrated. 6. *Chem.* (of a solution) a measure of the amount of dissolved substance contained per unit of volume.

concentration camp, 1. a guarded enclosure for the detention or imprisonment of political prisoners, prisoners of war, aliens, refugees, etc. 2. an area for the assembly of military personnel.

con·cen·tre (kŏn sĕn′tər), *v.t., v.i. Chiefly Brit.* concenter.

con·cen·tric (kən sĕn′trĭk), *adj.* having a common center, as circles or spheres. Also, **con·cen′tri·cal.** —**con·cen′tri·cal·ly,** *adv.* —**con·cen·tric·i·ty** (kŏn′sən trĭs′ə tĭ), *n.*

Con·cep·ción (kôn′sĕp syôn′), *n.* a city in central Chile, near the mouth of the Bio-Bio river. 85,813 (1940).

con·cept (kŏn′sĕpt), *n.* 1. a general notion; the predicate of a (possible) judgment. 2. a complex of characters. 3. the immediate object of thought in simple apprehension. [t. L: s. *conceptus* a conceiving]

con·cep·ta·cle (kən sĕp′tə kəl), *n. Biol.* an organ or cavity enclosing reproductive bodies. [t. L: m.s. *conceptāculum* receptacle]

con·cep·tion (kən sĕp′shən), *n.* 1. act of conceiving. 2. state of being conceived. 3. fertilization; inception of pregnancy. 4. that which is conceived. 5. beginning. 6. act or power of forming notions, ideas, or concepts. 7. a notion; idea; concept. 8. a design; plan. —**con·cep′tion·al,** *adj.* —**con·cep′tive,** *adj.*

con·cep·tu·al (kən sĕp′chŏŏ əl), *adj.* pertaining to the forming of concepts or to concepts. [t. ML: s. *conceptuālis*] —**con·cep′tu·al·ly,** *adv.*

con·cep·tu·al·ism (kən sĕp′chŏŏ ə lĭz′əm), *n.* the philosophical doctrine, midway between nominalism and realism, that concepts enable the mind to grasp objective reality. It is often ambiguous as to the existence and status of universals. —**con·cep′tu·al·ist,** *n.* —**con·cep′tu·al·is′tic,** *adj.*

con·cern (kən sûrn′), *v.t.* **1.** to relate to; be connected with; be of interest or importance to; affect: *the problem concerns us all.* **2.** to interest, engage, or involve (used reflexively or in the passive, often fol. by *with* or *in*): *to concern oneself with a matter, to be concerned in a plot.* **3.** to disquiet or trouble (used in the passive): *to be concerned about a person's health.* —*n.* **4.** that which relates or pertains to one; business; affair. **5.** a matter that engages one's attention, interest, or care, or that affects one's welfare or happiness: *it's no concern of mine.* **6.** solicitude or anxiety. **7.** important relation or bearing. **8.** a commercial or manufacturing firm or establishment. **9.** *Colloq.* any material object or contrivance. [t. ML: s. *concernere* relate to, in LL mix, f. L: *con-* CON- + *cernere* separate, have respect to] —**Syn. 6.** CONCERN, CARE, WORRY connote an uneasy and burdened state of mind. CONCERN implies an anxious sense of interest in, or responsibility for, something: *concern over a friend's misfortune.* CARE suggests a heaviness of spirit caused by dread, or by the constant pressure of burdensome demands: *poverty weighs one down with care.* WORRY is an active state of agitated uneasiness and restless apprehension: *he was disturbed by worry over the stock market.* —**Ant. 6.** indifference.

con·cerned (kən sûrnd′), *adj.* **1.** interested. **2.** troubled or anxious: *a concerned look.*

con·cern·ing (kən sûr′nĭng), *prep.* relating to; regarding; about.

con·cern·ment (kən sûrn′mənt), *n.* **1.** importance or moment. **2.** interest or participation. **3.** relation or bearing. **4.** anxiety or solicitude. **5.** a concern or affair. **6.** *Archaic.* a thing in which one is concerned.

con·cert (*n.* kŏn′sûrt, -sərt; *v.* kən sûrt′), *n.* **1.** a public musical performance in which several singers or players, or both, participate. **2.** agreement of two or more in a design or plan; combined action; accord or harmony. [t. F, t. It.: m. *concerto,* der. *concertare* be in accord] —*v.t.* **3.** to contrive or arrange by agreement. **4.** to plan; devise. —*v.i.* **5.** to plan or act together. [t. F: s. *concerter,* t. It.: m. *concertare* be in accord, g. L *concertāre* contend; influenced in meaning by *consertus,* pp., joined]

con·cert·ed (kən sûr′tĭd), *adj.* **1.** contrived or arranged by agreement; prearranged; planned or devised: *concerted action.* **2.** *Music.* arranged in parts for several voices or instruments. —**con·cert′ed·ly,** *adv.*

concert grand piano. See **piano** (def. 2).

con·cer·ti·na (kŏn′sər tē′nə), *n.* a small hexagonal accordion. [f. CONCERT + -INA]

con·cer·ti·no (kôn′chĕr tē′nô), *n., pl.* **-ni** (-nē), a short concerto. [It.]

con·cert·mas·ter (kŏn′sərt-mäs′tər, -mäs′tər), *n.* the leader, usually the first violinist, of an orchestra, ranking next to the conductor. Also, *Ger.,* **con·cert·meis·ter** (kôn tsĕrt′mīs′tər). Man playing a concertina

con·cer·to (kŏn chĕr′tō; *It.* kôn chĕr′tô), *n., pl.* **-tos,** *It.* **-ti** (-tē). *Music* a composition for one or more principal instruments, with orchestral accompaniment, now usually in symphonic form. [t. It.]

concert pitch, *Music.* a pitch slightly higher than the ordinary pitch, used in tuning instruments for concert use.

con·ces·sion (kən sĕsh′ən), *n.* **1.** act of conceding or yielding, as a right or privilege, or as a point or fact in an argument. **2.** the thing or point yielded. **3.** something conceded by a government or a controlling authority, as a grant of land, a privilege, or a franchise. **4.** *U.S.* a space or privilege within certain premises for a business: *the popcorn concession at the theater.* [t. L: s. *concessio,* der. *concēdere.* See CONCEDE]

con·ces·sion·aire (kən sĕsh′ə nâr′), *n.* one to whom a concession has been granted, as by a government. Also, **con·ces′sion·er.** [t. F: m. *concessionnaire*]

con·ces·sion·ar·y (kən sĕsh′ə nĕr′ĭ), *adj., n., pl.* **-aries.** —*adj.* **1.** pertaining to concession; of the nature of a concession. —*n.* **2.** a concessionaire.

con·ces·sive (kən sĕs′ĭv), *adj.* **1.** tending or serving to concede. **2.** *Gram.* expressing concession, as the English conjunction *though.* [t. L: m.s. *concessīvus*]

conch (kŏngk, kŏnch), *n., pl.* **conchs** (kŏngks), **conches** (kŏn′chĭz). **1.** the spiral shell of a gastropod, often used as a trumpet. **2.** any of several marine gastropods, esp. *Strombus gigas.* **3.** the fabled shell trumpet of the Tritons. **4.** *Archit.* **a.** the concave surface of a dome or half dome. **b.** apse. [t. L: s. *concha,* t. Gk.: m. *kónchē* mussel or cockle, shell-like part or thing, external ear]

con·cha (kŏng′kə), *n., pl.* **-chae** (-kē). **1.** *Anat.* a shell-like structure, esp. the external ear. See diag. under **ear.** **2.** *Archit.* a conch. [see CONCH]

con·chif·er·ous (kŏng kĭf′ər əs), *adj.* shell-bearing.

Con·cho·bar (kŏng′kō wər, kŏn′ōōr), *n.* See **Deirdre.**

con·choid (kŏng′koid), *n. Geom.* a plane curve such that if a straight line be drawn from a certain fixed point, called the pole of the curve, to the curve, the part of the line intersected between the curve and its asymptote is always equal to a fixed distance. [see CONCHOIDAL]

con·choi·dal (kŏng koi′dəl), *adj. Mineral.* having convex elevations and concave depressions like shells. [f. m. s. Gk. *konchoeidēs* shell-like + -AL¹]

con·chol·o·gy (kŏng kŏl′ə jĭ), *n.* the branch of zoology dealing with mollusks. [f. *concho-* (t. Gk.: m. *koncho-,* comb. form of *kónchē* mussel) + -LOGY] —**con·cho·log·i·cal** (kŏng′kə lŏj′ə kəl), *adj.* —**con·chol′o·gist,** *n.*

con·chy (kŏn′chĭ), *n., pl.* **-chies.** *Slang.* conscientious objector. [short for CONSCIENTIOUS]

con·ci·erge (kŏn′sĭ ûrzh′; *Fr.* kôn syĕrzh′), *n.* **1.** (in France, etc.) one who has charge of the entrance of a building; a janitor or doorkeeper. **2.** *Obs.* a custodian or warden. [t. F]

con·cil·i·ate (kən sĭl′ĭ āt′), *v.t.,* **-ated, -ating. 1.** to overcome the distrust or hostility of, by soothing or pacifying means; placate; win over. **2.** to win or gain (regard or favor). **3.** to render compatible; reconcile. [t. L: m. s. *conciliātus,* pp., brought together] —**con·cil′i·a′tion,** *n.* —**con·cil′i·a′tor,** *n.* —**Syn. 1.** propitiate. See **appease.**

con·cil·i·a·to·ry (kən sĭl′ĭ ə tôr′ĭ), *adj.* tending to conciliate: *a conciliatory manner.* Also, **con·cil·i·a·tive** (kŏn sĭl′ĭ ā′tĭv). —**con·cil′i·a·to′ri·ly,** *adv.* —**con·cil′i·a·to′ri·ness,** *n.*

con·cin·ni·ty (kən sĭn′ə tĭ), *n., pl.* **-ties. 1.** *Rhet.* **a.** a close harmony of tone as well as logic among the elements of a discourse. **b.** an instance of this effect. **2.** any harmonious adaptation of parts. [t. L: m.s. *concinnitas,* der. *concinnus* well put together]

con·cise (kən sīs′), *adj.* expressing much in few words; brief and comprehensive; succinct; terse: *a concise account.* [t. L: m.s. *concīsus,* pp., cut up or off] —**con·cise′ly,** *adv.*

con·cise·ness (kən sīs′nĭs), *n.* quality of being concise. —**Syn.** See **brevity.**

con·ci·sion (kən sĭzh′ən), *n.* **1.** concise quality; brevity; terseness. **2.** a cutting up or off; mutilation.

con·clave (kŏn′klāv, kŏng′-), *n.* **1.** any private meeting. **2.** the place in which the cardinals of the Roman Catholic Church meet in private for the election of a pope. **3.** the assembly or meeting of the cardinals for the election of a pope. **4.** the body of cardinals; the Sacred College. [ME, t. L: lockable place]

con·clav·ist (kŏn′klā vĭst, kŏng′-), *n.* either of two persons who attend upon a cardinal in conclave.

con·clude (kən klōōd′), *v.,* **-cluded, -cluding.** —*v.t.* **1.** to bring to an end; finish; terminate: *to conclude a speech.* **2.** to say in conclusion. **3.** to bring to a decision or settlement; settle or arrange finally: *to conclude a treaty.* **4.** to determine by reasoning; deduce; infer. **5.** to decide, determine, or resolve. **6.** *Obs.* to shut up or enclose. **7.** *Obs.* to restrict or confine. —*v.i.* **8.** to come to an end; finish. **9.** to arrive at an opinion or judgment; come to a decision; decide. [ME *conclude*(n), t. L: m. *conclūdere* shut up] —**con·clud′er,** *n.*

con·clu·sion (kən klōō′zhən), *n.* **1.** the end or close; the final part. **2.** the last main division of a discourse, containing a summing up of the points. **3.** a result, issue, or outcome: *a foregone conclusion.* **4.** final settlement or arrangement. **5.** **try conclusions with,** to engage (a person) in a contest or struggle for victory or mastery. **6.** final decision. **7.** a deduction or inference: *to jump to a conclusion.* **8.** *Logic.* a proposition concluded or inferred from the premises of an argument. **9.** *Law.* **a.** the effect of an act by which he who did it is bound not to do anything inconsistent therewith; an estoppel. **b.** the end of a pleading or conveyance. **10.** *Gram.* apodosis. [ME, t. L: s. *conclūsio*] —**Syn. 1.** ending, termination, completion, finale. See **end.**

con·clu·sive (kən klōō′sĭv), *adj.* serving to settle or decide a question; decisive; convincing: *conclusive evidence.* —**con·clu′sive·ly,** *adv.* —**con·clu′sive·ness,** *n.*

con·coct (kŏn kŏkt′, kən-), *v.t.* **1.** to make by combining ingredients, as in cookery: *to concoct a soup or a dinner.* **2.** to prepare; make up; contrive: *to concoct a story.* [t. L: s. *concoctus,* pp., cooked together, digested] —**con·coct′er, con·coc′tor,** *n.* —**con·coc′tive,** *adj.*

con·coc·tion (kŏn kŏk′shən, kən-), *n.* **1.** act or process of concocting. **2.** something concocted. [t. L: s. *concoctio*]

con·com·i·tant (kŏn kŏm′ə tənt, kən-), *adj.* **1.** accompanying; concurrent; attending. —*n.* **2.** a concomitant quality, circumstance, or thing. [t. LL: s. *concomitans,* ppr., accompanying] —**con·com′i·tance, con·com′i·tan·cy,** *n.* —**con·com′i·tant·ly,** *adv.*

con·cord (kŏn′kôrd, kŏng′-), *n.* **1.** agreement between persons; concurrence in opinions, sentiments, etc.; unanimity; accord. **2.** peace. **3.** a compact or treaty. **4.** agreement between things; mutual fitness; harmony. **5.** *Gram.* agreement. **6.** *Music.* consonance. [ME *concorde,* t. F, t. L: m. *concordia* agreement]

Con·cord (kŏng′kərd *for 1–3; also for 3* kŏn′kôrd), *n.* **1.** a town in E Massachusetts, NW of Boston: the second battle of the Revolution was fought here, April 19, 1775. 2299 (1950). **2.** the capital of New Hampshire, in the S part. 27,988 (1950). **3.** Concord grape.

---

b., blend of, blended; **c.,** cognate with; **d.,** dialect, dialectal; **der.,** derived from; **f.,** formed from; **g.,** going back to; **m.,** modification of; **r.,** replacing; **s.,** stem of; **t.,** taken from; **?,** perhaps. See the full key on inside cover.

con·cord·ance (kŏn kôr/dəns, kən-), *n.* **1.** state of being concordant; agreement; harmony. **2.** an alphabetical index of the principal words of a book, as of the Bible, with a reference to the passage in which each occurs and usually some part of the context. **3.** an alphabetical index of subjects or topics.

con·cord·ant (kŏn kôr/dənt, kən-), *adj.* agreeing; harmonious. **—con·cord/ant·ly,** *adv.*

con·cor·dat (kŏn kôr/dăt), *n.* **1.** an agreement; a compact. **2.** an agreement between the Pope and a secular government regarding the regulation of ecclesiastical matters. [t. F, t. ML: s. *concordātum,* prop. pp. neut. of L *concordāre* agree]

Concord coach, *U.S.* a type of stagecoach.

Con·cord grape (kŏng/kərd, kŏn/kôrd), a large, dark-blue, eastern U.S. grape, grown largely for unfermented juice.

con·course (kŏn/kōrs, kŏng/-), *n.* **1.** an assemblage; a throng: *a mighty concourse of people.* **2.** a driveway or promenade in a park. **3.** an open space in a railroad station. **4.** grounds for racing, athletic sports, etc. **5.** a running or coming together; confluence. [ME *concours,* t. OF, g. L *concursus* running together]

con·cres·cence (kŏn krĕs/əns), *n.* **1.** a growing together, as of parts, cells, etc.; coalescence. **2.** *Embryol.* the moving together and growing together of embryonic parts which give origin to the left and right halves of an embryo or of an organ. [t. L: m. s. *concrescentia* a condensing]

con·crete (kŏn/krēt, kŏn krēt/ for 1–11, 14; kŏn krēt/ for 12, 13), *adj., n., v.,* **-creted, -creting. —***adj.* **1.** constituting an actual thing or instance; real: *a concrete example.* **2.** pertaining to or concerned with realities or actual instances rather than abstractions; particular as opposed to general: *concrete ideas.* **3.** representing or applied to an actual substance or thing as opposed to an abstract quality: *a concrete noun.* **4.** made of concrete: *a concrete pavement.* **5.** formed by coalescence of separate particles into a mass; united in a coagulated, condensed, or solid state. **—***n.* **6.** a concrete idea or term; a concrete object or thing. **7.** a mass formed by coalescence or concretion of particles of matter. **8.** an artificial stonelike material used for foundations, etc., made by mixing cement, sand, and broken stones, etc., with water, and allowing the mixture to harden. **9.** this material strengthened by a system of embedded iron or steel bars, netting, or the like, used for building; *reinforced concrete.* **10.** any of various other artificial building or paving materials, as those containing tar. **—***v.t.* **11.** to treat or lay with concrete. **12.** to form into a mass by coalescence of particles; render solid. **—***v.i.* **13.** to coalesce into a mass; become solid; harden. **14.** to use or apply concrete. [t. L: m.s. *concrētus,* pp., grown together, hardened] **—con·crete/ly,** *adv.* **—con·crete/ness,** *n.* **—con·cre/tive,** *adj.* **—con·cre/tive·ly,** *adv.* **—Ant.** 1, 2. abstract.

concrete number, *Arith.* a number which relates to a particular object or thing.

con·cre·tion (kŏn krē/shən), *n.* **1.** act or process of concreting. **2.** state of being concreted. **3.** a solid mass formed by or as by coalescence or cohesion. **4.** *Pathol.* a solid or calcified mass in the body formed by a disease process. **5.** *Geol.* a rounded mass of mineral matter occurring in sandstone, clay, etc., often in concentric layers about a nucleus.

con·cre·tion·ar·y (kŏn krē/shə nĕr/ĭ), *adj.* formed by concretion; consisting of concreted matter or masses.

con·cu·bi·nage (kŏn kū/bə nĭj), *n.* **1.** cohabitation without legal marriage. **2.** the condition of a concubine.

con·cu·bi·nar·y (kŏn kū/bə nĕr/ĭ), *adj.* **1.** of a concubine. **2.** living in concubinage.

con·cu·bine (kŏng/kyə bīn, kŏn/-), *n.* **1.** a woman who cohabits with a man without being married to him. **2.** (among polygamous peoples) a secondary wife. [ME, t. L: m. *concubīna*]

con·cu·pis·cence (kŏn kū/pə səns), *n.* **1.** sensual appetite; lust. **2.** eager or illicit desire.

con·cu·pis·cent (kŏn kū/pə sənt), *adj.* **1.** eagerly desirous. **2.** lustful; sensual. [t. L: s. *concupiscens,* ppr.]

con·cur (kən kûr/), *v.i.,* **-curred, -curring. 1.** to accord in opinion; agree. **2.** to coöperate; combine; be associated. **3.** to coincide. **4.** to come together, as lines; unite. **5.** *Obs.* to run together. [late ME, t. L: m.s. *concurrere* run together] **—Syn.** 1. See consent.

con·cur·rence (kən kûr/əns, -kŭr/-), *n.* **1.** act of concurring. **2.** accordance in opinion; agreement. **3.** coöperation, as of agents or causes. **4.** simultaneous occurrence; coincidence. **5.** *Geom.* a point which is in three or more lines simultaneously. **6.** competition. **7.** *Law.* a power equally held or a claim shared equally. Also, **con·cur/ren·cy** for 1–4, 6.

con·cur·rent (kən kûr/ənt, -kŭr/-), *adj.* **1.** occurring or existing together or side by side. **2.** acting in conjunction; coöperating. **3.** having equal authority or jurisdiction. **4.** accordant or agreeing. **5.** tending to or intersecting in the same point: *four concurrent lines.* **—***n.* **6.** something joint or contributory. **7.** a rival or competitor. **—con·cur/rent·ly,** *adv.*

concurrent resolution, a resolution adopted by both branches of a legislative assembly which, unlike a joint resolution, does not require the signature of the chief executive.

con·cus·sion (kən kŭsh/ən), *n.* **1.** act of shaking or shocking, as by a blow. **2.** shock occasioned by a blow or collision. **3.** *Pathol.* jarring of the brain, spinal cord, etc., from a blow, fall, etc. [t. L: s. *concussio* shock] **—con·cus·sive** (kən kŭs/ĭv), *adj.*

Con·dé (kôn dā/), *n.* **Louis II de Bourbon** (lwē, də bŏr bôn/), **Prince of,** (*Duc d'Enghien,* "*the Great Condé*") 1621–86, French general.

con·demn (kən dĕm/), *v.t.* **1.** to pronounce adverse judgment on; express strong disapproval of; censure. **2.** to afford occasion for convicting: *his very looks condemn him.* **3.** to pronounce to be guilty; sentence to punishment; doom. **4.** to judge or pronounce to be unfit for use or service: *the old ship was condemned.* **5.** to declare incurable. **6.** *U.S. Law.* to acquire ownership of for a public purpose, under the right of eminent domain. [ME *condem(p)ne,* t. OF: m. *condem(p)ner,* g. L *condem(p)nāre*] **—con·dem·na·ble** (kən dĕm/nə bəl), *adj.* **—con·demn·er** (kən dĕm/ər), *n.* **—con·demn/ing·ly,** *adv.* **—Syn.** 1. See blame.

con·dem·na·tion (kŏn/dĕm nā/shən, -dəm-), *n.* **1.** act of condemning. **2.** strong censure; disapprobation; reproof. **3.** state of being condemned. **4.** cause or reason for condemning. **5.** *U.S.* the seizure (of property) for public use.

con·dem·na·to·ry (kən dĕm/nə tōr/ĭ), *adj.* serving to condemn.

con·den·sa·ble (kən dĕn/sə bəl), *adj.* capable of being condensed. Also, **condensible. —con·den/sa·bil/i·ty,** *n.*

con·den·sate (kən dĕn/sāt), *n.* something formed by condensation.

con·den·sa·tion (kŏn/dĕn sā/shən), *n.* **1.** act of condensing. **2.** condensed state or form. **3.** a condensed mass. **4.** *Chem.* a reaction between two or more like or unlike organic molecules, leading to the formation of a larger molecule and the splitting out of a simple molecule such as water or alcohol. **5.** act of reducing a gas or vapor to a liquid or solid form. **6.** *Psychoanal.* the representation of two or more ideas, memories, feelings, or impulses by one word or image, as in wit, slips, allegories, and dreams.

con·dense (kən dĕns/), *v.,* **-densed, -densing. —***v.t.* **1.** to make more dense or compact; reduce the volume or compass of. **2.** to reduce to another and denser form, as a gas or vapor to a liquid or solid state. **—***v.i.* **3.** to become denser or more compact. **4.** to become liquid or solid, as a gas or vapor. [late ME, t. L: m.s. *condensāre* make thick] **—Syn.** 1. compress, concentrate. See contract. **—Ant.** 1, 3. expand.

condensed milk, whole milk reduced by evaporation to a thick consistency with sugar added.

condensed type, a kind of type narrow in proportion to its height.

con·dens·er (kən dĕn/sər), *n.* **1.** one who or that which condenses. **2.** an apparatus for condensing. **3.** any device for reducing gases or vapors to liquid or solid form. **4.** a lens or combination of lenses, used to gather and concentrate the rays of light and direct them upon the object. **5.** *Elect.* a device for accumulating and holding a charge of electricity, consisting of two conducting surfaces separated by a nonconductor or dielectric and used esp. in radio apparatus, as for modifying the electrical capacity in a circuit, for blocking the flow of a direct current, etc.; a capacitor.

con·den·si·ble (kən dĕn/sə bəl), *adj.* condensable.

con·de·scend (kŏn/dĭ sĕnd/), *v.i.* **1.** to waive ceremony voluntarily and assume equality with an inferior. **2.** to stoop or deign (to do something). **3.** to behave as if one is conscious of descending from a superior position, rank, or dignity. **4.** *Obs.* to yield. **5.** *Obs.* to assent. [ME *condescende(n),* t. F: m. *condescendre,* t. LL: m. *condēscendere* stoop] **—con/de·scend/ence,** *n.*

con·de·scend·ing (kŏn/dĭ sĕn/dĭng), *adj.* showing or implying a gracious descent from dignity; patronizing. **—con/de·scend/ing·ly,** *adv.*

con·de·scen·sion (kŏn/dĭ sĕn/shən), *n.* act of condescending; gracious or patronizing complaisance.

con·dign (kən dīn/), *adj.* (chiefly of punishment, etc.) well-deserved; fitting; adequate. [ME *condigne,* t. F, t. L: m. *condignus* wholly worthy] **—con·dign/ly,** *adv.*

Con·dil·lac (kôn dē yåk/), *n.* **Étienne Bonnot de** (ē tyĕn/ bô nô/ də), 1715–80, French philosopher.

con·di·ment (kŏn/də mənt), *n.* something used to give flavor and relish to food, as a sauce or seasoning. [t. L: s. *condīmentum* spice] **—con/di·men/tal,** *adj.*

con·di·tion (kən dĭsh/ən), *n.* **1.** particular mode of being of a person or thing; situation with respect to circumstances; existing state or case. **2.** state of health. **3.** fit or requisite state. **4.** social position. **5.** a restricting, limiting, or modifying circumstance. **6.** a circumstance indispensable to some result; a prerequisite; that on which something else is contingent. **7.** something demanded as an essential part of an agreement. **8.** *Law.* **a.** a stipulation in a contract making some liability contingent on the happening of a future uncertain event. **b.** the event. **9. on condition that, if;** provided that. **10.** *U.S.* **a.** a requirement imposed on a college student who fails to reach the prescribed standard in a study at the end of the regular period of instruction, permitting credit to be established by later performance. **b.** the study or subject to which the requirement is attached. **11.** *Gram.* protasis. **12.** *Logic.* antecedent. **—***v.t.* **13.** to put in fit or proper state. **14.** to form or be a condition of; determine, limit, or restrict as a condition. **15.** to subject to something as a condition; make conditional (fol. by *on* or *upon*). **16.** to subject to particular conditions or circumstances. **17.** *U.S.* to impose a condition on (a student). **18.** to test (a commodity) to ascertain its condition. **19.** to make it a condition; stipulate. **20.** *Psychol.* to cause a conditioned response in. —*v.i.* **21.** to make conditions. [ME *condicion*, t. L: s. *condicio* (erroneously *conditio*) agreement, stipulation, circumstances] —**con·di'tion·er,** *n.* —**Syn. 1.** See **state. 6.** prerequisite. **7.** requirement, provision, proviso.

con·di·tion·al (kən dĭsh′ən əl), *adj.* **1.** imposing, containing, or depending on a condition or conditions; not absolute; made or granted on certain terms: *a conditional agreement, sale, etc.* **2.** *Gram.* (of a sentence, clause, or mood) involving or expressing a condition. For example: *If the suit is expensive* (conditional clause), *don't buy it.* **3.** *Logic.* **a.** (of a proposition) asserting that one state of affairs is or will be realized if some other state of affairs is realized, as in *if Smith is 21 years old, he is eligible to vote.* **b.** (of a syllogism) containing a conditional proposition as a premise. **4.** (in certain languages) a mood, tense, or other category used in expressing conditions, often corresponding to an English verb preceded by *if:* Spanish *"comería"* (*he would eat*) *is in the conditional.* —**con·di'tion·al'i·ty,** *n.* —**con·di'tion·al·ly,** *adv.*
conditional probability, *Statsitics.* the probability of the occurrence of an event under the condition that only a portion of the cases or alternatives are to be considered.

con·di·tioned (kən dĭsh′ənd), *adj.* existing under or subject to conditions. —**Ant.** free, absolute.
conditioned response, *Psychol.* a learned response resulting from the fact that whenever a stimulus has a motor outlet, another stimulus occurring at the same time will tend to acquire the same outlet. Also, **conditioned reflex.**

con·dole (kən dōl′), *v.,* **-doled, -doling.** —*v.i.* **1.** to express sympathy with one in affliction; grieve (fol. by *with*). —*v.t.* **2.** *Obs.* to grieve with (another) or over (another's misfortune). [t. LL: m.s. *condolēre* suffer greatly] —**con·do·la·to·ry** (kən dō′lə tōr′ĭ), *adj.* —**con·dol'er,** *n.* —**con·dol'ing·ly,** *adv.*
con·do·lence (kən dō′ləns), *n.* expression of sympathy with a person in affliction. Also, **con·dole'ment.**
con do·lo·re (kôn dô lō′rĕ), *Music.* sorrowfully. [It.]
con·do·min·i·um (kŏn′də mĭn′ĭ əm), *n.* **1.** joint or concurrent dominion. **2.** *Internat. Law.* joint sovereignty over a territory by several foreign states. [t. NL, f. L: *con-* CON- + *dominium* lordship]
con·do·na·tion (kŏn′dō nā′shən), *n.* act of condoning; the overlooking or implied forgiving of an offense.
con·done (kən dōn′), *v.t.,* **-doned, -doning. 1.** to pardon or overlook (an offense). **2.** to cause the condonation of. **3.** *Law.* to forgive, or act so as to imply forgiveness of (a violation of the marriage vow). [t. L: m. s. *condōnāre* give up] —**con·don'er,** *n.*
con·dor (kŏn′dər), *n.* **1.** a large vulture of the New World, as the **Andean condor** (*Sarcorhamphus gryphus*) and **California condor** (*Gymnogyps californianus*). **2.** a gold coin of South American countries, bearing the figure of a condor, that of Chile being worth about $2.05 and that of Ecuador about $8.49. [t. Sp., t. Kechua: m. *cuntur*]
Con·dor·cet (kôn dôr sĕ′), *n.* **Marie Jean Antoine Nicolas Caritat,** (mä rē′ zhäN äN twän′ nē kô lä′ kä rē tä′), **Marquis de,** 1743–94, French mathematician and philosopher.
con·dot·tie·re (kôn′dôt tyĕ′rĕ), *n., pl.* **-ri** (-rē). (in Italy and elsewhere, esp. in the 14th and 15th centuries) a professional military captain or leader of mercenaries, in the service of princes or states at war. [It.: leader, der. *condotto* mercenary (soldier), g. L *conductus,* pp., led together, hired]
con·duce (kən dūs′, -dōōs′), *v.i.,* **-duced, -ducing.** to lead or contribute to a result (fol by *to*). [late ME, t. L: m. s. *condūcere* lead together, hire] —**Ant.** hinder.
con·du·cive (kən dū′sĭv, -dōō′-), *adj.* conducing; contributive; helpful (fol. by *to*). —**con·du'cive·ness,** *n.*
con·duct (*n.* kŏn′dŭkt; *v.* kən dŭkt′), *n.* **1.** personal behavior; way of acting; deportment: *good conduct.* **2.** direction or management; execution: *the conduct of a business.* **3.** act of conducting; guidance; escort. **4.** *Obs.* a guide; an escort. —*v.t.* **5.** to behave (oneself). **6.** to direct in action or course; manage; carry on: *to conduct a campaign.* **7.** to direct as leader: *to conduct an orchestra.* **8.** to lead or guide; escort. **9.** to serve as a channel or medium for (heat, electricity, sound, etc.). —*v.i.* **10.** to lead. **11.** to act as conductor. **12.** *U.S. Obs.* to behave. [t. LL: s. *conductus,* n., escort, der. L *condūcere* bring together; r. ME *conduyt,* t. OF: m. *conduit*] —**con·duct'i·ble,** *adj.* —**con·duct'i·bil'i·ty,** *n.* —**Syn. 1.** See **behavior. 6.** superintend, supervise, regulate, control. **8.** See **guide.**
con·duct·ance (kən dŭk′təns), *n.* *Elect.* the conducting power of a conductor (the reciprocal of *resistance*).

con·duc·tion (kən dŭk′shən), *n.* **1.** a conducting, as of water through a pipe. **2.** *Physics.* **a.** transmission through a conductor. **b.** conductivity. **3.** *Physiol.* the carrying of an impulse by a nerve or other tissue.
con·duc·tive (kən dŭk′tĭv), *adj.* having the property of conducting.
con·duc·tiv·i·ty (kŏn′dŭk tĭv′ə tē), *n., pl.* **-ties. 1.** *Physics.* the property or power of conducting heat, electricity, or sound. **2.** *Elect.* the conductance between opposite faces of a one centimeter cube of a given material (the reciprocal of *resistivity*).
con·duc·tor (kən dŭk′tər), *n.* **1.** one who conducts; a leader, guide, director, or manager. **2.** the official in charge of a railroad train, bus, or streetcar (in England, only of a bus or streetcar). **3.** the director of an orchestra or chorus, who communicates to the performers by motions of a baton, etc. his interpretation of the music. **4.** that which conducts. **5.** a substance, body, or device that readily conducts heat, electricity, sound, etc. **6.** a lightning rod. —**con·duc'tor·ship',** *n.* —**con·duc·tress** (kən dŭk′trĭs), *n., esp. Brit. n.fem.*
con·duit (kŏn′dĭt, -dōō′ĭt), *n.* **1.** a pipe, tube, or the like, for conveying water or other fluid. **2.** some similar natural passage. **3.** *Elect.* a structure containing one or more ducts. **4.** *Archaic.* a fountain. [ME *condit,* t. OF: m. *conduit,* g. LL *conductus.* See CONDUCT]
con·du·pli·cate (kŏn dū′plə kĭt, -dōō′-), *adj.* *Bot.* (of a leaf in the bud) folded lengthwise with the upper face of the blade within.
con·dyle (kŏn′dĭl), *n.* *Anat.* a rounded protuberance on a bone, serving to form an articulation with another bone. [t. F., t. L: m.s. *condylus,* t. Gk.: m. *kóndylos* knuckle, bony knob] —**con'dy·lar,** *adj.*
con·dy·loid (kŏn′dəloid′), *adj.* resembling, or pertaining to, a condyle.
con·dy·lo·ma (kŏn′dəlō′mə), *n., pl.* **-mata** (-mətə). *Pathol.* a wartlike excrescence on the skin, usually in the region of the anus or genitals. [t. L, t. Gk.: m. *kondýlōma,* der. *kóndylos* CONDYLE] —**con·dy·lom·a·tous** (kŏn′də lŏm′ə təs, -lō′mə-), *adj.*
cone (kōn), *n., v.,* **coned, coning.** —*n.* **1.** *Geom.* a solid whose surface is generated by the straight lines joining a fixed point to the points of a plane curve whose plane does not contain the fixed point. When the plane curve is a circle and the fixed point lies on the perpendicular to the plane of the circle through its center the cone is a **right circular cone.** When the plane curve is a circle and the fixed point is not so situated the cone is an **oblique circular cone. 2.** *Mach.* a mechanical part having the shape of a cone or conoid. **3.** *Bot.* **a.** the more or less conical multiple fruit of the pine, fir, etc., consisting of imbricated or valvate scales bearing naked ovules or seeds; a strobile. **b.** a similar fruit, as in cycads, club mosses, etc. **4.** anything cone-shaped: *an ice cream cone.* —*v.t.* **5.** to shape like a cone or the segment of a cone. [t. L: m.s. *cōnus,* t. Gk.: m. *kōnos*]

Cone

cone·flow·er (kōn′flou′ər), *n.* **1.** a rudbeckia. **2.** any of various allied plants.
cone·nose (kōn′nōz′), *n.* assassin bug.
Con·es·to·ga wagon (kŏn′ə stō′gə), a large, heavy, broad-wheeled covered wagon, used esp. for transporting goods, the principal freighting medium westward prior to railroads in North America.
co·ney (kō′nĭ, kŭn′ĭ), *n., pl.* **-neys.** cony.
Co·ney Island (kō′nĭ), an island in New York City, off the S shore of Long Island: seaside resort and amusement center. 5 mi. long.
conf., (L *confer*) compare.
con·fab (kŏn′făb), *n., v.,* **-fabbed, -fabbing.** *Colloq.* —*n.* **1.** a confabulation. —*v.i.* **2.** to confabulate.
con·fab·u·late (kən făb′yə lāt′), *v.i.,* **-lated, -lating.** to talk together; converse. [t. L: m. s. *confābulātus,* pp.] —**con·fab'u·la'tion,** *n.*
con·far·re·a·tion (kŏn′făr′ĭ ā′shən), *n.* (among the ancient Romans) the highest form of marriage, marked by the offering of a cake made of spelt. [t. L: s. *confarreātio*]
con·fect (*v.* kən fĕkt′, *n.* kŏn′fĕkt), *v.t.* **1.** to make up, compound, or prepare from ingredients or materials. **2.** to make into a preserve or confection. **3.** to construct, form, or make. —*n.* **4.** a preserved, candied, or other sweet confection. [t. L: s. *confectus,* pp., put together]
con·fec·tion (kən fĕk′shən), *n.* **1.** the process of compounding, preparing, or making. **2.** a sweet preparation (liquid or dry) of fruit or the like, as a preserve or candy. **3.** a candy or bonbon. **4.** a medicinal preparation, now one made with the aid of sugar, honey, or syrup. **5.** a ready-made garment, esp. a woman's frilly garment. —*v.t.* **6.** to prepare as a confection. [ME, t. L: s. *confectio* a making ready]
con·fec·tion·ar·y (kən fĕk′shə nĕr′ĭ), *n., pl.* **-aries,** *adj.* —*n.* **1.** a place where confections are kept or made. **2.** a confection or sweetmeat. **3.** *Obs.* a confectioner. —*adj.* **4.** pertaining to or of the nature of confections or their making.
con·fec·tion·er (kən fĕk′shən ər), *n.* one who makes or sells candies or bonbons, and sometimes ice cream, cakes, etc.
confectioners' sugar, a finely ground powdered sugar.

---

b., blend of, blended; **c.,** cognate with; **d.,** dialect, dialectal; **der.,** derived from; **f.,** formed from; **g.,** going back to; **m.,** modification of; **r.,** replacing; **s.,** stem of; **t.,** taken from; **?,** perhaps. See the full key on inside cover.

con·fec·tion·er·y (kənfĕk/shənĕr/Y), *n.*, *pl.* **-eries.**
1. confections or sweetmeats collectively. **2.** the work or business of a confectioner. **3.** a confectioner's shop, sometimes used in England for a bakery.

con·fed·er·a·cy (kənfĕd/ər ə sĬ, -fĕd/rə sĬ), *n.*, *pl.* **-cies. 1.** a body of confederated persons, parties, or states. **2.** a union of confederated persons, parties, etc. **3.** a combination for unlawful purposes; a conspiracy. **4. the Confederacy,** the Confederate States of America.

con·fed·er·ate (*adj.*, *n.* kən fĕd/ər Ĭt, -fĕd/rĬt; *v.* kən-fĕd/ə rāt/), *adj.*, *n.*, *v.*, **-ated, -ating. —adj. 1.** confederated; united in a league or alliance, or a conspiracy. **2.** (*cap.*) denoting or pertaining to the Confederate States of America: *the Confederate army.* —*n.* **3.** one united with others in a confederacy; an ally. **4.** an accomplice. **5.** (*cap.*) an adherent of the Confederate States of America. —*v.t.*, *v.i.* **6.** to unite in a league or alliance, or a conspiracy. [ME, t. LL: m. s. *confoederātus*, pp., united in a league]

Confederate States of America, the name assumed by the eleven Southern States which seceded from the American Union in 1860-61.

con·fed·er·a·tion (kən fĕd/ə rā/shən), *n.* **1.** act of confederating. **2.** state of being confederated. **3.** a league or alliance. **4.** a body of confederates, esp. of states more or less permanently united for common purposes. **5. the Confederation,** the union of the American colonies from 1781 to 1789 under the Articles of Confederation. —**Syn. 3.** See **alliance.**

con·fed·er·a·tive (kənfĕd/ə rā/tĬv), *adj.* pertaining to a confederation.

con·fer (kən fûr/), *v.t.*, **-ferred, -ferring. —*v.t.* 1.** to bestow as a gift, favor, honor, etc. (fol. by *on* or *upon*). **2.** to compare. —*v.i.* **3.** consult together; compare opinions; carry on a discussion or deliberation. [t. L: s. *cŏnferre* bring together] —**con·fer/ment,** *n.* —**con·fer/ra·ble,** *adj.* —**con·fer/rer,** *n.* —**Syn. 1.** See **give. 3.** See **consult.**

con·fer·ee (kŏn/fə rē/), *n.* **1.** *U.S.* one who is conferred with or takes part in a conference. **2.** one on whom something is conferred. Also, **con/fer·ree/.**

con·fer·ence (kŏn/fər əns), *n.* **1.** a meeting for consultation or discussion. **2.** act of conferring or consulting together; consultation, esp. on an important or serious matter. **3.** *Govt.* a meeting (usually of committees) to settle disagreements between the two legislative groups. **4.** *Eccles.* **a.** an official assembly of clergy, or of clergy and laymen, customary in many Christian denominations. **b.** a group of churches the representatives of which regularly meet in such an assembly. **5.** *U.S. Sports.* an organization of teams. —**con·fer·en·tial** (kŏn/fə rĕn/shəl), *adj.* —**Syn. 1.** See **convention.**

con·fer·va (kŏn fûr/və), *n.*, *pl.* **-vae** (-vē), **-vas.** any simple filamentous green alga. [t. L: kind of water plant] —**con·fer·void** (kŏn fûr/void), *adj.*, *n.*

con·fess (kən fĕs/), *v.t.* **1.** to acknowledge or avow: *to confess a secret, fault, crime, debt, etc.* **2.** to own or admit; admit the truth or validity of: *I must confess that I haven't read it.* **3.** to acknowledge one's belief in; declare adherence to. **4.** to declare (one's sins) or declare the sins of (oneself), esp. to a priest, for the obtaining of absolution. **5.** (of a priest) to hear the confession of. **6.** *Archaic.* to reveal by circumstances. —*v.i.* **7.** to make confession; plead guilty; own (fol. by *to*). **8.** to make confession of sins, esp. to a priest. [ME *confesse*(*n*), t. LL: m. *confessāre*, der. L *confessus*, pp.] —**Syn. 1.** See **acknowledge. —Ant. 1.** conceal. **2.** deny.

con·fess·ed·ly (kən fĕs/Ĭd lĬ), *adv.* by confession or acknowledgment; admittedly.

con·fes·sion (kən fĕsh/ən), *n.* **1.** acknowledgment or avowal; admission or concession: *a confession of guilt.* **2.** acknowledgment of sin or sinfulness. **3.** a disclosing of sins to a priest to obtain forgiveness. **4.** that which is confessed. **5.** Also, **confession of faith.** a formal profession of belief and acceptance of church doctrines, as before being admitted to church membership. **6.** the tomb of a martyr or confessor, or the altar or shrine connected with it. [ME, t. L: s. *confessio*]

con·fes·sion·al (kən fĕsh/ən əl), *adj.* **1.** of, or of the nature of, confession. —*n.* **2.** the place set apart for the hearing of confessions by a priest.

con·fes·sion·ar·y (kən fĕsh/ə nĕr/Ĭ), *adj.* of or pertaining to confession, esp. auricular confession of sins.

con·fes·sor (kən fĕs/ər), *n.* **1.** one who confesses. **2.** a priest authorized to hear confessions. **3.** one who confesses and adheres to the Christian religion, esp. in spite of persecution and torture: *Edward the Confessor.* Also, **con·fess/er.**

con·fet·ti (kən fĕt/Ĭ; *It.* kôn fĕt/tē), *n. pl.*, *sing.* **-fetto** (-fĕt/tō). **1.** small bits of colored paper, thrown at carnivals, weddings, etc. **2.** confections; bonbons. [t. It., pl. of *confetto* comfit]

con·fi·dant (kŏn/fə dănt/, kŏn/fə dănt/), *n.* one to whom secrets are confided. [t. F, t. It.: m. *confidente*, t. L: m. s. *confīdens*, ppr., trusting] —**con/fi·dante/,** *n. fem.*

con·fide (kən fīd/), *v.*, **-fided, -fiding. —*v.i.* 1.** to show trust by imparting secrets (fol. by *in*). **2.** to have full trust: *confiding in that parting promise.* —*v.t.* **3.** to tell in assurance of secrecy. **4.** to entrust; commit to the charge, knowledge, or good faith of another. [late ME, t. L: m.s. *confīdere* trust altogether] —**con·fid/er,** *n.*

con·fi·dence (kŏn/fə dəns), *n.* **1.** full trust; belief in the trustworthiness or reliability of a person or thing. **2. in confidence,** as a secret or private matter, not to be divulged or communicated to others: *I told him in confidence.* **3.** *Brit. Pol.* the wish to retain the incumbent government in office, as shown by a vote on a particular issue: *this issue is a question of confidence.* **4.** self-reliance, assurance, or boldness. **5.** presumption. **6.** certitude or assured expectation. **7.** a confidential communication. **8.** a ground of trust. —**Syn. 1.** See **trust. 4.** CONFIDENCE, ASSURANCE both imply a faith in oneself. CONFIDENCE may imply trust in oneself or arrogant self-conceit. ASSURANCE implies even more sureness of oneself; this may be shown as undisturbed calm or as offensive boastfulness or headstrong conduct.

confidence game, the crime of obtaining money or property by fraud, after obtaining the victim's confidence. Also, *Brit.,* **confidence trick.**

confidence limits, *Statistics.* a pair of numbers used to estimate a characteristic of a population from a sample, which are such that it can be stated with a specified probability that the pair of numbers calculated from a sample will include the value of the population characteristic between them.

confidence man, one who swindles by a confidence game.

con·fi·dent (kŏn/fə dənt), *adj.* **1.** having strong belief or full assurance; sure: *confident of victory.* **2.** sure of oneself; bold: *a confident bearing.* **3.** overbold. **4.** *Obs.* trustful or confiding. —*n.* **5.** a confidant. —**con/fi·dent·ly,** *adv.* —**Syn. 1.** certain, positive. See **sure.**

con·fi·den·tial (kŏn/fə dĕn/shəl), *adj.* **1.** spoken or written in confidence; secret: *a confidential communication.* **2.** betokening confidence or intimacy; imparting private matters: *a confidential tone.* **3.** enjoying another's confidence; entrusted with secrets or private affairs: *a confidential secretary.* —**con/fi·den/ti·al/i·ty, con/fi·den/tial·ness,** *n.* —**con/fi·den/tial·ly,** *adv.* —**Syn. 3.** See **familiar.**

confidential communication, *Law.* a confidential statement made to a lawyer, doctor, or priest, or to one's husband or wife, privileged against disclosure in court if the privilege is claimed by the client, patient, penitent, or spouse.

con·fid·ing (kən fī/dĬng), *adj.* trustful; credulous or unsuspicious. —**con·fid/ing·ly,** *adv.*

con·fig·u·ra·tion (kən fĭg/yə rā/shən), *n.* **1.** the relative disposition of the parts or elements of a thing. **2.** external form, as resulting from this; conformation. **3.** *Astron.* **a.** the relative position or aspect of heavenly bodies. **b.** a group of stars. **4.** *Physics, Chem.* the relative position in space of the atoms in a molecule. [t. LL: s. *configūrātio*, der. L *configūrāre* shape after some pattern] —**con·fig/u·ra/tion·al, con·fig·u·ra·tive** (kən-fĭg/yə rə tĬv, -rā/-), *adj.*

con·fig·u·ra·tion·ism (kən fĭg/yə rā/shə nĬz/əm), *n.* Gestalt psychology.

con·fine (kən fīn/ *for 1-3, 5, 6b;* kŏn/fīn *for 4, 6a*), *v.*, **-fined, -fining,** *n.* —*v.t.* **1.** to enclose within bounds; limit or restrict. **2.** to shut or keep in; imprison. **3.** to be in childbed, or be delivered of a child (used in the passive). [t. F: m. s. *confiner*, t. It.: m. *confinare*, der. *confīno* bordering, g. L *confīnis*] —*n.* **4.** (*usually pl.*) a boundary or bound; a border or frontier. **5.** *Poetic.* confinement. **6.** *Obs.* **a.** (*usually pl.*) a region. **b.** a place of confinement. [t. F: m. *confīns* (pl.), g. L *confīnia*, pl. of *confīnium* a border] —**con·fin/er,** *n.* —**Syn. 1.** circumscribe. —**Ant. 1, 2.** free.

con·fine·ment (kən fīn/mənt), *n.* **1.** act of confining. **2.** state of being confined. **3.** the lying-in of a woman in childbed. **4.** *Mil.* state of being held in a guard house or prison, while awaiting trial or as punishment (as distinguished from *arrest*). [t. F, der. *confiner* CONFINE, v.]

con·firm (kən fûrm/), *v.t.* **1.** to make certain or sure; corroborate; verify: *this confirmed my suspicions.* **2.** to make valid or binding by some formal or legal act; sanction; ratify: *to confirm an agreement, appointment, etc.* **3.** to make firm or more firm; add strength to; settle or establish firmly: *the news confirmed my resolution.* **4.** to strengthen (a person) in habit, resolution, opinion, etc. **5.** *Eccles.* to administer the rite of confirmation to. [t. L: s. *confirmāre* make firm; r. ME *conferme*(*n*), t. OF: m. *confermer*] —**con·firm/a·ble,** *adj.* —**con·firm/-er;** *Law,* **con·firm·or** (kŏn/fər môr/, kən fûr/mər), *n.* —**Syn. 1.** substantiate, authenticate. —**Ant. 1.** disprove. **2.** invalidate. **3.** shake.

con·fir·ma·tion (kŏn/fər mā/shən), *n.* **1.** act of confirming. **2.** that which confirms, as a corroborative statement. **3.** *Eccles.* **a.** a rite administered to baptized persons, in some churches as a sacrament for confirming and strengthening the recipient in the Christian faith, in others as a rite without sacramental character by which the recipient is admitted to full communion with the church. **b.** (among American Jews) a solemn form of initiation of the Jewish youth into their ancestral faith. In the case of boys, it is used as a substitution for the bar mizvah ceremony, or as supplementary to it, or as the equivalent of it.

con·firm·a·to·ry (kən fûr/mə tôr/Ĭ), *adj.* serving to confirm; corroborative. Also, **con·firm/a·tive.**

con·firmed (kən fûrmd/), *adj.* **1.** made firm; settled; ratified. **2.** firmly established in a habit or condition; inveterate: *a confirmed drunk.* **3.** (of a disease) chronic.

con·fis·ca·ble (kən fĭs′kə bəl), *adj.* liable to be confiscated.

con·fis·cate (kŏn′fĭs kāt′, kən fĭs′kāt), *v.*, **-cated, -cating,** *adj.* —*v.t.* **1.** to seize as forfeited to the public treasury; appropriate, by way of penalty, to public use. **2.** to seize as if by authority; appropriate summarily. —*adj.* **3.** confiscated. [t. L: m.s. *confiscātus*, pp., put away in a chest] —**con′fis·ca′tion**, *n.* —**con′fis·ca′tor**, *n.*

con·fis·ca·to·ry (kən fĭs′kə tōr′ĭ), *adj.* characterized by or effecting confiscation.

Con·fit·e·or (kən fĭt′ĭ ōr′), *n. Rom. Cath. Ch.* a form of prayer beginning with "Confiteor," in which a general confession of sinfulness is made, used at the beginning of the mass and on other occasions. [t. L: I confess]

con·fi·ture (kŏn′fĭ chŏŏr′), *n.* a confection; a preserve, as of fruit. [ME, t. F, der. *confit* comfit, pp. of *confire* preserve, prepare, g. L *conficere*]

con·fla·gra·tion (kŏn′flə grā′shən), *n.* a large and destructive fire. [t. L: s. *conflagrātio*] —**Syn.** See **flame.**

con·fla·tion (kən flā′shən), *n. Bibliog.* **1.** the combination of two variant texts into a new one. **2.** the result. [t. LL: s. *conflātio*, der. L *conflāre* blow together]

con·flict (*v.* kən flĭkt′; *n.* kŏn′flĭkt), *v.i.* **1.** to come into collision; clash, or be in opposition or at variance. **2.** to contend; do battle. —*n.* **3.** a battle or struggle, esp. a prolonged struggle; strife. **4.** controversy; a quarrel: *conflicts between church and state.* **5.** discord of action, feeling, or effect; antagonism, as of interests or principles: *a conflict of ideas.* **6.** a striking together; collision. [t. L: s. *conflictus*, pp., struck together] —**con·flic′tion,** *n.* —**con·flic′tive,** *adj.* —**Syn.** 3. See **fight.** **5.** contention, opposition, variance. —**Ant.** 4. accord.

con·flu·ence (kŏn′flōō əns), *n.* **1.** a flowing together of two or more streams. **2.** the place of junction. **3.** the body of water so formed. **4.** a coming together of people or things. **5.** a throng; an assemblage. Also, **con·flux** (kŏn′flŭks).

con·flu·ent (kŏn′flōō ənt), *adj.* **1.** flowing or running together; blending into one. **2.** *Pathol.* **a.** running together: *confluent efflorescences.* **b.** characterized by confluent efflorescences: *confluent smallpox.* —*n.* **3.** one of two or more confluent streams. **4.** a tributary stream. [t. L: s. *confluens*, ppr., flowing together]

con·fo·cal (kŏn fō′kəl), *adj. Math.* having the same focus or foci.

con·form (kən fôrm′), *v.i.* **1.** to act in accord or harmony; comply (fol. by *to*). **2.** to become similar in form or character. **3.** to comply with the usages of the Established Church of England. —*v.t.* **4.** to make similar in form or character. **5.** to bring into correspondence or harmony. [ME *conforme(n)*, t. F: m. *conformer*, t. L: m. *conformāre* fashion] —**con·form′er,** *n.* —**Syn.** 5. adapt, adjust, accommodate. —**Ant.** 1, 3. dissent. 4. differ.

con·form·a·ble (kən fôr′mə bəl), *adj.* **1.** corresponding in form or character; similar. **2.** exhibiting agreement or harmony (usually fol. by *to*). **3.** compliant, acquiescent, or submissive. **4.** *Geol.* (of strata or beds) having the same dip and strike as a result of successive depositions uninterrupted by crustal movement. —**con·form′a·bil′i·ty,** **con·form′a·ble·ness,** *n.* —**con·form′a·bly,** *adv.*

con·form·ance (kən fôr′məns), *n.* act of conforming; conformity.

con·for·ma·tion (kŏn′fôr mā′shən), *n.* **1.** manner of formation; structure; form. **2.** symmetrical disposition or arrangement of parts. **3.** act of conforming; adaptation; adjustment. **4.** state of being conformed.

Conformable and unconformable strata

A and B, two sets of unconformable strata; CD. line of junction of A and B

con·form·ist (kən fôr′mĭst), *n.* **1.** one who conforms to a usage or practice. **2.** one who conforms to the usages of the Established Church of England.

con·form·i·ty (kən fôr′mə tĭ), *n., pl.* **-ties. 1.** correspondence in form or character; agreement, congruity, or accordance. **2.** compliance or acquiescence. **3.** compliance with the usages of the Church of England.

con·found (kŏn found′, kən-; *for 7 usually* kŏn′found′), *v.t.* **1.** to mingle so that the elements cannot be distinguished or separated. **2.** to treat or regard erroneously as identical; mix or associate by mistake. **3.** to throw into confusion or disorder: *confusion worse confounded.* **4.** to perplex, as with sudden disturbance or surprise. **5.** *Archaic.* to put to shame; abash. **6.** *Archaic.* to defeat or overthrow; bring to ruin or naught. **7.** (in mild imprecations) to damn: *confound it!* **8.** *Obs.* to spend uselessly, or waste. [ME *confounde(n)*, t. OF: m. *confondre*, g. L *confundere* pour together, mix, confuse] —**con·found′er,** *n.*

con·found·ed (kŏn foun′dĭd, kən-), *adj.* **1.** damned (a euphemism): *a confounded lie.* **2.** *Colloq.* execrable; odious; detestable. —**con·found′ed·ly,** *adv.*

con·fra·ter·ni·ty (kŏn′frə tûr′nə tĭ), *n., pl.* **-ties. 1.** a lay brotherhood devoted to some particular religious or charitable service. **2.** a society or body of men united for some purpose or in some profession. [late ME *confraternite*, t. ML: m.s. *confrāternitas* brotherhood, der. *confrāter.* See CONFRERE]

con·frere (kŏn′frâr), *n.* a fellow member of a fraternity, profession, etc.; a colleague. [ME, t. F, trans. of ML *confrāter* colleague]

con·front (kən frŭnt′), *v.t.* **1.** to stand or come in front of; stand or meet facing. **2.** to face in hostility or defiance; oppose. **3.** to set face to face. **4.** to bring together for examination or comparison. [t. F: s. *confronter*, t. ML: m. s. *confrontārī*, f. L: *con-* CON- + s. *frons* forehead + -*ārī*, inf. ending] —**con·fron·ta·tion** (kŏn′frən tā′shən), **con·front′ment,** *n.* —**con·front′er,** *n.*

Con·fu·cius (kən fū′shəs), *n.* (Chin. *Kung-fu-tse*) 551-478 B.C., Chinese philosopher and teacher of principles of conduct. His highest standards of conduct were treating others as you wish to be treated, loyalty, intelligence, and the fullest development of the individual in the five chief relationships of life: ruler and subject, father and son, elder and younger brother, husband and wife, friend and friend. —**Con·fu′cian,** *adj., n.* —**Con·fu′cian·ism,** *n.* —**Con·fu′cian·ist,** *n., adj.*

con·fuse (kən fūz′), *v.t.,* **-fused, -fusing. 1.** to combine without order or clearness; jumble; render indistinct. **2.** to throw into disorder. **3.** to fail to distinguish between; associate by mistake; confound: *to confuse dates.* **4.** to perplex or bewilder. **5.** to disconcert or abash. **6.** *Obs.* to bring to ruin or naught. [back formation from *confused,* f. ME *confus* (t. F, t. L: s. *confūsus*, pp., confounded) + -ED²] —**con·fus·ed·ly** (kən fū′zĭd lĭ, -fūzd′lĭ), *adv.* —**con·fus′ed·ness,** *n.* —**con·fus′ing·ly,** *adv.* —**Syn.** 4. CONFUSE, DISCONCERT, EMBARRASS imply temporary interference with the working of one's mind. To CONFUSE is to produce a general bewilderment: *to confuse by giving complicated directions.* To DISCONCERT is quickly or violently to disturb one's mind by irritation, perplexities, etc., making it difficult for him to collect his thoughts: *to disconcert by asking irrelevant questions.* To EMBARRASS is to cause one to be ill at ease or uncomfortable, so that his usual judgment and presence of mind desert him: *to embarrass by treating with unexpected rudeness.* —**Ant.** 5. compose.

con·fu·sion (kən fū′zhən), *n.* **1.** act of confusing. **2.** state of being confused. **3.** disorder. **4.** lack of clearness or distinctness. **5.** embarrassment or abashment. **6.** perplexity; bewilderment. **7.** *Psychiatry.* a disturbed mental state; a clouding of consciousness; disorientation. [ME, t. L: s. *confūsio*] —**Syn.** 3. turmoil.

con·fu·ta·tion (kŏn′fyōō tā′shən), *n.* **1.** act of confuting. **2.** that which confutes. **3.** (in the classically arranged speech) the fourth section, given over to direct refutation. —**con·fut·a·tive** (kən fū′tə tĭv), *adj.*

con·fute (kən fūt′), *v.t.,* **-futed, -futing. 1.** to prove to be false or defective; disprove: *to confute an argument.* **2.** to prove to be wrong; convict of error by argument or proof: *to confute one's opponent.* **3.** to confound or bring to naught. [t. L: m. s. *confūtāre*] —**con·fut′er,** *n.*

Cong., **1.** Congress. **2.** Congressional.

cong., (L *congius*) gallon.

con·gé (kŏn′zhā; *Fr.* kôɴ zhě′), *n.* **1.** leave to depart, or dismissal; leave or permission; leave-taking. **2.** a bow or obeisance. **3.** *Archit.* a type of concave molding. [F. See CONGEE]

con·geal (kən jēl′), *v.t., v.i.* **1.** to change from a fluid or soft to a solid or rigid state, as by freezing or cooling. **2.** to stiffen or coagulate, as blood. **3.** to make or become fixed, as sentiments, principles, etc. [ME *congele(n)*, t. L: m. *congelāre* cause to freeze together] —**con·geal′a·ble,** *adj.* —**con·geal′er,** *n.* —**con·geal′ment,** *n.*

con·gee (kŏn′jē), *n., v.,* **-geed, -geeing.** *Obsolesc.* —*n.* **1.** congé. —*v.i.* **2.** to take one's leave. **3.** to bow. [ME *congye,* t. OF: m. *congie* (F *congé*), g. L *commeātus* a going to and fro, leave of absence]

con·ge·la·tion (kŏn′jə lā′shən), *n.* **1.** act or process of congealing. **2.** state of being congealed. **3.** the product of congealing; a concretion; a coagulation.

con·ge·ner (kŏn′jə nər), *n.* **1.** one of the same kind or class. **2.** a fellow member of a genus, as of plants or animals. [t. L: of the same kind]

con·ge·ner·ic (kŏn′jə něr′ĭk), *adj.* of the same kind or genus. Also, **con·gen·er·ous** (kən jěn′ər əs).

con·gen·ial (kən jēn′yəl), *adj.* **1.** suited or adapted in spirit, feeling, temper, etc.: *congenial companions.* **2.** agreeable or pleasing; agreeing or suited in nature or character: *a congenial task.* [f. CON- + s. L *genius* spirit + -AL¹] —**con·ge·ni·al·i·ty** (kən jē′nĭ ǎl′ə tĭ), *n.* —**con·gen′ial·ly,** *adv.* —**Syn.** 1. kindred, sympathetic.

con·gen·i·tal (kən jěn′ə təl), *adj.* existing at or from one's birth: *a congenital defect.* [f. s. L *congenitus* born together with + -AL¹] —**con·gen′i·tal·ly,** *adv.*

con·ger (kŏng′gər), *n.* **1.** a large marine eel, *Conger conger,* sometimes growing to a length of 10 feet, which is caught for food along the coast of Europe. **2.** any other species of the family *Congridae.* Also, **conger eel.** [ME *congre,* t. OF, g. L *conger, congrus,* t. Gk.: m. *góngros*]

con·ge·ries (kŏn jĭr′ēz), *n. sing. and pl.* a collection of several particles or bodies in one mass; an assemblage; aggregation; heap. [t. L: heap, pile]

con·gest (kən jěst′), *v.t.* **1.** to fill to excess; overcrowd. **2.** *Pathol.* to cause an unnatural accumulation of blood in the vessels of (an organ or part). **3.** *Obs.* to heap together. —*v.i.* **4.** to become congested. [t. L: s. *congestus,* pp., brought together] —**con·ges′tion,** *n.* —**con·ges′tive,** *adj.*

con·gi·us (kŏn′jĭ əs), *n., pl.* **congii** (kŏn′jĭ ī′). **1.** *Pharm.* a gallon. **2.** an ancient Roman unit of liquid measure, equal to about 5 U.S. gallon. [t. L]

b., blend of, blended; c., cognate with; d., dialect, dialectal; der., derived from; f., formed from; g., going back to; m., modification of; r., replacing; s., stem of; t., taken from; ?, perhaps. See the full key on inside cover.

con·glo·bate (kŏn·glō′bāt, kŏng′glō bāt′), *adj.*, *v.*, **-bated, -bating.** —*adj.* **1.** formed into a ball. —*v.t.*, *v.i.* **2.** to collect or form into a ball or rounded mass. [t. L: m.s. *conglobātus*, pp.] —**con′glo·ba′tion,** *n.*

con·globe (kŏn glōb′), *v.t.*, *v.i.*, **-globed, -globing.** to conglobate.

con·glom·er·ate (*adj.*, *n.* kən glŏm′ər ĭt; *v.* -ə rāt′), *n.*, *adj.*, *v.*, **-ated, -ating.** —*n.* **1.** anything composed of heterogeneous materials or elements. **2.** *Geol.* a rock consisting of rounded and waterworn pebbles, etc., embedded in a finer cementing material; consolidated gravel. —*adj.* **3.** gathered into a rounded mass; consisting of parts so gathered; clustered. **4.** *Geol.* of the nature of a conglomerate. —*v.t.* **5.** to bring together into a cohering mass. **6.** to gather into a ball or rounded mass. —*v.i.* **7.** to collect or cluster together. [t. L: m. s. *conglomerātus*, pp., rolled together] —**con·glom·er·at·ic** (kən glŏm′ə răt′ĭk), **con·glom·er·it·ic** (kən glŏm′ə rĭt′ĭk), *adj.*

con·glom·er·a·tion (kən glŏm′ə rā′shən), *n.* **1.** act of conglomerating. **2.** state of being conglomerated. **3.** a cohering mass; a cluster. **4.** a heterogeneous combination.

con·glu·ti·nate (kən glōō′tə nāt′), *v.*, **-nated, -nating,** *adj.*, *v.t.*, *v.i.* **1.** to join or become joined as with glue. —*adj.* **2.** conglutinated. [t. L: m. s. *conglūtinātus*, pp., glued together] —**con·glu·ti·na′tion,** *n.* —**con·glu′ti·na·tive,** *adj.*

Con·go (kŏng′gō), *n.* **1.** a river in central Africa, flowing in a large arc through the Belgian Congo and along a portion of the border of French Equatorial Africa into the Atlantic. ab. 3000 mi. **2.** See **Belgian Congo.**

Congo colors, a group of azo dyes derived from benzidine which will dye cotton and other vegetable fibers without the aid of a mordant. Also, **Congo dyes.**

Congo Free State, former name of **Belgian Congo.**

Congo red, one of the Congo colors, used esp. to dye cotton, etc., red. Since it is not acid-fast or light-fast, it is often used as a chemical indicator.

congo snake, either of two eel-shaped salamanders: **a.** *Siren,* of the southern U.S., with small forelimbs but no hind ones. **b.** *Amphiuma,* of the southeastern U.S., having four minute limbs, and sometimes attaining a length of 3 feet. Also, **congo eel.**

con·gou (kŏng′gōō), *n.* a kind of black tea from China. Also, **con·go** (kŏn′gō). [t. Chinese: m. *kung-fu* labor]

con·grat·u·lant (kən grăch′ə lənt), *adj.* **1.** congratulating. —*n.* **2.** one who congratulates.

con·grat·u·late (kən grăch′ə lāt′), *v.t.*, **-lated, -lating.** **1.** to express sympathetic joy to (a person), as on a happy occasion; compliment with expressions of sympathetic pleasure; felicitate. **2.** *Obs.* **a.** to express sympathetic joy or satisfaction at (an event, etc.). **b.** to salute. [t. L; m.s. *congrātulātus*, pp.] —**con·grat′u·la·tor,** *n.*

con·grat·u·la·tion (kən grăch′ə lā′shən), *n.* **1.** act of congratulating. **2.** (*usually pl.*) a congratulatory expression; felicitation.

con·grat·u·la·to·ry (kən grăch′ə lə tōr′ĭ), *adj.* **1.** conveying congratulations: *a congratulatory speech.* **2.** inclined to congratulate: *a congratulatory mood.*

con·gre·gate (kŏng′grə gāt′), *v.*, **-gated, -gating,** *adj.* —*v.i.* **1.** to come together; assemble, esp. in large numbers. —*v.t.* **2.** to bring together in a crowd, body, or mass; assemble; collect. —*adj.* **3.** congregated; assembled. **4.** collective. [ME, t. L: m.s. *congregātus*, pp., collected into a flock] —**con′gre·ga′tive,** *adj.* —**con′gre·ga′tive·ness,** *n.* —**con′gre·ga′tor,** *n.*

con·gre·ga·tion (kŏng′grə gā′shən), *n.* **1.** act of congregating. **2.** a congregated body; an assemblage. **3.** an assembly of persons met for common religious worship. **4.** an organization formed for the purpose of providing for worship of God, religious education, and other church activities; a local church society. **5.** (in the Old Testament) the whole body of the Hebrews. **6.** (in the New Testament) the Christian church in general. **7.** *Rom. Cath. Ch.* **a.** a committee of cardinals or other ecclesiastics. **b.** a community of men or women who observe the simple vows of poverty, chastity, and obedience: *Congregation of the Holy Cross.* **8.** (at English Universities) the general assembly of the doctors, fellows, etc. **9.** (in colonial North America) a parish, hundred, town, plantation, or other settlement.

con·gre·ga·tion·al (kŏng′grə gā′shən əl), *adj.* **1.** of or pertaining to a congregation: *congregational singing.* **2.** (*cap.*) pertaining or adhering to a form of church government in which each congregation or local church acts as an independent, self-governing body, while maintaining fellowship with other like congregations.

con·gre·ga·tion·al·ism (kŏng′grə gā′shən ə lĭz′əm), *n.* **1.** the type of church government in which each local religious society is independent and self-governing. **2.** (*cap.*) the system of government and doctrine of the Congregational churches. —**con′gre·ga′tion·al·ist,** *n.*, *adj.*

con·gress (kŏng′grĭs), *n.* **1.** (*cap.*) **a.** the national legislative body of the U.S., consisting of the Senate (upper house) and the House of Representatives (lower house), as a continuous institution. **b.** this body as it exists for the two years during which the representatives hold their seats: *the 69th Congress.* **c.** the session of this body. **2.** the national legislative body of a nation, esp. of a republic. **3.** a formal meeting or assembly of representatives, as envoys of independent states, for the

discussion, arrangement, or promotion of some matter of common interest. **4.** act of coming together; an encounter. **5.** social relations; converse. —*v.i.* **6.** to meet in congress. [t. L: s. *congressus* a meeting] —**Syn. 3.** assembly, conference, council, convention.

congress boot, *U.S.* a high shoe with elastic sides, by the stretching of which it is drawn onto the foot.

con·gres·sion·al (kən grĕsh′ən əl), *adj.* of a congress, esp. (*cap.*) the Congress of the U.S.

con·gress·man (kŏng′grĭs mən), *n.*, *pl.* **-men.** (*often cap.*) a member of the U.S. Congress, esp. of the House of Representatives. —**con·gress·wom·an** (kŏng′grĭs wŏŏm′ən), *n. fem.*

Congress of Industrial Organizations, a federation of affiliated industrial labor unions, originally (1935) within the American Federation of Labor, but independent from it since 1938. *Abbr.:* CIO or C.I.O.

Congress of Vienna, an international conference (1814–15) held at Vienna after Napoleon I's banishment to Elba, with Metternich as the dominant figure, aimed at territorial resettlement and restoration to power of the crowned heads of Europe.

Con·greve (kŏn′grēv, kŏng′-), *n.* **William,** 1670–1729, British dramatist.

Con·greve (kŏn′grēv, kŏng′-), *n.* **1.** a kind of friction match (**Congreve match**). **2.** a kind of rocket formerly used in warfare (**Congreve rocket**). [named after Sir W. *Congreve* (1772–1828), British inventor]

con·gru·ent (kŏng′grōō ənt), *adj.* **1.** agreeing; accordant; congruous. **2.** *Geom.* coinciding exactly when superposed. [t. L: s. *congruens,* ppr. agreeing] —**con′gru·ence, con′gru·en·cy,** *n.* —**con′gru·ent·ly,** *adv.*

con·gru·i·ty (kən grōō′ə tĭ), *n.*, *pl.* **-ties.** **1.** state or quality of being congruous; agreement; harmony; appropriateness. **2.** *Geom.* equality; capacity of figures of being exactly superposed. **3.** a point of agreement.

con·gru·ous (kŏng′grōō əs), *adj.* **1.** agreeing or harmonious in character; accordant; consonant; consistent (fol. by *with* or *to*). **2.** exhibiting harmony of parts. **3.** appropriate or fitting. [t. L: m. *congruus* fit] —**con′gru·ous·ly,** *adv.* —**con′gru·ous·ness,** *n.*

con·ic (kŏn′ĭk), *adj.* **1.** Also, **con′i·cal.** having the form of, resembling, or pertaining to a cone. —*n.* **2.** *Math.* a conic section. [t. Gk.: m.s. *kōnikós* cone-shaped] —**con′i·cal·ly,** *adv.*

conic projection, *Cartog.* a map projection based on the concept of projecting the earth's surface on a conical surface, which is then unrolled to a plane surface.

con·ics (kŏn′ĭks), *n.* the branch of mathematics dealing with conic sections.

conic section, *Math.* a curve formed by the intersection of a plane with a right circular cone; an ellipse, a parabola, or a hyperbola.

conic sections, the branch of mathematics dealing with the ellipse, the parabola, and the hyperbola.

Conic sections
The two principal forms are fig. H, hyperbola, and fig. E, ellipse. Fig P, parabola, is the intermediate case. The degenerate form of the hyperbola is a pair of straight lines, fig. S. Fig. C, circle, is a special case of the ellipse in which the plane becomes perpendicular to the axis of the cone.

co·nid·i·o·phore (kō nĭd′ĭ ə fōr′), *n. Bot.* (in fungi) a special stalk or branch of the mycelium, bearing conidia. [f. *conidio-* (combining form of CONIDIUM) + -PHORE]

co·nid·i·um (kō nĭd′ĭ əm), *n.*, *pl.* **-nidia** (-nĭd′ĭ ə). *Bot.* (in fungi) an asexual spore formed by abstriction at the top of a hyphal branch, usually thin-walled and windborne. [NL, f. m.s. Gk. *kónis* dust + dim. *-ium*] —**co·nid′i·al, co·nid′i·an,** *adj.*

co·ni·fer (kō′nə fər, kŏn′ə-), *n.* **1.** any of the (mostly evergreen) trees and shrubs constituting the gymnospermous order or group (*Coniferales* or *Coniferae*), including the pine, fir, spruce, and other cone-bearing trees and shrubs, and also the yews and their allies, which bear drupelike seeds. **2.** a plant producing naked seeds in cones, or single naked seeds as in yews, but with pollen always borne in cones. [t. L: cone-bearing]

co·nif·er·ous (kō nĭf′ər əs), *adj. Bot.* belonging or pertaining to the conifers. See **conifer** (def. 1).

co·ni·ine (kō′nĭ ēn′, -ĭn, -nēn), *n.* a highly poisonous volatile alkaloid, $C_3H_7\cdot C_5H_9NH$, constituting the active principle of *Conium maculatum,* the poison hemlock. Also, **co·nin** (kō′nĭn), **co·nine** (kō′nēn, -nĭn). [f. CONIINE (UM) + -INE²]

co·ni·um (kō′nĭ əm), *n.* the poison hemlock, *Conium maculatum.* [t. L, t. Gk.: m. *kōneicn* hemlock]

conj., **1.** conjugation. **2.** conjunction. **3.** conjunctive.

con·jec·tur·al (kən jĕk′chər əl), *adj.* **1.** of, of the nature of, or involving conjecture; problematical: *a conjectural opinion.* **2.** given to making conjectures. —**con·jec′tur·al·ly,** *adv.*

con·jec·ture (kən jĕk′chər), *n.*, *v.*, **-tured, -turing.** —*n.* **1.** the formation or expression of an opinion without sufficient evidence for proof. **2.** an opinion so formed or expressed. **3.** *Obs.* the interpretation of signs or omens. —*v.t.* **4.** to conclude or suppose from grounds or evidence insufficient to ensure reliability. —*v.i.* **5.** to form conjectures. [ME, t. L: m. *conjectūra* a throwing together, inference] —**con·jec′tur·a·ble,** *adj.* —**con·jec′-tur·a·bly,** *adv.* —**con·jec′tur·er,** *n.* —**Syn.** 2. surmise, inference, supposition, theory, hypothesis. 4. surmise, suppose, presume. See **guess.**

con·join (kən join′), *v.t.. v.i.* to join together; unite; combine; associate. [ME *conjoigne*(n), t. F: m. *conjoign-*, s. *conjoindre*, g. L *conjungere* join together] —**con·join′er,** *n.* —**Ant.** disjoin.

con·joint (kən joint′), *adj.* 1. joined together; united; combined; associated. 2. pertaining to or formed by two or more in combination; joint. [t. F, pp. of *conjoindre*, g. L *conjungēre* join together] —**con·joint′ly,** *adv.*

con·ju·gal (kŏn′jə gəl), *adj.* 1. of, or of the nature of, marriage. 2. pertaining to the relation of husband and wife. [t. L: s. *conjugālis*, der. *conjux, conjunx* husband or wife] —**con′ju·gal′i·ty,** *n.* —**con′ju·gal·ly,** *adv.*

con·ju·gate (*v.* kŏn′jə gāt′; *adj., n.* kŏn′jə gĭt, -gāt′), *v.,* **-gated, -gating,** *adj., n.* —*v.t.* 1. *Gram.* **a.** to inflect (a verb). **b.** to recite or display all, or some subset of, the inflected forms of (a verb), in a fixed order: *conjugate the present tense verb "be" as I am, you are, he is, we are, you are, they are.* 2. *Obs.* to join together, esp. in marriage. —*v.i.* 3. *Biol.* to unite temporarily. 4. *Gram.* to be characterized by conjugation: *the Latin verb "esse" does not conjugate in the passive voice.* —*adj.* 5. joined together, esp. in a pair or pairs; coupled. 6. *Bot.* (of a pinnate leaf) having only one pair of leaflets. 7. (of words) having a common derivation. 8. *Bibliog.* (of two leaves in a book) forming one sheet. 9. *Math.* of two points, lines, etc., so related as to be interchangeable in the enunciation of certain properties. —*n.* 10. one of a group of conjugate words. 11. a conjugate number or axis. [t. L: m.s. *conjugātus,* pp., joined together, yoked] —**con′ju·ga′tive,** *adj.*

con·ju·ga·tion (kŏn′jə gā′shən), *n.* 1. *Gram.* **a.** the inflection of verbs. **b.** the whole set of inflected forms of a verb, or the recital or display thereof in a fixed order: *the conjugation of Latin "amo" begins amō, amas, amat.* **c.** a class of verbs having similar sets of inflected forms, as the Latin *second conjugation.* 2. act of joining. 3. state of being joined together; union; conjunction. 4. *Biol.* **a.** the sexual process in ciliate protozoans in which two animals adhere and exchange nuclear material through a temporary area of fusion. **b.** the temporary union or fusion of two cells or individuals, as in certain plants. —**con′ju·ga′tion·al,** *adj.* —**con′ju·ga′tion·al·ly,** *adv.*

con·junct (kən jŭngkt′, kŏn′jŭngkt), *adj.* 1. conjoined; associate. 2. formed by conjunction. 3. *Gram.* **a.** occurring only in combination with an immediately preceding or following form of a particular class, and constituting with this form a single phonetic unit, as *'ll* in English *he'll,* and *n't* in *isn't.* **b.** (of a pronoun) having enclitic or proclitic form and occurring with a verb, as French *me, le, se.* **c.** pertaining to a word so characterized. [late ME, t. L: s. *conjunctus,* pp., joined together] —**con·junct′ly,** *adv.*

con·junc·tion (kən jŭngk′shən), *n.* 1. act of conjoining; combination. 2. state of being conjoined; union; association. 3. a combination of events or circumstances. 4. *Gram.* **a.** (in some languages) one of the major form classes, or "parts of speech," comprising words used to link together words, phrases, clauses, or sentences. **b.** such a word, as English *and* or *but.* **c.** any form of similar function or meaning. 5. *Astron.* **a.** the meeting of heavenly bodies in the same longitude or right ascension. **b.** the situation of two or more heavenly bodies when their longitudes are the same. —**con·junc′-tion·al,** *adj.* —**con·junc′tion·al·ly,** *adv.*

con·junc·ti·va (kŏn′jŭngk tī′və), *n., pl.* **-vas, -vae** (-vē). *Anat.* the mucous membrane which lines the inner surface of the eyelids and is reflected over the fore part of the sclera and the cornea. See diag. under **eye.** [t. NL, short for *membrāna conjunctīva* membrane serving to connect] —**con·junc·ti′val,** *adj.*

con·junc·tive (kən jŭngk′tĭv), *adj.* 1. connective. 2. conjoined; joint. 3. *Gram.* **a.** (of a mode) subjunctive. **b.** (of a pronoun) conjunct. **c.** of the nature of a conjunction. —*n.* 4. *Gram.* a conjunctive word; a conjunction. —**con·junc′tive·ly,** *adv.*

con·junc·ti·vi·tis (kən jŭngk′tə vī′tĭs), *n. Pathol.* inflammation of the conjunctiva. [t. NL. See **CONJUNC-TIVA, -ITIS**]

con·junc·ture (kən jŭngk′chər), *n.* 1. a combination of circumstances or affairs; a particular state of affairs. 2. a critical state of affairs; a crisis. 3. *Obs.* conjunction; meeting. [f. **CON-** + **JUNCTURE**]

con·jur·a·tion (kŏn′jŏŏ rā′shən), *n.* 1. act of calling on or invoking by a sacred name. 2. an incantation; a spell or charm. 3. supernatural accomplishment by invocation or spell. 4. the practice of legerdemain. 5. *Archaic.* supplication; solemn entreaty.

con·jure (kŭn′jər, kŏn′- for 1–4, 7–9; kən jŏŏr′ for 5, 6, 10), *v.,* **-jured, -juring.** —*v.t.* 1. to call upon or command (a devil or spirit) by invocation or spell. 2. to affect or influence by, or as by, invocation or spell. 3. to effect, produce, bring, etc., by, or as by, magic. 4. **conjure up, a.** to call, raise up, or bring into existence by magic. **b.** to bring to mind or recall. 5. to appeal to solemnly or earnestly. 6. to charge solemnly. —*v.i.* 7. to call upon or command a devil or spirit by invocation or spell. 8. to practice magic. 9. to practice legerdemain. 10. *Obs.* to conspire. [ME *conjure*(n), t. OF: m. *conjurer,* t. L: m.s. *conjūrāre* swear together]

con·jur·er (kŭn′jər ər, kŏn′- for 1, 2; kən jŏŏr′ər for 3), *n.* 1. one who conjures spirits or practices magic; magician. 2. one who practices legerdemain; juggler. 3. one who solemnly charges or entreats. Also, **con′jur·or.**

conn (kŏn), *v.t.* to direct the steering of (a ship).

Conn., Connecticut.

con·nate (kŏn′āt), *adj.* 1. existing in a person or thing from birth or origin; inborn; congenital. 2. associated in birth or origin. 3. allied or agreeing in nature; cognate. 4. *Biol.* congenitally or firmly united into one body. [t. LL: m.s. *connātus,* pp., born at the same time] —**con′nate·ly,** *adv.* —**con·na·tion** (kə nā′shən), *n.*

con·nat·u·ral (kə nǎch′ə rəl), *adj.* 1. belonging to a person or thing by nature or from birth or origin. 2. of the same or like nature. [t. ML: s. *connātūrālis*] —**con·nat′u·ral·ly,** *adv.*

Con·naught (kŏn′ôt), *n.* a province in NW Eire. 500,339 pop. (est. 1943); 6839 sq. mi. Irish, **Con·nacht** (kŏn′ŭкнt, -ŭt).

con·nect (kə nĕkt′), *v.t.* 1. to bind or fasten together; join or unite; link. 2. to establish communication between; put in communication (fol. by *with*). 3. to associate or attach: *the pleasures connected with music.* 4. to associate mentally. —*v.i.* 5. to become connected; join or unite. 6. (of trains, buses, etc.) to run so as to make connections (*with*). [t. L: s. *connectere,* var. of *cōnectere* join, tie] —**con·nect′ed·ly,** *adv.* —**con·nect′er, con·nec′tor,** *n.* —**Syn.** 1. See **join.** —**Ant.** 1. divide. 3, 4. dissociate.

Con·nect·i·cut (kə nĕt′ə kət), *n.* 1. a State in the NE United States. 2,007,280 pop. (1950); 5009 sq. mi. *Cap.:* Hartford. *Abbr.:* Conn. 2. a river forming the boundary between Vermont and New Hampshire, flowing S through Massachusetts and Connecticut into Long Island Sound. 407 mi.

connecting rod, a rod or bar connecting movable parts, as in an engine.

con·nec·tion (kə nĕk′shən), *n.* 1. act of connecting. 2. state of being connected. 3. anything that connects; a connecting part. 4. association; relationship. 5. a circle of friends or associates, or a member of such a circle. 6. union in due order or sequence of words or ideas. 7. contextual relation. 8. the meeting of means of conveyance for transfer of passengers without delay. 9. a person related to another or others, esp. by marriage or distant consanguinity. 10. a body of persons connected as by political or religious ties. 11. a religious denomination. 12. communication. 13. sexual relation. Also, *Brit.,* **con·nex′ion.** [t. L: m.s. *connexio*] —**con·nec′tion·al,** *adj.* —**Syn.** 1. junction, conjunction, union. 3. bond, tie, link, coupling. 4. affiliation, alliance, combination. 9. relation, relative, kinsman.

con·nec·tive (kə nĕk′tĭv), *adj.* 1. serving or tending to connect. —*n.* 2. that which connects. 3. *Gram.* a word used to connect words, phrases, clauses, and sentences, as a conjunction. 4. *Bot.* the tissue joining the two cells of the anther. —**con·nec′tive·ly,** *adv.* —**con·nec·tiv·i·ty** (kŏn′ĕk tĭv′ə tĭ), *n.*

connective tissue, *Anat.* a tissue, usually of mesoblastic origin, which connects, supports or surrounds other tissues, organs, etc., and occurs in various forms throughout the body.

Con·nel·ly (kŏn′ə lĭ), *n.* **Marc,** born 1890, U.S. dramatist.

conning tower (kŏn′ĭng), the low, dome-shaped, armored pilothouse of a warship, used esp. during battle.

con·nip·tion (kə nĭp′shən), *n. U.S. Colloq.* a fit of hysterics or hysterical excitement.

con·niv·ance (kə nī′vəns), *n.* 1. act of conniving. 2. *Law.* **a.** tacit encouragement or assent (without participation) to wrongdoing by another. **b.** the consent by a person to a spouse's conduct, esp. adultery, which is later made the basis of a divorce proceeding or other complaint. Also, **con·niv′ence.**

con·nive (kə nīv′), *v.i.,* **-nived, -niving.** 1. to avoid noticing that which one should oppose or condemn but secretly approves; give aid to wrongdoing, etc., by forbearing to act or speak; be secretly accessory (fol. by *at*): *conniving at their escape.* 2. to coöperate secretly (fol. by *with*). [t. L: s. *connīvēre,* var. of *cōnīvēre* shut the eyes] —**con·niv′er,** *n.*

con·niv·ent (kə nī′vənt), *adj. Bot., Zool.* converging, as petals. [t. L: s. *connīvens,* ppr., winking at]

con·nois·seur (kŏn′ə sûr′), *n.* one competent to pass critical judgments in an art, esp. one of the fine arts, or in matters of taste. [t. F (now *connaisseur*), der. *connaître,* older *connoître,* g. L *cognoscere* come to know]

Con·nor (kŏn′ər), *n.* **Ralph,** (*Charles William Gordon*) 1860–1937, Canadian novelist and clergyman.

con·no·ta·tion (kŏn′ə tā′shən), *n.* 1. act or fact of connoting. 2. that which is connoted; secondary implied or associated meanings (as distinguished from *denotation*): *"It takes a heap o' living to make a house a home."* 3. *Logic.* the set of attributes constituting the meaning of a term, and thus determining the range of objects to which that term may be applied; comprehension; intension. —**con·no·ta·tive** (kŏn′ə tā′tĭv, kə nō′tə·), *adj.* —**con′no·ta′tive·ly,** *adv.*

con·note (kə nōt′), *v.t.,* **-noted, -noting.** 1. to denote secondarily; signify in addition to the primary meaning; imply. 2. to involve as a condition or accompaniment. [t. ML: m.s. *connotāre* mark with, f. L: *con-* **CON-** + *notāre* mark. See **NOTE, v.**]

---

b., blend of, blended; c., cognate with; d., dialect, dialectal; der., derived from; f., formed from; g., going back to; m., modification of; r., replacing; s., stem of; t., taken from; ?, perhaps. See the full key on inside cover.

con·nu·bi·al (kə nū′bĭ əl, -nōō′-), *adj.* of marriage or wedlock; matrimonial; conjugal. [t. L: s. *connūbiālis,* der. *connūbium* marriage] —**con·nu′bi·al·i·ty,** *n.* —**con·nu′bi·al·ly,** *adv.*

co·noid (kō′noid), *adj.* **1.** Also, **co·noi′dal.** resembling or approaching a cone in shape. —*n.* **2.** a geometrical solid formed by the revolution of a conic section about one of its axes. [t. Gk.: m.s. *kōnoeidēs* cone-shaped]

co·no·scen·te (kō′nō shěn′tě), *n., pl.* **-ti** (-tē) cognoscente.

con·quer (kŏng′kər), *v.t.* **1.** to acquire by force of arms; win in war: *to conquer territories.* **2.** to overcome by force; subdue: *to conquer an enemy.* **3.** to gain or obtain by effort. **4.** to gain the victory over; surmount. —*v.i.* **5.** to make conquests; gain the victory. [ME *conquere(n),* t. OF: m. *conquerre,* g. L *conquaerere, conquīrere* seek for] —**con′quer·a·ble,** *adj.* —**con′quer·ing·ly,** *adv.* —Syn. **2.** vanquish, overpower, overthrow, subjugate. See **defeat.**

con·quer·or (kŏng′kər ər), *n.* **1.** one who conquers. **2. the Conqueror,** William I of England.

con·quest (kŏn′kwěst, kŏng′-), *n.* **1.** act of conquering. **2.** captivation, as of favor or affections. **3.** vanquishment. **4.** territory acquired by conquering. **5.** a person whose favor or affections have been captivated. **6. the Conquest,** the conquering of England by William, Duke of Normandy, in 1066. [ME, t. OF: m. *conqueste,* fem. collective of *conquest,* pp. of *conquerre* conquer] —Syn. **3.** See **victory.**

con·qui·an (kŏng′kĭ ən), *n.* a card game of the rummy family for two players. [orig. uncert.]

con·quis·ta·dor (kŏn kwĭs′tə dôr′; *Sp.* kông kēs′tä-dôr′), *n., pl.* **-dors,** *Sp.* **-dores** (-dō′rĕs). one of the Spanish conquerors of Mexico and Peru in the 16th century. [t. Sp.]

Con·rad (kŏn′răd), *n.* **Joseph** (*Teodor Jozef Konrad Korzeniowski*), 1857-1924, Polish-born British novelist.

con·san·guin·e·ous (kŏn′săng gwĭn′Y əs), *adj.* related by birth; akin. Also, **con·san·guine** (kŏn-săng′gwĭn). [t. L: m. *consanguineus*] —**con′san-guin′e·ous·ly,** *adv.*

con·san·guin·i·ty (kŏn′săng gwĭn′ə tY), *n.* **1.** relationship by blood; kinship. **2.** relationship or affinity.

con·science (kŏn′shəns), *n.* **1.** the internal recognition of right and wrong as regards one's actions and motives; the faculty which decides upon the moral quality of one's actions and motives, enjoining one to conformity with the moral law. **2.** conscientiousness. **3.** *Obs.* consciousness. **4.** *Obs.* inmost thought. **5. in** (all) **conscience,** a. in (all) reason and fairness; in truth. b. most certainly; assuredly. [ME, t. OF, t. L: m.s. *conscientia* joint knowledge] —**con′science·less,** *adj.*

conscience clause, a clause or article in an act or law which relieves persons whose conscientious or religious scruples forbid their compliance with it.

conscience money, money paid to relieve the conscience, as for obligations previously evaded.

con·sci·en·tious (kŏn′shY ĕn′shəs, kŏn′sY-), *adj.* controlled by or done according to conscience; scrupulous: *a conscientious judge, conscientious conduct.* —**con′sci-en′tious·ly,** *adv.* —**con′sci·en′tious·ness,** *n.* —Syn. just, upright, honest, faithful, careful, particular, painstaking.

conscientious objector, one who, when called upon in time of war to fight for his country, refuses to do so because of conscientious scruples, as of religion, morality, etc.

con·scion·a·ble (kŏn′shən ə bəl), *adj.* conformable to conscience; just. —**con′scion·a·bly,** *adv.*

con·scious (kŏn′shəs), *adj.* **1.** awake to one's own existence, sensations, cognitions, etc.; endowed with consciousness. **2.** inwardly sensible or awake to something: *conscious of one's own faults.* **3.** having the mental faculties awake. **4.** present to consciousness; known to oneself; felt: *conscious guilt.* **5.** aware of what one is doing: *a conscious liar.* **6.** aware of oneself; self-conscious. **7.** deliberate or intentional. **8.** *Obs.* inwardly sensible of wrongdoing. [t. L: m. *conscius* knowing] —**con′scious·ly,** *adv.*
—Syn. **2.** CONSCIOUS, AWARE refer to an individual sense of recognition of something. CONSCIOUS implies to be awake or awakened to an inner realization of a fact, a truth, a condition, etc.: *he was conscious of an extreme weariness.* AWARE lays the emphasis on sense perceptions which lead to consciousness: *he was aware of the odor of tobacco.*

con·scious·ness (kŏn′shəs nĭs), *n.* **1.** state of being conscious. **2.** inward sensibility of something; knowledge of one's own existence, sensations, cognitions, etc. **3.** the thoughts and feelings, collectively, of an individual, or of an aggregate of people: *the moral consciousness of a nation.* **4.** activity of mental faculties: *to regain consciousness after a swoon.*

con·script (*adj., n.* kŏn′skrĭpt; *v.* kən skrĭpt′), *adj.* **1.** enrolled or formed by conscription; drafted: *a conscript soldier or army.* —*n.* **2.** a recruit obtained by conscription. —*v.t.* **3.** to draft for military or naval service. [t. L: s. *conscriptus,* pp., enrolled]

conscript fathers, 1. the senators of ancient Rome. **2.** any legislators.

con·scrip·tion (kən skrĭp′shən), *n.* **1.** compulsory enrollment of men for military or naval service; a draft. **2.** a compulsory monetary payment exacted by a government during war.

con·se·crate (kŏn′sə krāt′), *v.,* **-crated, -crating,** *adj.* —*v.t.* **1.** to make or declare sacred; set apart or dedicate to the service of the Deity. **2.** to devote or dedicate to some purpose: *a life consecrated to science.* **3.** to make an object of veneration: *a custom consecrated by time.* —*adj.* **4.** *Archaic.* consecrated; sacred. [ME, t. L: m.s. *consecrātus,* pp., dedicated] —**con′se·cra′tor,** *n.* —**con·se·cra·to·ry** (kŏn′sĕ kra tōr′Y), *adj.* —Syn. **2.** devote. **3.** sanctify. **4.** See **holy.**

con·se·cra·tion (kŏn′sə krā′shən), *n.* **1.** act of consecrating; dedication to the service and worship of God. **2.** act of giving the sacramental character to the Eucharistic elements of bread and wine. **3.** ordination to a sacred office, esp. to the episcopate.

con·se·cu·tion (kŏn′sə kū′shən), *n.* **1.** succession; sequence. **2.** logical sequence; inference. [t. L: s. *consecūtio,* der. *consequī* follow after]

con·sec·u·tive (kən sĕk′ya tĭv), *adj.* **1.** following one another in uninterrupted succession; uninterrupted in course or succession; successive. **2.** marked by logical sequence. **3.** *Gram.* expressing consequence or result: *a consecutive clause.* [t. F: m. *consécutif,* der. L *consecūtus,* pp., having followed after] —**con·sec′u·tive·ly,** *adv.* —**con·sec′u·tive·ness,** *n.* —Syn. **1.** See **successive.**

con·sen·su·al (kən sĕn′shōō əl), *adj.* **1.** formed or existing by mere consent: *a consensual marriage.* **2.** *Physiol.* (of an action) involuntarily correlative with a voluntary action, as the contraction of the iris when the eye is opened. [f. L *consensu(s)* agreement + -AL¹] —**con·sen′su·al·ly,** *adv.*

con·sen·sus (kən sĕn′səs), *n.* general agreement or concord: *the consensus is against revision.* [t. L: agreement]

con·sent (kən sĕnt′), *v.i.* **1.** to give assent; agree; comply or yield (fol. by *to* or infinitive). **2.** *Obs.* to agree in sentiment, opinion, etc.; be in harmony. —*n.* **3.** assent; acquiescence; permission; compliance. **4.** agreement in sentiment, opinion, a course of action, etc.: *by common consent.* **5.** *Archaic.* accord; concord; harmony. [ME *consente(n),* t. OF: m. *consentir,* g. L *consentīre* feel together] —**con·sent′er,** *n.*
—Syn. **1.** CONSENT, ASSENT, CONCUR imply agreeing with someone. CONSENT, applying to somewhat important matters, conveys an active and positive idea; it implies making a definite decision to comply with someone's expressed wish: *to consent to become engaged.* ASSENT conveys a more passive idea; it suggests agreeing intellectually or merely verbally with someone's assertion, request, etc.: *to assent to a speaker's theory, to a proposed arrangement.* To CONCUR is to show accord in matters of opinion, as of minds independently running along the same channels: *to concur in a judgment about an art exhibit.*

con·sen·ta·ne·ous (kŏn′sĕn tā′nY əs), *adj.* **1.** agreeing or accordant. **2.** done by common consent; unanimous. [t. L: m. *consentāneus* agreeing, fit] —**con·sen·ta′ne·ous·ly,** *adv.* —**con·sen·ta·ne·i·ty** (kən sĕn′tə nē′ə tY), **con′sen·ta′ne·ous·ness,** *n.*

con·sen·tient (kən sĕn′shənt), *adj.* **1.** agreeing; accordant. **2.** acting in agreement or harmony. **3.** unanimous, as an opinion. —**con·sen′tience,** *n.*

con·se·quence (kŏn′sə kwěns′), *n.* **1.** act or fact of following as an effect or result upon something antecedent. **2.** that which so follows; an effect or result. **3. in consequence,** as a result. **4.** the conclusion of an argument or inference. **5.** importance or significance: *a matter of no consequence.* **6.** importance in rank or position; distinction. —Syn. **2.** outcome, issue, upshot, sequel. See **effect.** **5.** moment, weight. See **importance.** —Ant. **2.** cause.

con·se·quent (kŏn′sə kwěnt′), *adj.* **1.** following as an effect or result; resulting. **2.** following as a logical conclusion. **3.** logically consistent. —*n.* **4.** anything that follows upon something else, with or without implication of causal relation. **5.** *Logic.* the second member of a conditional or hypothetical proposition, as the proposition expressed by the second clause in *If Jones is ill, he will remain indoors.* **6.** *Arith.* the second term of a ratio. [t. L: s. *consequens,* ppr.]

con·se·quen·tial (kŏn′sə kwěn′shəl), *adj.* **1.** of the nature of a consequence; following as an effect or result, or as a logical conclusion or inference; consequent; resultant. **2.** self-important; pompous. **3.** logically consistent. **4.** of consequence or importance. —**con′se-quen′ti·al′i·ty, con′se·quen′tial·ness,** *n.* —**con′se-quen′tial·ly,** *adv.*

con·se·quent·ly (kŏn′sə kwěnt′lY), *adv.* by way of consequence; in consequence of something; therefore. —Syn. See **therefore.**

con·serv·a·ble (kən sûr′və bəl), *adj.* capable of being conserved; preservable.

con·serv·an·cy (kən sûr′vən sY), *n., pl.* **-cies. 1.** (in England) a commission regulating navigation, fisheries, etc. **2.** conservation of natural resources.

con·ser·va·tion (kŏn′sər vā′shən), *n.* **1.** act of conserving; preservation. **2.** official supervision of rivers, forests, etc. **3.** a district under such supervision. [t. L: s. *conservātio*] —**con′ser·va′tion·al,** *adj.*

con·ser·va·tion·ist (kŏn′sər vā′shən Yst), *n.* one who advocates or promotes conservation, esp. of the natural resources of a country.

conservation of energy, *Physics.* the principle that the total energy of the universe is constant, no energy being created or destroyed in any of the processes of nature.

con·serv·a·tism (kən sûr′və tĭz′əm), *n.* 1. the disposition to preserve what is established; opposition to innovation or change. 2. the principles and practices of political conservatives as (*cap.*) those of the English Conservative Party.

con·serv·a·tive (kən sûr′və tĭv), *adj.* 1. disposed to preserve existing conditions, institutions, etc. 2. cautious or moderate: *a conservative estimate.* 3. having the power or tendency to conserve; preservative. 4. (*often cap.*) noting or pertaining to a political party whose characteristic principle is opposition to change in the institutions of a country. —*n.* 5. a person of conservative principles. 6. a member of a conservative party in politics, esp. (*cap.*) in England. 7. a preservative. —**con·serv′a·tive·ly,** *adv.* —**con·serv′a·tive·ness,** *n.*

Conservative Party, (in Brit. politics) a party now characterized by a tendency to oppose change in prevailing institutions, esp. those associated with capitalism.

con·ser·va·toire (kən sûr′və twär′, -sûr′və wär′; *Fr.* kôn sĕr vȧ twàr′), *n.* a conservatory (of music, etc.). [t. F]

con·ser·va·tor (kŏn′sər vā′tər, kən sûr′və tər), *n.* 1. one who conserves or preserves; a preserver. 2. *Law.* a guardian; a custodian. 3. *Brit.* one who has duties in conservancy (def. 1).

con·serv·a·to·ry (kən sûr′və tôr′ĭ), *n., pl.* **-ries,** *adj.* —*n.* 1. *Chiefly Brit.* a greenhouse, usually a glass-covered house or room for growing and displaying plants. 2. *U.S.* a place for instruction in music and theatrical arts; a school of music. 3. *Obs.* a place where things are preserved. —*adj.* 4. serving or adapted to conserve; preservative.

con·serve (*v.* kən sûrv′; *n.* kŏn′sûrv, kən sûrv′), *v.,* -**served, -serving,** *n.* —*v.t.* 1. to keep in a safe or sound state; preserve from loss, decay, waste, or injury; keep unimpaired. 2. to preserve, as fruit, with sugar, etc. [ME, t. L: m.s. *conservāre* preserve] —*n.* 3. (*often pl.*) a mixture of several fruits, cooked to jamlike consistency with sugar, often with nuts and raisins. [t. F, der. *conserver* CONSERVE, v.] —**con·serv′-er,** *n.*

con·sid·er (kən sĭd′ər), *v.t.* 1. to contemplate mentally; meditate or reflect on. 2. to regard as or deem to be: *I consider him a rascal.* 3. to think; suppose. 4. to make allowance for. 5. to pay attention to; regard: *he never considers others.* 6. to regard with consideration or respect; hold in honor; respect. 7. to think about (a position, purchase, etc.) with a view to accepting or buying. 8. *Archaic.* to view attentively, or scrutinize. 9. *Obs.* to recompense or remunerate. —*v.i.* 10. to think deliberately or carefully; reflect. 11. *Obs. or Archaic.* to look attentively. [ME *considere(n)*, t. L: s. *consīderāre* examine closely] —**Syn.** 1. ponder, deliberate, weigh, revolve. See **study.**

con·sid·er·a·ble (kən sĭd′ər ə bəl), *adj.* 1. worthy of consideration; important; of distinction. 2. (of an amount, extent, etc.) worthy of consideration; fairly large or great. —*n.* 3. *U.S. Colloq.* much; not a little: *he has done considerable for the community, I found considerable to detain me.* —**con·sid′er·a·bly,** *adv.*

con·sid·er·ate (kən sĭd′ər ĭt), *adj.* 1. showing consideration or regard for another's circumstances, feelings, etc. 2. marked by consideration or reflection; deliberate. 3. *Archaic.* given to consideration or reflection; prudent. —**con·sid′er·ate·ly,** *adv.* —**con·sid′-er·ate·ness,** *n.* —**Syn.** 1. See **thoughtful.**

con·sid·er·a·tion (kən sĭd′ər ā′shən), *n.* 1. act of considering; meditation or deliberation. 2. regard or account; something taken, or to be taken, into account. 3. a thought or reflection. 4. a recompense for service rendered, etc.; a compensation. 5. *Law.* something which suffices to make an informal promise legally binding, usually some value given in exchange for the promise. 6. thoughtful or sympathetic regard or respect; thoughtfulness for others; 7. importance or consequence. 8. estimation; esteem. 9. **in consideration of,** a. in view of. b. in return for. 10. **take into consideration,** to consider; take into account. 11. **under consideration,** being considered. —**Syn.** 1. contemplation, advisement, attention. 8. See **honor.**

con·sid·er·ing (kən sĭd′ər ĭng), *prep.* taking into account; in view of.

con·sign (kən sīn′), *v.t.* 1. to hand over or deliver formally; commit (fol. by *to*). 2. to transfer to another's custody or charge; entrust. 3. to set apart, as to a purpose or use. 4. *Commerce.* a. to transmit, as by public carrier, esp. for sale or custody. b. to address for such transmission. 5. *Obs.* to mark with a sign or seal. —*v.i. Obs.* 6. to yield or submit. 7. to agree or assent. [t. F: m. *consigner,* t. L: m. *consignāre* furnish or mark with a seal] —**con·sign′a·ble,** *adj.* —**con·sig·na·tion** (kŏn′sĭg nā′shən), *n.*

con·sign·ee (kŏn′sī nē′, -sī nē′), *n.* the person or party to whom merchandise is consigned.

con·sign·ment (kən sīn′mənt), *n.* 1. act of consigning. 2. that which is consigned. 3. *Com.* a. property sent to an agent for sale, storage, or shipment. b. **on consignment,** (of goods) sent to an agent for sale, title being held by the consignor until they are sold.

con·sign·or (kən sī′nər, kŏn′sī nôr′), *n.* one who consigns goods, etc. Also, **con·sign·er** (kən sī′nər).

con·sist (kən sĭst′), *v.i.* 1. to be made up or composed (fol. by *of*). 2. to be comprised or contained (fol. by *in*). 3. to be compatible, consistent, or harmonious (fol. by

with). 4. *Obs.* to exist together or be capable of existing together. 5. *Obs.* to stand together; be supported and maintained. [t. L: s. *consistĕre* place oneself] —**Syn.** 1, 2. CONSIST OF, CONSIST IN are often confused. With CONSIST OF, parts, materials, or ingredients are spoken of: *bread consists of flour, yeast, etc.* With CONSIST IN, something resembling a definition is given: *coöperation consists in helping one another and in sharing losses or gains.*

con·sist·en·cy (kən sĭs′tən sĭ), *n., pl.* **-cies.** 1. material coherence with retention of form; solidity or firmness. 2. degree of density or viscosity: *the consistency of cream.* 3. constant adherence to the same principles, course, etc. 4. agreement, harmony, or compatibility; agreement among themselves of the parts of a complex thing. Also, **con·sist′ence.**

con·sist·ent (kən sĭs′tənt), *adj.* 1. agreeing or accordant; compatible; not self-opposed or self-contradictory. 2. constantly adhering to the same principles, course, etc. 3. holding firmly together; cohering. 4. *Obs.* fixed; firm; solid. —**con·sist′ent·ly,** *adv.* —**Syn.** 1. congruous, consonant, harmonious. —**Ant.** 2. contradictory.

con·sis·to·ry (kən sĭs′tər ĭ), *n., pl.* **-ries.** 1. any of various ecclesiastical councils or tribunals. 2. the place where it meets. 3. the meeting of any such body. 4. *Rom. Cath. Ch.* an ecclesiastical senate, consisting of the whole body of cardinals, which deliberates upon the affairs of the church. 5. *Ch. of Eng.* a diocesan court held before the bishop or the bishop's chancellor or commissary in the cathedral church for the trial of ecclesiastical questions. 6. (in certain Reformed churches) the governing board of a local church or congregation. 7. an assembly or council. 8. *Obs.* a council chamber. [ME *consistorie,* t. ONF, t. L: m. *consistōrium* place of assembly] —**con·sis·to·ri·al** (kŏn′sĭs tōr′ĭəl), **con·sis·to′ri·an,** *adj.*

con·so·ci·ate (*adj., n.* kən sō′shĭ ĭt, -āt′; *v.* kən sō′shĭ-āt′), *adj., n., v.i.,* -**ated, -ating.** associate. [t. L: m. s. *consociātus,* pp.] —**con·so·ci·a·tion** (kən sō′sĭ ā′shən, -shĭ-), *n.*

con·so·la·tion (kŏn′sə lā′shən), *n.* 1. act of consoling. 2. state of being consoled. 3. one who or that which consoles. [ME, t. L: s. *consōlātio*] —**Syn.** 3. comfort, solace.

con·sol·a·to·ry (kən sŏl′ə tōr′ĭ), *adj.* affording consolation; consoling.

con·sole¹ (kən sōl′), *v.t.,* -**soled, -soling.** to alleviate the grief or sorrow of; comfort; solace; cheer. [t. L: m. *consōlārī* comfort] —**con·sol′a·ble,** *adj.* —**con·sol′er,** *n.* —**con·sol′ing·ly,** *adv.* —**Syn.** See **comfort.**

con·sole² (kŏn′sōl), *n.* 1. a desklike structure containing the keyboards, pedals, etc., of an organ, from which the organ is played. 2. a floor-model radio cabinet. 3. a console table. 4. *Archit.* an ornamental bracketlike member, as for supporting a cornice, bust, etc. 5. a bracket or bracketlike support. [t. F; orig. uncert.]

con·sole table (kŏn′sōl), 1. a table supported by consoles or brackets fixed to a wall. 2. a table, often with bracketlike legs, designed to fit against a wall.

con·sol·i·date (kən sŏl′ə dāt′), *v.,* -**dated, -dating,** *adj.* —*v.t.* 1. to make solid or firm; solidify; strengthen: *to consolidate gains.* 2. *Mil.* to strengthen by rearranging the position of ground combat troops after a successful attack. 3. to bring together compactly in one mass or connected whole; unite; combine: *to consolidate two companies.* —*v.i.* 4. to unite or combine. 5. to become solid or firm. —*adj.* 6. *Archaic.* consolidated. [t. L: m. s. *consolidātus,* pp., made solid] —**con·sol′i·da′tor,** *n.*

con·sol·i·da·tion (kən sŏl′ə dā′shən), *n.* 1. act of consolidating; unification. 2. state of being consolidated; combination. 3. a consolidated whole. 4. *Law.* a statutory combination of two or more corporations.

con·sols (kŏn′sŏlz, kən sŏlz′), *n.pl.* the funded government securities of Great Britain, which originated in the consolidation in 1751 of various public securities, chiefly in the form of annuities, into a single debt issue without maturity. [short for *consolidated annuities*]

con·som·mé (kŏn′sə mā′; *Fr.* kôn sô mĕ′), *n.* a strong, clear soup made by boiling meat long and slowly until most of the nutritive properties are extracted. [t. F, prop. pp. of *consommer,* t. L: m. *consummāre* finish]

con·so·nance (kŏn′sə nəns), *n.* 1. accord or agreement. 2. correspondence of sounds; harmony of sounds. 3. *Music.* a simultaneous combination of tones conventionally accepted as being in a state of repose (opposite of *dissonance*). Also, **con′so·nan·cy.**

con·so·nant (kŏn′sə nənt), *n.* 1. *Phonet.* a. (as a member of a syllable) a sound subordinated to another sound that has greater sonority; *w* and *g* in *wig* are subordinate to *i,* the sound of greatest sonority in the syllable, and by virtue of this subordination they are called consonants. b. (as a member of an articulation class) a sound made with more or less obstruction of the breath stream in its passage outward, as the *l, s,* and *t* of *list,* each an example of a consonantal subclass: *l* is a *sonorant* (relatively slight obstruction), *s* a *fricative* (relatively great obstruction), and *t* a *stop* (complete obstruction). 2. a letter which usually represents a consonant sound. —*adj.* 3. in agreement; agreeable or accordant; consistent (fol. by *to* or *with*). 4. corresponding in sound, as words. 5. harmonious, as sounds. 6. *Music.* constituting a consonance. 7. consonantal. [ME, t. L: s. *consonans* sounding together] —**con′so·nant·ly,** *adv.* —**Ant.** 6. dissonant.

con·so·nan·tal (kŏn′sə năn′təl), *adj.* **1.** of, or of the nature of, a consonant. **2.** marked by consonant sounds.

con·sort (*n.* kŏn′sôrt, *v.* kən sôrt′), *n.* **1.** a husband or wife; a spouse. **2.** one vessel or ship accompanying another. **3.** *Obs.* **a.** a companion or partner. **b.** company or association. **c.** accord or agreement. **d.** harmony of sounds. —*v.i.* **4.** to associate; keep company. **5.** to agree or harmonize. —*v.t.* **6.** to associate. **7.** *Obs.* **a.** to accompany; espouse. **b.** to sound in harmony. [late ME, t. F: mate, t. L: s. *consors* partner, sharer, orig. adj., sharing]

con·sor·ti·um (kən sôr′shĭ əm), *n.*, *pl.* **-tia** (-shĭ ə). **1.** a combination of financial institutions, capitalists, etc. for carrying into effect some financial operation requiring large resources of capital. **2.** an association or union. [t. L: partnership]

con·spec·tus (kən spĕk′təs), *n.* **1.** a general or comprehensive view. **2.** a digest; a résumé. [t. L: survey]

con·spic·u·ous (kən spĭk′yŏŏ əs), *adj.* **1.** easy to be seen. **2.** readily attracting the attention. [t. L: m. *conspicuus* visible, striking] —**con·spic′u·ous·ly,** *adv.* —**con·spic′u·ous·ness,** *n.* —**Syn. 1.** visible, manifest, noticeable, clear, marked, salient. **2.** prominent, striking, noteworthy.

con·spir·a·cy (kən spĭr′ə sĭ), *n.*, *pl.* **-cies. 1.** act of conspiring. **2.** a combination of persons for an evil or unlawful purpose; a plot. **3.** *Law.* an agreement by two or more persons to commit a crime, fraud, or other wrongful act. **4.** *Archaic.* any concurrence in action; combination in bringing about a given result. [f. CONSPIR(E) + -ACY] —**con·spir′a·tor,** *n.* —**con·spir·a·tress** (kən spĭr′ə trĭs), *n. fem.*

con·spire (kən spīr′), *v.*, **-spired, -spiring.** —*v.i.* **1.** to agree together, esp. secretly, to do something reprehensible or illegal; combine for an evil or unlawful purpose. **2.** to act in combination; contribute jointly to a result. —*v.t.* **3.** to plot (something evil or unlawful). [ME *conspire(n),* t. L: m. *conspīrāre,* lit., breathe together] —**con·spir′er,** *n.* —**con·spir′ing·ly,** *adv.* —**Syn. 1.** complot, intrigue. See **plot. 2.** combine, concur, coöperate.

con·sta·ble (kŏn′stə bəl, kŭn′-), *n.* **1.** any of various officers of the peace, as one who executes the processes of a justice of the peace. **2.** *Eng.* a policeman. **3.** an officer of high rank in medieval monarchies, usually the commander of all armed forces, particularly in the absence of the ruler. **4.** the keeper or governor of a royal fortress or castle. [ME *conestable,* t. OF, g. LL *comes stabuli* count of the stable, master of the horse] —**con′sta·ble·ship′,** *n.*

Con·sta·ble (kŭn′stə bəl), *n.* **John,** 1776–1837, British painter of landscapes.

con·stab·u·lar·y (kən stăb′yə lĕr′ĭ), *n.*, *pl.* **-laries,** *adj.* —*n.* **1.** the body of constables of a district or locality. **2.** a body of officers of the peace organized on a military basis. **3.** a district under a constable. —*adj.* **4.** pertaining to constables or their duties. [t. ML: m.s. *constabulāria*]

Con·stance (kŏn′stəns), *n.* **1. Lake of,** German, **Boden See.** a lake bounded by Germany, Austria, and Switzerland. 46 mi. long; 207 sq. mi. **2.** German, **Konstanz.** a city in SW Germany, on this lake: important church council, 1414–18. 37,700 (1939).

con·stan·cy (kŏn′stən sĭ), *n.* **1.** quality of being constant; firmness or fortitude; faithfulness to a person or cause. **2.** invariableness, uniformity, or regularity. [t. L: m. s. *constantia* firmness] —**Syn. 1.** steadfastness, fidelity, fealty, loyalty.

con·stant (kŏn′stənt), *adj.* **1.** invariable; uniform; always present. **2.** continuing without intermission. **3.** regularly recurrent; continual; persistent. **4.** steadfast, as in attachment; faithful. **5.** standing firm in mind or purpose; resolute. **6.** *Obs.* certain or confident. —*n.* **7.** something constant, invariable, or unchanging. **8.** *Physics.* a numerical quantity expressing a relation or value that remains unchanged under certain conditions. **9.** *Math.* a quantity assumed to be unchanged throughout a given discussion. [ME, t. L: s. *constans,* ppr., standing firm] —**con′stant·ly,** *adv.* —**Syn. 2.** perpetual, unremitting, uninterrupted. **3.** incessant, ceaseless. See **continual. 4.** loyal, stanch, true. See **faithful. 5.** steady, unwavering, unswerving, unshaken. —**Ant. 1.** changeable. **2.** fitful. **3.** sporadic. **4.** unreliable. **5.** wavering.

Con·stant (kôn stän′), *n.* **Jean Joseph Benjamin** (zhän zhô zĕf′ băn zhà măn′), 1845–1902, French portrait painter.

Con·stan·ta (kôn stän′tsä), *n.* a seaport in SE Rumania, on the Black Sea. 80,178 (est. 1943).

con·stant·an (kŏn′stən tăn′), *n.* an alloy containing 60% copper and 40% nickel, used for electrical resistance heating and thermocouples.

Con·stant de Re·becque (kôn stän′ də rə bĕk′), **Henri Benjamin** (än rē′ băn zhä măn′), (**Benjamin Constant**), 1767–1830, French statesman and author.

Con·stan·tine (kŏn′stən tēn′; *Fr.* kôn stän tēn′), *n.* a city in NE Algeria. 113,777 (1936).

Con·stan·tine I (kŏn′stən tīn′, -tēn′), **1.** ("*the Great*"), A.D. 288?–337, Roman emperor, A.D. 324–337: built Constantinople as new capital; made Christian worship lawful. **2.** 1868–1923, king of Greece, 1913–1917 and 1920–22.

Con·stan·ti·no·ple (kŏn′stăn tə nō′pəl), *n.* a city built on the site of ancient Byzantium by Constantine the Great, A.D. 330: capital of the Eastern Roman Empire and later of the Ottoman Empire. See **Istanbul.**

con·stel·late (kŏn′stə lāt′), *v.i., v.t.,* **-lated, -lating.** to cluster together, as stars in a constellation.

con·stel·la·tion (kŏn′stel lā′shən), *n.* **1.** *Astron.* **a.** any of various groups of stars to which definite names have been given, as Ursa Major, Ursa Minor, Boötes, Cancer, Orion. **b.** a division of the heavens occupied by such a group. **2.** *Astrol.* **a.** the grouping or relative position of the stars as supposed to influence events, esp. at a person's birth. **b.** *Obs.* character as supposed to be determined by the stars. **3.** any brilliant assemblage. [ME, t. LL: s. *constellātio* group of stars]

con·ster (kŏn′stər), *v.t., v.i. Obs.* construe.

con·ster·nate (kŏn′stər nāt′), *v.t.,* **-nated, -nating.** to dismay; terrify (usually used in the passive).

con·ster·na·tion (kŏn′stər nā′shən), *n.* amazement and dread tending to confound the faculties; paralyzing dismay. [t. L: s. *consternātio*] —**Syn.** bewilderment, alarm, terror, fear, panic. —**Ant.** equanimity.

con·sti·pate (kŏn′stə pāt′), *v.t.,* **-pated, -pating. 1.** to cause constipation in; make costive. **2.** *Obs.* to crowd or pack closely together. [t. L: m. s. *constīpātus,* pp., pressed together] —**con′sti·pat′ed,** *adj.*

con·sti·pa·tion (kŏn′stə pā′shən), *n.* **1.** a condition of the bowels marked by defective or difficult evacuation. **2.** *Obs.* act of crowding anything into a smaller compass; condensation.

con·stit·u·en·cy (kən stĭch′ŏŏ en sĭ), *n.*, *pl.* **-cies. 1.** a body of constituents; the body of voters, or, loosely, of residents, in a district represented by an elective officer. **2.** the district itself. **3.** any body of supporters, customers, etc.; a clientele.

con·stit·u·ent (kən stĭch′ŏŏ ənt), *adj.* **1.** serving to make up a thing; component; elementary: *constituent parts.* **2.** having power to frame or alter a political constitution or fundamental law (as distinguished from lawmaking power): *a constituent assembly.* —*n.* **3.** a constituent element, material, etc.; a component. **4.** a voter, or (loosely) a resident, in a district represented by an elective officer. **5.** *Gram.* an element that forms part of a construction. The **immediate constituents** are the largest parts (usually two) into which a construction is divisible, any or all of them sometimes further divisible into constituents of their own: the **ultimate constituents** are all the parts of a construction which are not further divisible. The sentence *John's hat looked slightly stained* has the immediate constituents *John's hat* (subject) and *looked slightly stained* (predicate), and the ultimate constituents *John, -'s, hat, look, -ed, slight, -ly, stain,* and *-ed.* [t. L: s. *constituens,* ppr., setting up] —**Syn. 3.** See **element.**

con·sti·tute (kŏn′stə tūt′, -tŏŏt′), *v.t.,* **-tuted, -tuting. 1.** (of elements, etc.) to compose; form. **2.** to appoint to an office or function; make or create. **3.** to set up or establish (laws, etc.); found (an institution, etc.). **4.** to give legal form to (an assembly, court, etc.). **5.** to make up or form of elements, material, etc.; frame. **6.** *Obs.* to set or place. [t. L: m. s. *constitūtus,* pp., set up, established] —**con′sti·tut′er, con′sti·tu′tor,** *n.*

con·sti·tu·tion (kŏn′stə tū′shən, -tŏŏ′-), *n.* **1.** the way in which anything is constituted; make-up or composition: *the physical constitution of the sun.* **2.** the physical character of the body as to strength, health, etc.: *a strong constitution.* **3.** character or condition of mind; disposition; temperament. **4.** act of constituting; establishment. **5.** state of being constituted; formation. **6.** any established arrangement or custom. **7.** the system of fundamental principles according to which a nation, state, corporation, etc., is governed: *the British constitution.* **8.** the document embodying these principles. [ME, t. L: s. *constitūtio*]

Con·sti·tu·tion (kŏn′stə tū′shən, -tŏŏ′-), *n.* **The,** an American 44-gun frigate, famous for its exploits in the War of 1812, popularly called "Old Ironsides."

con·sti·tu·tion·al (kŏn′stə tū′shən əl, -tŏŏ′-), *adj.* **1.** belonging to or inherent in a person's constitution of body or mind: *a constitutional weakness.* **2.** beneficial to, or designed to benefit. the bodily constitution: *a constitutional walk.* **3.** pertaining to the constitution or composition of a thing; essential. **4.** pertaining to, in accordance with, or subject to the constitution of a state, etc.: *a constitutional monarchy.* **5.** having the power of, or existing by virtue of and subject to, a constitution or fundamental organic law: *a constitutional government.* **6.** forming a part of, or authorized by, the constitution or fundamental organic law of a nation or state. —*n.* **7.** a walk or other exercise taken for the benefit of the health. —**con′sti·tu′tion·al·ly,** *adv.*

con·sti·tu·tion·al·ism (kŏn′stə tū′shən ə lĭz′əm. -tŏŏ′-). *n.* **1.** the principles of constitutional government, or adherence to them. **2.** constitutional rule or authority.

con·sti·tu·tion·al·ist (kŏn′stə tū′shən əl ĭst, -tŏŏ′-), *n.* **1.** an adherent or advocate of constitutionalism, or of an existing constitution. **2.** a student of or writer on a political constitution.

con·sti·tu·tion·al·i·ty (kŏn′stə tū′shən năl′ə tĭ, -tŏŏ′-), *n.* **1.** quality of being constitutional. **2.** accordance with the constitution of a state, etc. (as a measure or norm of lawmaking power).

Constitution of the United States, The, the fundamental or organic law of the U. S., framed in 1787 by the Constitutional Convention. It went into effect March 4, 1789.

con·sti·tu·tive (kŏn′stə tū/tĬv, -tōō/-), *adj.* **1.** constituent; making a thing what it is; essential. **2.** having power to establish or enact. **—con′sti·tu′tive·ly,** *adv.*

con·strain (kən strān′), *v.t.* **1.** to force, compel, or oblige; bring about by compulsion: *to constrain obedience.* **2.** to confine forcibly, as by bonds. **3.** to repress or restrain. [ME *constreign(en),* t. OF: m. *constreindre,* g. L *constringere* draw together] **—con·strain′a·ble,** *adj.* **—con·strain′er,** *n.* **—Syn.** 3. check, bind, confine.

con·strained (kən strānd′), *adj.* forced; cramped; restrained; stiff or unnatural: *a constrained smile or manner.* **—con·strain·ed·ly** (kən strā′nĬd lĬ), *adv.*

con·straint (kən strānt′), *n.* **1.** confinement or restriction. **2.** repression of natural feelings and impulses. **3.** unnatural restraint in manner, etc.; embarrassment. **4.** something that constrains. **5.** act of constraining. **6.** condition of being constrained. [ME *constreinte,* t. OF, prop. pp. fem. of *constreindre* CONSTRAIN]

con·strict (kən strĬkt′), *v.t.* to draw together; compress; cause to contract or shrink. [t. L: s. *constrictus,* pp., drawn together] **—Syn.** cramp, squeeze, bind, tighten. **—Ant.** expand.

con·stric·tion (kən strĬk′shən), *n.* **1.** act of constricting. **2.** state of being constricted. **3.** a constricted part. **4.** something that constricts.

con·stric·tive (kən strĬk′tĬv), *adj.* **1.** constricting, or tending to constrict. **2.** pertaining to constriction.

con·stric·tor (kən strĬk′tər), *n.* **1.** a snake that crushes its prey in its coils. **2.** *Anat.* a muscle that constricts a hollow part of the body, as the pharynx. **3.** one who or that which constricts. [t. NL]

con·stringe (kən strĬnj′), *v.t.,* -stringed, -stringing. to constrict; compress; cause to contract. [t. L: m.s. *constringere,* Cf. CONSTRAIN]

con·strin·gent (kən strĬn′jənt), *adj.* **1.** constringing. **2.** causing constriction. **—con·strin′gen·cy,** *n.*

con·struct (*v.* kən strŭkt′, *n.* kŏn′strŭkt), *v.t.* **1.** to form by putting together parts; build; frame; devise. **2.** *Geom., etc.* to draw, as a figure, so as to fulfill given conditions. **—n.** 3. something constructed. 4. a complex image or idea resulting from a synthesis by the mind. [t. L: s. *constructus,* pp., constructed, piled or put together] **—con·struc′tor, con·struct′er,** *n.* **—Syn.** 1. erect, form. See make.

con·struc·tion (kən strŭk′shən), *n.* **1.** act or art of constructing. **2.** the way in which a thing is constructed; structure: *objects of similar construction.* **3.** that which is constructed; a structure. **4.** *Gram.* **a.** the arrangement of two or more forms in a grammatical unit. Constructions involving bound forms are called morphological, as the bound forms *fif-* and *-teen* in *fifteen.* Those involving only free forms are called syntactic, as *the good man, in the house.* Cf. **bound form, free form. b.** a word or phrase consisting of two or more forms arranged in a particular way. **5.** explanation or interpretation, as of a law or a text, or of conduct or the like. **—con·struc′tion·al,** *adj.*

con·struc·tion·ist (kən strŭk′shən Ĭst), *n.* one who construes or interprets, esp. laws or the like.

con·struc·tive (kən strŭk′tĬv), *adj.* **1.** constructing, or tending to construct: *constructive (as opposed to destructive) criticism.* **2.** of, pertaining to, or of the nature of construction; structural. **3.** deduced by construction or interpretation; inferential: *constructive permission.* **4.** *Law.* not actually existing, but having the same legal effects as one that does: *a constructive contract.* **—con·struc′tive·ly,** *adv.* **—con·struc′tive·ness,** *n.*

con·strue (kən strōō′ *or, esp. Brit.* kŏn′strōō), *v.,* -strued, -struing. **—v.t.** 1. to show the meaning or intention of; explain; interpret; put a particular interpretation on. 2. to deduce by construction or interpretation; infer. 3. to translate, esp. orally. 4. to explain the syntax of: *in construing the sentence* "He caught a fish" *one says* "he" *is the subject,* "caught a fish" *is the predicate,* "(a) fish" *is the direct object of the verb* "caught," *etc.* 5. to arrange or combine (words, etc.) syntactically. **—v.i.** 6. to admit of grammatical analysis or interpretation. [ME *construe(n),* t. L: m. *construere* build up, pile together] **—con·stru′a·ble,** *adj.* **—con·stru′a·bil′i·ty,** *n.* **—con·stru′er,** *n.*

con·sub·stan·tial (kŏn′səb stăn′shəl), *adj.* of one and the same substance, essence, or nature. [t. LL: s. *consubstantiālis,* f. L: con- CON- + s. *substantia* substance + *-ālis* -AL¹] **—con′sub·stan′ti·al′i·ty,** *n.* **—con′sub·stan′tial·ly,** *adv.*

con·sub·stan·ti·ate (kŏn′səb stăn′shĬ āt′), *v.,* -ated, -ating. **—v.i.** 1. to profess the doctrine of consubstantiation. 2. to become united in one common substance or nature. **—v.t.** 3. to unite in one common substance or nature. 4. to regard as so united. [t. ML: m.s. *consubstantiātus,* pp., identified in substance]

con·sub·stan·ti·a·tion (kŏn′səb stăn′shĬ ā′shən), *n.* *Theol.* the doctrine that the substance of the body and blood of Christ coexist in and with the substance of bread and wine of the Eucharist.

con·sue·tude (kŏn′swĬ tūd′, -tōōd′), *n.* custom, esp. as having legal force. [ME, t. L: m. *consuētūdo* custom]

con·sue·tu·di·nar·y (kŏn′swĬ tū/də nĕr′Ĭ, -tōō/-), *adj.* customary.

con·sul (kŏn′səl), *n.* **1.** an agent appointed by an independent state to reside in a foreign state and discharge certain administrative duties. **2.** either of the two chief magistrates of the ancient Roman republic. **3.** one of the three supreme magistrates of the French republic from 1799 to 1804. [t. L] **—con′su·lar,** *adj.* **—con′sul·ship′,** *n.*

consular agent, an officer performing the duties of a consul at a place of small commercial importance.

con·su·late (kŏn′sə lĬt), *n.* **1.** the premises officially occupied by a consul. **2.** consulship. **3.** *(often cap.)* a government by consuls, as in France from 1799 to 1804. [t. L: m.s. *consulātus*]

consul general, a consular officer of the highest rank, as one stationed at a place of considerable commercial importance.

con·sult (*v.* kən sŭlt′; *n.* kŏn′sŭlt, kən sŭlt′), *v.t.* **1.** to seek counsel from; ask advice of. **2.** to refer to for information. **3.** to have regard for (a person's interest, convenience, etc.) in making plans. **—v.i.** 5. to consider or deliberate; take counsel; confer (fol. by *with*). **—n.** 6. *Rare.* **a.** consultation. **b.** a council. [t. L: s. *consultāre,* freq. of *consulere* deliberate, take counsel. Cf. COUNSEL, n., CONSUL] **—con·sult′a·ble,** *adj.* **—con·sult′er,** *n.* **—Syn.** 1. CONSULT, CONFER imply talking over a situation or a subject with someone to decide points in doubt. To CONSULT is to seek from a presumably qualified personal or an impersonal source advice, opinion, etc.: *to consult an authority.* To CONFER is to interchange views in order to throw light on a subject under consideration: *the partners conferred concerning their business policy.*

con·sult·ant (kən sŭl′tənt), *n.* **1.** one who consults. **2.** one who gives professional or expert advice.

con·sul·ta·tion (kŏn′səl tā/shən), *n.* **1.** act of consulting; conference. **2.** a meeting for deliberation.

con·sult·a·tive (kən sŭl′tə tĬv), *adj.* of consultation; advisory. Also, **con·sul·ta·to·ry** (kən sŭl′tə tōr′Ĭ).

con·sult·ing (kən sŭl′tĬng), *adj.* employed in giving professional advice, either to the public or to those practicing the profession: *a consulting physician.*

con·sume (kən sōōm′), *v.,* -sumed, -suming. **—v.t.** 1. to destroy or expend by use; use up. 2. to eat or drink up; devour. 3. to destroy, as by decomposition or burning. 4. to spend (money, time, etc.) wastefully. 5. to absorb; engross. **—v.i.** 6. to be consumed; suffer destruction; waste away. [ME *consume(n),* t. L: m. *consūmere* take up completely] **—con·sum′a·ble,** *adj.,* *n.* **—Syn.** 1. exhaust, expend. 4. squander, dissipate.

con·sum·ed·ly (kən sōō′mĬd lĬ), *adv.* excessively; extremely.

con·sum·er (kən sōō′mər), *n.* **1.** one who or that which consumes. **2.** *Econ.* one who uses up a commodity or service (opposed to *producer*).

consumers' goods, *Econ.* goods ready for consumption in satisfaction of human wants, as clothing, food, etc., and which are not utilized in any further production.

con·sum·mate (*v.* kŏn′sə māt′, *adj.* kən sŭm′Ĭt), *v.,* -mated, -mating. *adj.* **—v.t.** 1. to bring to completion or perfection. 2. to complete (a marriage) by sexual intercourse. **—adj.** 3. complete or perfect; supremely qualified; of the highest quality. [late ME, t. L: m. s. *consummātus,* pp., brought to the highest degree] **—con·sum′mate·ly,** *adv.* **—con′sum·ma′tive,** *adj.* **—con′sum·ma′tor,** *n.* **—Syn.** 1. complete, perfect, fulfill, accomplish, achieve. 3. excellent, finished, supreme.

con·sum·ma·tion (kŏn′sə mā′shən), *n.* the act of consummating, or the state of being consummated; completion; perfection; fulfillment.

con·sump·tion (kən sŭmp′shən), *n.* **1.** act of consuming; destruction or decay. **2.** destruction by use. **3.** the amount consumed. **4.** *Econ.* the using up of goods and services having an exchangeable value. **5.** *Pathol.* **a.** a wasting disease, esp. tuberculosis of the lungs. **b.** progressive wasting of the body. [ME, t. L: s. *consumptio* a wasting]

con·sump·tive (kən sŭmp′tĬv), *adj.* **1.** tending to consume; destructive; wasteful. **2.** pertaining to consumption by use. **3.** *Pathol.* **a.** pertaining to or of the nature of consumption. **b.** disposed to or affected with consumption. **—n.** 4. one who suffers from consumption. **—con·sump′tive·ly,** *adv.* **—con·sump′tive·ness,** *n.*

cont., **1.** containing. **2.** contents. **3.** continent. **4.** continental. **5.** continued.

con·tact (kŏn′tăkt), *n.* **1.** state or fact of touching; a touching or meeting of bodies. **2.** immediate proximity or association. **3.** *Elect.* **a.** a junction, usually surface, between electric conductors, usually solids, which may be presumed to permit current flow. **b.** a conducting part which acts together with another part to complete or to interrupt a circuit. **4.** *Med.* **a.** one who has lately been exposed to an infected person. **b.** inflammation of the skin due to contact with an irritating agent. **5.** *Sociol.* **a.** a condition in which two or more individuals or groups are placed in communication with one another. **b.** categoric contact, acting toward one on the basis of the type or group of people he represents rather than on the basis of his personal make-up. **c.** primary contact, a contact characterized by intimacy and personal familiarity. **d.** secondary contact, a contact characterized by impersonal and detached interest on the part of the participants, such as between strangers. **e. sympathetic contact**, acting toward an individual on the basis of his personal or individual make-up instead of on the basis of his group membership. —*v.t.* **6.** to put or bring into contact. **7.** *Colloq.* to get in touch with(a person). —*v.i.* **8.** to enter into or be in contact. [t. L: s. *contactus* a touching]

contact flight, *Aeron.* a flight in which the pilot always sees land or water over which he passes.

con·tac·tor (kŏn′tăk tər), *n.* *Elect.* a device, operated other than by hand, for repeatedly establishing and interrupting an electric power circuit.

con·ta·gion (kən tā′jən), *n.* **1.** the communication of disease by direct or indirect contact. **2.** a disease so communicated. **3.** the medium by which a contagious disease is transmitted. **4.** pestilential influence; hurtful contact or influence. **5.** the communication of any influence, as enthusiasm, from one to another. [ME, t. L: s. *contāgio* a contact]

con·ta·gious (kən tā′jəs), *adj.* **1.** communicable to other individuals, as a disease. **2.** causing or involving contagion; noxious. **3.** tending to spread from one to another: *panic is contagious.* [ME, t. LL: m. s. *contāgiōsus*] —**con·ta′gious·ly,** *adv.* —**con·ta′gious·ness,** *n.* —**Syn. 3.** CONTAGIOUS, INFECTIOUS have scientific uses in which they are precisely defined; but in popular use in referring to disease, the words are often confused. In popular figurative use, in which both have favorable connotations, they are differentiated to some extent. CONTAGIOUS emphasizes the rapidity with which the "contagion" spreads: *contagious laughter ran through the hall.* INFECTIOUS suggests the pleasantly irresistible quality of the source of "contagion": *his infectious enthusiasm stimulated applause.*

con·tain (kən tān′), *v.t.* **1.** to have within itself; hold within fixed limits. **2.** to be capable of holding; have capacity for. **3.** to have as contents or constituent parts; comprise; include. **4.** to keep within proper bounds; restrain: *to contain oneself or one's feelings.* **5.** *Math.* to be divisible by, without a remainder. **6.** to be equal to: *a quart contains two pints.* [ME *conteine(n),* t. OF: m. *contenir,* g. L *continēre* hold together, hold back] —**con·tain′a·ble,** *adj.* —**Syn. 1.** CONTAIN, ACCOMMODATE, HOLD express the idea that something is so designed that something else can exist or be placed within it. CONTAIN refers to what is actually within a given container. HOLD emphasizes the idea of causing to remain in position, or keeping within bounds; it refers also to the greatest amount or number that can be kept within a given container. ACCOMMODATE means to contain comfortably or conveniently, or to meet the needs of a certain number. A passenger plane which ACCOMMODATES fifty passengers may be able to HOLD sixty, but at a given time may CONTAIN only thirty.

con·tain·er (kən tā′nər), *n.* **1.** one who or that which contains. **2.** a vessel, receptacle, or other containing or enclosing structure.

contam., contamination.

con·tam·i·nate (*v.* kən tăm′ə nāt′; *adj.* -nǐt, -nāt′), *v.,* **-nated, -nating,** *adj.* —*v.t.* **1.** to render impure by contact or mixture. —*adj.* **2.** *Archaic.* contaminated. [t. L: m. s. *contāminātus,* pp.] —**con·tam′i·na′tive,** *adj.* —**con·tam′i·na′tor,** *n.* —**Syn. 1.** defile, pollute, befoul, sully, taint, infect, poison, corrupt.

con·tam·i·na·tion (kən tăm′ə nā′shən), *n.* **1.** act of contaminating. **2.** state of being contaminated. **3.** something that contaminates.

contd., continued.

conte (kôNt), *n.,* *pl.* **contes** (kôNts; *Fr.* kôNt). a tale or short story, esp. of extraordinary and usually imaginary events. [t. F]

con·temn (kən těm′), *v.t.* to treat disdainfully or scornfully; view with contempt. [t. L: s. *contemnere* despise] —**con·temn′er,** *con·tem·nor* (kən těm′nər), *n.*

con·tem·plate (kŏn′təm plāt′, kən těm′plāt), *v.,* **-plated, -plating.** —*v.t.* **1.** to look at or view with continued attention; observe thoughtfully. **2.** to consider attentively; reflect upon. **3.** to have as a purpose; intend. **4.** to have in view as a future event. —*v.i.* **5.** to think studiously; meditate; consider deliberately. [t. L: m. s. *contemplātus,* pp., having surveyed] —**con′tem·pla′tor,** *n.* —**Syn. 1.** observe, regard. **2.** meditate on, ponder. **3.** purpose, design, plan.

con·tem·pla·tion (kŏn′təm plā′shən), *n.* **1.** act of contemplating; thoughtful observation or consideration; reflection. **2.** religious meditation. **3.** purpose or intention. **4.** prospect or expectation.

con·tem·pla·tive (kŏn′təm plā′tǐv, kən těm′plə-), *adj.* given to or characterized by contemplation. —**con′tem·pla′tive·ly,** *adv.* —**con′tem·pla′tive·ness,** *n.* —**Syn.** thoughtful, reflective, meditative. —**Ant.** active.

con·tem·po·ra·ne·ous (kən těm′pə rā′nǐ əs), *adj.* contemporary. [t. L: m. *contemporāneus*] —**con·tem′po·ra′ne·ous·ly,** *adv.* —**con·tem′po·ra′ne·ous·ness,** *n.*

con·tem·po·rar·y (kən těm′pə rěr′ǐ), *adj., n., pl.* **-raries.** —*adj.* **1.** belonging to the same time; existing or occurring at the same time. **2.** of the same age or date. —*n.* **3.** one belonging to the same time or period with another or others. **4.** a person of the same age as another. [f. CON- + TEMPORARY] —**Syn. 1.** contemporaneous, coeval, coexistent, synchronous, simultaneous.

con·tem·po·rize (kən těm′pə rīz′), *v.,* **-rized, -rizing.** —*v.t.* **1.** to place in, or regard as belonging to, the same age or time. —*v.i.* **2.** to be contemporary.

con·tempt (kən těmpt′), *n.* **1.** act of contemning or despising. **2.** the feeling with which one regards anything

considered mean, vile, or worthless; disdain; scorn. **3.** state of being despised; dishonor; disgrace. **4.** *Law.* **a.** disobedience to, or open disrespect of, the rules or orders of a court or legislature. **b.** an act showing this disrespect. [ME, t. L: s. *contemptus* scorn] —**Syn. 2.** CONTEMPT, DISDAIN, SCORN imply strong feelings of disapproval combined with disgust or derision. CONTEMPT is disapproval tinged with disgust for what seems mean, base, or worthless: *to feel contempt for a weakling.* DISDAIN is a feeling that something is beneath the level of one's own dignity or is unworthy of one's notice or acceptance: *disdain for crooked dealing.* SCORN denotes derisive, open, or undisguised contempt, as for a thing thought unworthy of considerate treatment: *scorn for attempted evasion of punishment by blaming others.* —**Ant. 2.** respect.

con·tempt·i·ble (kən těmp′tə bəl), *adj.* **1.** deserving of or held in contempt; despicable. **2.** *Obs.* contemptuous. —**con·tempt′i·bil′i·ty, con·tempt′i·ble·ness,** *n.* —**con·tempt′i·bly,** *adv.* —**Syn. 1.** mean, abject, low, base. —**Ant. 1.** admirable.

con·temp·tu·ous (kən těmp′chōō əs), *adj.* manifesting or expressing contempt or disdain; scornful. [f. L *contemptu(s)* scorn + -OUS] —**con·temp′tu·ous·ly,** *adv.* —**con·temp′tu·ous·ness,** *n.* —**Syn.** disdainful, sneering, insolent, arrogant, supercilious, haughty.

con·tend (kən těnd′), *v.i.* **1.** to struggle in opposition. **2.** to strive in rivalry; compete; vie. **3.** to strive in debate; dispute earnestly. —*v.t.* **4.** to assert or maintain earnestly. [t. L: s. *contendere* stretch out] —**con·tend′er,** *n.* —**Syn. 1.** wrestle, grapple, battle, fight. **2.** See **compete. 3.** argue, wrangle. —**Ant. 3.** agree.

con·tent¹ (kŏn′těnt; *rarely* kən těnt′), *n., pl.* **contents** (kŏn′těnts *or, esp. Brit.* kən těnts′). **1.** (*usually pl.*) that which is contained: *the contents of a cask, room, or book.* **2.** substance or purport, as of a document. **3.** the sum of the attributes or notions composing a given conception; the substance or matter of cognition, etc. **4.** power of containing; capacity; volume. **5.** area; extent; size. **6.** the amount contained. [t. L: s. *contentum* that which is contained, prop. pp. neut.]

con·tent² (kən těnt′), *adj.* **1.** having the desires limited to what one has; satisfied. **2.** easy in mind. **3.** willing or resigned; assenting. —*v.t.* **4.** to make content. —*n.* **5.** state or feeling of being contented; contentment. **6.** (in the British House of Lords) an affirmative vote or voter. [ME, t. L: s. *contentus* satisfied, prop. pp.] —**Syn. 4.** appease, gratify. See **satisfy.**

con·tent·ed (kən těn′tǐd), *adj.* satisfied, as with what one has or with something mentioned; content; resigned. —**con·tent′ed·ly,** *adv.* —**con·tent′ed·ness,** *n.*

con·ten·tion (kən těn′shən), *n.* **1.** a struggling together in opposition; strife. **2.** a striving in rivalry; competition; a contest. **3.** strife in debate; a dispute; a controversy. **4.** a point contended for or affirmed in controversy. [ME, t. L: s. *contentio* strife] —**Syn. 1.** struggle, conflict, combat. **3.** disagreement, dissension, debate, wrangle, altercation.

con·ten·tious (kən těn′shəs), *adj.* **1.** given to contention: *a contentious crew.* **2.** characterized by contention: *contentious issues.* **3.** *Law.* pertaining to causes between contending parties. [t. L: m.s. *contentiōsus*] —**con·ten′tious·ly,** *adv.* —**con·ten′tious·ness,** *n.*

con·tent·ment (kən těnt′mənt), *n.* **1.** state of being contented; satisfaction; ease of mind. **2.** *Archaic.* act of contenting. —**Syn. 1.** See **happiness.**

con·ter·mi·nous (kən tûr′mə nəs), *adj.* **1.** having a common boundary; bordering; contiguous. **2.** meeting at their ends. **3.** having the same boundaries or limits; coextensive. Also, **con·ter′mi·nal.** [t. L: m. *conterminus*] —**con·ter′mi·nous·ly,** *adv.*

con·test (*n.* kŏn′těst; *v.* kən těst′), *n.* **1.** struggle for victory or superiority. **2.** conflict between competitors; a competition. **3.** strife in argument; dispute; controversy. —*v.t.* **4.** to struggle or fight for, as in battle. **5.** to argue against; dispute. **6.** to call in question. **7.** to contend for in rivalry. —*v.i.* **8.** to dispute; contend; compete. [t. F: s. *contester,* t. L: m. *contestārī* call to witness, bring a legal action] —**con·test′a·ble,** *adj.* —**con·test′er,** *n.* —**Syn. 1.** See **fight. 2.** rivalry, match, tournament, game. **5.** controvert, oppose. **6.** challenge. **7.** strive, compete, vie. **8.** See **compete.**

con·test·ant (kən těs′tənt), *n.* **1.** one who takes part in a contest or competition. **2.** one who contests the result of an election. **3.** *Law.* the party who, in proceedings in the probate court, contests the validity of a will. [t. F, ppr. of *contester* contest, used as n.]

con·tes·ta·tion (kŏn′těs tā′shən), *n.* **1.** act of contesting. **2.** an assertion contended for.

con·text (kŏn′těkst), *n.* the parts of a discourse or writing which precede or follow, and are directly connected with, a given passage or word. [late ME, t. L: s. *contextus* connection]

con·tex·tu·al (kən těks′chōō əl), *adj.* of or pertaining to the context; depending on the context. [f. L *contextu(s)* connection + -AL¹] —**con·tex′tu·al·ly,** *adv.*

con·tex·ture (kən těks′chər, kŏn-), *n.* **1.** the disposition and union of the constituent parts of anything; constitution; structure. **2.** an interwoven structure; a fabric. **3.** act of weaving together. **4.** fact or manner of being woven together. [t. F, der. L *contexere* weave together. See CON-, TEXTURE.]

con·ti·gu·i·ty (kŏn′tə gū′ə tǐ), *n., pl.* **-ties. 1.** state of being contiguous. **2.** a series of things in continuous connection; a continuous mass or extent.

con·tig·u·ous (kən tĭg′yŏŏ əs), *adj.* **1.** touching; in contact. **2.** in close proximity without actually touching; near. [t. L: m. *contiguus* touching] —**con·tig′u·ous·ly**, *adv.* —**con·tig′u·ous·ness**, *n.*

con·ti·nence (kŏn′tə nəns). *n.* self-restraint, esp. in regard to sexual passion. Also, **con′ti·nen·cy**. [ME, t. L: m. s. *continentia*]

con·ti·nent (kŏn′tə nənt), *n.* **1.** one of the main land masses of the globe, usually reckoned as six in number (Europe, Asia, Africa, North America, South America and Australia). **2.** the mainland (as distinguished from islands or peninsulas). **3. the Continent,** the mainland of Europe (as distinguished from the British Isles). **4.** a continuous tract or extent, as of land. **5.** *Archaic.* that which contains, holds, or comprises. —*adj.* **6.** exercising restraint in relation to the desires or passions; temperate. **7.** characterized by self-restraint in regard to sexual passion; chaste. **8.** *Rare.* containing; being a container; capacious. **9.** *Obs.* restraining or restrictive. **10.** *Obs.* continuous; forming a continuous tract, as land. [ME, t. L: s. *continens*, pp., lit., holding together].

con·ti·nen·tal (kŏn′tə nĕn′təl), *adj.* **1.** of, or of the nature of, a continent. **2.** (*usually cap.*) of or pertaining to the mainland of Europe. **3.** (*cap.*) of the colonies during and immediately after the Revolutionary War: *the Continental Congress.* —*n.* **4.** (*cap.*) a soldier of the Continental army in the Revolutionary War. **5.** a piece of paper money issued by the Continental Congress during the war: *not worth a continental.* **6.** an inhabitant of a continent, esp. (*usually cap.*) of the mainland of Europe.

Continental Congress, one of the two American legislative congresses during and after the Revolutionary War, responsible for the Declaration of Independence and The Articles of Confederation.

continental divide, 1. a water parting between river systems that flow into different oceans. **2.** (*caps.*) (in North America) the line of summits of the Rocky Mountains, separating streams flowing toward the Gulf of California and the Pacific from those flowing toward the Gulf of Mexico, Hudson Bay, and the Arctic Ocean.

continental shelf, *Phys. Geog.* that portion of a continent submerged under relatively shallow sea, in contrast with the deep ocean basins from which it is separated by the relatively steep **continental slope.**

con·ti·nent·ly (kŏn′tə nənt lĭ), *adv.* in a continent manner; temperately.

con·tin·gence (kən tĭn′jəns), *n.* contact or tangency.

con·tin·gen·cy (kən tĭn′jən sĭ), *n., pl.* **-cies. 1.** fortuitousness; uncertainty; dependence on chance or on the fulfillment of a condition. **2.** a contingent event; a chance, accident, or possibility, conditional on something uncertain. **3.** something incidental to a thing.

contingency table, *Statist.* the frequency distribution for a two-way statistical classification.

con·tin·gent (kən tĭn′jənt), *adj.* **1.** dependent for existence, occurrence, character, etc., on something not yet certain; conditional (often fol. by *on* or *upon*). **2.** liable to happen or not; uncertain; possible. **3.** happening by chance or without known cause; fortuitous; accidental. **4.** *Logic.* (of a proposition) not involving any self-contradiction if denied, so that its truth or falsity can be established only by sensory observation (as opposed to *analytic* or *necessary* propositions). —*n.* **5.** the proportion that falls to one as a share to be contributed or furnished. **6.** a quota of troops furnished. **7.** any one of the representative groups composing an assemblage: *the New York contingent at a national convention.* **8.** something contingent; a contingency. [ME, t. L: s. *contigens*, ppr., touching, bordering on, reaching, befalling] —**con·tin′gent·ly**, *adv.*

con·tin·u·al (kən tĭn′yŏŏ əl), *adj.* **1.** proceeding without interruption or cessation; continuous in time. **2.** of regular or frequent recurrence; often repeated; very frequent. —**Syn. 1, 2.** unceasing, ceaseless, incessant, uninterrupted, unremitting, constant.

—**Syn. 1, 2.** CONTINUAL, CONSTANT, CONTINUOUS, all refer to a succession of occurrences. CONTINUAL implies that successive recurrences are very close together, with only small breaks between them, or none at all: *continual misunderstanding between nations.* CONSTANT implies always recurring in the same way, under uniform conditions, with similar results, and the like: *constant repetition of the same mistakes.* CONTINUOUS emphasizes the idea that the succession is unbroken: *the continuous life of the universe.*

con·tin·u·al·ly (kən tĭn′yŏŏ ə lĭ), *adv.* **1.** without cessation or intermission; unceasingly. **2.** very often; at regular or frequent intervals; habitually.

con·tin·u·ance (kən tĭn′yŏŏ əns), *n.* **1.** act or fact of continuing; continuation. **2.** a continuation or sequel. **3.** *Law.* adjournment of a step in a proceeding to a future day. [ME, t. OF, der. *continuer* CONTINUE]

con·tin·u·ant (kən tĭn′yŏŏ ənt), *n.* *Phonet.* a consonant, such as *f* or *m*, which may be prolonged without change of quality. [t. L: s. *continuans*, ppr., continuing]

con·tin·u·a·tion (kən tĭn′yŏŏ ā′shən), *n.* **1.** act or fact of continuing or prolonging. **2.** state of being continued. **3.** extension or carrying on to a further point: *the continuation of a story.* **4.** that by which anything is continued; a sequel, as to a story.

continuation school, a school in which instruction (special or general) is given in continuation or extension of that given in the lower schools, for the benefit of those who have left school while in the lower grades to work.

con·tin·u·a·tive (kən tĭn′yŏŏ ā′tĭv), *adj.* **1.** tending or serving to continue, or to cause continuation or prolongation. **2.** expressing continuance of thought. **3.** expressing a following event. In the sentence "They arrested a suspect, who gave his name as John Doe," the second clause is a continuative clause. —*n.* **4.** something continuative. **5.** a continuative word or expression. —**con·tin′u·a·tive·ly**, *adv.* —**con·tin′u·a′tive·ness**, *n.*

con·tin·u·a·tor (kən tĭn′yŏŏ ā′tər), *n.* one who or that which continues; the continuator of a story.

con·tin·ue (kən tĭn′ū), *v.,* **-tinued, -tinuing.** —*v.i.* **1.** to go forward or onward in any course or action; keep on. **2.** to go on after suspension or interruption. **3.** to last or endure. **4.** to remain in a place; abide; stay. **5.** to remain in a particular state or capacity. —*v.t.* **6.** to go on with or persist in: *to continue an action.* **7.** to extend from one point to another in space; prolong. **8.** to carry on from the point of suspension or interruption: *to continue a narrative.* **9.** to say in continuation. **10.** to cause to last or endure; maintain or retain, as in a position. **11.** to carry over, postpone, or adjourn; keep pending, as a legal proceeding. [ME *continue(n),* t. L: m. *continuāre* make continuous] —**con·tin′u·a·ble**, *adj.* —**con·tin′u·er**, *n.*

—**Syn. 3.** CONTINUE, ENDURE, LAST, REMAIN imply existing uninterruptedly for an appreciable length of time. CONTINUE implies duration or existence without break or interruption: *the rain continued two days.* ENDURE implies persistent continuance against influences that tend to weaken, undermine, or destroy: *brass endures through many years.* LAST often applies to that which holds out to a desired end, fresh, unimpaired, or unexhausted, sometimes under conditions that tend to produce the opposite effect: *they had provisions enough to last all winter.* REMAIN is esp. applied to what continues without change in its essential state: *he remained a bachelor.*

continued fraction, a fraction whose denominator contains a fraction whose denominator contains a fraction, and so on, as

$$2\cfrac{}{7+\cfrac{1}{9+\cfrac{3}{4+\ldots}}}$$

con·ti·nu·i·ty (kŏn′tə nū′ə tĭ, -nōō′-), *n., pl.* **-ties. 1.** state or quality of being continuous. **2.** a continuous or connected whole. **3.** a motion-picture scenario giving the complete action, scenes, etc., in detail and in the order in which they are to be shown on the screen. **4.** a radio script for the spoken parts.

con·tin·u·ous (kən tĭn′yŏŏ əs), *adj.* **1.** having the parts in immediate connection. **2.** uninterrupted in time; without cessation. [t. L: m. *continuus* hanging together] —**con·tin′u·ous·ly**, *adv.* —**con·tin′u·ous·ness**, *n.* —**Syn. 2.** See **continual.**

continuous waves, *Radio.* electric waves which are not intermittent or broken up into damped wave trains, but (unless intentionally interrupted) follow one another without any interval of time between.

con·tin·u·um (kən tĭn′yŏŏ əm), *n., pl.* **-tinua** (-tĭn′yŏŏ ə). **1.** a continuous extent, series, or whole. **2.** *Math.* an infinite set of objects such that between any two of them there is a third object: *the continuum of rational numbers.* [t. L, neut. of *continuus* CONTINUOUS]

con·to (kŏn′tō; *Port.* kôn′tŏŏ), *n., pl.* **-tos** (-tōz; *Port.* -tŏŏsh; *Brazil.* -tŏŏs). **1.** a Portuguese or Brazilian money of account, in which large sums are calculated, equal to 1,000,000 reis. The sign for the conto is (:) and the thousand conto is (.). One thousand milreis is written Rs. 1:000$000. **2.** *Portugal.* 1000 escudos. **3.** *Brazil.* 1000 milreis. [t. Pg., g. L *computus* calculated]

con·tort (kən tôrt′), *v.t.* to twist; bend or draw out of shape; distort. [t. L: s. *contortus*, pp., twisted] —**con·tor′tion**, *n.*

con·tor·tion·ist (kən tôr′shən ĭst), *n.* **1.** one who performs gymnastic feats involving contorted postures. **2.** one who practices contortion: *a verbal contortionist.*

con·tour (kŏn′tŏŏr), *n.* **1.** the outline of a figure or body; the line that defines or bounds anything. **2.** a contour line. —*v.t.* **3.** to mark with contour lines. **4.** to make or form the contour or outline of. **5.** to build (a road, etc.) in conformity to a contour. —*adj.* **6.** *Agric.* of or used in a system of plowing and sowing along the contour lines of the terrain, thereby preventing rain water from washing away the topsoil. [t. F, t. It.: m. *contorno,* der. *contornare,* f. L: *con-* CON + *tornāre* turn]

contour feathers, any of the feathers which form the surface plumage of a bird, apart from wings, tail, and specialized types, as filoplumes.

contour interval, the difference in elevation represented by each contour line on a map.

contour line, 1. a line joining points of equal elevation on a surface. **2.** the representation of such a line on a map.

contour map, a map on which irregularities of land surface are shown by contour lines, the relative spacing of the lines indicating the relative slope of the surface.

contr., 1. contracted. **2.** contraction.

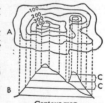
Contour map
A. Contour; B. Elevation;
C. Contour interval

contra-, a prefix meaning "against," "opposite," or "opposing." [t. L, prefix use of *contrā*, adv. and prep.]

con·tra·band (kŏn′trə bănd′), *n.* 1. anything prohibited by law from being imported or exported. 2. goods imported or exported illegally. 3. illegal or prohibited traffic; smuggling. 4. *Internal. Law.* goods which neutrals cannot supply to one belligerent except at the risk of seizure and confiscation by the other (**contraband of war**). 5. *U.S.* (during the Civil War) a Negro slave who escaped to or was brought within the Union lines. —*adj.* 6. prohibited from export or import. [t. Sp.: m. *contrabando*; r. *counterband* t. F: m. *contrebande*, t. It.: m. *contrabando*, f. *contra* against (g. L *contrā*) + *bando* proclamation (g. LL *bandum* BAN², n.)]

con·tra·band·ist (kŏn′trə băn′dĭst), *n.* a smuggler.

con·tra·bass (kŏn′trə băs′), *Music.* —*n.* 1. (in any family of instruments) the member below the bass. 2. (in the violin family) the double bass. —*adj.* 3. denoting such instruments: *a contrabass trombone.* —**con·tra·bass·ist** (kŏn′trə bā′sĭst, -băs′ĭst), *n.*

con·tra·bassoon (kŏn′trə), a bassoon larger in size and an octave lower in pitch than the ordinary bassoon; a double bassoon.

con·tra·cep·tion (kŏn′trə sĕp′shən), *n.* the prevention of conception by deliberate measures, in order to prevent childbirth. [f. CONTRA- + (CON)CEPTION]

con·tra·cep·tive (kŏn′trə sĕp′tĭv), *adj.* 1. tending or serving to prevent conception or impregnation. 2. pertaining to contraception. —*n.* 3. a contraceptive agent or device.

con·tra·clock·wise (kŏn′trə klŏk′wīz′), *adj., adv.* counterclockwise.

con·tract (*n.* and *usually for v.* 12 kŏn′trăkt; *otherwise v.* kən trăkt′), *n.* 1. an agreement between two or more parties for the doing or not doing of some definite thing. 2. an agreement enforceable by law. 3. the writing containing such an agreement. 4. the division of law dealing with contracts. 5. the formal agreement of marriage; betrothal. 6. Also, **contract bridge**. a modification of auction bridge in which the side which wins the bid can earn towards game only that number of tricks bid, all additional points being credited above the score line. 7. (in auction or contract bridge) a. the highest bid. b. the number of tricks so bid. [ME, t. LL: s. *contractus* agreement] —*v.t.* 8. to draw together or into smaller compass; draw the parts of together: *to contract a muscle.* 9. to wrinkle: *to contract the brows.* 10. to shorten (a word, etc.) by combining or omitting some of its elements. 11. to acquire, as by habit or contagion; incur, as a liability or obligation: *to contract a disease or debts.* 12. to settle or establish by agreement: *to contract an alliance.* 13. to enter into (friendship, acquaintance, etc.). 14. to betroth. —*v.i.* 15. to be drawn together or reduced in compass; become smaller; shrink. 16. to enter into an agreement. [t. L: s. *contractus*, pp., drawn together] —**con·tract′i·ble,** *adj.* —**con·tract′i·bil′i·ty, contract′i·ble·ness,** *n.*

—**Syn.** 1. See **agreement**. 8. reduce, shorten, lessen, narrow, shrivel, shrink. CONTRACT, COMPRESS, CONCENTRATE, CONDENSE imply retaining original content but reducing the amount of space occupied. CONTRACT means to cause to draw more closely together: *to contract a muscle.* COMPRESS suggests causing to become smaller by means of fairly uniform external pressure: *to compress gases into liquid form, clay into bricks.* CONCENTRATE implies causing to gather around a point, or eliminating nonessentials: *to concentrate troops near an objective, attention, strength.* CONDENSE implies increasing the compactness, or thickening the consistency of a homogeneous mass: *to condense milk.*—**Ant.** 8. expand.

con·tract·ed (kən trăk′tĭd), *adj.* 1. drawn together; shrunken. 2. condensed; abridged. 3. narrow or illiberal; restricted: *contracted circumstances.* —**con·tract′ed·ly,** *adv.* —**con·tract′ed·ness,** *n.*

con·trac·tile (kən trăk′təl, -tĭl), *adj.* capable of undergoing or of producing contraction. —**con·trac·til·i·ty** (kŏn′trăk tĭl′ə tĭ), *n.*

con·trac·tion (kən trăk′shən), *n.* 1. act of contracting. 2. state of being contracted. 3. a shortened form of a word, etc., as *e'er* for *ever, can't* for *cannot.* 4. *Physiol.* the change in a muscle by which it becomes thickened and shortened. 5. a restriction or withdrawal, as of currency or of funds available as call money. [t. L: s. *contractio* a drawing together]

con·trac·tive (kən trăk′tĭv), *adj.* serving or tending to contract. —**con·trac′tive·ly,** *adv.* —**con·trac′tive·ness,** *n.*

con·trac·tor (kŏn′trăk tər, kən trăk′tər), *n.* 1. one who contracts to furnish supplies or perform work at a certain price or rate. 2. one who or that which contracts. [t. LL]

con·trac·tu·al (kən trăk′chōō əl), *adj.* of, or of the nature of, a contract. [f. L *contractu(s)* contract + -AL¹]

con·tra·dance (kŏn′trə dăns′, -däns′), *n.* contredanse.

con·tra·dict (kŏn′trə dĭkt′), *v.t.* 1. to assert the contrary or opposite of; deny directly and categorically. 2. to deny the words or assertion of (a person). 3. (of a statement, action, etc.) to be directly contrary to. 4. *Obs.* to speak or declare against; oppose. —*v.i.* 5. to utter a contrary statement. [t. L: s. *contrādictus*, pp., said against] —**con′tra·dict′a·ble,** *adj.* —**con′tra·dict′er,** **con·tra·dic′tor,** *n.* —**Syn.** 1, 2. gainsay, impugn, controvert, dispute. See **deny**.

con·tra·dic·tion (kŏn′trə dĭk′shən), *n.* 1. act of contradicting; gainsaying or opposition. 2. assertion of the contrary or opposite; denial. 3. a statement or proposition that contradicts or denies another or itself. 4. direct opposition between things compared; inconsistency. 5. a contradictory act, fact, etc. 6. See **law of contradictions.**

con·tra·dic·tious (kŏn′trə dĭk′shəs), *adj.* 1. inclined to contradict; disputatious. 2. *Archaic.* self-contradictory. [f. CONTRADICTI(ON) + -OUS]

con·tra·dic·tive (kŏn′trə dĭk′tĭv), *adj.* tending to contradict; involving contradiction.

con·tra·dic·to·ry (kŏn′trə dĭk′tə rĭ), *adj., n., pl.* -ries. —*adj.* 1. of the nature of a contradiction; asserting the contrary or opposite; contradicting each other; inconsistent. 2. given to contradiction. —*n.* 3. *Logic.* a proposition so related to a second that it is impossible for both to be true or both to be false. —**con′tra·dic′to·ri·ly,** *adv.* —**con′tra·dic′to·ri·ness,** *n.* —**Syn.** 1. opposing, antagonistic, irreconcilable, paradoxical.

con·tra·dis·tinc·tion (kŏn′trə dĭs tĭngk′shən), *n.* distinction by opposition or contrast: *plants and animals in contradistinction to man.* —**con′tra·dis·tinc′tive, con′tra·dis·tinc′tive·ly,** *adv.*

con·tra·dis·tin·guish (kŏn′trə dĭs tĭng′gwĭsh), *v.t.* to distinguish by contrasting opposite qualities.

con·tra·in·di·cate (kŏn′trə ĭn′də kāt′), *v.t.,* -cated, -cating. *Med.* (of a symptom or condition) to give indication against the advisability of (a particular or usual remedy or treatment). —**con·tra·in·di·cant** (kŏn′trə ĭn′də kənt), *n.* —**con′tra·in′di·ca′tion,** *n.*

con·tral·to (kən trăl′tō), *n., pl.* -tos, *adj. Music.* —*n.* 1. the lowest female voice or voice part, intermediate between soprano and tenor. 2. the alto, or highest male voice or voice part. 3. a singer with a contralto voice. —*adj.* 4. pertaining to the contralto or its compass. [t. It., f. *contra* against, counter to + *alto* high]

con·trap·tion (kən trăp′shən), *n. Colloq.* a contrivance; a device.

con·tra·pun·tal (kŏn′trə pŭn′təl), *adj. Music.* 1. of or pertaining to counterpoint. 2. composed of two or more relatively independent melodies sounded together. [f. m. It. *contrappunto* counterpoint + -AL¹] —**con′tra·pun′tal·ly,** *adv.*

con·tra·pun·tist (kŏn′trə pŭn′tĭst), *n.* one skilled in the practice of counterpoint.

con·tra·ri·e·ty (kŏn′trə rī′ə tĭ), *n., pl.* -ties. 1. state or quality of being contrary. 2. something contrary or of opposite character; a contrary fact or statement. [t. LL: m.s. *contrārietas*]

con·trar·i·ous (kən trâr′ĭ əs), *adj. Now Rare.* 1. perverse. 2. adverse. [ME, t. ML: m. s. *contrāriōsus*]

con·tra·ri·wise (kŏn′trĕr ĭ wīz′), *adv.* 1. in the opposite way. 2. on the contrary. 3. perversely.

con·tra·ry (kŏn′trĕr ĭ; *for 5 also* kən trâr′ĭ), *adj., n., pl.* -ries, *adv.* —*adj.* 1. opposite in nature or character; diametrically opposed; mutually opposed: *contrary to fact, contrary propositions.* 2. opposite in direction or position. 3. being the opposite one of two. 4. untoward or unfavorable: *contrary winds.* 5. perverse; self-willed. 6. *Bot.* at right angles. —*n.* 7. that which is contrary or opposite: *to prove the contrary of a statement.* 8. either of two contrary things. 9. *Logic.* a proposition so related to a second that it is impossible for both to be true though both may be false. For example: *all judges are male* is the contrary of *no judges are male.* 10. by contraries, a. by way of opposition. b. contrary to expectation. 11. on the contrary, in extreme opposition to what has been stated. 12. to the contrary, to the opposite or a different effect. —*adv.* 13. contrarily; contrariwise. [ME *contrarie*, t. AF, t. L: m. *contrārius* opposite, hostile] —**con′tra·ri·ly,** *adv.* —**con′tra·ri·ness,** *n.*

—**Syn.** 1. contradictory, conflicting, discordant, counter. See **opposite**. 4. CONTRARY, ADVERSE both describe that which unfavorably opposes. CONTRARY conveys an idea of something impersonal and objective whose opposition happens to be unfavorable: *contrary winds.* ADVERSE suggests something more personally unfriendly or even hostile; it emphasizes the idea of the resulting misfortune to that which is opposed: *the judge rendered a decision adverse to the defendant.* 5. intractable, refractory, obstinate, headstrong.

contrary motion, *Music.* one part rising in pitch while the other descends, and vice versa.

con·trast (*v.* kən trăst′; *n.* kŏn′trăst), *v.t.* 1. to set in opposition in order to show unlikeness; compare by observing differences. 2. to afford or form a contrast to; set off. —*v.i.* 3. to exhibit unlikeness on comparison; form a contrast. —*n.* 4. act of contrasting. 5. state of being contrasted. 6. a striking exhibition of unlikeness. 7. something strikingly unlike. 8. opposition or juxtaposition of different forms, lines, or colors in a work of art to intensify each other's properties and produce a more dynamic expression. [t. F: s. *contraster,* t. It.: m. *contrastare,* g. LL: withstand, oppose] —**con·trast′a·ble,** *adj.* —**Syn.** 1. differentiate, discriminate, distinguish, oppose. See **compare**.

con·trast·y (kən trăs′tĭ), *adj. Photog.* having coarse or sharp gradations of tone, esp. between dark and light areas (opposed to *soft*).

con·tra·val·la·tion (kŏn′trə və lā′shən), *n. Fort.* a chain of redoubts and breastworks raised by besiegers about the place invested. [t. F: m. *contrevallation,* f. *contre-* CONTRA- + s. LL *vallātio* entrenchment]

con·tra·vene (kŏn′trə vēn′), *v.t.*, -vened, -vening.
1. to come or be in conflict with; go or act counter to;
oppose. **2.** to violate, infringe, or transgress: *to contravene the law*. [t. L: m. s. *contrāvenīre* oppose] —**con′tra-
ven′er**, *n.*

con·tra·ven·tion (kŏn′trə vĕn′shən), *n.* act of con-
travening; action counter to something; violation.

con·tra·yer·va (kŏn′trə yûr′və) *n.* the root of certain plants of the tropical American moraceous genus
Dorstenia, esp. *D. contrayerva*, used as a stimulant, tonic,
and diaphoretic. [t. Sp.: counter herb, antidote, f. L
contra- CONTRA- + Sp. *yerva* herb]

con·tre·danse (kôN trə däNs′), *n.* **1.** a variation of
the quadrille, in which the dancers face each other. **2.** a
piece of music suitable for such a dance. Also, **contra-
dance**. [F, mistranslation of COUNTRY-DANCE]

con·tre·temps (kôN trə täN′), *n., pl.* -temps (-tänz′;
Fr. -täN′). an inopportune occurrence; an embarrassing
mischance. [t. F, respelling of *contretant*, g. OF *contrestant*
opposing, ppr. of *contrester* oppose, g. L *contrāstāre*]

con·trib·ute (kən trĭb′ūt), *v.*, -uted, -uting. —*v.t.*
1. to give in common with others; give to a common
stock or for a common purpose: *to contribute money,
time, help.* **2.** to furnish to a magazine or journal. —*v.i.*
3. to make contribution; furnish a contribution. [t. L:
m. s. *contribūtus*, pp., brought together] —**con·trib′-
ut·a·ble**, *adj.* —**con·trib′u·tive**, *adj.* —**con·trib′u-
tive·ly**, *adv.* —**con·trib′u·tive·ness**, *n.*

con·tri·bu·tion (kŏn′trə bū′shən), *n.* **1.** act of contributing. **2.** something contributed. **3.** an article
contributed to a magazine or the like. **4.** an impost or
levy. **5.** the method of distributing liability, in case of
loss, among several insurers whose policies attach to the
same risk. [ME, t. L: s. *contribūtio*]

con·trib·u·tor (kən trĭb′yə tər), *n.* **1.** one that contributes. **2.** one who contributes articles to a newspaper,
magazine, or other joint literary work.

con·trib·u·to·ry (kən trĭb′yə tōr′ĭ), *adj., n., pl.* -ries.
—*adj.* **1.** pertaining to or of the nature of contribution;
contributing. **2.** furnishing something toward a result:
contributory negligence. **3.** subject to contribution or
levy. —*n.* **4.** one who or that which contributes.

con·trite (kən trīt′, kŏn′trīt), *adj.* **1.** broken in spirit
by a sense of guilt; penitent: *a contrite sinner.* **2.** proceeding from contrition: *contrite tears.* [ME *contrit*, t.
L: s. *contrītus*, pp., ground, worn down] —**con·trite′ly**,
adv. —**con·trite′ness**, *n.*

con·tri·tion (kən trĭsh′ən), *n.* **1.** sincere penitence.
2. *Theol.* sorrow for and detestation of sin with a true
purpose of amendment, arising from a love of God for his
own perfections (**perfect contrition**), or from some inferior motive, as fear of divine punishment (**imperfect
contrition**). [ME, t. L: s. *contrītio*]

con·triv·ance (kən trī′vəns), *n.* **1.** something contrived; a device, esp. a mechanical one. **2.** act or manner of contriving; the faculty or power of contriving.
3. a plan or scheme; an expedient.

con·trive (kən trīv′), *v.*, -trived, -triving. —*v.t.* **1.** to
plan with ingenuity; devise; invent. **2.** to plot (evil,
etc.). **3.** to bring about or effect by a device, stratagem,
plan, or scheme; manage (to do something). —*v.i.* **4.** to
form schemes or designs; plan. **5.** to plot. [ME
treve(n), controve(n), t. OF: m. *controver*, f. con- CON- +
trover find. See TROVER] —**con·triv′a·ble**, *adj.* —**con-
triv′er**, *n.* —**Syn. 1.** See prepare.

con·trol (kən trōl′), *v.*, -trolled, -trolling, *n.* —*v.t.*
1. to exercise restraint or direction over; dominate; command. **2.** to hold in check; curb. **3.** to test or verify (a
scientific experiment) by a parallel experiment or other
standard of comparison. **4.** to check or regulate (payments, etc.), orig. by means of a duplicate register. —*n.*
5. act or power of controlling; regulation; domination
or command. **6.** check or restraint. **7.** something that
serves to control; a check; a standard of comparison
in scientific experimentation. **8.** a person who acts as a
check; a controller. **9.** a device for regulating and guiding a machine, as a motor, airplane, etc. **10.** (*pl.*) a coördinated arrangement of such devices. **11.** *Auto Racing, etc.* that portion of the track which is not included in
the timing. [t. F: s. *contrôler*, in OF *contreroller*, der. con-
trerolle register. See COUNTER-, ROLL] —**con·trol′la-
ble**, *adj.* —**con·trol′la·bil′i·ty**, *n.* —**con·trol′ment**, *n.*
—**Syn. 1.** manage, govern, rule. **3.** See authority.

control chart, *Statistics.* a chart on which observations are plotted as ordinates in the order in which they
are obtained, and on which **control lines** are constructed
to indicate whether the population from which the observations are being drawn is remaining the same (used
particularly in industrial quality control work).

control experiment, an experiment in which the
variables are controlled so that the effects of varying one
factor at a time may be observed.

con·trol·ler (kən trō′lər), *n.* **1.** one employed to check
expenditures, etc.; a comptroller. **2.** one who regulates,
directs, or restrains. **3.** *Brit. Aeron.* the dispatcher.
4. a regulating mechanism. —**con·trol′ler·ship′**, *n.*

control stick, a lever which, by tubes or cables, controls the ailerons and elevator of an airplane.

con·tro·ver·sial (kŏn′trə vûr′shəl), *adj.* **1.** of, or of
the nature of, controversy; polemical. **2.** subject to controversy; debatable. **3.** given to controversy; disputatious. —**con′tro·ver′sial·ist**, *n.* —**con′tro·ver′-
sial·ly**, *adv.*

con·tro·ver·sy (kŏn′trə vûr′sĭ), *n., pl.* -sies. **1.** dispute, debate, or contention; disputation concerning a
matter of opinion. **2.** a dispute or contention. [t. L: m.
s. *controversia* debate, contention] —**Syn. 1.** disagreement, altercation. **2.** quarrel, wrangle. See argument.

con·tro·vert (kŏn′trə vûrt′, kŏn′trə vûrt′), *v.t.* **1.** to
contend against in discussion; dispute; deny; oppose.
2. to contend about in discussion; debate; discuss.
—**con′tro·vert′er**, *n.* —**con′tro·vert′i·ble**, *adj.*
—**con′tro·vert′i·bly**, *adv.*

con·tu·ma·cious (kŏn′tyŏŏ mā′shəs, -tŏŏ-), *adj.* stubbornly perverse or rebellious; willfully and obstinately
disobedient. [f. m. CONTUMACY + -OUS] —**con′tu·ma′-
cious·ly**, *adv.* —**con′tu·ma′cious·ness**, *n.*

con·tu·ma·cy (kŏn′tyŏŏ mə sĭ, -tŏŏ-), *n., pl.* -cies.
stubborn perverseness or rebelliousness; willful and obstinate resistance or disobedience to authority. [ME
contumacie, t. L: m. *contumācia*, der. *contumax* stubborn]

con·tu·me·ly (kŏn′tyŏŏ mə lĭ, -tŏŏ-; kən tū′mə lĭ,
-tŏŏ-; *formerly* kŏn′tyŏŏ mē′lĭ), *n., pl.* -lies. **1.** insulting manifestation of contempt in words or actions; contemptuous or humiliating treatment. **2.** a humiliating
insult. [ME *contumelie*, t. L: m. *contumēlia*] —**con-
tu·me·li·ous** (kŏn′tyŏŏ mē′lĭ əs, -tŏŏ-, *adj.* —**con′tu-
me′li·ous·ly**, *adv.* —**con′tu·me′li·ous·ness**, *n.*

con·tuse (kən tūz′, -tŏŏz′), *v.t.*, -tused, -tusing. to
injure as by a blow with a blunt instrument, without
breaking the skin; bruise. [t. L: m. s. *contūsus*, pp.,
beaten together] —**con·tu·sive** (kən tū′sĭv, -tŏŏ′-), *adj.*

con·tu·sion (kən tū′zhən, -tŏŏ′-), *n.* an injury as from
a blow with a blunt instrument, without breaking of the
skin; a bruise.

co·nun·drum (kə nŭn′drəm), *n.* **1.** a riddle the answer
to which involves a pun or play on words. **2.** anything
that puzzles. [orig. unknown]

con·va·lesce (kŏn′və lĕs′), *v.i.*, -lesced, -lescing. to
grow stronger after illness; make progress toward recovery of health. [t. L: m.s. *convalescere* grow strong]

con·va·les·cence (kŏn′və lĕs′əns), *n.* **1.** the gradual
recovery of health and strength after illness. **2.** the period during which one is convalescing.

con·va·les·cent (kŏn′və lĕs′ənt), *adj.* **1.** convalescing. **2.** of or pertaining to convalescence or convales-
cents. —*n.* **3.** a convalescent person.

con·val·lar·i·a·ceous (kŏn′və lâr′ĭ ā′shəs), *adj.* belonging to the *Convallariaceae*, a family of plants including the lily of the valley, asparagus, etc. [f. s. NL *Convallaria* the lily-of-the-valley genus (der. L *convallis*
valley inclosed on all sides) + -ACEOUS]

con·vec·tion (kən vĕk′shən), *n.* **1.** *Physics.* the transference of heat by the circulation or movement of the
heated parts of a liquid or gas. **2.** *Meteorol.* a mechanical
process thermally produced involving the upward or
downward transfer of a limited portion of the atmosphere. Convection is essential to the formation of many
types of clouds. **3.** conveyance. [t. LL: s. *convectio*, der.
L *convehere* carry together] —**con·vec′tion·al**, *adj.*
—**con·vec′tive**, *adj.* —**con·vec′tive·ly**, *adv.*

con·ve·nance (kŏn′və näns′; *Fr.* kôN və näNs′), *n.* **1.**
suitability; expediency; propriety. **2.** (*pl.*) the proprieties or conventionalities. [t. F: agreement, propriety,
der. *convenir* agree, be fitting, g. L *convenīre* come to-
gether]

con·vene (kən vēn′), *v.*, -vened, -vening. —*v.i.* **1.** to
come together; assemble, usually for some public purpose. —*v.t.* **2.** to cause to assemble; convoke. **3.** to
summon or convene, as before a judicial officer. [late ME,
t. L: m.s. *convenīre* come together] —**con·ven′er**, *n.*
—**Syn. 1.** congregate, meet, collect, gather.

con·ven·ience (kən vēn′yəns), *n.* **1.** quality of being
convenient; suitability. **2.** a situation of affairs or a
time convenient for one: *to await one's convenience.*
3. advantage, as from something convenient: *a shelter for
the convenience of travelers.* **4.** anything convenient; an
advantage; an accommodation; a convenient appliance,
utensil, or the like.

con·ven·ient (kən vēn′yənt), *adj.* **1.** agreeable to the
needs or purpose; well-suited with respect to facility or
ease in use; favorable, easy, or comfortable for use.
2. at hand; easily accessible. **3.** *Obs.* fitting or appropriate. [ME, t. L: s. *conveniens*, ppr., agreeing; suiting]
—**con·ven′ient·ly**, *adv.* —**Syn. 1.** suitable, adapted,
serviceable.

con·vent (kŏn′vĕnt), *n.* **1.** a community of persons
devoted to religious life under a superior. **2.** a society of
monks, friars, or nuns. **3.** (in popular usage) a society of
nuns. **4.** the building or buildings occupied by such a
society; a monastery or nunnery. **5.** (in popular usage)
a nunnery. [t. L: s. *conventus* meeting, assembly, company, in ML convent; r. ME *covent*, t. AF]

con·ven·ti·cle (kən vĕn′tə kəl), *n.* **1.** a secret or unauthorized meeting, esp. for religious worship, as those
held by Protestant dissenters in England when they were
prohibited by law. **2.** a place of meeting or assembly,
esp. a nonconformist meetinghouse. **3.** *Obs.* a meeting
or assembly. [ME, t. L: m. s. *conventiculum*, dim. of *conventus* meeting] —**con·ven′ti·cler**, *n.*

con·ven·tion (kən vĕn′shən), *n.* **1.** a meeting or assembly, esp., a formal assembly, as of representatives or
delegates, for action on particular matters. **2.** *U.S.
Pol.* a representative party assembly to nominate candidates, adopt platforms, and adopt party rules. **3.** an
agreement, compact, or contract. **4.** an international

b., blend of, blended; c., cognate with; d., dialect, dialectal; der., derived from; f., formed from; g., going back to;
m., modification of; r., replacing; s., stem of; t., taken from; ?, perhaps. See the full key on inside cover.

agreement, esp. one dealing with a specific matter, as postal service, copyright, arbitration, etc. **5.** general agreement or consent; accepted usage, esp. as a standard of procedure. **6.** conventionalism. **7.** a rule, method, or practice established by general consent or usage. [t. L: s. *conventio* a meeting]
—**Syn. 1.** CONVENTION, ASSEMBLY, CONFERENCE, CONVOCATION name meetings for particular purposes. CONVENTION usually suggests a meeting of delegates representing political, church, social, or fraternal organizations. ASSEMBLY usually implies a meeting for a settled or customary purpose, as for discussion, legislation, or participation in a social function. CONFERENCE suggests a meeting for consultation and discussion about business or professional problems. CONVOCATION denotes a (church) assembly, the members of which have been summoned for a special purpose; chapel services at some colleges are called CONVOCATIONS. **7.** custom, precedent.

con·ven·tion·al (kən věn′shən əl), *adj.* **1.** conforming or adhering to accepted standards, as of conduct or taste. **2.** pertaining to convention or general agreement; established by general consent or accepted usage; arbitrarily determined: *conventional symbols.* **3.** formal, rather than spontaneous or original: *conventional phraseology.* **4.** *Art.* **a.** in accordance with accepted manner, model, or tradition. **b.** (of figurative art) represented in a generalized or simplified manner. **5.** of or pertaining to a convention, agreement, or compact. **6.** *Law.* resting on consent, express or implied. **7.** of or pertaining to a convention or assembly. —**con·ven′tion·al·ist,** *n.* —**con·ven′tion·al·ly,** *adv.* —**Syn. 1.** See **formal.**

con·ven·tion·al·ism (kən věn′shə nə līz′əm), *n.* **1.** adherence or the tendency to adhere to that which is conventional. **2.** something conventional.

con·ven·tion·al·i·ty (kən věn′shə năl′ə tĭ), *n.*, *pl.* **-ties. 1.** conventional quality or character. **2.** adherence to convention. **3.** a conventional practice, principle, form, etc. **4. the conventionalities,** the conventional rules of propriety.

con·ven·tion·al·ize (kən věn′shən əl īz′), *v.t.*, **-ized, -izing. 1.** to make conventional. **2.** *Art.* to represent in a conventional manner. —**con·ven′tion·al·i·za′tion,** *n.*

con·ven·tu·al (kən věn′chōō əl), *adj.* **1.** of, belonging to, or characteristic of a convent. —*n.* **2.** (*cap.*) one of an order of Franciscan friars which in the 15th century was separated from the Observants, and which follows a mitigated rule. **3.** an inmate of a convent. [late ME, t. ML: s. *conventuālis,* der. *conventus* CONVENT]

con·verge (kən vûrj′), *v.,* **-verged, -verging.** —*v.i.* **1.** to tend to meet in a point or line; incline toward each other, as lines which are not parallel. **2.** to tend to a common result, conclusion, etc. —*v.t.* **3.** to cause to converge. [t. LL: m.s. *convergere* incline together]

con·ver·gence (kən vûr′jəns), *n.* **1.** act or fact of converging. **2.** convergent state or quality. **3.** degree of convergence, or point of convergence. **4.** *Physiol.* a turning of the eyes inward to bear upon a near point. **5.** *Meteorol.* a condition brought about by a net flow of air into a given region. **6.** *Biol.* similarity of form or structure caused by environment rather than heredity. Also, **con·ver′gen·cy** for 1–3. —**con·ver′gent,** *adj.*

convergent evolution, the appearance of apparently similar structures in organisms of different lines of descent.

con·vers·a·ble (kən vûr′sə bəl), *adj.* **1.** that may be conversed with, esp. easily and agreeably. **2.** able or disposed to converse. **3.** pertaining to or proper for conversation. —**con·vers′a·ble·ness,** *n.* —**con·vers′a·bly,** *adv.*

con·ver·sant (kŏn′vər sənt, kən vûr′-), *adj.* **1.** familiar by use or study (fol. by *with*): *conversant with a subject.* **2.** having regular or frequent conversation; intimately associating; acquainted. [ME, t. L: s. *conversans,* ppr., associating with] —**con′ver·sance, con′ver·san·cy,** *n.* —**con′ver·sant·ly,** *adv.* —**Syn. 1.** versed, learned, skilled, practiced, well-informed; proficient.

con·ver·sa·tion (kŏn′vər sā′shən), *n.* **1.** informal interchange of thoughts by spoken words; a talk or colloquy. **2.** association or social intercourse; intimate acquaintance. **3.** *Obs.* familiar acquaintance from using or studying. **4.** *Archaic.* behavior, or manner of living. [ME, t. OF, t. L: s. *conversātio* frequent use, intercourse]

con·ver·sa·tion·al (kŏn′vər sā′shən əl), *adj.* **1.** of, pertaining to, or characteristic of, conversation. **2.** able, or ready to converse; given to conversation. —**con′ver·sa′tion·al·ly,** *adv.* —**Syn. 1.** See **colloquial.**

con·ver·sa·tion·al·ist (kŏn′vər sā′shən əl ĭst), *n.* one given to or excelling in conversation.

conversational quality, (in public speaking and reading) a manner of utterance which sounds like spontaneous, direct communication.

conversation piece, a type of painting esp. popular in England in the 18th century, showing a group of more or less fashionable people in an appropriate setting.

con·ver·sa·zi·o·ne (kŏn′vər săt′sĭ ō′nĭ; *It.* kôn′věr sä tsyô′ně), *n., pl.* **-ziones** (-sĭ ō′něz), *It.* **-zioni** (-tsyô′ně). *Italian,* a social gathering for conversation, etc., esp. on literary or scholarly subjects.

con·verse[1] (*v.* kən vûrs′; *n.* kŏn′vûrs), *v.,* **-versed, -versing,** *n.* —*v.i.* **1.** to talk informally with another;

interchange thought by speech. **2.** to hold inward communion (fol. by *with*). —*n.* **3.** familiar discourse or talk; conversation. **4.** inward communion. [ME *converse(n),* t. OF: m. *converser,* g. L *conversārī* dwell or associate with] —**con·vers′er,** *n.* —**Syn. 1.** talk, chat. See **speak.**

con·verse[2] (*adj.* kən vûrs′, kŏn′vûrs; *n.* kŏn′vûrs), *adj.* **1.** turned about; opposite or contrary in direction or action. —*n.* **2.** a thing which is the opposite or contrary of another. **3.** *Logic.* **a.** a proposition obtained from another proposition by conversion. **b.** the relation between one term and a second when the second term is related in a certain manner to the first. For example: the relation *descendant of* is the converse of *ancestor of.* **4.** a group of words correlative with a preceding group but having a significant pair of terms interchanged. For example: *warm in winter but cold in summer* is the *converse* of *cold in winter but warm in summer.* [t. L: m.s. *conversus,* pp., turned about] —**con·verse·ly** (kən vûrs′lĭ, kŏn′vûrs-), *adv.*

con·ver·sion (kən vûr′zhən, -shən), *n.* **1.** act of converting. **2.** state of being converted. **3.** change in character, form, or function. **4.** spiritual change from sinfulness to righteousness. **5.** change from one religion, party, etc., to another. **6.** *Math.* a change in the form or units of an expression. **7.** *Logic.* the transposition of the subject and the predicate of a proposition, in accordance with certain rules, so as to form a new proposition. For example: *no good man is unhappy* becomes by conversion *no unhappy man is good.* **8.** *Law.* **a.** unauthorized assumption and exercise of rights of ownership over personal property belonging to another. **b.** change from realty into personalty, or vice versa, as in sale or purchase of land, mining coal, etc. **9.** *Psychoanal.* the process by which a repressed psychic event, idea, feeling, memory, or impulse is represented by a bodily change or symptom, thus simulating physical illnesses or their symptoms. —**con·ver′sion·al, con·ver·sion·ar·y** (kən vûr′zhə něr′ĭ, -shə-), *adj.*

con·vert (*v.* kən vûrt′, *n.* kŏn′vûrt), *v.t.* **1.** to change into something of different form or properties; transmute; transform. **2.** *Chem.* to cause (a substance) to undergo a chemical change: *to convert sugar into alcohol.* **3.** to cause to adopt a different religion, party, opinion, etc., esp. one regarded as better. **4.** to change in character; cause to turn from an evil life to a righteous one. **5.** to turn to another or a particular use or purpose; divert from the proper or intended use. **6.** to appropriate wrongfully to one's own use. **7.** *Law.* to assume unlawful rights of ownership of (personal property). **8.** to invert or transpose. **9.** *Logic.* to transpose the subject and predicate of (a proposition) by conversion. **10.** to exchange for an equivalent: *to convert banknotes into gold.* **11.** *Finance.* to exchange voluntarily (a bond or preferred share) into another security, usually common stock, because of the greater value of the latter. **12.** *Obs.* to turn about in position or direction. —*v.i.* **13.** to be converted. —*n.* **14.** one who has been converted, as to a religion or an opinion. [ME *converte(n),* t. L: m. *convertere* turn about, change] —**Syn. 1.** See **transform. 14.** proselyte, neophyte, disciple.

con·vert·er (kən vûr′tər), *n.* **1.** one who or that which converts. **2.** one engaged in converting textile fabrics, esp. cotton cloths, from the raw state into the finished product ready for the market, as by bleaching, dyeing, glossing, etc. **3.** *Elect.* See **synchronous converter. 4.** an oval vessel in which molten pig iron is converted into steel by forcing air through the metal. Also, **con·ver′tor.**

con·vert·i·ble (kən vûr′tə bəl), *adj.* **1.** capable of being converted. **2.** *Auto.* having a folding top. —*n.* **3.** *Colloq.* a convertible automobile. —**con·vert′i·bil′i·ty, con·vert′i·ble·ness,** *n.* —**con·vert′i·bly,** *adv.*

con·vert·ite (kŏn′vər tīt′), *n. Archaic.* a convert.

con·vex (*adj.* kŏn věks′, kən-; *n.* kŏn′věks), *adj.* **1.** curved like a circle or sphere when viewed from without; bulging and curved. —*n.* **2.** a convex surface, part, or thing. [t. L: s. *convexus* vaulted, arched; appar. earlier var. of *convectus,* pp., carried together] —**con·vex′ly,** *adv.*

con·vex·i·ty (kən věk′sə tĭ), *n., pl.* **-ties. 1.** state of being convex. **2.** a convex surface or thing.

con·vex·o-con·cave (kən věk′sō-kŏn kāv′), *adj.* convex on one side and concave on the other.

con·vex·o-con·vex (kən věk′sō kŏn-věks′), *adj.* convex on both sides.

con·vex·o-plane (kən věk′sō plān′), *adj.* plano-convex.

A. Convex or plano-convex lens; B. Concavo-concave lens; C. Convexo-convex lens

con·vey (kən vā′), *v.t.* **1.** to carry or transport from one place to another. **2.** to lead or conduct as a channel or medium; transmit. **3.** to communicate; impart; make known. **4.** *Law.* to transfer; pass the title to. **5.** *Obs.* to take away secretly. **6.** *Obs.* to steal. [ME *conveye(n),* t. OF: m. *conveier,* f. con- CON- + *veier,* der. *veie,* g. L *via* way, journey] —**con·vey′a·ble,** *adj.* —**Syn. 1.** See **carry.**

con·vey·ance (kən vā′əns), *n.* **1.** act of conveying; transmission; communication. **2.** a means of conveyance, esp. a vehicle; a carriage, auto, etc. **3.** *Law.* **a.** the transfer of property from one person to another. **b.** the instrument or document by which this is effected.

con·vey·anc·er (kən vā′ən sər), n. a person engaged in conveyancing.

con·vey·anc·ing (kən vā′ən sǐng), n. that branch of law practice consisting of examining titles, giving opinions as to their validity, and drawing of deeds, etc., for the conveyance of property from one person to another.

con·vey·or (kən vā′ər), n. 1. one who or that which conveys. 2. a contrivance for transporting material, as from one part of a building to another. Also, **con·vey′er.**

conveyor belt. See belt (def. 4b).

con·vict (v., adj. kən vǐkt′; n. kǒn′vǐkt), v.t. 1. to prove or declare guilty of an offense, esp. after a legal trial: to convict the prisoner of felony. 2. to impress with the sense of guilt. —n. 3. a person proved or declared guilty of an offense. 4. a convicted person serving a prison sentence. —adj. 5. Archaic. convicted. [ME, t. L: s. convictus, pp., overcome, convicted] —**con·vic′tive,** adj.

con·vic·tion (kən vǐk′shən), n. 1. act of convicting. 2. fact or state of being convicted. 3. act of convincing. 4. state of being convinced. 5. a fixed or firm belief. —**con·vic′tion·al,** adj. —**Syn.** 5. See **belief.** —**Ant.** 2. doubt, uncertainty.

con·vince (kən vǐns′), v.t., -vinced, -vincing. 1. to persuade by argument or proof; cause to believe in the truth of what is alleged (often fol. by of): to convince a man of his errors. 2. Obs. to prove or find guilty. 3. Obs. to overcome; vanquish. [t. L: m.s. convincere overcome by argument or proof, convict of error or crime, prove] —**con·vince′ment,** n. —**con·vinc′er,** n. —**con·vin′ci·ble,** adj. —**con·vinc′ing·ly,** adv. —**con·vinc′ing·ness,** n. —**Syn.** 1. See **persuade.**

con·viv·i·al (kən vǐv′ǐəl), adj. 1. fond of feasting, drinking, and merry company; jovial. 2. of or befitting a feast; festive. [t. L: s. convivialis pertaining to a feast] —**con·viv′i·al·ist,** n. —**con·viv′i·al·i·ty,** n. —**con·viv′i·al·ly,** adv.

con·vo·ca·tion (kǒn′və kā′shən), n. 1. act of convoking. 2. fact or state of being convoked. 3. a group of persons met in answer to a summons; an assembly. 4. Ch. of Eng. one of the two provincial synods or assemblies of the clergy. 5. Prot. Episc. Ch. a. an assembly of the clergy of part of a diocese. b. the area represented at such an assembly. [ME, t. L: s. convocātio] —**con′vo·ca′tion·al,** adj. —**Syn.** 3. See **convention.**

con·voke (kən vōk′), v.t., -voked, -voking. to call together; summon to meet; assemble by summons. [t. L: m.s. convocāre call together] —**con·vok′er,** n.

con·vo·lute (kǒn′və lōōt′), v., -luted, -luting, adj. —v.t. 1. to coil up; form into a twisted shape. —adj. 2. rolled up together, or one part over another. 3. Bot. coiled up longitudinally, so that one margin is within the coil and the other without, as the petals of cotton. [t. L: m.s. convolūtus, pp., rolled together] —**con′vo·lute′ly,** adv.

con·vo·lu·tion (kǒn′və lōō′shən), n. 1. a rolled up or coiled condition. 2. a rolling or coiling together. 3. a turn or winding of anything coiled; a whorl; a sinuosity. 4. Anat. one of the sinuous folds or ridges of the surface of the brain.

con·volve (kən vǒlv′), v.t., v.i., -volved, -volv′ng. to roll or wind together; coil; twist. [t. L: m.s. convolvere roll together]

con·vol·vu·la·ceous (kən vǒl′vyə lā′shəs), adj. belonging to the Convolvulaceae, or morning-glory family of plants, including the convolvuluses, ipomoeas, etc.

con·vol·vu·lus (kən vǒl′vyə ləs), n., pl. -luses, -li (-lī′). any plant of the genus Convolvulus, which comprises erect, twining, or prostrate herbs with trumpet-shaped flowers. The name has popular currency only in England. See **morning-glory.** [t. L: bindweed]

con·voy (v. kən voi′, kǒn′voi; n. kǒn′voi), v.t. 1. to accompany or escort, now usually for protection: a merchantship convoyed by a destroyer. [ME, t. F: s. convoyer, earlier conveier CONVEY] —n. 2. act of convoying. 3. the protection afforded by an escort. 4. an armed force, warship, etc., that escorts, esp. for protection. 5. a formation of ships, a train of vehicles, etc., usually accompanied by a protecting escort. 6. any group of military vehicles traveling together under the same orders. 7. a drag or friction brake, as for a wagon. [t. F: m. convoi, der. convoyer. See v. above] —**Syn.** 1. See **accompany.**

con·vulse (kən vǔls′), v.t., -vulsed, -vulsing. 1. to shake violently; cause violent agitation or disturbance in. 2. to cause to laugh violently. [t. L: m. s. convulsus, pp., shattered]

con·vul·sion (kən vǔl′shən), n. 1. Pathol. contortion of the body caused by violent muscular contractions of the extremities, trunk, and head. 2. violent agitation or disturbance; commotion. 3. a violent fit of laughter.

con·vul·sion·ar·y (kən vǔl′shə něr′ǐ), adj., n., pl. -aries. —adj. 1. pertaining to, of the nature of, or affected with, convulsion. —n. 2. one who is subject to convulsions.

con·vul·sive (kən vǔl′sǐv), adj. 1. of the nature of or characterized by convulsions or spasms. 2. producing or attended by convulsion: convulsive rage. —**con·vul′sive·ly,** adv. —**con·vul′sive·ness,** n.

co·ny (kō′nǐ, kǔn′ǐ), n., pl. -nies. 1. the fur of a rabbit, esp. when dyed to simulate Hudson seal. 2. the daman or some other animal of the same genus. 3. the

pika. 4. Archaic. a rabbit. Also, **coney.** [ME cunin, t. OF: m. conil, g. L cunīculus rabbit]

coo (kōō), v., cooed, cooing, n. —v.i. 1. to utter the soft, murmuring sound characteristic of pigeons or doves, or a similar sound. 2. to murmur or talk fondly or amorously. —v.t. 3. to utter by cooing. —n. 4. a cooing sound. —interj. 5. Cockney. an exclamation of surprise or amazement. [imit.] —**coo′er,** n. —**coo′ing·ly,** adv.

Co·o (kô′ô), n. Italian name of **Cos.**

Cooch Be·har (kōōch′ bə här′), 1. a state in NE India, in Bengal. 639,900 pop. (1941); 1318 sq. mi. 2. the capital of this state. 16,000 (1941).

coo·ee (kōō′ǐ, kōō′ē), n., v., cooeed, cooeeing. —n. 1. a prolonged, shrill, clear call or cry used as a signal by the Australian aborigines and adopted by the settlers in the country. —v.i. 2. to utter the call "cooee."

coo·ey (kōō′ǐ, kōō′ē), n., pl. cooeys, v., cooeyed, cooeying. cooee.

cook (kōōk), v.t. 1. to prepare (food) by the action of heat, as by boiling, baking, roasting, etc. 2. to subject (anything) to the action of heat. 3. Colloq. to concoct; invent falsely; alter surreptitiously or falsify (often fol. by up). 4. Slang. to ruin; spoil. —v.i. 5. to prepare food by the action of heat. 6. (of food) to undergo cooking. [v. use of n.] —n. 7. one whose occupation is the preparation of food for the table; one who cooks (commonly used in England without the): I'll tell (the) cook to prepare sandwiches. [ME; OE cōc, t. LL: m.s. cocus, L coquus] —**cook′er,** n.

Cook (kōōk), n. 1. Captain James, 1728–79, British navigator and explorer: expeditions to S Pacific, Antarctic oceans, and coasts of Australia and New Zealand. 2. Mount, a mountain in New Zealand, on South Island. 12,349 ft. Also, **Aorangi.**

cook·book (kōōk′bōōk′), n. a book containing recipes and instructions for cooking. Also, Brit., cookery book.

Cooke (kōōk), n. Jay, 1821–1905, U.S. financier.

cook·er·y (kōōk′ərǐ), n., pl. -eries. 1. the art or practice of cooking. 2. a place for cooking.

Cook Islands, a group of islands in the S Pacific, belonging to New Zealand. 14,506 pop. (est. 1945); 99 sq. mi.

Cook Strait, a strait between North and South Islands, in New Zealand.

cook·y (kōōk′ǐ), n., pl. cookies. 1. U.S. a small cake made from stiff sweet dough, dropped, rolled, or sliced, and then baked. 2. Scot. a bun. Also, U.S., **cook′ie.** [t. D: m. koekie, colloq. var. of koekje, dim. of koek cake]

cool (kōōl), adj. 1. moderately cold; neither warm nor very cold. 2. imparting or permitting a sensation of moderate coldness: a cool dress. 3. not excited; calm; unmoved; not hasty; deliberate. 4. deficient in ardor or enthusiasm. 5. lacking in cordiality: a cool reception. 6. calmly audacious or impudent. 7. Colloq. (of a number or sum) without exaggeration or qualification: a cool million dollars. 8. (of colors) with green, blue, or violet predominating. —adv. 9. Colloq. coolly. —n. 10. that which is cool; the cool part, place, time, etc. 11. coolness. —v.i. 12. to become cool. 13. to become less ardent, cordial, etc.; become more moderate. —v.t. 14. to make cool; impart a sensation of coolness to. 15. to lessen the ardor or intensity of; allay; calm; moderate. 16. cool one's heels, to be kept waiting. [ME; OE cōl; akin to COLD, CHILL] —**cool′ly,** adv. —**cool′ness,** n. —**Syn.** 1. See **cold.** 3. composed, collected; self-possessed, undisturbed, unruffled, unexcited, dispassionate. See **calm.** 5. indifferent, lukewarm.

cool·er (kōō′lər), n. 1. a container or apparatus for cooling or keeping cool: a water cooler. 2. anything that cools or makes cool; refrigerant. 3. Slang. a jail.

cool-head·ed (kōōl′hěd′ǐd), adj. not easily excited; calm.

Cool·idge (kōō′lǐj), n. Calvin, 1872–1933, 30th president of the U.S., 1923–29.

coo·lie (kōō′lǐ), n. 1. (in India, China, etc.) an unskilled native laborer. 2. (elsewhere) such a laborer employed for cheap service. [prob. var. of kōlī, name of tribe of Guzerat, but cf. Tamil kūli hire, wages]

cool·ish (kōō′lǐsh), adj. somewhat cool.

coo·ly (kōō′lǐ), n., pl. -lies. coolie.

coomb (kōōm, kōm), n. combe. [OE cumb valley, t. Celtic; cf. Welsh cwm valley]

coon (kōōn), n. 1. raccoon. 2. U.S. Slang. (in contemptuous use) a Negro.

coon·can (kōōn′kǎn′), n. a card game of the rummy family for two players.

coon's age, a long time.

coon·tie (kōōn′tǐ), n. 1. the arrowroot plant of Florida, Zamia integrifolia, the only species of the Cycadaceae native in the U.S. 2. the flour produced from its starch. [t. Seminole: m. kunti the flour]

coop (kōōp, kōop), n. 1. an enclosure, cage, or pen, usually with bars or wires on one side or more, in which fowls, etc., are confined for fattening, transportation, etc. 2. any small or narrow place. 3. Slang. a prison. 4. fly the coop, Slang. to escape from a prison, etc. —v.t. 5. to place in, or as in, a coop; confine narrowly (often fol. by up or in). [ME coupe basket, unexplained var. of kipe, ME cupe, OE cȳpe basket, c. LG kūpe]

co·öp (kō ǒp′, kō′ǒp), n. Colloq. a coöperative store or society. Also, **co-op′.**

coop·er (ko͞o′pər, ko͝op′ər), *n.* 1. one who makes or repairs vessels formed of staves and hoops, as casks, barrels, tubs, etc. —*v.t.* 2. to make or repair (casks, barrels, etc.). 3. to furnish or fix (fol. by *up*). —*v.i.* 4. to work as a cooper. [ME *couper*, t. MD or MLG: m. *kuper*, t. VL: m. s. *cūpārius*, der. L *cūpa* cask]

Coo·per (ko͞o′pər, ko͝op′ər), *n.* 1. **Anthony Ashley.** See **Shaftesbury.** 2. **James Fenimore** (fĕn′ə môr′), 1789–1851, U.S. novelist. 3. **Peter,** 1791–1883, U.S. inventor, manufacturer, reformer, and philanthropist.

coop·er·age (ko͞o′pəṙĭj, ko͝op′ər-), *n.* 1. the work or business of a cooper. 2. the place where it is carried on. 3. the price paid for coopers' work.

co·öp·er·ate (ko̅ŏp′ərāt′), *v.i.*, **-ated, -ating.** 1. to work or act together or jointly; unite in producing an effect. 2. to practice economic coöperation. Also, **co·op·er·ate, co·op·er·ate′.** [t. LL: m.s. *cooperātus,* pp., having worked together.] —**co·öp′er·a·tor,** *n.*

co·öp·er·a·tion (ko̅ŏp′ərā′shən), *n.* 1. act or fact of coöperating; joint operation or action. 2. *Econ.* the combination of persons for purposes of production, purchase, or distribution for their joint benefit: *producers' coöperation, consumers' coöperation.* 3. *Sociol.* activity shared for mutual benefit. 4. *Ecol.* the conscious or unconscious behavior of organisms living together and producing a result which has survival value for them. Also, **co·op′er·a′tion, co·op′er·a′tion.** —**co·öp′er·a′tion·ist,** *n.*

co·öp·er·a·tive (ko̅ŏp′ərā′tĭv, -ŏp′rətĭv), *adj.* 1. coöperating; of coöperation. 2. pertaining to economic coöperation: *a coöperative store.* —*n.* 3. a coöperative society or store. Also, **co·op′er·a·tive, co·op′er·a·tive.** —**co·öp′er·a·tive·ly,** *adv.* —**co·öp′er·a·tive·ness,** *n.*

coöperative store, 1. a retail store owned and managed by consumer-customers who supply the capital and share in the profits by patronage dividends. 2. a store operated by a farmers' coöperative organization or by a coöperative chain.

coop·er·y (ko͞o′pəṙĭ, ko͝op′əṙĭ), *n., pl.* **-eries.** 1. the work of a cooper. 2. a cooper's shop. 3. articles made by a cooper.

co·öpt (ko̅ŏpt′), *v.t.* to elect into a body by the votes of the existing members. Also, **co-opt′.** [t. L: s. *cooptāre*] —**co′öp·ta′tion,** *n.* —**co·öp·ta·tive** (ko̅ŏp′tətĭv), *adj.*

co·ör·di·nal (ko̅ôr′dənəl), *adj. Zool.* belonging to the same order. Also, **co-or′di·nal.**

co·ör·di·nate (*adj., n.* ko̅ôr′dənĭt, -nāt′; *v.* ko̅ôr′dənāt′), *adj., n., v.* **-nated, -nating.** —*adj.* 1. of the same order or degree; equal in rank or importance. 2. involving coördination. 3. *Math.* using or pertaining to systems of coördinates. —*n.* 4. one who or that which is equal in rank or importance; an equal. 5. *Math.* any of the magnitudes which define the position of a point, line, or the like, by reference to a fixed figure, system of lines, etc. —*v.t.* 6. to place or class in the same order, rank, division, etc. 7. to place or arrange in due order or proper relative position. 8. to combine in harmonious relation or action. —*v.i.* 9. to become coördinate. 10. to assume proper order or relation. 11. to act in harmonious combination. Also, **co-or′di·nate, co·or′di·nate.** [f. co- + ORDINATE] —**co·ör′di·nate·ly,** *adv.* —**co·ör′di·nate·ness,** *n.* —**co·ör′di·na′tive,** *adj.* —**co·ör′di·na′tor,** *n.*

co·ör·di·na·tion (ko̅ôr′dənā′shən), *n.* 1. act of coördinating. 2. state of being coördinated. 3. due ordering or proper relation. 4. harmonious combination. Also, **co-or′di·na′tion, co·or′di·na′tion.**

Coorg (ko̅ôrg), *n.* a province in SW India. 169,000 pop. (1941); 1593 sq. mi. *Cap.:* Mercara.

Coos (ko͞os), *n.* any of several Penutian languages of Oregon.

coot (ko͞ot), *n.* 1. any of the aquatic birds constituting the genus *Fulica*, characterized by lobate toes and short wings and tail, as the common coot (*F. atra*) of Europe. 2. any of various other swimming or diving birds, as the scoter. 3. *Colloq.* a fool; simpleton. [cf. D *koet*]

coot·ie (ko͞o′tĭ), *n. Orig. Brit. Colloq.* a louse.

cop¹ (kŏp), *n., v.,* **copped, copping.** —*n.* 1. *Colloq.* a policeman. —*v.t.* 2. *Slang.* to catch. 3. *Slang.* to steal. [OE *coppian* lop, steal]

Coot. *Fulica americana* (15 in. long)

cop² (kŏp), *n.* 1. a conical mass of thread, etc., wound on a spindle in a spinning machine. 2. *Obs. or Dial.* the top or crest of anything, esp. of a hill. [OE *cop, copp* top, summit. Cf. G *kopf* head]

co·pai·ba (ko̅pā′bə, -pī′bə), *n.* an oleoresin obtained from various tropical (chiefly South American) trees of the caesalpiniaceous genus *Copaiba,* used esp. as a stimulant and diuretic. [t. Sp., t. Guarani: m. *kupaiba*]

co·pal (ko̅′pəl, -păl), *n.* a hard, lustrous resin yielded by various tropical trees, used chiefly in making varnishes. [t. Sp., t. Nahuatl: m. *kopalli* resin]

Co·pán (ko̅ pän′), *n.* Santa Rosa de Copán.

co·par·ce·nar·y (ko̅ pär′sə nĕr′ĭ), *n. Law.* a special kind of joint ownership, esp. arising under common law upon the descent of real property to several female heirs. Also, **co·par·ce·ny** (ko̅ pär′sə nĭ).

co·par·ce·ner (ko̅ pär′sə nər), *n.* a member of a coparcenary. [f. co- + PARCENER]

co·part·ner (ko̅ pärt′nər), *n.* a partner; an associate. —**co·part′ner·ship′,** *n.*

cope¹ (kŏp), *v.,* **coped, coping.** —*v.i.* 1. to struggle or contend, esp. on fairly even terms or with a degree of success (fol. by *with*). 2. *Archaic.* to have to do (fol. by *with*). —*v.t.* 3. *Brit. Colloq.* to cope with. 4. *Obs.* to meet in contest. [ME *coupe*(*n*), t. F: m. *couper* strike, der. *coup* stroke, blow. See COUP, n.]

cope² (kŏp), *n., v.,* **coped, coping.** —*n.* 1. a long mantle of silk or other material worn by ecclesiastics over the alb or surplice in processions and on other occasions. 2. any cloaklike or canopylike covering. 3. the vault of heaven; the sky. 4. *Archit.* a coping. —*v.t.* 5. to furnish with or as with a cope or coping. [ME; OE *cāp* (in *cantel-cāp* cope), t. ML: s. *cāpa* cope]

A. Cope; B. Crosier

co·peck (ko̅′pĕk), *n.* kopeck.

Co·pen·ha·gen (ko̅′pənhā′gən), *n.* the capital of Denmark: a seaport on the E coast of Zealand. 890,130; with suburbs, 1,078,892 (1945). Danish, **Köbenhavn.**

copenhagen blue, gray blue.

co·pe·pod (ko̅′pəpŏd′), *n.* 1. any of the *Copepoda,* a large order of (mostly) minute freshwater and marine crustaceans. —*adj.* 2. pertaining to the *Copepoda.* [f. m. Gk. *kōpē* handle, oar + -POD]

Co·per·ni·cus (ko̅ pûr′nəkəs, kə-), *n.* **Nicolaus** (nĭk′-ə lā′əs), 1473–1543, Polish astronomer who promulgated the now accepted theory that the earth and the planets move about the sun (the **Copernican system**). Polish, **Kopernik.** —**Co·per′ni·can,** *adj.*

cope·stone (kŏp′stōn′), *n.* 1. the top stone of a building or the like. 2. a stone used for or in coping. 3. the crown or completion.

cop·i·er (kŏp′ĭ ər), *n.* one who copies; a copyist.

co·pi·lot (ko̅′pī′lət), *n.* the assistant or second pilot in an aircraft.

cop·ing (ko̅′pĭng), *n.* the uppermost course of a wall or the like, usually made sloping so as to carry off water.

coping saw, a saw with a short, narrow blade held at both ends in a deeply recessed handle, for cutting curved shapes.

co·pi·ous (ko̅′pĭ əs), *adj.* 1. large in quantity or number; abundant. 2. having or yielding an abundant supply. 3. exhibiting abundance or fullness, as of thoughts or words. [ME, t. L: m. s. *cōpiōsus* plentiful.] —**co′pi·ous·ly,** *adv.* —**co′pi·ous·ness,** *n.* —**Syn.** 1. plentiful, overflowing, profuse. See **ample.** —**Ant.** 1. scanty. 3. meager.

co·pla·nar (ko̅ plā′nər), *adj. Math.* (of figures) in the same plane.

Cop·land (kŏp′lənd), *n.* **Aaron** (âr′ən), born 1900, U.S. composer.

Cop·ley (kŏp′lĭ), *n.* **John Singleton** (sĭng′gəl tən), 1738–1815, U.S. historical and portrait painter.

co·pol·y·mer (ko̅ pŏl′ə mər), *n. Chem.* a compound made by polymerizing different compounds together.

co·pol·y·mer·ize (ko̅ pŏl′ə mə rīz′), *v.t., v.i.* **-ized, -izing.** to subject to or undergo a change analogous to polymerization but with a union of unlike molecules. —**co·pol′y·mer·i·za′tion,** *n.*

Cop·pée (ko̅ pā′), *n.* **François** (frän swä′), 1842–1908, French poet, dramatist, and novelist.

cop·per¹ (kŏp′ər), *n.* 1. *Chem.* a malleable, ductile metallic element having a characteristic reddish-brown color. *Symbol:* Cu; *at. wt.:* 63.57; *at. no.:* 29; *sp. gr.:* 8.92 at 20°C. 2. a copper coin, as the English penny or halfpenny or the U.S. cent. 3. a container made of copper. 4. *Brit.* a large boiler, as for cooking on shipboard. 5. a metallic reddish brown. —*v.t.* 6. to cover, coat, or sheathe with copper. 7. *Slang.* to bet against. [ME *coper,* OE *coper, copor* (c. G *kupfer*), t. LL: m.s. *cuprum,* for L *aes Cyprium* Cyprian metal. See CYPRUS]

cop·per² (kŏp′ər), *n. Slang.* a policeman. [see COP¹]

cop·per·as (kŏp′ər əs), *n.* green vitriol, or ferrous sulfate, used in dyeing, medicine, photography, making ink, etc. [ME *coperose,* t. OF *coperose,* t. ML: m.s. (*aqua*) *cuprōsa,* der. LL *cuprum.* See COPPER¹]

cop·per·head (kŏp′ər hĕd′), *n.* 1. a venomous snake, *Ancistrodon contortrix,* of the U.S., having a copper-colored head, and reaching a length of about 3 feet. 2. (*cap.*) a Northern sympathizer with the South during the U.S. Civil War.

Cop·per·mine (kŏp′ər mīn′), *n.* a river in the central Northwest Territories of Canada, flowing N to the Arctic Ocean. 525 mi.

cop·per·plate (kŏp′ər plāt′), *n.* 1. a plate of polished copper on which a writing, picture, or design is made by engraving or etching. 2. a print or an impression from such a plate. 3. engraving or printing of this kind.

copper pyrites, chalcopyrite.

cop·per·smith (kŏp′ər smĭth′), *n.* 1. a worker in copper; one who manufactures copper utensils. 2. the crimson-breasted barbet, *Megalaema haemacephala,* a common bird in India, etc.

copper sulfate, blue vitriol.

cop·per·y (kŏp′ər ĭ), *adj.* of, like, or containing copper.

cop·pice (kŏp′ĭs), *n. Chiefly Brit.* a wood or thicket of small trees or bushes. Also, **copse.** [t. OF: m. *copeiz,* f. m.s. *couper* cut + *-eiz* (g. L *-āticium*)]

cop·ra (kŏp/rə), *n.* the dried kernel or meat of the coconut, from which coconut oil is expressed. [t. Pg., t. Malayalam: m. *koppara*, in Hindī *khoprā* coconut]

cop·re·mi·a (kŏp·rē/mĭ·ə), *n. Pathol.* blood poisoning due to absorption of fecal matter. Also, **cop·rae/mi·a**. [f. *copr*(*o*)- (see COPROLITE) + -EMIA]

cop·ro·lite (kŏp/rə·līt/), *n.* a roundish, stony mass consisting of petrified fecal matter of animals. [f. *copro-* (t. Gk.: m. *kopro-*, comb. form of *kópros* dung) + -LITE]

cop·roph·a·gous (kŏp·rŏf/ə·gəs), *adj.* feeding on dung, as certain beetles. [f. *copro-* (see COPROLITE) + -PHAGOUS]

copse (kŏps), *n.* coppice.

Copt (kŏpt), *n.* 1. one of the natives of Egypt descended from the ancient Egyptians. 2. an Egyptian Christian of the sect of the Monophysites. [t. Ar.: m. *qibṭ*, *qubṭ* the Copts, t. Coptic: m. *gyptios*, aphetic var. of Gk. *Aigýptios* Egyptian]

'cop·ter (kŏp/tər), *n. Colloq.* helicopter.

Cop·tic (kŏp/tĭk), *n.* 1. the extinct language of Egypt which developed from the ancient Egyptian, used liturgically by the Egyptian Christians. —*adj.* 2. of or pertaining to the Copts.

Coptic Church, the native Christian church in Egypt, embracing about one twelfth of the population.

cop·u·la (kŏp/yə·lə), *n., pl.* -las, -lae (-lē/). 1. something that connects or links together. 2. *Gram., Logic.* a word or set of words (in English the verb *be*) which acts as a connecting link between the subject and the predicate. [t. L: a band, bond] —**cop/u·lar,** *adj.*

cop·u·late (*v.* -lŏp/yə·lāt/; *adj.* kŏp/yə·lĭt), *v.,* -lated, -lating, *adj.* —*v.i.* 1. to unite in sexual intercourse. —*adj.* 2. *Obs.* joined. [t. L: m.s. *copulātus*, pp., coupled]

cop·u·la·tion (kŏp/yə·lā/shən), *n.* 1. a joining together or coupling. 2. sexual union or intercourse.

cop·u·la·tive (kŏp/yə·lā/tĭv), *adj.* 1. serving to unite or couple. 2. involving or consisting of connected words or clauses. 3. of the nature of a copula: *a copulative verb.* 4. of or pertaining to copulation. —*n.* 5. a copulative word. —**cop/u·la/tive·ly,** *adv.*

cop·y (kŏp/ĭ), *n., pl.* copies, *v.,* copied, copying. —*n.* 1. a transcript, reproduction, or imitation of an original. 2. that which is to be transcribed, reproduced, or imitated. 3. written, typed, printed matter, or art work, intended to be reproduced in print. 4. one of the various examples or specimens of the same book, engraving, or the like. 5. an example of penmanship to be copied by a pupil. 6. *Brit. Colloq.* (in schools) a composition; a written assignment. —*v.t.* 7. to make a copy of; transcribe; reproduce: *to copy out a set of figures.* 8. to follow as a pattern or model; imitate. —*v.i.* 9. to make a copy or copies. 10. to make or do something in imitation of something else: *to copy after bad precedents.* [ME *copie,* t. F, L: m.s. *cōpia* plenty, ML transcript] —**Syn.** 1. duplicate. 8. See *imitate.* —**Ant.** 8. originate.

cop·y·book (kŏp/ĭ·bŏŏk/), *n.* 1. a book in which copies are written or printed for learners to imitate. 2. a book for or containing copies, as of documents.

copy desk, *Journalism.* the desk at which news stories, etc. are edited and prepared for printing.

cop·y·hold (kŏp/ĭ·hōld/), *n. Law.* (formerly) a type of ownership of land in England, evidenced by a copy of the manor roll establishing the title.

cop·y·hold·er (kŏp/ĭ·hōl/dər), *n.* 1. one who or that which holds copy. 2. a device for holding copy in its place, as on a printer's frame or on a typewriter. 3. a proofreader's assistant who reads copy aloud, or follows it while proof is read, for the detection of deviations from it in proof. 4. *Brit. Law.* one who holds an estate in copyhold.

cop·y·ist (kŏp/ĭ·ĭst), *n.* 1. a transcriber, esp. of documents. 2. an imitator.

cop·y·read·er (kŏp/ĭ·rē/dər), *n. Journalism.* one who edits and corrects material written by others.

cop·y·right (kŏp/ĭ·rīt/), *n.* 1. the exclusive right, granted by law for a certain term of years, to make and dispose of copies of, and otherwise to control, a literary, musical, or artistic work. —*adj.* 2. protected by copyright. —*v.t.* 3. to secure a copyright on. —**cop/y·right/·a·ble,** *adj.* —**cop/y·right/er,** *n.*

Co·que·lin (kôk·lăn/), *n.* **Benoît Constant** (bə·nwà/kôn·stän/), 1841–1909, French actor.

co·quet (kō·kĕt/), *v.,* -quetted, -quetting, *adj., n.* —*v.i.* 1. to trifle in love; flirt; play the coquette. 2. to act without seriousness or decision; trifle; dally. —*adj.* 3. coquettish. —*n.* 4. *Obs.* a male flirt. [t. F, dim. of *coq.* cock]

co·quet·ry (kō/kə·trĭ, kō·k't/rĭ), *n., pl.* -ries. 1. the behavior or arts of a coquette; flirtation. 2. trifling.

co·quette (kō·kĕt/), *n.* a woman who tries to gain the admiration and affections of men for mere self-gratification; a flirt. [t. F. See COQUET] —**co·quet/tish,** *adj.* —**co·quet/tish·ly,** *adv.* —**co·quet/tish·ness,** *n.*

co·quil·la nut (kō·kĭl/yə, -kē/yə), the elongated oval fruit or nut of a South American palm, *Attalea funifera,* having a very hard brown shell, used in turnery. [*coquilla,* t. Pg.: m. *coquilho,* dim. of *coco* coconut]

co·qui·na (kō·kē/nə), *n.* a soft, whitish rock made up of fragments of marine shells and coral, used to some extent as a building material. [t. Sp.: shellfish, cockle]

co·qui·to (kō·kē/tō), *n., pl.* -tos. a palm, *Jubaea spectabilis,* of Chile, bearing small edible nuts, which yield a

sweet syrup. Also, **coquito palm.** [t. Sp., dim. of *coco* coconut]

cor (kôr), *interj. Brit. Slang.* exclamation of surprise.

cor-, var. of **com-,** before *r,* as in *corrupt.*

Cor., 1. Corinthians. 2. Coroner.

cor., 1. corner. 2. corrected. 3. correction. 4. corresponding.

cor·a·ci·i·form (kôr/ə·sī/ə·fôrm/, kŏr/-), *adj.* belonging or pertaining to the *Coraciiformes,* the order of birds that includes the kingfishers, motmots, rollers, bee eaters, and hornbills. [f. s. NL *Coracia* genus of birds (der. Gk. *kórax* raven) + -(I)FORM]

cor·a·cle (kôr/ə·kəl, kŏr/-), *n. Brit.* (local to Wales and W England) a native boat nearly or quite as broad as long, made like a basket. [t. Welsh: m. *corwgl, cwrwgl,* der. *corwg, cwrwg* carcass, boat]

cor·a·coid (kôr/ə·koid/, kŏr/-), *Anat., Zool.* —*adj.* 1. pertaining to a bony process extending from the scapula toward the sternum in many *Vertebrata.* —*n.* 2. a coracoid bone. [t. Gk.: m.s. *korakoeidés* ravenlike]

cor·al (kôr/əl, kŏr/-), *n.* 1. the hard, calcareous (red, white, black, etc.) skeleton of any of various, mostly compound, marine coelenterate animals, the individual polyps of which come forth by budding. 2. such skeletons collectively, as forming reefs, islands, etc. 3. an animal of this kind. 4. something made of coral, as an ornament, child's toy, etc. 5. a reddish yellow; light yellowish red; pinkish yellow. 6. the unimpregnated roe or eggs of the lobster, which when boiled assume the color of red coral. —*adj.* 7. made of coral: *a coral reef, coral ornament.* 8. making coral: *a coral polyp.* 9. resembling coral, esp. in color. [ME, t. OF, g. L *corallum, coralium,* t. Gk.: m. *korállion* red coral]

cor·al·lif·er·ous (kôr/ə·lĭf/ər·əs, kŏr/-), *adj.* containing or bearing coral; producing coral.

cor·al·line (kôr/ə·lĭn, -līn/, kŏr/-), *adj.* 1. consisting of or containing deposits of calcium carbonate. 2. corallike. 3. coral-colored; reddish-yellow; light-yellowish red; pinkish-yellow. —*n.* 4. any alga having a red color and impregnated with lime. 5. any of various corallike animals, or calcareous algae.

cor·al·loid (kôr/ə·loid/, kŏr/-), *adj.* having the form or appearance of coral. Also, **cor/al·loi/dal.**

coral root, any of the species of the orchidaceous genus *Corallorrhiza,* native to the northern hemisphere.

Coral Sea, a part of the S Pacific, partially enclosed by NE Australia, New Guinea, the Solomon Islands, and the New Hebrides: U.S. naval victory over the Japanese, May, 1942.

coral snake, any of the brilliantly colored venomous snakes of the genus *Micrurus,* often with alternating black, yellow, and red rings, including forms found in the southern and southwestern U.S.

co·ram po·pu·lo (kōr/ăm pŏp/yə·lō/), *Latin.* before the public.

cor·ban (kôr/băn, kôr·băn/), *n.* (among the ancient Jews) an offering of any kind made to God, one kind of it being in fulfillment of a vow. [t. Heb.: m. *qorbān*]

cor·bel (kôr/bəl), *n., v.,* -beled, -beling or (*esp. Brit.*) -belled, -belling. *Archit.* —*n.* 1. a supporting projection of stone wood, etc., on the face of a wall. 2. a short horizontal timber supporting a girder. —*v.t.* 3. to furnish with or support by a corbel or corbels. [ME, t. OF, g. LL *corvellus,* dim. of L *corvus* raven]

cor·bel·ing (kôr/bəl·ĭng), *n. Archit.* 1. the construction of corbels. 2. an overlapping arrangement of stones, etc., each course projecting beyond the one below. Also, *esp. Brit.,* **cor/bel·ling.**

cor·bie (kôr/bĭ), *n. Scot.* a raven or crow. [ME *corbin,* t. OF, dim. of *corb* raven, g. L *corvus*]

Corbel (def. 1)

corbie gable, a gable with corbiesteps.

cor·bie·step (kôr/bĭ·stĕp/), *n.* one of a set of steplike projections on the sides of a gable.

cor·bi·na (kôr·bī/nə), *n.* 1. a fish, *Menticirrhus undulatus,* of the croaker family, the most prized game fish of the surf in southern California. 2. any of several other species of the family *Sciaenidae.*

Cor·cy·ra (kôr·sī/rə), *n.* ancient name of Corfu (def. 1).

cord (kôrd), *n.* 1. a string or small rope composed of several strands twisted or woven together. 2. a hangman's rope. 3. *Elect.* a small, very flexible insulated cable. 4. *Anat.* a cordlike structure: *the spinal cord, the vocal cords.* 5. a cordlike rib on the surface of cloth. 6. a ribbed fabric, esp. corduroy. 7. (*pl.*) corduroy breeches or trousers. 8. any influence which binds, restrains, etc. 9. a unit of volume used chiefly for fuel wood, now generally equal to 128 cubic feet, usually specified as 8 feet long, 4 feet wide, and 4 feet high. —*v.t.* 10. to furnish with a cord. 11. to bind or fasten with cords. 12. to pile or stack up (wood) in cords. [ME *corde,* t. OF, g. L *chorda,* t. Gk.: m. *chordé* gut. Cf. CHORD¹]

cord·age (kôr′dĭj), *n.* **1.** cords or ropes collectively, esp. in a ship's rigging. **2.** a quantity of wood measured in cords.

cor·date (kôr′dāt), *adj.* **1.** heart-shaped, as a shell. **2.** (of leaves) heart-shaped with the attachment at the notched end. [t. NL: m.s. *cordātus*, der. L *cor* heart] —**cor′date·ly,** *adv.*

Cordate leaf

Cor·day d'Ar·mont (kôr dĕ′ där mŏn′), (**Marie Anne**) **Charlotte** (mä-rē′ än shär lŏt′), 1768–93, French revolutionary heroine who assassinated Marat.

cord·ed (kôr′dĭd), *adj.* **1.** furnished with, made of, or in the form of cords. **2.** ribbed, as a fabric. **3.** bound with cords. **4.** (of wood) stacked up in cords.

Cor·de·lier (kôr′də lǐr′), *n.* **1.** a Franciscan friar (so called from his girdle of knotted cord). **2.** (*pl.*) a Parisian political club in the time of the French Revolution, which met in an old convent of the Cordeliers. [ME *cordilere,* t. F: m. *cordelier,* ult. der. *corde* CORD]

cor·dial (kôr′jəl), *adj.* **1.** hearty; warmly friendly. **2.** invigorating the heart; stimulating. **3.** *Obs.* of the heart. —*n.* **4.** anything that invigorates or exhilarates. **5.** a strong, sweetened, aromatic alcoholic liquor; a liqueur. **6.** a cordial or stimulating medicine. [ME, t. ML: s. *cordiālis,* der. L *cor* heart] —**cor′dial·ly,** *adv.* —**cor′dial·ness,** *n.*

cor·dial·i·ty (kôr jăl′ə tǐ or, esp. Brit., kôr′dǐ ăl′-), *n., pl.* **-ties. 1.** cordial quality or feeling. **2.** an instance or expression of cordial feeling.

cor·di·er·ite (kôr′dǐ ə rīt′), a blue mineral, consisting of a silicate of magnesium, aluminum, and iron.

cor·di·form (kôr′də fôrm′), *adj.* heart-shaped. [f. s. L *cor* heart + -(I)FORM]

cor·dil·le·ra (kôr′dǐl yâr′ə, kôr dǐl′ərə), *n.* a chain of mountains, usually the principal mountain system or mountain axis of a large land mass. [t. Sp.: mountain chain, ult. der. L *chorda* rope] —**cor′dil·le·ran,** *adj.*

Cor·dil·le·ras (kôr′dǐl yâr′əz, kôr dǐl′ərəz; *Sp.* kôr′-dē yĕ′räs), *n. pl.* **1.** a mountain system in W South America: the Andes and its component ranges. **2.** a mountain system in W North America, including the Sierra Nevada, Coast Range, Cascade Range, Rocky Mountains. etc. **3.** the entire chain of mountain ranges parallel to the Pacific coast, extending from Cape Horn to Alaska. —**Cor′dil·le′ran,** *adj.*

cord·ite (kôr′dīt), *n.* a smokeless powder composed of 30–58% nitroglycerin, 65–37% nitrocellulose, and 5–6% mineral jelly. [f. CORD + -ITE¹; so named from its cordlike or cylindrical form]

Cór·do·ba (kôr′dō bä), *n.* **1.** Also, **Cordova** (kĕr′də-və). a city in S Spain, on the Guadalquiver river: the capital of Spain under Moorish rule; famous cathedral. 143,206 (1940). **2.** a city in central Argentina. 339,375 (est. 1940). **3.** (*l.c.*) **a.** the Nicaraguan monetary unit equivalent to the U.S. gold dollar. **b.** the Nicaraguan silver coin equivalent to this unit.

cor·don (kôr′dən), *n.* **1.** a cord or braid worn for ornament or as a fastening. **2.** a ribbon worn, usually diagonally across the breast, as a badge of a knightly or honorary order. **3.** a line of sentinels, military posts, or the like, inclosing or guarding a particular area. **4.** *Fort.* a projecting course of stones at the base of a parapet. **5.** *Archit.* a stringcourse. [t. F, der. *corde* CORD]

cor·don bleu (kôr dōn blœ′), **1.** the sky-blue ribbon worn as a badge by knights of the highest order of French knighthood under the Bourbons. **2.** some similar high distinction. **3.** one entitled to wear the cordon bleu. **4.** any person of great distinction in his field.

Cor·do·van (kôr′də vən), *adj.* **1.** of Córdoba, Spain. **2.** (*l.c.*) designating or made of a leather made orig. at Córdoba, first of goatskin tanned and dressed, but later also of split horsehide, etc. —*n.* **3.** a native or inhabitant of Córdoba, Spain. **4.** (*l.c.*) cordovan leather.

cor·du·roy (kôr′də roi′, kôr′də roi′), *n.* **1.** a cotton pile fabric with lengthwise cords or ridges. **2.** (*pl.*) trousers or breeches made of this. —*adj.* **3.** of or like corduroy. **4.** constructed of logs laid together transversely, as a road across swampy ground. —*v.t.* **5.** to form, as a road, by laying logs together transversely. **6.** to make a corduroy road over. [cf. obs. *duroy,* a kind of coarse woolen fabric]

cord·wain (kôrd′wān), *n. Archaic.* cordovan leather. [ME *corduan,* t. OF: m. *cordoan,* t.m. *cordován*]

cord·wain·er (kôrd′wā nər), *n.* **1.** *Archaic.* a worker in cordovan leather. **2.** *Obs.* a shoemaker.

core (kôr), *n., v.,* **cored, coring.** —*n.* **1.** the central part of a fleshy fruit, containing the seeds. **2.** the central, innermost, or most essential part of anything. **3.** *Elect.* **a.** the piece of iron, bundle of iron wires, or the like, forming the central or inner portion of an electromagnet, induction coil, or the like. **b.** the armature core of a dynamo machine, consisting of the assembled armature laminations without the slot insulation or windings. **4.** *Founding.* a body of sand, usually dry, placed in a mold to form openings or give shape to a casting. **5.** the inside wood of a tree. **6.** the base to which veneer woods are attached, usually of a soft or inexpensive wood. —*v.t.* **7.** to remove the core of (fruit). **8.** to cut from the central part. [ME; orig. unknown] —**core′less,** *adj.*

Co·re·a (kō rē′ə), *n.* Korea.

co·re·li·gion·ist (kō′rǐ lǐj′ən ǐst), *n.* an adherent of the same religion as another.

co·re·op·sis (kôr′ǐ ŏp′sǐs), *n.* any plant of the composite genus *Coreopsis,* including familiar garden species with yellow, brownish, or parti-colored (yellow and red) flowers. [t. NL, f. m.s. Gk. *kóris* bug + -*opsis* -OPSIS; so called from the form of the seed]

cor·er (kôr′ər), *n.* a knife for coring apples, etc.

co·re·spond·ent (kōr′ǐ spŏn′dənt, kôr′-), *n. Law.* a joint defendant, esp. in a divorce proceeding, where one charged with adultery is made a joint defendant. —**co′re·spond′en·cy,** *n.*

corf (kôrf), *n., pl.* **corves** (kôrvz). *Brit.* a small wooden or iron freight wagon (formerly a wicker basket) used for carrying ore, coal, etc., in a mine. [t. MD, t. L: m. s. *corbis* basket]

Cor·fu (kôr′fū; *It.* kôr fōō′), *n.* **1.** Ancient, **Corcyra.** one of the Ionian Islands, off the NW coast of Greece. 111,355 pop. (est. 1940); 229 sq. mi. **2.** a seaport on this island. 32,221 (est. 1938). Greek, **Kerkyra.**

co·ri·a·ceous (kôr′ǐ ā′shəs, kōr′-), *adj.* of or like leather. [t. LL: m. *coriāceus* leathern]

co·ri·an·der (kôr′ǐ ăn′dər), *n.* **1.** a herbaceous plant, *Coriandrum sativum,* bearing aromatic seedlike fruit (**coriander seeds**) used in cookery and medicine. **2.** the fruit or seeds. [ME *coriandre,* t. F, t. L: m. *coriandrum,* t. Gk.: m. *koriandron,* var. of *koriannon*]

Cor·inth (kôr′ǐnth, kōr′-), *n.* **1.** an ancient city in Greece, strategically located on the Isthmus of Corinth: famed for its luxury. **2. Gulf of,** an arm of the Ionian Sea, N of the Peloponnesus. Also, **Gulf of Lepanto. 3. Isthmus of,** a narrow isthmus at the head of the Gulf of Corinth, connecting the Peloponnesus with central Greece: traversed by a ship canal.

Co·rin·thi·an (kə rǐn′thǐ ən), *adj.* **1.** of Corinth, noted in ancient times for its artistic adornment, luxury, and licentiousness. **2.** luxurious; licentious. **3.** ornate, as literary style. **4.** *Archit.* designating or pertaining to one of the three Greek orders, distinguished by a bell-shaped capital with rows of acanthus leaves and a continuous frieze. See fig. under **order.** —*n.* **5.** a native or inhabitant of Corinth. **6.** (*pl.*) the two books or epistles of the New Testament addressed by St. Paul to the Christian community at Corinth. **7.** a man of fashion.

Cor·i·o·la·nus (kôr′ǐ ə lā′nəs, kōr′-), *n.* **1. Gaius** (or **Gnaeus**) **Marcius** (gā′əs, or nē′əs, mär′shǐ əs), a legendary Roman general of the 5th century B.C. who, in revenge for being exiled, led an army against Rome, but was turned back by the appeals of his mother and his wife. **2.** a tragedy (about 1008) by Shakespeare.

co·ri·um (kōr′ǐ əm), *n., pl.* **coria** (kōr′ǐ ə). *Anat.* the sensitive vascular layer of the skin, beneath the epidermis; the derma. [t. L: skin, hide, leather]

cork (kôrk), *n.* **1.** the outer bark of a species of oak, *Quercus Suber,* of Mediterranean countries, used for making stoppers of bottles, floats, etc. **2.** the tree itself. **3.** something made of cork. **4.** a piece of cork, or of other material (as rubber), used as a stopper for a bottle, etc. **5.** *Angling.* a small float to buoy up a fishing line or to indicate when a fish bites. **6.** *Bot.* an outer tissue of bark produced by and exterior to the phellogen. —*v.t.* **7.** to provide or fit with cork or a cork. **8.** to stop with, or as with, a cork (often fol. by *up*). **9.** to blacken with burnt cork. [t. Sp.: aphetic m. *alcorque* shoe with cork, t. Ar.: m. *al qorq,* t. L: m. *quercus* oak; ? b. with Sp. *corcho* cork, ult. g. L *cortex* bark] —**cork′like′,** *adj.*

Cork (kôrk), *n.* **1.** a county in S Eire, in Munster. 346,548 pop. (est. 1943); 2881 sq. mi. **2.** its county seat: a seaport. 75,484 (est. 1943).

cork·age (kôr′kǐj), *n.* a charge made by hotelkeepers, etc., for serving liquor not supplied by the house.

cork cambium. *Bot.* phellogen.

corked (kôrkt), *adj.* **1.** stopped with a cork. **2.** (of wine) tasting of the cork; having the flavor spoiled by poor corking. **3.** blackened with burnt cork.

cork·er (kôr′kər), *n.* **1.** one who or that which corks. **2.** *Slang.* something that closes a discussion or settles a question. **3.** *Slang.* something striking or astonishing. **4.** *Slang.* something very good of its kind.

cork·ing (kôr′kǐng), *adj. Slang.* excellent; fine.

cork·screw (kôrk′skrōō′), *n.* **1.** an instrument consisting of a metal spiral with a sharp point and a transverse handle, used to draw corks from bottles. —*adj.* **2.** resembling a corkscrew; helical; spiral. —*v.t., v.i.* **3.** to move in a spiral or zigzag course.

cork·wood (kôrk′wood′), *n.* **1.** a stout shrub or small tree, *Leitneria floridana,* with shining deciduous leaves, densely pubescent aments, and a drupaceous fruit. **2.** any of certain trees and shrubs having a light and porous wood, as the balsa.

cork·y (kôr′kǐ), *adj.,* **corkier, corkiest. 1.** of the nature of cork; corklike. **2.** *Colloq.* buoyant, lively, or skittish. **3.** (of wine) corked (def. 2). —**cork′i·ness,** *n.*

corm (kôrm), *n. Bot.* an enlarged, fleshy bulblike base of a stem, as in the crocus. [t. NL: s. *cormus,* t. Gk.: m. *kormós* tree trunk with boughs lopped off]

Corm of crocus

cor·mo·phyte (kôr′mə fīt′), *n.* any of the *Cormophyta,* an old primary division or group of plants having an axis differentiated into stem and root, and including all phanerogams and the higher cryptogams. [f. *cormo-* (comb. form of CORM) + -PHYTE] —**cor·mo·phyt·ic** (kôr/mə fĭt/ĭk), *adj.*

cor·mo·rant (kôr/mə rənt), *n.* 1. any bird of the family *Phalacrocoracidae*, comprising large, voracious, totipalmate water birds with a long neck and a pouch under the beak in which they hold captured fish, as *Phalacrocorax carbo*, a common species of America, Europe, and Asia. 2. a greedy or rapacious person. —*adj.* 3. greedy; rapacious; insatiable. [ME *cormoraunte*, t. OF: m. *cormoran*, *cormaran*, f. *corp* raven + *marenc* marine (der. *mer* sea)]

Crested cormorant.
Phalacrocorax auritus
(2½ ft. long)

corn¹ (kôrn), *n.* 1. maize; Indian corn. 2. any edible grain, esp. wheat in England, and oats in Scotland. 3. a single seed of certain plants, esp. of cereal plants, as wheat, rye, barley, and maize; a grain. 4. *U.S. Colloq.* whiskey made from Indian corn. —*v.t.* 5. to granulate, as gunpowder. 6. to preserve and season with salt in grains. 7. to lay down in brine, as meat. 8. to plant (land) with corn. 9. to feed with corn. [ME and OE; c. G *korn*, akin to L *grānum* GRAIN]

corn² (kôrn), *n.* a horny induration or callosity of the epidermis, usually with a central core, caused by undue pressure or friction, esp. on the toes or feet. [t. OF: horn, g. L *cornū*]

cor·na·ceous (kôr nā/shəs), *adj.* belonging to the *Cornaceae*, a family of plants, mostly shrubs and trees, including the dogwood, etc. [f. NL *cornāce(ae)* (der. L *cornus* cornel) + -OUS]

Corn Belt, a region in the midwestern U.S., esp. Iowa, Illinois, and Indiana, excellent for raising corn and corn-fed livestock.

corn borer, the larva of a small moth, *Pyrausta nubilalis*, which feeds on corn and other grasses.

corn bread, a kind of bread made of corn meal.

corn cake, *U.S.* a cake made of Indian corn meal.

corn·cob (kôrn/kŏb/), *n. U.S.* 1. the elongated woody core in which the grains of an ear of maize are embedded. 2. a tobacco pipe with a bowl made of this.

corn cockle, a caryophyllaceous annual, *Agrostemma Githago*, bearing red or white flowers, common as a weed among crops of grain.

corn color, light ye ow. —**corn/-col/ored,** *adj.*

corn crake, the European land rail, *Crex crex*, a bird common in grain fields.

corn·crib (kôrn/krĭb/), *n.* a ventilated structure used for the storage of unshelled Indian corn.

corn dodger, *U.S.* a kind of bread made of corn meal, fried or baked hard.

cor·ne·a (kôr/nĭ ə), *n. Anat.* the transparent anterior part of the external coat of the eye, covering the iris and the pupil, and continuous with the sclera. See diag. under *eye*. [t. L, fem. sing. of *corneus* horny] —**cor/ne·al,** *adj.*

corn earworm, the larva of a noctuid moth, *Heliothis armigera*, destructive to corn, cotton, and other plants; bollworm.

corned (kôrnd), *adj.* preserved or cured with salt: *corned beef.*

Cor·neille (kôr nā/; *Fr.* kôr nĕ/y), *n.* **Pierre** (pyĕr), 1606–84, French dramatist and poet.

cor·nel (kôr/nəl), *n.* any of the trees or perennials constituting the genus *Cornus*, as *C. sanguinea*, the European dogwood, or *C. florida*, the flowering dogwood of America. [t. G, t. ML: m. *cornolius* cornel-tree, ult. der. L *cornus*]

Cor·ne·li·a (kôr nēl/yə), *n.* died after 121 B.C., the mother of Tiberius and Gaius Gracchus, champions of the rights of the Roman people.

cor·ne·li·an (kôr nēl/yən), *n.* carnelian.

Cor·ne·li·us (kôr nē/lĭ ŏos/), *n.* **Peter von** (pā/tər fən), 1783–1867, German painter, esp. of historical frescoes.

Cor·nell (kôr nĕl/), *n.* **Ezra,** 1807–74, U.S. capitalist and philanthropist.

cor·ne·ous (kôr/nĭ əs), *adj.* consisting of a horny substance; horny. [t. L: m. *corneus* horny]

cor·ner (kôr/nər), *n.* 1. the meeting place of two converging lines or surfaces. 2. the space between two converging lines or surfaces near their intersection; angle. 3. a projecting angle. 4. the place where two streets meet. 5. an end; margin; edge. 6. any narrow, secluded, or secret place. 7. an awkward or embarrassing position, esp. one from which escape is impossible. 8. any part, even the least or the most remote. 9. *Finance.* a monopolizing or a monopoly of the available supply of a stock or commodity, to a point permitting control of price (applied only when monopoly price is exacted). 10. a region; quarter: *all the corners of the earth.* 11. a piece to protect the corner of anything. —*v.t.* 12. to furnish with corners. 13. to place in, or drive into, a corner. 14. *Chiefly U.S.* to force into an awkward or difficult position, or one from which escape is impossible. 15. to form a corner in (a stock, etc.). —*v.i.* 16. *U.S.* to meet in, or be situated on or at, a corner. 17. to form a corner in a stock or commodity. [ME, t. AF, var. of OF *cornere*, ult. der. L *cornū* horn, corner]

cor·ner·stone (kôr/nər stōn/), *n.* 1. a stone which lies at the corner of two walls, and serves to unite them.

2. a stone built into a corner of the foundation of an important edifice as the actual or nominal starting point in building, usually laid with formal ceremonies, and often hollowed out and made the repository of documents, etc. 3. something of fundamental importance.

cor·ner·wise (kôr/nər wīz/), *adv.* 1. with the corner in front. 2. so as to form a corner. 3. from corner to corner; diagonally. Also, **cor·ner·ways** (kôr/nər wāz/).

cor·net (kôr nĕt/ *for 1;* kôr/nĭt, kôr nĕt/ *for 2–7*), *n.* 1. a wind instrument of the trumpet class, with valves or pistons. 2. a little cone of paper twisted at the end, used for enclosing small wares. 3. *Brit.* a cone, as for ice cream. 4. the great white cap worn by Sisters of Charity. 5. a headdress formerly worn by women. 6. *Naut.* a signal pennant. 7. (formerly) an officer in a troop of cavalry, who carried the colors. [ME *cornette*, t. OF: m. *cornet*, ult. der. L *cornū* horn] —**cor·net/ist, cor·net/tist,** *n.*

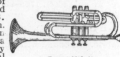
Cornet (def. 1)

cor·net-à-pis·tons (kôr nĕt/ə pĭs/tənz; *Fr.* kôr nĕ/à-pē stōN/), *n., pl.* **cornets-à-pistons** (kôr nĕts/-; *Fr.* kôr nĕ/zà pē stōN/). cornet. [t. F: cornet with pistons]

corn·flow·er (kôrn/flou/ər), *n.* 1. any of several plants growing in grain fields, as *Centaurea cyanus*, a composite plant with blue (varying to white) flowers, growing wild in Europe and often cultivated for ornament; bluebottle. 2. corn cockle. 3. *Brit.* cornstarch.

corn·husk (kôrn/hŭsk/), *n.* the husk of an ear of Indian corn.

cor·nice (kôr/nĭs), *n., v.,* **-niced, -nicing.** —*n.* 1. *Archit.* a. a horizontal molded projection which crowns or finishes a wall, building, etc. b. the uppermost division of an entablature, resting on the frieze. See diag. under **column.** c. the exposed exterior surface of a gutter. 2. the molding or moldings between the walls and ceiling of a room. 3. any of the various other ornamental horizontal moldings or bands, as for concealing hooks or rods from which curtains are hung or for supporting picture hooks. —*v.t.* 4. to furnish or finish with, or as with, a cornice. [t. F, t. It., t. MGk.: m.s. *korōnis* summit, Gk. anything curved or bent]

cor·nic·u·late (kôr nĭk/yə lāt/, -lĭt), *adj.* resembling a small horn in appearance. [f. s. L *corniculus* little horn + -ATE¹]

Cor·nish (kôr/nĭsh), *adj.* 1. of Cornwall (England), its inhabitants, or the language formerly spoken by them. —*n.* 2. the old Celtic language of Cornwall. 3. the dialect of English now spoken in Cornwall. —**Cor·nish·man** (kôr/nĭsh mən), *n.*

Corn Law, *Eng. Hist.* any one of a series of laws regulating the home and foreign grain trade, the last of which was repealed in 1846.

corn lily, any of several ornamental bulbous plants of the South African genus *Ixia*, family *Iridaceae.*

corn meal, 1. meal made of corn or grain. 2. *U.S.* Indian meal. 3. *Scot.* oatmeal. —**corn/-meal/,** *adj.*

corn picker, *U.S.* a machine for picking ears of corn from standing stalks and removing husks from the ears.

corn pit, an exchange devoted to trading in corn futures.

corn pone, *Southern U.S.* 1. corn bread, esp. of a plain or simple kind. 2. a cake or loaf of this.

corn poppy, the common Old World poppy, *Papaver rhoeas*, bearing bright red flowers, now the symbol of fallen soldiers.

corn rose, 1. the common red poppy, *Papaver rhoeas.* 2. the corn cockle, *Agrostemma Githago.*

corn salad, any of several plants of the genus *Valerianella*, esp. *V. olitoria* and *V. eriocarpa*, sometimes found wild in grainfields, and used for salad.

corn shock, a stack of upright cornstalks.

corn silk, the fresh styles and stigmas of *Zea mays*, used in medicine as a diuretic.

corn smut, a fungus, *Ustilago zeae*, growing on Indian corn, formerly used medicinally.

corn·stalk (kôrn/stôk/), *n.* the stalk or stem of corn, esp. Indian corn.

corn·starch (kôrn/stärch/), *n.* a starch, or a starchy flour made from corn, used for making puddings, etc.

corn sugar, a sugar made from corn, being the common form of glucose.

corn syrup, the syrup prepared from corn.

cor·nu (kôr/nū), *n., pl.* **-nua** (-nyŏō ə). a horn, esp. a process of bone resembling a horn. [See HORN]

cor·nu·co·pi·a (kôr/nə kō/pĭ ə), *n.* 1. the fabulous horn of the goat Amalthaea, which suckled Zeus, represented as overflowing with flowers, fruit, etc., and symbolizing plenty. 2. an overflowing supply. 3. a horn-shaped or conical receptacle or ornament. [t. LL, for L *cornū cōpiae* horn of plenty] —**cor/nu·co/pi·an,** *adj.*

cor·nus (kôr/nəs), *n.* a cornel. [t. L: dogwood tree]

cor·nut·ed (kôr nū/tĭd, -nŏō/-), *adj.* having horns.

Corn·wall (kôrn/wôl *or, esp. Brit.,* -wəl), *n.* a county in SW England. 321,000 pop. (est. 1946); 1357 sq. mi. *Co. seat:* Bodmin.

Corn·wal·lis (kôrn wŏl/ĭs, -wŏl/ĭs), *n.* **Charles, 1st Marquis,** 1738–1805, British general and statesman: surrendered to Washington at Yorktown, Virginia, October 19, 1781.

---

b., blend of, blended; c., cognate with; d., dialect, dialectal; der., derived from; f., formed from; g., going back to; m., modification of; r., replacing; s., stem of; t., taken from; ?, perhaps. See the full key on inside cover.

corn whiskey, whiskey made from corn.

corn·y (kôr′nĭ), *adj.,* **cornier, corniest. 1.** of or abounding in corn. **2.** *Colloq.* (of jazz) written or played with self-conscious emotionalism, lacking sophistication or spontaneity and enthusiasm. **3.** *Slang.* of poor quality: *corny radio programs.*

cor·o·dy (kôr′ə dĭ, kŏr′-), *n., pl.* **-dies.** *Chiefly Hist.* **1.** an allowance, as of food, etc., for one's maintenance. **2.** the right to this. [late ME, t. ML: m.s. *corrōdium,* var. of *corrēdium* provision. Cf. ARRAY]

co·rol·la (kə rŏl′ə), *n.* *Bot.* the internal envelope or floral leaves of a flower, usually of delicate texture and of some color other than green; the petals considered collectively. [t. L: garland, dim. of *corōna* crown]

cor·ol·la·ceous (kŏr′ə lā′shəs, kŏr′-), *adj.* *Bot.* having or resembling a corolla.

cor·ol·lar·y (kôr′ə lĕr′ĭ, kŏr′-, or, *esp.* *Brit.,* kə rŏl′ə rĭ), *n., pl.* **-laries. 1.** *Math.* a proposition incidentally proved in proving another. **2.** an immediate or easily drawn consequence. **3.** a natural consequence or result. [ME *corolarie,* t. LL: m. *corollārium* corollary, L gift, gratuity, orig. garland, der. L *corolla* garland]

Corollas
Polypetalous corollas: A, Unguiculate; B, Papilionaceous; C, Cruciate. Gamopetalous corollas: D, Personate; E, Ligulate; F, Labiate;

Cor·o·man·del Coast (kôr′ə măn′dəl, kŏr′-), that part of the coastline of SE India extending from Point Calimere (opposite the N end of Ceylon) to the mouth of the Kistna river.

co·ro·na (kə rō′nə), *n., pl.* **-nas, -nae** (-nē). **1.** a white or colored circle of light seen round a luminous body, esp. the sun or moon (in meteorology, restricted to those circles due to the diffraction produced by thin clouds or mist). **2.** *Astron.* a faintly luminous envelope outside of the sun's chromosphere, the inner part consisting of highly ionized elements. **3.** *Archit.* that part of a cornice supported by and projecting beyond the bed molding. See diag. under **column. 4.** *Anat.* the upper portion or crown of a part, as of the head. **5.** *Bot.* a crownlike appendage, esp. one on the inner side of a corolla, as in the narcissus. **6.** *Elect.* a discharge, frequently luminous, at the surface of a conductor, or between two conductors of the same transmission line, accompanied by ionization of the surrounding atmosphere and power loss; brush discharge. [t. L: garland, CROWN]

Co·ro·na Aus·tra·lis (kə rō′nə ô strā′lĭs), the Southern Crown, a southern constellation touching the southern part of Sagittarius. [t. L]

Co·ro·na Bo·re·al·is (kə rō′nə bōr′ĭ ăl′ĭs, -ā′lĭs), the Northern Crown, a northern constellation between Hercules and Boötes. [t. L]

cor·o·nach (kŏr′ə nəкн, kôr′-), *n.* (in Scotland and Ireland) a song or lamentation for the dead; a dirge. [t. Gaelic: m. *corranach* outcry, dirge]

Co·ro·na·do (kôr′ə nä′dō; *Sp.* kō′rō nä′dō), *n.* **Francisco Vásquez de** (frän thēs′kō väs′kĕth dě), 1510-1554?, Spanish explorer in the SW part of the U.S.

cor·o·nal (*n.* kôr′ə nəl, kŏr′-; *adj.* kə rō′nəl, kŏr′ə nəl, kŏr′-), *n.* **1.** *Anat.* the coronal suture. **2.** a crown; coronet. **3.** a garland. —*adj.* **4.** of or pertaining to a coronal. **5.** *Phonet.* retroflex. [t. LL: s. *corōnālis*]

coronal suture, *Anat.* a suture extending across the skull between the frontal bone and the parietal bones. See diag. under **cranium.**

cor·o·nar·y (kôr′ə nĕr′ĭ, kŏr′-), *adj.* **1.** of or like a crown. **2.** *Anat.* **a.** encircling like a crown, as certain blood vessels. **b.** pertaining to the arteries which supply the heart tissues and which originate in the root of the aorta. [t. L: m.s. *corōnārius*]

coronary thrombosis, *Pathol.* the occlusion of a coronary arterial branch by a blood clot within the vessel, usually at a site narrowed by arteriosclerosis.

cor·o·na·tion (kôr′ə nā′shən, kŏr′-), *n.* act or ceremony of investing a king, etc., with a crown.

cor·o·ner (kôr′ə nər, kŏr′-), *n.* an officer, as of a county or municipality, whose chief function is to investigate by inquest (often before a **coroner's jury**) any death not clearly due to natural causes. [ME, t. AF: m. *corouner* officer of the crown, der. *coroune.* See CROWN] —**cor′o·ner·ship′,** *n.*

cor·o·net (kôr′ə nĭt, -nĕt′, kŏr′-), *n.* **1.** a small or inferior crown. **2.** an insignia for the head, worn by peers or members of nobility. **3.** a crownlike ornament for the head, as of gold or jewels. **4.** the lowest part of the pastern of a horse, just above the hoof. [t. OF: m. *coronete,* dim. of *corone* CROWN]

cor·o·net·ed (kôr′ə nĭt ĭd, -nĕt′ĭd, kŏr′-), *adj.* wearing, or entitled to wear, a coronet. Also, **cor′o·net′ted.**

Co·rot (kō rō′), *n.* **Jean Baptiste Camille** (zhän bätēst′ kȧ mē′y), 1796-1875, French landscape painter.

Corp., 1. Corporal. 2. Corporation. Also, **corp.**

Corpl., Corporal.

cor·po·ra (kôr′pə rə), *n.* pl. of **corpus.**

cor·po·ral[1] (kôr′pə rəl), *adj.* **1.** of the human body; bodily; physical: *corporal pleasure.* **2.** personal: *corporal possession.* **3.** *Zool.* of the body proper (as distinguished from the head and limbs). **4.** *Obs.* corporeal. [ME, t. L: s. *corporālis* bodily] —**cor′po·ral′i·ty,** *n.* —**cor′po·ral·ly,** *adv.* —**Syn. 1.** See **physical.**

cor·po·ral[2] (kôr′pə rəl), *n.* **1.** (in the army) a noncommissioned officer of lowest rank. **2.** *Brit. Navy.* a petty officer whose duty is to assist the master-at-arms. [t. F, obs. var. of *caporal,* t. It.: m. *caporale,* der. *capo* (g. L *caput*) head] —**cor′po·ral·ship′,** *n.*

cor·po·ral[3] (kôr′pə rəl), *n.* *Eccles.* a fine cloth, usually of linen, on which the consecrated elements are placed during the celebration of the Eucharist. [ME, t. ML: s. *corporālis, corporāle,* der. L *corpus* body]

corporal punishment, *Law.* physical injury inflicted on the body of one convicted of a crime, including the death penalty, flogging, sentence to a term of years, etc.

cor·po·rate (kôr′pə rĭt, -prĭt), *adj.* **1.** forming a corporation. **2.** of a corporation. **3.** united in one body. **4.** pertaining to a united body, as of persons. [t. L: m.s. *corporātus,* pp., formed into a body] —**cor′po·rate·ly,** *adv.*

cor·po·ra·tion (kôr′pə rā′shən), *n.* **1.** an association of individuals, created by law or under authority of law, having a continuous existence irrespective of that of its members, and powers and liabilities distinct from those of its members. **2.** (*cap.*) (in England) the principal officials of a borough, etc. **3.** any group of persons united, or regarded as united, in one body. **4.** *Slang.* the abdomen, esp. when large and prominent.

cor·po·ra·tive (kôr′pə rā′tĭv), *adj.* *Pol. Econ.* of a political system under which the principal economic functions (banking, industry, labor, etc.) are organized as corporate unities.

cor·po·ra·tor (kôr′pə rā′tər), *n.* a member of a corporation, esp. one of the original members.

cor·po·re·al (kôr pōr′ĭ əl), *adj.* **1.** of the nature of the physical body; bodily. **2.** of the nature of matter; material; tangible: *corporeal property.* [f. s. L *corporeus* of the nature of body + -AL[1]] —**cor·po′re·al′i·ty, cor·po′re·al·ness,** *n.* —**cor·po′re·al·ly,** *adv.* —**Syn. 1.** See **physical.** —**Ant. 1.** spiritual. **2.** intangible.

cor·po·re·i·ty (kôr′pə rē′ə tĭ), *n.* material or physical nature or quality; materiality.

cor·po·sant (kôr′pə zănt′), *n.* a light, due to atmospheric electricity, sometimes seen on the mastheads, yardarms, etc., of ships and on church towers, treetops, etc. [t. Pg.: m. *corpo santo* holy body (L *corpus sanctum*)]

corps (kôr), *n., pl.* **corps** (kôrz). **1.** *Mil.* **a.** an organized military body consisting of officers and men, or of officers alone: *the U.S. Marine Corps, Corps of Cadets.* **b.** a military unit of ground combat forces consisting of two or more divisions and other troops. **2.** a group of persons associated or acting together: *the diplomatic corps.* **3.** *Obs.* corpse. [t. F. See CORPSE]

corps area, *Mil.* (formerly) one of the nine military subdivisions of the continental U.S.

corps de bal·let (kôr də bȧ lĕ′). *French.* the dancers in a ballet company who perform as a group and have no solo parts.

corpse (kôrps), *n.* **1.** a dead body, usually of a human being. **2.** *Obs.* a living body. [ME *corps, cors,* t. OF. g. L *corpus* body] —**Syn. 1.** See **body.**

corps·man (kôr′mən), *n., pl.* **-men. 1.** *U.S. Navy.* an enlisted man working as a pharmacist or hospital assistant. **2.** *U.S. Army.* an enlisted man of the Medical Department who accompanies combat troops into battle to give first aid, carry off the wounded, etc.

cor·pu·lence (kôr′pyə ləns), *n.* bulkiness or largeness of body; fatness; fleshiness; portliness. Also, **cor′pu·len·cy.** [late ME, t. F, t. L: m.s. *corpulentia*]

cor·pu·lent (kôr′pyə lənt), *adj.* large or bulky of body; portly; stout; fat. [ME, t. L: s. *corpulentus,* der. *corpus* body] —**cor′pu·lent·ly,** *adv.*

cor·pus (kôr′pəs), *n., pl.* **-pora** (-pə rə). **1.** the body of a man or animal. **2.** *Anat.* any of various bodies, masses, or parts of special character or function. **3.** a large or complete collection of writings, laws, etc. **4.** a principal or capital sum, as opposed to interest or income. [t. L]

cor·pus al·la·tum (kôr′pəs ə lā′təm), *pl.* **corpora allata** (kôr′pə rə ə lā′tə). *Entomol.* one of a pair of small ductless, hormone-secreting glands in the head of an insect behind the brain. [NL: added body]

cor·pus cal·lo·sum (kôr′pəs kə lō′səm), *pl.* **corpora callosa** (kôr′pə rə kə lō′sə). *Anat., Zool.* a great band of deeply situated transverse white fibers uniting the two halves of the cerebrum, peculiar to *Mammalia.* [NL: hard body]

cor·pus car·di·a·cum (kôr′pəs kär dĭ′ə kəm), *pl.* **corpora cardiaca** (kôr′pə rə kärdĭ′ə kə). *Entomol.* one of a pair of small cellular bodies associated with the corpora allata in the back of an insect's head, generally attached to the aorta, probably organs of hormone secretion.

Cor·pus Chris·ti (kôr′pəs krĭs′tĭ; *for 1 also* -tī). **1.** *Rom. Cath. Ch.* a festival in honor of the Eucharist, kept on the Thursday after Trinity Sunday. **2.** a seaport in S Texas, on **Corpus Christi Bay,** an inlet of the Gulf of Mexico. 108,287 (1950). [t. L: body of Christ]

cor·pus·cle (kôr′pəs əl, -pŭs əl), *n.* **1.** *Physiol.* one of the minute bodies which form a constituent of the blood (**blood corpuscles**, both red and white), the lymph (**lymph corpuscles**, white only), etc. **2.** a minute body forming a more or less distinct part of an organism. **3.** *Physics, Chem.* a minute or elementary particle of matter, as an electron, proton, or atom. **4.** a minute particle. Also, **cor·pus·cule** (kôr′pŭs′kūl). [t. L: m. s. *corpusculum*, dim. of *corpus* body] —**cor·pus·cu·lar** (kôr′pŭs′kyə lər), *adj.*

cor·pus de·lic·ti (kôr′pəs dĬ lĬk′tī), *Law.* the fact that a crime or offense has actually been committed. Except where the accused pleads guilty, corroboration of this fact by other evidence is usually required before he can be convicted. [t. L: body of the transgression]

cor·pus ju·ris (kôr′pəs jŏŏr′Ĭs), a compilation of law or the collected law of a nation or state. [t. L]

Corpus Juris Ca·no·ni·ci (kə nŏn′ə sī′), the collection of church law which remained in power until it was replaced in 1918 by the Codex Juris Canonici. [t. L]

Corpus Juris Ci·vi·lis (sĬ vī′lĬs), the collective title (since the 17th century) of the whole legislation of Justinian Code, promulgated in the 6th century, as the Digest, the Institutes, the Code, and the Novels. [t. L]

cor·pus lu·te·um (kôr′pəs lōō′tĬ əm), *pl.* **corpora lu·tea** (kôr′pə rə lōō′tĬ ə). **1.** *Anat.* a ductless gland developed within the ovary by the reorganization of a Graafian follicle following ovulation. **2.** *Pharm.* progesterone. [NL: yellow body]

cor·pus stri·a·tum (kôr′pəs strī ā′təm), *pl.* **corpora striata** (kôr′pə rə strī ā′tə). *Anat.* a mass of gray matter beneath the cortex and in front of the thalamus in each cerebral hemisphere. [NL: striped body]

cor·ral (kə rāl′), *n., v.,* **-ralled, -ralling.** —*n.* **1.** a pen or enclosure for horses, cattle, etc. **2.** an enclosure formed of wagons during an encampment, for defense against attack. —*v.t.* **3.** to confine in, or as in, a corral. **4.** *U.S. Colloq.* to seize; capture. **5.** to form (wagons) into a corral. [t. Sp.: enclosed yard, der. *corro* a ring]

cor·rect (kə rĕkt′), *v.t.* **1.** to set right; remove the errors or faults of. **2.** to point out or mark the errors in. **3.** to admonish or rebuke in order to improve. **4.** to counteract the operation or effect of (something hurtful). **5.** *Math., Physics., etc.* to alter or adjust so as to bring into accordance with a standard or with some required condition. —*adj.* **6.** conforming to fact or truth; free from error; accurate: *a correct statement.* **7.** in accordance with an acknowledged or accepted standard; proper: *correct behavior.* [ME *correcte(n)*, t. L: m. s. *correctus*, pp., made straight, directed] —**cor·rect′ly,** *adv.* —**cor·rect′ness,** *n.* —**cor·rec′tor,** *n.*
—**Syn. 1.** rectify, amend, emend, reform, remedy. **3.** discipline. See **punish. 6.** faultless, perfect, exact. CORRECT, ACCURATE, PRECISE imply conformity to fact, standard, or truth. A CORRECT statement is one free from error, mistakes, or faults. An ACCURATE statement is one which, as a result of an active effort to comprehend and verify, shows careful conformity to fact, truth, or spirit. A PRECISE statement shows scrupulously strict and detailed (sometimes excessive) conformity to fact. —**Ant. 6.** faulty, inaccurate. **7.** unconventional.

correcting plate, the thin lens used to correct incoming light rays in special forms of reflecting telescopes.

cor·rec·tion (kə rĕk′shən), *n.* **1.** act of correcting. **2.** that which is substituted or proposed for what is wrong; an emendation. **3.** punishment; chastisement; discipline; reproof. **4.** *Math., Physics, etc.* a subordinate quantity that has to be applied in order to ensure accuracy, as in the use of an instrument or the solution of a problem. —**cor·rec′tion·al,** *adj.*

cor·rect·i·tude (kə rĕk′tə tūd′, -tōōd′), *n.* correctness, esp. of manners and conduct. [f. CORRECT, v. + -*itude*, modeled on RECTITUDE]

cor·rec·tive (kə rĕk′tĬv), *adj.* **1.** tending to correct; having the quality of correcting. —*n.* **2.** a corrective agent. —**cor·rec′tive·ly,** *adv.*

Cor·reg·gio (kôr rĕd′jŏ), *n.* **Antonio Allegri da** (än-tō′nyŏ äl′lĕ′grĕ dä), 1494–1534, Italian painter.

Cor·reg·i·dor (kə rĕg′ə dôr′; *Sp.* kôr rĕ′hē dôr′), *n.* a fortified island in Manila Bay, in the Philippine Islands: surrendered to the Japanese after heroic resistance, May 6, 1942. 2 sq. mi.

cor·re·late (kôr′ə lāt′, kôr′-), *v.,* **-lated, -lating,** *adj., n.* —*v.t.* **1.** to place in or bring into mutual or reciprocal relation; establish an orderly connection. —*v.i.* **2.** to have a mutual or reciprocal relation; stand in correlation. —*adj.* **3.** mutually or reciprocally related; correlated. —*n.* **4.** either of two related things, esp. when one implies the other. [f. COR- + RELATE]

cor·re·la·tion (kôr′ə lā′shən, kôr′-), *n.* **1.** mutual relation of two or more things, parts, etc. **2.** act of correlating. **3.** state of being correlated. **4.** *Statistics.* the degree of relationship of two attributes or measurements on the same group of elements. **5.** *Physiol.* the interdependence or reciprocal relations of organs or functions.

correlation coefficient, *Statistics.* the measure of correlation, called r, having the value $+1$ for perfect positive linear correlation, -1 for perfect negative linear correlation, and a value of 0 for a complete lack of correlation.

correlation ratio, *Statistics.* a mathematical measure of the correlation between two sets of values not linearly correlated.

cor·rel·a·tive (kə rĕl′ə tĬv), *adj.* **1.** so related that each implies or complements the other. **2.** being in correlation; mutually related. **3.** having a mutual relation; answering to or complementing one another, as *either* and *or, where* and *there.* **4.** *Biol.* (of a typical structure of an organism) found in correlation with another. —*n.* **5.** either of two things, as two terms, which are correlative. **6.** a correlative expression. —**cor·rel′a·tive·ly,** *adv.* —**cor·rel′a·tive·ness, cor·rel′a·tiv′i·ty,** *n.*

cor·re·spond (kôr′ə spŏnd′, kôr′-), *v.i.* **1.** to be in agreement or conformity (often fol. by *with* or *to*): *his words and actions do not correspond.* **2.** to be similar or analogous; be equivalent in function, position, amount, etc. (fol. by *to*): *the U.S. Congress corresponds to the British Parliament.* **3.** to communicate by exchange of letters. [t. ML: s. *correspondēre* f. L: *cor-* (see COM-) + *respondēre* answer] —**cor′re·spond′ing·ly,** *adv.* —**Syn. 1.** harmonize, accord, match. See **agree.**

cor·re·spond·ence (kôr′ə spŏn′dəns, kôr′-), *n.* **1.** Also, **cor′re·spond′en·cy.** act or fact of corresponding. **2.** relation of similarity or analogy. **3.** agreement; conformity. **4.** communication by exchange of letters. **5.** letters that pass between correspondents.

correspondence course, the study materials issued by a correspondence school on a subject or topic.

correspondence school, a school which gives instruction by correspondence.

cor·re·spond·ent (kôr′ə spŏn′dənt, kôr′-), *n.* **1.** one who communicates by letters. **2.** one employed to contribute news, etc., regularly from a distant place. **3.** one who contributes letters to a newspaper. **4.** one who has regular business relations with another, esp. at a distance. **5.** a thing that corresponds to something else. —*adj.* **6.** corresponding; having a relation of correspondence. —**cor′re·spond′ent·ly,** *adv.*

cor·re·spon·sive (kôr′ə spŏn′sĬv, kôr′-), *adj.* responsive to effort or impulse; answering; corresponding.

cor·ri·dor (kôr′ə dər, -dôr′, kôr′-), *n.* **1.** a gallery or passage connecting parts of a building. **2.** a passage into which several rooms or apartments open. **3.** *Brit. Railroad.* a passageway on one side of a car into which the compartments open. **4.** a narrow tract of land forming a passageway, as one belonging to an inland country and affording an outlet to the sea: *the Polish Corridor.* [t. F: long passageway, t. It.: m. *corridore* covered way, t. Sp.: m. *corredor*, der. *correr* run, g. L *currere*]

cor·rie (kôr′Ĭ, kŏr′Ĭ), *n. Scot.* a circular hollow in the side of a hill or mountain. [t. Gaelic: m. *coire* caldron]

Cor·rie·dale (kôr′Ĭ dāl′, kŏr′-), *n.* a white-faced breed of sheep, orig. developed in New Zealand, noted for high quality wool and good market lambs of the mutton type.

Cor·ri·en·tes (kôr′rē ĕn′tĕs), *n.* a city in NE Argentina: a port on the Paraná river. 59,323 (est. 1940).

cor·ri·gen·dum (kôr′ə jĕn′dəm, kôr′-), *n., pl.* **-da** (-də). **1.** an error to be corrected, esp. an error in print. **2.** (*pl.*) a list of corrections of errors in a book, etc. [t. L, neut. gerundive of *corrigere* correct]

cor·ri·gi·ble (kôr′ə jə bəl, kôr′-), *adj.* **1.** capable of being corrected. **2.** submissive to correction. [t. LL: m.s. *corrigibilis*, der. L *corrigere* correct] —**cor′ri·gi·bil′i·ty,** *n.* —**cor′ri·gi·bly,** *adv.*

cor·ri·val (kə rī′vəl), *n., adj.* rival. [t. L: s. *corrīvālis* joint rival]

cor·rob·o·rant (kə rŏb′ər ənt), *adj.* **1.** corroborating; confirming. **2.** strengthening; invigorating. —*n.* **3.** something that corroborates or strengthens. **4.** *Obsolesc.* a strengthening medicine.

cor·rob·o·rate (*v.* kə rŏb′ə rāt′; *adj.* kə rŏb′ər Ĭt), *v.,* **-rated, -rating,** *adj.* —*v.t.* **1.** to make more certain; confirm. —*adj.* **2.** *Archaic.* corroborated. [t. L: m. s. *corrōborātus*, pp., strengthened] —**cor·rob′o·ra′tive, cor·rob·o·ra·to·ry** (kə rŏb′ə rə tōr′Ĭ), *adj.* —**cor·rob′o·ra′tive·ly,** *adv.* —**cor·rob′o·ra′tor,** *n.*

cor·rob·o·ra·tion (kə rŏb′ə rā′shən), *n.* **1.** act of corroborating. **2.** a corroboratory fact, statement, etc.

cor·rob·o·ree (kə rŏb′ə rĬ), *n.* **1.** a native Australian assembly of sacred, festive, or warlike character. **2.** *Australia.* any large or noisy gathering. **3.** a disturbance; an uproar. [t. native Australian]

cor·rode (kə rōd′), *v.,* **-roded, -roding.** —*v.t.* **1.** to eat away gradually as if by gnawing, esp. by chemical action. **2.** to impair; deteriorate: *jealousy corroded his character.* —*v.i.* **3.** to become corroded. [t. L: m. s. *corrōdere* gnaw away] —**cor·rod′i·ble,** *adj.* —**Syn. 1.** gnaw, eat, consume. **3.** canker, rust, crumble.

cor·ro·sion (kə rō′zhən), *n.* **1.** act or process of corroding. **2.** corroded condition. **3.** a product of corroding, as rust. [t. L: s. *corrōsio*]

cor·ro·sive (kə rō′sĬv), *adj.* **1.** having the quality of corroding, eating away, or consuming. —*n.* **2.** something corrosive, as an acid, drug, etc. —**cor·ro′sive·ly,** *adv.* —**cor·ro′sive·ness,** *n.*

corrosive sublimate, bichloride of mercury, $HgCl_2$, a strongly acrid, highly poisonous, white crystalline salt, prepared by sublimation, much used as an antiseptic.

cor·ru·gate (*v.* kôr′ə gāt′, kôr′-; *adj.* kôr′ə gĬt, -gāt′, kôr′-), *v.,* **-gated, -gating,** *adj.* —*v.t., v.i.* **1.** to draw or bend into folds or alternate furrows and ridges. **2.** to wrinkle, as the skin, etc. —*adj.* **3.** corrugated; wrinkled; furrowed. [t. L: m. s. *corrūgātus*, pp., wrinkled]

corrugated iron, a type of sheet iron or steel strengthened for use in construction by having a series

---

b., blend of, blended; c., cognate with; d., dialect, dialectal; der., derived from; f., formed from; g., going back to; m., modification of; r., replacing; s., stem of; t., taken from; ?, perhaps. See the full key on inside cover.

of alternating grooves and ridges forced into it, and usually galvanized for weather resistance.

cor·ru·gat·ed paper, heavy paper with alternating ridges and grooves for protection, etc.

cor·ru·ga·tion (kôr′ə gā′shən, kŏr′-), *n.* **1.** act of corrugating. **2.** state of being corrugated. **3.** a wrinkle; fold; furrow; ridge.

cor·rupt (kə rŭpt′), *adj.* **1.** dishonest; without integrity; guilty of dishonesty, esp. involving bribery: *a corrupt judge.* **2.** debased in character; depraved; perverted; wicked; evil. **3.** putrid. **4.** infected; tainted. **5.** made bad by errors or alterations, as a text. —*v.t.* **6.** to destroy the integrity of; cause to be dishonest, disloyal, etc., esp. by bribery. **7.** to lower morally; pervert; deprave. **8.** to infect; taint. **9.** to make putrid or putrescent. **10.** to alter (a language, text, etc.) for the worse; debase. **11.** *Archaic.* to mar; spoil. —*v.i.* **12.** to become corrupt. [ME, t. L: s. *corruptus,* pp., broken in pieces, destroyed] —**cor·rupt′er,** *n.* —**cor·rup′tive,** *adj.* —**cor·rupt′ly,** *adv.* —**cor·rupt′ness,** *n.* **Syn. 1.** CORRUPT, DISHONEST, VENAL apply to one, esp. in public office, who acts on mercenary motives, without regard to honor, right, or justice. A CORRUPT politician is one originally honest who has succumbed to temptation and begun questionable practices. A DISHONEST politician is one lacking native integrity and thoroughly untrustworthy. VENAL is a strongly opprobrious term; a VENAL politician is one so debased that he frankly sells his patronage. **6.** demoralize, bribe. **7.** debase. **8.** contaminate, pollute.

cor·rupt·i·ble (kə rŭp′tə bəl), *adj.* that may be corrupted. —**cor·rupt′i·bil′i·ty, cor·rupt′i·ble·ness,** *n.* —**cor·rupt′i·bly,** *adv.*

cor·rup·tion (kə rŭp′shən), *n.* **1.** act of corrupting. **2.** state of being corrupt. **3.** moral perversion; depravity. **4.** perversion of integrity. **5.** corrupt or dishonest proceedings. **6.** bribery. **7.** debasement, as of a language. **8.** a debased form of a word. **9.** putrefactive decay. **10.** any corrupting influence or agency. —**Syn. 4.** baseness, dishonesty. **9.** foulness, pollution.

cor·sage (kôr säzh′), *n.* **1.** a small bouquet worn by a woman at the waist, on the shoulder, etc. **2.** the body or waist of a dress; bodice. [t. F, der. *cors* body. See CORSE]

cor·sair (kôr′sâr), *n.* **1.** a privateer, esp. one of the Barbary Coast. **2.** a pirate. **3.** a fast vessel used for piracy. [t. F: m. *corsaire,* t. It.: m. *corsaro,* a runner, g. LL *cursārius,* der. *cursus* COURSE]

corse (kôrs), *n. Archaic.* corpse. [ME *cors,* t. OF, g. L *corpus* body]

cor·se·let (kôr′sə lĕt′ *for 1;* kôrs′lĭt *for 2*), *n.* **1.** a supporting undergarment with very few or no bones, worn by women. **2.** armor for the body, esp. the breast plate and the back piece together. Also, **corslet.** [t. F, dim. of OF *cors.* See CORSE]

cor·set (kôr′sĭt), *n.* **1.** (*often pl.*) a shaped, close-fitting inner garment stiffened with whalebone or the like and capable of being tightened by lacing, enclosing the trunk and extending for a distance above and below the waistline, worn, chiefly by women, to give shape and support to the body; stays. **2.** *Obs.* a close-fitting outer body garment. [ME, t. F, dim. of OF *cors.* See CORSE]

C. Corselet of German or Flemish pikeman (1600); M, morion

Cor·si·ca (kôr′sə kə), *n.* an island in the Mediterranean, SE of and forming a department in France. 267,971 pop. (1946); 3367 sq. mi. *Cap.:* Ajaccio. French, **Corse** (kôrs). See map under Elba. —**Cor′si·can,** *adj., n.*

cors·let (kôrs′lĭt), *n.* corselet.

cor·tege (kôr tĕzh′, -tēzh′), *n.* **1.** a train of attendants; retinue. **2.** a procession. Also, *French.,* **cor·tège** (kôr tĕzh′). [t. F, t. It.: m. *corteggio,* der. *corte* COURT]

Cor·tes (kôr′tĕz; *Sp.* -tĕs), *n.* the two houses constituting the national legislative body of Spain, or those of Portugal. [t. Sp., Pg., pl of *corte.* See COURT]

Cor·tés (kôr tĕz′; *Sp.* kôr tĕs′), *n.* **Hernando** or **Hernán** (ĕr nän′dô or ĕr nän′), 1485–1547, Spanish conqueror of Mexico. Also, **Cor·tez′.**

cor·tex (kôr′tĕks), *n., pl.* **-tices** (-tə sēz′). **1.** *Bot.* that portion of the stem between the epidermis and the vascular tissue; bark. **2.** *Anat., Zool.* **a.** the rind of an organ, such as the outer wall of the kidney. **b.** the layer of gray matter which invests the surface of the cerebral hemispheres and the cerebellum. [t. L: bark, rind, shell]

cor·ti·cal (kôr′tə kəl), *adj.* **1.** *Anat.* of, or of the nature of, cortex. **2.** *Physiol., Pathol.* due to or affecting the function or condition of the cerebral cortex. **3.** *Bot.* of the cortex. [t. NL: s. *corticālis.* See CORTEX] —**cor′ti·cal·ly,** *adv.*

cor·ti·cate (kôr′tə kĭt, -kāt′), *adj.* having a cortex. Also, **cor·ti·cat′ed.** [t. L: m. s. *corticātus* having bark]

cor·tin (kôr′tĭn), *n. Biochem.* a hormone essential to life, secreted by the adrenal glands. [f. CORT(EX) + -IN²]

cor·ti·sone (kôr′tə sōn′, -zōn′), *n.* a recently isolated adrenal-gland hormone, obtained by extraction from animal glands or prepared synthetically from strophanthus or other plants, and especially effective in the treatment of arthritic ailments.

Co·ru·ña (kō rōō′nyä), *n.* La Coruña.

co·run·dum (kə rŭn′dəm), *n.* a common mineral, aluminum oxide, Al_2O_3, notable for its hardness (=9). Transparent varieties, including the ruby and sapphire, are prized gems; translucent varieties are used as abrasives. [t. Tamil: m. *kurundam,* in Skt. *kuruvinda* ruby]

cor·us·cate (kôr′ə skāt′, kŏr′-), *v.i.,* **-cated, -cating.** to emit vivid flashes of light; sparkle; gleam. [t. L: m. s. *coruscātus,* pp., moved quickly, flashed]

cor·us·ca·tion (kôr′ə skā′shən, kŏr′-), *n.* **1.** act of coruscating. **2.** a flashing or a flash of light.

cor·vée (kôr vā′; *Fr.* kôr vĕ′), *n.* **1.** labor, as on the repair of roads, exacted by a feudal lord. **2.** an obligation imposed on inhabitants of a district to perform services, as repair of roads, etc., for little or no remuneration. [F, ult. der. L *corrogāre* bring together by entreaty]

corves (kôrvz), *n.* pl. of corf.

cor·vette (kôr vĕt′), *n.* **1.** a warship of the old sailing class, having a flush deck and usually only one tier of guns. **2.** *Brit.* a small lightly armed, fast vessel, used mostly for convoy escort, ranging between a destroyer and a gunboat in size. Also, **cor·vet** (kôr vĕt′, kôr′vĕt). [f. F, ult. g. L *corbīta* ship of burden]

cor·vine (kôr′vīn, -vĭn), *adj.* **1.** pertaining to or resembling a crow. **2.** belonging or pertaining to the *Corvidae,* a family of birds including the crows, ravens, jays, etc. [t. L: m. s. *corvīnus,* der. *corvus* raven]

Cor·vus (kôr′vəs), *n., gen.* **-vi** (-vī). a southern constellation between Virgo and Hydra. [t. L: a raven]

Cor·y·bant (kôr′ə bănt′, kŏr′-), *n., pl.* **Corybantes** (kôr′ə băn′tēz, kŏr′-), **Corybants.** one of the spirits or secondary divinities fabled to form the train of the ancient goddess Cybele, following her over the mountains by torchlight with wild music and dancing. [t. L: s. *Corybās,* t. Gk.: m. *Korýbās*] —**Cor·y·ban·tian** (kôr′ə băn′shən, kŏr′-), **Cor′y·ban′tic, Cor·y·ban·tine** (kôr′ə băn′tĭn, -tīn, kŏr′-), *adj.*

co·ryd·a·lis (kə rĭd′ə lĭs), *n.* any plant of the papaveraceous genus *Corydalis* (*Capnoides*), comprising erect or climbing herbs with divided leaves, tuberous or fibrous roots, and very irregular spurred flowers. [NL, t. Gk.: m. *korydallís* crested lark]

Cor·y·don (kôr′ə dən, -dŏn′, kŏr′-), *n.* (in pastoral literature) a name for a shepherd or rustic.

cor·ymb (kôr′ĭmb, -ĭm, kŏr′-), *n. Bot.* a form of inflorescence resembling a raceme but having a relatively shorter rachis and longer lower pedicles, so that the flowers form a flat-topped or convex cluster, the outermost flowers being the first to expand. [t. L: s. *corymbus,* t. Gk.: m. *kórymbos* head, top, cluster of fruit or flowers] —**cor′ymb·like′,** *adj.*

Corymb

co·rym·bose (kə rĭm′bōs), *adj.* characterized by or growing in corymbs; corymblike. —**co·rym′bose·ly,** *adv.*

cor·y·phae·us (kôr′ə fē′əs, kŏr′-), *n., pl.* **-phaei** (-fē′ī). **1.** the leader of the chorus in the ancient Greek drama. **2.** (in modern use) the leader of an operatic chorus, or of any band of singers. [t. L, t. Gk.: m. *koryphaios* leader, head man]

cor·y·phée (kôr′ə fā′, kŏr′-; *Fr.* kô rē fĕ′), *n.* a member of a ballet company ranking just above the corps de ballet. [t. F, t. L: m.s. *coryphaeus* CORYPHAEUS]

co·ry·za (kə rī′zə), *n.* **1.** *Pathol.* acute inflammation of the mucous membrane of the nasal cavities; cold in the head. **2.** *Vet. Sci.* a contagious disease of birds, esp. poultry, characterized by the secretion of a thick mucus in the mouth and throat. [t. LL, t. Gk.: m. *kóryza* catarrh]

Cos (kôs), *n.* one of the Dodecanese Islands, in the Aegean, off the SW coast of Turkey. 19,731 pop. (1936); 111 sq. mi. Italian, **Coo.**

cos (kôs, kŏs), *n. Chiefly Brit.* a kind of lettuce, including the romaine and other varieties, with erect oblong heads and generally crisp leaves. Also, **cos lettuce.** [named after Cos whence it orig. came]

cos, cosine.

cosec, cosecant.

co·se·cant (kō sē′kənt,-kănt), *n. Trig.* the secant of the complement, or the reciprocal of the sine, of a given angle or arc.

co·seis·mal (kō sīs′məl, -sīz′-), *adj.* denoting, pertaining to, or being in a line, curve, etc. connecting or comprising points on the earth's surface at which an earthquake wave arrives simultaneously. Also, **co·seis′mic.**

Cosecant
ACB being the angle, the ratio of LC to DC or AC is the cosecant; or, DC being equal to unity it is the line LC

co·sey (kō′zĭ), *adj.,* **-sier, -siest,** *n., pl.* **-seys.** cozy.

Cos·grave (kŏz′grāv), *n.* **William Thomas,** born 1880, Irish political leader: president of the executive Council of the Irish Free State, 1922–32.

cosh·er (kŏsh′ər), *v.t.* to pamper. [t. Irish: m. *coisir* feast]

co·sig·na·to·ry (kō sĭg′nə tôr′ĭ), *adj., n., pl.* **-ries.** —*adj.* **1.** signing jointly with another or others. —*n.* **2.** one who signs a document jointly with another or others.

co·sine (kō′sīn), *n. Trig.* the sine of the complement of a given angle or arc. See illus. on next page. *Abbr.:* cos.

cos lettuce, cos.

cosm-, var. of cosmo-, before vowels.

cos·met·ic (kŏz mĕt′ĭk), *n.* **1.** a preparation for beautifying the complexion, skin, etc. —*adj.* **2.** serving to beautify; imparting or improving beauty, esp. of the complexion. [t. Gk.: m. s. *kosmētikós* relating to adornment] —**cos·met′i·cal·ly,** *adv.*

ăct, āble, dâre, ärt; ĕbb, ēqual; ĭf, īce; hŏt, ōver, ôrder, oil, bŏŏk, ōōze, out; ŭp, ūse, ûrge; ə = a in alone; ch, chief; g, give; ng, ring; sh, shoe; th, thin; ŧh, that; zh, vision. See the full key on inside cover.

cos·mic (kŏz′mĭk), *adj.* **1.** of or pertaining to the cosmos: *cosmic philosophy.* **2.** characteristic of the cosmos or its phenomena; immeasurably extended in time and space; vast. **3.** forming a part of the material universe, esp. outside of the earth. **4.** orderly or harmonious. [t. Gk.: m.s. *kosmikós* of the world] —**cos′mi·cal·ly,** *adv.*

cosmic dust, *Astron.* matter in fine particles collected by the earth from space, like meteorites.

cosmic rays, rays of extremely high penetrating power that seem to originate beyond the earth's atmosphere, and that consist, at least in part, of particles moving in velocities approaching the speed of light.

cos·mism (kŏz′mĭz əm), *n.* the philosophy of cosmic evolution. —**cos′mist,** *n.*

cosmo-, a word element representing **cosmos.**

cos·mog·o·ny (kŏz mŏg′ə nĭ), *n., pl.* -**nies.** a theory or story of the genesis or origination of the universe. [t. Gk.: m. s. *kosmogonía* creation of the world. See COSMO-, -GONY] —**cos·mo·gon·ic** (kŏz′mə gŏn′ĭk), **cos·mo·gon′i·cal,** *adj.* —**cos·mog′o·nist,** *n.*

cos·mog·ra·phy (kŏz mŏg′rə fĭ), *n., pl.* -**phies. 1.** the science which describes and maps the main features of the heavens and the earth, embracing astronomy, geography, and geology. **2.** a description or representation of the universe in its main features. [t. Gk.: m. s. *kosmographía* description of the world. See COSMO-, -GRAPHY] —**cos·mog′ra·pher,** *n.* —**cos·mo·graph·ic** (kŏz′mə grăf′ĭk), **cos·mo·graph′i·cal,** *adj.*

cos·mo·line (kŏz′mə lēn′), *n., v.,* -**lined, -lining. —***n.* **1.** heavy grease used to preserve weapons from the elements. —*v.t.* **2.** to grease (weapons) against the elements. [f. COSM(ETIC) + -OL² + -INE²]

cos·mol·o·gy (kŏz mŏl′ə jĭ), *n.* the branch of philosophy that concerns itself with the origin and general structure of the universe, its parts, elements, and laws, esp. with such characteristics as space, time, causality, freedom. —**cos·mo·log·i·cal** (kŏz′mə lŏj′ə kəl), **cos′mo·log′ic,** *adj.* —**cos·mol′o·gist,** *n.*

cos·mo·pol·i·tan (kŏz′mə pŏl′ə tən), *adj.* **1.** belonging to all parts of the world; not limited to one part of the social, political, commercial, or intellectual world. **2.** *Bot., Zool.* widely distributed over the globe. **3.** free from local, provincial, or national ideas, prejudices, or attachments; at home all over the world. **4.** of or characteristic of a cosmopolite. —*n.* **5.** one who is free from provincial or national prejudices; a citizen of the world. [f. COSMOPOLITE + -AN] —**cos′mo·pol′i·tan·ism,** *n.*

cos·mop·o·lite (kŏz mŏp′ə lit′), *n.* **1.** a citizen of the world; one who is cosmopolitan in his ideas or life. **2.** an animal or plant of world-wide distribution. [t. Gk.: m. s. *kosmopolítēs* citizen of the world] —**cos·mop′o·lit·ism,** *n.*

cos·mo·ram·a (kŏz′mə răm′ə, -rä′mə), *n.* an exhibition of pictures of cities, buildings, landscapes, etc., in different parts of the world. [f. COSM- + m. Gk. *hórāma* view] —**cos′mo·ram′ic,** *adj.*

cos·mos (kŏz′məs, -mŏs), *n.* **1.** the world or universe as an embodiment of order and harmony (as distinguished from *chaos*). **2.** a complete and harmonious system. **3.** order; harmony. **4.** any plant of the composite genus *Cosmos,* of tropical America, some species of which, as *C. bipinnatus* and *C. sulphureus,* are cultivated for their showy flowers. [t. NL, t. Gk.: m. *kósmos* order, form, the world or universe as an ordered whole, ornament]

cos·mo·tron (kŏs′mə trŏn′), *n. Physics.* a type of electro-nuclear machine.

Cos·sack (kŏs′ăk, -ək), *n.* one of a people of the southern Soviet Union in Europe and adjoining parts of Asia, noted as horsemen or light cavalry. [t. Russ.: m. *kazak,* t. Turk.: m. *quzzāq* adventurer, freebooter]

cos·set (kŏs′ĭt), *v.t.* **1.** to treat as a pet; pamper; coddle. —*n.* **2.** a lamb brought up by hand; a pet lamb. **3.** a pet of any kind. [cf. OE *cossetung* kissing]

cost (kŏst, kôst), *n., v.,* **cost, costing.** —*n.* **1.** the price paid to acquire, produce, accomplish, or maintain anything. **2.** a sacrifice, loss, or penalty: *to work at the cost of one's health.* **3.** outlay or expenditure of money, time, labor, trouble, etc. **4. at all costs,** or **at any cost,** regardless of the cost. **5.** (*pl.*) *Law.* the sums which the successful party is usually entitled to recover for reimbursement of particular expenses incurred in the litigation. —*v.i.* **6.** to require the expenditure of money, time, labor, etc., in exchange, purchase, or payment; be of the price of; be acquired in return for: *it cost five dollars.* **7.** to result in a particular sacrifice, loss, or penalty: *it may cost him his life.* **8.** to estimate or determine the cost, as of production. —*v.t.* **9.** to estimate or determine the cost of (manufactured articles, etc.). [ME, t. OF, der. *coster,* g. L *constāre* stand together,] —**cost′less,** *adj.* —**Syn. 1.** charge, expense. See **price.**

cos·ta (kŏs′tə), *n., pl.* -**tae** (-tē). **1.** a rib or riblike part. **2.** the midrib of a leaf in mosses or a ridge. [t. L: rib, side]

cost accounting, 1. an accounting system indicating the cost items involved in production. **2.** the operation of such an accounting system. —**cost accountant.**

cos·tal (kŏs′təl, kôs′təl), *adj. Anat.* pertaining to the ribs or the side of the body: *costal nerves.* [t. LL: s. *costālis.*]

cos·tard (kŏs′tərd), *n.* **1.** a large English apple with prominent ribs. **2.** *Archaic and Humorous.* the head.

Cos·ta Ri·ca (kŏs′tə rē′kə, kôs′-, kōs′-), a republic in Central America between Panama and Nicaragua. 672,043 pop. (est. 1941); 19,238 sq. mi. *Cap.:* San José. —**Cos′ta Ri′can.**

cos·tate (kŏs′tāt, kôs′-), *adj.* **1.** *Anat.* bearing ribs. **2.** (of mosses) having a midrib or costa.

cos·ter·mon·ger (kŏs′tər mŭng′gər, kôs′-), *n. Chiefly Brit.,* a hawker of fruit, vegetables, fish, etc. Also, **cos′ter.** [earlier *costardmonger,* f. COSTARD + MONGER]

cos·tive (kŏs′tĭv, kôs′-), *adj.* **1.** suffering from constipation; constipated. **2.** slow in action or in expressing ideas, opinions, etc. [t. OF, g. L *constīpātus,* pp. See CONSTIPATE] —**cos′tive·ly,** *adv.* —**cos′tive·ness,** *n.*

cost·ly (kŏst′lĭ, kôst′-), *adj.,* -**lier, -liest. 1.** costing much; of great price or value. **2.** *Archaic.* lavish; extravagant. —**cost′li·ness,** *n.* —**Syn. 1.** dear, high-priced, valuable, sumptuous. See **expensive.**

cost·mar·y (kŏst′mâr′ĭ, kôst′-), *n., pl.* -**maries.** a perennial plant, *Chrysanthemum balsamita,* with fragrant leaves, used as a potherb and in salads, etc. [f. OE *cost* (t. L: s. *costus,* t. Gk.: m. *kóstos* kind of aromatic plant) + MARY]

costo-, *Anat., Zool.* a word element meaning "rib", as in *costoscapular.* [comb. form repr. L *costa*]

cos·to·cla·vic·u·lar (kŏs′tō klə vĭk′yə lər, kôs′-), *adj.* referring to both the ribs and the collarbone.

cost of living, the average cost of food, clothing, and other necessities paid by a person, family, etc.

cos·to·scap·u·lar (kŏs′tō skăp′yə lər, kôs′-), *adj. Anat.* pertaining to ribs and to the scapula.

cost-plus (kŏst′plŭs′, kôst′-), *n.* the cost of production plus an agreed rate of profit (often used as a basis of payment in government contracts).

cos·trel (kŏs′trəl), *n.* a bottle of leather, earthenware, or wood, often of flattened form and commonly having an ear or ears to suspend it by, as from the waist. [ME t. OF: m. *costerel,* appar. orig. a flask hung at the side, der. *coste* rib, side, g. L *costa*]

cos·tume (*n.* kŏs′tūm, -tōōm; *v.* kŏs tūm′, -tōōm′), *n., v.,* -**tumed, -tuming. —***n.* **1.** the style of dress, including ornaments and the way of wearing the hair, esp. that peculiar to a nation, class, or period. **2.** dress or garb belonging to another period, place, etc., as worn on the stage, at balls, etc. **3.** a set of garments, esp. for a woman. **4.** fashion of dress appropriate to a particular occasion or season: *winter costume.* —*v.t.* **5.** to dress; furnish with a costume; provide appropriate dress for: *to costume a play.* [t. F, t. It.: habit, fashion, t. OF, g. L *consuētūdo* custom] —**Syn. 1.** See **dress.**

cos·tum·er (kŏs tū′mər, -tōō′-), *n.* one who makes or deals in costumes. Also, **cos·tum·i·er** (kŏs tū′mĭ ər, -tōō′-; *Fr.* kôs tȳ myě′).

co·sy (kō′zĭ), *adj.,* -**sier, -siest,** *n., pl.* -**sies.** cozy. [orig. uncert.] —**co′si·ly,** *adv.* —**co′si·ness,** *n.*

cot¹ (kŏt), *n.* **1.** a light portable bed, esp. one of canvas stretched on a frame. **2.** *Brit.* a crib for a child. **3.** a light bedstead. **4.** *Naut.* a swinging bed made of canvas. [t. Anglo-Ind., t. Hind.: m. *khāt*]

cot² (kŏt), *n.* **1.** a small house; cottage; hut. **2.** a small place of shelter or protection. **3.** a sheath; covering. [ME and OE; orig. unknown]

cot, cotangent.

co·tan·gent (kō tăn′jənt), *n. Trig.* the tangent of the complement, or the reciprocal of the tangent, of a given angle or arc. *Abbr.:* cot or ctn. —**co·tan·gen·tial** (kō′tăn jěn′shəl), *adj.*

cote¹ (kōt), *n.* **1.** a shelter for sheep, pigs, pigeons, etc. **2.** *N. Eng.* a small house; cottage. [OE. See COT²]

cote² (kōt), *v.t.,* **coted, coting.** *Archaic.* to pass by; outstrip, surpass. [? var. of COAST, v.]

co·tem·po·ra·ne·ous (kō těm′pə rā′nĭ əs), *adj.* contemporaneous.

co·tem·po·rar·y (kō těm′pə rěr′ĭ), *adj., n., pl.* -**raries.** contemporary.

co·ten·ant (kō těn′ənt), *n.* a tenant in common with another or others; a joint tenant. —**co·ten′an·cy,** *n.*

co·te·rie (kō′tər ĭ), *n.* **1.** a set or circle of persons who are in the habit of associating together, esp. for social purposes; a clique. [t. F: set, association of people, earlier cotters' tenure, der. OF *cotier* cotter. See COTTER²] —**Syn. 1.** See **circle.**

co·ter·mi·nous (kō tûr′mə nəs), *adj.* conterminous.

co·thur·nus (kō thûr′nəs), *n., pl.* -**ni** (-nī). the high, thick-soled shoe worn by ancient Greek and Roman tragic actors, often symbolic of tragedy. Also, **co·thurn** (kō′thûrn, kō thûrn′). [t. L, t. Gk.: m. *kóthornos*]

co·tid·al (kō tī′dəl), *adj.* **1.** pertaining to a coincidence of tides. **2.** noting a line connecting points where it is high tide at the same time.

co·til·lion (kō tĭl′yən, kə-), *n.* **1.** a lively French social dance, originated in the 18th century, for two, eight, or even more performers, and consisting of a variety of steps and figures. **2.** any of various dances of the quadrille kind. **3.** music arranged or played for these dances. **4.** *U.S.* a complex dance, or entertainment of dancing, consisting of picturesque or elaborate figures, with changing of partners and giving of favors; a german. Also, **co·til·lon** (kō tĭl′yən, kə-; *Fr.* kô tē yôn′). [t. F: m. *cotillon,* orig., petticoat, dim. of *cotte* coat]

Diagram (right of cosmic entry): Cosine. ACB being the angle, the ratio ot FC to BC or that of BK to CD, is the cosine: or, CD being equal to unity, it is the line BK

Diagram (right of cotangent entry): Cotangent. ACB being the angle, the ratio of DL to DC, or that of AC to AH, is the cotangent; or DC being taken as unity, it is the line DL

Co·to·pax·i (kō'tə păk'sĭ; *Sp.* kô'tô pä'hē), *n.* a volcano in central Ecuador, in the Andes: the highest known active volcano in the world. 19,498 ft.

cot·quean (kŏt'kwēn'), *n. Obs.* **1.** a coarse hussy. **2.** a man who busies himself with women's household affairs. [f. COT² + QUEAN]

Cots·wold (kŏts'wōld, -wəld), *n.* a breed of large sheep with long wool (so called from the Cotswolds).

Cots·wolds (kŏts'wōldz, -wəldz), *n.* a range of hills in SW England, in Gloucestershire: sheep herding.

cot·ta (kŏt'ə), *n. Eccles.* **1.** a surplice. **2.** a short surplice, with short sleeves or sleeveless, worn esp. by choristers. [t. ML. See COAT]

cot·tage (kŏt'ĭj), *n.* **1.** a small, humble house. **2.** a small country residence or detached suburban house. **3.** *U.S.* a temporary residence at a vacation resort. [ME, var. of *cotage* (f. COT² + -AGE)]
—**Syn. 1-3.** COTTAGE, CABIN, LODGE, SHACK, HUT, SHANTY formerly meant small, simple, often crude dwellings. During recent years, the first four words have gained great currency as terms for the often elaborate structures built by the well-to-do for recreational purposes. HUT and SHANTY, however, still have the former meaning as their most frequent one.

cottage cheese, *U.S.* a kind of soft white cheese made of skim milk curds without rennet.

cottage pudding, a pudding made by covering some plain cake with a sweet (often fruit) sauce.

cot·tag·er (kŏt'ĭ jər), *n.* **1.** one who lives in a cottage. **2.** *Brit.* a laborer in a village or on a farm. **3.** *U.S.* a person having a private house at a vacation resort.

cot·ter¹ (kŏt'ər), *n.* **1.** a pin, wedge, key, or the like, fitted or driven into an opening in order to secure something or hold parts together. **2.** cotter pin. [orig. uncert.]

cot·ter² (kŏt'ər), *n.* **1.** *Scot.* a person occupying a plot of land under a system similar to cottier tenure. **2.** *Irish.* cottier. **3.** a cottager. Also, **cot'tar,** [t. ML.: m.s. *cotārius,* der. *cota,* Latinized form of COT²]

cotter pin, *Mech.* a cotter having a split end which is spread after being pushed through a hole, to prevent the cotter from working loose.

Cot·ti·an Alps (kŏt'ĭ ən), a range of the Alps on the boundary between France and Italy. Highest peak, Monte Viso, 12,602 ft.

cot·ti·er (kŏt'ĭ ər), *n.* **1.** an Irish peasant holding a portion of land directly from the owner, the amount of rent being fixed not by custom or private agreement but by public competition (**cottier tenure**). **2.** a cottager (def. 1). [ME *cotier,* t. OF, der. *cote* cot, t. Gmc.]

cot·ton (kŏt'ən), *n.* **1.** a soft, white, downy substance, consisting of the hairs or fibers attached to the seeds of plants of the malvaceous genus *Gossypium,* used in making fabrics, thread, wadding, guncotton, etc. **2.** a plant yielding cotton, as *G. hirsutum* (**upland cotton**) or *G. barbadense* (**sea-island cotton**). **3.** such plants collectively, as a cultivated crop. **4.** cloth, thread, etc., made of cotton. **5.** any soft, downy substance resembling cotton, but growing on some other plant. —*v.i.* **6.** *Colloq.* to become attached or friendly (fol. by *to* or *with*). **7.** *Colloq.* to become attached or friendly (fol. by *to* or *with*). **8.** *Colloq.* to get on together; agree. **9.** *Obs.* to prosper or succeed. [ME *coton,* t. OF, t. It.: m. *cotone,* t. Ar.: m. *qutn*]

Cot·ton (kŏt'ən), *n.* **John,** 1584-1652, U.S. clergyman, colonist, and author.

cotton belt, that part of the southern U.S. where cotton is grown.

cotton cake, *U.S.* a mass of compressed cottonseed after the oil has been extracted, used to feed cattle, etc.

cotton flannel, Canton flannel.

cotton gin, a machine for separating the fibers of cotton from the seeds.

cotton grass, any of the rushlike cyperaceous plants constituting the genus *Eriophorum,* common in swampy places and bearing spikes resembling tufts of cotton.

cot·ton·mouth (kŏt'ən mouth'), *n.* the water moccasin, a venomous snake of the southern U.S.

cotton picker, a machine for removing the ripe cotton fiber from the standing plant.

cot·ton·seed (kŏt'ən sēd'), *n., pl.* **-seeds,** (*esp. collectively*) **-seed.** the seed of the cotton plant, yielding an oil.

cottonseed meal, cotton cake.

cottonseed oil, a brown-yellow, viscid oil with a nutlike odor, obtained from the seed of the cotton plant, used in pharmacology and as an oil for salad dressing.

cotton stainer, any bug of the genus *Dysdercus* and related genera, which stains cotton an indelible reddish or yellowish color.

cot·ton·tail (kŏt'ən tāl'), *n.* the common rabbit, *Sylvilagus floridanus,* of the U.S., having a fluffy white tail.

cot·ton·weed (kŏt'ən wēd'), *n.* any of certain plants with stems and leaves covered with a soft, hoary pubescence, as those of the composite genus *Gnaphalium* or of various allied genera.

Cottontail.
Sylvilagus floridanus
(14 to 15 in. long)

cot·ton·wood (kŏt'ən wŏŏd'), *n.* any of several American species of poplar, as *Populus deltoides,* with cottonlike tufts on the seeds.

cotton wool, 1. cotton in its raw state, as on the boll or gathered for use. **2.** *Brit.* absorbent cotton.

cot·ton·y (kŏt'ən ĭ), *adj.* **1.** of or like cotton; soft. **2.** covered with a down or nap resembling cotton.

cot·y·le·don (kŏt'ə lē'dən), *n. Bot.* the primary or rudimentary leaf of the embryo of plants. See diag. under **hypocotyl.** [t. L: navelwort (a plant), t. Gk.: m. *kotylēdōn* any cup-shaped hollow] —**cot'y·le·don·al,** *adj.* —**cot·y·le·don·ar·y** (kŏt'ə lē'də nĕr'ĭ), *adj.*

couch (kouch), *n.* **1.** a bed or other place of rest; a lounge; any place used for repose. **2.** the lair of a wild beast. **3.** the frame on which barley is spread to be malted. **4.** a coat of paint, etc. [ME *couche,* t. OF, der. *coucher,* v. See below]
—*v.t.* **5.** to arrange or frame (words, a sentence, etc.); put into words; express. **6.** to express indirectly. **7.** to lower or bend down, as the head. **8.** to lower (a spear, etc.) to a horizontal position, as for attack. **9.** to lay or put down; cause to lie down; lay or spread flat. **10.** to overlay; embroider with thread laid flat on a surface and caught down at intervals. **11.** *Obs.* to place or lodge; conceal. **12.** *Surg.* to remove (a cataract) by inserting a needle and pushing the opaque crystalline lens downward in the vitreous humor below the axis of vision; remove a cataract from (a person) in this manner. —*v.i.* **13.** to lie at rest; repose; recline. **14.** to crouch; bend; stoop. **15.** to lie in ambush; lurk. **16.** to lie in a heap for decomposition or fermentation, as leaves. [ME *couche(n),* t. OF: m. *coucher,* g. L *collocāre* lay in its place]

couch·ant (kou'chənt), *adj.* **1.** lying down; crouching. **2.** *Her.* lying down, as of a lion. [t. F, ppr. of *coucher* lie]

couch grass (kouch, kōoch), any of various grasses, esp. *Agropyron repens,* known chiefly as troublesome weeds, characterized by creeping rootstocks which spread rapidly; quitch. [var. of QUITCH GRASS]

couch·ing (kou'chĭng), *n.* **1.** act of one who or that which couches. **2.** a method of embroidering in which a thread, often heavy, laid upon the surface of the material, is caught down at intervals by stitches taken with another thread through the material. **3.** work so made.

Cou·é (kōo ā'; *Fr.* kwĕ), *n.* **Émile** ē mēl'), 1857-1926, French psychologist: advocate of autosuggestion.

cou·gar (kōo'gər), *n. Zool.* a large tawny feline, *Felis concolor,* of North and South America; the puma; panther; mountain lion. [t. F: m. *couguar,* t. NL: m. s. *cuguacuara,* repr. Tupi *çuaçu ara,* Guarani *guaçu ara*]

Cougar, *Felis concolor*
(Total length 8 ft.,
2½ ft. high at the shoulder)

cough (kôf, kŏf), *v.i.* **1.** to expel the air from the lungs suddenly and with a characteristic noise. —*v.t.* **2.** to expel by coughing (fol. by *up* or *out*). **3. cough up,** *Slang.* **a.** to give; hand over. **b.** to blurt out. —*n.* **4.** act or sound of coughing. **5.** an illness characterized by frequent coughing. [ME *coghen,* back formation from OE *cohhetan* cough. Cf. G *keuchen* wheeze] —**cough'er,** *n.*

cough drop, a small medicinal lozenge for relieving a cough, sore throat, etc.

could (kŏŏd), *v.* pt. of **can¹.** [ME *coude,* OE *cūthe,* mod. *l* improperly inserted, after *would* and *should*]

could·n't (kŏŏd'nt), contraction of could not.

couldst (kŏŏdst), *v. Archaic or Poetic.* 2nd pers. sing. of **could.**

cou·lee (kōo'lĭ), *n.* **1.** *Western North America.* a deep ravine or gulch, usually dry, which has been worn by running water. **2.** a stream of lava. Also, *French,* **cou·lée** (kōo lā'). [t. F, der. *couler* flow, slide, g. L *colāre* strain]

cou·loir (kōo lwär'), *n.* a steep gorge or gully on the side of a mountain. [F, der. *couler.* See COULEE]

cou·lomb (kōo lŏm'), *n.* the usual unit of quantity of electricity; the quantity transferred by a current of one ampere in one second. [named after C. A. de *Coulomb,* 1736-1806, French physicist]

coul·ter (kōl'tər), *n.* colter.

Coul·ter (kōl'tər), *n.* **John Merle** (mûrl), 1851-1928, U.S. botanist.

cou·ma·rin (kōo'mə rĭn), *n.* a white crystalline substance, with a vanillalike odor, $C_9H_6O_2$, obtained from the tonka bean and certain other plants, or prepared synthetically, and used for flavoring and in perfumery. [t. F: m. *coumarine,* der. *coumarou,* repr. Guiana *kumarū* Tonka-bean tree]

coun·cil (koun'səl), *n.* **1.** an assembly of persons summoned or convened for consultation, deliberation, or advice. **2.** an ecclesiastical assembly for deciding matters of doctrine or discipline. **3.** (in the New Testament) the Sanhedrin or other body of authorities. **4.** a body of persons specially designated or selected to act in an advisory, administrative, or legislative capacity. **5.** (in many of the British colonies) a body assisting the governor in either an executive or a legislative capacity, or in both. [ME *counceil,* t. OF: m. *concile,* t. L: m.s. *concilium* assembly, union, but with sense affected by L *consilium* COUNSEL]

Council Bluffs, a city in SW Iowa, across the Missouri river from Omaha, Nebraska. 45,429 (1950).

council house, *Brit.* a low-rent dwelling house built by the local governing authority (county council, urban district council, or rural district council).

coun·cil·man (koun'səl mən), *n., pl.* **-men.** a member of a council, esp. the local legislative body of a city.

coun·cil·man·ag·er plan (koun'səl măn'ə jər), a system of municipal government in which the administrative powers of the city are entrusted to a manager selected by the city council.

Council of the Reich, Reichsrath (def. 1).

Council of Trent, the council of the Roman Catholic Church which met at Trent intermittently from 1545 to 1563, condemning the Reformation and defining church doctrines.

council of war, 1. a conference of high-ranking military or naval officers, usually to discuss war emergency problems. 2. any conference to make important plans.

coun·ci·lor (koun′sə lər), *n.* a member of a council. Also, *esp. Brit.,* **coun′cil·lor.** —**coun′ci·lor·ship′,** *n.*

council school, *Brit.* a public school (in U.S. sense).

coun·sel (koun′səl), *n., v.,* **-seled, -seling** or (*esp. Brit.*) **-selled, -selling.** —**n.** 1. advice; opinion or instruction given in directing the judgment or conduct of another. 2. interchange of opinions as to future procedure; consultation; deliberation: *to take counsel with one's partners.* 3. *Archaic.* wisdom; prudence. 4. deliberate purpose; plan; design. 5. a private or secret opinion or purpose; *to keep one's own counsel.* 6. the advoates or advocate engaged in the direction of a cause in court; a legal adviser, or counselor. 7. *Theol.* one of the advisory declarations of Christ, considered as not universally binding but as given for aid in attaining greater moral perfection. —*v.t.* 8. to give counsel or advice to; advise. 9. to urge the doing or adoption of; recommend (a plan, etc.). —*v.i.* 10. to give counsel or advice. 11. to take counsel. [ME *conseil,* t. OF, g. L *consilium* consultation, plan. Cf. COUNCIL] —**Syn.** 1. See **advice.**

coun·se·lor (koun′sə lər), *n.* 1. one who counsels or advises; an adviser. 2. *Law.* a lawyer, esp. a trial lawyer. 3. an adviser, esp. a legal adviser, of an embassy or legation. Also, *esp. Brit.,* **coun′sel·lor.** —**coun′se·lor·ship′,** *n.*

count[1] (kount), *v.t.* 1. to check over one by one (the individuals of a collection) in order to ascertain their total number; enumerate. 2. to reckon up; calculate; compute. 3. to list or name the numerals up to. 4. to include in a reckoning; take into account. 5. to reckon to the credit of another; ascribe; impute. 6. to esteem; consider. 7. **count out, a.** *Boxing.* to proclaim (one) a loser because of his inability to stand up after the referee has counted for ten seconds. **b.** to disqualify (some ballots) illegally in counting, in order to control the election.
—*v.i.* 8. to count the items of a collection one by one in order to know the total. 9. to list or name the numerals in order. 10. to reckon numerically, 11. to depend or rely (fol. by *on*). 12. to have a numerical value (as specified). 13. to be accounted or worth: *a book which counts as a masterpiece.* 14. to enter into consideration: *every effort counts.* 15. to be worth; amount (fol. by *for*). 16. to divide into groups by calling off numbers in order (fol. by *off*). 17. *Obs.* to take account (fol. by *of*).
—*n.* 18. act of counting; enumeration; reckoning; calculation. 19. the number representing the result of a process of counting; the total number. 20. an accounting. 21. *Law.* a distinct charge or theory of action in a declaration or indictment. 22. *Archaic.* regard; notice; consideration.
[ME *counte*(n), t. OF. m. *conter,* g. L *computāre* calculate, reckon] —**count′a·ble,** *adj.*

count[2] (kount), *n.* (in some European countries) a nobleman corresponding in rank to the English earl. [t. AF: m. *counte,* g. L *comes* companion]

coun·te·nance (koun′tə nəns), *n., v.,* **-nanced, -nancing.** —*n.* 1. aspect; appearance, esp. the look or expression of the face. 2. the face; visage. 3. composed expression of face. 4. **out of countenance,** visibly disconcerted, or abashed. 5. appearance of favor; encouragement; moral support. 6. *Obs.* bearing; behavior. —*v.t.* 7. to give countenance or show favor to; encourage; support. [ME, t. OF: m. *contenance* bearing, t. ML: m. s. *continentia* demeanor, L *restraint*] —**coun′te·nanc·er,** *n.* —**Syn.** 2. See **face.**

count·er[1] (koun′tər), *n.* 1. a table or board on which money is counted, business is transacted, or goods are laid for examination. 2. anything used in keeping account, as in games, esp. a round or otherwise shaped piece of metal, ivory, wood, or other material. 3. an imitation coin or token. 4. *Slang.* a piece of money. [ME, t. AF: m. *counteour* counting house, counting table, der. *conter* COUNT[1]]

count·er[2] (koun′tər), *n.* 1. one who counts. 2. an apparatus for counting revolutions or other movements. [f. COUNT[1] + -ER[1]]

coun·ter[3] (koun′tər), *adv.* 1. in the wrong way; contrary to the right course; in the reverse direction. 2. contrary; in opposition (chiefly with *run* or *go*): *to run counter to the rules.* —*adj.* 3. opposite; opposed; contrary. —*n.* 4. that which is opposite or contrary to something else. 5. a blow delivered in receiving or parrying another blow, as in boxing. 6. *Fencing.* a circular parry. 7. that portion of the stern of a boat or vessel extending from the water line to the full outward swell. 8. the piece of stiff leather forming the back of a shoe or boot around the heel. 9. that part of a horse's breast which lies between the shoulders and under the neck. —*v.t.* 10. to go counter to; oppose; controvert. 11. to meet or answer (a move, blow, etc.) by another

in return. —*v.i.* 12. to make a counter or opposing move. 13. to give a blow while receiving or parrying one, as in boxing. [t. F: m. *contre,* g. L *contrā,* adv. and prep., in opposition, against. Cf. COUNTER-]

coun·ter[4] (koun′tər), *n., v.t.* *Obs.* encounter.

counter-, a first element of compounds of various parts of speech signifying opposition to the latter element, which it modifies, as military opposition (*counterattack*), logical opposition (*counterproof*), reversal (*counterclockwise*), complementary position (*counterpoise*), etc. [see COUNTER[3]]

coun·ter·act (koun′tər ăkt′), *v.t.* to act in opposition to; frustrate by contrary action. —**coun′ter·ac′tion,** *n.* —**coun′ter·ac′tive,** *adj.* —**Syn.** neutralize, counterbalance, contravene, thwart, check.

coun·ter·at·tack (*n.* koun′tər ə tăk′; *v.* koun′tər ə tăk′), *n.* 1. an attack designed to counteract another attack; a responsive attack. 2. *Mil.* an attack by a ground combat unit to stop and drive back an enemy attack. —*v.t., v.i.* 3. to deliver a counterattack (to).

coun·ter·at·trac·tion (koun′tər ə trăk′shən), *n.* a rival or opposite attraction.

coun·ter·bal·ance (*n.* koun′tər băl′əns; *v.* koun′tər băl′əns), *n., v.,* **-anced, -ancing.** —*n.* 1. a weight balancing another weight; an equal weight, power, or influence acting in opposition; counterpoise. —*v.i.* 2. to weight or act against with an equal weight or force; offset.

coun·ter·blast (koun′tər blăst′, -blăst′), *n.* an opposing blast; a blast in opposition to another blast.

coun·ter·change (koun′tər chānj′), *v.t.,* **-changed, -changing.** 1. to cause to change places, qualities, etc.; interchange. 2. to diversify; checker.

coun·ter·charge (*n.* koun′tər chärj′; *v.* koun′tər chärj′), *n., v.,* **-charged, -charging.** —*n.* 1. a charge by an accused person against his accuser. 2. *Mil.* a retaliatory charge. —*v.t.* 3. to make an accusation against (one's accuser). 4. *Mil.* to charge in retaliation.

coun·ter·check (*n.* koun′tər chĕk′; *v.* koun′tər chĕk′), *n.* 1. a check that opposes or restrains. 2. a check controlling or confirming another check. —*v.t.* 3. to oppose or restrain (some obstacle, etc.) by contrary action. 4. to control or confirm by a second check.

coun·ter·claim (*n.* koun′tər klām′; *v.* koun′tər klām′), *n.* 1. a claim set up against another claim. —*v.i.* 2. to set up a counterclaim. —**coun′ter·claim′ant,** *n.*

coun·ter·clock·wise (koun′tər klŏk′wīz′), *adj., adv.* in a direction opposite to that of the rotation of the hands of a clock; from right to left in a circle.

coun·ter·cur·rent (koun′tər kûr′ənt), *n.* a current in an opposite direction.

coun·ter·dem·on·stra·tion (koun′tər dĕm′ən strā′shən), *n.* a demonstration intended to offset the effect of a preceding demonstration.

coun·ter·es·pi·o·nage (koun′tər ĕs′pĭ ə nĭj, -näzh′), *n.* the detection of enemy espionage.

coun·ter·feit (koun′tər fĭt), *adj.* 1. made to imitate. and pass for, something else; not genuine: *counterfeit coin.* 2. pretended: *counterfeit grief.* —*n.* 3. an imitation designed to pass as an original; a forgery. 4. *Archaic.* a copy. 5. a likeness; portrait; image. 6. an impostor. —*v.t.* 7. to make a counterfeit of; imitate fraudulently; forge. 8. to resemble. 9. to simulate. —*v.i.* 10. to make counterfeits, as of money. 11. to feign; dissemble. [ME *countrefet,* t. OF: m. *contrefait,* pp. of *contrefaire* imitate, der. *contre* CONTRA- + *faire* do (g. L *facere*)] —**coun′ter·feit′er,** *n.* —**Syn.** 1. spurious. See **false.** 2. sham, feigned, simulated, fraudulent.

coun·ter·foil (koun′tər foil′), *n.* *Chiefly Brit.* a complementary part of a bank check, etc., which is retained by the issuer, and on which particulars are noted. See U.S. **stub.**

coun·ter·ir·ri·tant (koun′tər ĭr′ə tənt), *n.* *Med.* an agent for producing irritation in one part to counteract irritation or relieve pain or inflammation elsewhere.

coun·ter·jump·er (koun′tər jŭmp′ər), *n.* *Slang.* a salesman at a counter.

coun·ter·mand (*v.* koun′tər mănd′, -mănd′; *n.* koun′tər mănd′, -mänd′), *v.t.* 1. to revoke (a command, order, etc.). 2. to recall or stop by a contrary order. —*n.* 3. a command, order, etc., revoking a previous one. [ME *countermaund*(en), t. OF: m. *contremander,* f. *contre* CONTRA- + *mander* command, g. L *mandāre* enjoin]

coun·ter·march (*n.* koun′tər märch′; *v.* koun′tər märch′), *n.* 1. a march back again. 2. a complete reversal of conduct or measures. —*v.i.* 3. to turn about and march back along the same route; execute a countermarch. —*v.t.* 4. to cause to countermarch.

coun·ter·meas·ure (koun′tər mĕzh′ər), *n.* an opposing or retaliatory measure.

coun·ter·mine (*n.* koun′tər mīn′; *v.* koun′tər mīn′), *n., v.,* **-mined, -mining.** —*n.* 1. *Mil.* a mine intended to intercept or destroy an enemy's mine. 2. a counterplot. —*v.t.* 3. to oppose by a countermine. —*v.i.* 4. to make a countermine. 5. *Mil.* to destroy enemy mines.

coun·ter·move (*n.* koun′tər mōōv′; *v.* koun′tər mōōv′), *n., v.,* **-moved, -moving.** —*n.* 1. an opposing or retaliatory move. —*v.i., v.t.* 2. to move in opposition or retaliation. —**coun·ter move·ment** (koun′tər mōōv′mənt), *n.*

coun·ter·of·fen·sive (koun′tər ə fĕn′sĭv), *n.* *Mil.* an attack by an army against an enemy force which has been and may still be attacking.

---

b., blend of, blended;   c., cognate with;   d., dialect, dialectal;   der., derived from;   f., formed from;   g., going back to; m., modification of;   r., replacing;   s., stem of;   t., taken from;   ?, perhaps.   See the full key on inside cover.

coun·ter·pane (koun/tər pān/), *n.* a quilt or coverlet for a bed. [var. of obs. *counterpoint* cover, t. OF]

coun·ter·part (koun/tər pärt/), *n.* **1.** a copy; duplicate. **2.** a part that answers to another, as each part of a document executed in duplicate. **3.** one of two parts which fit each other; a thing that complements something else. **4.** a person or thing closely resembling another.

coun·ter·plot (*n.,* v. koun/tər plŏt/; *v. also* koun/tər-plŏt/), *n., v.,* **-plotted, -plotting.** —*n.* **1.** a plot directed against another plot. —*v.i.* **2.** to devise a counterplot; plot in opposition. —*v.t.* **3.** to plot against (a plot or plotter); frustrate by a counterplot.

coun·ter·point (koun/tər point/), *n.* *Music.* **1.** the art of combining melodies. **2.** the texture resulting from the combining of individual melodic lines. **3.** a melody composed to be combined with another melody. [t. F: m. *contrepoint*. Cf. ML *punctum contrā punctum* note against note]

coun·ter·poise (koun/tər poiz/), *n., v.,* **-poised, -poising.** —*n.* **1.** a counterbalancing weight. **2.** any equal and opposing power or force. **3.** the state of being in equilibrium. —*v.t.* **4.** to balance by an opposing weight; counteract by an opposing force. **5.** to bring into equilibrium. **6.** *Archaic.* to weigh (one thing) against another. [ME *countrepeis*, t. OF, var. of *contrepois*, f. *contre* CONTRA- + *pois* weight (g. L *pensum*)]

coun·ter·poi·son (koun/tər poi/zən), *n.* **1.** an agent for counteracting a poison; an antidote. **2.** an opposite poison.

coun·ter·prop·a·gan·da (koun/tər prŏp/ə găn/də), *n.* propaganda to combat unfriendly or enemy propaganda.

coun·ter·ref·or·ma·tion (koun/tər rĕf/ər mā/shən), *n.* a reformation opposed to or counteracting a previous reformation.

Counter Reformation, the movement within the Roman Catholic Church which followed the Protestant Reformation of the 16th century.

coun·ter·rev·o·lu·tion (koun/tər rĕv/ə lōō/shən), *n.* a revolution opposed to a preceding one. —**coun·ter-rev·o·lu·tion·ar·y** (koun/tər rĕv/ə lōō/shə nĕr/ĭ), *adj.* —**coun·ter·rev·o·lu·tion·ist,** *n.*

coun·ter·scarp (koun/tər skärp/), *n.* *Fort.* **1.** the exterior slope or wall of the ditch of a fort, which supports the covered way. **2.** this slope with the covered way and glacis. [t. F: m. *contrescarpe*, t. It.: m. *contrascarpa*, f. *contra-* COUNTER- + *scarpa* slope of a wall]

coun·ter·shaft (koun/tər shäft/, -shăft/), *n.* *Mach.* an intermediate shaft driven from a main shaft.

coun·ter·sign (*n., v.* koun/tər sīn/; *v. also* koun/tər-sīn/), *n.* **1.** *Mil.* a password given by authorized persons in passing through a guard. **2.** a sign used in reply to another sign. **3.** a signature added to another signature, esp. for authentication. —*v.t.* **4.** to sign (a document) in addition to another signature, esp. in confirmation or authentication. [t. OF: m. *contresigne*, t. It.: m. *contrassegno*]

coun·ter·sig·na·ture (koun/tər sĭg/nə chər), *n.* a signature added by way of countersigning.

coun·ter·sink (*v., n.* koun/tər sĭngk/; *v. also* koun/tər-sĭngk/), *v.,* **-sunk, -sinking,** *n.* —*v.t.* **1.** to enlarge the upper part of (a hole or cavity), esp. by chamfering, to receive the cone-shaped head of a screw, bolt, etc. **2.** to cause (the head of a screw, bolt, etc.) to sink into a depression made for it, so as to be flush with or below the surface. —*n.* **3.** a tool for countersinking a hole. **4.** a countersunk hole.

coun·ter·state·ment (koun/tər stāt/mənt), *n.* a statement made to deny or refute another.

coun·ter·stroke (koun/tər strōk/), *n.* a stroke or blow given in return.

coun·ter·ten·den·cy (koun/tər tĕn/dən sĭ), *n., pl.* **-cies.** an opposing tendency.

coun·ter·ten·or (koun/tər tĕn/ər), *n.* *Music.* **1.** an adult male voice or voice part higher than the tenor. **2.** a singer with such a voice; a high tenor.

coun·ter·thrust (koun/tər thrŭst/), *n.* a thrust made in opposition or return.

coun·ter·type (koun/tər tīp/), *n.* **1.** a corresponding type. **2.** an opposite type.

coun·ter·vail (koun/tər vāl/), *v.t.* **1.** to act or avail against with equal power, force, or effect; counteract. **2.** to furnish an equivalent of or a compensation for; offset. **3.** *Archaic.* to equal. —*v.i.* **4.** to be of equal force in opposition; avail. [ME *countrevaile(n)*, t. AF: m. *countrevaloir*, f. *contre* against + *valoir* be strong, g. L *valēre*]

coun·ter·weight (koun/tər wāt/), *n.* a counterbalancing weight; a counterpoise. —**coun/ter·weight/ed,** *adj.*

coun·ter·work (*n.* koun/tər wûrk/; *v.* koun/tər wûrk/), *n.* **1.** opposing work or action; a work in opposition to another work. —*v.i.* **2.** to work in opposition. —*v.t.* **3.** to work in opposition to; hinder or frustrate. —**coun/ter-work/er,** *n.*

count·ess (koun/tĭs), *n.* **1.** the wife or widow of a count in the nobility of continental Europe, or of an earl in the British peerage. **2.** a woman having the rank of a count or earl in her own right. [ME *contesse*, t. OF, g. LL *comitissa*, fem. of L *comes*. See COUNT²]

counting house, *Chiefly Brit.* a building or office set aside for bookkeeping, etc., as in a factory.

counting room, a room used as a counting house.

count·less (kount/lĭs), *adj.* incapable of being counted; innumerable.

count palatine, 1. (orig. in Germany) a count having supreme jurisdiction in his fief or province. **2.** (formerly, in England) an earl, or other county proprietor, who exercised royal prerogatives within his county.

coun·tri·fied (kŭn/trĭ fīd/), *adj.* rustic or rural in appearance, conduct, etc.: *a countrified person, stretch of land, etc.* Also, **countryfied.**

coun·try (kŭn/trĭ), *n., pl.* **-tries,** *adj.* —*n.* **1.** a tract of land considered apart from geographical or political limits; region; district. **2.** any considerable territory demarcated by geographical conditions or by a distinctive population. **3.** the territory of a nation. **4.** a state. **5.** the people of a district, state, or nation. **6.** the public. **7.** *Law.* the public at large, as represented by a jury. **8.** the land of one's birth or citizenship. **9.** rural districts (as opposed to cities or towns). —*adj.* **10.** of the country; rural. **11.** rude; unpolished: *country manners.* **12.** of a country or one's own country. [ME *contree*, t. OF, g. LL *contrāta*, lit., what lies opposite, der. L *contrā* opposite to]

country club, a club in the country, often near a city, with a house, grounds, and facilities for outdoor sports, etc.

country cousin, a relative from the country to whom the sights and activities of a large city are novel and bewildering.

coun·try-dance (kŭn/trĭ dăns/, -däns/), *n.* a dance of rural (or native) English origin, esp. one in which the partners stand facing each other in two lines.

coun·try·fied (kŭn/trĭ fīd/), *adj.* countrified.

country gentleman, a wealthy man living in his country home or estate.

country house, a house on a country estate.

coun·try·man (kŭn/trĭ mən), *n., pl.* **-men. 1.** a man of one's own country. **2.** a native or inhabitant of a particular region. **3.** a man who lives in the country. —**coun·try·wom·an** (kŭn/trĭ wŏŏm/ən), *n. fem.* —**Syn. 1.** compatriot, fellow citizen. **3.** rustic, farmer.

coun·try·seat (kŭn/trĭ sēt/), *n.* *Chiefly Brit.* a country estate, esp. a fine one, often one used for only part of the year.

coun·try·side (kŭn/trĭ sīd/), *n.* **1.** a particular section of a country, esp. rural. **2.** its inhabitants.

coun·ty (koun/tĭ), *n., pl.* **-ties. 1.** the political unit next below the State in the U. S. **2.** one of the chief administrative divisions of a country or state, as in Great Britain and Ireland. **3.** one of the larger divisions for purposes of local administration, etc., in Canada, New Zealand, etc. **4.** the inhabitants of a county. **5.** *Obs. or Hist.* the domain of a count or an earl. [ME *counte*, t. AF, var. of OF *conte*, der. *conte* COUNT²]

county college, (in England) a part time continuation school with compulsory attendance for boys and girls from 15 to 18 years of age, created under the Education Act (1944).

county court, 1. *U.S.* **a.** an administrative board in counties in some States. **b.** a judicial tribunal in some States with jurisdiction extending over one or more counties. **2.** *England.* **a.** the lowest civil tribunal, but unconnected with county. **b.** *Hist.* a primary assembly, with varying composition, of inhabitants of a county.

county seat, *U.S.* the seat of government of a county. Also, **county town.**

coup (kōō), *n., pl.* **coups** (kōōz; *Fr.* kōō). an unexpected and successful stroke. [t. F, in OF *colp*, g. LL *colpus* blow, for L *colaphus*, t. Gk.: m. *kólaphos*]

coup de grâce (kōō də gräs/), **1.** a death blow, now usually a bullet in the head to make sure an executed person is dead. **2.** a finishing stroke. [F: grace-stroke]

coup de main (kōō də măn/), a surprise attack. [F: hand-stroke]

coup d'é·tat (kōō dĕ tä/), a sudden and decisive measure in politics, esp. one effecting a change of government illegally or by force. [F: lit., stroke of state]

coup de thé·â·tre (kōō də tĕ ä/tr), *French.* **1.** a theatrical hit. **2.** a surprising or sensational trick.

coup d'oeil (kōō dœ/y), *French.* a quick glance.

cou·pé (kōō pā/; *for 1, also* kōōp), *n.* **1.** a closed automobile with a body relatively shorter than that of a sedan of the same line, having a trunk compartment or rumble seat in the rear of the body. **2.** a short four-wheeled closed carriage with (usually) a single cross seat for two persons and with an outside seat for the driver. **3.** the end compartment in a European diligence or railroad car. [t. F, prop. pp. of *couper* cut]

couped (kōōpt), *adj.* *Her.* cut off, as of a cross cut off so as not to touch the edge of the shield, or an animal, cut off at its chest.

Cou·pe·rus (kōō pā/rəs), *n.* Louis (lōō ē/), 1863–1923, Dutch author.

cou·ple (kŭp/əl), *n., v.,* **-pled, -pling.** —*n.* **1.** a combination of two; a pair. **2.** two of the same sort connected or considered together. **3.** a man and a woman united by marriage or betrothal, associated as partners in a dance, etc. **4.** *Mech.* a pair of equal, parallel forces acting in opposite directions and tending to produce rotation. **5.** a leash for holding two hounds together. —*v.t.* **6.** to fasten, link, or associate together in a pair or pairs. **7.** to join; connect. **8.** *Colloq.* to unite in matrimony. —*v.i.* **9.** *Radio.* to join or associate by means of a coupler. **10.** to join in a pair; unite. **11.** to copulate. [ME, t. OF: m. *cople*, g. L *copula* band, bond] —**Syn. 1.** See **pair.**

cou·pler (kŭp/lər), *n.* **1.** one who or that which couples, or links together. **2.** a device in an organ for connecting keys, manuals, or a manual and pedals, so that they are played together when one is played. **3.** *Radio.* a device for transferring electrical energy from one circuit to another, as a transformer which joins parts of a radio apparatus together by induction.

cou·plet (kŭp/lĭt), *n.* **1.** a pair of successive lines of verse, esp. such as rhyme together and are of the same length. **2.** a pair; couple. [t. F, dim. of *couple* COUPLE]

cou·pling (kŭp/lĭng), *n.* **1.** act of one who or that which couples. **2.** any mechanical device for uniting or connecting parts or things. **3.** a device used in joining railroad cars, etc. **4.** *Elect.* **a.** the association of two circuits or systems in such a way that power may be transferred from one to the other. **b.** a device or expedient to insure coupling. **5.** the part of the body between the tops of the shoulder blades and the tops of the hip joints in a dog, etc.

cou·pon (kōō/pŏn, kū/-), *n.* **1.** a separable part of a certificate, ticket, advertisement, etc., entitling the holder to something. **2.** one of a number of such parts calling for periodical payments on a bond. **3.** a separate ticket or the like, for a similar purpose. [t. F, der. *couper* cut]

cour·age (kûr/ĭj, kŭr/-), *n.* **1.** the quality of mind that enables one to encounter difficulties and danger with firmness or without fear; bravery. **2 have the courage of one's convictions,** to act consistently with one's opinions. **3.** *Obs.* heart; mind; disposition. [ME *corage*, t. OF, der. *cor* heart, g. L] —**Syn. 1.** fearlessness, dauntlessness, intrepidity, fortitude, pluck, heroism, daring, hardihood. COURAGE, BRAVERY, VALOR, BRAVADO refer to qualities of spirit and conduct. COURAGE is that quality of mind which enables one to face dangers, difficulties, threats, pain, etc., without fear: *to take (or lose) courage.* BRAVERY implies true courage together with daring and an intrepid boldness: *bravery in a battle.* VALOR implies continuous, active bravery in the face of personal danger and a noble and lofty quality of courage: *valor throughout a campaign, in fighting for the right.* BRAVADO is now usually a boastful and ostentatious pretense of courage or bravery: *empty bravado.* —**Ant. 1.** cowardice.

cou·ra·geous (kə·rā/jəs), *adj.* possessing or characterized by courage; brave; valiant. —**cou·ra/geous·ly,** *adv.* —**cou·ra/geous·ness,** *n.* —**Syn.** See **brave.**

cou·rante (kōō·ränt/; *Fr.* kōō·ränt/), *n.* **1.** an old-fashioned dance dating back to the 17th century characterized by a running or gliding step. **2.** a piece of music for or suited to this dance. **3.** *Music.* a movement in the classical suite, following the allemande. Also, **cou·rant/.** [t. F, prop. fem. of *courant*, ppr. of *courir* run]

Cour·bet (kōōr bě/), *n.* **Gustave** (gystàv/), 1819–77, French painter.

Cour·be·voie (kōōr·b·vwä/), *n.* a city in N France, near Paris. 55,080 (1946).

cou·ri·er (kûr/ĭ·ər, kōōr/-), *n.* **1.** a messenger sent in haste. **2.** a person hired by travelers to take charge of the arrangements of a journey. [t. F, t. It.: m. *corriere* runner, der. *corre* run, g. L *currere*; r. ME *corour*, t. OF: m. *coreor*, g. LL *curritor* runner]

cou·lan (kōōr/lən), *n.* a bird of the tropical American genus *Aramus*, comprising one species, *A. guarauna*, a large, long-billed, raillike bird notable for its peculiar cry. [t. F, appar. repr. native name]

Cour·land (kōōr/lənd), *n.* a former duchy on the Baltic: later a province of Russia, and in 1918 incorporated into Latvia. Also, **Kurland.**

course (kōrs), *n.*, *v.*, **coursed, coursing.** —*n.* **1.** advance in a particular direction; onward movement. **2.** the path, route or channel along which anything moves: *the course of a stream, ship, etc.* **3.** the ground, water, etc., on which a race is run, sailed, etc. **4.** the continuous passage or progress through time or a succession of stages: *in the course of a year, a battle, etc.* **5.** customary manner of procedure; regular or natural order of events: *the course of a disease, argument, etc., a matter of course.* **6.** a mode of conduct; behavior. **7.** a particular manner of proceeding: *try another course with him.* **8.** a systematized or prescribed series: *a course of studies, lectures, medical treatments, etc.* **9.** any one of the studies in such a series: *the first course in algebra.* **10.** a part of a meal served at one time: *the main course was steak.* **11.** *Naut.* **a.** the point of the compass toward which a ship sails. **b.** the lowest square sail on any mast of a square-rigged ship, identified as **fore course, main course,** etc. **12.** a continuous horizontal (or inclined) range of stones, bricks, or the like, in a wall, the face of a building, etc. **13.** *Knitting.* the row of stitches going across from side to side (as opposed to *wale*). **14.** (*often pl.*) the menses. **15.** a charge, as in tilting. **16.** pursuit of game with dogs. **17.** *Archaic.* a race. **18. in due course,** in the proper or natural order; at the right time. **19. of course, a.** certainly; obviously. **b.** in the natural order. —*v.t.* **20.** to run through or over. **21.** to chase; pursue. **22.** to hunt (game) with hounds, esp. by sight and not by scent. **23.** to cause (dogs) to pursue game. —*v.i.* **24.** to follow a course; direct one's course. **25.** to run; move swiftly; race. **26.** to engage in coursing, in a hunt, a tilting match, etc. [t. F; r. ME *cors*, t. OF, g. L *cursus* a running] —**Syn.**

2. way, road, track, passage. **5.** process, career. **7.** method, mode. **8.** sequence, succession.

cours·er[1] (kōr/sər), *n.* **1.** one who or that which courses. **2.** a dog for coursing. [f. COURSE, v. + -ER[1]]

cours·er[2] (kōr/sər), *n. Chiefly Poetic.* a swift horse. [ME, t. F: m. *coursier*, der. *cours* COURSE]

cours·er[3] (kōr/sər), *n.* any of certain swift-footed, ploverlike birds constituting the genus *Cursorius*, of the desert regions of Africa and Asia, as *C. cursor*, occasionally found also in Europe. [t. L: m.s. *cursōrius* fitted for running]

cours·ing (kōr/sĭng), *n.* **1.** act of one who or that which courses. **2.** *Chiefly Brit.* the sport of pursuing hares, etc., with hounds, when the game is started in sight of the hounds.

court (kōrt), *n.* **1.** an open space wholly or partly enclosed by a wall, buildings, etc. **2.** a large building within such a space. **3.** *Chiefly Brit.* a stately dwelling. **4.** a short street. **5.** a smooth, level area on which to play tennis, handball, etc. **6.** one of the divisions of such an area. **7.** the residence of a sovereign or other high dignitary; palace. **8.** the collective body of persons forming his retinue. **9.** a sovereign and his councilors as the political rulers of a state. **10.** a formal assembly held by a sovereign. **11.** homage paid, as to a sovereign. **12.** assiduous attention directed to gain favor, affection, etc.: *to pay court to a king, a pretty woman, etc.* **13.** *Law.* **a.** a place where justice is administered. **b.** a judicial tribunal duly constituted for the hearing and determination of cases. **c.** a session of a judicial assembly. **14.** the body of qualified members of a corporation, council, board, etc. **15.** a branch or lodge of a fraternal society. **16. out of court,** not entitled to a hearing. —*v.t.* **17.** to endeavor to win the favor of. **18.** to seek the affections of; woo. **19.** to attempt to gain (applause, favor, a decision, etc.). **20.** to hold out inducements to; invite. —*v.i.* **21.** to make love; woo. [ME, t. OF: m. *cort*, g. L *co(ho)rs* enclosure, also division of troops (see COHORT)]

court card, *Brit. Cards.* face card.

court dress, the formal costume worn at court, for men including silk knee breeches and stockings.

cour·te·ous (kûr/tĭ əs), *adj.* having or showing good manners; polite. [ME *curteis*, t. OF, der. *cort* COURT] —**cour/te·ous·ly,** *adv.* —**cour/te·ous·ness,** *n.* —**Syn.** See **civil.** —**Ant.** rude.

cour·te·san (kōr/tə zən, kûr/-), *n.* a prostitute. Also, **cour/te·zan.** [t. F: m. *courtisane*, t. It.: m. *cortigiana* lewd woman, orig. woman of the court, der. *corte* COURT]

cour·te·sy (kûr/tə sĭ), *n., pl.* **-sies. 1.** excellence of manners or behavior; politeness. **2.** a courteous act or expression. **3.** favor; indulgence; consent: *a title by courtesy rather than by right.* **4.** a curtsy. [ME *cortesie*, t. OF, der. *corteis* COURTEOUS] —**Syn. 1.** courteousness, civility, urbanity.

courtesy title, *Brit.* a title allowed by custom, as to the children of dukes.

court hand, a style of handwriting formerly used in the English law courts.

court·house (kōrt/hous/), *n.* **1.** a building in which courts of law are held. **2.** *U.S.* a county seat.

cour·ti·er (kōr/tĭ ər), *n.* **1.** one in attendance at the court of a sovereign. **2.** one who seeks favor.

court·ly (kōrt/lĭ), *adj.,* **-lier, -liest,** *adv.* —*adj.* **1.** polite; elegant; refined. **2.** flattering; obsequious. **3.** of the court of a sovereign. —*adv.* **4.** in the manner of courts; elegantly; flatteringly. —**court/li·ness,** *n.*

court-mar·tial (kōrt/mär/shəl), *n., pl.* **courts-martial,** *v.,* **-tialed, -tialing** or (*esp. Brit.*) **-tialled, -tialling.** —*n.* **1.** a court consisting of military or naval officers appointed by a commander to try charges of offense against military or naval law. —*v.t.* **2.** to arraign and try by court-martial.

Court of St. James, the British royal court, so called from St. James's Palace, London, the former scene of royal receptions.

court plaster, cotton or other fabric coated on one side with an adhesive preparation, as of isinglass and glycerin, used for covering slight cuts, etc., on the skin.

Cour·trai (kōōr trě/), *n.* a city in W Belgium, on the Lys river: important medieval city. 41,548 (est. 1941).

court·room (kōrt/rōōm/, -rŏŏm/), *n.* a room in which the sessions of a law court are held.

court·ship (kōrt/shĭp), *n.* **1.** the wooing of a woman. **2.** solicitation, esp. of favors. **3.** *Obs.* courtly manners.

court tennis, tennis (def. 1).

court·yard (kōrt/yärd/), *n.* a space enclosed by walls, next to or within a castle, large house, etc.

cous·in (kŭz/ən), *n.* **1.** the son or daughter of an uncle or aunt. **2.** one related by descent in a diverging line from a known common ancestor. The children of brothers and sisters are called **cousins, cousins-german, first cousins,** or **full cousins;** children of **first cousins** are called **second cousins,** etc. Often, however, the term **second cousin** is loosely applied to the son or daughter of a **cousin-german,** more properly called a **first cousin once removed. 3.** a kinsman or kinswoman. **4.** a person or thing related to another by similar natures, languages, etc.: *our Canadian cousins.* **5.** a term of address from one sovereign to another or to a great noble. —*v.t.* **6.** to call "cousin"; claim kindred with. [t. F, g. L *consobrīnus* mother's sister's child; r. ME *cosin,* t. OF] —**cous/in·hood/, cous/in·ship/,** *n.*

Cou·sin (kŏŏ zăn′), *n.* **Victor** (vĕk tôr′), 1792–1867, French philosopher and educational reformer.

cous·in-ger·man (kŭz′ən jûr′mən), *n., pl.* **cousins-german.** a first cousin. See **cousin** (def. 2). [t. F: m. *cousin-germain.* See GERMAN, adj.]

cous·in·ly (kŭz′ən lĭ), *adj.* **1.** like or befitting a cousin. —*adv.* **2.** in the manner of a cousin; as a cousin.

cou·teau (kŏŏ tō′), *n., pl.* **-teaux** (-tōz′; *Fr.* -tō′). a knife, esp. a large double-edged one formerly carried as a weapon. [F, in OF *coutel,* g. L *cultellus,* dim. of *culter* knife]

cou·tu·rier (kŏŏ tẏ ryĕ′), *n.* a dressmaker (man). [F, der. *couture* sewing] —**cou·tu·rière** (kŏŏ tẏ ryĕr′), *n. fem.*

cou·vade (kŏŏ väd′; *Fr.* -väd′), *n.* a practice among some primitive peoples by which, at the birth of a child, the father takes to bed and performs other acts natural rather to the mother. [t. F, der. *couver* brood, incubate. See COVEY]

co·va·lence (kō vā′ləns), *n. Chem.* **1.** the number of electron pairs that an atom can share with those which surround it. **2.** the bond formed by the sharing of a pair of electrons by two atoms.

cove[1] (kōv), *n., v.,* **coved, coving.** —*n.* **1.** a small indentation or recess in the shoreline of a sea, lake, or river. **2.** a sheltered nook. **3.** a hollow or recess in a mountain; cave; cavern. **4.** a narrow pass between mountains. **5.** a sheltered area, usually prairie, between woods or hills. **6.** *Archit.* a concavity; a concave molding or member. —*v.t., v.i.* **7.** to form into a cove. [ME; OE *cofa* chamber, c. Icel. *kofi* hut]

cove[2] (kōv), *n. Brit. Slang.* a person; a fellow. [said to be t. Romany: m. *kova* creature]

cov·e·nant (kŭv′ə nənt), *n.* **1.** an agreement between two or more persons to do or refrain from doing some act; a compact; a contract. **2.** an incidental clause of agreement in such an agreement. **3.** *Eccles.* a solemn agreement between the members of a church, as that they will act together in harmony with the precepts of the gospel. **4.** (*cap.*) one of certain bonds of agreement signed by the Scottish Presbyterians for the defense or promotion of their religion, esp. the **National Covenant** of 1638, or the **Solemn League and Covenant** of 1643 (entered into with England). **5.** (in Biblical usage) the agreement or engagement of God with man as set forth in the Old and the New Testament. **6.** *Law.* **a.** a formal agreement of legal validity, esp. one under seal. **b.** an early English form of action in suits involving sealed contracts. **7.** (*cap.*) in full, **Covenant of the League of Nations,** the "Constitution" of the League of Nations, included as the first 26 articles in the Treaty of Versailles. —*v.i.* **8.** to enter into a covenant. —*v.t.* **9.** to agree to by covenant; stipulate. [ME, t. OF, der. *covenir,* g. L *convenīre* agree]

cov·e·nant·er (kŭv′ə nən tər; *for 2, also Scot.* kŭv′ə năn′tər), *n.* **1.** one who enters into a covenant. **2.** (*cap.*) adherent of the National Covenant. See **covenant,** def. 4.

cov·e·nan·tor (kŭv′ə nən tər). *n. Law.* the party who is to perform the obligation expressed in a covenant.

Cov·ent Garden (kŭv′ənt, kŏv′-), **1.** district in central London, England, noted for its vegetable and flower market. **2.** a theater in this district, first built in 1731, important in English theatrical history.

Cov·en·try (kŏv′ən trĭ, kŭv′-), *n.* **1.** a city in central England, in Warwickshire: heavily bombed, Nov., 1940. 233,000 (est. 1946). **2. send to Coventry,** to refuse to associate with.

cov·er (kŭv′ər), *v.t.* **1.** to put something over or upon, as for protection or concealment. **2.** to be or serve as a covering for; extend over; occupy the surface of. **3.** to put a cover or covering on; clothe. **4.** to put one's hat on (one's head). **5.** to bring upon or invest (oneself): *to cover oneself with honors.* **6.** to shelter; protect; serve as a defense to. **7.** *Mil.* **a.** to be in line with by occupying a position directly before or behind. **b.** to protect (a soldier, force, or military position) during an expected period of ground combat by taking a position from which any hostile troops can be fired upon who might shoot at the soldier, force, or position. **8.** to hide from view; screen. **9.** to aim directly at, as with a pistol. **10.** to have within range, as a fortress does certain territory. **11.** to include; comprise; provide for; take in: *this book covers all common English words.* **12.** to suffice to defray or meet (a charge, expense, etc.); offset (an outlay, loss, liability, etc.). **13.** to deposit the equivalent of (money deposited), as in wagering; accept the conditions of (a bet, etc.). **14.** to act as reporter of (occurrences, performances, etc.), as for a newspaper, etc. **15.** to pass or travel over. **16.** (of a male animal) to copulate with. **17.** to brood or sit on (eggs or chicks). —*n.* **18.** that which covers, as the lid of a vessel, the binding of a book, the wrapper of a letter, etc. **19.** protection; shelter; concealment. **20.** woods, underbrush, etc., serving to shelter and conceal wild animals or game; a covert. **21.** *Ecol.* vegetation which serves to protect or conceal animals, such as birds, from excessive sunlight or drying, or predators. **22.** something which veils, screens, or shuts from sight. **23.** a set of articles (plate, knife, fork, etc.) laid at table for one person. **24.** *Finance.* funds to cover liability or secure against risk of loss. **25.** *Philately.* **a.** an envelope or outer wrapping for mail. **b.** a letter folded so that the address may be placed on the outside and the missive mailed.

26. under cover, a. secret. **b.** secretly. [ME *cover(en),* t. OF: m. *covir,* g. L *cooperīre*] —**cov′er·er,** *n.* —**cov′er·less,** *adj.* —**Syn. 1.** overlay, overspread, envelop, enwrap. **8.** cloak, conceal. **12.** counterbalance, compensate for. **19.** COVER, PROTECTION, SCREEN, SHELTER mean a defense against harm or danger, and a provision for safety. The main idea in COVER is that of concealment, as in darkness, in a wood, behind something, etc.: *keep under cover, take cover, the ground troops were left without cover when the air force was withdrawn.* SCREEN refers especially to something behind which one can hide: *a heavy fire formed a screen for ground operations.* PROTECTION and SHELTER emphasize the idea of a guard or defense, a shield against injury or death. A PROTECTION is any such shield: *in World War II, an "air cover" of airplanes acted as a protection for troops.* A SHELTER is something which covers over, and acts as a place of refuge: *an abandoned monastery acted as a shelter.*

cov·er·age (kŭv′ər ĭj), *n.* **1.** *Insurance.* the total extent of risk, or the total number of risks, as fire, accident, etc., covered in a policy of insurance. **2.** *Finance.* the value of funds held to back up or meet liabilities.

cov·er·all (kŭv′ər ôl′), *n.* (*usually pl.*) a loose-fitting work garment with sleeves.

cover charge, an amount charged by a restaurant, night club, etc., for service or entertainment.

cover crop, a crop, preferably leguminous, planted to keep nutrients from leaching, soil from eroding, and land from weeding over, as during the winter.

Cov·er·dale (kŭv′ər dāl′), *n.* **Miles,** 1488–1569, British divine: translator of the Bible into English, 1535.

covered wagon, *U.S.* **1.** a large wagon with a canvas top, esp. a prairier schooner. **2.** *Brit. Railroads.* a boxcar.

cov·er·ing (kŭv′ər ĭng), *n.* **1.** something laid over or wrapped about a thing, esp. for concealment, protection, or warmth. **2.** *Com.* the operation of buying securities, etc., that one has sold short, in order to return them to the person from whom they were borrowed.

cov·er·let (kŭv′ər lĭt), *n.* **1.** the outer covering of a bed; a bedspread. **2.** any covering or cover. Also, **cov·er·lid** (kŭv′ər lĭd). [ME *coverlite,* appar. f. COVER + m. F *lit* bed]

Cov·er·ley (kŭv′ər lĭ), *n.* **Sir Roger de,** a literary figure representing the ideal of the early 18th century squire in the *Spectator* by Addison and Steele.

cov·er·point (kŭv′ər point′), *n. Cricket, Lacrosse, etc.* a player who supports the player called *point.*

covers., coversed sine.

co·versed sine (kō′vûrst), *Math.* the versed sine of the complement of an angle or arc.

cov·ert (kŭv′ərt), *adj.* **1.** covered; sheltered. **2.** concealed; secret; disguised. **3.** *Law.* under cover or protection of a husband. —*n.* **4.** a covering; cover. **5.** shelter; concealment; disguise; a hiding place. **6.** *Hunting.* a thicket giving shelter to wild animals or game. **7.** (*pl.*) *Ornith.* the smaller feathers that cover the bases of the large feathers of the wing and tail. **8.** covert cloth. [ME, t. OF, pp. of *covrir* COVER] —**cov′ert·ly,** *adv.* —**cov′ert·ness,** *n.*

covert cloth, a cotton or worsted fabric of twill weave. The warp is of ply yarns, one of which is white.

covert coat, *Brit.* a short, light overcoat; a duster.

cov·er·ture (kŭv′ər chər), *n.* **1.** a cover or covering; shelter; concealment. **2.** *Law.* the status of a married woman considered as under the protection and authority of her husband. [ME, t. OF]

cov·et (kŭv′ĭt), *v.t.* **1.** to desire inordinately, or without due regard to the rights of others; desire wrongfully. **2.** to wish for, esp. eagerly. —*v.i.* **3.** to have an inordinate or wrongful desire. [ME *coveiten,* t. OF: m. *cuveitier,* ult. der. L *cupiditas* desire] —**cov′et·a·ble** *adj.* —**cov′et·er,** *n.* —**Syn. 1.** See envy.

cov·et·ous (kŭv′ə təs), *adj.* **1.** inordinately or wrongly desirous. **2.** eagerly desirous. [ME, t. OF: m. *coveitos,* ult. der. L *cupiditas* desire] —**cov′et·ous·ly,** *adv.* —**cov′et·ous·ness,** *n.* —**Syn. 1.** greedy, grasping, rapacious, avaricious.

cov·ey (kŭv′ĭ), *n., pl.* **-eys.** **1.** a brood or small flock of partridges or similar birds. **2.** a company; a group. [ME, t. OF: m. *covee,* der. *cover,* incubate, g. L *cubāre* lie]

cov·in (kŭv′ĭn), *n.* **1.** *Obs. except Law.* a secret or collusive agreement between two or more to the prejudice of another. **2.** *Obs. or Archaic.* fraud. [ME, t. OF, ult. der. L *convenīre* agree]

Cov·ing·ton (kŭv′ĭng tən), *n.* a city in N Kentucky, on the Ohio river. 64,452 (1950).

cow[1] (kou), *n., pl.* **cows,** (*Archaic*) **kine. 1.** the female of a bovine animal, esp. of the genus *Bos,* that has produced a calf and is usually over three years of age. **2.** the female of various other large animals, as the elephant, whale, etc. [ME; OE *cū,* c. G *kuh*]

cow[2] (kou), *v.t.* to frighten with threats, etc.; intimidate. [t. Scand.; cf. Icel. *kūga* cow, tyrannize over]

cow·age (kou′ĭj), *n.* cowhage.

cow·ard (kou′ərd), *n.* **1.** one who lacks courage to meet danger or difficulty; one who is basely timid. —*adj.* **2.** lacking courage; timid. **3.** proceeding from or expressive of fear or timidity: *a coward cry.* [ME, t. OF: m. *coart,* der. *coe* tail, g. L *cauda,* through comparison with animal with tail between legs] —**Syn. 1.** craven, poltroon, dastard, milksop.

Cow·ard (kou′ərd), *n.* **Noel** (nō′əl), born 1899, British author, actor, and composer.

cow·ard·ice (kou′ər dĭs), *n.* lack of courage to face danger, difficulty, opposition, etc. —**Syn.** poltroonery, dastardliness, pusillanimity, timidity.

cow·ard·ly (kou′ərd lĭ), *adj.* 1. lacking courage; basely timid. 2. characteristic of or befitting a coward. —*adv.* 3. like a coward. —**cow′ard·li·ness,** *n.*
—**Syn.** 1. craven, poltroon, dastardly, pusillanimous, timorous, faint-hearted, white-livered, chicken-hearted. Cowardly, timid refer to a lack of courage or self-confidence. Cowardly means weakly and basely fearful in the presence of danger: *the cowardly wretch deserted his comrades in battle.* Timid means lacking in boldness or self-confidence even when there is no danger present: *a timid person stands in the way of his own advancement.*—**Ant.** 1. brave, self-confident.

cow·bane (kou′bān′), *n.* any of several umbelliferous plants supposed to be poisonous to cattle, as the European water hemlock, *Cicuta virosa,* or an American swamp plant, *Oxypolis rigidior.*

cow·bell (kou′bĕl′), *n.* 1. a bell hung round a cow's neck, to indicate her whereabouts. 2. an American name of the bladder campion, *Silene latifolia.*

cow·ber·ry (kou′bĕr′ĭ), *n., pl.* **-ries.** 1. the berry or fruit of any of various shrubs, as *Vaccinium vitis-idaea,* that grow in pastures. 2. any of these shrubs.

cow·bind (kou′bīnd′), *n.* either the black-berried white bryony, *Bryonia alba,* or the red-berried bryony, *B. dioica.*

cow·bird (kou′bûrd′), *n.* any of the American blackbirds of the genus *Molothrus,* esp. *M. ater* of North America (so called because they accompany cattle). Also, **cow blackbird, cow bunting.**

cow·boy (kou′boi′), *n.* *U.S.* 1. a man employed in the care of the cattle of a ranch, doing his work largely on horseback. 2. *Now Hist.* (during the Revolutionary War) a member of one of the Tory guerrilla bands that operated between the American and British lines near New York.

cow·catch·er (kou′kăch′ər), *n.* *U.S.* a triangular frame at the front of a locomotive, streetcar, etc., designed for clearing the track of obstructions.

cow·er (kou′ər), *v.i.* 1. to crouch in fear or shame. 2. to bend with the knees and back; stand or squat in a bent position. [ME *couren,* t. Scand.; cf. Icel. *kūra* sit moping, doze, c. G *kauern* cower, crouch]

Cowes (kouz), *n.* a seaport on the Isle of Wight, in S England: resort. 5542 (1939).

cow·fish (kou′fĭsh′), *n., pl.* **-fishes,** (*esp. collectively*) **-fish.** 1. any of various marine fishes with hornlike projections over the eyes, as *Lactophrys tricornis,* found along the southern Atlantic coast of the U.S., to Panama, Brazil, etc. 2. a sirenian, as the manatee. 3. any of various small cetaceans, as a porpoise or dolphin or the grampus, *Grampus griseus.*

cow·girl (kou′gûrl′), *n.* a girl who assists in herding and handling cattle on a ranch.

cow·hage (kou′ĭj), *n.* 1. the hairs on the pods of a tropical leguminous plant, *Stizolobium* (or *Mucuna*) *pruriens,* causing intense itching and sometimes used as a vermifuge. 2. the pods. 3. the plants. Also, **cowage.** [t. Hind.: m. *kawānch*]

cow hand, one employed on a cattle ranch; a cowboy.

cow·herd (kou′hûrd′), *n.* one whose occupation is the tending of cows.

cow·hide (kou′hīd′), *n., v.,* **-hided, -hiding.** —*n.* 1. the hide of a cow. 2. the leather made from it. 3. *U.S.* a strong, flexible whip made of rawhide or of braided leather. —*v.t.* 4. to whip with a cowhide.

cow killer, a wasp, *Dasymutilla occidentalis,* of the southern U.S., resembling a large ant.

cowl (koul), *n.* 1. a hooded garment worn by monks. 2. the hood of this garment. 3. a hood-shaped covering for a chimney or ventilating shaft, to increase the draft. 4. the forward part of the automobile body supporting the rear of the hood and the windshield, and housing the pedals and instrument panel. 5. *Aeron.* a cowling. 6. a wire netting fastened to the top of the smokestack of a locomotive, to prevent large sparks from being discharged; a spark arrester. —*v.t.* 7. to put a monk's cowl on. 8. to make a monk of. 9. to cover with, or as with, or as with, a cowl. [ME *couel,* OE *cūle, cug(e)le,* t. LL: m. *cuculla* cowl, var. of L *cucullus* hood]

cowled (kould), *adj.* 1. wearing a cowl. 2. shaped like a cowl; cucullate.

Cow·ley (kou′lĭ, kōō′lĭ), *n.* **Abraham,** 1618–67, British poet.

cow·lick (kou′lĭk′), *n.* a tuft of hair turned up, usually over the forehead.

cowl·ing (kou′lĭng), *n.* *Aeron.* a streamlined housing for an aircraft engine, usually forming a continuous line with the fuselage or wing.

cow·man (kou′mən), *n., pl.* **-men.** 1. *Western U.S.* an owner of cattle; a ranchman. 2. *Brit.* a farm laborer who takes care of cows.

co-work·er (kō wûr′kər), *n.* fellow worker.

cow parsnip, any plant of the umbelliferous genus *Heracleum,* as *H. spondylium,* of Europe, or *H. lanatum,* of North America.

cow·pea (kou′pē′), *n.* 1. an annual plant, *Vigna sinensis,* extensively cultivated in the southern U.S. for forage, soil im rovement, etc., the seeds sometimes being used for human food. 2. the seed.

Cow·per (kōō′ r, kou′pər), *n.* **William,** 1731–1800, British poet.

Cow·per's glands (kou′pərz, kōō′-), (in various animals) a pair of accessory prostate or urethral glands of lobulated or follicular structure, which during sexual excitement pour a mucous secretion into the urethra. [named after Wm. *Cowper,* 1666–1709, British anatomist who discovered them]

cow pilot, a small fish, *Abudefduf saxatilis,* with dark bars, common in the West Indies and along both coasts of tropical America; pintano; sergeant major.

Cow pony, *Western U.S.* a pony used in herding cattle.

cow·pox (kou′pŏks′), *n.* an eruptive disease appearing on the teats and udders of cows in which small pustules form which contain a virus used in the vaccination of man against smallpox.

cow·punch·er (kou′pŭn′chər), *n.* *U.S. Colloq.* a cowboy.

cow·rie (kou′rĭ), *n.* 1. the shell of any of the marine gastropods constituting the genus *Cypraea,* as that of *C. moneta,* a small shell with a fine gloss, used as money in certain parts of Asia and Africa, or that of *C. tigris,* a large, handsome shell often used as a mantel ornament. 2. the animal itself. [t. Hind.: m. *kaurī*]

cow·ry (kou′rĭ), *n., pl.* **-ries.** cowrie.

cow·skin (kou′skĭn′), *n.* 1. the skin of a cow. 2. the leather made from it.

cow·slip (kou′slĭp′), *n.* 1. an English primrose, *Primula officinalis* (*P. veris*), bearing yellow flowers. 2. *U.S.* the marsh marigold. [OE *cūslyppe* cowslime, var. of *cū-sloppe* (ME *couslop*) cow-slobber. Cf. OXLIP]

cox (kŏks), *n.* 1. *Colloq.* coxswain. —*v.t., v.i.* 2. to act as coxswain to (a boat).

cox·a (kŏk′sə), *n., pl.* **coxae** (kŏk′sē). 1. *Anat.* **a.** the innominate bone. **b.** the joint of the hip. 2. *Zool.* the first or proximal segment of the leg of insects and other arthropods. [t. L: hip] —**cox′al,** *adj.*

cox·al·gi·a (kŏk săl′jĭ ə), *n.* *Pathol.* pain in the hip. Also, **cox·al·gy** (kŏk′săl jĭ). [NL; f. cox(A) + -ALGIA] —**cox·al′gic,** *adj.*

Leg of beetle (enlarged) A. Coxa; B. Trochanter; C. Femur; D. Tibia; E. Tarsus

cox·comb (kŏks′kōm′), *n.* 1. a conceited dandy. 2. *Bot.* cockscomb. 3. *Obs.* the cap, resembling a cock's comb, formerly worn by professional fools. 4. *Obs. or Humorous.* the head. [var. of *cock's comb*] —**cox·comb·i·cal** (kŏks kŏm′ə kəl, -kŏm′mə-). *adj.* —**Syn.** 1. fop, dude, exquisite, beau, popinjay, jackanapes.

cox·comb·ry (kŏks′kōm′rĭ), *n., pl.* **-ries.** 1. the manners or behavior of a coxcomb. 2. a foppish trait.

cox·swain (kŏk′sən, -swān), *n.* 1. the steersman of a boat. 2. (on a ship) one who has charge of a boat and its crew. Also, **cockswain.** [f. *cock* ship's boat + swain servant]

coy (koi), *adj.* 1. shy; modest (now usually of girls). 2. affectedly shy or reserved. 3. *Obs.* disdainful. 4. *Obs.* quiet. —*v.i.* 5. *Archaic.* to act in a coy manner. —*v.t.* 6. *Obs.* to quiet; calm. 7. *Obs.* to pat; caress. [ME, t. F: m. *coi,* earlier *quei,* g. L *quiētus* at rest] —**coy′ly,** *adv.* —**coy′ness,** *n.* —**Syn.** 1. retiring, diffident, bashful, demure.

coy·o·te (kī ō′tĭ, kī′ōt), *n.* 1. a wild animal of the wolf kind, *Canis latrans,* of western North America, noted for loud and prolonged howling at night; the prairie wolf. 2. *Amer. Ind. Legend.* the culture hero and trickster of the American Indians of the West (sometimes human, sometimes animal). 3. *U.S.* a contemptible person. [t. Mex. Sp., t. Nahuatl: m. *koyotl*]

Coyote. *Canis latrans* (3½ to 4 ft. long)

co·yo·til·lo (kō′yō tēl′yō, kī′ō-; *Sp.* kô′yō tē′yô), *n., pl.* **-los.** any plant of the rhamnaceous genus *Karwinskia,* native to Mexico and some parts of southern U.S. and bearing fruits reported to be injurious to man. [t. Mex. Sp. (dim.). See COYOTE]

coy·pu (koi′pōō), *n., pl.* **-pus,** (*esp. collectively*) **-pu.** a large South American aquatic rodent, *Myocastor* (or *Myopotamus*) *coypus,* yielding the fur nutria. [t. Amer. Sp.: m. *coipu,* t. Araucan: m. *koypu*]

Coypu. *Myocastor coypus* (Total length ab. 3 ft. tail 14 in.)

coz (kŭz), *n.* *Colloq.* cousin.

coze (kōz), *v.,* **cozed, cozing,** *n.* —*v.i.* 1. to converse in a friendly way; chat. —*n.* 2. a friendly talk; a chat. [t. F: m.s. *causer*]

coz·en (kŭz′ən), *v.t., v.i.* to cheat; deceive; beguile. [orig. obscure] —**coz′en·er,** *n.*

coz·en·age (kŭz′ən ĭj), *n.* 1. the practice of cozening. 2. the fact of being cozened. 3. a fraud; a deception.

co·zy (kō′zĭ), *adj.,* **-zier, -ziest,** *n., pl.* **-zies.** —*adj.* 1. snug; comfortable. —*n.* 2. a padded covering for a teapot, etc., to retain the heat. Also, **cosy, co′zey, cosey.** [orig. Scot.; prob. t. Scand.; cf. Norw. *koselig*] —**co′zi·ly,** *adv.* —**co′zi·ness,** *n.*

cp., compare.
C.P., Common Prayer.

c.p., 1. candle power. 2. chemically pure.
C.P.A., 1. Certified Public Accountant. 2. Chartered Public Accountant. Also, **c.p.a.**

Cpl., Corporal. Also, **cpl.**
c.p.o., chief petty officer.
Cr, *Chem.* chromium.
cr., 1. credit. 2. creditor.
crab[1] (krăb), *n., v.,* **crabbed, crabbing.** —*n.* 1. any of the stalk-eyed decapod crustaceans constituting the sub-order *Brachyura* (**true crabs**), having a short, broad,

Crab, *Callinectes sapidus* (3 in. long)

more or less flattened body, the abdomen or so-called tail being small and folded under the thorax. 2. any of various other crustaceans (as the **hermit crab**), or other animals (as the **horseshoe crab**), resembling the true crabs. 3. (*cap.*) the zodiacal constellation or sign Cancer. 4. an ill-tempered or grouchy person. 5. **catch a crab,** to make a faulty stroke in rowing, so that the oar strikes the water forcibly on the backstroke. 6. any of various mechanical contrivances for hoisting or pulling. 7. (*pl.*) a losing throw, as two aces, in the game of hazard. —*v.i.* 8. to catch crabs. [ME *crabbe,* OE *crabba,* c. G *krabbe*]
crab[2] (krăb), *n.* a crab apple (fruit or tree). [ME *crabbe,* ? var. of d. *scrab* crab apple]
crab[3] (krăb), *v.,* **crabbed, crabbing.** —*v.i.* 1. (of hawks) to claw each other. 2. to find fault. —*v.t.* 3. to claw, as a hawk. 4. *Colloq.* to find fault with. 5. *Colloq.* to spoil. [cf. MD *krabben* scratch, quarrel; akin to CRAB[1]]
crab apple, 1. a small, sour wild apple. 2. any of various cultivated species and varieties of apple, small, sour, and astringent or slightly bitter, used for making jelly and preserves. 3. any tree bearing such fruit.
Crabb (krăb), *n.* **George,** 1778–1851, British author and philologist.
Crabbe (krăb), *n.* **George,** 1754–1832, British poet.
crab·bed (krăb′ĭd), *adj.* 1. perverse; contrary; grouchy; ill-natured; churlish; irritable. 2. perplexing; intricate: *a crabbed author, writings, etc.* 3. difficult to decipher, as handwriting. [ME; f. CRAB[1] + -ED[3]] —**crab′bed·ly,** *adv.* —**crab′bed·ness,** *n.*
crab·ber (krăb′ər), *n.* 1. one who catches crabs. 2. a boat used in catching crabs.
crab·by (krăb′ĭ), *adj.,* **-bier, -biest.** crabbed (def. 1).
crab grass, an annual grass, *Digitaria sanguinalis,* common in cultivated and waste grounds. It is a weedy pest in lawns.
crab·stick (krăb′stĭk′), *n.* 1. a stick, cane, or club made of wood, esp. of the crab tree. 2. an ill-tempered, crabbed person.
crab tree, a tree which bears crab apples.
crack (krăk), *v.i.* 1. to make a sudden, sharp sound in, or as in, breaking; snap, as a whip. 2. to break with a sudden, sharp sound. 3. to break without complete separation of parts; become fissured. 4. (of the v ice) to break abruptly and discordantly, esp. into an upper register. 5. *Colloq.* to fail; give way. 6. *Now Chiefly Dial.* to brag; boast. 7. *Chiefly Scot.* to chat; gossip. 8. **crack down,** *U.S. Colloq.* to take severe measures, esp. to enforce discipline. 9. **crack up, a.** to suffer a physical, mental, or moral breakdown. **b.** *Aeron.* to crash. —*v.t.* 10. *Colloq.* to cause to make a sudden, sharp sound; make a snapping sound with (a whip, etc.); strike with a sharp noise. 11. to break without complete separation of parts; break into fissures. 12. to break (a nut, etc.) with a sudden, sharp sound. 13. *Colloq.* to break into (a safe, vault, etc.). 14. to open and drink (a bottle of wine, etc.). 15. to damage (credit, etc.). 16. to make unsound mentally. 17. to make (the voice) harsh or unmanageable. 18. to break with grief; affect deeply. 19. to utter or tell, as a joke. 20. *Obs.* to boast. 21. to subject to the process of cracking in the distillation of petroleum, etc. 22. **crack up,** *a. Colloq.* to praise; extol. **b.** to crash: *to crack up a plane.*
—*n.* 23. a sudden, sharp noise, as of something breaking. 24. the snap of a whip, etc. 25. *Colloq.* a shot, as with a rifle. 26. *Colloq.* a resounding blow. 27. a break without complete separation of parts; a fissure; a flaw. 28. an opening between floor boards or in the floor. 29. a slight opening, as one between door and doorpost. 30. a mental flaw. 31. a broken or changing tone of the voice. 32. *Colloq.* a try; an opportunity or chance. 33. *Slang.* a joke; gibe. 34. *Colloq.* one who or that which excels in some respect. 35. *Colloq.* a moment; instant: *he was on his feet again in a crack.* 36. *Slang.* a burglary. 37. *Slang.* a burglar. 38. *Scot.* conversation; chat. 39. *Now Chiefly Dial.* a boast; a lie.
—*adj.* 40. *Colloq.* of superior excellence; first-rate. [unexplained var. of obs. *crake* creak, OE *cracian* resound. See CREAK. CROAK, all prob. imit. in orig.] —**Syn.** 23. snap, report. 27. crevice, cranny, chink, cleft, interstice.
crack-a-jack (krăk′ə jăk′), *n., adj.* crackerjack.
crack·brain (krăk′brān′), *n.* an insane person.
crack·brained (krăk′brānd′), *adj.* insane; crazy.
cracked (krăkt), *adj.* 1. broken. 2. broken without separation of parts; fissured. 3. damaged. 4. *Colloq.* mentally unsound. 5. broken in tone, as the voice.
crack·er (krăk′ər), *n.* 1. a thin, crisp biscuit. 2. a firecracker. 3. Also, **cracker bonbon,** a small paper roll containing an explosive, and usually a sweetmeat, motto,

etc., which explodes when pulled sharply at both ends. 4. one of a class of poor whites in parts of the south-eastern U.S. 5. *Obs.* or *Dial.* a boaster; a liar. 6. one who or that which cracks.
crack·er·jack (krăk′ər jăk′), *n. U.S. Slang.* 1. a person of marked ability; something exceptionally fine. —*adj.* 2. *Slang.* of marked ability; exceptionally fine. Also, **crackajack.**
crack·ing (krăk′ĭng), *n.* (in the distillation of petroleum or the like) the process of breaking down certain hydrocarbons into simpler ones of lower boiling points, by means of excess heat, distillation under pressure, etc., in order to give a greater yield of low-boiling products than could be obtained by simple distillation.
crack·le (krăk′əl), *v.,* **-led, -ling,** *n.* —*v.i.* 1. to make slight, sudden, sharp noises, rapidly repeated. —*v.t.* 2. to cause to crackle. 3. to break with a crackling noise. —*n.* 4. act of crackling. 5. a crackling noise. 6. a network of fine cracks, as in the glaze of some kinds of porcelain. 7. pottery ware with a network of fine cracks in the glaze. [freq. of CRACK]
crack·le·ware (krăk′əl wâr′), *n.* crackle (def. 7).
crack·ling (krăk′lĭng), *n.* 1. the making of slight cracking sounds rapidly repeated. 2. the crisp browned skin or rind of roast pork. 3. (*usually pl.*) *Dial.* the crisp residue left when fat, especially hogs' fat, is rendered.
crack·ly (krăk′lĭ), *adj.* apt to crackle.
crack·nel (krăk′nəl), *n.* 1. a hard, brittle cake or biscuit. 2. (*pl.*) small bits of fat pork fried crisp. [ME *crakenelle,* appar. t. F: m. *craquelin,* t. MD: m. *crakelinc*]
crack of doom, 1. the signal that announces the Day of Judgment. 2. the end of the world; doomsday.
crack·pot (krăk′pŏt′), *Slang.* —*n.* 1. an eccentric or insane person. —*adj.* 2. eccentric; insane.
cracks·man (krăks′mən), *n., pl.* **-men.** *Slang.* burglar.
crack·up (krăk′ŭp′), *n.* 1. a crash; collision. 2. *Colloq.* a breakdown in health. 3. collapse; defeat.
Crac·ow (krăk′ou, krä′kō; *Ger.* krä′kou), *n.* a city in S Poland, on the Vistula: the capital of Poland, 1320–1609. 300,000 (1946). Polish, **Kraków.**
-cracy, a noun termination meaning "rule," "government," "governing body," as in *autocracy, bureaucracy.* [t. F: m. *-cratie,* ult. t. Gk.: m. *-kratía,* der. *krátos* rule, strength]
cra·dle (krā′dəl), *n., v.,* **-dled, -dling.** —*n.* 1. a little bed or cot for an infant, usually built on rockers. 2. the place where anything is nurtured during its early existence. 3. any of various contrivances similar to a child's cradle, as the framework on which a ship rests during construction or repair, or a frame or case for protecting a broken limb. 4. a flat, movable framework with swivel wheels, on which a mechanic can lie while working beneath an automobile. 5. *Agric.* **a.** a frame of wood with a row of long curved teeth projecting above and parallel to a scythe, for laying grain in bunches as it is cut. **b.** a scythe together with the cradle in which it is set. 6. a kind of box on rockers used by miners for washing auriferous gravel or sand to separate the gold. 7. a docklike structure in which a rigid or semirigid airship is built or supported during inflation. 8. an engraver's tool for laying mezzotint grounds. —*v.t.* 9. to place or rock in or as in a cradle. 10. to nurture during infancy. 11. to cut (grain) with a cradle. 12. to place in a ship's cradle. 13. to wash in a miner's cradle. 14. to receive or hold as a cradle. —*v.i.* 15. to lie in, or as in, a cradle. 16. to use in mowing. [ME *cradel,* OE *cradol.* Cf. G *kratte* basket] —**cra′dler,** *n.*
cra·dle·song (krā′dəl sông′, -sŏng′), *n.* a lullaby.
craft (krăft, kräft), *n.* 1. skill; ingenuity; dexterity. 2. skill or art applied to bad purposes; cunning; deceit; guile. 3. an art, trade, or occupation requiring special skill, esp. manual skill; a handicraft. 4. the members of a trade or profession collectively; a guild. 5. (*construed as pl.*) boats, ships, and vessels collectively. 6. a single vessel. 7. (*construed as pl.*) aircraft collectively. 8. a single aircraft. [ME; OE *cræft,* c. G *kraft*] —**Syn.** 2. craftiness, subtlety, artifice. See **cunning.**
crafts·man (krăfts′mən, kräfts′-), *n., pl.* **-men.** 1. one who practices a craft; an artisan. 2. an artist. [f. *crafts* (poss. of CRAFT) + MAN] —**crafts′man·ship′,** *n.* —**Syn.** 1. artificer, mechanic, handicraftsman.
craft union, a labor union composed only of people in the same craft.
craft·y (krăf′tĭ, kräf′-), *adj.,* **craftier, craftiest.** 1. skillful in underhand or evil schemes; cunning; deceitful; sly. 2. *Archaic.* skillful; ingenious; dexterous. —**craft′i·ly,** *adv.* —**craft′i·ness,** *n.* —**Syn.** 1. artful, wily, insidious, tricky, designing, scheming, plotting.
crag[1] (krăg), *n.* a steep, rugged rock; a rough, broken, projecting part of a rock. [ME, t. Celtic; cf. Welsh *craig* rock] —**crag′gy, crag·ged** (krăg′ĭd), *adj.* —**crag′gi·ness,** *n.*
crag[2] (krăg), *n. Scot. and N Eng.* the neck; the throat; the craw. [t. MFlem.: m. *krage*]
crags·man (krăgz′mən), *n., pl.* **-men.** one accustomed to or skilled in climbing crags.
Craig·a·von (krāg ā′vən, -ăv′ən), *n.* **James Craig, 1st Viscount,** 1871–1940, first prime minister of Northern Ireland, 1921–40.
Crai·gie (krā′gĭ), *n.* **Sir William A.,** born 1867, British lexicographer.
Craik (krāk), *n.* **Dinah Maria Mulock** (mū′lŏk), 1826–87, British novelist.

Cra·io·va (krä yô′vä), *n.* a city in SW Rumania. 67,908 (est. 1943).

crake (krāk), *n.* any of various European birds of the rail family, esp. short-billed, as the corn crake (*Crex crex*). [ME, t. Scand.; cf. Icel. *krāka* crow]

cram (krăm), *v.,* **crammed, cramming,** *n.* —*v.t.* 1. to fill (something) by force with more than it can conveniently hold. 2. to force or stuff (fol. by *into, down,* etc.). 3. to fill with or as with excess of food. 4. *Colloq.* to prepare (a person), as for an examination, by hastily storing his memory with facts. 5. *Colloq.* to get a knowledge of (a subject) by so preparing oneself. 6. *Slang.* to tell lies or exaggerated stories to. —*v.i.* 7. to eat greedily or to excess. 8. *Colloq.* to cram a person, as for an examination. —*n.* 9. *Colloq.* act or result of cramming. 10. a crammed state. 11. *Colloq.* a dense crowd. 12. *Colloq.* information acquired by cramming. [OE *crammian,* der. *crimman* insert] —**cram′mer,** *n.* —**Syn.** 2. stuff, crowd, pack, squeeze, compress, overcrowd.

Cram (krăm), *n.* **Ralph Adams,** 1863–1942, U.S. architect and writer.

cram·bo (krăm′bō), *n.* 1. a game in which one person or side must find a rhyme to a word or a line of verse given by another. 2. (in contemptuous use) rhyme.

cram·oi·sy (krăm′oi zĭ, -ə zĭ), *adj.* 1. *Archaic.* crimson. —*n.* 2. *Obs.* crimson cloth. Also, **cram′oi·sie.** [t. F: m. *cramoisi,* t. It.: m. *chermisi,* t. Ar.: m. *qirmizī* CRIMSON]

cramp[1] (krămp), *n.* 1. a sudden involuntary, persistent contraction of a muscle or a group of muscles, esp. of the extremities, sometimes associated with severe pain. 2. **writer's cramp,** a professional or occupational disease involving some muscles of the fingers and hands: 3. (*often pl.*) piercing pains in the abdomen. —*v.t.* 4. to affect with, or as with, a cramp. [ME *crampe,* t. MD]

cramp[2] (krămp), *n.* 1. a small metal bar with bent ends, for holding together timbers, masonry, etc. 2. a portable frame or tool with a movable part which can be screwed up to hold things together; clamp. 3. anything that confines or restrains. 4. a cramped state or part. —*v.t.* 5. to fasten or hold with a cramp. 6. to confine narrowly; restrict; restrain; hamper. 7. to steer; to turn the front wheel of a motor vehicle by means of the steering gear. 8. **cramp one's style,** to hinder from showing one's best abilities, etc. —*adj.* 9. hard to decipher or understand; difficult; knotty. 10. contracted; narrow. [t. MD: hook, clamp]

cramp·fish (krămp′fĭsh′), *n., pl.* **-fishes,** (*esp. collectively*) **-fish.** an electric ray (fish).

cramp iron, a cramp, or piece of iron with bent ends, for holding together pieces of stone, etc.

cram·pon (krăm′pŏn), *n.* 1. a grappling iron, esp. one of a pair for raising heavy weights. 2. a spiked iron plate worn on the shoe to prevent slipping. Also, **crampoon** (krăm pōōn′). [t. F, der. *crampe* (t. Gmc. See CRAMP[2])]

cran·ber·ry (krăn′bĕr′ĭ), *n., pl.* **-ries.** 1. the red, acid fruit or berry of any plant of the ericaceous genus *Vaccinium,* as *V. oxycoccus* (**small cranberry** or **European cranberry**) or more commonly *V. macrocarpus* (**large cranberry** or **American cranberry**), used in making sauce, jelly, etc. 2. the plant itself. [t. LG: m. *kraanbere*; cf. G *kran(ich)beere* crane berry. See CRANE]

cranberry tree, a caprifoliaceous tree or shrub, *Viburnum Opulus,* bearing red berries and white cymose flowers, known in cultivated form as *snowball.* Also, **cranberry bush.**

crane (krān), *n., v.,* **craned, craning.** —*n.* 1. any of a group of large wading birds (family *Gruidae*) with very long legs, bill, and neck, and elevated hind toe. 2. (popularly) any of various similar birds of other families, as the great blue heron, *Ardea herodias.* 3. a device for moving heavy weights, having two motions, one a direct lift and the other a horizontal movement, and consisting in one of its simplest forms of an upright post turning on its vertical axis and bearing a projecting arm on which the hoisting tackle is fitted. 4. any of various similar devices, as a horizontally swinging arm by a fireplace, used for suspending pots, etc., over the fire. 5. (*pl.*) *Naut.* supports of iron or timber at a vessel's side for stowing boats or spars upon. —*v.t.* 6. to hoist, lower, or move by or as by a crane does. 7. to stretch (the neck) as a crane does. —*v.i.* 8. to stretch out one's neck. 9. *Colloq.* to hesitate at danger, difficulty, etc. [ME; OE *cran,* c. G *kran*]

Crane (def. 1),
Grus americana
(Ab. 4½ ft. long)

Crane (krān), *n.* 1. (Harold) **Hart,** 1899–1932, U.S. writer. 2. **Ichabod** (ĭk′ə bŏd′), an awkward, superstitious schoolmaster in Irving's *Legend of Sleepy Hollow.* 3. **Stephen,** 1871–1900, U. S. novelist, poet, and short-story writer.

crane fly, any of the dipterous insects constituting the family *Tipulidae,* characterized by very long legs; the daddy-longlegs of Great Britain.

crane's-bill (krānz′bĭl′), *n.* any plant of the genus *Geranium* (see **geranium**) with long, slender, beaked fruit. Also, **cranes′bill′, crane′bill′.** [f. CRANE('s) + BILL[2]; 16th cent. trans. of D *kranebek* geranium]

cra·ni·al (krā′nĭ əl), *adj.* of or pertaining to the cranium or skull. —**cra′ni·al·ly,** *adv.*

cranial index, *Craniom.* the ratio of the greatest breadth of the skull to the greatest length from front to back, multiplied by 100.

cra·ni·ate (krā′nĭ ĭt, -āt′), *adj.* 1. having a cranium or skull. 2. belonging to the *Craniata,* a primary division of vertebrates, comprising those which possess a skull and brain, and including the mammals, birds, reptiles, amphibians, and fishes. —*n.* 3. a craniate animal.

cranio-, a combining form of **cranium.** Also, **crani-.**

cra·ni·ol·o·gy (krā′nĭ ŏl′ə jĭ), *n.* the science that deals with the size, shape, and other characteristics of skulls. —**cra′ni·o·log′i·cal** (krā′nĭ ə lŏj′ə kəl), *adj.* —**cra′ni·ol′o·gist,** *n.*

craniom., craniometry.

cra·ni·om·e·ter (krā′nĭ ŏm′ə tər), *n.* an instrument for measuring the external dimensions of skulls.

cra·ni·om·e·try (krā′nĭ ŏm′ə trĭ), *n.* the science of measuring skulls. —**cra·ni·o·met·ric** (krā′nĭ ə mĕt′rĭk), **cra′ni·o·met′ri·cal,** *adj.* —**cra′ni·om′e·trist,** *n.*

cra·ni·ot·o·my (krā′nĭ ŏt′ə mĭ), *n., pl.* **-mies.** *Surg.* the operation of opening the skull, usually for operations on the brain.

cra·ni·um (krā′nĭ əm), *n., pl.* **-niums, -nia** (-nĭ ə). 1. the skull of a vertebrate. 2. that part of the skull which encloses the brain. [t. ML, t. Gk.: m. *krānion*]

Human cranium,
(from above)
F, P, O, frontal,
parietal, and
occipital bones;
C, S, L, coronal,
sagittal and
lambdoidal sutures

crank[1] (krăngk), *n.* 1. a device for communicating motion, or for changing rotary motion into reciprocating motion, or vice versa, consisting in its simplest form of an arm projecting from, or secured at right angles at the end of, the axis or shaft which receives or imparts the motion. 2. *U.S. Colloq.* an ill-tempered, grouchy person. 3. *U.S. Colloq.* an eccentric or impracticable person. 4. an eccentric notion. 5. a turn of speech; a verbal conceit. 6. *Obs.* a bend. —*v.t.* 7. to bend into or make in the shape of a crank. 8. to furnish with a crank. 9. to cause (a shaft) to revolve by applying force to a crank; turn a crankshaft in (an automobile engine, etc.) to start the engine. —*v.i.* 10. to turn a crank, as in starting an automobile engine. 11. *Obs.* to twist, wind. —*adj.* 12. unstable; shaky; unsteady. 13. *Brit. Dial.* sickly. [ME *cranke,* OE *cranc,* in *crancstæf* weaving implement, crank]

crank[2] (krăngk), *adj.* liable to lurch or capsize, as a ship. [short for *crank-sided*; cf. D *krengd* careened]

crank[3] (krăngk), *adj.* *Obs.* or *Dial.* lively; in high spirits; cheerful. [ME; orig. unknown]

crank·case (krăngk′kās′), *n.* (in an internal-combustion engine) the housing which encloses the crankshaft, connecting rods, and allied parts.

crank·le (krăng′kəl), *n., v.t., v.i.,* **-kled, -kling.** bend; turn. [freq. of CRANK[1], v.]

crank·ous (krăng′kəs), *adj.* *Scot.* irritated; cranky.

crank·pin (krăngk′pĭn′), *n.* *Mach.* a pin or cylinder at the outer end or part of a crank, as for holding a connecting rod.

crank·shaft (krăngk′shăft′, -shäft′), *n.* *Mach.* a shaft driving or driven by a crank.

crank·y[1] (krăng′kĭ), *adj.,* **crankier, crankiest.** 1. ill-tempered; cross. 2. eccentric; queer. 3. shaky; unsteady; out of order. 4. full of bends or windings; crooked. 5. *Brit. Dial.* sickly; infirm. —**crank′i·ly,** *adv.* —**crank′i·ness,** *n.* —**Syn.** 1. crotchety, cantankerous, perverse. —**Ant.** 1. good-natured.

crank·y[2] (krăng′kĭ), *adj.* liable to capsize.

Cran·mer (krăn′mər), *n.* **Thomas,** 1489–1556, first Protestant archbishop of Canterbury: a leader of the Protestant Reformation in England.

cran·nog (krăn′əg), *n.* an ancient Irish or Scottish lake dwelling, usually built on an artificial island. Also, **cran·noge** (krăn′əj). [t. Irish, der. *crann* tree, beam]

cran·ny (krăn′ĭ), *n., pl.* **-nies.** a small, narrow opening (in a wall, rock, etc.); a chink; crevice; fissure. [ME *crany,* f. F *cran* fissure (der. *crener* cut away, g. L *crēnāre*) + -Y[2], dim. suffix] —**cran′nied,** *adj.*

cran·reuch (krăn′rəkh), *n.* *Scot.* hoarfrost.

Cran·ston (krăn′stən), *n.* a city in E Rhode Island, near Providence. 55,060 (1950).

crap (krăp), *n.* *U.S.* 1. a losing throw, in which the total on the two dice is 2, 3, or 12, in craps. 2. craps.

crape (krāp), *n., v.t.,* **craped, craping.** crepe. [Anglicized sp. of CREPE]

crap·pie (krăp′ĭ), *n.* a small sunfish of the central U.S.: either the **black crappie,** *Pomoxis nigro-maculatus,* or the **white crappie,** *Pomoxis annularis.*

craps (krăps), *n. U.S.* a gambling game played with two dice, a modern and simplified form of hazard.

crap·shoot·er (krăp′shōō′tər), *n. U.S.* a person who plays the game of craps.

crap·u·lent (krăp′yŏŏ lənt), *adj.* sick from gross excess in drinking or eating. [t. L: s. *crāpulentus* drunk] —**crap′u·lence,** *n.*

crap·u·lous (krăp′yŏŏ ləs), *adj.* 1. given to or characterized by gross excess in drinking or eating. 2. suffering from or due to such excess. [t. LL: m.s. *crāpulōsus,* der. L *crāpula* intoxication] —**crap′u·lous·ness,** *n.*

b., blend of, blended; c., cognate with; d., dialect, dialectal; der., derived from; f., formed from; g., going back to; m., modification of; r., replacing; s., stem of; t., taken from; ?, perhaps. See the full key on inside cover.

crash¹ (krăsh), *v.t.* **1.** to break in pieces violently and noisily; shatter. **2.** to force or drive with violence and noise (fol. by *in, through, out,* etc.). **3.** *Colloq.* to come uninvited to (a party, etc.). **4.** *Colloq.* to enter without buying a ticket: *to crash the gate.* **5.** to cause (an aircraft) to make a landing in an abnormal manner, usually damaging or wrecking the apparatus. —*v.i.* **6.** to break or fall to pieces with noise. **7.** to make a loud, clattering noise, as of something dashed to pieces. **8.** to move or go with a crash; strike with a crash. **9.** *Aeron.* to land in an abnormal manner, usually damaging or wrecking the apparatus. —*n.* **10.** a breaking or falling to pieces with loud noise. **11.** the shock of collision and breaking. **12.** a sudden and violent falling to ruin. **13.** a sudden collapse of a financial enterprise or the like. **14.** a sudden, loud noise, as of something dashed to pieces; the sound of thunder, loud music, etc. **15.** *Aeron.* act of crashing. [ME; b. CRAZE and MASH] —**crash′er,** *n.* —**Syn. 1.** smash. **13.** failure, ruin.

crash² (krăsh), *n.* **1.** a fabric of plain weave, made of rough, irregular, or lumpy yarns. It may be used as linen or cotton toweling, rayon dress fabric, etc. **2.** *Bookbinding.* starched cotton fabric used to reinforce the spine of a bound book. [orig. unknown]

Crash·aw (krăsh′ô), *n.* **Richard,** 1613?–49, British religious poet.

crass (krăs), *adj.* **1.** gross; stupid: *crass ignorance.* **2.** thick; coarse. [t. L: s. *crassus* solid, thick, dense, fat] —**crass′ly,** *adv.* —**crass′ness,** *n.*

cras·si·tude (krăs′ə tūd′, -tōōd′), *n.* **1.** gross ignorance or stupidity. **2.** thickness; grossness.

cras·su·la·ceous (krăs′yōō lā′shəs), *adj.* belonging to the *Crassulaceae* family of plants, mostly fleshy or succulent herbs, including the houseleek, stonecrop, etc. [f. s. NL *Crassula* the typical genus, (der. L *crassus* thick) + -ACEOUS]

Cras·sus (krăs′əs), *n.* **Marcus Licinius** (mär′kəs lə-sĭn′ĭəs), c115–53 B.C., Roman general: member of the first triumvirate.

-crat, a noun termination meaning "ruler," "member of a ruling body," "advocate of a particular form of rule," as in *aristocrat, autocrat, democrat, plutocrat.* Cf. **-cracy.** [t. F: m. *-crate,* t. Gk.: m. *-kratēs* ruler]

cratch (krăch), *n. Archaic or Dial.* a crib to hold fodder; a manger. [ME *crecche,* t. OF: m. *cresche,* t. Gmc.]

crate (krāt), *n., v.,* **crated, crating.** —*n.* **1.** a box or framework, usually made of wooden slats, for packing and transporting fruit, furniture, etc. **2.** a basket of wickerwork, for the transportation of crockery, etc. —*v.t.* **3.** to put in a crate. [t. L: m.s. *crātis* wickerwork]

cra·ter (krā′tər), *n.* **1.** the cup-shaped depression or cavity marking the orifice of a volcano. **2.** the hole or pit in the ground where a military mine or shell has exploded. **3.** a large vessel or bowl used by the ancient Greeks and Romans, orig. for mixing wine with water. **4.** (*cap.*) *Astron.* a small southern constellation. [t. L, t. Gk.: m. *krātēr,* orig., bowl for mixing wine and water]

Crater Lake, a lake in the crater of an extinct volcano in SW Oregon. 5–6 mi. across; 1996 ft. deep.

craunch (krônch, krănch), *v.t., v.i., n.* crunch. [var. of *scranch, cranch.* Cf. D *schranzen* break]

cra·vat (krə văt′), *n.* **1.** *Orig. Brit. and still somewhat affected in U.S.* necktie. **2.** a scarf worn around the neck; neckcloth. [t. F: m. *cravate;* so called because adopted from the Croats (F *Cravates*)]

crave (krāv), *v.,* **craved, craving.** —*v.t.* **1.** to long for or desire eagerly. **2.** to need greatly; require. **3.** to ask earnestly for (something); beg for. **4.** to ask (a person) earnestly for something or to do something. —*v.i.* **5.** to beg or plead (fol. by *for*). **6.** to long (fol. by *for* or *after*). [ME *craven,* OE *crafian.* Cf. Icel. *krefja* demand] —**crav′er,** *n.* —**crav′ing·ly,** *adv.* —**Syn. 1.** want, yearn for, hunger for. **4.** beg, beseech, entreat, implore.

cra·ven (krā′vən), *adj.* **1.** cowardly; pusillanimous; mean-spirited. **2.** *Obs.* defeated. —*n.* **3.** a coward. —*v.t.* **4.** to make cowardly. [ME *cravant,* f. OF, b. *crav(ante)* overthrown and (*recre*)*ant* RECREANT] —**cra′ven·ly,** *adv.* —**cra′ven·ness,** *n.* —**Ant. 1.** brave.

crav·en·ette (krăv′ə nĕt′, krăv′və-), *n.* **1.** a finish for wool or cotton fabrics to render them water-repellent. **2.** (*cap.*) a trademark for this finish. [der. *Craven,* proper name]

crav·ing (krā′vĭng), *n.* eager or urgent desire; longing; yearning. —**Syn.** See **desire.**

craw (krô), *n.* **1.** the crop of a bird or insect. **2.** the stomach of an animal. [ME *crawe,* c. D *kraag* neck]

craw·fish (krô′fĭsh′), *n., pl.* **-fishes,** (*esp. collectively*) **-fish,** *v.* —*n.* **1.** any of numerous fresh-water decapod crustaceans of the suborder *Macrura,* closely related to the lobsters but smaller, as *Astacus fluviatilis,* of Europe, and various American species of the genus *Cambarus.* **2.** any of certain similar marine crustaceans. **3.** *U.S. Colloq.* one who backs out or retreats from a position or undertaking. —*v.i.* **4.** *U.S. Colloq.* to back out or retreat from a position or undertaking. Also, *esp. Brit.,* **crayfish** for 1, 2. [var. of CRAY-FISH]

Crawfish.
Cambarus diogenes
(3½ in. long)

Craw·ford (krô′fərd), *n.* **Francis Marion,** 1854–1909, U.S. novelist, long resident in Italy.

crawl¹ (krôl), *v.i.* **1.** to move slowly by dragging the body along the ground, as a worm. **2.** to progress slowly, laboriously, or timorously; go stealthily or abjectly: *the work crawled.* **3.** to be, or feel as if, overrun with crawling things. —*n.* **4.** act of crawling; a slow, crawling motion. **5.** *Swimming.* a stroke in prone position characterized by alternate overarm movements and a continuous up and down kick. [ME, t. Scand.; cf. Dan. *kravle* creep] —**crawl′er,** *n.* —**crawl′ing·ly,** *adv.* —**Syn. 1.** CRAWL, CREEP refer to methods of moving like reptiles or worms, or on all fours. They are frequently interchangeable, but CRAWL is used of a more prostrate movement than CREEP: *a dog afraid of punishment crawls toward his master.* CREEP expresses slow progress: *a baby creeps before walking.* —**Ant. 1.** stride.

crawl² (krôl), *n.* an enclosure in shallow water on the seacoast, for confining fish, turtles, etc. [t. D: m. *kraal,* t. Sp.: m. *corral* CORRAL]

crawl·y (krô′lĭ), *adj. Colloq.* creepy.

cray·fish (krā′fĭsh′), *n., pl.* **-fishes,** (*esp. collectively*) **-fish.** *Chiefly Brit.* crawfish (defs. 1, 2). [ME *crevice,* t. OF, t. OHG: m. *krebiz* crab]

cray·on (krā′ən, -ŏn), *n., v.,* **-oned, -oning.** —*n.* **1.** a pointed stick or pencil of colored clay, chalk, etc., used for drawing. **2.** a drawing in crayons. —*v.t.* **3.** to draw with a crayon or crayons. **4.** to sketch out (a plan, etc.). [t. F, der. *craie,* g. L *crēta* chalk] —**cray′on·ist,** *n.*

craze (krāz), *v.,* **crazed, crazing,** *n.* —*v.t.* **1.** to impair in intellect; make insane. **2.** to make small cracks on the surface of (pottery, etc.); to crackle. **3.** *Archaic or Dial.* to weaken or impair (health, etc.). **4.** *Obs. or Dial.* to crack. **5.** *Obs.* to break; shatter. —*v.i.* **6.** to become insane. **7.** to become minutely cracked, as the glaze of pottery. **8.** *Obs.* to break. —*n.* **9.** a mania; a popular fashion, etc., usually short-lived; a rage. **10.** insanity; an insane condition. **11.** a minute crack in the glaze of pottery, etc. **12.** *Obs. or Dial.* a crack. [ME *crase(n)* break, t. Scand.; cf. Sw. *krasa*]

crazed (krāzd), *adj.* **1.** insane; demented. **2.** having small cracks in the glaze, as pottery.

cra·zy (krā′zĭ), *adj.,* **-zier, -ziest. 1.** demented; insane; mad. **2.** *Colloq.* too excited or enthusiastic. **3.** liable to break or fall to pieces. **4.** weak; infirm. —**cra′zi·ly,** *adv.* —**cra′zi·ness,** *n.* —**Syn. 1.** crazed, deranged, lunatic. See **mad. 3.** rickety, shaky, tottering.

crazy bone, *U.S.* funny bone.

crazy quilt, *U.S.* a patchwork quilt made of irregular patches combined with little or no regard to pattern.

cra·zy·weed (krā′zĭ wēd′), *n.* locoweed.

creak (krēk), *v.i.* **1.** to make a sharp, harsh, grating, or squeaking sound. **2.** to move with creaking. —*v.t.* **3.** to cause to creak. —*n.* **4.** a creaking sound. [ME *creken.* Cf. OE *crǣcettan,* var. of *crǣcettan* CROAK]

creak·y (krē′kĭ), *adj.,* **creakier, creakiest.** creaking; apt to creak. —**creak′i·ly,** *adv.* —**creak′i·ness,** *n.*

cream (krēm), *n.* **1.** the fatty part of milk, which rises to the surface when the liquid is allowed to stand. **2.** something containing or resembling this substance, as a table delicacy, a cosmetic, etc. **3.** (*usually pl.*) a soft-centered confection of fondant or fudge coated with chocolate. **4.** a purée or soup containing cream sauce: *cream of tomato soup.* **5.** the best part of anything. **6.** yellowish white; light tint of yellow or buff. —*v.i.* **7.** to form cream. **8.** to froth; foam. —*v.t.* **9.** to work (butter and sugar, etc.) to a smooth, creamy mass. **10.** to prepare (chicken, oysters, vegetables, etc.) with cream, milk, or a cream sauce. **11.** to allow (milk) to form cream. **12.** to skim (milk). **13.** to separate as cream. **14.** to take the cream or best part of. **15.** to add cream to (tea, coffee, etc.). [ME *creme,* t. F, g. LL *chrisma* CHRISM]

cream cheese, a soft, white, smooth-textured, unripened cheese made of sweet milk and sometimes cream.

cream-col·ored (krēm′kŭl′ərd), *adj.* having a yellowish-white color. Also, *Brit.,* **cream′-col′oured.**

cream-cups (krēm′kŭps′), *n., pl.* **-cups.** a papaveraceous plant, *Platystemon californicus,* of California, bearing small pale-yellow or cream-colored flowers.

cream·er (krē′mər), *n.* **1.** one who or that which creams. **2.** a small jug, pitcher, etc., for holding cream. **3.** a refrigerator in which milk is placed to facilitate the formation of cream. **4.** a vessel or apparatus for separating cream from milk.

cream·er·y (krē′mə rĭ), *n., pl.* **-eries. 1.** an establishment engaged in the production of butter and cheese. **2.** a place for the sale of milk and its products. **3.** a place where milk is set to form cream.

cream ice, *Brit.* ice cream.

cream of tartar, purified and crystallized potassium bitartrate, used as a baking powder ingredient, etc. See **tartar¹** (def. 2).

cream sauce, a sauce made of cream or milk, flour, butter, etc.

cream·y (krē′mĭ), *adj.,* **creamier, creamiest. 1.** containing cream. **2.** resembling cream, as in appearance or consistency; soft and smooth. **3.** cream-colored. —**cream′i·ness,** *n.*

crease¹ (krēs), *n., v.,* **creased, creasing.** —*n.* **1.** a line or mark produced in anything by folding; a fold; a ridge; a furrow. **2.** *Cricket.* **a.** one of certain lines marked on the ground to define the positions of the bowler and the batsman. **b.** the space between such lines. —*v.t.* **3.** to make a crease or creases in or on; wrinkle. **4.** *U.S.* to wound or stun by a furrowing or superficial shot. —*v.i.* **5.** to become creased. [orig. unknown] —**creas′er,** *n.* —**creas′y,** *adj.*

crease[2] (krēs), *n.* creese.

crease-re·sist·ant (krēs′rĭ zĭs′tənt), *adj.* (of a fabric) able to resist normal wrinkling.

cre·ate (krē āt′), *v.,* **-ated, -ating** *adj.* —*v.t.* **1.** to bring into being; cause to exist; produce. **2.** to evolve from one's own thought or imagination. **3.** to be the first to represent (a part or role). **4.** to make by investing with new character or functions; constitute; appoint: *to create a peer.* **5.** to be the cause or occasion of; give rise to. —*adj.* **6.** *Poetic.* created. [t. L: m.s. *creātus,* pp. of *creāre* bring into being] —**Syn. 1.** originate, invent.

cre·a·tine (krē′ə tēn′, -tĭn), *n.* *Biochem.* an alkaloid or amino acid, $C_4H_9O_2N_3 + H_2O$, found in the muscles of vertebrates. Also, **cre·a·tin** (krē′ə tĭn). [f. m.s. Gk. *kréas* flesh + -INE[2]]

cre·a·tion (krē ā′shən), *n.* **1.** act of creating. **2.** fact of being created. **3. the Creation,** the original bringing into existence of the universe by the Deity. **4.** that which is created. **5.** the world; universe. **6.** creatures collectively. **7.** a product of inventive ingenuity; an original work, esp. of the imaginative faculty. —**cre·a′tion·al,** *adj.*

cre·a·tion·ism (krē ā′shə nĭz′əm), *n.* **1.** the doctrine that God immediately creates out of nothing a new human soul for each individual born. Cf. **traducianism. 2.** the doctrine that matter and all things were created, substantially as they now exist, by the fiat of an omnipotent Creator, and not gradually evolved or developed. —**cre·a′tion·ist,** *n.*

cre·a·tive (krē ā′tĭv), *adj.* **1.** having the quality or power of creating. **2.** originative; productive (fol. by *of*). —**cre·a′tive·ly,** *adv.* —**cre·a′tive·ness,** *n.*

cre·a·tor (krē ā′tər), *n.* **1.** one who or that which creates. **2. the Creator,** God. —**cre·a′tor·ship′,** *n.*

crea·tur·al (krē′chər əl), *adj.* of, pertaining to, or of the nature of a creature or creatures.

crea·ture (krē′chər), *n.* **1.** anything created, animate or inanimate. **2.** an animate being. **3.** an animal, as distinct from man: applied in the U.S. esp. to cattle, horses, etc. **4.** a human being (often used in contempt, commiseration, or endearment). **5.** a person owing his rise and fortune to another, or subject to the will or influence of another. **6.** *Humorous.* intoxicating liquor; whiskey. [ME, t. OF, t. LL: m. *creātūra* a thing created]

creature comforts, things, esp. food, which minister to bodily comfort.

crea·ture·ly (krē′chər lĭ), *adj.* creatural.

crèche (krāsh; *Fr.* krĕsh), *n.* **1.** *Chiefly Brit.* a nursery where children are cared for while their mothers work. Cf. *U.S.* **day nursery. 2.** an asylum for foundlings. **3.** a tableau of Mary, Joseph, and others around the crib of Jesus in the stable at Bethlehem, often built for display at Christmas. [t. F, t. OHG: m. *krippja* crib]

Cré·cy (krĕs′ĭ; *Fr.* krĕ sē′), *n.* a village in N France: scene of a famous English victory over the French, 1346. Also, **Cressy.**

cre·dence (krē′dəns), *n.* **1.** belief: *to give credence to a statement.* **2.** something giving a claim to belief or confidence: *letter of credence.* **3.** Also, **credence table.** a small side table, shelf, or niche for holding articles used in the eucharist service. [ME, t. ML: m.s. *crēdentia* belief, credit, sideboard, der. L *crēdens,* ppr., believing]

cre·den·dum (krĭ dĕn′dəm), *n.,* *pl.* **-da** (-də). that which is to be believed; an article of faith. [L, neut. of *crēdendus,* gerundive of *crēdere* believe]

cre·dent (krē′dənt), *adj.* **1.** believing. **2.** *Obs.* credible.

cre·den·tial (krĭ dĕn′shəl), *n.* **1.** that which gives a title to belief or confidence. **2.** (*usually pl.*) a letter or other testimonial attesting the bearer's right to confidence or authority. —*adj.* **3.** giving a title to belief or confidence. [f. ML *crēdentia* belief + -AL[1]]

cred·i·ble (krĕd′ə bəl), *adj.* **1.** capable of being believed; believable. **2.** worthy of belief or confidence; trustworthy. [ME, t. L: m.s. *crēdibilis*] —**cred′i·bil′i·ty, cred′i·ble·ness,** *n.* —**cred′i·bly,** *adv.*

cred·it (krĕd′ĭt), *n.* **1.** belief; trust. **2.** influence or authority resulting from the confidence of others or from one's reputation. **3.** trustworthiness; credibility. **4.** repute; reputation. **5.** favorable estimation. **6.** commendation or honor given for some action, quality, etc. **7.** a source of commendation or honor. **8.** the ascription or acknowledgment of something as due or properly attributable to a person, etc. **9.** *Educ.* **a.** official acceptance and recording of the work of a student in a particular course of study. **b.** a unit of a curriculum (short for **credit hour**): *he took the course for four credits.* **10.** time allowed for payment for goods, etc., obtained on trust. **11.** confidence in a purchaser's ability and intention to pay, displayed by entrusting him with goods, etc., without immediate payment. **12.** reputation of solvency and probity, entitling a person to be trusted in buying or borrowing. **13.** power to buy or borrow on trust. **14.** a sum of money due to a person; anything valuable standing on the credit side of an account. **15.** the balance in one's favor in an account. **16.** *Bookkeeping.* **a.** the acknowledgment or an entry of payment or value received, in an account. **b.** the side (right-

hand) of an account on which such entries are made (opposed to *debit*). **c.** an entry, or the total shown, on the credit side. **17.** any deposit or sum against which one may draw. —*v.t.* **18.** to believe; put confidence in; trust; have faith in. **19.** to reflect credit upon; do credit to; give reputation or honor to. **20.** to ascribe (something) to a person, etc.; make ascription of something to (a person, etc.) (fol. by *with*). **21. a.** *Bookkeeping.* to enter upon the credit side of an account; give credit for or to. **b.** to give the benefit of such an entry to (a person, etc.) **22.** *Educ.* to award educational credits to: *credited with three hours in history.* [t. F, t. It.: m. *credito,* g. L *creditus,* pp., believed]

—**Syn. 12.** CREDIT, REPUTE, REPUTATION, STANDING refer to one's status in the estimation of a community. CREDIT refers to business and financial status and the amount of money for which a man will be trusted: *his credit is excellent at all the stores.* REPUTE is particularly what is reported about someone, the favor in which he is held, etc.: *a man of fine repute among his acquaintances.* REPUTATION is the moral and other character commonly ascribed to someone: *of unblemished reputation.* STANDING is one's position in a community, or rank and condition in life: *a man of good standing and education.*—**Ant. 5.** disrepute.

cred·it·a·ble (krĕd′ĭt ə bəl), *adj.* bringing credit, honor, reputation, or esteem. —**cred′it·a·ble·ness,** *n.* —**cred′it·a·bly,** *adv.* —**Syn.** praiseworthy, meritorious, estimable, honorable, reputable, respectable.

credit memorandum, a record that the customer is entitled to an allowance or deduction. Also, **credit slip.**

cred·i·tor (krĕd′ĭ tər), *n.* **1.** one who gives credit in business transactions. **2.** one to whom money is due (opposed to *debtor*). **3.** *Bookkeeping.* credit. (def. 16 b, c).

credit standing, reputation for meeting financial obligations.

credit union, a coöperative group making low interest rate loans to its members.

cre·do (krē′dō, krā′dō), *n.,* *pl.* **-dos. 1.** the Apostles' or the Nicene Creed. **2.** a musical setting of the creed, usually of the Nicene Creed. **3.** any creed or formula of belief. [t. L: I believe, the first word of the Apostles' and the Nicene Creeds in Latin]

cre·du·li·ty (krə dū′lə tĭ, -dōō′-), *n.* a disposition arising from weakness or ignorance, to believe too readily. [late ME *credulite,* t. L: m.s. *crēdulitas*]

cred·u·lous (krĕj′ə ləs), *adj.* **1.** ready or disposed to believe, esp. on weak or insufficient evidence. **2.** marked by or arising from credulity. [t. L: m. *crēdulus* apt to believe] —**cred′u·lous·ly,** *adv.* —**cred′u·lous·ness,** *n.* —**Syn. 1.** believing, trustful, unsuspecting, gullible.

Cree (krē), *n.,* *pl.* **Cree, Crees. 1.** (*pl.*) an important North American Indian tribe belonging to the Algonquian linguistic stock, and located in Manitoba, Saskatchewan, etc. **2.** a member of this tribe. [short for F *Kristinaux,* m. *Kinistenoag,* given as one of their own names]

creed (krēd), *n.* **1.** an authoritative formulated statement of the chief articles of Christian belief, as the **Apostles',** the **Nicene,** or the **Athanasian Creed. 2.** the Apostles' Creed. **3.** any formula of religious belief, as of a denomination. **4.** an accepted system of religious belief. **5.** any system of belief or of opinion. [ME *crede,* OE *crēda,* t. L: m. *crēdo* I believe. See CREDO] —**creed′al,** *adj.* —**creed′less,** *adj.*

creek (krēk, krĭk), *n.* **1.** *U.S., Canada, and Australia.* a small stream, as a branch of a river. **2.** *Chiefly Brit.* a narrow recess in the shore of the sea, a river, etc.; a small inlet or bay. **3.** *Obs.* a narrow or winding passage. [ME *creke,* appar. north. var. of *crike* (short vowel), t. Scand.; cf. Icel. *kriki* crack; nook]

Creek (krēk), *n.* **1.** (*pl.*) a powerful confederacy of Muskhogean Indians which in historic times occupied the greater part of Alabama and Georgia. **2.** an Indian of this confederacy. [so called because of numerous streams in Creek territory]

creel (krēl), *n.* **1.** a wickerwork basket, esp. one used by anglers for holding fish. **2.** a wickerwork trap to catch fish, lobsters, etc. **3.** a framework, esp. one for holding bobbins in a spinning machine. [ME *crele.* ? t. F: m. *creil,* ult. der. L *crātis* wickerwork. Cf. GRILLE]

creep (krēp), *v.,* **crept, creeping,** *n.* —*v.i.* **1.** to move with the body close to the ground, as a reptile or an insect, or a child on hands and knees. **2.** to move slowly, imperceptibly, or stealthily. **3.** to move or behave timidly or servilely. **4.** to slip or move along gradually, as a railroad track under traffic. **5.** to have a sensation as of something creeping over the skin. **6.** to grow along the ground, a wall, etc., as a plant, esp. a creeper (def. 3). —*v.t.* **7.** *Poetic.* to creep along or over. —*n.* **8.** act of creeping. **9.** (*usually pl.*) a sensation as of something creeping over the skin. [ME *crepen,* OE *crēopan* c. D *kruipen*] —**Syn. 1.** See **crawl.**

creep·er (krē′pər), *n.* **1.** one who or that which creeps. **2.** (*pl.*) a loose garment, usually with attached pants, worn by infants. **3.** *Bot.* a plant which grows upon or just beneath the surface of the ground, or upon any other surface, sending out rootlets from the stem, as ivy and couch grass (often used in England where Americans say *vine*). **4.** any of various birds that creep or climb about on trees, esp. the several species of the family *Certhiidae* of Europe and North America, as the **tree creeper,** *Certhia familiaris.* **5.** one of a breed of domestic fowls with short legs. **6.** a grappling device for dragging a river, etc. **7.** a spiked piece of iron worn on the heel of the shoe to prevent slipping on ice, etc.

creep·ie (krē′pĭ, krĭp′ĭ), *n. Brit. Dial.* a low stool.

creep·y (krē′pĭ), *adj.* **creepier, creepiest. 1.** that creeps, as an insect. **2.** having or causing a creeping sensation of the skin, as from horror: *a creepy silence.* —**creep′i·ness,** *n.*

creese (krēs), *n.* a short sword or heavy dagger with a wavy blade, used by the Malays. Also, **crease, kris.** [t. Malay: m. *kris*]

creesh (krēsh), *n., v.t. Scot.* grease. [t. OF: m. *cresse, craisse,* g. L *crassa,* fem. of *crassus* thick, fat]

Cre·feld (krā′fĕld; *Ger.* -fĕlt), *n.* Krefeld.

cre·mate (krē′māt), *v.t.,* -**mated,** -**mating. 1.** to reduce (a corpse) to ashes. **2.** to consume by fire; burn. [t. L: m. s. *cremātus,* pp., consumed by fire] —**cre·ma′-tion,** *n.*

cre·ma·tion·ist (krĭ mā′shən ĭst), *n.* one who advocates cremation instead of burial of the dead.

cre·ma·tor (krē′mā tər), *n.* **1.** one who cremates. **2.** a furnace for cremating dead bodies. **3.** an incinerator for garbage, etc. [t. LL]

cre·ma·to·ri·um (krē′mə tōr′ĭəm, krĕm′ə-), *n. Chiefly Brit.* a crematory.

cre·ma·to·ry (krē′mə tōr′ĭ, krĕm′-), *adj., n., pl.* -**ries.** —*adj.* **1.** of or pertaining to cremation. —*n.* **2.** a furnace or an establishment for cremating.

crème (krĕm), *n. French.* **1.** cream. **2.** one of various liqueurs. [F. See CREAM]

crème de ca·ca·o (krĕm′ də kȧ kā ō′), *French.* a liqueur flavored with cacao and vanilla beans.

crème de la crème (krĕm′ də lȧ krĕm′), *French.* cream of the cream; the very best; the flower.

crème de menthe (krĕm də mänt′), *French.* liqueur flavored with mint.

Cre·mo·na (krĭ mō′nə; *It.* krĕ mō′nä), *n.* **1.** a city in N Italy, on the Po river. 69,952 (est. 1946). **2.** one of a class of violins of superior quality made there during the 16th, 17th, and 18th centuries.

cre·nate (krē′nāt), *adj.* having the margin notched or scalloped so as to form rounded teeth, as a leaf. Also, **cre′nat·ed.** [t. NL: m.s. *crēnātus,* der. *crēna* notch] —**cre′nate·ly,** *adv.*

Crenate and doubly crenate leaves

cre·na·tion (krĭ nā′shən), *n.* **1.** a rounded projection or tooth, as on the margin of a leaf. **2.** crenate state.

cren·a·ture (krĕn′ə chər, krē′nə-), *n.* **1.** a rounded tooth, as of a crenate leaf. **2.** a notch between teeth.

cren·el (krĕn′əl), *n., v.,* -**eled,** -**eling** or (*esp. Brit.*) -**elled,** -**elling.** —*n.* **1.** one of the open spaces between the merlons of a battlement. **2.** a crenature. —*v.t.* **3.** to crenelate. Also, **crenelle.** [t. OF, dim. of *cren* notch, der. *crener,* v., g. L *crēnāre*]

cren·e·late (krĕn′ə lāt′), *v.t.,* -**ated,** -**ating. 1.** to furnish with crenels or battlements. **2.** *Archit.* to form with square indentations, as a molding. Also, *esp. Brit.,* **cren′el·late′.** [f. s. F *créneler* (der. *crenel,* dim. of *cren* notch) + -ATE¹] —**cren′el·at·ed,** *adj.*

cren·el·a·tion (krĕn′ə lā′shən), *n.* **1.** act of crenelating. **2.** state of being crenelated. **3.** a battlement. **4.** a notch; indentation. Also, *esp. Brit.,* **cren′el·la′tion.**

cren·elle (krĭ nĕl′), *n., v.t.* -**nelled,** -**nelling.** crenel.

cren·u·late (krĕn′yə lāt′, -lĭt), *adj.* having the edge cut into very small scallops, as some leaves. Also, **cren′-u·lat′ed.** [t. NL: m.s. *crēnulātus,* der. *crēnula,* dim. of *crēna* notch]

cren·u·la·tion (krĕn′yə lā′shən), *n.* **1.** a minute crenation. **2.** crenulate state.

cre·o·dont (krē′ə dŏnt′), *n.* any of the *Creodonta,* a group of primitive carnivorous mammals, characterized by small brains. Certain creodonts are regarded as the ancestors of the modern carnivores. [t. NL: s. *Creodonta* (pl.), f. Gk.: m. *kréas* flesh + m.s. *odoús* tooth]

Cre·ole (krē′ōl), *n.* **1.** (in the West Indies and Spanish America) one born in the region but of European, usually Spanish, ancestry. **2.** (in Louisiana and elsewhere) a person born in the region but of French ancestry. **3.** a person born in a place but of foreign ancestry, as distinguished from the aborigines and half-breeds. **4.** the French language of Louisiana, especially that spoken by white persons in New Orleans. **5.** (*l.c.*) a person of mixed Creole and Negro ancestry speaking a form of French or Spanish. **6.** (*l.c.*) a native-born Negro, as distinguished from a Negro brought from Africa. —*adj.* **7.** of, pertaining to, or characteristic of a Creole or the Creoles. **8.** (*l.c.*) of, belonging to, or characteristic of the creoles: *a creole dialect, creole French.* **9.** bred or growing in a country, but of foreign origin, as an animal or plant. **10.** *Cookery.* denoting a sauce or dish made with stewed tomatoes, peppers, onions, etc. [t. F, t. Sp.: m. *criollo* native to the locality, t. Pg.: m. *crioulo,* der. *criar* bring up, g. L *creāre* create]

cre·o·lized (krē′ə līzd′), *adj.* (of a language) having become a jargon and then passed into use as a native language, as the English used by many Negroes of Dutch Guiana.

Cre·on (krē′ŏn), *n. Gk. Legend.* king of Thebes, after the fall of Oedipus. See **Antigone.**

cre·o·sol (krē′ə sōl′, -sŏl′), *n. Chem.* a colorless oily liquid, $C_8H_{10}O_2$, with an agreeable odor and burning taste, resembling carbolic acid, obtained from wood tar and guaiacum resin. [t. CREOS(OTE) + -OL²]

cre·o·sote (krē′ə sōt′), *n., v.,* -**soted,** -**soting.** —*n.* **1.** an oily liquid with a burning taste and a penetrating odor, obtained by the distillation of wood tar, and used as a preservative and antiseptic. **2.** coal-tar creosote. —*v.t.* **3.** to treat with creosote. [f. *creo-* (comb. form repr. Gk. *kréas* flesh + m. Gk. *sōtḗr* savior] —**cre·o·sot·ic** (krē′ə sŏt′ĭk), *adj.*

creosote bush, a zygophyllaceous evergreen shrub, *Covillea tridentata* (or *Larrea mexicana*), of northern Mexico and adjacent regions, bearing resinous foliage with a strong odor of creosote.

crepe (krāp), *n., v.,* **creped, creping.** —*n.* **1.** a thin, light fabric of silk, cotton, or other fiber, with a finely crinkled or ridged surface. **2.** Also, **crepe paper.** thin paper wrinkled to resemble crepe. **3.** a black (or white) silk fabric, used for mourning veils, trimmings, etc. **4.** a band or piece of this material, as for a token of mourning. —*v.t.* **5.** to cover, clothe, or drape with crepe. Also, **crêpe, crape.** [t. F, g. L *crispus* curled]

crepe de Chine (krāp′ də shēn′), a light, soft, thin silk or rayon fabric with minute irregularities of surface. [t. F: china crape]

crêpe su·zette (krāp′ sōō zĕt′), a thin dessert pancake usually rolled with hot orange or tangerine sauce, often flavored with curaçao or other liqueurs.

crep·i·tant (krĕp′ə tənt), *adj.* crackling.

crep·i·tate (krĕp′ə tāt′), *v.i.,* -**tated,** -**tating.** to make a crackling sound; crackle; rattle. [t. L: m. s. *crepitātus,* pp.] —**crep′i·ta′tion,** *n.*

crept (krĕpt), *v.* pt. and pp. of **creep.**

cre·pus·cu·lar (krĭ pŭs′kyə lər), *adj.* **1.** of, pertaining to, or resembling twilight; dim; indistinct. **2.** *Zool.* appearing or flying in the twilight.

cre·pus·cule (krĭ pŭs′kūl), *n.* twilight; dusk. [t. F, t. L: m. *crepusculum*]

cres., *Music.* crescendo (def. 3). Also, **cresc.**

cres·cat sci·en·ti·a vi·ta ex·co·la·tur (krĕs′kȧt sĭ ĕn′shĭ ə vī′tȧ ĕks′kō lā′tər), *Latin.* where knowledge increases life is ennobled.

cre·scen·do (krə shĕn′dō, -sĕn′dō; *It.* krĕ shĕn′dô), *n., pl.* -**dos** (-dōz; *It.* -dôs), *adj., adv.* —*n.* **1.** a gradual increase in force or loudness. **2.** *Music.* a crescendo passage. —*adj., adv.* **3.** gradually increasing in force or loudness. [It., ppr. of *crescere* increase, g. L *crescere*] —**Ant. 2.** diminuendo.

cres·cent (krĕs′ənt), *n.* **1.** the convexo-concave figure of the moon in its first quarter, or the similar figure of the moon in its last quarter, resembling a bow terminating in points. See diag. under **moon. 2.** a representation of this. **3.** the emblem of the Turkish Empire. **4.** the Turkish or Mohammedan power. **5.** any crescent-shaped object. **6.** a musical percussion instrument of Turkish origin used in military bands, consisting of a crescent-shaped metal plate hung with a set of little bells. **7.** *Chiefly Brit.* a curved street. —*adj.* **8.** shaped like the moon in its first quarter. **9.** increasing; growing. [t. L: s. *crescens,* ppr., increasing; r. ME *cressant,* t. OF: m. *creissant* (later *croissant*), ppr.]

cre·scit e·un·do (krĕs′ĭt ē ŭn′dō), *Latin.* it grows as it goes (motto of New Mexico). Lucretius, *De Rerum Natura* VI, 341.

cres·cive (krĕs′ĭv), *adj.* increasing; growing.

cre·sol (krē′sōl, -sŏl), *n. Chem.* any one of three isomeric methyl phenols, $CH_3C_6H_4OH$, occurring in coal tar and wood tar. [var. of CREOSOL]

cress (krĕs), *n.* **1.** any of various plants of the mustard family with pungent-tasting leaves, often used for salad and as a garnish, esp. the water cress. **2.** any of various similar plants. [ME and OE *cresse,* c. G *kresse*]

cres·set (krĕs′ĭt), *n.* a metal cup often mounted on a pole or suspended from above, containing oil, pitch, etc., which is burned for light or as a beacon. [ME, t. OF]

Cres·si·da (krĕs′ə də), *n.* a new character developed, in medieval redactions of the Troy story, out of Chryseis and Briseis and made the lover of the Trojan Troilus, who is deserted for the Greek Diomedes.

Cres·sy (krĕs′ĭ), *n.* Crécy.

cress·y (krĕs′ĭ), *adj.* abounding in cresses.

crest (krĕst), *n.* **1.** a tuft or other natural growth of the top of an animal's head, as the comb of a cock. **2.** anything resembling or suggesting such a tuft. **3.** the ridge of the neck of a horse, dog, etc. **4.** the mane growing from this ridge. **5.** a plume or other ornament on the top of a helmet. **6.** a helmet. **7.** the apex of a helmet. **8.** *Her.* a figure borne above the escutcheon in a coat of arms, and also used separately as a distinguishing device. **9.** the head or top of anything. **10.** the highest part of a hill or mountain range. **11.** a ridge or ridgelike formation. **12.** the foamy top of a wave.

Cresset

13. the highest or best of the kind. **14.** pride; high spirit; courage; daring. **15.** *Archit.* a cresting. —*v.t.* **16.** to furnish with a crest. **17.** to serve as a crest for; crown or top. **18.** to reach the crest or summit of (a hill, etc.). —*v.i.* **19.** to form or rise into a crest, as a wave. [ME *creste*, t. OF, g. L *crista* tuft] —**crest′ed,** *adj.* —**crest′less,** *adj.*

crested auklet, a small diving bird, *Aethia crista-tella,* found in various parts of the north Pacific Ocean.

crested flycatcher, a North American flycatcher. *Myiarchus crinitus,* famous for its use of castoff snake-skin as nest material.

crest·fall·en (krĕst′fô′lən), *adj.* **1.** dejected; dispir-ited; depressed. **2.** with drooping crest. —**crest′-fall′en·ly,** *adv.* —**crest′fall′en·ness,** *n.*

crest·ing (krĕs′tĭng), *n.* *Archit.* the ornamental part which surmounts a roof ridge, wall, etc.

cre·ta·ceous (krĭ tā′shəs), *adj.* **1.** of the nature of, resembling, or containing chalk. **2.** (*cap.*) *Stratig.* per-taining to a geological period or a system of rocks suc-ceeding the Jurassic and preceding the Tertiary. —*n.* **3.** (*cap.*) *Stratig.* the period or system comprising the youngest or uppermost part of the Mesozoic. [t. L: m. *crētāceus* chalklike]

Cre·tan (krē′tən), *adj.* **1.** of or pertaining to the island of Crete or its inhabitants. —*n.* **2. a native or in-habitant of Crete,** esp. one of the indigenous Grecian popu-lation of Crete.

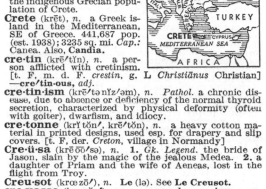

Crete (krēt), *n.* a Greek is-land in the Mediterranean, SE of Greece. 441,687 pop. (est. 1938); 3235 sq. mi. *Cap.:* Canea. Also, **Candia.**

cre·tin (krē′tĭn), *n.* a per-son afflicted with cretinism. [t. F, m. d. F. *crestin,* g. L *Christiānus* Christian] —**cre′tin·ous,** *adj.*

cre·tin·ism (krē′tə nĭz′əm), *n.* *Pathol.* a chronic dis-ease, due to absence or deficiency of the normal thyroid secretion, characterized by physical deformity (often with goiter), dwarfism, and idiocy.

cre·tonne (krĭ tŏn′, krē′tŏn), *n.* a heavy cotton ma-terial in printed designs, used esp. for drapery and slip covers. [t. F, der. *Creton,* village in Normandy]

Cre·ü·sa (krē ōō′sə), *n.* **1.** *Gk. Legend.* the bride of Jason, slain by the magic of the jealous Medea. **2.** a daughter of Priam and the wife of Aeneas, lost in the flight from Troy.

Creu·sot (krœ zō′), *n.* **Le** (lə). See **Le Creusot.**

cre·vasse (krə văs′), *n., v.,* **-vassed, -vassing.** —*n.* **1.** a fissure or deep cleft in the ice of a glacier. **2.** *U.S.* a breach in an embankment or levee. —*v.t.* **3.** to fissure with crevasses. [t. F. See CREVICE.]

Crève·coeur (krĕv kœr′), *n.* **Michel Guillaume Jean de** (mē shĕl′ gē yôm′ zhäN də), (*J. Hector St. John Crèvecoeur*) 1735–1813, French writer and agriculturist who became an American citizen.

crev·ice (krĕv′ĭs), *n.* a crack forming an opening; a cleft; a rift; a fissure. [ME *crevace,* t. OF, der. *crever* burst, g. L *crepāre* crack] —**crev′iced,** *adj.*

crew[1] (krōō), *n.* **1.** a group of persons engaged upon a particular work: *a train crew.* **2.** *Naut.* **a.** the company of men who man a ship or boat. **b.** the common sailors of a ship's company. **c.** a particular gang of a ship's company. **3.** any force or band of armed men. **4.** (often in derogatory use) a company; crowd. [late ME *crue,* t. OF: m. *creue* increase, ult. der. L *crescere* grow]

crew[2] (krōō), *v.* pt. of **crow[2].**

crew·el (krōō′əl), *n.* a kind of worsted yarn used for embroidery, etc. —**crew′el·work′,** *n.*

crib (krĭb), *n., v.,* **cribbed, cribbing.** —*n.* **1.** a child's bed with enclosed sides. **2.** a stall or pen for cattle. **3.** a rack or manger for fodder, as in a stable or house for cattle. **4.** a small house. **5.** a small room. **6.** any confined space. **7.** *Thieves' Slang.* a house, shop, etc. **8.** a wicker basket. **9.** any of various frameworks, as of logs or timbers, used in construction work. **10.** the wooden lining on the inside of a shaft. **11.** a bin for storing grain, salt, etc. **12.** *Colloq.* a petty theft, pla-giarism, etc. **13.** *Brit. Colloq.* a translation or other il-licit aid used by students. Cf. *U.S.* **pony** (def. 3). **14.** *Cribbage.* a set of cards made up by equal contributions from each player's hand, and belonging to the dealer. —*v.t.* **15.** to confine in, or as in, a crib. **16.** to provide with a crib or cribs. **17.** to line with timber or planking. **18.** *Colloq.* to pilfer or steal, as a passage from an author. —*v.i.* **19.** *Colloq.* to use a crib. **20.** to crib-bite. [OE *crib(b),* c. G *krippe*]

crib·bage (krĭb′ĭj), *n.* a game at cards, basically for two, but also played by three, or four players, a char-acteristic feature of which is the crib. [f. CRIB + -AGE]

crib·ber (krĭb′ər), *n.* **1.** one who cribs. **2.** a horse that practices cribbing.

crib·bing (krĭb′ĭng), *n.* **1.** Also, **crib-biting.** wind sucking by horses, an injurious habit in which the animal bites his manger and in the process swallows air. **2.** *Mining.* **a.** timber lining, closely spaced, as in a shaft or raise. **b.** pieces of timber for lining a shaft, raise, etc.

crib-bite (krĭb′bīt′), *v.i.,* **-bit, -bitten** or **-bit, -biting.** to practice cribbing, as a horse. —**crib′-bit′er,** *n.*

crib·ri·form (krĭb′rə fôrm′), *adj.* sievelike. Also, **crib·rous** (krĭb′rəs). [f. s. L *crībrum* sieve + -(I)FORM]

crib·work (krĭb′wûrk′), *n.* structural work consisting of layers of logs or beams one above another, with the logs of each layer at right angles to those below.

Crich·ton (krī′tən), *n.* **James,** ("the *Admirable Crich-ton*") 1560?–82, young Scottish scholar, poet, and ad-venturer who spoke many languages.

crick[1] (krĭk), *n.* **1.** a sharp, painful spasm of the muscles, as of the neck or back, making it difficult to move the part. —*v.t.* **2.** to give a crick or wrench to (the neck, etc.). [orig. uncert.]

crick[2] (krĭk), *n.* *U.S. Dial.* creek (def. 1).

crick·et[1] (krĭk′ĭt), *n.* any of the orthopterous insects comprising the family *Gryllidae,* characterized by their long antennae, ability to leap, and the ability of the males to pro-duce shrill sounds by friction of their leath-ery forewings. [ME *criket,* t. OF: m. *cri-quet;* ult. imit.]

House cricket. *Gryllus domesticus*

crick·et[2] (krĭk′ĭt), *n.* **1.** an open-air game played with ball, bats, and wickets, by two sides of eleven players each. **2.** *Colloq.* fair play. —*v.i.* **3.** to play cricket. [cf. OF *criquet* stick] —**crick′et·er,** *n.*

crick·et[3] (krĭk′ĭt), *n.* small, low stool. [orig. obscure]

cri·coid (krī′koid), *Anat.* —*adj.* **1.** having the shape of a seal ring: applied to a cartilage at the lower part of the larynx. —*n.* **2.** the cricoid cartilage. [t. Gk.: m.s. *krikoeidēs* ring-shaped]

cri·er (krī′ər), *n.* **1.** one who cries. **2.** a court or town official who makes public announcements. **3.** a hawker.

Crile (krīl), *n.* **George Washington,** 1864–1943, U.S. surgeon.

crim., criminal.

crime (krīm), *n.* **1.** an act committed or an omission of duty, injurious to the public welfare, for which pun-ishment is prescribed by law, imposed in a judicial pro-ceeding usually brought in the name of the state. **2.** serious violation of human law: *steeped in crime.* **3.** any offense, esp. one of grave character. **4.** serious wrong-doing; sin. **5.** *Colloq.* a foolish or senseless act: *it's a crime to have to work so hard.* [ME, t. OF, t. L: m.s. *crīmen* offense]

—**Syn. 2.** CRIME, OFFENSE, SIN agree in meaning a break-ing of law. CRIME usually means any serious violation of human laws: *the crime of treason, of robbery.* OFFENSE is used of an infraction of either human or divine law, and does not necessarily mean a serious one: *an offense leading to a jail sentence, an offense against morals.* SIN means a serious break-ing of moral or divine law: *the sin of hating one's neighbor.*

Cri·me·a (krī mē′ə, krī′-), *n.* **1.** a large peninsula in the SW Soviet Union, separat-ing the Black Sea from the Sea of Azov. **2.** an autono-mous republic of the Soviet Union coextensive with this peninsula. 1,126,824 pop. (1939); ab. 10,000 sq. mi. *Cap.:* Simferopol. Official name, **Crimean Autonomous Soviet Socialist Repub-lic.** —**Cri·me′an,** *adj.*

Crime and Punishment, a novel (1866) by Feodor Dostoevski.

Crimean War, a war between Great Britain, France, Turkey, and Sardinia on one side, and Russia on the other, chiefly in the Crimea, fought 1853–56.

crim·i·nal (krĭm′ə nəl), *adj.* **1.** of or pertaining to crime or its punishment: *criminal law.* **2.** of the nature of or involving crime. **3.** guilty of crime. —*n.* **4.** a per-son guilty or convicted of a crime. [t. L: s. *crīminālis*] —**crim′i·nal·ly,** *adv.* —**Syn. 2.** felonious, unlawful, il-legal, nefarious, flagitious, iniquitous, wicked, sinful, wrong. **4.** convict, malefactor, evildoer, transgressor, culprit. —**Ant. 2.** lawful. **3.** innocent.

criminal conversation, *Law.* adultery; illicit in-tercourse with a married woman, or, more recently, with a married man.

crim·i·nal·i·ty (krĭm′ə năl′ə tĭ), *n., pl.* **-ties. 1.** quality of being criminal. **2.** a criminal act or practice.

crim·i·nate (krĭm′ə nāt′), *v.t.,* **-nated, -nating. 1.** to charge with a crime. **2.** to incriminate. **3.** to censure (an act, etc.) as criminal; condemn. [t. L: m.s. *crīmin-ātus,* pp., accused] —**crim′i·na′tion,** *n.*

crim·i·na·tive (krĭm′ə nā′tĭv), *adj.* tending to or in-volving crimination; accusatory. Also, **crim·i·na·to·ry** (krĭm′ə nə tôr′ĭ).

crim·i·nol·o·gy (krĭm′ə nŏl′ə jĭ), *n.* the science deal-ing with the causes and treatment of crimes and crim-inals. [f. s. L *crīmen* crime + -(o)LOGY] —**crim·i·no-log·i·cal** (krĭm′ə nə lŏj′ə kəl), *adj.* —**crim′i·nol′o-gist,** *n.*

crim·mer (krĭm′ər), *n.* krimmer.

crimp[1] (krĭmp), *v.t.* **1.** to press into small regular folds; make wavy. **2.** to bend (leather) into shape. **3.** *Cookery.* to gash (the flesh of a live fish or of one just killed) with a knife to make it more crisp when cooked. —*n.* **4.** an act of crimping. **5.** crimped condition or form. **6.** (*usually pl.*) something crimped, as a lock of hair. **7.** the wavi-ness of wool fibers as naturally grown on sheep. **8.** a crease formed in sheet metal or plate metal to make the material less flexible, or for fastening purposes. **9. put a crimp in,** *Colloq.* to hinder. [OE *gecrympan* curl (der.

b., blend of, blended; **c.,** cognate with; **d.,** dialect, dialectal; **der.,** derived from; **f.,** formed from; **g.,** going back to; **m.,** modification of; **r.,** replacing; **s.,** stem of; **t.,** taken from; **?,** perhaps.   See the full key on inside cover.

crump crooked), c. LG *krümpen*, Dan. *krympe* shrink]
—**crimp′er**, *n.*

crimp² (krĭmp), *n.* **1.** an agent who procures seamen, soldiers, etc., by inducing, swindling, or coercing them. —*v.t.* **2.** to procure (seaman, soldiers, etc.) by such means. [special use of CRIMP¹]

crim·ple (krĭm′pəl), *v.i., v.t.,* **-pled, -pling.** to wrinkle, crinkle, or curl. [freq. of CRIMP¹]

crimp·y (krĭm′pĭ), *adj.,* **crimpier, crimpiest.** of a crimped form or appearance.

crim·son (krĭm′zən), *adj.* **1.** deep purplish-red. **2.** sanguinary. —*n.* **3.** a crimson color, pigment, or dye. —*v.t.* **4.** to make crimson. [ME *cremesin*, t. early It.: m. *cremesino*, der. *chermisi*, or t. Sp.: m. *cremesin*, der. *carmesi*; both t. Ar.: m. *qirmizī*]

cringe (krĭnj), *v.,* **cringed, cringing,** *n.* —*v.i.* **1.** to shrink, bend, or crouch, esp. from fear or servility; cower. **2.** to fawn. —*n.* **3.** servile or fawning obeisance. [ME *crengen*, der. OE *cringan* yield, fall (in battle). See CRINKLE, CRANK] —**cring′er,** *n.* —**cring′ing·ly,** *adj.*

crin·gle (krĭng′gəl), *n.* *Naut.* a ring or eye of rope or the like, esp. on the edge of a sail. It is usually made up around a metal thimble or grommet. [t. LG: m. *kringel*, dim. of *kring* circle, ring]

cri·nite¹ (krī′nīt), *adj.* **1.** hairy. **2.** *Bot., Entomol.* having long hairs, or tufts of long, weak hairs. [t. L: m. *crīnītus*, pp., provided with hair]

cri·nite² (krī′nīt, krĭn′īt), *n.* a fossil crinoid. [f. m. s. Gk. *krīnon* lily + -ITE¹]

crin·kle (krĭng′kəl), *v.,* **-kled, -kling,** *n.* —*v.t.* *v.i.* **1.** to wind or turn in and out. **2.** to wrinkle; crimple; ripple. **3.** to make slight, sharp sounds; rustle. —*n.* **4.** a turn or twist; a wrinkle; a ripple. **5.** a crinkling sound. [ME; freq. of OE *crincan* bend, yield. See CRINGE, CRANK] **crin′kly,** *adj.*

Cringle

crin·kle-root (krĭng′kəl rōōt′, -rŏŏt′), *n.* any of several species of the North American cruciferous perennials (genus *Dentaria*), esp. *Dentaria diphylla.*

crin·kum-cran·kum (krĭng′kəm krăng′kəm), *n.* *Colloq.* something full of twists and turns.

cri·noid (krī′noid, krĭn′oid), *adj.* **1.** lilylike. —*n.* **2.** one of the *Crinoidea.* [t. Gk.: m. s. *krinoeidēs* lilylike]

Cri·noi·de·a (krī noi′dĭ·ə, krĭ-), *n. pl.* *Zool.* a class of echinoderms with radiating arms usually borne mouthside up on an attached stalk, including the sea lilies, feather stars, and numerous fossil forms.

Unstalked crinoid, feather star.
Antendon rosacea

crin·o·line (krĭn′ə lĭn, -lēn′), **1.** a petticoat of haircloth or some other stiff material, formerly worn by women under a full dress skirt. **2.** a hoop skirt. **3.** stiff coarse cotton material for interlining. [t. F, t. It.: m. *crinolino*, f. *crino* hair + *lino* thread]

cri·num (krī′nəm), *n.* any plant of the tropical and subtropical amaryllidaceous genus *Crinum*, comprising tall bulbous plants, usually with umbels of large, showy flowers. [NL, t. Gk.: m. *krīnon* lily]

cri·o·sphinx (krī′ə sfĭngks′), *n.* a sphinx with the head of a ram. [f. m. Gk. *krió*(s) ram + *sphinx* sphinx]

crip·ple (krĭp′əl), *n., v.,* **-pled, -pling.** —*n.* **1.** one who is partially or wholly deprived of the use of one or more of his limbs; a lame person. **2.** *U.S. Dial.* a dense thicket in swampy or low land. —*v.t.* **3.** to make a cripple of; lame. **4.** to disable; impair. [ME *cripel*, OE *crypel*; akin to CREEP] —**crip′pler,** *n.*

—**Syn.** 3, 4. CRIPPLE, DISABLE mean to injure permanently or temporarily, to a degree which interferes with normal activities. To CRIPPLE is to injure in such a way as to deprive of the use of a member, particularly a leg or arm: *a broken arm cripples but does not disable a judge.* DISABLE, a more general word, implies such illness, injury, or impairment as makes a person incapable of engaging in his normal activities: *disabled by an attack of malaria, by a wound.*

Cripple Creek, a city in central Colorado, in the heart of one of the world's richest gold-producing areas: gold rush, 1891. 853 (1950); 9600 ft. high.

Cripps (krĭps), *n.* **Sir Stafford,** born 1889, British statesman and socialist leader.

cri·sis (krī′sĭs), *n., pl.* **-ses** (-sēz) **1.** a decisive or vitally important stage in the course of anything; a turning point; a critical time or occasion: *a political crisis, a business crisis.* **2.** the point in a play or story at which hostile elements are most tensely opposed to each other. **3.** *Pathol.* **a.** the point in the course of a disease at which a decisive change occurs, leading either to recovery or to death. **b.** the change itself. [t. L, t. Gk.: m. *krisis* decision] —**Syn. 1.** climax, juncture, exigency, strait, pinch. See **emergency.**

crisp (krĭsp), *adj.* **1.** hard but easily breakable; brittle: *crisp toast.* **2.** firm and fresh: *crisp leaf of lettuce.* **3.** brisk; sharp; decided: *crisp manner, reply, etc.* **4.** lively; pithy; sparkling: *crisp repartee.* **5.** bracing; invigorating: *crisp air.* **6.** crinkled, wrinkled, or rippled, as skin or water. **7.** in small, stiff or firm curls; curly. —*v.t., v.i.* **8.** to make or become crisp. **9.** to curl. —*n.* **10.** *Brit.* a potato chip. [OE, t. L: s. *crispus* curled] —**crisp′ly,** *adv.* —**crisp′ness,** *n.*

cris·pate (krĭs′pāt), *adj.* crisped or curled. Also, **cris′pat·ed.** [t. L: m. s. *crispātus*, pp., curled]

cris·pa·tion (krĭs pā′shən), *n.* **1.** act of crisping or curling. **2.** state of being crisped. **3.** a slight contraction or undulation.

crisp·er (krĭs′pər), *n.* one who or that which crisps, corrugates, or curls.

Cris·pi (krēs′pē), *n.* **Francesco** (frän chě′skô), 1819–1901, prime minister of Italy, 1887–91, and 1893–96.

Cris·pin (krĭs′pĭn), *n.* **1. Saint,** fl. 3rd century A.D., patron saint of shoemakers. **2.** a shoemaker.

crisp·y (krĭs′pĭ), *adj.* **crispier, crispiest. 1.** brittle; crisp. **2.** curly or wavy. **3.** brisk.

cris·sal (krĭs′əl), *adj.* of or pertaining to the crissum.

criss·cross (krĭs′krôs′, -krŏs′), *adj.* **1.** in crossing lines; crossed; crossing; marked by crossings. —*n.* **2.** a crisscross mark, pattern, etc. **3.** tick-tack-toe. —*adv.* **4.** in a crisscross manner; crosswise. —*v.t., v.i.* **5.** to mark with or form crossing lines. [var. of CHRISTCROSS]

criss·cross-row (krĭs′krôs′ rō′, -krŏs′-), *n.* *Archaic or Dial.* christcross-row.

cris·sum (krĭs′əm), *n., pl.* **crissa** (krĭs′ə), **1.** *Ornith.* the region surrounding the cloacal opening beneath the tail of a bird. **2.** the feathers of this region collectively. [NL, der. L *crissāre* move the haunches]

cris·tate (krĭs′tāt), *adj.* **1.** having a crest; crested. **2.** forming a crest. Also, **cris′tat·ed.** [t. L: m. s. *cristātus*, der. *crista* CREST]

Cris·to·bal (krĭs tō′bəl; *Sp.* krēs tô′bäl), *n.* a seaport in the Canal Zone at the Atlantic end of the Panama Canal, adjacent to Colón. 414 (prelim. 1950).

cri·te·ri·on (krī tĭr′ĭ ən), *n., pl.* **-teria** (-tĭr′ĭ ə), **-terions.** a standard of judgment or criticism; an established rule or principle for testing anything. [t. Gk.: m. *kritērion* test, standard] —**Syn.** measure, test, law, touchstone. See **standard.**

crit·ic (krĭt′ĭk), *n.* **1.** a person skilled in judging the qualities or merits of some class of things, esp. of literary or artistic work. **2.** one who judges captiously or with severity; one who censures or finds fault. **3.** *Obs.* a critique. [t. L: s. *criticus*, t. Gk.: m. *kritikós* skilled in judging, decisive, critical (as n., a critic)] —**Syn. 1.** reviewer, censor, judge, connoisseur. **2.** censurer, carper.

crit·i·cal (krĭt′ə kəl), *adj.* **1.** inclined to find fault or to judge with severity. **2.** occupied with or skilled in criticism. **3.** involving skillful judgment as to truth, merit, etc.; judicial: *a critical analysis.* **4.** of or pertaining to critics or criticism: *critical essays.* **5.** pertaining to, or of the nature of, a crisis; of decisive importance with respect to the outcome; crucial: *the critical moment.* **6.** involving suspense, risk, peril, etc.; dangerous: *a critical shortage.* **7.** *Physics.* denoting a constant value, as of temperature, frequency, etc., at which one or more related properties of a substance undergo an abrupt change: *critical pressure.* **8.** *Math.* indicating a point at which some transition or change takes place. —**crit′i·cal·ly,** *adv.* —**crit′i·cal·ness,** *n.* —**Syn. 1.** captious, censorious, carping, faultfinding, caviling. **3.** discriminating, fastidious, nice, exact. **5.** decisive, climacteric. **6.** hazardous, precarious.

critical angle. 1. *Optics.* the limiting angle of incidence for total reflection. **2.** *Aeron.* the angle of attack at which there is a sudden change in the airflow around an airfoil with subsequent decrease in lift and increase in drag.

critical constants, *Physics.* the critical temperature, pressure, density, and volume of a substance.

critical pressure, *Physics.* the vapor tension of a liquid at the critical temperature.

critical temperature, *Physics.* the temperature above which a gas cannot be liquefied by pressure alone.

crit·ic·as·ter (krĭt′ĭk ăs′tər), *n.* an inferior or incompetent critic. [f. CRITIC + -ASTER¹]

crit·i·cism (krĭt′ə sĭz′əm), *n.* **1.** act or art of criticizing, esp. of criticizing literary or artistic work. **2.** act of passing judgment as to the merits of anything. **3.** act of passing severe judgment; censure; faultfinding. **4.** a critical comment, article, or essay; a critique. **5.** investigation of the text, origin, etc., of literary, esp. Biblical, documents: *textual criticism.* —**Syn. 3.** stricture, animadversion, reflection. **4.** See **review.**

crit·i·cize (krĭt′ə sīz′), *v.,* **-cized, -cizing.** —*v.i.* **1.** to make judgments as to merits and faults. **2.** to find fault. —*v.t.* **3.** to judge or discuss the merits and faults of. **4.** to find fault with. Also, *Brit.,* **crit′i·cise′.** —**crit′i·ciz′a·ble,** *adj.* —**crit′i·ciz′er,** *n.*

cri·tique (krĭ tēk′), *n.* **1.** an article or essay criticizing a literary or other work; a review. **2.** art or practice of criticism. [t. F, t. Gk.: m. *kritikē* the critical art, prop. fem. of *kritikós*]

crit·ter (krĭt′ər), *n.* *Dial.* creature.

croak (krōk), *v.i.* **1.** to utter a low, hoarse, dismal cry, as a frog or a raven. **2.** to speak with a low, hollow voice. **3.** to talk despondingly; forebode evil; grumble. **4.** *Slang.* to die. —*v.t.* **5.** to utter or announce by croaking. **6.** *Slang.* to kill. —*n.* **7.** act or sound of croaking. [back formation from OE *crācettan.* Cf. CREAK]

croak·er (krō′kər), *n.* **1.** one who or that which croaks. **2.** any of various sciaenoid fishes that make a croaking noise, esp. *Micropogon undulatus*, a 'ood fish common on the Atlantic coast of the southern U.S.

croak·y (krō′kĭ), *adj.* making a croaking sound. **2.** given to croaking.

Cro·at (krō′ăt), *n.* **1.** a native or inhabitant of Croatia; a Croatian. **2.** Croatian (def. 3).

Cro·a·tia (krō ā′shə, -shĭ ə), *n.* a constituent republic of Yugoslavia, in the NW part: a medieval kingdom; now corresponding to the former Austrian crown land of **Croatia and Slavonia.** 3,360,500 pop. (1931); 19,817 sq. mi. *Cap.:* Zagreb.

Cro·a·tian (krō ā′shən, -shĭ ən), *adj.* **1.** of or pertaining to Croatia, the Croats, or their language. —*n.* **2.** a Croat. **3.** Serbo-Croatian.

Cro·ce (krō′chĕ), *n.* **Benedetto** (bĕ′nĕ dĕt′tô), born 1866, Italian statesman, philosopher, and historian.

cro·ce·in (krō′sĭ′ĭn), *n.* any of several acid azo dyes producing orange or scarlet colors. [f. s. L *croceus* saffron-colored + -IN²]

cro·chet (krō shā′), *n., v.,* **-cheted** (-shād′), **-cheting** (-shā′ĭng). —*n.* **1.** a kind of needlework done with a needle having at one end a small hook for drawing the thread or yarn into intertwined loops. **2.** the work or fabric so made. —*v.t., v.i.* **3.** to form by crochet. [t. F: hooked implement, dim. of OF *croc* hook]

cro·cid·o·lite (krō sĭd′ə līt′), *n.* a mineral of the amphibole group, essentially a sodium iron silicate, occurring in fibers of a delicate blue color, and appearing in altered form as the (golden-brown) tiger's-eye. [f. *crocido-* (comb. form repr. Gk. *krokís* nap, wool) + -LITE]

crock¹ (krŏk), *n.* **1.** an earthen pot, jar, or other vessel. **2.** a vessel of metal. [OE *croc(c)*, *crocca* pot. Cf. Icel. *krukka* jug]

crock² (krŏk), *n.* **1.** an old ewe. **2.** an old worn-out horse. **3.** *Brit. Slang.* or *Colloq.* a worn-out superannuated person. —*v.i.* **4.** *Brit. Slang.* to get injured (often fol. by *up*). [akin to CRACK, v.]

crock³ (krŏk), *n.* **1.** soot; smut. **2.** soil or marking from imperfectly dyed cloth. —*v...* **3.** to soil with crock. —*v.i.* **4.** to give off crock. [orig. uncert.]

crock·er·y (krŏk′ər ĭ), *n.* crocks or earthen vessels collectively; earthenware.

crock·et (krŏk′ĭt), *n. Archit.* a medieval ornament in the form of leafage curled out over a knot or knob placed on the angles of the inclined sides of pinnacles, under cornices, etc. [ME *croket*, t. AF. See CROCHET]

Crock·ett (krŏk′ĭt), *n.* **David,** 1786–1836, U.S. frontiersman and political figure, killed in the Texan defense of the Alamo.

crock·ing (krŏk′ĭng), *n. Textiles.* the surface dye which rubs off.

croc·o·dile (krŏk′ə dīl′), *n.* **1.** any of the large, thick-skinned reptiles, lizardlike in form, which constitute the genus *Crocodylus* (order *Crocodilia*), inhabiting the waters of tropical Africa, Asia, Australia, and America, esp. *C. niloticus* of the Nile. **2.** any animal of the order *Crocodilia*, including the alligators of America and the gavial of India. **3.** one who makes a hypocritical show of sorrow. **4.** *Brit. Colloq.* a file of persons, usually school girls, out for a walk. [t. L: m. s. *crocodīlus,* t. Gk.: m. *krokódeilos* lizard; r. ME *cocodrille,* t. OF]

Crocodile. *Crocodylus nilot cus* (16 ft long)

crocodile bird, an African plover, *Pluvianus aegyptius,* which often sits upon basking crocodiles and feeds on their insect parasites.

Crocodile River, Limpopo.

crocodile tears, 1. false or insincere tears, as the tears fabled to be shed by crocodiles over those they devour. **2.** hypocritical show of sorrow.

croc·o·dil·i·an (krŏk′ə dĭl′ĭ ən), *n.* **1.** any of the *Crocodilia,* an order of reptiles including the crocodiles, alligators, etc. —*adj.* **2.** of or pertaining to the crocodile. **3.** pertaining to the crocodilians. **4.** hypocritical.

cro·co·ite (krō′kōīt′), *n.* a mineral, lead chromate, PbCrO4. [f. m. Gk. *krokó(eis)* saffron-colored + -ITE¹]

cro·cus (krō′kəs), *n., pl.* **crocuses. 1.** any of the small bulbous plants constituting the iridaceous genus *Crocus,* much cultivated for their showy, solitary flowers. **2.** the flower or bulb of the crocus. **3.** a deep yellow; orangish yellow; saffron. **4.** a polishing powder consisting of iron oxide. [t. L, t. Gk.: m. *krókos* saffron]

Croe·sus (krē′səs), *n.* **1.** died 546 B.C., king of Lydia, 560–546 B.C., noted for his great wealth. **2.** a very rich man.

croft (krôft, krŏft), *n.* **1.** *Brit.* or *Scot.* a small piece of enclosed ground for tillage, pasture, etc. **2.** a very small agricultural holding, as one worked by a Scottish crofter. [OE. Cf. MD *kroft* field on high land]

croft·er (krôf′tər, krŏf′-), *n.* one who rents and tills a croft, as in parts of Scotland or northern England.

croix de guerre (krwä də gĕr′), a French military award for heroism in battle.

Cro-Mag·non (krō măg′nŏn; *Fr.* krō mà nyôn′), *adj. Anthropol.* belonging to a prehistoric race of Europe, believed to be of the same species as modern man. Remains found in the cave of Cro-Magnon in Dordogne, France, were characterized by a very long head, low face an l orbits, and tall stature.

Cro·mer (krō′mər), *n.* **Evelyn Baring, 1st Earl of,** 1841–1917, British statesman and diplomat.

crom·lech (krŏm′lĕk), *n. Archaeol.* **1.** a circle of upright stones or monoliths. **2.** a dolmen. [t. Welsh, f. *crom* bent, bowed + *llech* flat stone]

Cromp·ton (krŏmp′tən), *n.* **Samuel,** 1753–1827, British inventor of the spinning mule.

Crom·well (krŏm′wəl, -wĕl, krŭm′-), **1. Oliver,** 1599–1658, British general, Puritan statesman, and Lord Protector of the Commonwealth, 1653–58. **2.** his son, **Richard,** 1626–1712, British soldier, politician, Lord Protector of the Commonwealth, 1658–59. **3. Thomas,** (*Earl of Essex*) 1485?–1540, British statesman.

crone (krōn), *n.* an old woman. [t. MD: m. *croonje,* t. north. F: m. *carogne* carcass]

Cron·jé (krŏn′yä), *n.* **Piet Arnoldus** (pēt är nôl′dŏŏs), 1835?–1911, Boer general.

Cro·nus (krō′nəs), *n. Gk. Myth.* a Titan, son of Uranus and Gaea, who dethroned his father, and was dethroned by his own son Zeus. Saturn is his Roman counterpart. Also, **Cro·nos** (krō′nŏs), **Kronos.**

cro·ny (krō′nĭ), *n., pl.* **-nies.** an intimate friend or companion; a chum.

crook (krŏŏk), *n.* **1.** a bent or curved implement, piece, appendage, etc.; a hook; the hooked part of anything. **2.** an instrument or implement having a bent or curved part, as a shepherd's staff hooked at one end or as the crosier of a bishop or abbot. **3.** *Scot.* a pothook. **4.** act of crooking or bending. **5.** any bend, turn, or curve. **6.** *Colloq.* a dishonest person, esp. a sharper, swindler, or thief. **7.** a device on some musical wind instruments for changing the pitch, consisting of a piece of tubing inserted into the main tube. —*v.t.* **8.** to bend; curve; make a crook in. —*v.i.* **9.** to bend; curve. [ME *crok(e),* t. Scand.; cf. Icel. *krókr*]

crook·back (krŏŏk′băk′), *n.* a humpback. —**crook′-backed′,** *adj.*

crook·ed (krŏŏk′ĭd), *adj.* **1.** bent; not straight; curved. **2.** deformed. **3.** not straightforward or honest. [OE *gecrōcod*] —**crook′ed·ly,** *adv.* —**crook′ed·ness,** *n.* —**Syn. 1.** winding, devious, sinuous, flexuous, tortuous, spiral, twisted, askew, awry. **2.** misshapen. **3.** dishonest, unscrupulous, knavish, tricky, fraudulent. —**Ant. 1.** straight. **3.** honorable.

Crookes (krŏŏks), *n.* **Sir William,** 1832–1919, British chemist and physicist: discovered the element thallium and cathode rays.

Crookes space, *Physics.* the dark space in a vacuum tube between the cathode and the negative glow, occurring when pressure is very low. [named after Sir William CROOKES]

Crookes tube, a form of vacuum tube.

crook·neck (krŏŏk′nĕk′), *n. U.S.* a variety of squash with a long, recurved neck.

croon (krŏŏn), *v.i.* **1.** to sing softly, esp. with exaggerated feeling. **2.** to utter a low murmuring sound. **3.** *Scot. and N Eng.* to bellow; roar. —*v.t.* **4.** to sing softly, esp. with exaggerated feeling. —*n.* **5.** act or sound of crooning. [t. Scand.; cf. Icel. *krauna* murmur] —**croon′er,** *n.*

crop (krŏp), *n., v.,* **cropped, cropping.** —*n.* **1.** the cultivated produce of the ground, as grain or fruit, while growing or when gathered. **2.** the yield of such produce for a particular season. **3.** the yield of some other product in a season: *the ice crop.* **4.** a supply produced. **5.** the stock or handle of a whip. **6.** a short riding whip with a loop instead of a lash. **7.** an entire tanned hide of an animal. **8.** act of cropping. **9.** a mark produced by clipping the ears, as of an animal. **10.** a style of wearing the hair cut short. **11.** a head of hair so cut. **12.** an outcrop of a vein or seam. **13.** a special pouchlike enlargement of the gullet of many birds, in which food is held, and may undergo partial preparation for digestion. **14.** a digestive organ in other animals; the craw. —*v.t.* **15.** to cut off or remove the head or top of (a plant, etc.). **16.** to cut off the ends or a part of. **17.** to cut short. **18.** to clip the ears, hair, etc., of. **19.** to cause to bear a crop or crops. —*v.i.* **20.** to bear or yield a crop or crops. **21.** *Mining.* to come to the surface of the ground, as a vein of ore (usually fol. by *up* or *out*). **22.** to appear unintentionally or unexpectedly (fol. by *up* or *out*): *a new problem cropped up.* [OE *crop(p),* c. G *kropf;* orig. meaning protuberance. See CROUP²]

—**Syn. 1.** CROP, HARVEST, PRODUCE, YIELD refer to the return in food for men and animals obtained from land at the end of a season of growth. CROP, the term common in agricultural and commercial use, denotes the amount produced at one cutting or for one particular season: *the wheat crop, potato crop.* HARVEST denotes either the time of reaping and gathering, or the gathering, or that which is gathered: *the season of harvest; to work in a harvest; a ripe harvest.* PRODUCE esp. denotes household vegetables: *produce from the fields and gardens was taken to market.* YIELD emphasizes what is given by the land in return for expenditure of time and labor: *there was a heavy yield of grain this year.*

crop-eared (krŏp′ĭrd′), *adj.* **1.** having the ears cropped. **2.** having the hair cropped short, so that the ears are conspicuous.

crop·per (krŏp′ər), *n.* **1.** one who or that which crops. **2.** one who raises a crop. **3.** one who cultivates land for its owner in return for part of the crop. **4.** *Colloq.* a heavy fall, esp. from a horse: *to come a cropper.* **5.** a failure; collapse. **6.** a plant which furnishes a crop. **7.** a cloth-shearing machine.

cro·quet (krō kā′; *Brit.* krō′kā, -kǐ), *n.*, *v.*, -queted (-kād′; *Brit.* -kād, -kǐd), -queting (-kā′ǐng; *Brit.* -kā-ǐng, -kǐ ǐng). —*n.* **1.** an outdoor game played by knocking wooden balls through a series of iron arches by means of mallets. **2.** (in this game) act of driving away an opponent's ball by striking one's own when the two are in contact. —*v.t.* **3.** to drive away (a ball) by a croquet. [t. d. F: hockey stick]

cro·quette (krō kĕt′), *n.* a small mass of minced meat or fish, or of rice, potato, or other material, often coated with beaten egg and bread crumbs, and fried in deep fat. [t. F, der. *croquer* crunch]

crore (krōr), *n. India.* ten millions; one hundred lacs: *a crore of rupees.* [t. Hind.: m. k(a)rōr, g. Prakrit *krodi*]

cro·sier (krō′zhər), *n.* **1.** the pastoral staff of a bishop or an abbott, hooked at one end like a shepherd's crook. See illus. under **cope.** **2.** *Bot.* the circinate young frond of a fern. Also, **crozier.** [short for *crosier-staff* staff carried by the *crosier* crossbearer (t. F: m. *crosier* = ML *crociārius* crookbearer)]

cross (krôs, krŏs), *n.* **1.** a structure consisting essentially of an upright and a transverse piece, upon which persons were formerly put to death. **2. the Cross,** the cross upon which Jesus died. **3.** a figure of the cross as a Christian emblem, badge, etc. **4.** the cross as the symbol of Christianity. **5.** a small cross with a human figure attached to it, as a representation of Jesus crucified; a crucifix. **6.** the sign of the cross made with the right hand as an act of devotion. **7.** a structure or monument in the form of a cross, set up for prayer, as a memorial, etc. **8.** any of various conventional representations or modifications of the Christian emblem as used symbolically or for ornament, as in heraldry, art, etc.: *a Latin, Greek, St. George's, or Maltese cross.* **9.** the crucifixion of Jesus as the culmination of His redemptive mission. **10.** any suffering borne for Jesus' sake. **11.** the teaching of redemption gained by Jesus' death. **12.** Christian religion, or those who accept it; Christianity; Christendom. **13.** any object, figure, or mark resembling a cross, as two intersecting lines. **14.** such a mark made instead of a signature by a person unable to write. **15.** a fourway joint or connection used in pipe fitting, the connections being at right angles. **16.** a crossing. **17.** a place of crossing. **18.** an opposing; thwarting. **19.** any misfortune; trouble. **20.** a crossing of animals or plants; a mixing of breeds. **21.** an animal, plant, breed, etc. produced by crossing; a crossbreed. **22.** something intermediate in character between two things. **23.** *Slang.* a contest the result of which is dishonestly arranged beforehand. **24. the Southern Cross,** Crux, a constellation. —*v.t.* **25.** to make the sign of the cross upon or over, as in devotion. **26.** to mark with a cross. **27.** to cancel by marking with a cross or with a line or lines. **28.** to place in the form of a cross or crosswise. **29.** to put or draw (a line, etc.) across. **30.** to set (a yard, etc.) in position across a mast. **31.** to lie or pass across; intersect. **32.** to move, pass, or extend from one side to the other side of (a street, river, etc.). **33.** to transport across something. **34.** to meet and pass. **35.** *Archaic.* to encounter. **36.** to oppose; thwart. **37.** *Biol.* to cause (members of different genera, species, breeds, varieties, or the like) to produce offspring; cross-fertilize. —*v.i.* **38.** to lie or be athwart; intersect. **39.** to move, pass, extend from one side or place to another. **40.** to meet and pass. **41.** to interbreed. —*adj.* **42.** lying or passing crosswise or across each other; athwart; transverse; *cross beams, streets, etc.* **43.** involving interchange; reciprocal. **44.** contrary; opposite. **45.** adverse; unfavorable. **46.** ill-humored; snappish: *a cross word.* **47.** crossbred; hybrid. **48.** *Slang.* dishonest. [ME and OE *cros*, t. OIrish, t. L: m. *crux* (Icel. *kross*, also, t. OIrish or ? t. OE)] —**cross′·ly,** *adv.* —**cross′-ness,** *n.*

—**Syn. 36.** baffle, frustrate, foil, contradict. **46.** petulant, fractious, irascible, waspish, crabbed, churlish, sulky, cantankerous. CROSS, ILL-NATURED, PEEVISH, SULLEN refer to being in a bad mood or ill temper. CROSS means temporarily in an irritable or fretful state, and sometimes somewhat angry: *a cross reply, cross and tired.* ILL-NATURED implies a more permanent condition, without definite cause, and means unpleasant, unkind, inclined to snarl or be spiteful: *an ill-natured dog, ill-natured spite.* PEEVISH means complaining and snappish: *a peevish and whining child.* SULLEN suggests a kind of glowering silent gloominess and means refusing to speak because of bad humor, anger, or a sense of injury or resentment: *sullen and vindictive.* —**Ant. 36.** aid. **46.** good-natured.

Cross (krôs, krŏs), *n.* **Wilbur Lucius,** 1862–1948, U.S. educator: governor of Connecticut, 1931–39.

Forms of crosses

A. Latin cross; B. Tau cross or St. Anthony's cross; C. Cross of Calvary; D. Cross of Lorraine; E. Patriarchal cross; F. St. Andrew's cross; G. Greek cross, or St. George's cross; H. Papal cross; I. Maltese cross.

cross-, a first element of compounds, modifying the second part, meaning: **1.** going across: *crossroad.* **2.** counter: *cross-examination.* **3.** marked with a cross: *hot cross buns.* **4.** cruciform: *crossbones,* etc.

cross·bar (krôs′bär′, krŏs′-), *n.* a transverse bar, line, or stripe.

cross-bed·ded (krôs′bĕd′ǐd, krôs′-), *adj.* *Geol.* having irregular laminations, as strata of sandstone, inclining in various directions not coincident with the general stratification.

cross bench, *Brit.* a set of seats at the back of the halls of both houses of Parliament for those who belong neither to the government nor to opposition parties.

cross·bill (krôs′bǐl′, krŏs′-), *n.* any bird of the fringilline genus *Loxia,* characterized by mandibles curved so that the tips cross each other when the bill is closed.

cross·bones (krôs′bōnz′, krŏs′-), *n.pl.* two bones placed crosswise, usually below a skull, symbolizing death.

cross·bow (krôs′bō′, krŏs′-), *n.* an old weapon for shooting missiles, consisting of a bow fixed transversely on a stock having a groove or barrel to direct the missile. —**cross·bow·man** (krôs′bō′mən, krŏs′-), *n.*

cross·bred (krôs′brĕd′, krŏs′-), *adj.* **1.** produced by crossbreeding. —*n.* **2.** an animal or group of animals produced by hybridization.

cross·breed (krôs′brēd′, krŏs′-), *v.*, -bred, -breeding, *n.* —*v.t.* **1.** to produce (a hybrid) within a species, using two breeds or varieties. —*v.i.* **2.** to undertake or engage in hybridizing, esp. within a single species. —*n.* **3.** a crossbred.

cross bun, *Chiefly Brit.* a bun marked with a cross, eaten esp. on Good Friday.

cross-coun·try (krôs′kŭn′trǐ, krŏs′-), *adj.* **1.** directed across fields or open country; not following the roads or the great highways. **2.** from one end of the country to the other: *a cross-country flight.*

cross·cut (krôs′kŭt′, krŏs′-), *adj.*, *n.*, *v.*, -cut, -cutting. —*adj.* **1.** made or used for cutting crosswise: *a crosscut saw.* **2.** cut across the grain or on the bias: *crosscut crepe.* —*n.* **3.** a direct course between two points, as one diagonal to a main way. **4.** a transverse cut or course. **5.** *Mining.* an underground passageway, usually from shaft to a vein of ore or crosswise of a vein of ore. —*v.t.* **6.** to cut across.

crosscut saw, a saw used for sawing lumber in a direction perpendicular to the axis of the tree.

crosse (krôs, krŏs), *n.* a long-handled racket used in the game of lacrosse. [t. F; of Gmc. orig.]

cross-ex·am·ine (krôs′ǐg zăm′ǐn, krŏs′-), *v.t.*, -ined, -ining. **1.** to examine by questions intended to check a previous examination; examine closely or minutely. **2.** to examine (a witness called by the opposing side), as for the purpose of disproving his testimony. —**cross-ex·am·i·na·tion** (krôs′ǐg zăm′ə nā′shən, krŏs′-), *n.* —**cross′-ex·am′in·er,** *n.*

cross-eye (krôs′ī′, krŏs′-), *n.* strabismus, esp. the form in which both eyes turn toward the nose. —**cross′-eyed′,** *adj.*

cross-fer·ti·li·za·tion (krôs′fûr′tə lə zā′shən, krŏs′-), *n.* **1.** *Biol.* the fertilization of an organism by the fusion of an egg from one individual with a sperm (or male gamete) of a different individual. **2.** *Bot.* fertilization of one flower or plant by pollen from another (opposed to *self-fertilization*).

cross-fer·ti·lize (krôs′fûr′tə līz′, krŏs′-), *v.t.* -lized, -lizing. to cause the cross-fertilization of.

cross fire, *Mil.* lines of fire from two or more positions, crossing one another, or a single one of such lines.

cross-grained (krôs′grānd′, krŏs′-), *adj.* **1.** having the grain running transversely or diagonally, or having an irregular or gnarled grain, as timber. **2.** perverse.

cross hairs, fine wires, or strands of spider web or other material, crossing in a focal plane of an optical instrument, serving to define a line of sight.

cross-hatch (krôs′hăch′, krŏs′-), *v.t.* to hatch or shade with two or more intersecting series of parallel lines. —**cross′hatch′ing,** *n.*

cross·head (krôs′hĕd′, krŏs′-), *n.* **1.** *Print.* a title or heading filling a line or group of lines the full width of the column. **2.** the sliding and bearing member of a Diesel, steam, or gas engine, between the piston rod and the connecting rod.

cross·ing (krôs′ǐng, krŏs′ǐng), *n.* **1.** act of one who or that which crosses. **2.** a place where lines, tracks, etc., cross each other. **3.** the intersection of nave and transept in a cruciform church. **4.** a place at which a road, river, etc., may be crossed. **5.** act of opposing or thwarting; contradiction.

crossing over, *Biol.* the interchange of corresponding chromatid segments of homologous chromosomes with their linked genes.

cross·jack (krôs′jăk′, krŏs′-; *Naut.* krô′jǐk, krŏj′ǐk), *n.* *Naut.* a square sail on the lower yard of a mizzenmast. See illus. under **sail.**

cross-leg·ged (krôs′lĕg′ǐd, -lĕgd′, krŏs′-), *adj.* having the legs crossed; having one leg laid across the other.

cross·let (krôs′lǐt, krŏs′-), *n.* *Chiefly Heraldry.* a small cross.

cros·sop·te·ryg·i·an (krŏ sŏp′tə rǐj′ǐ ən), *n.* any fish of the group *Crossopterygii,* all fossil except *Latimeria chalumnae,* supposed to be ancestral to amphibians and other land vertebrates.

act, āble, dâre, ärt; ĕbb, ēqual; ǐf, īce; hŏt, ōver, ôrder, oil, bŏŏk, ōoze, out; ŭp, ūse, ûrge; ə = a in alone; ch, chief; g, give; ng, ring; sh, shoe; th, thin; ᵗħ, that; zh, vision. See the full key on inside cover.

cross·o·ver (krôs′ō′vər, krŏs′-), n. Biol. 1. crossing over. 2. a genotype resulting from crossing over.
cross·patch (krôs′păch′, krŏs′-), n. Colloq. an ill-humored person.
cross·piece (krôs′pēs′, krŏs′-), n. a piece of any material placed across something; a transverse piece.
cross·pol·li·nate (krôs′pŏl′ə nāt′, krŏs′-), v.t., -nat-ed, -nating, cross-fertilize. —**cross′-pol′li·na′tion**, n.
cross·pur·pose (krôs′pûr′pəs, krŏs′-), n. 1. an opposing or counter purpose. 2. **be at cross-purposes**, to misunderstand another's, or each other's, purpose, or act under such a misunderstanding. 3. (pl.) a kind of conversational game in which words are taken in different senses.
cross·ques·tion (krôs′kwĕs′chən, krŏs′-), v.t. 1. to cross-examine. —n. 2. a question asked by way of cross-examination.
cross·re·fer (krôs′rĭ fûr′, krŏs′-), v.t., v.i., -ferred, -ferring. to refer by a cross reference.
cross reference, a reference from one part of a book, etc., to a word, item, etc., in another part.
cross relation, Music. a relationship between two successive tones in different voices which normally occurs in one voice; false relation.
cross·road (krôs′rōd′, krŏs′-), n. 1. a road that crosses another road, or one that runs transversely to main roads. 2. a by-road. 3. (often pl., construed as sing.) the place where roads intersect.
cross·ruff (krôs′rŭf′, krŏs′-), n. Whist. a play in which each hand of a partnership trumps a different suit; a seesaw.
cross section, 1. a section made by a plane cutting anything transversely, esp. at right angles to the longest axis. See diag. under **section**. 2. a piece so cut off. 3. act of cutting anything across. 4. a typical selection; a sample showing all characteristic parts, etc.: a cross section of American opinion. 5. Survey. a vertical section of the ground surface taken at right angles to a survey line.
cross·stitch (krôs′stĭch′, krŏs′-), n. 1. a kind of stitching employing pairs of diagonal stitches of the same length crossing each other in the middle at right angles. —v.t., v.i. 2. to work in cross-stitch.
cross street, a street crossing another street, or one running transversely to main streets.
cross talk, 1. interference in a telephone or radio channel from one or more other telephone channels. 2. Brit. Parliament. an interchange of remarks across the hall between members of different parties.
cross·tie (krôs′tī′, krŏs′-), n. U.S. a timber placed transversely to form a foundation or support.
cross·town (krôs′toun′, krŏs′-), adj. U.S. that runs across the town: a cross-town bus.
cross·tree (krôs′trē′, krŏs′-), n. Naut. one of the horizontal transverse pieces of timber or metal fastened to the head of a lower mast or topmast in order to support the top, spread the shrouds, etc.
cross·way (krôs′wā′, krŏs′-), n. a cross-road.
cross wind, a wind blowing at right angles to the line of flight of an aircraft.
cross·wise (krôs′wīz′, krŏs′-), adv. 1. across; transversely. 2. in the form of a cross. 3. contrarily. Also, **cross·ways** (krôs′wāz′, krŏs′-).

C. Crosstree

cross·word puzzle (krôs′wûrd′, krŏs′-), a puzzle in which words corresponding to given meanings are to be supplied and fitted into a particular figure divided into spaces, the letters of the words being arranged across the figure, or vertically, or sometimes otherwise.
crotch (krŏch), n. 1. a forked piece, part, support, etc. 2. a forking or place of forking, as of the human body between the legs. [var. of CRUTCH] —**crotched** (krŏcht), adj.
crotch·et (krŏch′ĭt), n. 1. a small hook. 2. a hooklike device or part. 3. Entomol. a small hooklike process. 4. a curved surgical instrument with a sharp hook. 5. an odd fancy or whimsical notion. 6. Chiefly Brit. Music. a quarter note. See illus. under **note**. [ME crochet, t. OF. See CROCHET]
crotch·et·y (krŏch′ĭt ĭ), adj. 1. given to crotchets or odd fancies; full of crotchets. 2. of the nature of a crotchet. —**crotch·et·i·ness**, n.
cro·ton (krō′tən), n. 1. any of the chiefly tropical euphorbiaceous plants constituting the genus Croton, many species of which, as C. tiglium, have important medicinal properties. 2. (among florists) any plant of the related genus Codiaeum (or Phyllaurea) cultivated for the ornamental foliage. [NL, t. Gk.: m. krotōn a tick, also a plant having ticklike seeds]
Cro·ton bug (krō′tən), the common cockroach, Blatella germanica. [from the Croton Aqueduct water, introduced into New York City in 1842]
cro·ton·ic acid (krō tŏn′ĭk, -tō′nĭk), Chem. a colorless, crystalline compound, CH₃CHCHCOOH, used in organic synthesis.
croton oil, a powerful purgative oil from Croton tiglium (**croton-oil plant**), a euphorbiaceous shrub or tree of the East Indies.

crouch (krouch), v.i. 1. to stoop or bend low. 2. to bend close to the ground, as an animal preparing to spring, or shrinking with fear. 3. to bow or stoop servilely; cringe. —v.t. 4. to bend low. —n. 5. act of crouching; a stooping or bending low. [ME crouche(n), t. OF: m. crochir become bent, der. croche hook]
croup¹ (krōōp), n. Pathol. any affection of the larynx or trachea characterized by a hoarse cough and difficult breathing. [f. croup, v. (now dial.) cry hoarsely, b. CROAK and WHOOP]
croup² (krōōp), n. the rump or buttocks of certain animals, esp. of a horse. [ME croupe, t. F. Gmc.; cf. CROP]
crou·pi·er (krōō′pĭ ər; Fr. krōō pyĕ′), n. 1. an attendant who collects and pays the money at a gaming table. 2. one who at a public dinner sits at the lower end of the table as assistant chairman. [t. F; orig., one who rides behind on the croup of another's horse]
croup·ous (krōō′pəs), adj. Pathol. pertaining to, of the nature of, or resembling croup.
croup·y (krōō′pĭ), adj. 1. pertaining to or resembling croup. 2. affected with croup.
crouse (krōōs), adj. Scot. and N. Eng. bold; brisk; lively. [ME crus, crous(e), prob. t. Fris.: m. krus cocky, wild, etc.]
Crouse (krous), n. Russel, born 1893, U. S. dramatist and author.
crou·ton (krōō′tŏn), n. a small piece of fried or toasted bread, used in soups, etc. [t. F, der. croûte. See CRUST]
crow¹ (krō), n. 1. certain of the oscine birds constituting the genus Corvus (family Corvidae), with lustrous black plumage and a characteristic harsh cry of "caw", as the **carrion crow** (C. corone) of Europe and the **American crow** (C. brachyrhynchos). 2. certain birds of the family Corvidae, as the chough, or **Cornish crow**, Pyrrhocorax graculus. 3. any of various similar birds of other families, as the **pied crow** of Australia. 4. Astron. the southern constellation Corvus. 5. a crowbar. 6. **as the crow flies**, in a straight line. 7. **eat crow**, to be compelled to do or say something extremely unpleasant or humiliating. 8. **have a crow to pick with**, to have an unpleasant matter to discuss with. [ME; OE crāwe. See CROW,² v.]

American crow,
Corvus brachyrhynchos
(17 to 19 in. long)

crow² (krō), v., **crowed** (or **crew** for 1), **crowed**, **crowing**, n. —v.i. 1. to utter the characteristic cry of a cock. 2. to utter an inarticulate cry of pleasure, as an infant does. 3. to exult loudly; boast. —n. 4. the characteristic cry of the cock. [ME crowe(n), OE crāwan, c. D kraaien, G krähen; imit.]
Crow (krō), n. 1. a North American Indian Plains tribe, belonging to the Siouan linguistic stock, located in eastern Montana. 2. a member of this tribe. 3. a Siouan language closely related to Hidatsa. [trans. (through F gens de corbeaux) of their own name. Absaroke crow, sparrow-hawk, or bird people]
crow·bar (krō′bär′), n. a bar of iron, often with a wedge-shaped end, for use as a lever, etc.
crow·ber·ry (krō′bĕr′ĭ), n., pl. -ries. 1. the insipid black or reddish berry of an evergreen heathlike shrub, Empetrum nigrum, of northern regions. 2. the plant itself, of the family Empetraceae. 3. any of certain other fruits or the plants bearing them, as the bearberry.
crow blackbird, any of several North American birds of the genus Quiscalus (family Icteridae), as Q. quiscula, the purple grackle, noted for iridescent black plumage and trough-shaped tails.
crowd¹ (kroud), n. 1. a large number of persons gathered closely together; a throng. 2. any large number of persons. 3. people in general; the masses: far from the madding crowd's ignoble strife. 4. any group or set of persons: a jolly crowd. 5. a large number of things gathered or considered together. 6. Sociol. a group of persons acting together only through temporary stimulus, having no past or future continuity. [n. use of v.] —v.i. 7. to gather in large numbers; throng; swarm. 8. to press forward; advance by pushing. —v.t. 9. to push; shove. 10. to press closely together; force into a confined space. 11. to fill to excess; fill by crowding or pressing into. 12. Colloq. to urge; press by solicitation; annoy by urging: to crowd a debtor for immediate payment. 13. **crowd on sail**, Naut. to carry a press of sail. [ME crowde(n), OE crūdan, c. MD kruyden]
—**Syn.** 1. CROWD, MULTITUDE, SWARM, THRONG are terms referring to large numbers of people. CROWD suggests a jostling, uncomfortable, and possibly disordered company: a crowd gathered to listen to the speech. MULTITUDE emphasizes the great number of persons or things but suggests that there is space enough for all: a multitude of people at the market on Saturdays. SWARM as used of people is usually contemptuous, suggesting a moving, restless, often noisy, crowd: a swarm of dirty children played in the street. THRONG suggests a company that presses together or forward, often with some common aim: the throng pushed forward to see the cause of the excitement. 3. populace, commonalty 10. compress, pack, cram, squeeze, cramp. —**Ant.** 7. scatter.
crowd² (kroud), n. an ancient Celtic musical instrument related to the kithara, but bowed. [ME crowde, t. Welsh: m. crwth]

b., blend of, blended; c., cognate with; d., dialect, dialectal; der., derived from; f., formed from; g., going back to; m., modification of; r., replacing; s., stem of; t., taken from; ?, perhaps. See the full key on inside cover.

crowd·ed (krou′dĭd), *adj.* **1.** filled to excess; filled with a crowd; packed: *crowded streets.* **2.** uncomfortably close together: *crowded passengers on a bus.* —**crowd′ed·ly,** *adv.* —**crowd′ed·ness,** *n.*

crow·foot (krō′fŏŏt′), *n., pl.* **-foots** for 1 and 2, **-feet** for 3 and 4. **1.** any plant of the genus *Ranunculus,* esp. one with divided leaves suggestive of a crow's foot; a buttercup. **2.** any of various other plants with leaves or other parts suggestive of a bird's foot, as certain species of the genus *Geranium.* **3.** caltrop. **4.** *Naut.* a device consisting of small diverging lines or cords rove through a block of wood, used for suspending awnings, etc.

crow·keep·er (krō′kē′pər), *n.* *Now Dial.* a scare-crow.

crown (kroun), *n.* **1.** an ornamental wreath or garland for the head, conferred by the ancients as a mark of victory or distinction. **2.** honorary distinction; reward. **3.** a decorative fillet or covering for the head, worn as a symbol of sovereignty. **4.** the power or dominion of a sovereign. **5. the Crown,** the sovereign as head of the state, or the supreme governing power of a state under a monarchical government. **6.** any crownlike emblem or design, used in a heraldic crest, as a badge of rank in some armies, etc. **7.** a coin generally bearing a crown or a crowned head on the reverse. The English crown is worth five shillings. **8.** a krone or a krona. **9.** something having the form of a crown, as the corona of a flower. **10.** *Bot.* **a.** the leaves and living branches of a tree. **b.** the point at which the root of a seed plant joins the stem. **c.** a circle of appendages on the throat of the corolla, etc.; corona. **11.** the top or highest part of anything, as of the head, a hat, a mountain, etc. **12.** the head itself: *he broke his crown.* **13.** the crest, as of a bird. **14.** *Dentistry.* **a.** that part of a tooth which is covered by enamel. **b.** an artificial substitute, as of gold or porcelain, for the crown of a tooth. **15.** the highest or most perfect state of anything. **16.** an exalting or chief attribute. **17.** the acme or supreme source of honor, excellence, beauty, etc. **18.** crown glass. **19.** *Naut.* the part of an anchor where the arms join the shank. **20.** the part of a cut gem above the girdle. —*v.t.* **21.** to place a crown or garland upon the head of. **22.** to invest with a regal crown, or with regal dignity and power. **23.** to honor as with a crown; reward; invest with honor, dignity, etc. **24.** to surmount as with a crown; surmount as a crown does. **25.** to complete worthily; bring to a successful or effective conclusion. **26.** *Checkers.* to change (a checker) into a king after it has safely reached the last row by putting another piece on top of it. [ME *croune, coroune,* t. AF, g. L *corōna* garland, wreath, crown. Cf. CORONA] —**crown′er,** *n.*

crown colony, a colony in which the crown has the entire control of legislation and administration, as distinguished from one having a constitution and representative government.

crown·er (krou′nər, krōō′-), *n.* *Brit. Dial.* coroner.

crown glass, 1. an optical glass of low dispersion and generally low refractive index. **2.** an old form of window glass formed by blowing a globe and whirling it into a disk; composed essentially of soda, lime, and silica.

crown graft, *Hort.* a graft in which the scion is inserted at the crown of the stock.

crown land, 1. land belonging to the crown, the revenue of which goes to the reigning sovereign. **2.** Also, **crown′land′.** one of the provinces, or great administrative divisions of the former empire of Austria-Hungary.

crown·piece (kroun′pēs′), *n.* a piece or part forming or fitting the crown or top of anything.

Crown Point, a village in NE New York, on Lake Champlain: the site of a strategic fort in the French and Indian and Revolutionary wars.

crown prince, the heir apparent of a monarch.

crown princess, the wife of a crown prince.

crown saw, a rotary saw consisting of a hollow cylinder with teeth on its end or edge, as the surgeons' trephine.

crown wheel, *Horol.* a wheel next to the crown, having two sets of teeth, one at right angles to its plane.

crown·work (kroun′wûrk′), *n.* *Fort.* an outwork containing a central bastion with a curtain and demi-bastions, usually designed to cover some advantageous position.

crow's-foot (krōz′fŏŏt′), *n., pl.* **-feet. 1.** (*usually pl.*) a wrinkle at the outer corner of the eye. **2.** *Aeron.* a method by which one main cord exerts pressure or pull at several points simultaneously through smaller ropes. **3.** *Tailoring.* a three-pointed embroidered figure used as a finish, as at the end of a seam or opening.

crow's-nest (krōz′nĕst′), *n.* *Naut.* **1.** a box or shelter for the lookout man, secured near the top of a mast. **2.** a similar lookout station ashore.

Croy·don (kroi′dən), *n.* a city in SE England, near London: airport. 234,640 (est. 1946).

croze (krōz), *n.* **1.** the groove at the ends of the staves of a barrel, cask, etc., into which the edge of the head fits. **2.** a tool for cutting such a groove. [cf. F *creux* groove]

cro·zier (krō′zhər), *n.* crosier.

cru·ces (krōō′sēz), *n.* pl. of **crux.**

cru·cial (krōō′shəl), *adj.* **1.** involving a final and supreme decision; decisive; critical: *a crucial experiment.*

2. severe; trying. **3.** of the form of a cross; cross-shaped. [f. *cruci-* (t. L, comb. form of *crux* cross) + -AL¹] —**cru′-cial·ly,** *adv.*

cru·ci·ate (krōō′shĭ·ĭt, -āt′), *adj.* **1.** cross-shaped. **2.** *Bot.* having the form of a cross with equal arms, as the flowers of mustard, etc. **3.** *Entomol.* crossing each other diagonally in repose, as the wings of an insect. [t. NL: m. s. *cruciātus,* der. L *crux* CROSS]

Cruciate flower

cru·ci·ble (krōō′sə·bəl), *n.* **1.** a vessel of metal or refractory material employed for heating substances to high temperatures. **2.** (in a metallurgical furnace) the hollow part at the bottom, in which molten metal collects. **3.** a severe, searching test. [t. ML: m.s. *crucibulum* night lamp, melting pot; this ? m. *crucibolum* whale oil cruse (cf. L *bālaena* whale). See CRUSE]

crucible steel, steel made in a crucible, esp. a high-grade steel prepared by melting selected materials.

cru·ci·fer (krōō′sə·fər), *n.* **1.** one who carries a cross, as in ecclesiastical processions. **2.** *Bot.* a cruciferous plant. [t. LL]

cru·cif·er·ous (krōō·sĭf′ər·əs), *adj.* **1.** bearing a cross. **2.** *Bot.* belonging or pertaining to the family *Cruciferae* or *Brassicaceae,* whose members bear flowers having a crosslike, four-petaled corolla; brassicaceous. [f. LL *crucifer* cross-bearing + -OUS]

cru·ci·fix (krōō′sə·fĭks), *n.* **1.** a cross with the figure of Jesus crucified upon it. **2.** any cross. [ME, t. LL: s. *crucifixus,* pp., fixed to a cross]

cru·ci·fix·ion (krōō·sə·fĭk′shən), *n.* **1.** act of crucifying. **2.** (*cap.*) the death of Jesus by exposure upon a cross. **3.** a picture or other representation of this.

cru·ci·form (krōō′sə·fôrm′), *adj.* cross-shaped. [f. s. L *crux* cross + -(I)FORM] —**cru′ci·form′ly,** *adv.*

cru·ci·fy (krōō′sə·fī′), *v.t.,* **-fied, -fying. 1.** to put to death by nailing or binding the body to a cross. **2.** to torment; treat with severity. **3.** to subdue (passion, sin, etc.). [ME *crucifien,* t. OF: m. *crucifier,* t. LL: m. *crucifīgere* fix to a cross. See -FY]

crud (krŭd), *v.t., v.i.,* **crudded, crudding.** *Obs. or Dial.* to curd. [metathetic var. of CURD]

crude (krōōd), *adj.,* **cruder, crudest. 1.** in a raw or unprepared state; unrefined: *crude oil, sugar, etc.* **2.** unripe; not mature. **3.** lacking finish, polish, proper arrangement, or completeness: *a crude summary.* **4.** lacking culture, refinement, tact, etc.: *crude persons, behavior, speech,* etc. **5.** undisguised; blunt; bare: *a crude answer.* [ME, t. L: m. s. *crūdus* raw, crude, rough. Cf. CRUEL] —**crude′ly,** *adv.* —**crude′ness,** *n.* —**Syn. 1.** unfinished. See **raw. 2.** undeveloped. **3.** unpolished. **4.** uncouth, rough, rude, coarse, clumsy. —**Ant. 4.** cultivated.

cru·di·ty (krōō′də·tĭ), *n., pl.* **-ties. 1.** state or quality of being crude. **2.** an instance of this; anything crude.

cru·el (krōō′əl), *adj.* **1.** disposed to inflict suffering; indifferent to, or taking pleasure in, the pain or distress of another; hard-hearted; pitiless. **2.** causing, or marked by, great pain or distress: *a cruel remark.* [ME, t. OF, g. L *crūdēlis* hard, cruel, akin to *crūdus* CRUDE] —**cru′el·ly,** *adj.* —**cru′el·ness,** *n.* —**Syn. 1.** barbarous, bloodthirsty, ferocious, merciless, relentless, implacable. CRUEL, PITILESS, RUTHLESS, BRUTAL, SAVAGE imply readiness to cause pain to others, and being unmoved by their suffering. CRUEL implies willingness to cause pain, and indifference to suffering: *a cruel stepfather, cruel to animals.* PITILESS adds the idea of hard-heartedness and positive refusal to show compassion: *pitiless to captives, fate that seems pitiless.* RUTHLESS implies cruelty and unscrupulousness, letting nothing stand in one's way, and using any methods necessary: *ruthless in pressing an advantage, ruthless greed.* BRUTAL implies cruelty which takes the form of physical violence: *a brutal master.* SAVAGE suggests fierceness and brutality: *savage ba tles, jealousy.* —**Ant. 1.** kind, sympathetic, compassionate.

cru·el·ty (krōō′əl·tĭ), *n., pl.* **-ties. 1.** state or quality of being cruel. **2.** cruel disposition or conduct. **3.** a cruel act. —**Syn. 1.** harshness, brutality, ruthlessness, barbarity, inhumanity, atrocity. —**Ant. 2, 3.** kindness.

cru·et (krōō′ĭt), *n.* a glass bottle, esp. one for holding vinegar, oil, etc., for the table. [ME, t. OF, dim. of *crue* pitcher, pot, t. Gmc.; cf. G *krug* pot]

Cruik·shank (krŏŏk′shăngk′), *n.* **George,** 1792–1878, British artist and caricaturist.

cruise (krōōz), *v.,* **cruised, cruising,** *n.* —*v.i.* **1.** to sail to and fro, or from place to place, as in search of hostile ships, or for pleasure. **2.** *Colloq.* to move hither and thither on land. —*v.t.* **3.** to cruise over. —*n.* **4.** act of cruising; a voyage made by cruising. [t. D: m. *kruisen* cross, cruise, der. *kruis* cross]

cruis·er (krōō′zər), *n.* **1.** one who or that which cruises, as a person or a ship. **2.** one of a class of warships of medium tonnage, designed for high speed and long cruising radius. **3.** a boat, usually power-driven, adapted for pleasure trips.

cruis·ing (krōō′zĭng), *adj.* *Aeron.* of or denoting flight at practical rather than high speed: *cruising power.*

crul·ler (krŭl′ər), *n.* a light, sweet cake cut from a rolled dough and fried in deep hot fat, often having a ring-shaped or twisted form. Also, **kruller.** [f. m. LG *krull(koken)* + -ER¹]

crumb (krŭm), *n.* **1.** a small particle of bread, cake, etc., such as breaks or falls off. **2.** a small particle or portion of anything. **3.** the soft inner portion of a bread (distinguished from *crust*). —*v.t.* **4.** *Cookery.* to dress or prepare with bread crumbs; to bread. **5.** to break into crumbs or small fragments. Also, (formerly) **crum.** [ME *crumme*, OE *cruma*, akin to G *krume*]

crum·ble (krŭm′bəl), *v.*, **-bled, -bling,** *n.* —*v.t.* **1.** to break into small fragments or crumbs. —*v.i.* **2.** to fall into small pieces; break or part into small fragments. **3.** to decay; disappear piecemeal. —*n.* **4.** something crumbling or crumbled. **5.** *Now Dial.* a small or tiny crumb or fragment. [earlier *crimble,* freq. of OE *gecrymman* crumble (der. *cruma* crumb); assimilated in form to CRUMB]

crum·bly (krŭm′blĬ), *adj.,* **-blier, -bliest.** apt to crumble; friable.

crumb·y (krŭm′Ĭ), *adj.,* **crumbier, crumbiest. 1.** full of crumbs. **2.** soft.

crum·mie (krŭm′Ĭ, krŏŏm′Ĭ), *n.* a cow with crooked horns. Also, **crummy.** [der. obs. *crum* crooked, OE *crumb,* c. G *krumm*]

crum·my[1] (krŭm′Ĭ), *adj.,* **-mier, -miest.** *Slang.* very inferior, mean, or shabby.

crum·my[2] (krŭm′Ĭ, krŏŏm′Ĭ), *n., pl.* **-mies.** crummie.

crump (krŭmp, krŏŏmp), *v.t.* **1.** to crunch with the teeth. **2.** to strike heavily. —*v.i.* **3.** to make a crunching sound, as in walking over snow, or as snow when trodden on. —*n.* **4.** a crunching sound. **5.** a heavy blow. **6.** *Brit.* a soldiers' term for a large explosive shell.

crum·pet (krŭm′pĬt), *n. Chiefly Brit.* a kind of light, soft bread resembling a muffin, cooked on a griddle or the like, and often toasted. [short for *crumpet cake* curled cake, ME *crompid,* pp. of obs. *crump,* var. of CRIMP]

crum·ple (krŭm′pəl), *v.,* **-pled, -pling,** *n.* —*v.t.* **1.** to draw or press into irregular folds; rumple; wrinkle. —*v.i.* **2.** to contract into wrinkles; shrink; shrivel. **3.** *Colloq.* to collapse; give way. —*n.* **4.** an irregular fold or wrinkle produced by crumpling. [freq. of obs. *crump,* var. of CRIMP]

crunch (krŭnch), *v.t.* **1.** to crush with the teeth; chew with a crushing noise. **2.** to crush or grind noisily. —*v.i.* **3.** to chew with a crushing sound. **4.** to move or proceed with, a crushing noise. —*n.* **5.** act or sound of crunching. Also, **craunch.** [b. CRAUNCH and CRUSH]

cru·or (krŏŏ′ôr), *n.* coagulated blood, or that portion of the blood which forms the clot. [t. L: blood, gore]

crup·per (krŭp′ər, krŏŏp′-), *n.* **1.** a leather strap on the back of the saddle of a harness, and passing in a loop under a horse's tail, to prevent the saddle from slipping forward. See illus. under **harness. 2.** the rump or buttocks of a horse. [ME *cropere,* t. OF, der. *crope.* See CROUP[2]]

cru·ral (krŏŏr′əl), *adj.* **1.** of or pertaining to the leg or the hind limb. **2.** of or pertaining to the leg proper, or crus. [t. L: s. *crūrālis,* der. *crūs* leg]

crus (krŭs), *n., pl.* **crura** (krŏŏr′ə). **1.** *Anat., Zool.* **a.** that part of the leg or hind limb between the femur and thigh and the ankle or tarsus; the shank. **b.** a limb or process, as of a bone or other structure. **2.** any of various parts likened to a leg. [t. L: leg]

cru·sade (krŏŏ sād′), *n., v.,* **-saded, -sading.** —*n.* **1.** (*often cap.*) any of the military expeditions undertaken by the Christians of Europe in the 11th, 12th and 13th centuries for the recovery of the Holy Land from the Mohammedans. **2.** any war carried on under papal sanction. **3.** any vigorous, aggressive movement for the defense or advancement of an idea, cause, etc. —*v.i.* **4.** to go on or engage in a crusade. [b. earlier *crusada* (t. Sp.: m. *cruzada*) and *croisade* (t. F). See CROSS, -ADE[1]] —**cru·sad′er,** *n.*

cru·sa·do (krŏŏ sā′dō), *n., pl.* **-does, -dos.** an early Portuguese coin of gold or silver, bearing the figure of a cross. [t. Pg.: m. *cruzado,* prop. pp. of *cruzar* mark with a cross. Cf. CRUSADE]

cruse (krŏŏz, krŏŏs), *n.* an earthen pot, bottle, etc., for liquids. [t. MD]

crush (krŭsh), *v.t.* **1.** to press and bruise between two hard bodies; squeeze out of shape or normal condition. **2.** to break into small fragments or particles, as ore, stone, etc. **3.** to force out by pressing or squeezing. **4.** to drink (wine, etc.). **5.** to put down, overpower, or subdue completely; overwhelm. **6.** to oppress grievously. —*v.i.* **7.** to become crushed. **8.** to advance with crushing; press or crowd forcibly. —*n.* **9.** act of crushing. **10.** state of being crushed. **11.** *Colloq.* a large crowd; a crowded social gathering. [ME *crusch(en),* appar. t. OF: m. *croissir* crash, gnash, break, crush; prob. g. Gmc.] —**crush′er,** *n.* —**Syn. 1.** crumple, rumple. **2.** shatter, pulverize, mash. See **break. 5.** quell, subdue, overcome.

Cru·soe (krŏŏ′sō), *n.* **Robinson,** the shipwrecked seaman in Defoe's novel *Robinson Crusoe* (1719), who lives adventurously for years on a small uninhabited island.

crust (krŭst), *n.* **1.** the hard outer portion of a loaf of bread (distinguished from *crumb*). **2.** a piece of this. **3.** the outside covering of a pie. **4.** any more or less hard external covering or coating. **5.** the hard outer shell or covering of an animal or plant. **6.** the exterior portion of the earth, accessible to examination. **7.** a scab or eschar. **8.** deposit from wine, as it ripens, on the interior of bottles, consisting of tartar and coloring matter. —*v.t.* **9.** to cover with or as with a crust; encrust. **10.** to form (something) into a crust. —*v.i.* **11.** to form or contract a crust. **12.** to form into a crust. [ME, t. L: s. *crusta* rind; r. ME *crouste,* t. OF]

Crus·ta·ce·a (krŭs tā′shĬ ə, -shə), *n.pl.* See **crustacean.** [NL, neut. pl. of *crustāceus* hard-shelled]

crus·ta·cean (krŭs tā′shən), *adj.* **1.** belonging to the Crustacea, a class of (chiefly aquatic) arthropods, including the lobsters, shrimps, crabs, barnacles, wood lice, etc., commonly having the body covered with a hard shell or crust. —*n.* **2.** a crustacean animal.

crus·ta·ceous (krŭs tā′shəs), *adj.* **1.** of the nature of or pertaining to a crust or shell. **2.** belonging to the Crustacea. **3.** having a hard covering or crust.

crus·tal (krŭs′təl), *adj.* of or pertaining to a crust, as that of the earth.

crust·y (krŭs′tĬ), *adj.,* **crustier, crustiest. 1.** of the nature of or resembling a crust; having a crust. **2.** harsh; surly; crabbed: *a crusty person, manner, remark, etc.* —**crust′i·ly,** *adv.* —**crust′i·ness,** *n.*

crutch (krŭch), *n.* **1.** a staff or support to assist a lame or infirm person in walking, now usually with a crosspiece at one end to fit under the armpit. **2.** any of various devices resembling this in shape or use. **3.** a forked support or part. **4.** a forked rest for the legs in sidesaddle. **5.** the crotch of the human body. **6.** *Naut.* a forked support for the booms, when the sails are stowed. —*v.t.* **7.** to support on crutches; prop; sustain. [ME *crucche,* OE *crycc,* c. D *kruk* and G *krücke,* Cf. CROOK]

crutched (krŭcht), *adj.* having or bearing a cross: *a crutched friar.*

crux (krŭks), *n., pl.* **cruxes, cruces** (krŏŏ′sēz). **1.** a vital, basic, or decisive point. **2.** a cross. **3.** something that torments by its puzzling nature; a perplexing difficulty. [t. L: cross, torment, trouble]

Crux (krŭks), *n., gen.* **Crucis** (krŏŏ′sĬs). *Astron.* the Southern Cross.

crux an·sa·ta (krŭks′ ăn sā′tə), a T-shaped cross with a loop at the top; ankh. [L: cross with a handle]

cru·zei·ro (krŏŏ zâr′ō; *Port.* -zĕ′rô, -rŏŏ), *n., pl.* **-ros,** the gold unit of the Brazilian monetary system equivalent to a milreis, written Cr $1.00. [t. Pg., der. *cruz* cross]

cry (krī), *v.,* **cried, crying,** *n., pl.* **cries.** —*v.i.* **1.** to utter inarticulate sounds, esp. of lamentation, grief, or suffering, usually with tears. **2.** to weep; shed tears, with or without sound. **3.** to call loudly; shout. **4.** to give forth vocal sounds or characteristic calls, as animals; yelp; bark. —*v.t.* **5.** to utter or pronounce loudly; call out. **6.** to announce orally in public; sell by outcry. **7.** to beg for or implore in a loud voice. **8.** to disparage; belittle (fol. by *down*). **9.** to break a promise, agreement, etc. (fol. by *off*). **10.** to praise; extol (fol. by *up*). —*n.* **11.** act or sound of crying; any loud utterance or exclamation; a shout, scream, or wail. **12.** clamor; outcry. **13.** an entreaty; appeal. **14.** an oral proclamation or announcement. **15.** a call of wares for sale, etc., as by a street vendor. **16.** public report. **17.** an opinion generally expressed. **18.** a battle cry. **19.** a political or party slogan. **20.** a fit of weeping. **21.** the vocal utterance or characteristic call of an animal. **22.** a pack of hounds. [ME *crie(n),* t. OF: m. *crier,* g. L *quirītāre*] —**cry′ing·ly,** *adv.*

—**Syn. 1.** wail, bewail, weep, sob, squall, blubber, whimper, mewl, pule. **3.** clamor, vociferate, exclaim, ejaculate, bawl, scream, howl, yell, yowl. CRY, SHOUT, BELLOW, ROAR refer to kinds of loud articulate or inarticulate sounds. CRY is the general word: *to cry out.* To SHOUT is to raise the voice loudly in uttering words or other articulate sounds: *he shouted back to his companions.* BELLOW especially refers to the loud, deep cry of a bull, moose, etc., or, somewhat in deprecation, to human utterance which suggests such a sound: *the speaker bellowed his answer.* ROAR refers to a deep, hoarse, rumbling or vibrant cry; it often implies tumultuous volume: *the crowd roared approval.* **6.** proclaim, hawk. **11.** ejaculation, roar, howl, yell, whoop.

cry·ba·by (krī′bā′bĬ), *n., pl.* **-bies.** one given to crying like a baby, or to weak display of injured feeling.

cry·ing (krī′Ĭng), *adj.* **1.** that cries; clamorous; wailing; weeping. **2.** demanding attention or remedy: *a crying evil.* —**Syn. 2.** flagrant, notorious, urgent.

cryo-, a word element meaning "icy cold," "frost." [t. Gk.: m. *kryo-,* comb. form of *krýos*]

cry·o·gen (krī′ə jən), *n.* a substance for producing low temperatures; a freezing mixture.

cry·o·hy·drate (krī′ō hī′drāt), *n.* a mixture of ice and another substance in definite proportions such that a minimum melting or freezing point is attained.

cry·o·lite (krī′ə līt′), *n.* a mineral, sodium aluminum fluoride, Na$_3$AlF$_6$, occurring in white masses, used as a flux in the electrolytic production of aluminum and as an insecticide.

cry·om·e·ter (krī ŏm′ə tər), *n.* a thermometer for the measurement of low temperatures, as one containing alcohol instead of mercury.

cry·os·co·py (krī ŏs′kə pĬ), *n.* **1.** the determination of the freezing points of liquids or solutions, or of the lowering of the freezing points by dissolved substances. **2.** *Med.* the determination of the freezing points of certain bodily fluids, as urine, for diagnosis.

cry·o·stat (krī′ə stăt′), *n.* an apparatus, usually automatic, maintaining a very low constant temperature.

cry·o·ther·a·py (krī′ō thĕr′ə pĬ), *n. Med.* treatment by means of applications of ice.

crypt (krĬpt), *n.* **1.** a subterranean chamber or vault, esp. one beneath the main floor of a church, used as a burial place, etc. **2.** *Anat.* a slender pit or recess; a small glandular cavity. [t. L: s. *crypta,* t. Gk.: m. *kryptē,* prop. fem. of *kryptós* hidden]

---

b., blend of, blended; c., cognate with; d., dialect, dialectal; der., derived from; f., formed from; g., going back to; m., modification of; r., replacing; s., stem of; t., taken from; ?, perhaps. See the full key on inside cover.

cryp·tic (krĭp′tĭk), *adj.* **1.** hidden; secret; occult. **2.** *Zool.* fitted for concealing. Also, **cryp′ti·cal.** —**cryp′-ti·cal·ly,** *adv.*

crypto-, a word element meaning "hidden," as in *cryptoclastic.* Also, before vowels, **crypt-.** [comb. form repr. Gk. *kryptós*]

cryp·to·clas·tic (krĭp′tō klăs′tĭk), *adj. Petrog.* composed of fragments invisible to the unaided eye.

cryp·to·crys·tal·line (krĭp′tō krĭs′tə lĭn, -līn), *adj. Mineral.* indistinctly crystalline; having an indistinguishable crystalline structure.

cryp·to·gam (krĭp′tə găm′), *n. Bot.* **1.** any of the *Cryptogamia,* an old primary division of plants comprising those without true flowers and seeds, as the ferns, mosses, and thallophytes. **2.** a plant without a true seed (opposed to *phanerogam*). [back formation from NL *cryptogamia,* f. CRYPTO- + Gk. -*gamía* married state] —**cryp′to·gam′ic, cryp·tog·a·mous** (krĭp tŏg′ə məs), *adj.*

cryp·to·gen·ic (krĭp′tə jĕn′ĭk), *adj.* of obscure or unknown origin, as a disease.

cryp·to·gram (krĭp′tə grăm′), *n.* a message or writing in secret characters or otherwise occult; a cryptograph. —**cryp′to·gram′mic,** *adj.*

cryp·to·graph (krĭp′tə grăf′, -gräf′), *n.* **1.** a cryptogram. **2.** a system of secret writing; a cipher. **3.** a device for translating text into cipher.

cryp·tog·ra·phy (krĭp tŏg′rə fĭ), *n.* **1.** process or art of writing in secret characters or in cipher. **2.** anything so written. —**cryp·tog′ra·pher, cryp·tog′ra·phist,** *n.* —**cryp·to·graph·ic** (krĭp′tə grăf′ĭk), *adj.*

cryp·to·nym (krĭp′tə nĭm), *n.* a secret name. [f. CRYPT- + Gk. ónym(a) name]

cryp·ton·y·mous (krĭp tŏn′ə məs), *adj.* anonymous.

cryp·to·zo·ite (krĭp′tə zō′īt), *n. Parasitol.* the phase in the development of malaria parasites in their vertebrate hosts in which they live in cells other than red blood corpuscles.

cryst., crystallography. Also, **crystall.**

crys·tal (krĭs′təl), *n.* **1.** a clear, transparent mineral or glass resembling ice. **2.** the transparent form of crystallized quartz. **3.** *Chem., Mineral.* a solid body having a characteristic internal structure and enclosed by symmetrically arranged plane surfaces, intersecting at definite and characteristic angles. **4.** anything made of or resembling such a substance. **5.** a single grain or mass of a crystalline substance. **6.** glass of a high degree of brilliance. **7.** cut glass. **8.** the glass or plastic cover over the face of a watch. **9.** *Radio.* **a.** the piece of galena, carborundum, or the like, forming the essential part of a crystal detector. **b.** the crystal detector itself. **10.** a quartz crystal ground in the shape of a rectangular parallelepiped, which vibrates strongly at one frequency when electric voltages of that frequency are placed across opposite sides. It is used to control the frequency of an oscillator as for, example, the frequency of a radio transmitter. —*adj.* **11.** composed of crystal. **12.** resembling crystal; clear; transparent. **13.** *Radio.* pertaining to or employing a crystal detector. **14.** indicating the 15th event of a series, as a wedding anniversary. [ME *cristal,* t. OF; r. OE *cristalla,* t. L: m. *crystallum,* t. Gk.: m. *krýstallos* ice, crystal] —**crys′tal·like′,** *adj.*

crystal detector, *Radio.* a device for rectifying the alternating currents in a receiving apparatus, consisting essentially of a crystal, as of galena or carborundum, permitting a current to pass freely in one direction only.

crystal gazing, a steady staring at a crystal or glass ball or other clear object in order to arouse visual perceptions, as of distant happenings, the future, etc. —**crys·tal-gaz·er** (krĭs′təl gā′zər), *n.*

crystall-, var. of crystallo-, used before vowels.

crystall., crystallography.

crys·tal·lif·er·ous (krĭs′tə lĭf′ər əs), *adj.* bearing, containing, or yielding crystals. Also, **crys·tal·lig·er·ous** (krĭs′tə lĭj′ər əs). [f. s. L *crystallum* crystal + -(I)FEROUS]

crys·tal·line (krĭs′tə lĭn, -līn′), *adj.* **1.** of or like crystal; clear; transparent. **2.** formed by crystallization. **3.** composed of crystals, as rocks. **4.** pertaining to crystals or their formation. [ult. t. Gk.: m. *krystállinos*]

crystalline lens, *Anat.* a doubly convex, transparent, lenslike body in the eye, situated behind the iris and serving to focus the rays of light on the retina. See diag. under **eye.**

crys·tal·lite (krĭs′tə līt′), *n. Mineral.* a minute body in igneous rocks, marking an incipient stage in crystallization. [f. CRYSTALL- + -ITE[1]]

crys·tal·li·za·tion (krĭs′tə lə zā′shən), *n.* **1.** act of crystallizing; the process of forming crystals. **2.** a crystallized body or formation.

crys·tal·lize (krĭs′tə līz′), *v.* -lized, -lizing. —*v.t.* **1.** to form into crystals; cause to assume crystalline form. **2.** to give definite or concrete form to. —*v.i.* **3.** to form crystals; become crystalline in form. **4.** to assume definite or concrete form. —**crys′tal·liz′a·ble,** *adj.*

crystallo-, a word element meaning "crystal," as in *crystallographic.* Also, **crystall-.** [t. Gk.: m. *krystallo-,* comb. form of *krýstallos*]

crys·tal·lo·graph·ic (krĭs′tə lə grăf′ĭk), *adj.* of or pertaining to crystallography. Also, **crys′tal·lo·graph′i·cal.** —**crys′tal·lo·graph′i·cal·ly,** *adv.*

crys·tal·log·ra·phy (krĭs′tə lŏg′rə fĭ), *n.* the science

dealing with crystallization and the forms and structure of crystals. —**crys′tal·log′ra·pher,** *n.*

crys·tal·loid (krĭs′tə loid′), *adj.* **1.** resembling a crystal; of the nature of a crystalloid. —*n.* **2.** a substance (usually crystallizable), which, when dissolved in a liquid, will diffuse readily through vegetable or animal membranes (contrasted with *colloid*). **3.** *Bot.* one of certain minute crystallike granules of protein, found in the tissues of various seeds. [t. Gk.: m. s. *krystalloeidḗs.* See CRYSTAL, -OID] —**crys′tal·loi′dal,** *adj.*

crystal set, *Radio.* a tubeless receiving set with a crystal detector.

crystal violet, a dye derived from rosaniline used as an indicator in medicine and in Gram's method in bacteriology.

crystal vision, **1.** visual perception, as of distant happenings, the future, etc., supposed to be aroused by crystal gazing. **2.** that which seems to be perceived.

Cs, *Chem.* cesium.

C.S.A., Confederate States of America.

csc, cosecant.

C.S.T., Central Standard Time.

Ct., **1.** Connecticut. **2.** Count.

ct., **1.** cent. **2.** certificate. **3.** court.

cteno-, *Zool.* a word element referring to comblike scales, as in *ctenophore.* Also, before vowels, **cten-.** [t. Gk.: m. *kteno-,* comb form of *kteís* comb]

cte·noid (tē′noid, tĕn′oid), *adj. Zool.* **1.** comblike or pectinate; rough-edged. **2.** having rough-edged scales. [t. Gk.: m.s. *ktenoeidḗs* comb-shaped]

Cte·noph·o·ra (tĭ nŏf′ə rə), *n.pl.* a phylum of marine swimming invertebrates with rounded, oval or band-shaped gelatinous bodies and eight meridional rows of ciliated plates. —**cte·noph′o·ran,** *adj., n.*

cten·o·phore (tĕn′ə fôr′, tē′nə-), *n.* one of the Ctenophora or comb jellies.

Ctes·i·phon (tĕs′ə fŏn′), *n.* a ruined city in Iraq, on the Tigris, near Bagdad: an ancient capital of Parthia.

ctn, cotangent.

cts., **1.** cents. **2.** certificates.

Cu, cuprum.

cu., cubic.

cuar·ta (kwär′tə), *n. Southwestern U.S.* a long rawhide whip.

cub (kŭb), *n.* **1.** the young of certain animals, as the fox, bear, etc. **2.** *Humorous or Contemptuous.* an awkward or uncouth youth. **3.** *Colloq.* cub reporter. **4.** a member of the junior division (ages 8–11) of the Boy Scouts. [var. of COB] —**cub′bish,** *adj.* —**cub′bish·ness,** *n.*

Cu·ba (kū′bə; *Sp.* kōō′bä), *n.* a republic S of Florida, largest island in the West Indies. 4,778,583 pop. (1943); 44,218 sq. mi. *Cap.:* Havana. —**Cu′ban,** *adj., n.*

Cu·ba li·bre (kū′bə lē′brə), a drink consisting of rum and a kola drink.

cu·ba·ture (kū′bə chər), *n.* **1.** the determination of the cubic contents of a thing. **2.** cubic contents. [der. L *cubus* cube, on model of QUADRATURE]

cub·by (kŭb′ĭ), *n., pl.* -bies. a snug, confined place; a cubbyhole. [der. *cub* shed; cf. LG *kübje* shed]

cub·by·hole (kŭb′ĭ hōl′), *n.* a small enclosed space.

cube (kūb), *n., v.,* cubed, cubing. —*n.* **1.** a solid bounded by six equal squares, the angle between any two adjacent faces being a right angle. **2.** a piece of anything of this form. **3.** *Arith., Alg.* the third power of a quantity: *the cube of 4 is 4 × 4 × 4, or 64.* —*v.t.* **4.** to make into a cube or cubes. **5.** to measure the cubic contents of. **6.** to raise to the third power; find the cube of. [t. L: m.s. *cubus,* t. Gk.: m. *kýbos* die, cube]

cu·beb (kū′bĕb), *n.* the spicy fruit or drupe of an East Indian piperaceous climbing shrub, *Piper cubeba,* dried in an unripe but fully grown state, and used in the treatment of urinary and bronchial disorders. [ME *quibibe,* t. F: m. *cubèbe,* ult. t. Ar.: m. *kabāba*]

cube root, the quantity of which a given quantity is the cube: *4 is the cube root of 64.*

cu·bic (kū′bĭk), *adj.* **1.** of three dimensions, solid, or pertaining to solid content: *a cubic foot* (the volume of a cube whose edges are each a foot long). **2.** having the form of a cube. **3.** *Arith., Alg.,* etc., being of the third power or degree. **4.** *Crystall.* belonging or pertaining to the isometric system of crystallization. Also, **cu′bi·cal.** —**cu′bi·cal·ly,** *adv.* —**cu′bi·cal·ness,** *n.*

cu·bi·cle (kū′bə kəl), *n.* **1.** a bedroom, esp. one of a number of small ones in a divided dormitory, as in English public schools. **2.** any small space or compartment partitioned off. [t. L: m.s. *cubiculum* bedchamber]

cubic measure, **1.** the measurement of volume in cubic units. **2.** a system of such units, esp. that in which 1728 cubic inches = 1 cubic foot, 27 cubic feet = 1 cubic yard.

cu·bic·u·lum (kū bĭk′yə ləm), *n., pl.* -la (-lə). *Archaeol.* a burial chamber, as in catacombs. [t. L: bedroom]

cu·bi·form (kū′bə fôrm′), *adj.* formed like a cube.

cub·ism (kū′bĭz əm), *n. Art.* one of the aspects of post-impressionism, which aims to express the artist's emotions through arrangements on his canvas of geometrical forms in various colors and textures. —**cub′ist,** *n., adj.* —**cu·bis′tic,** *adj.* —**cu·bis′ti·cal·ly,** *adv.*

cu·bit (kū′bĭt), *n.* an ancient linear unit based on the length of the forearm, varying in extent, but usually from 17 to 21 inches. [ME, t. L: s. *cubitum* elbow, ell]

ăct, āble, dâre, ärt; ĕbb, ēqual; ĭf, īce; hŏt, ōver, ôrder, oil, bŏŏk, ōōze, out; ŭp, ūse, ûrge; ə = a in alone; ch, chief; g, give; ng, ring; sh, shoe; th, thin; ŧh, that; zh, vision. See the full key on inside cover.

cu·boid (kū′boid), *adj.* **1.** resembling a cube in form. **2.** *Anat.* noting or pertaining to the outermost bone of the distal row of tarsal bones. —*n.* **3.** *Math.* a rectangular parallelepiped. **4.** *Anat.* the cuboid bone. —**cuboi·dal**, *adj.*

cub reporter, *Colloq.* a reporter without experience.

cuck·ing stool (kŭk′ĭng), a former instrument of punishment consisting of a chair in which an offender, esp. a common scold, was strapped, to be jeered at and pelted by the crowd, or, sometimes, to be ducked.

cuck·old (kŭk′əld), *n.* **1.** the husband of an unfaithful wife. —*v.t.* **2.** to make a cuckold of (a husband). [ME *cokewold*; orig. uncert.]

cuck·old·ry (kŭk′əldrĭ), *n.* making a cuckold of one.

cuck·oo (kŏŏk′ŏŏ), *n., pl.* **-os,** *v.,* **-ooed, -ooing,** *adj.* —*n.* **1.** any bird of the family *Cuculidae,* esp. *Cuculus çanorus,* a common European migratory bird noted for its characteristic call, and for its loss of the instinct to build a nest. The females lay their eggs in the nests of various "host species," which rear the young cuckoos. **2.** the call of the cuckoo, or an imitation of it. **3.** a fool; simpleton. —*v.i.* **4.** to utter the call of the cuckoo or an imitation of it. —*v.t.* **5.** to repeat monotonously. —*adj.* **6.** *U.S. Slang.* crazy; silly; foolish. [ME *cucu* (imit. of its call). Cf. F *coucou,* G *kuckuk*]

cuckoo clock, a clock which announces the hours by a sound like the call of the cuckoo.

cuck·oo·flow·er (kŏŏk′ŏŏflou′ər), *n.* any of various plants, as the lady's-smock or the ragged robin.

cuck·oo·pint (kŏŏk′ŏŏpĭnt′), *n.* a common European species of arum, *Arum maculatum;* wake-robin.

cuck·oo·spit (kŏŏk′kŏŏspĭt′), *n.* **1.** a frothy secretion found on plants, exuded as a protective covering by the young of certain insects, as the froghoppers. **2.** an insect secreting this.

cu·cu·li·form (kūkū′lə fôrm′), *adj.* pertaining to or resembling the order *Cuculiformes,* containing the cuckoos, road runners, anis, etc. [f. s. L *cuculus* cuckoo + -(I)FORM]

cu·cul·late (kū′kəlāt′, kūkŭl′āt), *adj.* **1.** cowled; hooded. **2.** resembling a cowl or hood. Also, **cuc·u·lat·ed** (kū′kə lā′tĭd, kūkŭl′ātĭd). [t. LL: m.s. *cucullātus* hooded]

cu·cum·ber (kū′kŭmbər), *n.* **1.** a creeping plant, *Cucumis sativus,* occurring in many cultivated forms, yielding a long fleshy fruit which is commonly eaten green as a salad and used for pickling. **2.** the fruit of this plant. **3.** any of various allied or similar plants. **4.** its fruit. [t. OF: m. *cocombre,* g. s. L *cucumis;* r. ME *cucumer,* t. L: m.s. *cucumis*]

cucumber tree, 1. any of several American magnolias, esp. *Magnolia acuminata.* **2.** any of certain other trees, as an East Indian tree of the genus *Averrhoa.*

cu·cu·mi·form (kūkū′məfôrm′), *adj.* shaped like a cucumber; approximately cylindrical, with rounded or tapering ends. [f. L *cucumi(s)* cucumber + -FORM]

cu·cur·bit (kūkûr′bĭt), *n.* **1.** a gourd. **2.** any cucurbitaceous plant. [ME *cucurbite,* t. F, t. L: m. *cucurbita* gourd]

cu·cur·bi·ta·ceous (kūkûr′bə tā′shəs), *adj.* belonging to the *Cucurbitaceae,* or gourd family of plants which includes the pumpkin, squash, cucumber, muskmelon, watermelon, etc. [f. s. L *cucurbita* gourd + -ACEOUS]

cud (kŭd), *n.* the portion of food which a ruminating animal returns from the first stomach to the mouth to chew a second time. [ME; OE *cudu,* var. of *cwidu.* See QUID]

cud·bear (kŭd′bâr′), *n.* a violet coloring matter obtained from various lichens, esp. *Lecanora tartarea.*

cud·dle (kŭd′əl), *v.,* **-dled, -dling,** *n.* —*v.t.* **1.** to draw or hold close in an affectionate manner; hug tenderly; fondle. —*v.i.* **2.** to lie close and snug; nestle; curl up in going to sleep. —*n.* **3.** act of cuddling; a hug; an embrace. [f. *couth,* adj., comfortable, friendly + -le, freq. suffix. Cf. FONDLE] —**cud·dle·some** (kŭd′əl səm), *adj.* —**cud′dly,** *adj.*

cud·dy¹ (kŭd′ĭ), *n., pl.* **-dies. 1.** a small cabin on a ship or boat, esp. one under the poop. **2.** (in small vessels) the cookroom or pantry. **3.** a small room; a cupboard. [orig. unknown]

cud·dy² (kŭd′ĭ, kŏŏd′ĭ), *n., pl.* **-dies.** *Chiefly Scot.* **1.** a donkey. **2.** a stupid fellow. [orig. unknown]

cudg·el (kŭj′əl), *n., v.,* **-eled, -eling,** or (*esp. Brit.*) **-elled, -elling.** —*n.* **1.** a short, thick stick used as a weapon; a club. **2. take up the cudgels,** to engage in a contest. —*v.t.* **3.** to strike with a cudgel; beat. **4. cudgel one's brains,** to think hard. [ME *cuggel,* OE *cygel*] —**cudg′el·er,** *n.*

cud·weed (kŭd′wēd′), *n.* **1.** any of the woolly herbs constituting the composite genus *Gnaphalium.* **2.** any of various plants of allied genera.

cue¹ (kū), *n.* **1.** anything said or done on or behind the stage that is followed by a specific line or action: *each line of dialogue is a cue to the succeeding line; an off-stage door slam was his cue to enter.* **2.** a hint; an intimation; a guiding suggestion. **3.** the part one is to play; a prescribed or necessary course of action. **4.** humor; disposition. [? sp. of abbr. *q.* or *qu.* for L *quando* when]

cue² (kū), *n., v.,* **cued, cuing.** —*n.* **1.** a long tapering rod, tipped with a soft leather pad, used to strike the ball in billiards, pool, etc. **2.** a queue of hair. **3.** a queue or file, as of persons awaiting their turn. —*v.t.* **4.** to tie into a cue or tail. [var. of *queue,* t. F]

cue ball, *Billiards, etc.* the ball struck by the cue as distinguished from the other balls on the table.

Cuen·ca (kwĕng′kä), *n.* a city in SW Ecuador, 52,519 (est. 1944).

cues·ta (kwĕs′tə), *n.* *U.S.* a long low ridge presenting a relatively steep face or escarpment on one side and a long gentle slope on the other.

cuff¹ (kŭf), *n.* **1.** a fold, band, or variously shaped piece serving as a trimming or finish for the bottom of a sleeve. **2.** a turned-up fold at the bottom of trouser legs, etc. **3.** the part of a gauntlet or long glove that extends over the wrist. **4.** a separate or detachable band or piece of linen or other material worn about the wrist, inside or outside of the sleeve. [ME *cuffe, coffe* glove, mitten; orig. uncert.]

cuff² (kŭf), *v.t.* **1.** to strike with the open hand; beat; buffet. —*n.* **2.** a blow with the fist or the open hand; a buffet. **3.** a handcuff. [cf. Swed. *kuffa* thrust, push]

cuff button, the button for a man's shirt cuff.

cuff link, a link which fastens the cuff of a shirt.

cui bo·no (kwē′ bō′nō, kī′), *Latin.* **1.** for whose benefit? **2.** for what use? of what good?

cui·rass (kwĭ räs′), *n.* **1.** a piece of defensive armor for the body, combining a breastplate and a piece for the back. **2.** the breastplate alone. **3.** any similar covering, as the protective armor of a ship. **4.** *Zool.* a hard shell or other covering forming an indurated defensive shield. —*v.t.* **5.** to equip or cover with a cuirass. [t. F: m. *cuirasse,* b. *cuir(ie)* leather armor (der. *cuir,* g. L *corium* leather) and Pr. (*coir*)*assa* (g. LL *coriācea,* fem., made of leather)]

cui·ras·sier (kwĭr′ə sĭr′), *n.* a cavalry soldier wearing a cuirass. [t. F]

cui·sine (kwĭ zēn′), *n.* **1.** the kitchen; the culinary department of a house, hotel, etc. **2.** style of cooking; cookery. [t. F, g. L *cocīna, coquīna* kitchen. See KITCHEN]

cuisse (kwĭs), *n.* a piece of armor to protect the thigh. Also, **cuish** (kwĭsh). See illus. under **armor.** [t. F: thigh, g. L *coxa* hip]

cuit·tle (kĭt′əl), *v.t.,* **-tled, -tling.** *Scot.* to wheedle, cajole, or coax. Also, **cui′tle.**

Cul·bert·son (kŭl′bərt sən), *n.* **Ely** (ē′lĭ), born 1893, U.S. authority and writer on contract bridge.

culch (kŭlch), *n.* **1.** the stones, old shells, etc., forming an oyster bed and furnishing points of attachment for the spawn of oyster. **2.** the spawn. **3.** *Chiefly Dial.* rubbish; refuse. —*v.t.* **4.** to prepare (an oyster bed) with culch. Also, **cultch.** [t. OF: m. *culche* bed]

cul-de-sac (kŭl′də săk′, kŏŏl′-; *Fr.* kyd săk′), *n.* **1.** saclike cavity, tube, or the like, open only at one end, as the caecum. **2.** a street, lane, etc. closed at one end; blind alley. **3.** *Mil.* the situation of a military force hemmed in on all sides except behind. [t. F: bottom of sack]

-cule, a diminutive suffix of nouns, as in *animalcule, molecule.* Also, **-cle.** [t. F, or t. L: m. *-culus, -cula, -culum*]

Cu·ie·bra Cut (kŏŏlā′brə; *Sp.* kŏŏlĕ′brä), former name of **Gaillard Cut.**

cu·let (kū′lĭt), *n.* **1.** the small flat face forming the bottom of a brilliant. **2.** the part of medieval armor protecting the back of the body below the waist. [t. OF, dim. of *cul* bottom, g. L *cūlus.* Cf. F *culasse* culet]

cu·lex (kū′lĕks), *n., pl.* **-lices** (-lə sēz′), any mosquito of the genus *Culex,* including the common house mosquito, *Culex pipiens.* [t. L: a gnat]

cu·lic·id (kū′lĭs′ĭd), *n.* **1.** any of the dipterous family *Culicidae;* a mosquito. —*adj.* **2.** belonging or pertaining to the *Culicidae.*

cu·li·nar·y (kū′lə nĕr′ĭ), *adj.* pertaining to the kitchen or to cookery; used in cooking. [t. L: m. s. *culinārius,* der. *culina* kitchen]

Cu·lion (kŏŏlyôn′), *n.* one of the Philippine Islands, in the W part of the group, N of Palawan: leper colony. 7328 pop. (1939); 150 sq. mi.

cull¹ (kŭl), *v.t.* **1.** to choose; select; pick; gather the choice things or parts from. **2.** to collect; gather; pluck. —*n.* **3.** act of culling. **4.** something culled; esp. something picked out and put aside as inferior. [ME *culle(n),* t. OF: m. *coillir,* g. L *colligere* COLLECT]

cull² (kŭl), *n.* *Slang.* a fool; a dupe. [? short for CULLY]

Cul·len (kŭl′ən), *n.* **Countee** (koun tā′), 1903–46, U.S. poet.

cul·len·der (kŭl′ən dər), *n.* colander.

cul·let (kŭl′ĭt), *n.* broken or waste glass suitable for remelting.

cul·lion (kŭl′yən), *n.* *Obs.* a base or vile fellow. [ME *coillion,* t. F: m. *couillon,* der. L *cōleus* testicle]

cul·ly (kŭl′ĭ), *n., pl.* **-lies,** *v.,* **-lied, -lying.** *Slang* or *Colloq.* —*n.* **1.** a dupe. **2.** a man or fellow. —*v.t.* **3.** to trick; cheat; dupe. [short for CULLION]

culm¹ (kŭlm), *n.* **1.** coal dust; slack. **2.** anthracite, esp. of inferior grade. **3.** (*cap.*) *Geol.* a series of Lower Carboniferous rocks, mainly developed in parts of Europe, mostly dark-colored and siliceous. [var. of *coom* soot]

culm² (kŭlm), *n.* **1.** a stem or stalk, esp. t e jointed and usually hollow stem of grasses. —*v.i.* **2.** to grow or develop into a culm. [t. L: s. *culmus* stalk. Cf. HALM]

cul·mif·er·ous (kŭl mĭf′ər əs), *adj.* bearing culms.

cul·mi·nant (kŭl′mə nənt), *adj.* culminating; topmost.

cul·mi·nate (kŭl′mə nāt′), v.i. -nated, -nating. 1. to reach the highest point, the summit, or highest development (usually fol. by in). 2. Astron. (of a celestial body) to be on the meridian, or reach the highest or the lowest altitude. [t. LL: m.s. culminātus, pp., crowned]

cul·mi·na·tion (kŭl′mə nā′shən), n. 1. act or fact of culminating. 2. that in which anything culminates; the highest point; the acme. 3. Astron. the position of a celestial body when it is on the meridian. —Syn. 2. climax, zenith, peak.

cu·lottes (kū lŏts′; Fr. kylôt′), n.pl. a skirtlike garment, separated and sewn like trousers. [t. F]

cul·pa·ble (kŭl′pə bəl), adj. deserving blame or censure; blameworthy. [t. L: m.s. culpābilis blameworthy; r. ME coupable, t. OF] —cul′pa·bil′i·ty, cul′pa·ble·ness, n. —cul′pa·bly, adv. —Syn. censurable, reprehensible. —Ant. praiseworthy.

Cul·pep·er (kŭl′pĕp′ər), n. Thomas, died 1689, British governor of the colony of Virginia, 1680-83.

cul·prit (kŭl′prĭt), n. 1. a person arraigned for an offense. 2. one guilty of an offense or fault. [orig. uncert.]

cult (kŭlt), n. 1. a particular system of religious worship, esp. with reference to its rites and ceremonies. 2. an instance of an almost religious veneration for a person or thing, esp. as manifested by a body of admirers: a cult of Napoleon. 3. the object of such devotion. 4. Sociol. a group having an exclusive sacred ideology and a series of rites centering around their sacred symbols. [t. L: s. cultus care, worship]

cultch (kŭlch), n., v.t. culch.

cul·ti·va·ble (kŭl′tə və bəl), adj. capable of being cultivated. Also, cul·ti·vat·a·ble (kŭl′tə vā′tə bəl). [t. F, der. cultiver cultivate] —cul′ti·va·bil′i·ty, n.

cul·ti·vate (kŭl′tə vāt′), v.t., -vated, -vating. 1. to bestow labor upon (land) in raising crops; till; improve by husbandry. 2. to use a cultivator on. 3. to promote or improve the growth of (a plant, etc.) by labor and attention. 4. to produce by culture. 5. to develop or improve by education or training; train; refine. 6. to promote the growth or development of (an art, science, etc.); foster. 7. to devote oneself to (an art, etc.). 8. to seek to promote or foster (friendship, etc.). 9. to seek the acquaintance or friendship of (a person). [t. ML: m. s. cultīvātus, pp. of cultīvāre, der. cultīvus tilled, der. L cultus, pp. of colere till] —Ant. 8. neglect. 9. ignore.

cul·ti·vat·ed (kŭl′tə vā′tĭd), adj. 1. subjected to cultivation. 2. produced or improved by cultivation, as a plant. 3. educated; refined; cultured.

cul·ti·va·tion (kŭl′tə vā′shən), n. 1. act or art of cultivating. 2. state of being cultivated. 3. culture.

cul·ti·va·tor (kŭl′tə vā′tər), n. 1. one who or that which cultivates. 2. an implement for loosening the earth and destroying weeds when drawn between rows of growing plants.

cul·trate (kŭl′trāt), adj. sharp edged and pointed, as a leaf. Also, cul′trat·ed. [t. L: m.s. cultrātus, der. culter knife]

cul·tur·al (kŭl′chər əl), adj. of or pertaining to culture or cultivation. —cul′tur·al·ly, adv.

cultural change, culture change.

cultural lag, culture lag.

cul·ture (kŭl′chər), n., v., -tured, -turing. —n. 1. action or practice of cultivating the soil; tillage. 2. the raising of plants or animals, esp. with a view to their improvement. 3. the product or growth resulting from such cultivation. 4. development or improvement by education or training. 5. enlightenment or refinement resulting from such development. 6. a particular state or stage of civilization, as in the case of a certain nation or period: Greek culture. 7. Sociol. the sum total of ways of living built up by a group of human beings, which is transmitted from one generation to another. 8. Biol. a. the cultivation of microörganisms, as bacteria, or of tissues, for scientific study, medicinal use, etc. b. the product or growth resulting from such cultivation. —v.t. 9. to subject to culture; cultivate. 10. Biol. a. to develop (microörganisms, tissues, etc.) in an artificial medium. b. to introduce (living material) into a culture medium. [ME, t. F, t. L: m. cultūra tending, cultivation] —Syn. 5. See education.

culture area, Sociol. a region having a distinct pattern of culture.

culture change, Sociol. the process by which a culture is significantly modified for one or more various reasons, such as contact with another culture. Also, cultural change.

culture complex, Sociol. a group of culture traits all interrelated and dominated by one essential trait: political nationalism is a culture complex.

cul·tured (kŭl′chərd), adj. 1. cultivated. 2. enlightened; refined.

culture diffusion, Sociol. the spread of elements of culture from a point of origin.

culture factor, Sociol. the whole of a culture at a given time as it affects further cultural development.

culture lag, Sociol. a failure of one portion of culture of a group to keep abreast of the development of other portions of the culture. Also, cultural lag.

culture pattern, Sociol. a group of interrelated cultural traits of some continuity.

culture trait, Sociol. any fact in human activity acquired in social life and transmitted by communication.

cul·tur·ist (kŭl′chər ĭst), n. 1. a cultivator. 2. an advocate or devotee of culture.

cul·tus[1] (kŭl′təs), n. a cult. [t. L]

cul·tus[2] (kŭl′təs), n. a common marine food fish, Ophiodon elongatus, of the Pacific coast of the U.S. Also, cultus cod. [t. Chinook: worthless]

cul·ver (kŭl′vər), n. a dove; a pigeon. [ME colfre, OE culfre]

cul·ver·in (kŭl′vər ĭn), n. 1. a medieval form of musket. 2. a kind of heavy cannon, used in the 16th and 17th centuries. [t. F: m. couleurine, der. couleuvre, g. L colubra serpent. Cf. COBRA]

Cul·ver's root (kŭl′vərz), 1. the root of a tall scrophulariaceous herb, Veronica virginica, used in medicine as a cathartic and emetic. 2. the plant.

cul·vert (kŭl′vərt), n. a drain or channel crossing under a road, etc., a sewer; a conduit. [orig. uncert.]

cum (kŭm, kŏŏm), prep. 1. with; together with; including (used sometimes in financial phrases, as cum dividend, etc., which are often abbreviated simply cum). 2. Brit. closely related: the dwelling-cum-workshop was nearby. [t. L]

Cu·mae (kū′mē), n. an ancient city on the coast of Campania, in SW Italy: reputedly the earliest Greek colony in Italy or Sicily. —Cu·mae′an, adj.

Cumaean sibyl, one of the legendary women of antiquity whose authority in matters of divination was acknowledged by the Romans.

cum·ber (kŭm′bər), v.t. 1. to hinder; hamper. 2. to overload; burden. 3. to inconvenience; trouble. —n. 4. hindrance. 5. Archaic. embarrassment; trouble. 6. that which cumbers. [t. MFlem.: m. comber, c. G kummer trouble] —cum′ber·er, n.

Cum·ber·land (kŭm′bər lənd), n. 1. a county in NW England. 265,000 pop. (est. 1946); 1520 sq. mi. Co. seat: Carlisle. 2. a city in NW Maryland, on the Potomac. 37,679 (1950). 3. a river flowing from SE Kentucky through N Tennessee into the Ohio near Paducah, Kentucky. 687 mi.

Cumberland Gap, a pass in the Cumberland Mountains at the junction of the Virginia, Kentucky, and Tennessee boundaries. 1315 ft. high.

Cumberland Mountains, a W plateau of the Appalachian Mountains, largely in Kentucky and Tennessee. Highest point, ab. 4000 ft. Also, Cumberland Plateau.

cum·ber·some (kŭm′bər səm), adj. 1. burdensome; troublesome. 2. unwieldy; clumsy. —cum′ber·some·ly, adv. —cum′ber·some·ness, n.

cum·brance (kŭm′brəns), n. 1. trouble. 2. encumbrance.

cum·brous (kŭm′brəs), adj. cumbersome. —cum′brous·ly, adv. —cum′brous·ness, n.

cum gra·no sa·lis (kŭm grā′nō sā′lĭs), Latin. with a grain of salt (that is, not too seriously).

cum·in (kŭm′ən), n. 1. a small apiaceous plant, cuminum cyminum, bearing aromatic seed-like fruit used in cookery and medicine. 2. the fruit or seeds.

cum lau·de (kŭm lō′dē, kŏŏm lou′dě), Latin. with honor (used in diplomas to grant the lowest of three special honors for grades above the average). See magna cum laude and summa cum laude.

cum·mer (kŭm′ər), n. Scot. 1. a godmother. 2. a female companion. 3. a girl or woman. [Scot., ME commare, t. F: m. commère, g. LL commāter. See COM-, MATER]

cum·mer·bund (kŭm′ər bŭnd′), n. (in India and elsewhere) a shawl or sash worn as a belt. Also, kummerbund. [t. Hind., Pers.: m. kamarband loin band]

Cum·mings (kŭm′ĭngz), n. E(dward) E(stlin) (ĕst′-lĭn), born 1894, U. S. poet, writer, and painter.

cum·quat (kŭm′kwŏt), n. kumquat.

cum·shaw (kŭm′shô), n. (in Chinese ports) a present; gratuity; tip. [t. Chinese: m. Amoy kamsiā for Mandarin kan hsieh grateful thanks]

cu·mu·late (v. kū′myə lāt′; adj. kū′myə lĭt, -lāt′), v., -lated, -lating, adj. —v.t. 1. to heap up; amass; accumulate. —adj. 2. heaped up. [t. L: m. s. cumulātus, pp., heaped up]

cu·mu·la·tion (kū′myə lā′shən), n. 1. act of cumulating; accumulation. 2. a heap; mass.

cu·mu·la·tive (kū′myə lā′tĭv), adj. 1. increasing or growing by accumulation or successive additions. 2. formed by or resulting from accumulation or the addition of successive parts or elements. 3. Finance. of or pertaining to a dividend or interest which accumulates if not paid when due, and must be paid before those with an inferior claim to earnings can be paid. —cu′mu·la′tive·ly, adv. —cu′mu·la′tive·ness, n.

cumulative evidence, 1. evidence of which the parts reinforce one another, producing an effect stronger than any part taken by itself. 2. testimony repetitive of testimony earlier given.

cumulative voting, a system which gives each voter as many votes as there are persons to be elected from one representative district, allowing him to accumulate them on one candidate or to distribute them.

cu·mu·li·form (kū′myə lə fôrm′), adj. having the appearance or character of cumulus clouds.

cu·mu·lo-nim·bus (kū′myə lō nĭm′bəs), n. Meteorol. a heavy, tall mass of cloud whose summits rise in the form of mountains or towers, the upper parts having a fibrous texture characteristic of high clouds formed of ice

ăct, āble, dâre, ärt; ĕbb, ēqual; ĭf, īce; hŏt, ōver, ôrder, oil, bŏŏk, ōōze, out; ŭp, ūse, ûrge; ə = a in alone; ch, chief; g, give; ng, ring; sh, shoe; th, thin; ŧħ, that; zh, vision. See the full key on inside cover crystals. This cloud is characteristic of thunderstorm conditions.

cu·mu·lous (kū′myə ləs), *adj.* of the form of a cumulus (cloud); composed of cumuli.

cu·mu·lus (kū′myə ləs), *n., pl.* **-li** (-lī′), **1.** a heap; pile. **2.** *Meteorol.* a cloud with summit domelike or made up of rounded heaps, and with flat base, seen in fair weather and usually a brilliant white with a smooth, well-outlined structure.

Cu·nax·a (kū năk′sə), *n.* an ancient town in Babylonia, near the Euphrates: famous battle between Cyrus the Younger and Artaxerxes II, 401 B.C.

cunc·ta·tion (kŭngk tā′shən), *n.* delay. [t. L: s. *cunctātio*, der. *cunctārī* delay] —**cunc·ta·tive** (kŭngk′tə tĭv), *adj.*

cunc·ta·tor (kŭngk tā′tər), *n.* a delayer. [t. L] —**cunc·ta′tor·ship′**, *n.*

cu·ne·al (kū′nĭ əl), *adj.* wedgelike; wedge-shaped. [f. s. L *cuneus* wedge + -AL¹]

cu·ne·ate (kū′nĭ ĭt, -āt), *adj.* **1.** wedge-shaped. **2.** (of leaves) triangular and tapering to a po.nt at the base. Also, **cu′ne·at′ed.** [t. L: m.s. *cuneātus*, pp., made wedge-shaped]

Cuneate leaf

cu·ne·i·form (kū nē′ə fôrm′, kū′nĭ ə fôrm′), *adj.* **1.** having the form of a wedge; wedge-shaped, as the characters anciently used in writing in Persia, Assyria, etc. **2.** noting or pertaining to this kind of writing. **3.** *Anat.* noting or pertaining to any of various wedge-shaped bones, as of the tarsus. —*n.* **4.** cuneiform characters or writing. **5.** a cuneiform bone. Also, **cu·ni·form** (kū′nə fôrm′). [f. s. L *cuneus* wedge + -(ı)FORM]

Assyrian cuneiform characters

cun·ner (kŭn′ər), *n.* a small labrid fish, *Tautogolabrus adopersus*, common on the North Atlantic coast of the U. S.

cun·ning (kŭn′ĭng), *n.* **1.** ability; skill; expertness. **2.** skill employed in a crafty manner; skillfulness in deceiving; craftiness; guile. —*adj.* **3.** exhibiting or wrought with ingenuity. **4.** artfully subtle or shrewd; crafty; sly. **5.** *U.S. Colloq.* quaintly pleasing or attractive, as a child or something little. **6.** *Archaic.* skillful; expert. [ME; var. of OE *cunnung*, der. *cunnan* know (how). See CAN¹] —**cun′ning·ly**, *adv.* —**cun′ning·ness**, *n.* —**Syn. 2.** shrewdness, artfulness, wiliness, trickery, finesse, intrigue CUNNING, ARTIFICE, CRAFT imply an inclination toward deceit, slyness, and trickery. CUNNING implies a shrewd, often ınstinctive skill in concealing or disguising the real purposes of one's actions: *not intelligence but a low kind of cunning.* An ARTIFICE is a clever, unscrupulous ruse, used to mislead others: *a successful artifice to conceal one's motives.* CRAFT suggests underhand methods and the use of deceptive devices and tricks to attain one's ends: *craft and deceitfulness in every act* **4.** artful, wily, tricky, foxy.

cup (kŭp), *n., v.,* **cupped, cupping.** —*n.* **1.** a small, open container, esp. of porcelain or metal, used mainly to drink from. **2.** an ornamental cup or other article, esp. of precious metal, offered as a prize for a contest. **3.** the containing part of a goblet or the like. **4.** a cup with its contents. **5.** the quantity contained in a cup. **6.** a unit of capacity, equal to 8 fluid ounces, or 16 tablespoons. **7.** any of various beverages, as a mixture of wine and various ingredients: *claret cup.* **8.** the chalice used in the eucharist. **9.** the wine of the eucharist. **10.** something to be partaken of or endured, as suffering. **11.** (*pl.*) the drinking of intoxicating liquors. **12.** (*pl.*) a state of intoxication. **13.** any cuplike utensil, organ, part, cavity, etc. **14.** *Golf.* **a.** the metal receptacle within the hole. **b.** the hole itself. **15.** (*cap.*) *Astron.* the southern constellation Crater. **16.** a cupping glass. **17. in one's cups,** intoxicated; tipsy. —*v.t.* **18.** to take or place in or as in a cup. **19.** to use a cupping glass on. [OE *cuppe*, t. LL: m. *cuppa* cup, var. of L *cūpa* tub, cask] —**cup′like′,** *adj.*

cup·bear·er (kŭp′bâr′ər), *n.* an attendant who fills and hands the cups in which drink is served.

cup·board (kŭb′ərd), *n.* **1.** a closet with shelves for dishes, etc. **2.** *Brit.* any small closet or cabinet, for clothes, etc. [ME, f. CUP + BOARD]

cupboard love, love inspired by considerations of good feeding.

cup·cake (kŭp′kāk′), *n.* a small cake baked in a cup-shaped pan.

cu·pel (kū′pəl, kū pĕl′), *n., v.,* **-peled, -peling** or (*esp. Brit.*) **-pelled, -pelling.** *n.* **1.** a small cuplike porous vessel, usually made of bone ash, used in assaying, as for separating gold and silver from lead. **2.** a receptacle or furnace bottom in which silver is refined. —*v.t.* **3.** to heat or refine in a cupel. [t. F: m. *coupelle*, ult. der. LL *cuppa* CUP] —**cu·pel·la·tion** (kū′pə lā′shən), *n.*

cup·ful (kŭp′fŏŏl′), *n., pl.* **-fuls.** a quantity sufficient to fill a cup.

Cu·pid (kū′pĭd), *n.* **1.** the Roman god of love, son of Venus, commonly represented as a winged boy with bow and arrows. See EROS. **2.** (*l.c.*) a similar winged being, or a representation of one, esp. as symbolical of love. [ME *Cupide,* t. L: m. *Cupīdo,* lit., desire, passion]

cu·pid·i·ty (kū pĭd′ə tĭ), *n.* eager or inordinate desire, esp. to possess something. [t. L: m. s. *cupiditas* passionate desire]

cup of tea, *Brit. Colloq.* a favored object: *that show wasn't my cup of tea.*

cu·po·la (kū′pə lə), *n.* **1.** a rounded vault or dome constituting, or built upon, a roof; a small domelike or towerlike structure on a roof. **2.** a dome of relatively small size, esp. when forming part of a minor or decorative element of a larger building. **3.** any of various domelike structures, organs, etc. **4.** *Metall.* a vertical, circular furnace for melting cast iron. It uses coke as a fuel, a flux, and a forced blast. [t. It.: dome, t. LL: m. *cūpula,* dim. of *cūpa* tub, cask]

cupped (kŭpt), *adj.* hollowed out like a cup; cup-shaped.

cup·per (kŭp′ər), *n.* one who performs the operation of cupping.

cup·ping (kŭp′ĭng), *n.* the process of drawing blood from the body by scarification and the application of a cupping glass, or by the application of a cupping glass without scarification, as for relieving internal congestion.

cupping glass, a glass vessel in which a partial vacuum is created, as by heat, used in cupping.

cupr-, a word element referring to copper. Also, before consonants, **cupri-, cupro-.** [t. L, comb. form of *cuprum*]

cu·pre·ous (kū′prĭ əs), *adj.* **1.** copper-colored; metallic reddish-brown. **2.** consisting of or containing copper; copperlike. [t. L: m. *cupreus* of copper]

cu·pric (kū′prĭk), *adj. Chem.* of or containing copper, esp. in the divalent state (Cu⁺²), as *cupric oxide,* CuO.

cu·prif·er·ous (kū prĭf′ər əs), *adj.* yielding copper.

cu·prite (kū′prīt), *n.* a mineral, cuprous oxide, Cu_2O, occurring in red crystals and granular masses: an ore of copper.

cu·pro·nick·el (kū′prə nĭk′əl), *Metall.* —*n.* **1.** an alloy of copper containing nickel. —*adj.* **2.** containing copper and nickel.

cu·prous (kū′prəs), *adj. Chem.* containing monovalent copper (Cu⁺¹), as *cuprous oxide,* Cu_2O.

cu·prum (kū′prəm), *n.* copper. *Chem. abbr.:* Cu [t. L]

cu·pule (kū′pūl), *n.* **1.** *Bot.* a cup-shaped involucre consisting of indurated, cohering bracts, as in the acorn. **2.** *Zool.* a small cup-shaped sucker or similar organ or part. [t. L: m.s. *cūpula,* dim. of *cūpa* tub, cup]

Cupules (def. 1)
A, of acorn; B, of fungus

cur (kûr), *n.* **1.** a snarling, worthless, or outcast dog. **2.** a low, despicable person. [ME *curre;* imit.]

cur·a·ble (kyŏŏr′ə bəl), *adj.* that may be cured —**cur′a·bil′i·ty, cur′a·ble·ness,** *n.* —**cur′a·bly,** *adv.*

Cu·ra·çao (kyŏŏr′ə sō′, kōō′rä sou′), *n.* **1.** a Dutch colony in the West Indies, consisting of a group of, three islands off the NW coast of Venezuela and another group ab. 500 mi. to the NE in the Leeward Islands. 124,800 pop. (est. 1944); 403 sq. mi. *Cap.:* Willemstad. **2.** the main island of this colony, in the S group. 75,500 pop. (est. 1944); 210 sq. mi. **3.** (*l.c.*) Also **cu′ra·çoa′.** a cordial or liqueur flavored with the peel of the (bitter) **Curaçao orange.**

cu·ra·cy (kyŏŏr′ə sĭ), *n., pl.* **-cies.** the office or position of a curate.

cur·agh (kŭr′əKH, kŭr′ə), *n.* currach.

cu·ra·re (kyŏŏr ä′rĭ), *n.* **1.** a blackish resinlike substance from *Strychnos toxifera* and other tropical plants of the genus *Strychnos,* and from *Chondodendron tomentosum,* used by South American Indians for poisoning arrows, and employed in physiological experiments, etc., for arresting the action of the motor nerves. **2.** a plant yielding it. Also, **cu·ra′ri.** [t. Carib.: m. *kurare*]

cu·ra·rize (kyŏŏr′ə rīz′, kyŏŏr ä′rīz), *v.t.* **-rized, -rizing.** to administer curare to, as in vivisection. —**cu′ra·ri·za′tion,** *n.*

cu·ras·sow (kyŏŏr′ə sō′, kyŏŏr ăs′ō), *n.* any of various large, arboreal, gallinaceous South and Central American birds belonging to the family *Cracidae,* somewhat resembling the turkey and sometimes domesticated. [named after the island of *Curaçao*]

cu·rate (kyŏŏr′ĭt), *n.* **1.** *Chiefly Brit.* a clergyman employed as assistant or deputy of a rector or vicar. **2.** *Archaic.* any ecclesiastic entrusted with the cure of souls, as a parish priest. [ME *curat,* t. ML: s. *cūrātus,* der. *cūra.* See CURE, n.]

cur·a·tive (kyŏŏr′ə tĭv), *adj.* **1.** serving to cure or heal; pertaining to curing or remedial treatment; remedial. —*n.* **2.** a curative agent; a remedy. —**cur′a·tive·ly,** *adv.* —**cur′a·tive·ness,** *n.* —**Ant. 1.** injurious.

cu·ra·tor (kyŏŏr ā′tər for 1, 2; kyŏŏr′ə tər for 3), *n.* **1.** the person in charge of a museum, art collection, etc.; a custodian. **2.** a manager; overseer; superintendent. **3.** a guardian, as of a minor, lunatic, etc. [t. L: overseer, guardian; r. ME *curatour,* t. AF] —**cu·ra·to·ri·al** (kyŏŏr′ə tôr′ĭ əl), *adj.* —**cu·ra′tor·ship′,** *n.*

curb (kûrb), *n.* **1.** a chain or strap attached to the upper ends of the branches of a bit and passing under the horse's lower jaw, used in restraining the horse. See diag. under **harness. 2.** anything that restrains or controls; a restraint; a check. **3.** an enclosing framework or border. **4.** Also, *Brit.,* **kerb.** a line of joined stones, concrete, etc., at the edge of a street, wall, etc. **5.** the

---

b., blend of, blended; c., cognate with; d., dialect, dialectal; der., derived from; f., formed from; g., going back to; m., modification of; r., replacing; s., stem of; t., taken from; ?, perhaps. See the full key on inside cover.

framework round the top of a wall.   **6.** the sidewalk or street as a market for the sale of securities: *the New York Curb Market was formerly a street market.*   **7.** *Vet. Sci.* a swelling on the lower part of the back of the hock of a horse, often causing lameness.   —*v.t.* **8.** to control as with a curb; restrain; check.   **9.** to put a curb on (a horse).   **10.** Also, *Brit.,* **kerb.** to furnish with, or protect by a curb.   [t. F: m. *courbe* curved, g. L *curvus* bent, crooked]   —Syn. **8.** bridle, repress, control. See **check.**

curb bit, a bit for a horse, which, by slight effort, produces great pressure on the mouth to control the animal.

curb·ing (kûr′bĭng), *n.* the material forming a curb.

curb roof, a roof with two slopes to each face, the lower being the steeper.

Diagram of a curb roof

curb·stone (kûrb′stōn′), *n.* one of the stones, or a range of stones, forming a curb, as along the outer edge of a sidewalk, etc. Also, *Brit.,* **kerbstone.**

curch (kûrch), *n.* a kerchief.

cur·cu·li·o (kûr·kū′lĭ·ō′), *n., pl.* **-lios.** any of certain snout beetles or weevils, as the **plum curculio,** *Conotrachelus nenuphar,* injurious to fruit. [t. L: weevil]

cur·cu·ma (kûr′kyŏŏ·mə), *n.* any plant of the zingiberaceous genus *Curcuma,* of the East Indies, etc., as *C. longa* or *C. zedoaria,* the former yielding turmeric and the latter zedoary. [NL, t. Ar.: m. *kurkum* saffron, turmeric]

curd (kûrd), *n.* **1.** (*often pl.*) a substance consisting of casein, etc., obtained from milk by coagulation, used for making into cheese or eaten as food.   **2.** any substance resembling this.   —*v.t., v.i.* **3.** to turn into curd; coagulate; congeal. [ME *crud.* Cf. OE *crūdan* press, crowd]

curd cheese, *Chiefly Brit.* cottage cheese.

cur·dle (kûr′dəl), *v.t., v.i.* **-dled, -dling. 1.** to change into curd; coagulate; congeal.   **2. curdle the blood,** to terrify with horror or fear. [freq. of CURD]

curd·y (kûr′dĭ), *adj.* like curd; full of or containing curd; coagulated.

cure (kyŏŏr), *n., v.,* **cured, curing.** —*n.* **1.** a method or course of remedial treatment, as for disease.   **2.** successful remedial treatment; restoration to health.   **3.** a means of healing or curing; a remedy.   **4.** act or a method of curing meat, fish, etc.   **5.** spiritual charge of the people in a certain district.   **6.** the office or district of one exercising such oversight.   —*v.t.* **7.** to restore to health.   **8.** to relieve or rid of something troublesome or detrimental, as an illness, a bad habit, etc.   **9.** to prepare (meat, fish, etc.) for preservation, by salting, drying, etc.   —*v.i.* **10.** to effect a cure.   **11.** to become cured. [t. OF, g. L *cūra* care, treatment, concern, ML an ecclesiastical cure] —**cure′less,** *adj.* —**cure′less·ly,** *adv.* —**cur′er,** *n.*
—Syn. **8.** CURE, HEAL, REMEDY imply making well, whole, or right. CURE is especially applied to the eradication of disease or sickness: *to cure a fever, a headache.* HEAL suggests the making whole of wounds, sores, etc : *to heal a cut or a burn.* REMEDY is a more general word which includes both the others and applies also to making wrongs right: *to remedy a mistake, a misunderstanding.*

cu·ré (kyŏŏ·rā′; *Fr.* kṳ·rĕ′), *n.* (in French use) a parish priest. [t. F, g. VL *cūrātus.* See CURATE]

cure-all (kyŏŏr′ôl′), *n.* a cure for all ills; a panacea.

cu·ret·tage (kyŏŏr·ĕt′ĭj, kyŏŏr′ə·täzh′), *n.* the process of curetting. [t. F]

cu·rette (kyŏŏ·rĕt′), *n., v.,* **-retted, -retting.** —*n.* **1.** a scoop-shaped surgical instrument used for removing diseased tissue from body cavities such as the uterus, etc.   —*v.t.* **2.** to scrape with a curette. [t. F, der. *curer* cleanse, g. L *curāre*]

cur·few (kûr′fū), *n.* **1.** the ringing of a bell at a fixed hour in the evening as a signal for covering or extinguishing fires, as practiced in medieval Europe.   **2.** the ringing of an evening bell as later practiced.   **3.** the giving of a signal, esp. by a bell, at a certain hour in the evening, as for children to retire from the streets.   **4.** the time of ringing such a bell.   **5.** the bell itself.   **6.** its sound. [ME *corfew,* t. AF: m. *coeverfeu,* var. of OF *cuevreu* cover-fire]

cu·ri·a (kyŏŏr′ĭ·ə), *n., pl.* **curiae** (kyŏŏr′ĭ·ē′). **1.** one of the political subdivisions of each of the three tribes of ancient Roman citizens.   **2.** the building in which such a division or group met, as for worship or public deliberation.   **3.** the senate house in ancient Rome.   **4.** the senate of ancient Italian towns.   **5.** the Pope and those about him at Rome engaged in the administration of the papal authority (the **Curia Romana**).   **6.** the papal court. [L and ML] —**cu′ri·al,** *adj.*

cu·rie (kyŏŏr′ē, kyŏŏ·rē′), *n. Phys. Chem., Physics.* the amount of radioactivity associated with the radon in equilibrium with one gram of radium. [named after Marie CURIE]

Cu·rie (kyŏŏr′ē, kyŏŏ·rē′; *Fr.* kṳ·rē′), *n.* **1. Marie,** 1867–1934, Polish physicist and chemist, in France: with her husband, Pierre, discovered radium in 1898.   **2. Pierre,** 1859–1906, French physicist and chemist.

Curie constant, *Physics.* the constant relating absolute temperature to the magnetic susceptibility of a given substance.

Curie point, *Physics.* the temperature at which a substance loses its magnetic susceptibility.

Curie's law, *Physics.* the law that the magnetic susceptibility of a substance is inversely proportional to the absolute temperature. [named after Pierre CURIE]

cu·ri·o (kyŏŏr′ĭ·ō′), *n., pl.* **curios.** any article, object of art, etc., valued as a curiosity. [short for CURIOSITY]

cu·ri·o·sa (kyŏŏr′ĭ·ō′sə), *n.pl.* books, pamphlets, etc., dealing with unusual subjects, esp. pornographic ones (a term used by booksellers and collectors). [t. L: curious (things)]

cu·ri·os·i·ty (kyŏŏr′ĭ·ŏs′ə·tĭ), *n., pl.* **-ties. 1.** the desire to learn or know about anything; inquisitiveness.   **2.** curious or interesting quality, as from strangeness.   **3.** a curious, rare, or novel thing.   **4.** *Obs.* carefulness; fastidiousness. [t. L: m.s. *cūriōsitas*] —Syn. **3.** curio, rarity, wonder, marvel, phenomenon, freak.

cu·ri·ous (kyŏŏr′ĭ·əs), *adj.* **1.** desirous of learning or knowing; inquisitive.   **2.** prying; meddlesome.   **3.** *Archaic.* made or prepared with skill or art.   **4.** marked by special care or pains, as an inquiry or investigation.   **5.** exciting attention or interest because of strangeness or novelty.   **6.** *Colloq.* odd; eccentric.   **7.** (of books) indelicate, indecent, or obscene.   **8.** *Obs.* careful; fastidious.   **9.** *Obs.* marked by intricacy or subtlety. [ME, t. OF: m. *curios,* g. L *cūriōsus* careful, inquiring, inquisitive] —**cu′ri·ous·ly,** *adv.* —**cu′ri·ous·ness,** *n.*
—Syn. **1, 2.** CURIOUS, INQUISITIVE, MEDDLESOME, PRYING refer to taking an undue (and petty) interest in others' affairs. CURIOUS implies a desire to know what is not properly one's concern: *curious about a neighbor's habits.* INQUISITIVE implies asking impertinent questions in an effort to satisfy curiosity: *inquisitive in asking about a neighbor's habits.* MEDDLESOME implies thrusting oneself into and taking an active part in other people's affairs (or handling their possessions) entirely unasked and unwelcomed: *a meddlesome aunt who tries to run the affairs of a family.* PRYING implies a meddlesome and persistent inquiring into others' affairs: *prying into the secrets of a business firm.* **5.** strange, unusual, singular, novel, rare.

Cu·ri·ti·ba (kōō′rē·tē′bə), *n.* a city in S Brazil. 101,204 (1940). Also, **Cu/ri·ty/ba.**

cu·ri·um (kyŏŏr′ĭ·əm), *n. Chem.* an element not found in nature, but discovered in 1945 among the products of the bombardment of uranium and plutonium by very energetic helium ions. *Symbol:* Cm; *at. no.:* 96.

curl (kûrl), *v.t.* **1.** to form into ringlets, as the hair.   **2.** to form into a spiral or curved shape; coil.   **3.** *Obs.* to adorn with, or as with, curls or ringlets.   —*v.i.* **4.** to form curls or ringlets, as the hair.   **5.** to coil.   **6.** to become curved or undulated.   **7.** *Scot.* to play at curling.   —*n.* **8.** a ringlet of hair.   **9.** anything of a spiral or curved shape.   **10.** a coil.   **11.** act of curling.   **12.** state of being curled.   **13.** any of various diseases of plants with which the leaves are distorted, fluted, or puffed because of unequal growth. [ME *crolled, crulled,* ppl. adj., t. MD or MFlem.]

curl·er (kûr′lər), *n.* **1.** one who or that which curls.   **2.** a player at curling.

cur·lew (kûr′lōō), *n.* **1.** any of several shore birds of the genera *Numenius* and *Phaeopus,* with long slender downward curved bill, as the **common curlew** (*Numenius arquatus*) of Europe and the **Hudsonian curlew** (*Phaeopus hudsonicus*) of America.   **2.** any of certain superficially similar birds. [ME *corlewe,* t. OF: m. *courlieu;* imit.]

curl·i·cue (kûr′lĭ·kū′), *n.* a fantastic curl or twist. Also, **curl/y·cue/.**

curl·ing (kûr′lĭng), *n.* a Scottish game played on the ice, in which large, smooth, rounded stones are slid toward a mark called the tee.

Long-billed curlew.
Numenius americanus
(26 in. long)

curling iron, a rod of iron to be used when heated for curling the hair, which is twined around it. Also, **curling irons, curling tongs.**

curl·pa·per (kûrl′pā′pər), *n.* a piece of paper on which a lock of hair is rolled up tightly, to remain until the hair has become fixed in a curl.

curl·y (kûr′lĭ), *adj.,* **curlier, curliest. 1.** curling or tending to curl: *curly blonde hair.*   **2.** having curls: *curly-headed.* —**curl/i·ness,** *n.*

cur·mudg·eon (kər·mŭj′ən), *n.* an irascible, churlish fellow. —**cur·mudg′eon·ly,** *adj.*

curn (kûrn), *n. Scot.* **1.** a grain.   **2.** a small quantity or number.

curr (kûr), *v.i.* to make a low, murmuring sound, like the purring of a cat. [cf. Icel. *kurra* murmur]

cur·rach (kûr′əкн, kûr′ə), *n. Scot., Irish.* a coracle. Also, **curagh, cur′ragh.** [t. Gaelic or Irish: m. *curach.* Cf. Welsh *corwg*]

cur·ra·jong (kûr′ə·jŏng′), *n.* the native name of *Plagianthus sidoides,* a malvaceous shrub or tree of Australia and Tasmania.

cur·rant (kûr′ənt), *n.* **1.** a small seedless raisin, produced chiefly in California and in the Levant, used in cookery, etc.   **2.** the small, edible, acid, round fruit or berry of certain wild or cultivated shrubs of the genus *Ribes,* as *R. sativum* (**red currant** and **white currant**) and *R. nigrum* (**black currant**).   **3.** the shrub itself.   **4.** any of various similar fruits or shrubs. [ME (*raysons of*) *Coraunte,* t. AF: m. (*raisins de*) *Corauntz* (raisins of) Corinth; so called because orig. from Corinth in Greece]

cur·ren·cy (kûr'ən sĭ), n., pl. -cies. 1. that which is current as a medium of exchange; the money in actual use. 2. fact or quality of being passed on, as from person to person. 3. general acceptance; prevalence; vogue. 4. fact or state of passing in time. 5. circulation, as of coin. 6. Obs. or Rare. a running; flowing.

cur·rent (kûr'ənt), adj. 1. passing in time, or belonging to the time actually passing: the current month. 2. passing from one to another; circulating, as coin. 3. publicly reported or known. 4. prevalent. 5. generally accepted; in vogue. 6. Now Rare. running or flowing. 7. Obs. genuine; authentic. —n. 8. a flowing; flow, as of a river. 9. that which flows, as a stream. 10. a portion of a large body of water, or of air, etc., moving in a certain direction. 11. Elect. a. a movement or flow of electricity. b. the rate of flow, in amperes. 12. course, as of time or events; the main course; the general tendency. [t. L: s. currens, ppr., running; r. ME corant, t. OF] —cur'rent·ly, adv.
—Syn. 4. CURRENT, PRESENT, PREVAILING, PREVALENT, refer to something generally or commonly in use. That which is CURRENT is in general circulation or a matter of common knowledge or acceptance: current usage in English. PRESENT refers to that which is in general use now; it is more limited than CURRENT, as to time: present customs. That which is PREVAILING is that which has superseded others: prevailing fashion. That which is PREVALENT exists or is spread widely: a prevalent idea. 9. See stream. —Ant. 4. obsolete. 5. old-fashioned

current assets, Com. assets readily convertible into cash without serious sacrifice.

current collector, Elect. (on a trolley, subway, etc.) any device, as a pantograph (def. 2), for maintaining electrical contact between a contact conductor and the electrical circuit of the vehicle on which the collector is mounted.

current density, Elect. the rate of flow in amperes per unit of cross-sectional area at a given place in a conductor.

current expenses, regularly continuing expenditures for the maintenance and the carrying on of business.

current liabilities, Com. indebtedness maturing within one year.

cur·ri·cle (kûr'ə kəl), n. a light, two-wheeled, open carriage drawn by two horses abreast. [t. L: m. s. curriculum a running, course, race, race chariot]

cur·ric·u·lum (kə rĭk'yə ləm), n., pl. -lums, -la (-lə). 1. the aggregate of courses of study given in a school, college, university, etc. 2. the regular or a particular course of study in a school, college, etc. [t. L. See CURRICLE] —cur·ric'u·lar, adj.

cur·ri·er (kûr'ĭ ər), n. 1. one who dresses and colors leather after it is tanned. 2. one who curries (a horse, etc.). [ME corier, t. OF, g. L coriārius tanner]

Currier and Ives, the lithography firm of Nathaniel Currier and James Merritt Ives, founded originally by Currier (about 1834), which produced prints of American history, life, and manners.

cur·ri·er·y (kûr'ĭ ər ĭ), n., pl. -eries. 1. the occupation or business of a currier. 2. the place where it is carried on.

cur·rish (kûr'ĭsh), adj. 1. of or pertaining to a cur. 2. curlike; snarling; quarrelsome. 3. contemptible. —cur'rish·ly, adv. —cur'rish·ness, n.

cur·ry[1] (kûr'ĭ), n., pl. -ries, v., -ried, -rying. 1. an East Indian sauce or relish in many varieties, containing a mixture of spices, seeds, vegetables, fruits, etc., eaten with rice or combined with meat, fish, or other food. 2. a dish prepared with a curry sauce or with curry powder. —v.t. 3. to prepare (food) with a curry sauce or with curry powder. [t. Tamil: m. kari sauce]

cur·ry[2] (kûr'ĭ), v.t., -ried, -rying. 1. to rub and clean (a horse, etc.) with a comb; currycomb. 2. to dress (tanned hides) by soaking, scraping, beating, coloring, etc. 3. to beat; thrash. 4. **curry favor,** to seek favor by a show of kindness, courtesy, flattery, etc. [ME cory, t. OF: m. coreer, earlier conreder put in order, f. con- CON- + -reder make ready (ult. t. Gmc. See REDD)]

cur·ry·comb (kûr'ĭ kōm'), n. 1. a comb, usually with rows of metal teeth, for currying horses, etc. —v.t. 2. to rub or clean with such a comb.

curry powder, a powdered preparation of spices and other ingredients, notably turmeric, used for making curry sauce or for seasoning food.

curse (kûrs), n., v., cursed or curst, cursing. —n. 1. the expression of a wish that evil, etc., befall another. 2. an ecclesiastical censure or anathema. 3. a profane oath. 4. evil that has been invoked upon one. 5. something accursed. 6. the cause of evil, misfortune, or trouble. —v.t. 7. to wish or invoke evil, calamity, injury, or destruction upon. 8. to swear at. 9. to blaspheme. 10. to afflict with great evil. 11. to excommunicate. —v.i. 12. to utter curses; swear profanely. [ME curs, OE cūrs, der. cūrsian, v., curse, blame, reprove (whence ME cursen), t. OIrish: m.s. cūrsagim I blame] —curs'er, n.
—Syn. 1. imprecation, execration, fulmination, malediction. 6. bane, scourge, plague, affliction, torment. 7-9. CURSE, BLASPHEME, SWEAR are often interchangeable in the sense of using profane language. However, CURSE is the general word for the heartfelt invoking or violent or angry calling down of evil on another: they called down curses on their enemies. To BLASPHEME is to speak contemptuously or

with abuse of God or of sacred things: to blaspheme openly. To SWEAR is to use the name of God or of some holy person or thing as an exclamation to add force or show anger: to swear in every sentence. —Ant. 7. bless.

curs·ed (kûr'sĭd, kûrst), adj. 1. under a curse; damned. 2. deserving a curse; hateful; abominable. 3. Dial. cantankerous; ill-tempered; cross. —curs'ed·ly, adj. —curs'ed·ness, n. —Syn. 2. damnable, execrable.

cur·sive (kûr'sĭv), adj. 1. (of writing or printing type) in flowing strokes, with the letters joined together. —n. 2. a cursive letter or printing type. [t. ML: m. s. cursīvus, der. L cursus a running] —cur'sive·ly, adv.

cur·so·ri·al (kûr sōr'ĭ əl), adj. Zool. 1. adapted for running, as the feet and skeleton of dogs, horses, etc. 2. having limbs adapted for running, as certain birds, insects, etc.

cur·so·ry (kûr'sər ĭ), adj. going rapidly over something, without noticing details; hasty; superficial. [t. L: m. s. cursōrius pertaining to a runner or a race] —cur'so·ri·ly, adv. —cur'so·ri·ness, n.

curst (kûrst), v. 1. pt. and pp. of **curse.** —adj. 2. cursed.

curt (kûrt), adj. 1. short; shortened. 2. brief in speech, etc. 3. rudely brief in speech, manner, etc. [t. L: s. curtus cut short, clipped. Cf. SHORT] —curt'ly, adv. —curt'ness, n. —Syn. 2. See blunt.

cur·tail (kər tāl'), v.t. to cut short; cut off a part of; abridge; reduce; diminish. [var. (by assoc. with TAIL) of obs. curtal, v., dock. See CURTAL, adj.] —cur·tail'er, n. —cur·tail'ment, n. —Syn. lessen, dock. See **shorten.**

cur·tail step (kûr'tāl), the first or bottom step of a stair, when it is finished in a curved line at its outer end.

cur·tain (kûr'tən, -tĭn), n. 1. a hanging piece of fabric used to shut out the light from a window, adorn a room, etc. 2. anything that shuts off, covers, or conceals: a curtain of artillery fire. 3. Archit. a flat portion of a wall, connecting two towers, projecting structures, or the like. 4. Fort. the part of a wall or rampart connecting two bastions, towers, or the like. See diag. under **bastion.** —v.t. 5. to provide, shut off, conceal, or adorn with, or as with, a curtain. [ME curtine, t. OF, g. LL cortīna curtain]
—Syn. 1. drapery, portière, lambrequin, valance. CURTAIN, BLIND, SHADE, SHUTTER agree in being covers for a window, to shut out light or keep persons from looking in. CURTAIN, BLIND, and SHADE may mean a cover, usually of cloth, which can be rolled up and down inside the window. CURTAIN, however, may also refer to a drapery at a window; and a Venetian BLIND consists of slats mounted on tapes for drawing up or down and varying the pitch of the slats. BLIND and SHUTTER may mean a cover made of two wooden frames with movable slats, attached by hinges outside a window and pulled together or opened at will. SHUTTERS may mean also a set of panels (wooden or iron) put up outside small shops or stores at closing time.

curtain call, the appearance of performers at the conclusion of a performance in response to the applause of the audience.

curtain lecture, a private scolding, esp. one by a wife to her husband.

curtain raiser, a short play acted before a main play.

cur·tal (kûr'təl), Obs. or Archaic. —adj. 1. wearing a short frock: a curtal friar. —n. 2. anything docked or cut short. 3. a 16th century bassoon. [t. F: m. courtault, der. court short, g. L curtus]

cur·te·sy (kûr'tə sĭ), n., pl. -sies. Law. the life tenure formerly enjoyed by a husband in his wife's land inheritance after her death, provided they had issue able to inherit: a tenacy by the curtesy. [var. of COURTESY]

cur·ti·lage (kûr'tə lĭj), n. Law. the area of land occupied by a dwelling and its yard and outbuildings, actually enclosed or considered as enclosed. [ME, t. AF, der. OF courtil little court. See COURT]

Cur·tis (kûr'tĭs), n. George William, 1824–92, U.S. essayist, editor, and reformer.

Cur·tiss (kûr'tĭs), n. Glenn Hammond, 1878–1930, U.S. inventor: pioneer in aviation.

Cur·ti·us (kŏŏr'tsĭ ŏŏs), n. Ernst (ĕrnst), 1814–96, German archaeologist and historian.

curt·sey (kûrt'sĭ), n., pl. -seys, v., -seyed, -seying. curtsy.

curt·sy (kûrt'sĭ), n., pl. -sies, v., -sied, -sying. —n. 1. a bow by women in recognition or respect, consisting of bending the knees and lowering the body. —v.i. 2. to make a curtsy [var. of COURTESY]

cu·rule (kyŏŏr'ŏŏl), adj. 1. privileged to sit in a curule chair. 2. of the highest rank.

curule chair, Hist. a folding seat with curved legs and no back, often ornamented with ivory, etc., used only by certain high officials of ancient Rome.

cur·va·ceous (kûr vā'shəs), adj. Colloq. having a full figure. [f. CURVE + -ACEOUS]

cur·va·ture (kûr'və chər), n. 1. act of curving. 2. curved condition, often abnormal: curvature of the spine. 3. degree of curving. 4. something curved.

curve (kûrv), n., v., curved, curving, adj. —n. 1. a continuously bending line, without angles. 2. a curving. 3. any curved outline, form, thing, or part. 4. a curved ruler used by draftsmen. 5. Baseball. a. the curved course (other than one due to the force of gravity) given to a ball by the pitcher; a curved ball. b. the deflection itself. 6. Math. a collection of points whose coördinates are continuous functions of a single independent variable. —v.t., v.i. 7. to bend in a curve; take, or cause to take, the course of a curve. —*adj.* **8.** curved. [t. L: m. s. *curvus* bent, curved] —**curv·ed·ly** (kûr′vĭd lĭ′), *adv.* —**curv′ed·ness,** *n.*

cur·vet (*n.* kûr′vĭt; *v.* kər vĕt′, kûr′vĭt), *n., v.,* -**vet·ted,** -**vetting** or -**veted,** -**veting.** —*n.* **1.** a leap of a horse in which the forelegs are raised together and equally advanced, and then, as they are falling, the hindlegs are raised with a spring, so that all the legs are off the ground at once. —*v.i.* **2.** to leap in a curvet, as a horse; cause one's horse to do this. **3.** to leap and frisk. —*v.t.* **4.** to cause to make a curvet. [t. It.: m. *corvetta,* dim. of *corvo,* g. L *curvus* bent, curved]

curvi-, a combining form of **curve.**

cur·vi·lin·e·ar (kûr′və lĭn′ĭ ər), *adj.* **1.** consisting of or bounded by curved lines: *a curvilinear figure.* **2.** forming, or moving in, a curved line. **3.** formed, or characterized by, curved lines. Also, **cur′vi·lin·e·al.**

Cur·zon of Ked·le·ston (kûr′zən əv kĕd′əl stən, kĕl′stən), **George Nathaniel Curzon, 1st Marquis,** 1859–1925, British statesman: viceroy of India, 1899–1905.

Cus·co (kōōs′kô), *n.* Cuzco.

Cush (kŭsh), *n. Bible.* **1.** the eldest son of Ham. Gen. 10:6. **2.** (probably) Upper Egypt and the neighboring country.

cush·at (kŭsh′ət, kŏŏsh′-), *n.* the wood pigeon or ringdove, *Columba palumbus,* of Europe. [OE *cuscote*]

cu·shaw (kə shô′), *n.* any of various long-necked squashes, esp. varieties of *Cucurbita moschata;* cashaw.

Cush·ing (kŏŏsh′ĭng), *n.* **1. Caleb** (kā′ləb), 1800–79, U.S. statesman and diplomat. **2. Harvey,** 1869–1939, U.S. surgeon and author.

cush·ion (kŏŏsh′ən), *n.* **1.** a soft bag of cloth, leather, or rubber, filled with feathers, air, etc., used to sit, kneel, or lie on. **2.** anything similar in appearance or use. **3.** a pillow used in lacemaking. **4.** a pad worn under the hair by women. **5.** the elastic raised rim encircling the top of a billiard table. **6.** something to absorb or counteract a shock, jar, or jolt, as a body of air or steam. —*v.t.* **7.** to place on or support by a cushion. **8.** to furnish with a cushion or cushions. **9.** to cover or conceal with, or as with, a cushion. **10.** to check the motion of (a piston, etc.) by a cushion, as of steam. **11.** to form (steam, etc.) into a cushion. **12.** to suppress (complaints, etc.) quietly, as by ignoring. [ME *cushin,* t. OF: m. *coussin,* ? ult. der. L *culcita* cushion]
—**Syn. 1.** CUSHION, PILLOW agree in being cases filled with a material more or less resilient, intended to be used as supports for the body or parts of it. A CUSHION is a soft pad used to sit, lie, or kneel on, or to lean against: *a number of cushions on a sofa, cushions on pews in a church.* A PILLOW is a bag or case filled with feathers, down, or other soft material, usually to support the head: *to sleep with a pillow under one's head.*

Cush·it·ic (kə shĭt′ĭk), *n.* a group of Hamitic languages, including Somali and other languages of Somaliland and Ethiopia.

Cush·man (kŏŏsh′mən), *n.* **1. Charlotte Saunders,** 1816–76, U. S. actress. **2. Robert,** 1580?–1625, one of the Pilgrim founders of Plymouth, Massachusetts.

cush·y (kŏŏsh′ĭ), *adj.,* **cushier, cushiest.** *Chiefly Brit. Slang.* easy; pleasant. [f. CUSH(ION) + -Y¹]

cusk (kŭsk), *n., pl.* **cusks,** (*esp. collectively*) **cusk. 1.** an edible marine fish, *Brosmius brosme,* of both coasts of the northern Atlantic. **2.** a similar fish, as the American burbot, *Lota lota maculosa.* [var. of *tusk* fish]

cusp (kŭsp), *n.* **1.** a point; pointed end. **2.** *Anat., Zool., Bot.* a point, projection, or elevation, as on the crown of a tooth. **3.** *Geom.* a point where two branches of a curve meet, end, and are tangent. **4.** *Archit., etc.* a point or figure formed by the intersection of two small arcs or curved members, as one of the pointed projections sometimes decorating the internal curve of an arch or a traceried window. **5.** *Astron.* a point of a crescent, esp. of the moon. [t. L: m. *cuspis* point]

cusped (kŭspt), *adj.* having a cusp or cusps; cusplike. Also, **cus·pate** (kŭs′pĭt, -pāt), **cus·pat·ed.**

cus·pid (kŭs′pĭd), *n.* a tooth with a single projection point or elevation; a canine tooth (*cuspid* is preferred for a human canine tooth). [t. L: s. *cuspis* point]

cus·pi·dal (kŭs′pə dəl), *adj.* of, like, or having a cusp; cuspidate.

cus·pi·date (kŭs′pə dāt′), *adj.* **1.** having a cusp or cusps. **2.** furnished with or ending in a sharp and stiff point or cusp: *cuspidate leaves, cuspidate tooth.* Also, **cus′-pi·dat′ed.** [t. NL: m.s. *cuspidātus,* der. L *cuspis* point]

cus·pi·da·tion (kŭs′pə dā′shən), *n.* decoration with cusps, as in architecture.

cus·pi·dor (kŭs′pə dôr′), *n.* a bowl used as a receptacle for spit. [t. Pg.: spitter, spittoon, der. *cuspir,* g. L *conspuere* spit upon]

cuss (kŭs), *U.S. Colloq.* —*n.* **1.** a curse. **2.** a person or animal: *a queer but likable cuss.* —*v.t., v.i.* **3.** to curse. [early var. of CURSE]

cuss·ed (kŭs′ĭd), *adj. Colloq.* **1.** cursed. **2.** obstinate; perverse. —**cuss′ed·ly,** *adv.* —**cuss′ed·ness,** *n.*

cus·tard (kŭs′tərd), *n.* a dish made of eggs and milk, sweetened and baked or boiled. [earlier *crustarde* (with loss of first -r- by dissimilation), a kind of patty, der. OE *croste* CRUST]

custard apple, 1. the fruit of any of a group of shrubs and trees, native in tropical America, and possessing soft edible pulp; often confined to the single species, *Annona reticulata.* **2.** the tree itself. **3.** some

related tree, as *Asimina triloba,* the North American papaw. **6.** its fruit.

Cus·ter (kŭs′tər), *n.* **George Armstrong,** 1839–76, U.S. general and Indian fighter.

cus·to·di·al (kŭs tō′dĭ əl), *adj.* pertaining to custody.

cus·to·di·an (kŭs tō′dĭ ən), *n.* a person who has custody; a keeper; guardian. —**cus·to′di·an·ship′,** *n.*

cus·to·dy (kŭs′tə dĭ), *n., pl.* -**dies. 1.** keeping; guardianship; care: *in the custody of her father.* **2.** the keeping or charge of officers of the law: *the car was held in the custody of the police.* **3.** imprisonment: *he was taken into custody.* [t. L: m.s. *custōdia*]
—**Syn. 1, 2.** safekeeping, charge, watch. CUSTODY, KEEPING, POSSESSION imply a guardianship or care for something. CUSTODY denotes a strict keeping, as by a formally authorized and responsible guardian or keeper: *in the custody of the sheriff.* KEEPING denotes having in one's care or charge, as for guarding or preservation: *in a bank for safekeeping.* POSSESSION means holding, ownership, or mastery: *leave it in possession of its owner.*

cus·tom (kŭs′təm), *n.* **1.** a habitual practice; the usual way of acting in given circumstances. **2.** habits or usages collectively; convention. **3.** a long-continued habit which is so established that it has the force of law. **4.** such habits collectively. **5.** a customary tax, tribute, or service due by feudal tenants to their lord. **6.** *Sociol.* a group pattern of habitual activity usually transmitted from one generation to another. **7.** toll; duty. **8.** (*pl.*) duties imposed by law on imported or, less commonly, exported goods. **9.** (*pl.*) the government department that collects these duties. **10.** habitual patronage of a particular shop, etc.; business patronage. **11.** customers or patrons collectively. **12.** the aggregate of customers. —*adj.* **13.** made specially for individual customers: *custom shoes.* **14.** dealing in things so made, or doing work to order: *a custom tailor.* [ME *custume,* t. OF, ult. g. L *consuētūdo* custom. See CONSUETUDE. Cf. COSTUME]
—**Syn. 1, 2.** CUSTOM, HABIT, PRACTICE mean an established way of doing things. CUSTOM, applied to a community or to an individual, implies a (more or less permanent) continuance of a social usage: *it is the custom to give gifts at Christmas time.* HABIT, applied particularly to an individual, implies such repetition of the same action as to develop a natural, spontaneous, or rooted tendency or inclination to perform it: *make a habit of reading the newspapers.* PRACTICE applies to a set of fixed habits or an ordered procedure in conducting activities: *it is his practice to verify all statements, secret practice of a cult.*

cus·tom·a·ble (kŭs′təm ə bəl), *adj.* subject to customs or duties; dutiable.

cus·tom·ar·y (kŭs′tə mĕr′ĭ), *adj., n., pl.* -**aries.** —*adj.* **1.** according to or depending on custom; usual; habitual. **2.** of or established by custom rather than law. **3.** *Law.* defined by long continued practices: *the customary service due from land in a manor.* —*n.* **4.** a book or document containing the legal customs or customary laws of a locality. **5.** any body of such customs or laws. [t. ML: m. s. *customārius,* der. OF *custume* CUSTOM] —**cus′tom·ar′i·ly** or, for emphasis, **cus·tom·ar′i·ly,** *adv.* —**cus′tom·ar′i·ness,** *n.* —**Syn. 1.** wonted, accustomed, conventional. See **usual.** —**Ant. 1.** uncommon.

cus·tom-built (kŭs′təm bĭlt′), *adj.* made to individual order: *a custom-built limousine.*

cus·tom·er (kŭs′təm ər), *n.* **1.** one who purchases goods from another; a buyer; a patron. **2.** *Colloq.* a person one has to deal with; a fellow: *a queer customer.*

custom house, a government office, often at a seaport, for collecting customs, clearing vessels, etc.

cus·tom-made (kŭs′təm mād′), *adj.* made to individual order: *custom-made shoes.*

customs union, an arrangement between independent nations or tariff areas to remove customs barriers between them and to adopt a uniform tariff policy.

cus·tos (kŭs′tŏs), *n., pl.* **custodes** (kŭs tō′dēz). *Latin.* **1.** a custodian. **2.** a superior in the Franciscan order.

cus·tos mo·rum (kŭs′tŏs môr′əm), *Latin.* a custodian or guardian of morals; censor.

cus·tu·mal (kŭs′chōŏ məl), *n.* customary. [t. ML: s. *custumālis,* Latinization of OF *costumel* customary]

cut (kŭt), *v.,* **cut, cutting,** *adj., n.* —*v.t.* **1.** to penetrate with, or as with, a sharp-edged instrument: *he cut his finger.* **2.** to strike sharply, as with a whip. **3.** to wound severely the feelings of. **4.** to divide with, or as with, a sharp-edged instrument; sever; carve: *to cut a rope, bread into slices, etc.* **5.** to hew or saw down; fell: *to cut timber.* **6.** to detach with, or as with, a sharp-edged instrument; separate from the main body; lop off. **7.** to reap; mow; harvest: *to cut grain or hay.* **8.** to trim by clipping, shaving, paring, or pruning: *to cut the hair or the nails.* **9.** to intersect; cross: *one line cuts another at right angles.* **10.** to abridge or shorten by omitting a part: *to cut a speech.* **11.** to lower; reduce; diminish (sometimes fol. by *down*): *to cut rates.* **12.** to dissolve; dilute; make less thick: *to cut phlegm.* **13.** to make or fashion by cutting, as a statue, jewel, garment, etc. **14.** to hollow out; excavate; dig: *cut a trench.* **15.** *Colloq.* to renounce; give up. **16.** *Colloq.* to refuse to recognize socially. **17.** to perform or execute: *to cut a caper.* **18.** *Colloq.* to absent oneself from. **19.** *Cards.* **a.** to divide (a pack of cards) at random into two or more parts, by removing cards from the top. **b.** to take (a card) from a deck. **20.** *Sports.* to hit (a ball) either with the hand or some instrument so as to change its course and often to cause it to spin. **21.** *Cricket.* to strike and send off (a ball) in front of the batsman, and parallel to the wicket.

—*v.i.* **22.** to penetrate or divide something as with a sharp-edged instrument; make an incision: *the scissors cut well.* **23.** to admit of being cut, or turn out upon being cut. **24.** to pass, go, or come, esp. in the most direct way (fol. by *across, through, in,* etc.): *to cut across an empty lot.* **25.** to strike sharply, as with a whip. **26.** (of the teeth) to grow through the gums. **27.** *Cards.* to cut the cards. **28.** *Slang.* to run away; make off. **29.** (of a horse) to interfere. **30.** to interrupt (fol. by *in*). **31.** Some verb phrases are:

cut back, 1. to shorten by cutting off the end. **2.** (in a novel, movie, etc.) to return suddenly to earlier events. **3.** *Football.* to reverse direction suddenly by moving in the diagonally opposite course.

cut off, 1. to intercept. **2.** to interrupt. **3.** to bring to a sudden end. **4.** to shut out. **5.** to disinherit.

cut out, 1. to omit; delete; excise. **2.** to oust and replace; supplant (esp. a rival). **3.** to be fit for. **4.** to stop; cease. **5.** to plan or arrange; prepare. **6.** to fashion or shape; form; make. **7.** to move suddenly out of the lane or path in which one has been driving.

cut teeth, to have the teeth grow through the gums.

cut up, *Colloq.* **1.** to play pranks. **2.** to behave badly. —*adj.* **32.** that has been subjected to cutting; divided into pieces by cutting; detached by cutting: *cut flowers.* **33.** *Bot.* incised; cleft. **34.** fashioned by cutting; having the surface shaped or ornamented by grinding and polishing: *cut glass.* **35.** reduced by, or as by, cutting: *cut rates.* **36.** castrated; gelded. **37.** *Slang.* drunk. **38. cut and dried, a.** fixed or settled in advance. **b.** lacking freshness or spontaneity.

—*n.* **39.** act of cutting; a stroke or a blow as with a knife, whip, etc. **40.** a piece cut off, esp. of meat. **41.** *Butchering.* part of an animal usually cut as one piece. **42.** *U.S. Colloq.* share: *his cut was 20%.* **43.** quantity cut, esp. of lumber. **44.** the result of cutting, as an incision, wound, etc.; a passage, channel, etc., made by cutting or digging. **45.** manner or fashion in which anything is cut. **46.** style; manner; kind. **47.** a passage or course straight across: *a short cut.* **48.** an excision or omission of a part. **49.** a part excised or omitted. **50.** a reduction in price, salary, etc. **51.** an act, speech, etc., which wounds the feelings. **52.** an engraved block or plate used for printing, or an impression from it. **53.** *Colloq.* a refusal to recognize an acquaintance. **54.** *Colloq.* an absence when attendance is required. **55.** *Sports.* **a.** act of cutting a ball. **b.** the spin of the ball. **56.** *Cards.* a cutting of the cards. **57.** one of several pieces of straw, paper, etc., used in drawing lots. [ME *cutten, kytten, kitten;* akin to d. Sw. *kata* cut]

—**Syn. 1.** gash, slash, slit, lance. **4.** cleave, sunder, bisect. CUT, CHOP, HACK, HEW, refer to giving a sharp blow or stroke. CUT is a general word for this: *to cut the grass.* To CHOP is to cut by giving repeated blows with something sharp, for example, an ax. To CHOP and to HEW are practically interchangeable, but CHOP may refer to a more or less undirected action: whereas HEW, more formal, suggests keeping to a definite purpose: *to chop or hew down a tree, to hew to a line.* To HACK is to cut or chop roughly and unevenly: *hack off a limb.* **44.** gash, slash, slit.

cu·ta·ne·ous (kū tā′nĭ əs), *adj.* of, pertaining to, or affecting the skin. [t. ML: m. *cutāneus,* der. L *cutis* skin]

cut·a·way (kŭt′ə wā′), *adj.* **1.** (of a coat) having the skirt cut away from the waist in front in a curve or slope. —*n.* **2.** a cutaway coat.

cut·back (kŭt′băk′), *n.* **1.** a return in the course of a story, motion picture, etc. to earlier events. **2.** reduction to an earlier rate, as in production.

cutch (kŭch), *n.* catechu.

Cutch (kŭch), *n.* **1.** a state in western India. 500,800 pop. (1941); 8461 sq. mi. *Cap.:* Bhuj. **2. Rann of** (rŭn), a large salt marsh NE of this state. ab. 9000 sq. mi.

cut·cher·ry (kəchĕr′Y), *n.* **1.** *India.* a public administrative or judicial office. **2.** any administrative office. Also, **cutch·er·y** (kŭch′ə rY). [t. Hind.: m. *kacherī*]

cute (kūt), *adj.,* **cuter, cutest. 1.** *U.S. Colloq.* pleasingly pretty or dainty: *a cute child, hat, etc.* **2.** *Archaic or Dial.* mentally keen; clever; shrewd. [aphetic var. of ACUTE] —**cute′ly,** *adv.* —**cute′ness,** *n.*

cut glass, glass ornamented or shaped by cutting or grinding with abrasive wheels. —**cut′glass′,** *adj.*

cut-grass (kŭt′grăs′, -gräs′), *n.* any of various grasses with blades having rough edges, esp. grasses of the genus *Homalocenchrus.*

Cuth·bert (kŭth′bərt), *n.* **1. Saint,** died A.D. 687, English monk and bishop. **2.** *Hort.* a variety of high-quality red raspberry grown chiefly in the U. S.

cu·ti·cle (kū′tə kəl), *n.* **1.** the epidermis. **2.** a superficial integument, membrane, or the like. **3.** the nonliving epidermis which surrounds the edges of the finger nail or toenail. **4.** *Bot.* a very thin hyaline film covering the surface of plants, and derived from the outer surfaces of the epidermal cells. [t. L: m.s. *cutīcula,* dim. of *cutis* skin] —**cu·tic·u·lar** (kū tĭk′yə lər), *adj.*

cu·tic·u·la (kū tĭk′yə lə), *n., pl.* **-lae** (-lē′). the outer noncellular layer of the arthropod integument, composed of a mixture of chitin and protein, but commonly containing other hardening substances. [t. L: skin]

cu·tin (kū′tYn), *n.* a transparent waxy substance constituting together with cellulose the cuticle of plants. [f. s. L *cutis* skin + -IN²]

cu·tin·ize (kū′tə nīz′), *v.t., v.i.,* **-ized, -izing.** to make into or become cutin. —**cu′tin·i·za′tion,** *n.*

cu·tis (kū′tYs), *n. Latin.* the corium or true skin, beneath the epidermis. Also, **cutis ve·ra** (vY′ə).

cut·lass (kŭt′ləs), *n.* a short, heavy, slightly curved sword, formerly used esp. at sea. Also, **cut′las.** [t. F: m. *coutelas,* ult. der. L *cultellus* small knife]

cut·ler (kŭt′lər), *n.* one who makes, sells, or repairs knives and other cutting instruments. [ME *coteler,* t. F: m. *coutelier,* der. *coutel* small knife, g. L *cultellus*]

cut·ler·y (kŭt′lə rY), *n.* **1.** art or business of a cutler. **2.** cutting instruments collectively, esp. those for dinner table use. [t. F: m. *coutelerie.* See CUTLER]

cut·let (kŭt′lYt), *n.* **1.** a slice of meat for broiling or frying, orig. one, as of mutton, containing a rib, but now commonly one cut from the leg, esp. of veal or mutton. **2.** a flat croquette of minced chicken, lobster, or the like. [t. F: m. *côtelette,* double dim. of *côte,* rib g. L *costa*]

cut-off (kŭt′ôf′, -ŏf′), *n.* **1.** a cutting off, or something that cuts off; a shorter passage or way. **2.** a new and shorter channel formed for a river by the waters cutting across a bend in its course. **3.** the arresting of the passage of steam or working fluid to the cylinder of an engine, or the mechanims effecting it.

cut-out (kŭt′out′), *n.* **1.** something cut out from something else. **2.** a valve in the exhaust pipe of an internal-combustion engine, which when open permits the engine to exhaust directly into the air ahead of the muffler.

cut·purse (kŭt′pûrs′), *n.* **1.** one who stole by cutting purses from the girdle. **2.** a pickpocket.

cut rate, *U.S.* a price, fare, or rate below the standard charge. —**cut′-rate′,** *adj.*

cut·tage (kŭt′Yj), *n.* the process of propagating plants from separate vegetative parts.

cut·ter (kŭt′ər), *n.* **1.** one who or that which cuts. **2.** a type of small sailing vessel with a deep hull, square stern, and sloop rig. **3.** a medium-sized boat for rowing or sailing, or a launch, belonging to a warship. **4.** a light-armed government vessel or steamship (**revenue cutter**), used to prevent smuggling and enforce the customs regulations. **5.** a small, light, commonly single-seated sleigh, usually for one horse.

cut·throat (kŭt′thrōt′), *n.* **1.** one who cuts throats; a murderer. —*adj.* **2.** murderous. **3.** relentless: *cutthroat competition.* **4.** pertaining to a game participated in by three or more persons, each acting and scoring as an individual.

cut·ting (kŭt′Yng), *n.* **1.** act of one who or that which cuts. **2.** something cut off. **3.** *Hort.* a piece of plant, commonly a root, shoot, or leaf, cut from a plant to reproduce an entire new plant. **4.** *Brit.* a clipping from a newspaper, etc. **5.** *Now Brit.* something produced by cutting; an excavation through high ground, as in constructing a road, etc. —*adj.* **6.** that cuts; penetrating or dividing by, or as by, a cut. **7.** piercing, as a wind. **8.** wounding the feelings severely; sarcastic. —**cut′ting·ly,** *adv.* —**Syn. 7.** sharp, keen, incisive, trenchant. **8.** caustic, biting, mordant.

cut·tle·bone (kŭt′əl bōn′), *n.* the calcereous internal shell or plate of true cuttlefishes, used to make powder for polishing, and fed to canaries to supply the necessary lime, etc.

cut·tle·fish (kŭt′lə fYsh′), *n., pl.* **-fishes,** (esp. collectively) **-fish.** any of various decapod dibranchiate cephalopods, esp. of the genus *Sepia,* having sucker-bearing arms and the power of ejecting a black, inklike fluid when pursued. Also, **cut′tle.** [f. *cuttle* (ME *codulle,* OE *cudele* cuttlefish; akin to COD¹) + FISH]

Cuttlefish,
Sepia officinialis
(5 in. long)

cut·ty (kŭt′Y), *adj., n., pl.* **-ties.** *Chiefly Scot.* —*adj.* **1.** cut short; short. **2.** testy. —*n.* **3.** a short spoon. **4.** a short-stemmed tobacco pipe. **5.** an improper girl or woman. [der. CUT, v.]

cutty stool, *Scot.* **1.** a low stool. **2.** a seat in old churches, where offenders against chastity, or other delinquents, sat and received public rebuke.

cut-up (kŭt′ŭp′), *n. Colloq.* a showoff or prankster.

cut·wa·ter (kŭt′wô′tər, -wŏt′ər), *n.* **1.** the forepart of a ship's stem or prow, which cuts the water. **2.** the sharp edge of a pier of a bridge, which resists the action of water or ice.

cut·work (kŭt′wûrk′), *n.* openwork embroidery in which the ground fabric is cut out about the pattern.

cut·worm (kŭt′wûrm′), *n.* any of various caterpillars of certain noctuid moths, which feed at night on the young plants of corn, cabbage, etc., cutting them off at or near the ground.

Cu·vi·er (kū′vY ā′; *Fr.* ky vyē′), *n.* **Georges Léopold Chrétien Frédéric Dagobert** (zhôrzh lĕ ô pôld′ krā′tyăn′ frĕ dĕ rēk′ då gô bēr′), **Baron,** 1769–1832, French naturalist: founder of the science of paleontology.

Cux·ha·ven (kŏoks′hä′fən), *n.* a seaport in NW Germany at the mouth of the Elbe. 33,139 (1939).

Cu·ya·bá (kŏo′yä bä′), *n.* a city in W Brazil: a port on the Cuyabá river. 59,691 (est. 1944).

Cuy·a·hog·a Falls (kī′ə hŏg′ə; *older* -hō′gə), a city in NE Ohio, near Akron. 29,195 (1950).

Cuyp (koip), *n.* **Aalbert** (äl′bərt), 1620?–91, Dutch painter. Also, **Kuyp.**

Cuz·co (kŏos′kō), *n.* a city in S Peru: ancient Inca ruins. 45,158 (1940). Also, **Cusco.**

c.w.o., cash with order.

---

cwt., hundredweight.

-cy, 1. a suffix of abstract nouns, paired usually with adjectives ending in *-t, -te, -tic*, especially *-nt* (like the pair *-ant, -ance*), as *democracy, accuracy, expediency, necromancy*, also paired with other adjectives, as *fallacy*, or with a noun, as *lunacy*, sometimes forming (in extended suffixes) action nouns, as *vacancy* (*vacate*), *occupancy* (*occupy*). 2. a suffix of nouns denoting a rank or dignity, sometimes attached to the stem of a word rather than the word itself, as *captaincy, colonelcy, magistracy*. [repr. F -*cie, -tie,* L -*cia, -tia,* Gk. -*kia, -keia, -tia, -teia*]

cyan-¹, var. of **cyano-¹,** usually before vowels and *h*, as in *cyanamide*.

cyan-², var. of **cyano-²,** before vowels.

cyan-³, var. of **cyano-³,** before vowels.

cy·an·am·ide (sī′ə năm′īd, -ĭd, sī ăn′ə mīd′, -mĭd), *n. Chem.* 1. a white crystalline compound, H_2NCN, obtainable by the action of ammonia on cyanogen chloride or from calcium cyanamide. 2. an ester or salt of this substance. Also **cy·an·am·id** (sī′ə năm′ĭd, sī-ăn′ə mĭd). [f. CYAN(O)-¹ + AMIDE]

cy·a·nate (sī′ə nāt′), *n. Chem.* a salt of cyanic acid.

cy·an·ic (sī ăn′ĭk), *adj.* blue (applied esp. to a series of colors in flowers, including the blues and colors tending toward blue). [f. CYAN(O)-¹ + -IC]

cyanic acid, *Chem.* a poisonous compound, HOCN, isomeric with fulminic acid, but unstable except at low temperatures.

cy·a·nide (sī′ə nīd′, -nĭd), *n., v.,* **-nided, -niding.** —*n.* Also, **cy·a·nid** (sī′ə nĭd). 1. a salt of hydrocyanic acid, as *potassium cyanide*, KCN. —*v.t.* 2. to treat with a cyanide, as an ore in the process of extracting gold.

cy·a·nine (sī′ə nēn′, -nĭn), *n.* any of several groups of dyes which make silver halide photographic plates sensitive to a wider color range. Also, **cy·a·nin** (sī′ə nĭn).

cy·a·nite (sī′ə nīt′), *n.* a mineral aluminum silicate, Al_2SiO_5, occurring in blue or greenish bladed crystals, used as a refractory. Also, **kyanite.** [f. m.s. Gk. *kÿanos* blue + -ITE¹]

cyano-¹, a word element indicating dark-blue coloring. Also, **cyan-¹.** [t. Gk.: m. *kyano-*, comb. form of *kÿanos* dark blue]

cyano-², a combining form of cyanide. Also, **cyan-².**

cyano-³, *Chem.* a word element referring to the cyanogen group, CN. Also, **cyan-³.** [comb. form repr. CYANOGEN]

cy·an·o·gen (sī ăn′ə jən), *n.* 1. a poisonous, inflammable gas, C_2N_2. 2. a univalent radical, CN. [f. CYANO-² + -GEN]

cy·a·no·hy·drin (sī′ə nō hī′drĭn), *n.* one of a class of organic compounds which have both the CN and the OH radicals linked to the same carbon atom.

cy·a·no·sis (sī′ə nō′sĭs), *n. Pathol.* blueness or lividness of the skin, as from imperfectly oxygenated blood. Also, **cy·a·nop·a·thy** (sī′ə nŏp′ə thĭ). [NL., t. Gk.: m. *kyánosis* dark-blue color] —**cy·a·not·ic** (sī′ə nŏt′ĭk), *adj.*

cy·an·o·type (sī ăn′ə tīp′), *n.* 1. a process of photographic printing with ferric salts producing blue lines on a white background, used chiefly in printing tracings. 2. a print made by such a process. [f. CYANO-¹ + -TYPE]

cy·a·nu·ric acid (sī′ə nyōōr′ĭk, -nōōr′ĭk), *Chem.* a white, crystalline acid, $C_3H_3O_3N_3·2H_2O$, obtained by heating urea or by decomposing cyanogen chloride with water. [f. CYAN(O)-² + URIC]

Cyb·e·le (sĭb′ə lē′). *n.* a great nature goddess of Phrygia and Asia Minor whose worship was carried to Greece and Rome ("the Great Mother of the Gods").

cy·ber·net·ics (sī′bər nĕt′ĭks), *n.* the scientific study of those methods of control and communication which are common to living organisms and machines, esp. as applied to the analysis of the operations of machines such as computers. [f. s. Gk. *kybernētēs* helmsman + -ICS] —**cy′ber·net′ic,** *adj.*

cy·cad (sī′kăd), *n.* any of the *Cycadales*, an order of gymnospermous plants intermediate in appearance between ferns and the palms, many species having a thick, unbranched columnar trunk bearing a crown of large leathery pinnate leaves. [t. NL: s. *Cycas* the typical genus, t. Gk.: m. *kÿkās*, late spelling var. of *kóïkás*, acc. pl. of *kóïx* kind of palm]

cyc·a·da·ceous (sĭk′ə dā′shəs), *adj.* belonging or pertaining to the *Cycadales*. See **cycad.**

cycl-, a word element meaning "cycle," used especially in the chemical terminology of cyclic compounds, also in referring to wheel turns. Also, **cyclo-.** [t. Gk.: m. *kykl-* comb. form of *kÿklos* ring, circle, wheel]

Cyc·la·des (sĭk′lə dēz′), *n.pl.* a group of Greek islands in the S Aegean. 146,987 pop. (est. 1938); 1023 sq. mi.

cyc·la·men (sĭk′lə mən, -mĕn′), *n.* any plant of the primulaceous genus *Cyclamen*, comprising low-growing herbs with tuberous rootstocks and nodding white, purple, pink, or crimson flowers with reflexed petals. [t. NL, t. Gk.: m.s. *kyklāminos*]

cy·cle (sī′kəl), *n., v.,* **-cled, -cling.** —*n.* 1. a round of years or a recurring period of time, esp. one in which certain events or phenomena repeat themselves in the same order and at the same intervals. 2. any round of operations or events; a series which returns upon itself; any complete course or series. 3. any long period of years; an age. 4. a series of poetic or prose narratives about some mythical or heroic theme: *the Arthurian cycle.* 5. any group of poems about a central event,

figure, etc. 6. the aggregate of legendary or traditional matter with a common mythical or heroic theme. 7. a bicycle, tricycle, etc. 8. a period pertaining to the recurrence of astronomical phenomena. 9. *Physics.* a. a sequence of changes at the end of which the initial situation has been reëstablished. b. one of a succession of similar sequences of events or values. c. a complete or double alternation or reversal of an alternating electric current. —*v.i.* 10. to ride or travel by a bicycle, etc. 11. to move or revolve in cycles; pass through cycles. [t. L: m. *cyclus*, t. Gk.: m. *kÿklos* ring, circle]

cy·cle·car (sī′kəl kär′), *n.* a light automobile, open like a motorcycle but having three or four wheels.

cy·clic (sī′klĭk, sĭk′lĭk), *adj.* 1. of or pertaining to a cycle or cycles; revolving or recurring in cycles; characterized by recurrence in cycles. 2. *Chem.* of or noting a compound whose structural formula contains a closed chain or ring of atoms. *Bot.* a. arranged in whorls, as the parts of a flower. b. (of a flower) having the parts so arranged. Also, **cy·cli·cal.** [t. L: s. *cyclicus*, t. Gk.: m. *kyklikós* circular] —**cy·cli·cal·ly,** *adv.*

cy·clist (sī′klĭst), *n. Chiefly Brit.* one who rides or travels by a bicycle, tricycle, etc. Also, **cy′cler.**

cyclo-, var. of **cycl-,** before consonants, as in *cyclograph.*

cy·clo·graph (sī′klə grăf′, -gräf′), *n.* 1. arcograph. 2. *Photog.* a form of camera for obtaining a panoramic view of the periphery of an object, as a vase.

cy·clo·hex·ane (sī′klə hĕk′sān, sĭk′lə-), *n. Chem.* a colorless, hydrocarbon, ring compound, C_6H_{12}, composed of six methylene radicals (CH_2) united by single bonds. It is made by hydrogenation of benzene, and also occurs in some petroleum oils.

cy·cloid (sī′kloid), *adj.* 1. resembling a circle; circular. 2. (of fishes' scales) smooth-edged, more or less circular in form, with concentric striations. 3. having such scales, as a fish. —*n.* 4. a cycloid fish. 5. *Geom.* a curve generated by a point on the circumference of a circle which rolls, without slipping, on a straight line in its plane. [t. Gk.: m.s. *kykloeidēs* like a circle] —**cy·cloi′dal,** *adj.*

C, Cycloid; P, Point tracing cycloid on fixed circle

cy·clom·e·ter (sī klŏm′ə tər), *n.* 1. an instrument which measures circular arcs. 2. a device for recording the revolutions of a wheel and hence the distance traversed by a wheeled vehicle.

cy·clo·nal (sī klō′nəl), *adj.* of or like a cyclone.

cy·clone (sī′klōn), *n. Meteorol.* 1. an atmospheric pressure system characterized by relatively low pressure at its center, and by counterclockwise wind motion in the northern hemisphere, clockwise in the southern. 2. a tropical hurricane, esp. in the Indian Ocean. [t. Gk.: m.s. *kyklôn*, ppr., moving in a circle] —**cy·clon·ic** (sī-klŏn′ĭk), **cy·clon′i·cal,** *adj.* —**cy·clon′i·cal·ly,** *adv.*

cyclone cellar, a cellar or underground place for refuge from tornadoes, etc.

cy·clo·no·scope (sī klō′nə skōp′), *n.* a device for determining the center of a cyclone.

Cy·clo·pe·an (sī′klə pē′ən), *adj.* 1. of or characteristic of the Cyclops. 2. (*sometimes l.c.*) gigantic; vast. 3. *Archit.* of, like, or noting an early style of masonry employing massive stones, more or less irregular in shape.

cy·clo·pe·di·a (sī′klə pē′dĭə), *n.* a book having articles on subjects from all or certain branches of knowledge; an encyclopedia. Also, **cy′clo·pae′di·a.** [aphetic var. of ENCYCLOPEDIA] —**cy′clo·pe′dist,** *n.*

cy·clo·pe·dic (sī′klə pē′dĭk), *adj.* like a cyclopedia in character or contents; broad and varied; exhaustive. Also, **cy′clo·pae′dic.** —**cy′clo·pe′di·cal·ly,** *adv.*

cy·clo·pen·tane (sī′klə pĕn′tān, sĭk′lə-), *n. Chem.* a colorless liquid, C_5H_{10}, derived from some petroleums.

cy·clo·ple·gi·a (sī′klə plē′jĭ′ə, sĭk′lə-), *n. Pathol.* paralysis of the intraocular muscles.

cy·clo·pro·pane (sī′klə prō′pān, sĭk′lə-), *n. Chem.* a colorless gas, C_3H_6, used as an anesthetic.

Cy·clops (sī′klŏps), *n., pl.* **Cyclopes** (sī klō′pēz). *Gk. Myth.* one of a race of lawless giants with but one eye, which was circular and in the middle of the forehead, fabled to have forged thunderbolts for Zeus and to have assisted Hephaestus (Vulcan) in his workshops. [t. L, t. Gk.: m. *Kÿklôps*, lit., round-eyed]

cy·clo·ram·a (sī′klə răm′ə, -rä′mə), *n.* a pictorial representation, in natural perspective, of a landscape, a battle, etc. on the inner wall of a cylindrical room or hall, the spectators occupying a position in the center. [f. CYCL- + Gk. (*h*)*órama* view] —**cy′clo·ram′ic,** *adj.*

cy·clo·stom·a·tous (sī′klə stŏm′ə təs, -stō′mə-, sĭk′lə-), *adj.* 1. having a circular mouth. 2. belonging or pertaining to the *Cyclostomata*. See **cyclostome.** Also, **cy·clos·to·mate** (sī klŏs′tə mĭt, -māt′).

cy·clo·stome (sī′klə stōm′, sĭk′lə-), *adj.* 1. belonging or pertaining to the *Cyclostomata*, a group or class of eellike aquatic vertebrates (the lampreys and hagfishes) characterized by pouchlike gills and a circular suctorial mouth without hinged jaws. 2. having a circular mouth. —*n.* 3. a cyclostome vertebrate; a lamprey or a hagfish. [f. CYCLO- + m. Gk. *stóma* mouth]

cy·clo·style (sī′klə stīl′, sĭk′lə-), *n.* a manifolding device consisting of a kind of pen with a small toothed wheel at the end which cuts minute holes in a specially prepared paper stretched over a smooth surface, thus forming a stencil from which copies are printed.

ăct, āble, dâre, ärt; ĕbb, ēqual; ĭf, īce; hŏt, ōver, ôrder, oil, bŏŏk, ōōze, out; ŭp, ūse, ûrge; ə = a in alone; ch, chief; g, give; ng, ring; sh, shoe; th, thin; ₸ħ, that; zh, vision. See the full key on inside cover.

cy·clo·thy·mi·a (sī′klə thī′mī ə, sĭk′lə-), *n. Psychiatry.* a mild manic-depressive psychosis involving recurring cycles of exhilaration and depression. [f. CYCLO- + Gk. -*thymia* mindedness (der. *thymós* mind)] —**cy′clo·thy′mic,** *adj.*

cy·clo·thy·mi·ac (sī′klə thī′mī ăk′, sĭk′lə-), *n.* a person affected with cyclothymia.

cy·clo·tron (sī′klə trŏn′, sĭk′lə-), *n. Physics.* a device for imparting very high speed to electrified particles by successive electric impulses at high frequency, space requirements and applied voltage being kept relatively low by causing the particles to move in spiral paths in a strong magnetic field.

cy·der (sī′dər), *n. Brit.* cider.

Cyd·nus (sĭd′nəs), *n.* a historic river of Cilicia, in SE Asia Minor, flowing through ancient Tarsus.

cyg·net (sĭg′nĭt), *n.* a young swan. [ME, f. s. L *cygnus* swan (t. Gk.: m. *kŷknos*) + -ET]

Cyg·nus (sĭg′nəs), *n.,* gen. -**ni** (-nī). *Astron.* a northern constellation containing the star Deneb. [t. L: swan]

cyl, cylinder.

cyl·in·der (sĭl′ĭn dər), *n.* **1.** *Geom.* a solid which may be conceived as generated by the revolution of a rectangle about one of its sides (a **right circular cylinder**). **2.** a similar solid in which the elements of the curved surface are oblique to the circular bases (**oblique circular cylinder**). **3.** any solid bounded by two parallel planes and a curved surface generated by a moving straight line which intersects a given curve and is always parallel to its original position. **4.** a curved surface generated in this manner. **5.** any cylinderlike object or part, whether solid or hollow. **6.** the rotating part of a revolver, which contains the chambers for the cartridges. **7.** the body of a pump. **8.** the chamber in an engine in which the working medium acts upon the piston. **9.** (in certain printing presses) **a.** a rotating cylinder which produces the impression, under which a flat form to be printed from passes. **b.** either of two cylinders, one carrying a curved form or plate to be printed from, which rotate against each other in opposite directions. **10.** *Archaeol.* a cylindrical or somewhat barrel-shaped stone or clay object, bearing a cuneiform inscription or a carved design, worn by the Babylonians, Assyrians, and kindred peoples as a seal and amulet. —*v.t.* **11.** to furnish with a cylinder or cylinders. **12.** to subject to the action of a cylinder or cylinders. [t. L: m. s. *cylindrus,* t. Gk.: m. *kýlindros* roller, cylinder] —**cyl′in·der·like′,** *adj.*

Right circular cylinder

cylinder head, a detachable portion of an engine fastened securely to the cylinder block containing all or a portion of the combustion chamber.

cy·lin·dri·cal (sĭ lĭn′drə kəl), *adj.* of, pertaining to, or of the form of a cylinder. Also, **cy·lin′dric.** —**cy·lin′dri·cal·ly,** *adv.*

cyl·in·droid (sĭl′ĭn droid′), *n.* **1.** a solid having the form of a cylinder with equal and parallel elliptical bases. —*adj.* **2.** resembling a cylinder. [t. Gk.: m. s. *kylindroeidḗs* cylinderlike. See -OID]

cy·lix (sī′lĭks, sĭl′ĭks), *n., pl.* **cylices** (sĭl′ə sēz′). *Gk. Antiq.* a shallow drinking cup, usually with a stem and foot, and two handles; kylix. [t. Gk.: m. *kŷlix*]

Cyl·le·ni·an (sĭ lē′nĭ ən), *adj.* pertaining to Mount Cyllene, in Arcadia, Greece, or to the god Hermes, reputed to have been born there.

cy·ma (sī′mə), *n., pl.* -**mae** (-mē). **1.** *Archit.* a projecting molding whose profile is a compound concavo-convex curve. It is called a **cyma recta** when the projecting part is concave and a **cyma reversa** when the projecting portion is convex. See diag. under **column.** **2.** *Bot.* a cyme. [NL, t. Gk.: m. *kŷma* something swollen, wave, waved molding, sprout]

cy·mar (sĭ′mär′), *n.* simar.

cy·ma·ti·um (sĭ mā′shĭ əm), *n., pl.* -**tia** (-shĭ ə). *Archit.* the capping molding of a cornice, placed above the corona. commonly having a cyma recta as its most important feature. [t. L, t. Gk.: m. *kymátion,* dim. of *kŷma* wave]

cym·bal (sĭm′bəl), *n.* one of a pair of concave plates of brass or bronze which are struck together to produce a sharp, ringing sound. [OE, t. L: s. *cymbalum,* t. Gk.: m. *kŷmbalon,* der. *kŷmbē* cup, bowl] —**cym′bal·ist,** *n.*

Cym·be·line (sĭm′bə lēn′), *n.* a romantic drama (about 1610) by Shakespeare.

cyme (sīm), *n. Bot.* **1.** an inflorescence in which the primary axis bears a single terminal flower which develops first, the inflorescence being continued by secondary, tertiary, and other axes. **2.** a flat or convex inflorescence of this type. [t. L: m. s. *cŷma* sprout, t. Gk.: m. *kŷma.* See CYMA]

cy·mene (sī′mēn), *n. Chem.* a liquid hydrocarbon, $C_{10}H_{14}$, with a pleasant smell, occurring in the volatile oil of the common cumin, *Cuminum cyminum,* and existing in three isomeric forms, *ortho-, meta-,* and *para-cymene.* [f. *cym-* (comb. form repr. Gk. *kŷminon* cumin) + -ENE]

Cymes: A. of houseleek; B. of forget-me-not

cymo-, a word element meaning "wave." [t. Gk.: m. *kymo-,* comb. form of *kŷma* wave, embryo, sprout]

cy·mo·gene (sī′mə jēn′), *n. Chem.* a mixture of very volatile inflammable hydrocarbons, constituting the fraction boiling at about 0° C. obtained in distilling crude petroleum, and containing a large percentage of butane. [f. *cymo-* (comb. form repr. Gk. *kŷminon* cumin) + -GENE]

cy·mo·graph (sī′mə grăf′, -gräf′), *n.* kymograph.

cy·mom·e·ter (sī mŏm′ə tər), *n. Elect.* an instrument for measuring electromagnetic waves.

cy·mo·phane (sī′mə fān′), *n.* chrysoberyl.

cy·mo·scope (sī′mə skŏp′), *n.* a device for detecting the presence of electromagnetic waves.

cy·mose (sī′mōs, sī mōs′), *adj. Bot.* **1.** bearing a cyme or cymes. **2.** of or of the nature of a cyme. [t. L: m. s. *cŷmōsus* full of shoots. See CYME] —**cy′mose·ly,** *adv.*

Cym·ric (kĭm′rĭk, sĭm′-), *adj.* **1.** pertaining to the Cymry. —*n.* **2.** Welsh (the language). Also, **Kymric.** [f. m. Welsh *Cymru* Wales or *Cymry* the Welsh + -IC]

Cym·ry (kĭm′rĭ), *n.pl.* the Welsh, or the branch of the Celtic race to which the Welsh belong, comprising also the Cornish people and the Bretons. Also, **Kymry.** [t. Welsh, pl. of *Cymro* Welshman. Cf. Welsh *cymru* Wales]

cyn·ic (sĭn′ĭk), *n.* **1.** a sneering faultfinder; one who doubts or denies the goodness of human motives, and who often displays his attitude by sneers, sarcasm, etc. **2.** (*cap.*) one of a sect of Greek philosophers founded by Antisthenes of Athens (born about 444 B.C.), who sought to develop the ethical teachings of Socrates. The chief doctrines of the Cynics were that virtue is the only good, that the essence of virtue is self-control, and that surrender to any external influence is beneath the dignity of man. —*adj.* **3.** cynical. **4.** (*cap.*) of or pertaining to the Cynics or their doctrines. **5.** of or pertaining to the Dog Star: *the cynic year.* [t. L: s. *cynicus,* t. Gk.: m. *kynikós* doglike, churlish, Cynic]

cyn·i·cal (sĭn′ə kəl), *adj.* **1.** like or characteristic of a cynic; distrusting the motives of others. **2.** (*cap.*) cynic (def. 4). —**cyn′i·cal·ly,** *adv.*

—**Syn. 1.** CYNICAL, PESSIMISTIC, SARCASTIC, SATIRICAL, imply holding a low opinion of mankind. CYNICAL suggests a disbelief in the sincerity of human motives: *cynical about honesty.* PESSIMISTIC implies a more or less habitual disposition to look on the dark side of things, and to believe that the worst will happen: *pessimistic as to the future.* SARCASTIC refers to sneering or making cutting jibes: *sarcastic about a profession of faith.* SATIRICAL suggests expressing scorn or ridicule by saying the opposite of what one means: *satirical about the way in which actions and protestations differ.* —**Ant. 1.** optimistic.

cyn·i·cism (sĭn′ə sĭz′əm), *n.* **1.** cynical disposition or character. **2.** a cynical remark. **3.** (*cap.*) the doctrines or practices of the Cynics.

cy·no·sure (sī′nə shŏŏr′, sĭn′ə-), *n.* **1.** something that strongly attracts attention by its brilliance, etc.: *the cynosure of all eyes.* **2.** something serving for guidance or direction. **3.** (*cap.*) the constellation of the Little Bear (Ursa Minor). **4.** (*cap.*) the polestar. [t. L: m.s. *Cynosūra,* t. Gk.: m. *Kynósoura,* lit., dog's tail]

Cyn·thi·a (sĭn′thĭ ə), *n.* **1.** Artemis (Diana). **2.** *Poetic.* the moon, the emblem of Artemis (Diana).

cy·per·a·ceous (sī′pə rā′shəs, sĭp′ə-), *adj.* pertaining or belonging to, or resembling, the *Cyperaceae* or the sedge family of monocotyledonous plants, with solid, often triangular, stems and small, coriaceous, achenial fruit. [f. s. NL *Cyperus* the typical genus (t. Gk.: m. *kŷpeiros* kind of marsh plant) + -ACEOUS]

cy·pher (sī′fər), *n., v.i., v.t.* cipher.

cy pres (sē′ prā′), *Law.* **1.** as near as practicable. **2.** doctrine of cy pres, an equitable doctrine (applicable only to cases of charitable trusts or donations) which, in place of an impossible or illegal condition, limitation, or object, allows the nearest practicable one to be substituted. Also, **cy′pres′.** [t. late AF: as nearly]

cy·press¹ (sī′prəs), *n.* **1.** any of the evergreen trees constituting the coniferous genus *Cupressus,* distinguished by dark-green scalelike, overlapping leaves, often a very slender tree with a durable wood. **2.** any of various other coniferous trees allied to the true cypress, as *Taxodium distichum* (**swamp,** or **bald cypress**) of the southern U. S., *Chamaecyparis,* etc. **3.** any of various other plants in some way resembling the true cypress, as *Gilia coronopifolia* (**standing cypress**), a tall, slender, herb of the U. S. **4.** the wood of these trees. [t. LL: s. *cypressus,* t. Gk.: m. *kypárissos;* r. ME *cipres,* t. OF]

cy·press² (sī′prəs), *n. Obs.* a fine, thin fabric resembling lawn or crepe, which was formerly much used in black for mourning garments, etc. Also, **cyprus.** [ME *cipres,* prob. t. OF; appar. named from Cyprus]

cypress vine, a convolvulaceous garden plant, *Quamoclit pennata,* with finely parted leaves and scarlet or white tubular flowers.

Cyp·ri·an (sĭp′rĭ ən), *adj.* **1.** pertaining to Cyprus, famous as a center for the worship of Aphrodite (Venus). **2.** lewd; licentious. —*n.* **3.** a native or inhabitant of Cyprus. **4.** a lewd person, esp. a prostitute. [f. s. L *Cyprius* (t. Gk.: m. *Kŷprios* of Cyprus) + -AN]

Cyp·ri·an (sĭp′rĭ ən), *n.* **Saint,** A.D. 200?–258, a bishop of Carthage, writer, and martyr.

cy·pri·nid (sĭ prī′nĭd, sĭp′rə nĭd), *n.* **1.** any fish belonging to the *Cyprinidae,* or minnow family. —*adj.* **2.** carplike in form or structure.

cy·prin·o·dont (sĭ·prĭn′ə·dŏnt′, sĭ·prī′nə-), *n.* any of the *Cyprinodontidae,* a family of small soft-finned fishes, mostly inhabiting the fresh and brackish waters of America, including the killifishes, certain top minnows, the guppy, etc. [f. s. Gk. *kyprīnos* carp + s. *odoús* tooth]

cyp·ri·noid (sĭp′rə·noid′, sĭ·prī′noid), *adj.* **1.** resembling a carp; belonging to the *Cyprinoidea,* a group of fishes including the carps, suckers, loaches, etc. —*n.* **2.** a cyprinoid fish. [f. s. Gk. *kyprīnos* carp + -OID]

Cyp·ri·ote (sĭp′rĭ·ōt′), *n.* **1.** a native or inhabitant of Cyprus. **2.** the Greek dialect of Cyprus. —*adj.* **3.** Cyprian. Also, **Cyp·ri·ot** (sĭp′rĭ·ət). [t. Gk.: m. *Kypriótēs*]

cyp·ri·pe·di·um (sĭp′rə·pē′dĭ·əm), *n.* any plant of the genus *Cypripedium,* comprising orchids having large flowers with a protruding saclike labellum; a lady's-slipper. [NL, f. L *Cypri(s)* Venus + s. L *pēs* foot + -IUM]

Cy·prus (sī′prəs), *n.* an island in the Mediterranean, S of Turkey: a British colony. 395,000 pop. (est. 1943); 3572 sq. mi. *Cap.:* Nicosia.

cy·prus (sī′prəs), *n. Obs.* cypress[2].

cyp·se·la (sĭp′sə·lə), *n., pl.* **-lae** (-lē′). *Bot.* an achene with an adherent calyx, as in the composite plants. [NL, t. Gk.: m. *kypsélē* hollow vessel]

Cyr·e·na·ic (sĭr′ə·nā′ĭk, sī′rə-), *adj.* **1.** of or pertaining to Cyrenaica, or its chief city, Cyrene. **2.** noting or pertaining to a school of philosophy founded by Aristippus of Cyrene, who taught that pleasure is the only rational aim of life. —*n.* **3.** a native or inhabitant of Cyrenaica. **4.** a disciple of the Cyrenaic school of philosophy.

Cyr·e·na·i·ca (sĭr′ə·nā′ə·kə, sī′rə-) *n.* an ancient district in N Africa, W of Egypt. Also, **Barca.**

Cyrenaica, 350 B.C.

Cy·re·ne (sī·rē′nĭ), *n.* an ancient Greek city and colony in Cyrenaica, in N Africa.

Cyr·il (sĭr′əl), *n.* **Saint,** ("*Apostle of the Slavs*") A.D. 827–869, Greek missionary to the Moravians.

Cy·ril·lic (sĭ·rĭl′ĭk), *adj.* **1.** of or pertaining to an old Slavic alphabet reputed to have been invented by St. Cyril, and its modern forms as used in Serbia, Bulgaria, and the Soviet Union. **2.** of or pertaining to St. Cyril.

cyrto-, a word element meaning "curved." [t. Gk.: m. *kyrto-,* comb. form of *kyrtós*]

Cy·rus (sī′rəs), *n.* **1.** ("*the Elder*" or "*the Great*") died 529 B.C., king of Persia, 558?–529 B.C.; founder of Persian Empire. **2.** ("*The Younger*") died 401 B.C., Persian satrap: led army (including 10,000 Greeks) against his brother, Artaxerxes II, Persian king.

cyst (sĭst), *n.* **1.** *Pathol.* a closed bladderlike sac formed in animal tissues, containing fluid or semifluid morbid matter. **2.** a bladder, sac, or vesicle. **3.** *Bot.* **a.** a sporelike cell with a resistant protective wall. **b.** a cell or cavity enclosing reproductive bodies, etc. **4.** *Zool.* **a.** a sac, usually spherical, surrounding an animal that has passed into a dormant condition. **b.** such a sac plus the contained animal. **c.** a capsule or resistant covering. [t. NL: s. *cystis,* t. Gk.: m. *kýstis* bladder, bag, pouch]

cyst-, a combining form representing **cyst.** Also, **cysti-, cysto-.**

-cyst, a terminal combining form of **cyst.**

cys·tec·to·my (sĭs·tĕk′tə·mĭ), *n., pl.* **-mies.** *Surg.* excision of a cyst or bladder, usually the urinary bladder.

cys·te·ine (sĭs′tĭ·ēn′, -ĭn), *n. Biochem.* an amino acid, HSCH₂CH(NH₂)COOH, obtained from cystine and important for growth-stimulating characteristics.

cysti-, var. of **cyst-,** as in *cysticercoid.*

cyst·ic (sĭs′tĭk), *adj.* **1.** pertaining to, of the nature of, or having a cyst or cysts; encysted. **2.** *Anat.* belonging to or relating to the urinary bladder or the gall bladder.

cys·ti·cer·coid (sĭs′tə·sûr′koid), *n. Parasitol.* the larva of certain tapeworms, developing in insects, etc., in which a single head forms without a spacious bladder around it.

cys·ti·cer·cus (sĭs′tə·sûr′kəs), *n., pl.* **-cerci** (-sûr′sī). *Parasitol.* the bladderworm larva of certain tapeworms, with a single head (scolex) formed in a large bladder. [NL, f. Gk.: *cysti-* CYSTI- + m. *kérkos* tail]

cys·tine (sĭs′tēn, -tĭn), *n. Biochem.* one of the important sulfur-containing amino acids, C₆H₁₂O₄N₂S₂, found in proteins, esp., hair, wool, and horn. Also, **cystin** (sĭs′tĭn).

cys·ti·tis (sĭs·tī′tĭs), *n. Pathol.* inflammation of the urinary bladder.

cysto-, var. of **cyst-,** before consonants, as in *cystoscope.*

cys·to·carp (sĭs′tə·kärp′), *n.* the mass of carpospores formed as a result of fertilization in red algae (*Rhodophyta*), with or without a special envelope (pericarp).

cys·to·cele (sĭs′tə·sēl′), *n. Pathol.* hernia in which the urinary bladder protrudes into the vagina.

cyst·oid (sĭs′toid), *adj.* **1.** resembling a cyst but having no enclosing capsule. —*n.* **2.** a cystlike structure or formation.

cys·to·lith (sĭs′tə·lĭth), *n. Bot.* a mass of calcium carbonate on the cellulose wall.

cys·to·scope (sĭs′tə·skōp′), *n. Med.* a slender, cylindrical instrument for examining the interior of the urinary bladder and for the introduction of medication therein.

cys·tot·o·my (sĭs·tŏt′ə·mĭ), *n., pl.* **-mies.** *Surg.* the operation of cutting into the urinary bladder.

cy·tas·ter (sī·tăs′tər, sī′tăs′-), *n. Biol.* aster.

-cyte, a word element referring to cells or corpuscles, as in *leucocyte.* [comb. form repr. Gk. *kýtos* container]

Cy·the·ra (sĭ·thĭr′ə), *n.* a small island off S Greece, famous as a sanctuary of Aphrodite. Also, **Cerigo.**

Cyth·er·e·a (sĭth′ə·rē′ə), *n. Gk. Myth.* a surname of Aphrodite or Venus. —**Cyth′er·e′an,** *adj.*

cyto-, a word element referring to cells, as in *cytogenesis.* Also, before vowels, **cyt-.** [t. Gk.: m. *kyto-,* comb. form of *kýtos* container]

cy·to·gen·e·sis (sī′tō·jĕn′ə·sĭs), *n.* the genesis and differentiation of cells.

cy·to·ge·net·ics (sī′tō·jə·nĕt′ĭks), *n.* the part played by cells in causing phenomena of heredity, mutation, and evolution.

cy·to·ki·ne·sis (sī′tō·kĭ·nē′sĭs, -kī-), *n.* the changes in the cytoplasm during mitosis, meiosis, and fertilization.

cy·tol·o·gy (sī·tŏl′ə·jĭ), *n.* the scientific study of cells, esp. their formation, structure, and functions. —**cy·tol′o·gist,** *n.*

cy·tol·y·sis (sī·tŏl′ə·sĭs), *n. Physiol.* the dissolution or degeneration of cells.

cy·to·plasm (sī′tō·plăz′əm), *n. Biol.* the living substance or protoplasm of a cell exclusive of the nucleus. Also, **cy·to·plast** (sī′tə·plăst′). —**cy′to·plas′mic,** *adj.*

Cyz·i·cus (sĭz′ĭ·kəs), *n.* an ancient city of Mysia, in NW Asia Minor, on a peninsula in the Sea of Marmara.

C.Z., Canal Zone (Panama).

czar (zär), *n.* **1.** an emperor or king. **2.** (*usually cap.*) the emperor of Russia. **3.** (*often cap.*) an autocratic ruler or leader. Also, **tsar, tzar.** [t. Russ.: m. *tsar,* ult. t. L: m. *Caesar.*] —**czar·dom** (zär′dəm), *n.*

czar·das (chär′däsh), *n.* a Hungarian national dance in two movements, one slow and the other fast.

czar·e·vitch (zär′ə·vĭch), *n.* **1.** the son of a czar. **2.** (*later*) the eldest son. Also, **tsarevitch, tzarevitch.** [t. Russ.: m. *tsarevich*]

cza·rev·na (zär·ĕv′nə), *n.* a daughter of a czar. Also, **tsarevna.** [t. Russ.: m. *tsarevna*]

cza·ri·na (zä·rē′nə), *n.* the wife of a czar; a Russian empress. Also, **tsarina, tzarina.** [f. CZAR, TSAR | *-ina* (Latinization of G *-in,* fem. suffix, as in *zarin* wife of czar)]

czar·ism (zär′ĭzəm), *n.* dictatorship; autocratic government. Also, **tsarism, tzarism.**

cza·rit·za (zä·rĭt′sə), *n.* czarina. Also, **tsaritza, tzaritza.**

Czech (chĕk), *n.* **1.** a member of the most westerly branch of the Slavs, comprising the Bohemians (or Czechs proper), the Moravians, and the Slovaks. **2.** the language of Bohemia and Moravia, a Slavic language similar to Slovak. —**Czech′ic, Czech′ish,** *adj.*

Czech., Czechoslovakia. Also, **Czechosl.**

Czech·o·slo·vak (chĕk′ə·slō′văk, -văk), *n.* **1.** a member of the branch of the Slavic race comprising the Czechs proper, the Slovaks, etc. —*adj.* **2.** of or pertaining to the Czechoslovaks. Also, **Czech′o-Slo′vak.**

Czech·o·slo·va·ki·a (chĕk′ə·slō·vä′kĭ·ə, -văk′ĭ-), *n.* a republic in central Europe. 13,791,000 pop. (est. 1946); 49,379 sq. mi. (1938). *Cap.:* Prague. Also, **Czech′o-Slo·va′ki·a.** —**Czech′o·slo·vak′i·an,** *adj., n.*

Czer·no·witz (chĕr′nō·vĭts), *n.* Polish name of **Cernäuti.**

Czę·sto·cho·wa (chăN′stō·hô′vä), *n.* a city in S Poland. 101,000 (1946).

D

D, d (dē), *n., pl.* **D's** or **Ds, d's** or **ds. 1.** the 4th letter of the English alphabet. **2.** (used as a symbol) the fourth in order; the fourth in a series. **3.** the lowest passing mark for school or college work. **4.** *Music.* **a.** the second tone of the scale of C, or the fourth tone of the scale of A minor. **b.** a written or printed note representing this tone. **c.** a key, string, or pipe tuned to this note. **d.** (in solmization) the second note of the scale.

D, 1. Roman numeral for 500. **2.** *Chem.* deuterium. **3.** Dutch.

D., 1. December. **2.** Democrat. **3.** Democratic. **4.** *Physics.* density. **5.** *Chem.* dextro-. **6.** Dutch.

d., **1.** date. **2.** daughter. **3.** degree. **4.** delete. **5.** *Brit.* (L *denarius*) penny; (L *denarii*) pence: *3d = 6 cents.* **6.** *Physics.* density. **7.** *Chem.* dextro-. **8.** dialect. **9.** dialectal. **10.** diameter. **11.** died. **12.** dime. **13.** dividend. **14.** dollar. **15.** dose.

D.A., **1.** District Attorney. **2.** Delayed Action (bomb).

dab¹ (dăb), *v.*, dabbed, dabbing, *n.* —*v.t.* **1.** to strike, esp. lightly, as with the hand. **2.** to pat or tap gently, as with some soft or moist substance. **3.** to apply (a substance) by light strokes. —*v.i.* **4.** to strike lightly; peck. —*n.* **5.** a quick or light blow; a pat, as with the hand or something soft. **6.** a small moist lump or mass. **7.** a small quantity. [ME. Cf. Norw. *dabba* tap with the foot, G *tappe* footprint]

dab² (dăb), *n.* **1.** a European flatfish, *Limanda limanda*. **2.** a sand dab or other flatfish. [orig. unknown]

dab·ber (dăb′ər), *n.* **1.** one who or that which dabs. **2.** a cushionlike article used for applying ink, etc., as by printers and engravers.

dab·ble (dăb′əl), *v.*, -bled, -bling. —*v.t.* **1.** to wet slightly or repeatedly in or with a liquid; splash; spatter. —*v.i.* **2.** to play in water, as with the hands. **3.** to do anything in a slight or superficial manner: *to dabble in literature.* [t. Flem.: m. s. *dabbelen*] —**dab′bler**, *n.*

dab·chick (dăb′chĭk′), *n.* a small diving bird, esp. the little grebe, *Podiceps fluviatilis*, of Europe, or the pied-billed grebe, *Podilymbus podiceps*, of America.

dab·ster (dăb′stər), *n.* **1.** *Brit. Dial.* an expert. **2.** *Colloq.* a superficial worker; a dabbler.

da ca·po (dä kä′pō). *Music.* from the beginning (a direction to repeat). [It.]

Dac·ca (dăk′ə), *n.* the principal city of the E division of Pakistan, in E Bengal. 213,218 (1941).

dace (dās), *n.*, *pl.* **daces** (*esp. collectively*) **dace.** **1.** a small fresh-water cyprinoid fish, *Leuciscus leuciscus*, of Europe, with a stout, fusiform body. **2.** any of several similar or related fishes of the U.S. [ME *darse*, t. OF: m. *dars* DART]

Da·chau (dä′khou), *n.* a Nazi concentration camp, scene of mass murders, in S Germany, near Munich.

dachs·hund (dăks′hŏŏnd′, däsh′-; *Ger.* däks′hŏŏnt′), *n.* one of a German breed of small hounds with a long body and very short legs. [t. G: f. *dachs* badger + *hund* dog]

Dachshund
(8 in. or more high at the shoulder)

Da·ci·a (dā′shĭ·ə, -shə), *n.* an ancient kingdom and later a Roman province in S Europe between the Carpathian Mountains and the Danube, corresponding generally to modern Rumania and adjacent regions. —**Da·cian** (dā′shən), *adj.*, *n.*

da·coit (də·koit′), *n.* one of a class of robbers in India and Burma, who plunder in bands. [t. Hind.: m. *dākāit*, der. *dākā* gang robbery]

da·coit·y (də·koi′tĭ), *n.* gang robbery in India and Burma. [t. Hind.: m. *dākāitī*]

dac·tyl (dăk′təl, -tĭl), *n.* *Pros.* a foot of three syllables, one long followed by two short, or, in modern verse, one accented followed by two unaccented (– ˘ ˘), as in "Gēntly ănd|hūmănly." [ME *dactile*, t. L: m.s. *dactylus*, t. Gk.: m. *dáktylos* finger or toe, date (see DATE²), metrical foot]

dac·tyl·ic (dăk·tĭl′ĭk), *adj.* **1.** consisting of or characterized by dactyls. **2.** of a dactyl. —*n.* **3.** a dactylic verse.

dac·ty·lol·o·gy (dăk′tə·lŏl′ə·jĭ), *n.* the art of communicating ideas by signs made with the fingers, as in a manual alphabet used by the deaf.

dad (dăd), *n.* (in childish or familiar use) father. [earlier *dadde*, nursery substitute for FATHER]

da·da·ism (dä′də·ĭz′əm), *n.* a movement in art, literature, etc., which flourished during and just after World War I. It attempted to discredit all previous art by using the incongruous and the accidental. Also, **da·da** (dä′də). [t. F: m. *Dadaisme*, der. *Dada*, title of a review]

dad·dy (dăd′ĭ), *n.*, *pl.* **-dies.** a diminutive of **dad.**

dad·dy-long·legs (dăd′ĭ·lŏng′lĕgz′, -lông′-), *n.* **1.** *U.S.* a harvestman. See the illus. just above. **2.** *Brit. Dial.* a crane fly.

Daddy-longlegs,
Phalangium opilio

da·do (dā′dō), *n.*, *pl.* **-does, -dos.** **1.** *Archit.* the part of a pedestal between the base and the cornice or cap. **2.** the lower broad part of an interior wall finished in wallpaper, a fabric, paint, etc. [t. It.: die, cube, pedestal, g. L *datus*. See DIE²]

dae·dal (dē′dəl), *adj.* *Chiefly Poetic.* **1.** skillful or ingenious. **2.** showing skill or cunning. **3.** diversified. [t. L: s. *daedalus* skillful, t. Gk.: m. *daídalos*]

Daed·a·lus (dĕd′ə·ləs or, *esp. Brit.*, dē′də-), *n.* *Gk. Myth.* an Athenian architect who built the labyrinth for Minos and made wings for himself and his son Icarus. [t. L, t. Gk.: m. *Daídalos*, lit., the cunning worker] —**Dae·da·li·an, Dae·da·le·an** (dĭ·dā′lĭ·ən, -dāl′yən), *adj.*

A, Cornice; B, Dado; C, Base
Pedestal

dae·mon (dē′mən), *n.* **1.** *Gk. Myth.* **a.** a god. **b.** a subordinate deity, as the genius of a place or a man's attendant spirit. **2.** a demon. Also, **daimon.** [t. L, t. Gk.: m. *daímōn*] —**dae·mon·ic** (dē·mŏn′ĭk), *adj.*

daff¹ (dăf), *v.i.* *Scot.* to make sport; dally; play. [akin to DAFT]

daff² (dăf), *v.t.* **1.** to turn or thrust aside. **2.** *Obs.* to doff. [var. of DOFF]

daf·fo·dil (dăf′ə·dĭl), *n.* **1.** a plant, *Narcissus Pseudo-Narcissus*, of the genus *Narcissus*, with single or double yellow nodding flowers, blooming in the spring. **2.** (formerly) any plant of this genus. **3.** clear yellow; canary. [unexplained var. of ME *affodille*, t. VL: m. *affodillus*, var. of *asphodelus*, t. Gk.: m. *asphódelos*]

daf·fo·dil·ly (dăf′ə·dĭl′ĭ), *n.*, *pl.* **-lies.** *Poetic.* daffodil (def. 1, 2). Also, **daf·fa·down·dil·ly** (dăf′ə·doun·dĭl′ĭ), **daf·fy·down·dil·ly.**

daff·y (dăf′ĭ), *adj.*, **daffier, daffiest.** *U.S. Colloq.* or *Brit. Dial.* silly; weak-minded; crazy.

daft (dăft, däft), *adj.* **1.** insane; crazy. **2.** simple or foolish. **3.** *Scot.* frolicsome. [ME *dafte*, OE *gedæfte* mild, meek. Cf. DEFT] —**daft′ly**, *adv.* —**daft′ness**, *n.*

dag (dăg), *n.* a daglock. [ME *dagge*; orig. uncert.]

da Gam·a (də găm′ə; *Port.* də gä′mə), **Vasco.** See **Gama**, Vasco da.

Da·gan (dä′gän), *n.* the Babylonian earth god.

Dag·en·ham (dăg′ən·əm), *n.* a city in SE England, near London. 106,920 (est. 1946).

dag·ger (dăg′ər), *n.* **1.** a short-edged and pointed weapon, like a small sword, used for thrusting and stabbing. **2.** *Print.* a mark (†) used for references, etc.; the obelisk. —*v.t.* **3.** to stab with a dagger. **4.** *Print.* to mark with a dagger. [ME, der. obs. *dag* pierce, stab]

dag·gle (dăg′əl), *v.t.*, *v.i.*, **-gled, -gling.** to drag or trail through mud, water, etc.; draggle. [freq. of d. *dag* bemire. See DAG]

Da·ghe·stan (dä′gĕ·stän′), *n.* an autonomous republic in the SE Soviet Union in Europe, bordering on the Caspian Sea. 930,527 pop. (1939); ab. 13,500 sq. mi. *Cap.*: Makhach-Kala. Also, **Da/ge·stan/.**

dag·lock (dăg′lŏk′), *n.* a lock of wool on a sheep that hangs and drags in the wet. [see DAGGLE, LOCK²]

Da·go (dā′gō), *n.*, *pl.* **-gos, -goes.** *U.S. Slang.* (in contemptuous use) **1.** an Italian. **2.** a Spaniard. **3.** a Portuguese. [said to be t. Sp.: m. *Diego* James]

Dag·ö (dăg′ə), *n.* Danish name of Hiumaa.

da·go·ba (dä′gə·bə), *n.* a dome-shaped memorial alleged to contain relics of Buddha or a Buddhist saint.

Da·gon (dā′gŏn), *n.* the national god of the Philistines, represented as half man and half fish, originally a fish god and later the god of corn and grain. [t. L, t. Gk., t. Heb.: m. *dāghōn* little fish]

da·guerre·o·type (də·gĕr′ə·tīp′, -ĭ·ə·tīp′), *n.*, *v.*, **-typed, -typing.** —*n.* **1.** an early (1839) photographic process in which the impression was made on a silver surface sensitized to the action of light by iodine, and then developed by mercury vapor. **2.** a picture so made. —*v.t.* **3.** to photograph by this process. [named after L. J. M. *Daguerre* (1789–1851), French inventor. See -TYPE] —**da·guerre′o·typ′er, da·guerre′o·typ′ist**, *n.*

da·ha·be·ah (dä′hə·bē′ə), *n.* a kind of houseboat or passenger boat, used on the Nile. Also, **da/ha·bee/yah, da/ha·bi/ya.** [t. Ar.: m. *dhahabīyah*, lit., the golden]

dahl·ia (dăl′yə, däl′- or, *esp. Brit.*, dāl′-), *n.* **1.** any plant of the composite genus *Dahlia*, native in Mexico and Central America, widely cultivated for its showy, variously colored flowers. **2.** the flower or tuberous root of a dahlia. **3.** a violet coal-tar color. [t. NL; named after A. *Dahl*, Swedish botanist]

Da·ho·mey (də·hō′mĭ; *Fr.* dȧ̂·ô·mĕ′), *n.* a colony in French West Africa. 1,384,000 pop. (1940); 43,243 sq mi. *Cap.*: Porto Novo. See map under **Gold Coast.** —**Da·ho·man** (də·hō′mən), *adj.*, *n.*

Dail Eir·eann (dôl âr′ŏn; *Irish* t͡hôl), the lower house of parliament of Eire. See **Oireachtas.** Also, **Dail.** [Irish: *dail* assembly + *éireann*, gen. of *éire* Erin]

dai·ly (dā′lĭ), *adj.*, *n.*, *pl.* **-lies**, *adv.* —*adj.* **1.** of, done, occurring, or issued each day or each weekday. —*n.* **2.** a newspaper appearing each day or each weekday. **3.** *Brit.* a servant who comes to work every day. —*adv.* **4.** every day; day by day.

dai·ly-bread·er (dā′lĭ·brĕd′ər), *n.* *Brit.* commuter.

dai·men (dā′mĭn), *adj.* *Scot.* rare; occasional.

dai·mon (dī′mŏn), *n.* daemon. [see DEMON]

dai·myo (dī′myō), *n.*, *pl.* **-myo, -myos.** **1.** the class of greater nobles in Japanese feudalism; often the daimyo were descendants of younger sons of emperors. **2.** a member of this class. Also, **dai/mio.** [t. Jap., f. Chinese: *dai* great + *mio* name]

Dai Nip·pon (dī′ nĭp′ŏn; *Jap.* dī′ nēp′pôn′), Greater Japan. Once the watchword of Japanese expansionists, it is now against the law to use *Dai Nippon* in Japan. See **Japan.**

dain·ty (dān′tĭ), *adj.*, **-tier, -tiest.** *n.*, *pl.* **-ties.** —*adj.* **1.** of delicate beauty or charm; exquisite. **2.** pleasing to the palate; toothsome; delicious: *dainty food.* **3.** particular in discrimination or taste; fastidious. **4.** too particular; squeamish. —*n.* **5.** something delicious to the taste; a delicacy. [ME *deinte*, t. OF, g. L *dignitas* worthiness] —**dain′ti·ly**, *adv.* —**dain′ti·ness**, *n.* —**Syn. 1.** See **delicate. 3.** See **particular. 4.** finical, overnice.

dai·qui·ri (dī′kə rĭ, dăk′/ə-), n., pl. **-ris.** a vigorously shaken cocktail consisting of rum, lime juice, sugar, and ice.

Dai·ren (dī′rĕn′), n. a seaport in NE China: capital of the former Japanese leased territory of Kwantung in S Manchuria. 370,000 (est. 1939). Chinese, **Talien.** Formerly, **Dalny.**

dair·y (dâr′ĭ), n., pl. **dairies. 1.** a place, as a room or building, where milk and cream are kept and made into butter and cheese. **2.** a shop or company that sells milk, butter, etc. **3.** the business of producing milk, butter, and cheese. **4.** a dairy farm. **5.** the cows on a farm. [ME *deierie,* f. *dei* female servant, dairymaid (OE *dǣge* breadmaker) + *-erie* -ERY]

dairy cattle, cows raised mainly for their milk.

dairy farm, a farm devoted chiefly to the production of milk and the manufacture of butter and cheese.

dair·y·ing (dâr′ĭ ĭng), n. the business of a dairy.

dair·y·maid (dâr′ĭ mād), n. a female servant employed in a dairy.

dair·y·man (dâr′ĭ mən), n., pl. **-men. 1.** an owner or manager of a dairy. **2.** an employee in a dairy.

da·is (dā′ĭs, dās), n. a raised platform, as at the end of a room, for a throne, seats of honor, a lecturer's desk, etc. [ME *deis,* t. OF, g. LL *discus* table, L disk, dish. See DISCUS]

dai·sy (dā′zĭ), n., pl. **-sies,** adj. **—n. 1.** any of various composite plants, as *Chrysanthemum leucanthemum* (the common **oxeye daisy** of the U. S.) whose flower heads have a yellow disk and white rays, or *Bellis perennis* (the **English daisy**), etc. **2.** *Slang.* something fine or first-rate. **—adj. 3.** *Slang.* fine; first-class; excellent. [ME *daisye,* OE *dægesēage* day's eye] **—dai′sied,** adj.

dai·sy-cut·ter (dā′zĭ kŭt′ər), n. *Colloq.* (in baseball, tennis, etc.) a batted or served ball that skims along near the ground.

dak (dŏk, dăk), n. (in the East Indies) **1.** transportation by relays of men or horses. **2.** the mail. Also, **dawk.** [t. Hind.]

Da·kar (dä kär′), n. a seaport in and the capital of French West Africa. With dependencies, 141,000 pop. (1940); 68 sq. mi.

Da·kin's solution (dā′-kĭnz), a liquid antiseptic, an approximately neutral solution containing about 0.5 percent of sodium hypochlorite, used in treating infected wounds. [named after H. D. *Dakin* (1880-1952), chemist, the originator]

Da·ko·ta (də kō′tə), n. **1.** a former territory in the United States: divided into the States of North Dakota and South Dakota, 1889. **2.** North Dakota or South Dakota. **3.** a Sioux Indian. **4.** a division of the Siouan stock of North American Indians, whose former habitat was in and near North and South Dakota. **5.** any of several Siouan languages. **—Da·ko′tan,** adj., n.

Da·la·dier (dà là dyā′), n. **Édouard** (ĕ dwàr′), born 1884, premier of France, 1933, 1934, and 1938–40.

Da·lai La·ma (dä lī′ lä′mə), the Grand Lama, the chief pontiff and governmental ruler of Tibet. [f. Tibetan: *dalai* lit., ocean + *lama* priest]

dale (dāl), n. **1.** a vale; valley. **2.** *Phys. Geog.* a small, open, river valley partly enclosed by low hills. [ME; OE *dæl,* c. G *tal*]

Dale (dāl), n. **Sir Thomas,** died 1619, British governor of the colony of Virginia.

dales·man (dālz′mən), n., pl. **-men.** one living in a dale or valley, esp. in the northern counties of England.

Dal·hou·sie (dăl hōō′zĭ, -hou′-), n. **1. George Ramsay, Earl of,** 1770–1838, British general: governor of the Canadian colonies, 1819–28. **2. James Andrew Brown Ramsay** (răm′zĭ), **1st Marquis and 10th Earl of,** 1812–60, British statesman: viceroy of India, 1848–56.

Da·li (dä′lē), n. **Salvador** (säl′və dôr′; *Sp.* säl′vä dôr′), born 1904, Spanish painter in U.S.

Dal·las (dăl′əs), n. a city in NE Texas. 434,462 (1950).

dalles (dălz), n.pl. *Western U.S.* **1.** the precipice on either side of a deep ravine or canyon. **2.** rapids flowing over a flat rock bottom in a narrowed portion of a river, esp. (*cap.*) the rapids of the Columbia river. [t. Canadian F, special use of F *dalle* gutter, t. Gmc; cf. OE *dæl* gorge, DALE]

dal·li·ance (dăl′ĭ əns), n. **1.** a trifling away of time; dawdling. **2.** amorous toying; flirtation.

dal·ly (dăl′ĭ), v., **-lied, -lying. —v.i. 1.** to sport or play, esp. amorously. **2.** to play mockingly, trifle: *dally with danger.* **3.** to waste time; loiter; delay. **—v.t. 4.** to waste (time) (fol. by *away*). [ME *daly(en),* t. OF: m. *dalier* talk; ? of Gmc. orig.] **—dal′li·er, —dal′ly·ing·ly,** adv. **—Syn. 3.** See **loiter. —Ant. 3.** hasten.

Dal·ma·tia (dăl mā′shə), n. a region in W Yugoslavia, along the E coast of the Adriatic.

Dal·ma·tian (dăl mā′shən), adj. **1.** of or pertaining to Dalmatia or its people. **—n. 2.** an inhabi-

tant of Dalmatia, esp. a member of the native Slavic-speaking race. **3.** Also, **Dalmatian dog.** one of a breed of dogs resembling the pointer, and of a white color profusely marked with small black or liver-colored spots; coach dog.

dal·mat·ic (dăl măt′ĭk), n. an ecclesiastical vestment worn over the alb by the deacon, as at the celebration of the mass, and worn by bishops on certain occasions, as at a coronation. [t. L: s. *dalmatica,* prop. fem. of L *Dalmaticus* Dalmatian]

Dalmatian
(19 to 23 in. high at the shoulder)

Dal·ny (däl′nĭ), n. former name of **Dairen.**

Dal·rym·ple (dăl rĭm′pəl, däl′rĭm′-), n. **Sir James,** (*1st Viscount Stair*) 1619–95, British jurist.

dal se·gno (däl sĕ′nyō), *Music.* go back to the sign and repeat (a direction). [It.]

Dal·ton (dôl′tən), n. **John,** 1766–1844, British chemist and physicist.

dal·ton·ism (dôl′tə nĭz′əm), n. color blindness; esp., inability to distinguish red from green. [named after John DALTON, who was so afflicted]

Dalton System, a method of progressive education, whereby students contract to carry through on their own responsibility the year's work as divided up into monthly assignments. [from use in Dalton (Mass.) High Schools]

Da·ly (dā′lĭ), n. **John Augustin** (ô gŭs′tĭn), 1838–99, U.S. playwright, critic, and theatrical manager.

dam[1] (dăm), n., v., **dammed, damming. —n. 1.** a barrier to obstruct the flow of water, esp. one of earth, masonry, etc., built across a stream. **2.** a body of water confined by a dam. **3.** any barrier resembling a dam. **—v.t. 4.** to furnish with a dam; obstruct or confine with a dam. **5.** to stop up; block up. [ME, c. G *damm*]

dam[2] (dăm), n. a female parent (used esp. of quadrupeds). [ME *dam(me),* var. of DAME]

dam·age (dăm′ĭj), n., v., **-aged, -aging. —n. 1.** injury or harm that impairs value or usefulness. **2.** (*pl.*) *Law.* the estimated money equivalent for detriment or injury sustained. **3.** *Colloq.* cost; expense. **—v.t. 4.** to cause damage to; injure or harm; impair the usefulness of. **—v.i. 5.** to suffer damage. [ME, t. OF: f. *dam* (g. L *damnum* harm, loss) + *-age* -AGE] **—dam′age·a·ble,** adj. **—dam′ag·ing·ly,** adv.

—Syn. 1. DAMAGE, DETRIMENT, HARM, MISCHIEF refer to injuries of various kinds. DAMAGE is the kind of injury (or the effect of injury) which directly impairs appearance, value, usefulness, soundness, etc.: *fire causes damage to property, property suffers damage.* DETRIMENT is a falling off from an original condition as the result of damage, depreciation, devaluation, etc.: *detriment to health because of illness, to property because of neglect.* HARM is the kind of injury which connotes sorrow or a sense of evil; it may denote either physical hurt or mental, moral, or spiritual injury: *bodily harm, harm to one's self-confidence.* MISCHIEF may be damage, harm, trouble, or misfortune caused by a person, esp. if caused maliciously: *an enemy who would do one mischief.* **—Ant. 4.** improve. **5.** benefit.

dam·an (dăm′ən), n. **1.** a small mammal of the order *Hyracoidea, Procavia syriaca,* inhabiting Syria, Palestine, etc. (the *cony* of the English Bible). **2.** any hyrax. [t. Ar.: short for *daman isrāīl* lamb of Israel]

Da·man·hur (dä′măn hōōr′), n. a city in N Egypt, near Alexandria. 61,962 (1937).

Da·mão (dä moun′), n. a seaport in Portuguese India, on the Arabian Sea. 23,000 (1940). Also, **Da·man** (dä′män).

Da·ma·ra·land (dä mä′rə länd′), n. a region in the central part of South-West Africa.

Dam·a·scene (dăm′ə sēn′, dăm′ə sēn′), adj., n., v., **-scened, -scening. —adj. 1.** of or pertaining to the city of Damascus. **2.** (*l.c.*) of or pertaining to the art of damascening. **—n. 3.** an inhabitant of Damascus. **4.** (*l.c.*) work or patterns produced by damascening. **—v.t. 5.** (*l.c.*) to produce wavy lines on, as in the welding of iron and steel in the swords of Damascus. **6.** (*l.c.*) to ornament (objects of iron and steel) by inlaying with precious metals, or by etching. Also, **damaskeen** for 5, 6. [ME, t. L: m.s. *Damascēnus,* t. Gk.: m. *Damaskēnos* of Damascus]

Da·mas·cus (də măs′kəs), n. the capital of Syria, in the SW part: reputed to be the oldest continuously existing city in the world. 261,010 (est. 1942).

Damascus steel, a kind of steel with a wavy or variegated pattern, originally made in the East, chiefly at Damascus, and used for making sword blades.

dam·ask (dăm′əsk), n. **1.** a reversible fabric of linen, silk, cotton, or wool, woven with patterns. **2.** the napery of this material. **3.** Damascus steel. **4.** the peculiar pattern or wavy appearance on its surface. **5.** the pink color of the damask rose. **—adj. 6.** made of or like damask: *damask cloth.* **7.** pink (like the damask rose). **—v.t. 8.** to damascene. **9.** to weave or adorn with elaborate design, as in damask cloth. [ME *Damaske,* t. L: m. *Damascus,* t. Gk.: m. *Damaskōs* Damascus]

dam·a·skeen (dăm′ə skēn′), v.t. damascene.

damask rose, a fragrant pink rose, *Rosa damascena.*

dame (dām), n. **1.** *Archaic.* a woman of rank or authority, as a female ruler. **2.** (in Great Britain) **a.** the legal title of the wife of a knight or baronet. **b.** (since 1917) the distinctive title employed before the name of a woman upon whom a dignity corresponding to that of a knight has been conferred. **3.** a form of address to any woman of rank or authority. **4.** *U.S.* a married woman. **5.** *Slang.* a woman. **6.** *Archaic or Dial.* the mistress of a household. **7.** *Obsolesc.* the mistress of a school. [ME, t. OF, g. L *domina* mistress, lady]

Da·mien de Veus·ter (dȧ myăn′ də vœs tĕr′), **Joseph** (zhō zĕf′), known as **Father Damien** (dā′mĭ′ən), 1840–89, Belgian Roman Catholic missionary to the lepers of Molokai.

Dam·i·et·ta (dăm/ĭ ĕt′ə), *n.* a city in NE Egypt, in the Nile delta. 44,200 (est. 1941). Arabic, **Dumyat.**

dam·mar (dăm′ər), *n.* **1.** a copallike resin chiefly from dipterocarpaceous trees of southern Asia, esp. Malaya and Sumatra, much used for making colorless varnish. **2.** any of various similar resins from trees of other families. Also, **dam′mer.** [t. Malay: m. *damar* resin]

damn (dăm), *v.t.* **1.** to declare (something) to be bad, unfit, invalid, or illegal. **2.** to condemn as a failure: *damn a play.* **3.** to bring condemnation upon; ruin. **4.** to doom to eternal punishment, or condemn to hell. **5.** to swear at or curse, using the word "damn." —*v.i.* **6.** to use the word "damn"; swear. —*n.* **7.** the utterance of the word "damn" in swearing or for emphasis. [ME *damne*(n), t. OF: m. *damner*, t. L: m. *damnāre* condemn, doom]

dam·na·ble (dăm′nə bəl), *adj.* **1.** worthy of damnation. **2.** detestable, abominable, or outrageous. —**dam′na·ble·ness,** *n.* —**dam′na·bly,** *adv.*

dam·na·tion (dăm nā′shən), *n.* **1.** act of damning. **2** state of being damned. **3.** a cause or occasion of being damned. **4.** *Theol.* sin as incurring or deserving eternal punishment. **5.** an oath expressing anger, disappointment, etc.

dam·na·to·ry (dăm′nə tôr′ĭ), *adj.* conveying or occasioning condemnation; damning.

damned (dămd), *adj.* **1.** condemned, esp. to eternal punishment. **2.** detestable. —*adv.* **3.** extremely; very.

dam·ni·fy (dăm′nə fī′), *v.t.* **-fied, -fying.** *Law.* to cause loss or damage to. [t. OF: m. *damnifier*, t. L: m. *damnificare* injure]

damn·ing (dăm′ĭng, dăm′nĭng), *adj.* that damns or condemns; occasioning condemnation. —**damn′ing·ly,** *adv.*

Dam·o·cles (dăm′ə klēz′), *n.* *Gk. Legend.* a flatterer, who having extolled the happiness of Dionysius, tyrant of Syracuse, was placed at a banquet, with a sword suspended over his head by a single hair, to show him the perilous nature of that happiness. —**Dam·o·cle·an** (dăm′ə klē′ən), *adj.*

dam·oi·selle (dăm′ə zĕl′), *n.* *Archaic.* damsel. Also, **dam′o·sel′, dam′o·zel′.**

Da·mon (dā′mən), *n.* *Rom. Legend.* a Syracusan who barely escaped suffering the death penalty as voluntary hostage for his friend Pythias (Phintias).

damp (dămp), *adj.* **1.** moderately wet; moist. **2.** *Archaic.* dejected. —*n.* **3.** moisture; humidity; moist air. **4.** a noxious or stifling vapor or gas, esp. in a mine. **5.** depression of spirits; dejection. **6.** a check or discouragement. —*v.t.* **7.** to make damp; moisten. **8.** to check or retard the energy, action, etc., of. **9.** to stifle or suffocate; extinguish. **10.** *Acoustics, Music.* to check or retard the action of (a vibrating string, etc.); dull; deaden **11.** *Physics.* to cause a decrease in amplitude of (successive oscillations or waves). [ME *domp*, t. MFlem. vapor, c. G *dampf* steam] —**damp′ish,** *adj.* —**damp′ly,** *adv.* —**damp′ness,** *n.*

—**Syn. 1.** DAMP, HUMID, MOIST mean slightly wet. DAMP usually implies slight and extraneous wetness, generally undesirable or unpleasant unless the result of intention: *a damp cellar, to put a damp cloth on a patient's forehead.* HUMID is a literary or scientific word, applied to that which is so permeated with moisture that the moisture seems a part of it, esp. unpleasant dampness in the air in either hot or cold weather: *the air is oppressively humid today.* MOIST denotes that which is slightly wet, naturally or properly: *moist ground, leather.* —**Ant. 1.** dry.

damp·en (dăm′pən), *v.t.* **1.** to make damp; moisten. **2.** to dull or deaden; depress. —*v.i.* **3.** to become damp. —**damp′en·er,** *n.*

damp·er (dăm′pər), *n.* **1.** one who or that which damps. **2.** a movable plate for regulating the draft in a stove, furnace, etc. **3.** *Music.* **a.** a device in stringed keyboard instruments to deaden the vibration of the strings. **b.** the mute of a brass instrument, as a horn. **4.** *Elect.* an attachment to keep the indicator of a measuring instrument from oscillating excessively, usually a set of vanes in an air space or fluid, or a short-circuited winding in a magnetic field.

Dam·pi·er (dăm′pĭ′ər, dămp′yər), *n.* **William,** 1652–1715, British navigator, explorer, writer, and pirate.

Dam·rosch (dăm′rŏsh), *n.* **Walter Johannes** (jō hăn′əs), 1862–1950, U. S. musical conductor and composer, born in Germany.

dam·sel (dăm′zəl), *n.* a young woman; a girl; a maiden, originally one of gentle or noble birth. [ME *dameisele*, t. OF, ult. der. L *domina* mistress, lady. See DAME]

damsel fly, any of the more fragile, slow-flying insects of the order *Odonata,* distinguished from the dragonflies by having the wings closed while at rest.

dam·son (dăm′zən), *n.* **1.** the small dark-blue or purple fruit of a plum, *Prunus insititia,* introduced into Europe from Asia Minor. **2.** the tree bearing it. [ME

---

damascene, repr. L (*prunum*) *damascēnum* (plum) of Damascus. See DAMASCENE]

Dan (dăn), *n.* **1.** one of the twelve sons of Jacob. Gen. 30:6. **2.** one of the twelve Hebrew tribes. Josh. 19:40. **3.** a city at the northern end of Palestine; hence, the common phrase **from Dan to Beersheba** (the two limits of Palestine). Judges 20:1. [t. Heb.]

Dan (dăn), *n.* *Archaic.* a title of honor, equivalent to *master* or *sir: Dan Chaucer, Dan Cupid.* [ME, t. OF, g. L *dominus* master, lord]

Dan., **1.** Daniel. **2.** Danish.

Da·na (dā′nə), **1.** **Charles Anderson,** 1819–97, U.S. journalist. **2.** **Edward Salisbury,** 1849–1935, U.S. mineralogist and physicist. **3.** his father, **James Dwight,** 1813–95, U.S. geologist and mineralogist. **4.** **Richard Henry,** 1815–82, U.S. lawyer and writer.

Dan·a·ë (dăn′ĭ ē′), *n.* *Gk. Legend.* a maiden imprisoned in a brazen tower by her father Acrisius, King of Argos. Visited by Zeus in the form of a shower of gold, she became the mother of Perseus.

Da·na·i·des (də nā′ə dēz′), *n.pl.* *Gk. Myth.* daughters of Danaus, who for killing their husbands were condemned in Hades to pour water forever into a perforated or bottomless vessel. Also, **Da·na′i·des′.** —**Dan·a·id·e·an** (dăn′Ĭ ĭd′Ĭən, dăn′Ĭ ə dē′ən), *adj.*

Dan·a·üs (dăn′Ĭəs), *n.* *Gk. Myth.* the ruler of Argos who married his daughters, the Danaides, to their fifty cousins, the sons of Ægyptus, but made them slay their husbands on the wedding night. Also, **Dan′a·us.**

Dan·bur·y (dăn′bĕr′Ĭ, -bərĬ), *n.* a city in SW Connecticut. 22,067 (1950).

dance (dăns, däns), *v.,* **danced, dancing,** *n.* —*v.i.* **1.** to move with the feet or body rhythmically, esp. to music. **2.** to leap, skip, etc., as from excitement or emotion; move nimbly or quickly. **3.** to bob up and down. —*v.t.* **4.** to perform or take part in (a dance). **5.** to cause to dance. **6.** to bring about or cause to be by dancing. **7. dance attendance,** to attend constantly or solicitously. —*n.* **8.** a successive group of rhythmical steps, generally executed to music. **9.** an act or round of dancing. **10.** a social gathering for dancing; ball. **11.** a piece of music suited in rhythm to a particular form of dancing. [ME *daunse*(n), t. OF: m. *danser*; prob. of Gmc. orig.] —**danc′ing·ly,** *adv.*

dance of death. See macabre (def. 2).

danc·er (dăn′sər, dän′-), *n.* **1.** one who dances. **2.** one who dances professionally, as on the stage.

dan·de·li·on (dăn′də lī′ən), *n.* **1.** a common composite plant, *Taraxacum officinale,* abundant as a weed, characterized by deeply toothed or notched leaves and golden-yellow flowers. **2.** any other plant of the genus *Taraxacum.* [t. F: m. *dent de lion* lion's tooth (with allusion to the toothed leaves)]

dan·der (dăn′dər), *n.* *Colloq.* anger or temper. [? fig. use of *dander* DANDRUFF; or fig. use of *dander* ferment]

Dan·die Din·mont (dăn′dĬ dĬn′mŏnt), one of a breed of small terriers with a long body, short legs, and long pendulous ears. [from *Dandie* (Andrew) *Dinmont,* in Scott's "Guy Mannering," said to own the progenitors]

dan·di·fy (dăn′də fī′), *v.t.,* **-fied, -fying.** to make dandylike or foppish. —**dan′di·fi·ca′tion,** *n.*

dan·dle (dăn′dəl), *v.t.,* **-dled, -dling.** **1.** to move lightly up and down, as a child on the knees or in the arms. **2.** to pet; pamper. [b. DANCE and HANDLE] —**dan′dler,** *n.*

dan·druff (dăn′drəf), *n.* a scurf which forms on the scalp and comes off in small scales. Also, **dan·driff** (dăn′drĬf).

dan·dy[1] (dăn′dĬ), *n., pl.* **-dies,** *adj.* **-dier, -diest.** —*n.* **1.** a man who is excessively concerned about clothes and appearance; a fop. **2.** *Colloq.* something very fine or first-rate. **3.** *Naut. Brit.* **a.** a yawl with leg-of-mutton jigger. **b.** its small after-sail. —*adj.* **4.** foppish. **5.** *U.S. Colloq.* fine; first-rate. [? special use of *Dandy,* var. of *Andy* Andrew] —**dan′dy·ish** *adj.* —**dan′dy·ism,** *n.*

dan·dy[2] (dăn′dĬ), *n.* (in the West Indies) dengue.

dandy roll, a roller used in making some kinds of paper and in impressing water marks. Also, **dandy roller.**

Dane (dān), *n.* **1.** a native or inhabitant of Denmark. **2.** a person of Danish descent. **3.** a great Dane. [appar. back formation from OE *Dænemarc* Denmark; r. *Dene,* pl., the Danes; cf. Icel. *Danir*]

Dane·law (dān′lô′), *n.* **1.** the body of laws in force in that part of England to which the Danes were restricted in the ninth century. **2.** that part of England under this law. Also, **Dane·lagh** (dān′lô′). [f. DANE + LAW; r. OE *Denalagu* law of the Danes]

dan·ger (dān′jər), *n.* **1.** liability or exposure to harm or injury; risk; peril. **2.** an instance or cause of peril. **3.** *Obs.* power; jurisdiction; domain. [ME *daunger,* t. OF: m. *dangier,* g. LL deriv. of *dominium* lordship]

—**Syn. 1.** DANGER, HAZARD, PERIL, JEOPARDY imply some evil or harm which one may encounter. DANGER is the general word for liability to all kinds of injury or evil consequences, either near at hand and certain, or remote and doubtful: *to be in danger of catching cold or of being killed.* HAZARD suggests a danger which one can foresee but cannot avoid: *an aviator is exposed to many hazards.* PERIL usually denotes great and imminent danger: *the passengers on the disabled ship were in great peril.* JEOPARDY, a less common word, has essentially the same meaning as peril, but emphasizes exposure to the hazards and chances of a situation: *to save his friend he put his life in jeopardy.* —**Ant. 1.** safety.

---

b., blend of, blended; c., cognate with; d., dialect, dialectal; der., derived from; f., formed from; g., going back to; m., modification of; r., replacing; s., stem of; t., taken from; ?, perhaps. See the full key on inside cover.

dan·ger·ous (dān′jər əs), *adj.* full of danger or risk; causing danger; perilous; hazardous; unsafe. —**dan′ger·ous·ly**, *adv.* —**dan′ger·ous·ness**, *n.*

dan·gle (dăng′gəl), *v.*, **-gled**, **-gling**. *n.* —*v.i.* 1. to hang loosely with a swaying motion. 2. to hang about or follow a person, as if seeking favor. —*v.t.* 3. to cause to dangle; hold or carry swaying loosely. —*n.* 4. act of dangling. 5. something that dangles. [t. Scand; cf. Dan. *dangle* dangle, bob up and down] —**dan′gler**, *n.*

Dan·iel (dăn′yəl), *n.* 1. *Bible.* **a.** a Jewish captive and prophet living in Babylon. **b.** a canonical book in the Old Testament. 2. **Samuel**, 1562–1619, British poet and historian. [t. Heb.: m. *Dāni′ĕl*]

Dan·iels (dăn′yəlz), *n.* **Josephus** (jō sē′fəs), 1862–1948, U.S. editor and statesman.

Dan·ish (dā′nĭsh), *adj.* 1. of or pertaining to the Danes, their country, or their language. —*n.* 2. a Germanic language, the language of Denmark, closely related to Norwegian, Swedish, and Icelandic.

Danish West Indies, a former Danish colony in the Virgin Islands: purchased by the U. S., 1917.

Dan·ite (dăn′īt), *n.* 1. *Bible.* a descendant of Dan. Judges 13:2. 2. a member of an alleged secret order of Mormons supposed to have been formed about 1837.

dank (dăngk), *adj.* unpleasantly moist or humid; damp. [cf. Sw. *dank* marshy place, Icel. *dökk* pool] —**dank′ly** *adv.* —**dank′ness**, *n.*

dan·ke schön (dăng′kə shœn′), *German.* thank you.

D'An·nun·zi·o (dän nōōn′tsyō), *n.* **Gabriele** (gä′brē-ĕ′lĕ), 1863–1938, Italian author and soldier.

Da·no-Nor·we·gian (dā′nō nôr wē′jən), *n.* a standard literary and urban language of Norway, based on Danish.

danse ma·ca·bre (däns må kå′br), *French.* See **ma·cabre** (def. 2).

dan·seuse (dän sœz′), *n.*, *pl.* **-seuses** (-sœz′). a female ballet dancer. [t. F, fem. of *danseur* dancer, der. *danser* DANCE]

Dan·te (dän′tĭ; *It.* dän′tĕ), *n.* (*Dante Alighieri*) 1265–1321, Italian poet: author of the *Divine Comedy.*

Dan·te·an (dăn′tĭ ən, dän tē′ən), *adj.* 1. of Dante or his writings. 2. Dantesque.

Dan·tesque (dăn tĕsk′), *adj.* in the style of Dante; characterized by impressive elevation of style with deep solemnity or somberness of feeling.

Dan·ton (dän′tən; *Fr.* dän tôn′), *n.* **Georges Jacques** (zhôrzh zhäk), 1759–94, French Revolutionary leader.

Dan·ube (dăn′ūb), *n.* a river in Europe, flowing from SW Germany E to the Black Sea. 1725 mi. German, **Donau.** Hungarian, **Duna.** —**Dan·u·bi·an** (dăn ū′bĭ ən), *adj.*

Dan·ville (dăn′vĭl), *n.* 1. a city in E Illinois. 37,864 (1950). 2. a city in S Virginia. 35,066 (1950).

Dan·zig (dăn′sĭg; *Ger.* dän′tsĭкн), *n.* 1. a seaport in N Poland, on the Bay of Danzig, an inlet of the Baltic. 118,000 (1946). 2. **Free City of,** a former self-governing territory including the seaport of Danzig, constituted by the treaty of Versailles, 1920: a part of Germany, 1939–1945; now in Poland. 754 sq. mi. Polish, **Gdansk.**

dap (dăp), *v.i.* **dapped**, **dapping**. 1. to fish by letting the bait fall lightly on the water. 2. to dip lightly or suddenly into water. 3. to bounce. [ME *dop*. Cf. DIP]

Daph·ne (dăf′nĭ), *n.* 1. *Gk. Myth.* a nymph who, pursued by Apollo, was saved by being changed into a laurel tree. 2. (*l.c.*) **a.** the laurel, *Laurus nobilis.* **b.** any plant of the thymelaeaceous genus *Daphne*, of Europe and Asia, comprising small shrubs of which some species, as *D. Mezereum*, are cultivated for their fragrant flowers. [t. L, t. Gk.: laurel]

Daph·nis (dăf′nĭs), *n.* *Gk. Myth.* a son of Hermes by a nymph: the inventor of pastoral poetry.

Daphnis and Chlo·ë (klō′ĭ), two lovers in pastoral literature, esp. in a Greek romance attributed to Longus.

dap·per (dăp′ər), *adj.* 1. neat; trim; smart. 2. small and active. [late ME *dapyr* pretty, elegant; orig. uncert.] —**dap′per·ly**, *adv.* —**dap′per·ness**, *n.*

dap·ple (dăp′əl), *n.*, *adj.*, *v.*, **-pled**, **-pling**. —*n.* 1. mottled marking, as of an animal's skin or coat. 2. an animal with a mottled skin or coat. —*adj.* 3. dappled; spotted: *a dapple horse.* —*v.t.*, *v.i.* 4. to mark or become marked with spots. [orig. uncert. Cf. Icel. *depill* spot, dot]

dap·pled (dăp′əld), *adj.* having spots of different colors or shades; spotted.

dap·ple-gray (dăp′əl grā′), *adj.* gray with ill-defined mottling of a darker shade.

D.A.R., Daughters of the American Revolution.

d'Ar·blay (där′blā; *Fr.* där blā′), *n.* See **Burney.**

Dar·by and Joan (där′bĭ, jōn), the typical "old married couple" contentedly leading a life of placid, uneventful domesticity.

Dar·by·ites (där′bĭ īts′), *n.pl.* Plymouth Brethren.

Dar·dan (där′dən), *adj.*, *n.* Trojan. Also, **Dar·da·ni·an** (där dā′nĭ ən). [f. s. L *Dardanius* (t. Gk.: m. *Dardánios*) + -AN]

Dar·da·nelles (där′də-nĕlz′), *n.pl.* the strait between European and Asiatic Turkey, connecting the Aegean with the Sea of Marmara. 40 mi. long; 1–5 mi. wide. Ancient, **Hellespont.**

Dar·da·nus (där′də nəs), *n.* the mythical ancestor of the Trojans.

dare (dâr), *v.*, **dared** or **durst**, **dared** (p. subj. often *dare*), **daring**, *n.* —*v.i.* 1. to have the necessary courage or boldness for something; be bold enough. 2. **dare say,** to assume as probable; have no doubt. 3. to have the necessary courage for; venture on. 4. to meet defiantly. 5. to challenge or provoke to action, esp. by doubting one's courage; defy: *to dare a man to fight.* —*n.* 6. an act of daring; defiance; challenge. [ME *dar*, der. OE *dear(r)*, 1st and 3d pers. sing. pres. ind. of *durran*; akin to OHG *giturran*] —**dar′er**, *n.*
—**Syn.** 1. DARE, VENTURE imply involvement in risks and dangers. DARE emphasizes the state of mind that makes one willing to meet danger: *he dared to do what he knew was right.* VENTURE emphasizes the act of doing something which involves risk: *he ventured into deep water.*

dare·dev·il (dâr′dĕv′əl), *n.* 1. a recklessly daring person. —*adj.* 2. recklessly daring.

dare·dev·il·try (dâr′dĕv′əl trĭ), *n.* recklessness; venturesomeness. Also, **dare·dev·il·ry** (dâr′dĕv′əl rĭ).

Dar-es-Sa·laam (där′ĕs sə läm′), *n.* a seaport in and the capital of Tanganyika Territory. 22,732 (1931).

Dar·fur (där fōōr′), *n.* a province in the W Anglo-Egyptian Sudan. 715,543 pop. (est. 1940); 138,150 sq. mi. *Cap.:* El Fasher.

darg (därg), *n.* *Scot. and N. Eng.* a day's work. [ME *dawerk*]

dar·ic (dăr′ĭk), *n.* the gold coin unit of ancient Persia. [t. Gk.: m.s. *dāreikós*; from Pers.]

Dar·i·en (dâr′ĭ ĕn′, där′ĭ ĕn′; *Sp.* dä′rē ĕn′), *n.* 1. **Gulf of,** an arm of the Caribbean between the NE coast of Panama and Colombia. 2. **Isthmus of,** former name of the **Isthmus of Panama.**

dar·ing (dâr′ĭng), *n.* 1. adventurous courage; boldness. —*adj.* 2. that dares; bold; intrepid; adventurous. —**dar′ing·ly**, *adv.* —**dar′ing·ness**, *n.* —**Syn.** 2. dauntless, undaunted, venturesome, audacious. —**Ant.** 1. caution.

Da·ri·us I (də rī′əs). ("the Great," Darius Hystaspes) 558?–486? B.C., king of Persia, 521–486? B.C.

Dar·jee·ling (där jē′lĭng), *n.* a town in NE India, in Bengal: mountain resort. 25,900 (1941).

dark (därk), *adj.* 1. without light; with very little light: *a dark room.* 2. radiating or reflecting little light: *a dark color.* 3. approaching black in hue: *a dark brown.* 4. not pale or fair: *a dark complexion.* 5. gloomy; cheerless; dismal. 6. sullen; frowning. 7. morally or spiritually blind. 8. destitute of knowledge or culture; unenlightened. 9. hard to understand; obscure. 10. hidden; secret: *a dark purpose.* 11. silent; reticent. 12. *Phonet.* (of *l* sounds) resembling a back vowel in quality: *English l is darker than French l.* —*n.* 13. the absence of light; darkness. 14. night; nightfall. 15. a dark place. 16. a dark color. 17. obscurity. 18. secrecy. 19. ignorance. —*v.t.*, *v.i. Obs.* 20. to darken. [ME *derk*, OE *deorc*. Cf. MHG *terken*] —**dark′-ish**, *adj.*
—**Syn.** 1. DARK, DIM, GLOOMY, MURKY refer to absence or insufficiency of light. DARK implies a more or less complete absence of light: *a dark night.* DIM implies faintness of light or indistinctness of form (resulting from the lack of light or from imperfect vision): *a dim outline.* GLOOMY means cloudy, ill-lighted, dusky: *a gloomy hall.* MURKY implies a thick, cloudy, or misty darkness: *a murky cave* 4. dusky, swarthy, black. 9. recondite, abstruse. —**Ant.** 1. lighted. 2. bright. 5. cheerful. 6. pleasant. 9. clear.

Dark Ages, 1. the time in history from about A.D. 476 to about A.D. 1000. 2. (occasionally) the whole of the Middle Ages, from about A.D. 476 to the Renaissance.

Dark Continent, The, Africa: so called because it was formerly so little known.

dark·en (där′kən), *v.t.* 1. to make dark or darker; make obscure. 2. to make less white or clear in color. 3. to make gloomy; sadden. 4. to make blind. —*v.i.* 5. to become dark or darker. 6. to become obscure. 7. to become less white or clear in color. 8. to grow clouded, as with gloom or anger. 9. to become blind. —**dark′en·er**, *n.*

dark·ey (där′kĭ), *n.*, *pl.* **darkeys.** darky.

dark horse, 1. a race horse, competitor, etc., about whom little is known or who unexpectedly wins. 2. a person unexpectedly nominated, esp. in a political convention.

dark lantern, a lantern whose light can be obscured by a dark slide or cover at the opening.

dar·kle (där′kəl), *v.i.* **-kled**, **-kling**. 1. to appear dark; show indistinctly. 2. to grow dark, gloomy, etc. [back formation from DARKLING, *adv.*, taken as *ppr.*]

dark·ling (därk′lĭng), *adv.* 1. in the dark. —*adj.* 2. being or occurring in the dark; dark; obscure. [f. DARK + -LING²]

dark·ly (därk′lĭ), *adv.* 1. so as to appear dark. 2. mysteriously. 3. *Archaic.* imperfectly; faintly.

dark·ness (därk′nĭs), *n.* 1. state or quality of being dark. 2. absence or deficiency of light. 3. wickedness or evil. 4. obscurity; concealment. 5. blindness; ignorance.

dark·room (därk′rōōm′, -rŏŏm′), *n.* *Photog.* a room from which the actinic rays of light have been excluded, used in making, handling, and developing film, etc.

dark·some (därk′səm), *adj.* dark; darkish.

dark·y (där′kĭ), *n.*, *pl.* **darkies.** *Colloq.* (often offensive) a Negro. Also, **darkey.**

dar·ling (där'lĭng), *n.* **1.** a person very dear to another; person dearly loved. **2.** a person or thing in great favor. —*adj.* **3.** very dear; dearly loved. **4.** favorite. [ME *derling*, OE *dēorling*, f. *dēore* dear + -LING[1]]

Dar·ling River (där'lĭng), a river in SE Australia, flowing into the Murray river. 1160 mi.

Dar·ling·ton (där'lĭng tən), *n.* a city in NE England, in Durham. 83,460 (est. 1946).

Darm·stadt (därm'stät; *Ger.* därm'shtät), *n.* a city in W Germany: the capital of Hesse. 115,196 (1939).

darn[1] (därn), *v.t.* **1.** to mend (clothes, etc., or a rent or hole) with rows of stitches, sometimes with crossing and interwoven rows to fill up a gap. —*n.* **2.** a darned place in a garment, etc. **3.** act of darning. [? ME *dernen*, OE *dernan* hide] —**darn'er**, *n.* —**Syn. 1.** See **mend.**

darn[2] (därn), *adj., adv.* **1.** darned. —*v.t.* **2.** *U.S. Colloq.* to confound (used as a mild imprecation). —*n.* **3. not give a darn,** to be utterly indifferent. [var. of DAMN]

darned (därnd), *U.S. Colloq.* —*adj.* **1.** confounded; blessed. —*adv.* **2.** extremely; remarkably.

dar·nel (där'nəl), *n.* an annual grass, *Lolium temulentum*, found as a weed in grainfields. [ME. Cf. d. F *darnelle*, prob. of Gmc. orig.]

darn·ing (där'nĭng), *n.* **1.** act of one who darns. **2.** the result produced. **3.** articles darned or to be darned.

darning needle, 1. a long needle with a long eye used in darning. **2.** a dragonfly.

Darn·ley (därn'lĭ), *n.* **Henry Stewart, Lord,** 1545–1567, the second husband of Mary, Queen of Scots; father of James I of England.

dart (härt), *n.* **1.** a long, slender, pointed, missile weapon propelled by the hand or otherwise. **2.** something resembling such a weapon, as the sting of an insect. **3.** act of darting; a sudden, swift movement. **4.** (*pl.*) a game in which a pointed missile is thrown at a scoring board. **5.** a seam that is used where a wedge-shaped piece has been cut out to adjust the fit of a garment. —*v.i.* **6.** to move swiftly; spring or start suddenly and run swiftly. **7.** to throw a dart or other missile weapon. —*v.t.* **8.** to throw or thrust suddenly and rapidly. **9.** to throw with a sudden thrust, as a dart. [ME, t. OF, t. OG] —**dart'ing·ly**, *adv.* —**Syn. 6.** dash, bolt.

dart·er (där'tər), *n.* **1.** one who or that which darts or moves swiftly. **2.** a snakebird or anhinga. **3.** any percid fish of the American subfamily *Etheostomatinae*, small fresh-water fishes which dart quickly when disturbed.

dar·tle (där'təl), *v.t., v.i.,* **-tled, -tling.** to dart or shoot forth repeatedly. [freq. of DART]

Dart·moor (därt'mŏŏr', -mōr'), *n.* **1.** a rocky plateau in SW England, in Devonshire. ab. 25 mi. long. **2.** a famous prison located there.

Dar·win (där'wĭn), *n.* **1. Charles,** 1809–82, British naturalist. **2.** his grandfather, **Erasmus,** 1731–1802, British naturalist and poet.

Dar·win·i·an (där wĭn'ĭ ən), *adj.* **1.** pertaining to Charles Darwin or his doctrines. —*n.* **2.** a follower of Charles Darwin; one who accepts Darwinism.

Dar·win·ism (där'wə nĭz'əm), *n.* the body of biological doctrine maintained by Charles Darwin respecting the origin of species as derived by descent, with variation, from parent forms, through the natural selection, of those best adapted to survive in the struggle for existence. —**Dar'win·ist,** *n., adj.* —**Dar·win·ite** (där'wə nīt'), *n.*

das geht nicht (däs gāt' nĭкнт), *German.* that doesn't go; that won't do.

dash (dăsh), *v.t.* **1.** to strike violently, esp. so as to break to pieces. **2.** to throw or thrust violently or suddenly. **3.** to splash violently; bespatter (with water, mud, etc.). **4.** to apply roughly as by splashing. **5.** to throw something into so as to produce a mixture; mix; adulterate: *to dash wine with water.* **6.** to ruin or frustrate (hopes, plans, etc.). **7.** to depress or dispirit. **8.** to confound or abash. **9.** to write, make, sketch, etc., hastily (usually fol. by *off* or *down*). **10.** *Chiefly Brit.* to damn (used as a mild imprecation). —*v.i.* **11.** to strike with violence. **12.** to move with violence; rush. —*n.* **13.** a violent and rapid blow or stroke. **14.** a check or discouragement. **15.** the throwing or splashing of water, etc., against a thing. **16.** the sound of the splashing. **17.** a small quantity of anything thrown into or mixed with something else: *a dash of salt.* **18.** a hasty stroke, esp. of a pen. **19.** a horizontal line (—) used in writing and printing as a mark of punctuation to note an abrupt break or pause in a sentence, to begin and end a parenthetic clause, as an indication of omission of letters, words, etc., as a dividing line between distinct portions of matter, and for other purposes. **20.** an impetuous movement; a rush; a sudden onset. **21.** *Sports.* a short race decided in one attempt, not in heats: *a hundred-yard dash.* **22.** spirited action; vigor in action or style. **23.** a dashboard. **24.** *Teleg.* a signal of longer duration than a dot, used in groups of dots and dashes to represent letters, as in Morse code. —*interj.* **25.** *Chiefly Brit.* a mild exclamation. [ME *dasche(n)*, c. Dan. *daske* slap, flap] —**Syn. 12.** dart, bolt. See **rush**[1]. **17.** pinch, bit; touch, tinge. **22.** impetuosity, spirit, élan.

dash·board (dăsh'bōrd'), *n.* **1.** the instrument board of an automobile. **2.** a board or leather apron on the front of a vehicle to protect the occupants from mud, etc.

da·sheen (dă shēn'), *n.* the taro plant, *Colocasia esculenta*, native in tropical Asia, now cultivated in southern U.S. for its edible tubers. [t. F: m. *de Chine* of China]

dash·er (dăsh'ər), *n.* **1.** one who or that which dashes. **2.** the plunger of a churn. **3.** a dashboard (def. 2). **4.** *Colloq.* a dashing person.

dash·ing (dăsh'ĭng), *adj.* **1.** impetuous; spirited; lively. **2.** brilliant; showy; stylish. —**dash'ing·ly,** *adv.*

dash·y (dăsh'ĭ), *adj.,* **dashier, dashiest.** showy; stylish; dashing.

das·tard (dăs'tərd), *n.* **1.** a mean, sneaking coward. —*adj.* **2.** mean and sneaking; cowardly. [ME; f. *dast* (? var. of *dazed*, pp. of DAZE) + -ARD]

das·tard·ly (dăs'tərd lĭ), *adj.* cowardly; meanly base; sneaking. —**das'tard·li·ness,** *n.*

das·y·ure (dăs'ĭ yŏŏr'), *n.* **1.** any of the small, spotted, carnivorous marsupials constituting the genus *Dasyurus*, and related genera, native in Australia, Tasmania, etc. **2.** any of several related animals, as the Tasmanian devil or ursine dasyure. [t. NL: m.s. *Dasyūrus*, f. *dasy-* (comb. form of Gk. *dasýs* shaggy) + -*ūrus* (m. Gk. *ourá* tail)]

dat., dative.

da·ta (dā'tə, dăt'ə, dä'tə), *n.* **1.** pl. of **datum. 2.** facts, figures, etc., known or available; information.

da·ta·ry (dā'tər ĭ), *n., pl.* **-ries.** *Rom. Cath. Ch.* **1.** an officer, now cardinal, at the head of a certain office or department of the Curia who investigates the fitness of candidates for benefices in the gift of the papal see. **2.** this office or department. [t. ML: m.s. *datārius* (the officer), *datāria* (the office), der. *data* DATE[1]]

date[1] (dāt). *n., v.,* **dated, dating.** —*n.* **1.** a particular point or period of time when something happens or happened. **2.** an inscription on a writing, coin, etc., that shows the time, or time and place, of writing, casting, delivery, etc. **3.** the time or period of an event or to which anything belongs. **4.** the time during which anything lasts; duration. **5.** *U.S. Colloq.* an appointment made for a particular time. **6. down to date,** to the present time. **7. to date,** down to the present time. —*v.i.* **8.** to have a date: *the letter dates from 1873.* **9.** to belong to a particular period; have its origin. **10.** to reckon from some point in time. —*v.t.* **11.** to mark or furnish with a date. **12.** to ascertain or fix the date or time of; assign a date or time to. [ME, t. F, t. ML: m. *data*, prop. pp. fem. of L *dare* give] —**dat'er,** *n.*

date[2] (dāt), *n.* **1.** the oblong, fleshy fruit of the date palm, a staple food in northern Africa, Arabia, etc., and an important export. **2.** the date palm. [ME, t. OF, g. L *dactylus*, t. Gk.: m. *dáktylos* date, orig. finger]

dat·ed (dā'tĭd), *adj.* **1.** having or showing a date. **2.** out-of-date; old-fashioned.

date·less (dāt'lĭs), *adj.* **1.** without a date; undated. **2.** endless. **3.** so old as to be undatable. **4.** of permanent interest regardless of age.

date line, 1. a line in a letter, newspaper, article, or the like, giving the date (and often the place) of origin. **2.** a line, theoretically coinciding with the meridian of 180° from Greenwich, the regions on either side of which are counted as differing by one day in their calendar dates. It is occasioned by the difference in time between different points on the earth, due to the (apparent) movement of the sun.

date palm, the species of palm, *Phoenix dactylifera*, which bears dates, having a stem up to 60 feet high terminating in a crown of pinnate leaves.

da·tive (dā'tĭv), *adj.* **1.** *Gram.* denoting a case, in some inflected languages, having as one function indication of the indirect object of a verb. —*n.* **2.** the dative case. **3.** a word or form in that case, as *regi* in *regi haec dicite* meaning *tell this to the king*. [t. L: m.s. *datīvus* of or belonging to giving] —**da·ti·val** (dā tī'vəl), *adj.* —**da'tive·ly,** *adv.*

[Map: SOVIET UNION, ALASKA, TUESDAY, MONDAY, MIDWAY IS., HAWAIIAN ISLANDS, WAKE I., EQUATOR, INTERNATIONAL DATE LINE, Coral Sea, AUSTRALIA, Tasman Sea, NEW ZEALAND]

International date line

da·to (dä'tō; *Sp.* -tô), *n., pl.* **-tos** (-tōz; *Sp.* -tôs). **1.** (in the Philippines) a native chief. **2.** the headman of a barrio or Malay tribe. Also, **dat'to.** [t. Malay: m. *dātoq* title of respect]

da·tum (dā'təm), *n., pl.* **-ta** (-tə). **1.** any proposition assumed or given, from which conclusions may be drawn. **2.** (*often pl.*) any fact assumed to be a matter of direct observation. [t. L: given (pp. neut.)]

datum plane, level, line, etc. *Survey., Civ. Eng., etc.* a plane, level, line, etc., from which heights and depths are calculated or measured.

da·tu·ra (də tyŏŏr'ə, -tōŏr'ə), *n.* any plant of the solanaceous genus *Datura*, the species of which have funnel-shaped flowers, prickly pods, and narcotic properties. [NL, t. Hind.: m. *dhatūra*, native name of the plant]

---

b., blend of, blended; c., cognate with; d., dialect, dialectal; der., derived from; f., formed from; g., going back to; m., modification of; r., replacing; s., stem of; t., taken from; ?, perhaps.   See the full key on inside cover.

dau., daughter.

daub (dôb), *v.t.* **1.** to cover or coat with soft, adhesive matter, such as plaster, mud. etc. **2.** to spread (plaster, mud, etc.) on or over something. **3.** to smear. soil, or defile. **4.** to paint unskillfully. —*v.i.* **5.** to daub something. **6.** to paint unskillfully. —*n.* **7.** material, esp. of an inferior kind, for daubing walls, etc. **8.** anything daubed on. **9.** act of daubing. **10.** a crude, inartistic painting. [ME *daube*(n), t. OF: m. *dauber*, g. L *dealbāre* whiten, plaster] —**daub′er,** *n.*

daub·er·y (dô′bərĭ), *n.* unskillful painting or work. Also, **daub·ry** (dô′brĭ).

Dau·bi·gny (dō bē nyē′), *n.* **Charles François** (shärl frän swä′), 1817–78, French landscape painter.

Dau·det (dō dĕ′), *n.* **1.** **Alphonse** (àl fôns′), 1840–97, French novelist. **2.** **Léon** (lĕ ôN′), 1867–1942, French journalist and novelist; son of Alphonse.

Dau·ga·va (dou′gä vä), *n.* Lettish name of **Dvina.**

Dau·gav·pils (dou′gäf pēls′), *n.* a city in the W Soviet Union, in the Latvian Republic. 45,100 (1935). Russian, **Dvinsk.** German, **Dünaburg.**

daugh·ter (dô′tər), *n.* **1.** a female child or person in relation to her parents. **2.** any female descendant. **3.** one related as if by the ties binding daughter to parent: *daughter of the church.* **4.** anything (personified as female) considered with respect to its origin. [var. of ME *doughter,* OE *dohtor,* c. G *tochter,* Gk. *thygátēr*]

daugh·ter-in-law (dô′tər ĭn lô′), *n., pl.* **daughters-in-law.** the wife of one's son.

daugh·ter·ly (dô′tər lĭ), *adj.* pertaining to, befitting, or like a daughter. —**daugh′ter·li·ness,** *n.*

Daughters of the American Revolution, The, a patriotic society of women descended from Americans of the Revolutionary period, organized in 1890 in Washington, D. C.

daunt (dônt, dänt), *v.t.* **1.** to overcome with fear; intimidate. **2.** to lessen the courage of; dishearten. [ME *daunte*(n), t. OF: m. *danter,* ult. der. L *domāre* tame, subdue] —**Syn. 1.** frighten, cow, overawe. **2.** discourage, dispirit, dismay.

daunt·less (dônt′lĭs, dänt′-), *adj.* not to be daunted; fearless; intrepid; bold. —**daunt′less·ly,** *adv.* —**daunt′less·ness,** *n.* —**Syn.** daring, courageous, indomitable. —**Ant.** cowardly.

dau·phin (dô′fĭn; *Fr.* dō făN′), *n.* the distinctive title of the eldest son of the king of France, from 1349 to 1830. [t. F, appar. orig. a proper name used as a surname; often identified with L *delphīnus* dolphin]

dau·phin·ess (dô′fĭn ĭs), *n.* the wife of the dauphin. Also, **dau·phine** (dô′fēn; *Fr.* dō fēn′).

daut (dôt, dät), *v.t. Scot.* to fondle; caress. Also, **dawt.**

Da·vao (dä vou′), *n.* a seaport in the Philippine Islands, on Mindanao. 95,546 (1939).

D'Av·e·nant (dăv′ə nənt), *n.* **Sir William,** 1606–68, British dramatist and poet. Also, **Dav′e·nant.**

dav·en·port (dăv′ən pōrt′), *n.* **1.** *U.S.* a kind of large sofa, often one convertible into a bed. **2.** *Chiefly Brit.* a small writing table. [prob. from the maker's name]

Dav·en·port (dăv′ən pōrt′), *n.* **1.** **John,** 1597–1670, Puritan clergyman: one of the founders of New Haven. **2.** a city in E Iowa, on the Mississippi. 74,549 (1950).

Da·vid (dā′vĭd *for 1, 2;* dà vēd′ *for 3*), *n.* **1.** fl. c1000 B.C., the second king of the Hebrews, successor to Saul: united tribes of Israel into a nation with the capital at Jerusalem. **2. Saint,** (*Saint Dewi*) died A.D. 601?, Welsh bishop: patron saint of Wales. **3. Jacques Louis** (zhäk lwē), 1748–1825, French painter. [t. Heb.: m. *Dāwid*]

Da·vid I (dā′vĭd), 1084–1153, king of Scotland, 1124–53.

David Copperfield, a novel (1850) by Charles Dickens.

Da·vid d'An·gers (dà vēd′ dän zhē′), (*Pierre Jean David*) 1788–1856, French sculptor.

Da·vid·son (dā′vĭd sən), *n.* **1. Jo,** 1883–1952, U.S. sculptor. **2. John,** 1857–1909, British poet and dramatist.

da Vi·gno·la (dä vē nyô′lä). See **Vignola.**

da Vin·ci (dä vĭn′chĭ; *It.* dä vēn′chē). See **Vinci.**

Da·vis (dā′vĭs), *n.* **1. Jefferson,** 1808–89, U.S. statesman: president of the Confederate States of America, 1861–65. **2. John,** 1550?–1605, British navigator and explorer. **3. John William,** born 1873, U.S. lawyer and diplomat: Democratic candidate for president of the U.S. in 1924. **4. Richard Harding,** 1864–1916, U.S. journalist, novelist, and dramatist.

Da·vis·son (dā′və sən), *n.* **Clinton Joseph,** born 1881, U.S. physicist.

Davis Strait, a strait between Canada and Greenland, connecting Baffin Bay and the Atlantic. 200–500 mi. wide.

dav·it (dăv′ĭt, dā′vĭt), *n. Naut.* a projecting piece of wood or iron (frequently one of a pair) on the side or stern of a vessel, fitted with a tackle, etc., for raising, lowering, or suspending a small boat, anchor, or other weight. [ME *daviot,* t. AF, appar. dim. of *Davi* David]

D. Davit

Da·vout (dà vōō′), *n.* **Louis Nicolas** (lwē nē kô lä′), (*Duke of Auerstädt and Prince of Eckmühl*) 1770–1823,

marshal of France: one of Napoleon's leading generals.

Da·vy (dā′vĭ), *n.* **Sir Humphry,** 1778–1829, British chemist.

Da·vy Jones (dā′vĭ jōnz′), *Naut.* the spirit of the sea; the sailor's devil.

Davy Jones's locker, 1. the ocean's bottom, esp. as the grave of all who perish at sea. **2.** the ocean.

Davy lamp, an early safety lamp for miners.

daw (dô), *n.* **1.** a jackdaw. **2.** a simpleton. [ME *dawe.* Cf. OHG *tāha*]

daw·dle (dô′dəl), *v.,* **-dled, -dling** —*v.i.* **1.** to waste time; idle; trifle; loiter. —*v.t.* **2.** to waste (time) by trifling (usually fol. by *away*). [? var. of *daddle* TODDLE] —**daw′dler,** *n.* —**Syn. 1.** See **loiter.**

Dawes (dôz), *n.* **Charles Gates,** 1865–1951, U.S. financier and diplomat: vice-president of the U.S. 1925–29.

dawk (dôk, däk), *n.* dak.

dawn (dôn), *n.* **1.** the first appearance of daylight in the morning. **2.** the beginning or rise of anything; advent. —*v. i.* **3.** to begin to grow light in the morning. **4.** to begin to open or develop. **5.** to begin to be perceived (fol. by *on*): *the idea dawned on him.* —**Syn. 1.** daybreak, sunrise. [appar. alter. of *dawing,* der. *daw,* OE *dagian* become day]

Daw·son (dô′sən), *n.* **1. Sir John William,** 1820–99, Canadian geologist and educator. **2.** a town in NW Canada at the confluence of the Yukon and Klondike rivers: the capital of Yukon Territory. 1043 (1941).

Dawson Creek, a village in W Canada at the SE terminus of the Alaska Highway, which extends from E British Columbia to Fairbanks, Alaska.

dawt (dôt, dät), *v.t. Scot.* daut.

Dax (däks), *n.* a city in SW France: mineral hot springs. 10,168 (1936).

day (dā), *n.* **1.** the interval of light between two successive nights; the time between sunrise and sunset. **2.** the light of day; daylight. **3.** *Astron.* **a.** the period during which the earth (or a heavenly body) makes one revolution on its axis. **b.** the average length of this interval, twenty-four hours (**mean solar day**). **c.** the interval of time which elapses between two consecutive returns of the same terrestrial meridian to the sun (**solar day**). **d.** a period reckoned from midnight to midnight and equivalent in length to the mean solar day (**civil day**), as contrasted with a similar period reckoned from noon to noon (**astronomical day**). **4.** the portion of a day allotted to labor: *an eight-hour day.* **5.** a day as a point or unit of time, or on which something occurs. **6.** a day assigned to a particular purpose or observance: *New Year's Day.* **7.** a day of contest, or the contest itself: *to win the day.* **8.** (*often pl.*) a particular time or period: *the present day, in days of old.* **9.** (*often pl.*) period of life or activity. **10.** period of power or influence. [ME; OE *dæg,* c. G *tag*]

day bed, a narrow bed convertible to a couch by day.

day blindness, nyctalopia (def. 2).

day·book (dā′bŏŏk′), *n.* **1.** *Bookkeeping.* a book in which the transactions of the day are entered in the order of their occurrence. **2.** a diary.

day boy, *Chiefly Brit.* a boy who comes to school by day, as distinguished from those who live in the school.

day·break (dā′brāk′), *n.* the first appearance of light in the morning; dawn.

day coach, *U.S.* an ordinary railroad passenger car, as distinguished from a sleeping car, parlor car, etc.

day·dream (dā′drēm′), *n.* **1.** a visionary fancy indulged in while awake; reverie. —*v.i.* **2.** to indulge in daydreams. —**day′dream′er,** *n.*

day·flow·er (dā′flou′ər), *n.* any plant of the genus *Commelina,* of the spiderwort family, mostly bearing cymes of small blue flowers.

day·fly (dā′flī′), *n., pl.* **-flies.** mayfly.

day laborer, an unskilled worker paid by the day.

day letter, a telegram sent during the day, usually longer and slower, but cheaper, than a regular telegram.

day·light (dā′līt′), *n.* **1.** the light of day. **2.** openness; publicity. **3.** daytime. **4.** daybreak.

day·light-sav·ing time (dā′līt′ sā′vĭng), time one or more hours later than the standard time for a country or community, usually used during summer months to give more hours of daylight to the working day.

day lily, 1. any plant of the liliaceous genus *Hemerocallis,* with yellow or orange flowers which commonly last only for a day. **2.** any plant of the liliaceous genus *Niobe* (or *Funkia*), with white or blue flowers. **3.** the flower of any of these plants.

day nursery, *U.S.* a nursery for the care of small children during the day, esp. while their mothers are at work.

Day of Atonement, a Jewish fast day, Yom Kippur.

Day of Judgment, the day of the Last Judgment, at the end of the world.

day school, 1. a school held on weekdays (distinguished from *Sunday school*). **2.** a school held in the daytime (distinguished from *night school*). **3.** a private school for pupils living outside the school (distinguished from *boarding school*).

days·man (dāz′mən), *n. Archaic.* an umpire; mediator. [f. *day's* (poss. of DAY) + MAN]

days of grace, days (commonly three) allowed by law or custom for payment after a bill or note falls due.

day·spring (dā′sprĭng′), *n. Poetic.* dawn; daybreak.

day·star (dā'stär'), *n*. **1.** the morning star. **2.** *Poetic.* the sun.

day·time (dā'tīm'), *n*. the time between sunrise and sunset.

Day·ton (dā'tən), *n*. a city in SW Ohio. 243,872 (1950).

Day·to·na Beach (dā tō'nə), a city in NE Florida: seaside resort. 30,187 (1950).

daze (dāz), *v*., **dazed, dazing**, *n*. —*v.t.* **1.** to stun or stupefy with a blow, a shock, etc. **2.** to confuse; bewilder; dazzle. —*n*. **3.** a dazed condition. [ME *dase(n)*, t. Scand.; cf. Dan. *dase* doze, mope] —**daz·ed·ly** (dā'zĭd lY), *adv*.

daz·zle (dăz'əl), *v*., **-zled, -zling**, *n*. —*v.t.* **1.** to overpower or dim (the vision) by intense light. **2.** to bewilder by brilliancy or display of any kind. —*v.i.* **3.** to be overpowered by light. **4.** to excite admiration by brilliancy. —*n*. **5.** act or fact of dazzling. **6.** bewildering brightness. [freq. of DAZE] —**daz'zler**, *n*. —**daz'zling·ly**, *adv*.

db., decibel; decibels.

dbl., double.

DC, Dental Corps.

D.C., **1.** *Music*. da capo. **2.** *Elect*. direct current. **3.** District of Columbia.

d.c., *Elect*. direct current.

D.C.L., Doctor of Civil Law.

D.C.M., *Brit*. Distinguished Conduct Medal.

D.D., Doctor of Divinity.

D-day (dē'dā'), *n*. *Mil*. the day, usually unspecified, set for the beginning of a previously planned attack.

D.D.S., Doctor of Dental Surgery.

DDT, the symbol for a very powerful insecticide, p, p'-dichlorodiphenyl-trichloroethane.

de (da), *prep*. from; of: much used in French personal names, orig. to indicate place of origin. Also, **De**.

de-, a prefix meaning: **1.** privation and separation, as in *dehorn, dethrone, detrain*. **2.** negation, as in *demerit, derange*. **3.** descent, as in *degrade, deduce*. **4.** reversal, as in *detract*. **5.** intensity, as in *decompound*. [ME, t. L, repr. *de*, prep., from, away from, of, out of, etc.; in some words t. F, g. L *de-*, or g. L *dis-* (see DIS¹)]

dea·con (dē'kən), *n*. **1.** (in hierarchical churches) a member of the clerical order next below that of priest. **2.** (in other churches) an appointed or elected officer having variously defined duties. —*v.t.* **3.** *U.S. Colloq. or Dial*. to read out (a line of a psalm, hymn, etc.) before singing it. [ME *deacon, deken*, OE *dēacon, diacon*, t. LL: s. *diācōnus*, t. Gk.: m. *diákōnos* servant, minister, deacon] —**dea'con·ship'**, *n*.

dea·con·ess (dē'kən Ys), *n*. **1.** (in certain Protestant churches) one of an order of women who carry on educational, hospital, or social-service work. **2.** a woman elected by a church to assist the clergy.

dea·con·ry (dē'kən rY), *n*., *pl*. **-ries**. **1.** the office of a deacon. **2.** deacons collectively.

de·ac·ti·vate (dē ăk'tə vāt'), *v.t.*, **-vated, -vating**. to demobilize or disband (a military unit). —**de·ac'ti·va'tion**, *n*.

dead (dĕd), *adj*. **1.** no longer living; deprived of life. **2.** not endowed with life; inanimate: *dead matter*. **3.** resembling death: *a dead sleep*. **4.** bereft of sensation; insensible; numb: *dead to all sense of shame*. **5.** no longer in existence or use: *dead languages*. **6.** *Law*. deprived of civil rights so that one is in the state of civil death, esp. deprived of the rights of property. **7.** without spiritual life or vigor. **8.** *Colloq*. very tired; exhausted. **9.** infertile; barren. **10.** deprived of or lacking animation, motion, force, vigor, or any other characteristic quality: *dead air, water, machinery, affections*, etc. **11.** extinguished: *a dead fire*. **12.** tasteless or flat, as liquor. **13.** not glossy, bright, or brilliant. **14.** without resonance: *a dead sound*. **15.** without resiliency or bounce: *a dead tennis ball*. **16.** closed at one end: *a dead street*. **17.** dull or inactive: *a dead market*. **18.** complete; absolute: *dead loss, dead silence*. **19.** sure; unerring: *a dead shot*. **20.** direct; straight: *a dead line*. **21.** unproductive: *dead capital*. **22.** *Sports*. out of play: *a dead ball*. **23.** having been used or rejected, as type set up or copy for printing. **24.** *Elect*. **a.** free from any electric connection to a source of potential difference and from electric charge. **b.** not having a potential different from that of the earth. —*n*. **25.** one who is dead. **26.** (usually prec. by *the*) dead persons collectively. **27.** the period of greatest darkness, coldness, etc.: *the dead of night*. —*adv*. **28.** absolutely; completely: *dead right*. **29.** with abrupt and complete stoppage of motion, etc.: *he stopped dead*. **30.** directly; exactly; diametrically: *the wind was dead ahead*. [ME *deed*, OE *dēad*, c. G *tot*; orig. pp. See DIE] —**dead'ness**, *n*.

—**Syn. 1.** DEAD, DECEASED, EXTINCT, LIFELESS refer to something which does not have (or appear to have) life. DEAD is usually applied to that which had life but from which life is now gone: *dead trees, animals; they recovered the dead bodies*. DECEASED, a more formal word than DEAD, is applied to human beings who no longer have life: *a deceased member of the church*. EXTINCT is applied esp. to a race, species, or the like, no member of which is any longer alive: *mastodons are now extinct*. LIFELESS is applied to what may or may not have had life but which does not have it (or appear to have it) now: *the lifeless body of a child was taken out of the water, minerals consist of lifeless materials*. **4.** unfeeling, indifferent, callous. **10.** still, motionless, inert, inoperative. —**Ant. 1.** living, alive.

dead·beat (dĕd'bēt'), *adj*. *Physics*, etc. **1.** free from oscillation or recoil. **2.** having an index needle that comes to a stop with little or no oscillation.

dead beat, **1.** *U.S. Colloq*. one who has a reputation for not paying his bills. **2.** *Slang*. a loafer; sponger.

dead-beat (dĕd'bēt'), *adj*. *Colloq*. very tired; exhausted.

dead center, **1.** (in a gasoline engine, etc.) either of two positions of the crank in which the connecting rod has no power to turn it, occurring when the crank and connecting rod are in the same plane, at each end of a stroke. **2.** *Mach*. a stationary center which holds the work, as the tailstock of a lathe.

D. Dead center

dead·en (dĕd'ən), *v.t.* **1.** to make less sensitive, active, energetic, or forcible; dull; weaken: *to deaden sound, the force of a ball, the senses*. **2.** to lessen the velocity of; retard. **3.** to make impervious to sound, as a floor. —*v.i.* **4.** to become dead. —**dead'en·er**, *n*.

dead end, a street, water pipe, etc., that is closed at one end. —**dead'-end'**, *adj*.

dead·en·ing (dĕd'ən Yng), *n*. **1.** a device or material employed to deaden or render dull. **2.** a device or material preventing the transmission of sound.

dead·eye (dĕd'ī'), *n*. a round, laterally flattened block encircled by a rope or an iron band and pierced with three holes.

dead·fall (dĕd'fôl'), *n*. a trap, esp. for large game, in which a weight falls upon and crushes the prey.

dead hand, *Law*. mortmain.

dead·head (dĕd'hĕd'), *n*. *Colloq*. one who attends a theater, rides a streetcar, etc., without payment.

dead heat, a heat or race in which two or more competitors finish together.

dead letter, **1.** a law, ordinance, etc., which has lost its force, though not formally repealed or abolished. **2.** a letter which lies unclaimed for a certain time at a post office, or which, because of faulty address, etc., cannot be delivered. Such letters are sent to and handled in a special division or department (**dead letter office**) of the general post office. —**dead'-let'ter**, *adj*.

dead·light (dĕd'līt'), *n*. *Naut*. **1.** a strong wooden or iron shutter for a cabin window or porthole, to prevent water from entering. **2.** a thick pane of glass set in the hull or deck to admit light.

Deadeyes

dead·line (dĕd'līn'), *n*. **1.** a line or limit that must not be passed. **2.** the latest time for finishing something.

dead load, a load that is permanent and immovable, as the weight of a bridge.

dead·lock (dĕd'lŏk'), *n*. **1.** state of affairs in which progress is impossible; complete standstill. —*v.t.* **2.** to bring to a deadlock. —*v.i.* **3.** to come to a deadlock.

dead·ly (dĕd'lY), *adj*., **-lier, -liest**, *adv*. —*adj*. **1.** causing or tending to cause death; fatal: *a deadly poison*. **2.** aiming to kill or destroy; implacable: *a deadly enemy*. **3.** involving spiritual death: *a deadly sin*. **4.** like death: *a deadly pallor*. **5.** excessive: *deadly haste*. —*adv*. **6.** in a manner resembling or suggesting death: *deadly pale*. **7.** *Colloq*. excessively: *deadly dull*. —**dead'li·ness**, *n*. —**Syn. 1.** See fatal.

deadly nightshade, the belladonna.

deadly sins, pride, covetousness, lust, anger, gluttony, envy, and sloth.

dead march, a piece of solemn music for a funeral procession, esp. one played at a military funeral.

dead pan, *Slang*. **1.** a face completely lacking in expression. **2.** a person who assumes such a face, as a comedian. —**dead'-pan'**, *adj*.

dead point, dead center.

dead reckoning, *Naut*. **1.** the calculation of a ship's position without astronomical observations, by means of the distances sailed on the various courses as shown by the log and compass, with corrections for currents, etc. **2.** position as calculated.

Dead Sea, a salt lake on the E border of Palestine: the lowest lake in the world. 46 mi. long; 10 mi. wide; 1293 feet below sea level.

dead-stick landing (dĕd'stYk'), *Aeron*. a landing made with a dead engine.

dead weight, **1.** the heavy, unrelieved weight of anything inert. **2.** a heavy or oppressive burden. **3.** the weight of a railroad car, etc., as distinct from its load.

dead·wood (dĕd'wŏŏd'), *n*. **1.** the dead branches on a tree; dead branches or trees. **2.** anything useless.

deaf (dĕf; *now less often* dēf), *adj*. **1.** lacking or deprived of the sense of hearing, wholly or partially; unable to hear. **2.** refusing to listen; heedless of; inattentive: *deaf to advice, turn a deaf ear to a plea*. [ME *deef*, OE *dēaf*, c. G *taub*] —**deaf'ly**, *adv*. —**deaf'ness**, *n*.

deaf·en (dĕf'ən), *v.t.* **1.** to make deaf. **2.** to stun with noise. **3.** to render (a sound) inaudible, esp. by a louder sound. —**deaf'en·ing·ly**, *adv*.

deaf-mute (dĕf'mūt'), *n*. a person who is deaf and dumb, esp. one in whom inability to speak is due to congenital or early deafness.

deal[1] (dēl), *v.*, **dealt, dealing,** *n.* —*v.i.* **1.** to occupy oneself or itself (fol. by *with* or *in*): *deal with the first question, botany deals with the study of plants.* **2.** to take action with respect to a thing or person (usually fol. by *with*): *law courts must deal with lawbreakers.* **3.** to conduct oneself toward persons: *deal fairly.* **4.** to trade or do business: *to deal with a firm, to deal in an article.* **5.** to make a secret agreement or bargain (fol. by *with*). **6.** to distribute, esp. the cards required in a game. —*v.t.* **7.** to give to one as his share; apportion. **8.** to distribute among a number of recipients, as the cards required in a game. **9.** *Cards.* to give a player (a specific card) in dealing. **10.** to deliver (blows, etc.). —*n.* **11.** *Colloq.* a business transaction. **12.** a bargain or arrangement for mutual advantage, as in commerce or politics, often a secret or underhand one. **13.** treatment; arrangement: *a raw deal, a fair deal, a new deal.* **14.** a quantity, amount, extent, or degree. **15.** an indefinite but large amount or extent: *a deal of money.* **16.** act of dealing or distributing. **17.** *Cards.* **a.** the distribution to the players of the cards in a game. **b.** the set of cards in one's hand. **c.** the turn of a player to deal. **d.** the period of time during which a deal is played. **18.** *Obs.* portion or share. [ME *delen,* OE *dǣlan* (c. G *teilen,* etc.), der. *dǣl* part (c. G *teil*)] —**Syn.** 7. allot, assign.

deal[2] (dēl), *n.* **1.** a board or plank, esp. of fir or pine, in Britain usually more than 7 inches wide and 6 feet long, and less than 3 inches thick; in U. S. and Canada, 11 inches wide, 12 feet long, 2½ inches thick. **2.** such boards collectively. **3.** fir or pine wood. [ME *dele,* t. MLG or MD]

deal·er (dē′lər), *n.* **1.** one who buys and sells articles without altering their condition; trader or merchant. **2.** *Cards.* the player distributing the cards.

deal·fish (dēl′fĭsh′), *n., pl.* **-fishes,** (*esp. collectively*) **-fish.** any of the deep-sea fishes constituting the genus *Trachypterus,* characterized by a long, compressed, tape-like body. [f. DEAL[2] + FISH]

deal·ing (dē′lĭng), *n.* **1.** (*usually pl.*) relations; trading: *business dealings.* **2.** conduct in relation to others; treatment: *honest dealing.*

dealt (dĕlt), *v.* pt. and pp. of **deal**[1].

dean[1] (dēn), *n.* **1.** *Educ.* **a.** the head of a faculty, or sometimes its registrar or secretary, in a university or college. **b.** the official in charge of undergraduate students at an English university. **c.** an official in an American college or university having charge of student personnel services, such as counseling or discipline: *the dean of men.* **2.** *Eccles.* **a.** the head of the chapter of a cathedral or a collegiate church. **b.** any of various other ecclesiastical dignitaries, as the head of a division of a diocese. **3.** the senior member, in length of service, of any body. [ME *deen,* t. OF: m. *deien,* ult. der. L *decem* ten] —**dean′ship,** *n.*

dean[2] (dēn), *n.* *Brit.* dene.

dean·er·y (dē′nərĭ), *n., pl.* **-eries. 1.** the office, jurisdiction, or district of a dean. **2.** the residence of a dean.

dear[1] (dĭr), *adj.* **1.** beloved or loved: *a dear friend of mine.* **2.** (in the salutation of a letter) highly esteemed: *Dear Sirs.* **3.** precious in one's regard: *our dearest possessions.* **4.** high-priced; expensive. **5.** charging high prices. **6.** high: *a dear price to pay.* **7.** difficult to get. **8.** *Obs.* worthy. —*n.* **9.** one who is dear. **10.** a beloved one (often used in direct address): *my dear.* —*adv.* **11.** dearly; fondly. **12.** at a high price. —*interj.* **13.** an exclamation of surprise, distress, etc. [ME *dere,* OE *dēore,* c. G *teuer*] —**dear′ly,** *adv.* —**dear′ness,** *n.* —**Syn.** 4. See **expensive.** —**Ant.** 4. cheap.

dear[2] (dĭr), *adj. Archaic.* hard; grievous. Also, **dere.** [ME *dere,* OE *dēor;* cf. Icel. *dȳr* difficult, rigorous]

Dear·born (dĭr′bərn, -bôrn), *n.* **1.** a city in SE Michigan, near Detroit. 94,994 (1950). **2. Fort,** a former U.S. fort on the site of Chicago, 1803–37.

dearth (dûrth), *n.* **1.** scarcity or scanty supply; lack. **2.** scarcity and dearness of food; famine. [ME *derthe.* See DEAR[2], -TH[1]]

dear·y (dĭr′ĭ), *n., pl.* **dearies.** darling. Also, **dear′ie.**

death (dĕth), *n.* **1.** act of dying; the end of life; the total and permanent cessation of all the vital functions of an animal or plant. **2.** (*often cap.*) the annihilating power personified, usually represented as a skeleton: *"O Death, where is thy sting?"* **3.** state of being dead: *to lie still in death.* **4.** extinction; destruction: *it will mean the death of our hopes.* **5.** the time at which a person dies: *the letters may be published after my death.* **6.** manner of dying: *a hero's death.* **7.** loss or deprivation of civil life. **8.** loss or absence of spiritual life. **9.** bloodshed or murder. **10.** a cause or occasion of death. **11.** a pestilence: *the black death.* **12. do** or **put to death,** to kill. [ME *deeth,* OE *dēath,* c. G *tod*] —**Syn.** 1. decease, demise, passing, departure.

death·bed (dĕth′bĕd′), *n.* **1.** the bed on which a person dies. **2.** the last few hours before death.

death bell, the bell that announces a death.

death·blow (dĕth′blō′), *n.* a blow causing death.

death camass, 1. a perennial liliaceous herb, *Zygadenus,* with several species in the southern and western U. S. and in Canada. **2.** its root, poisonous to sheep and other animals.

death cup, 1. a poisonous mushroom of the genus *Amanita,* part of which persists around the base of the stipe as a definite membranous cup. **2.** the cup.

death duty, *Brit. Law.* an inheritance tax.

death·ful (dĕth′fəl), *adj.* **1.** fatal. **2.** deathlike.

death house, a building or part of a prison in which persons condemned to death await execution.

death·less (dĕth′lĭs), *adj.* **1.** not subject to death; immortal. **2.** perpetual. —**death′less·ly,** *adv.* —**death′less·ness,** *n.*

death·like (dĕth′līk′), *adj.* resembling death.

death·ly (dĕth′lĭ), *adj.* **1.** causing death; deadly; fatal. **2.** like death. **3.** *Poetic.* of death. —*adv.* **4.** in the manner of death. **5.** very; utterly: *deathly afraid.* [ME *dethlich,* OE *dēathlic*]

death mask, a cast of a person's face taken after death.

death rate, the number of deaths per unit (usually 1000) of population in a given place and time.

death's-head (dĕths′hĕd′), *n.* a human skull, esp. as a symbol of mortality.

deaths·man (dĕths′mən), *n., pl.* **-men.** *Archaic.* an executioner.

death·trap (dĕth′trăp′), *n.* a structure or situation involving imminent risk of death.

Death Valley, an arid basin in E California; lowest land in the Western Hemisphere. 276 ft. below sea level.

death warrant, 1. an official order authorizing the execution of the sentence of death. **2.** anything which ends hope, expectation, etc.

death·watch (dĕth′wŏch′, -wôch′), *n.* **1.** a vigil beside a dying or dead person. **2.** a guard set over a condemned person before execution. **3.** any of certain beetles of the family *Anobiidae* which infest timbers, esp. in Europe. The ticking sound caused by their heads tapping against wood was thought to presage death.

death·y (dĕth′ĭ), *adj., adv. Rare.* deathly.

Deau·ville (dō′vĭl; *Fr.* dō vēl′), *n.* a coastal resort in NW France, S of Le Havre. 4663 (1946).

deave (dēv), *v.t.,* **deaved, deaving.** *Dial.* to make deaf; deafen. [ME *deve,* OE *dēafian*]

deb., debenture.

de·ba·cle (dā bä′kəl, -băk′əl, dĭ-), *n.* **1.** a general breakup or rout; sudden overthrow or collapse. **2.** a breaking up of ice in a river. **3.** a violent rush of waters. [t. F, der. *débâcler* unbar, clear, f. *dé-* DIS-[1] + *bâcler* bar (der. L *baculum* stick, rod)]

de·bar (dĭ bär′), *v.t.,* **-barred, -barring. 1.** to bar out or exclude from a place or condition. **2.** to prevent or prohibit (an action, etc.). [t. F: m. s. *débarrer,* OF *desbarrer,* f. *des-* DIS-[1] + *barrer* BAR[1], v.] —**de·bar′ment,** *n.* —**Syn.** 1. See **exclude.** 2. interdict, hinder. —**Ant.** 1. admit. 2. permit.

de·bark (dĭ bärk′), *v.t., v.i.* to disembark. [t. F: m. s. *débarquer,* der. *dé-* DIS-[1] + *barque* BARK[3]] —**de·bar·ka·tion** (dē′bär kā′shən), *n.*

de·base (dĭ bās′), *v.t.,* **-based, -basing. 1.** to reduce in quality or value; adulterate. **2.** *Obs.* to lower in rank or dignity. [f. DE- + obs. *base* (aphetic var. of ABASE)] —**de·base′ment,** *n.* —**de·bas′er,** *n.* —**de·bas′ing·ly,** *adv.* —**Syn.** 1. lower, vitiate, corrupt, deteriorate.

de·bat·a·ble (dĭ bā′tə bəl), *adj.* **1.** capable of being debated. **2.** in dispute.

de·bate (dĭ bāt′), *n., v.,* **-bated, -bating.** —*n.* **1.** a discussion, esp. of a public question in an assembly. **2.** deliberation; consideration. **3.** a systematic contest of speakers in which two points of view of a proposition are advanced with proof. **4.** *Obs.* strife; contention. —*v.i.* **5.** to engage in discussion, esp. in a legislative or public assembly. **6.** to deliberate; consider; discuss or argue. **7.** *Obs.* to fight; quarrel. —*v.t.* **8.** to discuss or argue (a question) in a public assembly. **9.** to dispute about. **10.** to deliberate upon; consider. **11.** *Archaic.* to contend for or over. [ME *debate*(*n*), t. OF: m. *debatre,* f. *dé-* DE- + *batre* BEAT] —**de·bat′er,** *n.* —**Syn.** 1. argument, controversy, disputation. 6. See **argue.**

de·bauch (dĭ bôch′), *v.t.* **1.** to corrupt by sensuality, intemperance, etc.; seduce. **2.** to corrupt or pervert; deprave. **3.** *Obs.* to lead away, as from allegiance or duty. —*v.i.* **4.** to indulge in a debauch. —*n.* **5.** a period of debauchery. **6.** debauchery. [t. F: s. *débaucher,* OF *desbaucher* seduce from duty] —**de·bauch′er,** *n.* —**de·bauch′ment,** *n.*

deb·au·chee (dĕb′ô chē′, -shē′), *n.* one addicted to excessive indulgence in sensual pleasures; one given to debauchery. [t. F: m. *débauché,* pp. of *débaucher* DEBAUCH]

de·bauch·er·y (dĭ bô′chər ĭ), *n., pl.* **-eries. 1.** seduction from virtue or morality. **2.** excessive indulgence in sensual pleasures; intemperance. **3.** seduction from allegiance or duty.

de·ben·ture (dĭ bĕn′chər), *n.* **1.** a certificate of indebtedness, as a debenture bond (more widely used in England, where it often takes the place of *bond*). **2.** a certificate of drawback issued at a custom house. [t. L: m. *debentur* there are owing]

debenture bond, a corporation bond unsecured by any mortgage, dependent on the credit of the issuer.

de·bil·i·tate (dĭ bĭl′ə tāt′), *v.t.,* **-tated, -tating.** to make weak or feeble; weaken; enfeeble. [t. L: m. s. *dēbilitātus,* pp., weakened] —**de·bil′i·ta′tion,** *n.* —**de·bil′i·ta′tive,** *adj.*

de·bil·i·ty (dĭ bĭl′ə tĭ), *n., pl.* **-ties. 1.** state of being weak or feeble; weakness. **2.** *Pathol.* a condition of the body in which the vital functions are feebly discharged. [ME *debylite,* t. L: m.s. *dēbilitas* weakness]

---

deb·it (dĕb′ĭt), *n.* **1.** the recording or an entry of debt in an account. **2.** *Bookkeeping.* **a.** that which is entered in an account as a debt; a recorded item of debt. **b.** any entry, or the total shown, on the debit side. **c.** the side (left side) of an account on which such entries are made (opposed to *credit*). —*v.t.* **3.** to charge with a debt. **4.** to charge as a debt. **5.** *Bookkeeping.* to enter upon the debit side of an account. [t. L: s. *dēbitum* something owed. See DEBT]

deb·o·nair (dĕb′ə·nâr′), *adj.* **1.** of pleasant manners; courteous. **2.** gay; sprightly. Also, **deb′o·naire′**, **deb′-on·naire′**. [ME *debonere*, t. OF: m. *debonaire*, orig. phrase *de bon aire* of good disposition] —**deb′o·nair′ly**, *adv.* —**deb′o·nair′ness**, *n.*

de bonne grâce (də bôn gräs′), *French.* graciously.

Deb·o·rah (dĕb′ə·rə), *n. Bible.* a prophetess and judge of Israel. Judges 4, 5. [t. Heb.]

de·bouch (dĭ·bōōsh′), *v.i.* **1.** to march out from a narrow or confined place into open country, as a body of troops. **2.** *Phys. Geog.* **a.** to emerge from a relatively narrow valley upon an open plain: *a river or glacier debouches on the plains.* **b.** to flow from a small valley into a larger one. **3.** to issue; emerge. —*n.* **4.** débouché. [t. F: m.s. *déboucher*, der. *dé-* DIS-¹ + *bouche* mouth (g. L *bucca* cheek, mouth)]

dé·bou·ché (dě bōō shě′), *n. French.* **1.** *Fort.* an opening in works for passing troops. **2.** an outlet; an exit.

de·bouch·ment (dĭ·bōōsh′mənt), *n.* **1.** act or fact of debouching. **2.** a mouth or outlet, as of a river or pass.

De·bre·cen (dě′brě tsěn′), *n.* a city in E Hungary. 125,933 (1941).

de·bris (də·brē′, dā′brē *or, esp. Brit.,* dĕb′rē), *n.* **1.** the remains of anything broken down or destroyed; ruins; fragments; rubbish. **2.** *Geol.* an accumulation of loose fragments of rock, etc. Also, **dé·bris′**. [t. F: m. *débris*, der. OF *debrisier* break down, f. *de-* DE- + *brisier* break (cf. BRUISE)]

De Bro·glie (də brô glē′), **Louis Victor** (lwē vēk tôr′), born 1892, French physicist.

Debs (dĕbz), *n.* **Eugene Victor**, 1855–1926, U.S. labor leader; Socialist candidate for president 1900, 1904, 1908, 1912, and 1920.

debt (dĕt), *n.* **1.** that which is owed; that which one person is bound to pay to or perform for another. **2.** a liability or obligation to pay or render something. **3.** the condition of being under such an obligation. **4.** *Theol.* an offense requiring reparation; a sin; a trespass. [ME *det*, t. OF: m. *dete*, g. L *dēbitum* (thing) owed, prop. pp. neut.] —**Syn. 1.** obligation, duty, due.

debt of honor, a gambling debt.

debt·or (dĕt′ər), *n.* one who is in debt or under obligations to another (opposed to *creditor*).

de·bunk (dĭ·bŭngk′), *v.t. U.S. Colloq.* to remove false sentiments, opinions, etc., about.

De·bus·sy (də·bŭs′ĭ; *Fr.* də bv sē′), *n.* **Claude Achille** (klôd à shěl′), 1862–1918, French composer.

de·but (dĭ·bū′, dā-, dā′bū *or, esp. Brit.,* dĕb′ōō), *n.* **1.** a first public appearance on a stage, over the radio, etc. **2.** a formal introduction and entrance into society. **3.** the beginning of a professional career, etc. Also, *French,* **début** (dě BY′). [t. F, der. *débuter* make the first stroke in a game, make one's first appearance, f. *dé-* DE- + *but* goal, mark]

deb·u·tante (dĕb′yŏō tänt′, dĕb′yə tänt′), *n.* a woman making a debut. [t. F, fem. ppr. of *débuter*. See DEBUT] —**deb′u·tant′**, *n. masc.*

dec-, var. of **deca-**.

Dec., December.

dec., **1.** deceased. **2.** decimeter. **3.** declension. **4.** decrease. **5.** decrescendo.

deca-, a word element meaning "ten," specialized in the metric system so that *deca-* (deka-) gives the multiplication by 10, *deci-* the division by 10; e.g., *decaliter* (610.25 cu. in.), *liter* (61.025 cu. in.), *deciliter* (6.10 cu. in.). Cf. **deci-**. [t. Gk.: m. *deka-*, comb. form of *dĕka* ten]

dec·ade (dĕk′ād), *n.* **1.** a period of ten years. **2.** a group, set, or series of ten. [t. F, t. L: m. s. *decas*, t. Gk.: m. *dekás* a group of ten]

dec·a·dence (dĭ·kā′dəns, dĕk′ə-), *n.* act or process of falling into an inferior condition or state; decay; deterioration. Also, **dec·a·den·cy** (dĭ·kā′dən sĭ, dĕk′ə-). [t. F, ult. der L *dē-* DE- + *cadere* fall] —**Syn.** decline, degeneration, retrogression.

dec·a·dent (dĭ·kā′dənt, dĕk′ə-), *adj.* **1.** falling off or deteriorating. **2.** of or like the decadents. —*n.* **3.** one who is decadent. **4.** one of a group of French (and other) writers and artists toward the end of the 19th century whose work was characterized by great refinement or subtlety of style with a marked tendency toward the artificial and abnormal. [der. DECADENCE] —**dec·a′dent·ly**, *adv.*

dec·a·gon (dĕk′ə·gŏn′), *n. Geom.* a polygon having 10 angles and 10 sides. [t. ML: s. *decagōnum*. See DECA-, -GON] —**de·cag·o·nal** (dĭ·kăg′ə nəl), *adj.*

dec·a·gram (dĕk′ə·grăm′), *n. Metric System.* a unit of 10 grams, equivalent to 0.3527 ounce avoirdupois. Also, *esp. Brit.,* **dec′a·gramme′**. [t. F: m. *decagramme*. See DECA-, GRAM]

dec·a·he·dron (dĕk′ə hē′drən), *n., pl.* **-drons, -dra** (-drə). *Geom.* a solid figure having 10 faces. —**dec·a·he·dral** (dĕk′ə hē′drəl), *adj.*

Decagon

de·cal·ci·fy (dē·kăl′sə fī′), *v.t.,* **-fied, -fying.** to deprive of lime or calcareous matter, as a bone. —**de·cal·ci·fi·ca·tion** (dē kăl′sə fə kā′shən), *n.*

de·cal·co·ma·ni·a (dĭ′kăl′kə mā′nĭ·ə), *n.* **1.** the art or process of transferring pictures or designs from specially prepared paper to wood, metal, china, glass, etc. **2.** the paper bearing such a picture or design. Also, **de·cal** (dĭ′kăl′). [t. F: m. *décalcomanie*, f. *décalco-* (repr. *décalquer* transfer a tracing of) + *manie* MANIA]

de·ca·les·cence (dē′kə lĕs′əns), *n.* (in the heating of iron) the sudden absorption of heat observed as it passes a certain temperature. —**de·ca·les′cent**, *adj.*

dec·a·li·ter (dĕk′ə lē′tər), *n. Metric System.* a unit of 10 liters equivalent to 9.08 quarts U. S. dry measure, or 2.64 gallons U.S. liquid measure. Also, **dekaliter;** *esp. Brit.,* **dec′a·lit′re**. [t. F: m. *decalitre*. See DECA-, LITER]

Dec·a·logue (dĕk′ə lôg′, -lŏg′), *n.* the Ten Commandments. Ex. 20:2–17. Also, **dec′a·logue′**, **dec′a·log′**. [ME, t. LL: m.s. *decalogus*. t. Gk.: m. *dekálogos*, f. *dĕka* ten + *lógos* word]

De·cam·er·on (dĭ·kăm′ər ən), *n.* **The,** a famous collection of 100 tales (1353) by Boccaccio.

dec·a·me·ter (dĕk′ə mē′tər), *n. Metric System.* a measure of length equal to 10 meters. Also, **dekameter;** *esp. Brit.,* **dec′a·me′tre**. [t. F: m. *décamètre*. See DECA-, METER]

de·camp (dĭ·kămp′), *v.i.* **1.** to depart from a camp; break camp. **2.** to depart quickly, secretly, or unceremoniously. [t. F: m.s. *décamper*, f. *dé-* DIS-¹ + *camper* encamp] —**de·camp′ment**, *n.*

dec·ane (dĕk′ān), *n. Chem.* a hydrocarbon, $C_{10}H_{22}$, of the methane series, occurring in several isomeric forms.

de·cant (dĭ·kănt′), *v.t.* **1.** to pour off gently, as liquor, without disturbing the sediment. **2.** to pour from one container into another. [t. ML: m.s. *decanthāre*. See DE-, CANT²] —**de·can·ta·tion** (dē′kăn tā′shən), *n.*

de·cant·er (dĭ·kăn′tər), *n.* **1.** a bottle used for decanting. **2.** a vessel, usually an ornamental bottle, from which wine, water, etc., are served at table.

de·cap·i·tate (dĭ·kăp′ə tāt′), *v.t.,* **-tated, -tating.** to cut off the head of; behead; kill by beheading. [t. ML: m.s. *dēcapitāte,* pp. of *decapitāre,* der. L *caput* head] —**de·cap′i·ta′tion**, *n.* —**de·cap′i·ta′tor**, *n.*

dec·a·pod (dĕk′ə pŏd′), *n.* **1.** any crustacean of the order *Decapoda,* including crabs, lobsters, crayfish, prawns, shrimps, etc., characterized by their five pairs of walking legs. **2.** any ten-armed dibranchiate cephalopod, as the cuttlefish, squid, etc. —*adj.* **3.** belonging to the *Decapoda.* **4.** having ten feet or legs. —**de·cap·o·dous** (dĭ·kăp′ə dəs), *adj.*

de·car·bon·ate (dē·kär′bə nāt′), *v.t.,* **-ated, -ating.** to deprive of carbon dioxide.

de·car·bon·ize (dē·kär′bə nīz′), *v.t.,* **-ized, -izing.** decarburize. —**de·car′bon·i·za′tion**, *n.*

de·car·box·y·la·tion (dē′kär bŏk′sə lā′shən), *n. Chem.* the process of removing one or more carboxyl radicals, as carbon dioxide, from an organic acid.

de·car·bu·rize (dē·kär′byə rīz′), *v.t.,* **-rized, -rizing.** to remove carbon from (molten steel, automobile cylinders, etc.). —**de·car′bu·ri·za′tion**, *n.*

de·care (dĕk′âr, dĕ·kâr′), *n. Metric System.* a unit of area equal to 10 ares.

de·car·te·lize (dĭ·kär′tə līz), *v.t.,* **-lized, -lizing.** to break up or dissolve (a cartel, def. 1). —**de·car′te·li·za′-tion**, *n.*

dec·a·stere (dĕk′ə stĭr′), *n. Metric System.* a unit of volume equal to 10 steres.

dec·a·syl·lab·ic (dĕk′ə sĭ lăb′ĭk), *adj.* having ten syllables: *a decasyllabic verse.*

dec·a·syl·la·ble (dĕk′ə sĭl′ə bəl), *n.* a line or verse of ten syllables.

de·cath·lon (dĭ·kăth′lŏn), *n.* an athletic contest comprising ten different exercises or events, and won by the contestant having the highest total score. [f. DECA- + Gk. *áthlon* contest]

De·ca·tur (dĭ·kā′tər), *n.* **1.** a city in central Illinois. 66,269 (1950). **2.** **Stephen**, 1779–1820, U.S. naval officer.

de·cay (dĭ·kā′), *v.i.* **1.** to fall away from a state of excellence, prosperity, health, etc.; deteriorate; decline. **2.** to become decomposed; rot. —*v.t.* **3.** to cause to decay. —*n.* **4.** a gradual falling into an inferior condition; progressive decline. **5.** loss of strength, health, intellect, etc. **6.** decomposition; rotting. **7.** *Obs.* a wasting disease, esp. consumption. [ME *decay(en),* t. OF: m.s. *decair,* f. *de-* DE- + *cair* (g. L *cadere* fall)] —**Syn. 2.** DELAY, DECOMPOSE, DISINTEGRATE, ROT imply a deterioration or falling away from a sound condition. DECAY implies either entire or partial dissolution or deterioration by progressive natural changes: *teeth decay.* DECOMPOSE suggests the reducing of a substance, through natural change or human agency, to its component elements: *moisture makes some chemical compounds decompose.* DISINTEGRATE emphasizes the breaking up, going to pieces, or wearing away of anything, so that its original wholeness is impaired: *rocks disintegrate.* ROT is a stronger word than DECAY and is esp. applied to decaying vegetable matter, which may or may not emit offensive odors: *potatoes rot.* **4.** deterioration, decadence, impairment, dilapidation.

Dec·can (dĕk′ən), *n.* **1.** the entire peninsula of India S of the Narbuda river. **2.** the plateau region between the Narbuda and Kistna rivers.

---

de·cease (dĭ sēs′), *n.*, *v.*, **-ceased, -ceasing.** —*n.* **1.** departure from life; death. —*v.i.* **2.** to depart from life; die. [ME *deces*, t. OF, t. L: m.s. *dēcessus* departure, death] —Syn. 2. See **die**[1].

de·ceased (dĭ sēst′), *adj.* **1.** dead. —*n.* **2. the deceased,** the dead person. —Syn. 1. See **dead.**

de·ce·dent (dĭ sē′dənt), *n.* *Law.* a deceased person. [t. L: s. *dēcēdens*, ppr., departing, withdrawing]

decedent estate, *Law.* the estate left by a decedent.

de·ceit (dĭ sēt′), *n.* **1.** act or practice of deceiving; concealment or perversion of the truth for the purpose of misleading; fraud; cheating. **2.** an act or device intended to deceive; a trick; stratagem. **3.** deceiving quality; falseness. [ME *deceite*, t. OF, der. *deceveir* DECEIVE] —Syn. 1. DECEIT, GUILE, HYPOCRISY imply (usually) deliberate attempts to mislead someone. DECEIT is the habit or practice of intentionally concealing or perverting the truth for the purpose of misleading: *honest and without deceit.* GUILE implies craftiness in the use of deceit: *using guile and trickery to attain one's ends.* HYPOCRISY is the pretended possession of those qualities which would make others believe in one's sincerity, goodness, devotion, etc.: *it was sheer hypocrisy for him to go to church.* —Ant. 3. honesty, sincerity.

de·ceit·ful (dĭ sēt′fəl), *adj.* **1.** full of deceit; given to deceiving. **2.** misleading; fraudulent; deceptive. —**de·ceit′ful·ly,** *adv.* —**de·ceit′ful·ness,** *n.* —Syn. 1. insincere, disingenuous, false, hollow.

de·ceive (dĭ sēv′), *v.*, **-ceived, -ceiving.** —*v.t.* **1.** to mislead by a false appearance or statement; delude. **2.** *Obs.* to beguile or while away (time, etc.). —*v.i.* **3.** to practice deceit; act deceitfully. [ME *deceyve*(n), t. OF: m. *deceveir*, g. L *dēcipere* catch, ensnare, deceive] —**de·ceiv′er,** *n.* —**de·ceiv′ing·ly,** *adv.* —Syn. 1. See **cheat.** cozen, dupe, fool, gull, hoodwink, trick, defraud, outwit, entrap, ensnare, betray, bamboozle.

de·cel·er·ate (dē sĕl′ə rāt′), *v.t.*, *v.i.*, **-ated, -ating,** to decrease in velocity. [f. DE- + (AC)CELERATE] —**de·cel′er·a′tion,** *n.* —**de·cel′er·a′tor,** *n.*

De·cem·ber (dĭ sĕm′bər), *n.* the twelfth month of the year, containing 31 days. [t. L: the tenth month of the early Roman year; r. ME *decembre*, t. OF]

De·cem·brist (dĭ sĕm′brĭst), *n.* *Russian Hist.* a participant in the conspiracy and insurrection against the Emperor Nicholas on his accession, December, 1825.

de·cem·vir (dĭ sĕm′vər), *n.*, *pl.* **-virs, -viri** (-və rī′). **1.** a member of a permanent board or a special commission of ten members in ancient Rome, esp. the commission appointed to draw up Rome's first code of law. **2.** a member of any council or ruling body of ten. [t. L, orig. pl., *decemvirī*, f. *decem* ten + *virī* men] —**de·cem′vi·ral,** *adj.*

de·cem·vi·rate (dĭ sĕm′və rĭt, -rāt′), *n.* **1.** a body of decemvirs. **2.** the office or government of decemvirs.

de·cen·cy (dē′sən sĭ), *n.*, *pl.* **-cies. 1.** state or quality of being decent. **2.** conformity to the recognized standard of propriety, good taste, modesty, etc. **3.** something decent or proper. **4.** (*pl.*) the requirements or observances of decent life or conduct.

de·cen·na·ry (dĭ sĕn′ə rĭ), *n.*, *pl.* **-ries.** a decennium. [f. s. L *decennis* of ten years + -ARY[1]]

de·cen·ni·al (dĭ sĕn′ĭ əl), *adj.* **1.** of or for ten years. **2.** occurring every ten years. —*n.* **3.** a decennial anniversary. **4.** its celebration. —**de·cen′ni·al·ly,** *adv.*

de·cen·ni·um (dĭ sĕn′ĭ əm), *n.*, *pl.* **-cenniums, -cennia** (-sĕn′ĭ ə). a period of ten years; a decade. [t. L, der. *decennis* of ten years]

de·cent (dē′sənt), *adj.* **1.** fitting; appropriate. **2.** conforming to the recognized standard of propriety, good taste, modesty, etc., as in behavior or speech. **3.** respectable; worthy: *a decent family.* **4.** of seemly appearance: *decent clothes.* **5.** fair; tolerable; passable: *a decent fortune.* **6.** *Brit. Colloq.* kind; obliging: *thanks, that's frightfully decent of you.* [t. L: s. *decens*, ppr., fitting] —**de′cent·ly,** *adv.* —**de′cent·ness,** *n.* —Syn. 2. seemly, proper, decorous.

de·cen·ter (dē sĕn′tər), *v.t.* **1.** to put out of center. **2.** to make eccentric. Also, *Brit.*, **decentre.**

de·cen·tral·ize (dē sĕn′trə līz′), *v.t.*, **-ized, -izing.** to undo the centralization of (administrative powers, etc.). —**de·cen′tral·i·za′tion,** *n.*

de·cen·tre (dē sĕn′tər), *v.t.*, **-tred, -tring.** *Brit.* **decenter.**

de·cep·tion (dĭ sĕp′shən), *n.* **1.** act of deceiving. **2.** state of being deceived. **3.** something that deceives or is intended to deceive; an artifice; a sham; a cheat. [ME *decepcioun*, t. LL: m. s. *dēceptio*, der. L *dēcipere* DECEIVE] —Syn. 3. imposture, treachery, subterfuge, stratagem, ruse, hoax, fraud. See **trick.**

de·cep·tive (dĭ sĕp′tĭv), *adj.* apt or tending to deceive. [t. NL: m.s. *dēceptīvus*] —**de·cep′tive·ly,** *adv.* —**de·cep′tive·ness,** *n.* —Syn. misleading, delusive, fallacious, specious, false.

de·cern (dĭ sûrn′), *v.t.* **1.** *Scot. Law.* to decree by judicial sentence. **2.** to discern. [t. L: s. *dēcernere* decide, decree]

deci-, a word element meaning "ten," specialized in the metric system so that *deci-* gives division by 10, e.g. *deciliter* (6.10 cu. in.), *liter* (61.025 cu. in.). See **deca-.** [comb. form repr. L *decem* ten, *decimus* tenth]

dec·i·bel (dĕs′ə bĕl′), *n.* *Physics.* the unit of power ratio equal to one tenth of a bel.

de·cide (dĭ sīd′), *v.*, **-cided, -ciding.** —*v.t.* **1.** to determine or settle (a question, controversy, struggle, etc.) by giving victory to one side. **2.** to adjust or settle (anything in dispute or doubt). **3.** to bring (a person) to a decision. —*v.i.* **4.** to settle something in dispute or doubt. **5.** to pronounce a judgment; come to a conclusion. [ME *decide*(n), t. L: m. *dēcīdere* cut off, determine] —**de·cid′a·ble,** *adj.* —Syn. 1. DECIDE, RESOLVE, DETERMINE imply settling upon a purpose and being able to adhere to it. To DECIDE is to make up one's mind promptly, clearly, and firmly as to what shall be done and the way to do it: *he decided to go today.* To RESOLVE is usually positively or actively to show firmness of purpose: *he resolved to ask for a promotion.* To DETERMINE is to make up one's mind and then doggedly, and sometimes obstinately, to stick to a fixed or settled purpose: *determined to maintain his position at all costs.*

de·cid·ed (dĭ sī′dĭd), *adj.* **1.** free from ambiguity; unquestionable; unmistakable. **2.** free from hesitation or wavering; resolute; determined. —**de·cid′ed·ly,** *adv.* —**de·cid′ed·ness,** *n.* —Syn. 1. undeniable, indisputable, positive, certain, emphatic, pronounced.

de·cid·u·a (dĭ sĭj′ŏŏ ə), *n.* *Embryol.* the inner mucosal lining of the uterus which in some mammals is cast off at parturition. [NL, prop. fem. of L *dēciduus.* See DECIDUOUS] —**de·cid′u·al,** *adj.*

de·cid·u·ous (dĭ sĭj′ŏŏ əs), *adj.* **1.** shedding the leaves annually, as trees, shrubs, etc. **2.** falling off or shed at a particular season, stage of growth, etc., as leaves, horns, teeth, etc. **3.** not permanent; transitory. [t. L: m. *dēciduus* falling down] —**de·cid′u·ous·ly,** *adv.* —**de·cid′u·ous·ness,** *n.*

dec·i·gram (dĕs′ə grăm′), *n.* *Metric System.* a unit of weight of one tenth of a gram, equivalent to 1.543 grains. Also, *esp. Brit.,* **dec′i·gramme′.** [t. F: m. *décigramme.* See DECI-, GRAM]

dec·ile (dĕs′ĭl), *n.* *Statistics.* one of the values of a variable which divides the distribution of the variable into ten groups having equal frequencies. [f. L *dec*(*em*) ten + -ILE]

dec·i·li·ter (dĕs′ə lē′tər), *n.* *Metric System.* a unit of capacity of one tenth of a liter, equivalent to 6.102 cubic inches, or 3.381 U.S. fluid ounces. Also, *esp. Brit.,* **dec′i·li′tre.** [t. F: m. *décilitre.* See DECI-, LITER]

de·cil·lion (dĭ sĭl′yən), *n.* **1.** (in the U.S. and France) a cardinal number represented by one followed by 33 zeros. **2.** (in England and Germany) a cardinal number represented by one followed by 60 zeros. —*adj.* **3.** amounting to one decillion in number. [f. DECI- + (M)ILLION] —**de·cil′lionth,** *adj.*, *n.*

dec·i·mal (dĕs′ə məl), *adj.* **1.** pertaining to tenths, or to the number ten. **2.** proceeding by tens: *a decimal system.* —*n.* **3.** a decimal fraction. [f. s. L *decimus* tenth + -AL[1]] —**dec′i·mal·ly,** *adv.*

decimal fraction, a fraction whose denominator is some power of ten, usually indicated by a dot (the **decimal point**) written before the numerator: as 0.4 = $^4/_{10}$; 0.126 = $^{126}/_{1000}$.

dec·i·mal·ize (dĕs′ə mə līz′), *v.t.*, **-ized, -izing.** to reduce to a decimal system. —**dec′i·mal·i·za′tion,** *n.*

decimal system, any system of counting or measurement whose units are powers of ten.

dec·i·mate (dĕs′ə māt′), *v.t.*, **-mated, -mating. 1.** to destroy a great number or proportion of. **2.** to select by lot and kill every tenth man of. **3.** *Obs.* to take a tenth of or from. [t. L: m.s. *decimātus*, pp.] —**dec′i·ma′tion,** *n.* —**dec′i·ma′tor,** *n.*

dec·i·me·ter (dĕs′ə mē′tər), *n.* *Metric System.* a unit of length of one tenth of a meter. Also, *esp. Brit.,* **dec′i·me′tre.** [t. F: m. *décimètre.* See DECI-, -METER]

de·ci·pher (dĭ sī′fər), *v.t.* **1.** to make out the meaning of (poor or partially obliterated writing, etc.). **2.** to discover the meaning of (anything obscure or difficult to trace or understand). **3.** to interpret by the use of a key, as something written in cipher. **4.** *Obs.* to depict. —**de·ci′pher·a·ble,** *adj.* —**de·ci′pher·er,** *n.* —**de·ci′pher·ment,** *n.*

de·ci·sion (dĭ sĭzh′ən), *n.* **1.** act of deciding; determination (of a question or doubt). **2.** a judgment, as one formally pronounced by a court. **3.** a making up of one's mind. **4.** that which is decided; a resolution. **5.** the quality of being decided; firmness, as of character. [t. L: s. *dēcīsio* a cutting down, decision]

de·ci·sive (dĭ sī′sĭv), *adj.* **1.** having the power or quality of determining; putting an end to controversy: *a decisive fact, test, etc.* **2.** characterized by or displaying decision; resolute; determined. —**de·ci′sive·ly,** *adv.* —**de·ci′sive·ness,** *n.* —Syn. 1. conclusive, final.

dec·i·stere (dĕs′ə stĭr′), *n.* *Metric System.* a unit of volume equal to one tenth of a stere.

deck (dĕk), *n.* **1.** a platform extending from side to side of a ship or of a part of a ship, forming a covering for the space below and itself serving as a floor. **2.** a platform or part resembling this. **3.** a pack of playing cards. [t. MD: m. *dec* covering, roof] —*v.t.* **4.** to clothe or attire in something ornamental; array. **5.** *Naut.* to furnish with or as with a deck, as a vessel. [t. MD: s. *decken* cover, c. G *decken*] —Syn. 4. bedeck, garnish, trim, bedizen.

deck·er (dĕk′ər), *n.* **1.** one who or that which decks. **2.** a ship, vehicle, etc., having a certain number of decks: *a three-decker.*

Deck·er (dĕk′ər), *n.* Thomas. See **Dekker.**

deck hand, a sailor or workman employed on the deck of a vessel.

deck·house (dĕk′hous′), *n.* a small house erected on the deck of a ship for any purpose.

ăct, āble, dâre, ärt; ĕbb, ēqual; ĭf, īce; hŏt, ōver, ôrder, oil, bŏŏk, ōoze, out; ŭp, ūse, ûrge; ə = a in alone; ch, chief; g, give; ng, ring; sh, shoe; th, thin; ŧħ, that; zh, vision. See the full key on inside cover.

deck·le (dĕk′əl), n. 1. (in paper making) a frame which forms the paper pulp, fixing the size of a sheet of paper. 2. deckle edge. Also, **deck′el.** [t. G: (m.) *deckel*, dim. of *decke* cover]

deckle edge, the untrimmed edge of handmade paper, often used for ornamental effect in fine books.

deck·le-edged (dĕk′əl ĕjd′), adj. having a deckle edge.

decl., declension.

de·claim (dĭ klām′), v.i. 1. to speak aloud rhetorically; make a formal speech. 2. to inveigh (fol. by *against*). 3. to speak or write for oratorical effect, without sincerity or sound argument. —v.t. 4. to utter aloud in a rhetorical manner. [ME *declame*(n), t. L: m. *dēclāmāre* cry aloud] —**de·claim′er,** n.

dec·la·ma·tion (dĕk′lə mā′shən), n. 1. act or art of declaiming. 2. an exercise in oratory or elocution. 3. speech or writing for oratorical effect. 4. *Music.* the proper enunciation of the words, as in recitative.

de·clam·a·to·ry (dĭ klăm′ə tōr′ĭ), adj. 1. pertaining to or characterized by declamation. 2. merely rhetorical; stilted.

dec·la·ra·tion (dĕk′lə rā′shən), n. 1. a positive, explicit, or formal statement, announcement, etc. 2. a proclamation: *a declaration of war.* 3. that which is proclaimed. 4. the document embodying the proclamation. 5. *Law.* a. the formal statement in which a plaintiff presents his claim in an action. b. a complaint. 6. *Cards.* a. *Bridge.* a bid, esp. the successful bid. b. the statement during the game of the points earned by a player, in bezique or other games. 7. a statement of goods, etc., liable to duty.

Declaration of Independence, *U.S. Hist.* 1. the public act by which the Second Continental Congress, on July 4, 1776, declared the colonies to be free and independent of Great Britain. 2. the document embodying it.

de·clar·a·tive (dĭ klăr′ə tĭv), adj. serving to declare, make known, or explain. Also, **de·clar·a·to·ry** (dĭ klăr′ə tōr′ĭ).

de·clare (dĭ klâr′), v., **-clared, -claring.** —v.t. 1. to make known, esp. in explicit or formal terms. 2. to announce officially; proclaim. 3. to state emphatically; affirm. 4. to manifest; reveal. 5. to make due statement of (dutiable goods, etc.). 6. to make (a dividend) payable. 7. *Bridge.* to signify (a certain suit) as trumps or to establish the bid at no-trump. —v.i. 8. to make a declaration. 9. to proclaim oneself. [ME *declar*(en), t. L: m. *dēclārāre* make clear] —**de·clar′er,** n. —**Syn.** 3. DECLARE, AFFIRM, ASSERT, PROTEST imply making something known emphatically, openly, or formally. To DECLARE is to make known, sometimes in the face of actual or potential contradiction: *to declare someone the winner of a contest.* To AFFIRM is to make a statement based on one's reputation for knowledge or veracity, or so related to a generally recognized truth that denial is not likely: *to affirm the necessity of high standards.* To ASSERT is to state boldly, usually without other proof than personal authority or conviction: *to assert that the climate is changing.* To PROTEST is to affirm publicly, as if in the face of doubt: *to protest that a newspaper account is misleading.*

de·clared (dĭ klârd′), adj. avowed; professed. —**de·clar·ed·ly** (dĭ klâr′ĭd lĭ), adv.

de·class (dē klăs′, -kläs′), v.t. to remove or degrade from one's class (social or other).

dé·clas·sé (dā klà sĕ′), adj. fallen or lowered in social rank, class, etc. —**dé·clas·sée′,** adj. fem.

de·clen·sion (dĭ klĕn′shən), n. 1. act or fact of declining. 2. a bending, sloping, or moving downward. 3. deterioration; decline. 4. deviation, as from a standard. 5. *Gram.* a. the inflection of nouns, and of words similarly inflected, for categories such as case and number. Example (Latin): *puella, puellae, puellae, puellam, etc.* b. the whole set of inflected forms of such a word, or the recital thereof in a fixed order. c. a class of such words having similar sets of inflected forms, as the Latin *second declension.* [irreg. t. L: m.s. *dēclīnātio* a bending aside, inflection, prob. modeled on *dēscensio* descent] —**de·clen′sion·al** adj.

dec·li·na·tion (dĕk′lə nā′shən), n. 1. a bending, sloping, or moving downward. 2. deterioration; decline. 3. a swerving or deviating, as from a standard. 4. a polite refusal. 5. *Astron.* the angular distance of a heavenly body from the celestial equator, measured on a great circle passing through the celestial pole and the body. 6. the horizontal angle between the direction of true north and magnetic north at any place.

de·clin·a·to·ry (dĭ klī′nə tōr′ĭ), adj. expressing refusal; implying declination.

de·clin·a·ture (dĭ klī′nə chər), n. act of refusing.

de·cline (dĭ klīn′), v., **-clined, -clining,** n. —v.t. 1. to withhold consent to do; enter upon or accept; refuse: *he declined to say more about it, he declined the offer with thanks.* 2. to cause to slope or incline downward. 3. *Gram.* a. to inflect (a noun, pronoun, or adjective). In Latin, *puella* is declined *puella, puellae, puellae, puellam, puellā* in the five cases of the singular. b. to recite or display all, or some subset, of the inflected

forms of a noun, pronoun, or adjective in a fixed order. —v.i. 4. to express courteous refusal; refuse. 5. to bend or slant down; slope or trend downward; descend. 6. to draw toward the close, as the day. 7. to stoop (to an unworthy object); condescend. 8. to fail in strength, vigor, character, value, etc.; deteriorate. 9. *Gram.* to be characterized by declension. —n. 10. a downward incline or slope. 11. a failing or gradual loss, as in strength, character, value, etc.; deterioration; diminution. 12. progress downward or toward a close, as of the sun or the day. 13. a gradual diminution of the physical powers, as in later life or in disease. 14. the last part. [ME *decline*(n), t. OF: m. *decliner*, t. L: m. *dēclīnāre* bend from, avoid, inflect] —**de·clin′a·ble,** adj. —**de·clin′er,** n. —**Syn.** 1. reject. See **refuse**[1]. 8. degenerate, decay. 11. retrogression, degeneration.

dec·li·nom·e·ter (dĕk′lə nŏm′ə tər), n. an instrument for measuring declination. [f. *declino*- (comb. form repr. L *dēclīnāre*) + -METER]

de·cliv·i·tous (dĭ klĭv′ə təs), adj. rather steep.

de·cliv·i·ty (dĭ klĭv′ə tĭ), n., pl. **-ties.** a downward slope, as of ground (opposed to *acclivity*). [t. L: m. s. *dēclīvitas* slope]

de·cli·vous (dĭ klī′vəs), adj. sloping downward.

de·coct (dĭ kŏkt′), v.t. to boil (a medicinal substance, etc.) in water, etc.; to extract the essence or principles. [t. L: s. *dēcoctus*, pp., boiled down]

de·coc·tion (dĭ kŏk′shən), n. 1. act of boiling in water, in order to extract the peculiar properties or virtues. 2. an extract obtained by decocting. 3. water in which a substance, usually animal or vegetable, has been boiled, and which thus contains the constituents or principles of the substance soluble in boiling water.

de·code (dē kōd′), v.t., **-coded, -coding.** to translate from code into the original language or form.

de·col·late (dĭ kŏl′āt), v.t., **-lated, -lating.** to behead; decapitate. [t. L: m. s. *dēcollātus*, pp., beheaded] —**de·col·la·tion** (dē′kə lā′shən), n. —**de·col′la·tor,** n.

dé·colle·tage (dā′kŏl tăzh′; *Fr.* dĕ kôl tȧzh′), n. 1. the neckline of a dress cut low in the front and back and across the shoulders. 2. a décolleté garment or costume. [F, der. *décolleter.* See DECOLLETE]

dé·colle·té (dā′kŏl tā′; *Fr.* dĕ kôl tě′), adj. 1. (of a garment) low-necked. 2. wearing a low-necked garment. [t. F, pp. of *décolleter* bare the neck of, ult. der. *col.* neck]

de·col·or (dē kŭl′ər), v.t. to deprive of color; bleach. Also, *Brit.* **de·col′our.** [t. L: m. *dēcolōrāre* deprive of color] —**de·col·or·a′tion,** n.

de·col·or·ant (dē kŭl′ər ənt), adj. 1. having the property of removing color; bleaching. —n. 2. a decolorant substance or agent.

de·col·or·ize (dē kŭl′ə rīz′), v.t., **-ized, -izing.** decolor. Also, *Brit.,* **de·col′our·ize′.** —**de·col·or·i·za′tion,** n. —**de·col′or·iz′er,** n.

de·com·pose (dē′kəm pōz′), v.t., v.i., **-posed, -posing.** 1. to separate or resolve into constituent parts or elements; disintegrate. 2. to rot; putrefy. [t. F: s. *décomposer*, f. dé- DIS-[1] + *composer* COMPOSE] —**de′·com·pos′a·ble,** adj. —**Syn.** 2. See **decay**.

de·com·po·si·tion (dē′kŏm pə zĭsh′ən), n. 1. act or process of decomposing. 2. state of being decomposed; disintegration; decay.

de·com·pound (dē′kəm pound′), v.t. 1. to compound a second time or further, or of things already compound. 2. to decompose. —adj. 3. *Bot.* divided into compound divisions. 4. composed of things which are themselves compound.

de·con·tam·i·nate (dē′kən tăm′ə nāt′), v.t., **-nated, -nating.** to make (any object or area) safe for unprotected personnel by absorbing, making harmless, or destroying chemicals with which they have been in contact. —**de′con·tam′i·na′tion,** n.

de·con·trol (dē′kən trōl′), v., **-trolled, -trolling,** n. —v.t. 1. to remove controls, or from control. —n. 2. removal of control.

Decompound leaf

dé·cor (dā kôr′; *Fr.* dĕ kôr′), n. 1. decoration in general. 2. a decoration. 3. *Theat.* scenic decoration; scenery. [F, der. *décorer* decorate, t. L: m. *decorāre*]

dec·o·rate (dĕk′ə rāt′), v.t., **-rated, -rating.** 1. to furnish or deck with something becoming or ornamental; embellish. 2. to confer distinction upon by a badge, a medal of honor, etc. [t. L: m. s. *decorātus*, pp.]

Decorated style, *Archit.* the second style of English pointed architecture, in use from the end of the thirteenth to the beginning of the fifteenth century.

dec·o·ra·tion (dĕk′ə rā′shən), n. 1. act of decorating. 2. adornment; embellishment. 3. a badge of an order, medal, etc., conferred and worn as a mark of honor.

Decoration Day, *U.S.* Memorial Day.

dec·o·ra·tive (dĕk′ə rā′tĭv, dĕk′rə tĭv), adj. serving or tending to decorate. —**dec′o·ra′tive·ly,** adv. —**dec′o·ra′tive·ness,** n.

dec·o·ra·tor (dĕk′ə rā′tər), n. 1. one who decorates. 2. one who professionally decorates houses or buildings, particularly their interior.

Celestial diagram labels:
N A E / D / C S

A Star; DA, Declination of star; N, North celestial pole; S, South celestial pole; CE, Celestial equator

dec·o·rous (dĕk'ə rəs, dĭ kōr'əs), *adj.* characterized by propriety in conduct, manners, appearance, character, etc. [t. L: m. *decōrus* becoming, seemly] —**dec'o·rous·ly,** *adv.* —**dec'o·rous·ness,** *n.* —**Syn.** proper, seemly, becoming, decent, sedate, conventional. —**Ant.** undignified.

de·cor·ti·cate (dē kôr'tə kāt'), *v.t.,* **-cated, -cating.** to remove the bark, husk, or outer covering from. [t. L: m. s. *decorticātus,* pp.] —**de·cor'ti·ca'tion,** *n.* —**de·cor'ti·ca'tor,** *n.*

de·co·rum (dĭ kōr'əm), *n.* **1.** propriety of behavior; speech, dress, etc. **2.** that which is proper or seemly; fitness; congruity; propriety. **3.** an observance or requirement of polite society. [t. L, prop. neut. of *decōrus* DECOROUS] —**Syn. 1.** See **etiquette.**

de·coy (*n.* dĭ koi', dē'koi; *v.* dĭ koi'), *n.* **1.** one who entices or allures, as into a trap, danger, etc. **2.** anything used as a lure. **3.** a trained bird or other animal used to entice game into a trap or within gunshot. **4.** an image of a bird used for the same purpose. **5.** a pond into which wild fowl are lured to permit their capture. —*v.t.* **6.** to lure by or as by a decoy. —*v.i.* **7.** to be decoyed. [var. of *coy* (now d.), both t. D: m. *(de)kooi* (the) cage, t. L: m. s. *cavea* CAGE] —**de·coy'er,** *n.*

de·crease (*v.* dĭ krēs'; *n.* dē'krēs, dĭ krēs'), *v.,* **-creased, -creasing,** *n.* —*v.i.* **1.** to diminish gradually in extent, quantity, strength, power, etc. —*v.t.* **2.** to make less; cause to diminish. —*n.* **3.** a process of growing less, or the resulting condition; gradual diminution. **4.** the amount by which a thing is lessened. [ME *decrese(n),* t. OF: m. *decreiss-,* g. L *dēcrescere* grow less] —**de·creas'ing·ly,** *adv.* —**Syn. 1.** wane, lessen, fall off, decline, contract, abate. DECREASE, DIMINISH, DWINDLE, SHRINK imply becoming smaller or less in amount. DECREASE commonly implies a gradual and sustained reduction, esp. of bulk, size, volume, or quantity, often from some imperceptible cause or inherent process: *the swelling decreased daily.* DIMINISH usually implies the action of some external cause which keeps taking away: *disease caused the number of troops to diminish steadily.* DWINDLE implies an undesirable reduction by degrees, resulting in attenuation: *his followers dwindled to a mere handful.* SHRINK esp. implies contraction through an inherent property under specific conditions: *many fabrics shrink when wet.* **3.** abatement, reduction, decline. —**Ant. 1.** increase, expand.

de·cree (dĭ krē'), *n., v.,* **-creed, -creeing.** —*n.* **1.** an ordinance or edict promulgated by civil or other authority. **2.** *Law.* a judicial decision or order. **3.** *Theol.* one of the eternal purposes of God, by which events are foreordained. —*v.t., v.i.* **4.** to ordain or decide by decree. [ME *decre,* t. OF, var. of *decret,* t. L: s. *dēcrētum,* prop. pp. neut.]

decree ni·si (nī'sī), *Law.* a decree of divorce that will become absolute at a later date.

dec·re·ment (dĕk'rə mənt), *n.* **1.** the process or fact of decreasing; gradual diminution. **2.** the amount lost by diminution. **3.** *Math.* a negative increment.

de·crep·it (dĭ krĕp'ĭt), *adj.* broken down or weakened by old age; feeble; infirm. [t. L: s. *dēcrepitus,* lit., broken down] —**de·crep'it·ly,** *adv.* —**Syn.** See **weak.** —**Ant.** vigorous.

de·crep·i·tate (dĭ krĕp'ə tāt'), *v.,* **-tated, -tating.** —*v.t.* **1.** to roast or calcine (salt, etc.) so as to cause crackling or until crackling ceases. —*v.i.* **2.** to make a crackling noise, as salt in roasting. [t. NL: m.s. *dēcrepitātus* crackled down] —**de·crep'i·ta'tion,** *n.*

de·crep·i·tude (dĭ krĕp'ə tūd', -tōōd'), *n.* decrepit condition; feebleness, esp. from old age.

decresc., *Music.* decrescendo.

de·cres·cen·do (dē'krə shĕn'dō, dā'-; *It.* dě'krě shĕn'dô), *adj., n., pl.* **-dos.** *Music.* —*adj., n., adv.* **1.** gradually reducing force of loudness; diminuendo (opposed to *crescendo*). —*n.* **2.** a gradual reduction in force or loudness. **3.** a decrescendo passage. [t. It., ger. of *decrescere* DECREASE]

de·cres·cent (dĭ krĕs'ənt), *adj.* **1.** decreasing. **2.** waning, as the moon. [t. L: s. *dēcrescens,* ppr., decreasing]

de·cre·tal (dĭ krē'təl), *adj.* **1.** pertaining to, of the nature of, or containing a decree or decrees. —*n.* **2.** a papal document authoritatively determining some point of doctrine or church law. **3.** Decretals, the body or collection of such decrees as a part of the canon law. [ME *decretale,* t. ML, ult. der. L *dēcrētum* DECREE]

de·cre·tist (dĭ krē'tĭst), *n.* (in medieval universities) **1.** a student in the faculty of law. **2.** a student of the Decretals; one versed in the canon law.

de·cre·tive (dĭ krē'tĭv), *adj.* having the force of a decree; pertaining to a decree.

dec·re·to·ry (dĕk'rə tōr'ĭ), *adj.* **1.** pertaining to or following a decree. **2.** established by a decree; judicial; definitive.

de·cri·al (dĭ krī'əl), *n.* act of crying down.

de·cry (dĭ krī'), *v.t.,* **-cried, -crying. 1.** to speak disparagingly of; censure as faulty or worthless. **2.** to condemn or depreciate by proclamation, as foreign or obsolete coins. [t. F: m. *décrier,* f. *dé-* DIS-¹ + *crier* CRY] —**de·cri'er,** *n.* —**Syn. 1.** belittle, disparage, discredit.

dec·u·man (dĕk'yŏŏ mən), *adj.* **1.** large or immense, as a wave. **2.** every tenth in a series. [t. L: s. *decumānus,* var. of *decimānus* of the tenth, large (from the notion that every tenth wave is a large one)]

de·cum·bent (dĭ kŭm'bənt), *adj.* **1.** lying down; recumbent. **2.** *Bot.* (of stems, branches, etc.) lying or trailing on the ground with the extremity tending to ascend. [t. L: s. *decumbens,* ppr.] —**de·cum'bence, de·cum'ben·cy,** *n.* —**de·cum'bent·ly,** *adv.*

dec·u·ple (dĕk'yŏŏ pəl), *adj., n., v.,* **-pled, -pling.** —*adj.* **1.** tenfold; ten times as great. —*n.* **2.** a tenfold quantity or multiple. —*v.t.* **3.** to make ten times as great. [t. F, t. L: m. *decuplus* tenfold]

de·cu·ri·on (dĭ kyŏŏr'ĭ ən), *n.* **1.** *Rom. Hist.* the head of a decury. **2.** a member of the senate of an ancient Roman colony or municipality. [ME, t. L: s. *decurio*]

de·cur·rent (dĭ kûr'ənt), *adj. Bot.* extending down the stem below the place of insertion, as certain leaves. [t. L: s. *dēcurrens,* ppr., running down] —**de·cur'rent·ly,** *adv.*

Decurrent leaf of thistle

de·cu·ry (dĕk'yŏŏ rĭ), *n., pl.* **-ries. 1.** *Rom. Hist.* a division of a larger unit, nominally comprising ten persons, but frequently in excess of this number. **2.** a division, group, or class. [t. L: m. s. *decuria* a company of ten]

de·cus·sate (*v.* dĭ kŭs'āt, dĕk'ə sāt'; *adj.* dĭ kŭs'āt, -ĭt), *v.,* **-sated, -sating,** *adj.* —*v.t., v.i.* **1.** to cross in the form of the letter X; intersect. —*adj.* **2.** in the form of the letter X; crossed; intersected. **3.** *Bot.* (of leaves, etc.) arranged along the stem in pairs, each pair at right angles to the pair next above or below. [t. L: m. s. *decussātus,* pp., divided in the form of an X] —**de·cus·sa'tion** (dē'kə sā'shən, dĕk'ə-), *n.*

De·de A·gach (dĕ dĕ' ä gäch'), *n.* former name of Alexandroupolis.

Decussate leaf

ded·i·cate (dĕd'ə kāt'), *v.,* **-cated, -cating,** *adj.* —*v.t.* **1.** to set apart and consecrate to a deity or to a sacred purpose. **2.** to give up wholly or earnestly, as to some person or end; set apart or appropriate. **3.** to inscribe or address (a book, piece of music, etc.) to a patron, friend, etc., as in testimony of respect or affection. —*adj.* **4.** *Archaic.* consecrated. [t. L: m. s. *dēdicātus,* pp., proclaimed, devoted] —**ded'i·ca'tor,** *n.*

ded·i·ca·tion (dĕd'ə kā'shən), *n.* **1.** act of dedicating. **2.** fact of being dedicated. **3.** an inscription prefixed or attached to a book, etc., dedicating it to some person.

ded·i·ca·to·ry (dĕd'ə kə tōr'ĭ), *adj.* of or pertaining to dedication; serving as a dedication. Also, **ded·i·ca·tive** (dĕd'ə kā'tĭv), *n.*

de·duce (dĭ dūs', -dōōs'), *v.t.,* **-duced, -ducing. 1.** to derive as a conclusion from something known or assumed; infer. **2.** to trace the derivation of; trace the course of. [t. L: m.s. *dēdūcere* lead down, derive] —**de·duc'i·ble,** *adj.*

de·duct (dĭ dŭkt'), *v.t.* to take away, as from a sum or amount. [t. L: s. *dēductus,* pp., led down, withdrawn] —**de·duct'i·ble,** *adj.* —**Syn.** See **subtract.**

de·duc·tion (dĭ dŭk'shən), *n.* **1.** act of deducting; subtraction; abatement. **2.** that which is deducted. **3.** the process of drawing a conclusion from something known or assumed. **4.** *Logic.* inference by reasoning from generals to particulars (opposed to *induction*).

de·duc·tive (dĭ dŭk'tĭv), *adj.* based on inference from accepted principles; reasoning by deduction. —**de·duc'tive·ly,** *adv.* —**Syn.** DEDUCTIVE, INDUCTIVE, often confused, are not properly synonyms. They do agree in referring to processes of (formal or informal) reasoning, but the processes they describe are of opposite kinds. In DEDUCTIVE reasoning, an accepted general statement (true or false) is applied to an individual case; if formally, by the method of syllogism: *All dogs are animals; this is a dog; therefore this is an animal.* In INDUCTIVE reasoning, a set of individual cases is studied by the experimental method, and, from the observations made, a general principle is formed: *every metal I have tested expands when heated; therefore I can expect all metals to expand when heated.* When the general premise in deductive reasoning is true, the deduction from it will be certain for all possible instances. The principle formed in inductive reasoning is a workable theory but would be certain only when all possible instances had been examined.

Dee (dē), *n.* **1.** a river in NE Scotland, flowing into the North Sea at Aberdeen. **2.** a river in N Wales and W England, flowing into the Irish Sea.

deed (dēd), *n.* **1.** that which is done, performed, or accomplished; an act. **2.** an exploit or achievement. **3.** action or performance, often as contrasted with words. **4.** *Law.* a writing or document executed under seal and delivered to effect a conveyance, esp. of real estate. —*v.t.* **5.** to convey or transfer by deed. [ME *dede,* OE *dēd,* var. of *dǣd,* c. G *tat.* See DO¹] —**deed'less,** *adj.* —**Syn. 2.** See **achievement.**

deem (dēm), *v.i.* **1.** to form or have an opinion; judge; think. —*v.t.* **2.** to hold as an opinion; think; regard. [ME *demen,* OE *dēman,* c. Goth. *dōmjan.* See DOOM] —**Syn. 1.** See **think¹.**

deem·ster (dēm'stər), *n.* either of the two justices of the Isle of Man. Also, **dempster.** —**deem'ster·ship',** *n.*

deep (dēp), *adj.* **1.** extending far downward, inward, or backward. **2.** having a specified dimension downward, inward, or backward: *a tank 8 feet deep.* **3.** situated far or a certain distance down, in, or back. **4.** extending to or coming from a depth: *a deep dive, a deep breath.* **5.** lying below the surface. **6.** difficult to penetrate or understand; abstruse. **7.** not superficial; profound. **8.** grave or serious. **9.** heartfelt: *deep sorrow or prayer.*

10. absorbing: *deep study.* **11.** great in measure; intense; extreme: *deep sleep, color, etc.* **12.** low in pitch, as sound. **13.** having penetrating intellectual powers. **14.** profoundly cunning or artful. **15.** much involved: *deep in debt.* **16.** absorbed: *deep in thought.* **17. go off the deep end, a.** *U.S.* to go to extremes. **b.** *Brit.* to get into a dither; to become hysterical. —*n.* **18.** the deep part of the sea, a river, etc. **19.** any deep space or place. **20.** the part of greatest intensity, as of winter. **21.** *Naut.* the depth in fathoms between two successive marks on a lead line. **22.** the deep, *Poetic.* the sea or ocean. [ME *depe,* OE *dēop,* c. G. *tief.* See DIP, v.] —*adv.* **23.** to or at a considerable or specified depth. **24.** far on (in time). **25.** profoundly; intensely. [ME *depe,* OE *dēope*] —**deep′ly,** *adv.* —**deep′ness,** *n.* —**Syn. 6.** recondite, mysterious, obscure.

deep-dish (dēp′dĭsh′), *adj. Cookery.* baked in a deep dish, often with a pastry top, and usually in individual servings: *a deep-dish pie.*

deep·en (dē′pən), *v.t., v.i.* to make or become deep or deeper. —**deep′en·er,** *n.*

deep-freeze (dēp′frēz′), *n., v., -freezed, -freezing.* **1.** a locker or compartment in which foods are stored at a temperature of 0° F. **2.** (*cap.*) a trademark for this. —*v.t.* **3.** to store or freeze in a deep-freeze.

deep-fry (dēp′frī′), *v.t., -fried, -frying.* to cook in a deep pan of fat.

deep-laid (dēp′lād′), *adj.* carefully, cunningly, or secretly made: *deep-laid plot.*

deep-root·ed (dēp′rōō′tĭd, -rōōt′ĭd), *adj.* deeply rooted; firmly implanted.

deep-sea (dēp′sē′), *adj.* of, pertaining to, or in the deeper parts of the sea.

deep-seat·ed (dēp′sē′tĭd), *adj.* firmly implanted.

deer (dĭr), *n., pl.* **deer,** (*occasionally*) **deers. 1.** any animal of the family *Cervidae,* comprising ruminants most of which have solid deciduous horns or antlers (usually in the male only), as *Cervus elaphus* (of Europe), *Odocoileus virginianus* (of North America). **2.** any of the smaller species of this family, as distinguished from the moose, elk, etc. [ME *dere,* OE *dēor,* c. G *tier*]

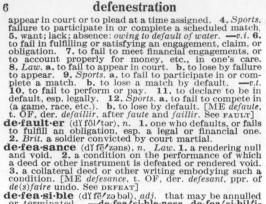

Virginia deer,
Odocoileus virginianus
(3½ ft. high at the shoulder,
total length ab. 6 ft.)

deer fly, any of the blood-sucking flies of the genus *Chrysops* (family *Tabanidae*).

deer·hound (dĭr′hound′), *n.* a hound of a Scottish breed allied to and resembling the greyhound but larger and having a shaggy coat.

deer lick, *U.S.* a spot of ground, naturally or artificially salty, where deer come to nibble or lick the earth.

deer mouse, any of several species of mice (family *Cricetidae*), esp. the widely distributed white-footed mouse, *Peromyscus leucopus,* of North America.

Scottish deerhound
(2½ ft. high at the shoulder)

deer·skin (dĭr′skĭn′), *n.* **1.** the skin of a deer. **2.** leather made from this. **3.** a garment made of such leather.

deer·stalk·er (dĭr′stô′kər), *n.* one who stalks deer; one who hunts deer by stealing upon them unawares. —**deer′stalk′ing,** *n.*

def., **1.** defective. **2.** defendant. **3.** deferred. **4.** defined. **5.** definite. **6.** definition.

de·face (dĭ·fās′), *v.t., -faced, -facing.* **1.** to mar the face or appearance of; disfigure. **2.** to blot out; obliterate; efface. [ME *deface(n),* t. F (obs.): m. *defacer,* earlier *desfacier,* der. *des-* DIS-¹ + *face* FACE] —**face′a·ble,** *adj.* —**de·face′ment,** *n.* —**de·fac′er,** *n.* —**Syn. 1.** See **mar.**

de fac·to (dē făk′tō). **1.** in fact; in reality. **2.** actually existing, whether with or without right. See **de jure.** [L: from the fact]

de·fal·cate (dĭ·făl′kāt, -fôl′-), *v.i., -cated, -cating. Law.* to be guilty of defalcation. [t. ML: m. s. *dēfalcātus,* pp.] —**de·fal′ca·tor,** *n.*

de·fal·ca·tion (dē′făl·kā′shən, -fôl-), *n. Law.* **1.** misappropriation of money, etc., held by a trustee or other fiduciary. **2.** the sum misappropriated.

def·a·ma·tion (dĕf′ə·mā′shən, dē′fə-), *n.* the wrong of injuring another's reputation without good reason or justification; calumny; slander or libel.

de·fam·a·to·ry (dĭ·făm′ə·tôr′ĭ), *adj.* containing defamation; injurious to reputation; slanderous.

de·fame (dĭ·fām′), *v.t., -famed, -faming.* **1.** to attack the good fame or reputation of, as by uttering or publishing maliciously anything injurious; slander; libel; calumniate. **2.** *Archaic.* to disgrace. **3.** *Obs.* to accuse. [ME *defamen,* t. ML: m. *dēfāmāre;* r. ME *diffamen,* t. OF: m. *diffamer,* t. L: m. *diffāmāre*] —**de·fam′er,** *n.*

de·fault (dĭ·fôlt′), *n.* **1.** failure to act; neglect. **2.** failure to meet financial obligations. **3.** *Law.* failure to perform an act or obligation legally required, esp. to

appear in court or to plead at a time assigned. **4.** *Sports.* failure to participate in or complete a scheduled match. **5.** want; lack; absence: *owing to default of water.* —*v.i.* **6.** to fail in fulfilling or satisfying an engagement, claim, or obligation. **7.** to fail to meet financial engagements, or to account properly for money, etc., in one's care. **8.** *Law.* **a.** to fail to appear in court. **b.** to lose by failure to appear. **9.** *Sports.* **a.** to fail to participate in or complete a match. **b.** to lose a match by default. —*v.t.* **10.** to fail to perform or pay. **11.** to declare to be in default, esp. legally. **12.** *Sports.* **a.** to fail to compete in (a game, race, etc.). **b.** to lose by default. [ME *defaute,* t. OF, der. *defaillir,* after *faute* and *faillir.* See FAULT]

de·fault·er (dĭ·fôl′tər), *n.* **1.** one who defaults, or fails to fulfill an obligation, esp. a legal or financial one. **2.** *Brit.* a soldier convicted by court martial.

de·fea·sance (dĭ·fē′zəns), *n. Law.* **1.** a rendering null and void. **2.** a condition on the performance of which a deed or other instrument is defeated or rendered void. **3.** a collateral deed or other writing embodying such a condition. [ME *defesance,* t. OF, der. *defesant,* ppr. of *de(s)faire* undo. See DEFEAT]

de·fea·si·ble (dĭ·fē′zə·bəl), *adj.* that may be annulled or terminated. —**de·fea·si·ble·ness, de·fea·si·bil·i·ty,** *n.*

de·feat (dĭ·fēt′), *v.t.* **1.** to overcome in a contest, battle, etc.; vanquish; win over. **2.** to frustrate; thwart. **3.** to deprive of something expected. **4.** *Law.* to annul. —*n.* **5.** act of overcoming in a contest. **6.** an overthrow; vanquishment. **7.** a bringing to naught; frustration. **8.** *Obs.* undoing; destruction; ruin. [ME *defete(n),* t. OF: m. *de(s)fait,* pp. of *desfaire* undo, f. *des-* DIS-¹ + *faire* (g. L *facere* do)] —**de·feat′er,** *n.* —**Syn. 1.** DEFEAT, CONQUER, OVERCOME, SUBDUE imply gaining a victory or control over an opponent. DEFEAT suggests temporarily, and often permanently, beating or frustrating: *to defeat an enemy in battle.* CONQUER, more formal, implies finally gaining control over, usually after a series of efforts or against systematic resistance: *to conquer a country, one's inclinations.* OVERCOME emphasizes surmounting difficulties in prevailing over an antagonist: *to overcome opposition, bad habits.* SUBDUE means to conquer so completely that the spirit of resistance is broken: *to subdue an uprising or a rebellious spirit.*

de·feat·ism (dĭ·fē′tĭz·əm), *n.* the spirit, policy, or procedure of those who desire or seek their country's defeat in war, as for the purpose of realizing their own theories or schemes, or of those who despair of their country's success. —**de·feat′ist,** *n., adj.*

de·fea·ture (dĭ·fē′chər), *n.* **1.** *Archaic.* disfigurement. **2.** *Obs.* defeat; ruin. [t. OF: m. *deffaiture.* See DEFEAT]

def·e·cate (dĕf′ə·kāt′), *v., -cated, -cating.* —*v.t.* **1.** to clear of dregs, impurities, etc.; purify; refine. —*v.i.* **2.** to become clear of dregs, impurities, etc. **3.** to void excrement. [t. L: m. s. *dēfaecātus,* pp., cleansed from dregs] —**def′e·ca′tion,** *n.* —**def′e·ca′tor,** *n.*

de·fect (dĭ·fĕkt′, dē′fĕkt), *n.* **1.** a falling short; a fault or imperfection. **2.** want or lack, esp. of something essential to perfection or completeness; deficiency. [t. L: s. *dēfectus* want, defect] —**Syn. 1.** DEFECT, BLEMISH, FLAW refer to faults which detract from perfection. DEFECT is the general word for any kind of shortcoming or imperfection, whether literal or figurative: *a defect in eyesight, in character, in a plan.* A BLEMISH is usually a defect on a surface, which mars the appearance: *a mole or scar on a cheek (or a scratch on a table) is a blemish.* FLAW is applied to a defect in quality, caused by imperfect structure (as in a diamond) or brought about during manufacture (as in texture of cloth, in tensile strength of metals, in clearness of glass, etc.).

de·fec·tion (dĭ·fĕk′shən), *n.* **1.** a falling away from allegiance, duty, virtue, etc.; desertion; backsliding; apostasy. **2.** failure; lack. —**Ant. 1.** loyalty.

de·fec·tive (dĭ·fĕk′tĭv), *adj.* **1.** having a defect; faulty; imperfect. **2.** *Psychol.* characterized by subnormal intelligence or behavior. **3.** *Gram.* (of an inflected word or its inflection) lacking one or more of the inflected forms proper to most words of the same class in the language, as English *must* (which occurs only in the present tense). —*n.* **4.** one who or that which is defective. —**de·fec′tive·ly,** *adv.* —**de·fec′tive·ness,** *n.* —**Ant. 1.** perfect, complete.

de·fence (dĭ·fĕns′), *n. Brit.* defense.

de·fend (dĭ·fĕnd′), *v.t.* **1.** to ward off attack from; guard against assault or injury (fol. by *from* or *against*). **2.** to maintain by argument, evidence, etc.; uphold. **3.** to contest (a legal charge, claim, etc.). —*v.i.* **4.** *Law.* to enter or make a defense. [ME *defende(n),* t. OF: m. *defendre,* g. L *dēfendere* ward off] —**de·fend′a·ble,** *adj.* —**de·fend′er,** *n.* —**Syn. 1.** garrison, fortify, shield shelter, screen. DEFEND, GUARD, PRESERVE, PROTECT all mean to keep safe. To DEFEND is to strive to keep safe by resisting attack: *to defend (a position) in battle, to defend one's country.* To GUARD is to watch over in order to keep safe: *to guard a camp, a secret.* To PRESERVE is to keep safe in the midst of danger, either in a single instance or continuously: *to preserve a city, a spirit of conciliation.* To PROTECT is to keep safe by interposing a shield or barrier: *to protect books by means of heavy paper covers, the reputation of a friend.* —**Ant. 1.** attack.

de·fend·ant (dĭ·fĕn′dənt), *n.* **1.** *Law.* the party against whom a claim or charge is brought in a proceeding. —*adj.* **2.** *Obs.* defensive.

de·fen·es·tra·tion (dē′fĕn′ə·strā′shən), *n.* act of throwing out of a window. [f. DE- + s. L *fenestra* window + -ATION]

de·fense (dĭ fĕns´), *n.* **1.** resistance against attack; protection. **2.** something that defends, esp. a fortification. **3.** the defending of a cause or the like by speech, argument, etc. **4.** a speech, argument, etc., in vindication. **5.** *Law.* **a.** the denial or pleading of the defendant in answer to the claim or charge against him. **b.** the proceedings adopted by a defendant, or his legal agents, for defending himself. **c.** a defendant and his legal agents collectively. **6.** the practice or art of defending oneself or one's goal against attack, as in fencing or boxing, soccer, etc. Also, *Brit.*, **defence.** [ME, t. OF, t. LL: m. *dēfensa* prohibition, der. L *dēfendere* ward off; r. ME *defens*, t. OF, t. L: s. *dēfensum* (thing) forbidden, prop. pp. of *dēfendere*] —**de·fense´less,** *adj.* —**de·fense´less·ly,** *adv.* —**de·fense´less·ness,** *n.*

defense mechanism, 1. *Physiol.* organic activity, as the formation of an antitoxin, as a defensive measure. **2.** *Psychoanal.* a group of unconscious processes which oppose the entrance into consciousness or the acting out of unacceptable or painful ideas and impulses.

de·fen·si·ble (dĭ fĕn´sə bəl), *adj.* **1.** capable of being defended against assault or injury. **2.** capable of being defended in argument; justifiable. —**de·fen´si·bil´i·ty, de·fen´si·ble·ness,** *n.* —**de·fen´si·bly,** *adv.*

de·fen·sive (dĭ fĕn´sĭv), *adj.* **1.** serving to defend; protective: *defensive armor.* **2.** made or carried on for the purpose of resisting attack. **3.** of or pertaining to defense: *a defensive attitude.* —*n.* **4.** something that serves to defend. **5.** defensive position or attitude. —**de·fen´sive·ly,** *adv.* —**de·fen´sive·ness,** *n.*

de·fer¹ (dĭ fûr´), *v.*, **-ferred, -ferring.** —*v.t.* **1.** to put off (action, etc.) to a future time. —*v.i.* **2.** to put off action; delay. [ME *differe(n)*, t. L: m. *differre* delay. See DIFFER] —**de·fer´rer,** *n.*
—**Syn. 1.** DEFER, DELAY, POSTPONE imply keeping something from occurring until a future time. To DEFER is to decide deliberately to do something later on: *to defer making a decision, a payment.* To DELAY is sometimes equivalent to DEFER, but usually it is to act in a dilatory manner and thus lay something aside until some indefinite future time: *to delay one's departure, answering a letter.* To POSTPONE a thing is to defer it to (usually) some particular time in the future, with the intention of beginning or resuming it then; the word is esp. used of official business, formal meetings, or the like: *to postpone an election.* —**Ant. 1.** accelerate.

de·fer² (dĭ fûr´), *v.i.,* **-ferred, -ferring.** to yield in judgment or opinion (fol. by *to*). [t. F: s. *déférer*, t. L: m. *deferre* carry from or down, report, accuse]

def·er·ence (dĕf´ər əns), *n.* **1.** submission or yielding to the judgment, opinion, wil., etc., of another. **2.** respectful or courteous regard: *in deference to his wishes.*

def·er·ent¹ (dĕf´ər ənt), *adj.* deferential. [t. L: s. *dēferens,* ppr., bringing down]

def·er·ent² (dĕf´ər ənt), *adj. Anat.* **1.** conveying away. **2.** pertaining to the vas deferens, the deferent duct of the testes. [see DEFERENT¹, DEFER²]

def·er·en·tial (dĕf´ə rĕn´shəl), *adj.* marked by or showing deference; respectful. —**def·er·en´tial·ly,** *adv.*

de·fer·ment (dĭ fûr´mənt), *n.* act of deferring or putting off; postponement.

de·ferred (dĭ fûrd´), *adj.* **1.** postponed or delayed, as property rights which do not vest until some future event has occurred. **2.** suspended or held back for a period: *deferred interest account of bondholders.*

de·fi·ance (dĭ fī´əns), *n.* **1.** a daring or bold resistance to authority or to any opposing force. **2.** open disregard: *in defiance of criticism.* **3.** a challenge to meet in combat or contest.

de·fi·ant (dĭ fī´ənt), *adj.* characterized by defiance, bold opposition, or antagonism. [t. F, ppr. of *défier* DEFY] —**de·fi´ant·ly,** *adv.* —**de·fi´ant·ness,** *n.*
—**Syn.** insubordinate, contumacious, refractory, recalcitrant, rebellious, insolent. —**Ant.** obedient.

de·fi·cien·cy (dĭ fĭsh´ən sĭ), *n., pl.* **-cies. 1.** state or fact of being deficient; lack; incompleteness; insufficiency. **2.** the amount lacked; a deficit.

deficiency disease, an illness due to an insufficient supply o one or more essential dietary constituents.

deficiency judgment, *Law.* a judgment in favor of a creditor who has not satisfied the full amount of his claim against a debtor.

de·fi·cient (dĭ fĭsh´ənt), *adj.* **1.** lacking some element or characteristic; defective. **2.** insufficient; inadequate. [t. L: s. *dēficiens,* ppr., wanting] —**de·fi´cient·ly,** *adv.*

def·i·cit (dĕf´ə sĭt; *Brit.* also dĭ fĭs´ĭt), *n.* the amount by which a sum of money falls short of the required amount. [t. L: there is wanting] —**Ant.** surplus.

de fi·de (dē fī´dĭ), *Latin.* of the faith (used to describe a teaching of the Roman Catholic Church).

de·fi·er (dĭ fī´ər), *n.* one who defies.

def·i·lade (dĕf´ə lād´), *v.,* **-laded, -lading,** *n. Fort.* —*v.t.* **1.** to arrange the plan and profile of (a fortification) so as to protect its lines from enfilading fire and its interior from plunging or reverse fire. —*n.* **2.** act or operation of defilading. [t. F, der. *défiler*, orig., unthread, f. *dé-* DIS-¹ + (*en*)*filer* thread (ult. der. L *filum* a thread)]

de·file¹ (dĭ fīl´), *v.t.,* **-filed, -filing. 1.** to make foul, dirty, or unclean; pollute; taint. **2.** to violate the chastity of. **3.** to make ceremonially unclean; desecrate. **4.** to sully (a reputation, etc.). [alter. of *befile*, OE *befȳlan* befoul)] —**de·file´ment,** *n.* —**de·fil´er,** *n.*

de·file² (dĭ fīl´, dē´fīl´), *n., v.,* **-filed, -filing.** —*n.* **1.** any narrow passage, esp. between mountains. —*v.i.* **2.** to

march in a line, or by files; file off. [t. F, n. use of pp. of *défiler* file off]

de·fine (dĭ fīn´), *v.t.,* **-fined, -fining. 1.** to state or set forth the meaning of (a word, phrase, etc.). **2.** to explain the nature or essential qualities of; describe. **3.** to determine or fix the boundaries or extent of. **4.** to make clear the outline or form of. **5.** to fix or lay down definitely; specify distinctly. [ME *deffyne(n)*, t. F: m. *dēfinir*, t. L: m. *dēfinire* limit, determine, explain, terminate] —**de·fin´a·ble,** *adj.* —**de·fin´a·bil´i·ty,** *n.* —**de·fin´a·bly,** *adv.* —**de·fin´er,** *n.*

def·i·nite (dĕf´ə nĭt), *adj.* **1.** clearly defined or determined; not vague or general; fixed; precise; exact. **2.** having fixed limits; bounded with precision. **3.** defining; limiting. **4.** *Bot.* (of an inflorescence) determinate. [t. L: m.s. *dēfinītus,* pp., limited, determined] —**def´i·nite·ly,** *adv.* —**def´i·nite·ness,** *n.* —**Syn. 2.** certain, clear, express. —**Ant. 1.** confused.

definite article, the article (Eng. *the*) which classes as "identified" the noun it modifies.

def·i·ni·tion (dĕf´ə nĭsh´ən), *n.* **1.** act of defining, or making definite or clear. **2.** the formal statement of the meaning or signification of a word, phrase, etc. **3.** condition of being definite. **4.** *Optics.* sharpness of the image formed by an optical system. **5.** *Radio.* the accuracy of sound reproduction through a receiver, or picture reproduction in a television receiver.

de·fin·i·tive (dĭ fĭn´ə tĭv), *adj.* **1.** having the function of deciding or settling; determining; conclusive; final. **2.** serving to fix or specify definitely. **3.** having its fixed and final form. —*n.* **4.** a defining or limiting word, as an article, a demonstrative, or the like. —**de·fin´i·tive·ly,** *adv.* —**de·fin´i·tive·ness,** *n.*

de·fin·i·tude (dĭ fĭn´ə tūd´, -tōōd´), *n.* definiteness; exactitude; precision.

def·la·grate (dĕf´lə grāt´, dē´flə-), *v.t., v.i.,* **-grated, -grating.** to burn, esp. suddenly and violently. [t. L: m.s. *dēflagrātus,* pp.] —**def´la·gra´tion,** *n.*

de·flate (dĭ flāt´), *v.t.,* **-flated, -flating. 1.** to release the air or gas from (something inflated, as a balloon). **2.** to reduce (currency, prices, etc.) from an inflated condition. [t. L: m.s. *dēflātus,* pp., prop. blown off]

de·fla·tion (dĭ flā´shən), *n.* **1.** act of deflating. **2.** an abnormal decline in the level of commodity prices, esp. one not accompanied by an equal reduction in the costs of production. —**de·fla·tion·ar·y** (dĭ flā´shə nĕr´ĭ), *adj.*

de·flect (dĭ flĕkt´), *v.t., v.i.* to bend or turn aside; turn from a true course or right line; swerve. [t. L: s. *dēflectere*] —**de·flec´tor,** *n.*

de·flec·tion (dĭ flĕk´shən), *n.* **1.** act of deflecting. **2.** state of being deflected. **3.** amount of deviation. **4.** *Physics.* the deviation or swing of the indicator of an instrument from the position taken as zero. **5.** *Optics.* the bending of rays of light from a straight line. Also, *Brit.,* **de·flex´ion.**

de·flec·tive (dĭ flĕk´tĭv), *adj.* causing deflection.

de·flo·ra·tion (dĕf´lə rā´shən, dē´flə-), *n.* act of deflowering. [ME *defloracion,* t. LL: m.s. *dēflōrātio*]

de·flow·er (dĭ flou´ər), *v.t.* **1.** to deprive or strip of flowers. **2.** to deprive (a woman) of virginity; ravish. **3.** to despoil of beauty, freshness, sanctity, etc. [f. DE- + FLOWER, r. ME *deflore(n)*, t. OF: m. *desflorer* remove the flower(s) from, ravish] —**de·flow´er·er,** *n.*

de·flux·ion (dĭ flŭk´shən), *n. Pathol.* a copious discharge of fluid matter, as in catarrh.

De·foe (dĭ fō´), *n.* **Daniel,** 1661?–1731, British novelist and essayist.

de·fo·li·ate (dē fō´lĭ āt´), *v.,* **-ated, -ating.** —*v.t.* **1.** to strip or deprive (a tree, etc.) of leaves. —*v.i.* **2.** to lose leaves. [t. ML: m. s. *dēfoliātus,* pp., of *dēfoliāre,* der. L *folium* leaf] —**de·fo´li·a´tion,** *n.*

de·force (dĭ fōrs´), *v.t.,* **-forced, -forcing.** *Law.* to withhold (something) by force or violence, as from the rightful owner. [t. AF: s. *deforcer,* f. *de-* DE- + *forcer* FORCE, v.] —**de·force´ment,** *n.*

de·for·ciant (dĭ fōr´shənt), *n. Law.* one who deforces.

de·for·est (dē fôr´ĭst, -fŏr´-), *v.t.* to divest of forests or trees. —**de·for´est·a´tion,** *n.* —**de·for´est·er,** *n.*

De For·est (dĭ fôr´ĭst, fŏr´-), **Lee,** born 1873, U.S. inventor, esp. in the field of electronics.

de·form¹ (dĭ fôrm´), *v.t.* **1.** to mar the natural form or shape of; put out of shape; disfigure. **2.** to make ugly, ungraceful, or displeasing; mar the beauty of; spoil. **3.** to change the form of; transform. **4.** *Mech.* to subject to deformation. [ME, t. L: s. *dēformāre* disfigure] —**de·form´er,** *n.* —**Syn. 1.** See **mar.**

de·form² (dĭ fôrm´), *adj. Archaic.* deformed; ugly. [ME *defourme,* t. L: m. *dēformis* misshapen]

de·form·a·ble (dĭ fôr´mə bəl), *adj.* capable of being deformed. —**de·form´a·bil´i·ty,** *n.*

de·for·ma·tion (dē´fôr mā´shən, dĕf´ər-), *n.* **1.** act of deforming; distortion; disfigurement. **2.** result of deforming; change of form, esp. for the worse. **3.** *Mech.* a change in the shape or dimensions of a body, resulting from stress; strain. **4.** an altered form.

de·formed (dĭ fôrmd´), *adj.* **1.** having the form changed, with loss of beauty, etc.; misshapen; disfigured. **2.** hateful; offensive. —**Syn. 1.** malformed, crippled.

de·form·i·ty (dĭ fôr´mə tĭ), *n., pl.* **-ties. 1.** quality or state of being deformed, disfigured, or misshapen. **2.** *Pathol.* an abnormally formed part of the body, etc. **3.** a deformed person or thing. **4.** hatefulness; ugliness.

de·fraud (dĭ frôd′), *v.t.* to deprive of a right or property by fraud; cheat. [ME *defraude*(*n*), t. L: m. *dēfraudāre*. Cf. FRAUD] **—de′frau·da′tion,** *n.* **—de·fraud′er,** *n.*

de·fray (dĭ frā′), *v.t.* to bear or pay (the costs, expenses, etc.). [t. F: s. *défrayer,* OF *desfraier* pay costs, der. *des-* DIS-¹ + *frai* cost, of Gmc. origin] **—de·fray′a·ble,** *adj.* **—de·fray′er,** *n.*

de·fray·al (dĭ frā′əl), *n.* payment of charges or expenses. Also, **de·fray′ment.**

de·frock (dē frŏk′), *v.t.* to unfrock.

de·frost (dē frôst′, -frŏst′), *v.t.* to remove the frost or ice from. **—de·frost′er,** *n.*

deft (dĕft), *adj.* dexterous; nimble; skillful; clever. [ME; var. of DAFT] **—deft′ly,** *adv.* **—deft′ness,** *n.*

de·funct (dĭ fŭngkt′), *adj.* **1.** deceased; dead; extinct. **—***n.* **2. the defunct,** the dead person. [t. L: s. *dēfunctus,* pp., discharged, finished] **—de·funct′ness,** *n.*

de·func·tive (dĭ fŭngk′tĭv), *adj.* of or pertaining to the dead; funereal.

de·fy (*v.* dĭ fī′; *n.* dĭ fī′, dē′fī), *v.,* **-fied, -fying,** *n., pl.* **-fies. —***v.t.* **1.** to challenge the power of; resist boldly or openly. **2.** to offer effective resistance to: *a fort which defies attacks.* **3.** to challenge (one) to do something deemed impossible. **4.** *Archaic.* to challenge to a combat or contest. **—***n.* **5.** *U.S. Slang.* a challenge; a defiance. [ME *defye*(*n*), t. OF: m. *defier,* f. *de-* DE- + *fier* (g. L *fīdere* trust)] **—Syn. 1.** dare, brave, flout, scorn.

deg., degree; degrees.

dé·ga·gé (dĕ gȧ zhĕ′), *adj.* *French.* unconstrained; easy, as in manner. [F, pp. of *dégager* disengage, put at ease]

de·gas (dĭ gȧs′), *v.t.,* **-gassed, -gassing. 1.** to free from gas. **2.** to treat with chemical agents to destroy a gas or its harmful properties. **3.** to complete the evacuation of gases in (a vacuum tube).

De·gas (də gȧs′; *Fr.* dĕ gä′), *n.* **Hilaire Germain Edgar** (ē lĕr′ zhĕr măN′ ĕd gär′), 1834–1917, French painter.

De Gaulle (də gōl′), **Charles André Joseph Marie** (shȧrl ȧN drĕ′ zhō sĕf′ mȧ rē′), born 1890, French general and statesman.

de·gauss·ing (dĭ gou′sĭng, -gô′zĭng), *n.* a demagnetizing process used esp. to neutralize a ship's magnetic field as a protection against magnetic mines. [f. DE- + *gauss* (from K. F. GAUSS) + -ING¹]

de·gen·er·a·cy (dĭ jĕn′ər ə sĭ), *n.* degenerate state or character; degeneration.

de·gen·er·ate (*v.* dĭ jĕn′ə rāt′; *adj., n.* dĭ jĕn′ər ĭt), *v.,* **-ated, -ating,** *adj., n.* **—***v.i.* **1.** to decline in physical, mental, or moral qualities; deteriorate. **2.** *Biol.* to revert to a less highly organized or simpler type. **—***adj.* **3.** having declined in physical or moral qualities; deteriorated; degraded: *a degenerate king.* **4.** having lost, or become impaired with respect to, the qualities proper to the race or kind: *a degenerate plant.* **5.** characterized by or associated with degeneracy: *degenerate times.* **—***n.* **6.** one who has retrograded from a normal type or standard, as in morals or character. **7.** one exhibiting morbid physical and mental traits or tendencies, esp. from birth. [t. L: m. s. *dēgenerātus,* pp., departed from its race] **—de·gen′er·ate·ly,** *adv.* **—de·gen′er·ate·ness,** *n.*

de·gen·er·a·tion (dĭ jĕn′ə rā′shən), *n.* **1.** process of degenerating. **2.** state of being degenerate. **3.** *Biol.* reversion to a less highly organized or a simpler type. **4.** *Pathol.* **a.** a process by which a tissue deteriorates, loses functional activity, and may become converted into or replaced by other kinds of tissue. **b.** the morbid condition produced by such a process.

de·gen·er·a·tive (dĭ jĕn′ə rā′tĭv), *adj.* **1.** tending to degenerate. **2.** characterized by degeneration.

de·glu·ti·nate (dē glōō′tə nāt′), *v.t.,* **-nated, -nating.** to extract the gluten from. [t. L: m. s. *dēglūtinātus,* pp., unglued]

de·glu·ti·tion (dē′glōō tĭsh′ən), *n.* *Physiol.* act or process of swallowing. [der. *deglute* swallow down (now OBS.), t. L: m.s. *dēglūtīre*]

deg·ra·da·tion (dĕg′rə dā′shən), *n.* **1.** act of degrading. **2.** state of being degraded. **3.** *Phys. Geog.* the wearing down of the land by the action of water, wind, or ice; erosion. **—Syn. 2.** humiliation, disgrace, dishonor, debasement.

de·grade (dĭ grād′), *v.t.,* **-graded, -grading. 1.** to reduce from a higher to a lower rank, degree, etc.; deprive of office, rank, degree, or title as a punishment. **2.** to lower in character or quality; debase; deprave. **3.** to lower in dignity or estimation; bring into contempt. **4.** to reduce in amount, strength, intensity, etc. **5.** *Phys. Geog.* to wear down by erosion, as hills (opposed to *aggrade*). [ME *degrade*(*n*), t. ecclesiastical LL: m. *dēgradāre* reduce in rank, der. L *gradus* GRADE] **—de·grad′er,** *n.* **—Syn. 1.** demote, depose. **3.** humiliate, disgrace, dishonor. See **humble. —Ant. 1.** promote. **2.** uplift.

de·grad·ed (dĭ grā′dĭd), *adj.* debased; degenerate. **—de·grad′ed·ly,** *adv.* **—de·grad′ed·ness,** *n.*

de·grad·ing (dĭ grā′dĭng), *adj.* that degrades; debasing: *degrading obsequiousness.* **—de·grad′ing·ly,** *adv.* **—de·grad′ing·ness,** *n.*

de·gree (dĭ grē′), *n.* **1.** a step or stage in an ascending or descending scale, or in a course or process. **2.** *Genetics, etc.* a certain distance or remove in the line of descent, determining the proximity of blood. **3.** a stage in a scale of rank or dignity; relative rank, station, etc. **4.** a stage

in a scale of intensity or amount: *to the last degree.* **5.** *Geom., etc.* the 360th part of a complete angle or turn (often indicated by the sign °, as 45°). **6.** *Alg.* the sum of the exponents of the variables in an algebraic expression: x^3 and $2x^2y$ are terms of degree three. **7.** a unit in the measurement of temperature. **8.** a unit on an arbitrary scale of measurement. **9.** *Geog., Astron.* a line or point on the earth or in the celestial sphere whose position is fixed by its angular distance measured in degrees from the equator (equinoctial) or a given meridian. **10.** *Law.* a relative measure of criminality; *esp. U.S.,* a distinctive grade of crime: *murder in the first degree.* **11.** *Educ.* an academic title conferred by universities and colleges as an indication of the completion of a course of study, or as an honorary recognition of achievement. **12.** *Gram.* one of the three parallel formations (positive, comparative, and superlative) of adjectives and adverbs, showing differences in quality, quantity, or intensity in the attribute referred to, as English *low, lower, lowest.* **13.** *Music.* a tone, or step, of the scale. **14.** *Obs.* a step, as of a stair. **15. by degrees,** gradually. **16. to a degree,** to an undefined but considerable extent. [ME *degre,* t. OF, f. *de-* DE- + *gre,* g. L *gradus* step, degree, GRADE]

Degrees (def. 5) of a circle

de·gree-day (dĭ grē′dā′), *n.* a unit of mean daily outdoor temperature representing one degree of difference from a standard temperature, usually 65°, used in reckoning fuel consumption.

degrees of freedom, *Phys. Chem.* variance.

de·gres·sion (dĭ grĕsh′ən), *n.* **1.** a going down; descent. **2.** the decrease in rate in degressive taxation.

de·gres·sive (dĭ grĕs′ĭv), *adj.* pertaining to a form of taxation in which the rate diminishes gradually on sums below a certain fixed amount.

De Groot (də grōt′), **Huig** (hoĭKH). See **Grotius.**

de·gum (dē gŭm′), *v.t.,* **-gummed, -gumming.** to free from gum.

de·gust (dĭ gŭst′), *v.t., v.i.* *Rare.* to taste. [t. L: s. *dēgustāre*] **—de′gus·ta′tion,** *n.*

de gus·ti·bus non est dis·pu·tan·dum (dē gŭs′tə bəs nŏn ĕst dĭs′pyŏō tăn′dəm), *Latin.* there is no disputing about tastes.

de·hisce (dĭ hĭs′), *v.i.,* **-hisced, -hiscing.** to gape; burst open, as capsules of plants. [t. L: m.s. *dēhiscere*]

de·his·cence (dĭ hĭs′əns), *n.* **1.** *Bot.* the natural bursting open of capsules, fruits, anthers, etc., for the discharge of their contents. **2.** *Biol.* the release of materials by the splitting open of an organ or tissue.

de·his·cent (dĭ hĭs′ənt), *adj.* gaping open; characterized by dehiscence.

de·horn (dē hôrn′), *v.t.* to deprive (cattle) of horns. **—de·horn′er,** *n.*

de·hort (dĭ hôrt′), *v.t., v.i.* *Now Rare or Obs.* to seek to dissuade. [t. L: s. *dehortārī*] **—de′hor·ta′tion,** *n.* **—de·hor·ta·tive** (dĭ hôr′tə tĭv), **de·hor·ta·to·ry** (dĭ hôr′tə tōr′ĭ), *adj., n.* **—de·hort′er,** *n.*

de·hu·man·ize (dē hū′mə nīz′), *v.t.,* **-ized, -izing.** to deprive of human character. **—de·hu′man·i·za′tion,** *n.*

de·hu·mid·i·fy (dē′hū mĭd′ə fī′), *v.t.,* **-fied, -fying.** to remove moisture from. **—de·hu·mid′i·fi·ca′tion,** *n.*

de·hy·drate (dē hī′drāt), *v.,* **-drated, -drating. —***v.t.* **1.** to deprive (a chemical compound) of water or the elements of water. **2.** to free (vegetables, etc.) from moisture for preservation. **—***v.i.* **3.** to lose water or moisture. [f. DE- + HYDR- + -ATE¹] **—de′hy·dra′tion,** *n.* **—Syn. 2.** See **evaporate.**

de·hy·dro·gen·ize (dē hī′drə jə nīz′), *v.t.,* **-ized, -izing.** *Chem.* to remove hydrogens from (a compound). **—de·hy·dro·gen·i·za·tion** (dē hī′drə jə nĭ zā′shən), *n.*

de·hyp·no·tize (dē hĭp′nə tīz′), *v.t.* **-tized, -tizing.** to bring out of the hypnotic state.

De·ia·ni·ra (dē′yə nī′rə), *n.* *Gk. Legend.* a sister of Meleager and wife of Hercules, whom she unwittingly killed by giving him the shirt of Nessus.

de·ic·er (dē ī′sər), *n.* a mechanical or exhaust-heat device preventing or removing ice formation.

de·i·cide¹ (dē′ə sīd′), *n.* one who kills a god. [t. NL: m.s. *deicīda*] **—de/i·ci′dal,** *adj.*

de·i·cide² (dē′ə sīd′), *n.* the killing of a god. [f. s. L *deus* god + -(i)CIDE²] **—de/i·ci′dal,** *adj.*

deic·tic (dīk′tĭk), *adj.* **1.** *Logic.* proving directly. **2.** *Gram.* pointing; demonstrative. [t. Gk.: m.s. *deiktikós*] **—deic′ti·cal·ly,** *adv.*

de·if·ic (dē ĭf′ĭk), *adj.* making divine; deifying. [t. LL: s. *deificus* god-making, sacred]

de·i·fi·ca·tion (dē′ə fə kā′shən), *n.* **1.** act of deifying. **2.** state of being deified. **3.** a deified embodiment.

de·i·form (dē′ə fôrm′), *adj.* godlike; divine. [t. ML: s. *deiformis,* der. L *deus* god. See -FORM]

de·i·fy (dē′ə fī′), *v.t.,* **-fied, -fying. 1.** to make a god of; exalt to the rank of a deity. **2.** to adore or regard as a deity: *to deify prudence.* [ME *deify*(*en*), t. OF: s. *deifier,* t. LL: m. *deificāre*] **—de′i·fi′er,** *n.*

deign (dān), *v.i.* **1.** to think fit or in accordance with one's dignity; condescend. **—***v.t.* **2.** to condescend to give or grant: *deigning no reply.* **3.** *Obs.* to condescend to accept. [ME *deine*(*n*), t. OF: m. *deignier,* g. L *dignārī* deem worthy]

---

b., blend of, blended; c., cognate with; d., dialect, dialectal; der., derived from; f., formed from; g., going back to; m., modification of; r., replacing; s., stem of; t., taken from; ?, perhaps.   See the full key on inside cover.

De·i gra·ti·a (dē′ī grā′shĭ ə), *Latin.* by the grace of God.

deil (dēl), *n. Scot.* devil.

De·iph·o·bus (dē′ĭf′ə bəs), *n. Gk. Legend.* a son of Priam and Hecuba, who married Helen after the death of Paris and was slain by Menelaus.

Deir·dre (dĭr′drĭ; *Irish* dâr′drä), *n.* heroine of an Irish legend: raised to be the wife of King Conchobar of Ulster, she fell in love with one of the sons of Usnach and escaped with him and his brothers to Scotland. Conchobar had the brothers killed and Deirdre killed herself, fulfilling a prenatal prophecy that she would bring sorrow and death. Deirdre is often used as a symbol for Ireland.

de·ism (dē′ĭz əm), *n.* **1.** belief in the existence of a God on the evidence of reason and nature only, with rejection of supernatural revelation (distinguished from *theism*). **2.** belief in a God who created the world but has since remained indifferent to his creation (distinguished from *atheism, pantheism,* and *theism*). [f. s. L *deus* god + -ISM]

de·ist (dē′ĭst), *n.* one who believes in deism. —**de·is′-tic, de·is′ti·cal,** *adj.* —**de·is′ti·cal·ly,** *adv.*

de·i·ty (dē′ə tĭ), *n., pl.* **-ties.** **1.** a god or goddess. **2.** divine character or nature. **3.** the estate or rank of a god. **4.** the character or nature of the Supreme Being. **5. the Deity,** God. [ME *deite,* t. OF, t. LL: m. s. *deitas*]

de·ject (dĭ jĕkt′), *v.t.* **1.** to depress the spirits of; dispirit; dishearten. —*adj.* **2.** *Obs. or Archaic.* dejected; downcast. [t. L: s. *dējectus,* pp., thrown down]

de·jec·ta (dĭ jĕk′tə), *n. pl.* excrements. [NL, prop. neut. pl. of L *dējectus,* pp., thrown down]

de·ject·ed (dĭ jĕk′tĭd), *adj.* depressed in spirits; disheartened; low-spirited. —**de·ject′ed·ly,** *adv.* —**de·ject′ed·ness,** *n.* —**Syn.** discouraged, despondent, dispirited, downhearted. See **sad.** —**Ant.** gay.

de·jec·tion (dĭ jĕk′shən), *n.* **1.** depression or lowness of spirits. **2.** *Med., Physiol.* **a.** evacuation of the bowels; fecal discharge. **b.** excrement. —**Ant. 1.** exhilaration.

dé·jeu·ner (dā′zhə nā′; *Fr.* dĕ zhœ nĕ′), *n.* **1.** breakfast. **2.** (in Continental use) lunch. [F, orig. inf., OF *desjeuner* break one's fast, der. *des-* DIS-¹ + *jeun* fasting, g. L *jējūnus* jejune]

de ju·re (dē jŏŏr′ĭ), *Latin.* by right; according to law.

dek-, var. of **dec-.**

deka-, var. of **deca-.**

De Kalb (dĭ kălb′), *n.* **Baron Johann** (yō′hän), 1721–1780, German general in the American Revolutionary Army.

dek·a·li·ter (dĕk′ə lē′tər), *n.* decaliter.

dek·a·me·ter (dĕk′ə mē′tər), *n.* decameter.

deki-, var. of **deci-.**

Dek·ker (dĕk′ər), *n.* **Thomas,** 1570?–1645?, British dramatist. Also, **Decker.**

De Ko·ven (dĭ kō′vən), **Henry Louis Reginald,** 1861–1920, U.S. composer.

De Kruif (də krīf′), **Paul,** born 1890, U.S. bacteriologist and author.

Del., Delaware.

del., delegate.

De·la·croix (də lȧ krwä′), *n.* **Ferdinand Victor Eugène** (fĕr dē nän′ vĕk tôr′ œ zhĕn′), 1798?–1863, French painter.

Del·a·go·a Bay (dĕl′ə gō′ə), an inlet of the Indian Ocean in S Mozambique. 55 mi. long.

de·laine (də lān′), *n.* mousseline de laine.

de la Mare (də lə mâr′, dĕl′ə mâr′), **Walter John,** born 1873, British poet and novelist.

de·lam·i·nate (dē lăm′ə nāt′), *v.i.,* **-nated, -nating.** to split into laminae or thin layers.

de·lam·i·na·tion (dē lăm′ə nā′shən), *n.* **1.** a splitting apart into layers. **2.** *Embryol.* the separation of a primitive blastoderm into two layers of cells.

De·land (dĭ lănd′), *n.* **Margaret** (*Mrs. Margaretta Wade Campbell Deland*), 1857–1945, U.S. novelist.

De·la·roche (də lȧ rôsh′), *n.* **Hippolyte Paul** (ē pô lēt′ pōl), 1797–1856, French painter.

de·late (dĭ lāt′), *v.t.,* **-lated, -lating.** **1.** to inform against; denounce or accuse. **2.** to relate or report (an offense, etc.). [t. L: m. s. *dēlātus,* pp., carried from or down, reported, accused] —**de·la′tion,** *n.* —**de·la′tor,** *n.*

De·la·vigne (də lȧ vēn′y), *n.* **Jean François Casimir** (zhän frän swȧ′ kȧ zē mēr′), 1793–1843, French poet and dramatist.

Del·a·ware (dĕl′ə wâr′), *n.* **1.** a State in the eastern United States, on the Atlantic coast. 318,085 pop. (1950); 2057 sq. mi. *Cap.:* Dover. *Abbr.:* Del. **2.** a river flowing from SE New York along the boundary between Pennsylvania and New Jersey into Delaware Bay. 296 mi. **3.** (*pl.*) a group of North American Indians, formerly occupying the drainage basin of the Delaware river and the greater part of New Jersey. **4.** a member of this group. **5.** their language, of the Algonquian stock. **6.** De La Warr. [named after Baron DE LA WARR] —**Del·a·war·e·an** (dĕl′ə wâr′ĭən), *adj., n.*

Delaware Bay, an estuary between E Delaware and S New Jersey. ab. 70 mi. long.

Delaware Water Gap, a scenic gorge cut by the Delaware river through the Appalachian Mountains, on the boundary between E Pennsylvania and NW New Jersey. ab. 1400 ft. deep.

De La Warr (dĕl′ə wâr′; *Brit.* -wər), **Thomas West, Baron,** 1577–1618, first British colonial governor of Virginia. Also, **Del′a·ware′.**

de·lay (dĭ lā′), *v.t.* **1.** to put off to a later time; defer; postpone. **2.** to impede the progress of; retard; hinder. —*v.i.* **3.** to put off action; linger; loiter: *Don't delay!* —*n.* **4.** act of delaying; procrastination; loitering. **5.** fact of being delayed. [ME *delaie*(n), t. OF: m. *delaier* put off, b. L *dīlātāre* (freq. of L *differre* DEFER¹) and L var. (unrecorded) of *dēliquāre* strain, clear off] —**de·lay′er,** *n.* —**Syn. 1.** See **defer. 5.** deferment, postponement, respite.

Del·cas·sé (dĕl kȧ sĕ′), *n.* **Théophile** (tĕ ô fēl′), 1852–1923, French statesman.

de·le (dē′lĭ), *v.t.,* **deled, deleing.** *Print.* **1.** (imperative) take out; omit: a direction (usually represented by a symbol) on a printer's proof. See page xxxviii. **2.** *Obs. or Rare.* to indicate for omission; delete. [t. L]

de·lec·ta·ble (dĭ lĕk′tə bəl), *adj.* delightful; highly pleasing; enjoyable. [ME, t. OF, t. L: m. s. *dēlectābilis*] —**de·lec′ta·ble·ness, de·lec′ta·bil′i·ty,** *n.* —**de·lec′ta·bly,** *adv.* —**Ant.** disagreeable, distasteful.

de·lec·tate (dĭ lĕk′tāt), *v.t.,* **-tated, -tating.** to please; charm; delight. [t. L: m. s. *dēlectātus,* pp. delighted]

de·lec·ta·tion (dē′lĕk tā′shən), *n.* delight.

De·led·da (dĕ lĕd′dä), *n.* **Grazia** (grä′tsyä), 1875–1936, Italian novelist.

del·e·ga·cy (dĕl′ə gə sĭ), *n., pl.* **-cies.** **1.** the position or commission of a delegate. **2.** the sending or appointing of a delegate. **3.** a body of delegates. **4.** (at English universities) a standing committee for certain duties.

de·le·gal·ize (dē lē′gə līz′), *v.t.,* **-ized, -izing.** to revoke the statutory authorization of.

del·e·gate (*n.* dĕl′ə gāt′, -gĭt; *v.* dĕl′ə gāt′), *n., v.,* **-gated, -gating.** —*n.* **1.** one delegated to act for or represent another or others; a deputy; a representative, as in a political convention. **2.** *U.S. Govt.* **a.** the representative of a Territory in the House of Representatives of the U.S. **b.** a member of the lower house of the State legislatures of Maryland, Virginia, and West Virginia. —*v.t.* **3.** to send or appoint (a person) as deputy or representative. **4.** to commit (powers, functions, etc.) to another as agent or deputy. [t. L: m. s. *dēlēgātus,* pp., sent, deputed] —**Syn. 4.** depute, entrust.

del·e·ga·tion (dĕl′ə gā′shən), *n.* **1.** act of delegating. **2.** fact of being delegated. **3.** the body of delegates chosen to represent a political unit in an assembly.

de·lete (dĭ lēt′), *v.t.,* **-leted, -leting.** to strike out or take out (anything written or printed); cancel; erase; expunge. [t. L: m. s. *dēlētus,* pp., done away with, destroyed] —**Syn.** See **cancel.**

del·e·te·ri·ous (dĕl′ə tĭr′ĭəs), *adj.* **1.** injurious to health. **2.** hurtful; harmful; injurious. [t. NL: m. *dēlētērius,* t. Gk.: m. *dēlētērios*] —**del′e·te′ri·ous·ly,** *adv.* —**del′e·te′ri·ous·ness,** *n.* —**Ant. 2.** beneficial.

de·le·tion (dĭ lē′shən), *n.* **1.** act of deleting. **2.** fact of being deleted. **3.** a deleted passage. [t. L: s. *dēlētio*]

delft (dĕlft), *n.* **1.** a kind of glazed earthenware decorated in colors, esp. in blue, made at Delft. **2.** any pottery resembling this. Also, **delf** (dĕlf), **delft′ware′.**

Delft (dĕlft), *n.* a city in W Netherlands. 59,925 (est. 1946).

Del·ga·do (dĕl gä′dô), *n.* **Cape,** a cape at the NE extremity of Mozambique.

Del·hi (dĕl′ĭ), **1.** a province in N India. 918,000 pop. (1941); 574 sq. mi. **2.** the capital of this province: former capital of the old Mogul Empire. Delhi was the administrative headquarters of British India from 1912 until 1929, when New Delhi became the capital. 521,849 (1941).

Delhi (def. 2)

De·li·an (dē′lĭ ən), *adj.* **1.** pertaining to Delos. —*n.* **2.** a native or inhabitant of Delos.

de·lib·er·ate (*adj.* dĭ lĭb′ər ĭt; *v.* dĭ lĭb′ə rāt′), *adj., v.,* **-ated, -ating.** —*adj.* **1.** carefully weighed or considered; studied; intentional. **2.** characterized by deliberation; careful or slow in deciding. **3.** leisurely in movement or action; slow; unhurried. —*v.t.* **4.** to weigh in the mind; consider: *to deliberate a question, a proposition, etc.* —*v.i.* **5.** to think carefully or attentively; reflect. **6.** to consult or confer formally. [t. L: m. s. *dēlīberātus,* pp., weighed well] —**de·lib′er·ate·ly,** *adv.* —**de·lib′er·ate·ness,** *n.* —**de·lib′er·a′tor,** *n.*

—**Syn. 1.** DELIBERATE, INTENTIONAL, PREMEDITATED, VOLUNTARY refer to something not happening by chance. DELIBERATE is applied to what is not done hastily but with full realization of what one is doing: *a deliberate attempt to evade justice.* INTENTIONAL is applied to what is definitely intended, or done on purpose: *an intentional omission.* PREMEDITATED is applied to what has been planned in advance: *a premeditated crime.* VOLUNTARY is applied to what is done by a definite exercise of the will and not because of outward pressures: *a voluntary enlistment.* **2.** thoughtful, circumspect, cautious. **3.** See **slow. 5.** weigh, ponder, cogitate. —**Ant. 1.** accidental. **2.** impulsive, precipitate.

de·lib·er·a·tion (dĭ lĭb′ə rā′shən), *n.* **1.** careful consideration before decision. **2.** formal consultation or discussion. **3.** deliberate quality; leisureliness of movement or action; slowness.

de·lib·er·a·tive (dĭ lĭb'ə rā'tĭv), *adj.* **1.** having the function of deliberating, as a legislative assembly. **2.** having to do with policy; dealing with the wisdom and expediency of a proposal: *a deliberative speech.* —**de·lib'er·a'tive·ly,** *adv.* —**de·lib'er·a'tive·ness,** *n.*

del·i·ca·cy (dĕl'ə kə sĭ), *n., pl.* **-cies. 1.** fineness of texture, quality, etc.; softness: *the delicacy of lace.* **2.** fineness of perception or feeling; sensitiveness. **3.** the quality of requiring or involving great care or tact: *negotiations of great delicacy.* **4.** nicety of action or operation; minute accuracy: *a surgeon's delicacy of touch.* **5.** fineness of feeling with regard to what is fitting, proper, etc. **6.** bodily weakness; liability to sickness. **7.** something delightful or pleasing, esp. to the palate. **8.** gratification; luxury. —**Ant. 1, 2.** coarseness.

del·i·cate (dĕl'ə kĭt), *adj.* **1.** fine in texture, quality, construction, etc. **2.** dainty or choice, as food. **3.** soft or faint, as color. **4.** so fine or slight as to be scarcely perceptible; subtle. **5.** easily damaged; fragile. **6.** requiring great care, caution, or tact. **7.** fine or exquisite in action or execution: *a delicate instrument.* **8.** regardful of what is becoming, proper, etc., or of the feelings of others. **9.** exquisite or refined in perception or feeling; sensitive. **10.** distinguishing subtle differences. **11.** *Obs.* fastidious. **12.** *Obs.* luxurious or voluptuous. —*n.* **13.** *Archaic.* a delicacy; a dainty. **14.** *Obs.* a luxury. [ME, t. L: m. s. *dēlicātus* delightful, luxurious, soft; akin to DELICIOUS] —**del'i·cate·ly,** —**del'i·cate·ness,** *n.*
—**Syn. 1.** DELICATE, DAINTY, EXQUISITE imply beauty such as belongs to rich surroundings or which needs careful treatment. DELICATE, used of an object, suggests fragility, small size, and often very fine workmanship: *a delicate piece of carving.* DAINTY, in concrete references, suggests a smallness, gracefulness, and beauty which forbid rough handling; there is a connotation of attractiveness: *a dainty handkerchief;* of persons, it refers to fastidious sensibilities: *dainty in eating habits.* EXQUISITE suggests an outstanding beauty, daintiness, and elegance, or a discriminating sensitivity and ability to perceive fine distinctions: *an exquisite sense of humor.* **5.** tender, frail. **6.** critical, precarious. **7.** exact, precise, accurate. —**Ant. 1-2.** coarse.

del·i·ca·tes·sen (dĕl'ə kə tĕs'ən), *n.* **1.** (*construed as sing.*) a store selling foods that are ready or require little preparation for serving. **2.** (*construed as pl.*) the foods sold. [t. G, pl. of *delicatesse* delicacy, t. F]

de·li·cious (dĭ lĭsh'əs), *adj.* **1.** highly pleasing to the senses, esp. to taste or smell. **2.** pleasing in the highest degree; delightful. —*n.* **3.** (*cap.*) a variety of red eating apple, widely grown in the U.S. [ME, t. OF, t. LL: m. s. *dēliciōsus,* der. L *dēlicia* delight] —**de·li'cious·ly,** *adv.* —**de·li'cious·ness,** *n.*
—**Syn. 1.** DELICIOUS, LUSCIOUS refer to that which is especially agreeable to the senses. That which is DELICIOUS is highly agreeable to the taste (or sometimes to the smell): *a delicious meal.* LUSCIOUS implies such a luxuriant fullness or ripeness as to make an object sweet and rich, sometimes to excess; it is often used in transferred or humorous senses: *a luscious banana, a luscious beauty, luscious music.* —**Ant. 1.** tasteless, insipid.

de·lict (dĭ lĭkt'), *n.* **1.** *Civil Law.* a misdemeanor. **2.** *Rom. Law.* a civil wrong permitting compensation or punitive damages. [t. L: s. *dēlictum* fault, orig. pp. neut.]

de·light (dĭ līt'), *n.* **1.** a high degree of pleasure or enjoyment; joy; rapture. **2.** something that gives great pleasure. —*v.t.* **3.** to give great pleasure, satisfaction, or enjoyment to; please highly. —*v.i.* **4.** to have great pleasure; take pleasure (fol. by *in* or an infinitive). [erroneous 16th cent. sp., after *light,* r. ME *delit,* t. OF: der. *delitier,* g. L *dēlectāre,* freq. of *dēlicere* to delight] —**de·light'er,** *n.* —**Syn. 1.** enjoyment, transport, delectation. See **pleasure.** —**Ant. 1.** distress. **2.** disappointment.

de·light·ed (dĭ lī'tĭd), *adj.* **1.** highly pleased. **2.** *Obs.* delightful. —**de·light'ed·ly,** *adv.*

de·light·ful (dĭ līt'fəl), *adj.* affording delight; highly pleasing. —**de·light'ful·ly,** —**de·light'ful·ness,** *n.* —**Syn.** pleasurable, enjoyable; charming, enchanting, delectable, agreeable. —**Ant.** obnoxious.

de·light·some (dĭ līt'səm), *adj.* delightful. —**de·light'some·ly,** *adv.* —**de·light'some·ness,** *n.*

De·li·lah (dĭ lī'lə), *n.* **1.** *Bible.* Samson's mistress, who betrayed him to the Philistines. Judges 16. **2.** a seductive and treacherous woman.

de·lim·it (dĭ lĭm'ĭt), *v.t.* to fix or mark the limits of; demarcate. [t. F: s. *délimiter,* t. L: m. *dēlīmitāre*]

de·lim·i·tate (dĭ lĭm'ə tāt'), *v.t.,* **-tated, -tating.** delimit. —**de·lim'i·ta'tion,** *n.* —**de·lim'i·ta'tive,** *adj.*

de·lin·e·ate (dĭ lĭn'ē āt'), *v.t.,* **-ated, -ating. 1.** to trace the outline of; sketch or trace in outline; represent pictorially. **2.** to portray in words; describe. [t. L: m. s. *dēlīneātus,* pp., sketched out]

de·lin·e·a·tion (dĭ lĭn'ē ā'shən), *n.* **1.** act or process of delineating. **2.** a chart or diagram; a sketch; a rough draft. **3.** a description. —**de·lin'e·a'tive,** *adj.*

de·lin·e·a·tor (dĭ lĭn'ē ā'tər), *n.* **1.** one who or that which delineates. **2.** a tailor's pattern which can be adjusted for cutting garments of different sizes.

de·li·ne·a·vit (dĭ lĭn'ē ā'vĭt), *Latin.* he (or she) drew (this).

de·lin·quen·cy (dĭ lĭng'kwən sĭ), *n., pl.* **-cies. 1.** failure in or neglect of duty or obligation; fault; guilt. **2.** a shortcoming; a misdeed or offense.

de·lin·quent (dĭ lĭng'kwənt), *adj.* **1.** failing in or neglectful of a duty or obligation; guilty of a misdeed or

offense. **2.** of or pertaining to delinquents: *delinquent taxes.* —*n.* **3.** one who is delinquent. [t. L: s. *dēlinquens,* ppr.] —**de·lin'quent·ly,** *adv.*

del·i·quesce (dĕl'ə kwĕs'), *v.i.,* **-quesced, -quescing. 1.** to melt away. **2.** to become liquid by absorbing moisture from the air, as certain salts. **3.** *Bot.* to form many small divisions or branches. [t. L: m. s. *dēliquescere* melt away]

del·i·ques·cence (dĕl'ə kwĕs'əns), *n.* **1.** act or process of deliquescing. **2.** the liquid produced when something deliquesces. —**del'i·ques'cent,** *adj.*

del·i·ra·tion (dĕl'ə rā'shən), *n.* mental derangement; raving; delirium. [t. L: s. *dēlīrātio*]

de·lir·i·ous (dĭ lĭr'ĭ əs), *adj.* **1.** *Pathol.* affected with delirium. **2.** characteristic of delirium. **3.** wild with excitement, enthusiasm, etc. —**de·lir'i·ous·ly,** *adv.* —**de·lir'i·ous·ness,** *n.*

de·lir·i·um (dĭ lĭr'ĭ əm), *n., pl.* **-liriums, -liria** (-lĭr'ĭ ə). **1.** a more or less temporary disorder of the mental faculties, as in fevers, disturbances of consciousness, or intoxication, characterized by restlessness, excitement, delusions, hallucinations, etc. **2.** a state of violent excitement or emotion. [t. L, der. *dēlīrāre* be deranged, lit., go out of the furrow]

delirium tre·mens (trē'mənz), a violent restlessness due to excessive indulgence in alcohol, characterized by trembling, terrifying visual hallucinations, etc. [NL trembling delirium]

del·i·tes·cent (dĕl'ə tĕs'ənt), *adj.* concealed. [t. L: s. *dēlitescens,* ppr.] —**del'i·tes'cence,** *n.*

De·li·us (dē'lĭ əs, dĕl'yəs), *n.* **Frederick,** 1862-1934, British composer.

de·liv·er (dĭ lĭv'ər), *v.t.* **1.** to give up or surrender; give into another's possession or keeping. **2.** to carry and turn over (letters, goods, etc.) to the intended recipients. **3.** *U.S. Colloq.* to bring (votes) to the support of a candidate or a cause. **4.** to give forth in words; utter or pronounce: *to deliver a verdict.* **5.** to give forth or emit; direct; cast. **6.** to set free; liberate. **7.** to release or save: *deliver us from evil.* **8.** to disburden (a woman) of a child in childbirth. **9.** to disburden (oneself) of thoughts, opinions, etc. **10.** *Obs.* to make known; assert. —*adj.* **11.** *Obs.* or *Archaic.* agile; active; quick. [ME *delivre*(*n*), t. F: m. *délivrer,* g. LL *dēlīberāre* set free] —**de·liv'er·a·ble,** *adj.* —**de·liv'er·er,** *n.* —**Syn. 1.** hand over, transfer, cede. **4.** communicate, impart. **6.** free, emancipate. **7.** redeem, rescue.

de·liv·er·ance (dĭ lĭv'ər əns), *n.* **1.** act of delivering. **2.** fact of being delivered. **3.** a thought or judgment expressed; a formal or authoritative pronouncement.

de·liv·er·ly (dĭ lĭv'ər lĭ), *adv. Obs.* or *Archaic.* quickly; deftly.

de·liv·er·y (dĭ lĭv'ər ĭ), *n., pl.* **-eries. 1.** the delivering of letters, goods etc. **2.** a giving up or handing over; surrender. **3.** the utterance or enunciation of words. **4.** vocal and bodily behavior during the presentation of a speech. **5.** act or manner of giving or sending forth, as of a ball by the pitcher in baseball. **6.** release or rescue. **7.** the being delivered of, or giving birth to a child; parturition. **8.** something delivered. **9.** *Com.* a shipment of goods from the seller to the buyer. **10.** *Law.* an act sometimes essential to a legally effective transfer of property: *a delivery of deed.*

dell (dĕl), *n. Literary in U.S.* a small valley; a vale. [ME *delle,* OE *dell;* akin to DALE]

del·la Rob·bia (dĕl'lä rôb'byä), **Luca** (lōō'kä). See **Robbia.**

de·lo·cal·ize (dē lō'kə līz'), *v.t.,* **-ized, -izing.** to remove from the proper or usual locality. —**de·lo'cal·i·za'tion,** *n.*

De·lorme (də lôrm'), *n.* **Philibert** (fē lē bĕr'), c1510-1570, French architect.

De·los (dē'lŏs), *n.* a tiny Greek island in the Cyclades, in the SW Aegean: the site of an oracle of Apollo.

de·louse (dē lous', -louz'), *v.t.,* **-loused, -lousing.** to free of lice; remove lice from.

Del·phi (dĕl'fī), *n.* an ancient city in central Greece, in Phocis: the site of an oracle of Apollo.

Del·phic (dĕl'fĭk), *adj.* **1.** pertaining to Delphi, to the temple and oracle of Apollo there, or to Apollo himself. **2.** ambiguous. Also, **Del·phi·an** (dĕl'fĭ ən). [t. L: s. *Delphicus,* t. Gk.: m. *Delphikós*]

Delphic oracle, the oracle of the temple of Apollo at Delphi which often gave ambiguous answers.

del·phi·nine (dĕl'fə nēn', -nĭn), *n. Chem.* a bitter, poisonous, crystalline alkaloid obtained from various species of larkspur, genus *Delphinium,* esp. *D. Staphisagria.* [f. DELPHIN(IUM) + -INE²]

del·phin·i·um (dĕl fĭn'ĭ əm), *n.* any of numerous garden varieties of ranunculaceous flowers, genus *Delphinium,* having handsome, usually blue, irregular flowers; larkspur. [t. NL, t. Gk.: m. *delphinion* larkspur, dim. of *delphín* dolphin; so called from the shape of the nectary]

Del·phi·nus (dĕl fī'nəs), *n., gen.* **-ni** (-nī). *Astron.* a northern constellation between Aquila and Pegasus. [t. L: dolphin]

Del·sarte (dĕl särt'; *Fr.* -sȧrt'), **François,** 1811-71, French musician and teacher.

Del·sar·ti·an (dĕl sär'tĭ ən), *adj.* pertaining to François Delsarte or to his system for developing bodily grace and improving musical and dramatic expression.

Del Sar·to (dĕl sär'tō), **Andrea** (än drē'ä). See **Sarto.**

---

b., blend of, blended; c., cognate with; d., dialect, dialectal; der., derived from; f., formed from; g., going back to; m., modification of; r., replacing; s., stem of; t., taken from; ?, perhaps. See the full key on inside cover.

del·ta (dĕl′tə), *n.* **1.** the fourth letter (Δ, δ, = English *D*, *d*) of the Greek alphabet. **2.** anything triangular, like the Greek capital Δ. **3.** a nearly flat plain of alluvial deposit between diverging branches of the mouth of a river, often, though not necessarily, triangular: *the delta of the Nile.*

del·ta·ic (dĕl tā′Ĭk), *adj.* **1.** forming a delta. **2.** having a delta.

del·toid (dĕl′toid), *n.* **1.** a large triangular muscle covering the joint of the shoulder and serving to raise the arm away from the side of the body. —*adj.* **2.** triangular. [t. Gk.: m. s. *deltoeidḗs* delta-shaped]

Deltoid leaf

de·lude (dĬ lōōd′), *v.t.,* **-lud·ed, -lud·ing. 1.** to mislead the mind or judgment of; deceive. **2.** *Obs.* to cheat the hopes of. **3.** *Obs.* to elude; evade. [t. L: m.s. *dēlūdere* play false] —**de·lud′er,** *n.* —Syn. **1.** beguile, cozen, dupe, cheat, defraud.

del·uge (dĕl′ūj), *n., v.,* **-uged, -ug·ing.** —*n.* **1.** a great overflowing of water; inundation; flood; downpour. **2.** anything that overwhelms like a flood. **3. the Deluge,** *Bible.* the great flood in the days of Noah. Gen. 7. —*v.t.* **4.** to flood; inundate. **5.** to overrun; overwhelm. [ME, t. OF, g. L *dīluvium*] —Syn. **1.** See **flood.** —Ant. **1.** drought. **2.** scarcity.

de·lu·sion (dĬ lōō′zhən), *n.* **1.** act of deluding. **2.** fact of being deluded. **3.** a false belief or opinion. **4.** *Psychiatry.* a fixed, dominating, or persistent false mental conception resistant to reason with regard to actual things or matters of fact: *a paranoiac delusion.* —**de·lu′sion·al,** *adj.* —Syn. **2.** See **illusion.**

de·lu·sive (dĬ lōō′sĬv), *adj.* **1.** tending to delude; deceptive. **2.** of the nature of a delusion; false; unreal. Also, **de·lu·so·ry** (dĬ lōō′sə rĬ). —**de·lu′sive·ly,** *adv.* —**de·lu′sive·ness,** *n.*

de luxe (də lŏoks′, lŭks′; *Fr.* də lŸks′), of special elegance, sumptuousness, or fineness. [t. F: of luxury]

delve (dĕlv), *v.,* **delved, delv·ing.** —*v.i.* **1.** to carry on intensive or thorough research for information, etc. **2.** *Archaic or Dial.* to dig, as with a spade. —*v.t.* **3.** *Archaic or Dial.* to dig. **4.** *Archaic.* to obtain by digging. [ME *delve(n),* OE *delfan,* c. D *delven*] —**delv′er,** *n.*

Dem., **1.** Democrat. **2.** Democratic.

de·mag·net·ize (dē măg′nə tīz′), *v.t.,* **-ized, -izing.** to remove magnetic properties from. —**de·mag′net·i·za′tion,** *n.* —**de·mag′net·iz′er,** *n.*

dem·a·gog·ic (dĕm′ə gŏj′Ĭk, -gŏg′Ĭk), *adj.* **1.** characteristic of a demagogue. **2.** of a demagogue. Also, **dem·a·gog′i·cal.**

dem·a·gogue (dĕm′ə gŏg′, -gôg′), *n.* **1.** a leader who uses the passions or prejudices of the populace for his own interests; an unprincipled popular orator or agitator. **2.** (historically) a leader of the people. Also, **dem·a·gog′.** [t. Gk.: m. s. *dēmagōgós,* f. s. *dêmos* people + *agōgós* leader]

dem·a·gogu·er·y (dĕm′ə gŏg′ər Ĭ, -gŏg′ər Ĭ), *n. Chiefly U.S.* the methods or practices of a demagogue.

dem·a·gogu·ism (dĕm′ə gŏg′Ĭzəm, -gôg′Ĭzəm), *n.* demagoguery. Also, **dem′a·gog′ism.**

dem·a·go·gy (dĕm′ə gō′jĬ, -gŏg′Ĭ, -gôg′Ĭ, -gô′jĬ), *n. Chiefly Brit.* **1.** demagoguery. **2.** the character of a demagogue. **3.** a body of demagogues.

de·mand (dĬ mănd′, -mänd′), *v.t.* **1.** to ask for with authority; claim as a right: *to demand something of or from a person.* **2.** to ask for peremptorily or urgently. **3.** to call for or require as just, proper, or necessary: *a task which demands patience.* **4.** *Law.* **a.** to lay formal legal claim to. **b.** to summon, as to court. —*v.i.* **5.** to make a demand; inquire or ask. —*n.* **6.** act of demanding. **7.** that which is demanded. **8.** an urgent or pressing requirement: *demands upon one's time.* **9.** an inquiry or question. **10.** a requisition; a legal claim. **11.** the state of being in request for purchase or use: *an article in great demand.* **12.** *Econ.* **a.** the desire to purchase and possess, coupled with the power of purchasing. **b.** the quantity of any goods which buyers will take at a particular price. See **supply.** **13. on demand,** subject to payment upon presentation and demand. [t. F: s. *demander,* g. L *dēmandāre* give in charge, intrust, ML demand] —**de·mand′a·ble,** *adj.* —**de·mand′er,** *n.* —Syn. **1.** DEMAND, CLAIM, REQUIRE imply making an authoritative request. To DEMAND is to ask in a bold, authoritative way: *to demand an explanation.* To CLAIM is to assert a right to something: *he claimed it as his due.* To REQUIRE is to ask for something as being necessary: to compel: *the Army requires absolute obedience of its soldiers.*

de·mand·ant (dĬ măn′dənt, -män′-), *n. Law.* **1.** the plaintiff in a real action. **2.** any plaintiff.

demand bill, draft, or **note,** a bill of exchange, note, etc., payable on demand or presentation.

demand deposit, *Banking.* a deposit withdrawable at the will of the depositor without prior notice.

demand loan, call loan.

de·mar·cate (dĬ mär′kāt, dē′mär kāt′), *v.t.,* **-cated, -cating. 1.** to mark off the boundaries of. **2.** to separate distinctly. [back formation from DEMARCATION]

de·mar·ca·tion (dē′mär kā′shən), *n.* **1.** the marking off of the boundaries of something. **2.** separation by distinct boundaries. **3.** the defining of boundaries. Also, **de′mar·ka′tion.** [Latinization of Sp. *demarcación,* der. *demarcar* mark out the bounds of]

dé·marche (dā märsh′), *n. French.* **1.** a plan or mode of procedure. **2.** a change in a course of action. [F, der. *démarcher* march]

de·ma·te·ri·al·ize (dē′mə tĬr′Ĭ ə līz′), *v.t., v.i.,* **-ized, -izing.** to deprive of or lose material character. —**de′ma·te′ri·al·i·za′tion,** *n.*

Dem·a·vend (dĕm′ə vĕnd′), *n.* a mountain′ peak of the Elburz Mountains in N Iran. 18,606 ft.

deme (dēm), *n.* one of the administrative divisions of ancient Attica and of modern Greece. [t. Gk.: m. s. *dêmos* district, country, people, commons]

de·mean[1] (dĬ mēn′), *v.t.* to lower in dignity or standing; debase. [f. DE- + MEAN[2], modeled on DEBASE]

de·mean[2] (dĬ mēn′), *v.t.* to conduct or behave (oneself) in a specified manner. [ME *demene(n),* t. OF: m. *demener,* f. de- DE- + *mener* lead, g. L *mināre* drive]

de·mean·or (dĬ mē′nər), *n.* conduct; behavior. Also, *Brit.,* **de·mean′our.** [ME *demenure,* der. *demene(n)* DEMEAN[2], v.]

de·ment (dĬ mĕnt′), *v.t.* to make mad or insane. [t. L: s. *dēmentāre* deprive of mind]

de·ment·ed (dĬ mĕn′tĬd), *adj.* out of one's mind; crazed; insane; affected with dementia. —**de·ment′ed·ly,** *adv.* —**de·ment′ed·ness,** *n.*

de·men·tia (dĬ mĕn′shə, -shĬ ə), *n. Pathol., Psychiatry.* a state of mental disorder characterized by impairment or loss of the mental powers; commonly an end result of several mental or other diseases. [t. L: madness]

dementia prae·cox (prē′kŏks), *Pathol., Psychiatry.* a form of insanity usually occurring or beginning at puberty and characterized by introversion, dissociation, and odd, distorted behavior. [t. L: precocious insanity]

de·mer·it (dē mĕr′Ĭt), *n.* **1.** censurable or punishable quality; fault. **2.** a mark against a person for misconduct or deficiency. **3.** *Obs.* merit or desert. [t. L: s. *dēmeritum* (in ML fault), prop. pp. neut. of *dēmerēri* deserve (esp. well)]

dem·e·rol (dĕm′ə rôl′, -rŏl′), *n.* **1.** a synthetic drug used as an analgesic and sedative. **2.** (*cap.*) a trademark for this drug.

de·mesne (dĬ mān′, -mēn′), *n.* **1.** possession (of land) as one's own. **2.** an estate possessed, or in the actual possession or use of the owner. **3.** the land attached to a manor house, reserved for the owner's use. **4.** the dominion or territory of a sovereign or state; a domain. **5.** a district; region. [ME *demeyne,* t. AF. See DOMAIN]

De·me·ter (dĬ mē′tər), *n. Gk. Myth.* the goddess of the fruitful earth, protectress of social order and marriage, identified by the Romans with Ceres. [t. L, t. Gk.]

demi-, a prefix meaning: **1.** half, as in *demiquaver.* **2.** inferior, as in *demigod.* [t. F: repr. *demi,* adj. (also n. and adv.), g. L *dīmedius,* r. *dīmidius* half]

dem·i·bas·tion (dĕm′Ĭ băs′chən), *n. Fort.* a work consisting of half a bastion, and hence having one face and one flank.

dem·i·god (dĕm′Ĭ gŏd′), *n.* **1.** one partly divine and partly human; an inferior deity. **2.** a deified mortal. —**dem·i·god·dess** (dĕm′Ĭ gŏd′Ĭs), *n. fem.*

dem·i·john (dĕm′Ĭ jŏn′), *n.* a large small-necked bottle, usually cased in wickerwork. [t. F: m. *dame-jeanne,* appar. a popular name, Dame Jane]

de·mil·i·ta·rize (dē mĬl′ə tə rīz′), *v.t.,* **-rized, -rizing. 1.** to deprive of military character; free from militarism. **2.** to place under civil instead of military control. —**de·mil′i·ta·ri·za′tion,** *n.*

dem·i·mon·daine (dĕm′Ĭ mŏn dān′; *Fr.* də mē môn-dĕn′), *n.* a woman of the demimonde. [t. F]

dem·i·monde (dĕm′Ĭ mŏnd′; *Fr.* də mē môN d′), *n.* the world or class of women who have become socially declassed, or of doubtful reputation and standing. [t. F: lit., half-world]

dem·i·pique (dĕm′Ĭ pēk′), *n.* an 18th century saddle having a peak about half the height of earlier styles. [f. DEMI- + *pique* (pseudo-F sp. of PEAK)]

dem·i·re·lief (dĕm′Ĭ rĬ lēf′), *n.* mezzo-rilievo.

dem·i·rep (dĕm′Ĭ rĕp′), *n.* a woman of doubtful or compromised reputation. [short for *demi-reputation*]

de·mise (dĬ mīz′), *n., v.,* **-mised, -mising.** —*n.* **1.** death or decease. **2.** *Law.* **a.** a death or decease occasioning the transfer of an estate. **b.** a conveyance or transfer of an estate. **3.** *Govt.* transfer of sovereignty, as by the death or deposition of the sovereign. —*v.t.* **4.** *Law.* to transfer (an estate, etc.) for a limited time; lease. **5.** *Govt.* to transfer (sovereignty), as by the death or abdication of the sovereign. —*v.i.* **6.** *Law.* to pass by bequest, inheritance, or succession to the Crown. [t. OF. prop. pp. fem. of *desmettre* send or put away. See DEMIT] —**de·mis′a·ble,** *adj.*

dem·i·sem·i·qua·ver (dĕm′Ĭ sĕm′Ĭ kwā′vər), *n. Music.* a note having half the time value of a semiquaver; a thirty-second note. See illus. under **note.**

de·mis·sion (dĬ mĬsh′ən), *n.* **1.** abdication. **2.** *Rare.* dismissal. [t. F. Cf. L *dīmissio* a sending away]

de·mit (dĬ mĬt′), *v.,* **-mitted, -mitting.** *Chiefly Scot.* —*v.t.* **1.** to give up, as a dignity or office; resign. **2.** *Archaic.* to dismiss. —*v.i.* **3.** to resign. [b. F *démettre* send or put away and L *dīmittere* send away]

dem·i·tasse (dĕm′Ĭ tăs′, -täs′; *Fr.* də mē täs′), *n.* **1.** a small cup for serving black coffee after dinner. **2.** the coffee contained in such a cup. [t. F: half cup]

dem·i·urge (dĕm′Ĭ ûrj′), *n.* **1.** *Philos.* **a.** (in Platonic philosophy) the artificer of the world. **b.** (in the Gnostic and certain other systems) a supernatural being imagined as creating or fashioning the world in subordination to the Supreme Being, and sometimes regarded as the originator of evil. **2.** (in many states of ancient Greece) a public official or magistrate. [t. Gk.: m. s. *dēmiourgós* worker for the people, artificer, maker] **—dem·i·ur·geous** (dĕm′Y ûr′jəs), **dem′i·ur′gic,** *adj.* **—dem′i·ur·gi·cal·ly,** *adv.*

dem·i·volt (dĕm′Y vōlt′), *n.* a half turn made by a horse with the forelegs raised. Also, **dem′i·volte′.** [t. F: m. *demi-volte*. See DEMI-, VOLT[1]]

demo-, a word element meaning "people," "population," "common people." [t. Gk., comb. form of *dēmos*]

de·mob (dē·mŏb′), *n., v.,* **-mobbed, -mobbing.** *Brit. Colloq.* **—n. 1.** demobilization. **2.** one who has been discharged from the army. **—v.t. 3.** to discharge (a soldier) from the army. [short for DEMOBILIZE]

de·mo·bi·lize (dē·mō′bə līz′), *v.t.,* **-lized, -lizing.** to disband (an army, etc.). **—de·mo′bi·li·za′tion,** *n.*

de·moc·ra·cy (dY·mŏk′rə sY), *n., pl.* **-cies. 1.** government by the people; a form of government in which the supreme power is vested in the people and exercised by them or by their elected agents under a free electoral system. **2.** a state having such a form of government. **3.** (in a restricted sense) a state in which the supreme power is vested in the people and exercised directly by them rather than by elected representatives. See **republic. 4.** a state of society characterized by formal equality of rights and privileges. **5.** political or social equality; democratic spirit. **6.** the common people of a community as distinguished from any privileged class; the common people with respect to their political power. **7.** (*cap.*) *U.S. Pol.* **a.** the principles of the Democratic party. **b.** the members of this party collectively. [t. F: m. *démocratie,* ult. t. Gk.: m. s. *dēmokratía* popular government, f. *dēmo-* DEMO- + *-kratía* rule, authority]

dem·o·crat (dĕm′ə krăt′), *n.* **1.** an advocate of democracy. **2.** one who maintains the political or social equality of men. **3.** (*cap.*) *U.S. Pol.* **a.** a member of the Democratic party. **b.** *Obs.* a member of the old Democratic-Republican party.

dem·o·crat·ic (dĕm′ə krăt′Yk), *adj.* **1.** pertaining to or of the nature of democracy or a democracy. **2.** pertaining to or characterized by the principle of political or social equality for all. **3.** advocating or upholding democracy. **4.** (*cap.*) *U.S. Pol.* **a.** of, pertaining to, or characteristic of the Democratic party. **b.** of, pertaining to, or belonging to the Democratic-Republican party. Also, **dem′o·crat′i·cal. —dem′o·crat′i·cal·ly,** *adv.*

Democratic party, one of the two major political parties in the U.S., founded in 1828.

Democratic-Republican party, *U.S. Hist.* a political party opposed to the old Federalist party.

de·moc·ra·tize (dY·mŏk′rə tīz′), *v.t., v.i.,* **-tized, -tizing.** to make or become democratic. **—de·moc′ra·ti·za′tion,** *n.*

De·moc·ri·tus (dY·mŏk′rə təs), *n.* ("*the Laughing Philosopher*") c460–c370 B.C., a Greek philosopher.

de·mod·ed (dē·mō′dYd), *adj.* no longer in fashion.

de·mod·u·late (dē·mŏj′ə lāt′), *v.t.,* **-lated, -lating.** *Radio.* detect (def. 4).

de·mod·u·la·tion (dē·mŏj′ə lā′shən), *n. Radio.* detection (def. 4b).

De·mo·gor·gon (dē′mə gôr′gən, dĕm′ə-), *n.* a vague, mysterious, infernal power or divinity of ancient mythology, variously represented, as an object of awe or fear. [t. LL, t. Gk. See DEMO-, GORGON]

de·mog·ra·phy (dY·mŏg′rə fY), *n.* the science of vital and social statistics, as of the births, deaths, diseases, marriages, etc., of populations. **—de·mog′ra·pher, de·mog′ra·phist,** *n.* **—de·mo·graph·ic** (dē′mə grăf′Yk), **de′mo·graph′i·cal,** *adj.* **—de′mo·graph′i·cal·ly,** *adv.*

dem·oi·selle (dĕm′wä zĕl′; *Fr.* də mwä zĕl′), *n.* **1.** a damsel. **2.** the Numidian crane, *Anthropoides virgo,* of northern Africa, Asia, and Europe, having long white plumes behind the eyes. **3.** any of various slender-bodied dragonflies. [F]

de·mol·ish (dY·mŏl′Ysh), *v.t.* **1.** to throw or pull down (a building, etc.); reduce to ruins. **2.** to put an end to; destroy; ruin utterly; lay waste. [t. F: m. *démoliss-,* s. *démolir,* t. L: m. *dēmōlīrī* throw down, destroy] **—de·mol′ish·er,** *n.* **—de·mol′ish·ment,** *n.* **—Syn. 2.** See **destroy. —Ant. 2.** restore.

dem·o·li·tion (dĕm′ə lYsh′ən, dē′mə-), *n.* **1.** act of demolishing. **2.** state of being demolished; destruction.

demolition bomb, *Mil.* a bomb containing a relatively large charge used to destroy material objects.

de·mon (dē′mən), *n.* **1.** an evil spirit; a devil. **2.** an evil passion or influence. **3.** an atrociously wicked or cruel person. **4.** a person of great energy, etc. **5.** daemon. [(defs. 1–4) used for L *daemonium,* t. Gk.: m. *daimónion* thing of divine nature (in Jewish and Christian writers, evil spirit); (def. 5) t. L: m. *daemon* spirit, evil spirit, t. Gk.: m. *daimōn* tutelary divinity, evil spirit]

demon-, a word element meaning "demon." [t. Gk., comb. form of *daimōn*]

de·mon·e·tize (dē·mŏn′ə tīz′, -mŭn′-), *v.t.,* **-tized, -tizing. 1.** to divest of value, as the monetary standard. **2.** to withdraw from use as money. **—de·mon′e·ti·za′tion,** *n.*

de·mo·ni·ac (dY·mō′nY ăk′), *adj.* Also, **de·mo·ni·a·cal** (dē′mə nī′ə kəl). **1.** of, pertaining to, or like a demon. **2.** possessed by an evil spirit; raging; frantic. **—n. 3.** one

seemingly possessed by a demon or evil spirit. [ME *demoniak,* t. LL: m.s. *daemoniacus,* t. Gk.: m. *daimoniakós*] **—de·mo·ni·a·cal·ly** (dē′mə nī′Yk lY), *adv.* **—Ant.** angelic.

de·mo·ni·an (dY·mō′nY ən), *adj.* pertaining to or of the nature of a demon.

de·mon·ic (dY·mŏn′Yk), *adj.* **1.** of, pertaining to, or of the nature of a demon. **2.** inspired as if by a demon, indwelling spirit, or genius. [t. L: m.s *daemonicus,* t. Gk.: m. *daimonikós*]

de·mon·ism (dē′mə nYz′əm), *n.* **1.** belief in demons. **2.** worship of demons. **3.** demonology. **—de′mon·ist,** *n.*

de·mon·ize (dē′mə nīz′), *v.t.,* **-ized, -izing. 1.** to turn into or make like a demon. **2.** to subject to the influence of demons.

demono-, var. of **demon-,** before consonants.

de·mon·o·la·ter (dē′mə nŏl′ə tər), *n.* a demon worshiper.

de·mon·o·la·try (dē′mə nŏl′ə trY), *n.* the worship of demons.

de·mon·ol·o·gy (dē′mə nŏl′ə jY), *n.* **1.** the study of demons or of beliefs about demons. **2.** the doctrine of demons. **—de′mon·ol′o·gist,** *n.*

de·mon·stra·ble (dY·mŏn′strə bəl, dĕm′ən-), *adj.* capable of being demonstrated. **—de·mon′stra·bil′i·ty, de·mon′stra·ble·ness,** *n.* **—de·mon′stra·bly,** *adv.*

de·mon·strant (dY·mŏn′strənt), *n.* demonstrator.

dem·on·strate (dĕm′ən strāt′), *v.,* **-strated, -strating. —v.t. 1.** to make evident by arguments or reasoning; prove. **2.** to describe and explain with the help of specimens or by experiment. **3.** to manifest or exhibit. **—v.i. 4.** to make, give, or take part in, a demonstration. **5.** *Mil.* to attack or make a show of force to deceive the enemy. [t. L: m. s. *dēmonstrātus,* pp., showed, proved]

dem·on·stra·tion (dĕm′ən strā′shən), *n.* **1.** the proving of anything conclusively, as by arguments, reasoning, evidence, etc. **2.** proof, or anything serving as a proof. **3.** a description or explanation, as of a process, given with the help of specimens or by experiment. **4.** act of exhibiting and explaining an article or commodity by way of advertising it. **5.** an exhibition, as of feeling; a display; manifestation. **6.** a public exhibition of sympathy, opposition, etc., as a parade or mass meeting. **7.** a show of military force or of offensive operations, made to deceive the enemy. **8.** *Math.* a logical presentation of the way in which given assumptions imply a certain result. **—dem′on·stra′tion·al,** *adj.* **—dem′on·stra′tion·ist,** *n.*

de·mon·stra·tive (dY·mŏn′strə tYv), *adj.* **1.** characterized by or given to open exhibition or expression of the feelings, etc. **2.** serving to demonstrate; explanatory or illustrative. **3.** serving to prove the truth of anything; indubitably conclusive. **4.** *Gram.* indicating or specifying the thing referred to. **—n. 5.** *Gram.* a demonstrative word, as *this* or *there.* **—de·mon′stra·tive·ly,** *adv.* **—de·mon′stra·tive·ness,** *n.*

dem·on·stra·tor (dĕm′ən strā′tər), *n.* **1.** one who or that which demonstrates. **2.** Also, **demonstrant.** one who takes part in a public demonstration. **3.** one who explains or teaches by practical demonstrations.

de·mor·al·ize (dY·môr′ə līz′, -mŏr′-), *v.t.,* **-ized, -izing. 1.** to corrupt or undermine the morals of. **2.** to deprive (a person, a body of soldiers, etc.) of spirit, courage, discipline, etc. **3.** to reduce to a state of weakness or disorder. [t. F: m.s. *démoraliser*] **—de·mor′al·i·za′tion,** *n.* **—de·mor′al·iz′er,** *n.*

De Mor·gan (dĕ môr′gən), **William Frend,** 1839–1917, British novelist and artist in stained glass and ceramics.

de mor·tu·is nil ni·si bo·num (dē môr′chŏŏ Ys nYl nī′sī bō′nəm), *Latin.* of the dead say nothing but good.

de·mos (dē′mŏs), *n.* **1.** the people or commons of an ancient Greek state. **2.** the common people; the populace. [t. Gk.: district, people]

De·mos·the·nes (dY·mŏs′thə nēz′), *n.* 384?–322 B.C., Athenian statesman and orator.

de·mote (dY·mōt′), *v.t.,* **-moted, -moting.** to reduce to a lower grade or class (opposed to *promote*). [f. DE- + *-mote,* modeled on PROMOTE]**—de·mo′tion,** *n.*

de·mot·ic (dY·mŏt′Yk), *adj.* **1.** of or pertaining to the common people; popular. **2.** noting or pertaining to the ancient Egyptian handwriting of ordinary life, a simplified form of the hieratic characters. [t. Gk.: m. s. *dēmotikós* popular, plebeian]

de·mot·ics (dY·mŏt′Yks), *n.* sociology.

de·mount (dē·mount′), *v.t.* to remove from its mounting, setting, or place of support, as a gun. **—de·mount′a·ble,** *adj.*

demp·ster (dĕmp′stər), *n.* deemster.

de·mul·cent (dY·mŭl′sənt), *adj.* **1.** soothing or mollifying, as a medicinal substance. **—n. 2.** a demulcent (often mucilaginous) substance or agent, as for soothing or protecting an irritated mucous membrane. [t. L: s. *dēmulcens,* ppr., stroking down, softening]

de·mur (dY·mûr′), *v.,* **-murred, -murring,** *n.* **—v.i. 1.** to make objection; take exception; object. **2.** *Law.* to interpose a demurrer. **3.** *Obs.* to linger; hesitate. **—n. 4.** act of making objection. **5.** an objection raised. **6.** *Obs., Law.* a demurrer. **7.** *Obs.* hesitation. [ME *demeore(n),* t. OF: m. *demeurer,* g. L *dēmorārī* linger] **—Ant. 1.** agree, accede.

de·mure (dY·myŏŏr′), *adj.,* **-murer, -murest. 1.** affectedly or unnaturally modest, decorous, or prim. **2.** sober;

serious; sedate; decorous. [ME, der. *mure* grave, discreet, t. OF: m. *meur*, g. L *mātūrus* MATURE]—**de-mure′ly**, *adv.* —**de-mure′ness**, *n.* —**Syn.** 1. See **modest.**

de·mur·rage (dǐ mûr′Ij), *n. Com.* 1. the detention of a vessel, as in loading or unloading, beyond the time agreed upon. 2. the similar detention of a railroad car, etc. 3. a charge for such detention.

de·mur·ral (dǐ mûr′əl), *n.* act of demurring; demur.

de·mur·rer (dǐ mûr′ər), *n.* 1. one who demurs; an objector. 2. *Law.* a pleading in effect that even if the facts are as alleged by the opposite party, they do not sustain the contention based on them. 3. an objection or demur. [t. AF, var. of OF *demourer*. See DEMUR]

de·my (dǐ mī′), *n.*, *pl.* **-mies.** 1. a foundation scholar at Magdalen College, Oxford (so called because orig. receiving half the allowance of a fellow). 2. a particular size of paper, 16 × 21 inches in America, 17½ × 22 inches in Great Britain. [free form of DEMI-, with change of final *i* to *y* in accordance with rules of English spelling]

den (dĕn), *n.*, *v.*, **denned, denning.** —*n.* 1. a retired place, as a cave, serving as the habitation of a beast. 2. a cave as a place of shelter, concealment, etc. 3. a squalid or vile abode or place: *dens of misery.* 4. a cozy or retired room for personal use. —*v.i.* 5. to live in or as in a den. [ME; OE *denn.* Cf. early mod. D *denne* floor, cave, den, G *tenne* floor]

Den., Denmark.

de·nar·i·us (dǐ nâr′Ĭ əs), *n.*, *pl.* **-narii** (-nâr′Ĭ ī′). 1. a Roman silver coin of varying intrinsic value. 2. (in English monetary reckoning) a penny. [t. L, orig. adj., containing ten (asses). See DENARY]

den·a·ry (dĕn′ə rǐ, dē′nə-), *adj.* 1. containing ten; tenfold. 2. proceeding by tens; decimal. [t. L: m. s. *dēnārius* containing ten, der. *dēnī* ten at a time]

de·na·tion·al·ize (dē nāsh′ən ə līz′), *v.t.*, **-ized, -izing.** to deprive of national status, attachments, or characteristics. —**de·na′tion·al·i·za′tion,** *n.*

de·nat·u·ral·ize (dē năch′ər ə līz′), *v.t.*, **-ized, -izing.** 1. to deprive of the original nature; make unnatural. 2. to deprive of the rights and privileges of citizenship or of naturalization. —**de·nat′u·ral·i·za′tion,** *n.*

de·na·ture (dē nā′chər), *v.t.*, **-tured, -turing.** 1. to deprive of its peculiar nature. 2. to render (alcohol, etc.) unfit for drinking or eating, as by adding an unwholesome substance, without altering the usefulness for other purposes. 3. *Biochem.* to treat, as a protein, by chemical or physical means so as to alter its original state. —**de·na′tur·ant,** *n.* —**de·na′tur·a′tion,** *n.*

de·na·tur·ize (dē nā′chər īz′), *v.t.*, **-ized, -izing.** to denature. —**de·na′tur·i·za′tion,** *n.*

de·na·zi·fy (dē năt′sə fī′, -năt′-), *v.t.*, **-fied, -fying.** to rid of Nazism or Nazi influences. —**de·na′zi·fi·ca′tion,** *n.*

Den·bigh·shire (dĕn′bǐ shĭr′, -shər), *n.* a county in N Wales. 165,000 pop. (est. 1946); 669 sq. mi. *Co. seat:* Denbigh. Also, **Den′high.**

dendr-, var. of dendro-, before vowels.

den·dri·form (dĕn′drə fôrm′), *adj.* treelike in form. [DENDR- +(I)FORM]

den·drite (dĕn′drīt), *n.* 1. *Geol.* **a.** a branching figure or marking, resembling moss or a shrub or tree in form, found on or in certain stones or minerals, and due to the presence of a foreign material. **b.** any arborescent crystalline growth. 2. *Anat., Physiol.* the branching portion of a neuron which picks up the stimulus and transmits it to the cyton. See diag. under **neuron.** [t. Gk.: m. s. *dendrītēs* of a tree]

Dendrite (def. 1a)

den·drit·ic (dĕn drĭt′Ĭk), *adj.* 1. formed or marked like a dendrite. 2. of a branching form; arborescent. Also, **den′drit′i·cal.** —**den·drit′i·cal·ly,** *adv.*

dendro-, a word element meaning "tree," as in *dendrology.* [t. Gk., comb. form of *dĕndron*]

den·droid (dĕn′droid), *adj.* treelike; branching like a tree; arborescent. Also, **den·droi′dal.** [t. Gk.: m. s. *dendroeidēs* treelike]

den·drol·a·try (dĕn drŏl′ə trĭ), *n.* the worship of trees.

den·drol·o·gy (dĕn drŏl′ə jĭ), *n.* the part of botany that treats of trees and shrubs. —**den·dro·log·i·cal** (dĕn′drə lŏj′ə kəl), **den·drol·o·gous** (dĕn drŏl′ə gəs), *adj.* —**den·drol·o·gist** (dĕn drŏl′ə jist), *n.*

-dendron, a word element meaning "tree," as in *rhododendron.* [repr. Gk. *dĕndron* tree]

dene (dēn), *n. Brit.* a bare sandy tract or low sand hill near the sea. Also, **dean.** [orig. uncert.]

Den·eb (dĕn′ĕb), *n. Astron.* a star of the first magnitude in the constellation Cygnus. [t. Ar.: m. *dhanab* tail]

den·e·ga·tion (dĕn′ə gā′shən), *n.* denial; contradiction. [t. LL: s. *dēnegātiō*]

den·gue (dĕng′gā, -gǐ), *n. Pathol.* an infectious, eruptive, usually epidemic fever of warm climates, characterized esp. by severe pains in the joints and muscles; breakbone fever. [t. Sp.; ? of African orig.]

Den·ham (dĕn′əm), *n.* **Sir John,** 1615–69, British poet, born in Ireland.

de·ni·al (dǐ nī′əl), *n.* 1. contradiction of a statement, etc. 2. refusal to believe a doctrine, etc. 3. disbelief in the existence or reality of a thing. 4. the refusal of a claim, request, etc., or of a person making a request. 5. refusal to recognize or acknowledge; a disowning or disavowal. 6. self-denial. [f. DENY + -AL³]

de·nic·o·tin·ize (dē nĭk′ə tǐ nīz′), *v.t.*, **-ized, -izing.** to remove nicotine from (tobacco).

de·ni·er¹ (dǐ nī′ər), *n.* one who denies. [f. DENY + -ER¹]

de·nier² (də nĭr′; *Fr.* də nyĕ′), *n.* 1. a unit of weight used to indicate the fineness of silk, rayon, or nylon yarn. 2. an obsolete French coin varying in value with time and locality. [t. OF, g. L *dēnārius* DENARIUS]

den·i·grate (dĕn′ə grāt′), *v.t.*, **-grated, -grating.** 1. to sully; defame. 2. to blacken. [t. L: m. s. *dēnigrātus*, pp., blackened] —**den′i·gra′tion,** *n.* —**den′i·gra′tor,** *n.*

De·ni·ker (dĕ nē′kĕr′), **Joseph** (zhô zĕf′), 1852–1918, French anthropologist and naturalist.

den·im (dĕn′əm), *n.* 1. a heavy twilled cotton for overalls, playsuits, etc. 2. a similar fabric of a finer quality used to make cushions, etc. [t. F: short for *serge de Nîmes* serge of Nîmes, city in southern France]

Den·is (dĕn′Ĭs; *Fr.* də nē′), *n.* **Saint,** died A.D. 280?, missionary bishop of Paris; patron saint of France. Also, **Denys.**

de·ni·trate (dē nī′trāt), *v.t.*, **-trated, -trating.** to free from nitric acid or nitrates; remove oxides of nitrogen from. —**de/ni·tra′tion,** *n.*

de·ni·tri·fy (dē nī′trə fī′), *v.t.*, **-fied, -fying.** to reduce (nitrates) to nitrites, ammonia, and free nitrogen, as in soil by microörganisms. —**de·ni′tri·fi·ca′tion,** *n.*

den·i·zen (dĕn′ə zən), *n.* 1. an inhabitant; resident. 2. *Brit.* an alien admitted to residence and to certain rights of citizenship in a country. 3. anything adapted to a new place, condition, etc., as a naturalized foreign word, or an animal or plant not indigenous to a place but successfully naturalized. —*v.t.* 4. to make a denizen of. [ME *deynseyn*, t. AF, m. *deinzein*, der. AF *deinz* within, der. L *intus*]

Den·mark (dĕn′märk), *n.* a kingdom in N Europe, on Jutland peninsula and the adjacent islands. 4,077,747 pop. (est. 1946); 16,576 sq. mi. *Cap.:* Copenhagen.

Denmark Strait, a strait between Iceland and Greenland. 130 mi. wide.

Den·nis (dĕn′Ĭs), *n.* **John,** 1657–1734, British critic and dramatist.

de·nom·i·nate (dǐ nŏm′ə nāt′), *v.t.*, **-nated, -nating.** to give a name to, esp. to call by a specific name. [t. L: m. s. *dēnōminātus*, pp.]

de·nom·i·na·tion (dǐ nŏm′ə nā′shən), *n.* 1. a name or designation, esp. one for a class of things. 2. a class or kind of persons or things distinguished by a specific name. 3. a religious sect. 4. act of denominating. 5. one of the grades or degrees in a series of designations of quantity, value, measure, weight, etc.: *money of small denominations.* —**de·nom′i·na′tion·al,** *adj.* —**de·nom′-i·na′tion·al·ly,** *adv.*

de·nom·i·na·tion·al·ism (dǐ nŏm′ə nā′shən ə lĭz′əm), *n.* denominational or sectarian spirit or policy; the tendency to divide into denominations or sects. —**de·nom′-i·na·tion·al·ist,** *n.*

de·nom·i·na·tive (dǐ nŏm′ə nā′tĭv, -nə tĭv), *adj.* 1. conferring or constituting a distinctive denomination or name. 2. *Gram.* (esp. of verbs) formed from a noun, as English *to man* from the noun *man.* —*n.* 3. *Gram.* a denominative verb or other word.

de·nom·i·na·tor (dǐ nŏm′ə nā′tər), *n.* 1. *Math.* that term of a fraction (usually under the line) which shows the number of equal parts into which the unit is divided; a divisor placed under a dividend. 2. one who or that which denominates or from which a name is derived.

de·no·ta·tion (dē′nō tā′shən), *n.* 1. the meaning of a term when it identifies something by naming it (distinguished from *connotation*). 2. act or fact of denoting; indication. 3. something that denotes; a mark; symbol. 4. *Logic.* **a.** the class of particulars to which a term is applicable. **b.** that which is represented by a sign.

de·no·ta·tive (dǐ nō′tə tĭv, dē′nō tā′tĭv), *adj.* having power to denote. —**de·no′ta·tive·ly,** *adv.*

de·note (dǐ nōt′), *v.t.*, **-noted, -noting.** 1. to be a mark or sign of; indicate: *a quick pulse often denotes fever.* 2. to be a name or designation for. 3. to represent by a symbol; stand as a symbol for. [t. F: m.s. *dēnoter,* t. L: m. *dēnōtāre* mark out] —**de·not′a·ble,** *adj.*

de·noue·ment (dā′nōō mäN′), *n.* 1. the final disentangling of the intricacies of a plot, as of a drama or novel. 2. the place in the plot at which this occurs. 3. outcome; solution. Also, *French,* **dé·noue·ment** (dē-nōō mäN′). [t. F, der. *dénouer* untie, f. *de-* DE- + *nouer,* g. L *nōdāre* knot, tie]

de·nounce (dǐ nouns′), *v.t.*, **-nounced, -nouncing.** 1. to condemn openly; assail with censure. 2. to make formal accusation against; inform against. 3. to give formal notice of the termination of (a treaty, etc.). 4. *Archaic.* to announce or proclaim (something evil). 5. *Obs.* to portend. [ME *denounse*(n), t. OF: m. *denoncier,* g. L *dēnuntiāre* threaten] —**de·nounce′ment,** *n.* —**de·nounc′er,** *n.* —**Ant.** 1. See **praise.**

de no·vo (dē nō′vō), *Latin.* from the beginning; anew.

dense (dĕns), *adj.*, **denser, densest.** 1. having the component parts closely compacted together; compact;

a dense forest, dense population, dense style. **2.** thick-headed; obtuse; stupid. **3.** intense: *dense ignorance.* **4.** *Photog.* (of a developed negative) relatively opaque; transmitting little light. [t. L: m. s. *densus* thick, thickly set] **—dense′ly,** *adv.* **—dense′ness,** *n.*

den·si·tom·e·ter (dĕn′sə tŏm′ə tər), *n.* *Photog.* an instrument for measuring the denseness of negatives.

den·si·ty (dĕn′sə tŭ), *n., pl.* **-ties.** **1.** state or quality of being dense; compactness; closely set or crowded condition. **2.** stupidity. **3.** *Physics.* the mass per unit of volume. **4.** *Elect.* **a.** the quantity of electricity per unit of volume at a point in space, or the quantity per unit of area at a point on a surface. **b.** current density.

dent[1] (dĕnt), *n.* **1.** a hollow or depression in a surface, as from a blow. **—v.t.** **2.** to make a dent in or on; indent. **3.** to impress as a dent. **—v.i.** **4.** to sink in, making a dent. **5.** to become indented. [ME *dente*; var. of DINT]

dent[2] (dĕnt), *n.* a toothlike projection, as a tooth of a gear wheel. [t. F, g. L *dens* tooth]

dent., **1.** dentist. **2.** dentistry.

den·tal (dĕn′təl), *adj.* **1.** of or pertaining to the teeth. **2.** of or pertaining to dentistry. **3.** *Phonet.* **a.** with the tongue tip touching or near the upper front teeth, as French *t.* **b.** alveolar, as English alveolar *t.* **—n.** **4.** *Phonet.* a dental sound. [t. ML: s. *dentālis,* der. L *dens* tooth]

den·tate (dĕn′tāt), *adj.* *Bot., Zool.* having a toothed margin, or toothlike projections or processes. [t. L: m. s. *dentātus,* der. *dens* tooth] **—den′tate·ly,** *adv.*

den·ta·tion (dĕn tā′shən), *n.* *Bot., Zool.* **1.** dentate state or form. **2.** an angular projection of a margin.

denti-, a word element meaning "tooth," as in *dentiform.* Also, before vowels, **dent-.** [t. L, comb. form of *dens*]

Dentate leaf

den·ti·cle (dĕn′tə kəl), *n.* a small tooth or toothlike part. [ME, t. L: m. s. *denticulus,* dim. of *dens* tooth]

den·tic·u·late (dĕn tĭk′yə lĭt, -lāt′), *adj.* **1.** *Bot., Zool.* finely dentate, as a leaf. **2.** *Archit.* having dentils. Also, **den·tic′u·lat′ed.** **—den·tic′u·late·ly,** *adv.*

den·tic·u·la·tion (dĕn tĭk′yə lā′shən), *n.* **1.** denticulate state or form. **2.** a denticle. **3.** a series of denticles.

den·ti·form (dĕn′tə fôrm′), *adj.* having the form of a tooth; tooth-shaped.

den·ti·frice (dĕn′tə frĭs), *n.* a powder, paste, or other preparation for cleaning the teeth. [t. F, t. L: m. s. *dentifricium* tooth powder. See DENTI-, FRICTION]

den·til (dĕn′təl, -tĭl), *n.* *Archit.* one of a series of small rectangular blocks arranged like a row of teeth, as in the lower part of a cornice. [t. F: m. *dentille* (obs.), fem. dim. of *dent* tooth]

den·ti·la·bi·al (dĕn′tə lā′bĭ əl), *adj., n.* labiodental.

den·ti·lin·gual (dĕn′tə lĭng′gwəl), *adj.* (of speech sounds) uttered with the tongue at the teeth, as the *th* in *thin* and *this.*

den·tin (dĕn′tĭn), *n.* *Anat.* the hard calcareous tissue beneath the enamel of the crown of the tooth and beneath the cementum of the root of the tooth. It contains less organic substance than cementum or bone and forms the greatest part of a tooth. Also, **den·tine** (dĕn′tēn, -tĭn). [f. DENT- + -INE[2]] **—den′tin·al,** *adj.*

den·ti·phone (dĕn′tə fōn′), *n.* an instrument held against the teeth to assist hearing by transmitting sound vibrations to the auditory nerve.

den·tist (dĕn′tĭst), *n.* one whose profession is dentistry. [t. F: m. *dentiste,* der. *dent* tooth]

den·tist·ry (dĕn′tĭs trĭ), *n.* the science or art dealing with the prevention and treatment of oral disease, esp. in relation to the health of the body as a whole, and including such operations as the filling and crowning of teeth, the construction of artificial dentures, etc.

den·ti·tion (dĕn tĭsh′ən), *n.* the kind, number, and arrangement of the teeth of an animal, including man. [t. L: s. *dentītio* teething]

D'En·tre·cas·teaux Islands (dän trə kàs tō′), a group of British islands in the Pacific, E of New Guinea.

den·ture (dĕn′chər), *n.* an artificial restoration of several teeth (**partial denture**) or of all the teeth of either jaw (**full denture**). [t. F, der. *dent* tooth]

den·u·date (*v.* dĕn′yŏŏ dāt′, dĭ nū′dāt, -nōō′-; *adj.* dĭ-nū′dāt -nōō′-, dĕn′yŏŏ dāt′), *v.,* **-dated, -dating,** *adj.* **—v.t.** **1.** to denude. **—adj.** **2.** denuded; bare.

den·u·da·tion (dĕn′yŏŏ dā′shən, dē′nyŏŏ-, -nŏŏ-), *n.* **1.** act of denuding. **2.** denuded or bare condition. **3.** *Geol.* the laying bare of rock by erosive processes.

de·nude (dĭ nūd′, -nōōd′), *v.t.,* **-nuded, -nuding.** **1.** to make naked or bare; strip. **2.** *Geol.* to subject to denudation. [t. L: m. s. *dēnūdāre* lay bare]

de·nun·ci·ate (dĭ nŭn′sĭ āt′, -shĭ āt′), *v.t., v.i.,* **-ated, -ating.** to denounce; condemn openly. [t. L: m. s. *dē-nuntiātus,* pp.] **—de·nun′ci·a′tor,** *n.*

de·nun·ci·a·tion (dĭ nŭn′sĭ ā′shən, -shĭ-), *n.* **1.** a denouncing as evil; open and vehement condemnation. **2.** an accusation of crime before a public prosecutor or tribunal. **3.** notice of the termination of an international agreement or part thereof. **4.** announcement of impending evil; threat; warning.

de·nun·ci·a·to·ry (dĭ nŭn′sĭ ə tōr′ĭ, -shĭ-), *adj.* characterized by or given to denunciation. Also, **de·nun′ci·a·tive** (dĭ nŭn′sĭ ā′tĭv, -shĭ-).

Den·ver (dĕn′vər), *n.* the capital of Colorado, in the central part. 415,786 (1950).

de·ny (dĭ nī′), *v.t.,* **-nied, -nying.** **1.** to assert the negative of; declare not to be true: *I deny the charge, I deny he has done it.* **2.** to refuse to believe (a doctrine, etc.); reject as false or erroneous. **3.** to refuse to grant (a claim, request, etc.): *he denied me this, I was denied this.* **4.** to refuse to recognize or acknowledge; disown; disavow; repudiate. **5.** to refuse access to (one visited). **6.** *Obs.* to refuse to accept. **7.** *Obs.* to refuse (to do something). **8. deny oneself,** to exercise self-denial. [ME *deny(n),* t. F: m. *dénier,* g. L *dēnegāre*]

—Syn. 1. dispute, controvert, oppose, gainsay. DENY, CONTRADICT both imply objecting to or arguing against something. To DENY is to say that something is not true, or that it would not hold in practice: *to deny an allegation.* To CONTRADICT is to declare that the contrary is true: *to contradict a statement.* **—Ant. 1.** admit. **2.** accept. **3.** allow.

Den·ys (dĕn′ĭs; *Fr.* da nē′), *n.* **Saint.** See **Denis.**

de·o·dand (dē′ə dănd′), *n.* *Eng. Law.* (formerly) an animal or article, which, having been the immediate occasion of the death of a human being, was forfeited to the crown to be applied to pious uses. [t. ML: s. *deōdandum* a thing to be given to God, f. L: dat. of *deus* god + neut. gerundive of *dare* give]

de·o·dar (dē′ə där′), *n.* a species of cedar, *Cedrus deodara,* a large Himalayan tree valued for its beauty and for its durable wood. [t. Hind., g. Skt. *devadāra* wood of the gods]

de·o·dor·ant (dē ō′dər ənt), *n.* **1.** an agent for destroying odors. **—adj.** **2.** capable of destroying odors.

de·o·dor·ize (dē ō′də rīz′), *v.t.,* **-ized, -izing.** to deprive of odor, esp. of the fetid odor arising from impurities. **—de·o′dor·i·za′tion,** *n.* **—de·o′dor·iz′er,** *n.*

De·o fa·ven·te (dē′ō fə vĕn′tĭ), *Latin.* God favoring (befriending, protecting).

De·o gra·ti·as (dē′ō grā′shĭ ăs), *Latin.* thanks be to God.

De·o ju·van·te (dē′ō jŏŏ văn′tĭ), *Latin.* God helping; if God gives aid.

de·on·tol·o·gy (dē′ŏn tŏl′ə jĭ), *n.* the science of duty or moral obligation; ethics. [f. Gk.: s. *déon* that which is binding or needful (prop. ppr. neut. of *dein* bind) + -(o)LOGY] **—de·on·to·log·i·cal** (dĭ ŏn′tə lŏj′ə kəl), *adj.* **—de·on′tol·o·gist,** *n.*

De·o vo·len·te (dē′ō vō lĕn′tĭ), *Latin.* God willing (it); if God wills it.

de·ox·i·dize (dē ŏk′sə dīz′), *v.t.,* **-dized, -dizing.** to remove oxygen from; reduce from the state of an oxide. **—de·ox′i·di·za′tion,** *n.* **—de·ox′i·diz′er,** *n.*

de·ox·y·gen·ate (dē ŏk′sə jə nāt′), *v.t.,* **-ated, -ating.** to remove oxygen from. **—de·ox′y·gen·a′tion,** *n.*

de·ox·y·gen·ize (dē ŏk′sə jə nīz′), *v.t.,* **-ized, -izing.** to deoxygenate.

dep., **1.** department. **2.** departs. **3.** deponent. **4.** deputy.

de·part (dĭ pärt′), *v.i.* **1.** to go away, as from a place; take one's leave. **2.** to turn aside or away; diverge; deviate (fol. by *from*). **3.** to pass away, as from life or existence. **—v.t.** **4.** to go away from or leave: *rare,* except in *to depart this life.* **—n.** **5.** *Obs.* departure; death. [ME *departe(n),* t. OF: m. *departir,* f. de- DE- + *partir* leave (g. L *partīre*)]

—Syn. 1. DEPART, RETIRE, RETREAT, WITHDRAW imply leaving a place. DEPART is a somewhat literary word, implying going away from a definite place: *to depart on a journey.* RETIRE emphasizes the reason or purpose for absenting oneself or drawing back from a place: *to retire from a position (in battle).* RETREAT implies a necessary withdrawal, esp. as a result of adverse fortune in war: *to retreat to secondary lines of defense.* WITHDRAW suggests leaving some specific place or situation, usually for some definite, and often unpleasant reason: *to withdraw from a hopeless task.* **—Ant. 1.** arrive.

de·part·ed (dĭ pär′tĭd), *adj.* **1.** deceased; dead. **2.** gone; past. **—n. 3. the departed, a.** the dead person. **b.** the dead collectively.

de·part·ment (dĭ pärt′mənt), *n.* **1.** a distinct part of anything arranged in divisions; a division of a complex whole or organized system. **2.** a division of official business or duties or functions. **3.** one of the (large) districts into which a country, as France, is divided for administrative purposes. **4.** one of the principal branches of a governmental organization. **5.** one of the sections of a school or college dealing with a particular field of knowledge: *the department of English.* **6.** *Mil.* **a.** a permanent military area, corresponding to the limits of a territory: *the Hawaiian department.* **b.** (formerly) one of the large geographical divisions of the United States as divided for military purposes. **—de·part·men·tal,** (dē′pärt mĕn′təl), *adj.* **—de′part·men′tal·ly,** *adv.*

department store, a large retail store handling several lines of goods, including dry goods, women's wear, etc., and organized in separate departments.

de·par·ture (dĭ pär′chər), *n.* **1.** a going away; a setting out or starting. **2.** divergence or deviation. **3.** *Naut.* **a.** the distance due east or west made by a ship when sailing on any course. **b.** the bearing or position of a point from which a vessel commences dead reckoning. **4.** *Archaic.* decease or death.

de·pas·ture (dĭ păs′chər, -päs′-), *v.,* **-tured, -turing.** **—v.t.** **1.** to consume the produce of (land) as pasture. **2.** to pasture (cattle). **—v.i. 3.** to graze.

de·pend (dĭ pĕnd′), *v.i.* **1.** to rely; trust: *you may depend on the accuracy of the report.* **2.** to rely for support,

---

b., blend of, blended; **c.,** cognate with; **d.,** dialect, dialectal; **der.,** derived from; **f.,** formed from; **g.,** going back to; **m.,** modification of; **r.,** replacing; **s.,** stem of; **t.,** taken from; **?,** perhaps. See the full key on inside cover.

maintenance, help, etc.: *children depend on their parents.*
3. to be conditioned or contingent: *it depends upon himself, his efforts, his knowledge.* **4.** *Gram.* (of a word or other linguistic form) to be subordinate (to another linguistic form in the same construction). **5.** to hang down; be suspended. **6.** to be undetermined or pending. [ME *depend(en)*, t. OF: m. *dependre*, t. L: m. *dēpendere* hang upon]

de·pend·a·ble (dĭ pĕn′də bəl), *adj.* that may be depended on; reliable; trustworthy. —**de·pend′a·bil′i·ty, de·pend′a·ble·ness,** *n.* —**de·pend′a·bly,** *adv.*

de·pend·ence (dĭ pĕn′dəns), *n.* **1.** state of depending for aid, support, etc. **2.** reliance; confidence; trust. **3.** state of being conditional or contingent on something; natural or logical sequence. **4.** subordination or subjection: *the dependence of the church upon the state.* **5.** an object of reliance or trust. **6.** the condition, as of a lawsuit, of awaiting settlement. Also, **de·pend′ance.**

de·pend·en·cy (dĭ pĕn′dən sĭ), *n., pl.* **-cies. 1.** state of being dependent; dependence. **2.** something dependent or subordinate; an appurtenance. **3.** an outbuilding or annex. **4.** a subject territory which is not an integral part of the ruling country. Also, **de·pend′an·cy.**

de·pend·ent (dĭ pĕn′dənt), *adj.* **1.** depending on something else for aid, support, etc. **2.** conditioned; contingent. **3.** subordinate; subject. **4.** (of linguistic forms) not used in isolation; used only in connection with other forms. **5.** hanging down; pendent. —*n.* **6.** one who depends on or looks to another for support, favor, etc. **7.** *Obs.* a subordinate part. Also, **de·pend′ant.**

De·pew (də pū′), *n.* **Chauncey Mitchell** (chôn′sĭ, chän′sĭ), 1834–1928, U.S. lawyer and politician.

de·phlo·gis·ti·cat·ed (dē′flə jĭs′tə kā′tĭd), *adj. Obs.* lacking phlogiston.

de·pict (dĭ pĭkt′), *v.t.* **1.** to represent by or as by painting; portray; delineate. **2.** to represent in words; describe. [t. L: s. *dēpictus,* pp., portrayed] —**de·pict′-er,** *n.* —**de·pic′tion,** *n.*

—**Syn. 1, 2.** DEPICT, PORTRAY, SKETCH imply an actual reproduction of an object or scene by colors or lines, or by words. DEPICT emphasizes vividness of detail: *to depict the confusion of departure.* PORTRAY emphasizes faithful representation: *could not portray the anguish of the exiles.* SKETCH suggests a drawing in which only the outlines of the most prominent features or fundamental facts are given, often in a preparatory way: *to sketch a scene so that it can later be painted; to sketch the plans for a community development.*

de·pic·ture (dĭ pĭk′chər), *v.t.,* **-tured, -turing.** to picture; depict.

dep·i·late (dĕp′ə lāt′), *v.t.,* **-lated, -lating.** to remove the hair from. [t. L: m. s. *dēpilātus,* pp.] —**dep′i·la′tion,** *n.*

de·pil·a·to·ry (dĭ pĭl′ə tōr′ĭ), *adj., n., pl.* **-ries.** —*adj.* **1.** capable of removing hair. —*n.* **2.** a depilatory agent.

de pla·no (dē plā′nō), *Latin.* **1.** without argument. **2.** by manifest right; plainly. **3.** *Law.* out of court.

de·plete (dĭ plēt′), *v.t.,* **-pleted, -pleting. 1.** to deprive of that which fills; decrease the fullness of; reduce the stock or amount of. **2.** *Med.* to empty or relieve (overcharged vessels, etc.), as by bloodletting or purging. [t. L: m. s. *dēplētus,* pp., emptied out] —**de·ple′tion,** *n.* —**de·ple′tive, de·ple·to·ry** (dĭ plē′tə rĭ), *adj.*

de·plor·a·ble (dĭ plōr′ə bəl), *adj.* **1.** lamentable. **2.** sad; calamitous; grievous; wretched. —**de·plor′a·ble·ness, de·plor′a·bil′i·ty,** *n.* —**de·plor′a·bly,** *adv.*

de·plore (dĭ plōr′), *v.t.,* **-plored, -ploring.** to feel or express deep grief for or in regard to; regret deeply. [t. L: m. s. *dēplōrāre* bewail] —**de·plor′er,** *n.* —**de·plor′ing·ly,** *adv.* —**Syn.** lament, bemoan, bewail.

de·ploy (dĭ ploi′), *Mil.* —*v.t.* **1.** to spread out (troops or military units) and form an extended front. —*v.i.* **2.** to spread out with extended front. [t. F: s. *déployer,* f. *dé-* DIS-¹ + *ployer,* g. L *plicāre* fold] —**de·ploy′ment,** *n.*

de·plume (dē ploom′), *v.t.,* **-plumed, -pluming. 1.** to deprive of feathers; pluck. **2.** to strip of honor, w alth, etc. [t. F: m.s. *déplumer,* der. *dé-* DIS-¹ + *plume* (g. L *pluma* feather)] —**de′plu·ma′tion,** *n.*

de·po·lar·ize (dē pō′lə rīz′), *v.t.,* **-ized, -izing.** to deprive of polarity or polarization. —**de·po′lar·i·za′tion,** *n.* —**de·po′lar·iz′er,** *n.*

de·pone (dĭ pōn′), *v.t., v.i.,* **-poned, -poning.** to testify under oath; depose. [t. L: m. s. *dēpōnere* put away or down, ML testify. See DEPOSIT]

de·po·nent (dĭ pō′nənt), *adj.* **1.** *Gk. and Lat. Gram.* (of a verb) appearing only in the passive (or Greek middle) voice forms, but with active meaning. —*n.* **2.** *Gram.* one who testifies under oath, esp. in writing. **3.** *Gk. and Lat. Gram.* a deponent verb: *a Latin form such as loqui is a deponent.* [t. L: s. *dēpōnens,* prp., laying aside, depositing, ML testifying]

de·pop·u·late (*v.* dē pŏp′yə lāt′; *adj.* dē pŏp′yə lĭt, -lāt′), *v.,* **-lated, -lating,** *adj.* —*v.t.* **1.** to deprive of inhabitants, wholly or in part, as by destruction or expulsion. —*adj.* **2.** *Archaic.* depopulated. [t. L: m. s. *dēpopulātus,* pp., having laid waste] —**de·pop′u·la′tion,** *n.* —**de·pop′u·la′tor,** *n.*

de·port (dĭ pōrt′), *v.t.* **1.** to transport forcibly, as to a penal colony or a place of exile. **2.** to bear, conduct, or behave (oneself) in a particular manner. —*n.* **3.** *Obs.* deportment. [t. F: s. *déporter,* g. L *dēportāre* carry away, transport, banish oneself]

de·por·ta·tion (dē′pōr tā′shən), *n. Law.* an expulsion of undesired aliens and other persons from a state.

de·por·tee (dē′pōr tē′), *n.* **1.** one who is deported, as from a country. **2.** a person awaiting deportation. [f. DEPORT, V. + -EE]

de·port·ment (dĭ pōrt′mənt), *n.* demeanor; conduct; behavior. —**Syn.** See **behavior.**

de·pos·al (dĭ pō′zəl), *n.* deposition, as from office.

de·pose (dĭ pōz′), *v.,* **-posed, -posing.** —*v.t.* **1.** to remove from office or position, esp. high office. **2.** to declare or testify, esp. under oath, usually in writing. —*v.i.* **3.** to bear witness; give sworn testimony, esp. in writing. [ME *depose(n),* t. OF: m. *deposer* put down, f. *de-* DE- + *poser* POSE¹] —**de·pos′a·ble,** *adj.* —**de·pos′er,** *n.*

de·pos·it (dĭ pŏz′ĭt), *v.t.* **1.** to put or lay down; place; put. **2.** to throw down or precipitate: *soil deposited by a river.* **3.** to place for safekeeping or in trust. **4.** to give as security or in part payment. —*n.* **5.** anything laid or thrown down, as matter precipitated from a fluid; sediment. **6.** a coating of metal deposited by an electric current. **7.** an accumulation, or occurrence, of ore, oil, etc., of any form or nature. **8.** anything laid away or entrusted to another for safekeeping. **9.** money placed in a bank. **10.** anything given as security or in part payment. **11.** a depository (def. 1). [t. L: s. *dēpositus,* pp., put away or down, deposited, ML testified. See DEPONE] —**Syn. 5.** precipitate, deposition.

de·pos·i·tar·y (dĭ pŏz′ə tĕr′ĭ), *n., pl.* **-taries. 1.** one to whom anything is given in trust. **2.** a depository.

dep·o·si·tion (dĕp′ə zĭsh′ən, dē′pə-), *n.* **1.** removal from an office or position. **2.** act of depositing. **3.** that which is deposited. **4.** *Law.* **a.** the giving of testimony under oath. **b.** the testimony so given. **c.** a statement under oath, taken down in writing, to be used in court in place of the production of the witness.

de·pos·i·tor (dĭ pŏz′ə tər), *n.* **1.** one who or that which deposits. **2.** one who deposits money in a bank.

de·pos·i·to·ry (dĭ pŏz′ə tōr′ĭ), *n., pl.* **-ries. 1.** a place where anything is deposited or stored for safekeeping; a storehouse. **2.** a depositary; trustee.

de·pot (dē′pō; *Mil. or Brit.* dĕp′ō), *n.* **1.** *U.S.* a railroad station. **2.** *Mil.* **a.** a place to which supplies and materials are shipped and stored for distribution. **b.** (formerly) a place where recruits receive their first training. **3.** *Chiefly Brit.* a depository; storehouse. [t. F, g. L *dēpositum* DEPOSIT, n.] —**Syn. 1.** See **station.**

de·prave (dĭ prāv′), *v.t.,* **-praved, -praving. 1.** to make bad or worse; vitiate; corrupt. **2.** *Obs.* to defame. [ME *deprave(n),* t. L: m. *dēprāvāre* pervert] —**dep·ra·va·tion** (dĕp′rə vā′shən), *n.* —**de·prav′er,** *n.*

de·praved (dĭ prāvd′), *adj.* corrupt or perverted, esp. morally; wicked. —**Syn.** See **immoral.**

de·prav·i·ty (dĭ prăv′ə tĭ), *n., pl.* **-ties. 1.** state of being depraved. **2.** a depraved act or practice.

dep·re·cate (dĕp′rə kāt′), *v.t.,* **-cated, -cating. 1.** to express earnest disapproval of; urge reasons against; protest against (a scheme, purpose, etc.). **2.** *Archaic.* to pray for deliverance from. [t. L: m. s. *dēprecātus,* pp., having prayed against] —**dep′re·cat′ing·ly,** *adv.* —**dep′re·ca′tion,** *n.* —**dep′re·ca′tor,** *n.*

dep·re·ca·tive (dĕp′rə kā′tĭv), *adj.* deprecatory. —**dep′re·ca′tive·ly,** *adv.*

dep·re·ca·to·ry (dĕp′rə kə tōr′ĭ), *adj.* of the nature of deprecation; expressing deprecation. —**dep′re·ca·to′ri·ly,** *adv.*

de·pre·ci·ate (dĭ prē′shĭ āt′), *v.,* **-ated, -ating.** —*v.t.* **1.** to reduce the purchasing value of (money). **2.** to lessen the value of. **3.** to represent as of little value or merit; belittle. —*v.i.* **4.** to decline in value. [t. LL: m. s. *dēpretiātus* (ML *dēpreciātus*) undervalued] —**de·pre′-ci·at′ing·ly,** *adv.* —**de·pre′ci·a′tor,** *n.*

de·pre·ci·a·tion (dĭ prē′shĭ ā′shən), *n.* **1.** decrease in value due to wear and tear, decay, decline in price, etc. **2.** a decrease in the purchasing or exchange value of money. **3.** a lowering in estimation; disparagement.

de·pre·ci·a·to·ry (dĭ prē′shĭ ə tōr′ĭ), *adj.* tending to depreciate. Also, **de·pre·ci·a·tive** (dĭ prē′shĭ ā′tĭv).

dep·re·date (dĕp′rə dāt′), *v.,* **-dated, -dating.** —*v.t.* **1.** to prey upon; plunder; lay waste. —*v.i.* **2.** to prey; make depredations. [t. L: m. s. *dēpraedātus,* pp., having pillaged] —**dep′re·da′tor,** *n.* —**dep·re·da·to·ry** (dĕp′-rə dā′tə rĭ, dĭ prĕd′ə tōr′ĭ), *adj.*

dep·re·da·tion (dĕp′rə dā′shən), *n.* a preying upon or plundering; robbery; ravage.

de·press (dĭ prĕs′), *v.t.* **1.** to lower in spirits; deject; dispirit. **2.** to lower in force, vigor, etc.; weaken; make dull. **3.** to lower in amount or value. **4.** to put into a lower position: *to depress the muzzle of a gun.* **5.** to press down. **6.** *Music.* to lower in pitch. [ME *depresse(n),* t. OF: m. *depresser,* der. L *dēpressus,* pp., pressed down] —**de·press′i·ble,** *adj.* —**de·press′ing·ly,** *adv.* —**Syn. 1.** See **oppress.** —**Ant. 4.** raise, elevate.

de·pres·sant (dĭ prĕs′ənt), *Med.* —*adj.* **1.** having the quality of depressing or lowering the vital activities; sedative. —*n.* **2.** a sedative.

de·pressed (dĭ prĕst′), *adj.* **1.** dejected; downcast. **2.** pressed down; lower than the general surface. **3.** lowered in force, amount, etc. **4.** *Bot., Zool.* flattened down; broader than high. —**Syn. 1.** See **sad.**

depressed area, *Brit.* a region where unemployment and a low standard of living prevail.

depressed classes, *Brit.* the lowest castes of India; untouchables (a euphemism).

de·pres·sion (dĭ prĕsh′ən), n. 1. act of depressing. 2. state of being depressed. 3. a depressed or sunken place or part; a hollow. 4. dejection of spirits. 5. *Psychiatry*. a morbid condition of emotional dejection and withdrawal; sadness greater and more prolonged than that warranted by any objective reason. 6. dullness or inactivity, as of trade. 7. period during which there is a decline in business. 8. *Pathol.* a low state of vital powers or functional activity. 9. *Astron., etc.* angular distance below the horizon. 10. *Survey.* the angle between the line from an observer to an object below him and a horizontal line. 11. *Meteorol.* an area of low atmospheric pressure. —**Syn.** 4. discouragement, despondency, gloom.

de·pres·sive (dĭ prĕs′ĭv), adj. 1. tending to depress. 2. characterized by depression, esp. mental depression. —**de·pres′sive·ly**, adv. —**de·pres′sive·ness**, n.

de·pres·so·mo·tor (dĭ prĕs′ō mō′tər), adj. *Physiol., Med.* causing a retardation of motor activity: *depressomotor nerves*.

de·pres·sor (dĭ prĕs′ər), n. 1. one who or that which depresses. 2. *Physiol., Anat.* **a.** a muscle that draws down a part. **b.** Also, **depressor nerve.** a nerve from the aorta to the centers controlling heart rate and blood pressure. 3. *Surg.* an instrument for pressing down a protruding part.

dep·ri·va·tion (dĕp′rə vā′shən), n. 1. act of depriving. 2. fact of being deprived. 3. dispossession; loss. Also, **de·priv·al** (dĭ prī′vəl).

de·prive (dĭ prīv′), v.t., **-prived, -priving.** 1. to divest of something possessed or enjoyed; dispossess; strip; bereave. 2. to keep (a person, etc.) from possessing or enjoying something withheld. [ME *deprive*(n), t. OF: m. *depriver*, der. *priver*, g. L *privāre* deprive] —**de·priv′-a·ble,** adj. —**de·priv′er,** n. —**Syn.** 1. See strip¹.

de pro·fun·dis (dē prō fŭn′dĭs), *Latin*. out of the depths (of sorrow, despair, etc.).

dep·side (dĕp′sīd, -sĭd), n. *Chem.* any of a group of esters formed from two or more phenol carboxylic acid molecules. [f. s. Gk. *dépsein* tan + -IDE]

dept., department.

Dept·ford (dĕt′fərd), n. a SE borough of London, England. 71,550 (est. 1946).

depth (dĕpth), n. 1. measure or distance downward, inward, or backward. 2. deepness, as of water, suited to or safe for a person or thing. 3. abstruseness, as of a subject. 4. gravity; seriousness. 5. emotional profundity: *depth of woe*. 6. intensity, as of silence, color, etc. 7. lowness of pitch. 8. intellectual penetration, sagacity, or profundity. 9. a deep part or place, as of the sea. 10. an unfathomable space, or abyss. 11. the remotest or extreme part, as of space. 12. a deep or underlying region, as of feeling. 13. the part of greatest intensity, as of night or winter. [ME *depth*(e), f. dep (OE *dēop* depth) + -TH¹] —**Ant.** 2. shallowness. 8. superficiality.

depth bomb, a depth charge, esp. when dropped from an airplane.

depth charge, a bomb dropped or thrown into the water from a ship or an airplane which explodes on reaching a certain depth, used to destroy submarines, etc.

dep·u·rate (dĕp′yə rāt′), v.t., v.i., **-rated, -rating.** to make or become free from impurities; purify; cleanse. [t. ML: m. s. *dēpūrātus*, pp.] —**dep′u·ra′tion,** n. —**dep′u·ra′tor,** n.

dep·u·ra·tive (dĕp′yə rā′tĭv), adj. 1. serving to depurate; purifying. —n. 2. a depurative agent or substance.

dep·u·ta·tion (dĕp′yə tā′shən), n. 1. appointment to represent or act for another or others. 2. the person or (usually) body of persons so appointed or authorized. Cf. *U.S. delegation* (def. 3).

de·pute (dĭ pūt′), v.t., **-puted, -puting.** 1. to appoint as one's substitute or agent. 2. to assign (a charge, etc.) to a deputy. [ME *depute*(n), t. OF: m. *deputer*, t. LL: m. *dēputāre* destine, allot, in L count as, reckon]

dep·u·tize (dĕp′yə tīz′), v., **-tized, -tizing.** —v.t. 1. to appoint as deputy. —v.i. 2. *Colloq.* to act as a deputy.

dep·u·ty (dĕp′yə tĭ), n., pl. **-ties,** adj. —n. 1. a person appointed or authorized to act for another or others. 2. a person appointed or elected as assistant to a public official, serving as successor in the event of a vacancy. 3. a person representing a constituency in any of certain legislative bodies, as in the French Chamber of Deputies. —adj. 4. acting as deputy for another. [ME *depute*, t. OF, prop. pp. of *deputer* DEPUTE]

De Quin·cey (dĭ kwĭn′sĭ), Thomas, 1785–1859, British essayist.

der., 1. derivation. 2. derivative. 3. derived.

de·rac·in·ate (dĭ răs′ə nāt′), v.t., **-nated, -nating.** to pull up by the roots; uproot; extirpate; eradicate. [f. s. F *déraciner* (der. *dé-* DIS-¹ + *racine,* der. L *rādix* root) + -ATE¹] —**de·rac′i·na′tion,** n.

de·raign (dĭ rān′), v.t. 1. *Law.* **a.** to dispute or contest (a claim, etc., of another). **b.** to maintain or vindicate a c'aim to (something). 2. *Hist.* to dispose troops for (battle). [ME *dereyne*(n), t. OF: m. *deraisnier* render an account, f. de- DE-¹ + *raisnier* discourse, der. *raison,* g. L *ratio* reckoning. Cf. ARRAIGN] —**de·raign′ment,** n.

de·rail (dē rāl′), v.t. 1. to cause (a train, etc.) to run off the rails. —v.i. 2. (of a train, etc.) to run off the rails of a track. [t. F: m. *dérailler,* der. *dé-* DIS-¹ + *rail* rail, t. E. See RAIL¹] —**de·rail′ment,** n.

De·rain (də răɴ′), n. André (äɴ drĕ′), born 1880, French painter.

de·range (dĭ rānj′), v.t., **-ranged, -ranging.** 1. to throw into disorder; disarrange. 2. to disturb the condition, action, or functions of. 3. to unsettle the reason of; make insane. [t. F: m. s. *déranger,* OF *desrengier,* f. *des-* DIS-¹ + *rengier* RANGE, V.]

de·ranged (dĭ rānjd′), adj. 1. disordered. 2. insane.

de·range·ment (dĭ rānj′mənt), n. 1. act of deranging. 2. disarrangement; disorder. 3. mental disorder; insanity.

de·ray (dĭ rā′), n. *Archaic or Dial.* disorderly merrymaking. [ME *derai,* t. OF: m. *desrei,* der. *desreer* put out of order, f. *des-* DIS-¹ + *rei* order. Cf. ARRAY, V.]

Der·bent (dĕr bĕnt′), n. a seaport in the SE Soviet Union in Europe, on the Caspian Sea. 23,097 (1926).

Der·by (dûr′bĭ; *Brit.* där′bĭ), n., pl. **-bies.** 1. a horse race in the United States, founded in 1875, run annually at Churchill Downs, Kentucky. 2. a horse race in England, founded 1780, run annually at Epsom Downs, near London. 3. some other important race, of horses, airplanes, foot runners, etc. 4. (*l.c.*) a stiff felt hat with rounded crown and narrow brim, worn chiefly by men. Cf. *Brit.* bowler.

Der·by (dûr′bĭ; *Brit.* där′bĭ), n. 1. a city in central England: the county seat of Derbyshire. 138,170 (est. 1946). 2. Derbyshire.

Der·by·shire (dûr′bĭ shĭr′, -shər; *Brit.* där′bĭ-), n. a county in central England. 790,000 pop. (est. 1946); 1006 sq. mi. *Co. seat:* Derby. Also, **Derby.**

dere (dĭr), adj. dear².

de rè·gle (də rĕ′gl), *French.* according to rule; following a pattern, principle, or law.

der·e·lict (dĕr′ə lĭkt), adj. 1. left or abandoned, as by the owner or guardian (said esp. of a ship abandoned at sea). 2. neglectful of duty; delinquent; unfaithful. —n. 3. personal property abandoned or thrown away by the owner. 4. a ship abandoned at sea. 5. a person forsaken or abandoned, esp. by society. 6. one guilty of neglect of duty. 7. *Law.* land left dry by a change of the water line. [t. L: s. *dērelictus,* pp., forsaken utterly]

der·e·lic·tion (dĕr′ə lĭk′shən), n. 1. culpable neglect, as of duty; delinquency; fault. 2. act of abandoning. 3. state of being abandoned. 4. *Law.* **a.** a leaving dry of land by recession of the water line. **b.** the land thus left dry. —**Syn.** 1. See neglect.

de·req·ui·si·tion (dē rĕk′wə zĭsh′ən), *Brit.* —n. 1. the return from military to civilian control. —v.t., v.i. 2. to return to civilian control.

de re·rum na·tu·ra (dē rĭr′əm nə tyōōr′ə, -tōōr′ə), *Latin.* on the nature of things.

de·ride (dĭ rīd′), v.t., **-rided, -riding.** to laugh at in contempt; scoff or jeer at; mock. [t. L: m. s. *dērīdēre* laugh] —**de·rid′er,** n. —**de·rid′ing·ly,** adv. —**Syn.** taunt, flout, gibe, banter, rally. See ridicule.

de ri·gueur (də rē gœr′), *French.* strictly required, as by etiquette or usage.

de·ris·i·ble (dĭ rĭz′ə bəl), adj. subject to or worthy of derision.

de·ri·sion (dĭ rĭzh′ən), n. 1. act of deriding; ridicule; mockery. 2. an object of ridicule. [t. L: s. *dērīsio*]

de·ri·sive (dĭ rī′sĭv), adj. characterized by derision; ridiculing; mocking. Also, **de·ri·so·ry** (dĭ rī′sə rĭ). —**de·ri′sive·ly,** adv. —**de·ri′sive·ness,** n.

deriv., 1. derivation. 2. derivative.

der·i·va·tion (dĕr′ə vā′shən), n. 1. act of deriving. 2. fact of being derived. 3. origination or origin. 4. *Math.* (of a theorem) **a.** development. **b.** differentiation. 5. *Gram.* **a.** the process of composing new words by the addition of prefixes or suffixes to already existing root words, as *atomic* from *atom, hardness* from *hard.* **b.** the systematic description of such processes in a particular language, as contrasted with *inflection* which consists of adding prefixes, infixes, or suffixes to make a different form of the same word: *hardness* is an example of derivation; *harder* of inflection. **c.** such processes collectively or in general. —**der′i·va′tion·al,** adj.

de·riv·a·tive (dĭ rĭv′ə tĭv), adj. 1. derived. 2. not original or primitive; secondary. —n. 3. something derived or derivative. 4. *Gram.* a form derived from another: *atomic* is a derivative of *atom.* 5. *Chem.* a substance or compound obtained from, or regarded as derived from, another substance or compound. 6. *Math.* the limit of the ratio of the increment of a function to the increment of a variable in it, as the latter becomes 0. —**de·riv′a·tive·ly,** adv.

de·rive (dĭ rīv′), v., **-rived, -riving.** —v.t. 1. to receive or obtain from a source or origin (fol. by *from*). 2. to trace, as from a source or origin. 3. to obtain by reasoning; deduce. 4. *Chem.* to produce (a compound) from another compound by replacement of elements or radicals. 5. *Obs.* to bring or direct (fol. by *to, on, upon,* etc.). —v.i. 6. to come from a source; originate. [t. F: m.s. *dériver,* t. L: m. *dērīvāre* lead off] —**de·riv′-a·ble,** adj. —**de·riv′er,** n.

derived unit, *Physics, etc.* any unit derived from primary units of length, time, mass, etc.

-derm, a word element meaning "skin," as in *endoderm.* [t. Gk.: s. *-dermos,* etc., having skin, skinned]

der·ma (dûr′mə), n. *Anat., Zool.* 1. the corium or true skin, beneath the epidermis. 2. the skin in general. [NL, t. Gk.: skin] —**der′mal,** adj.

---

b., blend of, blended; c., cognate with; d., dialect, dialectal; der., derived from; f., formed from; g., going back to; m., modification of; r., replacing; s., stem of; t., taken from; ?, perhaps. See the full key on inside cover.

der·ma·ti·tis (dûr′mə tī′tĭs), *n.* *Pathol.* inflammation of the skin.

dermato-, a word element meaning "skin," as in *dermatology.* Also, **derm-, dermat-, dermo-.** [t. Gk., comb. form of *dérma*]

der·mat·o·gen (dər măt′ə jən, dûr′mə tō′jən), *n.* *Bot.* a thin layer of meristem in embryos and growing ends of stems and roots, which gives rise to the epidermis.

der·ma·toid (dûr′mə toid′), *adj.* resembling skin; skinlike.

der·ma·tol·o·gy (dûr′mə tŏl′ə jĭ), *n.* the science of the skin and its diseases. —**der·ma·to·log·i·cal** (dûr′mə tə lŏj′ə kəl), *adj.* —**der′ma·tol′o·gist,** *n.*

der·ma·to·phyte (dûr′mə tō fīt′), *n.* *Pathol.,* *Vet. Sci.* any fungus parasitic on the skin and causing a skin disease, as ringworm.

der·ma·to·plas·ty (dûr′mə tō plăs′tĭ), *n.* plastic surgery of the skin. See **skin grafting.**

der·mis (dûr′mĭs), *n.* *Anat., Zool.* derma. [NL; abstracted from EPIDERMIS] —**der′mic,** *adj.*

der·moid (dûr′moid), *adj.* skinlike; dermatoid.

der·ni·er (dûr′nĭ ər; *Fr.* děr nyě′), *adj.* last; final; ultimate. [t. F]

der·nier cri (děr nyě krē′), *French.* **1.** the latest word. **2.** the latest fashion.

der·o·gate (*v.* děr′ə gāt′; *adj.* děr′ə gĭt, -gāt′), *v.,* **-gat·ed, -gat·ing,** *adj.* —*v.i.* **1.** to detract, as from authority, estimation, etc. (fol. by *from*). **2.** to fall away in character or conduct; degenerate (fol. by *from*). —*v.t.* **3.** *Archaic.* to take away (something) from a thing so as to impair it. —*adj.* **4.** *Obs.* or *Archaic.* debased. [t. L: m. s. *dērogātus,* pp., repealed, taken or detracted from] —**der′o·ga′tion,** *n.*

de·rog·a·tive (dĭ rŏg′ə tĭv), *adj.* lessening; belittling; derogatory. —**de·rog′a·tive·ly,** *adv.*

de·rog·a·to·ry (dĭ rŏg′ə tōr′ĭ), *adj.* tending to derogate or detract, as from authority or estimation; disparaging; depreciatory. —**de·rog′a·to′ri·ly,** *adv.* —**de·rog′a·to′ri·ness,** *n.*

der·rick (děr′ĭk), *n.* **1.** any of various devices for lifting and moving heavy weights. **2.** the towerlike framework over an oil well or the like. [named after *Derrick,* a hangman at Tyburn, London, about 1600]

der·ring-do (děr′ĭng dōō′), *n.* *Pseudoarchaic.* daring deeds; heroic daring. [ME *dorryng don* daring to do; erroneously taken as n. phrase by Spenser]

der·rin·ger (děr′ĭn jər), *n.* *U.S.* a short-barreled pistol of large caliber. [named after the inventor]

der·ris (děr′ĭs), *n.* an East Indian leguminous plant, *Derris elliptica* and allied species, the roots of which contain rotenone and are used as an insecticide.

Der·ry (děr′ĭ), *n.* Londonderry.

der·ry (děr′ĭ), *n.* a meaningless refrain or chorus in old songs. Also, **der·ry·down** (děr′ĭ doun′).

der Tag (děr tähн′), *German.* the day: used by German nationalists to refer to the day on which Germany would begin the "Drang nach Osten"; later, the day on which she would undertake a plan of conquest.

der·vish (dûr′vĭsh), *n.* a member of any of various Mohammedan ascetic orders, some of which carry on ecstatic observances, such as violent dancing and pirouetting (**dancing, spinning,** or **whirling dervishes**) or vociferous chanting or shouting (**howling dervishes**). [t. Turk., t. Pers.: m. *darvīsh* religious mendicant]

Der·went (dûr′wənt), *n.* **1.** one of three rivers in England. **2.** a river in Tasmania. ab. 130 mi.

De·saix de Vey·goux (děz ě′ də věgōō′), **Louis Charles Antoine** (lwē shårl än twän′), 1768–1800, French general.

des·cant (*n.* děs′kănt; *v.* děskănt′, dĭs-), *n.* **1.** *Music.* **a.** a melody or counterpoint accompanying a simple musical theme and usually written above it. **b.** (in part music) the soprano. **c.** a song or melody. **2.** a variation upon anything; comment on a subject. —*v.i.* **3.** *Music.* to sing. **4.** to make comments; discourse at length and with variety. Also, **discant.** [ME, t. ONF, f. *des-* DIS-1 + *cant* (g. L *cantus* song)] —**des·cant′er,** *n.*

Des·cartes (děkårt′), *n.* **René** (rə ně′), 1596–1650, French philosopher and mathematician.

de·scend (dĭ sěnd′), *v.i.* **1.** to move or pass from a higher to a lower place; go or come down; fall; sink. **2.** to pass from higher to lower in any scale. **3.** to go from generals to particulars. **4.** to slope or tend downward. **5.** to come down by transmission, as from ancestors. **6.** to be derived by birth or extraction. **7.** to come down in a hostile manner, as an army: *to descend upon the enemy.* **8.** to come down from a certain intellectual, moral, or social standard: *he would never descend to baseness.* **9.** *Astron.* to move toward the horizon, or toward the south, as a star. —*v.t.* **10.** to move downward upon or along; go down (stairs, a hill, etc.). [ME *descend(en),* t. OF: m. *descendre,* g. L *dēscendere*]

de·scend·ant (dĭ sěnd′dənt), *n.* **1.** one descended from an ancestor; an offspring, near or remote. —*adj.* **2.** descendent. [t. F, ppr. of *descendre* DESCEND]

de·scend·ent (dĭ sěnd′dənt), *adj.* **1.** descending; going or coming down. **2.** descending from an ancestor. [t. L: s. *dēscendens,* ppr., descending]

de·scend·er (dĭ sěnd′dər), *n.* **1.** one who or that which descends. **2.** *Print.* the part of such letters as *p, q, j,* and *y* that goes below the body of most lower case letters.

de·scend·i·ble (dĭ sěnd′də bəl), *adj.* capable of being transmitted by inheritance. Also, **de·scend′a·ble.**

de·scen·sion (dĭ sěn′shən), *n.* *Now Rare.* descent.

de·scent (dĭ sěnt′), *n.* **1.** act or fact of descending. **2.** a downward inclination or slope. **3.** a passage or stairway leading down. **4.** extraction; lineage. **5.** any passing from higher to lower in degree or state. **6.** a sudden incursion or attack. **7.** *Law.* transmission of real property by intestate succession. [ME, t. OF: m. *descente,* der. *descendre* DESCEND] —**Syn.** **1.** falling. sinking. **2.** decline, grade, declivity.

Des·chutes (dā shōōt′), *n.* a river flowing from the Cascade Range in central Oregon N to the Columbia river. ab. 250 mi.

de·scribe (dĭ skrīb′), *v.t.,* **-scribed, -scrib·ing.** **1.** to set forth in written or spoken words; give an account of: *to describe a scene, a person, etc.* **2.** *Geom.* to draw or trace, as an arc. [t. L: m. s. *dēscrībere* copy off, sketch off, describe] —**de·scrib′a·ble,** *adj.* —**de·scrib′er,** *n.* —**Syn.** **1.** DESCRIBE, NARRATE agree in the idea of giving an account of something. To DESCRIBE is to convey an image or impression in words designed to reveal the appearance, nature, attributes, etc., of the thing described. The word applies primarily to what exists in space (by extension, to what occurs in time) and often implies the vividness of personal observation: *to describe a scene, a sensation, a character, a room.* To NARRATE is to recount the occurrence of something, usually by giving the details of an event or events in the order of their happening. NARRATE thus applies only to that which happens in time: *to narrate an incident.*

de·scrip·tion (dĭ skrĭp′shən), *n.* **1.** representation by written or spoken words; a statement that describes. **2.** sort; kind; variety: *persons of that description.* **3.** *Geom.* act of describing a figure.

de·scrip·tive (dĭ skrĭp′tĭv), *adj.* **1.** having the quality of describing; characterized by description. **2.** *Gram.* **a.** (of an adjective) expressing a quality of the noun it modifies (opposed to *limiting* or *demonstrative*) as in *fresh milk.* **b.** (of any other expression) acting like a descriptive adjective. —**de·scrip′tive·ly,** *adv.* —**de·scrip′tive·ness,** *n.*

descriptive clause, a relative clause, in English writing usually set off in commas, which describes or supplements, but does not identify, the antecedent; nonrestrictive clause. In the sentence "this year, *which has been dry,* is bad for crops" the italicized part is a descriptive clause.

descriptive geometry, **1.** the theory of making projections of any accurately defined figure such that from them can be deduced not only its projective, but also its metrical, properties. **2.** geometry in general, treated by means of projections.

descriptive science, a science which classifies and describes the material in a particular field (usually opposed to *explanatory science,* which gives causes).

de·scry (dĭ skrī′), *v.t.,* **-scried, -scry·ing.** **1.** to make out by looking; espy: *the lookout descried land.* **2.** to discover by observation; perceive; detect. [ME *descry(en),* appar. t. OF: m. *descrier* proclaim. See DECRY] —**de·scri′er,** *n.*

des·e·crate (děs′ə krāt′), *v.t.,* **-crat·ed, -crat·ing.** to divest of sacred or hallowed character or office; divert from a sacred to a profane purpose; treat with sacrilege; profane. [f. DE- + *-secrate,* modeled on CONSECRATE] —**des′e·crat′er, des′e·cra′tor,** *n.* **des′e·cra′tion,** *n.*

de·sen·si·tize (dē sěn′sə tīz′), *v.t.,* **-tized, -tiz·ing.** **1.** to lessen the sensitiveness of. **2.** *Physiol.* to eliminate the natural or acquired reactivity or sensitivity of (an animal, organ, tissue, etc.) to an external stimulus, as an allergen. **3.** *Photog.* to make less sensitive or wholly insensitive to light, as the emulsion on a film. —**de·sen′si·ti·za′tion,** *n.* —**de·sen′si·tiz′er,** *n.*

des·ert¹ (děz′ərt), *n.* **1.** an area so deficient in moisture as to support only a sparse, widely spaced vegetation, or none at all. **2.** any area in which few forms of life can exist because of lack of water, permanent frost, or absence of soil. —*adj.* **3.** of, pertaining to, or like a desert; desolate; barren. [ME, t. OF, t. L (Eccl.): s. *dēsertum,* prop. neut. pp. of *dēserere* abandon, forsake] —**Syn.** **1.** DESERT, WASTE, WILDERNESS refer to areas which are uninhabited. DESERT emphasizes lack of water; it refers to a dry, barren, treeless region, usually sandy: *an oasis in a desert, the Sahara Desert.* WASTE emphasizes lack of inhabitants and of cultivation; it is used of wild, barren land, but fig. the word is also applied to turbulent seas: *a desolate waste, a terrifying waste of water.* WILDERNESS emphasizes the difficulty of finding one's way, whether because of barrenness or of luxuriant vegetation; this word, too, is applied to the ocean, especially in stormy weather: *a trackless wilderness, an ocean wilderness.*

de·sert² (dĭ zûrt′), *v.t.* **1.** to abandon or forsake; depart from: *he deserted his wife.* **2.** (of a soldier or sailor) to leave or run away from (the service, duty, etc.) with the intention of never coming back. **3.** to fail (one): *all hope deserted him.* —*v.i.* **4.** (esp. of a soldier or sailor) to forsake one's duty, etc. [t. F: m. s. *déserter,* t. LL: m. *dēsertāre,* freq. of L *dēserere*] —**de·sert′er,** *n.* —**Syn.** **1.** DESERT, ABANDON, FORSAKE mean to leave behind one persons, places, or things. DESERT implies intentionally violating an oath, formal obligation, or duty: *to desert campaign pledges.* ABANDON suggests giving up wholly and finally, whether of necessity, unwillingly, or through shirking responsibilities: *to abandon a hopeless task.* FORSAKE has emotional connotations, since it implies violating obligations of affection or association: *to forsake a noble cause.*

de·sert3 (dĭ zûrt′), *n.* **1.** that which is deserved; a due reward or punishment. **2.** worthiness of reward or punishment; merit or demerit. **3.** the fact of deserving well; merit; a virtue. [ME, t. OF: m. *deserte*, der. *deservir* DESERVE] **—Syn. 3.** See **merit.**

de·ser·tion (dĭ zûr′shən), *n.* **1.** act of deserting. **2.** state of being deserted. **3.** *Law.* willful abandonment, esp. of one's wife or husband without consent, in violation of legal or moral obligation.

de·serve (dĭ zûrv′), *v.*, **-served, -serving.** *—v.t.* **1.** to merit (reward, punishment, esteem, etc.) in return for actions, qualities, etc. *—v.i.* **2.** to be worthy of recompense. [ME *deserve(n)*, t. OF: m. *deservir*, g. L *dēservīre* serve zealously] **—de·serv′er,** *n.*

de·serv·ed·ly (dĭ zûr′vĭd lĭ), *adv.* justly; according to desert, whether of good or evil.

de·serv·ing (dĭ zûr′vĭng), *adj.* worthy of reward or praise; meritorious (often fol. by *of*). **—de·serv′ing·ly,** *adv.* **—de·serv′ing·ness,** *n.*

des·ha·bille (dĕz′ə bēl′), *n.* dishabille. [t. F]

des·ic·cant (dĕs′ə kənt), *adj.* **1.** desiccating or drying, as a medicine. *—n.* **2.** a desiccant substance or agent.

des·ic·cate (dĕs′ə kāt′), *v.t., v.i.*, **-cated, -cating. 1.** to dry thoroughly; dry up. **2.** to preserve by depriving of moisture, as foods. [t. L: m. s. *dēsiccātus*, pp., completely dried] **—des′ic·ca′tion,** *n.* **—des′ic·ca′tive,** *adj., n.*

des·ic·cat·ed (dĕs′ə kā′tĭd), *adj. Brit.* dehydrated or powdered: *desiccated milk or soup.*

des·ic·ca·tor (dĕs′ə kā tər), *n.* **1.** one who or that which desiccates. **2.** an apparatus for drying fruit, milk, etc., or for absorbing the moisture present in a chemical substance, etc.

de·sid·er·a·ta (dĭ sĭd′ə rā′tə), *n.* pl. of **desideratum.**

de·sid·er·ate (dĭ sĭd′ə rāt′), *v.t.*, **-ated, -ating.** to feel a desire for; long for; feel the want of. [t. L: m. s. *dēsīderātus*, pp., longed for] **—de·sid′er·a′tion,** *n.*

de·sid·er·a·tive (dĭ sĭd′ə rā′tĭv), *adj.* **1.** having or expressing desire. **2.** *Gram.* (of a verb derived from another) expressing desire to perform the action denoted by the underlying verb. Example: Sanskrit *vēda*, he knows; *vi-vid-is-ati*, he wishes to know. *—n.* **3.** *Gram.* a desiderative verb.

de·sid·er·a·tum (dĭ sĭd′ə rā′təm), *n., pl.* **-ta** (-tə). something wanted or needed. [t. L, prop. pp. neut.]

de·sign (dĭ zīn′), *v.t.* **1.** to prepare the preliminary sketch or the plans for (a work to be executed). **2.** to plan and fashion artistically or skillfully. **3.** to form or conceive in the mind; contrive; plan: *he is designing a plan to enlarge his garden.* **4.** to assign in thought or intention; purpose: *he is designing that his son shall help him in the garden.* **5.** *Obs.* to mark out, as by a sign; indicate. *—v.i.* **6.** to make drawings, preliminary sketches, or plans. **7.** to plan and fashion a work of art, etc. *—n.* **8.** an outline, sketch, or plan, as of a work of art, an edifice, or a machine to be executed or constructed. **9.** the combination of details or features of a picture, building, etc.; the pattern or device of artistic work. **10.** the art of designing: *a school of design.* **11.** a plan; a project; a scheme. **12.** a hostile plan; crafty scheme. **13.** the end in view; intention; purpose. **14.** evil or selfish intention: *have designs on* (*or against*) *a person.* **15.** adaptation of means to a preconceived end. **16.** an artistic work. [t. F: s. *dēsigner* designate, t. L: m. *dēsignāre* mark out] **—Syn. 4.** See **intend. 11.** See **plan.**

des·ig·nate (*v.* dĕz′ĭg nāt′; *adj.* dĕz′ĭg nĭt, -nāt′), *v.*, **-nated, -nating,** *adj. —v.t.* **1.** to mark or point out; indicate; show; specify. **2.** to name; entitle; style. **3.** to nominate or select for a duty, office, purpose, etc.; appoint; assign. *—adj.* **4.** designated. [t. L: m. s. *dēsignātus*, pp., marked out] **—des′ig·na′tive,** *adj.* **—des′ig·na′tor,** *n.*

des·ig·na·tion (dĕz′ĭg nā′shən), *n.* **1.** act of designating. **2.** fact of being designated. **3.** that which designates; a name. **4.** nomination; appointment.

de·sign·ed·ly (dĭ zī′nĭd lĭ), *adv.* by design; purposely.

de·sign·er (dĭ zī′nər), *n.* **1.** one who devises or executes designs, as for works of art, decorative patterns, dresses, machines, etc. **2.** a schemer or intriguer.

de·sign·ing (dĭ zī′nĭng), *adj.* **1.** contriving schemes; artful. **2.** showing forethought. *—n.* **3.** act or art of making designs. **—de·sign′ing·ly,** *adv.* **—Syn. 1.** wily, cunning, crafty, tricky, sly.

de·sign·ment (dĭ zīn′mənt), *n.* designation; design.

des·i·nence (dĕs′ĭ nəns), *n.* **1.** termination or ending, as a line of verse. **2.** *Gram.* a termination, ending, or suffix of a word.

de·sir·a·ble (dĭ zīr′ə bəl), *adj.* **1.** worthy to be desired; pleasing, excellent, or fine. *—n.* **2.** one who or that which is desirable. **—de·sir′a·bil′i·ty, de·sir′a·ble·ness,** *n.* **—de·sir′a·bly,** *adv.*

de·sire (dĭ zīr′), *v.*, **-sired, -siring,** *n. —v.t.* **1.** to wish or long for; crave; want: *he desires a college education.* **2.** to express a wish to obtain; ask for; request: *the king desired of him that he should return.* *—n.* **3.** a longing or craving. **4.** an expressed wish; a request. **5.** something desired. **6.** sensual appetite; lust. [ME *desire(n)*, t. OF: m. *desirer*, g. L *dēsīderāre* want] **—de·sir′er,** *n.*

—Syn. 1. See **wish. 3.** DESIRE, CRAVING, LONGING, YEARNING suggest feelings which impel one to the attainment or possession of something. DESIRE is a strong feeling, worthy or unworthy, that impels to the attainment or possession of something which is (in reality or imagination) within reach: *a desire for success.* CRAVING implies a deep and imperative wish for something, based on a sense of need and hunger (lit. or fig.): *a craving for food, companionship.* A LONGING is an intense wish, generally repeated or enduring, for something that is at the moment beyond reach but may be attainable at some future time: *a longing to visit Europe.* YEARNING suggests persistent, uneasy, and sometimes wistful or tender longing: *a yearning for one's native land.* **—Ant. 3.** indifference.

de·sir·ous (dĭ zīr′əs), *adj.* having or characterized by desire; desiring.

de·sist (dĭ zĭst′), *v.i.* to cease, as from some action or proceeding; stop. [t. OF: s. *desister*, t. L: m. *dēsistere* leave off] **—de·sist′ance, de·sist′ence,** *n.*

de Sit·ter (də sĭt′ər), **Willem** (vĭl′əm), 1872–1934, Dutch mathematician and astronomer.

desk (dĕsk), *n.* **1.** a table specially adapted for convenience in writing or reading, frequently made with a sloping top. **2.** a frame for supporting a book from which the service is read in a church. **3.** a pulpit. [ME *deske*, t. It.: m. *desco*, g. L *discus* disk, dish, ML table]

desk work, 1. work done at a desk. **2.** habitual writing, as that of a clerk or a literary man.

D. ès L., (F *Docteur ès Lettres*) Doctor of Letters.

des·man (dĕs′mən), *n., pl.* **-mans.** either of two aquatic, insectivorous mammals, related to shrews, *Myogale moschata*, of SE Russia, and *M. pyrenaica*, of the Pyrenees. [t. Sw.: short for *desman-ratta* muskrat]

des·mid (dĕs′mĭd), *n.* any of the microscopic freshwater algae belonging to the family *Desmidiaceae.* [t. NL: m. s. *Desmidium*, typical genus, dim. of Gk. *desmós* band, chain] **—des·mid′i·an,** *adj.*

des·moid (dĕs′moid), *adj. Anat.* **1.** resembling a fascia or fibrous sheet. **2.** resembling a ligament; ligamentous. *—n.* **3.** *Pathol.* a firm and tough tumor of woven fibrous tissue. [f. s. Gk. *desmós* band, chain, ligament+ -OID]

Des Moines (də moin′, moinz′), **1.** the capital of Iowa, in the central part, on the Des Moines river. 177,965 (1950). **2.** a river flowing from SW Minnesota, SE through Iowa to the Mississippi. ab. 450 mi.

Des·mou·lins (dĕ mo͞o lăN′), *n.* **Lucie Simplice Camille Benoît** (lY sē′ săN plēs′ kȧ mē′y bə nwȧ′), 1760–1794, one of the leaders of the French Revolution.

des·o·late (*adj.* dĕs′ə lĭt; *v.* dĕs′ə lāt′), *adj., v.*, **-lated, -lating.** *—adj.* **1.** barren or laid waste; devastated. **2.** deprived or destitute of inhabitants; deserted. **3.** left alone; lonely. **4.** having the feeling of being abandoned by friends or by hope. **5.** dreary; dismal. *—v.t.* **6.** to lay waste; devastate. **7.** to deprive of inhabitants; depopulate. **8.** to make disconsolate. **9.** to forsake or abandon. [ME, t. L: m. s. *dēsōlātus*, pp., left alone, forsaken] **—des′o·lat′er, des′o·la′tor,** *n.* **—des′o·late·ly,** *adv.* **—des′o·late·ness,** *n.*

—Syn. 4. miserable, wretched, woebegone. DESOLATE, DISCONSOLATE, FORLORN suggest one who is in a sad and wretched condition. The DESOLATE person or place gives a feeling or impression of isolation or of being deprived of human consolation, relationships, or presence: *desolate and despairing.* The DISCONSOLATE person is aware of the efforts of others to console and comfort him, but is unable to be relieved or cheered by them: *she remained disconsolate even in the midst of friends.* The FORLORN person has the feeling or gives the impression of being lost, deserted, or forsaken by friends: *wretched and forlorn in a strange city.*

des·o·la·tion (dĕs′ə lā′shən), *n.* **1.** act of desolating **2.** state of being desolated. **3.** depopulation; devastation; ruin. **4.** dreariness; barrenness. **5.** deprivation of companionship or comfort; loneliness; disconsolateness. **6.** a desolate place.

De So·to (də sō′tō; *Sp.* dĕ sô′tô), **Hernando** or **Fernando** (ĕr nän′dô *or* fĕr nän′dô), 1500–42, Spanish soldier-explorer in America: reached the Mississippi river, 1541.

de·spair (dĭ spâr′), *n.* **1.** loss of hope; hopelessness. **2.** that which causes hopelessness; that of which there is no hope. *—v.i.* **3.** to lose or give up hope; be without hope (fol. by *of*): *to despair of humanity.* *—v.t.* **4.** *Archaic.* to give up hope of. [ME *despeir(en)*, t. OF: m. s. *desperer*, g. L *dēspērāre* be without hope]

—Syn. 1. DESPAIR, DESPERATION, DESPONDENCY, DISCOURAGEMENT, HOPELESSNESS refer to a state of mind caused by circumstances which seem too much to cope with. DESPAIR suggests total loss or abandonment of hope, which may be passive or may drive one to furious efforts, even if at random: *in the depths of despair, courage born of despair.* DESPERATION is usually an active state, the abandonment of hope impelling to a furious struggle against adverse circumstances, with utter disregard of consequences: *an act of desperation when everything else had failed.* DESPONDENCY is usually a temporary state of deep gloom and disheartenment: *a spell of despondency.* DISCOURAGEMENT is a temporary loss of courage, hope, and ambition because of obstacles, frustrations, etc.: *his optimism resisted all discouragements.* HOPELESSNESS is a loss of hope so complete as to result in a more or less permanent state of passive despair: *a state of hopelessness and apathy.*

de·spair·ing (dĭ spâr′ĭng), *adj.* **1.** given to despair or hopelessness. **2.** indicating despair. **—de·spair′ing·ly,** *adv.* **—Syn. 1.** See **hopeless. —Ant. 1.** hopeful.

des·patch (dĭs păch′), *v.t., v.i., n.* dispatch. **—des·patch′er,** *n.*

des·per·a·do (dĕs′pə rā′dō, -rä′dō), *n., pl.* **-does, -dos.** a desperate or reckless criminal; one ready for any desperate deed. [prob. refashioning of *desperate* after Sp. words in *-ado.* Cf. OSp. *desperado*, g. L *dēspērātus* DESPERATE]

b., blend of, blended; c., cognate with; d., dialect, dialectal; der., derived from; f., formed from; g., going back to; m., modification of; r., replacing; s., stem of; t., taken from; ?, perhaps. See the full key on inside cover.

des·per·ate (dĕs'pər Ĭt), *adj.* **1.** reckless from despair; ready to run any risk. **2.** characterized by the recklessness of despair. **3.** leaving little or no hope; very serious or dangerous. **4.** extremely bad. **5.** extreme or excessive. **6.** having no hope. [t. L: m. s. *dēspērātus*, pp., given up] **—des'per·ate·ly**, *adv.* **—des'per·ate·ness**, *n.* **—Syn. 3.** See **hopeless. —Ant. 1.** cautious.

des·per·a·tion (dĕs'pər ā'shən), *n.* **1.** state of being desperate; the recklessness of despair. **2.** act or fact of despairing; despair. **—Syn. 1.** See **despair.**

des·pi·ca·ble (dĕs'pĬ kə bəl; *less often* dĕs pĬk'ə bəl), *adj.* that is to be despised; contemptible. [t. LL: m. s. *dēspicābilis*, der. L *dēspicārī* despise] **—des'pi·ca·bil'i·ty, des'pi·ca·ble·ness**, *n.* **—des'pi·ca·bly**, *adv.* **—Syn.** worthless, base, vile. **—Ant.** admirable.

de·spise (dĬ spīz'), *v.t.* **-spised, -spising.** to look down upon, as in contempt; scorn; disdain. [ME *despise(n)*, t. OF: m. *despis-*, s. *despire*, g. L *dēspicere* look down upon, despise] **—de·spis'er**, *n.* **—Ant.** admire.

de·spite (dĬ spīt'), *prep., n., v.* **-spited, -spiting. —prep. 1.** in despite of; notwithstanding. **—n. 2.** contemptuous treatment; insult. **3. in despite of,** in contempt or defiance of; in spite of; notwithstanding. **4.** *Archaic.* malice, hatred, or spite. **—v.t. 5.** *Obs.* to offend; vex; spite. [orig., *in despite of;* ME *despit*, t. OF, g. L *dēspectus* a looking down upon] **—Syn. 1.** See **notwithstanding.**

de·spite·ful (dĬ spīt'fəl), *adj. Archaic.* contemptuous; malicious; spiteful. **—de·spite'ful·ly**, *adv.* **—de·spite'ful·ness**, *n.*

des·pit·e·ous (dĕs pĬt'Ĭ əs), *adj. Archaic.* **1.** malicious; spiteful **2.** contemptuous. **—des·pit'e·ous·ly**, *adv.*

de·spoil (dĬ spoil'), *v.t.* to strip of possessions; rob; plunder; pillage. [ME *despoile(n)*, t. OF: m. s. *despoillier*, g. L *dēspoliāre* plunder, rob] **—de·spoil'er**, *n.* **—de·spoil'ment**, *n.*

de·spo·li·a·tion (dĬ spō'lĬ ā'shən), *n.* **1.** act of despoiling. **2.** fact of being despoiled.

de·spond (dĬ spŏnd'), *v.i.* **1.** to lose heart, courage, or hope. **—n. 2.** *Archaic.* despondency. [t. L: s. *dēspondēre* promise, give up, lose (heart)] **—de·spond'ing·ly**, *adv.*

de·spond·en·cy (dĬ spŏn'dən sĬ), *n.* a being despondent; depression of spirits from loss of courage or hope; dejection. Also, **de·spond'ence. —Syn.** discouragement, melancholy, gloom, desperation. See **despair. —Ant.** joy.

de·spond·ent (dĬ spŏn'dənt), *adj.* desponding; depressed or dejected. [t. L: s. *dēspondens*, ppr., giving up, despairing] **—de·spond'ent·ly**, *adv.* **—Syn.** discouraged, disheartened, downhearted, melancholy, low-spirited. See **hopeless. —Ant.** hopeful.

des·pot (dĕs'pət, -pŏt), *n.* **1.** an absolute ruler; an autocrat. **2.** a tyrant or oppressor. **3.** *Hist.* master or lord (a title of autocratic rulers, esp. the late Roman and Byzantine Emperors). [t. OF, t. Gk.: s. *despótēs* master]

des·pot·ic (dĕs pŏt'Ĭk), *adj.* of, pertaining to, or of the nature of a despot or despotism; autocratic; arbitrary; tyrannical. **—des·pot'i·cal·ly**, *adv.*

des·pot·ism (dĕs'pə tĬz'əm), *n.* **1.** the rule of a despot; the exercise of absolute authority. **2.** an absolute or autocratic government; a country ruled by a despot. **3.** absolute power or control; tyranny.

de·spu·mate (dĬ spū'māt, dĕs'pyŏŏ māt'), *v.,* **-mated, -mating. —v.t. 1.** to skim. **—v.i. 2.** to throw off froth, scum, or impurities. [t. L: m. s. *dēspūmātus*, pp., skimmed] **—des'pu·ma'tion**, *n.*

des·qua·mate (dĕs'kwə māt'), *v.i.,* **-mated, -mating.** *Pathol.* to come off in scales, as the skin in certain diseases; peel off. [t. L: m. s. *dēsquāmātus*, pp., scaled off] **—des'qua·ma'tion**, *n.*

D. ès S., (F. *Docteur ès Sciences*) Doctor of Sciences.

Des·sau (dĕs'ou), *n.* a city in central Germany: the capital of Anhalt. 119,099 (1939).

des·sert (dĬ zûrt'), *n.* **1.** *U.S.* a final course including pies, puddings, etc. **2.** *Eng.* a serving of fruits, sweetmeats, etc., at the end of a meal. [t. F, der. *desservir* clear the table, f. des- DIS-[1] + *servir*, g. L *servīre* serve]

des·sert·spoon (dĬ zûrt'spoon', -spŏŏn'), *n.* a spoon intermediate in size between a tablespoon and a teaspoon. **—des·sert·spoon·ful** (dĬ zûrt'spoon fŏŏl', -spŏŏn-), *n.*

des·sia·tine (dĕs'yə tēn'), *n.* a Russian unit of land measure equal to 2.7 English acres. [t. Russ.: m. *desyatína*, lit., tithe, tenth]

de·ster·i·lize (dē stĕr'ə līz'), *v.t.,* **-lized, -lizing.** to utilize an idle fund or commodity, as when a nation issues currency against gold previously unused.

Des·ter·ro (dĕs tĕr'rŏŏ), *n.* former name of **Florianópolis.**

des·ti·na·tion (dĕs'tə nā'shən), *n.* **1.** the predetermined end of a journey or voyage. **2.** the purpose for which anything is destined; ultimate end or design.

des·tine (dĕs'tĬn), *v.t.,* **-tined, -tining. 1.** to set apart for a particular use, purpose, etc.; design; intend. **2.** to appoint or ordain beforehand, as by divine decree; foreordain; predetermine. [ME *destenen*, t. OF: m. *destiner*, t. L: m. *dēstināre* make fast, establish, appoint]

des·tined (dĕs'tĬnd), *adj.* **1.** bound for a certain destination. **2.** designed; intended. **3.** foreordained; predetermined.

des·ti·ny (dĕs'tə nĬ), *n., pl.* **-nies. 1.** that which is to happen to a particular person or thing; one's lot or

fortune. **2.** the predetermined course of events. **3.** the power or agency which determines the course of events. **4.** (*cap.*) this power personified or represented as a goddess. **5. the Destinies,** the Fates. [ME *destinee*, t. OF, der. *destiner* DESTINE] **—Syn. 2.** See **fate.**

des·ti·tute (dĕs'tə tūt', -tōōt'), *adj.* **1.** bereft of means or resources; lacking the means of subsistence. **2.** deprived or devoid of (something) (fol. by *of*). **3.** *Obs.* abandoned or deserted. [t. L: m. s. *dēstitūtus*, pp., put away, abandoned] **—des'ti·tute'ness**, *n.* **—Syn. 1.** needy, poor, indigent, necessitous, penniless, poverty-stricken. **2.** lacking, deficient.

des·ti·tu·tion (dĕs'tə tū'shən, -tōō'-), *n.* **1.** want of the means of subsistence; utter poverty. **2.** deprivation; want; absence. **—Syn. 1.** See **poverty. —Ant. 1.** affluence.

des·tri·er (dĕs'trĬ ər, dĕs trĬr'), *n. Archaic.* a war horse; a charger. [ME *destrer*, t. AF, var. of OF *destrier*, g. LL *dextrārius*, lit., (horse) led at the right hand]

de·stroy (dĬ stroi'), *v.t.* **1.** to reduce to pieces or to a useless form; ruin; spoil; consume; demolish. **2.** to put an end to; extinguish. **3.** to kill; slay. **4.** to render ineffective; nullify; invalidate. [ME *destruy(en)*, t. OF: m. *destruire*, g. LL var. of L *dēstruere* pull down, destroy] **—de·stroy'a·ble**, *adj.* **—Syn. 1.** DESTROY, DEMOLISH, RAZE imply reducing a thing to uselessness. To DESTROY is to reduce something to nothingness or to take away its powers and functions so that restoration is impossible; the action is usually violent or sudden, but may be gradual and slow, esp. when it entails a reversal of natural processes: *fire destroys a building, disease destroys tissues.* To DEMOLISH is to destroy an organized body or structure by complete separation of parts: *to demolish a machine.* To RAZE is to level down to the ground: *to raze a fortress.* **—Ant. 1.** construct. **2.** establish. **3.** save. **4.** preserve.

de·stroy·er (dĬ stroi'ər), *n.* **1.** one who or that which destroys. **2.** a torpedo-boat destroyer.

de·struct·i·ble (dĬ strŭk'tə bəl), *adj.* that may be destroyed; liable to destruction. **—de·struct'i·bil'i·ty, de·struct'i·ble·ness**, *n.*

de·struc·tion (dĬ strŭk'shən), *n.* **1.** act of destroying. **2.** fact or condition of being destroyed; demolition; annihilation. **3.** a cause or means of destroying. [t. L: s. *dēstructio*] **—Syn. 1.** extinction, extermination. See **ruin.**

de·struc·tion·ist (dĬ strŭk'shən Ĭst), *n.* an advocate of the destruction of an existing political institution or the like.

de·struc·tive (dĬ strŭk'tĬv), *adj.* **1.** tending to destroy; causing destruction (fol. by *of* or *to*). **2.** tending to overthrow, disprove, or discredit: *destructive criticism.* **—de·struc'tive·ly**, *adv.* **—de·struc'tive·ness, de·struc·tiv'i·ty**, *n.* **—Syn. 1.** ruinous, baleful, pernicious, deleterious.

destructive distillation, *Chem.* the destruction or decomposition of a substance, as wood, coal, etc., by heat in a closed vessel, and the collection of the volatile matters evolved.

de·struc·tor (dĬ strŭk'tər), *n. Brit.* a furnace for the burning of refuse; an incinerator. [t. LL, der. L *dēstruere* destroy]

des·ue·tude (dĕs'wə tūd', -tōōd'), *n.* state of being no longer used or practiced. [t. F, t. L: m. *dēsuētūdo*]

de·sul·fur (dē sŭl'fər), *v.t.* to free from sulfur; desulfurize.

de·sul·fu·rize (dō sŭl'fə rīz'), *v.t.,* **-rized, -rizing.** to free from sulfur. **—de·sul'fu·ri·za'tion**, *n.*

des·ul·to·ry (dĕs'əl tōr'Ĭ), *adj.* **1.** veering about from one thing to another; disconnected, unmethodical, or fitful: *desultory reading or conversation.* **2.** random: *a desultory thought.* **3.** *m.* s. *dēsultōrius* of a leaper, superficial] **—des'ul·to·ri·ly**, *adv.* **—des'ul·to'ri·ness**, *n.* **—Ant. 1.** methodical. **2.** pertinent.

de·tach (dĬ tăch'), *v.t.* **1.** to unfasten and separate; disengage; disunite. **2.** to send away (a regiment, ship, etc.) on a special mission: *men were detached to defend the pass.* [t. F: s. *détacher*, der. OF *tache* (g. Rom. *tacca*) nail. Cf. ATTACH] **—de·tach'a·ble**, *adj.* **—de·tach'-a·bil'i·ty**, *n.* **—de·tach'er**, *n.*

de·tached (dĬ tăcht'), *adj.* **1.** standing apart; separate; unattached (usually applied to houses): *he lives in a detached house.* Cf. **semidetached. 2.** not interested; unconcerned.

de·tach·ment (dĬ tăch'mənt), *n.* **1.** act of detaching. **2.** condition of being detached. **3.** a state of aloofness, as from worldly affairs or from the concerns of others. **4.** freedom from prejudice or partiality. **5.** act of sending out a detached force of troops or naval ships. **6.** something detached, as a number of troops separated from a main force for some special combat or other task.

de·tail (*n.* dĬ tāl', dē'tāl; *v.* dĬ tāl'), *n.* **1.** an individual or minute part; an item or particular. **2.** particulars collectively; minutiae. **3.** a dealing with or treating part by part or item by item. **4.** a narrative or report of particulars. **5.** a detail drawing. **6.** any small section of a larger structure considered as a unit. **7.** *Mil.* **a.** a detailing or telling off, as of a small force or an officer, for a special service. **b.** the party or person so selected. **c.** a particular assignment of duty. **8. in detail,** circumstantially; item by item. **9.** to relate or report in particulars; tell fully and distinctly. **10.** *Mil.* to tell off or appoint for some particular duty, as a patrol, a guard, etc. [t. F, der. *détailler* cut in pieces, retail]

detail drawing, a drawing, at relatively large scale, of a part of a building, machine, etc., with dimensions or other information for use in construction.

de·tain (dǐ tān′), v.t. **1.** to keep from proceeding; keep waiting; delay. **2.** to keep under restraint or in custody. **3.** to keep back or withhold, as from a person. [late ME detaine(n), t. OF: m. detenir, L: m. dētinēre keep back] **—de·tain′ment,** n. **—Syn. 1.** retard, stop.

de·tain·er (dǐ tā′nər), n. Law. **1.** the wrongful detaining or withholding of what belongs to another. **2.** a writ for the further detention of a person already in custody. [t. AF: m. detener, var. of OF detenir]

de·tect (dǐ tĕkt′), v.t. **1.** to discover or catch (a person) in the performance of some act: to detect someone in a dishonest act. **2.** to find out the action or character of: to detect a hypocrite. **3.** to discover the presence, existence, or fact of. **4.** Radio. to subject to the action of a detector. [t. L: s. dētectus, pp., discovered, uncovered] **—de·tect′a·ble, de·tect′i·ble,** adj. **—Syn. 3.** See **learn.**

de·tec·tion (dǐ tĕk′shən), n. **1.** act of detecting. **2.** fact of being detected. **3.** discovery, as of error or crime. **4.** Radio. **a.** rectification of alternating currents in a radio receiver. **b.** the conversion of an alternating carrier wave or current into a direct pulsating current equivalent to the transmitted signal; demodulation.

de·tec·tive (dǐ tĕk′tǐv), n. **1.** a member of the police force whose function it is to obtain information and evidence, as of offenses against the law. **—adj. 2.** pertaining to detection or detectives: a detective story. **3.** serving to detect; detecting.

de·tec·tor (dǐ tĕk′tər), n. **1.** one who or that which detects. **2.** Radio. **a.** a device for detecting electric oscillations or waves. **b.** a device, as a crystal detector or a vacuum tube, which rectifies the alternating currents in a radio receiver. [t. LL]

de·tent (dǐ tĕnt′), n. a piece of a mechanism which, when disengaged, releases the operating power, or by which the action is prevented or checked; a catch, as in a lock; a pawl. [t. F: m. détente, der. détendre relax, f. dé- DIS-[1] + tendre (g. L tendere stretch)]

de·ten·tion (dǐ tĕn′shən), n. **1.** act of detaining. **2.** state of being detained. **3.** a keeping in custody; confinement. **4.** the withholding of what belongs to or is claimed by another.

de·ter (dǐ tûr′), v.t., **-terred, -terring.** to discourage or restrain (one) from acting or proceeding through fear, doubt, etc. [t. L: m. s. dēterrēre frighten from] **—de·ter′ment,** n. **—Syn.** dissuade, hinder, prevent, stop.

de·terge (dǐ tûrj′), v.t., **-terged, -terging. 1.** to wipe away. **2.** to cleanse by removing foul or morbid matter, as from a wound. [t. L: m. s. dētergēre wipe off]

de·ter·gen·cy (dǐ tûr′jən sǐ), n. cleansing or purging power. Also, **de·ter′gence.**

de·ter·gent (dǐ tûr′jənt), adj. **1.** cleansing; clearing away foul matter, as a medicinal substance. **—n. 2.** a detergent substance or agent.

de·te·ri·o·rate (dǐ tǐr′ǐ ə rāt′), v.t., v.i., **-rated, -rating.** to make or become worse; make or become lower in character or quality. [t. L: m. s. dēteriōrātus, pp.] **—de·te′ri·o·ra′tion,** n. **—de·te′ri·o·ra′tive,** adj.

de·ter·mi·na·ble (dǐ tûr′mə nə bəl), adj. **1.** capable of being determined. **2.** Law. subject to termination.

de·ter·mi·nant (dǐ tûr′mə nənt), n. **1.** a determining agent or factor. **2.** Math. an algebraic expression in the elements of any square matrix used in solving linear systems of equations.

de·ter·mi·nate (dǐ tûr′mə nǐt), adj. **1.** having defined limits; definite. **2.** settled; positive. **3.** determined upon; conclusive; final. **4.** determined; resolute. **5.** Bot. (of an inflorescence) having the primary and each secondary axis ending in a flower or bud, thus preventing further elongation. [ME, t. L: m. s. dēterminātus, pp., determined] **—de·ter′mi·nate·ly,** adv. **—de·ter′mi·nate·ness,** n.

de·ter·mi·na·tion (dǐ tûr′mə nā′shən), n. **1.** act of coming to a decision; the fixing or settling of a purpose. **2.** ascertainment, as after observation or investigation. **3.** a result ascertained; a solution. **4.** the settlement of a dispute, etc., by authoritative decision. **5.** the decision arrived at or pronounced. **6.** the quality of being determined or resolute; firmness of purpose. **7.** a fixed purpose or intention. **8.** the fixing or settling of amount, limit, character, etc. **9.** fixed direction or tendency toward some object or end. **10.** Chiefly Law. conclusion or termination. **11.** Embryol. the fixation of the nature of morphological differentiation in a group of cells before actual, visible differentiation. **12.** Logic. **a.** the rendering of a notion more definite by the addition of differentiating characters. **b.** the definition of a concept by citing its constituent elements.

de·ter·mi·na·tive (dǐ tûr′mə nā′tǐv), adj. **1.** serving to determine; determining. **—n. 2.** something that determines. **—de·ter′mi·na·tive·ly,** adv. **—de·ter′mi·na·tive·ness,** n.

de·ter·mine (dǐ tûr′mǐn), v., **-mined, -mining. —v.t. 1.** to settle or decide (a dispute, question, etc.) by an authoritative decision. **2.** to conclude or ascertain, as after reasoning, observation, etc. **3.** Geom. to fix the position of. **4.** to fix or decide causally; condition: demand determines supply. **5.** to give direction or tendency to; impel. **6.** Logic. to limit, as an idea, by adding differentiating characters. **7.** Chiefly Legal. to put an end to; terminate. **8.** to lead or bring (a person) to a

decision: it finally determined him to do it. **9.** to decide upon. **—v.i. 10.** to come to a decision or resolution; decide. **11.** Chiefly Legal. to come to an end. [ME determine(n), t. OF: m. determiner, L: m. dēterminäre limit] **—de·ter′min·er,** n. **—Syn. 1.** See **decide.**

de·ter·mined (dǐ tûr′mǐnd), adj. resolute; unflinching; firm. **—de·ter′mined·ly,** adv. **—de·ter′mined·ness,** n. **—Syn.** stanch, inflexible, unfaltering, unwavering.

de·ter·min·ism (dǐ tûr′mə nǐz′əm), n. the doctrine that neither outer events nor human choices are uncaused, but are the results of antecedent conditions, physical or psychological. **—de·ter′min·ist,** n., adj. **—de·ter′min·is′tic,** adj.

de·ter·rent (dǐ tûr′ənt, -tĕr′-), adj. **1.** deterring; restraining. **—n. 2.** something that deters. **—de·ter′rence,** n.

de·ter·sive (dǐ tûr′sǐv), adj. **1.** detergent. **—n. 2.** a detersive agent or medicine.

de·test (dǐ tĕst′), v.t. to feel abhorrence of; hate; dislike intensely. [t. F: s. détester, t. L: m. dētestārī, lit., curse while calling a deity to witness] **—de·test′er,** n. **—Syn.** abhor, loathe, abominate. See **hate.**

de·test·a·ble (dǐ tĕs′tə bəl), adj. deserving to be detested; abominable; hateful. **—de·test′a·bil′i·ty, de·test′a·ble·ness,** n. **—de·test′a·bly,** adv. **—Syn.** execrable, abhorrent, loathsome, odious, vile.

de·tes·ta·tion (dē′tĕs tā′shən), n. **1.** abhorrence; hatred. **2.** a person or thing detested.

de·throne (dē thrōn′), v.t., **-throned, -throning.** to remove from the throne; depose. **—de·throne′ment,** n. **—de·thron′er,** n.

det·i·nue (dĕt′ə nū′, -nōō′), n. Law. an old common-law form of action to recover possession or the value of articles of personal property wrongfully detained. [t. OF: m. detenue detention, orig. sup. fem. of detenir DE-TAIN]

det·o·nate (dĕt′ə nāt′, dē′tə-), v.i., v.t., **-nated, -nating.** to explode, esp. with great noise, suddenness, or violence. [t. L: m. s. dētonātus, pp., thundered forth]

det·o·na·tion (dĕt′ə nā′shən, dē′tə-), n. **1.** act of detonating. **2.** an explosion.

det·o·na·tor (dĕt′ə nā′tər, dē′tə-), n. **1.** a device, as a percussion cap or an explosive, used to make another substance explode. **2.** something that explodes.

de·tour (dē′tŏŏr, dǐ tŏŏr′), n. **1.** a roundabout or circuitous way or course, esp. one used temporarily instead of the main route. **—v.i. 2.** to make a detour; go by way of a detour. **—v.t. 3.** to cause to make a detour; send by way of a detour. Also, French, **dé·tour** (dē tŏŏr′). [t. F, der. détourner turn aside, f. dé- DIS-[1] + tourner turn]

de·tract (dǐ trăkt′), v.t. **1.** to take away (a part); abate (fol. by from). **2.** to draw away or divert. **—v.i. 3.** to take away a part, as from quality, value, or reputation. [t. L: s. dētractus, pp., drawn away or down] **—de·tract′ing·ly,** adv. **—de·trac′tor,** n.

de·trac·tion (dǐ trăk′shən), n. act of detracting, or of disparaging or belittling the reputation or worth of a person. **—Syn.** defamation, vilification.

de·trac·tive (dǐ trăk′tǐv), adj. tending or seeking to detract; depreciative. Also, **de·trac·to·ry** (dǐ trăk′tə rǐ). **—de·trac′tive·ly,** adv.

de·train (dē trān′), v.i., v.t. Chiefly Brit. to discharge or alight from a railroad train. **—de·train′ment,** n.

det·ri·ment (dĕt′rə mənt), n. **1.** loss, damage, or injury. **2.** a cause of loss or damage. [t. L: s. dētrīmentum loss, damage] **—Syn. 1.** harm, hurt, impairment, disadvantage, prejudice. See **damage.**

det·ri·men·tal (dĕt′rǐ mĕn′təl), adj. causing detriment; injurious; prejudicial. **—det′ri·men′tal·ly,** adv.

de·tri·tal (dǐ trī′təl), adj. composed of detritus.

de·tri·tion (dǐ trǐsh′ən), n. act of wearing away by rubbing.

de·tri·tus (dǐ trī′təs), n. **1.** Geol. particles of rock or other material worn or broken away from a mass, as by the action of water or glacial ice. **2.** any disintegrated material; debris. [t. L: a rubbing away]

De·troit (dǐ troit′), n. **1.** a city in SE Michigan, on the Detroit river. 1,849,568 (1950). **2.** a river flowing from Lake St. Clair into Lake Erie, forming a part of the boundary between the U.S. and Canada: the busiest inland waterway in the world. 25 mi.

de trop (də trō′), French. **1.** too much; too many. **2.** in the way; not wanted.

de·trude (dǐ trŏŏd′), v.t., **-truded, -truding. 1.** to thrust out or away. **2.** to thrust or force down. [t. L: m. s. dētrūdere]

de·trun·cate (dǐ trŭng′kāt), v.t., **-cated, -cating.** to reduce by cutting off a part; cut down. [t. L: m. s. dētruncātus, pp.] **—de′trun·ca′tion,** n.

de·tru·sion (dǐ trŏŏ′zhən), n. act of detruding. [t. LL: s. dētrūsio, der. L dētrūdere thrust away]

Deu·ca·li·on (dū kā′lǐ ən, dōō-), n. Gk. Legend. a son of Prometheus. He survived the deluge with his wife Pyrrha, and became the ancestor of the renewed human race.

deuce[1] (dūs, dōōs), n. **1.** Cards, Dice. a card, or the side of a die, having two pips. **2.** Tennis. a score in which each side has three points (the score 40) in a game, or five games in a set. [t. OF: m. deus, g. L duōs, acc. of duo two]

---

b., blend of, blended; **c.,** cognate with; **d.,** dialect, dialectal; **der.,** derived from; **f.,** formed from; **g.,** going back to; **m.,** modification of; **r.,** replacing; **s.,** stem of; **t.,** taken from; **?,** perhaps. See the full key on inside cover.

deuce[2] (dūs, dōōs), *n.* *Colloq.* bad luck; the mischief; the devil (used in mild imprecations and exclamations). [special use of *deuce*, prob. t. LG: m. *de duus!* the deuce, an unlucky throw at dice. Cf. G *der daus!*]

deu·ced (dū'sĭd, dōō'-; dūst, dōōst), *adj.* *Brit. Colloq.* confounded; excessive. **—deu′ced, deu′ced·ly,** *adv.*

de·us ex ma·chi·na (dē′əs ĕks măk′ə nə), *Latin.* a supernatural or unmotivated device for unraveling a plot, esp. in drama. [L: god from a machine]

De·us Mi·se·re·a·tur (dē′əs mĭz′ə rĭ ā′tər *or, esp. in Church Latin,* dā′ŏŏs mē′sā rā ä′tŏŏr), *Latin.* (May) God have mercy; God be merciful (title of Psalm 67).

De·us vult (dē′əs vŭlt′ *or, esp. in Church Latin,* dā′ŏŏs vŏŏlt′), *Latin.* God wills (it) (cry of the Crusaders).

deut-, var. of deuto-, before vowels.

Deut., Deuteronomy.

deuter-, a form of deutero- (def. 1) used before a vowel.

deu·te·ri·um (dū tĭr′ĭ əm, dōō-), *n.* *Chem.* an isotope of hydrogen, having twice the mass of ordinary hydrogen; heavy hydrogen. *Symbol:* D; *at. no.:* 1; *at. wt.:* 2.01. [NL, t. Gk.: m. *deutereîon*, neut. sing. of *deutereîos*, adj., having second place]

deuterium oxide, *Chem.* heavy water, D2O.

deutero-, a word element: **1.** meaning "second" or "later," as in *deuterogamy.* **2.** *Chem.* indicating the presence of deuterium. [t. Gk., comb. form of *deúteros* second]

deu·ter·o·ca·non·i·cal books (dū′tər ō kə nŏn′ə kəl, dōō′-), the books of the Bible regarded by the Roman Catholic Church as canonical but not universally acknowledged as such in the early church, including, in the Old Testament, most of the Protestant Apocrypha.

deu·ter·og·a·my (dū′tə rŏg′ə mĭ, dōō′-). *n.* **1.** a second marriage, after the death or divorce of a first husband or wife. **2.** the custom of contracting such marriage. [t. Gk.: m. s. *deuterogamía* second marriage] **—deu′ter·og′a·mist,** *n.*

deu·ter·on (dū′tə rŏn′, dōō′-), *n.* *Physics.* a deuterium nucleus, a particle with one positive charge.

Deu·ter·on·o·my (dū′tə rŏn′ə mĭ, dōō′-), *n.* *Bible.* the fifth book of the Pentateuch, containing a second statement of the Mosaic law. [t. LL: m. s. *Deuteronomium*, t. Gk.: m. *Deuteronómion* the second law]

deuto-, **1.** var. of deutero-. **2.** *Chem.* a prefix denoting the second in a series. Also, **deut-.**

deu·to·plasm (dū′tə plăz′əm, dōō′-). *n.* *Embryol.* that part of the ovocyte which furnishes the nourishment of the embryo.

Deut·sches Reich (doi′chəs rīκн′), former official name of Germany.

Deutsch·land (doich′länt′), *n.* German name of **Germany.**

de·va (dā′və), *n.* *Hindu Myth.* a god or divinity; one of an order of good spirits. [t. Skt.]

De Va·le·ra (dĕv′ə lâr′ə, -lĭr′ə; *Irish* dĕ vä lā′rä), Ea·mon (ā′mən), born 1882, Irish statesman: president of Executive Council of Irish Free State, 1932–37; prime minister of Eire, 1937–48.

de·val·u·ate (dē văl′yŏŏ āt′), *v.t.,* **-ated, -ating.** **1.** to deprive of value; reduce the value of. **2.** to fix a lower legal value on (a currency). [f. DE- + VALUE, n. + -ATE[1]] **—de·val′u·a′tion,** *n.*

de·val·ue (dē văl′ū), *v.t.,* **-valued, -valuing.** to devaluate.

De·va·na·ga·ri (dā′və nä′gə rē′), *n.* the syllabary invented for writing Sanskrit and widely employed for modern languages of India. [t. Skt.: lit., Nagari (an alphabet of India) of the gods]

dev·as·tate (dĕv′ə stāt′), *v.t.,* **-tated, -tating.** to lay waste; render desolate. [t. L: m.s. *dēvastātus*, pp.] **—dev′as·tat′ing·ly,** *adv.* **—dev′as·ta′tor,** *n.* **—Syn.** See ravage.

dev·as·ta·tion (dĕv′ə stā′shən), *n.* **1.** act of devastating; destruction. **2.** devastated state; desolation.

de Ve·ga (dĕ vě′gä), Lope (lō′pĕ), (*Lope Félix de Vega Carpio*) 1562–1635, Spanish dramatist and poet.

dev·el (dĕv′əl), *n.* *Scot.* a heavy blow.

devel., development.

de·vel·op (dĭ vĕl′əp), *v.t.* **1.** to bring out the capabilities or possibilities of; bring to a more advanced or effective state; cause to grow or expand; elaborate. **2.** to make known; disclose; reveal. **3.** to bring into being or activity; generate; evolve. **4.** *Biol.* to cause to go through the process of natural evolution from a previous and lower stage, or from an embryonic state to a later and more complex or perfect one. **5.** *Math.* to express in an extended form, as in a series. **6.** *Music.* to unfold, by various technical means, the inherent possibilities of (a theme). **7.** *Photog.* **a.** to render visible (the latent image) in the exposed sensitized film of a photographic plate, etc. **b.** to treat (a photographic plate, etc.) with chemical agents so as to bring out the latent image. **—v.i. 8.** to grow into a more mature or advanced state; advance; expand: *he is developing into a good citizen.* **9.** to come gradually into existence or operation; be evolved. **10.** to come out or be disclosed: *the plot of a novel develops.* **11.** *Biol.* to undergo differentiation in ontogeny or progress in phylogeny. **12.** to undergo developing, as a photographic plate. Also, **de·vel′ope.** [t. F: m.s. *développer*, f. dé- DIS-[1] + *voluper* wrap. Cf.

ENVELOP] —de·vel′op·a·ble, *adj.*

de·vel·op·er (dĭ vĕl′əp ər), *n.* **1.** one who or that which develops. **2.** *Photog.* the reducing agent or solution used to develop a photographic film or plate.

de·vel·op·ment (dĭ vĕl′əp mənt), *n.* **1.** act of developing. **2.** a developed state, form, or product. **3.** *Music.* the part of a movement or composition in which a theme or themes are developed. **—de·vel′op·men′tal,** *adj.* **—de·vel′op·men′tal·ly,** *adv.* **—Syn. 1.** expansion, elaboration, growth.

Dev·e·reux (dĕv′ə rōō′), *n.* Robert. See Essex.

de·vest (dĭ vĕst′), *v.t.* **1.** *Law.* to divest. **2.** *Obs.* to undress. [t. OF: s. *devester* (also *desvestir*), f. des- DIS-[1] + *vestir*, g. L *vestīre* clothe. See DIVEST]

De·vi (dā′vē), *n.* *Hinduism.* a female deity. [t. Skt.]

de·vi·ate (dē′vĭ āt′), *v.,* **-ated, -ating.** **—v.i. 1.** to turn aside (from the way or course); depart or swerve (from a course of action or procedure); digress (from a line of thought or reasoning). **—v.t. 2.** to cause to swerve; turn aside. [t. LL: m.s. *dēviātus*, pp. of *dēviāre*, der. L *dē-* DE- + *via* way] **—de′vi·a′tor,** *n.*

—Syn. 1. DEVIATE, DIGRESS, DIVERGE, SWERVE imply turning or going aside from a path. To DEVIATE is to turn or wander, often by slight degrees from what is considered the most direct or desirable approach to a given physical, intellectual, or moral end: *fear caused him to deviate from the truth.* To DIGRESS is primarily to wander from the main theme or topic in writing or speaking, esp. for explanation or illustration: *some authors digress to relate entertaining episodes.* Two paths DIVERGE when they proceed from a common point in such directions that the distance between them increases: *the sides of an angle diverge from a common point, their interests gradually diverged.* To SWERVE is to make a sudden or sharp turn from a line or course (and then, often, return to it): *the car swerved to avoid striking a pedestrian.*

de·vi·a·tion (dē′vĭ ā′shən), *n.* **1.** act of deviating; divergence. **2.** *Statistics.* the difference between one of a set of values and the mean of the set.

de·vi·a·tion·ism (dē′vĭ ā′shən ĭz əm), *n.* (in Communist ideology) departure from accepted party policies. **—de′vi·a′tion·ist,** *n.*

de·vice (dĭ vīs′), *n.* **1.** an invention or contrivance. **2.** a plan or scheme for effecting a purpose. **3.** a crafty scheme; a trick. **4.** an artistic figure or design used as a heraldic bearing (often accompanied by a motto), or as an emblem, badge, trademark, or the like. **5.** a motto. **6.** (*pl.*) will; desire; inclination: *left to his own devices.* **7.** something artistically or fancifully designed. **8.** *Archaic.* act or faculty of planning, contriving, or inventing. [b. ME *devis* division, discourse and *devise* heraldic device, will, both t. OF, g. L *dīvisus, -a*, pp., divided] **—Syn. 3.** wile, ruse, artifice, shift.

dev·il (dĕv′əl), *n., v.,* **-iled, -iling** or (*esp. Brit*) **-illed, -illing. —n. 1.** *Theol.* **a.** (*sometimes cap.*) the supreme spirit of evil; Satan. **b.** a subordinate evil spirit at enmity with God, and having power to afflict man both with bodily disease and with spiritual corruption. **2.** an atrociously wicked, cruel, or ill-tempered person. **3.** a person of great cleverness, energy, or recklessness. **4.** the errand boy or the youngest apprentice in a printing office. **5.** a fellow, esp. an unfortunate one. **6.** any of various mechanical devices, as a machine for tearing rags, etc. **7.** the devil, an emphatic expletive used in disgust, vexation, wonder, strong negation, etc. **8. the devil to pay,** great mischief afoot or trouble to be faced. **9. give the devil his due,** to do justice even to a bad person or one who is disliked. **—v.t. 10.** *Colloq.* to harass, torment, or plague. **11.** to tear (rags, etc.) to pieces with a devil (def. 6). **12.** *Cookery.* to prepare (food) with hot or savory seasoning. [ME *devel*, OE *deofol*, t. L: m.s. *diabolus*, t. Gk.: m. *diábolos* Satan, orig. slanderer]

devil dog, a nickname for a United States Marine.

dev·il·fish (dĕv′əl fĭsh′), *n., pl.* **-fishes,** (*esp. collectively*) **-fish. 1.** any of various marine animals, as the manta rays. **2.** any of various large cephalopods, as the octopus.

Devilfish (def. 1). *Manta hamiltoni* (Total length 20 ft.; tail 6 ft. width 20 ft.)

dev·il·ish (dĕv′əl ĭsh, dĕv′lĭsh), *adj.* **1.** of, like, or befitting a devil; diabolical; fiendish. **2.** *Colloq.* excessive; very great. **—adv. 3.** *Colloq.* excessively; extremely. **—dev′il·ish·ly,** *adv.* **—dev′il·ish·ness,** *n.* **—Syn. 1.** satanic, demoniac, infernal, hellish, impious, wicked, atrocious, nefarious.

dev·il·kin (dĕv′əl kĭn), *n.* a little devil; an imp.

dev·il·ment (dĕv′əl mənt), *n.* devilish action or conduct; mischief.

dev·il·ry (dĕv′əl rĭ), *n., pl.* **-ries.** deviltry.

devil's advocate, 1. an advocate of an opposing or bad cause. **2.** *Rom. Cath. Ch.* a person appointed to present the arguments against a proposed canonization as a saint. [trans. of L *advocātus diabolī*]

devil's darning needle, dragonfly.

devil's food cake, a rich, chocolate cake.

Devil's Island, one of the Safety Islands, off the coast of French Guiana: former French penal colony. French, Île du Diable.

devil's tattoo, a meaningless beating or drumming with the hands or feet.

dev·il·try (dĕv′əl trĭ), *n., pl.* **-tries. 1.** wicked or reckless mischief. **2.** extreme wickedness. **3.** diabolic magic or art. **4.** demonology. Also, **devilry.**

dev·il·wood (dĕv′əl wŏŏd′), *n.* a small oleaceous tree, *Osmanthus americanus*, of the U.S., with a hard, strong, close-grained wood.

de·vi·ous (dē′vĭ əs), *adj.* 1. departing from the direct way; circuitous: *a devious course.* 2. turning aside from the way; swerving; straying: *a devious comet.* 3. erring. [t. L: m. *dēvius* out of the way] —**de′vi·ous·ly,** *adv.* —**de′vi·ous·ness,** *n.*

de·vis·a·ble (dĭ vī′zə bəl), *adj.* 1. capable of being invented or contrived. 2. *Law.* capable of being bequeathed or assigned by will.

de·vis·al (dĭ vī′zəl), *n.* act of devising; contrivance.

de·vise (dĭ vīz′), *v.,* -**vised, -vising.** *n.* —*v.t.* 1. to order or arrange the plan of; think out; plan; contrive; invent. 2. *Law.* to assign or transmit (property, formerly specif. real property) by will. 3. *Obs.* to conceive or imagine. —*v.i.* 4. to form a plan; contrive. —*n.* 5. *Law.* **a.** act of disposing of property, esp. real property, by will. **b.** a will or clause in a will disposing of property, esp. real property. **c.** the property disposed of. [ME *devise*(n), t. OF: m. *deviser,* g. LL freq. of L *dividere* separate] —**de·vis′er,** *n.* —**Syn.** 1. See **prepare.**

de·vi·see (dĭ vĭ zē′, dĕv′ə zō′), *n. Law.* one to whom a devise is made.

de·vi·sor (dĭ vī′zər), *n. Law.* one who makes a devise.

de·vi·tal·ize (dē vī′tə līz′), *v.t.* -**ized, -izing.** to deprive of vitality or vital properties; make lifeless or weak. —**de·vi′tal·i·za′tion,** *n.* —**Ant.** invigorate.

de·vit·ri·fy (dē vĭt′rə fī′), *v.t.,* -**fied, -fying.** to deprive, wholly or partly, of vitreous character or properties. —**de·vit′ri·fi·ca′tion,** *n.*

de·vo·cal·ize (dē vō′kə līz′), *v.t.* -**ized, -izing.** *Phonet.* to deprive of vocal quality. —**de·vo′cal·i·za′tion,** *n.*

de·void (dĭ void′), *adj.* empty, void, or destitute (fol. by *of*). [orig. pp. of obs. *devoid,* v., t. OF: m. *desvuidier* empty out, f. *des-* DIS-[1] + *vuidier* empty, VOID, v.]

de·voir (də vwär′, dĕv′wär; *Fr.* də vwâr′), *n.* 1. an act of civility or respect. 2. (*pl.*) respects or compliments. 3. *Archaic.* duty. [t. F, orig. inf., g. L *dēbēre* owe]

dev·o·lu·tion (dĕv′ə lōō′shən), *n.* 1. act or fact of devolving; passage onward from stage to stage. 2. the passing on to a successor of an unexercised right. 3. *Law.* the passing of property upon death. 4. *Biol.* degeneration; retrograde evolution (opposed to *evolution*).

de·volve (dĭ vŏlv′), *v.,* -**volved, -volving.** —*v.t.* 1. to transfer or delegate (a duty, responsibility, etc.) to or upon another; pass on. 2. *Archaic.* to roll downward; roll. —*v.i.* 3. to fall as a duty or responsibility on a person. 4. *Archaic.* to roll down. [t. L: m.s. *dēvolvere* roll down] —**de·volve′ment,** *n.*

Dev·on (dĕv′ən), *n.* 1. one of a noted breed of dual-purpose cattle, usually red, originating in Devonshire, England. 2. Devonshire.

De·vo·ni·an (də vō′nĭ ən), *adj.* 1. *Stratig.* pertaining to a geological period or a system of rocks following the Silurian and preceding the Carboniferous or Mississippian. 2. of or pertaining to Devonshire, England. —*n.* 3. *Stratig.* the Devonian period or system. 4. a native or inhabitant of Devonshire.

Dev·on·shire (dĕv′ən shĭr′, -shər), *n.* a county in SW England. 738,000 pop. (est. 1946); 2612 sq. mi. *Co. seat:* Exeter. Also, **Devon.**

de·vote (dĭ vōt′), *v.,* -**voted, -voting,** *adj.* —*v.t.* 1. to give up or appropriate to a particular pursuit, occupation, purpose, cause, person, etc.: *devoting himself to science, evenings devoted to reading.* 2. to appropriate by or as by a vow; set apart or dedicate by a solemn or formal act; consecrate. 3. *Rare.* to pronounce a curse upon; doom. —*adj.* 4. *Archaic.* devoted. [t. L: m. s. *dēvōtus,* pp., vowed] —**Syn.** 1. assign, apply.

de·vot·ed (dĭ vō′tĭd), *adj.* 1. zealous or ardent in attachment: *a devoted friend.* 2. dedicated; consecrated. 3. *Archaic.* accursed or doomed. —**de·vot′ed·ly,** *adv.* —**de·vot′ed·ness,** *n.*

dev·o·tee (dĕv′ə tē′), *n.* 1. one ardently devoted to anything. 2. one zealously or fanatically devoted to religion.

de·vote·ment (dĭ vōt′mənt), *n.* devotion; dedication.

de·vo·tion (dĭ vō′shən), *n.* 1. dedication; consecration. 2. earnest attachment to a cause, person, etc. 3. a giving over or appropriating to any purpose, cause, etc. 4. *Theol.* the ready will to perform what belongs to the service of God. 5. (*often pl.*) *Eccles.* religious observance or worship; a form of prayer or worship for special use. [t. L: s. *dēvōtio*] —**Syn.** 2. See **love.**

de·vo·tion·al (dĭ vō′shən əl), *adj.* characterized by devotion; used in devotions. —**de·vo′tion·al·ly,** *adv.*

de·vour (dĭ vour′), *v.t.* 1. to swallow or eat up voraciously or ravenously. 2. to consume destructively, recklessly, or wantonly. 3. to swallow up or engulf. 4. to take in greedily with the senses or intellect. 5. to absorb or engross wholly: *devoured by fears.* [ME *devoure*(n), t. OF: m. *devorer,* t. L: m. *dēvorāre* swallow down] —**de·vour′er,** *n.* —**de·vour′ing·ly,** *adv.*

de·vout (dĭ vout′), *adj.* 1. devoted to divine worship or service; pious; religious. 2. expressing devotion or piety: *devout prayer.* 3. earnest or sincere; hearty. [ME, t. OF: m. *devot,* t. L: s. *dēvōtus,* pp., devoted] —**de·vout′·ly,** *adv.* —**de·vout′ness,** *n.* —**Syn.** 1. See **religious.**

De Vries (də vrēs′), **Hugo** (hy′gō), 1848–1935, Dutch botanist: proposed mutation theory of evolution.

dew (dū, dōō), *n.* 1. moisture condensed from the atmosphere, esp. at night, and deposited in the form of small drops upon any cool surface. 2. something likened to dew, as serving to refresh or as suggestive of morning or of youth. 3. moisture in small drops on a surface, as tears, perspiration, etc. —*v.t.* 4. to wet with or as with dew. [ME; OE *dēaw,* c. G *tau*] —**dew′less,** *adj.*

de·wan (dĭ wän′, -wŏn′), *n.* (in India) any of certain officials or servants. Also, **diwan.** [t. Hind.: minister (of state), t. Pers.: m. *dēvan* register. See DIVAN]

Dew·ar (dū′ər, dōō′-), *n.* **Sir James,** 1842–1923, Scottish chemist and physicist.

dew·ber·ry (dū′bĕr′ĭ, dōō′-), *n., pl.* -**ries.** 1. (in North America) the fruit of several species of running, trailing blackberries, principally *Rubus flagellaris.* 2. (in England) the fruit of *Rubus caesius.* 3. a plant bearing either fruit.

dew·claw (dū′klô′, dōō′-), *n.* 1. a functionless inner claw or digit in the foot of some dogs, not reaching the ground in walking. 2. an analogous false hoof of deer, hogs, etc.

dew·drop (dū′drŏp′, dōō′-), *n.* a drop of dew.

De Wet (də vĕt′), **Christian Rudolph** (krĭs′-tĭ än′ ry′dôlf), 1854–1922, Boer general.

Dew·ey (dū′ĭ, dōō′ĭ), *n.* 1. **George,** 1837–1917, U.S. admiral: defeated Spanish fleet in Manila Bay in the Spanish-American War. 2. **John,** born 1859, U.S. philosopher and educator. 3. **Melvil,** 1851–1931, U.S. librarian. 4. **Thomas Edmund,** born 1902, U.S. lawyer and political leader.

Dewey decimal system, *Library Science.* a system of classifying books and other publications into ten main classes of knowledge with further subdivision in these classes by use of the numbers (**Dewey decimals**) of a decimal system, devised by Melvil Dewey in 1876 and used in most libraries in the United States.

De Witt (də vĭt′), **Jan** (yän), 1625–72, Dutch statesman.

dew·lap (dū′lăp′, dōō′-), *n.* 1. the pendulous fold of skin under the throat of cattle. 2. any similar part, as the loose skin under the throat of some dogs, the wattle of fowls, etc. [f. dew, of uncert. meaning + lap, OE *læppa* pendulous piece. Cf. Dan. *doglæp*] —**dew′-lapped′,** *adj.*

dew plant, the ice plant.

dew point, the temperature of the air at which dew begins to be deposited; the temperature at which a given sample of air will have a relative humidity of 100%.

dew·y (dū′ĭ, dōō′ĭ), *adj.,* **dewier, dewiest.** 1. moist with or as with dew. 2. having the quality of dew: *dewy tears.* 3. *Poetic.* falling gently, or refreshing like dew: *dewy sleep.* 4. of dew. —**dew′i·ly,** *adv.* —**dew′i·ness,** *n.*

dex·ter (dĕk′stər), *adj.* 1. on the right side; right. 2. *Her.* situated to the right of the bearer and hence to the left of the spectator (opposed to *sinister*). 3. *Obs.* favorable. [t. L: right, favorable]

dex·ter·i·ty (dĕks tĕr′ə tĭ), *n.* 1. adroitness or skill in using the hands or body. 2. mental adroitness or skill; cleverness. 3. right-handedness. [f. DEXTER + -(I)TY[2]]

dex·ter·ous (dĕks′trəs, -tərəs), *adj.* 1. skillful or adroit in the use of the hands or body. 2. having mental adroitness or skill; clever. 3. done with dexterity. 4. right-handed. Also, **dextrous.** —**dex′ter·ous·ly,** *adv.* —**dex′ter·ous·ness,** *n.* —**Syn.** 1. adroit, deft, nimble, skillful. —**Ant.** 1. clumsy. 2. inept. 3. awkward.

dex·tral (dĕks′trəl), *adj.* 1. on the right-hand side; right. 2. right-handed. —**dex′tral·ly,** *adv.*

dex·tran (dĕks′trən), *n. Chem.* a white gummy material, produced from milk, molasses, etc., by bacterial action. [f. DEXTR(O)- + -AN(E)]

dex·trin (dĕks′trĭn), *n. Chem.* a soluble gummy substance formed from starch by the action of heat, acids, or ferments, occurring in various forms and having dextrorotatory properties, used as a substitute for gum arabic, as a mucilage, etc. Also, **dex·trine** (dĕks′trĭn, -trēn). [t. F: m. *dextrine,* der. L *dexter* right]

dex·tro (dĕks′trō), *adj. Chem.* turning clockwise.

dextro-, a word element meaning: 1. right. 2. *Chem.* turning clockwise. Also, **dextr-.** [t. L, comb. form of *dexter* right]

dex·tro·glu·cose (dĕks′trō glōō′kōs), *n. Chem.* See **glucose.**

dex·tro·gy·rate (dĕks′trō jī′rĭt, -rāt), *adj. Optics, Crystall., etc.* causing to turn toward the right hand: *a dextrogyrate crystal.*

dex·tro·ro·ta·tion (dĕks′trō rō tā′shən), *n. Optics, Chem., etc.* a turning of the plane of polarization of light to the right.

dex·tro·ro·ta·to·ry (dĕks′trō rō′rō′tə tôr′ĭ), *adj. Optics, Chem., etc.* turning the plane of polarization of light to the right, as certain crystals and compounds. Also, **dex·tro·ro·ta·ry** (dĕks′trō rō′tə rĭ).

dex·trorse (dĕks′trôrs, dĕks trôrs′), *adj. Bot.* rising spirally from left to right (from a point of view at the center of the spiral), as a stem (opposed to *sinistrorse*). Also, **dex·tror′sal.** [t. L: m.s. *dextrorsum* toward the right] —**dex′trorse·ly,** *adv.*

D, Dewclaw. Left forefoot of a terrier

Dextrorse stem

dex·trose (dĕks′trōs), *n.* *Chem.* dextroglucose, commercially obtainable from starch by acid hydrolysis. See **glucose.** [t. DEXTR(O)- + (GLUC)OSE]

dex·trous (dĕks′trəs), *adj.* dexterous. —**dex′trous·ly,** *adv.* —**dex′trous·ness,** *n.*

dey (dā), *n.* **1.** the title of the governor of Algiers before the French conquest in 1830. **2.** a title sometimes borne by the former rulers of Tunis and Tripoli. [t. F, t. Turk.: m. *dāī,* orig., maternal uncle]

Dezh·nev (dĕzh nyôf′), *n.* **Cape,** the NE tip of Asia, on Bering Strait. Also, **East Cape.**

de·zinc·i·fi·ca·tion (dē zĭng′kə fə kā′shən), *n.* *Metall.* a process of corrosion, in which the zinc of copper-zinc alloys becomes absorbed by the environment.

D.F., **1.** (L *Defensor Fidei*) Defender of the Faith. **2.** Distrito Federal.

dg., decigram; decigrams.

dhak (däk, dôk), *n.* an East Indian fabaceous tree, *Butea monosperma,* bearing orange-colored flowers and yielding an astringent gum or kino. [t. Hind.]

dhar·ma (där′mə; *native* dŭr′-), *n.* (in Hinduism and Buddhism) **1.** essential quality or character. **2.** law, esp. religious law. **3.** conformity to law; propriety. **4.** virtue. **5.** religion. [Skt.: decree, custom]

dhar·na (där′nə; *native* dŭr′-), *n.* the practice formerly common in India, etc., of fasting at a person's door until he complies with some demand. Also, **dhur·na** (dŭr′nə). [Hind.: placing]

Dhau·la·gi·ri (dou′lə gĭr′Ĭ), *n.* a peak of the Himalayas, in Nepal. 26,826 ft.

dhole (dōl), *n.* the Asiatic wild dog, a fierce, red-coated species, *Cuon rutilus,* of Asia, hunting in packs, and capable of running down large game.

dho·ti (dō′tĬ), *n., pl.* **-tis.** a loincloth worn by men in India. Also, **dhoo·ti** (dōō′tĬ). [t. Hind.]

dhow (dou), *n.* an Arab coasting vessel, usually lateen-rigged, used in the Arabian Sea, etc.

di (dē), *n.* *Music.* a tone in the scale between do and re, a half step above do.

di-[1], a prefix of Greek origin, meaning "twice," "doubly," "two," freely used (like *bi-*) as an English formative, as in *dicotyledon, dipolar,* and in many chemical terms, as *diatomic, disulfide.* Also, **dis-**[2]. Cf. **mono-.** [t. Gk., repr. *dís* twice, double; akin to Gk. *dýo* two; see BI-]

di-[2], var. of **dis-**[1], before *b, d, l, m, n, r, s,* and *v,* and sometimes *g* and *j,* as in *divide.*

di-[3], var. of **dia-,** before vowels, as in *diocese, diorama.* **Di,** *Chem.* didymium.

dia-, a prefix of learned words meaning: **1.** passing through, as in *diathermy.* **2.** thoroughly; completely, as in *diagnosis.* **3.** going apart, as in *dialysis.* **4.** opposed in moment, as in *diamagnetism.* Also, **di-**[3]. [t. Gk., repr. *diá,* prep., through, between, across, by, of; akin to *dýo* two, and di- DI-[1]]

di·a·base (dī′ə bās′), *n.* **1.** *U.S.* a dark igneous rock occurring as minor intrusives composed essentially of labradorite and pyroxene. **2.** *Brit.* a dark-colored igneous rock consisting essentially of augite and feldspar, an altered dolerite. **3.** *Obs.* diorite. [t. F, f. *dia-* (erron. for *di-* two) + *base* BASE[1]] —**di′a·ba′sic,** *adj.*

di·a·be·tes (dī′ə bē′tĬs, -tēz), *n.* *Pathol.* **1.** a disease in which the ability of the body to use sugar is impaired and sugar appears abnormally in the urine (**diabetes mellitus**). **2.** a disease in which there is a persistent abnormal amount of urine (**diabetes insipidus**). [t. NL, t. Gk.: a passer through]

di·a·bet·ic (dī′ə bĕt′Ĭk, -bē′tĬk), *adj.* **1.** of or pertaining to diabetes. **2.** having diabetes. —*n.* **3.** a person who has diabetes.

di·a·ble·rie (dĬ ä′blə rĬ; *Fr.* dyä blə rē′), *n.* **1.** diabolic magic or art; sorcery. **2.** the domain or realm of devils. **3.** the lore of devils; demonology. **4.** reckless mischief; deviltry. [t. F, der. *diable* DEVIL]

di·a·ble·ry (dĬ ä′blə rĬ), *n., pl.* **-leries.** diablerie.

di·a·bol·ic (dī′ə bŏl′Ĭk), *adj.* **1.** having the qualities of a devil; fiendish; outrageously wicked: *a diabolic plot.* **2.** pertaining to or actuated by the devil or a devil. Also, **di′a·bol′i·cal** (esp. for def. 1). [t. LL: s. *diabolicus,* t. Gk.: m. *diabolikós*] —**di′a·bol′i·cal·ly,** *adv.* —**di′a·bol′i·cal·ness,** *n.*

di·a·bo·lism (dī ăb′ə lĬz′əm), *n.* **1.** *Theol.* **a.** action aided or caused by the devil; sorcery; witchcraft. **b.** the character or condition of a devil. **c.** doctrine concerning devils; belief in or worship of devils. **2.** action befitting the devil; deviltry. —**di·ab′o·list,** *n.*

di·a·bo·lize (dī ăb′ə līz′), *v.t.,* **-lized, -lizing. 1.** to make diabolical or devilish. **2.** to represent as diabolical. **3.** to subject to diabolical influences.

di·a·caus·tic (dī′ə kôs′tĬk), *Math., Optics.* —*adj.* **1.** denoting a caustic surface or curve formed by refraction of light. See **catacaustic.** —*n.* **2.** a diacaustic surface or curve.

di·ach·y·lon (dī ăk′ə lŏn′), *n.* an adhesive plaster consisting essentially of lead oxide and oil. Also, **di·ach·y·lum** (dī ăk′ə ləm). [t. L, t. Gk.: m. *dià chýlōn* (something) made of juices; also Latinized as *diachýlum,* whence E sp. with *-um;* r. ME *diaculon,* t. ML, and ME *diaquilon,* t. F, both g. L *diachýlōn*]

di·a·cid (dī ăs′Ĭd), *adj.* *Chem.* **1.** capable of combining with two molecules of a monobasic acid. **2.** (of an acid or a salt) having two replaceable hydrogen atoms.

di·ac·o·nal (dī ăk′ə nəl), *adj.* pertaining to a deacon. [t. LL: s. *diāconālis,* der. *diāconus* DEACON]

di·ac·o·nate (dī ăk′ə nĬt, -nāt′), *n.* **1.** the office or dignity of a deacon. **2.** a body of deacons.

di·a·crit·ic (dī′ə krĬt′Ĭk), *n.* **1.** a diacritical mark, point, or sign. —*adj.* **2.** diacritical. **3.** *Med.* diagnostic. [t. Gk.: m. s. *diakritikós* that separates or distinguishes]

di·a·crit·i·cal (dī′ə krĬt′ə kəl), *adj.* **1.** distinctive. **2.** capable of distinguishing. —**di′a·crit′i·cal·ly,** *adv.*

diacritical mark, point, or **sign,** a mark, point, or sign added or attached to a letter or character to distinguish it from another of similar form, to give it a particular phonetic value, to indicate stress, etc.

di·ac·tin·ic (dī′ăk tĬn′Ĭk), *adj.* *Photog., etc.* capable of transmitting the actinic rays of light. —**di·ac′tin·ism,** *n.*

di·a·del·phous (dī′ə dĕl′fəs), *adj.* *Bot.* **1.** (of stamens) united into two sets by their filaments. **2.** (of plants) having the stamens so united. [f. DI-[1] + s. Gk. *adelphós* brother + -OUS]

di·a·dem (dī′ə dĕm′), *n.* **1.** a crown. **2.** a cloth headband, sometimes adorned with jewels, formerly worn by Oriental kings. **3.** royal dignity or authority. —*v.t.* **4.** to adorn with, or as if with, a diadem; crown. [t. L: m. *diadēma,* t. Gk.: fillet, band; r. ME *dyademe,* t. OF]

di·aer·e·sis (dī ĕr′ə sĬs), *n., pl.* **-ses** (-sēz′). dieresis. [t. L, t. Gk.: m. *diairesis* division]

diag., diagram.

Dia·ghi·lev (dyä′gĬ lĕf), *n.* **Sergei Pavlovich** (sĕr gā′Ĭ pä vlô vĬch), 1872–1929, Russian art critic, ballet master, and producer.

di·ag·nose (dī′əg nōs′, -nōz′), *v.t., v.i.,* **-nosed, -nosing.** to make a diagnosis of (a case, disease, etc.).

di·ag·no·sis (dī′əg nō′sĬs), *n., pl.* **-ses** (-sēz). **1.** *Med.* **a.** the process of determining by examination the nature and circumstances of a diseased condition. **b.** the decision reached from such an examination. **2.** *Biol.* scientific determination; a description which classifies precisely. **3.** any analogous examination or analysis. [t. NL, t. Gk.: a distinguishing]

di·ag·nos·tic (dī′əg nŏs′tĬk), *adj.* **1.** pertaining to a diagnosis. **2.** having value in diagnosis. —*n.* **3.** diagnosis (def. 1 a, b). **4.** a symptom or characteristic of value in diagnosis. [t. Gk.: m. s. *diagnōstikós*] —**di′ag·nos′ti·cal·ly,** *adv.*

di·ag·nos·ti·cate (dī′əg nŏs′tə kāt′), *v.t., v.i.,* **-cated, -cating.** to diagnose.

di·ag·nos·ti·cian (dī′əg nŏs tĬsh′ən), *n.* an expert in making diagnoses.

di·ag·nos·tics (dī′əg nŏs′tĬks), *n.* the art or science of diagnosis. [pl. of DIAGNOSTIC]

di·ag·o·nal (dī ăg′ə nəl), *adj.* **1.** *Math.* **a.** connecting, as a straight line, two nonadjacent angles or vertices of a quadrilateral, polygon, or polyhedron. **b.** extending, as a plane, from one edge of a solid figure to an opposite edge. **2.** having an oblique direction. **3.** having oblique lines, ridges, etc. —*n.* **4.** a diagonal line or plane. **5.** a diagonal row, plank, part, etc. **6.** diagonal cloth. [t. L: s. *diagōnālis,* der. Gk. *diagōnios* from angle to angle] —**di·ag′o·nal·ly,** *adv.*

di·a·gram (dī′ə grăm′), *n., v.,* **-gramed, -graming** or (*esp. Brit.*) **-grammed, -gramming.** —*n.* **1.** a figure, or set of lines, marks, etc., to accompany a geometrical demonstration, give the outlines or general features of an object, show the course or results of a process, etc. **2.** a chart, plan, or scheme. —*v.t.* **3.** to represent by a diagram; make a diagram of. [t. L: m. *diagramma,* t. Gk.: that which is marked out by lines]

di·a·gram·mat·ic (dī′ə grə măt′Ĭk), *adj.* **1.** in the form of a diagram. **2.** pertaining to diagrams. Also, **di′a·gram·mat′i·cal.** —**di′a·gram·mat′i·cal·ly,** *adv.*

di·a·graph (dī′ə grăf′, -gräf′), *n.* **1.** a device for drawing, used in reproducing outlines, plans, etc., mechanically on any desired scale. **2.** a combined protractor and scale. [t. F: m. *diagraphe,* t. Gk.: m. *di-graphē* marking out by lines. See DIAGRAM]

di·a·ki·ne·sis (dī′ə kī′nē′sĬs, -kĬ-), *n.* *Biol.* the prophase of the first meiotic division of a spermatocyte or ovocyte. [NL, f. *dia-* DIA- + Gk. *kīnēsis* movement]

di·al (dī′əl, dīl), *n., v.,* **dialed, dialing** or (*esp. Brit.*) **dialled, dialling.** —*n.* **1.** a face upon which time is indicated by hands, pointers, or shadows. **2.** a plate or disk with graduations or figures, as for the indication of pressure, number of revolutions, etc., as by the movements of a pointer. **3.** a rotatable plate or disk used for tuning a radio station in or out. **4.** a plate or disk with letters and numbers, used in making telephone connections. **5.** *Mining.* a compass used for underground surveying. —*v.t.* **6.** to measure with or as with a dial. **7.** to indicate on a telephone dial. **8.** to call by means of a telephone dial. **9.** *Mining.* to survey with the aid of a dial (def. 5) or compass. —*v.i.* **10.** to use a telephone dial. [ME, t. ML: s. *diālis* daily, der. L *dies* day]

dial., **1.** dialect. **2.** dialectal.

di·a·lect (dī′ə lĕkt′), *n.* **1.** the language of a particular district or class, esp. as distinguished from the standard language, as a provincial or rural substandard form of a language. **2.** a special variety or branch of a language, as Afrikaans if considered as a branch of Dutch. **3.** a language considered as one of a number of related languages: *the Romance dialects.* **4.** jargon. [t. L: s. *dia-lectus,* t. Gk.: m. *diálektos* discourse, language, dialect] —**Syn. 3.** See **language.**

di·a·lec·tal (dī/əlĕk′təl), *adj.* **1.** of a dialect. **2.** characteristic of a dialect. —**di/a·lec′tal·ly,** *adv.*

di·a·lec·tic (dī/əlĕk′tĭk), *adj.* **1.** of, pertaining to, or of the nature of logical argumentation. **2.** dialectal. —*n.* **3.** the art or practice of logical discussion as employed in investigating the truth of a theory or opinion. **4.** logical argumentation. **5.** logic, or a branch of logic. [t. L: s. *dialectica,* t. Gk.: m. *dialektikē* (*technē*) argumentative (art); r. ME *dialetike,* t. OF]

di·a·lec·ti·cal (dī/əlĕk′tə kəl), *adj.* **1.** dialectic. **2.** dialectal. —**di/a·lec′ti·cal·ly,** *adv.*

di·a·lec·ti·cian (dī/əlĕk tĭsh′ən), *n.* **1.** one skilled in dialectic; a logician. **2.** one who studies dialects.

dia·lec·ti·cism (dī/əlĕk′tə sĭz′əm), *n.* **1.** dialectal speech or influence. **2.** a dialectal word or expression.

di·a·lec·tics (dī/əlĕk′tĭks), *n.* dialectic (def. 5).

di·al·o·gism (dī ăl/ə jĭz′əm), *n.* the discussion of a subject in an imaginary dialogue. [t. Gk.: s. *dialogismós* consideration]

di·al·o·gist (dī ăl/ə jĭst), *n.* **1.** a speaker in a dialogue. **2.** a writer of dialogue. —**di·a·lo·gis·tic** (dī/ə lō jĭs′tĭk), *adj.*

di·al·o·gize (dī ăl/ə jīz′), *v.i.,* **-gized, -gizing.** to carry on a dialogue. [t. Gk.: m.s. *dialogízesthai* converse]

di·a·logue (dī/ə lôg′, -lŏg′), *n., v.,* **-logued, -loguing.** —*n.* **1.** conversation between two or more persons. **2.** the conversation between characters in a novel, drama, etc. **3.** a literary work in the form of a conversation. —*v.i.* **4.** to carry on a dialogue; converse. —*v.t.* **5.** to put into the form of a dialogue. Also, **di/a·log′.** [t. F, t. L: m.s. *dialogus,* t. Gk.: m. *diálogos;* r. ME *dialoge,* t. OF] —**di/a·logu′er,** *n.*

dial telephone system, a system in which a connection between two telephones (**dial telephones**) is ordinarily made without the help of an operator.

dial tone, (in a dial telephone) a steady humming sound which indicates that the line is ready for dialing.

di·al·y·sis (dī ăl/ə sĭs), *n., pl.* **-ses** (-sēz′). *Phys. Chem.* the separation of crystalloids from colloids in a solution by diffusion through a membrane. [t. Gk.: separation, dissolution]

di·a·lyt·ic (dī/ə lĭt′ĭk), *adj.* **1.** pertaining to dialysis. **2.** characterized by dialysis. —**di/a·lyt′i·cal·ly,** *adv.*

di·a·lyze (dī/ə līz′), *v.t.,* **-lyzed, -lyzing.** *Phys. Chem.* to subject to dialysis; separate or procure by dialysis. —**di/a·lyz′er,** *n.*

diam., diameter.

di·a·mag·net·ic (dī/ə măg nĕt′ĭk), *adj.* denoting or pertaining to a class of substances, as bismuth and copper, whose permeability is less than that of a vacuum. In a magnetic field their induced magnetism is in a direction opposite to that of iron (opposed to *paramagnetic* and *ferromagnetic*). —**di/a·mag·net/i·cal·ly,** *adv.* —**di·a·mag·net·ism** (dī/ə măg′nə tĭz′əm), *n.*

di·a·man·tif·er·ous (dī/ə măn tĭf′ər əs), *adj.* containing diamonds. [see DIAMOND, -FEROUS]

di·am·e·ter (dī ăm/ə tər), *n.* **1.** *Geom.* **a.** a straight line passing though the center of a circle or sphere and terminated at each end by the circumference or surface. **b.** a straight line passing from side to side of any figure or body, through its center. **2.** the length of such a line; thickness. [ME *diametre,* t. OF, t. L: m. s. *diametros,* t. Gk.: diagonal, diameter]

di·am·e·tral (dī ăm/ə trəl), *adj.* **1.** of a diameter. **2.** forming a diameter. —**di·am/e·tral·ly,** *adv.*

di·a·met·ri·cal (dī/ə mĕt/rə kəl), *adj.* **1.** pertaining to a diameter; along a diameter. **2.** direct; complete; absolute: *diametrical opposites.* Also, **di·a·met′ric.** —**di/a·met′ri·cal·ly,** *adv.*

di·am·ine (dī/ə mēn′, -mĭn, dī/ə mēn′), *n. Chem.* a compound containing two NH_2 radicals.

dia·mond (dī/mənd, dī/ə-), *n.* **1.** a pure or nearly pure form of carbon, crystallized in the isometric system, of extreme hardness and, when used as a precious stone, of great brilliancy. **2.** a piece of this stone. **3.** a tool provided with an uncut diamond, used for cutting glass. **4.** *Geom.* an equilateral quadrilateral, esp. as placed with its diagonals vertical and horizontal; a lozenge or rhombus. **5.** *Cards.* **a.** a red lozenge-shaped figure on a playing card. **b.** a card of the suit bearing such figures. **c.** (*pl.*) the suit. **6.** *Baseball.* **a.** the space enclosed by the home plate and three bases; the infield. **b.** the entire field. **7.** a printing type (4½ point) of a size between brilliant and pearl. —*adj.* **8.** made of or with a diamond or diamonds. **9.** indicating the 75th, or sometimes the 60th, event of a series, as of a wedding anniversary. —*v.t.* **10.** to adorn with or as with diamonds. [ME *diamant,* t. OF, t. LL: s. *diamas,* alter. of L *adamas* adamant, diamond. See ADAMANT]

Dia·mond (dī/mənd, dī/ə-), *n.* **Cape,** a hill overlooking the St. Lawrence at Quebec, Canada.

dia·mond·back (dī/mənd băk′, dī/ə-), *n.* **1.** any of the rattlesnakes with diamond-shaped marking, as the **Florida diamondback,** *Crotalus adamanteus.* **2.** Also, **diamondback terrapin.** any of several terrapins or edible turtles of the genus *Malaclemmys,* living in the salt-water marshes of the eastern and southern U.S. and characterized by diamond-shaped markings on the back.

Diamond Head, a promontory at Honolulu, in the Hawaiian Islands.

Di·an·a (dī ăn/ə), *n.* **1.** an ancient Italian deity, goddess of the moon and of hunting, and protectress of

women, identified by the Romans with the Greek Artemis. **2.** a young woman of fine physique and easy, graceful carriage. **3.** the moon.

di·an·drous (dī ăn′drəs), *adj Bot.* **1.** (of a flower) having two stamens. **2.** (of a plant) having flowers with two stamens. [t. NL: m. *diandrus.* See DI-, ANDROUS]

di·a·no·et·ic (dī/ə nō ĕt′ĭk), *adj.* pertaining to thought or reasoning, esp. discursive reasoning. [t. Gk.: s. *dianoētikós* pertaining to thinking]

di·an·thus (dī ăn′thəs), *n.* any plant of the caryophyllaceous genus *Dianthus,* as the carnation or the sweet william. [NL, f. Gk.: *Di*(ós) of Zeus + m. *ánthos* flower]

di·a·pa·son (dī/ə pā′zən, -sən), *n. Music.* **1.** a melody or strain. **2.** the compass of a voice or instrument. **3.** a fixed standard of pitch. **4.** either of two principal timbres or stops of a pipe organ: **a.** the **open diapason,** giving full, majestic tones. **b.** the **stopped diapason,** giving powerful flutelike tones. **5.** any of several other organ stops. **6.** a tuning fork. [t. L, t. Gk., short for *dià pasôn chordôn symphōnia* concord through all notes (of the scale)] —**di·a·pa·son·ic** (dī/ə pā zŏn′ĭk, -sŏn′-), *adj.*

di·a·per (dī/ə pər), *n.* **1.** a piece of cloth which forms part of a baby's underclothing; a baby's breechcloth. **2.** a linen or cotton fabric with a woven pattern of small constantly repeated figures, as diamonds. **3.** such a pattern (originally used in medieval weaving of silk and gold). —*v.t.* **4.** to put a diaper on (a baby). **5.** to ornament with a diaperlike pattern. [ME *diapre,* t. OF, var. of *diaspre,* ult. t. MGk.: m. *diaspros* pure white]

di·a·pha·ne·i·ty (dī/ə fə nē′ə tĭ), *n.* transparency.

di·aph·a·nous (dī ăf/ə nəs), *adj.* transparent; translucent. [t. NL: m. *diaphanus,* t. Gk.: m. *diaphanēs*] —**di·aph/a·nous·ly,** *adv.* —**di·aph/a·nous·ness,** *n.*

di·a·pho·re·sis (dī/ə fə rē′sĭs), *n. Med.* perspiration, esp. when artificially produced. [t. LL, t. Gk.: a sweat]

di·a·pho·ret·ic (dī/ə fə rĕt′ĭk), *Med.* —*adj.* **1.** producing perspiration. —*n.* **2.** a diaphoretic medicine.

di·a·phragm (dī/ə frăm′), *n.* **1.** *Anat.* **a.** a muscular, membranous or ligamentous wall separating two cavities or limiting a cavity. **b.** the partition separating the thoracic cavity from the abdominal cavity in mammals. **2.** *Phys. Chem., etc.* **a.** a porous plate separating two liquids, as in a galvanic cell. **b.** a semipermeable membrane or the like. **3.** a vibrating membrane or disk, as in a telephone. **4.** *Optics.* a ring, or a plate pierced with a circular hole so arranged as to fall in the axis of the instrument, used in optical instruments to cut off marginal beams of light, as in a camera or a telescope. —*v.t.* **5.** to furnish or act upon with a diaphragm. [t. LL: m. *diaphragma,* t. Gk.: midriff, barrier]

di·a·phrag·mat·ic (dī/ə frăg măt′ĭk), *adj.* **1.** of the diaphragm. **2.** like a diaphragm. —**di/a·phrag·mat/i·cal·ly,** *adv.*

di·aph·y·sis (dī ăf/ə sĭs), *n., pl.* **-ses** (-sēz′). *Anat.* the shaft of a long bone. [NL, t. Gk.: a growing through] —**di·a·phys·i·al** (dī/ə fĭz′ĭ əl), *adj.*

di·a·poph·y·sis (dī/ə pŏf/ə sĭs), *n., pl.* **-ses** (-sēz′). *Anat., Zool.* the transverse process proper of a vertebra. [NL. See DI³-, APOPHYSIS] —**di·ap·o·phys·i·al** (dī/ə p əf ĭz/ĭ əl), *adj.*

Di·ar·bek·r (dī är/bĕk′ər), *n.* Diyarbekir.

di·ar·chy (dī/är kĭ), *n., pl.* **-chies.** government or a government in which power is vested in two rulers or authorities. Also, **dyarchy.** [f. DI-¹ + m.s. Gk. *archia* rule]

di·a·rist (dī/ə rĭst), *n.* one who keeps a diary.

di·ar·rhe·a (dī/ə rē′ə), *n. Pathol.* an intestinal disorder characterized by morbid frequency and fluidity of fecal evacuations. Also, **di/ar·rhoe/a.** [t. LL: m. *diarrhoea,* t. Gk.: m. *diárrhoia* a flowing through] —**di/ar·rhe/al, di/ar·rhe/ic,** *adj.*

di·ar·thro·sis (dī/är thrō′sĭs), *n., pl.* **-ses** (-sēz). *Anat.* a form of articulation which permits maximal motion, as the knee joint. [NL, t. Gk.: division by joints. See DIA-, ARTHROSIS] —**di·ar·thro·di·al** (dī/är thrō′dĭ əl), *adj.*

di·a·ry (dī/ə rĭ), *n., pl.* **-ries.** **1.** a daily record, esp. of the writer's own experiences or observations. **2.** a book for keeping such a record. [t. L: m. s. *diārium* daily allowance, journal]

Di·as (dē′əs; *Port.* dē′əsh), *n.* **Bartholomeu** (bär tô′- lô mě/ōō), c1450–1500, Portuguese navigator and discoverer of the Cape of Good Hope. Also, **Diaz.**

Di·as·po·ra (dī ăs′pərə), *n.* **1.** the whole body of Jews living scattered among the Gentiles after the Babylonian captivity. **2.** (among the early Jewish Christians) the body of Jewish Christians outside Palestine. **3.** the dispersion of the Jews. [t. Gk.: a scattering]

di·a·spore (dī/ə spôr), *n.* a mineral, aluminum hydroxide, $HAlO_2$, occurring in crystals, or more usually in lamellar or scaly masses.

di·a·stase (dī/ə stās′), *n. Biochem.* an enzyme present in germinated barley, potatoes, etc., which converts starch into dextrin and maltose. [t. F, t. Gk.: m. *diástasis* separation]

di·a·stat·ic (dī/ə stăt′ĭk), *adj. Biochem.* **1.** pertaining to diastase. **2.** having the properties of diastase: *diastatic action.* Also, **di·a·sta·sic** (dī/ə stā′sĭk). [t. Gk.: m. s. *diastatikós* separating]

di·as·ter (dī ăs′tər), *n. Biol.* a stage in mitosis at which the chromosomes, after their division and separation, are grouped near the poles of the spindle. [f. DI-¹ + -ASTER²] —**di·as/tral,** *adj.*

---

di·as·to·le (dī·ăs′tə·lē′), *n.* **1.** *Physiol.*, *etc.* the normal rhythmical dilatation of the heart, esp. that of the ventricles. **2.** *Pros.* the lengthening of a syllable regularly short, esp. before a pause or at the ictus. [t. LL, t. Gk.: a putting asunder, dilatation, lengthening]

di·as·tol·ic (dī′ə·stŏl′Yk), *adj.* pertaining to or produced by diastole.

di·as·tro·phism (dī·ăs′trə·fYz′əm), *n.* *Geol.* **1.** the action of the forces which cause the earth's crust to be deformed, producing continents, mountains, changes of level, etc. **2.** any such deformation. [f. s. Gk. *diastrophē* distortion + -ISM] —**di·a·stroph·ic** (dī′ə·strŏf′Yk), *adj.*

di·a·tes·sa·ron (dī′ə·tĕs′ə·rŏn′), *n.* **1.** *Bible.* a harmony of the four Gospels, arranged to form a single narrative. **2.** *Gk. and Medieval Music.* the interval of a fourth. [t. L, t. Gk.: the interval of a fourth (lit., made of four, or through four)]

di·a·ther·man·cy (dī′ə·thûr′mən·sY), *n.* *Physics.* the property of transmitting radiant heat; quality of being diathermanous. [t. F: m. *diathermansie*, f. *dia-* DIA- + m. s. Gk. *thērmansis* heating]

di·a·ther·ma·nous (dī′ə·thûr′mə·nəs), *adj.* *Physics.* permeable to radiant heat.

di·a·ther·mic (dī′ə·thûr′mYk), *adj.* **1.** *Med.* pertaining to diathermy. **2.** *Physics.* diathermanous. [t. F: m. *diathermique*, f. *dia-* DIA- + s. Gk. *thērmē* heat + -*ique* -IC]

di·a·ther·my (dī′ə·thûr′mY), *n.* *Med.* the production of heat in body tissues by high currents for therapeutic purposes. Also, **di·a·ther·mi·a** (dī′ə·thûr′mY·ə).

di·ath·e·sis (dī·ăth′ə·sYs), *n., pl.* **-eses** (-ə·sēz′). *Pathol.* a constitutional predisposition or tendency, as to a particular disease or affection. [NL, t. Gk.: arrangement, disposition] —**di·a·thet·ic** (dī′ə·thĕt′Yk), *adj.*

di·a·tom (dī′ə·təm, -tŏm′), *n.* any of numerous microscopic, unicellular, marine or fresh-water algae, having siliceous cell walls. [NL: m. *Diatoma*, a genus of diatoms, der. LGk. *diátomos*, verbal adj. of Gk. *diatémnein* cut through]

di·a·to·ma·ceous (dī′ə·tə·mā′shəs), *adj.* consisting of or containing diatoms or their fossil remains.

diatomaceous earth, a fine siliceous earth composed chiefly of cell walls of diatoms: used in filtration, as an abrasive, etc. Also, **di·at·o·mite** (dī·ăt′ə·mīt′).

di·a·tom·ic (dī′ə·tŏm′Yk), *adj.* *Chem.* **1.** having two atoms in the molecule. **2.** containing two replaceable atoms or groups; bivalent.

di·a·ton·ic (dī′ə·tŏn′Yk), *adj.* *Music.* involving only the tones, intervals, or harmonies of a major or minor scale without chromatic alteration. [t. LL: s. *diatonicus*, t. Gk.: m. *diatonikós*, for *diátonos*] —**di·a·ton′i·cal·ly**, *adv.*

di·a·tribe (dī′ə·trīb′), *n.* a bitter and violent denunciation. [t. L: m. s. *diatriba*, t. Gk.: m. *diatribē* pastime, study, discourse]

di·at·ro·pism (dī·ăt′rə·pYz′əm), *n.* *Bot.* the tendency of some plant organs to take a transverse position to the line of action of an outside stimulus. —**di·a·trop·ic** (dī′ə·trŏp′Yk), *adj.*

Dí·az (dē′əs; *Port.* de′əsh), *n.* **Bartholomeu.** See **Dias.**

Dí·az (dē′äs), *n.* **Porfirio** (pôr·fē′ryō), 1830–1915, president of Mexico, 1877–80, 1884–1911.

di·a·zine (dī′ə·zēn′, dī′āz′ēn, -Yn), *n.* *Chem.* any of a group of three isomeric hydrocarbons, $C_4H_4N_2$, containing a ring of four carbon and two nitrogen atoms. Also, **di·a·zin** (dī′ə·zYn).

diazo-, *Chem.* a combining form denoting a diazo compound. [f. DI-[1] + AZO-]

di·az·o compound (dī·ăz′ō, -ā′zō), a compound containing a group of two nitrogen atoms, N_2, united with one hydrocarbon radical or with one hydrocarbon radical and another atom or group of atoms.

di·a·zole (dī′ə·zōl′, dī·ăz′ōl), *n.* *Chem.* any of a group of organic compounds containing three carbon and two nitrogen atoms arranged in a ring.

di·az·o·meth·ane (dī·ăz′ō·mĕth′ān, dī·ā′zō-), *n.* *Chem.* an odorless, yellow gas, CH_2N_2, which is poisonous, used as a methylating agent in organic syntheses.

di·a·zo·ni·um compounds (dī′ə·zō′nY·əm), *Chem.* a series of aromatic compounds which have the **diazonium** **radical** $(ArN \equiv N) +$.

diazonium salts, a group of acid salts, of the general formula $RXN:N$ (X being an acid radical); important intermediates in dye manufacture.

di·az·o·ti·za·tion (dī·ăz′ə·tə·zā′shən), *n.* the preparation of a diazo compound, as by treating an amine with nitrous acid.

di·az·o·tize (dī·ăz′ə·tīz′), *v.t.*, **-tized, -tizing.** *Chem.* to treat so as to convert into a diazonium salt.

dib (dYb), *v.i.*, **dibbed, dibbing.** to fish by letting the bait bob lightly on the water. [b. DIP and BOB[1]]

di·bas·ic (dī·bā′sYk), *adj.* *Chem.* **1.** containing two replaceable or ionizable hydrogen atoms, as dibasic acid. **2.** having two univalent, basic atoms, as *dibasic sodium phosphate*, Na_2HPO_4.

dib·ber (dYb′ər), *n.* a dibble.

dib·ble (dYb′əl), *n., v.,* **-bled, -bling.** —*n.* **1.** an implement for making holes in the ground for planting seeds, bulbs, etc. —*v.t.* **2.** to make a hole in (the ground) with or as with a dibble. [? akin to DIB] —**dib′bler,** *n.*

di·bran·chi·ate (dī·brăng′kY·Yt, -kY·āt′), *adj.* *Zool.* **1.** belonging or pertaining to the *Dibranchiata*, a subclass or order of cephalopods with two gills, including the

decapods and octopods. —*n.* **2.** a dibranchiate cephalopod. [t. NL: m. s. *Dibranchiāta*, pl. See DI-[1], BRANCHIATE]

di·bro·mide (dī·brō′mīd, -mYd), *n.* *Chem.* a compound containing two bromine atoms, as *ethylene dibromide*.

di·car·box·yl·ic acid (dī·kär′bŏk·sYl′Yk), *Chem.* any of the organic compounds which have two carboxyl radicals, -COOH.

di·cast (dī′kăst, dYk′ăst), *n.* (in ancient Athens) one of 6000 citizens over 30 years old, eligible to be chosen by lot to sit as judges. [t. Gk.: s. *dikastēs* juryman] —**di·cas′tic,** *adj.*

dice (dīs), *n. pl., sing.* **die,** *v.,* **diced, dicing.** —*n.* **1.** small cubes whose sides are marked with different numbers of spots, thrown from a box or the hand in gaming. **2.** the game played. **3.** any small cubes. —*v.t.* **4.** to cut into small cubes. **5.** to decorate with cubelike figures. —*v.i.* **6.** to play at dice. [see DIE[2]] —**dic′er,** *n.*

di·cen·tra (dī·sĕn′trə), *n.* any of the plants constituting the fumariaceous genus *Dicentra* (or *Bikukulla*), with racemes of drooping flowers, as the Dutchman's-breeches or the bleeding heart. [NL, t. Gk.: m. *dikentros* with two stings or points]

di·ceph·a·lous (dī·sĕf′ə·ləs), *adj.* having two heads. [t. Gk.: m. *diképhalos*]

di·cha·si·um (dī·kā′zhY·əm, -zY·əm), *n., pl.* **-si·a** (-zY·ə). *Bot.* a form of cymose inflorescence in which each axis produces a pair of lateral axes. [NL, f. s. Gk. *díchasis* division + -IUM] —**di·cha′si·al,** *adj.*

di·chlo·ride (dī·klōr′īd, -Yd), *n.* bichloride. *Dichloride* is more common in organic chemistry. Also, **di·chlo·rid** (dī·klōr′Yd).

di·chlo·ro·di·phen·yl·tri·chlor·o·eth·ane (dī·klōr′ō·dī·fĕn′Yl·trī·klōr′ō·ĕth′ăn), *n.* *Chem.* a white powdery compound having a faint, agreeable odor, used as a contact insecticide; commonly known as DDT.

dicho-, a word element meaning in "two parts," "in pairs." [t. Gk., comb. form of *dícha* in two, asunder]

di·chog·a·mous (dī·kŏg′ə·məs), *adj.* *Bot.* having the stamens and pistils maturing at different times (thus preventing self-fertilization), as a monoclinous flower (opposed to *homogamous*). Also, **di·cho·gam·ic** (dī′kō·găm′Yk).

di·chog·a·my (dī·kŏg′ə·mY), *n.* dichogamous condition.

di·chot·o·mize (dī·kŏt′ə·mīz′), *v.t., v.i.,* **-mized, -mizing. 1.** to divide or separate into two parts. **2.** to divide into pairs. —**di·chot′o·mist,** *n.* —**di·chot′o·mi·za′tion,** *n.*

di·chot·o·mous (dī·kŏt′ə·məs), *adj.* divided or dividing into two parts. Cf. dichotomy. Also, **di·cho·to·mic** (dī′kō·tŏm′Yk). —**di·chot′o·mous·ly,** *adv.*

di·chot·o·my (dī·kŏt′ə·mY), *n., pl.* **-mies. 1.** division into two parts or into twos; subdivision into halves or pairs. **2.** *Logic.* classification by division, or by successive subdivision, into two groups or sections. **3.** *Bot.* a mode of branching by constant bifurcation as in some stems, in veins of leaves, etc. **4.** *Astron.* the phase of the moon, or of an inferior planet, when half of its disk is visible. [t. Gk.: m. s. *dichotomía* a cutting in two]

Dichotomy (def. 3)

di·chro·ic (dī·krō′Yk), *adj.* **1.** characterized by dichroism: *a dichroic crystal.* **2.** dichromatic. Also, **di·chro·it·ic** (dī′krō·Yt′Yk). [f. s. Gk. *díchroos* of two colors + -IC]

di·chro·ism (dī′krō·Yz′əm), *n.* **1.** *Crystall.* a property possessed by many doubly refracting crystals of exhibiting different colors when viewed in different directions. **2.** *Chem.* the exhibition of essentially different colors by certain solutions in different degrees of dilution or concentration. [f. s. Gk. *díchroos* of two colors + -ISM]

di·chro·mate (dī·krō′māt), *n.* *Chem.* a salt of a theoretical acid, H_2Cr_7O, as *potassium dichromate*, $K_2Cr_2O_7$.

di·chro·mat·ic (dī′krō·măt′Yk), *adj.* **1.** having or showing two colors; dichromic. **2.** of or having dichromatism (def. 2). **3.** *Zool.* exhibiting two color phases within a species not due to age or season. [f. DI-[1] + m.s. Gk. *chrōmatikós* pertaining to color]

di·chro·mat·i·cism (dī′krō·măt′ə·sYz′əm), *n.* dichromism (def. 1).

di·chro·ma·tism (dī·krō′mə·tYz′əm), *n.* **1.** dichromatic condition. **2.** dichromic condition.

di·chro·mic[1] (dī·krō′mYk), *adj.* of or embracing two colors only. [f. s. Gk. *díchrōmos* two-colored + -IC]

di·chro·mic[2] (dī·krō′mYk), *adj.* *Chem.* of a compound containing two atoms of chromium. [f. DI-[1] + CHROM-(IUM) + IC]

dichromic acid, *Chem.* the hypothetical acid, $H_2Cr_2O_7$, from which the dichromates (sometimes called bichromates) are derived.

dichromic vision, *Pathol.* color blindness in which only two of the three primary colors are perceived.

di·chro·scope (dī′krə·skōp′), *n.* *Crystall.* an instrument for testing the dichroism (or pleochroism) of crystals. [f. s. Gk. *díchroos* of two colors + -SCOPE]

dick (dYk), *n.* **1.** *U.S. Slang.* a detective. **2.** *Colloq.* a man. [application of the proper name]

dick·cis·sel (dYk·sYs′əl), *n.* the black-throated bunting, *Spiza americana*, an open-country bird of the eastern and central U.S.

Dick·ens (dĭk/ĭnz), *n.* **Charles (John Huffam)** (hŭf/əm), 1812–70, British novelist. —**Dick·en·si·an** (dĭ-kĕn/zĭ ən), *adj.*

dick·ens (dĭk/ĭnz), *n., interj.* (prec. by *the*) devil; deuce (used as a mild imprecation).

dick·er[1] (dĭk/ər), *Chiefly U.S.* —*v.i., v.t.* **1.** to trade by barter or by petty bargaining; haggle. **2.** *U.S. Pol.* to try to arrange matters by mutual bargaining. —*n.* **3.** a petty bargain; barter. **4.** *U.S. Pol.* a deal. [? v. use of DICKER[2]]

dick·er[2] (dĭk/ər), *n. Hist.* the number or quantity ten, esp. a lot of ten hides or skins. [ME *dyker*, c. G *decher*; ult. akin to DECURY]

dick·ey (dĭk/ĭ), *n., pl.* **-eys. 1.** a waist for women, without sides or sleeves, to be worn under a dress or suit. **2.** a detachable shirt front. **3.** a linen shirt collar. **4.** a bib or pinafore worn by a child. **5.** a small bird. **6.** a donkey, esp. a male. **7.** (of a carriage) **a.** a rear seat for servants, etc. **b.** *Obsolesc.* the driver's seat on the outside. **8.** *Brit.* a rumble seat in an automobile. Also, **dicky, dick/ie.** [application of *Dicky*, dim. of *Dick*, proper name]

dick·ey·bird (dĭk/ĭ bûrd/), *n.* dickey (def. 5).

Dick·in·son (dĭk/ĭn sən), *n.* **1. Emily,** 1830–86, U.S. poet. **2. John,** 1732–1808, U.S. statesman and publicist.

dick·y (dĭk/ĭ), *n., pl.* **dickies.** dickey.

di·cli·nous (dī/klə nəs, dī klī/-), *adj. Bot.* **1.** (of a plant species, etc.) having the stamens and the pistils in separate flowers, either on the same plant or on different plants; either monoecious or dioecious. **2.** (of a flower) having only stamens or only pistils; unisexual. [f. DI-[1] + m. s. Gk. *klīnē* bed + -OUS]

di·cot·y·le·don (dī kŏt/ə lē/dən, dī/kŏt-), *n.* **1.** a plant with two cotyledons. **2.** a member of the group *Dicotyledones,* one of the two subclasses of angiospermous plants, characterized by producing seeds with two cotyledons or seed leaves, and by an exogenous mode of growth. Cf. **monocotyledon.**

di·cot·y·le·don·ous (dī kŏt/ə lē/dən əs, -lĕd/ən-, dī/kŏt-), *adj.* having two cotyledons; belonging or pertaining to the *Dicotyledones.* See **dicotyledon** (def. 2).

di·cou·ma·rin (dī kōō/mə rĭn), *n.* a drug occurring in spoiled clover and also synthesized, used to prevent the coagulation of blood and in the treatment of arterial thrombosis.

di·crot·ic (dī krŏt/ĭk), *adj. Physiol.* **1.** having two arterial beats for one heartbeat, as certain pulses. **2.** pertaining to such a pulse. [f. m.s. Gk. *díkrotos* double-beating + -IC] —**di·cro·tism** (dī/krə tĭz/əm), *n.*

dict., 1. dictation. **2.** dictator. **3.** dictionary.

dic·ta (dĭk/tə), *n.* pl. of **dictum.**

dic·ta·phone (dĭk/tə fōn/), *n.* **1.** a phonographic instrument that records and reproduces dictation. **2.** (*cap.*) a trademark for this device. [f. DICTA(TE) + -PHONE]

dic·tate (*v.* dĭk/tāt, dĭk tāt/; *n.* dĭk/tāt), *v.,* **-tated, -tating,** *n.* —*v.t.* **1.** to say or read aloud (something) to be taken down in writing or otherwise. **2.** to prescribe positively; command with authority. —*v.i.* **3.** to say or read aloud something to be taken down in writing. **4.** to give orders. —*n.* **5.** a positive order or command. [t. L: m. s. *dictātus,* pp., pronounced, dictated, composed, prescribed]

dic·ta·tion (dĭk tā/shən), *n.* **1.** act of dictating for reproduction in writing, etc. **2.** words dictated, or taken down as dictated. **3.** act of commanding positively or authoritatively. **4.** something commanded.

dic·ta·tor (dĭk/tā tər, dĭk tā/tər), *n.* **1.** a person exercising absolute power, esp. one who assumes absolute control in a government without hereditary right or the free consent of the people. **2.** (in ancient Rome) a person constitutionally invested with supreme authority during a crisis, the regular magistracy being subordinated to him until the crisis was met. **3.** a person who authoritatively prescribes conduct, usage, etc. **4.** one who dictates. [t. L] —**dic/ta·tor·ship/,** *n.* —**dic·ta·tress** (dĭk tā/trĭs), *n. fem.*

dic·ta·to·ri·al (dĭk/tə tōr/ĭ əl), *adj.* **1.** of a dictator. **2.** like that of a dictator; absolute; unlimited. **3.** inclined to dictate or command; imperious; overbearing: *a dictatorial tone.* —**dic/ta·to/ri·al·ly,** *adv.* —**dic/ta·to/ri·al·ness,** *n.*

dic·tion (dĭk/shən), *n.* **1.** style of speaking or writing as dependent upon choice of words: *good diction, a Latin diction.* **2.** the degree of distinctness with which speech sounds are uttered; enunciation. [t. L: s. *dictio* saying] —**Syn. 1.** DICTION, PHRASEOLOGY, WORDING refer to the means and the manner of expressing ideas. DICTION usually implies a high level of usage; it refers chiefly to the choice of words, their arrangement, and the force, accuracy, and distinction with which they are used: *the speaker was distinguished for his excellent diction, poetic diction.* PHRASEOLOGY refers more to the manner of combining the words into related groups, and esp. to the peculiar or distinctive manner in which certain technical, scientific, and professional ideas are expressed: *legal phraseology.* WORDING refers to the exact words or phraseology used to convey thought: *the wording of a will.*

dic·tion·ar·y (dĭk/shə nĕr/ĭ), *n., pl.* **-aries. 1.** a book containing a selection of the words of a language, or of a particular class of words, usually arranged alphabetically, with explanations of their meanings and other information concerning them, expressed either in the same

---

or in another language; a lexicon; a glossary. **2.** a book giving information on a particular subject, under alphabetically arranged headings: *a biographical dictionary.* [t. ML: m.s. *dictiōnārium,* lit., a wordbook, der. LL *dictio* word. See DICTION]

dic·to·graph (dĭk/tə grăf/, -gräf/), *n.* **1.** a telephonic device with a highly sensitive transmitter obviating the necessity of a mouthpiece, much used for secretly listening to conversations or obtaining a record of them. **2.** (*cap.*) a trademark for this device. [f. s. L *dictum* something said + -(o)GRAPH; modeled on PHONOGRAPH]

dic·tum (dĭk/təm), *n., pl.* **-ta** (-tə), **-tums. 1.** an authoritative pronouncement; judicial assertion. **2.** a saying; maxim. **3.** obiter dictum. [t. L: something said, a saying, a command, prop. pp. neut. of *dīcere* say]

di·cy·an·di·am·ide (dī sī/ən dī ăm/īd, -ĭd), *n. Chem.* a polymerization product of cyanamide, (H₂NCN)₂, used in the manufacture of plastics and resins, and as a chemical intermediate.

did (dĭd), *v.* pt. of **do.**

Did·a·che (dĭd/ə kē/), *n.* a Christian treatise of the second century, called more fully "The Teaching of the Twelve Apostles." [t. Gk.: teaching]

di·dac·tic (dī dăk/tĭk), *adj.* **1.** intended for instruction; instructive: *didactic poetry.* **2.** inclined to teach or lecture others too much: *a didactic old lady.* [t. Gk.: m. s. *didaktikós* apt at teaching] —**di·dac/ti·cal·ly,** *adv.* —**di·dac/ti·cism,** *n.*

di·dac·tics (dī dăk/tĭks), *n.* the art or science of teaching.

di·dap·per (dī/dăp/ər), *n.* a dabchick. [for *divedapper*]

did·dle[1] (dĭd/əl), *v.,* **-dled, -dling.** *Colloq.* —*v.t.* **1.** to cheat; swindle; victimize. —*v.i.* **2.** to waste time. [orig. uncert.] —**did/dler,** *n.*

did·dle[2] (dĭd/əl), *v.i., v.t.,* **-dled, -dling.** *Colloq.* to move rapidly up and down or backward and forward. [akin to DODDER]

Di·de·rot (dēd rō/), *n.* **Denis** (də nē/), 1713–84, French philosopher, critic, and encyclopedist.

did·n't (dĭd/ənt), contraction of *did not.*

Di·do (dī/dō), *n.* the legendary queen of Carthage who killed herself when abandoned by Aeneas. [t. L. t. Gk.]

di·do (dī/dō), *n., pl.* **-dos, -does.** (*often pl.*) *U.S. Colloq.* a prank; an antic. [orig. uncert.]

didst (dĭdst), *v. Archaic or Poetic.* 2nd pers. sing. pt. of **do.**

di·dy (dī/dĭ), *n., pl.* **-dies.** diaper (def. 1).

di·dym·i·um (dī dĭm/ĭ əm, dī-), *n. Chem.* a mixture of neodymium and praseodymium, formerly supposed to be an element (and called the "twin brother of lanthanum"). [NL, f. s. Gk. *dídymos* twin + -*ium* -IUM]

did·y·mous (dĭd/ə məs), *adj. Bot.* occurring in pairs; paired; twin. [t. Gk.: m. *dídymos* double, twin]

die[1] (dī), *v.i.,* **died, dying. 1.** to cease to live; suffer death: *to die by violence, from a wound.* **2.** to come to an end; pass out of existence: *the secret died with him.* **3.** to lose force, strength, or active qualities. **4.** to become less subject to: *to die to all sin.* **5.** to pass gradually; fade (fol. by *away, down, out,* etc.). **6.** *Theol.* to lose spiritual life. **7.** to sink; faint. **8.** to suffer as if dying. **9.** to pine with desire, love, etc. **10.** *Colloq.* to desire keenly or greatly: *he was dying to see her.* **11. die hard,** to die or yield only after a bitter struggle. [ME, c. Icel. *deyja.* Cf. DEAD, DEATH] —**Syn. 1, 2.** DIE, DECEASE, PASS AWAY (PASS ON), PERISH mean to relinquish life. To DIE is to become dead from any cause and in any circumstances. It is the simplest, plainest, and most direct word for this idea, and is used fig. of anything that has once displayed activity: *an echo, flame, storm, rumor dies.* DECEASE, now almost entirely a legal term, refers only to the death of a human being: *a person deceases or passes away (passes on).* PASS AWAY (or PASS ON) is a commonly used euphemism implying a continuation of life after the change called death. PERISH, a more literary term, implies death under harsh circumstances such as hunger, cold, neglect, etc.; fig. PERISH connotes utter extinction: *hardship caused many pioneers to perish, ancient Egyptian civilization has perished.* —**Ant. 1.** live. **2.** continue.

die[2] (dī), *n., pl.* **dies** for 1, 2, 5; **dice** for 3, 4, *v.,* **died, dieing.** —*n.* **1.** *Mach.* **a.** any of various devices for cutting or forming material in a press. **b.** a hollow device of steel, often composed of several pieces to be fitted into a stock, for cutting the threads of bolts, etc. **c.** one of the separate pieces of such a device. **d.** a steel block or plate with small conical holes through which wire, plastic rods, etc., are drawn. **2.** an engraved stamp for impressing a design, etc., upon some softer material, as in coining money. **3.** a small cube or block whose sides are marked with different numbers of spots, thrown from a box or the hand in gaming. **4.** any small cube or square block. **5.** *Archit.* the dado of a pedestal, esp. when cubical. **6. the die is cast,** the decision has been irrevocably made. —*v.t.* **7.** to impress, shape, or cut with a die. [ME *de,* t. OF, g. L *datum,* orig. pp. neut., lit., given (appar. in sense of given by fortune)]

die casting, *Metall.* **1.** a process in which metal is forced into metallic molds under hydraulic pressure. **2.** an article made by this process. —**die/-cast/ing,** *adj.*

di·e·cious (dī ē/shəs), *adj. Bot.* dioecious.

die-hard (dī/härd/), *n.* **1.** one who resists vigorously to the last, esp. a conservative in politics. —*adj.* **2.** resisting vigorously to the last.

di·e·lec·tric (dī/ĭ lĕk/trĭk), *Elect.* —*adj.* **1.** nonconducting. **2.** conveying electric effects otherwise than

---

b., blend of, blended;   c., cognate with;   d., dialect, dialectal;   der., derived from;   f., formed from;   g., going back to; m., modification of;   r., replacing;   s., stem of;   t., taken from;   ?, perhaps.   See the full key on inside cover.

by conduction, as a medium through which electricity acts in the process of induction. —n. 3. a dielectric substance. [f. DI-³ + ELECTRIC] —di·e·lec'tri·cal·ly, adv.

di·en·ceph·a·lon (dī'ĕn·sĕf'ə·lŏn'), n. Anat. the posterior section of the prosencephalon; the interbrain or middle brain. [f. DI-³ + ENCEPHALON]

-dienes, Chem. a suffix designating a compound containing two double bonds. [f. DI-¹ + -ENE + -s (pl.)]

Di·eppe (dĭ'ĕp'; Fr. dyĕp), n. a seaport in N France, on the English Channel: raided by an Allied expeditionary force, Aug., 1942. 21,770 (1946).

di·er·e·sis (dī·ĕr'ə·sĭs), n., pl. -ses (-sēz'). 1. the separation of two adjacent vowels. 2. a sign (··) placed over the second of two adjacent vowels to indicate separate pronunciation, as in coöperate. 3. Pros. the division made in a line or verse by coincidence of the end of a foot and the end of a word. Also, **diaeresis**. [t. L, t. Gk.: m. diaíresis separation, division]

di·es (dī'ēz or, esp. in Church Latin, dē'ās), n., sing. and pl. Latin. day.

Die·sel (dē'zəl), n. 1. Rudolf (rōō'dôlf), 1858–1913, German engineer who invented the Diesel engine. 2. a Diesel engine. 3. a locomotive, truck, ship, etc., driven by a Diesel engine.

Diesel cycle, Mach. an engine cycle, usually 4 strokes, as intake, compression, power, and exhaust, in which ignition occurs at constant pressure, and heat is rejected at constant volume.

Diesel engine, an ignition-compression type of internal-combustion engine in which fuel oil is sprayed into the cylinder after the air in it has been compressed to about 1000° F., thus causing the ignition of the oil, at substantially constant pressure. Also, **Diesel motor**. [named after Rudolf Diesel, of Munich, the inventor]

die·sink·er (dī'sĭngk'ər), n. an engraver of dies for stamping or embossing. —**die'sink'ing**, n.

Di·es I·rae (dī'ēz ī'rē or, esp. in Church Latin, dē'ās ē'rī), Latin. a famous medieval Latin hymn on the Day of Judgment (commonly ascribed to Thomas of Celano, a Franciscan of the first half of the 13th century), sung or recited in the mass for the dead. [ML: day of wrath (the first words of the hymn)]

di·e·sis (dī'ə·sĭs), n., pl. -ses (-sēz'). Print. the mark ‡; double dagger. [t. L, t. Gk.: a sending through]

di·es non (dī'ēz nŏn'), Law. a day on which no courts can be held or no legal business transacted. [short for L dies nōn jūridicus a day not juridical]

die·stock (dī'stŏk'), n. Mach. a device for holding the dies used in cutting threads on a rod or pipe.

di·et¹ (dī'ət), n., v., -eted, -eting. —n. 1. food considered in relation to its quality and effects: milk is a wholesome article of diet. 2. a particular selection of food, esp. one prescribed to improve the physical condition or cure a disease. 3. manner of living as regards food. —v.t. 4. to regulate the food of, esp. to improve the physical condition. 5. to feed. —v.i. 6. to adhere to a particular diet. 7. to eat; feed. [ME diete, t. OF, t. L: m. diaeta, t. Gk.: m. díaita way of living, diet] —**di'et·er**, n.

di·et² (dī'ət), n. a formal assembly for discussing or acting upon public or state affairs, as the general assembly of the estates of the former Holy Roman Empire, the German Reichstag, Japan, etc. [t. ML: m. s. diēta, diaeta public assembly, appar. the same word as L diaeta (see DIET¹), with sense affected by L dies day]

di·e·tar·y (dī'ə·tĕr'ĭ), adj., n., pl. -taries. —adj. 1. pertaining to diet: dietary laws. —n. 2. a system or course of diet. 3. a regulated allowance of food.

di·e·tet·ic (dī'ə·tĕt'ĭk), adj. pertaining to diet or to regulation of the use of food. Also, **di'e·tet'i·cal**. [t. L: m. s. diaetēticus, t. Gk.: m. diaitētikós] —**di'e·tet'i·cal·ly**, adv.

di·e·tet·ics (dī'ə·tĕt'ĭks), n. the art or science concerned with the regulation of diet.

di·eth·yl·stil·bes·trol (dī'ĕth'əl·stĭl'bĕs·trōl', -trōl), n. Chem. a synthetic substance, [HOC₆H₄C(C₂H₅)₂]₂, not itself an estrogen but having a more potent estrogenic activity than estrone; used in the treatment of menopausic symptoms, etc.

di·e·ti·tian (dī'ə·tĭsh'ən), n. Orig. U.S. one versed in the regulation of diet, or in the planning or supervision of meals. Also, **di'e·ti'cian**. [der. DIET¹, modeled on PHYSICIAN]

diet kitchen, an establishment for preparing and dispensing suitable diet for invalids, esp. among the poor.

Dieu a·vec nous (dyœ à·vĕk nōō'), French. God with us.

Dieu et mon droit (dyœ' ĕ môN drwä'), French. God and my right (motto on the royal arms of England).

diff., 1. difference. 2. different.

dif·fer (dĭf'ər), v.i. 1. to be unlike, dissimilar, or distinct in nature or qualities (fol. by from). 2. to disagree in opinion, belief, etc.; be at variance (fol. by with or from). 3. Obs. to dispute. [t. F: s. différer, t. L: m. differre carry part, put off, delay (see DEFER¹), be different]

dif·fer·ence (dĭf'ər·əns, dĭf'rəns), n., v., -enced, -encing. —n. 1. state or relation of being different; dissimilarity. 2. an instance or point of unlikeness or dissimilarity. 3. a distinguishing characteristic. 4. the degree in which one person or thing differs from another. 5. act of distinguishing; discrimination; distinction. 6. a disagreement in opinion; dispute; quarrel. 7. the amount by which one quantity is greater or less than

another. 8. Logic. a differentia. 9. Her. cadency. 10. **make a difference**, a. to alter or affect the case; matter. b. to make a distinction; discriminate. 11. **split the difference**, a. to compromise. b. to divide the remainder equally. —v.t. 12. to cause or constitute a difference in or between; make different. 13. to perceive the difference in or between; discriminate.

—**Syn. 1.** DIFFERENCE, DISCREPANCY, DISPARITY, DISSIMILARITY imply perceivable unlikeness, variation, or diversity. DIFFERENCE refers to a complete or partial lack of identity or a degree of unlikeness: a difference of opinion, a difference of six inches. DISCREPANCY usually refers to the difference or inconsistency between things that should agree, balance, or harmonize: a discrepancy between the statements of two witnesses. DISPARITY implies inequality, often where a greater approximation to equality might reasonably be expected: a great disparity between the ages of husband and wife. DISSIMILARITY indicates an essential lack of resemblance between things in some respect comparable: a dissimilarity between the customs in Asia and in America. 5. See **distinction**. —**Ant.** 1. likeness, similarity.

dif·fer·ent (dĭf'ər·ənt, dĭf'rənt), adj. 1. differing in character; having unlike qualities (unless used absolutely fol. by from, often to, sometimes than; use of to and than is considered improper by many; but the use of to is especially common in England): these two things are different; this is different from that. 2. not identical; separate; various; several: three different answers. 3. unusual; not ordinary. —**dif'fer·ent·ly**, adv. —**Syn.** 1. unlike, diverse, divergent, altered, changed. 2. sundry, divers, miscellaneous. See **various**.

dif·fer·en·ti·a (dĭf'ər·ĕn'shĭ·ə), n., pl. -tiae (-shĭ·ē'). Logic. the character or attribute by which one species is distinguished from all others of the same genus. [t. L: difference]

dif·fer·en·ti·a·ble (dĭf'ər·ĕn'shĭ·ə·bəl), adj. capable of being differentiated.

dif·fer·en·tial (dĭf'ər·ĕn'shəl), adj. 1. of or pertaining to difference or diversity. 2. constituting a difference; distinguishing; distinctive: a differential feature. 3. exhibiting or depending upon a difference or distinction. 4. Physics, Mach., etc. pertaining to or involving the difference of two or more motions, forces, etc.: a differential gear. 5. Math. pertaining to or involving differentials. —n. 6. Mach. an epicyclic train of gears designed to permit two or more shafts to revolve at different speeds, as a set of gears in an automobile permitting the rear wheels to revolve at different speeds when the car is turning. 7. Elect. a coil of wire in which the polar action produced is opposite to that of another coil. 8. Math. (of a function) a linear form whose coefficients are the derivatives of the function with respect to its arguments. 9. Com. a. the difference involved in a differential rate. b. differential rate. —**dif'fer·en'tial·ly**, adv.

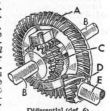

Differential (def. 6)
A. Ring gear; B. Axle;
C. Pinion gear; D. Drive shaft
gear; E. Drive shaft

differential calculus, the branch of mathematics which treats of differentials and derivatives.

differential coefficient, Math. the derivative of a function with respect to one of its arguments.

differential equation, Math. an equation involving differentials or derivatives.

differential gear, Mach. 1. differential (def. 6). 2. any of various analogous arrangements of gears.

differential quotient, derivative (def. 6).

differential rate, a special lower rate, as one charged by one of two or more businesses competing for the same traffic.

differential windlass, Mach. a windlass with a barrel composed of two parts of different diameter, its power being determined by the difference in the two diameters.

dif·fer·en·ti·ate (dĭf'ər·ĕn'shĭ·āt'), v., -ated, -ating. —v.t. 1. to mark off by differences; distinguish; alter; change. 2. to perceive the difference in or between; discriminate. 3. to make different by modification, as a biological species. 4. Math. to obtain the differential or the derivative of. —v.i. 5. to become unlike or dissimilar; change in character. 6. to make a distinction; discriminate. 7. Biol. (of cells or tissues) to change from relatively generalized to specialized kinds, during development. —**dif'fer·en'ti·a'tion**, n. —**dif'fer·en'ti·a'tor**, n. —**Syn.** 1. See **distinguish**.

dif·fi·cile (dĭf'ə·sēl'; Fr. dē·fē·sēl'), adj. hard to deal with, get on with, please, or satisfy; difficult. [t. F, t. L: m. difficilis hard to do]

dif·fi·cult (dĭf'ə·kŭlt', -kəlt), adj. 1. hard to do, perform, or accomplish; not easy; requiring much effort: a difficult task. 2. hard to understand or solve: a difficult problem. 3. hard to deal with or get on with. 4. hard to please or satisfy. 5. hard to persuade or induce. [earlier difficul (? t. L); -t from DIFFICULTY or difficulting making difficult] —**dif'fi·cult'ly**, adv. —**Syn.** 1. See **hard**. —**Ant.** 1. easy. 2. simple.

dif·fi·cul·ty (dĭf'ə·kŭl'tĭ, -kəl'tĭ), n., pl. -ties. 1. fact or condition of being difficult. 2. an embarrassing situation, esp. of financial affairs. 3. a trouble. 4. a cause of trouble or embarrassment. 5. reluctance; unwillingness. 6. a demur; objection. 7. that which is hard to do, understand, or surmount. [ME *difficulte*, t. L: m.s. *difficultas*] —Syn. 2. dilemma, predicament, quandary.

dif·fi·dence (dĭf′ə dəns), *n.* lack of confidence in one's own ability, worth, or fitness; timidity; shyness.

dif·fi·dent (dĭf′ə dənt), *adj.* 1. lacking confidence in one's own ability, worth, or fitness; timid; shy. 2. *Rare.* distrustful. [t. L: s. *diffidens*, ppr., mistrusting] —**dif′fi·dent·ly**, *adv.* —Syn. 1. See **shy**[1]. —Ant. 1. self-confident.

dif·flu·ent (dĭf′lōō ənt), *adj.* tending to flow apart; readily dissolving. [t. L: s. *diffluens*, ppr., flowing away]

dif·fract (dĭ frăkt′), *v.t.* to break up by diffraction. [t. L: s. *diffractus*, pp., broken in pieces]

dif·frac·tion (dĭ frăk′shən), *n.* *Physics.* 1. a modification that light or other radiation undergoes when it passes by the edge of an opaque body, or is sent through small apertures, resulting in the formation of a series of light and dark bands; prismatic colors, or spectra. This effect is an interference phenomenon due to the wave nature of radiation. 2. the analogous modification produced upon sound waves when passing by the edge of a building or other large body.

diffraction grating, *Physics.* a band of equidistant parallel lines (from 10,000 to 30,000 or more to the inch), ruled on a surface of glass or polished metal, used for obtaining optical spectra.

dif·frac·tive (dĭ frăk′tĭv), *adj.* causing or pertaining to diffraction. —**dif·frac′tive·ly**, *adv.* —**dif·frac′tive·ness**, *n.*

dif·fuse (*v.* dĭ fūz′; *adj.* dĭ fūs′), *v.*, **-fused**, **-fusing**, *adj.* —*v.t.* 1. to pour out and spread, as a fluid. 2. to spread or scatter widely; disseminate. 3. *Physics.* to spread by diffusion. —*v.i.* 4. to spread. 5. *Physics.* to intermingle or pass by diffusion. [t. L: m. s. *diffūsus*, pp., poured out] —*adj.* 6. characterized by great length or discursiveness in speech or writing; wordy. 7. widely spread or scattered; dispersed. [ME, t. L: m. s. *diffūsus*, pp., poured out] —**dif·fuse·ly** (dĭ fūs′lĭ), *adv.* —**dif·fuse′ness**, *n.* —**dif·fus·er**, **dif·fu·sor** (dĭ fū′zər), *n.*

dif·fus·i·ble (dĭ fū′zə bəl), *adj.* capable of being diffused. —**dif·fus·i·bil·i·ty** (dĭ fū′zə bĭl′ə tĭ), *n.*

dif·fu·sion (dĭ fū′zhən), *n.* 1. act of diffusing. 2. state of being diffused. 3. diffuseness or prolixity of speech or writing. 4. *Physics.* **a.** the gradual permeation of any region by a fluid, owing to the thermal agitation of its particles or molecules. **b.** the process of being scattered. See **scatter**. 5. *Anthrop., Sociol.* the transmission of elements from one culture to another.

dif·fu·sive (dĭ fū′sĭv), *adj.* 1. tending to diffuse. 2. characterized by diffusion. 3. diffuse; prolix. —**dif·fu′sive·ly**, *adv.* —**dif·fu′sive·ness**, *n.*

dif·fu·siv·i·ty (dĭf′yōō sĭv′ə tĭ), *n.* *Physics.* the property of a substance indicative of the rate at which a thermal disturbance will be transmitted.

dig (dĭg), *v.*, **dug** or **digged**, **digging**, *n.* —*v.i.* 1. to break up, turn over, or remove earth, etc., as with a spade; make an excavation. 2. to make one's way by, or as by, digging. 3. *Colloq.* to work hard, esp. at lessons (often fol. by *in*). 4. *Mil.* to dig a hole or trench for occupancy in a zone subject to the enemy's fire (fol. by *in*). —*v.t.* 5. to break up and turn over, or penetrate and loosen (the ground), with a spade, etc. (often fol. by *up*). 6. to make (a hole, tunnel, etc.) by removing material. 7. to obtain or remove by digging (often fol. by *up* or *out*). 8. to find or discover by effort or search. 9. to thrust, plunge, or force (fol. by *into*): *he dug his heel into the ground.* —*n.* *Colloq.* 10. a thrust; punch; poke. 11. a cutting, sarcastic remark. 12. *U.S.* a diligent student. 13. (*pl.*) *Brit.* lodgings. [ME *diggen*, prob. t. F: m. *diguer* of Gmc. orig.]

dig., digest.

di·gam·ma (dī găm′ə), *n.* a letter of the Greek alphabet, but early in disuse, corresponding in form to *F*, and having much the same sound as English *w*. [t. L, t. Gk.: f. *di-* DI-[1] + *gámma* gamma; from its likeness to two gammas (Γ) one above the other]

dig·a·my (dĭg′ə mĭ), *n.* second marriage; the practice of marrying again after the death of the first spouse. [t. LL: m. s. *digamia*, t. Gk.] —**dig′a·mous**, *adj.*

di·gas·tric (dī găs′trĭk), *adj.* 1. *Anat.* having two fleshy bellies with an intervening tendinous part, as certain muscles. —*n.* 2. a muscle of the lower jaw (so called because in man it has two bellies).

di·gen·e·sis (dī jĕn′ə sĭs), *n.* *Zool.* alternation of generations—**di·ge·net·ic** (dī′jə nĕt′ĭk), *adj.*

di·gest (*v.* dĭ jĕst′, dī-; *n.* dī′jĕst), *v.t.* 1. to prepare (food) in the alimentary canal for assimilation into the system. 2. to promote the digestion of (food). 3. to assimilate mentally; obtain mental nourishment or improvement from. 4. to arrange methodically in the mind; think over: *to digest a plan.* 5. to bear with patience; endure. 6. to arrange in convenient or methodical order; reduce to a system; classify. 7. *Chem.* to keep (a substance) in contact with a liquid to soften or to disintegrate it. —*v.i.* 8. to digest food. 9. to undergo digestion, as food. —*n.* 10. a collection or summary, esp. of literary, historical, legal, or scientific matter, often classified or condensed. 11. *Law.* **a.** a systematic abstract of some body of law. **b. the Digest,** a collection in fifty books, of excerpts compiled by order of Justinian in the sixth century, the largest part of the Corpus Juris Canonici; the Pandects. [t. L: s. *dīgestus*, pp., separated, arranged, dissolved] —Syn. 10. See **summary**.

di·gest·ant (dī jĕs′tənt, dī-), *n.* *Med.* an agent that promotes digestion.

di·gest·er (dī jĕs′tər, dī-), *n.* 1. one who or that which digests. 2. an apparatus in which substances are reduced or prepared by moisture and heat, chemical action, etc.

di·gest·i·ble (dī jĕs′tə bəl, dī-), *adj.* capable of being digested; easily digested. —**di·gest′i·bil′i·ty, di·gest′i·ble·ness**, *n.* —**di·gest′i·bly**, *adv.*

di·ges·tion (dī jĕs′chən, dī-), *n.* 1. the process by which food is digested. 2. the function or power of digesting food. 3. act of digesting. 4. the resulting state.

di·ges·tive (dī jĕs′tĭv, dī-), *adj.* 1. serving for or pertaining to digestion; having the function of digesting food. 2. promoting digestion. —*n.* 3. an agent or medicine promoting digestion. —**di·ges′tive·ly**, *adv.*

digestive biscuit, *Brit.* a graham cracker.

dig·ger (dĭg′ər), *n.* 1. a person or an animal that digs. 2. a tool, part of a machine, etc. for digging. 3. (*cap.*) any one of several Indian tribes of western North America, who subsist largely on roots dug from the ground. 4. *Colloq.* an Australian or New Zealand soldier (used also as a term of address).

digger wasp, any of the solitary wasps of the family *Sphecidae* which excavate holes in the ground and provision them with caterpillars, etc.

dig·gings (dĭg′ĭngz *for 1–3*; dĭg′ənz *for 4*), *n. pl.* 1. a place where digging is carried on. 2. a mining operation or locality. 3. that which is dug out. 4. *Chiefly Brit. Colloq.* living quarters; lodgings.

dight (dīt), *v.t.*, **dight** or **dighted**, **dighting**. *Archaic.* 1. to make ready; prepare. 2. to equip; furnish. 3. to dress; adorn. 4. *Dial.* to clean. [ME *dighte(n)*, OE *dihtan* compose, arrange, t. L: m. s. *dictāre* DICTATE. Cf. G *dichten* compose, Icel. *dikta* to write Latin]

dig·it (dĭj′ĭt), *n.* 1. a finger or toe. 2. the breadth of a finger used as a unit of linear measure, usually equal to three fourths of an inch. 3. any of the Arabic figures 0, 1, . . . 9. [t. L: s. *digitus* finger, toe]

dig·it·al (dĭj′ə təl), *adj.* 1. of or pertaining to a digit. 2. resembling a digit or finger. 3. having digits or digit-like parts. —*n.* 4. one of the keys or finger levers of instruments of the organ or piano class.

dig·i·tal·in (dĭj′ə tăl′ĭn, -tā/lĭn), *n.* *Pharm.* 1. a glucoside obtained from digitalis. 2. any of several extracts of mixtures of glucosides obtained from digitalis.

dig·i·tal·is (dĭj′ə tăl′ĭs, -tā′lĭs), *n.* 1. any plant of the scrophulariaceous genus *Digitalis*, esp. the common foxglove, *D. purpurea.* 2. the dried leaves of the common foxglove, used in medicine, esp. as a heart stimulant. [NL, the genus name (after G name *fingerhut* thimble; from the shape of the corolla), special use of L *digitālis* pertaining to the finger]

dig·i·tal·ism (dĭj′ə təlĭz′əm), *n.* *Pathol.* the morbid result of overconsumption of digitalis.

dig·i·tate (dĭj′ə tāt′), *adj.* 1. *Zool.* having digits or digitlike processes. 2. *Bot.* having radiating divisions or leaflets resembling the fingers of a hand. 3. like a digit or finger. Also, **dig′i·tat′ed.** —**dig′i·tate′ly**, *adv.*

dig·i·ta·tion (dĭj′ə tā′shən), *n.* *Biol.* 1. digitate formation. 2. a digitlike process or division.

Digitate leaf

dig·i·ti·form (dĭj′ə tə fôrm′), *adj.* fingerlike.

dig·i·ti·grade (dĭj′ə tə grād′), *adj.* *Zool.* walking on the toes, as most quadruped mammals. See **plantigrade.** [t. F, f. s. L *digitus* finger + *-(i)grade* -(I)GRADE]

dig·i·tox·in (dĭj′ə tŏk′sĭn), *n.* *Pharm.* a cardiac glucoside obtained from digitalis.

di·glot (dī′glŏt), *adj.* 1. bilingual. —*n.* 2. a bilingual book or edition. [t. Gk.: m. s. *díglōttos* speaking two languages] —**di·glot′tic**, *adj.*

dig·ni·fied (dĭg′nə fīd′), *adj.* marked by dignity of aspect or manner; noble; stately: *dignified conduct.* —**dig′ni·fied′ly**, *adv.* —Syn. stately, grave, august.

dig·ni·fy (dĭg′nə fī′), *v.t.*, **-fied**, **-fying**. 1. to confer honor or dignity upon; honor; ennoble. 2. to give high-sounding title or name to; confer unmerited distinction upon. [t. OF: m. *dignifier*, t. ML: m. s. *dignificāre*, f. L: *digni-* worthy + *-ficāre* make]

dig·ni·tar·y (dĭg′nə tĕr′ĭ), *n.*, *pl.* **-taries.** one who holds a high rank or office, esp. in the church.

dig·ni·ty (dĭg′nə tĭ), *n.*, *pl.* **-ties.** 1. nobility of manner or style; stateliness; gravity. 2. nobleness or elevation of mind; worthiness: *dignity of sentiments.* 3. honorable place; elevated rank. 4. degree of excellence, either in estimation or in the order of nature: *man is superior in dignity to brutes.* 5. relative standing; rank. 6. a high office or title. 7. the person holding it. 8. persons of high rank collectively. [t. L: m.s. *dignitas* worthiness, rank; r. ME *dignete*, t. OF]

di·graph (dī′grăf, -gräf), *n.* a group of two letters representing a single speech sound, as *ea* in *meat*, or *th* in *path.*

di·gress (dĭ grĕs′, dī-), *v.i.* 1. to deviate or wander away from the main purpose in speaking or writing, or from the principal line of argument, study, etc. 2. *Rare.* to turn aside. [t. L: s. *digressus*, pp., having departed] —**di·gress′er**, *n.* —Syn. 1. See **deviate.**

---

b., blend of, blended; c., cognate with; d., dialect, dialectal; der., derived from; f., formed from; g., going back to; m., modification of; r., replacing; s., stem of; t., taken from; ?, perhaps. See the full key on inside cover.

di·gres·sion (dĭ grĕsh′ən, dī-), n. **1.** act of digressing. **2.** a portion of a discourse, etc., deviating from the main theme. —**di·gres′sion·al**, adj.

di·gres·sive (dĭ grĕs′ĭv, dī-), adj. tending to digress; departing from the main subject. —**di·gres′sive·ly**, adv. —**di·gres′sive·ness**, n.

di·he·dral (dĭ hē′drəl), adj. Math. **1.** having, or formed by, two planes: a dihedral angle. **2.** pertaining to or having a dihedral angle or angles. —n. **3.** Also, **dihedral angle.** Math. the figure made by two planes which intersect. **4.** Aeron. the angle at which the right and left wings of an airplane or the like are inclined upward or downward with reference to the center section. [f. DI-[1] + s. Gk. hédra seat, base + -AL[1]]

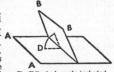

D. Dihedral angle included between planes AA and BB

Di·jon (dē zhôn′), n. a city in E France. 100,664 (1946).

dik-dik (dĭk′dĭk′), n. a diminutive antelope, genus Madoqua, native to eastern and southwestern Africa.

dike (dīk), n., v., **diked, diking.** —n. **1.** an embankment for restraining the waters of the sea or a river. **2.** a ditch. **3.** a ridge or bank of earth as thrown up in excavating. **4.** a causeway. **5.** Brit. Dial. a low wall or fence, esp. of earth or stone, for dividing or enclosing land. **6.** an obstacle; barrier. **7.** Geol. **a.** a long, narrow, cross-cutting mass of igneous or eruptive rock intruded into a fissure in older rock. **b.** a similar mass of rock composed of other kinds of material, as sandstone. —v.t. **8.** to furnish or drain with a dike. **9.** to enclose, restrain, or protect by a dike: to dike a tract of land. Also, **dyke.** [ME, t. Scand.; cf. Icel. dík, díki ditch; akin to DITCH] —**dik′er**, n.

di·ke·tone (dīke′tōn), n. Chem. a compound containing two OO groups.

di·lac·er·ate (dĭ lăs′ə rāt′, dī-), v.t., **-ated, -ating.** to rend asunder; tear in pieces. [t. L: m. s. dīlacerātus, pp.] —**di·lac′er·a′tion**, n.

di·lap·i·date (dĭ lăp′ə dāt′), v., **-dated, -dating.** —v.t. **1.** to bring (a building, etc.) into a ruinous condition, as by misuse or neglect. **2.** to squander; waste. —v.i. **3.** to fall into ruin or decay. [t. L: m. s. dīlapidātus, pp., thrown away, lit., scattered (orig. referring to stones)] —**di·lap′i·da′tion**, n.

di·lap·i·dat·ed (dĭ lăp′ə dā′tĭd), adj. reduced to or fallen into ruin or decay.

di·lat·ant (dĭ lā′tənt, dī-), adj. dilating; expanding. —**di·lat′an·cy**, n.

dil·a·ta·tion (dĭl′ə tā′shən, dī′lə-), n. **1.** act of dilating. **2.** state of being dilated. **3.** a dilated formation or part. **4.** Pathol. **a.** an abnormal enlargement of an aperture or a canal of the body, or one made for the purposes of surgical or medical treatment. **b.** a restoration to normal potency of an abnormally small body opening or passageway, as the anus or esophagus.

di·late (dī lāt′, dĭ-), v., **-lated, -lating.** —v.t. **1.** to make wider or larger; cause to expand. **2.** to enlarge upon. —v.i. **3.** to spread out; expand. **4.** to speak at length; expatiate (fol. by upon or on or used absolutely). [t. L: m.s. dīlātāre spread out] —**di·lat′a·ble**, adj. —**di·lat′a·bil′i·ty**, n. —Syn. **1.** See expand. —Ant. **1.** narrow.

di·la·tion (dī lā′shən, dĭ-), n. dilatation.

di·la·tive (dī lā′tĭv, dĭ-), adj. serving or tending to dilate.

dil·a·tom·e·ter (dĭl′ə tŏm′ə tər), n. an instrument for measuring the expansion of substances.

di·la·tor (dī lā′tər, dĭ-), n. **1.** one who or that which dilates. **2.** Anat. a muscle that dilates some cavity of the body. **3.** Surg. an instrument for dilating body canals, orifices, or cavities.

dil·a·to·ry (dĭl′ə tôr′ĭ), adj. **1.** inclined to delay or procrastinate; slow; tardy; not prompt. **2.** intended to bring about delay, gain time, or defer decision: a dilatory strategy. [t. L: m. s. dīlātōrius, der. dīlātor delayer] —**dil′a·to′ri·ly**, adv. —**dil′a·to′ri·ness**, n.

di·lem·ma (dĭ lĕm′ə), n. **1.** a situation requiring a choice between equally undesirable alternatives; an embarrassing situation. **2.** Logic. a form of argument in which two or more alternatives (**the horns of the dilemma**) are presented, each of which is indicated to have consequences (sometimes unfavorable) for the one who must choose. [t. LL, t. Gk.: double proposition] —**dil·em·mat·ic** (dĭl′ə măt′ĭk), adj. —Syn. **1.** See predicament.

dil·et·tan·te (dĭl′ə tăn′tĭ, -ə tänt′), n., pl. **-tes, -ti** (-tē), adj. —n. **1.** one who pursues an art or science desultorily or merely for amusement; a dabbler. **2.** a lover of an art or science, esp. of a fine art. —adj. **3.** of or pertaining to dilettantes. [t. It., prop. ppr. of dilettare, g. L dēlectāre DELIGHT, v.] —**dil′et·tan′tish**, **dil′et·tan′te·ish**, adj. —**dil·et·tant·ism** (dĭl′ə tăn′tĭzəm, -tän′-), n. the practice or characteristics of a dilettante. Also, **dil·et·tan·te·ism** (dĭl′ə tăn′tĭ ĭz′əm).

dil·i·gence[1] (dĭl′ə jəns), n. **1.** constant and earnest effort to accomplish what is undertaken; persistent exertion of body or mind. **2.** Obs. care; caution. —Syn. **1.** application, industry, assiduity, perseverance or persistence. [t. F, t. L: m. diligentia]

dil·i·gence[2] (dĭl′ə jəns; Fr. dē lē zhäNs′), n. a public stagecoach, esp. in France. [t. F: short for carrosse de diligence speed coach]

dil·i·gent (dĭl′ə jənt), adj. **1.** constant in effort to accomplish something; attentive and persistent in doing anything. **2.** pursued with persevering attention; painstaking. [ME, t. L: s. dīligens, prop. ppr., choosing, liking] —**dil′i·gent·ly**, adv. —Syn. **1.** industrious, assiduous. See busy. **2.** persevering, indefatigable, untiring, unremitting.

Diligence

dill (dĭl), n. **1.** an apiaceous plant, Anethum graveolens, bearing a seedlike fruit used in medicine and for flavoring pickles, etc. **2.** its aromatic seeds or leaves. [ME dille, dile, OE dile-; akin to G dill(e), Sw. dill]

dill pickle, a cucumber pickle flavored by dill.

dil·ly·dal·ly (dĭl′ĭ dăl′ĭ), v.i., **-lied, -lying.** to waste time, esp. by indecision; trifle; loiter.

di·lu·ent (dĭl′yōō ənt), adj. **1.** diluting; serving for dilution. —n. **2.** a diluting substance, esp. one that dilutes the blood. [t. L: s. dīluens, ppr., washing away]

di·lute (dĭ lōōt′, dī-; adj. also dī′lōōt), v., **-luted, -luting,** adj. —v.t. **1.** to make thinner or weaker by the addition of water or the like. **2.** to make (a color, etc.) fainter. **3.** to reduce the strength, force, or efficiency of by admixture. —v.i. **4.** to become diluted. —adj. **5.** reduced in strength, as a chemical by admixture; weak: a dilute solution. [t. L: m. s. dīlūtus, pp., washed to pieces, dissolved, diluted]

di·lu·tion (dĭ lōō′shən, dī-), n. **1.** act of diluting. **2.** state of being diluted. **3.** something diluted; a diluted form of anything.

di·lu·vi·al (dĭ lōō′vĭ əl), adj. **1.** pertaining to a deluge or flood. **2.** Geol. pertaining to or consisting of diluvium. Also, **di·lu′vi·an.** [t. L: s. dīluviālis]

di·lu·vi·um (dĭ lōō′vĭ əm), n., pl. **-via** (-vĭə). Geol. a coarse superficial deposit formerly attributed to a general deluge but now regarded as glacial drift. [t. L: deluge]

dim (dĭm), adj., **dimmer, dimmest,** v., **dimmed, dimming.** —adj. **1.** not bright; obscure from lack of light; somewhat dark: a dim room. **2.** not clearly seen; indistinct: a dim object. **3.** not clear to the mind; vague: a dim idea. **4.** not brilliant; dull in luster: a dim color. **5.** faint: a dim sound. **6.** not seeing clearly: eyes dim with tears. **7.** not clearly understanding. **8.** disparaging; adverse: to take a dim view. —v.t. **9.** to make dim. —v.i. **10.** to become or grow dim. [ME dim(e), OE dim(m), c. O Fris. dim, Icel. dimmr] —**dim′ly**, adv. —**dim′ness**, n. —Syn. **1.** See dark. **9.** darken, cloud. **10.** blur, dull, fade.

dim., **1.** diminuendo. **2.** diminutive. Also, **dimin.**

dime (dīm), n. a silver coin of the U.S., of the value of 10 cents or 1/10 dollar. [ME, t. OF, var. of disme, g. L decima tenth part, tithe, prop. fem. of decimus tenth]

dime novel, U.S. a melodramatic story designed for juvenile intelligence.

di·men·sion (dĭ mĕn′shən), n. **1.** magnitude measured in a particular direction, or along a diameter or principal axis. **2.** (usually pl.) measure; extent; size; magnitude. [t. F, t. L: s. dīmensio a measuring] —**di·men′sion·al**, adj. —**di·men′sion·less**, adj.

dim·er·ous (dĭm′ər əs), adj. **1.** consisting of or divided into two parts. **2.** Bot. (of flowers) having two members in each whorl. [f. s. Gk. dimerēs bipartite + -OUS] —**dim′er·ism**, n.

dim·e·ter (dĭm′ə tər), n. Pros. a verse or line of two measures or feet. For example: He is gone on the mountain, | He is lost to the forest. [t. LL, t. Gk.: m. s. dīmetros of two measures]

Dimerous flower

di·met·ric (dī mĕt′rĭk), adj. Crystall. tetragonal.

di·mid·i·ate (dĭ mĭd′ĭ āt′, dī-), v., **-ated, -ating,** adj. —v.t. **1.** to divide into halves; reduce to half. —adj. **2.** divided into halves. [t. L: m. s. dīmidiātus, pp., halved]

di·min·ish (dĭ mĭn′ĭsh), v.t. **1.** to make, or cause to seem, smaller; lessen; reduce. **2.** Archit., etc. to cause to taper. **3.** Music. to make smaller by a half step than the corresponding perfect or minor interval. **4.** Archaic. to detract from; disparage. —v.i. **5.** to lessen; decrease. [b. earlier diminue (t. ME: m.s. diminuen, for L dēminuere make smaller) and MINISH] —**di·min′ish·a·ble**, adj. —**di·min′ish·ing·ly**, adv. —Syn. **1.** See decrease. **5.** subside, ebb, dwindle, shrink, abate.

diminishing returns, Econ. the fact, often stated as a law or principle, that as any factor in production (as labor, capital, etc.) is increased, the output per unit factor will eventually decrease.

di·min·u·en·do (dĭ mĭn′ōō ĕn′dō; It. dē′mē nwĕn′dō), adj., n., pl. **-dos** (-dōz; It. -dōs). Music. —adj. **1.** gradually reducing in force or loudness; decrescendo (opposed to crescendo). —n. **2.** a gradual reduction of force or loudness. **3.** a diminuendo passage. Symbol: >. [t. It., ppr. of diminuire. See DIMINISH]

dim·i·nu·tion (dĭm′ə nū′shən, -nōō′-), n. **1.** act, fact or process of diminishing; lessening; reduction. **2.** Music. the repetition or imitation of a subject or theme in notes of shorter duration than those first used. [ME *diminucion*, t. AF: m. *diminuciun*, t. L: m. s. *dīminūtio*]

di·min·u·tive (dĭ mĭn′yə tĭv), *adj.* **1.** small; little; tiny: *a diminutive house.* **2.** *Gram.* pertaining to or productive of a form denoting smallness, familiarity, affection, or triviality: the suffix *-let*, as in *droplet* from *drop.* —*n.* **3.** a small thing or person. **4.** *Gram.* a diminutive element or formation. [ME, t. ML: m.s. *dīminutivus*, der. L *dī-*, *dēminutis*, pp., lessened] —**di·min′u·tive·ly**, *adv.* —**di·min′u·tive·ness**, *n.* —**Syn. 1.** See little. —**Ant. 1.** large.

dim·is·so·ry letter (dĭm′ə sôr′Y, dĭ mĭs′ər Y), a letter issued by a bishop, abbot, etc., permitting a subject to be ordained by another bishop. Also, **dim′is·so′ri·al letter**. [*dimissory*, f. s. LL *dimissōrius* (der. L *dīmissus*, pp., sent away) + -AL¹]

dim·i·ty (dĭm′ə tĭ), *n., pl.* **-ties**] a thin cotton fabric, white, dyed, or printed, woven with a stripe or check of heavier yarn. t. It.: m. *dimito* coarse cotton, t. Gk.: m. *dímitos* of double thread]

dim·mer (dĭm′ər), *n.* **1.** one who or that which dims. **2.** a rheostat, or similar device, by which the intensity of illumination, especially in stage lighting, is varied.

di·morph (dī′môrf), *n. Crystall.* either of the two forms assumed by a dimorphous substance.

di·mor·phism (dī môr′fĭz əm), *n.* **1.** *Zool.* the occurrence of two forms distinct in structure, coloration, etc., among animals of the same species. **2.** *Bot.* the occurrence of two different forms of flowers, leaves, etc., on the same plant or on distinct plants of the same species. **3.** *Crystall.* the property of some substances of crystallizing in two chemically identical but crystallographically distinct forms.

di·mor·phous (dī môr′fəs), *adj.* exhibiting dimorphism. Also, **di·mor′phic**. [t. Gk.: m. *dímorphos*]

dim-out (dĭm′out′), *n.* a reduction or concealment of night lighting, as of a city, a ship, etc., to make it less visible from the air or sea.

dim·ple (dĭm′pəl), *n., v.,* **-pled, -pling.** —*n.* **1.** a small natural hollow, permanent or transient, in some soft part of the human body, esp. one produced in the cheek in smiling. **2.** any slight depression like this. —*v.t.* **3.** to mark with, or as with, dimples; produce dimples in. —*v.i.* **4.** to form dimples. [ME *dympull*, c. MHG *tümpfil* pool] —**dim′ply**, *adj.*

dim·wit (dĭm′wĭt′), *n. Slang.* a stupid or slow-thinking person. —**dim′-wit′ted**, *adj.*

din (dĭn), *n., v.,* **dinned, dinning.** —*n.* **1.** a loud, confused noise; a continued loud or tumultuous sound; noisy clamor. —*v.t.* **2.** to assail with din. **3.** to sound or utter with clamor or persistent repetition. —*v.i.* **4.** to make a din. [ME *din(e)*, OE *dyne, dynn*, c. Icel. *dynr*] —**Syn. 1.** hubbub, uproar, racket. See **noise.**

di·nar (dĭ när′), *n.* **1.** any of certain Oriental coins, esp. gold coins of ancient Arab governments. **2.** a small monetary unit of Iran, equal to one thousandth part of a kran. **3.** a silver coin of Yugoslavia, worth about 19.3 U.S. cents. [t. Ar. and Pers., t. LGk.: m. s. *dēnárion*, t. L: m. *dēnārius* DENARIUS]

Di·nar·ic Alps (dĭ när′Yk), a mountain range along the Dalmatian coast in W Yugoslavia: a part of the E Alpine system.

din·dle (dĭn′dəl, dĭn′əl), *v.t., v.i.,* **-dled, -dling,** *n. Scot. and N. Eng.* tingle; thrill.

dine (dīn), *v.,* **dined, dining,** *n.* —*v.i.* **1.** to eat the principal meal of the day; take dinner. **2. dine out,** to eat dinner away from home. **3.** to take any meal. —*v.t.* **4.** to entertain at dinner. —*n.* **5.** *Obs.* dinner. [ME *dine(n)*, t. F: m. *dīner*, g. LL. *disjējūnāre* breakfast]

din·er (dī′nər), *n.* **1.** one who dines. **2.** *U.S.* a railroad dining car. **3.** a restaurant built like such a car.

di·nette (dī nĕt′), *n.* a small dining room.

ding (dĭng), *v.i., v.t.* **1.** to sound, as a bell; ring, esp. with wearisome continuance. **2.** *Colloq.* to keep repeating; impress by reiteration. —*n.* **3.** the sound of a bell or the like. [imit.]

ding-dong (dĭng′dông′, -dŏng′), *n.* **1.** the sound of a bell. **2.** any similar sound of repeated strokes. —*adj.* **3.** repeated in succession or alternation. **4.** *Colloq.* vigorously fought: *a ding-dong contest.* [imit.]

din·gey (dĭng′gĭ), *n., pl.* **-geys.** dinghy.

din·ghy (dĭng′gĭ), *n., pl.* **-ghies. 1.** a small boat used as a tender, as to a yacht. **2.** a small clinker-built pulling boat carried by men-of-war. **3.** any of various boats for rowing or sailing used in the East Indies. Also, **dingey, dingy, dinky**. [t. Hind.: m. *dīngī*]

din·gle (dĭng′gəl), *n. Chiefly Poetic and Dial.* a deep, narrow cleft between hills; a shady dell.

din·go (dĭng′gō), *n., pl.* **-goes.** a wolflike wild dog, *Canis dingo,* of Australia, believed to have been introduced by the aborigines. [native Australian name]

Dingo, *Canis dingo*
(Total length 3½ ft.,
tail 14 in., 21 in. high
at the shoulder)

ding·us (dĭng′əs), *n. Slang.* gadget; thing in general. [t. S Afr. D, der. D *ding* thing]

din·gy¹ (dĭn′jĭ), *adj.,* **-gier, -giest.** of a dark, dull, or dirty color or aspect; lacking brightness or freshness [orig. uncert.] —**din′gi·ly,** *adv.* —**din′gi·ness,** *n.*

din·gy² (dĭn′gĭ), *n., pl.* **-gies.** dinghy.

dining car, a railroad car equipped as a restaurant, and supplied with a kitchen, pantry, etc.

dining room, a room in which dinner and other meals are taken.

di·ni·tro·ben·zene (dī nī′trō bĕn′zĕn, -bĕn zēn′), *n. Chem.* one of three isomeric compounds, $C_6H_4(NO_2)_2$, the most important of which is made by nitration of benzene or nitrobenzene, and used in the manufacture of azo dyes.

dink (dĭngk), *Scot.* —*adj.* **1.** neatly dressed. —*v.t.* **2.** to deck; array. [? nasalized var. of *decked* adorned]

dink·ey (dĭngk′Y), *n., pl.* **dinkeys.** anything small, esp. a small locomotive. Also, **dinky**.

dink·y (dĭngk′Y), *adj.,* **dinkier, dinkiest,** *n., pl.* **dinkies.** —*adj.* **1.** *Colloq.* of small size. **2.** *Brit. Colloq.* neat; dainty; smart. —*n.* **3.** dinkey. **4.** dinghy.

din·ner (dĭn′ər), *n.* **1.** the main meal, esp. as taken about noon or (now) in the evening. **2.** a formal meal in honor of some person or occasion. [ME *diner*, t. F, orig. inf. See DINE] —**din′ner·less,** *adj.*

dinner coat or **jacket,** the coat or jacket of a tuxedo.

dino-, a word element meaning "terrible," as in *dinothere*. [t. Gk.: m. *deino-*, comb. form of *deinós*]

Di·noc·er·as (dī nŏs′ər əs), *n. Paleontol.* an extinct genus *Dinoceras,* comprising huge horned ungulate mammals of the Eocene of North America. [NL, f. *dino-* DINO- + m. Gk. *kéras* horn]

di·no·saur (dī′nə sôr′), *n. Paleontol.* any member of extinct groups of Mesozoic reptiles, mostly of gigantic size, known in modern classifications as the *Saurischia* and the *Ornithischia.* [t. NL: s. *dīnosaurus.* See DINO-, -SAUR]

Dinosaur, *Triceratops elatus*
(Ab. 24 ft. long)

di·no·sau·ri·an (dī′nə sôr′Y ən), *adj.* **1.** pertaining to or of the nature of a dinosaur. —*n.* **2.** a dinosaur.

di·no·there (dī′nə thĭr′), *n. Paleontol.* any animal of the extinct genus *Dinotherium,* comprising elephantlike mammals of the later Tertiary of Europe and Asia, characterized by downward curving tusks in the lower jaw. [t. NL: m.s. *dinotherium,* f. *dino-* DINO- + m. Gk. *thēríon* wild beast]

dint (dĭnt), *n.* **1.** force; power: *by dint of argument.* **2.** a dent. **3.** *Obs.* a blow; stroke. —*v.t.* **4.** to make a dint or dints in. **5.** to impress or drive in with force. [ME; OE *dynt,* c. Icel. *dyntr*] —**dint′less,** *adj.*

Din·wid·die (dĭn wĭd′Y, dĭn′wĭd Y), *n.* **Robert,** 1693?-1770, British official, lieutenant governor of Virginia.

di·oc·e·san (dī ŏs′ə sən, dī′ə sē′san), *adj.* **1.** of or pertaining to a diocese. —*n.* **2.** one of the clergy or people of a diocese. **3.** the bishop in charge of a diocese.

di·o·cese (dī′ə sēs′, -sĭs), *n.* the district, with its population, falling under the pastoral care of a bishop. [ME *diocise,* t. OF, t. ML: m. *diocēsis,* for L *dioecēsis* district, t. Gk.: m. *dioíkēsis* housekeeping, administration, province, diocese]

Di·o·cle·tian (dī′ə klē′shən), *n.* A.D. 245-313, Roman emperor, A.D. 284-305.

di·ode (dī′ōd), *n. Electronics.* a rectifier consisting of an electron tube having a heated cathode and a cold anode. [f. DI-¹ + -ODE²]

di·oe·cious (dī ē′shəs), *adj. Biol.* (esp. of plants) having the male and female organs in separate and distinct individuals; having separate sexes. [f. s. NL *dioecia* generic name (f. Gk.: *di-* DI-¹ + m. *oikíon* little house) + -OUS]

di·oes·trum (dī ĕs′trəm, -ēs′-), *n.* the period between the rutting periods, esp. of female animals. [NL. See DI¹-, OESTRUM]

Di·og·e·nes (dī ŏj′ə nēz′), *n.* c412-c323 B.C., Greek Cynic philosopher.

di·oi·cous (dī oi′kəs), *adj. Biol.* dioecious.

Di·o·me·des (dī′ə mē′dēz), *n. Gk. Legend.* the son of Tydeus and the next in prowess to Achilles among the Greeks before Troy. Also, **Di·o·mede** (dī′ə mēd′), **Di·o·med** (dī′ə mĕd′). [t. L, t. Gk.]

Di·o·nys·i·a (dī′ə nĭsh′Y ə, -nĭs′-), *n. pl. Gk. Antiq.* the orgiastic and dramatic festivals in honor of Dionysus or Bacchus, celebrated periodically in various parts of Greece, esp. those of Attica, out of which Greek comedy and tragedy developed. [t. L, t. Gk.]

Di·o·nys·i·ac (dī′ə nĭs′Y ăk), *adj.* pertaining to the Dionysia or to Dionysia; Bacchic. —**Di·o·ny·si·a·cal·ly** ((dī′ə nĭ sī′Yk lĭ), *adv.*

Di·o·ny·sian (dī′ə nĭsh′ən, -nĭs′Y ən), *adj.* **1.** pertaining to Dionysus or Bacchus. **2.** *(l.c.)* wild; orgiastic.

Di·o·ny·si·us (dī′ə nĭsh′Y əs, -nĭs′-), *n.* (the Elder) 430?-367 B.C., ruler of the ancient Greek city of Syracuse, on the island of Sicily.

Dionysius Ex·ig·u·us (ĕg zĭg′yŏŏ əs, ĕks Yg′-), fl. A.D. 530?, Roman monk and scholar: believed to have

b., blend of, blended; c., cognate with; d., dialect, dialectal; der., derived from; f., formed from; g., going back to; m., modification of; r., replacing; s., stem of; t., taken from; ?, perhaps. See the full key on inside cover.

founded system of reckoning dates as before or after the birth of Christ.

Di·o·ny·si·us of Hal·i·car·nas·sus, died 7? B.C., Greek rhetorician and historian, in Rome.

Di·o·ny·sus (dī/ə nī/səs), *n.* *Gk. Myth.* the youthful and beautiful god of wine and the drama, identified with the Roman god Bacchus. Also, **Di/o·ny/sos.**

di·op·side (dī ŏp/sīd, -sĭd), *n.* *Mineral.* a common variety of pyroxene, occurring in various colors, usually in crystals. [t. F, f. *di-* DI-[1] + m. s. Gk. *ŏpsis* appearance]

di·op·tase (dī ŏp/tās), *n.* a mineral, hydrous copper silicate, CuSiO₃H₂O, occurring in emerald-green crystals. [t. F, f. Gk.: *di-* DI-[3] + m.s. *optasía* view]

di·op·ter (dī ŏp/tər), *n.* *Optics.* the refractive power of a lens whose focal length is one meter. [t. F: m. *dioptre,* t. L: m. s. *dioptra,* t. Gk.: kind of leveling instrument]

di·op·tom·e·ter (dī/ŏp tŏm/ə tər), *n.* an instrument for measuring the eye's refraction.

di·op·tric (dī ŏp/trĭk), *adj.* 1. *Optics.* pertaining to dioptrics: *dioptric images.* 2. *Ophthalm.* assisting vision by refractive correction. Also, **di·op/tri·cal.** [t. Gk.: s. *dioptrikós* pertaining to the use of the *dióptra.* See DIOPTER] —**di·op/tri·cal·ly,** *adv.*

di·op·trics (dī ŏp/trĭks), *n.* the branch of geometrical optics dealing with the formation of images by lenses. Cf. catoptrics.

di·o·ram·a (dī/ə rǎm/ə, -rä/mə), *n.* 1. a miniature scene reproduced in three dimensions with the aid of lights, colors, etc. 2. a spectacular picture, partly translucent, for exhibition through an aperture, made more realistic by various illuminating devices. 3. a place where such pictures are exhibited. [t. F, f. *di-* DI-[3] + Gk. (h)órama view] —**di/o·ram/ic,** *adj.*

di·o·rite (dī/ə rīt/), *n.* a granular igneous rock consisting essentially of plagioclase feldspar and hornblende. [t. F, f. Gk. *dior(ízein)* distinguish + *-ite* -ITE[1]] —**di·o·rit·ic** (dī/ə rĭt/ĭk), *adj.*

Di·os·cu·ri (dī/ə skyŏŏr/ī), *n.pl.* Castor and Pollux.

di·os·mose (dī/ŏs/mōs, -ŏz/-), *v.t., -mosed, -mosing.* osmose. —**di·os·mo·sis** (dī/ŏs mō/sĭs, dī/ŏz-), *n.*

di·ox·ane (dī ŏk/sān), *n.* *Chem.* a colorless liquid, a cyclic ether with a faint, pleasant odor, C₄H₈O₂, used in the varnish and silk industries and as a dehydrator in histology.

di·ox·ide (dī ŏk/sīd, -sĭd), *n.* *Chem.* 1. an oxide containing two atoms of oxygen per molecule, as *manganese dioxide,* MnO₂. 2. (loosely) peroxide. Also, **di·ox·id** (dī ŏk/sĭd). [DI-[1] + OXIDE]

dip (dĭp), *v.,* **dipped** or **dipt, dipping,** *n.* —*v.t.* 1. to plunge temporarily into a liquid, as to wet or to take up some of the liquid. 2. to raise or take up by a dipping action; lift by bailing or scooping: *to dip water out of a boat.* 3. to lower and raise: *to dip a flag in salutation.* 4. to baptize by immersion. 5. to immerse (a sheep, etc.) in a solution to destroy germs, parasites, or the like. 6. to make (a candle) by repeatedly dipping a wick into melted tallow. 7. to moisten or wet as if by immersion. —*v.i.* 8. to plunge into water or other liquid and emerge quickly. 9. to plunge the hand, a dipper, etc., into water, etc., esp. in order to remove something. 10. to sink or drop down, as if plunging into water. 11. to incline or slope downward. 12. to engage slightly in a subject. 13. to read here and there in a book. —*n.* 14. the act of dipping; a plunge into water, etc. 15. that which is taken up by dipping. 16. a liquid into which something is dipped. 17. a lowering momentarily; a sinking down. 18. downward extension, inclination, or slope. 19. the amount of such extension. 20. a hollow or depression in the land. 21. *Geol., Mining.* the downward inclination of a stratum or vein, referred to a horizontal plane. 22. *Survey.* the angular amount by which the horizon lies below the level of the eye. 23. the angle which a freely poised magnetic needle makes with the plane of the horizon. 24. a short downward plunge of an airplane or the like. 25. a candle made by repeatedly dipping a wick into melted tallow. 26. *Gymnastics.* an exercise on parallel bars in which a person bends his elbow until his chin is on a level with the bars, then elevates himself by straightening out his arms. [ME *dippe(n),* OE *dyppan;* akin to G *taufen* baptize, and DEEP]

—**Syn.** 1. DIP, IMMERSE, PLUNGE refer literally to putting something into water (or any liquid). To DIP is to put down into a liquid quickly or partially and lift out again: *to dip a finger into water to test the temperature.* IMMERSE denotes a gradual lowering into a liquid until covered by it, sometimes for a moment only (as in one mode of baptism): *to immerse meat in salt water.* PLUNGE adds a suggestion of force or suddenness to the action of dipping: *to plunge a hen into boiling water before stripping off the feathers.*

di·pet·al·ous (dī pět/əl əs), *adj.* *Bot.* bipetalous.

di·phase (dī/fāz/), *adj.* *Elect.* having two phases. Also, **di·phas·ic** (dī fā/zĭk).

di·phen·yl (dī fěn/ĭl, -fē/nĭl), *n.* *Chem.* biphenyl.

di·phen·yl·a·mine (dī fěn/ĭl ə mēn/, -ǎm/ĭn, -fē/nĭl-), *n.* *Chem.* an aromatic crystalline benzene derivative, (C₆H₅)₂NH, used in the preparation of various dyes, as a reagent for oxidizing agents, and as a stabilizer in nitrocellulose propellants.

di·phos·gene (dī fŏs/jēn), *n.* *Chem.* a poison gas, ClCOOCCl₃, used in World War I.

diph·the·ri·a (dĭf thĭr/ĭ ə, dĭp-), *n.* *Pathol.* a febrile infectious disease caused by a specific bacillus, and characterized by the formation of a false membrane in the air passages, esp. the throat. [NL, f. Gk. *diphthéra* skin, leather + *-ia,* noun suffix]

diph·the·rit·ic (dĭf/thə rĭt/ĭk, dĭp/-), *adj.* *Pathol.* 1. pertaining to diphtheria. 2. affected by diphtheria. Also, **diph·the·ri·al** (dĭf thĭr/ĭ əl, dĭp-), **diph·ther·ic** (dĭf thěr/ĭk, dĭp-).

diph·the·roid (dĭf/thə roid/, dĭp/-), *adj.* *Pathol.* resembling diphtheria.

diph·thong (dĭf/thŏng, -thŏng, dĭp/-), *n.* 1. a speech sound of the vowel class that ends so differently from its beginning that two letters are needed to represent it adequately. 2. two contiguous vowel phonemes in the same syllable. [t. LL: s. *diphthongus,* t. Gk.: m. *díphthongos,* lit., having two sounds] —**diph·thon/gal,** *adj.*

diph·thong·ize (dĭf/thŏng īz/, -gīz/, -thŏng-, dĭp/-), *-ized, -izing.* —*v.t.* 1. to change into or pronounce as a diphthong. —*v.i.* 2. to become a diphthong. —**diph/thong·i·za/tion,** *n.*

di·phyl·lous (dī fĭl/əs), *adj.* *Bot.* having two leaves.

diph·y·o·dont (dĭf/ĭ ō dŏnt/), *adj.* *Zool.* having two successive sets of teeth, as most mammals. [f. s. Gk. *diphyés* double + -ODONT]

di·plex (dī/plěks), *adj.* noting or pertaining to a system of telegraphic or radio communication, for sending two messages simultaneously in the same direction, over a single wire or communications channel. [f. DI-[1] + *-plex,* modeled on DUPLEX]

diplo-, a word element referring to pairs, doubles, as in *diplocardiac.* Also, before vowels, **dipl-.** [t. Gk., comb. form of *diplóos* twofold]

dip·lo·car·di·ac (dĭp/lə kär/dĭ ǎk/), *adj.* *Zool.* pertaining to a condition whereby the right and left sides of the heart are somewhat or completely divided.

dip·lo·coc·cus (dĭp/lə kŏk/əs), *n., pl.* **-cocci** (-kŏk/sī). *Bacteriol.* any of certain bacterial species whose organisms occur in pairs, as in *diplococcus pneumoniae,* etc. [NL. See DIPLO-, COCCUS]

di·plod·o·cus (dī plŏd/ə kəs), *n.* *Paleontol.* any animal of the extinct genus *Diplodocus,* comprising gigantic dinosaurs of the upper Jurassic of western North America. [NL, f. *diplo-* DIPLO- + m. Gk. *dokós* beam]

dip·lo·ë (dĭp/lō ē/), *n.* *Anat.* the cancellate bony tissue between the hard inner and outer walls of the bones of the cranium. [t. Gk.: a fold]

dip·loid (dĭp/loid), *adj.* 1. double. 2. *Biol.* having two similar complements of chromosomes. —*n.* 3. *Biol.* an organism or cell with double the basic (haploid) number of chromosomes. 4. *Crystall.* a solid belonging to the isometric system, with 24 trapezoidal planes.

di·plo·ma (dĭ plō/mə), *n., pl.* **-mas,** *L* **-mata** (-mə tə), *v., -maed, -maing.* —*n.* 1. a document conferring some honor, privilege, or power, esp. one given by a university, etc., conferring a degree on a person or certifying to his qualifications. 2. a public or official document. —*v.t.* 3. to furnish with a diploma. [t. L, t. Gk.: paper folded double, letter of recommendation, license, etc.]

di·plo·ma·cy (dĭ plō/mə sĭ), *n., pl.* **-cies.** 1. the conduct by government officials of negotiations and other relations between states. 2. the science of conducting such negotiations. 3. skill in managing any negotiations; artful management. [t. F: m. *diplomatie* (with *t* pron. as *s*), der. *diplomate* diplomat]

dip·lo·mat (dĭp/lə mǎt/), *n.* one employed or skilled in diplomacy; a diplomatist.

dip·lo·mat·ic (dĭp/lə mǎt/ĭk), *adj.* 1. of, pertaining to, or engaged in diplomacy. 2. skilled in diplomacy; tactful. —**dip·lo·mat/i·cal·ly,** *adv.*

—**Syn.** 2. DIPLOMATIC, POLITIC, TACTFUL imply ability to avoid offending others or hurting their feelings, esp. in situations where this is important. DIPLOMATIC suggests a smoothness and skill in handling others, usually in such a way as to attain one's own ends and yet avoid any unpleasantness or opposition: *by diplomatic conduct he avoided antagonizing anyone.* POLITIC emphasizes expediency or prudence in looking out for one's own interests, thus knowing how to treat people of different types and on different occasions: *a truth which it is not politic to insist on.* TACTFUL suggests a nice touch in the handling of delicate matters or situations, and, unlike the other two, often suggests a sincere desire not to hurt the feelings of others: *a tactful wife.* —**Ant.** 2. blunt, blundering, tactless.

diplomatic corps, the entire body of diplomats accredited to and resident at a court or capital. Also, **diplomatic body.**

dip·lo·mat·ics (dĭp/lə mǎt/ĭks), *n.* the phase of paleography devoted to ancient documents.

di·plo·ma·tist (dĭ plō/mə tĭst), *n.* 1. *Brit.* a diplomat. 2. one who is astute and tactful in any negotiation.

di·plo·pi·a (dĭ plō/pĭ ə), *n.* *Ophthalm.* a morbid condition of vision in which a single object appears double. [NL. See DIPL-, -OPIA] —**di·plop·ic** (dĭ plŏp/ĭk), *adj.*

dip·lo·pod (dĭp/lə pŏd/), *n.* 1. of or pertaining to the *Diplopoda.* —*n.* 2. any member of the *Diplopoda;* a millipede. [f. DIPLO- + -POD]

Di·plop·o·da (dĭ plŏp/ə də), *n.pl.* *Zool.* a class of tracheate arthropods consisting of the millipedes.

di·plo·sis (dĭ plō/sĭs), *n.* *Biol.* the doubling of the chromosome number by the union of the haploid sets in the union of gametes. [t. Gk.: a doubling]

dip·lo·ste·mo·nous (dĭp/lə stē/mə nəs, -stěm/ə-), *adj.* *Bot.* having two series of stamens, or twice as many stamens as petals.

dip·no·an (dĭp/nō ən), *adj.* 1. belonging or pertaining to the *Dipnoi,* a class or group of fishes having both gills and lungs. —*n.* **2.** a dipnoan fish. [f. NL: s. *Dipnoi*, pl., genus type (t. Gk.: m. *dípnoos* (sing.) having two breathing apertures) + -AN]

dip·o·dy (dĭp/ə dĭ̄), *n.*, *pl.* **-dies.** *Pros.* a group of two feet.

di·pole (dī/pōl/), *n.* *Physics*, *Phys. Chem.* **1.** a pair of equal and opposite electric charges or magnetic poles, forces, etc., as on the surface of a body or in a molecule. **2.** a molecule having the effective centers of the positive and negative charges separated. —**di·po/lar**, *adj.*

dip·per (dĭp/ər), *n.* **1.** one who or that which dips. **2.** a container with a handle, used to dip liquids. **3.** (*cap.*) *Astron.* **a.** Also, **Big Dipper.** the group of seven bright stars in Ursa Major resembling such a vessel in outline. **b.** Also, **Little Dipper.** a similar group in Ursa Minor. **4.** any of various diving birds, esp. of the genus *Cinclus*, as *C. aquaticus*, the common European water ouzel. —**dip·per·ful** (dĭp/ər fo͝ol/), *n.*

dip·sa·ca·ceous (dĭp/sə kā/shəs), *adj.* belonging to the *Dipsacaceae*, or teasel family of plants. [f. s. NL *Dipsacus*, typical genus (t. Gk.: m. *dípsakos* teasel) + -ACEOUS]

dip·so·ma·ni·a (dĭp/sə mā/nĭ ə), *n.* an irresistible, generally periodic, craving for intoxicating drink. [NL, f. Gk.: *dípso(s)* thirst + *mania* MANIA]

dip·so·ma·ni·ac (dĭp/sə mā/nĭ ăk/), *n.* one who suffers from an irresistible and insatiable craving for intoxicants. —**dip·so·ma·ni·a·cal** (dĭp/sə mə nī/ə kəl), *adj.* —**Syn.** See **drunkard.**

dipt (dĭpt), *v.* pt. and pp. of **dip.**

dip·ter·al (dĭp/tər əl), *adj.* **1.** *Archit.* having two rows of columns on all sides. **2.** *Biol.* dipterous.

dip·ter·an (dĭp/tər ən), *adj.* **1.** dipterous. —*n.* **2.** a dipterous insect.

dip·ter·o·car·pa·ceous (dĭp/tər ō kär pā/shəs), *adj.* belonging to the *Dipterocarpaceae*, a family of trees, chiefly of tropical Asia.

dip·ter·on (dĭp/tər ŏn/), *n.* a dipterous insect; a fly. [t. Gk., neut. of *dípteros* two-winged]

dip·ter·ous (dĭp/tər əs), *adj.* **1.** *Entomol.* belonging or pertaining to the order *Diptera*, that includes the common houseflies, gnats, mosquitoes, etc., characterized typically by a single pair of membranous wings. **2.** *Bot.* having two winglike appendages, as seeds, stems, etc. [t. NL: m. *dípterus* two-winged, t. Gk.: m. *dípteros*]

dip·tych (dĭp/tĭk), *n.* **1.** *Archaeol.* a hinged two-leaved tablet used by the ancients for writing on with the stylus. **2.** *Fine Arts.* a pair of pictures or carvings on two panels hinged together. [t. LL: s. *diptycha*, neut. pl., double-folded, t. Gk.]

Di·rac (dĭ răk/), *n.* **Paul Adrien Maurice** (pôl ä/drĭ̄-ən môr/ĭs), born 1902, British physicist.

dir·dum (dĭr/dəm, dûr/-), *n.* *Scot.* and *N. Eng.* blame.

dire (dīr), *adj.*, *direr*, *direst.* causing or attended with great fear or suffering; dreadful; awful: *a dire calamity.* [t. L: m. s. *dīrus*] —**dire/ly**, *adv.* —**dire/ness**, *n.*

di·rect (dĭ rĕkt/, dī-), *v.t.* **1.** to guide with advice; regulate the course of; conduct; manage; control. **2.** to give authoritative instructions to; command; order or ordain (something): *I directed him to do it, or that he do it.* **3.** to tell or show (a person) the way to a place, etc. **4.** to point or aim toward a place or an object; cause to move, act, or work toward a certain object or end. **5.** to address (words, etc.) to a person. **6.** to mark (a letter, etc.) as intended for or sent to a particular person. —*v.i.* **7.** to act as a guide. **8.** to give commands or orders. —*adj.* **9.** proceeding in a straight line or by the shortest course; straight; undeviating; not oblique. **10.** proceeding in an unbroken line of descent; lineal, not collateral. **11.** following the natural order, as in mathematics. **12.** without intervening agency; immediate; personal. **13.** going straight to the point; straightforward; downright. **14.** absolute; exact: *the direct contrary.* **15.** *Gram.* (of quotation or discourse) consisting exactly of the words originally used. Example: *He said "I am coming."* **16.** *Govt.* of or by action of voters, which takes effect without any intervening agency such as representatives. **17.** *Elect.* of or pertaining to direct current. **18.** *Astron.* **a.** moving in an orbit in the same direction as the earth in its revolution round the sun. **b.** appearing to move in the zodiac according to the natural order of the signs, or from west to east (opposed to *retrograde*). **19.** *Dyeing.* working without the use of a mordant; substantive. —*adv.* **20.** in a direct manner; directly; straight. [ME *direct(en)*, t. L: s. *dīrectus*, pp.] —**di·rect/ness**, *n.* —**Syn. 1.** See **guide. 2.** DIRECT, ORDER, COMMAND mean to issue instructions. DIRECT suggests also giving explanations or advice; the emphasis is not on the authority of the director, but on steps necessary for the accomplishing of a purpose. ORDER connotes a personal relationship, in which one in a superior position imperatively instructs a subordinate (or subordinates) to do something. COMMAND, less personal and, often, less specific in detail suggests greater formality; and, sometimes, a more fixed authority on the part of the superior. **12.** DIRECT, IMMEDIATE imply relationships which are readily to be observed. A DIRECT result is one which is easily traceable to its cause or causes; there may be a number of steps in between, but the line from one to another is unbroken, simple, and quite evident. An IMMEDIATE result is one in which there is no medium or step (or practically none) intervening between cause and result; these are consecutive or side by side, so that it is possible to pass at once from one to the other. —**Ant. 13.** devious, roundabout.

direct action, any method of directly pitting the force of organized workers' strength against employers or capitalists, as strikes, picketing, sabotage, slowdowns, etc. —**direct actionist.**

direct carving, *Sculpture.* the art of carving directly in stone or wood without a finished model as a guide.

direct current, *Elect.* a relatively steady current in one direction in a circuit; a continuous stream of electrons through a conductor. Cf. **alternating current.**

direct discourse, *Rhet.* discourse in which the original words of a speaker are reported exactly (contrasted with *indirect discourse*).

direct evidence, evidence of a witness who testifies to the truth of the fact to be proved (contrasted with *circumstantial evidence*).

di·rec·tion (dĭ rĕk/shən, dī-), *n.* **1.** act of directing, pointing, aiming, etc. **2.** the line along which anything lies, faces, moves, etc., with reference to the point or region toward which it is directed. **3.** the point or region itself. **4.** a line of action, tendency, etc. **5.** guidance; instruction. **6.** order; command. **7.** management; control. **8.** a directorate. **9.** the superscription on a letter, etc., giving the name and address of the intended recipient. **10.** *Theat.* decisions in a stage or film production as to stage business, speaking of lines, lighting, and general presentation. **11.** *Music.* a symbol or phrase in a score which indicates the proper tempo, style of performance, mood, etc. —**Syn. 4.** See **tendency.**

di·rec·tion·al (dĭ rĕk/shən əl, dī-), *adj.* **1.** of or pertaining to direction in space. **2.** *Radio.* adapted for determining the direction of signals received, or for transmitting signals in a given direction: *a directional antenna.*

direction finder, *Radio.* a contrivance on a receiver usually based on a loop antenna rotating on a vertical axis, which ascertains the direction of incoming radio waves.

di·rec·tive (dĭ rĕk/tĭv, dī-), *adj.* **1.** serving to direct; directing. —*n.* **2.** an authoritative instruction or direction.

di·rect·ly (dĭ rĕkt/lĭ, dī-), *adv.* **1.** in a direct line, way, or manner; straight. **2.** *Chiefly Brit.* without delay; immediately. **3.** presently. **4.** absolutely; exactly; precisely. —*conj.* **5.** *Chiefly Brit.* as soon as: *directly he arrived, he mentioned the subject.* —**Syn. 2.** See **immediately.**

direct object, (in English and some other languages) the person or thing upon which the action of the verb is expended or toward which it is directed, in English expressed by a noun or pronoun without a preposition and generally coming after the verb. Example: *he hit the horse* has *the horse* as the direct object.

Di·rec·toire (dē rĕk twär/), *n.* **1.** *French Hist.* the French Directory. See **Directory.** —*adj.* **2.** (of costume) in the style of the period of the French Directory.

di·rec·tor (dĭ rĕk/tər, dī-), *n.* **1.** one who or that which directs. **2.** *Com.* one of a body of persons chosen to control or govern the affairs of a company or corporation. **3.** the manager of the interpretive aspects of a stage or film production who supervises such elements as the acting, photography, etc. **4.** *Mil.* a mechanical device that continuously calculates firing data for use against an airplane or other moving target. —**di·rec/-tor·ship/**, *n.* —**di·rec·tress** (dĭ rĕk/trĭs, dī-), *n. fem.*

di·rec·to·rate (dĭ rĕk/tər ĭt, dī-), *n.* **1.** the office of a director. **2.** a body of directors.

di·rec·to·ri·al (dĭ rĕk/tōr/ĭ əl, dī/rĕk-), *adj.* pertaining to a director or directorate.

di·rec·to·ry (dĭ rĕk/tər ĭ, dī-), *n.*, *pl.* **-ries**, *adj.* —*n.* **1.** a book or billboard containing an alphabetical list of the names and addresses of people in a city, district, building, etc., or of a particular class of persons, etc. **2.** a book of directions. **3.** the **Directory**, *French Hist.* the body of five directors forming the executives of France from 1795 to 1799. —*adj.* **4.** serving to direct; directing. [(defs. 1, 2, 4) t. L: m.s. *dīrectōrius* that directs (ML *dīrectōrium*, n.); (def. 3) t. F: m. *Directoire*, t. L, dir.]

direct primary, *Govt.* an election through which a political party nominates its candidates by direct vote.

di·rec·trix (dĭ rĕk/trĭks, dī-), *n.*, *pl.* **directrixes** (dĭ-rĕk/trĭk sĭz, dī-), **directrices** (dĭ/rĕk trī/sēz). **1.** *Math.* a fixed line used in the description of a curve or surface. See diag. under **parabola.** **2.** a directress. [t. NL]

direct tax, *Govt.* a tax demanded from the very persons who will bear the burden of it (not reimbursing themselves at the expense of others), as a poll tax, a general property tax, or an income tax.

dire·ful (dīr/fəl), *adj.* dreadful; awful; terrible. —**dire/ful·ly**, *adv.* —**dire/ful·ness**, *n.*

dirge (dûrj), *n.* **1.** a funeral song or tune, or one expressing mourning. **2.** *Eccles.* the office of the dead, or the funeral service as sung. [t. L, syncopated var. of *dīrige* (impv. of *dīrigere* direct), first word of the antiphon sung in the L office of the dead]

dir·hem (dĭr/hĕm/), *n.* a silver coin of the Mohammedans, usually equal to ¹⁄₁₀ dinar.

dir·i·gi·ble (dĭr/ə jə bəl), *n.* **1.** a dirigible balloon; an airship. —*adj.* **2.** that may be directed, controlled, or steered. [f. s. L. *dīrigere* DIRECT, v. + -IBLE] —**dir/i·gi·bil/i·ty**, *n.*

di·ri·go (dĭr/ĭ gō/), *Latin.* I direct (motto of Maine).

---

b., blend of, blended; c., cognate with; d., dialect, dialectal; der., derived from; f., formed from; g., going back to; m., modification of; r., replacing; s., stem of; t., taken from; ?, perhaps. See the full key on inside cover.

dir·i·ment (dĭr′ə mənt), *adj.* **1.** that renders absolutely void; nullifying. **2.** *Rom. Cath. Ch.* rendering marriage null and void from the very beginning. [t. L: s. *dirimens*, ppr., separating, breaking off]

dirk (dûrk), *n.* **1.** a stabbing weapon; a dagger. —*v.t.* **2.** to stab with a dirk. [orig. unknown]

dirl (dĭrl, dûrl), *v.i. Scot.* to vibrate; shake.

dirn·dl (dûrn′dəl), *n.* **1.** a type of woman's dress with full skirt and close-fitting bodice, commonly of colorful and strikingly patterned material, derived from Tyrolean peasant use. **2.** a skirt in such a style. [t. G: girl]

dirt (dûrt), *n.* **1.** any foul or filthy substance, as dust, excrement, mud, etc. **2.** *U.S. and Brit. Dial.* earth or soil, esp. when loose. **3.** something vile, mean, or worthless. **4.** moral filth; vileness. **5.** abusive or scurrilous language. **6.** gossip. **7.** *Mining.* **a.** crude broken ore or waste. **b.** (in placer mining) the material from which the gold is separated by washing. [metathetic var. of ME *drit*, t. Scand.; cf. Icel. *drit* excrement]

dirt-cheap (dûrt′chēp′), *adj.* very inexpensive.

dirt·y (dûr′tĭ), *adj.*, **dirtier, dirtiest,** *v.,* **dirtied, dirtying.** —*adj.* **1.** soiled with dirt; foul; unclean. **2.** imparting dirt; soiling. **3.** vile; mean. **4.** morally unclean; indecent. **5.** stormy; squally, as the weather: *it looks dirty to windward.* **6.** appearing as if soiled; dark-colored; dingy. —*v.t., v.i.* **7.** to make or become dirty. —**dirt′i·ly,** *adv.* —**dirt′i·ness,** *n.*
—Syn. **1.** DIRTY, FILTHY, FOUL, SQUALID refer to that which is not clean. DIRTY is applied to that which is filled or covered with dirt so that it is unclean or defiled: *dirty streets, dirty clothes.* FILTHY is an emphatic word suggesting that which is offensively defiled or is excessively soiled or dirty: *a filthy hovel.* FOUL implies an uncleanness that is grossly offensive to the senses: *a foul odor.* SQUALID, applied usually to dwellings or surroundings, implies dirtiness that results from the slovenly indifference often associated with poverty: *a whole family living in one squalid room.* **4.** obscene, nasty.

Dis (dĭs), *n. Rom. Myth.* **1.** the god of the lower world, Pluto. **2.** the infernal world.

dis-[1], a prefix of Latin origin, meaning "apart," "asunder," "away," "utterly," or having a privative, negative, or reversing force (see **de-** and **un-**[2]), used freely, esp. with these latter significations, as an English formative, as in *disability, disaffirm, disbar, disbelief, discontent, disentangle, dishearten, disinfect, dislike, disown, disrelish, disunion.* Also, **di-**. [t. L (akin to L *bis*, Gk. *dís* twice); before *f, dif-*; before some consonants, *di-*; often r. obs. *des-*, t. OF]

dis-[2], var. of **di-**[1], as in *dissyllable.*

dis·a·bil·i·ty (dĭs′ə bĭl′ə tĭ), *n., pl.* **-ties. 1.** lack of competent power, strength, or physical or mental ability; incapacity. **2.** legal incapacity; legal disqualification.
—Syn. **1.** DISABILITY, INABILITY imply a lack of power or ability. A DISABILITY is some qualifying deprivation or loss of power, physical or other: *excused because of a physical disability, a temporary disability.* INABILITY is a want of ability, usually because of an inherent lack of talent, power, etc.: *inability to talk, to do well in higher mathematics.*

disability clause, *Life Insurance.* a clause whereby a policy belonging to a totally and permanently disabled policyholder remains in full force and effect without payment of additional premiums, often providing for periodic payment of money to the assured during the period of disability.

dis·a·ble (dĭs ā′bəl), *v.t.,* **-bled, -bling. 1.** to make unable; weaken or destroy the capability of; cripple; incapacitate. **2.** to make legally incapable; disqualify. —**dis·a·ble·ment,** *n.* —Syn. **1.** See **cripple.**

dis·a·buse (dĭs′ə būz′), *v.t.,* **-bused, -busing.** to free from deception or error; undeceive; set right. [f. DIS-[1] + ABUSE, v.]

di·sac·cha·ride (dī săk′ə rīd′, -rĭd), *n. Chem.* any of a group of carbohydrates, as sucrose or lactose, which hydrolyze into two simple sugars (monosaccharides). [f. DI-[1] + SACCHARIDE]

dis·ac·cord (dĭs′ə kôrd′), *v.i.* **1.** to be out of accord; disagree. —*n.* **2.** lack of accord; disagreement. [ME *disacorde(n),* t. OF: m. *desac(c)orde,* f. *des-* DIS-[1] + *ac(c)order* ACCORD, v.]

dis·ac·cus·tom (dĭs′ə kŭs′təm), *v.t.* to cause to lose a habit.

dis·ad·van·tage (dĭs′əd văn′tĭj, -vän′-), *n., v.,* **-taged, -taging.** —*n.* **1.** absence or deprivation of advantage; any unfavorable circumstance or condition. **2.** injury to interest, reputation, credit, profit, etc.; loss. —*v.t.* **3.** to subject to disadvantage. —Syn. **1.** drawback, inconvenience, hindrance. **2.** detriment, hurt, harm, damage.

dis·ad·van·ta·geous (dĭs ăd′vən tā′jəs, dĭs′ăd-), *adj.* attended with disadvantage; unfavorable; detrimental. —**dis·ad′van·ta′geous·ly** *adv.* —**dis·ad′van·ta′geous·ness,** *n.*

dis·af·fect (dĭs′ə fĕkt′), *v.t.* to alienate the affection of; make ill-affected, discontented, or disloyal.

dis·af·fec·tion (dĭs′ə fĕk′shən), *n.* absence or alienation of affection or good will; estrangement; disloyalty.

dis·af·firm (dĭs′ə fûrm′), *v.t.* **1.** to deny; contradict. **2.** *Law.* to annul; reverse; repudiate. —**dis·af·firm′·ance, dis·af·fir·ma·tion** (dĭs′ăf ər mā′shən), *n.*

dis·af·for·est (dĭs′ə fôr′ĭst, -fŏr′-), *v.t.* **1.** to reduce from the legal status of a forest to that of common land. **2.** to strip of forests. [t. ML: s. *disafforestāre*] —**dis′·af·for′es·ta′tion, dis·af·for′est·ment,** *n.*

dis·a·gree (dĭs′ə grē′), *v.i.,* **-greed, -greeing. 1.** to fail to agree; differ (fol. by *with*): *the conclusions disagree with the facts.* **2.** to differ in opinion; dissent. **3.** to quarrel. **4.** to conflict in action or effect: *food that disagrees with one.*

dis·a·gree·a·ble (dĭs′ə grē′ə bəl), *adj.* **1.** contrary to one's taste or liking; unpleasant; offensive; repugnant. **2.** unpleasant in manner or nature; unamiable. —**dis′·a·gree′a·ble·ness, dis′·a·gree′a·bly,** *adv.*

dis·a·gree·ment (dĭs′ə grē′mənt), *n.* **1.** act, state, or fact of disagreeing. **2.** lack of agreement; diversity; unlikeness. **3.** difference of opinion; dissent. **4.** dissension; quarrel. **5.** unwholesome action or effect, as of food.

dis·al·low (dĭs′ə lou′), *v.t.* **1.** to refuse to allow. **2.** to refuse to admit the truth or validity of. —**dis′al·low′·ance,** *n.*

dis·an·nul (dĭs′ə nŭl′), *v.t.,* **-nulled, -nulling.** to annul utterly; make void. [f. DIS-[1] (intensive) + ANNUL] —**dis·an·nul′ment,** *n.*

dis·a·noint (dĭs′ə noint′), *v.t.* to invalidate the consecration of.

dis·ap·pear (dĭs′ə pĭr′), *v.i.* **1.** to cease to appear or be seen; vanish from sight. **2.** to cease to exist or be known; pass away; end gradually
—Syn. **1.** DISAPPEAR, FADE, VANISH suggest that something passes from sight. DISAPPEAR is used of whatever suddenly or gradually goes out of sight: *we watched him turn down a side street and then disappear.* FADE suggests a (complete or partial) disappearance that proceeds gradually and often by means of a blending into something else: *colors in the sky at sunrise quickly fade.* VANISH suggests complete, generally rapid, and often mysterious disappearance: *a mirage can vanish as suddenly as it appeared.*

dis·ap·pear·ance (dĭs′ə pĭr′əns), *n.* act of disappearing; a ceasing to appear or to exist.

dis·ap·point (dĭs′ə point′), *v.t.* **1.** to fail to fulfill the expectations or wishes of (a person): *his conduct disappointed us.* **2.** to defeat the fulfillment of (hopes, plans, etc.); thwart; frustrate. [t. OF: m. *desappointer,* f. *des-* DIS-[1] + *appointer* APPOINT] —**dis′ap·point′er,** *n.* —**dis′·ap·point′ing·ly,** *adv.*

dis·ap·point·ment (dĭs′ə point′mənt), *n.* **1.** act or fact of disappointing: *he has lost hope because of frequent disappointments.* **2.** state or feeling of being disappointed: *great was his disappointment.* **3.** something that disappoints: *the play was a disappointment.* —Syn. **1.** failure, defeat, frustration. **2.** mortification, frustration.

dis·ap·pro·ba·tion (dĭs′ăp rə bā′shən), *n.* disapproval.

dis·ap·prov·al (dĭs′ə prōō′vəl), *n.* act or state of disapproving; a condemnatory feeling or utterance; censure. —Syn. disapprobation, dislike, condemnation.

dis·ap·prove (dĭs′ə prōōv′), *v.,* **-proved, -proving.** —*v.t.* **1.** to think wrong or reprehensible; censure or condemn in opinion. **2.** to withhold approval from; decline to sanction: *the court disapproved the verdict.* —*v.i.* **3.** to have an unfavorable opinion (fol. by *of*). —**dis′·ap·prov′ing·ly,** *adv.* —Ant. **1.** praise.

dis·arm (dĭs ärm′), *v.t.* **1.** to deprive of arms. **2.** to deprive of means of attack or defense. **3.** to divest of hostility, suspicion, etc.; make friendly. —*v.i.* **4.** to lay down arms. **5.** (of a country) to reduce or limit the size, equipment, armament, etc., of the army, navy, or air forces. [t. OF: m.s. *desarmer,* f. *des-* DIS-[1] + *armer* ARM[2]] —**dis·arm′er,** *n.*

dis·ar·ma·ment (dĭs är′mə mənt), *n.* **1.** act of disarming. **2.** the reduction or limitation of the size, equipment, armament, etc., of the army, navy, or air forces.

dis·arm·ing (dĭs är′mĭng), *adj.* ingenuous. —**dis·arm′ing·ly,** *adv.*

dis·ar·range (dĭs′ə rānj′), *v.t.,* **-ranged, -ranging.** to disturb the arrangement of; disorder; unsettle. —**dis′·ar·range′ment,** *n.* —**dis′ar·rang′er,** *n.*

dis·ar·ray (dĭs′ə rā′), *v.t.* **1.** to put out of array or order; throw into disorder. **2.** to undress. —*n.* **3.** disorder; confusion. **4.** disorder of apparel; disorderly dress.

dis·ar·tic·u·late (dĭs′är tĭk′yə lāt′), *v.t., v.i.,* **-lated, -lating.** to take or come apart at the joints. —**dis′ar·tic′u·la′tion,** *n.* —**dis′ar·tic′u·la′tor,** *n.*

dis·as·sem·ble (dĭs′ə sĕm′bəl), *v.t.,* **-bled, -bling.** to take apart.

dis·as·sem·bly (dĭs′ə sĕm′blĭ), *n.* **1.** act of disassembling. **2.** state of being disassembled.

dis·as·so·ci·ate (dĭs′ə sō′shĭ āt′), *v.t.* **-ated, -ating,** to dissociate. —**dis′as·so′ci·a′tion,** *n.*

dis·as·ter (dĭ zăs′tər, -zäs′-), *n.* **1.** any unfortunate event; esp. a sudden or great misfortune. **2.** *Obs.* an unfavorable aspect of a star or planet. [t. F: m. *désastre,* t. It.: m. *disastro,* der. *disastrato* not having a (lucky) star, f. *dis-* DIS-[1] + *astro,* prop., ppl. ending] —Syn. **1.** mischance, misfortune, misadventure, blow, reverse. DISASTER, CALAMITY, CATASTROPHE refer to adverse happenings occurring often suddenly and unexpectedly. A DISASTER may be caused by carelessness, negligence, bad judgment, and the like; or by natural forces, as a hurricane, flood, etc.: *a railway disaster.* CALAMITY suggests great affliction, either personal or general; the emphasis is on the grief or sorrow caused: *the calamity of losing a dear child.* CATASTROPHE refers esp. to the tragic outcome of a personal or a public situation; the emphasis is on the destruction or irreplaceable loss: *the catastrophe of a defeat in battle.*

dis·as·trous (dĭ zăs′trəs, -zäs′-), *adj.* **1.** causing great distress or injury; ruinous; unfortunate; calamitous. **2.** *Archaic.* foreboding disaster. —**dis·as′trous·ly**, *adv.* —**dis·as′trous·ness**, *n.*

dis·a·vow (dĭs′ə vou′), *v.t.* to disclaim knowledge of, connection with, or responsibility for; disown; repudiate. [ME *desavoue*(*n*), t. OF: m. *desavouer*, f. *des-* DIS-¹ + *avouer* AVOW] —**dis′a·vow′er**, *n.*

dis·a·vow·al (dĭs′ə vou′əl), *n.* a disowning; repudiation; denial.

dis·band (dĭs bănd′), *v.t.* **1.** to break up or disorganize (a band or company); dissolve (a military force) by dismissing from service. —*v.i.* **2.** to break up, as a band or company. [t. MF: m. *desbander*, f. *des-* DIS-¹ + *bander* tie] —**dis·band′ment**, *n.* —**Syn. 1.** demobilize, dissolve, disperse.

dis·bar (dĭs bär′), *v.t.*, **-barred, -barring.** *Law.* to expel from the profession or from the bar of a particular court. [f. DIS-¹ + BAR¹] —**dis·bar′ment**, *n.*

dis·bos·om (dĭs bŏŏz′əm, -bōŏ′zəm), *v.t.* to make known; reveal; confess.

dis·bow·el (dĭs bou′əl), *v.t.*, **-eled, -eling** or (*esp. Brit.*) **-elled, -elling.** to disembowel.

dis·branch (dĭs brănch′, -bränch′), *v.t.* **1.** to deprive of branches, as a tree. **2.** to cut or break off, as a branch.

dis·bur·den (dĭs bûr′dən), *v.t.* **1.** to remove a burden from; rid of a burden. **2.** to relieve of anything oppressive or annoying. **3.** to get rid of (a burden); discharge. —*v.i.* **4.** to unload a burden. —**dis·bur′den·ment**, *n.*

dis·burse (dĭs bûrs′), *v.t.*, **-bursed, -bursing.** to pay out (money); expend. [t. OF: m. *desbourser*, f. *des-* DIS-¹ + *bourse* purse (g. LL *bursa.* See BURSA)] —**dis·burs′a·ble**, *adj.* —**dis·burs′er**, *n.* —**Syn.** See **spend.**

dis·burse·ment (dĭs bûrs′mənt), *n.* **1.** act of disbursing. **2.** that which is disbursed; money expended.

dis·bur·then (dĭs bûr′thən), *v.t.*, *v.i.* *Archaic.* to disburden.

disc (dĭsk), *n.* **1.** disk. **2.** *Anat., Zool.* **a. interarticular disc,** a plate of cartilage interposed between the articulating ends of bones. **b. intervertebral disc,** the plate of fibrocartilage interposed between the bodies of adjacent vertebrae. [see DISK, DISCUS]

disc., **1.** discount. **2.** discovered.

dis·calced (dĭs kălst′), *adj.* without shoes; unshod; barefooted: specif. applied to a branch of the Carmelite monks known as **Discalceati** (the barefooted). Also, **dis·cal·ce·ate** (dĭs kăl′sĭ ĭt, -āt′).

dis·cant (*n.* dĭs′kănt; *v.* dĭs kănt′), *n.*, *v.i.*, *v.t.* descant.

dis·card (*v.* dĭs kärd′; *n.* dĭs′kärd), *v.t.* **1.** to cast aside; reject; dismiss, esp. from use. **2.** *Cards.* **a.** to throw out (a card or cards) from one's hand. **b.** to play (a card, not a trump, of a different suit from that of the card led). —*v.i.* **3.** *Cards.* to discard a card or cards. —*n.* **4.** act of discarding. **5.** one who or that which is cast out or rejected. **6.** *Cards.* the card or cards discarded. —**dis·card′er**, *n.* —**Syn. 1.** See **reject.** —**Ant. 1.** retain.

dis·case (dĭs kās′), *v.t.*, **-cased, -casing.** to take the case or covering from; uncase.

dis·cept (dĭs ĕpt′), *v.i.* to dispute. [t. L: s. *disceptāre* contend] —**dis′cep·ta′tion**, *n.*

dis·cern (dĭ zûrn′, -sûrn′), *v.t.* **1.** to perceive by the sight or some other sense or by the intellect; see, recognize, or apprehend clearly. **2.** to distinguish mentally; recognize as distinct or different; discriminate: *he discerns good and bad, good from bad.* —*v.i.* **3.** to distinguish or discriminate. [ME *discerne*(*n*), t. F: m. *discerner*, t. L: m. *discernere*] —**dis·cern′er**, *n.* —**Syn. 1.** See **notice.**

dis·cern·i·ble (dĭ zûr′nə bəl, -sûr′-), *adj.* capable of being discerned; distinguishable. —**dis·cern′i·ble·ness**, *n.* —**dis·cern′i·bly**, *adv.*

dis·cern·ing (dĭ zûr′nĭng, -sûr′-), *adj.* showing discernment; discriminating. —**dis·cern′ing·ly**, *adv.*

dis·cern·ment (dĭ zûrn′mənt, -sûrn′-), *n.* **1.** faculty of discerning; discrimination; acuteness of judgment. **2.** act of discerning.

dis·cerp·ti·ble (dĭ sûrp′tə bəl), *adj.* capable of being torn apart; divisible. —**dis·cerp′ti·bil′i·ty**, *n.*

dis·charge (dĭs chärj′; *n. also* dĭs′chärj), *v.*, **-charged, -charging,** *n.* —*v.t.* **1.** to relieve of a charge or load; unload (a ship, etc.). **2.** to remove, send forth, or get rid of (a charge, lead, etc.). **3.** to fire; shoot: *discharge a gun, bow, bullet, etc.* **4.** to pour forth, as water. **5.** to relieve oneself of an (obligation, etc.). **6.** to relieve of obligation, responsibility, etc. **7.** to fulfill, perform, or execute (a duty, function, etc.). **8.** to relieve or deprive of office, employment, etc.; dismiss from service. **9.** to send away or allow to go (fol. by *from*). **10.** to pay (a debt). **11.** *Law.* to release, as bail or a defendant. **12.** *Elect.* to rid (something) of a charge of electricity. **13.** *Dyeing.* to free from a dye, as by chemical bleaching. —*v.i.* **14.** to get rid of a burden or load. **15.** to deliver a charge or load. **16.** to come or pour forth. **17.** to blur; run. **18.** *Elect.* to lose, or give up, a charge of electricity. —*n.* **19.** act of discharging a ship, load, etc. **20.** act of firing a missile weapon, as a bow by drawing and releasing the string, or a gun by exploding the charge of powder. **21.** a sending or coming forth, as of water from a pipe; ejection; emission. **22.** rate or amount of issue. **23.** something discharged or emitted. **24.** a relieving or ridding, or a getting rid, of something or of

the nature of a charge. **25.** *Law.* **a.** acquittal or exoneration. **b.** annulment, as of a court order. **c.** freeing of one held under legal process. **26.** a relieving or being relieved of obligation or liability; the fulfilling of an obligation. **27.** the payment of a debt. **28.** release or dismissal from office, employment, etc. **29.** a certificate of release, as from obligation or liability. **30.** *Elect.* **a.** the withdrawing or transference of an electric charge. **b.** the equalization of the difference of potential between two terminals or the like. [ME *discharge*(*n*), t. OF: m. *deschargier.* See DIS-¹, CHARGE] —**dis·charge′a·ble**, *adj.* —**dis·charg′er**, *n.* —**Syn. 4.** eject, expel, emit, exude. **6.** See **release. 7.** See **perform. 10.** settle, liquidate. **26.** fulfillment, execution, performance.

disci-, a combining form of **disk.**

dis·ci·flo·ral (dĭs′ĭ flôr′əl), *adj.* *Bot.* having flowers in which the receptacle is expanded into a conspicuous disk.

dis·ci·ple (dĭ sī′pəl), *n.*, *v.*, **-pled, -pling.** —*n.* **1.** one of the twelve personal followers of Jesus Christ. **2.** any follower of Christ. **3.** an adherent of the doctrines of another; a follower. —*v.t.* **4.** to convert into a disciple. **5.** *Obs.* to teach; train. [ME, t. OF, t. L: m. s. *discipulus;* r. ME *deciple*, t. OF; r. OE *discipul*, t. L (as above)] —**dis·ci′ple·ship′**, *n.* —**Syn. 3.** See **pupil¹.**

Disciples of Christ, a denomination of Christians, founded in the U.S. in the early part of the 19th century by Alexander Campbell (1788–1866), which seeking the unity of all Christians, rejects all creeds, accepts the Bible as a sufficient rule of faith and practice, and administers baptism by immersion.

dis·ci·plin·a·ble (dĭs′ə plĭn′ə bəl), *adj.* **1.** subject to or meriting correction. **2.** capable of being instructed.

dis·ci·pli·nal (dĭs′ə plĭ′nəl, dĭs′ə plĭn′əl), *adj.* of, pertaining to, or of the nature of discipline.

dis·ci·plin·ant (dĭs′ə plĭn′ənt), *n.* **1.** one who subjects himself to discipline. **2.** (*cap.*) *Eccles.* a member of a former Spanish religious order who scourged themselves publicly and inflicted upon themselves other severe tortures.

dis·ci·pli·nar·i·an (dĭs′ə plə när′ĭ ən), *n.* **1.** one who enforces or advocates discipline. —*adj.* **2.** disciplinary.

dis·ci·pli·nar·y (dĭs′ə plə nĕr′ĭ), *adj.* of or for discipline; promoting discipline.

dis·ci·pline (dĭs′ə plĭn), *n.*, *v.*, **-plined, -plining.** —*n.* **1.** training to act in accordance with rules; drill: *military discipline.* **2.** instruction and exercise designed to train to proper conduct or action. **3.** punishment inflicted by way of correction and training. **4.** the training effect of experience, adversity, etc. **5.** subjection to rules of conduct or behavior; a state of order maintained by training and control: *good discipline in an army.* **6.** a set or system of rules and regulations. **7.** *Eccles.* the system of government regulating the practice of a church as distinguished from its doctrine. **8.** a branch of instruction or learning. —*v.t.* **9.** to train by instruction and exercise; drill. **10.** to bring to a state of order and obedience by training and control. **11.** to subject to discipline or punishment; correct; chastise. [ME, t. L: m. *disciplīna* instruction] —**dis′ci·plin·er**, *n.* —**Syn. 11.** See **punish.**

dis·claim (dĭs klām′), *v.t.* **1.** to repudiate or deny interest in or connection with; disavow; disown: *disclaiming all participation.* **2.** *Law.* to renounce a claim or right to. **3.** to reject the claims or authority of. —*v.i.* **4.** *Law.* to renounce or repudiate a legal claim or right. **5.** *Obs.* to disavow interest. [t. AF: s. *disclaimer*, *desclamer*, f. *des-* DIS-¹ + *clamer* CLAIM]

dis·claim·er (dĭs klā′mər), *n.* **1.** act of disclaiming; the renouncing, repudiating, or denying of a claim; disavowal. **2.** one who disclaims. [t. AF]

dis·cla·ma·tion (dĭs′klə mā′shən), *n.* act of disclaiming; renunciation; disavowal.

dis·close (dĭs klōz′), *v.*, **-closed, -closing,** *n.* —*v.t.* **1.** to cause to appear; allow to be seen; make known; reveal: *to disclose a plot.* **2.** to uncover; lay open to view. **3.** *Obs.* to open up; unfold. —*n.* **4.** *Obs.* disclosure. [ME *disclose*(*n*), *desclose*(*n*), t. OF: m. *desclos-*, s. *desclore* unclose, f. *des-* DIS-¹ + *clore* (g. L *claudere* CLOSE)] —**dis·clos′er**, *n.* —**Syn. 1.** See **reveal.**

dis·clo·sure (dĭs klō′zhər), *n.* **1.** act of disclosing; exposure; revelation. **2.** that which is disclosed; a revelation. **3.** (in a patent application) the descriptive information imparted by the specification claims, drawings, and models.

dis·cob·o·lus (dĭs kŏb′ə ləs), *n.*, *pl.* **-li** (-lī′). **1.** *Class. Antiq.* a thrower of the discus. **2.** (*cap.*) a famous statue of a discus thrower by the Greek sculptor Myron (5th century B.C.). [t. L, t. Gk.: m. *diskobólos*]

dis·coid (dĭs′koid), *adj.* **1.** having the form of a discus or disk; flat and circular. **2.** *Bot.* (of a composite flower) consisting of a disk only, without rays. —*n.* **3.** something in the form of a disk. [t. LL: s. *discoīdēs*, t. Gk.: m. *diskoeídēs*]

dis·coi·dal (dĭs koi′dəl), *adj.* discoid.

dis·col·or (dĭs kŭl′ər), *v.t.* **1.** to change the color of; spoil the color of; stain. —*v.i.* **2.** to change color; become faded or stained. Also, *Brit.*, **dis·col′our.** [ME *discolour*(*en*), t. OF: m. *descolorer*, der. L: *dis-* DIS-¹ + *color* COLOR]

dis·col·or·a·tion (dĭs kŭl′ə rā′shən), *n.* **1.** act or fact of discoloring. **2.** state of being discolored. **3.** a discolored marking; a stain. Also, **dis·col′or·ment.**

---

b., blend of, blended; c., cognate with; d., dialect, dialectal; der., derived from; f., formed from; g., going back to; m., modification of; r., replacing; s., stem of: t., taken from; ?, perhaps. See the full key on inside cover.

dis·com·fit (dĭs·kŭm′fĭt), v.t. **1.** to defeat utterly; rout. **2.** to frustrate the plans of; thwart; foil. **3.** to throw into perplexity and dejection; disconcert. —n. **4.** Obs. rout; defeat. [ME, t. OF: m. desconfit, pp. of desconfire, f. des- DIS-¹ + confire make, accomplish (g. L conficere)]

dis·com·fi·ture (dĭs·kŭm′fĭ·chər), n. **1.** defeat in battle; rout. **2.** frustration of hopes or plans. **3.** disconcertion; confusion.

dis·com·fort (dĭs·kŭm′fərt), n. **1.** absence of comfort or pleasure; uneasiness; disturbance of peace; pain. **2.** anything that disturbs the comfort. —v.t. **3.** to disturb the comfort or happiness of; make uncomfortable or uneasy. [ME discomfort(en), t. OF: m. desconforter, f. des- DIS-¹ + conforter COMFORT]

dis·com·fort·a·ble (dĭs·kŭm′fərt·ə·bəl), adj. **1.** uncomfortable; uneasy. **2.** Archaic. discomforting.

dis·com·mend (dĭs′kə·mĕnd′), v.t. **1.** to express disapproval of. **2.** to bring into disfavor. —dis·com·mend′a·ble, adj. —dis·com·men·da·tion (dĭs′kŏm·ən·dā′shən), n. —dis·com·mend′er, n.

dis·com·mode (dĭs′kə·mōd′), v.t., -moded, -moding. to put to inconvenience; trouble; incommode. [f. DIS-¹ + m. s. L commodāre make fit]

dis·com·mod·i·ty (dĭs′kə·mŏd′ə·tĭ), n., pl. -ties. **1.** inconvenience; disadvantageousness. **2.** a source of inconvenience or trouble; disadvantage.

dis·com·mon (dĭs·kŏm′ən), v.t. **1.** (at Oxford and Cambridge) to prohibit (a tradesman or townsman who has violated the regulations of the university) from dealing with the undergraduates. **2.** Law. to deprive of the character of a common, as by enclosing a piece of land. [f. DIS-¹ + obs. common, v., participate, associate]

dis·com·pose (dĭs′kəm·pōz′), v.t., -posed, -posing. **1.** to bring into disorder; disarrange; unsettle. **2.** to disturb the composure of; agitate; perturb. —dis·com·pos′ed·ly, adv. —dis·com·pos′ing·ly, adv.

dis·com·po·sure (dĭs′kəm·pō′zhər), n. state of being discomposed; disorder; agitation; perturbation.

dis·con·cert (dĭs′kən·sûrt′), v.t. **1.** to disturb the self-possession of; confuse; perturb; ruffle. **2.** to throw into disorder or confusion; disarrange. —dis·con·cert′ing·ly, adv. —dis·con·cer′tion, dis·con·cert′ment, n. —Syn. **1.** See confuse.

dis·con·cert·ed (dĭs′kən·sûr′tĭd), adj. confused; abashed. —dis·con·cert′ed·ly, adv. —dis·con·cert′ed·ness, n.

dis·con·form·i·ty (dĭs′kən·fôr′mə·tĭ), n., pl. -ties. **1.** the lack of conformity; refusal or failure to conform. **2.** Geol. the surface of a division between parallel rock strata, indicating interruption of sedimentation (a type of unconformity).

dis·con·nect (dĭs′kə·nĕkt′), v.t. to sever or interrupt the connection of or between; detach.

dis·con·nect·ed (dĭs′kə·nĕk′tĭd), adj. **1.** disjointed; broken. **2.** incoherent. —dis·con·nect′ed·ly, adv. —dis·con·nect′ed·ness, n.

dis·con·nec·tion (dĭs′kə·nĕk′shən), n. **1.** act of disconnecting. **2.** state of being disconnected; lack of union. Also, Brit., dis·con·nex′ion.

dis·con·sid·er (dĭs′kən·sĭd′ər), v.t. to discredit.

dis·con·so·late (dĭs·kŏn′sə·lĭt), adj. **1.** without consolation or solace; unhappy; inconsolable. **2.** characterized by or causing discomfort; cheerless; gloomy. [t. ML: m.s. disconsōlātus, f. dis- DIS-¹ + L consōlātus, pp., having consoled] —dis·con′so·late·ly, adv. —dis·con·so·la·tion (dĭs′kŏn′sə·lā′shən), dis·con′so·late·ness, n. —Syn. **1.** See desolate.

dis·con·tent (dĭs′kən·tĕnt′), adj. **1.** not content; dissatisfied; discontented. —n. **2.** Also, dis·con′tent·ment. the lack of content; dissatisfaction. **3.** a malcontent. —v.t. **4.** to deprive of content; dissatisfy; displease. —Syn. **2.** uneasiness, inquietude, restlessness, displeasure. See dissatisfaction.

dis·con·tent·ed (dĭs′kən·tĕn′tĭd), adj. uneasy in mind; dissatisfied; restlessly unhappy. —dis·con′tent′ed·ly, adv. —dis·con·tent′ed·ness, n.

dis·con·tin·u·ance (dĭs′kən·tĭn′yo͞o·əns), n. **1.** lack of continued connection or cohesion of parts; lack of union; disruption. **2.** Law. the termination of a suit by the act of the plaintiff, as by notice in writing, or by neglect to take the proper adjournments to keep it pending.

dis·con·tin·u·a·tion (dĭs′kən·tĭn′yo͞o·ā′shən), n. breach or interruption of continuity or unity.

dis·con·tin·ue (dĭs′kən·tĭn′yo͞o), v., -tinued, -tinuing. —v.t. **1.** to cause to cease; put an end to. **2.** to cease to take, use, etc.: to discontinue a newspaper. **3.** Law. to terminate or abandon (a suit, etc.). —v.i. **4.** to come to an end or stop; cease; desist. —dis·con·tin′u·er, n. —Syn. **1.** See interrupt. —Ant. **1.** resume.

dis·con·ti·nu·i·ty (dĭs′kŏn·tə·nū′ə·tĭ, -no͞o′-), n. lack of continuity, uninterrupted connection, or cohesion.

dis·con·tin·u·ous (dĭs′kən·tĭn′yo͞o·əs), adj. not continuous; broken; interrupted; intermittent. —dis′con·tin′u·ous·ly, adv. —dis′con·tin′u·ous·ness, n.

dis·cord (n. dĭs′kôrd; v. dĭs·kôrd′), n. **1.** lack of concord or harmony between persons or things; disagreement of relations. **2.** difference of opinions. **3.** strife; dispute; war. **4.** Music. an inharmonious combination of musical tones sounded together. **5.** any confused or harsh noise; dissonance. —v.i. **6.** to disagree; be at variance. [ME discord(en), t. OF: m. discorder, t. L: m. discordāre be at variance]

dis·cord·ance (dĭs·kôr′dəns), n. discordant character; disagreement; discord or dissonance. Also, **dis·cord′an·cy**.

dis·cord·ant (dĭs·kôr′dənt), adj. **1.** being at variance; disagreeing; incongruous: discordant opinions. **2.** disagreeable to the ear; dissonant; harsh. —dis·cord′ant·ly, adv.

dis·count (v. dĭs′kount, dĭs·kount′; n. dĭs′kount), v.t. **1.** to reckon off or deduct, as a certain amount in settling a bill; make a reduction of. **2.** to advance money with deduction of interest on (commercial paper not immediately payable). **3.** to purchase or sell (a bill or note) before maturity at a reduction based on the interest for the time it still has to run. **4.** to leave out of account; disregard. **5.** to make a deduction from; allow for exaggeration in (a statement, etc.). **6.** to take (an event, etc.) into account in advance, esp. with loss of value, effectiveness, etc. —v.i. **7.** to advance money after deduction of interest. —n. **8.** act of discounting. **9.** amount deducted for prompt payment or other special reason. **10.** any deduction from the nominal value. **11.** a payment of interest in advance upon a loan of money. **12.** the amount of interest obtained by one who discounts. **13. at a discount, a.** Com. below par. **b.** in low esteem or regard. **c.** not in demand. [t. OF: m. desconter, f. des- DIS-¹ + conter COUNT¹] —dis′count·a·ble, adj. —dis′count·er, n.

dis·coun·te·nance (dĭs·koun′tə·nəns), v., -nanced -nancing, n. —v.t. **1.** to put out of countenance; disconcert; abash. **2.** to show disapproval of; treat with disfavor. —n. **3.** disapproval. [t. F (obs.): m. descontenancer, f. des- DIS-¹ + contenancer COUNTENANCE, v.]

discount rate, Finance. **1.** rate of interest charged in discounting commercial paper. **2.** rediscount rate.

dis·cour·age (dĭs·kûr′ĭj), v.t., -aged, -aging. **1.** to deprive of courage; dishearten; dispirit. **2.** to dissuade (fol. by from). **3.** to obstruct by opposition or difficulty; hinder: low prices discourage industry. **4.** to express disapproval of: to discourage the expression of enthusiasm. [t. OF: m. descoragier, der. des- DIS-¹ + corage COURAGE] —dis·cour′ag·er, n. —dis·cour′ag·ing·ly, adv. —Syn. **1.** daunt, depress, deject, overawe, cow, abash. DISCOURAGE, DISMAY, INTIMIDATE may imply the attempt to dishearten or frighten one so as to prevent some action, or any further action. To DISCOURAGE is to dishearten by expressing disapproval or by suggesting that a contemplated action or course will probably fail: he was discouraged from giving up his job. To DISMAY is to dishearten completely, by the disclosure of unsuspected facts, so that the action contemplated seems useless or dangerous: to dismay a prosecutor by revealing his brother's connection with a crime. To INTIMIDATE is to frighten, as by threats of force, violence, or dire consequences: to intimidate a prospective witness. —Ant. **1.** encourage.

dis·cour·age·ment (dĭs·kûr′ĭj·mənt), n. **1.** act of discouraging. **2.** state of being discouraged. **3.** something that discourages. —Syn. **2.** depression, dejection, hopelessness. See despair. **3.** deterrent, damper.

dis·course (n. dĭs′kōrs, dĭs·kōrs′; v. dĭs·kōrs′), n., v., -coursed, -coursing. —n. **1.** communication of thought by words; talk; conversation. **2.** a formal discussion of a subject in speech or writing, as a dissertation, treatise, sermon, etc. —v.i. **3.** to communicate thoughts orally; talk; converse. **4.** to treat of a subject formally in speech or writing. —v.t. **5.** to utter or give forth (musical sounds). [ME discours, t. F, t. L: m.s. discursus] —dis·cours′er, n.

dis·cour·te·ous (dĭs·kûr′tĭ·əs), adj. lacking courtesy; impolite; uncivil; rude. —dis·cour′te·ous·ly, adv. —dis·cour′te·ous·ness, n.

dis·cour·te·sy (dĭs·kûr′tə·sĭ), n., pl. -sies. **1.** lack or breach of courtesy; incivility; rudeness. **2.** a discourteous or impolite act.

dis·cov·er (dĭs·kŭv′ər), v.t. **1.** to get knowledge of, learn of, or find out; gain sight or knowledge of (something previously unseen or unknown). **2.** Archaic. to act so as to manifest unconsciously or unintentionally; betray. **3.** Archaic. to make known; reveal. [ME discover(en), t. OF: m. descovrir, f. des- DIS-¹ + covrir COVER] —dis·cov′er·a·ble, adj. —dis·cov′er·er, n. —Syn. **1.** detect, espy, descry, discern, ascertain, unearth, ferret out, notice. DISCOVER, INVENT, ORIGINATE suggest bringing to light something previously unknown. To DISCOVER may be to find something which had previously been in existence but had hitherto been unknown: to discover a new continent, a planet, electricity; it may also refer to devising a new use for something already known: to discover how to make synthetic rubber. To INVENT is to make or create something new, esp. something ingeniously devised to perform mechanical operations: to invent a device for detecting radioactivity. To ORIGINATE is to begin something new, esp. new ideas, methods, etc.: to originate a religious or political movement, the use of deep-freezing units. See learn.

dis·cov·ert (dĭs·kŭv′ərt), adj. Law. (of a woman) not covert; not under the protection of a husband. [t. OF: m. descovert, pp. of descouvrir DISCOVER]

dis·cov·er·y (dĭs·kŭv′ər·ĭ), n., pl. -eries. **1.** act of discovering. **2.** something discovered. **3.** Law. compulsory disclosure, as of facts or documents.

Discovery Day, Columbus Day.

Discovery Inlet, an inlet of the Ross Sea, in Antarctica.

dis·cred·it (dĭs·krĕd′ĭt), v.t. **1.** to injure the credit or reputation of. **2.** to show to be undeserving of credit or belief; destroy confidence in. **3.** to give no credit to;

disbelieve: *the report is discredited.* —*n.* **4.** loss or lack of belief, or confidence; disbelief; distrust. **5.** loss or lack of repute or esteem; disrepute. **6.** something that damages a good reputation. [f. DIS-¹ + CREDIT, v.]

dis·cred·it·a·ble (dĭs krĕd′ĭt ə bəl), *adj.* such as to bring discredit; disgraceful. —**dis·cred′it·a·bly**, *adv.*

dis·creet (dĭs krēt′), *adj.* wise or judicious in avoiding mistakes or faults; prudent; circumspect; cautious; not rash. [ME *discret*, t. OF, t. L: s. *discrētus*, pp., separated] —**dis·creet′ly**, *adv.* —**dis·creet′ness**, *n.* —Syn. See careful.

dis·crep·an·cy (dĭs krĕp′ən sĭ), *n.*, *pl.* **-cies.** **1.** state or quality of being discrepant; difference; inconsistency. **2.** an instance of difference or inconsistency. Also, **dis·crep′ance.** —Syn. **1.** See difference.

dis·crep·ant (dĭs krĕp′ənt), *adj.* differing; disagreeing; discordant; inconsistent. [t. L: s. *discrepans*, ppr., being discordant] —**dis·crep′ant·ly**, *adv.*

dis·crete (dĭs krēt′), *adj.* **1.** detached from others; separate; distinct. **2.** consisting of or characterized by distinct or individual parts; discontinuous. [t. L: m. s. *discrētus* separated] —**dis·crete′ly**, *adv.* —**dis·crete′ness**, *n.*

dis·cre·tion (dĭs krĕsh′ən), *n.* **1.** power or right of deciding, or of acting according to one's own judgment; freedom of judgment or choice. **2.** the quality of being discreet; discernment of what is judicious or expedient, esp. with reference to one's own actions or speech; prudence. **3. at discretion,** as one wishes or decides.

dis·cre·tion·al (dĭs krĕsh′ən əl), *adj.* discretionary. —**dis·cre′tion·al·ly**, *adv.*

dis·cre·tion·ar·y (dĭs krĕsh′ə nĕr′ĭ), *adj.* **1.** subject or left to one's discretion. **2.** of or pertaining to discretion.

dis·crim·i·nate (*v.* dĭs krĭm′ə nāt; *adj.* dĭs krĭm′ə nĭt), *v.*, **-nated, -nating,** *adj.* —*v.i.* **1.** to make a distinction, as in favor of or against a person or thing: *discriminate against a minority.* **2.** to note or observe a difference; distinguish accurately: *to discriminate between things.* —*v.t.* **3.** to make or constitute a distinction in or between; differentiate: *to discriminate one thing from another.* **4.** to note or distinguish as different. —*adj.* **5.** marked by discrimination; making nice distinctions. [t. L: m. s. *discrīminātus*, pp., divided, distinguished] —**dis·crim′i·nate·ly**, *adv.* —**dis·crim′i·na·tor**, *n.* —Syn. **3.** See distinguish.

dis·crim·i·nat·ing (dĭs krĭm′ə nā′tĭng), *adj.* **1.** differentiating; distinctive. **2.** noting differences or distinctions with nicety; possessing discrimination. **3.** differential, as a tariff. —**dis·crim′i·nat′ing·ly**, *adv.*

dis·crim·i·na·tion (dĭs krĭm′ə nā′shən), *n.* **1.** act of discriminating. **2.** the resulting state. **3.** the making of a difference in particular cases, as in favor of or against a person or thing. **4.** the power of making nice distinctions; discriminating judgment. **5.** *Rare.* something that serves to differentiate. **6.** *Lexicog.* the attempt to distinguish between synonyms.

dis·crim·i·na·tive (dĭs krĭm′ə nā′tĭv), *adj.* **1.** that marks distinction; constituting a difference; characteristic: *the discriminative features of men.* **2.** making distinctions; discriminating. **3.** (of a tariff, etc.) differential. Also, **dis·crim·i·na·to·ry** (dĭs krĭm′ə nə tōr′ĭ). —**dis·crim′i·na·tive·ly**, *adv.*

dis·crown (dĭs kroun′), *v.t.* to deprive of a crown.

dis·cur·sive (dĭs kûr′sĭv), *adj.* **1.** passing rapidly or irregularly from one subject to another; rambling; digressive. **2.** proceeding by reasoning or argument; not intuitive. —**dis·cur′sive·ly**, *adv.* —**dis·cur′sive·ness**, *n.*

dis·cus (dĭs′kəs), *n.*, *pl.* **discuses, disci** (dĭs′ī). *Gymnastics.* **1.** a circular stone or metal plate for throwing to a distance, as among the ancient Greeks and Romans. **2.** the exercise or game of throwing it. [t. L, t. Gk.: m. *dískos* discus, disk, dish]

dis·cuss (dĭs kŭs′), *v.t.* **1.** to examine by argument; sift the considerations for and against; debate; talk over. **2.** (in humorous use) to try the quality of (food or drink) by consuming. **3.** *Civil Law.* **a.** to collect a debt from (the person primarily liable) before proceeding against the person secondarily liable. **b.** to execute against the movable property of (a debtor) before proceeding against his immovable property, as land. **4.** *Obs.* to make known; reveal. [ME *discusse(n)*, t. L: m. s. *discussus*, pp., struck asunder] —**dis·cuss′er**, *n.* —Syn. **1.** reason, deliberate. See argue.

dis·cus·sion (dĭs kŭsh′ən), *n.* act of discussing; critical examination by argument; debate.

dis·dain (dĭs dān′), *v.t.* **1.** to look upon or treat with contempt; despise; scorn. **2.** to think unworthy of notice, performance, etc.; consider beneath oneself. —*n.* **3.** a feeling of contempt for anything regarded as unworthy; haughty contempt; scorn. [ME *desdaine(n)*, t. OF: m. *desdeigner*, f. *des-* DIS-¹ + *deignier* DEIGN] —Syn. **3.** contemptuousness, haughtiness, arrogance, superciliousness, contumely. See contempt.

dis·dain·ful (dĭs dān′fəl), *adj.* full of or showing disdain; scornful. —**dis·dain′ful·ly**, *adv.* —**dis·dain′ful·ness**, *n.* —Syn. contemptuous, haughty, supercilious, contumelious.

dis·ease (dĭ zēz′), *n.*, *v.*, **-eased, -easing.** —*n.* **1.** a morbid condition of the body, or of some organ or part; illness; sickness; ailment. **2.** a similar disorder in plants. **3.** any deranged or depraved condition of the mind, affairs, etc. —*v.t.* **4.** to affect with disease; make ill. [ME *disese*, t. OF: m. *desaise*, f. *des-* DIS-¹ + *aise* EASE] —Syn. **1.** DISEASE, AFFECTION, DISORDER, MALADY imply a deviation of the body, or an organ of it, from health or normality. DISEASE and MALADY apply to organic deviations involving structural change. A DISEASE is a serious, active, prolonged, and deep-rooted condition. A MALADY is a lingering, chronic disease, usually painful and often fatal. An AFFECTION is a seriously abnormal state of body or mind, esp. one that interferes with their functions. A DISORDER is usually a physical or mental derangement, frequently a slight or transitory one. —Ant. **1.** health. **4.** cure.

dis·em·bark (dĭs′ĕm bärk′), *v.t.*, *v.i.* to put or go on shore from a ship; land. —**dis·em·bar·ka·tion** (dĭs-ĕm′bär kā′shən), *n.*

dis·em·bar·rass (dĭs′ĕm băr′əs), *v.t.* **1.** to free from embarrassment. **2.** to relieve; rid. **3.** to disentangle; extricate. —**dis′em·bar′rass·ment**, *n.*

dis·em·bod·y (dĭs′ĕm bŏd′ĭ), *v.t.*, **-bodied, -bodying.** to divest (a soul, etc.) of the body. —**dis·em·bod′i·ment**, *n.*

dis·em·bogue (dĭs′ĕm bōg′), *v.*, **-bogued, -boguing.** —*v.i.* **1.** to empty or discharge by pouring forth the contents. **2.** *Geol.* to debouch. —*v.t.* **3.** to discharge; cast forth. [t. Sp.: m. *desembocar*, f. *des-* DIS-¹ + *embocar* enter by the mouth, f. *en-* in- + *boca* mouth (g. L *bucca*)] —**dis′em·bogue′ment**, *n.*

dis·em·bos·om (dĭs′ĕm bŏŏz′əm), *v.t.* **1.** to reveal; divulge. **2.** to relieve (oneself) of a secret.

dis·em·bow·el (dĭs′ĕm bou′əl), *v.t.*, **-eled, -eling** or (*esp. Brit.*) **-elled, -elling.** to remove the bowels or entrails from; eviscerate. —**dis′em·bow′el·ment**, *n.*

dis·em·broil (dĭs′ĕm broil′), *v.t.* to free from embroilment, entanglement, or confusion.

dis·en·a·ble (dĭs′ĕn ā′bəl), *v.t.*, **-bled, -bling.** to deprive of ability; make unable; prevent.

dis·en·chant (dĭs′ĕn chănt′, -chänt′), *v.t.* to free from enchantment; disillusion. —**dis′en·chant′er**, *n.* —**dis′en·chant′ment**, *n.*

dis·en·cum·ber (dĭs′ĕn kŭm′bər), *v.t.* to free from encumbrance; disburden.

dis·en·dow (dĭs′ĕn dou′), *v.t.* to deprive of endowment, esp. a church. —**dis′en·dow′er**, *n.* —**dis′en·dow′ment**, *n.*

dis·en·fran·chise (dĭs′ĕn frăn′chīz), *v.t.*, **-chised, -chising.** to disfranchise. —**dis·en·fran·chise·ment** (dĭs′ĕn frăn′chĭz mənt), *n.*

dis·en·gage (dĭs′ĕn gāj′), *v.*, **-gaged, -gaging.** —*v.t.* **1.** to release from attachment or connection; loosen; unfasten. **2.** to free from engagement, pledge, obligation, etc. **3.** *Mil.* to break off action with (an enemy). —*v.i.* **4.** to become disengaged; free oneself.

dis·en·gage·ment (dĭs′ĕn gāj′mənt), *n.* **1.** act or process of disengaging, or state of being disengaged. **2.** freedom from obligation or occupation; leisure.

dis·en·tail (dĭs′ĕn tāl′), *v.t.* *Law.* to free (an estate) from entail. —**dis′en·tail′ment**, *n.*

dis·en·tan·gle (dĭs′ĕn tăng′gəl), *v.t.*, *v.i.*, **-gled, -gling.** to free or become free from entanglement; untangle; extricate (fol. by *from*). —**dis·en·tan′gle·ment**, *n.*

dis·en·thral (dĭs′ĕn thrôl′), *v.t.*, **-thralled, -thralling.** disenthrall. —**dis′en·thral′ment**, *n.*

dis·en·thrall (dĭs′ĕn thrôl′), *v.t.* to free from thralldom. —**dis′en·thrall′ment**, *n.*

dis·en·throne (dĭs′ĕn thrōn′), *v.t.*, **-throned, -throning.** to dethrone. —**dis′en·throne′ment**, *n.*

dis·en·ti·tle (dĭs′ĕn tī′təl), *v.t.*, **-tled, -tling.** to deprive of title or right.

dis·en·tomb (dĭs′ĕn tōōm′), *v.t.* to take from the tomb; disinter. —**dis′en·tomb′ment**, *n.*

dis·en·trance (dĭs′ĕn trăns′, -träns′), *v.t.*, **-tranced, -trancing.** to bring out of an entranced condition. —**dis′en·trance′ment**, *n.*

dis·en·twine (dĭs′ĕn twīn′), *v.t.*, *v.i.*, **-twined, -twining.** to bring or come out of an entwined or intertwined state; untwine.

di·sep·a·lous (dī sĕp′ə ləs), *adj.* *Bot.* having two sepals.

dis·es·tab·lish (dĭs′ĕs tăb′lĭsh), *v.t.* **1.** to deprive of the character of being established. **2.** to withdraw exclusive state recognition or support from (a church). —**dis′es·tab′lish·ment**, *n.*

dis·es·teem (dĭs′ĕs tēm′), *v.t.* **1.** to hold in low esteem; think slightingly of. —*n.* **2.** lack of esteem; disregard.

di·seur (dē zœr′), *n.* a professional public entertainer who talks, recites, etc. [t. F: one who tells, says] —**di·seuse** (dē zœz′), *n. fem.*

dis·fa·vor (dĭs fā′vər), *n.* **1.** unfavorable regard; displeasure; disesteem: *the minister incurred the king's disfavor.* **2.** lack of favor; state of being regarded unfavorably: *in disfavor at court.* **3.** an act of disregard, dislike, or unkindness: *to dispense disfavors.* —*v.t.* **4.** to regard or treat with disfavor. Also, *Brit.,* **dis·fa′vour.**

dis·fea·ture (dĭs fē′chər), *v.t.*, **-tured, -turing.** to mar the features of; disfigure. —**dis·fea′ture·ment**, *n.*

dis·fig·ure (dĭs fĭg′yər), *v.t.*, **-ured, -uring.** **1.** to mar the figure, appearance, or beauty of; deform; deface. **2.** to mar the effect or excellence of. [ME *disfigure(n)*, t. OF: m. *desfigurer*, f. *des-* DIS-¹ + *figurer*, der. *figure* FIGURE, n.] —**dis·fig′ur·er**, *n.* —Syn. **1.** See mar.

dis·fig·ure·ment (dĭs fĭg′yər mənt), *n.* **1.** act of disfiguring. **2.** disfigured condition. **3.** something that disfigures. Also, **dis·fig·ur·a′tion.**

---

b., blend of, blended; c., cognate with; d., dialect, dialectal; der., derived from; f., formed from; g., going back to; m., modification of; r., replacing; s., stem of; t., taken from; ?, perhaps. See the full key on inside cover.

dis·for·est (dĭs fŏr′ĭst, -fôr′-), v.t. Law. to disafforest. —**dis·for′est·a′tion**, n.

dis·fran·chise (dĭs frăn′chīz), v.t., -chised, -chising. 1. to deprive (persons) of rights of citizenship, as of the right to vote. 2. to deprive of a franchise, privilege, or right. —**dis·fran·chise·ment** (dĭs frăn′chĭz mənt), n.

dis·frock (dĭs frŏk′), v.t. Eccles. to unfrock.

dis·fur·nish (dĭs fûr′nĭsh), v.t. to deprive of something with which a person or thing is furnished; strip. —**dis·fur′nish·ment**, n.

dis·gorge (dĭs gôrj′), v., -gorged, -gorging. —v.t. 1. to eject or throw out from or as from the gorge or throat; vomit forth; discharge. 2. to give up unwillingly. —v.i. 3. to disgorge something. [late ME, t. OF: m. desgorger, f. des- DIS-¹ + gorge throat] —**dis·gorge′ment**, n. —**dis·gorg′er**, n.

dis·grace (dĭs grās′), n., v., -graced, -gracing. —n. 1. state of being in dishonor; ignominy; shame. 2. a cause of shame or reproach; that which dishonors. 3. state of being out of favor; exclusion from favor, confidence, or trust. —v.t. 4. to bring or reflect shame or reproach upon. 5. to dismiss with discredit; put out of grace or favor; treat with disfavor. [t. F, t. It.: m. disgrazia. See DIS-¹, GRACE] —**dis·grac′er**, n. —Syn. 1. DISGRACE, DISHONOR, IGNOMINY, INFAMY imply a very low position in the opinion of others. DISGRACE implies the disfavor, with a greater or less degree of reproachful disapprobation, of others: he brought disgrace on his family, to be in disgrace. DISHONOR implies a stain on honor or honorable reputation: it relates esp. to the conduct of the person himself: he preferred death to dishonor. IGNOMINY is disgrace in which one's situation invites contempt: the ignominy of being discovered cheating. INFAMY is shameful notoriety, or baseness of action or character which is widely known and recognized: the children never outlived the father's infamy. —Ant. 1. honor.

dis·grace·ful (dĭs grās′fəl), adj. bringing or deserving disgrace; shameful; dishonorable; disreputable. —**dis·grace′ful·ly**, adv. —**dis·grace′ful·ness**, n.

dis·grun·tle (dĭs grŭn′təl), v.t., -tled, -tling. to put into a state of sulky dissatisfaction; make discontent. [f. DIS-¹ + gruntle, freq. of GRUNT] —**dis·grun′tle·ment**, n.

dis·guise (dĭs gīz′), v., -guised, -guising, n. —v.t. 1. to change the guise or appearance of so as to conceal identity or to mislead; conceal the identity of by means of a misleading garb, etc. 2. to conceal or cover up the real state or character of by a counterfeit form or appearance; misrepresent: to disguise one's intentions. —n. 3. that which disguises; something that serves or is intended for concealment of identity, character, or quality; a deceptive covering, condition, manner, etc. 4. the make-up, mask, or costume of an entertainer. 5. act of disguising. 6. state of being disguised. [ME desguise(n), t. OF: m. desguiser, f. des- DIS-¹ + guise GUISE] —**dis·guis′er**, n.

dis·gust (dĭs gŭst′), v.t. 1. to cause nausea or loathing in. 2. to offend the good taste, moral sense, etc. of; cause aversion or impatient dissatisfaction in. —n. 3. strong distaste; nausea; loathing. 4. repugnance caused by something offensive; strong aversion; impatient dissatisfaction. [t. MF: m. desgouster, f. des- DIS-¹ + gouster taste, relish] —**dis·gust′ed·ly**, adv. —Syn. 4. See dislike.

dis·gust·ful (dĭs gŭst′fəl), adj. causing disgust; nauseous; offensive.

dis·gust·ing (dĭs gŭs′tĭng), adj. causing disgust; offensive to the physical, moral, or aesthetic taste. —**dis·gust′ing·ly**, adv. —Syn. loathsome, sickening, nauseous, repulsive, revolting.

dish (dĭsh), n. 1. an open, more or less shallow container of pottery, glass, metal, wood, etc., used for various purposes, esp. for holding or serving food. 2. any container used at table. 3. that which is served or contained in a dish. 4. a particular article or preparation of food. 5. as much as a dish will hold; a dishful. 6. anything like a dish in form or use. 7. concave state, or the degree of concavity, as of a wheel. —v.t. 8. to put into or serve in a dish, as food: to dish up food. 9. to fashion like a dish; make concave. 10. Slang. to defeat; frustrate; cheat. [ME; OE disc dish, plate, bowl (cf. G tisch table), t. L: discus dish, DISCUS]

dis·ha·bille (dĭs ə bēl′), n. 1. undress or negligee. 2. a garment worn in undress. 3. a loose morning dress. Also, **deshabille**. [t. F: m. déshabillé, prop. pp. of deshabiller undress, f. dés- DIS-¹ + habiller dress]

dis·ha·bit·u·ate (dĭs hə bĭch′ōō āt′), v.t., -ated, -ating. to cause to be no longer habituated or accustomed.

dis·hal·low (dĭs hăl′ō), v.t. to profane; desecrate.

dis·har·mo·ni·ous (dĭs här mō′nĭ əs), adj. inharmonious; discordant.

dis·har·mo·nize (dĭs här′mə nīz′), v.t., v.i., -nized, -nizing. to make or be inharmonious.

dis·har·mo·ny (dĭs här′mə nĭ), n., pl. -nies. 1. discord. 2. something discordant.

dish·cloth (dĭsh′klôth′, -klŏth′), n. a cloth for use in washing dishes. Also, **dish·clout** (dĭsh′klout′).

dis·heart·en (dĭs här′tən), v.t. to depress the spirits of; discourage. —**dis·heart′en·ing·ly**, adv. —**dis·heart′en·ment**, n.

dished (dĭsht), adj. 1. concave: a dished face. 2. Slang. exhausted; worn out.

dis·helm (dĭs hĕlm′), v.t., v.i. Archaic. to divest of, or take off, the helmet.

dis·her·it (dĭs hĕr′ĭt), v.t. Obs. or Rare. to disinherit.

di·shev·el (dĭ shĕv′əl), v.t., -eled, -eling or (esp. Brit.) -elled, -elling. to let down (the hair); let hang in loose disorder. [ME dischevelen, t. OF: m. descheveler, der. des- DIS-¹ + chevel hair (g. L capillus)] —**di·shev′el·ment**, n.

di·shev·eled (dĭ shĕv′əld), adj. 1. hanging loosely or in disorder; unkempt: disheveled hair. 2. untidy; disarranged: disheveled appearance. Also, esp. Brit., **di·shev′elled**.

dish gravy, juice from cooked meat.

dis·hon·est (dĭs ŏn′ĭst), adj. 1. not honest; disposed to lie, cheat, or steal: a dishonest person. 2. proceeding from or exhibiting lack of honesty; fraudulent. —**dis·hon′est·ly**, adv. —Syn. 1. unscrupulous, knavish, thievish. See corrupt.

dis·hon·es·ty (dĭs ŏn′ĭs tĭ), n., pl. -ties. 1. lack of honesty; a disposition to lie, cheat, or steal. 2. a dishonest act; a fraud; theft.

dis·hon·or (dĭs ŏn′ər), n. 1. lack of honor; dishonorable character or conduct. 2. disgrace; ignominy; shame. 3. an indignity; insult. 4. a cause of shame; a disgrace. 5. Com. failure or refusal of the drawee or acceptor of a bill of exchange or note to accept it, or, if it is accepted, to pay and retire it. —v.t. 6. to deprive of honor; disgrace; bring reproach or shame on. 7. Com. to fail or refuse to honor (a draft, etc.) by payment. Also, Brit., **dis·hon′our**. [ME dishonour, t. OF: m. deshonor, f. des- DIS-¹ + honor honor (t. L)] —**dis·hon′or·er**, n. —Syn. 2. See disgrace.

dis·hon·or·a·ble (dĭs ŏn′ər ə bəl), adj. 1. showing lack of honor; ignoble; base; disgraceful; shameful: a dishonorable act. 2. having no honor or good repute: a dishonorable man. Also, Brit., **dis·hon′our·a·ble**. —**dis·hon′or·a·ble·ness**, n. —**dis·hon′or·a·bly**, adv. —Syn. 2. infamous, unscrupulous, unprincipled.

dish·pan (dĭsh′păn′), n. a pan in which dishes are washed.

dish·rag (dĭsh′răg′), n. dishcloth.

dish·tow·el (dĭsh′tou′əl), n. a towel for drying dishes.

dish·wa·ter (dĭsh′wô′tər, -wŏt′ər), n. water in which dishes are, or have been, washed.

dis·il·lu·sion (dĭs′ĭ lōō′zhən), v.t. 1. to free from illusion; disenchant. —n. 2. a freeing or a being freed from illusion; disenchantment. —**dis′il·lu′sion·ment**, n. —**dis·il·lu·sive** (dĭs′ĭ lōō′sĭv), adj.

dis·il·lu·sion·ize (dĭs′ĭ lōō′zhə nīz′), v.t., -ized, -izing. to disillusion.

dis·im·pas·sioned (dĭs′ĭm păsh′ənd), adj. calm; dispassionate; passionless.

dis·im·pris·on (dĭs′ĭm prĭz′ən), v.t. to release from imprisonment. —**dis′im·pris′on·ment**, n.

dis·in·cli·na·tion (dĭs ĭn′klə nā′shən), n. the absence of inclination; averseness; distaste; unwillingness.

dis·in·cline (dĭs′ĭn klīn′), v.t., v.i., -clined, -clining. to make or be averse or indisposed.

dis·in·fect (dĭs′ĭn fĕkt′), v.t. to cleanse (rooms, clothing, etc.) from infection; destroy disease germs in. —**dis′in·fec′tor**, n.

dis·in·fect·ant (dĭs′ĭn fĕk′tənt), n. 1. any chemical agent that destroys bacteria. —adj. 2. disinfecting.

dis·in·fec·tion (dĭs′ĭn fĕk′shən), n. the process of disinfecting.

dis·in·gen·u·ous (dĭs′ĭn jĕn′yōō əs), adj. not ingenuous; lacking in frankness, candor, or sincerity; insincere: disingenuous persons. —**dis′in·gen′u·ous·ly**, adv. —**dis′in·gen′u·ous·ness**, n.

dis·in·her·it (dĭs′ĭn hĕr′ĭt), v.t. 1. Law. to exclude from inheritance (an heir or a next of kin). 2. to deprive of the right to inherit. —**dis′in·her′it·ance**, n.

dis·in·te·grate (dĭs ĭn′tə grāt′), v., -grated, -grating. —v.t. 1. to reduce to particles, fragments, or parts; break up or destroy the cohesion of: rocks are disintegrated by frost and rain. —v.i. 2. to separate into its component parts; break up. —**dis·in·te·gra·ble** (dĭs ĭn′tə grə bəl), adj. —**dis·in′te·gra′tion**, n. —**dis·in′te·gra′tor**, n. —Syn. 2. See decay.

dis·in·ter (dĭs′ĭn tûr′), v.t., -terred, -terring. 1. to take out of the place of interment; exhume; unearth. 2. to bring from obscurity into view. —**dis′in·ter′ment**, n.

dis·in·ter·est (dĭs ĭn′tər ĭst, -trĭst), n. 1. absence of interest; indifference. —v.t. 2. to divest of interest or concern.

dis·in·ter·est·ed (dĭs ĭn′tər ĕs′tĭd, -trĭs′tĭd), adj. 1. unbiased by personal interest or advantage; not influenced by selfish motives. 2. U.S. Colloq. not interested; indifferent. —**dis·in′ter·est′ed·ly**, adv. —**dis·in′ter·est′ed·ness**, n. —Syn. 1. DISINTERESTED, UNINTERESTED are not properly synonyms. DISINTERESTED today stresses lack of prejudice or of selfish interests: a disinterested report. UNINTERESTED suggests aloofness and indifference: completely uninterested and taking no part in proceedings. See fair¹.

dis·ject (dĭs jĕkt′), v.t. to cast asunder; scatter; disperse. [t. L: s. disjectus, pp., thrown asunder]

dis·jec·ta mem·bra (dĭs jĕk′tə mĕm′brə), Latin. scattered members; disjointed portions or parts.

dis·join (dĭs join′), v.t. 1. to undo or prevent the junction or union of; disunite; separate. —v.i. 2. to become disunited; separate. [ME desjoyne(n), t. OF: m. desjoindre, g. L disjungere]

ăct, āble, dâre, ärt; ĕbb, ēqual; ĭf, īce; hŏt, ōver, ôrder, oil, bŏok, ōoze, out; ŭp, ūse, ûrge; ə = a in alone; ch, chief; g, give; ng, ring; sh, shoe; th, thin; ŧh, that; zh, vision. See the full key on inside cover.

dis·joint (dĭs joint′), *v.t.* **1.** to separate or disconnect the joints or joinings of. **2.** to put out of order; derange. —*v.i.* **3.** to come apart. **4.** to be dislocated; be put out of joint. —*adj.* **5.** *Obs.* disjointed; out of joint. [t. OF: m. *desjoint*, pp. of *desjoindre*, g. L *disjungere*]

dis·joint·ed (dĭs join′tĭd), *adj.* **1.** having the joints or connections separated: *a disjointed fowl.* **2.** disconnected; incoherent: *a disjointed discourse.* —**dis·joint′ed·ly,** *adv.* —**dis·joint′ed·ness,** *n.*

dis·junct (dĭs jŭngkt′), *adj.* **1.** disjoined; separated. **2.** *Music.* progressing melodically by intervals larger than a second. **3.** *Entomol.* having the head, thorax, and abdomen separated by deep constrictions. [t. L: s. *disjunctus*, pp., disjoined]

dis·junc·tion (dĭs jŭngk′shən), *n.* **1.** act of disjoining. **2.** state of being disjoined. **3.** *Logic.* **a.** a proposition in which two (or more) alternatives are asserted, only one of which can be true. **b.** the relation between the terms of a disjunctive proposition.

dis·junc·tive (dĭs jŭngk′tĭv), *adj.* **1.** serving or tending to disjoin; separating; dividing; distinguishing. **2.** *Gram.* **a.** syntactically setting two or more expressions in opposition to each other, as *but* in *poor but happy*, or expressing an alternative, as *or* in *this or that.* **b.** not syntactically dependent upon some particular expression. **3.** *Logic.* characterizing propositions which are disjunctions. —*n.* **4.** a statement, etc., involving alternatives. —**dis·junc′tive·ly,** *adv.*

dis·junc·ture (dĭs jŭngk′chər), *n.* **1.** act of disjoining. **2.** state of being disjoined.

dis·june (dĭs jōōn′), *n. Scot. Obs.* breakfast.

disk (dĭsk), *n.* **1.** any thin, flat, circular plate or object. **2.** a round, flat area. **3.** the apparently flat surface of the sun, etc. **4.** a phonograph record. **5.** a discus. **6.** *Bot., Zool., etc.* any of various roundish, flat structures or parts. **7.** *Bot.* (in the daisy and other composite plants) the central portion of the flower head, composed of tubular florets. Also, **disc.** [t. L: m. s. *discus* DISCUS]

disk harrow, a harrow having a number of sharp-edged concave disks set at such an angle that as the machine is drawn along they pulverize and turn the soil and destroy weeds.

disk jockey, a radio announcer on an all-record program.

disk wheel, a spokeless vehicular wheel, esp. on motor cars, having a heavy circular pressed-steel disk mounted on the wheel hub and supporting the tire rim on its outer edge.

dis·like (dĭs līk′), *v.*, **-liked, -liking,** *n.* —*v.t.* **1.** not to like; regard with displeasure or aversion: *I dislike him, I dislike his doing it, I dislike having to work.* —*n.* **2.** the feeling of disliking; distaste: *I have taken a strong dislike to him, of him, for him.* —**dis·lik′a·ble,** *adj.*
—**Syn. 2.** disrelish. DISLIKE, DISGUST, DISTASTE, REPUGNANCE imply antipathy toward something. DISLIKE is a general word, the strength of the feeling being indicated by the context. It expresses a positive (not necessarily strong), sometimes inherent or permanent feeling of antipathy for something: *to have a dislike for crowds, for someone, for noise.* DISGUST is a very strong word, expressing a feeling of loathing for what is offensive to the physical taste or to the feelings and sensibilities: *the taste of spoiled food fills one with disgust, to feel disgust at seeing snobbery and ostentation.* DISTASTE, though etymologically equal to DISGUST, is weaker; it implies a more or less settled dislike for what is naturally uncongenial or has been made so by association: *to have distaste for certain foods, for hard work, for unconventional art or music.* REPUGNANCE is a strong feeling of aversion for, and antagonism toward, something: *to feel repugnance for* (or *toward*) *low criminals, an idea or a kind of conduct.*

dis·limn (dĭs lĭm′), *v.t. Archaic or Poetic.* to obliterate (a picture); efface.

dis·lo·cate (dĭs′lō kāt′), *v.t.*, **-cated, -cating. 1.** to put out of place; displace; put out of proper relative position. **2.** *Surg.* to put out of joint or out of position, as a limb or an organ. **3.** to throw out of order; derange; upset; disorder. [t. ML: m. s. *dislocātus*, pp. of *dislocāre*, f. DIS-[1] + L *locāre* place] —**dis′lo·ca′tion,** *n.*

dis·lodge (dĭs lŏj′), *v.*, **-lodged, -lodging.** —*v.t.* **1.** to remove or drive from a place of lodgment; drive from a position occupied. —*v.i.* **2.** to go from a place of lodgment. —**dis·lodg′ment;** *esp. Brit.*, **dis·lodge′ment,** *n.*

dis·loy·al (dĭs loi′əl), *adj.* not loyal; false to one's obligations or allegiance; faithless; treacherous. [t. OF: m. *desloial*, f. *des-* DIS-[1] + *loial* law-abiding (g. L *lēgālis*)] —**dis·loy′al·ly,** *adv.* —**Syn.** unfaithful, false, perfidious, traitorous, treasonable. —**Ant.** constant.

dis·loy·al·ty (dĭs loi′əl tĭ), *n.*, *pl.* **-ties. 1.** quality of being disloyal; unfaithfulness. **2.** violation of allegiance or duty, as to a government. **3.** a disloyal act.
—**Syn. 1.** DISLOYALTY, PERFIDY, TREACHERY, TREASON imply betrayal of trust, and esp. traitorous acts against one's country or its government. DISLOYALTY applies to any violation of loyalty, whether to a person, a cause, or one's country, and whether in thought or in deeds: *to suspect disloyalty in a friend.* PERFIDY implies deliberate breaking of faith or of one's pledges and promises, on which others are relying: *it is an act of perfidy to cheat innocent persons.* TREACHERY implies being secretly traitorous but seeming friendly and loyal: *in treachery deceit is added to disloyalty.* TREASON is definitely wishing harm to one's country or government, and performing overt acts to help its enemies: *acting to aid a hostile power is treason.*

dis·mal (dĭz′məl), *adj.* **1.** causing gloom or dejection; gloomy; dreary; cheerless; melancholy. **2.** terrible; dreadful. **3.** *Now Rare.* disastrous; calamitous. **4.** *Obs.* evil; unlucky. —*n.* **5.** (*usually pl.*) *Colloq.* gloom; melancholy; dumps: *in the dismals.* **6.** something dismal. **7.** any of certain tracts of swampy land along or near the southern Atlantic coast of the U.S. [ME *dismall;* orig. uncert.] —**dis′mal·ly,** *adv.* —**dis′mal·ness,** *n.* —**Ant. 1.** gay.

Dis·mal Swamp (dĭz′məl), an extensive swamp in SE Virginia and NE North Carolina. ab. 30 mi. long.

dis·man·tle (dĭs măn′təl), *v.t.*, **-tled, -tling. 1.** to deprive or strip of apparatus, furniture, equipments, defenses, etc.: *to dismantle a ship or a fortress.* **2.** to pull down; take apart; take to pieces. **3.** to divest of dress, covering, etc. [t. F (obs.): m. s. *desmanteler.* See DIS-[1], MANTLE] —**dis·man′tle·ment,** *n.*

dis·mast (dĭs măst′, -mäst′), *v.t.* to deprive of masts; break off the masts of. —**dis·mast′ment,** *n.*

dis·may (dĭs mā′), *v.t.* **1.** to break down the courage of utterly, as by sudden danger or trouble; dishearten utterly; daunt. —*n.* **2.** sudden or complete loss of courage; utter disheartenment. [ME *desmaien*, prob. t. OF; cf. OF *esmaier* dismay] —**Syn. 1.** appall, terrify, horrify, frighten, disconcert. See **discourage. 2.** consternation, terror, panic, horror, fear.

dis·mem·ber (dĭs mĕm′bər), *v.t.* **1.** to deprive of members or limbs; divide limb from limb. **2.** to separate into parts; divide and distribute the parts of (a kingdom, etc.). [ME *dismembre(n)*, t. OF: m. *desmembrer*, der. *des-* DIS-[1] + *membre* MEMBER] —**dis·mem′ber·er,** *n.* —**dis·mem′ber·ment,** *n.*

dis·miss (dĭs mĭs′), *v.t.* **1.** to direct or allow (an assembly of persons, etc.) to disperse. **2.** to bid or allow (a person) to go; give permission to depart. **3.** to send forth (a thing); let go. **4.** to discharge or remove, as from office or service. **5.** to discard or reject. **6.** to put off or away; lay aside; esp., to put aside from consideration. **7.** to have done with (a subject) after summary treatment. **8.** *Law.* to put out of court, as a complaint or appeal. [t. ML: m. s. *dismissus*, pp., sent away, for L *dīmissus*] —**dis·miss′i·ble,** *adj.* —**Syn. 2.** See **release.** —**Ant. 5.** accept.

dis·miss·al (dĭs mĭs′əl), *n.* **1.** act of dismissing **2.** state of being dismissed. **3.** a spoken or written order of discharge. Also, **dis·mis·sion** (dĭs mĭsh′ən).

dis·mount (dĭs mount′), *v.i.* **1.** to get off or alight (from a horse, bicycle, truck, etc.). —*v.t.* **2.** to bring or throw down, as from a horse; unhorse. **3.** to remove (a thing) from its mounting, support, or setting, etc. **4.** to take (a piece of mechanism) to pieces. —*n.* **5.** act or manner of dismounting. —**dis·mount′a·ble,** *adj.*

dis·na·ture (dĭs nā′chər), *v.t.*, **-tured, -turing.** to deprive of its proper nature; make unnatural.

Dis·ney (dĭz′nĭ), *n.* **Walt**(**er E.**), born 1901, U.S. motion picture cartoon producer.

dis·o·be·di·ence (dĭs′ə bē′dĭ əns), *n.* lack of obedience; neglect or refusal to obey.

dis·o·be·di·ent (dĭs′ə bē′dĭ ənt), *adj.* neglecting or refusing to obey; refractory. —**dis′o·be′di·ent·ly,** *adv.* —**Syn.** insubordinate, contumacious, defiant.

dis·o·bey (dĭs′ə bā′), *v.t.*, *v.i.* to neglect or refuse to obey. [ME *disobey(en)*, t. OF: m. *desobeir*, f. *des-* DIS-[1] + *obeir* OBEY] —**dis′o·bey′er,** *n.* —**Syn.** transgress, violate, disregard, defy.

dis·o·blige (dĭs′ə blīj′), *v.t.*, **-bliged, -bliging. 1.** to refuse or neglect to oblige; act contrary to the desire or convenience of; fail to accommodate. **2.** to give offense to; affront. **3.** *Obs. or Dial.* to incommode; put to inconvenience. —**dis′o·blig′ing,** *adj.* —**dis′o·blig′ing·ly,** *adv.* —**dis′o·blig′ing·ness,** *n.*

dis·op·er·a·tion (dĭs ŏp′ə rā′shən), *n. Ecol.* the conscious or unconscious behavior of organisms living together and producing a result which is disadvantageous or harmful to the organisms concerned.

dis·or·der (dĭs ôr′dər), *n.* **1.** lack of order or regular arrangement; disarrangement; confusion. **2.** an irregularity. **3.** breach of order; disorderly conduct; a public disturbance. **4.** a derangement of physical or mental health or functions. —*v.t.* **5.** to destroy the order or regular arrangement of; disarrange. **6.** to derange the physical or mental health or functions of.
—**Syn. 1.** disorderliness, disarray, jumble, litter, clutter. **3.** DISORDER, BRAWL, DISTURBANCE, UPROAR are disruptions or interruptions of a peaceful situation. DISORDER refers to unrest within a city or state, and to any scene in which there is confusion or fighting among individuals or groups: *the police went to a scene of disorder.* A BRAWL is a noisy, unseemly quarrel, usually in a public place: *a tavern brawl.* A DISTURBANCE is disorder of such size as to inconvenience many people: *to cause a disturbance.* An UPROAR is a tumult, a bustle and clamor of many voices, often because of a disturbance: *a mighty uproar.* **4.** ailment, malady. See **disease.**

dis·or·dered (dĭs ôr′dərd), *adj.* **1.** in confusion. **2.** mentally ill.

dis·or·der·ly (dĭs ôr′dər lĭ), *adj.* **1.** characterized by disorder; irregular; untidy; confused. **2.** unruly; turbulent; tumultuous. **3.** *Law.* violating, or opposed to, constituted order; contrary to public order or morality. —*adv.* **4.** without order, rule, or method; irregularly; confusedly. —**dis·or′der·li·ness,** *n.*

disorderly conduct, *Law.* a petty misdemeanor, generally including nuisances, breaches of the peace, offensive or immoral conduct in public, etc.

b., blend of, blended; c., cognate with; d., dialect, dialectal; der., derived from; f., formed from; g., going back to; m., modification of; r., replacing; s., stem of; t., taken from; ?, perhaps. See the full key on inside cover.

dis·or·der·ly house, 1. a house of prostitution; brothel. 2. a gambling place.

dis·or·der·ly per·son, *Law.* 1. a person guilty of disorderly conduct. 2. a person guilty of a separate offense including loitering in public, vagrancy, etc.

dis·or·gan·i·za·tion (dĭs ôr′gən ə zā′shən), *n.* 1. a breaking up of order or system; disunion or disruption of constituent parts. 2. the absence of organization or orderly arrangement; disarrangement; disorder.

dis·or·gan·ize (dĭs ôr′gə nīz′), *v.t.,* **-ized, -izing.** to destroy the organization, systematic arrangement, or orderly connection of; throw into confusion or disorder. **—dis·or′gan·iz′er,** *n.*

dis·own (dĭs ōn′), *v.t.* to refuse to acknowledge as belonging or pertaining to oneself; deny the ownership of or responsibility for; repudiate; renounce.

dis·par·age (dĭs păr′ĭj), *v.t.,* **-aged, -aging.** 1. to bring reproach or discredit upon; lower the estimation of. 2. to speak of or treat slightingly; depreciate; belittle. [ME *desparage(n),* t. OF: m. *desparagier* match equally, der. *des-* DIS-[1] + *parage* equality, der. *parer* equalize (g. L *pariāre*)] **—dis·par′ag·er,** *n.* **—dis·par′ag·ing·ly,** *adv.*

dis·par·age·ment (dĭs păr′ĭj mənt), *n.* 1. act of disparaging. 2. something that causes loss of dignity or reputation.

dis·pa·rate (dĭs′pə rĭt), *adj.* distinct in kind; essentially different; dissimilar; unlike; having no common genus. [t. L: m. s. *disparātus,* pp., separated] **—dis′pa·rate·ly,** *adv.* **—dis′pa·rate·ness,** *n.*

dis·par·i·ty (dĭs păr′ə tĭ), *n., pl.* **-ties.** lack of similarity or equality; inequality; difference: *a disparity in age, rank, condition, etc.* **—Syn.** See **difference.**

dis·part (dĭs pärt′), *v.t., v.i.* to part asunder; separate; divide into parts. [appar. t. It.: s. *dispartire* part, separate, divide, g. L] **—dis·part′ment,** *n.*

dis·pas·sion (dĭs păsh′ən), *n.* freedom from passion; unemotional state or quality.

dis·pas·sion·ate (dĭs păsh′ən ĭt), *adj.* free from or unaffected by passion; devoid of personal feeling or bias; impartial; calm: *a dispassionate critic.* **—dis·pas′sion·ate·ly,** *adv.* **—dis·pas′sion·ate·ness,** *n.*

dis·patch (dĭs păch′), *v.t.* 1. to send off; put under way: *to dispatch a messenger, telegram, etc.* 2. to dismiss (a person), as after an audience. 3. to put to death; kill. 4. to transact or dispose of (business, etc.) promptly or speedily; execute quickly; settle. **—v.i.** 5. *Archaic.* to hasten; be quick. 6. *Obs.* to settle a matter. **—n.** 7. the sending off of a messenger, letter, etc., to a destination. 8. dismissal of a person after the transaction of his business. 9. a putting to death; killing. 10. prompt or speedy transaction, as of business. 11. expeditious performance, promptitude, or speed: *proceed with all possible dispatch.* 12. *Com.* **a.** a method of effecting a speedy delivery of goods. **b.** a conveyance or organization for the expeditious transmission of merchandise, etc. 13. a written message sent in haste. 14. an official communication sent by special messenger. 15. **mentioned in dispatches,** *Brit.* named in military reports for special bravery or acts of service. 16. *Journalism.* a news account transmitted by a reporter to his newspaper or other agency. 17. a telegram. Also, **despatch.** [t. It.: m. *dispacciare* hasten, speed, or t. Sp.: m. *despachar*] **—dis·patch′er,** *n.*

dis·pel (dĭs pĕl′), *v.t.,* **-pelled, -pelling.** to drive off in various directions; scatter; disperse; dissipate: *to dispel vapors, fear, etc.* [t. L: m. s. *dispellere* drive asunder] **—dis·pel′ler,** *n.* **—Syn.** See **scatter.** **—Ant.** gather.

dis·pend (dĭs pĕnd′), *v.t. Obs.* or *Archaic.* to pay out; expend; spend. [ME *despende(n),* t. OF: m. *despendre,* g. L *dispendere* weigh out]

dis·pen·sa·ble (dĭs pĕn′sə bəl), *adj.* 1. that may be dispensed with or done without; unimportant. 2. capable of being dispensed or administered. 3. admitting of dispensation, as an offense or a sin. 4. that may be declared not binding. **—dis·pen′sa·bil′i·ty,** *n.*

dis·pen·sa·ry (dĭs pĕn′sə rĭ), *n., pl.* **-ries.** 1. a place where something is dispensed, esp. medicines. 2. a charitable or public institution where medicines are furnished and medical advice is given gratuitously or for a small fee.

dis·pen·sa·tion (dĭs′pən sā′shən, -pĕn-), *n.* 1. act of dispensing; distribution; administration; management. 2. that which is distributed or given out. 3. a certain order, system, or arrangement. 4. *Theol.* **a.** the divine ordering of the affairs of the world. **b.** an appointment or arrangement, as by God. **c.** a divinely appointed order or system: *the old, Mosaic, or Jewish dispensation; the new, gospel, or Christian dispensation.* 5. a dispensing with, doing away with, or doing without something. 6. *Rom. Cath. Ch.* **a.** a relaxation of a law in a particular case granted by a competent superior or his delegate in laws which he has the power to make and enforce. **b.** the document containing this. **—dis·pen′sa·tion·al,** *adj.*

dis·pen·sa·tor (dĭs′pən sā′tər, -pĕn-), *n.* one who dispenses; a distributor; an administrator.

dis·pen·sa·to·ry (dĭs pĕn′sə tōr′ĭ), *n., pl.* **-ries.** 1. a book in which the composition, preparation, and uses of medicinal substances are described; a nonofficial pharmacopoeia. 2. a dispensary.

dis·pense (dĭs pĕns′), *v.,* **-pensed, -pensing,** *n.* **—v.t.** 1. to deal out; distribute: *to dispense justice, wisdom, etc.* 2. to administer (laws, etc.). 3. *Pharm.* to put up and distribute (medicine), esp. on prescription. 4. *Rom. Cath. Ch.* to grant a dispensation to, for, or from. **—v.i.** 5. to grant dispensation. 6. **dispense with, a.** to do without; forego. **b.** to do away with (a need, etc.). **c.** to grant exemption from (a law, promise, etc.). **—n.** 7. *Obs.* dispensation. [ME *dispense(n),* t. OF: m. *dispenser,* t. L: m. *dispensāre* weigh out, freq. of L *dispendere*] **—dis·pens′er,** *n.* **—Syn.** 1. See **distribute.**

dis·peo·ple (dĭs pē′pəl), *v.t.,* **-pled, -pling.** to deprive of people; depopulate.

di·sper·mous (dī spûr′məs), *adj. Bot.* two-seeded.

dis·per·sal (dĭs pûr′səl), *n.* dispersion (defs. 1 and 2).

dis·perse (dĭs pûrs′), *v.,* **-persed, -persing.** **—v.t.** 1. to scatter abroad; send or drive off in various directions. 2. to spread; diffuse: *the wise disperse knowledge.* 3. to dispel; cause to vanish: *the fog is dispersed.* **—v.i.** 4. to separate and move apart in different directions without order or regularity; become scattered: *the company dispersed at 10 o'clock.* 5. to be dispelled; be scattered out of sight; vanish. [t. F: m. s. *disperser,* ult. der. L *dispersus,* pp., scattered] **—dis·pers′ed·ly,** *adv.* **—dis·pers′er,** *n.* **—Syn.** 1. See **scatter.**

dis·per·sion (dĭs pûr′shən, -zhən), *n.* 1. act of dispersing. 2. state of being dispersed. 3. *Optics.* **a.** (of glass or other transparent substance) the variation of the refractive index with the wave length of light increasing as the wave length decreases. It is responsible for prism spectra. **b.** the separation of white or complex light into its constituent colors. 4. *Statistics.* the scattering of values of a variable around the mean or median of a distribution. 5. *Mil.* a scattered pattern of hits of bombs dropped under identical conditions, or of shots fired from the same gun with the same firing data.

dispersion error, *Mil.* the distance of one shot from the center of impact.

dis·per·sive (dĭs pûr′sĭv), *adj.* serving or tending to disperse.

dis·pir·it (dĭs pĭr′ĭt), *v.t.* to deprive of spirit; depress the spirits of; discourage; dishearten. **—dis·pir′it·ed,** *adj.* **—dis·pir′it·ed·ly,** *adv.* **—dis·pir′it·ed·ness,** *n.* **—dis·pir′it·ing,** *adj.* **—dis·pir′it·ing·ly,** *adv.*

dis·pit·e·ous (dĭs pĭt′ĭ əs), *adj. Chiefly Poetic.* malicious; cruel; pitiless.

dis·place (dĭs plās′), *v.t.,* **-placed, -placing.** 1. to put out of the usual or proper place: *to displace a wall.* 2. to take the place of; replace. 3. to remove from a position, office, or dignity. 4. *Obs.* to banish; remove. **—dis·place′a·ble,** *adj.* **—dis·plac′er,** *n.* **—Syn.** 1. DISPLACE, MISPLACE mean to put something in a different place from where it should be. To DISPLACE now often means to shift something solid and comparatively immovable, more or less permanently from its place: *the flood displaced houses from their foundations.* To MISPLACE is to put an object, usually an easily portable one, in a wrong place, so that it is difficult to find: *papers belonging in the safe were misplaced and temporarily lost.*

displaced person, (esp. in Europe) a person removed from his homeland for use as a slave laborer or driven from it by an invasion.

dis·place·ment (dĭs plās′mənt), *n.* 1. act of displacing. 2. state of being displaced. 3. *Physics.* **a.** the displacing or replacing of one thing by another, as of water by something immersed or floating in it. **b.** the weight or the volume of fluid displaced by a floating or submerged body, equivalent to the weight of the floating body or to the volume of the submerged body. 4. *Mach.* (of a cylinder) the volume swept out by the piston. 5. *Geol.* offset of rocks due to movement along a fault. 6. *Psychoanal.* the transfer of an emotion from the object about which it was originally experienced to another object.

displacement ton. See **ton**[1] (def. 4).

dis·plant (dĭs plănt′, -plänt′), *v.t. Obs.* 1. to dislodge. 2. to transplant.

dis·play (dĭs plā′), *v.t.* 1. to show; exhibit; make visible: *to display a flag.* 2. to reveal; betray: *to display fear.* 3. to unfold; open out; spread out: *to display a sail.* 4. to show ostentatiously. 5. *Print.* to give special prominence to (words, etc.) by choice and arrangement of type, etc. **—n.** 6. act of displaying; exhibition; show: *a display of radios, skill, etc.* 7. an ostentatious show: *a vulgar display of wealth.* 8. *Print.* **a.** the giving of prominence to particular words, etc., by the choice and arrangement of types and position, as in an advertisement, headline, or news story. **b.** printed matter thus displayed. [ME *desplay(en),* t. OF: m. *despleier, desploier* DEPLOY] **—dis·play′er,** *n.* **—Syn.** 1. DISPLAY, EVINCE, EXHIBIT, MANIFEST mean to show or bring to the attention of another or others. To DISPLAY is literally to spread something out so that it may be most completely and favorably seen: *to display goods for sale.* To EXHIBIT is to put something in plain view and usually in a favorable position for particular observation: *to exhibit the best flowers at a special show.* They may both be used of showing (off) one's qualities or feelings: *he displayed his wit, his ignorance; he exhibited great surprise.* To EVINCE and to MANIFEST have only this latter reference, MANIFEST being the stronger word: *to evince or manifest surprise, interest, sympathy.* 4. flourish, flaunt, parade, air. 6. See **show. —Ant.** 1. conceal.

dis·please (dĭs plēz′), *v.,* **-pleased, -pleasing.** **—v.t.** 1. to cause dissatisfaction or dislike to; offend; annoy. **—v.i.** 2. to be unpleasant; cause displeasure. **—dis·pleas′ing·ly,** *adv.*

dis·pleas·ure (dĭs plĕzh′ər), n., v., **-ured, -uring.** —n. **1.** dissatisfaction; annoyance; anger. **2.** Archaic. discomfort, uneasiness, or pain. **3.** Archaic. a cause of offense, annoyance, or injury. —v.t. **4.** Archaic. to displease. —Syn. **1.** See **dissatisfaction.**

dis·plode (dĭs plōd′), v.t., v.i., **-ploded, -ploding.** Obs. to explode. [t. L: m. s. displōdere burst asunder]

dis·plume (dĭs plōōm′), v.t., **-plumed, -pluming. 1.** to strip of plumes; deplume. **2.** to strip of honors.

dis·port (dĭs pōrt′), v.t. **1.** to divert or amuse (oneself); exercise or display (oneself) in a sportive manner. —v.i. **2.** to divert oneself; sport. —n. **3.** diversion; amusement; play; sport. [ME desporte(n), t. OF: m. desporter, deporter, f. des- DIS-¹, de- DE- + porter carry (g. L portāre)]

dis·pos·a·ble (dĭs pō′zə bəl), adj. capable of being disposed of; subject to disposal; inclined.

dis·pos·al (dĭs pō′zəl), n. **1.** act of disposing, or of disposing of, something; arrangement. **2.** a disposing of as by gift or sale; bestowal or assignment. **3.** power or right to dispose of a thing; control: left at his disposal.

dis·pose (dĭs pōz′), v., **-posed, -posing,** n. —v.t. **1.** to put in a particular or the proper order or arrangement; adjust by arranging the parts. **2.** to put in a particular or suitable place. **3.** to give a tendency or inclination to; incline. **4.** Archaic. to make fit or ready; prepare. —v.i. **5.** to arrange or decide matters. **6.** Obs. to make terms. **7.** dispose of, **a.** to deal with definitely; get rid of. **b.** to make over or part with, as by gift or sale. —n. **8.** Archaic. disposition; habit. **9.** Obs. arrangement; regulation; disposal. [ME dispose(n), t. OF: m. disposer, f. dis- DIS-¹ + poser POSE¹, but assoc. with derivs. of L dispōnere (cf. DISPOSITION)] —dis·pos′er, n.

dis·posed (dĭs pōzd′), adj. inclined or minded, esp. favorably (usually fol. by to or infinitive).

dis·po·si·tion (dĭs′pə zĭsh′ən), n. **1.** mental or moral constitution; turn of mind. **2.** mental inclination; willingness. **3.** physical inclination or tendency. **4.** arrangement, as of troops or buildings. **5.** final settlement of a matter. **6.** regulation; appointment; dispensation. **7.** bestowal, as by gift or sale. **8.** power to dispose of a thing; control. [t. L: s. dispositio]
—Syn. **1.** DISPOSITION, TEMPER, TEMPERAMENT refer to the aspects and habits of mind which one displays over a length of time. DISPOSITION is the natural or prevailing aspect of one's mind as shown in behavior and in relationships with others: a happy disposition, a selfish disposition. TEMPER sometimes denotes the essential quality of one's nature: a temper of iron; usually it has to do with propensity toward anger: an even temper, a quick or hot temper. TEMPERAMENT suggests the delicate balance of one's emotions, the disturbance of which determines one's moods: an artistic temperament, an unstable temperament.

dis·pos·sess (dĭs′pə zĕs′), v.t. to put (a person) out of possession, esp. of real property; oust. —**dis′pos·ses′-sion,** n. —**dis′pos·ses′sor,** n. —**dis·pos·ses·so·ry** (dĭs′pə zĕs′ə rĭ), adj. —Syn. See **strip¹.**

dis·po·sure (dĭs pō′zhər), n. disposal; disposition.

dis·praise (dĭs prāz′), v., **-praised, -praising,** n. —v.t. **1.** to speak of as undeserving; censure; disparage. —n. **2.** act of dispraising; censure. —**dis·prais′er,** n. —**dis·prais′ing·ly,** adv.

dis·pread (dĭs prĕd′), v.t., v.i., **-pread, -preading.** Archaic. to spread out; extend. Also, **disspread.**

dis·prize (dĭs prīz′), v.t., **-prized, -prizing.** Archaic. to hold in small esteem; disdain.

dis·proof (dĭs prōōf′), n. act of disproving; proof to the contrary; refutation.

dis·pro·por·tion (dĭs′prə pōr′shən), n. **1.** lack of proportion; want of due relation, as in size, number, etc. **2.** something out of proportion. —v.t. **3.** to make disproportionate. —**dis′pro·por′tion·a·ble,** adj. —**dis′-pro·por′tion·a·ble·ness,** n. —**dis′pro·por′tion·a·bly,** adv.

dis·pro·por·tion·al (dĭs′prə pōr′shə nəl), adj. disproportionate. —**dis′pro·por′tion·al·ly,** adv.

dis·pro·por·tion·ate (dĭs′prə pōr′shə nĭt), adj. not proportionate; out of proportion, as in size, number, etc. —**dis′pro·por′tion·ate·ly,** adv. —**dis′pro·por′tion·ate·ness,** n.

dis·pro·por·tion·a·tion (dĭs′prə pōr′shə nā′shən), n. Chem. the simultaneous oxidation and reduction of a substance reacting with itself, to form two dissimilar molecules, as $2C_2H_4 \rightarrow C_2H_6 + C_2H_2$.

dis·prove (dĭs prōōv′), v.t., **-proved, -proving.** to prove (an assertion, claim, etc.) to be false or wrong; refute; invalidate. [ME disprove(n), t. OF: m. desprover, f. des- DIS-¹ + prover PROVE] —**dis·prov′a·ble,** adj. —**dis·prov′al,** n.

dis·put·a·ble (dĭs pū′tə bəl, dĭs′pyŏŏ tə bəl), adj. that may be disputed; liable to be called in question; questionable. —**dis·put′a·bil′i·ty,** n. —**dis·put′a·bly,** adv.

dis·pu·tant (dĭs′pyŏŏ tənt, dĭs pū′tənt), adj. **1.** disputing. —n. **2.** one who disputes; a debater.

dis·pu·ta·tion (dĭs′pyŏŏ tā′shən), n. **1.** act of disputing or debating; verbal controversy; a discussion or debate. **2.** an academic exercise consisting of the arguing of a thesis between its maintainer and his opponents. **3.** Obs. conversation.

dis·pu·ta·tious (dĭs′pyŏŏ tā′shəs), adj. given to disputation; argumentative; contentious. Also, **dis·put·a·tive** (dĭs pū′tə tĭv). —**dis·pu·ta′tious·ly,** adv. —**dis·pu·ta′tious·ness,** n.

dis·pute (dĭs pūt′), v., **-puted, -puting,** n. —v.i. **1.** to engage in argument or discussion. **2.** to argue vehemently; wrangle or quarrel. —v.t. **3.** to argue or debate about; discuss. **4.** to argue against; call in question. **5.** to quarrel or fight about; contest. **6.** to strive against; oppose: to dispute an advance. —n. **7.** argumentation; verbal contention; a debate or controversy; a quarrel. [ME, t. L: m. s. disputāre; r. ME despute(n), t. OF] —**dis·put′er,** n. —Syn. **7.** See **argument.**

dis·qual·i·fi·ca·tion (dĭs kwŏl′ə fə kā′shən), n. **1.** act of disqualifying. **2.** state of being disqualified. **3.** something that disqualifies.

dis·qual·i·fy (dĭs kwŏl′ə fī′), v., **-fied, -fying.** —v.t. **1.** to deprive of qualification or fitness; render unfit; incapacitate. **2.** to deprive of legal or other rights or privileges; pronounce unqualified. **3.** Sports. to deprive of the right to engage or compete in a match because the rules have been broken.

dis·qui·et (dĭs kwī′ət), v.t. **1.** to deprive of quiet, rest, or peace; disturb; make uneasy: disquieting news. —n. **2.** lack of quiet; disturbance; unrest; uneasiness. —adj. **3.** Rare. unquiet; uneasy. —**dis·qui′et·ly,** adv.

dis·qui·e·tude (dĭs kwī′ə tūd′, -tōōd′), n. state of disquiet; uneasiness.

dis·qui·si·tion (dĭs′kwə zĭsh′ən), n. a formal discourse or treatise in which a subject is examined and discussed; a dissertation. [t. L: s. disquīsītio inquiry]

Dis·rae·li (dĭz rā′lĭ), n. **Benjamin,** (Earl of Beaconsfield) 1804–81, British statesman and novelist: prime minister, 1867, 1874–80.

dis·rate (dĭs rāt′), v.t., **-rated, -rating.** Naut. to reduce to a lower rating, as a petty officer, or a noncommissioned officer of marines. Cf. **degrade.**

dis·re·gard (dĭs′rĭ gärd′), v.t. **1.** to pay no attention to; leave out of consideration. **2.** to treat without due regard, respect, or attentiveness. —n. **3.** lack of regard or attention; neglect. **4.** lack of due or respectful regard. —**dis′re·gard′er,** n. —Syn. **2.** See **slight.**

dis·re·gard·ful (dĭs′rĭ gärd′fəl), adj. neglectful; careless.

dis·rel·ish (dĭs rĕl′ĭsh), v.t. **1.** to have a distaste for; dislike. —n. **2.** distaste; dislike.

dis·re·mem·ber (dĭs′rĭ mĕm′bər), v.t., v.i. Colloq. to fail to remember; forget.

dis·re·pair (dĭs′rĭ pâr′), n. state of being out of repair; impaired condition.

dis·rep·u·ta·ble (dĭs rĕp′yə tə bəl), adj. **1.** not reputable; having a bad reputation. **2.** discreditable; dishonorable. —**dis·rep′u·ta·bil′i·ty, dis·rep′u·ta·ble·ness,** n. —**dis·rep′u·ta·bly,** adv.

dis·re·pute (dĭs′rĭ pūt′), n. ill repute; discredit (usually prec. by in, into): that policy is in disrepute; this would bring the administration of justice into disrepute. Also, Archaic, **dis·rep·u·ta·tion** (dĭs rĕp′yə tā′shən).

dis·re·spect (dĭs′rĭ spĕkt′), n. **1.** lack of respect; disesteem; rudeness. —v.t. **2.** to regard or treat without respect; regard or treat with contempt or rudeness.

dis·re·spect·a·ble (dĭs′rĭ spĕk′tə bəl), adj. not respectable. —**dis′re·spect′a·bil′i·ty,** n.

dis·re·spect·ful (dĭs′rĭ spĕkt′fəl), adj. characterized by disrespect; having or showing disrespect. —**dis′-re·spect′ful·ly,** adv. —**dis′re·spect′ful·ness,** n. —Syn. discourteous, uncivil, impolite, rude, impudent.

dis·robe (dĭs rōb′), v.t., v.i., **-robed, -robing.** to undress. —**dis·robe′ment,** n. —**dis·rob′er,** n.

dis·root (dĭs rōōt′, -rŏŏt′), v.t. to uproot; dislodge.

dis·rupt (dĭs rŭpt′), v.t. **1.** to break or rend asunder; break up. —adj. **2.** disrupted; rent asunder. [t. L: s. disruptus, pp.] —**dis·rupt′er, dis·rup′tor,** n.

dis·rup·tion (dĭs rŭp′shən), n. **1.** forcible separation or division into parts. **2.** a disrupted condition.

dis·rup·tive (dĭs rŭp′tĭv), adj. disrupting; pertaining to disruption.

disruptive discharge, Elect. the sudden and large increase in current through an insulating medium due to complete failure of the medium under electrostatic stress.

dis·rup·ture (dĭs rŭp′chər), v.t., **-tured, -turing.** Rare. to disrupt.

dis·sat·is·fac·tion (dĭs′săt ĭs făk′shən), n. lack of satisfaction; state of not being satisfied.
—Syn. DISSATISFACTION, DISCONTENT, DISPLEASURE imply a sense of dislike for, or unhappiness in, one's surroundings and a wish for other conditions. DISSATISFACTION results from contemplating what falls short of one's wishes or expectations, and is usually only temporary: dissatisfaction with results of an afternoon's work. DISCONTENT is a sense of lack, and a general feeling of uneasy dislike for the conditions of one's life, which colors one's entire outlook: feeling a continual vague discontent. DISPLEASURE, a more positive word, suggests a certain amount of anger as well as dissatisfaction: displeasure at being kept waiting.

dis·sat·is·fac·to·ry (dĭs′săt ĭs făk′tə rĭ), adj. causing dissatisfaction.

dis·sat·is·fied (dĭs săt′ĭs fīd′), adj. **1.** discontented; not pleased; offended. **2.** showing dissatisfaction: a dissatisfied look. —**dis·sat′is·fied′ly,** adv.

dis·sat·is·fy (dĭs săt′ĭs fī′), v.t., **-fied, -fying.** to make ill-satisfied, ill-pleased, or discontented.

dis·seat (dĭs sēt′), v.t. to unseat.

dis·sect (dĭ sĕkt′), v.t. **1.** to cut apart (an animal body, plant, etc.) to examine the structure, relation of parts, or the like. **2.** to examine minutely part by part;

analyze. [t. L: s. *dissectus*, pp., cut asunder] —**dis-sec·ti·ble**, *adj.* —**dis·sec·tor**, *n.*

dis·sect·ed (dĭsĕk′tĭd), *adj.* **1.** *Bot.* deeply cut into numerous segments, as a leaf. **2.** *Phys. Geog.* cut up by many closely spaced valleys, as a plateau.

dis·sec·tion (dĭsĕk′shən), *n.* **1.** act of dissecting. **2.** something that has been dissected.

dis·seize (dĭssēz′), *v.t.*, **-seized, -seizing.** *Law.* to deprive (a person) of seizin, or of the possession, of a freehold interest in land, esp. wrongfully or by force; oust. Also, **dis·seise.** [ME *disseyse(n)*, t. AF: m. *disseisir* dispossess, f. dis-DIS-[1] + *saisir* SEIZE] —**dis·sei·zor**, *n.*

dis·sei·zee (dĭssēzē′, dĭssē′zē′), *n.* one who is disseized. Also, **dis·sei·see′.**

dis·sei·zin (dĭssē′zĭn), *n.* *Law.* **1.** act of disseizing. **2.** state of being disseized. Also, **dis·sei′sin.** [ME *dysseysyne*, t. AF: m. *disseisine*, f. dis-DIS-[1] + *saisine* possession, SEIZIN]

dis·sem·blance[1] (dĭssĕm′bləns), *n.* *Archaic.* dissimilarity; unlikeness. [t. OF: m. *dessemblance*, der. *dessembler* be unlike, f. des-DIS-[1] + *sembler* seem (g. L *simulāre*)]

dis·sem·blance[2] (dĭssĕm′bləns), *n.* *Archaic.* dissembling; dissimulation. [f. DISSEMBLE + -ANCE′]

dis·sem·ble (dĭssĕm′bəl), *v.*, **-bled, -bling.** —*v.t.* **1.** to give a false semblance to; conceal the real nature of. **2.** to put on the appearance of; feign. **3.** to let pass unnoticed; ignore. —*v.i.* **4.** to conceal one's motives, etc., under some pretense; speak or act hypocritically. [f. DIS- + -semble, modeled on RESEMBLE] —**dis·sem′-bler**, *n.* —**dis·sem′bling·ly**, *adv.*

dis·sem·i·nate (dĭssĕm′ənāt′), *v.t.*, **-nated, -nating.** to scatter, as seed in sowing; spread abroad; diffuse; promulgate. [t. L: m. s. *disseminātus*, pp.] —**dis·sem′-i·na′tion**, *n.* —**dis·sem′i·na′tor**, *n.*

dis·sen·sion (dĭssĕn′shən), *n.* **1.** violent disagreement; discord; a contention or quarrel. **2.** difference in sentiment or opinion; disagreement.

dis·sent (dĭssĕnt′), *v.i.* **1.** to differ in sentiment or opinion; disagree; withhold assent (fol. by *from*). **2.** to differ in religious opinion; reject the doctrines or authority of an established church. —*n.* **3.** difference in sentiment or opinion. **4.** separation from an established church, esp. that of England; nonconformity. [ME *dissente(n)*, t. L: m. *dissentīre* differ in opinion] —**dis·sent′ing**, *adj.* —**dis·sent′ing·ly**, *adv.*
—**Syn. 3.** DISSENT, DISSIDENCE mean disagreement with the majority opinion. DISSENT may express either withholding of agreement or open disagreement. DISSENTERS may withdraw from a group, but if so, they merely go their own way. DISSIDENCE, formerly much the same as DISSENT, has come to suggest not only strong dissatisfaction but a determined opposition. If dissidents withdraw, they continue actively to oppose the original group.

dis·sent·er (dĭssĕn′tər), *n.* **1.** one who dissents, as from an established church. **2.** (*sometimes cap.*) a person, now esp. a Protestant, who dissents from the Church of England.

dis·sen·tient (dĭssĕn′shənt), *adj.* **1.** dissenting, esp. from the opinion of the majority. —*n.* **2.** one who dissents. —**dis·sen′tience**, *n.*

dis·sen·tious (dĭssĕn′shəs), *adj.* contentious; quarrelsome.

dis·sep·i·ment (dĭssĕp′əmənt), *n.* **1.** a partition or septum. **2.** *Bot.* one of the partitions formed within ovaries and fruits by the coherence of the sides of the constituent carpels. [t. L: m. s. *dissaepīmentum* that which separates] —**dis·sep′-i·men′tal**, *adj.*

dis·sert (dĭssûrt′), *v.i.* *Obs.* or *Rare.* to discourse on a subject. [t. L: s. *dissertus*, pp., examined, discussed]

D. Dissepiment

dis·ser·tate (dĭs′ərtāt′), *v.i.*, **-tated, -tating.** to treat of a subject in discourse; make a dissertation. [t. L: m.s. *dissertātus*, pp., discussed] —**dis′ser·ta′tor**, *n.*

dis·ser·ta·tion (dĭs′ərtā′shən), *n.* **1.** a written essay, treatise, or thesis, esp. one written by a candidate for the Doctor's degree. **2.** a formal discourse.

dis·serve (dĭssûrv′), *v.t.*, **-served, -serving.** to serve ill; do an ill turn to.

dis·serv·ice (dĭssûr′vĭs), *n.* harm; injury; an ill turn.

dis·sev·er (dĭssĕv′ər), *v.t.* **1.** to sever; separate. **2.** to divide into parts. —*v.i.* **3.** to part; separate. —**dis·sev′er·ance, dis·sev′er·ment, dis·sev′er·a′tion**, *n.*

dis·si·dence (dĭs′ədəns), *n.* disagreement. See **dissent.**

dis·si·dent (dĭs′ədənt), *adj.* **1.** differing; disagreeing; dissenting. —*n.* **2.** one who differs; a dissenter. [t. L: s. *dissidens*, ppr., differing, sitting apart]

dis·sil·i·ent (dĭssĭl′Ĭənt), *adj.* flying or bursting asunder. [t. L: s. *dissiliens*, ppr.] —**dis·sil′i·en·cy, dis·sil′i·ence**, *n.*

dis·sim·i·lar (dĭssĭm′ələr), *adj.* not similar; unlike; different. —**dis·sim′i·lar·ly**, *adv.*

dis·sim·i·lar·i·ty (dĭssĭm′əlăr′ətĭ), *n.*, *pl.* **-ties.** **1.** unlikeness; difference. **2.** a point of difference. —**Syn. 1.** See **difference.**

dis·sim·i·late (dĭssĭm′əlāt′), *v.t.*, **-lated, -lating.** *Phonet.* to change (a speech sound) so that it is less like another sound in a neighboring syllable: Americans who pronounce *er* as an *r*-like vowel may fail to do so in the second syllable of *Northerner* and thus avoid a sequence of three *r* syllables. —**dis·sim′i·la′tive**, *adj.*

dis·sim·i·la·tion (dĭssĭm′əlā′shən), *n.* **1.** a making or becoming unlike. **2.** *Phonet.* act or process of dissimilating speech sounds. **3.** *Biol.* catabolism.

dis·si·mil·i·tude (dĭs′sĭmĭl′ĭtūd′, -tōōd′), *n.* **1.** unlikeness; difference. **2.** a point of difference.

dis·sim·u·late (dĭssĭm′yəlāt′), *v.*, **-lated, -lating.** —*v.t.* **1.** to disguise or conceal under a false semblance; dissemble. —*v.i.* **2.** to use dissimulation; dissemble. [t. L: m. s. *dissimulātus*, pp.] —**dis·sim′u·la′tive**, *adj.* —**dis·sim′u·la′tor**, *n.*

dis·sim·u·la·tion (dĭssĭm′yəlā′shən), *n.* **1.** act of dissimulating; feigning; hypocrisy. **2.** *Psychiatry.* the ability or the tendency to appear mentally normal when actually suffering from disorder: a characteristic of the paranoiac. Cf. **simulation.**

dis·si·pate (dĭs′əpāt′), *v.*, **-pated, -pating.** —*v.t.* **1.** to scatter in various directions; disperse; dispel; disintegrate. **2.** to scatter wastefully or extravagantly; squander. —*v.i.* **3.** to become scattered or dispersed; be dispelled; disintegrate. **4.** to indulge in extravagant, intemperate, or dissolute pleasure; practice dissipation. [t. L: m.s. *dissipātus*, pp., scattered, demolished] —**dis′si·pat′er, dis′si·pa′tor**, *n.* —**dis′si·pa′tive**, *adj.* —**Syn. 1.** See **scatter.**

dis·si·pat·ed (dĭs′əpā′tĭd), *adj.* indulging in or characterized by excessive devotion to pleasure; intemperate; dissolute. —**dis′si·pat′ed·ly**, *adv.* —**dis′si·pat′ed·ness**, *n.*

dis·si·pa·tion (dĭs′əpā′shən), *n.* **1.** act of dissipating. **2.** state of being dissipated; dispersion; disintegration. **3.** a wasting by misuse. **4.** mental distraction; a diversion. **5.** dissolute mode of living; intemperance.

dis·so·ci·a·ble (dĭssō′shĭəbəl, -shəbəl), *adj.* **1.** capable of being dissociated; separable. **2.** unsociable. **3.** incongruous; not reconcilable.

dis·so·cial (dĭssō′shəl), *adj.* unsocial; disinclined to or unsuitable for society.

dis·so·ci·ate (dĭssō′shĭāt′), *v.*, **-ated, -ating.** —*v.t.* **1.** to sever the association of; disunite; separate. **2.** *Chem.* to subject to dissociation. —*v.i.* **3.** to withdraw from association. **4.** *Chem.* to undergo dissociation. [t. L: m.s. *dissociātus*, pp.] —**dis·so′ci·a′tive**, *adj.*

dis·so·ci·a·tion (dĭssō′sĭā′shən, -shĭā′-), *n.* **1.** act of dissociating. **2.** state of being dissociated; disunion. **3.** *Phys. Chem.* **a.** the reversible resolution or decomposition of a complex substance into simpler constituents, due to variation in the physical conditions, as when water gradually decomposes into hydrogen and oxygen under great heat, in such a way that when the temperature is lowered the liberated elements recombine to form water. **b.** electrolytic dissociation. **4.** *Psychiatry.* the splitting off of certain mental processes from the main body of consciousness, with varying degrees of autonomy resulting.

dis·sol·u·ble (dĭssŏl′yəbəl), *adj.* capable of being dissolved. —**dis·sol′u·bil′i·ty**, *n.*

dis·so·lute (dĭs′əlōōt′), *adj.* indifferent to moral restraints; given over to dissipation; licentious. [t. L: m.s. *dissolūtus*, pp., loosened] —**dis′so·lute′ly**, *adv.* —**dis′so·lute′ness**, *n.*

dis·so·lu·tion (dĭs′əlōō′shən), *n.* **1.** act of resolving into parts or elements. **2.** the resulting state. **3.** the undoing or breaking up of a tie, bond, union, etc. **4.** the breaking up of an assembly or organization; dismissal; dispersal. **5.** *Govt.* an order issued by the head of the state terminating a parliament and necessitating a new election. **6.** death or decease. **7.** a bringing or coming to an end; destruction. **8.** the legal termination of business activity, including the distribution of assets and the fixing of liabilities. **9.** *Chem.* solution in a liquid substance. —**dis′so·lu′tive**, *adj.*

dis·solve (dĭzŏlv′), *v.*, **-solved, -solving.** —*v.t.* **1.** to make a solution of in a solvent. **2.** to undo (a tie or bond); break up (a connection, union, etc.). **3.** to break up (an assembly or organization); dismiss; disperse. **4.** *Govt.* to order the termination of a parliament, as in Great Britain, at five-year intervals (or less if the government is defeated). **5.** to bring to an end; destroy; dispel. **6.** to resolve into parts or elements; disintegrate. **7.** to destroy the binding power of: *dissolve a spell.* **8.** *Law.* to deprive of force; annul: *to dissolve a marriage or injunction.* —*v.i.* **9.** to become dissolved, as in a solvent. **10.** to break up or disperse. **11.** to lose force or strength; lose binding force. **12.** to disappear gradually; fade from sight or apprehension. **13.** *Motion Pictures.* to fade out one shot while simultaneously fading in the next shot, overlapping the two shots during the process. —*n.* **14.** *Motion Pictures.* a scene made by dissolving. [ME *dissolve(n)*, t. L: m. *dissolvere* loosen, disunite] —**dis·solv′a·ble**, *adj.* —**dis·solv′er**, *n.* —**dis·solv′ing**, *adj.* —**dis·solv′ing·ly**, *adv.* —**Syn. 1.** See **melt.**

dis·sol·vent (dĭzŏl′vənt), *adj., n.* solvent.

dissolving view, pictures thrown on a screen by a slide projector or magic lantern, which seem to dissolve one into another, without any interval between them.

dis·so·nance (dĭs′ənəns), *n.* **1.** an inharmonious or harsh sound; discord. **2.** *Music.* a simultaneous combination of tones conventionally accepted as being in a state of unrest and needing completion (opposed to *consonance*). **3.** disagreement or incongruity. Also, **dis′so·nan·cy.**

dis·so·nant (dĭs′ə nənt), *adj.* **1.** disagreeing or harsh in sound; discordant. **2.** out of harmony; incongruous; at variance. [t. L: s. *dissonans*, ppr., disagreeing in sound] **—dis′so·nant·ly,** *adv.*

dis·spread (dĭs prĕd′), *v.t., v.i.* dispread.

dis·suade (dĭ swād′), *v.t.,* **-suaded, -suading. 1.** to deter by advice or persuasion; persuade not to do something (fol. by *from*): *dissuade him from leaving home.* **2.** to advise or urge against (an action, etc.). [t. L: m.s. *dissuādēre* advise against] **—dis·suad′er,** *n.*

dis·sua·sion (dĭ swā′zhən), *n.* act of dissuading.

dis·sua·sive (dĭ swā′sĭv), *adj.* tending to dissuade. **—dis·sua′sive·ly,** *adv.*

dis·syl·la·ble (dĭ sĭl′ə bəl, dĭs′sĭl′-), *n.* disyllable. **—dis·syl·lab·ic** (dĭs′ĭ lăb′ĭk, dĭs′sĭ-), *adj.*

dis·sym·me·try (dĭ sĭm′ə trĭ), *n.* absence of symmetry. **—dis·sym·met·ric** (dĭs′ĭ mĕt′rĭk), **dis′sym·met′ri·cal,** *adj.*

dist., **1.** distance. **2.** distinguish. **3.** distinguished. **4.** district.

dis·taff (dĭs′tăf, -täf), *n.* **1.** a staff with a cleft end, formerly used for holding the wool, flax, etc., from which the thread was drawn in spinning by hand. **2.** an analogous part of a spinning wheel, for holding flax to be spun. **3.** the female sex. **4.** a female heir; a woman. [ME *distaf*, OE *distæf*, f. *dis-*, akin to LG *diesse* bunch of flax on a distaff (cf. DIZEN) + *stæf* STAFF]

distaff side, the female side of a family.

dis·tain (dĭs tān′), *v.t. Archaic.* to discolor; stain; sully. [ME *disteyne(n)*, t. OF: m. *desteindre*, f. *des-* DIS-¹ + *teindre* wet, dye (g. L *tingere*)]

dis·tal (dĭs′təl), *adj.* situated away from the point of origin or attachment, as of a limb or bone; terminal (opposed to *proximal*). [f. DIST(ANT) + -AL¹]

dis·tance (dĭs′təns), *n., v.,* **-tanced, -tancing. —n. 1.** the extent of space intervening between things or points. **2.** state or fact of being distant, as of one thing from another; remoteness. **3.** the interval between two points of time. **4.** remoteness in any respect. **5.** a distant point or place; the distant region. **6.** the distant part of a landscape, etc. **7.** reserve or aloofness; one's proper degree of aloofness: *to keep one's distance.* **8.** *Music.* interval (def. 7). **9.** *Sports.* the length, usually measured in furlongs (eighths of miles), to be run to the winning post on a race track. **10.** *Obs.* disagreement or dissension; a quarrel. **—v.t. 11.** to leave behind at a distance, as at a race; surpass. **12.** to place at a distance. **13.** to cause to appear distant.

dis·tant (dĭs′tənt), *adj.* **1.** far off or apart in space; not near at hand; remote (fol. by *from*). **2.** separate or apart in space: *a place a mile distant.* **3.** apart or far off in time. **4.** far apart in any respect: *a distant relative.* **5.** reserved; not familiar or cordial. **6.** to a distance: *a distant journey.* [t. F, t. L: s. *distans*, ppr., being distant, standing apart] **—dis′tant·ly,** *adv.*

dis·taste (dĭs tāst′), *n., v.,* **-tasted, -tasting. —n. 1.** dislike; disinclination. **2.** disrelish for food or drink. **—v.t. 3.** *Archaic.* to dislike. **—Syn. 1.** aversion, repugnance, disgust. See **dislike.**

dis·taste·ful (dĭs tāst′fəl), *adj.* **1.** causing dislike. **2.** unpleasant to the taste. **—dis·taste′ful·ly,** *adv.* **—dis·taste′ful·ness,** *n.* **—Syn. 1.** disagreeable, displeasing; offensive, repugnant, repulsive. **2.** unpalatable, unsavory.

Dist. Atty., District Attorney.

dis·tem·per¹ (dĭs tĕm′pər), *n.* **1.** *Vet. Sci.* **a.** a specific infectious disease of young dogs caused by a filterable virus. **b.** a disease of horses; strangles. **c.** (formerly) any of several diseases characterized by fever and catarrhal symptoms. **2.** deranged condition of mind or body; a disorder or disease. **3.** disorder or disturbance. **—v.t. 4.** to derange physically or mentally. [ME *distempre(n)*, t. ML: m. *distemperāre*. See DIS-¹, TEMPER]

dis·tem·per² (dĭs tĕm′pər), *n.* **1.** a method of painting in which the colors are mixed with some binding medium, as egg mixed with water, usually executed upon a gesso ground, used for murals, scene painting, or the like. **2.** a painting executed by this method. **3.** *Brit.* calcimine. **—v.t. 4.** to paint in distemper. **5.** *Brit.* to calcimine. [t. OF: m. *destemper*, f. *des-* DIS-¹ + *temper* dilute, soak (g. L *temperāre*)]

dis·tem·per·a·ture (dĭs tĕm′pər ə chər), *n.* distempered or disordered condition; disturbance of health, mind, or temper.

dis·tend (dĭs tĕnd′), *v.t., v.i.* **1.** to stretch apart or asunder; stretch out. **2.** to expand by stretching, as something hollow or elastic. [t. L: s. *distendere*] **—Syn. 2.** See **expand.**

dis·ten·si·ble (dĭs tĕn′sə bəl), *adj.* capable of being distended. **—dis·ten′si·bil′i·ty,** *n.*

dis·tent (dĭs tĕnt′), *adj. Rare.* distended. [t. L: s. *distentus*, pp.]

dis·ten·tion (dĭs tĕn′shən), *n.* **1.** act of distending. **2.** state of being distended. Also, **dis·ten′sion.**

dis·tich (dĭs′tĭk), *n. Pros.* **1.** a group of two lines of verse, usually making complete sense; a couplet. **2.** a rhyming couplet. [t. L: s. *distichon*, t. Gk., neut. of *distichos* of two rows or lines]

dis·tich·ous (dĭs′tĭk əs), *adj. Bot.* arranged alternately in two vertical rows on opposite sides of an axis, as leaves. See illus. under **alternate.** [t. L: m. *distichus* of two rows. See DISTICH] **—dis′tich·ous·ly,** *adv.*

dis·til (dĭs tĭl′), *v.t., v.i.,* **-tilled, -tilling.** *Chiefly Brit.* distill.

dis·till (dĭs tĭl′), *v.t.* **1.** to subject to a process of vaporization and subsequent condensation, as for purification or concentration. **2.** to extract the volatile components of by distillation; transform by distillation. **3.** to extract or obtain by distillation. **4.** to drive (*off* or *out*) by distillation. **5.** to let fall in drops; give forth in or as in drops. **—v.i. 6.** to undergo distillation. **7.** to become vaporized and then condensed in distillation. **8.** to drop, pass, or condense as a distillate. **9.** to fall in drops; trickle; exude. [ME *distille(n)*, t. L: m. *distillāre*, var. of *dēstillāre* drip down] **—dis·till′a·ble,** *adj.*

dis·til·late (dĭs′tə lĭt, -lāt′), *n.* the product obtained from the condensation of vapors in distillation.

dis·til·la·tion (dĭs′tə lā′shən), *n.* **1.** the volatilization or evaporation and subsequent condensation of a liquid, as when water is boiled in a retort and the steam is condensed in a cool receiver. **2.** the purification or concentration of a substance; the obtaining of the essence or volatile properties contained in it, or the separation of one substance from another, by such a process. **3.** a product of distilling; a distillate. **4.** act or process of distilling. **5.** fact of being distilled. **—dis·til·la·to·ry** (dĭs tĭl′ə tōr′ĭ), *adj.*

dis·tilled (dĭs tĭld′), *adj.* obtained or produced by distillation.

dis·till·er (dĭs tĭl′ər), *n.* **1.** an apparatus for distilling, as a condenser, or esp., one for distillation of salt water at sea. **2.** one whose business it is to extract spirituous liquors by distillation.

dis·till·er·y (dĭs tĭl′ə rĭ), *n., pl.* **-eries.** a place or establishment where distilling, esp. the distilling of spirituous liquors, is carried on.

dis·till·ment (dĭs tĭl′mənt), *n.* **1.** act or process of distilling. **2.** the product of distilling. Also, *esp. Brit.,* **dis·til′ment.**

dis·tinct (dĭs tĭngkt′), *adj.* **1.** distinguished as not being the same; not identical; separate (fol. by *from* or used absolutely). **2.** different in nature or qualities; dissimilar. **3.** clear to the senses or intellect; plain; definite; unmistakable. **4.** distinguishing clearly, as the vision. **5.** *Poetic.* decorated or adorned. [ME, t. L: s. *distinctus*, pp., separated] **—dis·tinct′ness,** *n.* **—Syn. 1.** See **various.**

dis·tinc·tion (dĭs tĭngk′shən), *n.* **1.** a marking off or distinguishing as different. **2.** the recognizing or noting of differences; discrimination. **3.** a discrimination made between things as different. **4.** the condition of being different; a difference. **5.** a distinguishing characteristic. **6.** a distinguishing or treating with special attention or favor. **7.** a mark of special favor. **8.** marked superiority; note; eminence. **9.** distinguished appearance. **10.** division. **—Syn. 3.** DISTINCTION and DIFFERENCE may both refer to perceivable dissimilarities and, in this meaning, may be used interchangeably: *there is a distinction (difference) between the two.* DISTINCTION, however, usually suggests the perception of dissimilarity, as the result of analysis and discrimination (*a carefully made distinction between two treatments of the same theme*) whereas DIFFERENCE refers only to the condition of being dissimilar: *the differences between Gothic and Roman architecture.* "A distinction without a difference" is a way of referring to an artificial or false discrimination. **7.** See **honor.—Ant. 4.** resemblance.

dis·tinc·tive (dĭs tĭngk′tĭv), *adj.* distinguishing; serving to distinguish; characteristic. **—dis·tinc′tive·ly,** *adv.* **—dis·tinc′tive·ness,** *n.*

dis·tinct·ly (dĭs tĭngkt′lĭ), *adv.* **1.** in a distinct manner; clearly. **2.** without doubt; unmistakably. **—Syn. 1.** See **clearly.**

dis·tin·gué (dĭs′tăng gā′, dĭs tăng′gā; *Fr.* dēs tăn gĕ′), *adj.* distinguished; having an air of distinction. [F, pp. of *distinguer* distinguish] **—dis′tin·guée′,** *adj. fem.*

dis·tin·guish (dĭs tĭng′gwĭsh), *v.t.* **1.** to mark off as different (fol. by *from*). **2.** to recognize as distinct or different; discriminate. **3.** to perceive clearly by sight or other sense; discern; recognize. **4.** to serve to separate as different; be a distinctive characteristic of; characterize. **5.** to make prominent, conspicuous, or eminent: *to distinguish oneself in battle.* **6.** to divide into classes; classify. **7.** *Archaic.* to single out for or honor with special attention. **—v.i. 8.** to indicate or show a difference (fol. by *between*). **9.** to recognize or note differences; discriminate. [f. s. L *distinguere* separate, distinguish + -ISH², modeled on EXTINGUISH] **—dis·tin′guish·a·ble,** *adj.* **—dis·tin′guish·a·ble·ness,** *n.* **—dis·tin′guish·a·bly,** *adv.* **—dis·tin′guish·er,** *n.* **—dis·tin′guish·ing·ly,** *adv.* **—Syn. 2.** DISTINGUISH, DIFFERENTIATE, DISCRIMINATE suggest a positive attempt to analyze characteristic features or qualities of things. To DISTINGUISH is to recognize the characteristic features belonging to a thing: *to distinguish a light cruiser from a heavy cruiser.* To DISCRIMINATE is to perceive the particular, nice, or exact differences between things, to determine wherein these differences consist, and to estimate their significance: *to discriminate prejudiced from unprejudiced testimony.* To DIFFERENTIATE is especially to point out exactly and in detail the differences (usually) between two things: *the symptoms of some diseases are so familiar that it is hard to differentiate one from another.* **—Ant. 2.** confuse.

dis·tin·guished (dĭs tĭng′gwĭsht), *adj.* **1.** conspicuous; marked. **2.** noted; eminent; famous. **3.** having an air of distinction; distingué. **—Syn. 2.** See **famous.**

---

b., blend of, blended; c., cognate with; d., dialect, dialectal; der., derived from; f., formed from; g., going back to; m., modification of; r., replacing; s., stem of; t., taken from; ?, perhaps.   See the full key on inside cover.

Distinguished Service Cross, *U.S. Army.* a bronze medal awarded to an officer or enlisted man for extraordinary heroism in military action against an armed enemy.

dis·tort (dĭs tôrt′), *v.t.* **1.** to twist awry or out of shape; make crooked or deformed. **2.** to pervert; misrepresent. [t. L: s. *distortus*, pp.] —**dis·tort′ed,** *adj.* —**dis·tort′ed·ly,** *adv.* —**dis·tort′ed·ness,** *n.* —**dis·tort′-er,** *n.*

dis·tor·tion (dĭs tôr′shən), *n.* **1.** act of distorting. **2.** state of being distorted. **3.** anything distorted. —**dis·tor′tion·al,** *adj.*

dis·tract (dĭs trăkt′), *v.t.* **1.** to draw away or divert, as the mind or attention. **2.** to divide (the mind, attention, etc.) between objects. **3.** to disturb or trouble greatly in mind. **4.** to rend by dissension or strife. —*adj.* **5.** *Archaic.* distracted. [t. L: s. *distractus*, pp., pulled asunder. Cf. DISTRAUGHT.] —**dis·tract′ed,** *adj.* —**dis·tract′ed·ly,** *adv.* —**dis·tract′er,** *n.* —**dis·tract′ing,** *adj.* —**dis·tract′ing·ly,** *adv.*

dis·trac·tion (dĭs trăk′shən), *n.* **1.** act of distracting. **2.** state of being distracted. **3.** violent disturbance of mind; mental derangement or madness. **4.** division or disorder due to dissention; tumult.

dis·trac·tive (dĭs trăk′tĭv), *adj.* tending to distract.

dis·train (dĭs trān′), *Law.* —*v.t.* **1.** to constrain by seizing and holding goods, etc., in pledge for rent, damages, etc., or in order to obtain satisfaction of a claim. **2.** to levy a distress upon. —*v.i.* **3.** to levy a distress. [ME *destreyne(n),* t. OF: m. *destreindre* constrain, g. L *distringere* draw asunder, detain, hinder] —**dis·train′-a·ble,** *adj.* —**dis·train′ment,** *n.* —**dis·train′or, dis·train′er,** *n.*

dis·traint (dĭs trānt′), *n.* *Law.* act of distraining; a distress.

dis·trait (dĭs trā′; *Fr.* dēs trĕ′), *adj.* absentminded in thought; absent-minded. [t. F, pp. of *distraire,* g. L *distrahere* pull asunder. See DISTRACT] —**dis·traite** (dĭs trāt′; *Fr.* dēs trĕt′), *n. fem.*

dis·traught (dĭs trôt′), *adj.* **1.** distracted; bewildered; deeply agitated. **2.** crazed. [var. of obs. *distract,* adj., by assoc. with *straught,* pp. of STRETCH]

dis·tress (dĭs trĕs′), *n.* **1.** great pain, anxiety, or sorrow; acute suffering; affliction; trouble. **2.** a state of extreme necessity. **3.** the state of a ship requiring immediate assistance, as because of accident. **4.** *Law.* **a.** act of distraining; the legal seizure and detention of the goods of another as security or satisfaction for debt, etc. **b.** the thing seized in distraining. —*v.t.* **5.** to afflict with pain, anxiety, or sorrow; trouble sorely; worry; bother. **6.** to subject to pressure, stress, or strain; embarrass or exhaust by strain. **7.** to constrain. [ME *destresse,* t. OF: m. *destrece,* der. L *districtus,* pp., distrained] —**dis·tress′ing,** *adj.* —**dis·tress′ing·ly,** *adv.* —**Syn. 1.** grief, agony, anguish, misery. See **sorrow.**

distressed area, *Brit.* a region where unemployment and a low standard of living prevail. Latterly called **special area.**

dis·tress·ful (dĭs trĕs′fəl), *adj.* **1.** causing or involving distress. **2.** full of distress; feeling or indicating distress. —**dis·tress′ful·ly,** *adv.* —**dis·tress′ful·ness,** *n.*

distress merchandise, *Com.* goods sold quickly, usually at less than the prevailing price, to secure cash.

dis·trib·ute (dĭs trĭb′ūt), *v.t.,* **-uted, -uting. 1.** to divide and bestow in shares; deal out; allot. **2.** to disperse through a space or over an area; spread; scatter. **3.** to divide into parts of distinct character. **4.** to divide into classes: *these plants are distributed into 22 classes.* **5.** *Logic.* to employ (a term) so as to refer to all the individuals denoted by it: *the term men is distributed in "all men are mortal" but not in "some men are old."* [t. L: m. s. *distribūtus,* pp.] —**dis·trib′ut·a·ble,** *adj.* —**Syn. 1.** assign, mete, apportion. DISTRIBUTE, DISPENSE, apply to giving out something. DISTRIBUTE implies apportioned, individualized, and, often, personal giving, esp. of something that is definite or limited in amount or number: *the prizes were distributed among ten winners.* DISPENSE formerly implied indiscriminate, general, and liberal giving, esp. of something that was more or less indefinite or unmeasured in amount: *to dispense largess.* It now applies chiefly to giving according to need or deserts, from an organized and official source: *to dispense medicines and food to the victims, justice to criminals.*

dis·trib·u·tee (dĭs trĭb′yŏŏ tē′), *n.* *Law.* a person who shares in a decedent estate.

dis·tri·bu·tion (dĭs′trə bū′shən), *n.* **1.** act of distributing. **2.** state or manner of being distributed. **3.** arrangement; classification. **4.** that which is distributed. **5.** the places where things of any particular category occur: *the distribution of coniferous forests in the world.* **6.** *Econ.* **a.** the division of the aggregate income of any society among its members, or among the factors of production. **b.** the system of dispersing goods throughout a community. **7.** *Statistics.* a set of values or measurements of a set of elements, each measurement being associated with an element. —**dis′tri·bu′tion·al,** *adj.*

distribution curve, *Statistics.* The curve or line of a graph whose axes or data are based upon a specific frequency distribution. See **frequency distribution.**

dis·trib·u·tive (dĭs trĭb′yə tĭv), *adj.* **1.** that distributes; characterized by or pertaining to distribution. **2.** *Gram.* treating the members of a group individually,

as the adjectives *each* and *every.* **3.** *Logic.* (of a term) distributed in a given proposition. —*n.* **4.** a distributive word or expression. —**dis·trib′u·tive·ly,** *adv.* —**dis·trib′u·tive·ness,** *n.*

dis·trib·u·tor (dĭs trĭb′yə tər), *n.* **1.** one who or that which distributes. **2.** *Com.* one engaged in the general distribution or marketing of some article or class of goods. **3.** *Mach.* a device in a multicylinder engine which distributes the igniting voltage to the spark plugs in a definite sequence. Also, **dis·trib′u·ter.**

dis·trict (dĭs′trĭkt), *n.* **1.** a division of territory, as of a country, state, county, etc., marked off for administrative, electoral, or other purposes. **2.** a region or locality. —*v.t.* **3.** to divide into districts. [t. ML: s. *districtus* territory under jurisdiction, special use of L *districtus,* pp., constrained]

district attorney, an officer who acts as attorney for the people or government within a specified district.

district council, *Brit.* a unit of local government.

district court, *U.S. Law.* **1.** (in many States) the court of general jurisdiction. **2.** the federal trial court sitting in each district of the United States.

District of Columbia, a federal area in the E United States, on the Potomac, coextensive with the federal capital, Washington: governed by Congress. 802,178 pop. (1950); 69 sq. mi. *Abbr.:* D. C.

Dis·tri·to Fe·de·ral (dēs trē′tô fĕ′dĕ räl′), Spanish name of **Federal District.** *Abbr.:* D.F.

dis·trust (dĭs trŭst′), *v.t.* **1.** to feel distrust of; regard with doubt or suspicion. —*n.* **2.** lack of trust; doubt; suspicion. —**dis·trust′er,** *n.* —**Syn. 2.** See **suspicion.**

dis·trust·ful (dĭs trŭst′fəl), *adj.* full of distrust; doubtful; suspicious. —**dis·trust′ful·ly,** *adv.* —**dis·trust′ful·ness,** *n.*

dis·turb (dĭs tûrb′), *v.t.* **1.** to interrupt the quiet, rest, or peace of. **2.** to interfere with; interrupt; hinder. **3.** to throw into commotion or disorder; agitate; disorder; disarrange; unsettle. **4.** to perplex; trouble. [t. L: s. *disturbāre* throw into disorder, disturb] —**dis·turb′er,** *n.* —**dis·turb′ing·ly,** *adv.*

dis·turb·ance (dĭs tûr′bəns), *n.* **1.** act of disturbing. **2.** state of being disturbed. **3.** an instance of this; a commotion. **4.** something that disturbs. **5.** an outbreak of disorder; a breach of public peace. **6.** *Geol.* a mountain-making crustal movement of moderate intensity and somewhat restricted in geographic extent. —**Syn. 2.** perturbation. See **agitation. 5.** confusion, tumult, riot. See **disorder.**

di·sul·fate (dī sŭl′fāt), *n.* **1.** *Chem.* a salt of pyrosulfuric acid, as *sodium disulfate,* Na₂S₂O₇. See **pyro-. 2.** bisulfate. Also, **di·sul′phate.** [f. DI-¹ + SULFATE]

di·sul·fide (dī sŭl′fīd, -fĭd), *n.* *Chem.* a sulfide containing two atoms of sulfur, as *carbon disulfide,* CS₂. Also, **di·sul′phide.**

di·sul·fu·ric (dī′sŭl fyŏŏr′ĭk), *n.* *Chem.* pyrosulfuric. See **pyro-.** Also, **di′sul·phu′ric.**

dis·un·ion (dĭs ūn′yən), *n.* **1.** severance of union; separation; disjunction. **2.** lack of union; dissension.

dis·un·ion·ist (dĭs ūn′yən ĭst), *n.* *U.S. Pol.* (during the Civil War period) an advocate of the disruption of the U.S. —**dis·un′ion·ism,** *n.*

dis·u·nite (dĭs′ū nīt′), *v.,* **-nited, -niting.** —*v.t.* **1.** to sever the union of; separate; disjoin. **2.** to set at variance, or alienate. —*v.i.* **3.** to part; fall asunder.

dis·u·ni·ty (dĭs ū′nə tĭ), *n., pl.* **-ties.** lack of unity.

dis·use (*n.* dĭs ūs′; *v.* dĭs ūz′), *n., v.,* **-used, -using.** —*n.* **1.** discontinuance of use or practice. —*v.t.* **2.** to cease to use.

dis·u·til·i·ty (dĭs′ū tĭl′ə tĭ), *n.* the quality of causing inconvenience or harm; injuriousness (the opposite of *utility*).

dis·val·ue (dĭs văl′ū), *v.t.,* **-ued, -uing.** *Rare.* to depreciate; disparage.

di·syl·la·ble (dī sĭl′ə bəl), *n.* a word of two syllables, as *virtue.* [t. L: m. s. *disyllabus,* t. Gk.: m. *disýllabos.* See SYLLABLE] —**dis·yl·lab·ic** (dĭs′ĭ lăb′ĭk), *adj.*

dis·yoke (dĭs yōk′), *v.t.,* **-yoked, -yoking.** to free from or as from a yoke.

di·tat De·us (dī′tăt dē′əs), *Latin.* God enriches (motto of Arizona).

ditch (dĭch), *n.* **1.** a long, narrow hollow made in the earth by digging, as one for draining or irrigating land; a trench. **2.** any open passage or trench, as a natural channel or waterway. —*v.t.* **3.** to dig a ditch or ditches in. **4.** to throw into or as into a ditch, as a railroad train. **5.** *Slang.* to get rid of; get away from. [ME *dich* OE *dīc,* c. G *teich.* See DIKE] —**ditch′er,** *n.*

di·the·ism (dī′thē ĭz′əm), *n.* *Relig.* **1.** the doctrine of, or belief in, two supreme gods. **2.** belief in the existence of two independent antagonistic principles, one good and the other evil. [f. DI-¹ + m. Gk. *theós* god + ISM] —**di′-the·ist,** *n.* —**di′the·is′tic,** *adj.*

dith·er (dĭth′ər), *n.* **1.** a trembling; vibration. **2.** *Colloq.* a state of trembling excitement or fear. —*v.i.* **3.** *Chiefly Dial.* to tremble with excitement or fear. [var. of *didder,* ME *diddir;* orig. obscure. Cf. DODDER.]

di·thi·on·ous (dī′thī ŏn′əs, dĭth′ĭ-), *adj.* *Chem.* hyposulfurous. [f. DI-¹ + m. Gk. *theîon* sulfur + -OUS]

dith·y·ramb (dĭth′ə răm′, -rămb′), *n.* **1.** a Greek choral song of vehement or wild character and usually irregular in form, orig. in honor of Dionysus or Bacchus.

ăct, āble, dâre, ärt; ĕbb, ēqual; ĭf, īce; hŏt, ōver, ôrder, oil, bŏŏk, ōōze, out; ŭp, ūse, ûrge; ə = a in alone; ch, chief; g, give; ng, ring; sh, shoe; th, thin; ŧh, that; zh, vision.   See the full key on inside cover.

2. any poem or other composition having similar characteristics. [t. L: s. *dīthyrambus*, t. Gk.: m. *dīthýrambos*]

dith·y·ram·bic (dĭth′ə·răm′bĭk), *adj.* **1.** of, pertaining to, or of the nature of a dithyramb. **2.** wildly irregular in form. **3.** wildly enthusiastic.

Dit·mars (dĭt′märz), *n.* Raymond Lee, 1876–1942, U. S. zoölogist and author.

dit·ta·ny (dĭt′ə·nĭ), *n., pl.* **-nies. 1.** a labiate plant, *Origanum dictamnus* (**dittany of Crete**), formerly in high repute for its alleged medicinal virtues. **2.** a labiate plant, *Cunila origanoides*, of North America, bearing clusters of purplish flowers. **3.** a rutaceous plant, *Dictamnus albus*, cultivated for its showy flowers. [ME *dittonye*, der. OF *ditan*, g. L *dictamnus*, t. Gk.: m. *dīktamnon*, said to be so called from Mount Dicte in Crete, where it abounded]

dit·tied (dĭt′ĭd), *adj.* composed or sung as a ditty.

dit·to (dĭt′ō), *n., pl.* **-tos,** *adv., v.,* **-toed, -toing.** —*n.* **1.** the aforesaid; the same (used in accounts, lists, etc., to avoid repetition). *Symbol:* ″; *abbr.:* do. **2.** the same thing repeated. **3.** *Colloq.* a duplicate or copy. —*adv.* **4.** as already stated; likewise. —*v.t.* **5.** to duplicate; copy. [t. It.: said, aforesaid, g. L *dictus,* pp., said]

dit·tog·ra·phy (dĭ·tŏg′rə·fĭ), *n.* **1.** unintentional repetition of one or more symbols in writing. **2.** the resulting passage or reading. [f. Gk. *dittó(s)* double + -GRAPHY] —**dit·to·graph·ic** (dĭt′ə·grăf′ĭk), *adj.*

ditto marks, two small marks (″) indicating the repetition of something, usually placed beneath the thing repeated.

dit·ty (dĭt′ĭ), *n., pl.* **-ties. 1.** a poem intended to be sung. **2.** a short, simple song. [ME *dite,* t. OF, g. L *dictātum* thing composed or recited]

ditty bag, a bag used by sailors to hold sewing implements and other necessaries.

ditty box, a small box used like a ditty bag.

di·u·re·sis (dī′ū·rē′sĭs), *n. Pathol.* excessive discharge of urine. [NL, f. Gk.: *di-* DI-³ + *ouŕēsis* urination]

di·u·ret·ic (dī′ŏŏ·rĕt′ĭk), *Med. adj.* **1.** increasing the volume of the urine, as a medicinal substance. —*n.* **2.** a diuretic medicine or agent. [t. LL: s. *diūrēticus* promoting urine, t. Gk.: m. *diouŕētikós*]

di·ur·nal (dī·ûr′nəl), *adj.* **1.** of or pertaining to each day; daily. **2.** of or belonging to the daytime. **3.** *Bot.* showing a periodic alteration of condition with day and night, as certain flowers which open by day and close by night. **4.** active by day, as certain birds and insects. —*n.* **5.** *Liturgy.* a service book containing the offices for the day hours of prayer. **6.** *Archaic.* a diary. **7.** *Archaic.* a daily or other newspaper. [t. LL: s. *diurnālis* daily] —**di·ur′nal·ly,** *adv.*

diurnal parallax. See **parallax** (def. 2).

div., **1.** divided. **2.** dividend. **3.** division. **4.** divisor.

di·va (dē′vä), *n., pl.* **-vas, -ve** (-vĕ). a distinguished female singer; a prima donna. [t. It., t. L: goddess]

di·va·gate (dī′və·gāt′), *v.i.* **-gated, -gating. 1.** to wander; stray. **2.** to digress in speech. [t. L: m. s. *dīvagātus,* pp., having wandered] —**di′va·ga′tion,** *n.*

di·va·lent (dī·vā′lənt), *adj. Chem.* having a valence of two, as the ferrous ion, Fe++.

di·van (dī·văn′, dĭ·văn′), *n.* **1.** a sofa or couch. **2.** a long, cushioned seat against a wall, as in Oriental countries. **3.** a council of state in Turkey and other Oriental countries. **4.** any council, committee, or commission. **5.** (in the Orient) **a.** a council chamber, judgment hall, audience chamber, or bureau of state. **b.** a large building used for some public purpose, as a custom house. **6.** a smoking room, as in connection with a tobacco shop. [t. Turk.: t. Pers.: m. *dīwān* (now *dīwān*)]

di·var·i·cate (*v.* dī·văr′ə·kāt′, dĭ-; *adj.* dī·văr′ə·kĭt, -kāt′, dĭ-), *v.,* **-cated, -cating,** *adj.* —*v.i.* **1.** to spread apart; branch; diverge. **2.** *Bot., Zool.* to branch at a wide angle. —*adj.* **3.** spread apart; widely divergent. **4.** *Bot., Zool.* branching at a wide angle. [t. L: m. s. *dīvāricātus,* pp., spread apart] —**di·var′i·cate·ly,** *adv.* —**di·var′i·ca′tion,** *n.* —**di·var′i·ca′tor,** *n.*

dive (dīv), *v.,* **dived** or *U.S. Colloq. and Brit. Dial.* **dove** (dōv); **dived; diving;** *n.* —*v.i.* **1.** to plunge, esp. head first, as into water. **2.** to go below the surface of the water, as a submarine. **3.** to plunge deeply. **4.** *Aeron.* (of an airplane) to plunge downward at a greater angle than when gliding. **5.** to penetrate suddenly into anything, as with the hand. **6.** to dart. **7.** to enter deeply into (a subject, business, etc.). —*n.* **8.** act of diving. **9.** *Colloq.* a disreputable place, as for drinking, gambling, etc. [ME *dive(n)* dive, dip, OE *dȳfan,* v.t., dip (causative of *dūfan,* v.i., dive, sink), c. Icel. *dȳfa* dip]

dive bomber, an airplane of the pursuit type which drops its bombs while diving at the target.

dive bombing, *Mil.* the releasing of a bomb load just before the bomber pulls out of a dive towards the target at an angle such that the pilot sights through his gun sights.

div·er (dī′vər), *n.* **1.** one who or that which dives. **2.** one who makes a business of diving, as for pearl oysters, to examine sunken vessels, etc. **3.** any of various birds that habitually dive, as loons, grebes, etc.

di·verge (dī·vûrj′, dĭ-), *v.i.,* **-verged, -verging. 1.** to move or lie in different directions from a common point; branch off. **2.** to differ in opinion or character; deviate. [t. NL: m.s. *dīvergere,* f. L *dī-* DIS-¹ + *vergere* incline, VERGE²] —**Syn. 2.** See **deviate.**

di·ver·gence (dĭ·vûr′jəns, dī-), *n.* **1.** act, fact, or amount of diverging. **2.** *Meteorol.* a condition brought about by a net flow of air from a given region.

di·ver·gen·cy (dĭ·vûr′jən·sĭ, dī-), *n., pl.* **-cies.** divergence.

di·ver·gent (dĭ·vûr′jənt, dī-), *adj.* **1.** diverging; deviating. **2.** pertaining to divergence. —**di·ver′gent·ly,** *adv.*

di·vers (dī′vərz), *adj.* several; sundry (sometimes used pronominally): *divers of them.* [ME, t. OF, g. L *dīversus,* pp., lit., turned different ways]

di·verse (dĭ·vûrs′, dī-, dī′vûrs), *adj.* **1.** of a different kind, form, character, etc.; unlike. **2.** of various kinds or forms; multiform. [var. of DIVERS, but now assoc. more directly with L *dīversus*] —**di·verse′ly,** *adv.* —**di·verse′ness,** *n.* —**Syn. 2.** See **various.**

di·ver·si·fied (dĭ·vûr′sə·fīd′, dī-), *adj.* **1.** distinguished by various forms, or by a variety of objects. **2.** varied; distributed among several types: *diversified investments.*

di·ver·si·form (dĭ·vûr′sə·fôrm′, dī-), *adj.* differing in form; of various forms. [f. s. L *dīversus* various + -(I)FORM]

di·ver·si·fy (dĭ·vûr′sə·fī′, dī-), *v.t.,* **-fied, -fying. 1.** to make diverse, as in form or character; give variety or diversity to; variegate. **2.** to vary (investments); invest in different types of (securities). [t. F: m. *diversifier,* t. ML: m.s. *dīversificāre,* f. L *dīversi-* diverse + *-ficāre* make] —**di·ver′si·fi·ca′tion,** *n.*

di·ver·sion (dĭ·vûr′zhən, -shən, dī-), *n.* **1.** act of diverting or turning aside, as from a course. **2.** *Brit.* a detour around a stoppage in a road. **3.** distraction from business, care, etc.; recreation; entertainment; amusement; a pastime. **4.** *Mil.* a feint intended to draw off attention from the point of main attack.

di·ver·si·ty (dĭ·vûr′sə·tĭ, dī-), *n., pl.* **-ties. 1.** the state or fact of being diverse; difference; unlikeness. **2.** variety; multiformity. **3.** a point of difference.

di·vert (dĭ·vûrt′, dī-), *v.t.* **1.** to turn aside or from a path or course; deflect. **2.** *Brit.* to set (traffic) on a detour. **3.** to draw off to a different object, purpose, etc. **4.** to distract from serious occupation; entertain or amuse. [t. OF: s. *divertir,* t. L: m. *dīvertere* turn aside, separate] —**di·vert′er,** *n.* —**di·vert′i·ble,** *adj.* —**Syn. 4.** See **amuse.**

di·ver·tic·u·lum (dī′vər·tĭk′yə·ləm), *n., pl.* **-la** (-lə). *Anat.* a blind tubular sac or process, branching off from a canal or cavity. [L: byway] —**di′ver·tic′u·lar,** *adj.*

di·ver·ti·men·to (dē·vĕr′tē·mĕn′tō), *n., pl.* **-ti** (-tē). *Music.* an instrumental composition in several movements, light and diverting in character, similar to a serenade. [It.]

di·vert·ing (dĭ·vûr′tĭng, dī-), *adj.* that diverts; entertaining; amusing. —**di·vert′ing·ly,** *adv.*

di·ver·tisse·ment (dē·vĕr·tēs·mäṅ′), *n.* **1.** a diversion or entertainment. **2.** *Music.* a divertimento. **3.** a short ballet or other performance given between or in the course of acts or longer pieces. **4.** a series of such performances. [F, der. *divertiss-,* s. of *divertir* DIVERT]

di·ver·tive (dĭ·vûr′tĭv, dī-), *adj.* diverting; amusing.

Dives (dī′vēz), *n.* **1.** *Bible.* the rich man of the parable in Luke 16:19–31. **2.** any rich man. [L: rich, rich man]

di·vest (dĭ·vĕst′, dī-), *v.t.* **1.** to strip of clothing, etc.; disrobe. **2.** to strip or deprive of anything; dispossess. **3.** *Law.* to take away or alienate (property, etc.). [t. ML: s. *dīvestīre,* var. of *disvestīre* (Latinization of OF *desvestir*)] —**Syn. 2.** See **strip².**

di·ves·ti·ble (dĭ·vĕs′tə·bəl, dī-), *adj.* capable of being divested, as an estate in land.

di·vest·i·ture (dĭ·vĕs′tə·chər, dī-), *n.* **1.** act of divesting. **2.** state of being divested. Also, **di·vest′ment, di·ves·ture** (dĭ·vĕs′chər, dī-).

di·vid·a·ble (dĭ·vī′də·bəl), *adj.* divisible.

di·vide (dĭ·vīd′), *v.,* **-vided, -viding,** *n.* —*v.t.* **1.** to separate into parts. **2.** to separate or part from each other or from something else; sunder; cut off. **3.** to deal out in parts; apportion; share. **4.** to separate in opinion or feeling; cause to disagree. **5.** to distinguish the kinds of; classify. **6.** *Math.* **a.** to separate into equal parts by the process of division. **b.** to be a divisor of, without a remainder. **c.** to graduate (a rule, etc.). **7.** *Brit. Govt.* to separate (a legislature, etc.) into two groups in ascertaining the vote on a question. —*v.i.* **8.** to become divided or separated. **9.** to share something with others. **10.** *Brit. Govt.* to vote by separating into two groups. —*n.* **11.** *Colloq.* act of dividing; a division. **12.** *Phys. Geog.* the line or zone separating the flow of water to either of two adjacent streams or drainage basins. [ME *divide(n),* t. L: m. *dīvidere* force asunder, cleave, part, distribute] —**Syn. 1.** See **separate.**

di·vid·ed (dĭ·vī′dĭd), *adj.* **1.** separated; separate; disunited; shared. **2.** *Bot.* (of a leaf) cut into distinct portions by incisions extending to the midrib or the base.

di·vi·de et im·pe·ra (dĭv′ə·dē′ ĕt ĭm′pə·rə), *Latin.* divide and rule (political maxim of Machiavelli, etc.).

div·i·dend (dĭv′ə·dĕnd′), *n.* **1.** *Math.* a number to be divided by another number (the divisor). **2.** *Law.* a sum out of an insolvent estate to be divided among the creditors. **3.** *Finance.* **a.** a pro-rata share in an amount to be distributed. **b.** a sum of money paid to shareholders of a corporation out of earnings. **4.** *Insurance.* a profit distribution by a company to an assured. **5.** a share of anything divided. [t. L: s. *dīvidendum* (thing) to be divided, neut. ger. of *dīvidere* DIVIDE]

---

b., blend of, blended; c., cognate with; d., dialect, dialectal; der., derived from; f., formed from; g., going back to; m., modification of; r., replacing; s., stem of; t., taken from; ?, perhaps. See the full key on inside cover.

di·vid·er (dǐ vī′dər), *n.* 1. one who or that which divides. 2. (*pl.*) a pair of compasses as used for dividing lines, measuring, etc.

div·i-div·i (dǐv′ǐ dǐv′ǐ), *n.* 1. a shrub or small tree, *Caesalpinia coriaria*, of tropical America, the astringent pods of which are much used in tanning and dyeing. 2. the related species *C. tinctoria*. 3. the pods of either plant. [native Carib or Galibi name]

di·vid·u·al (dǐ vǐj′ōō əl), *adj.* 1. divisible or divided. 2. separate; distinct. 3. distributed; shared. [f. s. L *dīviduus* divisible + -AL¹] —**di·vid′u·al·ly**, *adv.*

div·i·na·tion (dǐv′ə nā′shən), *n.* 1. the discovering of what is obscure or the foretelling of future events, as by supernatural means. 2. augury; a prophecy. 3. instinctive prevision. [t. L: s. *dīvīnātio*, der. *dīvīnāre* DIVINE, v.] —**di·vin·a·to·ry** (dǐ vǐn′ə tōr′ǐ), *adj.*

di·vine (dǐ vīn′), *adj., n., v.,* -vined, -vining. —*adj.* 1. of or pertaining to a god, esp. the Supreme Being. 2. addressed or appropriated to God; religious; sacred. 3. proceeding from God. 4. godlike; characteristic of or befitting deity. 5. heavenly; celestial. 6. being a god, or God. 7. pertaining to divinity or theology. 8. of superhuman or surpassing excellence. —*n.* 9. one versed in divinity; a theologian. 10. a priest or clergyman. —*v.t.* 11. to discover or declare (something obscure or future), as by supernatural means; prophesy. 12. to perceive by intuition or insight; conjecture. 13. *Obs.* or *Archaic.* to portend. —*v.i.* 14. to use or practice divination; prophesy. 15. to have perception by intuition or insight; conjecture. [ME, t. L: m. s. *dīvīnus*; r. ME *devine*, t. OF] —**di·vine′ly**, *adv.* —**di·vine′ness**, *n.*

di·vin·er (dǐ vī′nər), *n.* one who divines; a soothsayer; a prophet; a conjecturer.

divine right of kings, the right to rule derived directly from God, not from the consent of the people.

diving beetle, any of the predaceous beetles that constitute the family *Dytiscidae*, adapted for swimming and diving.

diving bell, a hollow vessel filled with air under pressure, in which persons may work under water.

diving suit, a watertight garment, consisting of a rubber or metal body covering and a helmet with an air-supply line attached, worn by divers.

divining rod, a rod used in divining, esp. a forked stick, commonly of hazel, supposed to be useful in locating spots where water, metal, etc., is underground.

di·vin·i·ty (dǐ vǐn′ə tǐ), *n., pl.* -ties. 1. the quality of being divine; divine nature. 2. deity; godhood. 3. a divine being, or god. 4. **the Divinity,** the Deity. 5. a deity below God but above man. 6. the science of divine things; theology. 7. godlike character; supreme excellence. 8. a fluffy white confection made usually of sugar, corn syrup, egg whites and flavoring, often with nuts.

div·i·nize (dǐv′ə nīz′), *v.t.,* -nized, -nizing. to make divine; deify. —**div′i·ni·za′tion**, *n.*

di·vis·i·bil·i·ty (dǐ vǐz′ə bǐl′ə tǐ), *n. Math.* the capacity of being exactly divided, without remainder.

di·vis·i·ble (dǐ vǐz′ə bəl), *adj.* capable of being divided. —**di·vis′i·ble·ness**, *n.* —**di·vis′i·bly**, *adv.*

di·vi·sion (dǐ vǐzh′ən), *n.* 1. act of dividing; partition. 2. state of being divided. 3. *Math.* the operation inverse to multiplication; the finding of a quantity (the quotient) which, when multiplied by a given quantity (the divisor) gives another given quantity (the dividend). 4. something that divides; a dividing line or mark. 5. one of the parts into which a thing is divided; a section. 6. separation by difference of opinion or feeling; disagreement; dissension. 7. *Govt.* the separation of a legislature, etc., into two groups, in taking a vote. 8. one of the parts into which a country or an organization is divided for political, administrative, judicial, military, or other purposes. 9. *Mil.* a major administrative and tactical unit, larger than a regiment or brigade, and smaller than a corps. It is usually commanded by a major general. 10. *Zool.* any subdivision of a classificatory group or category. [t. L: s. *dīvīsio*; r. ME *devisioun*, t. OF] —**di·vi′sion·al**, *adj.*

—**Syn.** 1. separation, apportionment, allotment, distribution. DIVISION, PARTITION suggest the operation of dividing into parts or of one part from another. DIVISION usually means little more than the marking off or separation of a whole into parts. PARTITION often adds the idea of sharing, of an allotting or assigning of parts following division: *partition of an estate, of a country.*

division sign, the symbol (÷) placed between two expressions, denoting division of the first by the second.

di·vi·sive (dǐ vī′sǐv), *adj.* 1. forming or expressing division or distribution. 2. creating division or discord. —**di·vi′sive·ly**, *adv.* —**di·vi′sive·ness**, *n.*

di·vi·sor (dǐ vī′zər), *n. Math.* 1. a number by which another number (the dividend) is divided. 2. a number contained in another given number a certain number of times, without a remainder.

di·vorce (dǐ vōrs′), *n., v.,* -vorced, -vorcing. —*n.* 1. *Law.* a. an absolute legal dissolution of the marriage bond (**absolute divorce**). b. a judicial separation of man and wife, or termination of cohabitation, without dissolution of the marriage bond (**limited divorce or divorce from bed and board**). c. a judicial declaration of the nullity of a supposed marriage. 2. any formal separation of man and wife according to established custom, as among uncivilized tribes. 3. a complete separation of any kind. —*v.t.* 4. to separate by divorce; put away (one's husband or wife) by divorce. 5. to

separate; cut off. [ME *divors*, t. F: m. *divorce*, g. L *dīvortium* separation, dissolution] —**di·vorce′a·ble**, *adj.* —**di·vorc′er**, *n.*

di·vor·cé (dǐ vōr′sā′), *n.* a divorced man. [t. F, prop. pp. of *divorcer*] —**di·vor′cée′**, *n. fem.*

di·vor·cee (dǐ vōr′sē′), *n.* a divorced person.

di·vorce·ment (dǐ vōrs′mənt), *n.* divorce.

div·ot (dǐv′ət), *n.* 1. *Golf.* a piece of turf cut out with a club in making a stroke. 2. *Scot.* a piece of turf; a sod.

di·vul·gate (dǐ vǔl′gāt), *v.t.,* -gated, -gating. to make publicly known; publish. [t. L: m. s. *dīvulgātus*, pp., divulged] —**di·vul′gat·er, di·vul′ga·tor,** *n.* —**div·ul·ga·tion** (dǐv′əl gā′shən), *n.*

di·vulge (dǐ vǔlj′), *v.t.,* -vulged, -vulging. 1. to disclose or reveal (something private, secret, or previously unknown): *I divulged the news.* 2. *Obs.* to make publicly known. [t. L: m. s. *dīvulgāre* make common] —**di·vulge′ment** —**di·vulg′er,** *n.* —**Syn.** 1. See **reveal.**

di·vul·gence (dǐ vǔl′jəns), *n.* a divulging.

di·vul·sion (dǐ vǔl′shən), *n.* a tearing asunder; violent separation. [t. F, t. L: s. *dīvulsio*] —**di·vul·sive** (dǐ vǔl′sǐv), *adj.*

di·wan (dǐ wän′, -wŏn′), *n.* dewan. [see DIVAN]

Dix·ie (dǐk′sǐ), *n.* 1. Also, **Dixie Land.** the Southern States of the United States. 2. any of several songs with this name, esp. the minstrel song (1859) by D. D. Emmett, popular as a Confederate war song. [orig. uncert.]

Dix·ie·crat (dǐk′sǐ krăt), *n.* a member of a minority in the Democratic party consisting of Democrats living in the Southern States. Under the name of the States' Rights party, the Dixiecrats nominated an independent ticket in the presidential election of 1948. [f. DIXIE + (DEMO)CRAT]

Dix·ie·land (dǐk′sǐ lǎnd′), *n. Jazz.* a style of composition and performance characterized by vigorous improvisation.

dix·it (dǐk′sǐt), *n.* an utterance. [t. L: he has said]

Di·yar·be·kir (dē yär′bě kǐr′), *n.* a city in SE Turkey, on the Tigris river. 42,555 (1940). Also, **Diarbekr.**

diz·en (dǐz′ən, dī′zən), *v.t.* to deck with clothes or finery; bedizen. [akin to *dis-* in DISTAFF] —**diz′en·ment**, *n.*

diz·zy (dǐz′ǐ), *adj.,* -zier, -ziest, *v.,* -zied, -zying. —*adj.* 1. affected with a sensation of whirling, with tendency to fall; giddy; vertiginous. 2. bewildered; confused. 3. causing giddiness: *a dizzy height.* 4. unsteady; thoughtless. 5. *Colloq.* foolish or stupid. —*v.t.* 6. to make dizzy. [ME and OE *dysig* foolish, c. LG *düsig* stupefied] —**diz′zi·ly**, *adv.* —**diz′zi·ness**, *n.*

Dji·bou·ti (jē bōō′tē), *n.* a seaport in and the capital of French Somaliland, on the Gulf of Aden. 16,600 (est. 1939). Also, **Jibuti.**

Djok·ja·kar·ta (jŏk′yä kär′tä), *n.* Dutch name of Jogjakarta.

dl., deciliter.

D. Lit., (L *Doctor Literarum*) Doctor of Literature.

D. Litt., (L *Doctor Litterarum*) Doctor of Letters.

D.L.S., Doctor of Library Science.

dm., decimeter.

D. Mus., Doctor of Music.

Dne·pro·dzer·zhinsk (dně′prŏ jěr zǐnsk′), *n.* a city in the SW Soviet Union, on the Dnieper. 147,829 (1939).

Dne·pro·pe·trovsk (dně′prŏ pě trŏfsk′), *n.* a city in the SW Soviet Union, on the Dnieper. 500,662 (1939). Formerly, **Ekaterinoslav.**

Dne·pro·stroi (dně′prŏ stroi′), *n.* the Dnieper dam and hydroelectric plant at Dnepropetrovsk.

Dnie·per (nē′pər), *n.* a river in the W Soviet Union, flowing S to the Black Sea. ab. 1400 mi. Russian, **Dne·pr** (dně′pər).

Dnies·ter (nē′stər), *n.* a river flowing from the Carpathian Mountains in the SW Soviet Union SE to the Black Sea. ab. 800 mi. Russian, **Dnes·tr** (dněs′tər). Rumanian, **Nistru.**

do¹ (dōō), *v., pres. sing.* 1 **do,** 2 (*Archaic*) **doest** or **dost,** 3 **does** or (*Archaic*) **doeth** or **doth;** *pl.* **do;** *pt.* **did;** *pp.* **done;** *ppr.* **doing;** *n.* —*v.t.* 1. to perform (acts, duty, penance, a problem, a part, etc.). 2. to execute (a piece or amount of work, etc.). 3. to accomplish; finish. 4. to put forth; exert: *do your best.* 5. to be the cause of (good, harm, credit, etc.); bring about; effect. 6. to render (homage, justice, etc.). 7. to deal with (anything) as the case may require: *to do (cook) meat, do (wash) the dishes.* 8. to cover; traverse: *we did thirty miles today.* 9. *Slang.* to cheat or swindle (often fol. by *out of*). 10. to serve; suffice for: *this will do us for the present.* 11. *Colloq.* to provide; prepare: *we do lunches here.* 12. **do in,** *Slang.* a. to ruin. b. to kill; murder. 13. **do up,** a. to wrap and tie up. b. to comb out and pin up (hair). c. to renovate; launder. d. *Colloq.* to tire out. —*v.i.* 14. to act, esp. effectively; be in action. 15. to behave or proceed (wisely, etc.). 16. to get along, or fare (well or ill); manage (with, without, etc.). 17. to be as to health: *how do you do?* 18. to serve or be satisfactory, as for the purpose; suffice, or be enough: *will this do?* 19. to deal with; treat (fol. by *by*): *to do well by a man.* 20. **do away with,** to put an end to; abolish. 21. **do for,** a. to accomplish defeat, ruin, death, etc., of. b. *Brit.* to cook and keep house for. c. to provide or manage for. 22. **make do,** to get along with what one has. 23. (used without special meaning in interrogative, negative, and inverted constructions; in imperatives

with *you* or *thou* expressed, and occasionally as a metrical expedient in verse): *do you think so? I don't agree.* 24. (used to lend emphasis to a principal verb): *do come!* 25. (used to avoid repetition of a verb or full verb expression): *I think as you do, make your application when we do, did you see him? I did.*
—*n.* 26. *Brit. Dial.* ado; action; work. 27. *Slang.* a swindle. 28. *Colloq.* a festivity or treat: *we're having a big do next week.*
[ME; OE *dōn*, c. D *doen*, G *tun*; akin to L *-dere*, Gk. *tithēnai*]
—**Syn.** 3. Do, ACCOMPLISH, ACHIEVE mean to bring some action to a conclusion. Do is the general word, carrying no implication of success or failure: *he did a great deal of hard work.* ACCOMPLISH and ACHIEVE both have a connotation of successful completion of an undertaking. ACCOMPLISH emphasizes attaining a desired purpose through effort, skill, and perseverance: *to accomplish what one has hoped for.* ACHIEVE emphasizes accomplishing something important, excellent, or great: *to achieve a beneficial service for mankind.*
do[2] (dō), *n. Music.* **1.** the syllable used for the first tone or keynote of a diatonic scale. **2.** (sometimes) the tone C. See **ut** and **sol-fa.** [see GAMUT]
do., ditto.
D.O., Doctor of Osteopathy.
do·a·ble (dōō′ə bəl), *adj.* that may be done.
do·all (dōō′ôl′), *n.* a factotum.
doat (dōt), *v.i.* dote.
dob·ber (dŏb′ər), *n. Local U.S.* a float for a fishing line; bob. [t. D]
dob·bin (dŏb′ĭn), *n.* **1.** a name for a horse, esp. a quiet, plodding horse for farm work or family use. **2.** a horse of this kind. [var. of *Robin,* familiar var. of *Robert,* man's name]
dob·by (dŏb′ĭ), *n., pl.* **-bies.** *Dial.* a sprite or goblin.
Do·ber·man pin·scher (dō′bər mən pĭn′shər), a breed of large smooth-coated terriers, usually black-and-tan or brown, with long forelegs, and wide hindquarters.
do·bie (dō′bĭ), *n., pl.* **-bies.** adobe.
do·bra (dō′brə), *n.* any of several former Portuguese coins, esp. a gold coin first issued by King John V and having twice the value of the johannes. [t. Pg., der. L *duplus* double]

Doberman pinscher
(24 to 27 in. high
at the shoulder)

Do·bru·ja (dō′brōō jə; *Bulg.* dô′brŏŏ jä′), *n.* a region in SE Rumania and NE Bulgaria, between the Danube and the Black Sea. Rumanian part, 531,317 pop. (est. 1943); 6120 sq. mi. (1946); Bulgarian part, 356,730 pop. (1946); 2970 sq. mi. Rumanian, **Do·bro·gea** (dō′brô jä′).
dob·son (dŏb′sən), *n.* **1.** a large, membranous-winged insect, *Corydalis cornutus,* possessing greatly elongated and hornlike mandibles. **2.** its large aquatic larva, the hellgrammite. [orig. uncert.]
Dob·son (dŏb′sən), *n.* (Henry) **Austin,** 1840–1921, British poet, biographer, and essayist.
dobson fly, any insect of the family *Corydalidae* (order *Megaloptera*), as the dobson.
doc., *pl.* **docs.** document.
do·cent (dō′sənt; *Ger.* dō tsĕnt′), *n.* **1.** Privatdocent. **2.** a college or university lecturer. [t. L: s. *docens,* ppr., teaching. Cf. G *privatdocent*] —**do′cent·ship′,** *n.*
doc·ile (dŏs′əl; *Brit.* dō′sīl), *adj.* **1.** readily trained or taught; teachable. **2.** easily managed or handled; tractable. [t. F, t. L: m. s. *docilis*] —**doc′ile·ly,** *adv.* —**do·cil·i·ty** (dō sĭl′ə tĭ, dŏs-), *n.*
dock[1] (dŏk), *n.* **1.** a wharf. **2.** the space or waterway between two piers or wharves, as for receiving a ship while in port. **3.** such a waterway, enclosed or open, together with the surrounding piers, wharves, etc. **4.** See **dry dock.** —*v.t.* **5.** to bring into a dock; lay up in a dock. **6.** to put into a dry dock for repairs, cleaning, or painting. —*v.i.* **7.** to come or go into a dock or dry dock. [cf. D *dok*; orig. uncert.]
dock[2] (dŏk), *n.* **1.** the solid or fleshy part of an animal's tail, as distinguished from the hair. **2.** the part of a tail left after cutting or clipping. —*v.t.* **3.** to cut off the end of (a tail, etc.). **4.** to deduct a part from (wages, etc.). **5.** to cut short the tail of. **6.** to deduct from the wages of. [OE *-docca,* in *fingerdocca* finger muscle]
dock[3] (dŏk), *n.* the place in a courtroom where a prisoner is placed during trial. [cf. Flem. *dok* cage]
dock[4] (dŏk), *n.* **1.** any of various plants of the polygonaceous genus *Rumex,* as *R. obtusifolius* (**bitter dock**) or *R. Acetosa* (**sour dock**), mostly troublesome weeds with long taproots. **2.** any of various other plants, mostly coarse weeds. [ME *dokke,* OE *docce*]
dock·age[1] (dŏk′ĭj), *n.* **1.** a charge for the use of a dock. **2.** docking accommodations. **3.** act of docking a vessel. [f. DOCK[1] + -AGE]
dock·age[2] (dŏk′ĭj), *n.* **1.** curtailment; deduction, as from wages. **2.** waste material in wheat and other grains which is easily removed. [f. DOCK[2] + -AGE]
dock·er[1] (dŏk′ər), *n. Brit.* a dock laborer; a longshoreman. [f. DOCK[1] + -ER[1]]
dock·er[2] (dŏk′ər), *n.* one who or that which docks, cuts short, or cuts off. [f. DOCK[2] + -ER[1]]
dock·et (dŏk′ĭt), *n., v.,* **-eted, -eting.** —*n.* **1.** a list of causes in court for trial, or the names of the parties who

have causes pending. **2.** *Chiefly Brit.* an official memorandum or entry of proceedings in a legal cause, or a register of such entries. **3.** *U.S.* the list of business to be transacted by court or assembly; the agenda; a list of projects or cases awaiting action. **4.** a writing on a letter or document, stating its contents; any statement of particulars attached to a package, etc.; a label or ticket. —*v.t.* **5.** *Law.* to make an abstract or summary of the heads of, as a document; abstract and enter in a book: *judgments regularly docketed.* **6.** to endorse (a letter, etc.) with a memorandum, as of contents. [ME *doket*; orig. obscure]
dock·mack·ie (dŏk′măk′ĭ), *n.* a caprifoliaceous shrub, *Viburnum acerifolium,* of North America, with yellowish-white flowers and ovoid, almost black berries. [t. Amer. Ind. (Delaware): m. *dogekumak,* c. Ojibwa *takaiamagad* it is cool]
dock·wal·lop·er (dŏk′wŏl′əp ər), *n. Slang.* a casual laborer about docks or wharves.
dock·yard (dŏk′yärd′), *n.* **1.** an enclosure containing docks, shops, warehouses, etc., where ships are repaired, fitted out, and built. **2.** *Eng.* a navy yard.
doc·tor (dŏk′tər), *n.* **1.** a person licensed to practice medicine, or some branch of medicine; a physician; a surgeon. In England, a surgeon is not called a doctor. **2.** a person who has received the highest degree conferred by a faculty of a univeristy. **3.** the academic title possessed by such a person, orig. implying qualification to teach, now generally based on at least three years of advanced study and research beyond the bachelor's degree. **4.** a man of great learning. **5.** *Colloq.* a cook, as on shipboard. **6.** any of various mechanical contrivances for particular purposes. **7.** a kind of artificial fly for angling, such as silver doctor. **8.** *Old Slang.* a false or loaded die. —*v.t.* **9.** to treat medicinally. **10.** *Colloq.* to repair or mend. **11.** *Colloq.* to tamper with; falsify; adulterate. —*v.i.* **12.** to practice medicine. **13.** to take medicine; receive medical treatment. [t. L: teacher; r. ME *doctour,* t. OF] —**doc′tor·al,** *adj.* —**doc′tor·ship′,** *n.* —**doc·tress** (dŏk′trĭs), (*Rare*) *n., fem.*
doc·tor·ate (dŏk′tər ĭt), *n.* the degree of doctor.
Doctors' Commons, a building in London, at one time the dining hall of the College of Doctors of Civil Law, and later housing ecclesiastical and Admiralty courts which applied primarily civil law.
Doctor's degree, *Colloq.* Ph.D.
doc·tri·naire (dŏk′trə nâr′), *n.* one who tries to apply some doctrine or theory without a sufficient regard to practical considerations; an impractical theorist. [t. F, der. *doctrine* DOCTRINE] —**doc′tri·nar′ism,** *n.* —**doc′-tri·nar′i·an,** *n.*
doc·tri·nal (dŏk′trə nəl; *Brit. also* dŏk trī′nəl), *adj.* of, pertaining to, or concerned with, doctrine. —**doc′-tri·nal·ly,** *adv.*
doc·trine (dŏk′trĭn), *n.* **1.** a particular principle taught or advocated. **2.** that which is taught; teachings collectively. **3.** a body or system of teachings relating to a particular subject. [ME, t. F, t. L: m. *doctrīna* teaching, learning] —**Syn.** 1. tenet, dogma, theory, precept, belief.
doc·u·ment (*n.* dŏk′yə mənt; *v.* dŏk′yə mĕnt′), *n.* **1.** a written or printed paper furnishing information or evidence, a legal or official paper. **2.** *Obs.* evidence; proof. —*v.t.* **3.** to furnish with documents, evidence, or the like. **4.** to support by documentary evidence. **5.** *Obs.* to instruct. [ME, t. L: s. *documentum* lesson, example]
doc·u·men·ta·ry (dŏk′yə mĕn′tə rĭ), *adj., n., pl.* **-ries.** —*adj.* **1.** Also, **doc·u·men·tal** (dŏk′yə mĕn′təl). pertaining to, consisting of, or derived from documents. —*n.* **2.** *Motion Pictures.* a film, usually nonfiction, in which the elements of dramatic conflict are provided by ideas, political or economic forces, etc.
doc·u·men·ta·tion (dŏk′yə mĕn tā′shən), *n.* **1.** the use of documentary evidence. **2.** a furnishing with documents.
Dodd (dŏd), *n.* **William Edward,** 1869–1940, U.S. historian and diplomat.
dod·der[1] (dŏd′ər), *v.i.* to shake; tremble; totter. [cf. DITHER, TOTTER, etc.]
dod·der[2] (dŏd′ər), *n.* any of the leafless parasitic plants comprising the genus *Cuscuta,* with yellowish, reddish, or white threadlike stems that twine about clover, flax, etc. [ME *doder,* c. G *dotter*]
dod·dered (dŏd′ərd), *adj.* infirm; feeble.
dod·der·ing (dŏd′ər ĭng), *adj.* that dodders; shaking; tottering; senile.
dodeca-, a word element meaning "twelve." Also, before vowels, **dodec-.** [t. Gk.: m. *dōdeka-,* comb. form of *dōdeka*]
do·dec·a·gon (dō dĕk′ə gŏn′, -gən), *n. Geom.* a polygon having twelve angles and twelve sides. [t. Gk.: s. *dōdekágōnon.* See DO- DECA-, -GON] —**do·de·cag·o·nal** (dō′dĕ kăg′ə nəl), *adj.*
do·dec·a·he·dron (dō′dĕk ə hē′drən), *n., pl.* **-drons, -dra** (-drə). *Geom.* a solid figure having twelve faces. [t. Gk.: m. *dōdekáedron*] —**do′-dec·a·he′dral,** *adj.*

Rhombic dodecahedron   Pentagonal dodecahedron

Do·dec·a·nese Islands (dō·dĕk′ə·nēs′, -nēz′, dō′-dĕk·ə-), a group of twelve Greek islands in the Aegean, off the SW coast of Turkey: formerly belonging to Italy. 140,848 pop. (1936); 1035 sq. mi.

dodge (dŏj), v., **dodged, dodging,** n. —v.i. **1.** to move aside or change position suddenly, as to avoid a blow or to get behind something. **2.** to use evasive methods; prevaricate. —v.t. **3.** to elude by a sudden shift of position or by strategy. —n. **4.** an act of dodging; a spring aside. **5.** Colloq. an ingenious expedient or contrivance; a shifty trick. [orig. uncert.] —**Syn. 2.** equivocate, quibble. **3.** evade, elude.

Dodge City, a city in SW Kansas, on the Arkansas river: it was an important frontier town and railhead on the old Santa Fe route. 11,262 (1950).

dodg·er (dŏj′ər), n. **1.** one who dodges. **2.** a shifty person. **3.** U.S. a small handbill. **4.** Southern U.S. a corn dodger.

Dodg·son (dŏj′sən), n. **Charles Lutwidge** (lŭt′wĬj), ("Lewis Carroll") 1832–98, British mathematician and author of books for children.

do·do (dō′dō), n., pl. **-does, -dos. 1.** a clumsy flightless bird of the genera Raphus and Pezophaps, about the size of a goose, related to the pigeons, formerly inhabiting the islands of Mauritius, Réunion and Rodriguez, but extinct since the advent of European settlers. **2.** Colloq. an old fogy. [t. Pg.: m. doudo silly]

Dodo, Raphus solitarius (Ab. 3 ft. long)

Do·do·na (dō·dō′nə), n. an ancient town in NW Greece, in Epirus: the site of a famous oracle of Zeus. —**Do·do·nae·an, Do·do·ne·an** (dō′də·nē′ən), adj.

doe (dō), n. the female of the deer, antelope, goat, rabbit, and certain other animals. [ME do, OE dā. Cf. L dāma, damma deer]

Doe (dō), n. **John,** a name referring to an avowedly fictitious person, used esp. in law for the plaintiff in action of ejectment.

do·er (dōō′ər), n. one who or that which does something; a performer; an actor.

Doe of Virginia deer, Odocoileus virginianus (5 ft. long)

does (dŭz), v. 3rd pers. sing. pres. ind. of **do.**

doe·skin (dō′skĬn′), n. **1.** the skin of a doe. **2.** leather made from this. **3.** (pl.) gloves made of sheepskin. **4.** a smoothly finished, closely woven, finely twilled woolen cloth.

does·n't (dŭz′ənt), contraction of does not.

do·eth (dōō′Ĭth), aux. v. Archaic. (now only in poetic or solemn use) 3rd pers. sing. pres. of **do.**

doff (dŏf, dôf), v.t. **1.** to put or take off, as dress. **2.** to remove (the hat) in salutation. **3.** to throw off; get rid of. [contr. of do off. Cf. DON²] —**doff′er,** n.

dog (dôg, dŏg), n., v., **dogged, dogging.** —n. **1.** a domesticated carnivore, Canis familiaris, bred in a great many varieties. **2.** any animal belonging to the same family, Canidae, including the wolves, jackals, foxes, etc. **3.** the male of such an animal (opposed to bitch). **4.** any of various animals suggesting the dog, as the prairie dog. **5.** a despicable fellow. **6.** a fellow in general: a gay dog. **7.** (cap.) Astron. either of two constellations, Canis Major (**Great Dog**) and Canis Minor (**Little Dog**), situated near Orion. **8.** Mech. any of various mechanical devices, as for gripping or holding something. **9.** an andiron. **10.** Meteorol. a sundog or fogdog. **11.** go to the **dogs,** Colloq. to go to ruin. **12.** put on the dog, U.S. Colloq. to behave pretentiously; put on airs. —v.t. **13.** to follow or track like a dog, esp. with hostile intent; hound. **14.** to drive or chase with a dog or dogs. [ME dogge, OE docga; orig. unknown]

Mechanical dogs (def. 8) A. Bench dog; B. Ring dog; C. Sling dog

dog·bane (dôg′bān′, dŏg′-), n. any of the genus Apocynum, esp. A. androsaemifolium, a perennial herb abounding in an acrid milky juice and having an intensely bitter root that has been used in medicine.

dog·ber·ry (dôg′bĕr′Ĭ, dŏg′-), n., pl. **-ries. 1.** the berry or fruit of any of various plants, as the European dogwood, Cornus sanguinea, the chokeberry, Aronia arbutifolia, or the mountain ash Sorbus americana. **2.** the plant itself. **3.** Local and Eng. any of several plants, esp. the dog rose, bearberry and guelder rose.

dog·cart (dôg′kärt′, dŏg′-), n. **1.** a light, two-wheeled vehicle for ordinary driving, with two transverse seats back to back. **2.** a cart drawn by dogs.

dog days, a sultry part of the summer supposed to occur about the time of the heliacal rising of one of the Dog Stars, now often reckoned from July 3 to Aug. 11.

doge (dōj), n. the chief magistrate of the old republics of Venice and Genoa, who had no real power. [t. It. (Venetian), g. L dux leader] —**doge′ship,** n.

dog-ear (dôg′Ĭr′, dŏg′-), n. **1.** the corner of a page in a book folded over like a dog's ear, as by careless use or to mark a place. —v.t. **2.** to disfigure with dog-ears. Also, **dog's-ear.** —**dog′-eared′,** adj.

dog fennel, mayweed.

dog·fight (dôg′fīt′, dŏg′-), n. **1.** Mil. a violent engagement of war planes at close quarters, esp. of small and highly maneuverable planes. **2.** any rough and tumble physical battle.

dog·fish (dôg′fĬsh′, dŏg′-), n., pl. **-fishes,** (esp. collectively) **-fish. 1.** any of various small sharks, as the spiny dogfish Squalus acanthias, common on both coasts of the northern Atlantic and destructive to food fishes, and the smooth dogfishes (genus Mustelus). **2.** any of various other fishes, as the bowfin.

dog fox, a male fox.

dog·ged (dôg′Ĭd, dŏg′-), adj. having the pertinacity of a dog; obstinate. [f. DOG + -ED³. Cf. CRABBED] —**dog′ged·ly,** adv. —**dog′ged·ness,** n. —**Syn.** mulish. persistent, inflexible, unyielding. See **stubborn.**

dog·ger (dôg′ər, dŏg′-), n. a two-masted Dutch fishing vessel with a blunt bow, used in the North Sea. [ME doggere. Cf. Icel. dugga small fishing vessel]

Dog·ger Bank (dôg′ər, dŏg′-), an extensive shoal in the North Sea, ab. 70 mi. E of N England: fishing grounds; naval battle, 1915. 36–120 ft. deep. [said to be named from DOGGER or from MD dogger trawler]

dog·ger·el (dôg′ər·əl, dŏg′-), adj. **1.** (of verse) comic or burlesque, and usually loose or irregular in measure. **2.** rude; crude; poor. —n. **3.** doggerel verse. Also, **dog·grel** (dôg′rəl, dŏg′-). [ME; orig. uncert.]

dog·ger·y (dôg′ər·Ĭ, dŏg′-), n., pl. **-geries. 1.** doggish behavior or conduct; mean or mischievous action. **2.** dogs collectively. **3.** rabble; canaille.

dog·gish (dôg′Ĭsh, dŏg′-), adj. **1.** canine. **2.** surly. **3.** stylish and showy. —**dog′gish·ly,** adv. —**dog′gish·ness,** n.

dog·gy (dôg′Ĭ, dŏg′Ĭ), n., pl. **-gies,** adj., **-gier, -giest.** —n. **1.** a little dog. **2.** a pet term for any dog. —adj. **3.** of or pertaining to a dog. **4.** fond of dogs. **5.** pretentious; ostentatious. Also, **dog′gie.**

dog·house (dôg′hous′, dŏg′-), n. **1.** a small shelter for a dog. **2.** in the doghouse, in disfavor.

do·gie (dō′gĬ), n. Western U.S. a motherless calf in a cattle herd.

dog in the manger, a person who, like the dog in the fable, churlishly keeps something of no particular use to himself so that others cannot use it.

dog Latin, mongrel or spurious Latin.

dog·ma (dôg′mə, dŏg′-), n., pl. **-mas, -mata** (-mə·tə). **1.** a system of principles or tenets, as of a church. **2.** a tenet or doctrine authoritatively laid down, as by a church. **3.** prescribed doctrine. **4.** a settled opinion; a belief; a principle. [t. L, t. Gk.]

dog·mat·ic (dôg·măt′Ĭk, dŏg-), adj. **1.** of, pertaining to, or of the nature of a dogma or dogmas; doctrinal. **2.** asserting opinions in an authoritative, positive, or arrogant manner; positive; opinionated. Also, **dog·mat′i·cal.** —**dog·mat′i·cal·ly,** adv.

dog·mat·ics (dôg·măt′Ĭks, dŏg-), n. the science which treats of the arrangement and statement of religious doctrines, esp. of the doctrines received in and taught by the Christian church; doctrinal theology.

dog·ma·tism (dôg′mə·tĬz′əm, dŏg′-), n. dogmatic character; authoritative, positive, or arrogant assertion of opinions.

dog·ma·tist (dôg′mə·tĬst, dŏg′-), n. **1.** one who asserts positively his own opinions; a dogmatic person. **2.** one who lays down dogmas.

dog·ma·tize (dôg′mə·tĬz′, dŏg′-), v., **-tized, -tizing.** —v.i. **1.** to make dogmatic assertions; speak or write dogmatically. —v.t. **2.** to assert or deliver as a dogma. [t. ML: m.s. dogmatizāre, t. Gk.: m. dogmatizein] —**dog′ma·ti·za′tion,** n. —**dog′ma·tiz′er,** n.

do-good·er (dōō′gŏŏd′ər), n. Colloq. a foolish, idealistic reformer.

dog rose, a species of wild rose, Rosa canina, having pale-red flowers, a common Old World plant.

dog's-ear (dôgz′Ĭr′, dŏgz′-), n., v.t. dog-ear. —**dog's′-eared′,** adj.

dog's-tail (dôgz′tāl′, dŏgz′-), n. any grass of the Old World genus Cynosurus, the species of which have the spikes fringed on one side only, esp. C. cristatus (crested dog's-tail). Also, **dog's-tail grass.**

Dog Star, 1. the bright star Sirius, in Canis Major. **2.** the bright star Procyon, in Canis Minor.

dog's-tongue (dôgz′tŭng′, dŏgz′-), n. hound's-tongue.

dog tag, 1. a small disk or strip attached to a dog's harness or collar stating owner, home, etc. **2.** Colloq. one of a pair of metal disks on a neckchain serving to identify men in the armed forces.

dog-tired (dôg′tĬrd′; dŏg′-), adj. very tired.

dog·tooth (dôg′tōōth′, dŏg′-), n., pl. **-teeth** (-tēth′). **1.** a canine tooth. **2.** Archit. a toothlike medieval ornament, or a molding cut in projecting teeth.

dogtooth violet, 1. a bulbous liliaceous plant, Erythronium dens-canis, of Europe, bearing purple flowers. **2.** any of several American plants of the same genus, as E. americanum, bearing yellow flowers, or E. albidum, bearing pinkish-white flowers. Also, **dog's-tooth violet.**

dog·trot (dôg′trŏt′, dŏg′-), n. a gentle trot, like that of a dog.

dog·vane (dôg′vān′,dŏg′-), n. Naut. a small vane, composed of bunting or the like, set on the weather gunwale of a vessel to show the direction of the wind.

dog·watch (dôg′wŏch′, -wôch′, dŏg′-), n. Naut. either of two short watches on shipboard, from 4 to 6 P.M. and from 6 to 8 P.M.

dog·wood (dôg′wŏŏd′, dŏg′-), n. **1.** any tree or shrub of the genus Cornus, esp. C. sanguinea, of Europe, or C. florida (**flowering dogwood**), an American ornamental tree with large white or pinkish flowers, widely planted. **2.** the wood of any such tree.

doiled (doild), adj. Scot. stupid; foolish; crazed.

doi·ly (doi′lĭ), n., pl. **-lies. 1.** a small ornamental napkin used at table at dessert, etc. **2.** any small ornamental mat, as of embroidery or lace. [named after a 17th century draper of London]

do·ing (dōō′ĭng), n. **1.** action; performance; execution. **2.** (pl.) deeds; proceedings.

doit (doit), n. **1.** a small copper coin formerly current among the Dutch. **2.** a bit or jot. [t. D: m. duit]

doit·ed (doi′tĭd, -tĭt), adj. Scot. enfeebled in mind, esp. by age; childish.

do·lab·ri·form (dō·lăb′rə fôrm′), adj. Bot., Zool. shaped like an ax or a cleaver. [f. s. L dolabra pickax, ax + -(I)FORM]

Dolabriform leaf

dol·ce (dōl′chĕ), Music. —adj. **1.** sweet; soft. —n. **2.** an instruction to the performer that the music is to be executed softly and sweetly. **3.** a soft-toned organ stop. [It.: sweet, g. L dulcis]

dol·ce far nien·te (dōl′chĕ fär nyĕn′tĕ), Italian. pleasing inactivity. [It.: lit., sweet doing nothing]

dol·drum (dōl′drəm), n. **1.** a calm, windless area, esp. on the ocean. **2.** a becalmed state. **3.** (pl.) Naut. **a.** the region of relatively calm winds near the equator. **b.** the calms or weather variations characteristic of those parts. **4.** (pl.) dullness; low spirits. [orig. uncert.]

dole[1] (dōl), n., v., doled, doling. —n. **1.** a portion of money, food, etc., given, esp. in charity or for maintenance. **2.** a dealing out or distributing, esp. in charity. **3.** a form of payment to the unemployed instituted by the British government in 1918. **4.** any similar payment by a government to an unemployed person. **5. go or be on the dole**, to receive such payments. **6.** Archaic. one's fate or destiny. —v.t. **7.** to distribute in charity. **8.** to give out sparingly or in small quantities (fol. by out). [ME; OE dāl part, portion. See DEAL[1]]

dole[2] (dōl), n. Archaic. grief or sorrow; lamentation. [ME dol, doel, t. OF, ult. der. L dolēre grieve]

dole·ful (dōl′fəl), adj. full of grief; sorrowful; gloomy. —**dole′ful·ly**, adv. —**dole′ful·ness**, n. —**Syn.** dolorous, mournful, woeful, lugubrious, plaintive, dismal.

dol·er·ite (dŏl′ə rīt′), n. **1.** a coarse-grained variety of basalt. **2.** any of various other igneous rocks, as diabase. **3.** U.S. any igneous rock resembling basalt whose composition cannot be determined without microscopic examination. [t. F, f. s. Gk. dolerós deceptive + -ITE[1]] —**dol·er·it·ic** (dŏl′ə rĭt′ĭk)

dole·some (dōl′səm), adj. Archaic or Dial. doleful.

dol·i·cho·ce·phal·ic (dŏl′ə kō sə făl′ĭk), adj. Cephalom. **1.** long-headed; having a breadth of head small in proportion to the length from front to back (opposed to brachycephalic). **2.** having a cephalic index of 76 and under. Also, **dol·i·cho·ceph·a·lous** (dŏl′ə kō sĕf′ə ləs). [f. Gk. dolichó(s) long + m.s. Gk. kephalē head + -IC] —**dol·i·cho·ceph·a·lism** (dŏl′ə kō sĕf′ə lĭz′əm), n. —**dol′i·cho·ceph′a·ly**, n.

dol·i·cho·cra·nic (dŏl′ə kō krā′nĭk), adj. Craniom. **1.** long-skulled; having a breadth of skull small in proportion to length from front to back (opposed to brachycranic). **2.** having a cranial index of 75 and under.

doll (dŏl), n. **1.** a toy puppet representing a child or other human being; a child's toy baby. **2.** a pretty but expressionless or unintelligent woman. —v.t., v.i. **3.** Slang. to dress in a smart or showy manner (fol. by up). [from Doll, Dolly, for Dorothy, woman's name] —**doll′ish**, adj. —**doll′ish·ly**, adv. —**doll′ish·ness**, n.

dol·lar (dŏl′ər), n. **1.** the monetary unit of the U.S., equivalent to 100 cents. **2.** a gold coin of this value, or a silver coin or a paper note having a corresponding legal value. **3.** a corresponding unit, coin, or note elsewhere, as in Canada, China, etc. **4.** the English name for the German thaler, a large silver coin of varying value, current in various German states from the 16th century. **5.** any of various similar coins, as the Spanish or Mexican peso. **6.** Levant dollar. [earlier daler, t. LG, and early mod. D, c. HG thaler, for Joachimsthaler coin of Joachimsthal, Bohemian city where they were coined]

dol·lar-a-year man (dŏl′ər ə yĭr′), a federal appointee serving for a token salary.

dollar diplomacy, a government policy designed to further the business interests of its citizens in other countries.

dol·lar·fish (dŏl′ər fĭsh′), n., pl. **-fishes**, (esp. collectively) **-fish. 1.** the butterfish. **2.** the moonfish.

Doll·fuss (dōl′fŏŏs), n. Engelbert (ĕng′əl bĕrt′), 1892–1934, Austrian statesman: premier, 1932–34.

dol·lop (dŏl′əp), n. Colloq. a lump; a mass; a large quantity.

doll·y (dŏl′ĭ), n., pl. dollies. **1.** a child's name for a doll. **2.** a low truck with small wheels for moving loads too heavy to be carried by hand. **3.** Mach. a tool for receiving and holding the head of a rivet while the other end is being headed. **4.** Bldg. Trades. an extension piece placed on the head of a pile while being driven. **5.** a small loco-

motive operating on narrow-gage tracks, esp. in quarries, construction sites, etc. **6.** a primitive apparatus for jerking cloths about while washing.

Doll·y Var·den (dŏl′ĭ vär′dən), **1.** a style of gay-flowered print gown. **2.** a broad-brimmed, flower-trimmed hat, formerly worn by women. **3.** a species of trout or charr, Salvelinus malma, ranging from Alaska to California. [named after character in Dickens' "Barnaby Rudge"; applied to fish in allusion to its coloring]

dol·man (dŏl′mən), n., pl. **-mans. 1.** a woman's mantle with capelike arm pieces instead of sleeves. **2.** a long outer robe worn by Turks. [ult. t. Turk.: m. dōlāmān]

dol·men (dŏl′mĕn), n. Archaeol. a structure usually regarded as a tomb, consisting of two or more large upright stones set with a space between and capped by a horizontal stone. Cf. **cromlech.** [t. F, made up by F writers as if from Breton taol, tol table + men stone]

Dolmen

dol·o·mite (dŏl′ə mīt′), n. **1.** a very common mineral, calcium magnesium carbonate, $CaMg(CO_3)_2$, occurring in crystals and in masses (called dolomite marble when coarse-grained). **2.** a rock consisting essentially or largely of this mineral. [named after D. G. de Dolomieu (1750–1801), French geologist] —**dol·o·mit·ic** (dŏl′ə mĭt′ĭk), adj.

Dol·o·mites (dŏl′ə mīts′), n.pl. a mountain range in N Italy: a part of the Alpine system. Highest peak, Marmolada, 11,020 feet. Also, **Dolomite Alps.**

do·lor (dō′lər), n. Now Chiefly Poetic. sorrow or grief. Also, Brit., **do′lour.** [ME doloure, t. OF: m. dolour, g. L dolor pain, grief]

do·lo·ro·so (dō′lô rô′sô), adj. Music. soft and pathetic; plaintive. [It.]

dol·or·ous (dŏl′ər əs, dō′lər-), adj. full of, expressing, or causing pain or sorrow; distressed; grievous; mournful. —**dol′or·ous·ly**, adv. —**dol′or·ous·ness**, n.

dol·phin (dŏl′fĭn), n. **1.** any of various cetaceans of the family Delphinidae, some of which are commonly called porpoises, esp. Delphinus delphis, which has a long, sharp nose and abounds in the Mediterranean and the temperate Atlantic. **2.** a large, thin-bodied ocean fish, Coryphaena hippurus or C. equisetis, notable for its rapid color change on death. **3.** Naut. a post, pile cluster, or buoy to which to moor a vessel. **4.** (cap.) Astron. the northern constellation Delphinus. [ME dalphyne, t. OF: m. daulphin, g. L delphinus, t. Gk.: m.s. delphis. Cf. DAUPHIN]

Dolphin, Delphinus delphis (Ab. 7½ ft. long)

dolphin striker, Naut. a martingale (def. 2).

dolt (dōlt), n. a dull, stupid fellow; a blockhead. —**dolt′ish**, adj. —**dolt′ish·ly**, adv. —**dolt′ish·ness**, n.

-dom, a noun suffix meaning: **1.** domain, as in kingdom. **2.** collection of persons, as in officialdom. **3.** rank or station as in earldom. **4.** general condition, as in freedom. [OE -dōm, suffix, repr. dōm, n. See DOOM]

dom., **1.** domestic. **2.** domain.

do·main (dō mān′), n. **1.** Law. ultimate ownership and control over the use of land. **2.** eminent domain. **3.** a territory under rule or influence; a realm. **4.** a field of action, thought, etc.: the domain of commerce or of science. [t. F: m. domaine, OF demeine (see DEMESNE), g. L dominicum, orig. neut. of dominicus of a lord]

dome (dōm), n., v., domed, doming. —n. **1.** Archit. **a.** a large, hemispherical, approximately hemispherical, or spheroidal vault, its form produced by rotating an arch on its vertical radius. **b.** a roof of domical shape. **c.** a vault or curved roof on a polygonal plan, as an octagonal dome. **2.** Poetic. a large, impressive, or fanciful structure. **3.** anything shaped like a dome. **4.** Crystall. a form whose planes intersect the vertical axis but are parallel to one of the lateral axes. —v.t. **5.** to cover with or as with a dome. **6.** to shape like a dome. —v.i. **7.** to rise or swell as a dome. [t. L: m.s. domus house; partly through F dôme cathedral church, t. It.: m. duomo cupola, dome, t. Pr.: m. doma cupola, t. Gk.: house]

Domes·day Book (dōōmz′dā′), a record of a survey of the lands of England made by order of William the Conqueror about 1086, giving ownership, extent, value, etc., of the properties. Also, **Doomsday Book.**

do·mes·tic (də mĕs′tĭk), adj. **1.** of or pertaining to the home, the household, or household affairs. **2.** devoted to home life or affairs. **3.** living with man; tame: domestic animals. **4.** of or pertaining to one's own or a particular country as apart from other countries. **5.** belonging, existing, or produced within a country; not foreign: domestic trade. —n. **6.** a hired household servant. **7.** (pl.) home manufacturers or goods. [t. L: s. domesticus belonging to the household] —**do·mes′ti·cal·ly**, adv.

do·mes·ti·cate (də mĕs′tə kāt′), v., **-cated, -cating.** —v.t. **1.** to convert to domestic uses; tame. **2.** to attach to home life or affairs. **3.** to cause to be or feel at home; naturalize. —v.i. **4.** to be domestic. —**do·mes′ti·ca′tion**, n. —**do·mes′ti·ca′tor**, n.

do·mes·tic·i·ty (dō′mĕs tĭs′ə tĭ), n., pl. **-ties.** state of being domestic; domestic or home life.

dom·i·cal (dō'mə kəl, dŏm'ə-), *adj.* **1.** domelike. **2.** having a dome or domes. —**dom'i·cal·ly,** *adv.*

dom·i·cile (dŏm'ə səl, -sīl'), *n., v.,* **-ciled, -ciling.** —*n.* Also, **dom'i·cil. 1.** a place of residence; an abode; a house or home. **2.** *Law.* a permanent legal residence. —*v.t.* **3.** to establish in a domicile. —*v.i.* **4.** to have one's domicile; dwell (fol. by *at, in,* etc.). [t. F, t. L: m.s. *domicilium* habitation, dwelling]

dom·i·cil·i·ar·y (dŏm'ə sĭl'ĭ ĕr'ĭ), *adj.* of or pertaining to a domicile.

dom·i·cil·i·ate (dŏm'ə sĭl'ĭ āt'), *v.t., v.i.,* **-ated, -ating.** domicile. —**dom'i·cil'i·a'tion,** *n.*

dom·i·nance (dŏm'ə nəns), *n.* **1.** rule; control; authority; ascendancy. **2.** the condition of being dominant. Also, **dom'i·nan·cy.**

dom·i·nant (dŏm'ə nənt), *adj.* **1.** ruling; governing; controlling; most influential. **2.** occupying a commanding position: *the dominant points of the globe.* **3.** *Genetics.* pertaining to or exhibiting a dominant, as opposed to a recessive. **4.** *Music.* pertaining to or based on the dominant: *the dominant chord.* —*n.* **5.** *Genetics.* a hereditary character resulting from a gene with a greater biochemical activity than another, termed the recessive. The dominant masks the recessive. **6.** *Music.* the fifth tone of a scale. [t. F, t. L: s. *dominans,* ppr.] —**dom'i·nant·ly,** *adv.*
—**Syn. 1.** prevailing, principal. DOMINANT, PREDOMINANT, PARAMOUNT, PREEMINENT describe something outstanding. DOMINANT describes that which is most influential or important: *the dominant characteristics of monkeys.* PREDOMINANT describes that which is dominant over all others, or is more widely prevalent: *curiosity is the predominant characteristic of monkeys.* PARAMOUNT applies to that which is first in rank or order: *safety is of paramount importance.* PREEMINENT applies to a prominence based on recognition of excellence: *his work was of preëminent quality.*

dominant tenement, *Law.* land in favor of which an easement or other servitude exists over another's land (the **servient tenement**). Also, **dominant estate.**

dom·i·nate (dŏm'ə nāt'), *v.,* **-nated, -nating.** —*v.t.* **1.** to rule over; govern; control. **2.** to tower above; overshadow. —*v.i.* **3.** to rule; exercise control; predominate. **4.** to occupy a commanding position. [t. L: m.s. *dominātus,* pp.] —**dom'i·na'tor,** *n.*

dom·i·na·tion (dŏm'ə nā'shən), *n.* **1.** act of dominating. **2.** rule or sway, often arbitrary. **3.** (*pl.*) an order of angels. See **angel.**

dom·i·na·tive (dŏm'ə nā'tĭv), *adj.* dominating; controlling.

dom·i·ne (dŏm'ə nĭ, dō'mə-), *n. Obs.* lord; master (used as a title of address). [vocative of L *dominus* master]

dom·i·ne, di·ri·ge nos (dŏm'ĭ nĭ, dĭr'ĭ jĭ nōs'), *Lat-in.* Master, guide us (motto of the City of London).

dom·i·neer (dŏm'ə nĭr'), *v.i., v.t.* **1.** to rule arbitrarily or despotically; tyrannize. **2.** to tower (over or above). [t. D: m.s. *domineren,* t. F: m. *dominer,* t. L: m. *dominārī* rule]

dom·i·neer·ing (dŏm'ə nĭr'ĭng), *adj.* inclined to domineer; overbearing; tyrannical. —**dom'i·neer'-ing·ly,** *adv.* —**dom'i·neer'ing·ness,** *n.*

Dom·i·nic (dŏm'ə nĭk), *n.* Saint, 1170–1221, Spanish priest: founder of the Dominican order.

Dom·i·ni·ca (dŏm'ə nē'kə, də mĭn'ə kə), *n.* an island in the British West Indies: a colony in the Windward Islands group. 54,500 pop. (est. 1944); 305 sq. mi. *Cap.:* Roseau.

do·min·i·cal (də mĭn'ə kəl), *adj.* **1.** of or pertaining to Jesus Christ as Lord. **2.** of or pertaining to the Lord's Day, or Sunday. [t. ML: s. *dominicālis* of or pertaining to the Lord or the Lord's Day (ML *dominica*), der. L *dominicus* belonging to a lord or (LL) the Lord]

dominical letter, that one of the seven letters *A* to *G* which is used in calendars to mark the Sundays throughout a particular year, and serving primarily to aid in determining the date of Easter.

Do·min·i·can (də mĭn'ə kən), *adj.* **1.** of or pertaining to St. Dominic (1170–1221), or to the mendicant religious order founded by him. **2.** of or pertaining to the Dominican Republic. —*n.* **3.** a member of the order of St. Dominic; a black friar. **4.** a native or inhabitant of the Dominican Republic. [t. Eccl. L: s. *Dominicānus,* der. *Dominicus,* Latin form of the name of Domingo de Guzmán, founder of the order]

Dominican Republic, a republic in the West Indies, occupying the E part of the island of Hispaniola. 2,059,113 pop. (est. 1946); 19,129 sq. mi. *Cap.:* Ciudad Trujillo. Also, **Santo Domingo.**

dom·i·nie (dŏm'ə nĭ, dō'mə-), *n.* **1.** *Chiefly Scot.* a schoolmaster. **2.** a clergyman, pastor, or parson (a title used specifically in the Reformed Church in America). [t. L: m. *domine,* vocative of *dominus* master, lord]

do·min·ion (də mĭn'yən), *n.* **1.** the power or right of governing and controlling; sovereign authority. **2.** rule or sway. **3.** control or influence. **4.** a territory, usually of considerable size, in which a single rulership holds sway. **5.** lands or domains subject to sovereignty or control. **6.** *Govt.* a territory constituting a self-governing commonwealth and being one of a number of such territories united in a community of nations, or empire (a term applied to self-governing divisions of the British Empire, as Canada, New Zealand, etc.). **7. the Dominion,** Canada. **8.** (*pl.*) *Theol.* dominations (def. 3). [ME, t. F (obs.), der. L *dominium* lordship, ownership]

Dominion Day, (in Canada) a legal holiday, July 1, celebrating the formation of the Dominion on July 1, 1867.

do·min·i·um (də mĭn'ĭ əm), *n. Law.* complete power to use, to enjoy, and to dispose of property at will. [t. L. See DOMINION]

dom·i·no¹ (dŏm'ə nō'), *n., pl.* **-noes, -nos. 1.** a large, loose cloak, usually hooded, worn with a small mask by persons in masquerade. **2.** the mask. **3.** a person wearing such dress. [t. Sp., t. L, dative of *dominus* master]

dom·i·no² (dŏm'ə nō'), *n., pl.* **-noes. 1.** (*pl. construed as sing.*) any of various games played with flat, oblong pieces of ivory, bone, or wood, the face of which is divided into two parts, each left blank or marked with pips, usually from one to six. **2.** one of these pieces. [orig. unknown]

Do·mi·nus vo·bis·cum (dŏm'ĭ nəs vō bĭs'kəm), *Lat-in.* the Lord (be or is) with you.

Do·mi·tian (də mĭsh'ən, -ĭ ən), *n.* A.D. 51–96, Roman emperor, A.D. 81–96.

Dom·re·my-la-Pu·celle (dôn rə mē' là py sĕl'), *n.* a village in NE France: birthplace of Joan of Arc. Also, **Dom·re·my'.**

don¹ (dŏn), *n.* **1.** (*cap.*). Mr., Sir (a Spanish title prefixed to a man's Christian name). **2.** a Spanish lord or gentleman. **3.** a person of great importance. **4.** *Colloq.* (in the English universities) a head, a fellow, or tutor of a college. [t. Sp., g. L *dominus* master, lord]

don² (dŏn), *v.t.,* **donned, donning.** to put on (clothing, etc.). [contr. of *do on.* Cf. DOFF]

Don (dŏn; *also for 1, Russ.* dôn), *n.* **1.** a river flowing from the central Soviet Union in Europe S through a wide arc to the Sea of Azov. ab. 1300 mi. **2.** a river in NE Scotland, in Aberdeen county, flowing E to the North Sea. 82 mi. **3.** a river in central England, in S Yorkshire, flowing NE to the Humber estuary. 60 mi.

do·na (dō'nə), *n.* Portuguese form of **doña.**

do·ña (dō'nyä), *n.* (in Spanish use) **1.** a lady. **2.** (*cap.*) a title of respect for a lady. [Sp., g. L *domina* lady, mistress. See DON¹]

Do·nar (dō'när), *n. German Myth.* the god of thunder. [OHG, c. OE *thunor,* Icel. *Thōr*]

do·nate (dō'nāt), *v.t.,* **-nated, -nating.** *Chiefly U.S.* to present as a gift; make a gift or donation of, as to a fund or cause. [t. L: m.s. *dōnātus,* pp.] —**do'na·tor,** *n.*

Don·a·tel·lo (dŏn'ə tĕl'ō; *It.* dō'nä tĕl'lō), *n.* c1386–1466, Italian sculptor. Also, **Do·na·to** (dō nä'tō).

do·na·tion (dō nā'shən), *n.* **1.** act of presenting something as a gift. **2.** a gift, as to a fund; a contribution. —**Syn. 2.** See present².

Don·a·tist (dŏn'ə tĭst), *n.* one of a Christian sect which arose in northern Africa in the year 311, and which maintained that it constituted the whole and only true church and that the baptisms and ordinations of the orthodox clergy were invalid. —**Don'a·tism,** *n.*

don·a·tive (dŏn'ə tĭv, dō'nə-), *n.* a gift or donation; a largess. [t. L: m.s. *dōnātivum* gift, prop. neut. of *dōnātivus,* adj.]

Do·na·tus (dō nā'təs), *n.* fl. A.D. c315, bishop of Casae Nigrae in Numidia and leader of a heretical group of African Christians.

Do·nau (dō'nou), *n.* German name of the **Danube.**

Don·cas·ter (dŏng'kăs tər; *Brit.* -kəs tər), *n.* a city in central England, in S Yorkshire. 75,690 (est. 1946).

done (dŭn), *v.* **1.** pp. of do¹. —*adj.* **2.** executed; completed; finished; settled. **3.** cooked. **4.** worn out; used up. **5.** *Chiefly Brit.* in conformity with fashion and good taste: *it isn't done.*

do·nee (dō nē'), *n. Law.* **1.** one to whom a gift is made. **2.** one who has a power of appointment in property. [f. DON(OR) + -EE]

Don·e·gal (dŏn'ĭ gôl', dŏn'ĭ gôl'), *n.* a county in N Eire, in Ulster. 136,035 pop. (est. 1943); 1865 sq. mi. *Co. Seat:* Lifford.

Don·el·son (dŏn'əl sən), *n.* Fort, a Confederate fort in NW Tennessee, on the Cumberland river: captured by Union forces, 1862.

Do·nets (dō nĕts'), *n.* **1.** a river in the SW Soviet Union, flowing SE to the Don river. ab. 660 mi. **2.** Also, **Donets Basin.** an area S of this river, in the E Ukrainian Republic: important coal mining region and recently developed industrial area. 9650 sq. mi.

Don·go·la (dŏng'gə lə), *n.* a province in the N Anglo-Egyptian Sudan. ab. 124,000 sq. mi. *Cap.:* Merowe.

Don·i·zet·ti (dŏn'ə zĕt'ĭ; *It.* dō'nē dzĕt'tē), *n.* **Gae-tano** (gä'ĕ tä'nō), 1797–1848, Italian operatic composer.

don·jon (dŭn'jən, dŏn'-), *n.* the inner tower, keep, or stronghold of a castle. [archaic var. of DUNGEON]

Don Ju·an (dŏn jōō'ən; *also for 1, 2, Sp.* dôn hwän'), **1.** a legendary Spanish nobleman of dissolute life. **2.** a libertine or rake. **3.** an incomplete romantic satirical poem (1819–24) by Byron.

don·key (dŏng'kĭ; *less often* dŭng'-), *n., pl.* **-keys. 1.** the ass. **2.** a stupid, silly, or obstinate person. [? familiar var. of *Duncan,* man's name.]

donkey engine, a small, usually subsidiary, steam engine.

donkey's years, *Brit. Colloq.* a long time; a coon's age: *I haven't seen him for donkey's years.*

don·na (dŏn'ə; *It.* dōn'nä), *n.* **1.** (in Italian use) a lady. **2.** (*cap.*) a title of respect for a lady. [It., g. L *domina* lady, mistress. See DON¹]

don·nard (dŏn′ərd), *adj. Chiefly Scot.* stunned; dazed. Also, **don·nered** (dŏn′ərd). [also *donnered*, f. Scot. v. *donner* stupefy (e. g., with a blow or loud noise) + -ED²]

Donne (dŭn), *n.* **John**, 1573–1631, British poet and clergyman.

don·nish (dŏn′ish), *adj.* resembling, or characteristic of, an English university don. **—don′nish·ness,** *n.*

Don·ny·brook Fair (dŏn′ĭ brŏŏk′), **1.** a fair which until 1855 was held annually at Donnybrook, County Dublin, Ireland, and which was famous for rioting and dissipation. **2.** any debauched or riotous occasion.

do·nor (dō′nər), *n.* **1.** one who gives or donates. **2.** *Med.* a person or animal furnishing blood for transfusion. **3.** *Law.* one who gives property by gift, legacy, or devise, or who confers a power of appointment. [ME *donour,* t. AF, der. *doner* give, g. L *dōnāre*]

Don Quix·ote (dŏn kwĭk′sət; *Sp.* dōn kē hō′tĕ), *Spanish.* **1.** the hero of Cervantes' romance who was inspired by lofty and chivalrous but impractical ideals. **2.** the romance itself (1605 and 1615).

don·sie (dŏn′sĭ), *adj. Scot.* unlucky. Also, **don′sy.**

don't (dōnt), *v.* contraction of *do not.*

don·zel (dŏn′zəl), *n. Archaic.* a young gentleman not yet knighted; a squire; a page. [t. It.: m. *donzello,* t. Pr.: m. *donsel,* g. LL *domnicellus,* dim. of L *dominus* master]

doo·dad (dōō′dăd), *n. Colloq.* any trifling ornament or bit of decorative finery.

doo·dle (dōō′dəl), *v.t., v.i.,* **-dled, -dling.** to draw or scribble idly.

doo·dle·bug¹ (dōō′dəl bŭg′), *n. Local U.S.* an ant lion larva. [f. *doodle* simpleton (cf. LG *dudeltopf*) + BUG]

doo·dle·bug² (dōō′dəl bŭg′), *n.* **1.** a divining rod or similar device supposedly useful in locating water, oil, minerals, etc., underground. **2.** *Brit. Colloq.* a buzz bomb. [appar. special uses of DOODLEBUG¹]

Doo·lit·tle (dōō′lĭt′əl), *n.* **Hilda,** ("H.D.") born 1886, U.S. poet.

doo·ly (dōō′lĭ), *n., pl.* **-lies.** a kind of litter used in India. Also, **doo′lie.** [t. Hind.: m. *dōlī* litter]

doom (dōōm), *n.* **1.** fate or destiny, esp. adverse fate. **2.** ruin; death. **3.** a judgment, decision, or sentence, esp. an unfavorable one. **4.** the Last Judgment, at the end of the world. **—v.t. 5.** to destine, esp. to an adverse fate. **6.** to pronounce judgment against; condemn. **7.** to ordain or fix as a sentence or fate. [ME *dome,* OE *dōm* judgment, sentence, law, authority, c. OHG *tuom,* Icel. *dōmr,* Goth. *dōms,* orig., that which is put or set; akin to DO, v., -DOM, suffix] **—Syn. 1.** See **fate.**

dooms (dōōmz), *adv. Scot. and N. Eng.* very; extremely.

dooms·day (dōōmz′dā′), *n.* **1.** the day of the Last Judgment, at the end of the world. **2.** any day of sentence or condemnation. [ME *domes dai,* OE *dōmes dæg* day of judgment]

Doomsday Book, Domesday Book.

Doon (dōōn), *n.* a river in SW Scotland, in Ayr county, flowing NW to the Firth of Clyde. ab. 30 mi.

door (dōr), *n.* **1.** a movable barrier of wood or other material, commonly turning on hinges or sliding in a groove, for closing and opening a passage or opening into a building, room, cupboard, etc. **2.** a doorway. **3.** the building, etc., to which a door belongs: *two doors down the street.* **4.** any means of approach or access, or of exit. [ME *dore,* OE *duru.* Cf. G *tür,* Icel. *dyrr,* also OE *dor* gate, c. G *tor;* akin to L *foris,* Gk. *thýra*]

door·bell (dōr′bĕl′), *n.* a bell at a door or connected with a door, rung by persons outside seeking admittance.

door·jamb (dōr′jăm′), *n.* a side or vertical piece of a door supporting the lintel.

door·keep·er (dōr′kē′pər), *n.* **1.** one who keeps or guards a door or entrance. **2.** *Brit.* janitor.

door·knob (dōr′nŏb′), *n.* the handle for opening a door.

door·man (dōr′măn′, -mən), *n., pl.* **-men** (-mĕn′, -mən). the door attendant of an apartment house, night club, etc., who performs minor duties for entering and departing guests.

Doorn (dōrn), *n.* a village in central Netherlands, SE of Utrecht: the residence of Wilhelm II of Germany after his abdication.

door·nail (dōr′nāl′), *n.* **1.** a large-headed nail formerly used for strengthening or ornamenting doors. **2. dead as a doornail,** dead beyond any doubt.

door·plate (dōr′plāt′), *n.* a plate on the door of a house or room, bearing a name, number, or the like.

door·post (dōr′pōst′), *n.* the jamb or upright sidepiece of a doorway.

door·sill (dōr′sĭl′), *n.* the sill of a doorway.

door·step (dōr′stĕp′), *n.* a step at a door, raised above the level of the ground outside; one of a series of steps leading from the ground to a door.

door·way (dōr′wā′), *n.* the passage or opening into a building, room, etc., closed and opened by a door.

door·yard (dōr′yärd′), *n.* a yard about the door of a house.

dope (dōp), *n., v.,* **doped, doping. —n. 1.** any thick liquid or pasty preparation, as a sauce, lubricant, etc. **2.** an absorbent material used to absorb and hold a liquid, as in the manufacture of dynamite. **3.** *Aeron.* **a.** any of various varnishlike products for coating the cloth fabric of airplane wings or the like, in order to make it waterproof, stronger, etc. **b.** a similar product used to coat the fabric of a balloon to reduce gas leak-

age. **4.** *Slang.* the molasseslike preparation of opium used for smoking. **5.** *Slang.* any stupefying drug. **6.** *Slang.* a person under the influence, or addicted to the use, of drugs. **7.** *Slang.* a stimulating drug, as one wrongfully given to a race horse to induce greater speed. **8.** *Slang.* information or data. **9.** *U.S. Slang.* a stupid person. **—v.t. 10.** *Slang.* to affect with dope or drugs. **11. dope out,** *Slang.* **a.** to work or make by calculation, inference, etc.: *to dope out a plan.* **b.** to deduce from information: *to dope out a story.* [t. D: m. *doop* a dipping, sauce, der. *dopen* dip, baptize. See DIP] **—dop′er,** *n.*

dope fiend, *Slang.* a person addicted to drugs.

dope·y (dō′pĭ), *adj.,* **dopier, dopiest.** *Slang.* affected by or as by a stupefying drug. Also, **dop′y.**

Dop·pel·gäng·er (dŏp′əl gĕng′ər), apparitional double or counterpart of a living person. Also, **doubleganger.** [G: double-goer. Cf. D *dubbelganger*]

Dop·pler effect (dŏp′lər), *Physics.* the apparent change in frequency and wave length of a train of sound or light waves if the distance between the source and the receiver is changing.

dor¹ (dōr), *n.* a common European dung beetle, *Geotrupes stercorarius.* Also, **dorr, dor·bee·tle** (dōr′bē′təl), **dorrbeetle.** [ME *dorre,* OE *dora*]

dor² (dōr), *n. Obs.* scoff; mockery. [cf. Icel. *dār* scoff]

Dor·cas (dōr′kəs), *n.* a Christian woman at Joppa who made clothing for the poor. Acts 9:36–41.

Dorcas society, a society of women of a church whose work it is to provide clothing for the poor.

Dor·ches·ter (dōr′chĕs′tər, -chĭs-), *n.* a town in S England: the county seat of Dorsetshire; named *Casterbridge* in Thomas Hardy's novels. 12,080 (1939).

Dor·dogne (dōr dōn′y), *n.* a river in SW France, flowing W to the Gironde estuary. ab. 300 mi.

Dor·drecht (dōr′drĕkʜt), *n.* a city in SW Netherlands, on the Waal. 65,962 (est. 1946). Also, **Dort.**

Dore (dōr), *n.* **Monts** (môN), a group of mountains in central France. Highest peak, 6188 ft.

Do·ré (dô rā′), *n.* **Paul Gustave** (pōl gŭs tȧv′), 1832?–83, French illustrator and artist.

do·ré (dô rā′), *n. Canadian Dial.* the walleye or pike perch of North America.

Do·ri·an (dōr′ĭ ən), *adj.* **1.** of or pertaining to Doris, a division of ancient Greece, or the race named from it, one of the principal divisions of the ancient Greeks. **—n. 2.** a Dorian Greek. [f. s. L *Dōrius* (t. Gk: m. *Dōrios* Dorian) + -AN]

Dor·ic (dōr′ĭk, dŏr′-), *adj.* **1.** of or pertaining to Doris, its inhabitants, or their dialect. **2.** rustic, as a dialect. **3.** *Archit.* noting or pertaining to the simplest of the three Greek orders, distinguished by low proportions, shaft without base, saucer-shaped capital (echinus) and frieze of metopes and triglyphs. See illus. under **order.** **—n. 4.** a dialect of ancient Greek. [t. L: s. *Dōricus,* t. Gk.: m. *Dōrikós*]

Do·ris (dōr′ĭs), *n.* an ancient region in central Greece.

Dor·king (dōr′kĭng), *n.* a breed of domestic fowls characterized by a long, low, full body and having five toes on each foot, esp. valued for the table. [named after *Dorking,* town in Surrey, southeastern England]

dorm (dōrm), *n. Colloq.* a dormitory.

dor·man·cy (dōr′mən sĭ), *n.* state of being dormant.

dor·mant (dōr′mənt), *adj.* **1.** lying asleep or as if asleep; inactive as in sleep; torpid. **2.** in a state of rest or inactivity; quiescent; inoperative; in abeyance. **3.** (of a volcano) not erupting. **4.** *Bot.* temporarily inactive: *dormant buds, dormant seeds.* **5.** *Her.* (of an animal) lying down with its head on its fore paws, as if asleep. [ME, t. OF, ppr. of *dormir,* g. L *dormīre* sleep, be inactive] **—Syn. 1.** See **inactive.**

dor·mer (dōr′mər), *n.* **1.** Also, **dormer window.** a vertical window in a projection built out from a sloping roof. **2.** the whole projecting structure. [orig., a sleeping chamber; t. OF: m. *dormeor,* g. L *dormūtōrium* DORMITORY]

dor·mered (dōr′mərd), *adj.* having dormer windows.

dor·mi·ent (dōr′mĭ ənt), *adj.* sleeping; dormant. [t. L: s. *dormiens,* ppr.]

dor·mi·to·ry (dōr′mə tōr′ĭ), *n., pl.* **-ries. 1.** *U.S.* a building containing a number of sleeping rooms. **2.** *Brit.* a sleeping apartment containing a number of beds. [t. L: m.s. *dormūtōrium,* prop. neut. of *dormūtōrius* or *dormītōrius*]

Dormer (def. 1)

dor·mouse (dōr′mous′), *n., pl.* **-mice** (-mīs′). any of the small, furry-tailed Old World rodents which constitute the family *Gliridae,* resembling small squirrels in appearance and habits. [? f. DOR(MANT) + MOUSE]

dor·my (dōr′mĭ), *adj. Golf.* (of a player or side) being in the lead by as many holes as are still to be played.

dor·nick (dōr′nĭk), *n. Obs.* a stout linen cloth, esp. a damask linen. Also, **dor·nock** (dōr′nək).

dorp (dōrp), *n.* a village; a hamlet. [t. D. See THORP]

Dor·pat (dōr′păt), *n.* German name of **Tartu.**

Dormouse,
Muscardinus avellanarius
(Total length 5½ to 6 in.)

dorr (dôr), *n.* dor[1]. Also, **dorr·bee·tle** (dôr′bē′tǝl).

dor·sal[1] (dôr′sǝl), *adj.* **1.** *Zool.* of, pertaining to, or situated on the back, as of an organ or part: *dorsal nerves.* **2.** *Bot.* pertaining to the surface away from the axis, as of a leaf; abaxial. [t. ML: s. *dorsālis,* der. L *dorsum* back] —**dor′sal·ly,** *adv.*

dor·sal[2] (dôr′sǝl), *n.* dossal.

dorsal fin, the fin or finlike integumentary expansion generally developed on the back of aquatic vertebrates.

Dor·set (dôr′sǐt), *n.* **1. Thomas Sackville, 1st Earl of** 1536–1608, British statesman and poet. **2.** Dorset-shire.

Dorset Horn, an English breed of a large-horned sheep bearing medium-length wool of close texture. [named after DORSETSHIRE.]

Dor·set·shire (dôr′sǐt shîr′, -shǝr), *n.* a county in S England. 260,000 pop. (est. 1946); 973 sq. mi. *Co. seat:* Dorchester. Also, **Dorset.**

dorsi-, a combining form of **dorsal, dorsum,** as in *dorsiferous.* Also, **dorso-.**

dor·sif·er·ous (dôr sĭf′ǝr ǝs), *adj. Bot.* borne on the back, as the sori on most ferns.

dor·si·ven·tral (dôr′sǐ vĕn′trǝl), *adj.* **1.** *Bot.* having distinct dorsal and ventral sides, as most foliage leaves. **2.** *Zool.* dorsoventral.

dor·so·ven·tral (dôr′sō vĕn′trǝl), *adj.* **1.** *Zool.* per-taining to the dorsal and ventral aspects of the body; extending from the dorsal to the ventral side: *the dorso-ventral axis.* **2.** *Bot.* dorsiventral.

dor·sum (dôr′sǝm), *n., pl.* **-sa** (-sǝ). *Anat., Zool.* **1.** the back, as of the body. **2.** the back or outer surface of an organ, part, etc. [t. L]

Dort (dôrt), *n.* Dordrecht.

Dort·mund (dôrt′mǝnd; *Ger.* dôrt′mŏŏnt), *n.* a city in W Germany. 542,261 (1939).

dort·y (dôr′tĭ), *adj. Scot.* sullen; sulky.

do·ry[1] (dōr′ĭ), *n., pl.* **-ries.** a boat with a narrow, flat bottom, high ends, and flaring sides. [first used in W Indies; native Central Amer. name for a dugout]

do·ry[2] (dōr′ĭ), *n., pl.* **-ries. 1.** a flattened, deep-bodied, spiny-rayed, marine food fish, *Zeus faber* (the John Dory), found both in European and in Australian seas. **2.** any of several related species. [ME *dore,* t. F: m. *dorée,* lit., gilded]

dos-à-dos (dō zá dō′; *n. in U.S. country dancing usu-ally,* dō′sē dō′), *adv., n., pl.* **-dos** (-dōz′; *Fr.* -dō′). —*adv.* **1.** back to back. —*n.* **2.** *Dancing.* an evolution in reels, etc., in which two persons advance, pass around each other back to back, and return to their places. [F]

dos·age (dō′sǐj), *n.* **1.** the administration of medicine in doses. **2.** the amount of a medicine to be given. **3.** the sugar syrup added to champagne to produce sec-ondary fermentation or to sweeten it.

dose (dōs), *n., v.,* **dosed, dosing.** —*n.* **1.** a quantity of medicine prescribed to be taken at one time. **2.** a defi-nite quantity of anything analogous to medicine, esp. of something nauseous or disagreeable. —*v.t.* **3.** to ad-minister in or apportion for doses. **4.** to give doses to. [t. F, t. ML: m.s. *dosis,* t. Gk.: giving, portion, dose]

do·sim·e·ter (dō sǐm′ǝ tǝr), *n.* an apparatus for meas-uring minute quantities of liquid; a drop meter. [f. Gk. *dósi(s)* DOSE + -METER]

do·sim·e·try (dō sǐm′ǝ trĭ), *n.* the measurement of the doses of medicines. —**do·si·met·ric** (dō′sǝ mĕt′rĭk), *adj.*

Dos Pas·sos (dōs päs′ōs), **John Roderigo** (rŏd rē′gō), born 1896, U.S. novelist and playwright.

doss (dŏs), *n. Brit. Slang.* **1.** a place to sleep, esp. in a cheap lodging house. **2.** sleep. [prob. t. F: m. *dos* back, through LL, g. L *dorsum*]

dos·sal (dŏs′ǝl), *n.* **1.** Also, **dorsal.** *Eccles.* an orna-mental hanging placed at the back of an altar or at the sides of the chancel. **2.** *Archaic.* dosser. Also, **dos′sel.** [t. ML: s. *dossālis* for *dorsālis,* L *dorsuālis* of the back]

dos·ser (dŏs′ǝr), *n.* **1.** a basket for carrying objects on the back; a pannier. **2.** an ornamental covering for the back of a seat, esp. a throne, etc. **3.** a hanging some-times richly embroidered for the walls of a hall, or the back or sides of a chancel. [ME *doser,* t. OF: m. *dossier,* der. *dos* back, g. L *dorsum*]

dos·si·er (dŏs′ĭ ā′, -ĭ ǝr; *Fr.* dô syě′), *n.* a bundle of documents all relating to the same matter or subject. [t. F. See DOSSER]

dost (dŭst), *v.* (now only in poetic or solemn use) 2nd pers. sing. pres. ind. of **do**[1].

Dos·to·ev·ski (dŏs′tǝ yĕf′skĭ; *Russ.* dŏ stŏ′-), *n.* **Feo-dor Mikhailovich** (fyô′dôr mĭ hī′lō vĭch), 1821–81, Russian novelist and short-story writer.

dot[1] (dŏt), *n., v.,* **dotted, dotting.** —*n.* **1** a minute or small spot on a surface; a speck. **2.** a small, roundish mark made with or as with a pen. **3.** anything relatively small or specklike. **4.** *Music.* **a.** a point placed after a note or rest, to indicate that the duration of the note or rest is to be increased one half. A double dot further in-creases the duration by one half the value of the single dot. **b.** a point placed under a note to indicate that it is to be played staccato, i.e., shortened. **5.** *Telegraphy.* a signal of shorter duration than a dash, used in groups of dots, dashes, and spaces, to represent letters in a Morse or a similar code. —*v.t.* **6.** to mark with or as with a dot or dots. **7.** to stud or diversify, as dots do. **8.** to place like dots. —*v.i.* **9.** to make a dot or dots. [OE *dott* head of a boil. Cf. D *dot* kind of knot] —**dot′ter,** *n.*

dot[2] (dŏt; *Fr.* dôt), *n. Mod. Civil Law.* dowry. [t. F, t. L: s. *dōs*] —**do·tal** (dō′tǝl), *adj.*

dot·age (dō′tǐj), *n.* **1.** feebleness of mind, esp. result-ing from old age; senility. **2.** excessive fondness; foolish affection. [f. DOTE, v. + -AGE]

do·tard (dō′tǝrd), *n.* one who is weak-minded, esp. from old age.

do·ta·tion (dō tā′shǝn), *n.* endowment.

dote (dōt), *v.i.,* **doted, doting. 1.** to bestow excessive love or fondness (fol. by *on* or *upon*). **2.** to be weak-minded, esp. from old age. Also, **doat.** [ME *doten,* c. MD *doten.* Cf. D *dutten* doze, dote, Icel. *dotta* nod from sleep, MHG *totzen* take a nap] —**dot′er,** *n.*

doth (dŭth), *v.* (now only in poetic or solemn use) 3rd per. sing. pres. ind. of **do**[1].

dot·ing (dō′tĭng), *adj.* **1.** extravagantly fond. **2.** weak-minded, esp. from old age. —**dot′ing·ly,** *adv.*

dot·ter·el (dŏt′ǝrǝl), *n.* **1.** a plover, *Eudromias mori-nellus,* of Europe and Asia, which allows itself to be ap-proached and readily taken. **2.** *Dial.* a dotard or silly fellow. Also, **dot·trel** (dŏt′rǝl). [f. DOTE + -REL]

dot·tle (dŏt′ǝl), *n.* the plug of half-smoked tobacco in the bottom of a pipe after smoking. Also, **dot′tel.**

dot·ty (dŏt′ĭ), *adj.,* **-tier, -tiest. 1.** *Chiefly Brit. Colloq.* crazy. **2.** *Colloq. or Dial.* feeble or unsteady in gait. **3.** marked with dots; placed like dots. [f. DOT, n.[1] + -Y[1]]

Dou (dou), *n.* **Gerard** (gā′rärt), 1613–75, Dutch painter. Also, **Dow.**

Dou·ai (dōō ā′; *Fr.* dwě), *n.* a city in N France. 37,258 (1946). Also, **Dou·ay′.**

Dou·a·la (dōō ä′lä), *n.* a seaport in Cameroun. 42,730 (1936).

Dou·ay Bible (dōō′ā), an English translation of the Bible, from the Latin Vulgate, prepared by Roman Cath-olic scholars, the Old Testament being published at Douay (Douai) in France, in 1609–10, and the New Testament at Rheims, in 1582. Also, **Douay Version.**

dou·ble (dŭb′ǝl), *adj., n., v.,* **-bled, -bling,** *adv.* —*adj.* **1.** twice as great, heavy, strong, etc.: *double pay, a double portion.* **2.** twofold in form, size, amount, ex-tent, etc.; of extra size, weight: *double blanket.* **3.** com-posed of two like parts or members; paired: *a double cherry.* **4.** *Bot.* (of flowers) having the number of petals largely increased. **5.** (of musical instruments) produc-ing a tone an octave lower than the notes indicate. **6.** twofold in character, meaning, or conduct; ambigu-ous: *a double interpretation.* **7.** deceitful; hypocritical; insincere. **8.** duple, as time or rhythm. —*n.* **9.** a twofold size or amount; twice as much. **10.** a duplicate; a counterpart. **11.** a fold or plait. **12.** a sud-den backward turn or bend. **13.** a shift or artifice. **14.** *Eccles.* one of the more important feasts of the year; so called because the antiphon is doubled, i.e., sung in full before each psalm as well as after (save for Little Hours). **15.** a substitute actor or singer ready to take another's place. **16.** *Motion Pictures.* a substitute who performs feats too hazardous or too difficult technically for a star to do. **17.** *Music. Rare.* a variation. **18.** *Mil.* double time. **19.** *Baseball.* a two-base hit. **20.** a game in which there are two players on each side. **21.** (in bridge or other card games) a challenge by an opponent that declarer cannot fulfill his contract, increasing the points to be won or lost. **22.** *Bridge.* **a.** a conventional bid informing partner that a player's hand is of certain strength. **b.** a hand which warrants such a challenge. —*v.t.* **23.** to make double or twice as great: *to double a sum, size, etc.* **24.** to be or have twice as much as. **25.** to bend or fold with one part upon another (often fol. by *over, up, back,* etc.). **26.** to clench (the fist). **27.** to sail or go round: *to double Cape Horn.* **28.** to couple; associate. **29.** *Music.* to reduplicate by means of a tone in another part, either at the unison or at an oc-tave above or below. **30.** *Bridge.* **a.** to increase (the points) to be won or lost on a declaration. **b.** to make increased, as a bid. —*v.i.* **31.** to become double. **32.** to bend or fold (often fol. by *up*). **33.** to turn back on a course (often fol. by *back*). **34.** to share quarters, etc. (fol. by *up*). **35.** *Mil.* to march at the double-time pace. **36.** to serve in two ca-pacities as: **a.** *Theat.* to play two stage roles in a small company. **b.** *Music.* to play two instruments in a band. **37.** *Bridge.* to become increased, as a bid. —*adv.* **38.** twofold; doubly. [ME, t. OF: m. *duble,* g. L *duplus*] —**dou′ble·ness,** *n.* —**dou′bler,** *n.*

dou·ble-act·ing (dŭb′ǝl ăk′tĭng), *adj.* (of any recip-rocating machine or implement) acting effectively in both directions (distinguished from *single-acting*).

double bar, *Music.* a double vertical line on a staff indicating the conclusion of a piece of music or a subdi-vision of it. See illus. under **bar.**

dou·ble-bar·reled (dŭb′ǝl băr′ǝld), *adj.* **1.** having two barrels, as a gun. **2.** serving a double purpose.

double bass, *Music.* **1.** Also, **double-bass viol.** the largest instrument of the violin family, now usually hav-ing 4 strings (sometimes 3), played resting vertically on the floor; the violone. **2.** contrabass.

double bassoon, *Music.* a bassoon an octave lower in pitch than the ordinary bassoon: the largest and deepest-toned instrument of the oboe class.

double boiler, a pair of interlocking pans, the bot-tom one containing water which while boiling gently heats the food in the upper pan.

dou·ble-breast·ed (dŭb/əl brĕs/tĭd), *adj.* (of a garment) overlapping sufficiently to form two thicknesses of considerable width on the breast, in men's clothes often with both buttonholes and buttons on each half of the front, to permit of buttoning on either side. See **single-breasted.**

double chin, a fold of fat beneath the chin.

double cloth, a fabric woven of two sets of yarns as double-faced coating or Jacquard blanket.

double cross, 1. *Slang.* an act of treachery; betrayal. 2. *Slang.* a proving treacherous to a person with reference to some dishonest arrangement made with him, as concerning the outcome of a contest. 3. *Genetics.* the first generation hybrid between two single crosses of inbred lines, thus involving four inbred lines.

dou·ble-cross (dŭb/əl krôs/, -krŏs/), *v.t.* to prove treacherous to; betray. **—dou/ble-cross/er,** *n.*

double dagger, a mark (‡) used for references, etc.; the diesis.

double date, *Colloq.* a social engagement or activity of two couples.

dou·ble-date (dŭb/əl dāt/), *v.i.,* **-dated, -dating.** (of two couples) to have a social engagement.

dou·ble-deal·ing (dŭb/əl dē/lĭng), *n.* 1. duplicity. **—adj.** 2. using duplicity; treacherous. **—dou/ble-deal/-er,** *n.*

dou·ble-deck·er (dŭb/əl dĕk/ər), *n.* something with two decks, tiers, or the like, as two beds one above the other, a ship with two decks above the water line, or a streetcar having a second floor for passengers.

double eagle, a United States gold coin worth two eagles, or $20.

dou·ble-edged (dŭb/əl ĕjd/), *adj.* 1. having two cutting edges. 2. acting both ways: *a double-edged charge.*

dou·ble-en·ten·dre (dŏŏ blän tän/dr), *n.* 1. a double meaning. 2. use of a word or expression with two meanings, one often indelicate. [F (obs.)]

double entry, *Bookkeeping.* a method in which each transaction is entered twice in the ledger, once to the debit of one account, and once to the credit of another. Cf. **single entry.**

dou·ble-faced (dŭb/əl fāst/), *adj.* 1. practicing duplicity; hypocritical. 2. having two faces or aspects.

double first, (at Oxford University) 1. one who gains first-class honors in two final examinations in different subjects. 2. the honor itself.

dou·ble-gang·er (dŭb/əl găng/ər), *n.* Doppelgänger.

dou·ble-head·er (dŭb/əl hĕd/ər), *n.* 1. the playing of two games, as of baseball, between the same teams on the same day in immediate succession. 2. a railroad train pulled by two locomotives.

dou·ble-joint·ed (dŭb/əl join/tĭd), *adj.* having unusually flexible joints which enable the appendages and spine to curve in extraordinary ways.

double magnum, wine bottle four times normal size.

dou·ble-mind·ed (dŭb/əl mīn/dĭd), *adj.* wavering or undecided in mind. **—dou/ble-mind/ed-ness,** *n.*

dou·ble-ness (dŭb/əl nĭs), *n.* 1. the quality or condition of being double. 2. deception or dissimulation.

double play, *Baseball.* a play in which two put-outs are registered before the ball again is put into play.

dou·ble-quick (dŭb/əl kwĭk/), *adj.* 1. very quick or rapid. **—adv.** 2. in a quick or rapid manner. **—n.** 3. double time. **—v.t., v.i.** 4. to double-time.

dou·ble-reed (dŭb/əl rēd/), *adj. Music.* of or pertaining to wind instruments producing sounds through two reeds fastened and beating together, as the oboe.

double refraction, *Physics.* the separation of a ray of light into two unequally refracted rays, as in passing through certain crystals.

dou·ble-rip·per (dŭb/əl rĭp/ər), *n.* a contrivance for coasting, consisting of two sleds, one behind the other, connected by a plank. Also, **dou/ble-run/ner.**

double salt, *Chem.* a salt which crystallizes as a single substance, but when dissolved ionizes as two distinct salts.

double standard, a moral code more lenient for men than for women.

double star, *Astron.* two stars so near to each other in the sky that they appear as one under certain conditions. **Optical double stars** are two stars at greatly different distances but nearly in line with each other and the observer. **Physical double stars** or **binary stars** are a physical system whose two components are at nearly the same distance from the earth.

double summer time, *Brit.* a setting of the clocks two hours ahead of Greenwich mean time.

dou·blet (dŭb/lĭt), *n.* 1. a close-fitting outer body garment, with or without sleeves, formerly worn by men. 2. a pair of like things; a couple. 3. one of a pair of like things; a duplicate. 4. one of two words in the same language, representing the same original, as the English *coy* and *quiet,* one taken from Old French, the other from Latin. 5. *Print.* an unintentional repetition in printed matter or proof. 6. (*pl.*) two dice on each of which the

Doublets (def. 1), Elizabethan period

same number of spots turns up at a throw. 7. *Jewelry.* a counterfeit gem made by the welding of two pieces of a different nature, usually a garnet top with a colored glass base. [ME, t. OF: f. *double* DOUBLE, adj. + *-et* -ET]

double tackle, a pulley having two grooved wheels.

double talk, *Colloq.* 1. speech using nonsense syllables along with words in a rapid patter. 2. evasive or ambiguous language.

double time, 1. *U.S. Army.* the fastest rate of marching troops, a slow jog in which 180 paces, each of 3 feet, are taken in a minute. 2. a slow run by troops in step. 3. *Colloq.* a run at any speed.

dou·ble-time (dŭb/əl tīm/), *v.,* **-timed, -timing. —v.t.** 1. to cause to march in double time. **—v.i.** 2. to march in double time. 3. to move or run at double time.

dou·ble-tongue (dŭb/əl tŭng/), *v.i.,* **-tongued, -tonguing.** *Music.* (in playing the flute, cornet, etc.) to apply the tongue rapidly to the teeth and the hard palate alternately, so as to ensure a brilliant execution of a staccato passage.

dou·ble-tongued (dŭb/əl tŭngd/), *adj.* deceitful.

dou·ble·tree (dŭb/əl trē/, -trĭ), *n.* (in a vehicle) a pivoted bar with a singletree attached to each end, used when two horses are harnessed abreast.

dou·bloon (dŭb lōōn/), *n.* a former Spanish gold coin, of varying value, orig. equal to 16 silver dollars, finally worth about $5. [t. F: m. *doublon,* or t. Sp.: m. *doblón,* aug. of *doble* DOUBLE, adj.]

dou·blure (dōō blyr/), *n.* an ornamental lining of a book cover. [F, der. *doubler* to line, DOUBLE]

dou·bly (dŭb/lĭ), *adv.* 1. in a double manner, measure, or degree. 2. in two ways. 3. *Obs. or Archaic.* with duplicity.

Doubs (dōō), *n.* a river in E France, flowing into the Saône river. ab. 270 mi.

doubt (dout), *v.t.* 1. to be uncertain in opinion about; hold questionable; hesitate to believe. 2. *Archaic or Prov.* to fear; suspect. **—v.i.** 3. to feel uncertainty as to something; be undecided in opinion or belief. **—n.** 4. undecidedness of opinion or belief; a feeling of uncertainty. 5. state of affairs such as to occasion uncertainty. 6. *Obs.* fear; dread. 7. **in doubt,** in uncertainty; in suspense. 8. **no doubt** or **without doubt,** without question; certainly. [ME *douten,* t. OF: m. *douter,* g. L *dubitāre* hesitate, doubt] **—doubt/a·ble,** *adj.* **—doubt/er,** *n.* **—doubt/ing·ly,** *adv.* **—Syn.** 1. distrust, mistrust, suspect, question. 4. faltering, indecision, irresolution, hesitation, hesitancy, vacillation.

doubt·ful (dout/fəl), *adj.* 1. admitting of or causing doubt; uncertain; ambiguous. 2. of uncertain issue. 3. of questionable character. 4. unsettled in opinion or belief; undecided; hesitating. **—doubt/ful·ly,** *adv.* **—doubt/ful·ness,** *n.*
—Syn. 2. undetermined, unsettled, indecisive, dubious. 4. irresolute, vacillating. DOUBTFUL, DUBIOUS, INCREDULOUS, SKEPTICAL imply reluctance or unwillingness to be convinced. To be DOUBTFUL about something is to feel that it is open to question or that more evidence is needed to prove it: *to be doubtful about the statements of witnesses.* DUBIOUS implies greater vacillation, vagueness, or suspicion: *dubious about suggested methods of manufacture, about future plans.* INCREDULOUS means actively unwilling or reluctant to believe, usually in a given situation: *incredulous at the good news.* SKEPTICAL implies a general disposition to doubt or question: *skeptical of human progress.* **—Ant.** 1. certain.

doubting Thomas, one who refuses to believe without proof.

doubt·less (dout/lĭs), *adv.* 1. without doubt; unquestionably. 2. probably or presumably. **—adj.** 3. free from doubt or uncertainty. **—doubt/less·ly,** *adv.* **—doubt/less·ness,** *n.*

douce (dōōs), *adj. Scot. and N. Eng.* quiet, sedate, or modest. [ME, t. OF, g. L *dulcis* sweet] **—douce/ly,** *adv.* **—douce/ness,** *n.*

dou·ceur (dōō sœr/), *n.* 1. a gratuity, fee, or tip. 2. a conciliatory gift or bribe. 3. sweetness; agreeableness. [F, der. *douce* (fem.) sweet, g. L *dulcis*]

douche (dōōsh), *n., v.,* **douched, douching. —n.** 1. a jet or current of water applied to a body part, organ, or cavity for medicinal purposes. 2. the application of such a jet. 3. an instrument for administering it. 4. a bath administered by such a jet. **—v.t.** 5. to apply a douche to; douse. **—v.i.** 6. to receive a douche. [t. F, t. It.: m. *doccia* conduit, shower, ult. der. L *dūcere* lead]

dough (dō), *n.* 1. flour or meal combined with water, milk, etc., in a mass for baking into bread, cake, etc.; paste of bread. 2. any soft, pasty mass. 3. *Slang.* money. [ME *dogh,* OE *dāh,* c. D *deeg,* G *teig*]

dough bird, the Eskimo curlew, *Numenius borealis,* of America.

dough·boy (dō/boi/), *n. U.S. Colloq.* an infantryman.

Dough·er·ty (dŏ/ər tĭ, dŏ/hər-), *n.* **Denis J.,** 1865-1951, U.S. Roman Catholic Cardinal since 1921.

dough·nut (dō/nət, -nŭt/), *n.* a small cake of sweetened or, sometimes, of unsweetened dough fried in deep fat. [f. DOUGH + NUT, in allusion to the original shape]

dought (dout), *v.* pt. of **dow.**

dough·ty (dou/tĭ), *adj.,* **-tier, -tiest.** *Now Archaic, and or Humorous,* strong; hardy; valiant. [ME; OE *dohtig,* unexplained var. of *dyhtig,* der. *dugan* be good, avail, c. G *tüchtig*] **—dough/ti·ly,** *adv.* **—dough/ti·ness,** *n.*

Dough·ty (dou/tĭ), *n.* **Charles Montagu** (mŏn/tə gū/), 1843-1926, British traveler and author.

---

b., blend of, blended; c., cognate with; d., dialect, dialectal; der., derived from; f., formed from; g., going back to; m., modification of; r., replacing; s., stem of; t., taken from; ?, perhaps. See the full key on inside cover.

dough·y (dō′ĭ), *adj.*, **doughier, doughiest.** of or like dough; half-baked; soft and heavy; pallid and flabby.

Doug·las (dŭg′ləs), *n.* 1. **Sir James,** (*"the Black Douglas"*) c1286–1330, Scottish military leader. 2. **James,** c1358–88, Scottish military leader. 3. **Stephen Arnold,** 1813–61, U.S. political leader who ran for president against Lincoln in 1860. 4. **William Orville,** born 1898, associate justice of the U.S. Supreme Court since 1939. 5. the capital of the Isle of Man: resort. 19,561 (est. 1938).

Douglas fir, a coniferous tree, *Pseudotsuga taxifolia* (*P. mucronata* or *P. douglasii*), of western North America, often over 200 feet high, and yielding a strong, durable timber. Also, **Douglas pine, Douglas spruce.** [named after David *Douglas* (1798–1834), Scottish botanist and traveler]

Doug·lass (dŭg′ləs), *n.* **Frederick,** 1817–95, U.S. Negro leader and orator who opposed slavery.

Dou·kho·bors (dōō′kō bôrz′), *n.* Dukhobors.

dou·ma (dōō′mä), *n.* duma.

Dou·mergue (dōō mĕrg′), *n.* **Gaston** (gȧs tôN′), 1863–1937, French statesman: president of France, 1924–31.

dour (dŏŏr, dour), *adj.* 1. sullen; gloomy; sour. 2. *Scot.* hard; severe; stern. 3. *Scot.* obstinate; stubborn. [ME *dowre*, t. L: m.s. *dūrus* hard] —**dour′ly,** *adv.* —**dour′ness,** *n.*

dou·ra (dŏŏr′ə), *n.* durra. Also, **dou′rah.**

dou·ri·cou·li (dŏŏr′ĭ kōō′lē), *n., pl.* **-lis.** a small nocturnal South American monkey, genus *Aotus*, with large owllike eyes.

dou·rine (dŏŏ rēn′), *n. Vet. Sci.* an infectious disease of horses, affecting chiefly the genitals and hind legs, due to a protozoan parasite, *Trypanosoma equiperdum.* [t. F: m. *dourin*]

Dou·ro (dō′rōō), *n.* a river flowing from N Spain W through N Portugal to the Atlantic. ab. 500 mi. Spanish, **Duero.**

douse (dous), *v.,* **doused, dousing.** —*v.t.* 1. to plunge into water or the like; drench: *to douse someone with water.* 2. *Slang.* to put out or extinguish (a light). 3. *Colloq.* to take off or doff. 4. *Naut.* to lower in haste, as a sail; slacken suddenly. —*v.i.* 5. to plunge or be plunged into a liquid. —*n.* 6. *Chiefly Dial.* a stroke or blow. Also, **dowse.** [orig. obscure] —**dous′er,** *n.*

douze·pers (dōōz′pârz′), *n.pl., sing.* **douzeper** (dōōz′-pâr′) 1. *French Legend.* the twelve peers or paladins represented in old romances as attendants of Charlemagne. 2. *French Hist.* twelve great spiritual and temporal peers of France, taken to represent those of Charlemagne. [ME *dusze pers, duspers,* t. OF: m. *douze pers* twelve peers]

dove[1] (dŭv), *n.* 1. any bird of the pigeon family (*Columbidae*), esp. certain small species of terrestrial habits, as the **ground dove,** *Columbigallina passerina,* of the southern U. S. and Mexico. 2. (in literature) the symbol of innocence, gentleness, and tenderness. 3. (*cap.*) *Theol.* the Holy Ghost. 4. an innocent, gentle, or tender person. [ME *dūfe*; c. D *duif,* G *taube,* Icel. *dūfa,* Goth. *dubō* dove, lit., diver; akin to DIVE, v.]

dove[2] (dōv), *v. U.S. Colloq. and Brit. Dial.* pt. of **dive.**

dove color (dŭv), warm gray with a slight purplish or pinkish tint. —**dove′-col′ored,** *adj.*

dove·cote (dŭv′kōt′), *n.* a structure, usually at a height above the ground, for domestic pigeons. Also, **dove·cot** (dŭv′kŏt′).

dove·kie (dŭv′kĭ), *n.* 1. the rotche, or little auk, *Plautus alle,* of Greenland, Novaya Zemlya, etc. 2. a European name for the black guillemot. Also, **dove′key.** [dim. of DOVE]

Do·ver (dō′vər), *n.* 1. a seaport in SE England, nearest to the coast of France. 30,500 (est. 1946). 2. **Strait of,** a strait between England and France, connecting the English Channel with the North Sea. Least width, 20 mi. French, **Pas de Calais.** 3. the capital of Delaware, in the central part. 6,223 (1950).

Dover's powder, *Med.* a powder containing ipecac and opium, used as an anodyne, diaphoretic, and antispasmodic. [named after T. *Dover* (1660–1742), English physician]

dove·tail (dŭv′tāl′), *n.* 1. *Carp.* a joint or fastening formed by one or more tenons and mortises spread in the shape of a dove's tail. —*v.t., v.i.* 2. *Carp.* to join or fit together by means of a dovetail or dovetails. 3. to join or fit together compactly or harmoniously.

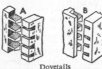
Dovetails
A. Common; B. Lapped

dow (dou, dō), *v.i.* **dowed** or **dought** (dout), **dowing.** *Scot. and N. Eng.* 1. to be able. 2. to do well, or thrive. [ME *dowen, doghen,* OE *dugan,* c. G *taugen.* Cf. DOUGHTY]

Dow (dou), *n.* **Gerard** (gā′rärt). See **Dou.**

Dow., Dowager.

dow·a·ble (dou′ə bəl), *adj. Law.* entitled to dower.

dow·a·ger (dou′ə jər), *n.* 1. a woman who holds some title or property from her deceased husband, esp. the widow of a king, duke, or the like. 2. *Colloq.* a dignified elderly lady. [t. OF: m. *douagiere,* der. *douage* dower, der. *douer* endow; g. L *dōtāre*]

Dow·den (dou′dən), *n.* **Edward,** 1843–1913, British critic and poet.

dow·dy (dou′dĭ), *adj.,* **-dier, -diest,** *n., pl.* **-dies.** —*adj.* 1. ill-dressed; not trim, smart, or stylish. —*n.* 2. an ill-dressed woman. 3. a deep-dish pie with a fruit filling. See **pandowdy.** [earlier *dowd,* ME *doude;* orig. obscure] —**dow′di·ly,** *adv.* —**dow′di·ness,** *n.* —**dow′dy·ish,** *adj.* —**Syn.** 1. frumpy, shabby.

dow·el (dou′əl), *n., v.,* **-eled, -eling** or (*esp. Brit.*) **-elled, -elling.** —*n.* 1. Also, **dowel pin.** *Carp.* a pin, usually round, fitting into corresponding holes in two adjacent pieces to prevent slipping or to align the two pieces. 2. a piece of wood driven into a hole drilled in masonry wall to receive nails of skirtings, etc. —*v.t.* 3. to reinforce with dowels; furnish with dowels. [cf. G *döbel* peg, plug, pin]

D. Dowel (def. 1)

dow·er (dou′ər), *n.* 1. *Law.* the portion of a deceased husband's real property allowed by the law to his widow for her life. 2. dowry (def. 1). 3. a natural gift or endowment. —*v.t.* 4. to provide with a dower or dowry. 5. to give as a dower or dowry. [ME, t. OF: m. *douaire,* g. LL *dōtārium,* der. L *dōs* dowry] —**dow′er·less,** *adj.*

dow·er·y (dou′ər ĭ), *n., pl.* **-eries.** dowry.

dowf (douf, dōōf), *adj. Scot. and N. Eng.* dull; stupid.

dow·ie (dou′ĭ, dō′ĭ), *adj. Scot. and N. Eng.* dull; melancholy; dismal. Also, **dowy.**

dow·itch·er (dou′ĭch ər), *n.* a long-billed, snipelike American shore bird, *Limnodromus griseus.* [orig. uncert.]

Dow·met·al (dou′mĕt′əl), *n.* 1. a trademark for any of many magnesium base alloys produced in the U. S. 2. **dowmetals,** the alloys themselves.

down[1] (doun), *adv.* 1. from higher to lower; in descending direction or order; into or in a lower position or condition. 2. on or to the ground. 3. to or in a position spoken of as lower, as the south, the country, a business district, etc. 4. to or at a low point, degree, rate, pitch, etc. 5. from an earlier to a later time. 6. from a greater to a less bulk, degree of consistency, etc.: *to boil down syrup.* 7. in due position or state: *to settle down to work.* 8. on paper or in a book: *to write down.* 9. in cash; at once: *to pay $40 down.* 10. confined to bed with illness. 11. *Colloq.* in a prostrate, depressed, or degraded condition. —*prep.* 12. in a descending direction on, over, or along. —*adj.* 13. downward; going or directed downward. 14. downcast; dejected: *a down expression.* 15. *Football.* pertaining to the ball which is not in play because it has stopped moving, or has been halted by the referee for any reason, or because the carrier shouts "down." 16. *Games.* losing or behind an opponent by a specified number of points, holes, etc. (opposed to *up*). 17. **down and out,** *a.* without friends, money, or prospects. *b. Boxing.* completely knocked out. 18. **down on,** *Colloq.* hostile to; disapproving of. —*n.* 19. a downward movement; a descent. 20. a reverse: *the ups and downs of fortune.* 21. *Football. a.* one of a series of four plays during which a team must advance the ball at least ten yards to keep possession of it. *b.* the declaring of the ball as down or out of play, or the play immediately preceding this. —*v.t.* 22. to put or throw down; subdue. 23. *Brit. Colloq.* to drink down: *to down a sconce.* —*v.i.* 24. to go down; fall. [ME *doune,* late OE *dūne,* aphetic var. of *adūne,* earlier *of dūne* from (the) hill. See DOWN[3]]

down[2] (doun), *n.* 1. the first feathering of young birds. 2. the soft under plumage of birds as distinct from the contour feathers. 3. a soft hairy growth as the hair on the human face when first beginning to appear. 4. *Bot. a.* a fine soft pubescence upon plants and some fruits. *b.* the light feather pappus or coma upon seeds by which they are borne upon the wind, as in the dandelion and thistle. [ME *downe,* t. Scand.; cf. Icel. *dūnn*]

down[3] (doun), *n.* 1. a hill; a sand hill or dune. 2. (*usually pl.,* applied esp. in S and SE England) open, rolling, upland country with fairly smooth slopes usually covered with grass. [ME; OE *dūn* hill, c. OD *dūna.* See DUNE. Not connected with OIrish *dūn* walled town]

Down (doun), *n.* a county in N Ireland, in SE Ulster. 227,800 pop. (est. 1946); 952 sq. mi.

down-bow (doun′bō′), *n. Music.* (in bowing on a stringed instrument) a stroke bringing the tip of the bow towards the strings, indicated in scores by the symbol ⊓ (opposed to *up-bow*).

down·cast (doun′kăst′, -käst′), *adj.* 1. directed downward, as the eyes. 2. dejected in spirit; depressed. —*n.* 3. overthrow or ruin. 4. a downward look or glance. 5. a shaft down which air passes, as into a mine.

down·come (doun′kŭm′), *n.* 1. descent; downfall. 2. a downcomer.

down·com·er (doun′kŭm′ər), *n.* a pipe, tube, or passage for conducting material downward.

down East, 1. New England. 2. Maine.

down·fall (doun′fôl′), *n.* 1. descent to a lower position or standing; overthrow; ruin. 2. a fall, as of rain or snow. 3. a kind of trap or deadfall, in which a weight or missile falls upon the prey. —**down′fall′en,** *adj.*

down·grade (doun′grād′), *n., adj., adv., v.,* **-graded, -grading.** —*n.* 1. a downward slope. 2. **on the downgrade,** headed for poverty, ruin, etc. —*adj., adv.* 3. downhill. —*v.t.* 4. to assign (a position) to a lower status with a smaller salary. —**down′grad′ing,** *n.*

down·haul (doun′hôl′), *n. Naut.* a rope for hauling down a sail.

down·heart·ed (doun′här′tĭd), *adj.* dejected; depressed; discouraged. —**down′heart′ed·ly**, *adv.* — **down′heart′ed·ness**, *n.* —**Syn.** downcast, despondent.

down·hill (doun′hĭl′), *adv.* 1. down the slope of a hill; downward. —*adj.* 2. going or tending downward on or as on a hill.

Down·ing Street (dou′nĭng), 1. a short street in W central London, Eng.: usual residence of the prime minister at No. 10; other important government offices here. 2. *Colloq.* the British prime minister and cabinet.

down·pour (doun′pōr′), *n.* a heavy, continuous fall of water, rain, etc.

down·right (doun′rīt′), *adj.* 1. thorough; absolute; out-and-out. 2. direct; straightforward. 3. directed straight downward: *a downright blow.* —*adv.* 4. completely or thoroughly: *he is downright angry.* —**down′-right′ly**, *adv.* —**down′right′ness**, *n.*

Downs (dounz), *n.pl.* **The,** 1. low ridges in S and SE England. 2. a roadstead in the Strait of Dover, between the SE tip of England and Goodwin Sands.

down·spout (doun′spout′), *n.* a pipe for conveying rain water from roofs to the drain or the ground.

down·stage (doun′stāj′), *adv. Theat.* at or toward the front of the stage.

down·stairs (doun′stârz′), *adv.* 1. down the stairs. 2. to or on a lower floor. —*adj.* 3. Also, **down′stair′.** pertaining to or situated on a lower floor. —*n.* 4. the lower floor of a house.

down·stream (doun′strēm′), *adv.* with or in the direction of the current of a stream.

down·throw (doun′thrō′), *n.* a throwing down or being thrown down; an overthrow.

down town, the business section of a city.

down·town (doun′toun′), *adv.* 1. to or in the business section of a city. —*adj.* 2. of, pertaining to, or situated in the business section of a city.

down·trod·den (doun′trŏd′an), *adj.* trodden down; trampled upon; tyrannized over. Also, **down′trod′.**

down under, Australia or New Zealand.

down·ward (doun′ward), *adv.* 1. Also, **down′wards.** from a higher to a lower place or condition; down from a head, source, or beginning. —*adj.* 2. moving or tending to a lower place or condition. 3. descending from a head or beginning. —**down′ward·ly**, *adv.* —**down′-ward·ness**, *n.*

down·y (dou′nĭ), *adj.*, **downier, downiest.** 1. of the nature of or resembling down; fluffy; soft. 2. made of down. 3. covered with down. 4. soft; soothing; calm. —**down′i·ness**, *n.*

downy woodpecker, a small North American woodpecker, *Dryobates pubescens.*

dow·ry (dou′rĭ), *n.*, *pl.* **-ries.** 1. the money, goods, or estate which a woman brings to her husband at marriage; dot. 2. any gift or reward given to or for a bride by a man in consideration for the marriage. 3. *Obs.* a widow's dower. 4. a natural gift or endowment: *a noble dowry.* Also, **dowery.** [ME *dowary*, t. AF: m. *dowarie*]

dow·sa·bel (dou′sa·bĕl′), *n. Obs.* sweetheart. [var. of *Dulcibella*, woman's name]

dowse¹ (dous), *v.t.*, *v.i.*, **dowsed, dowsing.** douse. —**dows′er**, *n.*

dowse² (douz), *v.i.*, **dowsed, dowsing.** to search for subterranean supplies of water, ore, etc., by the aid of a divining rod. [orig. unknown] —**dows′er**, *n.*

Dow·son (dou′son), *n.* **Ernest,** 1867–1900, British poet.

dow·y (dou′Ĭ, dō′Ĭ), *adj.* dowie.

dox·ol·o·gy (dŏks·ŏl′a·jĬ), *n.*, *pl.* **-gies.** a hymn or form of words containing an ascription of praise to God, as the Gloria in Excelsis (**great doxology** or **greater doxology**), the Gloria Patri (**lesser doxology**), or the metrical formula beginning "Praise God from whom all blessings flow." [t. ML: m. s. *doxologia*, t. Gk.: a praising] —**dox·o·log·i·cal** (dŏk′sa·lŏj′a·kal), *adj.* —**dox′o·log′i·cal·ly**, *adv.*

dox·y¹ (dŏk′sĬ), *n.*, *pl.* **doxies.** 1. opinion; doctrine. 2. religious views. Also, **dox′ie.** [abstracted from OR-THODOXY, HETERODOXY, etc.]

dox·y² (dŏk′sĬ), *n.*, *pl.* **doxies.** *Slang.* a mistress or paramour; a prostitute. [f. MFlem. *docke* doll + *-sy*, affectionate dim. suffix]

doy·en (doi′an; *Fr.* dwá yăN′), *n.* a dean; the senior member of a body, class, profession, etc. [F. See DEAN] —**doy·enne** (dwä yĕn′), *n. fem.*

Doyle (doil), *n.* **Sir Arthur Conan,** 1859–1930, British author of detective stories.

doz., dozen; dozens.

doze (dōz), *v.*, **dozed, dozing.** *n.* —*v.i.* 1. to sleep lightly or fitfully. 2. to fall into a light sleep unintentionally (often fol. by *off*). 3. to be dull or half asleep. —*v.t.* 4. to pass or spend (time) in drowsiness (often fol. by *away*). —*n.* 5. a light or fitful sleep. [cf. OE *dwǣsian* become stupid, Dan. *döse* make dull, heavy, drowsy] —**doz′-er**, *n.*

doz·en¹ (dŭz′an), *n.*, *pl.* **dozen, dozens.** a group of twelve units or things. [ME *dozein*, t. OF: m. *dozeine*, der. *douze* twelve, g. L *duodecim*]

doz·en² (dō′zan), *v.t. Scot.* to stun. [? akin to DOZE]

doz·enth (dŭz′anth), *adj.* twelfth.

doz·y (dō′zĬ), *adj.*, **dozier, doziest.** drowsy. —**doz′i-ly**, *adv.* —**doz′i·ness**, *n.*

D.P., displaced person. Also, **DP**

dpt., 1. department. 2. deponent.

D.P.W., Department of Public Works.

Dr., Doctor. Also, **Dr**

dr., 1. debtor. 2. dram; drams. 3. drawer.

drab¹ (drăb), *n.*, *adj.*, **drabber, drabbest.** —*n.* 1. dull gray; dull brownish or yellowish gray. —*adj.* 2. having a drab color. 3. dull; cheerless. [t. F: m. *drap* cloth. See DRAPE] —**drab′ly**, *adv.* —**drab′ness**, *n.*

drab² (drăb), *n.*, *v.*, **drabbed, drabbing.** —*n.* 1. a dirty, untidy woman; a slattern. 2. a prostitute. —*v.i.* 3. to associate with drabs. [cf. d. *drabbletail* slattern (der. DRABBLE, v.) and its synonym *draggletail*. Cf. also Irish *drabog*, Gaelic *dragbag* slattern]

drab·bet (drăb′ĭt), *n.* a coarse drab linen fabric used for making men's smock frocks, etc. [f. DRAB¹ + -ET]

drab·ble (drăb′al), *v.t.*, *v.i.*, **-bled, -bling.** to draggle; make or become wet and dirty. [ME *drabelen*, ? t. LG]

dra·cae·na (dra sē′na), *n.* 1. any tree of the liliaceous genus *Dracaena*, natives of tropical regions. 2. any of the closely related genus *Cordyline*. [NL, t. Gk.: m. *drákaina* she-dragon]

drachm (drăm), *n.* 1. *Brit.*; *Archaic in U.S.* dram. 2. drachma. [t. L: s. *drachma*, t. Gk.: m. *drachmḗ* an Attic weight and coin]

drach·ma (drăk′ma), *n.*, *pl.* **-mas, -mae** (-mē). 1. the monetary unit, or a silver coin, of modern Greece, equivalent to about U.S. $.00007 at present. 2. the principal silver coin of the ancient Greeks, varying in weight and value. 3. a small ancient Greek weight, approximately corresponding to the U.S. and British apothecaries' dram. 4. any of various modern weights, esp. a dram. [t. L, t. Gk.: m. *drachmḗ*, lit., handful]

Dra·co (drā′kō), *n.*, *gen.* **Draconis** (drā kō′nĬs). a northern circumpolar constellation between Ursa Major and Cepheus. [t. L, t. Gk.: m. *drákōn* serpent]

Dra·co (drā′kō), *n.* fl. 7th century B.C., Athenian statesman noted for the severity of his code of laws.

Dra·co·ni·an (drā kō′nĬ an), *adj.* 1. of, like, or befitting Draco. 2. rigorous; severe. —**Dra·co′ni·an·ism**, *n.*

dra·co·ni·an (drā kō′nĬ an), *adj.* draconic.

Dra·con·ic (drā kŏn′Ĭk), *adj. Hist.* Draconian. —**Dra·con′i·cal·ly**, *adv.*

dra·con·ic (drā kŏn′Ĭk), *adj.* of or like a dragon. [f. s. L *draco* DRAGON + -IC]

draff (drăf), *n.* refuse; lees; dregs. —**draff′y**, *adj.*

draft (drăft, dräft), *n.* (*Draft* is the common spelling for the following definitions. See also *draught*.) 1. a drawing, sketch, or design. 2. a first or preliminary form of any writing, subject to revision and copying. 3. act of drawing; delineation. 4. a current of air, esp. in a room, chimney, stove, or any enclosed space. 5. act of drawing or pulling, or that which is drawn; a pull; haul. 6. the taking of supplies, forces, money, etc., from a given source. 7. a selection or drawing of persons from the general body of the people, by lot or otherwise, for military service; a levy; conscription. 8. (formerly) a selection of persons already in service, to be sent from one post or organization to another, in either the army or the navy; a detachment. 9. a written order drawn by one person upon another; a writing directing the payment of money on account of the drawer; a bill of exchange. 10. a drain or demand made on anything. 11. *Obs.* an allowance for waste of goods sold by weight. 12. *Foundry.* the slight taper given to a pattern so that it may be drawn from the sand without injury to the mold. 13. *Masonry.* a line or border chiseled at the edge of a stone, to serve as a guide in leveling the surfaces. 14. the sectional area of the openings in a turbine wheel or in a sluice gate. —*v.t.* 15. to draw the outlines or plan of, or sketch. 16. to draw up in written form, as a first draft. 17. to draw or pull. 18. to take by draft, as for military service. 19. *Masonry.* to cut a draft on. —*adj.* 20. used or suited for drawing loads: *draft cattle.* [ME *draht*, later *draught*, *droft* (cf. OE *droht* pull, draught), verbal abstract of *draw* (OE *dragan*), c. G *tracht.* See DRAUGHT] —**draft′er**, *n.*

draft·ee (drăft tē′, dräf-), *n.* one who is drafted, as for military service.

drafts·man (drăfts′man, dräfts′-), *n.*, *pl.* **-men.** 1. one who draws sketches, plans, or designs. 2. one employed in making mechanical drawings, as of machines, structures, etc. 3. one who draws up documents. 4. draughtsman. —**drafts′man·ship′**, *n.*

draft tube, the flared passage leading vertically from a water turbine to its tailrace.

draft·y (drăf′tĬ, dräf′-), *adj.*, **draftier, draftiest.** characterized by or causing drafts (of air). Also, **draughty.** —**draft′i·ness**, *n.*

drag (drăg), *v.*, **dragged, dragging,** *n.* —*v.t.* 1. to draw with force, effort, or difficulty; pull heavily or slowly along; haul; trail. 2. to search with a drag, grapnel, or the like. 3. to break (land) with a drag or harrow. 4. to bring (*in*) as by main force, as an irrelevant matter. 5. to protract or pass tediously (often fol. by *out* or *on*). —*v.i.* 6. to be drawn or hauled along. 7. to trail on the ground. 8. to move heavily or with effort. 9. to proceed or pass with tedious slowness. 10. to use a drag or grapnel; dredge. —*n.* 11. *Naut.* a. something used by or for dragging, as a dragnet or a dredge. b. a grapnel, net, or other apparatus dragged through water in searching, as for dead bodies. **12.** *Agric.* a heavy harrow. **13.** a stout sledge or sled. **14.** a four-horse sporting and passenger coach with seats inside and on top. **15.** a metal shoe to receive a wheel of heavy wagons and serve as a wheel lock on steep grades. **16.** anything that retards progress. **17.** act of dragging. **18.** slow, laborious movement or procedure; retardation. **19.** *Aeron.* the force exerted on an airplane or airfoil or other aerodynamic body tending to reduce its forward motion, consisting partly of a component of the aerodynamic lift and partly of the effect of air eddies, friction, etc. **20.** *Hunting.* **a.** the scent or trail of a fox, etc. **b.** something, as aniseed, dragged over the ground to leave an artificial scent. **c.** a hunt with such a scent. **21.** *Angling.* **a.** a brake on a fishing reel. **b.** the sideways pull on a fishline as caused by a cross current. **22.** *Slang.* influence: *to have a drag.* [late ME; cf. MLG *dragge* grapnel] **—Syn. 1.** See **draw.**

dra·gée (drá zhē′), *n. French.* **1.** a sweetmeat in the form of a sugar-coated fruit or the like. **2.** a sugar-coated medicine.

drag·gle (drăg′əl), *v.,* **-gled, -gling.** **—v.t. 1.** to soil by dragging over damp ground or in the mud. **—v.i. 2.** to hang trailing; become draggled. **3.** to follow slowly; straggle. [b. DRAG and DRABBLE]

drag·gle·tail (drăg′əl tāl′), *n.* a bedraggled or untidy person; slut; slattern.

drag·gle·tailed (drăg′əl tāld′), *adj.* having the garments draggled as from trailing in the wet and dirt.

drag·hound (drăg′hound′), *n.* a hound trained to follow a drag or artificial scent.

drag hunt, a hunt with a drag or artificial scent.

drag·line (drăg′līn′), *n.* a dragrope (def. 2).

drag link, *Mach.* a link for connecting the cranks of two shafts.

drag·net (drăg′nĕt′), *n.* **1.** a net to be drawn along the bottom of a river, pond, etc., or along the ground, to catch something. **2.** anything that serves to catch or drag in, as a police system.

drag·o·man (drăg′ə mən), *n., pl.* **-mans, -men.** (in the Orient) a professional interpreter. [t. F, t. LGk.: m. *dragoúmanos,* t. Ar.: m. *targumān* interpreter. Cf. TARGUM]

drag·on (drăg′ən), *n.* **1.** a fabulous monster variously represented, generally as a huge winged reptile with crested head and terrible claws, and often spouting fire. **2.** *Now Rare.* a huge serpent or snake. **3.** (in the Bible) a large serpent, a crocodile, a great marine animal, or a jackal. **4.** a name for Satan. **5.** a fierce, violent person. **6.** a severely watchful woman; a duenna. **7.** any of the small flying lizards of the East Indian region. **8.** *Bot.* any of various araceous plants, as the jack-in-the-pulpit, *Arisaema atrorubens* (*Atriphyllum*). **9.** a short musket, carried by a dragoon (def. 2) in the 16th and 17th centuries. **10.** (*cap.*) *Astron.* the northern constellation Draco. [ME, t. OF, g. L *draco,* t. Gk.: m. *drákōn* serpent] **—drag·on·ess** (drăg′ən ĭs), *n. fem.* **—drag·on·ish,** *adj.*

drag·on·et (drăg′ən ĭt), *n.* **1.** a little or young dragon. **2.** any fish of the genus *Callionymus,* comprising small shore fishes which are often brightly colored. [ME, t. OF dim. of *dragon* DRAGON]

drag·on·fly (drăg′ən flī′), *n., pl.* **-flies.** any of the larger, harmless insects of the order *Odonata,* feeding on mosquitoes and other insects. Their immature forms are aquatic.

Common dragonfly, *Libellula trimaculata*

drag·on·head (drăg′ən hĕd′), *n.* any mint of the genera *Dracocephalum* (or *Moldavica*), esp. *D. parviflora.*

drag·on·nade (drăg′ə nād′), *n.* **1.** one of a series of persecutions of French Protestants, under Louis XIV, by dragoons quartered upon them. **2.** any persecution with the aid of troops. [t. F, der. *dragon* DRAGOON]

dragon's blood, 1. a red resin exuding from the fruit of *Daemonorops* (or *Calamus*) *Draco,* a palm of the Malay Archipelago, formerly used in medicine, but now chiefly in the preparation of varnishes, etc. **2.** any of various similar resins from other trees.

dragon tree, a liliaceous tree, *Dracaena Draco,* of the Canary Islands, yielding a variety of dragon's blood.

dragon withe, (in the West Indies) a malpighiaceous climber, *Heteropteris* (*Banisteria*) *laurifolia,* one of a large genus with winged fruits resembling maples.

dra·goon (drə gōōn′), *n.* **1.** a cavalryman of a particular type, as in the British army. **2.** *Obs.* a mounted infantryman armed with a short musket. **—v.t. 3.** to set dragoons or soldiers upon; to persecute by armed force; to oppress, harass. **4.** to force by rigorous and oppressive measures; coerce. [t. F: m. *dragon* dragoon (orig., dragon), referring first to the hammer of a pistol, then to the firearm and then to the troops carrying it]

drag·rope (drăg′rōp′), *n.* **1.** a rope for dragging something, as a piece of artillery. **2.** a rope dragging from something, as the guide rope from a balloon.

drag sail, *Naut.* sea anchor. Also, **drag sheet.**

drain (drān), *v.t.* **1.** to draw off gradually, as a liquid; remove by degrees, as by filtration. **2.** to draw off or take away completely. **3.** to withdraw liquid gradually from; make empty or dry by drawing off liquid. **4.** to deprive of possessions, resources, etc., by gradual withdrawal; exhaust. **—v.i. 5.** to flow off gradually. **6.** to become empty or dry by the gradual flowing off of

moisture. **—n. 7.** that by which anything is drained, as a pipe or conduit. **8.** *Surg.* a material or appliance for maintaining the opening of a wound to permit free exit of fluid contents. **9.** gradual or continuous outflow, withdrawal, or expenditure. **10.** act of draining. [OE *drēnian, dreahnian* drain, strain out; akin to DRY] **—drain·a·ble,** *adj.* **—drain·er,** *n.*

drain·age (drā′nĭj), *n.* **1.** act or process of draining. **2.** a system of drains, artificial or natural. **3.** drainage basin. **4.** that which is drained off. **5.** *Surg.* the draining of body fluids (bile, urine, etc.) or of pus and other morbid products from a wound.

drainage basin, the entire area drained by a river and all its tributaries. Also, **drainage area.**

drain·less (drān′lĭs), *adj. Poetic.* inexhaustible.

drain·pipe (drān′pīp′), *n.* a pipe receiving the discharge of waste pipes and soil pipes.

drake[1] (drāk), *n.* the male of any bird of the duck kind. [ME, c. d. G *draak;* orig. unknown]

drake[2] (drāk), *n. Obs.* **1.** a dragon. **2.** a small kind of cannon. [ME; OE *draca,* t. L: m. *draco* DRAGON]

Drake (drāk), *n.* **1.** Sir Francis, c1540–1596, British buccaneer, circumnavigator of the globe, and admiral. **2.** Joseph Rodman, 1795–1820, U.S. poet.

drake fly, a May fly used in angling.

Dra·kens·berg (drä′kĕnz bûrg′), *n.* a mountain range in the E part of the Union of South Africa. ab. 600 mi. long; highest peak, 10,988.

dram (drăm), *n., v.,* **drammed, dramming.** **—n. 1.** a unit of apothecaries' weight, equal to 60 grains, ⅛ ounce. **2.** *Obs.* ¹⁄₁₆ ounce, avoirdupois weight (27.34 grains). **3.** a fluid dram. **4.** a small drink of liquor. **5.** a small quantity of anything. **—v.i. 6.** to drink drams; tipple. **—v.t. 7.** to ply with drink. [ME *drame,* t. OF, g. L *drachma* DRACHMA]

dra·ma (drä′mə, drăm′ə), *n.* **1.** a composition in prose or verse presenting in dialogue or pantomime a story involving conflict or contrast of character, esp. one intended to be acted on the stage; a play. **2.** the branch of literature having such compositions as its subject; dramatic art or representation. **3.** that art which deals with plays from their writing to their final production. **4.** any series of events having dramatic interest or results. [t. LL: a play, t. Gk.: deed, play]

dram·a·mine (drăm′ə mēn′), *n. Pharm.* **1.** a recently developed synthetic antihistamine, used in the treatment of allergic disorders and as a preventive for seasickness and airsickness. **2.** (*cap.*) a trademark for this substance.

dra·mat·ic (drə măt′ĭk), *adj.* **1.** of or pertaining to the drama. **2.** employing the form or manner of the drama. **3.** characteristic of or appropriate to the drama, involving conflict or contrast. Also, *Rare,* **dra·mat′i·cal.** **—dra·mat′i·cal·ly,** *adv.*

dra·mat·ics (drə măt′ĭks), *n.* **1.** (construed as sing. or pl.) the art of producing or acting dramas. **2.** (construed as pl.) dramatic productions, esp. by amateurs.

dram·a·tis per·so·nae (drăm′ə tĭs pər sō′nē), *Latin.* the persons or characters in a drama.

dram·a·tist (drăm′ə tĭst), *n.* a writer of dramas or dramatic poetry; a playwright.

dram·a·ti·za·tion (drăm′ə tə zā′shən), *n.* **1.** act of dramatizing. **2.** construction or representation in dramatic form. **3.** a dramatized version, of another form of literature or of historic facts.

dram·a·tize (drăm′ə tīz′), *v.t.,* **-tized, -tizing. 1.** to put into dramatic form. **2.** to express or represent dramatically: *he dramatizes his woes.* **—dram′a·tiz′er,** *n.*

dram·a·turge (drăm′ə tûrj′), *n.* dramatist. Also, **dram·a·tur′gist.**

dram·a·tur·gy (drăm′ə tûr′jĭ), *n.* **1.** the science of dramatic composition. **2.** the dramatic art. **3.** dramatic representation. [t. Gk.: m. s. *dramatourgia* composition of dramas] **—dram′a·tur′gic, dram′a·tur′gi·cal,** *adj.*

dram·mock (drăm′ək), *n. Scot. and N. Eng.* meal mixed with water, without cooking.

dram. pers., dramatis personae.

dram·shop (drăm′shŏp′), *n.* a liquor saloon.

Drang nach Ost·en (dräng näκH ôs′tən), *German.* drive to the east: the German imperialistic foreign policy of extending influence to the east and south.

drank (drăngk), *v.* pt. and former pp. of **drink.**

drape (drāp), *v.,* **draped, draping.** **—v.t. 1.** to cover or hang with cloth or some fabric, esp. in graceful folds; adorn with drapery. **2.** to adjust (hangings, clothing, etc.) in graceful folds. **—v.i. 3.** to fall in folds, as drapery. **—n. 4.** a draped curtain or hanging. [t. F: s. *draper,* der. *drap* cloth, g. LL *drappus*]

drap·er (drā′pər), *n. Eng.* a dealer in dry goods, etc. [ME, t. AF, var. of F *drapier*]

Dra·per (drā′pər), *n.* **1.** Henry, 1837–82, U.S. astronomer. **2.** his father, John William, 1811–82, U.S. chemist, physiologist, and historian.

dra·per·y (drā′pər ĭ), *n., pl.* **-peries. 1.** coverings, hangings, clothing, etc., of some fabric, esp. as arranged in loose, graceful folds. **2.** the draping or arranging of hangings, clothing, etc., in graceful folds. **3.** *Art.* hangings, clothing, etc., so arranged as represented in sculpture or painting. **4.** cloths or textile fabrics collectively. **5.** *Brit.* the business of a draper. **—dra′per·ied,** *adj.*

dras·tic (drăs′tĭk), *adj.* acting with force or violence; violent. [t. Gk.: m. s. *drastikós* efficacious] **—dras′ti·cal·ly,** *adv.*

drat·ted (drăt′ĭd), *adj. Colloq.* or *Dial.* confounded.

draught (drăft, dräft), *n.* (*Draught* is the common spelling for the following definitions. See also *draft*.) **1.** a current of air, esp. in a room, chimney, stove, or any enclosed space. **2.** a device for regulating the flow of air or gas, as a damper in a stove. **3.** the drawing of a liquid from its receptacle, as of ale from a cask: *ale on draught.* **4.** drinking, or a drink or potion. **5.** a take of fish, etc. **6.** the depth a vessel sinks in water. **7.** (*pl.* construed as *sing.*) the game of checkers. —*adj.* **8.** being on draught; drawn as required: *draught ale.* [ME *draht,* c. D *dragt,* G *tracht,* Icel. *drättr.* See DRAFT] —**draught′er,** *n.*

draughts·man (drăfts′mən, dräfts′-), *n., pl.* -**men.** **1.** a checker. **2.** draftsman. —**draughts·man·ship′,** *n.*

draught·y (drăf′tĭ, dräf′-), *adj.,* **draughtier, draughtiest.** drafty. —**draught′i·ness,** *n.*

Dra·va (drä′vä), *n.* a river flowing from S Austria, along a portion of the boundary between Hungary and SE Yugoslavia into the Danube. ab. 450 mi. Also, **Dra·ve** (drä′və). German, **Drau** (drou).

drave (drāv), *v. Archaic.* pt. of **drive.**

Dra·vid·i·an (drə·vĭd′ĭ·ən), *n.* **1.** a great linguistic family of India, including Tamil, Telugu, Kanarese, and Malayalam, and, in Baluchistan, Brahui. It is wholly distinct from Indo-European. **2.** a member of the Dravidian race. —*adj.* **3.** Also, **Dra·vid′ic.** of or pertaining to this people or their language.

draw (drô), *v.,* **drew, drawn, drawing,** *n.* —*v.t.* **1.** to cause to come in a particular direction as by a pulling force; pull; drag; lead (often fol. by *along, away, in, out, off,* etc.). **2.** to bring or take out, as from a receptacle, or source: *to draw water, blood, tears, teeth.* **3.** to bring toward oneself or itself, as by inherent force or influence; attract. **4.** to sketch in lines or words; delineate; depict: *to draw a picture.* **5.** to mark out; trace. **6.** to write or draft (often fol. by *up*). **7.** to frame or formulate, as a distinction. **8.** to take in, as by sucking or inhaling. **9.** to get; derive; deduce: *to draw a conclusion.* **10.** to produce; bring in: *the deposits draw interest.* **11.** to disembowel (a fowl, etc.). **12.** to drain (a pond, etc.). **13.** to pull out to full or greater length; stretch; make by attenuating, as wire. **14.** to wrinkle or shrink by contraction. **15.** *Med.* to digest and cause to discharge: *to draw an abscess by a poultice.* **16.** *U.S. Army.* to obtain (rations, clothing, equipment, weapons, or ammunition) from an issuing agency, such as the quartermaster. **17.** *Naut.* (of a boat) to displace (a certain depth of water). **18.** *Games.* to leave (a contest) undecided. **19.** *Billiards.* to cause to recoil after impact, as if pulled back. **20.** *Chiefly Brit.* to search (cover) for game. **21.** *Cricket.* to play (a ball) with a bat held at an angle in order to deflect the ball between the wicket and the legs. **22.** *Curling.* to toss (the stone) gently. **23.** (of tea) see **steep²** (def. 1). —*v.i.* **24.** to exert a pulling, moving, or attracting force: *a sail draws by being filled with wind and properly trimmed.* **25.** to be drawn; move as under a pulling force (often fol. by *on, off, out, near,* etc.): *draw near.* **26.** to take out a sword, pistol, etc., for action (often fol. by *on*). **27.** to use or practice the art of tracing figures; practice drawing. **28.** to shrink or contract. **29.** to make a draft or demand (fol. by *on* or *upon*): *to draw on one's imagination.* **30.** to levy or call (*on*) for money, supplies, etc. **31.** *Med.* to act as an irritant or to cause blisters. **32.** to produce or have a draught of air, etc., as in a pipe or flue. **33.** *Games.* to leave a contest undecided. **34.** *Hunting.* **a.** (of a hound) to advance carefully toward the game, after indicating it by pointing. **b.** (of a hound) to follow the game animal by its scent. —*n.* **35.** act of drawing. **36.** something that draws or attracts. **37.** that which is drawn, as a lot or the movable part of a drawbridge. **38.** *Games.* a drawn or undecided contest. **39.** *Phys. Geog.* small, natural drainway, usually the upper part of a stream valley. [ME *drawen,* OE *dragan,* c. Icel. *draga* draw, G *tragen* carry, bear. Cf. DRAG]
—**Syn. 1.** DRAW, DRAG, HAUL, PULL imply causing movement of an object toward one by exerting force upon it. To DRAW is to move by a force, in the direction from which the force is exerted: *a magnet draws iron to it, horses draw a wagon.* To DRAG is to draw with greater force, necessary to overcome friction between the object drawn and the surface on which it rests: *to drag a sled to the top of a hill, a heavy piece of furniture across a room.* To HAUL is slowly to transport a heavy object by mechanical force or with sustained effort: *to haul a piano up to the seventh floor, to haul a large boat across a portage.* To PULL is to draw or tug, exerting varying amounts of force according to the effort needed: *to pull out an eyelash, to pull fighting dogs apart.* —**Ant. 1.** push.

draw·back (drô′băk′), *n.* **1.** a hindrance or disadvantage. **2.** *Com.* an amount paid back from a charge made. **3.** *Govt.* refund of tariff or other tax as when imported goods are reëxported. See **rebate¹.**

draw·bar (drô′bär′), *n. Railroads.* a metal rod or bar, for connecting locomotive, tender, and railway cars.

draw·bore (drô′bōr′), *n. Carp.* a hole in a tenon so that when a pin (**drawbore pin**) is driven in, the mortised and tenoned parts are drawn snugly together.

draw·bridge (drô′brĭj′), *n.* a bridge of which the whole or a part may be drawn up or aside, to prevent access or to leave a passage open for boats, etc.

draw·ee (drô·ē′), *n. Finance.* one on whom an order, draft, or bill of exchange is drawn.

draw·er (drôr *for 1, 2;* drô′ər *for 3–5*), *n.* **1.** a sliding compartment, as in a piece of furniture, that may be drawn out in order to get access to it. **2.** (*pl.*) a garment for the lower part of the body, with a separate portion for each leg. **3.** one who or that which draws. **4.** *Finance.* one who draws an order, draft, or bill of exchange. **5.** *Archaic.* a tapster.

draw·ing (drô′ĭng), *n.* **1.** act of a person or thing that draws. **2.** representation by lines; delineation of form without reference to color. **3.** a sketch, plan, or design, esp. one made with pen, pencil, or crayon. **4.** the art of making these.

drawing account, *Com.* **1.** an account used by a partner or employee for cash withdrawals. **2.** an account that is charged with advances of money for expenses, on salaries, against earnings, etc., esp. for salesmen.

drawing card, an entertainer, act, etc., which can be relied upon to produce a large audience.

drawing pin, *Brit.* a thumbtack.

drawing room, **1.** a room for the reception of company. **2.** *U.S.* a private compartment in a railway car. **3.** *Brit.* a formal reception, esp. at court. [f. obs. *drawing* withdrawing + ROOM]

draw·knife (drô′nīf′), *n. Carp., etc.* a knife with a handle at each end at right angles to the blade used by drawing over a surface. Also, **drawing knife.**

Drawknife

drawl (drôl), *v.t., v.i.* **1.** to say or speak with slow, lingering utterance. —*n.* **2.** act or utterance of one who drawls. [appar. a freq. form connected with DRAW. Cf. D *dralen,* LG *drauelen* loiter] —**drawl′er,** *n.* —**drawl′ing·ly,** *adv.* —**drawl′y,** *adj.*

drawn (drôn), *v.* **1.** pp. of **draw.** —*adj.* **2.** eviscerated, as a fowl.

drawn butter sauce, *U.S.* a sauce of melted butter, flour, seasonings and hot water.

drawn work, ornamental work done by drawing threads from a fabric, the remaining portions usually being formed into lacelike patterns by needlework.

draw·plate (drô′plāt′), *n. Mach.* a die plate with conical holes through which to draw wire and thus to regulate its size and shape.

draw·shave (drô′shāv′), *n. Carp., etc.* drawknife.

draw string, a string, cord, etc., which tightens or closes an opening, as of a bag, clothing, etc., when one or both ends are pulled.

draw·tube (drô′tūb′, -tōōb′), *n.* a tube sliding within another tube, as the tube carrying the eyepiece in a microscope.

dray (drā), *n.* **1.** a low, strong cart without fixed sides, for carrying heavy loads. **2.** a sledge or sled. —*v.t.* **3.** to convey on a dray. [ME *draye* sled without wheels. Cf. OE *dræg-* in *drægnett* dragnet, der. OE *dragan* draw]

dray·age (drā′ĭj), *n.* **1.** conveyance by dray. **2.** a charge made for it.

dray·man (drā′mən), *n., pl.* -**men.** a man who drives a dray.

Dray·ton (drā′tən), *n.* **Michael,** 1563–1631, British poet.

dread (drĕd), *v.t.* **1.** to fear greatly; be in shrinking apprehension or expectation of: *to dread death.* **2.** *Obs.* to hold in respectful awe. —*v.i.* **3.** to be in great fear. —*n.* **4.** terror or apprehension as to something future; great fear. **5.** deep awe or reverence. **6.** a person or thing dreaded. —*adj.* **7.** greatly feared; frightful; terrible. **8.** held in awe; revered. [OE *drǣdan,* aphetic var. of *adrǣdan, ondrǣdan,* c. OHG *intrātan* fear] —**Syn. 4.** See **fear.** —**Ant. 1.** welcome.

dread·ful (drĕd′fəl), *adj.* **1.** causing great dread, fear, or terror; terrible: *a dreadful storm.* **2.** venerable; awe-inspiring. **3.** *Colloq.* extremely bad, unpleasant, ugly, great, etc. —*n. Brit.* **4.** a cheap, lurid story, as of crime or adventure. **5.** a periodical given to highly sensational matter. —**dread′ful·ly,** *adv.* —**dread′ful·ness,** *n.* —**Syn. 1.** frightful, dire.

dread·nought (drĕd′nôt′), *n.* **1.** a type of battleship with the main battery consisting of heavy-caliber guns in turrets; so called from the British battleship, *Dreadnaught,* launched in 1906, the first of the type. **2.** one who fears nothing. **3.** an outer garment of heavy woolen cloth. **4.** a thick cloth with a long pile. Also, **dread′naught′.**

dream (drēm), *n., v.,* **dreamed** or **dreamt, dreaming.** —*n.* **1.** a succession of images or ideas present in the mind during sleep. **2.** the sleeping state in which this occurs. **3.** an object seen in a dream. **4.** an involuntary vision occurring to one awake: *a waking dream.* **5.** a vision voluntarily indulged in while awake; daydream; reverie. **6.** a wild or vain fancy. **7.** something of an unreal beauty or charm. —*v.i.* **8.** to have a dream or dreams. **9.** to indulge in daydreams or reveries. **10.** to think or conceive of something in a very remote way (fol. by *of*). **11.** to see or imagine in sleep or in a vision. **12.** to imagine as if in a dream; fancy; suppose. **13.** to pass or spend (time, etc.) in dreaming (often fol. by *away*). [ME *dreem* dream, OE *drēam* mirth, noise; change of meaning prob. due to Scand. influence. Cf. Icel. *draumr* dream] —**dream′er,** *n.* —**dream′ful,** *adj.* —**dream′ing·ly,** *adv.* —**dream′less,** *adj.*

dream·land (drēm′lănd′), *n.* the land of imagination or fancy; the region of reverie.

dreamt (drĕmt), *v.* pt. and pp. of **dream.**

dream world, the world of fancy, rather than of objective reality.

b., blend of, blended; c., cognate with; d., dialect, dialectal; der., derived from; f., formed from; g., going back to; m., modification of; r., replacing; s., stem of; t., taken from; ?, perhaps. See the full key on inside cover.

dream·y (drē'mĭ), *adj.*, **dreamier, dreamiest. 1.** full of dreams; characterized by or causing dreams. **2.** of the nature of or characteristic of dreams; visionary. **3.** vague; dim. **—dream'i·ly,** *adv.* **—dream'i·ness,** *n.*

drear·y (drĭr'ĭ), *adj.*, **drearier, dreariest. 1.** causing sadness or gloom. **2.** dull. **3.** *Archaic.* sad; sorrowful. Also, *Poetic.* **drear.** [ME *drery*, OE *drēorig* gory, cruel, sad] **—drear'i·ly,** *adv.* **—drear'i·ness,** *n.* **—dreari·some** (drĭr'ĭsəm), *adj.* **—Syn. 1.** gloomy, dismal, drear, cheerless. **2.** tedious, monotonous, wearisome. **—Ant. 2.** interesting.

dredge¹ (drĕj), *n., v.*, **dredged, dredging. —n. 1.** any of various powerful machines for dredging up or removing earth, etc., as from the bottom of a river, by means of a scoop, a series of buckets, a suction pipe, or the like. **2.** a dragnet or other contrivance for gathering material or objects from the bed of a river, etc. **—v.t. 3.** to clear out with a dredge; remove sand, silt, mud, etc., from the bottom of. **4.** to take, catch, or gather with a dredge; obtain or remove by a dredge. **—v.i. 5.** to use a dredge. [unrecorded OE deriv. of *drag-*, s. *dragan* draw]

dredge² (drĕj), *v.t.*, **dredged, dredging.** *Cookery.* to sprinkle or coat with some powdered substance, esp. flour. [appar. v. use of *dredge* mixed grain]

dredg·er¹ (drĕj'ər), *n.* *Brit.* **1.** dredge¹ (def. 1). **2.** one who uses a dredge. [f. DREDGE¹ + -ER¹]

dredg·er² (drĕj'ər), *n.* a container with a perforated top for sprinkling flour, etc. [f. DREDGE² + -ER¹]

dredging machine, dredge (def. 1).

dree (drē), *v.*, **dreed, dreeing,** *adj.* **—v.t. 1.** *Scot.* and *N. Eng.* to suffer; endure. **—adj. 2.** Also, **dreegh** (drēкн), **dreigh** (drēкн), **driegh.** *N. Eng.* tedious; dreary. [ME; OE *drēogan* endure].

dreg (drĕg), *n.* **1.** (*usually pl.*) the sediment of liquors; lees; grounds. **2.** any waste or worthless residue; refuse. **3.** a small remnant; any small quantity [ME, t. Scand.; cf. Icel. *dreggjar* dregs] **—dreg'gy,** *adj.*

Drei·bund (drī'boont'), *n.* **1.** the alliance between Germany, Austria-Hungary, and Italy, formed in 1882 and continuing until the withdrawal of Italy in May, 1915. **2.** (*l.c. or cap.*) a triple alliance. [G: f. *drei* three + *bund* alliance]

Drei·ser (drī'sər, -zər), *n.* Theodore, 1871–1945, U.S. novelist.

drench (drĕnch) *v.t.* **1.** to wet thoroughly; steep; soak: *garments drenched with rain, swords drenched in blood.* **2.** to cause to drink. **3.** *Vet. Sci.* to administer a draft of medicine to (an animal), esp. by force: *to drench a horse.* **—n. 4.** act of drenching. **5.** something that drenches: *a drench of rain.* **6.** a preparation for drenching or steeping. **7.** a large drink or draft. **8.** a draft of medicine, esp. one administered to an animal by force. [ME *drenche(n)*, OE *drencan*, causative of *drincan* drink] **—drench'er,** *n.* **—Syn. 1.** See **wet.**

Dres·den (drĕz'dən; *Ger.* drās'dən), *n.* **1.** a city in E Germany, on the Elbe. 630,216 (1939). **2.** an expensive china originally from Dresden.

dress (drĕs), *n., adj., v.*, **dressed or drest, dressing. —n. 1.** the garment worn by women, consisting of a skirt and a waist, made either separately or together. **2.** clothing; apparel; garb. **3.** fine clothes; formal costume: *full dress.* **4.** outer covering, as the plumage of birds. **—adj. 5.** of or for a dress or dresses. **6.** of or for a formal occasion: *a dress suit.* [n., adj. uses of v.] **—v.t. 7.** to equip with clothing, ornaments, etc.; deck; attire. **8.** to put formal or evening clothes on. **9.** to put best clothes on (fol. by *up*). **10.** to trim; ornament; adorn; *to dress a store window.* **11.** to prepare (food, skins, fabrics, timber, stone, ore, etc.) by special processes. **12.** to comb out and do up (hair). **13.** to cultivate (land, etc.). **14.** to treat (wounds or sores). **15.** to make straight; bring (troops) into line: *to dress ranks.* **16.** *Colloq.* to scold; thrash (fol. by *down*). **17. dress ship, a.** to decorate a ship by hoisting lines of flags running the full length of the ship. **b.** *U.S. Navy.* to display the national ensigns at each masthead and a larger ensign on the flagstaff. **—v.i. 18.** to clothe or attire oneself, esp. in formal or evening clothes: *she is dressing.* **19.** to put on one's best clothing (fol. by *up*). **20.** to come into line, as troops. [ME *dres(en)*, t. OF: m. *dresser* arrange, ult. der. L *directus* straight. See DIRECT v.] **—Syn. 1.** DRESS, COSTUME, GOWN refer to the outer garment of women. DRESS is the general term, esp. for a garment such as is used not only for covering but for adornment: *a black dress, a summer dress, a becoming dress.* COSTUME is used of the style of dress appropriate to some occasion, purpose, period, or character, esp. as used on the stage, at balls, at court, or the like: *an eighteenth century costume, an appropriate costume for the country, costumes worn at an important social event.* GOWN is usually applied to a dress more expensive and elegant than the ordinary, to be worn on a special occasion: *a wedding gown, an evening gown* (or *dress*). **2.** raiment, vesture, clothes, garments, vestments. **7.** clothe, apparel, array, robe.

dress circle, a circular or curving division of seats in a theater, etc., usually the first gallery, orig. set apart for spectators in evening dress.

dress coat, a man's close-fitting evening coat, with open front and with the skirts cut away over the hips.

dress·er¹ (drĕs'ər), *n.* **1.** one who dresses. **2.** one employed to help dress actors, etc. at a theater. **3.** any of several tools or devices used in dressing materials. **4.** *Brit.* an assistant to a surgeon. [f. DRESS + -ER¹]

dress·er² (drĕs'ər), *n.* **1.** a dressing table or bureau. **2.** a sideboard or set of shelves for dishes and cooking utensils. **3.** *Obs.* a table or sideboard on which food is dressed for serving. [ME *dressour*, t. OF: m. *decor*, der. *dresser* DRESS]

dress goods, cloth or material for dresses.

dress·ing (drĕs'ĭng), *n.* **1.** act of one who or that which dresses. **2.** that with which something is dressed. **3.** a sauce for food: *salad dressing.* **4.** stuffing for a fowl. **5.** an application for a wound. **6.** manure, compost, or other fertilizers for land.

dress·ing-down (drĕs'ĭng doun'), *n.* *Colloq.* **1.** a severe reprimand; scolding. **2.** a thrashing; beating.

dressing gown, a loose gown or robe worn while making the toilet or when in dishabille.

dressing room, a room for use in getting dressed, esp. backstage in a theater.

dressing sack, *U.S.* a woman's sack or jacket for wearing while making the toilet or when in dishabille.

dressing station, *Mil.* a post or center close to the combat area, which gives first aid to the wounded.

dressing table, a table or stand, usually surmounted by a mirror, for use in making the toilet.

dress·mak·er (drĕs'mā'kər), *n.* one whose occupation is the making of women's dresses, coats, etc. **—dress'mak'ing,** *n.*

dress parade, the ceremony at which soldiers in their dress uniforms take formation under arms.

dress rehearsal, a rehearsal of a play in costume and with scenery, properties, and lights arranged and operated as for a performance; the final rehearsal.

dress shield, a pad worn under the arms beneath the clothing to keep perspiration from showing or staining.

dress suit, a man's suit of evening clothes, with dress coat and open-fronted waistcoat.

dress·y (drĕs'ĭ), *adj.*, **dressier, dressiest.** *Colloq.* **1.** showy in dress; stylish. **2.** fond of dress. **—dress'i·ness,** *n.*

drest (drĕst), *v.* pt. and pp. of **dress.**

drew (drōō), *v.* pt. of **draw.**

Drew (drōō), *n.* **1.** John, 1827–62, U.S. actor, born in Ireland. **2.** his son John, 1853–1927, U.S. actor.

Drey·fus (drā'fəs, drī'-; *Fr.* drĕ'fŭs'), *n.* Alfred (ăl'frĭd; *Fr.* ăl frĕd'), 1859–1935, French army officer (Jewish) convicted of treason in 1894 and 1899, but proved innocent in 1906.

drib·ble (drĭb'əl), *v.*, **-bled, -bling,** *n.* **—v.i. 1.** to fall or flow in drops or small quantities; trickle. **2.** to drivel; slaver. **3.** (in men's basketball) to move about a court while bouncing the ball. **—v.t. 4.** to let fall in drops. **5.** *Sports.* **a.** (in men's basketball) to bounce (a basketball). **b.** (in some other games) to move (the ball) along by a rapid succession of short kicks or pushes. **—n. 6.** a small trickling stream, or a drop. **7.** a small quantity of anything. **8.** *Sports.* **a.** (in men's basketball) act of bouncing a basketball on the floor of the court as a player moves with the ball, it being a penalty to take more than two steps without such bouncing while in possession of the ball. **b.** (in some other games) act of dribbling. **9.** *Scot.* a drizzle. [freq. of obs. *drib* drip; in some senses influenced by DRIVEL] **—drib'bler,** *n.*

drib·let (drĭb'lĭt), *n.* **1.** a small portion or part. **2.** a small or petty sum. Also, **drib'blet.** [f. DRIBBLE + -ET]

dried (drīd), *v.* pt. and pp. of **dry.**

driegh (drēкн), *adj.* dree.

dri·er (drī'ər), *adj.* **1.** compar. of **dry. —n.** Also, **dryer. 2.** one who or that which dries. **3.** any substance added to paints, varnishes, etc., to make them dry quickly. **4.** mechanical contrivance or apparatus for removing moisture.

dri·est (drī'ĭst), *adj.* superl. of **dry.**

drift (drĭft), *n.* **1.** a driving movement or force; impulse; impetus; pressure. **2.** *Navig.* movement or course under the impulse of water (currents, wind, etc. **3.** *Phys. Geog.* a broad and shallow current which advances at a rate of ten or fifteen miles a day, like that which crosses the middle Atlantic. **4.** *Naut.* the speed in knots of an ocean current. **5.** *Aeron.* deviation of an aircraft from a set course, due to cross winds. **6.** the course of anything; tendency; aim: *the drift of an argument.* **7.** something driven, or formed by driving. **8.** a heap of any matter driven together: *a drift of snow.* **9.** *Geol.* **a.** a deposit of detritus. **b.** the deposit of a continental ice sheet. **10.** state or process of being driven. **11.** overbearing power or influence. **12.** an implement for cleaning the vent of ordnance after discharge. **13.** *Mach.* a round, tapering piece of steel for enlarging holes in metal, or for bringing holes in line to receive rivets, etc. **14.** *Civ. Eng.* a secondary tunnel between two main tunnels or shafts. **15.** *Mining.* an approximately horizontal passageway in underground mining, etc. **—v.i. 16.** to be carried along by currents of water or air, or by the force of circumstances. **17.** to be driven into heaps: *drifting sand.* **—v.t. 18.** to carry along: *the current drifted the boat to sea.* **19.** to drive into heaps: *drifted snow.* [ME *drift* act of driving, verbal abstract from OE *drīfan* drive] **—drift'er,** *n.*

drift·age (drĭf'tĭj), *n.* **1.** action or amount of drifting. **2.** drifted matter. **3.** *Naut.* the amount of deviation from a ship's course due to leeway. **4.** windage.

drift anchor, a sea anchor or drag.

drift ice, detached floating ice in masses which drift with the wind or ocean currents, as in the polar seas.

drift meter, *Aeron.* an instrument for measuring the drift of aircraft.

drift tube, *Radio.* a conducting enclosure, usually cylindrical, held at a constant potential so that electrons or charged particles within will experience no force, and hence no change in velocity. See **klystron.**

drift·wood (drĭft′wŏŏd′), *n.* wood floating on, or cast ashore by, the water.

drift·y (drĭf′tĭ), *adj.* of the nature of, or characterized by, drifts.

drill[1] (drĭl), *n.* **1.** a tool or machine for drilling or boring holes in metal, stone, or other hard substance. **2.** *Mil.* **a.** training in formal marching or other precise military or naval movements. **b.** an exercise in such training: *gun drill.* **3.** any strict, methodical training, instruction, or exercise. **4.** a gastropod, *Urosalpinx cinera,* destructive to oysters. —*v.t.* **5.** to pierce or bore a hole in (anything). **6.** to make (a hole) by boring. **7.** *Mil.* to instruct and exercise in formation marching and movement, the carrying of arms during formal marching, and the formal handling of arms for ceremonies and guard work. **8.** to impart (knowledge) by strict training or discipline. —*v.i.* **9.** to pierce or bore with a drill. **10.** to go through exercise in military or other training. [t. D: m. *drillen* bore, drill] —**drill′a·ble,** *adj.* —**drill′-er,** *n.* —Syn. 3. See **exercise.**

drill[2] (drĭl), *n.* **1.** a small furrow made in the soil, to sow seeds in. **2.** a machine for sowing seeds in rows and for covering the seeds when sown. **3.** a row of seeds or plants thus sown. —*v.t.* **4.** to sow (seed) or raise (crops) in drills. **5.** to plant (ground) in drills. —*v.i.* **6.** to sow seed in drills. [orig. uncert.] —**drill′er,** *n.*

drill[3] (drĭl), *n.* strong twilled cotton for a variety of uses. [short for DRILLING[2], t. G: triplet, confused with *drillich* ticking (f. *dri* three + *-lich*), t. L: m. s. *trilix* with three threads, *tri-* being translated]

drill[4] (drĭl), *n.* a baboon, *Papio leucophaeus,* of western Africa, smaller than the mandrill. [appar. native name. See MANDRILL]

drill bit, *Mach.* a boring tool for making round holes in metal or other hard substance.

drill·ing[1] (drĭl′ĭng), *n.* act of a person or thing that drills. [f. DRILL[1], v. + -ING[1]]

drill·ing[2] (drĭl′ĭng), *n.* drill[3].

drill·mas·ter (drĭl′măs′tər, -mäs′tər), *n.* **1.** one who trains others in anything, esp. in a mechanical manner. **2.** *Mil.* one who instructs in marching drill.

drill press, *Mach.* a machine tool for boring holes with a drill or drills.

dri·ly (drī′lĭ), *adv.* dryly.

Drin (drēn), *n.* a river flowing from S Yugoslavia through N Albania into the Adriatic. 180 mi.

Dri·na (drē′nä), *n.* a river in central Yugoslavia, flowing N to the Sava river. 160 mi.

drink (drĭngk), *v.,* **drank** (formerly also **drunk**); **drunk** (sometimes **drank,** formerly or as pred. adj. **drunken**); **drinking;** *n.* —*v.i.* **1.** to swallow water or other liquid; imbibe. **2.** to imbibe alcoholic liquors, esp. habitually or to excess; tipple. **3.** to salute in drinking; drink in honor of (fol. by *to*). —*v.t.* **4.** to swallow (a liquid). **5.** to take in (a liquid) in any manner; absorb. **6.** to take in through the senses, esp. with eagerness and pleasure. **7.** to swallow the contents of (a cup, etc.). **8.** to drink in honor of or with good wishes for. —*n.* **9.** any liquid which is swallowed to quench thirst, for nourishment, etc.; a beverage. **10.** alcoholic liquor. **11.** excessive indulgence in alcoholic liquor. **12.** a draft of liquid; a potion. [ME *drinke(n),* OE *drincan,* c. G *trinken*] —Syn. 1. DRINK, IMBIBE, SIP refer to swallowing liquids. DRINK is the general word: *to drink coffee.* IMBIBE is more formal and today is hardly used in reference to actual drinking except facetiously; it is used figuratively in the meaning to absorb: *to imbibe culture.* SIP implies drinking little by little, at short, succeeding intervals, often in a delicate, toying, or idle manner: *sip a cup of broth.*

drink·a·ble (drĭngk′ə bəl), *adj.* **1.** that may be drunk; suitable for drinking. —*n.* **2.** (*usually pl.*) something drinkable; a liquid for drinking.

drink·er (drĭngk′ər), *n.* **1.** one who drinks. **2.** one who drinks alcoholic liquors habitually or to excess.

Drink·wa·ter (drĭngk′wô′tər, -wŏt′ər), *n.* **John,** 1882–1937, British poet, dramatist, and critic.

drip (drĭp), *v.,* **dripped** or **dript, dripping,** *n.* —*v.i.* **1.** to let fall drops; shed drops. **2.** to fall in drops, as a liquid. —*v.t.* **3.** to let fall in drops. —*n.* **4.** act of dripping. **5.** the liquid that drips. **6.** *Archit.* **a.** a projecting part of a cornice or the like, so shaped as to throw off rain water and thus protect the parts below. **b.** a projecting metal strip having the same function. [ME *dryppe,* OE *dryppan,* der. OE *dropa* drop]

drip coffee, a beverage prepared in a vessel (**drip coffee maker**) in which boiling water filters from a top compartment through the coffee into a pot below.

drip·ping (drĭp′ĭng), *n.* **1.** act of anything that drips. **2.** (*often pl.*) the liquid that drips. **3.** fat exuded from meat in cooking and used as shortening.

dripping pan, a pan used under roasting meat to receive the dripping. Also, **drip pan.**

drip·stone (drĭp′stōn′), *n.* **1.** *Archit.* a projecting stone molding or cornice for throwing off rain water.

2. calcium carbonate, $CaCO_3$, occurring in the form of stalactites and stalagmites.

drive (drīv), *v.,* **drove** or (*Archaic*) **drave; driven; driving;** *n.* —*v.t.* **1.** to send along or away, off, in, out, back, etc., by compulsion; force along: *to drive someone to desperation, out of one's senses, to do something.* **2.** to overwork; overtask. **3.** to cause and guide the movement of (an animal, vehicle, etc.). **4.** to convey in a vehicle. **5.** to keep (machinery) going. **6.** to impel; constrain; urge; compel. **7.** to carry (business, a bargain, etc.) vigorously through. **8.** *Mining, etc.* to excavate horizontally (or nearly so). **9.** *Baseball, Tennis, etc.* to knock or throw (the ball) very swiftly. **10.** *Hunting.* **a.** to chase (game). **b.** to search (a district) for game. —*v.i.* **11.** to go along before an impelling force; be impelled: *the ship drove before the wind.* **12.** to rush or dash violently. **13.** to make an effort to reach or obtain; aim (fol. by *at*): *the idea he was driving at, what is he driving at?* **14.** to act as driver. **15.** to go or travel in a driven vehicle: *to drive away, back, in, out, from, to, etc.* **16. let drive (at),** to aim a blow, missile, etc., (at). —*n.* **17.** the act of driving. **18.** an impelling along, as of game, cattle, or floating logs, in a particular direction. **19.** the animals, logs, etc., thus driven. **20.** *Psychol.* a source of motivation: *the hunger drive.* **21.** *Sports.* a propelling or forcible stroke. **22.** a vigorous onset or onward course. **23.** a strong military offensive. **24.** a united effort to accomplish some purpose, esp. to raise money for a government loan or for some charity. **25.** vigorous pressure or effort, as in business. **26.** a trip in a driven vehicle. **27.** a road for driving. **28.** *Mach.* a driving mechanism, as of a motorcar: *gear drive, chain drive.* **29.** *Auto.* point or points of power application to the roadway: *front drive, rear drive, four-wheel drive.* **30.** *Trade Slang.* an attempt to force down the market price of a commodity by offering a quantity at a low price. **31.** *Baseball, Tennis, etc.* the knocking of a ball very swiftly. [ME *driven,* OE *drīfan,* c. G *treiben*] —Syn. 1. push, force. **15.** DRIVE, RIDE are used interchangeably to mean taking a trip in a private horse-drawn vehicle or an automobile. These two words are not synonyms in other connections. To DRIVE is to guide or steer the progress of a vehicle: *to drive a bus, a truck, an automobile, a horse, oxen.* To RIDE is to sit on the back of, and be carried about by, an animal; or to be carried as a passenger in a vehicle: *to ride a horse, in a train, on a bus, on a public conveyance.* **25.** energy. —Ant. 1. lead.

drive-in (drīv′ĭn′), *n.* a motion picture theater, refreshment stand, etc., catering to customers who remain in their automobiles.

driv·el (drĭv′əl), *v.,* **-eled, -eling** or (*esp. Brit.*) **-elled, -elling,** *n.* —*v.i.* **1.** to let saliva flow from the mouth or mucus from the nose; slaver. **2.** to issue like spittle. **3.** to talk childishly or idiotically. **4.** to act foolishly. —*v.t.* **5.** to utter childishly or idiotically. **6.** to waste foolishly. —*n.* **7.** saliva flowing from the mouth, or mucus from the nose; slaver. **8.** childish, idiotic, or silly talk; twaddle. [ME *dryvele, drevel(en),* OE *dreflian*] —**driv′el·er;** *esp. Brit.,* **driv′el·ler,** *n.*

driv·en (drĭv′ən), *v.* pp. of **drive.**

driv·er (drī′vər), *n.* **1.** one who or that which drives. **2.** one who drives an animal or animals, a vehicle, etc.; coachman; drover, chauffeur, etc. **3.** *Brit.* a locomotive engineer. **4.** *Mach.* a part that transmits force or motion. **5.** *Golf.* a long-shafted, wooden-headed club, used for making long shots, as from the tee. —**driv′er·less,** *adj.*

driver ant, any of the ants of the subfamily *Dorylinae,* occurring in tropical Africa and America, which live in temporary nests and travel as vast armies in long files, preying on other animals, chiefly insects. See **army ant.**

drive·way (drīv′wā′), *n.* **1.** a private road from a house to the street. **2.** a road for driving on.

driv·ing (drī′vĭng), *adj.* **1.** (of a person) effective in eliciting work from others; energetic. **2.** relaying or transmitting power.

driving wheel, 1. *Mach.* a main wheel which communicates motion to others. **2.** one of the propelling wheels of a locomotive; any wheel used to transform the force of the locomotive cylinder into tractive effort.

driz·zle (drĭz′əl), *v.,* **-zled, -zling,** *n.* —*v.i., v.t.* **1.** to rain gently and steadily in fine drops; sprinkle. —*n.* **2.** a light rain; mizzle; mist. **3.** *Meteorol.* precipitation consisting of numerous, minute droplets of water less than $1/50$ inch in diameter. [possibly dim. and freq. form of rare ME *dresen,* OE *drēosan* fall] —**driz′zly,** *adj.*

Drog·he·da (drŏ′hĭ da), *n.* a seaport in NE Eire, near the mouth of the Boyne river: town captured and the inhabitants massacred by Cromwell, 1649. 15,216 (1941).

droit (droit; *Fr.* drwä), *n.* **1.** a legal right or claim. **2.** that to which one has a legal right or claim. **3.** the body of rules constituting the law. **4.** *Finance.* duty; custom. [t. F, g. Rom. *dērectum,* r. L *dīrectum* right, prop. neut. of L *dīrectus* straight. See DIRECT, *adj.*]

droll (drōl), *adj.* **1.** amusingly queer; comical; waggish. —*n.* **2.** a waggish fellow; a jester; a buffoon. —*v.i.* **3.** to play the droll or buffoon; jest; joke. [t. F: m. *drôle,* t. MD: m. *drolle* little man] —**droll′ness,** *n.* —**drol′ly,** *adv.* —Syn. 1. See **amusing.**

droll·er·y (drō′lə rĭ), *n., pl.* **-eries. 1.** something amusingly queer or funny. **2.** a jest; a facetious tale. **3.** droll quality; humor. **4.** the action or behavior of a buffoon or wag; jesting. **5.** a comic picture. **6.** *Obs.* a puppet show.

-drome, a word element meaning "running," "course," "race course," as in *hippodrome*. [comb. form repr. Gk. *drómos*]

drom·e·dar·y (drŏm′ə dĕr′ĭ, drŭm′-), *n.*, *pl.* **-daries.** the one-humped or Arabian camel, *Camelus dromedarius*, light swift types of which are bred for riding and racing. [ME *dromedarye*, t. LL: m. *dromedārius* (sc. *camēlus*), der. L *dromas* dromedary, t. Gk.: running]

drom·ond (drŏm′ənd, drŭm′-), *n.* a large, fast-sailing vessel of the Middle Ages. [ME *dromon*, t. LL: s. *dromo*, t. LGk.: m. *drómōn* light vessel, der. Gk. *drómos* a running]

-dromous, an adjective termination corresponding to **-drome.** [f. -DROME + -OUS]

Dromedary,
Camelus dromedarius
(6 ft. high at the shoulder,
7 to 8 ft. high at the hump)

drone¹ (drōn), *n.* **1.** the male of the honeybee and other bees, stingless and making no honey. **2.** one who lives on the labor of others; an idler; a sluggard. **3.** a remotely controlled mechanism, as a radio-controlled airplane or boat. [earlier *drone(e)*, *drowne*, early ME *dron*, var. of ME and OE *dran* (cf. G *drohne*)] **—dron′ish,** *adj.*

drone² (drōn), *v.*, **droned, droning,** *n.* **—***v.i.* **1.** to make a dull, continued, monotonous sound; hum; buzz. **2.** to speak in a monotonous tone. **—***v.t.* **3.** to say in a dull, monotonous tone. **—***n.* **4.** *Music.* **a.** a continuous low tone produced by the bass pipes or bass strings of musical instruments. **b.** the pipes (esp. of the bagpipe) or strings producing this tone. **c.** a bagpipe equipped with such pipes. **5.** a monotonous tone; a humming; a buzzing. **6.** a monotonous speaker. [cf. DRONE¹; akin to ME *droun* roar] **—dron′ing·ly,** *adv.*

dron·go (drŏng′gō), *n.*, *pl.* **-gos.** any of the oscine passerine birds of the African and Asiatic family *Dicruridae*, usually black in color, with long forked tails, and insectivorous habits. [t. Malagasy]

drool (drool), *v.*, *n.* *Colloq.* drivel. [contr. of DRIVEL]

droop (droop), *v.i.* **1.** to sink, bend, or hang down, as from weakness or exhaustion. **2.** *Poetic.* to sink; descend, as the sun. **3.** to fall into a state of physical weakness; flag; fail. **4.** to lose spirit or courage. **—***v.t.* **5.** to let sink or drop. **—***n.* **6.** a drooping. [ME *droupe(n)*, t. Scand.; cf. Icel. *drūpa*; akin to DROOP] **—droop′ing·ly,** *adv.* **—droop′y,** *adj.* **—Syn. 1.** flag, languish.

drop (drŏp), *n.*, *v.*, **dropped** or **dropt, dropping.** **—***n.* **1.** a small quantity of liquid which falls or is produced in a more or less spherical mass; a liquid globule. **2.** the quantity of liquid contained in such a mass. **3.** a very small quantity of liquid. **4.** a minute quantity of anything. **5.** (*usually pl.*) liquid medicine given in drops. **6.** something like or likened to a drop. **7.** a lozenge (confection). **8.** a pendant. **9.** act of dropping; fall; descent. **10.** the distance or depth to which anything drops. **11.** a steep slope. **12.** that which drops or is used for dropping. **13.** a drop curtain. **14.** a trap door. **15.** gallows. **16.** a slit or aperture into which to drop mail, as a letter box. **17.** *Naut.* the vertical length of a course. See **holst. 18. get** or **have the drop on,** *Colloq.* **a.** to pull and aim a gun, etc., before an antagonist can. **b.** to get or have at a disadvantage. **—***v.i.* **19.** to fall in globules or small portions, as water or other liquid: *rain drops from the clouds.* **20.** to fall vertically like a drop; have an abrupt descent. **21.** to sink to the ground as if inanimate. **22.** to fall wounded, dead, etc. **23.** to come to an end; cease; lapse: *there the matter dropped.* **24.** to withdraw; disappear (fol. by *out*). **25.** to squat or crouch, as a dog at the sight of game. **26.** to fall lower in condition, degree, etc.; sink: *the prices dropped sharply.* **27.** to pass without effort into some condition: *to drop asleep, drop into the habit of doing it.* **28.** to move down gently, as with the tide or a light wind. **29.** to fall or move (*back, behind, to the rear,* etc.). **30.** to come or go casually or unexpectedly into a place; to visit informally: *he dropped in on us occasionally.* **31.** to give birth. **32. drop astern,** to pass or move toward the stern; move back; let another vessel pass ahead. **33. drop off, a.** to decrease; decline: *sales have dropped off.* **b.** to fall asleep. **—***v.t.* **34.** to let fall in drops or small portions: *drop a medicine.* **35.** *Archaic.* to sprinkle with or as with drops. **36.** to let fall; allow to sink to a lower position; lower: *to drop anchor.* **37.** to give birth to (young). **38.** to utter or express casually or incidentally, as a hint. **39.** to send (a note, etc.) in a casual or offhand manner: *drop me a line!* **40.** to bring to the ground by a blow or shot. **41.** to set down, as from a ship, car, etc. **42.** to omit (a letter or syllable) in pronunciation or writing: *he dropped his h's.* **43.** to lower (the voice) in pitch or loudness. **44.** to cease to keep up or have to do with: *I dropped the subject.* **45.** *U.S.* to cease to employ; to dismiss (from college, etc.). **46.** *Football.* to score (a goal) by a drop kick. **47.** *Naut.* to outdistance; pass out of sight of. **48.** *Cookery.* to poach. [ME *drope*, OE *dropa*, c. Icel. *dropi.*]

drop biscuit, a biscuit made by dropping baking powder biscuit dough from a spoon onto a pan for baking.

drop cooky, a cooky made by dropping batter from a spoon onto a greased cooky sheet for baking.

drop curtain, *Theat.* a curtain which is lowered into position from the flies.

drop-forge (drŏp′fôrj′), *v.t.,* **-forged, -forging.** *Metall.* to forge by the impact of a falling mass or weight, the hot piece of metal usually being placed between dies and subjected to the blow of a drop hammer or the like.

drop forging, *Metal.* a drop-forged forging.

drop hammer, an apparatus for forging, etc., in which a heavy weight is made to drop on the metal to be worked, which is placed on an anvil or in dies.

drop kick, *Football.* a kick given the ball as it rises from the ground after being dropped by the kicker.

drop-kick (drŏp′kĭk′), *v.i.*, *v.t. Football.* to give a drop kick. **—drop′-kick′er,** *n.*

drop leaf, *Furnit.* an extension attached to the end or side of a table and folded vertically when not needed. **—drop′-leaf′,** *adj.*

drop·let (drŏp′lĭt), *n.* a little drop.

drop letter, *U.S.* a letter to be delivered from or by the same post office in which it is posted.

drop·light (drŏp′līt′), *n.* a portable gas or electric lamp connected with a fixture above by a tube or wire.

drop·per (drŏp′ər), *n.* **1.** one who or that which drops. **2.** a glass tube with an elastic cap at one end and a small orifice at the other, for drawing in a liquid and expelling it in drops; medicine dropper.

drop·ping (drŏp′ĭng), *n.* **1.** act of one who or that which drops. **2.** that which drops or falls in drops. **3.** (*pl.*) dung of animals.

drop shipment, *Com.* an order shipped by a seller to the customer or his distributor, as a shipment by a manufacturer to a retailer that is billed to a wholesaler.

drop·si·cal (drŏp′sə kəl), *adj.* of, like, or affected with dropsy. **—drop′si·cal·ly,** *adv.*

drop·sy (drŏp′sĭ), *n. Pathol.* an excessive accumulation of serous fluid in a serous cavity or in the subcutaneous cellular tissue. [ME (*y*)*dropesie*, t. OF: m. *idropisie*, t. L: m.s. *hydrōpsis*, der. Gk. *hŷdrōps*] **—drop′sied** (drŏp′sĭd), *adj.*

dropt (drŏpt), *v.* pt. and pp. of **drop.**

drop·wort (drŏp′wûrt′), *n.* **1.** a European rosaceous herb, *Filipendula hexapetala*, bearing small, scentless, white or reddish flowers. **2.** any plant of the North American umbelliferous genus *Oxypolis* (*Tiedmania*), as *O. rigidior*, an herb of ditches and marshes.

drosh·ky (drŏsh′kĭ), *n.*, *pl.* **-kies. 1.** a light, low, four-wheeled, open vehicle, used in Russia, in which the passengers sit astride or sideways on a long, narrow bench. **2.** any of various other vehicles, as the ordinary cab, used mainly in Russia. Also, **dros·ky** (drŏs′kĭ). [t. Russ.: m. *drozhki*, dim. of *drogi* wagon]

dro·soph·i·la (drō sŏf′ə lə), *n.*, *pl.* **-lae** (lō′). a fly of the genus *Drosophila.*

Dro·soph·i·la (drō sŏf′ə lə), *n.pl.* a genus of flies of the family *Drosophilidae*, one species of which, the vinegar fly, *D. melanogaster*, is very widely used in laboratory studies of inheritance. [NL, f. Gk.: *drōso(s)* dew + *phíla*, fem. of *phílos* loving]

dross (drôs, drŏs), *n.* **1.** *Metall.* a waste product taken off molten metal during smelting, essentially metallic in character. **2.** waste matter; refuse. [ME and OE *drôs*, c. MD *droes* dregs. Cf. G *drusen* dregs, husks] **—dross′-y,** *adj.* **—dross′i·ness,** *n.*

drought (drout), *n.* **1.** dry weather; lack of rain. **2.** *Now Rare.* scarcity. **3.** *Dial.* thirst. Also, **drouth** (drouth). [ME *drought(h)*, etc., OE *drūgath*, akin to *drŷge* dry]

drought·y (drou′tĭ), *adj.* **1.** dry. **2.** lacking rain. **3.** *Dial.* or *Prov.* thirsty. Also, **drouth·y** (drou′thĭ).

drouk (drook), *v.t. Scot.* to drench; wet thoroughly. [t. Scand.; cf. Icel. *drukna* be drowned]

drove¹ (drōv), *v.* pt. of **drive.**

drove² (drōv), *n.*, *v.*, **droved, droving. —***n.* **1.** a number of oxen, sheep, or swine driven in a group; herd; flock. **2.** a large crowd of human beings, esp. in motion. **3.** *Bldg. Trades.* **a.** Also, **drove chisel.** a stonemason's chisel, from two to four inches broad, used in making droved work. **b.** drove work. **—***v.t.*, *v.i.* **4.** to drive or deal in (cattle) as a drover. **5.** *Bldg. Trades.* to work or smooth (stone, etc.) as with a stonemason's drove. [ME; OE *drāf* act of driving, herd, company. See DRIVE] **—Syn. 1.** See flock⁴.

dro·ver (drō′vər), *n.* **1.** one who drives cattle, sheep, etc., to market. **2.** a dealer in cattle.

drove work, *Bldg. Trades.* the surface of stone worked with a drove.

drown (droun), *v.i.* **1.** to be suffocated by immersion in water or other liquid. **—***v.t.* **2.** to suffocate (a person, etc.) by immersion in water or other liquid. **3.** to destroy; get rid of. **4.** to flood; inundate. **5.** to overwhelm as by a flood; overpower. [var. of obs. *drunken*, OE *druncnian*; ME *drounne* shows loss of *c* between the nasals; length of nasal later shifted to vowel]

drowse (drouz), *v.*, **drowsed, drowsing,** *n.* **—***v.i.* **1.** to be sleepy; be half-asleep. **2.** to be dull or sluggish. **—***v.t.* **3.** to make sleepy. **4.** to pass or spend (time) in drowsing. **—***n.* **5.** a sleepy condition; state of being half-asleep. [OE *drūsian* droop, become sluggish]

drow·si·head (drou′zĭ hĕd′), *n. Archaic.* drowsiness.

drow·sy (drou′zĭ), *adj.*, **-sier, -siest. 1.** inclined to sleep; half asleep. **2.** marked by or resulting from sleepiness. **3.** dull; sluggish. **4.** inducing sleepiness. **—drow′si·ly,** *adv.* **—drow′si·ness,** *n.*

drub (drŭb), v., **drubbed, drubbing,** n. —v.t. **1.** to beat with a stick or the like; cudgel; flog; thrash: to drub something into or out of a person. **2.** to defeat decisively. **3.** to stamp (the feet). —n. **4.** a blow with a stick or the like. [? t. Ar.: m. ḍarb stroke] —**drub′ber,** n.

drub·bing (drŭb′ĭng), n. **1.** a beating; a sound thrashing. **2.** a decisive defeat.

drudge (drŭj), n., v., **drudged, drudging.** —n. **1.** one who labors at servile or uninteresting tasks; a hard toiler. —v.i. **2.** to perform servile, distasteful, or hard work. [OE Drycg- bearer (in proper name); akin to DREE] —**drudg′er,** n. —**drudg′ing·ly,** adv.

drudg·er·y (drŭj′ər ĭ), n., pl. **-eries.** tedious, hard, or uninteresting work. —**Syn.** See **work.**

drug (drŭg), n., v., **drugged, drugging.** —n. **1.** a chemical substance given with the intention of preventing or curing disease or otherwise enhancing the physical or mental welfare of men or animals. **2.** a habit-forming medicinal substance; a narcotic. **3.** (formerly) any ingredient used in chemistry, pharmacy, dyeing, or the like. **4.** a commodity that is overabundant, or in excess of demand, in the market. —v.t. **5.** to mix (food or drink) with a drug, esp. a narcotic or poisonous drug. **6.** to stupefy or poison with a drug. **7.** to administer anything nauseous to; surfeit. [ME drogges (pl.), t. OF: m. drogue, ? t. D: m. drog dry thing]

drug·get (drŭg′ĭt), n. **1.** a rug from India made of coarse hair with cotton or jute. **2.** Obs. a fabric woven wholly or partly of wool, used for clothing. [t. F: m. droguet, der. drogue drug, cheap article]

drug·gist (drŭg′ĭst), n. Scot. and U.S. one who compounds or prepares drugs according to medical prescriptions; apothecary; pharmacist; dispensing chemist.

drug store, U.S. the place of business of a druggist or pharmacist, often also selling cosmetics, stationery, light meals, cigarettes, etc.

Dru·id (drōō′ĭd), n. (often l.c.) one of an order of priests or ministers of religion among the ancient Celts of Gaul, Britain, and Ireland. [t. F: m. druide, t. L: m. druidae, pl.] —**Dru·id·ess** (drōō′ĭd ĭs), n. fem. —**dru·id′ic, dru·id′i·cal,** adj.

dru·id·ism (drōō′ĭ dĭz′əm), n. the religion or rites of the Druids.

drum[1] (drŭm), n., v., **drummed, drumming.** —n. **1.** a musical instrument consisting of a hollow body covered at one or both ends with a tightly stretched membrane, or head, which is struck with the hand, a stick, or a pair of sticks. **2.** any hollow tree or similar device used in this way. **3.** the sound produced by either of these. **4.** any noise suggestive of it. **5.** one who plays the drum. **6.** a natural organ by which an animal produces a loud or bass sound. **7.** something resembling a drum in shape or structure, or in the noise it produces. **8.** Anat., Zool. **a.** the tympanum or middle ear. **b.** the eardrum or tympanic membrane. **9.** a cylindrical part of a machine. **10.** a cylindrical box or receptacle. **11.** drumfish. **12.** Obs. an assembly of fashionable people at a private house in the evening. —v.i. **13.** to beat or play a drum. **14.** to beat on anything rhythmically. **15.** to make a sound like that of a drum; resound. **16.** (of partridges and other birds) to produce a sound resembling drumming. —v.t. **17.** to beat rhythmically; perform (a tune) by drumming. **18.** to call or summon by, or as by, beating a drum. **19.** to drive or force by persistent repetition: to drum an idea into someone. **20.** to solicit or obtain (trade, customers, etc.) (often fol. by up). **21.** (formerly) to expel or dismiss in disgrace to the beat of a drum (fol. by out). [back formation from drumslade drummer, t. LG: m. trommelslag drumbeat (confused in E with trommelslager drummer); E d- ? by assoc. with dub-a-dub sound made in beating a drum]

drum[2] (drŭm), n. Irish, Scot. a long, narrow hill or ridge. [t. Irish and Gaelic: m. druim back, ridge]

drum·beat (drŭm′bēt′), n. the sound of a drum.

drum·ble (drŭm′bəl, drŭm′əl), v.i., **-bled, -bling.** Obs. or Prov. to move sluggishly.

drum corps, a body of drum players under the direction of a drum major or the like.

drum·fire (drŭm′fīr′), n. gunfire so heavy and continuous as to sound like the beating of drums.

drum·fish (drŭm′fĭsh′), n., pl. **-fishes,** (esp. collectively) **-fish.** any of various American sciaenoid fishes producing a drumming sound, as Pogonias cromis of the Atlantic coast of the United States, or the **fresh-water drumfish,** Aplodinotus grunniens, of the Great Lakes and the Mississippi valley.

drum·head (drŭm′hĕd′), n. **1.** the membrane stretched upon a drum. **2.** the top part of a capstan.

drumhead court-martial, a court-martial held (orig. round an upturned drum for a table) for the summary trial of charges of offenses committed during military operations.

drum·lin (drŭm′lĭn), n. Geol. a long narrow, or oval, smoothly rounded hill of unstratified glacial drift. [? var. of drumling, dim. of DRUM[2]]

drum·ly (drŭm′lĭ), adj. Scot. troubled; gloomy.

drum major, the leader of a drum corps or band in marching.

drum·mer (drŭm′ər), n. **1.** one who plays a drum. **2.** U.S. a commercial traveler or traveling salesman.

Drum·mond (drŭm′ənd), n. **1. Henry,** 1851–97, Scottish clergyman and writer. **2. William Henry,** 1854–1907, Canadian poet, born in Ireland.

Drummond light, the calcium light. [named after Capt. T. Drummond, R.E.]

drum·stick (drŭm′stĭk′), n. **1.** a stick for beating a drum. **2.** the lower part of the leg of a cooked chicken, duck, turkey, etc.

drunk (drŭngk), pred. adj. **1.** intoxicated with, or as with, strong drink: drunk with joy, success. —n. Colloq. **2.** a drunken person. **3.** a spree; a drinking party. —v. **4.** pp. and former pt. of **drink.**

drunk·ard (drŭngk′ərd), n. a person who is habitually or frequently drunk.
—**Syn.** toper, sot. DRUNKARD, INEBRIATE, DIPSOMANIAC are terms for a person who drinks hard liquors habitually. DRUNKARD connotes willful indulgence to excess. INEBRIATE, once a more formal word, is now applied only humorously. DIPSOMANIAC is the term for a person who, because of some psychological or physiological illness, has an irresistible craving for liquor. The dipsomaniac is popularly called an ALCOHOLIC.

drunk·en (drŭngk′ən), adj. **1.** intoxicated; drunk. **2.** given to drunkenness. **3.** pertaining to, proceeding from, or marked by intoxication: a drunken quarrel. —**drunk′en·ly,** adv. —**drunk′en·ness,** n. —**Syn. 1.** inebriated, tipsy, fuddled.

dru·pa·ceous (drōō pā′shəs), adj. Bot. **1.** resembling or relating to a drupe; consisting of drupes. **2.** producing drupes: drupaceous trees.

drupe (drōōp), n. Bot. a fruit, as the peach, cherry, plum, etc., consisting of an outer skin (epicarp), a (generally) pulpy and succulent layer (mesocarp), and a hard and woody inner shell or stone (endocarp) which incloses usually a single seed. [t. NL: m. s. drūpa drupe, L drūpa, druppa overripe olive, t. Gk.: m. drýppa]

drupe·let (drōōp′lĭt), n. Bot. a little drupe, as one of the individual pericarps composing the blackberry.

Druse (drōōz), n. one of a fanatical and warlike people and religious sect of Syria. [t. Ar.: m. Durūz, pl.] —**Dru·si·an, Dru·se·an** (drōō′zĭ ən), adj.

Dru·sus (drōō′səs), n. **Nero Claudius** (nĭr′ō klô′dĭ əs), ("Germanicus") 38 B.C.–9 B.C., Roman general.

dry (drī), adj., **drier, driest,** v., **dried, drying,** n., pl. **drys.** —adj. **1.** free from moisture; not moist; not wet. **2.** having little or no rain: a dry climate or season. **3.** characterized by absence, deficiency, or failure of natural or ordinary moisture. **4.** not under, in, or on water: dry land. **5.** not yielding water or other liquid: a dry well. **6.** not yielding milk: a dry cow. **7.** free from tears: dry eyes. **8.** wiped or drained away; evaporated: a dry river. **9.** desiring drink; thirsty. **10.** causing thirst: dry work. **11.** without butter or the like: dry toast. **12.** Art. hard and formal in outline, or lacking mellowness and warmth in color. **13.** plain; bald; unadorned: dry facts. **14.** dull; uninteresting: a dry subject. **15.** humorous or sarcastic in an unemotional or impersonal way: dry humor. **16.** indifferent; cold; unemotional: a dry answer. **17.** (of wines) not sweet. **18.** of or pertaining to nonliquid substances or commodities: dry measure. **19.** U.S. Colloq. characterized by or favoring prohibition of the manufacture and sale of alcoholic liquors for use as beverages. —v.t. **20.** to make dry; free from moisture: dry your eyes. —v.i. **21.** to become dry; lose moisture. **22. dry up, a.** to become completely dry. **b.** to become intellectually barren. **c.** Colloq. to stop talking. —n. **23.** U.S. Colloq. a prohibitionist. [ME drie, OE drȳge, akin to LG drög, G trocken] —**dry′ly, drily,** adv. —**dry′ness,** n.
—**Syn. 1.** DRY, ARID both mean without moisture. DRY is the general word indicating absence of water or freedom from moisture (which may be favorable): dry well, dry clothes or land. ARID suggests great or intense dryness in a region or climate, esp. such as results in bareness or in barrenness: arid tracts of desert. **20.** See **evaporate.** —**Ant. 1.** wet.

dry·ad (drī′əd, -ăd), n., pl. **-ads, -ades** (-ə dēz′). Gk. Myth. (often cap.) a deity or nymph of the woods; a nymph supposed to reside in trees or preside over woods. [t. L: s. Dryas (pl. Dryades), t. Gk., der. drýs tree, oak] —**dry·ad′ic** (drī ăd′ĭk), adj.

dry·as·dust (drī′əz dŭst′), n. one who deals with dry, uninteresting subjects; a dull pedant. —**dry′-as·dust′,** adj.

dry battery, Elect. a dry cell, or voltaic battery consisting of a number of dry cells.

dry-bone ore (drī′bōn′), smithsonite.

dry cell, Elect. a cell in which the electrolyte exists in the form of a paste or is absorbed in a porous medium, or is otherwise restrained from flowing from its original position.

dry-clean (drī′klēn′), v.t. to clean (garments, etc.) with benzine, gasoline, etc., rather than water. —**dry cleaner.**

dry-cleanse (drī′klĕnz′), v.t., **-cleansed, -cleansing.** dry-clean.

Dry·den (drī′dən), n. **John,** 1631–1700, British poet, dramatist, and critic.

dry distillation, Chem. destructive distillation.

dry dock, 1. a basinlike structure from which the water can be removed after the entrance of a ship: used when making repairs on a ship's bottom, etc. **2.** a floating structure which may be partially submerged to permit a vessel to enter, and then raised to lift the vessel out of the water for repairs, etc.

dry-dock (drī′dŏk′), v.t. **1.** to place in a dry dock. —v.i. **2.** to go into dry dock.

---

b., blend of, blended; c., cognate with; d., dialect, dialectal; der., derived from; f., formed from; g., going back to; m., modification of; r., replacing; s., stem of; t., taken from; ?, perhaps. See the full key on inside cover.

dry·er (drī′ər), *n.* drier.

dry farming, a mode of farming practised in regions of slight or insufficient rainfall, depending largely upon tillage methods which render the soil more receptive of moisture and reduce evaporation. **—dry farmer.**

dry-fly fishing (drī′flī′), fishing with an artificial fly in such a manner that the fly floats on the surface of the water.

dry fog, *Meteorol.* a haze due principally to the presence of dust or smoke in the air.

dry goods, textile fabrics and related articles of trade, in dictinction from groceries, hardware, etc.

dry ice, 1. solid carbon dioxide, having a temperature of 109° Fahr. below zero at atmospheric pressure. 2. (*cap.*) a trademark for this substance.

dry kiln, an oven for the controlled drying of cut lumber, boards, etc.

dry law, *U.S.* a law prohibiting general use of intoxicating liquors.

dry measure, the system of units of capacity ordinarily used in measuring dry commodities, such as grain, fruit, etc. In the U.S. 2 pints = 1 quart; 8 quarts = 1 peck; 4 pecks = 1 bushel or 2150.42 cubic inches. In Great Britain, the gallon of 4 quarts and the quarter of 8 bushels are added, the bushel being 2219.36 cubic inches.

dry nurse, 1. a nurse who takes care of a child but does not suckle it. 2. one who tutors and guides an inexperienced superior officer.

dry-nurse (drī′nûrs′), *v.t.,* **-nursed, -nursing.** to act as a dry nurse to.

dry plate, *Photog.* a glass plate coated with a sensitive emulsion of silver bromide and silver iodide in gelatin, upon which a negative or positive can be produced by exposure (as in a camera) and development.

dry point, 1. a stout, sharp-pointed needle used for ploughing into copper plates to produce furrows with raised edges that print with a fuzzy, velvety black. 2. the process of engraving in this way. 3. an engraving so made.

dry rot, 1. a decay of seasoned timber causing it to become brittle and to crumble to a dry powder, due to various fungi. 2. any of various diseases of vegetables with which the dead tissue is dry. 3. any concealed or unsuspected inward decay.

dry-shod (drī′shŏd′), *adj.* having or keeping the shoes dry.

Dry Tor·tu·gas (drī tôr tōō′gəz), a group of ten small islands at the N entrance to the Gulf of Mexico: a part of Florida; the site of Fort Jefferson.

dry wash, clothes, etc., washed and dried, but unironed.

Ds, *Chem.* dysprosium.

D.S., 1. Doctor of Science. 2. *Music.* dal segno.

d.s., 1. daylight saving. 2. Com. days after sight.

D. Sc., Doctor of Science.

D.S.C., Distinguished Service Cross.

D.S.M., *U.S.* Distinguished Service Medal.

D.S.O., *Brit.* (Companion of the) Distinguished Service Order.

D.S.T, Daylight Saving Time.

d.t., delirium tremens. Also, **d.t.'s.**

D. Th., Doctor of Theology. Also, **D. Theol.**

Du., 1. Duke. 2. Dutch.

du·ad (dū′ăd, dōō′-), *n.* a group of two. [b. DUAL and DYAD]

du·al (dū′əl, dōō′-), *adj.* 1. of or pertaining to two. 2. composed or consisting of two parts; twofold; double: *dual ownership, dual controls on a plane.* 3. *Gram.* (in some languages) designating a number category which implies two persons or things. **—n.** 4. *Gram.* **a.** the dual number. **b.** a form therein, as Greek *anthrōpō* two men, nominative dual of *anthrōpos* man, cf. *anthrōpoi* three or more men, or Old English *git* 'you two' as contrasted with *ge,* 'you' referring to three or more. [t. L: s. *duālis* containing two] **—du′al·ly,** *adv.*

Dual Alliance, 1. the alliance formed in 1891–94 between France and Russia, lasting until the Bolshevik revolution in 1917. 2. the alliance between Germany and Austria, 1879–1918, more frequently called the Austro-German alliance.

du·al·ism (dū′əlĭz′əm, dōō′-), *n.* 1. state of being dual or consisting of two parts; division into two. 2. *Philos.* a theory holding that there are two, and only two, basic and irreducible principles, as mind and body. 3. *Theol.* **a.** the doctrine that there are two independent divine beings or eternal principles, one good and the other evil. **b.** the belief that man embodies two parts, such as body and soul. **—du′al·ist,** *n.*

du·al·is·tic (dū′əlĭs′tĭk, dōō′-), *adj.* 1. of, pertaining to, or of the nature of dualism. 2. dual. **—du′al·is′-ti·cal·ly,** *adv.*

du·al·i·ty (dū ăl′ə tĭ, dōō-), *n.* dual state or quality.

du·al-pur·pose (dū′əl pûr′pəs, dōō′-), *adj.* 1. serving two functions. 2. (of cattle) bred for two purposes, as beef and milk.

dub[1] (dŭb), *v.t.,* **dubbed, dubbing.** 1. to strike lightly with a sword in the ceremony of conferring knighthood; make, or designate as, a knight: *the King dubbed his son a Knight.* 2. to invest with any dignity or title; style; name; call: *he dubbed me quack.* 3. to strike, cut, rub,

etc., to make smooth, or of an equal surface: *to dub leather, timber.* 4. to dress a fly for fishing. [ME *dubben,* OE *dubbian,* c. Icel. *dubba* equip, dub; akin to DOWEL]

dub[2] (dŭb), *n.* *Slang.* an awkward, unskillful person. [appar. back to DUB[1]]

dub[3] (dŭb), *v.,* **dubbed, dubbing,** *n.* **—v.t., v.i.** 1. to thrust; poke. **—n.** 2. a thrust; poke. 3. a drumbeat. [see DUB[1]. Cf. LG *dubben* thrust, beat]

dub[4] (dŭb), *v.,* **dubbed, dubbing,** *n.* *Motion Pictures.* **—v.t.** 1. to change the sound record on a film or to add sounds. **—n.** 2. the new sounds added. [shortened form of DOUBLE]

dub[5] (dŭb), *n.* *Scot. and N. Eng.* a pool of water; a puddle. [orig. uncertain]

Du Bar·ry (dū băr′ĭ, dōō; *Fr.* dy bȧ rē′), **Comtesse** (born *Marie Jeanne Bécu*) 1746–93, mistress of Louis XV of France.

dub·bing (dŭb′ĭng), *n.* 1. the conferring of knighthood; the accolade. 2. the materials used for the body of an angler's fly.

du·bi·e·ty (dū bī′ə tĭ, dōō-), *n., pl.* **-ties.** 1. doubtfulness; doubt. 2. a matter of doubt. Also, **du·bi·os·i·ty** (dū′bĭ ŏs′ə tĭ, dōō′-), *n.*

du·bi·ous (dū′bĭ əs, dōō′-), *adj.* 1. doubtful; marked by or occasioning doubt: *a dubious question.* 2. of doubtful quality or propriety; questionable: *a dubious transaction, a dubious compliment.* 3. of uncertain outcome: *in dubious battle.* 4. wavering or hesitating in opinion; inclined to doubt. [t. L: m. s. *dubiōsus* doubtful] **—du′bi·ous·ly,** *adv.* **—du′bi·ous·ness,** *n.* **—Syn.** 1. See doubtful.

du·bi·ta·ble (dū′bə tə bəl, dōō′-), *adj.* that may be doubted; doubtful; uncertain. **—du′bi·ta·bly,** *adv.*

du·bi·ta·tion (dū′bə tā′shən, dōō′-), *n.* doubt. [t. L: s. *dubitātio,* der. *dubitāre* doubt]

du·bi·ta·tive (dū′bə tā′tĭv, dōō′-), *adj.* 1. doubting; doubtful. 2. expressing doubt. [t. LL: m. s. *dubitātīvus* doubtful] **—du′bi·ta′tive·ly,** *adv.*

Dub·lin (dŭb′lĭn), *n.* 1. the capital of Eire, in the E part. 495,074 (est. 1943). 2. a country in E Eire. 618,997 pop. (est. 1943); 356 sq. mi. *Co. seat:* Dublin.

Du Bois (dōō bois′), *n.* **William Edward Burghardt** (bûrg′härd), born 1868, U.S. educator and writer.

Du·brov·nik (dōō′brôv nĭk), *n.* a seaport in SW Yugoslavia, on the Adriatic. 18,765 (1931). Italian, **Ragusa.**

Du·buque (də būk′), *n.* a city in E Iowa, on the Mississippi. 49,671 (1950).

duc (dyk), *n.* *French.* duke.

du·cal (dū′kəl, dōō′-), *adj.* of or pertaining to a duke. [t. LL: s. *ducālis,* der. *dux* leader. See DUKE] **—du′cal·ly,** *adv.*

duc·at (dŭk′ət), *n.* 1. any of various gold coins formerly in wide use in European countries, usually worth from $2.27 to $2.32. 2. an old silver coin of varying value; an old Venetian money of account. 3. (*pl.*) *Slang.* money; cash. 4. *Slang.* ticket. [ME, t. F, t. It.: m. *ducato* a coin (orig. one issued in 1140 by Roger II of Sicily as duke of Apulia), also duchy, der. *duca* DUKE]

du·ce (dōō′chĕ), *n.* 1. leader. 2. **il Duce,** the leader (applied esp. to Benito Mussolini as head of the Fascist Italian State). [It., g. L *dux* leader]

Du Chail·lu (dy shȧ yy′; *Fr.* pōl; **Paul Belloni** (pōl; *Fr.* pōl; bĕ lō nē′), 1835 or 1838–1903, U.S. explorer in Africa, traveler, and writer, born in France.

duch·ess (dŭch′ĭs), *n.* 1. the wife or widow of a duke. 2. *Hist.* a woman who holds in her own right the sovereignty or titles of a duchy. [ME *duchesse,* t. F, der. *duc* DUKE]

duch·y (dŭch′ĭ), *n., pl.* **duchies.** the territory ruled by a duke or duchess. [ME *duche,* t. OF, der. *duc* DUKE]

duck[1] (dŭk), *n.* 1. any of numerous wild or domesticated web-footed swimming birds of the family *Anatidae,* esp. of the genus *Anas* and allied genera, characterized by a broad, flat bill, short legs, and depressed body. 2. the female of this fowl, as distinguished from the male (or drake). 3. the flesh of a duck, eaten as food. 4. *Colloq.* a darling; pet. [ME *duk, doke,* OE *dūce,* lit., diver; akin to DUCK[2], v.]

duck[2] (dŭk), *v.i.* 1. to plunge the whole body or the head momentarily under water. 2. to stoop suddenly; bob. 3. to avoid a blow, unpleasant task, etc. **—v.t.** 4. to plunge or dip in water momentarily. 5. to lower (the head, etc.) suddenly. 6. to avoid (a blow, unpleasant task, etc). **—n.** 7. act of ducking. [ME *duke, douke,* c. MLG *duken,* G *tauchen* dive] **—Syn.** 1. dive, dip, souse. 2. bow, dodge.

duck[3] (dŭk), *n.* 1. heavy plain cotton fabric for tents, clothing, bags, mechanical uses, etc., in many weights and widths. 2. (*pl.*) clothes, esp. trousers, made of it. [t. D: m. *doek* cloth, c. G *tuch*]

duck[4] (dŭk), *n.* (in World War II) a military truck for amphibious use. [from *DUKW,* its code name]

duck·bill (dŭk′bĭl′), *n.* a small, aquatic, egg-laying monotreme mammal *Ornithorhynchus anatinus,* of Australia and Tasmania, having webbed feet and the muzzle like the beak of a duck. Also, **duck′billed′ platypus.**

Duckbill
Ornithorhynchus anatinus
(2 ft. long, tail 5½ in.)

duck board, a board or a section or structure of boarding laid as a floor or track over wet or muddy ground, as for military use.

duck call, *Hunting.* a tubular device into which a hunter blows to imitate the quack of a duck.

duck·er[1] (dŭk′ər), *n.* one who or that which ducks. [f. DUCK[2] + -ER[1]]

duck·er[2] (dŭk′ər), *n.* 1. one who raises ducks. 2. one who hunts ducks. [f. DUCK[1] + -ER[1]]

duck hawk, the American peregrine falcon, *Falco peregrinus anatum*, famous for its speed and audacity.

ducking stool, a stool or chair in which common scolds were formerly punished by being tied and plunged into water. See **cucking stool.**

Ducking stool

duck·ling (dŭk′lĭng), *n.* a young duck.

duck·pin (dŭk′pĭn′), *n.* 1. *Bowling.* a short pin of relatively large diameter, used in a game resembling tenpins, and bowled at with small balls. 2. (*pl. construed as sing.*) the game played with such pins.

ducks and drakes, 1. (*construed as sing.*) a pastime consisting in throwing shells, flat stones, etc., over the surface of water so as to strike and rebound repeatedly. 2. **make ducks and drakes of, play (at) ducks and drakes with,** to handle recklessly; squander.

duck·weed (dŭk′wēd′), *n.* any member of the family *Lemnaceae*, esp. of the genus *Lemna*, comprising small aquatic plants which float free on still water. [so called because it is eaten by ducks]

duck·y (dŭk′ĭ), *adj. Colloq.* dear; darling.

duct (dŭkt), *n.* 1. any tube, canal, or conduit by which fluid or other substances are conducted or conveyed. 2. *Anat., Zool.* a tube, canal, or vessel conveying a body fluid, esp. a glandular secretion or excretion. 3. *Bot.* a cavity or vessel formed by elongated cells or by many cells. 4. *Elect.* a single enclosed runway for conductors or cables. [t. L: s. *ductus* leading, conduct, conduit]

duc·tile (dŭk′təl, -tĭl), *adj.* 1. capable of being hammered out thin, as certain metals; malleable. 2. capable of being drawn out into wire or threads, as gold. 3. able to stand deformation under a load without fracture. 4. capable of being molded or shaped; plastic. 5. susceptible; compliant; tractable. [t. F, t. L: m.s. *ductilis* that may be led] **—duc·til·i·ty,** *n.*

duct·less gland (dŭkt′lĭs), *Anat., Zool.* a gland which possesses no excretory duct, but whose secretion is absorbed directly into the blood or lymph, as the thyroid, adrenals, pituitary gland, and parathyroids.

dud (dŭd), *n. Colloq.* 1. an article of clothing. 2. (*pl.*) clothes; often old or ragged clothes. 3. belongings in general. 4. any thing or person that proves a failure. 5. *Mil.* a shell that after being fired has failed to explode. [orig. unknown]

dud·dy (dŭd′ĭ), *adj. Scot.* ragged; tattered.

dude (dūd, dōōd), *n.* 1. an affected or fastidious man; fop. 2. *Slang.* a person raised in a large city. 3. *Western U.S.* an Easterner who vacations on a ranch. **—dud′ish,** *adj.*

du·deen (dōō dēn′), *n. Irish.* a short clay tobacco pipe.

dude ranch, a ranch operated also as a vacation resort.

Du·de·vant (dyd vän′), *n.* **Madame Amandine Lucile Aurore** (å mån dēn′ ly sēl′ ō rōr′). See **Sand, George.**

dudg·eon[1] (dŭj′ən), *n.* a feeling of offense or resentment; anger: *we left in high dudgeon.* [orig. unknown]

dudg·eon[2] (dŭj′ən), *n.* 1. *Obs.* a kind of wood used esp. for the handles of knives, daggers, etc. 2. *Archaic.* a dagger having such a hilt. 3. *Obs.* a handle or hilt made of this wood. [t. AF: m. *digeon*, ult. orig. unknown]

Dud·ley (dŭd′lĭ), *n.* 1. **Robert,** (*Earl of Leicester*) 1532?–88, British statesman and favorite of Queen Elizabeth. 2. a city in central England, near Birmingham. 61,940 (est. 1946).

due (dū, dōō), *adj.* 1. immediately payable. 2. owing, irrespective of whether the time of payment has arrived. 3. rightful; proper; fitting: *due care, in due time.* 4. adequate; sufficient: *a due margin for delay.* 5. attributable, as to a cause: *a delay due to an accident.* 6. under engagement as to time; expected to be ready, be present, or arrive. 7. that which is due or owed. 8. (*chiefly pl.*) a payment due, as a legal charge, a toll, a fee, etc. 9. **give a person his due,** to treat fairly. **—adv.** 10. directly or straight: *a due east course.* 11. *Archaic.* duly. [ME *dew,* t. OF: m. *deü,* orig. pp. of *devoir,* g. L *dēbēre* owe]

due bill, a brief written acknowledgment of indebtedness, not payable to order.

du·el (dū′əl, dōō′-), *n., v.,* **-eled, -eling** or (*esp. Brit.*) **-elled, -elling. —n.** 1. a prearranged combat between two persons, fought with deadly weapons according to an accepted code of procedure, esp. to settle a private quarrel. 2. any contest between two persons or parties. **—v.i., v.t.** 3. to fight in a duel. [t. F, t. ML: m.s. *duellum* a combat between two] **—du′el·er;** *esp. Brit.,* **du′el·ler,** *n.* **—du′el·ist;** *esp. Brit.,* **du′el·list,** *n.*

du·el·lo (dōō ĕl′lō), *n., pl.* **-los.** 1. the practice or art of dueling. 2. the code of rules regulating it. [It.]

du·en·na (dū ĕn′ə, dōō-), *n.* 1. (in Spain and Portugal) an older woman serving as escort or protector of a young lady. 2. a governess; chaperon. [t. Sp.: m. *dueña,* g. L *domina* mistress]

Due·ro (dwě′rō), *n.* Spanish name of **Douro.**

du·et (dū ĕt′, dōō-), *n. Music.* a composition for two voices or performers. [t. It.: m. *duetto,* dim. of *duo* two]

duff[1] (dŭf), *n.* a kind of organic surface horizon, consisting of matted peaty materials in forested soils. [fig. use of DUFF[2]]

duff[2] (dŭf), *n.* a flour pudding boiled, or sometimes steamed, in a bag. [var. of DOUGH]

duf·fel (dŭf′əl), *n.* 1. a sportsman's or camper's outfit. 2. a coarse woolen cloth having a thick nap. Also, **duf′fle.** [named after *Duffel,* town near Antwerp]

duffel bag, a canvas bag used esp. by military personnel for transporting personal effects. Also, **duffle bag.**

duff·er (dŭf′ər), *n.* 1. *Brit. Colloq.* a plodding, stupid, or incompetent person. 2. *Slang.* anything inferior, counterfeit, or useless. 3. *Slang or Dial.* a peddler, esp. one who sells cheap, flashy goods as valuable.

dug[1] (dŭg), *v.* pt. and pp. of **dig.**

dug[2] (dŭg), *n.* the mamma or the nipple of a female. [cf. Sw. *dägga,* Dan. *dægge* suckle]

du·gong (dōō′gŏng), *n.* the only member of the sirenian genus *Dugong,* a large herbivorous aquatic mammal of the East Indian and other waters, characterized by a fishlike body, flipperlike fore limbs, no hind limbs, and a rounded, paddlelike tail. [t. Malay: m. *dūyong*]

Dugong, *Dugong australis* (8 ft. long)

dug·out (dŭg′out′), *n.* 1. a rough shelter or dwelling formed by an excavation in the ground or in the face of a bank. 2. a boat made by hollowing out a log. 3. *Baseball.* a low, three-walled enclosure from which players and other members of the squad watch the game.

Du Gues·clin (dy gě klăn′), **Bertrand** (běr trän′), c1320–80, French military leader, constable of France.

dui·ker (dī′kər), *n.* any of the small African antelopes with spikelike horns, usually restricted to males, that plunge through and under bushes instead of leaping over them. They are included in two genera, *Cephalophus,* and *Syloicapra.* Also, **dui·ker·bok** (dī′kər bŏk′). [t. S Afr. D: diver]

Duis·burg-Ham·born (dys′bōōrκн häm′bôrn), *n.* a city in W Germany at the junction of the Rhine and Ruhr rivers: the largest river port in Europe; formerly the two cities of Duisburg and Hamborn. 434,646 (1939).

duke (dūk, dōōk), *n.* 1. a sovereign prince, the ruler of a small state called a duchy. 2. *Great Britain.* a nobleman of the highest rank after that of a prince and ranking next above a marquis. 3. a nobleman of corresponding rank in certain other countries. 4. (*chiefly pl.*) *Slang.* the hand or fist. [ME *duc,* t. OF, t. L: s. *dux* leader, ML *duke*]

duke·dom (dūk′dəm, dōōk′-), *n.* 1. the state or territory ruled by a duke. 2. the office or rank of a duke.

Du·kho·bors (dōō′kō bôrz′), *n.pl.* a Russian Christian religious sect of peasants, dating from the 18th century. A number of them, under persecution, migrated to Canada in 1899. [t. Russ.: m. *Dukhobortsy* spirit wrestlers, contenders against the Holy Spirit]

dul·ce et de·co·rum est pro pa·tri·a mo·ri (dŭl′sĭ ĕt dĭ kōr′əm ĕst prō pä′trĭ ə mōr′ĭ), *Latin.* sweet and fitting it is to die for one's country.

dul·cet (dŭl′sĭt), *adj.* 1. agreeable to the feelings, the eye, or, esp., the ear; pleasing; soothing; melodious. 2. *Archaic.* sweet to the taste or smell. **—n.** 3. an organ stop resembling the dulciana, but an octave higher. [ME *doucet,* t. OF, dim. of *dous* sweet, g. L *dulcis*]

dul·ci·an·a (dŭl′sĭ ăn′ə), *n.* an organ stop having metal pipes, and giving thin, incisive, somewhat stringlike tones. [NL, der. L *dulcis* sweet]

dul·ci·fy (dŭl′sə fī′), *v.t.,* **-fied, -fying.** 1. to make more agreeable; mollify; appease. 2. to sweeten. [t. LL: m.s. *dulcificāre,* f. L: *dulci-* sweet + *-ficāre* make] **—dul·ci·fi·ca′tion,** *n.*

dul·ci·mer (dŭl′sə mər), *n. Music.* 1. a trapezoidal zither with metal strings struck by light hammers. 2. a modern folk instrument related to the guitar and plucked with the fingers. [t. OF: m. *doulcemer,* var. of *doulcemele,* f. *doulce* sweet (see DULCET) + *-mele* (orig. uncert.)]

Dulcimer (def. 1)

dul·cin·e·a (dŭl sĭn′ĭ ə, dŭl′sə nē′ə; *Sp.* dōōl′thē ně′ä), *n.* a ladylove; a sweetheart. [from *Dulcinea* (der. Sp. *dulce,* g. L *dulcis* sweet), name given by Don Quixote, in Cervantes's romance, to his peasant ladylove]

du·li·a (dū lī′ə, dōō′-), *n. Rom. Cath. Theol.* veneration and invocation given to saints as the servants of God and friends of God. See **hyperdulia** and **latria.** [t. ML, t. Gk.: m. *douleía* servitude, service]

dull (dŭl), *adj.* 1. slow of understanding; obtuse; stupid. 2. lacking keenness of perception in the senses or feelings; insensible; unfeeling. 3. not intense or acute: *a dull pain.* 4. slow in motion or action; not brisk; sluggish. 5. listless; spiritless. 6. causing ennui or depression; tedious; uninteresting: *a dull sermon.* 7. not

sharp; blunt: *a dull knife.* **8.** having very little depth of color; lacking in richness or intensity of color. **9.** not bright, intense, or clear; dim: *a dull day or sound.* —*v.t., v.i.* **10.** to make or become dull. [ME *dul, dull;* akin to OE *dol* foolish, stupid, G *toll* mad] —**dull′ish,** *adj.* —**dull′ness, dul′ness,** *n.* —**dul′ly,** *adv.*
—**Syn. 1.** DULL, BLUNTED, SLOW, STUPID are applied figuratively to mental qualities. DULL implies obtuseness, inability to receive clear impressions, lack of imagination: *a dull child.* BLUNTED implies loss of original keenness of intelligence through disease, sad experience, and the like: *blunted wits or faculties.* SLOW applies to a sluggish intellect not able rapidly to take in or understand, though its eventual action may be good: *a slow mind.* STUPID implies slowness of mental processes, but also applies to lack of intelligence, wisdom, prudence, etc.: *a stupid person, thing to do.* **7.** DULL, BLUNT refer to the edge or point of an instrument, tool, or the like. DULL implies a lack or a loss of keenness or sharpness: *a dull razor or saw.* BLUNT may mean the same or may refer to an edge or point not intended to be keen or sharp: *a blunt or stub pen, a blunt foil.* —**Ant. 1.** keen, **7.** sharp.
dull·ard (dŭl′ərd), *n.* a dull or stupid person. [f. DULL, *adj.* + -ARD]
dulse (dŭls), *n.* coarse, edible, red seaweed, *Rhodymenia palmata.* [t. Irish and Gaelic: m. *duileasg*]
Du·luth (də lōōth′, dōō-), *n.* a city in E Minnesota: a port on Lake Superior. 104,511 (1950).
du·ly (dū′lĭ, dōō′-), *adv.* **1.** in a due manner; properly; fitly. **2.** in due season; punctually. **3.** adequately.
du·ma (dōō′mä), *n.* (in Russia prior to 1917) **1.** a council or official assembly. **2.** (*cap.*) an elective legislative assembly, constituting the lower house of parliament, which was established in 1905 by Nicholas II. Also, **douma.** [t. Russ.]
Du·mas (dy mä′), *n.* **1. Alexandre** (ȧ lĕk sän′dr), (*Dumas père*) 1802–70, French novelist and dramatist. **2.** his son, **Alexandre,** (*Dumas fils*) 1824–95, French dramatist and novelist.
Du Mau·ri·er (dū môr′ĭ ā′, dōō; *Fr.* dy môryĕ′), **George Louis Palmella Busson** (päl mĕl′ə bȳ sôN′), 1834–96, British illustrator and novelist.
dumb (dŭm), *adj.* **1.** without the power of speech. **2.** bereft of the power of speech temporarily: *dumb with astonishment.* **3.** that does not speak, or is little addicted to speaking. **4.** made, done, etc., without speech. **5.** lacking some usual property, characteristic, etc.: *dumb ague.* **6.** *U.S. Colloq.* stupid; dull-witted. [OE, c. G *dumm* stupid] —**dumb′ly,** *adv.* —**dumb′ness,** *n.*
—**Syn. 1, 2.** DUMB, MUTE, SPEECHLESS, VOICELESS describe a condition in which speech is absent. DUMB was formerly used to refer to persons unable to speak; it is now used almost entirely of the inability of animals to speak: *dumb beasts of the field.* The term MUTE is now the one more often applied to persons who, usually because of congenital deafness, have never learned to talk: *with training most mutes learn to speak well enough to be understood.* Either of the foregoing terms or SPEECHLESS may describe a temporary inability to speak, caused by emotion, etc.: *dumb with amazement, mute with terror, left speechless by surprise.* VOICELESS means literally having no voice, either from natural causes or from injury: *fish are voiceless, an operation to remove the larynx leaves one voiceless.*
dumb ague, an irregular form of intermittent malarial fever, lacking the usual chill.
Dum·bar·ton (dŭm bär′tən), *n.* **1.** Also, **Dum·bar·ton·shire** (dŭm bär′tən shĭr′, -shər). a county in W Scotland. 147,700 pop. (est. 1946); 241 sq. mi. **2.** its county seat, near the Clyde river: shipbuilding. 23,500 (est. 1946).
Dumbarton Oaks, the site in the District of Columbia where a series of conferences discussing tentative proposals for the United Nations organization was held Aug.–Oct. 1944.
dumb·bell (dŭm′bĕl′), *n.* **1.** gymnasium hand apparatus made of wood or metal, consisting of two balls joined by a barlike handle, used as weights, usually in pairs. **2.** *U.S. Slang.* a stupid, dull person.
dumb show, 1. a part of a dramatic representation given in pantomime, common in the early English drama. **2.** gesture without speech.
dumb·wait·er (dŭm′wā′tər), *n.* **1.** *Brit.* a small stand placed near a dining table. **2.** *U.S.* a conveyor of framework with shelves drawn up and down in a shaft.
dum·dum (dŭm′dŭm), *n.* a kind of hollow-nosed bullet that expands on impact, inflicting a severe wound. Also, **dumdum bullet.** [named after *Dum Dum,* town near Calcutta, India, where ammunition is made]
dum·found (dŭm found′), *v.t.* to strike dumb with amazement. Also, **dumb·found′.** [appar. b. DUMB and CONFOUND] —**dum·found′er,** *n.*
Dum·fries (dŭm frēs′), *n.* **1.** Also, **Dum·fries·shire** (dŭm frēs′shĭr, -shər). a county in S Scotland. 83,100 pop. (est. 1946); 1074 sq. mi. **2.** its county seat: burial place of Robert Burns. 25,600 (est. 1946).
dum·my (dŭm′ĭ), *n., pl.* **-mies,** *adj.* —*n.* **1.** an imitation or copy of something, as for display, to indicate appearance, exhibit clothing, etc. **2.** *Colloq.* a stupid person, dolt. **3.** one who has nothing to say or who takes no active part in affairs. **4.** one put forward to act for others while ostensibly acting for himself. **5.** a dumb person; a mute. **6.** *Cards.* **a.** (in bridge) the dealer's partner whose hand is exposed and played by the dealer. **b.** the cards so exposed. **c.** a game so played. **d.** an imaginary player represented by an exposed hand which is played by and serves as partner to one of the players.

7. *Railroads.* a type of steam switching locomotive having boiler and running gear completely enclosed, formerly used in city streets. **8.** *Print.* sheets folded and made up to show the size, shape, form, sequence, and general style of a contemplated piece of printing. —*adj.* **9.** put forward to act for others while ostensibly acting for oneself. **10.** counterfeit; sham; imitation. **11.** *Cards.* played with a dummy. [f. DUMB + -Y³]
du·mor·ti·er·ite (dū môr′tĭ ər īt′, dōō-), *n.* a mineral, aluminum borosilicate, used in making refractories. [named after M. Eugène *Dumortier.* See -ITE¹]
dump¹ (dŭmp), *v.t.* **1.** to throw down in a mass; fling down or drop heavily. **2.** to empty out, as from a cart by tilting. **3.** to empty out (a cart, etc.) by tilting or overturning. **4.** *Com.* **a.** to put (goods) on the market in large quantities and at a low price, esp. a low price to a large or favored buyer. **b.** to do this in a foreign country, as at a price below that charged in the home country. —*v.i.* **5.** to fall or drop down suddenly. **6.** to unload. **7.** to offer for sale at a low price esp. to offer low prices to favored buyers. —*n.* **8.** anything, as rubbish, dumped or thrown down. **9.** a place where it is deposited. **10.** *Mil.* a collection of ammunition, stores, etc., deposited at some point, as near a battle front, to be distributed for use. **11.** act of dumping. **12.** *Mining.* **a.** a runway or embankment, equipped with tripping devices, from which low-grade ore, rock, etc. are dumped. **b.** the pile of ore so dumped. **13.** *U.S. Slang.* a place, house, or town that is poorly kept up. —*adj.* **14.** (of a motor truck or railroad car, or the body of such a vehicle) equipped to haul loads of sand, coal, gravel, etc., and to spill the load by inclining the body. [ME, t. Scand.; cf. Dan. *dumpe* fall plump] —**dump′er,** *n.*
dump² (dŭmp), *n.* **1.** (*now only pl.*) *Colloq.* a dull, gloomy state of mind. **2.** *Obs.* a plaintive melody. **3.** *Obs.* a tune. **4.** *Obs.* a slow dance with a peculiar rhythm. [orig. obscure. Cf. MD *domp* haze]
dump³ (dŭmp), *n.* a clumsy leaden counter used by boys in games. [orig. uncert.; ? akin to DUMPY²]
dump·cart (dŭmp′kärt′), *n.* a cart the body of which can be tilted, or the bottom opened downward, to discharge the contents.
dump·ish (dŭmp′ĭsh), *adj.* **1.** dull; stupid. **2.** depressed; sad. —**dump′ish·ly,** *adv.* —**dump′ish·ness,** *n.*
dump·ling (dŭmp′lĭng), *n.* **1.** a rounded mass of steamed dough (often served with stewed meat, etc.). **2.** a kind of pudding consisting of a wrapping of dough inclosing an apple or other fruit, and boiled or baked. **3.** *Colloq.* a short and stout person or animal. [history obscure; ? orig. *lumpling* (f. LUMP¹ + -LING¹), with *d-* by dissimilation]
dump·y¹ (dŭmp′ĭ), *adj.* **dumpier, dumpiest.** dumpish; dejected; sulky. [f. DUMP² + -Y¹]
dump·y² (dŭmp′ĭ), *adj.* **dumpier, dumpiest.** short and stout; squat: *a dumpy woman.* [? akin to DUMPLING] —**dump′i·ly,** *adv.* —**dump′i·ness,** *n.*
dumpy level, *Survey.* an instrument consisting of a spirit level mounted under and parallel to a telescope, the latter being rigidly attached to its supports.
dum spi·ro, spe·ro (dŭm spī′rō, spĭr′ō), *Latin.* while I breathe, I hope (a second motto of South Carolina).
dum vi·vi·mus, vi·va·mus (dŭm vīv′ĭ məs, vī vä′məs), *Latin.* while we are living, let us live (to the full).
Dum·yat (dōōm yät′), *n.* Arabic name of **Damietta.**
dun¹ (dŭn), *v.,* **dunned, dunning,** *n.* —*v.t.* **1.** to make repeated and insistent demands upon, esp. for the payment of a debt. —*n.* **2.** one who duns; an importunate creditor. **3.** a demand for payment, esp. a written one. [special use of obs. *dun* din, t. Scand.; cf. Icel. *duna* boom, roar]
dun² (dŭn), *adj.* **1.** dull- or grayish-brown. **2.** dark; gloomy. —*n.* **3.** dun color. **4.** a May fly. **5.** a dun fly. [ME *dun*(ne), OE *dunn,* c. OS *dun* reddish brown]
Du·na (dōō′nô), *n.* Hungarian name of **Danube.**
Dü·na (dȳ′nä), *n.* German name of **Dvina.**
Dü·na·burg (dȳ′nä bŏŏrkh′), *n.* German name of **Daugavpils.**
Dun·bar (dŭn′bär *for def. 1;* dŭn bär′ *for defs 2, 3*), *n.* **1. Paul Laurence,** 1872–1906, U. S. poet. **2. William,** 1465?–1530?, Scottish poet. **3.** a town in SE Scotland at the mouth of the Firth of Forth: Cromwell defeated the Scots here, 1650. 4220 (1939).
Dun·can (dŭng′kən), *n.* **1. I,** died 1040, king of Scotland, 1034–40, murdered by Macbeth. **2. Isadora** (ĭz′ə dôr′ə), 1878–1927, U.S. dancer.
Dun·can Phyfe (dŭng′kən fīf′), of or like the furniture designed by Duncan Phyfe.
dunce (dŭns), *n.* a dull-witted or stupid person; a dolt [from John DUNS SCOTUS; his system was attacked as foolish by the humanists] —**Syn.** dullard, numbskull, blockhead, ignoramus, simpleton, nincompoop, ninny, booby, mooncalf.
dunce cap, a tall paper cone put on the head of a slow or lazy student. Also, **dunce's cap.**
dunch (dŭnsh), *n.* *Scot. and N. Eng.* a jog; shove.
Dun·ci·ad (dŭn′sĭ ăd′), *n.* **The,** a poem (1728–42) by Pope, satirizing various contemporary writers.
Dun·dee (dŭn dē′), *n.* a seaport in E Scotland, on the Firth of Tay. 170,500 (est. 1946).
dun·der·head (dŭn′dər hĕd′), *n.* a dunce; blockhead. Also, **dun·der·pate** (dŭn′dər pāt′). —**dun′der·head′ed,** *adj.*

dune (dūn, dōōn), *n.* a sand hill or sand ridge formed by the wind, usually in desert regions or near lakes and oceans. [t. F, t. MD, c. OE *dun*. See DOWN³]

Dun·e·din (dŭn ē′dĭn), *n.* a seaport in New Zealand, on South Island. 65,200; with suburbs, 82,200 (est. 1941).

Dun·ferm·line (dŭn fûrm′lĭn, -fĕrm′-), *n.* a city in E Scotland, in Fife county. 34,900 (1939).

dun fly, *Angling.* a dun-colored artificial fly attached to the leader to mimic the larvae stage of certain flies.

dung (dŭng), *n.* 1. manure; excrement, esp. of animals. —*v.t.* 2. to manure (ground) with, or as with, dung. [ME *dunge*, OE *dung*, c. G *dung*] —**dung′y,** *adj.*

dun·ga·ree (dŭng′gə rē′), *n.* 1. a coarse cotton fabric of East Indian origin, used esp. for sailors' clothing. 2. (*pl.*) work clothes, overalls, etc. made of this fabric. [t. Hind.: m. *dungrī*]

dung beetle, any of various scarabaeid beetles that feed upon or breed in dung, as the sacred Egyptian scarab *Scarabaeus sacer.*

dun·geon (dŭn′jən), *n.* any strong, close cell, esp. underground; donjon. [ME, t. OF: m. *donjon,* g. LL *dominio* dominion, tower, der. L *dominus* master, lord]

dung·hill (dŭng′hĭl′), *n.* 1. a heap of dung. 2. a mean or vile place, abode, condition, or person.

dun·ie·was·sal (dōō′nĭ wŏs′əl), *n.* a gentleman, esp. of secondary rank, among the Highlanders of Scotland; a cadet of a ranking family. [t. Gaelic: m. *duine uasal* gentleman (f. *duine* man + *uasal* of good birth)]

dunk (dŭngk), *v.t., v.i.* to dip (doughnuts, etc.) into coffee, milk, etc. [t. G: s. *dunken,* var. of *tunken* dip]

dunk·er (dŭngk′ər), *n.* one who dunks.

Dunk·er (dŭngk′ər), *n.* a popular name for a member of the German Baptist Brethren, now located chiefly in America, characterized by their Baptist practices, opposition to legal oaths and military service and by simplicity of life. Also, **Dunk·ard** (dŭngk′ərd). [var. of *Tunker,* t. G, der. *tunken* dip; with reference to baptism by immersion]

Dun·kirk (dŭn′kûrk), *n.* a seaport in N France: scene of the evacuation under German fire of the British expeditionary force of over 330,000 men, May 29–June 4, 1940. 10,575 (1946). Also, French, **Dunkerque** (dœ̃ kĕrk′).

dun·lin (dŭn′lĭn), *n.* a widely distributed sandpiper, *Erolia alpina,* which breeds in northern parts of the northern hemisphere. The American form is known as the **red-backed sandpiper,** *E. a. sakhalina.* [d. var. of *dunling,* f. DUN² + -LING¹]

Dun·more (dŭn mōr′), *n.* a borough in NE Pennsylvania, near Scranton. 20,305 (1950).

dun·nage (dŭn′ĭj), *n.* 1. baggage or personal effects. 2. *Naut.* loose material laid beneath or wedged among cargo to prevent injury from water or chafing: *dried brush for dunnage.* [t. D: m. *dunnetjes* loosely together]

Dunne (dŭn), *n.* **Finley Peter,** 1867–1936, U.S. humorist.

dunn·ite (dŭn′īt), *n.* an ammonium piorate explosive (officially known as explosive D) used as a bursting charge for armor-piercing projectiles and in high-explosive shells. [named after Colonel B. W. *Dunn* (1860–1936), of the U.S. Army, the inventor. See -ITE¹]

dun·nock (dŭn′ək), *n.* the common hedge sparrow, *Prunella modularis,* of Europe.

Du·nois (dy nwä′), *n.* **Jean** (zhäN), **Count de,** (*"Bastard of Orleans"*) c1403–68, French military leader, relieved by Joan of Arc and her troops when besieged at Orleans.

Dun·sa·ny (dŭn sā′nĭ), *n.* **Edward John Moreton Drax Plunkett, 18th Baron,** born 1878, Irish dramatist and writer of tales.

Dun·si·nane (dŭn′sə nān′, dŭn′sə nān′), *n.* a hill in central Scotland, NE of Perth: a ruined fort on its summit is traditionally called Macbeth's Castle. 1012 ft.

Duns Sco·tus (dŭnz skō′təs), **John,** c1265–c1308, Irish or Scottish scholastic theologian in Great Britain.

Dun·stan (dŭn′stən), *n.* **Saint,** A.D. 925?–988, archbishop of Canterbury and statesman.

dunt (dŭnt, dŏŏnt), *Scot. Dial.* —*n.* 1. a hard blow making a dull sound. 2. a wound from such a blow. —*v.t., v.i.* 3. to strike or knock with a dull sound. [var. of DINT. Cf. Swed. *dunt* dint]

du·o (dōō′ō), *n., pl.* **duos, dui** (dōō′ē). *Music.* a duet. [It., t. L: see DUO]

duo-, a word element meaning "two," as in *duologue.* [t. L, comb. form of *duo*]

du·o·dec·i·mal (dū′ō dĕs′ə məl, dōō′-), *adj.* 1. pertaining to twelfths, or to the number twelve. 2. proceeding by twelves. —*n.* 3. one of a system of numerals the base of which is twelve. 4. one of twelve equal parts. [f. L: s. *duodecimus* twelfth + -AL¹] —**du′o·dec′i·mal·ly,** *adv.*

du·o·dec·i·mo (dū′ō dĕs′ə mō′, dōō′-), *n., pl.* **-mos,** *adj.* —*n.* 1. a book size (about 5 x 7½ inches) determined by printing on sheets folded to form twelve leaves or twenty-four pages. *Abbr.:* 12mo or 12°. —*adj.* 2. in duodecimo. [t. L: (*in*) *duodecimō* in twelfth]

duoden-, a combining form representing **duodenum,** as in *duodenitis.* Also, **duodeno-.**

du·o·de·nal (dū′ə dē′nəl, dōō′-), *adj.* of or pertaining to the duodenum.

du·o·den·a·ry (dū′ə dĕn′ə rĭ, -dē′nə rĭ, dōō′-), *adj.* duodecimal. [t. L: ms. *duodēnārius* containing twelve]

du·o·de·ni·tis (dū′ə dĭ nī′tĭs, dōō′-), *n. Pathol.* inflammation of the duodenum.

du·o·de·num (dū′ə dē′nəm, dōō′-), *n. Anat., Zool.* the first portion of the small intestine, from the stomach to the jejunum. See diag. under **intestine.** [t. ML, der. L *duodēnī* twelve each; so called from its length, about twelve finger breadths]

du·o·logue (dū′ə lôg′, -lŏg′, dōō′-), *n.* 1. a conversation between two persons; a dialogue. 2. a dramatic performance or piece in the form of a dialogue limited to two speakers. [f. DUO- + -*logue,* modeled on MONOLOGUE]

duo·mo (dwô′mō), *n., pl.* **-mi** (-mē). *Italian.* cathedral. [see DOME]

dup (dŭp), *v.t.,* **dupped, dupping.** *Archaic or Eng. Dial.* to open (a door or gate). [contr. of *do up*]

dup., duplicate.

dupe (dūp, dōōp), *n., v.,* **duped, duping.** —*n.* 1. a person who is imposed upon or deceived; a gull. —*v.t.* 2. to make a dupe of; deceive; delude; trick. [t. F: prop., hoopoe, g. L *upupa*] —**dup′a·ble,** *adj.* —**dup′a·bil′i·ty,** *n.* —**dup′er,** *n.*

dup·er·y (dū′pər ĭ, dōō′-), *n., pl.* **-eries.** 1. act or practice of duping. 2. state of one who is duped.

du·ple (dū′pəl, dōō′-), *adj.* double; twofold. [t. L: m.s. *duplus* double]

Du·pleix (dy plĕks′), *n.* **Joseph François** (zhō zĕf′ fräN swä′), **Marquis,** 1697–1763, French Colonial governor in India, 1742–1754.

Du·ples·sis-Mor·nay (dy plĕ sē′môr nĕ′), *n.* Mornay.

duple time, *Music.* characterized by two beats to the measure.

du·plex (dū′plĕks, dōō′-), *adj.* 1. twofold; double. 2. *Mach.* including two identical working parts in a single framework, though one could operate alone. —*n.* 3. duplex house. [t. L: f. *duo* two + -*plex,* der. *plicāre* fold] —**du·plex′i·ty,** *n.*

duplex apartment, an apartment, or suite of rooms, on two floors or stories.

duplex house, *U.S.* a house for two families.

duplex telegraphy, a system for sending two messages simultaneously over the same wire, esp. in opposite directions.

du·pli·cate (*adj., n.* dū′plə kĭt, dōō′-; *v.* dū′plə kāt′, dōō′-), *adj., n., v.,* **-cated, -cating.** —*adj.* 1. exactly like or corresponding to something else. 2. double; consisting of or existing in two corresponding parts. 3. *Cards.* denoting a game in which a team tries for the best result on hands also played by competing partnerships: *duplicate bridge.* —*n.* 4. a copy exactly like an original. 5. anything corresponding in all respects to something else. 6. *Cards.* a duplicate game. 7. **in duplicate,** in two copies, exactly alike. —*v.t.* 8. to make an exact copy of; repeat. 9. to double; make twofold. [t. L: m.s. *duplicātus,* pp., doubled] —**du′pli·ca′tive,** *adj.* —**Syn.** 4. facsimile, replica, reproduction. 8. See imitate.

du·pli·ca·tion (dū′plə kā′shən, dōō′-), *n.* 1. act of duplicating. 2. state of being duplicated. 3. a duplicate. 4. a folding or doubling, as of a membrane.

du·pli·ca·tor (dū′plə kā′tər, dōō′-), *n.* a machine for making duplicates.

du·plic·i·ty (dū plĭs′ə tĭ, dōō-), *n., pl.* **-ties.** deceitfulness in speech or conduct; speaking or acting in two different ways concerning the same matter with intent to deceive; double-dealing. [t. LL: m.s. *duplicitas* doubleness, der. L *duplex,* base DUPLEX] —**Syn.** guile, hypocrisy, deception, dissimulation. —**Ant.** straightforwardness.

Du Pont (dū pŏnt′, dōō-, dū′pŏnt, dōō′-; *also Fr.* dy pôN′ *for 1*). 1. U.S. industrialist family, founded by **Éleuthère Irénée** (ĕ lœ tĕr′ ē rĕ nē′), 1771–1834. 2. **Samuel Francis,** 1803–65, U.S. rear admiral in the Union Navy in the Civil War.

Du·pré (dy prē′), *n.* **Jules** (zhyl), 1812–89, French landscape painter.

Du·quesne (dū kān′, dōō-; *also for 1, Fr.* dy kĕn′), *n.* 1. **Abraham** (á brá äm′), **Marquis,** 1610–88, French naval commander. 2. a city in SW Pennsylvania, on the Monongahela river. 17,620 (1950). 3. **Fort,** a French fort built on the site of Pittsburgh, 1754.

du·ra (dyŏŏr′ə, dŏŏr′ə), *n.* dura mater. —**du′ral,** *adj.*

du·ra·ble (dyŏŏr′ə bəl, dŏŏr′-), *adj.* having the quality of lasting or enduring; not easily worn out, decayed, etc. [t. F, t. L: m.s. *dūrābilis* lasting. See DURE²] —**du·ra·bil′i·ty, du′ra·ble·ness,** *n.* —**du′ra·bly,** *adv.* —**Syn.** permanent. —**Ant.** weak, transitory.

durable finish, any finish, as shrink-resistant or water-repellent, which endures washing and dry cleaning

du·ral·u·min (dyŏŏ răl′yə mĭn, dŏŏ-), *n.* 1. an aluminum base alloy containing copper, manganese, and sometimes, magnesium. It may be hardened and strengthened by heat treatment and was one of the first successful lightweight high-strength alloys: originally used in aircraft construction. 2. (*cap.*) a trademark for this alloy. [f. s. L *dūrus* hard + ALUMIN(UM)]

du·ra ma·ter (dyŏŏr′ə mā′tər, dŏŏr′ə), *n. Anat.* the tough, fibrous membrane forming the outermost of the three coverings of the brain and spinal cord. See **arachnoid** and **pia mater.** Also, **dura.** [t. ML: lit., hard mother]

---

b., blend of, blended; c., cognate with; d., dialect, dialectal; der., derived from; f., formed from; g., going back to; m., modification of; r., replacing; s., stem of; t., taken from; ?, perhaps. See the full key on inside cover.

du·ra·men (dyŏŏrā′mĭn, dŏŏ-), *n.* *Bot.* the hard central wood, or heartwood, of an exogenous tree. [t. L: hardness, a hardened vine branch]

dur·ance (dyŏŏr′əns, dŏŏr′-), *n.* **1.** forced confinement; imprisonment. **2.** *Archaic.* duration; endurance. [t. OF: duration, der. *durer*, g. L *dūrāre* last]

Du·ran·go (dŏŏ räng′gô), *n.* **1.** a state in N Mexico. 483,829 pop. (1940); 47,691 sq. mi. **2.** the capital of this state. 33,412 (1940).

du·ran·te vi·ta (dyŏŏrăn′tĭ vī′tə), *Latin.* during life.

du·ra·tion (dyŏŏrā′shən, dŏŏ-), *n.* **1.** continuance in time. **2.** the length of time anything continues. [t. LL: s. *dūrātio*, der. L *dūrāre* last]

dur·a·tive (dyŏŏr′ə tĭv, dŏŏr′-), *adj.* *Gram.* denoting a verb aspect, as in Russian, expressing incompleted, or continued, action, etc. Compare English *beat* which implies duration or continued action with *strike*, also *walk*, durative, with *step*.

Du·raz·zo (dŏŏ rät′tsô), *n.* a seaport in W Albania, on the Adriatic: important ancient city. 14,031 (1945). Albanian, **Durrës.**

Dur·ban (dûr′bən), *n.* a seaport in the E part of the Union of South Africa, in Natal. 259,606 (1936).

dur·bar (dûr′bär), *n.* (in India) **1.** the court of a native ruler. **2.** a public audience or levee held by a native prince or a British governor or viceroy; an official reception. **3.** the hall or place of audience. **4.** the audience itself. [t. Hind., Pers.: m. *darbār* court]

dure[1] (dyŏŏr, dŏŏr), *adj.* *Archaic.* hard; severe. [ME *dur*, t. OF, g. L *dūrus* hard. Cf. DOUR]

dure[2] (dyŏŏr, dŏŏr), *v.i., v.t.,* **dured, during.** *Archaic.* endure. [ME *dure(n)*, t. F: m. *durer*, g. L *dūrāre* endure]

Dü·rer (dy′rər), *n.* Albrecht (äl′brĕĸʜt) or Albert, (äl′bĕrt), 1471–1528, German painter and engraver.

du·ress (dyŏŏr′ĭs, dŏŏr′-, dyŏŏ rĕs′, dŏŏ-), *n.* **1.** constraint; compulsion. **2.** forcible restraint of liberty; imprisonment. **3.** *Law.* such constraint or coercion as will render void a contract or other legal act entered or performed under its influence. [ME *duresse*, t. OF, g. L *dūritia* hardness]

Dur·ham (dûr′əm), *n.* **1.** a county in NE England. 1,409,000 pop. (est. 1946); 1015 sq. mi. **2.** its county seat. 18,432 (1939). **3.** a city in N North Carolina. 71,311 (1950). **4.** one of a breed of beef cattle originating in Durham, England, at one time known as good milkers, but now bred largely for meat production.

du·ri·an (dŏŏr′ĭ ən), *n.* **1.** the edible fruit, with a hard, prickly rind, of a tree, *Durio zibethinus,* of southeastern Asia. It has extraordinary flavor and odor. **2.** the tree itself. Also, **du/ri·on.** [t. Malay, der. *duri* thorn]

dur·ing (dyŏŏr′ĭng, dŏŏr′-), *prep.* **1.** throughout the continuance of. **2.** in the course of. [orig. ppr. of DURE[2]]

dur·mast (dûr′măst, -məst), *n.* a European oak, *Quercus petraea,* with a heavy, elastic wood, highly valued by the builder and the cabinetmaker.

du·ro (dŏŏ′rō; *Sp.* -rō), *n., pl.* **-ros** (-rōz; *Sp.* -rôs). the Spanish silver dollar. [t. Sp., for *peso duro* hard piastre]

Du·roc (dyŏŏr′ŏk, dŏŏr′-), *n.* an American red hog of a breed developed for hardiness, weight, and quick growth. Also, **Du·roc-Jer·sey** (dyŏŏr′ŏk jûr′zĭ, dŏŏr′-).

dur·ra (dŏŏr′ə), *n.* a type of grain sorghum with slender stalks, cultivated in Asia, etc., and introduced into the U.S.; Indian millet; Guinea corn. Also, **doura, dourah.** [t. Ar.: m. *dhura*]

Dur·rës (dŏŏr′rəs), *n.* Albanian name of **Durazzo.**

durst (dûrst), *v.* pt. of **dare.**

du·rum wheat (dyŏŏr′əm, dŏŏr′-), an important species or variety of wheat, *Triticum durum,* the flour from which is largely used for macaroni, etc. Also, **durum.** [i.e. hard wheat. See DURE[1]]

Du·ruy (dy rwē′), *n.* Victor (vēk tôr′), 1811–94, French historian.

Du·se (dŏŏ′zĕ), *n.* Eleonora (ĕ′lĕ ô nô′rä), (*Signora Checchi*) 1859–1924, Italian actress.

dusk (dŭsk), *n.* **1.** partial darkness; a state between light and darkness; twilight; shade; gloom. **2.** the darker stage of twilight. —*adj.* **3.** dark; tending to darkness. —*v.t., v.i.* **4.** to make or become dusk; darken. [metathetic var. of OE *dux, dox* dark, c. L *fuscus* dark brown] —**dusk′ish,** *adj.*

dusk·en (dŭs′kən), *v.t., v.i.* *Rare.* to make or grow dusk; dim.

dusk·y (dŭs′kĭ), *adj.,* **duskier, duskiest. 1.** somewhat dark; dark-colored. **2.** deficient in light; dim. **3.** gloomy. —**dusk′i·ly,** *adv.* —**dusk′i·ness,** *n.*
—**Syn. 1.** DUSTY, SWARTHY both mean dark in color. They differ more in application than in meaning. DUSKY suggests shadiness or a veiled and dim light, as well as darkness of coloring: *dusky twilight shadows, a dusky grove, a dusky Ethiopian.* SWARTHY, which usually denotes a greater degree of darkness or blackness, is used only of the complexion: *a swarthy skin.*

dusky grouse, a gallinaceous game bird, *Dendragapus obscurus,* of western North America.

Düs·sel·dorf (dŏŏs′əl dôrf′; *Ger.* dys′əl-), *n.* a city in W Germany; a port on the Rhine. 541,410 (1939).

dust (dŭst), *n.* **1.** earth or other matter in fine, dry particles. **2.** any finely powdered substance, as sawdust. **3.** a cloud of finely powdered earth or other matter in the air. **4.** that to which anything, as the human body, is reduced by disintegration or decay. **5.** a dead body. **6.** *Now Rare.* a single particle or grain. **7.** *Brit.* ashes, refuse, etc. **8.** a low or humble condition. **9.** anything worthless. **10.** gold dust. **11.** *Slang.* money; cash. **12.** disturbance; turmoil. **13. bite the dust,** to be killed or wounded. **14. lick the dust, a.** to be killed or wounded. **b.** to grovel; humble oneself abjectly. **15. throw dust in one's eyes,** to mislead. —*v.t.* **16.** to free from dust; wipe the dust from: *to dust (or dust off) the table.* **17.** to sprinkle with dust or powder: *to dust plants with powder.* **18.** to strew or sprinkle as dust: *dust powder over plants.* **19.** to soil with dust; make dusty. —*v.i.* **20.** to wipe dust from a table, room, etc. **21.** to become dusty. [ME *doust,* OE *dūst,* c. G *dunst* vapor] —**dust′less,** *adj.*

dust bin, *Brit.* ash can; garbage can.

dust bowl, an area subject to dust storms.

dust cart, *Brit.* garbage wagon.

dust devil, a miniature whirlwind of considerable intensity that picks up dust and rubbish and carries it some distance into the air.

dust·er (dŭs′tər), *n.* **1.** one who or that which dusts. **2.** cloth, brush, etc., for removing dust. **3.** an apparatus for sprinkling dust or powder on something. **4.** a long, light overgarment to protect clothing from dust.

dust jacket, book jacket.

dust·man (dŭst′măn′, -mən), *n., pl.* **-men** (-mĕn′, -mən). **1.** *Brit.* one employed to remove dust and refuse. **2.** a popular personification of sleep. See **sandman.**

dust·pan (dŭst′păn′), *n.* a utensil in which dust is collected and removed.

dust storm, a storm of wind which raises dense masses of dust into the air, as in a desert region.

dust·y (dŭs′tĭ), *adj.,* **dustier, dustiest. 1.** filled, covered, or clouded with dust. **2.** of the nature of dust; powdery. **3.** of the color of dust; gray. —**dust′i·ly,** *adv.* —**dust′i·ness,** *n.*

Dutch (dŭch), *adj.* **1.** of, pertaining to, or characteristic of the natives or inhabitants of the Netherlands or Holland, or their country or language. **2.** *Archaic or Slang.* German; Teutonic. **3. go Dutch,** *Colloq.* to have each person pay his own expenses. **4. in Dutch,** *Slang.* in trouble or disfavor. —*n.* **5. the Dutch, a.** the people of the Netherlands or Holland. **b.** the German people. **6.** Pennsylvania Dutch. **7.** a Germanic language, the language of the Netherlands. **8.** *Obs.* the German language. [t. MD: m. *dutsch* German, Dutch, c. G *deutsch* German, orig., popular, national, trans. of L *vulgāris* vernacular]

Dutch Belted, one of a breed of dairy cattle originating in the Netherlands, and having a broad white belt circling an otherwise black body.

Dutch Borneo, former name for the southern and larger part of the island of Borneo: now part of the U.S. of Indonesia. 2,168,661 pop. (1930); 208,286 sq. mi.

Dutch cheese, 1. a small, globular, hard cheese made from skim milk. **2.** cottage cheese.

Dutch courage, courage inspired by liquor.

Dutch door, a door consisting of two units horizontally divided so that while the upper part is open the lower can be closed and act as a barrier.

Dutch East Indies, the former island possessions of the Netherlands in the Malay Archipelago, including Sumatra, Java, Celebes, parts of Borneo and New Guinea, the Moluccas, and other islands; constituted in Dec. 1949 the U.S. of Indonesia. 60,727,000 pop. (1930); 735,195 sq. mi. Also, **Netherlands Indies.**

Dutch gold, an alloy of copper and zinc in the form of thin sheets, used as a cheap imitation of gold leaf. Also, **Dutch foil, Dutch leaf, Dutch metal.**

Dutch Guiana, Surinam.

Dutch Harbor, a U.S. naval base in the Aleutian Islands, on Unalaska island.

Dutch·man (dŭch′mən), *n., pl.* **-men. 1.** a native or inhabitant of Holland. **2.** *Now Colloq.* a German. **3.** (*l.c.*) *Carp.,* etc. a piece or wedge inserted to hide the fault in a badly made joint, stop an opening, etc.

Dutch·man's-breech·es (dŭch′mənz brĭch′ĭz), *n. sing. and pl.* a delicate fumariaceous herb, *Dicentra* (or *Bicuculla*) *Cucullaria,* with pale-yellow, two-spurred flowers.

Dutch·man's-pipe (dŭch′mənz pīp′), *n.* an aristolochiaceous climbing vine, *Aristolochia Sipho,* with large leaves and flowers of a curved form suggesting a tobacco pipe.

Dutch New Guinea, the W part of the island of New Guinea: a part of the U.S. of Indonesia (after 1950). 330,000 pop. (est. 1930); ab. 159,000 sq. mi.

Dutchman's-pipe, *Aristolochia Sipho*

Dutch oven, 1. a heavily constructed kettle with a close-fitting lid, used for pot roasts, stews, etc. **2.** a metal utensil open in front, for roasting meat, etc., before an open fire. **3.** a brick oven in which the walls are preheated for cooking.

Dutch treat, *U.S. Colloq.* a meal or entertainment in which each person pays for himself.

Dutch uncle, a person who criticizes or reproves with unsparing severity and frankness.

Dutch West Indies, the six islands of Curaçao, and sometimes also Surinam.

du·te·ous (dū′tĭ əs, dŏŏ′-), *adj.* dutiful; obedient; submissive. —**du′te·ous·ly,** *adv.* —**du′te·ous·ness,** *n.*

du·ti·a·ble (dū′tǐ·ə·bəl, dōō′-), *adj.* subject to duty, as imported goods.

du·ti·ful (dū′tǐ·fəl, dōō′-), *adj.* 1. performing the duties required of one; obedient: *a dutiful child.* 2. required by duty; proceeding from or expressive of a sense of duty: *dutiful attention.* —**du′ti·ful·ly,** *adv.* —**du′ti·ful·ness,** *n.* —**Syn.** 1. respectful, docile, submissive.

du·ty (dū′tǐ, dōō′-), *n., pl.* **-ties.** 1. that which one is bound to do by moral or legal obligation. 2. the binding or obligatory force of that which is morally right; moral obligation. 3. action required by one's position or occupation; office; function: *the duties of a soldier or clergyman.* 4. the conduct due to a superior; homage; respect. 5. an act of respect, or an expression of respectful consideration. 6. *Com.* a specific or ad valorem levy imposed by law on the import or export of goods. 7. a payment, service, etc., imposed and enforceable by law or custom. 8. *Mach.* **a.** the amount of work done by an engine per unit amount of fuel consumed. **b.** the measure of effectiveness of any machine. 9. *Agric.* the amount of water necessary to provide for the crop in a given area. 10. **off duty,** not at work. 11. **on duty.** at work. [ME *duete.* t. AF, der. *du, due* DUE]
—**Syn.** 1. DUTY, OBLIGATION refer to what one feels bound to do. DUTY is what one performs, or avoids doing, in fulfillment of the permanent dictates of conscience, piety, right, or law: *duty to one's country, one's duty to tell the truth, to raise children properly.* An OBLIGATION is what one is bound to do to fulfill the dictates of usage, custom, or propriety, and to carry out a particular, specific, and often personal promise or agreement: *financial or social obligations.*

du·ty-free (dū′tǐ·frē′, dōō′-), *adj.* free of customs duty.

du·um·vir (dū·ŭm′vər, dōō-), *n., pl.* **-virs, -viri** (-vǐ·rī′). *Rom. Hist.* one of two officers or magistrates jointly exercising the same public function. [t. L: man of two]

du·um·vi·rate (dū·ŭm′və·rǐt, dōō-), *n.* 1. a union of two men in the same office, as in ancient Rome. 2. the office or government of two such persons.

du·ve·tyn (dōō′və·tēn′), *n.* a napped fabric, in a twilled or plain weave, of cotton, wool, silk, or rayon. Also, **du′ve·tine′, du′ve·tyne′.** [f. *duvet* kind of quilt (t. F) + *-yn,* var. of *-INE²*]

Du·vi·da (dōō′vē·də), *n.* **Río da** (rē′ōō da). See **Roosevelt, Río.**

D.V., Deo volente.

Dvi·na (dvǐ·nä′), *n.* 1. Lettish, **Daugava.** German, **Düna.** a river in the W Soviet Union, flowing NW to the Baltic at Riga. ab. 640 mi. 2. **Northern,** a river in the N Soviet Union in Europe, flowing NW to **Dvina Bay** (Gulf of Archangel), an arm of the White Sea. ab. 470 mi.

Dvinsk (dvēnsk), *n.* Russian name of **Daugavpils.**

D.V.M., Doctor of Veterinary Medicine.

D.V.M.S., Doctor of Veterinary Medicine and Surgery.

Dvo·řák (dvôr′zhäk), *n.* **Anton** (än′tôn), 1841–1904, Czech composer.

dwarf (dwôrf), *n.* 1. a human being much below the ordinary stature or size; a pygmy. 2. an animal or plant much below the ordinary size of its kind or species. —*adj.* 3. of unusually small stature or size; diminutive. —*v.t.* 4. to cause to appear or seem small in size, extent, character, etc. 5. to make dwarf or dwarfish; prevent the due development of. —*v.i.* 6. to become stunted or smaller. [ME *dwerf,* OE *dweorg,* c. D *dwerg,* G *zwerg*]
—**Syn.** 1. manikin, homunculus. DWARF, MIDGET, PYGMY are terms for a very small person. A DWARF is one checked in growth, or stunted; he usually has a large head or is in some way not properly formed: *in the past, dwarfs were considered very comical.* A MIDGET is one perfect in form and normal in function, but like a tiny replica of the ordinary species: *some midgets are like handsome dolls.* A PYGMY is properly a member of one of certain small-sized peoples of Africa and Asia, but the word is often used to mean dwarf or midget. 2. runt.

dwarf alder, the alder-leafed buckthorn (*Rhamnus alnifolia*).

dwarf cornel, the bunchberry, *Cornus canadensis,* a low herb bearing red berries, of the NE United States.

dwarf·ish (dwôr′fǐsh), *adj.* like a dwarf; below the ordinary stature or size; diminutive. —**dwarf′ish·ly,** *adv.* —**dwarf′ish·ness,** *n.* —**Syn.** pygmy, tiny, stunted, atrophied, runty.

dwarf mallow, a European herb, *Malva neglecta,* with roundish leaves and small pinkish-white flowers.

dwarf star, *Astron.* a star of moderate luminosity and mass, such as the sun.

dwell (dwĕl), *v.i.,* **dwelt or dwelled, dwelling.** 1. to abide as a permanent resident. 2. to continue for a time. 3. to linger over in thought, speech, or writing; to emphasize (often fol. by *on* or *upon*): *to dwell upon a subject, a point in argument.* [ME *dwellen* delay, tarry, abide, OE *dwellan, dwelian* lead astray, hinder, delay, c. Icel. *dvelja*] —**dwell′er,** *n.* —**Syn.** 1. stay, reside, live.

dwell·ing (dwĕl′ǐng), *n.* 1. a place of residence or abode; a house. 2. continued or habitual residence. —**Syn.** 1. See **house.**

dwelling house, a house occupied, or intended to be occupied, as a residence.

dwelling place, a place of residence or abode.

dwelt (dwĕlt), *v.* pt. and pp. of **dwell.**

dwin·dle (dwǐn′dəl), *v.,* **-dled, -dling.** —*v.i.* 1. to become smaller and smaller; shrink; waste away: *his vast fortune has dwindled away.* 2. to fall away, as in quality;

degenerate. —*v.t.* 3. to make smaller and smaller; cause to shrink: *failing health dwindles ambition.* [dim. of DWINE] —**Syn.** 1. diminish, decline. See **decrease.** —**Ant.** 1. increase. 3. magnify.

dwine (dwīn), *v.i.,* **dwined, dwining.** *Archaic or Dial.* to waste away; fade. [OE *dwīnan* languish]

dwt., pennyweight. [f. *d,* for DENARIUS (see def. 2) + *wt.* weight]

DX, *Radio.* distance; distant. Also, **D.X.**

Dy, *Chem.* dysprosium.

dy·ad (dī′ăd), *n.* 1. a group of two; a couple. 2. *Biol.* **a.** a secondary morphological unit, consisting of two monads: *chromosome dyad.* **b.** the double chromosomes resulting from the splitting of a tetrad. 3. *Chem.* an element, atom, or radical having a valence of two. —*adj.* 4. dyadic. [t. LL: s. *dyas,* t. Gk.: the number two]

dy·ad·ic (dī·ăd′ǐk), *adj.* of two parts; pertaining to the number two.

Dy·ak (dī′ăk), *n.* a member of a wild inland people of Borneo, notorious as head-hunters, of the same stock as the Malays, who found them there on first coming to the island.

dy·ar·chy (dī′är·kǐ), *n., pl.* **-chies.** diarchy. [t. Gk.: m.s. *dyarchia* rule of two] —**dy·ar′chic, dy·ar′chi·cal,** *adj.*

dye (dī), *n., v.,* **dyed, dyeing.** —*n.* 1. a coloring material or matter. 2. a liquid containing coloring matter, for imparting a particular hue to cloth, etc. 3. color or hue, esp. as produced by dyeing. 4. **of the deepest or blackest dye,** of the worst kind. [ME *die,* OE *dēag*] —*v.t.* 5. to color or stain; treat with a dye; color (cloth, etc.) by soaking in a liquid containing coloring matter: *to dye cloth red.* 6. to impart (color) by means of a dye. —*v.i.* 7. to impart color, as a dye: *this brand dyes well.* 8. to become colored when treated with a dye: *this cloth dyes easily.* [ME *dien,* OE *dēagian*] —**dy′er,** *n.*

dyed-in-the-wool (dīd′ǐn·thə·wōōl′), *adj.* 1. dyed before weaving. 2. through-and-through; complete: *a dyed-in-the-wool Republican.*

dye·ing (dī′ǐng), *n.* process of coloring fibers, yarns, or fabrics.

dy·er's-weed (dī′ərz·wēd′), *n.* any of various plants yielding dyes, as the weld, *Reseda Luteola,* or the dyeweed, *Genista tinctoria,* or the woad, *Isatis tinctoria.*

dye·stuff (dī′stŭf′), *n.* a material yielding, or used as, a dye.

dye·weed (dī′wēd′), *n.* a fabaceous shrub, *Genista tinctoria,* a native of the Old World, bearing yellow flowers and yielding a yellow dye.

dye·wood (dī′wōōd′), *n.* any wood yielding a coloring matter used for dyeing.

dy·ing (dī′ǐng), *adj.* 1. ceasing to live; approaching death: *a dying man.* 2. pertaining to or associated with death: *a dying hour.* 3. given, uttered, or manifested just before death: *dying words.* 4. drawing to a close: *the dying year.* —*n.* 5. death.

dyke (dīk), *n., v.,* **dyked, dyking.** dike.

dyn., dynamics. Also, **dynam.**

dyna-, a word element referring to power, as in *dynameter.* Also, **dynam-.** [t. Gk., comb. form of *dýnamis* power, *dýnasthai* be able]

dy·nam·e·ter (dī·năm′ə·tər), *n.* *Optics.* an instrument for determining the magnifying power of telescopes. [f. DYNA- + -METER; or shortened form of DYNAMOMETER]

dy·nam·ic (dī·năm′ǐk), *adj.* 1. of or pertaining to force not in equilibrium (opposed to *static*) or to force in any state. 2. pertaining to dynamics. 3. pertaining to or characterized by energy or effective action; active; forceful. Also, **dy·nam′i·cal.** [t. Gk.: m. s. *dynamikós* powerful] —**dy·nam′i·cal·ly,** *adv.*

dy·nam·ics (dī·năm′ǐks), *n.* 1. that branch of physics or mechanics which deals with force as producing or affecting motion (including *kinetics* but not *statics*), or, more comprehensively, with the action of force on bodies in motion or at rest (including *kinetics* and *statics*). 2. the science or principles of forces acting in any field. 3. (construed as *pl.*) the forces, physical or moral, at work in any field.

dynamic similarity, a principle whereby model airplanes, ships, and hydraulic structures are operated for test purposes under conditions exactly simulating full-scale performance.

dy·na·mism (dī′nə·mǐz′əm), *n.* any of various doctrines or philosophical systems which seek to explain phenomena of nature by the action of force (opposed to *mechanism*). —**dy·na·mist,** *n.* —**dy′na·mis′tic,** *adj.*

dy·na·mite (dī′nə·mīt′), *n., v.,* **-mited, -miting.** —*n.* 1. a high explosive consisting of nitroglycerin mixed with some absorbent substance such as kieselguhr. —*v.t.* 2. to blow up, shatter, or destroy with dynamite. 3. to mine or charge with dynamite. —**dy·na·mit·ic** (dī′nə·mǐt′ǐk), *adj.*

dy·na·mit·er (dī′nə·mī′tər), *n.* one who uses dynamite, esp. for revolutionary purposes. Also, **dy′·na·mit′ist.**

dy·na·mo (dī′nə·mō′), *n., pl.* **-mos.** any rotating machine in which either mechanical energy input may be converted into electrical energy output (a generator), or electrical input may be converted into mechanical output (a motor). The British use *dynamo* for the U.S. term *generator* as applied to an automobile. [short for *dynamoelectric machine*]

---

b., blend of, blended; c., cognate with; d., dialect, dialectal; der., derived from; f., formed from; g., going back to; m., modification of; r., replacing; s., stem of; t., taken from; ?, perhaps. See the full key on inside cover.

dynamo-, var. of **dyna-**, as in *dynamometer*.

dy·na·mo·e·lec·tric (dī′nə mō′ĭ lĕk′trĭk), *adj.* pertaining to the conversion of mechanical energy into electric energy, or vice versa: *a dynamoelectric machine.* Also, **dy′na·mo′e·lec′tri·cal.**

dy·na·mom·e·ter (dī′nə mŏm′ə tər), *n.* a device for measuring force or power. [f. DYNAMO + -METER]

dy·na·mom·e·try (dī′nə mŏm′ə trĭ), *n.* act or art of using the dynamometer. —**dy·na·mo·met·ric** (dī′nə mō mĕt′rĭk), **dy′na·mo·met′ri·cal,** *adj.*

dy·na·mo·tor (dī′nə mō′tər), *n.* a machine which combines both motor and generator action in one magnetic field either with two armatures or with one armature having two separate windings.

dy·nast (dī′năst, -nəst; *Brit. also* dĭn′ăst), *n.* a ruler or potentate, esp. a hereditary ruler. [t. L: s. *dynastes,* t. Gk.: lord, chief]

dy·nas·ty (dī′nəs tĭ; *Brit. also* dĭn′əs tĭ), *n., pl.* **-ties.** 1. a sequence of rulers from the same family or stock. 2. the rule of such a sequence. —**dy·nas·tic** (dī năs′tĭk), **dy·nas′ti·cal,** *adj.* —**dy·nas′ti·cal·ly,** *adv.*

dy·na·tron (dī′nə trŏn′), *n.* *Electronics.* a vacuum tube consisting of three electrodes, in which as the plate voltage increases there is a decrease in the plate current because of emission of electrons from the plate. It is frequently used as an oscillator in radio.

dyne (dīn), *n.* *Physics.* the unit of force in the centimeter-gram-second system, being that force which, acting on a body of mass of one gram for one second, gives it a velocity of one centimeter per second. [t. F, t. Gk.: m. *dýnamis* power]

dys-, a prefix, esp. medical, indicating difficulty, poor condition, as in *dysphoria.* [t. Gk.: hard, bad, unlucky; akin to Skt. *dus- dur-,* OE *tō-* HG *zer-*]

dys·en·ter·y (dĭs′ən tĕr′ĭ), *n.* *Pathol.* an infectious disease marked by inflammation and ulceration of the lower part of the bowels, with diarrhea that becomes mucous and hemorrhagic. [t. L: m.s. *dysenteria,* t. Gk.; r. ME *dissenterie,* t. OF] —**dys·en·ter′ic,** *adj.*

dys·func·tion (dĭs fŭngk′shən), *n.* *Med.* malfunctioning, as of a structure of the body.

dys·gen·ic (dĭs jĕn′ĭk), *adj.* pertaining to or causing degeneration in the type of offspring produced (opposed to *eugenic*).

dys·gen·ics (dĭs jĕn′ĭks), *n.* *Biol.* the study of the operation of factors that cause degeneration in offspring.

dys·lo·gis·tic (dĭs′lə jĭs′tĭk), *adj.* conveying disapproval or censure; opprobrious; not eulogistic. [f. DYS- + (EU)LOGISTIC] —**dys·lo·gis′ti·cal·ly,** *adv.*

dys·pep·sia (dĭs pĕp′shə, -sĭ ə), *n.* deranged or impaired digestion; indigestion (opposed to *eupepsia*). Also, **dys·pep·sy** (dĭs pĕp′sĭ). [t. L, t. Gk.]

dys·pep·tic (dĭs pĕp′tĭk), *adj.* 1. pertaining to, subject to, or suffering from dyspepsia. 2 morbidly gloomy or pessimistic. —*n.* 3 a person subject to or suffering from dyspepsia. Also, **dys·pep′ti·cal.** —**dys·pep′ti·cal·ly,** *adv.*

dys·pha·gi·a (dĭs fā′jĭ ə), *n.* *Pathol.* difficulty in swallowing. —**dys·phag·ic** (dĭs făj′ĭk), *adj.*

dys·pho·ni·a (dĭs fō′nĭ ə), *n.* disturbance of the normal functioning in the production of sound. [NL, t. Gk.: roughness of sound] —**dys·phon·ic** (dĭs fŏn′ĭk), *adj.*

dys·pho·ri·a (dĭs fōr′ĭ ə), *n.* *Pathol.* a state of dissatisfaction, anxiety, restlessness, or fidgeting. [NL, t. Gk.: agitation]

dysp·ne·a (dĭsp nē′ə), *n.* *Pathol.* difficult or labored breathing (opposed to *eupnea*). Also, **dysp·noe′a.** [t. L: m. *dyspnoea,* t. Gk.: m. *dýspnoia* difficulty of breathing] —**dysp·ne′al, dysp·ne′ic,** *adj.*

dys·pro·si·um (dĭs prō′zĭ əm, -shĭ-), *n.* *Chem.* a rare-earth metallic element found in small amounts in certain minerals together with other rare earths. *Symbol:* Dy; *at. wt.:* 162.46; *at. no.:* 66. [NL, der. Gk. *dysprósitos* hard to get at]

dys·u·ri·a (dĭs yŏŏr′ĭ ə), *n.* *Pathol.* difficult or painful urination. [t. LL, t. Gk.: m. *dysouría*]

Dyu·sham·be (dyŏŏ shäm′bĕ), *n.* former name of **Stalinabad.**

dz., dozen; dozens.

Dzher·zinsk (jĕr zĭnsk′), *n.* a city in the central Soviet Union in Europe. 103,415 (1939).

Dzu·gash·vi·li (jŏŏ′gäsh vē′lĕ), *n.* See **Stalin.**

E

E, e (ē), *n., pl.* **E's** or **Es, e's** or **es.** 1. the 5th letter of the English alphabet. 2. *Music.* **a.** the third tone in the scale of C major or the fifth in the relative minor scale of A minor. **b.** a printed or written note indicating this tone. **c.** a string, key, or pipe tuned to this note. **d.** (in solmization) the third tone of the scale, called *mi.* 3. (in medieval Roman numerals) 250.

e-, var. of **ex-**[1], used in words of Latin orig. before consonants except *c, f, p, q, s,* and *t,* as in *emit.*

E, 1. east. 2. eastern. 3. English. 4. Excellent.

e, 1. *Math.* a transcendental constant equal to 2.7182818 . . . , used as the base of natural logarithms. 2. erg.

E., 1. Earl. 2. east. 3. eastern. 4. English.

e., 1. eldest. 2. entrance. 3. *Baseball.* errors.

ea., each.

each (ēch), *adj.* 1. every, of two or more considered individually or one by one: *each stone in the building.* —*pron.* 2. each one: *each went his way.* —*adv.* 3. apiece: *they cost a dollar each.* [ME *ech(e),* etc., OE *ǣlc,* etc., f. *ā* ever + (ge)*līc* like, c. OHG *ēo-gilīh*] —**Syn.** 1. EACH, EVERY are alike in having a distributive meaning. Of two or more members composing a (usually) definite aggregate, EACH directs attention to the separate members in turn: *each child* (of those considered and enumerated) *received a large apple.* EVERY emphasizes the idea of inclusiveness or universality; it is also used of an indefinite number, all being regarded singly and separately: *every child present received an apple* (no child was omitted); *every child* (of all in existence) *likes to play.*

each other, each the other: *they struck each other;* that is, they struck, each striking the *other:* used also (like *one another*) as a compound reciprocal pronoun in oblique cases: *they struck at each other.*

Eads (ēdz), *n.* **James B.,** 1820–87, U.S. engineer.

ea·ger (ē′gər), *adj.* 1. keen or ardent in desire or feeling; impatiently longing: *I am eager for or about it, eager to do it.* 2. characterized by great earnestness: *an eager look.* 3. *Obs.* keen; sharp; biting. [ME *egre,* t. OF: m. *aigre,* g. L *ācer* sharp] —**ea′ger·ly,** *adv.* —**ea′ger·ness,** *n.* —**Syn.** 1. fervent, zealous, enthusiastic.

ea·gle (ē′gəl), *n.* 1. any of certain large diurnal birds of prey of the falcon family, esp. the **golden eagle,** *Aquila chrysaetos,* of the northern hemisphere, and the **bald eagle,** *Haliaetus leucocephalus,* of North America, noted for their size, strength, powerful flight, and keenness of vision. 2. a figure or representation of an eagle, much used as an emblem: *the Roman eagle.* 3. (*pl.*) insignia of a colonel in the U.S. Army. 4. a standard, seal,

etc., bearing such a figure, esp. the standard of the ancient Roman army. 5. a gold coin of the United States, of the value of ten dollars, having a figure of an eagle on the reverse. 6. (*cap.*) *Astron.* the northern constellation Aquila. 7. *Golf.* a score two below par on any but par-three holes. [ME *egle,* t. OF, g. L *aquila*]

ea·gle-eyed (ē′gəl īd′), *adj.* sharp-sighted.

eagle owl, a large, rapacious owl, *Bubo bubo,* of Europe.

ea·glet (ē′glĭt), *n.* a young eagle. [t. F: m. *aiglette,* dim. of *aigle* EAGLE]

ea·gre (ē′gər, ā′gər), *n.* *Brit. Dial.* bore[2]. [f. OE: *ēa* river + *gār* storm]

eal·dor·man (ôl′dər mən), *n.* *Early Eng. Hist.* 1. a chief. 2. (later) the chief magistrate of a county or group of counties.

Ea·ling (ē′lĭng), *n.* a city in SE England, near London. 178,590 (est. 1946).

EAM, National Liberation Front, a Greek underground resistance movement of World War II and political coalition of various leftist groups.

ear[1] (ĭr), *n.* 1. the organ of hearing, in man and mammals usually consisting of three parts (**external ear, middle ear,** and **internal ear**). 2. the external part alone. 3. the sense of hearing. 4. nice perception of the differences of sound; esp. sensitiveness to the quality and correctness of musical sounds: *an ear for music.* 5. attention; heed; esp. favorable attention: *gain a person's ear.* 6. any object resembling or suggestive of the external ear, as the handle of a pitcher or the part of a bell by which it is hung. 7. *Journalism.* either of the small spaces or boxes in the upper corners of

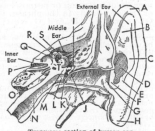

Transverse section of human ear
External ear: A, Helix; B, Fossa of antihelix; C, Antihelix; D, Concha; E, Antitragus; F, Tragus; G, External auditory meatus; H, Lobe. Middle ear: I, Incus; J, Tympanic membrane; K, Malleus; L, Tympanum; M, Stapes; N, Eustachian tube. Inner ear: O, Cochlea; P, Internal auditory meatus; Q, S, R, Anterior, posterior, external semicircular canals; T, Vestibule.

the front page of a newspaper, containing displayed matter, as, an indication of the edition, a weather bulletin, etc. [ME *ere*, OE *ēare*, c. G *ohr*; akin to L *auris*, Gk. *oûs*] —**ear′less**, *adj.*

ear² (ĭr), *n.* **1.** that part of a cereal plant, as corn, wheat, etc., which contains the flowers and hence the fruit, grains, or kernels. —*v.i.* **2.** to form or put forth ears. [ME *ere*, OE *ēar*, c. G *ähre*]

ear·ache (ĭr′āk′), *n.* pain in the ear; otalgia.

ear·drop (ĭr′drŏp′), *n.* an earring with a pendant.

ear·drum (ĭr′drŭm′), *n.* **1.** the tympanic membrane. **2.** the tympanum, or middle ear.

eared (ĭrd), *adj.* having ears or earlike appendages, as **eared owls** (having earlike feathers), **eared seals** (having outer ears as contrasted with those which do not).

ear·flap (ĭr′flăp′), *n.* one of a pair of pieces attached to a cap, for covering the ears in cold weather.

ear·ing (ĭr′ĭng), *n.* *Naut.* a small rope attached to a cringle of a sail and used in reefing, etc. [appar. f. EAR-¹ + -ING¹]

earl (ûrl), *n.* **1.** a British nobleman of a rank next below that of marquis and next above that of viscount. *Earl* is now a mere title unconnected with territorial jurisdiction. After the Norman Conquest earls were for a time called counts; the wife of an earl is called a countess. **2.** (before the Norman Conquest) the governor of one of the great divisions of Wessex, Mercia, etc. [ME *erl*, OE *eorl* (c. Icel. *jarl* JARL), orig., man, warrior, esp. one of good birth (contrasted with *ceorl* simple freeman, CHURL)]

ear·lap (ĭr′lăp′), *n.* **1.** earflap. **2.** the lobe of the ear. **3.** the whole external ear.

earl·dom (ûrl′dəm), *n.* **1.** the rank or title of an earl. **2.** *Obs.* the territory or jurisdiction of an earl.

Earl Marshal, a high officer of state in Great Britain, who is head of the Heralds' College, appointing its officers, and directing all great ceremonies of state. The office is now hereditary in the line of the dukes of Norfolk.

ear·ly (ûr′lĭ), *adv.,* **-lier, -liest,** *adj.* —*adv.* **1.** in or during the first part of some division of time, or of some course or series: *early in the year.* **2.** before the usual or appointed time; in good time: *come early.* **3.** far back in time. —*adj.* **4.** occurring in the first part of some division of time, or of some course or series: *an early hour.* **5.** occurring before the usual or appointed time: *an early dinner.* **6.** belonging to a period far back in time: *early English architecture.* **7.** occurring in the near future: *let us have an early reply.* [ME *erli*, etc., OE *ǣrlīce* (f. *ǣr* soon + -*līce* -LY)] —**ear′li·ness,** *n.* —**Ant. 1.** late. **6.** recent.

Ear·ly (ûr′lĭ), *n.* **Jubal Anderson** (jōō′bəl), 1816–94, Confederate general in the U.S. Civil War.

ear·mark (ĭr′märk′), *n.* **1.** a mark of identification made on the ear of an animal. **2.** any identifying or distinguishing mark or characteristic. —*v.t.* **3.** to mark with an earmark. **4.** to set aside for a specific purpose or use: *to earmark goods for export.*

ear·mind·ed (ĭr′mīn′dĭd), *adj.* responding strongly to auditory stimuli or showing a preference for them. —**ear′-mind′ed·ness,** *n.*

ear·muff (ĭr′mŭf′), *n.* *U.S.* one of a pair of adjustable coverings for protecting the ears in cold weather.

earn¹ (ûrn), *v.t.* **1.** to gain by labor or service: *to earn one's living.* **2.** to merit as compensation, as for service; deserve: *to receive more than one has earned.* **3.** to get as one's desert or due: *to earn a reputation for honesty.* **4.** to gain as due return or profit: *money well invested earns good interest.* **5.** to bring or procure as deserved: *fair dealing earns confidence.* [ME *ernie(n)*, OE *earnian*; akin to OHG *arnēn* earn] —**earn′er,** *n.* —**Syn. 1.** See **gain¹.**

earn² (ûrn), *v.i., v.t.* *Obs.* to yearn. [OE *eornian* murmur (? var. of *geornian*). See YEARN]

ear·nest¹ (ûr′nĭst), *adj.* **1.** serious in intention, purpose, or effort; sincerely zealous: *an earnest worker.* **2.** showing depth and sincerity of feeling: *earnest words.* **3.** having serious importance, or demanding serious attention: "*Life is real! Life is earnest!*" —*n.* **4.** seriousness, as of intention or purpose, as opposed to jest, play, or trifling, chiefly in the phrase: *in earnest.* [ME *ernest*, OE *eornost*, c. D and G *ernst*] —**ear′nest·ly,** *adv.* —**ear′nest·ness,** *n.*

—**Syn. 1.** EARNEST, RESOLUTE, SERIOUS, SINCERE imply having qualities of depth, firmness, and stability. EARNEST implies having a purpose and being steadily and soberly eager in pursuing it: *an earnest student.* RESOLUTE adds somewhat more of a quality of determination; one who is resolute is very difficult to sway or to turn aside from a purpose: *resolute in defending the right.* SERIOUS implies having depth and a soberness of attitude which contrasts with gaiety and frivolity; it may include the qualities of both earnestness and resolution: *serious and thoughtful.* SINCERE suggests genuineness, trustworthiness, and absence of deceit or superficiality: *a sincere interest in the common good.* —**Ant. 1.** frivolous.

ear·nest² (ûr′nĭst), *n.* **1.** a portion of something, given or done in advance as a pledge of the remainder. **2.** *Law.* earnest money. **3.** anything that gives pledge, promise, assurance, or indication of what is to follow. [ME *ernes*, alter. of earlier *erres* (orig., a pl. form, t. OF), appar. by assoc. with suffix -*ness*]

earnest money, *Law.* money given to bind a contract.

earn·ing (ûr′nĭng), *n.* **1.** act of one who earns. **2.** (*pl.*) money earned; wages; profits. [ME *erning,* OE *earnung*]

ear·phone (ĭr′fōn′), *n.* a receiver in a headset.

ear·ring (ĭr′rĭng′), *n.* a ring or other ornament worn in or on the lobe of the ear.

ear shell, abalone.

ear·shot (ĭr′shŏt′), *n.* reach or range of hearing.

ear stone, *n.* an otolith.

earth (ûrth), *n.* **1.** the planet which we inhabit, the third in order from the sun, having an equatorial diameter of 7926 miles. **2.** the inhabitants of this planet: *the whole earth rejoiced.* **3.** this planet as the habitation of man, often in contrast to heaven and hell. **4.** the surface of this planet. **5.** the solid matter of this planet: the dry land; the ground. **6.** the softer part of the land, as distinguished from rock; soil; dirt: *draw the earth up around the plant.* (The English often use this word where Americans say *dirt* or *ground.*) **7.** *Chiefly Brit.* the hole of a burrowing animal. **8.** worldly matters, as distinguished from spiritual. **9.** *Chem.* any of certain difficultly reducible metallic oxides, as alumina, zirconia, yttria, etc. (the alkaline earths). **10.** *Elect.* a ground. **11.** *Obs.* a land or country. —*v.i.* **12.** *Brit. Elect.* to ground. [ME *erthe,* OE *eorthe,* c. G *erde*]

—**Syn. 3.** EARTH, GLOBE, WORLD are terms applied to the planet on which we dwell. EARTH is used esp. in speaking of a condition of existence contrasted with that in heaven or hell: *those who are yet on earth.* GLOBE formerly emphasized merely the roundness of the earth: *to circumnavigate the globe.* It is now coming to be used more like WORLD, with especial application to the inhabitants of the earth and their activities, interests, and concerns. In this sense, both GLOBE and WORLD are more inclusive than EARTH and are used more abstractly: *the politics of the globe, the future of the world, One World.*

earth·born (ûrth′bôrn′), *adj.* **1.** born or sprung from the earth; of earthly origin. **2.** mortal.

earth·bound (ûrth′bound′), *adj.* **1.** firmly fixed in the earth. **2.** having only earthly interests.

earth·en (ûr′thən), *adj.* **1.** composed of earth. **2.** made of baked clay.

earth·en·ware (ûr′thən wâr′), *n.* **1.** earthen pottery; vessels, etc., of baked or hardened clay. **2.** the material of such vessels (usually the coarse, opaque varieties, the finer, translucent kinds being called *porcelain*).

earth inductor compass, *Aeron.* a compass actuated by induction from the earth's magnetic field.

earth·i·ness (ûr′thĭ nĭs), *n.* **1.** earthy nature or properties. **2.** earthliness.

earth·ling (ûrth′lĭng), *n.* **1.** an inhabitant of earth; a mortal. **2.** one attached to earthly or worldly things.

earth·ly (ûrth′lĭ), *adj.,* **-lier, -liest.** **1.** of or pertaining to the earth, esp. as opposed to heaven; worldly. **2.** possible or conceivable: *no earthly use.* [ME *erthly,* OE *eorthlīc*] —**earth′li·ness,** *n.*

—**Syn. 1.** EARTHLY, TERRESTRIAL, WORLDLY, MUNDANE refer to that which is concerned with the earth literally or figuratively. EARTHLY now almost always implies a contrast to that which is heavenly: *earthly pleasures, our earthly home.* TERRESTRIAL, the dignified Latin equivalent of EARTHLY, applies to the earth as a planet or to the land as opposed to the water, and is contrasted with that which is celestial: *terrestrial areas, the terrestrial globe.* WORLDLY is commonly used in the derogatory sense of being devoted to the vanities, cares, advantages, or gains of this present life to the exclusion of spiritual interests or the life to come: *worldly success, worldly standards.* MUNDANE, a formal Latin word, equivalent to WORLDLY, especially suggests that which is bound to the earth, is not exalted, and therefore is commonplace: *mundane affairs, pursuits, etc.*

earth·nut (ûrth′nŭt′), *n.* **1.** any of various roots, tubers, or underground growths, as the peanut and the truffle. **2.** any of the plants producing these.

earth·quake (ûrth′kwāk′), *n.* a vibration or movement of a part of the earth's surface, due to the faulting of rocks, to volcanic forces, etc.

earth·shine (ûrth′shīn′), *n.* *Astron.* the faint light on the part of the moon not illuminated by the sun, due to the light which the earth reflects on the moon.

earth·star (ûrth′stär′), *n.* a fungus of the genus *Geaster,* with an outer covering which splits into the form of a star.

earth·ward (ûrth′wərd), *adv.* **1.** Also, **earth′wards.** toward the earth. —*adj.* **2.** directed toward the earth.

earth·work (ûrth′wûrk′), *n.* **1.** the excavating and embanking of earth involved in engineering construction. **2.** *Mil.* a construction formed chiefly of earth, used in both defensive and offensive operations.

earth·worm (ûrth′wûrm′), *n.* **1.** any one of numerous annelid worms that burrow in soil and feed on soil and decaying organic matter. **2.** a mean or groveling person.

earth·y (ûr′thĭ), *adj.,* **earthier, earthiest.** **1.** of the nature of or consisting of earth or soil. **2.** characteristic of earth: *an earthy smell.* **3.** worldly. **4.** coarse or unrefined.

ear trumpet, a device for collecting and intensifying sounds, held to the ear as an aid in defective hearing.

ear·wax (ĭr′wăks′), *n.* cerumen.

ear·wig (ĭr′wĭg′), *n., v.,* **-wigged, -wigging.** —*n.* **1.** any insect of the order *Dermaptera,* characterized by the forceps or pincers at the end of the abdomen. These harmless insects were popularly supposed to injure the human ear. —*v.t.* **2.** to fill the mind of with prejudice by insinuations. [ME *erwyge,* OE *ēarwicga* ear insect]

---

b., blend of, blended; c., cognate with; d., dialect, dialectal; der., derived from; f., formed from; g., going back to; m., modification of; r., replacing; s., stem of; t., taken from; ?, perhaps. See the full key on inside cover.

ease (ēz), *n.*, *v.*, **eased, easing.** —*n.* **1.** freedom from labor, pain, or physical annoyance of any kind; tranquil rest; comfort: *to take one's ease.* **2.** freedom from concern, anxiety, or solicitude; a quiet state of mind: *be at ease.* **3.** freedom from difficulty or great labor; facility: *it can be done with ease.* **4.** freedom from stiffness, constraint, or formality; unaffectedness: *ease of manner, at ease with others.* **5. at ease,** *Mil.* a position of rest in which soldiers may relax, but may not leave their place or talk. —*v.t.* **6.** to give rest or relief to; make comfortable. **7.** to free from anxiety or care: *to ease one's mind.* **8.** to mitigate, lighten, or lessen: *to ease the pain.* **9.** to release from pressure, tension, or the like: *to ease off a rope.* **10.** to render less difficult; facilitate. **11.** *Naut.* **a.** to bring (the helm) slowly toward midships. **b.** to give (a ship) leeward helm or trim sails so as to present the bow to a wave. —*v.i.* **12.** to reduce severity, pressure, tension, etc. (often fol. by *off* or *up*). **13.** to become less painful, burdensome, etc. [ME *eise,* t. OF: m. *aise,* g. LL *adjacens* near]
—**Syn. 1.** EASE, COMFORT refer to a sense of relaxation or of well-being. EASE implies a relaxed condition with an absence of effort or pressure: *a life of ease, ease after the day's work.* COMFORT suggests a sense of well-being, along with ease, which produces a quiet happiness and contentment: *comfort in one's old age.* **7.** tranquilize, soothe. **8.** alleviate, assuage, allay. —**Ant. 1.** discomfort. **2.** anxiety. **3.** effort.
ease·ful (ēz′fəl), *adj.* comfortable; quiet; peaceful; restful. —**ease′ful·ly,** *adv.* —**ease′ful·ness,** *n.*
ea·sel (ē′zəl), *n.* a frame in the form of a tripod, for supporting an artist's canvas, a blackboard, or the like. [t. D: m. *ezel,* c. G *esel* easel, lit., ass; akin to ASS]
ease·ment (ēz′mənt), *n.* **1.** an easing; relief. **2.** something that gives ease; a convenience. **3.** *Law.* a right held by one person to make use of the land of another.
eas·er (ē′zər), *n.* one who or that which eases.
eas·i·ly (ē′zə lĭ, ēz′lĭ), *adv.* **1.** in an easy manner; with ease; without trouble. **2.** beyond question: *easily the best.*
eas·i·ness (ē′zĭ nĭs), *n.* **1.** quality or condition of being easy. **2.** ease of manner; carelessness; indifference.
east (ēst) *n.* **1.** a cardinal point of the compass (90 degrees to the right of North), corresponding to the point where the sun is seen to rise. **2.** the direction in which this point lies. **3.** (*l.c.* or *cap*) a quarter or territory situated in this direction. **4. the East, a.** the parts of Asia collectively (as lying east of Europe) where civilization has existed from early times, including Asia Minor, Syria, Arabia, India, China, etc.; the Orient. **b.** the whole eastern or Atlantic portion of the United States, esp. that north of Maryland. **c.** New England. [ME *est,* OE *ēaste,* g. G *osten*]
—*adj.* **5.** directed or proceeding toward the east. **6.** coming from the east: *an east wind.* **7.** lying toward the east or in the east: *the east side.* **8.** *Eccles.* toward the altar as situated with respect to the nave. —*adv.* **9.** toward or in the east: *he went east.* **10.** from the east. [ME *est,* OE *ēast,* c. MHG *ōst.* See EASTER]
East An·gli·a (ăng′glĭ ə), an early English kingdom in SE Britain; modern Norfolk and Suffolk. See map under Mercia.
east·bound (ēst′bound′), *adj.* **1.** traveling eastward. **2.** pertaining to eastward travel.
East·bourne (ēst′bôrn, -bərn), *n.* a seaport in SE England, in Sussex. 51,820 (est. 1946).
east by north, *Navig., Survey.* 11°15′ (one point) north of east; 78° 45′ from due north. *Abbr.:* E by N.
east by south, *Navig., Survey.* 11° 15′ (one point) south of east; 101° 15′ from due north. *Abbr.:* E by S.
East Cape. See Dezhnev, Cape.
East Chicago, a city in NW Indiana, near Chicago: a port on Lake Michigan. 54,263 (1950).
East China Sea, a part of the N Pacific, bounded by China, Korea, Japan, the Ryukyus, and Formosa.
East Cleveland, a city in NE Ohio, near Cleveland. 40,047 (1950).
East End, a large, thickly settled, and impoverished part of London, England, in the E part.
East·er (ēs′tər), *n.* **1.** an annual Christian festival in commemoration of the resurrection of Jesus Christ, observed on the first Sunday after the full moon that occurs on or next after March 21. **2.** the day on which this festival is celebrated. [ME *ester,* OE *ēastre,* pl. *ēastron,* (c. G *Ostern,* pl.), orig., name of goddess; akin to L *aurora* dawn, Gk. *eōs.* Cf. EAST]
Easter egg, a colored egg, or imitation of one, used at Easter as a gift or decoration.
Easter Island, an island in the S Pacific, ab. 2000 mi. W of and belonging to Chile: stone monuments. 45 sq. mi. Native name, **Rapa Nui.**
east·er·ling (ēs′tər lĭng), *n.* a native of some country lying eastward of another.
east·er·ly (ēs′tər lĭ), *adj.* **1.** moving, directed, or situated toward the east: *an easterly course.* **2.** coming from the east: *an easterly wind.* —*adv.* **3.** toward the east. **4.** from the east.
Easter Monday, the day after Easter.
east·ern (ēs′tərn), *adj.* **1.** lying toward or situated in the east: *the eastern side of town.* **2.** directed or proceeding toward the east: *an eastern route.* **3.** coming from the east: *an eastern wind.* **4.** (*l.c.* or *cap.*) of or pertaining to the East: *the Eastern Church, an Eastern Congressman.* **5.** (*usually cap.*) Oriental. [OE *ēasterne*]

Eastern Church, 1. the church of the countries comprised in the Eastern Roman Empire. **2.** any body of Christians owing allegiance to the Greek Church and observing the Greek rite rather than the Roman.
East·ern·er (ēs′tər nər), *n.* a person of or from the eastern U.S.
Eastern Hemisphere, the part of the world lying E of the Greenwich Meridian, including Asia, Africa, Australia, and Europe.
east·ern·most (ēs′tərn mōst′, -məst), *adj.* farthest east.
Eastern Roman Empire, the eastern division of the Roman Empire and after A.D. 476, the Roman Empire with its capital at Constantinople. Also, **Eastern Empire.**
Eastern shore, that part of Maryland along the eastern shores of Chesapeake Bay, sometimes including Delaware and parts of Virginia east of Chesapeake Bay.
Eastern time. See **standard time.**
East·er·tide (ēs′tər tīd′), *n.* **1.** Easter time. **2.** the week ushered in by and following Easter. **3.** the fifty days beween Easter and Whitsuntide.
East Ham, a city in SE England, near London. 114,420 (est. 1946).
East Indies, 1. a collective name of the two large peninsulas (India and Indo-China) of SE Asia, together with the Malay Archipelago. **2.** the Malay Archipelago. See the map just below. Also, **East India.** —**East Indian.**

East Indies (def. 2)

east·ing (ēs′tĭng), *n.* **1.** the distance due east made by a ship on any course tending eastward; easterly departure. **2.** a shifting eastward; easterly direction.
East Lansing, a city in S Michigan. 20,325 (1950).
East Liverpool, a city in E Ohio, on the Ohio river. 24,217 (1950).
East London, a seaport in the Union of South Africa, in SE Cape of Good Hope province. With suburbs, 78,530 (1946).
East Lo·thi·an (lō′thĭ ən), a county in SE Scotland. 48,400 pop. (est. 1946); 267 sq. mi. *Co. seat:* Haddington. Also, **Haddington.**
East·man (ēst′mən), *n.* **George,** 1854–1932, U.S. inventor (in field of photography) and philanthropist.
east-north-east (ēst′nôrth′ēst′), *n.* *Navig.* that point of the compass midway between east and northeast: 67° 30′ from north. *Abbr.:* ENE.
Eas·ton (ēs′tən), *n.* a city in E Pennsylvania, on the Delaware. 35,632 (1950).
East Orange, a city in NE New Jersey, near Newark. 79,340 (1950).
East Providence, a town in NE Rhode Island, near Providence. 35,871 (1950).
East Prussia, a former province in NE Germany: until 1939 it was an exclave separated from Germany by the Polish Corridor; now divided between Poland and the Soviet Union. (Prior to the annexation of the Polish Corridor) 2,186,413 (1939); 14,283 sq. mi. *Cap.:* Königsberg. German, **Ostpreussen.**
East Riding, an administrative county in Yorkshire, England. 473,000 pop. (est. 1946); 1172 sq. mi. *Co. seat:* Beverley.
East River, a strait in SE New York, separating Manhattan Island from Long Island, and connecting New York Bay and Long Island Sound.
East Saint Louis, a city in SW Illinois, across the Mississippi from St. Louis, Missouri. 82,295 (1950).
east-south-east (ēst′south′ēst′), *n.* *Navig.* that point of the compass midway between east and southeast; 112° 30′ from due north. *Abbr.:* ESE.
east·ward (ēst′wərd), *adv.* **1.** Also, **east′wards.** toward the east. —*adj.* **2.** moving, bearing, facing, or situated toward the east. —*n.* **3.** the eastward part, direction, or point.
east·ward·ly (ēst′wərd lĭ), *adj.* **1.** having an eastward direction or situation. **2.** coming from the east: *an eastwardly wind.* —*adv.* **3.** toward the east. **4.** from the east.
eas·y (ē′zĭ), *adj.*, **easier, easiest,** *adv.* —*adj.* **1.** not difficult; requiring no great labor or effort: *easy to read, an easy victory.* **2.** free from pain, discomfort, worry, or care: *he is resting easier this morning, easy in one's mind.* **3.** conducive to ease or comfort: *an easy chair.* **4.** fond of or given to ease; easygoing. **5.** not harsh or strict; lenient: *an easy master.* **6.** not burdensome or oppressive: *easy terms.* **7.** not difficult to influence; compliant. **8.** free from formality, constraint, or embarrassment: *an easy style or manners.* **9.** not tight; fitting loosely: *an easy fit.* **10.** not forced or hurried; moderate: *an easy*

pace. **11.** *Com.* **a.** (of a commodity) not difficult to obtain; in plentiful supply and (often) weak in price. **b.** (of the market) not characterized by eager demand. —*adv.* **12.** *Colloq.* in an easy manner; comfortably: *to go easy, take it easy.* [ME *aisie*, t. OF, pp. of *aisier* EASE, v.] —**Syn.** 2. tranquil, untroubled, comfortable, contented. 8. smooth, unconstrained. —**Ant.** 1. difficult. 2. agitated.

eas·y·go·ing (ē′zǐ gō′ǐng), *adj.* **1.** taking matters in an easy way; comfortably unconcerned. **2.** going easily, as a horse.

eat (ēt), *v.,* **ate** (āt; *esp. Brit,* ĕt) or (*Archaic*) **eat** (ĕt, ēt); **eaten** or (*Archaic*) **eat** (ĕt, ēt); **eating.** —*v.t.* **1.** to take into the mouth and swallow for nourishment; esp. to masticate and swallow, as solid food. **2.** to consume by or as by devouring. **3.** to ravage or devastate. **4.** to wear or waste away; corrode. **5.** to make (a hole, passage, etc.) as by gnawing or corrosion. **6. eat one's words,** to take back what one has said. —*v.i.* **7.** to consume food; take a meal. **8.** to make a way as by gnawing or corrosion. —*n.* **9.** (*pl.*) *Slang.* food. [ME *eten,* OE *etan,* c. G *essen*; akin to L *edere,* Gk. *edein*] —**eat′er,** *n.*

eat·a·ble (ē′tə bəl), *adj.* **1.** edible. —*n.* **2.** (*usually pl.*) an article of food.

eat·ing (ē′tǐng), *n.* **1.** act of one who or that which eats. **2.** food with reference to the quality perceived when eaten: *this fish is delicious eating.*

eau (ō), *n., pl.* **eaux** (ō). water. [F, g. L *aqua*]

Eau Claire (ō′ klâr′), a city in W Wisconsin. 36,058 (1950).

eau de Co·logne (ō′ də kə lōn′), **1.** cologne. **2.** (*cap.*) a trademark for a certain type of cologne. [t. F]

eau de Ja·velle (ō′ də zhä vĕl′), Javel water.

eau de vie (ō′ də vē′; *Fr.* ōd vē′), *French.* brandy, esp. the coarser and less purified varieties. [F: lit., water of life]

eaves (ēvz), *n.pl.* the overhanging lower edge of a roof. [ME *eves,* OE *efes,* c. OHG *obisa* hall]

eaves·drop (ēvz′drŏp′), *v.i.,* **-dropped, -dropping.** to listen clandestinely. [lit., he on the *eavesdrop* (of a house), earlier *eavesdrip* ground on which falls the drip from the eaves, OE *yfesdrype*] —**eaves′drop′per,** *n.*

ebb (ĕb), *n.* **1.** the reflux or falling of the tide (opposed to *flood* and *flow*). **2.** a flowing backward or away; decline or decay. **3.** a point of decline: *his fortunes were at a low ebb.* —*v.i.* **4.** to flow back or away, as the water of a tide (opposed to *flow*). **5.** to decline or decay; waste or fade away: *his life is ebbing.* [ME *ebbe,* OE *ebba,* c. D *ebbe, eb*] —**Syn.** 4. subside, abate. 5. sink, wane.

ebb tide, the reflux of the tide; the retiring tide.

E·bert (ā′bərt), *n.* **Friedrich** (frē′drǐKH), 1871–1925, first president of Germany, 1919–25.

Eb·lis (ĕb′lǐs), *n.* *Mohammedan Myth.* an evil spirit or devil, the chief of the wicked jinn. [t. Ar.: m. *Iblīs,* t. Gk.: m. *diábolos* (see DEVIL); dropping of *di-* through confusion with Aram. *di-* of]

E-boat (ē′bōt′), *n.* *Brit.* a very fast unarmored motorboat armed with torpedoes and small guns. [short for *enemy boat*]

eb·on·ite (ĕb′ə nīt′), *n.* vulcanite. [f. EBON(Y) + -ITE¹]

eb·on·ize (ĕb′ə nīz′), *v.t.,* **-ized, -izing.** to stain or finish in imitation of ebony.

eb·on·y (ĕb′ən ǐ), *n., pl.* **-onies,** *adj.* —*n.* **1.** a hard, heavy, durable wood, most highly prized when black, from various tropical trees of the genus *Diospyros,* as *D. Ebenum* of southern India and Ceylon, used for cabinetwork, etc. **2.** any tree yielding such wood. **3.** any of various similar woods or trees. —*adj.* **4.** made of ebony. **5.** like ebony, black. Also, *Poetic,* **eb′on.** [ME *hebenyf,* irreg. t. L: m.s. *hebeninus,* t. Gk.: m. *ebéninos* made of ebony]

Eb·o·ra·cum (ĕb′ə rā′kəm), *n.* ancient name of **York** (def. 4).

e·brac·te·ate (ē brăk′tǐ āt′), *adj.* *Bot.* without bracts.

E·bro (ē′brō; *Sp.* ā′brō), *n.* a river flowing from N Spain SE to the Mediterranean. ab. 470 mi.

e·bul·lience (ǐ bŭl′yəns), *n.* a boiling over; overflow. Also, **e·bul·lien·cy.**

e·bul·lient (ǐ bŭl′yənt), *adj.* **1.** seething or overflowing with fervor, enthusiasm, excitement, etc. **2.** boiling up; bubbling up like a boiling liquid. [t. L: s. *ēbulliens,* ppr., boiling out or up] —**e·bul′lient·ly,** *adv.*

eb·ul·li·tion (ĕb′ə lǐsh′ən), *n.* **1.** a seething or overflowing, as of passion or feeling; an outburst: *ebullition of feeling.* **2.** ebullient state. **3.** act or process of boiling up. **4.** a rushing forth of water, lava, etc., in a state of agitation. [t. L: s. *ēbullītio*]

e·bur·na·tion (ē′bər nā′shən, ĕb′ər-), *n.* *Pathol.* a morbid change in bone, by which it becomes hard and dense, like ivory. [f. s. L *eburnus* of ivory + -ATION]

ec-, var. of ex-³, before consonants, as in *eccentric.*

ECA, Economic Coöperation Administration. Also, **E.C.A.**

é·car·té (ā′kär tā′; *Brit.* ā kär′tā; *Fr.* ĕ kär tā′), *n.* a game at cards for two persons. [t. F, prop. pp. of *écarter* discard]

Ec·bat·a·na (ĕk băt′ə nə), *n.* an ancient city in W Asia, the capital of ancient Media. Modern, **Hamadan.**

ec·ce ho·mo (ĕk′sǐ hō′mō, ĕk′ē), *Latin.* **1.** "Behold the man!"—the words with which Pilate presented Christ, crowned with thorns, to his accusers. John 19:5. **2.** *Art.* a representation of Christ crowned with thorns.

ec·cen·tric (ǐk sĕn′trǐk, ĕk-), *adj.* **1.** deviating from the recognized or usual character, practice, etc.; irregular; erratic; peculiar; odd; queer: *eccentric conduct, an eccentric person.* **2.** *Math.* not having the same center, as two circles or spheres of which one is within the other or which intersect; not concentric. **3.** not situated in the center, as an axis. **4.** *Mach.* having the axis or support away from the center, as a wheel. **5.** *Astron.* deviating from a circular form, as an orbit. —*n.* **6.** one who or that which is unusual, peculiar, odd. **7.** *Mach.* a device for converting circular into reciprocating rectilinear motion, consisting of a disk fixed somewhat out of center to a revolving shaft, and working freely in a surrounding collar (**eccentric strap**), to which a rod (**eccentric rod**) is attached. [t. LL: s. *eccentricus,* t. Gk.: m. *ěkkentros* out of the center] —**ec·cen′tri·cal·ly,** *adv.* —**Ant.** 1. normal, ordinary.

Eccentric circles with eccentric axis A; B, Center of large circle

ec·cen·tric·i·ty (ĕk′sən trǐs′ə tǐ, ĕk′sĕn-), *n., pl.* **-ties.** **1.** an oddity or peculiarity, as of conduct. **2.** quality of being eccentric. **3.** the amount by which anything is eccentric. **4.** *Mach.* the throw of an eccentric. —**Syn.** 2. queerness, freakishness, aberration.

ec·ce sig·num (ĕk′sǐ sǐg′nəm, ĕk′ē), *Latin.* behold the sign (or proof).

ec·chy·mo·sis (ĕk′ə mō′sǐs), *n., pl.* **-ses** (-sēz). *Pathol.* a discoloration due to extravasation of blood, as in a bruise. [NL, t. Gk.: m. *ekchýmōsis,* der. *ekchymoûsthai* extravasate blood]

Eccl., Ecclesiastes. Also, **Eccles.**

eccl., ecclesiastical. Also, **eccles.**

Ec·cles (ĕk′əlz), *n.* **Marriner Stoddard,** born 1890, U. S. economist and banker.

ec·cle·si·a (ǐ klē′zhǐ ə, -zǐ ə), *n., pl.* **-siae** (-zhǐ ē′, -zǐ ē′). **1.** an assembly, esp. the popular assembly of ancient Athens. **2.** a congregation; a church. [t. L: assembly of the people, LL church, t. Gk.: m. *ekklēsía*]

Ec·cle·si·as·tes (ǐ klē′zǐ ăs′tēz), *n.* a book of the Old Testament traditionally ascribed to Solomon. [t. LL, t. Gk.: lit., preacher]

ec·cle·si·as·tic (ǐ klē′zǐ ăs′tǐk), *n.* **1.** a clergyman, or person in orders. —*adj.* **2.** ecclesiastical. [t. LL: s. *ecclēsiasticus,* t. Gk.: m. *ekklēsiastikós* of the assembly or church]

ec·cle·si·as·ti·cal (ǐ klē′zǐ ăs′tə kəl), *adj.* of or pertaining to the church or the clergy; churchly; clerical; not secular; not lay: *ecclesiastical discipline, affairs, ecclesiastical courts.* —**ec·cle′si·as′ti·cal·ly,** *adv.*

ecclesiastical society, (in the congregational churches of the U.S.) a legal corporation with power to sue and be sued, and to administer all of the temporalities of the church.

ec·cle·si·as·ti·cism (ǐ klē′zǐ ăs′tə sǐz′əm), *n.* **1.** ecclesiastical principles, practices, or spirit. **2.** devotion to the principles or interests of the church.

Ec·cle·si·as·ti·cus (ǐ klē′zǐ ăs′tə kəs), *n.* the book of the Apocrypha called also "The Wisdom of Jesus, the Son of Sirach." [t. LL. See ECCLESIASTIC]

ec·cle·si·ol·a·try (ǐ klē′zǐ ŏl′ə trǐ), *n.* worship of the church; excessive reverence for churchly forms and traditions. [f. ECCLESI(A) + -(O)LATRY]

ec·cle·si·ol·o·gy (ǐ klē′zǐ ŏl′ə jǐ), *n.* the science of church architecture and decoration. [f. ECCLES·(A) + -(O)LOGY] —**ec·cle·si·o·log·ic** (ǐ klē′zǐ ə lŏj′ǐk), **ec·cle′si·o·log′i·cal,** *adj.* —**ec·cle′si·ol′o·gist,** *n.*

Ecclus., Ecclesiasticus (Apocrypha).

ec·dy·sis (ĕk′də sǐs), *n., pl.* **-ses** (-sēz′), the shedding or casting off of an outer coat or integument by snakes, crustaceans, etc. [NL, t. Gk.: m. *ékdysis* a getting out]

e·ce·sis (ǐ sē′sǐs), *n.* *Ecol.* the establishment of an immigrant plant in a new location. [NL, t. Gk.: m. *oíkēsis* an inhabiting]

E·che·ga·ray (ĕ′chĕ gä rä′ē), *n.* **José** (hô sĕ′), 1833?–1916, Spanish dramatist and statesman.

ech·e·lon (ĕsh′ə lŏn′; *Fr.* ĕsh lôn′), *n.* **1.** a level of command: *in the higher echelons.* **2.** a formation of troops, ships, air planes, etc., in which groups are disposed in parallel lines, each to the right or left of the one in front, so that the whole presents the appearance of steps. **3.** one of the groups of a command so disposed. —*v.t., v.i.* **4.** to form in echelon. [t. F: lit., round of a ladder, der. *échelle* ladder, g. L *scāla* SCALE]

e·chid·na (ǐ kǐd′nə), *n., pl.* **-nas, -nae** (-nē). any of the spine-covered insectivorous monotreme mammals with claws and a slender snout, occurring in two genera, the curved-beaked echidna, *Zaglossus* (or *Proechidna*), of New Guinea, and the smaller, straight-beaked echidna, *Tachyglossus,* about 10 in. long, represented by several species in Australia, Tasmania, and southern New Guinea; spiny anteater. [NL, t. Gk.: viper]

ech·i·nate (ĕk′ə nāt′), *adj.* spiny; bristly. Also, **ech′i·nat′ed.**

Echidna, *Tachyglossus aculeatus* (Ab. 10 in. long)

b., blend of, blended; c., cognate with; d., dialect, dialectal; der., derived from; f., formed from; g., going back to; m., modification of; r., replacing; s., stem of; t., taken from; ?, perhaps. See the full key on inside cover.

e·chi·no·derm (ĭ kī′nə dûrm′, ĕk′ĭ nə-), *n.* any of the *Echinodermata*. [t. NL: m. *Echinodermata*. See ECHINUS, -DERM]

E·chi·no·der·ma·ta (ĭ kī′nə dûr′mə tə, ĕk′ĭ nə-), *n.pl.* a phylum of marine animals such as starfishes, sea urchins, sea cucumbers, etc., having a radiating arrangement of parts and a body wall stiffened by calcareous pieces that may protrude as spines.

e·chi·noid (ĭ kī′noid, ĕk′ə noid′), *adj.* 1. belonging to the *Echinoidea*. 2. resembling a sea urchin. —*n.* 3. one of the *Echinoidea;* a sea urchin. [f. ECHIN(US) + -OID]

Ech·i·noi·de·a (ĕk′ə noi′dĭ ə), *n.pl.* a class of echinoderms of rounded form covered with projecting spines, including the sea urchins, etc.

e·chi·nus (ĭ kī′nəs), *n.*, *pl.* **-ni** (-nī). 1. a sea urchin of the genus *Echinus.* 2. *Archit.* a rounded molding, as that supporting the abacus of a Doric capital. See diag. under **column.** [t. L, t. Gk.: m. *echinos*, orig. = hedgehog]

ech·o (ĕk′ō), *n.*, *pl.* **echoes,** *v.*, **echoed, echoing.** —*n.* 1. a repetition of sound, produced by the reflection of sound waves from an obstructing surface. 2. a sound heard again near its source, after reflection. 3. any repetition or close imitation, as of the ideas or opinions of another. 4. one who reflects or imitates another. 5. a sympathetic response, as to sentiments expressed. 6. (*cap.*) **a.** the personification of echo. **b.** *Class. Myth.* a mountain nymph who pined away for love of the beautiful youth Narcissus until only her voice remained. 7. *Music.* a part (**echo organ**) or stop (**echo stop**) of a large organ for the production of echolike effects. 8. *Cards.* (esp. in bridge or whist) a signal to a partner that the player wishes the suit continued. 9. *Electronics.* the reflection of a radio wave such as is used in radar or the like. —*v.i.* 10. to emit an echo; resound with an echo. 11. to be repeated by or as by an echo. —*v.t.* 12. to repeat by or as by an echo; emit an echo of: *the hall echoes even faint sounds.* 13. to repeat or imitate the words, sentiments, etc., of (a person). [t. L, t. Gk.: sound, echo] —**ech′o·er,** *n.* —Syn. 10, 12. reverberate.

e·cho·ic (ĕ kō′ĭk), *adj.* 1. echolike. 2. onomatopoetic.

ech·o·ism (ĕk′ō ĭz′əm), *n.* onomatopoeia.

ech·o·la·tion (ĕk′ō lā′shən), *n. Electronics.* the general method of locating objects by determining the time for an echo to return and the direction from which it returns, as by radar and sonar.

Eck·hart (ĕk′härt), *n.* **Johannes** (yō hän′əs) (*"Meister Eckhart"*), c1260–1327? the founder of German mysticism.

é·clair (ā klâr′; *Fr.* ĕ klĕr′), *n.* a light, finger-shaped cake having a cream or custard filling and coated with an icing. [t. F: lit., lightning, der. *éclairer* lighten. Cf. L *exclarare*]

é·clair·cisse·ment (ĕ klĕr sēs män′), *n. French.* a clearing up of something obscure; an explanation.

ec·lamp·si·a (ĕk lămp′sĭ ə), *n. Pathol.* a form of convulsions, esp. of a recurrent nature, as during pregnancy or parturition. [NL, der. Gk. *eklampein* shine forth]

é·clat (ā klä′; *Fr.* ĕ klä′), *n.* brilliance of success, reputation, etc: *the éclat of a great achievement.* [t. F: fragment, also burst (of light, etc.)]

ec·lec·tic (ĕk lĕk′tĭk), *adj.* 1. selecting; choosing from various sources. 2. made up of what is selected from diverse sources. 3. not following any one system, as of philosophy, medicine, etc., but selecting and using whatever is considered best in all systems. —*n.* 4. one who follows an eclectic method, as in philosophy. [t. Gk.: m.s. *eklektikós* selective] —**ec·lec′ti·cal·ly,** *adv.*

ec·lec·ti·cism (ĕk lĕk′tə sĭz′əm), *n.* 1. the use or advocacy of an eclectic method. 2. an eclectic system.

e·clipse (ĭ klĭps′), *n.*, *v.*, **eclipsed, eclipsing.** —*n.* 1. *Astron.* **a.** the obscuration of the light of a satellite by the intervention of its primary planet between it and the sun, as in a **lunar eclipse** when the moon is partially or wholly within the earth's shadow. **b. solar eclipse,** the interception of the light of the sun by the intervention of the moon between it and the observer. **c.** (in an eclipsing binary system) the partial or complete interception of the light of one component by the other. 2. any obscuration of light. 3. any obscuration or overshadowing; loss of brilliance or splendor. —*v.t.* 4. to cause to suffer eclipse: *the moon eclipses the sun.* 5. to cast a shadow upon; obscure; darken. 6. to make dim by comparison; surpass. [ME, t. OF, t. L: m.s. *eclipsis,* t. Gk.: m. *ēkleipsis,* lit., a failing]

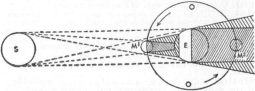

Diagram of eclipse
S, Sun; E, Earth; M¹, position of moon in a solar eclipse; M², position of moon in a lunar eclipse; O, Orbit of moon.

eclipsing variable, *Astron.* a variable star whose changes in brightness are caused by periodic eclipses of two stars in a binary system.

e·clip·tic (ĭ klĭp′tĭk), *n.* 1. the great circle formed by the intersection of the plane of the earth's orbit with the celestial sphere; the apparent annual path of the sun in the heavens. 2. an analogous great circle on a terrestrial globe. —*adj.* Also, **e·clip′ti·cal.** 3. pertaining to an eclipse. 4. pertaining to the ecliptic. [t. L: s. *eclipticus,* t. Gk.: m. *ekleiptikós* of or caused by an eclipse. See ECLIPSE] —**e·clip′ti·cal·ly,** *adv.*

Diagram of ecliptic
A, Ecliptic; B, Celestial equator; C, Orbit of earth; D, Sun

ec·lo·gite (ĕk′lə jīt′), *n.* a rock consisting of granular aggregate of green pyroxene and red garnet, often also containing cyanite, silvery mica, quartz, and pyrite. [f. s. Gk. *eklogē* selection + -ITE¹]

ec·logue (ĕk′lôg, -lŏg), *n.* a short poem, esp. pastoral or idyllic. [t. L: m. *ecloga,* t. Gk.: m. *eklogē* a selection.

ecol., ecology.

é·cole (ā kôl′), *n. French.* a school.

e·col·o·gy (ĭ kŏl′ə jĭ), *n.* 1. the branch of biology which treats of the relations between organisms and their environment; bionomics. 2. the branch of sociology concerned with the spacing of people and of institutions and their resulting interdependency. [f. m. Gk. *oîko(s)* house + -LOGY] —**ec·o·log·i·cal** (ĕk′ə lŏj′ə kəl, ē′kə-), **ec′o·log′ic,** *adj.* —**ec′o·log′i·cal·ly,** *adv.* —**e·col·o·gist** (ĭ kŏl′ə jĭst), *n.*

econ., 1. economic. 2. economics. 3. economy.

e·co·nom·ic (ē′kə nŏm′ĭk, ĕk′ə-), *adj.* 1. pertaining to the production, distribution, and use of income and wealth. 2. of or pertaining to the science of economics. 3. pertaining to an economy, or system of organization or operation, esp. of the process of production. 4. pertaining to the means of living; utilitarian: *economic entomology, botany, etc.* [t. L: m. s. *oeconomicus,* t. Gk.: m. *oikonomikós,* der. *oikonomía.* See ECONOMY]

e·co·nom·i·cal (ē′kə nŏm′ə kəl, ĕk′ə-), *adj.* 1. avoiding waste or extravagance; thrifty. 2. economic. —**Syn.** 1. saving, provident. ECONOMICAL, THRIFTY, FRUGAL imply careful and saving use of resources. ECONOMICAL implies prudent planning in the disposition of resources so as to avoid unnecessary waste or expense: *economical in budgeting household expenditures.* THRIFTY is a stronger word than ECONOMICAL, and adds to it the idea of industry and successful management: *a thrifty housewife looking for bargains.* FRUGAL emphasizes being saving, sometimes excessively saving, esp. in such matters as food, dress, or the like: *frugal almost to the point of being stingy.* —Ant. 1. wasteful, lavish.

e·co·nom·i·cal·ly (ē′kə nŏm′ĭk lĭ, ĕk′ə-), *adv.* 1. with economy; with frugality or moderation. 2. as regards the efficient use of income and wealth.

Economic Coöperation Administration, the U.S. government agency (established 1948) in charge of aid to foreign nations in their economic recovery.

e·co·nom·ics (ē′kə nŏm′ĭks, ĕk′ə-), *n.* the science treating of the production, distribution, and consumption of goods and services, or the material welfare of mankind; political economy.

e·con·o·mist (ĭ kŏn′ə mĭst), *n.* 1. one versed in the science of economics. 2. an economical person.

e·con·o·mize (ĭ kŏn′ə mīz′), *v.*, **-mized, -mizing.** —*v.t.* 1. to manage economically; use sparingly or frugally. —*v.i.* 2. to practice economy; avoid waste or extravagance. Also, *Brit.,* **e·con′o·mise′.** —**e·con′o·miz′er,** *n.*

e·con·o·my (ĭ kŏn′ə mĭ), *n.*, *pl.* **-mies.** 1. thrifty management; frugality in the expenditure or consumption of money, materials, etc. 2. an act or means of thrifty saving; a saving. 3. the management, or science of management, of the resources of a community, etc., with a view to productiveness and avoidance of waste: *national economy.* 4. the disposition or regulation of the parts or functions of any organic whole; an organized system or method. 5. *Theol.* **a.** the divine plan for man, his creation, redemption, final beatitude. **b.** the method of divine administration, as at a particular time or for a particular race. 6. *Archaic.* the management of household affairs. [t. L: m.s. *oeconomia,* t. Gk.: m. *oikonomía* management of a household or of the state] —Syn. 1. thriftiness, thrift, saving.

e·co·tone (ē′kə tōn′), *n.* the transition zone between two different plant communities, as that between forest and prairie. [f. Gk.: m. *oîko(s)* home + m. *tónos* stress]

é·cra·seur (ĕ krä zœr′), *n.* a surgical instrument used in an operation where hemorrhage is feared, as in removing certain types of tumors, by the gradual tightening of a chain or wire loop. [t. F, der. *écraser* crush]

ec·ru (ĕk′rōō, ā′krōō; *Fr.* ĕ krȳ′), *adj.* 1. very light brown in color, as raw silk, unbleached linen, etc. —*n.* 2. ecru color. Also, **é′cru.** [F: raw, unbleached, f. ē- thoroughly (g. L *ex*- EX-¹) + *cru* raw, g. L *crūdus*]

ec·sta·sy (ĕk′stə sĭ), *n.*, *pl.* **-sies.** 1. overpowering emotion or exaltation; a sudden access of intense feeling. 2. rapturous delight. 3. the frenzy of poetic inspiration. 4. mental transport or rapture from the contemplation of divine things. [ME *extasie,* t. ML: m. *extasis,* t. Gk.: m. *ékstasis* extension] —Syn. 1. rapture.

ec·stat·ic (ĕk stăt′ĭk), *adj.* 1. of, pertaining to, or characterized by ecstasy. 2. subject to or in a state of ecstasy; transported; rapturous. —*n.* 3. one subject to fits of ecstasy. 4. (*pl.*) ecstatic transports; raptures. —**ec·stat′i·cal·ly,** *adv.*

ec·thy·ma (ĕk/thə mə), v.⁻. *Vet. Sci.* a contagious virus disease of sheep and goats marked by vesicular and pustular lesions on the lips, and occasionally affecting man; sore mouth.

ecto-, a prefix (chiefly in biological words) meaning "outside," "outer," "external," "lying upon" (opposed to *endo-, ento-*), as in *ectoderm, Ectozoa*. [t. Gk.: m. *ekto-*, comb. form of *ektós* outside]

ec·to·blast (ĕk/tə blăst/), *n. Embryol.* the prospective ectoderm, before the separation of the germ layers. —ec/to·blas/tic, *adj.*

ec·to·derm (ĕk/tə dûrm/), *n. Embryol.* the outer germ layer in the embryo of any metazoan. —ec/to·der/mal, ec/to·der/mic, *adj.*

ec·to·mere (ĕk/tə mĭr/), *n. Embryol.* any one of the blastomeres which participates in the development of the ectoderm.

-ectomy, a combining form attached to the name of a part of the body and producing a word meaning an operation for the excision of that part. [f. *ec-*. t. Gk.: m. *ek-*, prefix form of *ek, ex-* out of) + -TOMY]

ec·to·par·a·site (ĕk/tō pär/ə sīt/), *n.* an external parasite (opposed to *endoparasite*).

ec·to·plasm (ĕk/tə plăz/əm), *n.* **1.** *Biol.* the outer portion of the cytoplasm in the cell of a protozoan or vegetable cell. **2.** *Spiritualism.* the supposed emanation from the body of a medium. —ec/to·plas/mic, *adj.*

ec·to·sarc (ĕk/tə särk/), *n. Biol.* the ectoplasm of a protozoan (opposed to *endosarc*).

ec·tos·to·sis (ĕk/tŏs tō/sĭs), *n. Anat.* the ossification of cartilage proceeding from without inward. [NL; f. ECT(o)- + *-ostosis* as in EXOSTOSIS]

ec·type (ĕk/tīp), *n.* a reproduction or copy (opposed to *prototype*). [t. Gk.: m.s. *ektypos* wrought in relief, formed in outline] —ec·ty·pal (ĕk/tə pəl), *adj.*

é·cu (ĕkY/), *n., pl.* **écus** (ĕkY/), *French.* **1.** the shield carried by a mounted man-at-arms in the middle ages. **2.** any of several gold and silver coins of France from the 14th century onward. [F: orig., shield, g. L *scūtum*]

Ecua., Ecuador.

Ec·ua·dor (ĕk/wə dôr/), *n.* a republic in NW South America. 3,171,367 pop. (est. 1944); 104,510 sq. mi. *Cap.:* Quito. —Ec/ua·do/ri·an, *adj., n.*

ec·u·men·i·cal (ĕk/yŏŏ mĕn/ə kəl *or, esp. Brit.,* ē/- kyŏŏ-), *adj.* **1.** general; universal. **2.** pertaining to the whole Christian church. Also, **œcumenical, ec/u·men/- ic.** [f. (m.) s. LL *oecūmenicus* (t. LGk.: m. *oikoumenikós* general, universal) + -AL¹] —ec/u·men/i·cal·ly, *adv.*

ec·ze·ma (ĕk/sə mə, ĕg zē/-), *n. Pathol.* an inflammatory disease of the skin attended with itching and the exudation of serous matter. [t. NL, t. Gk.: a cutaneous eruption] —ec·zem·a·tous (ĕg zĕm/ə təs), *adj.*

-ed¹, a suffix forming the past tense, as in *he crossed the river.* [OE *-de, -ede, -ode, -ade*]

-ed², a suffix forming **1.** the past participle, as in *he had crossed the river.* **2.** participial adjectives indicating a condition or quality resulting from the action of the verb, as *inflated balloons, illuminated windows.* [OE *-ed, -od, -ad*]

-ed³, a suffix serving to form adjectives from nouns, as *bearded, moneyed, tender-hearted.* [OE *-ede*]

ed., **1.** edited. **2.** edition. **3.** (*pl.,* **eds.**) editor.

e·da·cious (ĭ dā/shəs), *adj.* devouring; voracious; consuming. [f. EDACI(TY) + -OUS]

e·dac·i·ty (ĭ dăs/ə tĭ), *n. Humorous.* good appetite. [t. L: m.s. *edācitas* gluttony]

E·dam cheese (ē/dăm, -dəm; *Du.* ā däm/), a hard, round, fine-flavored yellow cheese, usually colored red on the outside. Also, **Edam.**

e·daph·ic (ĭ dăf/Yk), *adj. Ecol.* due to soil or topography rather than climate. [f. s. Gk. *édaphos* bottom + -IC]

Ed.B., Bachelor of Education.

Ed.D., Doctor of Education.

Ed·da (ĕd/ə), *n., pl.* **Eddas.** **1. Elder** or **Poetic Edda,** a collection of old Icelandic poems on mythical and religious subjects, erroneously ascribed to Saemund Sigfusson (about 1055–1133). **2. Younger** or **Prose Edda,** an old Icelandic work, compiled and partly written by Snorri Sturluson (1179–1241), containing ancient myths and legends of Scandinavia, rules and theories of versemaking, poems, etc. [t. Icel.] —Ed·da·ic (ĕ dā/Yk), Ed/dic, *adj.*

Ed·ding·ton (ĕd/Yng tən), *n.* **Sir Arthur Stanley,** 1882–1944, British astronomer, physicist, and author.

ed·does (ĕd/ōz), *n.pl.* the edible roots of the taro, or of any several related plants; dasheen. [t. West Afr.]

ed·dy (ĕd/Y), *n., pl.* **-dies,** *v.,* **-died, -dying.** —*n.* **1.** a current at variance with the main current in a stream of liquid or gas, esp. one having a rotary or whirling motion. **2.** any similar current, as of air, dust, fog, etc. —*v.i., v.t.* **3.** to move or whirl in eddies. [t. OE: *ed-* turning + *ēa* stream. Cf. Icel. *idha*]

Ed·dy (ĕd/Y), *n.* **Mrs. Mary Baker,** (*Mrs. Glover, Mrs. Patterson*), 1821–1910, U.S. religious leader: founder of the Christian Science Church.

Ed·dy·stone Rocks (ĕd/Y stən), dangerous rocks near the W end of the English Channel, SW of Plymouth, England: site of the **Eddystone Lighthouse.**

e·del·weiss (ā/dəl vīs/), *n.* a small composite herb, *Leontopodium alpinum,* with white woolly leaves and flowers, growing in the high altitudes of the Alps. [t. G: f. *edel* noble + *weiss* white]

e·de·ma (ĭ dē/mə), *n., pl.* **-mata** (-mə tə). *Pathol.* effusion of serous fluid into the interstices of cells in tissue spaces or into body cavities. [NL, t. Gk.: m. *oídēma* a swelling] —e·dem·a·tous (ĭ dĕm/ə təs), e·dem·a·tose (ĭ dĕm/ə tōs/), *adj.*

E·den (ē/dən), *n.* **1.** the garden which was the first home of Adam and Eve. **2.** any delightful region or abode. **3.** a state of perfect happiness. [t. Heb.: lit., pleasure, delight]

E·den (ē/dən), *n.* **(Robert) Anthony,** born 1897, British foreign minister, 1935–38 and 1940–45.

e·den·tate (ē dĕn/tāt), *adj.* **1.** belonging or pertaining to the *Edentata,* an order of New World mammals, comprising the armadillos, the sloths, and the South American anteaters. **2.** toothless. —*n.* **3.** an edentate mammal. [t. L: m.s. *ēdentātus,* pp., deprived of teeth]

EDES, Hellenic National Democratic army, a conservative Greek resistance coalition in World War II.

E·des·sa (ĭ dĕs/ə), *n.* an ancient city in NW Mesopotamia, an early center of Christianity; the capital of a principality under the Crusaders. Modern, **Urfa.**

edge (ĕj), *n., v.,* **edged, edging.** —*n.* **1.** the border or part adjacent to a line of division; a brim or margin: *the horizon's edge.* **2.** a brink or verge: *the edge of a precipice.* **3.** one of the narrow surfaces of a thin, flat object: *a book with gilt edges.* **4.** the line in which two surfaces of a solid object meet: *the edge of a box.* **5.** the thin, sharp side of the blade of a cutting instrument or weapon. **6.** the sharpness proper to a blade. **7.** sharpness or keenness of language, argument, appetite, desire, etc. **8.** *Brit. Local.* a hill or cliff. **9. have the edge,** *Colloq.* to have the advantage (usually fol. by *on* or *over*). **10. on edge, a.** acutely uncomfortable or sensitive: *nerves on edge, to set the teeth on edge.* **b.** eager or impatient. **11.** *Poker.* the prerogative or duty of the player at the dealer's left to put up the first stake. —*v.t.* **12.** to put an edge on; sharpen. **13.** to provide with an edge or border; border. **14.** to move edgewise; move or force gradually: *to edge one's way through a crowd.* —*v.i.* **15.** to move edgewise; advance gradually. [ME *egge,* OE *ecg,* c. G *ecke;* akin to L *aciēs* edge, point] —**edged,** *adj.* —**edge/less,** *adj.*

—Syn. **1.** EDGE, BORDER, MARGIN refer to a boundary. An EDGE is the boundary line of a surface or plane: *the edge of a table.* BORDER is the boundary of a surface or the strip adjacent to it, inside or out: *a border of lace.* MARGIN is a limited strip, generally unoccupied, at the extremity of an area: *the margin of a page.*

edge tool, a tool with a cutting edge.

edge·wise (ĕj/wīz/), *adv.* with the edge directed forward; in the direction of the edge. Also, **edge·ways** (ĕj/wāz/).

Edge·worth (ĕj/wûrth), *n.* **Maria,** 1767–1849, British novelist.

edg·ing (ĕj/Yng), *n.* **1.** act of one who edges. **2.** something that serves for an edge or border; trimming for edges.

edg·y (ĕj/Y), *adj.* **1.** sharp-edged; sharply defined, as outlines. **2.** on edge; irritable. —**edg/i·ness,** *n.*

edh (ĕth), *n.* eth.

ed·i·ble (ĕd/ə bəl), *adj.* **1.** fit to be eaten as food; eatable; esculent. **2.** (*usually pl.*) anything edible; an eatable. [t. LL: m.s. *edibilis,* der. L *edere* eat] —**ed/- i·bil/i·ty, ed/i·ble·ness,** *n.*

e·dict (ē/dYkt), *n.* **1.** a decree issued by a sovereign or other authority. **2.** any authoritative proclamation or command. [t. L: s. *ēdictum,* prop. pp. neut., declared, proclaimed; r. ME *edit,* t. OF] —**e·dic/tal,** *adj.* —**e·dic/tal·ly,** *adv.*

ed·i·fi·ca·tion (ĕd/ə fə kā/shən), *n.* **1.** act of edifying. **2.** state of being edified. **3.** moral improvement or benefit.

ed·i·fice (ĕd/ə fĭs), *n.* a building, esp. one of large size or imposing appearance: *a spacious edifice of brick.* [t. F, t. L: m.s. *aedificium* building] —**ed·i·fi·cial** (ĕd/ə fĭsh/əl), *adj.* —Syn. See **building.**

ed·i·fy (ĕd/ə fī/), *v.t.,* **-fied, -fying.** to build up or increase the faith, morality, etc., of; instruct or benefit, esp. morally. [ME *edifie(n),* t. OF: m. *edifier,* t. L: m.s. *aedificāre* build] —**ed/i·fi/er,** *n.* —**ed/i·fy/ing·ly,** *adv.*

e·dile (ē/dĭl), *n.* aedile.

Ed·in·burgh (ĕd/ən bûr/ō; *or, esp. Brit.,* -brə), *n.* **1.** the capital of Scotland, in the SE part. 463,100 (est. 1946). **2.** former name of Midlothian.

E·dir·ne (ĕ dēr/nĕ), *n.* Turkish name of **Adrianople.**

Ed·i·son (ĕd/ə sən), *n.* **Thomas Alva** (ăl/və), 1847– 1931, U.S. inventor, esp. of electrical devices.

ed·it (ĕd/Yt), *v.t.* **1.** to supervise or direct the preparation of (a newspaper, magazine, etc.); act as editor of; direct the policies of. **2.** to collect, prepare, and arrange (materials) for publication. [partly t. L: s. *ēditus,* pp., given forth; partly back formation from EDITOR]

edit., **1.** edited. **2.** edition. **3.** editor.

é·di·teur (ĕ dē tœr/), *n. French.* **1.** an editor. **2.** a publisher.

e·di·tion (ĭ dYsh/ən), *n.* **1.** one of a number of printings of the same book, newspaper, etc., issued at different times, and differing from another by alterations, additions, etc. (as distinguished from *impression*). **2.** the format in which a literary work is published: *a one- volume edition of Shakespeare.* **3.** the whole number of impressions or copies of a book, newspaper, etc., printed from one set of type at one time. [t. L: s. *ēditio*]

---

b., blend of, blended; c., cognate with; d., dialect, dialectal; der., derived from; f., formed from; g., going back to; m., modification of; r., replacing; s., stem of; t., taken from; ?, perhaps. See the full key on inside cover.

ed·i·tor (ĕd′ĭ tər), *n.* **1.** the supervising director of a newspaper or other periodical, or a special department of one. **2.** one who writes editorials. **3.** one who edits material for publication. [t. L] —**ed′i·tress**, *n. fem.*

ed·i·to·ri·al (ĕd′ə tōr′ĭ əl), *n.* **1.** an article, as in a newspaper presenting the opinion or comment of the periodical. —*adj.* **2.** of or pertaining to an editor. **3.** written by an editor.

ed·i·to·ri·al·ize (ĕd′ə tōr′ĭ ə līz′), *v.i.,* **-ized, -izing.** to set forth one's position or opinion on some subject in, or as if in, an editorial.

ed·i·to·ri·al·ly (ĕd′ə tōr′ĭ əlĭ), *adv.* **1.** in an editorial manner; as an editor does. **2.** in an editorial.

editor in chief, the policy-making executive or principal editor of a publishing house, publication, etc.

ed·i·tor·ship (ĕd′ĭ tər shĭp′), *n.* **1.** the office or function of an editor. **2.** editorial direction.

Ed. M., Master of Education.

Ed·mon·ton (ĕd′mən tən), *n.* **1.** a city in SW Canada: the capital of Alberta. 93,817 (1941). **2.** a city in SE England, near London. 104,590 (est. 1946).

E·dom (ē′dəm), *n.* **1.** Esau, the brother of Jacob. **2.** Greek, **Idumaea** or **Idumea.** an ancient region between the Dead Sea and the Gulf of Aqaba, bordering ancient Palestine. **3.** the nation living there.

E·dom·ite (ē′də mīt′), *n.* a descendant of Esau or Edom. Num. 20:14–21.

eds., editors.

Ed·sel Ford Range (ĕd′səl fōrd′), a mountain range in Antarctica, E of the Ross Sea.

E.D.T., Eastern daylight time. Also, **e.d.t.**

educ., **1.** educated. **2.** education. **3.** educational.

ed·u·ca·ble (ĕj′ŏŏ kə bəl), *adj.* capable of being educated.

ed·u·cate (ĕj′ŏŏ kāt′), *v.t.,* **-cated, -cating.** **1.** to develop the faculties and powers of by teaching, instruction, or schooling; qualify by instruction or training for a particular calling, practice, etc.; train: *to educate someone for something or to do something.* **2.** to provide education for; send to school. **3.** to develop or train (the ear, taste, etc.). [t. L: m.s. *ēducātus,* pp., brought up, trained, educated] —**Syn. 1.** teach, instruct, school, drill, indoctrinate.

ed·u·cat·ed (ĕj′ŏŏ kā′tĭd), *adj.* **1.** having undergone education. **2.** characterized by or displaying qualities of culture and learning.

ed·u·ca·tion (ĕj′ŏŏ kā′shən), *n.* **1.** act or process of educating; the imparting or acquisition of knowledge, skill, etc.; systematic instruction or training. **2.** the result produced by instruction, training, or study. **3.** the science or art of teaching; pedagogics. —**Syn. 1.** instruction, schooling, tuition. EDUCATION, TRAINING imply a discipline and development by means of study and learning. EDUCATION is the development of the special and general abilities of the mind (learning to know): *a liberal education.* TRAINING is practical education (learning to do) or practice, usually under supervision, in some art, trade, or profession: *training in art, teacher training.* **2.** learning, knowledge, enlightenment. EDUCATION, CULTURE are often used interchangeably to mean the results of schooling. EDUCATION, however, suggests chiefly the information acquired. CULTURE is a mode of thought and feeling encouraged by education (the process and the acquirement). It suggests an aspiration toward, and an appreciation of, high intellectual and esthetic ideals: *the level of culture in a country depends upon the education of its people.*

ed·u·ca·tion·al (ĕj′ŏŏ kā′shən əl), *adj.* **1.** pertaining to education. **2.** tending to educate. —**ed′u·ca′tion·al·ly,** *adv.*

ed·u·ca·tion·al·ist (ĕj′ŏŏ kā′shən əl ĭst), *n.* an expert in theories and methods of education. Also, **ed′u·ca′tion·ist.**

ed·u·ca·tive (ĕj′ŏŏ kā′tĭv), *adj.* **1.** serving to educate: *educative knowledge.* **2.** pertaining to education: *the educative process.*

ed·u·ca·tor (ĕj′ŏŏ kā′tər), *n.* one who or that which educates; a teacher. [t. L]

ed·u·ca·to·ry (ĕj′ŏŏ kə tōr′ĭ), *adj.* serving to educate.

e·duce (ĭ dūs′, ĭ dōōs′), *v.t.,* **educed, educing.** to draw forth or bring out; elicit; develop. [t. L: m.s. *ēdūcere* lead forth, bring up] —**e·duc′i·ble,** *adj.*

e·duct (ē′dŭkt), *n.* **1.** something educed. **2.** *Chem.* one substance extracted unchanged from another (distinguished from a *product*). [t. L: s. *ēductus,* pp., educed]

e·duc·tion (ĭ dŭk′shən), *n.* **1.** act of educing. **2.** something educed.

e·dul·co·rate (ĭ dŭl′kə rāt′), *v.t.,* **-rated, -rating.** *Chem.* to free from acids, salts, or impurities by washing; to purify. [t. L: m.s. *ēdulcorātus,* pp., sweetened.] —**e·dul′co·ra′tion,** *n.*

Ed·ward (ĕd′wərd), *n.* **1.** ("*the Black Prince*"), Prince of Wales, 1330–76; British military commander (son of Edward III). **2.** a lake in central Africa between Uganda and the Belgian Congo: a headwater of the Nile. ab. 830 sq. mi.

Edward I, ("*Edward Longshanks*"), 1239–1307, king of England, 1272–1307 (son of Henry III).

Edward II, 1284–1327, king of England, 1307–27 (son of Edward I).

Edward III, 1312–77, king of England, 1327–77 (son of Edward II).

Edward IV, 1442–83, king of England, 1461–70 and 1471–83 (successor of Henry VI, and son of Richard, Duke of York, and first king of the house of York).

Edward V, 1470–83, king of England in 1483; murdered in the Tower of London (son of Edward IV).

Edward VI, 1537–53, king of England and Ireland 1547–53 (son of Henry VIII and Jane Seymour).

Edward VII, (*Albert Edward*), 1841–1910, king of England; 1901–10 (son of Queen Victoria).

Edward VIII, (*Duke of Windsor*), born 1894, king of England in 1936 (son of George V and brother of George VI).

Ed·ward·i·an (ĕd wôr′dĭ ən), *adj.* pertaining to the time of Edward VII, often regarded latterly as ornate and overgenteel.

Ed·wards (ĕd′wərdz), *n.* **Jonathan,** 1703–58, colonial American clergyman and metaphysician.

Edward the Confessor, c1004–66, king of England, 1042–66.

-ee, a suffix of nouns denoting one who is the object of some action, or undergoes or receives something (often as opposed to the person acting), as in *assignee, donee, employee.* [t. F: m. *-é,* pp. ending, g. L *-ātus* -ATE¹]

E.E., Electrical Engineer.

e.e., errors excepted.

eel (ēl), *n.* **1.** an elongate, snakelike, apodal fish, esp. of the genus *Anguilla,* as *A. anguilla,* of European fresh waters, or the American eel, *A. bostoniensis.* **2.** any of several similar but unrelated fishes, as the lamprey. [ME *ele,* d. OE *ēl,* r. OE *ǣl,* c. D and G *aal*]

eel·grass (ēl′grăs′, -gräs′), *n.* *U.S.* any of several marine or sweet-water plants with ribbonlike leaves, as *Zostera marina* and *Vallisneria spiralis.*

eel·pout (ēl′pout′), *n.* **1.** any of the blennylike marine fishes constituting the family *Zoarcidae.* **2.** the burbot. [OE *ǣlepūte*]

eel·worm (ēl′wûrm′), *n.* any small nematode worm of the family *Anguillulidae,* including the minute vinegar eel, *Anguillula aceti.*

eel·y (ē′lĭ), *adj.* eellike; wriggling.

e'en (ēn), *adv.* *Poet.* or *Dial.* even.

e'er (âr), *adv.* *Poetic.* ever.

-eer, a suffix of nouns denoting one who is concerned with, or employed in connection with, or busies h mself with something, as in *auctioneer, engineer, profiteer.* Also, **-ier.** [t. F: m, *-ier,* g. L *-ārius.* See -ARY¹ and -ER²]

ee·rie (ĭr′ĭ), *adj.,* **-rier, -riest.** **1.** inspiring fear; weird, strange, or uncanny. **2.** affected with superstitious fear. [ME *eri,* d. var. of obs. *argh,* OE *earg* cowardly, c. G *arg* bad] —**ee′ri·ly,** *adv.* —**ee′ri·ness,** *n.* —**Syn. 1.** See **weird.**

ee·ry (ĭr′ĭ), *adj.,* **-rier, -riest.** eerie.

ef-, var. of **ex-,** (by assimilation) before *f* as in *efferent.*

ef·fa·ble (ĕf′ə bəl), *adj.* utterable; expressible.

ef·face (ĭ fās′), *v.t.,* **-faced, -facing.** **1.** to wipe out; destroy; do away with: *to efface a memory.* **2.** to rub out, erase, or obliterate (outlines, traces, inscriptions, etc.). **3.** to make inconspicuous or not noticeable: *to efface oneself.* [t. F: m.s. *effacer,* der. *ef-* (g. L *ex-* EX-¹) | *face* FACE] —**ef·face′a·ble,** *adj.* —**ef·face′ment,** *n.* —**ef·fac′er,** *n.*

ef·fect (ĭ fĕkt′), *n.* **1.** that which is produced by some agency or cause; a result; a consequence: *the effect of heat.* **2.** power to produce results; efficacy; force; validity; weight: *of no effect.* **3.** state of being operative; operation or execution; accomplishment or fulfillment: *to bring a plan into effect.* **4.** a mental impression produced, as by a painting, speech, etc. **5.** the result intended; purport or intent; tenor or significance: *he wrote to that effect.* **6.** (*pl.*) goods; movables; personal property. **7. in effect, a.** in fact or reality. **b.** in operation, as a law. **8. take effect,** to operate or begin to operate. —*v.t.* **9.** to produce as an effect; bring about; accomplish; make happen. **10.** to produce or make. [t. L: s. *effectus,* der. *efficere* bring about] —**ef·fect′er,** *n.* —**ef·fect′i·ble,** *adj.*
—**Syn. 1.** EFFECT, CONSEQUENCE(S), RESULT refer to something produced by an action or a cause. An EFFECT is that which is produced, usually more or less immediately and directly: *the effect of morphine is to produce sleep,* or *morphine produces the effect of sleep.* A CONSEQUENCE, something that follows naturally or logically, as in a train of events or sequence of time, is less intimately connected with its cause than is an effect: *punishment is the consequence of disobedience, take the consequences.* A RESULT may be near or remote, and often is the sum of effects or consequences as making an end or final outcome: *the English language is the result of the fusion of many different elements.* **6.** See **property.** **9.** accomplish, achieve, realize, fulfill. See **affect.**

ef·fec·tive (ĭ fĕk′tĭv), *adj.* **1.** serving to effect the purpose; producing the intended or expected result: *effective measures; effective aspect* (see **aspect**). **2.** actually in effect: *the law becomes effective at midnight.* **3.** producing a striking impression; striking: *an effective picture.* —*n.* **4.** a soldier or sailor fit for duty or active service. **5.** the effective total of a military force. —**ef·fec′tive·ly,** *adv.* —**ef·fec′tive·ness,** *n.*
—**Syn. 1.** capable, competent. EFFECTIVE, EFFICACIOUS, EFFICIENT refer to that which is able to produce a (desired) effect. EFFECTIVE is applied to that which has the power to, or which actually does, produce an (often lasting) effect: *an effective action, remedy, speech.* EFFECTUAL is used esp. of that which produces the effect desired or intended, or a decisive result: *an effectual bombardment silenced the enemy.* EFFICACIOUS suggests the capability of achieving a certain end, a capability often manifested only when actually employed: *an efficacious plan, medicine.* EFFICIENT

(applied also to persons) is the most active of these words, and implies the skillful use of energy or industry to accomplish desired results with little waste of effort: *efficient methods, an efficient manager.* —**Ant. 1.** futile.

ef·fec·tor (ĭfĕk′tər), *n.* **1.** *Physiol.* an organ tissue or cell that carries out a response to a nerve impulse, such as a muscle or gland. **2.** effecter. [t. L]

ef·fec·tu·al (ĭfĕk′chŏŏ əl), *adj.* **1.** producing, or capable of producing, an intended effect; adequate. **2.** valid or binding, as an agreement or document. [t. LL: s. *effectuālis*] —**ef·fec′tu·al′i·ty**, **ef·fec′tu·al·ness**, *n.* —**ef·fec′tu·al·ly**, *adv.* —**Syn. 1.** See **effective.**

ef·fec·tu·ate (ĭfĕk′chŏŏ āt′), *v.t.,* **-ated, -ating.** to bring about; effect. [f. s. F *effectuer* (der. L *effectus* EFFECT) + -ATE¹] —**ef·fec′tu·a′tion,** *n.*

ef·fem·i·na·cy (ĭfĕm′ə nə sĭ), *n.* state or quality of being effeminate.

ef·fem·i·nate (ĭfĕm′ə nĭt), *adj.* **1.** soft or delicate to an unmanly degree in traits, tastes, habits, etc.; womanish. **2.** characterized by unmanly softness, delicacy, self-indulgence, etc.: *an effeminate life.* [t. L: m. s. *effēminātus*, pp., made womanish] —**ef·fem′i·nate·ly,** *adv.* —**ef·fem′i·nate·ness,** *n.* —**Syn. 1.** See **female.**

ef·fen·di (ĭfĕn′dĭ), *n., pl.* **-dis.** a Turkish title of respect for government officials, etc. [t. Turk.: m. *efendi,* t. Gk.: m. *authéntēs* master, actual doer. See AUTHENTIC]

ef·fer·ent (ĕf′ər ənt), *adj. Anat., Physiol.* carrying away (opposed to *afferent*): *efferent impulses from the brain.* [t. L: s. *efferens,* ppr., bringing out, raising]

ef·fer·vesce (ĕf′ər vĕs′), *v.i.,* **-vesced, -vescing. 1.** to give off bubbles of gas, as fermenting liquors; bubble and hiss. **2.** to issue forth in bubbles. **3.** to exhibit fervor, excitement, liveliness, etc. [t. L: m.s. *effervescere* boil up] —**ef′fer·ves′cence, ef′fer·ves′cen·cy,** *n.*

ef·fer·ves·cent (ĕf′ər vĕs′ənt), *adj.* **1.** effervescing; bubbling. **2.** gay; lively; sparkling.

ef·fete (ĭfēt′), *adj.* **1.** that has lost its vigor or energy; exhausted; worn out. **2.** unable to produce. [t. L:m.s. *effētus* exhausted] —**ef·fete′ness,** *n.*

ef·fi·ca·cious (ĕf′ə kā′shəs), *adj.* having or showing efficacy; effective as a means, measure, remedy, etc. [f. s. L *efficācia* efficacy + -OUS] —**ef′fi·ca′cious·ly,** *adv.* —**ef′fi·ca′cious·ness,** *n.* —**Syn.** See **effective.**

ef·fi·ca·cy (ĕf′ə kə sĭ), *n., pl.* **-cies.** capacity for serving to produce effects; effectiveness: *the efficacy of a means, measure, expedient, remedy, etc.* [t. L: m.s. *efficācia*]

ef·fi·cien·cy (ĭfĭsh′ən sĭ), *n., pl.* **-cies. 1.** fact or quality of being efficient; competency in performance. **2.** the ratio of the work done or energy developed by a machine, engine, etc., to the energy supplied to it.

ef·fi·cient (ĭfĭsh′ənt), *adj.* **1.** adequate in operation or performance; having and using the requisite knowledge, skill, and industry; competent; capable. **2.** produc ng an effect, as a cause; causative. [t. L: s. *efficiens,* ppr., accomplishing] —**ef·fi′cient·ly,** *adv.* —**Syn. 1.** effectual, competent, capable. See **effective.**

ef·fi·gi·es (ĕfĭj′ĭ ēz′), *n.* Latin effigy. [L. See EFFIGY]

ef·fi·gy (ĕf′ə jĭ), *n., pl.* **-gies. 1.** a representation or image, esp. sculptured, as on a monument. **2.** a representation of an obnoxious person. **3. burn or hang in effigy,** to burn or hang an image of a person as an expression of public indignation, ridicule, or hatred. [t. F: m. *effigie,* t. L: m. *effigies* copy of an object]

ef·flo·resce (ĕf′lō rĕs′), *v.i.,* **-resced, -rescing. 1.** to burst into bloom; blossom. **2.** *Chem.* **a.** to change either throughout or on the surface to a mealy or powdery substance upon exposure to air, as a crystalline substance, through loss of water of crystallization. **b.** to become incrusted or covered with crystals of salt or the like through evaporation or chemical change. [t. L: m.s. *efflōrescere* blossom]

ef·flo·res·cence (ĕf′lō rĕs′əns), *n.* **1.** state or period of flowering. **2.** *Chem.* **a.** act or process of efflorescing. **b.** the resulting powdery substance or incrustation. **3.** *Pathol.* a rash or eruption.

ef·flo·res·cent (ĕf′lō rĕs′ənt), *adj.* **1.** efflorescing; blossoming. **2.** *Chem.* **a.** subject to efflorescence. **b.** covered with or forming an efflorescence. [t. L: s. *efflōrescens,* ppr.]

ef·flu·ence (ĕf′lŏŏ əns), *n.* **1.** outward flow; efflux. **2.** something that flows out; an emanation. [coinage modeled on *affluence.* See EFFLUENT]

ef·flu·ent (ĕf′lŏŏ ənt), *adj.* **1.** flowing out or forth. —*n.* **2.** that which flows out or forth; outflow. **3.** a stream flowing out of another stream, a lake, etc. [t. L: s. *effluens,* ppr.]

ef·flu·vi·um (ĭflŏŏ′vĭ əm), *n., pl.* **-via** (-vĭ ə), **-viums.** a slight or invisible exhalation or vapor, esp. one that is disagreeable or noxious. [t. L: a flowing out] —**ef·flu′vi·al,** *adj.*

ef·flux (ĕf′lŭks), *n.* **1.** outward flow, as of water. **2.** that which flows out; an effluence. [t. L: s. *effluxus,* der. *effluere* flow out]

ef·fort (ĕf′ərt), *n.* **1.** exertion of power, physical or mental: *an effort to reform.* **2.** a strenuous attempt. **3.** something done by exertion; an achievement, as in literature or art. **4.** *Brit.* a drive (for funds, etc.). **5.** *Mech.* a force independently exerted, opposed to the reaction arising in opposition to a force. [t. F, der. OF *esforcier,* der. *es-* (g. L *ex-* EX-¹) + *force* strength, ult. der. L *fortis* strong.]

—**Syn. 1.** EFFORT, APPLICATION, ENDEAVOR, EXERTION imply

actions directed or force expended toward a definite end. EFFORT is an expenditure of energy to accomplish some (usually single and definite) object: *he made an effort to control himself.* APPLICATION is continuous effort plus careful attention: *constant application to duties.* ENDEAVOR means a continued and sustained series of efforts to achieve some, often worthy and difficult, end: *a constant endeavor to be useful.* EXERTION is the vigorous and often strenuous expenditure of energy, frequently without conscious reference to a definite end: *out of breath from exertion.*

ef·fort·less (ĕf′ərt lĭs), *adj.* **1.** requiring or involving no effort; easy. **2.** making no effort; passive.

ef·fron·ter·y (ĭfrŭn′tə rĭ), *n., pl.* **-teries.** shameless or impudent boldness; barefaced audacity. [t. F: m. *effronterie,* der. OF *esfront* shameless, f. *es-* (g. L *ex-* EX-¹) + *front* brow, g. s. L *frons*]

ef·fulge (ĭfŭlj′), *v.t., v.i.,* **-fulged, -fulging.** to shine or send forth brilliantly. [t. L: m.s. *effulgēre* shine forth]

ef·ful·gent (ĭfŭl′jənt), *adj.* shining forth brilliantly; radiant. —**ef·ful′gence,** *n.* —**ef·ful′gent·ly,** *adv.*

ef·fuse (*v.* ĭfūz′; *adj.* ĭfūs′), *v.,* **-fused, -fusing,** *adj.* —*v.t.* **1.** to pour out or forth; shed; disseminate. —*v.i.* **2.** to exude. **3.** *Physics.* (of gas) to flow gradually through porous material or one or more tiny apertures. —*adj.* **4.** *Bot.* spread out loosely. **5.** (of certain shells) having the lips separated by a gap or groove. [t. L: m.s. *effūsus,* pp., poured forth]

ef·fu·sion (ĭfū′zhən), *n.* **1.** act of effusing or pouring forth. **2.** that which is effused. **3.** unrestrained expression of feelings, etc.: *poetic effusions.* **4.** *Pathol.* **a.** the escape of a fluid from its natural vessels into a body cavity. **b.** the fluid which escapes.

ef·fu·sive (ĭfū′sĭv), *adj.* **1.** unduly demonstrative; without reserve: *effusive emotion, an effusive person.* **2.** *Geol.* noting or pertaining to igneous rocks which have solidified near or on the surface of the earth (opposed to *plutonic*). —**ef·fu′sive·ly,** *adv.* —**ef·fu′sive·ness,** *n.*

eft (ĕft), *n.* **1.** *U.S.* the common newt in its land stage. **2.** *Obs.* a lizard or salamander. [ME *evete,* OE *efete.* See NEWT]

eft·soon (ĕft sŏŏn′), *adv. Archaic.* **1.** soon afterward. **2.** again. **3.** forthwith. Also, **eft·soons′.** [ME *eftsone,* OE *eftsōna,* f. *eft* again + *sōna* at once]

Eg., **1.** Egypt. **2.** Egyptian.

e.g., (L *exempli gratia*) for example.

e·gad (ĭgăd′, ē-), *interj.* an expletive or mild oath: *egad, that's true.* [alter. of *a God* oh God!]

e·gal·i·tar·i·an (ĭgăl′ə târ′ĭ ən), *n.* asserting the equality of all men.

é·ga·li·té (ĕgá lē tĕ′), *n. French.* equality.

Eg·bert (ĕg′bərt), *n.* died A.D. 839?, king of the West Saxons in England, A.D. 802–839: first overlord of England and Wales, A.D. 829–839.

E·ge·ri·a (ĭjĭr′ĭ ə), *n.* **1.** *Rom. Legend.* a nymph who instructed King Numa in religious worship. **2.** a woman counselor.

e·gest (ē jĕst′), *v.t.* to discharge, as from the body; void (opposed to *ingest*). [t. L: s. *ēgestus,* pp., brought out] —**e·ges′tive,** *adj.*

e·ges·ta (ē jĕs′tə), *n.pl.* matter egested from the body, as excrement. [t. L, neut. pl. of *ēgestus,* pp., brought out]

e·ges·tion (ē jĕs′chən), *n.* the process of egesting; the voiding of the refuse of digestion.

egg¹ (ĕg), *n.* **1.** the roundish reproductive body produced by the female of animals, consisting of the female reproductive cell and its envelopes. The envelopes may be albumen, jelly, membranes, egg case, or shell, according to species. **2.** the body of this sort produced by birds, esp. the domestic hen. **3.** anything resembling a hen's egg. **4.** Also, **egg cell.** *Biol.* the ovum or female reproductive cell. —*v.t.* **5.** to prepare (food) by dipping in beaten egg. [t. Scand. (cf. Icel. *egg*); r. ME *ey,* OE *ǣg,* c. G *ei.* Cf. L *ōvum,* Gk. *ōión*]

egg² (ĕg), *v.t.* to incite or urge; encourage (usually fol. by *on*). [t. Scand.; cf. Icel. *eggja,* der. *egg* EDGE]

egg and dart, egg and tongue, egg and anchor, an egg-shaped ornament alternating with a dart-like, tonguelike, or anchorlike ornament, used to enrich a molding.

egg cozy, *Brit.* a little hood to put over a boiled egg to keep it warm until it is eaten.

egg·er (ĕg′ər), *n.* a tent caterpillar.

Egg and dart molding

Eg·gle·ston (ĕg′əl stən), *n.* Edward, 1837–1902, U.S. author, editor, and clergyman.

egg·nog (ĕg′nŏg′), *n.* a drink made of eggs, milk, sugar, and, usually, wine or spirits. [f. EGG + *nog* strong ale]

egg·plant (ĕg′plănt′, -plänt′), *n.* **1.** a plant, *Solanum Melongena,* cultivated for its edible, more or less egg-shaped fruit, dark-purple (or sometimes white or yellow) in color. **2.** the fruit, used as a table vegetable.

egg-shaped (ĕg′shāpt′), *adj.* having elongated rounded (oval) form, esp. with one end broader than the other.

egg·shell (ĕg′shĕl′), *n.* **1.** the shell of an egg in birds, consisting of keratin fibers and calcite crystals. —*adj.* **2.** like an eggshell; thin and delicate; very brittle.

eggshell china, very thin, translucent porcelain.

e·gis (ē′jĭs), *n.* aegis.

eg·lan·tine (ĕg′lən tīn′, -tēn′), **1.** the sweetbrier,

Rosa eglanteria. **2.** the Austrian brier, *Rosa foetida.* Also, *Archaic,* **eg·la·tere** (ĕg/lə tîr/). [ME *eglentine,* t. F: m. *eglantine,* der. OF *aiglent* sweetbrier, ult. der. L *acus* needle]

e·go (ē/gō, ĕg/ō), *n., pl.* **egos.** **1.** the "I" or self of any person; a person as thinking, feeling, and willing, and distinguishing itself from the selves of others and from objects of its thought. **2.** (*often cap.*) *Philos.* **a.** the enduring and conscious element which knows experience. **b.** (in Scholasticism) the complete man comprising both body and soul. **3.** *Psychoanal.* that part of the psychic apparatus which experiences the outside world and re- acts to it, thus mediating between the primitive drives of the Id and the demands of the social and physical environment. **4.** *Colloq.* conceit; egotism. [t. L: I]

e·go·cen·tric (ē/gō sĕn/trĭk, ĕg/ō-), *adj.* **1.** having or regarding self as the center of all things, esp. as applied to the known world. **—n. 2.** an egocentric person. **—e·go·cen·tric·i·ty** (ē/gō sĕn trĭs/ə tĭ, ĕg/ō-), *n.*

ego ideal, *Psychoanal.* a more or less conscious criterion of personal excellence toward which an individ- ual strives. It is derived from a composite image of the characteristics of persons (initially the parents) with whom the individual identifies h mself.

e·go·ism (ē/gō ĭz/əm, ĕg/ō-), *n.* **1.** the habit of valuing everything only in reference to one's personal interest; pure selfishness. **2.** egotism or self-conceit. **3.** *Ethics.* the doctrine that the individual and his self-interest are the basis of all behavior. [f. EGO + -ISM] **—Syn. 1.** See **egotism. —Ant. 1.** altruism.

e·go·ist (ē/gō ĭst, ĕg/ō-), *n.* **1.** a self-centered or selfish person. **2.** an egotist. **3.** an adherent of the meta- physical principle of the ego; a solipsist. [f. EGO + -IST] **—e·go·is·tic, e·go·is·ti·cal,** *adj.* **—e·go·is·ti- cal·ly,** *adv.*

e·go·ma·ni·a (ē/gō mā/nĭ ə, ĕg/ō-), *n.* morbid egotism.

e·go·tism (ē/gə tĭz/əm, ĕg/ə-), *n.* **1.** the habit of talk- ing too much about oneself; self-conceit; boastfulness. **2.** selfishness. [f. EGO + hiatus-filling *-t-* + -ISM] **—Syn. 1.** EGOTISM, EGOISM refer to preoccupation with one's ego or self. EGOTISM is the common word for obtrusive and excessive reference to and emphasis upon oneself and one's own importance, in conversation and writing, often to the ex- tent of monopolizing attention and showing disregard for others' opinions: *his egotism alienated all his friends.* EGOISM, a less common word, is used especially in philosophy, ethics, or metaphysics where it emphasizes the importance of self in relation to other things: *sufficient egoism to understand one's place in the universe.* **—Ant. 1.** humility.

e·go·tist (ē/gə tĭst, ĕg/ə-), *n.* **1.** a conceited, boastful person. **2.** an egoist. **—e·go·tis/tic, e·go·tis/ti·cal,** *adj.* **—e·go·tis/ti·cal·ly,** *adv.*

e·gre·gious (ĭ grē/jəs, -jĭ əs), *adj.* **1.** remarkably or extraordinarily flagrant: *an egregious lie, an egregious fool.* **2.** *Obs.* distinguished or eminent. [t. L: m. *egregius* distinguished, lit., (standing) out from the herd] **—e·gre/gious·ly,** *adv.* **—e·gre/gious·ness,** *n.*

e·gress (ē/grĕs), *n.* **1.** act of going or passing out, esp. from an enclosed place. **2.** a means or place of going out; an exit. **3.** the right of going out. **4.** *Astron.* the passing of a star, planet, or satellite (except the moon) out from behind or before the disk of the sun, the moon, or a planet. [t. L: s. *ēgressus,* der. *ēgredī* go out]

e·gres·sion (ĭ grĕsh/ən), *n.* a going out; egress.

e·gret (ē/grĭt, ĕg/rĭt), *n.* **1.** any of various herons, as the great white heron, *Casmerodius albus,* of Europe and America and the **snowy egret,** *Leuco- phoyxt thula* of North America, bearing in the breeding season tufts of long plumes. **2.** plume of an egret; aigrette. [ME *egrete,* t. OF, var. of *aigrette*]

American great white egret, *Casmerodius albus egretta* (38 in. long)

E·gypt (ē/jĭpt), *n.* a kingdom in NE Africa: divided into **Lower Egypt** (the Nile delta) and **Upper Egypt** (from near Cairo S to the Sudan). 17,423,000 pop. (est. 1943); 386,100 sq. mi. (ab. 12,000 sq. mi. under cultiva- tion). *Cap.:* Cairo.

Egypt., Egyptian.

E·gyp·tian (ĭ jĭp/shən), *adj.* **1.** of or pertaining to Egypt or its people: *Egyptian architecture.* **2.** of or per- taining to the Gypsies. **—n. 3.** a native or inhabitant of Egypt. **4.** a Gypsy. **5.** the language of the ancient Egyptians, an extinct Hamitic language.

E·gyp·tol·o·gy (ē/jĭp tŏl/ə jĭ), *n.* the science of Egyp- tian antiquities. **—E·gyp·to·log·i·cal** (ĭ jĭp/tə lŏj/ə- kəl), *adj.* **—E/gyp·tol/o·gist,** *n.*

eh (ā, ĕ), *interj.* an interrogative utterance, sometimes expressing surprise or doubt: *wasn't it lucky, eh?*

Eh·ren·breit·stein (ā/rən brīt/shtīn), *n.* a famous Roman fortress overlooking the Rhine at Coblenz.

Eh·ren·burg (ā/rən bŏŏrkH/), *n.* **Ilya Grigorievich** (ĭl yä/ grĭ gōr/yə vĭch), born 1891, Russian author.

Ehr·lich (âr/lĭkH), *n.* **Paul** (poul), 1854–1915, German physician, bacteriologist, and chemist.

E.I., **1.** East Indian. **2.** East Indies.

ei·der (ī/dər), *n.* **1.** eider duck. **2.** eider down. [t. Sw. or G, ult. t. Icel. (see EIDER DOWN)]

eider down, 1. down or soft feathers from the breast of the eider duck. **2.** *U.S.* a fabric of cotton with wool nap. **3.** a heavy quilt or comfort, properly one filled with eider down (def. 1). [ult. t. Icel.: m. *ædardūn* (18th cent. spelling) down of the eider (gen. sing.); spelling *eider-* fol- lows (18th cent.) Sw. or G, repr. Icel. *æ* with *ei*]

eider duck, any of several large sea ducks of the genus *So- materia* and allied genera, of the northern hemisphere, generally black and white, and yielding eider down.

Eider duck. *Somateria v-nigra* (Ab. 22 in. long)

ei·det·ic imagery (ī dĕt/ĭk), a vivid and persistent type of imagery, esp. during childhood.

ei·do·lon (ī dō/lən), *n., pl.* **-la** (-lə). an image; a phan- tom; an apparition. [t. Gk.: image. Cf. IDOL]

Eif·fel Tower (ī/fəl), a tower of skeletal iron con- struction in Paris, France: built for the exhibition of 1889. 984 ft. high.

eight (āt), *n.* **1.** a cardinal number, seven plus one. **2.** a symbol for this number, as 8 or VIII. **3.** a set of this many persons or things, as the crew of an eight- oared racing shell. **—adj. 4.** amounting to eight in number. [ME *eighte, ehte,* OE *eahta,* c. D and G *acht;* akin to L *octō,* Gk. *oktō*]

eight·een (ā/tēn/), *n.* **1.** a cardinal number, ten plus eight. **2.** a symbol for this number, as 18 or XVIII. [ME *ehtetene,* OE *eahtatēne.* See EIGHT, -TEEN] **—eight- eenth** (ā/tēnth/), *adj., n.*

eight·een·mo (ā tēn/mō), *n.* octodecimo.

eight·fold (āt/fōld/), *adj.* **1.** comprising eight parts or members; eight times as great or as much. **—adv. 2.** in eightfold measure.

eighth (ātth), *adj.* **1.** next after the seventh. **2.** being one of eight equal parts. **—n. 3.** the eighth number of a series. **4.** an eighth part. **5.** *Music.* an octave.

eighth note, *Music.* a note having ⅛ of the time value of a whole note; a quaver. See illus. under **note.**

eight·y (ā/tĭ), *n., pl.* **eighties,** *adj.* **—n. 1.** a cardinal number, ten times eight. **2.** a symbol for this number, as 80 or LXXX or XXC. **—adj. 3.** amounting to eighty in number. [ME *eighteti,* OE *eahtatig*] **—eight·i·eth** (ā/tĭ ĭth), *adj., n.*

eight·y-nin·er (ā/tĭ nī/nər), *n.* one who began home- steading in Oklahoma in 1889.

ei·kon (ī/kŏn), *n.* icon.

Eind·ho·ven (īnt/hō/vən), *n.* a city in S Netherlands. 130,132 (est. 1940).

Ein' fes·te Burg ist un·ser Gott (īn fĕs/tə bŏŏrkH/ ĭst ŏŏn/zər gôt/), *German.* a mighty fortress is our God (first line of a hymn by Luther).

Ein·stein (īn/stīn; *Ger.* -shtīn), *n.* **Albert** (ăl/bərt; *Ger.* äl/bĕrt), born 1879, German physicist who formulated the theory of relativity, now a U.S. citizen. **—Ein- stein/i·an,** *adj.*

Einstein theory. See **relativity.**

Eir·e (âr/ə; *Gael.* ā/rə), *n.* a republic occupying most of Ireland: nominally associated with the British Common- wealth of Nations. 2,949,713 pop. (est. 1943); 27,137 sq. mi. *Cap.:* Dublin. Formerly (1922–37), **Irish Free State.** Officially (since 1949), **Republic of Ireland.**

Ei·sen·ach (ī/zə näkH/), *n.* a city in central Germany, in Thuringia. 53,116 (1939).

Ei·sen·how·er (ī/zən hou/ər), *n.* **Dwight David,** born 1890, U.S. general, supreme commander of the Allied Expeditionary Forces, 1943–45, Chief of Staff, 1945–48; president of Columbia University since 1948 (now on leave); Supreme Allied Commander of Atlantic Pact forces since 1950.

Eisk (āsk), *n.* a seaport in the SW Soviet Union, on the Sea of Azov. 38,094 (1926). Also, **Yeisk.**

eis·tedd·fod (ā stĕth/vŏd, ě-), *n., pl.* **eisteddfods, eisteddfodau** (ā/stĕth vŏd/ī, ĕs/tĕth-), a congress of Welsh bards and minstrels. [t. Welsh: session, der. *eistedd* sit]

ei·ther (ē/thər or, esp. *Brit.,* ī/thər), *adj.* **1.** one or the other of two: *you may sit at either end of the table.* **2.** each of the two; the one and the other: *there are trees on either side of the river.* **—pron. 3.** one or the other: *take either; either will do.* **—conj. 4.** used as one of two coördinate alternatives: *either come or write.* **—adv. 5.** used after negative sentences coördinated by *and, or, nor: he is not fond of parties and I am not either* (or *nor I either*), *I am not going and nobody can prevent it either;* after a neg. sub. clause: *if you do not come, he will not come either.* [ME; OE *ægther,* contr. of *æghwæther* each of two, both, f. *ā* always + *gehwæther* each of two. See WHETHER]

e·jac·u·late (ĭ jăk/yə lāt/), *v.t.,* **-lated, -lating. 1.** to utter suddenly and briefly; exclaim. **2.** to eject sud- denly and swiftly; discharge. [t. L: m.s. *ējaculātus,* pp., having cast out] **—e·jac/u·la/tor,** *n.*

e·jac·u·la·tion (ĭ jăk/yə lā/shən), *n.* **1.** an abrupt, exclamatory utterance. **2.** act of ejaculating. **3.** *Physiol.* the rhythmic discharge of seminal fluid from the male passages; an emission.

e·jac·u·la·to·ry (ĭ jăk/yə lə tōr/ĭ), *adj.* **1.** pertaining to or of the nature of an ejaculation or exclamatory utterance. **2.** *Physiol.* pertaining to ejaculation.

ăct, āble, dâre, ärt; ĕbb, ēqual; ĭf, īce; hŏt, ōver, ôrder, oil, bŏŏk, ōoze, out; ŭp, ūse, ûrge; ə = a in alone; ch, chief; g, give; ng, ring; sh, shoe; th, thin; ŧh, that; zh, vision. See the full key on inside cover.

e·ject (*v.* ĭjĕkt′; *n.* ē′jĕkt), *v.t.* **1.** to drive or force out; expel, as from a place or position. **2.** to dismiss, as from office, occupancy, etc. **3.** to evict, as from property. —*n.* **4.** *Psychol.* something whose existence is inferred as a reality, but which is outside of, and inaccessible to, the consciousness of the one making the inference: *the consciousness of one individual is an eject to that of any other.* [t. L: s. *ējectus*, pp., thrown out]

e·jec·ta (ĭjĕk′tə). *n.pl.* matter ejected, as from a volcano in eruption. [t. L, neut. pl. of *ējectus*. See EJECT]

e·jec·tion (ĭjĕk′shən), *n.* **1.** act of ejecting. **2.** state of being ejected. **3.** something ejected, as lava.

e·jec·tive (ĭjĕk′tĭv), *adj.* **1.** serving to eject. **2.** *Phonet.* (of a stop or fricative) produced with air compressed above the closed glottis. —*n.* **3.** *Phonet.* an ejective stop or fricative.

e·ject·ment (ĭjĕkt′mənt), *n.* **1.** act of ejecting. **2.** *Law.* a possessory action wherein the title to real property may be tried and the possession recovered, wherever the party claiming has a right of entry.

e·jec·tor (ĭjĕk′tər), *n.* **1.** one who or that which ejects. **2.** the mechanism in a firearm or gun which, after firing, throws out the empty cartridge or shell from the weapon.

E·ka·te·rin·burg (ĕkä′tĕrēnbŏŏrкн′), *n.* former name of **Sverdlovsk.**

E·ka·te·ri·no·dar (ĕkä′tĕrēnō̇där′), *n.* former name of **Krasnodar.**

E·ka·te·ri·no·slav (ĕkä′tĕrēnō̇släf′), *n.* former name of **Dnepropetrovsk.**

eke¹ (ēk), *v.t.*, **eked, eking. 1. eke out, a.** to supply what is lacking to; supplement. **b.** to contrive to make (a living) or support (existence) by various makeshifts. **2.** *Archaic or Dial.* to increase; enlarge; lengthen. [var. of obs. *ēche*, OE *ēcan*, with *k* from obs. n. *eke* addition (OE *ēaca*). Cf. *ēacen* augmented. Akin to Icel. *auka*, Goth. *aukan*, L *augēre* increase]

eke² (ēk), *adv.*, *conj.* *Archaic.* also. [ME *eek*, d. OE *ēc*; r. OE *ēac*, c. G *auch*]

el (ĕl), *n.* **1.** elevated railroad. **2.** ell¹.

e·lab·o·rate (*adj.* ĭlăb′ərĭt; *v.* ĭlăb′ərāt′), *adj.*, *v.*, **-rated, -rating.** —*adj.* **1.** worked out with great care and nicety of detail; executed with great minuteness: *elaborate preparations, care, etc.* —*v.t.* **2.** to work out carefully or minutely; work up to perfection. **3.** to produce or develop by labor. —*v.i.* **4.** to add details in writing, speaking, etc.; give additional or fuller treatment (fol. by *on* or *upon*): *to elaborate upon a theme or an idea.* [t. L: m.s. *ēlābōrātus*, pp., worked out] —**e·lab′o·rate·ly,** *adv.* —**e·lab′o·rate·ness,** *n.* —**e·lab′o·ra′-tive,** *adj.* —**e·lab′o·ra′tor,** *n.*
—**Syn. 1.** perfected, painstaking. ELABORATE, LABORED, STUDIED apply to that which is worked out in great detail. That which is ELABORATE is characterized by great, sometimes even excessive, nicety or minuteness of detail: *elaborate preparations for a banquet, an elaborate apology.* That which is LABORED is marked by excessive, often forced or uninspired, effort: *a labored explanation, style of writing.* That which is STUDIED is accomplished with care and deliberation, and is done purposely, sometimes even having been rehearsed: *a studied pose, effect of carelessness.* —**Ant. 1.** casual, simple.

e·lab·o·ra·tion (ĭlăb′ərā′shən), *n.* **1.** act of elaborating. **2.** state of being elaborated; elaborateness. **3.** something elaborated.

El·a·gab·a·lus (ĕl′əgăb′ələs, ē′lə-), *n.* (*Varius Avitus Bassanius*), A.D. 205?–222, Roman emperor, A.D. 218–222. Also, **Heliogabalus.**

E·laine (ĭlān′), *n.* the name of several characters in Arthurian legends, notably: **1.** the "lily maid of Astolat" who pined and died for Lancelot; the half sister of Arthur and mother of his son Modred. **2.** the daughter of King Pelles and mother of Sir Galahad.

El A·la·mein (ĕl ä′lämān′), a town on the N coast of Egypt, ab. 70 mi. W of Alexandria: decisive British victory, Oct., 1942.

E·lam (ē′ləm), *n.* an ancient country E of Babylonia and N of the Persian Gulf. *Cap.:* Susa. See map under **Chaldea.** —**E·lam·ite** (ē′ləmīt′), *n.*, *adj.*

é·lan (ĕläN′), *n.* dash; impetuous ardor. [F, der. *élancer* hurl, rush forth]

e·land (ē′lənd), *n.* a large, heavily built antelope, *Taurotragus oryx*, of southern and eastern Africa. [t. S Afr. D, special use of D *eland* elk, t. G: m. *elend*, said to be t. Lithuanian: m. *elnis* elk]

é·lan vi·tal (ĕ läN vētál′), *French.* (esp. in Bergsonian philosophy) the creative force within an organism, which is able to build physical form and to produce growth and necessary or desirable adaptations. [F: lit., living force]

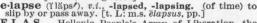
Eland, *Taurotragus oryx*
(6 ft. high at the shoulder, body 11½ ft. long, tail ab. 2 ft.)

e·lapse (ĭlăps′), *v.i.*, **-lapsed, -lapsing.** (of time) to slip by or pass away. [t. L: m.s. *ēlapsus*, pp.]

E.L.A.S., Hellenic People's Army of Liberation, the military organization of the EAM and the most powerful Greek resistance force in World War II. Also, **Elas** (ĕ′läs).

e·las·mo·branch (ĭlăs′məbrăngk′, ĭlăz′-), *adj.* **1.** of the *Elasmobranchii*, the group of vertebrates including the sharks and rays, with cartilaginous skeletons and five to seven pairs of gill openings. —*n.* **2.** an elasmobranch fish. [t. NL: m.s. *Elasmobranchiī*, pl., f. Gk.: *elasmó(s)* metal plate + *bránchia* gills]

e·las·tic (ĭlăs′tĭk), *adj.* **1.** having the property of recovering shape after deformation, as solids; spontaneously expansive, as gases. **2.** flexible, yielding, or accommodating: *an elastic conscience.* **3.** springing back or rebounding; springy: *an elastic step.* **4.** readily recovering from depression or exhaustion; buoyant: *an elastic temperament.* —*n.* **5.** webbing, or material in the form of a band, made elastic with strips of India rubber. **6.** a piece of this material. **7.** rubber band. [t. NL: s. *elasticus*, t. Gk.: m. *elastikós* propulsive] —**e·las′ti·cal·ly,** *adv.*

e·las·tic·i·ty (ĭlăs′tĭs′ətĭ, ē′lăs-), *n.* **1.** state or quality of being elastic. **2.** flexibility: *elasticity of meaning.* **3.** buoyancy; capacity for resisting or overcoming depression.

e·las·tin (ĭlăs′tĭn), *n.* *Biochem.* a protein constituting the basic substance of elastic tissue. [f. ELAST(IC) + -IN²]

e·late (ĭlāt′), *v.*, **elated, elating.** *adj.* —*v.t.* **1.** to put in high spirits; make proud. —*adj.* **2.** elated. [t. L: m.s. *ēlātus*, pp., brought out, raised, exalted]

e·lat·ed (ĭlā′tĭd), *adj.* in high spirits; proud. —**e·lat′ed·ly,** *adv.* —**e·lat′ed·ness,** *n.* —**Syn.** exhilarated, jubilant, exultant.

el·a·ter (ĕl′ətər), *n.* **1.** *Bot.* an elastic filament serving to disperse spores. **2.** *Zool.* elaterid. [NL, t. Gk.: driver]

el·at·er·id (ĭlăt′ərĭd), *n.* any of the click beetles, constituting the family *Elateridae*, most of which have the power of springing up when laid on their backs.

el·at·er·in (ĭlăt′ərĭn), *n.* *Chem.* a white crystalline substance obtained from and constituting the active principle of elaterium, used as a cathartic.

el·at·er·ite (ĭlăt′ərīt′), *n.* a brownish, elastic, rubberlike, naturally occurring asphalt.

el·a·te·ri·um (ĕl′ətĭr′ĭom), *n.* a powerful cathartic obtained from the juice of *Ecballium elaterium*, the squirting cucumber. [t. L, t. Gk.: m. *elatḗrion* an opening medicine]

e·la·tion (ĭlā′shən), *n.* exaltation of spirit, as from joy or pride; exultant gladness; high spirits.

El·ba (ĕl′bə), *n.* an Italian island in the Mediterranean between Corsica and Italy: the scene of Napoleon's first exile, 1814–15. 31,641 pop. (1936); 94 sq. mi.

El·be (ĕl′bə), *n.* a river flowing from W Czechoslovakia NW through Germany to the North Sea near Hamburg. 725 mi.

El·ber·feld (ĕl′bərfĕlt′), *n.* See **Wuppertal.**

El·ber·ta (ĕl bûr′tə), *n.* *Hort.* a yellow, freestone peach widely grown in eastern U.S.

El·bert Peak (ĕl′bərt), a mountain in central Colorado, in the Sawatch range: highest peak of the Rocky Mountains in the U.S. 14,431 ft.

El·bing (ĕl′bĭng), *n.* a seaport in N Poland: formerly in Germany (East Prussia). 85,952 (1939).

el·bow (ĕl′bō), *n.* **1.** the bend or joint of the arm between upper arm and forearm. **2.** something bent like the elbow, as a sharp turn in a road or river, or a piece of pipe bent, at an angle. **3. at one's elbow,** near at hand. **4. out at elbows** or **out at the elbow,** ragged or impoverished. **5. up to the elbows in,** very busy with; wholly engaged or engrossed in. —*v.t.* **6.** to push with or as with the elbow; jostle. **7.** to make (one's way) by so pushing. —*v.i.* **8.** to elbow one's way. [ME *elbowe*, OE *elneboga*, c. G *ellenbogen*, orig. arm bow. See ELL², BOW¹]

el·bow·room (ĕl′bōrŏŏm′, -rŏŏm′), *n.* ample room; free scope.

El·brus (ĕl′brŏŏs, āl′brŏŏs), *n.* a mountain in the S Soviet Union in Europe, in the Caucasus Mountains: the highest peak in Europe. 18,465 ft. Also, **El′bruz.**

El·burz Mountains (ĕl bŏŏrz′), a mountain range in N Iran, along the S coast of the Caspian Sea. Highest peak, Mt. Demavend, 18,606 ft.

El Cap·i·tan (ĕl kăp′ətăn′; *Sp.* ĕl kä′pētän′), a peak of the Sierra Nevada Mountains in E California, with a sheer precipice rising over 3300 ft. above Yosemite Valley.

El Cid Cam·pe·a·dor (ĕl thĕd′ käm′pĕ ä dôr′). See **Cid.**

eld (ĕld), *n.* *Archaic.* **1.** age. **2.** old age. **3.** antiquity. [ME *elde*, OE *eld(o)*, der. *eald, ald* old]

eld·er¹ (ĕl′dər), *adj.* **1.** older. **2.** senior: *an elder officer.* **3.** earlier: *in elder times.* —*n.* **4.** a person who is older than oneself; one's senior. **5.** an aged person. **6.** one of the older and more influential men of a tribe or community, often a chief or ruler. **7.** a presbyter. **8.** (in certain Protestant churches) a governing officer, either with or without teaching or pastoral functions. **9.** (in the Mormon church) one holding the higher or Melchisedek priesthood. [ME; OE *eldra*, etc. (compar. of *ald, eald* old), c. G *älter*] —**eld′er·ship′,** *n.* —**Syn. 1.** See **older.**

el·der[2] (ĕl′dər), *n.* any plant of the caprifoliaceous genus *Sambucus*, which comprises shrubs and small trees bearing clusters of small white or light-colored flowers and a blackish or red fruit, *Alnus glutinosa*, of Europe. [ME *eldre, elrene, ellerne*, OE *ellærn*, c. MLG *ellern, elderne*]

el·der·ber·ry (ĕl′dər bĕr′ĭ), *n., pl.* **-ries.** **1.** the drupaceous fruit of the elder, used in making wine, jelly, and in medicine for aperient and diuretic qualities. **2.** elder[2].

eld·er·ly (ĕl′dər lĭ), *adj.* **1.** somewhat old; between middle and old age. **2.** of or pertaining to persons in later life. —**eld′er·li·ness,** *n.* —**Syn. 1.** See old.

elder statesman, 1. (in Japan) a group of senior statesmen, with no legal status, and no defined membership, which toward the end of the Meiji era were a powerful influence on government policy; the genro. **2.** a similar group in any country or field.

eld·est (ĕl′dĭst), *adj.* oldest: now surviving only in *the eldest brother, sister, and eldest hand.* [OE *eldest*(*a*), superl. of *ald, eald* OLD, c. G. *ältest*(*e*)]

eldest hand, *Cards.* the player on the dealer's left.

El Do·ra·do (ĕl də rä′dō, -rä′-; *Sp.* ĕl dô rä′dō), **1.** a legendary treasure city of South America, probably based on myths of the Chibcha Indians of Colombia. **2.** any place of reputed fabulous wealth. [t. Sp.: the gilded]

el·dritch (ĕl′drĭch), *adj.* *Orig. Scot.* weird; uncanny; unearthly.

E·le·a (ē′lĭ ə), *n.* an ancient Greek city on the coast of Lucania in SW Italy.

El·ea·nor of Aquitaine (ĕl′ə nər), 1122?–1204, queen of Henry II of England.

E·le·at·ic (ĕl′ĭ ăt′ĭk), *adj.* **1.** pertaining to Elea. **2.** pertaining to the philosophical system of Xenophanes, Parmenides, and others who lived there. —*n.* **3.** a school of Greek philosophy founded by Xenophanes of Colophon, who resided in Elea, whose doctrines are developments of the conception of the universal unity of being. [t. L: s. *Eleāticus*, der. *Elea*, name of an ancient Greek city in SW Italy] —**El′e·at′i·cism,** *n.*

el·e·cam·pane (ĕl′ə kăm pān′), *n.* a composite plant, *Inula Helenium*, with large yellow flowers and aromatic leaves and root. [t. ML: m. *enula* (in L *inula*) *campāna*, prob., inula of the fields]

e·lect (ĭ lĕkt′), *v.t.* **1.** to select by vote, as for an office. **2.** to determine in favor of (a course of action, etc.) **3.** to pick out or choose. **4.** *Theol.* (of God) to select for divine mercy or favor, esp. for salvation. —*adj.* **5.** selected for an office, but not yet inducted (usually after the noun): *the governor-elect.* **6.** picked out; chosen. **7.** select or choice. **8.** *Theol.* chosen by God, esp. for eternal life. —*n.* **9.** a person or the persons chosen or worthy to be chosen. **10.** *Theol.* those chosen by God, esp. for eternal life. [t. L: s. *ēlectus*, pp., chosen, picked out] —**Syn. 3.** See **choose.**

elect., **1.** electric. **2.** electrical. **3.** electricity. Also, **elec.**

e·lec·tion (ĭ lĕk′shən), *n.* **1.** the selection of a person or persons for office by vote. **2.** a public vote upon a proposition submitted. **3.** act of electing. **4.** *Theol.* the choice by God of individuals, as for a particular work, or esp. for salvation of eternal life. —**Syn. 3.** selection, choice, preference, option.

e·lec·tion·eer (ĭ lĕk′shə nîr′), *v.i.* to work for the success of a candidate, party, ticket, etc., in an election. —**e·lec′tion·eer′er,** *n.*

e·lec·tive (ĭ lĕk′tĭv), *adj.* **1.** pertaining to the principle of electing to office, etc. **2.** appointed by election, as an officer. **3.** bestowed by or derived from election, as an office. **4.** having the power of electing to office, etc., as a body of persons. **5.** open to choice; optional; not required: *an elective subject in high school or college.* **6.** *Chem.* selecting for combination or action: *elective attraction* (tendency to combine with certain substances in preference to others). —*n.* **7.** an optional study, as in a course at college; a study which a student may select from among alternatives. —**e·lec′tive·ly,** *adv.* —**e·lec′tive·ness,** *n.*

e·lec·tor (ĭ lĕk′tər), *n.* **1.** one who elects or may elect, esp. a qualified voter. **2.** *U.S.* a member of the electoral college. **3.** (*usually cap.*) (in the Holy Roman Empire) one of the princes entitled to elect the emperor.

e·lec·tor·al (ĭ lĕk′tər əl), *adj.* **1.** pertaining to electors or election. **2.** consisting of electors.

electoral college, a body of electors chosen by voters in the several states to elect the president and vice-president of the United States.

e·lec·tor·ate (ĭ lĕk′tər ĭt), *n.* **1.** the body of persons entitled to vote in an election. **2.** the dignity or territory of an elector of the Holy Roman Empire.

electr-, var, of **electro-,** before vowels, as in *electrode.*

E·lec·tra (ĭ lĕk′trə), *n.* *Gk. Legend.* the daughter of Agamemnon and Clytemnestra. She incited her brother Orestes to avenge the murder of his father.

Electra complex, *Psychoanal.* the unresolved desire of a daughter for sexual gratification from her father.

e·lec·tress (ĭ lĕk′trĭs), *n.* **1.** a female elector. **2.** the wife or widow of an elector of the Holy Roman Empire.

e·lec·tric (ĭ lĕk′trĭk), *adj.* **1.** pertaining to, derived from, produced by, or involving electricity: *an electric current, an electric shock.* **2.** producing, transmitting, or operated by electric currents: *an electric bell.* **3.** electrifying; thrilling; exciting; stirring. —*n.* **4.** a railroad operated by electricity. **5.** a truck, etc. operated by electricity from storage batteries. [t. NL: s. *ēlectricus*, der. L *ēlectrum*, t. Gk.: m. *ēlektron* amber (as a substance that develops electricity under friction)]

e·lec·tri·cal (ĭ lĕk′trə kəl), *adj.* **1.** electric. **2.** concerned with electricity: *an electrical engineer.* —**e·lec′-tri·cal·ly,** *adv.*

electrical transcription, 1. a radio broadcast from a phonograph record made for the purpose. **2.** the phonograph record itself.

electric chair, 1. an electrified chair used to execute criminals. **2.** the electrocution.

electric eel, a fish, *Electrophorus electricus*, of eel-like form, having the power of giving strong electric discharges. It is found in the fresh waters of northern South America, and is sometimes over 6 feet long.

electric eye, a photoelectric cell.

electric field, a condition of space in the vicinity of an electric charge or a moving magnet which manifests itself as a force on an electric charge within that space.

electric furnace, a furnace in which the heat required is produced through electricity.

e·lec·tri·cian (ĭ lĕk′trĭsh′ən, ē′lĕk-), *n.* one who installs, operates, maintains, or repairs electrical devices.

e·lec·tric·i·ty (ĭ lĕk′trĭs′ə tĭ, ē′lĕk-), *n.* **1.** an agency producing various physical phenomena, as attraction and repulsion, luminous and heating effects, shock to the body, chemical decomposition, etc., which were originally thought to be caused by a kind of fluid, but are now regarded as being due to the presence and movements of electrons and other particles. **2.** the science dealing with this agency. **3.** electric current: *to install electricity, a machine run by electricity.*

electric organ, an organ with an electrophonic rather than a mechanical or a pneumatic, action.

electric ray, a ray of the family *Torpedinidae* which possesses a peculiar organ enabling it to stun its prey with electric shock.

e·lec·tri·fy (ĭ lĕk′trə fī), *v.t.,* **-fied, -fying. 1.** to charge with or subject to electricity; to apply electricity to. **2.** to equip for the use of electric power, as a railroad. **3.** to startle greatly; excite or thrill: *to electrify an audience.* [f. ELECTR(IC) + -(I)FY] —**e·lec′tri·fi·ca′tion,** *n.* —**e·lec′tri·fi′er,** *n.*

e·lec·trize (ĭ lĕk′trīz), *v.t.,* **-trized, -trizing.** electrify (defs. 1, 2). —**e·lec′tri·za′tion,** *n.* —**e·lec′triz·er,** *n.*

e·lec·tro (ĭ lĕk′trō), *n., pl.* **-tros.** electrotype.

electro-, a word element meaning "pertaining to or caused by electricity," as in *electromagnet, electrotype, electrochemistry, electrolysis, electrocute.* Also, **electr-.** [t. Gk.: m. *ēlektro-*, comb. form of *ēlektron* amber]

e·lec·tro·a·nal·y·sis (ĭ lĕk′trō ə năl′ə sĭs), *n.* chemical analysis by electrolysis.

e·lec·tro·chem·is·try (ĭ lĕk′trō kĕm′ĭs trĭ), *n.* the branch of chemistry that deals with the chemical changes produced by electricity and the production of electricity by chemical changes. —**e·lec·tro·chem·i·cal** (ĭ lĕk′-trō kĕm′ə kəl), *adj.,* **e·lec′tro·chem′i·cal·ly,** *adv.* —**e·lec′tro·chem′ist,** *n.*

e·lec·tro·cute (ĭ lĕk′trə kūt′), *v.t.,* **-cuted, -cuting. 1.** to kill by electricity. **2.** to execute (a criminal) by electricity. [f. ELECTRO- + -*cute* in EXECUTE]

e·lec·tro·cu·tion (ĭ lĕk′trə kū′shən), *n.* act of electrocuting.

e·lec·trode (ĭ lĕk′trōd), *n.* *Elect.* a conductor belonging to the class of metallic conductors, but not necessarily a metal, through which a current enters or leaves an electrolytic cell, arc furnace, vacuum tube, gaseous discharge tube, or any conductor of the nonmetallic class. [f. ELECTR(O)- + -ODE[2]]

e·lec·tro·de·pos·it (ĭ lĕk′trō dĭ pŏz′ĭt), *v.t.* **1.** to deposit (a metal, etc.) by electrolysis. —*n.* **2.** a deposit, as of metal, produced by electrolysis.

e·lec·tro·dy·nam·ic (ĭ lĕk′trō dī năm′ĭk), *adj.* **1.** pertaining to the force of electricity in motion. **2.** pertaining to electrodynamics. Also, **e·lec′tro·dy·nam′i·cal.**

e·lec·tro·dy·nam·ics (ĭ lĕk′trō dī năm′ĭks), *n.* the branch of electricity that deals with the mutual action of electric currents and the interaction of currents and magnets.

e·lec·tro·dy·na·mom·e·ter (ĭ lĕk′trō dī′nə mŏm′ə tər), *n.* an instrument in which the mechanical reactions between two parts of the same circuit are used for detecting or measuring an electric current.

e·lec·tro·en·ceph·a·lo·gram (ĭ lĕk′trō ĕn sĕf′ə lə grăm′), *n.* a record of the electrical potentials of the brain.

e·lec·tro·graph (ĭ lĕk′trō grăf′, -gräf′), *n.* **1.** a curve automatically traced, forming a record of the indications of an electrometer. **2.** an apparatus for engraving metal plates on cylinders used in printing. **3.** an apparatus used to transmit pictures, etc. electrically. —**e·lec′-tro·graph′ic,** *adj.* —**e·lec·trog·ra·phy** (ĭ lĕk′trŏg′rə-fĭ, ē′lĕk-), *n.*

e·lec·tro·ki·net·ics (ĭ lĕk′trō kĭ nĕt′ĭks, -kī-), *n.* the branch of electricity that deals with currents. —**e·lec′-tro·ki·net′ic,** *adj.*

e·lec·tro·lier (ĭ lĕk′trə lîr′), *n.* a chandelier or support for electric lamps. [f. ELECTRO- + -*lier* in CHANDELIER]

ăct, āble, dâre, ärt; ĕbb, ēqual; ĭf, īce; hŏt, ōver, ôrder, oil, bŏok, ōoze, out; ŭp, ūse, ûrge; ə = a in alone; ch, chief; g, give; ng, ring; sh, shoe; th, thin; ᵺ, that; zh, vision. See the full key on inside cover.

e·lec·trol·y·sis (ĭ lĕk/trŏl/ə sĭs), *n.* **1.** the decomposition of a chemical compound by an electric current. **2.** *Surg.* the destruction of tumors, hair roots, etc., by an electric current.

e·lec·tro·lyte (ĭ lĕk/trə līt/), *n.* **1.** *Elect.* a conducting medium in which the flow of current is accompanied by the movement of matter. **2.** *Chem.* any substance which dissociates into ions when dissolved in a suitable medium or when melted, thus forming a conductor of electricity.

e·lec·tro·lyt·ic (ĭ lĕk/trə lĭt/ĭk), *adj.* **1.** pertaining to or derived by electrolysis. **2.** pertaining to an electrolyte. Also, **e·lec/tro·lyt/i·cal.** —**e·lec/tro·lyt/i·cal·ly,** *adv.*

electrolytic cell. See cell (def. 9).

electrolytic dissociation, the separation of the molecule of an electrolyte into its constituent atoms.

e·lec·tro·lyze (ĭ lĕk/trə līz/), *v.t.,* **-lyzed, -lyzing.** to decompose by electrolysis. —**e·lec/tro·ly·za/tion,** *n.* —**e·lec/tro·lyz/er,** *n.*

e·lec·tro·mag·net (ĭ lĕk/trō-mǎg/nĭt), *n.* a device, consisting of an iron or steel core which is magnetized by electric current in a coil which surrounds it.

e·lec·tro·mag·net·ic (ĭ lĕk/trō-mǎg nĕt/ĭk), *adj.* **1.** pertaining to an electromagnet. **2.** pertaining to electromagnetism. —**e·lec/tro·mag·net/i·cal·ly,** *adv.*

e·lec·tro·mag·net·ism (ĭ lĕk/-trō mǎg/nə tĭz/əm), *n.* **1.** the phenomena collectively resting upon the relations between electric currents and magnetism. **2.** the science that deals with these relations.

Electromagnet
C, Coil carrying current;
A, Armature; L, Load

e·lec·tro·met·al·lur·gy (ĭ lĕk/trō mĕt/ə lûr/jĭ, -mə-tǎl/ər jĭ), *n.* the refining of metals and ores by an electric current. —**e·lec/tro·met/al·lur/gi·cal,** *adj.* —**e·lec/tro·met/al·lur/gist,** *n.*

e·lec·trom·e·ter (ĭ lĕk/trŏm/ə tər, ē/lĕk-), *n.* an instrument for detecting or measuring a potential difference by means of the mechanical forces exerted between electrically charged bodies.

e·lec·tro·mo·tive (ĭ lĕk/trə mō/tĭv), *adj.* pertaining to, producing, or tending to produce a flow of electricity.

electromotive force, the amount of energy supplied to an electric circuit in one second by a voltaic cell, dynamo, or other source of electrical energy when one ampere of current flows in the circuit.

e·lec·tro·mo·tor (ĭ lĕk/trə mō/tər), *n.* electric motor.

e·lec·tron (ĭ lĕk/trŏn), *n. Physics, Chem.* an extremely small, negatively charged particle, having about one thousandth the mass of a hydrogen atom, supposed to be or to contain the unit of negative electricity. [t. Gk.: m. *ēlektron.* See ELECTRUM] —**e·lec·tron·ic** (ĭ lĕk/trŏn/ĭk, ē/lĕk-), *adj.*

e·lec·tro·neg·a·tive (ĭ lĕk/trō nĕg/ə tĭv), *adj. Physics, Chem.* **1.** containing negative electricity; tending to pass to the positive pole in electrolysis. **2.** assuming negative potential when in contact with a dissimilar substance. **3.** nonmetallic.

electron gun, *Television.* the cathode in a cathode-ray tube which emits electrons, and the surrounding electrostatic or electromagnetic apparatus which controls and focuses the electron stream.

e·lec·tron·ics (ĭ lĕk/trŏn/ĭks, ē/lĕk-), *n.* the investigation and application of phenomena involving the movement of free electrons, as in radio, television, etc., now extended to include applications involving ions.

electron lens, a combination of static or varying electric and magnetic fields used to focus streams of electrons in a manner similar to that of an optical lens.

electron microscope, a microscope of extremely high power which uses beams of electrons focused by electron lenses instead of rays of light, the magnified image being formed on a fluorescent screen or recorded on a photographic plate. Its magnification is substantially greater than that of any optical microscope.

electron tube, *Electronics.* a vacuum tube (def. 1), or a gas-filled discharge tube.

e·lec·tro·nu·cle·ar machine (ĭ lĕk/trə nū/klĭ ər), a device for the production of very high energy beams of particles (protons, electrons, etc.) by acceleration in electric and magnetic fields. Examples are the cyclotron, synchrotron, bevatron, cosmotron, etc.

e·lec·tro·phon·ic (ĭ lĕk/trə fŏn/ĭk), *adj.* (of musical instruments) based on oscillating electric currents.

e·lec·tro·pho·re·sis (ĭ lĕk/trō fə rē/sĭs), *n. Physics., Chem.* the motion of colloidal particles suspended in a fluid medium, under the influence of an electric field. [f. ELECTRO- + Gk. *phórēsis* a carrying]

e·lec·troph·o·rus (ĭ lĕk/trŏf/ə rəs, ē/lĕk-), *n., pl.* **-ri** (-rī/). an instrument for generating static electricity by means of induction. [NL. See ELECTRO-, -PHOROUS]

e·lec·tro·plate (ĭ lĕk/trə plāt/), *v.,* **-plated, -plating,** *n.* —*v.t.* **1.** to plate or coat with a metal by electrolysis. —*n.* **2.** electroplated articles or ware. —**e·lec/tro·plat/er,** *n.* —**e·lec/tro·plat/ing,** *n.*

e·lec·tro·pos·i·tive (ĭ lĕk/trə pŏz/ə tĭv), *adj. Physics, Chem.* **1.** containing positive electricity; tending to pass to the negative pole in electrolysis. **2.** assuming positive

potential when in contact with another substance. **3.** basic, as an element or radical.

e·lec·tro·scope (ĭ lĕk/trə skōp/), *n.* a device for detecting the presence of electricity, and whether it is positive or negative, by means of electric attraction and repulsion. —**e·lec·tro·scop·ic** (ĭ lĕk/trə skŏp/ĭk), *adj.*

e·lec·tro·shock (ĭ lĕk/trə shŏk/), *n. Psychiatry.* shock therapy administered by electrical means.

e·lec·tro·stat·ics (ĭ lĕk/trə stăt/ĭks), *n.* the science of static electricity. —**e·lec/tro·stat/ic,** *adj.*

e·lec·tro·ther·a·peu·tics (ĭ lĕk/trō thĕr/ə pū/tĭks), *n.* therapeutics based upon the curative use of electricity. —**e·lec/tro·ther/a·peu/tic, e·lec/tro·ther/a·peu/ti·cal,** *adj.*

e·lec·tro·ther·a·pist (ĭ lĕk/trō thĕr/ə pĭst), *n.* one versed in electrotherapeutics. Also, **e·lec·tro·ther·a·peu·tist** (ĭ lĕk/trō thĕr/ə pū/tĭst).

e·lec·tro·ther·a·py (ĭ lĕk/trō thĕr/ə pĭ), *n.* treatment of diseases by means of electricity; electrotherapeutics.

e·lec·trot·o·nus (ĭ lĕk/trŏt/ə nəs, ē/lĕk-), *n. Physiol.* the altered state of a nerve during the passage of an electric current through it. [NL, f. Gk.: *ēlektro-* ELECTRO- + m. *tónos* tension] —**e·lec·tro·ton·ic** (ĭ lĕk/trə tŏn/ĭk), *adj.*

e·lec·tro·type (ĭ lĕk/trə tīp/), *n., v.,* **-typed, -typing.** —*n.* **1.** a facsimile, for use in printing, of a block of type, an engraving, or the like, consisting of a thin shell of metal (copper or nickel), deposited by electrolytic action in a wax, lead, or plastic mold of the original and backed with lead alloy. **2.** electrotypy. —*v.t.* **3.** to make an electrotype or electrotypes of. —**e·lec/tro·typ/er,** *n.*

e·lec·tro·typ·y (ĭ lĕk/trə tī/pĭ), *n.* the electrotype process.

e·lec·trum (ĭ lĕk/trəm), *n.* an amber-colored alloy of gold and silver known to the ancients. [t. L, t. Gk.: m. *ēlektron* amber, also gold-silver alloy. See ELECTRIC]

e·lec·tu·ar·y (ĭ lĕk/chŏŏ ĕr/ĭ), *n., pl.* **-aries.** a medicine composed usually of a powder mixed into a pasty mass with syrup or honey. [ME, t. LL: m. s. *ēlectuārium.* Cf. Gk. *ekleiktón* electuary, der. *ekleíchein* lick up (in passive, be taken as an electuary)]

el·ee·mos·y·nar·y (ĕl/ə mŏs/ə nĕr/ĭ, ĕl/ĭ ə-), *adj.* **1.** of or pertaining to alms, charity, or charitable donations; charitable. **2.** derived from or provided by charity. **3.** dependent on or supported by charity. [t. ML: m.s. *eleēmosynārius,* der. LL *eleēmosyna* alms. See ALMS]

el·e·gance (ĕl/ə gəns), *n.* **1.** elegant quality: *elegance of dress.* **2.** something elegant; a refinement.

el·e·gan·cy (ĕl/ə gən sĭ), *n., pl.* **-cies.** elegance.

el·e·gant (el/ə gənt), *adj.* **1.** tastefully fine or luxurious in dress, manners, etc.: *elegant furnishings.* **2.** gracefully refined, as in tastes, habits, literary style, etc. **3.** nice, choice, or pleasingly superior in quality or kind: as a contrivance, preparation, or process. **4.** *Colloq.* excellent; fine; superior. [t. L: s. *ēlegans* fastidious, nice, fine, elegant] —**el/e·gant·ly,** *adv.* —**Syn. 1.** See fine[1]. —**Ant. 1.** ordinary. **2.** common.

el·e·gi·ac (ĕl/ə jī/ăk, -ək, ĭ lē/jĭ ăk/), *adj.* Also, **el/e·gi/a·cal. 1.** *Ancient Pros.* noting a distich the first line of which is a dactylic hexameter and the second a pentameter, or a verse differing from the hexameter by suppression of the arsis or metrically unaccented part of the third and the sixth foot. **2.** belonging to an elegy or to elegy; having to do with elegies. **3.** expressing sorrow or lamentation: *elegiac strains.* —*n.* **4.** an elegiac or distich verse. **5.** a poem or poems in such distichs or verses. [t. LL: s. *elegīacus,* t. Gk.: m. *elegeiakós*]

el·e·gist (ĕl/ə jĭst), *n.* the author of an elegy.

el·e·git (ĭ lē/jĭt), *n. Law.* a writ of execution against a judgment debtor's goods or property held by the judgment creditor until payment of the debt. [L: he has chosen]

el·e·gize (ĕl/ə jīz/), *v.,* **-gized, -gizing.** —*v.t.* **1.** to lament in or as in an elegy. —*v.i.* **2.** to compose an elegy.

el·e·gy (ĕl/ə jĭ), *n., pl.* **-gies. 1.** a mournful, melancholy, or plaintive poem, esp. a funeral song or a lament for the dead, as Milton's *Lycidas.* **2.** poetry or a poem written in elegiac meter. **3.** *Music.* a sad or funeral composition, vocal or instrumental, whether actually commemorative or not. [t. L: m.s. *elegīa,* t. Gk.: m. *elegeīa,* prop. neut. pl. of *elegeīos* elegiac, der. *ēlegos* lament]

elem., 1. elementary. **2.** elements.

el·e·ment (ĕl/ə mənt), *n.* **1.** a component or constituent part of a whole. **2.** the rudimentary principles of an art, science, etc.: *the elements of grammar.* **3.** one of the simple substances, usually earth, water, air, and fire, early regarded as constituting the material universe. **4.** one of these four substances regarded as the natural habitat of something. **5.** the sphere or environment adapted to any person or thing: *to be in one's element.* **6.** *(pl.)* atmospheric agencies or forces: *exposed to the elements.* **7.** one of a class of substances (of which 99 are now recognized) which cannot be separated into substances of other kinds, or, at least, have hitherto resisted analysis by any known chemical means. **8.** *Math.* **a.** an infinitesimal part of a given quantity, similar in nature to it. **b.** any entity that satisfies the conditions of belonging to a class of objects, such as one of a number of objects arranged in a symmetrical or regular figure. **9.** *Geom.* one of the points, lines, planes, or other geometrical forms, of which a figure is composed. **10.** *Astron., etc.* one of the data required for the solution of a

problem: *the elements of a planetary orbit*, which determine the orientation, size and shape of the orbit, and the position of the planet in the orbit at any time. **11.** *Elect.* either of the two dissimilar substances which constitute a voltaic couple. **12.** *Radio.* one of the electrodes in a vacuum tube: *the grid is the control element.* **13.** *Gram.* any word, group of words, or part of a word, which recurs in various contexts in a language with relatively constant meaning. **14.** *(pl.)* the bread and wine used in the Eucharist. [ME, t. L: s. *elementum* a first principle, rudiment]
—**Syn. 1.** ELEMENT, COMPONENT, CONSTITUENT, INGREDIENT refer to the units which build up substances and compounds or mixtures. ELEMENT denotes a fundamental, ultimate part: *the elements of matter, of a discussion.* COMPONENT and CONSTITUENT denote that which goes into the making of a compound, COMPONENT suggesting one of a number of parts, and CONSTITUENT an active and necessary participation: *iron and carbon as components of steel; hydrogen and oxygen the constituents of water.* INGREDIENT denotes something essential or nonessential which enters into a mixture or compound: *the ingredients of a cake.*

el·e·men·tal (ĕl′ə mĕn′təl), *adj.* **1.** of the nature of an ultimate constituent; simple; uncompounded. **2.** pertaining to rudiments or first principles. **3.** of, pertaining to, or of the nature of the four elements or any one of them. **4.** pertaining to the agencies, forces, or phenomena of physical nature: *elemental gods, elemental worship.* **5.** comparable to the great forces of nature, as with reference to their power: *elemental grandeur.* **6.** pertaining to chemical elements. —**el′e·men·tal·ly**, *adv.*

el·e·men·ta·ry (ĕl′ə mĕn′tər)ĭ, -trĭ), *adj.* **1.** pertaining to or dealing with elements, rudiments, or first principles: *elementary education, an elementary grammar.* **2.** of the nature of an ultimate constituent; simple or uncompounded. **3.** pertaining to the four elements or to the great forces of nature; elemental. —**el′e·men′ta·ri·ly**, *adv.* —**el′e·men′ta·ri·ness**, *n.*
—**Syn. 1.** ELEMENTARY, PRIMARY, RUDIMENTARY refer to what is basic and fundamental. ELEMENTARY refers to the introductory, simple, easy facts, steps, or parts of a subject which must necessarily be learned first in order to understand succeeding ones: *elementary facts about geography, elementary arithmetic.* PRIMARY may mean much the same as ELEMENTARY; however, it usually emphasizes the idea of what comes first even more than that of simplicity: *the primary grades in school.* RUDIMENTARY applies to what is undeveloped or imperfect: *a rudimentary form of government.* —**Ant. 1.** advanced.

elementary school, the lowest school giving formal instruction, teaching the rudiments of learning and extending variously from six to eight years.

el·e·mi (ĕl′ə mĭ), *n., pl.* **-mis.** any of various fragrant resins used in medicine, varnish making, etc. [cf. F *élémi*, Sp. *elemi*, t. Ar.: m. *allāmī*]

e·len·chus (ĭ lĕng′kəs), *n., pl.* **-chi** (-kī). **1.** a logical refutation; an argument which refutes another argument, by proving the contrary of its conclusion. **2.** a false refutation; a sophistical argument. [t. L, t. Gk.: m. *élenchos* cross-examination] —**e·lenc·tic** (ĭ lĕngk′tĭk), *adj.*

el·e·op·tene (ĕl′ĭ ŏp′tēn), *Chem.* the liquid portion of volatile oils (opposed to the solid part, *stearoptene*). [f. Gk.: m. *élaio(n)* oil + m.s. *ptenós* winged, volatile]

African elephant,
Loxodonta africana
(10 ft. high at the shoulder)

el·e·phant (ĕl′ə fənt), *n., pl.* **-phants,** *(esp. collectively)* **-phant. 1.** any of the large five-toed mammals, with long prehensile trunk or proboscis and long tusks of ivory, constituting the family *Elephantidae*, comprising species of two existing genera, *Elephas* and *Loxodonta*, esp. *Elephas maximus*, of India and neighboring regions, with comparatively small ears, and *Loxodonta africana*, of Africa, with large, flapping ears. **2.** *U.S.* a representation of this animal as the emblem of the Republican party. **3.** a burdensome or perplexing possession. [t. L: s. *elephantus*, also s. *elephās*, t. Gk.: m. *eléphas* elephant, ivory; r. ME *olifount*, t. OF: m. *olifant*]

Indian elephant, *Elephas maximus*
(9 ft. high at the shoulder)

Elephant Butte, a dam and irrigation reservoir in SW New Mexico, on the Rio Grande. Dam, 306 ft. high; reservoir, 40 mi. long.

el·e·phan·ti·a·sis (ĕl′ə fən tī′ə sĭs, -făn-), *n. Pathol.* a chronic disease, due to lymphatic obstruction, characterized by enormous enlargement of the parts affected. [t. L, t. Gk., der. *eléphas* elephant]

el·e·phan·tine (ĕl′ə făn′tĭn, -tīn, -tēn), *adj.* **1.** pertaining to or resembling an elephant. **2.** huge; ponderous; clumsy: *elephantine movements, elephantine humor.*

el·e·phant′s-ear (ĕl′ə fənts ĭr′), *n.* the taro.

El·eu·sin·i·a (ĕl′yoo sĭn′ĭ ə), *n. Gk. Antiq.* the famous mysteries and festival celebrated at Eleusis, in honor of Demeter (Ceres). —**El′eu·sin′i·an,** *adj.*

E·leu·sis (ĭ loo′sĭs), *n.* a city in ancient Greece, in Attica.

el·e·vate (ĕl′ə vāt′), *v.,* **-vated, -vating,** *adj.* —*v.t.* **1.** to move or raise to a higher place or position; lift up. **2.** to raise to a higher state or station; exalt. **3.** to raise the spirits; put in high spirits. —*adj.* **4.** *Poetic.* raised; elevated. [t. L: m.s. *elevātus*, pp.]
—**Syn. 2.** ELEVATE, ENHANCE, EXALT, HEIGHTEN mean to raise or make higher in some respect. To ELEVATE is to raise something up to a relatively higher level, position, or state: *to elevate the living standards of a group.* To ENHANCE is to add to the attractions or desirability of something: *landscaping enhances the beauty of the grounds, paved streets enhance the value of real estate.* To EXALT is to raise very high in rank, character, estimation, mood, etc.: *a king is exalted above his subjects.* To HEIGHTEN is to increase the strength or intensity: *to heighten one's powers of concentration.* —**Ant. 2.** lower.

el·e·vat·ed (ĕl′ə vā′tĭd), *adj.* **1.** raised up, esp. above the ground: *an elevated platform.* **2.** exalted or noble. *elevated thoughts.* —*n.* **3.** *Colloq.* an elevated railroad.

elevated railway, a railway system operating on an elevated structure, as over streets. Also, **el.**

el·e·va·tion (ĕl′ə vā′shən), *n.* **1.** an elevated place; an eminence. **2.** the height to which anything is elevated. **3.** loftiness; grandeur or dignity; nobleness. **4.** act of elevating. **5.** state of being elevated. **6.** *Archit., etc.* a drawing or design which represents an object or structure as being projected geometrically on a vertical plane parallel to its chief dimension. **7.** *Survey.* the angle between the line from an observer to an object above him and a horizontal line. **8.** the ability of a dancer to stay in the air while executing a step. —**Syn. 2.** See **height.**

el·e·va·tor (ĕl′ə vā′tər), *n.* **1.** one who or that which elevates or raises. **2.** a moving platform or cage for conveying goods, persons, etc., from one level to another, as in a building. **3.** a mechanical device for raising articles. **4.** *U.S.* a building for storing grain, the grain being handled by means of mechanical elevating and conveying devices. **5.** a hinged horizontal plane on an airplane, etc., used to control the longitudinal inclination, generally placed at the tail end of the fuselage. [t. LL]

e·lev·en (ĭ lĕv′ən), *n.* **1.** a cardinal number, ten plus one. **2.** a symbol for this number, as 11 or XI. **3.** a set of this many persons or things, as a football team. —*adj.* **4.** amounting to eleven in number. [ME *elleven(e)*, etc., OE *ellefne, endleofan*, etc., lit., one left (after counting ten). Cf. OHG *einlif*, MHG *eilf*, G *elf*] —**e·lev′enth,** *adj., n.*

eleventh hour, the last possible hour for doing something.

elf (ĕlf), *n., pl.* **elves** (ĕlvz). **1.** one of a class of imaginary beings, esp. from mountainous regions, with magical powers, given to capricious interference in human affairs, and usually imagined to be a diminutive being in human form; a sprite; a fairy. **2.** a dwarf or a small child. **3.** a small, mischievous person. [ME; repr. OE var. of *ælf*, c. G *alp* nightmare (def. 3), incubus] —**elf′-like′,** *adj.* —**Syn. 1.** See **fairy.**

El Fai·yum (ĕl fī yoom′), a city in N Egypt. 63,703 (1937). Also, **El Fai·yûm′** or **El Fa·yûm′.**

El Fer·rol (ĕl fĕr rōl′), a seaport in NW Spain: naval arsenal and dockyard. 37,662 (1930). Also, **Ferrol.**

elf·in (ĕl′fĭn), *adj.* **1.** pertaining to elves. **2.** elflike: *an elfin smile.* —*n.* **3.** an elf.

elf·ish (ĕl′fĭsh), *adj.* elflike; elfin; small and mischievous. Also, **elvish.** —**elf′ish·ly,** *adv.* —**elf′ish·ness,** *n.* —**Syn.** prankish, impish.

elf·lock (ĕlf′lŏk′), *n.* a tangled lock of hair.

El·gar (ĕl′gər, -gär). *n.* **Sir Edward,** 1857–1934, British composer.

El·gin (ĕl′jĭn *for 1;* ĕl′gĭn *for 2*), *n.* **1.** a city in NE Illinois. 44,223 (1950). **2.** former name of **Moray.**

El Gi·za (ĕl gē′zə), a city in N Egypt, near Cairo: the pyramids and the Sphinx are located nearby. 37,779 (1937). Also, **El Gi′zeh, Giza,** or **Gizeh.**

El·gon (ĕl′gŏn), *n.* an isolated volcanic mountain in E Africa, on the boundary between Uganda and Kenya. 14,146 ft.

El Gre·co (ĕl grä′kō, grĕk′ō; *Sp.* ĕl grĕ′kô), ("the Greek") (*Domingo Theotocopuli*) 1548?–1614, painter, architect, and sculptor in Spain and Italy, born in Crete.

El Ha·sa (ĕl hä′sə), Hasa.

E·li (ē′lī), *n. Bible.* a Hebrew judge and high priest. I Sam. 1–3. [t. Heb.: m. '*Ēlī*]

E·li·a (ē′lĭ ə), *n.* the pen name of Charles Lamb.

E·li·as (ĭ lī′əs), *n.* (in the New Testament) Elijah. Matt. 16:14, etc.

e·lic·it (ĭ lĭs′ĭt), *v.t.* to draw or bring out or forth; educe; evoke: *to elicit information or approval, to elicit the truth.* [t. L: s. *ēlicitus*, pp.] —**e·lic′i·ta′tion,** *n.* —**e·lic′i·tor,** *n.* —**Syn.** extract, extort.

e·lide (ĭ līd′), *v.t.,* **elided, eliding. 1.** to omit (a vowel or syllable) in pronunciation. **2.** to suppress, or pass over in silence. **3.** *Law.* to annul or quash. [t. L: m.s. *ēlīdere* crush out]

el·i·gi·bil·i·ty (ĕl′ə bĭl′ə tĭ), *n.* **1.** worthiness or fitness to be chosen. **2.** legal qualification for election or appointment.

el·i·gi·ble (ĕl′ə jə bəl), *adj.* **1.** fit or proper to be chosen; worthy of choice; desirable. **2.** legally qualified to be elected or appointed to office. —*n.* **3.** a person or thing

---

ăct, āble, dâre, ärt; ĕbb, ēqual; ĭf, īce; hŏt, ōver, ôrder, oil, bŏŏk, ōōze, out; ŭp, ūse, ûrge; ə = a in alone; ch, chief; g, give; ng, ring; sh, shoe; th, thin; ŧh, that; zh, vision. See the full key on inside cover.

that is eligible. [t. F, der. L *ēligere* pick out] —**el'i-gi·bly,** *adv.*

E·li·jah (Ỹli'jə), *n.* a great Hebrew prophet of the 9th century B.C. I Kings 17, II Kings 2.

e·lim·i·nate (Ỹlĭm'ənāt/), *v.t.,* **-nated, -nating. 1.** to get rid of; expel; remove: *to eliminate errors.* **2.** to omit as irrelevant or unimportant; ignore. **3.** *Physiol.* to void or expel from an organism. **4.** *Math.* to remove (a quantity) from an equation by elimination. [t. L: m.s. *ēlimĭnātus,* pp., turned out of doors] —**e·lim'i·na/tive,** *adj.* —**e·lim'i·na·tor,** *n.* —**e·lim'i·na·to/ry,** *adj.* —**Syn. 1.** See **exclude.** —**Ant. 2.** include.

e·lim·i·na·tion (Ỹlĭm'ənā'shən), *n.* **1.** act of eliminating. **2.** state of being eliminated. **3.** *Math.* the process of solving a system of linear equations by a procedure in which variables are successively removed.

El·i·ot (ĕl'Ĭət), *n.* **1. Charles William,** 1834–1926, U.S. educator: president of Harvard University, 1869–1909. **2. George,** (*Mary Ann Evans*) 1819–80, British novelist. **3. John,** (*"the Apostle of the Indians"*) 1604–1690, colonial American missionary and translator. **4. Sir John,** 1592–1632, British statesman, patriot, and orator. **5. T(homas) S(tearns),** born 1888, British poet, critic, and essayist, born in the U. S.

E·lis (ē'lĬs), *n.* **1.** an ancient country in W Greece, in the Peloponnesus: site of the ancient Olympic games. **2.** the capital of this country.

E·li·sa·vet·grad (ĕlēzä vĕt'grät), *n.* former name of Kirovograd.

E·li·sa·vet·pol (ĕlēzä vĕt'pŏl'y), *n.* former name of Kirovabad.

E·li·sha (Ỹli'shə), *n.* a Hebrew prophet of the 9th century B.C., the successor of Elijah. II Kings 3–9.

e·li·sion (Ỹlĭzh'ən), *n.* **1.** the omission of a vowel in pronunciation. **2.** (in verse) the omission of a vowel at the end of one word when the next word begins with a vowel, as *th'orient.* [t. L: s. *ēlisio* a striking out]

e·lite (Ỹlēt', ā-), *n.* the choice or best part, as of a body or class of persons. Also, *French,* **é·lite** (ĕlēt'). [t. F, der. *élire* choose, g. L *ēligere*]

e·lix·ir (Ỹlĭk'sər), *n.* **1.** an alchemic preparation for transmuting base metals into gold, or for prolonging life: *elixir vitae,* or *elixir of life.* **2.** a sovereign remedy; panacea; cure-all. **3.** the quintessence or absolute embodiment of anything. **4.** *Pharm.* **a.** a tincture with more than one base, or some similar compound medicine. **b.** an aromatic, sweetened alcoholic liquid containing medicinal agents, or used as a vehicle for them. [ME, t. ML, t. Ar.: m. *el, al* the + *iksīr* philosopher's stone, prob. t. LGk.: m. *xērion* a drying powder for wounds]

E·liz·a·beth (Ỹlĭz'əbəth), *n.* **1. I,** 1533–1603, queen of England 1558–1603 (successor of Mary I; daughter of Henry VIII and Anne Boleyn). **2. II,** born 1926, queen of England since 1952; daughter of George VI. **3.** (*"Carmen Silva"*) 1843–1916, queen of Rumania, 1881–1914, and author. **4.** (in the New Testament) the mother of John the Baptist. Luke 1:5–25. **5.** a city in NE New Jersey. 112,817 (1950).

E·liz·a·be·than (Ỹlĭz'əbē'thən, -bĕth'ən), *adj.* **1.** of or pertaining to Elizabeth I, queen of England, or to her times. —*n.* **2.** one who lived in England during the Elizabethan period, esp. a poet or dramatist.

Elizabethan sonnet, a sonnet form rhyming *abab cdcd efef gg.*

elk (ĕlk), *n., pl.* **elks,** (*esp. collectively*) **elk. 1.** the largest existing European and Asiatic deer, *Alces alces,* the male of which has large palmate antlers. See **moose. 2.** (in America) the wapiti. **3.** a pliable leather used for sport shoes, and made orig. of elk hide, but now of calfskin or cowhide tanned and smoked to resemble elk hide. [appar. f. OE *ealh* elk (c. G *elch*) + -*k* suffix. Cf. OE *cranoc* crane (not dim.), L *alces,* Gk. *álkē* elk, of Gmc. orig.]

American elk, *Cervus canadensis*
(5 ft. high at the shoulder,
total length 9½ ft., female smaller)

Elk·hart (ĕlk'härt'; *commonly* ĕl'kärt), *n.* a city in N Indiana. 35,646 (1950).

ell[1] (ĕl), *n.* an extension to a building, usually at right angles to one end. Also, **el.** [from the shape of the letter L]

ell[2] (ĕl), *n.* a measure of length, now little used, varying in different countries: in England and her colonies equal to 45 inches. [ME and OE *eln,* c. D *el,* G *elle;* orig. meaning arm, forearm (see ELBOW), and akin to L *ulna,* Gk. *ōlénē*]

European elk, *Alces alces*
(Ab. 6 ft. high at the shoulder)

Elles·mere Island (ĕlz'mĬr), a large island in the Arctic Ocean, NW of Greenland: a part of the Canadian Northwest Territories. ab. 76,600 sq. mi.

El·lice Islands (ĕl'Ĭs), a group of islands in the central Pacific, S of the equator: a part of the British colony of Gilbert and Ellice islands. 4124 pop. (est. 1936); 16½ sq. mi. Also, **Lagoon Islands.**

el·lipse (Ỹlĭps'), *n. Geom.* a plane curve such that the sums of the distances of each point in its periphery from two fixed points, the foci, are equal. It is a conic section formed by the intersection of a right circular cone by a plane which cuts obliquely the axis and the opposite sides of the cone. See diag. under **conic section.** [t. L: m.s. *ellipsis.* See ELLIPSIS]

el·lip·sis (Ỹlĭp'sĬs), *n., pl.* **-ses** (-sēz). **1.** *Gram.* the omission from a sentence of a word or words which would complete or clarify the construction. **2.** *Print.* a mark or marks as ——, . . . , * * *, to indicate an omission or suppression of letters or words. [t. L, t. Gk.: m. *élleipsis* omission]

Ellipse
F, G, foci. FM + GM
equals FN + GN, M and N
being any points in the
curve

el·lip·soid (Ỹlĭp'soid), *n. Geom.* a solid figure all plane sections of which are ellipses or circles.

el·lip·soi·dal (Ỹlĭp'soi'dəl, ĕl'Ĭp-), *adj.* pertaining to, or having the form of, an ellipsoid.

el·lip·ti·cal (Ỹlĭp'təkəl), *adj.* **1.** pertaining to or having the form of an ellipse. **2.** pertaining to or marked by grammatical ellipsis. Also, **el·lip'tic.**

el·lip·ti·cal·ly (Ỹlĭp'tĬklĬ), *adv.* **1.** in the form of an ellipse. **2.** in an elliptical manner; with an ellipsis.

el·lip·tic·i·ty (Ỹlĭp'tĬs'ətĬ, ĕl'Ĭp-), *n.* the degree of divergence of an ellipse from the circle.

El·lis (ĕl'Ĭs), *n.* **1. Alexander John,** (orig. *Alexander John Sharpe*) 1814–90, British phonetician and mathematician. **2. (Henry) Havelock** (hăv'lŏk), 1859–1939, British scientific and miscellaneous writer.

El·lis Island (ĕl'Ĭs), a small island in upper New York Bay: a former U.S. immigrant examination station.

Ells·worth (ĕlz'wûrth), *n.* **Lincoln,** 1880–1951, U.S. polar explorer.

elm (ĕlm), *n.* **1.** any of the trees of the genus *Ulmus,* as *U. procera* (**English elm**), *U. americana* (**white or American elm**), *U. fulva* (**slippery elm**), etc., some of which are widely cultivated for shade and ornament. **2.** the wood of such a tree. [OE, c. OHG *elm;* akin to Icel. *ālmr,* L *ulmus*]

El·man (ĕl'mən), *n.* **Mischa** (mē'shə), born 1891, U.S. violinist, born in Russia.

El·mi·ra (ĕlmĬ'rə), *n.* city in S New York. 49,716 (1950).

El Mis·ti (ĕl mēs'tē), a volcanic mountain in S Peru, in the Andes. 19,200 ft. Also, **Misti.**

elm leaf beetle, a beetle, *Galerucella xanthomelena,* of the family *Chrysomelidae,* a destructive pest in the eastern U.S.

elm·y (ĕl'mĬ), *adj.* abounding in or consisting of elms.

el·o·cu·tion (ĕl'əkū'shən), *n.* **1.** manner of speaking or reading in public. **2.** *Speech.* the study and practice of delivery, including both the management of voice and gesture. **3.** (in a derogatory sense) a stilted, artificial manner of delivery. [t. L: s. *ēlocūtio* a speaking out] —**el·o·cu'tion·ar·y** (ĕl'əkū'shənĕr'Ĭ), *adj.* —**el·o·cu'tion·ist,** *n.* —**Syn. 2.** oratory, declamation.

E·lo·him (ĕlō'hĬm), *n.* the Hebrew word for God, often used in the Hebrew text of the Old Testament. [t. Heb.: m. *elōhim,* prop. pl. of *elōh* god, but often taken as sing.]

E·lo·hist (ĕlō'hĬst), *n.* the writer (or writers) of one of the major strands or sources of the Hexateuch in which God is characteristically referred to as Elohim instead of Yahweh (Jehovah). See **Yahwist.** —**El'o·his'tic,** *adj.*

e·loign (Ỹloin'), *v.t.* **1.** to remove (oneself) to a distance. **2.** *Law.* to remove out of legal jurisdiction, or conceal, as goods liable to distress. Also, **e·loin'.** [t. AF: m.s. *esloignier,* der. OF *es-* (See EX-[1]) + *loign* far away (g. L *longē*)]

e·lon·gate (Ỹlŏng'gāt, Ỹlŏng'-), *v.,* **-gated, -gating,** *adj.* —*v.t.* **1.** to draw out to greater length; lengthen; extend. —*v.i.* **2.** to increase in length; be comparatively long. —*adj.* **3.** elongated. [t. LL: m.s. *ēlongātus,* pp., removed, prolonged]

e·lon·ga·tion (Ỹlŏng'gā'shən, Ỹlŏng'-, ē'lŏng-, ē'lŏng-), *n.* **1.** act of elongating. **2.** state of being elongated. **3.** that which is elongated; an elongated part.

e·lope (Ỹlōp'), *v.i.,* **eloped, eloping. 1.** to run away with a lover. **2.** to run away from one's place of duty; escape. [t. AF: m.s. *aloper.* Cf. G *entlaufen* run away, elope] —**e·lope'ment,** *n.* —**e·lop'er,** *n.*

el·o·quence (ĕl'əkwəns), *n.* **1.** the action, practice, or art of using language with fluency, power, and aptness. **2.** eloquent language or discourse: *a flow of eloquence.*

el·o·quent (ĕl'əkwənt), *adj.* **1.** having or exercising the power of fluent, forcible, and appropriate speech: *an eloquent orator.* **2.** characterized by forcible and appropriate expression: *an eloquent speech.* **3.** movingly expressive: *eloquent looks.* [ME, t. L: s. *ēloquens,* ppr., speaking out] —**el'o·quent·ly,** *adv.*

El Pas·o (ĕl păs'ō), a city in W Texas, on the Rio Grande. 130,485 (1950).

El Sal·va·dor (ĕl săl'vədôr'; *Sp.* ĕl säl'vä dôr'), a republic in W Central America. 1,997,000 pop. (est. 1946); 13,176 sq. mi. *Cap.:* San Salvador. Also, **Salvador.**

else (ĕls), *adv.* **1.** (following as an appositive an indef. or interrog. pronoun) **a.** other than the person or the thing mentioned; instead: *somebody else; who else?* **b.** in addition: *what else shall I do? who else is going?* **2.** (following an indef. or interrog. pronoun and forming with it an indef. or compound pronoun with inflection at the end): *somebody else's child, nobody else's business, whose else* (older usage) or now usually *who else's child could it be?* **3.** otherwise: *run, else* (or *or else*) *you will be late, how else could I do it?* [ME and OE *elles* (c. OHG *elles*) adv. gen. of a pre-E word, c. L *alius* other]

El·se·ne (ĕl′sə nə), *n.* Flemish name of **Ixelles.**

El·se·vier (ĕl′zə vĭr′, -vər), *n., adj.* Elzevir.

else·where (ĕls′hwâr′), *adv.* somewhere else; in or to some other place.

El·si·nore (ĕl′sə nōr′), *n.* Helsingör.

e·lu·ci·date (ĭ lōō′sə dāt′), *v.t.,* **-dated, -dating.** to make lucid or clear; throw light upon; explain. [t. LL: m.s. *ēlūcidātus,* pp., made light] —**e·lu′ci·da′tion,** *n.* —**e·lu′ci·da′tive,** *adj.* —**e·lu′ci·da′tor,** *n.* —Syn. See **explain.**

e·lude (ĭ lōōd′), *v.t.,* **eluded, eluding. 1.** to avoid or escape by dexterity or artifice: *to elude pursuit.* **2.** to slip away from; evade: *to elude vigilance.* **3.** to escape the mind; baffle. [t. L: m.s. *ēlūdere* finish play, deceive] —**e·lud′er,** *n.* —Syn. **1.** shun, dodge. See **escape. 3.** foil, frustrate.

E·lul (ĕ lōōl′), *n.* (in the Jewish calendar) the twelfth month of the year. [t. Heb.]

e·lu·sion (ĭ lōō′zhən), *n.* act of eluding; evasion; clever escape. [t. ML: s. *ēlūsio.* See **ELUDE**]

e·lu·sive (ĭ lōō′sĭv), *adj.* **1.** eluding clear perception or complete mental grasp; hard to express or define. **2.** dexterously evasive. Also, **e·lu·so·ry** (ĭ lōō′sə rĭ). —**e·lu′sive·ly,** *adv.* —**e·lu′sive·ness,** *n.*

e·lu·tri·ate (ĭ lōō′trĭ āt′), *v.t.,* **-ated, -ating. 1.** to purify by washing and straining or decanting. **2.** to separate the light and heavy particles of by washing. [t. L: m.s. *ēlūtriātus,* pp.] —**e·lu′tri·a′tion,** *n.*

e·lu·vi·um (ĭ lōō′vĭ əm), *n., pl.* **-via** (-vĭ ə). *Geol.* a deposit of soil, dust, etc., originating in the place where found as through decomposition of rock (distinguished from *alluvium*). [NL, der. L *ēluere* wash out] —**e·lu′vi·al,** *adj.*

el·ver (ĕl′vər), *n.* a young eel, particularly when running up a stream from the ocean. [var. of *eel-fare* (f. **EEL** + **FARE**) passage of young eels up a river]

elves (ĕlvz), *n.* pl. of **elf.**

elv·ish (ĕl′vĭsh), *adj.* elfish. —**elv′ish·ly,** *adv.*

E·ly (ē′lĭ), *n.* **1.** Isle of, an administrative county in E England: formerly a part of Cambridgeshire. 84,000 pop. (est. 1946); 375 sq. mi. *Co. seat:* March. **2.** a town in this county: famous cathedral. 9972 (1939).

El·y·ot (ĕl′Yət, -yət), *n.* **Sir Thomas,** c1490–1546, British scholar and diplomat.

E·lyr·i·a (ĭ lĭr′Yə), *n.* a city in N Ohio. 30,307 (1950).

É·ly·sée (ĕ lē zě′), *n.* a palace in Paris: the official residence of the president of France.

E·ly·sian (ĭ lĭzh′ən), *adj.* **1.** pertaining to, or resembling, Elysium. **2.** blissful; delightful.

E·ly·si·um (ĭ lĭzh′Yəm, ĭ lĭz′-, ĭ lĭzh′əm), *n.* **1.** Also, **Elysian fields.** *Gk. Myth.* the abode of the blessed after death. **2.** any similarly conceived abode or state of the dead. **3.** any place or state of perfect happiness. [t. L, t. Gk.: short for *Elýsion (pedíon)* Elysian (plain or field)]

el·y·tra (ĕl′ə trə), *n.* pl. of **elytron, elytrum.**

el·y·troid (ĕl′ə troid′), *adj.* like an elytron.

el·y·tron (ĕl′ə trŏn′), *n., pl.* **-tra** (-trə). one of the pair of hardened forewings of certain insects, as beetles, forming a protective covering for the posterior wings. [NL, t. Gk.: cover, sheath]

el·y·trum (ĕl′ə trəm), *n., pl.* **-tra** (-trə). elytron.

El·ze·vir (ĕl′zə vĭr′, -vər), *n.* **1.** Louis, c1540–1617, founder of a Dutch printing firm at Leyden, carried on by his son, **Bonaventure,** 1583–1652, and his grandson, **Abraham,** (nephew of Bonaventure) 1592–1652. **2.** a book produced by the Elzevir printing house. **3.** a style of printing type with firm hairlines and stubby serifs. —*adj.* **4.** of or pertaining to the Elzevir family, famous for their small editions of the classics. **5.** indicating the type originated by this family. Also, **Elsevier, El′ze·vier′.** —**El·ze·vir·i·an** (ĕl′zə vĭr′Y ən), *adj.*

em[1] (ĕm), *n., pl.* **ems. 1.** the letter M, m. **2.** *Print.* the square of any size of type (orig. the portion of a line occupied by the letter M, used as the unit of measurement for printed matter. **3.** em pica, about one sixth of an inch, generally used as the unit of measurement in printing. —*adj.* **4.** having the size of an em: *em quad.* [name of the letter M]

em[2] (əm), *pron. pl. Colloq.* them (occurs only in unstressed position). Also, **'em.** [ME *hem,* dat. and acc. pl. of *HE;* now taken for weak form of *THEM*]

em-[1], var. of **en-**[1], before *b, p,* and sometimes *m,* as in *embalm.* Cf. **im-**[1].

em-[2], var. of **en-**[2], before *b, m, p, ph,* as in *embolism, emphasis.*

Em., *Chem.* emanation (def. 3).

e·ma·ci·ate (ĭ mā′shĭ āt′), *v.t.,* **-ated, -ating.** to make lean by a gradual wasting away of flesh. [t. L: m.s. *ēmaciātus,* pp.]

e·ma·ci·a·tion (ĭ mā′shĭ ā′shən, -sĭ-), *n.* abnormal thinness, caused by lack of nutrition or by disease.

em·a·nate (ĕm′ə nāt′), *v.i.,* **-nated, -nating.** to flow out, issue, or proceed as from a source or origin; come forth; originate. [t. L: m.s. *ēmānātus,* pp.] —**em′a·na′tive,** *adj.* —Syn. See **emerge.**

em·a·na·tion (ĕm′ə nā′shən), *n.* **1.** act or fact of emanating. **2.** something that emanates. **3.** *Chem.* a gaseous product of radioactive disintegration including radon, thoron, and actinon.

e·man·ci·pate (ĭ măn′sə pāt′), *v.t.,* **-pated, -pating. 1.** to free from restraint of any kind. **2.** *Roman and Civil Law.* **a.** to free (a slave). **b.** to terminate paternal control over. [t. L: m.s. *ēmancipātus,* pp.] —**e·man′ci·pa′tive,** *adj.*

e·man·ci·pa·tion (ĭ măn′sə pā′shən), *n.* **1.** act of emancipating. **2.** fact of being emancipated; freedom.

e·man·ci·pa·tor (ĭ măn′sə pā′tər), *n.* **1.** one who emancipates. **2.** the **Great Emancipator,** Abraham Lincoln. [t. LL]

e·mar·gi·nate (ĭ mär′jə nāt′), *adj.* **1.** notched at the margin. **2.** *Bot.* notched at the apex, as a petal or leaf. Also, **e·mar′gi·nat′ed.** [t. L: m.s. *ēmarginātus,* pp., deprived of an edge]

Emarginate leaves

e·mas·cu·late (*v.* ĭ măs′kyə lāt′; *adj.* ĭ măs′kyə lĭt, -lāt′), *v.,* **-lated, -lating,** *adj.* —*v.t.* **1.** to castrate. **2.** to deprive of strength or vigor; weaken; render effeminate. —*adj.* **3.** emasculated; effeminate. [t. L: m.s. *ēmasculātus,* pp.] —**e·mas′cu·la′tion,** *n.* —**e·mas′cu·la′tor,** *n.* —**e·mas·cu·la·to·ry** (ĭ măs′kyə lə tōr′Y), **e·mas′cu·la′tive,** *adj.*

em·balm (ĕm bäm′), *v.t.* **1.** to treat (a dead body) with balsams, spices, etc., or (now usually) with drugs or chemicals, in order to preserve from decay. **2.** to preserve from oblivion; keep in memory. **3.** *Poetic.* to impart a balmy fragrance to. [ME *enbaume(n),* t. F: m. *embaumer,* der. *em-* **EM-**[1] + *baume* **BALM**] —**em·balm′er,** *n.* —**em·balm′ment,** *n.*

em·bank (ĕm băngk′), *v.t.* to enclose, confine, or protect with a bank, mound, dike, or the like.

em·bank·ment (ĕm băngk′mənt), *n.* **1.** a bank, mound, dike, or the like, raised to hold back water, carry a roadway, etc. **2.** act of embanking.

em·bar·ca·tion (ĕm′bär kā′shən), *n.* embarkation.

em·bar·go (ĕm bär′gō), *n., pl.* **-goes,** *v.,* **-goed, -going.** —*n.* **1.** an order of a government prohibiting the movement of merchant vessels from or into its ports. **2.** an injunction from a government commerce agency to refuse freight for shipment, in case of insufficient facilities, congestion, etc. **3.** any restriction imposed upon commerce by law. **4.** a restraint or hindrance; a prohibition. —*v.t.* **5.** to impose an embargo on. [t. Sp., der. *embargar* restrain, ult. der. Rom. *barra* **BAR**[1]]

em·bark (ĕm bärk′), *v.t.* **1.** to put or receive on board a ship. **2.** to involve (a person) in an enterprise; venture or invest (money, etc.) in an enterprise. —*v.i.* **3.** to board a ship, as for a voyage. **4.** to engage in an enterprise, business, etc. [t. F: m.s. *embarquer,* der. *em-* **EM-**[1] (g. L *in-*) + *barque* **BARK**[3]]

em·bar·ka·tion (ĕm′bär kā′shən), *n.* act or process of embarking. Also, **embarcation.**

em·bar·rass (ĕm băr′əs), *v.t.* **1.** to disconcert; abash; make uncomfortable, self-conscious, etc.; confuse. **2.** to make difficult or intricate, as a question or problem; complicate. **3.** to put obstacles or difficulties in the way of; impede. **4.** to beset with financial difficulties; burden with debt. [t. F: s. *embarrasser,* lit., block, obstruct, der. *embarras* obstacle] —**em·bar′rass·ing,** *adj.* —**em·bar′rass·ing·ly,** *adv.* —Syn. **1.** discompose, discomfit, chagrin. See **confuse. 3.** hamper, hinder.

em·bar·rass·ment (ĕm băr′əs mənt), *n.* **1.** embarrassed state; disconcertment; abashment. **2.** act of embarrassing. **3.** that which embarrasses. —Syn. **1.** perplexity, discomposure, mortification, chagrin.

em·bas·sa·dor (ĕm băs′ə dər), *n.* ambassador.

em·bas·sy (ĕm′bə sĭ), *n., pl.* **-sies. 1.** a body of persons entrusted with a mission to a sovereign or government; an ambassador and his staff. **2.** the official headquarters of an ambassador. **3.** the function or office of an ambassador. **4.** the sending of ambassadors. [var. of *ambassy,* t. OF: m. *ambassée,* ult. der. L *ambactia* office]

em·bat·tle[1] (ĕm băt′əl), *v.t.,* **-tled, -tling. 1.** to arrange in order of battle; prepare for battle; arm. **2.** to fortify (a town, etc.). [ME *embataile(n),* t. OF: m. *embatailler,* der. *em-* **EM-**[1] + *bataille* **BATTLE**[1]]

em·bat·tle[2] (ĕm băt′əl), *v.t.,* **-tled, -tling.** to furnish with battlements. [f. **EM-**[1] + **BATTLE**[2]]

em·bay (ĕm bā′), *v.t.* to enclose in or as in a bay; surround or envelop.

em·bay·ment (ĕm bā′mənt), *n.* **1.** a bay. **2.** *Phys. Geog.* the process by which a bay is formed.

em·bed (ĕm bĕd′), *v.t.,* **-bedded, -bedding. 1.** to fix in a surrounding mass. **2.** to lay in or as in a bed. Also, **imbed.** —**em·bed′ment,** *n.*

em·bel·lish (ĕm bĕl′Ysh), *v.t.* **1.** to beautify by or as by ornamentation; ornament; adorn. **2.** to enhance (a statement or narrative) with fictitious additions; embroider. [ME *embelyss(en),* t. OF: m. *embelliss-,* s. *embellir,* der. *em-* **EM-**[1] + *bel* handsome] —**em·bel′lish·er,** *n.* —Syn. **1.** decorate, garnish, bedeck, embroider.

em·bel·lish·ment (ĕm bĕl′ĭsh mənt), *n.* **1.** an ornament or decoration. **2.** a fictitious addition, as in a statement. **3.** act of embellishing. **4.** state of being embellished.

em·ber[1] (ĕm′bər), *n.* **1.** a small live coal, brand of wood, etc., as in a dying fire. **2.** (*pl.*) the smoldering remains of a fire. [ME *eemer, emeri*, OE *æmerge*, c. Icel. *eimyrja*]

em·ber[2] (ĕm′bər), *adj.* pertaining to the three-day period of prayer and fasting that comes once in each season. See **Ember days.** [ME *ymber* (attrib.), OE *ymbren*, special use of OE *ymbrene, ymbryne* circuit, course, f. *ymb* around + *ryne* a running]

Ember days, a quarterly season of fasting and prayer (the Wednesday, Friday, and Saturday after the first Sunday in Lent, after Whitsunday, after Sept. 14, and after Dec. 13) observed in the Roman Catholic and other Western churches.

em·bez·zle (ĕm bĕz′əl), *v.t.*, **-zled, -zling.** to appropriate fraudulently to one's own use, as money or property entrusted to one's possession. [ME *enbesyl(en)*, t. AF: m. *enbesiler*, f. *en-* EM-[1] + *beseler* destroy, dissipate] —**em·bez′zle·ment,** *n.* —**em·bez′zler,** *n.*

em·bit·ter (ĕm bĭt′ər), *v.t.* to make bitter or more bitter. —**em·bit′ter·ment,** *n.*

em·bla·zon (ĕm blā′zən), *v.t.* **1.** to portray or inscribe on or as on a heraldic shield; to embellish or decorate. **2.** to proclaim; celebrate or extol. —**em·bla′zon·er,** *n.*

em·bla·zon·ment (ĕm blā′zən mənt), *n.* **1.** act of emblazoning. **2.** that which is emblazoned.

em·bla·zon·ry (ĕm blā′zən rĭ), *n.* **1.** act or art of emblazoning; heraldic decoration. **2.** brilliant representation or embellishment.

em·blem (ĕm′bləm), *n.* **1.** an object, or a representation of it, symbolizing a quality, state, class of persons, etc.; a symbol. **2.** an allegorical drawing or picture, often with explanatory writing. [t. L: m. *emblēma* inlaid work, ornamentation, t. Gk.: an insertion] —**Syn. 1.** token, sign, figure, image, device, badge.

cm·blem·at·ic (ĕm′blə măt′ĭk), *adj.* pertaining to, of the nature of, or serving as an emblem; symbolic. Also, **em′blem·at′i·cal.** —**em′blem·at′i·cal·ly,** *adv.*

em·blem·a·tist (ĕm blĕm′ə tĭst), *n.* a designer, maker, or user of emblems.

em·blem·a·tize (ĕm blĕm′ə tīz), *v.t.*, **-tized, -tizing.** to serve as an emblem of; represent by an emblem.

em·ble·ments (ĕm′blə mənts), *n. pl. Law.* the products or profits of land which has been sown or planted. [t. OF: m. *emblaement*, der. *emblaer*, der. *em-* EM-[1] + *blé* grain (t. Gmc. Cf. MD *blaad*, OE *blēd*)]

em·bod·i·ment (ĕm bŏd′ĭ mənt), *n.* **1.** act of embodying. **2.** state or fact of being embodied. **3.** that in which something is embodied; an incarnation. **4.** something embodied.

em·bod·y (ĕm bŏd′ĭ), *v.t.*, **-bodied, -bodying. 1.** to invest with a body, as a spirit; incarnate; make corporeal. **2.** to give a concrete form to; express or exemplify (ideas, etc.) in concrete form. **3.** to collect into or include in a body; organize; incorporate. **4.** to embrace or comprise.

em·bold·en (ĕm bōl′dən), *v.t.* to make bold or more bold; hearten or encourage.

em·bo·lec·to·my (ĕm′bə lĕk′tə mĭ), *n., pl.* **-mies.** the removal of an embolus from an artery, which it is obstructing, by surgery. [f. EMBOL(US) + -ECTOMY]

em·bol·ic (ĕm bŏl′ĭk), *adj.* **1.** *Pathol.* pertaining to an embolus or to embolism. **2.** *Embryol.* developing inwardly; related to a process of invagination.

em·bo·lism (ĕm′bə lĭz′əm), *n.* **1.** intercalation, as of a day in a year. **2.** a period of time intercalated. **3.** *Pathol.* the occlusion of a blood vessel by an embolus. [t. LL: s. *embolismus* intercalation, der. Gk. *embállein* throw in. See EMBLEM] —**em′bo·lis′mic,** *adj.*

em·bo·lus (ĕm′bə ləs), *n., pl.* **-li** (-lī′). *Pathol.* undissolved material carried by the blood current and impacted in some part of the vascular system, as thrombi or fragments of thrombi, tissue fragments, clumps of bacteria, protozoan parasites, fat globules, gas bubbles. [t. L: piston, t. Gk.: m. *émbolos* peg, stopper]

em·bon·point (äⁿ bôⁿ pwăⁿ′), *n. French.* exaggerated plumpness; stoutness. [F: lit., in good condition]

em·bos·om (ĕm bŏŏz′əm, -bōō′zəm), *v.t.* **1.** to enfold, envelop, or enclose. **2.** to take into or hold in the bosom; embrace. **3.** to cherish; foster.

em·boss (ĕm bôs′, -bŏs′), *v.t.* **1.** to raise or represent surface designs in relief. **2.** to cause to bulge out; make protuberant. **3.** to raise a design on a fabric by pressing. [ME *emboss(en)*, t. OF: m. *embocer* swell in protuberances, der. *em-* EM-[1] + *boce* swelling, BOSS[2]] —**em·boss′-er,** *n.* —**em·boss′ment,** *n.*

em·bou·chure (äm′bŏŏ shŏŏr′; Fr. äⁿ bōō shӱr′), *n.* **1.** the mouth of a river. **2.** the opening out of a valley into a plain. **3.** *Music.* **a.** the mouthpiece of a wind instrument, esp. when of metal. **b.** the adjustment of a player's mouth to such a mouthpiece. [t. F, der. *emboucher* put into the mouth, discharge by a mouth or outlet, der. *em-* EM-[1] + *bouche* mouth (g. L *bucca* cheek, mouth)]

em·bow·el (ĕm bou′əl -boul′), *v.t.*, **-eled, -eling** or (*esp. Brit.*) **-elled, -elling.** to disembowel.

em·bow·er (ĕm bou′ər), *v.t.*, *v.i.* to shelter in or as in a bower; cover or surround with foliage.

em·brace (ĕm brās′), *v.*, **-braced, -bracing.** *n.* —*v.t.* **1.** to take or clasp in the arms; press to the bosom; hug. **2.** to take or receive (an idea, etc.) gladly or eagerly; accept willingly. **3.** to avail oneself of (an opportunity, etc.). **4.** to adopt (a profession, a religion, etc.). **5.** to take in with the eye or the mind. **6.** to encircle; surround; enclose. **7.** to include or contain. —*v.i.* **8.** to join in an embrace. —*n.* **9.** act of embracing; a hug. [ME *enbrace(n)*, t. OF: m. *embracier*, der. *em-* EM-[1] + *bras* arm (g. L *brāchium*)] —**em·brace′a·ble,** *adj.* —**brace′ment,** *n.* —**em·brac′er,** *n.* —**Syn. 2.** adopt, espouse. **7.** comprise, comprehend. See **include.**

em·branch·ment (ĕm brănch′mənt, -bränch′-), *n.* **1.** a branching or ramification. **2.** a branch.

em·bra·sure (ĕm brā′zhər), *n.* **1.** an opening in a wall or parapet through which a gun may be fired, constructed with sides which flare outward. See diag. under **bartizan. 2.** *Archit.* an enlargement of the aperture of a door or window, at the inside face of the wall, by means of splayed sides. [t. F, der. *embraser, ébraser* to splay (an opening)]

em·bro·cate (ĕm′brō kāt′), *v.t.*, **-cated, -cating.** to moisten and rub with a liniment or lotion. [t. ML: m.s. *embrocātus*, pp. of *embrocāre*, der. LL *embrocha*, t. Gk.: m. *embroché* lotion]

em·bro·ca·tion (ĕm′brō kā′shən), *n.* **1.** act of embrocating a bruised or diseased part of the body. **2.** the liquid used for this; a liniment or lotion.

em·broi·der (ĕm broi′dər). *v.t.* **1.** to decorate with ornamental needlework. **2.** to produce or form in needlework. **3.** to adorn or embellish rhetorically, esp. with fictitious additions. —*v.i.* **4.** to do embroidery. [appar. f. EM-[1] + BROIDER] —**em·broi′der·er,** *n.*

em·broi·der·y (ĕm broi′dər ĭ), *n., pl.* **-deries. 1.** the art of working with the needle raised and ornamental designs in threads of silk, cotton, gold, silver, or other material, upon any woven fabric, leather, paper, etc. **2.** embroidered work or ornamentation.

em·broil (ĕm broil′), *v.t.* **1.** to bring into a state of discord; involve in contention or strife. **2.** to throw into confusion; complicate. [t. F: m. *embrouiller*, f. *em-* EM-[1] + *brouiller* BROIL[1]] —**em·broil′er,** *n.* —**em·broil′ment,** *n.*

em·brown (ĕm broun′), *v.t., v.i.* to make or become brown or dark.

em·brute (ĕm brōōt′), *v.t., v.i.* imbrute.

em·bry·ec·to·my (ĕm′brĭ ĕk′tə mĭ), *n., pl.* **-mies.** removal of an embryo by surgery. [f. EMBRY(O) + -ECTOMY]

em·bry·o (ĕm′brĭ ō′), *n., pl.* **-os. 1.** an organism in the earlier stages of its development, as before emergence from the egg or before metamorphosis. **2.** among mammals and other viviparous animals) a young animal during its earlier stages within the mother's body (including, in man, the developmental stages up to the end of the seventh week). **3.** *Bot.* the rudimentary plant usually contained in the seed. **4.** the beginning or rudimentary stage of anything. —*adj.* **5.** embryonic. [t. ML, t. Gk.: m. *ēmbryon*]

em·bry·og·e·ny (ĕm′brĭ ŏj′ə nĭ), *n.* the formation and development of the embryo, as a subject of scientific study. Also, **em·bry·o·gen·e·sis** (ĕm′brĭ ō jĕn′ə sĭs). [f. EMBRYO + -GENY] —**em·bry·o·ge·net·ic** (ĕm′brĭ ō-jə nĕt′ĭk), *adj.*

embryol., embryology.

em·bry·ol·o·gy (ĕm′brĭ ŏl′ə jĭ), *n.* the science of the embryo, its genesis, development, etc. [f. EMBRYO + -LOGY] —**em·bry·o·log·i·cal** (ĕm′brĭ ə lŏj′ə kəl), **em′-bry·o·log′ic,** *adj.* —**em′bry·ol′o·gist,** *n.*

em·bry·on·ic (ĕm′brĭ ŏn′ĭk), *adj.* **1.** pertaining to or in the state of an embryo. **2.** rudimentary; undeveloped. Also, **em·bry·o·nal** (ĕm′brĭ ə nəl), *adj.*

embryo sac, *Bot.* the megaspore of a seed-bearing plant, being situated within the ovule, giving rise to the endosperm or supposed female prothallium, and forming the cell in which the embryo is developed.

em·cee (ĕm′sē′), *n., v.i., v.t.*, **-ceed, -ceeing.** —*n.* **1.** master of ceremonies. —*v.i., v.t.* **2.** to act as master of ceremonies (for). [var. *M.C.* master of ceremonies]

Em·den (ĕm′dən), *n.* a seaport in NW Germany. 35,105 (1939).

e·meer (ə mĭr′), *n.* emir.

e·mend (ĭ mĕnd′), *v.t.* **1.** to free from faults or errors; correct. **2.** to amend (a text) by removing errors. [t. L: s. *ēmendāre* correct] —**e·mend′a·ble,** *adj.*

e·men·date (ē′mən dāt′), *v.t.*, **-dated, -dating.** to emend (a text). —**e·men·da·tor** (ē′mən dā′tər, ĕm′-ən-), *n.*

e·men·da·tion (ē′mĕn dā′shən, ĕm′ən-), *n.* **1.** a correction. **2.** act of emending. —**e·mend′a·to·ry,** *adj.*

em·er·ald (ĕm′ər əld, ĕm′rəld), *n.* **1.** a rare green variety of beryl, highly valued as a gem. **2.** clear deep green. **3.** *Brit.* a printing type of a size between nonpareil and minion. —*adj.* **4.** having a clear, deep-green color. [ME *emeraude*, t. OF, g. L *smaragdus* a green precious stone, t. Gk.: m. *smáragdos*]

Emerald Isle, Ireland.

e·merge (ĭ mûrj′), *v.i.*, **emerged, emerging. 1.** to rise or come forth from or as from water or other liquid. **2.** to come forth into view or notice, as from concealment or obscurity. **3.** to come up or arise, as a question or difficulty. [t. L: m.s. *ēmergere* rise out] —**Syn. 2.** EMERGE, EMANATE, ISSUE mean to come forth from a place or source. EMERGE is used of coming forth from something that envelops or encloses, from a place shut off from view, or from concealment, obscurity, retirement, or the like, into sight and notice: *the sun emerges from behind the clouds.* EMANATE is used esp. of intangible or immaterial things, as light, vapor, ideas, news, etc. spreading or streaming from a source: *rumors often emanate from irresponsible persons.* ISSUE is most often used of a number of persons, a mass of matter, or a volume of smoke, sound, or the like, coming forth through any outlet or outlets: *the crowd issued from the building.*

e·mer·gence (ĭ mûr′jəns), *n.* **1.** act or fact of emerging. **2.** an outgrowth, as a prickle, on the surface of an organ. **3.** *Biol., Philos.* the appearance of new properties in the course of development or evolution that could not have been foreseen in the earlier stage.

e·mer·gen·cy (ĭ mûr′jən sĭ), *n., pl.* **-cies.** an unforeseen occurrence; a sudden and urgent occasion for action. [t. L: m.s. *ēmergentia* a coming up] **—Syn.** EMERGENCY, CRISIS, STRAITS refer to situations in which quick action and judgment are necessary, though they may not avert undesirable consequences. An EMERGENCY is a situation demanding immediate action: *a power failure created an emergency in transportation.* A CRISIS is a vital or decisive turning point in a condition or state of affairs, and everything depends on the outcome of it: *help arrived when affairs had reached a crisis.* STRAIT (usually plural) suggests a pressing situation, often one of need or want, which usually makes necessary some difficult alternative or choice: *the family was in desperate straits for food and clothing.*

e·mer·gent (ĭ mûr′jənt), *adj.* **1.** emerging; rising from a liquid or other surrounding medium. **2.** coming into view or notice; issuing. **3.** arising casually or unexpectedly. **4.** calling for immediate action; urgent. **5.** *Biol., Philos.* displaying emergence (def. 3).

emergent evolution, *Biol., Philos.* the origin of entirely new properties at certain critical stages or levels in the course of evolution, e.g. the origin of multicellular organisms, of nervous systems, psychic processes, etc.

e·mer·i·tus (ĭ mĕr′ə təs), *adj.* retired or honorably discharged from active duty because of age, infirmity, or long service, but retained on the rolls: *a professor emeritus.* [t. L: pp., having served out one's time]

e·mersed (ĭ mûrst′), *adj.* **1.** having emerged. **2.** *Bot.* risen or standing out of water, surrounding leaves, etc. [f. s. L *ēmersus,* pp., emerged + -ED[2]]

e·mer·sion (ĭ mûr′shən, -zhən), *n.* **1.** act or fact of emerging; emergence. **2.** *Astron.* the reappearance of a heavenly body after an eclipse or occultation.

Em·er·son (ĕm′ər sən), *n.* **Ralph Waldo,** 1803–82, U.S. essayist and poet. **—Em·er·so·ni·an** (ĕm′ər sō′nĭ ən), *adj.*

em·er·y (ĕm′ə rĭ, ĕm′rĭ), *n.* a granular mineral substance consisting typically of corundum mixed with magnetite or hematite, used powdered, crushed, or consolidated for grinding and polishing. [t. F. m. *émeri,* t. It.: m. *smeriglio,* der. Gk. *smēris*]

emery cloth, emery-coated cloth used as an abrasive.

emery wheel, a wheel for grinding or polishing, consisting mostly of or faced with emery.

em·e·sis (ĕm′ə sĭs), *n. Pathol.* vomiting. [NL, t. Gk.]

e·met·ic (ĭ mĕt′ĭk), *adj.* **1.** inducing vomiting, as a medicinal substance. **—n. 2.** an emetic medicine or agent. [t. L: s. *emeticus,* t. Gk.: m. *emetikós*]

em·e·tine (ĕm′ə tēn′, -tĭn), *n.* a colorless crystalline, or white powdery substance, $C_{29}H_{40}N_2O_2$, the principal ingredient of ipecac, used as a specific against amoebic dysentery. Also, **em·e·tin** (ĕm′ə tĭn). [f. s. Gk. *ēmetos* vomiting + -INE[2]]

e·meu (ē′mū), *n.* emu.

E.M.F., electromotive force. Also, **e.m.f., emf**

-emia, *Med.* a suffix referring to the state of the blood, as in *hyperemia.* Also, **-aemia, -haemia.** [NL: also *-hemia, -haemia,* t. Gk.: m. *-aimia* (as in *anaimía* want of blood), der. *haîma* blood]

em·i·grant (ĕm′ə grənt), *n.* **1.** one who emigrates, as from his native country. **—adj. 2.** emigrating. [t. L: s. *ēmigrans,* ppr.]

em·i·grate (ĕm′ə grāt′), *v.i.,* **-grated, -grating.** to leave one country or region to settle in another; migrate. [t. L: s. *ēmigrātus,* pp.] **—Syn.** See **migrate.**

em·i·gra·tion (ĕm′ə grā′shən), *n.* **1.** act of emigrating. **2.** a body of emigrants; emigrants collectively.

é·mi·gré (ĕm′ə grā′; *Fr.* ĕ mē grĕ′), *n., pl.* **-grés** (-grāz′; *Fr.* -grĕ′). **1.** an emigrant, esp. one who flees from his native land to escape political persecution. **2.** a person who fled from France because of opposition to or fear of the revolution that began in 1789. [F, pp. of *émigrer,* t. L: m. *ēmigrāre* emigrate]

E·mi·lia (ĕ mē′lyä), *n.* a department in N Italy. 3,284,205 pop. (1936); 8547 sq. mi.

em·i·nence (ĕm′ə nəns), *n.* **1.** high station, rank, or repute. **2.** a high place or part; a hill or elevation; height. **3.** (*cap.*) *Rom. Cath. Ch.* the title of honor of a cardinal: *your Eminence.* **—Syn. 1.** distinction, prominence, celebrity, renown.

em·i·nen·cy (ĕm′ə nən sĭ), *n., pl.* **-cies.** *Now Rare.* eminence.

em·i·nent (ĕm′ə nənt), *adj.* **1.** high in station, rank, or repute; distinguished. **2.** conspicuous, signal, or noteworthy: *eminent services, eminent fairness.* **3.** lofty; high. **4.** prominent; projecting; protruding. [t. L: s. *ēminens,* ppr., standing out] **—em′i·nent·ly,** *adv.* **—Syn. 1.** prominent, celebrated, renowned, illustrious. See **famous. 2.** noted; noteworthy. **—Ant. 1.** unknown.

eminent domain, *Law.* the dominion of the sovereign power over all property within the state, by which it can appropriate private property for public use, compensation being given for it.

e·mir (ə mēr′), **1.** an Arabian chieftain or prince. **2.** a title of honor of the descendants of Mohammed. Also, **emeer.** [var. of AMIR]

em·is·sar·y (ĕm′ə sĕr′ĭ), *n., pl.* **-saries,** *adj.* **—n. 1.** an agent sent on a mission or errand. **2.** an agent sent on a mission of a secret nature. **—adj. 3.** sent forth, as on a mission. **4.** pertaining to one so sent forth. [t. L: m.s. *ēmissārius* sent out (adj.), scout (n).]

e·mis·sion (ĭ mĭsh′ən), *n.* **1.** act of emitting. **2.** that which is emitted; a discharge; an emanation. **3.** act of issuing (as of paper money). **4.** *Electronics.* a measure of the number of electrons emitted by the heated filament or cathode of a vacuum tube. [t. L: s. *ēmissio*]

e·mis·sive (ĭ mĭs′ĭv), *adj.* **1.** serving to emit. **2.** pertaining to emission.

em·is·siv·i·ty (ĕm′ə sĭv′ə tĭ), *n. Thermodynamics.* the relative ability of a surface to emit radiant energy compared to an ideal, black body at the same temperature and with the same area.

e·mit (ĭ mĭt′), *v.t.,* **emitted, emitting. 1.** to send forth; give out or forth (liquid, light, heat, sound, etc.); discharge. **2.** to issue, as an order or a decree. **3.** to issue formally for circulation, as paper money. **4.** to utter, as opinions. [t. L: m.s. *ēmittere* send out] **—e·mit′ter,** *n.* **—Syn. 1.** vent, exhale, exude, expel, eject.

Em·man·u·el (ĭ măn′yŏŏ əl), *n.* Christ. See **Immanuel.**

em·men·a·gogue (ə mĕn′ə gŏg′, -gŏg′, ə mē′nə-), *n.* a medicine that promotes the menstrual discharge. [f. Gk. *émmēn(a)* menses + -AGOGUE]

em·met (ĕm′ĭt), *n. Archaic or Dial.* an ant.

Em·met (ĕm′ĭt), *n.* **Robert,** 1778–1803, Irish patriot.

em·me·tro·pi·a (ĕm′ə trō′pĭ ə), *n.* the normal refractive condition of the eye, in which the rays of light are accurately focused on the retina. [NL, f. Gk.: s. *ĕmmetros* in measure + -ōpía eye state] **—em·me·trop·ic** (ĕm′ə trŏp′ĭk), *adj.*

e·mol·lient (ĭ mŏl′yənt), *adj.* **1.** having the power of softening or relaxing living tissues, as a medicinal substance; soothing, esp. to the skin. **—n. 2.** *Med.* an emollient medicine or agent. [t. L: s. *ēmolliens,* ppr.]

e·mol·u·ment (ĭ mŏl′yə mənt), *n.* profit arising from office or employment; compensation for services; salary or fees. [t. L: (m.) s. *ēmolumentum, ēmolimentum* profit]

e·mo·tion (ĭ mō′shən), *n.* **1.** an affective state of consciousness in which joy, sorrow, fear, hate, or the like, is experienced (distinguished from cognitive and volitional states of consciousness). **2.** any of the feelings of joy, sorrow, fear, hate, love, etc. [t. L: s. *ēmōtio,* der. *ēmōtus,* pp., moved out, stirred up] **—e·mo′tion·less,** *adj.* **—Syn. 1.** See **feeling.**

e·mo·tion·al (ĭ mō′shən əl), *adj.* **1.** pertaining to emotion or the emotions. **2.** subject to or easily affected by emotion. **3.** appealing to the emotions. **—e·mo′tion·al·ly,** *adv.*

e·mo·tion·al·ism (ĭ mō′shən ə lĭz′əm), *n.* **1.** emotional character. **2.** appeal to the emotions. **3.** tendency to emotion, esp. morbid emotion. **4.** expression of emotion.

e·mo·tion·al·ist (ĭ mō′shən əl ĭst), *n.* **1.** one who appeals to the emotions, esp. unduly. **2.** one easily affected by emotion. **3.** *Philos.* one who bases conduct or the theory of conduct upon feelings.

e·mo·tion·al·i·ty (ĭ mō′shə năl′ə tĭ), *n.* emotional state or quality.

e·mo·tion·al·ize (ĭ mō′shən ə līz′), *v.t.,* **-ized, -izing.** to make emotional; treat as a matter of emotion.

e·mo·tive (ĭ mō′tĭv), *adj.* **1.** characterized by or pertaining to emotion. **2.** exciting emotion. **—e·mo′tive·ly,** *adv.* **—e·mo′tive·ness, e·mo·tiv·i·ty** (ē′mō tĭv′ə tĭ), *n.*

Emp., 1. Emperor. **2.** Empress.

em·pale (ĕm pāl′), *v.t.,* **-paled, -paling.** impale.

em·pan·el (ĕm păn′əl), *v.t.,* **-eled, -eling** or (*esp. Brit.*) **-elled, -elling.** impanel.

em·pa·thy (ĕm′pə thĭ), *n. Psychol.* mental entering into the feeling or spirit of a person or thing; appreciative perception or understanding; motor mimicry. [t. Gk.: m.s. *empátheia.* Cf. G *einfühlung,* lit., infeeling] **—em·path·ic** (ĕm păth′ĭk), *adj.* **—em·path′i·cal·ly,** *adv.*

Em·ped·o·cles (ĕm pĕd′ə klēz′), *n.* c490–c430 B.C., Greek philosopher and statesman.

em·pen·nage (än pĕ näzh′), *n.* the rear part of an airplane or airship, usually comprising stabilizer, elevator, vertical fin, and rudder. [t. F, der. *empenner* feather, der. *em-* EM-[1] + *penne* (g. L *penna* feather)]

em·per·or (ĕm′pər ər), *n.* the sovereign or supreme ruler of an empire. [ME *emperour(e),* t. OF: m. *empereor,* g. L *imperātor* ruler] **—em′per·or·ship′,** *n.*

em·per·y (ĕm′pər ĭ), *n., pl.* **-peries.** *Poetic.* **1.** absolute dominion; empire. **2.** the territory of an emperor. [ME *emperie,* t. OF, der. *emperer* to rule, g. L *imperāre*]

em·pha·sis (ĕm′fə sĭs), *n., pl.* **-ses** (-sēz′). **1.** stress laid upon, or importance or significance attached to, anything. **2.** *Rhet.* **a.** special and significant stress of voice laid on particular words or syllables. **b.** stress laid on particular words, by means of position, repetition, or other indication. **3.** intensity or force of expression, action, etc. **4.** prominence, as of outline. [t. L, t. Gk.]

em·pha·size (ĕm'fə sīz'), v.t., **-sized, -sizing.** to give emphasis to; lay stress upon; stress.

em·phat·ic (ĕm făt'ĭk), adj. 1. uttered, or to be uttered, with emphasis; strongly expressive. 2. using emphasis in speech or action. 3. forcibly significant; strongly marked; striking. [t. Gk.: m.s. emphatikós, var. of emphantikós expressive] —**em·phat'i·cal·ly**, adv. —**Syn.** 3. positive, energetic, forcible, pronounced.

em·phy·se·ma (ĕm'fə sē'mə), n. Pathol., Vet. Sci. abnormal distention of an organ or a part of the body with air or other gas. [NL, t. Gk.: inflation] —**em·phy·sem·a·tous** (ĕm'fə sĕm'ə təs, -sē'mə-), adj.

em·pire (ĕm'pīr), n. 1. an aggregate of nations or peoples ruled over by an emperor or other powerful sovereign or government; usually a territory of greater extent than a kingdom ruled by a single sovereign: the Roman empire. 2. a government under an emperor: the first French empire. 3. supreme power in governing; imperial power; sovereignty. 4. supreme control; absolute sway. —adj. 5. (cap.) developed or in vogue during the first French empire (1804–15): applied esp. to certain styles of interior decoration, furniture, etc., and of women's dress (implying esp. a high waistline, with undraped skirts hanging loosely). [ME, t. F, g. L imperium a command, authority, realm] —**Syn.** 3. dominion, rule.

Empire Day, May 24, the anniversary of Queen Victoria's birth, observed throughout the British Empire.

Empire State, the State of New York.

em·pir·ic (ĕm pĭr'ĭk), n. 1. any one who follows an empirical method. 2. a quack; a charlatan. —adj. 3. empirical. [t. L: s. empīricus, t. Gk.: m. empeirikós, der. empeiria experience]

em·pir·i·cal (ĕm pĭr'ə kəl), adj. 1. derived from or guided by experience or experiment. 2. depending upon experience or observation alone, without using science or theory, esp. in medicine. —**em·pir'i·cal·ly**, adv.

empirical formula, Chem. See **formula.**

em·pir·i·cism (ĕm pĭr'ə sĭz'əm), n. 1. empirical method or practice. 2. Philos. the doctrine that all knowledge is derived from experience. 3. undue reliance upon experience; quackery. 4. an empirical conclusion. —**em·pir'i·cist**, n., adj.

em·place·ment (ĕm plās'mənt), n. 1. Fort. the space, platform, or the like for a gun or battery and its accessories. 2. a putting in place or position; location.

em·ploy (ĕm ploi'), v.t. 1. to use the services of (a person); have or keep in one's service; keep busy or at work: this factory employs thousands of men. 2. to make use of (an instrument, means, etc.); use; apply. 3. to occupy or devote (time, energies, etc.): I employ my spare time in reading. —n. 4. employment; service: to be in someone's employ. [t. F: s. employer, g. L implicāre enfold] —**em·ploy'a·ble**, adj. —**Syn.** 1. engage, hire. —**Ant.** 1. discharge.

em·ploy·ee (ĕm ploi'ē, ĕm'ploi ē'), n. a person working for another person or a business firm for pay. Also, **em·ploy'e, em·ploy'é.** [f. EMPLOY, v. + -EE; r. employe, t. F, pp. of employer employ] —**Syn.** See **servant.**

em·ploy·er (ĕm ploi'ər), n. one who employs, esp. for wages.

em·ploy·ment (ĕm ploi'mənt), n. 1. act of employing. 2. state of being employed; employ; services. 3. that on which one is employed; work; occupation; business.

em·poi·son (ĕm poi'zən), v.t. 1. to corrupt. 2. Obs. to poison. [ME empoyson(en), t. F: m. empoisoner, der. em- EM-1 + poison POISON]

Em·po·ri·a (ĕm pōr'ĭ ə), n. a city in E Kansas. 15,669 (1950).

em·po·ri·um (ĕm pōr'ĭ əm), n., pl. **-poriums, -poria** (-pōr'ĭ ə). 1. a place, town, or city of important commerce, esp. a principal center of trade. 2. a large store selling a great variety of articles. [t. L, t. Gk.: a trading place]

em·pov·er·ish (ĕm pŏv'ər ĭsh, -pŏv'rĭsh), v.t. impoverish.

em·pow·er (ĕm pou'ər), v.t. 1. to give power or authority to; authorize: I empowered him to make the deal for me. 2. to enable or permit. —**em·pow'er·ment**, n. —**Syn.** 1. warrant, commission, license, qualify.

em·press (ĕm'prĭs), n. 1. a woman ruler of an empire. 2. the consort of an emperor. 3. a supreme or sovereign ruler: empress of the seas. [ME empresse, t. OF: (m.) emper(er)esse, r. empereris, g. L imperātrix]

empress dowager, the widow of an emperor.

em·presse·ment (än prĕs män'), n. French. display of cordiality.

em·prise (ĕm prīz'), n. Archaic. 1. an adventurous enterprise. 2. knightly daring or prowess. Also, **emprize'.** [ME, t. OF, n. use of fem. pp. of emprendre undertake, f. em- EM-1 + prendre take (g. L prehendre)]

emp·ty (ĕmp'tĭ), adj., **-tier, -tiest,** v., **-tied, -tying,** n., pl. **-ties.** —adj. 1. containing nothing; void of the usual or appropriate contents: an empty bottle. 2. vacant; unoccupied: an empty house. 3. without burden or load: an empty wagon. 4. destitute of some quality or qualities; devoid (fol. by of): a life now as empty of happiness as it was full of it. 5. without force, effect, or significance; unsatisfactory; meaningless: empty compliments, empty pleasures. 6. Colloq. hungry. 7. without knowledge or sense; frivolous; foolish. —v.t. 8. to make empty; deprive of contents; discharge the contents of: to empty a bucket. 9. to discharge (contents): empty the water out of

a bucket. —v.i. 10. to become empty: the room emptied rapidly after the lecture. 11. to discharge contents, as a river: the river empties into the sea. —n. 12. Colloq. something empty, as a freight car, bottle, etc. [ME; OE ǣmtig, var. of ǣmettig, f. s. ǣmetta leisure + -ig -Y1] —**emp'ti·ly**, adv. —**emp'ti·ness**, n. —**Syn.** 1. EMPTY, VACANT, BLANK denote absence of content or contents. EMPTY means without appropriate or accustomed contents: empty barrel, the house is empty (has no furnishings). VACANT is usually applied to that which is temporarily unoccupied: vacant chair, house (uninhabited). BLANK applies to surfaces free from any marks or lacking appropriate markings, openings, etc.: blank paper, wall. 5. hollow, delusive, vain. 8. unload, unburden. —**Ant.** 1. full.

emp·ty-hand·ed (ĕmp'tĭ hăn'dĭd), adj. having nothing in the hands; bringing or taking nothing.

emp·ty-head·ed (ĕmp'tĭ hĕd'ĭd), adj. brainless; foolish.

em·pur·ple (ĕm pûr'pəl), v.t., **-pled, -pling.** to tinge or color with purple.

em·py·e·ma (ĕm'pī ē'mə, -pī-), n. Pathol. a collection of pus in some cavity of the body, esp. in the pleural cavity. [NL, t. Gk.: suppuration] —**em·py·e'mic**, adj.

em·pyr·e·al (ĕm pĭr'ĭ əl, ĕm'pə rē'əl, -pī-), adj. 1. pertaining to the highest heaven; empyrean. 2. pertaining to the sky; celestial. 3. formed of pure fire or light. [f. s. LL empyreus (t. Gk.: m. ĕmpyros fiery) + -AL1]

em·py·re·an (ĕm'pə rē'ən, -pī-), n. 1. the highest heaven, supposed by the ancients to contain the pure element of fire. 2. the visible heavens; the firmament. —adj. 3. empyreal.

e·mu (ē'mū), n. either of two large, flightless, three-toed Australian birds of the ratite genus Dromiceius, D. novae (or n.) hollandiae and D. diemenianus, closely related to the ostrich, but smaller. The latter species is now extinct. Also, **emeu.** [t. Moluccan: m. emeu cassowary]

em·u·late (v. ĕm'yə lāt'; adj. ĕm'yə lĭt), v., **-lated, -lating,** adj. —v.t. 1. to try to equal or excel; imitate with effort to equal or surpass. 2. to rival with some degree of success. —adj. 3. Obs. emulous. [t. L: m.s. aemulātus, pp., having rivaled] —**em'u·la'tive**, adj. —**em'u·la'tor**, n.

Emu,
Dromiceius novae hollandiae
(Total length ab. 6½ ft.)

em·u·la·tion (ĕm'yə lā'shən), n. 1. effort or desire to equal or excel others. 2. Obs. jealous rivalry. —**Syn.** 1. competition, rivalry.

em·u·lous (ĕm'yə ləs), adj. 1. desirous of equaling or excelling; filled with emulation. 2. arising from or of the nature of emulation, as actions, etc. 3. Obs. jealous; envious. [t. L: m. aemulus] —**em'u·lous·ly**, adv. —**em'u·lous·ness**, n.

e·mul·si·fy (ĭ mŭl'sə fī'), v.t., **-fied, -fying.** to make into an emulsion. —**e·mul'si·fi·ca'tion**, n. —**e·mul'si·fi'er**, n.

e·mul·sion (ĭ mŭl'shən), n. 1. a liquid preparation of the color and consistency of milk. 2. Phys. Chem. any colloidal suspension of a liquid in another liquid. 3. Pharm. a liquid preparation consisting of minute particles of an oily, fatty, resinous, or other substance held in suspension in an aqueous fluid by means of a gum or other viscous matter. 4. Photog. the light sensitive layer on a photographic film, plate, or paper, consisting of one or more of the silver halides in gelatin. [t. NL: s. ēmulsio, der L ēmulsus, pp., milked out] —**e·mul'sive**, adj.

e·munc·to·ry (ĭ mŭngk'tə rĭ), n., pl. **-ries,** adj. —n. 1. a part or organ of the body, as the skin, a kidney, etc., carrying off waste products. —adj. 2. excretory. [t. NL: m.s. ēmunctōrium, L a pair of snuffers]

en (ĕn), n. 1. the letter N, n. 2. Print. half of the width of an em; N quad.

en-1, a prefix meaning primarily "in," "into," first occurring in words from French, but now used freely as an English formative: 1. with the old concrete force of putting the object into or on something or of bringing the object into the specified condition, often serving to form transitive verbs from nouns or adjectives, as in enable, enact, endear, engulf, enshrine, enslave. 2. prefixed to verbs, to make them transitive, or, if already transitive, to give them the transitive sign, as in enkindle, entwine, engild, engird, engrave, enshield. Also, **em-1.** Cf. **in-2, im-1.** [t. F, g. L in-, repr. in, prep., in, into, on, to]

en-2, a prefix representing Greek en-, corresponding to **en-1** and occurring chiefly in combinations already formed in Greek, as energy, enthusiasm. Also, **em-2.**

-en1, a suffix, forming transitive and intransitive verbs from adjectives, as in fasten, harden, sweeten, or from nouns, as in heighten, lengthen, strengthen. [abstracted from old verbs like fasten (contrast listen, where -en has kept its nonmorphemic character)]

-en2, a suffix of adjectives indicating "material," "appearance," as in ashen, golden, oaken. [OE]

-en3, a suffix used to mark the past participle in many strong and some weak verbs, as in taken, proven. [OE]

-en4, a suffix forming the plural of some nouns, as in brethren, children, oxen, and other words, now mostly archaic, as eyen, hosen. [ME; OE -an, case ending of weak nouns, as in *oxan*, oblique sing. and nom. and acc. pl. of *oxa* ox]

-en[5], a diminutive suffix, as in *maiden, kitten*, etc. [OE]

en·a·ble (ĕn ā′bəl), *v.t.*, **-bled, -bling. 1.** to make able; give power, means, or ability to; make competent; authorize: *this will enable him to do it.* **2.** to make possible or easy: *aeronautics enables us to overcome great distances.*

enabling act or **statute**, an act or statute enabling a person or a corporation to do something otherwise illegal.

en·act (ĕn ăkt′), *v.t.* **1.** to make into an act or statute. **2.** to ordain; decree. **3.** to represent on or as on the stage; act the part of: *to enact Hamlet.* —**en·act′a·ble**, *adj.* —**en·ac′tor**, *n.*

en·ac·tive (ĕn ăk′tĭv), *adj.* having power to enact or establish, as a law.

en·act·ment (ĕn ăkt′mənt), *n.* **1.** act of enacting. **2.** state or fact of being enacted. **3.** that which is enacted; a law; a statute. **4.** a single provision of a law.

en·ac·to·ry (ĕn ăk′tə rĭ), *adj. Law.* of or pertaining to an enactment which creates new rights and obligations.

en·am·el (ĭ năm′əl), *n., v.,* **-eled, -eling** or (*esp. Brit.*) **-elled, -elling.** —*n.* **1.** a glassy substance, usually opaque, applied by fusion to the surface of metal, pottery, etc., as an ornament or for protection. **2.** enamelware. **3.** any of various enamellike varnishes, paints, etc. **4.** any enamellike surface with a bright luster. **5.** an artistic work executed in enamel. **6.** *Anat., Zool.* the hard, glossy, calcareous outer structure of the crowns of the teeth, containing only a slight amount of organic substance. **7.** a coating applied to the skin to simulate a beautiful complexion. —*v.t.* **8.** to inlay or overlay with enamel. **9.** to form an enamellike surface upon: *to enamel cardboard.* **10.** to decorate as with enamel; variegate with colors. [ME *enamayl,* t. AF, f. *en-* EN-[1] + *amayl,* OF *esmail,* c. It. *smalto* SMALT; akin to SMELT] —**e·nam′el·er**; *esp. Brit.,* **e·nam′el·ler**, *n.* —**e·nam′el·ist**; *esp. Brit.,* **e·nam′el·list**, *n.* —**e·nam′el·work′**, *n.*

en·am·el·ing (ĭ năm′əl ĭng), *n.* **1.** act or work of one who enamels. **2.** a decoration or coating of enamel. Also, *esp. Brit.,* **e·nam′el·ling.**

en·am·el·ware (ĭ năm′əl wâr′), *n.* metalware, as cooking utensils, covered with an enamel surface.

en a·mi (äN nà mē′), *French.* as a friend.

en·am·or (ĕn ăm′ər), *v.t.* to inflame with love; charm; captivate (usually passive fol. by *of*): *to be enamored of a lady.* Also, *Brit.,* **en·am′our.** [ME *enamor(en),* t. OF: m. *enamourer,* der. *en-* EN-[1] + *amour* (g. L *amor* love)] —**Syn.** fascinate, bewitch.

en ar·riè·re (äN nà ryěr′), *French.* backward.

en·ar·thro·sis (ĕn′är thrō′sĭs), *n., pl.* **-ses** (-sēz). *Anat.* a joint, as at the shoulder, in which a convex end of one bone is socketed in a concavity of another; a ball-and-socket joint. [NL, t. Gk.: jointing in]

en a·vant (äN nà väN′), *French.* forward; onward.

en bloc (ĕn blŏk′; *Fr.* äN blôk′), *French.* as a whole.

en bro·chette (äN brō shĕt′), *French.* See **brochette** (def. 2).

enc., 1. enclosed. **2.** enclosure.

en·cae·ni·a (ĕn sē′nyə, -nĭ′ə), *n.pl.* **1.** festive ceremonies commemorating the founding of a city or the consecration of a church. **2.** (*cap.*) ceremonies at Oxford University in honor of founders and benefactors. [t. L, t. Gk.: m. *enkainia* consecration feast]

en·cage (ĕn kāj′), *v.t.,* **-caged, -caging.** to confine in or as in a cage; coop up. Also, **incage.**

en·camp (ĕn kămp′), *v.i., v.t.* to settle or lodge in a camp.

en·camp·ment (ĕn kămp′mənt), *n.* **1.** act of encamping; lodgment in a camp. **2.** the place or quarters occupied in camping; a camp.

en·car·nal·ize (ĕn kär′nə līz′), *v.t.,* **-ized, -izing.** to invest with a carnal or fleshly form.

en·case (ĕn kās′), *v.t.,* **-cased, -casing.** incase.

en cas·se·role (äN kàs rôl′), *French.* See **casserole** (def. 5).

en·caus·tic (ĕn kôs′tĭk), *adj.* **1.** painted with wax colors fixed with heat, or with any process in which colors are burned in. —*n.* **2.** a work of art produced by an encaustic process. [t. L: s. *encausticus* of burning in, t. Gk.: m. *enkaustikōs*]

-ence, a noun suffix equivalent to -ance, and corresponding to -ent in adjectives, as in *abstinence, consistence, dependence, difference.* [t. F, alter. of -ance -ANCE by etymological assoc. with L -*entia* noun suffix]

en·ceinte[1] (ĕn sānt′; *Fr.* äN sănt′), *adj.* pregnant; with child. [F, g. LL *incincta,* pp. fem., ungirt]

en·ceinte[2] (ĕn sānt′; *Fr.* äN sănt′), *n.* **1.** a wall or enclosure, as of a fortified place. **2.** the place enclosed. [F, der. *enceindre,* g. L *incingere* enclose, as with a girdle]

en·ce·phal·ic (ĕn′sə făl′ĭk), *adj.* of or pertaining to the encephalon or brain.

en·ceph·a·li·tis (ĕn sĕf′ə lī′tĭs), *n. Pathol.* inflammation of the substance of the brain. [NL; see ENCEPHAL(O)-, -ITIS] —**en·ceph·a·lit·ic** (ĕn sĕf′ə lĭt′ĭk), *adj.*

encephalitis le·thar·gi·ca (lĭ thär′jə kə), sleeping sickness.

encephalo-, a word element meaning "brain," as in *encephalomyelitis.* Also, **encephal-.** [t. Gk., m. *enkephalo-,* comb. form of *enkephalos*]

en·ceph·a·lo·ma (ĕn sĕf′ə lō′mə), *n., pl.* **-mata** (-mə tə). *Pathol.* **1.** a brain tumor. **2.** hernia of the brain.

en·ceph·a·lo·my·e·li·tis (ĕn sĕf′ə lō mī′ə lī′təs), *n. Pathol., Vet. Sci.* any of several inflammatory diseases of the brain.

en·ceph·a·lon (ĕn sĕf′ə lŏn′), *n., pl.* **-la** (-lə). the brain. [NL, t. Gk.: (neut.) within the head, as n., the brain]

en·chain (ĕn chān′), *v.t.* **1.** to fasten with or as with a chain or chains; fetter; restrain. **2.** to hold fast, as the attention. [ME *encheinen,* t. OF: m. *enchainer,* der. *en-* EN-[1] + *chaine* CHAIN] —**en·chain′ment**, *n.*

en·chant (ĕn chănt′, -chänt′), *v.t.* **1.** to subject to magical influence; cast a spell over; bewitch. **2.** to impart a magic quality or effect to. **3.** to delight in a high degree; charm. [ME *enchaunt(en),* t. OF: m. *enchanter,* g. L *incantāre* chant a magic formula against] —**Syn. 3.** fascinate, captivate, enrapture, transport.

en·chant·er (ĕn chăn′tər, -chän′-), *n.* **1.** one who enchants. **2.** a magician.

en·chant·ing (ĕn chăn′tĭng, -chän′-), *adj.* charming; bewitching. —**en·chant′ing·ly**, *adv.*

en·chant·ment (ĕn chănt′mənt, -chänt′-), *n.* **1.** act or art of enchanting. **2.** that which enchants. —**Syn. 1.** magic, sorcery, fascination, witchery. **2.** spell, charm.

en·chant·ress (ĕn chăn′trĭs, -chän′-), *n.* **1.** a woman who enchants; a sorceress. **2.** a fascinating woman.

en·chase (ĕn chās′), *v.t.,* **-chased, -chasing. 1.** to place (gems) in an ornamental setting. **2.** to decorate with inlay, embossing, or engraving. [t. F: m. *enchâsser,* der. *en-* EN-[1] + *châsse* shrine (g. L *capsa* box. see CASE[2])]

en·chi·rid·i·on (ĕn′kī rĭd′ĭ ən, -kĭ′-), *n., pl.* **-ridions, -ridia** (-rĭd′ĭ ə). a handbook; a manual. [t. Gk.: f. *en-* EN-[2] + m. *cheir* hand + *-idion,* dim. suffix]

en·chon·dro·ma (ĕn′kən drō′mə), *n., pl.* **-mata** (-mə tə), **-dromas.** *Pathol.* a tumor which consists essentially of cartilage. [f. EN-[2] + s. Gk. *chóndros* cartilage + -OMA] —**en·chon·drom·a·tous** (ĕn′kən drŏm′ə təs, -drō′mə-), *adj.*

en·cho·ri·al (ĕn kōr′ĭəl), *adj.* (esp. of demotic writing) belonging to or used in a particular country; native; domestic. Also, **en·chor·ic** (ĕn kôr′ĭk, -kŏr′-). [f. s. Gk. *enchōrios* in or of a country + -AL[1]]

en·cir·cle (ĕn sûr′kəl), *v.t.,* **-cled, -cling. 1.** to form a circle round; surround; encompass. **2.** to make a circling movement about; make the circuit of. —**en·cir′cle·ment**, *n.* —**Syn. 1.** environ, gird, enfold, enclose.

encl., 1. enclosed. **2.** enclosure.

en·clasp (ĕn klăsp′, -kläsp′), *v.t.* to hold in or as in a clasp or embrace. Also, **inclasp.**

en·clave (ĕn′klāv; *Fr.* äN klàv′), *n.* a country, or, esp., an outlying portion of a country, entirely or mostly surrounded by the territory of another country. [t. F, der. *enclaver* shut in, g. Rom. *inclāvāre*]

en·clit·ic (ĕn klĭt′ĭk), *adj.* **1.** (of a word) so closely connected with a preceding word as to have no independent accent. —*n.* **2.** an enclitic word, as *que* (and) in Latin: *arma virumque,* arms and the man. [t. LL: s. *encliticus,* t. Gk.: m. *enklitikós,* lit., leaning on] —**en·clit′i·cal·ly**, *adv.*

en·close (ĕn klōz′), *v.t.,* **-closed, -closing. 1.** to shut in; close in on all sides. **2.** to surround as with a fence or wall: *to enclose land.* **3.** to insert in the same envelope, etc., with the main letter, etc.: *he enclosed a check.* **4.** to contain (the thing transmitted): *his letter enclosed a check.* Also, **inclose.** [f. EN-[1] + CLOSE, v., after OF *enclos,* pp. of *enclore*] —**Syn. 1.** surround, encircle, encompass.

en·clo·sure (ĕn klō′zhər), *n.* **1.** act of enclosing. **2.** the separation and appropriation of land by means of a fence. **3.** a tract of land surrounded by a fence. **4.** that which encloses, as a fence or wall. **5.** that which is enclosed, as a paper sent in a letter. Also, **inclosure.**

en·co·mi·ast (ĕn kō′mĭ ăst′), *n.* one who utters or writes an encomium; a eulogist. [t. Gk.: s. *enkōmiastēs*]

en·co·mi·as·tic (ĕn kō′mĭ ăs′tĭk), *adj.* eulogistic.

en·co·mi·um (ĕn kō′mĭ əm), *n., pl.* **-miums, -mia** (-mĭ′ə). a formal expression of praise; a eulogy. [t. L, t. Gk.: m. *enkōmion* eulogy, prop. neut. of *enkōmios* belonging to a Bacchic revel]

en·com·pass (ĕn kŭm′pəs), *v.t.* **1.** to form a circle about; encircle; surround. **2.** to enclose; contain. **3.** *Obs.* to outwit. —**en·com′pass·ment**, *n.*

en·core (äng′kōr, än′-), *interj. n., v.,* **-cored, -coring.** —*interj.* **1.** again; once more (used by an audience in calling for a repetition of a song, etc., or for an additional number or piece). —*n.* **2.** a demand, as by applause, for a repetition of a song, etc., or for an additional number or piece. **3.** that which is given in response to such a demand. —*v.t.* **4.** to call for a repetition of. **5.** to call for an encore from (a performer). [t. F: still, yet, besides, g. L *hanc hōram* within this hour]

en·coun·ter (ĕn koun′tər), *v.t.* **1.** to come upon; meet with, esp. unexpectedly. **2.** to meet with or contend against (difficulties, opposition, etc.). **3.** to meet (a person, military force, etc.) in conflict. —*v.i.* **4.** to meet, esp. in conflict. —*n.* **5.** a meeting with a person or thing, esp. casually or unexpectedly. **6.** a meeting in conflict or opposition; a battle; a combat. **7.** *Obs.* manner of meeting; behavior. [ME *encountre(n),* t. OF: m. *encontrer,* g. LL *incontrāre,* der. L *in-* IN-[2] + *contrā* against] —**Syn. 6.** conflict, skirmish.

en·cour·age (ĕn kûr′ĭj), *v.t.*, **-aged, -aging. 1.** to inspire with courage, spirit, or confidence. **2.** to stimulate by assistance, approval, etc. [ME *encorage(n)*, t. OF: m. *encoragier*, der. *en-* EN-¹ + *corage* COURAGE] —**en·cour′ag·er**, *n.* —**en·cour′ag·ing·ly**, *adv.* —**Syn. 1.** inspirit, embolden, hearten. **2.** urge, abet, second; foment, promote, advance, foster. —**Ant. 1.** dishearten.

en·cour·age·ment (ĕn kûr′ĭj mənt), *n.* **1.** act of encouraging. **2.** state of being encouraged. **3.** that which encourages. —**Ant. 1.** disapproval. **2.** depression.

en·crim·son (ĕn krĭm′zən), *v.t.* to make crimson.

en·cri·nite (ĕn′krə nīt′), *n.* **1.** a fossil crinoid. **2.** any crinoid. [f. EN-² + m.s. Gk. *krínon* lily + -ITE¹]

en·croach (ĕn krōch′), *v.i.* **1.** to advance beyond proper limits; make gradual inroads. **2.** to trespass upon the property or rights of another, esp. stealthily or by gradual advances. [ME *encroche(n)*, t. OF: m. *encrochier*, der. *en-* EN-¹ + *croc* hook] —**en·croach′er**, *n.* —**Syn. 1, 2.** See **trespass.**

en·croach·ment (ĕn krōch′mənt), *n.* **1.** act of encroaching. **2.** anything taken by encroaching.

en·crust (ĕn krŭst′), *v.t.* incrust. —**en′crus·ta′tion**, *n.*

en·cum·ber (ĕn kŭm′bər), *v.t.* **1.** to impede or hamper; retard; embarrass. **2.** to block up or fill with what is obstructive or superfluous. **3.** to burden with obligations, debt, etc. Also, **incumber.** [ME *encombre(n)*, t. OF: m. *encombrer*, der. *en-* EN-¹ + *combre* barrier (g. LL *combrus*, t. Gallic: m. *comberos* a bringing together)] —**Syn. 3.** oppress, overload.

en·cum·brance (ĕn kŭm′brəns), *n.* **1.** that which encumbers; something useless or superfluous; a burden; a hindrance. **2.** a dependent person, esp. a child. **3.** *Law.* a burden or claim on property, as a mortgage. Also, **incumbrance.**

en·cum·branc·er (ĕn kŭm′brən sər), *n. Law.* one who holds an encumbrance.

-ency, a noun suffix, equivalent to **-ence,** as in *consistency, dependency, exigency.* [t. L: m.s. *-entia*]

ency., encyclopedia. Also, **encyc.**

en·cyc·li·cal (ĕn sĭk′lə kəl, -sī′klə-), *n.* **1.** a letter addressed by the Pope to all the bishops of the world in communion with the Holy See. —*adj.* **2.** intended for wide or general circulation; general. Also, **en·cyc′lic.** [f. s. LL *encyclicus* (r. L *encyclios*, t. Gk.: m. *enkýklios* circular, general) + -AL¹]

en·cy·clo·pe·di·a (ĕn sī′klə pē′dī ə), *n.* **1.** a work treating separately various topics from all branches of knowledge, usually in alphabetical arrangement. **2.** a work treating exhaustively one art or science, esp. in articles arranged alphabetically; a cyclopedia. **3.** (*cap.*) the French work edited by Diderot and D'Alembert, published in the 18th century, distinguished by its advanced or radical character. Also, **en·cy′clo·pae′di·a.** [t. LL, t. pseudo-Gk. (occurring in mss. of Quintilian, Pliny, and Galen): m. *enkyklopaideía*, for *enkýklios paideía* general education, complete round or course of learning. See ENCYCLIC, CYCLOPEDIA]

en·cy·clo·pe·dic (ĕn sī′klə pē′dĭk), *adj.* pertaining to or of the nature of an encyclopedia; relating to all branches of knowledge. Also, **en·cy′clo·pae′dic, en·cy′clo·pe′di·cal.**

en·cy·clo·pe·dism (ĕn sī′klə pē′dĭzəm), *n.* **1.** encyclopedic learning. **2.** (*often cap.*) the doctrines and influence of the Encyclopedists. Also, **en·cy′clo·pae′dism.**

en·cy·clo·pe·dist (ĕn sī′klə pē′dĭst), *n.* **1.** a compiler of or contributor to an encyclopedia. **2.** (*often cap.*) one of the collaborators in the French Encyclopedia. Also, **en·cy′clo·pae′dist.**

en·cyst (ĕn sĭst′), *v.t.*, *v.i. Biol.* to enclose or become enclosed in a cyst. —**en·cyst′ment, en/cys·ta′tion,** *n.*

end¹ (ĕnd), *n.* **1.** an extremity of anything that is longer than it is broad: *the end of a street, rope, rod, etc.* **2.** an extreme or furthermost part of anything extended in space: *the ends of the earth.* **3.** anything that bounds an object at one of its extremities; a limit. **4.** act of coming to an end; termination. **5.** the concluding part. **6.** a purpose or aim: *to gain one's ends.* **7.** the object for which a thing exists: *the happiness of the people is the end of government.* **8.** issue or result. **9.** termination of existence; death. **10.** a cause of death, destruction, or ruin. **11.** a remnant or fragment: *odds and ends.* **12.** *Football, etc.* either of the players at the ends of the forward line. **13.** at loose ends, in disorder. **14.** make both ends meet, to keep within one's means. —*v.t.* **15.** to bring to an end, or natural conclusion. **16.** to put an end to by force. **17.** to form the end of. —*v.i.* **18.** to come to an end; terminate; cease: *he ended by settling down.* **19.** to issue or result: *extravagance ends in want.* [ME and OE *ende*, c. G *ende.* See and] —**end′er,** *n.* —**Syn. 3.** tip, bound, limit, terminus. **4.** END, CLOSE, CONCLUSION, OUTCOME refer to the termination of something. END implies a natural termination, completion of an action or process, or attainment of purpose: *the end of a day, of a race, to some good end.* CLOSE implies a planned rounding off of something in process: *the close of a conference.* CONCLUSION suggests a decision or arrangement: *all evidence leads to this conclusion, the conclusion of peace terms.* FINISH emphasizes completion of something begun: *a fight to the finish.* OUTCOME suggests the issue of something which was in doubt: *the outcome of a game.* FINISH. **6.** fate. **aim. 8.** outcome, consequence. **9.** destruction, extermination, annihilation, ruin. **15.** conclude, finish, complete, terminate. **16.** close, stop, discontinue. —**Ant. 4.** beginning. start. **15.** begin.

end² (ĕnd), *v.t. Now Dial.* to put (wheat, hay, etc.) into a barn, stack, etc. [? var. of *inn* to lodge, der. INN]

end-, var. of **endo-,** before vowels, as in *endamoeba.*

en·dam·age (ĕn dăm′ĭj), *v.t.*, **-aged, -aging.** damage.

en·da·moe·ba (ĕn′də mē′bə), *n.* a protozoan, genus *Endamoeba,* one species of which causes dysentery and liver abscess. Also, **en/da·me/ba.** [f. END- + AMOEBA]

en·dan·ger (ĕn dān′jər), *v.t.* to expose to danger; imperil. —**en·dan′ger·ment,** *n.*

end-blown (ĕnd′blōn′), *adj.* (of a flute) having a mouthpiece at the end of the tube, so that the player's breath is directed into the instrument.

en·dear (ĕn dĭr′), *v.t.* **1.** to make dear, esteemed, or beloved: *he endeared himself to his mother.* **2.** *Obs.* to make costly. —**en·dear′ing·ly,** *adv.*

en·dear·ment (ĕn dĭr′mənt), *n.* **1.** act of endearing. **2.** state of being endeared. **3.** action or utterance manifesting affection; a caress or an affectionate term.

en·deav·or (ĕn dĕv′ər), *v.i.* **1.** to exert oneself to do or effect something; make an effort; strive. —*v.t.* **2.** to attempt; try: *he endeavors to keep things nice about his place.* —*n.* **3.** a strenuous effort; an attempt. Also, *Brit.,* **en·deav′our.** [ME *endeavor(en),* der. EN-¹ + DEVOIR. Cf. F *en devoir* in duty] —**en·deav′or·er,** *n.* —**Syn. 1, 2.** struggle, labor, essay, undertake, seek, aim. See **try. 3.** exertion, struggle, essay. See **effort.**

en·dem·ic (ĕn dĕm′ĭk), *adj.* **1.** Also, **en·dem/i·cal,** peculiar to a particular people or locality, as a disease. —*n.* **2.** an endemic disease. [f. s. Gk. *éndēmos* belonging to a people + -IC] —**en·dem/i·cal·ly,** *adv.*

En·der·by Land (ĕn′dər bĭ), a part of the coast of Antarctica, in the central part of the **Enderby Quadrant** (the quadrant below Africa): discovered, 1831.

en·der·mic (ĕn dûr′mĭk), *adj.* acting through the skin, as a medicine. [f. EN-² + DERM(A) + -IC]

en dés·ha·bil·lé (än dĕ zȧ bē yĕ′), *French.* in dishabille or undress.

En·di·cott (ĕn′dĭ kət, -kŏt′), *n.* **John,** 1588?–1665, colonial governor of Massachusetts, born in England. Also **En/de·cott.**

end·ing (ĕn′dĭng), *n.* **1.** a bringing or coming to an end; termination; close. **2.** the final or concluding part. **3.** death. **4.** *Gram.* an inflexional morpheme at the end of a word form, as *-s* in *cuts.* **5.** (in popular use) any final word part, as the *-ow* of *widow.* [ME; OE *endung*]

en·dive (ĕn′dīv, än′dēv; *Fr.* än dēv′), *n.* **1.** *U.S.* a plant, *Cichorium endivia,* of two main types, one with finely divided, much curled leaves and one with broad, fleshy leaves, both used for salads. **2.** *Brit.* chicory (defs. 1, 2). [ME, t. F, t. ML: m.s. *endivia,* t. MGk.: m. *endiui,* t. L: m. *indivia, intibum*]

end·less (ĕnd′lĭs), *adj.* **1.** having no end, limit, or conclusion; boundless; infinite; interminable; incessant. **2.** made continuous, as by joining the two ends of a single length: *an endless chain or belt.* —**end′less·ly,** *adv.* —**end′less·ness,** *n.* —**Syn. 1.** limitless, illimitable, immeasurable, unending, unceasing, continuous, continual, perpetual, everlasting. See **eternal.**

end·long (ĕnd′lông′, -lŏng′), *adv. Archaic or Dial.* **1.** lengthwise. **2.** on end. [ME *endelong,* r. OE *andlang* ALONG]

end man, 1. a man at one end of a row or line. **2.** a man at either end of the line of performers of a minstrel troupe, who plays on the bones or tambourine and carries on humorous dialogue with the interlocutor.

end·most (ĕnd′mōst′), *adj.* furthest.

endo-, a word element meaning "internal," as in *endocardial.* Also, **end-.** [t. Gk., comb. form of *éndon* within]

en·do·blast (ĕn′dō blăst′), *n. Embryol.* the prospective endoderm; the blastemic cells which are to form the endoderm. —**en/do·blas/tic,** *adj.*

en·do·car·di·al (ĕn′dō kär′dĭ əl), *adj.* **1.** within the heart; intracardiac. **2.** pertaining to the endocardium.

en·do·car·di·tis (ĕn′dō kär dī′tĭs), *n. Pathol.* inflammation of the endocardium. [NL; f. ENDOCARD(IUM) + -ITIS] —**en·do·car·dit·ic** (ĕn′dō kär dĭt′ĭk), *adj.*

en·do·car·di·um (ĕn′dō kär′dĭ əm), *n. Anat.* the delicate serous membrane which lines the cavities of the heart and aids in forming the valves by duplication. [NL: f. *endo-* ENDO- + *-cardium* (comb. form repr. Gk. *kardía* heart)]

en·do·carp (ĕn′dō kärp′), *n. Bot.* the inner layer of a pericarp, as the stone of certain fruits.

Fruit of peach A, Endocarp; B, Epicarp; C, Mesocarp; ABC, Pericarp

en·do·cen·tric construction (ĕn′dō sĕn′trĭk), a grammatical construction which contains as one of its immediate constituents a word or other form (called the *head*) which belongs to the same form class and may play the same grammatical role as the construction itself (opposed to *exocentric construction*). Example: *cold water* (having the noun *water* as head), or *good work* where both constituents as a unit function as the word *work* would alone.

en·do·crine (ĕn′dō krĭn′, -krĭn), *n.* **1.** an endocrine gland or organ. **2.** an internal secretion. —*adj.* **3.** of or pertaining to the endocrine glands or their secretions: *endocrine function.* [f. ENDO- + m.s. Gk. *krínein* separate] —**en·do·cri·nal** (ĕn′dō krī′nəl), **en·do·crin·ic** (ĕn′dō krĭn′ĭk), **en·doc·ri·nous** (ĕn dŏk′rə nəs), *adj.*

---

b., blend of, blended; c., cognate with; d., dialect, dialectal; der., derived from; f., formed from; g., going back to; m., modification of; r., replacing; s., stem of; t., taken from; ?, perhaps. See the full key on inside cover.

endocrine gland, any of various glands or organs (as the thyroid gland, suprarenal bodies, pituitary body, etc.) which produce certain important internal secretions (products given up directly to the blood or lymph) acting upon particular organs, and which, through improper functioning, may cause grave disorders or death.

en·do·cri·nol·o·gy (ĕn/dō krī nŏl/ə jĭ, -krĬ-), n. the science that deals with the endocrine glands, esp. in their relation to bodily changes. —**en·do·cri·nol/o·gist,** n.

en·do·derm (ĕn/dō dûrm/), n. Embryol. the inner germ layer in the embryo of a metazoan. Also, **entoderm.** —**en/do·der/mal, en/do·der/mic,** adj.

en·dog·a·mous (ĕn dŏg/ə məs), adj. **1.** marrying customarily within the tribe or other social unit. **2.** pertaining to such marriage (opposed to exogamous). Also, **en·do·gam·ic** (ĕn/dō găm/ĭk).

en·dog·a·my (ĕn dŏg/ə mĭ), n. marriage within the tribe or other social unit, a custom among some savage peoples (opposed to exogamy).

en·do·gen (ĕn/də jĕn), n. Bot. any plant of the obsolete class Endogenae, including the monocotyledons, whose stems were erroneously supposed to grow from within.

en·dog·e·nous (ĕn dŏj/ə nəs), adj. **1.** Biol. growing or proceeding from within; originating within. **2.** Physiol., Biochem. pertaining to the anabolic processes of a cell. **3.** Anat. autogenous. —**en·dog/e·nous·ly,** adv.

en·do·lymph (ĕn/dō lĭmf/), n. Anat. the fluid contained within the membranous labyrinth of the ear.

en·do·morph (ĕn/dō môrf/), n. Mineral. a mineral enclosed within another mineral (opposed to perimorph).

en·do·mor·phic (ĕn/dō môr/fĭk), adj. Mineral. **1.** occurring in the form of an endomorph. **2.** of or relating to endomorphs. **3.** taking place within a rock mass.

en·do·mor·phism (ĕn/dō môr/fĭzəm), n. Mineral. a change brought about within the mass of an intrusive igneous rock.

en·do·par·a·site (ĕn/dō păr/ə sīt/), n. an internal parasite (opposed to ectoparasite).

en·do·pe·rid·i·um (ĕn/dō pĭ rĭd/Ĭəm), n. Bot. See **peridium** (def. 1).

en·do·phyte (ĕn/dō fīt/), n. Bot. a plant living within an animal or another plant, usually as a parasite.

en·do·plasm (ĕn/dō plăz/əm), n. Biol. **1.** the inner portion of the cytoplasm in the cell of a protozoan. **2.** the granular inner layer of cytoplasm in a vegetable cell (opposed to ectoplasm). —**en/do·plas/mic,** adj.

end organ, Physiol. one of several specialized structures found at the peripheral end of sensory or motor nerve fibers.

en·dorse (ĕn dôrs/), v.t., **-dorsed, -dorsing. 1.** to approve, support, or sustain: to endorse a statement. **2.** to write (something) on the back of a document, etc. **3.** to designate oneself as payee of (a check) by signing, usually on the reverse side of the instrument. **4.** to sign one's name on (a commercial document or other instrument). **5.** to designate another as payee by one's endorsement. **6.** to acknowledge (payment) by placing one's signature on a bill, draft, etc. Also, **indorse.** [partial Latinization of ME endosse, t. OF: m. endosser, der. en- on + dos (g. L dorsum back)] —**en·dors/a·ble,** adj. —**en·dors/er, en·dor/sor,** n.

en·dor·see (ĕn dôr/sē/, ĕn/dôr-), n. one to whom a negotiable document is endorsed. Also, **indorsee.**

en·dorse·ment (ĕn dôrs/mənt), n. **1.** approval or sanction. **2.** the placing of one's signature, etc., on a document. **3.** the signature, etc., placed on the reverse of a commercial document which assigns the interest therein to another. **4.** Insurance. a clause under which the stated coverage of an insurance policy may be altered. Also, **indorsement.**

en·do·sarc (ĕn/dō särk/), n. Biol. the endoplasm of a protozoan (opposed to ectosarc).

en·do·scope (ĕn/də skōp/), n. Med. a slender tubular instrument used to examine the interior of a body cavity or hollow viscus. —**en·dos·co·py** (ĕn dŏs/kə pĭ), n.

en·do·skel·e·ton (ĕn/dō skĕl/ə tən), n. Anat. the internal skeleton or framework of the body of an animal (opposed to exoskeleton). —**en/do·skel/e·tal,** adj.

en·dos·mo·sis (ĕn/dŏs mō/sĭs, -dŏz-), n. Phys. Chem. **1.** osmosis from without inward. **2.** (in osmosis) the flow of that fluid which passes with the greater rapidity into the other (opposed to exosmosis). [NL] —**en·dos·mot·ic** (ĕn/dŏs mŏt/Ĭk, -dŏz-), adj.

en·do·sperm (ĕn/dō spûrm/), n. Bot. nutritive matter in seed plant ovules, derived from the embryo sac.

en·do·spore (ĕn/dō spōr/), n. **1.** Bot. the inner coat of a spore. **2.** Bacteriol. a spore formed within a cell of a rod-shaped organism. —**en·dos·por·ous** (ĕn-dŏs/pər əs, ĕn/dō spôr/-), adj.

en·do·spo·ri·um (ĕn/dō spōr/Ĭəm), n., pl. **-sporia** (-spōr/Ĭ ə). Bot. endospore (def. 1). [NL]

en·dos·te·um (ĕn dŏs/tĬ əm), n., pl. **-tea** (-tĬ ə). Anat. the vascular membrane lining the medullary cavity of a bone. [NL, f. Gk.: end- ENDO- + m. ostéon bone]

en·dos·to·sis (ĕn/dŏs tō/sĬs), n. Anat. bone formation beginning in the substance of cartilage. [f. END(O)- + OSTOSIS]

en·do·the·ci·um (ĕn/dō thē/shĬ əm, -sĬ əm), n., pl. **-cia** (-shĬ ə, -sĬ ə). Bot. **1.** the lining of the cavity of an anther. **2.** (in mosses) the central mass of cells in the

rudimentary capsule, from which the archespore is generally developed. **3.** (in bryophytes) the central mass of cells in the capsule, including the spores and columella. [NL, f. Gk.: endo- ENDO- + m. thēkíon little case]

en·do·the·li·al (ĕn/dō thē/lĬ əl), adj. pertaining to endothelium.

en·do·the·li·oid (ĕn/dō thē/lĬ oid/), adj. resembling endothelium.

en·do·the·li·o·ma (ĕn/dō thē/lĬ ō/mə), n., pl. **-mata** (-mə tə), **-mas.** Pathol. a tumor (malignant or benign) originating from the endothelium. [f. ENDOTHELI(UM) + -OMA]

en·do·the·li·um (ĕn/dō thē/lĬ əm), n., pl. **-lia** (-lĬ ə). Anat. the tissue which lines blood vessels, lymphatics, serous cavities, and the like: a form of epithelium (in the broad sense). [NL, f. Gk.: endo- ENDO- + s. thēlē nipple + m. -ion]

en·do·ther·mic (ĕn/dō thûr/mĭk), adj. noting or pertaining to a chemical change which is accompanied by an absorption of heat (opposed to exothermic).

en·do·tox·in (ĕn/dō tŏk/sĬn), n. the toxic protoplasm of an organism which is liberated and causes its toxic action when the organism dies and disintegrates, as in Eberthella typhi, the causative agent of typhoid fever.

en·dow (ĕn dou/), v.t. **1.** to provide with a permanent fund or source of income: to endow a college. **2.** to furnish, as with some gift, faculty, or quality; equip: Nature has endowed him with great ability. **3.** Archaic. to provide with dower. [ME endow(en), t. OF: m. endouer, f. en- EN-¹ + douer, g. L dōtāre endow] —**en·dow/er,** n. —**Syn. 2.** invest, clothe, endue.

en·dow·ment (ĕn dou/mənt), n. **1.** act of endowing. **2.** that with which an institution, person, etc., is endowed, as property or funds. **3.** (usually pl.) an attribute of mind or body; a gift of nature. —**Syn. 3.** capacity, talent, faculties.

endowment insurance, a form of insurance providing for the payment of a fixed sum to the insured person at a specified time, or to his heirs, or a person designated, should he die before the time named.

end product, final or resulting product.

en·due (ĕn dū/, -dōō/), v.t., **-dued, -duing. 1.** to invest or endow with some gift, quality, or faculty: endued with life. **2.** to put on; assume. **3.** to clothe (fol. by with). Also, **indue.** [ME endew(en), t. OF: m. enduire, g. L indūcere lead into, confused with L induere put on]

en·dur·a·ble (ĕn dyŏor/ə bəl, -dōōr/-), adj. that may be endured. —**en·dur/a·bly,** adv. —**Syn.** bearable, tolerable.

en·dur·ance (ĕn dyŏor/əns, -dōōr/-), n. **1.** fact or power of enduring or bearing anything. **2.** lasting quality; duration. **3.** something endured, as a hardship. —**Syn. 1.** See **patience.**

en·dure (ĕn dyŏor/, -dōōr/), v., **-dured, -during.** —v.t. **1.** to hold out against; sustain without impairment or yielding; undergo. **2.** to bear without resistance or with patience; tolerate: I cannot endure to listen to that any longer. —v.i. **3.** to continue to exist; last. **4.** to support adverse force or influence of any kind; suffer without yielding; suffer patiently. [ME endure(n). t. OF: m. endurer, g. L indūrāre harden, ML endure] —**Syn. 2.** experience, stand. See **bear¹. 3.** abide, remain, persist. See **continue.**

en·dur·ing (ĕn dyŏor/Ĭng, -dōōr/-), adj. that endures; lasting; permanent. —**en·dur/ing·ly,** adv. —**en·dur/-ing·ness,** n.

end·ways (ĕnd/wāz/), adv. **1.** on end. **2.** with the end upward or forward. **3.** toward the ends or end; lengthwise. **4.** end to end. Also, **end·wise** (ĕnd/wĪz/).

En·dym·i·on (ĕn dĬm/Ĭ ən), n. Gk. Myth. a beautiful youth whom Selene caressed as he slept.

-ene, 1. a noun suffix used in chemistry, in names of hydro-carbons, as anthracene, benzene, napthhalene, specif. those of the olefine or ethylene series, as butylene. **2.** a generalized suffix used in trademarks for substances, often implying synthetic manufacture. [special use of -ene, adj. suffix (as in terrene), t. L: m. s. -ēnus (in Gk. -ēnos)]

ENE, east-northeast. Also, **E.N.E.**

en·e·ma (ĕn/ə mə), n., pl. enemas, enemata (ĕ nĕm/ə-tə). Med. a fluid injected into the rectum. [t. Gk.: injection, clyster]

en·e·my (ĕn/ə mĬ), n., pl. **-mies,** adj. —n. **1.** one who cherishes hatred or harmful designs against another; an adversary or opponent. **2.** an armed foe; an opposing military force. **3.** a hostile nation or state. **4.** a subject of such a state. **5.** something harmful or prejudicial. —adj. **6.** belonging to a hostile power or to any of its nationals: enemy property. **7.** Obs. inimical; ill-disposed. [ME, t. OF: m. enemi, g. L inimīcus unfriendly, hostile] —**Syn. 1.** ENEMY, FOE refer to a dangerous public or personal adversary. ENEMY emphasizes the idea of hostility: to overcome the enemy, a bitter enemy. FOE, a more literary word, may be used interchangeably with ENEMY, but emphasizes somewhat more the danger to be feared from such a one: deadly foe, arch foe of mankind (the Devil). —**Ant. 1.** friend. **2.** ally.

en·er·get·ic (ĕn/ər jĕt/Ĭk), adj. **1.** possessing or exhibiting energy; forcible; vigorous. **2.** powerful in action or effect; effective. [t. Gk.: m.s. energētikós active] —**en/er·get/i·cal·ly,** adv. —**Syn. 1.** See **active.** —**Aat. 1.** listless.

en·er·get·ics (ĕn/ər jĕt/Ĭks), n. the science of the laws of energy. [pl. of ENERGETIC. See -ICS]

en·er·gize (ĕn′ər jīz′), v., **-gized, -gizing.** —v.t. **1.** to give energy to; rouse into activity. —v.i. **2.** to be in operation; put forth energy. —**en′er·giz′er,** n.

en·er·gu·men (ĕn′ər gū′mən), n. **1.** one possessed by an evil spirit; a demoniac. **2.** a fanatical enthusiast. [t. LL: s. energūmenus, t. Gk.: m. energoúmenos, ppr. pass. of energein operate, influence]

en·er·gy (ĕn′ər jĭ), n., pl. **-gies. 1.** capacity or habit of vigorous activity. **2.** the actual exertion of power; operation; activity. **3.** power as exerted. **4.** ability to produce action or effect. **5.** vigor or forcefulness of expression. **6.** Physics. the property of a system which diminishes, when the system does work on any other system, by an amount equal to the work so done. [t. LL: m.s. energīa, t. Gk.: m. enérgeia agency, force] —**Syn. 1.** vigor, force, potency, zeal, push.

en·er·vate (v. ĕn′ər vāt′; adj. Ĭ nûr′vĬt), v., **-vated, -vating,** adj. —v.t. **1.** to deprive of nerve, force, or strength; destroy the vigor of; weaken. —adj. **2.** enervated. [t. L: m.s. ēnervātus, pp.] —**en′er·va′tion,** n. —**en′er·va′tor,** n.

en·face (ĕn fās′), v.t., **-faced, -facing. 1.** to write, print, or stamp something on the face of (a note, draft, etc.). **2.** to write, print, or stamp (something) on the face of a note, draft, etc. —**en·face′ment,** n.

en fa·mille (än fȧ mē′y), French. in the family.

en·fants per·dus (än fän pĕr dü′), French. a suicide squad or rear guard of soldiers. [F: lit., lost children]

en·fant ter·ri·ble (än fän tĕ rē′bl), French. **1.** a child that makes embarrassing remarks. **2.** an indiscreet and irresponsible person. [F: lit., terrible child]

en·fee·ble (ĕn fē′bəl), v.t., **-bled, -bling.** to make feeble; weaken. [ME enfeble(n), t. OF: m. enfeblir, der. en- EN-¹ + feble FEEBLE] —**en·fee′ble·ment,** n. —**en·fee′bler,** n.

en·feoff (ĕn fĕf′, -fēf′), v.t. **1.** to invest with a fief or fee. **2.** to give as a fief. **3.** to surrender. [ME enfeoffe(n), t. AF: m. enfeoffer. See EN-¹, FIEF] —**en·feoff′ment,** n.

en fête (än fět′), French. in festivity; in gala attire.

en·fet·ter (ĕn fět′ər), v.t. to bind with or as with fetters.

En·field (ĕn′fēld′), n. a city in SE England, in Middlesex, near London. 106,380 (est. 1946).

en·fi·lade (ĕn′fə lād′), n., v., **-laded, -lading.** Mil. —n. **1.** a situation of works, troops, etc., making them subject to a sweeping fire from along the length of a line of troops, a trench, a battery, etc. **2.** the fire thus directed. —v.t. **3.** to attack with an enfilade. [t. F, der. enfiler to thread, string, go through, rake with fire, der. en- EN-¹ + fil a thread]

en·fin (än fän′), adv. French. in conclusion; finally.

en·fleu·rage (än flœräzh′), n. a process of extracting perfumes by exposing inodorous oils or fats to the exhalations of flowers. [t. F, der. enfleurer impregnate with the scent of flowers, der. en- EN-¹ + fleur flower]

en·fold (ĕn fōld′), v.t. infold. —**en·fold′er,** n. —**en·fold′ment,** n.

en·force (ĕn fōrs′), v.t., **-forced, -forcing. 1.** to put or keep in force; compel obedience to: to enforce laws or rules. **2.** to obtain (payment, obedience, etc.) by force or compulsion. **3.** to impose (a course of action) upon a person; support (a demand, etc.) by force. **4.** to impress or urge (an argument, etc.) forcibly; lay stress upon. [ME enforce(n), t. OF: m. enforcier, ult. der. L. in- IN-¹ + fortis strong] —**en·force′a·ble,** adj. —**en·for·ced·ly** (ĕn fōr′sĬd lĬ), adv. —**en·forc′er,** n.

en·force·ment (ĕn fōrs′mənt), n. **1.** act or process of enforcing. **2.** Archaic. that which enforces.

en·fran·chise (ĕn frăn′chīz), v.t., **-chised, -chising. 1.** to grant a franchise to; admit to citizenship, esp. to the right of voting. **2.** to set free; liberate, as from slavery. [t. OF: m. enfranchiss-, s. enfranchir, der. en- EN-¹ + franc free, FRANK] —**en·fran·chise·ment** (ĕn frăn′chĬz mənt), n. —**en·fran′chis·er,** n.

Eng., 1. England. **2.** English.

eng., 1. engine. **2.** engineer. **3.** engineering. **4.** engraved. **5.** engraver. **6.** engraving.

En·ga·dine (ĕng′gə dēn′), n. the valley of the Inn river in E Switzerland: resorts. ab. 60 mi. long.

en·gage (ĕn gāj′), v., **-gaged, -gaging.** —v.t. **1.** to occupy the attention or efforts of (a person, etc.): he engaged her in conversation. **2.** to secure for aid, employment, use, etc.; hire: to engage a workman, to engage a room. **3.** to attract and hold fast: to engage the attention, interest, etc. **4.** to attract or please: his good nature engages everybody to him. **5.** to bind as by pledge, promise, contract, or oath; make liable: he engaged, verbally or by writing, to do it. **6.** to betroth (usually used in the passive). **7.** to bring (troops) into conflict; enter into conflict with: our army engaged the enemy. **8.** Mech. to cause to become interlocked; interlock with. **9.** Archaic. to entangle or involve. **10.** Archaic. to attach or secure. —v.i. **11.** to occupy oneself; become involved: to engage in business, politics. **12.** to take employment. **13.** to pledge one's word; assume an obligation. **14.** to cross weapons; enter into conflict. **15.** Mech. to interlock. [t. F: s. engager, der. en- EN-¹ + gage pledge, GAGE¹] —**en·gag′er,** n. —**Ant. 2.** discharge. **8.** release.

en·gaged (ĕn gājd′), adj. **1.** busy or occupied; involved. **2.** under engagement; pledged. **3.** betrothed. **4.** entered into conflict with. **5.** Mech. a. interlocked. b. (of wheels) in gear with each other. **6.** Archit. secured to, or (actually or apparently) partly sunk into, something else, as a column with respect to a wall.

en·gage·ment (ĕn gāj′mənt), n. **1.** act of engaging. **2.** state of being engaged. **3.** a pledge; an obligation or agreement. **4.** betrothal. **5.** employment, or a period or post of employment. **6.** an affair of business. **7.** an encounter, conflict, or battle. **8.** Mech. act or state of interlocking. **9.** (pl.) Com. financial obligations. —**Syn. 3.** contract, promise.

en·gag·ing (ĕn gā′jĬng), adj. winning; attractive; pleasing. —**en·gag′ing·ly,** adv. —**en·gag′ing·ness,** n.

en gar·çon (än gȧr sŏn′), French. as a bachelor.

en·gar·land (ĕn gär′lənd), v.t. encircle with a garland.

En·gels (ĕng′əls for 1; ĕng′gĕls for 2), n. **1.** Friedrich (frē′drĬkH), 1820–95, German socialist writer in England, associated with Karl Marx. **2.** a city in the E Soviet Union in Europe, on the Volga. 73,279 (1939).

en·gen·der (ĕn jĕn′dər), v.t. **1.** to produce, cause, or give rise to: hatred engenders violence. **2.** to beget; procreate. —v.i. **3.** to be produced or caused; come into existence. [ME engendre(n), t. OF: m. engendrer, g. L ingenerāre beget] —**en·gen′der·er,** n. —**en·gen′der·ment,** n. —**Syn. 1.** create, occasion, excite, stir up.

En·ghien (dän găn′; Belg. -gyän′), n. Duc d', (Louis Antoine Henry de Bourbon-Condé) 1772–1804, French prince, executed by Napoleon I.

engin., engineering.

en·gine (ĕn′jən), n. **1.** any mechanism or machine designed to convert energy into mechanical work: a steam engine, internal-combustion engine, etc. **2.** a railroad locomotive. **3.** any mechanical contrivance. **4.** a machine or instrument used in warfare, as a battering ram, catapult, piece of artillery, etc. **5.** Obs. an instrument of torture, esp. the rack. [ME engin, t. OF, g. L ingenium nature, invention]

engine driver, Brit. an engineer on a locomotive.

en·gi·neer (ĕn′jə nîr′), n. **1.** one versed in the design, construction, and use of engines or machines, or in any of the various branches of engineering: a mechanical engineer, an electrical, civil, etc. engineer. **2.** one who manages a stationary or locomotive engine. **3.** a member of the army or navy especially trained in engineering work. **4.** a skillful manager. —v.t. **5.** to plan, construct, or manage as an engineer. **6.** to arrange, manage, or carry through by skillful or artful contrivance.

en·gi·neer·ing (ĕn′jə nîr′Ĭng), n. **1.** the art or science of making practical application of the knowledge of pure sciences such as physics, chemistry, biology, etc. **2.** the action, work, or profession of an engineer. **3.** skillful or artful contrivance; maneuvering.

engineer's chain. See chain (def. 9).

engine house, a building in which a fire engine is stationed.

en·gine·ry (ĕn′jən rĬ), n. **1.** engines collectively. **2.** engines of war. **3.** skillful or artful contrivance.

en·gird (ĕn gûrd′), v.t., **-girt** or **-girded, -girding.** to encircle; encompass.

en·gir·dle (ĕn gûr′dəl), v.t., **-dled, -dling.** to engird.

en·gla·cial (ĕn glā′shəl), adj. Geol. **1.** within the ice of a glacier. **2.** believed to have been formerly within the ice of a glacier: englacial debris.

Eng·land (Ĭng′glənd), n. the largest division of the United Kingdom, occupying all of the island of Great Britain except Scotland and Wales. 38,468,000 pop. (est. 1946); 50,327 sq. mi. Cap.: London. Latin, **Anglia.** [ME Engeland, OE Englaland land of the English]

Eng·land·er (Ĭng′glən dər), n. a native of England.

Eng·lish (Ĭng′glĬsh), adj. **1.** of, perta ning to, or characteristic of England or its inhabitants, institutions, etc. **2.** belonging or pertaining to, or spoken or written in, the English language. —n. **3.** the people of England collectively, esp. as distinguished from the Scotch, Welsh, and Irish. **4.** the Germanic language of the British Isles, widespread and standard also in the U.S. and most of the British Empire, historically termed Old English or Anglo-Saxon (to 1150), Middle English (to 1450), and Modern English. **5.** (l.c.) U.S. Billiards. a spinning motion imparted to a ball by a quick stroke on one side of its center. **6.** a printing type (14 point) of a size between pica and Columbian. —v.t. **7.** to translate into English. **8.** to adopt (a foreign word) into English. **9.** (l.c.) U.S. Billiards. to impart english to (a ball). [ME; OE Englisc, der. Engle. Angle the English. See ANGLE]

English Channel, an arm of the Atlantic between England and France, connected with the North Sea by the Strait of Dover. ab. 350 mi. long; 20–100 mi. wide.

English daisy, Chiefly U.S. the common European daisy, Bellis perennis.

English horn, the alto of the oboe family, richer in tone, and a fifth lower in pitch than the oboe.

Eng·lish·ism (Ĭng′glĬsh Ĭz′əm), n. **1.** a Briticism. **2.** attachment to what is English.

English ivy. See ivy (def. 1).

Eng·lish·man (Ĭng′glĬsh mən), n., pl. **-men. 1.** a native or a naturalized citizen of England. **2.** an English ship.

Man playing an English horn

Englishman's tie, Naut. a method of tying two rope ends or pieces of gut together by making an overhand knot in each around the other.

---

b., blend of, blended; c., cognate with; d., dialect, dialectal; der., derived from; f., formed from; g., going back to; m., modification of; r., replacing; s., stem of; t., taken from; ?, perhaps. See the full key on inside cover.

Eng·lish·ness (Ĭng′glĭsh nĭs), *n.* quality of being English.

English Pale. See **pale** (def. 6).

English Revolution, The, *Eng. Hist.* the convulsion of 1688–89 by which James II was expelled and the sovereignty conferred on William and Mary.

Eng·lish·ry (ĭng′glĭsh rĭ), *n.* **1.** state of being English. **2.** a population that is English or of English descent.

English setter, a type of setter dog, usually black and white, tan and white, or pure white, with a rangy body.

English sonnet, the Elizabethan or Shakespearean sonnet.

English sparrow, sparrow (def. 1).

English setter
(23 to 25 in. high)

English walnut, 1. a walnut tree, *Juglans regia.* **2.** the nut of this tree, widely used in cookery.

Eng·lish·wom·an (ĭng′glĭsh wŏŏm′ən), *n., pl.* **-wom·en.** a woman who is a native or citizen of England.

en·gorge (ĕn gôrj′), *v.t.,* **-gorged, -gorging. 1.** to swallow greedily; glut or gorge. **2.** *Pathol.* to congest with blood. [t. F: m.s. *engorger,* der. en- EN-[1] + *gorge* GORGE] **—en·gorge′ment,** *n.*

engr., 1. engineer. **2.** engraved. **3.** engraver.

en·graft (ĕn grăft′, -gräft′), *v.t.* to insert, as a scion of one tree or plant into another, for propagation: *to engraft a peach on a plum.* Also, **ingraft.**

en·grail (ĕn grāl′), *v.t.* to ornament the edge of with curved indentations. [ME *engrele(n),* t. OF: m. *engresler,* der. en- EN-[1] + *gresle* hail] **—en·grail′ment,** *n.*

en·grain (ĕn grān′), *v.t., adj.* ingrain. [ME, f. EN-[1] + GRAIN. Cf. F *en graine* where *graine* means cochineal dye]

en·gram (ĕn′grăm), *n.* **1.** *Biol.* the durable mark caused by a stimulus upon protoplasm. **2.** *Psychol.* trace[1] (def. 6)

en·grave (ĕn grāv′), *v.t.,* **-graved, -graving. 1.** to chase (letters, designs, etc.) on a hard surface, as of metal, stone, or the end grain of wood. **2.** to print from such a surface. **3.** to mark or ornament with incised letters, designs, etc. **4.** to impress deeply; infix. [f. EN-[1] + GRAVE[3], v., modeled on F *engraver*] **—en·grav′er,** *n.*

en·grav·ing (ĕn grā′vĭng), *n.* **1.** the act or art of one that engraves. **2.** the art of forming designs by cutting, corrosion by acids, a photographic process, etc., on the surface of metal plates or of blocks of wood, etc., for purpose of taking off impressions or prints of the design so formed. **3.** the design engraved. **4.** an engraved plate or block. **5.** an impression or print from this.

en·gross (ĕn grōs′), *v.t.* **1.** to occupy wholly, as the mind or attention; absorb. **2.** to write or copy in a fair, large hand or in a formal manner, as a public document or record. **3.** to acquire the whole of (a commodity), in order to control the market; monopolize. [ME *engross-(en),* t. AF: m. *engrosser* write large; also t. OF, der. *en gros* in large quantities, g. L in- IN-[2] + LL *grossus* thick, GROSS] **—en·gross′er,** *n.*

en·gross·ing (ĕn grō′sĭng), *adj.* fully occupying the mind or attention; absorbing. **—en·gross′ing·ly,** *adv.*

en·gross·ment (ĕn grōs′mənt), *n.* **1.** act of engrossing. **2.** an engrossed copy of a document.

en·gulf (ĕn gŭlf′), *v.t.* to swallow up in or as in a gulf; submerge. Also, **ingulf.** **—en·gulf′ment,** *n.*

en·hance (ĕn hăns′, -häns′), *v.t.,* **-hanced, -hancing. 1.** to raise to a higher degree; intensify; magnify. **2.** to raise the value or price of. [ME *enhaunce(n),* t. AF: m. *enhauncer,* nasalized var. of OF *enhaucier,* f. en- EN-[1] + *haucier* raise. See HAWSER.] **—en·hance′ment,** *n.* **—en·hanc′er,** *n.* **—Syn. 2.** See **elevate.** **—Ant. 1.** diminish. **2.** reduce.

en·har·mon·ic (ĕn′här mŏn′ĭk), *adj. Music.* having the same pitch in the tempered scale but written in different notation, as G-sharp and A-flat. [t. LL: s. *enharmonicus* in accord, t. Gk.: m. *enarmonikós*] **—en′har·mon′i·cal·ly,** *adv.*

E·nid (ē′nĭd), *n.* **1.** a city in N Oklahoma. 36,017 (1950). **2.** *Arthurian Romance.* the beautiful wife of Sir Geraint in Tennyson's *Idylls of the King.*

e·nig·ma (ĭ nĭg′mə), *n.* **1.** something puzzling or inexplicable. **2.** a saying, question, picture, etc., containing a hidden meaning; a riddle. [t. L: m. *aenigma,* t. Gk.: m. *ainigma* riddle] **—Syn. 1.** See **puzzle.**

en·ig·mat·ic (ĕn′ĭg măt′ĭk, ē′nĭg-), *adj.* resembling an enigma; perplexing; mysterious. Also, **en′ig·mat′i·cal.** **—en′ig·mat′i·cal·ly,** *adv.*

en·isle (ĕn īl′), *v.t.,* **-isled, -isling.** *Poetic.* **1.** to make an island of. **2.** to place on an island. **3.** to isolate.

en·jamb·ment (ĕn jăm′mənt, -jämb′-; *Fr.* äɴ zhäɴbmäɴ′), *n. Pros.* the running on of the thought from one line or couplet to the next. Also, **en·jambe′ment.** [t. F: m. *enjambement,* der. *enjamber* stride over, project, der. en- EN-[1] + *jambe* leg]

en·join (ĕn join′), *v.t.* **1.** to order or direct (a person, etc.) to do something; prescribe (a course of action, etc.) with authority or emphasis. **2.** *Law.* to prohibit or restrain by an injunction. [ME *enjoyn(en),* t. OF: m. *enjoindre,* g. L *injungere* join into or to, impose, enjoin] **—en·join′er,** *n.* **—en·join′ment,** *n.* **—Syn. 1.** charge.

en·joy (ĕn joi′), *v.t.* **1.** to experience with joy; take pleasure in. **2.** to have and use with satisfaction; have

the benefit of. **3.** to find or experience pleasure for (oneself). [ME *enjoye(n),* t. OF: m. *enjoir,* f. en- EN-[1] + *joir* JOY, v.] **—en·joy′er,** *n.*

en·joy·a·ble (ĕn joi′ə bəl), *adj.* that may be enjoyed; affording enjoyment. **—en·joy′a·ble·ness,** *n.* **—en·joy′a·bly,** *adv.*

en·joy·ment (ĕn joi′mənt), *n.* **1.** the possession, use, or occupancy of anything with satisfaction or pleasure. **2.** a particular form or source of pleasure. **3.** *Law.* the exercise of a right: *the enjoyment of an estate.* **—Syn. 1.** delight, delectation, gratification. See **pleasure.**

en·kin·dle (ĕn kĭn′dəl), *v.t., v.i.,* **-dled, -dling.** to kindle into flame, ardor, activity, etc. **—en·kin′dler,** *n.*

enl., enlarged.

en·lace (ĕn lās′), *v.t.* **-laced, -lacing. 1.** to bind or encircle as with a lace or cord. **2.** to interlace; intertwine. [ME *enlase(n),* t. F: m. *enlacer,* f. en- EN-[1] + *lacier* LACE, v.] **—en·lace′ment,** *n.*

en·large (ĕn lärj′), *v.,* **-larged, -larging. —v.t. 1.** to make larger; increase in extent, bulk, or quantity; add to. **2.** to increase the capacity or scope of; expand. **3.** *Photog.* to make (a print) larger than the negative, by projection printing. **—v.i. 4.** to grow larger; increase; expand. **5.** to speak or write at large; expatiate: *to enlarge upon a point.* [ME *enlargen,* t. OF: m. *enlarger,* der. en- EN-[1] + *large* LARGE] **—en·large′a·ble,** *adj.* **—en·larg′er,** *n.* **—Syn. 1.** extend, augment, amplify, dilate. See **increase.** **—Ant. 1.** diminish. **2.** contract.

en·large·ment (ĕn lärj′mənt), *n.* **1.** act of enlarging; increase; expansion; amplification. **2.** anything, as a photograph, that is an enlarged form of something else. **3.** anything that enlarges something else; an addition.

en·light·en (ĕn lī′tən), *v.t.* **1.** to give intellectual or spiritual light to; instruct; impart knowledge to. **2.** *Archaic and Poetic.* to shed light upon. **—en·light′en·er,** *n.* **—Syn. 1.** illumine, edify, teach, inform.

en·light·en·ment (ĕn lī′tən mənt), *n.* **1.** act of enlightening. **2.** state of being enlightened. **3. the Enlightenment,** an 18th century philosophical movement characterized by rationalism.

en·list (ĕn lĭst′), *v.i.* **1.** to engage for military or naval service by enrolling after mutual agreement. **2.** to enter into some cause, enterprise, etc. **—v.t. 3.** to engage for military or naval service: *to enlist men for the army.* **4.** to secure (a person, services, etc.) for some cause, enterprise, etc. **—en·list′er,** *n.*

enlisted man, any male member of the U. S. armed services who is not a commissioned officer or a warrant officer, nurse, or cadet.

en·list·ment (ĕn lĭst′mənt), *n.* **1.** the period of years for which a man or woman engages to serve in the armed forces of his country. **2.** act of enlisting.

en·liv·en (ĕn lī′vən), *v.t.* **1.** to make vigorous or active; invigorate. **2.** to make sprightly, gay, or cheerful; brighten. [f. obs. *enlive* enliven (der. EN-[1] + LIVE, adj.) + -EN[1]] **—en·liv′en·er,** *n.* **—en·liv′en·ment,** *n.* **—Syn. 1.** animate, inspirit, vivify, stimulate, quicken. **2.** exhilarate, gladden. See **cheer.** **—Ant. 2.** depress.

en masse (ĕn măs′; *Fr.* äɴ mȧs′), *French.* in a mass or body; all together.

en·mesh (ĕn mĕsh′), *v.t.* to catch, as in a net; entangle. Also, **immesh, inmesh.**

en·mi·ty (ĕn′mə tĭ), *n., pl.* **-ties.** a feeling or condition of hostility; hatred; ill will; animosity; antagonism. [ME *enemyte,* t. OF: m. *ennemistie,* der. L *inimicus* enemy]

en·ne·ad (ĕn′ĭ ăd′), *n.* **1.** a group of nine persons or things. **2.** (*cap.*) nine gods in Egyptian religion. [t. Gk.: s. *enneás,* der. *ennéa* nine] **—en′ne·ad′ic,** *adj.*

En·ni·us (ĕn′ĭ əs), *n.* Quintus (kwĭn′təs), 239–169? B.C., Roman poet.

en·no·ble (ĕn nō′bəl), *v.t.,* **-bled, -bling. 1.** to elevate in degree, excellence, or respect; dignify; exalt. **2.** to confer a title of nobility on. **—en·no′ble·ment,** *n.* **—en·no′bler,** *n.*

en·nui (än′wē; *Fr.* äɴ nwē′), *n.* a feeling of weariness and discontent resulting from satiety or lack of interest; boredom. [t. F, g. L *in odiō.* See ANNOY, n.]

E·noch (ē′nək), *n. Bible.* **1.** the father of Methuselah. Gen. 5: 18–24. **2.** the eldest son of Cain. Gen. 4:17, 18.

e·nol (ē′nŏl, ē′nōl), *n. Chem.* an organic compound containing a hydroxyl group attached to a doubly linked carbon atom as in C=C-OH. [appar. f. Gk. (*h*)*ēn* (neut of *heis* one) + -OL[1]] **—e·nol·ic** (ē nŏl′ĭk), *adj.*

e·nor·mi·ty (ĭ nôr′mə tĭ), *n., pl.* **-ties. 1.** outrageous or heinous character; atrociousness: *the enormity of his offenses.* **2.** something outrageous or heinous, as an offense. [t. L: m.s. *ēnormitas* hugeness, irregularity]

e·nor·mous (ĭ nôr′məs), *adj.* **1.** greatly exceeding the common size, extent, etc.; huge; immense. **2.** outrageous or atrocious: *enormous wickedness.* [t. L: m. *ēnormis* huge] **—e·nor′mous·ly,** *adv.* **—e·nor′mous·ness,** *n.* **—Syn. 1.** vast, colossal, gigantic, mammoth, prodigious, stupendous. See **huge.**

E·nos (ē′nəs), *n. Bible.* the son of Seth. Gen. 5:6.

e·nough (ĭ nŭf′), *adj.* **1.** adequate for the want or need; sufficient for the purpose or to satisfy desire: *I've had enough of it, noise enough to wake the dead.* **—n. 2.** an adequate quantity or number; a sufficiency. **—adv. 3.** in a quantity or degree that answers a purpose or satisfies a need or desire; sufficiently. **4.** fully or quite: *ready enough.* **5.** tolerably or passably: *he sings well enough.* **—interj. 6.** it (or that) is enough! [ME *enogh,* OE *genōh,* c. G *genug*]

e·nounce (ĭ nouns´), *v.t.*, **enounced, enouncing.** **1.** to announce, declare, or proclaim. **2.** to state definitely, as a proposition. **3.** to utter or pronounce, as words. [t. F: m.s. *énoncer*, t. L: m. *ēnuntiāre*] —**e·nounce´ment**, *n.*

e·now (ĭ nou´; *formerly* ĭ nō´), *adj.*, *adv. Archaic.* enough. [ME; OE *genōg(e)* enough]

en pas·sant (än på sän´), *French.* **1.** in passing; by the way. **2.** *Chess.* a method of taking a pawn. When, on moving a pawn two squares, an adversary's pawn is in a position to take the pawn moved if it were moved but one square, the moving pawn may be taken *en passant.*

en·plane (ĕn plān´), *v.i.,* **-planed, -planing.** to enter an airplane.

en prise (än prēz´), *French.* (in chess) in line for capture; likely to be captured.

en·quire (ĕn kwīr´), *v.t., v.i.,* **-quired, -quiring.** inquire.

en·quir·y (ĕn kwīr´ĭ), *n., pl.* **-quiries.** inquiry.

en·rage (ĕn rāj´), *v.t.,* **-raged, -raging.** to put into a rage; infuriate. [t. OF: m.s. *enrager*, der. *en-* EN-[1] + *rage* RAGE] —**en·rage´ment**, *n.*
—**Syn.** ENRAGE, INCENSE, INFURIATE imply stirring to violent anger. To ENRAGE is to provoke a display of wrath: *enrage him by deliberate and continual injustice.* To INCENSE is to inflame with indignation or anger; the connotation is serious provocation present or prolonged: *to incense one by making insulting remarks.* To INFURIATE is to arouse suddenly to fury or fierce and vehement anger: *infuriate him by a false accusation.* —**Ant.** appease, pacify.

en rap·port (än rå pôr´), *French.* in sympathy or accord; in agreement; congenial.

en·rapt (ĕn răpt´), *adj.* rapt; transported; enraptured.

en·rap·ture (ĕn răp´chər), *v.t.,* **-tured, -turing.** to move to rapture; delight beyond measure.

en·reg·is·ter (ĕn rĕj´ĭs tər), *v.t.* to register; record.

en rè·gle (än rĕ´gl), *French.* according to rule; in due form.

en·rich (ĕn rĭch´), *v.t.* **1.** to supply with riches, wealth, abundant or valuable possessions, etc.: *commerce enriches a nation.* **2.** to supply with abundance of anything desirable: *to enrich the mind with knowledge.* **3.** to make finer in quality as by supplying desirable elements or ingredients: *to enrich bread or soil.* [ME *enrich(en)*, t. OF: m. *enrichir,* der. *en-* EN-[1] + *riche* RICH] —**en·rich´er,** *n.*

en·rich·ment (ĕn rĭch´mənt), *n.* **1.** act of enriching. **2.** state of being enriched. **3.** something that enriches.

en·robe (ĕn rōb´), *v.t.,* **-robed, -robing.** to dress; attire.

en·rol (ĕn rōl´), *v.t.,* **-rolled, -rolling.** enroll.

en·roll (ĕn rōl´), *v.t.* **1.** to write (a name), or insert the name of (a person), in a roll or register; place upon a list. **2.** to enlist (oneself). **3.** to put in a record; record. **4.** to roll or wrap up. [ME *enroll(en),* t. OF: m. *enroller,* der. *en-* EN-[1] + *rolle* ROLL, n.] —**en·roll´er,** *n.*

en·roll·ment (ĕn rōl´mənt), *n.* **1.** act of enrolling; process of being enrolled. **2.** the number of persons enrolled, as for a course or in a school. Also, **en·rol´ment.**

en·root (ĕn rōōt´, -rŏŏt´), *v.t.* **1.** to fix by the root. **2.** to fix fast; implant deeply.

en route (än rōōt´; *Fr.* än), on the way. [F]

ens (ĕnz), *n., pl.* **entia** (ĕn´shĭ ə). *Metaphys.* being, considered in the abstract. [t. LL, ppr. neut. of *esse* be]

Ens., Ensign.

en·sam·ple (ĕn săm´pəl), *n. Archaic.* example.

en·san·guine (ĕn săng´gwĭn), *v.t.,* **-guined, -guining.** to stain or cover with blood. [der. EN-[1] + SANGUINE]

En·sche·de (ĕn´sкнə dā´), *n.* a city in E Netherlands. 97,574 (est. 1946).

en·sconce (ĕn skŏns´), *v.t.,* **-sconced, -sconcing.** **1.** to cover or shelter; hide securely. **2.** to settle securely or snugly: *ensconce in an armchair.* [der. EN-[1] + SCONCE[2]]

en·sem·ble (än säm´bəl; *Fr.* än sän´bl), *n.* **1.** all the parts of a thing taken together, so that each part is considered only in relation to the whole. **2.** the entire costume of an individual, esp. when all the parts are in harmony. **3.** the general effect, as of a work of art. **4.** *Music.* **a.** the united performance of the full number of singers, musicians, etc. **b.** the group so performing: *a string ensemble.* —*adv.* **5.** together; all at once; simultaneously. [ME, t. F, g. LL *insimul* at the same time]

en·shrine (ĕn shrīn´), *v.t.,* **-shrined, -shrining.** **1.** to enclose in or as in a shrine. **2.** to cherish as sacred. Also, **inshrine.** —**en·shrine´ment,** *n.*

en·shroud (ĕn shroud´), *v.t.* to shroud; conceal.

en·si·form (ĕn´sə fôrm´), *adj. Biol.* sword-shaped; xiphoid. [f. L *ensi(s)* sword + -FORM]

en·sign (ĕn´sīn; *Mil.* ĕn´sən), *n.* **1.** a flag or banner, as of a nation. **2.** a badge of office or authority. **3.** any sign, token, or emblem. **4.** *U.S. Navy.* the lowest commissioned officer, ranking next below a lieutenant (junior grade), and equal to a second lieutenant in the Army. **5.** a standard bearer, formerly one in the British Army. [ME *ensaigne,* t. OF: m. *enseigne,* g. L *insignia* insignia] —**en´sign·ship´, en´sign·cy,** *n.*

en·si·lage (ĕn´sə lĭj), *n., v.,* **-laged, -laging.** —*n.* **1.** the preservation of green fodder in a silo or pit. **2.** fodder thus preserved. —*v.t.* **3.** ensile. [t. F, der. *ensiler* ENSILE]

en·sile (ĕn sīl´, ĕn´sīl), *v.t.,* **-siled, -siling.** **1.** to preserve (green fodder) in a silo. **2.** to make into ensilage. [t. F: m.s. *ensiler,* t. Sp.: m. *ensilar,* der. *en-* EN-[1] + *silo* SILO]

en·slave (ĕn slāv´), *v.t.,* **-slaved, -slaving.** to make a slave of; reduce to slavery. —**en·slave´ment,** *n.* —**en·slav´er,** *n.*

en·snare (ĕn snâr´), *v.t.,* **-snared, -snaring.** to capture in, or involve as in, a snare. Also, **insnare.** —**en·snare´ment,** *n.* —**en·snar´er,** *n.* —**Syn.** entrap, entangle, enmesh. —**Ant.** release.

en·soul (ĕn sōl´), *v.t.* to endow with a soul. Also, **insoul.**

en·sphere (ĕn sfĭr´), *v.t.,* **-sphered, -sphering.** to enclose in or as in a sphere. Also, **insphere.**

en·sta·tite (ĕn´stə tīt´), *n.* a mineral of the pyroxene group, occurring as an important constituent of basic igneous rocks. [f. s. Gk. *enstátēs* adversary + -ITE[1]; so called because of its refractory nature]

en·sue (ĕn sōō´), *v.i.,* **-sued, -suing.** **1.** to follow in order; come afterward, esp. in immediate succession. **2.** to follow as a consequence, or result. [ME *ensewe(n),* t. OF: m. *ensuivre,* g. L *insequī* follow close upon] —**Syn.** 1, 2. See **follow.** —**Ant.** 2. cause.

en suite (än swēt´; *Fr.* än), *French.* in succession; in a series or set.

en·sure (ĕn shŏŏr´), *v.t.,* **-sured, -suring.** **1.** to secure, or bring surely, as to a person: *this letter will ensure you a hearing.* **2.** to make sure or certain to come, occur, etc.: *measures to ensure the success of an undertaking.* **3.** to make secure or safe, as from harm. **4.** *Obsolesc.* to insure. [ME *ensure(n),* t. AF: m. *enseurer,* der. *en-* EN-[1] + OF *seur* SURE]

en·swathe (ĕn swāth´), *v.t.,* **-swathed, -swathing.** to swathe. Also, **inswathe.** —**en·swathe´ment,** *n.*

-ent, a suffix equivalent to **-ant,** in adjectives and nouns, as in *ardent, dependent, different, expedient.* [t. L: stem ending of ppr. in vbs. of conjugations 2, 3, 4]

en·tab·la·ture (ĕn tăb´lə chər), *n.* **1.** that part of a classic architectural order which rests horizontally upon the columns and consists of the architrave, frieze, and cornice. See diag. under **column.** **2.** a similar part in other constructions. [t. It.: m. *intavolatura,* der. *intavolare* board up]

en·tail (ĕn tāl´), *v.t.* **1.** to bring on or involve by necessity or consequences: *a loss entailing no regret.* **2.** to impose as a burden. **3.** to limit the inheritance of (a landed estate) to a specified line of heirs, so that it cannot be alienated, devised, or bequeathed. **4.** to cause (anything) to descend to a fixed series of possessors. —*n.* **5.** act of entailing. **6.** state of being entailed. **7.** any predetermined order of succession, as to an office. **8.** that which is entailed, as an estate. **9.** the rule of descent settled for an estate. [f. EN-[1] + TAIL[2]] —**en·tail´ment,** *n.*

en·tan·gle (ĕn tăng´gəl), *v.t.,* **-gled, -gling.** **1.** to make tangled; complicate (usually used in the passive). **2.** to involve in anything like a tangle; ensnare; enmesh. **3.** to involve in difficulties; embarrass; perplex. —**en·tang´ler,** *n.* —**Syn.** 3. bewilder, confuse. See **involve.**

en·tan·gle·ment (ĕn tăng´gəl mənt), *n.* **1.** act of entangling. **2.** state of being entangled. **3.** that which entangles; a snare; an embarrassment; a complication.

en·ta·sis (ĕn´tə sĭs), *n. Archit.* the swelling or outward curve of the shaft of a column. [t. NL, t. Gk.: a stretching]

En·teb·be (ĕn tĕb´ĕ), *n.* the capital of Uganda, in E Africa, on Lake Victoria. ab. 6000.

en·tel·e·chy (ĕn tĕl´ə kĭ), *n., pl.* **-chies.** **1.** a realization or actuality as opposed to a potentiality. **2.** (in vitalist philosophy) the vital force or principle directing growth and life. [t. L: m.s. *entelechīa,* t. Gk., der. *en telei echein* be in fulfillment or completion]

en·tel·lus (ĕn tĕl´əs), *n.* the sacred monkey or langur of India, *Semnopithecus entellus,* having a long tail, a beard, and a caplike growth of hair. [NL; appar. named after *Entellus,* character (elderly man) in "Aeneid"]

en·tente (än tänt´; *Fr.* än tänt´), *n.* **1.** understanding. **2.** the parties to an understanding. [t. F]

en·tente cor·diale (än tänt´ kôr dyäl´), *French.* a friendly understanding, esp. between two governments.

en·ter (ĕn´tər), *v.i.* **1.** to come or go in. **2.** to make an entrance, as on the stage. **3.** to be admitted. **4.** to make a beginning (often fol. by *on* or *upon*). **5.** enter into, **a.** to take an interest or part in; engage in. **b.** to take up the consideration of (a subject). **c.** to sympathize with (a person's feelings, etc.). **d.** to assume the obligation of. **e.** to become a party to. **f.** to make a beginning in. **g.** to form a constituent part or ingredient of: *lead enters into the composition of pewter.* —*v.t.* **6.** to come or go into. **7.** to penetrate or pierce: *the bullet entered the flesh.* **8.** to put in or insert: *to enter a wedge.* **9.** to become a member of, or join. **10.** to cause to be admitted, as into a school, competition, etc. **11.** to make a beginning of or in, or begin upon; engage or become involved in. **12.** to make a record of; record or register. **13.** *Law.* **a.** to place in regular form before a court, as a writ. **b.** to occupy or to take possession of (lands); make an entrance, entry, ingress in, under claim of a right to possession. **c.** to file an application for (public lands). **14.** to report (a vessel, etc.) at the customhouse. [ME *entre(n),* t. OF: m. *entrer,* g. L *intrāre* go into] —**en´ter·a·ble,** *adj.* —**en´ter·er,** *n.* —**Ant.** 1. leave. 8. remove.

en·ter·ic (ĕn tĕr´ĭk), *adj.* **1.** pertaining to the enteron; intestinal. **2.** *Brit.* typhoid fever. [t. Gk.: m.s. *enterikós,* der. *énteron* intestine]

---

b., blend of, blended; c., cognate with; d., dialect, dialectal; der., derived from; f., formed from; g., going back to; m., modification of; r., replacing; s., stem of; t., taken from; ?, perhaps. See the full key on inside cover.

enteric fever, typhoid fever.

en·ter·i·tis (ĕn'tərī'tĭs), *n.* *Pathol.* inflammation of the intestines.

entero-, a word element meaning "intestine," as in *enterotoxemia.* [t. Gk., comb. form of *énteron*]

en·ter·on (ĕn'tərŏn'), *n.,* *pl.* **-tera** (-tərə). *Anat., Zool.* the alimentary canal; the digestive tract. [NL, t. Gk.: intestine]

en·ter·os·to·my (ĕn'tərŏs'təmĭ), *n.,* *pl.* **-mies.** *Surg.* the making of an artificial opening into the small intestine, which opens onto the abdominal wall, for feeding or drainage.

en·ter·o·tox·e·mi·a (ĕn'tərōtŏksē'mĭə), *n.* *Vet. Sci.* a disease of sheep caused by severe systemic poisoning from bacterial toxins in the intestinal tract.

en·ter·prise (ĕn'tərprīz'), *n.* **1.** a project undertaken or to be undertaken, esp. one that is of some importance or that requires boldness or energy. **2.** engagement in such projects. **3.** boldness or readiness in undertaking, adventurous spirit, or energy. [ME, t. OF: m. *entreprise,* der. *entreprendre* take in hand, f. *entre-* INTER- + *prendre* seize, take (g. L *prehendere*)] —**Syn. 1.** plan, undertaking, venture.

en·ter·pris·ing (ĕn'tərprī'zĭng), *adj.* ready to undertake projects of importance or difficulty, or untried schemes; energetic in carrying out any undertaking. —**en'ter·pris'ing·ly,** *adv.* —**Syn.** See **ambitious.** —**Ant.** timid.

en·ter·tain (ĕn'tərtān'), *v.t.* **1.** to hold the attention of agreeably; divert; amuse. **2.** to receive as a guest, esp. at one's table; show hospitality to. **3.** to give admittance or reception to. **4.** to admit into the mind; consider. **5.** to hold in the mind; harbor; cherish. **6.** *Archaic.* to maintain or keep up. —*v.i.* **7.** to exercise hospitality; entertain company; provide entertainment for guests. [late ME *entertene(n),* t. F: m. *entretenir,* f. *entre-* INTER- + *tenir* (g. L *tenēre* hold)] —**Syn. 1.** See **amuse.**

en·ter·tain·er (ĕn'tərtā'nər), *n.* **1.** one who entertains. **2.** a singer, reciter, or the like, who gives, or takes part in, public entertainments.

en·ter·tain·ing (ĕn'tərtā'nĭng), *adj.* affording entertainment; amusing; diverting. —**en'ter·tain'ing·ly,** *adv.* —**en'ter·tain'ing·ness,** *n.*

en·ter·tain·ment (ĕn'tərtān'mənt), *n.* **1.** act of entertaining; agreeable occupation for the mind, diversion, or amusement. **2.** something affording diversion or amusement, esp. an exhibition or performance of some kind. **3.** hospitable provision for the wants of guests. **4.** *Obs.* maintenance in service.

en·thet·ic (ĕnthĕt'ĭk), *adj.* introduced from without, as diseases propagated by inoculation. [t. Gk.: m.s. *enthetikós* fit for implanting]

en·thral (ĕnthrôl'), *v.t.,* **-thralled, -thralling.** enthrall. —**en·thral'ment,** *n.*

en·thrall (ĕnthrôl'), *v.t.* **1.** to captivate; charm. **2.** to put or hold in thraldom; subjugate. Also, **enthrall, inthral.** —**en·thrall'er,** *n.* —**en·thrall'ment,** *n.*

en·throne (ĕnthrōn'), *v.t.,* **-throned, -throning. 1.** to place on or as on a throne. **2.** to invest with sovereign or episcopal authority. **3.** to exalt. Also, **inthrone.** —**en·throne'ment, en·thron·i·za·tion** (ĕnthrō'nəzā'shən), *n.*

en·thuse (ĕnthōōz'), *v.,* **-thused, -thusing.** *U.S. Colloq.* —*v.i.* **1.** to become enthusiastic; show enthusiasm. —*v.t.* **2.** to move to enthusiasm. [back formation from ENTHUSIASM]

en·thu·si·asm (ĕnthōō'zĭăz'əm), *n.* **1.** absorbing or controlling possession of the mind by any interest or pursuit; lively interest. **2.** *Archaic.* extravagant religious emotion. [t. LL: s. *enthūsiasmus,* t. Gk.: m. *enthousiasmós*] —**Syn. 1.** eagerness, warmth, fervor, zeal, ardor. —**Ant. 1.** indifference.

en·thu·si·ast (ĕnthōō'zĭăst'), *n.* **1.** one who is filled with enthusiasm for some principle, pursuit, etc.; a person of ardent zeal. **2.** a religious visionary or fanatic. —**Syn. 1.** zealot, devotee.

en·thu·si·as·tic (ĕnthōō'zĭăs'tĭk), *adj.* **1.** full of or characterized by enthusiasm; ardent. **2.** pertaining to or of the nature of enthusiasm. —**en·thu'si·as'ti·cal·ly,** *adv.* —**Syn. 1.** zealous, eager, fervent, passionate.

en·thy·meme (ĕn'thəmēm'), *n.* *Logic.* a syllogism in which one premise is unexpressed. [t. L: m.s. *enthȳmēma,* t. Gk.: thought, argument]

en·tice (ĕntīs'), *v.t.,* **-ticed, -ticing.** to draw on by exciting hope or desire; allure; inveigle. [ME *entyce(n),* t. OF: m. *enticier* incite, der. L *titio* firebrand] —**en·tic'er,** *n.* —**en·tic'ing·ly,** *adv.* —**Syn.** lure, attract, decoy, tempt.

en·tice·ment (ĕntīs'mənt), *n.* **1.** act or practice of enticing, esp. to evil. **2.** state of being enticed. **3.** that which entices; an allurement.

en·tire (ĕntīr'), *adj.* **1.** having all the parts or elements; whole; complete. **2.** not broken, mutilated, or decayed; intact. **3.** unimpaired or undiminished. **4.** being wholly of one piece; undivided; continuous. **5.** *Bot.* without notches or indentations, as leaves. **6.** full or thorough: *entire freedom of choice.* **7.** not gelded: *an entire horse.* **8.** *Obs.* wholly of one kind; unmixed or pure. —*n.* **9.** the whole; entirety. **10.** an entire horse; a stallion. **11.** *Brit.* a kind of malt liquor; porter. [ME *enter,* t. OF: m. *entier,* g. L *integrum,* acc. of *integer* untouched, whole] —**en·tire'ness,** *n.* —**Syn. 1.** See **complete.** —**Ant. 1.** partial. **2.** defective.

en·tire·ly (ĕntīr'lĭ), *adv.* **1.** wholly or fully; completely or unreservedly. **2.** solely or exclusively.

en·tire·ty (ĕntīr'tĭ), *n.,* *pl.* **-ties. 1.** state of being entire; completeness. **2.** that which is entire; the whole.

en·ti·tle (ĕntī'təl), *v.t.,* **-tled, -tling. 1.** to give (a person or thing) a title, right, or claim to something; furnish with grounds for laying claim. **2.** to call by a particular title or name; name. **3.** to designate (a person) by an honorary title. Also, **intitle.** [ME *entitle(n),* t. OF: m. *entituler,* t. LL: m. *intitulāre,* der. L *in-* IN-² + *titulus* TITLE] —**Syn. 1.** empower, qualify.

en·ti·ty (ĕn'tətĭ), *n.,* *pl.* **-ties. 1.** something that has a real existence; a thing. **2.** being or existence. **3.** essential nature. [t. LL: m.s. *entitas*]

ento-, var. of **endo-.**

en·to·derm (ĕn'tōdûrm'), *n.* endoderm.

en·toil (ĕntoil'), *v.t.* *Archaic.* to take in toils; ensnare.

entom., entomology. Also, **entomol.**

en·tomb (ĕntōōm'), *v.t.* **1.** to place in a tomb; bury; inter. **2.** to serve as a tomb for. Also, **intomb.** [t. OF: s. *entomber,* der. en- EN-¹ + *tombe* TOMB] —**en·tomb'-ment,** *n.*

entomo-, a word element meaning "insect." Also, before vowels, **entom-.** [comb. form repr. Gk. *éntomos,* lit., cut up, in neut. pl., insects]

en·to·mol·o·gize (ĕn'təmŏl'əjīz'), *v.i.,* **-gized, -gizing. 1.** to study entomology. **2.** to gather entomological specimens.

en·to·mol·o·gy (ĕn'təmŏl'əjĭ), *n.,* the branch of zoology that treats of insects. —**en·to·mo·log·i·cal** (ĕn'-təməlŏj'əkəl), *adj.* —**en'to·mol'o·gist,** *n.*

en·to·moph·a·gous (ĕn'təmŏf'əgəs), *adj.* feeding on insects; insectivorous.

en·to·mos·tra·can (ĕn'təmŏs'trəkən), *adj.* **1.** belonging to the *Entomostraca,* a subclass of mostly small crustaceans. —*n.* **2.** an entomostracan crustacean. [f. ENTOM(o)- + m.s. Gk. *óstrakon* shell + -AN]

en·to·phyte (ĕn'tōfīt'), *n.* *Bot.* a plant growing within an animal or another plant, usually as a parasite. [f. *ento-* (comb. form repr. Gk. *entós* within) + -PHYTE] —**en·to·phyt·ic** (ĕn'tōfĭt'ĭk), *adj.*

en·tou·rage (än'tōōräzh'; *Fr.* äntōōräzh'), *n.* **1.** attendants, as of a person of rank. **2.** surroundings; environment. [t. F, der. *entourer* surround. See EN-¹, TOUR]

en·tr'acte (änträkt'; *Fr.* änträkt'), *n.* **1.** the interval between two consecutive acts of a theatrical or operatic performance. **2.** a performance, as of music or dancing, given during such an interval. **3.** a piece of music or the like for such performance. [t. F: between-act]

en·trails (ĕn'trālz, -trəlz), *n.pl.* **1.** the internal parts of the trunk of an animal body. **2.** the intestines or bowels. **3.** the internal parts of anything. [ME *entraile,* t. F: m. *entrailles,* g. LL *intrālia* intestines, der. L *inter* within]

en·train (ĕntrān'), *v.t., v.i.* to put or go aboard a train. —**en·train'ment,** *n.*

en·trance¹ (ĕn'trəns), *n.* **1.** act of entering, as into a place or upon new duties. **2.** a point or place of entering; an opening or passage for entering. **3.** power or liberty of entering; admission. **4.** *Theat.* the moment, or place in the script, at which an actor comes on the stage. [t. OF, der. *entrer* ENTER] —**Syn. 1.** entry, ingress. **3.** ENTRANCE, ADMITTANCE, ADMISSION refer to the possibility of entering a place. ENTRANCE suggests the possibility of entering without supervision or permission: *entrance is by way of the side door.* ADMITTANCE refers to the act of admitting or allowing entry: *to give admittance to a building.* ADMISSION suggests entering by permission, special right or privilege, by ticket, and the like: *admission to a concert, a game.*

en·trance² (ĕnträns', -tráns'), *v.t.,* **-tranced, -trancing. 1.** to fill with delight or wonder; enrapture. **2.** to put into a trance. [f. EN-¹ + TRANCE, v.] —**en·trance'-ment,** *n.* —**en·tranc'ing·ly,** *adv.*

en·trant (ĕn'trənt), *n.* **1.** one who enters. **2.** a new member, as of an association, a university, etc. **3.** a competitor in a contest. [t. F, ppr. of *entrer* ENTER]

en·trap (ĕntrăp'), *v.t.,* **-trapped, -trapping. 1.** to catch in or as in a trap; ensnare. **2.** to bring unawares into difficulty or danger. **3.** to draw into contradiction or damaging admission. [t. OF: s. *entraper,* der. en- EN-¹ + *trape* trap] —**en·trap'ment,** *n.* —**en·trap'per,** *n.*

en·treas·ure (ĕntrĕzh'ər), *v.t.,* **-ured, -uring.** to lay up in or as in a treasury.

en·treat (ĕntrēt'), *v.t.* **1.** to make supplication to (a person); beseech; implore: *entreat a person for something.* **2.** to ask earnestly for (something). —*v.i.* **3.** to make an earnest request or petition. Also, **intreat.** [ME *entrete(n),* t. OF: m. *entraitier,* f. en- EN-¹ + *traitier* TREAT] —**en·treat'ing·ly,** *adv.* —**Syn. 1.** See **appeal.**

en·treat·y (ĕntrē'tĭ), *n.,* *pl.* **-treaties.** earnest request or petition; supplication. —**Syn.** appeal, suit, plea.

en·tre·chat (äNtrəshä'), *n.* (in ballet) a jump during which the dancer crosses his feet a number of times while in the air. [t. F, t. It: m. *(capriola) intrecciata* complicated (caper), der. *in-* IN-² + *treccia* tress, plait]

en·tre·côte (äNtrəkōt'), *n.* *French.* rib steak.

en·tree (än'trā; *Fr.* äntrĕ'), *n.* **1.** *U.S.* any food other than a roast, served as the main course. **2.** a dish served at dinner before the main course or between the regular courses. **3.** the right or privilege of entering. Also, **en'trée.** [t. F. See ENTRY]

en·tre·mets (än′trə mā′; *Fr.* än trə mĕ′), *n.*, *pl.* **-mets** (-māz′; *Fr.* -mĕ′). *French.* a dish served at dinner between the principal courses or with the roast; a side dish. [F: lit., between-dish]

en·trench (ĕn trĕnch′), *v.t.* **1.** to dig trenches for defensive purposes around (oneself, a military position, etc.). **2.** to establish in a strong position: *safely entrenched behind undeniable facts.* —*v.i.* **3.** to trench or encroach; trespass; infringe (fol. by *on* or *upon*): *to entrench on the domain or rights of another.* **4.** to verge (fol. by *on* or *upon*): *proceedings entrenching on impiety.* Also, **intrench.** —**en·trench′er,** *n.*

en·trench·ment (ĕn trĕnch′mənt), *n.* **1.** act of trenching. **2.** an entrenched position. **3.** (*usually pl.*) an earth breastwork or ditch for protection against enemy fire. Also, **intrenchment.**

en·tre nous (äṉ trə nōō′), *French.* between ourselves; confidentially.

en·tre·pôt (än′trə pō′; *Fr.* äṉ trə pō′), *n.* **1.** a warehouse. **2.** a commercial center to which goods are sent for distribution. [t. F, der. OF *entreposer* store up, f. *entre*- INTER- + *poser* place (g. L *pausāre* rest)]

en·tre·pre·neur (än′trə prə nûr′; *Fr.* äṉ trə prə nœr′), *n.* **1.** an employer of productive labor; a contractor. **2.** one who undertakes to carry out any enterprise. [t. F, der. *entreprendre* undertake. See ENTERPRISE]

en·tre·sol (ĕn′tər sŏl′, äṉ′trə-; *Fr.* äṉ trə sōl′), *n. Archit.* a low story between two other stories of greater height, usually one immediately above the chief or ground floor; a mezzanine. [t. F: between-floor]

en·tro·py (ĕn′trə pĭ′), *n. Physics.* a measure of the unavailable energy in a thermodynamic system, commonly expressed in terms of its changes on an arbitrary scale, being zero for water at 32° F. [t. Gk.: m.s. *entropía* transformation]

en·trust (ĕn trŭst′), *v.t.* **1.** to invest with a trust or responsibility; charge with a specified office or duty involving trust. **2.** to commit (something) in trust (*to*); confide, as for care, use, or performance: *to entrust a secret, money, powers, or work to another.* **3.** to commit as if with trust or confidence: *to entrust one's life to a frayed rope.* Also, **intrust.**

en·try (ĕn′trĭ), *n.*, *pl.* **-tries.** **1.** act of entering; entrance. **2.** a place of ingress or entrance, esp. an entrance hall or vestibule. **3.** act of entering or recording something in a book, register, list, etc. **4.** the statement, etc., so entered or recorded. **5.** one entered in a contest or competition. **6.** *Law.* act of taking possession of lands or tenements by entering or setting foot on them. **7.** the giving of an account of a ship's cargo at a customhouse, to obtain permission to land the goods. **8.** *Bookkeeping.* **a.** See **double entry. b.** See **single entry.** [ME *entree*, t. F, der. *entrer* ENTER]

en·try·way (ĕn′trĭ wā′), *n.* a passage for affording entrance.

en·twine (ĕn twīn′), *v.t.*, *v.i.*, **-twined, -twining.** to twine with, about, around, or together. Also, **intwine.** —**en·twine′ment,** *n.*

en·twist (ĕn twĭst′), *v.t.* to twist together or about. Also, **intwist.**

e·nu·cle·ate (v. ĭ nū′klĭ āt′, ĭ nōō′-; adj. ĭ nū′klĭ ĭt, -āt′, ĭ nōō′-), *v.t.* **-ated, -ating,** *adj.* —*v.t.* **1.** *Biol.* to deprive of the nucleus. **2.** to remove (a kernel, tumor, eyeball, etc.) from its enveloping cover. **3.** to bring out; disclose. —*adj.* **4.** having no nucleus. [t. L: m.s. *ēnūcleātus,* pp.] —**e·nu′cle·a′tion,** *n.*

e·nu·mer·ate (ĭ nū′mə rāt′, ĭ nōō′-), *v.t.*, **-ated, -ating.** **1.** to mention separately as if in counting; name one by one; specify as in a list. **2.** to ascertain the number of; count. [t. L: m.s. *ēnumerātus,* pp., counted out] —**e·nu′mer·a′tive,** *adj.* —**e·nu′mer·a′tor,** *n.* —**Syn. 1.** recapitulate, recount, rehearse.

e·nu·mer·a·tion (ĭ nū′mə rā′shən, ĭ nōō′-), *n.* **1.** act of enumerating. **2.** a catalogue or list.

e·nun·ci·ate (ĭ nŭn′sĭ āt′, -shĭ-), *v.t.*, *v.i.*, **-ated, ating.** **1.** to utter or pronounce (words, etc.), esp. in a particular manner: *he enunciates his words distinctly.* **2.** to state or declare definitely as a theory. **3.** to announce or proclaim. [t. L: m.s *ēnuntiātus,* pp.] —**e·nun′ci·a′tive, e·nun′ci·a·to′ry,** *adj.* —**e·nun′ci·a′tive·ly,** *adv.* —**e·nun′ci·a′tor,** *n.*

e·nun·ci·a·tion (ĭ nŭn′sĭ ā′shən, -shĭ-), *n.* **1.** act or the manner of enunciating. **2.** utterance or pronunciation. **3.** announcement; statement.

en·ure (ĕn yŏŏr′), *v.t.*, *v.i.*, **-ured, -uring.** inure.

en·u·re·sis (ĕn′yə rē′sĭs), *n. Pathol.* incontinence or involuntary discharge of urine; bed-wetting. [NL, der. Gk. *enourein* make water in]

en·vel·op (ĕn vĕl′əp), *v.*, **-oped, -oping,** *n.* —*v.t.* **1.** to wrap up in or as in a covering. **2.** to serve as a wrapping or covering for. **3.** to surround entirely. —*n.* **4.** envelope. [ME *envolupe(n)*, t. OF: m. *envoluper,* f. *en*- EN-[1] + *voluper* wrap. Cf. DEVELOP] —**en·vel′op·er,** *n.* —**Syn. 1.** enfold, cover, hide, conceal. **3.** encompass, enclose.

en·ve·lope (ĕn′və lōp′, än′-), *n.* **1.** a cover for a letter or the like, usually so made that it can be sealed or fastened. **2.** that which envelops; a wrapper, integument, or surrounding cover. **3.** *Bot.* a surrounding or enclosing part, as of leaves. **4.** *Geom.* a curve or surface tangent to each member of a family of curves or surfaces. **5.** the fabric structure enclosing the gas bag of an aerostat. **6.** the gas bag itself. [t. F: m. *enveloppe*]

en·vel·op·ment (ĕn vĕl′əp mənt), *n.* **1.** act of enveloping. **2.** state of being enveloped. **3.** a wrapping or covering.

en·ven·om (ĕn vĕn′əm), *v.t.* **1.** to impregnate with venom; make poisonous. **2.** to embitter. [ME *envenime(n)*, t. OF: m. *envenimer,* der. *en*- EN-[1] + *venim* VENOM]

en·vi·a·ble (ĕn′vĭ ə bəl), *adj.* that is to be envied; worthy to be envied. —**en′vi·a·ble·ness,** *n.* —**en′vi·a·bly,** *adv.*

en·vi·ous (ĕn′vĭ əs), *adj.* **1.** full of, feeling, or expressing envy: *envious of a person's success, an envious attack.* **2.** *Obs.* emulous: [ME, t. AF, var. of OF *envieus,* der. *envie* ENVY] —**en′vi·ous·ly,** *adv.* —**en′vi·ous·ness,** *n.*

en·vi·ron (ĕn vī′rən), *v.t.* to form a circle or ring round; surround; envelop. [ME *environ(en)*, t. F: m. *environner,* der. *environ* around]

en·vi·ron·ment (ĕn vī′rən mənt), *n.* **1.** the aggregate of surrounding things, conditions, or influences. **2.** act of environing. **3.** state of being environed. **4.** that which environs. —**en·vi′ron·men′tal,** *adj.*

en·vi·rons (ĕn vī′rənz, ĕn′və rənz), *n.pl.* surrounding parts or districts, as of a city; outskirts; suburbs. [t. F]

en·vis·age (ĕn vĭz′ĭj), *v.t.*, **-aged, -aging.** **1.** to contemplate; visualize. **2.** to look in the face of; face. [t. F: m.s. *envisager,* der. *en*- EN-[1] + *visage* VISAGE]

en·vi·sion (ĕn vĭzh′ən), *v.t.* to picture mentally, esp. some future event or events.

en·voy[1] (ĕn′voi), *n.* **1.** a diplomatic agent of the second rank, next in dignity after an ambassador, commonly called minister (title in full: **envoy extraordinary and minister plenipotentiary**). **2.** a diplomatic agent. **3.** any accredited messenger or representative. [t. F: m. *envoyé,* prop. pp. of *envoyer* send. See ENVOY[2]]

en·voy[2] (ĕn′voi), *n.* **1.** *Pros.* a short stanza concluding a poem in certain archaic metrical forms. **2.** a postscript to a poetical or prose composition, sometimes serving as a dedication. Also, **en′voi.** [ME *envoye,* t. OF, der. *envoier* send, der. *en voie* on the way]

en·vy (ĕn′vĭ), *n.*, *pl.* **-vies,** *v.*, **-vied, -vying.** —*n.* **1.** a feeling of discontent or mortification, usually with ill will, at seeing another's superiority, advantages, or success. **2.** desire for some advantage possessed by another. **3.** an object of envious feeling. **4.** *Obs.* ill will. —*v.t.* **5.** to regard with envy; be envious of. —*v.i.* **6.** *Obs.* to be affected with envy. [ME *envie,* t. OF, g. L *invidia*] —**en′vi·er,** *n.* —**en′vy·ing·ly,** *adv.* —**Syn. 5.** ENVY, BEGRUDGE, COVET refer to one's attitude concerning the possessions or attainments of others To ENVY is to feel resentful, spiteful, and unhappy because someone else possesses, or has achieved, what one wishes oneself to possess, or to have achieved: *to envy the wealthy, a girl's beauty, an honest man's reputation.* To BEGRUDGE is simply to be unwilling that another should have the possessions, honors, or credit he deserves: *to begrudge a man a reward for heroism.* To COVET is to long jealously to possess what someone else possesses: *I covet your silverware.*

en·weave (ĕn wēv′), *v.* inweave.

en·wind (ĕn wīnd′), *v.t.*, **-wound, -winding.** to wind or coil about; encircle. Also, **inwind.**

en·womb (ĕn wōōm′), *v.t.* to enclose in or as in the womb.

en·wrap (ĕn răp′), *v.t.*, **-wrapped, -wrapping. 1.** to wrap or envelop in something: *enwrapped in leaves.* **2.** to wrap in slumber, etc.: *enwrapped in fond desire.* **3.** to absorb or engross in thought, etc. Also, **inwrap.**

en·wreathe (ĕn rēth′), *v.t.*, **-wreathed, -wreathing.** to surround with or as if with a wreath: *peace enwreathes thy brow.* Also, **inwreathe.**

en·zo·ot·ic (ĕn′zō ŏt′ĭk), *adj.* **1.** (of diseases) prevailing among or afflicting animals in a particular locality. Cf. **endemic.** —*n.* **2.** an enzoötic disease. [f. EN-[2] + zo(o)- + -OTIC, modeled on EPIZOOTIC]

en·zy·mat·ic (ĕn′zī măt′ĭk, -zī-), *adj.* of or pertaining to an enzyme.

en·zyme (ĕn′zīm, -zĭm), *n.* any of various complex organic substances, as pepsin, originating from living cells, and capable of producing by catalytic action certain chemical changes in organic substances; unorganized ferment. Also, **en·zym** (ĕn′zĭm). [t. MGk.: m.s. *énzymos* leavened, f. *en*- EN-[2] + Gk. *zýmē* leaven]

eo-, a word element meaning "early," "primeval," as in *Eocene.* [t. Gk., comb. form of *ēōs* dawn]

E·o·cene (ē′ə sēn′), *adj.* **1.** pertaining to the second principal subdivision of the Tertiary period or system. —*n.* **2.** an early Tertiary epoch or series succeeding Paleocene and preceding Oligocene.

E·o·gene (ē′ə jēn′), *adj. Geol.* **1.** pertaining to a division of the Tertiary period or system that comprises Paleocene, Eocene, and Oligocene. —*n.* **2.** the time or rocks representing the earlier half of the Tertiary period or system.

e·o·hip·pus (ē′ō hĭp′əs), *n.* a horse of a fossil genus, *Eohippus,* from the Lower Eocene of the western U.S., the oldest type of the family *Equidae,* about as large as a fox, with four complete toes on each forefoot and three hoofed toes on each hindfoot. [NL, f. Gk.: *ēō-* EO- + m. *hippos* horse]

E·o·li·an (ē ō′lĭ ən), *adj.*, *n.* Aeolian.

E·ol·ic (ē ŏl′ĭk), *n.*, *adj.* Aeolic.

e·o·lith (ē′ə lĭth), *n.* a rude stone implement characteristic of the earliest stage of human culture, shaped by, rather than for, use.

---

e·o·lith·ic (ē/ə lĭth/ĭk), *adj.* noting or pertaining to the earliest stage of human culture, characterized by the use of amorphous stone implements.

e.o.m., *Chiefly Com.* end of the month.

e·on (ē/ən, ē/ŏn), *n.* **1.** an indefinitely long period of time; an age; aeon. **2.** the largest division of geologic time comprising two or more eras. [t. L: m. *aeon*, t. Gk.: m. *aiōn* lifetime, age]

E·os (ē/ŏs), *n.* the Greek goddess of the dawn, identified with the Roman Aurora. [t. L, t. Gk.: personification of *ēōs* dawn. Cf. EAST]

e·o·sin (ē/ə sĭn), *n.* **1.** a coal-tar product, C₂₀H₈O₅Br₄, used for dyeing silk, etc., rose-red. **2.** any of a variety of eosinlike dyes. Also, **e·o·sine** (ē/ə sĭn, -sēn/). [f. Gk. *ēōs* dawn + -IN²] —e·o·sin·like/, *adj.*

e·o·sin·o·phil (ē/ə sĭn/ə fĭl), *n. Anat.* a cell containing granules staining with acid dyes, whose numbers increase in allergic diseases and certain parasitic infections. [f. EOSIN + -(O)PHIL(E)]

-eous, var. of *-ous,* occurring in adjectives taken from Latin or (infrequently) derived from Latin nouns. [t. L: m. *-eus*]

E·o·zo·ic (ē/ə zō/ĭk), *n.* a division of pre-Cambrian time and rocks characterized by the dawn of life on the earth. [f. EO- + ZO(O)- + -IC]

ep-, var. of *epi-,* before vowels, as in *epaxial.*

Ep., Epistle.

e·pact (ē/păkt), *n.* **1.** the excess in days of a solar year over a lunar year. **2.** the age in days of the calendar moon at the beginning of the year (Jan. 1). [t. LL: s. *epacta,* t. Gk.: m. *epaktē,* prop. fem. of *epaktós,* vbl. adj., added]

E·pam·i·non·das (ĭ păm/ə nŏn/dəs), *n.* c418–362 B.C., general and statesman of ancient Thebes in Greece.

ep·arch (ĕp/ärk), *n.* **1.** the prefect or governor of an eparchy. **2.** any military prefect. [t. Gk.: s. *éparchos* commander]

ep·ar·chy (ĕp/är kĭ), *n., pl.* **-chies. 1.** (in modern Greece) one of the administrative subdivisions of a province. **2.** (in ancient Greece) a province. **3.** *Gk. Ch.* a diocese or archdiocese. —ep·ar/chi·al, *adj.*

ep·au·let (ĕp/ə lĕt/ -lĭt), *n.* an ornamental shoulder piece worn on uniforms, chiefly by military and naval officers. Also, **ep/au·lette/.** [t. F: m. *épaulette,* der. *épaule* shoulder, g. L *spatula* blade]

ep·ax·i·al (ĕp ăk/sĭ əl), *adj. Anat.* above or posterior to an axis. —ep·ax/i·al·ly, *adv.*

é·pée (ā pā/; *Fr.* ĕ pě/), *n. Fencing.* a long narrow weapon with blunted edges and a sharp point. [F, g. L *spatha,* t. Gk.: m. *spáthē* blade]

é·pée·ist (ā pā/ĭst), *n. Fencing.* one who uses an épée.

ep·ei·rog·e·ny (ĕp/ī rŏj/ə nĭ), *n. Geol.* vertical or tilting movement of the earth crust, generally affecting broad areas of a continent. Also, **epirogeny.** [f. Gk. *ēpeiro(s)* land, mainland, continent + -GENY] —e·pei·ro·gen·ic (ĭ pī/rō jĕn/ĭk), *adj.*

ep·en·ceph·a·lon (ĕp/ən sĕf/ə lŏn/), *n., pl.* **-la** (-lə). *Anat.* the hindbrain. —ep·en·ce·phal·ic (ĕp/ən sə făl/ĭk), *adj.*

ep·en·the·sis (ĕp ĕn/thə sĭs), *n., pl.* **-ses** (-sēz/). (in linguistic process) the insertion of one or more sounds in the middle of a word, as the schwa in the substandard pronunciation (ĕl/əm) of *elm.* [t. LL, t. Gk.: insertion] —ep·en·thet·ic (ĕp/ĕn thĕt/ĭk), *adj.*

e·pergne (ĭ pûrn/, ā pârn/), *n.* an ornamental piece for the center of a dinner table, often elaborate in design, for holding fruit, flowers, etc. [? t. F: m. *épargne* saving, treasury]

ep·ex·e·ge·sis (ĕp ĕk/sə jē/sĭs), *n. Rhet.* **1.** the addition of a word or words to explain a preceding word or sentence. **2.** the word or words so added.

ep·ex·e·get·ic (ĕp ĕk/sə jĕt/ĭk), *adj.* of or like an epexegesis. Also, **ep·ex/e·get/i·cal.** —ep·ex/e·get/i·cal·ly, *adv.*

eph-, var. of *epi-,* before an aspirate, as in *ephemera.*

Eph., Ephesians.

e·phah (ē/fə), *n.* a Hebrew unit of dry measure, equal to about a bushel. Also, **e/pha.** [t. Heb.]

e·phebe (ĭ fēb/, ĕf/ēb), *n.* (among the ancient Greeks) a youth just entering upon manhood or just enrolled as a citizen. [t. Gk.: m. *éphēbos*] —e·phe/bic, *adj.*

e·phed·rine (ĭ fĕd/rĭn; *Chem.* ĕf/ə drēn/, -drĭn), *n. Pharm.* a crystalline alkaloid, C₁₀H₁₅NO, found in species of *Ephedra,* used esp. for colds, asthma, and hay fever. Also, **e·phed·rin** (ĭ fĕd/rĭn; *Chem.* ĕf/ə drĭn). [f. s. NL *ephedra* (L horsetail, a plant, t. Gk.) + -INE²]

e·phem·er·a (ĭ fĕm/ər ə), *n., pl.* **-erae** (-ə rē/), **-eras. 1.** anything short-lived or transitory. **2.** an ephemerid. [t. NL, orig., pl. of *ephēmeron* (t. Gk., neut. sing of *ephēmeros* or for only one day), but now treated as sing.]

e·phem·er·al (ĭ fĕm/ər əl), *adj.* **1.** lasting but a day or a very short time; short-lived; transitory. —*n.* **2.** an ephemeral entity, as certain insects. —e·phem/er·al·ly, *adv.* —**Syn. 1.** fleeting, evanescent, transient.

e·phem·er·id (ĭ fĕm/ər ĭd), *n.* a May fly. [t. NL: s. *Ephēmeridae.* See EPHEMERA]

e·phem·er·is (ĭ fĕm/ər ĭs), *n., pl.* **ephemerides** (ĕf/ə mĕr/ə dēz/). **1.** a table showing the positions of a heavenly body on a number of dates in an orderly sequence. **2.** an astronomical almanac containing such tables. **3.** *Obs.* an almanac or calendar. [t. L, t. Gk.: diary, calendar, record]

e·phem·er·on (ĭ fĕm/ər ŏn, -ər ən), *n., pl.* **-era** (-ər ə), **-erons.** anything short-lived or ephemeral. [t. Gk.: a short-lived insect. See EPHEMERA]

Ephes., Ephesians.

E·phe·sian (ĭ fē/zhən), *adj.* **1.** of or pertaining to Ephesus. —*n.* **2.** a native or inhabitant of Ephesus. **3.** (*pl.*) the book of the New Testament called in full *The Epistle of Paul the Apostle to the Ephesians.*

Eph·e·sus (ĕf/ə səs), *n.* an ancient city in W Asia Minor, S of Smyrna: famous temple of Artemis (Diana).

eph·od (ĕf/ŏd, ē/fŏd), *n.* a kind of Hebrew priestly vestment, esp. that worn by the high priest. [t. Heb.; in some passages appar. meaning "idol"]

eph·or (ĕf/ôr, ĕf/ər), *n., pl.* **-ors, -ori** (-ə rī/). one of a body of magistrates in various ancient Dorian states, esp. at Sparta, where a body of five was annually elected by the people. [t. Gk.: s. *éphoros* overseer] —eph/or·al, *adj.*

E·phra·im (ē/frĭ əm), *n. Old Testament.* **1.** the younger son of Joseph. Gen. 41:52. **2.** the tribe of Israel traditionally descended from him. Gen. 48:1, etc. **3.** the Kingdom of Israel. [t. Heb.]

epi-, a prefix meaning "on," "to," "against," sometimes used as an English formative, chiefly in scientific words, as *epiblast, epicalyx, epizoön.* Also, **ep-, eph-.** [t. Gk., repr. *epí,* prep. and adv., *ep-* before vowel, *eph-* before rough breathing]

ep·i·blast (ĕp/ə blăst/), *n. Embryol.* the outer layer of a gastrula, consisting of ectoblast and various portions of mesoblast and endoblast, according to species. —ep/i·blas/tic, *adj.*

ep·ib·o·ly (ĭ pĭb/ə lĭ), *n. Embryol.* the development of one part so that it surrounds another. [t. Gk.: m. *epibolē* a throwing on] —ep·i·bol·ic (ĕp/ə bŏl/ĭk), *adj.*

ep·ic (ĕp/ĭk), *adj.* Also, **ep/i·cal. 1.** denoting or pertaining to poetic composition in which a series of heroic achievements or events, usually of a hero, is dealt with at length as a continuous narrative in elevated style: *Homer's Iliad is an epic poem.* **2.** resembling or suggesting such poetry; of heroic character; imposing. —*n.* **3.** an epic poem. **4.** any epiclike composition. **5.** something worthy to form the subject of an epic poem: *that life was a Christian epic.* [t. L: s. *epicus,* t. Gk.: m. *epikós,* der. *épos* EPOS] —ep/i·cal·ly, *adv.* —ep/ic·like/, *adj.*

ep·i·ca·lyx (ĕp/ə kā/lĭks, -kăl/ĭks), *n., pl.* **-calyxes, -calyces** (-kăl/ə sēz/, -kā/lə-). *Bot.* an involucre resembling an outer calyx, as in the mallow.

ep·i·car·di·um (ĕp/ə kär/dĭ əm), *n., pl.* **-dia** (-dĭ ə). *Anat.* the inner serous layer of the pericardium, lying directly upon the heart. [t. NL: f. *epi-* EPI- + *-cardium* (comb. form repr. Gk. *kardía* heart] —ep/i·car/di·al, *adj.*

A. Epicalyx; B. Calyx

ep·i·carp (ĕp/ə kärp/), *n. Bot.* the outermost layer of a pericarp, as the rind or peel of certain fruits. See diag. under endocarp.

ep·i·ce·di·um (ĕp/ə sē/dĭ əm, -sə dī/əm), *n., pl.* **-sedia** (-sē/dĭ ə, -sə dī/ə). a funeral song; a dirge. [t. L, t. Gk.: m. *epikēdeion,* prop. neut. adj., of or for a funeral]

ep·i·cene (ĕp/ə sēn/), *adj.* **1.** belonging to, or partaking of the characteristics of, both sexes. **2.** (of Greek and Latin nouns) of the same gender class regardless of the sex of the being referred to, as Latin *vulpēs,* fox or vixen, always grammatically feminine. —*n.* **3.** an epicene person. [t. L: m.s. *epicoenus,* t. Gk.: m. *epíkoinos* common]

ep·i·cen·ter (ĕp/ə sĕn/tər), *n. Geol.* a point from which earthquake waves seem to go out, directly above the true center of disturbance. Also, *Brit.,* **ep·i·cen·trum** (ĕp/ə sĕn/trəm), **ep/i·cen/tre.** [t. NL: m. *epicentrum,* t. Gk.: m. *epíkentros* on the center] —ep/i·cen/tral, *adj.*

ep·i·cot·yl (ĕp/ə kŏt/əl, -ĭl), *n. Bot.* (in the embryo of a plant) that part of the stem above the cotyledons.

ep·i·crit·ic (ĕp/ə krĭt/ĭk), *adj. Physiol.* referring or pertaining to cutaneous nerve fibers perceiving fine sensational variations, or to such perception (opposed to *protopathic*). [t. Gk.: m. s. *epikritikós* determining]

Ep·ic·te·tus (ĕp/ĭk tē/təs), *n.* A.D. 60?–120?, Greek Stoic philosopher, who taught in Rome.

ep·i·cure (ĕp/ə kyŏor/), *n.* **1.** one who cultivates a refined taste in eating and drinking. **2.** one given up to sensual enjoyment, esp. in eating; a glutton. [orig. Anglicized form of EPICURUS] —**Syn. 1.** gastronome, gourmet, gourmand.

ep·i·cu·re·an (ĕp/ə kyŏo rē/ən), *adj.* **1.** given or adapted to luxury, or indulgence in sensual pleasures; of luxurious tastes or habits, esp. in eating and drinking. **2.** fit for an epicure. **3.** (*cap.*) of or pertaining to Epicurus or Epicureanism. —*n.* **4.** one devoted to the pursuit of pleasure or luxury; an epicure. **5.** (*cap.*) a disciple of Epicurus.

Ep·i·cu·re·an·ism (ĕp/ə kyŏo rē/ə nĭz/əm), *n.* **1.** the philosophical system of Epicurus, or attachment to his doctrines, the chief of which were that the external world resulted from a fortuitous concourse of atoms, and that the highest good in life is pleasure, which consists in freedom from disturbance or pain. **2.** (*l.c.*) epicurean indulgence or habits. Also, **Ep·i·cur·ism** (ĕp/ə kyŏo rĭz/əm, ĕp/ə kyŏor/ĭz əm).

Ep·i·cu·rus (ĕp/ə kyŏor/əs), *n.* 342?–270 B.C., Greek philosopher.

ep·i·cy·cle (ĕp′ə sī′kəl), *n.* **1.** a small circle the center of which moves round in the circumference of a larger circle, used in ptolemaic astronomy to account for observed periodic irregularities in planetary motions. **2.** *Math.* a circle which rolls (externally or internally), without slipping, on another circle, generating an epicycloid or a hypocycloid. [t. LL: m.s. *epicyclus*, t. Gk.: m. *epikýklos*]

ep·i·cy·clic (ĕp′ə sī′klĭk, -sĭk′lĭk), *adj.* of or pertaining to an epicycle. Also, **ep′i·cy′cli·cal.**

epicyclic train, *Mach.* any train of gears the axes of the wheels of which revolve around a common center.

ep·i·cy·cloid (ĕp′ə sī′kloid), *n.* *Geom.* a curve generated by the motion of a point on the circumference of a circle which rolls externally, without slipping, on a fixed circle. **—ep′i·cy·cloi′dal,** *adj.*

epicycloidal wheel, one of the wheels in an epicyclic train.

E, Epicycloid; P, Point tracing epicycloid on fixed circle

ep·i·deic·tic (ĕp′ə dīk′tĭk), *adj.* *Rhet.* displaying the skill of the speaker: *epideictic orations.* Also, **epidictic.** [t. Gk.: m.s. *epideiktikós* displaying]

ep·i·dem·ic (ĕp′ə dĕm′ĭk), *adj.* **1.** Also, **ep′i·dem′i·cal.** affecting at the same time a large number of persons in a locality, and spreading from person to person, as a disease not permanently prevalent there. **—n. 2.** a temporary prevalence of a disease. [der. obs. *epidemy*, t. LL: m.s. *epidēmia*, t. Gk.: prevalence of an epidemic] **—ep′i·dem′i·cal·ly,** *adv.* **—ep·i·de·mic·i·ty** (ĕp′ə də mĭs′ə tĭ), *n.*

ep·i·de·mi·ol·o·gy (ĕp′ə dē′mĭ ŏl′ə jĭ), *n.* the branch of medicine dealing with epidemic diseases. **—ep·i·de·mi·o·log·i·cal** (ĕp′ə dē′mĭ ə lŏj′ə kəl), *adj.* **—ep′i·de·mi·ol′o·gist,** *n.*

ep·i·der·mis (ĕp′ə dûr′mĭs), *n.* **1.** *Anat.* the outer, nonvascular, nonsensitive layer of the skin, covering the true skin or corium (dermis). **2.** *Zool.* the outermost living layer of an animal, usually composed of one or more layers of cells. **3.** *Bot.* a thin layer of cells forming the outer integument of seed plants and ferns. [t. LL, t. Gk.: outer skin] **—ep′i·der′mal, ep·i·der′mic,** *adj.*

ep·i·der·moid (ĕp′ə dûr′moid), *adj.* resembling epidermis. Also, **ep′i·der·moi′dal.**

ep·i·dic·tic (ĕp′ə dĭk′tĭk), *adj.* epideictic.

ep·i·did·y·mis (ĕp′ə dĭd′ə mĭs), *n., pl.* **-didymides** (-dĭ′dĭm′ə dēz′). *Anat.* an elongated organ applied to the posterior surface of the testis, in which the spermatozoa ripen; chiefly the convoluted beginning of the deferent duct. [NL, t. Gk.] **—ep′i·did′y·mal,** *adj.*

ep·i·dote (ĕp′ə dōt′), *n.* a mineral, calcium aluminum iron silicate, $Ca_2(Al,Fe)_3Si_3O_2(OH)$, occurring in yellowish-green prismatic crystals. [t. F, der. Gk. *epidídōnai* increase] **—ep·i·dot·ic** (ĕp′ə dŏt′ĭk), *adj.*

ep·i·fo·cal (ĕp′ə fō′kəl), *adj.* *Geol.* epicentral.

ep·i·gas·tric (ĕp′ə găs′trĭk), *adj.* *Anat.* lying upon, distributed over, or pertaining to, the abdomen or the stomach.

ep·i·gas·tri·um (ĕp′ə găs′trĭ əm), *n.* *Anat.* the upper and median part of the abdomen, lying over the stomach. [NL, t. Gk.: m. *epigástrion* (neut.) over the belly]

ep·i·ge·al (ĕp′ə jē′əl), *adj.* **1.** *Entomol.* living near the surface of the ground, as on low herbs or on other surface vegetation. **2.** *Bot.* epigeous. Also, **ep′i·ge′an.** [f. EPIGE(OUS) + -AL[1]]

ep·i·gene (ĕp′ə jēn′), *adj.* *Geol.* formed or originating on the earth's surface (opposed to *hypogene*). [t. F, t. Gk.: m.s. *epigenēs* growing after or later]

ep·i·gen·e·sis (ĕp′ə jĕn′ə sĭs), *n.* *Biol.* **1.** a theoretical concept of generation according to which the embryo is formed by a series of new formations or successive differentiations (opposed to *preformation*). **2.** *Geol.* the processes of ore deposition effective during a period subsequent to the original formation of the enclosing rock. **—ep·i·ge·net·ic** (ĕp′ə jə nĕt′ĭk), *adj.*

e·pig·e·nous (ĭ pĭj′ə nəs), *adj.* *Bot.* growing on the surface, esp. the upper surface, as fungi on leaves.

ep·i·ge·ous (ĕp′ə jē′əs), *adj.* *Bot.* **1.** growing on or close to the ground. **2.** (of cotyledons) lifted above ground in germination. [t. Gk.: m. *epígeios* on earth]

ep·i·glot·tis (ĕp′ə glŏt′ĭs), *n.* *Anat.* a thin, valvelike cartilaginous structure that covers the glottis during swallowing, preventing the entrance of food and drink into the larynx. See diag. under **larynx.** [t. NL, t. Gk.]

E·pig·o·ni (ĭ pĭg′ə nī′), *n.pl.* See **Seven Against Thebes.**

ep·i·gram (ĕp′ə grăm′), *n.* **1.** any witty, ingenious, or pointed saying tersely expressed. **2.** epigrammatic expression. **3.** a short poem dealing concisely with a single subject, usually ending with a witty or ingenious turn of thought, and often satirical. [t. L: m. *epigramma*, t. Gk.: an inscription]

ep·i·gram·mat·ic (ĕp′ə grə măt′ĭk), *adj.* **1.** of or like an epigram; terse and ingenious in expression. **2.** given to epigrams. **—ep′i·gram·mat′i·cal·ly,** *adv.*

ep·i·gram·ma·tism (ĕp′ə grăm′ə tĭz′əm), *n.* epigrammatic character or style.

ep·i·gram·ma·tist (ĕp′ə grăm′ə tĭst), *n.* a maker of epigrams.

ep·i·gram·ma·tize (ĕp′ə grăm′ə tīz′), *v.t., v.i.,* **-tized, -tizing.** to express by epigrams, or make epigrams.

ep·i·graph (ĕp′ə grăf′, -gräf′), *n.* **1.** an inscription, esp. on a building, statue, or the like. **2.** an apposite quotation at the beginning of a book, chapter, etc. [t. Gk.: s. *epigraphē*]

ep·i·graph·ic (ĕp′ə grăf′ĭk), *adj.* **1.** pertaining to epigraphs. **2.** pertaining to epigraphy. Also, **ep′i·graph′i·cal. —ep·i·graph′i·cal·ly,** *adv.*

e·pig·ra·phy (ĭ pĭg′rə fĭ), *n.* **1.** the study or science of epigraphs or inscriptions. **2.** inscriptions collectively. **—e·pig′ra·phist, e·pig′ra·pher,** *n.*

e·pig·y·nous (ĭ pĭj′ə nəs), *adj.* *Bot.* **1.** (of flowers) having all floral parts conjoint and generally divergent from the ovary at or near its summit. **2.** having stamens, etc., so arranged, as a flower. [f. EPI- + m.s. Gk. *gynē* woman, female + -OUS]

e·pig·y·ny (ĭ pĭj′ə nĭ), *n.* an epigynous condition.

Epigynous stamens

ep·i·lep·sy (ĕp′ə lĕp′sĭ), *n.* *Pathol.* a nervous disease usually characterized by convulsions and practically always by loss of consciousness. [t. LL: m.s. *epilēpsia*, t. Gk.: lit., a seizure]

ep·i·lep·tic (ĕp′ə lĕp′tĭk), *adj.* **1.** pertaining to epilepsy: *epileptic state.* **—n. 2.** one affected with epilepsy.

ep·i·lep·toid (ĕp′ə lĕp′toid), *adj.* resembling epilepsy. Also, **ep·i·lep·ti·form** (ĕp′ə lĕp′tə fôrm′).

e·pil·o·gist (ĭ pĭl′ə jĭst), *n.* the writer or speaker of an epilogue.

ep·i·logue (ĕp′ə lôg′, -lŏg′), *n.* **1.** a speech, usually in verse, by one of the actors after the conclusion of a play. **2.** the person or persons speaking this. **3.** a concluding part added to a literary work. Also, **ep′i·log′.** [t. F, t. L: m.s. *epilogus*, t. Gk.: m. *epílogos* a conclusion]

Ep·i·me·theus (ĕp′ə mē′thōos, -thy əs), *n.* *Gk. Myth.* the brother of Prometheus and husband of Pandora.

ep·i·mor·pho·sis (ĕp′ə môr fō′sĭs), *n.* *Zool.* a form of development in segmented animals in which body segmentation is completed before hatching.

ep·i·nas·ty (ĕp′ə năs′tĭ), *n.* *Bot.* (esp. of leaves) increased growth on the upper surface of an organ or part, causing it to bend downward. [f. EPI- + s. Gk. *nastós* pressed close, compact + -Y[3]] **—ep′i·nas′tic,** *adj.*

ep·i·neph·rine (ĕp′ə nĕf′rĭn, -rēn), *n.* *Chem.* adrenalin. Also, **ep·i·neph·rin** (ĕp′ə nĕf′rĭn). [f. EPI- + s. Gk. *nephrós* kidney + -INE[2]]

ep·i·neu·ri·um (ĕp′ə nyōor′ĭ əm, -nōor′-), *n., pl.* **-neu·ria** (-nyōor′ĭ ə, -nōor′-). *Anat.* the dense sheath of connective tissue which surrounds the trunk of a nerve. [NL, f. Gk.: epi- EPI- + m. *neûron* sinew, tendon]

Epiph., Epiphany.

E·piph·a·ny (ĭ pĭf′ə nĭ), *n., pl.* **-nies. 1.** a Christian festival, observed on Jan. 6, commemorating the manifestation of Christ to the Gentiles in the persons of the Magi. **2.** (*l.c.*) an appearance or manifestation, esp. of a deity. [ME *epiphanie*, t. OF, t. LL: m. *epiphania*, t. LGk.: the Epiphany, ult. der. *epiphaínein* manifest]

ep·i·phe·nom·e·nal·ism (ĕp′ə fə nŏm′ə nə lĭz′əm), *n.* *Philos.* automatism (def. 2).

ep·i·phe·nom·e·non (ĕp′ə fə nŏm′ə nŏn′, -nən), *n., pl.* **-na** (-nə). **1.** *Pathol.* a secondary or additional symptom or complication arising during the course of a malady. **2.** any secondary phenomenon.

e·piph·y·sis (ĭ pĭf′ə sĭs), *n., pl.* **-ses** (-sēz′). *Anat.* **1.** a part or process of a bone which is separated from the main body of the bone by a layer of cartilage, and which finally becomes united with the bone through further ossification. **2.** the pineal body of the brain. [NL, t. Gk.: an outgrowth] **—ep·i·phys·i·al** (ĕp′ə fĭz′ĭ əl), *adj.*

ep·i·phyte (ĕp′ə fīt′), *n.* *Bot.* a plant which grows upon another but does not get food, water, or minerals from it; an air plant or aerophyte. **—ep·i·phyt·ic** (ĕp′ə fĭt′ĭk), **ep′i·phyt′i·cal,** *adj.* **—ep′i·phyt′i·cal·ly,** *adv.*

ep·i·phy·tot·ic (ĕp′ə fĭ tŏt′ĭk), *adj.* (of a disease or parasite) epidemic on plants. [f. EPI- + -PHYTE + -OTIC]

ep·i·plo·ön (ĭ pĭp′lō ŏn), *n.* *Anat.* the great omentum.

e·pi·rog·e·ny (ĕp′ī rŏj′ə nĭ), *n.* epeirogeny. **—e·pi·ro·gen·ic** (ĕp′ī rō jĕn′ĭk), *adj.*

E·pi·rus (ĭ pī′rəs), *n.* **1.** a country of ancient Greece, corresponding to what is now NW Greece and S Albania. **2.** a modern region in NW Greece. 363,041 pop. (est. 1938); 3688 sq. mi.

Epis., Episcopal. Also, **Episc.**

e·pis·co·pa·cy (ĭ pĭs′kə pə sĭ), *n., pl.* **-cies. 1.** government of the church by bishops; church government in which there are three distinct orders of ministers, namely bishops, priests or presbyters, and deacons. **2.** the office or incumbency of a bishop. **3.** the order of bishops.

e·pis·co·pal (ĭ pĭs′kə pəl), *adj.* **1.** pertaining to a bishop. **2.** (*sometimes cap.*) based on or recognizing a governing order of bishops: *the Methodist Episcopal Church.* **3.** (*cap.*) designating the Anglican Church or some branch of it: *the Protestant Episcopal Church in the U.S.* [t. LL: s. *epíscopālis,* der. *epíscopus* BISHOP] **—e·pis′co·pal·ly,** *adv.*

E·pis·co·pa·lian (ĭ pĭs′kə pāl′yən), *adj.* **1.** pertaining or adhering to the Episcopal Church (of the Anglican communion). **2.** (*l.c.*) pertaining or adhering to the episcopal form of church government. **—n. 3.** a member of the Episcopal Church. **4.** (*l.c.*) an adherent of the episcopal system. **—E·pis′co·pa′lian·ism,** *n.*

e·pis·co·pal·ism ((Ỹpĭs′kə·pəlĭz′əm), *n.* the theory of church polity according to which the supreme ecclesiastical authority is vested in the episcopal order as a whole, and not in any individual except by delegation.

e·pis·co·pate (Ỹpĭs′kəpĭt, -pāt′), *n.* **1.** the office and dignity of a bishop; a bishopric. **2.** the order or body of bishops. **3.** the incumbency of a bishop.

ep·i·sode (ĕp′ə·sōd′, -zōd′), *n.* **1.** an incident in the course of a series of events, in a person's life or experience, etc. **2.** an incidental narrative or digression in the course of a story, poem, or other writing. **3.** a part in an old Greek tragedy between two choric songs. **4.** *Music.* an intermediate or digressive passage, esp. in a contrapuntal composition. [t. Gk.: m.s. *epeisódion* a parenthetic addition, prop. neut. of *epeisódios* coming in besides] **—Syn. 1.** See **event.**

ep·i·sod·ic (ĕp′ə·sŏd′ĭk, -zŏd′-), *adj.* pertaining to or of the nature of an episode; incidental. Also, **ep/i·sod/i·cal.** **—ep/i·sod/i·cal·ly,** *adv.*

ep·i·spas·tic (ĕp′ə·spăs′tĭk), *adj.* **1.** raising a blister. **—n. 2.** a blistering agent; a vesicatory. [t. Gk.: m.s. *epispastikós*, lit., drawing towards]

e·pis·ta·sis (Ỹ pĭs′tə·sĭs), *n.* Genetics. a form of interaction between nonallelic genes in which one combination of such genes exerts a dominant effect over other combinations. [t. Gk.] **—ep·i·stat·ic** (ĕp′ə·stăt′ĭk), *adj.*

ep·i·stax·is (ĕp′ə·stăk′sĭs), *n.* Pathol. bleeding from the nose. [NL, der. Gk. *epistázein* drop on]

e·pis·te·mol·o·gy (Ỹ pĭs′tə·mŏl′ə·jĭ), *n.* the branch of philosophy which investigates the origin, nature, methods, and limits of human knowing. [f. s. Gk. *epistēmē* knowledge + -(o)LOGY] **—e·pis·te·mo·log·i·cal** (Ỹ pĭs′tə·mə·lŏj′ə·kəl), *adj.* **—e·pis/te·mo·log/i·cal·ly,** *adv.* **—e·pis/te·mol/o·gist,** *n.*

ep·i·ster·num (ĕp′ə·stûr′nəm), *n., pl.* **-na** (-nə). **1.** Anat. the manubrium. **2.** Entomol. the principal anterior subdivision of a thoracic pleuron. **—ep/i·ster/nal,** *adj., n.*

e·pis·tle (Ỹpĭs′əl), *n.* **1.** a written communication; a letter, esp. one of formal or didactic character. **2.** (usually cap.) one of the apostolic letters found in the New Testament. **3.** (often cap.) an extract, usually from one of the Epistles of the New Testament, forming part of the Eucharistic service in certain churches. [ME; OE *epistol*, t. L: s. *epistola*, t. Gk.: m. *epistolē* message, letter]

e·pis·tler (Ỹpĭs′lər, Ỹpĭst′lər), *n.* **1.** a writer of an epistle. **2.** the one who reads the epistle in the Eucharistic service. Also, **e·pis·to·ler** (Ỹ pĭs′tə·lər).

e·pis·to·lar·y (Ỹ pĭs′tə·lĕr′Ỹ), *adj.* **1.** contained in or carried on by letters. **2.** of or pertaining to letters.

ep·i·style (ĕp′ə·stīl′), *n.* Archit. an architrave. [t. L: m.s. *epistylium*, t. Gk.: m. *epistýlion*]

ep·i·taph (ĕp′ə·tăf′, -täf′), *n.* **1.** a commemorative inscription on a tomb or mortuary monument. **2.** any brief writing resembling such an inscription. [ME *epitaphe*, t. L: m.s. *epitaphium*, t. Gk.: m. *epitáphion* funeral oration, neut. of *epitáphios* over or at a tomb] **—ep·i·taph·ic** (ĕp′ə·tăf′Ỹk), *adj.* **—ep/i·taph/ist,** *n.*

e·pit·a·sis (Ỹ pĭt′ə·sĭs), *n.* the part of an ancient drama (following the protasis) in which the action is developed, before the catastrophe. [NL, t. Gk.: an intensifying, a stretching]

ep·i·tha·la·mi·on (ĕp′ə·thə·lā′mỸ·ən), *n., pl.* **-mia** (-mỸ·ə). epithalamium.

ep·i·tha·la·mi·um (ĕp′ə·thə·lā′mỸ·əm), *n., pl.* **-miums, -mia** (-mỸ·ə), a nuptial song or poem; a poem in honor of a bride and bridegroom. [t. L, t. Gk.: m. *epithalámion* (neut. adj.) nuptial]

ep·i·the·li·al (ĕp′ə·thē′lỸ·əl), *adj.* pertaining to epithelium.

ep·i·the·li·oid (ĕp′ə·thē′lỸ·oid′), *adj.* resembling epithelium.

ep·i·the·li·o·ma (ĕp′ə·thē′lỸ·ō′mə), *n., pl.* **-mata** (-mə·tə), **-mas.** Pathol. a cancer or malignant growth consisting chiefly of epithelial cells. [NL; f. EPITHELI(UM) + -OMA]

ep·i·the·li·um (ĕp′ə·thē′lỸ·əm), *n., pl.* **-liums, -lia** (-lỸ·ə). Biol. any tissue which covers a surface, or lines a cavity or the like, and which performs protective, secreting, or other functions, as the epidermis, the lining of blood vessels, etc. [NL, f. Gk.: epi- EPI- + m. *thēlē* nipple + m. -ion, dim. suffix]

ep·i·thet (ĕp′ə·thĕt′), *n.* **1.** an adjective or other term applied to a person or thing to express an attribute, as in Alexander the Great. **2.** a meaningful name. [t. L: s. *epitheton*, t. Gk., prop. neut. of *epithetos* added] **—ep/i·thet/ic, ep/i·thet/i·cal,** *adj.*

e·pit·o·me (Ỹ pĭt′ə·mỸ), *n.* **1.** a summary or condensed account, esp. of a literary work; an abstract. **2.** a condensed representation of something: the epitome of all mankind. [t. L, t. Gk., der. *epitémnein* cut into, abridge]

e·pit·o·mist (Ỹ pĭt′ə·mỸst), *n.* one who makes an epitome.

e·pit·o·mize (Ỹ pĭt′ə·mīz′), *v.t.,* **-mized, -mizing. 1.** to make an epitome of. **2.** to contain in small compass. **—e·pit/o·miz/er,** *n.*

ep·i·zo·ic (ĕp′ə·zō′Ỹk), *adj.* Zool. externally parasitic.

ep·i·zo·ön (ĕp′Ỹ·zō′ŏn, -ən), *n., pl.* **-zoa** (-zō′ə). an external parasite; an ectozoön. [f. EPI- + ZOON]

ep·i·zo·öt·ic (ĕp′ə·zōŏt′Ỹk), *Vet. Sci.* **—adj. 1.** (of diseases) prevalent temporarily among animals. **—n. 2.** an epizoötic disease. [f. EPI- + zo(o)- + -OTIC. Cf. F *epizoötique*]

ep·i·zo·ö·ty (ĕp′ə·zō′ə·tỸ), *n., pl.* **-ties.** an epizoötic disease.

e plu·ri·bus u·num (ē plōōr′ə·bəs ū′nəm), Latin. one out of many (motto of the United States).

ep·och (ĕp′ək or, esp. Brit., ē′pŏk), *n.* **1.** a particular period of time as marked by distinctive character, events, etc. **2.** the beginning of any distinctive period in the history of anything. **3.** a point of time distinguished by a particular event, or state of affairs. **4.** Geol. the main division of a geological period, representing the time required for making a geological series. **5.** Astron. **a.** an arbitrarily fixed instant of time or date (usually the beginning of a century or half century) used as a reference in giving the elements of a planetary orbit or the like. **b.** the mean longitude of a planet as seen from the sun at such an instant or date. [t. ML: s. *epocha*, t. Gk.: m. *epochē* check, pause, position, epoch] **—Syn. 1.** See **age.**

ep·och·al (ĕp′ək·əl), *adj.* **1.** of or pertaining to an epoch or epochs. **2.** of the nature of an epoch. **3.** epochmaking.

ep·och·mak·ing (ĕp′ək·mā′kỸng), *adj.* opening a new era, as in human history, thought, or knowledge: an epoch-making discovery.

ep·ode (ĕp′ōd), *n.* Anc. Pros. **1.** a kind of lyric poem, invented by Archilochus (about 650 B.C.), in which a long verse is followed by a short one. **2.** the part of a lyric ode following the strophe and antistrophe. [t. F, t. L: m.s. *epōdos*, t. Gk.: m. *epōidós* after song, incantation]

ep·o·nym (ĕp′ə·nỸm), *n.* **1.** a person, real or imaginary, from whom a tribe, place, institution, etc., takes, or is supposed to take, its name, as Britons from Brut (supposed to be the grandson of Aeneas). **2.** any ancient official whose name was used to designate his year of office. [t. Gk.: s. *epōnymon* (neut.) named after] **—ep/o·nym/ic,** *adj.*

e·pon·y·mous (ĕ pŏn′ə·məs), *adj.* giving one's name to a tribe, place, etc. [t. Gk.: m. *epōnymos*]

e·pon·y·my (ĕ pŏn′ə·mỸ), *n.* the derivation of names from eponyms. [t. Gk.: m.s. *epōnymia* surname]

ép·o·pée (ĕp′ə·pē′, ĕp′ə·pē′), *n.* **1.** an epic. **2.** epic poetry. Also, **ep·o·poe·ia** (ĕp′ə·pē′ə). [t. F, t. Gk.: m. *epopoiía* epic poetry]

ep·os (ĕp′ŏs), *n.* **1.** an epic. **2.** epic poetry. [t. L, t. Gk.: word, tale, song, pl. epic poetry]

Ep·ping Forest (ĕp′Ỹng), a former royal forest in E England, at one time nearly coextensive with Essex: now a park NE of London. 8¾ sq. mi.

ep·si·lon (ĕp′sə·lŏn′, -lən or, esp. Brit., ĕp sī′lən), *n.* the fifth letter (E, ε, English short E, e) of the Greek alphabet. [t. Gk.: m. ĕ *psīlón* e simple]

Ep·som (ĕp′səm), *n.* a town in SE England, in Surrey, S of London: site of **Epsom Downs,** a famous race track where the annual Derby is held.

Epsom salt, (often pl.) hydrated magnesium sulfate, used as a cathartic, etc. [so called because first prepared from the water of the mineral springs at EPSOM]

Ep·stein (ĕp′stīn), *n.* Jacob, born 1880, English sculptor, born in New York of Russian-Polish parents.

eq., **1.** equal. **2.** equation. **3.** equivalent.

eq·ua·ble (ĕk′wə·bəl, ē′kwə-), *adj.* **1.** free from variations; uniform, as motion or temperature. **2.** uniform in operation or effect, as laws. **3.** tranquil, even, or not easily disturbed, as the mind. [t. L: m.s. *aequābilis* that can be made equal] **—eq/ua·bil/i·ty, eq/ua·ble·ness,** *n.* **—eq/ua·bly,** *adv.* **—Syn. 1, 3.** See **even.** **—Ant. 1.** variable.

e·qual (ē′kwəl), *adj., n., v.,* **equaled, equaling** or (esp. Brit.) **equalled, equalling. —adj. 1.** as great as another (fol. by to or with): the velocity of sound is not equal to that of light. **2.** like or alike in quantity, degree, value, etc.: of the same rank, ability, merit, etc. **3.** evenly proportioned or balanced: an equal mixture, an equal contest. **4.** uniform in operation or effect: equal laws. **5.** adequate or sufficient in quantity or degree: the supply is equal to the demand. **6.** having adequate powers, ability, or means: he was not equal to the task. **7.** level, as a plain. **8.** Archaic. tranquil or undisturbed. **9.** Archaic. impartial or equitable. **—n. 10.** one who or that which is equal. **—v.t. 11.** to be or become equal to; match. **12.** to make or do something equal to. **13.** to recompense fully. **14.** Archaic. to make equal; equalize. [t. L: m.s. *aequālis* like, equal] **—Syn. 2.** proportionate, commensurate, coördinate, correspondent. EQUAL, EQUIVALENT, TANTAMOUNT imply a correspondence between two or more things. EQUAL indicates a correspondence in all respects, unless a particular respect (or respects) is stated or implied: a dime is equal to ten cents (that is, in purchasing power, which is implied) EQUIVALENT indicates a correspondence in one or more respects, but not in all: an egg is said to be the equivalent of a pound of meat (that is, in nutritive value). TANTAMOUNT, a word of limited application, is used esp. of immaterial things which are equivalent to such an extent as to be practically identical: the prisoner's refusal to answer was tantamount to an admission of guilt. **4.** even, uniform, regular, unvarying. **10.** peer, compeer, match, mate. **—Ant. 1, 3, 4.** unequal. **2.** different. **5.** disproportionate. **6.** inadequate.

e·qual·i·tar·i·an (Ỹ kwŏl′ə·târ′Ỹən), *adj.* **1.** pertaining or adhering to the doctrine of equality among men. **—n. 2.** one who adheres to the doctrine of equality among men. **—e·qual/i·tar·i·an·ism,** *n.*

e·qual·i·ty (Ỹ kwŏl′ə·tỸ), *n., pl.* **-ties. 1.** state of being equal; correspondence in quantity, degree, value, rank, ability, etc. **2.** uniform character, as of motion or surface.

e·qual·ize (ē′kwə līz′), *v.t.*, **-ized, -izing. 1.** to make equal: *to equalize tax burdens.* **2.** to make uniform. —e′qual·i·za′tion, *n.*

e·qual·iz·er (ē′kwə lī′zər), *n.* **1.** one who or that which equalizes. **2.** any of various devices or appliances for equalizing strains, pressures, etc. **3.** *Elect.* an electrical connection established between two points in a network to secure some constant relation between the two points, as potential, impedance, phase angle.

e·qual·ly (ē′kwəl ĭ), *adv.* in an equal manner; to an equal degree.

e·qua·nim·i·ty (ē′kwə nĭm′ə tĭ, ĕk′wə-), *n.* evenness of mind or temper; calmness; composure; self-possession. [t. L: m.s. *aequanimitas,* der. *aequanimis* of an even mind]

e·quate (ĭ kwāt′), *v.t.,* **equated, equating. 1.** to state the equality of or between; put in the form of an equation. **2.** to reduce to an average; make such correction or allowance in as will reduce to a common standard of comparison. **3.** to regard, treat, or represent as equivalent. [t. L: m.s. *aequātus,* pp., made equal]

e·qua·tion (ĭ kwā′zhən, -shən), *n.* **1.** act of making equal; equalization. **2.** equally balanced state; equilibrium. **3.** *Math.* **a.** an expression of, or a proposition asserting, the equality of two quantities, employing the sign = between them. **b.** a mathematical formula interpreted as a question asking for what values of a variable two expressions in that variable are equal, as $3x^2 - 2x + 4 = 0$. **4.** *Chem.* a symbolic representation of a reaction. **5.** See **personal equation.** —e·qua′tion·al, *adj.*

e·qua·tor (ĭ kwā′tər), *n.* **1.** that great circle of a sphere or any heavenly body which has a center at each pole and lies equidistant between them, its plane being perpendicular to the axis of the sphere or heavenly body. **2.** the great circle of the earth, equidistant from the North and South Poles. **3.** a circle separating a surface into two congruent parts. [t. LL: m. *aequātor,* lit., equalizer (of day and night), as when the sun is on the equator)]

e·qua·to·ri·al (ē′kwə tōr′ĭ əl, ĕk′wə-), *adj.* **1.** of, pertaining to, or near an equator, esp. the equator of the earth. **2.** of or like the regions at the earth's equator: *equatorial vegetation.* —n. **3.** a telescope mounting having two axes of motion, one parallel to the earth's axis, and one at right angles to it. —e′qua·to′ri·al·ly, *adv.*

eq·uer·ry (ĕk′wə rĭ), *n., pl.* **-ries. 1.** an officer of a royal or similar household, charged with the care of the horses. **2.** an officer who attends on the British sovereign. [t. F: m. *écurie,* OF *escuirie,* der. *escuier* SQUIRE]

e·ques·tri·an (ĭ kwĕs′trĭ ən), *adj.* **1.** of or pertaining to horsemen or horsemanship. **2.** mounted on horseback. **3.** of or pertaining to the Roman equites: *the equestrian order.* **4.** representing a person on horseback: *an equestrian statue.* **5.** pertaining to or composed of knights. —n. **6.** a rider or performer on horseback. [f. L *equestri(s)* of a horseman + -AN]

e·ques·tri·enne (ĭ kwĕs′trĭ ĕn′), *n.* a female rider or performer on horseback. [pseudo-F fem. of EQUESTRIAN]

equi-, a word element meaning "equal," as in *equidistant, equivalent.* [comb. form repr. L *aequus* equal]

e·qui·an·gu·lar (ē′kwĭ ăng′gyə lər), *adj.* having all the angles equal.

e·qui·dis·tance (ē′kwə dĭs′təns), *n.* equal distance.

e·qui·dis·tant (ē′kwə dĭs′tənt), *adj.* equally distant. —e′qui·dis′tant·ly, *adv.*

e·qui·lat·er·al (ē′kwə lăt′ər əl), *adj.* **1.** having all the sides equal. —n. **2.** a figure having all its sides equal. **3.** a side equivalent, or equal, to others. [t. LL: s. *aequi·laterālis*] —e′qui·lat′er·al·ly, *adv.*

Equilateral triangle

e·quil·i·brant (ĭ kwĭl′ə brənt), *n. Physics.* a counterbalancing force or system of forces.

e·quil·i·brate (ē′kwə lī′brāt, ĭ kwĭl′ə brāt′), *v.,* **-brated, -brating.** —v.t. **1.** to balance equally; keep in equipoise or equilibrium. **2.** to be in equilibrium with; counterpoise. —v.i. **3.** to balance. [t. LL: m.s. *aequilībrātus* in equilibrium, f. L: *aequi-* EQUI- + *lībrātus* balanced] —e·qui·li·bra·tion (ē′kwə lĭ brā′shən, ĭ kwĭl′ə-), *n.* —e·qui·li·bra·tor (ē′kwə lĭ brā′tər), *n.*

e·quil·i·brist (ĭ kwĭl′ə brĭst), *n.* one who practices balancing in unnatural positions and hazardous movements, as a ropedancer. [f. EQUILIBR(IUM) + -IST] —e·quil′i·bris′tic, *adj.*

e·qui·lib·ri·um (ē′kwə lĭb′rĭ əm), *n.* **1.** a state of rest due to the action of forces that counteract each other. **2.** equal balance between any powers, influences, etc., equality of effect. **3.** mental balance. [t. L: m. *aequilībrium,* f. *aequi-* EQUI- + s. *lībra* balance + *-ium* -IUM]

e·quine (ē′kwīn), *adj.* **1.** of, pertaining to, or resembling a horse. —n. **2.** a horse. [t.L: m.s. *equīnus,* der. *equus* horse]

e·qui·noc·tial (ē′kwə nŏk′shəl), *adj.* **1.** pertaining to an equinox or the equinoxes, or to the equality of day and night. **2.** pertaining to the celestial equator. **3.** occurring at or about the time of an equinox: *an equinoctial storm.* **4.** *Bot.* (of a flower) opening regularly at a certain hour. —n. **5.** equinoctial line. **6.** a gale or storm at or near the time of an equinox. [t. L: m. s. *aequinoctiālis,* der. *aequinoctium* EQUINOX]

equinoctial line, the celestial equator. Also, **equinoctial circle.**

equinoctial point, either of the two points in which the celestial equator and the ecliptic intersect each other, reached by the sun's center at the equinoxes.

e·qui·nox (ē′kwə nŏks′), *n.* **1.** the time when the sun crosses the plane of the earth's equator, making night and day all over the earth of equal length, occurring about March 21 (**vernal equinox**) and Sept. 22 (**autumnal equinox**). **2.** either of the equinoctial points. [t. ML: m.s. *equinoxium,* L *aequinoctium* equality between day and night]

e·quip (ĭ kwĭp′), *v.t.* **equipped, equipping. 1.** to furnish or provide with whatever is needed for service or for any undertaking; to fit out, as a ship. **2.** to dress out; array. [t. F: m. *équiper,* OF *esquiper,* prob. t. Scand.; cf. Icel. *skipa* put in order, arrange, man (a ship, etc.)] —e·quip′per, *n.* —**Syn. 1.** See **furnish.**

eq·ui·page (ĕk′wə pĭj), *n.* **1.** a carriage. **2.** a completely equipped carriage, with horses and servants. **3.** outfit, as of a ship, an army, or a soldier; equipment. **4.** a set of small household articles, as of china. **5.** a collection of articles for personal ornament or use.

e·quip·ment (ĭ kwĭp′mənt), *n.* **1.** anything used in or provided for equipping. **2.** act of equipping. **3.** state of being equipped. **4.** a person's knowledge and skill necessary for a task, etc.: *a man's equipment for the law, for medicine.* **5.** *Railroads.* rolling stock. —**Syn. 1.** apparatus, paraphernalia.

e·qui·poise (ē′kwə poiz′, ĕk′wə-), *n.* **1.** an equal distribution of weight; even balance; equilibrium. **2.** a counterpoise.

e·qui·pol·lent (ē′kwə pŏl′ənt), *adj.* **1.** equal in power, effect, etc.; equivalent. **2.** *Logic.* (of two propositions, etc.) logically deductible from each other, as "All men are mortal" and "No men are immortal." —n. **3.** an equivalent. [t. L: m.s. *aequipollens* of equal value] —e′qui·pol′lence, e′qui·pol′len·cy, *n.*

e·qui·pon·der·ance (ē′kwə pŏn′dər əns), equality of weight; equipoise. Also, **e′qui·pon′der·an·cy.** —e′qui·pon′der·ant, *adj.*

e·qui·pon·der·ate (ē′kwə pŏn′də rāt′), *v.t.,* **-ated, -ating.** to equal or offset in weight, force, importance, etc.; counterbalance. [t. ML: m.s. *aequiponderātus,* pp. of *aequiponderāre,* f. L: *aequi-* EQUI- + *ponderāre* weigh]

e·qui·po·tent (ē′kwə pō′tənt), *adj.* equal in power.

e·qui·po·ten·tial (ē′kwə pō tĕn′shəl), *adj. Physics.* of the same potential.

e·qui·ro·tal (ē′kwə rō′təl), *adj.* having wheels all of the same size or diameter, as a vehicle.

eq·ui·se·tum (ĕk′wə sē′təm), *n., pl.* **-tums, -ta** (-tə). any plant of the genus *Equisetum*; a horsetail or scouring rush. [NL, m. L *equisaetum,* f. *equi-* horse + m. *saeta* bristle]

eq·ui·ta·ble (ĕk′wə tə bəl), *adj.* **1.** characterized by equity or fairness; just and right; fair, reasonable. **2.** *Law.* pertaining to or valid in equity, as distinguished from the common law. —**eq′ui·ta·ble·ness,** *n.* —**eq′ui·ta·bly,** *adv.*

eq·ui·tant (ĕk′wə tənt), *adj. Bot.* straddling or overlapping, as leaves whose bases overlap the leaves above or within them. [t. L: s. *equitans,* ppr., riding]

eq·ui·ta·tion (ĕk′wə tā′shən), *n.* horsemanship. [t. L: s. *equitātio,* der. *equitāre* ride]

eq·ui·tes (ĕk′wə tēz′), *n., pl.* **1.** (in ancient Rome) **a.** the mounted military units; the cavalry. **b.** the equestrian order of knights. **2.** (later) a privileged or imperial class. [t. L, pl. of *eques* a horseman, knight]

eq·ui·ty (ĕk′wə tĭ), *n., pl.* **-ties. 1.** the quality of being fair or impartial; fairness; impartiality. **2.** that which is fair and just. **3.** *Law.* **a.** the application of the dictates of conscience or the principles of natural justice to the settlement of controversies. **b.** a system of jurisprudence or a body of doctrines and rules developed in England and followed in the United States, serving to supplement and remedy the limitations and the inflexibility of the common law. **c.** an equitable right or claim. **d.** an equity of redemption. **4.** the interest of a shareholder as distinguished from that of a bondholder. [ME *equite,* t. L: m.s. *aequitas* equality, justice]

equity of redemption, 1. the right of a mortgagor or pledgor by absolute deed to redeem the property by paying the debt, even after forfeiture, but before sale under foreclosure or transfer of title, or before this right is barred by statutes of limitation. **2.** the interest of an owner of land which is subject to a mortgage.

equiv., equivalent.

e·quiv·a·lence (ĭ kwĭv′ə ləns), *n.* **1.** state or fact of being equivalent; equality in value, force, significance, etc. **2.** *Chem.* the quality of having equal valence. Also, **e·quiv′a·len·cy.**

e·quiv·a·lent (ĭ kwĭv′ə lənt), *adj.* **1.** equal in value, measure, force, effect, significance, etc. **2.** corresponding in position, function, etc. **3.** *Geom.* having the same extent, as a triangle and a square of equal area. **4.** *Chem.* having the same capacity to combine or react chemically. —n. **5.** that which is equivalent. [ME, t. LL: s. *aequivalens,* ppr., having equal power] —**e·quiv′a·lent·ly,** *adv.* —**Syn. 1.** See **equal.**

e·quiv·o·cal (ĭ kwĭv′ə kəl), *adj.* **1.** of uncertain significance; not determined: *an equivocal attitude.* **2.** of doubtful nature or character; questionable; dubious;

suspicious.　**3.** having different meanings equally possible, as a word or phrase; susceptible of double interpretation; ambiguous. [f. ME *equivoc* (t. LL: m.s. *aequivocus* ambiguous) + -AL¹] —**e·quiv′o·cal·ly,** *adv.* —**e·quiv′o·cal·ness,** *n.* —**Syn. 3.** See **ambiguous.**

e·quiv·o·cate (ĭkwĭv′əkāt′), *v.i.,* **-cated, -cating.** to use equivocal or ambiguous expressions, esp. with a view to misleading; prevaricate. [back formation from EQUIVOCATION] —**e·quiv′o·cat′ing·ly,** *adv.* —**e·quiv′o·ca′tor,** *n.*

e·quiv·o·ca·tion (ĭkwĭv′ə·kā′shən), *n.* **1.** the use of equivocal or ambiguous expressions, esp. in order to mislead; prevarication. **2.** *Logic.* a fallacy depending on the double meaning of a word. [ME, t. LL: m.s. *aequivocātiō*]

eq·ui·voque (ĕk′wəvōk′, ē′kwə-), *n.* **1.** an equivocal term; an ambiguous expression. **2.** a play upon words; a pun. **3.** double meaning; ambiguity. Also, **eq′ui·voke′.** [t. F, r. ME *equivoc.* See EQUIVOCAL]

-er¹, a suffix: **a.** forming nouns designating persons from the object of their occupation or labor, as in *hatter, tiler, tinner, moonshiner,* or from their place of origin or abode, as in *Icelander, southerner, villager,* or designating either persons or things from some special characteristic or circumstance, as in *six-footer, three-master, teetotaler, fiver, tenner.* **b.** serving as the regular English formative of agent nouns (being attached to verbs of any origin), as in *bearer, creeper, distributer, employer, harvester, poker, ruler, teacher, theorizer.* [OE *-ere.* c. G *-er,* etc.; akin to L *-ārius*]

-er², a suffix of nouns denoting persons or things concerned or connected with something, as in *butler, grocer, officer, garner.* [ME, t. AF, OF: *-er, -ier,* g. L *-ārius,* neut. *-ārium.* Cf. -ARY¹]

-er³, termination of certain nouns denoting action or process, as in *dinner, rejoinder, remainder, trover.* [t. F; orig. sign of inf.]

-er⁴, a suffix forming the comparative degree of adjectives, as in *harder, smaller.* [OE *-ra, -re,* c. G *-er*]

-er⁵, a suffix forming the comparative degree of adverbs, as in *faster.* [OE *-or,* c. OHG *-or,* G *-er*]

-er⁶, a suffix forming frequentative verbs, as *flicker, flutter, glimmer, patter.* [OE *-r-,* c. G *-(e)r-*]

Er, *Chem.* erbium.

E.R., **1.** East Riding (Yorkshire). **2.** East River (New York City). **3.** (L *Eduardus Rex*), King Edward.

e·ra (ĭr′ə, ē′rə), *n.* **1.** a period of time marked by distinctive character, events, etc.: *an era of progress.* **2.** the period of time to which anything belongs or is to be assigned. **3.** a system of chronologic notation reckoned from a given date. **4.** a period during which years are numbered and dates reckoned from a particular point of time in the past: *the Christian era.* **5.** a point of time from which succeeding years are numbered, as at the beginning of a system of chronology. **6.** a date or an event forming the beginning of any distinctive period. **7.** *Geol.* a major division of geological time: *Paleozoic era.* [t. LL, var. of *aera* number or epoch by which reckoning is made, era, prob. the same word as L *aera* counters, pl. of *aes* copper, bronze] —**Syn. 1.** See **age.**

e·ra·di·a·tion (ĭrā′dĭ·ā′shən), *n.* act or process of shooting forth (light rays, etc.); radiation.

e·rad·i·ca·ble (ĭrăd′əkəbəl), *adj.* that may be eradicated.

e·rad·i·cate (ĭrăd′əkāt′), *v.t.,* **-cated, -cating. 1.** to remove or destroy utterly, extirpate. **2.** to pull up by the roots. [t. L, m.s. *ērādīcātus,* pp. rooted out] —**e·rad′i·ca′tion,** *n.* —**e·rad′i·ca′tive,** *adj.* —**e·rad′i·ca′tor,** *n.* —**Syn. 1.** See **abolish.**

e·rase (ĭrās′), *v.t.,* **erased, erasing.** to rub or scrape out, as letters or characters written, engraved, etc.; efface. [t. L: m.s. *ērāsus,* pp., scratched out] —**e·ras′a·ble,** *adj.* —**Syn.** expunge, obliterate. See **cancel.**

e·ras·er (ĭrā′sər), *n.* an instrument, as a piece of rubber or cloth, for erasing marks made with pen, pencil, chalk, etc.

E·ras·mus (ĭrăz′məs), *n.* **Desiderius** (dĕz′ə·dĭr′Yəs), (*Gerhard Gerhards*) 1466?–1536, Dutch humanist, scholar, theologian, and satirist.

E·ras·tian (ĭrăs′chən, -tYən), *adj.* **1.** pertaining to Thomas Erastus, or to his doctrines, advocating the supremacy of the state in ecclesiastical matters. —*n.* **2.** an advocate of the doctrines of Erastus. —**E·ras′tian·ism,** *n.*

E·ras·tus (ĭrăs′təs; *Ger.* ā·räs′tŏŏs), *n.* **Thomas** (tŏm′əs; *Ger.* tō′mäs), 1524–83, a Swiss-German theologian.

e·ras·ure (ĭrā′shər), *n.* **1.** act of erasing. **2.** a place where something has been erased.

Er·a·to (ĕr′ə·tō′), *n. Gk. Myth.* the Muse of love poetry. [t. L, t. Gk.: lit., lovesome]

Er·a·tos·the·nes (ĕr′ə·tŏs′thə·nēz′), *n.* 276?–195? B.C., Greek mathematician and astronomer, at Alexandria.

er·bi·um (ûr′bĭ·əm), *n. Chem.* a rare-earth metallic element, having pink salts. *Symbol:* Er; *at. w..:* 167.2; *at. no.:* 68. [t. NL: f. (*Ytt*)*erb*(*y*) (see YTTERBIUM) + *-ium* -IUM]

Erck·mann-Cha·tri·an (ĕrk·män′ shä·trē·än′), *n.* the joint pen name of **Émile** (ē mēl′) **Erckmann,** 1822–99, and **Alexandre** (à·lĕk·sän′dr) **Chatrian,** 1826–90, collaborating French novelists and dramatists.

ere (âr), *prep.* **1.** before (in time). —*conj.* **2.** before. **3.** sooner than; rather than. [ME; OE *ǣr,* er (c. G *eher*), comparative of OE *ār* soon, early, c. Goth. *air.* See ERST, EARLY]

Er·e·bus (ĕr′ə·bəs), *n.* **1.** *Gk. Myth.* a place of nether darkness through which the shades of the dead pass on their way to Hades: *dark as Erebus.* **2. Mount,** a volcano on Ross Island, in Antarctica. ab. 13,370 ft.

Er·ech·the·um (ĕr′ək·thē′əm), *n.* a temple of Ionic order on the Acropolis of Athens, built c420 B.C., and one of the most perfect examples of Greek architecture, notable for its porches of different height, supported by caryatides.

e·rect (ĭrĕkt′), *adj.* **1.** upright in position or posture: *to stand or si erect.* **2.** raised or directed upward: *a dog with ears erect.* **3.** *Bot.* vertical throughout; not spreading or declined: *an erect stem, an erect leaf or ovule.* —*v.t.* **4.** to build; construct; raise: *to erect a house.* **5.** to raise and set in an upright or perpendicular position: *to erect a telegraph pole.* **6.** *Geom.* to draw or construct (a line or figure) upon a given line, base, or the like. **7.** *Optics.* to change (an inverted image) to a normal position. **8.** to form (fol. by *into*): *to erect a territory into a state.* **9.** to set up or establish, as an institution; found. **10.** *Mach.* to assemble; make ready for use. [t. L: s. *ērectus,* pp., set upright, built] —**e·rect′a·ble,** *adj.* —**e·rect′er,** *n.* —**e·rect′ly,** *adv.* —**e·rect′ness,** *n.* —**Syn. 1.** standing, vertical. See **upright. 5.** upraise, uprear, set up.

e·rec·tile (ĭrĕk′təl, -tYl), *adj.* **1.** capable of being erected or set upright. **2.** *Anat.* susceptible of being distended with blood and becoming rigid, as tissue. —**e·rec·til·i·ty** (ĭrĕk′tYl′ə·tY, ē′rĕk-), *n.*

e·rec·tion (ĭrĕk′shən), *n.* **1.** act of erecting. **2.** state of being erected. **3.** something erected, as a building or other structure. **4.** *Physiol.* a turgid and rigid state of an organ or part containing erectile tissue.

e·rec·tive (ĭrĕk′tYv), *adj.* tending to erect.

e·rec·tor (ĭrĕk′tər), *n.* **1.** erecter. **2.** *Anat.* a muscle which erects the body or one of its parts.

erc·long (âr·lông′, -lŏng′), *adv.* before long; soon: *erelong the knight did come to court.*

er·e·mite (ĕr′ə·mīt′), *n.* a religious solitary; a hermit. [ME, t. LL: m. *erēmīta,* t. Gk.: m. *erēmítēs* a hermit] —**er·e·mit·ic** (ĕr′ə·mĭt′Yk), **er′e·mit′i·cal,** **er·e·mit·ish** (ĕr′ə·mī′tYsh), *adj.*

ere·now (âr·nou′), *adv.* ere now; before this time.

er·e·thism (ĕr′ə·thYz′əm), *n. Physiol.* an unusual or excessive degree of irritation or stimulation in an organ or tissue. [t. Gk.: s. *erethismós* irritation]

ere·while (âr·hwīl′), *adv. Archaic.* a while before; formerly.

Er·furt (ĕr′fŏŏrt), *n.* a city in central Germany. 165,615 (1939).

erg (ûrg), *n. Physics.* the unit of work or energy in the cgs system, being the work done by a force of one dyne when its point of application moves through a distance of one centimeter. [t. Gk.: s. *érgon* work. See WORK, n.]

er·go (ûr′gō; *older* ĕr′gō), *conj., adv. Latin.* therefore; accordingly; consequently.

er·gos·ter·ol (ərgŏs′tərōl′, -rŏl′), *n. Biochem.* a sterol derived from ergot and contained in yeast, converted into vitamin D by exposure to ultraviolet rays. [f. ERGO(T) + STEROL]

er·got (ûr′gət, -gŏt), *n.* **1.** a disease of rye and other cereals, due to a fungus (in rye, *Claviceps purpurea*) which replaces the grain by a long, hard, hornlike, dark-colored body. **2.** a body so produced. **3.** the sclerotium of *C. purpurea,* developed on rye plants, and used medicinally as a hemostatic, etc. [t. F, in OF *argot* cock's spur]

er·got·ine (ûr′gətYn), *n.* any of various extracts of ergot (def. 3) used in medicine.

er·got·ism (ûr′gətYz′əm), *n.* a disease due to eating food prepared from rye, etc., affected with ergot.

er·i·ca·ceous (ĕr′Ykā′shəs), *adj.* belonging to the Ericaceae, or heath family of plants, which includes the heath, arbutus, azalea, rhododendron, American laurel, etc. [f. m.s. NL *Erĭcācĭae* (der. *Erĭca* the heath genus, t. Gk.: m. *ereĭkē* heath) + -OUS]

Er·ic·son (ĕr′Yk sən), *n.* **Leif** (lēf; *Scan.* lāf), fl. A.D. 1000, a Scandinavian navigator (son of Eric the Red); probable discoverer of "Vineland" or Nova Scotia.

Er·ics·son (ĕr′Yk sən), *n.* **1. John,** 1803–89, a Swedish-American engineer and inventor. **2.** Ericson.

Er·ic the Red (ĕr′Yk), born A.D. about 950, Norseman who discovered Greenland A.D. about 982 and later colonized it. Also, **Eric.**

E·rie (ĭr′Y), *n.* **1. Lake,** one of the five Great Lakes, between the U.S. and Canada: the southernmost and most shallow of the group: Commodore Perry's defeat of the British, 1813. 239 mi. long; 9940 sq. mi. **2.** a city in NW Pennsylvania: a port on Lake Erie. 130,803 (1950). **3.** a member of a tribe of American Indians formerly living along the southern shore of Lake Erie. The Senecas conquered (1653) and absorbed them.

Erie Canal, a canal in New York, extending from Albany to Buffalo and connecting the Hudson with Lake Erie: completed in 1825. See **New York State Barge Canal.**

ăct, āble, dâre, ärt; ĕbb, ēqual; Yf, īce; hŏt, ōver, ôrder, oil, bŏŏk, ōōze, out; ŭp, ūse, ûrge; ə = a in alone; ch, chief; g, give; ng, ring; sh, shoe; th, thin; ŧħ, that; zh, vision.　See the full key on inside cover.

e·rig·er·on (ĭ·rĭj′ə·rŏn′), *n.* any plant of the composite genus *Erigeron*, with flower heads resemb'ing those of the asters but having narrower and usually more numerous (white or purple) rays. [t. L, t. Gk.: groundsel]

Er·in (âr′ĭn, ĭr′ĭn), *n.* *Poetic.* Ireland. [t. OIrish: m. *Erinn*, dat. of *Eriu*, later *Eire* Ireland]

er·i·na·ceous (ĕr′ĭ·nā′shəs), *adj.* of the hedgehog kind or family.

e·rin·go (ĭ·rĭng′gō), *n.* eryngo.

E·rin·ys (ĭ·rĭn′ĭs, ĭ·rī′nĭs), *n.*, *pl.* **Erinyes** (ĭ·rĭn′ĭ·ēz′). *Gk. Myth.* one of the Furies.

E·ris (ĭr′ĭs, ĕr′ĭs), *n.* *Gk. Myth.* the goddess of discord, and, sometimes, sister of Ares. See **apple of discord**.

er·is·tic (ĕ·rĭs′tĭk), *adj.* pertaining to controversy or disputation; controversial. [t. Gk.: m.s. *eristikós*, der *erizein* wrangle]

Er·i·tre·a (ĕr′ĭ·trē′ə; *It.* ĕ′rē·trĕ′ä), *n.* a former Italian colony in NE Africa, on the Red Sea: in 1936 it became a part of Italian East Africa. 865,000 pop. (est. 1946); 45,900 sq. mi. *Cap.:* Asmara. —**Er′i·tre′an,** *adj.*, *n.*

Er·i·van (ĕr′ĭ·vän′y), *n.* a city in the S Soviet Union, in Caucasia: the capital of the Armenian Republic. 200,031 (1939).

erl·king (ûrl′kĭng′), *n.* (in German and Scandinavian mythology) a spirit or personified natural power which works mischief, esp. to children. [repr. G *erlkönig* alderking, itself a mistrans. of Dan. *ellerkonge*, var. of *elverkonge* king of the elves]

er·mine (ûr′mĭn), *n.*, *pl.* **-mines,** (*esp. collectively*) **-mine.** **1.** an Old World weasel, *Mustela erminea*, which turns white in winter. The brown summer phase is called the stoat. **2.** *U.S.* any of a number of weasels that are white in winter. **3.** the lustrous white winter fur of the ermine, having a black tail tip. **4.** the office or dignity of a judge. [ME, t. OF: m. (h)*ermine*, t. Gmc.; cf. OHG *harmīn* pertaining to the ermine]

Ermine. *Mustela erminea*
(10 to 11 in. l ong, tail ab. 4 in.)

er·mined (ûr′mĭnd), *adj.* covered or adorned with ermine.

-ern, *adj.* suffix occurring in *northern*, etc. [ME and OE *-erne*, c. OHG *-rōni* (as in *nordrōni* northern)]

erne (ûrn), *n.* a sea eagle. Also, **ern.** [ME; OE *earn*, c. MLG *arn* eagle]

e·rode (ĭ·rōd′), *v.t.*, **eroded, eroding.** **1.** to eat out or away; destroy by slow consumption. **2.** to form (a channel, etc.) by eating or wearing away (used esp. in geology, to denote the action of all the forces of nature that wear away the earth's surface). [t. L: m.s. *ērōdere* gnaw off]

e·rod·ent (ĭ·rō′dənt), *adj.* eroding; erosive: *the erodent power of wind.*

e·rog·e·nous (ĭ·rŏj′ə·nəs), *adj.* arousing or tending to arouse sexual desire.

E·ros (ĭr′ŏs, ĕr′ŏs), *n.* the Greek god of love, identified by the Romans with Cupid. [t. L, t. Gk.: lit., love]

e·rose (ĭ·rōs′), *adj.* **1.** uneven as if gnawed away. **2.** *Bot.* having the margin irregularly incised as if gnawed, as a leaf. [t. L: m.s. *ērōsus*, pp., gnawed off]

e·ro·sion (ĭ·rō′zhən), *n.* **1.** act of eroding. **2.** state of being eroded. **3.** *Geol.* the process by which the surface of the earth is worn away by the action of water, glaciers, winds, waves, etc.

e·ro·sive (ĭ·rō′sĭv), *adj.* serving to erode; causing erosion.

Section of stratified rock bent into a low anticline by erosion

Erosion

e·rot·ic (ĭ·rŏt′ĭk), *adj.* **1.** of or pertaining to sexual love: *amatory.* —*n.* **2.** an erotic poem. **3.** an erotic person. [t. Gk.: m.s. *erōtikós* pertaining to love. See **Eros**] —**e·rot′i·cal·ly,** *adv.*

e·rot·i·cism (ĭ·rŏt′ə·sĭz′əm), *n.* **1.** erotic character or tendency. **2.** *Psychoanal.* erotism.

e·ro·tism (ĕr′ə·tĭz′əm), *n.* *Psychoanal.* the arousal and satisfaction of sexual desire.

ERP, European Recovery Program. Also, **E.R.P.**

err (ûr), *v.i.* **1.** to go astray in thought or belief; be mistaken; be incorrect. **2.** to go astray morally; sin. **3.** to deviate from the true course, aim, or purpose. [ME *erre(n)*, t. OF: m. *errer*, t. L: m. *errāre* wander]

er·rand (ĕr′ənd), *n.* **1.** a trip to convey a message or execute a commission; a short journey for a specific purpose: *he was sent on an errand.* **2.** a special business entrusted to a messenger; a commission. **3.** the purpose of any trip or journey: *his errand was to bribe the chieftain into releasing the captives.* [ME; OE *ærende*, c. OHG *ārunti.* Cf. OE *ār* messenger]

er·rant (ĕr′ənt), *adj.* **1.** journeying or traveling, as a medieval knight in quest of adventure; roving adventurously. **2.** deviating from the regular or proper course; erring. [ME *erraunte*, t. F: m. *errant*, prop. ppr. of *errer*, OF *esrer* travel (g. VL *iterāre* journey), but b. with F *errant*, ppr. of *errer* **err**] —**er′rant·ly,** *adv.*

er·rant·ry (ĕr′ən·trĭ), *n.*, *pl.* **-ries.** conduct or performance like that of a knight-errant.

er·ra·re hu·ma·num est (ĕ·rär′ĭ hū·mä′nəm ĕst′), *Latin.* to err is human.

er·ra·ta (ĭ·rā′tə, ĭ·rä′-), *n.* pl. of **erratum.**

er·rat·ic (ĭ·răt′ĭk), *adj.* **1.** deviating from the proper or usual course in conduct or opinion; eccentric; queer. **2.** having no certain course; wandering; not fixed: *an erratic star* (a planet). **3.** *Geol.* **a.** (of boulders, etc.) transported from the original site to an unusual location, as by glacial action. **b.** pertaining to such boulders, etc. —*n.* **4.** an erratic or eccentric person. **5.** *Geol.* an erratic boulder or block of rock. [ME, t. L: s. *errāticus*, der. *errāre* wander, **err**] —**er·rat′i·cal·ly,** *adv.*

er·ra·tum (ĭ·rā′təm, ĭ·rä′-), *n.*, *pl.* **-ta** (-tə). an error in writing or printing. [t. L: prop. pp. neut., erred]

er·rhine (ĕr′ĭn, ĕr′ĭn), *Med.* —*adj.* **1.** designed to be snuffed into the nose. **2.** occasioning discharges from the nose. —*n.* **3.** a medicine to be snuffed up the nostrils to promote sneezing and increased discharges. [t. NL: m.s. *errhīnum*, t. Gk.: m. *érrhīnon*, der. *en-* **en-**[2] + *rhís* nose]

err·ing (ûr′ĭng, ĕr′-), *adj.* **1.** going astray; in error; wrong. **2.** sinning. —**err′ing·ly,** *adv.*

erron., **1.** erroneous. **2.** erroneously.

er·ro·ne·ous (ə·rō′nĭ·əs, ĕ-), *adj.* **1.** containing error; mistaken; incorrect. **2.** *Obs.* or *Archaic.* straying from the right. [ME, t. L: m. *errōneus* straying] —**er·ro′ne·ous·ly,** *adv.* —**er·ro′ne·ous·ness,** *n.* —**Syn. 1.** inaccurate, wrong, untrue, false.

er·ror (ĕr′ər), *n.* **1.** deviation from accuracy or correctness; a mistake, as in action, speech, etc. **2.** the belief of what is not true. **3.** condition of believing what is not true: *in error about the date.* **4.** a moral offense; wrongdoing. **5.** *Math.*, *etc.* the difference between the observed or approximately determined value and the true value of a quantity. **6.** *Baseball.* any faulty play (except certain misplays by the pitcher or catcher, as a wild pitch or a passed ball) which prolongs a batsman's time at bat or leaves a runner safe, or allows him to advance one or more bases when he should have been put out. [t. L; r. ME *errour*, t. OF] —**er′ror·less,** *adj.* —**Syn. 1.** blunder, slip, oversight. See **mistake.**

error of closure, *Survey.* **1.** the amount by which a closed traverse fails to satisfy the requirements of a true mathematical figure as the length of line joining the true and computed position of the same point. **2.** the ratio of this linear error to the perimeter of the traverse. **3.** (for angles) the amount by which the sum of the observed angles fails to equal the true sum.

er·satz (ĕr·zäts′), *adj.* **1.** serving as a substitute: *an ersatz meat dish made of eggplant and oatmeal.* —*n.* **2.** a substitute. [t. G]

Erse (ûrs), *n.* **1.** Gaelic, esp. Scotch Gaelic. —*adj.* **2.** of or pertaining to the Celts in the Highlands of Scotland, or their language. [Scot. var. of **Irish**]

Ers·kine (ûr′skĭn), *n.* **1. John,** 1695–1768, Scottish writer on law. **2. John,** 1879–1951, U.S. author.

erst (ûrst), *adv.* *Archaic.* before the present time; formerly. [ME OE *ærst*, syncopated var. of *ærest* (c. G *erst*), superl. of *ær.* See **ere**]

erst·while (ûrst′hwīl′), *adj.* **1.** former: *erstwhile enemies.* —*adv.* **2.** *Archaic.* formerly; erst.

er·u·bes·cent (ĕr′ōō·bĕs′ənt), *adj.* becoming red or reddish; blushing. [t. L: s. *ērubescens*, ppr., reddening] —**er′u·bes′cence,** *n.*

e·ruct (ĭ·rŭkt′), *v.t.*, *v.i.* **1.** to belch forth, as wind from the stomach. **2.** to emit or issue violently, as matter from a volcano. [t. L: s. *ēructāre* belch forth]

e·ruc·tate (ĭ·rŭk′tāt), *v.t.*, *v.i.*, **-tated, -tating.** eruct. —**e·ruc·ta·tion** (ĭ·rŭk′tā′shən, ē′rŭk-), *n.*

er·u·dite (ĕr′ōō·dīt′, ĕr′yōō-), *adj.* characterized by erudition; learned or scholarly: *an erudite professor, an erudite commentary.* [t. L: m.s. *ērudītus*, pp., instructed] —**er′u·dite′ly,** *adv.* —**er′u·dite′ness,** *n.*

er·u·di·tion (ĕr′ōō·dĭsh′ən, ĕr′yōō-), *n.* acquired knowledge, esp. in literature, languages, history, etc; learning; scholarship. —**Syn.** See **learning.**

e·rum·pent (ĭ·rŭm′pənt), *adj.* **1.** bursting forth. **2.** *Bot.* prominent, as if bursting through the epidermis.

e·rupt (ĭ·rŭpt′), *v.i.* **1.** to burst forth, as volcanic matter. **2.** (of a volcano, geyser, etc.) to eject matter. **3.** (of teeth) to break through surrounding hard and soft tissues and become visible in the mouth. —*v.t.* **4.** to cause to burst forth. **5.** (of a volcano, etc.) to eject (matter). [t. L: s. *ēruptus*, pp.]

e·rup·tion (ĭ·rŭp′shən), *n.* **1.** an issuing forth suddenly and violently; an outburst; an outbreak. **2.** *Geol.* the ejection of molten rock, water, etc., as from a volcano, geyser, etc. **3.** *Pathol.* **a.** the breaking out of a rash or the like. **b.** a rash or exanthema. [t. L: s. *ēruptio*]

e·rup·tive (ĭ·rŭp′tĭv), *adj.* **1.** bursting forth, or tending to burst forth. **2.** pertaining to or of the nature of an eruption. **3.** *Geol.* (of rocks) formed by the eruption of molten material. **4.** *Pathol.* causing or attended with an eruption or rash. —*n.* **5.** *Geol.* an eruptive rock.

-ery, a suffix of nouns denoting occupation, business, calling, or condition, place or establishment, goods or products, things collectively, qualities, actions, etc., as in *archery, bakery, cutlery, fishery, grocery, nunnery, pottery, finery, foolery, prudery, scenery, tracery, trickery, witchery.* [ME, t. OF: m. *-erie*, f. *-ier* **-er**[2] + *-ie* **-y**[3]]

Er·y·man·thi·an boar (ĕr′ĭ·man′thĭ·ən), *Gk. Legend.* a savage beast fabled to have infested Arcadia and to have been caught by Hercules.

e·ryn·go (ĭ·rĭng′gō), *n.*, *pl.* **-goes.** any plant of the umbelliferous genus *Eryngium*, consisting of coarse herbs, esp. *E. maritimum*, the sea holly, whose root was formerly candied as a sweetmeat. Also, **eringo**. [? t. It.: m. *eringio*, der. L *ēryngion*, t. Gk., dim. of *ēryngos*]

er·y·sip·e·las (ĕr′ə·sĭp′ə·ləs, ĭr′ə-), *n.* *Pathol.* an acute, febrile, infectious disease, due to a specific streptococcus, and characterized by diffusely spreading, deep-red inflammation of the skin or mucous membranes. [t. L, t. Gk.; r. ME *herisipila*, etc., t. ML] **—er·y·si·pel·a·tous** (ĕr′ə·sĭ·pĕl′ə·təs, ĭr′-), *adj.*

er·y·sip·e·loid (ĕr′ə·sĭp′ə·loid′, ĭr′ə-), *n.* *Pathol.* a disease of man contracted by contact with the swine erysipelas bacillus characterized by a painful local ulcer generally on one of the hands.

er·y·the·ma (ĕr′ə·thē′mə), *n.* *Pathol.* abnormal redness of the skin due to local congestion, as in inflammation. [NL, t. Gk.: redness or flush] **—er·y·the·mat·ic** (ĕr′ə·thĭ·măt′ĭk), **er·y·them·a·tous** (ĕr′ə·thĕm′ə·təs, -thē′mə-), *adj.*

e·ryth·rin (ĭ·rĭth′rĭn), *n.* *Chem.* **1.** a crystalline compound, $C_{20}H_{22}O_{10}$, obtained from certain lichens. **2.** a coal-tar color used to dye silk a fluorescent red.

e·ryth·rism (ĭ·rĭth′rĭz·əm), *n.* abnormal redness, as of plumage or hair. **—er·y·thris·mal** (ĕr′ə·thrĭz′·məl), *adj.*

e·ryth·rite (ĭ·rĭth′rīt), *n.* **1.** cobalt bloom. **2.** erythritol.

e·ryth·ri·tol (ĭ·rĭth′rə·tōl′, -tŏl′), *n.* *Chem.* a tetrahydric crystalline alcohol, $H(CHOH)_4H$, related to carbohydrates, derived from certain lichens.

erythro-, a word element meaning "red," as in *erythrocyte.* Also, **crythr-.** [t. Gk., comb. form of *erythrós*]

e·ryth·ro·blast (ĭ·rĭth′rō·blăst′), *n.* *Anat.* a nucleated cell in the bone marrow from which red blood cells develop.

e·ryth·ro·cyte (ĭ·rĭth′rō·sīt′), *n.* *Anat.* one of the red corpuscles of the blood.

e·ryth·ro·cy·tom·e·ter (ĭ·rĭth′rō·sī·tŏm′ə·tər), *n.* an apparatus used to make a red blood cell count.

Erz Ge·bir·ge (ĕrts′ gə·bĭr′gə), a mountain range on the boundary between E Germany and NW Czechoslovakia. Highest point, Keilberg, 4080 ft.

Er·zu·rum (ĕr′zə·rŏŏm′), *n.* a city in NE Turkey. 47,613 (1940). Also, **Er′ze·rum**.

es-. For words with initial **es-,** see also **aes-.**

E·sau (ē′sô), *n.* *Bible.* a son of Isaac and Rebecca, older brother of Jacob, to whom he sold his birthright. Gen. 25:21–25.

es·ca·drille (ĕs′kə·drĭl′; *Fr.* ĕs·kå·drē′y). *n.* **1.** a squadron or divisional unit of airplanes: *the Lafayette Escadrille* of World War I. **2.** a small naval squadron. [t. F, t. Sp.: m. *escadrilla*, dim. of *escuadra* squadron, t. It.: m. *squadra* square, der. *squadrare* to square, g. L *exquadrāre*]

es·ca·lade (ĕs′kə·lād′), *n.*, *v.*, **-laded, -lading.** **—n.** **1.** a scaling or mounting by means of ladders, esp. in an assault upon a fortified place. **—v.t.** **2.** to mount, pass, or enter by means of ladders. [t. F, t. It.: m. *scalata*, der. *scalare* climb, der. *scala* steps, SCALE³] **—es·ca·lad′er,** *n.*

es·ca·la·tor (ĕs′kə·lā′tər), *n.* **1.** a moving inclined continuous stairway or runway used for raising or lowering passengers. **2.** (*cap.*) a trademark for this device. [? b. ESCALADE and ELEVATOR]

escalator clause, a provision in a contract between a labor union and a company permitting wage increases or decreases under specified conditions.

es·cal·lop (ĕs·kŏl′əp, ĕs·kăl′-), *v.t.* **1.** to bake (food, usually cut in pieces) in a sauce or other liquid, often with crumbs on top; scallop. **2.** to bake (fish, etc.) in scallop shells. **3.** to bake (as potatoes or fish) in a sauce. **—n.** **4.** scallop. Also, **es·cal′op.** [t. OF: m. *escalope* shell, of Gmc. orig.; cf. D *schelp* shell] **—es·cal′loped,** *adj.*

es·ca·pade (ĕs′kə·pād′, ĕs′kə·pād′), *n.* **1.** a reckless proceeding; a wild prank. **2.** an escape from confinement or restraint. [t. F, t. Sp.: m. *escapada*, der. *escapar* escape, or t. It.: m. *scappata* (der. *scappare*)]

es·cape (ĕs·kāp′), *v.*, **-caped, -caping.** **—v.i.** **1.** to slip or get away, as from confinement or restraint; gain or regain liberty. **2.** to slip away from pursuit or peril; avoid capture, punishment, or any threatened evil. **3.** to issue from a confining enclosure, as a fluid. **4.** *Bot.* (of an introduced plant) to grow wild. **—v.t.** **5.** to slip away from or elude (pursuit, etc.); succeed in avoiding (any threatened or possible evil). **6.** to elude (notice, search, etc., or one's memory); fail to be noticed or recollected by (a person). **7.** to slip from (a person) inadvertently, as a remark. **—n.** **8.** act of escaping. **9.** fact of having escaped. **10.** a means of escaping: *a fire escape.* **11.** avoidance of reality. **12.** leakage, as of water, gas, etc. **13.** *Bot.* a plant originally cultivated, now growing wild. [ME *escape(n)*, t. ONF: m. *escaper*, der. L: *ex-* EX-¹ + *cappa* cloak] **—es·cap′a·ble,** *adj.* **—es·cap′er,** *n.*

—Syn. 1. flee, abscond, decamp. **5.** shun, fly. ESCAPE, ELUDE, EVADE mean to keep free of something. To ESCAPE is to succeed in keeping away from danger, pursuit, observation, etc.: *to escape punishment.* To ELUDE implies s ipping through an apparently tight net, thus avoiding, often by a narrow margin, whatever threatens; it imp ies, also, us ng vigi ance, adroitness, dexterity, or slyness, so as to baffle

or foil: *a fox managed to e ude the hounds.* To EVADE is to turn aside from or go out of reach of a person or thing (at least temporarily), usually by using artifice or stratagem to direct attention elsewhere: *to evade the police.* See **avoid.**

es·cape·ment (ĕs·kāp′mənt), *n.* **1.** a way of escape; an outlet. **2.** *Horol.* the portion of a watch or clock which measures beats and controls the speed of the time train. **3.** a mechanism consisting of a notched wheel and ratchet for regulating the motion of a typewriter carriage.

escape wheel, *Horol.* a revolving toothed wheel which transmits impulses to a vibrating fork.

es·cap·ism (ĕs·kā′pĭz·əm), *n.* the avoidance of reality by absorption of the mind in entertainment, or in an imaginative situation, activity, etc. **—es·cap′ist,** *adj.*, *n.*

Two forms of escapement (def. 2)

es·car·got (ĕs·kär·gō′), *n.* *French.* an edible snail.

es·ca·role (ĕs′kə·rōl′; *Fr.* ĕs·kå·rôl′), *n.* a broad-leaved kind of endive, used for salads. [t. F]

es·carp (ĕs·kärp′), *n.* **1.** *Fort.* the inner slope or wall of the ditch surrounding a rampart. **2.** any similar steep slope. **—v.t.** **3.** to make into an escarp; give a steep slope to; furnish with escarps. [t. F: m. *escarpe*, t. It.: m. *scarpa*, of Gmc. orig. See SHARP, and cf. SCARP]

es·carp·ment (ĕs·kärp′mənt), *n.* **1.** a long, preciptous, clifflike ridge of land, rock, or the like, commonly formed by faulting or fracturing of the earth's crust. **2.** ground cut into an escarp about a fortification or defensive position.

Es·caut (ĕs·kō′), *n.* French name of **Scheldt.**

-esce, a suffix of verbs meaning to begin to be or do something, become, grow, or be somewhat (as indicated by the rest of the word), as in *convalesce, putresce.* [t. L: m.s. *-escere*, with inchoative force]

-escence, a suffix of nouns denoting action or process, change, state, or condition, etc., and corresponding to verbs ending in *-esce* or adjectives ending in *-escent,* as in *convalescence, deliquescence, luminescence, recrudescence.* [t. L: m.s. *-escentia.* See -ESCE, -ENCE]

-escent, a suffix of adjectives meaning beginning to be or do something, becoming or being somewhat (as indicated), as in *convalescent, deliquescent, recrudescent:* often associated with verbs ending in *-esce* or nouns ending in *-escence.* [t. L: s. *-escens,* ppr. ending]

esch·a·lot (ĕsh′ə·lŏt′, ĕsh′ə·lŏt′), *n.* shallot.

es·char (ĕs′kär, -kər), *n.* *Pathol.* a hard crust or scab, as from a burn. [t. LL: s. *eschara,* t. Gk.: hearth, scar]

es·cha·rot·ic (ĕs′kə·rŏt′ĭk), *Med.* **—adj. 1.** producing an eschar, as a medicinal substance; caustic. **—n. 2.** a caustic application. [t. LL: s. *escharōticus,* t. Gk.: m. *escharōtikós*]

es·cha·tol·o·gy (ĕs′kə·tŏl′ə·jĭ), *n.* *Theol.* **1.** the doctrines of the last or final things, as death, the judgment, the future state, etc. **2.** the branch of theology dealing with them. [f. Gk. *éschato(s)* last + -LOGY] **—es·cha·to·log·i·cal** (ĕs′kə·tə·lŏj′ə·kəl), *adj.* **—es′cha·tol′o·gist,** *n.*

es·cheat (ĕs·chēt′), *n.* *Law.* **1.** the "return" of property to the state or some agency of the state, or, as in England, to the crown, when there is a failure of persons legally qualified to inherit or to claim. **2.** property or a possession which reverts by escheat. **3.** the right to take property subject to escheat. **—v.i. 4.** to revert by escheat, as to the crown or the state. **—v.t. 5.** to make an escheat of; confiscate. [ME *eschete,* t. OF, der. *escheoir* fall to one's share, f. *es-* EX-¹ + *cheoir* (g. L *cadere* fall)] **—es·cheat′a·ble,** *adj.*

es·cheat·age (ĕs·chē′tĭj), *n.* the right of succeeding to an escheat.

es·cheat·or (ĕs·chē′tər), *n.* an officer in charge of escheats.

es·chew (ĕs·chōŏ′), *v.t.* to abstain from; shun; avoid: *to eschew evil.* [ME *eschewen,* t. OF: m. *eschiver,* ult. t. Gmc.; cf. SHY and see SKEW] **—es·chew′al,** *n.* **—es·chew′er,** *n.*

es·clan·dre (ĕs·klän′dr), *n.* *French.* a scandalous scene; unbecoming conduct.

Es·co·ri·al (ĕs·kōr′ĭ·əl; *Sp.* ĕs·kô·rē·äl′), *n.* a famous building in central Spain, 27 miles NW of Madrid, containing a monastery, palace, church, and mausoleum of the Spanish sovereigns: erected 1563–84. Also, **Escurial.** [t. Sp.: lit., a refuse heap, der. *escoria,* t. L: m.s. *scōria*]

es·cort (*n.* ĕs′kôrt; *v.* ĕs·kôrt′), *n.* **1.** a body of persons, or a single person, accompanying another or others for protection, guidance, or courtesy. **2.** an armed guard. **3.** protection, safeguard, or guidance on a journey. **—v.t. 4.** to attend or accompany as an escort. [t. F: m. *escorta,* t. It.: m. *scorta,* der. *scorgere* guide, f. L: *ex-* EX-¹ + *corrigere* CORRECT] **—Syn. 4.** conduct, usher, guard, convoy. See **accompany.**

es·cri·toire (ĕs′krĭ·twär′), *n.* a writing desk. [t. F, g. LL *scriptōria,* for *scriptōrium*]

es·crow (ĕs′krō, ĕs·krō′), *n.* *Law.* a contract, deed, bond, or other written agreement deposited with a third person, by whom it is to be delivered to the grantee or promisee on the fulfillment of some condition. [t. AF: m. *escrowe,* OF of *escroe* piece of cloth, parchment, SCROLL; of Gmc. orig.; akin to SHRED]

es·cu·age (ĕs′kyŏŏ·ĭj), *n.* *Feudal Law.* scutage. [t. AF, der. OF *escu,* g. L *scūtum* shield]

es·cu·do (ĕskōō′dō; *Port.* -dŏ̄; *Sp.* -dô), *n.*, *pl.* **-dos** (-dōz; *Port.*, *Sp.* -dôs). **1.** the gold monetary unit (established in 1911) of Portugal, divided into 100 centavos, and equivalent in value at that time to about $1.08. **2.** a Portuguese gold or silver coin having this value. **3.** any of various gold and silver coins of Spain, Chile, etc. [t. Sp., Pg., g. L *scūtum* shield. Cf. ECU, SCUDO]

es·cu·lent (ĕs′kyələnt), *adj.* **1.** suitable for use as food; edible. —*n.* **2.** something edible, esp. a vegetable. [t. L: s. *esculentus* good to eat]

Es·cu·ri·al (ĕskyōōr′Yəl), *n.* Escorial.

es·cutch·eon (ĕskŭch′ən), *n.* **1.** the shield or shield-shaped surface, on which armorial bearings are depicted; a hatchment. **2.** blot on the escutcheon, a stain on one's honor or reputation. **3.** a plate for protecting the keyhole of a door, or to which the handle is attached. **4.** the panel on a ship's stern bearing her name. [t. ONF: m. *escuchon*, ult. der. L *scūtum* shield] —**es·cutch′eoned**, *adj.*

Esd., Esdras (Apocrypha).

Es·dra·e·lon (ĕs′drā ē′lŏn, ĕz′-), *n.* a plain in N Palestine: the scene of many ancient battles. Also, **Plain of Jezreel**. See Megiddo.

Es·dras (ĕz′drəs), *n.* either of the first two books of the Apocrypha.

-ese, a noun and adjective suffix referring to locality, nationality, language, literary style, etc., as in *Bengalese*, *Chinese*, *Johnsonese*, *journalese*. [t. OF: m. *-eis*, g. L *-ēnsis*]

ESE, east-southeast. Also, **E.S.E.**

es·ker (ĕs′kər), *n.* Geol. a serpentine ridge of gravelly and sandy drift, believed to have been formed by streams under or in glacial ice. Also, **es·kar** (ĕs′kär, -kər). [t. Irish: m. *eiscir*]

Es·ki·mo (ĕs′kəmō′), *n.*, *pl.* **-mos, -mo**, *adj.* —*n.* **1.** one of a race or people, characterized by short stature, muscular build, light-brown complexion, and broad, flat face, inhabiting the arctic coasts of America from Greenland to Alaska and a small part of the adjacent Asiatic coast. **2.** their language, of Eskimoan stock. —*adj.* **3.** of or pertaining to the Eskimos or their language. Also, **Esquimau**. [t. Dan., t. F: m. *Esquimaux* (pl.), t. N Amer. Ind.: m. Algonquian name for the people, meaning eaters of raw flesh; cf. Abnaki *eskimantsi̇s*, Ojibwa *aškimek*. Cf. *Innuit* men, name applied by Eskimos to themselves]

Es·ki·mo·an (ĕs′kəmō′ən), *adj.* **1.** of or pertaining to the Eskimos or their language. —*n.* **2.** a linguistic stock including Eskimo and Aleut. Also, **Es′ki·mau′an**.

Eskimo dog, one of a breed of strong dogs used by the Eskimos to draw sledges.

Es·ki·şe·hir (ĕskē′shĕ hŸr′), *n.* a city in W Turkey. 60,742 (1940). Also, **Es·ki′she·hir′**.

e·so·phag·e·al (ē′sŏ făj′Yəl), *adj.* pertaining to the esophagus: *esophageal glands*. Also, **oesophageal**.

e·soph·a·gus (ē sŏf′əgəs), *n.*, *pl.* **-gi** (-jī′). Anat., Zool. a tube connecting the mouth or pharynx with the stomach in invertebrate and vertebrate animals; gullet. Also, **oesophagus**. [t. NL: m. *oesophagus*, t. Gk.: m. *oiso-phágos*]

es·o·ter·ic (ĕs′ə tĕr′Yk), *adj.* **1.** understood by or meant for a select few; profound; recondite. **2.** belonging to the select few. **3.** private; secret, confidential. **4.** (of philosophical doctrine, etc.) intended to be communicated only to the initiated (orig. applied to certain writings of Aristotle, and afterward to the secret teachings of Pythagoras). [t. Gk.: m. s. *esōterikós* inner] —**es′o·ter′i·cal·ly**, *adv.*

ESP, extrasensory perception; perception or communication outside of normal sensory activity, as in telepathy and clairvoyance.

esp., especially.

es·pal·ier (ĕs păl′yər), *n.* **1.** a trellis or framework on which fruit trees or shrubs are trained to grow flat. **2.** a tree or plants so trained. —*v.t.* **3.** to train on an espalier. **4.** to furnish with an espalier. [t. F, t. It.: m. *spalliera* support, der. *spalla* shoulder]

Es·pa·ña (ĕs pä′nyä), *n.* Spanish name of **Spain**.

Es·par·te·ro (ĕs′pär tĕ′rō), *n.* Joaquín Baldomero (hwä kēn′ bäl′dō mĕ′rō), 1792–1879, a Spanish general and statesman.

es·par·to (ĕs pär′tō), *n.* any of several grasses, esp. *Stipa tenacissima*, of S Europe and N Africa, used for making paper, cordage, etc. Also, **esparto grass**. [t. Sp., g. L *spartum*, t. Gk.: m. *spárton* a rope made of *spártos* a broomlike plant]

espec., especially.

es·pe·cial (ĕs pĕsh′əl), *adj.* **1.** special; exceptional; outstanding: *of no especial importance, an especial friend*. **2.** of a particular kind, or peculiar to a particular one: *your especial case*. [ME, t. OF, t. L: m.s. *speciālis* pertaining to a particular kind]

es·pe·cial·ly (ĕs pĕsh′əlY), *adv.* particularly; principally; unusually: *be especially watchful*.

—**Syn.** ESPECIALLY, CHIEFLY, PARTICULARLY, PRINCIPALLY refer to those cases of a class or kind which seem to be significant. ESPECIALLY and PARTICULARLY single out the most prominent case or example (often in order to particularize a general statement): *winter is especially severe on old people; corn grows well in the Middle West, particularly*

in Iowa. CHIEFLY and PRINCIPALLY imply that the general statement applies to a majority of the cases in question, and have a somewhat comparative force: *owls fly chiefly at night, crime occurs principally in large cities*.

es·per·ance (ĕs′pər əns), *n.* Obs. hope. [ME *esperaunce*, t. OF: m. *esperance*, der. *esperer*, g. L *spērāre* hope]

Es·pe·ran·to (ĕs′pə rän′tō, -rän′tō), *n.* an artificial language invented in 1887 by Dr. Zamenhof and intended for international auxiliary use. It is based on the commonest words in the most important European languages. [t. Sp.: m. *esperanza* hope, used by Zamenhof as a pseudonym] —**Es′pe·ran′tist**, *n.*, *adj.*

es·pi·al (ĕs pī′əl), *n.* **1.** act of spying. **2.** act of keeping watch.

es·pie·gle (ĕs pyĕ′gl), *adj.* French. roguish; playful. [F, alter. of *Ulespiegel*, t. D: m. (*Till*) *Uilenspiegel*, name of famous trickster]

es·pie·gle·rie (ĕs pyĕglə rē′), *n.* French. a roguish or playful trick. [F., der. *espiègle* ESPIEGLE]

es·pi·o·nage (ĕs′pī ən Yj, əspī′-, ĕs′pī ə näzh′), *n.* **1.** practice of spying on others. **2.** the systematic use of spies by a government to discover the military and political secrets of other nations. [t. F: m. *espionnage*, der. *espionner* spy upon, der. *espion* spy, t. It.: m. *spione*, aug. of *spia*, t. Gmc.; cf. G *spähe* spying]

es·pla·nade (ĕs′plə nād′, -näd′), *n.* any open, level space, esp. one serving for public walks or drives. [t. F, t. Sp.: m. *esplanada*, der. *esplanar*, g. L *explānāre* level]

es·pous·al (ĕs pou′zəl), *n.* **1.** adoption or advocacy, as of a cause or principle. **2.** (*sometimes pl.*) a marriage (or sometimes an engagement) ceremony. [ME *espousaile*, t. OF, g. L *sponsālia*, neut. pl. of *sponsālis* pertaining to betrothal]

es·pouse (ĕs pouz′), *v.t.*, **-poused, -pousing. 1.** to make one's own, adopt, or embrace, as a cause. **2.** to take in marriage; marry. **3.** to give (a woman) in marriage. [t. OF: m.s. *espouser*, g. L *sponsāre* betroth, espouse] —**es·pous′er**, *n.*

es·prit (ĕs prē′), *n.* French. wit; sprightliness; lively intelligence. [F, t. L: m.s. *spīritus* SPIRIT]

es·prit de corps (ĕs prē′ də kôr′), French. a sense of union and of common interests and responsibilities, as developed among a group of persons associated together.

es·py (ĕs pī′), *v.t.*, **-pied, -pying.** to see at a distance; catch sight of. [ME *espy*(*en*), t. OF: m. *espier*, ult. t. Gmc.; cf. G *spähen* spy] —**es·pi′er**, *n.* —**Syn.** discern, descry, discover, perceive, make out.

Esq., Brit., latterly borrowed in U.S. as an affectation. Esquire. *Henry Adams, Esq. = Mr. Henry Adams.*

-esque, an adjective suffix indicating style, manner, or distinctive character, as in *arabesque, picturesque, statuesque, Romanesque*. [t. F, t. It.: m. *-esco*; of Gmc. orig. Cf. -ISH¹]

Es·qui·line (ĕs′kwə lĭn′), one of the seven hills on which ancient Rome was built. [t. L: m.s. *Esquilīnus* (sc. *mons* hill)]

Es·qui·mau (ĕs′kə mō′), *n.*, *pl.* **-maux** (-mō′, -mōz′), *adj.* Eskimo. [t. F]

es·quire (ĕs kwīr′), *n.*, *v.* **-quired, -quiring.** —*n.* **1.** Brit. a polite title (usually abbreviated to *Esq.*) after a man's last name (*Mr.* or *Dr.* is omitted when it is used): *John Smith, Esq.* **2.** (in the Middle Ages) a squire, or aspirant to knighthood, attendant upon a knight. **3.** a man belonging to the order of English gentry ranking next below a knight. **4.** Archaic. an English country "squire." —*v.t.* **5.** to raise to the rank of esquire. **6.** to address as "Esquire." [ME *esquier*, t. OF, g. LL *scūtārius* shieldbearer, der. L *scūtum* shield]

ess (ĕs), *n.* **1.** the letter S, s. **2.** something shaped like an S.

-ess, a suffix forming distinctively feminine nouns, as *countess, hostess, lioness*. [t. F: m. *-esse*, g. L *-issa*, t. Gk.]

es·say (*n.* ĕs′ā for 1; ĕs′ā, ĕ sā′ for 2, 3; *v.* ĕ sā′), *n.* **1.** a short literary composition, on a particular subject. **2.** an effort to perform or accomplish something; an attempt. **3.** Obs. a tentative effort. —*v.t.* **4.** to try; attempt. **5.** to put to the test; make trial of. [t. OF: m. *essai*, g. LL *exagium* a weighing. Cf. ASSAY] —**es·say′er**, *n.*

es·say·ist (ĕs′ā Yst), *n.* **1.** a writer of essays. **2.** Rare. one who makes essays or trials.

es·se (ĕs′Y), *n.* Latin. being; existence. [L: to be]

Es·sen (ĕs′ən), *n.* a city in W Germany: the chief city of the Ruhr; Krupp works. 666,743 (1939).

es·sence (ĕs′əns), *n.* **1.** that by which a thing is what it is; intrinsic nature; important elements or features of a thing. **2.** a substance obtained from a plant, drug, or the like, by distillation or other process, and containing its characteristic properties in concentrated form. **3.** an alcoholic solution of an essential oil. **4.** a perfume. **5.** Philos. the inward nature, true substance, or constitution of anything. **6.** something that is, esp. a spiritual or immaterial entity. [t. L: m.s. *essentia*]

Es·sene (ĕs′ēn, ĕ sēn′), *n.* one of an ascetic, celibate brotherhood of Jews in ancient Palestine, first appearing in the 2d century B.C. [sing. of *Essenes*, Anglicized form of L *Essēnī*, pl., t. Gk.: m. *Essēnoí*] —**Es·se·ni·an** (ĕ sē′nYən), **Es·sen·ic** (ĕ sĕn′Yk), *adj.*

es·sen·tial (ə sĕn′shəl), *adj.* **1.** absolutely necessary; indispensable: *discipline is essential in an army*. **2.** pertaining to or constituting the essence of a thing. **3.** having the nature of an essence of a plant, etc. **4.** being such by its very nature, or in the highest sense: *es-*

sential happiness, essential poetry. —*n.* **5.** an indispensable element; a chief point: *concentrate on essentials rather than details.* [ME, t. LL: s. *essentiālis.* See ESSENCE] —**es·sen'tial·ly,** *adv.* —**es·sen'tial·ness,** *n.* —**Syn. 1.** fundamental, basic, inherent, intrinsic. See **necessary. 2.** ESSENTIAL, INHERENT INTRINSIC refer 'o that which is in the natural composition of a thing. ESSENTIAL suggests that which is in the very essence or constitution of a thing: *oxygen and hydrogen are essential in water.* INHERENT means inborn or fixed from the beginning as a permanent quality or constituent of a thing: *properties inherent in iron.* INTRINSIC implies belonging to the nature of a thing itself, and comprised within it, without regard to external considerations or accidentally added properties: *the intrinsic value of diamonds.* —**Ant. 2.** accidental, extrinsic.

es·sen·ti·al·i·ty (ə sĕn'shĭ ăl'ə tĭ), *n., pl.* -**ties. 1.** the quality of being essential; essential character. **2.** an essential element or point.

essential oil, any of a class of oils obtained from plants, possessing the odor and other properties of the plant, and volatilizing completely when heated; used in making perfumes, flavors, etc.

es·se quam vi·de·ri (ĕs'ĭ kwăm vĭ dâr'ī), *Latin.* to be rather than (merely) to seem (motto of North Carolina).

Es·se·qui·bo (ĕs'ĭ kē'bō), *n.* a river flowing from S British Guiana N to the Atlantic. ab. 550 mi.

Es·sex (ĕs'ĭks), *n.* **1.** a county in SE England. 1,858,000 pop. (est. 1946); 1528 sq. mi. *Co. seat:* Chelmsford. **2. Robert Devereux** (dĕv'ə rōō'), **Earl of,** 1567–1601, British soldier; favorite of Queen Elizabeth.

-est, a suffix forming the superlative degree of adjectives and adverbs, as in *warmest, fastest, soonest.* [OE *-est, -ost.* Cf. Gk. *-isto-*]

EST, Eastern Standard Time. Also, **E.S.T., e.s.t.**

est., **1.** established. **2.** estate. **3.** estimated. **4.** estuary.

estab., established.

es·tab·lish (ĕs tăb'lĭsh), *v.t.* **1.** to set up on a firm or permanent basis; institute; found: *to establish a government, a business, a university, etc.* **2.** to settle or install in a position, business, etc.: *to establish one's son in business.* **3.** to settle (oneself) as if permanently. **4.** to cause to be permanently accepted: *to establish a custom or a precedent.* **5.** to show to be valid or well grounded; prove: *to establish a fact, theory, claim, etc.* **6.** to appoint or ordain for permanence, as a law; fix unalterably. **7.** to set up or bring about permanently: *establish order.* **8.** to make (a church) a national or state institution. **9.** *Cards.* to obtain control of (a suit) so that one can win all the subsequent tricks in that suit. [ME *establisse(n)*, t. OF: m. *establiss-*, s. *establir*, g. L *stabilīre* make stable] —**es·tab'lish·er,** *n.* —**Syn. 1.** form, organize. See **fix. 5.** verify, substantiate. —**Ant. 1.** abolish. **5.** disprove.

established church, a church recognized and sometimes partly supported by the state, as (*caps.*) the Church of England.

es·tab·lish·ment (ĕs tăb'lĭsh mənt), *n.* **1.** act of establishing. **2.** state or fact of being established. **3.** something established; a constituted order or system. **4.** a household; a place of residence with everything connected with it. **5.** the building and equipment occupied by a business concern. **6.** a permanent civil, military, or other force or organization. **7.** institution. **8.** the recognition by the state of a church as the state church. **9.** the church so recognized, esp. the Church of England. **10.** fixed or settled allowance or income.

Es·taing, d' (dĕs tăn'), **Charles Hector, Comte,** 1729–94, French admiral.

es·ta·mi·net (ĕs tá mē nĕ'), *n. French.* a taproom. [F, t. Walloon: m. *staminé*, der. *stamon* post, t. Gmc.; cf. G *stamm* STEM]

es·tan·cia (ĕs tän'syä), *n.* (in Spanish America) a landed estate; a stock farm.

es·tate (ĕs tāt'), *n., v.,* -**tat·ed, -tat·ing.** —*n.* **1.** a piece of landed property, esp. one of large extent: *to have an estate in the country.* **2.** *Law.* **a.** property or possessions. **b.** the legal position or status of an owner, considered with respect to his property in land or other things. **c.** the degree or quantity of interest which a person has in land with respect to the nature of the right, its duration, or its relation to the rights of others. **d.** interest, ownership, or property in land or other things. **e.** the property of a deceased person, a bankrupt, etc., viewed as an aggregate. **3.** *Brit.* a housing development. **4.** period or condition of life: *to attain to man's estate.* **5.** a political or social group or class, as in France, the clergy, nobles, and commons, or in England, the lords spiritual, lords temporal, and commons (the three **estates of the realm**). **6.** condition or circumstances with reference to worldly prosperity, estimation, etc.; social status or rank. **7.** high rank or dignity. **8.** *Archaic.* pomp or state. —*v.t.* **9.** *Now Rare or Obs.* to establish in or as in an estate. [ME, t. OF: m. *estat*, t. L: m.s. *status.* See STATE] —**Syn. 1.** See **property.**

estate agent, *Brit.* **1.** the steward or manager of a landed estate. **2.** a real estate agent; a realtor.

Estates General, *French Hist.* the States-General.

es·teem (ĕs tēm'), *v.t.* **1.** to regard as valuable; regard highly or favorably: *I esteem him highly.* **2.** to consider as of a certain value; regard: *I esteem it worthless.* **3.** to set a value on; value: *to esteem lightly.* —*n.* **4.** favorable opinion or judgment; respect or regard: *to hold a person or thing in high esteem.* **5.** opinion or judgment of merit

or demerit; estimation. [ME *estyme(n)*, t. OF: m. *estimer*, t. L: m.s. *aestimāre.* See ESTIMATE, and cf. AIM] —**Syn. 1.** prize, honor, revere. See **appreciate. 4.** favor, admiration, honor, reverence, veneration. See **respect.** —**Ant. 1.** disdain.

es·ter (ĕs'tər), *n. Chem.* a compound formed by the reaction between an acid and an alcohol with the elimination of a molecule of water. [coined by L. Gmelin (1788–1853), German chemist]

es·ter·ase (ĕs'tə rās'), *n. Biochem.* any fement or enzyme which saponifies an ester.

es·ter·i·fy (ĕs tĕr'ə fī'), *v.t., v.i.,* -**fied, -fying.** *Chem.* to convert into an ester. —**es·ter'i·fi·ca'tion,** *n.*

Es·tes Park (ĕs'tĭz), a summer resort in N Colorado.

Esth., **1.** Esther. **2.** Esthonia.

Es·ther (ĕs'tər), *n.* one of the books of the Old Testament, named from its principal character. [t. L (Vulgate), t. Gk. (Septuagint), t. Heb. See ISHTAR]

es·the·sia (ĕs thē'zhə, -zhĭ'ə), *n.* sensitivity; feeling; perceptibility. Also, **aesthesia.** [NL, t. Gk.: m. *-aisthēsia* perceptive state]

es·the·sis (ĕs thē'sĭs), *n.* esthesia. Also, **aesthesis.** [t. Gk.: m. *aisthēsis* a perceiving]

es·thete (ĕs'thēt), *n.* aesthete.

es·thet·ic (ĕs thĕt'ĭk), *adj.* aesthetic.

es·thet·i·cal (ĕs thĕt'ə kəl), *adj.* aesthetical; —**es·thet'i·cal·ly,** *adv.*

es·the·ti·cian (ĕs'thə tĭsh'ən), *n.* aesthetician;

es·thet·i·cism (ĕs thĕt'ə sĭz'əm), *n.* aestheticism;

es·thet·ics (ĕs thĕt'ĭks), *n.* aesthetics.

Es·tho·ni·a (ĕs tō'nĭ ə, -thō'-), *n.* Estonia. —**Es·tho'ni·an,** *adj., n.*

Es·tienne (ĕs tyĕn'), *n.* a French printing firm famous for its scholarship, founded by **Henri** (än rē'), 1460?–1520, and carried on by his son **Robert** (rô bĕr'), 1503–1559, and by his grandson **Henri,** 1528–98.

es·ti·ma·ble (ĕs'tə məbəl), *adj.* **1.** worthy of esteem; deserving respect. **2.** capable of being estimated. —**es'ti·ma·ble·ness,** *n.* —**es'ti·ma·bly,** *adv.* —**Syn. 1.** reputable, respectable, worthy, meritorious. —**Ant. 1.** contemptible.

es·ti·mate (*v.* ĕs'tə māt'; *n.* ĕs'tə mĭt, -māt'), *v.,* -**mated -mating,** *n.* —*v.t.* **1.** to form an approximate judgment or opinion regarding the value, amount, size, weight, etc., of; calculate approximately. **2.** to form an opinion of; judge. —*v.i.* **3.** to submit approximate figures, as of the cost of work to be done. —*n.* **4.** an approximate judgment or calculation, as of the value, amount, etc., of something. **5.** a judgment or opinion, as of the qualities of a person or thing; estimation or judgment. **6.** an approximate statement of what would be charged for certain work to be done, submitted by one ready to undertake the work. [t. L: m. s. *aestimātus*, pp., valued, rated. Cf. ESTEEM] —**es'ti·ma'tor,** *n.* —**Syn. 1.** compute, count, reckon, gage.

es·ti·ma·tive (ĕs'tə mā'tĭv), *adj.* **1.** capable of estimating. **2.** based upon or pertaining to estimation.

es·ti·ma·tion (ĕs'tə mā'shən), *n.* **1.** judgment or opinion: *in my estimation.* **2.** esteem; respect: *to hold in high estimation.* **3.** approximate calculation; estimate: *to make an estimation of one's resources.* —**Syn. 2.** appreciation, regard, honor, veneration.

es·tip·u·late (ĕ stĭp'yə lĭt, -lāt'), *adj.* exstipulate.

es·ti·val (ĕs'tə vəl, ĕs tī'vəl), *adj.* pertaining or appropriate to summer. Also, **aestival.** [t. L: m.s. *aestivālis*]

es·ti·vate (ĕs'tə vāt'), *v.i.,* -**vated, -vating. 1.** to spend the summer. **2.** *Zool.* to pass the summer in a torpid condition. Also, **aestivate.** —**es'ti·va'tor,** *n.*

es·ti·va·tion (ĕs'tə vā'shən), *n.* **1.** *Zool.* act of estivating. **2.** *Bot.* the arrangement of the parts of a flower in the bud. Also, **aestivation.**

est mo·dus in re·bus (ĕst mō'dəs ĭn rē'bəs), *Latin.* there is a due measure in things. Horace, *Satires* I, 1, 106.

Es·to·ni·a (ĕs tō'nĭ ə), *n.* a constituent republic of the Soviet Union, on the Baltic, S of the Gulf of Finland: an independent republic, 1918–40; annexed by the Soviet Union, 1940. 1,126,413 pop. (1934); 18,300 sq. mi. *Cap.:* Tallinn. Also, **Esthonia.** Official name, **Estonian Soviet Socialist Republic.**

Es·to·ni·an (ĕs tō'nĭ ən), *adj.* **1.** of or pertaining to Estonia and its people. —*n.* **2.** one of a Finnish people inhabiting Estonia, Livonia, and other districts of Russia. **3.** the Finno-Ugric language of Estonia, very closely related to Finnish. Also, **Esthonian.**

es·top (ĕs tŏp'), *v.t.,* -**topped, -topping. 1.** *Law.* to hinder or prevent by estoppel. **2.** *Archaic.* to stop. [t. OF: m. *estoper* stop up, AF *estopper* (in law), der. OF *estoupe*, g. L *stuppa* tow. Cf. STOP, v.]

es·to per·pe·tu·a (ĕs'tō pər pĕch'ōō ə), *Latin.* may she endure (live) forever (motto of Idaho).

es·top·page (ĕs tŏp'ĭj), *n.* condition of being estopped.

es·top·pel (ĕs tŏp'əl), *n. Law.* a bar or impediment preventing a party from asserting a fact or a claim inconsistent with a position he previously took, either by conduct or words, esp. where a representation has been relied or acted upon by others. [appar. t. OF: m. *estoupail* stopple, stopper, der. *estouper* ESTOP]

es·to·vers (ĕs tō'vərz), *n.pl. Law.* necessaries allowed by law, as wood and timber to a tenant, alimony to a wife, etc. [t. OF: m. *estovoir* necessity, as inf., be necessary, g. Rom. *estopēre*, der. L *est opus* it is necessary]

ăct, āble, dâre, ärt; ĕbb, ēqual; ĭf, īce; hŏt, ōver, ôrder, oil, bŏŏk, ōōze, out; ŭp, ūse, ûrge; ə = a in alone; ch, chief; g, give; ng, ring; sh, shoe; th, thin; ŧh, that; zh, vision. See the full key on inside cover.

es·trange (ĕs·trānj′), *v.t.*, **-tranged, -tranging. 1.** to turn away in feeling or affection; alienate the affections of. **2.** to remove to or keep (usually oneself) at a distance. **3.** to divert from the original use or possessor. [t. OF: m. *estrangier,* g. L *extrāneāre,* der. *extrāneus* foreign. See STRANGE] —**es·trange′ment,** *n.* —**es·trang′-er,** *n.*

es·tray (ĕs·trā′), *n.* **1.** anything strayed away. **2.** *Law.* a domestic animal, as a horse or a sheep, found wandering or without an owner. —*v.i. Archaic.* **3.** to stray. [t. OF: m. *estraier.* See STRAY, v.]

es·treat (ĕs·trēt′), *Eng. Law.* —*n.* **1.** a true copy or extract of an original writing or record, as of a fine. —*v.t.* **2.** to make an estreat of (a fine, etc.) for prosecution. **3.** to levy (fines) under an estreat; exact (anything) by way of fine or levy. [t. AF: m. *estrete,* var. of *estraite,* prop. fem. pp. of *estraire,* g. L *extrahere.* See EXTRACT]

Es·tre·ma·du·ra (ĕs′trĕ mä dōō′rä), *n.* a region in W Spain. 1,253,924 pop. (1940); 16,054 sq. mi.

es·tri·ol (ĕs′trĭ ōl′, -ŏl′), *n. Biochem.* an estrogenic hormone, $C_{18}H_{21}(OH)_3$, occurring in pregnancy urine. Also, **oestriol.**

es·tro·gen (ĕs′trə jən), *n. Biochem.* any one of a group of female hormones which induce estrus in immature, spayed mammals. Also, **oestrogen.**

es·tro·gen·ic (ĕs′trə jĕn′ĭk), *adj. Biochem.* promoting or producing estrus.

es·trone (ĕs′trōn), *n. Biochem.* an estrogenic hormone, $C_{18}H_{22}O_2$, manufactured by the ovarian follicles and found in pregnancy urine and placental tissue. Also, **oestrin.**

es·trous (ĕs′trəs), *adj.* involving or pertaining to the estrus. Also, **oestrous.**

estrous cycle, *Zool.* a recurrent series of physiological changes in sexual and other organs extending from one previous period to the next. Also, **oestrous cycle.**

es·trus (ĕs′trəs), *n. Zool.* **1.** the estrous cycle in mammals other than primates, terminating with ovulation. **2.** the rut of animals. Also, **es·trum** (ĕs′trəm), **oestrus.** [t. L: m. *oestrus* frenzy]

es·tu·a·rine (ĕs′chŏŏ ə rĭn, -rĭn′), *adj.* **1.** formed in an estuary. **2.** found in estuaries.

es·tu·a·ry (ĕs′chŏŏ ĕr′ĭ), *n., pl.* **-aries. 1.** that part of the mouth or lower course of a river in which its current meets the sea's tides, and is subject to their effects. **2.** an arm or inlet of the sea. [t. L: m.s. *aestuārium,* der. *aestus* a heaving motion, surge, tide] —**es·tu·a·ri·al** (ĕs′chŏŏ âr′ĭ əl), *adj.*

e·su·ri·ent (ĭ sŏŏr′ĭ ənt), *adj.* hungry; greedy. [t. L: s. *ēsuriens,* ppr., desiring to eat] —**e·su′ri·ence, e·su′-ri·en·cy,** *n.* —**e·su′ri·ent·ly,** *adv.*

-et, a noun suffix having properly a diminutive force (now lost in many words), as in *islet, bullet, facet, midget, owlet, plummet.* [t. OF: *-et* masc., *-ette,* fem.]

e·ta (ā′tə, ē′tə), *n.* the seventh letter (H, η, English long E, e) of the Greek alphabet.

é·ta·gère (ā tȧ zhĕr′), *n. French.* a series of open shelves for bric-a-brac, etc.

et al., 1. (L *et alibi*) and elsewhere. **2.** (L *et aliī*) and others.

etc., et cetera.

et cet·er·a (ĕt sĕt′ər ə, -sĕt′rə), *Latin.* and others; and so forth; and so on (used to indicate that more of the same sort or class might have been mentioned, but for shortness are omitted). *Abbr.:* etc. [L, *et cētera* (sometimes *caetera*) and the rest]

et·cet·er·a (ĕt sĕt′ər ə, -sĕt′rə), *n., pl.* **-ras. 1.** other things or persons unspecified. **2.** (*pl.*) extras or sundries.

etch (ĕch), *v.t.* **1.** to cut, bite, or corrode with an acid or the like; engrave (metals, etc.) with an acid or the like, esp. to form a design in furrows which when charged with ink will give an impression on paper. **2.** to produce or copy by this method, as on copper. —*v.i.* **3.** to practice the art of etching. [t. D: m. *etsen,* t. G: m. *ätzen* feed, corrode, etch; akin to EAT] —**etch′er,** *n.*

etch·ing (ĕch′ĭng), *n.* **1.** a process of making designs or pictures on a metal plate, glass, etc., by the corrosion of an acid instead of by a burin. **2.** an impression, as on paper, taken from an etched plate.

E·te·o·cles (ĭ tē′ə klēz′), *n. Gk. Legend,* a son of Oedipus, and brother of Polynices, by whom he was slain. His breach of an agreement made with his brother led to the expedition of the Seven against Thebes.

e·ter·nal (ĭ tûr′nəl), *adj.* **1.** lasting throughout eternity; without beginning or end: *eternal life.* **2.** perpetual; ceaseless: *eternal quarreling, chatter,* etc. **3.** enduring; immutable: *eternal principles.* **4.** *Metaphys.* existing outside of all relations of time; not subject to change. —*n.* **5.** that which is eternal. **6. the Eternal,** God. [ME, t. LL: m.s. *aeternālis,* der. L *aeternus.* See ETERNE] —**e·ter′nal·ly,** *adv.* —**e·ter′nal·ness,** *n.*

—**Syn. 1.** ETERNAL, ENDLESS, EVERLASTING, PERPETUAL imply lasting or going on without ceasing. That which is ETERNAL is, by its nature, without beginning or ending: *God, the eternal father.* That which is ENDLESS never stops but goes on continually as if in a circle: *an endless succession of years.* That which is EVERLASTING will endure through all future time: *a promise of everlasting life.* PERPETUAL implies continuous renewal and lasting as far into the future as one can foresee: *perpetual strife between nations.* **3.** timeless, immortal, deathless, undying. —**Ant. 2.** temporary.

Eternal City, the, Rome.

e·terne (ĭ tûrn′), *adj. Archaic.* eternal. [ME, t. OF, t. L: m.s. *aeternus,* for *aeviternus* eternal]

e·ter·ni·ty (ĭ tûr′nə tĭ), *n., pl.* **-ties. 1.** infinite time; duration without beginning or end. **2.** eternal existence, esp. as contrasted with mortal life. **3.** an endless or seemingly endless period of time. [ME *eternite,* t. OF, t. L: m.s. *aeternitas,* der. *aeternus.* See ETERNE]

e·ter·nize (ĭ tûr′nīz), *v.t.,* **-nized, -nizing. 1.** to make eternal; perpetuate. **2.** to immortalize.

e·te·sian (ĭ tē′zhən), *adj.* recurring annually (applied to certain Mediterranean winds). [f. s. L *etēsius* (t. Gk.: m. *etēsios,* lit., annual) + -AN]

eth (ĕth), *n.* name of a letter formerly used in the English alphabet, and still used in Icelandic and in phonetic alphabets. It is a crossed *d* in form, and represents (1) in Old English, both surd and sonant *th;* (2) in phonetics, the sonant *th* only. See **thorn** (def. 5). Also, **edh.**

-eth,[1] an ending of the third person singular present indicative of verbs, now occurring only in archaic forms or used in solemn or poetic language, as in *doeth* or *doth, hath, hopeth, sitteth.* [OE *-eth, -ath, -oth, -th;* akin to L *-t*]

-eth,[2] the form of *-th,* the ordinal suffix, after a vowel, as in *twentieth, thirtieth,* etc. See **-th**[2].

Eth., Ethiopia.

eth·ane (ĕth′ān), *n. Chem.* an odorless, gaseous hydrocarbon, C_2H_6, of the methane series, present in illuminating gas and crude petroleum. [f. ETH(ER) + -ANE]

eth·a·nol (ĕth′ə nōl′, -nŏl′), *n. Chem.* ethyl alcohol. [f. ETHAN(E) + -OL[1]]

Eth·el·red II (ĕth′əl rĕd′), ("*the Unready*") 968?–1016, king of the English, 978–1016.

e·ther (ē′thər), *n.* **1.** *Chem.* **a.** a highly volatile and inflammable colorless liquid (**ethyl ether**), $(C_2H_5)_2O$, obtained by the action of sulfuric acid on alcohol, and used as a solvent and anesthetic. **b.** one of a class of organic compounds in which any two organic radicals are attached directly to oxygen, having the general formula R_2O, as diethyl ether $(C_2H_5)_2O$. **2.** the upper regions of space; the clear sky; the heavens. **3.** the medium anciently supposed to fill the upper regions. **4.** an all-pervading medium postulated for the transmission of light, heat, etc. by the older elastic solid theory. Also, **aether** (for defs. 2–4). [t. L: m. *aether,* t. Gk.: m. *aithēr* upper air, sky]

e·the·re·al (ĭ thĭr′ĭ əl), *adj.* **1.** light, airy, or tenuous. **2.** extremely delicate or refined: *ethereal beauty.* **3.** heavenly or celestial. **4.** of or pertaining to the ether or upper regions of space. **5.** *Chem.* pertaining to, containing, or resembling ethyl ether. Also, **aethereal** (for defs. 1–4). —**e·the′re·al′i·ty, e·the′re·al·ness,** *n.* —**e·the′re·al·ly,** *adv.*

e·the·re·al·ize (ĭ thĭr′ĭ ə līz′), *v.t.,* **-ized, -izing.** to make ethereal. **-e·the′re·al·i·za′tion,** *n.*

Eth·er·ege (ĕth′ər ĭj), *n.* **Sir George,** 1635?–91, British dramatist.

e·ther·i·fy (ĭ thĕr′ə fī′, ē′thər ə fī′), *v.t.,* **-fied, -fying.** *Chem.* to convert into ether or one of the ethers. —**e·ther′i·fi·ca′tion,** *n.*

e·ther·ize (ē′thə rīz′), *v.t.,* **-ized, -izing.** *Med.* to put under the influence of ether. —**e′ther·i·za′tion,** *n.* —**e′ther·iz′er,** *n.*

eth·ic (ĕth′ĭk), *adj.* **1.** pertaining to morals; ethical. —*n.* **2.** *Rare.* ethics. [t. L: s. *ēthicus,* t. Gk.: m. *ēthikós* of morals, moral]

eth·i·cal (ĕth′ĭ kəl), *adj.* **1.** pertaining to or dealing with morals or the principles of morality; pertaining to right and wrong in conduct. **2.** in accordance with the rules or standards for right conduct or practice, esp. the standards of a profession: *it is not considered ethical for physicians or dentists to advertise.* —**eth′i·cal·ly,** *adv.* —**eth′i·cal·ness,** *n.*

eth·i·cize (ĕth′ə sīz′), *v.t.,* **-cized, -cizing.** to make ethical; treat or regard as ethical.

eth·ics (ĕth′ĭks), *n.pl.* **1.** the principles of morality, including both the science of the good and the nature of the right. **2.** the rules of conduct recognized in respect to a particular class of human actions: *medical ethics.* **3.** moral principles, as of an individual. **4.** (*usually construed as sing.*) the science of the human character in its ideal state. —**Syn. 2.** See **moral.**

E·thi·op (ē′thĭ ŏp′), *adj., n.* Ethiopian. [t. L: s. *Aethiops,* t. Gk.: m. *Ae-thiops*]

E·thi·o·pi·a (ē′thĭ ō′pĭ ə), *n.* **1.** Also, **Abyssinia.** a kingdom in E Africa: formerly a part of Italian East Africa, 1936–41. 6,800,000 pop. (est. 1946); ab. 350,000 sq. mi. *Cap.:* Addis Ababa. **2.** an ancient region in NE Africa, bordering on Egypt and the Red Sea.

Ethiopia (def 1)

E·thi·o·pi·an (ē′thĭ ō′pĭ ən), *adj.* **1.** pertaining to Ethiopia or to its inhabitants. **2.** Negro. **3.** belonging to Africa south of the tropic of Cancer. —*n.* **4.** a native of Ethiopia. **5.** *Ethnol.* a member of the Ethiopian race, one of the five racial divisions originally recognized, including the African Negro and Negrito. **6.** a Negro.

---

b., blend of, blended; c., cognate with; d., dialect, dialectal; der., derived from; f., formed from; g., going back to; m., modification of; r., replacing; s., stem of; t., taken from; ?, perhaps. See the full key on inside cover.

E·thi·op·ic (ē'thĭ ŏp'ĭk, -ō'pĭk), *adj.* **1.** Ethiopian. **—n. 2.** the ancient Semitic language of Ethiopia.

eth·moid (ĕth'moid), *Anat. adj.* **1.** designating or pertaining to a bone of the skull at the root of the nose, containing numerous perforations for the filaments of the olfactory nerve. **—n. 2.** the ethmoid bone. [t. Gk.: m.s. *ethmoeidēs* sievelike] **—eth·moi'dal,** *adj.*

eth·narch (ĕth'närk), *n.* the ruler of a people, tribe, or nation. [t. Gk.: s. *ethnárchēs*. See ETHNO-, -ARCH]

eth·nar·chy (ĕth'när kĭ), *n.*, *pl.* **-chies.** the government, office or jurisdiction of an ethnarch.

eth·nic (ĕth'nĭk), *adj.* **1.** pertaining to or peculiar to a population, esp. to a speech group, loosely also to a race. **2.** referring to the origin, classification, characteristics, etc. of such groups. **3.** pertaining to nations not Jewish or Christian; heathen or pagan: *ancient ethnic revels.* Also, **eth'ni·cal.** [ME, t. LL: s. *ethnicus*, t. Gk.: m. *ethnikós* national, gentile, heathen, der. *éthnos* nation] **—eth'ni·cal·ly,** *adv.*

ethnic group, *Sociol.* a group of people, racially or historically related, having a common and distinctive culture, as an Italian or Chinese colony in a large American city.

ethno-, a word element meaning "race," "nation," as in *ethnology.* [t. Gk., comb. form of *éthnos*]

eth·no·cen·trism (ĕth'nō sĕn'trĭz əm), *n.* *Sociol.* the belief in the inherent superiority of one's own group and culture accompanied by a feeling of contempt for other groups and cultures. **—eth'no·cen'tric,** *adj.*

ethnog., ethnography.

eth·nog·e·ny (ĕth nŏg'ə nĭ), *n.* *Anthropol.* the branch of ethnology which studies the origin of distinctive populations or races.

eth·nog·ra·phy (ĕth nŏg'rə fĭ), *n.* **1.** the scientific description and classification of the various cultural and racial groups of mankind. **2.** ethnology, esp. as descriptive. **—eth·nog'ra·pher,** *n.* **—eth·no·graph·ic** (ĕth'nə grăf'ĭk), **eth'no·graph'i·cal,** *adj.* **—eth'no·graph'i·cal·ly,** *adv.*

ethnol., **1.** ethnological. **2.** ethnology.

eth·nol·o·gy (ĕth nŏl'ə jĭ), *n.* the science that treats of the distinctive subdivisions of mankind, their origin, relations, speech, institutions, etc. **—eth·no·log·i·cal** (ĕth'nə lŏj'ə kəl), **eth'no·log'ic,** *adj.* **—eth'no·log'i·cal·ly,** *adv.* **—eth·nol'o·gist,** *n.*

et hoc (or id) ge·nus om·ne (ĕt hŏk' (or ĭd) jē'nəs ŏm'nē), *Latin.* and all this (or that) sort of thing.

e·thos (ē'thŏs), *n.* **1.** character or disposition. **2.** *Sociol.* the fundamental spiritual characteristics of a culture. **3.** *Art.* the inherent quality of a work which produces, or is fitted to produce, a high moral impression, noble, dignified, and universal (opposed to *pathos*). [t. NL, t. Gk.: character]

eth·yl (ĕth'əl), *n.* **1.** *Chem.* a univalent radical, C_2H_5, from ethane. **2.** a type of antiknock fluid, containing tetraethyl lead and other ingredients for a more even combustion. **3.** gasoline to which this fluid has been added. **4.** (*cap.*) a trademark for the antiknock fluid (def. 2) or the gasoline (def. 3). [f. ETH(ER) + -YL] **—e·thyl·ic** (ĭ thĭl'ĭk), *adj.*

ethyl alcohol. See alcohol.

eth·yl·ate (ĕth'ə lāt), *v.*, **-ated, -ating,** *n.* *Chem.* **—v.t. 1.** to introduce one or more ethyl radicals into (a compound). **—n. 2.** a metallic derivative of ethyl alcohol, as potassium ethylate (KOC_2H_5).

eth·yl·ene (ĕth'ə lēn), *n.* *Chem.* a colorless, inflammable gas, C_2H_4, with an unpleasant odor, the first member of the ethylene series.

ethylene glycol, *Chem.* glycol.

ethylene series, *Chem.* a series of unsaturated aliphatic hydrocarbons having one double bond, with the general formula, C_nH_{2n}.

ethyl ether. See ether (def. 1a).

e·ti·o·late (ē'tĭ ə lāt'), *v.*, **-lated, -lating. —v.t. 1.** to cause (a plant) to whiten by excluding light. **—v.i. 2.** (of plants) to whiten through lack of light. [f. s. F *étioler* blanch (der. *tiolé* many-colored, inoculate, der. *tieule* tile, g. L *tēgula*) + -ATE¹] **—e'ti·o·la'tion,** *n.*

e·ti·ol·o·gy (ē'tĭ ŏl'ə jĭ), *n.* the study of the causes of diseases. Also, **aetiology.** [t. L: m.s. *aetiologia*, t. Gk.: m. *aitiología*, der. *aitía* cause. See -LOGY] **—e·ti·o·log·i·cal** (ē'tĭ ə lŏj'ə kəl), *adj.* **—e'ti·o·log'i·cal·ly,** *adv.* **—e'ti·ol'o·gist,** *n.*

et·i·quette (ĕt'ə kĕt'), *n.* **1.** conventional requirements as to social behavior; proprieties of conduct as established in any class or community or for any occasion. **2.** a prescribed or accepted code of usage in matters of ceremony, as at a court or in official or other formal observances. [t. F, in OF *estiquette* TICKET, of Gmc. orig.; cf. STICK²]

—Syn. 1. ETIQUETTE, DECORUM, PROPRIETY imply observance of the formal requirements governing behavior in polite society. ETIQUETTE refers to conventional forms and usages: *the rules of etiquette.* DECORUM suggests dignity and a sense of what is becoming or appropriate for a person of good breeding: *a fine sense of decorum.* PROPRIETY (usually plural) implies established conventions of morals and good taste: *she never fails to observe the proprieties.*

Et·na (ĕt'nə), *n.* **1.** Also, **Aetna. Mount,** an active volcano in E Sicily. 10,758 ft. **2.** (*l.c.*) a small vessel for heating liquids, consisting of a cup for the liquid with a fixed saucer surrounding it in which alcohol is burned.

E·ton (ē'tən), *n.* a town in S England, on the Thames, W of London: the site of Eton College. 4399 (1939).

Eton collar, a broad stiff collar folded outside an Eton jacket.

Eton College, an educational establishment at Eton, England, founded in 1440 by Henry VI.

E·to·ni·an (ē tō'nĭ ən), *n.* **1.** one who is or has been a pupil at Eton College. **—adj. 2.** of or pertaining to Eton College.

Eton jacket, 1. a boys' short jacket reaching to the waistline, as worn by students at Eton College, England. **2.** a similar short jacket worn by women.

Boy wearing an Eton jacket

E·tru·ri·a (ĭ trŏŏr'ĭ ə), *n.* an ancient country in W Italy, centering between the Arno and the Tiber and roughly corresponding to modern Tuscany.

E·trus·can (ĭ trŭs'kən), *adj.* **1.** pertaining to Etruria, its inhabitants, civilization, art, or language. **—n. 2.** an inhabitant of ancient Etruria. **3.** the extinct language of Etruria. Also, **E·tru·ri·an** (ĭ trŏŏr'ĭ ən). [f. s. L *Étruscus* of Etruria + -AN]

et seq., *pl.* **et seqq, et sqq.** (L *et sequens*) and the following.

et seqq., (L *et sequentes, et sequentia*) and those following. Also, **et sqq.**

et sic de si·mi·li·bus (ĕt sĭk dē sĭ mĭl'ə bəs), *Latin.* and thus concerning (all) similar (ones).

-ette, a noun suffix, the feminine form of *-et,* occurring esp.: **1.** with the original diminutive force, as in *cigarette.* **2.** as a distinctively feminine ending, as in *coquette,* and various colloquial or humorous formations, such as *usherette, farmerette.* **3.** in trademarks of imitations or substitutes, as in *leatherette.* [t. F, fem. of *-et* -ET]

et tu, Bru·te! (ĕt tū brŏŏ'tĭ), *Latin.* and thou, Brutus! (reproachful exclamation of Julius Caesar on seeing his friend Brutus among his assassins).

é·tude (ā tūd', ā tŏŏd'; *Fr.* ĕ tyd'), *n.* *Music.* **1.** a composition intended mainly for the practice of some point of technique. **2.** a composition performed for its aesthetic appeal which also embodies a specific technical exercise. [F. See STUDY, n.]

e·tui (ā twē', ĕt'wē), *n.*, *pl.* **etuis.** a small case, esp. one for small objects, as needles, toilet articles, etc. Also, **e·twee'.** [t. F, der. OF *etuier* keep, g. L *studiāre* care for]

etym., 1. etymological. **2.** etymology. Also, **etymol.**

et·y·mol·o·gize (ĕt'ə mŏl'ə jīz'), *v.*, **-gized, -gizing. —v.t. 1.** to trace the history of (a word). **—v.i. 2.** to study etymology. **3.** to give or suggest the etymology of words.

et·y·mol·o·gy (ĕt'ə mŏl'ə jĭ), *n.*, *pl.* **-gies. 1.** the study of historical linguistic change, esp. as applied to individual words. **2.** an account of the history of a particular word. **3.** the derivation of a word. [t. L: m.s. *etymologia,* t. Gk. See ETYMON, -LOGY] **—et·y·mo·log·i·cal** (ĕt'ə mə lŏj'ə kəl), **et'y·mo·log'ic,** *adj.* **—et'y·mo·log'i·cal·ly,** *adv.* **—et·y·mol'o·gist,** *n.*

et·y·mon (ĕt'ə mŏn'), *n.*, *pl.* **-mons, -ma** (-mə). a primary linguistic form, from which derivatives are formed. [t. L, t. Gk.: the original sense, form, or element of a word, prop. neut. of *étymos* true, real]

Et·zel (ĕt'səl), *n.* *German Legend.* Attila.

eu-, a prefix meaning "good," "well," occurring chiefly in words of Greek origin, as in *eupepsia.* [t. Gk., comb. form of *eûs,* adj., good, neut. *eû* (used as adv., well)]

Eu, *Chem.* curopium.

Eu·boe·a (ū bē'ə), *n.* an island in the Aegean, off the E coast of, and belonging to, Greece. 140,851 pop. (1928); 1457 sq. mi. *Cap.* Chalcis. Modern Greek, **Evvoia.** Also, **Negropont. —Eu·boe'an,** *adj.*

eu·caine (ū kān'), *n.* **1.** a crystalline organic compound used, in the form of a salt, as a local anesthetic (**alpha eucaine**). **2.** a similar but less used compound (**beta eucaine**); betaeucaine. [f. EU- + (CO)CAINE]

eu·ca·lyp·tol (ū'kə lĭp'tōl, -tŏl), *n.* cineole. [f. EUCALYPT(US) + -OL²]

eu·ca·lyp·tus (ū'kə lĭp'təs), *n.*, *pl.* **-ti** (-tī), **-tuses.** any member of the myrtaceous genus *Eucalpytus,* including many tall trees, esp. the blue gum, *E. globulus,* native in and around Australia and cultivated elsewhere, which yields a valuable timber and bears leaves containing an oil used in medicine. Also, **eu·ca·lypt** (ū'kə lĭpt'). [t. NL, f. *eu-* EU- + m. Gk. *kaplytós* covered (with allusion to the cap covering the bud)]

eu·cha·ris (ū'kə rĭs), *n.* any of the amaryllidaceous plants constituting the South American genus *Eucharis,* some of which are cultivated for their large, fragrant white flowers. [NL, t. Gk.: pleasing]

Eu·cha·rist (ū'kə rĭst), *n.* **1.** the sacrament of the Lord's Supper; the communion; the sacrifice of the Mass. **2.** the consecrated elements of the Lord's Supper, esp. the bread. **3.** (*l.c.*) the giving of thanks; thanksgiving. [t. LL: m.s. *eucharistia,* t. Gk.: gratefulness, thanksgiving, the eucharist] **—Eu·cha·ris'tic, Eu'cha·ris'ti·cal,** *adj.* **—Eu'cha·ris'ti·cal·ly,** *adv.*

eu·chre (ū'kər), *n.*, *v.*, **-chred, -chring. —n. 1.** *Cards.* a game played usually by two, three, or four persons, with the 32 (or 28 or 24) highest cards in the pack. **2.** an instance of euchring or being euchred. **—v.t. 3.** to get the better of (an opponent) in a hand at euchre by his failure to win three tricks after having made the trump. **4.** *U.S. Colloq.* to outwit; get the better of, as by scheming (usually fol. by *out*). [orig. uncert.]

ăct, āble, dâre, ärt; ĕbb, ēqual; ĭf, īce; hŏt, ōver, ôrder, oil, bŏŏk, ōoze, out; ŭp, ūse, ûrge; ə = a in alone; ch, chief; g, give; ng, ring; sh, shoe; th, thin; ŧħ, that; zh, vision. See the full key on inside cover.

Euck·en (oi′kən), *n.* **Rudolph Christoph** (rōō′dôlf krĭs′tôf), 1846–1926, German philosopher.

eu·clase (ū′klās), *n.* a green or blue mineral, beryllium aluminum silicate, HBeAl(SiO₅), occurring in prismatic crystals. [t. F, f. Gk. *eu-* EU- + m.s. Gk. *klásis* a breaking]

Eu·clid (ū′klĭd), *n.* 1. fl. c300 B.C., Greek geometer at Alexandria. 2. the works of Euclid, esp. his treatise on geometry. 3. Euclidean geometry. 4. a city in NE Ohio, near Cleveland. 41,396 (1950).

Eu·clid·e·an (ū klĭd′ĭ ən), *adj.* of or pertaining to Euclid, or adopting his postulates: *Euclidean geometry.* Also, **Eu·clid′i·an.**

eu·de·mon (ū dē′mən), *n.* a good demon or spirit. Also, **eu·dae′mon.** [f. EU- + m. Gk. *daímōn* DEMON]

eu·de·mo·ni·a (ū′dĭ mō′nĭ ə), *n.* 1. happiness; welfare. 2. (in Aristotelian philosophy) happiness as the result of an active life governed by reason. Also, **eu′dae·mo′ni·a.** [f. Gk.: m. *eudaimonía*]

eu·de·mon·ic (ū′dĭ mŏn′ĭk), *adj.* 1. pertaining or conducive to happiness. 2. pertaining to eudemonics. Also, **eu′dae·mon′ic.**

eu·de·mon·ics (ū′dĭ mŏn′ĭks), *n.* 1. the science of happiness. 2. eudemonism. Also, **eu′dae·mon′ics.**

eu·de·mon·ism (ū dē′mə nĭz′əm), *n.* the system of ethics which holds that the basis of moral obligations lies in their relation to the production of happiness. Also, **eu·dae′mon·ism.** [f. EUDEMON(IA) + -ISM] —**eu·de′mon·ist,** *n.* —**eu·de·mon·is′tic, eu·de·mon·is·ti·cal,** *adj.*

eu·di·om·e·ter (ū′dĭ ŏm′ə tər), *n. Chem.* a graduated glass measuring tube for gas analysis. [f. Gk. *eúdio(s)* fine, clear, as weather + -METER] —**eu·di·o·met·ric** (ū′dĭ ə mĕt′rĭk), **eu·di·o·met·ri·cal,** *adj.* —**eu·di·o·met′ri·cal·ly,** *adv.*

eu·di·om·e·try (ū′dĭ ŏm′ə trĭ), *n. Chem.* the measurement and analysis of gases with the eudiometer.

Eu·gene (ū jēn′), *n.* a city in W Oregon. 35,879 (1950).

Eu·gène (œ zhĕn′), *n.* **Prince,** *(François Eugène de Savoie-Carignan)* 1663–1736, Austrian general, born in France.

eu·gen·ic (ū jĕn′ĭk), *adj.* 1. of or bringing about improvement in the type of offspring produced. 2. having good inherited characteristics. Also, **eu·gen′i·cal.** [f. s. Gk. *eugenḗs* well born + -IC] —**eu·gen′i·cal·ly,** *adv.*

eu·gen·i·cist (ū jĕn′ə sĭst), *n.* 1. a specialist in eugenics. 2. an advocate of eugenic measures. Also, **eu·ge·nist** (ū′jə nĭst).

eu·gen·ics (ū jĕn′ĭks), *n.* 1. the science of improving the qualities of the human race, esp. the careful selection of parents. 2. the science of improving offspring.

Eu·gé·nie (œ zhĕ nē′), *n.* **Empress,** *(Marie Eugénie de Montijo de Guzmán)* 1826–1920, empress of the French, born in Spain (wife of Napoleon III).

eu·ge·nol (ū′jə nōl′, -nŏl′), *n. Chem.* a colorless, aromatic, oily compound, C₁₀H₁₂O₂, contained in certain essential oils, as that of cloves. [f. NL *Eugen(ia)* genus of myrtaceous plants + -OL²]

Eu·gle·na (ū glē′nə), *n.* a green type of flagellate protozoan with one flagellum and a red eyespot, much used for class and experimental study.

eu·he·mer·ism (ū hē′mə rĭz′əm, ū hĕm′ə-), *n.* 1. the theory held by Euhemerus that polytheistic mythology arose out of the deification of dead heroes. 2. mythological interpretation which reduces the gods to the level of distinguished men; the derivation of mythology from history. —**eu·he′mer·ist,** *n.* —**eu·he′mer·is·tic,** *adj.* —**eu·he′mer·is·ti·cal·ly,** *adv.*

eu·he·mer·ize (ū hē′mə rīz′, ū hĕm′ə-), *v.t., v.i.,* -ized, -izing. to treat or explain (myths) by euhemerism.

Eu·he·mer·us (ū hē′mər əs), *n.* fl. c300 B.C., Greek writer. See **euhemerism.**

eu·la·chon (ū′lə kŏn′), *n.* candlefish.

Eu·ler (oi′lər), *n.* **Leonhard** (lā′ôn härt′), 1707–83, Swiss mathematician.

eu·lo·gi·a (ū lō′jĭ ə), *n. Eccles.* the unconsecrated bread not needed in the Eucharist, but blessed and distributed among those members of the congregation who did not commune. This custom still exists in the Greek Church. [t. Eccl. L, t. Gk. See EULOGY]

eu·lo·gist (ū′lə jĭst), *n.* one who eulogizes.

eu·lo·gis·tic (ū′lə jĭs′tĭk), *adj.* pertaining to or containing eulogy; laudatory. Also, **eu′lo·gis′ti·cal.** —**eu′lo·gis′ti·cal·ly,** *adv.*

eu·lo·gi·um (ū lō′jĭ əm), *n., pl.* -giums, -gia (-jĭ ə). 1. eulogy. 2. eulogistic language. [t. ML. See EULOGY]

eu·lo·gize (ū′lə jīz′), *v.t.,* -gized, -gizing. to praise highly; speak or write a eulogy about. —**eu′lo·giz′er,** *n.* —**Syn.** extol, laud, commend, panegyrize.

eu·lo·gy (ū′lə jĭ), *n., pl.* -gies. 1. a speech or writing in praise of a person or thing, esp. a set oration in honor of a deceased person. 2. high praise or commendation. [t. ML: m.s. *eulogium,* var. of L *eulogia* (t. Gk.: praise), by assoc. with *ēlogium* short saying]

Eu·men·i·des (ū mĕn′ə dēz′), *n.pl. Class. Myth.* a euphemistic name for the Furies or Erinyes. [t. L, t. Gk.: lit., the gracious goddesses]

eu·nuch (ū′nək), *n.* a castrated man, esp. one formerly employed as a harem attendant or officer of state by Oriental rulers. [t. L: s. *eunŭchus,* t. Gk.: m. *eunoûchos* chamber attendant]

eu·on·y·mus (ū ŏn′ə məs), *n.* any of a celastraceous genus *Euonymus,* of shrubs and small trees, of northern temperate regions, usually bearing crimson or rose-colored capsules, which on opening disclose the seed. Also, **evonymus.** [t. Gk.: m. *euṓnymos* spindle tree, lit., of good name]

eu·pa·to·ri·um (ū′pə tōr′ĭ əm), *n.* any plant of the large composite genus *Eupatorium,* mostly American, with heads of white or purplish flowers, as thoroughwort and joe-pye weed, and esp. a garden species, the mistflower. [NL, t. Gk.: m. *eupatórion;* named after Mithridates *Eupator,* king of Pontus (120?–63 B.C.)]

eu·pat·rid (ū păt′rĭd, ū′pə trĭd), *n.* 1. one of the hereditary aristocrats of ancient Athens and other states of Greece, who at one time formed the ruling class. 2. any aristocrat or patrician. [t. Gk.: s. *eupatrídēs*]

eu·pat·ri·dae (ū păt′rə dē′), *n.pl.* the eupatrids. [NL, t. Gk.: m. *eupatrídai,* pl. of *eupatrídēs* of noble family]

Eu·pen and Mal·mé·dy (oi′pən; mál mĕ dē′), two districts on the Belgian-German border: ceded to Belgium, 1919; reannexed to Germany, 1940; now in Belgium.

eu·pep·sia (ū pĕp′shə, -sĭ ə), *n.* good digestion (opposed to *dyspepsia*). [t. NL, t. Gk.: good digestion] —**eu·pep·tic** (ū pĕp′tĭk), *adj.*

eu·phe·mism (ū′fə mĭz′əm), *n. Rhet.* 1. the substitution of mild, indirect, or vague expression for a harsh or blunt one. 2. the expression so substituted: "*To pass away*" *is a euphemism for "to die."* [t. Gk.: s. *euphēmismós,* der. *euphēmízein* use fair words] —**eu′phe·mist,** *n.* —**eu′phe·mis′tic, eu′phe·mis′ti·cal,** *adj.* —**eu′phe·mis′ti·cal·ly,** *adv.*

eu·phe·mize (ū′fə mīz′), *v.,* -mized, -mizing. —*v.t.* 1. to refer to by means of euphemism. —*v.i.* 2. to employ euphemism.

eu·phon·ic (ū fŏn′ĭk), *adj.* pertaining to or characterized by euphony. Also, **eu·phon′i·cal.** —**eu·phon′i·cal·ly,** *adv.* —**eu·phon′i·cal·ness,** *n.*

eu·pho·ni·ous (ū fō′nĭ əs), *adj.* characterized by euphony; well-sounding; agreeable to the ear. —**eu·pho′ni·ous·ly,** *adv.* —**eu·pho′ni·ous·ness,** *n.*

eu·pho·ni·um (ū fō′nĭ əm), *n. Music.* a baritone tuba, used in bands. [t. NL, der. Gk. *eúphōnos* well-sounding]

eu·pho·nize (ū′fə nīz′), *v.t.,* -nized, -nizing. to make euphonious.

eu·pho·ny (ū′fə nĭ), *n., pl.* -nies. 1. agreeableness of sound; pleasing effect to the ear, esp. of speech sounds as uttered or as combined in utterance. 2. a tendency to change speech sounds for ease and economy of utterance: an explanation formerly given of phonetic change. [t. LL: m.s. *euphōnia,* t. Gk., der. *eúphōnos* well-sounding]

eu·phor·bi·a (ū fôr′bĭ ə), *n.* any of the plants of the widespread genus *Euphorbia,* which vary greatly, but consist mostly of herbs and shrubs with an acrid milky juice; a spurge. [NL, for L *euphorbea* an African plant; named after *Euphorbus,* a Greek physician]

eu·phor·bi·a·ceous (ū fôr′bĭ ā′shəs), *adj.* belonging to the *Euphorbiaceae,* or spurge family of plants, which includes the spurges, the cascarilla, castor oil, and cassava plants, several that yield rubber, and others.

eu·pho·ri·a (ū fōr′ĭ ə), *n. Psychol.* a feeling or state of well-being. [t. NL, t. Gk., der. *eúphoros* bearing well]

eu·phra·sy (ū′frə sĭ), *n.* eyebright, *Euphrasia officinalis.* [t. ML: m.s. *euphrasia,* t. Gk.: delight]

Eu·phra·tes (ū frā′tēz), *n.* a river flowing from E Turkey through Syria and Iraq, joining the Tigris to form the Shatt al Arab near the Persian Gulf. 1700 mi.

eu·phroe (ū′frō, ū′vrō), *n. Naut.* an oblong or oval piece of wood perforated with holes through which small lines are rove, forming a crowfoot, from which an awning is suspended. Also, **uphroe.** [t. D: pseudo-learned spelling of *juffrouw,* lit., young woman]

Eu·phros·y·ne (ū frŏs′ə nē′), *n. Gk. Myth.* one of the Graces.

Eu·phu·es (ū′fū ēz′), *n.* the main character in John Lyly's works *Euphues, the Anatomy of Wit* (1579), and *Euphues and his England* (1580). [t. Gk.: well grown]

eu·phu·ism (ū′fū ĭz′əm), *n.* 1. an affected style in imitation of that of Lyly (see **Euphues**), fashionable in England about the end of the 16th century, characterized chiefly by long series of antitheses, frequent similes relating to fabulous natural history, alliteration, etc. 2. any similar ornate style of writing or speaking; high-flown language. 3. an instance of such style or language. —**eu′phu·ist,** *n.* —**eu′phu·is′tic, eu′phu·is′ti·cal,** *adj.* —**eu′phu·is′ti·cal·ly,** *adv.*

eu·plas·tic (ū plăs′tĭk), *adj. Physiol.* capable of being transformed into organized tissue. [f. s. Gk. *eúplastos* easy to mold + -IC]

eup·ne·a (ūp nē′ə), *n. Pathol.* easy or normal breathing (opposed to *dyspnea*). Also, **eup·noe′a.** [NL, t. Gk.: m. *eúpnoia,* der. *eúpnoos* breathing well]

Eur., 1. Europe. 2. European.

Eur·a·sia (yŏŏ rā′zhə, -shə), *n.* Europe and Asia considered as a whole.

Eur·a·sian (yŏŏ rā′zhən, -shən), *adj.* 1. pertaining to Europe and Asia taken together. 2. of mixed European and Asiatic descent. —*n.* 3. a person one of whose parents is European, and the other Asiatic.

eu·re·ka (yŏŏ rē′kə), *interj.* 1. I have found (it): the reputed exclamation of Archimedes when, after long study, he discovered a method of detecting the amount of alloy in the crown of the king of Syracuse. 2. an exclamation of triumph at a discovery or supposed discovery (motto of California). [t. Gk.: m. *heúrēka*]

eu·rhyth·mic (yŏŏ rĭ*th*′mĭk), *adj.* characterized by a pleasing rhythm; harmoniously ordered or proportioned. Also, **eurythmic**.

eu·rhyth·mics (yŏŏ rĭ*th*′mĭks), *n.* the art of interpreting in bodily movements the rhythm of musical compositions: applied to a method invented by Émile Jaques-Dalcroze, a Swiss composer, aiming to develop the sense of rhythm and symmetry. Also, **eurythmics**.

eu·rhyth·my (yŏŏ rĭ*th*′mĭ), *n.* rhythmical movement or order; harmonious proportion. Also, **eurythmy**. [t. Gk.: m.s. *eurhythmía* rhythmical order]

Eu·rip·i·des (yŏŏ rĭp′ə dēz′), *n.* 480?–406? B.C., Athenian tragic poet.

eu·ri·pus (yŏŏ rī′pəs), *n., pl.* **-pi** (-pī). a strait, esp. one in which the flow of water in both directions is violent, as (*cap.*) that between the island of Euboea and Boeotia in Greece. [t. L, t. Gk.: m. *eúripos*, f. *eu-* EU- + m. *rhīpē* impetus, rush]

Eu·roc·ly·don (yŏŏ rŏk′lə dŏn′), *n.* a stormy northeast or north-northeast wind. [t. Gk.: m. *euroklýdon*]

Eu·ro·pa (yŏŏ rō′pə), *n. Gk. Myth.* sister of Cadmus, borne to Crete by Zeus disguised in the form of a white bull; the mother by him of Rhadamanthus, Minos, and Sarpedon. [t. L, t. Gk.: m. *Európē*]

Eu·rope (yŏŏr′əp), *n.* a continent in the W part of Eurasia, separated from Asia by the Ural Mountains on the E and the Caucasus Mountains and the Black and Caspian Seas on the SE. In British usage, *Europe* sometimes contrasts with *England.* ab. 550,000,000 pop.; ab. 3,754,-000 sq. mi.

Eu·ro·pe·an (yŏŏr′ə pē′ən), *adj.* **1.** pertaining to Europe or its inhabitants. **2.** native to or derived from Europe. —*n.* **3.** a native or inhabitant of Europe. **4.** a person of European descent or connections.

Eu·ro·pe·an·ism (yŏŏr′ə pē′ə nĭz′əm), *n.* **1.** European characteristics, ideas, methods, sympathies, etc. **2.** a European trait or practice.

Eu·ro·pe·an·ize (yŏŏr′ə pē′ə nīz′), *v.t.,* **-ized, -izing.** to make European. —**Eu′ro·pe·an·i·za′tion,** *n.*

European plan, *U.S.* that method of conducting a hotel according to which the fixed charge per day covers only lodging and service.

European Recovery Program, a broad plan for aiding the European nations in their economic recovery, first proposed by Secretary of State George C. Marshall in 1947.

eu·ro·pi·um (yŏŏ rō′pĭ əm), *n. Chem.* a rare-earth metallic element with light pink salts. *Symbol:* Eu; *at. wt.:* 152; *at no.:* 63. [t. NL, der. L *Európa* Europe]

Eu·rus (yŏŏr′əs), *n. Class. Myth.* the easterly or south-easterly wind personified. [t. L, t. Gk.]

eury-, a word element meaning "broad," as in *euryp-terid.* [t. Gk., comb. form of *eurýs*]

Eu·ry·a·le (ū rī′ə lē′), *n. Gk. Leg.* one of the Gorgons.

Eu·ryd·i·ce (yŏŏ rĭd′ə sē′), *n. Gk. Myth.* the wife of Orpheus, permitted by Pluto to follow her husband out of Hades, but lost to him because he disobediently looked back at her. See **Orpheus.**

eu·ryp·ter·id (yŏŏ rĭp′tər ĭd), *n. Paleontol.* any of the *Eurypterida,* a group of Paleozoic arthropods resembling in some respects the horseshoe crabs. [t. NL: s. *Eurypterida,* pl., f. Gk. *eury-* EURY- + s. Gk. *pterón* wing + *-ida* (see ID-²)]

Eu·rys·theus (yŏŏ rĭs′thōos, -thĭ əs), *n. Gk. Legend.* a king of Mycenae, who imposed the twelve labors upon Hercules.

eu·ryth·mic (yŏŏ rĭ*th*′mĭk), *adj.* eurhythmic. —**eu·ryth′mics,** *n.* —**eu·ryth′my,** *n.*

Eu·se·bi·us (ū sē′bĭ əs), *n.* (*Eusebius Pamphili*) A.D. 260?–340?, Christian bishop in Palestine and historian of the early Christian church. —**Eu·se′bi·an,** *adj.*

eu·spo·ran·gi·ate (ū′spō răn′jĭ āt′), *adj. Bot.* having sporangia derived from a group of cells.

Eu·sta·chi·an tube (ū stā′kĭ ən, -stā′shən), *Anat.* a canal extending from the middle ear to the pharynx; auditory canal. See diag. under **ear.** [Eustachian, f. Eustachi(o) + -an]

Eu·sta·chio (ĕ′ŏŏ stā′kyō), *n.* **Bartolommeo** (bär′tō-lôm mě′ō), (*Eustachius*), died 1574, Italian anatomist.

eu·tax·y (ū′tăk sĭ), *n.* good or right order. [t. F: m. *eutaxie,* t. Gk.: m. *eutaxía* good arrangement]

eu·tec·tic (ū tĕk′tĭk), *adj. Chem.* **1.** of greatest fusibility: said of an alloy or mixture whose melting point is lower than that of any other alloy or mixture of the same ingredients. **2.** denoting or pertaining to such a mixture or its properties: *a eutectic melting point.* —*n.* **3.** a eutectic substance. [f. s. Gk. *eútēktos* easily melted + -IC]

eu·tec·toid (ū tĕk′toid), *adj.* **1.** resembling a eutectic. —*n.* **2.** eutectoid alloy. [f. EUTECT(IC) + -OID]

Eu·ter·pe (ū tûr′pĭ), *n. Class. Myth.* the Muse of music and lyric poetry. [t. L, t. Gk.: lit., well-pleasing]

eu·tha·na·sia (ū′thə nā′zhə), *n.* **1.** painless death. **2.** the putting of a person to death painlessly, esp. a person suffering from an incurable and painful disease. [t. NL, t. Gk.: an easy death]

eu·then·ics (ū thĕn′ĭks), *n.* the science of bettering the environment or living conditions, esp. to improve the race. [f. s. Gk. *euthēnía* plenty, well-being + -ICS]

eux·e·nite (ūk′sə nīt′), *n.* a brownish-black mineral of complex composition, containing yttrium, columbium, titanium, uranium, etc. [f. s. Gk. *eúxenos* hospitable (in allusion to its many constituents) + -ITE¹]

Eux·ine Sea (ūk′sĭn, -sīn), Black Sea.

e·vac·u·ant (ĭ văk′yŏŏ ənt), *Med.* —*adj.* **1.** evacuating; promoting evacuation, esp. from the bowels. —*n.* **2.** an evacuant medicine or agent.

e·vac·u·ate (ĭ văk′yŏŏ āt′), *v.,* **-ated, -ating.** —*v.t.* **1.** to leave empty; vacate. **2.** *Mil.* **a.** to remove (troops, wounded soldiers, inhabitants, etc.) from a place. **b.** to withdraw from or quit (a town, fort, etc., which has been occupied). **3.** *Physiol.* to discharge or eject as through the excretory passages, esp. from the bowels. —*v.i.* **4.** to leave a town because of air raid threats, etc.: *they had evacuated into the country.* [t. L: m.s. *ēvacuātus,* pp., emptied out] —**e·vac′u·a′tor,** *n.*

e·vac·u·a·tion (ĭ văk′yŏŏ ā′shən), *n.* **1.** act or process of evacuating. **2.** condition of being evacuated. **3.** a making empty of contents; expulsion, as of contents. **4.** *Physiol.* discharge, as of waste matter through the excretory passages, esp. from the bowels. **5.** that which is evacuated or discharged. **6.** *Mil.* **a.** clearance by removal of troops, etc. **b.** the withdrawal or removal of troops, wounded soldiers, inhabitants, etc.

e·vac·u·ee (ĭ văk′yŏŏ ē′, ĭ văk′yŏŏ ē′), *n.* a person who is withdrawn or removed from a place of danger.

e·vade (ĭ vād′), *v.,* **evaded, evading.** —*v.t.* **1.** to escape from by trickery or cleverness: *evade pursuit.* **2.** to get around by trickery: *evade the law, the rules.* **3.** to avoid doing or fulfilling: *evade a duty, obligation, etc.* **4.** to avoid answering directly: *evade a question.* **5.** to baffle, elude: *a word that evades definition, the solution evaded him.* —*v.i.* **6.** to practice evasion. [t. L: m.s. *ēvādere* pass over, go out] —**e·vad′a·ble, e·vad′i·ble,** *adj.* —**e·vad′er,** *n.* —**e·vad′ing·ly,** *adv.* —**Syn. 1.** elude, avoid, shun, dodge. **3.** See **escape. 6.** prevaricate.

e·vag·i·nate (ĭ văj′ə nāt′), *v.t.,* **-nated, -nating.** to turn inside out, or cause to protrude by eversion, as a tubular organ. [t. L: m.s. *ēvāginātus,* pp., unsheathed] —**e·vag′i·na′tion,** *n.*

e·val·u·ate (ĭ văl′yŏŏ āt′), *v.t.,* **-ated, -ating. 1.** to ascertain the value or amount of; appraise carefully. **2.** *Math.* to ascertain the numerical value of. [f. s. F *évaluer* (der. OF *value,* pp., of *valoir* be worth, g. L *valēre*) + -ATE¹] —**e·val′u·a′tion,** *n.*

ev·a·nesce (ĕv′ə něs′), *v.i.,* **-nesced, -nescing.** to disappear gradually; vanish; fade away. [t. L: m.s. *ēvānescere*] —**ev′a·nes′cence,** *n.*

ev·a·nes·cent (ĕv′ə něs′ənt), *adj.* **1.** vanishing; passing away; fleeting. **2.** tending to become imperceptible; scarcely perceptible. —**ev′a·nes′cent·ly,** *adv.*

Evang., Evangelical.

e·van·gel¹ (ĭ văn′jəl), *n.* **1.** the good tidings of the redemption of the world through Jesus Christ; the Gospel. **2.** (*usually cap.*) any of the four Gospels. **3.** doctrine taken as a guide or regarded as of prime importance. [t. LL: m.s. *evangelium,* t. Gk.: m. *euangélion* good tidings; r. ME *evangile,* t. OF]

e·van·gel² (ĭ văn′jəl), *n.* an evangelist. [t. Gk.: m.s. *euángelos* good messenger]

e·van·gel·i·cal (ē′văn jĕl′ə kəl, ĕv′ən-), *adj.* Also, **e′van·gel′ic. 1.** pertaining to or in keeping with the Gospel and its teachings. **2.** belonging to or designating those Christian churches which emphasize the teachings and authority of the Scriptures, esp. of the New Testament, in opposition to that of the church itself or of reason. **3.** pertaining to certain movements in the Protestant churches in the 18th and 19th centuries which stressed the importance of personal experience of guilt for sin, and of reconciliation to God through Christ. **4.** evangelistic. —*n.* **5.** an adherent of evangelical doctrines; a member of an evangelical church or party, as of the Low Church party of the Church of England. —**e′van·gel′i·cal·ly,** *adv.*

e·van·gel·i·cal·ism (ē′văn jĕl′ə kə lĭz′əm, ĕv′ən-), *n.* **1.** evangelical doctrines or principles. **2.** adherence to them, or to an evangelical church or party.

e·van·ge·lism (ĭ văn′jə lĭz′əm), *n.* **1.** the preaching or promulgation of the Gospel; the work of an evangelist. **2.** evangelicalism.

e·van·ge·list (ĭ văn′jə lĭst), *n.* **1.** a preacher of the Gospel. **2.** (*cap.*) any of the writers (Matthew, Mark, Luke, and John) of the four Gospels. **3.** one of a class of teachers in the early church, next in rank after apostles and prophets. **4.** a revivalist. **5.** an occasional or itinerant preacher. **6.** (*cap.*) *Mormon Ch.* a patriarch.

e·van·ge·lis·tic (ĭ văn′jə lĭs′tĭk), *adj.* **1.** pertaining to evangelists, or preachers of the Gospel. **2.** evangelical. **3.** seeking to evangelize; striving to convert sinners. **4.** designed or fitted to evangelize. **5.** (*often cap.*) of or pertaining to the four Evangelists. —**e·van′ge·lis′ti·cal·ly,** *adv.*

e·van·ge·lize (ĭ văn′jə līz′), *v.,* **-lized, -lizing.** —*v.t.* **1.** to preach the gospel to. **2.** to convert to Christianity. —*v.i.* **3.** to preach the gospel; act as an evangelist. —**e·van′ge·li·za′tion,** *n.* —**e·van′ge·liz′er,** *n.*

e·van·ish (ĭ văn′ĭsh), *v.i. Poetic.* **1.** to vanish or disappear. **2.** to cease to be.

Ev·ans (ĕv′ənz), *n.* **1. Sir Arthur John,** 1851–1941, British archaeologist. **2. Herbert McLean** (mə klān′), born 1882, U.S. embryologist. **3. Mary Ann** (*Mrs. J. W. Cross*). See **Eliot, George.**

Ev·ans·ton (ĕv′ən stən), *n.* a city in NE Illinois, on Lake Michigan, near Chicago. 73,641 (1950).

Ev·ans·ville (ĕv′ənz vĭl′), *n.* a city in SW Indiana, on the Ohio river. 128,636 (1950).

e·vap·o·ra·ble (ĭ văp′ər ə bəl), *adj.* capable of being converted to gas by evaporation. —e·vap′o·ra·bil′i·ty, *n.*

e·vap·o·rate (ĭ văp′ə rāt′), *v.,* -rated, -rating. —*v.i.* 1. to turn to vapor; pass off in vapor. 2. to give off moisture. 3. to disappear; vanish; fade: *as soon as his situation became clear to him, his hopes quickly evaporated.* —*v.t.* 4. to convert into a gaseous state or vapor; drive off or extract in the form of vapor. 5. to extract moisture or liquid from, as by heat, so as to make dry or to reduce to a denser state: *to evaporate fruit.* [t. LL: m.s. ēvapōrātus, pp., dispersed in vapor] —e·vap′o·ra′tive, *adj.* —e·vap′o·ra′tor, *n.*
—**Syn.** 5. EVAPORATE, DEHYDRATE, DRY mean to abstract moisture from. To EVAPORATE is to remove moisture by means of heat, and thus to produce condensation or shriveling: *to evaporate milk, sliced apples* To DEHYDRATE is to remove all vestiges of moisture by means of a mechanical process: *to dehydrate foods makes them easier to preserve and to transport.* To DRY may mean to wipe moisture off the surface or to withdraw moisture by exposure to air or heat; the object dried is left unchanged: *to dry a dish, clothes.*

evaporated milk, thick, unsweetened, canned milk made by removing some of the water from whole milk.

e·vap·o·ra·tion (ĭ văp′ə rā′shən), *n.* 1. act or process of evaporating. 2. state of being evaporated. 3. matter, or the quantity of matter, evaporated or passed off in vapor. —e·vap′o·ra′tive, *adj.*

Ev·arts (ĕv′ərts), *n.* **William Maxwell,** 1818–1901, U.S. lawyer and statesman.

e·va·sion (ĭ vā′zhən), *n.* 1. act of escaping something by trickery or cleverness: *evasion of one's duty, responsibilities, etc.* 2. the avoiding of an argument, accusation, question or the like, as by a subterfuge. 3. a means of evading; a subterfuge; an excuse or trick to avoid or get around something. [t. LL: s. ēvāsiō] —**Syn.** 1. avoidance, dodging. 2. prevarication, equivocation, quibbling.

e·va·sive (ĭ vā′sĭv), *adj.* 1. tending or seeking to evade; characterized by evasion: *an evasive answer.* 2. elusive or evanescent. —e·va′sive·ly, *adv.* —e·va′sive·ness, *n.*

eve (ēv), *n.* 1. the evening, or often the day, before a church festival, and hence before any date or event. 2. the period just preceding any event, etc.: *the eve of a revolution.* 3. *Chiefly Poetic.* the evening. [var. of EVEN²]

Eve (ēv), *n.* *Bible.* the first woman. Gen. 3:20. [ME; OE *Efe,* t. L: m. *Eva,* t. Gk. (Septuagint), t. Heb.: m. *ḥawwāh,* explained as "mother of the living" (*ḥāy*), but meaning uncert.]

e·vec·tion (ĭ vĕk′shən), *n.* *Astron.* a periodic inequality in the moon's motion caused by the attraction of the sun. [t. L: s. ēvectiō, der. ēvehere carry forth or up] —e·vec′tion·al, *adj.*

Ev·e·lyn (ĕv′ə lĭn, ēv′lĭn), *n.* **John,** 1620–1706, British diarist.

e·ven¹ (ē′vən), *adj.* 1. level; flat; without irregularities; smooth: *an even surface, even country.* 2. on the same level; in the same plane or line; parallel: *even with the ground.* 3. free from variations or fluctuations; regular: *even motion.* 4. uniform in action, character, or quality: *an even color; to hold an even course.* 5. equal in measure or quantity: *even quantities of two substances, letters of even date* (letters of the same date). 6. divisible by 2: thus, 2, 8, and 12 are *even* numbers (opposed to *odd,* as 1, 3, etc.). 7. denoted by such a number: *the even pages of a book.* 8. exactly expressible in integers, or in tens, hundreds, etc., without fractional parts: *an even mile, an even hundred.* 9. leaving no balance of debt on either side, as accounts; square, as one person with another. 10. calm; placid; not easily excited or angered: *an even temper.* 11. equitable, impartial, or fair: *an even bargain, an even chance.* —*adv.* 12. evenly. 13. still; yet (used to emphasize a comparative): *even more suitable.* 14. (used to suggest that something mentioned as a possibility constitutes an extreme case, or one that might not be expected): *the slightest noise, even, disturbs him; even if he goes, he may not take part.* 15. just: *even now.* 16. fully or quite: *even to death.* 17. indeed (used as an intensive for stressing identity or truth of something): *he is willing, even eager, to do it.* 18. *Archaic.* exactly or precisely: *it was even so.* 19. **break even,** *Colloq.* to have one's profits equal one's losses. 20. **get even,** to get one's revenge; square accounts. —*v.t.* 21. to make even; level; smooth. 22. to place in an even state as to claim or obligation; balance: *to even, or even up, accounts.* [ME; OE *efen,* c. G *eben*] —e′ven·er, *n.* —e′ven·ly, *adv.* —e′ven·ness, *n.*
—**Syn.** 1. See **level.** 3. EVEN, EQUABLE, UNIFORM imply a steady sameness. EVEN implies freedom from inequalities or irregularities: *even breathing, an even flow.* EQUABLE suggests the inherent quality of regularity or, in a nonmaterial reference, that of being well-balanced, not easily disturbed, and impartial in judgment: *an equable temperament.* UNIFORM emphasizes sameness and conformity to a standard: *uniform height or practice.* —**Ant.** 1. irregular, changeable.

e·ven² (ē′vən), *n.* *Archaic.* evening; eve. [ME; OE *ēfen, æfen;* akin to G *abend*]

e·ven·fall (ē′vən fôl′), *n.* the beginning of evening.

e·ven-hand·ed (ē′vən hăn′dĭd), *adj.* impartial; equitable: *even-handed justice.* —e′ven-hand′ed·ness, *n.*

eve·ning (ēv′nĭng), *n.* 1. the latter part of the day and early part of the night. 2. the period from sunset to bedtime. 3. *Southern U.S.* the time between noon and dark, including afternoon and twilight. 4. any concluding or declining period: *the evening of life.* 5. an evening's reception or entertainment. —*adj.* 6. of or pertaining to evening; occurring or seen in the evening. [ME; OE *æfnung,* der. *æfnian* draw toward evening] —**Syn.** 1. eventide, dusk, twilight, gloaming, nightfall.

evening dress, formal evening clothes.

evening gown, a woman's formal dress.

evening primrose, 1. a plant, *Oenothera biennis,* family *Onagraceae,* with yellow flowers that open at nightfall. 2. any of various plants of the same or related genera.

evening star, a bright planet seen in the west after sunset, esp. Venus.

e·ven-mind·ed (ē′vən mīn′dĭd), *adj.* not easily ruffled, disturbed, prejudiced, etc.; calm; equable. —e′ven-mind′ed·ness, *n.*

e·ven·song (ē′vən sông′, -sŏng′), *n.* 1. *Anglican Ch.* a form of worship appointed to be said or sung at evening. 2. *Rom. Cath. Ch.* vespers. 3. *Archaic.* evening. [ME; OE *æfensang,* f. *æfen* evening + *sang* song]

e·vent (ĭ vĕnt′), *n.* 1. anything that happens or is regarded as happening; an occurrence, esp. one of some importance. 2. fact of happening (chiefly in the phrase *in the event of*). 3. the outcome, issue, or result of anything (chiefly in the phrase *after the event*). 4. *Philos.* something which occurs in a certain place during a particular interval of time. 5. *Sports.* **a.** each of the items in a program of races, etc. **b.** something on the outcome of which money is at stake. 6. **at all events** or **in any event,** whatever happens; in any case. [t. L: s. ēventus occurrence, issue] —e·vent′less, *adj.*
—**Syn.** 1. happening, affair, case, circumstance. EVENT, EPISODE, INCIDENT, OCCURRENCE are terms for a happening. An EVENT is usually an important happening, esp. one that comes out of and is connected with previous happenings: *historical events.* An EPISODE is one of a progressive series of happenings, frequently distinct from the main course of events but arising naturally from them and having a continuity and interest of its own: *an episode in one's life.* An INCIDENT is usually a happening which takes place in connection with an event or a series of events of greater importance: *an amusing incident in a play.* An OCCURRENCE is something (usually of an ordinary nature) that happens, having no particular connection with (or causation by) antecedent happenings: *his arrival was an unexpected occurrence.*

e·ven-tem·pered (ē′vən tĕm′pərd), *adj.* not easily ruffled or disturbed; calm.

e·vent·ful (ĭ vĕnt′fəl), *adj.* 1. full of events or incidents, esp. of a striking character: *an eventful period.* 2. having important issues or results; momentous. —e·vent′ful·ly, *adv.* —e·vent′ful·ness, *n.*

e·ven·tide (ē′vən tīd′), *n.* *Now Poetic.* evening.

eventu-, a word element meaning "event." [comb. form repr. L *eventus*]

e·ven·tu·al (ĭ vĕn′chōō əl), *adj.* 1. pertaining to the event or issue; consequent; ultimate. 2. depending upon uncertain events; contingent.

e·ven·tu·al·i·ty (ĭ vĕn′chōō ăl′ə tĭ), *n.,* *pl.* -ties. 1. a contingent event; a possible occurrence or circumstance. 2. state or fact of being eventual; contingent character.

e·ven·tu·al·ly (ĭ vĕn′chōō ə lĭ), *adv.* finally; ultimately.

e·ven·tu·ate (ĭ vĕn′chōō āt′), *v.i.,* -ated, -ating. 1. to have issue; result. 2. to be the issue or outcome; come about. —e·ven′tu·a′tion, *n.*

ev·er (ĕv′ər), *adv.* 1. at all times: *he is ever ready to excuse himself.* 2. continuously: *ever since then.* 3. at any time: *did you ever see anything like it?* 4. (with emphatic force, in various idiomatic constructions and phrases) in any possible case; by any chance; at all: *how did you ever manage to do it?* In England it sometimes appears in an order strange to U.S.: *we must try as hard as ever we can, why ever not?* 5. **ever and again** or **ever and anon,** every now and then; continually. 6. **ever so,** to whatever extent or degree; greatly; exceedingly: *ever so long, be he ever so bold.* 7. **for ever,** (usually one word) for eternity; eternally; always; continually. 8. **for ever and a day,** forever; eternally. [ME; OE *æfre,* prob. akin to ā ever. See AY¹] —**Syn.** 1. eternally, perpetually, constantly. See **always.**

Ev·er·est (ĕv′ər ĭst), *n.* **Mount,** a peak of the Himalayas, in E Nepal: the highest mountain in the world. 29,-141 ft.

Ev·er·ett (ĕv′ər ĭt), *n.* 1. **Edward,** 1794–1865, U.S. statesman, orator, and writer. 2. a city in E Massachusetts, near Boston. 45,982 (1950). 3. a seaport in NW Washington, on Puget Sound. 33,849 (1950).

ev·er·glade (ĕv′ər glād′), *n.* *Southern U.S.* a tract of low, swampy land characterized by clumps of tall grass and numerous branching waterways.

Ev·er·glades (ĕv′ər glādz′), *n.* a swampy and partly forested region in S Florida, mostly S of Lake Okeechobee. Over 5000 sq. mi.

ev·er·green (ĕv′ər grēn′), *adj.* 1. (of trees, shrubs,

etc.) having green leaves throughout the entire year, the leaves of the past season not being shed until after the new foliage has been completely formed. **2.** (of leaves) belonging to such a tree, shrub, etc. —*n.* **3.** an evergreen plant. **4.** (*pl.*) evergreen twigs or branches used for decoration.

ev·er·last·ing (ĕv′ər lăs′tĭng, -läs′-), *adj.* **1.** lasting forever; eternal. **2.** lasting or continuing indefinitely. **3.** incessant; constantly recurring. **4.** wearisome: *to tire of someone's everlasting puns.* —*n.* **5.** eternal duration; eternity. **6.** the Everlasting, the Eternal Being; God. **7.** any of various plants or flowers which retain their shape, color, etc., when dried, as certain species of the asteraceous genus *Helichrysum*, and various species of cudweed, genus *Gnaphalium.* —**ev′er·last′ing·ly,** *adv.* —**ev′er·last′ing·ness,** *n.* —**Syn. 1.** See **eternal.**

everlasting flower, *Brit.* the immortelle.

ev·er·more (ĕv′ər mōr′), *adv.* **1.** always; forever; eternally (often prec. by *for*). **2.** at all times; continually.

e·ver·si·ble (ĭ vûr′sə bəl), *adj.* capable of being everted.

e·ver·sion (ĭ vûr′shən, -zhən), *n.* a turning or being turned outward, or inside out.

e·vert (ĭ vûrt′), *v.t.* to turn outward, or inside out. [t. L: s. *ēvertere* overturn]

e·ver·tor (ĭ vûr′tər), *n.* *Anat.* a muscle which turns a part toward the outside.

eve·ry (ĕv′rĭ), *adj.* **1.** each (referring one by one to all the members of an aggregate): *we go there every day, be sure to remember every word he says.* **2.** all possible; the greatest possible degree of: *every prospect of success.* **3.** every bit, *Colloq.* in every respect; in all points: *every bit as good.* **4.** every now and then or every now and again or every once in a while, repeatedly; frequently; from time to time. **5.** every other, every second; every alternate. [ME *every, everich,* etc., OE *ǣfre ǣlc* EVER, EACH] —**Syn. 1.** See **each.**

eve·ry·bod·y (ĕv′rĭ bŏd′ĭ), *pron.* every person.

eve·ry·day (ĕv′rĭ dā′), *adj.* **1.** of or pertaining to every day; daily: *an everyday occurrence.* **2.** of or for ordinary days, as contrasted with Sundays or special occasions: *everyday clothes.* **3.** such as is met with every day; ordinary; commonplace: *an everyday scene.*

Eve·ry·man (ĕv′rĭ măn′), *n.* a 15th century English morality play translated from the Dutch *Elkerlijk.*

eve·ry·one (ĕv′rĭ wŭn′, -wən), *n.* every person; everybody. Also, **every one.**

eve·ry·thing (ĕv′rĭ thĭng′), *pron.* **1.** every thing or particular of an aggregate or total; all. **2.** something extremely important: *this news means everything to us.*

eve·ry·way (ĕv′rĭ wā′), *adv.* in every way; in every direction, manner, or respect.

eve·ry·where (ĕv′rĭ hwâr′), *adv.* In every place or part; in all places.

Eve·sham (ēv′shəm, ēv′zəm), *n.* a town in W England, SE of Worcester: battle, 1265. 12,805 (1939).

e·vict (ĭ vĭkt′), *v.t.* **1.** to expel (a person, esp. a tenant) from land, a building, etc. by legal process. **2.** to recover (property, etc.) by virtue of superior legal title. [t. L: s. *ēvictus,* pp., overcome completely, (property) recovered by judicial decision] —**e·vic′tion,** *n.* —**e·vic′tor,** *n.*

ev·i·dence (ĕv′ə dəns), *n., v.,* **-denced, -dencing.** —*n.* **1.** ground for belief; that which tends to prove or disprove something, proof. **2.** something that makes evident; an indication or sign. **3.** *Law.* the data, in the form of testimony of witnesses, or of documents or other objects (such as a photograph, a revolver, etc.) identified by witnesses, offered to the court or jury in proof of the facts in issue. **4.** one who bears testimony or witness. **5.** turn state's, or king's or queen's, evidence, (of an accomplice in a crime) to become a witness for the prosecution against the others involved. **6.** in evidence, in a situation to be readily seen; plainly visible; conspicuous. —*v.t.* **7.** to make evident or clear; show clearly; manifest. **8.** to support by evidence. —**Syn. 3.** information, deposition, affidavit. EVIDENCE, EXHIBIT, TESTIMONY, PROOF refer to information furnished in a legal investigation to support a contention. EVIDENCE is any information so given, whether furnished by witnesses or derived from documents or from any other source: *hearsay evidence is not admitted in a trial.* An EXHIBIT in law, is a document or article which is presented in court as evidence: *the signed contract is Exhibit A.* TESTIMONY is usually evidence given by witnesses under oath: *the jury listened carefully to the testimony.* PROOF is evidence that is so complete and convincing as to put a conclusion beyond reasonable doubt: *proof of the innocence of the accused.*

ev·i·dent (ĕv′ə dənt), *adj.* plain or clear to the sight or understanding: *an evident mistake.* [t. L: s. *ēvidens*] —**Syn.** obvious, manifest, palpable, patent, unmistakable. See **apparent.**

ev·i·den·tial (ĕv′ə dĕn′shəl), *adj.* of or having the nature of, serving as, or based on evidence.

ev·i·dent·ly (ĕv′ə dənt lĭ, -dĕnt′-; *emph.* ĕv′ə dĕnt′lĭ), *adv.* obviously; apparently. —**Syn.** See **clearly.**

e·vil (ē′vəl), *adj.* **1.** violating or inconsistent with the moral law; wicked: *evil deeds, an evil life.* **2.** harmful; injurious: *evil laws.* **3.** characterized or accompanied by misfortune or suffering; unfortunate; disastrous: *to be fallen on evil days.* **4.** due to (actual or imputed) bad character or conduct: *an evil reputation.* **5.** the evil one, the devil; Satan. —*n.* **6.** that which is evil; evil quality,

intention, or conduct: *to choose the lesser of two evils.* **7.** harm; mischief; misfortune: *to wish one evil.* **8.** anything causing injury or harm. **9.** a disease: *king's evil* (scrofula). —*adv.* **10.** in an evil manner; badly; ill: *it went evil with his house.* [ME; OE *yfel,* c. G *übel*] —**e′vil·ly,** *adv.* —**e′vil·ness,** *n.* —**Syn. 1.** sinful, iniquitous, depraved, vicious, corrupt, immoral, base. See **bad¹. 6.** wickedness, depravity, iniquity, unrighteousness. **7.** disaster, calamity. —**Ant. 1.** righteous.

e·vil·do·er (ē′vəl dōō′ər), *n.* one who does evil. —**e·vil·do·ing** (ē′vəl dōō′ĭng), *n.*

evil eye, the power superstitiously attributed to certain persons, of inflicting injury or bad luck by a look. —**e′vil-eyed′,** *adj.*

e·vil-mind·ed (ē′vəl mīn′dĭd), *adj.* **1.** having an evil mind; malignant. **2.** excessively sexminded.

e·vince (ĭ vĭns′), *v.t.,* **evinced, evincing. 1.** to show clearly; make evident or manifest; prove. **2.** to reveal the possession of (a quality, trait, etc.). [t. L: m.s. *ēvincere* overcome completely, prove, demonstrate] —**e·vin′ci·ble,** *adj.* —**Syn. 1.** See **display.**

e·vin·cive (ĭ vĭn′sĭv), *adj.* serving to evince; indicative.

e·vis·cer·ate (ĭ vĭs′ə rāt′), *v.,* **-ated, -ating,** *adj.* —*v.t.* **1.** to disembowel. **2.** to deprive of vital or essential parts. —*adj.* **3.** *Surg.* disemboweled, usually after a surgical operation on the abdomen when the wound breaks open due to a technical error or poor healing. [t. L: m.s. *ēviscerātus,* pp., disemboweled] —**e·vis′cer·a′tion,** *n.*

ev·i·ta·ble (ĕv′ə tə bəl), *adj.* avoidable. [t. L: m.s. *ēvītābilis* avoidable]

e·vite (ĭ vīt′), *v.t.,* **evited, eviting.** *Archaic.* to avoid; shun. [t. L: m.s. *ēvītāre*]

ev·o·ca·ble (ĕv′ə kə bəl), *adj.* that may be evoked.

ev·o·ca·tion (ĕv′ō kā′shən), *n.* **1.** act of evoking; a calling forth. **2.** *Civil Law.* the power of a higher court to decide finally on an entire case when it is appealed, even if the court below decided only incidental matters and even if the appeal is based merely on procedural errors. [t. L: s. *ēvocātio,* der. *ēvocāre* call forth]

e·voc·a·tive (ĭ vŏk′ə tĭv, -vō′kə-), *adj.* tending to evoke.

ev·o·ca·tor (ĕv′ə kā′tər), *n.* **1.** *Embryol.* a morphogenic substance, or a piece of tissue, generally not living, which contains morphogenic substances. **2.** one who evokes, esp., one who calls up spirits.

e·voke (ĭ vōk′), *v.t.,* **evoked, evoking. 1.** to call up, produce (memories, feelings, etc.): *to evoke a memory, a smile, etc.* **2.** to call up; cause to appear; summon: *to evoke a spirit from the dead.* [t. L: m.s. *ēvocāre* call forth] —**e·vok′er** *n.*

ev·o·lute (ĕv′ə lōōt′), *n.* *Geom.* the locus of the centers of curvature of, or the envelope of the normals to, another curve (called the *involute*). [t. L: m.s. *ēvolūtus,* pp., rolled out]

ABC, Evolute of parabolic arc OPQ

ev·o·lu·tion (ĕv′ə lōō′shən; *Brit. also* ē′və-), *n.* **1.** any process of formation or growth; development: *the evolution of man, the drama, the airplane, etc.* **2.** something evolved; a product. **3.** *Biol.* the continuous genetic adaptation of organisms or species to the environment by the integrating agencies of selection, hybridization, inbreeding, and mutation. **4.** a movement, or one of a series of movements, of troops, ships, etc., as for disposition in order of battle or in line on parade. **5.** any similar movement, esp. in close-order drill. **6.** a motion incomplete in itself, but combining with coördinated motions to produce a single action, as in a machine. **7.** an evolving or giving off of gas, heat, etc. **8.** *Math.* the extraction of roots from powers (the inverse of *involution*). [t. L: s. *ēvolūtio,* der. *ēvolvere* roll out] —**ev′o·lu′tion·al,** *adj.* —**ev′o·lu′tion·al·ly,** *adv.*

ev·o·lu·tion·ar·y (ĕv′ə lōō′shə nĕr′ĭ; *Brit. also* ē′və-), *adj.* **1.** pertaining to evolution or development; developmental: *the evolutionary origin of species.* **2.** in accordance with the theory of evolution. **3.** pertaining to or performing evolutions (def. 4).

ev·o·lu·tion·ist (ĕv′ə lōō′shən ĭst; *Brit. also* ē′və-), *n.* a believer in the doctrine of evolution.

ev·o·lu·tion·is·tic (ĕv′ə lōō′shə nĭs′tĭk; *Brit. also* ē′və-), *adj.* **1.** tending to support the theory of evolution. **2.** tending to cause evolution.

e·volve (ĭ vŏlv′), *v.,* **evolved, evolving.** —*v.t.* **1.** to develop gradually: *to evolve a scheme, a plan, a theory, etc.* **2.** *Biol.* to develop, as by a process of differentiation, to a more highly organized condition. **3.** to give off or emit, as odors, vapors, etc. —*v.i.* **4.** to come forth gradually into being; develop; undergo evolution. [t. L: m.s. *ēvolvere* roll out, unroll, unfold] —**e·volv′a·ble,** *adj.* —**e·volve′ment,** *n.* —**e·volv′er,** *n.*

ev·on·y·mus (ĕv ŏn′ə məs), *n.* euonymus.

e·vul·sion (ĭ vŭl′shən), *n.* act of plucking or pulling out; forcible extraction. [t. L: s. *ēvulsio,* der. *ēvellere* pluck out]

Ev·voi·a (ĕ′vēä′), *n.* modern Greek name of Euboea.

ewe (ū; *dial.* yō), *n.* a female sheep. [ME and OE, c. D *ooi;* akin to L *ovis,* Gk. *ŏis,* Skt. *avi* sheep]

E·we (ā′vā), *n.* a language of western Africa, spoken in parts of Togoland.

Ew·ell (ū'əl), *n.* Richard Stoddert, 1817–72, Confederate lieutenant general in the U.S. Civil War.

ewe-neck (ū'nĕk'), *n.* a thin hollow neck, low in front of the shoulder, as of a horse or other animal. **—ewe-necked** (ū'nĕkt'), *adj.*

ew·er (ū'ər), *n.* 1. a pitcher with a wide spout, esp. one to hold water for ablutions. 2. *Decorative Art.* a vessel having a spout and a handle; esp., a tall, slender vessel with a base. [ME, t. AF, g. L *aquāria* vessel for water]

Ewer and basin

E·wig-Weib·li·che (ā'vYKH vīp'lYKHə), *n. German.* the eternal feminine (used in Goethe's *Faust*).

ex[1] (ĕks), *prep.* 1. *Finance.* without, not including, or without the right to have: *ex dividend, ex interest, ex rights.* 2. *Com.* out of; free out of: *ex elevator, ex ship, etc.* (free of charges until the time of removal out of the elevator, ship, etc.). 3. (in U.S. colleges and universities) from, but not graduated with, the class of: *ex '47.* [t. L. See EX-[1]]

ex[2] (ĕks), *n.* the letter X, x.

ex-[1], a prefix meaning "out of," "from," and hence "utterly," "thoroughly," and sometimes serving to impart a privative or negative force or to indicate a former title, status, etc.; freely used as an English formative, as in *exstipulate, exterritorial,* and esp. in such combinations as *ex-president* (former president), *ex-member, ex-wife;* occurring before vowels and *c, p, q, s, t.* Also, **e-, ef-.** [t. L, comb. form of *ex, ē,* prep., out of, from, beyond]

ex-[2], var. of exo-.

ex-[3], a prefix identical in meaning with **ex-**[1], occurring before vowels in words of Greek orig., as in *exarch, exegis.* Also, **ec-.** [t. Gk., also before consonants *ek-* EC-; becoming *ec-* in L derivatives]

Ex., Exodus.

ex., 1. examination. 2. examined. 3. example. 4. except. 5. exception. 6. exchange. 7. excursion. 8. executed. 9. executive.

ex·ac·er·bate (Yg zăs'ər bāt', Yk săs'-), *v.t.,* **-bated, -bating.** 1. to increase the bitterness or violence of (disease, ill feeling, etc.); aggravate. 2. to embitter the feelings of (a person); irritate; exasperate. [t. L: m.s. *exacerbātus,* pp., irritated] **—ex·ac·er·ba'tion,** *n.*

ex·act (Yg zäkt'), *adj.* 1. strictly accurate or correct: *an exact likeness, description, or translation.* 2. precise, as opposed to approximate: *the exact sum due, the exact date.* 3. admitting of no deviation, as laws, discipline, etc.; strict or rigorous. 4. characterized by or using strict accuracy or precision: *exact instruments, an exact thinker.* —*v.t.* 5. to call for, demand, or require: *to exact obedience, respect.* 6. to force or compel the payment, yielding, or performance of: *to exact money, tribute, etc.* [t. L: s. *exactus,* pp., forced out, required, measured by a standard] **—ex·act'a·ble,** *adj.* **—ex·act'er, ex·ac'-tor,** *n.* **—ex·act'ness,** *n.* **—Syn.** 3. rigid, severe. 4. methodical, careful, punctilious. 5. force, compel. 6. extort, wrest, wring. See **extract.**

ex·act·ing (Yg zăk'tYng), *adj.* 1. severe, or unduly severe, in demands or requirements, as a person. 2. requiring close application or attention, as a task. 3. given to or characterized by exaction; extortionate. **—ex·act'ing·ly,** *adv.* **—ex·act'ing·ness,** *n.*

ex·ac·tion (Yg zăk'shən), *n.* 1. act of exacting; extortion. 2. something exacted.

ex·act·i·tude (Yg zăk'tə tūd', -tōod'), *n.* the quality of being exact; exactness; preciseness; accuracy.

ex·act·ly (Yg zăkt'lY), *adv.* 1. in an exact manner; precisely, according to rule, measure, fact, etc. accurately. 2. quite so; that's right.

exact science, a science (such as mathematics) which permits of accurate analysis.

ex ae·quo et bo·no (ĕks ē'kwō ĕt bō'nō), *Latin.* according to the principle of fairness and good.

ex·ag·ger·ate (Yg zăj'ə rāt'), *v.,* **-ated, -ating.** —*v.t.* 1. to magnify beyond the limits of truth; overstate; represent disproportionately: *to exaggerate one's importance, the difficulties of a situation, the size of one's house, etc.* 2. to increase or enlarge abnormally. —*v.i.* 3. to employ exaggeration, as in speech or writing: *a person who is always exaggerating.* [t. L: m.s. *exaggerātus,* pp., heaped up] **—ex·ag'ger·at'ing·ly,** *adv.* **—ex·ag'ger·a'tor,** *n.* **—Ant.** 1. minimize.

ex·ag·ger·at·ed (Yg zăj'ə rā'tYd), *adj.* 1. unduly magnified: *to have an exaggerated opinion of oneself.* 2. abnormally increased or enlarged: *a heart greatly exaggerated by disease.* **—ex·ag'ger·at'ed·ly,** *adv.*

ex·ag·ger·a·tion (Yg zăj'ə rā'shən), *n.* 1. act of exaggerating. 2. state of being exaggerated. 3. an exaggerated statement.

ex·ag·ger·a·tive (Yg zăj'ə rā'tYv), *adj.* given to or characterized by exaggeration. Also, **ex·ag·ger·a·to·ry** (Yg zăj'ə rə tōr'Y).

ex·alt (Yg zôlt'), *v.t.* 1. to elevate in rank, honor, power, character, quality, etc.: *exalted to the position of President.* 2. to praise; extol: *to exalt someone to the skies.* 3. to elate, as with pride or joy. 4. to stimulate, as the imagination. 5. to intensify, as a color. 6. *Archaic or Rare.* to raise up. [t. L: s. *exaltāre* lift up] **—ex·alt'er,** *n.* **—Syn.** 1. promote, dignify. See **elevate.** 2. glorify. **—Ant.** 1. humble. 2. depreciate.

ex·al·ta·tion (ĕg'zôl tā'shən), *n.* 1. act of exalting. 2. state of being exalted. 3. elation of mind, or feeling, sometimes abnormal or morbid in character; rapture. 4. abnormal intensification of the action of an organ.

ex·alt·ed (Yg zôl'tYd), *adj.* 1. elevated, as in rank or character; of high station: *an exalted personage.* 2. noble or elevated, lofty: *an exalted style, mind, etc.* 3. rapturously excited. **—ex·alt'ed·ly,** *adv.* **—ex·alt'ed·ness,** *n.* **—Syn.** 1. sublime, grand.

ex·am (Yg zăm'), *n. Colloq.* an examination.

exam., 1. examination. 2. examined. 3. examinee. 4. examiner.

ex·a·men (Yg zā'mĕn), *n. Eccles.* an examination, as of conscience. [t. L: a weighing, consideration]

ex·am·i·nant (Yg zăm'ə nənt), *n.* an examiner.

ex·am·i·na·tion (Yg zăm'ə nā'shən), *n.* 1. act of examining; inspection; inquiry; investigation. 2. state of being examined. 3. act or process of testing pupils, candidates, etc., as by questions. 4. the test itself; list of questions asked. 5. the statements, etc., made by one examined. 6. *Law.* formal interrogation. [t. L: s. *exāminātio*] **—ex·am'i·na'tion·al,** *adj.* **Syn.** 1. EXAMINATION, INSPECTION, SCRUTINY refer to a scanning of something. An EXAMINATION may mean a careful noting of details or may mean little more than a casual glance over something: *a thorough examination of the plumbing revealed a defective pipe.* An INSPECTION is a formal and official examination: *an inspection of records, a military inspection.* SCRUTINY implies a critical and minutely detailed examination: *the papers seemed to be in good order but they would not stand close scrutiny.* See **investigation.**

ex·am·ine (Yg zăm'Yn), *v.t.,* **-ined, -ining.** 1. to inspect or scrutinize carefully; inquire into or investigate. 2. to test the knowledge, reactions, or qualifications of (a pupil, candidate, etc.), as by questions or assigned tasks. 3. to subject to legal inquisition; put to question in regard to conduct or to knowledge of facts; interrogate: *to examine a witness or a suspected person.* [ME *examine(n),* t. F: m. *examiner,* t. L: m. *exāmināre* weigh accurately, test] **—ex·am'in·a·ble,** *adj.* **—ex·am'in·er,** *n.* **—Syn.** 1. search, probe, explore. 2. catechize.

ex·am·i·nee (Yg zăm'ə nē'), *n.* one who is examined.

ex·am·ple (Yg zăm'pəl, -zäm'-), *n., v.,* **-pled, -pling.** —*n.* 1. one of a number of things, or a part of something, taken to show the character of the whole. 2. something to be imitated; a pattern or model: *to set a good example.* 3. an instance serving for illustration; a specimen. 4. an instance illustrating a rule or method, as a mathematical problem proposed for solution. 5. an instance, esp. of punishment, serving for a warning; a warning. 6. a precedent; a parallel case: *an action without example.* —*v.t.* 7. to give or be an example of (chiefly in pp.). [ME, t. OF: m. *essample,* g. L *exempla,* pl. of *exemplum*] **—Syn.** 1. EXAMPLE, SAMPLE, SPECIMEN refer to an individual phenomenon taken as representative of a type, or to a part representative of the whole. EXAMPLE is used of an object, activity, condition, etc., which is assumed to illustrate a certain principle, law, or standard: *a good example of baroque architecture.* SAMPLE, used mainly in a concrete reference, refers to a small portion of a substance, or to a single representative of a group or type, which is intended to show what the rest of the substance, or the group, is like: *a sample of yarn.* SPECIMEN usually suggests that the "sample" chosen is intended to serve a scientific or technical purpose: *a blood specimen, zoological specimens.* 2. See **ideal.** 3. See **case**[1].

ex·an·i·mate (Yg zăn'ə mYt, -māt'), *adj.* 1. inanimate or lifeless. 2. spiritless; disheartened. [t. L: m.s. *exanimātus,* pp., deprived of breath, life, or spirit]

ex a·ni·mo (ĕks ăn'ə mō'), *Latin.* from the heart; sincerely.

ex·an·the·ma (ĕk'săn thē'mə), *n., pl.* **-themata** (-thĕm'ə tə, -thē'mə tə). 1. *Pathol.* an eruptive disease, esp. one attended with fever, as smallpox or measles. 2. See **vesicular exanthema.** [t. LL, t. Gk.: a bursting into flower] **—ex·an·the·mat·ic** (ĕk'săn'thə măt'Yk), **ex·an·them·a·tous** (ĕk'săn thĕm'ə təs), *adj.*

ex·arch (ĕk'särk), *n.* 1. (in the Eastern Church) a. a patriarch's deputy. b. (formerly) a bishop ranking below a patriarch and above a metropolitan. c. (orig.) patriarch. 2. the ruler of a province in the Byzantine Empire. [t. LL: s. *exarchus,* t. Gk.: m. *exarchos* leader]

ex·ar·chate (ĕk'sär kāt', ĕk sär'kāt), *n.* the office, jurisdiction, or province of an exarch.

ex·as·per·ate (Yg zăs'pə rāt'), *v.t.,* **-ated, -ating.** 1. to irritate to a high degree; annoy extremely; infuriate. 2. to increase the intensity or violence of (disease, pain, feelings, etc.). [t. L: m.s. *exasperātus,* pp., roughened] **—ex·as'per·at'ed·ly,** *adv.* **—ex·as'per·at'er,** *n.* **—ex·as'per·at'ing·ly,** *adv.* **—Syn.** 1. exacerbate, incense, anger. See **irritate.** **—Ant.** 1. mollify.

ex·as·per·a·tion (Yg zăs'pə rā'shən), *n.* 1. act of exasperating; provocation. 2. state of being exasperated; irritation; extreme annoyance: *his exasperation was understandable.*

Exc., Excellency.

exc., 1. except. 2. exception. 3. excursion.

Ex·cal·i·bur (ĕks kăl'ə bər), *n.* the magic sword of King Arthur.

ex ca·the·dra (ĕks kə thē'drə, kăth'Y drə), *Latin.* from the seat of authority; with authority. [t. L: from the chair] **—ex'-ca·the'dra,** *adj.*

ex·cau·date (ĕks kô'dāt), *adj. Zool.* tailless; destitute of a tail or taillike process.

ex·ca·vate (ĕks′kə vāt′), *v.t.*, **-vated, -vating. 1.** to make hollow by removing the inner part; make a hole or cavity in; form into a hollow, as by digging. **2.** to make (a hole, tunnel, etc.) by removing material. **3.** to dig or scoop out (earth, etc.). **4.** to expose or lay bare by digging; unearth: *to excavate an ancient city.* [t. L: m.s. *excavātus*, pp., hollowed out]

ex·ca·va·tion (ĕks′kə vā′shən), *n.* **1.** act of excavating. **2.** a hole or cavity made by excavating. **—Syn. 2.** See **hole.**

ex·ca·va·tor (ĕks′kə vā′tər), *n.* **1.** one who or that which excavates. **2.** a power-driven machine for digging, moving, or transporting loose gravel, sand, or soil.

ex·ceed (ĭk sēd′), *v.t.* **1.** to go beyond the bounds or limits of: *to exceed one's powers.* **2.** to go beyond in quantity, degree, rate, etc.: *to exceed the speed limit.* **3.** to surpass; be superior to; excel. **—v.i. 4.** to be greater, as in quantity or degree. **5.** to surpass others, excel, or be superior. [ME *excede(n)*, t. F: m. *excēder*, t. L: m. *excēdere* go out] **—ex·ceed′er,** *n.* **—Syn. 1.** overstep, transcend.

ex·ceed·ing (ĭk sē′dĭng), *adj.* **1.** extraordinary; excessive. **—adv. 2.** *Archaic.* exceedingly.

ex·ceed·ing·ly (ĭk sē′dĭng lĭ), *adv.* to an unusual degree; extremely.

ex·cel (ĭk sĕl′), *v.,* **-celled, -celling. 1.** to surpass; be superior to; outdo. **—v.i. 2.** to surpass others or be superior in some respect. [t. L: m.s. *excellere*] **—Syn. 1.** outstrip, eclipse, transcend. EXCEL, OUTDO, SURPASS imply being better than others or being superior in achievement. To EXCEL is to be superior to others in some (usually) good or desirable quality, attainment, or performance: *to excel competitors at playing chess.* To OUTDO is to make more successful effort than others: *to outdo competitors in the high jump.* To SURPASS is to go beyond others (who are definitely pointed out) esp. in a contest as to quality or ability: *to surpass one's classmates in knowledge of corporation law.*

ex·cel·lence (ĕk′sə ləns), *n.* **1.** fact or state of excelling; superiority; eminence. **2.** an excellent quality or feature. **3.** *(usually cap.)* Excellency (def. 1). **—Syn. 1.** preëminence, transcendence. **2.** merit, virtue.

ex·cel·len·cy (ĕk′sə lən sĭ), *n., pl.* **-cies. 1.** *(usually cap.)* a title of honor given to certain high officials, as governors and ambassadors. **2.** *(usually cap.)* a person so entitled. **3.** excellence. [t. L: m.s. *excellentia*]

ex·cel·lent (ĕk′sə lənt), *adj.* **1.** possessing excellence or superior merit; remarkably good. **2.** *Obs.* extraordinary; superior. [ME, t. L: s. *excellens*, ppr.] **—ex′cel·lent·ly,** *adv.* **—Syn. 1.** worthy, estimable, choice, fine, first-rate.

ex·cel·si·or (*n.* ĭk sĕl′sĭ ər; *adj.* -sĭ ôr′), *n.* **1.** a kind of fine wood shavings, used for stuffing, packing, etc. **2.** a printing type (3 point) smaller than brilliant. **—adj. 3.** *Latin.* higher (motto of New York State). [t. L, compar. of *excelsus* high, prop. pp., risen above others]

ex·cept¹ (ĭk sĕpt′), *prep.* **1.** with the exclusion of; excluding; save; but: *they were all there except me.* **—conj. 2.** with the exception (that): *parallel cases except that A is younger than B.* **3.** otherwise than; but (fol. by an adv., phrase, or clause): *well fortified except here.* **4.** *Archaic.* unless. [t. L: s. *exceptus*, pp., taken out] **—Syn. 1.** EXCEPT (more rarely EXCEPTING), BUT, SAVE point out something excluded from a general statement. EXCEPT emphasizes the excluding: *take any number except 12.* BUT merely states the exclusion: *we ate all but one.* SAVE is now mainly found in poetic use: *nothing in sight save sky and sea.*

ex·cept² (ĭk sĕpt′), *v.t.* **1.** to exclude; leave out: *present company excepted.* **—v.i. 2.** to object: *to except against a statement, a witness, etc.* [ME *excepte(n)*, t. F: m. *excepter*, der. L *exceptus*, pp.]

ex·cept·ing (ĭk sĕp′tĭng), *prep.* **1.** excluding; barring; saving; except. **—conj. 2.** *Archaic.* except; unless; save. **—Syn. 1.** See **except¹.**

ex·cep·tion (ĭk sĕp′shən), *n.* **1.** act of excepting. **2.** fact of being excepted. **3.** something excepted; an instance or case not conforming to the general rule. **4.** an adverse criticism, esp. on a particular point; opposition of opinion; objection; demurral: *a statement liable to exception.* **5. take exception, a.** to make objection; demur with respect to something (usually fol. by *to*). **b.** to take offense (often fol. by *at*). **6.** *Law.* **a.** an objection, as to a ruling of the court in the course of a trial. **b.** a notation that an objection is preserved for purposes of appeal: *saving an exception.* [t. L: s. *exceptio*]

ex·cep·tion·a·ble (ĭk sĕp′shən ə bəl), *adj.* liable to exception or objection; objectionable. **—ex·cep′tion·a·ble·ness,** *n.* **—ex·cep′tion·a·bly,** *adv.*

ex·cep·tion·al (ĭk sĕp′shən əl), *adj.* forming an exception or unusual instance; unusual; extraordinary. **—ex·cep′tion·al·ly,** *adv.* **—ex·cep′tion·al·ness,** *n.* **—Syn.** uncommon, peculiar, singular, superior. See **irregular.** **—Ant.** average.

ex·cep·tive (ĭk sĕp′tĭv), *adj.* **1.** that excepts; making an exception. **2.** disposed to take exception; objecting.

ex·cerpt (*n.* ĕk′sûrpt; *v.* ĭk sûrpt′), *n.* **1.** a passage taken out of a book or the like; an extract. **—v.t. 2.** to take out (a passage) from a book or the like; extract. [t. L: s. *excerptus*, pp. picked out] **—ex·cerp′tion,** *n.*

ex·cess (*n.* ĭk sĕs′; *adj.* ĕk′sĕs, ĭk sĕs′), *n.* **1.** the fact of exceeding something else in amount or degree. **2.** the amount or degree by which one thing exceeds another. **3.** an extreme or excessive amount or degree; superabundance: *have an excess of energy.* **4.** a going beyond ordinary or proper limits. **5.** immoderate indulgence; intemperance in eating and drinking. **—adj. 6.** more than or above what is necessary, usual, or specified; extra: *excess baggage, excess profits.* [ME *excesse*, t. L: m. *excessus* a departure] **—Syn. 3.** overplus, surplus, surplusage. **—Ant. 3.** deficiency.

ex·ces·sive (ĭk sĕs′ĭv), *adj.* exceeding the usual or proper limit or degree; characterized by excess: *excessive charges, excessive indulgence.* **—ex·ces′sive·ly,** *adv.* **—ex·ces′sive·ness,** *n.* **—Syn.** immoderate, extravagant, extreme, inordinate, exorbitant.

ex·cess-prof·its tax (ĕk′sĕs prŏf′ĭts), a tax on the profits of a business enterprise in excess of the average profits for a number of base years, or of a specified rate of return on capital.

exch., 1. exchange. **2.** exchequer.

ex·change (ĭks chānj′), *v.,* **-changed, -changing,** *n.* **—v.t. 1.** to part with for some equivalent; to give up (something) for something else. **2.** to replace by another or something else; change for another: *to exchange a purchase.* **3.** to give and receive reciprocally; interchange: *to exchange blows, gifts, etc.* **4.** to part with in return for some equivalent; transfer for a recompense; barter: *to exchange goods with foreign countries.* **5.** *Chess.* to capture (an enemy piece) in return for a capture by the opponent generally of pieces of equal value. **—v.i. 6.** to make an exchange. **7.** to pass or be taken in exchange or as an equivalent. **—n. 8.** act or process of exchanging: *an exchange of gifts, prisoners of war, etc.* **9.** that which is given or received in exchange or substitution for something else: *the car was a fair exchange.* **10.** a place for buying and selling commodities, securities, etc., typically open only to members. **11.** a central office or central station: *a telephone exchange.* **12.** the method or system by which debits and credits in different places are settled without the actual transference of money, by means of documents (bills of exchange) representing money values. **13.** the discharge of obligations in different places by the transfer of credits. **14.** the amount or percentage charged for exchanging money, collecting a draft, etc. **15.** the reciprocal transference of equivalent sums of money, as in the currencies of two different countries. **16.** the giving or receiving of a sum of money in one place for a bill ordering the payment of an equivalent sum in another. **17.** the varying rate or sum, in one currency, given for a fixed sum in another currency; rate of exchange. **18.** the amount of the difference in value between two or more currencies, or between the values of the same currency at two or more places. **19.** the checks, drafts, etc. exchanged at a clearinghouse. **20.** *Brit.* labor exchange. [ME *eschaunge*, t. AF, g. LL *excambium*] **—ex·chang′er,** *n.* **—Syn. 1.** interchange, commute, barter, trade, swap. **8.** interchange, trade, traffic.

ex·change·a·ble (ĭks chān′jə bəl), *adj.* that can be exchanged. **—ex·change′a·bil′i·ty,** *n.* **—Syn.** EXCHANGEABLE, INTERCHANGEABLE apply to something which may replace something else. That is EXCHANGEABLE which may be taken or sent back to the place at which it was purchased, to be exchanged for money, credit, or other purchases to the amount of the original purchase: *these dishes are exchangeable if you find they are not satisfactory.* INTERCHANGEABLE applies to those things which are capable of being reciprocally put in each other's place: *standard parts are interchangeable.*

ex·cheq·uer (ĭks chĕk′ər, ĕks′chĕk ər), *n.* **1.** a treasury, as of a state or nation. **2.** (in Great Britain) **a.** *(often cap.)* the governmental department in charge of the public revenues. **b.** (formerly) an office which administered the royal revenues and determined all cases affecting them. **c.** *(cap.)* an ancient common law court of civil jurisdiction (**Court of Exchequer**) in which all cases affecting the revenues of the crown were tried, now merged in the King's Bench Division of the High Court. **3.** *Colloq.* funds; finances. [ME *escheker*, t. OF: m. *eschequier* chess board (so called with reference to the table cover marked with squares on which accounts were reckoned with counters). See CHECKER]

ex·cide (ĭk sīd′), *v.t.,* **-cided, -ciding.** to excise.

ex·cip·i·ent (ĭk sĭp′ĭ ənt), *n. Pharm.* a more or less inert substance, as sugar, jelly, etc., used as the medium or vehicle for the administration of an active medicine. [t. L: s. *excipiens*, ppr., taking out]

ex·cis·a·ble (ĭk sī′zə bəl), *adj.* subject to excise duty.

ex·cise¹ (*n.* ĭk sīz′, ĕk′sīz; *v.* ĭk sīz′), *n., v.,* **-cised, -cising. —n. 1.** an inland tax or duty on certain commodities, as spirits, tobacco, etc., levied on their manufacture, sale, or consumption within the country. **2.** a tax levied for a license to carry on certain employments, pursue certain sports, etc. **3.** *Brit.* that branch of the civil service which collects excise duties. **—v.t. 4.** to impose an excise on. [prob. t. MD: m. *excijs*, t. OF: m. *acceis* a tax, ult. der. LL *accēnsāre* tax] **—ex·ci·sion** (ĭk sĭzh′ən), *n.*

ex·cise² (ĭk sīz′), *v.t.,* **-cised, -cising. 1.** to expunge, as a passage or sentence. **2.** to cut out or off, as a tumor. [t. L: m.s. *excīsus*, pp., cut out.]

ex·cise·man (ĭk sīz′mən), *n., pl.* **-men.** *Brit.* an officer who collects excise taxes and enforces excise laws.

ex·cit·a·bil·i·ty (ĭk sī′tə bĭl′ə tĭ), *n.* **1.** quality of being excitable. **2.** *Physiol.* irritability.

ex·cit·a·ble (ĭk sī′tə bəl), *adj.* capable of being excited; easily excited. **—ex·cit′a·ble·ness,** *n.* **—ex·cit′a·bly,** *adv.* **—Syn.** emotional, passionate, fiery. **—Ant.** placid.

ex·cit·ant (Ĭk sī'tənt, ĕk'sə tənt), *adj.* **1.** exciting; stimulating. —*n.* **2.** *Physiol.* something that excites; a stimulant.

ex·ci·ta·tion (ĕk'sī tā'shən), *n.* **1.** act of exciting. **2.** state of being excited. **3.** *Elect.* the relative strength of the magnetic field in a dynamo: *normal excitation.*

ex·ci·ta·tive (Ĭk sī'tə tĭv), *adj.* tending to excite. Also, **ex·ci·ta·to·ry** (Ĭk sī'tə tôr'Ĭ).

ex·cite (Ĭk sīt'), *v.t.*, **-cited, -citing. 1.** to arouse or stir up the feelings of: *to excite jealousy or hatred.* **2.** to cause; awaken: *to excite interest or curiosity.* **3.** to stir to action; stir up: *to excite a dog.* **4.** *Physiol.* to stimulate: *to excite a nerve.* **5.** *Elect.* to produce electric activity or a magnetic field in: *to excite a dynamo.* [ME *excite(n),* t. L: m.s. *excitāre,* freq. of *exciere* call forth, rouse] —**Syn. 1.** stir, arouse, awaken, stimulate, animate, kindle, inflame. **3.** provoke. —**Ant. 1.** soothe.

ex·cit·ed (Ĭk sī'tĭd), *adj.* **1.** stirred emotionally; agitated. **2.** stimulated to activity; brisk. **3.** *Physics.* (of an atom or nucleus) in a state of higher energy than the normal state. —**ex·cit·ed·ly,** *adv.* —**Syn. 1.** ruffled, discomposed, stormy, perturbed, impassioned.

ex·cite·ment (Ĭk sīt'mənt), *n.* **1.** excited state or condition. **2.** something that excites. —**Syn. 1.** perturbation, commotion, ado. See **agitation.**

ex·cit·er (Ĭk sī'tər), *n.* **1.** one who or that which excites. **2.** *Elect.* an auxiliary generator which supplies energy for the excitation of another electric machine.

ex·cit·ing (Ĭk sī'tĭng), *adj.* producing excitement; stirring. —**ex·cit'ing·ly,** *adv.*

ex·ci·tor (Ĭk sī'tər, -tôr), *n.* **1.** *Physiol.* a nerve whose stimulation excites greater action. **2.** exciter.

ex·claim (Ĭk sklām'), *v.i.* **1.** to cry out or speak suddenly and vehemently, as in surprise, strong emotion, protest, etc. —*v.t.* **2.** to cry out; say loudly or vehemently. [t. F: m.s. *exclamer,* t. L: m. *exclāmāre* call out] —**ex·claim'er,** *n.*

exclam·, **1.** exclamation. **2.** exclamatory.

ex·cla·ma·tion (ĕks'klə mā'shən), *n.* **1.** act of exclaiming; an outcry; a loud complaint or protest. **2.** an interjection. —**Syn. 1.** cry, ejaculation.

exclamation point, a punctuation mark (!) used after an exclamation. Also, **exclamation mark.**

ex·clam·a·to·ry (Ĭk sklăm'ə tō'rĬ), *adj.* **1.** using, containing, or expressing exclamation. **2.** pertaining to exclamation.

ex·clude (Ĭk sklōōd'), *v.t.*, **-cluded, -cluding. 1.** to shut or keep out; prevent the entrance of. **2.** to shut out from consideration, privilege, etc. **3.** to expel and keep out; thrust out; eject. [ME *exclude(n),* t. L: m. *exclūdere*] —**ex·clud'a·ble,** *adj.* —**ex·clud'er,** *n.* —**Syn. 2.** EXCLUDE, DEBAR, ELIMINATE mean to remove from a certain place, or from consideration in a particular situation. To EXCLUDE is to set aside as unwanted, unusable, etc.: *words excluded from polite conversation.* To DEBAR is to prohibit, esp. in a legal sense, from a place or from the enjoyment of privileges, rights, or the like: *to debar all candidates lacking the necessary preparation.* To ELIMINATE is to select and take out or remove, esp. as irrelevant, unnecessary, or undesirable: *to eliminate such objections.* —**Ant. 2.** admit.

excluded middle, law of, *Logic.* the law which states that a proposition is either true or false, or that a thing either has or does not have a given property.

ex·clu·sion (Ĭk sklōō'zhən), *n.* **1.** act of excluding. **2.** state of being excluded. **3.** *Physiol.* a keeping apart; blocking entrance. [t. L: s. *exclūsio*]

ex·clu·sion·ism (Ĭk sklōō'zhən Ĭz'əm), *n.* the principle, policy, or practice of exclusion, as from rights or privileges.

ex·clu·sion·ist (Ĭk sklōō'zhən Ĭst), *n.* one who favors exclusion; one who could exclude another from some right or privilege.

ex·clu·sive (Ĭk sklōō'sĬv), *adj.* **1.** not admitting of something else; incompatible: *mutually exclusive ideas.* **2.** excluding from consideration or account: *from 100 to 121 exclusive* (excluding 100 and 121, and including from 101 to 120). **3.** limited to the object or objects designated: *exclusive attention to business.* **4.** shutting out all others from a part or share: *an exclusive grant.* **5.** in which no others have a share: *exclusive information.* **6.** single or sole: *the exclusive means of communication between two places.* **7.** disposed to resist the admission of outsiders to association, intimacy, etc.: *an exclusive clique.* **8.** *Colloq.* fashionable: *an exclusive club.* **9.** *Logic.* excluding all except what is specified: *an exclusive proposition.* [t. ML: m.s. *exclūsivus,* der. L *exclūsus,* pp., excluded] —**ex·clu'sive·ly,** *adv.* —**ex·clu'sive·ness,** *n.* —**Syn. 7.** select, narrow, clannish, snobbish.

exclusive representation, *Labor.* the right of a union chosen by a majority of the employees in a plant, craft, industry or department of a shop or business, to represent all the employees in the unit, regardless of whether they are members of the union or not.

ex·cog·i·tate (ĕks kŏj'ə tāt'), *v.t.*, **-tated, -tating.** to think out; devise; invent. [t. L: m.s. *excōgitātus,* pp., found out by thinking] —**ex·cog'i·ta'tion,** *n.* —**ex·cog'i·ta'tive,** *adj.* —**ex·cog'i·ta'tor,** *n.*

ex·com·mu·ni·ca·ble (ĕks'kə mū'nə kə bəl), *adj.* **1.** liable or deserving to be excommunicated, as a person. **2.** punishable by excommunication, as an offense.

ex·com·mu·ni·cate (ĕks'kə mū'nə kāt'), *v.*, **-cated, -cating,** *n.*, *adj.* —*v.t.* **1.** to cut off from communion or

membership, esp. from the sacraments and fellowship of the church by ecclesiastical sentence. —*n.* **2.** an excommunicated person. —*adj.* **3.** excommunicated. [t. LL: m.s. *excommūnicātus,* pp., lit., put out of the community] —**ex'com·mu'ni·ca'tor,** *n.*

ex·com·mu·ni·ca·tion (ĕks'kə mū'nə kā'shən), *n.* **1.** act of excommunicating. **2.** state of being excommunicated. **3.** the ecclesiastical sentence by which a person is excommunicated.

ex·com·mu·ni·ca·tive (ĕks'kə mū'nə kā'tĬv), *adj.* disposed or serving to excommunicate.

ex·com·mu·ni·ca·to·ry (ĕks'kə mū'nə kə tôr'Ĭ), *adj.* relating to or causing excommunication.

ex·co·ri·ate (Ĭk skôr'Ĭ āt'), *v.t.*, **-ated, -ating. 1.** *Physiol.* to strip off or remove the skin from. **2.** to flay verbally; denounce; censure. [t. L: m.s. *excoriātus,* pp. of *excoriāre* strip off the hide]

ex·co·ri·a·tion (Ĭk skôr'Ĭ ā'shən), *n.* **1.** act of excoriating. **2.** state of being excoriated. **3.** an excoriated place on the body.

ex·cre·ment (ĕks'krə mənt), *n.* waste matter discharged from the body, esp. the feces. [t. L: s. *excrēmentum* what is evacuated] —**ex·cre·men·tal** (ĕks'-krə mĕn'təl), *adj.*

ex·cre·men·ti·tious (ĕks'krə mĕn tĬsh'əs), *adj.* of or like excrement.

ex·cres·cence (Ĭk skrĕs'əns), *n.* **1.** abnormal growth or increase. **2.** an abnormal outgrowth, usually harmless, on an animal or vegetable body. **3.** a normal outgrowth, such as hair. **4.** any disfiguring addition.

ex·cres·cen·cy (Ĭk skrĕs'ən sĬ), *n.*, *pl.* **-cies.** state of being excrescent.

ex·cres·cent (Ĭk skrĕs'ənt), *adj.* **1.** growing abnormally out of something else; superfluous. **2.** *Phonet.* added without grammatical or historical justification, as in the *t* often heard at the end of *once* or *twice.* [t. L: s. *excrescens,* ppr., growing out]

ex·cre·ta (Ĭk skrē'tə), *n.pl.* excreted matters, as sweat, urine, etc. [t. L, neut. pl. of *excrētus,* pp., separated] —**ex·cre'tal,** *adj.*

ex·crete (Ĭk skrēt'), *v.t.*, **-creted, -creting.** to separate and eliminate from an organic body; separate and expel from the blood or tissues, as waste or harmful matters. [t. L: m.s. *excrētus,* pp., sifted out, discharged] —**ex·cre'tive,** *adj.*

ex·cre·tion (Ĭk skrē'shən), *n.* **1.** act of excreting. **2.** the substance excreted, as sweat or urine, or certain plant products.

ex·cre·to·ry (ĕks'krə tōr'Ĭ, Ĭk skrē'tə rĬ), *adj.* pertaining to or concerned in excretion; having the function of excreting: *excretory organs.*

ex·cru·ci·ate (Ĭk skrōō'shĬ āt'), *v.t.*, **-ated, -ating.** to inflict severe pain upon; torture. [t. L: m.s. *excruciātus,* pp., tortured greatly]

ex·cru·ci·at·ing (Ĭk skrōō'shĬ ā'tĬng), *adj.* extremely painful; causing extreme suffering; torturing. —**ex·cru'ci·at'ing·ly,** *adv.*

ex·cru·ci·a·tion (Ĭk skrōō'shĬ ā'shən), *n.* **1.** act of excruciating. **2.** state of being excruciated. **3.** an instance of this; torture.

ex·cul·pate (ĕks'kŭl pāt', Ĭk skŭl'pāt), *v.t.*, **-pated, -pating.** to clear from a charge of guilt or fault; free from blame; vindicate. [f. EX-¹ + s. L *culpa* fault, blame + -ATE¹] —**ex·cul·pa·ble** (Ĭk skŭl'pə bəl), *adj.* —**ex'-cul·pa'tion,** *n.*

ex·cul·pa·to·ry (Ĭk skŭl'pə tō'rĬ), *adj.* tending to clear from a charge of fault or guilt.

ex·cur·rent (Ĭk skŭr'ənt), *adj.* **1.** running out or forth. **2.** *Zool.* giving passage outward; affording exit: *the excurrent canal of certain sponges.* **3.** *Bot.* **a.** having the axis prolonged so as to form an undivided main stem or trunk, as the stem of the spruce. **b.** projecting beyond the apex, as the midrib in certain leaves. [t. L: s. *excurrens,* ppr., running out]

ex·cur·sion (Ĭk skŭr'zhən, -shən), *n.* **1.** a short journey or trip to some point for a special purpose, with the intention of speedy return: *a pleasure excursion, a scientific excursion.* **2.** a trip on a train, ship, etc. at a reduced rate: *week-end excursions to seashore or mountain resorts.* **3.** the persons who make such a journey. **4.** deviation or digression. **5.** *Physics.* the departure of a body from its mean position or proper course. **6.** *Mach.* **a.** the range of stroke of any moving part. **b.** the stroke itself. **7.** *Obs.* a sally or raid. [t. L: s. *excursio* a running out] —**Syn. 2.** EXCURSION, JAUNT, JUNKET, TOUR are trips made primarily for pleasure. An EXCURSION is a short trip, often no more than a day's outing, made usually by a number of people, as a result of special inducements (low fare, a special event, etc): *an excursion at reduced rates.* JAUNT is a familiar term for a short, agreeable trip, now esp. by automobile: *take a little jaunt to the country, over to a cousin's house.* JUNKET, with a still stronger suggestion of pleasure-seeking, is frequently applied to trips made ostensibly on official business, enjoyed at public expense: *the junket of a congressional committee.* A TOUR is a planned trip to celebrated places, to see interesting scenery, etc.: *a tour of Europe.*

ex·cur·sion·ist (Ĭk skŭr'zhən Ĭst, -shən-), *n.* one who goes on an excursion.

excursion ticket, a ticket to a particular point and back, at a reduced fare.

ex·cur·sive (Ĭk skŭr'sĬv), *adj.* **1.** given to making excursions; wandering; digressive. **2.** of the nature of an

---

excursion; rambling; desultory. —**ex·cur′sive·ly,** *adv.* —**ex·cur′sive·ness,** *n.*

ex·cur·sus (ĕks kûr′səs), *n., pl.* **-suses, -sus.** a detailed discussion of some point in a book (usually added as an appendix). [t. L, der. *excurrere* run out]

ex·cus·a·to·ry (ĭk skū′zə tōr′Y), *adj.* serving or intended to excuse.

ex·cuse (*v.* ĭk skūz′; *n.* ĭk skūs′), *v.,* **-cused, -cusing,** *n.* —*v.t.* **1.** to regard or judge with indulgence; pardon or forgive; overlook (a fault, etc.). **2.** to offer an apology for; apologize for; seek to remove the blame of. **3.** to serve as an apology or justification for; justify: *ignorance of the law excuses no man.* **4.** to release from an obligation or duty: *to be excused from attending a meeting.* **5.** to seek or obtain exemption or release for (oneself): *to excuse oneself from duty.* **6.** to refrain from exacting; remit; dispense with: *to excuse a fine.* —*n.* **7.** that which is offered as a reason for being excused; a plea offered in extenuation of a fault, or for release from an obligation, etc. **8.** something serving to excuse; a ground or reason for excusing. **9.** act of excusing. **10.** a pretext or subterfuge. [ME *excuse*(*n*), t. L: m. *excūsāre* allege in excuse] —**ex·cus′a·ble,** *adj.* —**ex·cus′a·ble·ness,** *n.* —**ex·cus′a·bly,** *adv.* —**ex·cus′er,** *n.*

—**Syn. 1.** EXCUSE, FORGIVE, PARDON imply being lenient or giving up the wish to punish. EXCUSE means to overlook some (usually) slight offense, because of circumstance, realization that it was unintentional, or the like: *to excuse bad manners.* FORGIVE is applied to excusing more serious offenses; the person wronged not only overlooks the offense but harbors no ill feeling against the offender: *to forgive and forget.* PARDON usually applies to a specific act of lenience or mercy by an official or superior in remitting all or the remainder of the punishment that belongs to a serious offense or crime: *the governor was asked to pardon the condemned criminal.* **3.** extenuate, palliate. **7.** EXCUSE, APOLOGY both imply an explanation of some failure or failing. EXCUSE implies a desire to avoid punishment or rebuke. APOLOGY usually implies acknowledgment that one has been, at least seemingly, in the wrong; it may aim at setting matters right by either alleging extenuating circumstances, or expressing regret for an error. —**Ant. 1.** blame, punish.

exec., **1.** executive. **2.** executor.

ex·e·cra·ble (ĕk′sə krə bəl), *adj.* **1.** deserving to be execrated; detestable; abominable. **2.** *Colloq.* very bad: *an execrable pun.* —**ex′e·cra·bly,** *adv.*

ex·e·crate (ĕk′sə krāt′), *v.,* **-crated, -crating.** —*v.t.* **1.** to detest utterly; abhor; abominate. **2.** to curse; imprecate evil upon. —*v.i.* **3.** to utter curses. [t. L: m.s. *ex*(*s*)*ecrātus,* pp., having cursed] —**ex′e·cra′tor,** *n.*

ex·e·cra·tion (ĕk′sə krā′shən), *n.* **1.** act of execrating. **2.** a curse or imprecation. **3.** the object execrated; a thing held in abomination.

ex·e·cra·tive (ĕk′sə krā′tĭv), *adj.* **1.** pertaining to or characterized by execration. **2.** prone to execrate.

ex·e·cra·to·ry (ĕk′sə krə tōr′Y, -krā′tə rY), *adj.* **1.** pertaining to execration. **2.** having the nature of or containing an execration.

ex·e·cu·tant (Yg zĕk′yə tənt), *n.* one who executes or performs, esp. musically.

ex·e·cute (ĕk′sə kūt′), *v.t.,* **-cuted, -cuting. 1.** to carry out; accomplish: *to execute a plan or order.* **2.** to perform or do: *to execute a maneuver or gymnastic feat.* **3.** to inflict capital punishment on; put to death according to law. **4.** to produce in accordance with a plan or design: *to execute a statue or a picture.* **5.** to perform or play (a piece of music). **6.** *Law.* **a.** to give effect or force to (a law, decree, judicial sentence, etc.): carry out the terms of (a will). **b.** to transact or carry through (a contract, mortgage, etc.) in the manner prescribed by law; complete and give validity to (a legal instrument) by fulfilling the legal requirements, as by signing, sealing, etc. [ME *execute*(*n*), t. ML: m. *execūtāre,* der. L *ex*(*s*)*ecūtus,* pp., having followed out] —**ex′e·cut′a·ble,** *adj.* —**ex′e·cut′er,** *n.* —**Syn. 2.** See **perform. 3.** See **kill¹. 6. a.** administer, enforce.

ex·e·cu·tion (ĕk′sə kū′shən), *n.* **1.** act or process of executing. **2.** state or fact of being executed. **3.** the infliction of capital punishment, or, formerly, of any legal punishment. **4.** mode or style of performance; technical skill, as in music. **5.** effective action, esp. of weapons. **6.** effective work, or the result attained by it (generally after *do*): *every shot did execution.* **7.** *Law.* a judicial writ directing the enforcement of a judgment.

ex·e·cu·tion·er (ĕk′sə kū′shən ər), *n.* **1.** one who executes. **2.** an official who inflicts capital punishment in pursuance of a legal warrant.

ex·e·cu·tive (Yg zĕk′yə tĭv), *adj.* **1.** suited for execution or carrying into effect; of the kind requisite for practical performance or direction: *executive ability.* **2.** charged with or pertaining to execution of laws, or administration of affairs. —*n.* **3.** a person or body charged with or skilled in administrative work. **4.** the person or persons in whom the supreme executive power of a government is vested. **5.** the executive branch of a government. —**ex·ec′u·tive·ly,** *adv.*

Executive Mansion, (in the U.S.) the official residence of the President at Washington, D.C. (the White House), or of the governor of one of the States.

executive order, (*usually cap.*) an order issued by the President of the U.S. to the army, navy, or other part of the executive branch of the Government.

ex·ec·u·tor (Yg zĕk′yə tər), *n.* **1.** one who executes, or carries out, performs, fulfills, etc. **2.** *Law.* a person named by a decedent in his will to carry out the provisions of his will. [ME *executour,* t. AF, t. L: m.s. *ex*(*s*)*ecūtor,* lit., one who follows out]

ex·ec·u·to·ry (Yg zĕk′yə tōr′Y), *adj.* **1.** executive. **2.** *Law.* intended, or of such a nature as, to take effect on a future contingency.

ex·ec·u·trix (Yg zĕk′yə trĭks′), *n., pl.* **executrices** (Yg-zĕk′yə trī′sēz), **executrixes.** *Law.* a female executor.

ex·e·ge·sis (ĕk′sə jē′sĭs), *n., pl.* **-ses** (-sēz). critical explanation or interpretation, esp. of Scripture. [t. NL, t. Gk.: explanation]

ex·e·gete (ĕk′sə jēt′), *n.* one skilled in exegesis.

ex·e·get·ic (ĕk′sə jĕt′Yk), *adj.* pertaining to exegesis; expository. Also, **ex′e·get′i·cal.** [t. Gk.: s. *exēgētikós* explanatory] —**ex′e·get′i·cal·ly,** *adv.*

ex·e·get·ics (ĕk′sə jĕt′Yks), *n.* the science of exegesis; exegetical theology.

ex·e·gi mo·nu·men·tum ae·re pe·ren·ni·us (ĕk sē′jĭ mōn′yōō mĕn′təm Yr′Y pə rĕn′Y əs). *Latin.* I have made a monument more lasting than brass. Horace, Odes, III, 30.

ex·em·plar (Yg zĕm′plər, -plär), *n.* **1.** a model or pattern to be copied or imitated. **2.** an example; typical instance. **3.** an original or archetype. [t. L: copy, model; r. ME *exemplaire,* t. OF]

ex·em·pla·ry (Yg zĕm′plə rY, ĕg′zəm plĕr′Y), *adj.* **1.** worthy of imitation; commendable: *exemplary conduct.* **2.** such as may serve for a warning: *an exemplary penalty.* **3.** serving for a model or pattern. **4.** serving for an illustration or specimen; illustrative; typical. —**ex·em′pla·ri·ly,** *adv.* —**ex·em′pla·ri·ness,** *n.*

ex·em·pli·fi·ca·tion (Yg zĕm′plə fə kā′shən), *n.* **1.** act of exemplifying. **2.** that which exemplifies; an illustration or example. **3.** *Law.* an attested copy of a document, under official seal.

ex·em·pli·fi·ca·tive (Yg zĕm′plə fə kā′tYv), *adj.* serving to exemplify.

ex·em·pli·fy (Yg zĕm′plə fī′), *v.t.,* **-fied, -fying. 1.** to show or illustrate by example. **2.** to furnish, or serve as, an example of. **3.** *Law.* to transcribe or copy; make an attested copy of (a document) under seal. [ME *exemplyfy*(*en*), t. ML: m.s. *exemplificāre,* f. L: *exempli-* example + *-ficāre* make] —**ex·em′pli·fi′er,** *n.*

ex·em·pli gra·ti·a (Yg zĕm′plī grā′shY ə), *Latin.* for the sake of example; for example. *Abbr.:* e.g.

ex·empt (Yg zĕmpt′), *v.t.* **1.** to free from an obligation or liability to which others are subject; release: *to exempt someone from military service, from an examination,* etc. —*adj.* **2.** released from, or not subject to, an obligation, liability, etc.: *exempt from taxes.* —*n.* **3.** one who is exempt from, or not subject to, an obligation, duty, etc. [ME, t. L: s. *exemptus,* pp.]

ex·emp·tion (Yg zĕmp′shən), *n.* **1.** act of exempting. **2.** state of being exempted; immunity.

—**Syn. 2.** EXEMPTION, IMMUNITY, IMPUNITY imply special privilege or freedom from requirements imposed upon others. EXEMPTION implies release or privileged freedom from sharing with others some (usually arbitrarily imposed) duty, tax, etc.: *exemption from military service.* IMMUNITY implies freedom from a penalty or from some natural or common liability, esp one that is disagreeable or threatening: *immunity from disease.* IMPUNITY (limited mainly to the fixed expression *with impunity*) primarily suggests freedom from punishment: *the police force was so inadequate that crimes could be committed with impunity.* —**Ant. 2.** liability.

ex·e·qua·tur (ĕk′sə kwā′tər), *n.* **1.** a written recognition of a consul by the government of the state in which he is stationed authorizing him to exercise his powers. **2.** an authorization granted by a secular ruler for the publication of papal bulls or other ecclesiastical enactments to give them binding force. [t. L: let him execute]

ex·e·quies (ĕk′sə kwYz), *n.pl. Now Rare.* a funeral rite or ceremony. [ME *exequiēs* (pl.), t. OF, t. L: m. *exequiae* funeral procession]

ex·er·cise (ĕk′sər sīz′), *n., v.,* **-cised, -cising.** —*n.* **1.** bodily or mental exertion, esp. for the sake of training or improvement. **2.** something done or performed as a means of practice or training: *exercises for the piano.* **3.** a putting into action, use, operation, or effect: *the exercise of caution or care, the exercise of will power.* **4.** (*often pl.*) a ceremony: *graduating exercises.* **5.** a religious observance or service. —*v.t.* **6.** to put through exercises, or forms of practice or exertion, designed to train, develop, condition, etc.: *to exercise troops, a horse, the voice,* etc. **7.** to put (faculties, rights, etc.) into action, practice, or use: *to exercise one's strength, one's sight,* etc. **8.** to use or display in one's action or procedure: *to exercise caution, patience, judgment.* **9.** to make use of (one's privileges, powers, etc.): *to exercise one's rights.* **10.** to discharge (a function); perform: *to exercise the duties of one's office.* **11.** to have as an effect: *to exercise an influence on someone.* **12.** to worry; make uneasy; annoy: *to be much exercised about one's health.* —*v.i.* **13.** to go through exercises; take bodily exercise. [ME *exercice,* t. OF, g. L *exercitium*] —**ex′er·cis′a·ble,** *adj.* —**ex′er·cis′er,** *n.*

—**Syn. 2.** EXERCISE, DRILL, PRACTICE refer to activities undertaken for training in some skill. An EXERCISE may be either physical or mental, and may be more or less irregular in time and varied in kind: *an exercise in arithmetic.* DRILL is disciplined repetition of set exercises, often performed in a group, directed by a leader: *military drill.* PRACTICE is methodical exercise, usually characterized by much repetition, with a view to becoming perfect in some operation or pursuit and to acquiring further skills: *even great musicians require constant practice.* **3.** employment, application. **6.** discipline. **8.** employ, apply, exert.

ex·er·ci·ta·tion (ĕg zûr′sə tā′shən), *n.* **1.** exercise or exertion, as of faculties or powers. **2.** practice or training. **3.** a performance. **4.** a disquisition or discourse. [ME *exercitacion*, t. L: m.s. *exercitātio* exercise, practice]

ex·ergue (ĭg zûrg′, ĕk′sûrg), *n. Numismatics.* the space below the base line on a coin or medal. [t. F, f. Gk.: *ex-* EX-³ + m.s. * érgon* work]

ex·ert (ĭg zûrt′), *v.t.* **1.** to put forth, as power; exercise, as ability or influence; put into vigorous action. **2.** **exert oneself,** to put forth one's powers; use one's efforts; strive. [t. L: s. *ex(s)ertus*, pp.] —**ex·er′tive,** *adj.*

ex·er·tion (ĭg zûr′shən), *n.* **1.** vigorous action or effort. **2.** an effort. **3.** exercise, as of power or faculties. **4.** an instance of this. —**Syn. 1.** endeavor, struggle, attempt. See **effort.**

Ex·e·ter (ĕk′sə tər), *n.* a city in SW England, in Devonshire: cathedral. 73,990 (est. 1946).

ex·e·unt (ĕk′sĭ ənt), *Latin.* they (or the persons named) go out (instruction for actors in plays).

ex·e·unt om·nes (ĕk′sĭ ənt ŏm′nēz), *Latin.* all go out; all go offstage (used in plays).

ex·fo·li·ate (ĕks fō′lĭ āt′), *v.,* **-ated, -ating.** —*v.t.* **1.** to throw off in scales. **2.** to remove the surface of (a bone, etc.) in scales or laminae. —*v.i.* **3.** to throw off scales or flakes; peel off in thin fragments: *the exfoliating bark of a tree.* **4.** *Geol.* **a.** to split or swell into a scaly aggregate, as certain minerals when heated. **b.** to separate into rudely concentric layers or sheets, as certain rocks during weathering. **5.** *Surg.* to separate and come off in scales, as scaling skin or any structure separating in flakes. [t. LL: m.s. *exfoliātus*, pp., stripped of leaves] —**ex·fo′li·a·tive,** *adj.*

ex·fo·li·a·tion (ĕks fō′lĭ ā′shən), *n.* **1.** act or process of exfoliating. **2.** state of being exfoliated. **3.** that which is exfoliated, or scaled off.

ex·hal·ant (ĕks hā′lənt, ĭg zā′lənt), *adj.* **1.** exhaling; emitting. —*n.* **2.** that which exhales.

ex·ha·la·tion (ĕks′hə lā′shən, ĕg′zə-), *n.* **1.** act of exhaling. **2.** that which is exhaled; a vapor; an emanation.

ex·hale (ĕks hāl′, ĭg zāl′), *v.,* **-haled, -haling.** —*v.i.* **1.** to emit breath or vapor. **2.** to pass off as vapor; pass off as an effluence. —*v.t.* **3.** to breathe out; emit (air, etc.). **4.** to give off as vapor. **5.** to draw out as a vapor or effluence; evaporate. [ME *exale(n)*, t. F: m. *exhaler*, t. L: m. *exhālāre* breathe out] —**ex·hal′a·ble,** *adj.*

ex·haust (ĭg zôst′), *v.t.* **1.** to empty by drawing out the contents. **2.** to create a vacuum in. **3.** to draw out or drain off; draw or drain off completely. **4.** to use up or consume completely; expend the whole of. **5.** to drain of strength or energy, wear out, or fatigue greatly, as a person: *I have exhausted myself working.* **6.** to draw out all that is essential in (a subject, topic, etc.); treat or study thoroughly. **7.** to deprive wholly of useful or essential properties, possessions, resources, etc. **8.** to deprive of ingredients by the use of solvents, as a drug. —*v.i.* **9.** to pass out or escape, as spent steam from the cylinder of an engine. —*n.* **10.** *Mach.* **a.** the escape of the gases from the cylinder of an engine after expansion. **b.** the steam or gases ejected. **c.** the parts of an engine through which the exhaust is ejected. [t. L: s. *exhaustus*, pp., drained out] —**ex·haust′er,** *n.* —**ex·haust′i·ble,** *adj.* —**ex·haust′i·bil′i·ty,** *n.* —**Syn. 5.** tire, enervate, prostrate. See **tired¹.** —**Ant. 5.** invigorate.

exhaust fan, the fan in a ventilation system used to remove vitiated or excess air.

ex·haus·tion (ĭg zôs′chən), *n.* **1.** act or process of exhausting. **2.** state of being exhausted. **3.** extreme weakness or fatigue. —**Syn. 3.** weariness, lassitude.

ex·haus·tive (ĭg zôs′tĭv), *adj.* **1.** exhausting a subject, topic, etc.; comprehensive; thorough. **2.** tending to exhaust or drain, as of resources or strength. —**ex·haus′tive·ly,** *adv.* —**ex·haus′tive·ness,** *n.*

ex·haust·less (ĭg zôst′lĭs), *adj.* inexhaustible. —**ex·haust′less·ly,** *adv.* —**ex·haust′less·ness,** *n.*

ex·hib·it (ĭg zĭb′ĭt), *v.t.* **1.** to offer or expose to view; present for inspection. **2.** to manifest or display: *to exhibit anger.* **3.** to place on show: *to exhibit paintings.* **4.** *Law.* to submit (a document, etc.) in evidence in a court of law; present (a petition, charge, etc.) for consideration. **5.** *Med.* to administer (a remedy, etc.). —*v.i.* **6.** to make or give an exhibition; present something to public view. —*n.* **7.** an exhibiting or exhibition. **8.** that which is exhibited. **9.** an object or a collection of objects shown in an exhibition, fair, etc. **10.** *Law.* a document or other object exhibited in court and referred to and identified in written evidence. [t. L: s. *exhibitus*, pp.] —**ex·hib′i·tor, ex·hib′it·er,** *n.* —**Syn. 1.** See **display. 2.** evince, disclose, betray. **8, 10.** See **evidence.** —**Ant. 2.** conceal.

ex·hi·bi·tion (ĕk′sə bĭsh′ən), *n.* **1.** an exhibiting, showing, or presenting to view. **2.** a public display, as of works of art, manufactures, etc., or of feats of skill, etc. **3.** *Brit.* an exposition; a big fair of extended duration. **4.** *Med.* administration, as of a remedy. **5.** an allowance given to a student in an English college or university or school, usually upon the result of a competitive examination.

ex·hi·bi·tion·er (ĕk′sə bĭsh′ən ər), *n.* a student who receives an exhibition (def. 5).

ex·hi·bi·tion·ism (ĕk′sə bĭsh′ə nĭz′əm), *n.* **1.** a tendency to display one's abilities or to behave in such a way as to attract attention. **2.** *Psychiatry.* the attaining of sexual gratification by exhibiting and attracting attention to the genitals.

ex·hi·bi·tion·ist (ĕk′sə bĭsh′ən ĭst), *n.* **1.** one who desires to make an exhibition of himself or his powers, personality, etc. **2.** *Psychiatry.* one affected with the compulsions of exhibitionism. —**ex′hi·bi′tion·is′tic,** *adj.*

ex·hib·i·tive (ĭg zĭb′ə tĭv), *adj.* serving for exhibition; tending to exhibit.

ex·hib·i·to·ry (ĭg zĭb′ə tôr′ĭ), *adj.* pertaining to or intended for exhibition or display.

ex·hil·a·rant (ĭg zĭl′ə rənt), *adj.* **1.** exhilarating. —*n.* **2.** something that exhilarates.

ex·hil·a·rate (ĭg zĭl′ə rāt′), *v.t.,* **-rated, -rating.** to make cheerful or merry. [t. L: m.s. *exhilarātus*, pp.] —**ex·hil′a·rat′ing,** *adj.* —**ex·hil′a·rat′ing·ly,** *adv.* —**ex·hil′a·ra′tor,** *n.* —**Syn.** cheer, gladden, enliven, animate, inspirit.

ex·hil·a·ra·tion (ĭg zĭl′ə rā′shən), *n.* **1.** exhilarated condition or feeling. **2.** act of exhilarating. —**Syn. 1.** animation, joyousness, gaiety, jollity, hilarity.

ex·hil·a·ra·tive (ĭg zĭl′ə rā′tĭv), *adj.* tending to exhilarate. Also, **ex·hil′a·ra·to·ry** (ĭg zĭl′ə rə tôr′ĭ).

ex·hort (ĭg zôrt′), *v.t.* **1.** to urge, advise, or caution earnestly; admonish urgently. —*v.i.* **2.** to make exhortation; give admonition. [ME *exhort(en)*, t. L: m. *exhortārī* urge, encourage] —**ex·hort′er,** *n.*

ex·hor·ta·tion (ĕg′zôr tā′shən, ĕk′sôr-), *n.* **1.** act or process of exhorting. **2.** an utterance, discourse, or address conveying urgent advice or recommendations.

ex·hor·ta·tive (ĭg zôr′tə tĭv), *adj.* **1.** serving or intended to exhort. **2.** pertaining to exhortation. Also, **ex·hor·ta·to·ry** (ĭg zôr′tə tôr′ĭ).

ex·hume (ĭg zūm′, ĕks hūm′), *v.t.,* **-humed, -huming.** to dig (something buried, esp. a dead body) out of the earth; disinter. [t. ML: m.s. *exhumāre*, f. L *ex-* EX-¹ + *humus* earth, ground] —**ex·hu·ma·tion** (ĕks′hyŏŏ mā′shən), *n.* —**ex·hum′er,** *n.*

ex·i·geant (ĕk′sə jənt; *Fr.* ĕg zē zhäN′), *adj.* exacting; overdemanding. —**ex·i·geante** (ĕg zē zhäNt′), *adj. fem.*

ex·i·gen·cy (ĕk′sə jən sĭ), *n., pl.* **-cies.** **1.** exigent state or character; urgency. **2.** (*usually pl.*) a circumstance that renders prompt action necessary; a need, demand, or requirement. **3.** a case or situation which demands prompt action or remedy; an emergency. Also, **ex′i·gence.**

ex·i·gent (ĕk′sə jənt), *adj.* **1.** requiring immediate action or aid; urgent; pressing. **2.** requiring a great deal, or more than is reasonable. [t. L: s. *exigens*, ppr., requiring, lit., driving out] —**ex′i·gent·ly,** *adv.*

ex·i·gi·ble (ĕk′sə jə bəl), *adj.* that may be exacted; requirable.

ex·ig·u·ous (ĭg zĭg′yŏŏ əs, ĭk sĭg′-), *adj.* scanty; small; slender. [t. L: m. *exiguus*] —**ex·i·gu·i·ty** (ĕk′sə gū′ə tĭ), **ex·ig′u·ous·ness,** *n.*

ex·ile (ĕg′zīl, ĕk′sīl), *n., v.,* **-iled, -iling.** —*n.* **1.** prolonged separation from one's country or home, as by stress of circumstances. **2.** any one separated from his country or home. **3.** expulsion from one's native land by authoritative decree. **4.** fact or state of such expulsion. **5.** a person banished from his native land. **6. the Exile,** the Babylonian captivity of the Jews in the 6th century B.C. —*v.t.* **7.** to separate from country, home, etc. **8.** to expel or banish (a person) from his country; expatriate. [ME *exil*, t. OF, t. L: m.s. *ex(s)ilium* banishment]

ex·il·ic (ĕg zĭl′ĭk, ĕk sĭl′ĭk), *adj.* pertaining to exile, as that of the Jews in Babylon. Also, **ex·il′i·an.**

ex·im·i·ous (ĕg zĭm′ĭ əs), *adj. Now Rare.* distinguished; eminent; excellent. [t. L: m. *eximius* select]

ex int., ex (without) interest.

ex·ist (ĭg zĭst′), *v.i.* **1.** to have actual being; be. **2.** to have life or animation; live. **3.** to continue to be or to live. **4.** to have being in a specified place or under certain conditions; be found; occur. [t. L: s. *existere* stand forth, arise, be]

ex·ist·ence (ĭg zĭs′təns), *n.* **1.** state or fact of existing; being. **2.** continuance in being or life; life: *a struggle for existence.* **3.** mode of existing. **4.** all that exists. **5.** something that exists, an entity, or a being.

ex·ist·ent (ĭg zĭs′tənt), *adj.* **1.** existing; having existence. **2.** now existing. —*n.* **3.** one who or that which exists.

ex·is·ten·tial (ĕg′zĭs tĕn′shəl, ĕk′sĭs-), *adj.* pertaining to existence. —**ex′is·ten′tial·ly,** *adv.*

ex·is·ten·tial·ism (ĕg′zĭs tĕn′shə lĭz′əm, ĕk′sĭs-), *n. Philos.* **1.** the doctrine that there is no difference between the external world and the internal world of the mind, and that the source and the elements of knowledge have their existence in states of the mind. **2.** a recent movement which claims to represent a middle way between the traditional materialism and idealism and stresses personal decision in the face of a universe without purpose.

ex·it (ĕg′zĭt, ĕk′sĭt), *n.* **1.** a way or passage out. **2.** a going out or away; a departure: *to make one's exit.* **3.** the departure of a player from the stage. —*v.* **4.** he (or she, or the person named) goes out (used in the text of plays, with reference to an actor). [special use of stage direction *exit* he goes out, influenced by assoc. with L *exitus* a going out]

ex lib., ex libris.

ex li·bris (ĕks lī′brĭs, lē′-), *pl.* **-bris** for 2. *Latin.* **1.** from the library (of) (a phrase inscribed in or on a book, before the name of the owner). **2.** an inscription in or on a book, to indicate the owner; a bookplate.

Ex·moor (ĕks′mŏŏr), *n.* a high moorland in SW England, in Somersetshire and Devonshire: the scene of Blackmore's *Lorna Doone.*

ex ni·hi·lo ni·hil fit (ĕks nī′hĭ lō′ nī′hĭl fĭt′), *Latin.* (only) nothing is created from nothing; that is, all that exists has always existed.

exo-, a prefix meaning "external." Also, **ex-²**. [t. Gk.: outside]

ex·o·carp (ĕk′sō kärp′), *n. Bot.* epicarp.

ex·o·cen·tric construction (ĕk′sō sĕn′trĭk), *Ling.* a grammatical construction which as a unit does not function in the same manner as any one of its immediate constituents (opposed to *endocentric construction*): "*in the garden,*" "*for her,*" "*Tom played*" are exocentric constructions.

Exod., Exodus.

ex·o·der·mis (ĕk′sō dûr′mĭs), *n. Bot.* a temporary, protective layer of cells in some roots, as in certain orchids.

ex·o·don·tia (ĕk′sō dŏn′sha, -shĭ·a), *n.* the branch of dentistry dealing with the extraction of teeth. [NL, f. Gk.: *ex-* ᴇx-³ + s. *odoús* tooth + *-ia* -ɪᴀ. Cf. Gk. *exodontizomai* have one's tusks removed]

ex·o·dus (ĕk′sə dəs), *n.* **1.** a going out; a departure or emigration, usually of a large number of people. **2.** (*often cap.*) the departure of the Israelites from Egypt under Moses. **3.** (*cap.*) the second book of the Old Testament, containing an account of this departure. [ME, t. L, t. Gk.: m. *éxodos* a going out]

ex off., ex officio.

ex of·fi·ci·o (ĕks əf ĭsh′ĭ ō′), by virtue of office or official position. —**ex′-of·fi′ci·o′,** *adj.* [t. L: from office]

ex·og·a·my (ĕks ŏg′ə mĭ), *n.* **1.** the custom of marrying outside the tribe or blood group (opposed to *endogamy*). **2.** *Biol.* the union of gametes of unrelated parents. —**ex·og·a·mous** (ĕks ŏg′ə məs), **ex·o·gam·ic** (ĕk′sō găm′ĭk), *adj.*

ex·o·gen (ĕk′sə jĕn), *n. Bot.* any plant of the obsolete class *Exogenae,* including the dicotyledons. [t. F: m. *exogène.* See ᴇxo-, -ɢᴇɴ]

ex·og·e·nous (ĕks ŏj′ə nəs), *adj.* **1.** having its origin external; derived externally. **2.** *Bot.* **a.** (of plants, as the dicotyledons) having stems which grow by the addition of an annual layer of wood to the outside beneath the bark. **b.** pertaining to plants having such stems. **c.** belonging to the exogens. **3.** *Physiol., Biochem.* of or denoting the metabolic assimilation of proteins, in which the elimination of nitrogenous catabolites is in direct proportion to the amount of protein taken in. [t. NL: m. *exōgenus* growing on the outside. See ᴇxo-, -ɢᴇɴous] —**ex·og′e·nous·ly,** *adv.*

Parts of an Exogen
Section of a branch of three years' growth: A, Medulla or pith; B, Medullary sheath; C, Circles of annual growth; D, Bark; E, Medullary ray

ex·on·er·ate (ĭg zŏn′ə rāt′), *v.t.,* **-ated, -ating. 1.** to clear, as of a charge; free from blame; exculpate. **2.** to relieve, as from an obligation, duty, or task. [t. L: m.s. *exonerās,* pp., disburdened] —**ex·on′er·a′tion,** *n.* —**ex·on′er·a′tive,** *adj.* —**Syn. 1.** See **absolve.**

ex·o·per·id·i·um (ĕks′ō pĭ rĭd′ĭ əm), *n. Bot.* See **peridium** (def. 1).

ex·oph·thal·mos (ĕk′sŏf thăl′mŏs), *n. Pathol.* protrusion of the eyeball from the orbit, caused by disease or injury. Also, **ex·oph·thal·mus** (ĕk′sŏf thăl′məs), **ex·oph·thal·mi·a** (ĕk′sŏf thăl′mĭ a). [NL, t. Gk.: as adj., with prominent eyes] —**ex′oph·thal′mic,** *adj.*

ex·o·ra·ble (ĕk′sə rə bəl), *adj.* susceptible of being persuaded or moved by entreaty. [t. L: m.s. *exōrābilis*] —**ex′o·ra·bil′i·ty,** *n.*

ex·or·bi·tance (ĭg zôr′bə təns), *n.* quality of being exorbitant; excessiveness. Also, **ex·or′bi·tan·cy.**

ex·or·bi·tant (ĭg zôr′bə tənt), *adj.* exceeding the bounds of custom, propriety, or reason, esp. in amount or extent: *to charge an exorbitant price for something.* [t. LL: s. *exorbitans,* ppr., going out of the track] —**ex·or′bi·tant·ly,** *adv.* —**Syn.** inordinate, excessive, extravagant, unreasonable, unconscionable. —**Ant.** fair.

ex·or·cise (ĕk′sôr sīz′), *v.t.,* **-cised, -cising. 1.** to seek to expel (an evil spirit) by adjuration or religious or solemn ceremonies. **2.** to deliver (a person, place, etc.) from evil spirits or malignant influences. Also, **ex′or·cize′.** [t. LL: m.s. *exorcīzāre,* t. Gk.: m. *exorkīzein*] —**ex′or·cise′ment,** *n.* —**ex′or·cis′er,** *n.*

ex·or·cism (ĕk′sôr sĭz′əm), *n.* **1.** act or process of exorcising. **2.** the ceremony or the formula used. —**ex′or·cist** (ĕk′sôr sĭst), *n.*

ex·or·di·um (ĭg zôr′dĭ əm, ĭk sôr′-), *n., pl.* **-diums, -dia** (-dĭ a). **1.** the beginning of anything. **2.** the introductory part of an oration or discourse. [t. L: a beginning] —**ex·or′di·al,** *adj.*

ex·o·skel·e·ton (ĕk′sō skĕl′ə tən), *n. Anat.* an external protective covering or integument, esp. when hard, as the shell of crustaceans, the scales and plates of fishes, etc. (opposed to *endoskeleton*).

ex·os·mo·sis (ĕk′sŏs mō′sĭs, ĕk′sŏz-), *n. Phys. Chem., etc.* **1.** osmosis from within outward. **2.** (in osmosis) the flow of that fluid which passes with the lesser rapidity into the other (opposed to *endosmosis*). Also, **ex·os·mose** (ĕk′sŏs mōs′, ĕk′sŏz-). [f. ᴇx³- + osmosis] —**ex·os·mot·ic** (ĕk′sŏs mŏt′ĭk, ĕk′sŏz-), **ex·os·mic** (ĕk′sŏs′mĭk, -sŏz′-), *adj.*

ex·o·spore (ĕk′sō spōr′), *n. Bot.* the outer coat of a spore.

ex·os·to·sis (ĕk′sŏs tō′sĭs), *n., pl.* **-ses** (-sēz). *Pathol.* the morbid formation of bone, or a morbid bony growth, on a bone. [NL, t. Gk.: outgrowth of bone]

ex·o·ter·ic (ĕk′sə tĕr′ĭk), *adj.* **1.** suitable for or communicated to the general public. **2.** not belonging or pertaining to the inner or select circle, as of disciples. **3.** popular; simple; commonplace. [t. LL: s. *exōtericus* external, t. Gk. m. *exōterikós*] —**ex′o·ter′i·cal·ly,** *adv.*

ex·o·ther·mic (ĕk′sō thûr′mĭk), *adj. Chem.* noting or pertaining to a chemical change which is accompanied by a liberation of heat (opposed to *endothermic*).

ex·ot·ic (ĭg zŏt′ĭk), *adj.* **1.** of foreign origin or character; not native; introduced from abroad, but not fully naturalized or acclimatized. **2.** *Colloq.* strikingly unusual or colorful in appearance or effect. —*n.* **3.** anything exotic, as a plant. [t. L: s. *exōticus,* t. Gk.: m. *exōtikós* foreign, alien] —**ex·ot′i·cal·ly,** *adv.*

ex·ot·i·cism (ĭg zŏt′ə sĭz′əm), *n.* **1.** tendency to adopt what is exotic. **2.** exotic quality or character. **3.** anything exotic, as a foreign word or idiom.

ex·o·tox·in (ĕk′sō tŏk′sĭn), *n. Biochem.* a toxin secreted during the life of an organism, either in the body tissues or in food. The organism itself is nontoxic.

exp., **1.** expenses. **2.** expired. **3.** export. **4.** exportation. **5.** exported. **6.** exporter. **7.** express.

ex·pand (ĭk spănd′), *v.t.* **1.** to increase in extent, size, volume, scope, etc: *heat expands metal.* **2.** to spread or stretch out; unfold: *a bird expands its wings.* **3.** to express in fuller form or greater detail; develop: *to expand a short story into a novel.* —*v.i.* **4.** to increase or grow in extent, bulk, scope, etc.: *most metals expand with heat, the mind expands with experience.* **5.** to spread out; unfold; develop: *the buds had not yet expanded.* [t. L: s. *expandere* spread out] —**ex·pand′er,** *n.*
—**Syn. 1.** extend, swell, enlarge. ᴇxᴘᴀɴᴅ, ᴅɪʟᴀᴛᴇ, ᴅɪsᴛᴇɴᴅ, ɪɴꜰʟᴀᴛᴇ imply becoming larger and filling more space. To ᴇxᴘᴀɴᴅ is to spread out, usually in every direction, so as to occupy more space or have more capacity: *to expand one's chest.* To ᴅɪʟᴀᴛᴇ is esp. to increase the width or circumference, and applies to space enclosed within confines or to hollow bodies: *to dilate the pupils of the eyes.* To ᴅɪsᴛᴇɴᴅ is to stretch, often beyond the point of natural expansion: *to distend an artery.* To ɪɴꜰʟᴀᴛᴇ is to blow out or swell a hollow body with air or gas of some kind: *to inflate a balloon.* **2.** spread, unfurl. —**Ant. 1.** contract.

ex·pand·ed (ĭk spăn′dĭd), *adj.* **1.** increased in area, bulk, or volume; enlarged. **2.** spread out; extended. **3.** (of printing type) wider than usual for its height.

ex·panse (ĭk spăns′), *n.* **1.** that which is expanded; an uninterrupted space or area; a wide extent of anything: *an expanse of water, of sky, etc.* **2.** expansion. [t. L: m.s. *expansum,* prop. pp. neut.]

ex·pan·si·ble (ĭk spăn′sə bəl), *adj.* capable of being expanded.

ex·pan·sile (ĭk spăn′sĭl), *adj.* **1.** capable of expanding; such as to expand. **2.** pertaining to expansion.

ex·pan·sion (ĭk spăn′shən), *n.* **1.** act of expanding. **2.** state of being expanded. **3.** the amount or degree of expanding. **4.** an expanded, dilated, or enlarged portion or form of a thing. **5.** anything spread out; an expanse. **6.** *Math.* the development at length of an expression indicated in a contracted form. **7.** *Mach.* that part of the operation of an engine in which the volume of the working medium increases and its pressure decreases. [t. LL: s. *expansio*]

ex·pan·sion·ism (ĭk spăn′shə nĭz′əm), *n.* policy of expansion, as of territory or currency. —**ex·pan′sion·ist,** *n.*

ex·pan·sive (ĭk span′sĭv), *adj.* **1.** tending to expand or capable of expanding. **2.** having a wide range or extent, comprehensive; extensive. **3.** (of a person's character, or speech) effusive, unrestrained, free, or open. **4.** *Psychiatry.* marked by an abnormal euphoristic state and by delusions of grandeur. —**ex·pan′sive·ly,** *adv.* —**ex·pan′sive·ness,** *n.*

ex par·te (ĕks pär′tĭ), *Latin.* from or on one side only, as in a controversy; in the interest of one party.

ex·pa·ti·ate (ĭk spā′shĭ āt′), *v.i.,* **-ated, -ating. 1.** to enlarge in discourse or writing; copious in description or discussion: *to expatiate upon a theme.* **2.** *Now Rare.* to move or wander about without restraint. [t. L: m.s. *ex(s)patiātus,* pp., extended, spread out] —**ex·pa′ti·a′tion,** *n.* —**ex·pa′ti·a′tor,** *n.*

ex·pa·tri·ate (*v.* ĕks pā′trĭ āt′; *adj., n.* ĕks pā′trĭ ĭt, -āt′), *v.,* **-ated, -ating,** *adj., n.* —*v.t.* **1.** to banish (a person) from his native country. **2.** to withdraw (oneself) from residence in one's native country. **3.** to withdraw (oneself) from allegiance to one's country. —*adj.* **4.** expatriated. —*n.* **5.** an expatriated person. [t. LL: m.s. *expatriātus,* pp.] —**ex·pa′tri·a′tion,** *n.*

ex·pect (ĭk spĕkt′), *v.t.* **1.** to look forward to; regard as likely to happen; anticipate the occurrence or the

coming of: *I expect to do it, I expect him to come, that he will come.* **2.** to look for with reason or justification: *we cannot expect obedience; expect him to do that.* **3.** *Colloq.* to suppose or surmise. **4.** *Obs.* to await or wait for. [t. L: s. *ex(s)pectāre* look for]
—**Syn. 1.** Expect, anticipate, hope, await all imply looking to some future event. Expect implies confidently believing, usually for good reasons, that an event will occur: *to expect a visit from a friend.* Anticipate is to look forward eagerly to an event and even to picture it: *to anticipate seeing a play.* Hope implies a wish that an event may take place and an expectation that it will: *to hope for the best.* Await (wait for) implies being alert and ready, whether for good or evil: *to await news after a cyclone.*

ex·pect·an·cy (ĭk·spĕk′tən·sĭ), *n.*, *pl.* **-cies. 1.** quality or state of expecting; expectation; anticipatory belief or desire. **2.** state of being expected. **3.** an object of expectation; something expected. Also, **ex·pec′tance.**

ex·pect·ant (ĭk·spĕk′tənt), *adj.* **1.** having expectations; expecting. **2.** expecting the birth of a child: *an expectant mother or father.* **3.** characterized by expectations. **4.** expected or anticipated. —*n.* **5.** one who expects; one who waits in expectation. —**ex·pect′ant·ly,** *adv.*

ex·pec·ta·tion (ĕk′spĕk·tā′shən), *n.* **1.** act of expecting. **2.** state of expecting: *wait in expectation.* **3.** state of being expected. **4.** expectant mental attitude. **5.** something expected; a thing looked forward to. **6.** (*often pl.*) a prospect of future good or profit: *to have great expectations.* **7.** the degree of probability of the occurrence of something. —**Syn. 2., 4.** expectancy, anticipation, hope, trust.

expectation of life, the average duration of life beyond any age, of persons who have attained that age, as shown by mortality tables.

ex·pect·a·tive (ĭk·spĕk′tə·tĭv), *adj.* **1.** of or pertaining to expectation. **2.** characterized by expectation.

ex·pec·to·rant (ĭk·spĕk′tə·rənt), *Med.* —*adj.* **1.** promoting the secretion of fluid from the respiratory tract. —*n.* **2.** an expectorant medicine.

ex·pec·to·rate (ĭk·spĕk′tə·rāt′), *v.*, **-rated, -rating.** —*v.t.* **1.** to eject or expel (phlegm, etc.) from the throat or lungs by coughing or hawking and spitting; spit. —*v.i.* **2.** to spit. [t. L: m.s. *expectorātus,* pp., banished from the breast] —**ex·pec′to·ra′tor,** *n.*

ex·pec·to·ra·tion (ĭk·spĕk′tə·rā′shən), *n.* **1.** act of expectorating. **2.** matter that is expectorated.

ex pe·de Her·cu·lem (ĕks pē′dĭ hûr′kyōō·lĕm), *Latin.* from the foot (we may know) Hercules; from a part or sample we may judge the whole.

ex·pe·di·en·cy (ĭk·spē′dĭ·ən·sĭ), *n.*, *pl.* **-cies. 1.** quality of being expedient; advantageousness; advisability. **2.** a regard for what is politic or advantageous rather than for what is right or just; a sense of self interest. **3.** something expedient. Also, **ex·pe′di·ence.**

ex·pe·di·ent (ĭk·spē′dĭ·ənt), *adj.* **1.** tending to promote some proposed or desired object; fit or suitable for the purpose; proper under the circumstances: *it is expedient that you go.* **2.** conducive to advantage or interest, as opposed to right. **3.** acting in accordance with expediency. —*n.* **4.** a means to an end. **5.** a means devised or employed in an exigency; a resource; a shift: *to resort to expedients to achieve one's purpose.* [ME, t. L: s. *expediens,* ppr., despatching] —**ex·pe′di·ent·ly,** *adv.* —**Syn. 1.** advantageous, profitable, advisable. **5.** device, contrivance.

ex·pe·di·en·tial (ĭk·spē′dĭ·ĕn′shəl), *adj.* pertaining to or regulated by expediency.

ex·pe·dite (ĕks′pə·dīt′), *v.*, **-dited, -diting,** *adj.* —*v.t.* **1.** to speed up the progress of; hasten: *to expedite matters.* **2.** to accomplish promptly, as a piece of business; dispatch. **3.** to issue officially, as a document. —*adj.* **4.** ready; alert. [t. L: m.s. *expedītus,* pp., extricated, helped forward, sent off or dispatched] —**ex′pe·dit′er,** *n.* —**Syn. 1.** quicken, speed, push. —**Ant. 1.** delay.

ex·pe·di·tion (ĕks′pə·dĭsh′ən), *n.* **1.** an excursion, journey, or voyage made for some specific purpose, as of war or exploration. **2.** the body of persons or ships, etc., engaged in it. **3.** promptness or speed in accomplishing something. —**Syn. 1.** See **trip. 3.** haste, quickness, dispatch.

ex·pe·di·tion·ar·y (ĕks′pə·dĭsh′ə·nĕr′ĭ), *adj.* pertaining to or composing an expedition: *an expeditionary force.*

ex·pe·di·tious (ĕks′pə·dĭsh′əs), *adj.* characterized by expedition or prompt dispatch; quick. —**ex′pe·di′tious·ly,** *adv.* —**ex′pe·di′tious·ness,** *n.*

ex·pel (ĭk·spĕl′), *v.t.,* **-pelled, -pelling. 1.** to drive or force out or away; discharge or eject: *to expel air from the lungs, an invader from a country.* **2.** to cut off from membership or relations: *to expel a student from a college.* [ME *expelle(n),* t. L: m. *expellere* drive out] —**ex·pel′la·ble,** *adj.* —**ex·pel′ler,** *n.* —**Syn. 2.** oust, dismiss.

ex·pel·lant (ĭk·spĕl′ənt), *adj.* **1.** expelling or having the power to expel. —*n.* **2.** an expellant medicine. Also, **ex·pel′lent.**

ex·pend (ĭk·spĕnd′), *v.t.* **1.** to use up: *to expend energy, time, care, etc.,* on something. **2.** to pay out; disburse; spend. [t. L: s. *expendere* weigh out, pay out] —**ex·pend′a·ble,** *adj.* —**ex·pend′er,** *n.* —**Syn. 1.** See **spend.**

ex·pend·i·ture (ĭk·spĕn′dĭ·chər), *n.* **1.** act of expending; disbursement; consumption. **2.** that which is expended; expense.

ex·pense (ĭk·spĕns′), *n.* **1.** cost or charge. **2.** a cause or occasion of spending: *owning a car is a great expense.* **3.** act of expending; expenditure. **4.** loss or injury due to any detracting cause (prec. by *at*): *quantity at the expense of quality.* **5.** (*pl.*) *Com.* a. charges incurred in the execution of an undertaking or commission. b. money paid as reimbursement for such charges: *to receive a salary and expenses.* [ME, t. AF, t. LL: m. *expensa,* prop, pp. fem., paid or weighed out] —**Syn. 1.** See **price.**

ex·pen·sive (ĭk·spĕn′sĭv), *adj.* entailing great expense; costly. —**ex·pen′sive·ly,** *adv.* —**ex·pen′sive·ness,** *n.*
—**Syn.** Expensive, costly, dear apply to that which is higher in price than the average person's usual purchases. Expensive is applied to whatever entails (usually considerable) expense; it suggests a price beyond a thing's worth and beyond what the person can properly afford to pay: *an expensive automobile.* Costly implies that the price is a large sum, usually because of the fineness, preciousness, etc. of the object: *a costly jewel.* Dear is commonly applied in England to that which is selling beyond its usual or just price. In the U. S., high-priced is the usual equivalent: *buy cheap and sell dear.* —**Ant.** cheap.

ex·pe·ri·ence (ĭk·spĭr′ĭ·əns), *n.*, *v.*, **-enced, -encing.** —*n.* **1.** a particular instance of personally encountering or undergoing something: *a strange experience.* **2.** the process or fact of personally observing, encountering, or undergoing something: *business experience.* **3.** the observing, encountering, or undergoing of things generally as they occur in the course of time: *to learn from experience, the range of human experience.* **4.** knowledge or practical wisdom gained from what one has observed, encountered, or undergone· *men of experience.* **5.** *Philos.* the totality of the cognitions given by perception; all that is perceived, understood, and remembered. —*v.t.* **6.** to have experience of; meet with; undergo; feel. **7.** *Rare.* to learn by experience. [ME, t. OF, t. L: m.s. *experientia* trial, proof, knowledge]
—**Syn. 6.** Experience, undergo refer to encountering situations, conditions, etc. in life, or to having certain sensations, feelings. Experience implies being affected by what one meets with (pleasant or unpleasant), so that to a greater or less degree one suffers a change: *to experience a change of heart, bitter disappointment.* Undergo usually refers to the bearing or enduring of something hard, difficult, disagreeable, or dangerous: *to undergo severe hardships, an operation.*

ex·pe·ri·enced (ĭk·spĭr′ĭ·ənst), *adj.* **1.** having had experience. **2.** having learned through experience; taught by experience. **3.** wise or skillful through experience: *an experienced teacher, general, etc.* —**Syn. 3.** skilled, expert, practiced, veteran.

experience table, *Life Insurance.* actuarial tables. See **mortality table.**

ex·pe·ri·en·tial (ĭk·spĭr′ĭ·ĕn′shəl), *adj.* pertaining to or derived from experience. —**ex·pe′ri·en′tial·ly,** *adv.*

ex·per·i·ment (*n.* ĭk·spĕr′ə·mənt; *v.* -mĕnt′), *n.* **1.** a test or trial; a tentative procedure; an act or operation for the purpose of discovering something unknown or testing a principle, supposition, etc.: *a chemical experiment.* **2.** the conducting of such operations; experimentation: *a product that is the result of long experiment.* **3.** *Obs.* experience. —*v.i.* **4.** to try or test in order to find something out: *to experiment with drugs in order to find a cure for a certain disease.* [ME, t. L: s. *experīmentum* a trial, test] —**ex·per′i·ment′er,** *n.* —**Syn. 1.** See **trial.**

ex·per·i·men·tal (ĭk·spĕr′ə·mĕn′təl), *adj.* **1.** pertaining to, derived from, or founded on experiment: *an experimental science.* **2.** based on or derived from experience; empirical: *experimental religion.* **3.** of the nature of an experiment; tentative. —**ex·per′i·men′tal·ist,** *n.* —**ex·per′i·men′tal·ly,** *adv.*

experimental evolution, the artificial production of new races and even species by experimental transformation of genes and genotypes and by hybridization.

ex·per·i·men·ta·tion (ĭk·spĕr′ə·mĕn·tā′shən), *n.* act or practice of making experiments; the process of experimenting.

experiment station, an establishment in which experiments in a particular line of research or activity, as agriculture or mining, are systematically carried on.

ex·pert (*n.* ĕks′pûrt; *adj.* ĭk·spûrt′, ĕks′pûrt), *n.* **1.** a person who has special skill or knowledge in some particular field; a specialist; authority: *a language· expert, an expert on mining.* —*adj.* **2.** possessing special skill or knowledge; trained by practice; skillful or skilled (*often fol.* by *in* or *at*): *an expert driver,* to be expert at driving a car. **3.** pertaining to, coming from or characteristic of an expert: *expert work, expert advice.* [ME, t. L: s. *expertus,* pp., having tried] —**ex·pert′ly,** *adv.* —**ex·pert′ness,** *n.* —**Syn. 1.** authority, specialist, connoisseur, master. **2.** experienced, trained, proficient, dexterous, adroit. See **skillful.** —**Ant. 1.** novice. **2.** clumsy.

ex·per·to cre·di·te (ĕks·pûr′tō krĕd′ə·tē′), *Latin.* believe in the expert; trust one who has had experience.

ex·pi·a·ble (ĕks′pĭ·ə·bəl), *adj.* that may be expiated.

ex·pi·ate (ĕks′pĭ·āt′), *v.t.,* **-ated, -ating.** to atone for; make amends or reparation for. [t. L: m.s. *expiātus,* pp.] —**ex′pi·a′tor,** *n.*

ex·pi·a·tion (ĕks′pĭ·ā′shən), *n.* **1.** act of expiating. **2.** the means by which atonement or reparation is made.

ex·pi·a·to·ry (ĕks′pĭ·ə·tōr′ĭ), *adj.* able to make atonement or expiation; offered by way of expiation.

---

b., blend of, blended; **c.,** cognate with; **d.,** dialect, dialectal; **der.,** derived from; **f.,** formed from; **g.,** going back to; **m.,** modification of; **r.,** replacing; **s.,** stem of; **t.,** taken from; **?,** perhaps. See the full key on inside cover.

ex·pi·ra·tion (ĕk/spə rā/shən), *n.* **1.** a coming to an end; termination; close. **2.** act of expiring, or breathing out; emission of air from the lungs. **3.** *Obs.* death.
ex·pir·a·to·ry (ĭk spīr/ə tōr/ĭ), *adj.* pertaining to the expiration of air from the lungs.
ex·pire (ĭk spīr/), *v.*, **-pired, -piring.** —*v.i.* **1.** to come to an end; terminate. **2.** to die out, as a fire. **3.** to emit the last breath; die. —*v.t.* **4.** to breathe out; emit (air) from the lungs. **5.** to emit or eject. [ME *expire(n)*, t. L: m. *ex(s)pīrāre* breathe out] —**ex·pir/er,** *n.*
ex·pi·ry (ĭk spī/rĭ, ĕk/spə rĭ), *n.*, *pl.* **-ries.** expiration.
ex·plain (ĭk splān/), *v.t.* **1.** to make plain or clear; render intelligible: *to explain an obscure point.* **2.** to make known in detail: *to explain how to do something, to explain a process.* **3.** to assign a meaning to; interpret. **4.** to make clear the cause or reason of; account for. **5.** to dispel (difficulties, etc.) by explanation; nullify the significance, or the apparent significance, of (words, facts, occurrences, etc.) by explanation (fol. by *away*). —*v.i.* **6.** to give an explanation. [t. L: m.s. *explānāre* make plain, flatten out] —**ex·plain/a·ble,** *adj.* —**ex·plain/er,** *n.*
—**Syn. 1.** EXPLAIN, ELUCIDATE, EXPOUND, INTERPRET imply making the meaning of something clear or understandable. To EXPLAIN is to make plain, clear, or intelligible something that is not known or understood: *to explain a theory or a problem.* To ELUCIDATE is to throw light on what before was dark and obscure, usually by illustration and commentary and sometimes by elaborate explanation: *they asked him to elucidate his statement.* To EXPOUND is to give a methodical, detailed, scholarly explanation of something, usually Scriptures, doctrines, or philosophy: *to expound the doctrine of free will.* To INTERPRET is to give the meaning of something by paraphrase, by translation, or by an explanation (sometimes involving one's personal opinion and therefore original), which is often of a systematic and detailed nature: *to interpret a poem or a symbol.*
ex·pla·na·tion (ĕk/splə nā/shən), *n.* **1.** act or process of explaining. **2.** that which explains; a statement made to clarify something and make it understandable; an exposition. **3.** a meaning or interpretation: *to find an explanation of a mystery.* **4.** a mutual declaration of the meaning of words spoken, actions, motives, etc., with a view to adjusting a misunderstanding or reconciling differences. [t. L: s. *explānātio*] —**Syn. 1.** elucidation, explication, exposition, definition, interpretation. **3.** solution, key, answer.
ex·plan·a·to·ry (ĭk splăn/ə tōr/ĭ), *adj.* serving to explain. Also, **ex·plan/a·tive.** —**ex·plan/a·to/ri·ly,** *adv.*
ex·plant (ĕks plănt/, -plänt/), *v.t.* **1.** to take living material from an animal or plant and place it in a culture medium. —*n.* **2.** a piece of explanted tissue. [f. EX-[1] + PLANT]
ex·ple·tive (ĕks/plə tĭv), *adj.* **1.** Also, **ex·ple·to·ry** (ĕks/plə tōr/ĭ). added merely to fill out a sentence or line, give emphasis, etc. —*n.* **2.** an expletive syllable, word, or phrase. **3.** an interjectory word or expression, frequently profane; an exclamatory oath. [t. LL: m.s. *explētīvus* serving to fill out] —**ex/ple·tive·ly,** *adv.*
ex·pli·ca·ble (ĕks/plĭ kə bəl), *adj.* capable of being explained.
ex·pli·cate (ĕks/plə kāt/), *v.t.*, **-cated, -cating.** **1.** to develop (a principle, etc.). **2.** to make plain or clear; explain; interpret. [t. L: m.s. *explicātus*, pp., unfolded]
ex·pli·ca·tion (ĕks/plə kā/shən), *n.* **1.** act of explicating. **2.** an explanation; interpretation.
ex·pli·ca·tive (ĕks/plə kā/tĭv, ĭk splĭk/ə tiv), *adj.* explanatory; interpretative. Also, **ex/pli·ca·to/ry.**
ex·plic·it (ĭk splĭs/ĭt), *adj.* **1.** leaving nothing merely implied; clearly expressed; unequivocal: *an explicit statement, instruction, etc.* **2.** clearly developed or formulated: *explicit knowledge or belief.* **3.** definite and unreserved in expression; outspoken: *he was quite explicit on that point.* [t. L: s. *explicitus*, var. of *explicātus*, pp., unfolded] —**ex·plic/it·ly,** *adv.* —**ex·plic/it·ness,** *n.* —**Syn. 1.** express, definite, precise, exact, unambiguous. —**Ant. 1.** vague.
ex·plode (ĭk splōd/), *v.*, **-ploded, -ploding.** —*v.i.* **1.** to expand with force and noise because of rapid chemical change or decomposition, as gunpowder, nitroglycerine etc. **2.** to burst, fly into pieces, or break up violently with a loud report, as a boiler from excessive pressure of steam. **3.** to burst forth violently, esp. with noise, laughter, violent speech, etc. **4.** *Phonet.* (of stop consonants) to end with an explosion so that the end of the consonant is audible, as *t* in *ten.* In *Where's my hat?* the *t* usually does not explode. —*v.t.* **5.** to cause (gunpowder, a boiler, etc.) to explode. **6.** to cause to be rejected, destroy the repute of; discredit or disprove: *to explode a theory.* **7.** *Phonet.* to end with an explosion (def. 6). **8.** *Obs.* to drive (a player, play, etc.) from the stage by loud expressions of disapprobation. [t. L: m.s. *explōdere* drive out by clapping] —**ex·plod/er,** *n.*
ex·ploit[1] (ĕks/ploit, ĭk sploit/), *n.* a striking or notable deed; a feat; a spirited or heroic act. [ME *esploit*, t. OF, g. L *explicitum*, pp. neut., unfolded] —**Syn.** See **achievement.**
ex·ploit[2] (ĭk sploit/), *v.t.* **1.** to turn to practical account; utilize for profit. **2.** to use selfishly for one's own ends. [ME *exploiten*, t. F: m. *exploiter*, g. L freq. of *explicāre* unfold] —**ex·ploit/a·ble,** *adj.* —**ex·ploit·a·tive** (ĭk sploi/tə tĭv), *adj.*
ex·ploi·ta·tion (ĕks/ploi tā/shən), *n.* **1.** utilization for profit. **2.** selfish utilization.
ex·ploit·er (ĭk sploi/tər), *n.* **1.** one who exploits. —*v.t.* **2.** exploit[2].
ex·plo·ra·tion (ĕks/plə rā/shən), *n.* **1.** act of exploring. **2.** the investigation of unknown regions.
ex·plor·a·to·ry (ĭk splōr/ə tōr/ĭ), *adj.* **1.** pertaining to or concerned with exploration. **2.** inclined to make explorations. Also, **ex·plor/a·tive.**
ex·plore (ĭk splōr/), *v.*, **-plored, -ploring.** —*v.t.* **1.** to traverse or range over (a region, etc.) for the purpose of discovery. **2.** to look into closely; scrutinize; examine. **3.** *Surg.* to investigate into, esp. mechanically, as with a probe. **4.** *Obs.* to search for; search out. —*v.i.* **5.** to engage in exploration. [t. L: m.s. *explōrāre*]
ex·plor·er (ĭk splōr/ər), *n.* **1.** one who or that which explores, esp., one who investigates unknown regions. **2.** any instrument used in exploring or sounding a wound, or a cavity in a tooth, etc.
ex·plo·sion (ĭk splō/zhən), *n.* **1.** act of exploding; a violent expansion or bursting with noise, as of gunpowder or a boiler. **2.** the noise itself. **3.** a violent outburst of laughter, anger, etc. **4.** any violent bursting forth. **5.** the burning of the fuel and air mixture in an internal-combustion engine. **6.** *Phonet.* the audible end of a stop consonant at break of closure. See **explode,** def. 4. [t. L: s. *explōsio* a driving off by clapping]
ex·plo·sive (ĭk splō/sĭv), *adj.* **1.** tending or serving to explode: *an explosive substance.* **2.** pertaining to or of the nature of an explosion. **3.** *Phonet.* (of stop consonants) ending with an explosion. See **explode** (def. 4). —*n.* **4.** an explosive agent or substance, as dynamite. **5.** *Phonet.* a stop consonant that ends with an explosion. —**ex·plo/sive·ly,** *adv.* —**ex·plo/sive·ness,** *n.*
ex·po·nent (ĭk spō/nənt), *n.* **1.** one who or that which expounds or explains. **2.** one who or that which stands as a representative, type, or symbol of something: *the exponent of Republican principles.* **3.** *Alg.* a symbol placed above and at the right of another symbol (the base), to denote to what power the latter is to be raised, as in X^3. [t. L: s. *expōnens*, ppr., putting forth]
ex·po·nen·tial (ĕks/pō nĕn/shəl), *adj.* *Alg.* of or pertaining to an exponent or exponents.
ex·po·ni·ble (ĭk spō/nə bəl), *adj.* *Logic.* (esp. of an obscure proposition) admitting of or requiring exposition.
ex·port (*v.* ĭk spōrt/, ĕks/pōrt; *n.* ĕks/pōrt), *v.t.* **1.** to send (commodities) to other countries or places for sale, exchange, or gift. —*n.* **2.** act of exporting; exportation. **3.** that which is exported; an article exported. —*adj.* **4.** of or pertaining to exportation of goods or to exportable goods. [t. L: s. *exportāre* carry away] —**ex·port/a·ble,** *adj.* —**ex·port/er,** *n.*
ex·por·ta·tion (ĕks/pōr tā/shən), *n.* **1.** act of exporting; the sending of commodities out of a country, typically in trade. **2.** something exported.
ex·pos·al (ĭk spō/zəl), *n.* exposure.
ex·pose (ĭk spōz/), *v.t.*, **-posed, -posing.** **1.** to lay open to danger, attack, harm, etc.: *to expose soldiers to gunfire, to expose one's character to attack.* **2.** to lay open to something specified: *to expose oneself to misunderstanding.* **3.** to uncover or bare to the air, cold, etc., *to expose one's head to the rain.* **4.** to present to view; exhibit; display: *the beggar who exposes his sores.* **5.** to make known, disclose, or reveal (intentions, secrets, etc.); unmask (crime, fraud, an imposter, etc.). **6.** to hold up to public reprehension or ridicule (fault, folly, a fool, etc.). **7.** to put out into an unsheltered or open place, as a child. **8.** to subject, as to the action of something: *to expose photographic plate to light.* [t. OF: m.s. *exposer*, f. *ex-* EX[1] + *poser* put (see POSE[2]), but assoc. with deriv. of L *expōnere* set forth] —**ex·pos/er,** *n.* —**Syn. 1.** subject (to), endanger, imperil, jeopardize. **5.** uncover, unveil, betray. —**Ant. 2.** protect *(from).* **5.** conceal.
ex·po·sé (ĕks/pō zā/), *n.* an exposure, as of something discreditable. [t. F, orig. pp. of *exposer* expose]
ex·posed (ĭk spōzd/), *adj.* **1.** left or being without shelter or protection. **2.** laid open to view; unconcealed. —**ex·pos·ed·ness** (ĭk spō/zĭd nĭs), *n.*
ex·po·si·tion (ĕks/pə zĭsh/ən), *n.* **1.** an exhibition or show, as of the products of art and manufacture. **2.** act of expounding, setting forth, or explaining. **3.** a detailed statement or explanation; an explanatory treatise. **4.** the act of presenting to view; display. **5.** act of putting out or abandoning in an unsheltered place: *the exposition of children.* **6.** state of being exposed. —**Syn. 3.** explanation, elucidation, commentary.
ex·pos·i·tor (ĭk spŏz/ə tər), *n.* one who expounds, or gives an exposition. [t. L; r. ME *exposit(o)ur*, t. AF]
ex·pos·i·to·ry (ĭk spŏz/ə tōr/ĭ), *adj.* serving to expound, set forth, or explain. Also, **ex·pos/i·tive.**
ex post fac·to (ĕks/ pōst/ făk/tō), *Latin.* from or by subsequent action; subsequently; retrospectively;
ex post facto law, one passed after an alleged crime has been committed which, if applied in the case of an accused person, would work to his disadvantage.
ex·pos·tu·late (ĭk spŏs/chə lāt/), *v.i.*, **-lated, -lating.** to reason earnestly with a person against something he intends to do or has done; remonstrate (fol. by *about, for, on,* or *upon*): *to expostulate with him on* (or *about*) *the impropriety.* [t. L: m.s. *expostulātus*, pp.] —**ex·pos/tu·lat/ing·ly,** *adv.* —**ex·pos/tu·la/tor,** *n.*
ex·pos·tu·la·tion (ĭk spŏs/chə lā/shən), *n.* **1.** act of expostulating; remonstrance; earnest and kindly protest. **2.** an expostulatory remark or address.

ăct, āble, dâre, ärt; ĕbb, ēqual; ĭf, īce; hŏt, ōver, ôrder, oil, bo͝ok, o͞oze, out; ŭp, ūse, ûrge; ə = a in alone; ch, chief; g, give; ng, ring; sh, shoe; th, thin; th, that; zh, vision. See the full key on inside cover.

ex·pos·tu·la·to·ry (Ĭk spŏs/chə lə tōr/Ĭ), *adj.* expostulating; conveying expostulation. Also, **ex·pos/tu·la/tive.**

ex·po·sure (Ĭk spō/zhər), *n.* **1.** act of exposing. **2.** disclosure, as of something private or secret; unmasking, as of crime, fraud, an impostor, etc. **3.** presentation to view, esp. in an open or public manner. **4.** a laying open or subjecting to the action or influence of something *exposure to the weather, to danger, or to ridicule.* **5.** *Photog.* act of presenting a sensitive material as film, plate, or paper, to the action of the actinic rays of light: *the exposure was too long.* **6.** a putting out without shelter or protection, as of an abandoned child. **7.** state of being exposed. **8.** situation with regard to sunlight or wind; aspect: *a southern exposure.* **9.** something exposed, as to view; an exposed surface. [f. EXPOS(E) + -URE] —**Syn. 2.** divulgement, revelation, exposé.

exposure meter, *Photog.* an instrument which measures the light intensity and indicates the proper exposure for a given scene.

ex·pound (Ĭk spound/), *v.t.* **1.** to set forth or state in detail: *to expound theories, principles, etc.* **2.** to explain; interpret. [ME *expoune(n), expounde(n),* t. OF: m. *espondre,* g. L *expōnere* put out, expose, set forth, explain] —**ex·pound/er,** *n.* —**Syn. 2.** See **explain.**

ex·pres·i·dent (ĕks/prĕz/ə dənt), *n.* a former president.

ex·press (Ĭk sprĕs/), *v.t.* **1.** to put (thought) into words: *to express an idea clearly.* **2.** to show, manifest, or reveal: *to express one's feeling.* **3. express oneself,** to set forth one's opinion, meaning, feeling, etc., in words. **4.** to represent by a symbol, character, figure, or formula, or as a symbol or the like does. **5.** *U.S.* to send express: *to express a package or merchandise.* **6.** to press or squeeze out: *to express the juice of grapes.* **7.** to exude or emit (a liquid, odor, etc.) as if under pressure. —*adj.* **8.** clearly indicated; distinctly stated (rather than implied); definite, explicit; plain. **9.** special: *an express purpose.* **10.** duly or exactly formed or represented: *an express image.* **11.** pertaining to an express: *an express agency.* **12.** specially direct or fast, as a train, highway, etc. —*adv.* **13.** by express: *to travel express.* **14.** specially; for a particular purpose. —*n.* **15.** an express train, bus, elevator, etc. **16.** a messenger or a message specially sent. **17.** a system or method of sending parcels, money, etc.: *to send a package by express.* **18.** a company engaged in this business. **19.** that which is sent by express. [ME *expresse,* t. L: m.s. *expressus,* pp., pressed out, described] —**ex·press/er,** *n.* —**ex·press/i·ble,** *adj.* —**Syn. 1.** utter, declare, state. **4.** indicate, designate. —**Ant. 1.** imply.

ex·press·age (Ĭk sprĕs/Ĭj), *n.* **1.** the business of transmitting parcels, money, etc., by express. **2.** the charge for such transmission.

express delivery, *Brit.* special delivery.

ex·pres·sion (Ĭk sprĕsh/ən), *n.* **1.** act of expressing or setting forth in words: *the expression of opinions, facts, etc.* **2.** a particular word, phrase, or form of words: *archaic expressions.* **3.** the manner or form in which a thing is expressed in words; wording; phrasing. **4.** power of expressing in words: *joy beyond expression.* **5.** indication of feeling, spirit, character, etc., as on the face, in the voice, or in artistic execution. **6.** a look or intonation as expressing feeling, etc.: *a sad expression.* **7.** quality or power of expressing feeling, etc.: *a face that lacks expression.* **8.** act of expressing or representing, as by symbols. **9.** *Math.* a symbol or a combination of symbols serving to express something. **10.** act of expressing or pressing out. —**ex·pres/sion·less,** *adj.* —**Syn. 1.** utterance, declaration, assertion, statement. **2.** phrase, term. **3.** language, diction, phraseology. **5.** manifestation, sign. **6.** aspect, air.

ex·pres·sion·ism (Ĭk sprĕsh/ə nĬz/əm), *n.* a theory of art originating in Europe about the time of World War I, which aimed at the free expression of the artist's emotional reactions rather than the representation of the natural appearance of objects. —**ex·pres/sion·ist,** *n., adj.* —**ex·pres/sion·is/tic,** *adj.*

ex·pres·sive (Ĭk sprĕs/Ĭv), *adj.* **1.** serving to express; indicative of power to express: *a look expressive of gratitude.* **2.** full of expression, as the face or voice. **3.** pertaining to or concerned with the expression. —**ex·pres/sive·ly,** *adv.* —**ex·pres/sive·ness,** *n.* —**Syn. 1.** EXPRESSIVE, MEANING, SIGNIFICANT, SUGGESTIVE imply the conveying of a thought, indicating an attitude of mind, or the like, by words or otherwise. EXPRESSIVE suggests conveying, or being capable of conveying a thought, intention, emotion, etc. in an effective or vivid manner: *an expressive shrug.* MEANING and SIGNIFICANT imply an underlying and unexpressed thought whose existence is plainly shown although its precise nature is left to conjecture. MEANING implies a more secret and intimate understanding between the persons involved: *meaning looks passed between them.* SIGNIFICANT suggests calling the attention of a person or persons to a happening which is important in some way to them or to others: *on hearing this statement, he gave the officers a significant glance.* SUGGESTIVE implies an indirect or covert conveying of a meaning, sometimes mentally stimulating, sometimes verging on impropriety or indecency: *a suggestive story or remark.*

express letter, *Brit.* a special delivery letter.

ex·press·ly (Ĭk sprĕs/lĬ), *adv.* **1.** in an express manner; explicitly. **2.** for the express purpose; specially.

ex·press·man (Ĭk sprĕs/mən), *n., pl.* **-men. 1.** one engaged in the express business. **2.** a man who makes collections or deliveries for an express company.

ex·press·way (Ĭk sprĕs/wā), *n.* a highway designed for express traffic.

ex·pro·pri·ate (ĕks prō/prĬ āt/), *v.t.,* **-ated, -ating. 1.** to take or condemn, esp. for public use by the right of eminent domain, thus divesting the title of the private owner. **2.** to dispossess (a person) of ownership. [t. LL: m.s. *expropriātus,* pp., deprived of property, der. L *ex-* EX-[1] + *proprium* property] —**ex·pro/pri·a/tion,** *n.* —**ex·pro/pri·a/tor,** *n.*

ex·pul·sion (Ĭk spŭl/shən), *n.* **1.** act of driving out or expelling. **2.** state of being expelled. [t. L: s. *expulsio*]

ex·pul·sive (Ĭk spŭl/sĬv), *adj.* tending or serving to expel.

ex·punc·tion (Ĭk spŭngk/shən), *n.* act of expunging; an erasure. [f. s. L *expunctus,* pp., struck out + -ION]

ex·punge (Ĭk spŭnj/), *v.t.,* **-punged, -punging. 1.** to strike or blot out; erase; obliterate. **2.** to efface; wipe out or destroy. [t. L: m.s. *expungere* prick out, strike out] —**ex·pung/er,** *n.*

ex·pur·gate (ĕks/pər gāt/, Ĭk spûr/gāt), *v.t.,* **-gated, -gating. 1.** to amend by removing offensive or objectionable matter: *to expurgate a book.* **2.** to purge or cleanse. [t. L: m.s. *expurgātus,* pp., purged] —**ex/pur·ga/tion,** *n.* —**ex/pur·ga/tor,** *n.*

ex·pur·ga·to·ri·al (Ĭk spûr/gə tōr/Ĭ əl), *adj.* pertaining to an expurgator or to expurgation.

ex·pur·ga·to·ry (Ĭk spûr/gə tō′rĬ), *adj.* serving to expurgate; of or pertaining to expurgation.

Expurgatory Index. See index (def. 10).

ex·qui·site (ĕks/kwĬ zĬt, Ĭk skwĬz/Ĭt), *adj.* **1.** of peculiar beauty or charm, or rare and appealing excellence, as a face, a flower, coloring, music, poetry, etc. **2.** extraordinarily fine, admirable, or consummate. **3.** intense, acute, or keen, as pleasure, pain, etc. **4.** keenly or delicately sensitive or responsive: *an exquisite ear for music.* **5.** of rare excellence of production or execution, as works of art, workmanship, or the artist or worker. **6.** of peculiar refinement or elegance, as taste, manners, etc., or persons. **7.** *Obs.* carefully sought out, chosen, ascertained, devised, etc. —*n.* **8.** a person, esp. a man, who is overnice in dress, etc.; a dandy; a coxcomb. [ME, t. L: m.s. *exquisitus,* pp., sought out] —**ex/qui·site·ly,** *adv.* —**ex/qui·site·ness,** *n.* —**Syn. 1.** dainty, beautiful, elegant, rare. See **delicate. 2.** perfect, matchless. See **fine**[1]. —**Ant. 1.** gross. **2.** ordinary.

exr., executor.

ex·san·guine (ĕks săng/gwĬn), *adj.* anemic.

ex·scind (ĕk sĬnd/), *v.t.* to cut out or off. [t. L: s. *exscindere*]

ex·sect (ĕk sĕkt/), *v.t.* to cut out. [t. L: s. *exsectus,* pp.] —**ex·sec/tion,** *n.*

ex·sert (ĕks sûrt/), *v.t.* **1.** to thrust out. —*adj.* **2.** exserted. [t. L: s. *exsertus,* pp., put forth] —**ex·ser/tion,** *n.*

ex·sert·ed (ĕks sûr/tĬd), *adj. Biol.* projecting beyond the surrounding parts, as a stamen.

ex·ser·tile (ĕks sûr/təl, -tĬl), *adj. Biol.* capable of being exserted or protruded.

ex·ser·vice·man (ĕks/sûr/vĬs măn/), *n., pl.* **-men** (-mĕn/). one who has served in one of the armed services, esp. during wartime. Ex-serviceman has greater currency in England, where *veteran* is not used in this sense.

ex·sic·cate (ĕk/sə kāt/), *v.t.,* **-cated, -cating. 1.** to dry or remove the moisture from, as a substance. **2.** to dry up, as moisture. [t. L: m.s. *exsiccātus,* pp.] —**ex/sic·ca/tion,** *n.* —**ex/sic·ca/tive,** *adj.* —**ex/sic·ca/tor,** *n.*

ex·stip·u·late (ĕks stĬp/yŏŏ lĬt, -lāt/), *adj. Bot.* without stipules. Also, **estipulate.**

ext., 1. extension. **2.** external. **3.** extinct. **4.** extra.

ex·tant (ĕks/tənt, Ĭk stănt/), *adj.* **1.** in existence; still existing; not destroyed or lost. **2.** *Archaic.* standing out; protruding. [t. L: s. *ex(s)tans,* ppr., standing out]

ex·tem·po·ral (Ĭk stĕm/pə rəl), *adj. Obs.* or *Archaic* extemporaneous; extempore. [t. L: s. *extemporālis*]

ex·tem·po·ra·ne·ous (Ĭk stĕm/pə rā′nĬ əs), *adj.* **1.** done or spoken extempore; impromptu: *an extemporaneous speech.* **2.** speaking or performing extempore. **3.** made for the occasion, as a shelter. [t. LL: m. *extemporāneus,* r. L *extemporālis*] —**ex·tem/po·ra/ne·ous·ly,** *adv.* —**ex·tem/po·ra/ne·ous·ness,** *n.* —**Syn. 1.** EXTEMPORANEOUS (EXTEMPORARY, EXTEMPORE), IMPROMPTU, IMPROVISED are used of (artistic) expression given without preparation or based on only partial preparation. EXTEMPORANEOUS, though often used interchangeably with IMPROMPTU, is applied esp. to an unmemorized speech given from an outline or notes: *an extemporaneous discussion.* IMPROMPTU is applied to a speech (poem, song, etc.) delivered without preparation and at a moment's notice: *called upon without warning, she nevertheless gave an excellent impromptu speech.* IMPROVISED is applied to that which is composed (recited, sung, acted) on a particular occasion, and is made up, at least in part, as one goes along: *an improvised piano accompaniment.* —**Ant. 1.** memorized.

ex·tem·po·rar·y (Ĭk stĕm/pə rĕr′i), *adj.* **1.** extemporaneous; extempore. **2.** *Obs.* sudden; unexpected. —**ex·tem/po·rar/i·ly,** *adv.* —**ex·tem/po·rar/i·ness,** *n.* —**Syn. 1.** See **extemporaneous.**

ex·tem·po·re (Ĭk stĕm/pə rĬ), *adv.* **1.** on the spur of the moment; without premeditation or preparation; offhand. **2.** without notes: *to speak extempore.* **3.** (of musical performance) by improvisation. —*adj.* **4.** extemporaneous. [t. L: *ex tempore,* lit., out of the time] —**Syn. 4.** See **extemporaneous.**

---

b., blend of, blended; c., cognate with; d., dialect, dialectal; der., derived from; f., formed from; g., going back to; m., modification of: r., replacing; s., stem of; t., taken from; ?, perhaps. See the full key on inside cover.

ex·tem·po·rize (Ĭk stĕm/pə rīz/), v., **-rized, -rizing.** —v.i. **1.** to speak extempore. **2.** to sing, or play on an instrument, composing the music as one proceeds; improvise. —v.t. **3.** to make or devise for the occasion. **4.** *Music.* to compose offhand; improvise. —**ex·tem/po·ri·za/tion,** n. —**ex·tem/po·riz/er,** n.

ex·tend (Ĭk stĕnd/), v.t. **1.** to stretch out; draw out to the full length. **2.** to stretch, draw, or arrange in a given direction, or so as to reach a particular point, as a cord or a line of troops. **3.** to stretch forth or hold out, as the arm or hand. **4.** to place at full length, esp. horizontally, as the body, limbs, etc. **5.** to increase the length or duration of; lengthen; prolong. **6.** to stretch out in various or all directions; expand; spread out in area. **7.** to enlarge the scope of, or make more comprehensive, as operations or influence. **8.** to hold forth as an offer or grant; offer; grant; give. **9.** *Finance.* to postpone (the payment of a debt) beyond the time originally agreed upon. **10.** *Com.* to transfer (figures) from one column to another in bookkeeping, invoices, etc. **11.** *Law.* **a.** to assess or value. **b.** to make a seizure or levy upon, as land, by a writ of extent. **12.** *Obs.* to take by seizure. **13.** *Obs.* to exaggerate. —v.i. **14.** to be or become extended; stretch out; to be continued in length or duration, or in various or all directions. **15.** to reach, as to a particular point. **16.** to increase in length, area, scope, etc. [ME *extend(en),* t. L: m. *extendere*] —**ex·tend/i·ble,** adj. —**Syn. 5.** prolong, protract, continue. See **lengthen. 6.** spread, enlarge, widen. **8.** bestow, impart.

ex·tend·ed (Ĭk stĕn/dĬd), adj. **1.** stretched out. **2.** continued or prolonged. **3.** spread out. **4.** widespread or extensive; having extension or spatial magnitude. **5.** outstretched. **6.** *Print.* (of type) expanded. —**ex·tend/ed·ly,** adv.

ex·ten·si·ble (Ĭk stĕn/sə bəl), adj. capable of being extended. —**ex·ten/si·bil/i·ty, ex·ten/si·ble·ness,** n.

ex·ten·sile (Ĭk stĕn/səl), adj. *Chiefly Zool., Anat.* capable of being extended; adapted for stretching out; extensible; protrusible.

ex·ten·sim·e·ter (ĕks/tĕn sĬm/ə tər), n. extensometer.

ex·ten·sion (Ĭk stĕn/shən), n. **1.** act of extending. **2.** state of being extended. **3.** that by which something is extended; a prolongation, as an addition to a house. **4.** something extended; an extended object or space. **5.** range of extending; degree of extensiveness; extent. **6.** *Com.* a written engagement on the part of a creditor, allowing a debtor further time to pay a debt. **7.** *Physics,* etc. that property of a body by which it occupies a portion of space. **8.** *Anat.* **a.** act of straightening a limb. **b.** the position which a limb assumes when it is straightened. **9.** *Surg.* act of pulling the broken or dislocated part of a limb in a direction from the trunk, in order to bring the ends of the bone into their natural situation. **10.** *Logic.* the class of things to which a term is applicable; denotation: *the extension of the term "man" consists of the class, of such individuals as "Socrates," "Plato," "Aristotle,"* etc. [t. L: s. *extensio*] —**ex·ten/sion·al,** adj. —**Syn. 1.** stretching, expansion, enlargement. —**Ant. 1.** contraction.

extension courses, (in many universities and colleges) a program for persons not regularly enrolled as students, frequently provided through evening classes or classes in off-campus centers, or by correspondence.

ex·ten·si·ty (Ĭk stĕn/sə tĬ), n. **1.** the quality of having extension. **2.** *Psychol.* that attribute of sensation from which the perception of extension is developed.

ex·ten·sive (Ĭk stĕn/sĬv), adj. **1.** of great extent; wide; broad: *an extensive area.* **2.** far-reaching; comprehensive; thorough: *extensive knowledge, extensive inquiries.* **3.** pertaining to a system of agriculture involving the use or cultivation of large areas of land (as where land is cheap) with a minimum of labor and expense (opposed to *intensive*). —**ex·ten/sive·ly,** adv. —**ex·ten/sive·ness,** n. —**Syn. 1.** extended, large, spacious, ample, vast. —**Ant. 1.** limited. **2.** intensive.

ex·ten·som·e·ter (ĕks/tĕn sŏm/ə tər), n. *Mach.* an apparatus for measuring minute degrees of expansion, contraction, or deformation. Also, **extensimeter.** [f. s. L *extensus,* pp., extended + -(o)METER]

ex·ten·sor (Ĭk stĕn/sər, -sôr), n. a muscle which serves to extend or straighten a part of the body (opposed to *flexor*). [t. LL: one who or that which stretches]

ex·tent (Ĭk stĕnt/), n. **1.** the space or degree to which a thing extends; length, area, or volume: *the extent of a line, to the full extent of his power.* **2.** something extended; an extended space; a particular length, area, or volume; something having extension. **3.** *U.S. Law.* a writ, or a levy, by which a creditor has his debtor's lands valued and transferred to himself, absolutely or for a term of years. **4.** *Eng. Law.* **a.** a writ to recover debts of record due to the crown, under which land, etc., may be seized. **b.** a seizure made under such a writ. **5.** *Brit. Hist.* assessment or valuation, as of land. **6.** *Logic.* extension. [ME *extente,* t. AF, ult. der. L *extendere* extend] —**Syn. 1.** magnitude, measure, amount, scope, compass, range, expanse, stretch, reach. See **size.**

ex·ten·u·ate (Ĭk stĕn/yŏŏ āt/), v.t., **-ated, -ating. 1.** to represent (fault, offense, etc.) as less serious: *to extenuate a crime.* **2.** to serve to make (fault, offense, etc.) seem less serious: *extenuating circumstances.* **3.** to underestimate, underrate, or make light of. **4.** *Archaic.* **a.** to make thin, lean, or emaciated. **b.** to reduce the consistence or density of. [t. L: m.s. *extenuātus,* pp., made thin] —**ex·ten/u·at/ing·ly,** adv. —**ex·ten/u·a/tive,** adj. —**ex·ten/u·a/tor,** n.

ex·ten·u·a·tion (Ĭk stĕn/yŏŏ ā/shən), n. **1.** act of extenuating **2.** state of being extenuated. **3.** that which extenuates; a partial excuse.

ex·ten·u·a·to·ry (Ĭk stĕn/yŏŏ ə tōr/Ĭ), adj. tending to extenuate; characterized by extenuation.

ex·te·ri·or (Ĭk stĬr/Ĭ ər), adj. **1.** outer; being on the outer side: *the exterior side or surface, exterior decorations.* **2.** situated or being outside; pertaining to or connected with what is outside: *the exterior possessions of a country.* **3.** *Geom.* (of an angle) outer, as an angle formed outside two parallel lines when cut by a third line. See diag. under **interior.** —n. **4.** the outer surface or part; the outside. **5.** (pl.) externals. [t. L, compar. of *exter, exterus* outer, outward] —**ex·te/ri·or·ly,** adv. —**Syn. 1.** outward, outside. **2.** outlying, extraneous. —**Ant. 1.** interior.

ex·ter·mi·nate (Ĭk stûr/mə nāt/), v.t., **-nated, -nating.** to get rid of by destroying; destroy totally; extirpate. [t. L: m.s. *exterminātus,* pp., driven beyond the boundaries] —**ex·ter/mi·na/tion,** n. —**ex·ter/mi·na/tor,** n. —**Syn.** eradicate, abolish, annihilate.

ex·ter·mi·na·to·ry (Ĭk stûr/mə nə tōr/Ĭ), adj. serving or tending to exterminate. Also, **ex·ter·mi·na·tive** (Ĭk stûr/mə nā/tĬv).

ex·tern (ĕks/tûrn, Ĭk stûrn/), n. *Brit.* a person connected with an institution but not residing in it. [t. L: s. *externus* outward]

ex·ter·nal (Ĭk stûr/nəl), adj. **1.** of or pertaining to the outside or outer part; outer. **2.** to be applied to the outside of a body, as a remedy. **3.** situated or being outside of something; acting or coming from without. **4.** pertaining to the outward or visible appearance or show: *external acts of worship.* **5.** pertaining to or concerned with what is outside or foreign: *external commerce.* **6.** *Zool., Anat.* on the side farthest away from the body, from the median line, or from the center of a radially symmetrical form. **7.** *Metaphys.* belonging or pertaining to the world of things, considered as independent of the perceiving mind. —n. **8.** the outside; outer surface. **9.** that which is external. **10.** (pl.) external features, circumstances, etc.: *the externals of religion.* [f. EXTERN + -AL[1]] —**ex·ter/nal·ly,** adv.

ex·ter·nal-com·bus·tion (Ĭk stûr/nəl kəm bŭs/chən), adj. of or pertaining to an engine in which the ignition of the fuel mixture takes place outside the engine cylinder (as distinct from an *internal-combustion engine*).

ex·ter·nal·ism (Ĭk stûr/nə lĬz/əm), n. **1.** attention or devotion to externals; undue regard to externals, esp. in religion. **2.** *Philos.* realism. —**ex·ter/nal·ist,** n.

ex·ter·nal·i·ty (ĕk/stər năl/ə tĬ), n., pl.-ties. **1.** state or quality of being external. **2.** something external; an outward feature. **3.** undue regard to externals.

ex·ter·nal·ize (Ĭk stûr/nə līz/), v.t., **-ized, -izing.** to make external; embody in an outward form. —**ex·ter/nal·i·za/tion,** n.

ex·ter·o·cep·tive (ĕk/stər ə sĕp/tĬv), adj. *Physiol.* pertaining to exteroceptors, the stimuli impinging upon them, and the nerve impulses initiated by them. [f. *extero-* (comb. form of L *exterus* exterior) + *-ceptive,* as in RECEPTIVE]

ex·ter·o·cep·tor (ĕk/stər ə sĕp/tər), n. *Physiol.* a sense organ, as the nose, eyes, ears, or skin, responding to and conveying stimuli from the external environment. [f. *extero-* + *-CEPTOR* as EXTEROCEPTIVE]

ex·ter·ri·to·ri·al (ĕks/tĕr ə tōr/Ĭ əl), adj. extraterritorial. —**ex·ter/ri·to/ri·al/i·ty,** n. —**ex/ter·ri·to/ri·al·ly,** adv.

ex·tinct (Ĭk stĬngkt/), adj. **1.** extinguished; quenched; having ceased eruption, as a volcano. **2.** obsolete, as an institution. **3.** having come to an end; without a living representative, as a species. [ME *extincte,* t. L: m.s. *extinctus,* pp., destroyed, put out] —**Syn. 3.** See **dead.**

ex·tinc·tion (Ĭk stĬngk/shən), n. **1.** act of extinguishing. **2.** fact of being extinguished; condition of being extinct. **3.** suppression; abolition; annihilation. **4.** *Biol.* a becoming extinct; a coming to an end or dying out.

ex·tinc·tive (Ĭk stĬngk/tĬv), adj. tending or serving to extinguish.

ex·tin·guish (Ĭk stĬng/gwĬsh), v.t. **1.** to put out (a fire, light, etc.); put out the flame of (something burning or lighted). **2.** to put an end to or bring to an end; wipe out of existence: *to extinguish a hope, a life, etc.* **3.** to obscure or eclipse, as by superior brilliancy. **4.** *Law.* to discharge (a debt), as by payment. [f. s. L *ex(s)tinguere* put out, quench, destroy + -ISH[2]] —**ex·tin/guish·a·ble,** adj. —**ex·tin/guish·ment,** n.

ex·tin·guish·er (Ĭk stĬng/gwĬsh ər), n. **1.** one who or that which extinguishes. **2.** any of various portable apparatuses for extinguishing fire: *a chemical extinguisher.*

ex·tir·pate (ĕk/stər pāt/, Ĭk stûr/pāt), v.t., **-pated, -pating. 1.** to remove utterly; destroy totally; exterminate; do away with. **2.** to pull up by the roots; root up. [t. L: m.s. *ex(s)tirpātus,* pp., rooted out] —**ex/tir·pa/tion,** n. —**ex/tir·pa/tive,** adj. —**ex/tir·pa/tor,** n.

ex·tol (Ĭk stōl/, -stŏl/), v.t., **-tolled, -tolling.** to praise highly; laud; eulogize. Also, esp. *Brit.,* **ex·toll/.** [t. L: m.s. *extollere,* lit., lift out or up] —**ex·tol/ler,** n. —**ex·tol/ment,** n. —**Syn.** commend, glorify. —**Ant.** disparage.

ex·tort (ĭk stôrt′), v.t. **1.** Law. **a.** to wrest or wring (something) from a person by violence, intimidation, or abuse of authority; obtain (money, information, etc.) by force, torture, threat, or the like. **b.** to take illegally under cover of office. **2.** to charge excessively for. [t. L: s. extortus, pp., twisted or wrested out] —**ex·tort′er,** n. —**ex·tor′tive,** adj. —**Syn. 1.** See extract.

ex·tor·tion (ĭk stôr′shən), n. **1.** act of extorting. **2.** Law. the crime of obtaining money or other things of value under color of office, when none is due or not so much is due, or before it is due. **3.** oppressive or illegal exaction, as of excessive price or interest. **4.** anything extorted.

ex·tor·tion·ar·y (ĭk stôr′shə nĕr′ĭ), adj. characterized by or given to extortion.

ex·tor·tion·ate (ĭk stôr′shən ĭt), adj. **1.** exorbitant; grossly excessive: extortionate prices. **2.** characterized by extortion, as persons. —**ex·tor′tion·ate·ly,** adv.

ex·tor·tion·er (ĭk stôr′shən ər), n. one who practices extortion. Also, **ex·tor′tion·ist.**

ex·tra (ĕks′trə), adj. **1.** beyond or more than what is usual, expected, or necessary; additional: an extra edition of a newspaper, an extra price. **2.** larger or better than what is usual: an extra binding. —n. **3.** something extra or additional. **4.** an additional expense. **5.** an edition of a newspaper other than the regular edition or editions. **6.** something of superior quality. **7.** Motion Pictures. a person hired by the day to play a minor part, as a member of a mob or crowd. **8.** an additional worker. **9.** (usually pl.) Cricket. a score or run not made from the bat, as a bye or a wide. —adv. **10.** in excess of the usual or specified amount: an extra high price. **11.** beyond the ordinary degree; unusually; uncommonly: done extra well. [prob. orig. short for EXTRAORDINARY. Cf. EXTRA-]

extra-, a prefix meaning "outside," "beyond," "besides," freely used as an English formative, as in extra-judicial, extraterritorial, and many other words mostly self-explanatory, as extra-atmospheric, etc. Also, **extro-.** [t. L, comb. form of extrā, adv. and prep., outside (of), without]

ex·tra·bold (ĕks′trə bōld′), n. Print. unusually heavy boldface.

ex·tra·ca·non·i·cal (ĕks′trə kə nŏn′ə kəl), adj. Eccles. not included in the canon of Scripture.

ex·tra·cel·lu·lar (ĕks′trə sĕl′yə lər), adj. Biol. outside a cell or cells.

ex·tra·con·densed (ĕks′trə kən dĕnst′), adj. Print. (of type) having an extremely narrow face.

ex·tract (v. ĭk străkt′; n. ĕks′trăkt), v.t. **1.** to draw forth or get out by force: to extract a tooth. **2.** to deduce (a doctrine, principle, etc.). **3.** to derive or obtain (pleasure, comfort, etc.) from a particular source. **4.** to take or copy out (matter from a book, etc.), or make excerpts from (the book, etc.). **5.** to extort (information, money, etc.). **6.** to separate or obtain (a juice, ingredient, principle, etc.) from a mixture by pressure, distillation, treatment with solvents, or the like. **7.** Math. to determine (the root of a quantity). —n. **8.** something extracted. **9.** a passage taken from a book, etc.; an excerpt; a quotation. **10.** a solution or preparation containing the active principles of a drug, plant juice, or the like. **11.** a solid or viscid substance extracted from a drug, plant, or the like. [t. L: s. extractus, pp., drawn out] —**ex·tract′a·ble, ex·tract′i·ble,** adj. —**Syn. 1.** pull out, pry out. **5.** evoke, educe, draw out, elicit. EXTRACT, EXACT, EXTORT, WREST imply using force to remove something. To EXTRACT is to draw forth something as by pulling, importuning, and the like: to extract a confession by using third degree methods. To EXACT is to impose a penalty, or to obtain by force or authority, something to which one lays claim: to exact payment, obedience. To EXTORT is usually to wring something by intimidation or threats from an unwilling person: to extort money by threats of blackmail. To WREST is to take by force or violence in spite of active resistance: the courageous minority wrested the power from their oppressors. **6.** withdraw, distill.

ex·trac·tion (ĭk străk′shən), n. **1.** act of extracting. **2.** state or fact of being extracted. **3.** descent or lineage: to be of foreign extraction. **4.** something extracted; an extract.

ex·trac·tive (ĭk străk′tĭv), adj. **1.** tending or serving to extract. **2.** that may be extracted. —n. **3.** something extracted.

ex·trac·tor (ĭk străk′tər), n. **1.** a person or a thing that extracts. **2.** the mechanism in a firearm or cannon which, after firing, pulls an empty or unfired cartridge or shell case out of the chamber of the weapon and brings it into place for action by the ejector.

ex·tra·cur·ric·u·lar (ĕks′trə kə rĭk′yə lər), adj. **1.** outside the regular curriculum. **2.** referring, designating, or pertaining to those phases of school activities not taught in the classroom, though functioning under the guidance of the faculty, as sports, clubs, etc.

ex·tra·dit·a·ble (ĕks′trə dī′tə bəl), adj. subject to extradition: an extraditable offense.

ex·tra·dite (ĕks′trə dīt), v.t., -dited, -diting. **1.** to give up (a fugitive or prisoner) to another nation or authority. **2.** to obtain the extradition of. [back formation from EXTRADITION]

ex·tra·di·tion (ĕks′trə dĭsh′ən), n. the surrender of a fugitive from justice or a prisoner by one state or authority to another. [t. F, f. L: ex- EX-[1] + s. trāditio a giving over]

ex·tra·dos (ĕks trā′dŏs), n. Archit. the exterior curve or surface of an arch or vault. See diag. under **arch.** [t. F, f. L extra- EXTRA- + F dos back (g. L dorsum)]

ex·tra·ju·di·cial (ĕks′trə jōō dĭsh′əl), adj. outside of judicial proceedings; beyond the action or authority of a court. —**ex′tra·ju·di·cial·ly,** adv.

ex·tra·mun·dane (ĕks′trə mŭn′dān), adj. beyond our world or the material universe.

ex·tra·mu·ral (ĕks′trə myōōr′əl), adj. outside the walls or boundaries, as of a city or town or a university.

ex·tra·ne·ous (ĭk strā′nĭ əs), adj. introduced or coming from without; not belonging or proper to a thing; external; foreign. [t. L: m. extrāneus that is without, foreign] —**ex·tra′ne·ous·ly,** adv. —**ex·tra′ne·ous·ness,** n. —**Syn.** extrinsic, adventitious, alien.

ex·traor·di·nar·y (ĭk strôr′də nĕr′ĭ, ĕks′trə ôr′də nĕr′ĭ), adj. **1.** beyond what is ordinary; out of the regular or established order: extraordinary power or expenses. **2.** exceptional in character, amount, extent, degree, etc.; unusual; remarkable: extraordinary weather, weight, speed, an extraordinary man or book. **3.** (of officials, etc.) outside of, additional to, or ranking below an ordinary one: an extraordinary professor. [t. L: m.s. extrāordinārius out of the common order] —**ex·traor′di·nar′i·ly,** adv. —**ex·traor′di·nar′i·ness,** n. —**Syn. 2.** uncommon, exceptional, singular, rare, phenomenal.

ex·tra·po·late (ĕks′trə pə lāt′, ĕks trăp′ə lāt′), v.i., -lated, -lating. Statistics. to estimate a quantity which depends on one or more variables by extending the variables beyond their established ranges. —**ex·tra·po·la·tion** (ĕks′trə pōlā′shən, ĕks trăp′ə-), n.

ex·tra·pro·fes·sion·al (ĕks′trə prə fĕsh′ən əl), adj. outside ordinary limits of professional interest or duty.

ex·tra·sen·so·ry (ĕks′trə sĕn′sər ĭ), adj. outside of the normal sense perception.

ex·tra·ter·ri·to·ri·al (ĕks′trə tĕr′ə tōr′ĭ əl), adj. **1.** beyond local territorial jurisdiction, as the status of persons resident in a country but not subject to its laws. **2.** pertaining to such persons. Also, **exterritorial.** [f. NL extrā territōri(um) outside the domain + -AL[1]] —**ex′tra·ter′ri·to′ri·al·ly,** adv.

ex·tra·ter·ri·to·ri·al·i·ty (ĕks′trə tĕr′ə tōr′ĭ ăl′ə tĭ), n. the possession or exercise of political rights by a foreign power within a state having its own government.

ex·tra·u·ter·ine (ĕks′trə ū′tər ĭn, -tə rīn′), adj. being beyond or outside of the uterus.

ex·trav·a·gance (ĭk străv′ə gəns), n. **1.** excessive expenditure or outlay of money. **2.** an instance of this. **3.** unrestrained or fantastic excess, as of actions, opinions, etc. **4.** an extravagant action, notion, etc. —**Syn. 2.** lavishness, profusion. —**Ant. 1.** frugality.

ex·trav·a·gan·cy (ĭk străv′ə gən sĭ), n., pl. -cies. extravagance.

ex·trav·a·gant (ĭk străv′ə gənt), adj. **1.** going beyond prudence or necessity in expenditure; wasteful: an extravagant person. **2.** exorbitant: extravagant expenses or prices. **3.** exceeding the bounds of reason, as actions, demands, opinions, passions, etc. **4.** Obs. wandering beyond bounds. [t. ML: s. extrāvagans, ppr. of extrāvagārī wander beyond, f. L extrā- EXTRA- + vagārī wander] —**ex·trav′a·gant·ly,** adv. —**ex·trav′a·gant·ness,** n. —**Syn. 2.** immoderate, excessive, inordinate. **3.** unrestrained, fantastic, wild. —**Ant. 2.** reasonable.

ex·trav·a·gan·za (ĭk străv′ə găn′zə), n. a musical or dramatic composition, as comic opera or musical comedy, marked by wildness and irregularity in form and feeling and elaborateness in staging and costume. [b. EXTRAVAGANCE and It. stravaganza queer behavior]

ex·trav·a·gate (ĭk străv′ə gāt′), v.i., -gated, -gating. **1.** to wander beyond bounds; stray; roam at will. **2.** to go beyond the bounds of propriety or reason.

ex·trav·a·sate (ĭk străv′ə sāt′), v., -sated, -sating. —v.t. **1.** Pathol. to force out from the proper vessels, as blood, esp. so as to diffuse through the surrounding tissues. **2.** Geol. to pour forth, as lava from a subterranean source in a molten state. —v.i. **3.** Pathol. to be extravasated, as blood; escape from the proper vessels. **4.** Geol. to pour forth lava, etc. [f. EXTRA + L vās vessel + -ATE[1]]

ex·trav·a·sa·tion (ĭk străv′ə sā′shən), n. **1.** act of extravasating. **2.** the matter extravasated.

ex·tra·vas·cu·lar (ĕks′trə văs′kyə lər), adj. Anat. situated outside of a blood vessel or vessels.

ex·tra·ver·sion (ĕks′trə vûr′zhən, -shən), n. Psychol. extroversion.

ex·tra·vert (ĕks′trə vûrt′), n. extrovert.

ex·treme (ĭk strēm′), adj., -tremer, -tremest, n. —adj. **1.** of a character or kind farthest removed from the ordinary or average: an extreme case, extreme measures. **2.** utmost or exceedingly great in degree: extreme joy. **3.** farthest from the center or middle; outermost; endmost. **4.** farthest, utmost, or very far in any direction. **5.** going to the utmost lengths, or exceeding the bounds of moderation: extreme fashions. **6.** going to the utmost or very great lengths in action, habit, opinion, etc.: an extreme socialist. **7.** last or final: extreme unction. —n. **8.** the utmost or highest degree, or a very high degree: showy in the extreme, or to an extreme. **9.** one of two things as remote or different from each other as possible: the extremes of joy and grief. **10.** the furthest or utmost length, or an excessive length, beyond the ordinary or average: to go to extremes in dress. **11.** Math.

the first or the last term, as of a proportion or series. **12.** *Logic.* the subject or the predicate of the conclusion of a syllogism; either of two terms which are separated in the premises and brought together in the conclusion. **13.** *Obs. or Rare.* the utmost point, or extremity, of something. [ME, t. L: m.s. *extrēmus*, superl. of *exter* outer, outward] —**ex·treme′ness,** *n.* —**Syn. 6.** immoderate, excessive, fanatical, uncompromising. See **radical.** —**Ant. 6.** lukewarm.

ex·treme·ly (ĭk strēm′lĭ), *adv.* in an extreme degree; exceedingly.

extreme unction, *Rom. Cath. Ch.* a sacrament in which a dying person is anointed with oil by a priest for the health of his soul and body.

ex·trem·ism (ĭk strē′mĭz əm), *n.* tendency or disposition to go to extremes.

ex·trem·ist (ĭk strē′mĭst), *n.* **1.** one who goes to extremes. **2.** a supporter of extreme doctrines or practices. —*adj.* **3.** belonging or pertaining to extremists.

ex·trem·i·ty (ĭk strēm′ə tĭ), *n., pl.* **-ties.** **1.** the extreme or terminal point, limit, or part of something. **2.** a limb of the body. **3.** (*chiefly pl.*) the end part of a limb, as a hand or foot. **4.** (*often pl.*) a condition, or circumstances, of extreme need, distress, etc. **5.** the utmost or any extreme degree: *the extremity of joy.* **6.** (*chiefly pl.*) an extreme measure: *to be forced to extremities.* **7.** extreme character, as of views. **8.** (*chiefly pl.*) a person's last moments. —**Syn. 1.** end, termination, extreme, verge, border, boundary.

ex·tri·ca·ble (ĕks′trə kə bəl), *adj.* that may be extricated.

ex·tri·cate (ĕks′trə kāt′), *v.t.,* **-cated, -cating. 1.** to disentangle; disengage; free: *to extricate one from a dangerous or embarrassing situation.* **2.** to liberate (gas, etc.) from combination, as in a chemical process. [t. L: m.s. *extrīcātus,* pp., disentangled] —**ex′tri·ca′-tion,** *n.*

ex·trin·sic (ĕks trĭn′sĭk), *adj.* **1.** extraneous; not inherent; unessential. **2.** being outside of a thing; outward or external; operating or coming from without. **3.** *Anat.* (of certain muscles, nerves, etc.) originating outside the anatomical limits of a part. Also, **ex·trin′-si·cal.** [f. EX-¹ + (IN)TRINSIC. Cf. F *extrinsèque,* adj., L *extrinsecus,* adv.] —**ex·trin′si·cal·ly,** *adv.*

extro-, var. of **extra-** (used to contrast with **intro-**).

ex·trorse (ĕks trôrs′), *adj. Bot.* turned or facing outward, as anthers which open toward the perianth. [t. LL: m.s. *extrorsus* in an outward direction] —**ex·trorse′ly,** *adv.*

ex·tro·ver·sion (ĕks′trō vûr′zhən, -shən), *n.* **1.** Also, **extraversion.** *Psychol.* interest directed outward or to things outside the self (opposed to *introversion*). **2.** *Pathol.* a turning inside out, as of the eyelids or of the bladder. **3.** act of extroverting. **4.** extroverted state.

ex·tro·vert (ĕks′trō vûrt′), *Psychol.* —*n.* **1.** one characterized by extroversion; a person concerned chiefly with what is external or objective (opposed to *introvert*). —*adj.* **2.** marked by extroversion. —*v.t.* **3.** to direct (the mind, etc.) outward, or to things outside the self. Also, **extravert.** [f. EXTRO- + s. L *vertere* turn. See INTROVERT]

ex·trude (ĭk strood′), *v.,* **-truded, -truding.** —*v.t.* **1.** to thrust out; force or press out; expel. **2.** (in molding or making metals, plastics, etc.) to form into a desired cross-sectional shape by ejecting through a shaped opening: *to extrude tubing.* —*v.i.* **3.** to protrude. [t. L: m.s. *extrūdere* thrust out] —**ex·tru·sion** (ĭk-strōō′zhən), *n.*

ex·tru·sive (ĭk strōō′sĭv), *adj.* **1.** tending to extrude. **2.** pertaining to extrusion. **3.** *Geol.* (of rocks) having been forced out in a molten or plastic condition at the surface of the earth.

ex·u·ber·ance (ĭg zōō′bər əns), *n.* **1.** Also, **ex·u·ber·an·cy.** state of being exuberant. **2.** an instance of this. —**Syn.** 1. superabundance, excess, copiousness, profusion, luxuriance, lavishness. —**Ant.** 1. scarcity.

ex·u·ber·ant (ĭg zōō′bər ənt), *adj.* **1.** lavish; effusive; *exuberant health; an exuberant welcome.* **2.** profuse in growth or production; luxuriant; superabundant: *exuberant vegetation.* [t. L: s. *exūberans,* ppr., being fruitful] —**ex·u′ber·ant·ly,** *adv.* —**Syn. 2.** copious, rank. —**Ant. 2.** sparse.

ex·u·ber·ate (ĭg zōō′bə rāt′), *v.i.,* **-ated, -ating.** to be exuberant; superabound; overflow.

ex·u·date (ĕks′yōō dāt′), *n.* a substance exuded.

ex·u·da·tion (ĕks′yōō dā′shən), *n.* **1.** act of exuding. **2.** that which is exuded. **3.** a sweatlike issue or discharge through pores or small openings. —**ex·u·da·tive** (ĕks ū′də tĭv), *adj.*

ex·ude (ĭg zōōd′, ĭk sōōd′), *v.,* **-uded, -uding.** —*v.i.* **1.** to come out gradually in drops like sweat through pores or small openings; ooze out. —*v.t.* **2.** to send out like sweat; emit through pores or small openings. [t. L: m.s. *ex(s)ūdāre*]

ex·ult (ĭg zŭlt′), *v.i.* **1.** to show or feel a lively or triumphant joy; rejoice exceedingly; be highly elated; be jubilant (fol. by *in, at, over,* or an infinitive): *he exulted to find that he had won.* **2.** *Obs.* to leap, esp. for joy. [t. L: s. *ex(s)ultāre,* freq. of *exsilīre* leap out or up] —**ex·ult′ing·ly,** *adv.*

ex·ult·ant (ĭg zŭl′tənt), *adj.* exulting; highly elated; triumphant. —**ex·ult′ant·ly,** *adv.*

ex·ul·ta·tion (ĕg′zŭl tā′shən, ĕk′sŭl-), *n.* act of exulting; lively or triumphant joy, as over success or victory. Also, **ex·ult·an·cy** (ĭg zŭl′tən sĭ), **ex·ult′ance.**

ex·u·vi·ae (ĭg zōō′vĭ ē′, ĭk sōō′-), *n.pl.* the cast skins, shells, or other coverings of animals. [t. L: garments stripped off, skins of animals] —**ex·u′vi·al,** *adj.*

ex·u·vi·ate (ĭg zōō′vĭ āt′, ĭk sōō′-), *v.i., v.t.,* **-ated, -ating.** to cast off or shed (exuviae); to molt. —**ex·u′vi·a′tion,** *n.*

ex vo·to (ĕks vō′tō), *Latin.* from, or in pursuance of, a vow.

-ey¹, var. of **-y**¹, used esp. after *y,* as in *clayey.*

-ey², var. of **-y²,** used esp. after *y.*

e·ya·let (ā′yä lĕt′), *n.* vilayet.

ey·as (ī′əs), *n.* a nestling. [ME, var. of *nyas, nias* (*a nyas* being taken as *an eyas*), t. F: m. *niais* a nestling, der. L *nīdus* nest]

Eyck (īk), *n.* **1.** Hubert or Huybrecht van (hȳ′bĕrt *or* hoi′brĕкнt vän), 1366–1426, Flemish painter. **2.** his brother, **Jan van** (yän vän), (*Jan van Brugge*) 1385?–1440, Flemish painter.

eye (ī), *n., pl.* **eyes,** (*Archaic*) **eyen,** *v.,* **eyed, eying** or **eyeing,** *interj.* —*n.* **1.** the organ of sight or vision. **2.** all the structures situated within or near the orbit which assist the organ of vision. **3.** this organ with respect to the color of the iris: *blue eyes.* **4.** the region surrounding the eye: *a black eye.* **5.** sight; vision. **6.** power of seeing; appreciative or discriminating visual perception: *an eye for color.* **7.** (*often pl.*) look, glance, or gaze: *to cast one's eye on a thing.* **8.** (*often pl.*) attentive look, close observation, or watch: *to keep an eye on a person, to be all eyes.* **9.** regard, respect, view, aim, or intention: *to have an eye to one's own advantage, with an eye to win favor.* **10.** (*often pl.*) manner or way of looking at a thing, estimation, or opinion: *in the eyes of the law.* **11.** mental view: *in my mind's eye.* **12.** a center of light, intelligence, influence, etc. **13.** something resembling or suggesting the eye in appearance, shape, etc., as the bud of a tuber, the central spot of a target, one of the round spots on the tail feathers of a peacock, the hole of a needle, a hole pierced in a thing for the insertion of some object, a metal or other ring as for a rope to pass through, or the loop into which a hook is inserted (forming together with the hook a hook and eye). **14.** *Meteorol.* the central region of low pressure in a tropical hurricane, where calm conditions prevail, often with clear skies. **15.** eye of the wind, *Naut.* the precise direction from which the wind is blowing. **16.** make eyes at, to throw amorous or covetous glances at. **17.** set or lay eyes on, *Colloq.* to catch sight of; see. —*v.t.* **18.** to fix the eyes upon; view. **19.** to observe or watch narrowly. **20.** to make an eye in: *to eye a needle.* —*v.i.* **21.** *Obs.* to appear to the eye. —*interj.* **22.** mild exclamation of contradiction or surprise: *my eye!* [ME; OE *ēge,* d. var. of *ēage,* c. G *auge.* Cf. L *oculus*]

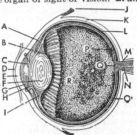

Human Eye
A, Ciliary muscle; B, Ciliary processes; C, Iris; D, Conjunctiva; E, Cornea; F, Crystalline lens; G, Anterior chamber; H, Posterior chamber; I, Suspensory ligament; J, Ocular muscles; K, Sclera; L, Choroid; M, Optic nerve; N, Retinal artery; O, Retina; P, Yellow spot; Q, Blind spot; R, Vitreous humor.

eye·ball (ī′bôl′), *n.* the ball or globe of the eye.

eye·beam (ī′bēm′), *n.* a beam or glance of the eye.

eye·bright (ī′brīt′), *n.* **1.** any of various scrophulariaceous herbs of the genus *Euphrasia,* as *E. officinalis* of Europe, formerly used for diseases of the eye. **2.** scarlet pimpernel.

eye·brow (ī′brou′), *n.* **1.** the arch or ridge forming the upper part of the orbit of the eye. **2.** the fringe of hair growing upon it.

eye·cup (ī′kŭp′), *n.* a device for applying lotions to the eye, consisting of a cup or glass with a rim shaped to fit snugly about the orbit of the eye. Also, **eye bath.**

eyed (īd), *adj.* **1.** having eyes. **2.** having eyelike spots.

eye·glass (ī′glås′, ī′gläs′), *n.* **1.** (*pl.*) a pair of lenses to correct a refractive error of the eye, esp. when kept in position by a spring which compresses the nose (as distinguished from *spectacles,* which have bows for the ears). **2.** the eyepiece of an optical instrument; an ocular. **3.** an eyecup.

eye·hole (ī′hōl′), *n.* **1.** eye socket. **2.** a hole to look through, as in a mask or a curtain. **3.** a circular opening for the insertion of a pin, hook, rope, etc.

eye·lash (ī′lăsh′), *n.* one of the short, thick, curved hairs growing as a fringe on the edge of an eyelid.

eye·less (ī′lĭs), *adj.* **1.** lacking eyes. **2.** blind.

eye·let (ī′lĭt), *n.* **1.** a small, typically round hole, esp. one finished at the edge, as in cloth or leather, for the passage of a lace or cord; or in embroidery, for ornament. **2.** a metal ring for lining a small hole. **3.** an eyehole in a wall, mask, etc. **4.** a small eye. —*v.t.* **5.** to make eyelets (holes) in. **6.** to insert metal eyelets in. [ME *oilet,* t. F: m. *œillet,* dim. of *œil* eye]

eye·let·eer (ī/lə tïr/), *n.* a small pointed instrument for making eyelet holes.

eye·lid (ī/lĭd/), *n.* the movable lid of skin which serves to cover and uncover the eyeball.

ey·en (ī/ən), *n. Archaic.* pl. of **eye.**

eye opener, *U.S.* **1.** something that causes the eyes to open, as an enlightening or startling disclosure or experience. **2.** *Colloq.* a drink of liquor, esp. one taken early in the day.

eye·piece (ī/pēs/), *n.* (in an optical instrument) the lens or combination of lenses to which the eye is applied.

eye·serv·ant (ī/sûr/vənt), *n.* a servant or other who attends to his duty only when watched by his employer. Also, **eye/serv/er.**

eye·serv·ice (ī/sûr/vĭs), *n.* **1.** service performed only under the eye or watch of the employer. **2.** homage paid with the eyes; admiring looks.

eye·shot (ī/shŏt/), *n.* **1.** range of vision; view. **2.** a glance.

eye·sight (ī/sīt/), *n.* **1.** the power or faculty of seeing. **2.** action or fact of seeing. **3.** the range of the eye.

eye socket, the socket or orbit of the eye.

eye·some (ī/səm), *adj.* pleasant to look at.

eye·sore (ī/sōr/), *n.* something unpleasant to look at: *the broken window was an eyesore to the neighbors.*

eye·spot (ī/spŏt/), *n. Zool.* **1.** a sensory organ of lower animals, having a light-perceiving function. **2.** an eyelike spot, as on the tail of a peacock.

eyes right or **left,** *Mil.* the command given to turn the head and eyes to the right or to the left as a salute while marching at ceremonies.

eye·stalk (ī/stôk/), *n. Zool.* the stalk or peduncle upon which the eye is borne in lobsters, shrimps, etc.

eye·stone (ī/stōn/), *n.* a small calcareous body, flat on one side and convex on the other passed between the eye and the eyelid to bring out cinders, etc.

eye·strain (ī/strān/), *n.* a sensation of discomfort produced in the eyes by their excessive or faulty use.

eye·tooth (ī/tooth/), *n., pl.* **-teeth** (-tēth/). **1.** a canine tooth, esp. of the upper jaw (so named from its position under the eye). **2. cut one's eyeteeth,** to become old and experienced enough to understand things.

eye·wash (ī/wŏsh/, ī/wôsh/), *n.* **1.** Also, **eye·wa·ter** (ī/wô/tər, ī/wŏt/ər). a lotion for the eyes. **2.** *Slang.* deceitful excuse; applesauce.

eye·wink (ī/wĭngk/), *n.* **1.** a wink of the eye. **2.** a look or glance.

eye·wink·er (ī/wĭngk/ər), *n.* eyelash.

eye·wit·ness (ī/wĭt/nĭs), *n.* one who actually beholds some act or occurrence, and hence can give testimony concerning it.

eyne (īn), *n. Archaic.* pl. of **eye.**

ey·ot (ī/ət, āt), *n. Brit. Local.* a small island.

ey·ra (âr/ə, ī/rə), *n.* jaguarundi. [t. Tupi]

eyre (âr), *n.* **1.** a journey in a circuit. **2.** *Eng. Law.* **a.** a journey made by judges to hold court throughout a circuit, under royal commission, superseded prior to the time of Edward III by Commission of Assize. **b. justices in eyre,** the judges holding the commission. **c.** the court held by justices in eyre. [ME, t. OF: m. *eire* journey, circuit, der. *errer,* v., journey, g. LL *iterāre*]

Eyre (âr), *n.* **Lake,** a shallow salt lake in S Australia. ab. 4000 sq. mi.

Eyre's Peninsula (ârz), a peninsula in S Australia, E of the Great Australian Bight.

ey·rie (âr/ĭ, ĭr/ĭ), *n.* aerie. Also, **ey/ry.**

Ez., Ezra. Also, **Ezr.**

Ezek., Ezekiel.

E·ze·ki·el (ĭ zē/kĭ əl), *n.* **1.** fl. 6th century B.C., one of the major Hebrew prophets. **2.** the 26th book of the Old Testament, written by him. **3. Moses Jacob,** 1844–1917, U.S. sculptor, in Rome. [t. Gk. (Septuagint): m. *Iezekiél,* t. Heb.: m. *Yeḥezqēl;* r. *Ezechiel,* t. L (Vulgate)]

Ez·ra (ĕz/rə), *n.* **1.** fl. 5th century B.C., Hebrew scribe and priest who with Nehemiah led the revival of Judaism in Palestine. **2.** a short book of chronicles of the Old Testament. [t. Heb.: m. *'Ezrā*]

F

F, f (ĕf), *n., pl.* **F's** or **Fs, f's** or **fs.** **1.** the sixth letter of the English alphabet. **2.** the sixth in order or in a series. **3.** *Music.* **a.** the fourth tone in the scale of C major or the sixth in the relative scale of A minor. **b.** a printed or written note indicating this tone. **c.** a string, key, or pipe tuned to this note. **d.** (in solmization) the fourth tone of the scale of C, called fa.

F, 1. failure (a grade or mark in school). **2.** *Elect.* farad. **3.** *Math.* field. **4.** *Genetics.* (with a subscript number following) a generation of filial offspring from a given parent: F_1 is the first generation of offspring, F_2 is the second, etc. **5.** *Chem.* fluorine. **6.** French. **7.** *Math.* function (of).

F, *Photog.* See **F number.** Also, **f, F:, f:, F/, f/.**

F., 1. Fahrenheit. **2.** February. **3.** French. **4.** Friday.

f., 1. *Music.* forte. **2.** *Math.* function (of). **3.** *Elect.* farad. **4.** farthing. **5.** fathom. **6.** female. **7.** feminine. **8.** fluid (ounce). **9.** (*pl.* **ff.**) folio. **10.** following. **11.** formed of. **12.** franc.

fa (fä), *n. Music.* the syllable used for the fourth tone of a scale. [see GAMUT]

fa·ba·ceous (fə bā/shəs), *adj. Bot.* belonging to the *Fabaceae,* or bean family of plants, sometimes included in the *Leguminosae,* including many herbs, shrubs, and trees, as the bean, pea, lentil, furze, broom, locust, etc., which bear seeds in pods or legumes. [t. L: m. *fabāceus,* der. *faba* bean]

Fa·bi·an (fā/bĭ ən), *adj.* **1.** avoiding battle; purposely delaying; cautiously dilatory: *Fabian policy.* See **Fabius Maximus. 2.** of the Fabian Society. —*n.* **3.** a member of or sympathizer with the Fabian Society. —**Fa/bi·an·ism,** *n.* —**Fa/bi·an·ist,** *n., adj.*

Fabian Society, a socialist society founded in England in 1884 favoring the gradual spread of socialism by peaceful means.

Fa·bi·us Max·i·mus (fā/bĭ əs măk/sə məs), **Quintus** (kwĭn/təs), died 203 B.C., Roman general who harassed Hannibal's army without risking a pitched battle.

fa·ble (fā/bəl), *n., v.,* **-bled, -bling.** —*n.* **1.** a short tale to teach a moral, often with animals or inanimate objects as characters; apologue: *the fable of the tortoise and the hare.* **2.** a story not founded on fact. **3.** a story about supernatural or extraordinary persons or incidents; a legend. **4.** legends or myths collectively: *Mohammedan fable.* **5.** an untruth; a falsehood. **6.** *Archaic.* the plot of an epic, a dramatic poem, or a play. **7.** *Archaic.* idle talk: *old wives' fables.* —*v.i.* **8.** to tell or write fables. **9.** to speak falsely; lie. —*v.t.* **10.** to invent (stories); talk about as if true. [ME, t. OF, t. L: m.s. *fābula* narrative] —**fa/bler,** *n.* —**Syn. 2.** See **legend.**

fa·bled (fā/bəld), *adj.* **1.** celebrated in fables; mythical; legendary: *fabled goddess of the wood.* **2.** having no real existence; fictitious: *fabled chest of gold.*

fab·li·au (făb/lĭ ō/; *Fr.* fà blē ō/), *n., pl.* **-aux** (-ōz/; *Fr.* -ō/), one of the short metrical tales of the medieval French poets, usually rough and humorous. [t. F, orig.. d., dim. of *fable* FABLE]

Fa·bre (fä/bər; *Fr.* fà/br), *n.* **Jean Henri** (zhän än rē/), 1823–1915, French entomologist and popular writer on insect life.

fab·ric (făb/rĭk), *n.* **1.** a cloth made by weaving, knitting, or felting fibers: *woolen fabrics.* **2.** the texture of the woven, knitted, or felted material: *cloths of different fabric.* **3.** framework; structure: *fabric of society.* **4.** a building; edifice. **5.** the method of construction. [t. OF: m. *fabrique,* t. L: m.s. *fabrica* workshop, art, fabric]

fab·ri·cant (făb/rə kənt), *n.* a maker; artisan.

fab·ri·cate (făb/rə kāt/), *v.t.,* **-cated, -cating. 1.** to make by art and labor; construct. **2.** to make by assembling standard parts or sections. **3.** to devise or invent (a legend, lie, etc.). **4.** to fake; forge (a document). [t. L: m.s. *fabricātus,* pp., having made] —**fab/ri·ca/tor,** *n.* —**Syn. 1.** See **manufacture.**

fab·ri·ca·tion (făb/rə kā/shən), *n.* **1.** the process of fabricating; manufacture. **2.** something fabricated, esp. an untruthful statement. —**Syn. 2.** See **fiction.**

fab·ri·koid (făb/rə koid/), *n.* **1.** a waterproof fabric having a cloth foundation and a pyroxylin surface, used as a substitute for leather, cloth, etc. **2.** (*cap.*) a trademark for it. [f. m. FABRIC + -OID]

fab·u·list (făb/yə lĭst), *n.* **1.** a person who invents or relates fables. **2.** a liar.

fab·u·lous (făb/yə ləs), *adj.* **1.** almost unbelievable: *fabulous price.* **2.** told about in fables; not true or real: *the fabulous exploits of Hercules.* **3.** known about only through myths or legends: *the fabulous age in Greek history.* **4.** based on fables. [t. L: m.s. *fābulōsus*] —**fab/u·lous·ly,** *adv.* —**fab/u·lous·ness,** *n.* —**Syn. 1.** incredible, amazing, astonishing. **2.** fabled, fictitious, imaginary. —**Ant. 1.** moderate. **2.** historical.

fac., 1. facsimile. **2.** factor. **3.** factory.

fa·çade (fə säd/, fä-; *Fr.* fà sàd/), *n.* **1.** *Archit.* a face or front, or the principal face, of a building. **2.** the front part (of anything): *a façade of wealth.* [t. F, der. *face,* after It. *facciata,* der. *faccia* FACE]

face (fās), *n., v.,* **faced, facing.** —*n.* **1.** the front part of the head, from the forehead to the chin. **2.** sight; presence: *to one's face.* **3.** a look or expression on the face: *sad face.* **4.** an expression, indicating ridicule, disgust, etc.: *to make faces.* **5.** *Colloq.* boldness; impudence: *to have the face to ask.* **6.** outward appearance: *old problems with new faces.* **7.** outward show; pretense: *to put a good face on a matter.* **8.** good name; prestige: *to save one's face.* **9.** the amount specified in a bill or note, exclusive of interest. **10.** (of a document) the manifest sense or express terms. **11.** the geographic characteristics or general appearance (of a land surface). **12.** the surface: *face of the earth.* **13.** the side or part of a side upon which the use of a thing depends: *the face of a cloth, document, playing card, watch, etc.* **14.** the most important side; the front: *the face of a building, arch, etc.* **15.** the acting, striking, or working surface of an implement, tool, etc. **16.** *Geom.* any one of the bounding surfaces of a solid figure: *a cube has six faces.* **17.** *Mining.* the front or end of a drift or excavation, where the material is being or was last mined. **18.** *Print.* **a.** the working surface of a type, plate, etc. See diag. under **type. b.** the style or appearance of type: *broad or narrow face.* **19.** *Fort.* either of the two outer sides which form the salient angle of a bastion or the like. See diag. under **bastion. 20. in (the) face of, a.** notwithstanding: *in the face of many obstacles.* **b.** when confronted with: *to keep up prices in the face of a falling market.* **c.** *Brit.* in front of: *in the face of the sea.* —*v.t.* **21.** to look toward: *face the light.* **22.** to front toward: *the statue faces the park.* **23.** to meet face to face; confront: *faced with a problem.* **24.** to confront with impudence: *to face a thing out.* **25.** to oppose confidently or defiantly: *to face fearful odds.* **26.** to cover or partly cover with a different material in front: *wooden house faced with brick.* **27.** to cover some part of (a garment) with another material. **28.** to turn the face of (a playing card) upwards. **29.** to dress or smooth the surface of (a stone, etc.). **30.** to cause (soldiers) to turn to the right, left, or in the opposite direction. —*v.i.* **31.** to be turned (often fol. by *to, toward*). **32.** to be placed (fol. by *on, to, toward*). **33.** to turn to the right, left, or in the opposite direction. [ME, t. F, g. VL *facia,* r. L *facies* form, face] —**face/a·ble,** *adj.* —**face/less,** *adj.*
—**Syn. 1.** FACE, COUNTENANCE, VISAGE refer to the front of the (usually human) head. The FACE is the combination of the features: *a face with broad cheekbones.* COUNTENANCE, a more formal word, denotes the face as it is affected by or reveals the state of mind, and hence often signifies the look or expression on the face: *an expressive countenance.* VISAGE, still more formal, refers to the face as seen in a certain aspect, esp. as revealing seriousness or severity: *a stern visage.*

face card, the king, queen, or jack of playing cards.

face-hard·en (fās/här/dən), *v.t.* to harden the face or surface (of steel or other metal or a metallic object) by chilling, case hardening, or the like. Cf. **caseharden.**

face lifting, plastic surgery on the face for the elimination of wrinkles, etc.

fac·er (fā/sər), *n.* **1.** one who or that which faces, esp. a cutter for smoothing a surface. See **face** (defs. 26, 29). **2.** *Colloq.* a blow in the face. **3.** *Chiefly Brit. Colloq.* a sudden and severe check.

face-sav·ing (fās/sā/vĭng), *adj.* that saves one's prestige.

fac·et (făs/ĭt), *n., v.,* **-eted, -eting** or (*esp. Brit.*) **-etted, -etting.** —*n.* **1.** one of the small plane polished surfaces of a cut gem. **2.** aspect; phase: *a facet of the mind.* **3.** *Archit.* a filled-in flute sometimes seen at the bottom of columnar shafts. **4.** *Zool.* one of the corneal lenses of a compound arthropod eye. —*v.t.* **5.** to cut facets on. [t. F: m. *facette,* dim. of *face* FACE]

Compound eye of a housefly showing facets (highly magnified)

fa·cete (fə sēt/), *adj. Archaic.* facetious; witty. [t. L: m.s. *facētus* fine, elegant, witty]

fa·ce·ti·ae (fə sē/shĭ ē/), *n.pl.* **1.** amusing writings or witty remarks. **2.** coarsely witty books. [t. L, pl. of *facētia* a witticism. See FACETE]

fa·ce·tious (fə sē/shəs), *adj.* **1.** amusing; humorous: *a facetious remark.* **2.** trying to be amusing: *a facetious person.* [f. FACETI(AE) + -OUS] —**fa·ce/tious·ly,** *adv.* —**fa·ce/tious·ness,** *n.* —**Syn. 1.** See humorous.

face value, 1. par value; the value printed on the face of a financial instrument or document. **2.** apparent value: *accept promises at face value.*

fa·cial (fā/shəl), *adj.* **1.** of the face: *facial expression.* **2.** for the face: *a facial cream.* —*n.* **3.** *Colloq.* a massage or treatment for the face. —**fa/cial·ly,** *adv.*

facial angle, *Craniom.* the angle formed by a line from nasion to prosthion at its intersection with the plane of the Frankfort horizontal.

Orthognathous Skull   Prognathous Skull

ACD, Facial angle: AB, Axis of face; CD, Axis of the skull

facial index, *Craniom.* the ratio of the breadth of a face to its height.

-facient, a suffix forming adjectives meaning "that makes or causes (something)" and nouns meaning "one that makes or causes (something)," as in *absorbifacient,* n. and adj. [t. L: s. *faciens* ppr., doing, making]

fa·ci·es (fā/shĭ ēz/), *n.* **1.** general appearance. **2.** *Geol.* the composite nature of sedimentary deposits reflecting the conditions and environment of their origin. [t. L]

fac·ile (făs/ĭl), *adj.* **1.** moving, acting, working, proceeding, etc., with ease: *a facile hand, tongue, pen, etc., facile expression.* **2.** easily done, performed, used, etc.: *a facile victory, method, etc.* **3.** easy or unconstrained, as manners or persons; affable, agreeable, or complaisant; easily influenced. [t. L: m.s. *facilis* easy to do, easy] —**fac/ile·ly,** *adv.* —**fac/ile·ness,** *n.*

fa·ci·le prin·ceps (făs/ə lĭ prĭn/sĕps), *Latin.* easily the first or best.

fa·ci·lis de·scen·sus A·ver·ni (făs/ə lĭs dĭ sĕn/səs ə vûr/nī), *Latin.* (the) descent to hell is easy; it is easy to take the downward path. Vergil, *Aeneid,* 6, 126.

fa·cil·i·tate (fə sĭl/ə tāt/), *v.t.,* **-tated, -tating. 1.** to make easier or less difficult; help forward (an action, a process, etc.). **2.** to assist the progress of (a person).

fa·cil·i·ta·tion (fə sĭl/ə tā/shən), *n.* **1.** act or process of facilitating. **2.** *Psychol.* the tendency of a stimulus to reinforce another stimulus.

fa·cil·i·ty (fə sĭl/ə tĭ), *n., pl.* **-ties. 1.** something that makes possible the easier performance of any action; advantage: *transportation facilities, to afford someone every facility for doing something.* **2.** freedom from difficulty; ease: *facility of understanding.* **3.** readiness because of skill or practice; dexterity: *compose with great facility.* **4.** an easy-flowing manner: *facility of style.* **5.** ready compliance. [t. L: m.s. *facilitas.* See FACILE]

fac·ing (fā/sĭng), *n.* **1.** a covering in front, for ornament, protection, etc., as an outer layer of different stone forming the face of a wall. **2.** material applied on the edge of a garment for ornament or protection. **3.** (*pl.*) coverings of a different color applied on the collar, cuffs, or other parts of a military coat. **4.** *Mil.* act of turning to face in a given direction in response to a command.

facing tool, a lathe tool for smoothing a plane surface at right angles to the axis of rotation.

fa·cin·o·rous (fə sĭn/ə rəs), *adj. Now Rare.* atrociously wicked. [t. L: m.s. *facinorōsus,* der. *facinus* (bad) deed]

facsim., facsimile.

fac·sim·i·le (făk sĭm/ə lĭ, -lē/), *n., adj., v.,* **-led, -leing.** —*n.* **1.** an exact copy. **2.** *Radio.* **a.** a method of transmitting pictures by radio telegraph. See **phototelegraphy. b.** a picture so sent. —*adj.* **3.** of a facsimile. **4.** producing facsimiles. —*v.t.* **5.** to reproduce in facsimile; make a fascimile of. [f. L: *fac,* impv., make + *simile* (neut.) like]

fact (făkt), *n.* **1.** what has really happened or is the case; truth; reality: *in fact rather than in theory, the fact of the matter is,* **2.** something known to have happened; a truth known by actual experience or observation: *scientists working with facts.* **3.** something said to be true or supposed to have happened: *the facts are as follows.* **4.** *Law.* **a.** an actual or alleged physical or mental event or existence, as distinguished from a legal effect or consequence. Thus, whether certain words were spoken is *a question of fact;* whether, if spoken, they constituted a binding promise, is usually *a question of law.* **b.** an evil deed (now only in certain legal phrases): *before the fact, after the fact.* **5. in fact,** really; indeed. [t. L: s. *factum* (thing) done, prop. pp. neut.].

fact-find·ing (făkt/fīn/dĭng), *adj.* engaged in determining facts.

fac·tice (făk/tĭs), *n.* a rubberlike substance produced by vulcanizing vegetable oils with sulfur or sulfur chloride. [t. F, t. L: m.s. *factītius* artificial]

fac·tion (făk/shən), *n.* **1.** a smaller group of people within a larger group, often one using unscrupulous methods to accomplish selfish purposes. **2.** party strife or intrigue: *faction has no regard for national interests.* [t. L: s. *factio* a doing or making, action, party]

fac·tion·al (făk/shən əl), *adj.* of a faction or factions; self-interested; partisan. —**fac/tion·al·ism,** *n.*

fac·tious (făk/shəs), *adj.* **1.** inclined to act for party purposes: *factious opposition.* **2.** caused by party spirit or strife: *factious quarrels.* [t. L: m.s. *factiōsus*] —**fac/tious·ly,** *adv.* —**fac/tious·ness,** *n.*

fac·ti·tious (făk tĭsh/əs), *adj.* **1.** artificial; not spontaneous or natural: *a factitious value, factitious enthusiasm.* **2.** made; manufactured. [t. L: m. *factītius* made by art] —**fac·ti/tious·ly,** *adv.* —**fac·ti/tious·ness,** *n.*

fac·ti·tive (făk/tə tĭv), *adj. Gram.* **1.** used to designate verbs which convey the idea of making or rendering according to order or specification; such verbs are accompanied not only by the direct object but by an additional word indicating the result of the process. For example: They *made* him their *ruler;* to *paint* the house *red.* **2.** pertaining to such a verb. [t. NL: m.s. *factītīvus,* der. L *factitāre* declare (a person) to be, freq. of *facere* do, make] —**fac/ti·tive·ly,** *adv.*

fac·tor (făk/tər), *n.* **1.** one of the elements that contribute to bring about any given result. **2.** *Math.* one of two or more numbers, algebraic expressions, or the like, which when multiplied together produce a given product; a divisor: *6 and 3 are factors of 18.* **3.** *Biol.* a gene, allele, or determiner for hereditary characters. **4.** *Brit.* one who acts, or transacts business, for another. **5.** *Brit.* a commission merchant. **6.** *Brit.* an agent entrusted with the possession of goods for sale. **7.** *Law.* (in some of the United States) a person charged as a garnishee. **8.** *Now only Scot.* the steward or bailiff of an estate. —*v.t.* **9.** to express (a mathematical quantity) as a product of two or more quantities of like kind; thus: $30 = 2 \cdot 3 \cdot 5$, or $x^2 - y^2 = (x + y)(x - y)$. [t. L: doer, maker] —**fac′tor·ship′**, *n.*

fac·tor·age (făk′tər ĭj), *n.* **1.** the action or business of a factor. **2.** the allowance or commission paid to a factor.

fac·to·ri·al (făk tōr′ĭ əl), *n.* **1.** *Math.* the product of an integer multiplied by all the lower integers: *the factorial of 4 (written 4! or |4) is $4 \times 3 \times 2 \times 1 = 24$.* —*adj.* **2.** *Math.* of or pertaining to factors or factorials. **3.** of or pertaining to a factor or a factory.

fac·tor·ing (făk′tər ĭng), *n.* *Com.* the business of purchasing and collecting accounts receivable.

fac·tor·ize (făk′tə rīz′), *v.t.*, **-ized, -izing. 1.** *Math.* to resolve into factors. **2.** *Law.* to garnish. —**fac′tor·i·za′tion**, *n.*

fac·to·ry (făk′tə rĭ), *n.*, *pl.* **-ries. 1.** a building or group of buildings, usually with equipment, where goods are manufactured. **2.** (formerly) an establishment for factors and merchants carrying on business in a foreign country. [t. ML: m.s. *factōria*, der. L *factor*] —**fac′to·ry·like′**, *adj.* —**Syn. 1.** manufactory, mill, workshop.

fac·to·tum (făk tō′təm), *n.* one employed to do all kinds of work for another. [t. ML, f. L *fac*, impv., do + *tōtum* (neut.) all]

fac·tu·al (făk′chŏŏ əl), *adj.* pertaining to facts; of the nature of fact; real. —**fac′tu·al·ly**, *adv.*

fac·ture (făk′chər), *n.* **1.** act, process, or manner of making anything; construction. **2.** the thing made. [ME, t. L: m.s. *factūra*, der. *facere* do, make]

fac·u·la (făk′yə lə), *n.*, *pl.* **-lae** (-lē′). *Astron.* one of the irregular patches on the sun's disk, brighter than the general surface. [t. L, dim. of *fax* torch] —**fac′u·lar**, *adj.*

fac·ul·ta·tive (făk′əl tā′tĭv), *adj.* **1.** conferring a faculty, privilege, or permission, or the power of doing or not doing something: *a facultative enactment.* **2.** left to one's option or choice; optional. **3.** that may or may not take place; that may or may not assume a specified character. **4.** *Biol.* having the capacity to live under more than one specific set of environmental conditions, as an animal or plant that can lead either a parasitic or a nonparasitic life (opposed to *obligate*).

fac·ul·ty (făk′əl tĭ), *n.*, *pl.* **-ties. 1.** an ability, natural or acquired, for a particular kind of action. **2.** one of the powers of the mind, as memory, reason, speech, etc.: *the mental faculties, be in full possession of all one's faculties.* **3.** an inherent capability of the body: *the faculties of sight and hearing.* **4.** *U.S. Colloq.* executive ability; efficiency. **5.** *Educ.* **a.** one of the departments of learning, as theology, medicine, or law, in a university. **b.** the teaching body, sometimes with the students, in any of these departments. **c.** the entire teaching and administrative force of a university, college, or school. **6.** the members of a learned profession, esp. the medical profession. **7.** a power or privilege conferred. **8.** *Eccles.* a dispensation, license, or authorization. [ME *faculte*, t. L: m. s. *facultas* ability, means] —**Syn. 1.** capacity, capability, aptitude, knack, turn, talent. See **ability.**

fad (făd), *n.* a temporary, usually irrational, pursuit, fashion, etc. by numbers of people of some action that excites attention and has prestige. [n. use of *fad*, v., be busy about trifles, itself back formation from obs. *faddle*, v., fondle. Cf. FIDDLE v., and FIDDLE-FADDLE] —**fad′like′**, *adj.*

fad·dish (făd′ĭsh), *adj.* **1.** fadlike. **2.** given to fads.

fad·dist (făd′ĭst), *n.* one who has a fad or is given to fads.

fad·dy (făd′ĭ), *adj.*, **-dier, -diest.** faddish.

fade (fād), *v.*, **faded, fading.** —*v.i.* **1.** to lose freshness, vigor, strength, or health: *the flower faded.* **2.** to lose brightness or vividness, as light or color. **3.** to disappear or die gradually (often fol. by *away* or *out*): *a fading smile, sound, etc.* **4.** *Motion Pictures.* to appear (**fade in**) or disappear (**fade out**) by gradually becoming lighter or darker. —*v.t.* **5.** to cause to fade: *sunshine faded the tapestry.* **6.** *Colloq.* (in dice throwing) to make a wager against (the caster). [ME *fade(n)*, t. OF: m. *fader*, der. *fade* pale, weak, g. b. L *vapidus* flat and *fatuus* insipid] —**Syn. 1.** wither, droop, languish. **2.** blanch, bleach, pale. **3.** See **disappear.**

fade-in (fād′ĭn′), *n.* a progressive lighting of a scene in a motion picture as it appears.

fade·less (fād′lĭs), *adj.* unfading. —**fade′less·ly**, *adv.*

fade-out (fād′out′), *n.* **1.** a progressive darkening of a scene in a motion picture as it disappears. **2.** a disappearance, esp. a gradual one.

fadge (făj), *v.i.*, **fadged, fadging.** *Obs.* or *Dial. Eng.* **1.** to fit; suit; agree. **2.** to succeed; thrive.

Fad·i·man (făd′ə mən), *n.* **Clifton**, born 1904, U. S. writer and critic.

fae·ces (fē′sēz), *n.pl.* feces. —**fae·cal** (fē′kəl), *adj.*

Fa·en·za (fä ĕn′tsä), *n.* a city in N Italy, SE of Bologna. 23,823 (1936).

fa·ër·ie (fā′ər ĭ, fâr′ĭ), *n.* **1.** fairyland. **2.** *Archaic.* a fairy. —*adj.* **3.** *Archaic.* fairy. [var. of FAIRY]

Faerie Queene (kwēn), a chivalric romance in verse (1590–1611), by Edmund Spenser, containing an intricate allegory.

Faer·oe Is·lands (fâr′ō), a group of 21 islands in the N Atlantic between Great Britain and Iceland: independence from Denmark proclaimed Sept. 18, 1946. 29,178 pop. (1945); 540 sq. mi. *Cap.:* Torshaven. Also, **the Faeroes** or **Faroe Islands.** Danish, **Faer·ö·er·ne** (fĕr œ′ĕr nə).

fa·ër·y (fā′ər ĭ, fâr′ĭ), *n.*, *pl.* **faëries**, *adj.* faërie.

Faf·nir (făv′nĭr, fäf′-), *n.* (in the Icelandic version of the Siegfried story) the guardian dragon of the Nibelungs' hoard, slain by Sigurd. [Icel.]

fag (făg), *v.*, **fagged, fagging**, *n.* —*v.i.* **1.** *Brit.* to work till wearied; work hard: *to fag away at French.* **2.** *Brit.* to act as a fag. —*v.t.* **3.** to tire by labor; exhaust (often fol. by *out*): *we were fagged out.* **4.** *Brit.* to make a fag of. —*n.* **5.** drudgery; toil. **6.** *Brit. Colloq.* a younger pupil in English public schools required to perform certain services for an older pupil. **7.** a drudge. **8.** a fag end, as of cloth. **9.** *Chiefly Brit. Slang.* a cigarette. [special use of obs. *fag*, n., flap, which occurs only in expression *fag feathers*, ? for *wag feathers* by allit. assimilation; cf. FIELDFARE]

fa·ga·ceous (fə gā′shəs), *adj.* belonging to the *Fagaceae*, or beech family of trees and shrubs, which includes the beech, chestnut, oak, etc. [f. m.s. NL *Fāgāceae* genus type (der. L *fāgus* beech) + -OUS]

fag end, 1. the last part or very end of something, esp. a remnant. **2.** the unfinished end of a piece of cloth.

Fa·gin (fā′gĭn), *n.* (in Dickens' *Oliver Twist*) a villainous old man who employs young boys as thieves.

fag·ot (făg′ət), *n.* **1.** a bundle of sticks, twigs, or small branches, etc. bound together, used for fuel, as a fascine, etc. **2.** a collection. **3.** a bundle of pieces of iron or steel to be welded. —*v.t.* **4.** to bind or make into a fagot. **5.** to ornament with fagoting. Also, *Brit.*, **fag′got.** [ME, t. OF; orig. uncert.]

fag·ot·ing (făg′ət ĭng), *n.* a type of decorative joining used to combine cloth or lace. Also, *Brit.*, **fag′got·ing.**

Fagoting

fahl·band (fäl′bänd′; *Ger.* fäl′bänt′), *n.* *Mining.* a belt or zone of rock impregnated with metallic sulfides. [G: f. *fahl* ash-colored + *band* band, stripe]

Fahr., Fahrenheit (thermometer).

Fahr·en·heit (fâr′ən hīt′; *Ger.* fär′-), *adj.* **1.** denoting or pertaining to a thermometric scale in which the melting point of ice is 32 degrees above the zero, and the boiling point of water 212 degrees above the zero. See illus. under **thermometer.** —*n.* **2. Gabriel Daniel** (gä′brē ĕl′ dä′nē ĕl′), 1686–1736, German physicist who devised this scale and introduced the use of mercury in thermometers.

fa·ïence (fī äns′, fā-; *Fr.* fà yäṅs′), *n.* glazed earthenware or pottery, esp. a fine variety with highly colored designs. [t. F, orig. pottery of Faenza]

fail (fāl), *v.i.* **1.** to come short or be wanting in action, detail, or result; disappoint or prove lacking in what is attempted, expected, desired, or approved: *the crop failed, the experiment failed of success, he failed in history.* **2.** to be or become deficient or lacking; fall short; be insufficient or absent: *our supplies failed.* **3.** to fall off; dwindle; pass or die away. **4.** to lose strength or vigor; become weaker. **5.** to become unable to meet one's engagements, especially one's debts or business obligations; become insolvent or bankrupt. —*v.t.* **6.** to neglect to perform or observe: *he failed to come.* **7.** to prove of no use or help to, as some expected or usual resource: *his friends failed him, words failed him.* **8.** to declare (a person) unsuccessful in a test, course of study, etc. **9.** failure as to performance, occurrence, etc.: *pay him without fail.* [ME *faile(n)*, t. OF: m. *faillir*, g. var. of L *fallere* deceive, disappoint] —**Syn. 4.** decline, sink, wane. **7.** desert, forsake. —**Ant. 4.** improve. **7.** support.

fail·ing (fā′lĭng), *n.* **1.** act or state of one who or that which fails; failure. **2.** a defect; shortcoming; weakness. —*prep.* **3.** in the absence or default of: *failing payment, we shall sue.* —**fail′ing·ly**, *adv.* —**Syn. 2.** See **fault.**

faille (fīl; fāl; *Fr.* fà′y), *n.* a soft, transversely ribbed silk or rayon fabric. [t. F]

fail·ure (fāl′yər), *n.* **1.** act of failing; a proving unsuccessful; lack of success: *his effort ended in failure, the campaign was a failure.* **2.** nonperformance of something due or required: *a failure to do what one has promised, a failure to appear.* **3.** running short; insufficiency: *failure of crops, of supplies.* **4.** loss of strength, or vigor, etc.: *the failure of health.* **5.** condition of being bankrupt by reason of insolvency. **6.** a becoming insolvent or bankrupt: *the failure of a bank.* **7.** one who or that which proves unsuccessful. [t. AF: m. *failer*, orig. inf., var. of OF *faillir* FAIL] —**Syn. 2.** neglect, omission, dereliction. **4.** decline, decay, deterioration.

fain (fān), *adv.* **1.** *Poetic.* gladly; willingly (only with *would*, fol. by simple infinitive): *I would fain be with you.* —*adj.* **2.** *Rare.* content; willing (fol. by an infinitive). **3.** *Rare.* constrained; obliged. **4.** *Archaic* or *Dial.* glad; pleased. **5.** *Archaic* or *Dial.* desirous; eager. [ME; OE *fægn*, var. of *fægen.* Cf. Icel. *feginn* glad]

fai·né·ant (fā′nĭ ənt; *Fr.* fĕ nĕ äṅ′), *adj.* **1.** that does nothing; idle; indolent. —*n.* **2.** an idler. [F: f. s. *faire* do + *néant* nothing] —**fai′ne·an·cy**, *n.*

faint (fānt), *adj.* **1.** lacking brightness, vividness, clearness, loudness, strength, etc.: *a faint light, color, resemblance.* **2.** feeble; half-hearted: *faint resistance, faint* *praise.* **3.** feeling weak, dizzy, or exhausted; about to swoon: *faint with hunger.* **4.** lacking courage; cowardly; timorous: *faint heart.* —*v.i.* **5.** to lose consciousness temporarily; swoon. **6.** *Now Rare.* to lose brightness, vividness, etc. **7.** *Archaic.* to grow weak; lose spirit or courage. —*n.* **8.** temporary loss of consciousness; a swoon. [ME *faint, feint,* t. OF: feigned; hypocritical, sluggish, spiritless, pp. of *feindre* FEIGN] —**faint′er,** *n.* —**faint′ish,** *adj.* —**faint′ly,** *adv.* —**faint′ness,** *n.* —Syn. **1.** indistinct, ill-defined, dim, faded. **2.** faltering, irresolute, weak. **3.** feeble, languid.

faint-heart·ed (fānt′här′tĭd), *adj.* lacking courage; cowardly; timorous. —**faint′-heart′ed·ly,** *adv.* —**faint′-heart′ed·ness,** *n.*

faints (fānts), *n.pl.* the impure spirit which comes over first and last in distilling whiskey, etc. Also, **feints.**

fair[1] (fâr), *adj.* **1.** free from bias, dishonesty, or injustice: *a fair decision or judge.* **2.** that is legitimately sought, pursued, done, given, etc.; proper under the rules: *fair game, stroke, hit, etc.* **3.** moderately good, large, or satisfactory; not undesirable, but not excellent: *a fair income, appearance, reputation.* **4.** marked by favoring conditions; likely; promising: *in a fair way to succeed.* **5.** *Meteorol.* **a.** (of the sky) bright ; sunny; cloudless to half cloudy. **b.** (of the weather) fine; with no aspect of rain, snow, or hail; not stormy. **6.** unobstructed; not blocked up. **7.** without irregularity or unevenness: *a fair surface.* **8.** free from blemish, imperfection, or anything that impairs the appearance, quality, or character: *a fair copy.* **9.** clear; easy to read: *fair handwriting.* **10.** of a light hue; not dark: *fair skin.* **11.** beautiful; pleasing in appearance; attractive. **12.** seemingly good or sincere but not so: *fair promises.* **13.** courteous; civil: *fair words.* —*adv.* **14.** in a fair manner: *he doesn't play fair.* **15.** straight; directly, as in aiming or hitting. **16.** favorably; auspiciously: *to bid fair.* **17. fair and square,** honestly; justly; straightforwardly. —*n.* **18.** *Archaic.* that which is fair. **19.** *Archaic.* a woman. **20.** *Archaic.* a beloved woman, sweetheart. —*v.t.* **21** *Obs.* to make fair. —*r.i.* **22.** *Brit. Dial. and U.S. Colloq.* (of the weather) to clear. [ME; OE *fæger,* c. OHG *fagar*] —**fair′ness,** *n.* —Syn. **1.** unbiased, equitable, just, honest. FAIR, IMPARTIAL, DISINTERESTED, UNPREJUDICED refer to lack of bias in opinions, judgments, etc. FAIR implies the treating of all sides alike, justly and equitably: *fair play.* IMPARTIAL, like fair, implies showing no more favor to one side than another, but suggests particularly a judicial consideration of a case: *an impartial judge.* DISINTERESTED implies a fairness arising particularly from lack of desire to obtain a selfish advantage: *the motives of her guardian were entirely disinterested.* UNPREJUDICED means not influenced or swayed by bias, or by prejudice caused by irrelevant considerations: *an unprejudiced decision.* **3.** passable, tolerable, average, middling. **8.** clean, spotless, pure, untarnished, unsullied. **9.** legible, distinct. **10.** blond, pale. **11.** pretty, comely, lovely.

fair[2] (fâr), *n.* **1.** a competitive exhibition of farm products, live stock, etc. **2.** *Chiefly Brit.* a periodic gathering of buyers and sellers in an appointed place. **3.** an exhibition and sale of fancy articles to raise money, often for some charitable purpose. [ME *feire,* t. OF, g. L *feria* holiday]

fair ball, *Baseball.* any batted ball other than a foul.

Fair·banks (fâr′băngks′), *n.* **1.** a town in central Alaska, on the Tanana river. 5625 (prelim. 1950). **2. Douglas,** 1883–1939, U.S. motion picture actor.

fair catch, *Football.* a catch of the kickoff, or of a punt, wherein the catcher signals that he will not advance the ball and is therefore not interfered with.

fair copy, 1. a copy of a document made after final correction. **2.** the condition of such a copy.

Fair Deal, the principles of the liberal wing of the Democratic party under the leadership of President Harry S. Truman, consisting largely of a continuation and development of the principles of the New Deal.

Fair·fax (fâr′făks), *n.* **1. Thomas, 3rd Baron,** 1612–1671, British general and commander in chief of the army of Parliament against Charles I in the English Civil War. **2. Thomas, 6th Baron,** 1692–1782, British colonist in Virginia.

fair green, *Golf.* fairway (def. 2).

fair·ground (fâr′ground′), *n.* (*often pl.*) a place where fairs, horse races, etc., are held.

fair-haired (fâr′hârd′), *adj.* **1.** having light-colored hair. **2.** favorite: *to be someone's fair-haired boy.*

fair·ing[1] (fâr′ĭng), *n.* an exterior part of an airplane, etc., which reduces eddying and resulting drag. [f. FAIR[1], adj. (def. 7) + -ING[1]]

fair·ing[2] (fâr′ĭng), *n.* *Archaic.* a gift, esp. one given at or bought at a fair. [f. FAIR[2] + -ING[1]]

fair·ish (fâr′ĭsh), *adj.* moderately good, large, or well.

fair-lead (fâr′lēd′), *n.* *Naut.* a fitting such as a ring, thimble, or block, or a strip of board with holes in it, through which running rigging is passed to be guided and kept clear of obstructions and chafing. Also, **fair′-lead′-er.** [f. FAIR[1], adj. (def. 7) + LEAD[1]]

fair·ly (fâr′lĭ), *adv.* **1.** in a fair manner; justly; impartially. **2.** moderately; tolerably: *fairly good.* **3.** actually; completely: *the wheels fairly spun.* **4.** properly; legitimately. **5.** clearly; distinctly. **6.** *Obs.* softly. **7.** *Obs.* courteously.

fair-mind·ed (fâr′mīn′dĭd), *adj.* fair in mind or judgment; impartial; unprejudiced: *a wise and fair-minded judge.* —**fair′-mind′ed·ness,** *n.*

Fair·mont (fâr′mŏnt), *n.* a city in N West Virginia. 29,346 (1950).

Fair Oaks, a locality in E Virginia, near Richmond: battle (also called "Seven Pines"), 1862.

fair sex, women.

fair-spo·ken (fâr′spō′kən), *adj.* courteous, civil, or plausible in speech; smooth-tongued.

fair to middling, *U.S. Colloq.* tolerably good in appearance or quality; so so.

fair·way (fâr′wā′), *n.* **1.** an unobstructed passage or way. **2.** *Golf.* that part of the links between tees and putting greens where the grass is kept short. **3.** *Naut.* **a.** (in a harbor, river, etc.) the navigable portion or channel for vessels. **b.** the usual course taken by vessels, as in making a port.

fair-weath·er (fâr′wĕth′ər), *adj.* **1.** for fair weather only. **2.** weakening or failing in time of trouble: *he was surrounded by fair-weather friends.*

Fair-weath·er (fâr′wĕth′ər), *n.* **Mount,** a mountain in SE Alaska. 15,292 ft.

fair·y (fâr′ĭ), *n., pl.* **fairies,** *adj.* —*n.* **1.** one of a class of supernatural beings, generally conceived as of diminutive human form, having magical powers capriciously exercised for good or evil in human affairs. **2.** such beings collectively. —*adj.* **3.** having to do with fairies. **4.** of the nature of a fairy; fairylike. [ME, t. OF: m. *faerie,* der. *fae* FAY[1]] —**fair′y·like′,** *adj.* —Syn. **1.** fay, pixy, leprechaun, nix, nixie. FAIRY, BROWNIE, ELF, SPRITE are terms for imaginary beings usually less than human size thought to be helpful or harmful to mankind. FAIRY is the most general name for such beings: *a good fairy as a godmother, misadventures caused by an evil fairy.* A BROWNIE is a good-natured tiny man who appears usually at night to do household tasks: *perhaps the brownies will come and help us tonight.* ELF suggests a young, mischievous or roguish fairy: *that child is a perfect little elf.* SPRITE suggests a fairy of pleasing appearance, older than an elf, to be admired for ease and lightness of movement: it may, however, be impish or even hostile: *a dainty sprite.*

fair·y·hood (fâr′ĭhŏŏd′), *n.* **1.** fairy state or nature. **2.** fairies collectively.

fair·y·ism (fâr′ĭiz′əm), *n.* **1.** fairylike quality. **2.** belief in fairies.

fair·y·land (fâr′ĭländ′), *n.* **1.** the imaginary realm of the fairies. **2.** any enchanting, beautiful region: *the island was a veritable fairyland.*

fairy ring, a circle formed on the grass in a field by the growth of certain fungi, formerly supposed to be caused by fairies in their dances.

fairy tale, 1. a story about fairies. **2.** a statement or account of something imaginary, or incredible.

Fai·sal (fī′səl), *n.* 1885–1933, king of Syria in 1920, and king of Iraq, 1921–33. Also, **Feisal, Feisul.**

fait ac·com·pli (fĕ tå kôn plē′), *French.* an accomplished fact; a thing already done.

faith (fāth), *n.* **1.** confidence or trust in a person or thing. **2.** belief which is not based on proof. **3.** belief in the doctrines or teachings of religion. **4.** the doctrines which are or should be believed. **5.** a system of religious belief: *the Christian faith, the Jewish faith.* **6.** the obligation of loyalty or fidelity (to a person, promise, engagement, etc.): *to keep or break faith with.* **7.** the observance of this obligation: *to act in good or bad faith.* **8.** *Theol.* that trust in God and in his promises as made through Christ by which man is justified or saved. —*interj.* **9. in faith,** *Archaic.* in truth; indeed. [ME, t. OF: m. *feit,* g. L *fides*] —Syn. **5.** doctrine, tenet, creed, dogma, persuasion, religion.

faith cure, 1. a method of attempting to cure disease by prayer and religious faith. **2.** a cure thus effected.

faith·ful (fāth′fəl), *adj.* **1.** strict or thorough in the performance of duty. **2.** true to one's word, promises, vows, etc. **3.** full of or showing loyalty or fidelity. **4.** that may be relied upon, trusted, or believed. **5.** adhering or true to fact or an original: *a faithful account, a faithful copy.* **6.** *Obs.* full of faith; believing. —*n.* **7.** the body of loyal members of any party or group. **8. the faithful,** the believers, esp. **a.** the believing members of the Christian church or of some branch of it. **b.** the adherents of the Mohammedan faith. —**faith′-ful·ly,** *adv.* —**faith′ful·ness,** *n.* —Syn. **1.** true, devoted, stanch. **3.** FAITHFUL, CONSTANT, LOYAL imply qualities of stability, dependability, and devotion. FAITHFUL implies long-continued and steadfast fidelity to whatever one is bound to by a pledge, duty, or obligation: *a faithful friend.* CONSTANT suggests firmness and steadfastness in attachment: *a constant affection.* LOYAL implies unswerving allegiance to a person, organization, cause, or idea: *loyal to one's associates, one's country.* **4.** trustworthy, trusty, reliable. **5.** accurate, precise, exact. —Ant. **1.** irresponsible. **4.** undependable.

faith·less (fāth′lĭs), *adj.* **1.** not adhering to allegiance, promises, vows, or duty: *a faithless wife or servant.* **2.** that cannot be relied on or trusted: *faithless coward.* **3.** without trust or belief. **4.** without religious faith. **5.** (among Christians) without Christian faith. —**faith′-less·ly,** *adv.* —**faith′less·ness,** *n.* —Syn. **1.** false, inconstant, fickle; disloyal, perfidious, treacherous.

fai·tour (fā′tər), *n.* *Obs.* an impostor, esp. a vagabond. [ME, t. AF: impostor, var. of OF *faitor* doer, maker, g. L *factor*]

Fai·yum (fī yōōm′), *n.* See **El Faiyum.**

fake (fāk), *v.,* **faked, faking,** *n., adj. Colloq.* —*v.t.* **1.** to get up, prepare, or make (something specious, deceptive, or fraudulent). **2.** to conceal the defects of, usually in order to deceive. **3.** to pretend; simulate: *to fake illness.* —*v.i.* **4.** to fake something; pretend. —*n.* **5.** something faked up; anything made to appear otherwise than it actually is. **6.** one who fakes. —*adj.* **7.** designed to deceive or cheat. [orig. obscure; ? var. of obs. *feak, feague,* t. D: m. *vegen* furbish up]

fake[2] (fāk), *n., v.,* **faked, faking.** *Naut.* —*n.* **1.** one of the rings or windings of a coiled cable or hawser. —*v.t.* **2.** to lay (a rope, cable, etc.) in a coil to prepare it for running. [orig. obscure]

fak·er (fā′kər), *n. Colloq.* **1.** one who fakes. **2.** a petty swindler. **3.** a peddler or street vendor.

fa·kir (fəkĭr′, fā′kər), *n.* **1.** a Mohammedan or Hindu religious ascetic or mendicant monk. **2.** a member of any Islamic religious order. Also, **fa·keer′.** [t. Ar.: m. *faqīr* poor]

fa-la (fä lä′), *n.* **1.** a text or refrain in old songs. **2.** an old kind of part song or madrigal. Also, **fal la.**

Fa·lange (fā′lănj; *Sp.* fä län′hě), *n.* the Fascist party in power in Spain since the Civil War of 1936–39.

Fa·lan·gist (fə lăn′jĭst), *n.* a member of the Falange.

fal·ba·la (făl′bə lə), *n.* a flounce; a furbelow. [t. F; orig. uncert.]

fal·cate (făl′kāt), *adj.* hooked; curved like a scythe or sickle; falciform: *a falcate part or organ.* [t. L: m.s. *fal-cātus,* der. *falx* sickle]

fal·chion (fôl′chən, -shən), *n.* **1.** a broad, short sword having a convex edge curving sharply to the point. **2.** *Poetic.* a sword. [t. It.: m. *falcione* (der. *falce* sickle, g. L *falx*); r. ME *fauchoun,* t. OF]

fal·ci·form (făl′sə fôrm′), *adj.* sickle-shaped; falcate. [f. s. L *falx* sickle + -(I)FORM]

fal·con (fôl′kən, fô′kən), *n.* **1.** any of various diurnal birds of prey of the family *Falconidae,* esp. of the genus *Falco,* as the **peregrine falcon** (*F. peregrinus*), having long, pointed wings and a notched bill, and taking its quarry as it moves. **2.** any of various hawks used in falconry, and trained to hunt other birds and game (properly, the female only, the male being known as a *tercel*). **3.** an old kind of cannon. [t. LL: s. *falco* (der. L *falx* sickle); r. ME *faucon,* t. OF]

Peregrine falcon,
Falco peregrinus
(16½ in. long)

fal·con·er (fôl′kən ər, fô′kən-), *n.* **1.** one who hunts with falcons; one who follows the sport of hawking. **2.** one who breeds and trains hawks for hunting.

fal·co·net[1] (fôl′kə nĕt′, fô′kə-), *n.* any of several very small Asiatic birds of prey principally of the genus *Microhierax.* [f. FALCON + -ET]

fal·co·net[2] (fôl′kə nĕt′, fô′kə-), *n.* an old kind of light cannon. [t. It.: m. *falconetto,* dim. of *falcone* FALCON]

fal·con-gen·tle (fôl′kən jĕn′təl, fô′kən-), *n.* **1.** the female of the peregrine falcon. **2.** any female falcon. [trans. of F *faucon gentil*]

fal·con·i·form (făl′kən ə fôrm′), *adj. Ornith.* of or belonging to the family *Falconidae,* which includes falcons, hawks, etc. [f. FALCON + -(I)FORM]

fal·con·ry (fôl′kən rĭ, fô′-), *n.* **1.** the art of training falcons to attack wild fowl or game. **2.** the sport of hawking.

fal·de·ral (făl′də răl′), *n.* **1.** meaningless syllables forming the refrain of various old songs. **2.** mere nonsense; foolish talk or ideas. **3.** a trifle; gimcrack; gewgaw. Also, **fal·de·rol** (făl′də rŏl′), **folderol.**

fald·stool (fôld′stōōl′), *n.* **1.** a chair or seat, orig. one capable of being folded, used by a bishop or other prelate when officiating in his own church away from the throne, or in a church not his own. **2.** a movable folding stool or desk at which worshipers kneel during certain acts of devotion. **3.** such a stool placed at the south side of the altar, at which the kings or queens of England kneel at their coronation. **4.** a desk at which the litany is said or sung. [OE *fealdestōl,* c. OHG *faltistuol* folding chair. See FOLD[1], STOOL]

Fa·lie·ri (fä lyĕ′rē), *n.* **Marino** (mä rē′nô), c1278–1355, doge of Venice in 1354.

Fal·ken·hayn (făl′kən hīn′), *n.* **Erich von** (ā′rĭKH fən), 1861–1922, German general of World War I.

Fal·kirk (fôl′kûrk, fô′kûrk), *n.* a city in central Scotland, in Stirling county: site of the defeat of the Scots under Wallace by the English, 1298. 36,707 (1939).

Falk·land Islands (fôk′lənd), a group of about 200 islands in the S Atlantic, ab. 300 mi. E of the Strait of Magellan: a British crown colony; the British defeated the Germans in a naval battle near here, 1914. 2239 pop. (est. 1946); 4618 sq. mi. *Cap.:* Stanley.

Falk·ner (fôk′nər), *n.* **William.** See **Faulkner.**

fall (fôl), *v.,* **fell, fallen, falling,** *n.* —*v.i.* **1.** to descend from a higher to a lower place or position through loss or lack of support; drop. **2.** to come down suddenly from a standing or erect position: *to fall*

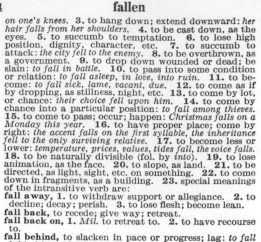

on one's knees. **3.** to hang down; extend downward: *her hair falls from her shoulders.* **4.** to be cast down, as the eyes. **5.** to succumb to temptation. **6.** to lose high position, dignity, character, etc. **7.** to succumb to attack: *the city fell to the enemy.* **8.** to be overthrown, as a government. **9.** to drop down wounded or dead; be slain: *to fall in battle.* **10.** to pass into some condition or relation: *to fall asleep, in love, into ruin.* **11.** to become: *to fall sick, lame, vacant, due.* **12.** to come as if by dropping, as stillness, night, etc. **13.** to come by lot, or chance: *their choice fell upon him.* **14.** to come by chance into a particular position: *to fall among thieves.* **15.** to come to pass; occur; happen: *Christmas falls on a Monday this year.* **16.** to have proper place; come by right: *the accent falls on the first syllable, the inheritance fell to the only surviving relative.* **17.** to become less or lower: *temperature, prices, values, tides fall, the voice falls.* **18.** to be naturally divisible (fol. by *into*). **19.** to lose animation, as the face. **20.** to slope, as land. **21.** to be directed, as light, sight, etc. on something. **22.** to come down in fragments, as a building. **23.** special meanings of the intransitive verb are:

fall away, 1. to withdraw support or allegiance. **2.** to decline; decay; perish. **3.** to lose flesh; become lean.

fall back, to recede; give way; retreat.

fall back on, 1. *Mil.* to retreat to. **2.** to have recourse to.

fall behind, to slacken in pace or progress; lag: *to fall behind in work, payments, etc.*

fall down, *Colloq.* to fail: *to fall down on the job.*

fall for, *Colloq.* **1.** to be deceived by. **2.** to fall in love with.

fall foul, 1. to come into collision, as ships; become entangled. **2.** to come into conflict; have trouble. **3.** to make an attack.

fall in, 1. to sink inward; fall to pieces inwardly. **2.** to take one's proper place in line, as a soldier. **3.** to come together; meet; agree.

fall off, 1. to drop off. **2.** to separate or withdraw. **3.** to become estranged; withdraw from allegiance. **4.** to decline in vigor, interest, etc. **5.** to decrease in number, amount, intensity, etc.; diminish. **6.** *Naut.* to deviate from the course to which the head of the ship was directed; fall to leeward.

fall on or **upon, 1.** to assault; attack. **2.** to light upon; chance upon.

fall out, 1. to drop out of one's place in line, as a soldier. **2.** to disagree; quarrel. **3.** to occur; happen; turn out.

fall short, 1. to fail to reach a particular amount, degree, standard, etc. **2.** to prove insufficient; give out.

fall through, to come to naught; fail; miscarry.

fall to, to betake or apply oneself; begin: *to fall to work, argument, blows, etc.*

fall under, to be classed as; be included in.

—*v.t.* **24.** to chop down or fell, as a tree.

—*n.* **25.** act of falling, or dropping from a higher to a lower place or position; descent, as of rain, snow, etc. **26.** the quantity that descends. **27.** *Chiefly U.S.* autumn. **28.** a becoming less; a lowering; a sinking to a lower level. **29.** the distance through which anything falls. **30.** (*usually pl.*) a cataract or waterfall: *Niagara Falls.* **31.** downward slope or declivity. **32.** a falling from an erect position, as to the ground: *to have a bad fall.* **33.** a hanging down; a dropping. **34.** a succumbing to temptation; lapse into sin. **35.** *Theol.* the lapse of mankind into a state of natural or innate sinfulness through the transgression of Adam and Eve: *the fall of man.* **36.** surrender or capture, as of a city. **37.** proper place: *the fall of an accent on a syllable.* **38.** *Wrestling.* **a.** the fact or a method of being thrown on one's back by an opponent. **b.** a bout: *to try a fall.* **39.** a loosely hanging veil. **40.** *Mach., etc.* the part of the rope of a tackle to which the power is applied in hoisting. **41.** (*pl.*) *Naut.* **a.** the apparatus used in lowering or hoisting a ship's boat, cargo, etc. **b.** the break in the line of a ship between decks of different levels. **42.** *Hunting.* a deadfall. [ME *falle(n),* OE *feallan* c. G *fallen*]

fal la, fa-la.

Fal·la (fä′lyä), *n.* **Manuel de** (mä nwĕl′ dĕ), 1876–1946, Spanish composer.

fal·la·cious (fə lā′shəs), *adj.* **1.** deceptive; misleading: *fallacious evidence.* **2.** containing a fallacy; logically unsound: *fallacious arguments, reasoning, etc.* **3.** disappointing; delusive: *a fallacious peace.* —**fal·la′cious·ly,** *adv.* —**fal·la′cious·ness,** *n.*

fal·la·cy (făl′ə sĭ), *n., pl.* **-cies.** **1.** a deceptive, misleading, or false notion, belief, etc.: *a popular fallacy.* **2.** a misleading or unsound argument. **3.** deceptive, misleading, or false nature. **4.** *Logic.* any of various types of erroneous reasoning that render arguments logically unsound. **5.** *Obs.* deception. [ME *falacye,* t. L: m. *fallācia* deceit; r. ME *fallace,* t. OF]

fal·lal (făl′lăl′), *n.* **1.** a bit of finery; a showy article of dress. **2.** a piece of ribbon, worn with streaming ends as an ornament in the 17th century. —*adj.* **3.** finicky; foppish; trifling. [? var. of FALBALA]

fal·lal·er·y (făl′lăl′ər ĭ), *n.* fallals collectively; finery.

fall dandelion, a chicoriaceous herb, *Leontodon autumnalis,* with yellow flowers, a native of Europe naturalized in the U.S.

fall·en (fô′lən), *v.* **1.** pp. of **fall.** —*adj.* **2.** that has dropped or come down from a higher place or level, or from an upright position. **3.** on the ground; prostrate;

down flat. **4.** degraded: *a fallen woman.* **5.** overthrown; destroyed: *a fallen city.* **6.** dead: *fallen in battle.*

fall·er (fôl′ər), *n.* **1.** one who or that which falls. **2.** any of various devices that operate by falling.

fall-fish (fôl′fĭsh′), *n., pl.* **-fishes,** (*esp. collectively*) **-fish.** a large minnow, *Leucosomus corporalis,* of the eastern U.S.

fall guy, *U.S. Slang.* an easy victim; scapegoat.

fal·li·ble (făl′ə bəl), *adj.* **1.** liable to be deceived or mistaken; liable to err. **2.** liable to be erroneous or false. [t. ML: m.s. *fallibilis,* der. L *fallere* deceive] **—fal′-li·bil′i·ty, fal′li·ble·ness,** *n.* **—fal′li·bly,** *adv.*

falling sickness, *Now Rare.* epilepsy.

falling star, an incandescent meteor; a shooting star.

Fal·lo·pi·an tubes (fə lō′pʹĭ ən), *Anat., Zool.* the uterine tubes, a pair of slender oviducts leading from the body cavity to the uterus, for transport and fertilization of ova. [named after *Fallopius,* Italian anatomist (1523–62)]

fal·low¹ (făl′ō), *adj.* **1.** plowed and left unseeded for a season or more; uncultivated. **—n.** **2.** land that has lain unseeded for a season or more after plowing and harrowing. **3.** the method of allowing land to lie for a season or more untilled in order to increase its productivity. **—v.t.** **4.** to make (land) fallow for agricultural purposes. [ME *falwe,* OE *fealga,* pl., fallow land]

fal·low² (făl′ō), *adj.* pale-yellow; light-brown; dun. [ME *fal(o)we,* OE *fealu,* c. G *fahl, falb* fallow]

fallow deer, a Eurasian deer, *Dama dama,* with a fallow or yellowish coat.

Fall River, a seaport in SE Massachusetts, on an arm of Narragansett Bay. 111,963 (1950).

Fal·mouth (făl′məth), *n.* a seaport in SW England, in Cornwall. 16,211 (1939).

Fallow deer, Dama dama (3 ft. high at the shoulder, antlers ab. 2 ft. long)

false (fôls), *adj.,* **falser, falsest. 1.** not true or correct; erroneous: *a false statement or accusation.* **2.** uttering or declaring what is untrue: *false prophets, a false witness.* **3.** deceitful; treacherous; faithless: *a false friend.* **4.** deceptive; used to deceive or mislead: *false weights, to give a false impression.* **5.** not genuine: *a false signature, false diamonds, false teeth.* **6.** substitute or supplementary, esp. temporarily: *false supports for a bridge.* **7.** *Biol.* improperly so called, as from deceptive resemblance to something that properly bears the name: *the false acacia.* **8.** not properly adjusted, as a balance. **9.** inaccurate in pitch, as a musical note. [ME and OE *fals,* t. L: s. *falsus* feigned, deceptive, false, orig. pp] **—false′ly,** *adv.* **—false′ness,** *n.* **—Syn. 1.** mistaken, incorrect, wrong, untrue. **2.** untruthful, lying, mendacious. **3.** insincere, hypocritical, disingenuous, disloyal, unfaithful, inconstant, recreant, perfidious, traitorous. **4.** misleading, fallacious. **5.** artificial, spurious, bogus, forged. FALSE, SHAM, COUNTERFEIT agree in referring to something that is not genuine. FALSE is used mainly of imitations of concrete objects; it often implies an intent to deceive: *false teeth, false hair.* SHAM is rarely used of concrete objects and has nearly always the suggestion of intent to deceive: *sham title, sham tears.* COUNTERFEIT always has the implication of cheating; it is used particularly of spurious imitation of coins, paper money, etc.

false bottom, a horizontal partition in the lower part of a box, trunk, vessel, etc., esp. one forming a secret compartment.

false cirrus, *Meteorol.* cirruslike clouds found over thunder clouds.

false colors, 1. another nation's flag. **2.** deceptive appearance; pretense.

false face, a mask.

false foxglove, any plant of the North American scrophulariaceous genus *Gerardia* (*Dasistoma, Aureolaria*), related to the foxglove.

false-heart·ed (fôls′här′tĭd), *adj.* having a false or treacherous heart; deceitful; perfidious.

false·hood (fôls′hŏŏd), *n.* **1.** lack of conformity to truth or fact. **2.** something false; an untrue idea, belief, etc. **3.** a false statement; a lie. **4.** act of lying or making false statements. **5.** *Rare.* falseness. **6.** *Obs.* deception. **—Syn. 3.** FALSEHOOD, FIB, LIE, UNTRUTH refer to something untrue or incorrect. A FALSEHOOD is a statement that distorts or suppresses the truth, in order to deceive: *to tell a falsehood about one's ancestry, in order to escape punishment.* A FIB denotes a trivial falsehood, and is often used to characterize that which is not strictly true: *a polite fib.* A LIE is a vicious falsehood: *to tell a lie about one's neighbor.* An UNTRUTH is an incorrect statement, either intentionally misleading (less harsh, however, than falsehood or lie) or arising from misunderstanding or ignorance: *I'm afraid you are telling an untruth.* **4.** untruthfulness, insincerity, mendacity. **—Ant. 3.** truth.

false imprisonment, *Law.* the imprisonment of a person contrary to law.

false keel, a narrow extension of the keel, to protect a ship's bottom and reduce the leeway.

false pretenses, *Law.* the obtaining of title to money or property by the use of false representations, forged documents, or similar illegal device.

false relation, *Music.* cross relation.

false ribs, *Anat.* the five lower pairs of ribs, which are not attached to the sternum.

false step, 1. a stumble. **2.** an unwise act.

fal·set·to (fôl sĕt′ō), *n., pl.* **-tos,** *adj., adv.* **—n. 1.** an unnaturally or artificially high-pitched voice or register, esp. in a man. **2.** one who sings with such a voice. **—adj. 3.** having the quality and compass of, or pertaining to, such a voice. **4.** singing in a falsetto. **—adv. 5.** in a falsetto: *to speak falsetto.* [t. It., dim. of *falso* FALSE]

false vampire, a bat of any of the three Old World genera, *Megaderma, Macroderma,* and *Lyroderma,* large carnivorous forms erroneously reputed to suck blood.

fal·si·fy (fôl′sə fī′), *v.,* **-fied, -fying. —v.t. 1.** to make false or incorrect, esp. so as to deceive. **2.** to alter fraudulently. **3.** to represent falsely; misrepresent. **4.** to show or prove to be false; disprove. **—v.i. 5.** to make false statements. [t. F: m. *falsifier,* t. LL: m. *falsificāre,* der. L *falsificus* that acts falsely] **—fal·si·fi·ca·tion** (fôl′sə fə kā′shən), *n.* **—fal′si·fi′er,** *n.*

fal·si·ty (fôl′sə tĭ), *n., pl.* **-ties. 1.** the quality of being false; incorrectness; untruthfulness; deceitfulness; treachery. **2.** something false; a falsehood. [t. L: m.s. *falsitas*]

Fal·staff (fôl′stăf, -stäf), *n.* the jovial fat knight of brazen assurance and few scruples in Shakespeare's *Henry IV* and *Merry Wives of Windsor.* **—Fal·staff·i·an** (fôl stăf′ĭ ən), *adj.*

Fal·ster (fäl′stər), *n.* an island in SE Denmark. 44,198 pop. (1940); 198 sq. mi.

falt·boat (fält′bōt′), *n.* a folding boat similar to a kayak but more easily carried about. Also, **foldboat.** [t. G: m. *faltboot*]

fal·ter (fôl′tər), *v.i.* **1.** to hesitate or waver in action, purpose, etc.; give way. **2.** to speak hesitatingly or brokenly. **3.** to become unsteady in movement, as a person, an animal, or the legs, steps, etc.: *with faltering steps.* **—v.t. 4.** to utter hesitatingly or brokenly. **—n. 5.** act of faltering; an unsteadiness of gait, voice, action, etc. **6.** a faltering sound. [ME, ? t. Scand.; cf. Icel. *faltrask,* refl., be cumbered] **—fal′ter·ing·ly,** *adv.* **—Syn. 1.** vacillate. **2.** stammer, stutter.

F.A.M., Free and Accepted Masons. Also, **F. & A.M.**

fame (fām), *n., v.,* **famed, faming. —n. 1.** widespread reputation, esp. of a favorable character: *literary fame, to seek fame.* **2.** reputation; common estimation; opinion generally held. **—v.t. 3.** to spread the fame of; make famous: *a place famed throughout the world.* [ME, t. obs. F, t. L: m. *fāma* report, fame] **—fame′less,** *adj.* **—Syn. 1.** repute, notoriety, celebrity, renown, eminence, honor, glory. **—Ant. 1.** obscurity; ignominy.

famed (fāmd), *adj.* famous.

Fa·meuse (fə mūz′; *Fr.* fȧ mœz′), *n.* an American variety of red apple which ripens in the early winter. [t. F. fem. of *fameux* famous]

fa·mil·ial (fə mĭl′yəl), *adj.* **1.** of or pertaining to a family. **2.** appearing in individuals by heredity: *a familial disease.*

fa·mil·iar (fə mĭl′yər), *adj.* **1.** commonly or generally known or seen: *a familiar sight, a sight familiar to us all.* **2.** well-acquainted; thoroughly conversant: *to be familiar with a subject, book, method, tool, etc.* **3.** easy; informal; unceremonious; unconstrained: *to write in a familiar style.* **4.** closely intimate: *a familiar friend, to be on familiar terms.* **5.** unduly intimate; taking liberties; presuming. **6.** domesticated; tame. **7.** *Rare.* of or pertaining to a family or household. **—n. 8.** a familiar friend or associate. **9.** a familiar spirit. **10.** *Rom. Cath. Ch.* **a.** an officer of the Inquisition, employed to arrest accused or suspected persons. **b.** one who belongs to the household of the Pope or of a bishop, rendering domestic though not menial service. [t. L: s. *familiāris* belonging to a household, private; r, ME *familier,* t. OF] **—fa·mil′iar·ly,** *adv.* **—Syn. 1.** common, well-known, frequent. **4.** close, friendly, fraternal. FAMILIAR, CONFIDENTIAL, INTIMATE suggest a long association between persons. FAMILIAR means well acquainted with another person: *a familiar friend.* CONFIDENTIAL suggests a sense of mutual trust which extends to the sharing of confidences and secrets: *a confidential advisor.* INTIMATE suggests close acquaintance or connection, often based on interest, sympathy, or affection: *intimate and affectionate letters.* **5.** free, forward, intrusive, bold. **—Ant. 1.** strange. **2.** unacquainted. **5.** well-bred.

fa·mil·i·ar·i·ty (fə mĭl′ĭ ăr′ə tĭ), *n., pl.* **-ties. 1.** close acquaintance; thorough knowledge of (a thing, subject, etc.). **2.** undue intimacy; freedom of behavior justified only by the most intimate friendly relations. **3.** (*often pl.*) an instance or manifestation of such freedom, as in action or speech. **4.** absence of formality or ceremony: *to be on terms of familiarity with someone.* **—Syn. 1.** intimacy, friendship, fellowship. **2.** liberty, unreserve, disrespect. **4.** informality, freedom, unconstraint.

fa·mil·iar·ize (fə mĭl′yər īz′), *v.t.,* **-ized, -izing. 1.** to make (a person) familiarly acquainted or conversant, as with something. **2.** to make (something) well-known; bring into common knowledge or use. **3.** *Rare.* to make familiar; establish (a person) in friendly intimacy. **—v.i. 4.** *Now Rare.* to associate in a familiar way. **—fa·mil′iar·i·za′tion,** *n.*

familiar spirit, a supernatural spirit or demon supposed to attend on or serve a person.

fam·i·ly (făm′ə lĭ, făm′lĭ), *n., pl.* **-lies. 1.** parents and their children, whether dwelling together or not. **2.** one's children collectively. **3.** any group of persons closely related by blood, as parents, children, uncles, aunts, and cousins. **4.** all those persons descended from a common progenitor. **5.** *Chiefly Brit.* descent, esp. good or noble descent: *young men of family.* **6.** *Biol.* the usual major subdivision of an order or suborder, commonly comprising a plurality of genera: e.g. *Equidae* (horses), *Formicidae* (the ants), *Orchidaceae* (the orchids). Names of animal families end in *-idae*, of plant families in *-aceae.* **7.** the group of persons who form a household under one head, including parents, children, servants, etc. **8.** the staff, or body of assistants, of an official. **9.** a group of related things. **10.** (in the classification of languages) a number of languages all of which are more closely related to each other than any of them are to any language outside the group, usually a major grouping admitting of subdivisions: *English is of the Indo-European family.* [ME *familie,* t. L: m.s. *familia* the servants of a household, household, family]

family circle, 1. the closely related members of a family as a group: *a scandal known only within the family circle.* **2.** a gallery in a theater, etc., esp. the topmost one.

family name, 1. the hereditary surname of a family. **2.** a frequent Christian, or first name, in a family.

family skeleton, a secret or hidden source of shame to a family.

family tree, a genealogical chart showing the ancestry, descent, and relationship of all members of a family.

fam·ine (făm′ĭn), *n.* **1.** extreme and general scarcity of food. **2.** any extreme and general scarcity. **3.** extreme hunger; starvation. [ME, t. F, der. *faim* hunger, g. L *fames*]

fam·ish (făm′ĭsh), *v.t., v.i.* **1.** to suffer, or cause to suffer, extreme hunger; starve. **2.** to starve to death. [f. ME *fame*(n) famish (ult. der. L *fames* hunger) + -ish²] —**fam′ish·ment,** *n.*

fam·ished (făm′ĭsht), *adj.* very hungry. —Syn. See **hungry.**

fa·mous (fā′məs), *adj.* **1.** celebrated in fame or public report; renowned; well-known: *a famous victory.* **2.** *Colloq.* first-rate; excellent. **3.** *Obs.* notorious (in an unfavorable sense). [ME, t. AF, t. L: m.s. *fāmōsus,* der. *fāma* fame] —**fa′mous·ly,** *adv.* —**fa′mous·ness,** *n.* —Syn. **1.** famed, notable. FAMOUS, CELEBRATED, EMINENT, DISTINGUISHED refer to someone or something widely and favorably known. FAMOUS is the general word: *a famous lighthouse.* CELEBRATED originally referred to something commemorated, but now usually refers to someone or something widely known for conspicuous merit, services, etc.: *a celebrated writer.* EMINENT implies high standing among one's contemporaries, esp. in his own profession or craft: *an eminent physician.* DISTINGUISHED adds to *eminent* the idea of honors conferred more or less publicly: *a distinguished scientist.* —Ant. **1.** unknown, obscure.

fam·u·lus (făm′yə ləs), *n., pl.* **-li** (-lī′). a servant or attendant, esp. of a scholar or a magician. [t. L]

fan¹ (făn), *n., v.,* **fanned, fanning.** —*n.* **1.** any device for causing a current of air by the movement of a broad surface or a number of such surfaces. **2.** an object of feathers, leaves, paper, cloth, etc., for causing a cooling current of air. **3.** anything resembling such an implement, as the tail of a bird. **4.** any of various devices consisting essentially of a series of radiating vanes or blades attached to and revolving with a central hublike portion, and used to produce a current of air. **5.** a series of revolving blades supplying air for winnowing or cleaning grain. —*v.t.* **6.** to move or agitate (the air) with, or as with, a fan. **7.** to cause air to blow upon, as from a fan; cool or refresh with, or as with, a fan. **8.** to stir to activity with, or as with, a fan: *fan a flame, emotions, etc.* **9.** (of a breeze, etc.) to blow upon, as if driven by a fan. **10.** to spread out like a fan. **11.** *Agric.* to winnow, esp. by an artificial current of air. **12.** *Baseball.* to strike out (a batter). —*v.i.* **13.** to spread out like a fan (fol. by *out*). **14.** *Baseball.* to strike out. [ME; OE *fann,* t. L: m.s. *vannus* fan for winnowing grain] —**fan′like′,** *adj.*

fan² (făn), *n. Colloq.* an enthusiastic devotee or follower: *a baseball fan, a movie fan.* [short for FANATIC]

fa·nat·ic (fə năt′ĭk), *n.* **1.** a person with an extreme and unreasoning enthusiasm or zeal, esp. in religious matters. —*adj.* **2.** fanatical. [t. L: s. *fānāticus* pertaining to a temple, inspired by a divinity, frantic]

fa·nat·i·cal (fə năt′ə kəl), *adj.* **1.** actuated or characterized by an extreme, unreasoning enthusiasm or zeal, esp. in religious matters. **2.** pertaining to or characteristic of a fanatic. —**fa·nat′i·cal·ly,** *adv.* —Syn. **1.** See **intolerant. 2.** See **radical.**

fa·nat·i·cism (fə năt′ə sĭz′əm), *n.* fanatical character, spirit, or conduct.

fa·nat·i·cize (fə năt′ə sīz′), *v.,* **-cized, -cizing.** —*v.t.* **1.** to make fanatical. —*v.i.* **2.** to act with or show fanaticism.

fan·cied (făn′sĭd), *adj.* imaginary: *fancied grievances.*

fan·ci·er (făn′sĭ ər), *n.* **1.** a person having a liking for or interest in something, as some class of animals or plants. **2.** one who breeds and sells birds, dogs, etc. **3.** one who is under the influence of his fancy.

fan·ci·ful (făn′sĭ fəl), *adj.* **1.** exhibiting fancy; quaint or odd in appearance: *a fanciful design.* **2.** suggested by fancy; imaginary; unreal. **3.** led by fancy rather than by reason and experience; whimsical: *a fanciful mind.* —**fan′ci·ful·ly,** *adv.* —**fan′ci·ful·ness,** *n.*

fan·ci·less (făn′sĭ lĭs), *adj.* without fancy or imagination.

fan·cy (făn′sĭ), *n., pl.* **-cies,** *adj.,* **-cier, -ciest,** *v.,* **-cied, -cying,** *interj.* —*n.* **1.** imagination, esp. as exercised in a capricious or desultory manner. **2.** the faculty of creating illustrative or decorative imagery, as in poetical or literary composition, as distinct from the power of producing ideal creations consistent with reality (imagination). **3.** a mental image or conception. **4.** an idea or opinion with little foundation; a hallucination. **5.** a caprice; whim; vagary. **6.** capricious preference; inclination; a liking: *to take a fancy to something.* **7.** critical judgment; taste. **8.** the breeding of animals to develop points of beauty or excellence. **9.** *Obs.* love. —*adj.* **10.** adapted to please the taste or fancy; of superfine quality: *fancy goods, work, fruits, etc.* **11.** ornamental. **12.** imaginative. **13.** depending on fancy or caprice; whimsical; irregular. **14.** bred to develop points of beauty or excellence, as an animal. —*v.t.* **15.** to form a conception of; picture to oneself: *fancy living with him all your life!* **16.** to believe without being sure or certain. **17.** to take a liking to; like. **18.** to breed to develop a special type of animal. —*interj.* **19.** an expression of mild surprise. [contr. of FANTASY] —Syn. **2.** FANCY, FANTASY, IMAGINATION refer to qualities in literary or other artistic composition. The creations of FANCY are casual, whimsical, and often amusing, being at once less profound and less inspirational than those of imagination: *letting one's fancy play freely on a subject, an impish fancy.* FANTASY now usually suggests an unrestrained or extravagant fancy, bordering on caprice: *the use of fantasy in art brings strange results.* The name and concept of creative IMAGINATION are less than two hundred years old; previously only the *reproductive* aspect had been recognized, hardly to be distinguished from memory. "Creative imagination" suggests that the memories of sights and experiences may so blend in the mind of the writer or artist as to produce something that has never existed before—often a hitherto unperceived vision of the realities of life: *to use imagination in portraying character and action.*

fancy ball, a ball at which costumes are worn.

fancy dress, dress chosen in accordance with the wearer's fancy, for wear at a ball or the like, as that characteristic of a particular period or place, class of persons, or historical or fictitious character.

fan·cy-free (făn′sĭ frē′), *adj.* free from any influence, esp. love.

fan·cy·work (făn′sĭ wûrk′), *n.* ornamental needlework.

fan·dan·go (făn dăng′gō), *n., pl.* **-gos. 1.** a lively Spanish or Spanish-American dance in triple time. **2.** a piece of music for such a dance or with its rhythm. **3.** a ball or dance. [t. Sp., from W Ind.]

fan delta, an alluvial cone, partially submerged.

fane (fān), *n. Archaic or Poetic.* **1.** a temple. **2.** a church. [t. L: m.s. *fānum* temple]

fa·ne·ga (fä nĕ′gä), *n.* **1.** a unit of dry measure in Spanish-speaking countries, equal in Spain to 1.58 U.S. bushels. **2.** a Mexican unit of land measure, equal to 8.81 acres. [t. Sp.]

fa·ne·ga·da (fä′nĕ gä′dä), *n.* a unit of land measure in Spanish-speaking countries varying from 1¼ to 1¾ acres. [t. Sp.]

Fan·euil (făn′əl, -yəl), *n.* **Peter,** 1700–43, colonial American merchant, founder of Faneuil Hall, in Boston.

Faneuil Hall, a market house and hall in Boston, Massachusetts, called "the Cradle of Liberty" because it was used as a meeting place by American patriots in the Revolutionary period.

fan·fare (făn′fâr), *n.* **1.** a flourish or short air played on trumpets or the like. **2.** an ostentatious flourish or parade. [t. F, der. *fanfarer* blow a fanfare, der. s. *fanfaron* FANFARON]

fan·fa·ron (făn′fə rŏn′), *n.* **1.** a braggart. **2.** a fanfare. [t. F, t. Sp.: m. *fanfarrón,* der. Ar. *farfâr* talkative]

fan·fa·ron·ade (făn′fə rə năd′), *n.* bragging; bravado; bluster. [t. F: m. *fanfaronnade,* t. Sp.: m. *fanfarronada,* der. *fanfarrón* FANFARON]

fang (făng), *n.* **1.** one of the long, sharp, hollow or grooved teeth of a snake, by which venom is injected. **2.** a canine tooth. **3.** the root of a tooth. **4.** a doglike tooth. **5.** a pointed tapering part of a thing. **6.** *Mach.* a tang of a tool. [ME and OE, c. G *fang*] —**fanged** (făngd), *adj.* —**fang′less,** *adj.* —**fang′like′,** *adj.*

Head of rattlesnake
F, Fangs; P, Poison sac; D, Poison duct; M, Muscle

fan·gle (făng′gəl), *n.* a fashion: *new fangles of dress.*

fan·light (făn′līt′), *n.* a fan-shaped or other window above a door or other opening. (In British usage *fanlight* often equals U.S. *transom.*)

fan·ner (făn′ər), *n.* one who or that which fans.

fanning mill, a machine for cleaning grain by the action of riddles and sieves and an air blast.

fan·on (făn′ən), *n. Eccles.* **1.** a maniple. **2.** a striped scarflike vestment worn by the pope over the alb when celebrating solemn pontifical mass. [ME, t. F, t. ML: s. *fano,* t. OHG: flag, cloth, c. VANE]

fan palm, any palm with fan-shaped leaves, as the talipot and numerous others.

fan·tail (făn′tāl′), *n.* **1.** a tail, end, or part shaped like a fan. **2.** a fancy breed of domestic pigeons with a fan-shaped tail. **3.** any of various small birds having fanlike tails, as the Old World flycatchers of the genus *Rhipidura* and the American wood warblers of the genus *Euthlypis*. **4.** an artificially bred variety of goldfish with double anal and caudal fins. **5.** an American fresh-water fish, a darter of the perch family, *Poecilichthys flabellaris*, or a related species. **6.** *Archit.* **a.** a member, or piece of a construction, having the shape of a fan. **b.** a substructure of radiating supports, as of an arch.

fan-tan (făn′tăn′), *n.* **1.** *Cards.* a game in which the cards are played in sequence, the winner being the player who first gets rid of his cards. **2.** a Chinese gambling game in which a pile of coins or counters is placed under a bowl and bets are made on what the remainder will be after they have been divided by four. [t. Chinese (Mandarin): m. *fan t'an* repeated divisions]

fan-ta-si-a (făn tā′zhĭ·ə, -zhə, făn′tə zē′ə), *n.* **1.** *Music.* **a.** a composition in fanciful or irregular rather than strict form or style. **b.** a potpourri of well-known airs arranged with interludes and florid decorations. **2.** a literary work that is not curbed by a fixed plan. [t. It., g. L *phantasia*. See FANTASY]

fan-tasm (făn′tăzəm), *n.* phantasm.

fan-tas-ma-go-ri-a (făn tăz′mə gōr′Ĭ·ə), *n.* phantasmagoria.

fan-tast (făn′tăst), *n.* a visionary.

fan-tas-tic (făn tăs′tĭk), *adj.* **1.** odd, quaint, eccentric, or grotesque in conception, design, character, movement, etc.: *fantastic ornaments.* **2.** fanciful or capricious, as persons or their ideas, actions, etc. **3.** imaginary; groundless; not real: *fantastic fears.* **4.** extravagantly fanciful; irrational: *fantastic reasons.* Also, **fan-tas′ti-cal.** [ME *fantastik*, t. ML: m.s. *fantasticus* imaginary, LL *phantasticus*, t. Gk.: m. *phantastikós* able to represent (to the mind)] **—fan-tas′ti-cal-ly,** *adv.* **—fan-tas′-ti-cal-ness, fan-tas′ti-cal-i-ty,** *n.*

fan-ta-sy (făn′tə sĬ, -zĬ), *n., pl.* **-sies. 1.** imagination, esp. when unrestrained. **2.** the forming of grotesque mental images. **3.** a mental image, esp. when grotesque. **4.** *Psychol.* an imaginative sequence fulfilling a psychological need; a daydream. **5.** a hallucination. **6.** a supposition based on no solid foundation; a visionary idea. **7.** caprice; whim. **8.** an ingenious or odd thought, design, or invention. **9.** *Music.* a fantasia. Also, **phantasy.** [ME *fantasie*, t. OF, t. L: m. *phantasia* idea, fancy, t. Gk.: impression, image] **—Syn. 1.** See **fancy.**

fan-toc-ci-ni (făn′tə chē′nĬ), *n.pl.* **1.** puppets operated by concealed wires or strings. **2.** dramatic representations in which they are used. [t. It., pl. of *fantoccino,* dim. of *fantoccio* puppet, der. *fante* boy, g. L *infans* child]

fan-tom (făn′təm), *n., adj.* phantom.

fan tracery, *Archit.* tracery which rises from a capital or a corbel and diverges like the folds of a fan, spreading over the surface of a vault.

fan vaulting, *Archit.* a complicated mode of roofing, in which the vault is covered by ribs and veins of tracery, diverging from a single point.

fan window, *Archit.* a fan-shaped window whose sash is formed with radial bars; a fanlight.

fan-wort (făn′wûrt′), *n.* a plant, *Cabomba caroliniana,* of the water-lily family, found in ponds, etc.

far (fär), *adv., adj.,* **farther, farthest. —adv. 1.** at or to a great distance; a long way off; to a remote point: *far ahead.* **2.** very remote in time, degree, scope, purpose, desire, etc.: *far from successful.* **3.** to a great degree; very much: *far better, worse, different.* **4.** at or to a definite distance, point of progress, or degree. **5.** Some special adverb phrases are:
as far as, to the distance, extent, or degree that.
by far, very much.
far and away, very much.
far and wide, to great distances.
far be it from me, I do not wish or dare.
from far, from a distance.
go far, 1. to be successful; do much. **2.** to tend greatly.
how far, to what distance, extent, or degree.
in so far, to such an extent.
so far, 1. up to now. **2.** up to that point, extent, etc.
so far so good, no trouble yet.
—adj. **6.** at a great distance. **7.** to a great distance. **8.** more distant of the two: *the far side.* **9.** greatly different or apart. [ME *far, fer,* etc., OE *feor,* c. OHG *fer;* akin to Gk. *pérā*]

far-ad (făr′əd, -ăd), *n. Elect.* a unit of capacitance equal to the change in the number of coulombs of charge per volt of change of potential. [named after FARADAY]

Far-a-day (făr′ə dĬ, -dā′), *n.* **1.** a unit of quantity used in electrolysis, equal to about 96,500 coulombs. **2. Michael,** 1791–1867, British physicist and chemist: discoverer of electromagnetic induction.

fa-rad-ic (fə răd′Ĭk), *adj. Elect.* of or pertaining to induction or the phenomena connected with it. [var. of *faradaic,* der. FARADAY]

far-a-dism (făr′ə dĬz′əm), *n.* **1.** induced electricity. **2.** *Med.* its application for therapeutic purposes.

far-a-dize (făr′ə dĬz′), *v.t.* **-dized, -dizing.** *Med.* to stimulate or treat, as a muscle, with induced electric currents. **—far′a-di-za′tion,** *n.* **—far′a-diz′er,** *n.*

far-and (făr′ənd), *adj.* farrand.

far-an-dole (făr′ən dōl; *Fr.* fȧ rȧn dōl′), *n.* **1.** a lively dance, of Provençal origin, in which all the dancers join hands and execute various figures. **2.** the music for this

dance. [t. F, t. Pr.: m. *farandoulo,* prob. f. *fa* make + *roundelo* round dance, ult. der. L *rotundus* round]

far-a-way (fär′ə wā′), *adj.* **1.** distant; remote. **2.** abstracted or dreamy, as a look.

farce (färs), *n., v.,* **farced, farcing. —n. 1.** a play, light in tone, in which the plot depends upon situation rather than character. **2.** foolish show; mockery; a ridiculous sham. *—v.t.* **3.** to season (a speech or composition), as with scraps of wit. **4.** *Obs.* to stuff; cram. [ME *farse*(n), t. F: m. *farcir,* g. L *farcīre* stuff]

farce-meat (färs′mēt′), *n. Cookery.* forcemeat.

far-ceur (fär sœr′), *n. French.* **1.** a writer or player of farces. **2.** a joker or wag.

far-ci (fär sē′; *Fr.* fär-), *adj. Cookery.* stuffed. [t. F]

far-ci-cal (fär′sə kəl), *adj.* **1.** pertaining to or of the nature of farce. **2.** resembling farce; ludicrous; absurd. **—far′ci-cal′i-ty, far′ci-cal-ness,** *n.* **—far′ci-cal-ly,** *adv.*

far cry, a great distance.

far-cy (fär′sĬ), *n. Vet. Sci.* a form of the disease glanders chiefly affecting the superficial lymphatics and the skin of horses and mules. [var. of *farcin,* t. F, g. L *farcīminum* disease of horses]

farcy bud, *Vet. Sci.* an ulcerated swelling, produced in farcy. Also, **farcy button.**

far-del (fär′dəl), *n. Archaic.* a bundle; a burden. [ME, t. OF, dim. of *farde* pack, t. Ar.: m. *farda* bundle]

fare (fär), *n., v.,* **fared, faring. —n. 1.** the price of conveyance or passage. **2.** the person or persons who pay to be conveyed in a vehicle. **3.** food. **4.** *Archaic.* state of things. *—v.i.* **5.** to be entertained, esp. with food and drink. **6.** to experience good or bad fortune, treatment, etc.; get on: *he fared well.* **7.** to go; turn out; happen (used impersonally): *it fared ill with him.* **8.** *Archaic.* to go; travel. [ME *fare*(n), OE *faran,* c. G *fahren;* akin to Gk. *perân* pass, *póros* passage] **—far′er,** *n.* **—Syn. 3.** See **food.**

Far East, the countries of E and SE Asia: China, Japan, Korea, Siam, etc.

Far Eastern Region, former name of **Khabarovsk** (def. 1).

fare-well (fâr′wĕl′), *interj.* **1.** may you fare well; good-by; adieu. *—n.* **2.** an expression of good wishes at parting. **3.** leave-taking; departure: *a fond farewell.* *—adj.* **4.** parting; valedictory: *a farewell sermon or performance.* [orig. two words, *fare well.* See FARE, v.]

Fare-well (fâr′wĕl′), *n.* **Cape,** the S tip of Greenland.

far-fetched (fär′fĕcht′), *adj.* remotely connected; forced; strained: *a far-fetched example.*

far-flung (fär′flŭng′), *adj.* flung or extending over a great distance: *our far-flung battle line.*

Far-go (fär′gō), *n.* a city in SE North Dakota. 38,256 (1950).

fa-ri-na (fə rē′nə), *n.* **1.** flour or meal made from cereal grains, cooked as cereal or used in puddings, etc. **2.** starch. [t. L, der. *far* spelt]

far-i-na-ceous (făr′ə nā′shəs), *adj.* **1.** consisting or made of flour or meal, as food. **2.** containing or yielding starch, as seeds. **3.** mealy in appearance or nature.

far-i-nose (făr′ə nōs′), *adj.* **1.** yielding farina. **2.** resembling farina. **3.** covered with a mealy powder.

far-kle-ber-ry (fär′kəl bĕr′Ĭ), *n., pl.* **-ries.** a shrub or small tree, *Vaccinium* (*Batodendron*) *arboreum,* of the southern U.S., bearing a black, many-seeded berry.

farl (färl), *n.* a thin circular cake of flour or oatmeal.

Far-ley (fär′lĬ), *n.* **James Aloysius** (ăl′ō Ĭsh′əs), born 1888, U.S. political leader.

farm (färm), *n.* **1.** a tract of land devoted to agriculture. **2.** a tract of land or water devoted to some other industry: *a chicken farm, an oyster farm.* **3.** the system, method, or act of collecting revenue by letting out a territory in districts. **4.** *Rare.* a country or district let out for the collection of revenue. **5.** a fixed amount accepted from a person in lieu of taxes or the like which he is authorized to collect. **6.** *Eng. Hist.* **a.** the rent or income from leased property or rights such as lands or revenues. **b.** the state of leased property or rights; a lease; possession under lease. **7.** *Obs.* a fixed yearly amount payable in the form of rent, taxes, or the like. *—v.t.* **8.** to cultivate (land). **9.** to take the proceeds or profits of (a tax, undertaking, etc.) on paying a fixed sum. **10.** to let or lease (taxes, revenues, an enterprise, etc.) to another for a fixed sum or a percentage (often fol. by *out*). **11.** to let or lease the labor or services of (a person) for hire. **12.** to contract for the maintenance of (a person, institution, etc.). *—v.i.* **13.** to cultivate the soil; operate a farm. [ME *ferme,* t. F, der. *fermer* fix, g. L *firmāre*]

farm-er (fär′mər), *n.* **1.** one who farms; one who cultivates land or operates a farm. **2.** one who undertakes some service, as the care of children, at a fixed price. **3.** one who undertakes the collection of taxes, etc., paying a fixed sum for the privilege of retaining them.

farm-er-ette (fär′mə rĕt′), *n. Colloq.* a girl or woman working on a farm.

farm-er-gen-er-al (fär′mər jĕn′ər əl), *n., pl.* **farmers-general.** (in France, under the old monarchy) a member of a company of capitalists that farmed certain taxes. [trans. of F *fermier-général*]

Farm-er-La-bor Party (fär′mər lā′bər), a political party in the U.S. attempting to unite farmers and industrial workers for the protection of their interests.

farmers' coöperative, an organization of farmers for marketing their products or buying supplies.

farm·er·y (fär'mər ĭ), n., pl. **-eries.** Brit. the buildings, yards, etc., of a farm.

farm hand, person who works on a farm.

farm·house (färm'hous'), n. a house on a farm.

farm·ing (fär'mĭng), n. 1. the business of operating a farm. 2. the practice of letting or leasing taxes, revenue, etc., for collection. 3. the business of collecting taxes. —adj. 4. of, for, or pertaining to farms: farming tools, land, etc.

farm·stead (färm'stĕd), n. Chiefly Brit. a farm with its buildings.

farm·yard (färm'yärd'), n. a yard or enclosure surrounded by or connected with farm buildings.

Far·ne·se (fär nā'sĕ) n. **Alessandro** (ä'lĕs sän'drō), (Duke of Parma) 1545–92, Italian general, statesman, and diplomat in the service of Philip II of Spain.

far·ne·sol (fär'nə sōl', -sŏl'), n. Chem. an extract, $C_{15}H_{26}O$, from the flowers of the acacia, cassia oil, etc., used in the perfume industry.

far·o (fâr'ō), n. Cards. a gambling game in which the players bet on the cards of the dealer's or banker's pack. [alter. of PHARAOH]

Far·oe Islands (fâr'ō), Faeroe Islands.

Far·o·ese (fâr'ō ēz', -ēs'), n., pl. **-ese.** 1. a native or an inhabitant of the Faeroes. 2. a Scandinavian dialect spoken in the Faeroes, closely related to Icelandic.

far-off (fär'ôf', -ŏf'), adj. distant; remote.

fa·rouche (fä rōōsh'), adj. French. 1. fierce. 2. unsociable; shy. 3. sullen. [F, alter. of forasche, g. L forasticus foreign, der. foras outside]

Fa·rouk I (fä rōōk'), born 1920, king of Egypt since 1936. Also, **Faruk.**

Far·quhar (fär'kwər, -kwär, -kər), n. **George,** 1678–1707, British writer of comedies.

far·rag·i·nous (fə răj'ə nəs), adj. Now Rare. formed of various materials. [f. s. L farrāgo mixed fodder + -ous]

far·ra·go (fə rā'gō, -rä'-), n., pl. **-goes.** a confused mixture; a hodgepodge; a medley: a farrago of doubts, fears, hopes, wishes. [t. L: mixed fodder, medley]

Far·ra·gut (făr'ə gət), n. **David Glasgow,** 1801–70, U.S. admiral: won the battles of New Orleans and Mobile Bay for the Union in the U.S. Civil War.

far·rand (făr'ənd), adj. having a (fair, ugly, evil, etc.) nature or appearance. Also, **farand.** [ME farand comely, orig. ppr. (North.) of FARE, v.]

Far·rar (fə rär'), n. **Geraldine** (Mrs. Lou Tellegen), born 1882, U.S. operatic soprano.

far-reach·ing (fär'rē'chĭng), adj. extending far in influence, effect, etc.

Far·rell (făr'əl), n. **James Thomas,** born 1904, U.S. novelist.

far·ri·er (făr'ĭ ər), n. Brit. 1. a blacksmith who shoes horses. 2. a doctor for horses; a veterinarian. [t. OF: m. ferrier, g. L ferrārius, der. ferrum iron]

far·ri·er·y (făr'ĭ ər ĭ), n., pl. **-eries.** the art or the establishment of a farrier.

far·row¹ (făr'ō), n. 1. a litter of pigs. —v.t. 2. (of swine) to bring forth (young). —v.i. 3. to produce a litter of pigs. [ME far, OE fearh; akin to G ferkel pig, L porcus]

far·row² (făr'ō), adj. (of a cow) not pregnant. [orig. uncert. Cf. Flem. verwekoe barren cow]

far-see·ing (fär'sē'ĭng), adj. 1. having foresight; sagacious; discerning. 2. able to see far; far-sighted.

far-sight·ed (fär'sī'tĭd), adj. 1. seeing to a great distance. 2. seeing objects at a distance more clearly than those near at hand; hypermetropic. 3. foreseeing future results wisely: a far-sighted statesman. —**far'-sight'ed·ly,** adv. —**far'-sight'ed·ness,** n.

far·ther (fär'thər), compar. of **far.** —adv. 1. at or to a greater distance. 2. at or to a more advanced point. 3. to a greater degree or extent. 4. additionally. —adj. 5. more distant or remote. 6. extending or tending to a greater distance. 7. additional; further. [ME ferther; orig. var. of further, but now taken as an irreg. formed compar. (prop. farrer) of far, with superl. farthest]

Farther India, Indo-China.

far·ther·most (fär'thər mōst', -məst), adj. most distant or remote; farthest.

far·thest (fär'thĭst), superl. of **far.** —adj. 1. most distant or remote. 2. longest. —adv. 3. to or at the greatest distance. [ME ferthest, orig. var. of furthest. See FARTHER]

far·thing (fär'thĭng), n. 1. an English coin of bronze, worth one fourth of a penny, or about half a U.S. cent. 2. something of very small value. [ME ferthing, OE fēorthung, der. fēortha fourth]

far·thin·gale (fär'thĭng gāl'), n. a kind of hoop skirt or framework for expanding a woman's skirt, worn in the 16th and 17th centuries. [t. OF: m. verdugale, t. Sp.: m. verdugado, der. verdugo shoot, rod]

Fa·ruk I (fä rōōk'), Farouk I.

Far West, 1. the area of the Rocky Mountains and the Pacific Coast.

Farthingale, Elizabethan period

2. U.S. Hist. the Middle West, esp. the area west of the Mississippi river. —Far Western.

F.A.S., free alongside ship (which see). Also, **f.a.s.**

fas·ces (făs'ēz), n.pl., sing. **fascis.** a bundle of rods containing an ax with the blade projecting, borne before Roman magistrates as an emblem of official power. [t. L, pl. of fascis bundle] —**fas·ci·al** (făsh'ĭ əl), adj.

fas·ci·a (făsh'ĭ ə), n., pl. **fasciae** (făsh'ĭ ē'). 1. a band or fillet. 2. Surg. a bandage. 3. Archit. a. a long, flat member or band. b. a triple horizontal division of an architrave in Ionic, Corinthian, and composite orders. See diag. under **column.** 4. Anat., Zool. a. a band or sheath of connective tissue investing, supporting, or binding together internal organs or parts of the body. b. tissue of this kind. 5. Zool. a distinctly marked band of color. [t. L: band] —**fas·ci·al,** adj.

fas·ci·ate (făsh'ĭ āt'), adj. 1. bound with a band, fillet, or bandage. 2. Bot. a. compressed into a band or bundle. b. grown together, as stems. 3. Zool. a. composed of bundles or bound together in a bundle. b. marked with a band or bands. Also, **fas'ci·at'ed.** [t. L: m.s. fasciātus, pp., enveloped with bands]

fas·ci·a·tion (făsh'ĭ ā'shən), n. 1. act of binding up or bandaging. 2. the process of becoming fasciated. 3. resulting state.

fas·ci·cle (făs'ə kəl), n. 1. a small bundle. 2. a part of a printed work; a number of printed or written sheets bound together, as an installment for convenience in publication. 3. Bot. a close cluster, as of flowers or leaves. 4. Anat. a small bundle of fibers within a nerve or the central nervous system. [t. L: m.s. fasciculus, dim. of fascis bundle] —**fas'ci·cled,** adj.

fas·cic·u·lar (fə sĭk'yə lər), adj. pertaining to or forming a fascicle; fasciculate.

as·cic·u·late (fə sĭk'yə lĭt, -lāt'), adj. arranged in a fascicle or fascicles. Also, **fas·cic'u·lat'ed.** —**fas·cic'-u·late·ly,** adv.

fas·cic·u·la·tion (fə sĭk'yə lā'shən), n. fascicular condition.

fas·ci·cule (făs'ə kūl'), n. a fascicle, esp. of a book. [t. L: m.s. fasciculus little bundle]

fas·cic·u·lus (fə sĭk'yə ləs), n., pl. **-li** (-lī'). 1. a fascicle, as of nerve or muscle fibers. 2. a fascicle of a book. [t. L: little bundle]

fas·ci·nate (făs'ə nāt'), v.t., **-nated, -nating.** 1. to attract and hold irresistibly by delightful qualities. 2. to deprive of the power of resistance, as through terror. 3. Obs. to bewitch. 4. Obs. to cast under a spell by a look. [t. L: m.s. fascinātus, pp., enchanted] —**Syn.** 1. bewitch, charm, enchant, entrance, enrapture, captivate, allure, infatuate, enamor. —**Ant.** 1. repel.

fas·ci·nat·ing (făs'ə nā'tĭng), adj. bewitching; enchanting; charming; captivating: a fascinating poem. —**fas'ci·nat'ing·ly,** adv.

fas·ci·na·tion (făs'ə nā'shən), n. 1. act of fascinating. 2. state of being fascinated. 3. fascinating quality; powerful attraction; charm.

fas·ci·na·tor (făs'ə nā'tər), n. 1. one who or that which fascinates. 2. a kind of scarf of crochet work, lace, etc., narrowing towards the ends, worn as a head covering by women.

fas·cine (fă sēn', fə-), n. 1. a fagot. 2. Fort. a long bundle of sticks bound together, used in building earthworks and batteries and in strengthening ramparts, etc. [t. F, t. L: m. fascīna bundle of sticks]

fas·cis (făs'ĭs), n. sing. of **fasces.**

fas·cism (făsh'ĭz əm), n. 1. (often cap.) a governmental system with strong centralized power, permitting no opposition or criticism, controlling all affairs of the nation (industrial, commercial, etc.), emphasizing an aggressive nationalism, and (often) anticommunist. Fascism was established in Italy by Mussolini in 1922, whence its influence spread to Germany and elsewhere; it was dissolved in Italy in 1943. 2. (often cap.) the philosophy, principles, or methods of fascism. 3. (cap.) a fascist movement, esp. the one in Italy. Also, Italian, **Fa·scis·mo** (fä shēs'mō). [t. It.: m. Fascismo, der. fascio group, bundle, g. s. L fascis bundle (of sticks, as lictors' emblem). See FASCES]

fas·cist (făsh'ĭst), n. 1. anyone who believes in or sympathizes with fascism. 2. a member of a fascist movement or party, esp. (cap.) in Italy. —adj. 3. of or like fascism or fascists.

Fa·scis·ti (fə shĭs'tĭ; It. fä shē'stē), n.pl. Italian. Fascists.

fash (făsh), n., v.t., v.i. Scot. trouble; worry. [t. OF: m.s. fascher]

fash·ion (făsh'ən), n. 1. a prevailing custom or style of dress, etiquette, procedure, etc.: the latest fashion in hats. 2. conventional usage in dress, manners, etc., esp. of polite society, or conformity to it: dictates of fashion, out of fashion. 3. fashionable people collectively. 4. manner; way; mode: in a warlike fashion. 5. after or in a fashion, in some manner or other, but not particularly well. 6. the make or form of anything. 7. a kind; sort. 8. Obs. workmanship. 9. Obs. act or process of making. —v.t. 10. to give a particular shape or form to; make. 11. to accommodate; adapt: doctrines fashioned to the varying hour. 12. Obs. to contrive;

manage. [ME *facioun*, t. OF: m. *façon*, g. s. L *factio* a doing or making]
—Syn. 1. fad, rage, craze. FASHION, STYLE, VOGUE imply popularity or widespread acceptance of manners, customs, dress, etc. FASHION is that which characterizes or distinguishes the habits, manners, dress, etc. of a period or group: *the fashions of the eighteenth century.* STYLE is sometimes the equivalent of FASHION, but also denotes conformance to a prevalent standard: *to be in style, a chair in the Queen Anne style.* VOGUE suggests the temporary popularity of certain fashions: *this year's vogue in popular music.* **6.** shape, cut, pattern. **10.** frame, construct, mold.

fash·ion·a·ble (fǎsh′ən ə bəl), *adj.* **1.** observant of or conforming to the fashion. **2.** of, characteristic of, or patronized by the world of fashion. **—***n.* **3.** a fashionable person. **—fash′ion·a·ble·ness,** *n.* **—fash′ion·a·bly,** *adv.*

fash·ioned (fǎsh′ənd), *adj.* (of knitted garments) shaped: *full-fashioned hose.*

fash·ion·er (fǎsh′ən ər), *n.* **1.** one who fashions, forms, or gives shape to anything. **2.** *Obs.* a tailor or modiste.

fashion plate, 1. a pictorial design showing a prevailing or new mode of dress. **2.** *Colloq.* a person who wears the latest style in dress.

Fa·sho·da (fə shō′də), *n.* a town in the SE Anglo-Egyptian Sudan, on the White Nile: British and French colonial interests came into conflict here in the "Fashoda incident," 1898. Now called **Kodok.**

fast[1] (fǎst, fäst), *adj.* **1.** moving or able to move quickly; quick; swift; rapid: *a fast horse.* **2.** done in comparatively little time: *a fast race, fast work.* **3.** indicating a time in advance of the correct time, as a clock. **4.** adapted to or productive of rapid movement: *a fast track.* **5.** extremely energetic and active, esp. in pursuing pleasure immoderately or without restraint, as a person. **6.** characterized by such energy or pursuit of pleasure, as a mode of life. **7.** resistant: *acid-fast.* **8.** firmly fixed in place; not easily moved; securely attached. **9.** that cannot escape or be extricated. **10.** firmly tied, as a knot. **11.** closed and made secure, as a door. **12.** such as to hold securely: *to lay fast hold on a thing.* **13.** firm in adherence: *fast friends.* **14.** permanent; lasting: *a fast color.* **15.** deep or sound, as sleep. **16.** deceptive, insincere, inconstant, or unreliable. **17.** *Photog.* permitting very short exposure, as by having a wide shutter opening or high film sensitivity: *a fast lens or film.* **—***adv.* **18.** tightly: *to hold fast.* **19.** soundly: *fast asleep.* **20.** quickly, swiftly, or rapidly. **21.** in quick succession. **22.** in an energetic or dissipated way. **23.** *Archaic.* close; near: *fast by.* [ME; OE *fæst*, c. D *vast*, Icel. *fastr* fast, firm] **—Syn. 1, 2.** fleet, speedy. See **quick. 6.** dissipated, dissolute, profligate, immoral. **8.** secure, tight. **13.** loyal, faithful, steadfast. **18.** fixedly, firmly, tenaciously. **—Ant. 1, 2.** slow. **6.** well-behaved. **8.** loose.

fast[2] (fǎst, fäst), *v.i.* **1.** to abstain from all food. **2.** to eat only sparingly or of certain kinds of food, esp. as a religious observance. **—***n.* **3.** a fasting; an abstinence from food, or a limiting of one's food, esp. when voluntary and as a religious observance. **4.** a day or period of fasting. [ME *faste(n)*, OE *fæstan*, c. G *fasten*]

fast day, a day on which fasting is observed, esp. such a day appointed by some ecclesiastical or civil authority.

fas·ten (fǎs′ən, fäs′-), *v.t.* **1.** to make fast; fix firmly or securely in place or position; attach securely to something else. **2.** to make secure, as an article of dress with buttons, clasps, etc. or a door with a lock, bolt, etc. **3.** to enclose securely, as a person or an animal (fol. by *in*). **4.** to attach by any connecting agency: *to fasten a nickname or a crime upon one.* **5.** to direct (the eyes, thoughts, etc.) intently. **—***v.i.* **6.** to become fast, fixed, or firm. **7.** to take firm hold; seize (usually fol. by *on*). [ME *fasten(en)*, *fastne(n)*, OE *fæstnian*, der. *fæst*, adj., FAST] **—fas′ten·er,** *n.* **—Syn. 2.** attach, connect, link, hook, clasp, clinch, rivet, clamp, secure, bind, tie, tether.

fas·ten·ing (fǎs′ən ǐng, fäs′-), *n.* something that fastens, as a lock or clasp.

fas·tid·i·ous (fǎs tǐd′ǐ əs), *adj.* hard to please; excessively critical: *a fastidious taste.* [t. L: m.s. *fastīdiōsus*, der. *fastīdium* loathing, disgust] **—fas·tid′i·ous·ly,** *adv.* **—fas·tid′i·ous·ness,** *n.* **—Syn.** See **particular.**

fas·tig·i·ate (fǎs tǐj′ǐ ǐt, -āt′), *adj.* **1.** rising to a pointed top. **2.** *Zool.* joined together in a tapering adhering group. **3.** *Bot.* **a.** erect and parallel, as branches. **b.** having such branches. Also, **fas·tig′i·at′ed.** [f. s. L *fastīgium* gable top, summit, slope + -ATE[1]]

fast·ness (fǎst′nǐs, fäst′-), *n.* **1.** a secure or fortified place. **2.** state of being fixed or firm. **3.** state of being rapid. **4.** quality of being energetic or dissipated, as in behavior.

fat (fǎt), *adj.*, **fatter, fattest,** *n.*, *v.*, **fatted, fatting. —***adj.* **1.** having much flesh other than muscle; fleshy; plump. **2.** consisting of, resembling, or containing fat. **3.** abounding in a particular element: *fat pine* (pine rich in resin). **4.** fertile, as land. **5.** profitable, as an office. **6.** affording good opportunities: *a fat profit.* **7.** thick; broad; extended. **8.** plentiful. **9.** plentifully supplied. **10.** dull; stupid. **—***n.* **11.** any of several white or yellowish substances, greasy to the touch, forming the chief part of the adipose tissue of animals and also found in plants. When pure, the fats are odorless, tasteless, and colorless and may be either solid or liquid. They are insoluble in water or cold alcohol but easily soluble in ether, chloroform, or benzene. They are compound esters of various fatty acids with glycerol, the pure fats being composed of carbon, hydrogen, and oxygen. **12.** animal tissue containing much of this substance. **13.** the richest or best part of anything. **14.** especially profitable or advantageous work. **15.** action or lines in a dramatic part which permit an actor to display his abilities. **—***v.t., v.i.* **16.** to make or become fat. [ME; OE *fǣtt*, orig. pp., fatted, c. G *feist*] **—fat′less,** *adj.* **—fat′like′,** *adj.* **—Syn. 1.** corpulent, obese, adipose, chubby, pudgy. See **stout. 2.** oily, greasy. **5.** lucrative, remunerative. **—Ant. 1.** thin. **5.** ill-paying.

fa·tal (fā′təl), *adj.* **1.** causing death: *a fatal accident.* **2.** causing destruction or ruin: *an action that is fatal to the success of a project.* **3.** decisively important; fateful: *the fatal day finally arrived.* **4.** influencing fate: *the fatal sisters.* **5.** proceeding from or decreed by fate; inevitable. **6.** *Obs.* doomed. **7.** *Obs.* prophetic. [ME, t. L: s. *fātālis* of or belonging to fate] **—fa′tal·ness,** *n.*
—Syn. 1. FATAL, DEADLY, MORTAL refer to something which has caused or is capable of causing death. FATAL may refer to either the future or the past; in either case, it emphasizes inevitability and the inescapable—the disastrous, whether death or dire misfortune: *the accident was fatal, such a mistake would be fatal.* DEADLY looks to the future, and suggests that which is likely to cause death (though not inevitably so): *a deadly poison, disease.* MORTAL looks to the past, and refers to death which has actually occurred: *he received a mortal wound, the disease proved to be mortal.*

fa·tal·ism (fā′təl ǐz′əm), *n.* **1.** *Philos.* the doctrine that all events are subject to fate or inevitable predetermination. **2.** the acceptance of all things and events as inevitable; submission to fate. **—fa′tal·ist,** *n.* **—fa′tal·is′tic,** *adj.* **—fa′tal·is′ti·cal·ly,** *adv.*

fa·tal·i·ty (fā tǎl′ə tǐ, fə-), *n.*, *pl.* **-ties. 1.** a disaster resulting in death; a calamity or misfortune. **2.** the quality of causing death or disaster; deadliness; a fatal influence. **3.** predetermined liability to disaster. **4.** the quality of being predetermined by or subject to fate. **5.** the fate or destiny of a person or thing. **6.** a fixed, unalterably predetermined course of things.

fa·tal·ly (fā′tə lǐ), *adv.* **1.** in a manner leading to death or disaster. **2.** by a decree of fate or destiny; by inevitable predetermination.

Fa·ta Mor·ga·na (fä′tä môr gä′nä), **1.** a mirage seen esp. in the Strait of Messina, formerly attributed to fairy agency. **2.** Morgan le Fay. [t. It.: fairy Morgana. See FAY[1]]

fat cat, *U.S. Slang.* a wealthy person from whom large political campaign contributions are expected.

fate (fāt), *n.*, *v.*, **fated, fating. —***n.* **1.** fortune; lot; destiny. **2.** a divine decree or a fixed sentence by which the order of things is prescribed. **3.** that which is inevitably predetermined; destiny. **4.** a prophetic declaration of what must be. **5.** death, destruction, or ruin. **—***v.t.* **6.** to predetermine as by the decree of fate; destine (now only in the passive). [ME, t. L: m.s. *fātum* a prophetic declaration, fate, prop. pp. neut., (thing) said]
—Syn. 1. FATE, DESTINY, DOOM refer to the idea of a fortune, usually adverse, which is predetermined and unescapable. The three words are frequently interchangeable. FATE stresses the irrationality and impersonal character of events: *it was Napoleon's fate to be exiled.* The word is often lightly used, however: *it was my fate to meet him that very afternoon.* DESTINY emphasizes the idea of an unalterable course of events, and is often used of a propitious fortune: *a man of destiny; it was his destiny to save his nation.* DOOM esp. applies to the final ending, always unhappy or terrible, brought about by destiny or fate: *he met his doom bravely.*

fat·ed (fā′tǐd), *adj.* **1.** subject to, guided by, or predetermined by fate. **2.** destined. **3.** doomed.

fate·ful (fāt′fəl), *adj.* **1.** involving momentous consequences; decisively important. **2.** fatal, deadly, or disastrous. **3.** controlled by irresistible destiny. **4.** prophetic; ominous. **—fate′ful·ly,** *adv.* **—fate′ful·ness,** *n.*

Fates (fāts), *n.pl. Gk. and Roman Myth.* the three goddesses of destiny. Clotho spins the thread of life, Lachesis measures it, and Atropos severs it.

fat·head (fǎt′hěd′), *n.* a stupid person. **—fat′head′ed,** *adj.*

fa·ther (fä′thər), *n.* **1.** a male parent. **2.** any male ancestor, esp. the founder of a race, family, or line. **3.** *Colloq.* a father-in-law, stepfather, or adoptive father. **4.** one who exercises paternal care over another; a fatherly protector or provider: *a father to the poor.* **5.** a title of respect for an old man. **6.** *Chiefly Brit.* the oldest member of a society, profession, etc. Cf. *U.S.* **dean** (def. 3). **7.** one of the leading men of a city, etc. **8.** a person or thing who originates or establishes something. **9.** (*cap.*) *Theol.* the Supreme Being and Creator; God. **10. the Father,** the first person of the Trinity. **11.** *Ch. Hist.* any of the chief early Christian writers, whose works are the main sources for the history, doctrines, and observances of the church in the early ages. **12.** *Eccles.* **a.** a title of reverence in ecclesiastical use, as for church dignitaries, officers of monasteries, monks, confessors, and priests. **b.** a person bearing this title. **13.** (*pl.*) *Rom. Hist.* conscript fathers. **—***v.t.* **14.** to beget. **15.** to originate; be the author of. **16.** to act as a father toward. **17.** to acknowledge oneself the father of. **18.** to assume as one's own; take the responsibility of. **19.** to charge with the begetting of. [ME *fader*, OE *fæder*, c. G *vater;* akin to L *pater*, Gk. *patēr*]

Father Christmas, *Brit.* Santa Claus.

father confessor, *Eccles.* a confessor.

fa·ther·hood (fä′thər hŏŏd′), *n.* state of being a father.

fa·ther-in-law (fä′thər ĭn lô′), *n., pl.* **fathers-in-law. 1.** the father of one's husband or wife. **2.** *Brit. Colloq.* a stepfather.

fa·ther·land (fä′thər lănd′), *n.* **1.** one's native country. **2.** the land of one's ancestors.

fa·ther·less (fä′thər lĭs), *adj.* **1.** without a living father. **2.** without a known or legally responsible father.

fa·ther·ly (fä′thər lĭ), *adj.* **1.** of, like, or befitting a father. —*adv.* **2.** in the manner of a father. —**fa′ther·li·ness,** *n.*
—**Syn. 1.** FATHERLY, PATERNAL refer to the relationship of a male parent to his children. FATHERLY has emotional connotations; it always suggests a kind, protective, tender, or forbearing attitude: *fatherly advice.* PATERNAL may suggest a kindly, more proprietary attitude: *paternal interest;* but it may also be used objectively, as a legal and official term: *his paternal grandmother, paternal estate.*

fath·om (făth′əm), *n., pl.* **fathoms,** (*esp. collectively*) **fathom,** *v.* —*n.* **1.** a unit of length equal to 6 feet: used chiefly in nautical and mining measurements. —*v.t.* **2.** to reach in depth by measurement in fathoms; sound; try the depth of; penetrate to or find the bottom or extent of. **3.** to measure the depth of by sounding. **4.** to penetrate to the bottom of; understand thoroughly. [ME *fathme,* OE *fæthm,* c. G *faden;* akin to Gk. *pétalos* spreading] —**fath′om·a·ble,** *adj.* —**fath′om·er,** *n.*

fath·om·less (făth′əm lĭs), *adj.* impossible to fathom. —**fath′om·less·ly,** *adv.*

fa·tid·ic (fā tĭd′ĭk, fə-), *adj.* prophetic. Also, **fa·tid′i·cal.** [t. L: s. *fātidicus* prophesying]

fat·i·ga·ble (făt′ə gə bəl), *adj.* easily fatigued or tired.

fa·tigue (fə tēg′), *n., v.,* **-tigued, -tiguing,** *adj.* —*n.* **1.** weariness from bodily or mental exertion. **2.** a cause of weariness; labor; exertion. **3.** *Physiol.* temporary diminution of the excitability or functioning of organs, tissues, or cells after excessive exertion or stimulation. **4.** *Mech.* the weakening of material subjected to stress, esp. a continued series of stresses. **5.** Also, **fatigue duty.** *Mil.* **a.** labor of a generally nonmilitary kind done by soldiers, such as cleaning up an area, or digging drainage ditches, or raking up leaves. **b.** state of being engaged in fatigue: *on fatigue.* **c.** (*pl.*) fatigue clothes. —*v.t.* **6.** to weary with bodily or mental exertion; exhaust the strength of. —*adj.* **7.** of or pertaining to fatigue: *fatigue detail.* [t. F, der. *fatiguer,* t. L: m. *fatīgāre* tire] —**fa·tigue′less,** *adj.*

fatigue clothes, a soldier's uniform for fatigue duty.

fa·tigued (fə tēgd′), *adj.* wearied. —**Syn.** See tired[1].

fatigue party, a group or detail of soldiers engaged on fatigue.

Fat·i·ma (făt′ĭ mə, fä′tē mä′), *n.* **1.** A.D. c606–632, daughter of Mohammed. **2.** the seventh and last wife of Bluebeard, popularly a synonym of feminine curiosity.

Fat·i·mid (făt′ə mĭd), *n.* **1.** caliph of the North African dynasty, 909–1171, claiming descent from Fatima (def. 1) and Ali. **2.** any descendant of Fatima and Ali. Also, **Fat·i·mite** (făt′ə mīt′).

fat·ling (făt′lĭng), *n.* a young animal, as a calf or a lamb, fattened for slaughter. [f. FAT + -LING[1]]

fat·ly (făt′lĭ), *adv.* **1.** in a fat manner; plumply. **2.** clumsily.

fat·ness (făt′nĭs), *n.* **1.** condition of being fat. **2.** corpulence. **3.** oiliness. **4.** richness; fertility.

Fat·shan (făt′shän′), *n.* a city in SE China, in Kwantung province, near Canton. ab. 500,000.

fat-sol·u·ble (făt′sŏl′yə bəl), *adj. Chem.* soluble in oils or fats.

fat·ten (făt′ən), *v.t.* **1.** to make fat. **2.** to feed for slaughter. **3.** to enrich; make fertile. **4.** *Poker.* to increase the number of chips in (a pot). —*v.i.* **5.** to grow fat. —**fat′ten·er,** *n.*

fat·ti ma·schi·i, pa·ro·le fe·mi·ne (făt′tē mä′skē ē′, pä rô′lĕ fĕ′mē nĕ), *Italian.* deeds (are) manly, words womanish (one of the mottoes of Maryland).

fat·tish (făt′ĭsh), *adj.* somewhat fat.

fat·ty (făt′ĭ), *adj.,* **-tier, -tiest. 1.** consisting of, containing, or resembling fat: *fatty tissue.* **2.** *Pathol.* characterized by over production or accumulation of fat. —**fat′ti·ness,** *n.*

fatty acid, *Chem.* any of a class of aliphatic acids, esp., one such as palmitic, stearic, oleic, etc., present in animal and vegetable fats and oils as glycerides.

fatty degeneration, *Med.* deterioration of the cells of the body accompanied by the formation of fat globules within the diseased cells.

fatty tumor, lipoma.

fa·tu·i·tous (fə tū′ə təs, -tōō′-), *adj.* characterized by fatuity.

fa·tu·i·ty (fə tū′ə tĭ, -tōō′-), *n., pl.* **-ties. 1.** foolishness; complacent stupidity. **2.** something foolish. [t. L: m.s. *fatuitas*]

fat·u·ous (făch′ŏŏ əs), *adj.* **1.** foolish, esp. in an unconscious, complacent manner; silly. **2.** unreal; illusory. [t. L: m. *fatuus*] —**fat′u·ous·ly,** *adv.* —**fat′u·ous·ness,** *n.* —**Syn. 1.** See foolish.

fat-wit·ted (făt′wĭt′ĭd), *adj.* dull; stupid.

fau·bourg (fō′bŏŏr, -bŏŏrg; *Fr.* fō bŏŏr′), *n.* a part of a city outside of, or orig. outside of, the walls; suburb.

fau·cal (fô′kəl), *adj.* **1.** pertaining to the fauces or opening of the throat. **2.** *Phonet.* **a.** (of the explosion of a stop) produced by lowering the velum: the *t* of *button* has faucal explosion if no vowel is pronounced before the *n.* **b.** laryngal. [f. s. L *fauces* throat + -AL[1]]

fau·ces (fô′sēz), *n.pl. Anat.* the cavity at the back of the mouth, leading into the pharynx. [t. L] —**fau·cial** (fô′shəl), *adj.*

fau·cet (fô′sĭt), *n.* any device for controlling the flow of liquid from a pipe or the like by opening or closing an orifice; a tap; a cock. [ME, t. OF: m. *fausset,* der. *fausser* force in, damage, g. L *falsāre* falsify]

faugh (fô), *interj.* an exclamation of disgust.

Faulk·ner (fôk′nər), *n.* **William,** born 1897, U.S. novelist, short-story writer, and poet. Also, **Falkner.**

fault (fôlt), *n.* **1.** a defect or imperfection; a flaw; a failing. **2.** an error or mistake. **3.** a misdeed or transgression. **4.** delinquency; culpability; cause for blame. **5.** *Geol., Mining.* a break in the continuity of a body of rock or of a vein, with dislocation along the plane of fracture. **6.** *Elect.* a partial or total local failure, in the insulation or continuity of a conductor, or in the functioning of an electric system. **7.** *Tennis, Rackets, etc.* **a.** a failure to serve the ball legitimately within the prescribed limits. **b.** a ball which when served does not land in the proper section of the opponent's court. **8.** *Hunting.* a break in the line of scent; a losing of the scent. **9.** *Obs.* lack; want. **10. at fault, a.** open to censure; blamable. **b.** puzzled; astray. **11. in fault,** open to censure; blamable. **12. find fault,** find something wrong; complain. **13. to a fault,** excessively. —*v.i.* **14.** *Geol.* to undergo a fault or faults. **15.** *Archaic.* to commit a fault. —*v.t.* **16.** *Geol.* to cause a fault in. **17.** *Now Rare or Dial.* to find fault with, blame, or censure. [ME *faute,* t. OF, g. LL *fallita,* der. L *fallere* deceive]
—**Syn. 1.** FAULT, FAILING, FOIBLE, WEAKNESS, VICE imply moral shortcomings or imperfections in a person. FAULT is the common word used to refer to any of the average shortcomings of a person; when it is used, condemnation is not necessarily implied: *of his many faults the greatest is vanity.* FOIBLE, FAILING, WEAKNESS all tend to excuse the person referred to. Of these, FOIBLE is the mildest, suggesting a weak point that is slight and often amusing, manifesting itself in eccentricity rather than in wrongdoing: *the foibles of artists.* WEAKNESS suggests that the person in question is unable to control a particular impulse, and gives way to self-indulgence: *a weakness for pretty women.* FAILING is closely akin to FAULT, except that it is particularly applied to humanity at large, suggesting common, often venial, shortcomings: *procrastination and making excuses are common failings.* VICE (which may also apply to a sin in itself, apart from a person: *the vice of gambling*) is the strongest term, and designates a habit that is truly evil and corrupt: *he is very unruly, but he has no vices.* —**Ant. 1.** virtue, merit.

Section of strata displaced by a fault. F, Fault line; A and A, formerly, a continuous mass of rock

fault·find·er (fôlt′fīn′dər), *n.* one who finds fault; one who complains or objects.

fault·find·ing (fôlt′fīn′dĭng), *n.* **1.** act of pointing out faults; carping; picking flaws. —*adj.* **2.** given to finding fault; disposed to complain or object.

fault·less (fôlt′lĭs), *adj.* without fault or defect; perfect. —**fault′less·ly,** *adv.* —**fault′less·ness,** *n.*

fault plane, *Geol.* the plane of fracture in a fault.

fault·y (fôl′tĭ), *adj.,* **faultier, faultiest. 1.** having faults or defects: *faulty workmanship.* **2.** *Rare.* of the nature of a fault; morally blamable: *whatever is faulty with the Church.* **3.** *Obs.* culpable; at fault. —**fault′i·ly,** *adv.* —**fault′i·ness,** *n.* —**Syn. 1.** defective, imperfect, wrong, incomplete. **2.** blameworthy, reprehensible, censurable.

faun (fôn), *n. Rom. Myth.* one of a class of rural deities represented as men with the ears, horns, and tail, and later also the hind legs, of a goat. [ME. See FAUNUS.] —**faun′like′,** *adj.*

fau·na (fô′nə), *n.* **1.** the animals of a given region or period, taken collectively (as distinguished from the plants or *flora*). **2.** a treatise on the animals of a given region or period. [NL, special use of *Fauna,* name of sister of FAUNUS] —**fau′nal,** *adj.*

Fau·nus (fô′nəs), *n. Rom. Relig.* a woodland deity, identified with Pan. [t. L]

Faust (foust), *n.* **1.** the chief character in a famous German story; he is represented as selling his soul to the devil for power or knowledge. **2.** a tragedy by Goethe (Part 1, 1808, Part 2, 1833). **3.** an opera (1859) by Gounod.

fau·teuil (fō′tĭl; *Fr.* fō tœ′y), *n. French.* an easy chair.

faux pas (fō pä′), *pl.* **faux pas** (fō päz′; *Fr.* pä′). *French.* a false step; a slip in manners or conduct; a breach of etiquette or propriety.

fa·ve·o·late (fə vē′ə lāt′), *adj.* honeycombed; alveolate; pitted. [f. s. NL *faveolus* (dim. of L *favus* honeycomb) + -ATE[1]]

fa·vo·ni·an (fə vō′nĭ ən), *adj.* **1.** of or pertaining to the west wind. **2.** mild; favorable; propitious. [t. L: s. *favōniānus,* der. *Favōnius,* the west wind]

fa·vor (fā′vər), *n.* **1.** a kind act; something done or granted out of good will, rather than from justice or for

remuneration: *ask a favor.* **2.** kindness; kind approval. **3.** state of being approved, or held in regard: *in favor, out of favor.* **4.** excessive kindness; unfair partiality: *show undue favor to someone.* **5.** a gift bestowed as a token of good will, kind regard, love, etc. **6.** a ribbon, badge, etc., worn in evidence of good will or loyalty. **7.** a letter, esp. a commercial one. **8.** *(pl.)* consent to sexual intimacy. **9. in favor of, a.** in support of; on the side of. **b.** to the advantage of; (of a check, etc.) payable to. —*v.t.* **10.** to regard with favor. **11.** to have a preference for; treat with partiality. **12.** to show favor to; oblige. **13.** to be favorable to; facilitate. **14.** *Now Rare.* to deal with gently: *favor a lame leg.* **15.** to aid or support. **16.** *Colloq.* to resemble. Also, *Brit.,* **fa'vour.** [ME, t. OF, g. L] —**fa'vor·er,** *n.* —**fa'vor·ing·ly,** *adv.*
—**Syn. 2.** Favor, good will imply a kindly regard or friendly disposition shown by an individual or group. Favor may be merely an attitude of mind: *to look with favor on a proposal.* Good will is more active and leads often to outward manifestations of friendly approval: *by frequent applause the audience showed its good will toward the speaker.* —**Ant. 2.** animosity, malice.

fa·vor·a·ble (fā'vər ə bəl), *adj.* **1.** affording aid, advantage, or convenience: *a favorable position.* **2.** manifesting favor; inclined to aid or approve. **3.** (of an answer) granting what is desired. **4.** promising well: *the signs are favorable.* Also, *Brit.,* **fa'vour·a·ble.** —**fa'vor·able·ness,** *n.* —**fa'vor·a·bly,** *adv.*

fa·vored (fā'vərd), *adj.* **1.** regarded or treated with favor. **2.** enjoying special advantages. **3.** of specified appearance: *ill-favored.* Also, *Brit.,* **fa'voured.**

fa·vor·ite (fā'vər ĭt), *n.* **1.** a person or thing regarded with special favor or preference. **2.** *Sports.* a competitor considered likely to win. **3.** a person treated with special (esp. undue) favor by a prince, etc. —*adj.* **4.** regarded with particular favor or preference: *a favorite child.* Also, *Brit.,* **fa'vour·ite.** [t. F: m. *favorit,* var. of *favori,* t. It.: m. *favorito,* ult. der. *favore* favor, g. L *favor*]

fa·vor·it·ism (fā'vər ə tĭz'əm), *n.* **1.** the favoring of one person or group over others having equal claims. **2.** state of being a favorite. Also, *Brit.,* **fa'vour·it·ism.**

fa·vus (fā'vəs), *n.* *Pathol.* a skin disease, esp. of the scalp, characterized by dry incrustations due to the fungus *Achorion schonleinii.* [t. L: honeycomb]

Fawkes (fôks), *n.* **Guy,** 1570–1606, British conspirator and leader in the Gunpowder Plot to blow up the Houses of Parliament.

fawn[1] (fôn), *n.* **1.** a young deer. **2.** a buck or doe of the first year. **3.** a fawn color. —*adj.* **4.** light yellowish-brown. —*v.i.* **5.** (of deer) to bring forth young. [ME *foun,* t. OF: m. *faon,* ult. der. L *fetus* offspring, young] —**fawn'like',** *adj.*

fawn[2] (fôn), *v.i.* **1.** to seek notice or favor by servile demeanor. **2.** to show fondness by crouching, wagging the tail, licking the hand, etc. (said esp. of dogs). [ME *faghne(n),* OE *fagnian,* var. of *fægnian* rejoice, fawn, der. *fægen* glad, fain] —**fawn'er,** *n.* —**fawn'ing·ly,** *adv.*

Fawn of Virginia deer, *Odocoileus virginianus*

fay[1] (fā), *n.* a fairy. [ME, t. OF: m. *fae, fee,* g. L *fāta* the Fates, pl. of *fātum* FATE]

fay[2] (fā), *v.t., v.i.* to fit, esp. together closely, as timbers in shipbuilding. [ME *feien, fey,* OE *fēgan,* c. G *fügen*]

fay[3] (fā), *n.* *Archaic.* faith. [ME *fei,* t. OF. See FAITH]

Fa·yal (fä yäl'), *n.* an island in the Azores, in the N Atlantic. 23,579 pop. (1940); 66 sq. mi.

fay·al·ite (fā'ə līt', fī ä'līt), *n.* a black, greenish, or brownish mineral of the olivine group, ferrous orthosilicate, Fe$_2$SiO$_4$. [f. FAYAL + -ITE[1]]

Fa·yette·ville (fā'ət vĭl), *n.* a city in S North Carolina. 34,715 (1950).

faze (fāz), *v.t.,* **fazed, fazing.** *U.S. Colloq.* to disturb; discomfit; daunt. [var. of FEEZE]

f.b., *Football.* fullback.

FBI, Federal Bureau of Investigation.

f.c., *Print.* follow copy.

FCC, Federal Communications Commission.

F clef, *Music.* a bass clef. See illus. under **clef.**

fcp., foolscap.

F.D., Fidei Defensor.

Fe, *Chem.* (L *ferrum*) iron.

feal (fēl), *adj.* *Archaic.* faithful; loyal. [back formation from FEALTY]

fe·al·ty (fē'əl tĭ), *n., pl.* **-ties. 1.** *Hist.* **a.** fidelity to a lord. **b.** the obligation or the engagement to be faithful to a lord, usually sworn to by the vassal. **2.** fidelity; faithfulness. [ME *feaute,* t. OF, g. s. L *fidēlitas* fidelity]

fear (fîr), *n.* **1.** a painful feeling of impending danger, evil, trouble, etc.; the feeling or condition of being afraid. **2.** a specific instance of such a feeling. **3.** anxiety; solicitude. **4.** reverential awe, esp. toward God. **5.** a cause for fear. **6. for fear of,** in order to avoid or prevent. —*v.t.* **7.** to regard with fear; be afraid of. **8.** to have reverential awe of. **9.** *Archaic.* to be afraid (used reflexively). **10.** *Archaic and Dial.* to frighten. —*v.i.* **11.** to have fear; be afraid. [ME *fere,* OE *fǣr* sudden attack, sudden danger, c. OS *fār* ambush; akin to G *gefahr* danger] —**fear'er,** *n.*

—**Syn. 1.** apprehension, consternation, dismay, terror, fright, panic. FEAR, ALARM, DREAD all imply a painful emotion experienced when one is confronted by threatening danger or evil. ALARM implies an agitation of the feelings caused by awakening to imminent danger; it names a feeling of fright or panic: *he started up in alarm.* FEAR and DREAD usually refer more to a condition or state than to an event. FEAR is often applied to an attitude toward something which, when experienced, will cause the sensation of fright: *fear of falling.* DREAD suggests an attitude of anticipating something, usually a particular event, which, when experienced, will be disagreeable rather than frightening: *she lives in dread of losing her money.* (The same is often true of FEAR, when used in a negative statement: *she has no fear she'll lose her money.*)

Fear (fîr), *n.* **Cape, 1.** a river in SE North Carolina. 202 mi. **2.** a cape at the mouth of this river.

fear·ful (fîr'fəl), *adj.* **1.** causing, or apt to cause, fear. **2.** feeling fear, dread, apprehension, or solicitude: *I am fearful of his doing it,* or *lest he should do it.* **3.** full of awe or reverence. **4.** showing or caused by fear. **5.** *Chiefly Colloq.* extremely bad, large, etc. —**fear'ful·ly,** *adv.* —**fear'ful·ness,** *n.*

fear·less (fîr'lĭs), *adj.* without fear; bold. —**fear'-less·ly,** *adv.* —**fear'less·ness,** *n.* —**Syn.** See **brave.**

fear·nought (fîr'nôt'), *n.* a kind of stout woolen cloth. Also, **fear/naught/.**

fear·some (fîr'səm), *adj.* **1.** causing fear. **2.** afraid; timid. —**fear'some·ly,** *adv.* —**fear'some·ness,** *n.*

fea·sance (fē'zəns), *n.* *Law.* doing or performance, as of a condition or duty. [t. AF: m. *fesance,* der. *faire* do]

fea·si·ble (fē'zə bəl), *adj.* **1.** capable of being done, effected, or accomplished: *a feasible plan.* **2.** suitable: *a road feasible for travel.* **3.** likely; probable: *a feasible theory.* [ME *fesable,* t. OF, der. *faire,* g. L *facere* do, make] —**fea'si·bil'i·ty, fea'si·ble·ness,** *n.* —**fea'si·bly,** *adv.* —**Syn. 1.** See **possible.**

feast (fēst), *n.* **1.** a periodical celebration, or day or time of celebration, of religious or other character, in commemoration of some event or person, or having some other special significance: *feasts of the church, the medieval feast of fools, the Chinese feast of lanterns.* **2.** a sumptuous entertainment or meal for many guests. **3.** any rich or abundant meal. **4.** something highly agreeable. —*v.i.* **5.** to have, or partake of, a feast; eat sumptuously. **6.** to dwell with gratification or delight, as on a picture. —*v.t.* **7.** to provide or entertain with a feast. **8.** to gratify; delight. [ME *feste,* t. OF, g. L *festa,* fem. sing. of *festus* festal] —**feast'er,** *n.*
—**Syn. 2.** FEAST, BANQUET imply large social events, with an abundance of food. A FEAST is a meal with a plenteous supply of food and drink for a large company: *to provide a feast for all company employees.* A BANQUET is an elaborate feast for a formal and ceremonious occasion: *the main speaker at a banquet.*

feast·ful (fēst'fəl), *adj.* festive; joyful.

Feast of Weeks, Pentecost (def. 2).

feat[1] (fēt), *n.* **1.** a noteworthy or extraordinary act or achievement, usually displaying boldness, skill, etc. **2.** an action; deed. [ME *fait,* t. OF, g. L *factum* (thing) done, prop. pp. neut.] —**Syn. 1.** See **achievement.**

feat[2] (fēt), *adj.* *Archaic or Dial.* **1.** apt; skillful; dexterous. **2.** suitable. **3.** neat. [ME *fete,* appar. t. OF: m. *fait,* pp. of *faire,* g. L *facere* do, make]

feath·er (fĕth'ər), *n.* **1.** one of the epidermal appendages which together constitute the plumage of birds, being typically made up of a hard, tubelike portion (the quill) attached to the body of the bird, which passes into a thinner, stemlike distal portion (the rachis) bearing a series of slender processes (barbs) which unite in a bladelike structure (web) on each side. **2.** plumage. **3.** attire. **4.** condition, as of health, spirits, etc.: *in fine feather, in high feather.* **5.** kind or character. **6.** something like a feather, as a tuft or fringe of hair. **7.** a featherlike flaw, as in a precious stone. **8.** *Archery.* **a.** a feather or feathers attached to the nock (rear) end of an arrow to direct its flight. **b.** the feathered end or string end of an arrow. **9.** something very light, weak, or small. **10.** *Rowing.* the act of feathering. **11. a feather in one's cap,** a mark of distinction; an honor. —*v.t.* **12.** to provide with feathers, as an arrow. **13.** to clothe or cover with, or as with, feathers. **14.** *Rowing.* to turn (an oar) after a stroke so that the blade becomes nearly horizontal, and hold it thus as it is moved back into position for the next stroke. **15. feather one's nest,** to provide for or enrich oneself. —*v.i.* **16.** to grow feathers. **17.** to be or become feathery in appearance. **18.** to move like feathers. **19.** *Rowing.* to feather an oar. [ME and OE *fether,* c. G *feder;* akin to Gk. *pterón* wing] —**feath'er·less,** *adj.* —**feath'er·like',** *adj.*

feath·er·bed·ding (fĕth'ər bĕd'ĭng), *n.* a type of coercion of an employer by a labor union, in which the employer is forced to pay for services not performed, esp. by hiring unnecessary employees.

feath·er·bone (fĕth'ər bōn'), *n.* a substitute for whalebone, made from the quills of domestic fowls.

feath·er·brain (fĕth'ər brān'), *n.* a giddy or weak-minded person. —**feath'er·brained',** *adj.*

feath·ered (fĕth'ərd), *adj.* **1.** clothed, covered, or provided with feathers. **2.** winged; swift.

feath·er·edge (fĕth'ər ĕj'), *n.* **1.** an edge which thins out like a feather. **2.** the thinner edge of a wedge-shaped board or plank. **3.** the shallow edge of the furrow of a millstone, etc. —**feath'er·edged',** *adj.*

feather grass, any grass of the American genus *Stipa*.

feath·er·head (fĕ*th*'ər hĕd'), *n.* **1.** a silly or light-headed person. **2.** a light or empty head. **—feath'er·head'ed,** *adj.*

feath·er·ing (fĕ*th*'ər ĭng), *n. Music.* a very light and delicate use of the violin bow.

feather star, sea lily or crinoid.

feath·er·stitch (fĕ*th*'ər stĭch'), *n.* **1.** an embroidery stitch producing work in which a succession of branches extend alternately on each side of a central stem. **—v.t. 2.** to ornament by featherstitch.

feath·er·veined (fĕ*th*'ər vānd'), *adj. Bot.* (of a leaf) having a series of veins branching from each side of the midrib toward the margin.

feath·er·weight (fĕ*th*'ər wāt'), *n.* **1.** a boxer or other contestant lighter in weight than a lightweight. **2.** a fighter's weight when between 118 and 126 lbs. **3.** a very light or insignificant person or thing. **—adj. 4.** belonging to the class of featherweights. **5.** trifling; slight.

feath·er·weight·ed (fĕ*th*'ər wā'tĭd), *adj.* (of a race horse) assigned the least weight by the handicapper.

feath·er·y (fĕ*th*'ə rĭ), *adj.* **1.** clothed or covered with feathers; feathered. **2.** resembling feathers; light; airy; unsubstantial. **—feath'er·i·ness,** *n.*

feat·ly (fēt'lĭ), *adv. Archaic or Dial.* **1.** in a feat manner; fitly. **2.** skillfully; nimbly. **3.** neatly; elegantly. [f. FEAT² + -LY] **—feat'li·ness,** *n.*

fea·ture (fē'chər), *n., v.,* **-tured, -turing. —n. 1.** any part of the face, as the nose, chin, etc. **2.** (*pl.*) the face. **3.** the form or cast of the face. **4.** a prominent or conspicuous part or characteristic. **5.** the main picture in a movie program. **6.** a special article, column, cartoon, etc., in a newspaper or magazine. **7.** *Obs. or Archaic.* make, form, or shape. **—v.t. 8.** to be a feature or distinctive mark of. **9.** to make a feature of; or give prominence to: *to feature a story or picture in a newspaper.* **10.** to delineate the features of; depict; outline. **11.** *Colloq.* to resemble in features; favor. [ME *feture,* t. OF, g. L *factūra* making, formation] **—Syn. 4.** FEATURE, CHARACTERISTIC, PECULIARITY refer to a distinctive trait of an individual, or of a class. FEATURE suggests an outstanding or marked property which attracts attention: *complete harmony was a feature of the convention.* CHARACTERISTIC means a distinguishing mark or quality (or one of such) always associated in one's mind with a particular person or thing: *defiance is one of his characteristics, arrogance is a characteristic of bad consciences.* PECULIARITY means that distinct or unusual characteristic which marks off an individual in the class to which he (or it) belongs: (among flowers) *the arrangement of the petals is a peculiarity of pansies.*

fea·tured (fē'chərd), *adj.* **1.** made a feature of; given prominence to. **2.** having features, or a certain cast of features. **3.** *Obs.* formed; fashioned.

fea·ture·less (fē'chər lĭs), *adj.* without distinctive features; uninteresting.

feature story, *Journalism.* a story printed for reasons other than its news value.

feaze¹ (fēz), *v.t., v.i.,* **feazed, feazing.** to unravel. [t. LG: m. *fäsen.* Cf. OE *fæs* fringe]

feaze² (fēz, fāz), *n., v.i., v.t.,* **feazed, feazing.** feeze.

Feb., February.

febri-, a word element meaning "fever," as in *febrifuge.* [t. L, comb. form of *febris*]

fe·bric·i·ty (fĭ brĭs'ə tĭ), *n.* feverishness.

fe·bric·u·la (fĭ brĭk'yə lə), *n.* a slight and short fever, especially when of obscure causation. [t. L, dim. of *febris* fever]

feb·ri·fa·cient (fĕb'rə fā'shənt), *adj.* **1.** producing fever. **—n. 2.** something that produces fever.

fe·brif·er·ous (fĭ brĭf'ər əs), *adj.* producing fever.

fe·brif·ic (fĭ brĭf'ĭk), *adj.* producing or marked by fever. [f. FEBRI- + -FIC]

feb·rif·u·gal (fĭ brĭf'yə gəl, fĕb'rə fū'gəl), *adj.* of or like a febrifuge.

feb·ri·fuge (fĕb'rə fūj'), *adj.* **1.** serving to dispel or reduce fever, as a medicine. **—n. 2.** a febrifuge medicine or agent. **3.** a cooling drink. [t. F, t. L: m.s. *febrifugia,* f. *febri-* FEBRI- + *-fugia* -FUGE]

fe·brile (fē'brəl, fĕb'rəl), *adj.* pertaining to or marked by fever; feverish. [t. L: m.s. *febrīlis* pertaining to fever]

Feb·ru·ar·y (fĕb'rŏŏ ĕr'ĭ), *n.* the second month of the year, containing ordinarily 28 days, in leap years 29. [t. L: m.s. *Februārius,* der. *februa,* pl., the Roman festival of purification, celebrated Feb. 15; r. ME *feverer,* t. OF: m. *feverier,* g. L *Februārius*]

fec., fecit.

fe·ces (fē'sēz), *n. pl.* **1.** waste matter discharged from the intestines; excrement. **2.** dregs; sediment. Also, **faeces.** [t. L: m. *faecēs,* pl. of *faex* dregs] **—fe·cal** (fē'kəl), *adj.*

Fech·ner (fĕкн'nər), *n.* **Gustav Theodor** (gŏŏs'täf tā'ō dōr'), 1801–87, German physicist, psychologist, and philosopher.

fe·cit (fē'sĭt), *v. Latin.* he (or she) made (it, a work of art, etc.).

feck (fĕk), *n. Scot. and N. Eng.* **1.** effect; efficacy; value. **2.** amount; quantity. [var. of *fect,* aphetic var. of EF-FECT]

feck·less (fĕk'lĭs), *adj. Orig. Scot. and N. Eng.* **1.** ineffective; feeble. **2.** spiritless; worthless. **—feck'less·ly,** *adv.* **—feck'less·ness,** *n.*

fec·u·la (fĕk'yə lə), *n., pl.* **-lae** (-lē'). starch obtained by washing the comminuted roots, grains, or other parts of plants. [t. L: m. *faecula* crust of wine, dim. of *faex* dregs]

fec·u·lent (fĕk'yə lənt), *adj.* abounding in dregs or foul matter; turbid; muddy; foul. [t. L: s. *faeculentus* abounding in dregs, impure] **—fec'u·lence,** *n.*

fe·cund (fē'kŭnd, fĕk'ŭnd), *adj.* capable of producing offspring, or fruit, vegetation, etc., in abundance; prolific; fruitful; productive. [t. L: s. *fēcundus* fruitful; r. ME *fecounde,* t. OF: m. *fecond*]

fe·cun·date (fē'kən dāt', fĕk'ən-), *v.t.,* **-dated, -dating. 1.** to make prolific or fruitful. **2.** *Biol.* to impregnate. [t. L: m.s. *fēcundātus,* pp., made fruitful] **—fe'·cun·da'tion,** *n.*

fe·cun·di·ty (fĭ kŭn'də tĭ), *n.* **1.** the quality of being fecund; the capacity, esp. in female animals, of producing young in great numbers. **2.** fruitfulness or fertility, as of the earth. **3.** capacity of abundant production: *fecundity of imagination.*

fed (fĕd), *v.* pt. and pp. of **feed.**

Fed., Federal.

fed·er·a·cy (fĕd'ər ə sĭ), *n.* a confederacy.

fed·er·al (fĕd'ər əl), *adj.* **1.** of or pertaining to a compact or a league, esp. a league between nations or states. **2.** *Govt.* **a.** pertaining to or of the nature of a union of states under a central government distinct from the individual governments of the separate states: *the federal government of the U.S.* **b.** favoring a strong central government in such a union. **c.** pertaining to such a central government: *federal offices.* **3.** (*cap.*) *U.S. Hist.* **a.** noting or pertaining to a party in early U.S. history advocating a strong central government. **b.** (in the Civil War) pertaining to or supporting the Union government. **c.** relating to, or adhering to, the support of the Constitution. **—n. 4.** an advocate of federation or federalism. **5.** (*cap.*) *U.S. Hist.* **a.** a Federalist. **b.** an adherent of the Union government during the Civil War; a Unionist. **c.** a soldier in the Federal army. [early mod. E *foederal,* f. s. L *foedus* compact, league (akin to *fides* faith) + -AL¹] **—fed'er·al·ly,** *adv.*

Federal Bureau of Investigation, a federal agency charged with investigations for the attorney general of the U.S. and with the safeguarding of national security.

Federal Capital Territory, former name of **Australian Capital Territory.**

Federal Constitution, the Constitution of the United States government. See **Constitution.**

Federal District, a district in which the national government of a particular country is located, esp. among the republics of Latin America. Spanish, **Distrito Federal.**

fed·er·al·ism (fĕd'ər ə lĭz'əm), *n.* **1.** the federal principle of government. **2.** (*cap.*) *U.S. Hist.* the principles of the Federalist party.

fed·er·al·ist (fĕd'ər əl ĭst), *n.* **1.** an advocate of federalism. **2.** (*cap.*) *U.S. Hist.* **a.** a member or supporter of the Federalist party. **b. The,** a collection of essays written by Hamilton, Madison, and Jay supporting the adoption of the Constitution. **—adj. 3.** Also, **fed'·er·al·is'tic.** of federalism or the Federalists.

Federalist party, *U.S. Hist.* **1.** a political group that favored the adoption by the States of the Constitution. **2.** a political party in early U.S. history advocating a strong central government. Also, **Federal party.**

fed·er·al·ize (fĕd'ər ə līz'), *v.t.,* **-ized, -izing.** to make federal; unite in a federal union, as different states. **—fed'er·al·i·za'tion,** *n.*

Federal Republic of Germany. See **Germany.**

Federal Reserve System, a system of banks (**Federal Reserve Banks**) in the U.S., forming 12 districts under the control of a central board of governors (**Federal Reserve Board**) and 12 central banks, which regulate the making of loans, the amount of reserves, etc., of member banks, and, in general, attempt to adjust banking practices to the needs of the nation's industry and agriculture.

fed·er·ate (*v.* fĕd'ə rāt'; *adj.* fĕd'ər ĭt), *v.,* **-ated, -ating,** *adj.* **—v.t., v.i. 1.** to unite in a league or federation. **2.** to organize on a federal basis. **—adj. 3.** federated; allied: *federate nations.* [t. L: m.s. *foederātus,* pp., leagued together]

Federated Malay States, a former federation of four native states in British Malaya. 2,212,000 pop. (est. 1941); 27,540 sq. mi. See **Malaya, Federation of.**

fed·er·a·tion (fĕd'ə rā'shən), *n.* **1.** act of federating, or uniting in a league. **2.** the formation of a political unity, with a central government, out of a number of separate states, etc., each of which retains control of its own internal affairs. **3.** a league or confederacy. **4.** a federated body formed by a number of states, societies, etc., each retaining control of its own internal affairs.

fed·er·a·tive (fĕd'ə rā'tĭv), *adj.* **1.** pertaining to or of the nature of a federation. **2.** inclined to federate. **—fed'er·a'tive·ly,** *adv.*

fe·do·ra (fĭ dōr'ə), *n.* a soft felt hat with a curled brim, worn with the crown creased lengthwise. [said to be from *Fédora,* drama by Sardou]

Fed. Res. Bd., Federal Reserve Board.

Fed. Res. Bk., Federal Reserve Bank.

---

b., blend of, blended; c., cognate with; d., dialect, dialectal; der., derived from; f., formed from; g., going back to; m., modification of; r., replacing; s., stem of; t., taken from; ?, perhaps. See the full key on inside cover.

fee (fē), *n.; v.*, **feed, feeing.** —*n.* **1.** a payment for services: *a doctor's fee.* **2.** sum paid for a privilege: *an admission fee.* **3.** a gratuity; tip. **4.** a charge allowed by law for the service of a public officer. **5.** possession; ownership. **6.** *Law.* a. an estate of inheritance in land, either absolute and without limitation to any particular class of heirs (**fee simple**) or limited to a particular class of heirs (**fee tail**). **b.** an estate in land held of a feudal lord on condition of the performing of certain services; **c.** a territory held in fee. **7. hold in fee**, to have full ownership in (land). —*v.t.* **8.** to give a fee to. **9.** *Chiefly Scot.* to hire; employ. [ME, t. AF; of Gmc. orig.] —**fee´less,** *adj.*

fee·ble (fē´bəl), *adj.,* **-bler, -blest. 1.** physically weak, as from age, sickness, etc. **2.** weak intellectually or morally: *a feeble mind.* **3.** lacking in volume, loudness, brightness, distinctness, etc.: *a feeble voice, light.* **4.** lacking in force, strength, or effectiveness: *feeble resistance, arguments, barriers.* [ME *feble,* t. OF, g. L *feēbilis* lamentable] —**fee´ble·ness,** *n.* —**fee´blish,** *adj.* —**fee´bly,** *adv.* —**Syn. 1.** infirm, frail, sickly. See **weak.** —**Ant.** 1–4. strong.

fee·ble-mind·ed (fē´bəl mīn´dĭd), *adj.* **1.** feeble in intellect; lacking the normal mental powers. **2.** lacking firmness of mind. —**fee´ble-mind´ed·ness,** *n.*

feed (fēd), *v.,* **fed, feeding,** *n.* —*v.t.* **1.** to give food to; supply with nourishment. **2.** to provide with the requisite materials for development, maintenance, or operation. **3.** to yield, or serve as, food for. **4.** to provide as food. **5.** to furnish for consumption. **6.** to satisfy; minister to; gratify. **7.** to supply for maintenance or to be operated upon, as to a machine. **8.** to use (land) as pasture. **9.** *Colloq.* to provide cues to (an actor, esp. a comedian). **10. be fed up,** *Colloq.* to have more than enough of something. —*v.i.* **11.** to take food; eat. **12.** to be nourished or gratified; subsist. —*n.* **13.** food, esp. for cattle, horses, etc. **14.** an allowance of such food. **15.** *Colloq.* a meal. **16.** act of feeding. **17.** the act or process of feeding a furnace, machine, etc. **18.** the material, or the amount of it, so fed or supplied. **19.** a feeding mechanism. **20.** *Theat. Chiefly Brit. Colloq.* a line spoken by one actor to which another actor responds with a line which causes a laugh. [ME *fede(n),* OE *fēdan,* der. *fōda* food] —**Syn. 13.** FEED, FODDER, FORAGE, PROVENDER mean food for animals. FEED is the general word: *pig feed, chicken feed.* FODDER is esp. applied to dry or green feed, as opposed to pasturage, fed to horses, cattle, etc.: *cornstalks are good fodder, fodder for winter feeding.* FORAGE is food which an animal obtains (usually grass, leaves, etc.) by searching about for it: *lost cattle can usually live on forage.* PROVENDER denotes dry feed, such as hay, oats, or corn: *a supply of provender in the haymow and corn cribs.*

feed·back (fēd´bǎk´), *adj.* **1.** *Electronics.* denoting or pertaining to a system in which some of the energy of the plate circuit of a vacuum tube is returned (fed back) to the grid circuits. When this opposes the input, it is called *inverse,* when it aids the input it is called *regenerative.* —*n.* **2.** a feedback system.

feed·bag (fēd´bǎg´), *n.* a bag for feeding horses, placed before the mouth with straps around the head.

feed·er (fē´dər), *n.* **1.** one who or that which supplies food or feeds something. **2.** one who or that which takes food or nourishment. **3.** a lamb or sheep to be fed for fattening. **4.** a person or device that feeds a machine, printing press, etc. **5.** a tributary stream, a branch railroad, etc. **6.** *Elect.* a conductor, or group of conductors, connecting primary equipment in an electric power system. **7.** *Brit.* a bib.

feeder line, the branch line of an airline system.

feel (fēl), *v.,* **felt, feeling,** *n.* —*v.t.* **1.** to perceive or examine by touch. **2.** to have a sensation (other than sight, hearing, taste, and smell) of. **3.** to find or pursue (one's way) by touching, groping, or cautious moves. **4.** to be or become conscious of. **5.** to be emotionally affected by: *to feel one's disgrace keenly.* **6.** to experience the effects of: *the whole region felt the storm.* **7.** to have a particular sensation or impression of (fol. by an adjunct or complement): *to feel oneself slighted.* **8.** to have a general or thorough conviction of. —*v.i.* **9.** to have perception by touch or by any nerves of sensation other than those of sight, hearing, taste, and smell. **10.** to make examination by touch; grope. **11.** have mental sensations or emotions. **12.** to be consciously, in emotion, opinion, etc.: *to feel happy, angry, sure.* **13.** to have sympathy or compassion (fol. by *with* or *for*). **14.** to have a sensation of being: *to feel warm, free.* **15.** to seem in the impression produced: *how does it feel to be rich?* —*n.* **16.** a quality of an object that is perceived by feeling or touching: *a soapy feel.* **17.** a sensation of something felt; a vague mental impression or feeling. **18.** the sense of touch: *soft to the feel.* [ME *fele(n),* OE *fēlan,* c. G *fühlen*]

feel·er (fē´lər), *n.* **1.** one who or that which feels. **2.** a proposal, remark, hint, etc., designed to bring out the opinions or purposes of others. **3.** *Zool.* an organ of touch, as an antenna or a tentacle.

feel·ing (fē´lĭng), *n.* **1.** the function or the power of perceiving by touch; physical sensation not connected with sight, hearing, taste, or smell. **2.** a particular sensation of this kind: *a feeling of warmth, pain, or drowsiness.* **3.** *Psychol.* consciousness itself without regard to thought or a perceived object, as excitement—calm, strain—relaxation. **4.** a consciousness or impression: *a*

feeling of inferiority. **5.** an emotion: *a feeling of joy, sorrow, fear.* **6.** capacity for emotion; pity. **7.** a sentiment; opinion: *to have a feeling that something will succeed, the general feeling was in favor of the proposal.* **8.** (*pl.*) sensibilities; susceptibilities: *to hurt one's feelings.* **9.** fine emotional endowment. **10.** *Music., etc.* a. emotional or sympathetic perception revealed by an artist in his work. **b.** the general impression conveyed by a work. **c.** sympathetic appreciation, as of music. **11.** that feels; sentient; sensitive, as nerves. **12.** accessible to emotion; sympathetic: *a feeling heart.* **13.** indicating emotion: *a feeling retort.* —**feel´ing·ly,** *adv.* —**Syn. 5.** FEELING, EMOTION, PASSION, SENTIMENT refer to pleasurable or painful sensations experienced when one is stirred to sympathy, anger, fear, love, grief, etc. FEELING is a general term for a subjective point of view as well as for specific sensations: *to be guided by feeling rather than by facts, a feeling of sadness, of rejoicing.* EMOTION is applied to an intensified feeling: *agitated by emotion.* PASSION is strong or violent emotion, often so overpowering that it masters the mind or judgment: *stirred to a passion of anger.* SENTIMENT is a mixture of thought and feeling, esp. refined or tender feeling: *recollections are often colored by sentiment.*

fee simple. See fee (def. 6a).

feet (fēt), *n.* pl. of foot. —**feet´less,** *adj.*

fee tail. See fee (def. 6a).

feeze (fēz, fāz), *n., v.,* **feezed, feezing.** *Obs.* or *Dial.* —*n.* **1.** *U.S.* a state of vexation or worry. **2.** a rush; a violent impact. —*v.i.* **3.** to fret; worry. —*v.t.* **4.** to disturb. **5.** to beat; flog. Also, **feaze.** [ME *fese(n),* OE *fēs(i)an* drive, c. Sw. *fōsa*]

feign (fān), *v.t.* **1.** to invent fictitiously or deceptively, as a story or an excuse. **2.** to represent fictitiously; put on an appearance of: *to feign sickness.* **3.** to imitate deceptively: *to feign another's voice.* —*v.i.* **4.** to make believe; pretend: *she feigns to be ill.* [ME *feigne(n),* t. OF: m. *feign-,* s. *feindre,* g. L *fingere* form, conceive, devise] —**feign´er,** *n.* —**feign´ing·ly,** *adv.* —**Syn. 4.** See **pretend.**

feigned (fānd), *adj.* **1.** pretended; sham; counterfeit. **2.** assumed, as a name. **3.** disguised, as a voice. **4.** fictitiously invented. —**feign·ed·ly** (fā´nĭd lǐ), *adv.*

feint (fānt), *n.* **1.** a movement made with the object of deceiving an adversary; an appearance of aiming at one part or point when another is the real object of attack. **2.** a feigned or assumed appearance. —*v.i.* **3.** to make a feint. [t. F: m. *feinte,* der. *feindre* FEIGN]

feints (fānts), *n.pl.* faints.

Fei·sal (fī´sȯl), *n.* Faisal. Also, **Fei´sul.**

feist (fīst), *n.* a small dog.

feld·spar (fĕld´spär´, fĕl´-), *n.* any of a group of minerals, principally aluminosilicates of potassium, sodium, and calcium, and characterized by two cleavages at nearly right angles. They are among the most important constituents of igneous rocks. Also, *esp. Brit.,* **felspar.** [half-taken, half-translated from G *feldspath*] —**feld·spath·ic** (fĕld spǎth´ĭk, fĕl´-), *adj.*

feld·spath·ose (fĕld´spǎth ōs´), *adj. Mineral.* of, pertaining to, consisting of, or containing feldspar.

fe·lic·i·fic (fē´lə sĭf´ĭk), *adj.* making happy; productive of happiness. [t. L: s. *fēlicificus* making happy]

fe·lic·i·tate (fī lĭs´ə tāt´), *v.,* **-tated, -tating,** *adj.* —*v.t.* **1.** to compliment upon a happy event; congratulate: *to felicitate a friend on his good fortune.* **2.** *Now Rare,* to make happy. —*adj.* **3.** *Obs.* made happy. [t. LL: m.s. *fēlicitātus,* pp. of *fēlicitāre* make happy, der. L *fēlix* happy] —**fe·lic´i·ta´tor,** *n.*

fe·lic·i·ta·tion (fī lĭs´ə tā´shən), *n.* expression of good wishes; congratulation.

fe·lic·i·tous (fī lĭs´ə təs), *adj.* **1.** apt or appropriate, as action, manner, or expression. **2.** apt in manner or expression, as a person. —**fe·lic´i·tous·ly,** *adv.* —**fe·lic´i·tous·ness,** *n.*

fe·lic·i·ty (fī lĭs´ə tǐ), *n., pl.* **-ties. 1.** state of being happy, esp. in a high degree. **2.** an instance of this. **3.** a source of happiness. **4.** a skillful faculty: *felicity of expression.* **5.** an instance or display of this. **6.** *Now Rare.* good fortune. [ME *felicite,* t. L: m.s. *fēlicitas* happiness] —**Syn. 1.** See **happiness.**

fe·lid (fē´lĭd), *n.* one of the cat family, *Felidae.*

fe·line (fē´līn), *adj.* **1.** belonging or pertaining to the cat family, *Felidae,* which includes, besides the domestic cat, the lions, tigers, leopards, lynxes, jaguars, etc. **2.** catlike; characteristic of animals of the cat family: *feline softness of step.* **3.** sly; stealthy; treacherous. —*n.* **4.** an animal of the cat family. [t. L: m.s. *fēlinus* of a cat] —**fe´line·ly,** *adv.* —**fe´line·ness, fe·lin·i·ty** (fī lǐn´ə tǐ), *n.*

feline agranulocytosis, *Vet. Sci.* a highly fatal, contagious virus disease of domestic cats characterized by fever, somnolence, and diarrhea.

fell¹ (fĕl), *v.* pt. of fall.

fell² (fĕl), *v.t.* **1.** to cause to fall; knock, strike, or cut down: *to fell a moose, a tree, etc.* **2.** *Sewing.* to finish (a seam) by sewing the edge down flat. —*n.* **3.** *Lumbering.* the timber cut down in one season. **4.** *Sewing.* a seam finished by felling. [ME *felle(n),* OE *fellan,* causative of *feallan* fall] —**fell´er,** *n.*

fell³ (fĕl), *adj.* **1.** fierce; cruel; dreadful. **2.** destructive; deadly: *fell poison or disease.* [ME, t. OF: m. *fel* base. See FELON] —**fell´ness,** *n.*

fell⁴ (fĕl), *n.* the skin or hide of an animal; a pelt. [ME and OE, c. G *fell;* akin to L *pellis* skin]

fell[5] (fĕl), *n. Scot. and N. Eng.* a stretch of elevated waste land or pasture; a down. [ME, t. Scand.; cf. Icel. *fiall* mountain]

fell·a·ble (fĕl'ə bəl), *adj.* capable of being or fit to be felled.

fel·lah (fĕl'ə), *n., pl.* **fellahs.** *Ar.* **fellahin, fellaheen** (fĕl'ə hēn'). a native peasant or laborer in Egypt, Syria, etc. [t. Ar.: husbandman]

fell·mon·ger (fĕl'mŭng'gər), *n.* a dealer in skins or hides of animals, esp. sheepskins.

fel·loe (fĕl'ō), *n.* the circular rim, or a part of the rim of a wheel, into which the outer ends of the spokes are inserted. Also, **felly.** [ME *fely, felwe,* OE *felg, c.* G *felge*]

Wheel
F, Felloe; S, Spoke; H, Hub

fel·low (fĕl'ō), *n.* **1.** a man; boy. **2.** *Colloq.* beau; suitor. **3.** *Colloq.* a person. **4.** a person of small worth or no esteem. **5.** a companion; comrade. **6.** one belonging to the same class; an equal; peer. **7.** one of a pair; a mate or match. **8.** *Educ.* a graduate student of a university or college, to whom an allowance is granted for special study. **b.** *Brit.* an incorporated member of a college, entitled to certain privileges. **c.** a member of the corporation or board of trustees of certain universities or colleges. **9.** a member of any of certain learned societies: *a fellow of the British Academy.* **10.** *Obs.* a partner. **11.** hail fellow well met, a boon companion. —*v.t.* **12.** to make, or represent as, equal with another. **13.** to produce a fellow to; match. —*adj.* **14.** belonging to the same class or group; united by the same occupation, interests, etc.; being in the same condition: *fellow students, citizens,* etc., *fellow sufferers.* [ME *felowe, felawe,* late OE *fēolaga,* t. Scand.; cf. Icel. *fēlagi* companion (f. *fē* money + *-lagi* one who lays (something) down)]

fellow creature, a creature produced by the same Creator (now used chiefly of human beings): *he was ashamed of his fellow creatures.*

fellow feeling, 1. sympathetic feeling; sympathy. **2.** sense of joint interest.

fellow servant rule, the common law rule that the employer was not liable to a servant for injuries caused by the negligence of a fellow servant.

fellow servants, *Law.* workers engaged by the same employer.

fel·low·ship (fĕl'ō shĭp'), *n., v.,* **-shiped, -shiping** or (*esp. Brit.*) **-shipped, -shipping.** —*n.* **1.** the condition or relation of being a fellow. **2.** community of interest, feeling, etc. **3.** communion, as between members of the same church. **4.** friendliness. **5.** an association of persons having similar tastes, interests, etc. **6.** a company; a guild or corporation. **7.** *Educ.* **a.** the body of fellows in a college or university. **b.** the position or emoluments of a fellow of a university, etc., or the sum of money he receives. **c.** a foundation for the maintenance of a fellow in a college or university. —*v.t.* **8.** *Chiefly U.S.* to admit to fellowship, esp. religious fellowship. —*v.i.* **9.** *Chiefly U.S.* to join in fellowship, esp. religious fellowship.

fellow traveler, a nonmember who supports or sympathizes with a party, usually the Communist party.

fel·ly[1] (fĕl'ĭ), *n., pl.* **-lies.** felloe.

fel·ly[2] (fĕl'ĭ), *adv. Archaic.* in a fell manner; fiercely; ruthlessly. [f. FELL[3] + -(L)Y]

fe·lo-de-se (fē'lō də sē', fĕl'ō-), *n., pl.* **felones-de-se** (fĕl'ō nēz'də sē') or **felos-de-se** (fē'lōz də sē', fĕl'ōz-). *Latin.* **1.** one who commits suicide. **2.** suicide. [Anglo-L: a felon with respect to oneself]

fel·on[1] (fĕl'ən), *n.* **1.** *Law.* one who has committed a felony. **2.** *Obs.* a wicked person. —*adj.* **3.** wicked; malicious; treacherous. [ME *felun,* t. OF: m. *felon* base, der. L *fellāre* to suck (obscene)]

fel·on[2] (fĕl'ən), *n. Pathol.* an acute and painful inflammation of the deeper tissues of a finger or toe, usually near the nail; a form of whitlow. [orig. uncert.]

fe·lo·ni·ous (fĭ lō'nĭ əs), *adj.* **1.** *Law.* pertaining to, of the nature of, or involving a felony: *felonious homicide, felonious intent.* **2.** *Now Rare.* wicked; base; villainous. —**fe·lo'ni·ous·ly,** *adv.* —**fe·lo'ni·ous·ness,** *n.*

fel·on·ry (fĕl'ən rĭ), *n.* **1.** the whole body or class of felons. **2.** the convict population of a penal colony.

fel·o·ny (fĕl'ə nĭ), *n., pl.* **-nies.** *Law.* **1.** any of various offenses, as murder, burglary, etc., of graver character than those called misdemeanors, and commonly punished in the U.S. by death or imprisonment for more than a year. **2.** (in early English law) any crime punishable by loss of life or member and forfeiture of goods and chattels, and which could be prosecuted by appeal.

felony murder, a murder while committing an independent felony, as robbery.

fel·site (fĕl'sīt), *n.* a dense, igneous rock consisting typically of feldspar and quartz, both of which may appear as phenocrysts. [f. FELS(PAR) + -ITE[1]] —**fel·sit·ic** (fĕl sĭt'ĭk), *adj.*

fel·spar (fĕl'spär'), *n. Chiefly Brit.* feldspar.

felt[1] (fĕlt), *v.* pt. and pp. of feel.

felt[2] (fĕlt), *n.* **1.** a nonwoven fabric of wool, fur, or hair, matted together by pressure. **2.** any article of this material, as a hat. **3.** any matted fabric or material. —*adj.* **4.** pertaining to or made of felt. —*v.t.* **5.** to make

into felt; mat or press together. **6.** to cover with, or as with, felt. —*v.i.* **7.** to become matted together. [ME and OE; akin to G *filz.* See FILTER]

felt·ing (fĕl'tĭng), *n.* **1.** felted material. **2.** act or process of making felt. **3.** the materials of which felt is made.

fe·luc·ca (fē lŭk'ə), *n.* a long, narrow vessel propelled by oars or lateen sails, or both, used in the Mediterranean. [t. It., t. Ar.]

Felucca

fe·male (fē'māl), *n.* **1.** a human being of the sex which conceives and brings forth young; a woman or girl. **2.** any animal of corresponding sex. **3.** *Bot.* a pistillate plant. —*adj.* **4.** belonging to the sex which brings forth young, or any division or group corresponding to it. **5.** pertaining to or characteristic of this sex; feminine. **6.** *Bot.* **a.** designating or pertaining to a plant or its reproductive structure which produces or contains elements that need fertilization. **b.** (of seed plants) pistillate. **7.** *Mech.* designating some part, etc., into which a corresponding part fits: *a female outlet.* **8.** *Obs.* womanish; weakly. [ME *female* (a form due to assoc. with *male*), var. of *femelle,* t. OF, g. L *fēmella,* dim. of *fēmina* woman] —**Syn. 1.** See **woman. 5.** FEMALE, EFFEMINATE, FEMININE refer to attributes of women. FEMALE, referring to anything not male, is the scientific word, and was once the general word, to designate one of the two sexes: *female organs in a plant or animal, a female seminary.* EFFEMINATE is applied reproachfully or contemptuously to qualities which, when possessed by men, are unmanly and weak, though these same qualities might be proper and becoming in women: *effeminate gestures, an effeminate voice.* FEMININE, corresponding to masculine, applies to the attributes particularly appropriate to women, esp. the softer and more delicate qualities. The word is seldom used merely to denote sex, and, if applied to men, suggests the delicacy and weakness of women: *a feminine figure, point of view, features.* —**Ant. 5.** male, masculine.

female rhyme, *Pros.* feminine rhyme.

female suffrage, woman suffrage.

feme (fĕm), *n. Law.* a woman or wife. [t. AF, OF. See FEMME]

feme cov·ert (kŭv'ərt), *Law.* a married woman. [t. AF: a woman covered, i.e., protected]

feme sole (sōl), *Law.* **1.** an unmarried woman, whether spinster, widow, or divorcée. **2.** a married woman who is independent of her husband with respect to property. [t. AF: a woman alone]

feme-sole trader (fĕm'sōl'), *Law.* a married woman who is entitled to carry on business on her own account and responsibility, independently of her husband.

fem·i·ne·i·ty (fĕm'ə nē'ə tĭ), *n.* feminine nature; womanliness. Also, **fe·mal·i·ty** (fĭ mäl'ə tĭ), **fem·i·nal·i·ty** (fĕm'ə näl'ə tĭ). [f. s. L *fēmineus* feminine + -ITY]

fem·i·nie (fĕm'ə nĭ), *n.* women collectively. [ME, t. OF, der. L *fēmina* woman]

fem·i·nin (fĕm'ə nĭn), *n. Biochem.* estrone.

fem·i·nine (fĕm'ə nĭn), *adj.* **1.** pertaining to a woman. **2.** like a woman; weak; gentle. **3.** effeminate. **4.** belonging to the female sex. **5.** *Gram.* denoting or pertaining to one of the three genders of Latin, Greek, German, etc., or one of the two of French, Spanish, etc. (so termed because many nouns denoting females belong to it). For example, in Latin, *puella* "girl" is feminine, but so is *stella* 'star'. In German, *Frau* "woman" is feminine, but so is *Zeit* 'time'. —*n.* **6.** *Gram.* **a.** the feminine gender. **b.** a noun of that gender. **c.** another element marking that gender, as *la* (the feminine article in French and Spanish). [ME, t. L: m.s. *fēmininus,* der. *fēmina* woman] —**fem'i·nine·ly,** *adv.* —**fem'i·nine·ness,** *n.* —**Syn. 2.** See **female.**

feminine cadence, *Music.* a cadence in which the chord falls on a weak beat.

feminine ending, 1. *Pros.* an ending in which a line closes with an extra unaccented syllable in addition to the normal accented syllable. **2.** *Gram.* a termination or final syllable marking a feminine word: *"-ā" in Latin is a feminine ending for the ablative case in the singular.*

feminine rhyme, *Pros.* a rhyme of two syllables of which the second is unstressed: *motion, notion* (double rhyme), or of three syllables of which the second and third are unstressed: *fortunate, importunate* (triple rhyme).

fem·i·nin·i·ty (fĕm'ə nĭn'ə tĭ), *n.* **1.** the quality of being feminine; womanliness: *she kept her femininity even in greasy overalls.* **2.** women collectively. Also, **fe·min·i·ty** (fĭ mĭn'ə tĭ).

fem·i·nism (fĕm'ə nĭz'əm), *n.* **1.** the doctrine advocating extension of the activities of women in social and political life. **2.** feminine character. —**fem'i·nist,** *n., adj.* —**fem'i·nis'tic,** *adj.*

fem·i·nize (fĕm'ə nīz'), *v.t., v.i.,* **-nized, -nizing.** to make or become feminine. —**fem'i·ni·za'tion,** *n.*

femme de cham·bre (fàm də shän'br), *French.* **1.** a lady's maid. **2.** a chambermaid.

fem·o·ral (fĕm'ə rəl), *adj.* of or pertaining to the thigh or femur. [f. s. L *femur* thigh + -AL[1]]

fe·mur (fē′mər), *n.*, *pl.* **femurs, femora** (fĕm′ə rə).
1. *Anat.* a bone in the limb of an animal, extending from
the pelvis to the knee; the thigh bone. See diag. under
skeleton. 2. *Entom.* the third segment of an insect's
leg (counting from the base), situated between the
trochanter and the tibia. See diag. under **coxa.** [t. L:
thigh]

fen (fĕn), *n.* **1.** *Brit.* low land covered wholly or partially
with water; boggy land; a marsh. **2. the Fens,** marshy
region W and S of The Wash, in E England. [ME and
OE, c. Icel. *fen* quagmire]

fence (fĕns), *n.*, *v.*, **fenced, fencing.** —*n.* **1.** an enclosure
or barrier, as around or along a field, yard, etc. **2. on
the fence,** *U.S. Colloq.* undecided or neutral. **3.** the
act, practice, or art of fencing; swordplay. **4.** skill in
argument, repartee, etc. **5.** a person who receives and
disposes of stolen goods, or the place of business of such
a person. **6.** *Mach.* a guard or guide, as for regulating
the movements of a tool or machine. **7.** *Archaic.* a
means of defense; a bulwark. —*v.t.* **8.** to enclose by
some barrier, thus asserting exclusive right to possession. **9.** to separate by, or as by, a fence or fences.
10. *Archaic.* to ward off; keep out. **11.** to defend; protect; guard. —*v.i.* **12.** to use a sword, foil, etc., in defense and attack, or in exercise or exhibition of skill in
that art. **13.** to parry arguments; strive to evade giving
direct answers. **14.** (of a horse) to leap over a fence.
15. *Obs.* to raise a defense. [aphetic var. of DEFENCE]
—**fence′less,** *adj.* —**fence′less·ness,** *n.* —**fence′-
like′,** *adj.*

fenc·er (fĕn′sər), *n.* **1.** one who fences. **2.** one who
practices the art of fencing with a sword, foil, etc.
3. *Austral.* a person who makes or mends fences.

fen·ci·ble (fĕn′sə bəl), *n.* **1.** *Archaic.* a soldier enlisted
for defensive service in his own country only. —*adj.*
2. *Scot.* capable of being defended or of making defense.

fenc·ing (fĕn′sĭng), *n.* **1.** act, practice, or art of using
a sword, foil, etc., for defense and attack. **2.** a parrying
of arguments; an evading of direct answers. **3.** an enclosure or railing. **4.** fences collectively. **5.** material
for fences.

fend (fĕnd), *v.t.* **1.** to ward off (often fol. by *off*): *to fend
off blows.* **2.** *Archaic.* to defend. —*v.i.* **3.** to make defense; offer resistance. **4.** to parry. **5.** *Colloq.* to shift;
provide: *to fend for oneself.* [aphetic var. of DEFEND]

fend·er (fĕn′dər), *n.* **1.** one who or that which wards
something off. **2.** the pressed and formed sheet metal
part mounted over the road wheel of an automobile, etc.
3. *Chiefly Brit.* a device attached to the front or rear of
a locomotive, electric car, or the like, for holding off
persons or objects, or cushioning the shock in case of a
collision. Cf. *U.S.* **bumper** (def. 2). **4.** a mudguard or
splashboard on a horse-drawn vehicle. **5.** *Naut.* a piece
of timber, bundle of rope, or the like, hung over the side
of a vessel to lessen shock or prevent chafing. **6.** a low
metal guard before an open fireplace, to keep back falling
coals. [aphetic var. of DEFENDER]

Fé·ne·lon (fĕn lôn′), *n.* **François de Salignac de La
Mothe** (frän swä′ də sä lē nyák′ də lä môt′), 1651–
1715, French theologian, writer, and archbishop of
Cambrai.

fen·es·tel·la (fĕn′ĭs tĕl′ə), *n.*, *pl.* **-tellae** (-tĕl′ē). *Archit.* **1.** a small window or windowlike opening. **2.** a
small windowlike niche in the wall on the south side of
an altar, containing the piscina, and frequently also the
credence. [t. L, dim. of *fenestra* window]

fe·nes·tra (fĭ nĕs′trə), *n.*, *pl.* **-trae** (-trē). **1.** *Anat.*,
Zool. a small opening or perforation, as in a bone.
2. *Entom.* a transparent spot in an otherwise opaque
surface, as in the wings of certain butterflies and moths.
3. *Archit.* a windowlike opening. [t. L: window] —**fe-
nes′tral,** *adj.*

fe·nes·trat·ed (fĭ nĕs′trā tĭd), *adj.* *Archit.* having
windows; windowed; characterized by windows. Also,
fe·nes′trate. [f. m.s. L *fenestrātus,* pp., furnished with
windows + -ED²]

fen·es·tra·tion (fĕn′ĭs trā′shən), *n.* *Archit.* the disposition of windows in a building.

Feng·tien (fŭng′tyĕn′), *n.* **1.** Mukden. **2.** former
name of **Liaoning.**

Fe·ni·an (fē′nĭ ən, fĕn′yən), *n.* **1.** a member of an Irish
revolutionary organization (Irish Republican Brotherhood) founded in New York in 1858, which had for its
aim the establishment of an independent Irish republic.
2. *Irish Hist.* a member of any of several bands of Scots
and Picts (Fianna), fighting the Romans along Hadrian's
Wall in Britain. **3.** *Later Irish Legend.* a member of a
roving band of warriors, the center of numerous legends
comparable to those of King Arthur and the Round
Table. [appar. b. OIrish *fēn(e)* Irishman and OIrish
(f)iann legendary band of warriors in service of Finn
MacCool] —**Fe′ni·an·ism,** *n.*

fen·nec (fĕn′ĕk), *n.* a small North African fox, *Vulpes
zerda,* of a pale-fawn color, and having large pointed
ears. [t. Ar.: m. *fenek*]

fen·nel (fĕn′əl), *n.* **1.** an umbelliferous plant, *Foeni-
culum vulgare,* having yellow flowers, and bearing aromatic fruits used in cookery and medicine. **2.** the fruits
(**fennel seed**) of this plant. **3.** any of various more or
less similar plants, as *Ferula communis* (**giant fennel**), a
tall ornamental apiaceous herb. [ME *fenel,* etc., OE
fenol, finol, finugl, t. VL: m.s. *fēnuclum,* var. of L
faeniculum fennel, dim. of *faenum* hay]

fen·nel·flow·er (fĕn′əl flou′ər), *n.* **1.** any of the ranunculaceous herbs constituting the genus *Nigella,* esp.
N. sativa, whose seeds are used in the East as a condiment and medicine. **2.** the flower of this plant.

fen·ny (fĕn′ĭ), *adj.* **1.** having the character of a fen;
marshy. **2.** inhabiting, or growing in, fens. [ME; OE
fennig, der. *fenn* fen]

Fen·rir (fĕn′rĭr), *n.* *Scand. Myth.* a gigantic wolflike
water demon, son of Loki: slayer of Odin and slain by
Vidar. Also, **Fen·ris** (fĕn′rĭs).

fen·u·greek (fĕn′yŏŏ grēk′), *n.* a plant, *Trigonella
Foenum-Graecum,* indigenous to western Asia, but extensively cultivated elsewhere, chiefly for forage and for
its mucilaginous seeds, which are used in medicine.
[ME *fenegrek,* OE *fenogrǣcum,* t. L: m. *faenugraecum,*
for *faenum graecum* Greek hay]

feod (fūd), *n.* feud². See **fee** (def. 6, 7).

feoff (fĕf *for 1*; fēf, fĕf *for 2*), *n.* **1.** a fief or fee. —*v.t.*
2. to invest with a fief or fee; enfeoff. [ME *feoff(en),* t.
AF: m. *feoffer,* var. of OF *fefier, fieffer,* der. *fieu* FEE]
—**feoff′ment,** *n.* —**feof′for, feof′fer,** *n.*

feoff·ee (fĕf ē′, fēf ē′), *n.* a person invested with a fief.

-fer, a noun suffix with a corresponding adjective in
-ferous, as *conifer* (a coniferous tree). [t. L: bearing, der.
ferre bear]

fe·ra·cious (fə rā′shəs), *adj.* fruitful; productive. [f.
FERACI(TY) + -OUS]

fe·rac·i·ty (fə rǎs′ə tĭ), *n.* fruitfulness. [t. L: m.s.
ferācitas]

fe·ral (fĭr′əl), *adj.* **1.** wild, or existing in a state of
nature, as animals (or, sometimes, plants). **2.** having
reverted to the wild state, as from domestication. **3.** pertaining to or characteristic of wild animals: *the feral
state.* [f. s. L *fera* wild beast (prop. fem. of *ferus* wild)
+ -AL¹]

Fer·ber (fûr′bər), *n.* **Edna,** born 1887, U.S. novelist,
short-story writer, and dramatist.

fer-de-lance (fĕr də läns′), *n.* a large, very venomous
snake, *Trimeresurus atrox,* of tropical America. [F: lit.,
iron (head) of a lance]

Fer·di·nand I (fûr′dĭ nǎnd′; *Ger.* fĕr′dĭ nänt′), **1.**
1503–64, emperor of the Holy Roman Empire, 1558–64,
and king of Bohemia and of Hungary, 1526–64 (brother
of Emperor Charles V). **2.** (*Prince of Saxe-Coburg-
Gotha*) born 1861, ruling prince of Bulgaria, 1887–1908
and tsar, 1908 until he abdicated in 1918. **3.** (''*Ferdinand
the Great*''), died 1065, king of Castile, 1035?–65, and
Leon, 1037–65; recognized as emperor of Spain, 1038–65.

Ferdinand II, 1. 1578–1637, emperor of the Holy
Roman Empire, 1619–37, king of Bohemia, 1617–37, and
king of Hungary, 1618–37. **2.** 1452–1516, king of
Aragon, 1479–1516 and of Sicily, 1408–1516. See **Ferdinand V.**

Ferdinand III, 1452–1516, king of Naples, 1502–16.
See **Ferdinand V.**

Ferdinand V, (''*the Catholic*''), 1452–1516, Spanish
king who founded the Spanish monarchy. He commissioned Christopher Columbus to make his voyages. (As
Ferdinand II, king of Aragon, 1479–1516, and king of
Sicily, 1468–1516; as **Ferdinand III,** king of Naples,
1502–16; as **Ferdinand V,** joint ruler of Castile with his
wife Isabella I, 1474–1504, and sole ruler of United
Spain, 1506–16).

fere (fĭr), *n.* *Obs.* a companion; a mate. [ME; OE
gefēra, der. *fōr* journey; akin to FARE]

fer·e·to·ry (fĕr′ə tōr′ĭ), *n.*, *pl.* **-ries. 1.** a shrine, usually portable, designed to hold the relics of saints. **2.** a
room or chapel in which shrines were kept. [b. *ferē-
(trum)* bier and (REPOSI)TORY; r. ME *fertre,* t. OF]

fe·ri·al (fĭr′ĭ əl), *adj.* **1.** pertaining to a holiday. **2.** *Eccles.* pertaining to weekdays not set apart as festivals.
[t. ML: s. *fēriālis,* der. L *fēria* holiday]

fe·rine (fĭr′ĭn, -ĭn), *adj.* feral. [t. L: m.s. *ferīnus*]

Fe·rin·gi (fə rĭng′gĭ), *n.* (in India, usually in contemptuous use) **1.** a European or a person of European descent. **2.** a Portuguese born in India. Also,
Fe·rin′ghee. [ult. t. Pers.: m. *Farangī,* in Ar. *Faranjī,*
lit., Frank]

fer·i·ty (fĕr′ə tĭ), *n.* **1.** wild, untamed, or uncultivated
state. **2.** savagery; ferocity. [t. L: m.s. *feritas* wildness]

Fer·man·agh (fər mǎn′ə), *n.* a county in Northern
Ireland, in SW Ulster. 54,000 pop. (est. 1946); 653 sq. mi.
Co. seat: Enniskillen.

fer·ment (*n.* fûr′mĕnt; *v.* fər mĕnt′), *n.* **1.** any of
various agents or substances which cause fermentation,
esp.: **a.** any of various living organisms (**organized ferments**), as yeasts, molds, certain bacteria, etc. **b.** any
of certain complex substances derived from living cells
(**unorganized ferments or enzymes**), as pepsin, etc.
2. fermentation. **3.** agitation; excitement; tumult.
—*v.t.* **4.** to act upon as a ferment. **5.** to cause to undergo
fermentation. **6.** to inflame; foment. **7.** to agitate;
excite. —*v.i.* **8.** to be fermented; undergo fermentation.
9. to seethe with agitation or excitement. [t. L: s. *fer-
mentum* leaven, agitation] —**fer·ment′a·ble,** *adj.*

fer·men·ta·tion (fûr′mĕn tā′shən), *n.* **1.** act or process of fermenting. **2.** *Chem.* a change, as effervescence
or decomposition, brought about by a ferment, such as
yeast which converts grape sugar into alcohol and carbon
dioxide, etc. **3.** agitation; excitement.

fer·ment·a·tive (fər mĕn′tə tĭv), *adj.* **1.** tending to produce or undergo fermentation. **2.** pertaining to or of the nature of fermentation.

Fer·mi (fĕr/mē), *n.* **Enrico** (ĕn rē/kō), born 1901, Italian physicist, in U.S. since 1939.

fern (fûrn), *n.* *Bot.* any of the pteridophytes constituting the order *Filicales*, distinguished from other pteridophytes in having few leaves, large in proportion to the stems, and bearing sporangia on the undersurface or margin. [ME *ferne*, OE *fearn*, c. G *farn*; akin to Skt. *parna* feather] —**fern/like/**, *adj.*

Fer·nán·dez (fər nän/dĕz; *Sp.* fĕr nän/dĕth), *n.* **Juan** (hwän), fl. c1570, Spanish navigator and explorer of the western coast of South America and islands of the Pacific.

Fer·nan·do (fĕr nän/dō), *n.* Spanish for **Ferdinand.**

Fer·nan·do de No·ro·nha (fĕr nän/dŏŏ də nô rō/nyə), an island in the S Atlantic, ab. 125 mi. E of the easternmost tip of Brazil: a Brazilian penal colony. 1166 pop. (est. 1944); 10 sq. mi.

Fer·nan·do Po (fər nän/dō pō/), an island in the Bight of Biafra, near the W coast of Africa: a part of Spanish Guinea. 33,818 pop. (1942); ab. 800 sq. mi.

Fern·dale (fûrn/dāl/), *n.* a city in SE Michigan, near Detroit. 29,675 (1950).

fern·er·y (fûr/nə rĭ), *n., pl.* **-eries.** a place or a glass case in which ferns are grown for ornament.

fern seed, the spores of ferns, formerly supposed to have the power to make persons invisible.

fern·y (fûr/nĭ), *adj.* **1.** pertaining to, consisting of, or like ferns. **2.** abounding in or overgrown with ferns.

fe·ro·cious (fə rō/shəs), *adj.* savagely fierce, as a wild beast, person, action, aspect, etc.; violently cruel. [f. FEROCI(TY) + -OUS] —**fe·ro/cious·ly,** *adv.* —**fe·ro/cious·ness,** *n.* —**Syn.** See **fierce.**

fe·roc·i·ty (fə rŏs/ə tĭ), *n.* ferocious quality or state; savage fierceness. [t. L: m.s. *ferōcitas*]

-ferous, an adjective suffix meaning "bearing," "producing," "yielding," "containing," "conveying," as in *auriferous, coniferous, pestiferous.* [f. -FER producing, + -OUS]

Fer·ra·ra (fĕr rä/rä), *n.* a city in N Italy, near the Po: medieval university and cathedral. 131,014 (est. 1946).

fer·rate (fĕr/āt), *n.* *Chem.* a salt of the hypothetical ferric acid. [f. s. L *ferrum* iron + -ATE²]

Fer·re·ro (fĕr rĕ/rō), *n.* **Guglielmo** (gŏŏ lyĕl/mô), 1871–1942, Italian historian and sociologist.

fer·ret¹ (fĕr/ĭt), *n.* **1.** a domesticated, albinistic, red-eyed form of the polecat, employed in Europe for hunting the burrows of rabbits and rats. **2.** a wild species, *Mustela nigripes*, **(black-footed ferret)** yellowish-brown with the tip of the tail and the legs black, inhabiting the plains of Nebraska and Kansas, and feeding largely on prairie dogs. —*v.t.* **3.** to

Black-footed ferret. *Mustela nigripes* (21 to 23 in. long, tail 5 in.)

drive out by, or as by, means of a ferret. **4.** to hunt with ferrets. **5.** to search out or bring to light: *to ferret out the facts.* —*v.i.* **6.** to search about. [ME *fyrette*, t. OF: m. *fuiret*, der. L *fur* thief] —**fer/ret·er,** *n.*

fer·ret² (fĕr/ĭt), *n.* a narrow tape or ribbon, as of silk or cotton, used for binding, etc. [t. It.: m. *fioretto*, dim. of *fiore*, g. L *flōs* flower; conformed to FERRET¹]

ferret badger, any of the small carnivores constituting the genus *Helictis*, of southern and eastern Asia.

ferri-, *Chem.* a word element meaning "iron," implying esp. combination with ferric iron. [var. of FERRO-]

fer·ri·age (fĕr/ĭ ĭj), *n.* **1.** conveyance by a ferryboat or the like. **2.** the price charged for ferrying.

fer·ric (fĕr/ĭk), *adj.* *Chem.* of or containing iron, esp. in the trivalent state (Fe+³). [f. FERR(I)- + -IC]

fer·ri·cy·a·nide (fĕr/ĭ sī/ə nīd/), *n.* *Chem.* a salt containing the radical Fe(CN)₆-³, a complex of ferric iron and cyanide, as *potassium ferricyanide*, K₃Fe(CN)₆.

fer·rif·er·ous (fĕ rĭf/ər əs), *adj.* producing or yielding iron.

Fer·ris wheel (fĕr/ĭs), an amusement device consisting of a large upright wheel rotating about a fixed axis with seats suspended at intervals around its rim. [named after G.W.G. Ferris (1859–96), U.S. engineer]

fer·rite (fĕr/īt), *n.* **1.** *Chem.* a compound formed when ferric oxide is combined with a more basic metallic oxide, as NaFeO₂. **2.** *Metall.* the pure iron constituent of steel, etc., as distinguished from the iron carbides, etc. **3.** *Petrog.* any of certain indeterminable mineral substances (probably iron compounds) frequently observed in the microscopic examination of certain igneous rocks.

ferro-, a word element meaning "iron." In *Chem., ferro-* implies esp. combination with ferrous iron as opposed to ferric iron. Also, **ferri-.** [comb. form repr. L *ferrum* iron]

fer·ro·con·crete (fĕr/ō kŏn/krēt, -kŏn krēt/), *n.* reinforced concrete.

fer·ro·cy·a·nide (fĕr/ō sī/ə nīd/, -nĭd), *n.* *Chem.* a salt containing the radical Fe(CN)₆-⁴, a complex of ferrous iron and cyanide, as, *potassium ferrocyanide*, K₄Fe(CN)₆.

Fer·rol (fĕr rôl/), *n.* El Ferrol.

fer·ro·mag·ne·sian (fĕr/ō măg nē/shən), *adj.* *Geol.* (of minerals and rocks) containing iron and magnesium.

fer·ro·mag·net·ic (fĕr/ō măg nĕt/ĭk), *adj.* *Physics.* paramagnetic to a high degree; behaving like iron in a

magnetic field. —**fer·ro·mag·net·ism** (fĕr/ō măg/nətĭz/əm), *n.*

fer·ro·type (fĕr/ō tīp/), *v.,* **-typed, -typing,** *n.* *Photog.* —*v.t.* **1.** to put a glossy surface on (a print) by pressing it while wet on a metal sheet **(ferrotype tin).** —*n.* **2.** a photograph taken on a sensitized sheet of enameled iron or tin; a tintype. **3.** the process itself.

fer·rous (fĕr/əs), *adj.* *Chem.* of or containing iron, esp. in the divalent state (Fe+²).

fer·ru·gi·nous (fĕ rōō/jə nəs), *adj.* iron-bearing. [t. L: m. *ferrūginus*, der. *ferrūgo* iron rust]

fer·rule (fĕr/əl, -ōōl), *n., v.,* **-ruled, -ruling.** —*n.* **1.** a metal ring or cap put round the end of a post, cane, etc., for strength or protection. **2.** (in steam boilers) a bushing for expanding the end of a flue. —*v.t.* **3.** to furnish with a ferrule. Also, **ferule.** [earlier *verrel*, t. OF: m. *virelle*, g. L *viriola*, dim. of *viriae* bracelets]

fer·ry (fĕr/ĭ), *n., pl.* **-ries,** *v.,* **-ried, -rying.** —*n.* **1.** an establishment with terminals and floating equipment, for transport from shore to shore across a body of water. **2.** a ferryboat. **3.** the legal right to ferry passengers, etc., and to charge toll for the service. —*v.t.* **4.** to carry or convey over a river, strait, etc., in a boat. —*v.i.* **5.** to pass over water in a boat or by ferry. [ME *feri(en)*, OE *ferian*, akin to *faran* fare]

fer·ry·boat (fĕr/ĭ bōt/), *n.* a boat used to convey passengers, vehicles, etc., across a river or the like.

Ferrying Command, *Mil.* a command for transporting planes from the factory to place of use.

fer·ry·man (fĕr/ĭ mən), *n., pl.* **-men.** one who owns or runs a ferry.

fer·tile (fûr/təl or, *esp. Brit.*, -tīl), *adj.* **1.** bearing or producing vegetation, crops, etc., abundantly, as land or soil. **2.** bearing offspring freely; prolific. **3.** abundantly productive: *a fertile imagination.* **4.** producing an abundance (fol. by *of* or *in*): *a land fertile of wheat.* **5.** conducive to productiveness: *fertile showers.* **6.** *Biol.* **a.** fertilized, as an egg or ovum; fecundated. **b.** capable of growth or development, as seeds or eggs. **7.** *Bot.* **a.** capable of producing sexual reproductive structures. **b.** capable of causing fertilization, as an anther with fully developed pollen. **c.** having spore-bearing organs, as a frond. **8.** *Obs.* produced in abundance. [ME, t. L: m.s. *fertilis* fruitful] —**fer/tile·ly,** *adv.* —**fer/tile·ness,** *n.* —**Syn. 1.** See **productive.**

Fertile Crescent, 1. an arc-shaped region favorable for agriculture extending from the Levant to Iraq. **2.** an area in the Middle and Near East, once fertile but now partly desert, in which it is believed that man first practiced agriculture.

fer·til·i·ty (fər tĭl/ə tĭ), *n.* **1.** state or quality of being fertile. **2.** *Biol.* the ability to produce offspring; power of reproduction. **3.** (of soil) the quality of supplying nutrients in proper amounts for plant growth when other factors are favorable.

fer·ti·li·za·tion (fûr/tə lə zā/shən), *n.* **1.** act or process of fertilizing. **2.** state of being fertilized. **3.** *Biol.* **a.** the union of male and female gametic nuclei. **b.** fecundation or impregnation of animals or plants. **4.** the enrichment of soil for the production of crops, etc.

fer·ti·lize (fûr/tə līz/), *v.t.,* **-lized, -lizing. 1.** *Biol.* **a.** to render (an egg, ovum, or female cell) capable of development by union with the male element, or sperm. **b.** to fecundate or impregnate (an animal or plant). **2.** to make fertile; enrich (soil, etc.) for crops, etc. **3.** to make productive. —**fer/ti·liz/a·ble,** *adj.*

fer·ti·liz·er (fûr/tə lī/zər), *n.* **1.** any material used to fertilize the soil, esp. a commercial or chemical manure. **2.** one who or that which fertilizes an animal or plant.

fer·u·la (fĕr/yŏŏ lə, fĕr/ŏŏ-), *n., pl.* **-lae** (-lē/). **1.** *Bot.* any plant of an umbelliferous genus, *Ferula*, chiefly of the Mediterranean region and central Asia, generally tall and coarse with dissected leaves, many of the Asiatic species yielding strongly scented, medicinal gum resins. **2.** a rod; a ferule. [t. L: rod, giant fennel]

fer·u·la·ceous (fĕr/yŏŏ lā/shəs, fĕr/ŏŏ-), *adj.* pertaining to reeds or canes; having a stalklike reed: *ferulaceous plants.* [t. L: m. *ferulāceus*, der. *ferula* giant fennel]

fer·ule¹ (fĕr/əl, -ōōl), *n., v.,* **-uled, -uling.** —*n.* **1.** a rod, cane, or flat piece of wood for the punishment of children, by striking them, esp. on the hand. —*v.t.* **2.** to punish with a ferule. [OE *ferele* rod, t. L: m. *ferula*]

fer·ule² (fĕr/əl, -ōōl), *n., v.t.,* **-uled, -uling.** ferrule.

fer·ven·cy (fûr/vən sĭ), *n.* warmth of feeling; ardor.

fer·vent (fûr/vənt), *adj.* **1.** having or showing great warmth and earnestness of feeling: *a fervent admirer, plea, etc.* **2.** hot; burning; glowing. [ME, t. L: s. *fervens*, ppr., boiling, glowing] —**fer/vent·ly,** *adv.* —**fer/vent·ness,** *n.* —**Syn. 1.** fervid, fiery, ardent, eager, earnest, zealous, vehement, impassioned, passionate.

fer·vid (fûr/vĭd), *adj.* **1.** heated or vehement in spirit, enthusiasm, etc.: *a fervid orator.* **2.** burning; glowing; hot. [t. L: s. *fervidus* burning] —**fer/vid·ly,** *adv.* —**fer/vid·ness,** *n.*

fer·vor (fûr/vər), *n.* **1.** great warmth and earnestness of feeling: *to speak with great fervor.* **2.** intense heat. Also, *Brit.,* **fer/vour.** [ME, t. OF, t. L: heat, passion. —**Syn. 1.** ardor, intensity, eagerness, enthusiasm.

Fes·cen·nine (fĕs/ə nīn/, -nĭn), *adj.* scurrilous; licentious; obscene: *Fescennine verse.* [t. L: m.s. *Fescennīnus* pertaining to *Fescennia* in Etruria]

fes·cue (fĕs/kū), *n.* **1.** any grass of the genus *Festuca*, some species of which are cultivated for pasture or lawns. **2.** a straw, slender twig, etc., used to point out the letters in teaching children to read. [ME *festue*, t. OF, g. L *festūca* stalk, straw]

fess (fĕs), *n.* *Her.* a wide horizontal band across the middle of an escutcheon. Also, **fesse**. [t. OF: m. *fesse*, *faisse*, g. L *fascia* band]

Fes·sen·den (fĕs′ən dən), *n.* **William Pitt,** 1806–69, U.S. statesman.

fess point, *Her.* the central point of an escutcheon. See diag. under **escutcheon.**

fess·wise (fĕs′wīz′), *adv.* *Her.* in the manner of a fess; across the shield. Also, **fesse′wise′.**

fes·ta (fĕs′tə), *n.* a feast, festival, or holiday. [It.]

fes·tal (fĕs′təl), *adj.* pertaining to or befitting a feast, festival, or gala occasion. [t. OF, der. L *festum* a festival, feast] —**fes′tal·ly,** *adv.*

fes·ter (fĕs′tər), *v.i.* **1.** to generate purulent matter; suppurate. **2.** to cause ulceration, or rankle, as a foreign body in the flesh. **3.** to putrefy or rot. **4.** to rankle, as a feeling of resentment. —*v.t.* **5.** to cause to fester. —*n.* **6.** an ulcer; a rankling sore. **7.** a small, purulent, superficial sore. [ME *festre*, t. OF, g. L *fistula* ulcer]

fes·ti·na len·te (fĕs tī′nə lĕn′tī), *Latin.* make haste slowly.

fes·ti·na·tion (fĕs′tə nā′shən), *n.* *Pathol.* a type of gait marked by an involuntary hurrying in walking, observed in certain nervous diseases. [t. L: s. *festīnātio* haste]

fes·ti·val (fĕs′tə vəl), *n.* **1.** a periodic religious or other feast: *the festival of Christmas, a Roman festival.* **2.** any time of feasting; an anniversary for festive celebration. **3.** any course of festive activities: *a music festival.* **4.** *Archaic.* merrymaking; revelry. —*adj.* **5.** of, pertaining to, or befitting a feast or holiday; festal. [ME, t. ML: s. *festivālis*, der. L *festivus* FESTIVE]

fes·tive (fĕs′tĭv), *adj.* pertaining to or suitable for a feast or festival. Also, *Rare,* **fes·ti·vous** (fĕs′tĭ vəs). [t. L: m.s. *festivus* merry, lively] —**fes′tive·ly,** *adv.* —**fes′tive·ness,** *n.*

fes·tiv·i·ty (fĕs tĭv′ə tĭ), *n.,* *pl.* **-ties. 1.** a festive celebration or occasion. **2.** (*pl.*) festive proceedings. **3.** festive character; festive gaiety or pleasure.

fes·toon (fĕs tōōn′), *n.* **1.** a string or chain of flowers, foliage, ribbon, etc., suspended in a curve between two points. **2.** a decorative representation of this, as in architectural work or on pottery. —*v.t.* **3.** to adorn with, or as with, festoons. **4.** to form into festoons. **5.** to connect by festoons. [t. F: m. *feston*, t. It.: m. *festone*, der. *festa* festival, FEAST]

festoon cloud, *Meteorol.* a mammato-cumulus.

fes·toon·er·y (fĕs tōō′nə rĭ), *n.* **1.** a decoration of festoons. **2.** festoons collectively.

fe·tal (fē′təl), *adj.* *Embryol.* of, pertaining to, or having the character of a fetus. Also, **foetal.**

fe·ta·tion (fē tā′shən), *n.* *Embryol.* pregnancy; gestation. Also, **foetation.**

fetch (fĕch), *v.t.* **1.** to go and bring to the speaker, or to or from a particular place: *to fetch a book from another room.* **2.** to cause to come to a particular place or condition; succeed in bringing: *to fetch a doctor.* **3.** to bring (a price, etc.). **4.** *Colloq.* to charm; captivate. **5.** to take (a breath). **6.** to utter (a sigh, groan, etc.). **7.** to deal or deliver (a stroke, blow, etc.). **8.** to perform or execute (a movement, step, leap, etc.). **9.** *Chiefly Naut. or Dial.* to reach; arrive at. **10.** *Hunting.* (as a command to a dog) to retrieve (game). **11. fetch up,** to bring up a child, etc. —*v.i.* **12** to go and bring things. **13.** *Chiefly Naut.* **a.** to move, go, or take a course: *to fetch about.* **b.** to reach; attain; get. **14.** *Hunting.* to retrieve game. **15. fetch and carry,** to do minor menial jobs. **16.** to arrive; reach. —*n.* **17.** act of fetching. **18.** the distance of fetching. **19.** the reach or stretch of a thing (specif. with reference to the traveling of waves of the sea). **20.** a trick; dodge. **21.** the apparition of a living person; a wraith. **22.** *Archaic.* a stroke; effort: *a fetch of the imagination.* [ME *fecche(n)*, OE *feccan*, prob. var. of *fetian*] —**fetch′er,** *n.* —**Syn. 1.** See **bring.**

fetch·ing (fĕch′ĭng), *adj.* *Colloq.* charming; captivating. —**fetch′ing·ly,** *adv.*

fete (fāt; *Fr.* fĕt), *n.,* *v.,* **feted, feting.** —*n.* **1.** a feast or festival. **2.** a festal day; a holiday. **3.** a festive celebration or entertainment. —*v.t.* **4.** to entertain at or honor with a fete. Also, **fête.** [t. F. See FEAST]

fête cham·pê·tre (fĕt shän pĕ′tr), *French.* an outdoor festival; a garden party.

fete day, a festival day.

fet·e·ri·ta (fĕt′ə rē′tə), *n.* a grain sorghum, a variety of *Sorghum vulgare*, cultivated for grain and forage. [prob. t. native African]

fe·tial (fē′shəl), *adj.* **1.** pertaining to fetiales. **2.** concerned with declarations of war and treaties of peace: *fetial law.* **3.** heraldic. —*n.* **4.** one of the fetiales. [t. L]

fe·ti·a·les (fē′shĭ ā′lēz), *n.pl.* (in ancient Rome) a college of priests who acted as heralds and representatives of the people in disputes with foreign nations and in the declaration of war and the ratification of peace. [t. L]

fe·tich·ism (fē′tĭsh ĭz′əm, fĕt′ĭsh-), *n.* fetishism. —**fe′tich·ist,** *n.* —**fe′tich·is′tic,** *adj.*

fe·ti·cide (fē′tə sīd′), *n.* the destruction of the life of a fetus. Also, **foeticide.** [f. s. L *fētus* (see FETUS) + -(I)-CIDE²] —**fe′ti·cid′al,** *adj.*

fet·id (fĕt′ĭd, fē′tĭd), *adj.* having an offensive odor; stinking. Also, **foetid.** [t. L: s. *fetidus,* var. of *foetidus*] —**fet′id·ly,** *adv.* —**fet′id·ness, fe·tid′i·ty,** *n.*

fe·tish (fē′tĭsh, fĕt′ĭsh), *n.* **1.** a material, commonly an inanimate object regarded with awe as being the embodiment or habitation of a potent spirit, or as having magical potency because of the materials and methods used in compounding it. **2.** any object of blind reverence. Also, **fe′tich.** [t. F: m. *fétich,* t. Pg.: m. *feitiço* orig. adj., artificial, g. L *factīcius* factitious] —**fe′tish·like′,** *adj.*

fe·tish·ism (fē′tĭsh ĭz′əm, fĕt′ĭsh-), *n.* **1.** belief in or use of fetishes. **2.** *Psychiatry.* the compulsive use of some inanimate object in attaining sexual gratification, such as a shoe, a lock of hair, stockings, underclothes, a neckpiece, etc. **3.** blind devotion. Also, **fetichism.** —**fe′tish·is′tic,** *adj.*

fe·tish·ist (fē′tĭsh ĭst, fĕt′ĭsh-), *n.* a user of fetishes. Also, **fetichist.**

fet·lock (fĕt′lŏk), *n.* **1.** a part of a horse's leg situated behind the joint between the cannon bone and the great pastern bone, and bearing a tuft of hair. See illus. under **horse.** **2.** this tuft of hair. **3.** the joint at this point (**fetlock joint**). [ME *fet(e)lok,* etc., c. G *fissloch*; orig. obscure]

fe·tor (fē′tər), *n.* any strong offensive smell; a stench. Also, **foetor.** [t. L]

fet·ter (fĕt′ər), *n.* **1.** a chain or shackle placed on the feet. **2.** (*usually pl.*) anything that confines or restrains. —*v.t.* **3.** to put fetters upon. **4.** to confine; restrain. [ME and OE *feter,* c. OHG *fezzera*; akin to FOOT]

fet·ter·bush (fĕt′ər bŏŏsh′), *n.* **1.** an ericaceous evergreen shrub *Lyonia lucida,* of the southern U.S., with fragrant white flowers. **2.** a similar shrub, *Pieris floribunda,* with white campanulate flowers. **3.** any of several heathlike shrubs in the southern U.S.

fet·ter·less (fĕt′ər lĭs), *adj.* without fetters; unfettered.

fet·ter·lock (fĕt′ər lŏk′), *n.* fetlock.

fet·tle (fĕt′əl), *n.* state; condition: *in fine fettle.* [n. use of *fettle* make ready, ME *fetlen,* der. OE *fetel* belt]

fet·tling (fĕt′lĭng), *n.* *Metall.* the material with which the hearth of a puddling furnace or the like is lined, as a substance rich in oxides of iron. [der. *fettle,* v. See FETTLE]

fe·tus (fē′təs), *n.* *Embryol.* the young of an animal in the womb or in the egg, esp. in its later stages. Also, **foetus.** [t. L: a bringing forth, offspring, young]

feu (fū), *n.,* *v.t.* *Scot. Law.* fee (defs. 6, 7). [ME *few,* t. OF: m. *fieu.* See FEE]

feu·ar (fū′ər), *n.* *Scot. Law.* one who holds land in fee.

Feucht·wang·er (foikнt′väng′ər), *n.* **Lion** (lē′ŏn), born 1884, German novelist and dramatist.

feud¹ (fūd), *n.* **1.** a bitter, continuous hostility, esp. between two families, clans, etc. **2.** a quarrel or contention. [var. of *foad* (a being misread as *u*), earlier *fede,* t. OF: m. *fe(i)de,* t. OHG: m. *fēhida* (G *fehde*), c. OE *fǣhth* enmity. Cf. FOE] —**Syn. 2.** See **quarrel**¹.

feud² (fūd), *n.* *Law.* fee (defs. 6, 7). Also, **feod.** [t. ML: s. *feudum,* var. of *feodum.* See FEE]

feu·dal (fū′dəl), *adj.* **1.** of, pertaining to, or of the nature of a fief or fee: *a feudal estate.* **2.** of or pertaining to the holding of land in a fief or fee. **3.** of or pertaining to the feudal system: *feudal law.* —**feu′dal·ly,** *adv.*

feudal investiture, (in the feudal system) the public grant of the land by the lord to the tenant.

feu·dal·ism (fū′dəl ĭz′əm), *n.* the feudal organization, or its principles and practices. —**feu′dal·ist,** *n.* —**feu′dal·is′tic,** *adj.*

feu·dal·i·ty (fū dăl′ə tĭ), *n.,* *pl.* **-ties. 1.** state or quality of being feudal; the principles and practices of feudalism. **2.** a fief or fee.

feu·dal·ize (fū′də līz′), *v.t.* **-ized, -izing.** to make feudal; bring under the feudal system. —**feu′dal·i·za′tion,** *n.*

feudal system, the organization in Europe during the Middle Ages, based on the holding of lands in fief or fee, and on the resulting relations between lord and vassal.

feu·da·to·ry (fū′də tōr′ĭ), *n.,* *pl.* **-ries. 1.** one who holds his lands by feudal tenure; a feudal vassal. **2.** a fief or fee.

feud·ist¹ (fū′dĭst), *n.* *U.S.* a person who fights in a feud. [f. FEUD¹ + -IST]

feud·ist² (fū′dĭst), *n.* a writer or authority on feudal law. [f. FEUD² + -IST]

Feuil·lant (fœ yän′), *n.* a member of a club of constitutional royalists in the French Revolution, which disintegrated as the Revolution grew radical, violent, and antimonarchical. [t. F]

feuil·le·ton (fœ yə tôn′), *n.* *French.* **1.** a part of a newspaper (usually the bottom of one or more pages, marked off by a rule) devoted to light literature, fiction, criticism, etc. **2.** an item printed in the feuilleton.

fe·ver (fē′vər), *n.* **1.** a morbid condition of the body characterized by undue rise of temperature, quickening of the pulse, and disturbance of various bodily functions. **2.** any of a group of diseases in which high temperature is a prominent symptom: *scarlet fever.* **3.** intense nervous excitement. —*v.t.* **4.** to affect with or as with fever. [ME; OE *fefer,* t. L: m.s. *febris*] —**fe′vered,** *adj.* —**fe′ver·less,** *adj.*

ăct, āble, dâre, ärt; ĕbb, ēqual; ĭf, īce; hŏt, ōver, ôrder, oil, bŏŏk, ōōze, out; ŭp, ūse, ûrge; ə = a in alone; ch, chief; g, give; ng, ring; sh, shoe; th, thin; ŧħ, that; zh, vision. See the full key on inside cover.

fe·ver·few (fē′vər·fū′), *n.* a perennial composite plant, *Chrysanthemum Parthenium*, bearing small white flowers, formerly used as a febrifuge. [ME *fevyrfue*, OE *feferfug(i)e*, t. LL: m.s. *febrifugia* kind of plant, f. L: *febri(s)* fever + *-fugia*. See -FUGE]

fever heat, 1. the heat of fever; bodily heat exceeding 98.6 degrees F. 2. feverish excitement.

fe·ver·ish (fē′vər·ĭsh), *adj.* 1. excited or restless, as if from fever. 2. having fever, esp. a slight degree of fever. 3. pertaining to, of the nature of, or resembling fever. 4. infested with fever, as a region. 5. having a tendency to produce fever, as food. —**fe′ver·ish·ly**, *adv.* —**fe′ver·ish·ness**, *n.*

fe·ver·ous (fē′vər·əs), *adj.* feverish. —**fe′ver·ous·ly**, *adv.*

fe·ver·root (fē′vər·rōōt′, -rŏŏt′), *n.* a North American caprifoliaceous herb, *Triosteum perfoliatum*, having a purgative and emetic root.

fever sore, a cold sore.

fever tree, any of several trees, which produce or are supposed to produce a febrifuge, as: 1. the blue gum (tree), which is supposed to prevent malaria. 2. a small rubiaceous tree, *Pinckneya pubens* of the southeastern U.S., with a bark used as a tonic and febrifuge.

fe·ver·weed (fē′vər·wēd′), *n.* any plant of the genus *Eryngium* used medicinally, esp. the *Eryngium foetidum* of the West Indies or the *Eryngium campestre* of Europe.

fe·ver·wort (fē′vər·wûrt′), *n.* 1. the feverroot. 2. the thoroughwort or boneset.

few (fū), *adj.* 1. not many. —*n.* 2. **the few,** the minority. 3. **quite a few,** *Colloq.* a fairly large number. [ME; OE *fēawe*, pl., c. OHG *fōhe*; akin to L *paucus*, Gk. *paûros* little, in pl., few] —**few′ness,** *n.*

few·er (fū′ər), *adj.*, *comp. of* **few.** a smaller number of. —**Syn.** FEWER, LESS are sometimes confused because both imply a comparison with something larger (in number or in amount). FEWER applies only to number: *fewer street cars are running now than ten years ago.* LESS is used in various ways. It is commonly applied to material in bulk, in reference to amount: *less gasoline in the tank than we thought.* It is also used frequently with abstractions, esp. where the idea of amount is figuratively present: *less courage, less wealth.* LESS applies where such attributes as value degree, etc. (but not size or number) are concerned: *a nickel is less than a dime* (in value); *a corporal is less than a sergeant* (in rank). —**Ant.** more.

fey (fā), *adj. Now Chiefly Scot.* 1. fated to die. 2. dying. 3. appearing to be under a spell. [ME; OE *fǣge* doomed to die, timid, c. G *feige* cowardly]

fez (fĕz), *n.*, *pl.* **fezzes.** a felt cap, usually of a red color, having the shape of a truncated cone, and ornamented with a long black tassel, formerly the national headdress of the Turks. [t. Turk.; named after the city of *Fez*]

Turkish fez

Fez (fĕz), *n.* a city in N Morocco, in the French Zone: one of the traditional capitals of the sultanate. 144,424 pop. (1936).

Fez·zan (fĕz·zän′), *n.* a region in SW Libya: a portion of the Sahara with numerous oases. 50,000–80,000 pop.; ab. 150,000 sq. mi. *Chief town:* Murzuq.

ff., 1. folios. 2. and the following (pages, verses, etc.). 3. *Music.* fortissimo.

F.F.A., free from alongside (ship). Also, **f.f.a.**

FHA, Federal Housing Administration.

F.I., Falkland Islands.

fi·a·cre (fĭ·ä′kər; *Fr.* fyȧ′kr), *n.* a hackney coach. [t. F, named after the Hotel de St. *Fiacre* in Paris]

fi·an·cé (fē′än·sā′, fē·än′sā; *Fr.* fē·än·sā′), *n.* a man engaged to be married; a man to whom a girl is engaged. [t. F, pp. of *fiancer* betroth, ult. der. *fier* trust, g. L *fīdere*] —**fi′an·cée′,** *n. fem.*

Fi·an·na (fē′ə·nə), *n.* the Fenians (def. 2).

Fianna Fail (foil′, fīl′), an Irish nationalist party, organized in 1927 by Eamon de Valera, advocating establishment of an Irish Republic. [t. Irish: f. *Fianna* Fenians + *Fáil*, gen. sing. of *fál* sod]

fi·ar (fē′ər), *n. Scot. Law.* the owner of land in fee simple.

fi·as·co (fĭ·ăs′kō), *n.*, *pl.* **-cos, -coes.** an ignominious failure. [t. It.: lit., bottle; sense development obscure]

fi·at (fī′ət, -ăt), *n.* 1. an authoritative decree, sanction, or order. 2. a formula containing the word *fiat*, by which a person in authority gave his sanction. [t. L: let it be done, or made]

fiat lux (fī′ăt lŭks′), *Latin.* let there be light.

fiat money, *U.S.* paper currency made legal tender by a fiat of the government, but not based on or convertible into coin.

fib¹ (fĭb), *n.*, *v.*, **fibbed, fibbing.** —*n.* 1. a trivial falsehood. —*v.i.* 2. to tell a fib. [short for *fibble-fable*, redupl. of FABLE] —**fib′ber,** *n.* —**Syn.** 1. See **falsehood.**

fib² (fĭb), *v.t.*, **fibbed, fibbing.** *Slang.* to strike; beat. [orig. unknown]

fi·ber (fī′bər), *n.* 1. a fine threadlike piece, as of cotton, jute, or asbestos. 2. a slender filament. 3. filaments collectively. 4. matter composed of filaments. 5. fibrous structure. 6. character: *moral fiber.* 7. *Bot.* **a.** filamentous matter from the bast tissue or other parts of plants, used for industrial purposes. **b.** a slender, threadlike root of a plant. **c.** a slender, threadlike bast cell. 8. *Chem.* vulcanized fiber. Also, **fi′bre.** [ME *fibre*, t. F, t. L: m. *fibra* fiber, filament] —**fi′ber·less,** *adj.*

fi·ber·board (fī′bər·bōrd′), *n.* 1. a building material made of wood or other plant fibers compressed and cemented into rigid sheets. 2. a sheet of fiberboard.

fi·ber·glas (fī′bər·glăs′, -gläs′), *n.* 1. a material consisting of extremely fine filaments of glass which are combined in yarn and woven into fabrics, or are used in masses as an insulator. 2. (*cap.*) a trademark for this material.

fibr-, a word element meaning "fiber," as in *fibrin.* Also, **fibri-, fibro-.** [comb. form repr. L *fibra*]

fi·bri·form (fī′brə·fôrm′), *adj.* of the form of a fiber or fibers. [f. FIBRI- + -FORM]

fi·bril (fī′brəl), *n.* 1. a small or fine fiber. 2. *Bot.* one of the delicate hairs on the young roots of some plants. [t. NL: m.s. *fibrilla*, dim. of L *fibra* fiber]

fi·bril·lar (fī′brə·lər), *adj.* of, pertaining to, or of the nature of fibrils.

fi·bril·li·form (fī·brĭl′ə·fôrm′), *adj.* of the form of a fibril.

fi·bril·lose (fī′brə·lōs′), *adj.* composed of or furnished with fibrils.

fi·brin (fī′brĭn), *n.* 1. *Physiol.* a white, tough, strongly elastic, fibrous proteid, formed in the coagulation of blood. 2. *Bot.* a substance like fibrin found in some plants; gluten. [f. FIBR- + -IN²]

fibrino-, a word element representing **fibrin.**

fi·brin·o·gen (fī·brĭn′ə·jən), *n. Physiol.* a globulin occurring in blood and yielding fibrin in the coagulation of blood.

fi·brin·o·gen·ic (fī′brə·nō·jĕn′ĭk), *adj. Physiol.* producing fibrin. Also, **fi·bri·nog·e·nous** (fī′brə·nŏj′ə·nəs).

fi·brin·ous (fī′brə·nəs), *adj.* containing, composed of, or of the nature of fibrin.

fibro-, var. of **fibr-,** before consonants.

fi·broid (fī′broid), *adj.* 1. resembling fiber or fibrous tissue. 2. composed of fibers, as a tumor. —*n.* 3. *Pathol.* a tumor largely composed of smooth muscle.

fi·bro·in (fī′brō′ĭn), *n. Biochem.* an indigestible protein, a principal component of spider webs and silk.

fi·bro·ma (fī·brō′mə), *n.*, *pl.* **-mata** (-mə·tə), **-mas.** *Pathol.* a tumor consisting essentially of fibrous tissue. [NL: f. s. L *fibra* fiber + -*oma* -OMA]

fi·bro·sis (fī·brō′sĭs), *n. Pathol.* the development in an organ of excess fibrous connective tissue. [NL: f. s. L *fibra* fiber + -*osis* -OSIS]

fi·brous (fī′brəs), *adj.* containing, consisting of, or resembling fibers. [t. NL: m.s. *fibrōsus*, der. L *fibra* fiber]

fib·ster (fĭb′stər), *n. Colloq.* one who tells fibs.

fib·u·la (fĭb′yə·lə), *n.*, *pl.* **-lae** (-lē′), **-las.** 1. *Anat.* the outer and thinner of the two bones of the lower leg, extending from the knee to the ankle. See diag. under **skeleton.** 2. *Zool.* a corresponding bone (often rudimentary, or ankylosed with the tibia) of the leg or hind limb of other animals. 3. *Archaeol.* a clasp or brooch, usually more or less ornamented. [t. L: clasp, buckle, pin] —**fib′u·lar,** *adj.*

-fic, an adjective suffix meaning "making," "producing," "causing," as in *colorific, frigorific, horrific, pacific, prolific, soporific.* [t. L: s. -*ficus* making. Cf. F -*fique*]

-fication, a suffix of nouns of action or state corresponding to verbs ending in -*fy*, as in *deification, pacification.* [t. L: s. -*ficātio*, der. -*ficāre.* See -FY]

Fich·te (fĭKH′tə; *Ger.* **Johann Gottlieb** (yō′hän gôt′-lēp), 1762–1814, German philosopher. —**Fich·te·an** (fĭKH′tĭ′ən, fĭk′-), *adj.*

fich·u (fĭsh′ōō; *Fr.* fē shÿ′), *n.* a kind of kerchief of muslin, lace, or the like, generally triangular in shape, worn about the neck by women, with the ends drawn together or crossed on the breast. [t. F, der. *ficher* to throw on in haste]

fick·le (fĭk′əl), *adj.* likely to change from caprice, irresolution, or instability. [ME *fikel*, OE *ficol* deceitful, treacherous, akin to *gefic* deceit, *befician* deceive, *ficung* fraud] —**fick′le·ness,** *n.* —**Syn.** unstable, unsteady, inconstant, changeable, variable, capricious, fitful.

fi·co (fē′kō), *n.*, *pl.* **-coes.** 1. *Archaic.* the merest trifle. 2. *Obs.* fig (def. 5). [t. It., g. L *fīcus* fig]

fict., fiction.

fic·tile (fĭk′təl; *Brit.* -tīl), *adj.* 1. capable of being molded; plastic. 2. molded into form by art. 3. made of earth, clay, etc., by a potter. 4. having to do with pottery. [t. L: m.s. *fictilis*, der. *fingere* form]

fic·tion (fĭk′shən), *n.* 1. the branch of literature comprising works of imaginative narration, esp. in prose form. 2. works of this class, as novels or tales. 3. something feigned, invented, or imagined; a made-up story. 4. act of feigning, inventing, or imagining. 5. *Law.* an allegation that a fact exists which is known not to exist, made by authority of law to bring a case within the operation of a rule of law. [ME, t. L: s. *fictio* a making, fashioning, feigning] —**Syn.** 3. FICTION, FABRICATION, FIGMENT suggest a story which is without basis in reality. FICTION suggests a story invented and fashioned either to entertain or to deceive: *clever fiction, pure fiction.* FABRICATION applies particularly to a false but carefully invented statement or series of statements, in which some truth is sometimes interwoven, the whole usually intended to deceive: *fabrications to lure speculators.* FIGMENT applies to a tale, idea, or statement often made up to explain, justify, or glorify oneself: *his rich uncle was a figment of his imagination.* —**Ant.** 3. fact.

fic·tion·al (fĭk′shən·əl), *adj.* of, pertaining to, or of the nature of fiction. —**fic′tion·al·ly,** *adv.*

---

b., blend of, blended; c., cognate with; d., dialect, dialectal; der., derived from; f., formed from; g., going back to; m., modification of; r., replacing; s., stem of; t., taken from; ?, perhaps. See the full key on inside cover.

fic·tion·ist (fĭk´shən ĭst), *n.* a writer of fiction.

fic·ti·tious (fĭk tĭsh´əs), *adj.* **1.** counterfeit; false; not genuine: *fictitious names*. **2.** pertaining to or consisting of fiction; imaginatively produced or set forth; created by the imagination: *a fictitious hero*. [t. L: m. *fictīcius* artificial] —**fic·ti´tious·ly**, *adv.* —**fic·ti´tious·ness**, *n.*

fictitious person, *Law.* a legal entity or artificial person, as a corporation.

fic·tive (fĭk´tĭv), *adj.* **1.** fictitious; imaginary. **2.** pertaining to the creation of fiction. —**fic´tive·ly**, *adv.*

fid (fĭd), *n. Naut.* **1.** a square bar or support to hold in place a topmast, etc. **2.** a conical wooden pin used to open strands of rope in splicing. **3.** a bar or pin to support or steady something. [orig. obscure]

-fid, an adjective suffix meaning "divided," "lobed," as in *bifid, trifid, multifid, pinnatifid*. [t. L: s. *-fidus*, der. *findere* cleave]

fid·dle (fĭd´əl), *n., v.,* **-dled, -dling.** —*n.* **1.** a stringed musical instrument of the viol class, esp. a violin (now only in familiar or contemptuous use, or to denote bowed instruments of the Orient and the Middle Ages). **2.** *Naut.* a device to prevent things from rolling off the table in bad weather. **3. fit as a fiddle,** in excellent health. **4. play second fiddle,** to take a minor part. —*v.i.* **5.** *Colloq.* to play on the fiddle. **6.** to make aimless movements, as with the hands. **7.** to trifle. —*v.t.* **8.** *Colloq.* to play (a tune) on a fiddle. **9.** to trifle: *to fiddle time away*. [ME (and prob. OE) *fithele* (see FIDDLER), c. G *fiedel*, Icel. *fidhla*. Cf. ML *vitula, vidula* VIOL]

fiddle bow, a bow strung with horsehair with which the strings of the violin or a similar instrument are set in vibration.

fid·dle-de-dee (fĭd´əl dĭ dē´), *interj., n.* nonsense.

fid·dle-fad·dle (fĭd´əl făd´əl), *n., v.,* **-dled, -dling.** *Colloq.* —*n.* **1.** nonsense; something trivial. —*v.i.* **2.** to fuss with trifles. [redupl. of FIDDLE, v.]

fid·dle-head (fĭd´əl hĕd´), *n.* an ornament at the bow of a ship, containing a scroll somewhat like that at the head of a violin.

fid·dler (fĭd´lər), *n.* **1.** a violinist. **2.** one who trifles, etc. [ME and OE *fithelere,* c. Icel. *fithlari*]

fiddler crab, any small burrowing crab of the genus *Gelasimus*, the male of which has one greatly enlarged claw.

Fiddler crab, *Gelasimus annulipes*

fid·dle·stick (fĭd´əl stĭk´), *n.* **1.** a fiddle bow. **2.** a mere nothing.

fid·dle·sticks (fĭd´əl stĭks´), *interj.* nonsense.

fid·dle·wood (fĭd´əl wŏŏd´), *n.* **1.** the heavy, hard, durable wood of various West Indian and other trees. **2.** any of the trees.

fid·dling (fĭd´lĭng), *adj.* trifling; trivial.

fi·de·i·com·mis·sar·y (fĭ´dĭ ĭ kŏm´ə sĕr´ĭ), *n., pl.* **-saries,** *adj. Civil Law.* —*n.* **1.** the recipient of a fideicommissum. —*adj.* **2.** of, pertaining to, or resembling a fideicommissum. [t. L: m. s. *fidei commissārius*. See -ARY¹]

fi·de·i·com·mis·sum (fĭ´dĭ ĭ kə mĭs´əm), *n., pl.* **-missa** (-mĭs´ə). *Civil Law.* a request by a testator that his heir convey a specified part of the estate to another person, or permit another person to enjoy such a part. [t. L, prop. neut. pp. of *fidei committere* entrust to faith]

Fi·de·i De·fen·sor (fĭ´dĭ ī´ dĭ fĕn´sôr), *Latin.* Defender of the Faith, one of the titles of English sovereigns.

Fi·de·lio (fĭ dā´lyō), *n.* an opera (1805) by Beethoven.

fi·del·i·ty (fĭ dĕl´ə tĭ, fə-), *n., pl.* **-ties.** **1.** strict observance of promises, duties, etc. **2.** loyalty. **3.** conjugal faithfulness. **4.** adherence to fact. **5.** *Radio.* the ability of a transmitter or receiver to produce radio waves or sound which reproduce its input accurately (often in combination): *a high-fidelity receiver*. [t. L: m.s. *fidēlitas* faithfulness] —**Syn. 2.** See **loyalty.**

fidge (fĭj), *v.i.,* **fidged, fidging,** *n. Now Rare.* fidget. [var. of d. *fitch* v., c. Icel. *fikja* move restlessly, be eager]

fidg·et (fĭj´ĭt), *v.i.* **1.** to move about restlessly or impatiently; be uneasy. —*v.t.* **2.** to cause to fidget; make uneasy. —*n.* **3.** (*often pl.*) condition of restlessness or uneasiness. **4.** one who fidgets. [der. FIDGE]

fidg·et·y (fĭj´ə tĭ), *adj.* restless; uneasy. —**fidg´et·i·ness,** *n.*

fi·du·cial (fĭ dū´shəl, -dōō´-), *adj.* **1.** *Physics, etc.* accepted as a fixed basis of reference or comparison: *a fiducial point*. **2.** based on or having trust: *fiducial dependence upon God*. [t. ML: s. *fīdūciālis*, der. L *fīdūcia* trust] —**fi·du´cial·ly,** *adv.*

fi·du·ci·ar·y (fĭ dū´shĭ ĕr´ĭ, -dōō´-), *adj., n., pl.* **-aries.** —*adj.* **1.** *Law.* of or pertaining to the relation between a fiduciary and his principal: *a fiduciary capacity, a fiduciary duty*. **2.** depending on public confidence for value or currency, as fiat money. **3.** *Obs.* like or based on trust or reliance. —*n.* **4.** *Law.* a person to whom property is entrusted to hold, control, or manage for another.

fi·dus A·cha·tes (fĭ´dəs ə kā´tēz), *Latin.* **1.** faithful Achates (the comrade of Aeneas). **2.** a devoted, trustworthy friend.

fie (fī), *interj.* an exclamation expressing: **1.** disgust, disapprobation, etc. **2.** humorous pretense of being shocked. [ME *fi,* t. OF, g. L *fi,* but cf. Icel. *fȳ*]

fief (fēf), *n.* **1.** a fee or feud, or estate in land held of a feudal lord; a tenure of land subject to feudal obligations. **2.** a territory held in fee. [t. F. See FEE]

field (fēld), *n.* **1.** a piece of open or cleared ground, esp. one suitable for pasture or tillage. **2.** *Sports.* **a.** a piece of ground devoted to sports or contests. **b.** sports played on it, collectively. **c.** all the contestants not individually favored in betting: *to bet on the field in a horse race*. **d.** the players on the field, in football: *to dodge through a broken field*. **3.** *Baseball.* **a.** that part of the ground on which the fielders play, and known as *infield, outfield, right, center,* and *left field,* according to the station or the corresponding players. **b.** the outfield. **4.** *Baseball, Cricket, etc.* the team in the field, as opposed to the one which is at bat. **5.** *Mil.* **a.** the scene or area of active military operations. **b.** a battleground. **c.** a battle. **d.** *Colloq.* (in the U.S. Army) the locations of the parts of the army not in Washington: *out in the field*. **6.** an expanse of anything: *a field of ice*. **7.** any region characterized by a particular feature or product: *a gold field*. **8.** the surface of a canvas, shield, etc., on which something is portrayed. **9.** (in a flag) the ground of each division. **10.** a sphere, or range of interest, opportunity, etc. **11.** *Physics.* a region of space influenced by some agent: *electric field, temperature field.* **12.** *Optics.* the entire area visible through or projected by an optical instrument at a given time. **13.** *Elect.* **a.** the main magnetic field of an electric motor or generator. **b.** the structure in a dynamo designed to establish magnetic lines of force in an armature. **14.** *Math.* a number system which has the same properties relative to the operations of addition, subtraction, multiplication, and division as the number system of all real numbers: *the field of all rational numbers*. **15.** *Obs.* open country. —*v.t.* **16.** *Baseball, Cricket, etc.* **a.** to stop, or catch, and throw (the ball) as a fielder. **b.** to place (a player or group of players) into the field to play. —*v.i.* **17.** *Baseball, Cricket, etc.* **a.** to act as a fielder; field the ball. **b.** to take to the field. —*adj.* **18.** *Sports, etc.* of, or happening on, or competed on, a field rather than a track. **19.** *Mil.* of or pertaining to campaign and active combat service as distinguished from service in rear areas or at headquarters: *a field soldier*. [ME and OE *feld,* c. G *feld*]

Field (fēld), *n.* **1. Cyrus West,** 1819–92, U.S. capitalist; projector of first Atlantic cable. **2. Eugene,** 1850–95, U.S. poet and journalist.

field artillery, *Mil.* **1.** artillery mobile enough to accompany troops in the field. **2.** (*caps.*) a branch of the U.S. Army that is armed with various types of field guns and cannons.

field bag, *Mil.* a musette bag.

field battery, *Mil.* a battery of field guns.

field corn, maize or Indian corn grown for stock feed.

field day, **1.** a day devoted to outdoor sport or athletic contests. **2.** any day of unusual activity or display.

field·er (fēl´dər), *n.* **1.** *Baseball, Cricket, etc.* a player who fields the ball. **2.** *Baseball.* any of the players of the infield or the outfield, esp. an outfielder.

fielder's choice, *Baseball.* a fielder's attempt to put out a base runner rather than the batter, when a throw to first base would have put out the batter.

field·fare (fēld´fâr´), *n.* a large European thrush, *Turdus pilaris,* of reddish-brown color, with a blackish tail and ashy head. [ME *feldefare* (with two *f*'s by allit. assim.), late OE *feldeware* inhabitant of the fields]

field glass, a compact binocular telescope for use out of doors.

field goal, **1.** *Football.* a goal earned by a kick from the field. **2.** *Basketball.* a goal made while the ball is in play.

field gun, a cannon mounted on a carriage for service in the field.

field hockey, a hockey game which takes place on a field.

Field·ing (fēl´dĭng), *n.* **Henry,** 1707–54, British novelist.

field lark, either of two North American meadow larks, the eastern species, *Sturnella magna,* or the western, *S. neglecta.*

field magnet, a magnet for producing a magnetic field.

field marshal, an officer of the highest military rank in the British and certain other armies, and of the second highest rank in the French army.

field mouse, any of various short-tailed mice or moles inhabiting fields and meadows.

field music, *Mil.* **1.** trumpeters and drummers organized to play as a band. **2.** the music they play.

field officer, *Mil.* an officer above the rank of captain and below that of a brigadier general, as a colonel.

field of force, *Physics.* field (def. 11).

field of honor, the scene of a battle or duel.

field·piece (fēld´pēs´), *n. Mil.* a field gun.

field ration, *U.S. Army.* ration issued only in actual articles, not in money, and authorized for troops in the field.

fields·man (fēldz´mən), *n., pl.* **-men.** *Brit.* a fielder in cricket.

ăct, āble, dâre, ärt; ĕbb, ēqual; ĭf, īce; hŏt, ōver, ôrder, oil, bŏŏk, ōōze, out; ŭp, ūse, ûrge; ə = a in alone; ch, chief; g, give; ng, ring; sh, shoe; th, thin; th, that; zh, vision. See the full key on inside cover.

field sparrow, a common North American finch *Spizella pusilla*, found in brushy pasture lands.

field trial, a trial of animals, as hunting dogs, in actual performance in the field.

field trip, an investigation of facts away from the classroom.

field winding, *Elect.* the electrically conducting circuit, usually a number of coils wound on individual poles and connected in series, which produces excitation in a motor or generator.

field·work (fēld/wûrk/), *n.* *Fort.* a temporary fortification constructed in the field.

field work, work done in the field, as by a surveyor, geologist, etc.

fiend (fēnd), *n.* **1.** Satan; the devil. **2.** any evil spirit. **3.** a diabolically cruel or wicked person. **4.** *Colloq.* a person or thing that causes mischief or annoyance. **5.** *Colloq.* one who is hopelessly addicted to some pernicious habit: *an opium fiend.* **6.** *Colloq.* one who is excessively interested in some game, sport, etc.: *a bridge fiend.* [ME *feend*, OE *feond*, c. G *feind*, all orig. ppr. of a verb meaning hate; cf. OE *feo(ga)n*] **—fiend/like/,** *adj.*

fiend·ish (fēn/dĭsh), *adj.* diabolically cruel and wicked. **—fiend/ish·ly,** *adv.* **—fiend/ish·ness,** *n.*

fierce (fîrs), *adj.,* **fiercer, fiercest. 1.** wild or vehement in temper, appearance, or action: *fierce animals, fierce looks.* **2.** violent in force, intensity, etc.: *fierce winds.* **3.** furiously eager or intense: *fierce competition.* **4.** *Slang.* extremely bad, unpleasant, etc. [ME *fers, fiers,* t. OF., g. L *ferus* wild, fierce, cruel] **—fierce/ly,** *adv.* **—fierce/ness,** *n.*

—Syn. 1. savage, cruel, fell, brutal; bloodthirsty, murderous. FIERCE, FEROCIOUS, TRUCULENT suggest vehemence and violence of manner and conduct. FIERCE suggests violence of temper, manner, or action: *fierce in repelling a foe.* FEROCIOUS implies fierceness or cruelty, esp. of a bloodthirsty kind, in disposition or action: *a ferocious glare, ferocious brutality toward helpless refugees.* TRUCULENT suggests an intimidating or bullying fierceness of manner or conduct: *his truculent attitude kept them terrified and submissive.* **—Ant. 1.** tame, mild.

fi·e·ri fa·ci·as (fī/ərī/ fā/shĭ ăs/), *Latin.* a writ commanding the sheriff to levy upon the goods, or the goods and lands, of a judgment debtor for the collection of the amount due. [L: lit., cause it to be done]

fier·y (fîr/ĭ, fī/ərĭ), *adj.,* **fierier, fieriest. 1.** consisting of, attended with, characterized by, or containing fire: *a fiery discharge.* **2.** intensely hot, as winds, desert sands, etc. **3.** like or suggestive of fire: *a fiery heat, a fiery red.* **4.** flashing or glowing, as the eye. **5.** intensely ardent, impetuous, or passionate: *fiery courage, zeal, speech, etc.* **6.** easily angered; irritable. **7.** inflammable, as gas in a mine. **8.** containing inflammable gas, as a mine. **9.** inflamed, as a tumor or sore. **10.** causing a burning sensation, as liquors or condiments. **—fier/i·ly,** *adv.* **—fier/i·ness,** *n.* **—Syn. 3.** flaming, glowing, burning. **5.** fervid, fervent, vehement, spirited, impassioned.

fiery cross, a burning cross, the emblem of several organizations, notably the Ku Klux Klan.

Fie·so·le (fyě/zō lě), *n.* **1.** a town in central Italy, near Florence. 3013 (1936). **2. Giovanni da** (jō vän/nē dä), (*Fra Angelico*) 1387-1455, Italian painter.

fi·es·ta (fĭ es/tə; *Sp.* fyěs/tä), *n.* *Spanish.* **1.** a religious celebration; a saint's day. **2.** a holiday or festival.

fife (fīf), *n., v.,* **fifed, fifing. —*v.i., v.t.* 2.** to play on a fife. [t. HG: m. *pfeife* PIPE] **—fif/er,** *n.*

Fife (fīf), *n.* a county in E Scotland. 287,100 pop. (est. 1946); 505 sq. mi. *Co. Seat:* Cupar. Also, **Fife·shire** (fīf/shĭr, -shər).

Man playing a fife

fife rail, *Naut.* a rail round the lower part of a mast, for securing belaying pins.

fif·teen (fĭf/tēn/), *n.* **1.** a cardinal number, ten plus five. **2.** a symbol for this number, as 15 or XV. **—*adj.* 3.** amounting to fifteen in number. [ME and OE *fīftene,* f. *fīf* FIVE + *-tēne* -TEEN]

fif·teenth (fĭf/tēnth/), *adj.* **1.** next after the fourteenth. **2.** being one of fifteen equal parts. **—*n.* 3.** a fifteenth part, esp. of one (1/15). **4.** the fifteenth member of a series.

fifth (fĭfth), *adj.* **1.** next after the fourth. **2.** being one of five equal parts. **—*n.* 3.** a fifth part, esp. of one (1/5). **4.** the fifth member of a series. **5.** *Music.* **a.** a tone on the fifth degree from another tone (counted as the first). **b.** the interval between such tones. **c.** the harmonic combination of such tones. [earlier *fift,* ME *fifte,* OE *fifta;* mod. *-th* from *fourth,* etc.] **—fifth/ly,** *adv.*

fifth column, a body of persons residing in a country who are in sympathy with its enemies, and who are serving enemy interests or are ready to assist an enemy attack. **2.** (originally) Franco sympathizers in Madrid during the civil war in allusion to a statement in 1936 that the insurgents had four columns marching on Madrid and a fifth column of sympathizers in the city ready to rise and betray it. **—fifth columnist.**

fifth wheel, 1. a horizontal ring (or segment of a ring) consisting of two bands which slide on each other, placed above the front axle of a carriage and designed to support the fore part of the body while allowing it to turn freely in a horizontal plane. **2.** an extra wheel for a four-wheeled vehicle. **3.** any extra or superfluous thing or person.

fif·ty (fĭf/tĭ), *n., pl.* **-ties,** *adj.* **—*n.* 1.** a cardinal number, ten times five. **2.** a symbol for this number, as 50 or L. **—*adj.* 3.** amounting to fifty in number. [ME; OE *fīftig,* f. *fīf* FIVE + *-tig* -TY1] **—fif/ti·eth,** *adj.*

fif·ty-fif·ty (fĭf/tĭ fĭf/tĭ), *adv., adj. Colloq.* with equality of shares, as of profits.

fig1 (fĭg), *n.* **1.** any tree or shrub of the moraceous genus *Ficus,* esp. a small tree, *F. Carica,* native in southwestern Asia, bearing a turbinate or pear-shaped fruit which is eaten fresh or preserved or dried. **2.** the fruit of such a tree or shrub, or of any related species. **3.** any of various plants having a fruit somewhat resembling the fig. **4.** the value of a fig; the merest trifle; the least bit. **5.** a gesture of contempt; a fico. [ME *fige,* t. OF., t. OPr.; m. *figa,* ult. der. L *ficus*]

fig2 (fĭg), *v.,* **figged, figging,** *n.* *Colloq.* **—*v.t.* 1.** to dress or array (fol. by *out*). **2.** to furbish (fol. by *up*). **—*n.* 3.** dress or array. **4.** condition. [orig. uncert.]

fig., 1. figurative. **2.** figuratively. **3.** figure; figures.

fig·eat·er (fĭg/ē/tər), *n.* *Southern U.S.* a scarabaeid beetle, *Cotinis nitida.*

fight (fīt), *n., v.,* **fought, fighting. —*n.* 1.** a battle or combat. **2.** any contest or struggle. **3.** ability or inclination to fight: *there was no fight left in him, to show fight.* **4.** *Naval.* (formerly) a bulkhead or other screen for the protection of the men during a battle. **—*v.i.* 5.** to engage in battle or in single combat; attempt to defeat, subdue, or destroy an adversary. **6.** to contend in any manner; strive vigorously for or against something. **—*v.t.* 7.** to contend with in battle or combat; war against. **8.** to contend with or against in any manner. **9.** to carry on (a battle, duel, etc.). **10.** to maintain (a cause, quarrel, etc.) by fighting or contending. **11.** to make (one's way) by fighting or striving. **12.** to cause or set (a boxer, dog, etc.) to fight. **13.** to manage or maneuver (troops, ships, guns, planes, etc.) in battle. **14. fight it out,** to struggle till a decisive result is obtained. **15. fight shy of,** to keep carefully aloof from (a person, affair, etc.). [ME; OE *fe(o)htan,* c. G *fechten*] **—fight/a·ble,** *adj.*

—Syn. 1, 2. encounter, engagement, affray, fray; mêlée, scuffle, tussle. FIGHT, COMBAT, CONFLICT, CONTEST denote a struggle of some kind. FIGHT connotes a hand-to-hand struggle for supremacy, literally or in a figurative sense. COMBAT suggests an armed encounter, to settle a dispute. CONFLICT implies a bodily, mental, or moral struggle caused by opposing views, beliefs, etc. CONTEST applies to either a friendly or a hostile struggle for a definite prize or aim. **5, 6.** struggle.

fight·er (fī/tər), *n.* **1.** one who fights. **2.** *Mil.* an aircraft designed to seek out and destroy enemy aircraft in the air, and to protect bomber aircraft.

fight·er-bomb·er (fī/tər bŏm/ər), *n.* *Mil.* an aircraft that combines the functions of a fighter and a bomber.

fighting chance, a possibility of success culminating a struggle.

fighting cock, 1. a gamecock. **2.** *Colloq.* a pugnacious person.

fighting fish, a small brilliantly colored aquarium fish, a species of *Betta,* noted for the fighting habits of the males.

fighting top, (in a warship) a platform on or near the top of a mast, from which rapid-fire guns, etc., are fired. It is also used for observation, lookouts, fire control, etc.

fig leaf, 1. the leaf of a fig tree, esp. in allusion to the first covering of Adam and Eve. Gen. 3:7. **2.** something designed to conceal what is shameful or indecorous.

fig marigold, any of various herbs of the genus *Mesembryanthemum,* with showy white, yellow, or pink flowers.

fig·ment (fĭg/mənt), *n.* **1.** a mere product of the imagination; a pure invention. **2.** a feigned, invented, or imagined story, theory, etc. [t. L: s. *figmentum* image, fiction, anything made] **—Syn. 2.** See **fiction.**

fig·u·line (fĭg/yŏolĭn), *n.* a piece of pottery. [t. L: m.s. *figulīna,* fem. of *figulīnus* of a potter]

fig·u·rant (fĭg/yŏȯränt/; *Fr.* fē gy rän/), *n.* a ballet dancer who dances only with others in groups or figures. [t. F, ppr. of *figurer,* t.: L m.s. *figūrāre* form] **—fig·u·rante** (fĭg/yŏȯränt/; *Fr.* fē gy ränt/), *n. fem.*

fig·ur·ate (fĭg/yərĭt), *adj.* **1.** of a certain determinate figure or shape. **2.** *Music.* characterized by the use of passing notes or other embellishments; florid. [t. L: m.s. *figūrātus,* pp.. figured]

fig·ur·a·tion (fĭg/yərā/shən), *n.* **1.** act of shaping into a particular figure. **2.** the resulting figure or shape. **3.** act of representing figuratively. **4.** a figurative representation. **5.** act of marking or adorning with figures or designs. **6.** *Music.* **a.** the employment of passing notes or other embellishments. **b.** the figuring of a bass part.

fig·ur·a·tive (fĭg/yərə tĭv), *adj.* **1.** of the nature of or involving a figure of speech, esp. a metaphor; metaphorical; not literal: *a figurative expression.* **2.** metaphorically so called: *this remark was a figurative boomerang.* **3.** abounding in or addicted to figures of speech. **4.** representing by means of a figure or likeness, as in drawing or sculpture. **5.** representing by a figure or emblem; emblematic. **—fig/ur·a·tive·ly,** *adv.* **—fig/ur·a·tive·ness,** *n.*

figure 451 **filibuster**

fig·ure (fĭg′yər; *Brit.* fĭg′ər), *n., v.,* **-ured, -uring.** —*n.*
1. a written symbol other than a letter. 2. a numerical symbol, esp. an Arabic numeral. 3. an amount or value expressed in numbers. 4. (*pl.*) the use of numbers in figuring: *poor at figures.* 5. form or shape, as determined by outlines or exterior surfaces: *round, square, or cubical in figure.* 6. the bodily form or frame: *a slender or graceful figure.* 7. an individual bodily form, or a person with reference to form or appearance: *a tall figure stood in the doorway.* 8. a person as he appears or as presented before the eyes of the world: *political figures.* 9. a character or personage, esp. one of distinction: *a figure in society.* 10. the appearance or impression made by a person, or sometimes a thing. 11. a representation, pictorial or sculptured, of something, specif. of the human form. 12. an emblem or type: *the dove is a figure of peace.* 13. *Rhet.* a figure of speech. 14. a device or pattern, as in cloth. 15. a movement, pattern, or series of movements in skating. 16. a distinct movement or division of a dance. 17. *Music.* a short succession of musical notes, either as melody or as a group of chords, which produces a single, complete, and distinct impression. 18. *Geom.* a combination of geometrical elements disposed in a particular form or shape: *the circle, square, and polygon are plane figures, the sphere, cube, and polyhedron are solid figures.* 19. *Logic.* any of the forms of the syllogism with respect to the relative position of the middle term. 20. *Optics.* the precise curve required on the surface of an optical element, esp. the mirror of a reflecting telescope. 21. *Obs.* a phantasm or illusion. —*v.t.* 22. to compute or calculate. 23. to express in figures. 24. to mark or adorn with figures, or with a pattern or design. 25. to portray by speech or action. 26. to represent or express by a figure of speech. 27. to represent by a pictorial or sculptured figure, a diagram, or the like; picture or depict; trace (an outline, etc.). 28. *Colloq.* to conclude or judge: *I figured she was jealous.* 29. *Music.* **a.** to embellish with passing notes or other decorations. **b.** to write figures above or below (a bass part) to indicate accompanying chords. 30. **figure out,** *Chiefly U.S. Colloq.* **a.** to make a calculation of. **b.** to solve; understand; make out. —*v.i.* 31. to compute or work with numerical figures. 32. to make a figure or appearance; be conspicuous: *his name figures in the report.* 33. **figure on,** *Colloq.* **a.** to count or rely on. **b.** to take into consideration. [ME, t. F, t. L: m.s. *figūra* form, shape] —**fig′ure·less,** *adj.* —**fig′ur·er,** *n.* —Syn. 5. See **form.**

fig·ured (fĭg′yərd), *adj.* 1. formed or shaped. 2. represented by a pictorial or sculptured figure. 3. ornamented with a device or pattern: *figured silk, figured wallpaper.* 4. *Music.* **a.** florid. **b.** having the accompanying chords indicated by figures. 5. figurative, as language.

fig·ure·head (fĭg′yər hĕd′), *n.* 1. a person who is nominally the head of a society, community, etc., but has no real authority or responsibility. 2. *Naut.* an ornamental figure, as a statue or bust, placed over the cutwater of a ship.

figure of eight, a kind of knot. See illus. under **knot.**

figure of speech, *Rhet.* a literary mode of expression as a metaphor, simile, personification, antithesis, etc., in which words are used out of their literal sense, or out of ordinary locutions, to suggest a picture or image, or for other special effect; a trope.

fig·ur·ine (fĭg′yərēn′), *n.* a small ornamental figure of pottery, metalwork, etc.; statuette. [t. F, t. It.: m. *figurina,* dim. of *figura* FIGURE]

fig·wort (fĭg′wûrt′), *n.* 1. any of numerous, usually coarse, herbs of the genus *Scrophularia.* 2. any scrophulariaceous plant.

Fi·ji (fē′jē), *n.* 1. a British colony in the S Pacific, N of New Zealand, comprising the **Fiji Islands** and a dependent group to the NW. 234,000 pop. (est. 1942); 7435 sq. mi. *Cap.:* Suva. See the map just below. 2. a native of the Fiji Islands. —**Fi·ji·an** (fē′jĭ ən, fĭ jē′ĭn), *adj., n.*

fikh (fĭk), *n.* Mohammedan jurisprudence: the legal foundations of religious, political, and civil life.

fil·a·gree (fĭl′ə grē′), *n., adj., v.t.* filigree.

fil·a·ment (fĭl′ə mənt), *n.* 1. a very fine thread or threadlike structure; a fiber or fibril. 2. a single element of textile fiber (as silk), or mechanically produced fiber (as rayon, or nylon). 3. *Bot.* **a.** the stalklike portion of a stamen, supporting the anther. **b.** a long slender cell or series of attached cells, as in some algae, fungi, etc. 4. *Ornith.* the barb of a down feather. 5. *Elect.* (in an incandescent lamp) the threadlike conductor in the bulb which is raised to incandescence by the passage of current. 6. *Electronics,* the heating element (sometimes also acting as a cathode) of a vacuum tube. It resembles an incandescent electric-lamp filament. 7. *Pathol.* a threadlike substance sometimes contained in urine, or

in fluids of inflammation. [t. LL: s. *filāmentum,* der. L *filum* thread]

fil·a·men·ta·ry (fĭl′ə mĕn′tə rĭ), *adj.* pertaining to or of the nature of a filament or filaments.

fil·a·men·tous (fĭl′ə mĕn′təs), *adj.* 1. composed of or containing filaments. 2. resembling a filament. 3. bearing filaments. 4. pertaining to filaments.

fi·lar (fī′lər), *adj.* 1. of or pertaining to a thread or threads. 2. having threads or the like. [f. s. L *filum* thread + -AR¹]

fi·lar·i·a (fĭ lâr′ĭ ə), *n., pl.* **-lariae** (-lâr′ĭ ē). any of the slender, threadlike nematode worms (family *Filariidae*), parasitic as adults in the blood or tissues of vertebrates, and development as larvae in insects, etc., which become infected by sucking the embryos from the blood. [NL, der. L *filum* thread]

fi·lar·i·al (fĭ lâr′ĭ əl), *adj.* 1. belonging to the genus *Filaria* and allied genera of the family *Filariidae.* 2. pertaining to infection by filariae: *filarial disease.*

fil·a·ri·a·sis (fĭl′ə rī′ə sĭs), *n. Pathol.* the presence of filarial worms in the blood and lymph channels, in the lymph glands, and other tissues. [t. NL. See FILARIA, -ASIS]

fil·a·ture (fĭl′ə chər), *n.* 1. act of forming into threads. 2. a reel for drawing off silk from cocoons. 3. the reeling of silk from cocoons. 4. an establishment for reeling silk. [t. F, der. LL *filāre* spin]

fil·bert (fĭl′bərt), *n.* 1. the thick-shelled, edible nut of certain cultivated varieties of hazel, esp. of *Corylus avellana* of Europe. 2. a tree or shrub bearing such nuts. [ME; short for *filbert nut,* nut of (St.) Philibert, so called because ripe about this saint's day, Aug. 22]

filch (fĭlch), *v.t., v.i.* to steal (esp. something of small value); pilfer. —**filch′er,** *n.*

file¹ (fīl), *n., v.,* **filed, filing.** —*n.* 1. any device, as a cabinet, in which papers, etc., are arranged or classified for convenient reference. 2. a collection of papers so arranged or classified; any orderly collection of papers, etc. 3. a string or wire on which papers are strung for preservation and reference. 4. **on file,** on or in a file, or in orderly arrangement for convenient reference, as papers. 5. a line of persons or things arranged one behind another. 6. *Mil.* **a.** a man in front of or behind another in a military formation. **b.** one step on a promotion list. 7. one of the vertical lines of squares on a chess board. 8. a list or roll. —*v.t.* 9. to arrange (papers, etc.) methodically for preservation and convenient reference. —*v.i.* 10. to march in a file or line, one after another, as soldiers. 11. to make application: *to file for a civil service job.* [repr. F *fil* thread, string (g. L *filum*) and F *file* file, row, der. L *filum* thread] —**fil′er,** *n.*

file² (fīl), *n., v.,* **filed, filing.** —*n.* 1. a metal (usually steel) tool of varying size and form, with numerous small cutting ridges or teeth on its surface, for smoothing or cutting metal and other substances. 2. *Brit. Slang.* a cunning, shrewd, or artful person. —*v.t.* 3. to reduce, smooth, cut, or remove with or as with a file. [ME; d. OE *fīl,* r. OE *fēol,* c. G *feile*] —**fil′er,** *n.*

file³ (fīl), *v.t.,* **filed, filing.** *Archaic or Dial.* defile. [ME; OE *fȳlan* befoul, defile, der. *fūl* foul]

file clerk, an employee who works primarily with office files.

file·fish (fīl′fĭsh′), *n., pl.* **-fishes,** (*esp. collectively*) **-fish.** 1. any of various fishes with rough, granular skin, as *Alutera schoepfi* of the Atlantic coast of the U.S. and southward. 2. triggerfish.

fi·let (fĭ lā′, fĭl′ā; *Fr.* fē lĕ′), *n., v.t.* fillet (defs. 6, 10).

fi·let de sole (fĭl′ā də sōl′; *Fr.* fē lĕ də sôl′), *French.* a fillet of any of certain flatfishes used for food.

filet lace, a square mesh net or lace, originally knotted by hand but now copied by machine.

fi·let mi·gnon (fĭ lā′ mēn′yŏn; *Fr.* fē lĕ mē nyôN′), a round beef fillet to which pork or bacon is added before cooking. [t. F]

fil·i·al (fĭl′ĭ əl), *adj.* 1. pertaining to or befitting a son or daughter: *filial obedience.* 2. bearing the relation of a child to a parent. 3. *Genetics.* indicating the sequence of generations from an original parent. First filial is shown as F_1, second filial as F_2, etc. [t. LL: s. *filiālis,* f. s. L *filius* son, *filia* daughter + *-ālis* -AL¹] —**fil′i·al·ly,** *adv.*

fil·i·ate (fĭl′ĭ āt′), *v.t.,* **-ated, -ating.** 1. to affiliate. 2. *Law.* to determine judicially the paternity of, as a bastard child. [t. LL: m.s. *filiātus,* pp. of *filiāre* have a child, der. L *filius* son, *filia* daughter. Cf. AFFILIATE]

fil·i·a·tion (fĭl′ĭ ā′shən), *n.* 1. the fact of being the child of a certain parent. 2. descent as if from a parent; derivation. 3. *Law.* the judicial determination of the paternity of a child, especially of a bastard. 4. the relation of one thing to another from which it is derived. 5. act of filiating. 6. state of being filiated. 7. an affiliated branch, as of a society. [t. LL: s. *filiātio,* der. *filiāre* have a child]

fil·i·beg (fĭl′ə bĕg′), *n.* the kilt or plaited skirt worn by Scottish Highlanders. Also, **philibeg.** [t. Gaelic: m. *feileadh-beag* small kilt (as distinguished from the large one formerly worn)]

fil·i·bus·ter (fĭl′ə bŭs′tər), *n.* 1. *U.S.* **a.** a member of a minority in a legislative assembly who resorts to irregular or obstructive tactics to prevent the adoption of a measure generally favored or to force a decision almost unanimously disliked. **b.** a course of legislative filibustering. 2. an irregular military adventurer; a freebooter or buccaneer. **3.** one who engages in an unlawful military expedition into a foreign country to inaugurate or to aid a revolution. —*v.i.* **4.** *U.S.* to impede legislation by irregular or obstructive tactics. esp. by making long speeches. **5.** to act as a freebooter, buccaneer, or irregular military adventurer. [t. Sp.: m. *filibustero*, t. D: m. *vrijbuiter* freebooter] —**fil′i·bus′ter·er,** *n.*

fil·i·cide[1] (fĭl′ə·sīd′), *n.* one who kills his son or daughter. [f. s. L *filius* son, *filia* daughter + -CIDE[1]] —**fil′i·cid′al,** *adj.*

fil·i·cide[2] (fĭl′ə·sīd′), *n.* act of killing one's son or daughter. [f. s. L *filius* son, *filia* daughter + -CIDE[2]] —**fil′i·cid′al,** *adj.*

fil·i·form (fĭl′ə·fôrm′, fī′lə-), *adj.* threadlike; filamentous. [f. s. L *filum* thread + -(I)FORM]

fil·i·gree (fĭl′ə·grē′), *n., adj., v.,* **-greed, -greeing.** —*n.* **1.** ornamental work of fine wires, esp. lacy jewelers′ work of scrolls and arabesques. **2.** anything very delicate or fanciful. —*adj.* **3.** composed of or resembling filigree. —*v.t.* **4.** to adorn with or form into filigree. Also, **filagree, fillagree.** [var. of *filigrane*, t. F, t. It.: m. *filigrana.* See FILE[1], GRAIN] —**fil′i·greed′,** *adj.*

fil·i·greed (fĭl′ə·grēd′), *adj.*having filigree decorations.

fil·ings (fī′lĭngz), *n.pl.* particles removed by a file.

Fil·i·pine (fĭl′ə·pēn′), *adj.* Philippine.

Fil·i·pi·no (fĭl′ə·pē′nō; *Sp.* fē′lē·pē′nō), *n., pl.* **-nos** (-nōz; *Sp.* -nōs), *adj.* —*n.* **1.** a native of the Philippine Islands, esp. a member of a Christianized native tribe. —*adj.* **2.** Philippine. [t. Sp., der. *Felipe* Philip]

fill (fĭl), *v.t.* **1.** to make full; put as much as can be held into. **2.** to occupy to the full capacity: *water filled the basin, the crowd filled the hall.* **3.** to supply to fullness or plentifully: *to fill a house with furniture, to fill the heart with joy.* **4.** to satisfy, as food does. **5.** to put, as contents, into a receptacle. **6.** to be plentiful throughout: *fish filled the rivers.* **7.** to extend throughout; pervade completely: *the odor filled the room.* **8.** to furnish (a vacancy or office) with an occupant or incumbent. **9.** to execute (a business order). **10.** to supply (a blank space) with written matter, decorative work, etc. **11.** to meet (requirements, etc.) satisfactorily: *the book fills a longfelt want.* **12.** to make up or compound (a medical prescription). **13.** to stop up or close: *to fill a tooth or a crevice.* **14.** to occupy and perform the duties of (a vacancy, position, post, etc.). **15.** *Naut.* **a.** to distend (a sail) by pressure of the wind so as to impart headway to a vessel. **b.** to brace (a yard) so that the sail will catch the wind on its after side. **16.** to adulterate: *filled soaps.* **17.** *Civil Eng.* to build up with fill (def. 24): *to fill low ground with gravel, sand, or earth.* —*v.i.* **18.** to become full: *the hall filled rapidly, her eyes filled with tears.* **19.** to become distended, as sails with the wind. **20.** to fill a cup or other receptacle; pour out drink, as into a cup. **21.** Some special verb phrases are: **fill away,** *Naut.* **1.** to fall off the wind and proceed on a board. **2.** to brace the yards, so that sails which have been aback will stand full. **fill in, 1.** to fill (a hole, hollow, blank, etc.) with something put in. **2.** *Chiefly Brit.* to complete (a document, design, etc.) by filling blank spaces. **3.** to put in or insert so as to fill: *to fill in omitted names.* **fill out, 1.** to complete (a document, list, etc.) by filling blanks, or fill (blanks) in a document, etc. **2.** to distend (sails, etc.). **3.** to round out (the cheeks, figure, etc.). **4.** to become rounded, as the cheeks, figure, etc. **fill the bill,** *Colloq.* to satisfy the requirements of the case: be or do what is wanted. **fill up,** to fill completely. —*n.* **22.** a full supply; enough to satisfy want or desire: *to eat one's fill.* **23.** an amount of something sufficient for filling; a charge. **24.** a mass of earth, stones, etc., used to fill a hollow, etc. [ME *fille*(n), OE *fyllan*, c. G *füllen*; der. FULL[1]]

fill·a·gree (fĭl′ə·grē′), *n., adj., v.t.* filigree.

filled gold (fĭld), a gold plate mechanically welded to a backing of brass or other base metal and rolled, in which the gold is ¹/₂₀ or more of the total weight.

filled milk, milk containing a substitute for the butter fat.

fill·er[1] (fĭl′ər), *n.* **1.** one who or that which fills. **2.** a thing or quantity of a material put in to fill something, or to fill out a gap. **3.** a liquid, paste, or the like used to coat a surface or to give solidity, bulk, etc., to a substance. **4.** the tobacco forming the body of a cigar, as distinguished from the wrapper. **5.** *Journalism.* something used to fill a vacant space. **6.** *Bldg. Trades, etc.* a sheet or plate inserted in a gap between two structural members. **7.** an implement used in filling, as a funnel. [f. FILL + -ER[1]]

fil·lér[2] (fĕl′lār), *n., pl.* **-ler,** a Hungarian minor bronze coin formerly equal to ¹/₁₀₀ of a pengö, and now equal to ¹/₁₀₀ of a forint. [t. Hung.]

fil·let (fĭl′ĭt; *usually* fĭl′ā *for* 6, 10), *n.* **1.** a narrow band of ribbon or the like bound round the head or hair. **2.** any narrow strip, as wood or metal. **3.** a strip of any material used for binding. **4.** *Bookbinding.* **a.** a decorative line impressed on a book's cover, usually at the top and bottom of the back. **b.** a rolling tool for impressing such lines. **5.** *Archit., etc.* **a.** a relatively narrow molding with a plane face, as between other moldings. **b.** the flat top of the ridge between two flutes of a column. **6.** *Cookery.* **a.** a strip or long (flat or thick) piece of meat or fish, esp. such as is easily detached from the bones or adjoining parts. **b.** a thick slice of meat, etc. **c.** a piece of

veal or other meat boned, rolled, and tied, for roasting. **7.** *Anat.* a band of fibers, esp. of white nerve fibers in the brain. **8.** a raised rim or ridge, as a ring on the muzzle of a gun. —*v.t.* **9.** to bind or adorn with or as with a fillet. **10.** *Cookery.* **a.** to cut or prepare (meat or fish) as a fillet. **b.** to cut fillets from. Also, filet for 6, 10. [ME *filet*, t. F, dim. of *fil* thread, string, g. L *filum*]

fill·ing (fĭl′ĭng), *n.* **1.** that which is put in to fill something: *the filling of a pie.* **2.** a substance in plastic form, as cement, amalgam, or gold foil, used to close a cavity in a tooth. **3.** act of one who or that which fills; a making or becoming full.

filling station, a place where gasoline and oil are retailed for automobiles.

fil·lip (fĭl′əp), *v.t.* **1.** to strike with the nail of a finger snapped from the end of the thumb. **2.** to tap or strike smartly. **3.** to drive by or as by a fillip. —*v.i.* **4.** to make a fillip with the fingers. —*n.* **5.** act or movement of filliping; a smart tap or stroke. **6.** anything that tends to rouse, excite, or revive; a stimulus. [appar. imit. Cf. FLIP]

fil·li·peen (fĭl′ə·pēn′), *n.* *Games.* philopena.

fil·lis·ter (fĭl′ĭs·tər), *n.* *Carp.* a rabbet or groove, as one on a window sash to hold the glass and putty.

fillister plane, *Carp.* a plane for cutting rabbets or grooves.

Fill·more (fĭl′mōr), *n.* **Millard** (mĭl′ərd), 1800–74. 13th president of the United States, 1850–53.

fil·ly (fĭl′ĭ), *n., pl.* **-lies. 1.** a female colt or foal; a young mare. **2.** *Colloq.* a lively young girl. [t. Scand.; cf. Icel. *fylja* female foal. See FOAL]

film (fĭlm), *n.* **1.** a thin layer or coating. **2.** a thin sheet of any material. **3.** *Photog.* **a.** the sensitive coating, as of gelatin and silver bromide, on a photographic plate. **b.** a strip or roll of cellulose nitrate or cellulose acetate composition coated with a sensitive emulsion, used instead of a photographic plate. **4.** *Motion Pictures.* **a.** the film strip containing the photographs exhibited in a motion-picture machine. **b.** a motion picture. **c.** (*pl.*) motion pictures collectively. **d.** (*pl.*) the motion-picture industry, or its productions, operations, etc. **5.** a thin skin or membrane. **6.** a delicate web of filaments or fine threads. —*v.t.* **7.** to cover with a film, or thin skin or pellicle. **8.** *Motion Pictures.* **a.** to photograph with a motion-picture camera. **b.** to reproduce in the form of motion pictures: *to film a novel.* —*v.i.* **9.** to become covered by a film. **10.** *Motion Pictures.* **a.** to be reproduced in a motion picture, esp. in a specified manner: *this story films easily.* **b.** to direct, make, or otherwise engage in the production of motion pictures. [ME *fylme*, OE *filmen*; akin to FELL[4]]

film library, *Library Sci.* an organized collection of films for private or public use, including reproductions of printed materials on film, slides, motion-picture reels, etc.

film pack, *Photog.* camera film so arranged in a stack that individual sheets can be brought successively in place.

film·y (fĭl′mĭ), *adj.,* **filmier, filmiest.** of the nature of, resembling, or covered with a film. —**film′i·ly,** *adv.* —**film′i·ness,** *n.*

fil·o·plume (fĭl′ə·plōōm′, fī′lə-), *n.* *Ornith.* a degenerate feather with a shaft but few or no barbs.

fi·lose (fī′lōs), *adj.* **1.** threadlike. **2.** ending in a threadlike process. [f. s. L *filum* thread + -OSE[1]]

fils (fēs), *n.* French. son: sometimes used after a name in meaning of *Jr.,* as in *Dumas fils.* Cf. **père.**

fil·ter (fĭl′tər), *n.* **1.** any device in which cloth, paper, porous porcelain, or a layer of charcoal or sand, is held and through which liquid is passed to remove suspended impurities or to recover solids. **2.** any of various analogous devices, as for removing dust from air or eliminating certain kinds of light rays. **3.** *Photog.* a screen of dyed gelatin or glass used to control the rendering of color or to diminish the intensity of light. **4.** *Physics.* a device for selecting waves or currents of certain frequencies only out of an aggregation including others. —*v.t.* **5.** to remove by the action of a filter. **6.** to act as a filter for. **7.** to pass through, or as through, a filter. —*v.i.* **8.** to percolate; pass through or as through a filter. [ME *filtre*, t. OF, t. ML: m.s. *feltrum* felt (used as a filter), ult. t. Gmc.; cf. FELT[2]] —**fil′ter·er,** *n.*

fil·ter·a·ble (fĭl′tər·ə·bəl), *adj.* **1.** capable of being filtered. **2.** *Bacteriol.* capable of passing through bacteria-retaining filters: *a filterable virus.* Also, **fil·tra·ble** (fĭl′trə·bəl).

filter bed, a pond or tank having a false bottom covered with sand, and serving to filter river or pond waters.

filth (fĭlth), *n.* **1.** foul matter; offensive or disgusting dirt. **2.** foul condition. **3.** moral impurity, corruption, or obscenity. **4.** foul language. [ME; OE *fŷlth,* der. *fūl* foul]

filth·y (fĭl′thĭ), *adj.,* **filthier, filthiest. 1.** foul with, characterized by, or having the nature of filth; disgustingly dirty. **2.** vile; obscene. **3.** (as a general epithet of strong condemnation) highly offensive or objectionable. —**filth′i·ly,** *adv.* —**filth′i·ness,** *n.* —**Syn. 1.** See **dirty.**

fil·trate (fĭl′trāt), *v.,* **-trated, -trating,** *n.* —*v.t., v.i.* **1.** to filter. —*n.* **2.** liquid which has been passed through a filter. —**fil·tra′tion,** *n.*

fi·lum (fī′ləm), *n., pl.* **-la** (-lə). *Latin.* a threadlike structure or part; a filament.

fim·ble (fĭm′bəl), *n.* the male or staminate plant of hemp, which is harvested before the female or pistillate plant. [t. LG: m. *fimel*, t. F: m. (*chanvre*) *femelle*, lit., female hemp]

fim·bri·a (fĭm′brĭ·ə), *n., pl.* **-bri·ae** (-brĭ·ē′). (*often pl.*) *Bot., Zool.* a fringe or fringed border. [t. L: thread, fringe] —**fim′bri·al,** *adj.*

fim·bri·ate (fĭm′brĭ·ĭt, -āt′), *adj. Bot., Zool.* fringed; bordered with hairs or with filiform processes. Also, **fim′bri·at·ed.**

fim·bri·a·tion (fĭm′brĭ·ā′shən), *n. Bot., Zool.* **1.** fimbriate or fringed condition. **2.** a fringe or fringelike part.

fim·bril·late (fĭm·brĭl′ĭt, -āt), *adj. Bot., Zool.* bordered with, or having, a small or fine fringe. [f. NL *fimbrilla* (dim. of L *fimbria* FIMBRIA) + -ATE[1]]

Fimbriate petals

fin (fĭn), *n., v.,* **finned, finning.** —*n.* **1.** a membranous winglike or paddlelike organ attached to any of various parts of the body of fishes and certain other aquatic animals, used for propulsion, steering, or balancing. **2.** *Naut.* **a.** a fin-shaped plane on a submarine or boat. **b.** a fin keel. **3.** *Aeron.* any of certain small, subsidiary planes on an aircraft, in general placed parallel to the plane of symmetry. **4.** an external rib for cooling, used on radiators, the cylinders of air-cooled internal-combustion engines, etc. **5.** any part, as of a mechanism, resembling a fin. **6.** *Slang.* the arm or hand. —*v.t.* **7.** to cut off the fins from (a fish); carve or cut up, as a chub. —*v.i.* **8.** to move the fins; lash the water with the fins, as a whale when dying. [ME *finne*, OE *finn*, c. D *vin*, LG *finne*. Cf. L *pinna*] —**fin′less,** *adj.* —**fin′like′,** *adj.*

Fin., 1. Finland. **2.** Finnish.

fin., financial.

fi·na·gle (fĭ·nā′gəl), *v.,* **-gled, -gling.** *Colloq.* —*v.i.* **1.** to practice deception or fraud. —*v.t.* **2.** to trick or cheat (a person); get (something) by guile or trickery. **3.** wangle: *to finagle free tickets.* [var. of *fainaigue*; orig. uncert.] —**fi·na′gler,** *n.*

fi·nal (fī′nəl), *adj.* **1.** pertaining to or coming at the end; last in place, order, or time. **2.** ultimate: *the final goal.* **3.** conclusive, or decisive. **4.** *Law.* **a.** precluding further controversy on the questions passed upon: *the decision of the Supreme Court is final.* **b.** determining completely the rights of the parties, so that no further decision upon the merits of the issues is necessary: *a final judgment or decree.* **5.** constituting the end or purpose: *a final cause.* **6.** pertaining to or expressing end or purpose: *a final clause.* **7.** *Phonet.* coming at the end of a word or syllable: *"t" is final in the word "fit."* —*n.* **8.** that which is last; that which forms an end or termination. **9.** (*often pl.*) something final, as a last and decisive examination or athletic contest after preliminary ones. **10.** *Colloq.* the last edition of a newspaper during the day. [ME, t. LL: s. *finālis*, der. L *finis* end] —**Syn. 1.** See **last[1].**

final causes, *Philos.* the doctrine that the course of events in the universe is explicable mainly by reference to ends or purposes by which all events are controlled.

fi·na·le (fĭ·nä′lĭ; *It.* fē·nä′lĕ), *n.* **1.** *Music.* the last piece, division, or movement of a concert, opera, or composition. **2.** the concluding part of any performance, course of proceedings, etc. [t. It., *adj.* used as n. See FINAL]

fi·nal·ism (fī′nəl·ĭz′əm), *n. Philos.* the doctrine that nothing exists or was made except for a determinate end; the doctrine of final causes; teleology.

fi·nal·ist (fī′nəl·ĭst), *n.* one who is entitled to take part in the final trial or round, as of an athletic contest.

fi·nal·i·ty (fī·năl′ə·tĭ), *n., pl.* **-ties. 1.** state, quality, or fact of being final; conclusiveness or decisiveness. **2.** something that is final; a final act, utterance, etc.

fi·nal·ly (fī′nəl·ĭ), *adv.* **1.** at the final point or moment; in the end. **2.** in a final manner; conclusively or decisively.

fi·nance (fĭ·năns′, fī′năns), *n., v.,* **-nanced, -nancing.** —*n.* **1.** the management of public revenues; the conduct or transaction of money matters generally, esp. such as affect the public, as in the fields of banking and investment. **2.** (*pl.*) pecuniary resources, as of a sovereign, state, corporation, or an individual; revenues. —*v.t.* **3.** to supply with means of payment; provide capital for; to obtain or furnish credit for. **4.** to manage financially. —*v.i.* **5.** to conduct financial operations; manage finances. [ME, t. OF: ending, payment, revenue, der. OF *finer* finish, settle, pay, der. *fin* end, settlement. See FINE[2]]

finance bill, *Govt.* a bill or act of a legislature to obtain public funds.

fi·nan·cial (fĭ·năn′shəl, fī-), *adj.* **1.** pertaining to monetary receipts and expenditures; pertaining or relating to money matters; pecuniary: *financial operations.* **2.** of or pertaining to those commonly engaged in dealing with money and credit. —**fi·nan′cial·ly,** *adv.*
—**Syn. 1.** FINANCIAL, FISCAL, MONETARY, PECUNIARY refer to matters concerned with money. FINANCIAL usually refers to money matters or transactions of some size or importance: *a financial wizard.* FISCAL is used esp. in connection with government funds, or those of any organization: *the end of the fiscal year.* MONETARY relates especially to money as such: *a monetary system or standard.* PECUNIARY refers to money as used in making ordinary payments: *a pecuniary obligation or reward.*

fin·an·cier (fĭn′ən·sïr′, fī·nən-; *Brit.* fī·năn′sï·ər), *n.* **1.** one skilled or engaged in financial operations, whether public, corporate, or individual. —*v.t.* **2.** to finance. —*v.i.* **3.** *Rare.* to act as a financier. [t. F, der. *finance* FINANCE]

fin·back (fĭn′băk), *n.* any whalebone whale of the genus *Balaenoptera* having a prominent dorsal fin, as *B. musculus* of the northern Atlantic, or *B. physalus,* which attains a length of 60 or even 80 feet; a rorqual. Also, **finback whale.**

finch (fĭnch), *n.* **1.** any of numerous small passerine birds of the family *Fringillidae,* including the buntings, sparrows, crossbills, linnets, grosbeaks, etc., most of which have heavy, conical seed-cracking bills. **2.** any of various nonfringilline birds. [ME; OE *finc,* c. D *vink,* G *fink*]

Purple finch. *Carpodacus purpureus* (6 in. long)

find (fīnd), *v.,* **found, finding,** *n.* —*v.t.* **1.** to come upon by chance; meet with. **2.** to learn, attain, or obtain by search or effort. **3.** to discover. **4.** to recover (something lost). **5.** to gain or regain the use of: *to find one's tongue.* **6.** to succeed in attaining; gain by effort: *find safety in flight, to find occasion for revenge.* **7.** to discover by experience or to perceive: *to find something to be true, find something new to be developing.* **8.** to ascertain by study or calculation: *to find the sum of several numbers.* **9.** *Law.* **a.** to determine after judicial inquiry: *find a person guilty.* **b.** to pronounce as an official act (an indictment, verdict, or judgment). **10.** to provide or furnish. **11. find fault,** to find cause of blame or complaint; express dissatisfaction. **12. find oneself,** to discover the right place or conditions for oneself. **13. find out, a.** to discover in the course of time or experience; discover by search or inquiry; ascertain by study. **b.** to detect, as in an offense; discover the actions or character of; discover or detect (a fraud, imposture, etc.). **c.** to discover the identity of (a person). —*v.i.* **14.** to determine an issue after judicial inquiry: *the jury found for the plaintiff.* **15.** *Brit. Hunting.* to come upon game. —*n.* **16.** act of finding; a discovery. **17.** something found; a discovery, esp. a valuable or gratifying discovery: *our cook was a find.* [ME *finde(n),* OE *findan,* c. G *finden*] —**find′a·ble,** *adj.*

find·er (fīn′dər), *n.* **1.** one who or that which finds. **2.** *Photog.* a camera attachment enabling a photographer to determine what will be included in the picture. **3.** *Astron.* a small telescope attached to a larger for the purpose of finding an object more readily.

fin de siè·cle (făn də syĕ′kl), *French.* **1.** end of the century. **2.** a period freed from social and moral traditions. —*attributive.* **3.** (toward the close of the 19th century) **a.** modern; up-to-date. **b.** decadent.

find·ing (fīn′dĭng), *n.* **1.** act of one who or that which finds; discovery. **2.** that which is found or ascertained. **3.** *Law.* a decision or verdict after judicial inquiry. **4.** (*pl.*) tools, materials, etc., used by artisans.

Find·lay (fĭnd′lĭ, fīnd′-), *n.* a city in NW Ohio. 23,-845 (1950).

fine[1] (fīn), *adj.,* **finer, finest,** *adv., v.,* **fined, fining** —*adj.* **1.** of the highest or of very high grade or quality; free from imperfections or impurities. **2.** choice, excellent, or admirable: *a fine sermon.* **3.** consisting of minute particles: *fine sand.* **4.** very thin or slender: *fine thread.* **5.** keen or sharp, as a tool. **6.** delicate in texture: *fine linen.* **7.** delicately fashioned. **8.** highly skilled or accomplished: *a fine musician.* **9.** trained down to the proper degree, as an athlete. **10.** characterized by or affecting refinement or elegance: *a fine lady.* **11.** polished or refined: *fine manners.* **12.** affectedly ornate or elegant: *fine writing.* **13.** delicate or subtle: *a fine distinction.* **14.** showy or smart; smartly dressed. **15.** good-looking or handsome. **16.** (of gold, silver, etc.) having a high proportion of pure metal, or having the proportion as specified. —*adv.* **17.** *Colloq.* in a fine manner; excellently, or very well; elegantly; delicately; with nicety. **18.** *Billiards, Pool.* in such a way that the driven ball barely touches the object ball in passing. —*v.i.* **19.** to become fine or finer. —*v.t.* **20.** to make fine or finer. **21.** to clarify (wines or spirits) by filtration. [ME *fin,* t. OF, g. Common Rom. *fino,* back formation from L *finīre* FINISH]
—**Syn. 1.** superior; finished, consummate, perfect. FINE, CHOICE, ELEGANT, EXQUISITE are terms of praise with reference to quality. FINE is a general term: *a fine horse, person, book.* CHOICE implies a discriminating selection of the object in question: *a choice piece of steak.* ELEGANT suggests a refined and graceful superiority as is generally associated with luxury and a cultivated taste: *elegant furnishings.* EXQUISITE suggests an admirable delicacy, finish, or perfection: *an exquisite piece of lace.* **3.** powdered, pulverized. —**Ant. 1.** inferior.

fine[2] (fīn), *n., v.,* **fined, fining.** —*n.* **1.** a sum of money exacted as a penalty for an offense or dereliction; a mulct. **2.** *Law.* **a.** a fee paid by a feudal tenant to the landlord, as on the renewal of tenure. **b.** a sum of money paid by a tenant on the commencement of his tenancy so that his rent may be small or nominal. **3.** *Eng. Law.* a conveyance of land through decree of a court, based upon a simulated law suit. **4. in fine,** finally; in short. **5.** *Archaic.* a penalty of any kind. —*v.t.* **6.** to subject to a fine, or pecuniary penalty; punish by a fine. [ME *fin*, t. OF, g. L *fīnis* boundary, end, ML settlement, fine]

fi·ne³ (fē′ně), *n. Music.* **1.** the end of a repeated section, whether *da capo* or *dal segno.* **2.** the end of a composition comprising several movements. [It.: end]

fine arts, those arts which seek expression through beautiful or significant modes; specif., architecture, sculpture, painting, and engraving.

fine-cut (fīn′kŭt′), *adj.* (of tobacco) cut fine, and used for chewing or smoking.

fine-draw (fīn′drô′), *v.t.*, **-drew, -drawn, -drawing.** **1.** *Sewing.* to sew together or up so finely or nicely that the joining is not noticeable. **2.** to draw out to extreme fineness, tenuity, or subtlety.

fine-drawn (fīn′drôn′), *adj.* drawn out to extreme fineness or thinness: *a fine-drawn wire* or *distinction.*

fine·ly (fīn′lĭ), *adv.* in a fine manner; excellently; elegantly; delicately; minutely; nicely; subtly.

fine·ness (fīn′nĭs), *n.* **1.** state or quality of being fine. **2.** the proportion of pure metal (gold or silver) in an alloy, often expressed by the number of parts in 1,000.

fin·er·y¹ (fī′nər ĭ), *n.*, *pl.* **-eries. 1.** fine or showy dress, ornaments, etc. **2.** *Rare.* smartness, or elegance. [f. FINE¹, adj. + -ERY]

fin·er·y² (fī′nər ĭ), *n.*, *pl.* **-eries.** *Metall.* a hearth on which cast iron is converted into wrought iron. [t. F: m. *finerie*, der. *finer* fine, v.]

fines herbes (fēn zĕrb′), *Cookery.* a combination of finely chopped herbs for flavoring soups, sauces, etc. [F]

fine-spun (fīn′spŭn′), *adj.* **1.** spun or drawn out to a fine thread. **2.** highly or excessively refined or subtle.

fi·nesse (fĭ něs′), *n.*, *v.*, **-nessed, -nessing.** —*n.* **1.** delicacy of execution; subtlety of discrimination. **2.** artful management; craft; strategy; an artifice or stratagem. **3.** *Cards.* an attempt to win a trick with a card while holding a higher card not in sequence with it, in the hope that the card or cards between will not be played. —*v.i.* **4.** to use finesse or artifice. **5.** to make a finesse at cards. —*v.t.* **6.** to bring by finesse or artifice. **7.** to make a finesse with (a card). [t. F, der. *fin* FINE¹, adj.]

fin·foot (fīn′fŏŏt′), *n.*, *pl.* **-foots.** any of certain pinnatiped or lobately webbed aquatic birds, family *Heliornithidae*, of South America, Asia, and Africa, related to the rails and coots.

fin-foot·ed (fīn′fŏŏt′ĭd), *adj. Ornith.* **1.** web-footed. **2.** having feet whose toes are separately furnished with flaps, as the finfoots and coots.

Fin·gal's Cave (fĭng′gəlz), an unusual cavern on the island of Staffa, in the Hebrides, Scotland. 227 ft. long; 42 ft. wide.

fin·ger (fĭng′gər), *n.* **1.** any of the terminal members of the hand, esp. one other than the thumb. **2.** a part of a glove made to receive a finger. **3.** the breadth of a finger as a unit of length; a digit. **4.** the length of finger, 4½ in., or approximately that. **5.** something like or likened to a finger, or serving the purpose of a finger: *the finger of a clock.* **6.** any of various projecting parts of machines. **7.** Some special noun phrases are:

burn one's fingers, to get hurt or suffer loss from meddling with or engaging in anything.

have a finger in the pie, to have a share in the doing of something.

lay or **put one's finger on**, to indicate exactly. —*v.t.* **8.** to touch with the fingers; handle; toy or meddle with. **9.** to pilfer; filch. **10.** *Music.* **a.** to play on (an instrument) with the fingers. **b.** to perform or mark (a passage of music) with a certain fingering (def. 2b). —*v.i.* **11.** to touch or handle something with the fingers. **12.** *Music.* **a.** to have its keys arranged for playing with the fingers, as a piano, clarinet, etc. **b.** to use the fingers in playing. [ME and OE; c. G *finger*; akin to FIVE, FIST] —**fin′ger·er**, *n.* —**fin′ger·less**, *adj.*

finger board, **1.** (in a violin, guitar, etc.) the strip of wood on the neck against which the strings are stopped by the fingers. **2.** (in a piano, organ, etc.) the keyboard.

finger bowl, a small bowl to hold water for rinsing the fingers at table.

fin·ger·ing (fĭng′gər ĭng), *n.* **1.** act of one who fingers. **2.** *Music.* **a.** the action or method of using the fingers in playing on an instrument. **b.** the indication of the way the fingers are to be used in performing a piece of music.

Finger Lakes, a series of elongated glacial lakes in central and W New York: a resort region.

fin·ger·ling (fĭng′gər lĭng), *n.* **1.** a young or small fish, esp., a very small salmon or a small trout. **2.** something very small. [f. FINGER + -LING¹. Cf. G *fingerling* thimble]

finger mark, a mark, esp. a smudge or stain, made by a finger.

fin·ger·nail (fĭng′gər nāl′), *n.* the nail at the end of a finger.

finger post, a guidepost with an arm terminating, in the shape of an index finger.

fin·ger·print (fĭng′gər prĭnt′), *n.* **1.** an impression of the markings of the inner surface of the last joint of the thumb or a finger. **2.** such an impression made with ink for purposes of identification. —*v.t.* **3.** to take the fingerprints of.

finger wave, *Hairdressing.* a wave set by impressing the fingers into hair dampened with lotion.

fin·i·al (fĭn′ĭ əl, fī′nĭ-), *n. Archit.* **1.** the ornamental termination of a pinnacle, gable, etc., usually foliated. **2.** a vertical termination; a cast, carved, or turned ornament capping another form. [ME, f. s. L *finis* end + -IAL]

fin·i·cal (fĭn′ə kəl), *adj.* **1.** overfastidious; too particular or fussy. **2.** (of things) overelaborate; containing too much unimportant detail. [f. FINE¹ + -ICAL] —**fin′i·cal·i·ty**, **fin′i·cal·ness**, *n.* —**fin′i·cal·ly**, *adv.*

fin·ick·y (fĭn′ə kĭ), *adj.* finical. Also, **fin·i·kin** (fĭn′ə kĭn), **fin·ick·ing** (fĭn′ə kĭng). [unexplained var. of FINICAL]

fin·ing (fī′nĭng), *n.* **1.** the process by which fused glass becomes free from undissolved gases. **2.** the process of clarifying or filtering a wine or spirit to render it brilliant in appearance. [der. FINE¹, v.]

fi·nis (fī′nĭs), *n. Latin.* end; conclusion (often used at the end of a book).

fin·ish (fĭn′ĭsh), *v.t.* **1.** to bring (action, speech, work, affairs, etc.) to an end or to completion. **2.** to come to the end of (a course, period of time, etc.). **3.** to use up completely: *to finish a plate of food.* **4.** *Colloq.* to overcome completely; destroy or kill. **5.** to complete and perfect in detail; put the final touches on. **6.** to perfect (a person) in education, accomplishments, social graces, etc. —*v.i.* **7.** to come to an end. **8.** to complete a course, etc. **9.** *Obs.* to die. —*n.* **10.** the end or conclusion; the last stage. **11.** the end of a hunt, race, etc. **12.** a decisive ending: *a fight to a finish.* **13.** the quality of being finished or completed with smoothness, elegance, etc. **14.** educational or social polish. **15.** the manner in which a thing is finished in preparation, or an effect imparted in finishing: *a soft or dull finish.* **16.** something used or serving to finish, complete, or perfect a thing. **17.** woodwork, etc., esp. in the interior of a building, not essential to the structure, but used for purposes of ornament, neatness, etc. **18.** a final coat of plaster or paint. **19.** a material for application in finishing. [ME *finisch(en)*, t. F: m. *finiss-*, s. *finir*, g. L *fīnīre* bound, end] —**fin′ish·er**, *n.* —**Syn. 10.** See end¹.

fin·ished (fĭn′ĭsht), *adj.* **1.** ended or completed. **2.** completed or perfected in all details, as a product. **3.** polished to the highest degree of excellence: *a finished poem.* **4.** highly accomplished, as a person. —**Syn. 4.** talented, skilled, gifted; trained.

finishing school, a school for completing the education of young women and preparing them for entrance into society.

Fin·is·terre (fĭn′ĭs târ′; Sp. fē′nēs tĕr′rĕ), *n.* **Cape, a** headland in NW Spain: the westernmost point of Spain.

fi·nite (fī′nīt), *adj.* **1.** having bounds or limits; not too great or too small to be measurable. **2.** *Math.* **a.** (of a class or integral number) capable of being completely counted. **b.** not infinite or infinitesimal. **3.** subject to limitations or conditions, as of space, time, circumstances, or the laws of nature: *finite existence.* —*n.* **4. the finite, a.** that which is finite. **b.** finite things collectively. [t. L: m.s. *fīnītus*, pp., bounded] —**fi′nite·ly**, *adv.* —**fi′nite·ness**, *n.*

finite verb, a verb limited by person, number, tense, mood, and aspect, opposed to the infinite forms, participle, infinitive, and gerund, which have only a few limitations.

fin·i·tude (fĭn′ə tūd′, -tōōd′, fī′nə-), *n.* state of being finite.

fink (fĭngk), *n. U.S. Slang.* **1.** a strikebreaker. **2.** a labor spy.

fin keel, *Naut.* a finlike projection extending downward from the keel of a sailboat, serving to prevent lateral motion and acting as additional ballast.

Fin·land (fĭn′lənd), *n.* **1.** Finnish, **Suomi.** a republic in N Europe: formerly a province of the Russian Empire. 3,816,000 pop. (est. 1945); ab. 118,000 sq. mi. (1945). *Cap.*: Helsinki. **2. Gulf of**, an arm of the Baltic, S of Finland. —**Fin′land·er**, *n.*

fin·let (fĭn′lĭt), *n.* a small detached finlike appendage in certain fishes, as the mackerel.

Finn (fĭn), *n.* **1.** an inhabitant or native of Finland. **2.** any native speaker of Finnish, as in America or Russia. **3.** *Rare.* a speaker of any Finnic language.

fin·nan had·die (fĭn′ən hăd′ĭ), smoked haddock; lit., haddock of Findhorn, fishing port in Scotland. Also, **finnan haddock.**

finned (fĭnd), *adj.* having a fin or fins.

Finn·ic (fĭn′ĭk), *adj.* **1.** designating Finnish and the languages most closely related to it, as Estonian, Lapp, and some minor languages of the northwestern Soviet Union. **2.** designating all Finno-Ugric languages except the Ugric, or all except Ugric and Permian.

Finn·ish (fĭn′ĭsh), *n.* **1.** the principal language of Finland, a Finno-Ugric language, closely related to Estonian. —*adj.* **2.** of or pertaining to Finland or its inhabitants. **3.** Finnic.

Fin·no-U·gri·an (fĭn′ō ōō′grĭ ən), *adj.* pertaining to the Finns and the Ugrians.

Fin·no-U·gric (fĭn′ō ōō′grĭk), *n.* an important linguistic family of eastern Europe and western Siberia, including Finnish, Estonian, and Lapp, farther east the Zyrian and Votyak, and also the Ugric languages, such as Hungarian and Vogul. It is related to Samoyed.

fin·ny (fĭn′ĭ), *adj.* **1.** pertaining to or abounding in fish. **2.** having fins; finned. **3.** finlike.

---

b., blend of, blended; c., cognate with; d., dialect, dialectal; der., derived from; f., formed from; g., going back to; m., modification of; r., replacing; s., stem of; t., taken from; ?, perhaps. See the full key on inside cover.

Fin·ster·aar·horn (fĭn'stər är'hôrn), *n.* a mountain in SW Switzerland: the highest peak of the Bernese Alps. 14,026 ft.

fiord (fyôrd; *Nor.* fyôr, fyôor), *n.* a long, relatively narrow arm of the sea, bordered by steep cliffs, as on the coast of Norway. Also, **fjord.** [t. Norw. See FIRTH]

fip·pen·ny bit (fĭp'ən ĭ, fĭp'nĭ), *U.S.* the Spanish half real, the value of which was about 6 cents. Also, **fippenny piece.** [var. of *fivepenny bit*]

fip·ple (fĭp'əl), *n. Music.* a plug, stopping the upper end of a pipe.

fipple flute, *Music.* a flute equipped with a fipple.

fir (fûr), *n.* 1. any of the pyramidal coniferous trees constituting the genus *Abies,* as *A. balsamea,* the balsam fir. 2. the wood of such a tree. [ME *firr*(e), OE *fyrh.* Cf. OE *furh*(*wudu*) pine, Icel. *fura* fir; akin to L *quercus* oak]

Fir·dau·si (fĭr dou'sē), *n.* (*Abul Kasim Mansur*), A.D. c940–1020, Persian poet who wrote the greatest Persian epic poem. Also, **Fir·du·si** (fĭr doo'sē).

fire (fīr), *n., v.,* **fired, firing.** —*n.* 1. the active principle of burning or combustion, manifested by the evolution of light and heat. 2. a burning mass of material, as on a hearth or in a furnace. 3. the destructive burning of a building, town, forest, etc.; a conflagration. 4. a composition or device for producing a conflagration or a fiery display: *Greek fire.* 5. flashing light; luminous appearance. 6. brilliancy, as of a gem. 7. burning passion; ardor; enthusiasm. 8. liveliness of imagination. 9. fever; inflammation. 10. severe trial or trouble. 11. exposure to fire by way of torture or ordeal. 12. heating quality, as of strong drink. 13. a spark or sparks. 14. the discharge of firearms: *to open fire.* 15. the effect of firing military weapons: *to place fire upon the enemy.* 16. *Archaic.* lightning, or a thunderbolt. 17. *Poetic.* a luminous object, as a star: *heavenly fires.* 18. Special noun phrases are:
between two fires, being attacked from both directions.
catch fire, to become ignited.
hang fire, 1. to be slow in exploding. **2.** to be irresolute or slow in acting.
lay a fire, to arrange fuel to be lit.
miss fire, 1. to fail to explode or discharge. **2.** to be unsuccessful; fail.
on fire, 1. ignited; burning. **2.** eager; ardent, zealous.
play with fire, to meddle carelessly or lightly with a dangerous matter.
set fire to or **set on fire, 1.** to cause to burn. **2.** to excite violently; inflame.
take fire, to become ignited.
under fire, 1. exposed to enemy fire. **2.** under criticism or attack.
—*v.t.* **19.** to set on fire. **20.** to supply (a furnace, etc.) with fuel; attend to the fire of (a boiler, etc.). **21.** to expose to the action of fire; subject to heat. **22.** to apply heat in a kiln for baking or glazing; burn. **23.** to heat very slowly for the purpose of drying, as tea. **24.** to inflame, as with passion; fill with ardor. **25.** to inspire. **26.** to light or cause to glow as if on fire. **27.** to discharge, as a gun. **28.** to project (a missile) by discharging from a gun, etc. **29.** to subject to explosion or explosive force, as a mine. **30.** *Colloq.* to hurl; throw: *to fire a stone through a window.* **31.** *Slang.* to eject or dismiss forcibly or peremptorily. **32.** *Vet. Sci.* to apply a heated iron to (the skin) in order to create a local inflammation of the superficial structures, thus favorably affecting deeper inflammatory processes. **33.** *Obs.* to drive out or away by, or as by, fire.
—*v.i.* **34.** to take fire; be kindled. **35.** to glow as if on fire. **36.** to become inflamed with passion; become excited. **37.** to go off, as a gun. **38.** discharge a gun, etc.: *to fire at a fleeing enemy.* **39.** *Colloq.* to hurl a missile. **40.** (of grain crops) to lose green coloring and become yellow before ripening.
[ME *fȳr,* c. D *vier,* G *feuer;* akin to Gk. *pŷr*]

fire alarm, 1. an alarm of fire. **2.** an apparatus for giving the alarm.

fire·arm (fīr'ärm'), *n.* 1. a gun from which a projectile is fired. 2. small arms.

fire·ball (fīr'bôl'), *n.* 1. a ball filled with explosive or combustible material, used as a projectile, to injure the enemy by explosion or to set fire to their works. 2. a ball of fire, as the sun. 3. a luminous meteor, sometimes exploding. 4. lightning having the appearance of a globe of fire.

fire bay, *Brit. Fort.* that section of a fire trench occupied by riflemen, usually one squad to a bay.

fire beetle, any of the click beetles of the genus *Pyrophorus,* of tropical America, which emit reddish or greenish light from luminous spots.

fire·bird (fīr'bûrd'), *n.* the Baltimore oriole.

fire·board (fīr'bôrd'), *n.* a board used to close a fireplace.

fire·boat (fīr'bōt'), *n.* a powered vessel fitted for fire fighting.

fire·box (fīr'bŏks'), *n.* 1. the box or chamber in which the fire of a steam boiler, etc., is placed. 2. the furnace of a locomotive, where coal, oil, or other fuel is burned for the purpose of generating steam. 3. *Obs.* a tinderbox.

fire·brand (fīr'brănd'), *n.* 1. a piece of burning wood or other material. 2. one who or that which kindles strife, inflames the passions, etc.

fire·break (fīr'brāk'), *n. U.S.* a strip of ploughed or cleared land made to check the spread of a prairie or forest fire.

fire·brick (fīr'brĭk'), *n.* a brick made of fire clay.

fire brigade, *Brit.* a company of firemen.

fire·bug (fīr'bŭg'), *n. U.S. Colloq.* an incendiary.

fire clay, a kind of clay capable of resisting high temperature, used for making crucibles, firebricks, etc.

fire company, 1. a company of firemen. **2.** a fire-insurance company.

fire control, *Mil.* technical supervision of artillery fire.

fire·crack·er (fīr'krăk'ər), *n.* a paper or cardboard cylinder filled with an explosive and having a fuse to be discharged to make a noise.

fire-cure (fīr'kyoor'), *v.t.,* **-cured, -curing.** to cure (tobacco) by means of open fires, the smoke and flame imparting a creosotic flavor.

fire·damp (fīr'dămp'), *n.* 1. a combustible gas, consisting chiefly of methane, formed esp. in coal mines, and dangerously explosive when mixed with certain proportions of atmospheric air. 2. the explosive mixture itself.

fire department, 1. the department of a municipal government charged with the prevention and extinction of fire. **2.** the men in this department.

fire direction, *Mil.* tactical supervision of artillery fire.

fire·dog (fīr'dôg', -dŏg'), *n.* andiron.

fire·drake (fīr'drāk'), *n.* a mythical fiery dragon. [OE *fȳrdraca,* f. *fȳr* fire + *draca* dragon]

fire drill, 1. a practice drill for a company of firemen, the crew of a ship, etc., to accustom them to their duties in case of fire. **2.** a drill for pupils in a school, employees in a factory, etc., to train them in the manner of exit to be followed in case of fire.

fire-eat·er (fīr'ē'tər), *n.* 1. a juggler who pretends to eat fire. 2. one who seeks occasion to fight or quarrel.

fire engine, a motor truck equipped for fire fighting, now usually having a motor-driven pump for shooting water from fire hydrants, etc., or chemical solutions at high pressure.

fire escape, an apparatus or structure used to escape from a burning building.

fire extinguisher, a portable apparatus, usually containing chemicals, for putting out a fire.

fire·flaught (fīr'flôt'; *Scot.* -fläкht'), *n. Chiefly Scot.* lightning. [f. FIRE, n. + *flaught* flash]

fire·fly (fīr'flī'), *n., pl.* **-flies.** any of the soft-bodied, nocturnal beetles of the family *Lampyridae,* which possess abdominal light-producing organs. The luminous larvae or wingless females are called *glow-worms.*

fire·guard (fīr'gärd'), *n.* a framework of wire placed in front of a fireplace as a protection.

fire·house (fīr'hous'), *n.* a building where fire-fighting apparatus or firemen are stationed.

fire insurance, insurance covering loss or damage through fire.

fire·less (fīr'lĭs), *adj.* 1. lacking fire; without a fire. 2. without life or animation.

fireless cooker, an insulated container which seals in heat for a long enough time to cook food.

fire·light (fīr'līt'), *n.* the light from a fire, as on a hearth.

fire·lock (fīr'lŏk'), *n.* 1. the flintlock musket, in whose lock the priming is ignited by sparks struck from flint and steel. 2. (formerly) a soldier armed with such a gun.

fire·man (fīr'mən), *n., pl.* **-men.** 1. a man employed to extinguish or prevent fires. 2. a man employed to tend fires; a stoker.

fire-new (fīr'nū', -noo'), *adj. Archaic.* brand-new.

Fi·ren·ze (fē rĕn'tsĕ), *n.* Italian name of **Florence.**

fire opal, a red Mexican opal, with or without a color play.

fire pink, a caryophyllaceous plant, *Silene virginica,* with brilliant scarlet flowers.

fire·place (fīr'plās'), *n.* 1. that part of a chimney which opens into an apartment and in which fuel is burned. 2. any open structure, usually of masonry, for containing fire, as at a camp site.

fire·plug (fīr'plŭg'), *n.* a hydrant for use in case of fire.

fire pot, that part of a household furnace in which the fire is made.

fire power, *Mil.* the ability to deliver fire; the amount of fire delivered by a unit or weapon.

fire·proof (fīr'proof'), *adj.* 1. proof against fire; comparatively incombustible. —*v.t.* 2. to make fireproof.

fire·proof·ing (fīr'proo'fĭng), *n.* 1. act or process of rendering fireproof. 2. material for use in making anything fireproof.

fir·er (fīr'ər), *n.* 1. one who fires, sets on fire, treats with fire or heat, discharges a firearm, etc. 2. a firearm with reference to its firing: *a single-firer, a rapid-firer.*

fire sale, *U.S.* a special sale of merchandise supposedly injured by fire.

fire screen, a metal screen placed in front of a fireplace for protection.

Firefly.
Photuris pennsylvanica
A, Larva (line shows actual size); B, Adult beetle

fire ship, a vessel freighted with combustibles and explosives and set adrift to destroy an enemy's ships, etc.

fire·side (fīr′sīd′), *n.* **1.** the space about a fire or hearth. **2.** home; home life.

fire step, *Fort.* a board or narrow ledge above the bottom of a fire trench from which men can fire, observe enemy movements, etc.

fire·stone (fīr′stōn′), *n.* a fire-resisting stone, esp. a kind of sandstone used in fireplaces, furnaces, etc. [OE *fȳrstān,* f. *fȳr* fire + *stān* stone]

fire·trap (fīr′trăp′), *n.* a building which, because of the material or arrangement of the structure, is especially dangerous in case of fire.

fire trench, *Fort.* a trench from which men can fire rifles and other small arms and in which they are relatively well protected.

fire wall, 1. a wall made of fireproof material to prevent the spread of a fire from one part of a building to another. **2.** *Aeron.* a wall made of stainless steel and asbestos to isolate the engine compartment from the rest of an aircraft.

fire·ward·en (fīr′wôr′dən), *n.* a person having authority in the prevention or extinguishing of fires, as in towns or camps.

fire·wa·ter (fīr′wô′tər, -wŏt′ər), *n.* strong liquor.

fire·weed (fīr′wēd′), *n.* any of various plants appearing in recently burned clearings or districts, as the willow herb, *Epilobium angustifolium,* or the composite weed, *Erechtites hieracifolia,* of North America.

fire·wood (fīr′wŏŏd′), *n.* wood for fuel.

fire·work (fīr′wûrk′), *n.* **1.** (*usually pl.*) a combustible or explosive device for producing a striking display of light or a loud noise, often also used in signaling at night, etc. **2.** (*pl.*) a pyrotechnic display.

fir·ing (fīr′ĭng), *n.* **1.** act of one who or that which fires. **2.** material for a fire; fuel.

firing battery, *Mil.* that part of a battery actually at the firing position when the battery is prepared for action.

firing data, *Mil.* precise calculations in set formula by which cannon are aimed and fired.

firing line, *Mil.* **1.** the positions at which troops are stationed to fire upon the enemy or targets. **2.** the troops firing from this line.

firing pin, *Ordn.* a plunger in the firing mechanism of a firearm or cannon that strikes the primer and thus ignites the propelling charge of a projectile.

firing squad, a military or naval detachment assigned to fire a salute at the burial of an honored person or to execute a condemned person.

fir·kin (fûr′kĭn), *n.* **1.** a unit of capacity, usually the fourth part of a barrel. **2.** a small wooden vessel for butter, etc. [ME *ferdekyn,* t. MD: m. *ferdelkijn,* dim. of *ferdel* firkin (lit., fourth part)]

firm[1] (fûrm), *adj.* **1.** comparatively solid, hard, stiff, or rigid: *firm ground, flesh, texture.* **2.** securely fixed in place. **3.** steady; not shaking or trembling: *a firm hand or voice.* **4.** fixed, settled, or unalterable, as a belief or conviction, a decree, etc. **5.** steadfast or unwavering, as persons or principles. **6.** indicating firmness: *a firm countenance.* **7.** not fluctuating or falling, as prices or the market. —*v.t., v.i.* **8.** to make or become firm. —*adv.* **9.** firmly: *stand firm.* [t. L: s. *firmus;* r. ME *ferme,* t. OF] —**firm′ly,** *adv.* —**firm′ness,** *n.*
—**Syn. 1.** FIRM, HARD, SOLID, STIFF are applied to substances that tend to retain their form unaltered in spite of pressure or force. FIRM often implies that something has been brought from a more yielding state to a fixed or elastic one: *an increased amount of pectin makes jellies more firm.* HARD is applied to substances so resistant that it is difficult to make any impression upon their surface or to penetrate their interior: *as hard as a stone.* SOLID is applied to substances that without external support retain their form and resist pressure: *water in the form of ice is solid;* it sometimes denotes the opposite of hollow: *a solid block of marble.* STIFF implies rigidity that resists a bending force: *as stiff as a poker.* **5.** determined, immovable, resolute. —**Ant. 1.** yielding.

firm[2] (fûrm), *n.* **1.** a partnership or unincorporated association of two or more persons for carrying on a business. **2.** the name or title under which associated parties transact business: *the firm of Jones & Co.* [t. It., Sp.: m. *firma* signature, der. L *firmāre* confirm]

fir·ma·ment (fûr′mə mənt), *n.* the vault of heaven; the sky. [ME, t. LL: s. *firmāmentum* firmament, L a support, prop] —**fir′ma·men′tal,** *adj.*

fir·man (fûr′mən, fər män′), *n., pl.* **-mans.** an edict or administrative order issued by or in the name of an Oriental sovereign (formerly by an Ottoman Turkish sultan). [t. Pers.: m. *fermān*]

firm·er chisel (fûr′mər), a carpenter's chisel with a blade thin in proportion to its width, fixed to the handle by a tang, usually pushed by the hand and not driven with a mallet. [*firmer,* t. F: m. *fermoir,* b. *formoir* former (der. *former* form, t. L: m. *formāre*) and *fermer* make firm (g. L *firmāre*)]

firn (fĭrn), *n.* névé. [t. G: (prop. adj.) of last year]

fir·ry (fûr′ĭ), *adj.* of or pertaining to the fir; made of fir; abounding in firs.

first (fûrst), *adj.* **1.** being before all others with respect to time, order, rank, importance, etc. (used as the ordinal of *one*). **2.** *Music.* highest or chief among several voices or instruments of the same class: *first alto, first horn.*

3. *Auto.* of or pertaining to low transmission gear ratio. **4. at first blush,** at the first view; on first consideration. **5. at first hand,** from the first or original source. —*adv.* **6.** before all others or anything else in time, order, rank, etc. **7.** before some other thing, event, etc. **8.** for the first time. **9.** in preference to something else; rather; sooner. **10.** in the first place; firstly. **11. first and last,** altogether; in all. **12. first off,** in the first place. **13. first or last,** at one time or another; sooner or later. —*n.* **14.** that which is first in time, order, rank, etc. **15.** the beginning. **16.** the first part; the first member of a series. **17.** *Music.* **a.** the voice or instrument that takes the highest or chief part in its class, especially in an orchestra or chorus. **b.** a leader of a part or group of performers. **18.** *Auto.* the lowest forward gear ratio, as in passenger cars. **19.** the first place in a race, etc. **20.** *Brit.* the highest class in an examination for honors: *he got a first in mathematics.* **21.** (*pl.*) the best quality of certain articles of commerce. **22. at** (**the**) **first,** at the beginning or outset. **23. from the first,** from the beginning or outset. [ME; OE *fyrst,* c. OHG *furist,* G *fürst* prince; a superl. form akin to FORE[1]]

first aid, emergency aid or treatment given to persons suffering from accident, etc., before the services of a physician can be obtained.

first base, 1. *Baseball.* **a.** the first of the bases from the home plate. **b.** playing this position. **2. get to first base,** *Colloq.* to make a slight amount of progress.

first baseman, *Baseball.* the player stationed at first base.

first-born (fûrst′bôrn′), *adj.* **1.** first in the order of birth; eldest. —*n.* **2.** a first-born child. **3.** a first result or product.

first cause, 1. a cause which does not depend upon any other: *God is the first cause.* **2.** any prime mover.

first-class (fûrst′klăs′, -kläs′), *adj.* **1.** of the highest or best class or quality. **2.** best-equipped and most expensive: *a first-class coach.* —*adv.* **3.** by first-class conveyance: *to travel first-class.*

First day, Sunday (used by the Quakers).

first fruit, (*usually pl.*) **1.** the earliest fruit of the season. **2.** the first product or result of anything.

first-hand (fûrst′hănd′), *adv.* **1.** from the first or original source. —*adj.* **2.** of or pertaining to the first or original source. **3.** obtained directly from the original source.

first lady, *U.S.* the wife of the president of the U.S., or of the governor of a State.

first lieutenant, *Mil.* an officer ranking next above a second lieutenant and next below a captain. See **lieutenant** (def. 1a).

first·ling (fûrst′lĭng), *n.* **1.** the first of its kind to be produced or to appear. **2.** first offspring. **3.** the first product or result.

first·ly (fûrst′lĭ), *adv.* in the first place; first.

first mortgage, a mortgage having priority over all other mortgages on property.

first-night·er (fûrst′nī′tər), *n.* one who makes a practice of attending the theater on the nights of the first public performance of plays.

first papers, *U.S.* the first documents of record in the naturalization of a foreigner.

first person, *Gram.* the class of a pronoun or verb in which the speaker is the subject. See **person** (def. 13a).

first-rate (fûrst′rāt′), *adj.* **1.** of the first rate or class. **2.** excellent; very good. —*adv.* **3.** *Colloq.* excellently; very well.

First Reich. See **Reich** (def. 1).

first sergeant, *U.S. Army.* the noncommissioned officer of highest rank in a company or other unit of similar size.

first speed, *Brit.* low gear.

first water, 1. the highest degree of fineness in a diamond or other precious stone. **2.** the highest rank.

firth (fûrth), *n. Chiefly Scot.* a long, narrow indentation of the sea coast. Also, **frith.** [t. Scand.; cf. Icel. *firdh-,* s. *fjördhr* firth. Cf. FIORD]

fisc (fĭsk), *n.* a royal or state treasury; an exchequer. [t. L: s. *fiscus* basket, purse, treasury]

fis·cal (fĭs′kəl), *adj.* **1.** of or pertaining to the public treasury or revenues. **2.** pertaining to financial matters in general. —*n.* **3.** (in some countries) an official having the function of public prosecutor. [t. L: s. *fiscālis* belonging to the state treasury] —**fis′cal·ly,** *adv.* —**Syn. 2.** See **financial.**

fiscal agent, a person or organization serving as another's financial agent.

fiscal year, any yearly period at the end of which a firm determines its financial condition without regard to the calendar year.

fish (fĭsh), *n., pl.* **fishes,** (*esp. collectively*) **fish. 1.** any of various cold-blooded, completely aquatic vertebrates, having gills, commonly fins, and typically an elongated body usually covered with scales. **2.** any of various other aquatic animals. **3.** the flesh of fishes used as food. **4. other fish to fry,** *Colloq.* other matters requiring attention. **5. the Fishes,** *Astron.* the Zodiacal constellation or sign Pisces. **6.** *Colloq.* (with an adjective) a person: *a queer fish, a poor fish.* **7.** a long strip of wood, iron, etc., used to strengthen a mast, joint, etc. —*v.t.* **8.** to catch or attempt to catch (fish or the like). **9.** to try to catch fish in (a stream, etc.). **10.** to draw as by fishing

(fol. by *up*, *out*, etc.). **11.** to search through as by fishing. **12.** *Naut.* **a.** to strengthen (a mast, joint, etc.) by a fish (def. 7). **b.** to hoist the flukes of (an anchor) up to the gunwale or rail by means of a tackle. **13. fish out, a.** to exhaust of fish by fishing. **b.** to obtain by careful search or by artifice. —*v.i.* **14.** to catch or attempt to catch fish, as by angling or drawing a net. **15.** to search for or attempt to catch onto something under water, in mud, etc., by the use of a dredge, rake, hook, or the like. **16.** to seek to obtain something by artifice or indirectly: *to fish for compliments, information, etc.* [ME; OE *fisc*, c. D *visch*, G *fisch*; akin to L *piscis*] —**fish′a·ble,** *adj.* —**fish′less,** *adj.* —**fish′like′,** *adj.*
Fish (fĭsh), *n.* **Hamilton**, 1808–93, U.S. statesman; secretary of state, 1869–77.
fish and chips, *Chiefly Brit.* fried fish fillets and fried potatoes.
fish·bolt (fĭsh′bōlt′), *n.* a bolt that secures a fishplate to the rail in a railway track.
fish cake, a fried ball or cake of shredded fish, esp. salt codfish, and mashed potato. Also, **fish ball.**
fish crow, a North American crow, *Corvus ossifragus,* found along the entire Atlantic coast, fond of fish, mollusks, etc.
fish·er (fĭsh′ər), *n.* **1.** a fisherman. **2.** an animal that catches fish for food. **3.** a dark-brown or blackish, somewhat foxlike marten, *Martes pennanti,* of northern North America. **4.** its fur.

Fisher, *Martes pennanti*
(3 ft. long)

Fish·er (fĭsh′ər), *n.* **1.** **Dorothy Canfield,** (*Dorothea Frances Canfield, Mrs. Fisher*) born 1879, U.S. novelist. **2.** **Irving,** 1867–1947, U.S. political economist.
fish·er·man (fĭsh′ər mən), *n., pl.* **-men. 1.** one engaged in fishing, whether for profit or pleasure. **2.** a vessel employed in fishing.
fisherman's bend, a knot, consisting of two round turns and a half hitch around them and the standing part, used commonly to bend a rope to an anchor or similar object.
Fisher of Kil·ver·stone (kĭl′vər stən), **John Arbuthnot** (är′bəth nət, -nŏt′), **1st Baron,** 1841–1920, British admiral.
fish·er·y (fĭsh′ə rĭ), *n., pl.* **-eries. 1.** the occupation or industry of catching fish or taking other products of the sea or streams from the water. **2.** a place where such an industry is regularly carried on. **3.** a fishing establishment. **4.** *Law.* the right of fishing in certain waters.
fish hawk, osprey.
fish·hook (fĭsh′hŏŏk′), *n.* a hook used with fishing tackle.
fish·ing (fĭsh′ĭng), *n.* **1.** the art or practice of catching fish. **2.** a place or facilities for catching fish.
fishing rod, a long, flexible pole supporting a line used in fishing.
fishing smack, any of various small vessels used for deep-sea fishing.
fishing tackle, the equipment used to catch fish.
fish joint, a splice formed by fastening one or more fishplates to the sides of rails, beams, etc., which meet end to end: used esp. in connecting railroad rails.
fish-line (fĭsh′līn′), *n.* a line used in fishing.
fish louse, *Zool.* any of numerous small crustaceans, esp. certain copepods, parasitic on fish.
fish·mon·ger (fĭsh′mŭng′gər), *n. Chiefly Brit.* a dealer in fish.
fish·plate (fĭsh′plāt′), *n.* one of the splicing plates used in a fish joint.

Fishplate

fish·pound (fĭsh′pound′), *n. U.S.* a submerged net used by commercial fishermen for capturing fish.
fish slice, 1. a kitchen implement with a broad, thin blade and a long handle, for turning fish in frying. **2.** *Chiefly Brit.* a broad-bladed implement for serving fish at table.
fish spear, a spear or lance, often with several tines, for spearing fish through ice or from a boat or shore.
fish story, *Colloq.* an exaggerated or incredible story.
fish tackle, the tackle used for fishing an anchor.
fish·tail (fĭsh′tāl′), *Colloq.* —*v.i.* **1.** to slow an airplane by causing its tail to move rapidly from side to side. —*n.* **2.** such a maneuver.
fish·wife (fĭsh′wīf′), *n., pl.* **-wives. 1.** a woman who sells fish. **2.** a woman who uses abusive language.
fish·worm (fĭsh′wûrm′), *n.* an earthworm.
fish·y (fĭsh′ĭ), *adj.,* **fishier, fishiest. 1.** fishlike in shape, smell, taste, etc. **2.** consisting of fish. **3.** abounding in fish. **4.** *Colloq.* improbable, as a story. **5.** *Colloq.* of questionable character. **6.** dull and expressionless: *fishy eyes.* —**fish′i·ly,** *adv.* —**fish′i·ness,** *n.*
Fiske (fĭsk), *n.* **1.** **John,** (orig. *Edmund Fiske Green*) 1842–1901, U.S. historian and writer on philosophy and science. **2. Mrs.,** (*Minnie Davey*), known as *Minnie Maddern,* 1865–1932, U.S. actress.

fissi-, a word element meaning "cleft." [t. L; comb. form of *fissus*, pp.]
fis·sile (fĭs′əl), *adj.* capable of being split or divided; cleavable. [t. L: m.s. *fissilis*] —**fis·sil·i·ty** (fĭ sĭl′ə tĭ), *n.*
fis·sion (fĭsh′ən), *n.* **1.** act of cleaving or splitting into parts. **2.** *Biol.* the division of an organism into new organisms as a process of reproduction. [t. L: s. *fissio* a cleaving]
fis·sion·a·ble material (fĭsh′ən ə bəl), *Physics.* a substance capable of undergoing nuclear fission.
fis·sip·a·rous (fĭ sĭp′ə rəs), *adj.* reproducing by fission.
fis·si·ros·tral (fĭs′ĭ rŏs′trəl), *adj. Ornith.* **1.** having a broad, deeply cleft beak or bill, as the swallows and goatsuckers. **2.** (of the bill) deeply cleft.

Fissirostral bill of goatsucker.
Caprimulgus europaeus

fis·sure (fĭsh′ər), *n., v.,* **-sured, -suring.** —*n.* **1.** a narrow opening produced by cleavage or separation of parts; a cleft. **2.** act of cleaving. **3.** state of being cleft; cleavage. **4.** *Surg., Anat.* a natural division or groove between adjoining parts of like substance. —*v.t.* **5.** to make fissures in; cleave; split. —*v.i.* **6.** to open in fissures; become split. [t. F, t. L: m.s. *fissūra* a cleft]
fist (fĭst), *n.* **1.** the hand closed tightly, with the fingers doubled into the palm. **2.** *Colloq.* the hand. **3.** *Colloq.* a person's handwriting. **4.** *Print.* the index sign (☞). —*v.t.* **5.** to strike with the fist. **6.** to grasp with the fist. [ME *fiste*, OE *fȳst*, c. G *faust*]
fist·ic (fĭs′tĭk), *adj.* pertaining to boxing; pugilistic: *fistic exploits, fistic heroes.*
fist·i·cuff (fĭs′tə kŭf′), *n.* **1.** a cuff or blow with the fist. **2.** (*pl.*) combat with the fists. —*v.t., v.i.* **3.** to strike or fight with the fists. —**fist′i·cuff′er,** *n.*
fis·tu·la (fĭs′chŏŏ lə), *n., pl.* **-las, -lae** (-lē), *n.* **1.** *Pathol.* a narrow passage or duct formed by disease or injury, as one leading from an abscess to a free surface, or from one cavity to another. **2.** *Vet. Sci.* any of various suppurative inflammations, as in the withers of a horse, characterized by the formation of passages or sinuses through the tissues and to the surface of the skin. **3.** *Obs.* a pipe, as a flute. [t. L: pipe, tube, reed, ulcer. Cf. FESTER]
fis·tu·lous (fĭs′chŏŏ ləs), *adj.* **1.** *Pathol.* pertaining to or of the nature of a fistula. **2.** tubelike; tubular. **3.** containing tubes or tubelike parts. Also, **fis′tu·lar.**
fit¹ (fĭt), *adj.,* **fitter, fittest,** *v.,* **fitted, fitting,** *n.* —*adj.* **1.** well adapted or suited: *a fit choice or opportunity, fit to be eaten.* **2.** proper or becoming. **3.** qualified or competent, as for an office or function. **4.** worthy or deserving: *not fit to be seen.* **5.** prepared or ready: *crops fit for gathering.* **6.** in good physical condition, as an athlete, a race horse, military troops, etc. **7.** in good health. **8.** *U.S. Colloq.* in a condition; ready: *dressed up fit to kill; fit to be tied.* —*v.t.* **9.** to be adapted to or suitable for (a purpose, object, occasion, etc.). **10.** to be proper or becoming for. **11.** to be of the right size or shape for. **12.** to conform or adjust to something: *to fit a ring to the finger.* **13.** to make qualified or competent: *qualities that fit one for leadership.* **14.** to prepare: *this school fits students for college.* **15.** to put with nice adjustment (fol. by *in, into, on, over, together,* etc.). **16.** to provide; furnish; equip: *fit a door with a new handle.* **17. fit out** or **up,** to furnish with clothing, equipment, furniture, fixtures, or other requisites. —*v.i.* **18.** to be suitable or proper. **19.** to be of the right size or shape, as a garment for the wearer, or any object or part for a thing to which it is applied. —*n.* **20.** the manner in which a thing fits: *a perfect fit.* **21.** something that fits: *the coat is a poor fit.* **22.** the process or a process of fitting. [ME *fyt*; orig. uncert.] —**fit′ness,** *n.*
fit² (fĭt), *n.* **1.** a sudden, acute attack or manifestation of a disease: *fit of epilepsy.* **2.** an access, spell, or period of emotion or feeling, inclination, activity, idleness, etc. **3. by fits,** or **by fits and starts,** by irregular spells; fitfully; intermittently. [ME; OE *fitt* fight, struggle]
fit³ (fĭt), *n.* **1.** a song, ballad, or story. **2.** a division of a song, ballad, or story. [ME; OE *fitt*]
fitch (fĭch), *n.* **1.** the European polecat, *Mustela putorius.* **2.** its fur. Yellow fitch is often dyed to imitate other furs. Also, **fitch·et** (fĭch′ĭt), **fitch·ew** (fĭch′ŏŏ). [t. MD: m. *vitsche* polecat]
Fitch (fĭch), *n.* **1.** **John,** 1743–98, American who invented a steamboat in 1790. **2. William Clyde,** 1865–1909, U.S. playwright.

Fitch, *Mustela putorius*
(Total length 2 ft., tail 7 in.)

Fitch·burg (fĭch′bûrg′), *n.* a city in N Massachusetts. 42,691 (1950).
fit·ful (fĭt′fəl), *adj.* coming, appearing, acting, etc., in fits or by spells; irregularly intermittent. [f. FIT² + -FUL] —**fit′ful·ly,** *adv.* —**fit′ful·ness,** *n.*
fit·ly (fĭt′lĭ), *adv.* **1.** in a fit manner. **2.** at a fit time.
fit·ter (fĭt′ər), *n.* **1.** one who or that which fits. **2.** one who fits garments. **3.** one who fits together or adjusts

the parts of machinery. **4.** one who supplies and fixes fittings or fixtures. **5.** one who furnishes or equips with whatever is necessary for some purpose.

fit·ting (fĭt′ĭng), *adj.* **1.** suitable or appropriate; proper or becoming. —*n.* **2.** act of one who or that which fits. **3.** anything employed in fitting up. **4.** (*pl.*) furnishings, fixtures, etc. —**fit′ting·ly,** *adv.* —**fit′ting·ness,** *n.*

Fitz·Ger·ald (fĭts jĕr′əld), *n.* **1.** Edward, 1809–83, British poet who translated some of the poems of Omar Khayyam. **2.** F(rancis) Scott (Key), 1896–1940, U.S. novelist and short-story writer.

Fiu·me (fū′mĕ), *n.* a seaport in NW Yugoslavia at the head of the Gulf of Quarnero: seized by d'Annunzio, 1919; a part of Italy, 1924–47.

five (fīv), *n.* **1.** a cardinal number, four plus one. **2.** a symbol for this number, as 5 or V. **3.** a set of this many persons or things. **4.** a playing card, etc., with five pips. —*adj.* **5.** amounting to five in number. [ME; OE *fīf*, c. D *vijf*, G *fünf*; akin to L *quinque*, Gk. *pénte*]

five-fin·ger (fīv′fĭng′gər), *n.* **1.** any of certain species of potentilla with leaves of five leaflets, as *Potentilla canadensis.* **2.** bird's-foot trefoil. **3.** oxlip. **4.** Virginia creeper.

five·fold (fīv′fōld′), *adj.* **1.** comprising five parts or members. **2.** five times as great or as much. —*adv.* **3.** in fivefold measure.

five hundred, *Cards.* a modification of euchre in which a joker and a widow are included and in which 500 points win.

Five Nations, *U.S. Hist.* a confederacy of Iroquoian Indians: the Mohawks, Oneidas, Onondagas, Cayugas, and Senecas.

fiv·er (fī′vər), *n.* *Colloq.* **1.** a five-dollar bill or a five-pound note. **2.** anything that counts as five.

fives (fīvz), *n.* *Brit.* a game similar to handball.

fix (fĭks), *v.,* **fixed** or **fixt, fixing,** *n.* —*v.t.* **1.** to make fast, firm, or stable. **2.** to place definitely and more or less permanently. **3.** to settle definitely; determine: *to fix a price.* **4.** to direct (the eyes, the attention, etc.) steadily. **5.** to attract and hold (the eye, the attention, etc.). **6.** to make set or rigid. **7.** to put into permanent form. **8.** to put or place (responsibility, blame, etc.) on a person. **9.** to assign or refer to a definite place, time, etc. **10.** to repair. **11.** to put in order or in good condition; adjust or arrange (common in U.S., but not considered good usage in England). **12.** *Colloq.* to arrange matters with, or with respect to, esp. privately or dishonestly, so as to secure favorable action: *to fix a jury or a game.* **13.** *U.S.* to get (a meal); prepare (food). **14.** *Colloq.* to put in a condition or position to make no further trouble. **15.** *Colloq.* to get even with; get revenge upon. **16.** *Chem.* to make stable in consistence or condition; reduce from fluidity or volatility to a more permanent state. **17.** *Photog.* to remove the light-sensitive silver halides from (a photographic image), rendering it permanent. **18.** *Microscopy.* to kill, make rigid, and preserve for microscopic study. **19. fix up,** *U.S.* **a.** to clear up. **b.** to punish. —*v.i.* **20.** to become fixed. **21.** to become set; assume a rigid or solid form. **22.** to become stable or permanent. **23.** to settle down. **24. fix on,** to decide on. —*n.* **25.** *Colloq.* a position from which it is difficult to escape; a predicament. [t. ML: s. *fixāre,* freq. of L *fīgere* fix] —**fix′a·ble,** *adj.* —**fix′er,** *n.*

—**Syn. 1, 2.** Fix, ESTABLISH imply making firm or permanent. To FIX is to fasten in position securely or to make more or less permanent against change, esp. something already existing: *to fix a bayonet on a gun, fix a principle.* To ESTABLISH is to make firm or permanent something (usually newly) originated, created, or ordained: *to establish a business, a claim to property.*

fix·ate (fĭk′sāt), *v.,* **-ated, -ating.** —*v.t.* **1.** to fix; make stable, as a sensation. —*v.i.* **2.** to become fixed. [appar. back formation from FIXATION]

fix·a·tion (fĭk sā′shən), *n.* **1.** act of fixing. **2.** state of being fixed. **3.** *Chem.* **a.** reduction from a volatile or fluid to a stable or solid form. **b.** the process of converting atmospheric nitrogen into a useful compound, as a nitrate fertilizer. **4.** *Psychoanal.* a partial arrest of emotional and instinctual development at an early point in life, due to a severe traumatic experience or an overwhelming gratification. [ME, t. ML: s. *fixātio,* der. *fixāre,* freq. of L *fīgere* fix]

fix·a·tive (fĭk′sə tĭv), *adj.* **1.** serving to fix; making fixed or permanent. —*n.* **2.** a fixative substance, esp.: **a.** a gummy liquid sprayed on a drawing or pastel to prevent blurring. **b.** a solution for killing, hardening, and preserving material for microscopic study.

fixed (fĭkst), *adj.* **1.** made fast or firm; firmly implanted. **2.** rendered stable or permanent, as color. **3.** set or intent upon something; steadily directed; set or rigid. **4.** definitely and permanently placed: *the fixed stars.* **5.** definite; not fluctuating or varying: *fixed charges.* **6.** put in order. **7.** *Colloq.* arranged with, or arranged, privately or dishonestly. **8.** *Chem.* **a.** (of an element) taken into a compound from its free state. **b.** nonvolatile, or not easily volatilized: *a fixed oil.* —**fix·ed·ly** (fĭk′sĭd lĭ), *adv.* —**fix′ed·ness,** *n.*

fixed charge, 1. an expense which must be met. **2.** periodic obligation as taxes, interest on bonds issued, etc. **3.** (*pl.*) such charges as depreciation, rent, interest, etc., arising out of the maintenance of fixed assets.

fixed idea, 1. a persistent or obsessing idea, often delusional, from which a person cannot escape. **2.** *Psychiatry.* a delusional idea which dominates the mind in certain forms of insanity.

fixed oil, *Chem.* a natural oil which is fixed (def. 8b), as lard oil, linseed oil, etc. Fixed oils occur in the cellular membranes, etc., of animals, and in the seeds, capsules, etc., of plants.

fixed star, *Astron.* any of the stars which apparently always retain the same position with respect to one another.

fix·ing (fĭk′sĭng), *n.* **1.** act of one who or that which fixes. **2.** (*pl.*) *U.S. Colloq.* appliances; trimmings.

fix·i·ty (fĭk′sə tĭ), *n., pl.* **-ties. 1.** state or quality of being fixed; stability; permanence. **2.** something fixed.

fixt (fĭkst), *v.* pt. and pp. of **fix.**

fix·ture (fĭks′chər), *n.* **1.** something securely fixed in position; a permanently attached part or appendage of a house, etc.: *an electric-light fixture.* **2.** a person or thing long established in the same place or position. **3.** *Mach.* a device for holding the work in a machine tool, esp. where the machining is to be done in straight surfaces, as in a planer or a milling machine. **4.** *Law.* a movable chattel (such as a machine, heating plant, etc.) which, by reason of **(a)** annexation to real property and **(b)** adaptation to continuing use in connection with the realty, is considered a part of the realty. **5.** *Rare.* act of fixing. **6.** *Rare.* state of being fixed. [var. of *fixture* (t. LL: m.s. *fixūra*) modeled on MIXTURE] —**fix′ture·less,** *adj.*

fiz (fĭz), *v.i.,* **fizzed, fizzing,** *n.* fizz.

fiz·gig (fĭz′gĭg′), *n.* **1.** a frivolous, gadding girl or woman. **2.** a kind of hissing firework. **3.** a kind of whirling toy that makes a whizzing noise. **4.** a fish spear.

fizz (fĭz), *v.i.* **1.** to make a hissing or sputtering sound. —*n.* **2.** a hissing sound; effervescence. **3.** *U.S.* **a.** soda water or other effervescent water. **b.** an iced mixed drink made of liquor, lemon juice, sugar, and soda. **4.** *Brit.* champagne. [back formation from FIZZLE]

fiz·zle (fĭz′əl), *v.,* **-zled, -zling,** *n.* —*v.i.* **1.** to make a hissing or sputtering sound, esp. one that dies out weakly. **2.** *Colloq.* to fail ignominiously after a more or less brilliant start (often fol. by *out*). —*n.* **3.** a fizzling, hissing, or sputtering. **4.** *Colloq.* a fiasco; a failure. [f. obs. *fise* (t. Scand.; cf. Icel. *fīsa* break wind) + *-le,* freq. and dim. suffix]

fizz·y (fĭz′ĭ), *adj.,* **fizzier, fizziest.** that fizzes; fizzing.

fjeld (fyĕld; *Nor.* fyĕl), *n.* a high, bleak plateau on the Scandinavian peninsula. [t. Norw. See FELL[2]]

fjord (fyôrd; *Nor.* fyôr, fyôör), *n.* fiord.

Fl, *Chem.* fluorine.

fl., 1. florin. **2.** (L *floruit*) flourished. **3.** fluid.

Fla., Florida.

flab·ber·gast (flăb′ər găst′), *v.t. Colloq.* to overcome with surprise and bewilderment; astound. [? f. FLABB(Y) + AGHAST]

flab·by (flăb′ĭ), *adj.,* **-bier, -biest. 1.** hanging loosely or limply, as flesh, muscles, etc., or having such flesh. **2.** lacking firmness, as character, persons, principles, utterances, etc.; feeble. [cf. earlier *flappy* (f. FLAP + -Y[1]) in same sense] —**flab′bi·ly,** *adv.* —**flab′bi·ness,** *n.*

fla·bel·late (flə bĕl′ĭt, -āt), *adj. Bot., Zool.* fan-shaped. Also, **fla·bel·li·form** (flə bĕl′ə fôrm′).

fla·bel·lum (flə bĕl′əm), *n., pl.* **-bella** (-bĕl′ə). **1.** a fan, esp. one used in religious ceremonies. **2.** a fan-shaped part. [t. L: fan]

flac·cid (flăk′sĭd), *adj.* soft and limber; flabby; limp; not firm: *flaccid muscles.* [t. L: s. *flaccidus*] —**flac·cid′i·ty, flac′cid·ness,** *n.* —**flac′cid·ly,** *adv.*

fla·con (flȧ kôn′), *n. French.* a small bottle or flask with a stopper.

flag[1] (flăg), *n., v.,* **flagged, flagging.** —*n.* **1.** a piece of cloth, commonly bunting, of varying size, shape, color, and device, usually attached by one edge to a staff or cord, and used as an ensign, standard, symbol, signal, etc. **2.** *Ornith.* the tuft of long feathers on the leg of falcons and most other hawks; the lengthened feathers on the crus or tibia. **3.** *Hunting.* the tail of a deer or of a setter dog. **4.** *Journalism.* the name or title of a newspaper as it appears on the first page. **5.** *Music.* hook (def. 12). —*v.t.* **6.** to place a flag or flags over or on; decorate with flags. **7.** to signal or warn (a person, etc.), or communicate (information) by, or as by, a flag. **8.** to decoy, as game, by waving a flag or the like to excite attention or curiosity. [appar. b. FLAP, n., and obs. *fag,* n., flap, flag; corresp. words in G, D, etc., t. E] —**flag′less,** *adj.*

flag[2] (flăg), *n.* **1.** any of various plants with long, sword-shaped leaves, as the sweet flag. **2.** the blue flag. **3.** the long, slender leaf of such a plant or of a cereal. [ME *flagge*; orig. uncert. Cf. D *vlag*]

flag[3] (flăg), *v.i.,* **flagged, flagging. 1.** to hang loosely or limply; droop. **2.** to fall off in vigor, energy, activity, interest, etc. [appar. b. FLAP, v., and FAG, v., in obs. sense of droop. See FLAG[1], n.]

flag[4] (flăg), *n., v.,* **flagged, flagging.** —*n.* **1.** a flat slab of stone used for paving, etc. **2.** (*pl.*) a walk paved with such slabs. —*v.t.* **3.** to lay or pave with flags. [unexplained doublet of FLAKE[1]] —**flag′less,** *adj.*

Flag Day, June 14, the anniversary of the day (June 14, 1777) when Congress adopted the Stars and Stripes as the national emblem of the United States.

flag·el·lant (flăj′ə lənt, flə jĕl′ənt), *n.* **1.** one who flagellates. **2.** one who flagellates or scourges himself for religious discipline. **3.** (*often cap.*) one of a medieval European sect of fanatics that practiced scourging in public. —*adj.* **4.** flagellating. [t. L: s. *flagellans*, ppr.]

Flag·el·la·ta (flăj′ə lā′tə), *n.pl. Zool.* a class of *Protozoa* distinguished by having one or more long mobile filaments as locomotory organs.

flag·el·late (flăj′ə lāt′), *v.,* -lated, -lating, *adj., n.* —*v.t.* **1.** to whip; scourge; flog; lash. —*adj.* **2.** Also, **flag·el·lat·ed.** *Biol.* having flagella. See **flagellum.** **3.** *Bot.* producing filiform runners or runnerlike branches, as the strawberry. —*n.* **4.** any of the *Flagellata.* [t. L: m.s. *flagellātus,* pp., whipped] —**flag′el·la′tion,** *n.* —**flag′el·la′tor,** *n.*

fla·gel·li·form (flə jĕl′ə fôrm′), *adj. Biol.* long, slender, and flexible, like the lash of a whip. [f. s. L *flagellum* a whip + -(I)FORM]

fla·gel·lum (flə jĕl′əm), *n., pl.* -gella (-jĕl′ə), -gellums. **1.** *Biol.* a long, lashlike appendage serving as an organ of locomotion in certain reproductive bodies, bacteria, protozoa, etc. **2.** *Bot.* a runner. **3.** a whip or lash. [t. L: whip, scourge]

flag·eo·let (flăj′ə lĕt′), *n.* a small end-blown flute with four finger holes in front and two in the rear. [t. F, dim. of OF *flajol* flute, ult. der. L *flāre* blow]

Flagg (flăg), *n.* James Montgomery, born 1877, U.S. painter and illustrator.

flag·ging[1] (flăg′ĭng), *adj.* drooping; failing. —**flag′ging·ly,** *adv.* [f. FLAG[3] + -ING[2]]

flag·ging[2] (flăg′ĭng), *n.* **1.** flagstones collectively. **2.** a pavement of flagstones. [f. FLAG[4] + -ING[1]]

flag·gy[1] (flăg′ĭ), *adj.* flagging; drooping; limp. [f. FLAG[3] + -Y[1]]

flag·gy[2] (flăg′ĭ), *adj.* consisting of or resembling flags or flagstone; laminate. [f. FLAG[4] + -Y[1]]

flag·gy[3] (flăg′ĭ), *adj.* abounding in, consisting of, or resembling the plants called flags. [f. FLAG[2] + -Y[1]]

fla·gi·tious (flə jĭsh′əs), *adj.* **1.** shamefully wicked, as persons, actions, times, etc. **2.** heinous or flagrant, as crime; infamous. [ME, t. L: m.s. *flāgitiōsus*] —**fla·gi′tious·ly,** *adv.* —**fla·gi′tious·ness,** *n.*

flag·man (flăg′mən), *n., pl.* -men. **1.** one who has charge of or carries a flag. **2.** one who signals with a flag, as at a railroad crossing.

flag officer, 1. a naval officer, as an admiral, vice-admiral, or rear admiral, entitled to display a flag indicating his rank. **2.** an officer in command of a fleet, squadron, or group of ships.

flag of truce, *Mil.* a white flag displayed as an invitation to the enemy to confer, or carried as a sign of peaceful intention by one sent to deal with the enemy.

flag·on (flăg′ən), *n.* **1.** a large bottle for wine, etc. **2.** a vessel for holding liquids, as for use at table, esp. one with a handle, a spout, and usually a cover. [ME *flakon,* t. OF: m. *fla(s)con*; cf. ML *flasca* FLASK]

flag·pole (flăg′pōl′), *n.* a staff or pole on which a flag is displayed. Also, **flag·staff** (flăg′stăf′, -stäf′).

fla·grant (flā′grənt), *adj.* **1.** glaring; notorious; scandalous: *a flagrant crime, a flagrant offender.* **2.** *Rare.* blazing, burning, or glowing. [t. L: s. *flagrans,* ppr. blazing, burning] —**fla′gran·cy, fla′grance,** *n.* —**fla′grant·ly,** *adv.*

fla·gran·te de·lic·to (flə grăn′tĭ dĭ lĭk′tō), *Law.* while the crime is, or was, being committed. [L]

flag·ship (flăg′shĭp′), *n.* a ship which bears a flag officer of a fleet, squadron, or the like, and displays his flag.

Flag·staff (flăg′stăf′, -stäf′), *n.* a city in central Arizona. 7663 (1950). ab. 6900 ft. high.

flag station, a railroad station where trains stop only when a flag or other signal is displayed or when one or more passengers are to be discharged.

flag·stone (flăg′stōn′), *n.* **1.** a flat slab of stone used for paving, etc. **2.** (*pl.*) a walk paved with such slabs. **3.** rock, such as sandstone, shale, etc., which can be split up into slabs for paving.

flail (flāl), *n.* **1.** an instrument for threshing grain by hand, consisting of a staff or handle to one end of which is attached a freely swinging stick or bar. **2.** *Mil.* an implement derived from the threshing flail used as a weapon of war in the Middle Ages. —*v.t.* **3.** to strike with, or as if with, a flail. [ME *flegl,* OE *flygel;* akin to FLY]

flair (flâr), *n.* **1.** talent; aptitude; keen perception. **2.** fondness; inclination; bent. **3.** *Hunting.* scent; sense of smell. [t. F, der. *flairer* smell, g. L *frāgrāre*]

flak (flăk), *n.* anti-aircraft fire, esp. as experienced by the crews of combat airplanes at which the fire is directed. [prop. *Fl.A.K.,* t. G, abbrev. of *flieger-abwehr-kanone* anti-aircraft cannon]

flake[1] (flāk), *n., v.,* flaked, flaking. —*n.* **1.** a small, flat, thin piece of anything. **2.** a small, detached piece or mass: *a flake of cloud.* **3.** a stratum or layer. —*v.i.* **4.** to peel off or separate in flakes. **5.** to fall in flakes, as snow. —*v.t.* **6.** to remove in flakes. **7.** to break flakes or chips from. **8.** to cover with or as with flakes. **9.** to form into flakes. [ME, appar. der. OE *flac-,* which occurs in *flacor* flying (said of arrows). Cf. also Icel. *flaka* be loose] —**flak′-**

flake[2] (flāk), *n.* a frame, as for drying fish. [ME *flake, fleke.* Cf. Icel. *flaki, fleki* hurdle, wickerwork shield]

flake[3] (flāk), *n. Naut.* one fake of a cable or hawser laid in coils. [var. of FAKE[2]. Cf. G *flechte*]

flake white, a pigment made from pure white lead.

flak·y (flā′kĭ), *adj.,* flakier, flakiest. **1.** consisting of flakes. **2.** lying or cleaving off in flakes or layers. **3.** flakelike. [f. FLAKE[1] + -Y[1]] —**flak′i·ly,** *adv.* —**flak′i·ness,** *n.*

flam (flăm), *n., v.,* flammed, flamming. *Dial. or Colloq.* —*n.* **1.** a falsehood. **2.** a deception or trick. —*v.t., v.i.* **3.** to deceive; delude; cheat. [see FLIMFLAM]

flam·beau (flăm′bō), *n., pl.* -beaux (-bōz), -beaus. **1.** a flaming torch. **2.** a torch for use at night in illuminations, processions, etc. **3.** a large decorated candlestick, as of bronze. [t. F, der. OF *flambe* flame, earlier *flamble,* g. L *flammula,* dim. of *flamma* flame]

flam·boy·ant (flăm boi′ənt), *adj.* **1.** flaming; gorgeous: *flamboyant colors.* **2.** florid; ornate; showy: *flamboyant rhetoric.* **3.** *Archit.* characterized by wavy, flamelike tracery, as in windows and openwork: applied to the highly ornate style of French Late Gothic architecture of the 15th century. [t. F, ppr. of *flamboyer* to flame, flare, der. OF *flambe.* See FLAMBEAU] —**flam·boy′ance, flam·boy′an·cy,** *n.* —**flam·boy′ant·ly,** *adv.*

flame (flām), *n., v.,* flamed, flaming. —*n.* **1.** burning gas or vapor, as from wood, etc., undergoing combustion; a portion of ignited gas or vapor. **2.** (*often pl.*) state or condition of blazing combustion: *to burst into flames.* **3.** any flamelike condition; glow; inflamed condition. **4.** brilliant light; scintillating luster. **5.** bright coloring; a streak or patch of color. **6.** heat or ardor, as of zeal or passion. **7.** *Slang.* an object of the passion of love; sweetheart. —*v.i.* **8.** to burn with a flame or flames; burst into flames; blaze. **9.** to glow like flame; shine brilliantly; flash. **10.** to burn as with flame, as passion; break into open anger, indignation, etc. (often fol. by *out* or *up*). —*v.t.* **11.** to subject to the action of flame or fire. [ME, t. OF: m. *flamme,* g. L *flamma*] —**flame′less,** *adj.* —**flame·let** (flām′lĭt), *n.*
—Syn. **1.** FLAME, BLAZE, CONFLAGRATION refer to the light and heat given off by combustion. FLAME is the common word, referring to a combustion of any size: *the light of a match flame.* BLAZE usually denotes a quick, hot, bright, and comparatively large flame: *the fire burst into a blaze.* CONFLAGRATION refers to destructive flames which spread over a considerable area: *a conflagration destroyed Chicago.*

flame color, bright reddish-orange. —**flame′-col′ored,** *adj.*

fla·men (flā′mĕn), *n., pl.* flamens, flamines (flăm′ə nēz′). *Rom. Antiq.* a priest devoted to the service of one particular deity. [t. L; r. ME *flamin(e)*]

flame thrower, *Mil.* an apparatus, either portable or mounted on a tank, that throws a spray of oil that ignites in the air.

flam·ing (flā′mĭng), *adj.* **1.** emitting flames; blazing; fiery. **2.** glowing; brilliant. **3.** violent; vehement; passionate. —**flam′ing·ly,** *adv.*

fla·min·go (flə mĭng′gō), *n., pl.* -gos, -goes. any of the aquatic birds constituting the family *Phoenicopteridae,* with very long neck and legs, webbed feet, bills bent downward, and pinkish to scarlet plumage. [t. Pg., t. Sp.: m. *flamenco,* t. Pr.: m. *flamenc,* f. *flama* (g. L *flamma* FLAME) + suffix *-enc* (t. Gmc.: m. *-ing*)]

Florida flamingo,
Phoenicopterus ruber
(Ab. 4 ft. long)

Fla·min·i·an Way (flə mĭn′ĭ ən), an ancient Roman road extending from Rome N to Ariminum (Rimini) on the Adriatic coast. 215 mi.

Fla·min·i·us (flə mĭn′ĭ əs), *n.* **Ga·ius** (gā′əs), died 217 B.C., Roman general and statesman, defeated by Hannibal.

flam·ma·ble (flăm′ə bəl), *adj.* easily set on fire; combustible; inflammable. —**flam′ma·bil′i·ty,** *n.*

flam·y (flā′mĭ), *adj.* pertaining to, consisting of, or like flame.

flan (flăn; *Fr.* flän), *n.* **1.** a cheese-, cream-, or fruit-filled cake. **2.** a piece of metal shaped ready to form a coin, but not yet stamped by the die. **3.** the metal of which a coin is made, as distinct from its design. [t. F]

Flan·ders (flăn′dərz), *n.* a medieval county in W Europe, extending along the North Sea from the Strait of Dover to the mouth of the Scheldt river: the corresponding modern regions include the provinces of **East Flanders** and **West Flanders** in W Belgium, and the adjacent parts of N France and SW Netherlands.

flange (flănj), *n., v.,* flanged, flanging. —*n.* **1.** a projecting rim, collar, edge, ridge, or the like, on an object, for keeping it in place, attaching it to another object, strengthening it, etc. See illus. in col. 1 of next page. **2.** the horizontal portion or portions of steel shapes, such as the top and bottom flange of an I-beam. **3.** a device or tool for making flanges. —*v.i.* **4.** to project like, or take the form of, a flange. [var. of *flanch,* n., from *flanch,* v., t. OF: s. *flanchir* bend, b. *flanc* FLANK and *flechier* (g. Rom. *flecticāre,* der. L *flectere*)] —**flange′less,** *adj.*

flank (flăngk), *n.* **1.** the side of an animal or a human being between the ribs and hip. **2.** the thin piece of flesh constituting this part. **3.** a slice of meat from the flank. **4.** the side of anything, as of a building. **5.** *Mil., Naval.* the extreme right or left side of an army or fleet, or a subdivision of an army or fleet. **6.** *Fort.* **a.** the right or left side of a work or fortification. **b.** a part of a work that defends another work by a fire along the outside of its parapet. **c.** the part of a bastion which extends from the curtain to the face and protects the curtain, opposite face, etc. See diag. under **bastion.** —*v.t.* **7.** to stand or be placed or posted at the flank or side of. **8.** to defend or guard at the flank. **9.** to pass round or turn the flank of. —*v.i.* **10.** to occupy a position at the flank or side. **11.** to present the flank or side. [ME *flanke*, OE *flanc*, t. OF, t. Gmc.; cf. OHG *hlancha*]

Three forms of flanges (def. 1)

flank·er (flăngk′ər), *n.* **1.** one who or that which flanks. **2.** *Mil.* one of a body of soldiers employed on the flank of an army to guard a line of march. **3.** *Fort.* a fortification projecting so as to defend another work, or to command the flank of an assailing body.

flan·nel (flăn′əl), *n., v.,* **-neled, -neling** or (*esp. Brit.*) **-nelled, -nelling.** —*n.* **1.** a warm, soft fabric of wool or blends of wool and cotton, wool and rayon, or cotton warp with wool filling. **2.** (*pl.*) an outer garment, esp. trousers, made of flannel. **3.** (*pl.*) woolen undergarments. —*v.t.* **4.** to cover or clothe with flannel. **5.** to rub with flannel. [orig. uncert.]

flannel cake, a tender, thin pancake.

flan·nel·et (flăn′ə lĕt′), *n.* a cotton fabric, plain or printed, napped on one side. Also, **flan′nel·ette′.**

flan·nel·ly (flăn′ə lĭ), *adj.* made of or resembling flannel.

flap (flăp), *v.,* **flapped, flapping,** *n.* —*v.i.* **1.** to swing or sway about loosely, esp. with noise: *a curtain or flag flaps in the wind.* **2.** to move up and down, as wings; flap the wings, or make similar movements. **3.** to strike a blow with something broad and flexible. —*v.t.* **4.** to move (wings, etc.) up and down. **5.** to cause to swing or sway loosely, esp. with noise. **6.** to strike with something broad and flexible. **7.** *Colloq.* to toss, fold, shut, etc., smartly, roughly, or noisily. —*n.* **8.** a flapping motion. **9.** the noise produced by something that flaps. **10.** a blow given with something broad and flexible. **11.** something broad and flexible, or flat and thin, that hangs loosely, attached at one side only. **12.** *Surg.* a portion of skin or flesh partially separated from the body which may subsequently be transposed by grafting. [ME *flappe(n)*, prob. of imit. orig.; cf. G *flappen* clap] —**flap′less,** *adj.*

flap·doo·dle (flăp′dōō′dəl), *n. Slang.* nonsense; bosh.

flap·drag·on (flăp′drăg′ən), *n.* **1.** an old game in which the players snatch raisins, plums, etc., out of burning brandy, and eat them. **2.** the object so caught and eaten.

flap·jack (flăp′jăk′), *n.* griddlecake.

flap·per (flăp′ər), *n.* **1.** something broad and flat for striking with, or for making a noise by striking. **2.** broad, flat, hinged or hanging piece; flap. **3.** a young bird just learning to fly. **4.** *Colloq.* a young, half-grown girl, often one who tries to appear sophisticated. **5.** *Slang.* the hand.

flare (flâr), *v.,* **flared, flaring,** *n.* —*v.i.* **1.** to burn with an unsteady, swaying flame, as a torch or candle in the wind. **2.** to blaze with a sudden burst of flame (often fol. by *up*). **3.** to start up or burst out in sudden fierce activity, passion, etc. (usually fol. by *up* or *out*). **4.** to shine or glow. **5.** to spread gradually outward as the end of a trumpet, or a ship's sides or bows. —*v.t.* **6.** to cause (a candle, etc.) to burn with a swaying flame. **7.** to display conspicuously or ostentatiously. **8.** to signal by flares of fire or light. **9.** to cause (something) to spread gradually outward in form. **10.** *Metall.* to heat (a high-zinc brass) to such a high temperature that the zinc vapors begin to burn. —*n.* **11.** a flaring or swaying flame or light, as of torches in the wind. **12.** a sudden blaze or burst of flame. **13.** a sudden blaze of fire or light used as a signal or for illumination or guidance, or a substance burned to produce such a blaze. **14.** a sudden burst, as of zeal or of temper. **15.** a gradual spread outward in form; outward curvature: *the flare of a skirt.* **16.** something that spreads out. **17.** *Optics.* light reflected by the surfaces of an optical system. [orig. meaning spread out, display; b. FLY[1] and BARE[1], but cf. Norw. *flara* blaze]

flare·back (flâr′băk′), *n.* **1.** a blast of flame that sometimes issues from the breech of a large gun or cannon when it is opened after firing. **2.** an outburst of something coming back: *a flareback of winter.*

flare-up (flâr′ŭp′), *n.* **1.** a sudden flaring up of flame or light. **2.** *Colloq.* a sudden outburst of anger.

flar·ing (flâr′ĭng), *adj.* **1.** that flares; flaming. **2.** glaringly bright or showy. **3.** spreading gradually outward in form. —**flar′ing·ly,** *adv.*

flash (flăsh), *n.* **1.** a sudden, transitory outburst of flame or light: *a flash of lightning.* **2.** a sudden, brief outburst or display of joy, wit, etc. **3.** the time occupied by a flash of light; an instant: *to do something in a flash.*

4. ostentatious display. **5.** *Journalism.* a brief telegraphic dispatch, usually transmitting preliminary news of an important story or development. **6.** *Colloq.* the cant or jargon of thieves, vagabonds, etc. **7.** *Naut., etc.* **a.** an extra volume or rush of water, as that produced by a dam or sluiceway, utilized to float a boat over shoals or for other purposes. **b.** the device, as a lock or sluice, used for this purpose. —*v.i.* **8.** to break forth into sudden flame or light, esp. transiently or intermittently (often used as a copula): *he flashed crimson with anger.* **9.** to gleam. **10.** to burst suddenly into view or perception: *the answer flashed into his mind.* **11.** to move like a flash. **12.** to break into sudden action. **13.** *Colloq. or Slang.* to make a flash or sudden display. **14.** *Rare.* to dash or splash, as the sea or waves. —*v.t.* **15.** to emit or send forth (fire or light) in sudden flashes. **16.** to cause to flash, as powder by ignition or a sword by waving. **17.** to send forth like a flash. **18.** to communicate instantaneously, as by telegraph. **19.** *Colloq.* to make a sudden or ostentatious display of: *to flash one's diamonds.* **20.** to increase the flow of water in (a river, etc.). **21.** *Rare.* to dash or splash (water). **22.** *Glassmaking.* **a.** to coat (plain glass or a glass object) with a film of colored, opal, or white glass. **b.** to apply (such a coating). **23.** *Bldg. Trades.* to protect by flashing (def. 1). —*adj.* **24.** showy or ostentatious. **25.** counterfeit or sham. **26.** belonging or pertaining to sporting men. **27.** *Colloq.* belonging to or connected with thieves, vagabonds, etc., or their cant or jargon. [ME *flasche(n)* rise and dash (said of tidal waters); b. FLOW (or FLOOD) and WASH] —**flash′er,** *n.* —**Syn. 8.** FLASH, GLANCE, GLINT, GLITTER mean to send forth a sudden gleam (or gleams) of bright light. To FLASH is to send forth light with a sudden, transient brilliancy: *a shooting star flashed briefly.* To GLANCE is to emit a brilliant flash of light as a reflection from a smooth surface: *sunlight glanced from the glass windshield.* GLINT suggests a hard bright gleam of reflected light as from something polished or burnished: *light glints from silver or from burnished copper.* To GLITTER is to reflect (intermittently) from a hard surface flashes of light like bright coins: *ice glitters in moonlight.*

flash·back (flăsh′băk′), *n.* a representation, during the course of a novel, motion picture, etc., of some event or scene occurring at a previous time.

flash·board (flăsh′bôrd′), *n. Civ. Eng.* a board, or one of a series of boards, as on a milldam, used to increase the depth of the impounded water.

flash bulb, *Photog.* a glass bulb filled with oxygen and thin sheet magnesium or aluminum, giving a momentary bright light when ignited, used as a light source.

flash flood, *Phys. Geog.* a sudden, destructive rush of water down a narrow gully or over a sloping surface in desert regions, due to heavy rains in the mountains or foothills. —**Syn.** See **flood.**

flash gun, *Photog.* a device which simultaneously discharges a flash bulb and operates the camera shutter.

flash·ing (flăsh′ĭng), *n.* **1.** *Bldg. Trades.* pieces of sheet metal, etc., used to cover and protect certain joints and angles, as where a roof comes in contact with a wall or chimney. **2.** act of creating an artificial flood in a conduit or stream, as in a sewer for cleansing it.

flash·light (flăsh′līt′), *n.* **1.** a small portable electric lamp powered by dry batteries or a tiny generator. **2.** a flash of light, or a light that flashes. **3.** any source of artificial light as used in flashlight photography.

flashlight photography, the process of picture making which uses a brilliant flash of artificial light as the source of illumination.

flash·o·ver (flăsh′ō′vər), *Elect.* —*n.* **1.** a disruptive discharge around or over the surface of a solid or liquid insulator. —*v.i.* **2.** to establish a flashover.

flash point, the lowest temperature at which a volatile oil will give off explosive or ignitable vapors.

flash·y (flăsh′ĭ), *adj.,* **flashier, flashiest. 1.** sparkling or brilliant, esp. in a superficial way or for the moment. **2.** pretentiously smart; showy; gaudy. **3.** *Rare.* flashing with light. —**flash′i·ly,** *adv.* —**flash′i·ness,** *n.* —**Syn. 2.** See **gaudy[1].**

flask[1] (flăsk, fläsk), *n.* **1.** a bottle-shaped container made of glass, metal, etc.: *a flask of oil, a brandy flask.* **2.** an iron container for shipping mercury. It holds 76 lbs. **3.** *Foundry.* a container of sand in which sand is rammed to form a mold. [OE *flasce, flaxe.* Cf. FLAGON]

flask[2] (flăsk, fläsk), *n. Ordn.* **1.** the armored plates making up the sides of a gun-carriage trail. **2.** *Obs.* the bed of a gun carriage. [t. d. F: m. *flasque* cheek of a gun carriage, g. LL *flasca* FLASK[1], t. Gmc. See FLAGON]

flask·et (flăs′kĭt, fläs′-), *n.* **1.** a small flask. **2.** a long, shallow basket. [ME *flaskett*, t. OF: m. *flasquet* small flask, der. *flasque* FLASK[1]]

flat[1] (flăt), *adj.,* **flatter, flattest,** *n., v.,* **flatted, flatting,** *adv.* —*adj.* **1.** horizontally level: *a flat roof.* **2.** level, even, or without inequalities of surface, as land, areas, surfaces, etc. **3.** comparatively lacking in projection or depression of surface: *a broad, flat face.* **4.** lying at full length, as a person. **5.** lying wholly on or against something: *a ladder flat against a wall.* **6.** thrown down, laid low, or level with the ground, as fallen trees or buildings. **7.** having a generally level shape or appearance; not deep or thick: *a flat plate.* **8.** spread out, as an unrolled map, the open hand, etc. **9.** collapsed; deflated: *a flat tire.* **10.** without qualification; unqualified, downright; or positive: *a flat denial*. **11.** without modification: *a flat price*. **12.** uninteresting, dull, or tedious. **13.** having lost its flavor, sharpness, or life, as wine, beer, etc.; stale; tasteless or insipid, as food. **14.** pointless, as a remark, joke, etc. **15.** commercially dull, as trade or the market. **16.** lacking relief, contrast, or shading, as a painting. **17.** *Painting.* without gloss; mat. **18.** not clear, sharp, or ringing, as sound, a voice, etc. **19.** *Music.* **a.** (of a tone) lowered a half step in pitch: *B flat*. **b.** below an intended pitch, as a note; too low (opposed to *sharp*). **c.** (of an interval) diminished. **20. flat a,** the *a* sound in *glad*. **21.** *Gram.* derived without change in form, as English *to brush* from the noun *brush* and adverbs which do not add *-ly* to the adjective form as *fast, cheap, slow*, etc. **22.** *Naut.* (of a sail) **a.** cut with little or no fullness. **b.** trimmed as nearly fore-and-aft as possible, for sailing to windward. —*n.* **23.** something flat. **24.** a flat surface, side, or part of anything: *the flat of a blade, the flat of the hand*. **25.** flat or level ground; a flat area. **26.** a marsh; a shallow. **27.** *Music.* **a.** (in musical notation) the character *b*, which when attached to a note or to a staff degree lowers its significance one chromatic half step. **b.** a tone one chromatic half step below another: *the flat of B is B flat*. **c.** (on keyboard instruments, with reference to any given key) the key next below or to the left. **28.** *Theat.* a piece of scenery consisting of a wooden frame, usually rectangular, covered with lightweight board or fabric. **29.** *Colloq.* a deflated automobile tire. —*v.t.* **30.** to make flat. **31.** *Music.* to lower (a pitch) esp. one half step. —*v.i.* **32.** to become flat. —*adv.* **33.** in a flat position; horizontally; levelly. **34.** in a flat manner; positively; absolutely. **35.** exactly. **36.** *Music.* below the true pitch. **37.** *Finance.* without interest. **38. brace a yard flat aback,** *Naut.* to set a yard so that the wind is nearly at right angles to the forward surface of the sail. **39. fall flat,** to fail completely; fail to succeed in attracting interest, purchasers, etc. [ME, t. Scand.; cf. Icel. *flatr*, Sw. *flat*; akin to OE *flet* floor. See FLAT²] —**flat′ly,** *adv.* —**flat′ness,** *n.* —**flat′tish,** *adj.* —**Syn. 1.** See **level.**

flat² (flăt), *n.* **1.** a floor, or a suite of rooms on one floor, forming a complete residence, as for a family. **2.** *Chiefly Brit.* a floor or story of a building. [var. of obs. *flet*, OE *flet* floor, house, hall; akin to FLAT¹]

flat·boat (flăt′bōt′), *n.* a large flat-bottomed boat for use in shallow water, esp. for floating down a river.

flat·car (flăt′kär′), *n.* *U.S.* a railroad car consisting of a platform without sides or top; a platform car.

flat-cyl·in·der press (flăt′sĭl′ĭn·dər). See **press¹** (def. 30a).

flat·fish (flăt′fĭsh′), *n., pl.* **-fishes,** (*esp. collectively*) **-fish.** any of a group of fishes (often considered as constituting the suborder *Heterosomata*), including the halibut, flounder, sole, etc., having a greatly compressed body, and swimming on one side, and (in the adult) having both eyes on the upper side.

flat·foot (flăt′fŏŏt′), *n., pl.* **-feet. 1.** *Pathol.* **a.** a condition in which the arch of the foot is flattened so that the entire sole rests upon the ground. **b.** a foot with such an arch. **2.** *Slang.* a policeman.

flat-foot·ed (flăt′fŏŏt′ĭd), *adj.* **1.** having flat feet. **2.** *Colloq.* taking or showing an uncompromising stand in a matter; firm and explicit. —**flat′-foot′ed·ly,** *adv.* —**flat′-foot′ed·ness,** *n.*

Flat·head (flăt′hĕd′), *n.* **1.** one of a tribe of Salishan Indians of northwest Montana. **2.** a Chinook Indian.

flat·i·ron (flăt′ī′ərn), *n.* an iron with a flat face, for smoothing cloth.

flat knot, reef knot.

flat·ling (flăt′lĭng), *Archaic or Dial.* —*adv.* **1.** in a flat position; with the flat side, as of a sword. **2.** flatly or positively. —*adj.* **3.** dealt with the flat side.

flat silver, flatware (def. 2).

flat·ten (flăt′ən), *v.t., v.i.* **1.** to make or become flat. **2. flatten out,** *Aeron.* to fly into a horizontal position, as after a dive. —**flat′ten·er,** *n.*

flat·ter¹ (flăt′ər), *v.t.* **1.** to seek to please by complimentary speech or attentions; compliment or praise insincerely. **2.** to represent too favorably, as in portrayal. **3.** to play upon the vanity or susceptibilities of; cajole, wheedle, or beguile. **4.** to gratify by compliments or attentions, or as a compliment does: *to feel flattered by an invitation*. **5.** to beguile with hopes; encourage (hopes); please (oneself) with the thought or belief (fol. by *that* and a clause): *he flattered himself (that) he might become the head of the school*. —*v.i.* **6.** to use flattery. [ME *flat(t)eren* float, flutter, fawn upon, OE *floterian* float, flutter; for sense development, cf. E *flicker*, Icel. *fladhra* flutter; not connected with F *flatter* flatter] —**flat′ter·er,** *n.* —**flat′ter·ing·ly,** *adv.*

flat·ter² (flăt′ər), *n.* **1.** one who or that which makes something flat. **2.** a hammer with a broad face, used by smiths. **3.** a drawplate with a flat orifice for drawing flat metal strips, as for watch springs, etc. [f. FLAT¹, v. + -ER¹]

flat·ter·y (flăt′ər·ĭ), *n., pl.* **-teries. 1.** act of flattering. **2.** a flattering compliment or speech; excessive, insincere praise. [ME *flaterie*, t. OF, der. *flatere* a flatterer, der. *flater*. Cf. FLATTER¹]

flat·top (flăt′tŏp′), *n.* *U.S. Navy.* an aircraft carrier.

flat·u·lent (flăch′ə·lənt), *adj.* **1.** generating gas in the alimentary canal, as food. **2.** attended with or caused by, or suffering from, such an accumulation of gas. **3.** pretentious; empty. [t. F, der. L *flātus* a blowing] —**flat′u·lence, flat′u·len·cy,** *n.* —**flat′u·lent·ly,** *adv.*

fla·tus (flā′təs), *n.* an accumulation of gas in the stomach, intestines, or other body cavity. [t. L: a blowing]

flat·ware (flăt′wâr′), *n.* **1.** vessels for the table, or for other use, that are more or less flat, as plates, saucers, etc. (distinguished from *hollowware*). **2.** silver utensils, knives, forks, etc.

flat·wise (flăt′wīz′), *adv.* with the flat side (not the edge) foremost or in contact. Also, **flat·ways** (flăt′-wāz′).

flat·worm (flăt′wûrm′), *n.* any platyhelminth.

Flau·bert (flō bĕr′), *n.* **Gustave** (gȳs täv′), 1821–80, French novelist.

flaunt (flônt), *v.i.* **1.** to parade or display oneself conspicuously or boldly. **2.** to wave conspicuously in the air. —*v.t.* **3.** to parade or display ostentatiously. —*n.* **4.** act of flaunting. **5.** *Obs.* something flaunted. [t. Scand.; cf. Norw. *flanta* gad about, der. *flana* roam; akin to Gk. *plānē* roaming (see PLANET)] —**flaunt′er,** *n.* —**flaunt′ing·ly,** *adv.* —**flaunt′y,** *adj.*

flau·tist (flô′tĭst), *n.* a flutist. [t. It.: m. *flautista*, der. *flauto* flute]

fla·ves·cent (flə·vĕs′ənt), *adj.* turning yellow; yellowish. [t. L: s. *flāvescens*, ppr.]

fla·vin (flā′vĭn), *n.* *Chem.* **1.** a complex heterocyclic ketone which is common to the nonprotein part of several important yellow enzymes, the flavoproteins. **2.** quercetin. [f. s. L *flāvus* yellow + -IN²]

-flavin, *Chem.* a word element indicating any of a number of natural derivatives of flavin, as *riboflavin*.

flavo-, a word element meaning "yellow," as in *flavoprotein*. Also, before vowels, **flav-.** [comb. form repr. L *flāvus*]

fla·vone (flā′vōn), *n.* *Chem.* **1.** an organic compound, $C_{15}H_{10}O_2$, the parent substance of various yellow dyes. **2.** a derivative of this compound.

fla·vo·pro·te·in (flā′vō·prō′tĭ·ən, -tēn), *n.* *Biochem.* an enzyme, containing riboflavin and linked chemically with a protein, active in the oxidation of foods in animal cells.

fla·vo·pur·pu·rin (flā′vō·pûr′pyə·rĭn), *n.* *Chem.* a yellowish crystalline compound, $C_{14}H_8O_5$ (isomeric with purpurin), used in dyeing.

fla·vor (flā′vər), *n.* **1.** taste, esp. a characteristic taste, or a noticeable element in the taste, of a thing. **2.** a flavoring substance or extract. **3.** the characteristic quality of a thing: *a book which has the flavor of the sea*. **4.** a particular quality noticeable in a thing: *language with a strong nautical flavor*. **5.** smell, odor, or aroma. —*v.t.* **6.** to give flavor. Also, *Brit.*, **fla′vour.** [ME, t. OF: m. *flaur*, ult. der. L *frāgrāre* emit an odor] —**fla′-vor·er,** *n.* —**fla′vor·less,** *adj.* —**Syn. 1.** See **taste.**

fla·vor·ing (flā′vər·ĭng), *n.* something that gives flavor; a substance or preparation used to give a particular flavor to food or drink. Also, *Brit.*, **fla′vour·ing.**

fla·vor·ous (flā′vər·əs), *adj.* **1.** full of flavor. **2.** pleasant to the smell or taste.

flaw¹ (flô), *n.* **1.** a marring feature; a defect; a fault. **2.** a defect impairing legal soundness or validity: *flaw in a lease or a will.* **3.** a crack, break, breach, or rent. —*v.t.* **4.** to produce a flaw in. —*v.i.* **5.** to contract a flaw; become cracked or defective. [ME, t. Scand.; cf. Sw. *flaga* flake, flaw] —**flaw′less,** *adj.* —**flaw′less·ly,** *adv.* —**flaw′less·ness,** *n.* —**Syn. 1.** See **defect.**

flaw² (flô), *n.* **1.** a sudden gust or brief sharp storm of wind. **2.** a short spell of rough weather. **3.** *Obs.* a burst of feeling, fury, etc. [t. Scand.; cf. Sw. *flaga* gust]

flaw·y (flô′ĭ), *adj.* characterized by gusts, as wind.

flax (flăks), *n.* **1.** any plant of the genus *Linum*, esp. *L. usitatissimum*, a slender, erect annual plant with narrow, lance-shaped leaves and blue flowers, much cultivated for its fiber and seeds. **2.** the fiber of this plant, manufactured into linen yarn for thread or woven fabrics. **3.** any of various plants resembling flax. [ME; OE *fleax*, c. D and LG *vlas*, G *flachs*]

flax·en (flăk′sən), *adj.* **1.** made of flax. **2.** resembling flax. **3.** pertaining to flax. **4.** of the pale-yellowish color of dressed flax. Also, **flax′y.**

flax·seed (flăks′sēd′), *n.* the seed of flax, yielding linseed oil; linseed.

flay (flā), *v.t.* **1.** to strip off the skin or outer covering of. **2.** to criticise or reprove with scathing severity. **3.** to strip of money or property; fleece. [ME *flen*, etc., OE *flēan*, c. MD *vlaen*, Icel. *flā*] —**flay′er,** *n.*

flea (flē), *n.* **1.** any of numerous small, wingless, bloodsucking insects of the order *Siphonaptera*, parasitic upon mammals and birds, and noted for their powers of leaping. **2.** any of various small beetles and crustaceans which leap like a flea, or swim in a jumpy manner, as the water flea and beach flea. **3. flea in one's ear,** a discomfiting rebuke or rebuff; a sharp hint. [ME *fle*, OE *flēah*, *flēa*, c. G *floh*; akin to FLEE]

Dog flea.
Ctenocephalus canis
(Line shows actual length)

flea·bane (flē′bān′), *n.* any of various composite plants, as *Pulicaria dysenterica* of Europe or *Erigeron philadelphicus* of the U.S., reputed to destroy or drive away fleas.

ăct, āble, dâre, ärt; ĕbb, ēqual; ĭf, īce; hŏt, ōver, ôrder, oil, bŏŏk, ōōze, out; ŭp, ūse, ûrge; ə = a in alone; ch, chief; g, give; ng, ring; sh, shoe; th, thin; ŧħ, that; zh, vision. See the full key on inside cover.

flea beetle, any of certain leaf beetles, noted for their ability to leap.

flea·bite (flē′bīt′), *n.* **1.** the bite of a flea. **2.** the red spot caused by it. **3.** a trifling wound, annoyance, etc.

flea-bit·ten (flē′bĭt′ən), *adj.* **1.** bitten by a flea or fleas. **2.** (of a horse, etc.) having small reddish spots or streaks upon a lighter ground.

fleam (flēm), *n. Surg.* a kind of lancet, as for opening veins. [t. OF: m. *fieme*, ult. der. LL *phlebotomus* lancet, t. Gk.: m. *phlebotómos* opening veins. Cf. PHLEBOTOMY]

flea·wort (flē′wûrt′), *n.* **1.** a rough-leaved composite herb of Europe, *Inula Conyza.* **2.** a European plantain, *Plantago Psyllium,* whose seeds resemble fleas and are used in medicine.

flèche (flāsh; *Fr.* flĕsh), *n.* **1.** *Archit.* **a.** a spire, esp. a small light spire decorating a roof. **b.** a slender spire rising from the junction of the nave and transepts of a church, or sometimes crowning the apse. **2.** *Fort.* a fieldwork consisting of two faces forming a salient angle, open at the gorge. [t. F: arrow, prob. t. Gmc.; cf. FLY¹]

flé·chette (flā shĕt′; *Fr.* flĕ-), *n. Mil.* a steel dart thrown from an airplane, used chiefly in World War I in personnel strafing. [t. F, dim. of *flèche* arrow]

fleck (flĕk), *n.* **1.** a spot or mark on the skin, as a freckle. **2.** any spot or patch of color, light, etc. **3.** a speck; a small bit. [n. use of FLECK, v., or back formation from *flecked,* ppl. adj., ME *flekked;* cf. *G fleck* spot] —*v.t.* **4.** to mark with a fleck or flecks; spot; dapple. [t. Scand.; cf. Icel. *flekka*]

fleck·less (flĕk′lĭs), *adj.* without flecks or spots.

flec·tion (flĕk′shən), *n.* **1.** act of bending. **2.** state of being bent. **3.** a bend; a bent part. **4.** *Anat.* flexion. **5.** *Gram.* inflection. Also, *esp. Brit.,* flexion for 1–3. [t. L: m.s. *flexio* a bending] —**flec′tion·al,** *adj.* —**flec′tion·less,** *adj.*

fled (flĕd), *v.* pt. and pp. of flee.

fledge (flĕj), *v.,* **fledged, fledging,** —*v.t.* **1.** to bring up (a young bird) until it is able to fly. **2.** to furnish with or as with feathers or plumage; feather (an arrow). —*v.i.* **3.** (of a young bird) to acquire the feathers necessary for flight. —*adj.* **4.** (of young birds) able to fly; having the wings developed for flight. [ME *flegge,* OE *-fligge,* in *unfligge* unfledged]

fledg·ling (flĕj′lĭng), *n.* **1.** a young bird just fledged. **2.** an inexperienced person. Also, *esp. Brit.,* **fledge′ling.**

fledg·y (flĕj′ĭ), *adj. Rare.* feathered or feathery.

flee (flē), *v.,* **fled, fleeing.** —*v.i.* **1.** to run away, as from danger, pursuers, etc.; take flight. **2.** to move swiftly; fly; speed. —*v.t.* **3.** to run away from (a place, person, etc.). [ME *flee(n),* OE *flēon,* c. *G fliehen*]

fleece (flēs), *n., v.,* **fleeced, fleecing.** —*n.* **1.** the coat of wool that covers a sheep or some similar animal. **2.** the wool shorn from a sheep at one time. **3.** something resembling a fleece: *a fleece of hair.* **4.** a fabric with a soft, silky pile, used for warmth, as for lining garments. **5.** the soft nap or pile of such a fabric. —*v.t.* **6.** to deprive (a sheep) of the fleece. **7.** to strip of money or belongings; plunder; swindle. **8.** to overspread as with a fleece; fleck with fleecelike masses. [ME *flees,* OE *flēos,* c. *G fliess*] —**fleece′a·ble,** *adj.* —**fleeced** (flēst), *adj.* —**fleece′less,** *adj.* —**fleec′er,** *n.*

fleec·y (flē′sĭ), *adj.,* **fleecier, fleeciest.** covered with, consisting of, or resembling a fleece or wool. —**fleec′i·ly,** *adv.* —**fleec′i·ness,** *n.*

fleer¹ (flĭr), *Dial.* —*v.i.* **1.** to grin or laugh coarsely or mockingly. —*v.t.* **2.** to fleer at; deride. —*n.* **3.** a fleering look; a jeer or gibe. [ME *flery(e), flire.* Cf. Norw. *flire* grin] —**fleer′ing·ly,** *adv.*

fle·er² (flē′ər), *n.* one who flees. [f. FLEE + -ER³]

fleet¹ (flēt), *n.* **1.** the largest organized unit of naval ships grouped for tactical or other purposes. **2.** the largest organization of warships under the command of a single officer (usually called the Commander in Chief). **3.** a number of naval vessels, or vessels carrying armed men. **4.** a large number of vessels of a commercial steamship company. **5.** a number of airplanes, automobiles, etc., moving or operating in company. [ME *flete,* OE *flēot* ship, craft, der. *flēotan* float]

fleet² (flēt), *adj.* **1.** swift; rapid: *fleet of foot, a fleet horse.* [adj. use of v. Cf. Icel. *fliótr*] —*v.i.* **2.** to move swiftly; fly. **3.** *Naut.* to change position; shift. **4.** *Archaic.* to glide away like a stream. **5.** *Archaic.* to fade; vanish. **6.** *Obs.* to float; drift. **7.** *Obs.* to swim; sail. —*v.t.* **8.** to cause (time) to pass lightly or swiftly. **9.** *Naut.* to change the position of; shift. [ME *flete(n),* v., OE *flēotan* float, *G fliessen* flow] —**fleet′ly,** *adv.* —**fleet′ness,** *n.*

fleet³ (flēt), *n.* **1.** *Dial. or in Place Names.* an arm of the sea; an inlet; a creek. **2.** the Fleet, a former London prison, long used for debtors. [ME *flete,* OE *flēot* flowing water, c. *G fliess* brook]

Fleet Admiral, *U.S. Navy.* the highest ranking naval officer, ranking next above admiral (equivalent to *General of the Army* of the U.S. Army).

fleet-foot·ed (flēt′foot′ĭd), *adj.* swift of foot.

fleet·ing (flē′tĭng), *adj.* gliding swiftly away; passing swiftly; transient; transitory. —**fleet′ing·ly,** *adv.* —**fleet′ing·ness,** *n.*

Fleet Street, a famous old street in central London, now the location of many newspaper offices: often used figuratively for the English newspaper world.

Flem·ing (flĕm′ĭng), *n.* **1.** a native of Flanders. **2.** a Flemish-speaking Belgian.

Flem·ing (flĕm′ĭng), *n.* **Sir Alexander,** born 1881, British bacteriologist; discoverer of penicillin, 1929.

Flem·ish (flĕm′ĭsh), *adj.* **1.** of or pertaining to Flanders, its people, or their language. —*n.* **2.** the people of Flanders, the Flemings. **3.** one of the official languages of Belgium, a Germanic language very similar to Dutch.

flense (flĕns), *v.t.,* **flensed, flensing.** **1.** to strip the blubber or the skin from (a whale, seal, etc.). **2.** to strip off (blubber or skin). Also, **flench** (flĕnch), **flinch.** [t. D]

flesh (flĕsh), *n.* **1.** the soft substance of an animal body, consisting of muscle and fat. **2.** muscular tissue. **3.** fatness; weight: *to put on flesh.* **4.** such substance of animals as an article of food, usually excluding fish and sometimes fowl; meat. **5.** the body, esp. as distinguished from the spirit or soul. **6.** man's physical or animal nature, as distinguished from his moral or spiritual nature. **7.** mankind. **8.** living creatures generally. **9.** one's kindred or family, or a member of it. **10.** *Bot.* the soft pulpy portion of a fruit, vegetable, etc., as distinguished from the core, skin, shell, etc. **11.** the surface of the body, esp. with respect to color. **12.** flesh color; pinkish white with a tinge of yellow; pinkish cream. **13. in the flesh, a.** alive. **b.** in bodily form; in person. —*v.t.* **14.** to plunge (a weapon) into the flesh. **15.** *Hunting.* to feed (a hound or hawk) with flesh in order to make it more eager for the chase. **16.** to incite and accustom (persons) to bloodshed or battle by an initial experience. **17.** to inflame the ardor or passions of by a taste of indulgence. **18.** to feed full with flesh, and hence with fleshly enjoyments, spoil, etc. **19.** to clothe (a skeleton, etc.) with flesh; make fleshy. **20.** to remove adhering flesh from (hides), for leather and for manufacture. [ME; OE *flǣsc,* c. *G fleisch*] —**flesh′-less,** *adj.*

flesh and blood, 1. offspring or relatives: *one's own flesh and blood.* **2.** human nature: *more than flesh and blood can endure.*

flesh color, a pinkish-white color with a tinge of yellow; a pinkish-cream color. —**flesh′-col′ored,** *adj.*

flesh·er (flĕsh′ər), *n.* **1.** one who fleshes hides. **2.** a tool for fleshing hides.

flesh fly, any fly of the dipterous family *Sarcophagidae* which deposits its larvae in the flesh of living animals.

flesh·hook (flĕsh′hŏŏk′), *n.* **1.** a hook for use in lifting meat, as from a pot. **2.** a hook to hang meat on.

flesh·ings (flĕsh′ĭngz), *n.pl.* flesh-colored tights.

flesh·ly (flĕsh′lĭ), *adj.,* **-lier, -liest.** **1.** of or pertaining to the flesh or body; bodily, corporeal, or physical. **2.** carnal; sensual. **3.** worldly, rather than spiritual. **4.** *Obs.* having much flesh; fleshy. —**flesh′li·ness,** *n.*

flesh·pot (flĕsh′pŏt′), *n.* **1.** a pot or vessel containing flesh or meat. **2.** (*pl.*) good living; luxuries.

flesh wound, a wound which does not extend beyond the flesh; a slight wound.

flesh·y (flĕsh′ĭ), *adj.,* **fleshier, fleshiest.** **1.** having much flesh; plump; fat. **2.** consisting of or resembling flesh. **3.** *Bot.* consisting of fleshlike substance; pulpy, as a fruit; thick and tender, as a leaf. —**flesh′i·ness,** *n.*

fletch (flĕch), *v.t.* **1.** to provide (an arrow) with a feather. —*n.* **2.** (*pl.*) the feathers on an arrow.

fletch·er (flĕch′ər), *n. Archaic.* one who makes or deals in arrows, or bows and arrows. [t. OF: m. *flechier,* der. *fleche* arrow]

Fletch·er (flĕch′ər), *n.* **1. John,** 1579–1625, British dramatist who collaborated with Francis Beaumont. **2. John Gould,** 1886–1950, U.S. poet.

Fletch·er·ism (flĕch′ər ĭz′əm), *n.* the practice of chewing food until it is reduced to a finely divided, liquefied mass, as advocated by Horace Fletcher (1849–1919) as a nutritional measure.

Fletch·er·ize (flĕch′ə rīz′), *v.i., v.t.,* **-ized, -izing.** to masticate (food) thoroughly.

fleur-de-lis (flœr′də lē′), *n., pl.* **fleurs-de-lis** (flœr′-də lēz′). **1.** a heraldic device somewhat resembling three petals or floral segments of an iris tied by an encircling band. **2.** the distinctive bearing of the royal family of France. **3.** the iris (flower or plant). [t. F: lily flower; r. ME *flour-de-lys,* t. OF]

Three forms of fleur-de-lis

Fleu·ry (flœrē′), *n.* **1. André Hercule de** (än drĕ′ĕr kyl′ də), 1653–1743, French cardinal and statesman. **2. Claude** (klōd), 1640–1723, French ecclesiastical historian.

flew¹ (flōō), *v.* pt. of fly¹.

flew² (flōō), *n.* flue³.

flews (flōōz), *n.pl.* the large pendulous upper lip of certain dogs, as bloodhounds.

flex (flĕks), *v.t., v.i.* to bend, as a part of the body. [t. L: s. *flexus,* pp.]

flex·i·ble (flĕk′sə bəl), *adj.* **1.** capable of being bent; easily bent. **2.** susceptible of modification or adaptation; adaptable. **3.** willing or disposed to yield. [t. L: m.s. *flexibilis*] —**flex′i·bil′i·ty, flex′i·ble·ness,** *n.* —**flex′i·bly,** *adv.*

—**Syn. 1.** FLEXIBLE, LIMBER, PLIANT refer to that which bends easily. FLEXIBLE refers to that which is capable of

b., blend of, blended; c., cognate with; d., dialect, dialectal; der., derived from; f., formed from; g., going back to; m., modification of; r., replacing; s., stem of; t., taken from; ?, perhaps. See the full key on inside cover.

being bent and adds sometimes the idea of compressibility or expansibility: *a flexible piece of rubber hose*. LIMBER is esp. applied to the body to refer to ease of movement; it also resembles FLEXIBLE except that there is an idea of even greater ease in bending: *a young and limber body, a limber willow wand*. PLIANT stresses an inherent quality or tendency to bend which does not require force or pressure from the outside; it may mean merely adaptable or may have a derogatory sense: *a pliant mind, character*. **—Ant. 1.** stiff.

flex·ile (flĕk′sĭl), *adj.* flexible; pliant; tractable; adaptable. [t. L: m.s. *flexilis*]

flex·ion (flĕk′shən), *n.* **1.** *Anat.* **a.** the motion of a joint which brings the connected parts continually nearer together; the action of any flexor muscle (opposed to *extension*). **b.** state of a part so moved. **2.** *Chiefly Brit.* flection (defs. 1, 2, 3). [t. L: s. *flexio* a bending] **—flex′-ion·al,** *adj.* **—flex′ion·less,** *adj.*

Flex·ner (flĕks′nər), *n.* **1.** **Abraham,** born 1866, U.S. educator. **2.** his brother, **Simon,** 1863–1946, U.S. physician.

flex·or (flĕk′sər), *n. Anat.* a muscle which serves to flex or bend a part of the body. [NL. See FLEX, -OR²]

flex·u·os·i·ty (flĕk′shŏŏ ŏs′ə tĭ), *n.* quality or condition of being flexuous.

flex·u·ous (flĕk′shŏŏ əs), *adj.* full of bends or curves; winding; sinuous. Also, **flex·u·ose** (flĕk′shŏŏ ōs′). [t. L: m.s. *flexuōsus,* der. *flexus* a bending] **—flex′u·ous·ly,** *adv.*

flex·ure (flĕk′shər), *n.* **1.** act of flexing or bending. **2.** state of being flexed or bent. **3.** the part bent; a bend; a fold. [t. L: m.s. *flexūra* a bending] **—flex′ur·al,** *adj.*

flib·ber·ti·gib·bet (flĭb′ər tĭ jĭb′ĭt), *n.* **1.** a chattering or flighty person, usually a woman. **2.** *(cap.) Obs.* the name of a fiend.

flic-flac (flĭk′flăk′), *n.* a step in dancing in which the feet strike rapidly together. [t. F; imit. of the sound]

flick (flĭk), *n.* **1.** a sudden light blow or stroke, as with a whip or the finger. **2.** the sound thus made. **3.** something thrown off with or as with a jerk: *a flick of spray.* **4.** *(usually pl.) Brit. Slang.* motion pictures. **—v.t. 5.** to strike lightly with a whip, the finger, etc. **6.** to remove with such a stroke: *to flick dust from one's coat, to flick away a crumb.* **7.** to move (something) with a sudden stroke or jerk. **—v.i. 8.** to move with a jerk or jerks. **9.** to flutter. [appar. imit.]

flick·er¹ (flĭk′ər), *v.i.* **1.** to burn unsteadily; shine with a wavering light. **2.** to wave to and fro; vibrate; quiver. **3.** to flutter. **—v.t. 4.** to cause to flicker. **—n. 5.** an unsteady flame or light. **6.** a flickering; flickering movement. **7.** a brief spark: *a flicker of hope.* [ME *flickeren,* OE *flicorian* flutter] **—flick′er·ing·ly,** *adv.*

flick·er² (flĭk′ər), *n.* any of several North American woodpeckers of the genus *Colaptes* with bright wing and tail linings, esp. *C. auratus,* of eastern parts of the continent. [imit. of the bird's note]

fli·er (flī′ər), *n.* **1.** something that flies, as a bird or insect. **2.** one who or that which moves with great speed. **3.** an aviator. **4.** some part of a machine having a rapid motion. **5.** a flying jump or leap. **6.** *U.S. Colloq.* a financial venture outside of one's ordinary business. **7.** *Archit.* **a.** a single step or a straight flight of steps or stairs. **b.** *(pl.)* stairs of straight flights (opposed to *winding stairs*). **8.** *U.S.* a small handbill. Also, **flyer.**

flight¹ (flīt), *n.* **1.** act, manner, or power of flying. **2.** the distance covered or the course pursued by a flying object. **3.** a number of beings or things flying or passing through the air together: *a flight of swallows.* **4.** a journey by air, esp. by airplane. **5.** a scheduled trip on an air line. **6.** the basic tactical unit of military air forces, consisting of two or more aircraft. **7.** act, principles, or art of flying an airplane. **8.** swift movement in general, as of a missile. **9.** a soaring above or transcending ordinary bounds: *a flight of fancy.* **10.** *Archit.* **a.** the series of steps or stairs between two adjacent landings. **b.** a series of steps, ascending without change of direction. **11.** *Archery.* **a.** a light arrow for long-distance shooting. **b.** a contest with such arrows. **—v.i. 12.** (of wild fowl) to fly in flights. [ME; OE *flyht,* c. G *flucht;* akin to FLY, v.]

flight² (flīt), *n.* **1.** act of fleeing; hasty departure. **2. put to flight,** to force to flee; rout. **3. take (to) flight,** to flee. [ME; c. G *flucht;* akin to FLEE]

flight arrow, *Archery.* **1.** an arrow having a conical or pyramidal head without barbs. **2.** a long and light arrow in general; a shaft or arrow for the longbow, as distinguished from the bolt.

flight deck, *Naval.* the upper deck of an aircraft carrier, constructed and equipped for the landing and take-off of aircraft.

flight feather, *Ornith.* one of the large, stiff feathers which form most of the extent of a bird's wing, and which are essential to flight.

flight formation, two or more airplanes flying in some set arrangement.

flight·less (flīt′lĭs), *adj.* incapable of flying.

flight·y (flī′tĭ), *adj.,* **flightier, flightiest. 1.** given to flights or sallies of fancy, caprice, etc.; volatile; frivolous. **2.** slightly delirious; light-headed; mildly crazy. **3.** *Rare.* swift or fleet. [f. FLIGHT¹ + -Y¹] **—flight′i·ly,** *adv.* **—flight′i·ness,** *n.*

flim-flam (flĭm′flăm′), *n., v.,* **-flammed, -flamming.** *Colloq.* **—n. 1.** a piece of nonsense; mere nonsense.

2. a trick or deception; humbug. **—v.t. 3.** to trick; delude; humbug; cheat. [cf. Icel. *flimska* mockery] **—flim′flam′mer,** *n.*

flim·sy (flĭm′zĭ), *adj.,* **-sier, -siest,** *n., pl.* **-sies. —adj. 1.** without material strength or solidity: *a flimsy material, a flimsy structure.* **2.** weak; inadequate; not carefully thought out: *a flimsy excuse or argument.* **—n. 3.** a thin kind of paper, esp. for use in making several copies of a writing, telegraphic dispatch, etc., at once, as in newspaper work. **4.** *Brit.* a copy of a report or dispatch on such paper. **5.** *Slang.* a bank note. [f. FILM (by metathesis) + -sy, adj. suffix] **—flim′si·ly,** *adv.* **—flim′-si·ness,** *n.*

flinch¹ (flĭnch), *v.i.* **1.** to draw back or shrink from what is dangerous, difficult, or unpleasant. **2.** to shrink under pain; wince. **3.** *Croquet.* to let the foot slip from the ball in the act of croqueting. **—v.t. 4.** to draw back or withdraw from. **—n. 5.** act of flinching. **6.** *Cards.* a game in which the cards are accumulated on the table. [prob. t. OF: m.s. *flenchir,* der. *flechier* bend, turn aside, g. Rom. *flecticāre* bend, der. L *flectere*] **—flinch′er,** *n.* **—flinch′ing·ly,** *adv.*

flinch² (flĭnch), *v.t.* flense. [var. of FLENSE]

flin·ders (flĭn′dərz), *n. pl.* splinters; small pieces or fragments. [cf. Norw. *flindra* splinter]

fling (flĭng), *v.,* **flung, flinging,** *n.* **—v.t. 1.** to throw, cast, or hurl; throw with force or violence; throw with impatience, disdain, etc. **2.** to put suddenly or violently: *to fling one into jail.* **3.** to send forth suddenly and rapidly: *to fling fresh troops into a battle.* **4.** to throw aside or off. **5.** to throw to the ground, as in wrestling or from horseback. **—v.i. 6.** to move with haste or violence; rush; dash. **7.** to fly into violent and irregular motions, as a horse; throw the body about, as a person. **8.** to utter harsh or abusive language (usually fol. by *out*). **—n. 9.** act of flinging. **10.** a spell of unrestrained indulgence of one's impulses: *to have one's fling.* **11.** an attack upon or attempt at something, as in passing. **12.** a severe or contemptuous remark or gibe. **13.** a lively Scotch dance characterized by flinging movements of the legs and arms (commonly called **Highland fling**). [ME. Cf. Sw. *flänga* fly, race] **—fling′er,** *n.*

flint (flĭnt), *n.* **1.** a hard kind of stone, a form of silica resembling chalcedony but more opaque, less pure, and less lustrous. **2.** a piece of this, esp. as used for striking fire. **3.** something very hard or obdurate. **—v.t. 4.** to furnish with flint. [ME and OE, c. MD *vlint,* Dan. *flint.* Cf. PLINTH]

Flint (flĭnt), *n.* **1.** a city in SE Michigan. 163,143 (1950). **2.** Flintshire. **3.** **Austin,** 1812–1886, U.S. physician. **4.** his son, **Austin,** 1836–1915, U.S. physiologist and physician.

flint corn, a variety of maize, *Zea mays indurata,* having very hard-skinned kernels not subject to shrinkage.

flint glass, 1. an optical glass of high dispersion and relatively high index of refraction. **2.** a glass containing alkalis, lead oxide, and silica, with or without other bases. **3.** a colorless glass.

flint·head (flĭnt′hĕd′), *n.* the wood ibis (*Mycteria americana*) of North and South America (so named because the naked head is hard in appearance).

flint·lock (flĭnt′lŏk′), *n.* **1.** a gunlock in which a piece of flint striking against steel produces sparks which ignite the priming. **2.** a firearm with such a lock.

Flintlock fowling piece
A, Steel struck by flint; B, Powder pan; C, Touchhole; D, Flint; E, Cock

Flint·shire (flĭnt′shĭr, -shər), *n.* a county in NE Wales. 131,000 pop. (est. 1946); 256 sq. mi. *Co. seat:* Mold. Also, **Flint.**

flint·y (flĭn′tĭ), *adj.,* **flintier, flintiest. 1.** composed of, containing, or resembling flint; hard as flint. **2.** obdurate; cruel; unmerciful: *a flinty heart.* **—flint′-i·ly,** *adv.* **—flint′i·ness,** *n.*

flip¹ (flĭp), *v.,* **flipped, flipping,** *n.* **—v.t. 1.** to toss or put in motion with a snap of a finger and thumb; fillip; flick. **2.** to move (something) with a jerk or jerks. **—v.i. 3.** to make a fillip; strike smartly at something. **4.** to move with a jerk or jerks. **5. flip up,** to toss a coin. **—n. 6.** a fillip; a smart tap or strike. **7.** a sudden jerk. [prob. imit.]

flip² (flĭp), *n.* a mixed drink made with liquor or wine, sugar, and egg, powdered with nutmeg. [n. use of FLIP¹]

flip³ (flĭp), *adj.,* **flipper, flippest.** *Colloq.* smart; pert; flippant. [adj. use of FLIP¹]

flip·pant (flĭp′ənt), *adj.* **1.** smart or pert in speech. **2.** characterized by a shallow or disrespectful levity. **3.** *Obs.* voluble; talkative. **4.** *Obs. or Dial.* nimble, limber, or pliant. [orig. obscure, but cf. Icel. *fleipa* babble] **—flip′pan·cy, flip′pant·ness,** *n.* **—flip′pant·ly,** *adv.*

flip·per (flĭp′ər), *n.* **1.** a broad, flat limb, as of a seal, whale, etc., especially adapted for swimming. **2.** *Slang.* the hand.

flirt (flûrt), *v.i.* **1.** to trifle in love; play at love; coquet. **2.** to trifle or toy (with an idea, etc.). **3.** to move with a jerk or jerks; dart about. **—v.t. 4.** to give a sudden or brisk motion to; wave smartly, as a fan. **5.** to throw or propel with a toss or jerk; fling suddenly. **—n. 6.** a person (woman or man) given to flirting. **7.** a quick throw or toss; a sudden jerk; a darting motion. [imit.] —**flirt′er,** n. —**flirt′ing·ly,** adv.

flir·ta·tion (flûr·tā′shən), n. **1.** act or practice of flirting; coquetry. **2.** a love affair which is not serious.

flir·ta·tious (flûr·tā′shəs), adj. **1.** given to flirtation. **2.** pertaining to flirtation. Also, **flirt′y.** —**flir·ta′-tious·ly,** adv. —**flir·ta′tious·ness,** n.

flit (flĭt), v., **flitted, flitting,** n. —v.i. **1.** to move lightly and swiftly; fly, dart, or skim along. **2.** to flutter, as a bird. **3.** to pass away quickly, as time. **4.** Chiefly Scot. and N. Eng. **a.** to depart or die. **b.** to change one's residence. —v.t. **5.** Archaic. to remove; transfer; oust or dispossess. —n. **6.** a light, swift movement; a flutter. **7.** Chiefly Scot. and N. Eng. a removal. [ME flitten, t. Scand.; cf. Icel. flytja carry, convey] —**Syn.** 1. See fly[1].

flitch (flĭch), n. **1.** the side of a hog (or, formerly, some other animal) salted and cured: a flitch of bacon. **2.** a steak cut from a halibut. —v.t. **3.** to cut into flitches. [ME flicche, OE flicce, c. MLG vlike, Icel. flikki]

flite (flīt), v., **flited, fliting,** n. Now Scot. and N. Eng. —v.i. **1.** to dispute; wrangle; scold; jeer. —n. **2.** a dispute or wrangle; a scolding. Also, **flyte.** [ME flite(n), OE flītan strive, contend]

flit·ing (flī′tĭng), n. **1.** contention. **2.** war of words, in versified dialogue.

flit·ter[1] (flĭt′ər), v.i., v.t. to flutter. [freq. of FLIT]

flit·ter[2] (flĭt′ər), n. one who or that which flits. [f. FLIT, v. + -ER[1]]

flit·ter·mouse (flĭt′ər·mous′), n., pl. **-mice.** Obs. a bat (animal). [f. FLITTER[1] + MOUSE. Cf. G fledermaus]

flit·ting (flĭt′ĭng), adj. moving lightly and swiftly; passing quickly; fluttering. —**flit′ting·ly,** adv.

fliv·ver (flĭv′ər), n. **1.** Slang. something of unsatisfactory quality or inferior grade, as an automobile. **2.** Humorous. any automobile. [orig. meaning a failure; ? b. flopper (der. FLOP) and fizzler (der. FIZZLE)]

float (flōt), v.i. **1.** to rest on the surface of a liquid; be buoyant. **2.** to move gently on the surface of a liquid; drift along. **3.** to rest or move in a liquid, the air, etc. **4.** to move or hover before the eyes or in the mind. **5.** to pass from one to another, as a rumor. **6.** to move or drift about free from attachment. **7.** to be launched or floated, as a company, scheme, etc. **8.** Com. to be in circulation, as an acceptance; be awaiting maturity. —v.t. **9.** to cause to float. **10.** to cover with water; flood; irrigate. **11.** to launch (a company, scheme, etc.); set going. **12.** to sell on the market, as a stock or a bond. **13.** to make smooth or level, as the surface of plaster. —n. **14.** something that floats, as a raft. **15.** something for buoying up. **16.** an inflated bag to sustain a person in water; a life preserver. **17.** Plumbing, Mach., etc. (in certain apparatus, cisterns, etc.) a device, as a hollow ball, which through its buoyancy automatically regulates the level, supply, or outlet of a liquid. **18.** Naut. a floating platform fastened to a wharf or the shore, from which to embark in or land from boats, as a landing place at a ferry. **19.** Aeron. a hollow, boatlike part under the wing or fuselage of an airplane enabling it to float on water. **20.** Angling. a piece of cork for supporting a baited line in the water and showing by its movement when a fish bites. **21.** Zool. an inflated organ that supports an animal in the water. **22.** a platform on wheels, bearing a display, and drawn in a procession. **23.** a low-bodied dray for transporting heavy goods. **24.** any of various tools for smoothing, leveling, or the like, as a kind of file, a plasterer's trowel, etc. **25.** the loose yarn on the back of cloth due to a figure weave or brocading. **26.** Banking. uncollected checks and commercial paper in process of transfer from bank to bank. **27.** (pl.) Theat. the footlights. [ME flotie(n), OE flotian, c. Icel. flota, MD vloten. See FLEET[2], v.]

float·a·ble (flō′tə·bəl), adj. **1.** capable of floating; that may be floated. **2.** that can be floated on, as a river.

float·age (flō′tĭj), n. flotage.

float·a·tion (flō·tā′shən), n. Brit. flotation.

float·er (flō′tər), n. **1.** one who or that which floats. **2.** Colloq. one who is continually changing his place of abode, employment, etc. **3.** U.S. a voter not attached to any party, esp. one whose vote may be purchased. **4.** U.S. one who fraudulently votes, usually for pay, in different places in the same election.

float-feed (flōt′fēd′), adj. Mach. equipped with a float to control the feed.

float·ing (flō′tĭng), adj. **1.** that floats. **2.** free from attachment, or having but little attachment. **3.** Pathol. away from its proper position, esp. in a downward direction: a floating kidney. **4.** not fixed or settled in a definite place or state: floating population. **5.** Finance. **a.** in circulation or use, or not permanently invested, as capital. **b.** composed of sums due within a short time and not requiring frequent renewal or refinancing: a floating debt. **6.** Mach. having a vibration-free suspension; working smoothly. —**float′ing·ly,** adv.

floating dock, a floating structure which may be lowered in the water to admit a ship and then raised to leave the ship dry for repairs, etc.; a floating dry dock.

floating heart, any of certain perennial aquatic herbs of the genus Nymphoides, esp. N. lacunosum, with floating, more or less heart-shaped leaves.

floating island, **1.** a dish consisting of boiled custard

with portions of meringue or whipped cream, and often bits of jelly, etc., floating upon it. **2.** a floating, islandlike mass of earth and partly decayed vegetation held together by interlacing roots, sometimes built artificially on wooden platforms as in the Orient, or resulting naturally from the accumulation of plant litter on a water surface.

floating ribs, Anat. the two lowest pairs of ribs in man, which are attached neither to the sternum nor to the cartilages of other ribs.

floating stock, stock not held for permanent investment and hence available for speculation; stock held by brokers and speculators rather than investors.

floating supply, the aggregate supply of ready-to-market goods or securities.

floating vote, U.S. the voters collectively who are not permanently attached to any political organization, and whose votes therefore cannot be counted upon by party managers.

float·y (flō′tĭ), adj. **1.** able to float; buoyant. **2.** (of a boat) drawing little water.

floc (flŏk), n. a tuftlike mass, as in a chemical precipitate. Also, **flock.** [short for FLOCCULE]

floc·cil·la·tion (flŏk′sə·lā′shən), n. Pathol. a delirious picking of the bedclothes, etc., by the patient, as in certain fevers. [f. s. *floccillus (assumed dim. of L floccus flock of wool) + -ATION]

floc·cose (flŏk′ōs), adj. **1.** Bot. consisting of or bearing woolly tufts or long soft hairs. **2.** flocculent. [t. LL: m.s. floccōsus, der. L floccus flock of wool]

floc·cu·late (flŏk′yə·lāt′), v., **-lated, -lating.** —v.t. **1.** to form into flocculent masses. —v.i. **2.** to form flocculent masses, as cloud, a chemical precipitate, etc.; form aggregated or compound masses of particles. —**floc′cu·la′tion,** n.

floc·cule (flŏk′ūl), n. **1.** something resembling a small flock or tuft of wool. **2.** a bit of flocculent matter, as in a liquid. [t. NL: m.s. flocculus. See FLOCCULUS]

floc·cu·lent (flŏk′yə·lənt), adj. **1.** like a flock or flocks of wool; covered with a soft woolly substance. **2.** consisting of or containing loose woolly masses. **3.** flaky. —**floc′cu·lence,** n. —**floc′cu·lent·ly,** adv.

flocculent precipitate, Chem. a woolly-looking precipitate, like that of aluminum hydroxide, from the solution of an aluminum salt to which ammonia is added.

floc·cu·lus (flŏk′yə·ləs), n., pl. **-li** (-lī′). **1.** floccule. **2.** Astron. one of the bright or dark patches which mottle the sun's chromosphere, visible in spectroheliograms. [NL, dim. of L floccus flock of wool]

floc·cus (flŏk′əs), n., pl. **flocci** (flŏk′sī). a small tuft of woolly hairs. [t. L]

flock[1] (flŏk), n. **1.** a number of animals of one kind keeping, feeding, or herded together, now esp. of sheep or goats, or of birds. **2.** a crowd; large number of people. **3.** (in New Testament and ecclesiastical use) **a.** the Christian church in relation to Christ. **b.** a single congregation in relation to its pastor. **4.** Now Rare. a band or company of persons. —v.i. **5.** to gather or go in a flock, company, or crowd. [ME; OE floc, c. Icel. flokkr] —**flock′less,** adj.

—**Syn.** 1, 2. bevy, covey, flight, gaggle; brood, hatch, litter; shoal, school, swarm. FLOCK, DROVE, HERD, PACK refer to a company of animals, often under the care or guidance of someone. FLOCK is the popular term, which applies to groups of animals, esp. of sheep or goats, and companies of birds: this lamb is the choicest of the flock, a flock of wild geese flew overhead. DROVE is esp. applied to a number of oxen, sheep, or swine when driven in a group: a drove of oxen was taken to market, a large drove of swine filled the roadway. HERD is usually applied to large animals such as cattle, originally under the charge of someone; but by extension, to other animals feeding or driven together: a buffalo herd, a herd of elephants. PACK applies to a number of animals kept together; or herding together for offense or defense: a pack of hounds kept for hunting, a pack of wolves. As applied to crowds of people, DROVE, HERD, and PACK carry a contemptuous implication.

flock[2] (flŏk), n. **1.** a lock or tuft of wool, hair, etc. **2.** (pl. or sing.) wool refuse, shearings of cloth, old cloth torn to pieces, etc., used for stuffing mattresses, upholstering furniture, etc. **3.** (sing. or pl.) finely powdered wool, cloth, etc., used in making wallpaper. **4.** floc. —v.t. **5.** to stuff with flock, as a mattress. **6.** to cover or coat with flock, as wallpaper. [ME flokke, appar. t. OF: m. floc, g. L floccus flock of wool. Cf. OHG floccho]

flock dot, a pattern of dots or figures not woven but fastened to cloth with adhesive.

flock·y (flŏk′ĭ), adj. like flocks or tufts; flocculent.

Flod·den (flŏd′ən), n. a hill in NE England, in Northumberland county: the invading Scots were disastrously defeated here by the English in a famous battle, 1513.

floe (flō), n. **1.** a field of floating ice formed on the surface of the sea, etc. **2.** a detached floating portion of such a field. [? t. Norw.: m. flo. Cf. Icel. flō]

flog (flŏg, flôg), v.t., **flogged, flogging.** to beat hard with a whip, stick, etc.; whip. [? b. FLAY and jog, var. of JAG[1]. v., prick, slash (but cf. FLAGELLATE)] —**flog′ger,** n.

flog·ging (flŏg′ĭng, flôg′ĭng), n. punishment by beating or whipping.

flood (flŭd), n. **1.** a great flowing or overflowing of water, esp. over land not usually submerged. **2. the Flood,** the universal deluge recorded as having occurred in the days of Noah. Gen. 7. **3.** Poetic. the sea; a river;

a lake; any large body of water in general. **4.** any great outpouring or stream: *a flood of words, tears, light, lava, etc.* **5.** the flowing in of the tide (opposed to *ebb*). —*v.t.* **6.** to overflow in or cover with a flood; fill to overflowing. **7.** to cover as with a flood. **8.** to overwhelm with an abundance of something. —*v.i.* **9.** to flow or pour in or as in a flood. **10.** to rise in a flood; overflow. **11.** *Med.* **a.** to suffer uterine hemorrhage, esp. in connection with parturition. **b.** to have an excessive menstrual flow. [ME; OE *flōd*, c. G *flut*] —**flood'a·ble,** *adj.* —**flood'-er,** *n.* —**flood'less,** *adj.*
—**Syn. 1.** FLOOD, FLASH FLOOD, DELUGE, FRESHET, INUNDA- TION refer to the overflowing of normally dry areas, usually after heavy rains. FLOOD is usually applied to the overflow of a great body of water, as for example a river, though it may refer to any water which overflows an area: *a flood along the river, a flood in a basement.* A FLASH FLOOD is one which comes so suddenly that no preparation can be made against it; it is usually destructive, but begins almost at once to subside: *a flash flood caused by a downpour.* DELUGE suggests a great downpouring of water, usually with much destruc- tion: *the rain came down in a deluge.* FRESHET suggests a small, quick overflow such as that caused by heavy rains: *a freshet in an abandoned watercourse.* INUNDATION, a literary word, suggests the covering of a great area of land by water: *the inundation of thousands of acres.*
flood control, *Civ. Eng.* the technique of controlling river flow with dams, dikes, artificial channels, etc., so as to minimize the occurrence of floods.
flood·gate (flŭd'gāt'), *n.* **1.** *Civ. Eng.* a gate designed to regulate the flow of water. **2.** anything serving to control indiscriminate flow or passage.
flood·light (flŭd'līt'), *n.* **1.** an artificial light so directed or diffused as to give a comparatively uniform illumination over a given area. **2.** a floodlight lamp or projector. —*v.t.* **3.** to illuminate with floodlight.
floodlight projector, a powerful lamp having a reflector curved to produce a floodlight.
flood plain, *Phys. Geog.* a nearly flat plain along the course of a stream that is naturally subject to flooding at high water.
flood tide, the inflow of the tide; the rising tide.
floor (flōr), *n.* **1.** that part of a room or the like which forms its lower enclosing surface, and upon which one walks. **2.** a story of a building. **3.** a level supporting sur- face in any structure: *the floor of a bridge.* **4.** a platform or prepared level area for a particular use: *a threshing floor.* **5.** the flat bottom of any more or less hollow place: *the floor of the ocean.* **6.** a flat extent of surface. **7.** the part of a legislative chamber, etc., where the members sit, and from which they speak. **8.** the right of one member to speak from such a place in preference to other mem- bers: *to get or have the floor.* **9.** the main part of an ex- change or the like, in distinction from galleries, etc. **10.** *Mining.* **a.** the bottom of a horizontal passageway. **b.** an underlying stratum, as of ore, usually flat. **11.** *Naut.* that part of the bottom of a vessel on each side of the keelson which is most nearly horizontal. **12.** the bottom, base, or minimum charged or paid: *a price or wage floor.* —*v.t.* **13.** to cover or furnish with a floor. **14.** to bring down to the floor or ground; knock down. **15.** *Colloq.* to beat or defeat. **16.** *Colloq.* to confound or nonplus: *to be floored by a problem.* [ME *flore,* OE *flōr,* c. G *flur*] —**floor'less,** *adj.*
floor·age (flōr'ĭj), *n.* floor space.
floor·cloth (flōr'klôth', -klŏth'), *n.* **1.** a cloth for washing or wiping floors. **2.** a piece of cloth, as crash, drugget, linoleum, etc., used with or without a carpet for covering a floor.
floor·er (flōr'ər), *n.* **1.** one who lays floors. **2.** a person or thing, as a blow, that knocks to the floor. **3.** *Colloq.* something that beats, overwhelms, or confounds.
floor·ing (flōr'ĭng), *n.* **1.** a floor. **2.** floors collectively. **3.** materials for making floors.
floor leader, *U.S. Govt.* the party member in either the Senate or the House who directs the activities of his party on the floor.
floor show, an entertainment given in a night club or cabaret, usually consisting of a series of singing, dancing, and/or comic episodes.
floor·walk·er (flōr'wô'kər), *n.* a person employed in a store to direct customers, supervise salespeople, etc.
flop (flŏp), *v.,* **flopped, flopping,** *n. Colloq.* —*v.i.* **1.** to fall or plump down suddenly, esp. with noise; drop or turn with a sudden bump or thud. **2.** to change sud- denly, as from one side or party to another (often fol. by *over*). **3.** to yield or break down suddenly; fail. **4.** to flap, as in the wind. —*v.t.* **5.** to drop, throw, etc., with a sudden bump or thud. **6.** to flap clumsily and heavily, as wings. —*n.* **7.** act of flopping. **8.** the sound of flopping; a thud. **9.** a failure. [var. of FLAP] —**flop'- per,** *n.*
flop·house (flŏp'hous'), *n.* a cheap hotel, usually for men only.
flop·py (flŏp'ĭ), *adj.,* **-pier, -piest.** *Colloq.* tending to flop. —**flop'pi·ly,** *adv.* —**flop'pi·ness,** *n.*
flor., (L *floruit*) flourished.
flo·ra (flōr'ə), *n., pl.* **floras, florae** (flōr'ē). **1.** the plants of a particular region or period, listed by species. **2.** a work systematically describing such plants. **3.** (*cap.*) the Roman goddess of flowers. [t. L, der. *flōs* flower]
flo·ral (flōr'əl), *adj.* **1.** pertaining to or consisting of flowers. **2.** (*cap.*) of or pertaining to the goddess Flora. [t. L: s. *Flōrālis* (def. 2)] —**flo'ral·ly,** *adv.*

floral envelope, *Bot.* the calyx and corolla of a flower.
Flo·ré·al (flô·rē·äl'), *n.* (in the calendar of the first French republic) the eighth month of the year, extending from April 20 to May 19.
flo·re·at·ed (flōr'ĭ·ā'tĭd), *adj.* floriated.
Flor·ence (flôr'əns, flŏr'-), *n.* a city in central Italy, on the Arno river: capital of the former grand duchy of Tuscany. 307,945 (est. 1946). Italian, **Firenze.**
Flor·en·tine (flôr'ən·tēn', flŏr'-; *less often* -tīn'), *adj.* **1.** of or pertaining to Florence, Italy: *the Florentine painters.* —*n.* **2.** a native or inhabitant of Florence.
Flo·res (flō'rĕs *for 1;* flô'rĭsh *for 2*), *n.* **1.** one of the Lesser Sunda Islands in the U.S. of Indonesia, sep- arated from Celebes by the **Flores Sea.** With adjacent islands, 717,300 pop. (1930); 7753 sq. mi. **2.** the western- most island of the Azores, in the N Atlantic. 7372 pop. (1940); 55 sq. mi.
flo·res·cence (flō·rĕs'əns), *n.* act, state, or period of flowering; bloom. [t. NL: m.s. *flōrescentia,* der. L *flōrescens,* ppr., beginning to flower] —**flo·res'cent,** *adj.*
flo·ret (flōr'ĭt), *n.* **1.** a small flower. **2.** *Bot.* one of the closely clustered small flowers that make up the flower head of a composite flower, as the daisy. [t. OF: m. *florete,* dim. of *flor,* g. L *flōs* flower]
Flo·ri·a·nóp·o·lis (flōr'ĭ·ə·nŏp'ə·lĭs; *Pg.* flōr'yə·nô'- pŏō·lēs'), *n.* a seaport on an island off the S coast of Brazil. 25,253 (1940). Formerly, **Desterro.**
flo·ri·at·ed (flōr'ĭ·ā'tĭd), *adj.* decorated with floral ornamentation: *floriated columns.* Also, **floreated.**
flo·ri·cul·ture (flōr'ə·kŭl'chər), *n.* the cultivation of flowers or flowering plants, esp. under glass. [f. L *flōri-* (comb. form of *flōs* flower) + CULTURE] —**flo'ri·cul'- tur·al,** *adj.* —**flo'ri·cul'tur·ist,** *n.*
flor·id (flōr'ĭd, flŏr'-), *adj.* **1.** high-colored or ruddy, as complexion, cheeks, persons, etc. **2.** flowery; exces- sively ornate; showy: *a florid prose style, florid music.* **3.** *Archit.* abounding in decorative features, as in baroque or rococo styles. **4.** *Archaic or Rare.* abounding in or consisting of flowers. [t. L: s. *flōridus* flowery] —**flo- rid·i·ty** (flō·rĭd'ə·tĭ), **flor'id·ness,** *n.* —**flor'id·ly,** *adv.*
Flor·i·da (flōr'ə·də, flŏr'-), *n.* a State in the SE United States between the Atlantic and the Gulf of Mexico. 2,771,305 pop. (1950); 58,560 sq. mi. *Cap.:* Tallahassee. *Abbr.:* Fla. —**Flo·rid·i·an** (flō·rĭd'ĭ·ən),**Flor'i·dan,** *adj.,n.*
Florida Keys, a chain of small islands and reefs off S Florida. ab. 225 mi. long.
Florida moss, a bromeliaceous epiphytic plant, *Tillandsia usneoides,* of the southern U.S., growing in long festoons which drape the branches of trees; Spanish moss.
Florida Strait, a strait separating Florida from Cuba and the Bahama Islands and connecting the Gulf of Mexico with the Atlantic.
flo·rif·er·ous (flō·rĭf'ər·əs), *adj.* flower-bearing. [f. L *flōrifer* bearing flowers + -OUS]
flor·in (flōr'ĭn, flŏr'-), *n.* **1.** an English silver coin worth 2 shillings, first minted in 1849. **2.** the gulden of the Netherlands. **3.** a former gold coin weighing about 54 grains, first issued at Florence in 1252. **4.** a former English gold coin of Edward III, worth 6 shillings. [ME, t. F, t. It.: m. *florino* a Florentine coin stamped with a lily, der. *fiore,* g. L *flōs* flower]
Flo·ri·o (flōr'ĭ·ō'), *n.* **John,** 1553?–1625, British lex- icographer and translator.
flo·rist (flōr'ĭst, flŏr'-), *n.* one who cultivates flowers, esp. for sale; a dealer in flowers.
flo·ris·tic (flō·rĭs'tĭk), *adj.* pertaining to a flora.
-florous, an adjectival suffix meaning "flower," as in *uniflorous.* [t. L: m. *-flōrus* flowered]
flos fer·ri (flŏs' fĕr'ī), *Mineral.* a coralloid variety of aragonite. [t. L: flower of iron]
floss (flôs, flŏs), *n.* **1.** the cottony fiber yielded by the silk-cotton trees. **2.** silk filaments with little or no twist, used in weaving as brocade or in embroidery. **3.** any silky filamentous matter, as the silk of maize. Also, **floss silk.** [t. Scand.; cf. Icel. *flos* shag of velvet]
floss·y (flôs'ĭ, flŏs'ĭ), *adj.,* **flossier, flossiest.** made of or resembling floss.
flo·tage (flō'tĭj), *n.* **1.** act of floating. **2.** state of floating. **3.** floating power; buoyancy. **4.** *Colloq.* any- thing that floats; flotsam. **5.** the ships, etc., afloat on a river. **6.** the part of a ship above the water line. Also, **floatage.** [f. FLOAT, n. + -AGE. Cf. F *flottage*]
flo·ta·tion (flō·tā'shən), *n.* **1.** act of floating. **2.** the floating or launching of a commercial venture, a loan, etc. **3.** *Metall.* a process for separating the different crystalline phases in a mass of powdered ore based on their ability to sink in, or float on, a given liquid. **4.** the science of floating bodies. **5.** state of floating. Also, *Brit.,* **floatation.** [var. of *floatation.* Cf. F *flottaison* (see FLOTSAM)]
flo·til·la (flō·tĭl'ə), *n.* **1.** number of small naval vessels; a subdivision of a fleet. **2.** a small fleet. [t. Sp., dim. of *flota* fleet, t. F: m. *flotte,* t. OE: m. *flota*]
Flo·tow (flō'tō), *n.* **Friedrich von** (frē'drĭKH fən), 1812–83, German operatic composer.
flot·sam (flŏt'səm), *n.* such part of the wreckage of a ship and its cargo as is found floating on the water. Cf. jetsam. [t. AF: m. *floteson,* der. *floter* float, t. OE: m. *flotian*]

flotsam and jetsam,   1. the wreckage of a ship and its cargo found either floating upon the sea or washed ashore.   2. odds and ends.

flounce[1] (flouns), *v.,* **flounced, flouncing,** *n.* —*v.i.* 1. to go with an impatient or angry fling of the body (fol. by *away, off, out,* etc.): *to flounce out of a room in a rage.* 2. to throw the body about, as in floundering or struggling; twist; turn; jerk. —*n.* 3. action of flouncing; a flouncing movement. [t. Scand.; cf. Norw. *flunsa* hurry]

flounce[2] (flouns), *n., v.,* **flounced, flouncing.** —*n.* 1. a strip of material, wider than a ruffle, gathered and attached at one edge and with the other edge left hanging: used for trimming, esp. on women's skirts. —*v.t.* 2. to trim with a flounce or flounces. [var. of FROUNCE]

flounc·ing (floun'sǐng), *n.*   1. material for flounces. 2. trimming consisting of a flounce.

floun·der[1] (floun'dər), *v.i.* 1. to struggle with stumbling or plunging movements (fol. by *along, on, through,* etc.). 2. to struggle clumsily or helplessly in embarrassment or confusion. —*n.* 3. action of floundering; a floundering movement. [? b. FLOUNCE[1] and FOUNDER[2]]

floun·der[2] (floun'dər), *n., pl.* **-ders,** (*esp. collectively*) **-der.** 1. a European marine flatfish, *Platichthys flesus,* widely caught for food. 2. any of a number of similar or closely related non-European flatfishes. 3. any flatfish other than soles. [ME, t. AF: m. *floundre,* t. Scand.; cf. Norw. *flundra*]

flour (flour), *n.* 1. the finely ground meal of grain, esp. the finer meal separated by bolting. 2. the finely ground and bolted meal of wheat. 3. any fine, soft powder: *flour of emery.* —*v.t.* 4. to make (grain, etc.) into flour; grind and bolt. 5. to sprinkle or dredge with flour, as food or utensils in cookery. 6. *Mining.* to break up (mercury, in amalgamation) into fine globules, which, owing to some impurity, do not unite with a precious metal. [ME; special use of FLOWER. Cf. F *fleur de farine* the flower or finest part of the meal] —**flour′less,** *adj.*

flour·ish (flûr'ǐsh), *v.i.* 1. to be in a vigorous state; thrive; prosper; be successful: *during this period art flourished.* 2. to be in its or one's prime; be at the height of fame or excellence. 3. to grow luxuriantly, or thrive in growth, as a plant. 4. to make strokes or flourishes with a brandished weapon or the like. 5. to make a parade or ostentatious display. 6. to add embellishments or flourishes to writing, letters, etc. 7. to speak or write in flowery or pretentious language. 8. *Music.* **a.** to play a showy passage. **b.** to play in a showy manner. **c.** to sound a trumpet call or fanfare. —*v.t.* 9. to brandish or wave (a sword, a stick, the limbs, etc.) about in the air. 10. to parade, flaunt, or display ostentatiously: *to flourish one's wealth.* 11. to embellish (writing, etc.) with sweeping or fanciful curves or lines. 12. to adorn with decorative designs, color, etc. —*n.* 13. a brandishing or waving, as of a sword, a stick, or the like. 14. a parade or ostentatious display. 15. a decoration or embellishment in writing. 16. *Rhet.* a parade of fine language; an expression used merely for effect. 17. *Music.* **a.** an elaborate passage or addition largely for display. **b.** a trumpet call or fanfare. 18. *Rare.* the condition of flourishing or thriving: *in full flourish.* 19. *Obs.* state of flowering. [ME *florish(en),* t. OF: m. *floriss-,* s. *florir,* ult. der. L *flōrēre* bloom] —**flour′ish·er,** *n.* —**Syn.** 2. See **succeed.**

flour·ish·ing (flûr'ǐsh ǐng), *adj.* that flourishes; vigorous in growth; thriving; prosperous. —**flour′ish·ing·ly,** *adv.*

flour mill, a mill for making flour.

flour·y (flour'ǐ), *adj.* 1. of, pertaining to, or resembling flour. 2. covered or white with flour.

flout (flout), *v.t.* 1. to mock; scoff at; treat with disdain or contempt. —*v.i.* 2. to mock, gibe, or scoff (often fol. by *at*). —*n.* 3. a flouting speech or action; a mocking insult; a gibe. [ME *floute(n),* var. of FLUTE, v. Cf. D *fluiten* play the flute, mock, impose upon] —**flout′er,** *n.* —**flout′ing·ly,** *adv.*

flow (flō), *v.i.* 1. to move along in a stream, as a liquid; circulate, as the blood. 2. to stream or well forth; issue or proceed from a source; discharge a stream, as of blood. 3. to come or go as in a stream, as persons or things. 4. to proceed continuously and smoothly, like a stream, as thought, speech, or verse. 5. to fall or hang loosely at full length, as hair. 6. to overflow or abound with something: *a land flowing with milk and honey.* 7. to rise and advance, as the tide (opposed to ebb). —*v.t.* 8. to cause or permit to flow. 9. to cover with water or other liquid; flood. —*n.* 10. act of flowing. 11. movement in or as in a stream; any continuous movement, as of thought, speech, trade, etc., like that of a stream of water. 12. the rate of flowing. 13. the volume of fluid that flows through a passage of any given section in a unit of time. 14. that which flows; a stream. 15. an outpouring or discharge of something, as in a stream: *a flow of blood.* 16. an overflowing. 17. the rise of the tide (opposed to ebb). [ME *flowen,* OE *flōwan,* c. LG *flojen,* Icel. *flōa*]

—**Syn.** 1. FLOW, GUSH, SPOUT, SPURT refer to certain of the movements characteristic of fluids. FLOW is the general term: *water flows, a steam of blood flows.* To GUSH is to rush forth copiously from a cavity, in as large a volume as can issue therefrom, as the result of some strong impelling force: *the water will gush out if the main breaks.* SPOUT and SPURT both imply the ejecting of a liquid from a cavity by some internal impetus given to it. SPOUT implies a rather steady,

---

possibly well-defined, jet or stream, not necessarily of long duration but always of considerable force: *a whale spouts.* SPURT implies a forcible, possibly sudden, spasmodic, or intermittent issue or jet: *the liquid spurted out suddenly when the bottle cap was pushed in, juice is likely to spurt from oranges or grapefruit.* SPOUT applies only to liquids; the other terms apply also to gases.

flow·age (flō'ǐj), *n.* 1. act of flowing; flow; state of being flooded. 2. the flowing or overflowing liquid. 3. *Mech.* gradual internal motion or deformation, without fracture, of a viscous solid such as asphalt.

flow·er (flou'ər), *n.* 1. the blossom of a plant. 2. *Bot.* **a.** that part of a seed plant comprising the reproductive organs and their envelopes (if any), esp. when such envelopes are more or less conspicuous in form and color. **b.** an analogous reproductive structure in other plants, as the mosses. 3. a plant considered with reference to its blossom or cultivated for its floral beauty. 4. state of efflorescence or bloom: *plants in flower.* 5. an ornament representing a flower. 6. any ornament or adornment. 7. a figure of speech. 8. the finest or most flourishing state or period, as of life or beauty. 9. the best or finest member or part of a number, body, or whole. 10. the finest or choicest product or example. 11. (*pl.*) *Chem.* a substance in the form of a fine powder, esp. as obtained by sublimation: *flowers of sulfur.* —*v.i.* 12. to produce flowers, or blossom, as a plant; to come to full bloom. 13. to abound in flowers. 14. to come out into full development or display (often fol. by *out*). —*v.t.* 15. to cover or deck with flowers. 16. to decorate with a floral design. [ME *flour,* t. OF, g. L *flōs*]

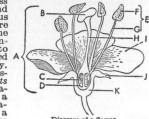

Diagram of a flower
A, Pistil; B, Stigma; C, Ovule; D, Ovary;
E, Stamen; F, Anther; G, Filament;
H, Style; I, Petal; J, Sepal; K, Receptacle

flow·er·age (flou'ər ǐj), *n.* 1. flowers collectively. 2. floral ornament or decoration. 3. *Rare.* the process or state of flowering.

flow·er-de-luce (flou'ər də lōōs'), *n.* the iris (flower or plant). [old var. of *fleur-de-lis,* influenced by FLOWER]

flow·ered (flou'ərd), *adj.* 1. having flowers. 2. decorated with flowers, or a floral pattern.

flow·er·er (flou'ər·ər), *n.* a plant that flowers at a specific time, etc.: *a late flowerer, an abundant flowerer.*

flow·er·et (flou'ər ǐt), *n.* a small flower; a floret.

flower girl, *Brit.* a woman of any age who sells flowers in the streets.

flower head, *Bot.* an inflorescence consisting of a dense cluster of sessile florets; a capitulum.

flow·er·ing (flou'ər ǐng), *adj.* bearing flowers.

flowering dogwood, a North American tree, *Cornus florida,* widely planted, bearing in the spring a profusion of white or pale pink flowers.

flowering maple, any member of the malvaceous genus *Abutilon,* shrubs with large bright-colored flowers; abutilon.

flow·er·less (flou'ər lǐs), *adj.* 1. without flowers. 2. *Bot.* without a true seed; cryptogamic.

flow·er·pot (flou'ər pǒt'), *n.* a pot to hold earth for a plant to grow in.

flow·er·y (flou'ər ǐ), *adj.,* **-erier, -eriest.** 1. abounding in or covered with flowers. 2. containing highly ornate language: *a flowery style.* 3. decorated with floral designs. —**flow′er·i·ly,** *adv.* —**flow′er·i·ness,** *n.*

flow·ing (flō'ǐng), *adj.* 1. that flows; moving in or as in a stream: *flowing water.* 2. proceeding smoothly or easily: *flowing language.* 3. smoothly and gracefully continuous throughout the length: *flowing lines or curves.* 4. falling or hanging loosely at full length: *flowing hair, draperies,* etc. —**flow′ing·ly,** *adv.*

flown[1] (flōn), *v.* pp. of fly[1].

flown[2] (flōn), *adj.* 1. decorated by means of color freely blended or flowed, as a glaze. 2. *Archaic.* filled to excess. 3. *Obs.* swollen, as a river in flood. [ME *flowen,* OE *flōwen,* pp. of *flōwan* flow]

flow sheet, (in a factory, etc.) a detailed diagram or chart of the operations and equipment through which material passes.

fl. oz., fluid ounce; fluid ounces.

flu (flōō), *n.* *Colloq.* influenza.

flub·dub (flŭb'dŭb'), *n.* *Colloq.* pretentious nonsense or show; airs.

fluc·tu·ant (flŭk'chōō ənt), *adj.* fluctuating; varying. [t. L: s. *fluctuans,* ppr., undulating]

fluc·tu·ate (flŭk'chōō āt'), *v.,* **-ated, -ating.** —*v.i.* 1. to change continually, as by turns, from one course, position, condition, amount, etc., to another, as the mind, opinion, policy, prices, temperature, etc.; vary irregularly; be unstable. 2. to move in waves or like waves. —*v.t. Rare.* 3. to cause to fluctuate. [t. L: m.s. *fluctuātus,* pp., undulated] —**Syn.** 1. See **waver.**

fluc·tu·a·tion (flŭk'chōō ā'shən), *n.* 1. continual change from one course, position, condition, etc., to another; alternating variation; vacillation; wavering; instability. 2. wavelike motion. 3. *Biol.* a body variation which is not inherited.

---

b., blend of, blended;   c., cognate with;   d., dialect, dialectal;   der., derived from;   f., formed from;   g., going back to; m., modification of;   r., replacing;   s., stem of;   t., taken from;   ?, perhaps.   See the full key on inside cover.

flue[1] (floo), *n.* **1.** the smoke passage in a chimney. **2.** any duct or passage for air, gases, or the like. **3.** (in certain steam boilers) any of the pipes or tubes through which hot gases, etc., are conveyed in order to heat surrounding or adjacent water. **4.** *Music.* **a.** a flue pipe. **b.** the air passage in a flue pipe between the blowing end and the lateral hole. [earlier *flew,* ? repr. OE *flēwsa* a flowing, the form *flews* being taken for a plural]

flue[2] (floo), *n.* downy matter; fluff. [? OE *flug-* in *flugol* swift, fleeting (akin to FLY, v.). Cf. LG *flug*]

flue[3] (floo), *n.* a kind of fishing net. Also, **flew.** [ME *flowe.* Cf. MD *vluwe* fishing net]

flue[4] (floo), *n.* **1.** a barb of a feather. **2.** the fluke of an anchor. [orig. obscure. Cf. Sw. *fly*]

flu·ent (floo'ənt), *adj.* **1.** flowing smoothly and easily: *to speak fluent French.* **2.** able to speak or write readily: *a fluent speaker.* **3.** easy; graceful: *fluent motion, curves, etc.* **4.** flowing, as a stream. **5.** *Rare.* capable of flowing, or fluid, as liquids or gases. **6.** *Rare.* not fixed or stable in form. [t. L: s. *fluens,* ppr., flowing] —**flu′en·cy, flu′ent·ness,** *n.* —**flu′ent·ly,** *adv.*
—**Syn. 1.** FLUENT, GLIB, VOLUBLE may refer to a flow of words. FLUENT suggests an easy and ready flow and is usually a term of commendation: *a fluent and interesting speech.* GLIB implies an excessive fluency divorced from sincerity or profundity; it often suggests talking smoothly and hurriedly to cover up or deceive, not giving the audience a chance to stop and think; it may also imply a plausible, prepared, and well-rehearsed lie: *he had a glib answer for everything.* VOLUBLE implies the overcopious, and often rapid flow of words, characteristic of a person who loves to talk and will spare his audience no details: *she overwhelmed him with her voluble answer.* —**Ant. 1.** hesitant.

flue pipe, *Music.* an organ pipe in which a current of air striking a mouth or aperture produces the tone.

flue stop, *Music.* an organ stop whose sound is produced by flue pipes: a generic name for all but reed stops.

fluff (fluf), *n.* **1.** light, downy particles, as of cotton. **2.** a downy mass; something downy or fluffy. —*v.t.* **3.** to make into fluff; shake or puff out (feathers, hair, etc.) into a fluffy mass. —*v.i.* **4.** to become fluffy; move, float, or settle down like fluff. [? b. FLUE[2] and PUFF]

fluff·y (fluf'ĭ), *adj.,* **fluffier, fluffiest.** of, like, or covered with fluff. —**fluff′i·ly,** *adv.* —**fluff′i·ness,** *n.*

flu·id (floo'ĭd), *n.* **1.** a substance, as a liquid or a gas, which is capable of flowing, and which usually does not resist forces tending to change its shape but not its volume. —*adj.* **2.** capable of flowing; liquid or gaseous. **3.** consisting of or pertaining to fluids. **4.** changing readily; shifting; not fixed, stable, or rigid. [t. L: s. *fluidus,* der. *fluere* flow] —**flu·id′ic,** *adj.* —**flu·id′i·ty, flu′id·ness,** *n.* —**flu′id·ly,** *adv.* —**Syn. 1.** See liquid.

fluid dram, the eighth part of a fluid ounce. Also, **fluid drachm.**

flu·id·ex·tract (floo'ĭd·ĕks'trăkt), *n.* *Pharm.* an alcoholic solution of a vegetable drug when one cc. of the preparation is equivalent, in activity, to one gram of the drug in powdered form.

fluid mechanics, an applied science embodying the basic principles of both gaseous and liquid flow.

fluid ounce, *n.* a measure of capacity equal to $1/16$ pint in the U.S., and to $1/20$ of an imperial pint in Great Britain.

fluid pressure, *Physics, etc.* pressure within a fluid or at the confines of a restrained fluid.

fluke[1] (flook), *n.* **1.** the flat triangular piece at the end of each arm of an anchor, which catches in the ground. **2.** a barb, or the barbed head, of a harpoon, etc. **3.** either half of the triangular tail of a whale. [? special use of FLUKE[3]]

fluke[2] (flook), *n., v.,* **fluked, fluking.** —*n.* **1.** any accidental advantage; a lucky chance. **2.** an accidentally successful stroke in billiards or other sports. —*v.t.* **3.** *Colloq.* to hit, make, or gain by a fluke. [orig. unknown. Cf. d. E *fluke* a guess]

fluke[3] (flook), *n.* **1.** the flounder, *Platichthys flesus.* **2.** any flounder. **3.** a trematode. [ME, var. of *flook,* OE *flōc*]

fluk·ey (floo'kĭ), *adj.,* **flukier, flukiest.** fluky.

fluk·y (floo'kĭ), *adj.,* **flukier, flukiest. 1.** *Colloq.* obtained by chance rather than skill. **2.** uncertain, as a wind. [f. FLUKE[2] + -Y[1]] —**fluk′i·ness,** *n.*

flume (floom), *n., v.,* **flumed, fluming.** —*n.* **1.** a deep, narrow defile, esp. one containing a mountain torrent. **2.** an artificial channel or trough for conducting water, as one in which logs, etc., are transported. —*v.t.* **3.** to transport, as lumber, in a flume. **4.** to divert (a river, etc.) by a flume. [ME., t. OF: m. *flum,* g. L. *flūmen* stream]

flum·mer·y (flŭm'ə·rĭ), *n., pl.* **-meries. 1.** oatmeal or flour boiled with water until thick. **2.** any of various dishes made of flour, milk, eggs, sugar, etc. **3.** agreeable humbug; empty compliment. [t. Welsh: m. *llymru*]

flum·mox (flŭm'əks), *v.t.* *Slang.* to bewilder; confuse.

flump (flŭmp), *Colloq.* —*v.i., v.t.* **1.** to plump down suddenly or heavily; flop. —*n.* **2.** act or sound of flumping. [b. FALL and PLUMP[2]]

flung (flŭng), *v.* pt. and pp. of **fling.**

flunk (flŭngk), *U.S. Colloq.* —*v.i.* **1.** to fail, as a student in a recitation or examination. **2.** to give up; back out (fol. by *out*). —*v.t.* **3.** to fail in (a recitation, etc.). **4.** to remove (a student) as unqualified from a school, course, etc. —*n.* **5.** a failure, as in a recitation or examination. [? akin to FLINCH[1], FUNK]

flun·key (flŭng'kĭ), *n., pl.* **-keys.** flunky.

flun·ky (flŭng'kĭ), *n., pl.* **-kies. 1.** (in contemptuous use) a male servant in livery; a lackey. **2.** a servile follower; a toady. [? alter. of FLANKER]

flun·ky·ism (flŭng'kĭ·ĭz'əm), *n.* servility; toadying. Also, **flun′key·ism.**

flu·o·phos·phate (floo'ə·fŏs'fāt), *n.* a substance containing both fluorine and phosphorus.

flu·or (floo'ôr), *n.* fluorite. [t. L: a flowing (so called from its use as a flux)]

fluor-[1], a word element indicating the presence of fluorine. [comb. form of FLUORINE]

fluor-[2], a word element indicating fluorescence. [comb. form of FLUORESCENCE]

flu·o·resce (floo'ə·rĕs'), *v.i.,* **-resced, -rescing.** to exhibit the phenomena of fluorescence.

flu·o·res·ce·in (floo'ə·rĕs'ĭn), *n.* *Chem.* an orange-red water-insoluble compound, $C_{20}H_{12}O_5$, whose solutions in alkalis produce an orange color and a green fluorescence. It is used as an indicator and in dyes. Also, **flu′o·res′ce·ine.**

flu·o·res·cence (floo'ə·rĕs'əns), *n.* *Physics, Chem.* **1.** the property possessed by certain substances of emitting light upon exposure to external radiation or bombardment by a stream of particles. **2.** the light or luminosity so produced.

flu·o·res·cent (floo'ə·rĕs'ənt), *adj.* possessing the property of fluorescence; exhibiting fluorescence.

fluorescent lamp, an electric discharge lamp in which light is produced by the passage of electricity through a metallic vapor or gas enclosed in a tube or bulb.

flu·or·ic (floo·ôr'ĭk, -ŏr'-), *adj.* **1.** *Chem.* pertaining to or obtained from fluorine. **2.** *Mineral.* pertaining to or obtained from fluor. [t. F: m. *fluorique,* der. *fluor* fluid acid, t. L; a flowing]

flu·o·ride (floo'ə·rīd'), *n.* *Chem.* a compound, usually of two elements, one of which is fluorine, as *sodium fluoride,* NaF. Also, **flu·o·rid** (floo'ə·rĭd).

flu·o·rine (floo'ə·rēn' -rĭn), *n.* *Chem.* a nonmetallic element, a pale yellow corrosive gas, occurring combined, esp. in fluorite, cryolite, phosphate rock, and other minerals. *Symbol:* F; *at. wt.:* 19.0; *at. no.:* 9. Also, **flu·o·rin** (floo'ə·rĭn).

flu·o·rite (floo'ə·rīt'), *n.* a common mineral, calcium fluoride, CaF_2, occurring in colorless, green, blue, purple, and yellow crystals, usually in cubes: the principal source of fluorine. It is also used as a flux in metallurgy and for ornamental purposes. Also, **fluor, fluorspar.**

flu·o·ro·car·bon (floo'ə·rə·kär'bən), *n.* *Chem.* any of a class of compounds made by substituting fluorine for hydrogen in a hydrocarbon, and characterized by great chemical stability. They are used as lubricants, fire extinguishers, and in a number of industrial applications in which resistance to heat, radioactivity, etc., is essential.

fluor·o·scope (floor'ə·skōp', floo'ə·rə-), *n.* a tube or box, fitted with a screen coated with a fluorescent substance, used for viewing objects exposed to x-rays or other radiation directed to, or focused upon, the screen. [f. FLUOR-[2] + -(O)SCOPE]

fluor·o·scop·ic (floor'ə·skŏp'ĭk, floo'ə·rə-), *adj.* pertaining to the fluoroscope or to fluoroscopy. —**fluor′o·scop′i·cal·ly,** *adv.*

fluor·os·co·py (floor·ŏs'kə·pĭ, floo'ə·rŏs'-), *n.* the act of using the fluoroscope, or of examining by means of a fluorescent screen, the shadows of bodies being examined by means of x-rays.

flu·or·spar (floo'ôr·spär', -ər-), *n.* fluorite. Also, **fluor spar.**

flur·ry (flûr'ĭ), *n., pl.* **-ries,** *v.,* **-ried, -rying.** —*n.* **1.** a sudden gust of wind. **2.** a light gusty shower or snowfall. **3.** commotion; sudden excitement or confusion; nervous hurry. **4.** *Stock Exchange.* a brief agitation in prices. —*v.t.* **5.** to put (a person) into a flurry; make nervous; confuse; fluster. [b. FLUTTER and HURRY]

flush[1] (flŭsh), *n.* **1.** a blush; a rosy glow. **2.** a rushing or overspreading flow, as of water. **3.** a rush of emotion; elation: *the first flush of success, of victory.* **4.** glowing freshness or vigor: *the flush of youth.* **5.** the hot stage of a fever. —*v.t.* **6.** to redden; cause to blush or glow. **7.** to flood with water, as for cleansing purposes; wash out (a sewer, etc.). **8.** to animate or elate. —*v.i.* **9.** to blush; redden. **10.** to flow with a rush; flow and spread suddenly. [b. FLASH and GUSH; in some senses further blended with BLUSH] —**flush′er,** *n.*

flush[2] (flŭsh), *adj.* **1.** even or level, as with a surface; in one plane. **2.** well-supplied, as with money; affluent; prosperous. **3.** abundant or plentiful, as money. **4.** flushed with color; blushing. **5.** full of vigor; lusty. **6.** quite full; full to overflowing. **7.** *Naut.* (of a deck) unbroken by deckhouses, etc., and having an even surface fore and aft or from stem to stern. **8.** *Print.* even or level with the right or left margins of the type page; without an indentation. —*adv.* **9.** so as to be flush or even. —*v.t.* **10.** to make flush or even. —*v.i.* **11.** to send out shoots, as plants in spring. —*n.* **12.** a fresh growth, as of shoots and leaves. [? adj. use of FLUSH[1]]

flush[3] (flŭsh), *Hunting.* —*v.t.* **1.** to rouse and cause to start up or fly off: *to flush a woodcock.* —*v.i.* **2.** to fly out or start up suddenly. —*n.* **3.** a flushed bird, or flock of birds. [ME *flussh,* orig. uncert.]

flush⁴ (flŭsh), *Cards.* —*adj.* **1.** consisting entirely of cards of one suit: *a flush hand.* —*n.* **2.** a hand or set of cards all of one suit. See **royal flush, straight flush.** [cf. F (obs.) *flus,* var. of *flux* flow, flush (cf. E *run* of cards), t. L: s. *fluxus* FLUX]

Flush·ing (flŭsh′ĭng), *n.* a seaport in SW Netherlands, on Walcheren island. 21,753 (est. 1937). Dutch, **Vlissingen.**

flus·ter (flŭs′tər), *v.t.* **1.** to confuse; make nervous. **2.** to excite and confuse with drink. —*v.i.* **3.** to become confused; become agitated or flurried. —*n.* **4.** confusion; flurry; nervous excitement. [cf. Icel. *flaustr* hurry, bustle and cf. BLUSTER]

flus·trate (flŭs′trāt), *v.t.*, **-trated, -trating.** fluster. —**flus·tra′tion,** *n.*

flute (flōot), *n.*, *v.*, **fluted, fluting.** —*n.* **1.** a musical wind instrument consisting of a tube with a series of finger holes or keys, in which the wind is directed against a sharp edge, either directly, as in the modern transverse flute, or through a flue, as in the re-

Flute

corder. **2.** an organ stop with wide flue pipes, having a flutelike tone. **3.** *Archit., etc.* a channel or furrow with a rounded section, as in a pillar. **4.** a groove in any material, as in a woman's ruffle. —*v.i.* **5.** to produce or utter flutelike sounds. **6.** to play on a flute. —*v.t.* **7.** to utter in flutelike tones. **8.** to form longitudinal flutes, depressions, or furrows in. [ME *flowte,* t. OF: m. *fleüte,* t. Pr.: m. *flauta,* ult. der. L *flātus,* pp., blown] —**flute′like′,** *adj.*

flut·ed (flōo′tĭd), *adj.* **1.** fine, clear, and mellow; flutelike: *fluted notes.* **2.** having flutes or grooves, as a pillar.

flut·er (flōo′tər), *n.* **1.** one who makes flutings. **2.** *Rare.* a flutist.

flut·ing (flōo′tĭng), *n.* **1.** act of playing on the flute. **2.** the sound made by such playing; a flutelike sound. **3.** fluted work. **4.** act of making flutes. **5.** a flute, groove, or furrow.

fluting iron, a specially shaped iron for pressing ruffles, etc., into a fluted form.

flut·ist (flōo′tĭst), *n.* a flute player. Also, **flautist.** [cf. F *flûtiste*]

flut·ter (flŭt′ər), *v.i.* **1.** to toss or wave in air, as a flag. **2.** (of birds, etc.) to flap the wings, or fly with flapping movements. **3.** to move in quick, irregular motions. **4.** to beat fast and irregularly, as the heart. **5.** to be tremulous or agitated. **6.** to go with irregular motions or aimless course. —*v.t.* **7.** to cause to flutter; vibrate; agitate. **8.** to confuse; throw into a state of nervous excitement, mental agitation, or tremulous excitement. —*n.* **9.** a fluttering movement. **10.** a state of nervous excitement or mental agitation. **11.** sensation; stir: *to cause or make a flutter.* **12.** *Swimming.* flutter kick. [ME *floteren,* OE *floterian,* freq. of *flotian* float] —**flut′-ter·er,** *n.* —**flut′ter·ing·ly,** *adv.* —**Syn. 2.** see **fly¹.**

flutter kick, *Swimming.* the up-and-down movements of the legs in the crawl.

flut·ter·y (flŭt′ərĭ), *adj.* fluttering; apt to flutter.

flut·y (flōo′tĭ), *adj.* flutelike, as in tone.

flu·vi·al (flōo′vĭ əl), *adj.* of, pertaining to, or produced by a river. [t. L: s. *fluviālis,* der. *fluvius* river]

flu·vi·a·tile (flōo′vĭ ə tīl; *Brit.* -tĭl), *adj.* pertaining or peculiar to rivers; found in or near rivers. [t. L: m.s. *fluviātilis,* der. *fluvius* river]

flux (flŭks), *n.* **1.** a flowing or flow. **2.** the flowing in of the tide. **3.** continuous passage; continuous change: *to be in a state of flux.* **4.** *Pathol.* **a.** an abnormal or morbid discharge of blood or other matter from the body. **b.** dysentery (**bloody flux**). **5.** *Physics.* **a.** the rate of flow of a fluid, heat, or the like. **b.** luminous flux. **c.** magnetic flux. **6.** *Chem. Metall., etc.* **a.** a substance, as borax or fluorspar, used to promote the fusion of metals or minerals. **b.** a nonmetallic substance, as a salt or mixture of salts, used to protect the surface of molten metal from oxidation. **c.** (in the refining of scrap or other metal) a salt or mixture of salts which combines with nonmetallic impurities, causing them to float or coagulate. **7.** fusion. —*v.t.* **8.** to melt; fuse; make fluid. **9.** *Obs.* to purge. —*v.i.* **10.** to flow. [ME, t. L: s. *fluxus* a flowing]

flux density, *Physics.* the magnetic or electric flux per unit of cross-sectional area.

flux·ion (flŭk′shən), *n.* **1.** act of flowing; a flow or flux. **2.** *Math. Obs.* the derivative relative to the time. —**flux′ion·al, flux·ion·ar·y** (flŭk′shə nĕr′ĭ), *adj.* —**flux′ion·al·ly,** *adv.*

flux·me·ter (flŭks′mē′tər), *n.* *Physics.* an instrument for measuring magnetic flux.

fly¹ (flī), *v.*, **flew** or (for def. 7) **flied; flown; flying;** *n., pl.* **flies.** —*v.i.* **1.** to move through the air on wings, as a bird. **2.** to be borne through the air by the wind or any other force or agency. **3.** to float or flutter in the air, as a flag, the hair, etc. **4.** to travel through an aircraft or as an aircraft does. **5.** to move or pass swiftly; move with a start or rush. **6.** *Archaic.* to attack by flying, as a hawk does. **7.** *Baseball.* to bat a fly ball: *he flied into right field.* —*n.* **8.** a strip sewn along one edge of a garment, to aid in concealing the buttons or other fasteners. **9.** a flap forming the door of a tent. **10.** a piece of canvas extending over the ridgepole of a tent and forming an

outer roof. **11.** act of flying; a flight. **12. on the fly,** during flight, before reaching the ground. **13.** the course of a flying object, as a ball. **14.** *Baseball and Cricket.* a ball knocked high in the air. **15.** *Brit.* a light public carriage for passengers. **16.** *Mach.* a flywheel. **17.** *Horol.* a regulating device for chime and striking mechanisms, consisting of an arrangement of vanes on a revolving axis. **18.** *Print.* **a.** a contrivance for receiving and delivering separately printed sheets from a press. **b.** (formerly) one who removed printed matter from a press. **19.** the extent of a flag from the staff to the outer end, or the outer end itself. **20.** (*pl.*) *Theat.* the space and apparatus above the stage. [ME *flien,* OE *flēogan,* c. D *vliegen,* G *fliegen*] —**Syn. 1.** FLY, FLIT, FLUTTER, HOVER, SOAR refer to moving through the air as on wings. FLY is the general term: *birds fly, airplanes fly.* To FLIT is to make short rapid flights from place to place: *a bird flits from tree to tree.* To FLUTTER is to agitate the wings tremulously, either without flying or in flying only short distances: *a young bird flutters out of a nest and in again.* To HOVER is to linger in the air, or to move over or about something within a narrow area or space: *hovering clouds, a hummingbird hovering over a blossom.* To SOAR is to (start to) fly upward to a great height usually with little advance in any other direction, or else to (continue to) fly at a lofty height without visible movement of the wings: *above our heads great birds were soaring.*

fly² (flī), *n., pl.* **flies.** **1.** any of the two-winged insects constituting the order *Diptera* (**true flies**), especially one of the family *Muscidae,* as the common housefly, *Musca domestica.* **2.** any of a number of other winged insects, as the May fly or firefly. **3.** *Angling.* a fishhook dressed with silk, tinsel, etc., so as to resemble an insect. [ME *flye,* OE *flēoge, flȳge,* c. G *fliege*] —**fly′less,** *adj.*

fly³ (flī), *adj. Slang.* knowing; sharp; smart. [? special use of FLY¹]

fly agaric, a very poisonous mushroom, *Amanita muscaria,* sometimes used for making a poison for flies.

fly·a·way (flī′ə wā′), *adj.* **1.** fluttering; streaming. **2.** flighty; volatile; frivolous.

fly·blow (flī′blō′), *v.t.* **1.** to deposit eggs or larvae on meat. —*n.* **2.** the egg or young larva (maggot) of a blowfly, deposited on meat, etc.

fly·blown (flī′blōn′), *adj.* **1.** tainted with flyblows. **2.** spoiled; corrupt.

fly·boat (flī′bōt′), *n.* a fast vessel. [t. D: m. *vlieboot*]

fly book, *Angling.* a booklike case for artificial flies.

fly·by·night (flī′bī nīt′), *adj.* **1.** irresponsible; unreliable. —*n.* **2.** a person who leaves secretly at night in order to avoid paying his debts.

fly·catch·er (flī′kăch′ər), *n.* any of numerous small, insectivorous birds of the Old World family *Muscicapidae,* (as the **spotted flycatcher,** *Muscicapa grisola,* of Europe) or of the American family *Tyrannidae* (as the kingbird).

fly·er (flī′ər), *n.* flier.

fly·fish (flī′fĭsh′), *v.i. Angling.* to fish with artificial flies as bait. —**fly′-fish′er,** *n.* —**fly′-fish′ing,** *n.*

fly·ing (flī′ĭng), *adj.* **1.** that flies; making flight or passing through the air: *a flying insect, a flying boat.* **2.** floating, fluttering or waving, or hanging or moving freely, in the air: *flying banners, flying hair.* **3.** extending through the air. **4.** moving swiftly. **5.** made while moving swiftly: *a flying start.* **6.** hasty: *a flying trip.* **7.** designed for swiftness: *a flying squad.* **8.** fleeing, running away, or taking flight. **9.** *Naut.* (of a sail) having none of its edges bent to spars or stays. —*n.* **10.** act of moving through the air on wings; flight.

flying boat, an aircraft whose main body consists of a single hull or boat.

flying buttress, (in Gothic architecture) a segmental arch which carries the thrust of the nave wall over the aisle to a solid pier buttress. See illus. under **buttress.**

flying circus, a squadron of airplanes operating together, esp. any of several squadrons of famous World War I aviators.

flying column, *Mil.* (formerly) a force of troops equipped and organized to move swiftly and independently of a principal unit to which it is attached.

Flying Dutchman, 1. a legendary spectral Dutch ship supposed to be seen at sea, esp. near the Cape of Good Hope. **2.** the captain of this ship, supposed to have been condemned to sail the sea, beating against the wind, till the day of judgment.

flying field, *Aeron.* a small landing field with short runways and facilities for servicing airplanes on a lesser scale than an airport.

flying fish, any of certain fishes with winglike pectoral fins which help them to glide for some distance through the air after leaping from the water, esp. of the family *Exocoetidae,* as *Exocoetus volitans.*

flying fox, any large fruit-eating bat of the family *Pteropodidae,* esp. of the genus *Pteropus,* as *P. edulis,* of Old World tropical regions, having a foxlike head.

flying gurnard, any of several fishes of the family *Dactylopteridae,* esp. *Dactylopterus volitans,* having winglike pectoral fins, though apparently not able to fly.

flying jib, a triangular sail set outside of the jib. See illus. under **sail.**

flying lemur, a lemurlike mammal having a broad fold of skin on each side of the body to act as a wing in

---

b., blend of, blended; c., cognate with; d., dialect, dialectal; der., derived from; f., formed from; g., going back to; m., modification of; r., replacing; s., stem of; t., taken from; ?, perhaps. See the full key on inside cover.

gliding from tree to tree. The species *Cynocephalus temminckii* is distributed over southeastern Asia and the East Indies, *Cynocephalus volans* in the Philippine area. They are the only representatives of the order *Dermoptera.*

flying lizard, any of the arboreal lizards of the genus *Draco* of southeastern Asia and the East Indies, with extensible membranes along the sides by means of which they make long gliding leaps from tree to tree.

flying machine, a contrivance which sustains itself in, and propels itself through, the air; an airplane or the like.

flying mare, *Wrestling.* a method of attack in which a wrestler grasps the wrist of his opponent, turns in the opposite direction, and throws him over his shoulder and down.

Flying phalanger, *Schoinobates volans* (Total length 3 ft., tail 1½ ft.)

flying phalanger, any of a number of small phalangers of Australia and New Guinea having a parachutelike fold of skin at each side, to give gliding assistance in leaping.

flying squirrel, a squirrellike animal, esp. of the genus *Glaucomys* as *G. volans* of the eastern U.S., with folds of skin connecting the fore and hind legs, enabling it to take long gliding leaps.

fly in the ointment, a trifle that spoils or lessens the pleasure or value of something else.

Flying squirrel, *Glaucomys volans* (Total length 9 to 9½ in., tail 3½ to 4 in.)

fly·leaf (flī′lēf′), *n., pl.* **-leaves** (-lēvz′). a blank leaf in the front or the back of a book.

fly loft, the portion of a theater building above the stage into which scenery may be raised.

fly·man (flī′mən), *n., pl.* **-men.** *Theat.* a stage hand, esp. one who operates the apparatus in the flies.

fly net, a fringe or net to protect a horse from flies.

fly·pa·per (flī′pā′pər), *n.* paper prepared to destroy flies by poisoning them or by catching them on its sticky surface.

Fly River (flī), a river flowing from central New Guinea SE to the Gulf of Papua. ab. 800 mi.

fly·speck (flī′spĕk′), *n.* **1.** a speck or tiny stain from the excrement of a fly. **2.** a minute spot. —*v.t.* **3.** to mark with flyspecks.

flyte (flīt), *v.i.,* **flyted, flyting,** *n.* *Now Scot. and N. Eng.* flite.

fly·trap (flī′trăp′), *n.* **1.** any of various plants which entrap insects, esp. Venus's-flytrap. **2.** a trap for flies.

fly·weight (flī′wāt′), *n.* a boxer of 112 pounds or less, lighter than a featherweight and a bantamweight.

fly·wheel (flī′hwēl′), *n.* *Mach.* **1.** a heavy wheel which by its momentum tends to equalize the speed of machinery with which it is connected. **2.** a wheel used to carry the piston over dead center.

FM, *Radio.* frequency modulation.

fm., **1.** fathom. **2.** from.

F number, *Photog.* the focal distance divided by the effective diameter of the lens aperture; the relative aperture. It is a numerical indication of the relative exposure required by a lens, and is used in numbering diaphragm openings.

F.O., **1.** Field Officer. **2.** *Brit.* Foreign Office.

foal (fōl), *n.* **1.** the young of the horse, ass, or any allied animal; a colt or filly. —*v.t., v.i.* **2.** to bring forth (a foal). [ME *fole,* OE *fola,* c. OHG *folo*]

foam (fōm), *n.* **1.** an aggregation of minute bubbles formed on the surface of a liquid by agitation, fermentation, etc. **2.** the froth of perspiration formed on the skin of a horse or other animal from great exertion. **3.** froth formed in the mouth, as in epilepsy and rabies. —*v.i.* **4.** to form or gather foam; emit foam; froth. —*v.t.* **5.** to cause to foam. [ME *fome,* OE *fām,* c. G *feim*] —**foam′ing·ly,** *adv.* —**foam′less,** *adj.*

foam·flow·er (fōm′flou′ər), *n.* a North American saxifragaceous herb, *Tiarella cordifolia,* which bears white flowers in the spring.

foam·y (fō′mī), *adj.,* **foamier, foamiest. 1.** covered with or full of foam. **2.** consisting of foam. **3.** resembling foam. **4.** of or pertaining to foam. —**foam′i·ness,** *n.*

fob¹ (fŏb), *n.* **1.** a small pocket just below the waistline in trousers or breeches, to hold a watch, etc. **2.** a short chain or ribbon with a seal or the like, attached to a watch and worn hanging from the pocket. [orig. unknown. Cf. d. HG *fuppe* pocket, *fuppen* to pocket stealthily]

fob² (fŏb), *v.t.,* **fobbed, fobbing. 1.** to palm off (fol. by *off*): *to fob off something inferior or spurious on a person.* **2.** to put off (fol. by *off*): *to fob someone off with promises.* **3.** *Archaic.* to cheat; deceive. [akin to FOB¹. Cf. G *foppen* deceive]

F.O.B., free on board (a price F.O.B. is a price which does not include carriage charges from the seller to the buyer). Also, **f.o.b.**

fo·cal (fō′kəl), *adj.* of or pertaining to a focus. —**fo′cal·ly,** *adv.*

focal distance, *Optics.* **1.** (of a mirror or lens) the distance from a point near its center to the focal point. **2.** (of a telescope) the distance between the object glass and the focal plane. Also, **focal length.**

focal infection, *Pathol., Dentistry.* an infection in which the bacteria are localized in some region, as the tissue around a tooth or a tonsil, from which they often spread to some other organ or structure of the body.

fo·cal·ize (fō′kə līz′), *v.t.,* **-ized, -izing.** focus. —**fo′cal·i·za′tion,** *n.*

focal plane, *Optics.* the transverse plane in a telescope where the real image of a distant view is in focus.

Foch (fôsh), *n.* **Ferdinand** (fĕr dē nän′), 1851–1929, French marshal.

fo·cus (fō′kəs), *n., pl.* **-cuses, -ci** (-sī), *v.,* **-cused, -cusing** or (*esp. Brit.*) **-cussed, -cussing.** —*n.* **1.** *Physics.* a point at which rays of light, heat, or other radiation, meet after being refracted or reflected. **2.** *Optics.* **a.** a point from which diverging rays appear to proceed, or a point at which converging rays would meet if they could be prolonged in the same direction (**virtual focus**). **b.** the focal distance of a lens. **c.** clear and sharply defined condition of an image. **d.** the position of a viewed object, or the adjustment of an optical device, necessary to produce a clear image: *in focus, out of focus.* **3.** a central point, as of attraction, attention, or activity. **4.** *Geom.* one of the points from which the distances to any point of a given curve are in a linear relation. See diag. under **parabola. 5.** *Seismology.* the point where an earthquake starts. **6.** *Pathol.* the primary center from which a disease develops or in which it localizes. —*v.t.* **7.** to bring to a focus or into focus. **8.** to concentrate: *to focus one's thoughts.* —*v.i.* **9.** to become focused. [t. L: hearth, fireplace] —**fo′cus·er,** *n.*

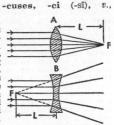

F, Focus; L, Focal distance; A, Convex lens; B, Concave lens.

fod·der (fŏd′ər), *n.* **1.** coarse roughages used as feed for livestock, composed of entire plant, including leaves, stalks, and grain of such forages as corn (maize) and sorghum. —*v.t.* **2.** to feed with or as with fodder. [ME; OE *fodder, fōdor,* c. G *futter;* akin to FOOD] —**Syn. 1.** See **feed.**

fodg·el (fŏj′əl), *adj.* *Scot.* fat; stout; plump.

foe (fō), *n.* **1.** one who entertains enmity, hatred, or malice against another; an enemy. **2.** an enemy in war; hostile army. **3.** one belonging to a hostile army or nation. **4.** an opponent in a game or contest. **5.** a person who is opposed in feeling, principle, etc., to something: *a foe to progress.* **6.** a thing that is opposed to or destructive of: *cleanliness is a foe to infection.* [ME *foo,* OE *(ge)fā(h)* enemy (absolute use of adj. meaning hostile). See FEUD¹] —**Syn. 1.** See **enemy.**

F.O.E., Fraternal Order of Eagles.

foehn (fān; *Ger.* fœn), *n.* *Meteorol.* föhn.

foe·man (fō′mən), *n., pl.* **-men.** *Archaic.* an enemy in war.

foe·ta·tion (fē tā′shən), *n.* fetation.

foe·ti·cide (fē′tə sīd′), *n.* feticide.

foe·tid (fē′tĭd, fĕt′ĭd), *adj.* fetid.

foe·tor (fē′tər), *n.* fetor.

foe·tus (fē′təs), *n.* fetus. —**foe′tal,** *adj.*

fog¹ (fŏg, fôg), *n., v.,* **fogged, fogging.** —*n.* **1.** *Meteorol.* a cloudlike mass or layer of minute globules of water in the air near the earth's surface; thick mist. **2.** any darkened state of the atmosphere, or the diffused substance which causes it. **3.** a state of mental confusion or obscurity: *a fog of doubt.* **4.** *Photog.* a darkening of the whole or of parts of a developed plate or print from sources other than image-forming light in the camera. **5.** *Phys. Chem.* a colloidal system consisting of liquid particles dispersed in a gaseous medium. —*v.t.* **6.** to envelop with, or as with, fog. **7.** *Photog.* to affect (a negative or print) by fog. **8.** to confuse; perplex; bewilder. —*v.i.* **9.** to become enveloped or obscured with, or as with, fog. **10.** *Photog.* to be affected by fog. [back formation from FOGGY. See FOG²] —**fog′less,** *adj.* —**Syn. 1.** See **cloud.**

fog² (fŏg, fôg), *n.* **1.** a second growth of grass, as after mowing. **2.** long grass left standing in fields during the winter. [ME *fogge,* t. Scand.; cf. Norw. *fogg* long grass on damp ground, and obs. E *foggy* marshy]

fog bank, a stratum of fog as seen from a distance.

fog·bound (fŏg′bound′, fôg′-), *adj.* *Naut.* unable to navigate due to heavy fog.

fog·dog (fŏg′dôg′, -dŏg′, fôg′-), *n.* a bright spot sometimes seen in a fog bank.

fo·gey (fō′gĭ), *n., pl.* **-geys.** fogy.

fog·gage (fŏg′ĭj), *n.* *Chiefly Dial.* fog².

Fog·gia (fôd′jä), *n.* a city in S Italy. 65,155 (est. 1946).

fog·gy (fŏg′ĭ, fôg′ĭ), *adj.,* **-gier, -giest. 1.** abounding in or thick with fog; misty. **2.** resembling fog; dim; obscure. **3.** *Photog.* affected by fog. [der. FOG²; orig. meaning marshy, thick, murky] —**fog′gi·ly,** *adv.* —**fog′gi·ness,** *n.*

fog·horn (fŏg′hôrn′, fôg′-), *n.* **1.** a horn for sounding warning signals, as to vessels, in foggy weather. **2.** a deep, loud voice.

fo·gy (fō′gĭ), *n.*, *pl.* **-gies. 1.** an old-fashioned or excessively conservative person: *the old fogy.* **2.** a slow or dull person. **—fo′gy·ish,** *adj.* **—fo′gy·ism,** *n.*

föhn (fān; *Ger.* fœn), *n. Meteorol.* a warm, dry wind descending a mountain, in the valleys on the north side of the Alps. Also, **foehn.** [t. G, t. Romansch: m. *favugn,* g. L *Favōnius*]

foi·ble (foi′bəl), *n.* **1.** a weak point or whimsy; a weakness or failing of character. **2.** the weaker part of a sword blade, between the middle and the point. [t. F, obs. form of *faible* FEEBLE] **—Syn. 1.** See **fault.**

foil[1] (foil), *v.t.* **1.** to frustrate (a person, an attempt, a purpose); baffle; check. **2.** *Archaic.* to defeat; repulse; check. **—n. 3.** *Archaic.* a defeat; check; repulse. [ME *foile(n),* t. OF: m. *fuler* trample, full (cloth). See FULL[2]]

foil[2] (foil), *n.* **1.** a metallic substance formed into very thin sheets by rolling and hammering: *gold, tin,* or *lead foil.* **2.** the metallic backing applied to glass to form a mirror. **3.** a thin layer of metal placed under a gem in a closed setting, to improve its color or brilliancy. **4.** anything that serves to set off another thing distinctly or to advantage by contrast. **5.** *Archit.* an arc or a rounded space between cusps, as in the tracery of a window or in other ornamentation. **—v.t. 6.** to cover or back with foil. **7.** *Archit.* to ornament with foils. **8.** to set off by contrast. [ME *foile,* t. OF: m. *foil,* g. L *folium* leaf; akin to Gk. *phýllon*]

Architectural foils
A, Trefoil; B, Quatrefoil

foil[3] (foil) *n.* **1.** a blunt sword with a button at the point, for use in fencing. **2.** (*pl.*) the art of exercise or fencing with such swords. [orig. uncert.]

foils·man (foilz′mən), *n.*, *pl.* **-men.** one who is expert at fencing with foils.

foin (foin), *Obs.* or *Archaic.* **—n 1.** a thrust with a weapon. **—v.i. 2.** to thrust with a weapon; lunge. [appar. t. OF: m. *foine* fish spear, g. L *fuscina*]

foi·son (foi′zən), *n. Archaic.* **1.** abundance; plenty. **2.** abundant harvest. [ME, t. OF, ult. der. L *fūsio* a pouring out]

foist (foist), *v.t.* **1.** to palm off or impose fraudulently or unwarrantably (fol. by *on* or *upon*): *to foist inferior goods on a customer.* **2.** to bring or put surreptitiously or fraudulently (fol. by *in* or *into*). [prob. t. D: m. *vuisten* to take in hand]

Fo·kine (Fr. fô kēn′; Russ. fô′kĭn), *n.* **Michel** (mē-shĕl′), 1880–1942, U.S. choreographer, born in Russia.

Fok·ker (fŏk′ər), *n.* **1.** an airplane manufactured by, or according to the designs of, A. H. G. Fokker. **2.** trademark for such craft. **3. Anthony Herman Gerard** (än tō′nē hĕr′män gā′rärt), 1890–1939, Dutch airplane designer and builder.

fol., 1. folio. **2.** following. **3.** followed.

fold[1] (fōld), *v.t.* **1.** to double or bend (cloth, paper, etc.) over upon itself. **2.** to bring into a compact form, or shut, by bending and laying parts together (often fol. by *up*): *to fold up a map.* **3.** to bring together (the arms, hands, legs, etc.) with one around or within another: *to fold one's arms on one's chest.* **4.** to bend or wind (fol. by *about, round,* etc.): *to fold one's arms about a person's neck.* **5.** to bring (the wings) close to the body, as a bird on alighting; wrap: *to fold something in paper.* **7.** to clasp or embrace: *to fold someone in one's arms.* **8.** *Cookery.* to mix (*in*), as beaten egg whites added to a batter or the like, by gently turning one part over another with a spoon, etc. **9.** *Poetic.* to be disposed about, surround, or cover. **—v.i. 10.** to be folded or be capable of folding: *the doors fold back.* **11. fold up, a.** to collapse. **b.** to fail in business. **—n. 12.** a part that is folded; pleat; layer: *to wrap something in folds of cloth.* **13.** a hollow made by folding: *to carry something in the fold of one's dress.* **14.** a hollow place in undulating ground: *a fold of the hills or mountains.* **15.** *Geol.* a portion of strata which is folded or bent (as an anticline or syncline), or which connects two horizontal or parallel portions of strata of different levels (as a monocline). **16.** a coil of a serpent, string, etc. **17.** act of folding or doubling over. [ME *folde(n),* d. OE *faldan,* r. OE *fealdan,* c. G *falten*]

fold[2] (fōld), *n.* **1.** an enclosure for domestic animals, esp. sheep. **2.** the sheep contained in it. **3.** a flock of sheep. **4.** the church, or a particular church. **—v.t. 5.** to confine (sheep, etc.) in a fold. [ME *folde,* OE *fald, falod,* c. LG *falt* enclosure, yard]

-fold, a suffix attached to numerals and other quantitative words or stems to denote multiplication by or division into a certain number, as in *twofold, manifold.* [ME; d. OE *-fald,* r. OE *-feald,* c. G *-falt;* akin to Gk. *-paltos,* as in *dípaltos* double]

fold·boat (fōld′bōt′), *n.* faltboat.

fold·er (fōl′dər), *n.* **1.** one who or that which folds. **2.** a folded printed sheet, as a circular or a timetable. **3.** an outer cover, usually a folded sheet of light cardboard, for papers.

fol·de·rol (fŏl′də rŏl′), *n.* falderal.

folding doors, a set of doors hinged together to fold flat against one another when opened.

fo·li·a (fō′lĭ ə), *n.* pl. of **folium.**

fo·li·a·ceous (fō′lĭ ā′shəs), *adj.* **1.** of the nature of a leaf; leaflike. **2.** bearing leaves or leaflike parts. **3.** pertaining to or consisting of leaves. **4.** consisting of leaflike plates or laminae; foliated. [t. L: m. *foliāceus* leafy]

fo·li·age (fō′lĭ ĭj), *n.* **1.** the leaves of a plant, collectively; leafage. **2.** leaves in general. **3.** the representation of leaves, flowers, and branches in architectural ornament, etc. [t. F: alter. (to conform to L *folium*) of *feuillage,* der. *feuille,* g. L *folium* leaf] **—fo′li·aged,** *adj.*

fo·li·ar (fō′lĭ ər), *adj.* of, pertaining to, or having the nature of a leaf or leaves.

fo·li·ate (*adj.* fō′lĭ ĭt, -āt′; *v.* fō′lĭ āt′), *adj., v.,* **-ated, -ating. —adj. 1.** having or covered with leaves. **2.** leaflike. **—v.i. 3.** to put forth leaves. **4.** to split into thin leaflike layers or laminae. **—v.t. 5.** to shape like a leaf or leaves. **6.** to decorate with foils or foliage. **7.** to form into thin sheets. **8.** to spread over with a thin metallic backing. **9.** to number leaves (not pages) of (a book). [t. L: m. s. *foliātus* leafy]

fo·li·at·ed (fō′lĭ ā′tĭd), *adj.* **1.** shaped like a leaf or leaves. **2.** *Crystall.* consisting of thin and separable laminae.

fo·li·a·tion (fō′lĭ ā′shən), *n.* **1.** act of foliating or putting forth leaves. **2.** state of being in leaf. **3.** *Bot.* the arrangement of leaves within the bud. **4.** leaves or foliage. **5.** the consecutive numbering of the leaves (not pages) of a book or manuscript. **6.** the total number of such leaves. **7.** *Geol.* the splitting up or the arrangement of certain rocks, or certain kinds of rocks, in leaflike layers. **8.** ornamentation with foliage, or an arrangement of foliage. **9.** *Archit.* ornamentation with foils, or tracery so formed. **10.** formation into thin sheets. **11.** the application of foil to glass.

fo·li·a·ture (fō′lĭ ə chər), *n.* a cluster of leaves; foliage.

fo·lic acid (fō′lĭk), *Biochem.* a synthetic form of one of the B complex of vitamins, said to be especially effective in curing anemia. [f. L FOL(IUM) leaf + -IC]

fo·li·o (fō′lĭ ō′), *n., pl.* **-lios,** *adj., v.,* **-lioed, -lioing. —n. 1.** a sheet of paper folded once to make two leaves (four pages) of a book. **2.** a volume having pages of the largest size, esp. one more than 30 cm. in height. **3.** a leaf of a manuscript or book numbered only on the front side. **4.** *Print.* the page number of a book. **5.** *Bookkeeping.* a page of an account book or a left-hand page and a right-hand page facing each other and having the same serial number. **6.** *Law.* a certain number of words (in the U.S. generally 100) taken as a unit for computing the length of a document. **—adj. 7.** pertaining to or having the format of a folio: *a folio volume.* **—v.t. 8.** to number the leaves of (a book) on one side only. **9.** *Law.* to mark each folio in (a pleading, etc.) with the proper number. [t. L, abl. of *folium* leaf]

fo·li·o·late (fō′lĭ ə lāt′, fō lī′ə lĭt, -lāt′), *adj. Bot.* pertaining to or consisting of leaflets (often used in compounds, as *bifoliolate, trifoliolate,* etc.). [t. NL: m.s. *foliolātus,* der. *foliolum* a leaflet, dim. of L *folium* leaf]

fo·li·ose (fō′lĭ ōs′), *adj. Bot.* leafy. Also, **fo·li·ous** (fō′lĭ əs). [t. L: m.s. *foliōsus*]

-folious, *Bot.* an adjective suffix meaning "leafy." [t. L: m.s. *foliōsus*]

fo·li·um (fō′lĭ əm), *n., pl.* **-lia** (-lĭ ə). **1.** a thin leaflike stratum or layer; a lamella. **2.** *Geom.* a loop; part of a curve terminated at both ends by the same node. [t. L: leaf. See FOIL[2]]

folk (fōk), *n., pl.* **folk, folks,** *adj.* **—n. 1.** (*often pl.*) people in general. **2.** (*usually pl.*) people of a specified class or group: *poor folks.* **3.** (*pl.*) *Colloq.* the persons of one's own family; one's relatives. **4.** *Archaic.* a people or tribe. **—adj. 5.** originating among the common people. [ME; OE *folc,* c. D and G *volk,* Sw. and Dan. *folk* people]

folk dance, 1. a dance which originated among, and has been transmitted through, the common people. **2.** a piece of music for such a dance.

Folke·stone (fōk′stən), *n.* a seaport in SE England, on the Strait of Dover. 37,560 (est. 1946).

Fol·ke·ting (fŏl′kə tĭng′), *n.* the lower house of the Danish parliament or Rigsdag.

folk etymology, a type of pseudolearned modification of linguistic forms according to a falsely assumed etymology, as in *Welsh rarebit* from *Welsh rabbit.*

folk·lore (fōk′lōr′), *n.* **1.** the lore of the common people; the traditional beliefs, legends, customs, etc., of a people. **2.** the study of such lore. **—folk′lor·ist,** *n.* **—folk′lor·is′tic,** *adj.*

folk·moot (fōk′mōōt′), *n.* (formerly, in England) a general assembly of the people of a shire, town, etc. Also, **folk·mote** (fōk′mōt′), **folk′mot′.** [ME; OE *folc-mōt* folk meeting]

folk music, music, usually of simple character, originating and handed down among the common people.

folk·right (fōk′rīt′), *n. Early Eng. Hist.* the right of the people under the customary law.

folk·say (fōk′sā′), *n.* informal verbal expressions, such as proverbs and exclamations, among a relatively unsophisticated group of people, as *Was I ever,* instead of *I certainly was.*

folk song, 1. a song, usually of simple or artless character, originating and handed down among the common people. **2.** a song in imitation of this type.

folk·sy (fōk/sĭ), *adj.* sociable.

folk tale, a tale or legend originating and handed down among the common people. Also, **folk story.**

folk·ways (fōk/wāz/), *n.pl. Sociol.* the ways of living and acting in a human group, built up without conscious design but serving as compelling guides of conduct.

foll., following.

fol·li·cle (fŏl/ə kəl), *n.* **1.** *Bot.* a dry one-celled seed vessel consisting of a single carpel, and dehiscent only by the ventral suture, as the fruit of larkspur. **2.** *Anat.* a small cavity, sac, or gland. [t. L: m.s. *folliculus*, dim. of *follis* bellows, bag]

fol·lic·u·lar (fə lĭk/yə lər), *adj.* **1.** pertaining to, consisting of, or resembling a follicle or follicles; provided with follicles. **2.** *Pathol.* affecting or originating in a follicle or follicles. Also, **fol·lic·u·late** (fə lĭk/yə lāt/), **fol·lic/u·lat/ed.**

fol·lic·u·lin (fə lĭk/yə lĭn), *n.* **1.** estrone. **2.** (*cap.*) a trademark for it.

Follicle of larkspur

fol·low (fŏl/ō), *v.t.* **1.** to come after in natural sequence, order of time, etc.; succeed. **2.** to go or come after; move behind in the same direction: *go on ahead and I'll follow you.* **3.** to accept as a guide or leader; accept the authority or example of, or adhere to, as a person. **4.** to conform to, comply with, or act in accordance with: *to follow a person's advice.* **5.** to move forward along (a path, etc.). **6.** to come after as a result or consequence; result from: *it follows from this that he must be innocent.* **7.** to go after or along with (a person, etc.) as a companion. **8.** to go in pursuit of: *to follow an enemy.* **9.** to endeavor to obtain or to attain to. **10.** to engage in or be concerned with as a pursuit: *to follow the sea.* **11.** to watch the movements, progress, or course of. **12.** to keep up with and understand (an argument, etc.): *do you follow me?* **13. follow suit, a.** *Cards.* to play a card of the same suit as that first played. **b.** to follow the example of another. **14. follow up, a.** to pursue closely. **b.** to pursue to a conclusion. **c.** to prosecute with energy. **d.** to increase the effect of by further action. —*v.i.* **15.** to come next after something else in natural sequence, order of time, etc. **16.** to happen or occur after something else; come next as an event. **17.** to attend. **18.** to go or come after a person or thing in motion: *go on ahead and I'll follow.* **19.** to result as an effect; occur as a consequence. —*n.* **20.** act of following. **21.** *Billiards.* a stroke causing the player's ball to roll after the ball struck by it. [ME *folwe(n)*, OE *folgian*, c. G *folgen*] —**fol/low·a·ble,** *adj.*

—**Syn. 8.** pursue, chase; trail, track, trace. **15.** FOLLOW, ENSUE, RESULT, SUCCEED imply coming after something else, in a natural sequence. FOLLOW is the general word: *we must wait to see what follows, a detailed account follows.* ENSUE implies a logical sequence, what might be expected normally to come after a given act, cause, etc., and indicates some duration: *when the power lines were cut, a paralysis of transportation ensued.* RESULT emphasizes the connection between a cause or event and its effect, consequence, or outcome: *the accident resulted in injuries to those involved.* SUCCEED implies coming after in time, particularly coming into a title, office, etc.: *a son often succeeds to his father's title.* —**Ant. 1.** precede. **19.** cause.

fol·low·er (fŏl/ō ər), *n.* **1.** one who or that which follows. **2.** one who follows another in regard to his ideas or belief; disciple or adherent. **3.** an attendant or servant. **4.** *Brit. Colloq.* a male admirer, esp. of a maidservant. **5.** *Mach.* a part of a machine that receives motion from, or follows the motion of, another part.

—**Syn. 2.** FOLLOWER, ADHERENT, PARTISAN refer to one who demonstrates allegiance to a person, a doctrine, a cause, and the like. FOLLOWER often has an implication of personal relationship or of slavish acquiescence. ADHERENT, a more formal word, has also implications of more active championship of a person or a point of view. PARTISAN, ordinarily meaning a person prejudiced and unreasoning in adherence to a party, during World War II took on the meaning of a member of certain groups in occupied countries of Europe, who carried on underground resistance to Fascists.

fol·low·ing (fŏl/ō ĭng), *n.* **1.** a body of followers, attendants, adherents, etc. **2. the following,** things, lines, pages, etc. that follow. —*adj.* **3.** that follows. **4.** that comes after or next in order or time: *the following day.* **5.** that is now to follow; now to be mentioned, described, related, or the like.

fol·low-through (fŏl/ō thrōō/), *n. Sports.* **1.** the completion of a motion, as in the stroke of a tennis racket. **2.** the portion of such a motion after the ball has been hit.

fol·low-up (fŏl/ō ŭp/), *n.* **1.** act of following up. **2.** a letter or circular sent to a person to increase the effectiveness of a previous one, as in advertising. —*adj.* **3.** (of business letters, etc.) sent to a prospective customer to obtain an additional order or offer.

fol·ly (fŏl/ĭ), *n.*, *pl.* **-lies. 1.** state or quality of being foolish; lack of understanding or sense. **2.** a foolish action, practice, idea, etc.; an absurdity. **3.** a costly but foolish undertaking, structure, etc. **4.** (*pl.*) a theatrical revue. **5.** *Obs.* wickedness; wantonness. [ME *folie*, t. OF, der. *fol* mad. See FOOL[1]]

Fol·som man (fōl/səm), a member of a hypothetical New World prehistoric people which may have inhabited North America during the most recent (Pleistocene) glacial epoch. [so named from Folsom, New Mexico, where implements were discovered in 1925]

fo·ment (fō mĕnt/), *v.t.* **1.** to promote the growth or development of; instigate or foster (discord, rebellion, etc.). **2.** to apply warm water or medicated liquid, cloths dipped in such liquid, or the like, to (the surface of the body). [t. LL: s. *fōmentāre*, der. L *fōmentum* a warm application] —**fo·ment/er,** *n.*

fo·men·ta·tion (fō/mĕn tā/shən), *n.* **1.** instigation; encouragement of discord, rebellion, etc. **2.** the application of warm liquid, etc., to the surface of the body. **3.** the liquid, etc., so applied.

fond[1] (fŏnd), *adj.* **1.** liking (fol. by *of*): *fond of children, fond of drink.* **2.** loving: *give someone a fond look.* **3.** foolishly tender; overaffectionate; doting: *a fond parent.* **4.** cherished with strong or unreasoning affection: *nourish fond hopes.* **5.** foolishly credulous or trusting. **6.** *Archaic or Dial.* foolish or silly. [ME *fonned*, pp. of *fonnen* be foolish; orig. uncert. Cf. FUN]

fond[2] (fŏnd), *n.* **1.** a background or groundwork, esp. of lace. **2.** *Obs.* fund; stock. [F. See FUND]

fon·dant (fŏn/dənt; *Fr.* fôn dän/), *n.* a thick, creamy sugar paste, the basis of many candies. [t. F, prop. ppr. of *fondre* melt]

Fond du Lac (fŏn/ də lăk/, jŏŏ lăk/), a city in E Wisconsin, on Lake Winnebago. 29,936 (1950).

fon·dle (fŏn/dəl), *v.*, **-dled, -dling.** —*v.t.* **1.** to handle or touch fondly; caress. **2.** *Obs.* to treat with fond indulgence. —*v.i.* **3.** to show fondness, as by manner, words, or caresses. [freq. of obs. *fond*, v.] —**fon/dler,** *n.*

fond·ly (fŏnd/lĭ), *adv.* **1.** in a fond manner; lovingly or affectionately. **2.** with complacent credulity.

fond·ness (fŏnd/nĭs), *n.* **1.** state or quality of being fond. **2.** affectionateness or tenderness. **3.** doting affection. **4.** complacent credulity. **5.** instinctive liking.

fon·due (fŏn/dōō, fŏn dōō/; *Fr.* fôn dy/), *n.* a baked dish composed of grated cheese melted with butter, eggs, etc. [t. F, fem. pp. of *fondre* melt]

font[1] (fŏnt), *n.* **1.** a receptacle, usually of stone, as in a baptistery or church, for the water used in baptism. **2.** a receptacle for holy water; stoup. **3.** the reservoir for oil in a lamp. **4.** *Archaic.* a fountain. [ME and OE, *t.* L: s. *fons* baptismal font, spring, fountain]

font[2] (fŏnt), *n. Print.* a complete assortment of type of one style and size. Also, *esp. Brit.*, **fount.** [t. F: m. *fonte*, der. *fondre* melt, cast. See FOUND[3]]

Baptismal font

Fon·taine·bleau (fŏn/tĭn blō/; *Fr.* fôn těn blō/), *n.* a town in N France, SE of Paris: site of a famous palace, long a favorite residence of French kings, and an extensive forest. 15,008 (1946).

Fontainebleau School, a group of painters, many of them Italian and Flemish, who worked on the decorations of the palace of Fontainebleau in the sixteenth century.

font·al (fŏn/tal), *adj.* **1.** pertaining to or issuing as from a fount or spring. **2.** pertaining to or being the source of something. **3.** of or pertaining to a font, as of baptism.

fon·ta·nel (fŏn/tə něl/), *n.* **1.** *Anat.* one of the spaces, closed by membrane, between the bones of the fetal or young skull. **2.** *Pathol. Obs.* an opening for the discharge of pus. Also, **fon/ta·nelle/.** [t. F: m. *fontanelle*, dim. of *fontaine* FOUNTAIN]

Fon·tanne (fŏn tăn/), *n.* **Lynn,** born 1887?, U.S. actress, born in England.

Foo·chow (fōō/chou/; *Chin.* -jō/), *n.* a seaport in SE China: the capital of Fukien province. 348,280 (est. 1938). Also, **Minhow.**

food (fōōd), *n.* **1.** what is eaten, or taken into the body, for nourishment. **2.** more or less solid nourishment (as opposed to *drink*). **3.** a particular kind of solid nourishment: *a breakfast food.* **4.** whatever supplies nourishment to organic bodies: *the food of plants.* **5.** anything serving as material for consumption or use. [ME *fode*, OE *fōda.* Cf. FEED, FODDER, FOSTER] —**food/less,** *adj.*

—**Syn. 1.** FOOD, FARE, PROVISIONS, RATION(s) refer to nutriment for any organism, whether of man, animal, or plant. FOOD is the general word: *breakfast foods have become very popular, many animals prefer grass as food.* FARE refers to the whole range of foods which may nourish person, animal, or plant: *an extensive bill of fare, the fare of some animals is limited in range.* PROVISIONS is applied to a store or stock of necessary things, esp. food, prepared beforehand: *provisions for a journey.* RATION implies an allotment or allowance of provisions: *a daily ration for each man of a company.* RATIONS often mean food in general: *to be on short rations.*

food chain, *Ecol.* a series of organisms interrelated in their feeding habits, the smallest being fed upon by a larger one, which in turn feeds a still larger one, etc.

food·stuff (fōōd/stŭf/), *n.* a substance or material suitable for food.

food web, *Ecol.* a series of organisms related by predator-prey activities; a series of interrelated food chains.

fool[1] (fōōl), *n.* **1.** one who lacks sense; a silly or stupid person. **2.** a professional jester, formerly kept by a person of rank for amusement. **3.** one who is made to appear a fool; one who has been imposed on by others: *to make a fool of someone.* **4.** a weak-minded or idiotic person. —*v.t.* **5.** to make a fool of; impose on; trick; deceive. **6.** to spend foolishly, as time or money (fol. by *away*). —*v.i.* **7.** to act like a fool; joke; play. **8.** to potter aimlessly; waste time: *to fool around with minor details.* **9.** to play or meddle foolishly (fol. by *with*): *to fool with a loaded gun.* **10.** to jest; make believe: *I was only fooling.* [ME *fol*, t. OF (n. and adj.), ? g. L *follis* bellows, LL bag] —**Syn. 1.** simpleton, dolt, dunce, blockhead, numskull, ignoramus, dunderhead, ninny, nincompoop, booby, saphead, sap. **2.** buffoon, droll. **5.** delude, hoodwink, trick, cheat, gull, hoax, cozen. **8.** play, trifle, toy, dally, idle, dawdle, loiter, tarry.

fool² (fool), *n.* *Brit.* *Cookery.* a dish made of fruit scalded or stewed, crushed, and mixed with cream, etc.: *gooseberry fool.* [prob. special use of FOOL¹]

fool·er·y (foo′lər ĭ), *n.*, *pl.* **-er·ies.** **1.** foolish action or conduct. **2.** a foolish action, performance, or thing.

fool·har·dy (fool′här′dĭ), *adj.*, **-dier, -diest.** bold without judgment; foolishly rash or venturesome. —**fool′har′di·ly,** *adv.* —**fool′har′di·ness,** *n.*

fool hen, *U.S.* a grouse which is confiding, hence easily killed, esp. the blue grouse, *Dendragapus obscurus,* and spruce grouse, *Canachites canadensis.*

fool·ish (foo′lĭsh), *adj.* **1.** silly; without sense: *a foolish person.* **2.** resulting from or evidencing folly; ill-considered; unwise: *a foolish action, speech, etc.* **3.** *Obs.* or *Archaic.* trifling, insignificant, or paltry. —**fool′ish·ly,** *adv.* —**fool′ish·ness,** *n.*
—**Syn. 1, 2.** FOOLISH, FATUOUS, SILLY, STUPID imply weakness of intellect and lack of judgment. FOOLISH implies lack of common sense or good judgment or, sometimes, weakness of mind: *a foolish decision, the child seems foolish.* FATUOUS implies being foolish, dull, and vacant in mind, but complacent and highly self-satisfied: *fatuous and self-important, fatuous answers.* SILLY denotes extreme and conspicuous foolishness; it may also refer to pointlessness of jokes, remarks, etc.: *silly and senseless behavior, a perfectly silly statement.* STUPID implies natural slowness or dullness of intellect, or, sometimes, a benumbed or dazed state of mind; it is also used to mean foolish or silly: *well-meaning but stupid, rendered stupid by a blow, it is stupid to do such a thing.* —**Ant. 1.** wise, intelligent.

fool·proof (fool′proof′), *adj.* *Colloq.* **1.** involving no risk or harm, even when tampered with. **2.** never-failing: *a foolproof method.*

fools·cap (foolz′kăp′), *n.* **1.** writing paper, usually folded, varying in size from 12 x 15 to 12½ x 16 inches. **2.** an English printing paper size, 13½ x 17 inches (so called from its former watermark, the outline of a fool's cap). **3.** fool's cap.

fool's cap, 1. a kind of cap or hood, usually hung with bells, formerly worn by professional jesters. **2.** a conical paper cap sometimes worn by dunces at school as punishment.

fool's errand, an absurd or useless errand.

fool's gold, iron pyrites, sometimes mistaken for gold.

fool's paradise, state of illusory happiness; enjoyment based on false beliefs or hopes.

fool's-par·sley (foolz′pärs′lĭ), *n.* a fetid, poisonous umbelliferous herb, *Aethusa Cynapium,* resembling parsley.

foot (foot), *n.*, *pl.* **feet** or (often for def. 17) **foots**; *v.* —*n.* **1.** (in vertebrates) the terminal part of the leg, below the ankle joint, on which the body stands and moves. **2.** (in invertebrates) any part similar in position or function. **3.** such a part considered as the organ of locomotion. **4.** a unit of length derived from the length of the human foot. In English-speaking countries it is divided into 12 inches and equal to 30.48 centimeters. **5.** infantry. **6.** walking or running motion. **7.** step; pace. **8.** any thing or part resembling a foot, as in function. **9.** the part of a stocking, etc., covering the foot. **10.** the lowest part, or bottom, as of a hill, ladder, page, etc. **11.** the part of anything opposite the top or head. **12.** the end of a bed, grave, etc., toward which the feet are placed. **13.** *Print.* the part of the type body which forms the sides of the groove, at the base. **14.** the last, as of a series. **15.** that which is written at the bottom, as the total of an account. **16.** *Pros.* a group of syllables constituting a metrical unit of a verse. **17.** (often in *pl.* **foots**) sediment or dregs. **18.** Some special noun phrases are:
have one foot in the grave, to be near death.
on foot, 1. on one's feet, rather than riding or sitting. **2.** in motion; astir. **3.** in active existence or operation.
put one's best foot forward, 1. to make as good an impression as possible. **2.** to do one's very best. **3.** to walk as fast as possible.
put one's foot down, to take a firm stand.
put one's foot in it, to make an embarrassing blunder.
—*v.i.* **19.** to walk; go on foot (often fol. by indefinite *it*). **20.** to move the feet to measure or music, or dance (often fol. by indefinite *it*). **21.** to total, as an account (often fol. by *up*). **22.** (esp. of vessels) to move. —*v.t.* **23.** to set foot on; walk or dance on. **24.** to traverse on foot. **25.** to make or attach a foot to: *to foot a stocking.* **26.** *Colloq.* and *Dial.* to add, as a column of figures, and set the sum at the foot (fol. by *up*). **27.** *Colloq.* to pay or settle, as a bill. **28.** to seize with talons, as a hawk. **29.** to establish. **30.** *Obs.* to kick. [ME; OE *fōt,* c. G *fuss;* akin to L *pēs,* Gk. *poús*]

foot·age (foot′ĭj), *n.* **1.** length or extent in feet: *the footage of lumber, motion-picture film, etc.* **2.** *Mining.* **a.** payment by the running foot of work done. **b.** amount so paid.

foot-and-mouth disease (foot′ən mouth′), *Vet. Sci.* a contagious virus disease of cattle and other cloven-footed animals, characterized by a vesicular eruption about the hoofs and mouth. The disease very rarely affects man.

foot·ball (foot′bôl′), *n.* **1.** a game played with a large, inflated leather ball on a field at either end of which there is a goal post. Each team, consisting of eleven players, tries to score touchdowns by running or passing the ball to its opponents' goal line and field goals by kicking the ball over the crossbars of the opponents' goal post. **2.** the ball itself. **3.** *Brit.* Rugby football. **4.** *Brit.* soccer; association football. **5.** any thing or person treated roughly, casually, etc.

foot·board (foot′bôrd′), *n.* **1.** a board or small platform on which to support the foot or feet. **2.** an upright piece across the foot of a bedstead. **3.** a treadle.

foot·boy (foot′boi′), *n.* a boy in livery employed as a servant; page; lackey.

foot brake, a brake which is applied by pressure on a foot pedal.

foot·bridge (foot′brĭj′), *n.* a bridge intended for pedestrians only.

foot·can·dle (foot′kăn′dəl), *n.* *Photom.* a unit of illumination equivalent to that produced by a standard candle at the distance of one foot.

foot·cloth (foot′klôth′, -klŏth′), *n.* **1.** a carpet or rug. **2.** *Obs.* a richly ornamented caparison for a horse, hanging down to the ground.

foot·ed (foot′ĭd), *adj.* provided with a foot or feet: *a four-footed animal.*

foot·er (foot′ər), *n.* **1.** one who goes on foot; a walker. **2.** (with a numeral prefixed) a person or thing of the height or length in feet indicated: *a six-footer.*

foot·fall (foot′fôl′), *n.* **1.** a footstep. **2.** the sound of footsteps.

foot·gear (foot′gîr′), *n.* covering for the feet, as shoes, boots, etc.

foot·hill (foot′hĭl′), *n.* a minor elevation at the base of a mountain or mountain range.

foot·hold (foot′hōld′), *n.* **1.** a hold or support for the feet; a place where one may stand or tread securely. **2.** firm footing; secure position.

foot·ing (foot′ĭng), *n.* **1.** secure position; foothold. **2.** the basis or foundation on which anything is established. **3.** place or support for the feet; surface to stand on. **4.** act of one that foots, or moves on foot, as in walking or dancing. **5.** a firm placing or stable position of the feet. **6.** the part of the foundation of wall, column, etc. that is in direct contact with the ground. **7.** position or status assigned to a person, etc., in estimation or treatment. **8.** mutual standing; reciprocal relation: *to be on a friendly footing with someone.* **9.** entrance into a new position or relationship. **10.** a fee demanded from a person upon his entrance into a trade, society, etc. **11.** act of putting a foot to anything, as a stocking. **12.** that which is added as a foot. **13.** act of adding up a column of figures. **14.** the amount of such a column as footed up.

foot·le (foot′əl), *v.*, **-led, -ling,** *n.* —*v.i.* **1.** to talk or act in a silly way. —*n.* **2.** nonsense; silliness. [orig. obscure. Cf. FOOTY]

foot·less (foot′lĭs), *adj.* **1.** without a foot or feet. **2.** unsupported or unsubstantial. **3.** *Colloq.* awkward, helpless, or inefficient.

foot·lights (foot′līts′), *n.pl.* **1.** *Theat.* a row of lights at the front of the stage, nearly on a level with the feet of the performers. **2.** the stage; acting profession.

foot·ling (foot′lĭng), *adj.* *Colloq.* foolish; silly; trifling. [f. FOOTLE, v. + -ING²]

foot-loose (foot′loos′), *adj.* free to go or travel about; not confined by responsibilities, etc.

foot·man (foot′mən), *n.*, *pl.* **-men.** **1.** a male servant in livery who attends the door or the carriage, waits at table, etc. **2.** a metal stand before a fire, to keep something hot.

foot·mark (foot′märk′), *n.* a footprint.

foot·note (foot′nōt′), *n.* a note or comment at the foot of a page, referring to a specific part of the text on the page.

foot·pace (foot′pās′), *n.* **1.** a walking pace. **2.** a raised portion of a floor. **3.** a landing or resting place at the end of a short flight of steps.

foot·pad (foot′păd′), *n.* a highwayman who robs on foot.

foot·path (foot′păth′, -päth′), *n.* **1.** a path for pedestrians only. **2.** *Brit.* a sidewalk.

foot-pound (foot′pound′), *n.* *Mech.* a unit of energy or work, the equivalent to that produced by a force of one pound moving through a distance of one foot.

foot-pound·al (foot′poun′dəl), *n.* *Mech.* a unit of energy equivalent to that produced by a force of one poundal moving through a distance of one foot.

foot-pound-sec·ond system (foot′pound′sĕk′-ənd), a system of units employed in science, based on the foot, pound, and second as the fundamental units of length, mass, and time.

foot·print (foot′prĭnt′), *n.* a mark left by the foot.

foot·rest (foot′rĕst′), *n.* a short bench or stool used to support one's feet.

foot·rope (foot′rōp′), *n.* *Naut.* **1.** the portion of the boltrope to which the lower edge of a sail is sewn. **2.** a

GARDEN FLOWERS

Zinnia

Hardy Aster

Columbine

Campanula

Regal Lily

Veronica

Darwin and
Cottage Tulips

Phlox

Gladiolus

Peony

Delphinium

Hybrid
Tea Rose

China Aster

Dahlia

Chrysanthemum

Snapdragon

Japanese
Iris

Bearded Iris

Pansy

Trollius

A.H.WINKLER

AMERICAN WILDFLOWERS

Wild Iris
American Senna
Lotus
Moccasin Flower
Lupine
Rose Mallow
Wild Geranium
Greater Bindweed
Fringed Gentian
Jacob's Ladder
Tuberous Water Lily
Pitcher Plant
Sneezeweed
Black-eyed Susan
Bee Balm
Yellow Pond Lily
Red Trillium
Meadow Lily
Butterfly Weed
Swamp Milkweed

H.H. WINKLER

rope extended under a yard, for the men to stand on while reefing or furling.

foot rot, *Vet. Sci.* an infection of the feet of sheep, causing inflammatory changes of the toes and lameness.

foot soldier, an infantryman.

foot·sore (foŏt'sōr'), *adj.* having sore or tender feet, as from much walking.

foot·stalk (foŏt'stôk'), *n. Bot., Zool.* a pedicel; peduncle.

foot·stall (foŏt'stôl'), *n.* **1.** the stirrup of a woman's sidesaddle. **2** *Archit.* the plinth or base of a pillar.

foot·step (foŏt'stĕp'), *n.* **1.** a step or tread of the foot, or the sound produced by it; footfall. **2.** the distance traversed by the foot in stepping; a pace. **3.** a footprint. **4.** follow in one's footsteps, to succeed or imitate another. **5.** a step by which to ascend or descend.

foot·stone (foŏt'stōn'), *n.* a stone placed at the foot of a grave.

foot·stool (foŏt'stōol'), *n.* a low stool upon which to rest one's feet.

foot-ton (foŏt'tŭn'), *n. Mech.* a unit of work equivalent to the energy expended in raising a ton of 2,240 pounds one foot.

foot·wall (foŏt'wôl'), *n. Mining.* the top of the rock stratum underlying a vein or bed of ore.

foot warmer, any of various contrivances for keeping the feet warm.

foot·way (foŏt'wā'), *n.* **1.** a way or path for pedestrians only. **2.** *Brit.* a sidewalk.

foot·wear (foŏt'wâr'), *n.* articles for wearing on the feet, esp. shoes, slippers, gaiters, etc.

foot·work (foŏt'wûrk'), *n.* the use of the feet, as in tennis, boxing, etc.

foot·worn (foŏt'wôrn'), *adj.* **1.** worn by the feet: *a footworn pavement.* **2.** footsore.

foot·y (foō'tĭ), *adj.* **-ti·er, -ti·est.** *Dial.* or *Colloq.* poor; worthless; paltry. [der. FOOT (def. 17)]

foo·zle (foō'zəl), *v.,* **-zled, -zling,** *n.* —*v.t., v.i.* **1.** to bungle; play clumsily: *to foozle a stroke in golf.* —*n.* **2.** act of foozling, esp. a bad stroke in golf. [cf. d. G *fuseln* work badly]

fop (fŏp), *n.* a man who is excessively concerned about his manners and appearance. [orig. uncert. Cf. FOP²]

fop·per·y (fŏp'ər·ĭ), *n., pl.* **-per·ies. 1.** the manners, actions, dress, etc., of a fop. **2.** something foppish.

fop·pish (fŏp'ĭsh), *adj.* resembling or befitting a fop. —**fop'pish·ly,** *adv.* —**fop'pish·ness,** *n.*

for (fôr; *unstressed* fər), *prep.* **1.** with the object or purpose of: *to go for a walk.* **2.** intended to belong to, suit the purposes or needs of, or be used in connection with: *a book for children, a box for gloves.* **3.** in order to obtain: *a suit for damages.* **4.** with inclination or tendency toward: *to long for a thing, to have an eye for beauty.* **5.** in consideration of, or in return for: *three for a dollar, to be thanked for one's efforts.* **6.** appropriate or adapted to: *a subject for speculation.* **7.** with regard or respect to: *pressed for time, too warm for April.* **8.** during the continuance of: *for a long time.* **9.** in favor of, or on the side of: *to stand for honest government.* **10.** in place of, or instead of: *a substitute for butter.* **11.** in the interest of: *to act for a client.* **12.** as an offset to: *blow for blow.* **13.** in honor of: *to give a dinner for a person.* **14.** with the purpose of reaching: *to start for London.* **15.** conducive to: *for the advantage of everybody.* **16.** in order to save: *to flee for one's life.* **17.** in order to become: *to go for a soldier.* **18.** in assignment or attribution to: *an engagement for this evening, it is for you to decide.* **19.** to allow of; to require: *too many for separate mention.* **20.** such as results in: *his reason for going.* **21.** as affecting the interests or circumstances of: *bad for one's health.* **22.** in proportion or with reference to: *tall for his age.* **23.** in the character of, or as being: *to know a thing for a fact.* **24.** by reason of, or because of: *to shout for joy, famed for its beauty.* **25.** in spite of: *for all that.* **26.** to the extent or amount of: *to walk for a mile.* **27.** (sometimes used to govern a noun or pronoun followed by an infinitive, in a construction equivalent to a clause with *that* and the auxiliary *should,* etc.): *it is time for him to go,* or *that he should go.* —*conj.* **28.** seeing that; since. **29.** because. [ME and OE; c. OS *for;* akin to *fore,* adv. and prep.] —**Syn. 29.** See **because.**

for-, a prefix meaning "away," "off," "to the uttermost," "extremely," "wrongly," or imparting a negative or privative force, occurring in words of Old or Middle English origin, many of which are now obsolete or archaic, as in *forswear, forbid.* [ME and OE. Cf. G *ver-,* Gk. *peri-,* L *per-*]

for., 1. foreign. **2.** forestry.

F.O.R., free on rails. Also, **f.o.r.**

for·age (fôr'ĭj, fŏr'-), *n., v.,* **-aged, -aging.** —*n.* **1.** food for horses and cattle; fodder; provender. **2.** the seeking or obtaining such food. **3.** act of searching for provisions of any kind. **4.** a raid. —*v.i.* **5.** to wander in search of supplies. **6.** to hunt or search about. **7.** to make a raid. —*v.t.* **8.** to collect forage from; strip of supplies; plunder. **9.** to supply with forage. **10.** to obtain by foraging. [ME, n. F: m. *fourrage,* der. OF *fuerre* fodder, t. Gmc. (see FODDER)] —**for'ag·er,** *n.* —**Syn. 1.** See **feed.**

forage cap, *Brit.* a small, low, undress military cap.

For·a·ker (fôr'ə·kər, fŏr'-), *n.* **Mount,** a peak in central Alaska, near Mt. McKinley. ab. 17,000 ft.

fo·ra·men (fō·rā'mən), *n., pl.* **-ram·i·na** (-răm'ə·nə). an opening, orifice, or short passage, as in a bone or in the integument of the ovule of a plant. [t. L: hole]

foramen mag·num (măg'nəm), *Latin.* the great hole in the occipital bone forming the passage from the cranial cavity to the spinal canal. [L: lit., great hole]

fo·ram·i·nate (fō·răm'ə·nĭt, -nāt'), *adj. Rare.* full of holes or foramina.

fo·ram·i·fer (fôr'ə·mĭn'ə·fər, fôr'-), *n.* any of the *Foraminifera,* an extensive order of small, mostly marine rhizopods commonly having a calcareous shell perforated in many species by small holes or pores. [f. s. L *forāmen* hole + -(I)FER] —**fo·ram·i·nif·er·al** (fō·răm'ə·nĭf'ər·əl), **fo·ram'i·nif'er·ous,** *adj.*

for·as·much (fôr'əz·mŭch'), *conj.* in view of the fact that; seeing that; since (fol. by *as*).

for·ay (fôr'ā, fŏr'ā), *n.* **1.** a raid for the purpose of taking plunder. —*v.i.* **2.** to make a raid; forage; pillage. —*v.t.* **3.** to ravage in search of plunder. [ME *forrei(en)*, back formation from *forreier* FORAYER]

for·ay·er (fôr'ā·ər, fŏr'-), *n.* a marauder. [ME *forreier*, t. OF: m. *forrier* forager]

forb (fôrb), *n.* any herb that is not a grass or grasslike.

for·bade (fər·băd'), *v.* pt. of **forbid.** Also, **for·bad'.**

for·bear¹ (fôr·bâr'), *v.,* **-bore, -borne, -bearing.** —*v.t.* **1.** to refrain from; desist from; cease. **2.** to refrain from using, etc.; keep back; withhold. **3.** *Archaic.* to endure. —*v.i.* **4.** to refrain; hold back. **5.** to be patient; show forbearance. [ME *forbere(n)*, OE *forberan.* See FOR-, BEAR¹] —**for·bear'er,** *n.* —**for·bear'ing·ly,** *adv.*

for·bear² (fôr'bâr'), *n.* forebear.

for·bear·ance (fôr·bâr'əns), *n.* **1.** act of forbearing; a refraining from something. **2.** forbearing conduct or quality; patient endurance; lenity. **3.** an abstaining from the enforcement of a right. **4.** a creditor's giving of indulgence after the day originally fixed for payment.

Forbes-Rob·ert·son (fôrbz'rŏb'ərt·sən), *n.* **Sir Johnston,** 1853–1937, British actor and theater manager.

for·bid (fər·bĭd'), *v.t.,* **-bade** or **-bad, -bidden** or **-bid, -bidding. 1.** to command (a person, etc.) not to do, have, use, etc., something, or not to enter some place. **2.** to put an interdiction against (something); prohibit **3.** to hinder or prevent; make impossible. **4.** to exclude; repel. [ME *forbede(n)*, OE *forbēodan*] —**for·bid'der,** *n.*

—**Syn. 1.** FORBID, INHIBIT, PROHIBIT, TABOO indicate a command to refrain from some action. FORBID, a common and familiar word, usually denotes a direct or personal command of this sort: *I forbid you to go, to forbid children to play in the park.* INHIBIT, besides indicating ecclesiastical prohibition, implies a checking or hindering of impulses by the mind: *to inhibit one's desires.* PROHIBIT, a formal or legal word, means usually to forbid by official edict, enactment, or the like: *to prohibit the sale of liquor.* TABOO, primarily associated with primitive superstition, means to prohibit by common disapproval and by social custom: *to taboo a subject in polite conversation.* —**Ant. 1.** permit.

for·bid·dance (fər·bĭd'əns), *n. Rare.* **1.** act of forbidding. **2.** state of being forbidden.

for·bid·den (fər·bĭd'ən), *v.* **1.** pp. of **forbid.** —*adj.* **2.** prohibited.

forbidden fruit, unlawful pleasure.

for·bid·ding (fər·bĭd'ĭng), *adj.* **1.** causing dislike or fear: *a forbidding countenance.* **2.** repellent; dangerous-looking: *forbidding cliffs, clouds, etc.* —**for·bid'ding·ly,** *adv.* —**for·bid'ding·ness,** *n.*

for·bore (fôr·bōr'), *v.* pt. of **forbear¹.**

for·borne (fôr·bōrn'), *v.* pp. of **forbear¹.**

for·by (fôr·bī'), *prep., adv. Now Chiefly Scot. and Dial.* **1.** close by; near. **2.** besides. Also, **for·bye'.** [f. FOR- + BY]

force (fōrs), *n., v.,* **forced, forcing.** —*n.* **1.** strength; impetus; intensity of effect. **2.** might, as of a ruler or realm; strength for war. **3.** strength or power exerted upon an object; physical coercion; violence: *to use force in order to do something, to use force on a person.* **4.** *Law.* violence offered to persons or things, as the use of force in breaking into a house. **5.** power to influence, affect, or control; power to convince: *the force of an argument, the force of circumstances.* **6.** mental or moral strength; power of effective action or of overcoming resistance. **7.** *(often pl.)* a large body of armed men; an army. **8.** any body of persons combined for joint action: *a police force, an office force.* **9.** operation: *a law now in force.* **10.** *Physics.* **a.** an influence which produces or tends to produce motion or change of motion. **b.** the intensity of such an influence. **11.** any influence or agency analogous to physical force: *social forces.* **12.** binding power, as of an agreement. **13.** value; significance; meaning. —*v.t.* **14.** to compel; constrain, or oblige (oneself or someone) to do something: *force someone to confess.* **15.** to drive or propel against resistance. **16.** to bring about or effect by force; bring about of necessity or as a necessary result: *force a passage, to force a smile, etc.* **17.** to put or impose (something) forcibly on or upon a person: *force something on someone's attention.* **18.** to compel by force; overcome the resistance of. **19.** to obtain or draw forth by or as by force; extort: *force a confession.* **20.** to overpower; enter or take by force. **21.** to break open (a door, lock, etc.). **22.** to cause plants, fruits, etc.) to grow or mature at an increased rate by artificial means. **23.** to press, urge, or exert to violent effort or to the utmost. **24.** to use force upon.

25. *Baseball.* **a.** to retire (a base runner) who has had to leave his base to make room for an advancing runner, or for a batter who has not been given a base on balls. **b.** (of a pitcher) to allow a score by walking (a batter) with the bases full which automatically brings home the runner on third. **26.** *Cards.* **a.** to compel (a player) to trump by leading a suit of which he has no cards. **b.** to compel a player to play (a particular card). **c.** to compel (a player) to play so as to make known the strength of his hand. **27.** *Obs.* to enforce (a law, etc.). **28.** *Obs.* to give force to; strengthen; reinforce. —*v.i.* **29.** *Rare.* to make one's way by force. [ME, t. F, g. VL *fortia*, der. L *fortis* strong] —**force'**-**less,** *adj.* —**forc'er,** *n.* —**Syn. 1.** See **strength.**

forced (fōrst), *adj.* **1.** enforced or compulsory: *forced labor.* **2.** strained, unnatural, or affected: *a forced smile.* **3.** subjected to force. **4.** emergency: *forced landing of an airplane.* —**for·ced·ly** (fōr'sĭd lĭ), *adv.*

forced march, *Mil.* any march longer than troops are usually expected to travel, and maintained with little time for resting or for servicing vehicles.

force feed, a means of lubrication used on most internal-combustion engines, characterized by the use of a pressure pump.

force·ful (fōrs'fəl), *adj.* **1.** full of force; powerful; vigorous; effective. **2.** acting or driven with force. —**force'ful·ly,** *adv.* —**force'ful·ness,** *n.*

force majeure (fôrs mȧ zhœr'), *French.* **1.** a superior force. **2.** *Law.* **a.** an unexpected and disruptive event operating to excuse a party from a contract. **b.** (of a clause) providing that a party to a contract shall be excused in case of war, strikes, etc.

force·meat (fōrs'mēt'), *n. Cookery.* meat chopped fine and seasoned, used as stuffing, etc. Also, **farcemeat.** [f. *force,* var. of obs. *farce* stuffing + MEAT]

for·ceps (fōr'səps), *n., pl.* **-ceps, -cipes** (-sə pēz'). an instrument, as pincers or tongs, for seizing and holding objects, as in surgical operations. [t. L] —**for'ceps-like',** *adj.*

Surgical forceps
A. For compression of an artery to control hemorrhage: B. For removing stone from the bladder in lithotomy

force pump, any pump which delivers a liquid under pressure, so as to eject it forcibly (opposed to *lift pump*).

for·ci·ble (fōr'sə bəl), *adj.* **1.** effected by force. **2.** having force; producing a powerful effect; effective. **3.** convincing, as reasoning. **4.** characterized by the use of force or violence. —**for'ci·ble·ness,** *n.* —**for'ci·bly,** *adv.*

ford (fōrd), *n.* **1.** a place where a river or other body of water may be crossed by wading. —*v.t.* **2.** to cross (a river, etc.) by a ford. [ME and OE, c. G *furt;* akin to FARE, PORT] —**ford'a·ble,** *adj.* —**ford'less,** *adj.*

Ford (fōrd), *n.* **1. Ford Madox** (fōrd măd'əks), (*Ford Madox Hueffer*) 1873–1939, British author. **2. Henry,** 1863–1947, U.S. automobile manufacturer. **3. John,** 1586–1640?, British dramatist.

for·do (fōr dōō'), *v.t.,* **-did, -done, -doing.** *Archaic.* **1.** to do away with; kill; destroy. **2.** to ruin; undo. Also, **foredo.** [ME *fordon,* OE *fordon.* See FOR-, DO]

for·done (fōr dŭn'), *adj. Archaic.* exhausted with fatigue; worn out.

fore[1] (fōr), *adj.* **1.** situated at or toward the front, as compared with something else. **2.** first in place, time, order, rank, etc.; forward; earlier. —*adv.* **3.** *Naut.* at or toward the bow. **4.** *Dial.* before. **5.** *Dial.* forward. —*n.* **6.** the fore part of anything; the front. **7.** *Naut.* the foremast. **8. to the fore, a.** to or at the front; to or in a conspicuous place or position. **b.** ready at hand. **c.** still alive. —*prep.* and *conj.* **9.** *Now Only Dial.* before. [special use of FORE-, detached from words like *forepart, forefather,* etc.]

fore[2] (fōr), *interj. Golf.* a cry of warning to persons on a course who are liable to be struck by the ball. [prob. aphetic var. of BEFORE]

fore-, a prefix form of **before** meaning "front" (*forehead, forecastle*), "ahead of time" (*forecast, foretell*), "superior" (*foreman*), etc. [ME and OE *for(e)*]

fore and aft, *Naut.* in, at, or to both ends of a ship.

fore-and-aft (fōr'ənd äft'), *adj. Naut.* **1.** in a line with the keel of a ship: *a fore-and-aft sail.* **2.** denoting a rig in which the principal sails are set on gaffs, stays, or masts, on the center line of the vessel.

fore-and-af·ter (fōr'ənd äf'tər), *n. Naut.* a vessel with fore-and-aft sails, as a schooner.

fore-and-aft sail, *Naut.* any sail not set on a yard, usually bent to a gaff or set on a stay in the centerline. See **sail** (def. 1).

fore·arm[1] (fōr'ärm'), *n.* the part of the arm between the elbow and the wrist. [f. FORE- + ARM[1]]

fore·arm[2] (fōr ärm'), *v.t.* to arm beforehand. [f. FORE- + ARM[2]]

fore·bear (fōr'bâr'), *n.* (*usually pl.*) an ancestor; forefather. Also, **forbear.** [ME (Scot.); f. FORE- + *bear* being (var. of *beer,* f. BE, v. + -ER[1])]

fore·bode (fōr bōd'), *v.,* **-boded, -boding.** —*v.t.* **1.** to foretell or predict; portend; be an omen of; indicate beforehand: *clouds that forebode a storm.* **2.** to have a presentiment of (esp. evil). —*v.i.* **3.** to prophesy. **4.** to have a presentiment. —**fore·bod'er,** *n.*

fore·bod·ing (fōr bō'dĭng), *n.* **1.** a prediction; portent. **2.** a presentiment. —*adj.* **3.** that forbodes, esp. evil. —**fore·bod'ing·ly,** *adv.*

fore·brain (fōr'brān'), *n. Anat.* **1.** that portion of the adult brain which develops from the prosencephalon. **2.** the prosencephalon. **3.** the telencephalon.

fore·cast (fōr'kăst', -käst'), *v.,* **-cast** or **-casted, -casting,** *n.* —*v.t.* **1.** to conjecture beforehand; predict. **2.** to make a forecast of (the weather, etc.). **3.** to serve as a forecast of; foreshadow. **4.** to cast, contrive, or plan beforehand; prearrange. —*v.i.* **5.** to conjecture beforehand; make a forecast. **6.** to plan or arrange beforehand. —*n.* **7.** a conjecture as to something in the future. **8.** a prediction, esp. as to the weather. **9.** act, practice, or faculty of forecasting. **10.** foresight in planning. —**fore·cast'er,** *n.* —**Syn. 1.** See **predict.**

fore·cas·tle (fōk'səl, -kăs'əl), *n. Naut.* **1.** the seamen's quarters in the forward part of a merchant vessel. **2.** that part of the upper deck forward of the foremast. **3.** Also, **forecastle deck** or **head.** a short raised deck in the fore part of a ship.

G
M F B
L

Diagram of a ship's bow
B, Bowsprit; F. Forecastle (def. 1). G. Forecastle (def. 2); L. Lower deck; M, Main deck or spar deck

fore·cit·ed (fōr'sī'tĭd), *adj.* previously cited.

fore·close (fōr klōz'), *v.,* **-closed, -closing.** —*v.t.* **1.** *Law.* **a.** to deprive (a mortgagor or pledgor) of the right to redeem his property. **b.** to take away the right to redeem (a mortgage or pledge). **2.** to shut out; exclude or bar. **3.** to hinder or prevent, as from doing something. **4.** to establish an exclusive claim to. **5.** to close, settle, or answer beforehand. —*v.i.* **6.** to foreclose a mortgage or pledge. [ME *forclose(n),* t. OF: m. *forclos,* pp. of *forclore* exclude, f. *for-* out + *clore* shut, g. L *claudere*] —**fore·clos'a·ble,** *adj.*

fore·clo·sure (fōr klō'zhər), *n. Law.* act of foreclosing a mortgage or pledge.

fore·course (fōr'kōrs'), *n. Naut.* the course set on the foremast (the foresail in a square-rigged vessel).

fore·date (fōr'dāt'), *v.t.,* **-dated, -dating.** antedate.

fore·deck (fōr'děk'), *n. Naut.* the forward part of the spar deck.

fore·do (fōr dōō'), *v.t.,* **-did, -done, -doing.** fordo.

fore·doom (*v.* fōr dōōm'; *n.* fōr'dōōm'), *v.t.* **1.** to doom beforehand. —*n.* **2.** a doom ordained beforehand.

fore edge, the front outer edge of a book, opposite the bound edge.

fore·fa·ther (fōr'fä'thər), *n.* an ancestor.

Forefathers' Day, the anniversary of the day (Dec. 21, 1620, in Old Style Dec. 11) on which the Pilgrims landed at Plymouth, Massachusetts. Owing to an error in changing the date from the Old Style to the New, it is generally observed on Dec. 22.

fore·feel (fōr fēl'), *v.,* **-felt, -feeling,** *n.* —*v.t.* **1.** to feel or perceive beforehand; have a presentiment of. —*n.* **2.** a feeling beforehand.

fore·fend (fōr fěnd'), *v.t.* forfend.

fore·fin·ger (fōr'fĭng'gər), *n.* the first finger, next to the thumb.

fore·foot (fōr'fŏŏt'), *n., pl.* **-feet** (-fēt'). **1.** *Zool.* one of the front feet of a quadruped, or of an insect, etc. **2.** *Naut.* the forward end of the keel.

fore·front (fōr'frŭnt'), *n.* the foremost part or place.

fore·gath·er (fōr găth'ər), *v.i.* forgather.

fore·go[1] (fōr gō'), *v.t., v.i.,* **-went, -gone, -going.** to go before; precede. [OE *foregān* go before, f. *fore-* FORE- + *gān* go] —**fore·go'er,** *n.*

fore·go[2] (fōr gō'), *v.t.,* **-went, -gone, -going.** forgo. —**fore·go'er,** *n.*

fore·go·ing (fōr gō'ĭng), *adj.* going before; preceding: *the foregoing passage.*

fore·gone (fōr gôn', -gŏn', fōr'gôn', -gŏn'), *adj.* that has gone before; previous; past. —**fore·gone'ness,** *n.*

foregone conclusion, 1. an inevitable conclusion or result. **2.** a conclusion, opinion, or decision formed in advance.

fore·ground (fōr'ground'), *n.* the ground or parts situated, or represented as situated, in the front; the nearer portion of a scene (opposed to *background*).

fore·gut (fōr'gŭt'), *n. Embryol., Zool.* the upper part of the embryonic digestive canal from which the pharynx, esophagus, stomach, and part of the duodenum develop.

fore·hand (fōr'hănd'), *adj.* **1.** made to the right side of the body (when the player is right-handed). **2.** being in front or ahead. **3.** foremost or leading. **4.** done beforehand; anticipative; given or made in advance, as a payment. —*n.* **5.** position in front or above; superior position; adventure. **6.** *Tennis, etc.* **a.** a forehand stroke. **b.** that type of playing, or the stance taken when making such strokes. **7.** the part of a horse which is in front of the rider.

fore·hand·ed (fōr'hăn'dĭd), *adj.* **1.** forehand, as a stroke in tennis, etc. **2.** providing for the future; prudent; thrifty. **3.** in easy circumstances; well-to-do. —**fore'hand'ed·ness,** *n.*

fore·head (fōr'ĭd, fōr'-, fōr'hěd'), *n.* **1.** the fore or front upper part of the head; the part of the face above the eyes; the brow.   2. the fore or front part of anything. [ME *forehe(v)ed*, OE *forhēafod*, f. *for(e)*- FORE- + *hēafod* head]

for·eign (fôr′ĭn, fŏr′-), *adj.*   1. pertaining to, characteristic of, or derived from another country or nation; not native or domestic.   2. pertaining to relations or dealings with other countries.   3. external to one's own country or nation: *a foreign country.*   4. carried on abroad, or with other countries: *foreign trade.*   5. belonging to or coming from another district, province, society, etc.   6. situated outside a district, province, etc.   7. *Law.* outside the legal jurisdiction of the state; alien.   8. belonging to or proceeding from other persons or things: *a statement supported by foreign testimony.*   9. not belonging to the place or body where found: *a foreign substance in the eye.*   10. not related to or connected with the thing under consideration: *foreign to our discussion.*   11. alien in character; irrelevant or inappropriate; remote.   12. strange or unfamiliar. [ME *forene*, t. OF: m. *forain*, ult. der. L *foras* out of doors, outside] —**for′eign·ness**, *n.*

foreign affairs, international relations; activities of a nation arising from its dealings with other nations.

for·eign·er (fôr′ĭn·ər, fŏr′-), *n.*   1. a person not native or naturalized in the country or jurisdiction under consideration; an alien.   2. a thing produced in or brought from a foreign country.   3. *Naut.* a foreign vessel. —**Syn. 1.** See **stranger**.

foreign exchange,   1. the process of striking a balance in commercial transactions between businessmen of different nations.   2. commercial paper drawn on a person or corporation in a foreign nation.

for·eign·ism (fôr′ĭnĭz′əm, fŏr′-), *n.*   1. a foreign custom, etc.   2. any trait or deviation from accepted speech standards that comes from the influence of a foreign language.   3. imitation of anything foreign.   4. foreign quality.

foreign legion,   1. a military body in the service of a state, consisting of foreign volunteers.   2. (*caps.*) a military body in the French Army, consisting of foreigners of all nationalities, including Frenchmen, used mainly for military operations and duties in northern Africa.

foreign office, *Brit.* the department of a government concerned with the conduct of international relations.

fore·judge[1] (fōr·jŭj′), *v.t.*, **-judged**, **-judging**.   to judge beforehand; prejudge. [f. FORE- + JUDGE, v.]

fore·judge[2] (fōr·jŭj′), *v.t.*, **-judged**, **-judging**. forjudge.

fore·know (fōr·nō′), *v.t.*, **-knew**, **-known**, **-knowing**.   to know beforehand. —**fore·know′a·ble**, *adj.*

fore·knowl·edge (fōr′nŏl′ĭj, fōr·nŏl′ĭj), *n.*   knowledge of a thing before it exists or happens; prescience: *had you any foreknowledge of the banquet?*

fore·la·dy (fōr′lā′dĭ), *n., pl.* **-dies**. forewoman.

fore·land (fōr′lănd′), *n.*   1. a cape, headland, or promontory.   2. land or territory lying in front.

fore·leg (fōr′lĕg′), *n.*   one of the front legs of a quadruped, or of an insect, etc.

fore·limb (fōr′lĭm′), *n.*   a front limb of an animal.

fore·lock[1] (fōr′lŏk′), *n.*   1. the lock of hair that grows from the fore part of the head.   2. a prominent or somewhat detached lock above the forehead. [f. FORE- + LOCK[2]]

fore·lock[2] (fōr′lŏk′), *n.*   a round or flat wedge of iron passed through a hole in the inner end of a bolt to prevent its withdrawal when a strain is placed on it. [f. FORE- + LOCK[1]]

fore·man (fōr′mən), *n., pl.* **-men**.   1. a man in charge of a group of workers.   2. the chairman of a jury. —**fore′man·ship**, *n.*

fore·mast (fōr′măst′, -mäst′; *Naut.* -məst), *n. Naut.* the mast nearest the bow of a ship.

fore·most (fōr′mōst′, -məst), *adj., adv.*   first in place, order, rank, etc. [f. FORE, adj. + -MOST, r. ME and OE *formest*, f. *forma* first (var. of *frum(a)*. Cf. L *prīmus*) + -EST]

fore·name (fōr′nām′), *n.*   a name that precedes the family name or surname; a first name.

fore·named (fōr′nāmd′), *adj.*   named before; mentioned before in the same writing or discourse.

fore·noon (*n.* fōr′nōōn′; *adj.* fōr′nōōn′), *n.*   1. the period of daylight before noon.   2. the latter part of the morning, esp. the part ordinarily employed in transacting business. —*adj.* 3. of or pertaining to the forenoon.

fo·ren·sic (fərĕn′sĭk), *adj.*   1. pertaining to, connected with, or used in courts of law or public discussion and debate.   2. adapted or suited to argumentation; argumentative. [f. L *forens(is)* of the forum + -IC] —**fo·ren′si·cal·ly**, *adv.*

fore·or·dain (fōr′ôrdān′), *v.t.*   to ordain or appoint beforehand; predestinate. —**fore·or·dain′ment**, *n.*

fore·or·di·na·tion (fōr′ôrdənā′shən), *n.*   previous ordination or appointment; predestination.

fore·part (fōr′pärt′), *n.*   the fore, front, or early part.

fore·peak (fōr′pēk′), *n. Naut.* the part of the hold in the angle formed by the bow.

fore·quar·ter (fōr′kwôr′tər), *n.*   (in cutting meat) the forward end of half of a carcass.

fore·reach (fōr·rēch′), *v.i.*   1. to gain, as one ship on another. —*v.t.* 2. to gain upon; overhaul and pass.

fore·run (fōr·rŭn′), *v.t.*, **-ran**, **-run**, **-running**.   1. to run in front of; precede; be the precursor of.   2. to anticipate or forestall.   3. to outrun or outstrip.

fore·run·ner (fōr′rŭn′ər, fōr·rŭn′ər), *n.*   1. a predecessor; ancestor.   2. one who or that which foreruns; a herald or harbinger.   3. a prognostic or portent.   4. the Forerunner, John the Baptist.

fore·said (fōr′sĕd′), *adj.* forementioned; aforesaid.

fore·sail (fōr′sāl′; *Naut.* -səl), *n. Naut.* 1. the sail bent to the foreyard of a square-rigged vessel. See illus. under **sail**.   2. the principal sail on the foremast of a schooner.   3. the forestaysail of a sloop, cutter, etc.

fore·see (fōr·sē′), *v.*, **-saw**, **-seen**, **-seeing**. —*v.t.* 1. to see beforehand; have prescience of; foreknow. —*v.i.* 2. to exercise foresight. [ME; OE *foresēon*, f. fore- FORE- + *sēon* SEE[1]] —**fore·see′a·ble**, *adj.* —**fore·se′er**, *n.* —**Syn. 1.** See **predict**.

fore·shad·ow (fōr·shăd′ō), *v.t.*   to shadow or indicate beforehand; prefigure. —**fore·shad′ow·er**, *n.*

fore·sheet (fōr′shēt′), *n. Naut.* 1. a sheet of a foresail.   2. (*pl.*) the forward part of an open boat.

fore·shore (fōr′shōr′), *n.*   1. the forepart of the shore; the part of the shore between the ordinary high-water mark and low-water mark.   2. the ground between the water's edge and the land cultivated or built upon.

fore·short·en (fōr·shôr′tən), *v.t. Drawing.* to reduce the length of (a line, part, object, or the like, which lies in a plane not perpendicular to the line of sight) in order to give the proper impression to the eye by means of perspective.

fore·show (fōr·shō′), *v.t.*, **-showed**, **-shown**, **-showing**.   to show beforehand; foretell; foreshadow. [ME *forescewen*, OE *foresceāwian*, f. *fore-* FORE- + *sceāwian* show]

fore·side (fōr′sīd′), *n.*   1. the front side or part.   2. the upper side.   3. *U.S.* a stretch of land fronting the sea.

fore·sight (fōr′sīt′), *n.*   1. care or provision for the future; provident care.   2. act or power of foreseeing; prevision; prescience.   3. act of looking forward.   4. perception gained by or as by looking forward; prospect; a view into the future.   5. *Survey.* a. a sight or reading taken on a forward point.   b. (in leveling) a rod reading on a point the elevation of which is to be determined.   6. a sight on the muzzle of a gun. —**fore′sight′ed**, *adj.* —**fore′sight′ed·ness**, *n.* —**Syn. 1.** See **prudence**.

fore·skin (fōr′skĭn′), *n. Anat.* the prepuce.

for·est (fôr′ĭst, fŏr′-), *n.*   1. a large tract of land covered with trees; an extensive wood.   2. the trees alone: *to cut down a forest.*   3. *Eng. Law.* a tract of woody grounds and pastures, generally belonging to the sovereign, set apart for game. —*v.t.* 4. to cover with trees; convert into a forest. [ME, t. OF, g. VL *forestis* an unenclosed wood (as opposed to a park), der. L *foris* outside. See FOREIGN] —**for′est·ed**, *adj.* —**for′est·less**, *adj.* —**for′est·like′**, *adj.* —**Syn. 1.** FOREST, GROVE, WOOD refer to an area covered with trees. A FOREST is an extensive wooded area, preserving some of its primitive wildness and usually having game or wild animals in it: *Sherwood Forest, the Black Forest.* A GROVE is a group or cluster of trees, usually not very large in area and cleared of underbrush; it may consist of fruit or nut trees: *a shady grove, a grove of pines, an orange grove, a walnut grove.* A WOOD (WOODS) is a wooded tract smaller than a forest and resembling one, but less wild in character and nearer to civilization: *a wood covering several acres, lost in the woods.*

fore·stall (fōr·stôl′), *v.t.*   1. to prevent, hinder, or thwart by action in advance; take measures concerning or deal with (a thing) in advance.   2. to deal with, meet, or realize in advance of the natural or proper time; be beforehand with or get ahead of (a person, etc.) in action.   3. to buy up (goods) in advance, in order to enhance the price.   4. to prevent sales at (a fair, market etc.) by buying up or diverting goods. [ME *forstalle*, der. OE *foresteall* intervention (to defeat justice), waylaying. See FORE-, STALL[2]] —**fore·stall′er**, *n.* —**fore·stall′ment**, **fore·stal′ment**, *n.*

for·est·a·tion (fôr′ĭstā′shən, fŏr′-), *n.*   the planting of forests.

fore·stay (fōr′stā′), *n. Naut.* a strong rope (now generally of wire) extending forward from the head of the foremast to the knightheads or stem to support the mast.

fore·stay·sail (fōr′stā′sāl′; *Naut.* -səl), *n. Naut.* a triangular sail set on the forestay, being the first sail in front of the forward (or single) mast.

for·est·er (fôr′ĭstər, fŏr′-), *n.*   1. one who practices, or is versed in, forestry.   2. an officer having charge of a forest.   3. *Zool.* an animal of the forest.   4. the great gray kangaroo, *Macropus canguru.*   5. any of various moths of the family *Zygaenidae*, as *Alypia octomaculata*, the **eight-spotted forester**, a moth whose larva devours grapevines.

For·est·er (fôr′ĭstər, fŏr′-), *n.*   **Cecil Scott**, born 1899, British novelist.

forest reserve, *U.S.* an area of forest set aside by the government as a reserve.

for·est·ry (fôr′ĭstrĭ, fŏr′-), *n.*   1. the science of planting and taking care of forests.   2. act of establishing and managing forests.   3. forest land.

fore·taste (*n.* fōr′tāst′; *v.* fōr·tāst′), *n., v.*, **-tasted**, **-tasting**. —*n.* 1. a taste beforehand; anticipation. —*v.t.* 2. to taste beforehand; enjoy by anticipation.

fore·tell (fōr·tĕl′), *v.*, **-told**, **-telling**. —*v.t.* 1. to tell of beforehand; predict or prophesy.   2. (of things) to

foreshow. —*v.i.* 3. to utter a prediction or a prophecy. —**fore·tell′er,** *n.*

fore·thought (fōr′thôt′), *n.* 1. provident care; prudence. 2. a thinking of something beforehand; previous consideration; anticipation. —**Syn.** 1. See **prudence.**

fore·thought·ful (fōr′thôt′fəl), *adj.* full of or having forethought; provident. —**fore·thought′ful·ly,** *adv.* —**fore·thought′ful·ness,** *n.*

fore·time (fōr′tīm′), *n.* former or past time; the past.

fore·to·ken (*n.* fōr′tō′kən; *v.* fōr tō′kən), *n.* 1. a premonitory token or sign. —*v.t.* 2. to foreshadow. [ME *foretokne,* OE *foretācn,* f. *fore-* FORE- + *tācn* token]

fore·top (fōr′tŏp′; *for 1 also Naut.* -tŏp), *n.* 1. *Naut.* a platform at the head of a foremast. 2. the front seat on the top of a vehicle. 3. the forelock of an animal, esp. a horse. 4. *Obs.* a human forelock, or a lock of hair on the front of a wig.

fore·top·gal·lant (fōr′tŏp găl′ənt; *Naut.* -təgăl′-), *adj. Naut.* (of a mast, sail, yard, etc.) next above the foretopmast. See illus. under **sail.**

fore·topgallant mast, *Naut.* the mast next above the foretopmast.

fore·top·mast (fōr′tŏp′măst′, -măst′; *Naut.* -məst), *n. Naut.* the mast erected at the head of the foremast, above the foretop.

fore·top·sail (fōr′tŏp′sāl′; *Naut.* -səl), *n. Naut.* the sail set on the foretopmast. See illus. under **sail.**

for·ev·er (fōrĕv′ər), *adv.* 1. eternally; without ever ending: *to last forever, go away forever.* 2. continually; incessantly: *he's forever complaining.* [prop. phrase]

for·ev·er·more (fōrĕv′ərmōr′), *adv.* for ever hereafter.

fore·warn (fōr wôrn′), *v.t.* to warn beforehand.

fore·wom·an (fōr′wŏŏm′ən), *n., pl.* **-women.** 1. a woman in charge of a group of workwomen. 2. the chairlady of a jury.

fore·word (fōr′wûrd′), *n.* a preface or introductory statement in a book, etc. —**Syn.** See **introduction.**

fore·worn (fōr wôrn′), *adj. Archaic.* forworn.

fore·yard (fōr′yärd′), *n. Naut.* the lower yard on the foremast.

For·far (fôr′fər, -fär), *n.* former name of **Angus.**

for·feit (fôr′fĭt), *n.* 1. a fine; a penalty. 2. act of forfeiting; forfeiture. 3. something to which the right is lost by the commission of a crime or misdeed, the neglect of a duty, a breach of contract, etc. 4. an article deposited in a game because of a mistake and redeemable by a fine or penalty. 5. (*pl.*) a game so played. —*v.t.* 6. to lose as a forfeit. 7. to lose, or become liable to lose, in consequence of crime, fault, breach of engagement, etc. —*adj.* 8. forfeited. [ME *forfet,* t. OF, pp. of *forfaire,* f. *for-* outside, wrongly + *faire* do] —**for′feit·a·ble,** *adj.*—**for′feit·er,** *n.*

for·fei·ture (fôr′fĭ′chər), *n.* 1. act of forfeiting. 2. that which is forfeited; a fine or mulct.

for·fend (fôr fĕnd′), *v.t.* 1. to defend, secure, or protect. 2. *Archaic.* to fend off, avert, or prevent. Also, **forefend.** [f. FOR- + FEND]

for·fi·cate (fôr′fəkĭt, -kāt′), *adj.* deeply forked, as the tail of certain birds. [f. s. L *forfex* scissors + -ATE[1]]

for·gat (fərgăt′), *v. Archaic.* pt. of **forget.**

for·gath·er (fôr găth′ər), *v.i.* 1. to gather together; convene; assemble. 2. to encounter or meet, esp. by accident. 3. to associate or fraternize (fol. by *with*). Also, **foregather.**

for·gave (fərgāv′), *v.* pt. of **forgive.**

forge[1] (fôrj), *n., v.,* **forged, forging.** —*n.* 1. the special fireplace, hearth, or furnace in which metal is heated before shaping. 2. a smithy. —*v.t.* 3. to form by heating and hammering; beat into shape. 4. to form or make in any way. 5. to invent (a fictitious story, a lie, etc.). 6. to imitate (a signature, etc.) fraudulently; fabricate by false imitation. —*v.i.* 7. to commit forgery. 8. to work at a forge. [ME, t. OF, ult. g. L *fabrica* workshop] —**forge′a·ble,** *adj.* —**forg′er,** *n.*

forge[2] (fôrj), *v.i.,* **forged, forging.** to move ahead slowly, with difficulty, or by mere momentum (usually fol. by *ahead*). [orig. uncert.]

for·ger·y (fôr′jərĭ), *n., pl.* **-geries.** 1. the making of a fraudulent imitation of a thing, or of something spurious which is put forth as genuine, as a coin, a work of art, a literary production, etc. 2. something, as a coin, a work of art, a writing, etc., produced by forgery. 3. *Law.* the false making or alteration of a writing by which the legal rights or obligations of another person are apparently affected; simulated signing of another person's name to any such writing (whether or not it is also the forger's name). 4. act of fabricating or producing falsely. 5. *Now Poetic.* fictitious invention; deception or artifice.

for·get (fərgĕt′), *v.,* **-got** or (*Archaic*) **-gat; -got; -gotten** or **-got; -getting.** —*v.t.* 1. to cease to remember; fail to remember; be unable to recall. 2. to omit or neglect unintentionally (to do something). 3. to omit to take; leave behind inadvertently: *to forget one's keys.* 4. to omit to mention; leave unnoticed. 5. to omit to think of; take no note of. 6. to neglect willfully; overlook, disregard, or slight. 7. **forget oneself, a.** to say or do something improper. **b.** to fail to remember one's station, position, or character. **c.** to neglect or slight oneself. **d.** to become absent-minded. **e.** to lose conscious-

ness, as in sleep. —*v.i.* 8. to cease or omit to think of something. [f. FOR- + GET; r. ME *forgete(n),* OE *forg(i)etan*] —**for·get′ta·ble,** *adj.* —**for·get′ter,** *n.*

for·get·ful (fərgĕt′fəl), *adj.* 1. apt to forget; that forgets: *a forgetful person.* 2. heedless or neglectful (often fol. by *of*): *to be forgetful of others.* 3. *Poetic.* causing to forget. —**for·get′ful·ly,** *adv.* —**for·get′ful·ness,** *n.*

for·ge·tive (fôr′jətĭv), *adj. Archaic.* inventive; creative. [? b. FORGE[1], *v.* and CREATIVE]

for·get-me-not (fərgĕt′mĭ′nŏt′), *n.* 1. a small boraginaceous Old World plant, *Myosotis palustris,* bearing a light-blue flower commonly regarded as an emblem of constancy and friendship. 2. any of several other plants of the same genus. 3. any of various similar plants.

forg·ing (fôr′jĭng), *n.* 1. something forged; a piece of forged work in metal. 2. (in horses) the act of striking and injuring the forelegs with the shoes of the hind legs while racing.

for·give (fərgĭv′), *v.* **-gave, -given, -giving.** —*v.t.* 1. to grant free pardon for or remission of (an offense, debt, etc.). 2. to give up all claim on account of; remit (a debt, etc.). 3. to grant free pardon to (a person). 4. to cease to feel resentment against: *to forgive one's enemies.* —*v.i.* 5. to pardon an offense or an offender. [f. FOR- + GIVE: r. ME *foryiven,* OE *forgiefan*] —**for·giv′a·ble,** *adj.* —**for·giv′er,** *n.* —**Syn.** 1. See **excuse.**

for·give·ness (fərgĭv′nĭs), *n.* 1. act of forgiving. 2. state of being forgiven. 3. disposition or willingness to forgive.

for·giv·ing (fərgĭv′ĭng), *adj.* that forgives; disposed to forgive; indicating forgiveness. —**for·giv′ing·ly,** *adv.* —**for·giv′ing·ness,** *n.*

for·go (fôrgō′), *v.t.,* **-went, -gone, -going.** 1. to abstain or refrain from; do without; give up, renounce, or resign. 2. *Archaic.* to neglect or overlook. 3. *Archaic.* to quit or leave. 4. *Obs.* to go or pass by. Also, **forego.** [ME *forgon,* OE *forgān.* See FOR-, GO] —**for·go′er,** *n.*

for·got (fərgŏt′), *v.* pt. and pp. of **forget.**

for·got·ten (fərgŏt′ən), *v.* pp. of **forget.**

for·int (fôr′ĭnt), *n.* the standard monetary unit of Hungary, equal to about $.085.

for·judge (fôr jŭj′), *v.t.,* **-judged, -judging.** *Law.* to exclude, expel, dispossess, or deprive by a judgment. Also, **forejudge.** [ME *forjuge(n),* t. OF: m. *forjugier,* f. *for-* out + *jugier* JUDGE, v.]

fork (fôrk), *n.* 1. an instrument having two or more prongs or tines, for holding, lifting, etc., as any of various agricultural tools, or an implement for handling food at table or in cooking. 2. something resembling or suggesting this in form. 3. a tuning fork. 4. a forking, or dividing into branches. 5. the point or part at which a thing, as a river or a road, divides into branches. 6. each of the branches into which a thing forks. 7. *Chiefly U.S.* a principal tributary of a river. 8. *Obs.* the barbed head of an arrow. —*v.t.* 9. to make fork-shaped. 10. to pierce, raise, pitch, dig, etc., with a fork. 11. *Chess.* to assail (two pieces) at the same time. 12. *Slang.* to hand (fol. by *over* or *out*). —*v.i.* 13. to form a fork; divide into branches. [ME *forke,* OE *forca,* t. L: m. *furca*] —**fork′less,** *adj.* —**fork′like′,** *adj.*

forked (fôrkt, fôr′kĭd), *adj.* 1. having a fork or bifurcation, or forking branches. 2. zigzag, as lightning. Also, **fork′y.** —**fork·ed·ly** (fôr′kĭd lĭ), *adv.* —**fork′ed·ness,** *n.*

For·lì (fôrlē′), *n.* a city in N Italy. 72,251 (est. 1946).

for·lorn (fôrlôrn′), *adj.* 1. abandoned, deserted, or forsaken (sometimes fol. by *of*). 2. desolate or dreary; unhappy, miserable, or wretched, as in feeling, condition, or appearance. 3. desperate or hopeless. 4. bereft (fol. by *of*). [var. of *forlore(n),* pp. of (obs.) *forlese,* v., OE *forlēosan* lose, destroy. See FOR-, LORN] —**for·lorn′ly,** *adv.* —**for·lorn′ness,** *n.* —**Syn.** 1. See **desolate.**

forlorn hope, 1. a vain hope; an undertaking almost certain to fail. 2. a perilous or desperate enterprise. 3. a group of soldiers for some unusually perilous service. [t. D: alter. of *verloren hoop,* lit., lost troop]

form (fôrm), *n.* 1. definite shape; external shape or appearance considered apart from color or material; configuration. 2. the shape of a thing or person. 3. a body, esp. that of a human being. 4. something that gives or determines shape; a mold. 5. a particular structural condition, character, or mode of being exhibited by a thing: *water in the form of ice.* 6. the manner or style of arranging and coördinating parts for a pleasing or effective result, as in literary or musical composition. 7. any assemblage of similar things constituting a component of a group, especially of a zoölogical group. 8. *Crystall.* the combination of all the like faces possible on a crystal of given symmetry. 9. due or proper shape; orderly arrangement of parts; good order. 10. *Philos.* **a.** the structure, pattern, organization, or essential nature of anything. **b.** form or pattern considered in distinction from matter. **c.** (in Platonic use) an idea (def. 7c). **d.** (in Aristotelian use) that which gives to a thing its particular species or kind. 11. *Logic.* the abstract relations of terms in a proposition, and of propositions to one another. 12. a set, prescribed, or customary order or method of doing something. 13. a set order of words, as for use in religious ritual or in a legal document. 14. a document with blank spaces to be filled in with particulars before it is executed: *a tax*

form. **15.** a typical document to be used as a guide in framing others for like cases: *a form for a deed*. **16.** a conventional method of procedure or behavior. **17.** a formality or ceremony, often with implication of absence of real meaning. **18.** procedure, according to a set order or method. **19.** formality; ceremony; conformity to the usages of society. **20.** mere outward formality or ceremony; conventional observance of social usages. **21.** procedure or conduct, as judged by social standards. **22.** manner or method of performing something. **23.** condition, esp. good condition, with reference to fitness for performing. **24.** *Gram.* **a.** any word, part of a word, or group of words arranged in a construction, which recurs in various contexts in a language with relatively constant meaning. **b.** a particular shape of a form (sense a) when it occurs in several: in *I'm, 'm* is a form of *am.* **c.** a word with a particular inflectional ending or other modification, as *goes* is a form of *go*. **25.** *Brit.* a grade or class of pupils in a school. **26.** *Brit.* a bench or long seat. **27.** Also, *Brit.*, **forme.** an assemblage of types, etc., secured in a chase to print from. —*v.t.* **28.** to construct or frame. **29.** to make or produce. **30.** to serve to make up, or compose; serve for, or constitute. **31.** to place in order; arrange; organize. **32.** to frame (ideas, opinions, etc.) in the mind. **33.** to contract (habits, friendships, etc.). **34.** to give form or shape to; shape; fashion. **35.** to give a particular form to, or fashion in a particular manner. **36.** to mold by discipline or instruction. **37.** *Gram.* to stand in relation to (a particular derivative or other form) by virtue of the absence or presence of an affix or other grammatical element or change: *"man" forms its plural by the change of -a- to -e-.* **38.** *Mil.* to draw up in lines or in formation. —*v.i.* **39.** to take or assume form. **40.** to be formed or produced. **41.** to take a particular form or arrangement. [ME *forme*, t. OF, t. L: m.s. *forma* form, figure, model, mold, sort, ML seat]

—**Syn. 1.** FORM, FIGURE, OUTLINE, SHAPE refer to an appearance which can be recognized. FORM, FIGURE, and SHAPE are often used to mean recognizable lines as contrasted with color and material; SHAPE is more colloquial than the others. OUTLINE refers to the line which delimits a form, figure, or shape: *the outline of a hill*. FIGURE always refers to a concrete object, but FORM and SHAPE may also be applied to abstractions: *the figure of a man, the shape of a cow, of the future*. FORM is the most widely applied to physical objects, mental images, methods of procedure, etc.: *the form of a cross, of a ceremony, of a poem*. —**Ant. 1.** substance.

-form, a suffix meaning "having the form of," as in *cruciform*. [t. L: s. *-formis*]

for·mal (fôr′məl), *adj.* **1.** being in accordance with conventional requirements; conventional. **2.** marked by form or ceremony: *a formal occasion*. **3.** observant of form, as persons; ceremonious. **4.** excessively ceremonious. **5.** being a matter of form only; perfunctory. **6.** made or done in accordance with forms ensuring validity: *a formal authorization*. **7.** being in accordance with prescribed or customary forms: *a formal siege*. **8.** academic; rigorously methodical. **9.** excessively regular or symmetrical. **10.** *Speech.* denoting language whose grammar and syntax are correct, and speech whose sounds are carefully formed without sounding stilted: *the language and speech of formal occasions*. See *informal* (def. 3). **11.** *Philos.* **a.** pertaining to form. **b.** (in Aristotelian use) not material; essential. **12.** pertaining to the form, shape, mode of being of a thing, esp. as distinguished from the matter. **13.** being such in form, esp. in mere outward form. —**for′mal·ness,** *n.*

—**Syn. 2.** FORMAL, ACADEMIC, CONVENTIONAL may have either favorable or unfavorable implications. FORMAL may mean in proper form, or may imply excessive emphasis on empty form. In the favorable sense, ACADEMIC applies to scholars or higher institutions of learning; it may, however, imply slavish conformance to mere rules, or to belief in impractical theories. CONVENTIONAL, in a favorable sense, applies to desirable conformity with accepted conventions or customs; but it may apply to arbitrary, forced, or superficial conformance.

form·al·de·hyde (fôr·măl′də·hīd′), *n. Chem.* a gas, CH₂O, used most often in the form of a 40% aqueous solution, as a disinfectant and preservative, and in the manufacture of various resins and plastics. Also, **form·al′de·hyd′.** [f. FORM(IC) + ALDEHYDE]

for·ma·lin (fôr′mə·lĭn), *n. Chem.* an aqueous solution of formaldehyde.

for·mal·ism (fôr′məl·ĭz′əm), *n.* **1.** strict adherence to, or observance of, prescribed or customary forms. **2.** (in religion) excessive attachment to external forms and observances. —**for′mal·ist,** *n.* —**for′mal·is′tic,** *adj.*

for·mal·i·ty (fôr·măl′ə·tĭ), *n., pl.* **-ties.** **1.** condition or quality of being formal; accordance with prescribed, customary, or due forms; conventionality. **2.** rigorously methodical character. **3.** excessive regularity, or stiffness. **4.** observance of form or ceremony. **5.** marked or excessive ceremoniousness. **6.** an established order or mode of proceeding: *the formalities of judicial process*. **7.** a formal act or observance. **8.** something done merely for form's sake; a requirement of custom or etiquette.

for·mal·ize (fôr′mə·līz′). *v.,* **-ized, -izing.** —*v.t.* **1.** to make formal. **2.** to give a definite form or shape to. —*v.i.* **3.** to be formal; act with formality. —**for′mal·i·za′tion,** *n.*

formal logic, the branch of logic concerned exclusively with the principles of deductive reasoning, and in

consequence with the forms (as distinct from the content) of propositions.

for·mal·ly (fôr′məl·ĭ), *adv.* **1.** in a formal manner. **2.** as regards form; in form.

for·mat (fôr′măt), *n.* **1.** the shape and size of a book as determined by the number of times the original sheet has been folded to form the leaves. See **folio** (def. 2), **quarto, octavo, duodecimo,** etc. **2.** the general physical appearance of a book, such as the type face, binding, quality of paper, margins, etc. [t. F, t. L: s. (*liber*) *formātus* (a book) formed (in a certain way)]

for·mate (fôr′māt), *n. Chem.* a salt or ester of formic acid. [f. FORM(IC) + -ATE²]

for·ma·tion (fôr·mā′shən), *n.* **1.** act or process of forming. **2.** state of being formed. **3.** the manner in which a thing is formed; disposition of parts; formal structure or arrangement. **4.** *Mil.* **a.** a particular disposition of troops, as in columns, squares, etc. **b.** any required assembling of the soldiers of a unit. **5.** something formed. **6.** *Geol.* **a.** a body of rocks classed as a unit for geologic mapping. **b.** the process of depositing rock or mineral of a particular composition or origin.

form·a·tive (fôr′mə·tĭv), *adj.* **1.** giving form or shape; forming; shaping; fashioning; molding. **2.** pertaining to formation or development: *the formative period of a nation*. **3.** *Biol.* **a.** capable of developing new cells or tissue by cell division and differentiation: *formative tissue*. **b.** concerned with the formation of an embryo, organ, or the like. **4.** *Gram.* pertaining to a formative. —*n.* **5.** *Gram.* a derivational affix, particularly one which determines the part of speech of the derived word, such as *-ness*, in *loudness, hardness*, etc. —**form′a·tive·ly,** *adv.* —**form′a·tive·ness,** *n.*

formative element, *Gram.* **1.** a morpheme which serves as an affix, not as a base (or root) in word formation. **2.** any noninflectional morpheme, whether base or affix.

form class, *Gram.* a class of words or forms in a language with one or more grammatical features in common, as (in Latin) all masculine nouns in the nominative singular, or all masculine singular nouns, or all masculine nouns, or all singular nouns, or all nouns.

form drag, *Hydraulics, etc.* that portion of the resisting force encountered by a body moving through a fluid which is due to irregularity of shape and hence can be reduced to a minimum by streamlining.

forme (fôrm), *n. Brit.* form (def. 27).

for·mer¹ (fôr′mər), *adj.* **1.** preceding in time; prior or earlier. **2.** past, long past, or ancient. **3.** preceding in order; being the first of two. **4.** being the first mentioned of two. **5.** having held a particular office in the past: *a former president*. [ME, f. obs. *forme* (OE *forma* fîrst) + -ER⁴. Cf. ME and OE *formest* foremost]

form·er² (fôr′mər), *n.* one who or that which forms or serves to form. [f. FORM + -ER¹]

for·mer·ly (fôr′mər·lĭ), *adv.* **1.** in time past; heretofore; of old. **2.** *Obs.* in time past; just now.

for·mi·ca (fôr′mə·kə), *n.* a thermosetting plastic usually used in transparent or printed sheets as a chemical-proof and heatproof covering for furniture, wall panels, etc.

for·mic acid (fôr′mĭk), *Chem.* a colorless irritant liquid, HCOOH, once obtained from ants and other insects, but now manufactured synthetically. [*formic*, irreg. t. L: s. *formica* ant]

for·mi·car·i·um (fôr′mə·kâr′ĭ·əm), *n., pl.* **-caria** (-kâr′-ĭ·ə). formicary. [t. ML, der. L *formica* ant]

for·mi·car·y (fôr′mə·ker′ĭ), *n., pl.* **-caries.** an ants' nest.

for·mi·cate (fôr′mə·kāt′), *v.i.,* **-cated, -cating.** to swarm with moving beings, as ants. [t. L: m.s. *formicātus*, pp. of *formicāre* creep like ants]

for·mi·da·ble (fôr′mĭ·də·bəl), *adj.* **1.** that is to be feared or dreaded, esp. in encounters or dealings. **2.** of alarming strength, size, difficulty, etc. **3.** such as to inspire apprehension of defeat or failure. [t. F, t. L: m.s. *formīdābilis* causing fear] —**for′mi·da·ble·ness,** *for′-mi·da·bil′ity,* *n.* —**for′mi·da·bly,** *adv.* —**Syn. 1.** dread, dreadful, appalling, threatening, menacing.

form·less (fôrm′lĭs), *adj.* wanting form or shape; shapeless; without a determinate or regular form. —**form′less·ly,** *adv.* —**form′less·ness,** *n.*

form letter, a letter, printed, processed, or typed, copies of which are sent to a number of readers.

For·mo·sa (fôr·mō′sə), *n.* a Chinese island separated from the SE coast of China by **Formosa Strait**: a possession of Japan, 1895–1945. 5,895,864 pop. (1939); 13,807 sq. mi. Also, **Taiwan.**

for·mu·la (fôr′myə·lə), *n., pl.* **-las, -lae** (-lē′). **1.** a set form of words, as for stating or declaring something definitely or authoritatively, for indicating procedure to be followed, or for prescribed use on some ceremonial occasion. **2.** *Math.* a rule or principle frequently expressed in algebraic symbols. **3.** *Chem.* an expression of the constituents of a compound by symbols and figures, as an **empirical formula,** which merely indicates the number of each kind of atom in the molecule, a-CH₂O, or a **structural formula,** which represents diagrammatically the linkage of each atom in the molecules as H—O—H. **4.** a recipe or prescription. **5.** a formal statement of religious doctrine. [t. L, dim. of *forma* FORM. *n.*]

for·mu·lar·ize (fôr′myələrīz′), v.t., -ized, -izing. formulate. —**for′mu·lar·i·za′tion,** n.

for·mu·lar·y (fôr′myəlĕr′ĭ), n., pl. -laries, adj. —n. 1. a collection or system of formulas. 2. a set form of words; formula. 3. Pharm. a book listing pharmaceutical substances, formulas, and prescriptions. 4. Eccles. a book containing prescribed forms used in the services of a church. —adj. 5. of or pertaining to a formula or formulas. 6. of the nature of a formula.

for·mu·late (fôr′myəlāt′), v.t., -lated, -lating. 1. to express in precise form; state definitely or systematically. 2. to reduce to or express in a formula. —**for′mu·la′tion,** n. —**for′mu·la′tor,** n.

for·mu·lism (fôr′myəlĭz′əm), n. 1. adherence to or systematic use of formulas. 2. a system of formulas. —**for′mu·lis′tic,** adj.

for·mu·lize (fôr′myəlīz′), v.t., -lized, -lizing. formulate. —**for′mu·li·za′tion,** n. —**for′mu·liz′er,** n.

for·myl (fôr′mĭl), n. Chem. the radical, HCO, derived from formic acid. [f. FORM(IC) + -YL]

for·ni·cate (fôr′nəkāt′), v.i., -cated, -cating. to commit fornication. [t. LL: m.s. fornicātus, pp. of fornicārī, der. L fornix (underground) brothel, arch, vault] —**for′ni·ca′tor,** n.

for·ni·ca·tion (fôr′nəkā′shən), n. 1. voluntary sexual intercourse on the part of an unmarried person with a person of the opposite sex. 2. Bible. **a.** adultery. **b.** idolatry.

for·nix (fôr′nĭks), n., pl. -nices (-nəsēz′). Anat. any of various arched or vaulted structures, as an arching fibrous formation in the brain. [t. L: arch, vault]

For·rest (fôr′ĭst, fŏr′-), n. 1. Edwin, 1806–72, U.S. actor. 2. John, Baron, 1847–1918, Australian explorer and statesman. 3. Nathan Bedford, 1821–77, Confederate cavalry general in the U.S. Civil War.

for·sake (fôr·sāk′), v.t., -sook, -saken, -saking. 1. to quit or leave entirely; desert: forsake one's friends. 2. to give up or renounce (a habit, way of life, etc.). [ME forsake(n), OE forsacan deny, give up, f. for- FOR- + sacan dispute] —**Syn.** 1. See desert².

for·sak·en (fôr·sā′kən), v. 1. pp. of forsake. —adj. 2. deserted; abandoned; forlorn. —**for·sak′en·ly,** adv.

For·se·ti (fôr′sĕ tē′), n. Scand. Myth. the god of justice, son of Balder.

for·sook (fôr·sŏŏk′), v. pt. of forsake.

for·sooth (fôr·sōōth′), adv. in truth; in fact; indeed (now commonly used ironically or derisively). [ME forsoth(e), OE forsōth for sooth]

for·spend (fôr·spĕnd′), v.t., -spent, -spending. to spend or use up completely, as strength; wear out or exhaust, as with exertion (occurs chiefly in pp.). [ME forspend(en), OE forspendan. See FOR-, SPEND]

For·ster (fôr′stər), n. Edward Morgan, born 1879, British novelist.

for·ster·ite (fôr′stərīt′), n. a mineral of the olivine group, a silicate of magnesium, Mg₂SiO₄, occurring usually as white, greenish, or yellowish grains in basic igneous rocks.

for·swear (fôr·swâr′), v., -swore, -sworn, -swearing. —v.t. 1. to reject or renounce upon oath or with protestations. 2. to deny upon oath or with strong asseveration. 3. to perjure (oneself). —v.i. 4. to swear falsely; commit perjury. [ME forsweren, OE forswerian; see FOR-, SWEAR] —**for·swear′er,** n.

for·sworn (fôr·swôrn′), v. 1. pp. of forswear. —adj. 2. perjured.

for·syth·i·a (fôr·sĭth′ĭ ə, -sī′thĭ ə), n. any shrub of the oleaceous genus Forsythia, native in China and southeastern Europe, species of which are much cultivated for their showy yellow flowers, appearing in early spring before the leaves. [NL, named after W. Forsyth (1737–1804), British horticulturist.]

fort (fôrt), n. 1. a strong or fortified place; any armed place surrounded by defensive works and occupied by troops; a fortification; a fortress. 2. (in North America) a trading post. [t. F, g. L fortis strong]

Fort, for forts, see under the second word, as Sumter, Fort; when "Fort" is a part of the name of a city, see under the first word, as Fort Worth.

fort., 1. fortification. 2. fortified.

For·ta·le·za (fôr′tä lĕ′zə), n. a seaport in E Brazil. 142,453 (1940). Also, Ceará.

for·ta·lice (fôr′tə lĭs), n. 1. a small fort; an outwork. 2. Obs. a fortress. [ME, t. ML: m.s. fortalitia, fortalitium, der. L fortis strong]

Fort-de-France (fôr də fräns′), n. a seaport in and the capital of Martinique, in the French West Indies. 52,051 (1936).

Fort Dodge (dŏj′), a city in central Iowa, on the Des Moines river. 25,115 (1950).

forte¹ (fôrt), n. 1. a strong point, as of a person; that in which one excels. 2. the stronger part of a sword blade between the middle and the hilt (opposed to foible). [t. F: m. fort, n. use of fort, adj. See FORT]

for·te² (fôr′tĕ), Music. —adj. 1. loud; with force (opposed to piano). —adv. 2. loudly. —n. 3. a passage that is loud and forcible, or is intended to be so. [It., g. L fortis strong]

forth (fôrth), adv. 1. forward; onward or outward in place or space. 2. onward in time, in order, or in a se-

ries: from that day forth. 3. out, as from concealment or inaction; into view or consideration. 4. away, as from a place or country; abroad. 5. and so forth, and so on; and others; et cetera. —prep. 6. Archaic. out of; forth from. [ME and OE, c. G fort; akin to FURTHER]

forth·com·ing (fôrth′kŭm′ĭng), adj. 1. coming forth, or about to come forth; about to appear; approaching in time. 2. ready or available when required or expected. —n. 3. a coming forth; appearance.

Forth (fôrth), **Firth of,** an arm of the North Sea, in SE Scotland: the estuary of the Forth river, traversed by a railroad bridge, 5330 ft. long. 48 mi. long.

forth·right (adj., n. fôrth′rīt′; adv. fôrth′rīt′, fôrth′-rīt′), adj. 1. going straight to the point; outspoken. 2. proceeding in a straight course; direct; straightforward. —adv. 3. straight or directly forward; in a direct manner. 4. straightway; at once; immediately. —n. 5. Archaic. a straight course or path. —**forth′right′-ness,** n.

forth·with (fôrth′wĭth′, -wĭth′), adv. 1. immediately; at once; without delay. 2. as soon as can reasonably be expected.

for·ti·eth (fôr′tĭ ĭth), adj. 1. next after the thirty-ninth. 2. being one of forty equal parts. —n. 3. a fortieth part, esp. of one (1/40). 4. the fortieth member of a series.

for·ti·fi·ca·tion (fôr′təfəkā′shən), n. 1. act of fortifying or strengthening. 2. that which fortifies or protects. 3. art or science of constructing defensive military works. 4. a military work constructed for the purpose of strengthening a position; fortified place; fort; castle. —**Syn.** 4. fortress, citadel, stronghold.

for·ti·fy (fôr′təfī′), v., -fied, -fying. —v.t. 1. to strengthen against attack; surround with defenses; provide with defensive military works; protect with fortifications. 2. to furnish with a means of resisting force or standing strain, wear, etc. 3. to make strong; impart strength or vigor to, as the body. 4. to strengthen mentally or morally. 5. to confirm or corroborate. 6. to add alcohol to (wines, etc.). —v.i. 7. to set up defensive works; erect fortifications. [ME fortifie(n), t. F: m. fortifier, t. LL: m. fortificāre, f. forti- strong + -ficāre make] —**for′ti·fi′a·ble,** adj. —**for′ti·fi′er,** n.

for·tis (fôr′tĭs), adj., n., pl. -tes (-tēz). —adj. 1. Phonet. pronounced with considerable muscular tension and breath pressure, resulting in a strong fricative or explosive sound: f and p are fortis, as compared to lenis v and b. —n. 2. a fortis consonant. [t. L: strong]

for·tis·si·mo (fôr·tĭs′ə mō′; It. fôr·tēs′sē mô′), Music. —adj. 1. very loud. —adv. 2. very loudly. [t. It., superl. of forte. See FORTE²]

for·ti·tude (fôr′tə tūd′, -tōōd′), n. patient courage under affliction, privation, or temptation; moral strength or endurance. [t. L: m. fortitūdo] —**Syn.** See patience.

Fort Lau·der·dale (lô′dər dāl′), a city in SE Florida: a seaside resort. 36,328 (1950).

fort·night (fôrt′nīt′, -nĭt), n. Chiefly Brit., in U.S. literary only. the space of fourteen nights and days; two weeks. [ME fourtenight, contr. of OE fēowertēne niht fourteen nights]

fort·night·ly (fôrt′nīt′lĭ), adj., adv., n., pl. -lies. —adj. 1. occurring or appearing once a fortnight. —adv. 2. once a fortnight. —n. 3. a periodical issued every two weeks.

for·tress (fôr′trĭs), n. 1. a large fortified place; a fort or group of forts, often including a town. 2. any place of security. —v.t. 3. to furnish with or defend by a fortress: the city is heavily fortressed. [ME forterresse, t. OF, der. fort strong]

Fort Smith, a city in W Arkansas, on the Arkansas river. 47,942 (1950).

for·tu·i·tism (fôr tū′ə tĭz′əm, -tōō′-), n. Philos. the doctrine or belief that adaptations in nature come about by chance, and not by design. —**for·tu′i·tist,** n., adj.

for·tu·i·tous (fôr tū′ə təs, -tōō′-), adj. happening or produced by chance; accidental. [t. L: m. fortuitus casual] —**for·tu′i·tous·ly,** adv. —**for·tu′i·tous·ness,** n. —**Syn.** See accidental.

for·tu·i·ty (fôr tū′ə tĭ, -tōō′-), n., pl. -ties. 1. fortuitous character; the fact of being accidental or casual. 2. accident or chance. 3. an accidental occurrence.

For·tu·na (fôr tū′nə, -tōō′-), n. Rom. Myth. the goddess of fortune and chance, the counterpart of the Greek Tyche.

for·tu·nate (fôr′chə nĭt), adj. 1. having good fortune; receiving good from uncertain or unexpected sources; lucky. 2. bringing or presaging good fortune; resulting favorably; auspicious. [ME, t. L: m.s. fortūnātus, pp., made prosperous or happy] —**for′tu·nate·ly,** adv. —**for′tu·nate·ness,** n. —**Syn.** 1, 2. FORTUNATE, HAPPY, LUCKY refer to persons who enjoy, or events which produce, good fortune. FORTUNATE implies that the success is obtained by the operation of favorable circumstances more than by direct effort; it is usually applied to grave or large matters (esp. those happening in the ordinary course of things): fortunate in one's choice of a wife, a fortunate investment. HAPPY emphasizes a pleasant ending or something which happens by chance at just the right moment: by a happy accident I received the package on time. LUCKY, a more colloquial word, is applied to situations of minor moment that turn out well by chance: lucky at cards, my lucky day.

---

b., blend of, blended; c., cognate with; d., dialect, dialectal; der., derived from; f., formed from; g., going back to; m., modification of; r., replacing; s., stem of; t., taken from; ?, perhaps. See the full key on inside cover.

for·tune (fôr′chən), *n., v.,* **-tuned, -tuning.** —*n.*
1. position in life as determined by wealth: *to make one's fortune, a man of fortune.* **2.** amount or stock of wealth. **3.** great wealth; ample stock of wealth. **4.** a person of wealth, esp. a woman; an heiress. **5.** chance; luck. **6.** (*often pl.*) that which falls or is to fall to one as his portion in life or in any particular proceeding. **7.** lot; destiny. **8.** (*often cap.*) chance personified, commonly regarded as a goddess distributing arbitrarily or capriciously the lots of life. **9.** good luck; success; prosperity. —*v.t.* **10.** to endow with a fortune. —*v.i.* **11.** *Rare.* to chance or happen; come by chance. [ME, t. F, t. L: m.s. *fortūna* chance, luck, fortune] —**for′tune·less,** *adj.*

fortune hunter, one who seeks to win a fortune, esp. through marriage. —**for′tune-hunt′ing,** *adj.*

for·tune·tell·er (fôr′chən tĕl′ər), *n.* one who professes to tell people what will happen in the future. —**for′tune·tell′ing,** *adj., n.*

Fort Wayne (wān), a city in NE Indiana. 133,607 (1950).

Fort William, a city in S Canada, in Ontario: a port on Lake Superior. 30,585 (1941).

Fort Worth (wûrth), a city in N Texas. 278,778 (1950).

for·ty (fôr′tĭ), *n., pl.* **-ties,** *adj.* —*n.* **1.** a cardinal number, ten times four. **2.** a symbol for this number, as 40 or XL or XXXX. —*adj.* **3.** amounting to forty in number. [ME *fourti,* OE *fēowertig,* f. *fēower* four + *-tig* -TY¹]

for·ty-nin·er (fôr′tĭ nī′nər), *n.* (*sometimes cap.*) *U.S. Hist.* one of those who went to California in 1849, during the gold rush, in search of fortune.

Forty Thieves, The, one of the tales of the *Arabian Nights' Entertainments,* often called *Ali Baba and the Forty Thieves.* See **Ali Baba.**

forty winks, a short nap, esp. in the daytime.

fo·rum (fôr′əm), *n., pl.* **forums, fora** (fôr′ə). **1.** the market place or public square of an ancient Roman city, the center of judicial and other business and a place of assembly for the people. **2.** a court or tribunal: *the forum of public opinion.* **3.** an assembly for the discussion of questions of public interest. [t. L]

for·ward (fôr′wərd), *adv.* Also, **forwards. 1.** toward or at a place, point, or time in advance; onward; ahead: *to move forward, from this day forward, to look forward.* **2.** towards the front. **3.** out; forth; into view or consideration: *to come or bring forward.* —*adj.* **4.** directed toward a point in advance; moving ahead; onward: *a forward motion.* **5.** being in a condition of advancement; well-advanced. **6.** ready, prompt, or eager. **7.** presumptuous, pert, or bold. **8.** situated in the front or fore part. **9.** lying in advance; fore. **10.** of or pertaining to the future: *forward buying.* **11.** radical or extreme, as persons or opinions. —*n.* **12.** *Sports.* a player stationed in advance of others on his team: **a,** *Football.* any player in the forward line. **b,** *Basketball.* one of two (or in women's rules, three) offensive players on a team. —*v.t.* **13.** to send forward; transmit, esp. to a new address: *to forward a letter.* **14.** to advance or help onward; hasten; promote. **15.** *Bookbinding.* to prepare (a book) for the finisher. See **forwarding** (def. 1). [ME and OE *for(e)-ward.* See FORE¹, WARD] —**for′ward·ly,** *adv.*
—**Syn. 1.** FORWARD, ONWARD both indicate a direction toward the front or a movement in a frontward direction. FORWARD applies to any movement toward what is or is conceived to be the front or a goal: *to face forward, to move forward in the aisles.* ONWARD applies to any movement in continuance of a course: *to march onward toward a goal.* **7.** See **bold.** —**Ant. 4.** backward.

forward delivery, *Com.* delivery at a future date.

for·ward·er (fôr′wər dər), *n.* **1.** one who forwards or sends forward. **2.** one who undertakes to see that the goods of another are transported, without himself incurring the liability of a carrier to deliver.

for·ward·ing (fôr′wər dĭng), *n.* **1.** *Bookbinding.* a stage which involves stitching, fitting the back, pasting, etc., just before the pages are placed in the completed book cover. **2.** *Engraving.* the process of starting a copper plate by etching and of finishing with a graver.

for·ward·ness (fôr′wərd nĭs), *n.* **1.** overreadiness to push oneself forward; presumption; boldness; lack of due modesty. **2.** cheerful readiness; promptness; eagerness. **3.** condition of being forward or in advance.

forward pass, *Football.* a pass in which the ball is thrown towards the opponent's goal.

forward quotation, *Com.* the price quoted on a forward delivery.

for·wards (fôr′wərdz), *adv.* forward. [f. FORWARD + adv. genitive *-s*]

for·worn (fôr wôrn′), *adj. Archaic.* worn out; exhausted. Also, **foreworn.**

for·zan·do (fôr tsän′dō), *adv. Music.* sforzando. [It., ger. of *forzare* force]

Fos·dick (fŏz′dĭk), *n.* **Harry Emerson,** born 1878, U.S. preacher and author.

fos·sa (fŏs′ə), *n., pl.* **fossae** (fŏs′ē). *Anat.* a pit, cavity, or depression in a bone, etc. [t. L: ditch, trench]

fosse (fôs, fŏs), *n.* **1.** a moat or defensive ditch in a fortification, usually filled with water. **2.** any ditch, trench, or canal. Also, **foss.** [ME, t. F, g. L *fossa* ditch]

fos·sette (fŏ sĕt′), *n.* a little hollow; a depression; a dimple. [t. F, dim. of *fosse* FOSSE]

fos·sick (fŏs′ĭk), *Australia.* —*v.i.* **1.** *Mining.* to undermine another's digging; search for waste gold in relinquished workings, washing places, etc. **2.** to search for any object by which to make gain: *to fossick for clients.* —*v.t.* **3.** to dig; hunt. [cf. d. *fossick* troublesome person, *fussick* bustle about, appar. f. FUSS + *-ick,* var. of -OCK] —**fos′sick·er,** *n.*

fos·sil (fŏs′əl), *n.* **1.** any remains, impression, or trace of an animal or plant of a former geological age, as a skeleton or a footprint. **2.** *Colloq.* an outdated or old-fashioned person or thing. **3.** *Obs.* anything dug out of the earth. —*adj.* **4.** of the nature of a fossil: *fossil insects.* **5.** dug out of the earth, or obtained by digging: *fossil fuel.* **6.** belonging to a past epoch or discarded system; antiquated. [t. L: s. *fossilis* dug up; r. earlier *fossile,* t. F] —**fos′sil·like′,** *adj.*

fos·sil·if·er·ous (fŏs′ə lĭf′ər əs), *adj.* bearing or containing fossils, as rocks or strata.

fos·sil·ize (fŏs′ə līz′), *v.,* **-ized, -izing.** —*v.t.* **1.** *Geol.* to convert into a fossil; replace organic substances with mineral in the remains of an organism. **2.** to change as if into mere lifeless remains or traces of the past. **3.** to make rigidly antiquated, as persons, ideas, etc. —*v.i.* **4.** to become a fossil. —**fos′sil·i·za′tion,** *n.*

fos·so·ri·al (fŏ sôr′ĭ əl), *adj. Zool.* **1.** digging or burrowing. **2.** adapted for digging, as the hands, feet, and skeleton of moles, armadillos, and aardvarks. [f. s. LL *fossōrius* (der. L *fossor* digger) + -AL¹]

fos·ter (fôs′tər, fŏs′-), *v.t.* **1.** to promote the growth or development of; further; encourage: *to foster foreign trade.* **2.** to bring up or rear, as a foster child. **3.** to care for or cherish. **4.** *Obs.* to feed or nourish. —*n.* **5.** a cherisher. **6.** nourishment. [ME; OE *fōster* nourishment, *fōstrian* nourish; akin to FOOD] —**fos′ter·er,** *n.* —**Syn. 3.** See **cherish.**

Fos·ter (fôs′tər, fŏs′-), *n.* **1. Stephen Collins,** 1826–64, U.S. song writer and composer of "Old Folks at Home" and other popular songs. **2. William Z.,** born 1881, U.S. Communist party leader and labor organizer.

fos·ter·age (fôs′tər ĭj, fŏs′-), *n.* **1.** act of fostering or rearing another's child as one's own. **2.** condition of being a foster child. **3.** act of promoting or encouraging.

foster brother, a boy brought up with another child of different parents.

foster child, a child raised by someone not its own mother or father.

foster daughter, a girl raised like one's own daughter, though not such by birth.

foster father, one who takes the place of a father in raising a child.

fos·ter·ling (fôs′tər lĭng, fŏs′-), *n.* a foster child. [ME; OE *fōstorling.* See FOSTER, *n.,* -LING¹]

foster mother, **1.** a woman who takes the place of the mother in raising a child. **2.** a nurse.

foster parent, a foster father or foster mother.

foster sister, a girl brought up with another child of different parents.

foster son, a boy raised like one's own son, though not such by birth.

fos·tress (fôs′trĭs, fŏs′-), *n.* a woman who fosters.

Foth·er·ing·hay (fŏth′ər ĭng gā′), *n.* a village in E England, near Peterborough: Mary Queen of Scots was imprisoned and executed (1587) in the castle here.

Fou·cault (foō kō′), *n.* **Jean Bernard Léon** (zhän bĕr nàr′ lĕ ôN′), 1819–68, French physicist.

fou·droy·ant (foō droi′ənt; *Fr.* foō drwà yäN′), *adj.* **1.** striking as with lightning; sudden and overwhelming in effect; stunning; dazzling. **2.** *Pathol.* (of disease) beginning in a sudden and severe form. [t. F, ppr. of *foudroyer* strike with lightning, der. *foudre* lightning, g. L *fulgur*]

fought (fôt), *v.* pt. and pp. of **fight.**

fought·en (fô′tən), *adj. Archaic.* that has been the scene of fighting: *a foughten field.*

foul (foul) *adj.* **1.** grossly offensive to the senses; disgustingly loathsome; noisome: *a foul smell.* **2.** charged with or characterized by offensive or noisome matter: *foul air.* **3.** filthy or dirty, as places, vessels, or clothes. **4.** muddy, as a road. **5.** clogged or obstructed with foreign matter: *a foul chimney.* **6.** unfavorable or stormy, as weather. **7.** contrary, as the wind. **8.** grossly offensive in a moral sense. **9.** abominable, wicked, or vile, as deeds, crime, slander, etc. **10.** scurrilous, profane, or obscene, as language. **11.** contrary to the rules or established usages, as of a sport or game; unfair. **12.** *Baseball.* pertaining to a foul ball or a foul line. **13.** in collision or obstructing contact: *a ship foul of a rock.* **14.** entangled, caught, or jammed: *a foul anchor.* **15.** abounding in errors or in marks of correction, as a printer's proof. **16.** *Dial.* not fair; ugly or unattractive. **17.** *Obs.* disfigured. —*adv.* **18.** in a foul manner; foully; unfairly. —*n.* **19.** that which is foul. **20.** a collision or entanglement. **21.** a violation of the rules of a sport or game. **22.** *Baseball.* a foul ball. —*v.t.* **23.** to make foul; defile; soil. **24.** to clog or obstruct, as a chimney or the bore of a gun. **25.** to collide with. **26.** to cause to become entangled or caught, as a rope. **27.** to defile; dishonor; disgrace. **28.** *Naut.* to encumber (a ship's bottom) with seaweed, barnacles, etc. —*v.i.* **29.** to become foul. **30.** *Naut.* to come into collision, as two boats. **31.** to become entangled or clogged.

the rope fouled. **32.** *Sports.* to make a foul play; give a foul blow. **33.** *Baseball.* to knock a foul ball, etc. **34. foul out,** *Baseball.* to be retired, through the catching of a foul ball by one of the opposite nine. [ME; OE *fūl*, c. G *faul*; akin to L *pūs* pus, *pūtere* to stink] —**foul′ly,** *adv.* —**Syn. 3.** See **dirty.**

fou·lard (foō lärd′, fə-), *n.* a soft lightweight silk or rayon of twill weave with printed design, for neckties, trimmings, etc. [t. F, t. Swiss F: m. *foulat* fulled cloth, c. F *fouler* to full, g. L *fullāre*]

foul ball, *Baseball.* a ball struck so that it falls outside of the foul lines.

foul line, 1. *Baseball.* either of two lines connecting the "home" with the first and third bases respectively, or their continuation. **2.** *Basketball.* a line 15 feet from the backboard from which free throws are made.

foul-mind·ed (foul′mīn′dĭd), *adj.* having unclean thoughts. —**foul′-mind′ed·ness,** *n.*

foul-mouthed (foul′mouтнd′, -moutht′), *adj.* using scurrilous, profane, or obscene language; given to filthy or abusive speech.

foul·ness (foul′nĭs), *n.* **1.** state or quality of being foul. **2.** that which is foul; foul matter; filth. **3.** wickedness. [ME; OE *fūlness.* See FOUL, adj., -NESS]

foul play, 1. any unfair or treacherous dealing, often such as involves murder. **2.** unfair conduct in a game.

fouls (foulz), *n.* *Vet. Sci.* an infection of the feet of cattle causing a foul-smelling inflammation between the toes and around the coronary band.

foul shot, *Basketball.* **1.** a free throw given a member of one team after a penalty has been called against an opponent. **2.** a score of one point.

foul tip, *Baseball.* a ball that glances off the bat directly into the catcher's glove. The player is out on such a play if he has two strikes on him.

found[1] (found), *v.* pt. and pp. of **find.** [ME; OE *funde, fundon* p.t., *funden* pp.]

found[2] (found), *v.t.* **1.** to set up or establish on a firm basis or for enduring existence: *to found a dynasty.* **2.** to lay the lowest part of, fix, or build (a structure) on a firm base or ground: *a house founded upon a rock.* **3.** to base or ground (fol. by *on* or *upon*): *a story founded on fact.* **4.** to afford a basis or ground for. —*v.i.* **5.** to be founded or based (fol. by *on* or *upon*). **6.** to base one's opinion (fol. by *on* or *upon*). [ME *founde(n),* t. OF: m. *fonder,* g. L *fundāre* lay the bottom of, found]

found[3] (found), *v.t.* **1.** to melt and pour (metal, etc.) into a mold. **2.** to form or make (an article) of molten material in a mold; cast. [ME *fond(en),* t. OF: m. *fondre* melt, cast, g. L *fundere* pour, melt, cast]

foun·da·tion (foun dā′shən), *n.* **1.** that on which something is founded. **2.** the basis or ground of anything. **3.** the natural or prepared ground or base on which some structure rests. **4.** the lowest division of a building, wall, or the like, usually of masonry and partly or wholly below the surface of the ground. **5.** act of founding, setting up, establishing, etc. **6.** state of being founded. **7.** a donation or legacy for the support of an institution; endowment. **8.** an endowed institution. —**Syn. 3.** See **base**[1].

Foundation Day, a legal holiday in Australia, usually January 26, to commemorate the British landings in 1788.

found·er[1] (foun′dər), *n.* one who founds or establishes. [f. FOUND[2] + -ER[1]]

foun·der[2] (foun′dər), *v.i.* **1.** to fill with water and sink, as a ship. **2.** to fall or sink down, as buildings, ground, etc. **3.** to suffer wreck, or fail utterly. **4.** to stumble, break down, or go lame, as a horse. **5.** *Vet. Sci.* (of a horse) to suffer from founder. —*v.t.* **6.** to cause to fill with water and sink, as a ship. **7.** *Vet. Sci.* to cause (a horse, etc.) to break down, go lame, or suffer from founder. **8.** *Golf.* to drive (the ball) into the ground. —*n.* **9.** *Vet. Sci.* laminitis. [ME *foundren,* t. OF: m. *fondrer,* ult. der. L *fundus* bottom]

found·er[3] (foun′dər), *n.* one who founds or casts metal, etc. [f. FOUND[3] + -ER[1]]

foun·der·ous (foun′dər əs), *adj.* *Now Chiefly Dial.* miry; swampy.

founders' shares, *Finance.* shares of stock given, at least nominally, for consideration to the organizers or original subscribers of a corporation, sometimes carrying special voting privileges, but likely to receive dividends after other classes of stock.

found·ling (found′lĭng), *n.* an infant found abandoned; a child without a parent or guardian. [ME *found(e)ling,* f. *founde(n),* pp. of FIND, v. + -LING[1]]

found·ry (foun′drĭ), *n.,* *pl.* **-ries. 1.** an establishment for the production of castings, in which molten metal is poured into molds to shape the castings. **2.** the founding of metal, etc. **3.** things made by founding; castings. **4.** *Obs.* the casting of metals. [t. F: m. *fonderie,* der. *fondre* FOUND[3]]

foundry proof, *Print.,* a proof pulled for a final checking before printing plates are made.

fount[1] (fount), *n.* **1.** a spring of water; fountain. **2.** a source or origin. [short for FOUNTAIN]

fount[2] (fount, fŏnt), *n.* *Print., Chiefly Brit.* font[2].

foun·tain (foun′tən), *n.* **1.** a spring or source of water; the source or head of a stream. **2.** the source or origin of anything. **3.** a jet or stream of water (or other liquid) made by mechanical means to spout or rise from an

opening or structure, as to afford water for use, or to cool the air, or to serve for ornament. **4.** a structure for discharging such a jet or a number of jets, often an elaborate or artistic work with basins, sculptures, etc. **5.** a soda fountain. **6.** a reservoir for a liquid to be supplied gradually or continuously. [late ME *fontayne,* t. OF: m. *fontaine,* g. LL *fontāna,* prop. fem. of L *fontānus* of or from a spring] —**foun′tain·less,** *adj.* —**foun′-tain·like,** *adj.*

foun·tain·head (foun′tən hĕd′), *n.* **1.** a fountain or spring from which a stream flows; the head or source of a stream. **2.** a primary source.

Fountain of Youth, a mythical spring, sought in the Bahama Islands and Florida by Ponce de Leon, Narváez, De Soto, and others. Indians of Central America believed that it was to the northward, and that its waters would cure ills and renew youth.

fountain pen, a writing pen with a reservoir for supplying ink continuously.

Fou·qué (foō kā′), *n.* **Friedrich Heinrich Karl** (frē′-drĭкн hīn′rĭкн kärl), (*Baron de La Motte-Fouqué*) 1777–1843, German novelist and poet.

Fou·quet (foō kĕ′), *n.* **Nicolas** (nē kô lä′), (*Marquis de Belle-Isle*) 1615–80, French minister under Louis XIV.

Fou·quier-Tin·ville (foō kyĕ tăn vēl′), *n.* **Antoine Quentin** (ăn twän′/ kän tän′), 1747?–95, French revolutionist: prosecutor during the Reign of Terror.

four (fôr), *n.* **1.** a cardinal number, three plus one. **2.** a symbol of this number, 4 or IV or IIII. **3.** a set of this many persons or things. **4.** a playing card, etc., with four pips. **5. on all fours,** on the hands and feet (or knees). —*adj.* **6.** amounting to four in number. [ME; OE *fēower,* c. D and G *vier* four; akin to L *quattuor,* Gk. *téttares*]

four·chette (foŏr shĕt′), *n.* **1.** *Anat.* the fold of skin which forms the posterior margin of the vulva. **2.** *Ornith.* the furcula or united clavicles of a bird; the wishbone of a fowl. **3.** *Zool.* the frog of an animal's foot. **4.** a strip of leather or fabric joining front and back sections of a glove finger. [t. F, dim. of *fourche,* g. L *furca* fork]

four·cy·cle (fôr′sī′kəl), *n.* (In an internal-combustion engine) a cycle in which one piston stroke out of every four is a power stroke.

four-di·men·sion·al (fôr′dĭ mĕn′shən əl), *adj.* *Math.* of a space having points, or a set having elements, which require four coördinates for their unique determination.

Four·drin·i·er (foŏr drĭn′ĭ ər), *n.* **Henry,** 1766–1854, British inventor (of papermaking machinery).

four flush, (in poker) **1.** four cards of a possible flush, which, with one card of a different suit, make up a hand. **2.** an imperfect flush.

four-flush (fôr′flŭsh′), *v.i.* *Slang.* to act as a four-flusher.

four-flush·er (fôr′flŭsh′ər), *n.* *Slang.* one who makes pretensions that he cannot or does not bear out.

four-fold (fôr′fōld′), *adj.,* *adv.* four times as great or as much.

four-foot·ed (fôr′fŏŏt′ĭd), *adj.* having four feet.

four freedoms, freedom of speech, freedom of worship, freedom from want, and freedom from fear: listed by Franklin D. Roosevelt.

four·gon (foŏr gôn′), *n.* *French.* a long covered wagon for carrying baggage, goods, military supplies, etc.; a van or tumbril. [F, ? identical with *fourgon* oven fork, der. OF *forgier* search, ult. der. L *forāre* bore]

four-hand·ed (fôr′hăn′dĭd), *adj.* **1.** involving four hands or players, as a game at cards. **2.** intended for four hands, as a piece of music for the piano. **3.** having four hands, or four feet adapted for use as hands; quadrumanous.

four hundred, the, the *U.S.* the exclusive social set.

Fou·rier (foō ryĕ′), *n.* **1. François Marie Charles** (frän swä′ má rē′ shárl), 1772–1837, French socialist, writer, and reformer. **2. Jean Baptiste Joseph** (zhän bá tēst′ zhô zĕf′), 1768–1830, French mathematician and physicist.

Four·i·er analysis (foŏr′ĭ ā′, -ĭ ər), *Physics.* the decomposition of any periodic function such as a complex sound or electromagnetic wave form into the sum of a number of sine and cosine functions.

Fou·ri·er·ism (foŏr′ĭ ə rĭz′əm), *n.* the communistic system propounded by François Marie Charles Fourier, under which society was to be organized into phalanxes or associations, each large enough for all industrial and social requirements. —**Fou′ri·er·ist, Fou·ri·er·ite** (foŏr′ĭ ə rīt′), *n.* —**Fou′ri·er·is′tic,** *adj.*

four-in-hand (fôr′ĭn hănd′), *n.* **1.** a long scarf or necktie to be tied in a slipknot with the ends left hanging. **2.** a vehicle drawn by four horses and driven by one person. **3.** a team of four horses. —*adj.* **4.** having to do with a four-in-hand.

four-mast·ed (fôr′măs′tĭd, -mäs′-), *adj.* *Naut.* carrying four masts.

four-o'clock (fôr′ə klŏk′), *n.* **1.** a common nyctaginaceous garden plant, *Mirabilis jalapa,* with red, white, yellow, or variegated flowers which open late in the afternoon. **2.** a similar red-flowered plant, *M. laevis,* common in California. **3.** any plant of the same genus. **4.** the Australian friarbird.

four·pence (fôr′pəns), *n.* *Brit.* **1.** a sum of money of the value of four English pennies, or about 8 U.S. cents; **2.** a silver coin of this value.

---

b., blend of, blended; c., cognate with; d., dialect, dialectal; der., derived from; f., formed from; g., going back to; m., modification of; r., replacing; s., stem of; t., taken from; ?, perhaps. See the full key on inside cover.

four·pen·ny (fôr/pĕn/ĭ, -pənĭ), *adj.* *Brit.* of the amount or value of fourpence.

four-post·er (fôr/pōs/tər), *n.* a bed with four posts, as for supporting curtains.

four·ra·gère (foō rå zhĕr/), *n.* (in French and U.S. military use) **1.** an ornament of cord worn on the shoulder. **2.** such a cord awarded as an honorary decoration, as to members of a regiment or other unit that has received a requisite number of citations. [F]

four·score (fôr/skôr/), *adj.* four times twenty; eighty.

four·some (fôr/səm), *n.* **1.** *Golf, etc.* a match played by four persons, two on each side. **2.** a company or set of four. —*adj.* **3.** consisting of four; performed by four persons together. [f. FOUR + -SOME²]

four·square (fôr/skwâr/), *adj.* **1.** square. **2.** firm; steady. **3.** frank; blunt. —*adv.* **4.** without equivocation.

four·teen (fôr/tēn/), *n.* **1.** a cardinal number, ten plus four. **2.** a symbol for this number, as 14 or XIV or XIIII. —*adj.* **3.** amounting to fourteen in number. [ME *fourtene*, OE *fēowertēne*. See FOUR, -TEEN]

Fourteen Points, The, a statement of the war aims of the Allies, made by President Wilson on January 8, 1918.

four·teenth (fôr/tēnth/), *adj.* **1.** next after the thirteenth. **2.** being one of fourteen equal parts. —*n.* **3.** a fourteenth part, esp. of one (¹/₁₄). **4.** the fourteenth member of a series.

fourth (fôrth), *adj.* **1.** next after the third. **2.** being one of four equal parts. —*n.* **3.** a fourth part, esp. of one (¼). **4.** the fourth member of a series. **5.** *Music.* **a.** a tone on the fourth degree from a given tone (counted as the first). **b.** the interval between such tones. **c.** the harmonic combination of such tones. **6. the Fourth,** the Fourth of July. [ME; OE *fēo(we)rtha*. See FOUR, -TH²]

fourth-class matter (fôrth/klăs/, -kläs/), (in the U. S. postal system) mail matter consisting of merchandise, not written or printed matter.

fourth dimension, *Math.* an assumed dimension in addition to length, breadth, and thickness.

fourth estate, the public press, the newspapers, or the body of journalists.

fourth·ly (fôrth/lĭ), *adv.* in the fourth place.

Fourth of July, *U.S.* the date of the adoption of the Declaration of Independence, in 1776, observed as a legal holiday.

four-wheel (fôr/hwēl/), *adj.* **1.** having four wheels. **2.** functioning on or by four wheels: *a four-wheel drive.*

fou·ter (foō/tər), *n.* a word formerly used in expressions of contemptuous indifference: "*a fouter for the world!*" Also, **fou/tre.** [t. F: m. (*se*) *foutre* (*de*) care nothing for, g. L *futuere* have sexual intercourse with]

fo·ve·a (fō/vĭ ə), *n., pl.* **-veae** (-vĭ ē/). *Biol.* a small pit or depression in a bone or other structure. [t. L: small pit] —**fo/ve·al,** *adj.*

fovea cen·tra·lis (sĕn trā/lĭs), *Anat.* a small pit or depression at the back of the retina forming the point of sharpest vision. [L]

fo·ve·ate (fō/vĭ ĭt, -āt/), *adj.* *Biol.* having foveae; pitted.

fo·ve·o·la (fō vē/ə lə), *n., pl.* **-lae** (-lē/). *Biol.* a small fovea; a very small pit or depression. [NL., dim. of L *fovea.* See FOVEA]

fo·ve·o·late (fō/vĭ ə lāt/), *adj.* *Biol.* having foveolae, or very small pits. Also, **fo/ve·o·lat/ed.**

fowl (foul), *n., pl.* **fowls,** (*esp. collectively*) **fowl,** *v.* —*n.* **1.** the domestic or barnyard hen or rooster (**domestic fowl**), a gallinaceous bird (often designated as *Gallus domesticus*) of the pheasant family, descended from wild species of *Gallus* (**jungle fowl**). **2.** any of various other gallinaceous or similar birds, as the turkey or duck. **3.** (in market and household use) a full-grown domestic fowl for food purposes (as distinguished from a chicken, or young fowl). **4.** the flesh or meat of a domestic fowl. **5.** any bird (now chiefly in combination): *water fowl, wild fowl.* —*v.i.* **6.** to hunt or take wild fowl. [ME *foule*, OE *fugel*, c. D and G *vogel*] —**fowl/er,** *n.*

fowl cholera, a specific, acute, diarrheal disease of fowls, especially chickens, caused by a bacterium, *Pasteurella multocida.*

fowl·ing (fou/lĭng), *n.* the practice or sport of shooting or snaring birds.

fowling piece, a shotgun for shooting wild fowl.

fowl pox, a virus disease of chickens and other birds characterized by warty excrescences on the comb and wattles, and often by diphtherialike changes in the mucous membranes of the head.

fox (fŏks), *n.* **1.** any of certain carnivores of the dog family (*Canidae*), esp. those constituting the genus *Vulpes,* smaller than the wolves, characterized by pointed muzzle, erect ears, and long, bushy tail. **2.** a cunning or crafty person. **3.** *Naut.* a seizing made by twisting several rope yarns together and rubbing them down. **4.** (*cap.*) **a.** a tribe of North American Algonquian Indians,

Red fox, *Vulpes fulva*
(Total length 3½ ft., tail 16 in.)

formerly in Wisconsin, later merged with the Sac tribe. **b.** a member of this tribe. **5.** *Bible.* (sometimes) the jackal. —*v.t.* **6.** *Colloq.* to deceive or trick. **7.** to intoxicate or befuddle. **8.** to cause (papers, etc.) to discolor with reddish brown spots of mildew. **9.** to make sour, as beer. **10.** to repair or make (a shoe) with leather or other material applied so as to cover or form part of the upper front. —*v.i.* **11.** to act cunningly or craftily. **12.** (of papers, etc.) to become foxed. [ME and OE, c. G *fuchs*. See VIXEN] —**fox/like/,** *adj.*

Fox (fŏks), *n.* **1. Charles James,** 1749–1806, British statesman and orator. **2. George,** 1624–91, British preacher and writer, founder of the Society of Friends. **3. John.** See **Foxe.**

Foxe (fŏks), *n.* **John,** 1516–87, British clergyman and writer.

fox·glove (fŏks/glŭv/), *n.* any plant of the scrophulariaceous genus *Digitalis,* esp. *D. purpurea* (the common foxglove), a native of Europe, bearing drooping, tubular, purple or white flowers, and leaves that are used as digitalis in medicine. [ME *foxes glove*, OE *foxes glōfa*]

fox grape, either of two species of grape, *Vitis labrusca* of the northern U.S. or *V. rotundifolia* of the southern U.S., from which various cultivated varieties have been derived.

fox·hole (fŏks/hōl/), *n.* a small pit, usually for one or two men, used for cover in a battle area.

fox·hound (fŏks/hound/), *n.* one of a breed of fleet, keen-scented hounds trained to hunt foxes.

English foxhound
(23 in. high at the shoulder, 27½ in. long)

fox hunt, a sport in which the hunters follow a fox that is being pursued by a hound or hounds.

fox squirrel, any of several North American arboreal squirrels varying in color and remarkable for large size.

fox·tail (fŏks/tāl/), *n.* **1.** the tail of a fox. **2.** any of various grasses with soft, brushlike spikes of flowers.

foxtail millet, an annual grass, *Cetaria italica,* of numerous varieties, introduced into the U.S. from Europe and Asia, and grown chiefly for emergency hay crops.

fox terrier, one of a breed of small, active terriers, sometimes used for driving foxes from their holes, but kept chiefly as pets.

fox trot, 1. a social dance, in 4/4 time, performed by couples, characterized by various combinations of short, quick steps. **2.** a pace, as of a horse, consisting of a series of short steps, as in slackening from a trot to a walk.

fox-trot (fŏks/trŏt/), *v.i.,* **-trotted, -trotting.** to dance a fox trot.

Fox terrier
(15 in. high at the shoulder)

fox·y (fŏk/sĭ), *adj.,* **foxier, foxiest. 1.** foxlike; cunning or crafty. **2.** discolored or foxed. **3.** yellowish- or reddish-brown; of the color of the common red fox. **4.** impaired or defective in quality. **5.** (of wines) having the pronounced flavor natural to native American grape varieties, as that of Concord grapes. —**fox/i·ly,** *adv.* —**fox/i·ness,** *n.*

foy (foi), *n.* *Dial.* **1.** a feast, gift, etc., given by or to a person about to start on a journey. **2.** a feast held on some special occasion, as at the end of the harvest. [t. MD: m. *foye*, prob. t. OF: m. *voie*, g. L *via* way]

foy·er (foi/ər, foi/ā; Fr. fwà yē/), *n.* **1.** the lobby of a theater or hotel. **2.** an entrance hall in a house. [t. F: hearth, fireside (orig. a room to which theater audiences went for warmth between the acts), g. Rom. *focārium,* der. L *focus* hearth]

F.P., foot-pound. Also, **f.p.**

f.p., freezing point.

f.p.s. system, foot-pound-second system.

Fr., 1. Father. **2.** France. **3.** frater¹. **4.** French. **5.** Friar. **6.** Friday.

fr., 1. fragment. **2.** (*pl.* **fr., frs.**) franc. **3.** from.

Fra (frä), *n.* brother (a title of a friar): *Fra Giovanni.* [t. It., abbr. of *frate* brother]

fra·cas (frā/kəs; *Brit.* fräk/ä), *n.* a disorderly noise, disturbance, or fight; uproar. [t. F, t. It.: m. *fracasso,* der. *fracassare* smash, f. *fra-* (g. L *infrā* among) completely + *cassare* (ult. g. L *quassāre* to shake)]

frac·tion (frăk/shən), *n.* **1.** *Math.* **a.** one or more aliquot parts of a unit or whole number; the ratio between any two numbers. **b.** a ratio of algebraic quantities analogous to the arithmetical vulgar fraction, and similarly expressed. **2.** a part as distinct from the whole of anything: *only a fraction of the regiment came back.* **3.** a piece broken off; fragment or bit. **4.** act of breaking. —*v.t.* **5.** to divide into fractions. [ME, t. LL: s. *fractio,* der. L *frangere* break]

frac·tion·al (frăk/shən əl), *adj.* **1.** pertaining to fractions; comprising a part or the parts of a unit; constituting a fraction: *fractional numbers.* **2.** partial, inconsiderable, or insignificant. **3.** *Chem.* of or denoting a process, as distillation, crystallization, or oxidation, by which the component substances of a mixture are sep-

arated according to differences in certain of their properties, as boiling point, critical temperature, solubil-
ity, etc. Also, **frac·tion·ar·y** (frăk/shə nĕr/ĭ) for 1, 2.
—**frac/tion·al·ly,** adv.

fractional currency, coins or paper money of a
smaller denomination than the monetary unit.

frac·tion·ate (frăk/shə nāt/), v.t., **-ated, -ating. 1.** to
separate (a mixture) into its ingredients, or into portions
having different properties, as by distillation or crystallization; subject to fractional distillation, crystallization, or the like. **2.** to obtain by such a process.
—**frac/tion·a/tion,** n.

frac·tion·ize (frăk/shə nīz/), v.t., v.i., **-ized, -izing.** to
divide into fractions.

frac·tious (frăk/shəs), adj. **1.** cross, fretful, or peevish.
2. refractory or unruly. [f. FRACTI(ON) (in obs. sense of
discord) + -OUS, modeled on CAPTIOUS, etc.] —**frac/-
tious·ly,** adv. —**frac/tious·ness,** n.

fracto-, a word element meaning "broken." [comb.
form repr. L *fractus,* pp.]

frac·to·cu·mu·lus (frăk/tō kū/myə ləs), n., pl. **-li** (-lī/).
Meteorol. very low, ragged clouds, slightly cumuliform,
which often appear beneath nimbostratus clouds during
active precipitation.

frac·to·stra·tus (frăk/tō strā/təs), n., pl. **-ti** (-tī).
Meteorol. very low, ragged clouds of stratiform appearance which often appear beneath nimbostratus clouds
during active precipitation; scud clouds.

frac·ture (frăk/chər), n., v., **-tured, -turing.** —n.
1. the breaking of a bone, cartilage, etc., or the resulting
condition (in a bone, called *simple* when the bone does
not communicate with the exterior, and *compound* when
there is also a laceration of the integuments permitting
communication with the exterior). **2.** the characteristic
manner of breaking. **3.** the characteristic appearance
of a broken surface, as of a mineral. **4.** act of breaking.
5. state of being broken. **6.** a break, breach, or split.
—v.t. **7.** to break or crack. **8.** to cause or to suffer a
fracture in (a bone, etc.). —v.i. **9.** to undergo fracture;
break. [t. F, t. L: m. *fractūra* breach] —**frac/tur·al,** adj.

frae (frā), prep., adv. *Scot.* from.

frae·num (frē/nəm), n., pl. **-na** (-nə). *Anat., Zool.*
frenum.

frag·ile (frăj/əl; *Brit.* frăj/īl), adj. easily broken, shattered, or damaged; delicate; brittle; frail. [t. L: m.s.
fragilis] —**frag/ile·ly,** adv. —**fra·gil·i·ty** (frə jĭl/-
ə tĭ), **frag/ile·ness,** n. —**Syn.** See **frail¹.**

frag·ment (frăg/mənt), n. **1.** a part broken off or
detached: *scattered fragments of rock.* **2.** a portion that is
unfinished or incomplete: *fragments of a letter.* **3.** an odd
piece, bit, or scrap. [t. L: s. *fragmentum*]

frag·men·tal (frăg mĕn/təl), adj. **1.** fragmentary.
2. *Geol.* clastic.

frag·men·tar·y (frăg/mən tĕr/ĭ), adj. composed of
fragments; broken; disconnected; incomplete: *fragmentary evidence, remains, etc.* —**frag/men·tar/i·ly,** adv.
—**frag/men·tar/i·ness,** n.

frag·men·ta·tion (frăg/mən tā/shən), adj. *Mil.* denoting a bomb, grenade, etc., that scatters fragments of
its case or contents over a wide area.

frag·ment·ed (frăg/mən tĭd), adj. reduced to fragments.

Fra·go·nard (frȧ gô nȧr/), n. **Jean Honoré** (zhän ô-
nô rā/), 1732–1806, French painter.

fra·grance (frā/grəns), n. fragrant quality or odor;
sweet scent. —**Syn.** See **perfume.**

fra·gran·cy (frā/grən sĭ), n., pl. **-cies.** fragrance.

fra·grant (frā/grənt), adj. **1.** having a pleasant odor;
sweet-smelling; sweet-scented. **2.** delightful; pleasant:
fragrant memories. [t. L: s. *frāgrans,* ppr., emitting an
odor, smelling sweet] —**fra/grant·ly,** adv. —**Syn.**
perfumed, odorous, redolent.

frail¹ (frāl), adj. **1.** weak; not robust; having delicate
health. **2.** easily broken or destroyed; fragile. **3.** morally weak; not strong against temptation. [ME *frele,* t.
OF, var. of *fraile,* g. L *fragilis* fragile] —**frail/ly,** adv.
—**frail/ness,** n.
—**Syn. 1, 2.** FRAIL, BRITTLE, FRAGILE imply a delicacy or
weakness of substance or construction. FRAIL applies particularly to health, and immaterial things: *a frail constitution,
frail hopes.* BRITTLE implies a hard outside finish but delicate
material which snaps or breaks to pieces easily: *brittle as
glass.* FRAGILE implies that the object must be handled
carefully to avoid breakage or damage: *fragile bric-à-brac.*
—**Ant. 1.** sturdy.

frail² (frāl), n. **1.** a flexible basket made of rushes, used
esp. for dried fruits, as dates, figs, or raisins. **2.** a certain
quantity of raisins, about 75 pounds, contained in such
a basket. [ME *frayel,* t. OF: m. *fraiel*]

frail·ty (frāl/tĭ), n., pl. **-ties. 1.** quality or state of
being frail. **2.** moral weakness; liability to yield to
temptation. **3.** a fault proceeding from moral weakness.

fraise (frāz), n. **1.** *Fort.* a defense consisting of pointed
stakes projecting from the ramparts in a horizontal or an
inclined position. **2.** a ruff worn around the neck in the
16th century. [t. F, der. *fraiser* to frizzle, curl, t. Pr.: m.
frezar, ult. der. Gmc.; cf. OE *frīs* curled]

Frak·tur (frȧk toor/), n. *Print.* German text, a style
of type.

fram·be·sia (frăm bē/zhə), n. *Pathol.* a contagious
disease resembling syphilis, prevalent in certain tropical
regions, characterized by an eruption of raspberrylike
excrescences; yaws. Also, **fram·boe/sia.** [NL: Latin-

ization of F *framboise* raspberry, g. Rom. *frambosia,*
contr. of *frāga ambrosia* ambrosia strawberry]

frame (frām), n., v., **framed, framing.** —n. **1.** an
enclosing border or case, as for a picture. **2.** anything
composed of parts fitted and joined together; a structure.
3. the sustaining parts of a structure fitted and joined
together; framework or skeleton. **4.** the body, esp. the
human body, with reference to its make or build. **5.** a
structure for admitting or enclosing something. **6.** any
of various machines operating on or within a framework.
7. a particular state, as of the mind: *an unhappy frame
of mind.* **8.** form, constitution, or structure in general;
system; order. **9.** *Shipbuilding.* **a.** one of the transverse
structural members of a ship's hull, extending from the
gunwale to the bilge or to the keel. **b. square frame,**
a frame set perpendicularly to the vertical plane of the
keel. **c. cant frame,** a frame set at an acute angle to
the vertical plane of the keel. **10.** *Colloq.* (in baseball) an
inning. **11.** *American Bowling.* a turn to bowl, each
player usually having ten turns, of two (or, if a strike is
made, three) shots each, in a game. **12.** *Pool.* **a.** the
triangular form used to set up the balls for a game. **b.**
the balls as so set up. **c.** the period of play required to
pocket them. **13.** *Movies.* one of the successive small
pictures on a strip of film.
—v.t. **14.** to form or make, as by fitting and uniting parts
together; construct. **15.** to contrive, devise, or compose,
as a plan, law, poem, etc. **16.** to conceive or imagine, as
ideas, etc. **17.** to fashion or shape. **18.** to shape or to
adapt to a particular purpose. **19.** *Colloq.* to contrive or
prearrange fraudulently or falsely, as a plot, a race, etc.
20. *Colloq.* to incriminate unjustly by a plot, as a person.
21. to provide with or put into a frame, as a picture.
22. *Obs.* to direct, as one's steps.
—v.i. **23.** to betake oneself, or resort. **24.** to prepare,
attempt, give promise, or manage to do something.
[ME *frame(n),* OE *framian* avail, profit, der. *fram* for-
ward] —**frame/less,** adj. —**fram/er,** n.

frame house, *U.S.* a house constructed with a skeleton frame of timber, as the ordinary wooden house.

frame-up (frām/ŭp/), n. *Orig. U.S. Slang.* **1.** that
which is framed, as a plot, or a contest whose result is
fraudulently prearranged. **2.** act of framing up.

frame·work (frām/wûrk/), n. **1.** a structure composed of parts fitted and united together. **2.** one designed to support or enclose something; frame or skeleton. **3.** frames collectively. **4.** work done in, on, or
with a frame.

fram·ing (frā/mĭng), n. **1.** act, process, or manner of
constructing anything. **2.** act of providing with a frame.
3. framed work; a frame or a system of frames.

Fram·ing·ham (frā/mĭng hăm/), n. a town in E Massachusetts. 28,086 (1950).

franc (frăngk; *Fr.* frän), n. **1.** a French monetary unit
and coin, equal at present to .0028 U.S. dollar. **2.** the
corresponding coin and unit of Switzerland, Belgium,
Italy, etc. **3.** either of two old coins and units of France,
one of gold and the other of silver. [ME *frank,* t. OF:
m. *franc,* so called from the ML legend *Francōrum rex*
king of the Franks (or French), on the first coin]

France (frăns, fräns), n. a republic in W Europe,
40,517,923 pop. (1946); 212,736 sq. mi. *Cap.:* Paris.

France (fräns), n. **Anatole** (ȧ nȧ tôl/), (*Jacques Anatole Thibault*) 1844–1924, French novelist and essayist.

Fran·ces·ca (frän chĕs/kä), n. **Piero della** (pyĕ/rô
dĕl/lä), (*Piero de' Franceschi*) c1420–92, Italian painter.

Franche-Com·té (fränsh kôn tā/), n. a former province in E France: once a part of Burgundy.

fran·chise (frăn/chīz), n. **1.** the right to vote. **2.** a
privilege arising from the grant of a sovereign or government, or from prescription, which presupposes a grant.
3. a privilege of a public nature conferred on an individual or body of individuals by a governmental grant:
a franchise for a street railway. **4.** permission granted by
a manufacturer to a distributor or retailer to sell his
products. **5.** the district or jurisdiction to which the
privilege of an individual or corporation extends. **6.**
(orig.) a legal immunity or exemption from a particular
burden, exaction, or the like. [ME, t. OF, der. *franc*
free, FRANK]

Fran·cis (frăn/sĭs, frän/-), **Saint,** (*Francis of Assisi*)
1181?–1226, Italian friar: founded Franciscan order.

Francis I, 1. 1494–1547, king of France, 1515–47.
2. title of Francis II as emperor of Austria.

Francis II, 1768–1835, last emperor of the Holy
Roman Empire, 1792–1806. As Francis I, he was the
first emperor of Austria, 1804–35.

Fran·cis·can (frăn sĭs/kən), adj. **1.** of or pertaining to
St. Francis of Assisi or the mendicant religious order
founded by him (authorized by the Pope in 1209;
formally ratified in 1223). —n. **2.** a member of this
order.

Francis Ferdinand, 1863–1914, Archduke of Austria, heir to the thrones of Austria and Hungary, nephew
of Francis Joseph I. His assassination June 28, 1914, led
to the outbreak of World War I.

Francis Joseph I, 1830–1916, emperor of Austria,
1848–1916, and king of Hungary and Bohemia.

Francis of Pa·u·la (pä/ōō lä/), **Saint,** 1416–1507,
Italian monk: founder of order of Minims.

Francis of Sales (sälz; *Fr.* säl), **Saint,** 1567–1622,
French Roman Catholic bishop of Geneva, Switzerland.

Francis Xa·vi·er (zā'vĭ ər, zăv'ĭ-). See **Xavier.**

Franck (frängk), *n.* **César Auguste** (sĕ zär' ō gyst'), 1822–1890, French composer, born in Belgium.

Fran·co (fräng'kō), *n.* **Francisco** (frän thēs'kō), born 1892, Spanish chief of state, 1939–47; regent of the kingdom of Spain since 1947.

Franco-, a word element meaning "French" or "France," as in *Franco-American.* [comb. form repr. ML *Francus* a Frank, a Frenchman]

fran·co·lin (fräng'kə lĭn), *n.* any of numerous Old World gallinaceous birds of the genus *Francolinus* and allied genera, esp. *F. vulgaris*, a species formerly common in southern Europe but now chiefly confined to Asia. [t. F, t. It.: *m. francolino*]

Fran·co·ni·a (fräng kō'nĭ ə), *n.* a medieval duchy in Germany, largely in the valley of the Main river.

Fran·co·phile (fräng'kə fĭl'), *adj.* **1.** friendly to France or the French. —*n.* **2.** one who is friendly to France or the French. Also, **Fran·co·phil** (fräng'kə fĭl).

Fran·co·phobe (fräng'kə fōb'), *adj.* **1.** fearing or hating France. —*n.* **2.** one who fears or hates France.

franc-ti·reur (frän tē rœr'), *n., pl.* **francs-tireurs** (frän tē rœr'). a sharpshooter in the French Army. [F: lit., free shooter]

fran·gi·ble (frăn'jə bəl), *adj.* capable of being broken; breakable. [ME *frangebyll*, t. OF: *m. frangible*, der. L *frangere* break] —**fran'gi·bil'i·ty,** *n.*

fran·gi·pane (frăn'jə pān'), *n.* **1.** a kind of pastry cake, filled with cream, almonds, and sugar. **2.** frangipani. [t. F; said to be from *Frangipani*, the inventor]

fran·gi·pan·i (frăn'jĭ păn'ĭ, -pä'nĭ), *n., pl.* **-panis. 1.** a perfume prepared from or imitating the odor of the flower of the red jasmine, *Plumeria rubra*, an apocynaceous tree or shrub of tropical America. **2.** the tree or shrub itself. [said to be named after the inventor]

frank (frăngk), *adj.* **1.** open or unreserved in speech; candid or outspoken; sincere. **2.** undisguised; avowed; downright: *frank mutiny.* **3.** *Rare.* liberal or generous. **4.** *Obs.* free. —*n.* **5.** a signature or mark affixed by special privilege to a letter, package, or the like, to ensure its transmission free of charge, as by mail. **6.** the privilege of franking letters, etc. **7.** a franked letter, package, etc. —*v.t.* **8.** to mark (a letter, package, etc.) for transmission free of the usual charge, by virtue of official or special privilege; send free of charge, as mail. **9.** to facilitate the coming of (a person); convey (a person) free of charge. **10.** to enable to pass or go freely. **11.** to secure exemption for. [ME, t. OF: *m. franc*, g. LL *francus* free, orig. Frank] —**frank'a·ble,** *adj.* —**frank'er,** *n.*

—**Syn. 1.** FRANK, CANDID, OPEN, OUTSPOKEN imply a freedom and boldness in speaking. FRANK is applied to one unreserved in expressing the truth and his real opinions and sentiments: *a frank disagreement.* CANDID suggests one (sometimes unpleasantly) sincere and truthful or impartial and fair in judgment: *a candid expression of opinion.* OPEN implies a lack of reserve or of concealment: *open antagonism.* OUTSPOKEN applies to one who expresses himself freely, even when this is inappropriate: *outspoken disapproval.* —**Ant. 1.** reticent.

Frank (frăngk), *n.* **1.** a member of a group of ancient Germanic peoples dwelling in the regions of the Rhine, one division of whom, the Salians, conquered Gaul about A.D. 500, founded an extensive kingdom, and gave origin to the name France. **2.** (in the Levant) any native or inhabitant of western Europe. [ME *Franke*, OE *Franca*, c. OHG *Franko*; usually said to be from the name of the national weapon. Cf. OE *franca* spear, javelin. See FRANK]

Frank·en·stein (frăngk'ən stīn'), *n.* **1.** one who creates a monster or a destructive agency that he cannot control or that brings about his own ruin. **2.** the monster or destructive agency itself. [from the hero of Mary Shelley's novel, "Frankenstein," a student who created such a monster]

Frank·fort (frăngk'fərt), *n.* the capital of Kentucky, in the N part. 11,973 (1950).

Frankfort on the Main (mān), a city in W Germany, on the Main river. 553,464 (1939). German, **Frank·furt am Main** (frängk'fŏŏrt äm mīn'), **Frankfurt.**

Frankfort on the O·der (ō'dər), a city in NE Germany, on the Oder. 83,669 (1939). German, **Frankfurt an der O·der** (frängk'fŏŏrt än dər ō'dər), **Frankfurt.**

frank·furt·er (frăngk'fər tər), *n.* a reddish variety of sausage made of beef and pork, commonly cooked by steaming or boiling. Also, **frank'furt.** [t. G: Frankfurt (sausage)]

Frank·furt·er (frăngk'fər tər), *n.* **Felix,** born 1882, U.S. jurist: associate justice U.S. Supreme Court since 1939, born in Austria.

Frankfurt horizontal (frăngk'fərt), **1.** *Craniom.* the plane established when right and left poria and left orbitale are in the same horizontal plane. **2.** *Cephalom.* the plane established when right and left tragia and left orbitale are in the same horizontal plane.

frank·in·cense (frăngk'ĭn sĕns'), *n.* an aromatic gum resin from various Asiatic and African trees of the genus *Boswellia*, esp. *B. carteri*: used chiefly for burning as incense or ceremonially. [ME *franc ensens*, t. OF: *m. franc encens* pure incense. See FRANK, INCENSE[2]]

Frank·ish (frăngk'ĭsh), *adj.* **1.** of or pertaining to the Franks. —*n.* **2.** the language of the Franks (def. 1).

Frank·lin (frăngk'lĭn), *n.* **1. Benjamin,** 1706–90. American statesman, diplomat, author, scientist, and inventor. **2. Sir John,** 1786–1847, British explorer. **3.** a district in extreme N Canada, in the Northwest Territories, including Baffin Island, other Arctic islands, and Boothia and Melville peninsulas. 549,253 sq. mi.

frank·lin (frăngk'lĭn), *n.* (in the late Middle Ages) a non-noble freeholder of the middle class. [ME *frankeleyn*, ult. der. ML *francus* free, FRANK]

frank·lin·ite (frăngk'lĭ nīt'), *n.* a mineral of the spinel group, an oxide of zinc, manganese, and iron, occurring in black octahedral crystals or in masses: an ore of zinc. [named after *Franklin*, N. J., where it is found. See -ITE[1]]

Franklin stove, *U.S.* **1.** a type of iron fireplace designed by Benjamin Franklin. **2.** an open stove of various types.

frank·ly (frăngk'lĭ), *adv.* in a frank manner; freely; openly; unreservedly; candidly; plainly.

frank·ness (frăngk'nĭs), *n.* plainness of speech; candor; openness.

frank·pledge (frăngk'plĕj'), *n. Early Eng. Law.* **1.** a system by which the inhabitants of a community were divided into groups of ten or more, whose members had to produce one of their number charged with a breach of the law or pay a fine. **2.** a member of such a group. **3.** the group itself. [t. AF: *m. franc plege*, mistranslation of OE *frithborg* peace pledge]

fran·tic (frăn'tĭk), *adj.* **1.** wild with excitement, passion, fear, pain, etc.; frenzied; characterized by or pertaining to frenzy. **2.** *Archaic.* insane or mad. [ME *frentik*, t. OF: *m. frenetique*, t. L: *m. phreneticus* delirious, t. Gk.: *m. phrenetikós*] —**fran'ti·cal·ly, fran'tic·ly,** *adv.* —**fran'tic·ness,** *n.*

Franz Jo·sef Land (fränts' yō'zĕf), an archipelago in the Arctic Ocean, E of Spitzbergen and N of Novaya Zemlya, belonging to the Soviet Union. Also, **Fridtjof Nansen Land.**

frap (frăp), *v.t.,* **frapped, frapping.** *Naut.* to bind securely. [ME *frap(en).* t. OF: *m. fraper* strike. Cf. FRAPPE]

frap·pé (fră pā'; *Fr.* frà pĕ'), *n.* *U.S.* **1.** a fruit juice mixture frozen to a mush, to be sipped as an appetizer. —*adj.* **2.** chilled; iced; frozen. [t. F, pp. of *frapper* ice (drinks), orig., beat, t. Gmc.; cf. RAP]

Fra·ser (frā'zər), *n.* a river in SW Canada, flowing S through British Columbia to the Pacific. 695 mi.

frat (frăt), *n.* *U.S. College Slang.* a fraternity (def. 1).

fra·ter[1] (frā'tər), *n.* a brother; comrade. [L: brother]

fra·ter[2] (frā'tər), *n.* *Obs. except Hist.* the refectory of a religious house. [ME *freitur*, t. OF: *m. fraitur*, short for *refreitor*, repr. ML *refectōrium* REFECTORY]

fra·ter·nal (frə tûr'nəl), *adj.* **1.** of, pertaining to, or befitting a brother or brothers; brotherly. **2.** being, or pertaining to, a society of men associated in brotherly union, as for mutual aid or benefit: *a fraternal society.* [f. s. L *frāternus* brotherly + -AL[1]] —**fra·ter'nal·ism,** *n.* —**fra·ter'nal·ly,** *adv.*

fraternal insurance, insurance underwritten by a fraternal society, under either a legal reserve plan or an assessment plan.

fra·ter·ni·ty (frə tûr'nə tĭ), *n., pl.* **-ties. 1.** *U.S.* a student society organized for social and other purposes, commonly composed of affiliated branches or chapters in various institutions and designated by two or more letters of the Greek alphabet: commonly applied to men's or to coeducational organizations, women's organizations being called sororities. **2.** a body of persons associated as by ties of brotherhood. **3.** any body or class of persons having common purposes, interest, etc.: *the medical fraternity.* **4.** an organization of laymen for pious or charitable purposes. **5.** the relation of persons associated on the footing of brothers: *liberty, equality, and fraternity.* **6.** the relation of a brother or between brothers; brotherhood. [ME *fraternite*, t. L: m.s. *frāternitas* brotherhood]

fraternity house, a house occupied by a fraternity.

frat·er·nize (frăt'ər nīz'), *v.,* **-nized, -nizing.** —*v.i.* **1.** to associate in a fraternal or friendly way. **2.** to associate intimately with citizens of an enemy or conquered country. —*v.t.* **3.** to bring into fraternal association or sympathy. —**frat'er·ni·za'tion,** *n.* —**frat'er·niz'er,** *n.*

frat·ri·cide[1] (frăt'rə sīd', frā'trə-), *n.* one who kills his or her brothers. [t. L: m.s. *frātricīda*] —**frat'ri·cid'al,** *adj.*

frat·ri·cide[2] (frăt'rə sīd', frā'trə-), *n.* act of killing one's own brother. [t. L: m.s. *frātricīdium*] —**frat'ri·cid'al,** *adj.*

Frau (frou), *n., pl.* **Fraus** (frouz), *Ger.* **Frauen** (frou'ən). *German.* a married woman; a wife; a lady (as title, equivalent to *Mrs.*).

fraud (frôd), *n.* **1.** deceit, trickery, sharp practice, or breach of confidence, by which it is sought to gain some unfair or dishonest advantage. **2.** a particular instance of such deceit or trickery: *election frauds.* **3.** any deception, artifice or trick. **4.** *U.S. Colloq.* a person who makes deceitful pretenses; imposter. [ME *fraude*, t. OF, t. L: m.s. *fraus* cheating, deceit] —**Syn. 1.** See **trick.**

fraud·u·lent (frô'jə lənt), *adj.* **1.** given to or using fraud, as a person; cheating; dishonest. **2.** characterized by, involving, or proceeding from fraud, as actions, enterprises, methods, gains, etc. [t. OF, t. L: s. *fraudulentus* cheating] —**fraud'u·lence, fraud'u·len·cy,** *n.* —**fraud'u·lent·ly,** *adv.*

fraught (frôt), *adj.* **1.** involving; attended with; full of: *an undertaking fraught with danger, a heart fraught with grief.* **2.** *Archaic or Poetic.* filled or laden with: *ships fraught with precious wares.* —*n.* **3.** *Obs. or Scot.* a load; cargo; freight (of a ship). [ME, t. MD or MLG: m. *vracht* freight money, FREIGHT. Cf. OHG *frēht* earnings]

Fräu·lein (froi′līn), *n., pl.* **Fräuleins,** *Ger.* **Fräulein.** *German.* an unmarried woman; a young lady (as a title, equivalent to *Miss*).

Fraun·ho·fer (froun′hō′fər), *n.* **Joseph von** (yō′zĕf fən), 1787–1826, German optician and physicist.

Fraunhofer lines, the dark lines of the solar spectrum. [named after Joseph von FRAUNHOFER]

frax·i·nel·la (frăk′sə něl′ə), *n.* dittany (def. 3). [NL, dim. of L *fraxinus* ash tree]

fray[1] (frā), *n.* **1.** a noisy quarrel; brawl; fight, skirmish, or battle. **2.** *Obs. or Scot.* fright. —*v.t.* **3.** *Archaic.* to frighten. —*v.i.* **4.** *Archaic or Dial.* to fight; brawl. [aphetic var. of AFFRAY]

fray[2] (frā), *v.t.* **1.** to wear (cloth, rope, etc.) to loose, raveled threads or fibers at the edge or end; cause to ravel out. **2.** to rub. **3.** to wear by rubbing (sometimes fol. by *through*). —*v.i.* **4.** to become frayed, as cloth, etc.; ravel out. **5.** to rub against something. —*n.* **6.** a frayed part, as in cloth. [t. F: s. *frayer*, g. L *fricāre* rub]

Fra·zer (frā′zər), *n.* **Sir James George,** 1854–1941, British anthropologist.

fraz·zle (frăz′əl), *v.,* **-zled, -zling,** *n.* *Chiefly U.S.* —*v.i., v.t.* **1.** to fray; wear to threads or shreds. **2.** to weary; tire out. —*n.* **3.** state of being frazzled or worn out. **4.** a remnant; shred. [b. FRAY[2] and *fazzle,* ME *faseln* unravel, c. G *faseln*]

FRC, Federal Radio Commission.

freak[1] (frēk), *n.* **1.** a sudden and apparently causeless change or turn of the mind; a capricious notion; a whim. **2.** capriciousness. **3.** any abnormal product or curiously unusual object; monstrosity. **4.** a person or animal on exhibition as an example of some strange deviation from nature. —*adj.* **5.** unusual; odd; irregular: *a freak copy of a book.* [? akin to OE *frīcian* dance]

freak[2] (frēk), *v.t.* **1.** to fleck, streak, or variegate. —*n.* **2.** a fleck or streak of color. [? v. use of FREAK[1]; appar. coined by Milton]

freak·ish (frē′kĭsh), *adj.* **1.** given to or full of freaks; whimsical; capricious. **2.** resembling a freak; queer, odd; grotesque. —**freak′ish·ly,** *adv.* —**freak′ish·ness,** *n.*

freak·y (frē′kĭ), *adj.,* **freakier, freakiest.** freakish. —**freak′i·ness,** *n.*

Fré·chette (frĕ shĕt′), *n.* **Louis Honoré** (lwē ônô′rē′), 1839–1908, Canadian poet, journalist, and politician.

freck·le (frĕk′əl), *n., v.,* **-led, -ling.** —*n.* **1.** a small brownish-yellow spot in the skin, esp. on the face, neck, or arms. **2.** any small spot or discoloration. —*v.t.* **3.** to cover with freckles or produce freckles on. —*v.i.* **4.** to become freckled. [b. obs. *frecken* freckle (t. Scand.; cf. Icel. *freknur,* pl.) and SPECKLE, n.] —**freck′led,** *adj.*

freck·ly (frĕk′lĭ), *adj.* full of freckles.

Fred·er·ick I (frĕd′ər ĭk, frĕd′rĭk), **1.** Frederick Barbarossa. **2.** 1657–1713, first king of Prussia, 1701–13.

Frederick II, 1. 1194–1250, German king, king of Sicily, and emperor of the Holy Roman Empire, 1218–1250. **2.** Frederick the Great.

Frederick III, (*"the Wise"*) 1463–1525, elector of Saxony, 1486–1525: protector of Martin Luther.

Frederick Bar·ba·ros·sa (bär′bə rŏs′ə), (*Frederick I*) c1123–1190, German king and emperor of the Holy Roman Empire, 1152–90.

Fred·er·icks·burg (frĕd′rĭks bûrg′), *n.* a city in NE Virginia, on the Rappahannock river: scene of a Confederate victory in the Civil War, 1862. 12,158 (1950).

Frederick the Great, (*Frederick II*) 1712–86, king of Prussia, 1740–86.

Frederick William, 1. (*"the Great Elector"*) 1620–1688, elector of Brandenburg who increased the power and importance of Prussia. **2.** 1882–1951, former crown prince of Germany, 1888–1918; German general (son of William II of Germany).

Frederick William I, 1688–1740, king of Prussia, 1713–40.

Frederick William II, 1744–97, king of Prussia, 1786–97.

Frederick William III, 1770–1840, king of Prussia, 1797–1840.

Frederick William IV, 1795–1861, king of Prussia, 1840–61.

Fred·er·ic·ton (frĕd′ər ĭk tən), *n.* a city in SE Canada, on the St. John river: the capital of New Brunswick. 10,062 (1941).

Fred·er·iks·berg (frĕth′ə rĕks bĕrкн′), *n.* a city in E Denmark, near Copenhagen. 113,208 (1940).

free (frē), *adj.,* **freer, freest,** *adv., v.,* **freed, freeing.** —*adj.* **1.** enjoying personal rights or liberty, as one not in slavery. **2.** pertaining to or reserved for those who enjoy personal liberty: *free soil.* **3.** possessed of, characterized by, or existing under civil liberty as opposed to arbitrary or despotic government, as a country or state, or its citizens, institutions, etc. **4.** enjoying political liberty or independence, as a people or country not under foreign rule. **5.** exempt from external authority, interference, restriction, etc., as a person, the will,

thought, choice, action, etc.; independent; unfettered. **6.** at liberty, permitted, or able at will (to do something): *free to choose.* **7.** not subject to special regulation or restrictions, as trade: *free trade.* **8.** not literal, as a translation. **9.** not subject to rules, set forms, etc.: *the free song of a bird, free verse.* **10.** clear of obstructions or obstacles, as a corridor. **11.** exempt or released from something specified that controls, restrains, burdens, etc. (fol. by *from* or *of*): *free from matrimonial ties, free of taxes.* **12.** having immunity or being safe (usually fol. by *from*): *free from criticism.* **13.** uncombined chemically: *free oxygen.* **14.** open (fol. by *to* or *for*): *a race free for all competitors, a free port.* **15.** general: *a free fight.* **16.** unimpeded, as motion or movements; easy, firm, or swift in movement: *a free step.* **17.** loose, or not held fast or attached: *to get one's arm free.* **18.** not joined to or in contact with something else: *a free surface.* **19.** acting without self-restraint or reserve: *too free with one's tongue.* **20.** frank and open; unconstrained, unceremonious, or familiar. **21.** unrestrained by decency; loose, or licentious. **22.** ready in giving, liberal, or lavish: *to be free with one's advice.* **23.** given readily or in profusion, or unstinted. **24.** given without consideration of a return, as a gift. **25.** provided without, or not subject to a charge or payment: *free schools.* **26.** admitted to entry and enjoyment at will (fol. by *of*): *to be free of a friend's house.* **27.** easily worked, as stone or land. **28.** *Naut.* (of a wind) blowing so that a boat can sail with sheets eased or yards squared; fair. **29.** *Phonet.* a. (of a vowel) situated in an open syllable. b. belonging to a class of vowels which need not be followed by a consonant: the vowel of *see* is one of the English free vowels. **30. free and clear,** *Law.* denoting real property without any encumbrance, such as a mortgage, on it. **31. make free with,** to treat or use too familiarly; take liberties with. —*adv.* **32.** in a free manner; freely. **33.** without cost or charge. **34.** *Naut.* further from the wind than when close hauled: *to sail free.* —*v.t.* **35.** make free; set at liberty; release from bondage, imprisonment, or restraint. **36.** to exempt or deliver (fol. by *from*). **37.** to relieve or rid (fol. by *of*). **38.** to disengage (fol. by *from* or *of*). [ME; OE *frēo,* c. G *frei,* orig., dear, favored. Cf. FRIEND] —**Syn. 35.** See **release.**

free alongside ship, a term of sale meaning that the seller agrees to deliver the merchandise alongside ship without extra charge to buyer.

free·board (frē′bōrd′), *n.* *Naut.* the part of a ship's side between the water line and the deck or gunwale.

free·boot (frē′boot′), *v.i.* to act as a freebooter.

free·boot·er (frē′boo′tər), *n.* one who goes about in search of plunder; a pirate or buccaneer. [t. D: Anglicization of *vrijbuiter,* f. *vrij* free + *buit* booty + *-er* -ER[1]]

free·born (frē′bôrn′), *adj.* **1.** born free, rather than in slavery, bondage, or vassalage. **2.** pertaining to or befitting persons born free.

free city, a city having an independent government and forming a sovereign state by itself.

free coinage, the unrestricted coinage of bullion, or of a specified metal, as silver, into money for any person bringing it to the mint, either with or without charge for expenses of minting.

free companion, a member of a band of mercenary soldiers of the Middle Ages.

free company, a band of free companions.

free delivery, *U.S.* the delivery of mail matter without charge.

freed·man (frēd′mən), *n., pl.* **-men.** a man who has been freed from slavery. —**freed′wom′an,** *n. fem.*

free·dom (frē′dəm), *n.* **1.** civil liberty, as opposed to subjection to an arbitrary or despotic government. **2.** political or national independence. **3.** a particular immunity or other privilege enjoyed, as by a city or corporation. **4.** personal liberty, as opposed to bondage or slavery. **5.** state of being at liberty rather than in confinement or under physical restraint. **6.** exemption from external control, interference, regulation, etc. **7.** power of determining one's or its own action. **8.** *Philos.* the condition of the will as the volitional instigator of human actions; relative self-determination. **9.** absence of or release from ties, obligations, etc. **10.** exemption or immunity: *freedom from taxation.* **11.** exemption from the presence of anything specified (fol. by *from*): *freedom from fear.* **12.** ease or facility of movement or action. **13.** frankness of manner or speech. **14.** absence of ceremony or reserve; familiarity. **15.** a liberty taken. **16.** the right of enjoying all the privileges or peculiar rights of citizenship, membership, or the like: *the freedom of the city.* **17.** the right of frequenting, enjoying, or using at will: *to have the freedom of a friend's library.* [ME; OE *frēodōm.* See FREE, -DOM] —**Syn. 1.** FREEDOM, INDEPENDENCE, LIBERTY refer to an absence of undue restrictions and an opportunity to exercise one's rights and powers. FREEDOM emphasizes the large opportunity given for the exercise of one's rights, powers, desires, or the like: *freedom of speech or conscience, freedom of movement.* INDEPENDENCE implies not only lack of restrictions but also the ability to stand alone, unsustained by anything else: *independence of thought promotes invention and discovery.* LIBERTY, though often interchanged with FREEDOM, is commonly used to refer to past or possible restriction, confinement, or subjection: *give me liberty or give me death.* —**Ant. 1.** oppression.

---

b., blend of, blended; c., cognate with; d., dialect, dialectal; der., derived from; f., formed from; g., going back to; m., modification of; r., replacing; s., stem of; t., taken from; ?, perhaps. See the full key on inside cover.

freedom of the press, the right of printing and publishing whatever is desired, without governmental permission or censorship.

freedom of the seas, *Internat. Law.* the doctrine that ships of neutral countries may sail anywhere on the high seas during a war without interference by the warring powers.

free energy, *Physics.* that portion of the energy of a system which is the maximum available for doing work.

free enterprise, the doctrine or practice of a minimum amount of government control of private business and industry.

free-for-all (frē/fər ôl/), *n.* a fight, game, contest, etc., open to everyone.

free form, a linguistic form which occurs sometimes or always by itself, not having the limitation of a bound form (which see), as *fire.*

free gold, 1. *U.S.* treasury gold, including the legal reserve, not restricted to the redemption of gold certificates or other specific uses. **2.** *Mining.* gold found in a pure state in nature, as in placer mining.

free-hand (frē/hănd/), *adj.* done by the hand without guiding instruments, measurements, or other aids.

free hand, unrestricted authority.

free-hand-ed (frē/hăn/dĭd), *adj.* **1.** open-handed; generous; liberal. **2.** having the hands free.

free-heart-ed (frē/här/tĭd), *adj.* having a free heart; light-hearted; spontaneous; frank; generous.

free-hold (frē/hōld/), *n.* *Law.* an estate in fee simple, in fee tail, or for life.

free-hold-er (frē/hōl/dər), *n.* the owner of a freehold.

free lance, 1. a contributor to periodicals, etc., who is not regularly employed by them. **2.** one who contends in a cause, or in a succession of various causes, as he chooses, without personal attachment or allegiance. **3.** a mercenary soldier or military adventurer of the Middle Ages, often of knightly rank, who offered his services to any state, party, or cause.

free-lance (frē/lăns/, -läns/), *v.i.,* **-lanced, -lancing.** to act or work as a free lance.

free list, *U.S. Com.* a list or register of articles that may be brought into a country duty-free.

free liver, one who in his mode of life freely indulges his appetites. **—free/-liv/ing,** *adj.*

free love, the doctrine or practice of free choice in sexual relations, without restraint of legal marriage or of any continuing obligations independent of individual will.

free lunch, *U.S.* food given without charge in a saloon, to attract customers.

free-ly (frē/lĭ), *adv.* in a free manner.

free-man (frē/mən), *n., pl* **-men. 1.** a man who is free; a man who enjoys personal, civil, or political liberty. **2.** one who enjoys or is entitled to citizenship, franchise, or other peculiar privilege: *a freeman of a city.*

Free-man (frē/mən), *n.* **1. Douglas Southall** (sou/-thôl), born 1886, U.S. journalist and biographer. **2. Edward Augustus,** 1823–92, British historian. **3. Mary Wilkins,** 1862–1930, U.S. writer.

free-mar-tin (frē/mär/tən), *n.* a generally sterile heifer calf twinborn with a bull. [orig. uncert.]

Free-ma-son (frē/mā/sən, frē/mā/-), *n.* **1.** a member of a widely distributed secret order **(Free and Accepted Masons),** having for its object mutual assistance and the promotion of brotherly love among its members. **2.** (*l.c.*) *Hist.* **a.** one of a class of skilled stoneworkers of the Middle Ages, possessed of secret signs and pass words. **b.** a member of a society composed of such workers, with honorary members (known as *accepted masons*) who were not connected with the building trades. **—free-ma-son-ic** (frē/mə sŏn/ĭk), *adj.*

free-ma-son-ry (frē/mā/sən rĭ), *n.* **1.** secret or tacit brotherhood; instinctive sympathy. **2.** (*cap.*) the principles, practices, and institutions of Freemasons.

free-ness (frē/nĭs), *n.* state or quality of being free.

free on board, *Com.* a term of sale meaning that the seller agrees to deliver the merchandise aboard the carrier without extra charge to buyer.

free port, 1. a port open under equal conditions to all traders. **2.** a part or all of a port not included in customs territory so as to expedite transshipment of what is not to be imported.

Free-port (frē/pōrt/), *n.* **1.** a city in NW Illinois. 22,467 (1950). **2.** a village in SE New York, on Long Island. 24,680 (1950).

free radical, *Chem.* an organic compound in which an atom utilizes less than its normal valence, as CH₃·, the methyl radical in which carbon has a valence of three instead of four.

free-si-a (frē/zhĭ ə, -sĭ ə), *n.* any plant of the iridaceous genus *Freesia,* native in South Africa, esteemed for its fragrant white, yellow, or sometimes rose-colored, tubular flowers. [NL; named after E.M. *Fries* (1794–1878), Swedish botanist]

free silver, *Econ.* the free coinage of silver; esp., at a fixed ratio with gold.

free-soil (frē/soil/), *adj.* *U.S. Hist.* **1.** pertaining to or in favor of the nonextension of slavery into the Territories, or those parts of the country not yet elected into states. **—n. 2.** (*cap.*) a political party supporting the free-soil principle, active 1848–56. **—free/-soil/-er,** *n.*

free-spo-ken (frē/spō/kən), *adj.* given to speaking freely or without reserve. **—free/-spo/ken-ness,** *n.*

Free State, 1. *U.S.* any nonslavery State prior to the Civil War. **2.** Irish Free State.

free-stone (frē/stōn/), *n.* **1.** any stone, as sandstone, which can be freely worked or quarried, esp. one which cuts well in all directions without splitting. **2.** a freestone fruit, esp. a peach or plum. **—adj. 3.** having a stone from which the pulp is easily separated, as certain peaches and plums.

free-swim-mer (frē/swĭm/ər), *n.* *Zool.* an animal, as a fish, that swims about freely.

free-swim-ming (frē/swĭm/ĭng), *adj.* *Zool.* (of aquatic animals) not fixed or attached; capable of swimming about freely.

free-think-er (frē/thĭng/kər), *n.* one who forms his opinions independently of authority or tradition, esp. in matters of religion. **—free/think/ing,** *n., adj.*

free thought, thought unrestrained by deference to authority, esp. in matters of religion.

free throw, *Basketball.* **1.** a throw from the foul line given a player after a penalty has been called against an opponent for a foul. **2.** a score of one point.

Free-town (frē/toun/), *n.* a seaport in and the capital of Sierra Leone, in W Africa. 55,358 (1931).

free trade, 1. trade between different countries, free from governmental restrictions or duties. **2.** international trade free from protective duties, etc., and subject only to such tariffs as are needed for revenue. **3.** the system, principles, or maintenance of such trade. **4.** *Obs.* smuggling.

free-trad-er (frē/trā/dər), *n.* **1.** an advocate of the principle or system of free trade. **2.** *Obs.* a smuggler. Also, **free trader.**

free verse, *Pros.* verse unhampered by fixed metrical forms, in extreme instances consisting of little more than rhythmic prose in lines of irregular length.

free-wheel (frē/hwēl/), *n.* **1.** an overrunning clutch device in connection with the transmission gear box of a motor vehicle which automatically disengages the drive shaft whenever it tends to rotate more rapidly than the shaft driving it. **2.** a form of rear bicycle wheel which has a device freeing it from the driving mechanism, as when the pedals are stopped in coasting.

free will, 1. free choice; voluntary decision. **2.** the doctrine that the conduct of human beings expresses personal choice and is not simply determined by physical or divine forces.

free-will (frē/wĭl/), *adj.* **1.** made or done freely or of one's own accord; voluntary: *a freewill offering.* **2.** of or pertaining to the metaphysical doctrine of the freedom of the will: *the freewill controversy.*

freeze (frēz), *v.,* **froze, frozen, freezing,** *n.* **—v.i. 1.** to become hardened into ice or into a solid body; to change from the liquid to the solid state by loss of heat. **2.** to become hard or rigid because of loss of heat, as objects containing moisture. **3.** to become obstructed by the formation of ice, as pipes. **4.** to become fixed to something by or as by the action of frost. **5.** to be of the degree of cold at which water freezes: *it is freezing tonight.* **6.** to suffer the effects of intense cold; have the sensation of extreme cold. **7.** to die of frost or cold. **8.** to lose warmth of feeling; be chilled with fear, etc. **—v.t. 9.** to congeal; harden into ice; change from a fluid to a solid form by loss of heat. **10.** to form ice on the surface of, as a river or pond. **11.** to obstruct or close by the formation of ice, as pipes (often fol. by *up*). **12.** to fix fast in ice (fol. by *in* or *up*). **13.** to harden or stiffen by cold, as objects containing moisture. **14.** to cause to suffer the effects of intense cold; produce the sensation of extreme cold in. **15.** to kill by frost or cold. **16.** to congeal as if by cold; chill with fear; dampen the enthusiasm of. **17.** *U.S. Colloq.* to exclude, or compel to withdraw, from society, business, etc., as by chilling behavior, severe competition, etc. (fol. by *out*). **18.** *Finance, Colloq.* to render impossible of liquidation or collection: *bank loans are frozen in business depressions.* **19.** to fix (rents, prices, etc.) at a specific amount, usually by government order. **20.** *Med.* to insensitize (a part of the body) by artificial freezing, as for surgery. **—n. 21.** act of freezing. **22.** state of being frozen. **23.** a frost. [ME *frese(n),* OE *frēosan,* c. G *frieren*]

freez-er (frē/zər), *n.* **1.** one who or that which freezes or chills. **2.** a machine containing cold brine, etc. for freezing ice-cream mix or the like. **3.** a refrigerator or cabinet held at temperatures at or below zero degrees Centigrade.

freezing point, the temperature at which a liquid freezes: *the freezing point of water is 32°F., 0°C.*

free zone, a free port area.

Frei-burg (frī/bŏŏrκн), *n.* **1.** a city in SW Germany. 110,110 (1939). **2.** German name of Fribourg.

freight (frāt), *n.* **1.** the ordinary conveyance or means of transport of goods afforded by common carriers (as opposed to *express*). **2.** the price paid for such transportation. **3.** the cargo, or any part of the cargo, of a vessel. **4.** *U.S. and Canada.* **a.** cargo or lading carried for pay either by water, land, or air. **b.** a train of cars for transporting goods or merchandise. **5.** transportation of goods by water or (esp. in the U.S. and Canada) by land. **—v.t. 6.** to load; burden. **7.** to load or lade with goods or merchandise for transportation. **8.** to transport as freight; send by freight. **9.** to let out for the transportation of freight. [ME *freyght,* t. MD or MLG: m. *vrecht,* var. of *vracht.* See FRAUGHT, n.] —**freight′less,** *adj.*

—**Syn. 3.** FREIGHT, CARGO, SHIPMENT refer to goods being transported from place to place. FREIGHT is now applied only to goods carried on land or in the air: *to send freight from New York to New Orleans.* CARGO is the term used for goods carried by ship: *to send a cargo to Europe.* SHIPMENT is a quantity of goods destined for a particular place, no matter how sent: *a shipment of potatoes.*

freight·age (frā′tĭj), *n.* **1.** the transportation of goods. **2.** the price for this. **3.** freight, cargo, or lading.

freight car, a railroad car for carrying freight, commonly a boxcar.

freight engine, *U.S.* a locomotive used for drawing freight trains.

freight·er (frā′tər), *n.* **1.** a vessel engaged chiefly in the transportation of goods. **2.** one whose occupation it is to receive and forward freight. **3.** one for whom freight is transported.

freight house, *U.S.* depot or storage place for freight.

freight ton. See ton[1] (def. 2).

freight train, *U.S.* a train of freight cars.

Fre·ling·huy·sen (frē′lĭng hī′zən), *n.* **Frederick Theodore,** 1817–85, U. S. statesman.

Fre·man·tle (frē′măn′tel), *n.* a seaport in SW Australia, near Perth. 17,006 (1933).

fremd (frĕmd, frămd), *adj. Dial.* **1.** foreign; strange; unusual or unnatural. **2.** unfriendly. [ME and OE *fremde,* c. G *fremd*]

frem·i·tus (frĕm′Ĭ təs), *n., pl.* **-tus.** *Pathol.* palpable vibration, as of the walls of the chest. [t. L: a roaring, murmuring]

Fré·mont (frē′mŏnt), *n.* **John Charles,** 1813–90, U. S. explorer, general, and political leader; first presidential candidate of the Republican Party, in 1856.

French (frĕnch), *adj.* **1.** of, pertaining to, or characteristic of France, its inhabitants, or their language. —*n.* **2.** the people of France and their immediate descendants elsewhere, collectively. **3.** a Romance language, the language of France, official also in Belgium, Switzerland, and Canada. [ME; OE *Frencisc,* der. *Franca* FRANK]

French (frĕnch), *n.* **1. Daniel Chester,** 1850–1931, U.S. sculptor. **2. Sir John Denton Pinkstone,** (*1st Earl of Ypres*) 1852–1925, British field marshal in World War I.

French Academy, an association of forty scholars and men of letters, formally established in 1635 by Cardinal Richelieu for the purpose of controlling the French language and regulating literary taste.

French and Indian War, the war between France and England in America, 1754–60, in which the French were aided by Indian allies.

French chalk, a talc for marking lines on cloth, etc.

French Chamber of Deputies, the second (or lower) house of the national assembly of France.

French doors, a pair of doors hinged to the doorjambs and opening in the middle.

French dressing, salad dressing prepared from oil, vinegar, salt, spices, etc.

French Equatorial Africa, a French territory in central Africa, comprising Chad, Gabon, Middle Congo, and Ubangi-Shari. 3,423,000 pop. (1936); 960,230 sq. mi. *Cap.:* Brazzaville. Formerly, **French Congo.**

French fried potatoes, thin strips of potatoes fried in deep fat.

French Gui·an·a (gĭ ăn′ə, gĭ ä′nə), a French possession on the NE coast of South America: formerly a colony; now administered as a department of France. 31,000 pop. (1936); 7720 sq. mi. (with the dependent territory of Inini, 34,740 sq. mi.). *Cap.:* Cayenne. See map under **Guiana.**

French Guin·ea (gĭn′Ĭ), a colony in French West Africa, on the Atlantic coast, N of Sierra Leone. 2,100,-000 pop. (1940); ab. 96,900 sq. mi. *Cap.:* Conakry.

French horn, a mellow-toned brass-wind instrument derived from the hunting horn and consisting of a long, coiled tube ending in a flaring bell. See illus. under **horn.**

French·i·fy (frĕn′chə fī′), *v.t.* **-fied, -fying.** to make French; imbue with French qualities. Also, **french′i·fy′.**

French India, the five small French provinces of Chandernagor, Karikal, Mahé, Pondichéry, and Yanaon, scattered along or near the coast of India. 323,295 pop. (1941); 197 sq. mi. *Cap.:* Pondichéry.

French Indo-China, a territory in SE Asia, formerly a French colonial federation of Cochin-China, the protectorates of Annam, Cambodia, Tonkin, and Laos, and the leased territory of Kwangchowan: now (1950) it comprises the three states of Viet Nam, Cambodia, and Laos within the French Union, Kwangchowan having reverted to the Chinese. 23,030,000 pop. (1936); ab. 285,900 sq. mi. (1936). Its capital was Hanoi.

French leave, departure without ceremony, permission, or notice.

French·man (frĕnch′mən), *n., pl.* **-men. 1.** a man belonging to the French nation. **2.** a French ship. —**French·wom·an** (frĕnch′wŏŏm′ən), *n., fem.*

French Morocco. See **Morocco.**

French Oceania, a French colony in the S Pacific, including the Society Islands, Marquesa Islands, and other widely scattered island groups. 44,000 pop. (1936); 1544 sq. mi. *Cap.:* Papeete.

French pancake, a light pancake which has been rolled and covered with sugar, eaten as a dessert.

French pastry, pastry made from the shortened paste used for pie crusts and filled with rich creams, preserves, etc.

French Revolution, *French Hist.* the movement that, beginning in 1789, overthrew the absolute monarchy of the Bourbons and the system of class privilege, and ended in the seizure of power by Napoleon in 1799.

French seam, *Sewing.* a seam in which the edges of the cloth are sewn first on the right side, then on the wrong, so as to be completely covered.

French Somaliland, a French colony in E Africa, on the Gulf of Aden. 46,000 pop. (1936); 8380 sq. mi. *Cap.:* Djibouti.

French Sudan, a colony in French West Africa, E of Senegal and Mauritania. 3,755,000 pop. (1940); 591,220 sq. mi. *Cap.:* Bamako.

French telephone, a telephone with the receiver and transmitter at the ends of a handle.

French toast, bread covered with an egg and milk mixture and sautéed.

French Union, an administrative division of France (under the 1946 constitution), having jurisdiction over the French territories overseas, as the departments, colonies, protectorates, territories, etc.

French West Africa, a French territory in W Africa, comprising the eight colonies of Dahomey, French Guinea, French Sudan, Ivory Coast, Mauritania, Niger, Senegal, and Dakar and dependencies. 15,336,000 pop. (1940); 1,815,278 sq. mi. *Cap.:* Dakar.

French West Indies, the French islands in the West Indies, comprising Guadeloupe and dependencies, and Martinique. 551,000 pop. (1936); 1114 sq. mi.

French window, a long window having two sashes hinged at the sides and opening in the middle.

French·y (frĕn′chĬ), *adj.,* **Frenchier, Frenchiest,** *n. Colloq.* —*adj.* **1.** characteristic or suggestive of the French. —*n.* **2.** a Frenchman.

Fre·neau (frĭ nō′), *n.* **Philip,** 1752–1832, American poet and editor.

fre·net·ic (frə nĕt′Ĭk), *adj.* frantic; frenzied. Also, **phrenetic.** [var. of PHRENETIC] —**fre·net′i·cal·ly,** *adv.*

fren·u·lum (frĕn′yə ləm), *n., pl.* **-la** (-lə). **1.** *Anat., Zool.* a small frenum. **2.** *Entomol.* a strong spine or group of bristles on the hind wing of moths and butterflies, projecting beneath the forewing and serving to hold the two wings together in flight. [NL, dim. of L *frēnum* curb]

fre·num (frē′nəm), *n., pl.* **-na** (-nə). *Anat., Zool.* a little fold of membrane which checks or restrains the motion of a part, as the one which binds down the under side of the tongue. Also, **fraenum.** [t. L: bridle, curb]

fren·zied (frĕn′zĬd), *adj.* wildly excited or enthusiastic; frantic. Also, **phrensied.**

fren·zy (frĕn′zĬ), *n., pl.* **-zies,** *v.* **-zied, -zying.** —*n.* **1.** violent mental agitation; wild excitement or enthusiasm. **2.** the violent excitement of a paroxysm of mania; mental derangement; delirium. —*v.t.* **3.** to affect with or drive to frenzy; make frantic. Also, **phrensy.** [ME *frenesie,* t. OF, t. LL: m. *phrenēsis,* t. LGk., r. Gk. *phrenitis.* See PHRENITIS] —**Syn. 2.** madness, rage, fury, raving.

fre·on (frē′ŏn), *n.* an odorless, colorless gas, CCl_2F_2, boiling at $-29°$ C., used as a refrigerating agent.

freq., **1.** frequent. **2.** frequentative. **3.** frequently.

fre·quen·cy (frē′kwən sĬ), *n., pl.* **-cies. 1.** Also, **fre′-quence.** state or fact of being frequent; frequent occurrence. **2.** rate of recurrence. **3.** *Physics.* **a.** the number of periods or regularly recurring events of any given kind in unit time, usually in one second; the reciprocal of the period. **b.** (of an alternating electric current) the number of cycles, or completed alternations, per second. **4.** *Math.* the number of times an event occurs. **5.** *Statistics.* the number of items occurring in a given category. See **relative frequency.** [t. L: m.s. *frequentia*]

frequency distribution. *Statistics.* the set of frequencies associated with the different categories, intervals, or values to which items or variates in a group belong.

frequency modulation, *Electronics.* a broadcasting system, relatively free from static, in which the frequency of the transmitted wave is modulated or varied in accordance with the amplitude and pitch of the signal (distinguished from *amplitude modulation*).

fre·quent (*adj.* frē′kwənt; *v.* frĬ kwĕnt′), *adj.* **1.** happening or occurring at short intervals: *to make frequent trips to a place.* **2.** constant, habitual, or regular: *a frequent guest.* **3.** at short distances apart: *a coast with frequent lighthouses.* —*v.t.* **4.** to visit often; go often to; be often in. [t. L: s. *frequens* crowded] —**fre·quent′er,** *n.*

fre·quen·ta·tion (frē′kwən tā′shən), *n.* the practice of frequenting; habit of visiting often.

fre·quen·ta·tive (frĬ kwĕn′tə tĬv), *Gram.* —*adj.* **1.** (of a derived verb, or of an aspect of verb inflection) expressing repetition of the action denoted by the underlying verb. —*n.* **2.** a frequentative or iterative verb. **3.** the frequentative or iterative aspect. **4.** a verb therein, as *wrestle* from *wrest.*

fre·quent·ly (frē′kwənt lĬ), *adv.* often; many times; at short intervals. —**Syn.** See **often.**

frère (frĕr), *n., pl.* **frères** (frĕr). *French.* **1.** brother; fellow member of an organization. **2.** friar; monk.

fres·co (frĕs′kō), *n.*, *pl.* **-coes, -cos,** *v.*, **-coed, -coing.** **—n. 1.** a method of painting on a wall, ceiling, or the like, made before the plaster is dry so that the colors become incorporated (**true fresco**), or, less properly, after the plaster has dried (**dry fresco**). **2.** a picture or design so painted. **—v.t. 3.** to paint in fresco. [t. It.: cool, FRESH; t. Gmc.] **—fres′co·er,** *n.*

fresh (frĕsh), *adj.* **1.** newly made, arrived, obtained, etc.: *fresh footprints.* **2.** new; not previously known, met with, etc.; novel. **3.** additional or further: *fresh supplies.* **4.** not salt, as water. **5.** retaining the original properties unimpaired; not deteriorated. **6.** not preserved by pickling, salting, drying, etc. **7.** not fatigued; brisk; vigorous. **8.** not faded, worn, obliterated, etc. **9.** looking youthful and healthy. **10.** pure, cool, or refreshing, as air. **11.** *Meteorol.* (of wind) moderately strong or brisk; blowing at a velocity within the range of 19–24 miles per hour. **12.** inexperienced. **13.** *Slang.* forward or presumptuous. **14.** (of a cow) having recently given birth to a calf. **—n. 15.** the fresh part or time. **16.** a freshet. **—v.t., v.i. 17.** *Obs.* to make or become fresh. **—adv. 18.** freshly. [ME; OE *fersc*, c. G *frisch*] **—fresh′ly,** *adv.* **—fresh′ness,** *n.* **—Syn. 1.** See **new. 12.** artless, untrained, raw, green. **—Ant. 1.** old. **12.** sophisticated.

fresh·en (frĕsh′ən), *v.t.* **1.** to make fresh; refresh, revive, or renew. **2.** to remove saltness from. **3.** *Naut.* to relieve, as a rope, by altering the position of a part exposed to friction. **—v.i. 4.** to become or grow fresh. **5.** to give birth to a calf. **—fresh′en·er,** *n.*

fresh·et (frĕsh′ĭt), *n.* **1.** a sudden rise in the level of a stream, or a flood, due to heavy rains or the rapid melting of snow and ice. **2.** a fresh-water stream flowing into the sea. [dim. of FRESH, used as n.] **—Syn. 1.** See **flood.**

fresh·man (frĕsh′mən), *n.*, *pl.* **-men. 1.** a student in the first year of the course at a university, college, or school. **2.** a novice. Also, *Brit. Slang.*, **fresh′er.**

fresh-wa·ter (frĕsh′wô′tər, -wŏt′ər), *adj.* **1.** of or living in water that is fresh, or not salt (opposed to *salt-water* or *marine*). **2.** accustomed to fresh water only, and not to the sea. **3.** of little experience. **4.** *U.S.* small or little known: *a fresh-water college.*

Fres·no (frĕz′nō), *n.* a city in central California. 91,669 (1950).

fret¹ (frĕt), *v.*, **fretted, fretting,** *n.* **—v.i. 1.** to give oneself up to feelings of irritation, resentful discontent, regret, worry, or the like. **2.** to cause corrosion; gnaw. **3.** to make a way by gnawing or corrosion. **4.** to become eaten, worn, or corroded. **5.** to move in agitation or commotion, as water. **—v.t. 6.** to torment; irritate, annoy, or vex. **7.** to wear away or consume by gnawing, friction, rust, corrosives, etc. **8.** to form or make by wearing away a substance. **9.** to agitate (water). **—n. 10.** an irritated state of mind; annoyance; vexation. **11.** erosion; corrosion; gnawing. **12.** a worn or eroded place. [ME *frete(n)*, OE *fretan*, c. G *fressen*] **—Syn. 6.** worry, harass. **—Ant. 6.** soothe.

fret² (frĕt), *n.*, *v.*, **fretted, fretting.** **—n. 1.** an interlaced, angular design; fretwork. **2.** an angular design of bands within a border. **—v.t. 3.** to ornament with a fret or fretwork. [ME *frette*, of uncert. orig.; cf. OF *frete* interlaced work, OE *frettewian*, var. of *fretwian*, *frætwian* adorn]

fret³ (frĕt), *n.*, *v.*, **fretted, fretting. —n. 1.** any of the ridges of wood, metal, or string, set across the finger board of a lute or similar instrument which help the fingers to stop the strings at the correct points. **—v.t. 2.** to provide with frets. [orig. uncert.]

Greek frets

fret·ful (frĕt′fəl), *adj.* disposed to fret; irritable or peevish. **—fret′ful·ly,** *adv.* **—fret′ful·ness,** *n.* **—Syn.** petulant, querulous, impatient. **—Ant.** patient.

fret saw, a long, narrow-bladed saw used to cut ornamental work from thin wood.

fret·ted (frĕt′ĭd), *adj.* ornamented with frets.

fret·work (frĕt′wûrk′), *n.* **1.** ornamental work consisting of interlacing parts; esp. work in which the design is formed by perforation. **2.** any pattern of dark and light, such as that of perforated fretwork.

Freud (froid; *Ger.* froit), *n.* **Sigmund** (sĭg′mənd; *Ger.* zēкн′mŏont), 1856–1939, Austrian physician and psychoanalyst.

Freud·i·an (froi′dĭ ən), *adj.* **1.** of or pertaining to Sigmund Freud or his doctrines, esp. in respect to the causes and treatment of neurotic and psychopathic states, the interpretation of dreams, etc. **—n. 2.** an adherent of the essential doctrines of Freud. **—Freud′i·an·ism,** *n.*

Frey (frā), *n. Scand. Myth.* god of earth's fruitfulness and dispenser of wealth. [t. Icel.: m. *Freyr*]

Frey·a (frā′ə), *n. Scand. Myth.* goddess of fruitfulness and sexual love; the daughter of Njord and sister of Frey. [t. Icel.: m. *Freyja*]

Frey·tag (frī′täкн), *n.* **Gustav** (gōōs′täf), 1816–95, German novelist and dramatist.

F.R.G.S., Fellow of the Royal Geographical Society.

Fri., Friday.

fri·a·ble (frī′ə bəl), *adj.* easily crumbled or reduced to powder; crumbly: *friable rock.* [t. L: m.s. *friābilis*] **—fri′a·bil′i·ty, fri′a·ble·ness,** *n.*

fri·ar (frī′ər), *n. Rom. Cath. Ch.* a brother or member of one of certain religious orders, esp. the mendicant orders of Franciscans (**Gray Friars**), Dominicans (**Black Friars**), Carmelites (**White Friars**), and Augustinians (**Austin Friars**). [ME *frere*, t. OF, g. L *frāter* brother] **—Syn.** See **monk.**

fri·ar·bird (frī′ər bûrd′), *n.* any of various Australasian honey eaters (*Meliphagidae*), esp. of genus *Philemon.*

friar's lantern, the ignis fatuus or will-o'-the-wisp.

fri·ar·y (frī′ər ĭ), *n.*, *pl.* **-aries. 1.** a convent of friars. **2.** a brotherhood of friars.

frib·ble (frĭb′əl), *v.*, **-bled, -bling,** *n.* **—v.i. 1.** to act in a trifling or frivolous manner. **—v.t. 2.** to waste foolishly. **—n. 3.** a trifler. **4.** anything trifling or frivolous. **5.** frivolousness. [orig. uncert.]

Fri·bourg (frē boōr′), *n.* a city in W Switzerland. 26,045 (1941). German, **Freiburg.**

fric·an·deau (frĭk′ən dō′), *n.* veal or other meat larded, stewed, and served with a sauce. [t. F]

fric·as·see (frĭk′ə sē′), *n.*, *v.*, **-seed, -seeing. —n. 1.** meat, as chicken or veal, cut up, sometimes browned, stewed, and served in a sauce made of its own gravy. **—v.t. 2.** to prepare as a fricassee. [t. F, der. *fricasser* to sauté and serve with sauce, t. Pr.: m. *fricassá*, der. *fricar* fry, g. Rom. *frigicāre*, intensive of L *frigere*]

fric·a·tive (frĭk′ə tĭv), *Phonet.* **—adj. 1.** (of consonants) characterized by a noise produced by air being forced through an opening, as in *f*, *v*, *s*, etc. **—n. 2.** a fricative consonant. [t. NL: m.s. *fricātīvus*, der. L *fricāre* rub]

Frick (frĭk), *n.* **Henry Clay,** 1849–1919, U.S. manufacturer and philanthropist.

fric·tion (frĭk′shən), *n.* **1.** *Mech.*, *Physics.* the resistance to the relative motion (sliding or rolling) of surfaces of bodies in contact. **2.** the rubbing of the surface of one body against that of another. **3.** clashing or conflict, as of opinions, etc. [t. L: s. *frictio* a rubbing] **—fric′tion·less,** *adj.*

fric·tion·al (frĭk′shən əl), *adj.* **1.** of, pertaining to, or of the nature of friction. **2.** moved, worked, or produced by friction. **—fric′tion·al·ly,** *adv.*

friction match, a kind of match tipped with a compound that ignites by friction.

Fri·day (frī′dĭ), *n.* **1.** the sixth day of the week, following Thursday. **2.** the native companion of Defoe's Robinson Crusoe. **3.** a devoted or servile follower. [ME; OE *Frīgedæg* Freo's day, f. *Frīge*, gen. sing. of *Frēo* (OE goddess identified with Venus) + *dæg* day; *Freo* is identical with OE adj. *frēo* free]

Fridt·jof Nan·sen Land (frĭt′yôf nän′sən), Franz Josef Land.

fried (frīd), *adj.* **1.** cooked in fat. **—v. 2.** pt. and pp. of **fry¹.**

fried·cake (frīd′kāk′), *n.* a kind of small cake, cooked in deep fat, esp. a doughnut.

friend (frĕnd), *n.* **1.** one attached to another by feelings of personal regard. **2.** a well-wisher, patron, or supporter. **3.** one who is on good terms with another; one not hostile. **4.** a member of the same nation, party, etc. **5.** (*cap.*) a member of the Society of Friends, the Christian sect opposed to taking oaths and to war, founded by George Fox about 1650; Quaker. [ME; OE *frēond*, c. D *vriend*, G *freund*, Goth. *frijōnds*, all orig. ppr. of a verb meaning love (in OE, *frēogan*). Cf. FRIDAY, FREE] **—friend′less,** *adj.* **—friend′less·ness,** *n.* **—Syn. 1.** companion, comrade, chum, crony. See **acquaintance.**

friend at court, a friend who is in a position to further one's interests with others.

friend·ly (frĕnd′lĭ), *adj.*, **-lier, -liest,** *adv.* **—adj. 1.** characteristic of or befitting a friend; showing friendship: *a friendly greeting.* **2.** like a friend; kind. **3.** favorably disposed; inclined to approve, help, or support. **4.** not hostile or at variance; amicable. **—adv. 5.** in a friendly manner; like a friend. [ME *frendly*, OE *frēondlīc*] **—friend′li·ly,** *adv.* **—friend′li·ness,** *n.* **—Syn. 1.** companionable, neighborly. **3.** amiable, cordial, genial, kindly. **—Ant. 3.** antagonistic.

Friendly Islands, Tonga Islands.

friend·ship (frĕnd′shĭp), *n.* **1.** friendly feeling or disposition. **2.** state of being a friend; association as friends. **3.** a friendly relation or intimacy. **—Syn. 2.** companionship, comradeship. **3.** friendliness, amity.

fri·er (frī′ər), *n.* fryer.

Frie·sian (frē′zhən), *adj.*, *n.* Frisian. Also, **Fries·ic** (frē′zĭk).

Fries·land (frēz′lənd; *Du.* frēs′länt′), *n.* a province in N Netherlands. 453,173 pop. (est. 1946); 1431 sq. mi. *Cap.*: Leeuwarden.

frieze¹ (frēz), *n.* **1.** that part of an entablature between the architrave and the cornice, commonly ornamented with sculpture. See diag. under **column. 2.** any similar decorative band or feature, as on a wall. [t. F: m. *frise*, ult. orig. uncert.]

frieze² (frēz), *n.* heavy, napped woolen cloth for overcoats. [t. MD: m. *frise* coarse, hairy cloth. Cf. FRAISE, FRIZZ]

frig·ate (frĭg′ĭt), *n.* an old type of sailing war vessel, designed for high speed and used primarily for scouting. [t. F: m. *frégate*, t. It.: m. *fregata*]

frigate bird, either of two species of rapacious totipalmate marine birds, *Fregata aquila* and *F. minor*, noted for their powers of flight; man-o'-war bird.

Frigg (frĭg), *n. Scand. Myth.* wife of Odin and queen of the gods (often confused with Freya). Also, **Frig·ga** (frĭg′ə). [t. Icel.]

fright (frīt), *n.* **1.** sudden and extreme fear; a sudden terror. **2.** a person or thing of shocking, grotesque, or ridiculous appearance. —*v.t.* **3.** *Poetic.* to frighten. [ME *frighte*, OE *fryhto*, metathetic var. of *fyrhto*; akin to G *furcht*] —**Syn. 1.** dismay, consternation. See **terror.**

fright·en (frī′tən), *v.t.* **1.** to throw into a fright; terrify; scare. **2.** to drive (fol. by *away, off,* etc.) by scaring. —**fright′en·er,** *n.* —**fright′en·ing·ly,** *adv.* —**Syn. 1.** FRIGHTEN, ALARM, SCARE, TERRIFY, APPAL mean to arouse fear in a person or animal. To FRIGHTEN is to shock with sudden, startling, but usually short-lived fear, especially that arising from the apprehension of physical harm: *to frighten someone by a sudden noise.* To ALARM is to arouse the feelings through the realization of some imminent or unexpected danger: *to alarm someone by a scream.* To SCARE is to frighten into a loss of poise or dignity, often in fun: *a sudden noise may scare any one.* To TERRIFY is to strike with violent, overwhelming, or paralyzing fear: *to terrify a city by lawless acts.* To APPAL is to overcome or confound by dread, dismay, or horror: *the suffering caused by the earthquake appalled him.*

fright·ened (frī′tənd), *adj.* **1.** thrown into a fright. **2.** afraid (fol. by *of*). —**Syn. 2.** See **afraid.**

fright·ful (frīt′fəl), *adj.* **1.** such as to cause fright; dreadful, terrible, or alarming. **2.** horrible, shocking, or revolting. **3.** *Colloq.* unpleasant, disagreeable: *we had a frightful time.* **4.** *Colloq.* very great. —**fright′-ful·ly,** *adv.* —**fright′ful·ness,** *n.* —**Syn. 1.** fearful, awful. **2.** hideous. —**Ant. 1.** reassuring.

frig·id (frĭj′ĭd), *adj.* **1.** very cold in temperature: *a frigid climate.* **2.** without warmth of feeling; without ardor or enthusiasm. **3.** stiff or formal. [t. L: s. *frīgidus*] —**fri·gid′i·ty, frig′id·ness,** *n.* —**frig′id·ly,** *adv.*

Frigid Zone, the regions between the poles and the polar circles.

frig·o·rif·ic (frĭg′ərĭf′ĭk), *adj.* causing or producing cold. [t. L: s. *frīgorificus* cooling]

fri·jol (frē′hōl; *Sp.* frē·hōl′), *n., pl.* **frijoles** (frē′hōlz; *Sp.* frē·hō′lĕs). a cultivated bean of the genus *Phaseolus,* much used for food in Mexico, etc. Also, **fri·jo·le** (frē-hō′lĭ; *Sp.* frē·hō′lĕ). [t. Sp.]

frill (frĭl), *n.* **1.** a trimming consisting of a strip of cloth or lace, gathered at one edge and left loose at the other; a ruffle. **2.** something resembling such a trimming, as the fringe of hair on the chest of some dogs. **3.** *Colloq.* affectation of manner, style, etc. **4.** *Photog.* a loosening of the gelatin on a negative or positive, usually the result of high temperature in developing, fixing, etc. —*v.t.* **5.** to trim or ornament with a frill or frills. **6.** to form into a frill [? t. Flem.: m. *frul* frill (of a collar), *frullen* have frills] —**frill′y,** *adj.*

frill·ing (frĭl′ĭng), *n.* frilled edging.

Fri·maire (frē·mĕr′), *n.* (in the calendar of the first French republic) the third month of the year, from Nov. 21 to Dec. 20. [t. F, der. *frimas* hoarfrost, der. OF *frim,* t. Gmc. See RIME[2]]

fringe (frĭnj), *n., v.,* **fringed, fringing.** —*n.* **1.** an ornamental bordering having projecting lengths of thread, cord, etc., either loose or variously arranged or combined. **2.** anything resembling or suggesting this: *a fringe of trees about a field.* **3.** *Optics.* one of the alternate light and dark bands produced by diffraction or interference. —*v.t.* **4.** to furnish with or as with a fringe. **5.** to serve as a fringe for. [ME *frenge,* t. OF, g. LL *fimbria* border, fringe] —**fringe′less,** *adj.* —**fringe′like′,** *adj.* —**fring′y,** *adj.*

fringed gentian, a gentian of eastern North America, *Gentiana crinita,* with a blue fringed corolla.

fringed orchis, one of several species of American orchid, genus *Blephariglottis,* with cut fringed lip.

fringe tree, an oleaceous shrub or small tree, *Chionanthus virginicus,* of the southern U.S., bearing panicles of white flowers with long, narrow petals.

frin·gil·line (frĭn·jĭl′īn, -ĭn), *adj.* belonging or pertaining to the *Fringillidae,* the finch family which includes the sparrows, canaries, linnets, etc., as well as various finches. [f. s. L *fringilla* kind of bird + -INE[1]]

frip·per·y (frĭp′ərĭ), *n., pl.* **-peries. 1.** finery in dress, esp. when tawdry. **2.** empty display; ostentation. **3.** trifles. [t. F: m. *friperie,* OF *freperie,* der. *frepe* rag]

Fris., Frisian.

Frisch (frĭsh), *n.* **Otto Robert** (ŏt′ō rō′bărt), born 1904, Danish physicist.

Frisch·es Haff (frĭsh′əs häf′), a lagoon on the Baltic coast of Poland. 52 mi. long; 4–12 mi. wide.

Fris·co (frĭs′kō), *n. Colloq.* San Francisco.

fri·sé (frĭ·zā′), *n.* a rug or upholstery fabric made with pile in uncut loops or in a combination of cut and uncut.

fri·sette (frĭ·zĕt′), *n.* a fringe of curled or frizzed hair, esp. artificial, worn on the forehead by women. Also, **frizette.** [t. F: little curl, frizz, der. *friser* to curl]

fri·seur (frē·zœr′), *n. French.* a hairdresser.

Fri·sian (frĭzh′ən), *adj.* **1.** of or pertaining to Friesland, its inhabitants, or their language. —*n.* **2.** one of the people of Friesland. **3.** the Germanic language most closely related to English, spoken in Friesland and nearby islands. Also, **Friesian, Friesic.**

frisk (frĭsk), *v.i.* **1.** to dance, leap, skip, or gambol, as in frolic. —*v.t.* **2.** *Slang.* to search (a person) for concealed weapons, etc., by feeling his clothing. **3.** *Slang.*

to steal something from (someone) in this way. —*n.* **4.** a leap, skip, or caper. **5.** a frolic. [orig. adj., t. OF: m. *frisque,* t. Gmc.; cf. G *frisch* lively] —**frisk′er,** *n.*

frisk·y (frĭs′kĭ), *adj.,* **friskier, friskiest.** lively; frolicsome; playful. —**frisk′i·ly,** *adv.* —**frisk′i·ness,** *n.*

frit (frĭt), *n., v.,* **fritted, fritting.** —*n.* **1.** *Ceramics.* **a.** a fused or partially fused material used as a basis for glazes or enamels. **b.** the composition from which artificial soft porcelain is made. **2.** (in medieval glassmaking) fused or calcined material, ready to serve as part of the batch for glassmaking. —*v.t.* **3.** to fuse (materials) in making a frit. Also, **fritt.** [t. F: m. *fritte,* t. It.: m. *fritta,* der. *friggere* (g. L *frīgere*) roast, fry]

frit fly, a minute fly, *Oscinosoma frit,* whose larva is an injurious pest to wheat and other cereals.

frith (frĭth), *n. Chiefly Scot.* a firth. [metathetic var. of FIRTH]

frit·il·lar·i·a (frĭt′əlâr′ĭə), *n.* any plant of the liliaceous genus *Fritillaria,* comprising bulbous herbs with drooping, bell-shaped flowers, as *F. imperialis,* the crown imperial.

frit·il·lar·y (frĭt′əlĕr′ĭ), *n., pl.* **-laries.** any of several orange-brown butterflies which are silver-spotted beneath, of the genus *Argynnis* and allies. [t. NL: m.s. *fritillāria,* der. L *fritillus* dicebox]

frit·ter[1] (frĭt′ər), *v.t.* **1.** to disperse or squander piecemeal, or waste little by little (usually fol. by *away*): *to fritter away one's money.* **2.** to break or tear into small pieces or shreds. —*n.* **3.** a small piece, fragment, or shred. [earlier *fitter,* der. *fit* part] —**frit′ter·er,** *n.*

frit·ter[2] (frĭt′ər), *n.* a small cake of batter, sometimes containing fruit, clams, or some other ingredient, fried in deep fat or sautéed in a frying pan. [ME *frytour,* t. OF: m. *friture,* der. *frire* FRY]

Fri·u·li·an (frĭ·ōō′lĭ·ən), *n.* a Rhaeto-Romanic language spoken by about half a million people in NE Italy.

friv·ol (frĭv′əl), *v.,* **-oled, -oling** or (*esp. Brit.*) **-olled, -olling.** *Colloq.* —*v.i.* **1.** to behave frivolously; trifle. —*v.t.* **2.** to spend frivolously (fol. by *away*). [back formation from FRIVOLOUS] —**friv′ol·er,** *esp. Brit.* **friv′ol·ler,** *n.*

fri·vol·i·ty (frĭ·vŏl′ə·tĭ), *n., pl.* **-ties. 1.** quality or state of being frivolous. **2.** a frivolous act or thing.

friv·o·lous (frĭv′ələs), *adj.* **1.** of little or no weight, worth, or importance; not worthy of serious notice: *a frivolous objection.* **2.** characterized by lack of seriousness or sense: *frivolous conduct.* **3.** given to trifling or levity, as persons. [t. L: m. *frivolus* silly, trifling, paltry] —**friv′o·lous·ly,** *adv.* —**friv′o·lous·ness,** *n.* —**Syn. 1.** trifling, petty, paltry, trivial. **3.** idle, silly, foolish. —**Ant. 1.** weighty. **3.** serious.

friz (frĭz), *v.,* **frizzed, frizzing,** *n., pl.* **frizzes.** —*v.t., v.i.* **1.** to form into small, crisp curls or little tufts. —*n.* **2.** state of being frizzed. **3.** something frizzed; frizzed hair. Also, **frizz.** [back formation from FRIZZLE[1]]

fri·zette (frĭ·zĕt′), *n.* frisette.

friz·zle[1] (frĭz′əl), *v.,* **-zled, -zling,** *n.* —*v.t.* **1.** to friz. —*n.* **2.** a short, crisp curl. [orig. obscure. Cf. OE *frīs* curled] —**friz′zler,** *n.*

friz·zle[2] (frĭz′əl), *v.,* **-zled, -zling.** —*v.i.* **1.** to make a sizzling or sputtering noise in frying or the like. —*v.t.* **2.** to crisp (meat, etc.) by frying. [b. FRY and FIZZLE]

friz·zly (frĭz′lĭ), *adj.* curly: *frizzly hair.* Also, **friz′zy.**

fro (frō), *adv.* **1.** from; back. **2.** to and fro, **a.** back and forth. **b.** hither and thither. [ME, earlier *frā,* t. Scand.; cf. Icel. *frā,* c. OE *fram* from]

Fro·bish·er (frō′bĭsh·ər, frŏb′ĭsh-), *n.* **Sir Martin,** 1535?-94, British navigator and explorer.

frock (frŏk), *n.* **1.** a gown or dress. **2.** a loose outer garment worn by peasants and workmen; smock. **3.** a coarse outer garment with large sleeves, worn by monks. **4.** a frock coat. —*v.t.* **5.** to provide with or clothe in a frock. **6.** to invest with priestly or clerical office. [ME *froke,* t. OF: m. *froc;* ult. orig. uncert.] —**frock′less,** *adj.*

frock coat, a man's close-fitting coat, usually double-breasted, extending to about the knees.

froe (frō), *n. Chiefly U.S.* frow.

Froe·bel (frœ′bəl), *n.* **Friedrich** (frē′drĭKH), 1782-1852, German educational reformer; founder of the kindergarten system.

frog[1] (frŏg, frôg), *n., v.,* **frogged, frogging.** —*n.* **1.** any of various tailless amphibians (order *Salientia*) esp. of the web-footed aquatic species constituting the genus *Rana* and allied genera. **2.** any of various froglike amphibians. **3.** a slight hoarseness due to mucus on the vocal cords: *a frog in the throat.* **4.** (*cap.*) *Contemptuous.* Frenchman. **5.** a small, heavy holder placed in a bowl or vase to hold flower stems in position. —*v.i.* **6.** to catch, or search for, frogs. [ME *frogge,* OE *frogga;* akin to G *frosch*] —**frog′like′,** *adj.*

Bullfrog,
Rana catesbeiana
(7½ in. long)

frog[2] (frŏg, frôg), *n.* **1.** an ornamental fastening for the front of a coat, consisting of a button and a loop through which it passes. **2.** a device at the intersection of two railway tracks to permit the wheels and flanges on one track to cross or branch from the other. [? t. Pg.: m. *froco,* g. L *floccus* FLOCK[2]]

Ornamental frog (def. 1)

frog[3] (frŏg, frôg), *n.* a triangular mass

---

b., blend of, blended; c., cognate with; d., dialect, dialectal; der., derived from; f., formed from; g., going back to; m., modification of; r., replacing; s., stem of; t., taken from; ?, perhaps. See the full key on inside cover.

of elastic, horny substance in the middle of the sole of the foot of a horse or related animal. [special use of FROG[1]]

frog·eye (frôg/ī/, frŏg/ī/), *n.* a disease, attributed to a fungus, which affects tobacco leaves, producing small white spots.

frog·fish (frôg/fĭsh/, frŏg/-), *n., pl.* **-fishes**, (*esp. collectively*) **-fish.** **1.** any of the anglers (def. 3) constituting the family *Antennariidae,* characterized by a wide froglike mouth and broad limblike fins. **2.** an angler (def. 2).

frog·hop·per (frôg/hŏp/ər, frŏg/-), *n.* any of various small, leaping, homopterous insects (family *Cercopidae*) whose young live in a spittlelike secretion on plants.

frog kick, *Swimming.* a type of kick in which the legs are bent at the knees, extended outward, and then brought together forcefully.

frog lily, a yellow pond lily.

frog·mouth (frôg/mouth/, frŏg/-), *n.* any of the Australian and East Indian goatsuckers (birds) constituting the family *Podargidae,* or, according to some classifications, the subfamily *Podarginae:* so called from their wide, flat, froglike mouth.

frog spit, any of several filamentous fresh-water green algae forming floating masses. Also, **frog spittle.**

Froh·man (frō/mən), *n.* **Charles,** 1860-1915, U.S. theatrical producer.

Frois·sart (froi/särt; *Fr.* frwà sàr/), *n.* **Jean** (zhäɴ), c1337-c1410, French historian and poet.

frol·ic (frŏl/ĭk), *n., v.,* **-icked, -icking,** *adj.* —*n.* **1.** merry play; gay prank; gaiety; fun. **2.** a merrymaking. —*v.i.* **3.** to play merrily; have fun; play merry pranks. —*adj.* **4.** gay; merry; full of mirth or pranks; full of fun. [t. D: m. *vrolijk* joyful (c. G *fröhlich*), f. *vro* glad + *lijk* like] —**frol/ick·er,** *n.*

frol·ic·some (frŏl/ĭk səm), *adj.* merrily playful; full of fun —**frol/ic·some·ly,** *adv.* —**frol/ic·some·ness,** *n.*

from (frŭm; *unstressed* frəm), *prep.* a particle specifying a starting point, and hence used to express removal or separation in space, time, order, etc., discrimination or distinction, source or origin, instrumentality, and cause or reason: *a train running west from New York, from that time onward, to wander from one's purpose, to refrain from laughing, sketches drawn from nature.* [ME and OE, var. of *fram,* prep., from, as adv., forward, forth, c. OHG and Goth. *fram,* prep. and adv., Icel. *frā,* prep. (cf. FRO), *fram,* adv.]

fro·men·ty (frō/mən tĭ), *n.* *Chiefly Brit. Dial.* frumenty.

frond (frŏnd), *n.* *Bot.* **1.** a finely divided leaf, often large, properly applied to the ferns and some of the palms. **2.** a leaflike expansion not differentiated into stem and foliage, as in lichens. [t. L: s. *frons* leafy branch] —**frond/ed,** *adj.* —**frond/less,** *adj.*

Fronde (frŏɴd), *n.* *French.* **1.** a parliamentary and aristocratic rebellion against the court party and Cardinal Mazarin during the minority of Louis XIV of France. **2.** the groups which waged this rebellion.

fron·des·cence (frŏn dĕs/əns), *n.* **1.** the process or period of coming into leaf. **2.** foliage. [t. NL: m.s. *frondescentia,* der. s. L *frondescens,* ppr. of *frondescere,* freq. of *frondēre* put forth leaves] —**fron·des/cent,** *adj.*

frons (frŏnz), *n.* the facial area of an insect's head above or behind the clypeus.

front (frŭnt), *n.* **1.** the foremost part or surface of anything. **2.** the part or side of anything, as a house, which seems to look out or be directed forward. **3.** any side or face, as of a house. **4.** a place or position directly before anything. **5. Front!** *U.S.* ellip. command meaning (come to the) front, (come) forward, which a hotel clerk calls out to a bellhop. **6.** *Mil.* **a.** the foremost line or part of an army, etc. **b.** a line of battle. **c.** the place where active operations are carried on. **7.** land facing a road, river, etc. **8.** *Brit.* a promenade along a seashore. **9.** *Colloq.* a distinguished person listed as an official of an organization, for the sake of prestige, and usually inactive. **10.** *Colloq.* outward impression of rank, position, or weath. **11.** bearing or demeanor in confronting anything: *a calm front.* **12.** cool assurance, or impudence. **13.** the forehead, or the entire face. **14.** a coalition or movement to achieve a particular end, usually political: *people's front.* **15.** something attached or worn at the forepart, as a shirt front, a dicky, etc. **16.** a necktie or cravat. **17.** *Meteorol.* a surface of discontinuity separating two dissimilar air masses. **18.** *Theat.* the auditorium. —*adj.* **19.** of or pertaining to the front. **20.** situated in or at the front. **21.** *Phonet.* pronounced with the tongue relatively far forward in the mouth: *the vowels of "beet" and "gait" are front vowels.* —*v.t.* **22.** to have the front toward; face: *our house fronts the lake.* **23.** to meet face to face; confront. **24.** to face in opposition, hostility, or defiance. **25.** to furnish or supply with a front. **26.** to serve as a front to. —*v.i.* **27.** to have or turn the front in some specified direction: *our house fronts on the lake.* [ME, t. L: s. *frons* forehead, front] —**front/less,** *adj.*

front·age (frŭn/tĭj), *n.* **1.** the front of a building or lot. **2.** the lineal extent of this front. **3.** the direction it faces. **4.** land abutting on a river, street, etc. **5.** the space lying between a building and the street, etc.

fron·tal (frŭn/təl), *adj.* **1.** of, in, or at the front: a

frontal attack. **2.** noting or pertaining to the bone (or pair of bones) forming the forehead, or to the forehead in general. —*n.* **3.** *Eccles.* a movable cover or hanging for the front of an altar. **4.** *Anat.* a bone of the forehead; frontal bone. See diag. under **cranium.** [t. LL: s. *frontālis,* der. L *frons* front; r. ME *frountel,* t. OF: m. *frontel*] —**front/al·ly,** *adv.*

front bench, *Brit.* (in Parliament) the seats near the Speaker, on which the leaders of the parties sit.

Fron·te·nac (frŏn/tə năk/, *Fr.* frôɴt nåk/), *n.* **Louis de Buade de** (lwē də bɣàd/ də), c1620-98, French governor of Canada.

front foot, *U.S.* a foot measured along the front of a lot.

fron·tier (frŭn tĭr/, frŏn/tĭr), *n.* **1.** that part of a country which borders another country; the border. **2.** *U.S.* that part of a country which forms the border of its settled or inhabited regions. **3.** the incompletely developed region of a field of knowledge, feeling, etc.: *frontiers of philosophy.* —*adj.* **4.** of or on the frontier: *a frontier town.* [ME *frountere,* t. OF: m. *frontiere,* der. *front* in sense of opposite side]

fron·tiers·man (frŭn tĭrz/mən), *n., pl.* **-men.** a man who lives on the frontier.

fron·tis·piece (frŭn/tĭs pēs/, frŏn/-), *n.* **1.** an illustrated leaf preceding the title page of a book. **2.** *Archit.* **a.** the most richly decorated and usually central portion of the principal face of a building. **b.** the pediment over a door, gate, etc. [alter. (conformed to *piece*) of earlier *frontispice,* t. F, t. ML: m.s. *frontispicium,* f. L. *fronti-* front + *-spicium* look]

front·let (frŭnt/lĭt), *n.* **1.** the forehead of an animal. **2.** *Ornith.* the forehead when marked by a different color or texture of the plumage. **3.** something worn on the head. **4.** (among the Jews) a phylactery worn on the head. [ME *frontlette,* t. OF: m. *frontelet,* dim. of *frontel* FRONTAL, n.]

front matter, *U.S. Printing.* all matter in a book that precedes the text proper.

front-page (frŭnt/pāj/), *adj.* of consequence; worth putting on the first page of a newspaper.

Front Range, the easternmost range of the Rocky Mountains, extending from central Colorado to S Wyoming. Highest peak, Grays Peak, 14,341 ft.

frore (frōr), *adj.* **1.** *Archaic.* frozen. **2.** *Poetic.* frosty; intensely cold. [old pp. of FREEZE]

frost (frôst, frŏst), *n.* **1.** a state of the temperature which occasions the freezing of water. **2.** *Brit.* **degrees of frost,** degrees below the freezing point: *we had ten degrees of frost* (i.e., 22° Fahr.). **3.** a covering of minute ice needles, formed from the atmosphere at night upon the ground and exposed objects when these have cooled by radiation below the dew point, and when the dew point is below the freezing point (**white frost** or **hoarfrost**). **4.** act or process of freezing. **5.** coldness of manner or temperature. **6.** *Colloq.* a coolness between persons. **7.** *Slang.* a failure. —*v.t.* **8.** to cover with frost. **9.** to give a frostlike surface to (glass, etc.). **10.** to ice (a cake, etc.). **11.** to kill or injure by frost. [ME and OE *frost, forst,* c. D *vorst,* G and Icel. *frost;* akin to FREEZE] —**frost/less,** *adj.* —**frost/like/,** *adj.*

Frost (frôst, frŏst), *n.* **Robert,** born 1875, U.S. poet.

frost·bite (frôst/bīt/, frŏst/-), *n., v.,* **-bit, -bitten, -biting.** —*n.* **1.** the inflamed, gangrenous effect of excessive exposure to extreme cold. —*v.t.* **2.** to injure by frost or extreme cold.

frost·bit·ten (frôst/bĭt/ən, frŏst/-), *adj.* injured by frost or extreme cold.

frost·fish (frôst/fĭsh/, frŏst/-), *n., pl.* **-fishes,** (*esp. collectively*) **-fish.** the tomcod, *Microgadus tomcod,* which appears on the northeastern coast of North America, as frost sets in.

frost·flow·er (frôst/flou/ər, frŏst/-), *n.* **1.** a liliaceous plant, *Milla biflora,* of the southwestern U.S. and Mexico. **2.** its waxy-white, starlike flower. **3.** any aster.

frost·ing (frôs/tĭng, frŏs/-), *n.* **1.** a preparation of confectioner's sugar beaten together with egg whites or cream, etc., or a preparation of sugar, water, etc., cooked together, for covering cakes. **2.** a lusterless finish, as of metal or glass. **3.** a material used for decorative work, as signs, etc., made from coarse, powdered glass flakes.

frost·work (frôst/wûrk/, frŏst/-), *n.* **1.** the delicate tracery formed by frost, esp. on glass. **2.** similar ornamentation, as on metal.

frost·y (frôs/tĭ, frŏs/-), *adj.,* **frostier, frostiest.** **1.** attended with or producing frost; freezing; very cold: *frosty weather.* **2.** consisting of or covered with a frost. **3.** lacking warmth of feeling. **4.** resembling frost; white or gray, as the hair. **5.** pertaining to or characteristic of old age. —**frost/i·ly,** *adv.* —**frost/i·ness,** *n.* —**frost/less,** *adj.*

froth (frôth, frŏth), *n.* **1.** an aggregation of bubbles, as on a fermented liquid or at the mouth of a hard-driven horse; foam. **2.** a foam of saliva or fluid resulting from disease. **3.** something unsubstantial or evanescent, as idle talk; trivial ideas. —*v.t.* **4.** to cover with froth. **5.** to cause to foam. **6.** to emit like froth. —*v.i.* **7.** to give out froth; foam. [ME *frothe,* ? t. Scand.; cf. Icel. *frodha.* Cf. also OE *āfrēothan* froth from froth]

froth·y (frôth/ĭ, frŏth/ĭ), *adj.,* **frothier, frothiest.** **1.** of, like, or having froth; foamy. **2.** unsubstantial; trifling; shallow. —**froth/i·ly,** *adv.* —**froth/i·ness,** *n.*

Froude (frŏŏd), *n.* James Anthony, 1818–94, British historian.

frou-frou (frōō′frōō′), *n.* a rustling, particularly the rustling of silk, as in a woman's dress. [t. F]

frounce (frouns), *n., v.,* **frounced, frouncing.** —*n.* 1. *Archaic.* affectation; empty show. —*v.t.* 2. to curl the hair of. 3. *Obs.* to pleat. —*v.i.* 4. *Obs.* to frown. [ME *fronce*(n), t. OF: m. *froncier,* der. *fronce* a wrinkle, fold, t. Gmc.; cf. Icel. *hrukka,* G *runzel* wrinkle]

frouz-y (frou′zĭ), *adj.* **frouzier, frouziest.** frowzy.

frow (frō), *n.* U.S. a cleaving tool having a wedged-shaped blade, with a handle set at right angles to it. Also, **froe.** [special use of FROW(ARD) turned away from]

fro-ward (frō′wərd, frō′ərd), *adj.* perverse; willfully contrary; refractory; not easily managed. [ME. See FRO, -WARD] —**fro′ward-ly,** *adv.* —**fro′ward-ness,** *n.* —**Syn.** obstinate, willful, disobedient. —**Ant.** docile.

frown (froun), *v.i.* 1. to contract the brow as in displeasure or deep thought; scowl. 2. to look displeased; have an angry look. 3. to look disapprovingly (fol. by *on* or *upon*): *to frown upon a scheme.* —*v.t.* 4. to express by a frown. —*n.* 5. a frowning look; scowl. 6. any expression or show of disapproval. [ME *froune*(n), t. OF: m. *froignier,* der. *froigne* surly expression; of Celtic orig.] —**frown′er,** *n.* —**frown′ing-ly,** *adv.*

frowst-y (frou′stĭ), *adj.* Brit. Dial. and Colloq. ill-smelling; musty.

frowz-y (frou′zĭ), *adj.* **frowzier, frowziest.** 1. dirty and untidy; slovenly. 2. ill-smelling; musty. Also, **frows′y, frouzy.** [akin to FROWSTY] —**frowz′i-ly,** *adv.* —**frowz′i-ness,** *n.*

froze (frōz), *v.* pt. of **freeze.**

fro-zen (frō′zən), *v.* 1. pp. of **freeze.** —*adj.* 2. congealed by cold; covered with ice, as a stream. 3. frigid; very cold. 4. injured or killed by frost or cold. 5. obstructed by ice, as pipes. 6. chilly or cold in manner; unfeeling: *a frozen stare.* 7. *Finance, Colloq.* rendered impossible of liquidation, as by business conditions: *frozen loans.* [pp. of FREEZE] —**fro′zen-ly,** *adv.* —**fro′zen-ness,** *n.*

F.R.S., Fellow of the Royal Society.

frt., freight.

Fruc-ti-dor (frŭk tē dôr′), *n.* (in the calendar of the first French republic) the twelfth month of the year, extending from Aug. 18 to Sept. 16. [t. F, f. L *fructi-* fruit + s. Gk. *dōron* gift]

fruc-tif-er-ous (frŭk tĭf′ər əs), *adj.* fruit-bearing; producing fruit. [f. L *fructifer* fruit-bearing + -OUS]

fruc-ti-fi-ca-tion (frŭk′tə fə kā′shən), *n.* 1. act of fructifying; the fruiting of a plant. 2. the fruit of a plant. 3. the organs of fruiting.

fruc-ti-fy (frŭk′tə fī′), *v.,* **-fied, -fying.** —*v.i.* 1. to bear fruit. —*v.t.* 2. to make fruitful or productive; fertilize. [ME *fructifie*(n), t. F: m. *fructifier,* t. L: m. *fructificāre* bear fruit]

fruc-tose (frŭk′tōs), *n.* Chem. a levorotatory ketose sugar, $C_6H_{12}O_6$, known also as levulose. It is an intensely sweet carbohydrate occurring in honey and invert sugar. [f. s. L *fructus* fruit + -OSE²]

fruc-tu-ous (frŭk′chŏŏ əs), *adj.* fruitful; profitable.

fru-gal (frōō′gəl), *adj.* 1. economical in use or expenditure; prudently saving or sparing. 2. entailing little expense; costing little. [t. L: s. *frūgālis* economical] —**fru-gal-i-ty** (frōō găl′ə tĭ), **fru′gal-ness,** *n.* —**fru′gal-ly,** *adv.* —**Syn.** 1. self-denying, thrifty, chary, provident. See economical. —**Ant.** 1. extravagant.

fruit (frōōt), *n.* 1. any product of vegetable growth useful to men or animals. 2. *Bot.* **a.** the developed ovary of a seed plant with its contents and accessory parts, as the pea pod, nut, tomato, pineapple, etc. **b.** the edible part of a plant developed from a flower, with any accessory tissues, as the peach, mulberry, banana, etc. **c.** the spores and accessory organs of a cryptogram. 3. anything produced or accruing; product, result, or effect; return or profit. —*v.i., v.t.* 4. to bear or bring to bear fruit. [ME, t. OF, g. L *fructus* enjoyment, proceeds, fruit] —**fruit′like′,** *adj.*

fruit-age (frōō′tĭj), *n.* 1. the bearing of fruit or result. 2. fruits collectively. 3. product or result.

fruit cake, a rich cake containing raisins, nuts, citron, etc.

fruit cup, an assortment of fruits served in a glass or a cup as an appetizer or dessert.

fruit-er (frōō′tər), *n.* 1. a ship employed in transporting fruit. 2. a fruitgrower.

fruit-er-er (frōō′tər ər), *n.* Chiefly Brit. a dealer in fruit.

fruit fly, 1. any small fly of the dipterous family *Trypetidae,* which includes many seriously destructive pests, as the Mediterranean fruit fly. 2. any member of the genus *Drosophila,* the vinegar flies.

fruit-ful (frōōt′fəl), *adj.* 1. abounding in fruit, as trees or other plants; bearing fruit abundantly. 2. conducing to abundance of fruit, as soil or showers. 3. productive of results; profitable: *fruitful investigations.* —**fruit′ful-ly,** *adv.* —**fruit′ful-ness,** *n.* —**Syn.** 3. prolific, fertile. See productive. —**Ant.** 3. barren.

fru-i-tion (frōō ĭsh′ən), *n.* 1. attainment of anything desired; realization of results: *the fruition of one's labors.* 2. enjoyment, as of something attained or realized. 3. state of bearing fruit. [late ME, t. LL: s. *fruitio* enjoyment]

fruit jar, a large-mouthed bottle, usually with an airtight cap, for preserving fruit.

fruit-less (frōōt′lĭs), *adj.* 1. useless; unproductive; vain; without results. 2. without fruit; barren. —**fruit′-less-ly,** *adv.* —**fruit′less-ness,** *n.* —**Syn.** 1. ineffective, abortive, unprofitable, bootless, futile.

fruit ranch, a farm where fruit is the main produce.

fruit sugar, Chem. levulose.

fruit tree, a tree bearing edible fruit.

fruit-y (frōō′tĭ), *adj.* **fruitier, fruitiest.** resembling fruit; having the taste or flavor of fruit.

fru-men-ta-ceous (frōō′mən tā′shəs), *adj.* of the nature of or resembling wheat or other grain. [t. LL: m. *frūmentāceus* of grain]

fru-men-ty (frōō′mən tĭ), *n.* Chiefly Brit. Dial. hulled wheat boiled in milk and seasoned with sugar, etc. Also, **fromenty, furmenty, furmety.** [ME *frumentee,* t. OF, der. *frument,* g. L *frūmentum* grain]

frump (frŭmp), *n.* a dowdy, sometimes cross, woman. [orig. unknown]

frump-ish (frŭmp′ĭsh), *adj.* dowdy, and sometimes cross. —**frump′ish-ly,** *adv.* —**frump′ish-ness,** *n.*

frump-y (frŭmp′ĭ), *adj.,* **frumpier, frumpiest.** frumpish. —**frump′i-ly,** *adv.* —**frump′i-ness,** *n.*

Frun-ze (frōōn′zĕ), *n.* a city in the SW Soviet Union in Asia: the capital of Kirghiz Republic. 92,659 (1939).

frus-trate (frŭs′trāt), *v.,* **-trated, -trating,** *adj.* —*v.t.* 1. to make (plans, efforts, etc.) of no avail; defeat, baffle, nullify. 2. to disappoint or thwart (a person). —*adj.* 3. *Archaic.* frustrated. [t. L: m.s. *frustrātus,* pp., having disappointed or deceived] —**Syn.** 1. balk, foil, circumvent. See thwart. —**Ant.** 1. assist.

frus-tra-tion (frŭs trā′shən), *n.* state or quality of being frustrated; nullification.

frus-tule (frŭs′chōōl), *n.* Bot. the siliceous cell wall of a diatom. [t. LL: m.s. *frustulum,* dim. of *frustum* piece, bit.]

frus-tum (frŭs′təm), *n., pl.* **-tums, -ta** (-tə). Geom. 1. the part of a conical solid left after cutting off a top portion by a plane parallel to the base. 2. the part of a conical solid between two cutting planes. [t. L: piece, bit]

F. Frustum of a cone

fru-tes-cent (frōō tĕs′ənt), *adj.* Bot. tending to be shrublike; shrubby. [irreg. f. L *frut*(ex) shrub, bush + -ESCENT] —**fru-tes′cence,** *n.*

fru-ti-cose (frōō′tĭ kōs′), *adj.* Bot. having the form of a shrub; shrublike. [t. L: m.s. *fruticōsus* bushy]

fry¹ (frī), *v.,* **fried, frying,** *n., pl.* **fries.** —*v.t.* 1. to cook in fat, usually over direct heat. —*v.i.* 2. to undergo cooking in fat. —*n.* 3. a dish of something fried. 4. *U.S.* an occasion at which the chief food is fried, frequently outdoors: *a fish fry.* [ME *frye*(n), t. F: m. *frire,* g. L *frīgere*]

fry² (frī), *n., pl.* **fry.** 1. the young of fishes, as of some other animals, as frogs. 2. young or small fishes or other young creatures, as children, collectively. [ME; cf. Icel. *frjō,* Sw. *frö,* Goth. *fraiw* seed]

fry-er (frī′ər), *n.* 1. one who or that which fries. 2. something, as a young chicken, for frying. Also, **frier.**

frying pan, a shallow pan with a long handle, in which food is fried.

f.s., foot-second.

ft., 1. feet. 2. foot. 3. fort. 4. fortification.

FTC, Federal Trade Commission.

fth., fathom. Also, **fthm.**

ft-lb., foot-pound.

Fu-ad I (fŏŏ äd′), (Ahmed Fuad) 1868–1936, king of Egypt, 1922–36.

fuch-sia (fū′shə), *n.* 1. any plant of the onagraceous genus *Fuchsia,* which includes many varieties cultivated for their handsome drooping flowers. 2. Also, **California fuchsia.** a herbaceous shrub, *Zauschneria californica,* with large crimson flowers. [NL, named after Leonhard *Fuchs* (1501–66), German botanist. See -IA]

fuch-sin (fŏŏk′sĭn), *n.* a coal-tar dye obtained by oxidizing a mixture of aniline and the toluidines; magenta. The dye is a greenish solid which forms deep-red solutions. Also, **fuch-sine** (fŏŏk′sĭn, -sēn). [f. FUCHS(IA) + -IN²; so named from its likeness to the flower in color]

fu-coid (fū′koid), *adj.* 1. resembling, or allied to, seaweeds of the genus *Fucus.* See fucus. —*n.* 2. a fucoid seaweed. [f. FUC(US) + -OID]

fu-cus (fū′kəs), *n., pl.* **-ci** (-sī), **-cuses.** any seaweed of the genus *Fucus,* olive-brown algae with branching fronds and often air bladders. [t. L: rock lichen]

fud-dle (fŭd′əl), *v.,* **-dled, -dling.** —*v.t.* 1. to intoxicate. 2. to muddle or confuse. —*v.i.* 3. to tipple.

fudge¹ (fŭj), *n.* a kind of candy (often homemade) composed of sugar, butter, milk, and chocolate. [orig. uncert.]

fudge² (fŭj), *n., v.,* **fudged, fudging.** —*n.* 1. nonsense or bosh (sometimes used as a contemptuous interjection). —*v.i.* 2. to talk nonsense. [orig. unknown]

fudge³ (fŭj), *n., v.,* **fudged, fudging.** —*n.* 1. a small stereotype or a few lines of specially prepared type which may replace a detachable part of the page plate of a newspaper in order to admit a late bulletin without replating the whole page. 2. the bulletin thus printed, often in color. 3. a machine or attachment for printing such a bulletin. —*v.t.* 4. to adjust or perform clumsily.

---

b., blend of, blended; c., cognate with; d., dialect, dialectal; der., derived from; f., formed from; g., going back to; m., modification of; r., replacing; s., stem of; t., taken from; ?, perhaps. See the full key on inside cover.

perfunctorily, or dishonestly; make or get (*up*). [var. of FADGE]

Fu·e·gi·an (fū·ē′jĬ′ən, fwā′jĬ′ən), *adj.* **1.** of or belonging to Tierra del Fuego or its indigenous Indians. —*n.* **2.** a native or inhabitant of Tierra del Fuego.

fu·el (fū′əl), *n.*, *v.*, **-eled, -eling** or (*esp. Brit.*) **-elled, -elling.** —*n.* **1.** combustible matter used to maintain fire, as coal, wood, oil, etc. **2.** means of sustaining or increasing passion, ardor, etc. —*v.t.* **3.** to supply with fuel. —*v.i.* **4.** to procure or take in fuel. [ME *fuelle,* t. OF: m. *feuaile,* ult. der. L *focus* hearth, fireplace]

fuel oil, an oil used for fuel, esp. one used as a substitute for coal, as crude petroleum.

fu·ga·cious (fū·gā′shəs), *adj.* **1.** *Bot.* falling or fading early. **2.** fleeting; transitory. [f. obs. *fugacy* flight + -OUS] —**fu·gac·i·ty** (fū·găs′ə tĬ), *n.*

fu·gal (fū′gəl), *adj. Music.* of or pertaining to a fugue, or composed in the style of a fugue. —**fu′gal·ly,** *adv.*

fu·gate (fū′gāt), *n. Music.* a piece composed in fugue style, but not according to strict rules.

-fuge, a word element referring to "flight," as in *refuge.* [comb. form repr. L -*fugia,* der. *fugāre* put to flight]

fu·gi·tive (fū′jətĬv), *n.* **1.** a person who is fleeing; a runaway. —*adj.* **2.** having taken flight, or run away: *a fugitive slave.* **3.** fleeting; transitory. **4.** dealing with subjects of passing interest, as writings; ephemeral. **5.** wandering, roving, or vagabond. [t. L: m.s. *fugitīvus* fleeing; r. ME *fugitif,* t. F] —**fu′gi·tive·ly,** *adv.* —**fu′gi·tive·ness,** *n.*

fu·gle·man (fū′gəl mən), *n., pl.* **-men. 1.** a well-drilled soldier placed in front of a military company as a model for the others. **2.** anyone serving as an example. [t. G: m. *flügelmann,* lit., wing man]

fugue (fūg), *n. Music.* a polyphonic composition based upon one, two, or even more themes, which are enunciated by the several voices or parts in turn, subjected to contrapuntal treatment, and gradually built up into a complex form having somewhat distinct divisions or stages of development and a marked climax at the end. [t. F, t. It.: m. *fuga,* g. L *fuga* flight] —**fugue′like′,** *adj.*

Füh·rer (fy′rər), *n. German.* **1.** leader. **2.** der (dĕr) **Führer,** the leader (applied esp. to Adolph Hitler, head of the Nazi German State).

Fu·ji (foo′jē), *n.* an extinct volcano in central Japan, on Honshu island: it is the highest mountain in Japan and is renowned for its beautiful symmetry. 12,395 ft. Also, **Fu·ji·ya·ma** (foo′jē yä′mä) or **Fu·ji·san** (foo′jē-sän′).

Fu·kien (foo′kyĕn′), *n.* a maritime province in SE China. 11,654,200 pop. (est. 1944); 45,845 sq. mi. *Cap.:* Foochow.

Fu·ku·o·ka (foo′koo ō′kä), *n.* a city in SW Japan, on Kyushu island. 288,794 (1940).

Ful (fool), *n.* a language of Senegal related to Wolof.

-ful, a suffix meaning: **1.** full or of characterized by: *shameful, beautiful, careful, thoughtful.* **2.** tending or able to: *wakeful, harmful.* **3.** as much as will fill: *spoonful, handful.* [ME and OE -*full,* -*ful,* repr. *full, ful* FULL[1]]

Fu·lah (foo′lä), *n., pl.* **-lah.** an African people, probably of mixed Berber and Negro origin, scattered through the Sudan from Senegal eastward. Also, **Fu′la.**

ful·crum (fŭl′krəm), *n., pl.* **-crums, -cra** (-krə). **1.** the support, or point of rest, on which a lever turns in moving a body. **2.** a prop. [t. L: bedpost]

ful·fil (fool fĬl′), *v.t.,* **-filled, -filling. fulfill.**

ful·fill (fool fĬl′), *v.t.* **1.** to carry out, or bring to consummation, as a prophecy, promise, etc. **2.** to perform or do, as

F Fulcrum; L, Lever

duty; obey or follow, as commands. **3.** to satisfy (requirements, etc.). **4.** to bring to an end, finish, or complete, as a period of time. [ME *fulfil(en),* OE *fullfyllan,* f. *full,* adj., full + *fyllan,* v., fill] —**ful·fill′er,** *n.* —**Syn. 2.** execute, discharge.

ful·fill·ment (fool fĬl′mənt), *n.* a fulfilling or carrying out; performance; completion. Also, **ful·fil′ment.**

ful·gent (fŭl′jənt), *adj.* shining brightly; resplendent. [ME, t. L: s. *fulgens,* ppr.] —**ful′gent·ly,** *adv.*

ful·gu·rant (fŭl′gyə rənt), *adj.* flashing like lightning. [t. L: s. *fulgurans,* ppr.]

ful·gu·rate (fŭl′gyə rāt′), *v.i.,* **-rated, -rating. 1.** to flash or dart like lightning. **2.** *Med.* to destroy (as an abnormal growth) by electricity. [t. L: m.s. *fulgurātus,* pp.] —**ful′gu·ra′tion,** *n.*

ful·gu·rat·ing (fŭl′gyə rā′tĬng), *adj. Med.* (of pains) sharp and piercing, like lightning.

ful·gu·rite (fŭl′gyə rĬt′), *n.* a tube formed in sand or rock by lightning. [f. L *fulgur* lightning + -ITE[1]]

ful·gu·rous (fŭl′gyə rəs), *adj.* lightninglike.

fu·lig·i·nous (fū·lĬj′ə nəs), *adj.* **1.** sooty; smoky. **2.** dull or brownish dark-gray. [t. LL: m.s. *fulīginōsus* full of soot]

full[1] (fool), *adj.* **1.** filled; containing all that can be held; filled to utmost capacity: *a full cup.* **2.** complete; entire; maximum: *a full supply.* **3.** of the maximum size, amount, extent, volume, etc.: *a full mile, full pay, the full moon.* **4.** (of garments, etc.) wide, ample, or

having ample folds. **5.** abundant; well-supplied; *a pocket full of money.* **6.** filled or rounded out, as in form. **7.** *Music.* ample and complete in volume or richness of sound. **8.** (of wines) having considerable body. **9. in full cry,** in hot pursuit, as dogs in the chase. —*adv.* **10.** fully, completely, or entirely. **11.** exactly or directly: *the blow struck him full in the face.* **12.** *Chiefly Poetic.* very: *full well.* —*v.t.* **13.** *Sewing.* to bring (the cloth) on one side of a seam to a little greater fullness than on the other by gathering or tucking very slightly. —*v.i.* **14.** to become full. —*n.* **15.** in full, a. without reduction; to or for the full amount: *a receipt in full.* **b.** without abbreviation or contraction. **16. to the full,** in full measure; to the utmost extent. **17.** (of the moon) the stage of complete illumination. See diag. under **moon.** [ME and OE *full, ful,* c. G *voll;* akin to L *plēnus,* Gk. *plērēs*] —**full′ness,** *n.* —**ful′ly,** *adv.*

full[2] (fool), *v.t.* **1.** to cleanse and thicken (cloth, etc.) by special processes in manufacture. —*v.i.* **2.** (of cloth, etc.) to become compacted or felted. [back formation from FULLER[1]]

full·back (fool′băk′), *n. Football.* the player usually farthest behind the line of scrimmage.

full binding, a complete binding of a volume in any one material, generally leather.

full blood, 1. an individual of unmixed ancestry; a purebred. **2.** relationship through both parents.

full-blood·ed (fool′blŭd′Ĭd), *adj.* **1.** of unmixed ancestry; thoroughbred. **2.** vigorous; virile; hearty.

full-blown (fool′blōn′), *adj.* **1.** in full bloom: *a full-blown rose.* **2.** completely developed.

full-bod·ied (fool′bŏd′Ĭd), *adj.* with all the flavor and strength possible.

full dress, 1. a ceremonial style of dress. **2.** the formal attire customarily worn in the evening.

full·er[1] (fool′ər), *n.* one who fulls cloth. [ME; OE *fullere,* f. L *full(o)* fuller + -*ere* -ER[1]]

full·er[2] (fool′ər), *n.* a half-round set hammer used for grooving and spreading iron. [appar. f. *full,* v., to make full + -ER[1]]

Ful·ler (fool′ər), *n.* **1.** Melville Weston, 1833–1910, chief justice of the U.S. Supreme Court, 1888–1910. **2.** (Sarah) Margaret, (Marchioness Ossoli) 1810–50, U.S. author and literary critic. **3.** Thomas, 1608–61, British clergyman and historian.

fuller's earth, an absorbent clay, used for removing grease from cloth, etc., in fulling, as a filter and, in medicine, as a dusting powder.

fuller's teasel, the teasel, *Dipsacus fullonum.*

full-faced (fool′fāst′), *adj.* **1.** having a plump or round face. **2.** facing squarely toward the spectator or in a given direction. **3.** *Printing.* (of type) bold-faced.

full-fash·ioned (fool′făsh′ənd), *adj.* knitted in the shape of the foot or leg.

full-fledged (fool′flĕjd′), *adj.* **1.** fully developed. **2.** of full rank or standing: *a full-fledged professor.*

full gainer, *Swimming.* a type of dive in which the diver takes off facing forward and performs a complete back somersault before entering the water.

full-grown (fool′grōn′), *adj.* fully grown; mature.

full house, *Poker.* a hand consisting of three of a kind and a pair, as three queens and two tens.

full moon, the moon when the whole of its disk is illuminated. See **moon** (def. 2c).

fullness of time, the proper or destined time.

full-rigged (fool′rĬgd′), *adj.* **1.** *Naut.* carrying complete rigging. **2.** having all equipment.

full stop, a period.

ful·mar (fool′mər), *n.* any of certain oceanic birds of the petrel family, esp. *Fulmarus glacialis,* a gull-like arctic species. [? lit., foul gull (with allusion to its stench), t. Scand; cf. Icel. *fūll* foul, *mār* gull]

ful·mi·nant (fŭl′mə nənt), *adj.* **1.** fulminating. **2.** *Pathol.* developing or progressing suddenly: *fulminant plague.* [t. L: s. *fulminans,* ppr., lightening]

ful·mi·nate (fŭl′mə nāt′), *v.,* **-nated, -nating,** *n.* —*v.i.* **1.** to explode with a loud noise; detonate. **2.** to issue denunciations or the like (fol. by *against*). —*v.t.* **3.** to cause to explode. **4.** to denounce vehemently. —*n.* **5.** *Chem.* one of a group of unstable, explosive compounds derived from fulminic acid; esp. the mercury salt of fulminic acid which is a powerful detonating agent. [t. L: m.s. *fulminātus,* pp., lightened] —**ful′mi·na′tor,** *n.*

fulminating compound, *Chem.* a fulminate.

fulminating powder, *Chem.* **1.** powder which explodes by percussion. **2.** a fulminate.

ful·mi·na·tion (fŭl′mə nā′shən), *n.* **1.** a violent denunciation or censure. **2.** violent explosion.

ful·min·ic acid (fŭl mĬn′Ĭk), *Chem.* an acid, HONC, an isomer of cyanic acid, found only in its salts, the fulminates.

ful·ness (fool′nĬs), *n.* fullness.

ful·some (fool′səm, fŭl′-), *adj.* **1.** offensive to good taste, esp. as being excessive; gross: *fulsome praise.* **2.** disgusting. [ME *fulsum;* f. FULL[1] + -SOME[1]; evidence of assoc. with FOUL] —**ful′some·ly,** *adv.* —**ful′some·ness,** *n.*

Ful·ton (fool′tən), *n.* **Robert,** 1765–1815, American inventor: built the first profitable steamboat.

ful·vous (fŭl′vəs), *adj.* tawny; dull yellowish-gray or brown. [t. L: m. *fulvus* deep yellow]

fu·mar·ic acid (fū mǎr/Ĭk), *Chem.* a dibasic acid, $C_2H_2(COOH)_2$, isomeric with maleic acid and occurring in several plants.

fu·ma·role (fū/mə rōl/), *n.* a hole in or near a volcano, from which vapor issues. [t. F: m. *fumerolle*, g. LL *fūmāriolum*, dim. of L *fūmārium* smoke chamber]

fum·ble (fŭm/bəl), *v.*, **-bled, -bling,** *n.* —*v.i.* **1.** to feel or grope about clumsily (fol. by *at, with, after, for*). **2.** *Sports.* to fumble the ball. —*v.t.* **3.** to handle clumsily. **4.** *Sports.* to fail to catch and hold (a ball). —*n.* **5.** act of fumbling. [cf. Sw. *fumla* grope] —**fum/bler,** *n.* —**fum/bling,** *adj.* —**fum/bling·ly,** *adv.*

fume (fūm), *n., v.,* **fumed, fuming.** —*n.* **1.** (*often pl.*) any smokelike or vaporous exhalation from matter or substances. **2.** an odorous exhalation, as from flowers. **3.** an irritable or angry mood: *to be in a fume.* —*v.t.* **4.** to send forth as fumes. **5.** to disperse or drive away in vapors; send up as vapor. **6.** to treat with fumes. —*v.i.* **7.** to rise, or pass off, as fumes. **8.** to emit fumes. **9.** to show irritation or anger. [ME, t. OF: m. *fum*, g. L *fūmus* smoke, steam, fume] —**fume/less,** *adj.* —**fume/like/,** *adj.* —**fum/ing·ly,** *adv.* —**Syn. 9.** chafe, fret, rage.

fumed (fūmd), *adj.* darkened or colored by exposure to ammonia fumes, as oak and other wood.

fu·mi·gate (fū/mə gāt/), *v.t.,* **-gated, -gating.** to expose to smoke or fumes, as in disinfecting. [t. L: m.s. *fūmigātus,* pp., smoked] —**fu/mi·ga/tion,** *n.*

fu·mi·ga·tor (fū/mə gā/tər), *n.* **1.** one who or that which fumigates. **2.** a structure in which plants are fumigated to destroy insects.

fu·mi·to·ry (fū/mə tōr/Ĭ), *n., pl.* **-ries.** any plant of the genus *Fumaria,* of the family *Fumariaceae,* esp. a delicate herb, *F. officinalis,* with finely dissected leaves and racemes of purplish flowers. [ME *fumeter,* t. OF: m. *fumeterre,* t. ML: m. *fūmus terrae* smoke of the earth]

fum·y (fū/mĬ), *adj.,* **fumier, fumiest.** full of fumes; fumelike.

fun (fŭn), *n., v.,* **funned, funning.** —*n.* **1.** mirthful sport or diversion; merry amusement; joking; playfulness. **2.** **for** or **in fun,** as a joke; playfully; not seriously. **3. make fun of,** to ridicule. —*v.i.* **4.** *Colloq.* to make fun; joke. [? d. var of obs. *fon,* v., befool] —**Syn. 1.** merriment, enjoyment.

fu·nam·bu·list (fū năm/byə lĬst), *n.* a tightrope walker. [f. s. L *fūnambulus* rope-dancer + -IST] —**fu·nam/bu·lism,** *n.*

Fun·chal (fōŏn shäl/), *n.* a seaport in and the capital of the Madeira Islands: winter resort. 39,558 (1940).

func·tion (fŭngk/shən), *n.* **1.** the kind of action or activity proper to a person, thing, or institution. **2.** any ceremonious public or social gathering or occasion. **3.** *Math.* a mathematical quantity whose value depends upon the values of other quantities, called the arguments or independent variables of the function. **4.** *Gram.* **a.** the grammatical role which a linguistic form plays, or the position which it occupies in a particular construction. **b.** the grammatical roles or the positions of a linguistic form or form class collectively. —*v.i.* **5.** to perform a function, or one's or its functions; act; serve; operate; carry out normal work, activity, or processes. **6.** *Gram.* to have or exercise a function: *in earlier English the present tense often functioned as the future.* [t. L: s. *functio* performance] —**func/tion·less,** *adj.*

func·tion·al (fŭngk/shən əl), *adj.* **1.** of or pertaining to a function or functions. **2.** designed or adapted primarily to perform some operation or duty: *a functional building.* **3.** capable of operating or functioning. **4.** pertaining to an algebraical operation: *a functional symbol.* —**func/tion·al·ly,** *adv.*

functional disease, *Pathol.* a disease in which there is a morbid change in the function of an organ, but no structural alteration in the tissues involved (opposed to *organic disease*).

func·tion·al·ism (fŭngk/shən əl Ĭz/əm), *n.* the doctrine or practice in furniture design, architecture, etc., under which such factors as material and form are determined primarily by functional considerations.

func·tion·ar·y (fŭngk/shə něr/Ĭ), *n., pl.* **-aries.** an official.

fund (fŭnd), *n.* **1.** a stock of money or pecuniary resources, as for some purpose. **2.** a store or stock of something, now often of something immaterial: *a fund of knowledge.* **3.** (*pl.*) money in hand; pecuniary resources. —*v.t.* **4.** to provide a fund to pay the interest or principal of (a debt). **5.** to convert (general outstanding debts) into a more or less permanent debt or loan, represented by interest-bearing bonds. [t. L: s. *fundus* bottom, estate; r. FOND[2] in most of its meanings]

fun·da·ment (fŭn/də mənt), *n.* **1.** the physical characteristics of a geographical region, as land forms, drainage, climate, soils, etc. **2.** the buttocks. [t. L: s. *fundāmentum* foundation; r. ME *fondement,* t. OF]

fun·da·men·tal (fŭn/də měn/təl), *adj.* **1.** serving as, or being a component part of, a foundation or basis; basic; underlying: *fundamental principles.* **2.** of or affecting the foundation or basis: *a fundamental change.* **3.** original. **4.** *Music.* (of a chord) having its root as its lowest note. —*n.* **5.** a leading or primary principle, rule, law, or the like, which serves as the groundwork of a system; essential part. **6.** Also, **fundamental note** or **tone.** *Music.* **a.** the root of a chord. **b.** the generator of a series of harmonics. **7.** *Physics.* the component of lowest frequency in a composite wave. [t. NL: s.

fundāmentālis, der. L *fundāmentum* foundation] —**fun/da·men·tal/i·ty,** *n.* —**fun/da·men/tal·ly,** *adv.* —**Syn. 1.** indispensable, necessary, first, primary, elementary. —**Ant. 1.** accidental, secondary, nonessential.

fundamental bass, *Music.* a bass consisting of the roots of the chords employed.

fun·da·men·tal·ism (fŭn/də měn/tə lĬz/əm), *n.* **1.** a movement in American Protestantism which stresses the inerrancy of the Bible not only in matters of faith and morals but also as literal historical record and prophecy, e. g., of creation, the virgin birth of Christ, his second advent, etc. (opposed to *modernism*). **2.** the faith in the Bible so stressed. —**fun/da·men/tal·ist,** *n., adj.*

fundamental unit, *Physics.* one of the units (esp. those of mass, length, and time) taken as a basis for a system of units.

fun·dus (fŭn/dəs), *n.* *Anat.* the base of an organ, or the part opposite to or remote from an aperture. [t. L: bottom]

Fun·dy (fŭn/dĬ), *n.* **Bay of,** a deep inlet of the Atlantic in SE Canada between New Brunswick and Nova Scotia: noted for its swift tidal currents, sometimes rising 70 ft.

Fü·nen (fY/nən), *n.* German name of **Fyn.**

fu·ner·al (fū/nər əl), *n.* **1.** the ceremonies connected with the disposition of the body of a dead person; obsequies. **2.** a funeral procession. [ME, t. ML: m.s. *fūnerālia,* neut. pl. of the adj.] —*adj.* **3.** of or pertaining to a funeral. [ME, t. ML: s. *fūnerālis,* der. L *fūnus* funeral, death]

fu·ner·ar·y (fū/nə rěr/Ĭ), *adj.* of or pertaining to a funeral or burial: *a funerary urn.*

fu·ne·re·al (fū nĬr/Ĭ əl), *adj.* **1.** of or pertaining to a funeral. **2.** mournful; gloomy; dismal. [f. s. L *funereus* of a funeral + -AL[1]] —**fu·ne/re·al·ly,** *adv.*

Fünf·kir·chen (fYnf/kĬr/ʍən), *n.* German name of **Pécs.**

fun·gal (fŭng/gəl), *adj.* **1.** fungous. —*n.* **2.** a fungus.

fun·gi (fŭn/jī), *n.* pl. of **fungus.**

fun·gi·ble (fŭn/jə bəl), *Law.* —*adj.* **1.** of such a nature that one instance or portion may be replaced by another in respect of function, office, or use: usually confined to goods. —*n.* **2.** a fungible thing, as money or grain. [t. ML: m.s. *fungibilis,* der. L *fungī* fulfill the office of]

fun·gi·cide (fŭn/jə sĭd/), *n.* an agent, such as a spray or dust, used for destroying fungi. [f. *fungi-* (comb. form of FUNGUS) + -CIDE[1]] —**fun/gi·cid/al,** *adj.*

fun·gi·form (fŭn/jə fôrm/), *adj.* having the form of a fungus or mushroom. [f. *fungi-* (comb. form of FUNGUS) + -FORM]

fun·goid (fŭng/goid), *adj.* **1.** resembling a fungus; of the nature of a fungus. **2.** *Pathol.* characterized by funguslike morbid growths.

fun·gous (fŭng/gəs), *adj.* **1.** of, pertaining to, or caused by fungi; fungal. **2.** of the nature of or resembling a fungus. [ME, t. L: m.s. *fungōsus,* der. *fungus* sponge, mushroom, fungus]

fun·gus (fŭng/gəs), *n., pl.* **fungi** (fŭn/jī), **funguses,** *adj.* —*n.* **1.** any of the *Fungi,* a group of thallophytes including the mushrooms, molds, mildews, rusts, smuts, etc., characterized chiefly by absence of chlorophyll and by subsisting upon dead or living organic matter. **2.** *Pathol.* a spongy morbid growth, as proud flesh formed in a wound. —*adj.* **3.** fungous. [t. L: mushroom, fungus] —**fun/gus·like/,** *adj.*

fu·ni·cle (fū/nə kəl), *n.* *Bot.* the stalk of an ovule or seed. [t. L: m.s. *fūniculus,* dim. of *fūnis* rope]

fu·nic·u·lar (fū nĬk/yə lər), *adj.* **1.** of or pertaining to a rope or cord, or its tension. **2.** worked by a rope or the like. [f. s. L *fūniculus* little rope + -AR[1]]

funicular railway, a railway system of short length operating up steep grades, in which cable-linked trains move up and down simultaneously, thus minimizing the pull of gravity.

fu·nic·u·late (fū nĬk/yə lĬt, -lāt/), *adj.* *Bot.* having a funicle.

fu·nic·u·lus (fū nĬk/yə ləs), *n., pl.* **-li** (-lī/). **1.** *Anat.* a conducting cord such as a nerve cord, spermatic cord, umbilical cord, etc. **2.** *Bot.* a funicle. [t. L, dim. of *fūnis* rope]

funk (fŭngk), *Colloq.* —*n.* **1.** cowering fear; state of fright or terror. —*v.t.* **2.** to be afraid of. **3.** to frighten. **4.** to shrink from; try to shirk. —*v.i.* **5.** to shrink or quail in fear. [cf. OF *funicle* terrible, g. L *phrenēticus.* See FRANTIC]

fun·nel (fŭn/əl), *n., v.,* **-neled, -neling** or (*esp. Brit.*) **-nelled, -nelling.** —*n.* **1.** a cone-shaped utensil with a tube at the apex, for conducting liquid, etc., through a small opening, as into a bottle. **2.** a smokestack, esp. of a steamship or a locomotive. **3.** a flue, tube, or shaft, as for ventilation. —*v.t.* **4.** to converge or concentrate: *to funnel all one's energies into a job.* [ME *fonel,* t. OF, ult. g. LL *fundibulum,* L *infundibulum*] —**fun/nel·like/,** *adj.*

fun·nies (fŭn/Ĭz), *n.pl.* *U.S. Colloq.* **1.** comic strips. **2.** the section of a newspaper containing them.

fun·ny (fŭn/Ĭ), *adj.,* **-nier, -niest. 1.** affording fun; amusing; comical. **2.** *Colloq.* curious; strange; queer; odd. [f. FUN, n. + -Y[1]] —**fun/ni·ly,** *adv.* —**fun/ni·ness,** *n.* —**Syn. 1.** comic, farcical, absurd, ridiculous, droll, witty, facetious, humorous. FUNNY, LAUGHABLE, LUDICROUS refer to that which excites laughter. FUNNY and LAUGHABLE are both applied to that which provokes laughter or deserves to be laughed at; FUNNY is a colloquial term loosely applied

---

b., blend of, blended; c., cognate with; d., dialect, dialectal; der., derived from; f., formed from; g., going back to; m., modification of; r., replacing; s., stem of; t., taken from; ?, perhaps. See the full key on inside cover.

and in popular use is commonly interchangeable with the other terms: *a funny story, scene, joke, a laughable incident, mistake*. That which is LUDICROUS excites laughter by its incongruity and foolish absurdity: *the monkey's attempts to imitate the woman were ludicrous*. —**Ant. 1.** solemn, serious.

funny bone, the part of the elbow where the ulnar nerve passes by the internal condyle of the humerus, which when struck causes a peculiar, tingling sensation in the arm and hand; the crazy bone.

Fun·ston (fŭn′stən), *n.* **Frederick**, 1865–1917, U.S. general.

fur (fûr), *n., v.,* **furred, furring.** —*n.* **1.** the skin of certain animals (as the sable, ermine, beaver, etc.), covered with a fine, soft, thick, hairy coating, used for lining or trimming garments or for entire garments. **2.** (*usually pl.*) an article of apparel made of or with such material, as a fur scarf or tippet. **3.** any coating resembling or suggesting fur, as one of morbid matter on the tongue. —*v.t.* **4.** to line, face, or trim (a garment, etc.) with fur. **5.** to clothe (a person) with fur. **6.** to coat with foul or deposited matter. [ME *furre,* t. OF: m. *forrer* line with fur, orig. encase, der. *forre* sheath, t. Gmc.; cf. G *futter* sheath] —**fur′less,** *adj.*

fu·ran (fyŏŏr′ăn, fyōō răn′), *n.* *Chem.* a colorless liquid, C₄H₄O, an unsaturated five-membered ring compound derived from furfural. [short for *furfurane,* t. G: m. *furfuran,* f. L *furfur* bran + *-an* -ANE]

fur·be·low (fûr′bəlō′), *n.* **1.** a plaited or gathered trimming on a woman's gown or the like; flounce. **2.** any bit of showy trimming or finery. —*v.t.* **3.** to ornament with or as with furbelows. [var. of FALBALA]

fur·bish (fûr′bĭsh), *v.t.* **1.** to restore to freshness of appearance or condition (often fol. by *up*). **2.** to rub or scour (armor, weapons, etc.) to brightness; polish; burnish. [ME *furbish(en),* t. OF: m. *forbiss-,* s. *forbir* polish, clean, t. Gmc.; cf. OHG *furban*] —**fur′bish·er,** *n.*

fur·cate (*adj.* fûr′kāt, -kĭt; *v.* fûr′kāt), *adj., v.,* **-cated, -cating.** —*adj* **1.** forked. —*v.i.* **2.** to form a fork; divide into branches. [t. ML: m.s. *furcātus* cloven, der. L *furca* fork]

fur·cu·la (fûr′kyələ), *n., pl.* **-lae** (-lē′). the forked clavicular bone of a bird; wishbone. [t. L, dim. of *furca* fork]

fur·cu·lum (fûr′kyələm), *n., pl.* **-la** (-lə). furcula. [NL, incorrectly formed dim. of L *furca* fork]

fur·fu·ra·ceous (fûr′fyərā′shəs), *adj.* **1.** branlike. **2.** scaly; scurfy. [t. LL: m. *furfurāceus*]

fur·fur·al (fûr′fərăl′), *n.* *Chem.* an oily liquid aldehyde, C₅H₄O₂, with an aromatic odor, obtained by distilling bran, sugar, wood, corncobs, etc., with dilute sulfuric acid: used in the manufacture of plastics and in refining lubricating oils. [f. L *furfur* bran + AL- (DEHYDE)]

Fu·ries (fyŏŏr′ĭz), *n.pl.* *Class. Myth.* See **fury** (def. 3).

fu·ri·ous (fyŏŏr′əs), *adj.* **1.** full of fury, violent passion, or rage. **2.** intensely violent, as wind, storms, etc. **3.** of unrestrained energy, speed, etc.: *furious activity*. [ME, t. L: m.s. *furiōsus* raging] —**fu′ri·ous·ly,** *adv.* —**fu′ri·ous·ness,** *n.*

furl (fûrl), *v.t.* **1.** to draw into a compact roll, as a sail against a spar or a flag against its staff. —*v.i.* **2.** to become furled. —*n.* **3.** act of furling. **4.** a roll resulting from being furled. [cf. F *ferler,* OF *ferlier,* f. *fer* firm (g. L *firmus*) + *lier* to bind (g. L *ligāre*)]

furl., furlough.

fur·long (fûr′lông, -lŏng), *n.* a unit of distance, equal to 220 yards or ⅛ mi. [ME; OE *furlang,* f. *furh* furrow + *lang* long]

fur·lough (fûr′lō), *Mil.* —*n.* **1.** vacation granted to an enlisted man (in the U.S. Army, one month per year). —*v.t.* **2.** to grant a furlough to. [var. of *furloff,* t. D: m. *verlof* leave, furlough. Cf. G *verlaub* leave, permission; current pronunciation due to assoc. with *dough, though*]

fur·men·ty (fûr′məntĭ), *n.* frumenty. Also, **fur·me·ty** (fûr′mətĭ).

fur·nace (fûr′nĭs), *n.* **1.** a structure or apparatus in which to generate heat, as for heating houses, smelting ores, producing steam, etc. **2.** a place of burning heat. **3.** a place of severe trial. [ME *furneise,* OF: m. *fornais, fornaise,* g. s. L *fornax* oven] —**fur′nace·like′,** *adj.*

Fur·ness (fûr′nĭs), *n.* **Horace Howard,** 1833–1912, U.S. scholar.

fur·nish (fûr′nĭsh), *v.t.* **1.** to provide or supply. **2.** to fit up (a house, room, etc.) with necessary appliances, esp. furniture. [ME *furnisshe(n),* t. OF: m. *furniss-,* s. *furnir* accomplish, furnish, t. Gmc.; cf. OHG *frumjan* provide] —**fur′nish·er,** *n.*

—**Syn. 1, 2.** FURNISH, APPOINT, EQUIP all refer to providing something necessary. FURNISH emphasizes the idea of providing necessary or customary services or appliances in living quarters: *to furnish board, a room.* APPOINT (now found only in WELL-APPOINTED) means to furnish completely with all requisites or accessories or in an elegant style: *a well-appointed house.* EQUIP means to supply with necessary materials or apparatus for some service, action, or undertaking; it emphasizes preparation: *to equip a vessel, a soldier.*

fur·nish·ing (fûr′nĭshĭng), *n.* **1.** that with which anything is furnished. **2.** (*pl.*) fittings, appliances, articles of furniture, etc., for a house or room. **3.** (*pl.*) accessories of dress: *men's furnishings.*

furnit., furniture.

fur·ni·ture (fûr′nəchər), *n.* **1.** the movable articles, as tables, chairs, bedsteads, desks, cabinets, etc., required for use or ornament in a house, office, or the like.

2. fittings, apparatus, or necessary accessories for something. **3.** *Print.* pieces of wood or metal, less than type-high, set in and about pages of type to fill them out and hold the type in place. [t. F: m. *fourniture,* der. *fournir* FURNISH]

Fur·ni·vall (fûr′nəval), *n.* **Frederick James,** 1825–1910, British philologist and editor.

fu·ror (fyŏŏr′ôr), *n.* **1.** a general outburst of enthusiasm or excitement. **2.** a prevailing mania or craze. **3.** fury; rage; madness. [t. L: a raging; r. late ME *fureur,* t. F]

furred (fûrd), *adj.* **1.** having fur. **2.** made with or of fur, as garments. **3.** clad in fur or furs, as persons. **4.** coated with morbid matter, as the tongue.

fur·ri·er (fûr′ĭər), *n.* a dealer in or dresser of furs.

fur·ri·er·y (fûr′ĭərĭ), *n., pl.* **-eries. 1.** furs in general. **2.** the business or trade of a furrier.

fur·ring (fûr′ĭng), *n.* **1.** act of lining, trimming, or clothing with fur. **2.** the fur used. **3.** the formation of a coating of matter on something, as on the tongue. **4.** *Bldg. Trades.* **a.** the nailing on of thin strips of board, as to furnish a level surface for lathing or plastering, to provide air space between a wall and plastering, etc. **b.** materials so used.

fur·row (fûr′ō), *n.* **1.** a narrow trench made in the ground, esp. by a plow. **2.** a narrow, trenchlike depression in any surface: *the furrows of a wrinkled face.* —*v.t.* **3.** to make a furrow or furrows in; plow (land, etc.). **4.** to make wrinkles in (the face, etc.). [ME *forwe, furgh(e),* OE *furh,* c. G *furche;* akin to L *porca* ridge between furrows] —**fur′row·er,** *n.* —**fur′row·less,** *adj.* —**fur′row·like′,** *adj.* —**fur′row·y,** *adj.*

fur·ry (fûr′ĭ), *adj.,* **-rier, -riest. 1.** made of or with fur. **2.** covered with fur; wearing fur. **3.** consisting of or resembling fur. —**fur′ri·ness,** *n.*

Northern fur seal,
Callorhinus alascanus
(Male 7 ft. long,
female ab. 4 ft.)

fur seal, any of various species of eared seal, as *Callorhinus alascanus,* which have under the outer hair a thick coat of fur of great commercial value (distinguished from *hair seal*).

Fürth (fyrt), *n.* a city in S Germany, near Nuremberg. 82,315 (1939).

fur·ther (fûr′thər), *compar. adv. and adj., superl.* **furthest,** *v.* —*adv.* **1.** at or to a greater distance; farther. **2.** at or to a more advanced point; to a greater extent. **3.** in addition; moreover. —*adj.* **4.** more distant or remote; farther. **5.** more extended. **6.** additional; more. —*v.t.* **7.** to help forward (a work, undertaking, cause, etc.); promote; advance; forward. [ME *further(e), furthra,* c. G *vordere* more advanced] —**fur′ther·er,** *n.*

fur·ther·ance (fûr′thərəns), *n.* act of furthering; promotion; advancement.

fur·ther·more (fûr′thərmôr′), *adv.* moreover; besides; in addition.

fur·ther·most (fûr′thərmōst′), *adj.* most distant.

fur·thest (fûr′thĭst), *adj., adv.* superl. of **further.** [ME, coined as a superl. of FURTHER. Cf. FARTHEST]

fur·tive (fûr′tĭv), *adj.* **1.** taken, done, used, etc., by stealth; secret: *a furtive glance.* **2.** sly; shifty: *a furtive manner.* [t. L: m.s. *furtivus* stolen] —**fur′tive·ly,** *adv.* —**fur′tive·ness,** *n.*

fu·run·cle (fyŏŏr′ĭngkəl), *n.* a boil or inflammatory sore. [t. L: m.s. *fūrunculus* a petty thief, a boil]

fu·run·cu·lo·sis (fyŏŏrŭng′kyəlō′sĭs), *n.* *Pathol.* the morbid state characterized by the presence of furuncles.

fu·ry (fyŏŏr′ĭ), *n., pl.* **-ries. 1.** frenzied or unrestrained violent passion, esp. anger. **2.** violence; vehemence; fierceness. **3.** (*cap.*) one of the avenging deities of classical mythology (in female form, with serpents twined in her hair), in later accounts three in number and called Alecto, Megaera, and Tisiphone. **4.** a fierce and violent person, esp. a woman. **5.** like **fury,** *Colloq.* furiously; violently. [ME, t. L: m.s. *furia* rage, madness] —**Syn. 1.** furor, frenzy, rage, ire, wrath. See **anger.**

furze (fûrz), *n.* any plant of the leguminous genus *Ulex,* esp. *U. europaeus,* a low, much-branched, spiny shrub with yellow flowers, common on waste lands in Europe; gorse. [ME *furse, firse,* OE *fyrs*]

fur·zy (fûr′zĭ), *adj.* *Brit.* **1.** of or pertaining to furze. **2.** overgrown with furze.

fu·sain (fū zăn′; *Fr.* fy zăn′), *n.* **1.** a fine charcoal used in drawing, made from the wood of the spindle tree. **2.** a drawing made with it. [t. F: spindle tree, charcoal made from its wood, der. L *fūsus* spindle]

Furze.
Ulex europaeus

Fu·san (fōō′sän′), *n.* a seaport in SE Korea. 222,690 (est. 1939).

fus·cous (fŭs′kəs), *adj.* dark brownish-gray; dark; dusky. [t. L: m. *fuscus* dark]

fuse¹ (fūz), *n., v.,* **fused, fusing.** —*n.* **1.** *Elect.* an over-current protective device, with a circuit-opening fusible member directly heated and destroyed by the passage of overcurrent through it. **2.** a tube, ribbon, or the like, filled or saturated with combustible matter, for igniting an explosive. **3.** fuze. —*v.i.* **4.** *Chiefly Brit.* to blow a fuse. [t. It.: m. *fuso,* g. L *fūsus* spindle] —**fuse′less,** *adj.* —**fuse′like′,** *adj.*

fuse² (fūz), v., **fused, fusing.** —v.t. **1.** to combine or blend by melting together; melt. **2.** to unite or blend into a whole, as if by melting together. —v.i. **3.** to become liquid under the action of heat; melt. **4.** to become united or blended, as if by melting together. [t. L: m.s. *fūsus*, pp., poured, melted, cast] —Syn. **2.** amalgamate, merge, liquefy, dissolve, smelt. See **melt.**

fu·see (fū zē′), n. **1.** a kind of match with a large head, for igniting by friction. **2.** a red flare light, used on a railroad as a warning signal to approaching trains. **3.** *Horology.* a spirally grooved, conical pulley and chain arrangement for counteracting the diminishing power of the uncoiling mainspring. **4.** a fuse. Also, **fuzee.** [t. F: spindleful, der. OF *fus* spindle, g. L *fūsus*]

fu·se·lage (fū′zə lĭj, fū′zə läzh′, -sə-), n. the framework of the body of an airplane. [t. F, der. *fuselé* spindleshaped, der. *fuseau* spindle, der. L *fūsus*]

fuse link, *Elect.* an element, made of fusible wire or cast from fusible metal, inserted in a fuse receptacle.

fu·sel oil (fū′zəl, -səl), a mixture of amyl alcohols obtained as a by-product in the fermentation of grains. [*fusel*, t. G: inferior liquor or spirits]

fu·si·bil·i·ty (fū′zə bĭl′ə tĭ), n. **1.** quality of being fusible, or convertible from a solid to a fluid state by heat. **2.** the degree to which a substance is fusible.

fu·si·ble (fū′zə bəl), adj. capable of being fused or melted. —**fu′si·ble·ness,** n.

fusible metal, *Metall.* any of various alloys, as one of bismuth, lead, and tin, which melt at comparatively low temperatures, and hence can be used for making various safety devices. Also, **fusible alloy.**

fu·si·form (fū′zə fôrm′), adj. spindle-shaped; rounded and tapering from the middle toward each end, as some roots. [t. s. L *fūsus* spindle + -(I)FORM]

fu·sil (fū′zəl, -sĭl), n. a light flintlock musket. [t. F, in OF *foisil* steel for striking fire, ult. der. L *focus* hearth]

fu·sil·ier (fū′zĭ lĭr′), n. **1.** a term used in the names of certain British regiments. **2.** a soldier armed with a fusil. Also, **fu′sil·eer′.** [t. F, der. *fusil* musket]

fu·sil·lade (fū′zə lād′), n., v., **-laded, -lading.** —n. **1.** a simultaneous or continuous discharge of firearms. **2.** a general discharge or outpouring of anything: *a fusillade of questions.* —v.t. **3.** to attack or shoot by a fusillade. [t. F, der. *fusiller* shoot, der. *fusil* FUSIL]

fu·sion (fū′zhən), n. **1.** act or process of fusing. **2.** state of being fused. **3.** that which is fused. **4.** *Pol.* **a.** the coalition of parties or factions. **b.** the body resulting from such coalition. [t. L: s. *fusio* a pouring out]

fu·sion·ism (fū′zhə nĭz′əm), n. *Pol.* the principle, policy, or practice of fusion. —**fu′sion·ist,** n., adj.

fuss (fŭs), n. **1.** an excessive display of anxious activity; needless or useless bustle. **2.** a person given to fussing. —v.i. **3.** to make a fuss; make much ado about trifles. —v.t. **4.** to put into a fuss; disturb with trifles; bother. [orig. unknown] —**fuss′er,** n. —Syn. **1.** pother, to-do, stir, commotion.

fuss-budg·et (fŭs′bŭj′ĭt), n. *Colloq.* a fussy person.

fuss·y (fŭs′ĭ), adj., **fussier, fussiest. 1.** excessively busy with trifles; anxious or particular about petty details. **2.** (of clothes, etc.) elaborately made or trimmed. **3.** full of details. —**fuss′i·ly,** adv. —**fuss′i·ness,** n.

fus·tian (fŭs′chən), n. **1.** a stout fabric of cotton and flax. **2.** a stout twilled cotton fabric with a short nap or pile. **3.** inflated or turgid language in writing or speaking; bombast; rant; claptrap. —adj. **4.** made of fustian. **5.** pompous or bombastic, as language. **6.** worthless; cheap. [ME, t. OF: m. *fustaigne*, g. LL *fustaneum*, der. L *fustis* cudgel), translation of Gk. *xylinon*, der. *xylon* wood]

fus·tic (fŭs′tĭk), n. **1.** the wood of a large moraceous tree, *Chlorophora tinctoria*, of tropical America, yielding a light-yellow dye. **2.** the tree itself. **3.** the dye. **4.** any of several other dyewoods. [t. F: m. *fustoc*, t. Sp., t. Ar.: m. *fustuq*; akin to Gk. *pistákē* pistachio tree; from Pers.]

fus·ti·gate (fŭs′tə gāt′), v.t., **-gated, -gating.** to cudgel; beat. [t. L: m.s. *fustīgātus*, pp., cudgeled to death] —**fus′ti·ga′tion,** n. —**fus′ti·ga′tor,** n.

fust·y (fŭs′tĭ), adj., **fustier, fustiest. 1.** moldy; musty; having a stale smell; stuffy. **2.** old-fashioned; fogyish. **3.** stubbornly old-fashioned and out-of-date. [der. *fust*, n., t. OF: wine cask, log, g. L *fustis* cudgel] —**fust′i·ly,** adv. —**fust′i·ness,** n.

fut., future.

fu·thorc (fōō′thôrk), n. the runic alphabet. Also, **fu′thork, fu·tharc** (fōō′thärk), **fu′thark.**

fu·tile (fū′təl, -tĭl; *Brit.* fū′tīl), adj. **1.** incapable of producing any result; ineffective; useless; not successful. **2.** trifling; not important. [t. L: m.s. *fut(t)ilis* untrustworthy, vain, lit., that easily pours out] —**fu′tile·ly,** adv. —**fu′tile·ness,** n. —Syn. **1.** ineffectual, unavailing, vain, idle, profitless, unprofitable, bootless. See **useless. 2.** trivial, frivolous. —Ant. **1.** effectual.

fu·til·i·tar·i·an (fū tĭl′ə târ′Ĭ ən), adj. **1.** believing that human hopes are vain and human strivings unjustified. —n. **2.** one who holds this belief. [der. FUTILITY, modeled on UTILITARIAN]

fu·til·i·ty (fū tĭl′ə tĭ), n., pl. **-ties. 1.** quality of being futile; ineffectiveness; uselessness. **2.** unimportance. **3.** a futile act or event.

fut·tock (fŭt′ək), n. *Naut.* one of the curved timbers which form the middle sections of a compound rib in a ship. [said to be for *foothook*]

futtock plates, *Naut.* iron plates at the top of a lower mast, into which are fastened the upper ends of the futtock shrouds.

futtock shrouds, *Naut.* the short iron rods extending from the futtock plates to an iron band on the mast.

fu·ture (fū′chər), n. **1.** time that is to be or come hereafter. **2.** what will exist or happen in future time. **3.** a future condition, esp. of success or prosperity. **4.** *Gram.* **a.** the future tense. **b.** another future formation or construction. **c.** a form therein, as *he will come.* **5.** (*usually pl.*) a speculative purchase or sale of commodities for future receipt or delivery. —adj. **6.** that is to be or come hereafter: *future events, at some future day.* **7.** pertaining to or connected with time to come: *one's future prospects, future hopes.* **8.** *Gram.* designating a tense, or other verb formation or construction, which refers to events or states in time to come. [ME *futur*, t. L: s. *futūrus*, future participle of *esse* be]

fu·ture·less (fū′chər lĭs), adj. without a future; having no prospect of future betterment or prosperity.

future life, a form of life which follows mortal death.

future perfect, *Gram.* **1.** perfect with respect to a temporal point of reference in the future. **2.** designating a tense, or other verb formation or construction, with such meaning. **3. a.** the future perfect tense. **b.** another verb formation or construction with future perfect meaning. **c.** a form therein, as *he will have come.*

fu·tur·ism (fū′chər ĭz′əm), n. a relatively recent artistic doctrine or movement (orig. Italian) requiring complete abandonment of traditional usage and reconstruction of art and life on the basis of the dynamic, revolutionary, mechanical present and the future.

fu·tur·ist (fū′chər ĭst), adj. **1.** of or pertaining to work of futurism. —n. **2.** a futurist artist or writer. —**fu′tur·is′tic,** adj.

fu·tu·ri·ty (fū tyŏŏr′ə tĭ, -tōŏr′-), n., pl. **-ties. 1.** future time. **2.** a future state or condition; a future event. **3.** quality of being future. **4.** a futurity race.

futurity race, *U.S. Racing.* a race, as for horses, for which the entries are nominated long before the running.

futurity stakes, *U.S. Racing.* **1.** the stakes in a futurity race. **2.** a futurity race.

fuze (fūz), n. **1.** a mechanical or electronic device to detonate an explosive charge. **2.** fuse¹.

fu·zee (fū zē′), n. fusee.

fuzz (fŭz), n. **1.** loose, light, fibrous or fluffy matter. **2.** a mass or coating of such matter. [cf. D *voos* spongy]

fuzz·y (fŭz′ĭ), adj., **fuzzier, fuzziest. 1.** of the nature of or resembling fuzz. **2.** covered with fuzz. **3.** indistinct; blurred. —**fuzz′i·ly,** adv. —**fuzz′i·ness,** n.

f.v., (L *folio verso*) on the back of the page.

fwd., forward.

-fy, a suffix meaning: **1.** to make; cause to be; render: *simplify, beautify.* **2.** to become; be made: *liquefy.* Also, **-ify.** [t. F: m. *-fier*, g. L *-ficāre* do, make]

fyke (fīk), n. a bag-shaped fish trap. [t. D: m. *fuik*]

fyl·fot (fĭl′fŏt), n. swastika. [? var. of *fill-foot* foot filler]

Fyn (fȳn), n. an island in S Denmark. 325,905 pop. (1940); 1149 sq. mi. German, **Fünen.**

Fyz·a·bad (fī′zä bäd′), n. a city in N India, in the United Provinces. 55,200 (1941).

G

G, g (jē), n., pl. **G's** or **Gs, g's** or **gs. 1.** the 7th letter of the English alphabet. **2.** *Music.* **a.** the fifth tone in the scale of C major or the seventh in the relative minor scale of A minor. **b.** a printed or written note indicating this tone. **c.** a string, key, or pipe tuned to this note. **d.** (in the fixed system of solmization) the 5th tone of the scale, called *sol.* **3.** (in medieval Roman numerals) 400.

G, German.

g, 1. *Psychol.* general intelligence. **2.** *Physics, etc.* (acceleration of) gravity.

G., 1. German. 2. (specific) gravity. 3. Gulf.

g., 1. *Elect.* conductance. 2. gauge. 3. gender. 4. genitive. 5. going back to. 6. gram. 7. *Brit.* guinea.

Ga, *Chem.* gallium.

Ga., Georgia.

G.A., 1. General Agent. 2. General Assembly.

g.a., general average.

gab (găb), v., **gabbed, gabbing**, n. *Colloq.* —v.i. 1. to talk idly; chatter. —n. 2. idle talk; chatter. 3. glib speech: *the gift of gab.* [var. of *gob* mouth, t. Gaelic or Irish]

gab·ar·dine (găb'ər dēn', găb'ər dēn'), n. 1. firm, woven fabric of worsted, cotton, or spun rayon, with steep twill. 2. a man's long, loose cloak or frock, worn in the Middle Ages. Also, **gab'er·dine'.** [t. Sp.: m. *gabardina,* ult. der. MHG *wallevart* pilgrimage]

gab·ble (găb'əl), v., **-bled, -bling**, n. —v.i. 1. to talk rapidly and unintelligibly; jabber. 2. (of geese, etc.) to cackle. —v.t. 3. to utter rapidly and unintelligibly. —n. 4. rapid, unintelligible talk. [freq. of GAB] —**gab'-bler,** n.

gab·bro (găb'rō), n., pl. **-bros.** *Petrog.* a granular igneous rock composed essentially of labradorite and augite. [t. It.]

gab·by (găb'ĭ), adj., **-bier, -biest.** loquacious.

ga·belle (gə bĕl'), n. 1. a tax; an excise. 2. (in France before 1790) a tax on salt. [t. F, t. Pr.: m. *gabela,* t. It.: m. *gabella* tax, t. Ar.: m. *qabāla* the impost]

Ga·bès (gä'bĕs), n. Gulf of, a gulf of the Mediterranean on the E coast of Tunisia.

ga·bi·on (gā'bĭ ən), n. 1. a cylinder of wickerwork filled with earth, used as a military defense. 2. a cylinder filled with stones and sunk in water, used in laying the foundations of a dam or jetty. [t. F, t. It.: m. *gabbione,* aug. of *gabbia,* g. L *cavea* cage]

ga·bi·on·ade (gā'bĭ ə nād'), n. 1. a work formed of or with gabions. 2. a row of gabions sunk in a stream to control the current. [t. F: m. *gabionnade.* See GABION]

ga·ble (gā'bəl), n., v., **-bled, -bling.** *Archit.* —n. 1. the end of a ridged roof cut off at its extremity in a vertical plane, together with the triangular expanse of wall from the level of the eaves to the apex of the roof. 2. a similar end, as of a gambrel roof, not triangular. 3. an architectural member resembling the triangular end of a roof. 4. an end wall. —v.t. 5. to build with a gable or gables; form as a gable (chiefly in **gabled,** *pp.*). [ME, prob. t. Scand.; cf. Icel. *gafl.* Cf. also OHG *gabala,* G *gabel* fork] —**ga'ble·like',** adj.

Gables (def. 1 and 2)

gable end, (in a gabled building) the triangular wall space between the eaves level and the ridge, or the decorative wall carried up past the ends of a gable roof, and sloped, stepped, or scrolled to follow at a higher level its approximate shape.

gable roof, a ridged roof terminating at one or both ends in a gable.

gable window, 1. a window in or under a gable. 2. a window having its upper part shaped like a gable.

Ga·bon (gà bôn'), n. 1. a colony in the SW part of French Equatorial Africa. 410,000 pop. (1936); 91,506 sq. mi. *Cap.:* Libreville. 2. an estuary in this colony. Also, **Ga·bun** (gà bōōn').

Ga·bo·riau (gà bô ryō'), n. Émile (ĕ mēl'), 1833 or 1835–73, French novelist.

Ga·bri·el (gā'brĭ əl), n. one of the archangels, appearing usually as a divine messenger. Dan. 8:16, 9:21. Luke, 1: 19, 26. [t. Heb.: m. *Gabrī'ēl* the man of God]

Ga·bri·lo·witsch (gä'brĭ lŭv'ĭch; *Russ.* gä'vrĭ lô'vĭch), n. **Ossip** (ô'sĭp), 1878–1936, Russian pianist and conductor, in America.

ga·by (gā'bĭ), n., pl. **-bies.** *Colloq.* a fool. [orig. uncert.]

gad[1] (găd), v., **gadded, gadding**, n. —v.i. 1. to move restlessly or idly about. —n. 2. act of gadding. [? special use of GAD[2]] —**gad'der,** n.

gad[2] (găd), n., v., **gadded, gadding**. —n. 1. a goad for driving cattle. 2. a pointed mining tool for breaking up rock, coal, etc. —v.t. 3. to break up with a mining gad. [ME, t. Scand.; cf. Icel. *gaddr* spike]

Gad (găd), n., interj. *Archaic.* a euphemistic form of *God* used as a mild oath. Also, **gad.**

Gad (găd), n. 1. son of Jacob by Zilpah. Gen. 30:11, etc. 2. a Hebrew prophet and chronicler at the court of David. 2 Sam. 24:11–19. 3. one of the twelve tribes of Israel. 4. its territory east of the Jordan.

gad·a·bout (găd'ə bout'), n. *Colloq.* one who gads, esp. for curiosity or gossip.

gad·fly (găd'flī'), n., pl. **-flies.** any fly that goads or stings domestic animals, as many voracious, blood-sucking flies of the dipterous family *Tabanidae.* [f. GAD[2] + FLY]

gadg·et (găj'ĭt), n. *Colloq.* a mechanical contrivance or device; any ingenious article. [orig. uncert. Cf. F *gâchette*]

Ga·dhel·ic (gə dĕl'ĭk, -dē'lĭk), adj., n. Goidelic.

Gadfly, *Tabanus ruficornis* (Ab. 1½ in. long)

ga·did (gā'dĭd), n. a fish of the cod family, *Gadidae.* [f. s. NL *gadus* cod + -ID[2]]

ga·doid (gā'doid), adj. 1. belonging to or resembling the *Anacanthini,* an order of soft-finned fishes including the cod, haddock, etc. —n. 2. a gadoid fish. [f. s. NL *gadus* cod (t. Gk.: m. *gádos* kind of fish) + -OID]

gad·o·lin·ite (găd'ə lĭ nīt'), n. a silicate ore from which the rare-earth metals gadolinium, holmium, and rhenium are extracted. [named after J. Gadolin (1760–1852), Finnish chemist. See -ITE[1]]

gad·o·lin·i·um (găd'ə lĭn'ĭ əm), n. *Chem.* a rare-earth metallic element. *Symbol:* Gd; *at. wt.:* 156.9; *at. no.:* 64. [f. GADOLIN(ITE) + -IUM]

ga·droon (gə drōōn'), n. 1. *Archit.* an elaborately carved or indented convex molding. 2. a decorative series of curved inverted flutings, or of convex and concave flutings, as on silversmith's work. Also, **godroon.** [t. F: m. *godron,* der. *goder* crease, pucker] —**ga·drooned',** adj.

Gads·den (gădz'dən), n. 1. **James,** 1788–1858, U.S. railroad promoter and diplomat. 2. a city in NE Alabama. 55,725 (1950).

Gadsden Purchase, The, a tract of 45,535 sq. mi., now contained in New Mexico and Arizona, purchased from Mexico for $10,000,000 in 1853, the treaty being negotiated by James Gadsden.

Gadsden Purchase, 1853

gad·wall (găd'wôl), n., pl. **-walls,** (esp. collectively) **-wall.** a wild duck, *Anas strepera,* found in temperate parts of the Northern Hemisphere.

Gae·a (jē'ə), n. *Gk. Myth.* earth goddess who bore Oceanus, Cronus, and the Titans. [t. Gk.: m. *Gaîa*]

Gaek·war (gīk'wär), n. title of the ruler of Baroda. Also, **Gaikwar.** [t. Marathi: lit., cowherd]

Gael (gāl), n. 1. a Scottish Celt or Highlander. 2. *Rare.* an Irish Celt. [t. Scot. Gaelic: m. *Gaidheal,* OIrish *Gaidel*]

Gael., Gaelic.

Gael·ic (gā'lĭk), n. 1. the Celtic language of ancient Ireland and any of the languages that developed from it (Irish, Scotch Gaelic, and Manx). 2. Goidelic. —adj. 3. of or pertaining to the Gaels or their language.

gaff[1] (găf), n. 1. a strong hook with a handle, used for landing large fish. 2. a metal spur for a gamecock. 3. **stand the gaff,** *U.S. Slang.* to endure hardship or strain. 4. *Naut.* the spar extending the upper edge of a fore-and-aft sail. —v.t. 5. to hook or land with a gaff. [ME *gaffe,* t. OF: boat hook, prob. of Celtic orig.]

gaff[2] (găf), n. *Brit. Slang.* a cheap place of amusement. [? orig., a place of outcry or humbug, special use of d. *gaff* loud, rude talk (OE *gaf* in *gafspræc* foolish speech, scurrility)]

G. Gaff (def. 4)

gaf·fer (găf'ər), n. *Brit.* 1. a rustic title or term for an old man. 2. an overseer or foreman. [var. of late ME *godfar* (contracted form of GODFATHER)]

gaff-top·sail (găf'tŏp'sāl'; *Naut.* -səl), n. *Naut.* a light triangular sail above a gaff, which extends its foot.

gag[1] (găg), v., **gagged, gagging**, n. —v.t. 1. to stop up the mouth so as to prevent sound or speech. 2. to restrain by force or authority from freedom of speech. 3. to fasten open the jaws of, as in surgical operations. 4. to cause to heave with nausea. —v.i. 5. to heave with nausea. —n. 6. something thrust into the mouth to prevent speech. 7. any violent or authoritative suppression of freedom of speech. 8. a surgical instrument for holding the jaws open. [prob. imit. of the sound made in choking] —**gag'ger,** n.

gag[2] (găg), v., **gagged, gagging**, n. —v.t. *Slang.* 1. to introduce interpolations into (an actor's stage part) (fol. by *up*). 2. to deceive; hoax. —v.i. *Slang.* 3. to introduce interpolations or gags in acting. 4. to play on one's credulity by false stories, etc. —n. 5. *U.S. Colloq.* **a.** a joke; an interpolation introduced by an actor into his part. **b.** any contrived piece of wordplay or horseplay. [cf. Icel. *gagg* yelp] —**gag'ger,** n.

gage[1] (gāj), n., v., **gaged, gaging.** —n. 1. something, as a glove, thrown down in token of challenge to combat. 2. a challenge. 3. a pledge or pawn; security. —v.t. 4. *Archaic.* to pledge, stake, or wager. [ME, t. OF: pledge, security; of Gmc. orig. Cf. WAGE]

gage[2] (gāj), n., v.t., **gaged, gaging.** gauge. —**gag'er,** n.

gage[3] (gāj), n. any of several plums, varieties of *Prunus domestica.* [short for GREENGAGE]

Gage (gāj), n. **Thomas,** 1721–87, British general in America, 1763–76.

gag·gle (găg'əl), v., **-gled, -gling**, n. —v.i. 1. to cackle. —n. 2. a flock of geese. 3. a cackle. [imit.]

gag·root (găg'rōōt', -rŏŏt'), n. a plant, *Lobelia inflata,* with emetic properties; Indian tobacco.

gahn·ite (gä'nīt), n. a dark-green to black mineral of the spinel group, zinc aluminate, $ZnAl_2O_4$. [named after J. G. *Gahn* (1745–1818), Swed. chemist. See -ITE[1]]

gai·e·ty (gā′ə tĭ), *n., pl.* **-ties.** **1.** state of being gay or cheerful; gay spirits. **2.** (*often pl.*) merrymaking or festivity: *the gaieties of the New Year season.* **3.** showiness; finery: *gaiety of dress.* Also, **gayety.** [t. F: m. *gaieté, gaité,* der. *gai* GAY] —**Syn. 1.** merriment, mirth, glee, jollity, joyousness, liveliness, sportiveness, hilarity, vivacity. —**Ant. 1.** sadness.

Gaik·war (gīk′wär), *n.* Gaekwar.

Gail·lard Cut (gĭl yärd′, gä′lärd), an artificial defile excavated for the Panama Canal, 10 mi. NW of the city of Panama. ab. 8 mi. long. Formerly, **Culebra Cut.**

gail·lar·di·a (gā lär′dǐ ə), *n.* any plant of the American composite genus *Gaillardia,* several species of which are cultivated for their showy flowers. [NL: named after M. *Gaillard* de Marentonneau]

gai·ly (gā′lǐ), *adv.* **1.** merrily. **2.** showily. Also, **gayly.**

gain[1] (gān), *v.t.* **1.** to obtain; secure (something desired); acquire: *gain time.* **2.** to win; get in competition: *gain the prize.* **3.** to acquire as an increase or addition: *to gain weight, speed, etc.* **4.** to obtain as a profit: *he gained ten dollars by this deal.* **5.** to reach by effort; get to; arrive at: *to gain a good harbor.* —*v.i.* **6.** to improve; make progress; advance. **7.** to get nearer, as in pursuit (fol. by *on* or *upon*). —*n.* **8.** profit; advantage. **9.** (*pl.*) profits; winnings. **10.** an increase or advance. **11.** act of gaining; acquisition. [t. F: m. *gagner,* of Gmc. orig.] —**gain′a·ble,** *adj.*

—**Syn. 1.** GAIN, ATTAIN, EARN, WIN imply obtaining a reward or something advantageous. GAIN carries the least suggestion of method or of effort expended. ATTAIN emphasizes the reaching of a goal. EARN emphasizes the exertions and labor expended which deserve reward. WIN emphasizes attainment in spite of competition or opposition. **10.** addition, increment, acquisition. —**Ant. 1.** lose.

gain[2] (gān), *n.* **1.** a notch or dado cut across the edge of a board, usually made to support a cross board. —*v.t.* **2.** to make a gain or gains in. [? akin to obs. *gane,* OE *ganian,* c. Icel. *gana* gape]

gain·er (gā′nər), *n.* **1.** one who or that which gains. **2.** a type of dive in which the diver takes off facing forward, and jumps upward and backward to enter the water facing the board.

gain·ful (gān′fəl), *adj.* profitable; lucrative. —**gain′ful·ly,** *adv.* —**gain′ful·ness,** *n.*

gain·ly (gān′lǐ), *adj. Obs. or Dial.* agile; handsome. [der. *gain,* obs. adj., t. Scand.; cf. Icel. *gegn* straight, favorable, c. OE *gegn–,* in *gegnum,* adv., straight on, *gegnunga,* adv., directly] —**gain′li·ness,** *n.*

gain·say (gān′sā′), *v.t.,* **-said, -saying. 1.** to deny. **2.** to speak or act against. [f. *gain–* against + SAY]

Gains·bor·ough (gānz′bŭr′ō; *Brit.* -bərə), *n.* **Thomas,** 1727–88, British painter, esp. of portraits and landscapes.

'gainst (gĕnst *or, esp. Brit.,* gānst), *prep., conj.* against. Also, **gainst.**

Gaines·ville (gānz′vĭl), *n.* a city in N Florida. 26,861 (1950).

gait (gāt), *n.* **1.** the manner of walking or stepping, esp. of a horse, as the walk, trot, canter, gallop, single-foot, etc. —*v.t.* **2.** to teach a uniform gait to. [Scot. and N Eng. sp. of GATE in various senses, incl. those above]

gait·ed (gā′tĭd), *adj.* having a specified gait: *slow-gaited, heavy-gaited oxen.*

gai·ter (gā′tər), *n.* **1.** a covering of cloth, leather, etc., for the ankle and instep, and sometimes also the lower leg, worn over the shoe, etc. **2.** a cloth or leather shoe with elastic insertions at the sides. [t. F: m. *guêtre*]

Ga·ius (gā′əs), *n.* A.D. c110–c180, Roman jurist.

gal (găl), *n. Slang.* girl.

Gal., Galatians.

gal., gallon; gallons.

ga·la (gā′lə, găl′ə; *Brit.* gä′lə), *adj.* **1.** festive; festal; showy: *his visits were always gala occasions.* —*n.* **2.** a celebration; festive occasion. **3.** festal pomp or dress. [t. F, t. It.: festal pomp, finery, t. OF: m. *gale* joy, pleasure, t. MD: m. *wale* riches]

ga·lac·ta·gogue (gə lăk′tə gôg′, -gŏg′), *adj.* **1.** increasing the amount of milk collected, either with or without increasing the amount secreted. —*n.* **2.** a galactagogue agent or medicine. [f. Gk.: m. *galakt-* milk (s. *gála*) + m.s. *-agōgós* bringing]

ga·lac·tic (gə lăk′tǐk), *adj. Astron.* pertaining to the Galaxy or Milky Way. [t. Gk.: m.s. *galaktikós* milky]

galactic circle, *Astron.* that great circle which most nearly coincides with the middle of the Milky Way.

galactic latitude. See **latitude** (def. 3).

galactic poles, the two opposite points of the heavens situated at 90° from the galactic circle.

ga·lac·to·poi·et·ic (gə lăk′tə poi ĕt′ĭk), *adj.* **1.** increasing the secretion of milk, though not necessarily the amount collected. —*n.* **2.** a galactopoietic agent or medicine. [f. Gk.: m. *galakto-* milk (comb. form of *gála*) + m.s. *poiētikós* making]

ga·lac·tose (gə lăk′tōs), *n. Chem.* a hexose sugar, $C_6H_{12}O_6$, either levo- or dextrorotatory, the latter being derived from milk sugar by hydrolysis. [f. m.s. Gk. *gála* milk + -OSE[2]]

Gal·a·had (găl′ə hăd′), *n.* **Sir, 1.** *Arthurian Romance.* the noblest and purest knight of the Round Table, son of Lancelot and Elaine and fated to retrieve the Holy Grail. **2.** a man of ideal purity of heart and life.

ga·lan·gal (gə lăng′gəl), *n.* the aromatic, medicinal rhizome of certain plants of the ginger family, esp. *Alpinia officinarum,* of China and the East Indies. [see GALINGALE]

Ga·lá·pa·gos Islands (gə lä′pə gōs′; *Sp.* gä lä′pä gōs′), an archipelago on the equator in the Pacific, ab. 600 mi. W of and belonging to Ecuador: many unique species of animal life. 661 pop. (est. 1944); 3029 sq. mi.

GALÁPAGOS ISLANDS

gal·a·te·a (găl′ə tē′ə), *n.* a strong striped cotton fabric used for clothing. [from the name of a British man-of-war]

Gal·a·te·a (găl′ə tē′ə), *n. Gk. Legend.* an ivory statue of a maiden, brought to life by Aphrodite in response to the prayers of the sculptor, Pygmalion, who had fallen in love with his work.

Ga·la·ti (gä läts′), *n.* a city in E Rumania: a port on the Danube. 94,490 (est. 1943). Also, **Ga·latz** (gä′läts).

Ga·la·tia (gə lā′shə, -shǐ ə), *n.* an ancient country in central Asia Minor: later a Roman province. —**Ga·la′tian,** *adj., n.*

Ga·la·tians (gə lā′shənz), *n. pl.* the book of the New Testament called in full "The Epistle of Paul the Apostle to the Galatians."

gal·a·vant (găl′ə vănt′), *v.i.* gallivant.

ga·lax (gā′lăks), *n.* an evergreen herb, *Galax aphylla,* of southeastern U.S., with small white flowers. [NL, der. Gk. *gála* milk; so called from the white flowers]

gal·ax·y (găl′ək sǐ), *n., pl.* **-axies. 1.** *Astron.* **a.** (*usually cap.*) the Milky Way. **b.** any galactic system including those outside of the Milky Way. **2.** any brilliant or splendid assemblage. [ME *galaxye,* t. ML: m. *galaxia,* var. of *galaxias,* t. Gk., der. *gála* milk]

Gal·ba (găl′bə), *n.* **Servius Sulpicius** (sûr′vǐ əs sŭl·pĭsh′əs), 5? B.C.–A.D. 69, Roman emperor, A.D. 68–69.

gal·ba·num (găl′bə nəm), *n.* a gum resin with a peculiar disagreeable odor, obtained from certain Asiatic plants of the apiaceous genus *Ferula:* used in medicine and the arts. [t. L (Vulgate); answering to Gk. *chalbáne* (Septuagint), rendering Heb. *ḥelbĕnāh*]

gale[1] (gāl), *n.* **1.** a strong wind. **2.** *Meteorol.* a wind with a velocity between about 30 and about 65 miles per hour. **3.** *Colloq.* a noisy outburst: *a gale of laughter.* **4.** *Poetic.* a gentle breeze. [orig. uncert.]

gale[2] (gāl), *n.* a shrub, *Myrica gale,* with a pleasant aromatic odor, growing in marshy places; sweet gale. [ME *gayl,* OE *gagel,* c. D and G *gagel*]

Gale (gāl), *n.* **Zona** (zō′nə), 1874–1938, U.S. novelist.

ga·le·a (gā′lǐ ə), *n., pl.* **-leae** (-lǐ ē′). *Bot.* any part of the calyx or corolla in the form of a helmet, as the upper lip of the corolla of the monkshood. [t. L: helmet]

ga·le·ate (gā′lǐ āt′), *adj. Bot.* having a galea. Also, **ga′le·at′ed.**

ga·le·i·form (gə lē′ə fôrm′), *adj.* helmet-shaped; resembling a galea. [f. s. L *galea* helmet + -(I)FORM]

Ga·len (gā′lən), *n.* **1. Claudius** (klô′dǐ əs), A.D. c130–c200, Greek physician and writer on medicine. **2.** (in humorous use) a physician.

ga·le·na (gə lē′nə), *n.* a very common heavy (sp. gr. 7.6) mineral, lead sulfide, PbS, occurring in lead-gray crystals, usually cubes, and cleavable masses: the principal ore of lead. Also, **ga·le·nite** (gə lē′nīt). [t. L: lead ore]

Ga·len·ic (gā lĕn′ĭk, -lē′nĭk), *adj.* of or pertaining to Galen, or his principles, or his methods.

Ga·len·ism (gā′lə nǐz′əm), *n.* the medical system or principles of Galen. —**Ga′len·ist,** *n.*

Gales·burg (gālz′bûrg), *n.* a city in NW Illinois. 31,425 (1950).

Ga·li·cia (gə lǐsh′ə, -lǐsh′ǐ ə), *n.* **1.** a former crownland of Austria, included in S Poland after World War I, and now partly in the Soviet Union. ab. 30,500 sq. mi. **2.** a maritime region in NW Spain: a former kingdom, and later a province. 2,495,860 pop. (1940); 11,256 sq. mi. —**Ga·li′cian,** *adj., n.*

Gal·i·le·an (găl′ə lē′ən), *adj.* **1.** of or pertaining to Galilee. —*n.* **2.** a native or inhabitant of Galilee. **3.** a Christian. **4. the Galilean,** Jesus. [f. GALILE(E) + -AN]

Gal·i·le·an (găl′ə lē′ən), *adj.* of or pertaining to Galileo: *the Galilean telescope.* [f. GALILE(O) + -AN]

Gal·i·lee (găl′ə lē′), *n.* **1.** an ancient Roman province in N Palestine. **2. Sea of,** a lake in NE Israel through which the river Jordan flows. 14 mi. long; 682 ft. below sea level. Also, **Sea of Tiberias.**

SEA OF GALILEE

gal·i·lee (găl′ə lē′), *n.* a porch or vestibule, often on the ground floor of a tower, at the entrance of some English churches. [t. OF, t. ML: m.s. *galilaea,* a galilee, orig. (L) the province of Galilee; said to refer to the "Galilee of the Gentiles" in Mat. 4:15]

Gal·i·le·o (găl′ə lē′ō; *It.* gä/lē lĕ′ō), *n.* (*Galileo Galilei*) 1564–1642, Italian physicist and astronomer.

gal·i·ma·ti·as (găl′ə mā′shǐ əs, -măt′ǐ əs), *n.* confused or unintelligible talk; gibberish. [t. F: f. m. *Galli* term

---

b., blend of, blended; c., cognate with; d., dialect, dialectal; der., derived from; f., formed from; g., going back to; m., modification of; r., replacing; s., stem of; t., taken from; ?, perhaps.   See the full key on inside cover.

applied to doctoral candidates + m. Gk. *-matheia* knowledge, a humorous 16th cent. formation]

gal·in·gale (găl'ĭn gāl'), *n.* any sedge of the genus *Cyperus*, esp. *C. longus*, an English plant with aromatic roots. [ME, t. OF: m. *galingal*, t. Ar.: m. *khalanjān*, said to be (through Pers.) from Chinese *Ko-liang-kiang*, lit., wild ginger from Ko, a prefecture in Canton province]

gal·i·ot (găl'ĭ ət), *n.* a small galley propelled by both sails and oars. Also, **galliot**. [ME *galiote*, t. OF, dim. of *galie* GALLEY]

gal·i·pot (găl'ə pŏt'), *n.* a kind of turpentine exuded on the stems of certain species of pine. Also, **gallipot**. [t. F, earlier *garipot* resin, prob. t. D: m. *harpuis*, c. MLG *harpois* boiled and skimmed resin]

gall[1] (gôl), *n.* **1.** something very bitter or severe. **2.** bitterness of spirit; rancor. **3.** bile, esp. that of the ox. **4.** *Anat.* gall bladder. **5.** *U.S. Slang.* impudence; effrontery. [ME; d. OE *gealla*, r. OE *gealla*, c. G *galle*; akin to L *fel*, Gk. *cholē* gall, bile]

gall[2] (gôl), *v.t.* **1.** to make sore by rubbing; chafe severely. **2.** to vex; irritate: *galled by sarcasm.* —*v.i.* **3.** to be or become chafed. —*n.* **4.** a sore on the skin, esp. of a horse, due to rubbing; excoriation. **5.** something irritating. **6.** a state of irritation. [special use of GALL[1]]

gall[3] (gôl), *n.* any abnormal vegetable growth or excrescence on plants, caused by various agents, including insects, nematodes, fungi, bacteria, viruses, chemicals, and mechanical injuries. [ME *galle*, t. F, g. L *galla* the oak apple]

gal·lant (*adj.* găl'ənt *for* 1-3; gə länt', găl'ənt *for* 4, 5; *n.* găl'ənt, gə länt'), *adj.* **1.** brave, high-spirited, or chivalrous. **2.** stately: *a gallant sight.* **3.** gay or showy, as in dress. **4.** polite and attentive to women; courtly. **5.** amorous. —*n.* **6.** a man of spirit or mettle. **7.** a gay and dashing man. **8.** a man particularly attentive to women. **9.** a suitor or lover. **10.** a paramour. [ME *galaunt*, t. OF: m. *galant*, der. *gale* GALA] —**gal'lant·ly**, *adv.* —**gal'lant·ness**, *n.* **1.** valiant, courageous, heroic. See **brave**. —**Ant.** 1. cowardly, craven.

gal·lant·ry (găl'ən trĭ), *n., pl.* -**ries**. **1.** dashing courage; heroic bravery. **2.** gallant or courtly attention to women. **3.** a gallant action or speech. —**Syn. 1.** bravery, valor, heroism. **2.** chivalry, courtliness.

Gal·la·tin (găl'ə tĭn), *n.* **Albert**, 1761-1849, U.S. statesman, Secretary of the Treasury, 1801-13.

gall bladder, *Anat.* a vesicle attached to the liver which receives bile from the hepatic ducts, concentrates it, and discharges it after meals. See diag. under **stomach**.

Galle (gäl), *n.* a seaport in SW Ceylon. 38,400 (1931).

gal·le·ass (găl'ĭ ăs'), *n.* a large war galley formerly used in the Mediterranean, generally with three masts and rowed by slaves. Also, **galliass**. [t. OF: m. *galcace*, t. It.: m. *galeazza*, aug. of *galea* GALLEY]

gal·le·on (găl'ĭ ən, găl'yən), *n.* a kind of large sailing vessel formerly used by the Spaniards and others. [t. Sp.: m. *galeón*, aug. of *galea* GALLEY]

gal·ler·y (găl'ə rĭ, găl'rĭ), *n., pl.* -**leries**. **1.** a covered walk or promenade. **2.** *Southern U.S.* a piazza or portico; veranda. **3.** a long narrow apartment; corridor. **4.** a raised platform or passageway along the outside or inside of the wall of a building; balcony. **5.** a platform projecting from the interior walls of a church, theater, etc. to provide seats or room for a part of the audience. **6.** the highest of such platforms in a theater. **7.** the occupants of a gallery in a theater. **8.** any body of spectators or auditors, as the spectators of a golf match. **9.** a room, series of rooms, or building devoted to the exhibition of works of art. **10.** a collection of art for exhibition. **11.** a room or building in which to take pictures, practice shooting, etc. **12.** *Naut.* a balconylike structure or platform at the stern or quarters of old ships. **13.** a passageway made by an animal. **14.** *Fort.* an underground or covered passage to another part of a fortified position or to a mine. **15.** *Mining.* a level or drift. [t. It.: m.s. *galleria*, t. ML: m. *galilaea* GALILEE]

gal·ley (găl'ĭ), *n., pl.* -**leys**. **1.** an early sea-going vessel propelled by oars or by oars and sails. **2.** a large rowboat. **3.** the kitchen of a ship. **4.** *Print.* **a.** a long, narrow tray, usually of metal, for holding type which has been set. **b.** galley proof. **c.** a rough unit of measurement for type composition (about 22 inches). [ME *galeie*, t. ML: m. *galeia*, t. LGk.: m. *galaia*]

galley proof, *Print.* proof from type on a galley.

galley slave, **1.** a person condemned to work at the oar on a galley. **2.** an overworked person; drudge.

galley west, *U.S. Colloq.* out completely: *knock galley west.* [alter. of d. *collywest* (Brit.)]

gall·fly (gôl'flī'), *n., pl.* -**flies**. a gall wasp.

gal·liard (găl'yərd), *n.* **1.** a spirited dance for two dancers in triple rhythm, common in the 16th and 17th centuries. —*adj.* **2.** *Archaic.* lively or gay. [ME, t. OF, prob. der. Celtic *galli-* might, ability]

gal·li·ass (găl'ĭ ăs'), *n.* galleass.

Gal·lic (găl'ĭk), *adj.* **1.** pertaining to the Gauls or Gaul. **2.** pertaining to the French or France. [t. L: s. *Gallicus*, der. *Gallus* a Gaul]

gal·lic[1] (găl'ĭk), *adj. Chem.* of or containing gallium, esp. in the trivalent state (Ga+3). [f. GALL(IUM) + -IC]

gal·lic[2] (găl'ĭk), *adj.* pertaining to or derived from plant galls: *gallic acid.* [f. GALL[3] + -IC]

gallic acid, *Chem.* an acid, $C_6H_2(OH)_3CO_2H$, a white or yellowish crystalline powder found in nutgalls, mangoes, and other plants.

Gal·li·can (găl'ə kən), *adj.* **1.** Gallic. **2.** *Eccles.* **a.** pertaining to the Roman Catholic Church in France. **b.** pertaining to a school or party of French Roman Catholics, before 1870, advocating restricting papal authority in favor of the authority of general councils, the bishops, and temporal rulers.

Gal·li·can·ism (găl'ə kə nĭz'əm), *n. Eccles.* a religious opinion peculiar to France opposing the Papal authority in favor of that of the bishops and the temporal order.

Gallican liberties, parliamentary form of Gallicanism which augmented the rights of the state to the prejudice of the church.

Gal·li·ce (găl'ə sĭ), *adv.* in French. [ML]

Gal·li·cism (găl'ə sĭz'əm), *n.* **1.** a French linguistic peculiarity. **2.** a French idiom or expression used in another language. Also, **gal'li·cism**.

Gal·li·cize (găl'ə sīz'), *v.t., v.i.* -**cized**, -**cizing**. to make or become French, in language, character, etc. Also, **gal'li·cize'**.

Gal·li-Cur·ci (găl'ĭ kûr'chĭ; *It.* gäl'lē koor'chē), *n.* **Amelita** (ä'mĕ lē'tä), born 1889, Italian soprano in the U.S.

gal·li·gas·kins (găl'ĭ găs'kĭnz), *n.pl.* **1.** a kind of loose hose or breeches worn in the 16th and 17th centuries. **2.** loose breeches in general. **3.** leggings or gaiters of leather. [appar. alter. of F *garguesque*, metathetic var. of *greguesque*, t. It.: m. *grechesa*, from *alla grechesa* in the Greek manner]

gal·li·mau·fry (găl'ĭ mô'frĭ), *n., pl.* -**fries**. **1.** a hodgepodge; jumble; confused medley. **2.** a ragout or hash. [t. F: m. *galimafrée*, orig. unknown]

gal·li·na·cean (găl'ə nā'shən), *n.* **1.** a gallinaceous bird. —*adj.* **2.** gallinaceous.

gal·li·na·ceous (găl'ə nā'shəs), *adj.* **1.** pertaining to or resembling the domestic fowls. **2.** belonging to the group or order *Galliformes*, which includes the domestic fowls, pheasants, grouse, partridges, etc. [t. L: m. *gallinaceus* pertaining to poultry]

Gal·li·nas (gä yē'näs), *n.* **Punta** (poon'tä), a cape in NE Colombia: northernmost point of South America.

gall·ing (gô'lĭng), *adj.* that galls; chafing; irritating; exasperating. —**gall'ing·ly**, *adv.*

gal·li·nip·per (găl'ə nĭp'ər), *n.* a large American mosquito, *Psorophora ciliata.* [orig. uncert.]

gal·li·nule (găl'ə nūl', nool'), *n.* any of certain longtoed aquatic birds of the rail family, as the **Florida gallinule**, *Gallinula chloropus cachinnans*, and the European moor hen, *G. c. chloropus.* [t. NL: m.s. *Gallinula*, the typical genus (LL: chicken), dim. of L *gallīna* hen]

gal·li·ot (găl'ĭ ət), *n.* galiot.

Gal·lip·o·li Peninsula (gə lĭp'ə lĭ), a peninsula in European Turkey between the Dardanelles and the Aegean: the scene of a disastrous British naval and land campaign, 1915-16. ab. 60 mi. long.

gal·li·pot[1] (găl'ə pŏt'), *n.* a small glazed pot used by druggists for medicines, etc. [? f. GALLEY + POT[1] (as if brought or imported in galleys)]

gal·li·pot[2] (găl'ə pŏt'), *n.* galipot.

gal·li·um (găl'ĭ əm), *n. Chem.* a rare, bluish-white easily fusible trivalent metallic element, used in high temperature thermometers on account of its high boiling point, (1700°C.) and low melting point (30°C.). *Sym.*: Ga; *at. wt.*: 69.72; *at. no.*: 31; *sp. gr.*: 5.91 at 20°C. [NL, said to be der. L *gallus* cock, trans. of F *coq*, from the name of the discoverer, *Lecoq* de Boisbaudran]

gal·li·vant (găl'ə vănt'), *v.i.* to gad gaily or frivolously. Also, **galavant**. [? humorous alter. of GALLANT]

gall midge, any small fly of the family *Cecidomyidae* which makes galls on plants.

gall·nut (gôl'nŭt'), *n.* a nutlike gall on plants.

Gallo-, a word element meaning "Gallic." [t. L, comb. form of *Gallus* a Gaul]

gal·lon (găl'ən), *n.* a common unit of capacity (= 4 quarts) in English-speaking countries, the U.S. standard gallon being equal to 231 cu. in. (3.7853 liters), and the British imperial gallon 277.42 cu. in. (4.546 liters). [ME *galun*, t. ONF, ult. der. Gallic *galla* vessel, bowl]

gal·loon (gə loon'), *n.* a braid or trimming of worsted, silk or rayon tinsel, gold or silver, etc. [t. F: m. *galon*, der. *galonner* trim with *galloon*, orig. adorn (the head or hair) with bands or ribbons, der. OF *gale* GALA]

gal·loot (gə loot'), *n. U.S. Slang.* galoot.

gal·lop (găl'əp), *v.i.* **1.** to ride a horse at a gallop; ride at full speed. **2.** to run rapidly by leaps, as a horse; go at a gallop. **3.** to go fast, race, or hurry, as a person, the tongue, time, etc. —*v.t.* **4.** to cause (a horse, etc.) to gallop. —*n.* **5.** a fast gait of the horse (or other quadruped) in which in the course of each stride all four feet are off the ground at once. **6.** a run or ride at this gait. **7.** a rapid rate of going, or a course of going at this rate. [t. F: m.s. *galoper*, t. OLG: m. *wala hlōpan* run well] —**gal'lop·er**, *n.*

gal·lo·pade (găl'ə pād'), *n.* **1.** a sprightly kind of dance. **2.** the music for it. [t. F: m. *galopade*, der. *galoper* GALLOP]

Gallo-Rom., Gallo-Romance.

Gal·lo-Ro·mance (găl/ō rō mǎns/), *n.* the vernacular language, a development from Latin, spoken in France from about A.D. 600–900.

gal·lous (găl/əs), *adj. Chem.* containing divalent gallium (Ga+2).

Gal·lo·way (găl/ə wā/), *n.* 1. a region in SW Scotland, comprising the counties of Wigtown and Kircudbright. 2. one of a breed of beef cattle originating in this region, with a coat of curly black hair. 3. one of a breed of small strong horses first raised in Galloway, Scotland.

gal·lows (găl/ōz, -əz), *n., pl.* **-lowses, -lows.** 1. a wooden frame, consisting of a crossbeam on two uprights, on which condemned persons are executed by hanging. 2. a similar structure, as for suspending something or for gymnastic exercise. [ME *galwes,* OE *galgan,* pl. of *g(e)alga* gallows, c. G *galgen*]

gallows bird, *Colloq.* one who deserves to be hanged.

gallows bitts, *Naut.* a frame on the deck of a ship for supporting spare topmasts, etc.

gall·stone (gôl/stōn/), *n. Pathol.* a calculus or stone formed in the bile or gall passages.

Gal·lup (găl/əp), *n.* **George Horace,** born 1901, U.S. statistician.

gal·lus·es (găl/əs ̄ɪz), *n.pl. Chiefly Dial.* suspenders for trousers.

gall wasp, an insect of the hymenopterous family *Cynipidae,* whose larvae cause galls on plants.

ga·loot (gə lōōt/), *n. U.S. Slang.* an awkward, silly fellow. Also, **galloot.**

gal·op (găl/əp), *n.* 1. a lively round dance in duple time. 2. music for, or in the rhythm of, this dance. [t. F]

ga·lore (gə lōr/), *adv.* 1. in abundance. —*n.* 2. *Obs.* or *Rare.* abundance. [t. Irish: m. *go leōr* (Gaelic *guleōr*) to sufficiency]

ga·losh (gə lŏsh/), *n.* (*usually pl.*) an overshoe or rubber. Also, **galoshe, golosh.** [ME *galoche,* t. F, prob. g. L *gallicula* Gallic (sandal), b. *gallica* Gallic and *caligula* soldier's boot]

gals., gallons.

Gals·wor·thy (gôlz/wûr/t̸hĭ, gălz/-), *n.* **John,** 1867–1933, British novelist, dramatist, and short-story writer.

Gal·ton (gôl/tən), *n.* **Sir Francis,** 1822–1911, British scientist and writer. —**Gal·to·ni·an** (gôl tō/nĭ ən), *adj.*

Gal·va·ni (găl vä/nē), *n.* **Luigi** (lōō ē/jē), 1737–98, an Italian physiologist whose experiments led to the discovery that electricity may result from chemical action.

gal·van·ic (găl văn/ĭk), *adj.* 1. pertaining to or produced by galvanism; producing or caused by an electric current. 2. affecting or affected as if by galvanism. [f. GALVAN(I) + -IC] —**gal·van/i·cal·ly,** *adv.*

galvanic battery, a voltaic battery.

galvanic cell, *Elect.* an electrolytic cell capable of producing electric energy by electrochemical action.

gal·va·nism (găl/və nĭz/əm), *n.* 1. *Elect.* electricity, esp. as produced by chemical action. 2. *Med.* the therapeutic application of electricity to the body.

gal·va·nize (găl/və nīz/), *v.t.,* **-nized, -nizing.** 1. to stimulate by or as by a galvanic current. 2. to startle into sudden activity. 3. to coat (metal, esp. iron or steel) with zinc. Also, *esp. Brit.* **gal/va·nise/.** —**gal/va·ni·za/tion,** *n.* —**gal/va·niz/er,** *n.*

galvanized iron, iron coated with zinc to prevent rust.

galvano-, a combining form representing **galvanic, galvanism,** as in *galvanocautery.*

gal·va·no·cau·ter·y (găl/və nō kô/tər ĭ, găl văn/ō-), *n., pl.* **-teries.** *Med.* 1. a cautery heated by a galvanic current. 2. cauterization by such means.

gal·va·nom·e·ter (găl/və nŏm/ə tər), *n.* an instrument for detecting the existence and determining the strength and direction of an electric current.

gal·va·nom·e·try (găl/və nŏm/ə trĭ), *n.* art or process of determining the strength of electric currents. —**gal·va·no·met·ric** (găl/və nō mĕt/rĭk, găl văn/ō-), *adj.*

gal·va·no·plas·tic (găl/və nō plăs/tĭk, găl văn/ō-), *adj.* pertaining to reproduction by electrotypy.

gal·va·no·plas·ty (găl/və nō plăs/tĭ, găl văn/ō-), *n.* electrotypy. Also, **gal/va·no·plas/tics.**

gal·va·no·scope (găl/və nə skōp/, găl văn/ə-), *n.* an instrument for detecting the existence and determining the direction of an electric current. —**gal·va·no·scop·ic** (găl/və nə skŏp/ĭk, găl văn/ə-), *adj.*

gal·va·not·ro·pism (găl/və nŏt/rə pĭz/əm), *n. Bot.* the movements in growing organs induced by the passage of electric currents.

Gal·ves·ton (găl/vəs tən), *n.* a seaport in SE Texas, on an island at the mouth of **Galveston Bay,** an inlet of the Gulf of Mexico. 66,568 (1950).

Gal·way (gôl/wā), *n.* 1. a county in W Eire, in Connaught. 166,231 pop. (est. 1943); 2293 sq. mi. 2. its county seat: a seaport. 20,437 (1946).

gam (găm), *n.* 1. (in whalers' speech) a herd or school of whales. 2. *U.S. Local.* a social meeting, visit, or the like, as between vessels at sea. [var. of GAME¹]

Ga·ma (găm/ə; *Port.* gä/mə), *n.* **Vasco da** (väs/kō də; *Port.* väsh/kōō), c1469–1524, Portuguese navigator and discoverer of the sea route from Portugal around the continent of Africa to India.

ga·ma grass (gä/mə), a tall, stout grass, *Tripsacum dactyloides,* one of the largest in the United States.

gam·ba·do (găm bā/dō), *n., pl.* **-dos, -does.** 1. one of a pair of large protective boots or gaiters fixed to a saddle instead of stirrups. 2. any long gaiter or legging. [f. It. *gamba* leg + suffix -ado. See GAMBOL]

gam·be·son (găm/bə sən), *n.* a medieval, military garment of linen, padded, and worn under mail, but also worn as the principal garment of defense. [ME *gambisoune,* t. OF: m. *gambison,* of Gmc. orig.]

Gam·bet·ta (găm bĕt/ə; *Fr.* gän bĕ tá/), *n.* **Léon** (lě ôN/), 1838–82, French statesman.

Gam·bi·a (găm/bĭ ə), *n.* 1. a large river in W Africa, flowing W to the Atlantic. ab. 500 mi. 2. a British crown colony and protectorate extending inland along both sides of this river. 205,000 pop. (est. 1938); 4068 sq. mi. *Cap.:* Bathurst.

gam·bier (găm/bĭr), *n.* an astringent extract obtained from the leaves and young shoots of *Uncaria Gambir,* a tropical Asiatic rubiaceous shrub: used in medicine, dyeing, tanning, etc. [t. Malay: m. *gambĭr*]

gam·bit (găm/bĭt), *n. Chess.* an opening in which the player seeks by sacrificing a pawn or piece to obtain some advantage. [t. F, t. Pr.: m. *cambi* an exchange]

gam·ble (găm/bəl), *v.,* **-bled, -bling,** *n.* —*v.i.* 1. to play at any game of chance for stakes. 2. to stake or risk money or anything of value, on the outcome of something involving chance: *gamble on the result of a race.* —*v.t.* 3. to lose or squander by betting (usually fol. by *away*). —*n.* 4. *Colloq.* any matter or thing involving risk or uncertainty. 5. *Colloq.* a venture in or as in gambling. [? d. var. of ME *gamenen,* OE *gamenian* to sport, play] —**gam/bler,** *n.* —**gam/bling,** *n.*

gam·boge (găm bōj/, -bōozh/), *n.* 1. Also **cambogia.** a gum resin from various trees of the genus *Garcinia,* esp. *G. Hanburyi,* of Cambodia, Siam, etc.: used as a yellow pigment and as a cathartic. 2. yellow or yellow orange. [t. NL: m.s. *gambogium,* der. *Camboja, Cambodia,* in Indo-China]

gam·bol (găm/bəl), *v.,* **-boled, -boling** or (*esp. Brit.*) **-bolled, -bolling.** —*v.i.* 1. to skip about, as in dancing or playing; frolic. —*n.* 2. a skipping or frisking about; frolic. [earlier *gambald,* t. F: m. *gambade* a leap, t. It.: m. *gambata* a kick, der. *gamba* leg] —**Syn.** 1. spring, caper, frisk, romp.

gam·brel (găm/brəl), *n.* the hock of an animal, esp. of a horse. [t. OF (Norman): m. *gamberel* butcher's gambrel, der. *gambe,* g. LL *gamba* hoof, leg]

gambrel roof, a roof whose ends are cut off in a vertical plane, and whose sides have two slopes (likened to a horse's gambrel), the lower one being the steeper. See diag. under **roof.** —**gam/brel-roofed/,** *adj.*

Gam·bri·nus (găm brī/nəs), *n.* mythical Flemish king, reputed inventor of beer.

game¹ (gām), *n., adj.,* **gamer, gamest,** *v.,* **gamed, gaming.** —*n.* 1. an amusement or pastime: *children's games.* 2. the apparatus employed in playing any of certain games: *a store selling toys and games.* 3. a contest for amusement in the form of a trial of chance, skill, or endurance, according to set rules: *games of golf, etc.* 4. a single contest at play, or a definite portion of play in a particular game: *a rubber of three games at bridge.* 5. the number of points required to win a game. 6. a particular manner or style of playing a game. 7. a proceeding carried on like a game: *the game of diplomacy.* 8. a trick; strategy: *to see through someone's game.* 9. fun; sport of any kind; joke: *to make game of a person.* 10. wild animals, including birds and fishes, such as are hunted or taken for sport or profit. 11. the flesh of wild animals or game, used for food. 12. any object of pursuit or attack; prey. 13. fighting spirit; pluck. —*adj.* 14. pertaining to animals hunted or taken as game. 15. having the fighting spirit of a gamecock; plucky: *a game sportsman.* 16. *Colloq.* having the spirit or will (fol. by *for* or an infinitive). —*v.i.* 17. to play games of chance for stakes; gamble. —*v.t.* 18. to squander in gaming (fol. by *away*). [ME; OE *gamen,* c. OHG *gaman* glee] —**game/ly,** *adv.* —**game/ness,** *n.* —**Syn.** 1. sport, contest; diversion. See **play.** 8. scheme, artifice, stratagem. 10. prey, quarry.

game² (gām), *adj. Colloq.* lame: *a game leg.* [orig. uncert.]

game bird, a bird hunted for sport or profit, or protected by law.

game·cock (gām/kŏk/), *n.* a cock bred and trained for fighting, or one of a fighting breed.

game fish, an edible fish, capable of affording sport to the angler in its capture.

game fowl, 1. a fowl of any species regarded as game or the object of hunting. 2. a domestic fowl of a breed much used for fighting.

game·keep·er (gām/kē/pər), *n. Chiefly Brit.* a person employed, as on an estate, to take care of game, prevent poaching, etc.

game law, a law enacted for the preservation of game, as by restricting open seasons and the manner of taking.

game·some (gām/səm), *adj.* full of play; frolicsome. —**game/some·ly,** *adv.* —**game/some·ness,** *n.*

game·ster (gām/stər), *n.* a person who gambles habitually: gambler. [f. GAME¹ + -STER]

gam·e·tan·gi·um (găm/ə tăn/jĭ əm), *n., pl.* **-gia** (-jĭ ə). *Bot.* an organ or body producing gametes. [NL, f. Gk.: s. *gametē* wife, *gametēs* husband, + m. *angeion* vessel]

gam·ete (găm/ēt, gə mēt/), *n. Biol.* either of the two germ cells which unite to form a new organism; a mature reproductive cell. [t. NL: m.s. *gameta,* t. Gk.: m.

---

b., blend of, blended; c., cognate with; d., dialect, dialectal; der., derived from; f., formed from; g., going back to; m., modification of; r., replacing; s., stem of; t., taken from; ?, perhaps.   See the full key on inside cover.

gametê wife or m. *gamêtēs* husband] —**ga·met·ic** (gə-mĕt′ĭk), *adj.*

gam·e·to·gen·e·sis (găm′ə tō jĕn′ə sĭs), *n. Biol.* the development of gametes.

gam·e·to·phore (gə mē′tə fōr′), *n. Bot.* a part or structure producing gametes.

gam·e·to·phyte (gə mē′tə fīt′), *n. Bot.* the sexual form of a plant in the alternation of generations (opposed to *sporophyte*).

game warden, an official who enforces game laws.

gam·ic (găm′ĭk), *adj. Biol.* sexual (opposed to *agamic*). [t. Gk.: m.s. *gamikós* of or for marriage]

gam·in (găm′ĭn; *Fr.* gȧ mȧN′), *n.* a neglected boy left to run about the streets; street Arab: *a string of gamins followed him down the street.* [t. F; orig. uncert.]

gam·ing (gā′mĭng), *n.* act or practice of playing games of chance for stakes; gambling.

gam·ma (găm′ə), *n.* 1. the third letter (Γ, γ, = English G, g) of the Greek alphabet. 2. the third of any series (used esp. in scientific classification).

gam·ma·di·on (gə mā′dĭ ən), *n., pl.* **-di·a** (-dĭ ə). an ornamental figure consisting of combinations of the Greek capital gamma, esp. in the form of a swastika or fylfot, or of a voided Greek cross. [t. MGk., var. of *gammátion*, dim. of Gk. *gámma* gamma]

gamma rays, *Physics.* rays similar to x-rays, but of higher frequency and penetrating power, forming part of the radiation of radioactive substance.

gam·mer (găm′ər), *n. Brit.* a rustic title or term for an old woman. [var. of late ME *godmor* (contr. of GODMOTHER)]

gam·mon[1] (găm′ən), *n.* 1. the game of backgammon. 2. *Backgammon.* a victory in which the winner throws off all his men before his opponent throws off any. —*v.t.* 3. *Backgammon.* to win a gammon over. [? special use of ME and OE *gamen*. See GAME[1]]

gam·mon[2] (găm′ən), *n.* 1. a smoked or cured ham. 2. the lower end of a side of bacon. [ME *gambon*, t. ONF: ham, der. *gambe* hoof, leg, g. LL *gamba*]

gam·mon[3] (găm′ən), *Brit. Colloq.* —*n.* 1. deceitful nonsense; bosh. —*v.i.* 2. to talk gammon. 3. to make pretense. —*v.t.* 4. to impose upon; humbug. [see GAMMON[1]]

gam·mon[4] (găm′ən), *v.t. Naut.* to fasten (a bowsprit) to the stem of a ship. [? akin to GAMMON[2]]

gamo-, *Biol.* a word element meaning "sexual union." [comb. form repr. Gk. *gámos* marriage]

gam·o·gen·e·sis (găm′ō jĕn′ə sĭs), *n. Biol.* sexual reproduction. —**gam·o·ge·net·ic** (găm′ō jə nĕt′ĭk), *adj.* —**gam·o·ge·net′i·cal·ly,** *adv.*

gam·o·pet·al·ous (găm′ə pĕt′əl əs), *adj. Bot.* having the petals united.

gam·o·phyl·lous (găm′ə fĭl′əs), *adj. Bot.* having leaves united by their edges.

gam·o·sep·al·ous (găm′ə sĕp′əl əs), *adj. Bot.* having the sepals united. See illus. under **calyx.**

-gamous, an adjectival word element corresponding to the noun element **-gamy,** as in *polygamous.* [t. Gk.: m. *-gamos* marrying]

Gamopetalous flower

gamp (gămp), *n. Chiefly Brit.* (in humorous use) an umbrella. [said to be from the umbrella of Mrs. Sarah *Gamp* in Dickens' "Martin Chuzzlewit"]

gam·ut (găm′ət), *n.* 1. the whole scale or range. 2. *Music.* **a.** the whole series of recognized musical notes. **b.** the major scale. [t. ML: contr. of *gamma ut*, f. *gamma*, used to represent the first or lowest tone (G) in the medieval scale + *ut* (later *do*); the notes of the scale being named from a L hymn to St. John: *Ut* queant *laxis* resonare *fibris*, *Mira* gestorum *famuli* tuorum, *Solve* polluti *labi* reatum, *Sancte Iohannes.* See GUIDO D'AREZZO]

gam·y (gā′mĭ), *adj.*, **gamier, gamiest.** 1. having the flavor of game, esp. game kept uncooked until slightly tainted, as preferred by connoisseurs: *the meat had a delightfully gamy flavor.* 2. game or plucky. —**gam′i·ly,** *adv.* —**gam′i·ness,** *n.*

-gamy, 1. a word element meaning "marriage," as in *polygamy.* 2. *Biol.* a word element meaning "sexual union," as in *allogamy.* [t. Gk.: m. *-gamía*, der. *-gamos* marrying, married]

gan (găn), *v. Archaic and Poetic.* began.

Gand (gäN), *n.* French name of Ghent.

gan·der (găn′dər), *n.* the male of the goose. [ME; OE *gan(d)ra*, c. MLG *ganre*, D *gander*, g. Vernerian var. of Gmc. *gans-* goose]

Gan·dhi (gän′dē), *n.* **Mohandas Karamchand** (mō′hən däs′ kŭr′əm chŭnd′), (*Mahatma Gandhi*) 1869–1948, Hindu religious and political leader and social reformer.

Gand·zha (gänd′zhä), *n.* former name of **Kirovabad.**

gang (găng), *n.* 1. a band or group: *a gang of boys.* 2. a group of persons working together; squad; shift: *a gang of laborers.* 3. a group of persons associated for a particular purpose (used esp. in a contemptuous sense or of disreputable persons): *a gang of thieves.* 4. a set of tools, etc. arranged to work together or simultaneously. [ME and OE; orig. "a going"; sense of "group" from OE *gang* in *gangdæg* processional day.] —*v.t.* 5. to arrange in gangs; form into a gang. 6. *Colloq.* to attack in a gang. —*v.i.* 7. *Colloq.* to form or act as a gang (often fol. by *up*): *to gang up on Sam and Ned.*

8. *Brit. Dial.* to walk; go. [ME *gong(e)*, *gang(en)*, OE *gongan*, *gangan*, c. OHG *gangan*] —**Syn.** 1. company, crowd, crew.

gang[2] (găng), *n.* gangue.

gang cultivator, a cultivator having several shares or shovels mounted to be operated as a gang.

map: TIBET, INDIA, HIMALAYA MTS., GANGES RIVER, BURMA, Calcutta, Bay of Bengal, Bombay

Gan·ges (găn′jēz), *n.* a river flowing from the Himalayas in N India SE to the Bay of Bengal: sacred to the Hindus. ab. 1500 mi.

gang hook, *Angling.* a hook made by joining back to back the shanks of two or three hooks.

gan·gli·a (găng′glĭ ə), *n.* pl. of **ganglion.**

gan·gli·at·ed (găng′glĭ ā′tĭd), *adj.* having ganglia. Also, **gan·gli·ate** (găng′glĭ ĭt, -āt′).

gan·gling (găng′glĭng), *adj.* awkwardly tall and spindly; lank and loosely built. Also, **gan·gly.** [akin to obs. *gangrel* gangling person, der. GANG[1]]

gan·gli·on (găng′glĭ ən), *n., pl.* **-glia** (-glĭ ə), **-glions.** 1. *Anat.* gray matter outside the brain and spinal cord. 2. *Pathol.* a cyst or enlargement in connection with the sheath of a tendon, usually at the wrist. 3. a center of intellectual or industrial force, activity, etc. [t. LL: kind of swelling, t. Gk.: tumor under the skin, on or near a tendon] —**gan·gli·on·ic** (găng′glĭ ŏn′ĭk), *adj.*

gan·gli·on·ec·to·my (găng′glĭ ə nĕk′tə mĭ), *n., pl.* **-mies.** *Surg.* the excision of a ganglion.

gang·plank (găng′plăngk′), *n.* a plank, often with cleats, or a long, narrow, flat structure, used as a temporary bridge in passing into and out of a ship, etc.

gang plow, 1. a plow with several bottoms. 2. a combination of plows in one frame.

gan·grene (găng′grēn, găng grēn′), *n., v.,* **-grened, -grening.** *Pathol.* —*n.* 1. the dying of tissue, as from interruption of circulation; mortification. —*v.i.* 2. to affect or become affected with gangrene. [t. L: m.s. *gangraena*, t. Gk.: m. *gángraina* an eating sore] —**gan·gre·nous** (găng′grə nəs), *adj.*

gang·ster (găng′stər), *n. Colloq.* a member of a gang of criminals.

gangue (găng), *n.* the stony or earthy minerals occurring with the metallic ore in a vein or deposit. Also, **gang.** [t. F, t. G: m. *gang* mineral vein, lode]

gang·way (găng′wā′), *n.* 1. a passageway. 2. *Naut.* **a.** any of various passageways on a ship, as that between the rail and the cabins or houses on the deck. **b.** an opening or removable section of a ship's rail for the gangplank. **c.** a platform and ladder or stairway slung over the side of a ship. 3. *Brit.* **a.** an aisle in a theater, restaurant, etc. **b.** an aisle in Parliament separating the responsible members of the parties from the younger or uncertain members. 4. *Mining.* a main passage or level. 5. the inclined plane up which logs are moved into a sawmill. —*interj.* 6. *Chiefly Naut.* clear the way! [OE *gangweg*]

Gan·is (găn′ĭs), *n.* Bors de. See Bors (def. 1).

gan·is·ter (găn′ĭs tər), *n.* a highly refractory, siliceous rock, used to line furnaces, sometimes artificially made by mixing ground quartz with a bonding material. [orig. uncert.]

gan·net (găn′ĭt), *n.* any of several large totipalmate pelagic birds of the family *Sulidae,* which includes the boobies; esp., the common gannet, *Moris bassana,* of the Atlantic coasts of North America and Europe. [ME and OE *ganet,* akin to D *gent* gander]

gan·oid (găn′oid), *adj.* 1. belonging or pertaining to the *Ganoidei,* a composite and artificial grouping of fishes, many of which have hard, smooth scales, as the sturgeons, etc. 2. (of fish scales) having a smooth, shining surface. [f. s. Gk. *gános* brightness + -OID]

gant·let[1] (gănt′lĭt, gônt′-), *n.* 1. a former punishment, chiefly military, in which the offender ran between two rows of men who struck at him with switches or other weapons as he passed: *to run the gantlet.* 2. an attack from both or all sides; trying conditions. 3. a section of two-way railroad track, as through a tunnel or over a bridge, in which the inner rails overlap, so as to narrow the roadbed without switching to a single track. —*v.t.* 4. to lay down as a gantlet: *to gantlet tracks.* Also, **gauntlet.** [earlier *gantlope,* t. Sw.: m. *gatlopp,* lit., lane run, f. *gata* way, lane + *lopp* a running course]

Gantlet (def. 3)

gant·let[2] (gănt′lĭt, gônt′-), *n.* gauntlet[1].

gant·line (gănt′lĭn′), *n. Naut.* a rope temporarily made fast or rove through a block, as for hoisting rigging, raising a man to the rigging, etc. [alter. of *girtline*]

gan·try (găn′trĭ), *n., pl.* **-tries.** 1. a spanning framework, as a bridgelike portion of certain cranes. 2. a frame supporting a barrel or cask. Also, **gauntry.** [f. *gaun* (contr. of GALLON) + m. *-tree* supporting frame]

Gan·y·mede (găn′ə mēd′), *n.* 1. *Class. Myth.* a Trojan youth carried off (according to one legend, by an eagle) to become cupbearer to Zeus. 2. (in humorous use) a young waiter. 3. *Astron.* the largest satellite of Jupiter.

ăct, āble, dâre, ärt; ĕbb, ēqual; ĭf, īce; hŏt, ōver, ôrder, oil, bŏok, ōoze, out; ŭp, ūse, ûrge; ə = a in alone; ch, chief; g. give; ng, ring; sh, shoe; th, thin; ŧħ, that; zh, vision. See the full key on inside cover.

gaol (jāl), *n.*, *v.t.*   *Brit.* jail. [ME *gay(h)ole, gaile,* t. ONF: m. *gaiole, gaole,* ult. der. L *cavea* cavity, cage] —**gaol/er**, *n.*

gap (găp), *n.*, *v.*, **gapped, gapping.** —*n.* 1. a break or opening, as in a fence, wall, or the like; breach. 2. a vacant space or interval. 3. a wide divergence. 4. a deep, sloping ravine or cleft cutting a mountain ridge. 5. *Aeron.* the distance from one supporting plane of an airplane and another directly above or below it. —*v.t.* 6. to make a gap, opening, or breach in. [ME, t. Scand.; cf. Sw. *gap* opening chasm, *gapa* GAPE] —**gap/less**, *adj.*

gape (gāp, găp), *v.*, **gaped, gaping,** *n.* —*v.i.* 1. to open the mouth involuntarily or as the result of hunger, sleepiness, or absorbed attention. 2. to stare with open mouth, as in wonder. 3. to open as a gap; split or become open wide. —*n.* 4. a breach or rent; wide opening. 5. act of gaping. 6. a stare, as with open mouth. 7. astonishment. 8. *Zool.* the width of the open mouth. [ME *gapen,* t. Scand.; cf. Icel. and Sw. *gapa* open the mouth, c. G *gaffen*] —**gap/er,** *n.* —**gap/ing·ly,** *adv.* —**Syn.** 2. See gaze.

gapes (gāps, găps), *n.pl.* 1. a disease of poultry and other birds, attended with frequent gaping, due to infestation of the trachea and bronchi with gapeworms. 2. a fit of yawning.

gape·worm (gāp/wûrm/, găp/-), *n.* a nematode worm, *Syngamus trachea,* which causes gapes.

gar (gär), *n.*, *pl.* **gars,** (*esp. collectively*) **gar.** 1. a predaceous fish of the genus *Lepisosteus* (including several species, all of North American fresh waters), covered with very hard diamond-shaped ganoid scales and having a beak armed with large teeth. 2. needlefish (def. 1). [short for GARFISH]

G.A.R., Grand Army of the Republic.

ga·rage (gərazh/, -räj/ *or, esp. Brit.,* gär/ĭj), *n.*, *v.*, **-raged, -raging.** —*n.* 1. a building for sheltering, cleaning, or repairing motor vehicles. —*v.t.* 2. to put or keep in a garage. [t. F, der. *garer* put in shelter. t. Pr.: m. *garar* keep, heed, t. Gmc.; cf. OHG *warōn* heed]

Gar·a·mond (gär/ə mŏnd/), *n.* a kind of type designed in 1540 by Claude Garamond, French type founder.

Gar·and rifle (găr/ənd), a semiautomatic, gas-operated, clip-fed rifle, having a caliber of .30 inch and weighing 8.56 pounds. It has been adopted as standard equipment in the U. S. Army.

garb (gärb), *n.* 1. fashion or mode of dress, esp. of a distinctive kind. 2. clothes. 3. covering, semblance, or form. —*v.t.* 4. to dress; clothe. [t. F: m. *garbe,* t. It., m. *garbo* grace, t. Gmc.; cf. MHG *garwe* GEAR] —**Syn.** 2. dress, costume, attire, apparel, habiliments, garments.

gar·bage (gär/bĭj), *n.* 1. refuse animal and vegetable matter from a kitchen. 2. any foul refuse; vile or worthless matter. [ME; prob. der. Rom. root *garb-* mess]

gar·ble (gär/bəl), *v.*, **-bled, -bling,** *n.* —*v.t.* 1. to make unfair or misleading selections from (facts, statements, writings, etc.); corrupt: *a garbled account.* 2. *Rare.* to take out the best of: *to garble coins.* —*n.* 3. the process of garbling. [t. It.: m. *garbellare,* t. Ar.: m. *gharbala* sift, ʔ t. LL: m. *crĕbellăre,* der. *crĕbellum* little sieve] —**gar/bler,** *n.*

gar·board (gär/bōrd/), *n. Shipbuilding.* the strake of planks laid next to the keel. Also, **garboard strake.** [t. D: m. *gaarboord*]

gar·çon (gàr sôN/), *n.*, *pl.* **-çons** (-sôN/). *French.* 1. a boy; young unmarried man. 2. a male employee or servant. 3. a waiter, esp. at a public table.

Gar·da (gär/dä), *n.* **Lago di** (lä/gô dē), a lake in N Italy: largest of Italian lakes. 35 mi. long; 143 sq. mi.

gar·den (gär/dən), *n.* 1. a plot of ground devoted to the cultivation of useful or ornamental plants. 2. a piece of ground, or other space, commonly with ornamental plants, trees, etc., used as a place of public resort: *a botanical garden, a roof garden.* 3. a fertile and delightful spot or region. —*adj.* 4. pertaining to or produced in a garden. —*v.i.* 5. to lay out or cultivate a garden. —*v.t.* 6. to cultivate as a garden. [ME *gardin,* t. ONF, of Gmc. orig.; cf. G *garten*] —**gar/den·like/,** *adj.*

Gar·den (gär/dən), *n.* **Mary,** born 1877, U.S. soprano.

garden cress. See peppergrass.

gar·den·er (gärd/nər), *n.* 1. a person employed to take care of a garden. 2. one who gardens.

gar·de·nia (gär dē/nyə, -nĭ ə), *n.* any of the evergreen trees and shrubs of the rubiaceous genus *Gardenia,* native in the warmer parts of the Eastern Hemisphere, including species, as *G. jasminoides,* the Cape jasmine, cultivated for their fragrant, waxlike, white flowers. [NL; named after Dr. Alexander *Garden* (1730–91)]

gar·den·ing (gärd/nĭng), *n.* 1. act of cultivating a garden. 2. the work or art of a gardener.

garden warbler, any of various small birds esteemed in Italy for the table, as the warblers of the family *Sylvidae,* esp. *Sylvia hortensis.*

Gar·di·ner (gär/dĭ nər, gärd/nər), *n.* **Samuel Rawson,** 1829–1902, British historian.

Gard·ner (gärd/nər), *n.* a city in N Massachusetts. 19,581 (1950).

Gar·eth (găr/ĭth), *n. Arthurian Romance.* nephew of King Arthur.

Gar·field (gär/fēld), *n.* 1. **James Abram** (ā/brəm), 1831–81, twentieth president of the United States, in 1881. 2. a city in NE New Jersey. 27,550 (1950).

gar·fish (gär/fĭsh/), *n.*, *pl.* **-fishes,** (*esp. collectively*) **-fish.** gar. [late ME *garfysshe,*, f. *gar* (OE *gār* spear) + *fysshe* FISH]

gar·ga·ney (gär/gə nĭ), *n.* a small Old World species of duck, *Anas querquedula.* [erroneous var. of It. *garganello,* der. Rom. root *garg-* throat]

Gar·gan·tu·a (gär găn/chŏŏ ə), *n.* the amiable giant and king, of enormous capacity for eating and drinking, in Rabelais' *Gargantua and Pantagruel.*

Gar·gan·tu·an (gär găn/chŏŏ ən), *adj.* gigantic; enormous; prodigious.

gar·get (gär/gĭt), *n. Vet. Sci.* inflammation of the udder of cows, etc., caused by bacteria; mastitis. [ME, t. OF: m. *gargate* throat, der. Rom. root *garg-*]

gar·gle (gär/gəl), *v.*, **-gled, -gling,** *n.* —*v.t.* 1. to wash or rinse (the throat or mouth) with a liquid held in the throat and kept in motion by a stream of air from the lungs. —*v.i.* 2. to gargle the throat or mouth. —*n.* 3. any liquid used for gargling. [t. F: m. *gargouiller,* der. *gargouille* throat. Cf. L *gurgulio* gullet]

gar·goyle (gär/goil), *n.* a spout, often terminating in a grotesque head (animal or human) with open mouth, projecting from the gutter of a building for carrying off rain water. [ME *gargulye,* t. OF: m. *gargouille, gargoule,* appar. the same word as *gargouille* throat. See GARGLE]

Gargoyle. 13th century

Gar·i·bal·di (găr/ə bôl/dĭ, -bäl/-; *It.* gä/rē bäl/dē), *n.* **Giuseppe** (jōō sĕp/pĕ), 1807–82, Italian patriot and general. -**Gar/i·bal/di·an,** *adj.*, *n.*

gar·i·bal·di (găr/ə bôl/dĭ), *n.* a loose waist worn by women and children in mid-19th century, made in imitation of the red shirts worn by the soldiers of Garibaldi.

gar·ish (gâr/ĭsh), *adj.* 1. glaring, or excessively bright. 2. crudely gay or showy, as dress, etc. 3. excessively ornate, as structures, writings, etc. [earlier *gaurish,* der. obs. *gaure* stare] —**gar/ish·ly,** *adv.* —**gar/ish·ness,** *n.* —**Syn.** 2. See gaudy[1].

gar·land (gär/lənd), *n.* 1. a wreath or string of flowers, leaves, or other material, worn for ornament or as an honor, or hung on something as a decoration. 2. a representation of such a wreath or festoon. 3. a collection of short literary pieces, usually poems and ballads; a miscellany. 4. *Naut.* a band, collar, or grommet, as of rope, for various purposes. —*v.t.* 5. to crown with a garland; deck with garlands. [ME *garlande,* t. OF]

Gar·land (gär/lənd), *n.* **Hamlin** (hăm/lĭn), 1860–1940, U.S. novelist, short-story writer, and poet.

gar·lic (gär/lĭk), *n.* 1. a hardy liliaceous plant, *Allium sativum,* whose strong-scented, pungent bulb is used in cookery and medicine. 2. any of various other species of the same genus. 3. the bulb of any such plant. [ME *garlec,* OE *gārlēac,* f. *gār* spear + *lēac* leek]

gar·lick·y (gär/lĭk ĭ), *adj.* like or containing garlic.

gar·ment (gär/mənt), *n.* 1. any article of clothing. 2. outer covering; outward appearance. —*v.t.* 3. to clothe. [ME, t. OF: m. *garnement,* der. *garnir* equip. See GARNISH] —**gar/ment·less,** *adj.*

gar·ner (gär/nər), *v.t.* 1. to collect or deposit in or as in a garner; hoard. [v. use of GARNER, *n.*] —*n.* 2. a granary. 3. a store of anything. [ME, t. OF: m. *gernier, grenier,* g. L *grānārium* GRANARY]

Gar·ner (gär/nər), *n.* **John Nance,** born 1869, vice-president of the United States, 1933–41.

gar·net[1] (gär/nĭt), *n.* 1. any of a group of hard, vitreous minerals, silicates of calcium, magnesium, iron, or manganese with aluminum or iron, varying in color. A deep-red transparent variety is used as a gem and as an abrasive (**garnet paper**). 2. deep red, as of a garnet. [ME *gernet,* t. OF: m. *grenat,* t. ML: m. s. *grānātum* garnet, also pomegranate, prop. neut. of *grānātus* having grains or seeds] —**gar/net·like/,** *adj.*

gar·net[2] (gär/nĭt), *n. Naut.* a form of hoisting tackle. [orig. uncert. Cf. D *granaat*]

gar·ni·er·ite (gär/nĭ ər ĭt/), *n.* a mineral, hydrous nickel magnesium silicate, occurring in earthy, green masses: an important ore of nickel. [named after Jules *Garnier,* French geologist. See -ITE[1]]

gar·nish (gär/nĭsh), *v.t.* 1. to fit out with something that adorns or decorates. 2. to decorate (a dish) for the table. 3. *Law.* a. to warn; give notice. b. to summon in, so as to take part in litigation already pending between others. c. to attach, as money due or property belonging to a debtor, while it is in the hands of a third person, by warning the latter not to pay it over or surrender it. —*n.* 4. something placed around or added to a dish for decorative effect or relish. 5. adornment or decoration. [ME *garnisshe(n),* t. OF: m. *garniss-,* s. *garnir* prepare, WARN; of Gmc. orig.] —**gar/nish·er,** *n.* —**Syn.** 1. embellish, ornament, beautify, trim.

gar·nish·ee (gär/nĭ shē/), *v.*, **-nisheed, -nisheeing,** *n. Law.* —*v.t.* 1. to attach (money or property) by garnishment. 2. to make (a person) a garnishee. —*n.* 3. a person served with a garnishment.

gar·nish·ment (gär/nĭsh mənt), *n.* 1. adornment; decoration. 2. *Law.* a. a warning or notice. b. a summons to appear in litigation pending between others. c. a warning served on a person, at the suit of a creditor plaintiff, to hold, subject to the court's direction, money or property of the defendant in his possession.

gar·ni·ture (gär'nĭ chər), *n.* anything that garnishes; decoration; adornment. [t. F, der. *garnir*. See GARNISH]

Ga·ronne (gȧ·rôn'), *n.* a river in SW France, flowing from the Pyrenees NW to the Gironde. ab. 350 mi.

ga·rote (gȧ·rōt', -rŏt'), *n., v.t.,* **-roted, -roting.** garrote. Also, **ga·rotte'.**

gar pike, a gar.

gar·ret (găr'ĭt), *n.* attic (def. 1). [ME *garite,* t. OF: watchtower, der. *garir* defend. See GARRISON]

gar·ret·eer (găr'ə tĭr'), *n.* a person living in a garret, esp. a literary hack.

Gar·rick (găr'ĭk), *n.* **David,** 1717–79, British actor and theatrical manager.

gar·ri·son (găr'ə sən), *n.* **1.** a body of troops stationed in a fortified place. **2.** the place where they are stationed. —*v.t.* **3.** to provide (a fort, town, etc.) with a garrison. **4.** to occupy (a fort, post, station, etc.). **5.** to put on duty in a fort, post, station, etc. [ME *garison,* t. OF: defense, der. *garir* defend, of Gmc. orig.]

Gar·ri·son (găr'ə sən), *n.* **William Lloyd,** 1805–79, U.S. leader in the abolition movement.

garrison cap, U.S. military dress headgear of felt, or woolen or cotton cloth, with leather visor.

gar·rot (găr'ət), *n.* the goldeneye (duck). [t. F]

gar·rote (gȧ·rōt', -rŏt'), *n., v.,* **-roted, -roting.** —*n.* **1.** a Spanish mode of capital punishment, orig. by means of an instrument causing death by strangulation, later by one injuring the spinal column at the base of the brain. **2.** the instrument used. **3.** strangulation or throttling, esp. for the purpose of robbery. —*v.t.* **4.** to execute by the garrote. **5.** to throttle, esp. for the purpose of robbery. Also, **garote, garotte, gar·rotte'.** [t. Sp.: orig. a stick (formerly used in drawing cord tight), t. Pr.: m. *garrot* cudgel, stick for tightening the cord about a pack, der. Celtic *garra* leg] —**gar·rot'er,** *n.*

gar·ru·li·ty (gȧ·rōō'lə tĭ), *n.* the quality of being garrulous; talkativeness; loquacity.

gar·ru·lous (găr'ə ləs, -yə ləs), *adj.* **1.** given to much talking, esp. about trifles. **2.** wordy or diffuse, as speech. [t. L: m. *garrulus* talkative] —**gar'ru·lous·ly,** *adv.* —**gar'ru·lous·ness,** *n.* —**Syn. 1.** See **talkative.**

gar·ter (gär'tər), *n.* **1.** a fastening, often in the form of a band passing round the leg, to keep up the stocking. **2.** *Brit.* the badge of the **Order of the Garter,** the highest order of knighthood. **3.** *Brit.* membership in the order. **4.** (*cap.*) *Brit.* the order itself. —*v.t.* **5.** to fasten with a garter. [ME, t. ONF: m. *gartier,* der. *garet* the bend of the knee, der. Celtic *garra* leg]

garter snake, any of various harmless snakes of the genus *Thamnophis,* usually with three light stripes on body and tail.

garth (gärth), *n.* **1.** the open court enclosed by a cloister (in full, **cloister garth**). **2.** *Archaic.* or *Dial.* a yard or garden. [ME, t. Scand.; cf. Icel. *gardhr,* c. YARD²]

Gar·y (gâr'ĭ), *n.* **1.** a city in NW Indiana; a port on Lake Michigan. 133,911 (1950). **2. Elbert Henry,** 1846–1927, U.S. financier.

gas (găs), *n., pl.* **gases,** *v.,* **gassed, gassing.** —*n.* **1.** *Physics.* a substance possessing perfect molecular mobility and the property of indefinite expansion. **2.** any such fluid or mixture of fluids except air, as laughing gas, or some combustible fluid burned for illumination and heating. **3.** *U.S. Colloq.* gasoline. **4.** *Coal Mining.* an explosive mixture of firedamp with air. **5.** an aeriform fluid, or a mistlike assemblage of fine particles suspended in air, used in warfare to asphyxiate, poison, or stupefy the enemy. **6.** *Slang.* empty talk. —*v.t.* **7.** to supply with gas. **8.** to affect, overcome, or asphyxiate with gas or fumes. **9.** to singe (yarns or fabrics) with a gas flame to remove superfluous fibers. **10.** to treat or impregnate with gas. **11.** *Slang.* to talk nonsense or falsehood to. —*v.i.* **12.** to give off gas, as a storage battery being charged. **13.** *Slang.* to indulge in empty talk idly. [coined by J. B. van Helmont, (1577–1644), Flemish chemist; suggested by Gk. *cháos* chaos] —**gas'less,** *adj.*

gas attack, an attack in which asphyxiating or poisonous gases are employed, as by liberating the gases and allowing the wind to carry the fumes, or by gas shells.

gas·bag (găs'băg'), *n.* **1.** a bag for holding gas, as in a balloon or dirigible, or for the use of dentists. **2.** *Slang.* an empty, voluble talker; a windbag.

gas black, the soot of a natural gas flame, used in paints; fine carbon.

gas burner, the tip, jet, or endpiece of a gas fixture, from which the gas issues to be ignited.

Gas·con (găs'kən), *n.* **1.** a native of Gascony, the inhabitants of which were noted for their boastfulness. **2.** (*l.c.*) a boaster or braggart. —*adj.* **3.** pertaining to Gascony and its people. [t. F, g. s. L *Vasco* Basque]

gas·con·ade (găs'kə nād'), *n., v.,* **-aded, -ading.** —*n.* **1.** extravagant boasting; boastful talk. —*v.i.* **2.** to boast extravagantly; bluster. [t. F: m. *gasconnade,* der. *gascon* GASCON]

Gas·co·ny (găs'kə nĭ), *n.* a former province in SW France. French, **Gas·cogne** (gȧs·kôn'y).

gas engine, an internal-combustion engine operated by illuminating gas, natural gas, or other gas from without.

gas·e·ous (găs'ĭ əs), *adj.* having the nature of, in the form of, or pertaining to gas. —**gas'e·ous·ness,** *n.*

[map: Bay of Biscay, FRANCE, GASCONY, SPAIN, MEDIT. SEA]

gas fitter, one whose business is the fitting up of buildings with apparatus for the use of gas.

gas fitting, 1. the work or business of a gas fitter. **2.** (*pl.*) fittings for the employment of gas for illuminating and heating purposes.

gas fixture, a permanent fixture attached to a gas pipe in the ceiling or wall of a room, as a more or less ornamental pipe (without or with branches) bearing a burner (or burners) and regulating devices.

gas gangrene, a gangrenous infection developing in wounds, esp. deep wounds with closed spaces, due to bacteria which form gases in the subcutaneous tissues.

gash (găsh), *n.* **1.** a long, deep wound or cut, esp. in the flesh; a slash. —*v.t.* **2.** to make a long, deep cut in; slash. [earlier *garsh,* t. ONF: m.s. *garser* scarify]

gas helmet, *Mil.* a type of gas mask.

gas·i·form (găs'ə fôrm'), *adj.* gaseous.

gas·i·fy (găs'ə fī'), *v.t., v.i.,* **-fied, -fying.** to convert into or become a gas. —**gas'i·fi·ca'tion,** *n.*

Gas·kell (găs'kəl), *n.* **Mrs.,** (*Elizabeth Cleghorn Stevenson Gaskell*) 1810–65, British novelist.

gas·ket (găs'kĭt), *n.* **1.** anything used as a packing, as a rubber or metal ring or disk. **2.** *Naut.* one of several bands or lines used to bind a furled sail to a yard, etc. [orig. uncert. Cf. It. *gassetta* gasket]

gas·light (găs'līt'), *n.* **1.** light produced by the combustion of illuminating gas. **2.** a gas burner.

gas mask, a masklike device worn to protect against noxious gases, fumes, etc., as in warfare or in certain industries, the air inhaled by the wearer being filtered through charcoal and chemicals.

gas meter, an apparatus for measuring and recording the amount of gas produced or consumed.

gas·o·line (găs'ə lēn, găs'ə lēn'), *n.* a volatile, inflammable, liquid mixture of hydrocarbons, obtained in the distillation of petroleum, and used as a solvent, as fuel for internal-combustion engines, etc. Also, **gas'o·lene'.** [f. GAS + -OL² + -INE²]

gas·om·e·ter (găs·ŏm'ə tər), *n.* **1.** an apparatus for measuring or storing gas. **2.** *Brit.* a tank for storing gas. [t. F: m. *gazomètre.* See GAS METER]

gasp (găsp, gäsp), *n.* **1.** a sudden, short breath; convulsive effort to breathe. **2.** a short, convulsive utterance. —*v.i.* **3.** to catch the breath, or struggle for breath, with open mouth; breathe convulsively. **4.** to long with breathless eagerness; desire; crave (fol. by *for* or *after*). —*v.t.* **5.** to utter with gasps (often fol. by *out, forth, away,* etc.). **6.** to breathe or emit with gasps (often fol. by *away*). [ME *gaspe(n), gayspe(n),* t. Scand.; cf. Icel. *geispa,* metathetic var. of *geipsa* yawn; akin to OE *gipian* yawn, *gipung* open mouth] —**Syn. 3.** See **pant.**

Gas·pé Peninsula (găs·pā'; *Fr.* gȧs·pē'), a peninsula in SE Canada, in Quebec province, between New Brunswick and the St. Lawrence.

gas·per (găs'pər, gäs'-), *n. Brit. Slang.* a cheap cigarette.

gas range, a cooking range using gas as fuel.

gas·ser (găs'ər), *n.* **1.** one who or that which gasses. **2.** a well or boring yielding natural gas.

gas shell, *Mil.* an explosive shell containing a liquid or other material which, when the shell bursts, is converted into an asphyxiating or poisonous gas or vapor.

gas·sing (găs'ĭng), *n.* **1.** act of one who or that which gasses. **2.** an affecting or overcoming with gas or fumes, as in battle. **3.** the evolution of gases during electrolysis. **4.** a process by which a material is gassed.

gas·sy (găs'ĭ), *adj.,* **-sier, -siest. 1.** full of or containing gas. **2.** like gas.

gas·ter·o·pod (găs'tər ə pŏd'), *n.* gastropod.

gas thermometer, a device for measuring temperature by observing the change in either pressure or volume of an enclosed gas.

gas·tight (găs'tīt'), *adj.* **1.** not penetrable by a gas. **2.** not admitting a given gas under a given pressure.

Gas·to·ni·a (găs·tō'nĭ ə), *n.* a city in S North Carolina, W of Charlotte. 23,069 (1950).

gastr-, var. of **gastro-,** before vowels, as in *gastralgia.*

gas·tral·gi·a (găs·trăl'jĭ ə), *n. Pathol.* **1.** neuralgia of the stomach. **2.** any pain in the stomach. [f. GASTR- + -ALGIA]

gas·trec·to·my (găs·trĕk'tə mĭ), *n., pl.* **-mies.** *Surg.* the excision of a portion of the stomach.

gas·tric (găs'trĭk), *adj.* pertaining to the stomach.

gastric juice, *Biochem.* the digestive fluid secreted by the glands of the stomach, and containing pepsin and other enzymes.

gastric ulcer, *Pathol.* an erosion of the stomach's inner wall, caused in part by the corrosive action of the gastric juice upon the mucous membrane.

gas·trin (găs'trĭn), *n. Biochem.* a hormone which stimulates the secretion of gastric juice.

gas·tri·tis (găs·trī'tĭs), *n. Pathol.* inflammation of the stomach, esp. of its mucous membrane. [f. GASTR- + -ITIS] —**gas·trit·ic** (găs·trĭt'ĭk), *adj.*

gastro-, a word element meaning "stomach," as in *gastropod.* Also, **gastr-.** [t. Gk., comb. form of *gastḗr*]

gas·tro·en·ter·i·tis (găs'trō en'tər ī'tĭs), *n. Pathol.* inflammation of the stomach and intestines. [f. GASTRO- + ENTER(O)- + -ITIS]

gastroentero-, a combining form meaning "gastric and enteric," as in *gastroenterology.* [f. GASTRO- + ENTERO-]

ăct, āble, dâre, ärt; ĕbb, ēqual; ĭf, īce; hŏt, ōver, ôrder, oil, bŏŏk, ōōze, out; ŭp, ūse, ûrge; ə = a in alone; ch, chief; g, give; ng, ring; sh, shoe; th, thin; ᵺ, that; zh, vision. See the full key on inside cover.

gas·tro·en·ter·ol·o·gy (găs′trō ĕn′tə rŏl′ə jĭ′), n. the study of the structure and diseases of digestive organs.

gas·tro·en·ter·os·to·my (găs′trō ĕn′tə rŏs′tə mĭ′), n., pl. **-mies.** Surg. the making of a new opening between the stomach and the small intestine.

gas·tro·lith (găs′trə lĭth), n. Pathol. a calculus or stony concretion in the stomach.

gas·trol·o·gy (găs trŏl′ə jĭ′), n. the study of the structure, functions, and diseases of the stomach.

gas·tro·nome (găs′trə nōm′), n. a gourmet; epicure. Also, **gas·tron·o·mer** (găs trŏn′ə mər). [t. F, der. gastronomie GASTRONOMY]

gas·tron·o·my (găs trŏn′ə mĭ′), n. the art or science of good eating. [t. F: m. gastronomie, t. Gk.: m.s. gastronomīa] —**gas·tro·nom·ic** (găs′trə nŏm′ĭk), **gas′tro·nom′i·cal,** adj. —**gas′tro·nom′i·cal·ly,** adv. —**gas·tron′o·mist,** n.

gas·tro·pod (găs′trə pŏd′), n. any of the Gastropoda. Also, **gasteropod.** [t. NL: s. Gastropoda, pl. See GASTRO-, -POD]

Gas·trop·o·da (găs trŏp′ə də), n.pl. a class of mollusks comprising the snails, having a shell of a single valve, usually spirally coiled, and a ventral muscular foot on which they glide about. [NL]

gas·tro·scope (găs′trə skōp′), n. Med. an instrument for inspecting the interior of the stomach. —**gas·tro·scop·ic** (găs′trə skŏp′ĭk), adj.

gas·tros·co·py (găs trŏs′kə pĭ′), n. Med. examination with a gastroscope to detect disease.

gas·tros·to·my (găs trŏs′tə mĭ′), n., pl. **-mies.** Surg. the operation of cutting into the stomach and leaving a more or less permanent opening for feeding or drainage.

gas·trot·o·my (găs trŏt′ə mĭ′), n., pl. **-mies.** Surg. the operation of cutting into the stomach.

gas·tro·vas·cu·lar (găs′trō văs′kyə lər), adj. Zool. serving for digestion and circulation, as a cavity.

gas·tru·la (găs′trŏŏ lə), n., pl. **-lae** (-lē′). Embryol. a metazoan embryo, consisting in typical cases of a cup-like body (formed from the blastula) with a wall formed by two layers of cells, the epiblast and hypoblast. [NL. dim. of Gk. gastēr belly,stomach] —**gas′tru·lar,** adj.

gas·tru·late (găs′trŏŏ lāt′), v.i., **-lated, -lating.** Embryol. to undergo gastrulation.

gas·tru·la·tion (gas′trŏŏ lā′shən), n. Embryol. 1. the formation of a gastrula. 2. any process (as that of invagination) by which a blastula or other form of embryo is converted into a gastrula.

gas turbine. See **turbine** (def. 2).

gat[1] (găt), v. Archaic. pt. of **get.**

gat[2] (găt), n. Slang. a gun, pistol, or revolver. [abbr. of Gatling gun]

gate (gāt), n., v., **gated, gating.** —n. 1. the movable barrier, as a swinging frame, often of openwork, in a fence or wall, or to close any passageway. 2. an opening for passage into an enclosure such as a fenced yard or walled city. 3. a structure built about such an opening and containing the barrier. 4. any narrow means of access or entrance. 5. a device for regulating the passage of water, steam, or the like, as in a dam, pipe, etc.; valve. 6. the number of persons who pay for admission to an athletic contest or other exhibition. 7. gate money. 8. a sash or frame for a saw or gang of saws. 9. Metall. a channel or opening in a mold through which molten metal enters the mold cavity to form a casting. —v.t. 10. (at British universities) to punish by restricting (a student) within the college gates. [ME gat, gate, OE gatu gates, pl. of geat opening in a wall, c. LG D gat hole, breach] —**gate′less,** adj. —**gate′like′,** adj. —**gate′man,** n.

gâ·teau (gä tō′), n., pl. **-teaux** (-tō′). French. a cake.

gate·house (gāt′hous′), n. 1. a house at or over a gate, used as the keeper's quarters, a fortification, etc. 2. a house or structure at the gate of a dam, reservoir, etc., with apparatus for regulating the flow of water.

gate·keep·er (gāt′kē′pər), n. one in charge of a gate.

gate-leg table (gāt′lĕg′), a table having drop leaves which are supported when open by legs which swing out and are usually connected by crosspieces. Also, **gate-legged table.**

gate money, the receipts taken in for admission to an athletic contest or other exhibition.

gate·post (gāt′pōst′), n. the post on which a gate is hung, or the one against which it is closed.

Gates (gāts), n. Horatio, 1728–1806, American Revolutionary general, born in England.

Gates·head (gāts′hĕd′), n. a seaport in NE England, on the Tyne opposite Newcastle. 112,600 (est. 1946).

gate·way (gāt′wā′), n. 1. a passage or entrance which is closed or may be closed by a gate. 2. a frame or arch in which a gate is hung; structure built at or over a gate. 3. any means of entering or leaving a place.

gath·er (găth′ər), v.t. 1. to bring (persons, animals, or things) together into one company or aggregate. 2. to get together from various places or sources; collect gradually. 3. to learn or infer from observation: I gather that he'll be leaving. 4. to pick (any crop or natural yield) from its place of growth or formation: to gather grain, fruit, or flowers. 5. to take: to gather a person into one's arms. 6. **be gathered to one's fathers,** to die. 7. to take by selection from among other things; sort out; cull. 8. to assemble or collect

(one's energies or oneself) as for an effort (often fol. by up). 9. to contract (the brow) into wrinkles. 10. to draw up (cloth) on a thread in fine folds or puckers by means of even stitches. 11. Bookbinding. to assemble (the printed sheets of a book) in their proper sequence to be bound. 12. Naut. to gain (way) from a dead stop or extremely slow speed. —v.i. 13. to come together or assemble: to gather around a fire, to gather in crowds. 14. to collect or accumulate. 15. to grow as by accretion; increase. 16. to become contracted into wrinkles, as the brow. 17. to come to a head, as a sore in suppurating. —n. 18. a drawing together; contraction. 19. (usually pl.) a fold or pucker in gathered cloth, etc. [ME gader(en), OE gaderian, der. geador together, akin to gæd fellowship. Cf. TOGETHER, GOOD] —**gath′er·a·ble,** adj. —**gath′er·er,** n.

—**Syn.** 2. GATHER, ASSEMBLE, COLLECT, MUSTER, MARSHAL imply bringing or drawing together. GATHER expresses the general idea usually with no implication of arrangement: to gather seashells. ASSEMBLE is used of objects or facts brought together preparatory to arranging them: to assemble data for a report. COLLECT implies purposeful accumulation to form an ordered whole: to collect evidence. MUSTER, primarily a military term, suggests thoroughness in the process of collection: to muster all his resources. MARSHAL, another term primarily military, suggests rigorously ordered, purposeful arrangement: to marshal facts for effective presentation. 3. deduce, conclude, assume. 4. pluck, crop, reap, glean, garner, harvest. —**Ant.** 1. disperse.

gath·er·ing (găth′ər ĭng), n. 1. act of one who or that which gathers. 2. that which is gathered together. 3. an assembly or meeting; a crowd. 4. a collection or assemblage of anything. 5. an inflamed and suppurating swelling. 6. Bookbinding. a section in a book: usually a sheet cut into several leaves. —**Syn.** 3. assemblage, assembly, convocation, congregation, concourse, company, throng. 5. boil, abscess, carbuncle.

Gat·ling gun (găt′lĭng), an early type of machine gun consisting of a revolving cluster of barrels around a central axis, each barrel being automatically loaded and fired during every revolution of the cluster. [named after R. J. Gatling (1818–1903), American inventor]

Ga·tun (gä tōōn′), n. 1. a town in the N Canal Zone. 2271 (prelim. 1950). 2. a large dam near this town. 1½ mi. long.

Gatun Lake, an artificial lake in the Canal Zone, created by Gatun dam. 164 sq. mi.

gauche (gōsh), adj. awkward; clumsy; tactless: her reply was typically gauche. [t. F]

gau·che·rie (gō′shə rē′; Fr. gōsh rē′), n. 1. awkwardness; clumsiness; tactlessness. 2. an awkward or tactless movement, act, etc. [t. F, der. gauche awkward, lit., left (hand)]

Gau·cho (gou′chō; Sp. -chô), n., pl. **-chos** (-chōz; Sp. -chôs). a native of the South American pampas, of mixed Spanish and Indian descent. [t. Sp.]

gaud (gôd), n. a showy ornament. [ME gaude, ? t. AF, der. gaudir rejoice, jest, t. L: m. gaudēre]

gaud·er·y (gô′də rĭ′), n., pl. **-eries.** 1. ostentatious show. 2. finery; fine or showy things: she stood in the doorway resplendent in her gaudery.

gaud·y[1] (gô′dĭ′), adj., **gaudier, gaudiest.** 1. brilliant; excessively showy. 2. showy without taste; vulgarly showy; flashy. [orig. attributive use of GAUDY[2] large bead of rosary, feast; later taken as der. GAUD, n.] —**gaud′i·ly,** adv. —**gaud′i·ness,** n.

—**Syn.** 2. tawdry. GAUDY, FLASHY, GARISH, SHOWY agree in the idea of conspicuousness and, often, bad taste. That which is GAUDY challenges the eye, as by brilliant colors or evident cost, and is not in good taste: a gaudy hat. FLASHY suggests insistent and vulgar display, in rather a sporty manner: a flashy necktie. GARISH suggests a glaring brightness, or crude vividness of color, and too much ornamentation: garish decorations. SHOWY applies to that which is strikingly conspicuous, but not necessarily offensive to good taste: a garden of showy flowers, a showy dress. —**Ant.** 2. modest, sober.

gaud·y[2] (gô′dĭ′), n., pl. **gaudies.** Brit. a festival or merrymaking, esp. an annual college feast. [t. L: m.s. gaudium joy]

gauf·fer (gō′fər, gôf′ər), n., v.t. goffer.

gauge (gāj), v., **gauged, gauging,** n. —v.t. 1. to appraise, estimate, or judge. 2. to determine the dimensions, capacity, quantity, or force of; measure, as with a gauge. 3. to make conformable to a standard. 4. Plastering. to prepare (plaster) in a certain gauge, as for hardness. 5. to cut or rub (bricks or stones) to a uniform size or shape. —n. 6. a standard of measure; standard dimension or quantity. 7. a means of estimating or judging; criterion; test. 8. extent; scope; capacity. 9. Ordn. the internal diameter of a gun bore. 10. the distance between the rails of a railroad. In the United States the **standard gauge** is 4 feet 8½ inches; **broad gauge** is wider, and **narrow gauge** narrower, than this. 11. the position of one ship with reference to another and to the wind. 12. Plastering. the quantity of plaster of Paris mixed with common plaster to accelerate its setting. Also, **gage.** [late ME, t. ONF: m.s. gauger, ult. der. gal- measuring rod; of Celtic orig.] —**gauge′a·ble,** adj.

gaug·er (gā′jər), n. 1. one who or that which gauges. 2. an officer who ascertains the contents of casks, etc. 3. an exciseman. Also, **gager.**

Gau·guin (gō găn′), n. Paul (pōl), 1848–1903, French painter.

---

b., blend of, blended; c., cognate with; d., dialect, dialectal; der., derived from; f., formed from; g., going back to; m., modification of; r., replacing; s., stem of; t., taken from; ?, perhaps. See the full key on inside cover.

Gaul (gôl), *n.* **1.** a vast ancient region in W Europe, including what is now N Italy, France, Belgium, and parts of the Netherlands, Germany, and Switzerland: divided by the Alps into **Cisalpine Gaul** (N Italy) and **Transalpine Gaul. 2.** an inhabitant of this country. **3.** a Frenchman. [t. F: m. *Gaule*, t. Gmc. (cf. OHG *walh* foreigner, esp. Gaul), b. with L *Gallus, Gallia* Gaul]

Gau·lei·ter (gou′lī′tər), *n.* a Nazi official, head of a political district.

Gaul·ish (gô′lĭsh), *n.* the extinct language of ancient Gaul, a Celtic language.

gaul·the·ri·a (gôl·thĭr′Ĭə), *n.* any of the aromatic evergreen shrubs constituting the ericaceous genus *Gaultheria*, as *G. procumbens*, the American wintergreen. [NL; named after Dr. *Gaultier*, Canadian physician]

gaunt (gônt), *adj.* **1.** abnormally thin; emaciated; haggard. **2.** bleak, desolate, or grim, as places or things. [? t. d. F: m. *gaunet* yellowish] **—gaunt′ly,** *adv.* **—gaunt′ness,** *n.* **—Syn. 1.** lean, spare, scrawny, lank; angular, bony, raw-boned. See **thin. —Ant. 1.** stout.

Gaunt (gônt, gänt), *n.* **John of,** (Duke of Lancaster) 1340–99, British soldier and statesman; fourth son of Edward III and founder of the royal house of Lancaster.

gaunt·let[1] (gônt′lĭt, gänt′-), *n.* **1.** a medieval glove, as of mail or plate, to protect the hand. **2.** a glove with a cufflike extension for the wrist. **3.** the cuff itself. **4. the gauntlet,** a challenge. Also, **gantlet.** [ME, t. OF: m. *gantelet*, dim. of *gant* glove, t. Gmc.; cf. OSw. *wante*]

gaunt·let[2] (gônt′lĭt, gänt′-), *n., v.t.* gantlet[1].

gaun·try (gôn′trĭ), *n., pl.* **-tries.** gantry.

gauss (gous), *n. Physics.* **1.** a unit of magnetic induction such that an induction of one gauss will result in one volt per centimeter of length in a linear conductor moved perpendicularly across the induction at a speed of one centimeter per second. **2.** *Obs.* oersted (def. 1). [named after K. F. *Gauss*]

Gauss (gous), *n.* **Karl Friedrich** (kärl frē′drĭ×н), 1777–1855, German mathematician. **—Gauss·i·an** (gou′sĬ ən), *adj.*

Gau·ta·ma (gô′təmə, gou′-), *n.* 563?–483? B.C., Buddha. Also, **Siddhartha, Gotama.**

Gau·tier (gō tyĕ′), *n.* **Théophile** (tĕ·ô fēl′), 1811–72, French poet, novelist, and critic of art and literature.

gauze (gôz), *n.* **1.** any thin transparent fabric made from any fiber in a plain or leno weave. **2.** some similar open material, as of wire. **3.** a thin haze. [t. F: m. *gaze* named after city of *Gaza* in Palestine] **—gauze′like′,** *adj.*

gauz·y (gô′zĬ), *adj.* **gauzier, gauziest.** like gauze; thin as gauze. **—gauz′i·ness,** *n.*

ga·vage (gə väzh′; Fr. gȧ vȧzh′), *n.* forced feeding, as of poultry or human beings, as by a flexible tube and a force pump. [t. F, der. *gaver* to gorge]

gave (gāv), *v.* pt. of **give.**

gav·el (găv′əl), *n.* a small mallet used by a presiding officer to signal for attention or order. [back formation from *gavelock*, OE *gafeluc* spear]

gav·el·kind (găv′əl kīnd′), *n. Early Eng. Law.* **1.** a customary system of land tenure, whose chief feature was equal division of inherited land among the heirs. **2.** a tenure of land in which the tenant was liable for money rent rather than labor or military service. **3.** the land so held. [ME *gavelkynde, gavelikind*, f. OE *gafol* tax, tribute + *gecynd* KIND[2]]

ga·vi·al (gā′vĬ əl), *n.* a large crocodilian, *Gavialis gangeticus*, with elongated jaws, found in India. [t. F, t. Hind.: m. *ghariyal*]

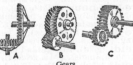
Head of gavial, *Gavialis gangeticus* (Total length ab. 20 ft.)

ga·votte (gə vŏt′), *n.* **1.** an old French dance in moderately quick ¾ time. **2.** a piece of music for, or in the rhythm of, this dance, often forming one of the movements in the classical suite, usually following the saraband. Also, **ga·vot′.** [t. F, t. Pr.: m. *gavoto* dance of the Gavots (Alpine mountaineers), fem. of *gavot* hillbilly, der. pre-Rom. *gav-* mountain stream]

Ga·wain (gä′wĭn, gô′-), *n. Arthurian Romance.* one of the knights of the Round Table.

gawk (gôk), *n.* **1.** an awkward, foolish person. **—***v.i.* **2.** *Colloq.* to act like a gawk; stare stupidly. [appar. repr. OE word meaning fool, f. *gagol* foolish + *-oc* -OCK; used attributively in *gawk hand, gallock* left hand]

gawk·y (gô′kĬ), *adj.* **gawkier, gawkiest.** awkward; ungainly; clumsy. **—gawk′i·ly,** *adv.* **—gawk′i·ness,** *n.*

gay (gā), *adj.* **gayer, gayest. 1.** having or showing a joyous mood: *gay spirits, music, scenes, etc.* **2.** bright or showy: *gay colors, flowers, ornaments, etc.* **3.** given to or abounding in social or other pleasures: *a gay social season.* **4.** dissipated; licentious: *to lead a gay life.* [ME, t. OF: m. *gai*; orig. uncert.] **—gay′ness,** *n.* **—Syn. 1.** gleeful, jovial, glad, joyous, light-hearted; lively, vivacious, frolicsome, sportive, hilarious. GAY, JOLLY, JOYFUL, MERRY describe a happy or light-hearted mood. GAY suggests a lightness of heart or liveliness of mood that is openly manifested: *when hearts were young and gay.* JOLLY indicates a good-humored, natural, expansive gaiety of mood or disposition: *a jolly crowd at a party.* JOYFUL suggests gladness, happiness, rejoicing: *joyful over the good news.* MERRY is often interchangeable with GAY: *a merry disposition, a merry party;* it suggests, even more than the latter, convivial animated enjoyment. **—Ant. 1.** solemn. **2.** sedate, sober.

Gay (gā), *n.* **John,** 1685–1732, British poet and dramatist.

Ga·ya (gä′yə, gī′ə), *n.* a city in NE India: a famous place of Hindu pilgrimage. 105,223 (1941).

gay·e·ty (gā′ə tĬ), *n., pl.* **-ties.** gaiety.

Gay-Lus·sac (gā ly săk′), *n.* **Joseph Louis** (zhô zĕf′ lwē), 1778–1850, French chemist.

gay·ly (gā′lĬ), *adv.* gaily.

Gay-Pay-Oo (gā′pā′ōō′; *Russ.* gĕ′pĕ′ōō′), *n. U.S.S.R.* the secret service from 1922, when Cheka was reorganized, until 1935, when the N.K.V.D., the official state police, was formed; the Ogpu. [attempt to give the names of the Russian letters transliterated as *G.P.U.*]

gay·wings (gā′wĬngz′), *n.* the fringed milkwort, *Polygala paucifolia*, whose aerial flowers have paired, large, usually pink-purple petals.

gaz., 1. gazette. **2.** gazetteer.

Ga·za (gā′zə), *n.* a seaport in SW Palestine: ancient trade route center. 34,170 (est. 1940).

gaze (gāz), *v.,* **gazed, gazing,** *n.* **—***v.i.* **1.** to look steadily or intently; look with curiosity, wonder, etc. **—***n.* **2.** a steady or intent look. [ME, t. Scand.; cf. d. Sw. *gasa* gape, stare] **—gaz′er,** *n.* **—Syn. 1.** GAZE, STARE, GAPE suggest looking fixedly at something. To GAZE is to look steadily and intently at something; esp. at that which excites admiration, curiosity, or interest: *to gaze at scenery, at a scientific experiment.* To STARE is to gaze with eyes wide open, as from surprise, wonder, alarm, stupidity, or impertinence: *to stare unbelievingly or rudely.* GAPE is a word with uncomplimentary connotations; it suggests open-mouthed, often ignorant or rustic wonderment or curiosity: *to gape at a high building, at a circus parade.*

ga·ze·bo (gə zē′bō), *n., pl.* **-bos, -boes.** a structure commanding an extensive prospect, esp. a pavilion or summerhouse. [? f. GAZE, *v.* + L (*vid*)*ēbō* I shall see]

gaze·hound (gāz′hound′), *n.* a hound that hunts by sight rather than scent.

ga·zelle (gə zĕl′), *n.* any of various small antelopes of the genus *Gazella* and allied genera, noted for their graceful movements and lustrous eyes. [t. F, t. Ar.: m. *ghazāl*] **—gazelle′like′,** *adj.*

Gazelle, *Gazella dama ruficollis* (3 ft. high at the shoulder)

ga·zette (gə zĕt′), *n., v.,* **-zetted, -zetting.** **—***n.* **1.** a newspaper (now common only in newspaper titles). **2.** an official government journal, esp. in Great Britain, containing lists of government appointments and promotions, bankruptcies, etc. **—***v.t.* **3.** *Chiefly Brit.* to publish, announce, or list in a gazette. [t. F, t. It.: m. *gazzetta*, var. of Venetian *gazeta*, orig. a Venetian coin (the price of the gazette), dim. of *gaza* magpie]

gaz·et·teer (găz′ə tĬr′), *n.* **1.** a geographical dictionary. **2.** a journalist, esp. appointed and paid by the government. [t. F (obs.): m. *gazettier*]

Ga·zi·an·tep (gä′zĬ än tĕp′), *n.* a city in S Turkey. 26,558 (1940). Also, **Aintab.**

G.B., Great Britain.

G.C.B., (Knight) Grand Cross of the Bath.

G.C.D., greatest common divisor. Also, **g.c.d.**

G.C.F., greatest common factor. Also, **g.c.f.**

G clef, *Music.* treble clef. See illus. under **clef.**

G.C.M., greatest common measure. Also, **g.c.m.**

G.C.V.O., Knight Grand Cross of the Royal Victorian Order.

Gd, *Chem.* gadolinium.

Gdansk (gdänsk), *n.* Polish name of **Danzig.**

gds., goods.

Gdy·nia (gdĬ′nyä), *n.* a seaport in N Poland, on the Bay of Danzig. 79,000 (1946).

Ge, *Chem.* germanium.

ge·an·ti·cli·nal (jē′ăn tĬ klī′nəl), *Geol.* **—***adj.* **1.** pertaining to an anticlinal fold extending over a relatively large part of the earth's surface. **—***n.* **2.** a geanticline. [f. Gk. *gê* earth + ANTICLINAL]

ge·an·ti·cline (jē ăn′tə klīn′), *n. Geol.* a geanticlinal fold. [f. Gk. *gê* earth + ANTICLINE]

gear (gĬr), *n.* **1.** *Mach.* **a.** a mechanism for transmitting or changing motion, as by toothed wheels. **b.** a toothed wheel which engages with another wheel or part. **c.** the connection or engagement of toothed wheels with each other: *in gear, out of gear, in high gear, in low gear.* **d.** a group of parts in a complex machine that operates for a single purpose. **e.** the diameter of an imaginary wheel whose circumference is equal to the distance traversed by a bicycle during a single revolution of the pedals. **2.** implements, tools, or apparatus, esp. as used for a particular occupation; harness; tackle. **3.** *Naut.* **a.** the ropes, blocks, etc., belonging to a particular sail or spar. **b.** the tools and equipment used on a ship. **c.** a sailor's personal baggage. **4.** *Archaic.* property. **5.** *Archaic.*

Gears
A. Bevel gears; B, Herringbone gears; C. Spur gears

armor or arms. —*v.t.* **6.** to provide with gearing; connect by gearing; put (machinery) into gear. **7.** to provide with gear; supply; fit; harness. —*v.i.* **8.** to fit exactly, as one part of gearing into another; come into or be in gear. [ME *gere*, t. Scand.; cf. Icel. *gervi*, *görvi* gear, apparel; akin to OE *gearwe*, pl., equipment, *gearu* ready] —**gear·less**, *adj.*

gear·box (gîr′bŏks′), *n.* *Brit.* transmission.

gear·ing (gîr′ĭng), *n.* **1.** the parts collectively by which motion is transmitted in machinery, esp. a train of toothed wheels. **2.** act of equipping with gears. **3.** the method of installation of such gears.

gear·shift (gîr′shĭft′), *n.* a device for selecting or connecting gears for transmitting power. Also, *Brit.*, **gear lever.**

gear·wheel (gîr′hwēl′), *n.* a wheel having teeth or cogs which engage with those of another wheel or part; cogwheel. Also, **gear wheel.**

geb., (Ger. *geboren*) born.

geck·o (gĕk′ō), *n.*, *pl.* **geckos, geckoes.** a small, harmless lizard of the family *Geckonidae*, mostly nocturnal, many with adhesive pads on the toes. [t. Malay: m. *gēkoq*; imit.]

Burmese gecko, *Gecko gecko*
(10 in. long)

Ged·des (gĕd′ēz), *n.*, **Norman Bel**, born 1893, U.S. industrial and stage designer and architect.

gee (jē), *interj.*, *n.*, *v.*, **geed, geeing.** —*interj.* **n. 1.** a word of command to horses, etc., directing them to turn to the right or (fol. by *up*) to go faster. —*v.i.* **2.** to turn to the right. —*v.t.* **3.** to turn (something) to the right. **4.** to evade. [orig. uncert.]

Gee·long (jĭ′lông′), *n.* a seaport in SE Australia, in Victoria. 16,931; with suburbs, 39,223 (1933).

Geel·vink Bay (KHĀl′vĭngk), a large bay on the NW coast of New Guinea.

geese (gēs), *n.* pl. of **goose.**

geest (gēst), *n.* *Geol.* old deposits produced by flowing water. [t. LG: dry or sandy soil]

gee·zer (gē′zər), *n.* *Slang.* a queer character. [var. of *guiser* (f. GUISE (def. 7) + -ER¹), repr. d. pronunciation]

Ge·hen·na (gĭ·hĕn′ə), *n.* **1.** *Old Test.* the valley of Hinnom, near Jerusalem, regarded as a place of abomination (II Kings 23:10), and used as a dumping place for refuse, with fires kept burning to prevent pestilence. **2.** *New Test. and Rabbinical literature.* hell. **3.** any place of extreme torment or suffering. [t. LL, t. Gk.: m. *Géenna*, t. Heb.: m. *Gē-Hinnōm* hell, short for *gē ben Hinnōm*, lit., valley of son of Hinnom. See Jer. 19:5]

Gei·ger counter (gī′gər), an instrument for detecting and counting ionizing particles, consisting of a tube which conducts electricity when the gas within is ionized by such a particle. It is used in measuring the degree of radio-activity in an area left by the explosion of an atom bomb, in investigations of cosmic rays, etc.

Gei·kie (gē′kĭ), *n.* **Sir Archibald**, 1835–1924, Scottish geologist.

gei·sha (gā′shə), *n.*, *pl.* **-sha, -shas.** a Japanese singing and dancing girl. [t. Jap.]

Geiss·ler tube (gīs′lər), a sealed glass tube with platinum connections at the ends, containing rarefied gas made luminous by an electrical discharge. [named after H. *Geissler* (1814–79), the (German) inventor]

gel (jĕl), *n.*, *v.*, **gelled, gelling.** *Phys. Chem.* —*n.* **1.** a semirigid colloidal dispersion of a solid with a liquid or gas, as jelly, glue, or silica gel. —*v.i.* **2.** to form or become a gel. [short for GELATIN]

gel·a·tin (jĕl′ə·tĭn), *n.* **1.** a brittle, nearly transparent, faintly yellow, odorless, and almost tasteless organic substance, obtained by boiling in water the ligaments, bones, skin, etc., of animals, and forming the basis of jellies, glues, and the like. **2.** any of various similar substances, as vegetable gelatin. **3.** a preparation or product in which gelatin (1 or 2) is the essential constituent. Also, **gel′a·tine.** [t. F: (m.) *gélatine*, t. It.: m. *gelatina*, der. *gelata* jelly, d. L *gelāta*, pp. fem., frozen, congealed]

ge·lat·i·nize (jĭ·lăt′ə·nīz′), *v.*, **-nized, -nizing.** —*v.t.* **1.** to make gelatinous. **2.** to coat with gelatin, as paper. —*v.i.* **3.** to become gelatinous. —**ge·lat′i·ni·za′tion**, *n.*

ge·lat·i·noid (jĭ·lăt′ə·noid′), *adj.* **1.** resembling gelatin; gelatinous. —*n.* **2.** a gelatinoid substance.

ge·lat·i·nous (jĭ·lăt′ə·nəs), *adj.* **1.** having the nature of jelly; jellylike. **2.** pertaining to or consisting of gelatin. —**ge·lat′i·nous·ly**, *adv.* —**ge·lat′i·nous·ness**, *n.*

ge·la·tion (jĭ·lā′shən), *n.* solidification by cold; freezing. [t. L: s. *gelātio* freezing]

geld¹ (gĕld), *v.t.*, **gelded** or **gelt, gelding.** to castrate (esp. animals). [ME *gelde*(n), t. Scand.; cf. Icel. *gelda*]

geld² (gĕld), *n.* *Eng. Hist.* **1.** a payment; tax. **2.** a tax paid to the crown by landholders under the Saxon and Norman kings. [t. ML: s. *geldum*, t. OE: m. *geld*, *gield*, *gyld* payment, tribute, c. D and G *geld* money; akin to YIELD, v.]

Gel·der·land (gĕl′dər·länd′; *Du.* KHĕl′dər·länt′), *n.* a province in E Netherlands. 998,030 pop. (est. 1946); 1965 sq. mi. *Cap.* Arnhem. Also, **Guelders.**

geld·ing (gĕl′dĭng), *n.* a castrated animal, esp. a horse. [ME, t. Scand.; cf. Icel. *geldingr*]

Ge·lée (zhə·lē′), *n.* **Claude** (klōd). See **Lorrain.**

gel·id (jĕl′ĭd), *adj.* very cold; icy. [t. L: s. *gelidus* icy cold] —**ge·lid′i·ty, gel·id′ness**, *n.* —**gel′id·ly**, *adv.*

gel·se·mi·um (jĕl·sē′mĭəm), *n.* **1.** a twining shrub of the loganiaceous genus *Gelsemium*, esp. the yellow jasmine, *G. sempervirens*, of the southern U.S. **2.** the root of the yellow jasmine, or the tincture from it, used a drug. [NL, der. It. *gelsomino* JASMINE]

Gel·sen·kir·chen (gĕl′zən·kîr′KHən), *n.* a city in W Germany, in the Ruhr. 317,568 (1939).

gelt (gĕlt), *v.* pt. and pp. of **geld.**

gem (jĕm), *n.*, *v.*, **gemmed, gemming.** —*n.* **1.** a stone used in jewelry, fashioned to bring out its beauty. **2.** something likened to, or prized as, a gem because of its beauty or worth, esp. something small: *the gem of the collection.* **3.** *Cookery.* a kind of muffin. **4.** *Brit.* a printing type (4 point) between brilliant and diamond. —*v.t.* **5.** to adorn with or as with gems. [ME, t. F: m. *gemme*, g. L **gemma** bud, jewel; r. OE *gim* (c. OHG *gimma*), t. L] —**gem·like′**, *adj.*

Ge·ma·ra (gə·mä′rä, -mô′rä), *n.* *Jewish Lit.* a commentary on the Mishnah; the Talmud. [t. Aram.: completion]

gem·i·nate (*adj.* jĕm′ə·nĭt, -nāt′; *v.* jĕm′ə·nāt′), *v.*, **-nated, -nating**, *adj.* —*v.t.*, *v.i.* **1.** to make or become double or paired. —*v.i.* **2.** twin; combined in pairs; coupled. [t. L: m.s. *gemīnātus*, pp., doubled] —**gem′i·nate·ly**, *adv.*

gem·i·na·tion (jĕm′ə·nā′shən), *n.* **1.** a doubling; duplication; repetition. **2.** *Phonetics.* the doubling of an originally single consonant. **3.** *Rhet.* the immediate repetition of a word, phrase, etc., for rhetorical effect.

Gem·i·ni (jĕm′ə·nī′), *n.*, *pl.* gen. **Geminorum** (jĕm′ə·nōr′əm). **1.** *Astron.* the Twins, a zodiacal constellation containing the bright stars Castor and Pollux. **2.** the third sign of the zodiac. See diag. under **zodiac.** [t. L, pl. of *geminus* twin]

gem·ma (jĕm′ə), *n.*, *pl.* **gemmae** (jĕm′ē). *Bot.* **1.** a cell or cluster of cells, or a leaf- or budlike body, which separates from the parent plant and forms a new plant, as in mosses, liverworts, etc. **2.** a bud, esp. a leaf bud. [t. L: bud, germ. Cf. GEM]

gem·mate (jĕm′āt), *adj.*, *v.*, **-mated, -mating.** *Bot.* —*adj.* **1.** having buds; increasing by budding. —*v.i.* **2.** to put forth buds; increase by budding. [t. L: m. s. *gemmātus*, pp., increased by budding, set with gems]

gem·ma·tion (jĕm·ā′shən), *n.* *Bot.* the process of reproduction by gemmae.

gem·mule (jĕm′ūl), *n.* **1.** *Bot.* gemma. **2.** *Zool.* an asexually produced mass of cells that will develop into an animal. **3.** *Biol.* one of the hypothetical living units conceived by Darwin as the bearers of the hereditary attributes. [t. L: m. *gemmula*, dim. of *gemma* bud]

ge·mot (gə·mōt′), *n.* *Early Eng. Hist.* a meeting or an assembly, as for judicial purposes. Also, **ge·mote′.** [OE *gemōt*, f. ge- together + *mōt* meeting. Cf. MOOT]

gems·bok (gĕmz′bŏk′), *n.* a large antelope, *Oryx gazella*, of South Africa, having long, straight horns and a long, tufted tail. [t. S Afr. D: chamois buck]

Gemsbok, *Oryx gazella*
(4 ft. high at the shoulder)

-gen, a suffix meaning: **1.** something produced, or growing: *acrogen, endogen, exogen.* **2.** something that produces: *hydrogen, oxygen.* [t. F: m. *-gène*, ult. t. Gk.: m. *-genēs* born, produced, der. *gen*- bear, produce]

Gen., 1. *Mil.* General. **2.** Genesis. **3.** Geneva.

gen., 1. gender. **2.** general. **3.** genitive. **4.** genus.

gen·darme (zhän′därm; *Fr.* zhän·därm′), *n.*, *pl.* **-darmes** (-därmz; *Fr.* -därm′). one of a corps of military police, esp. in France. [t. F, formed as sing. from *gens d'armes* men of arms]

gen·dar·me·rie (zhän·därm·rē′), *n.* gendarmes collectively. Also, **gen·darm·er·y** (zhän·där′mə·rĭ).

gen·der (jĕn′dər), *n.* **1.** *Gram.* **a.** (in many languages) a set of classes which together include all nouns, membership in a particular class being shown by the form of the noun itself or by the form or choice of words that modify, replace, or otherwise refer to the noun; e.g., in Eng., the choice of *he* to replace *the man*, of *she* to replace *the woman*, of *it* to replace *the table*, of *it* or *she* to replace *the ship.* The number of genders in different languages varies from two to more than twenty; often the classification correlates in part with sex or animateness. The most familiar sets of genders are of three classes (e.g. Latin and German, *masculine, feminine, neuter*) or of two (e.g. French and Spanish, *masculine* and *feminine*; Dutch, *common* and *neuter*). **b.** one class of such a set. **c.** such classes or sets collectively or in general. **2.** *Colloq.* sex. **3.** *Obs.* kind, sort, or class. [ME *gendre*, t. OF, t. L: m.s. *genus* race, kind, sort, gender. Cf. GENUS, GENRE] —**gen′der·less**, *adj.*

gene (jēn), *n.* *Biol.* the unit of inheritance, probably biochemical in nature, which is located on and transmitted by the chromosome, and which develops into a hereditary character as it reacts with the environment and with the other genes. [t. Gk.: s. *geneá* breed, kind]

b., blend of, blended; c., cognate with; d., dialect, dialectal; der., derived from; f., formed from; g., going back to; m., modification of; r., replacing; s., stem of; t., taken from; ?, perhaps. See the full key on inside cover.

genealogical tree, family tree.

ge·ne·al·o·gy (jē′nĭ ăl′ə jĭ, jĕn′Y-, -ŏl′-), *n., pl.* **-gies.** 1. an account of human family pedigrees of ancestors or relatives. 2. the investigation of pedigrees as a department of knowledge. [ME, t. LL: m.s. *geneālogia,* t. Gk.: tracing of descent] —**ge·ne·a·log·i·cal** (jē′nY ə lŏj′ə kəl, jĕn′Y-), **ge′ne·a·log′ic,** *adj.* —**ge′ne·a·log′i·cal·ly,** *adv.* —**ge·ne·al·o·gist** (jē′nY ăl′ə jĭst, jĕn′Y-, -ŏl′-), *n.* —Syn. 2. See **pedigree.**

gen·e·ra (jĕn′ər ə), *n.* pl. of **genus.**

gen·er·al (jĕn′ər əl), *adj.* 1. pertaining to, affecting, including, or participated in by all members of a class or group; not partial or particular: *a general election.* 2. common to many or most of a community; prevalent; usual: *the general practice.* 3. not restricted to one class or field; miscellaneous: *the general public.* 4. not limited to a detail of application; not specific or special: *general instructions.* 5. indefinite or vague: *to refer to a matter in a general way.* 6. having extended command, or superior or chief rank (often follows noun): *a general officer, governor general.* —*n.* 7. *Mil.* **a.** *U.S. Army.* brigadier general, major general, lieutenant general, general, general of the army, or general of the armies. **b.** *U.S. Army.* an officer with the rank between lieutenant general and general of the army (or armies); a full general. **c.** (in numerous foreign armies) an officer in the second or third highest rank, as in Great Britain, where he ranks just below a field marshal. 8. *Eccles.* the chief of a religious order. 9. a general statement or principle. 10. **in general, a.** with respect to the whole class referred to. **b.** as a general rule; commonly. 11. *Archaic.* the general public. [ME, t. L: s. *generālis,* of or belonging to a (whole) race, kind, the opposite of *speciālis* special, particular. See GENUS] —**gen′er·al·ness,** *n.* —Syn. 1. 2. customary, regular, ordinary. GENERAL, COMMON, POPULAR, UNIVERSAL agree in the idea of being nonexclusive and widespread. GENERAL means belonging to, or prevailing throughout, a whole class or body collectively, irrespective of individuals: *a general belief.* COMMON means shared by all, and belonging to one as much as another: *a common fund, interests.* POPULAR means belonging to, or adapted for, or favored by the people or the public generally, rather than by a particular (esp. a superior) class: *the popular conception, a popular candidate.* UNIVERSAL means found everywhere, and with no exceptions: *a universal longing.* —Ant. 1. special, limited.

General American Speech, the pronunciation of English typical of American speakers not native to New England, New York City, or the South.

General Assembly, the legislature in certain States of the United States.

General Court, *U.S.* a State legislature, which, during colonial administration, had judicial authority: now used only in Massachusetts and New Hampshire.

gen·er·al·ìs·si·mo (jĕn′ər əl ĭs′ə mō′), *n., pl.* **-mos.** 1. (in certain foreign armies) the supreme commander of several armies acting together. 2. (in China and U.S. S.R.) the supreme commander of all the forces of the country. [t. It., superl. of *generale* general, der. L *generālis.* See GENERAL]

gen·er·al·i·ty (jĕn′ər ăl′ə tĭ), *n., pl.* **-ties.** 1. a general or vague statement: *to speak in vague generalities.* 2. general principle; general rule or law. 3. the greater part or majority: *the generality of people.* 4. state or quality of being general.

gen·er·al·i·za·tion (jĕn′ər əl ə zā′shən), *n.* 1. act or process of generalizing. 2. a result of this process; general statement, idea, or principle. 3. *Logic.* **a.** a proposition asserting something to be true either of all members of a certain class or of an indefinite part of that class. **b.** the process of obtaining such propositions.

gen·er·al·ize (jĕn′ər ə līz′), *v.,* **-ized, -izing.** —*v.t.* 1. to give a general (rather than specific or special) character to. 2. to infer (a general principle, etc.) from facts, etc. 3. to make general; bring into general use or knowledge. —*v.i.* 4. to form general notions. 5. to deal in generalities. 6. to make general inferences.

gen·er·al·ly (jĕn′ər ə lĭ), *adv.* 1. with respect to the larger part, or for the most part: *a claim generally recognized.* 2. usually; commonly; ordinarily: *he generally comes at noon.* 3. without reference to particular persons or things: *generally speaking.* —Syn. 2. See **often.**

General of the Armies, *U.S. Army.* a special rank held by John J. Pershing, equivalent to General of the Army.

General of the Army, *U.S. Army.* the highest ranking military officer; the next rank above general (equivalent to *Admiral of the Fleet* of the U.S. Navy).

general paralysis, *Pathol.* a syphilitic brain disorder characterized by chronic inflammation and degeneration of cerebral tissue, resulting in mental and physical deterioration. Also, **general paresis.**

gen·er·al-pur·pose (jĕn′ər əl pûr′pəs), *adj.* of broad usage; not restricted in function, as a horse.

gen·er·al·ship (jĕn′ər əl shĭp′), *n.* 1. skill as commander of a large military force or unit. 2. management or tactics. 3. the rank or functions of a general.

general staff, *Mil.* a group of officers without command, whose duties are to assist high commanders in planning and carrying out orders in peace and war.

general strike, a mass strike in all or many trades and industries in a section or in all parts of a country.

gen·er·ate (jĕn′ə rāt′), *v.t.,* **-ated, -ating.** 1. to bring into existence; cause to be: *to generate electricity.* 2. to produce; procreate. 3. *Math.* to trace out (a figure) by the motion of another figure. [t. L: m. s. *generātus,* pp., begotten]

gen·er·a·tion (jĕn′ə rā′shən), *n.* 1. the whole body of individuals born about the same time: *the rising generation.* 2. the age or average lifetime of a generation; term of years (commonly 30) accepted as the average difference of age between one generation of a family and the next. 3. a single step in natural descent, as of human beings, animals, or plants. 4. act or process of generating; procreation. 5. the fact of being generated. 6. production by natural or artificial processes; evolution, as of heat or sound. 7. the offspring of a given parent or parents, considered as a single step in descent. 8. *Biol.* a form or phase of a plant or animal, with reference to the manner of its reproduction. 9. *Math.* the production of a geometrical figure by the motion of another figure. [t. L: s. *generātio*]

gen·er·a·tive (jĕn′ə rā′tĭv), *adj.* 1. pertaining to the production of offspring. 2. capable of producing.

gen·er·a·tor (jĕn′ə rā′tər), *n.* 1. a machine which converts mechanical energy into electrical energy; dynamo. 2. *Chem.* an apparatus for producing a gas or vapor. 3. one who or that which generates. [t. L]

gen·er·a·trix (jĕn′ə rā′trĭks), *n., pl.* **gen·er·a·tri·ces** (jĕn′ər ə trī′sēz). *Math.* an element generating a figure. [t. L]

ge·ner·ic (jĭ nĕr′ĭk), *adj.* 1. pertaining to a genus. 2. applicable or referring to all the members of a genus or class. Also, **ge·ner′i·cal.** [f. s. L *genus* kind + -IC. Cf. F *générique*] —**ge·ner′i·cal·ly,** *adv.*

gen·er·os·i·ty (jĕn′ə rŏs′ə tĭ), *n., pl.* **-ties.** 1. readiness or liberality in giving. 2. freedom from meanness or smallness of mind or character. 3. a generous act. —Syn. 1. munificence. 2. nobleness. —Ant. 1. stinginess.

gen·er·ous (jĕn′ər əs), *adj.* 1. munificent or bountiful; unselfish: *a generous giver or gift.* 2. free from meanness or smallness of mind or character. 3. furnished liberally; abundant: *a generous portion.* 4. rich or strong, as wine. 5. fertile, as soil. [t. L: m. s. *generōsus* of noble birth] —**gen′er·ous·ly,** *adv.* —**gen′er·ous·ness,** *n.* —Syn. 1. liberal, open-handed, free. 2. highminded, noble. 3. ample, plentiful. —Ant. 1. selfish. 2. mean. 3. meager.

Gen·e·see (jĕn′ə sē′), *n.* a river flowing from N Pennsylvania through W New York into Lake Ontario. 144 mi.

Gen·e·sis (jĕn′ə sĭs), *n.* the first book of the Old Testament, telling of the beginnings of the world and of man. [special use of Gk. *génesis* origin, creation]

gen·e·sis (jĕn′ə sĭs), *n., pl.* **-ses** (-sēz′). origin; production; creation. [ME, t. L, t. Gk.: origin, creation]

gen·et[1] (jĕn′Yt, jY nĕt′), *n.* 1. any of the small Old World carnivores constituting the genus *Genetta,* esp. *G. vulgaris,* allied to the civets but without a scent pouch, yielding a soft fur. 2. the fur. Also, **ge·nette′.** [ME *genete,* t. OF, t. Sp.: m. *gineta,* t. Ar.: m. *jarnaiṭ*]

gen·et[2] (jĕn′Yt), *n.* jonnet.

ge·net·ic (jə nĕt′ĭk), *adj.* 1. *Biol.* pertaining or according to genetics. 2. pertaining to genesis or origin. Also, **ge·net′i·cal.** [t. Gk.: m. s. *genetikós* generative] —**ge·net′i·cal·ly,** *adv.*

ge·net·i·cist (jY nĕt′ə sĭst), *n.* one versed in genetics.

ge·net·ics (jY nĕt′Yks), *n. Biol.* the science of heredity, dealing with resemblances and differences of related organisms flowing from the interaction of their genes and the environment. [pl. of GENETIC (def. 2). See -ICS]

Ge·ne·va (jə nē′və), *n.* 1. a city in SW Switzerland, on the Lake of Geneva: seat of the League of Nations, 1920–46. 132,200 (est. 1944). 2. **Lake of.** Also, **Lake Leman.** a lake between SW Switzerland and France. 45 mi. long; 225 sq. mi. French, **Ge·nève** (zhə nĕv′).

ge·ne·va (jə nē′və), *n.* Hollands gin. [t. D: m. *genever,* t. OF: m. *genevre,* g. L *jūniperus* juniper]

Geneva bands, two bands, or pendent strips, worn at the throat as part of a clerical garb: worn orig. by the Swiss Calvinist clergy.

Geneva Convention, *Mil.* an international agreement establishing rules for the treatment during war of the sick, the wounded, and prisoners of war.

Geneva cross, a red Greek cross on a white ground, displayed in war, etc., to distinguish ambulances, hospitals, and persons serving them; red cross.

Geneva gown, a loose, large-sleeved, black preaching gown worn by Protestant clergymen: so named from its use by the Genevan Calvinist clergy.

Ge·ne·van (jə nē′vən), *adj.* 1. of or pertaining to Geneva. 2. Calvinistic. —*n.* 3. a native or inhabitant of Geneva. 4. a Calvinist.

Gen·e·vieve (jĕn′ə vēv′; *Fr.* zhən vyĕv′), *n.* **Saint,** A.D. c422–512, French nun, patron saint of Paris.

Gen·ghis Khan (jĕng′gĭs kän′), 1162–1227, Mongol conqueror of most of Asia and of E Europe to the Dnieper river. Also, **Jenghis Khan, Jenghiz Khan.**

gen·ial[1] (jēn′yəl), *adj.* 1. sympathetically cheerful; cordial: *a genial disposition, a genial host.* 2. enlivening; supporting life; pleasantly warm, or mild. 3. *Rare.* characterized by genius. [t. L: s. *geniālis* festive, jovial, pleasant, lit., pertaining to generation or to marriage] —**gen′ial·ly,** *adv.* —**gen′ial·ness,** *n.* —Syn. 1. friendly, hearty, pleasant, agreeable. —Ant. 1. sullen.

ge·ni·al[2] (jə nī′əl), *adj. Anat., Zool.* of or pertaining to the chin. [f. m. s. Gk. *géneion* chin + -AL[1]]

ge·ni·al·i·ty (jē/nĭ ăl/ə tĭ), *n.* genial quality; sympathetic cheerfulness or kindliness.

gen·ic (jĕn/ĭk), *adj. Biol.* of, relating to, resembling, or arising from a gene or genes.

ge·nic·u·late (jə nĭk/yə lĭt, -lāt/), *adj. Biol.* 1. having kneelike joints or bends. 2. bent at a joint like a knee. [t. L: m. s. *geniculātus* knotted]

ge·nic·u·la·tion (jə nĭk/yə lā/shən), *n.* 1. geniculate state. 2. a geniculate formation. [t. LL: s. *geniculātio* a bending of the knee]

ge·nie (jē/nĭ), *n.* a jinni or spirit of Mohammedan mythology. [t. F, t. L: m. *genius*. See GENIUS]

ge·ni·i (jē/nĭ ī/), *n.* pl. of **genius**.

gen·i·pap (jĕn/ə păp/), *n.* 1. the edible fruit of a tropical American rubiaceous tree, *Genipa americana*, about the size of an orange. 2. the plant. [t. Pg.: m. *genipapo*; of Tupian orig.]

gen·i·tal (jĕn/ə təl), *adj.* pertaining to generation or the organs of generation. [t. L: s. *genitālis*]

gen·i·ta·lia (jĕn/ə tāl/yə), *n.pl.* the genitals. [t. L]

gen·i·tals (jĕn/ə təlz), *n.pl.* the reproductive organs, esp. the external organs.

gen·i·tive (jĕn/ə tĭv), *Gram.* —*adj.* 1. (in some inflected languages) denoting the case of nouns generally used to modify other nouns, often indicating possession, but used also in expressions of measure, origin, characteristic: *Examples: John's hat, his book, week's vacation, duty's call.* 2. denoting the affix or other element characteristic of this case, or a word containing such an element. 3. similar to such a case form in function or meaning. —*n.* 4. the genitive case. 5. a word in that case. 6. a construction of similar meaning. [t. L: m.s. *genitīvus*, lit., pertaining to generation] —**gen·i·ti·val** (jĕn/ə tī/vəl), *adj.* —**gen/i·ti/val·ly**, *adv.*

gen·i·to·u·ri·nar·y (jĕn/ə tō yŏŏr/ə nĕr/ĭ), *adj. Anat. Physiol.* noting or pertaining to the genital and urinary organs; urogenital. [f. *genito-* (comb. form of GENITAL) + URINARY]

gen·ius (jēn/yəs), *n.,* pl. **geniuses** for 1–4, 7, **genii** (jē/nĭ ī/) for 5, 6, 8. 1. exceptional natural capacity for creative and original conceptions. 2. a person having such capacity. 3. natural ability or capacity: *a task suited to one's genius.* 4. distinctive character or spirit, as of a nation, period, language, etc. 5. the guardian spirit of a place, institution, etc. 6. either of two mutually opposed spirits, one good and the other evil, supposed to attend a person throughout his life. 7. a person who strongly influences the character, conduct, or destiny of another. 8. any demon or spirit, esp. a genie or jinni (now chiefly or only in *pl.*). [t. L: tutelary spirit, any spiritual being, disposition, orig. a male generative or creative principle. c. GENIAL[1], GENITAL, GENUS, GENESIS, KIN] —**Syn.** 3. gift, talent, aptitude, faculty.

ge·ni·us lo·ci (jē/nĭ əs lō/sī), *Latin.* 1. guardian of a place. 2. the peculiar character of a place with reference to the impression that it makes on the mind.

Genl., General.

Gen·o·a (jĕn/ə wə), *n.* a seaport in NW Italy. 648,480 (est. 1946). Italian, **Ge·no·va** (jě/nô vä/).

gen·o·cide (jĕn/ə sīd/), *n.* extermination of a national or racial group as a planned move. [f. Gk. *gėno(s)* race + -CIDE[2]; coined by Dr. Raphael Lemkin, 1944] —**gen/o·cid/al**, *adj.*

Gen·o·ese (jĕn/ō ēz/, -ēs/), *adj., n.,* pl. **-ese.** —*adj.* 1. of or pertaining to Genoa. —*n.* 2. a native or inhabitant of Genoa.

gen·o·type (jĕn/ə tīp/), *n. Genetics.* 1. the fundamental hereditary constitution of an organism. 2. its breeding formula of genes. 3. a group of organisms with a common heredity. [f. Gk. *gėno(s)* origin, race + -TYPE]

-genous, an adjective suffix derived from nouns in **-gen** and **-geny.** [f. -GEN + -OUS] —**gen·o·typ·ic** (jĕn/ə tĭp/ĭk), *adj.* —**gen/o·typ/i·cal·ly**, *adv.*

gen·re (zhän/r), *n.* 1. genus; kind; sort; style. 2. the category of subject matter, as in painting, that represents scenes from ordinary life (as distinguished from landscapes, etc.). [t. F: kind. See GENDER]

gen·ro (gĕn/rō/), *n., pl.* **-ros.** See **elder statesman.** [t. Jap.: old men]

gens (jĕnz), *n., pl.* **gentes** (jĕn/tēz). 1. a group of families in ancient Rome claiming descent from a common ancestor and united by a common name and common religious rites. 2. *Anthropol.* a patrilineal descent group. [t. L: also race, people]

Gen·san (gĕn/sän/), *n.* a seaport in E Korea. 79,320 (1940). Japanese, **Wŏnsan.**

Gen·ser·ic (jĕn/sər ĭk, gĕn/-), *n.* A.D. c390–477, king of the Vandals, conqueror in northern Africa and Italy.

gent (jĕnt), *n.* (in humorous or vulgar use) gentleman.

Gent (кнĕnt), *n.* Flemish name of **Ghent.**

Gent., gentleman; gentlemen. Also, **gent.**

gen·teel (jĕn tēl/), *adj.* 1. belonging or suited to polite society. 2. well-bred or refined; polite; elegant; stylish. 3. affected in manner. [t. F: m. *gentil*. See GENTLE] —**gen·teel/ly**, *adv.* —**gen·teel/ness**, *n.*

gen·tian (jĕn/shən), *n.* 1. any plant of the large genus *Gentiana*, comprising herbs having commonly blue flowers, less frequently yellow, white, or red; esp, *G. crinita* (one of the *fringed gentians*), of eastern North America, with blue, delicately fringed corolla, and *G. lutea*, a yellow-flowered European species. 2. any of various plants resembling the gentian. 3. the root of *G. lutea*, a prep-

aration of it, used as a stomachic and tonic. [ME *gencian*, t. L: m. s. *gentiana*; said to be named after *Gentius*, an Illyrian king]

gen·ti·a·na·ceous (jĕn/shĭ ə nā/shəs), *adj.* belonging to the *Gentianaceae*, or gentian family of plants.

gentian violet, crystal violet.

gen·tile (jĕn/tīl), *adj.* 1. of or pertaining to any people not Jewish. 2. Christian as distinguished from Jews. 3. heathen or pagan. 4. (of a linguistic expression) expressing nationality or local extractions. —*n.* 5. a person belonging to a non-Jewish nation, esp. a Christian. 6. (among Mormons) one not a Mormon. 7. a heathen or pagan. Also, **Gen/tile.** [ME *gentil*, t. L: s. *gentīlis* belonging to a people, national, LL foreign]

gen·til·i·ty (jĕn tĭl/ə tĭ), *n., pl.* **-ties.** 1. superior refinement or elegance, possessed or affected. 2. (*usually pl.*) an instance of this. 3. gentle birth.

gen·tle (jĕn/təl), *adj.,* **-tler, -tlest,** *v.,* **-tled, -tling.** —*adj.* 1. mild, kindly, or amiable: *gentle words.* 2. not severe, rough, or violent: *a gentle wind, a gentle tap.* 3. moderate; gradual: *gentle heat, a gentle slope.* 4. of good birth or family; wellborn. 5. characteristic of good birth; honorable; respectable. 6. easily handled or managed: *a gentle animal.* 7. soft or low: *a gentle sound.* 8. polite; refined. 9. *Archaic.* noble; chivalrous: *a gentle knight.* —*v.t.* 10. *Colloq.* to tame; render tractable. 11. *Rare.* to mollify (a person). 12. *Obs.* to ennoble; dignify. [ME *gentil*, t. OF: of good family, noble, excellent, g. L *gentīlis*. See GENTILE] —**gen/tle·ness,** *n.* —**gen/tly**, *adv.*
—**Syn.** 1. soft, bland, peaceful, pacific, soothing; kind, tender, humane, lenient, merciful. GENTLE, MEEK, MILD, refer to an absence of bad temper or belligerence. GENTLE has reference esp. to disposition and behavior, and often suggests a deliberate or voluntary kindness or forbearance in dealing with others: *a gentle pat, gentle with children.* MEEK implies a submissive spirit, and may even indicate undue submission in the face of insult or injustice: *meek and even servile or weak.* MILD suggests absence of harshness or severity, rather because of natural character or temperament than conscious choice: *a mild rebuke, a mild manner.* —**Ant.** 1. arrogant.

gentle breeze, *Meteorol.* a wind of Beaufort scale #3, i.e. one within the range of 8–12 miles per hour.

gen·tle·folk (jĕn/təl fōk/), *n.pl.* persons of good family and breeding. Also, **gen/tle·folks/.**

gen·tle·man (jĕn/təl mən), *n., pl.* **-men.** 1. a man of good breeding, education, and manners. 2. (as a polite form of speech) any man. 3. a male personal servant, or valet, esp. of a man of social position. 4. a man of good or gentle birth. 5. *Hist.* a man above the social rank of yeoman. —**gen/tle·man·like/,** *adj.*

gen·tle·man-at-arms (jĕn/təl mən ət ärmz/), *n., pl.* **gentlemen-at-arms.** (in England) one of a guard of forty gentlemen with their officers who attend the sovereign on state occasions.

gen·tle·man-com·mon·er (jĕn/təl mən kŏm/ən ər), *n., pl.* **gentlemen-commoners.** a member of a class of commoners enjoying special privileges, formerly but no longer, at Oxford University.

gen·tle·man·ly (jĕn/təl mən lĭ), *adj.* like or befitting a gentleman; well-bred. —**gen/tle·man·li·ness,** *n.*

gentlemen's agreement, an agreement binding as a matter of honor alone, not enforceable at law.

gentle reader, courteous or kind reader: used in writing by the author in addressing the reader.

gentle sex, women.

gen·tle·wom·an (jĕn/təl wŏŏm/ən), *n., pl.* **-women.** 1. a woman of good family or breeding; a lady. 2. a woman who attends upon a lady of rank. —**gen/tle·wom/an·ly,** *adj.* —**gen/tle·wom/an·li·ness,** *n.*

gen·try (jĕn/trĭ), *n.* 1. wellborn and well-bred people. 2. (in England) the upper middle class. 3. (in humorous use) people; folks. [ME, f. *gent* noble + -RY]

ge·nu (jē/nū, -nōō), *n., pl.* **genua** (jĕn/yŏŏ ə). *Anat., Zool.* 1. the knee. 2. a kneelike part or bend. [L]

gen·u·flect (jĕn/yŏŏ flĕkt/), *v.i.* to bend the knee in reverence. [t. ML: s. *genūflectere*, f. L *genū* knee + *flectere* bend] —**gen/u·flec/tor,** *n.*

gen·u·flec·tion (jĕn/yŏŏ flĕk/shən), *n.* act of bending the knee or knees in worship. Also, *esp. Brit.*, **gen/u·flex/ion.** [t. ML: m. s. *genūflexio*, der. ML *genūflectere* bend the knee]

gen·u·ine (jĕn/yŏŏ ĭn), *adj.* 1. being truly such; real; authentic: *genuine regret, genuine worth.* 2. properly so called: *genuine leprosy.* 3. sincere; free from pretense or affectation: *a genuine person.* 4. proceeding from the original stock; pure in breed: *a genuine Celtic people.* [t. L: m. s. *genuīnus* native, natural, authentic, genuine] —**gen/u·ine·ly,** *adv.* —**gen/u·ine·ness,** *n.*

ge·nus (jē/nəs), *n., pl.* **genera** (jĕn/ərə), **genuses.** 1. a kind; sort; class. 2. *Biol.* the usual major subdivision of a family or subfamily, usually consisting of more than one species, essentially very similar to one another and regarded as phylogenetically very closely related. The genus designation is the first part of the scientific name of a species, as *Lynx canadensis*, the Canadian lynx. 3. *Logic.* a class or group of individuals including subordinate groups called *species*. [t. L: race, stock, kind, sort, gender (c. Gk. *gėnos*)]

-geny, a suffix meaning "origin," as in *phylogeny*. [t. Gk.: m. s. *-geneia*, der. *-genēs* born, produced. See -GEN]

geo-, a word element meaning "the earth," as in *geocentric.* [t. Gk., comb. form of *gē*]

---

b., blend of, blended; c., cognate with; d., dialect, dialectal; der., derived from; f., formed from; g., going back to; m., modification of; r., replacing; s., stem of; t., taken from; ?, perhaps. See the full key on inside cover.

Geo., George.

ge·o·cen·tric (jē′ō sĕn′trĭk), *adj.* **1.** *Astron.* as viewed or measured from the center of the earth: *the geocentric altitude of a star.* **2.** having or representing the earth as a center: *a geocentric theory of the universe.* Also, **ge′o·cen′tri·cal.** —**ge′o·cen′tri·cal·ly,** *adv.*

geocentric parallax. See **parallax** (def. 2).

ge·o·chem·is·try (jē′ō kĕm′ĭs trĭ), *n.* the science dealing with the chemical changes in, and the composition of, the earth's crust. —**ge·o·chem·i·cal** (jē′ō-kĕm′ə kəl), *adj.*

geod., **1.** geodesy. **2.** geodetic.

ge·ode (jē′ōd), *n.* *Geol.* a hollow concretionary or nodular stone frequently lined with crystals. [t. F, t. L: m. s. *geōdes* precious stone, t. Gk.: adj., earthlike]

ge·o·des·ic (jē′ə dĕs′ĭk, -dē′sĭk), *adj.* **1.** Also, **ge′o·des′i·cal.** pertaining to the geometry of curved surfaces, in which geodesic lines take the place of the straight lines of plane geometry. —*n.* **2.** a geodesic line.

geodesic line, *Math.* the shortest line lying on a given surface and connecting two given points.

ge·od·e·sy (jĭ ŏd′ə sĭ), *n.* that branch of applied mathematics which determines the shape and area of large tracts of country, the exact position of geographical points, and the curvature, shape, and dimensions of the earth. Also, **ge·o·det·ics** (jē′ə dĕt′ĭks). [t. NL: m. s. *geodaesia,* t. Gk.: m. *geōdaisía* art of mensuration] —**ge·od′e·sist,** *n.*

ge·o·det·ic (jē′ə dĕt′ĭk), *adj.* **1.** pertaining to geodesy. **2.** geodesic. Also, **ge′o·det′i·cal.** —**ge′o·det′i·cal·ly,** *adv.*

Geof·frey of Monmouth (jĕf′rĭ), 1100?–1154, British chronicler.

geog., **1.** geographer. **2.** geographic; geographical. **3.** geography.

ge·og·no·sy (jĭ ŏg′nə sĭ), *n.* that branch of geology which treats of the constituent parts of the earth, its envelope of air and water, its crust, and the condition of its interior. [f. GEO- + m. s. Gk. *-gnōsía* knowledge]

ge·og·ra·pher (jĭ ŏg′rə fər), *n.* one who specializes in the study and writing of geography.

ge·o·graph·i·cal (jē′ə grăf′ə kəl), *adj.* **1.** of or pertaining to geography. **2.** referring to or characteristic of a certain locality, esp. in reference to its location in relation to other places. Also, **ge′o·graph′ic.** —**ge′o·graph′i·cal·ly,** *adv.*

geographical mile, mile (def. 16).

geographic determinism, *Sociol.* the doctrine which regards geographical conditions as the determining or molding agency of group life.

geographic environment, *Sociol.* the entire natural surroundings of mankind, independent of his activity but underlying and conditioning it.

ge·og·ra·phy (jĭ ŏg′rə fĭ), *n.,* *pl.* **-phies.** **1.** the study of the areal differentiation of the earth surface, as shown in the character, arrangement, and interrelations over the world of elements such as climate, relief soil, vegetation, population, land use, industries, or states, and of the unit areas formed by the complex of these individual elements. **2.** the topographical features of a region, usually of the earth, but sometimes of Mars, the moon, etc. [t. L: m. s. *geōgraphía,* t. Gk.]

ge·oid (jē′oid), *n.* **1.** an imaginary surface which coincides with the mean sea level over the ocean and its extension under the continents. **2.** the geometrical figure formed by this surface, an ellipsoid flattened at the poles. [t. Gk.: m.s. *geōeidḗs* earthlike]

geol., **1.** geologic; geological. **2.** geologist. **3.** geology.

ge·o·log·ic (jē′ə lŏj′ĭk), *adj.* of or pertaining to geology. Also, **ge′o·log′i·cal.** —**ge′o·log′i·cal·ly,** *adv.*

ge·ol·o·gize (jĭ ŏl′ə jīz′), *v.,* **-gized, -gizing.** —*v.i.* **1.** to study geology. —*v.t.* **2.** to examine geologically.

ge·ol·o·gy (jĭ ŏl′ə jĭ), *n.,* *pl.* **-gies.** the science which treats of the earth, the rocks of which it is composed, and the changes which it has undergone or is undergoing. [t. NL: m. s. *geōlogia.* See GEO-, -LOGY] —**ge·ol′o·gist,** *n.*

geom., **1.** geometric. **2.** geometrical. **3.** geometry.

ge·o·mag·net·ic (jē′ō măg nĕt′ĭk), *adj.* of or pertaining to terrestrial magnetism.

ge·o·man·cer (jē′ə măn′sər), *n.* one versed in or practicing geomancy.

ge·o·man·cy (jē′ə măn′sĭ), *n.* divination by means of the figure made by a handful of earth thrown down at random, or, by figures or lines formed by a number of dots made at random. [ME *geomancie,* t. ML: m. *geōmantia,* f. Gk. (see GEO-, -MANCY)]

ge·om·e·ter (jĭ ŏm′ə tər), *n.* geometrician. [t. L: m. s. *geōmetra, geōmetrēs,* t. Gk.: (m.) *geōmétrēs* land measurer, geometer]

ge·o·met·ric (jē′ə mĕt′rĭk), *adj.* **1.** of or pertaining to geometry; according to the principles of geometry. **2.** resembling or employing the lines or figures in geometry. **3.** of or pertaining to painting, sculpture, or ornamentation of predominantly geometrical characteristics or figures. Also, **ge′o·met′ri·cal,** —**ge′o·met′-ri·cal·ly,** *adv.*

ge·om·e·tri·cian (jĭ ŏm′ə trĭsh′ən, jē′ə mə-), *n.* an expert in geometry.

geometric mean, *Math.* the means of n positive numbers obtained by taking the n-th root of the product of the numbers: *the geometric mean of 6 and 24 is 12.*

geometric progression, *Math.* a sequence of

terms in which the ratio of any term to its predecessor is a constant; e.g., 1, 3, 9, 27, 81 and 2187; 144, 12, 1, $^1/_{12}$.

geometric ratio, *Math.* the ratio of consecutive terms in a geometric progression.

ge·om·e·trid (jĭ ŏm′ə trĭd), *adj.* **1.** of or relating to the moths of the family *Geometridae,* the larvae of which are called measuring worms. —*n.* **2.** a geometrid moth. [t. NL: s. *Geometridae,* der. L *geōmetra* GEOMETER]

Geometrid
A, Larva; B, Moth
(Slightly enlarged)

ge·om·e·trize (jĭ ŏm′ə trīz′), *v.,* **-trized, -trizing.** —*v.i.* **1.** to work by geometrical methods. —*v.t.* **2.** to put into geometric form.

ge·om·e·try (jĭ ŏm′ə trĭ), *n.* that branch of mathematics which deduces the properties of figures in space from their defining conditions. by means of assumed properties of space. [ME *geometrie,* t. L: m. *geōmetria,* t. Gk.]

ge·o·mor·phic (jē′ə môr′fĭk), *adj.* **1.** of or pertaining to the figure of the earth, or the forms of its surface. **2.** resembling the earth in form.

ge·o·mor·phol·o·gy (jē′ə môr fŏl′ə jĭ), *n.* the study of the characteristics, origin, and development of land forms.

ge·oph·a·gy (jĭ ŏf′ə jĭ), *n.* the practice of eating earthy matter, esp. clay or chalk. [f. GEO- + -PHAGY]

ge·oph·i·lous (jĭ ŏf′ə ləs), *adj.* *Bot., Zool.* terrestrial, as certain snails, or any plant fruiting underground.

ge·o·phys·ics (jē′ō fĭz′ĭks), *n.* the physics of the earth, dealing esp. with the study of inaccessible portions of the earth by instruments and apparatus such as the torsion balance, seismograph, and magnetometer. —**ge′o·phys′i·cal,** *adj.* —**ge′o·phys′i·cist,** *n.*

ge·o·phyte (jē′ə fīt′), *n.* *Bot.* a plant with underground buds.

ge·o·pol·i·tics (jē′ō pŏl′ə tĭks), *n.* the application of political and economic geography to the external political problems of states, notably problems of national power, frontiers, and possibilities for expansion.

ge·o·pon·ic (jē′ə pŏn′ĭk), *adj.* of or pertaining to tillage or agriculture; agricultural. [t. Gk.: m. s. *geōponikós*]

ge·o·pon·ics (jē′ə pŏn′ĭks), *n.* the art or science of agriculture.

ge·o·ram·a (jē′ō răm′ə, -rä′mə), *n.* a large hollow globe on the inside of which is depicted a map of the earth's surface, to be viewed by a spectator within the globe. [t. F, f. Gk.: *gê* earth + *(h)órama* view]

George (jôrj), *n.* **1.** David Lloyd. See Lloyd George. **2. Henry,** 1839–97, U.S. economist, advocate of a single tax. **3. Saint,** died A.D. 303? Christian martyr, patron saint of England. **4. Lake,** a lake in E New York. "Lake Horicon" of Cooper's novels. 36 mi. long.

George I, **1.** 1660–1727, king of England, 1714–27; first king of the House of Hanover. **2.** 1845–1913, king of Greece, 1863–1913.

George II, **1.** 1683–1760, king of England, 1727–60 (son of George I). **2.** 1890–1947, king of Greece, 1922–1923 and 1935–47.

George III, 1738–1820, king of England, 1760–1820 (grandson of George II).

George IV, 1762–1830, king of England, 1820–30 (son of George III).

George V, 1865–1936, king of England, 1910–36 (son of Edward VII).

George VI, 1895–1952, king of England, 1936–1952 (second son of George V; brother of Edward VIII).

George·town (jôrj′toun′), *n.* a seaport in and the capital of British Guiana. 38,946 (1931).

George Town, a seaport in and the capital of the British settlement of Penang. 149,408 (1931). Also, **Georgetown** or **Penang.**

Geor·gette (jôr jĕt′), *n.* sheer silk or rayon crepe of dull texture. Also, **Georgette crepe.** [named after Mme. *Georgette,* French modiste]

Geor·gia (jôr′jə), *n.* **1.** a State in the SE United States. 3,444,578 pop. (1950); 58,876 sq. mi. *Cap.:* Atlanta. *Abbr.:* Ga. **2.** Official name, **Georgian Soviet Socialist Republic.** a constituent republic of the Soviet Union in Caucasia, bordering on the Black Sea: it was an independent kingdom for ab. 2000 years. 3,542,289 pop. (1939); ab. 26,800 sq. mi. *Cap.:* Tiflis. **3. Strait of,** an inlet of the Pacific in SW Canada between Vancouver Island and the mainland of British Columbia.

Georgia (def. 2)

Geor·gian (jôr′jən), *adj.* **1.** pertaining to the four Georges, kings of England (1714–1830), or the period of their reigns. **2.** pertaining to George V (1910–36), or the period of his reign. **3.** of or pertaining to the State of Georgia in the U.S. **4.** pertaining to Georgia in the Soviet Union. —*n.* **5.** a person, esp. a writer, of either of the Georgian periods in England. **6.** the styles or character of a Georgian period. **7.** a native or inhabitant of the State of Georgia. **8.** a native or inhabitant of of Georgia in the Soviet Union. **9.** the most important South Caucasian language.

Geor·gian Bay, the NE part of Lake Huron, in Ontario, Canada. ab. 6000 sq. mi.

Georgia pine, longleaf pine.

geor·gic (jôr′jĭk), *adj.* **1.** agricultural. —*n.* **2.** a poem on agricultural matters. [t. L: s. *geōrgicus* agricultural, t. Gk.: m. *geōrgikós*]

ge·o·syn·cli·nal (jē′ō sĭn klī′nəl), *adj. Geol.* **1.** pertaining to a synclinal fold which involves a relatively large part of the earth's surface. —*n.* **2.** a geosyncline.

ge·o·syn·cline (jē′ō sĭn′klīn), *n. Geol.* a portion of the earth's crust subjected to downward warping during a large fraction of geologic time; a geosynclinal fold.

ge·o·tax·is (jē′ō tăk′sĭs), *n. Biol.* a movement of an organism toward or away from a gravitational force. [f. GEO- + -TAXIS]

ge·o·tec·ton·ic (jē′ō tĕk tŏn′ĭk), *adj.* pertaining to the structure of the earth's crust or to the arrangement and form of its constituents.

ge·o·therm·al (jē′ō thûr′məl), *adj.* of or pertaining to the internal heat of the earth.

ge·o·trop·ic (jē′ə trŏp′ĭk), *adj. Biol.* taking a particular direction with reference to the earth: **a.** positively geotropic, directed downward. **b.** negatively geotropic, directed upward. **c.** transversely geotropic, directed horizontally. —**ge′o·trop′i·cal·ly,** *adv.*

ge·ot·ro·pism (jĭ ŏt′rə pĭz′əm), *n. Biol.* a tropism oriented with respect to gravitation, as the direction of growth of plants or the ability of some animals to avoid an upside-down position in the air.

Ger., **1.** German. **2.** Germany.

ger., **1.** gerund. **2.** gerundive.

ge·rah (gē′rə), *n.* a Hebrew weight and coin, equal to $^{1}/_{20}$ of a shekel. [t. Heb.: m. *gērāh*, t. Akkadian: m. *girū*]

Ge·raint (jĭ rānt′), *n. Arthurian Romance.* one of the knights of the Round Table, husband of Enid.

ge·ra·ni·a·ceous (jĭ rā′nĭ ā′shəs), *adj.* belonging to the *Geraniaceae,* or geranium family of plants.

ge·ra·ni·al (jĭ rā′nĭ əl), *n. Chem.* citral.

ge·ra·ni·um (jĭ rā′nĭ əm), *n.* **1.** any of the plants of the genus *Geranium,* most of which have pink or purple flowers, and some of which, as *G. maculatum,* have an astringent root used in medicine; crane's-bill. **2.** a plant of the allied genus *Pelargonium,* of which many species are well known in cultivation for their showy flowers (as the **scarlet geraniums**) or their fragrant leaves (as the **rose geraniums**). [t. L, t. Gk.: m. *gerānion* crane's-bill]

ger·a·tol·o·gy (jĕr′ə tŏl′ə jĭ), *n.* the study of the decline of life, as in old age or in animals approaching extinction. [f. s. Gk. *gēras* old age + -(o)LOGY]

ger·bil (jûr′bĭl), *n.* any of numerous jerboalike rodents (genus *Gerbillus,* etc.) of Asia, Africa, and southern Russia, belonging to the mouse family, and forming the subfamily *Gerbillinae.* Also, **ger′bille.** [t. F: m. *gerbille,* t. NL: m. s. *gerbillus,* dim. of *gerbo* JERBOA]

ge·rent (jĭr′ənt), *n.* a ruling power; manager. [t. L: s. *gerens,* ppr., bearing, conducting, managing]

ger·fal·con (jûr′fôl′kən, -fŏ′/-), *n.* any of various large arctic and subarctic falcons, as the **white gerfalcon,** *Falco rusticolus obsoletus.* Also, **gyrfalcon.** [ME, t. OF: m. *gerfaucon;* of Gmc. orig.]

ger·i·at·rics (jĕr′ĭ ăt′rĭks), *n.* the science of the medical and hygienic care of, or the diseases of, aged persons. —**ger·i·a·tri·cian** (jĕr′ĭ ə trĭsh′ən), **ger′i·at′rist,** *n.*

Gerfalcon,
Falco rusticolus
(21 in. long)

germ (jûrm), *n.* **1.** a microörganism, esp. when disease-producing; microbe. **2.** that from which anything springs as if from a seed; **3.** *Embryol.* **a.** a bud, offshoot or seed. **b.** the rudiment of a living organism; an embryo in its early stages. **4.** *Biol.* the initial stage in development or evolution, as a germ cell or ancestral form. [t. F: m. *germe,* g. L *germen* sprout] —**germ′-less,** *adj.*

Ger·man (jûr′mən), *adj.* **1.** of or pertaining to Germany, its inhabitants, or their language. —*n.* **2.** a native or inhabitant of Germany; a High German or a Low German. **3.** a Germanic language, the language of Germany and Austria and an official language of Switzerland. **4.** *Ling.* High German. **5.** (*l.c.*) an elaborate kind of dance; cotillion. **6.** (*l.c.*) a party at which only the german is danced. [t. L: s. *Germānus;* orig. uncert.]

ger·man (jûr′mən), *adj.* **1.** sprung from the same father and mother (always placed after the noun): *a brother-german.* **2.** sprung from the brother or sister of one's father or mother, or from brothers or sisters: *a cousin-german.* **3.** germane. [t. L: s. *germānus* having the same father (and mother); r. ME *germain,* t. OF]

Ger·man-A·mer·i·can (jûr′mən ə mĕr′ə kən), *adj.* **1.** pertaining to Americans of German birth or descent. —*n.* **2.** an American of German birth or descent.

German Baptist Brethren. See Dunker.

ger·man·der (jər măn′dər), *n.* **1.** any of the herbs or shrubs constituting the labiate genus *Teucrium,* as *T. Chamaedrys,* a purple-flowered European species, and *T. canadense,* an American species. **2.** a species of speedwell (**germander speedwell**). See speedwell. [t. ML:

m. s. *germandra,* t. LGk.: m. *chamándra,* alter. of Gk. *chamaídrys,* lit., ground oak]

ger·mane (jər mān′), *adj.* closely related; pertinent: *a remark germane to the question.* [var. of GERMAN]

German East Africa, a former German territory in E Africa, now divided into trusteeships of Britain (Tanganyika Territory) and Belgium (Ruanda-Urundi).

Ger·man·ic (jər măn′ĭk), *adj.* **1.** pertaining to the Teutonic race or any of the peoples belonging to it, or to the group of languages spoken by these peoples; Teutonic. **2.** of or pertaining to the Germans; German. —*n.* **3.** a group of Indo-European languages, including English, German, Dutch, and the Scandinavian languages. [t. L: s. *Germānicus*]

ger·man·ic (jər măn′ĭk), *adj. Chem.* of or containing germanium, esp. in the tetravalent state (Ge +4). [f. GERMAN(IUM) + -IC]

Ger·man·i·cus Caesar (jər măn′ĭ kəs), 15 B.C.–A.D. 19, Roman general.

Ger·man·ism (jûr′mə nĭz′əm), *n.* **1.** a German characteristic, usage, or idiom. **2.** German modes of thought, action, etc. **3.** attachment to what is German.

ger·ma·ni·um (jər mā′nĭ əm), *n. Chem.* a rare metallic element, normally tetravalent, with a grayish-white color. *Symbol:* Ge; *at. wt.:* 72.6; *at. no.:* 32; *sp. gr.:* 5.36 at 20°C. [NL, der. L *Germānia* country of the Germans]

Ger·man·ize (jûr′mə nīz′), *v.t.* -ized, -izing. **1.** to make German in character, sentiment, etc. **2.** to translate into German. —*v.i.* **3.** to become German in habits, sympathies, etc. —**Ger′man·i·za′tion,** *n.*

German measles, *Pathol.* a contagious disease, usually mild, accompanied by fever, often some sore throat, and a rash resembling that of scarlet fever; rubella.

German Ocean, the North Sea.

ger·man·ous (jər măn′əs), *adj. Chem.* containing divalent germanium (Ge+2).

German shepherd dog, police dog (def. 1).

German silver, a white alloy of copper, zinc, and nickel, used for making utensils, drawing instruments, wire of high electrical resistance, etc.

German Southwest Africa, a former German protectorate, now under mandate to the Union of South Africa. See South-West Africa.

German text, *Print.* the modern German type.

Ger·man·town (jûr′mən toun′), *n.* the NW part of Philadelphia, Pa.: American defeat by British, 1777.

Ger·ma·ny (jûr′mə nĭ), *n.* a country in central Europe. 65,285,900 pop. (est. 1945); 137,975 sq. mi. Now divided into four zones of occupation: **British Zone,** 23,026,000 pop. (est. 1946); 37,877 sq. mi.; **French Zone,** 5,787,081 pop. (est. 1946); 16,491 sq. mi.; **Russian Zone,** 19,693,600 pop. (est. 1945); 42,235 sq. mi.; **U.S. Zone,** 16,980,763 pop. (est. 1947); 41,371 sq. mi. *Cap.:* Berlin. The British, French, and U.S. zones were combined in 1949 as the **Federal Republic of Germany** (capital: Bonn). German, **Deutschland.** Former official name, **Deutsches Reich.**

germ cell, *Biol.* the sexual reproductive cell at any stage from the primordial cell to the mature gamete.

ger·mi·cide (jûr′mə sĭd′), *n.* an agent that kills germs or microörganisms. [f. GERM + -(I)CIDE[1]] —**ger′mi·cid′al,** *adj.*

ger·mi·nal (jûr′mə nəl), *adj.* **1.** pertaining to a germ or germs. **2.** of the nature of a germ or germ cell. **3.** in the earliest stage of development: *germinal ideas.*

germinal disk, *Embryol.* blastodisc.

germinal vesicle, *Embryol.* the large, vesicular nucleus of an ovum before the polar bodies are formed.

ger·mi·nant (jûr′mə nənt), *adj.* germinating.

ger·mi·nate (jûr′mə nāt′), *v.,* -nated, -nating. —*v.i.* **1.** to begin to grow or develop. **2.** *Bot.* **a.** to develop into a plant or individual, as a seed, or as a spore, bulb, or the like. **b.** to sprout; put forth shoots. —*v.t.* **3.** to cause to develop; produce. [t. L: m.s. *germinātus,* pp.] —**ger′mi·na′tion,** *n.* —**ger′mi·na′tor,** *n.*

ger·mi·na·tive (jûr′mə nā′tĭv), *adj.* capable of germinating or developing; pertaining to germination.

Ger·mis·ton (jûr′mĭs tən), *n.* a city in the NE Union of South Africa, in Transvaal. 128,971 (1946).

germ layer, one of the three primary embryonic cell layers, i.e., ectoderm, endoderm, and mesoderm.

germ plasm, the protoplasm of the germ cells containing the units of heredity (chromosomes and genes).

germ theory, 1. *Biol.* the theory that living matter cannot be produced by evolution or development from nonliving matter, but is necessarily produced from germs or seeds; the doctrine of biogenesis. **2.** *Pathol.* the theory that infectious diseases, etc., are due to the agency of germs or microörganisms.

Gé·rôme (zhā rōm′), *n.* Jean Léon (zhän lĕ ôn′), 1824–1904, French painter and sculptor.

Ge·ron·i·mo (jĭ rŏn′ə mō′), *n.* c1834–1909, Apache Indian chief.

ger·on·toc·ra·cy (jĕr′ŏn tŏk′rə sĭ), *n., pl.* -cies. **1.** government by old men. **2.** a governing body consisting of old men. [f. s. Gk. *gérōn* old man + -(o)CRACY]

ger·on·tol·o·gy (jĕr′ŏn tŏl′ə jĭ), *n.* the science that treats of the decline of life.

-gerous, a combining form meaning "bearing" or "producing," as in *setigerous.* [f. L -*ger* bearing + -OUS]

Ger·ry (gĕr′ĭ), *n.* Elbridge (ĕl′brĭj), 1744–1814, vice-president of the U.S., 1813–14.

---

b., blend of, blended; c., cognate with; d., dialect, dialectal; der., derived from; f., formed from; g., going back to; m., modification of; r., replacing; s., stem of; t., taken from; ?, perhaps. See the full key on inside cover.

ger·ry·man·der (gĕr/Ĭmăn/dər, jĕr/-), v.t. **1.** U.S. Pol. to subject (a State, county, etc.) to a gerrymander. **2.** to manipulate unfairly. —n. **3.** U.S.Pol. an arbitrary arrangement of the political divisions of a State, county, etc., made so as to give one party an unfair advantage in elections. [f. Gerry (gov. of Massachusetts, whose party in 1812 redistricted Massachusetts) + (sala)mander (from a fancied resemblance of the map of Essex Co., Mass., to this animal, after the redistricting)]

Gersh·win (gûrsh/wĭn), n. George, 1898–1937, U.S. composer.

ger·und (jĕr/ənd), n. Gram. **1.** (in Latin and some other languages) a derived noun form of verbs, having (in Latin) all case forms but the nominative. Example: Latin dicendī gen., dicendō, dat., abl., dicendum, acc., "saying." No nominative form occurs. **2.** Gram. (sometimes, from similarity of meaning) the English ing-form of a verb (loving) when in nominal function. Hunting and writing are gerunds in the sentences "Hunting is good exercise" and "writing is easy." **3.** (sometimes, in other languages) a form similar to the Latin gerund in meaning or function. [t. LL: m. s. gerundium, der. L gerundum, var. of gerendum, ger. of L gerere bear, conduct] —**ge·run·di·al** (jĬrŭn/dĬəl), adj.

ge·run·dive (jĬrŭn/dĬv), n. **1.** (in Latin) the future passive participle, similar to the gerund in formation. Example: Haec dicendum est "This must be said." —adj. **2.** resembling a gerund. [t. LL: m. s. gerundīvus, der. gerundium GERUND] —**ger·un·di·val** (jĕr/ən dī/vəl), adj. —**ge·run/dive·ly**, adv.

Ge·ry·on (jĬr/Ĭ ən, gĕr/Ĭ-), n. Class. Legend. a monster king of Cadiz, whose cattle Hercules carried off.

ges·so (jĕs/ō), n. **1.** gypsum, or plaster of Paris, prepared with glue for use as a surface for painting. **2.** any plasterlike preparation to fit a surface for painting, gilding, etc. **3.** a prepared surface of plaster or plasterlike material for painting, etc. [t. It., g. L gypsum GYPSUM]

gest (jĕst), n. Archaic. **1.** a metrical romance or history. **2.** a story or tale. **3.** a deed or exploit. Also, **geste**. [ME geste, t. OF, t. L: m. s. gesta deeds, prop. pp. neut. pl.]

gest., (Ger. gestorben) died; deceased.

Ge·stalt (gəshtält/), n., pl. **-stalten** (-shtäl/tən). Psychol. an organized configuration or pattern of experiences or of acts: the Gestalt of a melody is distinct from the separate tones. [t. G: form]

Gestalt psychology, a school of psychology which believes that experiences and conduct do not occur through the summation of reflexes or other individual elements but through configurations called Gestalten, which operate individually or mutually interact.

Ge·sta·po (gəstä/pō; Ger. -shtä/-), n. Secret State Police of Nazi Germany. [G: g(eheime) Sta(ats) po(lizei)]

Ges·ta Ro·ma·no·rum (jĕs/tə rō/mə nōr/əm), a popular collection of stories in Latin, compiled late in the 13th century.

ges·tate (jĕs/tāt), v.t., **-tated, -tating.** to carry in the womb during the period from conception to delivery. [t. L: m. s. gestātus, pp., carried]

ges·ta·tion (jĕs tā/shən), n. act or period of gestating. [t. L: s. gestātio a carrying]

ges·tic (jĕs/tĭk), adj. pertaining to bodily motions, esp. dancing. Also, **ges/ti·cal.** [f. s. L gestus gesture + -IC]

ges·tic·u·late (jĕs tĭk/yə lāt/), v.i., **-lated, -lating. 1.** to make or use gestures, esp. in an animated or excited manner with or instead of speech. —v.t. **2.** to express by gesturing. [t. L: m.s. gesticulātus, pp., having made mimic gestures] —**ges·tic/u·la/tor,** n.

ges·tic·u·la·tion (jĕs tĭk/yə lā/shən), n. **1.** act of gesticulating. **2.** an animated or excited gesture.

ges·tic·u·la·to·ry (jĕs tĭk/yə lə tōr/Ĭ), adj. characterized by or making gesticulations. Also, **ges·tic/u·la/tive.**

ges·ture (jĕs/chər), n., v., **-tured, -turing.** —n. **1.** movement of the body, head, arms, hands, or face expressive of an idea or an emotion: the gestures of an orator, a gesture of impatience. **2.** any action or proceeding intended for effect or as a formality; demonstration: a gesture of friendship. —v.i. **3.** to make or use gestures. —v.t. **4.** to express by gestures. [ME, t. ML: m. gestūra, der. L gerere bear, conduct] —**ges/tur·er,** n.

Ge·sund·heit (gə zŏŏnt/hīt), n. German. soundness; health (used after a person has sneezed or as a toast).

get (gĕt), v., **got** or (Archaic) **gat; got** or **gotten; getting;** n. —v.t. **1.** to obtain, gain, or acquire by any means: to get favor by service, get a good price. **2.** to obtain by labor; earn: to get one's living, get coal. **3.** to acquire a mental grasp or command of; learn: get a lesson. **4.** to cause to be or do: to get a friend appointed, get one's hair cut, get the fire to burn. **5.** to capture; seize upon. **6.** Colloq. to be under an obligation to; be obliged to: you have got to go. **7.** to prevail on: get him to speak. **8.** to prepare; get ready: to get dinner. **9.** to beget (now usually of animals). **10.** Slang. to hit: the bullet got him in the leg. **11.** Colloq. to kill. **12.** Colloq. to puzzle; irritate: that gets me. **13.** Chiefly U.S. Colloq. to understand: I get you. —v.i. **14.** to come to or arrive: to get home. **15.** to become; grow: to get tired. **16.** to succeed in coming or going (fol. by away, in, into, out, over, through, etc.). **17.** to earn money; gain. **18.** to bribe; influence by surreptitious means (fol. by at). **19.** Some special verb phrases are:

get across, to make understood.
get along, 1. to go; go off. **2.** See **get on.**

get at, to bribe; influence by surreptitious means.
get even with, to square accounts with.
get off, 1. to escape; evade consequences. **2.** to start a journey; leave. **3.** to dismount from (a horse or train). **4.** to say or express (a joke).
get on or **along, 1.** to make progress; proceed; advance. **2.** to succeed; manage well. **3.** to agree with a person; be congenial.
get over, 1. to overcome (a difficulty, etc.). **2.** to recover from: to get over a shock or illness.
get round, 1. to outwit. **2.** to cajole.
get up, 1. to arise; sit up or stand. **2.** to rise from bed. **3.** to ascend or mount. **4.** (in the command, "Get up!" to a horse) go! go ahead! go faster! **5.** to prepare, arrange, or organize. **6.** to acquire a knowledge of: to get up a subject. **7.** to do up: to get up the linen. **8.** to produce in a specified style, as a book. **9.** to work up (a feeling, etc.).
—n. **20.** (in some games, such as tennis) a return of a stroke which under normal circumstances would be a point for the opponent. [ME geten, t. Scand.; cf. Icel. geta, c. OE gietan (G -gessen in vergessen forget): akin to L -hendere in prehendere seize, take, and to Gk. chandánein hold, contain] —**get/ta·ble, get/a·ble,** adj. —**get/ter,** n. —**Syn. 1-3.** GET, OBTAIN, ACQUIRE, PROCURE, SECURE imply gaining possession of something. GET may apply to coming into possession in any manner, and either voluntarily or not. OBTAIN suggests putting forth effort to gain possession, and ACQUIRE stresses the possessing after an (often prolonged) effort. PROCURE suggests the method of obtaining as that of search or choice. SECURE, considered in bad taste as a would-be-elegant substitute for GET, is, however, when used with discrimination, a perfectly proper word. It suggests making possession sure and safe, after obtaining something by competition or the like.

get·a·way (gĕt/ə wā/), n. Colloq. **1.** a getting away; an escape. **2.** the start of a race.

Geth·sem·a·ne (gĕth sĕm/ə nĬ), n. **1.** a garden east of Jerusalem, near the brook Kedron: the scene of Christ's agony and betrayal. Matt. 26:36, etc. **2.** (l.c.) a scene or occasion of suffering.

Get·tys·burg (gĕt/Ĭz bûrg/), n. a borough in S Pennsylvania: the Confederate forces were defeated in a crucial battle of the Civil War fought near here. July, 1, 2, and 3, 1863; national cemetery and military park. 7046 (1950).

get·up (gĕt/ŭp/), n. Colloq. **1.** style of production; appearance: getup of a book. **2.** style of dress; costume.

gew·gaw (gū/gô), n. **1.** a bit of gaudy or useless finery. —adj. **2.** showy, but without value.

gey·ser (gī/zər, -sər for 1; gē/zər for 2), n. **1.** a hot spring which intermittently sends up fountainlike jets of water and steam into the air. **2.** Brit. a hot-water heater. [t. Icel.: m. Geysir, i.e. gusher, name of a hot spring in Iceland, der. geysa rush furiously, gush]

gey·ser·ite (gī/zə rīt/), n. a variety of opaline silica deposited about the orifices of geysers and hot springs.

g.gr., great gross.

ghast·ly (găst/lĬ, gäst/-), adj., **-lier, -liest,** adv. —adj. **1.** frightful; dreadful; horrible: a ghastly murder. **2.** deathly pale: a ghastly look. **3.** Colloq. bad; unpleasant; shocking: a ghastly failure. —adv. **4.** in a ghastly manner; horribly. **5.** with a deathlike aspect: ghastly pale. [ME gastly, OE gāstlic spectral, f. gāst spirit + lic -LY] —**ghast/li·ness,** n. —**Syn. 1.** hideous, grisly, gruesome, grim. **2.** deathlike, pallid, cadaverous.

ghat (gôt), n. (in India) **1.** a passage or stairway descending to a river. **2.** a mountain pass. **3.** a mountain range. Also, **ghaut.** [t. Hind.]

Ghats (gôts), n. two low mountain ranges in S India, along the E and W margins of the Deccan plateau: the **Eastern Ghats,** parallel to the coast of the Bay of Bengal, and the **Western Ghats,** bordering on the Arabian Sea.

gha·zi (gä/zē), n., pl. **-zis. 1.** a Mohammedan warrior fighting against non-Mohammedans. **2.** (cap.) a title given in Turkey to a victorious sultan or president. [t. Ar., ppr., of ghazā fight]

ghee (gē), n. (in the East Indies) a kind of liquid butter, clarified by boiling, made from the milk of cows and buffaloes. [t. Hind.: m. ghī]

Ghent (gĕnt), n. a city in NW Belgium: a port at the confluence of the Scheldt and Lys rivers: treaty, 1814. 160,141 (est. 1941). French, **Gand.** Flemish, **Gent.**

gher·kin (gûr/kĭn), n. **1.** the small, immature fruit of some common variety of cucumber, used in pickling. **2.** the small, spiny fruit of a cucurbitaceous vine, Cucumis Anguria, of the West Indies, the southern U.S., etc., used in pickling. **3.** the plant yielding it. [var. of gurchen (t. G), with substitution of -KIN for G dim. -chen. Cf. D gurkje, Pol. ogurek, etc., ult. der. LGk. angoúrion watermelon]

ghet·to (gĕt/ō), n., pl. **ghettos, ghetti** (gĕt/ē). **1.** any quarter inhabited chiefly by Jews. **2.** a quarter in a city in which Jews were formerly required to live. [t. It. (Venetian): b. Heb. ghēt separation and It. ge(t)to foundry (der. getar cast, ult. der. L jacere throw), as name of Jewish quarter in Venice in the 16th cent.]

Ghib·el·line (gĭb′ə lĭn, -lēn′), *n.* **1.** a member of the imperial and aristocratic party of medieval Italy, opposed to the Guelphs. —*adj.* **2.** of or pertaining to the Ghibellines. [t. It.: m. *Ghibellino*, t. G: m. *Waiblingen*, name of an estate belonging to the imperial family]

Ghi·ber·ti (gē bĕr′tē), *n.* **Lorenzo** (lô rĕn′tsō), 1378?–1455, Florentine sculptor.

Ghir·lan·da·io (gēr′län dä′yō), *n.* (*Domenico di Tommaso Curradi di Doffo Bigordi*) 1449–94, Italian painter.

ghost (gōst), *n.* **1.** the soul of a dead person, a disembodied spirit imagined as wandering among or haunting living persons. **2.** a mere shadow or semblance: *ghost of a chance.* **3.** (*cap*). a spiritual being: *Holy Ghost.* **4.** spirit; principle of life. **5.** **give up the ghost,** to die. **6.** *Colloq.* ghost writer. **7.** *Optics.* a bright spot or secondary image, from a defect of the instrument. —*v.t.* **8.** to write for someone else who is publicly known as the author. **9.** to haunt. [ME *goost*, OE *gāst*, c. G *geist* spirit. Cf. GHASTLY.] —**ghost′like′,** *adj.*
—**Syn. 1.** apparition, phantom, phantasm, wraith, revenant; shade, spook. GHOST, SPECTER, SPIRIT all refer to the disembodied soul of a person. A GHOST is the soul or spirit of a deceased person, which appears or otherwise makes its presence known to man: *the ghost of a drowned child.* A SPECTER is a ghost or apparition of more or less weird, unearthly, or terrifying aspect: *a frightening specter.* SPIRIT is often interchangeable with GHOST but may mean a supernatural being, usually with an indication of good or malign intent toward man: *the spirit of a friend, an evil spirit.*

ghost dance, a religious movement of western North American Indian tribes, originating in connection with a Messianic doctrine which was put forth about 1888 and led to serious disturbances in 1890, and which prophesied the return of the dead and the extinction of the whites.

ghost·ly (gōst′lĭ), *adj.,* **-lier, -liest. 1.** of or pertaining to a ghost; spectral; shadowy. **2.** *Archaic or Literary.* spiritual: *ghostly father.* —**ghost′li·ness,** *n.*

ghost writer, one who does literary work for someone else who takes the credit.

ghoul (gōōl), *n.* **1.** an evil demon of Oriental legend, supposed to feed on human beings, and esp. to rob graves, prey on corpses, etc. **2.** anyone who preys upon the dead; body snatcher; grave robber. **3.** one who revels in what is revolting. [t. Ar.: m. *ghūl*] —**ghoul′ish,** *adj.* —**ghoul′ish·ly,** *adv.* —**ghoul′ish·ness,** *n.*

G.H.Q., *Mil.* General Headquarters.

gi·, gill; gills.

G.I., *Colloq.* **1.** an enlisted man of the U.S. Army. **2.** an enlisted man or former enlisted man of any of the U.S. armed services. **3.** *U.S. Army.* government issue. —*attributive.* **4.** of or standardized by the Army: *G.I. shoes.* **5.** according to the letter of military regulations.

gi·ant (jī′ənt), *n.* **1.** one of a race of beings in Greek mythology, of more than human size and strength, who were subdued by the Olympian gods. **2.** an imaginary being of human form but superhuman size, strength, etc. **3.** a person or thing of unusually great size, endowments, importance, etc.: *an intellectual giant.* —*adj.* **4.** gigantic; of extraordinary size: *the giant cactus.* **5.** great or eminent above others. [ME *geant*, t. OF: r. OE *gīgant*, t. L: s. *gigās*, t. Gk.] —**gi·ant·ess** (jī′ən tĭs, -ĕs′), *n. fem.*

gi·ant·ism (jī′ən tĭz′əm), *n. Pathol.* gigantism.

giant panda, panda (def. 2).

giant powder, a form of dynamite composed of nitroglycerin and kieselguhr.

giant star, *Astron.* a star of great luminosity and mass such as Arcturus or Betelgeuse.

giaour (jour), *n.* a Turkish word for an unbeliever or non-Mohammedan, esp. a Christian. [t. Turk.: m. *giaur*, t. Pers.: m. *gaur*, var. of *gabr*]

gib·ber (jĭb′ər, gĭb′-), *v.i.* **1.** to speak inarticulately; chatter. —*n.* **2.** gibbering utterance. [? freq. of obs. *gib* v., caterwaul, behave like a cat; sense devel. and pronunciation influenced by assoc. with *jabber*]

gib·ber·ish (jĭb′ər ĭsh, gĭb′-), *n.* rapid, unintelligible talk. [f. GIBBER + -ISH¹ (modeled on *English*)]

gib·bet (jĭb′ĭt), *n., v.,* **-beted, -beting.** —*n.* **1.** gallows with a projecting arm at the top, from which formerly the bodies of criminals were hung in chains and left suspended after execution. —*v.t.* **2.** to hang on a gibbet. **3.** to put to death by hanging on a gibbet. **4.** to hold up to public scorn. [ME *gibet*, t. OF, appar. dim. of *gibe* staff]

gib·bon (gĭb′ən), *n.* any of the small, slender, long-armed anthropoid apes, genus *Hylobates*, of arboreal habits, found in the East Indies and southern Asia. [t. F, appar. from a dialect of India]

Gib·bon (gĭb′ən), *n.* **Edward,** 1737–94, British historian.

gib·bos·i·ty (gĭ bŏs′ə tĭ), *n., pl.* **-ties. 1.** state of being gibbous. **2.** a protuberance or swelling.

gib·bous (gĭb′əs), *adj.* **1.** humpbacked. **2.** (of a heavenly body) so viewed as to appear convex on both margins, as the moon when more than half-full but less than full. See diag. under **moon.** Also, **gib·bose** (gĭb′ōs). [t. L: m.s. *gibbōsus* humped] —**gib′bous·ly,** *adv.* —**gib′bous·ness,** *n.*

Gibbon. *Hylobates lar* (3½ ft. high)

Gibbs (gĭbz), *n.* **Josiah Willard,** 1839–1903, U.S. mathematical physicist.

gibbs·ite (gĭbz′īt), *n.* a mineral, hydrated aluminum oxide, Al₂O₃·3H₂O, occurring in whitish or grayish crystals and masses, an important constituent of bauxite ore. [named after G. Gibbs, U.S. mineralogist. See -ITE¹]

gibe (jīb), *v.,* **gibed, gibing,** *n.* —*v.i.* **1.** to utter mocking words; scoff; jeer. —*v.t.* **2.** to taunt; deride; flout. —*n.* **3.** a taunting or sarcastic remark. Also, **jibe.** [? t. OF: m.s. *giber*, handle roughly, shake, der. *gibe* staff, bill hook] —**gib′er,** *n.* —**gib′ing·ly,** *adv.*

Gib·e·on (gĭb′ĭ ən), *n.* an ancient town in Palestine, near Jerusalem. Josh. 9:3, etc. See **Gibeonite.**

Gib·e·on·ite (gĭb′ĭ ə nīt′), *n. Bible.* one of the inhabitants of Gibeon, who were condemned by Joshua to be hewers of wood and drawers of water for the Israelites. Joshua 9.

gib·let (jĭb′lĭt), *n.* (*usually pl.*) the heart, liver, or gizzard from a fowl, cooked separately. [ME *gibelet*, t. OF: dish of game]

Gi·bral·tar (jĭ brôl′tər), *n.* **1.** a British crown colony comprising a fortress and seaport located on a narrow promontory near the S tip of Spain. 20,000 pop. (est. 1938); 1⅞ sq. mi. **2. Rock of,** a long, precipitous mountain nearly coextensive with this colony: one of the Pillars of Hercules. 1396 ft. high; 2½ mi. long. **3. Strait of,** a strait between Europe and Africa at the Atlantic entrance to the Mediterranean. 8½–23 mi. wide.

Gib·son (gĭb′sən), *n.* **Charles Dana** (dā′nə), 1867–1944, U.S. artist and illustrator.

gid (gĭd), *n. Vet. Sci.* staggers in sheep, etc., due to infestation of the brain with larvae of the tapeworm, *Multiceps multiceps.* [back formation from GIDDY, adj.]

gid·dy (gĭd′ĭ), *adj.,* **-dier, -diest,** *v.,* **-died, -dying.** —*adj.* **1.** frivolously light; impulsive; flighty: *a giddy mind, a giddy girl.* **2.** affected with vertigo; dizzy. **3.** attended with or causing dizziness: *a giddy climb.* —*v.t., v.i.* **4.** to make or become giddy. [ME *gidy*, OE *gydig* mad, der. *god;* orig. sense presumably godpossessed, in a state of divine frenzy] —**gid′di·ly,** *adv.* —**gid′di·ness,** *n.* —**Syn. 1.** unstable, volatile. **2.** light-headed, vertiginous. —**Ant. 1.** steady, stable.

Gide (zhēd), *n.* **André** (än drĕ′), 1869–1951, French novelist, essayist, and critic.

Gid·e·on (gĭd′ĭ ən), *n. Bible.* Hebrew liberator and religious leader, conqueror of the Midianites and judge in Israel for forty years. Judges 6–8. [var. of *Gedeon* (Septuagint), t. Heb.: m. *Gid′ōn*]

gift (gĭft), *n.* **1.** something given; a present. **2.** act of giving. **3.** the power or right of giving. **4.** a quality, or special ability; natural endowment; talent. —*v.t.* **5.** to present with as a gift; bestow gifts upon; endow with. [ME, t. Scand.; cf. Icel. *gift,* c. OE *gift* payment for a wife (pl., marriage), G *gift* poison, etc.; akin to GIVE, v.] —**Syn. 1.** donation, contribution, offering, benefaction, bounty, boon, largess, alms, gratuity, premium, allowance, subsidy, bequest, legacy. See **present².** **4.** faculty, aptitude, bent, turn, knack.

gift·ed (gĭf′tĭd), *adj.* endowed with natural gifts; talented: *a gifted artist.*

Gi·fu (gē′fōō′), *n.* a city in central Japan, on Honshu island. 148,637 (1946).

gig¹ (gĭg), *n., v.,* **gigged, gigging.** —*n.* **1.** *Naut.* **a.** a long, fast-pulling boat used esp. for racing. **b.** the boat reserved for a ship's captain. **2.** a light, two-wheeled one-horse carriage. —*v.i.* **3.** to ride in a gig. [orig. uncert.]

gig² (gĭg), *n., v.,* **gigged, gigging.** —*n.* **1.** a device, commonly four hooks secured back to back, for dragging through a school of fish to hook them through the body. —*v.t., v.i.* **2.** to catch (fish) with a gig. [short for *fizgig,* t. Sp.: m. *fisga* harpoon]

Gig

gi·gan·te·an (jī′găn tē′ən) *adj.* gigantic. [f. s. L *giganteus* + -AN. See GIANT]

gi·gan·tesque (jī′găn tĕsk′), *adj.* of a gigantic kind; suited to a giant. [t. F, t. It.: m. *gigantesco,* der. *gigante,* t. L: m.s. *gigās* GIANT]

gi·gan·tic (jī găn′tĭk), *adj.* **1.** of, like, or befitting a giant. **2.** very large; huge. [f. s. L *gigās* GIANT + -IC] —**gi·gan′ti·cal·ly,** *adv.* —**gi·gan′tic·ness,** *n.*
—**Syn. 2.** enormous, immense, prodigious, herculean, cyclopean, titanic. GIGANTIC, COLOSSAL, MAMMOTH, MONSTROUS are used of whatever is physically or metaphorically of great magnitude. GIGANTIC refers to the size of a giant: *a gigantic stalk of corn.* COLOSSAL to that of a colossus: *a colossal skeleton of a brontosaurus.* MAMMOTH to that of the animal of that name: *a mammoth jaw of a prehistoric animal.* MONSTROUS means unusual or out of the normal in some striking way, as in size: *a monstrous blunder.* —**Ant. 2.** tiny.

gi·gan·tism (jī găn′tĭz′əm, jī′găn tĭz′-), *n. Pathol.* abnormally great development in size or stature of the whole body, or of parts of body, most often due to dysfunction of the pituitary gland. Also, **giantism.**

gi·gan·to·ma·chi·a (jī găn′tō mā′kĭ ə), *n.* **1.** a war of giants, esp. the war of the giants of Greek mythology against the Olympian gods. 2. a representation of this, as in sculpture. [t. LL, t. Gk.: the battle of the giants]

gig·gle (gǐg'əl), v., -gled, -gling, n. —v.i. 1. to laugh in a silly undignified way, as from youthful spirits or ill-controlled amusement; titter. —n. 2. a silly, spasmodic laugh; a titter. [appar. back formation from obs. *giglet* giddy, laughing girl, der. obs. *gig* flighty, giddy girl. Cf. D *gigelen*, G *gickeln* giggle] —**gig'gler**, n.

gig·gly (gǐg'lǐ), adj. inclined to giggle.

gig·o·lo (jǐg'əlō'), n., pl. -los. 1. a man supported by a woman. 2. a male professional dancing partner. [t. F]

gig·ot (jǐg'ət), n. 1. a leg-of-mutton sleeve. 2. a leg of mutton. [t. F, dim. of d. F *gigue* leg, der. *giguer* hop, dance, der. OF *gigue* fiddle, t. Gmc.; cf. G *geige*]

gigue (zhēg), n. 1. *Dance*. jig (def. 1). 2. *Music*. a jig (def. 2), often forming the concluding movement in the classical suite. [t. F. See JIG]

G.I. Joe, *Colloq.* the common enlisted U.S. Army soldier.

Gi·la (hē'lə), n. a river flowing from SW New Mexico W across S Arizona to the Colorado river. 630 mi.

Gila monster, a large, venomous lizard, *Heloderma suspectum*, of the southwestern U.S., having the skin studded with yellow- or orange-and-black beadlike tubercles. [named after the *Gila* river, in Arizona]

Gila monster,
Heloderma suspectum

Gila woodpecker, a dull-colored woodpecker, *Centurus uropygialis*, of the southwestern United States and Mexico.

gil·bert (gǐl'bərt), n. *Elect.* the c.g.s. unit of magneto-motive force, equal to .7958 ampere turns. [named after W. *Gilbert* (1540–1603), British scientist]

Gil·bert (gǐl'bərt), n. 1. **Cass,** 1859–1934, U.S. architect. 2. **Sir Humphrey,** 1539?–83, British soldier, navigator, and colonizer in America. 3. **Sir William Schwenck,** 1836–1911, British dramatist, humorist, and poet; collaborator with Sir Arthur Sullivan.

Gilbert and El·lice Islands (ĕl'ǐs), a British colony in the central Pacific, comprising the Gilbert and Ellice groups and other widely scattered islands. 35,000 pop. (est. 1940); 203 sq. mi. *Cap.*: Ocean Island.

gild[1] (gǐld), v.t., **gilded** or **gilt, gilding.** 1. to coat with gold, gold leaf, or gold-colored substance. 2. to give a bright, pleasing, or specious aspect to. 3. *Obs.* to make red, as with blood. [ME *gilden*, OE *gyldan*, der. GOLD]

gild[2] (gǐld), n. guild. —**gilds·man** (gǐldz'mən), n.

gild·er[1] (gǐl'dər), n. one who or that which gilds. [f. GILD[1] + -ER[1]]

gil·der[2] (gǐl'dər), n. guilder.

gild·hall (gǐld'hôl'), n. guildhall.

gild·ing (gǐl'dǐng), n. 1. the application of gilt. 2. the gold leaf or other material with which anything is gilded. 3. the golden surface produced. 4. any deceptive coating or aspect used to give a fine appearance.

Gil·e·ad (gǐl'ǐəd), n. 1. an ancient district of Palestine, E of the Jordan, in present Trans-Jordan. 2. **Mount,** a mountain in NW Trans-Jordan. 3596 ft.

Gil·ga·mesh (gǐl'gəmĕsh'), n. a mythical Babylonian king who is the hero of a Babylonian epic.

gill[1] (gǐl), n. 1. an aquatic respiratory organ, either external or internal, usually feathery, platelike, or filamentous. 2. one of the radiating vertical plates on the under side of the cap of an agaric. 3. the ground ivy. —v.t. 4. to catch (fish) by the gills in a gill net. 5. to gut or clean (fish). [ME *gile*, t. Scand.; cf. Sw. *gäl*, Dan. *gælle*] —**gilled,** adj. —**gill'-like',** adj.

gill[2] (jǐl), n. a unit of liquid measure equal to ¼ pint. [ME *gille*, t. OF: wine measure. Cf. GALLON]

gill fungus (gǐl), an agaricaceous fungus.

gil·lie (gǐl'ǐ), n. *Scot.* 1. a sportsman's attendant. 2. a male attendant on a Highland chieftain. [t. Gaelic: m. *gille* lad, servant]

gill net (gǐl), a curtainlike net, suspended vertically in the water, with meshes of such a size as to catch by the gills a fish that has thrust its head through.

gil·ly (gǐl'ǐ), n., pl. -lies. *Scot.* gillie.

gil·ly·flow·er (jǐl'ǐflou'ər), n. 1. the name for various flowers, as for example, the wallflower, *Cheiranthus Cheiri*, the common stock gillyflower, *Matthiola incana*, etc. 2. *Archaic* or *Dial.* the clove pink. Also, **gil'li·flow'er.** [alter. of ME *gilofre*, t. OF: clove, g. L *caryophyllon*, t. Gk.: m. *karyóphyllon* clove tree]

Gil·man (gǐl'mən), n. **Daniel Coit,** 1831–1908, U.S. educator.

gil·son·ite (gǐl'sənīt'), n. an extremely pure asphalt particularly valuable for the manufacture of paints and varnishes, the chief deposits being in Utah; uintaite. [named after S. H. *Gilson* of Salt Lake City. See -ITE[1]]

gilt[1] (gǐlt), v. 1. pt. and pp. of **gild.** —adj. 2. gilded; golden in color. —n. 3. the gold or other material applied in gilding; gilding.

gilt[2] (gǐlt), n. a female swine that has not produced pigs and that has not reached an evident stage of pregnancy. [ME *gilte*, t. Scand.; cf. Icel. *gylta*]

gilt-edged (gǐlt'ĕjd'), adj. 1. having the edges gilded: *gilt-edged paper.* 2. of the highest order or quality: *gilt-edged securities.*

gim·bals (jǐm'bəlz, gǐm'-), n. a contrivance for keeping a suspended object, as a ship's compass, horizontal. [pl. of *gimbal* (now used only attributively and in composition), var. of *gimmal*, orig. *gemel*, t. OF]

gim·crack (jǐm'krăk'), n. 1. a showy, useless trifle; gewgaw. —adj. 2. showy but useless. [orig. uncert.]

gim·let (gǐm'lǐt), n. 1. a small tool for boring holes, consisting of a shaft with a pointed screw at one end and a handle at the other. —v.t. 2. to pierce with or as with a gimlet. [ME *gymlet*, t. OF: m. *guimbelet*, dim. of unrecorded *guimbel* WIMBLE]

gim·mick (gǐm'ǐk), n. *U.S. Slang.* a device by which a magician or carnival pitchman works a trick. [? b. *gimmer* trick finger ring and MAGIC]

Gimlet

gimp (gǐmp), n. a flat trimming of silk, wool, or other cord, sometimes stiffened with wire, for garments, curtains, furniture, etc. [appar. t. D; ult. orig. unknown]

gin[1] (jǐn), n. an alcoholic beverage obtained by redistilling spirits with flavoring agents, esp. juniper berries, orange peel, angelica root, etc. [short for GENEVA]

gin[2] (jǐn), n., v., **ginned, ginning.** —n. 1. a machine for separating cotton from its seeds, as a cotton gin. 2. a trap or snare for game, etc. —v.t. 3. to clear (cotton) of seeds with a gin. 4. to catch (game, etc.) in a gin. [ME; aphetic var. of OF *engin* ENGINE] —**gin'ner,** n.

gin[3] (gǐn), v.i., v.t., **gan, gun, ginning.** *Archaic* or *Poetic.* begin. [ME *ginnen*, OE *ginnan*, aphetic var. of *onginnan*. Cf. OE *beginnan*]

gin[4] (jǐn), n. *Cards.* a rummy game in which a player with a total of 10 unmatched points or less may end the game. [? a pun: *gin* = *rum*]

gin·gal (jǐn'gôl), n. jingal. Also, **gin'gall.**

gin·ge·li (jǐn'jəlǐ), n. gingili. Also, **gin'gel·ly.**

gin·ger (jǐn'jər), n. 1. the pungent, spicy rhizome of any of the reedlike plants of the genus *Zingiber*, esp. of *Z. officinale*, variously used in cookery and medicine. 2. any of these plants, native in the East Indies, but now cultivated in most tropical countries. 3. a dull-yellowish or tawny color. In England often used for red, especially for the color of the hair. 4. *Colloq.* piquancy; animation. —v.t. 5. to treat or flavor with ginger. 6. *Colloq.* to impart spiciness or piquancy to; make lively. [ME *gingivere*, OE *gingifere*, t. LL: m. *gingiber*, L *zingiberi*, t. Gk.: m. *zingiberis* ginger, appar. t. Prakrit: m. *singabēra*]

ginger ale, a drink similar to ginger beer.

ginger beer, a nonalcoholic effervescing drink of water, sugar or molasses, yeast, etc., flavored with ginger.

gin·ger·bread (jǐn'jərbrĕd'), n. 1. a kind of cake flavored with ginger and molasses. 2. a rolled cookie similarly flavored, often cut in fanciful shapes, and sometimes frosted. 3. something showy but unsubstantial and inartistic. —adj. 4. showy but unsubstantial and inartistic. [alter. of ME *gingimbrut* preserved ginger, t. ML, der. s. *gingiber* GINGER]

gingerbread tree, a tree, *Parinarium macrophyllum* of western Africa, with a large, edible farinaceous fruit (**gingerbread plum**).

gin·ger·ly (jǐn'jərlǐ), adv. 1. with extreme care or caution; warily. 2. *Obs.* mincingly; daintily. —adj. 3. cautious or wary. —**gin'ger·li·ness,** n.

gin·ger·snap (jǐn'jərsnăp'), n. a small, thin, brittle cookie spiced with ginger.

gin·ger·y (jǐn'jərǐ), adj. 1. gingerlike; pungent; spicy. 2. of the color of ginger.

ging·ham (gǐng'əm), n. yarn-dyed, plain-weave cotton fabric, usually striped or checked. [t. F: m. *guingan*, ult. t. Malay: m. *ginggang*, lit., striped]

gin·gi·li (jǐn'jəlǐ), n., pl. -lis. 1. the sesame plant. 2. its oil. Also, **gingeli, gingelly.** [t. Hind.: m. *jinjalī*, ult. t. Ar.: m. *juljulān*]

gin·gi·val (jǐn jī'vəl, jǐn'jəvəl), adj. 1. of or pertaining to the gums. 2. *Phonet.* made at the gums. [f. s. L *gingīva* gum + -AL[1]]

gin·gi·vi·tis (jǐn'jəvī'tǐs), n. *Pathol.* inflammation of the gums.

gink·go (gǐngk'gō, jǐngk'gō), n., pl. -goes. a large, ornamental, gymnospermous tree, *Ginkgo biloba*, native to China, with fan-shaped leaves, fleshy fruit, and edible nuts. Also, **ging'ko.** [t. Jap.]

gin·ner·y (jǐn'ərǐ), n., pl. -neries. a mill for ginning cotton.

gin rummy, gin[4].

gin·seng (jǐn'sĕng), n. 1. either of two araliaceous plants, *Panax schinseng* of China, Korea, etc., and *P. quinquefolium* of North America, yielding an aromatic root which is extensively used in medicine by the Chinese. 2. the root itself. 3. a preparation made from it. [t. Chinese (Mandarin): m. *jên shên*, f. *jên* man + *shên*, of obscure meaning]

Gior·gio·ne (jôr jō'ně), n. (Giorgione da Castelfranco, Giorgio Barbarelli) 1478?–1511, Italian painter.

Giot·to (jŏt'ō; *It.* jôt'tō), n. c1266–1337, Florentine painter and architect.

gip (jǐp), v.t., **gipped, gipping,** n. gyp[1]. —**gip'per,** n.

Gip·sy (jǐp'sǐ), n., pl. -sies, adj. *Chiefly Brit.* Gypsy.

gi·raffe (jərăf'), n. 1. a tall, long-necked, spotted ruminant, *Giraffa camelopardalis*, of Africa, the tallest of existing quadrupeds. See illus. on next page. 2. (*cap.*) *Astron.* the northern constellation Camelopardal. [t. F (now *girafe*), t. Ar.: m. *zarāfah*, prob. of African orig.]

gir·an·dole (jǐr'əndōl'), n. 1. a rotating and radiating firework. 2. *Fort.* a group of connected mines. 3. an ornate branched support for candles or other lights. Also, **gi·ran·do·la** (jĭ răn′də lə). [t. F, t. It.: m. *girandola*, der. *girare* turn, g. L *gȳrāre*. See GYRATE]

Gi·rard (jə rärd′), *n.* **Stephen**, 1750–1831, American merchant, banker, and philanthropist.

gir·a·sol (jĭr′ə sŏl′, -sōl′), *n.* **1.** a variety of opal which reflects a floating luminous glow. **2.** Jerusalem artichoke. Also, **gir′a·sole′**, **girosol**. [t. F, t. It.: m. *girasole*, f. *gira(re)* turn + *sole* sun, in imitation of Gk. *hēliotrópion*]

Gi·raud (zhē rō′), *n.* **Henri Honoré** (äN rē′ ô nô rē′), 1879–1949, French general.

gird[1] (gûrd), *v.t.*, **girt** or **girded**, **girding**. **1.** to encircle with a belt or girdle. **2.** to surround; hem in. **3.** to prepare (oneself) mentally for action (often fol. by *up*). **4.** to endue. [ME *girde(n)*, OE *gyrdan*, c. G *gürten*]

gird[2] (gûrd), *v.i.* **1.** to gibe; jeer (fol. by *at*). —*v.t.* **2.** *Obs.* to gibe or jeer at; taunt. —*n.* **3.** *Archaic.* a gibe. [ME; orig. obscure]

Giraffe,
*Giraffa
camelopardalis*
(17 to 19 ft. high)

gird·er (gûr′dər), *n.* **1.** (in structural work) any main horizontal supporting member or beam, as of wood or iron. **2.** one of the principal horizontal timbers which support the joists in certain floors. [f. GIRD[1] + ER[1]]

gir·dle (gûr′dəl), *n.*, *v.*, **-dled**, **-dling**. —*n.* **1.** a belt, cord, sash, or the like, worn about the waist. **2.** a lightweight undergarment which supports the abdominal region of the body. **3.** any encircling band; compass; limit. **4.** *Gems.* the edge about a brilliant or other cut stone at the junction of the upper and lower faces. **5.** *Anat.* the bony framework which unites the upper or lower extremities to the axial skeleton. **6.** a ring made about a tree trunk, etc., by cutting the bark. —*v.t.* **7.** to encircle with a belt; gird. **8.** to encompass; enclose; encircle. **9.** to cut away the bark in a ring about (a tree, branch, etc.), thus causing death. [ME; OE *gyrdel*, der. *gyrdan* gird[1]] —**gir′dle·like′**, *adj.* —**gir′dler**, *n.*

G, Steel girder;
C, Cross section of girder

Gir·gen·ti (jēr jěn′tē), *n.* former name of **Agrigento**.

girl (gûrl), *n.* **1.** a female child or young person. **2.** a young unmarried woman. **3.** a female servant. **4.** *Colloq.* a sweetheart. **5.** *Colloq.* a woman. [ME *gurle*, *girle* child, young person, OE *gyrl-* in *gyrlgyden* virgin goddess. Cf. LG *gör(e)* young person]

girl guide, a member of an organization of girls (**Girl Guides**) in England and elsewhere: a sister organization of the Girl Scouts.

girl·hood (gûrl′hŏŏd), *n.* **1.** state or time of being a girl. **2.** girls collectively.

girl·ish (gûr′lĭsh), *adj.* of, like, or befitting a girl: *girlish laughter.* —**girl′ish·ly**, *adv.* —**girl′ish·ness**, *n.*

girl scout, a member of an organization of girls (**Girl Scouts**), founded in the U.S. in 1912, to develop health, citizenship, character, and homemaking ability.

gi·ro (jĭ′rō), *n.*, *pl.* **-ros.** autogiro.

Gi·ronde (jə rŏnd′; *Fr.* zhē rôNd′), *n.* **1.** an estuary in SW France, formed by the junction of the Garonne and Dordogne rivers. ab. 45 mi. long. **2. the Gironde,** the party of the Girondists taken collectively.

Gi·ron·dist (jə rŏn′dĭst), *n.* a member of a French political party of moderate republicans (1791–1793), whose leaders were deputies from the department of Gironde, in SW France.

gir·o·sol (jĭr′ə sŏl′, -sōl′), *n.* girasol.

girt[1] (gûrt), *v.* pt. and pp. of **gird**[1].

girt[2] (gûrt), *v.t.*, **gird**[1] (def. 1).

girth (gûrth), *n.* **1.** the measure around anything; circumference. **2.** a band passed under the belly of a horse, etc., to secure a saddle or pack on its back. **3.** a band or girdle. —*v.t.* **4.** to bind or fasten with a girth. **5.** to girdle; encircle. [ME *girth*, *gerth*, t. Scand.; cf. Icel. *gjörth* girdle, hoop; akin to GIRD[1]]

gi·sarme (gĭ zärm′), *n.* a medieval shafted weapon with a scythelike cutting blade from the back edge of which emerges a long slender blade with a sharp point. [ME *gisharme(e)*, t. OF: m. *g(u)isarme*; orig. uncert.]

Gis·sing (gĭs′ĭng), *n.* **George Robert**, 1857–1903, British novelist.

gist (jĭst), *n.* **1.** the substance or pith of a matter; essential part: *the gist of an argument.* **2.** the ground on which a legal action rests. [t. OF, 3rd pers. sing. pres. ind. of *gesir* lie, rest, g. L *jacēre*]

git·tern (gĭt′ərn), *n.* cittern. [ME *gitern(e)*, t. OF: m. *guiterne*. Cf. GUITAR]

Giu·ba (jōō′bä), *n.* Italian name of **Juba**.

Giu·lio Ro·ma·no (jōōl′yô rō mä′nô), (*Giulio Pippi*) 1492?–1546, Italian painter and architect.

give (gĭv), *v.*, **gave**, **given**, **giving**, *n.* —*v.t.* **1.** to deliver freely; bestow; hand over: *give someone a present.* **2.** to deliver to another in exchange for something; pay. **3.** to grant permission or opportunity to; enable; assign; award. **4.** to set forth or show; present; offer. **5.** to assign as a basis of calculation or reasoning; suppose; assume: *given these facts.* **6.** to furnish or provide: *give aid, evidence, etc.* **7.** to afford or yield; produce: *give satisfaction, good results, etc.* **8.** to make, do, or perform: *give a start, a lurch, etc.* **9.** to issue; put forth, emit, or utter: *to give a cry, a command, etc.* **10.** to impart or communicate: *give advice, give someone a cold.* **11.** to deal or administer: *give one a blow, a medicine, the sacrament, etc.* **12.** to relinquish or surrender: *to give ground, place, etc.* **13.** to put forth; emit (fol. by *off* or *out*). **14.** to produce; present: *to give a play.* —*v.i.* **15.** to make a gift or gifts. **16.** to yield, as to pressure or strain; draw back; relax. **17.** to break down; fail. **18.** Some special verb phrases are:

give away, 1. to give as a present. **2.** to hand over (the bride) to the bridegroom at a wedding. **3.** *Slang.* to let (a secret) be known. **4.** to betray (a person).

give birth to, 1. to bear. **2.** to be the origin of.

give in, 1. to yield; acknowledge defeat. **2.** to hand in.

give out, 1. to become worn out or used up. **2.** to send out; emit. **3.** to distribute; issue.

give rise to, to give origin to; cause; result in.

give up, 1. to lose all hope. **2.** to abandon as hopeless. **3.** to desist from; forsake: *give up a task.* **4.** to surrender. **5.** to devote entirely.

—*n.* **19.** act or fact of yielding to pressure; elasticity. [ME, t. Scand. (cf. Dan. *give*); r. ME *yeve(n)*, *yive(n)*, OE *gefan*, *gi(e)fan*, c. D *geven*, G *geben*, Goth. *giban*. Cf. GIFT] —**giv′er**, *n.*

—Syn. **1.** offer, vouchsafe, impart, accord, furnish, provide, supply, donate, contribute. GIVE, CONFER, GRANT, PRESENT may mean that something concrete or abstract is bestowed on one person by another. GIVE is the general word: *to give someone a book, permission, etc.* CONFER usually means to give an honor or a favor; it implies courteous and gracious giving: *to confer a degree.* GRANT is limited to the idea of acceding to a request; it may apply to the bestowal of privileges, or the fulfillment of an expressed wish: *to grant a charter, a prayer, permission, etc.* PRESENT, a more formal word than GIVE, usually implies a certain ceremony in the giving: *to present a citation to a regiment.*

give-and-take (gĭv′ən tāk′), *n.* **1.** a method of dealing by compromise or mutual concession; coöperation. **2.** good-humored exchange of talk, ideas, etc.

give·a·way (gĭv′ə wā′), *n.* **1.** a betrayal, usually unintentional. **2.** a premium given with various articles to promote sales, etc. —*adj.* **3.** (of a radio program, etc.) characterized by the awarding of prizes, money, etc., to recipients chosen, usually, through a question-and-answer contest.

giv·en (gĭv′ən), *adj.* **1.** stated, fixed, or specified: *at a given time.* **2.** addicted or disposed (often fol. by *to*), *given to drink.* **3.** bestowed as a gift; conferred. **4.** assigned as a basis of calculation, reasoning, etc.: *given A and B, C follows.* **5.** *Math.* known or determined: *a given magnitude.* **6.** (on official documents) executed and delivered as of the date given.

given name, the name given to one, not inherited; first name.

Gi·za (gē′zə), *n.* El Giza. Also, **Gi′zeh**.

giz·zard (gĭz′ərd), *n.* the grinding or muscular stomach of birds, the organ in which food is triturated after leaving the glandular stomach; ventriculus. [ME *giser*, t. OF, ult. g. L *gigēria* cooked entrails of poultry]

Gk., Greek.

Gl, *Chem.* glucinum.

gla·bel·la (glə běl′ə), *n.*, *pl.* **-bellae** (-běl′ē). *Anat.* the flat area of bone between the eyebrows, used as a craniometric point. [NL, prop. fem. of L *glabellus* smooth, hairless, dim. of *glaber*. See GLABROUS]

gla·bel·lum (glə běl′əm), *n.*, *pl.* **-bella.** glabella.

gla·brate (glā′brāt, -brĭt), *adj.* **1.** *Zool.* smooth; glabrous. **2.** *Bot.* becoming glabrous; somewhat glabrous.

gla·brous (glā′brəs), *adj.* *Zool., Bot.* smooth; having a surface devoid of hair or pubescence. [f. s. L *glaber* smooth, hairless + -OUS]

gla·cé (glá sě′), *adj.* **1.** frozen. **2.** frosted or iced, as cake. **3.** candied, as fruits. **4.** finished with a gloss, as kid or silk. [F, pp. of *glacer*, der. *glace* ice, ult. g. L *glacies*]

gla·cial (glā′shəl), *adj.* **1.** characterized by the presence of ice in extensive masses or glaciers. **2.** due to or associated with the action of ice or glaciers. **3.** of or pertaining to glaciers or ice sheets. **4.** cold as ice; icy. **5.** *Chem.* of or tending to assume an icelike form, as certain acids. [t. L: s. *glaciālis* icy] —**gla′cial·ly**, *adv.*

glacial acetic acid, a 99.5% concentration of acetic acid.

glacial epoch, 1. the geologically recent Pleistocene epoch, during which much of the northern hemisphere was covered by great ice sheets. **2.** any one of the Eocene, Permian, Carboniferous, Cambrian, and pre-Cambrian glaciations.

gla·cial·ist (glā′shəl ĭst), *n.* one who studies geological phenomena involving the action of ice.

gla·ci·ate (glā′shĭ āt′), *v.t.*, **-ated**, **-ating**. **1.** to cover with ice or glaciers. **2.** to affect by glacial action. —**gla·ci·a·tion** (glā′sĭ ā′shən, -shĭ-), *n.*

gla·cier (glā′shər), *n.* an extended mass of ice formed from snow falling and accumulating over the years and moving very slowly, either descending from high mountains, as in valley glaciers, or moving outward from centers of accumulation, as in continental glaciers. [t. F, der. *glace* ice, ult. g. L *glacies*] —**gla′ciered**, *adj.*

Glacier National Park, a scenic mountain and forest reserve in NW Montana, with numerous glaciers and lakes. 1534 sq. mi.

b., blend of, blended; c., cognate with; d., dialect, dialectal; der., derived from; f., formed from; g., going back to; m., modification of; r., replacing; s., stem of; t., taken from; ?, perhaps. See the full key on inside cover.

gla·cis (glā′sĭs, glăs′ĭs), *n.* **1.** a gentle slope. **2.** *Fort.* a bank of earth in front of the counterscarp or covered way of a fort, having an easy slope toward the field or open country. [t. F: orig., icy or slippery place, der. OF *glacier* slip. See GLACE]

glad (glăd), *adj.*, **gladder, gladdest. 1.** delighted or pleased (fol. by *of*, *at*, etc., or an infinitive or clause): *to be glad at the news, glad to go, glad that one has come.* **2.** characterized by or showing cheerfulness, joy, or pleasure, as looks, utterances, etc. **3.** attended with or causing joy or pleasure: *a glad occasion, glad tidings.* —*v.t.* **4.** *Archaic.* to make glad. [ME; OE glæd, c. Icel. *gladhr* bright, glad, D *glad* and G *glatt* smooth; akin to L *glaber* smooth] —**glad′ly**, *adv.* —**glad′ness**, *n.* —**Syn. 1.** elated, delighted, gratified. **2.** merry, joyous, cheerful. —**Ant.** sad.

glad·den (glăd′ən), *v.t.* **1.** to make glad. —*v.i.* **2.** *Obs.* to be glad. —**glad′den·er**, *n.* —**Syn. 1.** See **cheer.**

glade (glād), *n.* an open space in a forest. [akin to GLAD (in obs. sense "bright")]

glad·i·ate (glăd′ĭ ĭt, -āt′, glā′dĭ-), *adj. Bot.* sword-shaped. [f. s. L *gladius* sword + -ATE¹]

glad·i·a·tor (glăd′ĭ ā′tər), *n. Rom. Hist.* a person, often a slave or captive, who fought in public with a sword or other weapon to entertain the people. [t. L]

glad·i·a·to·ri·al (glăd′ĭ ə tōr′ĭ əl), *adj.* pertaining to gladiators or to their combats.

glad·i·o·la (glăd′ĭ ō′lə, glə dī′ə lə), *n.* gladiolus. [t. L, neut. pl. treated as if fem. sing. See GLADIOLUS]

glad·i·o·lus (glăd′ĭ ō′ləs *for the plant;* glə dī′ə ləs *for the genus*), *n., pl.* **-li** (-lī), **-luses.** any plant of the iridaceous genus *Gladiolus*, native esp. in South Africa, with erect, gladiate leaves, and spikes of variously colored flowers. [t. L, dim. of *gladius* sword]

glad·some (glăd′səm), *adj.* **1.** making joyful; delightful. **2.** glad. —**glad′some·ly**, *adv.* —**glad′some·ness**, *n.*

Glad·stone (glăd′stōn, -stən), *n.* **1. William Ewart** (ū′ərt), 1809–98, British statesman: prime minister four times between 1868 and 1894. **2.** a Gladstone bag. **3.** a four-wheeled pleasure carriage with a calash top, two inside seats, and driver and dickey seats.

Gladstone bag, a light traveling bag hinged to open into two compartments. [named after W. E. *Gladstone* (1809–98), British statesman]

glair (glâr), *n.* **1.** the white of an egg. **2.** a glaze or size made of it. **3.** any viscous substance like egg white. [ME *glaire*, t. OF, ult. der. L *clārus* clear]

glair·y (glâr′ĭ), *adj.* **1.** of the nature of glair; viscous. **2.** covered with glair. Also, **glair·e·ous** (glâr′ĭ əs). —**glair′i·ness**, *n.*

glaive (glāv), *n. Archaic.* a sword or broadsword. [ME *gleyve*, t. OF: m. *glaive* lance, sword, g. L *gladius* sword]

Gla·mor·gan·shire (glə môr′gən shĭr′, -shər), *n.* a county in SE Wales. 1,155,000 pop. (est. 1946); 816 sq. mi. *Co, seat:* Cardiff. Also, **Gla·mor′gan.**

glam·or·ous (glăm′ər əs), *adj.* full of glamour or charm. Also, **glam′our·ous.** —**glam′or·ous·ly**, *adv.*

glam·our (glăm′ər), *n.* **1.** alluring and often illusory charm; fascination. **2.** magic or enchantment; spell; witchery. Also, **glam′or.** [earlier *glammar*, dissimilated var. of GRAMMAR in sense of "occult learning," "magic"]

glance¹ (glăns, gläns), *v.*, **glanced, glancing,** *n.* —*v.i.* **1.** to look quickly or briefly. **2.** to gleam or flash. **3.** to go off in an oblique direction from an object struck: *a missile glances away.* **4.** to allude briefly in passing. —*v.t.* **5.** to cast a glance or brief look at; catch a glimpse of. **6.** to cast or reflect, as a gleam. —*n.* **7.** a quick or brief look. **8.** a gleam or flash of light. **9.** a glancing off, as of a missile after striking. **10.** a reference in passing. **11.** *Cricket.* a stroke in which the ball is allowed to glance off the bat. [nasalized var. of ME *glacen* strike a glancing blow, t. OF: m. *glacer* slip] —**Syn. 2.** See **flash.**

glance² (glăns, gläns), *n. Mining, Mineral.* any of various minerals having a luster which indicates their metallic nature. [t. G: m. *glanz*, lit., brightness, luster]

gland (glănd), *n.* **1.** *Anat.* **a.** an organ by which certain constituents are separated from the blood for use in the body or for ejection from it, or by which certain changes are produced in the blood or lymph. **b.** any of various organs or structures likened to true glands. **2.** *Bot.* a secreting organ or structure, esp. one on or near a surface. [t. F: m. *glande*, m. OF *glandre*, g. L *glandula*, dim. of *glans* acorn] —**gland′less**, *adj.* —**gland′like′**, *adj.*

glan·dered (glăn′dərd), *adj.* affected with glanders.

glan·ders (glăn′dərz), *n. Vet. Sci.* a contagious disease of horses, mules, etc., communicable to man, due to a microörganism (*Bacillus mallei*), and characterized by swellings beneath the jaw and a profuse mucous discharge from the nostrils. [t. OF: m. *glandres*, g. L *glandulae* (swollen) glands] —**glan′der·ous**, *adj.*

glan·du·lar (glăn′jə lər), *adj.* **1.** consisting of, containing, or bearing glands. **2.** of, pertaining to, or resembling a gland.

glandular fever, *Pathol.* an acute infectious disease characterized by sudden fever, a benign swelling of lymph nodes, and increase in leucocytes having only one nucleus in the blood stream; infectious mononucleosis.

glan·du·lous (glăn′jə ləs), *adj.* glandular. [t. L: m. s. *glandulōsus*]

glans (glănz), *n., pl.* **glandes** (glăn′dēz). *Anat.* the head of the penis (**glans penis**) or of the clitoris (**glans clitoridis**). [t. L: lit., acorn]

glare¹ (glâr), *n., v.,* **glared, glaring.** —*n.* **1.** a strong, dazzling light; brilliant luster. **2.** dazzling or showy appearance; showiness. **3.** a fierce or piercing look. —*v.i.* **4.** to shine with a strong, dazzling light. **5.** to be too brilliantly ornamented. **6.** to be intensely bright in color. **7.** to be conspicuous. **8.** to look with a fierce or piercing stare. —*v.t.* **9.** to express with a glare. [ME *glaren*, c. MD and MLG *glaren*; akin to GLASS (cf. OE *glæren* glassy)] —**Syn. 7.** GLARE, GLOWER, GLOAT agree in having connotations of emotion which accompany an intense gaze. To GLARE is to look piercingly or angrily: *a tiger glares at its victims.* To GLOWER is to look fiercely and threateningly, as from wrath; it suggests a scowl along with a glare: *to glower at a persistently mischievous child.* To GLOAT meant originally to look with exultation, avaricious or malignant, on something or someone: *a tyrant gloating over the helplessness of his victim.* Today, however, it may imply simply inner exultation. **2.** See **shine.**

glare² (glâr), *n.* **1.** a bright, smooth surface, as of ice. —*adj.* **2.** bright and smooth; glassy: *glare ice.* [special uses of GLARE¹]

glar·ing (glâr′ĭng), *adj.* **1.** that glares; brilliant; dazzling. **2.** excessively bright; garish. **3.** very conspicuous: *glaring defects.* **4.** staring fiercely. —**glar′ing·ly**, *adv.* —**glar′ing·ness**, *n.*

glar·y¹ (glâr′ĭ), *adj.* brilliant; glaring. [f. GLARE¹ + -Y¹]

glar·y² (glâr′ĭ), *adj.* U.S. smooth and slippery, as ice. [early mod. E *glarie* icy. Cf. OE *glæren* glassy]

Glas·gow (glăs′gō, -kō, glăs′-), *n.* a seaport in SW Scotland, on the Clyde. 1,061,000 pop. (est. 1946).

Glas·gow (glăs′gō), *n.* **Ellen Anderson Gholson** (gōl′sən), 1874–1945, U.S. novelist.

glass (glăs, gläs), *n.* **1.** a hard, brittle, more or less transparent substance produced by fusion, usually consisting of mutually dissolved silica and silicates (the ordinary variety used for windows, bottles, and the like, containing silica, soda, and lime). See **crown glass** and **flint glass. 2.** any artificial or natural substance having similar properties and composition, as fused borax, obsidian, etc. **3.** something made of glass, as a window, mirror, lens, barometer, etc. **4.** (*pl.*) eyeglasses. **5.** things made of glass, collectively; glassware. **6.** a glass container for drinking water, etc. **7.** quantity or contents of a drinking glass; glassful. —*adj.* **8.** made of glass. **9.** furnished or fitted with panes of glass; glazed. —*v.t.* **10.** to fit with panes of glass; cover with or encase in glass. **11.** *Poetic.* to reflect: *trees glass themselves in the lake.* [ME *glas*, OE *glæs*, c. D and G *glas*] —**glass′-less**, *adj.*

Glass (glăs, gläs), *n.* **Carter**, 1858–1946, U.S. statesman.

glass blowing, 1. the art or process of forming glass into ware by blowing by mouth or mechanically. **2.** the operation of working glass in a flame, starting with tubing, rod, or cane, and forming laboratory apparatus, ornaments, or knickknacks. —**glass blower.**

glass·ful (glăs′fŏŏl′, gläs′-), *n., pl.* **-fuls.** as much as a glass holds.

glass harmonica, an instrument consisting of a series of glass bowls graduated in size which can be played by the friction of the moistened finger.

glass·house (glăs′hous′, gläs′-), *n.* **1.** an establishment where glass is made. **2.** *Chiefly Brit.* a greenhouse.

glass·ine (glă sēn′), *n.* a glazed, semitransparent paper, used for book jackets, etc.

glass·mak·ing (glăs′māk′ĭng, gläs′-), *n.* the art of making glass or glassware.

glass·man (glăs′mən, gläs′-), *n., pl.* **-men. 1.** one who makes or sells glass. **2.** a glazier.

glass snake, 1. a limbless, snakelike lizard, *Ophisaurus ventralis*, of the southern U.S., having an extremely fragile tail. **2.** any of certain similar lizards of Europe and Asia.

glass tank, a reverberatory furnace in which glass is melted directly under the flames.

glass·ware (glăs′wâr′, gläs′-), *n.* articles of glass.

glass·work (glăs′wûrk′, gläs′-), *n.* **1.** the manufacture of glass and glassware. **2.** the fitting of glass; glazing. **3.** articles of glass collectively; glassware.

glass·work·er (glăs′wûr′kər, gläs′-), *n.* one who works in glass.

glass·works (glăs′wûrks′, gläs′-), *n. pl. or sing.* glasshouse (def. 1).

glass·wort (glăs′wûrt′, gläs′-), *n.* **1.** any of the herbs with succulent leafless stems constituting the chenopodiaceous genus *Salicornia*, and formerly much used (when burned to ashes) as a source of soda for glassmaking. **2.** the saltwort, *Salsola Kali* (**prickly glasswort**).

glass·y (glăs′ĭ, gläs′ĭ), *adj.*, **glassier, glassiest. 1.** resembling glass, as in transparency, smoothness, etc. **2.** having a fixed, unintelligent stare. **3.** of the nature of glass; vitreous. —**glass′i·ly**, *adv.* —**glass′i·ness**, *n.*

Glau·ber salt (glou′bər), sodium sulfate, used as a cathartic, etc. Also, **Glau′ber's salt.** [named after J. R. *Glauber* (1604–68), German chemist]

glau·co·ma (glô kō′mə), *n. Pathol.* a disease of the eye, characterized by increased pressure within the eyeball with progressive loss of vision. [t. Gk.: m. *glaukōma* opacity of the crystalline lens. See GLAUCOUS] —**glau·co·ma·tous** (glô kō′mə təs, -kŏm′ə-), *adj.*

glau·co·nite (glô′kə nīt′), *n.* a greenish micaceous mineral, essentially of a hydrous silicate of potassium, aluminum, and iron, and occurring in greensand, clays, etc. [f. m. Gk. *glaukón*, neut. adj., bluish-green + -ITE[1]]

glau·cous (glô′kəs), *adj.* **1.** light bluish-green or greenish-blue. **2.** *Bot.* covered with a whitish bloom, as a plum. [t. L: m. *glaucus*, t. Gk.: m. *glaukós* gleaming, silvery, gray, bluish-green]

glaucous gull, a large white and pale-gray gull, *Latus hyperboreus*, of arctic regions.

glaze (glāz), *v.*, **glazed, glazing,** *n.* —*v.t.* **1.** to furnish or fit with glass; cover with glass. **2.** to produce a vitreous or glossy surface on (pottery, biscuit, etc.). **3.** to cover with glaze. **4.** *Painting.* to cover (a painted surface or parts of it) with a thin layer of transparent color in order to modify the tone. **5.** to cover with a smooth lustrous coating; give a glassy surface to, as by polishing. —*v.i.* **6.** to become glazed or glassy. —*n.* **7.** a smooth, glossy surface or coating. **8.** the substance for producing it. **9.** *Ceramics.* **a.** the vitreous or glossy surface or coating on glazed pottery. **b.** the substance or material used to produce such a surface. **10.** *Painting.* a thin layer of transparent color, spread over a painted surface. **11.** *Cookery.* **a.** something used to coat a food, esp. sugar or sugar syrup. **b.** stock cooked down to a thin paste, for applying to the surface of meats. **12.** *U.S. Weather Bureau.* a smooth coating of ice on terrestrial objects due to the freezing of rain. [ME *glasen*, der. *glas* GLASS] —**glaz′er,** *n.* —**glaz′y,** *adj.*

gla·zier (glā′zhər), *n.* one who fits windows, etc., with glass. [ME *glasier*, f. *glas* GLASS + -IER]

gla·zier·y (glā′zhə rĭ), *n.* glaziers' work.

glaz·ing (glā′zĭng), *n.* **1.** act of furnishing or fitting with glass; business of a glazier. **2.** glass set, or to be set, in frames, etc. **3.** act of applying a glaze. **4.** the glassy surface of anything glazed.

gleam (glēm), *n.* **1.** a flash or beam of light. **2.** dim or subdued light. **3.** a brief or slight manifestation: *a gleam of hope.* —*v.i.* **4.** to send forth a gleam or gleams. **5.** to appear suddenly and clearly, like a flash of light. —*v.t.* **6.** *Rare.* to send forth in gleams. [ME *glem(e)*, OE *glǣm*, c. OHG *gleimo* glowworm; akin to OS *glīmo* brightness, etc. See GLIMMER, GLIMPSE]
—**Syn. 1.** GLEAM, RAY, GLIMMER are terms for a stream of light. GLEAM denotes a not very brilliant, and often intermittent, stream of light: *the distant gleam from a lighted window.* RAY usually implies a smaller amount of light than a beam; a single line of light: *a ray through a pinprick in a window shade.* GLIMMER indicates a feeble, unsteady light: *a faint glimmer of moonlight.*

glean (glēn), *v.t.* **1.** to gather slowly and laboriously in bits. **2.** to gather (grain, etc.) after the reapers or regular gatherers. —*v.i.* **3.** to collect or gather anything little by little or slowly. **4.** to gather what is left by reapers. [ME *glene(n)*, t. OF: m. *glener*, g. LL *glenāre*, of Celtic orig.] —**glean′er,** *n.*

glean·ing (glē′nĭng), *n.* **1.** act of one who gleans. **2.** (*usually pl.*) that which is gleaned.

glebe (glēb), *n.* **1.** *Poetic.* soil; field. **2.** *Brit.* the cultivable land owned by a parish church or ecclesiastical benefice. [ME, t. L: m.s. *glēba*, *glaeba* clod, soil, land]

glede (glēd), *n.* the common European kite, *Milvus ictinus.* Also, **gled** (glĕd). [ME; OE *glida*, c. Icel. *gledha;* akin to GLIDE]

glee (glē), *n.* **1.** demonstrative joy; exultation. **2.** a kind of unaccompanied part song, grave or gay, for three or more voices. [ME; OE *glēo*, c. Icel. *glȳ*] —**Syn. 1.** merriment, jollity, hilarity. See **mirth.**

glee club, a club or group for singing choral music.

glee·ful (glē′fəl), *adj.* full of glee; merry; exultant. —**glee′ful·ly,** *adv.* —**glee′ful·ness,** *n.*

glee·man (glē′mən), *n.*, *pl.* **-men.** *Archaic.* a strolling professional singer or minstrel. [OE *glēomann*]

glee·some (glē′səm), *adj.* gleeful. —**glee′some·ly,** *adv.* —**glee′some·ness,** *n.*

gleet (glēt), *n.* *Pathol.* **1.** a thin, morbid discharge, as from a wound. **2.** a persistent or chronic gonorrhea. [ME *glette*, t. OF: slime, mucus, pus, foul matter]

glen (glĕn), *n.* a small, narrow, secluded valley. [ME, t. Gaelic: m. *gle(a)nn*, c. Welsh *glyn*] —**glen′like′,** *adj.*

Glen·dale (glĕn′dāl′), *n.* a city in SW California, near Los Angeles. 95,702 (1950).

Glen·dow·er (glĕn dou′ər, glĕn′dou ər), *n.* **Owen,** 1359?–1416?, Welsh rebel against Henry IV of England.

glen·gar·ry (glĕn găr′ĭ), *n.*, *pl.* **-ries.** a Scotch cap, with straight sides, a crease along the top, and sometimes short ribbon streamers at the back, worn by Highlanders as part of military dress. [named after *Glengarry*, valley in Invernesshire, Scotland]

gle·noid (glē′noid), *adj.* *Anat.* **1.** shallow or slightly cupped, as the articular cavities of the scapula and the temporal bone. **2.** pertaining to such a cavity. [t. Gk.: m.s. *glēnoeidēs* like a shallow joint socket. See -OID]

glib (glĭb), *adj.*, **glibber, glibbest. 1.** ready and fluent, often thoughtlessly or insincerely so: *glib speakers, a glib tongue.* **2.** easy, as action or manner. [back formation from obs. *glibbery* slippery, t. D: m. *glibberig*] —**glib′ly,** *adv.* —**glib′ness,** *n.* —**Syn. 1.** See **fluent.**

glide (glīd), *v.*, **glided, gliding,** *n.* —*v.i.* **1.** to move smoothly along, as if without effort or difficulty, as a flying bird, a boat, a skater, etc. **2.** to pass by gradual or insensible change (often fol. by *along, away, by,* etc.). **3.** to go quietly or unperceived; slip (fol. by *in, out,* etc.). **4.** *Aeron.* to move in the air, esp. at an easy angle downward, by the action of gravity or by virtue of momentum already acquired. **5.** *Music.* to pass from tone to tone without a break; slur. —*v.t.* **6.** to cause to glide. —*n.* **7.** a gliding movement, as in dancing. **8.** a dance in which such movements are employed. **9.** *Music.* a slur (def. 8a). **10.** *Phonet.* **a.** a transitional sound produced while passing from the articulation required by one speech sound to that required by the next, such as the *k* often heard before the *th* of *length.* **b.** a semivowel, such as *w* in *wet.* [ME *glide(n)*, OE *glīdan*, c. G *gleiten*] —**glid′ing·ly,** *adv.* —**Syn. 1.** See **slide.**

glid·er (glī′dər), *n.* **1.** one who or that which glides. **2.** *Aeron.* a motorless heavier-than-air craft for gliding from a higher to a lower level by the action of gravity, or from a lower to a higher level by the action of air currents. **3.** a swing made of an upholstered seat suspended from a steel framework by links or springs.

glim·mer (glĭm′ər), *n.* **1.** a faint or unsteady light; gleam. **2.** a dim perception; inkling. —*v.i.* **3.** to shine faintly or unsteadily; twinkle; flicker. **4.** to appear faintly or dimly. [ME *glemer(en)* gleam, c. G *glimmern.* Cf. OE *gleomu* splendor] —**Syn. 1.** See **gleam.**

glim·mer·ing (glĭm′ər ĭng), *n.* **1.** a faint or unsteady light; a glimmer. **2.** a faint glimpse; inkling. —*adj.* **3.** that glimmers. —**glim′mer·ing·ly,** *adv.*

glimpse (glĭmps), *n.*, *v.*, **glimpsed, glimpsing.** —*n.* **1.** a momentary sight or view. **2.** a momentary or slight appearance. **3.** a vague idea; inkling. **4.** *Archaic.* a gleam, as of light. —*v.t.* **5.** to catch a glimpse of. —*v.i.* **6.** to look briefly, or glance (fol. by *at*). **7.** *Poetic.* to come into view; appear faintly. [ME *glymsen*, c. MHG *glimsen* glow; akin to GLIMMER] —**glimps′er,** *n.*

Glin·ka (glēn′kä), *n.* **Mikhail Ivanovich** (mĭ hä ēl′ ĭ vä′nŏ vĭch), 1803?–57, Russian composer.

glint (glĭnt), *n.* **1.** a gleam or glimmer; flash. **2.** glinting brightness; luster. —*v.i.* **3.** to gleam or flash. **4.** to move suddenly; dart. —*v.t.* **5.** to cause to glint; reflect. [ME *glynt*, var. of obs. *glent*, t. Scand.; cf. d. Sw. *glänta, glinta* slip, shine] —**Syn. 3.** See **flash.**

gli·o·ma (glī ō′mə), *n.*, *pl.* **-mata** (-mə tə), **-mas.** *Pathol.* a tumor arising from and consisting largely of neuroglia. [NL, f. s. Gk. *glía* glue + *-oma* -OMA] —**gli·o·ma·tous** (glī ō′mə təs, -ŏm′ə-), *adj.*

glis·sade (glĭ säd′, -sād′), *n.*, *v.*, **-saded, -sading.** —*n.* **1.** a skillful glide over snow or ice in descending a mountain. **2.** *Dancing.* a sliding or gliding step. —*v.i.* **3.** to perform a glissade. [t. F, der. *glisser* slip, slide, b. OF *glacier* slip and *glier* slide (t. Gmc.; cf. GLIDE)]

glis·san·do (glĭ sän′dō), *adj.*, *n.*, *pl.* **-di** (-dē). —*adj.* **1.** performed with a gliding effect by sliding one finger rapidly over the keys of a piano or strings of a harp. —*n.* **2.** a glissando passage. **3.** (in string playing) a slide. [pseudo-It., t. F: m. *glissant*, ppr. of *glisser* slide]

glis·ten (glĭs′ən), *v.i.* **1.** to shine with a sparkling light or a faint intermittent glow. —*n.* **2.** a glistening; sparkle. [ME *glis(t)nen*, OE *glisnian*, der. *g isian* glitter. See -EN[1]] —**glis′ten·ing·ly,** *adv.*
—**Syn. 1.** GLISTEN, SHIMMER, SPARKLE refer to different ways in which light is reflected from surfaces. GLISTEN refers to a lustrous light as from something sleek or wet, or it may refer to myriads of tiny gleams reflected from small surfaces: *wet fur glistens, snow glistens in the sunlight* SHIMMER refers to the changing play of light on a (generally moving) surface, as of water or silk: *moonbeams shimmer on water, silk shimmers in a high light.* To SPARKLE is to give off sparks or small ignited particles, or to send forth small but brilliant gleams: *a diamond sparkles as with numerous points of light.*

glis·ter (glĭs′tər), *v.i.* **1.** *Archaic.* to glisten; glitter. —*n.* **2.** *Archaic or Dial.* a glistering; glitter. [ME; freq. of obs. v. *glist* glitter, var. of GLISTEN (? back formation)]

glit·ter (glĭt′ər), *v.i.* **1.** to shine with a brilliant, sparkling light or luster. **2.** to make a brilliant show: *glittering scenes of a court.* —*n.* **3.** glittering light or luster; splendor. [ME, t. Scand.; cf. Icel. *glitra*, freq. of *glita* shine; cf. OE *glitenian*, G *gleissan* shine, glitter] —**glit′ter·ing·ly,** *adv.* —**Syn. 1.** See **flash.**

glit·ter·y (glĭt′ər ĭ), *adj.* glittering; sparkling.

gloam·ing (glō′mĭng), *n.* *Poetic.* twilight; dusk. [ME *gloming*, OE *glōmung*, der. *glōm* twilight; mod. *-oa-* (instead of *-oo-*) presumably by contam. with GLOW]

gloat (glōt), *v.i.* to gaze with exultation; dwell mentally upon something with intense (and usually evil) satisfaction: *to gloat over another's misfortunes.* [cf. Icel. *glotta* grin, smile scornfully, d. Sw. *glotta* peep, G *glotzen* stare] —**gloat′er,** *n.* —**gloat′ing·ly,** *adv.* —**Syn.** See **glare**[1].

glob·al (glō′bəl), *adj.* **1.** spherical; globe-shaped. **2.** pertaining to the whole world. —**glob′al·ly,** *adv.*

glo·bate (glō′bāt), *adj.* shaped like a globe. Also, **glo′bat·ed.** [t. L: m.s. *globātus*, pp., formed into a ball]

globe (glōb), *n.*, *v.*, **globed, globing.** —*n.* **1.** the earth (usually prec. by *the*). **2.** a planet or other celestial body. **3.** a sphere on which is depicted a map of the earth (**terrestrial globe**) or of the heavens (**celestial globe**). **4.** a spherical body; sphere. **5.** anything more or less spherical, as a lamp shade or a glass fish bowl. **6.** *Hist.* a golden ball borne as an emblem of sovereignty. —*v.t.* **7.** to form into a globe. —*v.i.* **8.** to take the form of a globe. [t. F, t. L: m. *globus* round body or mass, ball, globe] —**globe′like′,** *adj.* —**Syn. 1.** See **earth. 4.** See **ball**[1].

globe·fish (glōb′fĭsh′), *n.*, *pl.* **-fishes,** (*esp. collectively*) **-fish.** a puffer (def. 2).

globe·flow·er (glōb′flou′ər), *n.* **1.** a ranunculaceous plant, *Trollius europaeus*, of Europe, having pale-yellow globelike flowers. **2.** an American species, *T. laxus.*

b., blend of, blended; c., cognate with; d., dialect, dialectal; der., derived from; f., formed from; g., going back to; m., modification of; r., replacing; s., stem of; t., taken from; ?, perhaps. See the full key on inside cover.

globe·trot·ter (glōb′trŏt′ər), *n. Colloq.* one who travels widely, esp. for sightseeing. —**globe′trot′ting,** *n., adj.*

Glo·big·er·i·na (glō bĭj′ər ī′nə), *n., pl.* **-nae** (-nē). a marine protozoan belonging to the *Foraminifera,* the shell of which, falling to the ocean floor upon death, forms a mud known as the **globigerina ooze.**

glo·bin (glō′bĭn), *n. Biochem.* a protein contained in hemoglobin. [f. s. L *globus* GLOBE + -IN²]

glo·boid (glō′boid), *adj.* 1. approximately globular. —*n.* 2. a globoid figure or body.

glo·bose (glō′bōs, glō bōs′), *adj.* globelike; globe-shaped, or nearly so. Also, **glo·bous** (glō′bəs). [t. L: m.s. *globōsus* round as a ball] —**glo′bose·ly,** *adv.* —glo·bos·i·ty (glō bŏs′ə tĭ), *n.*

glob·u·lar (glŏb′yə lər), *adj.* 1. globe-shaped; spherical. 2. composed of globules. —**glob′u·lar′i·ty,** *n.* —**glob′u·lar·ly,** *adv.*

glob·ule (glŏb′ūl), *n.* a small spherical body. [t. F, t. L: m. *globulus,* dim. of *globus* GLOBE]

glob·u·lin (glŏb′yə lĭn), *n. Biochem.* any of a group of proteins insoluble in pure water. [f. GLOBULE + -IN²]

glock·en·spiel (glŏk′ən spēl′; *Ger.* glô′kən shpēl′), *n. Music.* 1. a set of steel bars mounted in a frame and struck with hammers, used by military bands. 2. a small keyboard instrument, imitating the sound of bells. 3. a set of bells; carillon. [t. G: f. *glocken-,* comb. form of *glocke* bell + *spiel* play]

glom·er·ate (glŏm′ər ĭt), *adj.* compactly clustered. [t. L: m. s. *glomerātus,* pp., wound or formed into a ball]

glom·er·a·tion (glŏm′ə rā′shən), *n.* 1. glomerate condition; conglomeration. 2. a glomerate mass.

glom·er·ule (glŏm′ər ōōl′), *n. Bot.* a cyme condensed into a headlike cluster. [t. F, t. NL: m. s. *glomerulus,* dim. of L *glomus* ball (of yarn, thread, etc.)]

glo·mer·u·lus (glō měr′yŏō ləs, -ōō ləs), *n., pl.* **-li** (-lī′). *Anat.* a compact cluster of capillaries. [NL. See GLOMERULE]

glon·o·in (glŏn′ō ĭn), *n.* nitroglycerin: esp. so called in medicine. Also, **glon·o·ine** (glŏn′ō ĭn, -ēn′). [said to be f. GL(YCERIN) + chemical symbols *O* (oxygen) and *NO₃* (nitric anhydride) + -IN²]

gloom¹ (glōōm), *n.* 1. darkness; dimness. —*v.i.* 2. to appear or become dark or gloomy. —*v.t.* 3. to make dark or somber. [OE *glōm* twilight. See GLOAMING, GLOW] —**Syn.** 1. shadow, shade. —**Ant.** 1. brightness.

gloom² (glōōm), *n.* 1. a state of melancholy or depression; low spirits. 2. a despondent look or expression. —*v.i.* 3. to look dismal or dejected; frown. —*v.t.* 4. to fill with gloom; make gloomy or sad. [ME *gloum(b)e, glomme* frown, lower. See GLUM] —**Syn.** 1. dejection, despondency. —**Ant.** 1. cheerfulness.

gloom·y¹ (glōō′mĭ), *adj.,* **gloomier, gloomiest.** dark; deeply shaded. [f. GLOOM¹ + -Y¹] —**Syn.** See **dark.**

gloom·y² (glōō′mĭ), *adj.,* **gloomier, gloomiest.** 1. causing gloom; depressing: *a gloomy prospect.* 2. affected with or expressive of gloom; melancholy. [f. GLOOM² + -Y¹] —**gloom′i·ly,** *adv.* —**gloom′i·ness,** *n.* —**Syn.** 2. dejected, downcast, downhearted, sad, despondent.

Gloos·cap (glōōs′kăp), *n.* a divinity or legendary hero among the northeastern Algonquian Indians.

Glo·ri·a (glōr′ĭ ə), *n.* 1. (in Christian liturgical worship) the great, or greater, doxology beginning "Gloria in excelsis Deo" (Glory be to God on high), the lesser doxology beginning "Gloria Patri" (Glory be to the Father), or the response "Gloria tibi, Domine" (Glory be to thee, O Lord). 2. (*l.c.*) a repetition of one of these. 3. (*l.c.*) a musical setting for one of these, esp. the first. 4. (*l.c.*) a halo, nimbus, or aureola, or an ornament in imitation of one. 5. (*l.c.*) a silk and wool (or cotton) fabric for umbrellas, dresses, etc. [t. L: glory]

Glo·ri·a in Ex·cel·sis De·o (glōr′ĭ ə ĭn ĕk sĕl′sĭs dē′ō), the hymn beginning, in Latin, "*Gloria in Excelsis Deo*" (Glory in the highest to God), and, in the English version, "Glory be to God on high."

Glo·ri·a Pa·tri (glōr′ĭ ə păt′rĭ), the short hymn "Glory be to the Father, and to the Son, and to the Holy Ghost. As it was in the beginning, is now, and ever shall be, world without end. Amen."

glo·ri·fi·ca·tion (glōr′ə fə kā′shən), *n.* 1. act of glorifying; exaltation to the glory of heaven. 2. state of being glorified. 3. *Colloq.* a celebration or jubilation. 4. *Colloq.* a glorified or more splendid form of something.

glo·ri·fy (glōr′ə fī), *v.t.,* **-fied, -fying.** 1. to magnify with praise; extol. 2. to transform into something more splendid. 3. to make glorious; invest with glory. 4. to promote the glory of (God); ascribe glory and praise in adoration to (God). [ME *glorify(en),* t. OF: m. *glorifier,* t. LL: m. *glorificāre.* See GLORY, -FY] —**glo′ri·fi′a·ble,** *adj.* —**glo′ri·fi′er,** *n.*

glo·ri·ole (glōr′ĭ ōl′), *n.* a halo, nimbus, or aureola. [t. F, t. L: m. s. *glōriola,* dim. of *glōria* GLORY, n.]

glo·ri·ous (glōr′ĭ əs), *adj.* 1. admirable; delightful: *to have a glorious time.* 2. conferring glory: *a glorious victory.* 3. full of glory; entitled to great renown: *England is glorious in her poetry.* 4. brilliantly beautiful: *the glorious heavens.* [ME, t. AF, t. L: m.s. *glōriōsus* full of glory] —**glo′ri·ous·ly,** *adv.* —**glo′ri·ous·ness,** *n.* —**Syn.** 3. famous, renowned; illustrious.

glo·ry (glōr′ĭ), *n., pl.* **glories,** *v.,* **gloried, glorying.** —*n.* 1. exalted praise, honor, or distinction, accorded by common consent: *paths of glory.* 2. something that makes honored or illustrious; a distinguished ornament;

an object of pride. 3. adoring praise or thanksgiving: *give glory to God.* 4. resplendent beauty or magnificence: *the glory of God.* 5. state of splendor, magnificence, or greatest prosperity. 6. the splendor and bliss of heaven; heaven. 7. a ring, circle, or surrounding radiance of light represented about the head or the whole figure of a sacred person, as Christ, a saint, etc.; a halo, nimbus, or aureola. —*v.i.* 8. to exult with triumph; rejoice proudly. 9. to be boastful; exult arrogantly (fol. by *in*). [ME, t. OF: m. *glorie,* t. L: m. *glōria* glory, fame, vainglory, boasting] —**Syn.** 1. fame, eminence. 5. grandeur, pomp. —**Ant.** 1. disgrace.

gloss¹ (glôs, glŏs), *n.* 1. a superficial luster: *gloss of satin.* 2. an external show; specious appearance. —*v.t.* 3. to put a gloss upon. 4. to give a specious appearance to (often fol. by *over*). [t. Scand.; cf. Icel. *glossi* spark] —**gloss′er,** *n.* —**gloss′less,** *adj.* —**Syn.** 1. sheen, polish, glaze. See **polish.**

gloss² (glôs, glŏs), *n.* 1. an explanation, by means of a marginal or interlinear note, of a technical or unusual expression in a manuscript text. 2. a series of verbal interpretations of a text. 3. an artfully misleading interpretation. —*v.t.* 4. to insert glosses on; annotate. 5. to give a specious interpretation of; explain away (often fol. by *over*): *to gloss over a mistake.* —*v.i.* 6. to make glosses. [t. L: s. *glossa* (explanation of) hard word, t. Gk.: lit., tongue. Cf. GLOZE] —**gloss′er,** *n.*

gloss., glossary.

Glos·sa (glŏs′ə), *n.* **Cape,** a promontory in SW Albania.

glos·sal (glŏs′əl, glôs′əl), *adj.* of or pertaining to the tongue.

glos·sa·ry (glŏs′ə rĭ, glôs′ə-), *n., pl.* **-ries.** a list of basic technical, dialectal, and difficult terms in a subject or field, with definitions. [t. L: m.s. *glossārium,* der. *glossa* GLOSS²] —**glos·sar·i·al** (glŏ sâr′ĭ əl, glô-), *adj.* —**glos′sa·rist,** *n.*

glos·sa·tor (glŏ sā′tor, glô-), *n.* one of the early medieval interpreters (not later than 1250) of the Roman and canon laws. [t. ML, ult. der. L *glossa* GLOSS²]

glos·sec·to·my (glŏ sĕk′tə mĭ, glô-), *n., pl.* **-mies.** *Surg.* the removal of all or of a portion of the tongue.

glos·si·tis (glŏ sī′tĭs, glô-), *n. Pathol.* inflammation of the tongue. [f. *glosso-* (see GLOSSOLOGY) + -ITIS]

glos·sol·o·gy (glŏ sŏl′ə jĭ, glô-), *n. Obs.* linguistics. [f. *glosso-* (t. Gk., comb. form of *glôtta* tongue) + -LOGY]

gloss·y (glôs′ĭ, glŏs′ĭ), *adj.,* **glossier, glossiest.** 1. having a gloss; lustrous. 2. having a specious appearance; plausible. [t. GLOSS¹, n. + -Y¹] —**gloss′i·ly,** *adv.* —**gloss′i·ness,** *n.* —**Syn.** 1. shining, polished, glazed; smooth, sleek. —**Ant.** 1. dull.

glost (glôst, glŏst), *n. Ceramics.* glaze or glazed ware.

-glot, a suffix indicating proficiency in language, as in *polyglot.* [t. Gk.: m.s. *glôtta* tongue]

glot·tal (glŏt′əl), *adj.* 1. pertaining to the glottis. 2. *Phonet.* articulated in the glottis.

glottal stop, *Phonet.* stop consonant made by closing the glottis so tightly that no breath can pass through, as in *yep* yes, *nope* no.

glot·tic (glŏt′ĭk), *adj.* 1. pertaining to the glottis; glottal. 2. *Obs.* linguistic.

glot·tis (glŏt′ĭs), *n.* the opening at the upper part of the larynx, between the vocal cords. [t. NL, t. Gk.: the mouth of the windpipe]

glot·tol·o·gy (glŏ tŏl′ə jĭ), *n. Obs.* linguistics. [f. *glotto-* (t. Gk., comb. form of *glôtta* tongue) + -LOGY] —**glot·to·log·ic** (glŏt′ə lŏj′ĭk), **glot′to·log′i·cal,** *adj.* —**glot·tol′o·gist,** *n.*

Glou·ces·ter (glŏs′tər, glôs′-), *n.* 1. a city in SW England: port on Severn. 63,500 (est. 1946). 2. a seaport in NE Massachusetts. 25,167 (1950). 3. Gloucestershire.

Glou·ces·ter (glŏs′tər, glôs′-), *n.* **Duke of,** 1. See **Humphrey.** 2. See **Richard III.** 3. See **Thomas of Woodstock.**

Glou·ces·ter·shire (glŏs′tər shĭr′, -shər, glôs′-), *n.* a county in SW England. 903,000 pop. (est. 1946); 1255 sq. mi. Co. seat: Gloucester. Also, **Gloucester.**

glove (glŭv), *n., v.,* **gloved, gloving.** —*n.* 1. a covering for the hand, now made with a separate sheath for each finger and for the thumb. 2. a boxing glove. —*v.t.* 3. to cover with or as with a glove; provide with gloves. 4. to serve as a glove for. [ME; OE *glōf,* c. Icel. *glōfi*] —**glove′less,** *adj.* —**glove′like′,** *adj.*

glov·er (glŭv′ər), *n.* one who makes or sells gloves.

Glov·ers·ville (glŭv′ərz vĭl′), *n.* a city in E New York. 23,634 (1950).

glow (glō), *n.* 1. light emitted by a substance heated to luminosity; incandescence. 2. brightness of color. 3. a state of bodily heat. 4. warmth of emotion or passion; ardor. —*v.i.* 5. to emit bright light and heat without flame; be incandescent. 6. to shine like something intensely heated. 7. to exhibit a strong, bright color; be lustrously red or brilliant. 8. to be excessively hot. 9. to be animated with emotion. [ME *glowe(n),* OE *glōwan,* akin to G *glühen,* Icel. *glōa*]

glow·er (glou′ər), *v.i.* 1. to look angrily; stare with sullen dislike or discontent. —*n.* 2. a glowering look; frown. [freq. of obs. *glow* stare, of uncert. orig.] —**glow′er·ing·ly,** *adv.* —**Syn.** 1. See **glare¹.**

glow·ing (glō′ĭng), *adj.* 1. incandescent. 2. rich and warm in coloring: *glowing colors.* 3. exhibiting the glow of health, excitement, etc. 4. ardent or impassioned: *a glowing account.* —**glow′ing·ly,** *adv.*

glow·worm (glō'wûrm'), *n.* **1.** any of the fireflies of the family *Lampyridae* or their larvae. **2.** a European beetle, *Lampyris noctiluca*, the wingless female of which emits a greenish light from the end of the abdomen.

glox·in·i·a (glŏk·sĭn'ĭ·ə), *n.* the garden name of tuberous-rooted plants of the genus *Sinningia*, esp. a widely cultivated species, *S. speciosa*, having large white, red, or purple bell-shaped flowers. [NL; named after B. P. *Gloxin*, German botanist]

gloze (glōz), *v.*, **glozed, glozing,** *n.* —*v.t.* **1.** to explain away; extenuate; gloss over (usually fol. by *over*). **2.** to palliate with specious talk. —*v.i.* **3.** *Obs.* to make glosses; comment. —*n.* **4.** *Rare.* flattery or deceit. **5.** *Obs.* a specious show. [ME *glose*, t. OF. See GLOSS²]

glu·ci·num (glōō·sī'nəm), *n.* *Chem.* beryllium. *Sym.:* Gl. Also, **glu·cin·i·um** (glōō·sĭn'ĭ·əm). [NL, der. Gk. *glykýs* sweet (some of the salts having a sweet taste)]

Gluck (glŏŏk), *n.* **1.** Alma, (*Reba Fiersohn, Mme. Efrem Zimbalist*) 1884–1938, U.S. operatic soprano, born in Rumania. **2.** Christoph Willibald von (krĭs'tôf vĭl'ĭ bält' fən), 1714–87, German operatic composer.

glu·co·pro·te·in (glōō'kō prō'tĭ ĭn, -tēn), *n.* glycoprotein.

glu·cose (glōō'kōs), *n.* **1.** *Chem.* a sugar, $C_6H_{12}O_6$, having several optically different forms, the common or dextrorotatory form (d-glucose) occurring in many fruits, animal tissues and fluids, etc., and having a sweetness about one half that of ordinary sugar. The levorotatory form (l-glucose) is rare and not naturally occurring. **2.** *Com.* a syrup containing dextrose, maltose, and dextrine, obtained by the incomplete hydrolysis of starch. [t. F; f. m.s. Gk. *glykýs* sweet + *-ose* -OSE²]

glu·co·side (glōō'kə sīd'), *n.* *Chem.* one of an extensive group of compounds which yield glucose and some other substance or substances when treated with a dilute acid or when decomposed by a ferment or enzyme. [f. GLU-COS(E) + -IDE]

glu·co·su·ri·a (glōō'kō sōōr'ĭ ə), *n.* *Pathol.* glycosuria.

glue (glōō), *n.*, *v.*, **glued, gluing.** —*n.* **1.** an impure gelatin obtained by boiling skins, hoofs, and other animal substances in water, and used for various purposes in the arts, esp. as an adhesive medium in uniting substances. **2.** any of various preparations of this substance. **3.** any similar adhesive material. —*v.t.* **4.** to join or fasten with glue. **5.** to fix or attach firmly, as if with glue; make adhere closely. [ME, t. OF: m. *glu*, g. LL *glus.* Cf. GLUTEN] —**glue'like'**, *adj.* —**glu'er,** *n.*

glue·y (glōō'ĭ), *adj.*, **gluier, gluiest. 1.** like glue; viscid; sticky. **2.** full of or smeared with glue.

glum (glŭm), *adj.*, **glummer, glummest.** gloomily sullen or silent; dejected. [cf. LG *glum* turbid, muddy; akin to GLOOM²] —**glum'ly,** *adv.* —**glum'ness,** *n.*

glu·ma·ceous (glōō mā'shəs), *adj.* **1.** glumelike. **2.** consisting of or having glumes.

glume (glōōm), *n.* *Bot.* one of the characteristic bracts of the inflorescence of grasses, sedges, etc., esp. one of the pair of bracts at the base of a spikelet. [t. L: m.s. *gluma* hull or husk (of grain)] —**glume'like'**, *adj.*

glut (glŭt), *v.*, **glutted, glutting,** *n.* —*v.t.* **1.** to feed or fill to satiety; sate: *to glut the appetite.* **2.** to feed or fill to excess; cloy. **3. glut the market,** to overstock the market; furnish a supply of any article largely in excess of the demand, so that the price is unusually low. **4.** to choke up: *glut a channel.* —*v.i.* **5.** to eat to satiety. —*n.* **6.** a full supply. **7.** a surfeit. **8.** act of glutting. **9.** state of being glutted. [ME *glotye(n)*, appar. der. obs. *glut*, n., glutton, t. OF: adj., greedy. See GLUTTON¹]

glu·tam·ic acid (glōō tăm'ĭk), *Chem.* a colorless solid, $HOOCCH_2CH_2CH(NH_2)COOH$, found in the proteins of seeds and beets.

glu·ta·mine (glōō'tə mēn', -mĭn), *n.* *Chem.* a crystalline amino acid, $HOOCCH(NH_2)CH_2CH_2CONH_2$, related to glutamic acid. [f. GLUT(EN) + -AMINE]

glu·ta·thi·one (glōō'tə thī'ōn, -thī'ən), *n.* *Biochem.* a peptide found in blood and animal tissues, in embryos and germinating seedlings: important in metabolic actions.

glu·te·al (glōō tē'əl, glōō'tĭ əl), *adj.* *Anat.* pertaining to buttock muscles or the buttocks. [f. GLUTE(US) + -AL¹]

glu·te·lins (glōō'tə lĭnz), *n.pl.* *Biochem.* a group of simple proteins of vegetable origin, esp. from wheat.

glu·ten (glōō'tən), *n.* **1.** the tough, viscid nitrogenous substance remaining when the flour of wheat or other grain is washed to remove the starch. **2.** glue, or some gluey substance. [t. L: glue, akin to LL *glus* GLUE]

gluten bread, bread made from gluten flour.

gluten flour, wheat flour from which a large part of the starch has been removed, thus increasing the proportion of gluten.

glu·te·nous (glōō'tə nəs), *adj.* **1.** like gluten. **2.** containing gluten, esp. in large amounts.

glu·te·us (glōō tē'əs), *n.*, *pl.* **-tei** (-tē'ī). *Anat.* any of several muscles of the buttocks. [NL, der. Gk. *gloutós* rump, pl. buttocks]

glu·ti·nous (glōō'tə nəs), *adj.* of the nature of glue; gluey; viscid; sticky. [t. L: m. s. *glūtinōsus* gluey, viscous] —**glu'ti·nous·ly,** *adv.* —**glu'ti·nous·ness,** *n.* **glu·ti·nos·i·ty** (glōō'tə nŏs'ə tĭ), *n.*

glu·tose (glōō'tōs), *n.* an ingredient of the syrupy mixture obtained by the action of alkali on levulose, or in the unfermentable reducing portion of cane molasses.

glut·ton¹ (glŭt'ən), *n.* **1.** one who eats to excess; a

gormandizer. **2.** one who indulges in something excessively. [ME *glutun*, t. OF: m. *glouton*, g. L *glūto, glutto*]

glut·ton² (glŭt'ən), *n.* *Zool.* a thick-set, voracious mammal, *Gulo luscus*, of the weasel family, measuring from 2 to 3 feet in length, and inhabiting northern regions. The kind found in America is usually called the **wolverine**, and is practically identical with that of Europe and Asia. [ult. t. Sw.: trans. of *fjällfräs* (through G *vielfrass*), whence also NL name of animal, *gulo*]

glut·ton·ize (glŭt'ə nīz'), *v.*, **-ized, -izing.** —*v.i.* **1.** to eat like a glutton. —*v.t.* **2.** to feast gluttonously on.

glut·ton·ous (glŭt'ən əs), *adj.* **1.** given to excessive eating; voracious. **2.** greedy; insatiable. —**glut'ton·ous·ly,** *adv.* —**glut'ton·ous·ness,** *n.*

glut·ton·y (glŭt'ən ĭ), *n.*, *pl.* **-tonies.** excess in eating.

gly·cer·ic (glĭ sĕr'ĭk, glĭs'ər ĭk), *adj.* *Chem.* pertaining to or derived from glycerin.

glyceric acid, *Chem.* a colorless, syrupy fluid, $CH_2OHCHOHCOOH$, produced during the fermentation of alcohol.

glyc·er·ide (glĭs'ə rīd', -ər ĭd), *n.* *Chem.* one of a group of esters obtained from glycerol in combination with acids. [f. GLYCER(IN) + -IDE]

glyc·er·in (glĭs'ər ĭn), *n.* glycerol. Also, **glyc·er·ine** (glĭs'ər ĭn, -ə rēn'). [t. F: m. *glycérine*, f. m.s. Gk. *glykerós* sweet + *-ine* -IN²]

glyc·er·ol (glĭs'ə rōl', -rŏl'), *n.* *Chem.* a colorless, odorless, liquid alcohol, $HOCH_2CHOHCH_2OH$, of syrupy consistency and sweet taste, obtained by the saponification of natural fats and oils, and used in the arts, in medicine, etc.

glyc·er·yl (glĭs'ər ĭl) *adj.* *Chem.* denoting or pertaining to the trivalent radical (C_3H_5) derived from glycerin. [f. GLYCER(IN) + -YL]

gly·cine (glĭ'sēn, glĭ sēn'), *n.* *Chem.* a sweet-tasting, colorless, crystalline compound, H_2NCH_2COOH, the simplest amino acid, obtained by hydrolysis of proteins. [f. m. Gk. *glyk(ýs)* sweet + -INE²]

gly·co·gen (glĭ'kə jən), *n.* *Biochem.* a white, tasteless, polysaccharide ($C_6H_{10}O_5)_x$, usually stored in the liver, and easily hydrolyzed into glucose. [f. m.s. Gk. *glykýs* sweet + -GEN]

gly·co·gen·ase (glĭ'kə jə nās'), *n.* *Biochem.* a liver enzyme which changes glycogen to glucose, **gly·co·gen·ol·y·sis** (glĭ'kō jə nŏl'ə sĭs), or which imitates the reverse process, **gly·co·gen·e·sis** (glĭ'kə jĕn'ə sĭs), depending on conditions.

gly·co·gen·ic (glĭ'kə jĕn'ĭk), *adj.* *Biochem.* of or pertaining to glycogen.

gly·col (glĭ'kōl, -kŏl), *n.* *Chem.* **1.** a colorless, sweet-tasting liquid, CH_2OHCH_2OH, used as an antifreeze in automobiles. **2.** any of a group of alcohols containing two hydroxyl groups. [b. GLYC(ERIN) and (ALCOH)OL]

gly·col·ic (glĭ kŏl'ĭk), *adj.* *Chem.* pertaining to or derived from glycol, as **glycolic acid,** $HOCH_2COOH$.

gly·co·pro·te·in (glĭ'kō prō'tĭ ĭn, -tēn), *n.* *Biochem.* any of a group of complex proteins containing a carbohydrate combined with a simple protein, as mucin, etc. Also, **glucoprotein.** [f. m.s. Gk. *glykýs* sweet + PROTEIN]

gly·co·su·ri·a (glĭ'kō sōōr'ĭ ə), *n.* *Pathol.* excretion of glucose in the urine, as in diabetes. Also, **glucosuria.** [NL, f. F *glycose* GLUCOSE + -uria -URIA] —**gly·co·su'ric,** *adj.*

gly·ox·a·lin (glĭ ŏk'sə lĭn), *n.* *Chem.* imidazole.

glyph (glĭf), *n.* **1.** *Archit.* an ornamental channel or groove, usually vertical, as in a Doric frieze. **2.** a sculptured figure. **3.** *Archaeol.* a pictograph or hieroglyph. [t. Gk.: s. *glyphē* carving] —**glyph'ic,** *adj.*

glyp·tic (glĭp'tĭk), *adj.* of or pertaining to carving or engraving, esp. on precious stones. [t. Gk.: m.s. *glyptikós* of engraving]

glyp·tog·ra·phy (glĭp tŏg'rə fĭ), *n.* **1.** the description or study of engraved gems, etc. **2.** the art or process of engraving on gems or the like. [f. Gk. *glyptó(s)* carved + -GRAPHY]

gm., gram; grams.

G.M., 1. Grand Marshal. **2.** Grand Master.

G-man (jē'măn'), *n.* an agent for the FBI.

Gmc., Germanic.

gnar (när), *v.i.*, **gnarred, gnarring.** to snarl; growl.

gnarl (närl), *n.* **1.** a knotty protuberance on a tree; knot. —*v.t.* **2.** to twist. [back formation from GNARLED]

gnarled (närld), *adj.* **1.** (of trees) full of or covered with gnarls. **2.** (of persons) **a.** having a rugged, weather-beaten appearance. **b.** cross-grained; perverse; cantankerous. Also, **gnarl'y.** [var. of KNURLED]

gnash (năsh), *v.t.* **1.** to grind (the teeth) together, esp in rage or pain. **2.** to bite with grinding teeth. —*v.i.* **3.** to gnash the teeth. —*n.* **4.** act of gnashing. [unexplained var. of obs. *gnast*, t. Scand.; cf. Icel. *gnastan* gnashing of teeth]

gnat (năt), *n.* **1.** any of certain small flies, esp. the biting gnats or punkies (*Ceratopogonidae*), the midges (*Chironomidae*), and the buffalo gnats or black flies (*Simulidae*). **2.** *Eng.* any of certain small dipterous insects (mosquitoes) of the family *Culicidae*, esp. *Culex pipiens*. [ME; OE *gnæt(t)*, c. d. G *gnatze*] —**gnat'like',** *adj.*

Gnat (def. 2), *Culex pipiens* (Small figure shows natural size)

gnat·catch·er (năt'kăch'ər), *n.* any of various small American insectivorous birds of the genus *Polioptila*, as the blue-gray gnatcatcher, *P. caerulea.*

gnath·ic (năth'ĭk), *adj.* of or pertaining to the jaw. [f. s. Gk. *gnáthos* jaw + -ɪC]

gnathic index, *Craniol.* the ratio of the distance from basion to prosthion to the distance from basion to nasion, expressed in per cent of the latter.

gna·thi·on (nā'thĭ ŏn', năth'ĭ-), *n. Craniol.* the lowest point on the anterior margin of the lower jaw in the mid-sagittal plane. [NL, dim. of Gk. *gnáthos* jaw]

-gnathous, an adjectival word element referring to the jaw, as in *prognathous.* [f. s. Gk. *gnáthos* jaw + -ous]

gnaw (nô), *v.,* **gnawed, gnawed** or **gnawn, gnawing.** —*v.t.* **1.** to wear away or remove by persistent biting. **2.** to make by gnawing. **3.** to corrode; consume. **4.** to consume with passion; torment. —*v.i.* **5.** to bite persistently. **6.** to cause corrosion. **7.** to act as if by corrosion. [ME *gnawe(n),* OE *gnagan,* c. G *nagen,* Icel. *gnaga*] —**gnaw'er,** *n.*

gnaw·ing (nô'ĭng), *n.* **1.** act of one who or that which gnaws. **2.** a persistent pain suggesting gnawing: *the gnawings of hunger.* —**gnaw'ing·ly,** *adv.*

gneiss (nīs), *n.* a metamorphic rock, generally made up of bands which differ in color and composition, some bands being rich in feldspar and quartz, others rich in hornblende or mica. [t. G] —**gneiss'ic,** *adj.*

gneiss·oid (nī'soid), *adj.* resembling gneiss.

gnome[1] (nōm), *n.* one of a species of diminutive beings fabled to inhabit the interior of the earth and to act as guardians of its treasures, usually thought of as shriveled little old men; a troll. [t. F, t. NL (Paracelsus): m.s. *gnomus*] —**gnom'ish,** *adj.* —**Syn.** See **goblin, sylph.**

gnome[2] (nōm), *n.* a short, pithy expression of a general truth; aphorism. [t. Gk.: judgment, opinion, maxim]

gno·mic (nō'mĭk, nŏm'ĭk), *adj.* **1.** like or containing gnomes or aphorisms. **2.** of, pertaining to, or denoting a writer of aphorisms, esp. certain Greek poets. Also, **gno'mi·cal.** [t. Gk.: m.s. *gnōmikós*] —**gno'mi·cal·ly,** *adv.*

gno·mist (nō'mĭst), *n.* a writer of aphorisms.

gno·mon (nō'mŏn), *n.* **1.** a vertical shaft, column, obelisk, or the like, used (esp. by the ancients) as an astronomical instrument for determining the altitude of the sun, the position of a place, etc., by noting the length of the shadow cast at noon. **2.** the vertical triangular plate of a sundial. **3.** *Geom.* the part of a parallelogram which remains after a similar parallelogram has been taken away from one of its corners. [t. L, t. Gk.: one who knows, an indicator]

EFGBCD Gnomon (def. 3)

gno·sis (nō'sĭs), *n.* a knowledge of spiritual things; mystical knowledge. [NL, t. Gk.: knowledge]

-gnosis, a suffix referring to recognition, esp. of a morbid condition, as in *prognosis.* [t. Gk.: knowledge]

gnos·tic (nŏs'tĭk), *adj.* Also, **gnos'ti·cal. 1.** pertaining to knowledge. **2.** possessing knowledge, esp. esoteric knowledge of spiritual things. **3.** *(cap.)* pertaining to or characteristic of the Gnostics. —*n.* **4.** *(cap.)* a member of any of certain sects among the early Christians who claimed to have superior knowledge of spiritual things, and explained the world as created by powers or agencies arising as emanations from the Godhead. [t. LL: s. *Gnosticus,* t. Gk.: m. *gnōstikós* pertaining to knowledge] —**Gnos'ti·cism,** *n.*

Gnos·ti·cize (nŏs'tə sīz'), *v.,* **-cized, -cizing.** —*v.i.* **1.** to adopt or maintain Gnostic views. —*v.t.* **2.** to explain on Gnostic principles; give a Gnostic coloring to.

gnu (nōō, nū), *n., pl.* **gnus,** *(esp. collectively)* **gnu.** any of several African antelopes constituting the genus *Connochaetes,* characterized by an oxlike head, curved horns, and a long, flowing tail; a wildebeest. [t. Kaffir: m. *nqu*]

Brindled gnu,
Connochaetes taurinus
(4½ ft. high at the shoulder)

go (gō), *v.,* **went, gone, going,** *n., pl.* **goes.** —*v.i.* **1.** to move or pass along; proceed. **2.** to move away or out; depart (opposed to *come* or *arrive*). **3.** to keep or be in motion; act, work, or run. **4.** to become; assume another state or condition: *to go mad.* **5.** to continue; be habitually: *to go in rags.* **6.** to move toward a point or a given result or in a given manner; proceed; advance. **7.** to be known: *to go by a name.* **8.** to reach or extend: *this road goes to the city.* **9.** (of time) to pass; elapse. **10.** to be awarded, transferred, or applied to a particular recipient or purpose. **11.** to be sold: *the property went for a song.* **12.** to conduce or tend: *this only goes to prove the point.* **13.** to turn out; result: *how did the game go?* **14.** to belong; have a place: *this book goes on the top shelf.* **15.** (of colors, etc.) to harmonize; be compatible; be suited. **16.** to act or operate with sound, as a bell or a gun; make a certain sound: *the gun goes bang.* **17.** to be discharged, or explode (fol. by *off*). **18.** to be phrased: *how do the words go?* **19.** to resort; have recourse: *to go to court.* **20.** to get the facts; find out (fol. by *behind*). **21.** to be given up; be worn out; be lost or

ended. **22.** to die. **23.** to fail; give way. **24.** to be overwhelmed; be ruined (fol. by *under*). **25.** to begin; come into action: *here goes!* **26.** to attack (fol. by *at*). **27.** to be contained (fol. by *into*): *4 goes into 12.* **28.** to contribute in amount or quantity; be requisite: *16 ounces go to the pound.* **29.** to share equally (fol. by a complementary substantive): *to go partners.* **30.** to contribute to a result: *the items which go to make up a total.* **31.** to be about, intending, or destined (used in the pres. part. fol. by an infinitive): *he is going to write.* **32.** *Naut.* to change course by tacking or wearing (fol. by *about*). —*v.t.* **33.** *Colloq.* to endure or tolerate: *I can't go his preaching.* **34.** *Colloq.* to risk or wager. **35.** Some special verb phrases are:

go around, 1. to move about; circulate. **2.** to be enough for all.

go back on, *Colloq.* **1.** to fail (someone); let (someone) down. **2.** to fail to keep (one's word, promise, etc.).

go by, 1. to pass. **2.** to be guided by.

go down, 1. to descend; slope down. **2.** to be defeated. **3.** *Brit.* to leave the University at the end of the term or permanently (according to context).

go in for, to make (a thing) one's particular interest.

go on, 1. to go ahead; proceed. **2.** to manage; do. **3.** to behave; act.

go out, 1. to come to a stop; end: *the light went out.* **2.** to go to social affairs, etc.

go over, 1. to reread. **2.** to repeat. **3.** to look at; scan.

go through with, to complete; bring to a finish.

go up, 1. to rise or ascend; advance. **2.** *Brit.* to go to the University at the beginning of term.

go with, *Colloq.* **1.** to harmonize with. **2.** to frequent the society of.

—*n.* **36.** act of going: *the come and go of the seasons.* **37.** *Colloq.* energy, spirit, or animation: *to be full of go.* **38.** *Eng.* the first or preliminary examination at Cambridge University for the degree of A.B. **39.** *Colloq.* a try at something; attempt: *to have a go at something.* **40.** *Colloq.* something that goes well; a success: *to make a go of something.* **41.** *Colloq.* a bargain: *it's a go!* **42.** on the go, *Colloq.* constantly going; very active. [ME *go(n),* OE *gān;* akin to D *gaan,* MLG *gān,* OHG *gān, gēn,* G *gehen.* Cf. GANG[2], v.] —**go'er,** *n.* —**Syn. 1.** walk, run, ride, travel, advance. —**Ant. 1.** stay.

G.O., general order.

go·a (gō'ə), *n.* the black-tailed gazelle, *Procapra picticaudata,* of the Tibetan plateau. [t. Tibetan: m. *dgoba*]

Gō·a (gō'ə), *n.* a district of Portuguese India, on the Arabian Sea, ab. 250 mi. S of Bombay. 624,177 pop. (1940); 1538 sq. mi. *Cap.:* Panjim.

Goa, *Procapra picticaudata*
(2 ft. high at the shoulder)

goad (gōd), *n.* **1.** a stick with a pointed end, for driving cattle, etc. **2.** anything that pricks or wounds like such a stick; a stimulus. —*v.t.* **3.** to prick or drive with or as with a goad; incite. [ME *gode,* OE *gād,* c. Langobardic *gaida* arrowhead] —**goad'like',** *adj.* —**Syn. 3.** spur, stimulate, instigate, impel.

goal (gōl), *n.* **1.** that toward which effort is directed; aim or end. **2.** the terminal point in a race. **3.** a pole or other object by which this is marked. **4.** a bound or structure toward which the players strive to advance the ball, etc. **5.** act of throwing or kicking the ball through or over the goal. **6.** the score made by accomplishing this. [ME *gol* boundary, limit. Cf. OE *gǣlan* hinder, impede] —**goal'less,** *adj.*

goal·ie (gō'lĭ), *n.* the goalkeeper on a hockey team.

goal·keep·er (gōl'kē'pər), *n. Sports.* a player whose special duty it is to prevent the ball from going through or over the goal.

goal line, *Sports.* the line which bounds the goal.

goal post, either of the two posts which support a bar across them, and form the football or soccer goal.

goat (gōt), *n.* **1.** any animal of the genus *Capra* (family *Bovidae*), comprising various agile hollow-horned ruminants closely related to the sheep, found native in rocky and mountainous regions of the Old World, and including domesticated forms common throughout the world. **2.** any of various allied animals, as *Oreamnos montanus* (**Rocky Mountain goat**), a ruminant of western North America. **3.** *(cap.) Astron.* the zodiacal constellation or sign Capricorn. **4.** *U.S. Slang.* the scapegoat; one who is the butt of a joke. **5.** **get one's goat,** *U.S. Slang.* to make one lose his temper. [ME *gote, goot,* OE *gāt,* c. G *geiss;* akin to L *haedus* kid] —**goat'-like',** *adj.*

Domestic goat, *Capra hircus*
(2½ ft. high at the shoulder)

goat antelope, 1. a goatlike antelope of the genus *Naemorhedus,* as the goral, *N. goral,* or *N. crispus* of Japan. **2.** any antelope of the tribe *Rupicaprini,* a subdivision of the sheep and goat family, and including the chamois, goral, serow, and Rocky Mountain goat.

goat·ee (gō tē'), *n.* a man's beard trimmed to a tuft.

goat·fish (gōt′fĭsh′), *n.*, *pl.* **-fishes**, (*esp. collectively*) **-fish**. any fish of the tropical and subtropical marine family *Mullidae*, having a pair of long barbels below the mouth, and including species highly esteemed as a delicacy by the ancient Romans; surmullet; red mullet.

goat god, any deity with the legs and feet of a goat, as Pan or the satyrs.

goat·herd (gōt′hûrd′), *n.* one who tends goats.

goat·ish (gō′tĭsh), *adj.* like a goat; lustful. —**goat′-ish·ly**, *adv.* —**goat′ish·ness**, *n.*

goats·beard (gōts′bĭrd′), *n.* **1.** a composite plant, *Tragopogon pratensis*. **2.** a rosaceous herb, *Aruncus sylvester*, with long, slender spikes of small flowers.

goat·skin (gōt′skĭn′), *n.* **1.** the skin or hide of a goat. **2.** leather made from it.

goat's-rue (gōts′rōō′), *n.* **1.** an American leguminous herb, *Telphrosia virginiana*. **2.** a European leguminous herb, *Galega officinalis*, formerly used in medicine.

goat·suck·er (gōt′sŭk′ər), *n.* **1.** a nonpasserine nocturnal bird, *Caprimulgus europaeus*, of Europe, with flat head and wide mouth, formerly supposed to suck the milk of goats. **2.** any of the group of chiefly nocturnal or crepuscular birds to which this species belongs, usually regarded as including two families, the *Caprimulgidae* (**true goatsuckers**) and the *Podargidae* (**frogmouths**).

gob[1] (gŏb), *n.* a mass or lump. [ME *gobbe* lump, mass, appar. t. OF: m. *go(u)be*, ult. of Gallic derivation]

gob[2] (gŏb), *n.* *Slang.* a seaman in the U.S. naval service. [appar. akin to GOB[1]]

gob·bet (gŏb′ĭt), *n.* **1.** a fragment or hunk, esp. of raw flesh. **2.** *Archaic or Dial.* a lump or mass. [ME *gobet*, t. OF, dim of *gobe* GOB[1]]

gob·ble[1] (gŏb′əl), *v.*, **-bled**, **-bling**. —*v.t.* **1.** to swallow hastily in large pieces; gulp. **2.** *U.S. Slang.* to seize upon greedily or eagerly. —*v.i.* **3.** to eat hastily. [der. GOB[1]] —**gob′bler**, *n.* —**Syn. 1.** bolt. devour.

gob·ble[2] (gŏb′əl), *v.*, **-bled**, **-bling**. —*v.i.* **1.** to make the characteristic throaty cry of a turkey cock. —*n.* **2.** this sound. [var. of GABBLE, taken as imit. of the cry]

gob·ble·de·gook (gŏb′əl dĭ gōōk′), *n.* *Colloq.* language characterized by circumlocution and jargon: *the gobbledegook of government reports.* [intentionally grotesque coinage (by Rep. Maury Maverick, b. 1895), modeled on HOBBLEDEHOY. Final element *gook* may be slang word for tramp, var. of GOWK. Cf. GOBBLE, GOO]

gob·bler (gŏb′lər), *n.* a male turkey.

Gob·e·lin (gŏb′ə lĭn; *Fr.* gô blăn′), *adj.* **1.** made at the tapestry factory of the Gobelins in Paris. **2.** resembling the tapestry made at the Gobelins.

go-be·tween (gō′bə twēn′), *n.* one who acts as agent between persons or parties.

Go·bi (gō′bĭ), *n.* a desert in E Asia, mostly in Mongolia. ab. 500,000 sq. mi. Chinese, **Shamo.**

go·bi·oid (gō′bĭ oid′), *adj.* **1.** of or resembling a goby. —*n.* **2.** a gobioid fish.

gob·let (gŏb′lĭt), *n.* **1.** a drinking glass with a foot and stem. **2.** *Archaic.* a bowl-shaped drinking vessel. [ME *gobelet*, t. OF, dim. of *gobel* cup; ult. of Celtic orig.]

gob·lin (gŏb′lĭn), *n.* a grotesque, mischievous sprite or elf. [ME *gobelin*, t. F (obs.), t. MHG: m. *kobold* goblin] —**Syn.** GOBLIN, GNOME, GREMLIN refer to imaginary beings, thought to be malevolent to man. GOBLINS are demons of any size, usually in human or animal forms, which are supposed to assail, afflict, and even torture human beings: "*Be thou a spirit of health or goblin damn'd, . . .*" (Shak. Hamlet I, iv). GNOMES are small beings, like ugly little old men, who live in the earth, guarding mines, treasures, etc. They are mysteriously malevolent and terrify human beings by causing dreadful mishaps to occur. GREMLINS are invisible beings who were said by pilots in World War II to cause all sorts of things to go wrong with airplanes.

go·by (gō′bĭ), *n.*, *pl.* **-bies**, (*esp. collectively*) **-by**. **1.** any member of the *Gobiidae*, a family of marine and freshwater fishes, mostly small and having the pelvic fins united to form a suctorial disk that enables them to cling to rocks, as *Baleosoma basci*, common on the South Atlantic coast of the U.S. **2.** any member of the closely related family, *Eleotridae*, in which the pelvic fins are separate. [t. L: m. s. *gōbius, cōbius*, t. Gk.: m. *kōbiós* kind of fish]

go-by (gō′bī′), *n.* *Colloq.* a going by without notice; intentional passing by: *to give one the go-by.*

go·cart (gō′kärt′), *n.* **1.** a small, wheeled vehicle for small children to ride in. **2.** a small framework with casters, in which children learn to walk. **3.** a handcart.

God (gŏd), *n.* **1.** the one Supreme Being, the creator and ruler of the universe. **2.** the Supreme Being considered with reference to a particular attribute: *the God of justice.* **3.** (*l.c.*) a deity, esp. a male deity, presiding over some portion of wordly affairs. **4.** (*cap. or l.c.*) a supreme being according to some particular conception: *the God of pantheism.* **5.** (*l.c.*) an image of a deity; an idol. **6.** (*l.c.*) any deified person or object. [ME and OE, c. D *god*, G *gott*, Icel. *godh*, Goth. *guth*]

Go·da·va·ri (gō dä′və rē′), *n.* a river flowing from W India SE to the Bay of Bengal. ab. 900 mi.

god·child (gŏd′chīld′), *n.*, *pl.* **-children**. one for whom a person (godparent) stands sponsor at baptism.

god·daugh·ter (gŏd′dô′tər), *n.* a female godchild.

god·dess (gŏd′ĭs), *n.* **1.** a female god or deity. **2.** a woman of extraordinary beauty. **3.** an adored woman. —**god′dess·hood′, god′dess·ship′,** *n.*

Go·de·froy de Bouil·lon (gôd frwä′ də bōō yôN′), c1060–1100, French crusader.

go-dev·il (gō′dĕv′əl), *n.* **1.** a movable-jointed apparatus forced through a pipe line to free it from obstructions. **2.** a dart dropped into a well to explode a charge of dynamite or nitroglycerin previously placed in a desired position. **3.** *Railway Slang.* a handcar.

god·fa·ther (gŏd′fä′thər), *n.* **1.** a man who stands sponsor for a child at baptism or confirmation. —*v.t.* **2.** to act as godfather to; be sponsor for.

God·head (gŏd′hĕd′), *n.* **1.** the essential being of God; the Supreme Being. **2.** (*l.c.*) godhood or godship. **3.** (*l.c.*) *Rare.* a deity; god or goddess.

god·hood (gŏd′hŏŏd), *n.* divine character; godship.

Go·di·va (gō dī′və), *n.* wife of Leofric, Earl of Mercia (11th century). According to legend, she rode naked through the streets of Coventry, England, to win relief for the people from a burdensome tax.

god·less (gŏd′lĭs), *adj.* **1.** having or acknowledging no God. **2.** wicked. —**god′less·ly**, *adv.* —**god′less·ness**, *n.*

god·like (gŏd′līk′), *adj.* like or befitting a god, or God. —**god′like′ness**, *n.*

god·ly (gŏd′lĭ), *adj.*, **-lier, -liest. 1.** conforming to God's laws; pious. **2.** *Archaic.* coming from God; divine. —**god′li·ly**, *adv.* —**god′li·ness**, *n.* —**Syn. 1.** devout, religious; saintly. —**Ant. 1.** wicked, ungodly.

god·moth·er (gŏd′mŭth′ər), *n.* **1.** a woman who sponsors a child at baptism. **2.** a female sponsor. —*v.t.* **3.** to act as godmother to; sponsor.

Go·dol·phin (gō dŏl′fĭn), *n.* **Sidney, 1st Earl of,** 1645–1712, British statesman and financier.

go·down (gō doun′), *n.* (in India and eastern Asia) a warehouse. [t. Malay: m. *godong*]

god·par·ent (gŏd′pâr′ənt), *n.* a godfather or godmother.

go·droon (gō drōōn′), *n.* gadroon.

God's acre, a burial ground; cemetery.

god·send (gŏd′sĕnd′), *n.* something unexpected but particularly welcome and timely, as if sent by God. [earlier *God's send*, var. (under influence of *send*, v.) of *God's sond* or *sand*, OE *sond, sand* message, service]

god·ship (gŏd′shĭp), *n.* the rank or character of a god.

god·son (gŏd′sŭn′), *n.* a male godchild.

God·speed (gŏd′spēd′), *n.* God speed you: a wish of success to one setting out on a journey or undertaking.

Go·du·nov (gō dŏŏ nôf′), *n.* **Boris Fëdorovich** (bŏ-rēs′ fyô′dô rô′vĭch), 1552–1605, Russian regent and czar, 1598–1605.

God·ward (gŏd′wərd), *adv.* **1.** Also, **God′wards.** toward God. —*adj.* **2.** directed toward God.

God·win (gŏd′wĭn), *n.* **1.** (*Earl of Wessex*) died 1053, English statesman. **2. Mrs.,** (*Mary Wollstonecraft*) 1759–97, British writer (wife of William). **3. William,** 1756–1836, British political philosopher and writer.

God·win Aus·ten (gŏd′wĭn ôs′tĭn). See K2.

god·wit (gŏd′wĭt), *n.* any of several large New and Old World shore birds of the genus *Limosa*, all with long, slightly upcurved bills, as the **Hudsonian godwit,** *L. haemastica*, of America.

Goeb·bels (gœb′əls), *n.* **Paul Joseph** (poul yō′zĕf), 1897–1945, German Nazi propaganda leader.

Goe·ring (gœ′rĭng), *n.* **Hermann** (hĕr′män), 1893–1946, German field marshal and Nazi party leader.

goes (gōz), *v.* **1.** 3rd pers. sing. pres. of go. —*n.* **2.** pl. of go.

Goe·thals (gō′thəlz), *n.* **George Washington,** 1858–1928, U.S. major general and army engineer, in charge of building the Panama Canal.

Goe·the (gœ′tə), *n.* **Johann Wolfgang von** (yō′hän vôlf′gäng fən), 1749–1832, German poet, dramatist, novelist, and philosopher.

goe·thite (gō′thīt, gō′tīt), *n.* a very common mineral, iron hydroxide, FeO(OH), occurring in crystals, but more commonly in yellow or brown earthy masses, an ore of iron. Also, **göthite.** [named after the poet GOETHE. See -ITE[1]]

gof·fer (gŏf′ər), *n.* **1.** an ornamental plaiting used for the frills and borders of women's caps, etc. —*v.t.* **2.** to flute (a frill, etc.), as with a heated iron. **3.** to impress (book edges, etc.) with an ornamental pattern. Also, **gauffer.** [t. F: m. *gauffer* stamp cloth, paper, etc., der. *gaufre* honeycomb, waffle, t. D: m. *wafel*. See WAFER]

go-get·ter (gō′gĕt′ər), *n.* *U.S. Colloq.* an enterprising, aggressive person.

gog·gle (gŏg′əl), *n.*, *v.*, **-gled, -gling.** —*n.* **1.** (*pl.*) spectacles so devised as to protect the eyes from injury. **2.** a goggling look. —*v.i.* **3.** to roll the eyes; stare. **4.** (of the eyes) to roll; bulge and stare. —*v.t.* **5.** to roll (the eyes). [ME *gogelen* look aside; orig. uncert.]

gog·gle-eyed (gŏg′əl īd′), *adj.* having prominent, rolling eyes, esp. as a mark of astonishment.

Gogh (gō, gôKH; *Du.* KHôKH), *n.* **Vincent van** (văn; *Du.* vĭn sĕnt′ vän′), 1853–90, Dutch painter.

gog·let (gŏg′lĭt), *n.* (in India, etc.) a long-necked vessel, usually of porous earthenware to permit evaporation, used as a water cooler. [earlier *gurglet*, t. Pg.: m. *gorgoleta*, ult. der. L *gurga*, abyss; throat]

Go·gol (gō′gôl), *n.* **Nikolai Vasilievich** (nĭ kŏ lī′ vä-sē′lyə vĭch), 1809–52, Russian novelist, short-story writer, and dramatist.

---

b., blend of, blended; c., cognate with; d., dialect, dialectal; der., derived from; f., formed from; g., going back to; m., modification of; r., replacing; s., stem of; t., taken from; ?, perhaps. See the full key on inside cover.

Goi·del·ic (goiˈdĕlˈĭk), *adj.* **1.** of or pertaining to the Gaels or their language. —*n.* **2.** *Ling.* the Gaelic subgroup of Celtic. Also, **Gadhelic**. [f. m. OIrish *Goideal* a Gael + -IC]

go·ing (gōˈĭng), *n.* **1.** a going away; departure: *a safe going and return.* **2.** condition of surfaces and roads for walking or driving: *the going was bad.* **3.** (*usually pl.*) way; deportment. —*adj.* **4.** moving or working, as machinery. **5.** that goes; in existence. **6.** continuing to do business: *a going concern.* **7.** having to do with a going business: *the going value of a company.* **8.** departing. **9. going on,** getting to be nearly: *it is going on four o'clock.*

goings on, *Colloq.* actions; conduct; behavior: used chiefly with depreciative force.

goi·ter (goiˈtər), *n.* *Pathol.* an enlargement of the thyroid gland, on the front and sides of the neck. Also, **goi·tre.** [t. F: (m.) *goitre*, ult. der. L *guttur* throat]

goi·trous (goiˈtrəs), *adj.* pertaining to or affected with goiter.

Gol·con·da (gŏlkŏnˈdə), *n.* **1.** an ancient city of India, the ruins of which are near the capital city of Hyderabad state: once the capital of a powerful Mohammedan kingdom, it was renowned for its wealth and diamond cutting. **2.** (*often l.c.*) a mine or source of wealth.

gold (gōld), *n.* **1.** a precious yellow metal, highly malleable and ductile, and free from liability to rust. *Sym.:* Au; *at. wt.:* 197.2; *at. no.:* 79; *sp. gr.:* 19.3, at 20°C. **2.** coin made of it. **3.** money; wealth. **4.** something likened to this metal in brightness, preciousness, etc.: *a heart of gold.* **5.** bright metallic yellow sometimes tending toward brown. —*adj.* **6.** consisting of gold. **7.** pertaining to gold. **8.** like gold. **9.** of the color of gold. [ME and OE, c. G *gold*; akin to Russ. *zoloto*]

gold basis, adaptation of prices to a gold standard.

goldbeater's skin, the prepared outside membrane of the large intestine of the ox, used by goldbeaters to lay between the leaves of the metal while they beat it.

gold beating, art or process of beating out gold into gold leaf. —**gold′beat′er,** *n.*

gold beetle, any of certain beetles characterized by a golden luster, as *Coptocycla aurichalcea,* a small beetle which feeds on plants. Also, **gold bug.**

gold brick, *Colloq.* **1.** a brick-shaped mass of gold, or an imitation of it, sold by a swindler who then delivers a spurious substitute. **2.** *Colloq.* anything of supposed value which turns out to be worthless. **3.** a loafer.

gold-brick (gōldˈbrĭkˈ), *Colloq.* —*v.t.* **1.** to swindle. —*v.i.* **2.** to loaf on the job or evade responsibility. —**gold′-brick′er,** *n.*

gold certificate. See **certificate** (def. 4).

Gold Coast, a British territory in W Africa, comprising Gold Coast Colony, Ashanti, the Northern Territories, and Togoland. 3,572,000 pop. (est. 1940); 91,843 sq. mi. *Cap.:* Accra.

Gold Coast Colony, a British colony in W Africa, on the Gulf of Guinea. 1,573,000 pop. (1931); 23,937 sq. mi. *Cap.:* Accra.

gold digger, 1. one who digs or seeks for gold in a gold field. **2.** *Colloq.* a woman who uses her feminine arts to extract profit from men.

gold digging, 1. the work of digging for gold. **2.** (*pl.*) a region where digging or seeking for gold, esp. by placer mining, is carried on.

gold dust, gold in fine particles.

gold·en (gōlˈdən), *adj.* **1.** of the color of gold; yellow; bright, metallic, or lustrous like gold. **2.** made or consisting of gold: *golden keys.* **3.** resembling gold in value; most excellent: *a golden opportunity.* **4.** flourishing; joyous: *the golden hours.* **5.** indicating the 50th event of a series, as a wedding anniversary. —**gold′en·ly,** *adv.* —**gold′en·ness,** *n.*

golden age, 1. (in Greek and Roman mythology) the first and best age of the world, when mankind lived in innocence and happiness. **2.** the most flourishing period in the history of a nation, literature, etc.

golden aster, any plant of a North American genus, *Chrysopsis,* of asterlike composites with bright golden-yellow flowers, esp., a wild flower species, *C. mariana,* abundant in eastern U.S.

golden buck, a dish consisting of Welsh rabbit topped by a poached egg.

golden calf, *Bible.* **1.** a golden idol set up by Aaron. Ex. 32. **2.** either of the two similar idols set up by Jeroboam. I Kings, 12:28,29.

golden chain, laburnum.

Golden Delicious, *Hort.* a variety of yellow apple grown in the U.S.

golden eagle, a large eagle, *Aquila chrysaëtos,* of both eastern and western hemispheres (so called because of the golden-brown feathers on the back of the neck).

gold·en·eye (gōlˈdənīˈ), *n., pl.* -eyes, (*esp. collectively*) -eye. a diving duck of the subfamily *Aythyinae* and genus *Glaucionetta* with bright-yellow eyes, as G. *clangula,* of Europe and America; whistler; garrot.

Golden Fleece, *Gk. Legend.* the fleece of gold taken

from the ram on which Phrixus was carried to Colchis, recovered from King Aeëtes by the Argonautic expedition under Jason. See **Medea.**

Golden Gate, a strait in W California between San Francisco Bay and the Pacific: spanned by the **Golden Gate Bridge,** whose channel span of 4200 ft. is the longest single span in the world.

golden glow, a tall coneflower, *Rudbeckia laciniata,* with abundant yellow flowers and a yellow conical disk.

golden goose, *Gk. Legend.* a goose which laid one golden egg a day and was killed by its impatient owner who wanted all the gold immediately.

Golden Horn, an inlet of the Bosporus in European Turkey, which forms the inner harbor of Istanbul.

golden mean, the happy medium between extremes; moderate course of action. [trans. of L *aurea mediocritas* (Horace)]

golden pheasant, an Asiatic pheasant, *Chrysolophus pictus,* with rich yellow and orange tones in the head and neck plumage of the male.

golden plover, either of two plovers with yellow spotting above; the European species is *Pluvialis apricaria;* the American, *P. dominica.*

golden robin, Baltimore oriole.

gold·en·rod (gōlˈdənrŏdˈ), *n.* **1.** any plant of the composite genus, *Solidago,* most species of which bear numerous small yellow flowers. **2.** any of various related composite plants, as *Brachychaeta sphacelata* (false goldenrod).

golden rule, the rule of conduct: *Whatsoever ye would that men should do to you, do ye even so to them,* Matt. 7:12.

Dwarf goldenrod. *Solidago nemoralis* (2 ft. high)

gold·en·seal (gōlˈdənsēlˈ), *n.* **1.** a ranunculaceous herb, *Hydrastis canadensis,* with a thick yellow rootstock. **2.** the rhizomes and roots of this plant, formerly much used in medicine.

golden wattle, 1. a broad-leafed Australian acacia, *Acacia pycnantha,* yielding useful gum and tanbark. Its yellow flower is the unofficial Australian Commonwealth flower. **2.** any similar acacia, esp. *A. longifolia,* of Australia and Tasmania.

golden wedding, the 50th anniversary of a wedding.

gold-ex·change standard (gōldˈĭksˈchānjˈ), a monetary system whose monetary unit is kept at a fixed relation with that of a country on the gold standard.

gold·eye (gōldˈī′), *n., pl.* -eyes, (*esp. collectively*) -eye. a silvery, herringlike fish, *Amphiodon alosoides,* of the fresh waters of central North America, of some note as a game fish.

gold field, a district in which gold is mined.

gold-filled (gōldˈfĭldˈ), *adj.* containing a filling of cheaper metal within a layer of gold.

gold·finch (gōldˈfĭnchˈ), *n.* **1.** a European fringilline songbird, *Carduelis carduelis,* having a crimson face and wings marked with yellow. **2.** any of certain small American finches, esp. *Spinus tristis,* the male of which has yellow body plumage in summer. [ME; OE *goldfinc.* See GOLD, FINCH.]

gold·fish (gōldˈfĭshˈ), *n., pl.* -fishes, (*esp. collectively*) -fish. a small fish, *Carassius auratus,* of the carp family, and orig. native in China, prized for aquariums and pools because of its golden coloring and odd form (produced by artificial selection).

gold foil, gold beaten into thin sheets (many times thicker than gold leaf), esp. for the use of dentists.

gold·i·locks (gōlˈdĭˈlŏksˈ), *n.* **1.** a person with golden hair. **2.** an Old World species of buttercup, *Ranunculus auricomus.* **3.** a European plant, *Linosyris vulgaris,* resembling goldenrod, with small heads of yellow flowers. [f. obs. *goldy* golden + LOCK(S)[2]]

gold leaf, gold beaten into a very thin sheet, used for gilding, etc.

gold mine, 1. a mine yielding gold. **2.** a source of great wealth.

gold note, *U.S.* a bank note payable in gold coin.

gold-of-pleas·ure (gōldˈəvˈplĕzhˈər), *n.* a brassicaceous herb, *Camelina sativa,* with small yellowish flowers.

Gol·do·ni (gōldôˈnē), *n.* **Carlo** (kärˈlō), 1707–93, Italian dramatist.

gold point, the point at which it is equally expensive to buy (sell), exchange, or export (import) gold in adjustment of foreign claims (counterclaims).

gold reserve, that part of the U.S. federal gold supply held to maintain the value of governmental promissory notes.

gold rush, a large-scale emigration of people to a region where gold has been discovered, as that to California in 1849.

gold·smith (gōldˈsmĭthˈ), *n.* one who makes or sells articles of gold (down to the 18th cent., often acting also as a banker). [ME and OE]

Gold·smith (gōldˈsmĭthˈ), *n.* **Oliver,** 1728–74, British poet, novelist, and dramatist.

goldsmith beetle, a brilliant golden scarabaeid beetle of Europe, *Cetonia aurata.*

gold standard, a monetary system with gold of specified weight and fineness as the unit of value.

äct, āble, dâre, ärt; ĕbb, ēqual; ĭf, īce; hŏt, ōver, ôrder, oil, bŏŏk, ōōze, out; ŭp, ūse, ûrge; ə = a in alone; ch, chief; g, give; ng, ring; sh, shoe; th, thin; ŧh, that; zh, vision. See the full key on inside cover.

gold stick, (in England) **1.** the gilded rod carried on state occasions by certain members of the royal household. **2.** the bearer of it.

gold·stone (gōld'stōn'), *n.* aventurine (def. 1).

gold·thread (gōld'thrĕd'), *n.* **1.** a white-flowered ranunculaceous herb, *Coptis groenlandica*, with a slender yellow root. **2.** the root itself, used in medicine.

go·lem (gō'lĕm), *n.* **1.** *Jewish Legend.* a figure constructed to represent a human being, and endowed with life, by human agency. **2.** an automaton. [t. Heb.]

golf (gŏlf, gôlf; *Brit.* gŏf, gôf), *n.* **1.** an outdoor game, in which a small resilient ball is driven with special clubs into a series of holes, distributed at various distances over a course having natural or artificial obstacles, the object being to get the ball into each hole in as few strokes as possible. —*v.i.* **2.** to play golf. [ME (Scot.); orig. uncert.] —**golf'er,** *n.*

golf club, 1. any of the various implements for striking the ball in golf. **2.** an organization of golf players. **3.** *Brit.* a country club.

golf links, (*pl. sometimes construed as sing.*) the ground or course over which golf is played.

Gol·go·tha (gŏl'gə thə), *n.* **1.** Calvary. **2.** a place of suffering or sacrifice. [t. L (Vulgate), t. Gk. (N.T.), t. Aram.: m. *goghaltā,* Heb. *gulgōlĕth* skull; see John 19:17]

gol·iard (gōl'yərd), *n.* one of a class of wandering students in Germany, France, and England, chiefly in the 12th and 13th centuries, noted for their rioting and intemperance, and as the authors of satirical Latin verse. [t. OF: appar. lit., glutton, der. *gole,* g. L *gula* throat, palate, gluttony] —**gol·iar·dic** (gōl yär'dĭk), *adj.*

gol·iar·der·y (gōl yär'dər ĭ), *n.* the poems of the goliards.

Go·li·ath (gə lī'əth), *n.* the giant champion of the Philistines whom David is reputed to have killed with a stone from a sling. I Sam. 17:4. Cf. II Sam. 21:19 and I Chron. 20:5. [t. L (Vulgate), t. Gk. (Septuagint,) repr. Heb. *Golyath*]

gol·ly (gŏl'ĭ), *interj.* *Colloq.* a mild expletive expressing surprise, etc. [a euphemistic var. of *God!*]

go·losh (gə lŏsh'), *n.* galosh.

Goltz (gōlts), *n.* **Baron Colmar von der** (kôl'mär fən dər), 1843–1916, German field marshal.

gom·bo (gŭm'bō), *n.* gumbo.

gom·broon (gŏm brōōn'), *n.* a type of Persian pottery ware. [named after a town on the Persian Gulf]

Go·mel (gô'mĕl), *n.* a city in the W Soviet Union, on a tributary of the Dnieper. 144,169 (1939).

gom·er·el (gŏm'ər əl), *n.* *Scot. and N. Eng.* a fool. Also, **gom'er·al, gom·er·il** (gŏm'ər əl). [f. obs. *gome* man (OE *guma,* c. L *homo*) + -REL]

Go·mor·rah (gə môr'ə, -mŏr'ə), *n.* **1.** an ancient city destroyed (with Sodom) for the wickedness of its inhabitants. Gen. 18–19. **2.** any extremely wicked place. Also, **Go·mor'rha.**

Gom·pers (gŏm'pərz), *n.* **Samuel,** 1850–1924, U.S. labor leader; one of the founders of the American Federation of Labor and its president, 1886–94, 1896–1924.

gom·pho·sis (gŏm fō'sĭs), *n.* *Anat.* an immovable articulation in which one bone or part is received in a cavity in another, as a tooth in its socket. [NL, t. Gk.: a bolting together]

go·mu·ti (gə mōō'tĭ), *n., pl.* **-tis. 1.** Also, **gomuti palm.** a sago palm, *Arenga pinnata,* of the East Indies: source of palm sugar. **2.** a black, horsehairlike fiber obtained from it, used for making cordage, etc. [t. Malay]

-gon, a suffix denoting geometrical figures having a certain number or kind of angles, as in *polygon, pentagon.* [t. Gk.: m. *-gōnos* (neut. *-gōnon*) -angled, -angular]

gon·ad (gŏn'ăd), *n.* *Anat.* the sex gland, male or female, in which germ cells develop and appropriate sex hormones are produced. [t. Gk.: s. *gonár* womb] —**gon'ad·al, go·na·di·al** (gō nā'dĭ əl), **go·nad·ic** (gō năd'ĭk), *adj.*

gon·a·do·trop·ic (gŏn'ə dō trŏp'ĭk, gə năd'ō-), *adj.* *Biochem.* pertaining to substances formed in the hypophysis or the placenta which affect the activity of the ovary or testis. Also, **gon·a·do·troph·ic** (gŏn'ə dō trŏf'ĭk, gə năd'ō-).

Gon·court (gôN kōōr'), *n.* **Edmond Louis Antoine Huot de** (ĕd môN' lwē äN twän' y ō' də), 1822–96, and his brother, **Jules Alfred Huot de** (zhɪl ál frĕd'), 1830–1870, French art critics, historians, and novelists, who collaborated in writing novels until the death of Jules.

Gond (gŏnd), *n.* one of an aboriginal nationality of Dravidian stock in central India and the Deccan.

Gon·dar (gŏn'där), *n.* a city in NW Ethiopia, N of Lake Tana: a former capital of Ethiopia.

gon·do·la (gŏn'də lə), *n.* **1.** a long, narrow boat with a high peak at each end and often a small cabin near the middle, used on the Venetian canals and usually propelled at the stern by a single oar or pole. **2.** *U.S.* (locally) a heavy boat. **3.** the car of a dirigible. [t. It. (Venetian), der. *gondolar, gongolarsi,* ult. der. Rom. root *dond-* to rock]

Venetian gondola

gondola car, *U.S.* a railway freight car with sides but no top, used for transporting bulk commodities.

gon·do·lier (gŏn'də lĭr'), *n.* a man who rows or poles a gondola. [t. F, t. It.: m. *gondoliere,* der. *gondola*]

Gon·do·mar (gŏn'dô mär'), *n.* **Diego Sarmiento de Acuña** (dyĕ'gô sär myĕn'tô dĕ äkōō'nyä), **Count of,** 1567–1626, Spanish diplomat.

Gond·wa·na (gŏnd wä'nə), *n.* *Geol.* a great land mass in the Southern Hemisphere that in Paleozoic and part of Mesozoic time joined South America, Africa, southern Asia, and Australia.

gone (gŏn, gôn), *v.* **1.** pp. of go. —*adj.* **2.** departed; left. **3.** lost, or hopeless. **4.** that has departed or passed away; dead. **5.** weak and faint: *a gone feeling.* **6. far gone, a.** much advanced; deeply involved. **b.** dying. **7. gone on,** *Colloq.* very much in love with.

gone·ness (gŏn'nĭs, gôn'-), *n.* sinking sensation; faintness.

gon·er (gŏn'ər, gôn'ər), *n.* *Colloq.* a person or thing that is dead, lost, or past recovery.

gon·fa·lon (gŏn'fə lən), *n.* **1.** a banner suspended from a crossbar, often with several streamers or tails. **2.** the standard used esp. by the medieval Italian republics. [t. It.: m. *gonfalone,* t. OHG: m. *gundfano,* lit., war flag]

gon·fa·lon·ier (gŏn'fə lə nĭr'), *n.* **1.** the bearer of a gonfalon. **2.** chief magistrate or some other elected official in several medieval Italian republics. [t. It.: m. *gonfaloniere*]

gong (gŏng, gŏng), *n.* *Music.* **1.** an oriental bronze disk with the rim turned up, to be struck with a soft-headed stick. **2.** a saucer-shaped bell sounded by a hammer. [t. Malay] —**gong'like',** *adj.*

Gón·go·ra y Ar·go·te (gông gô' rä ē ärgô'tĕ), **Luis de** (lōō ēs'dĕ), 1561–1627, Spanish poet.

Gon·go·rism (gŏng'gə rĭz'əm), *n.* affected elegance of style introduced into Spanish literature in imitation of the Spanish poet, Gongora y Argote.

go·nid·i·um (gə nĭd'ĭ əm), *n., pl.* **-nidia** (-nĭd'ĭ ə). *Bot.* (among algae): **1.** any one-celled asexual reproductive body, as a tetraspore or zoöspore. **2.** an algal cell, or a filament of an alga, growing within the thallus of a lichen. [NL, f. Gk.: s. *gónos* offspring, seed + m. *-idion* -IDION] —**go·nid'i·al,** *adj.*

go·ni·om·e·ter (gō'nĭ ŏm'ə tər), *n.* **1.** an instrument for measuring solid angles, as of crystals. **2.** a radiogoniometer. [t. F: m. *goniomètre,* f. Gk. *gōnio-* angle + *mètre* METER] —**go·ni·o·met·ric** (gō'nĭ ə mĕt'rĭk), **go·ni·o·met'ri·cal,** *adj.* —**go'ni·om'e·try,** *n.*

go·ni·on (gō'nĭ ŏn'), *n., pl.* **-nia** (-nĭ ə). *Craniol.* the point on either side of the lower jaw at the mandibular angle, marked by the intersection of a plane tangent to the lower border of the body and the posterior border of the ascending ramus. [NL, der. Gk. *gōnía* angle]

go·ni·um (gō'nĭ əm), *n., pl.* **-nia** (-nĭ ə). *Biol.* the germ cell during the phase marked by mitosis. [NL]

-gonium, *Bot., Biol.* a word element referring to reproductive cells. [t. NL, t. Gk.: m. *-gonia,* comb. form repr. *goneía* generation]

gono-, a word element meaning "sexual" or "reproductive," as in *gonococcus.* [t. Gk., comb. form of *gónos, gonē* seed, generation, etc.]

gon·o·coc·cus (gŏn'ə kŏk'əs), *n., pl.* **-cocci** (-kŏk'sī). a cell of the micrococcus found in the pus cells of the gonorrheal discharge. [see GONO-, -COCCUS]

gon·o·cyte (gŏn'ə sīt'), *n.* *Biol.* a germ cell, esp. during the maturation phase; oöcyte; spermatocyte.

gon·o·phore (gŏn'ə fōr'), *n.* **1.** *Zool.* a sexually produced bud in hydrozoans that gives rise to a medusa or its equivalent. **2.** *Bot.* a prolongation of the axis of a flower above the perianth, bearing the stamens and pistil.

gon·or·rhe·a (gŏn'ə rē'ə), *n.* *Pathol.* a contagious, purulent inflammation of the urethra or the vagina, due to the gonococcus. Also, *esp. Brit.,* **gon·or·rhoe·a.** [t. LL: m. *gonorrhoea,* t. Gk.: m. *gonórrhoia,* f. *gono-* GONO- + *rhoía* a flow] —**gon·or·rhe'al,** *adj.*

-gony, a word element meaning "production," "genesis," "origination," as in *cosmogony, theogony.* [t. L: m. s. *-gonia,* t. Gk. See -GONIUM and -GENY]

goo (gōō), *n.* *U.S. Slang.* sticky matter. [short for BURGOO]

goo·ber (gōō'bər), *n.* *U.S.* the peanut. Also, **goober pea.** [t. Angolan: m. *nguba*]

good (gŏod), *adj.,* **better, best,** *n., interj., adv.* —*adj.* **1.** morally excellent; righteous; pious: *a good man.* **2.** satisfactory in quality, quantity, or degree; excellent: *good food, good health.* **3.** right; proper; qualified; fit: *do whatever seems good to you, his credit is good.* **4.** well-behaved: *a good child.* **5.** kind, beneficent, or friendly: *to do a good turn.* **6.** honorable or worthy; in good standing: *a good name, Mr. Hood and his good lady.* **7.** reliable; safe: *good securities.* **8.** genuine; sound or valid: *good judgment, good reasons.* **9.** agreeable; pleasant; genial: *have a good time.* **10.** satisfactory for the purpose; advantageous: *a good day for fishing.* **11.** sufficient or ample: *a good supply.* **12.** full: *a good day's journey.* **13.** competent or skilful; clever: *a good manager, good at arithmetic.* **14.** fairly great: *a good deal.* **15. as good as,** in effect; practically: *he as good as promised it to me.*
—*n.* **16.** profit; worth; advantage; benefit: *what good will that do? to work for the common good.* **17.** excellence or merit; righteousness; kindness: *to be a power for good, do good.* **18.** a good, commendable, or desirable thing. **19.** (*pl.*) possessions, esp. movable effects or personal

chattels. **20.** (*pl.*) articles of trade; wares; esp. in England, freight. **21.** (*pl.*) *U.S. Colloq.* what has been promised or is expected: *to deliver the goods.* **22.** (*pl.*) *U.S. Colloq.* the genuine article. **23.** (*pl.*) *U.S. Colloq.* evidence of guilt, as stolen articles: *to catch with the goods.* **24.** (*pl.*) *U.S.* cloth or textile material: *will these goods wash well?* **25. for good** or **for good and all,** finally and permanently; forever: *to leave a place for good (and all).* **26. make good, a.** to make recompense for; pay for. **b.** to keep to an agreement; fulfill. **c.** to be successful. **d.** to prove the truth of; substantiate. —*interj.* **27.** an expression of approval or satisfaction. —*adv.* **28.** *Colloq.* well.
[ME; OE *gōd*, c. D *goed*, G *gut*, Icel. *gōdhr*, Goth. *gōths* good; ? orig. meaning fitting, suitable, and akin to GATHER] **—Syn. 1.** pure, moral, virtuous; conscientious, meritorious, worthy, exemplary. **2.** commendable, admirable. **10.** favorable, auspicious, propitious, fortunate; profitable, useful. **11.** full, adequate. **13.** efficient, proficient, capable, dexterous, adroit, apt. **19.** See **property. —Ant. 1.** bad, evil.
Good Book, the Bible.
good-by (gŏŏd'bī'), *interj., n., pl.* **-bys.** —*interj.* **1.** farewell: a conventional expression used at parting. —*n.* **2.** a farewell. [contr. of *God be with you (ye)*]
good-bye (gŏŏd'bī'), *interj., n., pl.* **-byes.** good-by.
good cheer, 1. cheerful spirits; courage: *to be of good cheer.* **2.** feasting and merrymaking: *to make good cheer.* **3.** good fare or food; feasting: *to be fond of good cheer.*
good form, *Chiefly Brit.* good or proper conduct.
good-for-noth·ing (gŏŏd'fər nŭth'ĭng), *adj.* **1.** worthless. —*n.* **2.** a worthless person.
Good Friday, the Friday before Easter, a holy day of the Christian church, observed as the anniversary of the crucifixion of Jesus.
good-heart·ed (gŏŏd'här'tĭd), *adj.* kind; considerate. **—good'-heart'ed·ly,** *adv.* **—good'-heart'ed·ness,** *n.*
Good Hope, Cape of. See **Cape of Good Hope.**
good humor, a cheerful or amiable mood.
good-hu·mored (gŏŏd'hū'mərd, -ū'mərd), *adj.* having or showing a pleasant, amiable mood: *good-humored man, a good-humored remark.* **—good'-hu'mored·ly,** *adv.* **—good'-hu'mored·ness,** *n.*
good·ish (gŏŏd'ĭsh), *adj.* rather good; fairly good.
good-look·ing (gŏŏd'lŏŏk'ĭng), *adj.* of good appearance; handsome.
good looks, handsome personal appearance.
good·ly (gŏŏd'lĭ), *adj.,* **-lier, -liest. 1.** of a good quality: *a goodly gift.* **2.** of good or fine appearance. **3.** of good size or amount: *a goodly sum.* **—good'li·ness,** *n.*
good·man (gŏŏd'mən), *n., pl.* **-men.** *Archaic or Dial.* **1.** the master of a household; husband. **2.** title of respect used for those below the rank of gentleman, esp. a farmer or yeoman.
good nature, pleasant disposition; cheerful nature.
good-na·tured (gŏŏd'nā'chərd), *adj.* having or showing good nature or a pleasant or complaisant disposition or mood; good-humored. **—good'-na'tured·ly,** *adv.* **—good'-na'tured·ness,** *n.*
Good Neighbor Policy, a diplomatic policy of the U.S., first presented in 1933 by President Roosevelt for the encouragement of friendly relations and mutual defense by the nations of the Western Hemisphere.
good·ness (gŏŏd'nĭs), *n.* **1.** moral excellence; virtue. **2.** kindly feeling; kindness; generosity. **3.** excellence of quality: *goodness of workmanship.* **4.** the best part of anything; essence; strength. **5.** (used in various exclamatory or emphatic expressions): *thank goodness!* **—Syn. 1.** GOODNESS, MORALITY, VIRTUE refer to qualities of character or conduct which entitle the possessor to approval and esteem. GOODNESS is the simple word for the general quality recognized in character or conduct: *many could tell of her goodness and kindness.* MORALITY implies conformity to the recognized standards of right conduct: *a citizen of the highest morality.* VIRTUE is a rather formal word, and suggests usually GOODNESS that is consciously or steadily maintained, often in spite of temptations or evil influences: *of unassailable virtue, firm and of unwavering virtue.* **—Ant. 1.** badness, evil, vice.
good Samaritan, a person who is compassionate and helpful to one in distress. See Luke 10: 30–37.
Good Shepherd, Jesus Christ.
good-sized (gŏŏd'sīzd'), *adj.* of ample size; largish.
good speed, good fortune, or success: *to wish a person good speed.*
goods train, *Brit.* a freight train.
good-tem·pered (gŏŏd'tĕm'pərd), *adj.* good-natured; amiable. **—good'-tem'pered·ly,** *adv.*
good use, (in a language) standard use or usage.
good·wife (gŏŏd'wīf'), *n., pl.* **-wives** (-wīvz'). *Archaic or Dial.* **1.** the mistress of a household. **2.** a title of respect for a woman.
good will, 1. friendly disposition; benevolence; favor. **2.** cheerful acquiescence. **3.** *Com.* an intangible, salable asset arising from the reputation of a business and its relations with its customers, distinct from the value of its stock, etc. Also, **good-will** (gŏŏd'wĭl'). **—Syn. 1.** See **favor.**
Good·win Sands (gŏŏd'wĭn), a dangerous line of shoals at the N entrance to the Strait of Dover, ab. 6 mi. off the SE coast of England. ab. 10 mi. long.
good·y¹ (gŏŏd'ĭ), *n., pl.,* **goodies,** *adj., interj. Colloq.* —*n.* **1.** (*pl.*) sweet food; candy. —*adj.* **2.** weakly or

sentimentally good; affecting goodness. —*interj.* **3.** wonderful! how nice! [f. GOOD, adj. + -Y¹]
good·y² (gŏŏd'ĭ), *n., pl.* **goodies.** a polite term formerly applied to a woman in humble life. [var. of GOODWIFE]
Good·year (gŏŏd'yĭr), *n.* **Charles,** 1800–60, U.S. inventor (of vulcanized rubber).
good·y-good·y (gŏŏd'ĭ gŏŏd'ĭ), *adj., n., pl.* **-goodies.** —*adj.* **1.** goody. —*n.* **2.** a goody person.
goo·ey (gŏŏ'ĭ), *adj.,* **gooier, gooiest.** *Slang.* like goo; sticky; viscid.
goof (gŏŏf), *n. Slang.* a foolish or stupid person. [appar. var. of obs. *goff* dolt, t. F: m. *goffe*] **—goof'y,** *adj.* **—goof'i·ly,** *adv.* **—goof'i·ness,** *n.*
goo·gly (gŏŏ'glĭ), *n., pl.* **-glies.** *Cricket.* a bowled ball that swerves first one way and then breaks in the other.
goo·gol (gŏŏ'gŏl), *n.* a number, usually 1, followed by 100 zeros. [fanciful, based on *goose-egg* zero]
goon (gŏŏn), *n. U.S. Slang.* **1.** a stupid person. **2.** a hired thug used by one side or the other in a labor dispute. **3.** a roughneck.
goop (gŏŏp), *n. U.S. Slang.* a bad-mannered person.
goos·an·der (gŏŏs ăn'dər), *n.* **1.** a saw-billed fish-eating duck, *Mergus merganser,* of Europe and North America. **2.** any merganser.
goose (gŏŏs), *n., pl.* **geese** for 1–4, 6; **gooses** for 5. **1.** any of numerous wild or domesticated web-footed birds of the family *Anatidae,* most of them larger and with a longer neck than the ducks: the principal genera are *Anser, Branta,* and *Chen.* **2.** the female of this bird, as distinguished from the male (or gander). **3.** the flesh of the goose. **4.** a silly or foolish person; simpleton. **5.** a tailors' smoothing iron with a curved handle. **6.** *Obs.* a game played with counters. [ME *gos(e), goos,* OE *gōs* (pl. *gēs*), c. D and G *gans,* Icel. *gās* goose; akin to L *anser,* Gk. *chēn*] **—goose'like',** *adj.*
goose·ber·ry (gŏŏs'bĕr'ĭ, gŏŏz'-, -bə rĭ), *n., pl.* **-ries. 1.** the small, edible, acid, globular fruit or berry of certain prevailingly prickly shrubs of the genus *Ribes,* esp. *R. Grossularia.* **2.** the shrub itself.
goose flesh, a rough condition of the skin, resembling that of a plucked goose, induced by cold or fear.
goose·foot (gŏŏs'fŏŏt'), *n., pl.* **-foots. 1.** any plant of the genus *Chenopodium,* containing many widely distributed herbs and shrubs with minute green flowers. **2.** any chenopodiaceous plant.
goose grass, cleavers.
goose grease, the melted fat of the goose, used in domestic medicine as an ointment.
goose·herd (gŏŏs'hûrd'), *n.* one who tends geese.
goose·neck (gŏŏs'nĕk'), *n.* something curved like the neck of a goose, as an iron hook for attaching a boom to a mast, or a flexible stand for a desk lamp.
goose pimples, goose flesh. Also, **goose skin.**
goose step, 1. a military exercise in which the body is balanced on one foot (without advancing) while the other foot is swung forward and back. **2.** marching step of the German and other foreign infantry, in which the legs are swung high with straight, stiff knees.
goose-step (gŏŏs'stĕp'), *v.i.,* **-stepped, -stepping.** *Colloq.* to walk in a goose step.
G.O.P., the "Grand Old Party," an epithet for the Republican party since 1880.
go·pher (gō'fər), *n.* **1.** any of various ground squirrels of western North America, as *Citellus* (or *Spermophilus*) *tridecemlineatus* (a destructive rodent common in the prairie states), and *Citellus* (or *Spermophilus*) *richardsoni,* a similar species prevalent in North Dakota. **2.** any of various burrowing rodents of the genera *Geomys, Thomomys,* etc. (family *Geomyidae*), of western and southern

Common pocket gopher.
Geomys bursarius
(10½ to 11½ in. long)

North America and Central America, with large external fur-lined cheek pouches (also called *pocket gopher* and *pouched rat*). **3.** an edible, burrowing land tortoise, *Gopherus* (or *Testudo*) *polyphemus,* of the southeastern U.S. **4.** Also, **gopher snake.** a burrowing snake, *Compsosoma corais,* of the southern U.S. **5.** (*cap.*) a nickname for a Minnesotan. [? t. F: m. *gaufre* honeycomb. See GOFFER]
go·pher·wood (gō'fər wŏŏd'), *n.* **1.** yellowwood. **2.** an unidentified wood used in building Noah's ark. See Gen. 6:14. [f. *gopher,* a tree (t. Heb.) + WOOD¹]
go·ral (gōr'əl), *n.* a goat antelope, *Naemorhedus goral,* of mountainous southeastern Asia, having small horns shorter than the distance apart at their bases.
gor·cock (gôr'kŏk'), *n.* the moor cock, or male red grouse, *Lagopus scoticus,* of Great Britain. [orig. obscure]
Gor·di·an (gôr'dĭ ən), *adj.* **1.** pertaining to Gordius, ancient king of Phrygia, who tied a knot (the **Gordian knot**) which was to be undone only by one who should rule Asia, and which was summarily cut by Alexander the Great. **2.** resembling the Gordian knot; intricate. **3. cut the Gordian knot,** to devise and use instantly a drastic way out of a difficulty.
Gor·don (gôr'dən), *n.* **Charles George,** ("*Chinese Gordon*") 1833–85, British general and administrator in China and Egypt.
Gordon setter, a black, long-haired variety of setter dog with red or tan marks on the muzzle, neck, and legs.

gore[1] (gōr), *n.* blood that is shed, esp. when clotted. [ME; OE *gor* dung, dirt, c. D *goor*, OHG *gor* filth]

gore[2] (gōr), *v.t.*, **gored, goring.** (of an animal) to pierce with the horns or tusks. [ME *goren*. Cf. GORE[3]]

gore[3] (gōr), *n.*, *v.*, **gored, goring.** —*n.* **1.** a triangular piece of cloth, etc., inserted in a garment, a sail, etc., to give greater width or secure the desired shape or adjustment. **2.** one of the breadths (mostly tapering, or shaped) of a woman's skirt. —*v.t.* **3.** to make or furnish with a gore or gores. [ME; OE *gāra* corner (c. G *gehre* gusset), der. *gār* spear] —**gored,** *adj.* —**gor'ing,** *n.*

Gor·gas (gôr′gəs), *n.* **William Crawford,** 1854–1920, surgeon general in the U.S. Army; chief sanitation expert in the building of the Panama Canal.

gorge (gôrj), *n.*, *v.*, **gorged, gorging.** —*n.* **1.** a narrow cleft with steep, rocky walls, esp. one through which a stream runs. **2.** a gorging or gluttonous meal. **3.** that which is swallowed; contents of the stomach. **4.** strong disgust; repulsion: *one's gorge rises in resentment.* **5.** a choking mass. **6.** *Fort.* the rear entrance or part of a bastion or similar outwork. See diag. under **bastion**. **7.** *Archaic.* the throat; gullet. —*v.t.* **8.** to stuff with food (mainly reflexive and passive): *gorged with food, he gorged himself.* **9.** to swallow, esp. greedily. **10.** to choke up (mainly passive). —*v.i.* **11.** to eat greedily. [ME, t. OF: throat, g. LL *gurga*, b. L *gurges* stream, abyss and *gula* throat] —**gorg'er,** *n.* —**Syn. 8.** glut, stuff. **9.** bolt, gulp, gobble.

gor·geous (gôr′jəs), *adj.* sumptuous; magnificent; splendid in appearance or coloring. [t. OF: m. *gorgias* fashionable, gay; orig. uncert.] —**gor'geous·ly,** *adv.* —**gor'geous·ness,** *n.* —**Syn.** rich, superb, grand; brilliant, resplendent. See **magnificent**.

gor·ger·in (gôr′jər ĭn), *n. Archit.* the necklike portion of a capital of a column, or a feature forming the junction between a shaft and its capital. [t. F, der. *gorge* throat]

gor·get (gôr′jĭt), *n.* **1.** a piece of armor for the throat. **2.** a form of wimple, or neck and chest covering, worn by women in the Middle Ages. **3.** a patch on the throat of a bird or other animal, distinguished by its color or otherwise. [t. OF: m. *gorgete,* dim. of *gorge* throat]

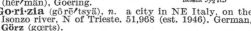

G. Gorget (def. 1), 15th century
A. Attached to the brigandine
B. Worn over mail

Gor·gon (gôr′gən), *n.* **1.** *Gk. Legend.* any of three sisters, Stheno, Euryale, and Medusa, whose heads were covered with snakes instead of hair, and whose glance turned the beholder to stone. **2.** (*l.c.*) a terrible or repulsive woman. —**gor·go·ni·an** (gôr gō′nĭ ən), *adj.*

gor·go·nei·on (gôr′gə nē′ŏn), *n.*, *pl.* **-neia** (-nē′ə). a representation of the head of a Gorgon, esp. that of Medusa. [t. Gk.]

Gor·gon·zo·la (gôr′gən zō′lə), *n.* a strongly flavored, Italian, semihard variety of milk cheese veined with mold. [named after *Gorgonzola,* town in N Italy]

gor·hen (gôr′hĕn′), *n.* the female red grouse. [cf. GORCOCK]

go·ril·la (gə rĭl′ə), *n.* **1.** the largest of the anthropoid apes, *Gorilla gorilla,* ground-living and vegetarian, of western equatorial Africa and the Kivu highlands. **2.** an ugly, brutal fellow. [t. NL, t. Gk.; said to be of African orig.] —**go·ril'la·like',** *adj.*

Gorilla (def. 1), *Gorilla gorilla* (6 ft. high; standing height 5½ ft.)

Gö·ring (gœ′rĭng), *n.* **Hermann** (hĕr′män), Goering.

Go·ri·zia (gō rē′tsyä), *n.* a city in NE Italy, on the Isonzo river, N of Trieste. 51,968 (est. 1946). German, **Görz** (gœrts).

Gor·ki (gôr′kĭ), *n.* **1. Maxim** (mäk sēm′), (*Aleksyey Maksimovich Pyeshkov*) 1868–1936, Russian novelist, short-story writer, and dramatist. **2.** Formerly, **Nizhni Novgorod.** a city in the central Soviet Union in Europe, on the Volga. 644,116 (1939).

Gör·litz (gœr′lĭts), *n.* a city in E Germany, on the Neisse river (the Polish boundary). 93,808 (1939).

Gor·lov·ka (gôr lôf′kä), *n.* a city in the SW Soviet Union. 108,693 (1939).

gor·mand (gôr′mənd), *n.* gourmand.

gor·mand·ize (gôr′mən dīz′), *v.*, **-ized, -izing,** *n.* —*v.i.*, *v.t.* **1.** to eat like a glutton. [v. use of n.] —*n.* **2.** *Rare.* the habits of a glutton. [t. F: m. *gourmandise* gluttony] —**gor'mand·iz'er,** *n.*

gorse (gôrs), *n. Chiefly Brit.* furze. [ME *gorst,* OE *gors(t)*; akin to G *gerst,* L *hordeum* barley] —**gors'y,** *adj.*

gor·y (gôr′ĭ), *adj.*, **gorier, goriest. 1.** covered or stained with gore; bloody. **2.** resembling gore. —**gor'i·ly,** *adv.* —**gor'i·ness,** *n.*

gosh (gŏsh), *interj.* an exclamation or mild oath. [a euphemistic var. of *God!*]

gos·hawk (gŏs′hôk′), *n.* any of various powerful, short-winged hawks formerly much used

Goshawk. *Astur atricapillus* (20 to 23 in. long)

in falconry, as *Accipiter gentilis* of Europe and America. [ME *goshawke,* OE *gōshafoc* goosehawk]

Go·shen (gō′shən), *n.* **1.** a pastoral region in Lower Egypt, colonized by the Israelites before the Exodus. Gen. 45:10, etc. **2.** a land or place of plenty and comfort.

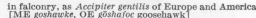

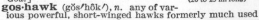
Goshen (def. 1), 1450 B.C.

gos·ling (gŏz′lĭng), *n.* **1.** a young goose. **2.** a foolish, inexperienced person. [ME *goselyng,* var. (by assoc. with GOOSE) of *geslyng,* t. Scand.; cf. Icel. *gæslingr,* f. *gās* goose + *-lingr,* dim. suffix (see -LING[1])]

gos·pel (gŏs′pəl), *n.* **1.** the body of doctrine taught by Christ and the apostles; Christian revelation. **2.** glad tidings, esp. concerning salvation and the kingdom of God as announced to the world by Christ. **3.** the story of Christ's life and teachings, esp. as contained in the first four books of the New Testament. **4.** (*usually cap.*) one of these books. **5.** (*often cap.*) *Eccles.* an extract from one of the four Gospels, forming part of the Eucharistic service in certain churches. **6.** *Colloq.* something regarded as true and implicitly believed: *to take for gospel.* **7.** a doctrine regarded as of prime importance: *political gospel.* —*adj.* **8.** pertaining to the gospel. **9.** in accordance with the gospel; evangelical. [ME *go(d)spel,* OE *gōdspel,* f. *gōd* GOOD + *spell* tidings (SPELL[2]), trans. of L *evangelium.* See EVANGEL]

gos·pel·er (gŏs′pəl ər), *n. Eccles.* one who reads or sings the Gospel (def. 5). Also, *esp. Brit.,* **gos'pel·ler.**

Gos·plan (gŏs plän′), *n. U.S.S.R.* official planning organization, which draws up plans embracing trade and industry, agriculture, education, and public health. [f. *gos(udar)* national + *plan* PLAN]

gos·sa·mer (gŏs′ə mər), *n.* **1.** a fine filmy cobweb, seen on grass and bushes, or floating in the air in calm weather, esp. in autumn. **2.** a thread or a web of this substance. **3.** an extremely delicate variety of gauze. **4.** any thin, light fabric. **5.** a thin, waterproof outer garment, esp. for women. —*adj.* **6.** Also, **gos·sa·mer·y** (gŏs′ə mo rĭ), or like gossamer; thin and light. [ME *gos(e)-somer.* See GOOSE, SUMMER; possibly first used as name for late mild autumn (Indian summer), time when goose was a favorite dish (cf. G *gänsemonat* November), then transferred to the filmy matter also frequent at that time of year]

Gosse (gôs, gŏs), *n.* **Sir Edmund William,** 1849–1928, British critic and poet.

gos·sip (gŏs′əp), *n.*, *v.*, **-siped, -siping.** —*n.* **1.** idle talk, esp. about the affairs of others. **2.** light, familiar talk or writing. **3.** a person, esp. a woman, given to tattling or idle talk. **4.** *Archaic.* a friend, esp. a woman. **5.** *Archaic or Dial.* a godparent. —*v.i.* **6.** to talk idly, esp. about the affairs of others; go about tattling. —*v.t.* **7.** to repeat like a gossip. **8.** *Archaic.* to stand godparent to. [ME *gossib,* OE *godsibb,* orig., godparent, f. *god* GOD + *sibb* related (see SIB[1], adj.] —**gos'sip·er,** *n.* —**gos'-sip·ing,** *n.* —**gos'sip·ing·ly,** *adv.*

—**Syn. 1.** GOSSIP, SCANDAL apply to idle talk and newsmongering about the affairs of others. GOSSIP is light chat or talk: *gossip about the neighbors.* SCANDAL is rumor or general talk that is damaging to reputation; it is usually more or less malicious: *a scandal involving bribes.*

gos·sip·mon·ger (gŏs′əp mŭng′gər), *n.* one especially addicted to gossiping.

gos·sip·y (gŏs′ə pĭ), *adj.* **1.** given to or fond of gossip. **2.** full of gossip.

gos·soon (gŏ sōōn′), *n. Anglo-Irish.* **1.** a boy. **2.** a male servant. [alter. of GARCON]

got (gŏt), *v.* pt. and pp. of **get**.

Go·ta·ma (gō′tə mə, gō′-), *n.* Buddha. See **Gautama**.

Gö·te·borg (yœ′tə bôr′y), *n.* a seaport in SW Sweden, on the Kattegat. 315,474 (est. 1945). Also, **Goth·en·burg** (gŏt′ən bûrg′).

Goth (gŏth), *n.* **1.** one of a Teutonic people who, in the 3rd to 5th century, invaded and settled in parts of the Roman Empire. **2.** a barbarian; rude person. [ME *Gothe,* t. LL: m.s. *Gothī,* pl.; r. OE *Gotan,* pl. (*Gota,* sing.), c. Goth. *Gut-* in *Gut-thiuda* Goth people]

Goth., Gothic.

Go·tha (gō′tä), *n.* a city in central Germany, in Thuringia. 54,639 (1939).

Goth·am (gŏth′əm, gō′thəm *for 1;* gŏt′əm *for 2*), *n.* **1.** the city of New York. **2.** an English village, proverbial for the foolishness of its inhabitants.

Goth·ic (gŏth′ĭk), *adj.* **1.** *Archit.* denoting or pertaining to a style originating in France and spreading over western Europe from the 12th to the 16th century, characterized by a design emphasizing skeleton construction, the elimination of wall planes, the comparatively great height of the buildings, the pointed arch, rib vaulting, and the flying buttress. **2.** (orig. in derogatory use) denoting all European art of this period. **3.** (sometimes in disparagement) pertaining to the Middle Ages; barbarous; rude. **4.** (esp. in literature) stressing irregularity and details, usually of a grotesque or horrible nature: *a Gothic novel.* —*n.* **5.** Gothic architecture, sculpture, or decoration. **6.** an extinct Germanic language, preserved especially in Ulfilas' Bible (4th cent.). **7.** *Brit.* black letter. **8.** (*l.c.*) *U.S.* a square-cut printing type, without serifs or hairlines. [t. LL: s. *Gothicus*] —**Goth'i·cal·ly,** *adv.*

b., blend of, blended; c., cognate with; d., dialect, dialectal; der., derived from; f., formed from; g., going back to; m., modification of; r., replacing; s., stem of; t., taken from; ?, perhaps. See the full key on inside cover.

Goth·i·cism (gŏth'ə sĭz'əm), *n*. **1.** conformity or devotion to the Gothic style of architecture. **2.** a mixture of the elevated and the bizarre, often with many details, as distinct from the unity and simplicity of classicism. **3.** adherence to aspects of Gothic culture. **4.** (*also l.c.*) barbarism; rudeness. **5.** a Gothic idiom.

Goth·i·cize (gŏth'ə sīz'), *v.t.*, **-cized, -cizing. 1.** to make Gothic, as in style. **2.** to make pseudomedieval.

gö·thite (gœ'tīt), *n*. goethite.

Got·land (gŏt'lənd; *Swed.* gôt'lŭnd, gôl'lŭnd), *n*. an island in the Baltic, forming a province of Sweden. 59,566 pop. (est. 1946); 1212 sq. mi. *Cap.*: Visby. Also, **Gott'land.**

got·ten (gŏt'ən), *v*. a pp. of **get**.

Göt·ter·däm·mer·ung (gœt'ər dĕm'ə rŏŏng'), *n*. See **Ring of the Nibelung**. [G: twilight of the gods]

Göt·tin·gen (gœt'ĭng ən), *n*. a city in central Germany. 51,214 (1939).

Gott mit uns (gôt' mĭt ŏŏns'), *German*. God is (or be) with us.

gouache (gwȧsh), *n*. **1.** a method of painting with opaque water colors prepared with gum. **2.** an opaque color used in painting a gouache. **3.** a work executed in this medium. [F, t. It.: m. *guazzo* puddle, spray of water, g. L *aquātio* a watering, der. *aqua* water]

Gou·da (gou'də; *Du.* ᴋʜᴏu'dä), *n*. a city in W Netherlands, NE of Rotterdam: noted for its cheese. 36,622 (est. 1946).

Gouda cheese, a cheese made in Holland from whole milk or partly skimmed milk, colored with saffron, and marketed in bladders or in colored wax skins. Also, **Gouda.**

Gou·dy (gou'dĭ), *n*. **Frederic William,** 1865–1947, U.S. designer of printing types.

gouge (gouj), *n., v.,* **gouged, gouging.** —*n.* **1.** a chisel whose blade has a concavo-convex cross section, the bevel being ground on either the inside or the outside of the cutting end of the tool. **2.** *U.S. Colloq.* act of gouging. **3.** groove or hole made by gouging. **4.** *U.S. Colloq.* an imposition or swindle. —*v.t.* **5.** to scoop out or turn with or as with a gouge: *gouge a channel, gouge holes.* **6.** to dig or force out with or as with a gouge: *to gouge out an eye.* **7.** *U.S. Colloq.* to impose upon or swindle. [t. F, g. LL *gu(l)bia*; of Celtic orig.] —**goug'er,** *n*.

Carpenter's gouges

gou·lash (gŏŏ'lȧsh, -läsh), *n*. a stew of beef, veal, vegetables, etc., with paprika or other seasoning. [t. Hung.: m. *gulyas*, short for *gulyas hus* herdsman's meat]

Gould (gŏŏld), *n*. **Jay,** 1836–92, U.S. financier and capitalist.

Gou·nod (gŏŏ'nō; *Fr.* gŏŏ nō'), *n*. **Charles François** (shȧrl frȧn swä'), 1818–93, French composer.

gou·ra·mi (gŏŏr'ə mĭ), *n., pl.* **-mis. 1.** a large, air-breathing, nest-building, fresh-water Asiatic fish, *Osphronemus goramy*, highly prized for food. **2.** any of a number of smaller, air-breathing, nest-building, Asiatic fishes (genera *Trichogaster, Colisa,* and *Trichopsis*) widely cultivated in home aquaria in the U.S., as the **dwarf gourami,** *Colisa lalia.*

gourd (gōrd, gŏŏrd), *n*. **1.** the fruit of any of various cucurbitaceous plants, esp. that of *Lagenaria Siceraria* (**bottle gourd**), whose dried shell is used for bottles, bowls, etc., or that of certain forms of *Cucurbita Pepo* sometimes cultivated for ornament. **2.** a plant bearing such a fruit. **3.** a dried and excavated gourd shell used as a bottle, dipper, flask, etc. **4.** a gourd-shaped, small-necked bottle or flask. [ME, t. F: m. *gourde,* g. L *cucurbita*] —**gourd'like',** *adj*. —**gourd-shaped** (gōrd'-shȧpt', gŏŏrd'-), *adj*.

gourde (gŏŏrd), *n*. the monetary unit of Haiti since 1920, equal to 20 cents in U.S. [t. F, fem. of *gourd* numb, slow, heavy, g. L *gurdus* dull, obtuse]

gour·mand (gŏŏr'mənd; *Fr.* gŏŏr män'), *n*. one fond of good eating. Also, **gormand.** [t. F: gluttonous, der. *gourmet* GOURMET]

gour·met (gŏŏr'mā; *Fr.* gŏŏr mĕ'), *n*. a connoisseur in the delicacies of the table; an epicure. [t. F, in OF also *groumet* wine taster, wine merchant's man. Cf. GROOM]

Gour·mont (gŏŏr môN'), *n*. **Remy de** (rə mē' də), 1858–1915, French critic and novelist.

gout (gout), *n*. **1.** a constitutional disease characterized by painful inflammation of the joints (chiefly those in the feet and hands, and esp. in the great toe), and by excess of uric acid in the blood. **2.** *Archaic or Poetic.* a drop, splash, or spot, esp. of blood. [ME *goute,* t. OF, g. L *gutta* a drop, ML gout]

goût (gŏŏ), *n. French.* taste; perception. [F, g. L *gustus* taste]

gout·y (gou'tĭ), *adj.,* **goutier, goutiest. 1.** pertaining to or having the nature of gout. **2.** causing gout. **3.** diseased with or subject to gout. **4.** swollen as if from gout. —**gout'i·ly,** *adv*. —**gout'i·ness,** *n*.

gou·ver·nante (gŏŏ vĕr näNt'), *n. French.* **1.** a chaperon. **2.** a governess.

Gov., governor.

gov., **1.** governor. **2.** government.

gov·ern (gŭv'ərn), *v.t.* **1.** to rule by right of authority, as a sovereign does: *to govern a state.* **2.** to exercise a directing or restraining influence over; guide: *the motives governing a decision.* **3.** to hold in check: *to govern one's temper.* **4.** to serve as or constitute a law for: *the principles governing a case.* **5.** *Gram.* to be accompanied by

(a particular form) as in *"they helped us,"* not *"they helped we,"* the verb *"helped"* is said to govern the objective case of the pronoun. —*v.i.* **6.** to exercise the function of government. **7.** to have predominating influence. [ME *governe(n),* t. OF: m. *governer,* g. L *gubernāre,* t. Gk.: m. *kybernān* steer, guide, govern] —**gov'ern·a·ble,** *adj*. —**Syn. 1.** See **rule.**

gov·ern·ance (gŭv'ər nəns), *n*. **1.** government; exercise of authority; control. **2.** method or system of government or management.

gov·ern·ess (gŭv'ər nĭs), *n*. a woman who directs the education of children, generally in their own homes.

gov·ern·ment (gŭv'ərn mənt, -ər-), *n*. **1.** the authoritative direction and restraint exercised over the actions of men in communities, societies, and states; direction of the affairs of a state, etc.; political rule and administration: *government is necessary to the existence of society.* **2.** the form or system of rule by which a state, community, etc., is governed: *monarchical government, episcopal government.* **3.** the governing body of persons in a state, community, etc.; the executive power; the administration: *the government was* (or in England, *were*) *defeated in the last election.* **4.** direction; control; rule: *the government of one's conduct.* **5.** the district governed; a province. **6.** *Gram.* the established usage which requires that one word in a sentence should cause another to be of a particular form. —**gov·ern·men·tal** (gŭv'ərn mĕn'təl, -ər-), *adj*. —**gov'ern·men'tal·ly,** *adv*.

gov·er·nor (gŭv'ər nər), *n*. **1.** the executive head of a State in the U.S. **2.** *Chiefly Brit.* one charged with the direction or control of an institution, society, etc.: *governors of a bank, governor of a prison.* **3.** the representative of the crown in a British colony or dependency. **4.** a ruler or chief magistrate appointed to govern a province, town, fort, or the like. **5.** *Mach.* a device for regulating a supply of fuel for ensuring uniform speed regardless of the load. **6.** *Chiefly Brit. Colloq.* **a.** master or employer. **b.** one's father. [ME *governour,* t. OF: m. *governeor,* g. L *gubernātor* steersman, director]

governor general, *pl.* **governors general.** a governor who has under him subordinate or deputy governors. Also, *esp. Brit.,* **governor-general.** —**gov'er·nor-gen'er·al·ship',** *n*.

gov·er·nor·ship (gŭv'ər nər shĭp'), *n*. a governor's duties, term in office, etc.

Governors Island, a small island in New York Bay at the S end of the East river: U.S. military post.

Govt., government. Also, **govt.**

gow·an (gou'ən), *n. Scot. and N. Eng.* any of various yellow or white field flowers, esp. the English daisy. [? var. of obs. *gollan,* t. Scand.; cf. Icel. *gullinn* golden]

Gow·er (gou'ər, gōr), *n*. **John,** c1325–1408, British poet.

gowk (gouk, gōk), *n*. **1.** the cuckoo. **2.** a fool or simpleton. [ME *goke,* t. Scand.; cf. Icel. *gaukr,* c. OE *gēac* cuckoo, G *gauch* cuckoo, fool]

gown (goun), *n*. **1.** a woman's dress or robe, comprising waist and skirt (either joined or separate). **2.** a loose, flowing, outer garment in various forms, worn by men or women as distinctive of office, profession, or status: *a judge's gown, an academic gown.* **3.** the student and teaching body in British university towns, as contrasted to the town, or townfolk. —*v.t., v.i.* **4.** to dress in, or put on, a gown. [ME *goune,* t. OF, g. LL *gunna*; of Celtic orig.] —**Syn. 1.** See **dress.**

gowns·man (gounz'mən), *n., pl.* **-men.** a man who wears a gown indicating his office, profession, or status.

Go·ya (gō'yä), *n*. **Francisco de** (frän thēs'kô dĕ), (**Francisco José de Goya y Lucientes**) 1746–1828, Spanish painter and etcher.

G.P., 1. Gloria Patri. **2.** Graduate in Pharmacy. **3.** *Chiefly Brit.* General Practitioner.

GPO, Government Printing Office.

G.P.O., General Post Office.

G.P.U., Gay-Pay-Oo.

Gr., 1. Grecian. **2.** Greece. **3.** Greek.

gr., 1. grade. **2.** grain; grains. **3.** gram; grams. **4.** gross.

G.R., *Brit.* Georgius Rex.

Graaf·i·an follicle (grä'fĭən), *Anat.* one of many small vesicles within the ovary which, at the time of ovulation, discharge an ovum. Also, **Graafian vesicle.** [der. name of R. de *Graaf,* Dutch anatomist (1641–73)]

grab (grăb), *v.,* **grabbed, grabbing,** *n*. —*v.t.* **1.** to seize suddenly and eagerly; snatch. **2.** to take illegal possession of; seize forcibly or unscrupulously: *to grab land.* —*n.* **3.** a sudden, eager grasp or snatch. **4.** seizure or acquisition by violent or unscrupulous means. **5.** that which is grabbed. **6.** a mechanical device for gripping objects. [c. MD and MLG *grabben,* Sw. *grabba*] —**grab'ber,** *n*.

grab bag, *n. U.S. Colloq.* a receptacle from which one draws without knowing what he is getting.

grab·ble (grăb'əl), *v.i.,* **-bled, -bling. 1.** to feel or search with the hands; grope. **2.** to sprawl; scramble. [freq. of GRAB.[1] Cf. D *grabbelen*]

gra·ben (grä'bən), *n*. a portion of the earth's crust, bounded on at least two sides by faults, that has been moved downward in relation to adjacent portions. [t. G: ditch]

grab rope, *Naut.* any of certain lines or ropes on a ship for taking hold of, as one for boatmen to hold on to when coming alongside. Also, **grab line.**

Grac·chi (grăk'ī), *n.pl.* Gaius and Tiberius Gracchus.

Grac·chus (grăk′əs), *n.* **1. Gaius Sempronius** (gā′əs sĕm prō′nĭ əs), 153?–121 B.C., Roman political reformer and orator. **2.** his brother, **Tiberius Sempronius** (tī-bĭr′ĭ əs), 163?–133 B.C., Roman reformer and orator.

grace (grās), *n., v.,* **graced, gracing.** —*n.* **1.** elegance or beauty of form, manner, motion, or act. **2.** a pleasing or attractive quality or endowment. **3.** favor or good will. **4.** manifestation of favor, esp. as by a superior. **5.** mercy; clemency; pardon. **6.** favor shown in granting a delay or temporary immunity. **7.** *Law.* an allowance of time to a debtor before suit can be brought against him after his debt has by its terms become payable: *days of grace.* **8.** *Theol.* **a.** the free, unmerited favor and love of God. **b.** the influence or spirit of God operating in man to regenerate or strengthen. **c.** a virtue or excellence of divine origin: *the Christian graces.* **9. state of grace,** *Theol.* **a.** condition of being in God's favor. **b.** condition of being one of the elect. **10.** moral strength: *the grace to perform a duty.* **11.** a short prayer before or after a meal, in which a blessing is asked and thanks are given. **12.** (*usually cap.*) a formal title used in addressing or mentioning a duke, duchess, or archbishop, and formerly also a sovereign (prec. by *your, his,* etc.). **13.** (*cap.*) *Class. Myth.* one of three sister goddesses, commonly given as **Aglaia** (brilliance), **Euphrosyne** (joy), and **Thalia** (bloom), presiding over all beauty and charm in nature and humanity. **14.** *Music.* an embellishment consisting of a note or notes not essential to the harmony or melody, as an appoggiatura, an inverted mordent, etc. —*v.t.* **15.** to lend or add grace to; adorn. **16.** to favor or honor: *to grace an occasion with one's presence.* **17.** *Music.* to add grace notes, cadenzas, etc., to. [ME, t. OF, t. L: m. s. *grātia* favor, gratitude, agreeableness] —**Syn. 1.** attractiveness, charm, gracefulness. **4.** kindness. **5.** lenity. **15.** embellish, beautify; honor, enhance.

grace cup, 1. a cup, as of wine, passed round at the end of the meal for the final health or toast. **2.** the drink.

grace·ful (grās′fəl), *adj.* characterized by grace of form, manner, movement, or speech; elegant; easy or effective. —**grace′ful·ly,** *adv.* —**grace′ful·ness,** *n.*

grace·less (grās′lĭs), *adj.* **1.** wanting grace, pleasing elegance, or charm. **2.** without any sense of right or propriety. —**grace′less·ly,** *adv.* —**grace′less·ness,** *n.*

grace note, *Music.* a note not essential to the harmony or melody, added as an embellishment, esp. an appoggiatura.

grac·ile (grās′ĭl), *adj.* **1.** gracefully slender. **2.** slender; thin. [t. L: m. s. *gracilis* slender] —**gra·cil′i·ty,** *n.*

gra·ci·o·so (grä′shĭ ō′sō; *Sp.* grä thyō′sō), *n., pl.* **-sos. 1.** a character in Spanish comedy, resembling the English clown. **2.** a low comic character. **3.** *Obs.* a favorite. [Sp., der. *gracia* wit, grace, t. L: m. *grātia*]

gra·cious (grā′shəs), *adj.* **1.** disposed to show grace or favor; kind; benevolent; courteous. **2.** indulgent or beneficent in a condescending or patronizing way, esp. to inferiors. **3.** merciful or compassionate. **4.** *Obs.* fortunate or happy. —*interj.* **5.** an exclamation of surprise, etc. [ME, t. OF, t. L: m.s. *grātiōsus* enjoying or showing favor] —**gra′cious·ly,** *adv.* —**gra′cious·ness, gra·ci·os·i·ty** (grā′shĭ ŏs′ə tY), *n.* —**Syn. 1.** kindly, benign. See kind¹. —**Ant. 1.** churlish, surly.

grack·le (grăk′əl), *n.* any of various birds of the Old World family *Sturnidae* (starlings), or of the American family *Icteridae* (American starlings, blackbirds, etc.), as the crow blackbird or **purple grackle** (*Guiscalus quiscula*). [t. L: m.s. *grāculus* jackdaw]

grad., **1.** graduate. **2.** graduated.

gra·date (grā′dāt), *v.,* **-dated, -dating.** —*v.i.* **1.** to pass by insensible degrees, as one color into another. —*v.t.* **2.** to cause to gradate. **3.** to arrange in grades.

gra·da·tion (grā dā′shən), *n.* **1.** any process or change taking place through a series of stages, by degrees, or gradually. **2.** (*usually pl.*) a stage, degree, or grade in such a series. **3.** the passing of one tint or shade of color to another, or one surface to another, by very small degrees, as in painting, sculpture, etc. **4.** act of grading. **5.** ablaut (def. 2). —**gra·da′tion·al,** *adj.* —**gra·da′tion·al·ly,** *adv.*

grade (grād), *n., v.,* **graded, grading.** —*n.* **1.** a degree in a scale, as of rank, advancement, quality, value, intensity, etc. **2.** a class of persons or things of the same relative rank, quality, etc. **3.** a step or stage in a course or process. **4.** a single division of a school classified according to the progress of the pupils (American public schools commonly being divided into eight grades below the high school division). **5.** *U.S.* the pupils themselves in such a division. **6.** (*pl.*) *U.S.* the divisions of an elementary school or the school itself. **7.** *U.S.* a number, letter, etc., indicating the relative quality of a student's work in a course, examination, or special assignment. **8.** inclination with the horizontal of a road, railroad, etc., usually expressed by stating the vertical rise or fall as a percentage of the horizontal distance. **9. at grade,** on the same level: *a railroad crosses a highway at grade.* **10.** an animal resulting from a cross between a parent of common stock and one of a pure breed. —*v.t.* **11.** to arrange in a series of grades; class; sort. **12.** to determine the grade of. **13.** to cause to pass by degrees, as from one color or shade to another. **14.** to reduce to a level or to practicable degrees of inclination: *to grade a road.* **15.** to cross (a nondescript animal or a low grade one) with one of a pure breed. —*v.i.* **16.** to be graded. **17.** to

be of a particular grade or quality. [t. F, t. L: m. s. *gradus* step, stage, degree]

-grade, a word element meaning "walking," "moving," "going," as in *retrograde.* [comb. form repr. L *gradus* step, or *gradī,* v., walk. See GRADE, GRADIENT]

grade crossing, a crossing of a railroad and a highway or another railroad at grade.

grade labeling, a method of giving information on a label about the quality of the merchandise.

grad·er (grā′dər), *n.* **1.** one who or that which grades. **2.** *Orig. U.S.* a pupil of a certain grade at school: *a fourth grader.* **3.** *U.S.* a machine for grading.

grade school, an elementary school that has its pupils grouped or classified into grades according to their advancement. Also, **graded school.**

gra·di·ent (grā′dĭ ənt), *n.* **1.** the degree of inclination, or the rate of ascent or descent, in a railroad, etc.; grade. **2.** an inclined surface; grade; ramp. **3.** *Physics.* **a.** change in a variable quantity, as temperature or pressure, per unit distance. **b.** curve representing such a rate of change. —*adj.* **4.** rising or descending by regular degrees of inclination. **5.** progressing by walking as an animal; gressorial. **6.** of a type suitable for walking, as some birds' feet. [t. L: s. *gradiens,* ppr., walking, going]

gra·din (grā′dĭn; *Fr.* grȧ dăn′), *n.* **1.** one of a series of steps or seats raised one above another. **2.** *Eccles.* a shelf or one of a series of shelves behind and above an altar. Also, **gra·dine** (grə dēn′). [t. F, t. It.: m. *gradino,* der. *grado* GRADE]

grad·u·al (grăj′ōō əl), *adj.* **1.** taking place, changing, moving, etc., by degrees or little by little: *gradual improvement in health.* **2.** rising or descending at an even, moderate inclination: *a gradual slope.* —*n.* **3.** *Eccles.* **a.** an antiphon sung between the epistle and the gospel in the eucharistic service. **b.** a book containing the words and music of the parts of the liturgy which are sung by the choir. [t. ML: s. *graduālis* (as n., *graduāle*), der. L *gradus* step, grade] —**grad′u·al·ly,** *adv.* —**grad′u·al·ness,** *n.* —**Syn. 1.** slow.

grad·u·ate (*adj., n.* grăj′ōō ĭt, -āt′; *v.* grăj′ōō āt′), *n., adj., v.,* **-ated, -ating.** —*n.* **1.** one who has received a degree or diploma on completing a course of study, as in a university, college, or school. **2.** a student who holds the first or bachelor's degree and is studying for an advanced degree. **3.** a cylindrical or tapering graduated vessel of glass, for measuring. —*adj.* **4.** that has been graduated: *a graduate student.* **5.** of or pertaining to graduates: *a graduate school.* —*v.i.* **6.** to receive a degree or diploma on completing a course of study. **7.** to pass by degrees; change gradually. —*v.t.* **8.** to confer a degree upon, or to grant a diploma to, at the close of a course of study, as in a university, college, or school. **9.** to arrange in grades or gradations; establish gradation in. **10.** to divide into or mark with degrees or other divisions, as the scale of a thermometer. [t. ML: m.s. *graduātus,* pp. of *graduāre* admit to an academic degree, der. L *gradus* step, grade] —**grad′u·a·tor,** *n.*

grad·u·a·tion (grăj′ōō ā′shən), *n.* **1.** act of graduating. **2.** state of being graduated. **3.** ceremony of conferring degrees or diplomas, as at a college or school. **4.** marks or a mark on an instrument or a vessel for indicating degree, quantity, etc.

gra·dus (grā′dəs), *n.* *Music.* a work consisting wholly, or in part, of exercises of increasing difficulty. [t. L: short for *gradus ad Parnassum* step to Parnassus]

Grae·ae (grē′ē), *n.pl.* *Gk. Myth.* three old sea deities, who had but one eye and one tooth among them and were the protectresses of the Gorgons, their sisters. Also, **Graiae.**

Grae·ci·a Mag·na (grē′shĭ ə măg′nə), Magna Graecia.

Grae·cize (grē′sīz), *v.t., v.i.,* **-cized, -cizing.** *Chiefly Brit.* Grecize. —**Grae′cism,** *n,*

Graeco-, *Chiefly Brit.* var. of Greco-.

Graf (gräf), *n., pl.* **Grafen** (grä′fən) a count; a title of nobility in Germany, Austria, and Sweden, which corresponds to English earl and French comte. [cf. BURGRAVE, LANDGRAVE, MARGRAVE]

graf·fi·to (grə fē′tō), *n., pl.* **-ti** (-tē) *Archaeol.* an ancient drawing or writing scratched on a wall or other surface. [t. It., der. *graffio* a scratch, ult. der. Gk. *grȧphein* mark, draw, write]

graft¹ (grȧft, gräft), *n.* **1.** *Hort.* **a.** a shoot or part of a plant (the scion) inserted in a groove, slit, or the like in another plant or tree (the stock) so as to become nourished by and united with it. **b.** the plant or tree (the united stock and scion) resulting from such an operation. **c.** the place where the scion is inserted. **2.** *Surg.* a portion of living tissue surgically transplanted from one part of an individual to another, or from one individual to another, with a view to its adhesion and growth. **3.** act of grafting. —*v.t.* **4.** to insert (a graft) into a plant or tree; insert a scion of (one plant) into another plant. **5.** to cause (a plant) to reproduce through grafting. **6.** *Surg.* to transplant (a portion of living tissue) as a graft. **7.** to insert as if by grafting: *to graft a pagan custom upon*

Types of grafting
A. Splice; B. Saddle; C. Cleft; D, E. Whip or tongue

Christian institutions. —*v.i.* **8.** to insert scions from one tree, or kind of tree, into another. **9.** to become grafted. [earlier *graff*, ME *grafe*, t. OF: orig., stylus, pencil, t. LL: m.s. *graphium*, t. Gk.: m. *grapheion* stylus] —**graft′er**, *n.* —**graft′ing**, *n.*

graft² (gråft, gräft), *n.* *U.S. Colloq.* —*n.* **1.** the acquisition of gain or advantage by dishonest, unfair, or sordid means, esp. through the abuse of one's position or influence in politics, business, etc. **2.** a particular instance, method, or means of thus acquiring gain. **3.** the gain or advantage acquired. —*v.t.* **4.** to obtain by graft. —*v.i.* **5.** to practice graft. [cf. prov. Eng. or slang *graft* work, a job or trade, ? identical with *graft* in expression *spade(s) graft*, var. of *spade(s)-graff*, lit., spade's digging (depth of earth thrown up at a single spading), OE *græf* trench. See GRAVE¹] —**graft′er**, *n.*

graft·age (gråf′tĭj, gräf′-), *n.* the art of inserting a part of one plant into another plant in such a way that the two will unite and continue their growth.

gra·ham (grā′əm), *adj.* made of graham flour.

graham flour, unbolted wheat flour, containing all of the wheat grain; whole-wheat flour. [named after S. *Graham* (1794–1851), U.S. reformer of dietetics]

Gra·ham Land (grā′əm), Palmer Peninsula.

Gra·iae (grā′ē, grī′ē), *n.pl.* Graeae.

grail (grāl), *n.* a cup (also taken as a chalice) which according to medieval legend was used by Jesus at the Last Supper, and in which Joseph of Arimathea received the last drops of Jesus' blood at the cross: used often as a symbol for a lost, pure kind of Christianity; Holy Grail. [ME *grayle*, t. OF: m. *graal*, t. ML: m. s. *gradāle* plate, or der. L *crātēr* bowl, t. Gk.: m. *krātēr*]

grain (grān), *n.* **1.** a small hard seed, esp. a seed of one of the cereal plants, wheat, rye, oats, barley, maize, or millet. **2.** the gathered seeds of cereal plants in the mass. **3.** the plants themselves, whether standing or gathered. **4.** any small, hard particle, as of sand, gold, pepper, gunpowder, etc. **5.** the smallest unit of weight in most systems, originally determined by the weight of a plump grain of wheat. In the U.S. and British systems —avoirdupois, troy, and apothecaries' —the grain is identical. In an avoirdupois ounce there are 437.5 grains; in the troy and apothecaries' ounces there are 480 grains. **6.** the smallest possible amount of anything: *a grain of truth*. **7.** **with a grain of salt**, with some reserve; without wholly believing. **8.** the arrangement or direction of fibers in wood, or the resulting appearance or markings. **9.** the side of leather from which the hair has been removed. **10.** a stamped pattern to imitate natural grain of leather: used either on leather to simulate a different type of natural leather, or on coated cloth. **11.** the fibers or yarn in a piece of fabric as differentiated from the fabric itself. **12.** lamination or cleavage of stone, coal, etc. **13.** *Gems.* unit of weight for pearls equal to 50 mg, or ¼ carat. **14.** (in diamond polishing) the cleavage directions. **15.** the size of constituent particles of any substance; texture: *sugar of fine grain*. **16.** granular texture or appearance: *a stone of coarse grain*. **17.** state of crystallization: *boiled to the grain*. **18.** temper or natural character: *to go against the grain*. **19.** *Obs.* color or hue. —*v.t.* **20.** to form into grains, granulate. **21.** to give a granular appearance to. **22.** to paint in imitation of the grain of wood, stone, etc. **23.** *Tanning.* to remove the hair from (skins); soften and raise the grain of (leather). [coalescence of two ME words: ME *grevn*, t. OF: m. *grain*, g. L *grānum* grain, seed; and ME *grayne* red dye, t. OF: m. *graine*, g. L *grāna*, pl. of *grānum* grain]. —**grain′er**, *n.* —**grain′less**, *adj.*

grain alcohol, alcohol made from grain; ethyl alcohol.

grain elevator, a building where grain is stored.

Grain·ger (grān′jər), *n.* **Percy Aldridge** (ôl′drĭj), born 1882, Australian pianist and composer.

grains (grānz), *n.pl.* (*often construed as sing.*) an iron instrument with barbed prongs, for spearing or harpooning fish. [earlier also *grainse*, t. Icel.: m. *grein* division, branch; cf. Sw. *gren*]

grains of paradise, the pungent, peppery seeds of either of two zingiberaceous plants, *Aframomum Melegueta* and *A. granum-paradisi*, of Africa: used to strengthen cordials, etc., and in veterinary medicine.

grain·y (grā′nĭ), *adj.*, **grainier**, **grainiest**. **1.** grainlike or granular. **2.** full of grains or grain. **3.** resembling the grain of wood, etc. —**grain′i·ness**, *n.*

gral·la·to·ri·al (grål′ə tōr′ĭ əl), *adj.* belonging or pertaining to the wading birds, as the snipe, cranes, storks, herons, etc., many species of which have very long legs. [f. L *grallātor* one who goes on stilts + -IAL]

gram¹ (gråm), *n.* a metric unit of mass, defined as one thousandth of a kilogram and equal to 15.432 grains. Also, *esp. Brit.*, **gramme**. [t. F: m. *gramme*, t. LL: m. *gramma*, t. Gk.: a small weight, orig. something drawn]

gram² (gråm), *n.* **1.** (in the Orient) the chick-pea, there used as a food for man and cattle. **2.** any of various other plants, as *Phaseolus aureus* (**green gram**) and *P. mungo* (**black gram**), beans cultivated in India as a food crop. [t. Pg.: m. *grao*, g. L *grānum* GRAIN¹]

-gram¹, a word element meaning something drawn or written, as in *diagram, epigram, telegram, monogram*. [t. Gk.: m. *-gramma* something drawn or written, or m. *-grammon* pertaining to a stroke or line]

-gram², a word element meaning grams; of or per-

taining to a gram, as in *kilogram*. [t. Gk.: m. *grámma* small weight]

gram., **1.** grammar. **2.** grammatical.

gra·ma grass (grä′mə), any range grass of the western and southwestern U.S. of the genus *Bouteloua*, as *B. gracilis* (**blue grama**), the commonest species. [*grama*, t. Sp.: kind of grass, g. L *grāmen* grass]

gram·a·rye (gråm′ə rĭ), *n.* *Archaic.* occult learning; magic. Also **gram′a·ry**. [ME *grammarie, gramarye*, t. OF: GRAMMAR, magic]

gram atom, *Chem.* that quantity of an element whose weight in grams is numerically equal to the atomic weight of the element.

gram calorie. See **calorie** (def. 1a).

gra·mer·cy (grə mûr′sĭ), *interj.* *Archaic.* **1.** many thanks. **2.** an exclamation of surprise or sudden feeling. [ME, t. OF: m. *grant merci*. See GRAND, MERCY]

gra·min·e·ous (grə mĭn′ĭ əs), *adj.* **1.** grasslike. **2.** pertaining or belonging to the *Gramineae* (or *Poaceae*) family, the grass family of plants. [t. L: m. *grāmineus* pertaining to grass]

gram·i·niv·o·rous (gråm′ə nĭv′ə rəs), *adj.* **1.** feeding on seeds or like food. **2.** adapted for feeding on grain, as the jaws, teeth, etc., of gophers and other rodents.

gram·mar (gråm′ər), *n.* **1.** the features of a language (sounds, words, formation and arrangement of words, etc.) considered systematically as a whole, especially with reference to their mutual contrasts and relations: *English grammar*. **2.** an account of the preceding. **3.** a similar account comparing two or more languages, or different stages of the same language. **4.** speech or writing in accordance with standard usage: *he knows his grammar*. **5.** the elements of any science, art, or subject. **6.** a book treating them. [ME *grammer*, t. OF: m. *grammaire*, t. L: m. *grammatica*, t. Gk.: m. *grammatikē* grammar, prop. fem. of *grammatikós* pertaining to letters or literature] —**gram′mar·less**, *adj.*

gram·mar·i·an (grə mâr′ĭ ən), *n.* **1.** a specialist in the study of grammar. **2.** a person who claims, or is reputed to establish, standards of usage in a language.

grammar school, **1.** *U.S.* a graded school intermediate between a primary school and a high school. **2.** *Brit.* a secondary school corresponding to an American high school. **3.** a secondary school in which Latin and Greek are among the principal subjects taught.

gram·mat·i·cal (grə măt′ə kəl), *adj.* **1.** of or pertaining to grammar: *grammatical analysis*. **2.** conforming to standard usage: *grammatical speech*. —**gram·mat′i·cal·ly**, *adv.* —**gram·mat′i·cal·ness**, *n.*

gramme (gråm), *n.* *Chiefly Brit.* gram¹.

gram molecule, *Chem.* that quantity of a substance whose weight in grams is numerically equal to the number which expresses the molecular weight of the substance. Also, **gram′-mo·lec′u·lar weight**.

Gra·mont (grá môN′), *n.* **Philibert de** (fē lā bĕr′ dɔ), 1621 1707, French courtier, soldier, and adventurer.

gram·o·phone (gråm′ə fōn′), *n.* **1.** a phonograph. **2.** (*cap.*) a trade name for this. [inverted var. of PHONOGRAM. See PHONO-, -GRAM¹]

Gram·pi·ans (gråm′pĭ ənz), *n.pl.* **The**, a range of low mountains in central Scotland, separating the Highlands from the Lowlands. Highest peak, Ben Nevis, 4406 ft. Also, **Gram′pi·an Hills.**

gram·pus (gråm′pəs), *n.* **1.** a cetacean, *Grampus griseus*, of the dolphin family, widely distributed in northern seas. **2.** any of various related cetaceans, as the killer, *Orca orca*. [earlier *graundepose*, alter. of *grapays*, t. OF: m. *graspeis*, g. ML *crassus piscis* fat fish]

Gram's method (gråmz), a method of bacterial staining in which the film is first stained with crystal violet and then with Gram's iodine solution. It permits the classification of bacteria, **Gram-positive** species keeping the violet dye, and **Gram-negative** species being decolorized. [named after H. C. J. *Gram*, Danish physician (1853–1938)]

Grampus. *Grampus griseus* (10 to 13 ft. long)

Gra·na·da (grə nä′də; *Sp.* grä nä′dä), *n.* **1.** a medieval kingdom along the Mediterranean coast of S Spain. See map under **Castile**. **2.** a city in S Spain: the capital of this former kingdom and the last stronghold of the Moors in Spain; site of the Alhambra. 155,405 (1940).

gran·a·dil·la (grån′ə dĭl′ə), *n.* **1.** the edible fruit of certain species of passionflower, esp. *Passiflora edulis* (**purple granadilla**) and *P. quadrangularis* (**giant granadilla**). **2.** any of the plants yielding these fruits. [t. Sp., dim. of *granada* pomegranate. See GRENADE]

gran·a·ry (grån′ə rĭ, grā′nə-), *n.*, *pl.* **-ries.** **1.** a storehouse or repository for grain, esp. after it has been threshed or husked. **2.** a region abounding in grain. [t. L: m. s. *grānārium*]

Gran Ca·na·ri·a (grän kä nä′rĭ ä), one of the Canary Islands. 216,853 pop. (1930); 650 sq. mi. *Cap.:* Las Palmas. Also, **Grand Canary.**

Gran Cha·co (grän chä′kō), an extensive subtropical region in Argentina, Bolivia, and Paraguay. ab. 300,000 sq. mi. See **Chaco.**

grand (gränd), *adj.* **1.** imposing in size or appearance or general effect: *grand mountain scenery*. **2.** stately, majestic, or dignified. 3. lofty: *grand ideas*. 4. magnificent or splendid: *a grand palace, display, etc.* 5. noble or fine: *a grand old man.* 6. highest, or very high, in rank or official dignity: *a grand jury*. 7. main or principal; chief: *the grand staircase.* 8. of great importance, distinction, or pretension: *grand personages*. 9. complete or comprehensive: *a grand total.* 10. *Colloq.* first-rate; very good; splendid: *to have a grand time, grand weather.* 11. *Music.* **a.** written on a large scale or for a large ensemble: *a grand fugue.* **b.** applied to compositions which contain all the regular parts or movements in a complete form. 12. *Genealogy.* one degree more remote in ascent or descent (used in compounds), as in *grandaunt, grandchild, etc.* [ME *graunt*, t. OF, g. L *grandis* large, full-grown, great, grand] **—grand′ly,** *adv.* **—grand′ness,** *n.* —Syn. 4. great, large, palatial. —Ant. 1. insignificant.

Grand Army of the Republic, a society, founded in 1866, composed of men who served in the U.S. army or navy during the Civil War.

grand·aunt (grănd′ănt′, -änt′), *n.* a great-aunt.

Grand Banks, an extensive shoal SE of Newfoundland: one of the world's greatest fishing grounds. ab. 300 mi. long; ab. 40,000 sq. mi. Also, **Grand Bank.**

Grand Canal, 1. a canal in E China, extending from Tientsin S to Hangchow. ab. 900 mi. 2. a large canal in Venice, Italy, forming the main thoroughfare.

Grand Canary, Gran Canaria.

Grand Canyon, a gorge of the Colorado river in N Arizona. Over 200 mi. long; 2000 to 6000 ft. deep.

Grand Canyon National Park, a national park in N Arizona, including a part of the Grand Canyon and the area around it. 1009 sq. mi.

grand·child (grănd′chīld′), *n., pl.* **-children.** a child of one's son or daughter.

Grand Cou·lee (kōō′lē), 1. a dry canyon in central Washington, cut by the Columbia river in the glacial period. 52 mi. long; over 400 ft. deep. 2. a dam on the Columbia river at the N end of this canyon: the largest concrete dam in the world. 550 ft. high.

grande dame (grä̈nd dȧm′), *French.* a great lady.

grand·daugh·ter (grănd′dô′tər), *n.* a daughter of one's son or daughter.

grand duchess, 1. the wife or widow of a grand duke. 2. a woman who governs a grand duchy in her own right. 3. a daughter of a czar or of a czar's son.

grand duchy, a territory ruled by a grand duke or grand duchess.

grand duke, 1. the sovereign of a territory called a grand duchy, ranking next below a king. 2. a son of a czar or of a czar's son.

Gran·de (*Texas* rē′ō grän′dā, rē′ō grănd′; *Brazil* rē′ōō grän′də), *n.* Rio. See **Rio Grande.**

gran·dee (grăndē′), *n.* a Spanish nobleman of the highest rank. [t. Sp., Pg.: m. *grande* great (person). See GRAND]

gran·deur (grăn′jər, -jōōr), *n.* state or quality of being grand; imposing greatness; exalted rank, dignity, or importance. [t. F, der. *grand* GRAND] **—Syn.** stateliness, majesty, sublimity; pomp, splendor, state.

Grand Falls, a great waterfall of the Hamilton river, in Labrador. ab. 200 ft. wide; 316 ft. high.

grand·fa·ther (grănd′fä′ᵺər), *n.* 1. the father of one's father or mother. 2. a forefather.

grandfather clause, *U.S. Hist.* a state constitutional clause disfranchising Negroes, held void in 1915.

grand·fa·ther·ly (grănd′fä′ᵺərlĭ), *adj.* 1. of, or in the manner of, a grandfather. 2. indulgent; kindly.

Grand Forks, a town in E North Dakota. 26,836 (1950).

Grand Island, a city in S Nebraska. 22,682 (1950).

gran·dil·o·quence (grăndĭl′əkwəns), *n.* lofty speech, bombast. [f. s. L *grandiloquus* speaking loftily + -ENCE]

gran·dil·o·quent (grăndĭl′əkwənt), *adj.* speaking or expressed in a lofty or pompous style; bombastic. **—gran·dil′o·quent·ly,** *adv.* —Ant. simple, sincere.

gran·di·ose (grăn′dĭōs′), *adj.* 1. grand in an imposing or impressive way. 2. affectedly grand or stately; pompous. [t. F, t. It.: m. *grandioso,* der. L *grandis* GRAND. See -OSE[1]] **—gran′di·ose′ly,** *adv.* **—gran·di·os·i·ty** (grăn′dĭŏs′ə tĭ′), *n.*

grand jury, a jury of from 12 to 23 persons designated to inquire into alleged violations of the law in order to ascertain whether the evidence is sufficient to warrant trial by a petty jury.

Grand Lama. See **Dalai Lama.**

grand larceny. See **larceny.**

grand·ma (grănd′mä′, grăn′mä′, grăm′ə), *n.* grandmamma.

grand·mam·ma (grănd′məmä′, -mä′mə), *n.* grandmother.

Grand Ma·nan (mənăn′), a Canadian island at the entrance to the Bay of Fundy: a part of New Brunswick; summer resort. 2457 pop. (1941); 57 sq. mi.

grand monde (grä̈n mônd′), *French.* the fashionable world; the best society. [F: lit., the great world]

grand·moth·er (grănd′mŭᵺ′ər), *n.* 1. the mother of one's father or mother. 2. an ancestress.

grand·moth·er·ly (grănd′mŭᵺ′ərlĭ), *adj.* 1. of or in the manner of a grandmother. 2. like a grandmother.

Grand Mufti, the head of the Moslem Arab community in Jerusalem, long chosen from the Husseini family.

grand·neph·ew (grănd′nĕf′ū, -nĕv′ū), *n.* a son of one's nephew or niece.

grand·niece (grănd′nēs′), *n.* a daughter of one's nephew or niece.

Grand Old Party. See **G.O.P.**

grand opera, a drama interpreted by music, the text being sung throughout.

grand·pa (grănd′pä′, grăm′pä′, grăm′pə), *n.* grandpapa.

grand·pa·pa (grănd′pəpä′, -pä′pə), *n.* grandfather.

grand·par·ent (grănd′pâr′ənt), *n.* a parent of a parent.

grand piano. See **piano** (def. 2).

Grand Pré (grä̈n prē′), a village in central Nova Scotia, on Minas Basin: locale of Longfellow's "Evangeline."

grand prix (grä̈n prē′), *French.* a great prize.

Grand Rapids, city in SW Michigan. 176,515 (1950).

Grand River, 1. former name of the **Colorado** above its junction with the Green river. ab. 350 mi. 2. a river in SW Michigan, flowing W to Lake Michigan. 260 mi. 3. Hamilton (def. 10).

grand·sire (grănd′sīr′), *n. Archaic.* 1. a grandfather. 2. a forefather. 3. an old man.

grand·son (grănd′sŭn′), *n.* a son of one's son or daughter.

grand·stand (grănd′stănd′), *n.* the principal stand for spectators at a racecourse, athletic field, etc.

grand tour, an extended tour on the continent of Europe, esp. as the finishing course in the education of British young men of good family.

grand·un·cle (grănd′ŭng′kəl), *n.* an uncle of one's father or mother; a great-uncle.

grand vizier, the chief officer of state of various Moslem countries, as in the former Turkish Empire.

grange (grānj), *n.* 1. a farm. 2. *Chiefly Brit.* a country dwelling house with its various farm buildings; dwelling of a yeoman or gentleman farmer. 3. (formerly) an outlying farmhouse with barns, etc., belonging to a feudal manor or a religious establishment, where crops and tithes in kind were stored. 4. (*cap.*) *U.S.* a lodge or local branch of the "Patrons of Husbandry," an association for promoting the interests of agriculture. 5. **the Grange,** the association itself. [ME *graunge*, t. AF, var. of OF *grange,* g. LL *grānica,* der. L *grānum* grain]

grang·er (grān′jər), *n.* 1. a farmer. 2. a farm steward. 3. (*cap.*) *U.S.* a member of a Grange.

grang·er·ize (grān′jəriz′), *v.t.* **-ized, -izing.** 1. to augment the illustrative content of (a book) by inserting additional prints, drawings, engravings, etc., not included in the original volume. 2. to mutilate (books) in order to get illustrative material for such a purpose. [der. J. *Granger,* whose "Biographical History of England" (1769) was arranged for such illustration]

gran·ite (grăn′ĭt), *n.* 1. a granular igneous rock composed chiefly of feldspar (orthoclase) and quartz, usually with one or more other minerals, as mica, hornblende, etc.: much used in building, and for monuments, etc. 2. great hardness or firmness. [t. It.: m. *granito,* orig. pp., grained, of *granire,* der. *grano,* g. L *grānum* grain] **—gran′ite·like′,** *adj.* **—gra·nit′ic,** *adj.*

Granite City, a city in SW Illinois, near St. Louis, Missouri. 29,465 (1950).

gran·ite·ware (grăn′ĭt wâr′), *n.* 1. a kind of ironware with a gray, stonelike enamel. 2. pottery with a speckled appearance like granite. 3. a semivitreous white pottery somewhat harder than earthenware.

gran·it·ite (grăn′ĭtīt′), *n.* a granite rich in biotite.

gra·niv·o·rous (grănĭv′ərəs), *adj.* feeding on grain and seeds.

Gran·jon (grăn′jən), *n. Print.* a style of type originally cut by the French designer Robert Granjon.

gran·ny (grăn′ĭ), *n., pl.* **-nies.** *Colloq.* 1. a grandmother. 2. an old woman. 3. a fussy person. 4. *Southern U.S.* a nurse or midwife. 5. granny's knot. Also, **gran′nie.**

granny's knot, *Naut.* a reef or square knot in which the second part is crossed the wrong way: derided by seamen because it is difficult to untie when jammed, yet likely to slip under strain. See illus. under **knot.**

gran·o·phyre (grăn′əfīr′), *n.* a fine-grained or porphyritic granitic rock with a micrographic intergrowth of the minerals of the groundmass. [t. G: m. *granophyr,* f. *grano-* (comb. form of *granit* GRANITE) + (*por*)*phyr* porphyry] **—gran′o·phy′ric,** *adj.*

grant (grănt, gränt), *v.t.* 1. to bestow or confer, esp. by a formal act: *to grant a right.* 2. to give or accord: *to grant permission.* 3. to agree or accede to: *to grant a request.* 4. to admit or concede; accept for the sake of argument: *I grant that point.* 5. to transfer or convey, esp. by deed or writing: *to grant property.* **—n.** 6. that which is granted, as a privilege or right, a sum of money, or a tract of land. 7. act of granting. 8. *Law.* an instrument which conveys property. 9. a geographical unit in Vermont, Maine, and New Hampshire, originally a grant of land to a person or group of people. [ME *grant(en),* t. OF: m. *granter* promise, authorize, confirm, approve, ult. der. L *crēdens,* ppr., of *crēdere* trust, believe] **—grant′a·ble,** *adj.* **—grant′er,** *n.* —Syn. 2. See **give.**

Grant (grănt), *n.* Ulysses Simpson, 1822–85, U.S. general in the Civil War and 18th president of the U.S., 1869–77.

---

b., blend of, blended; c., cognate with; d., dialect, dialectal; der., derived from; f., formed from; g., going back to; m., modification of; r., replacing; s., stem of; t., taken from; ?, perhaps. See the full key on inside cover.

gran·tee (grăn tē′, grăn-), *n.* *Law.* one to whom a grant is made.

Granth (grŭnt), *n.* the sacred scripture of the Sikhs.

grant·or (grăn′tər, grăn tôr′, grän-), *n.* *Law.* one who makes a grant.

gran·u·lar (grăn′yə lər), *adj.* **1.** of the nature of granules. **2.** composed of or bearing granules or grains. **3.** showing a granulated structure. —**gran′u·lar′·i·ty**, *n.* —**gran′u·lar·ly**, *adv.*

gran·u·late (grăn′yə lāt′), *v.*, -lated, -lating. —*v.t.* **1.** to form into granules or grains. **2.** to raise in granules; make rough on the surface. —*v.i.* **3.** to become granular. **4.** *Pathol.* to form granulation tissue. [f. GRANUL(E) + -ATE¹] —**gran′u·la′tor**, *n.*

gran·u·la·tion (grăn′yə lā′shən), *n.* **1.** act or process of granulating. **2.** granulated condition. **3.** one of the grains of a granulated surface. **4.** *Pathol.* **a.** the formation of granulation tissue, esp. in healing. **b.** granulation tissue. **5.** *Astron.* one of the small short-lived features of the solar surface which in the aggregate give it a mottled appearance when viewed with a telescope.

granulation tissue, tissue formed in early wound healing and repair, composed largely of newly growing capillaries and so called from its irregular surface in open wounds; proud flesh.

gran·ule (grăn′ūl), *n.* **1.** a little grain. **2.** a small particle; pellet. **3.** a corpuscle; sporule. [t. LL: m. s. *grānulum*, dim. of L *grānum* GRAIN]

gran·u·lite (grăn′yə līt′), *n.* *Petrog.* a metamorphic rock composed of granular minerals of uniform size, such as quartz, feldspar, pyroxene, and showing a definite banding. —**gran·u·lit·ic** (grăn′yə lĭt′ĭk), *adj.*

gran·u·lose (grăn′yə lōs′), *n.* that portion of the starch granule acted upon by diastase and the saliva.

Gran·ville (grăn′vĭl), *n.* **John Carteret, Earl of,** 1690–1763, British statesman.

Gran·ville-Bar·ker (grăn′vĭl bär′kər), *n.* **Harley,** 1877–1946, British dramatist, actor, and critic.

grape (grāp), *n.* **1.** the edible, pulpy, smooth-skinned berry or fruit which grows in clusters on vines of the genus *Vitis*, and from which wine is made. **2.** any vine bearing this fruit. **3.** dull, dark purplish-red. **4.** (*pl.*) *Vet. Sci.* a morbid growth on the fetlock of a horse, resembling a bunch of grapes. **5.** *Archaic.* grapeshot. [ME, t. OF, var. of *crape* cluster of fruit or flowers, orig. hook; of Gmc. orig. (cf. G *krapf* hook). Cf. GRAPNEL, GRAPPLE] —**grape′less**, *adj.* —**grape′like′**, *adj.*

grape·fruit (grāp′frōōt′), *n.* **1.** a large roundish, yellow-skinned edible citrus fruit with a juicy, acid pulp, grown mainly in the U. S. **2.** the tropical or semitropical rutaceous tree, *Citrus paradisi*, yielding it.

grape hyacinth, any plant of the liliaceous genus *Muscari*, as *M. botryoides*, a species whose globular blue flowers resemble minute grapes.

grap·er·y (grā′po rĭ), *n.*, *pl.* -eries. **1.** a building where grapes are grown. **2.** a plantation of grapevines.

grape·shot (grāp′shŏt′), *n.* *Archaic.* a cluster of small cast-iron balls used as a charge for a cannon.

grape sugar, dextrose.

grape·vine (grāp′vīn′), *n.* **1.** a vine that bears grapes. **2.** *U.S. Colloq.* **a.** Also, **grapevine telegraph.** a person-to-person method of relaying secret reports which cannot be had through regular channels. **b.** an unauthenticated report.

graph (grăf, gräf), *n.* **1.** a diagram representing a system of connections or interrelations among two or more things by a number of distinctive dots, lines, bars, etc. **2.** *Math.* a curve as representing a given function. —*v.t.* **3.** to draw (a curve) as representing a given function. [short for *graphic formula*. See GRAPHIC] —**Syn. 1.** See **map.**

graph-, var. of grapho- before vowels.

-graph, a word element meaning: **1.** drawn or written, as in *autograph.* **2.** something drawn or written, as in *lithograph, monograph.* **3.** an apparatus for drawing, writing, recording, etc., as in *phonograph.* [t. Gk.: s. *-graphos* (something) drawn or written, also one who draws or writes. See GRAPHIC]

graph·ic (grăf′ĭk), *adj.* **1.** lifelike; vivid: *a graphic description of a scene.* **2.** pertaining to the use of diagrams, graphs, mathematical curves, or the like; diagrammatic. **3.** pertaining to writing: *graphic symbols.* **4.** *Geol.* possessing that kind of texture produced in a rock when certain constituents crystallize in such a way as to appear like written characters on the surfaces or sections of the rock. **5.** *Math.* pertaining to the de-

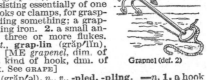

Line graph

Bar graph

termination of values, solving of problems, etc., by direct measurement on diagrams instead of by ordinary calculations. **6.** pertaining to the graphic arts. Also, **graph′i·cal.** [t. L: s. *graphicus*, t. Gk.: m. *graphikós*, der. *graphē* drawing, writing] —**graph′i·cal·ly, graph′-ic·ly,** *adv.* —**graph′i·cal·ness,** *n.* —**Syn. 1.** See **picturesque.**

graphic accent, *Gram.* **1.** any mark written above a letter, esp. one indicating stress in pronunciation, as in *rápido*, in Spanish. **2.** any of the written or printed signs used as diacritics to indicate an accent, esp. the acute accent used to mark stress.

graphic arts, drawing, engraving, etching, painting, and other arts involving the use of lines and strokes to express or convey ideas in terms of forms.

graph·ics (grăf′ĭks), *n.* **1.** the art of drawing, esp. as concerned with mathematics, engineering, etc. **2.** the science of calculating by diagrams. [f. GRAPH + -ICS]

graph·ite (grăf′īt), *n.* a very common mineral, soft native carbon, occurring in black to dark-gray foliated masses with metallic luster and greasy feel: used in "lead" pencils, as a lubricant, for making crucibles and other refractories, etc.; plumbago; black lead. [t. G: m. *graphit*, f. s. Gk. *gráphein* mark, draw, write + -*it* -ITE¹] —**gra·phit·ic** (grə fĭt′ĭk), *adj.*

graph·i·tize (grăf′ə tīz′), *v.t.*, -tized, -tizing. **1.** to convert into graphite. **2.** to cover (the surface of an object) with graphite. —**graph′i·ti·za′tion,** *n.*

grapho-, a word element meaning "writing," as in *graphology.* Also, **graph-.** [t. Gk., comb. form of *graphē*]

graph·ol·o·gy (grăf ŏl′ə jĭ), *n.* the study of handwriting, esp. as regarded as an expression of the writer's character. —**graph·ol′o·gist,** *n.*

graph·o·ma·ni·a (grăf′ə mā′nĭ ə), *n.* a mania for writing.

graph·o·mo·tor (grăf′ō mō′tər), *adj.* *Med.* pertaining to the muscular movements in writing.

-graphy, a combining form denoting some process or form of drawing, representing, writing, recording, describing, etc., or an art or science concerned with some such thing, as in *biography, choreography, geography, orthography, photography, telegraphy.* [t. Gk.: m.s. *-graphia*, der. *gráphos*. See -GRAPH, -Y³]

grap·nel (grăp′nəl), *n.* **1.** a device consisting essentially of one or more hooks or clamps, for grasping or holding something; a grapple; grappling iron. **2.** a small anchor with three or more flukes. Also, *Naut.*, **grap·lin** (grăp′lĭn), **grap′line.** [ME *grapenel*, dim. of OF *grapin* kind of hook, dim. of *grape* hook. See GRAPE]

Grapnel (def. 2)

grap·ple (grăp′əl), *n.*, *v.*, -pled, -pling. —*n.* **1.** a hook or an iron instrument by which one thing, as a ship, fastens on another; a grapnel. **2.** a seizing or gripping. **3.** a grip or close hold in wrestling or hand-to-hand fighting. —*v.t.* **4.** to seize, hold, or fasten with or as with a grapple. **5.** to engage in a struggle or close encounter with. —*v.i.* **6.** to hold or make fast to something as with a grapple. **7.** to use a grapple. **8.** to seize another, or each other, in a firm grip, as in wrestling; clinch. **9.** to try to overcome or deal (fol. by *with*): *to grapple with a problem.* [appar. a dim. of OF *grape* hook. See GRAPE, GRAPNEL] —**grap′pler,** *n.*

grap·pling (grăp′lĭng), *n.* **1.** that by which anything is seized and held. **2.** a grapnel.

grappling iron, a grapnel. Also, **grappling hook.**

grap·y (grā′pĭ), *adj.* of, like, or composed of grapes.

Gras·mere (gräs′mĭr, gräs′-), *n.* **1.** a lake in NW England, in Westmoreland. 1 mi. long. **2.** a village on this lake: Wordsworth's home, 1799–1808.

grasp (grăsp, gräsp), *v.t.* **1.** to seize and hold by or as by clasping with the fingers. **2.** to seize upon; hold firmly. **3.** to lay hold of with the mind; comprehend; understand. —*v.i.* **4.** to make the motion of seizing; seize something firmly or eagerly. **5.** to catch at; try to seize (fol. by *at*): *a drowning man grasps at a straw.* —*n.* **6.** a grasping or gripping; grip of the hand. **7.** power of seizing and holding; reach: *to have a thing within one's grasp.* **8.** hold, possession, or mastery: *to wrest power from the grasp of a usurper.* **9.** mental hold or comprehension: *a subject beyond one's grasp.* **10.** broad or thorough comprehension: *a good grasp of a subject.* [ME *graspen, grapsen* c. LG *grapsen*; akin to OE *gegræppian* seize] —**grasp′a·ble,** *adj.* —**grasp′er,** *n.* —**Syn. 1.** grip, clutch; grab, snatch. See **catch. 6.** GRASP, REACH refer to the power of seizing, either concretely or figuratively. GRASP suggests actually seizing and closing the hand upon something (or figuratively thoroughly comprehending something) and therefore refers to something within one's possession or immediate possibility of possession: *a good grasp of a problem immense mental grasp.* REACH suggests a stretching out of (usually) the hand to touch, strike, or if possible, seize something; it therefore refers to a potentiality of possession which requires an effort. Figuratively, it implies perhaps a faint conception of something still too far beyond one to be definitely and clearly understood: *"Ah, but a man's reach should exceed his grasp, or what's a heaven for?"* (Browning). —**Ant. 1.** release.

grasp·ing (grăs′pĭng, gräs′-), *adj.* **1.** that grasps. **2.** greedy. —**grasp′ing·ly,** *adv.* —**grasp′ing·ness,** *n.*

grass (grăs, gräs), *n.* **1.** any plant of the family *Gramineae* (or *Poaceae*), characterized by jointed stems, sheathing leaves, flower spikelets, and fruit consisting of a seedlike grain or caryopsis (**true grasses**). **2.** herbage in general, or the plants on which grazing animals pasture or which are cut and dried as hay. **3.** the grass-covered ground. **4.** pasture: *half of the farm is grass, to put animals to grass.* **5.** (*pl.*) stalks or sprays of grass: *filled with dried grasses.* **6.** the season of the new growth of grass. —*v.t.* **7.** to cover with grass or turf. **8.** to feed with growing grass; pasture. **9.** to lay on the grass, as for the purpose of bleaching. —*v.i.* **10.** to feed on growing grass; graze. **11.** to produce grass; become covered with grass. [ME *gras*, OE *græs*, c. D, G, Icel. and Goth. *gras*; akin to GROW and GREEN] —**grass′less**, *adj.* —**grass′like′**, *adj.*

Grasse (gräs), *n.* **François Joseph Paul, Count de** (frän swä′ zhō zĕf′ pōl), (*Marquis de Grasse-Tilly*) 1722–1788, French admiral.

grass finch, **1.** the vesper sparrow, *Poöcetes gramineus*, of North America. **2.** any of various Australian weaverbirds, esp. of the genus *Poëphila*.

grass-green (grăs′grēn′, gräs′-), *adj.* yellowish-green.

grass·hop·per (grăs′hŏp′ər, gräs′-), *n.* any of numerous orthopterous insects which are terrestial, herbivorous, and have their hind legs fitted for leaping. Many are very destructive to vegetation, as the locusts, certain katydids, etc.

Red-legged grasshopper. *Melanoplus femur-rubrum*

grass·land (grăs′lănd′, gräs′-), *n.* an area in which the natural vegetation consists largely of perennial grasses, whereas trees are either limited to stream valleys or are widely spotted, characteristic of subhumid and semiarid climates.

grass-of-Par·nas·sus (grăs′əv pär năs′əs, gräs′-), *n.* any of the genus *Parnassia* (family *Saxifragaceae* or *Parnassiaceae*) of perennials of marshy areas, having broad, smooth leaves and single pale flowers.

grass·quit (grăs′kwĭt′, gräs′-), *n.* any of several small fringilline birds, esp. of the genus *Tiaris*, as the **melodious grassquit**, *Tiaris canora*, of Cuba.

grass-roots (grăs′rōōts′, -rŏōts′, gräs′-), *adj. U.S. Colloq.* close to, or emerging spontaneously from, the people.

grass snipe, the pectoral sandpiper.

grass tree, **1.** any member of the Australian liliaceous genus *Xanthorrhoea*, comprising plants with a stout woody stem bearing a tuft of long grasslike leaves and a dense flower spike. **2.** any of various similar plants of Australasia.

grass widow, a woman who is separated, divorced, or lives apart from her husband.

grass widower, a man who is separated, divorced, or lives apart from his wife.

grass·y (grăs′ĭ, gräs′ĭ), *adj.*, **grassier, grassiest.** **1.** covered with grass. **2.** pertaining to or consisting of grass; grasslike. —**grass′i·ness**, *n.*

grate[1] (grāt), *n., v.*, **grated, grating.** —*n.* **1.** a frame of metal bars for holding fuel when burning, as in a fireplace or furnace. **2.** a framework of parallel or crossed bars used as a partition, guard, cover, or the like. **3.** a fireplace. —*v.t.* **4.** to furnish with a grate or grates. [ME, ult. t. It., g. L *crātis* wickerwork, hurdle. Cf. CRATE] —**grate′less**, *adj.* —**grate′like′**, *adj.*

grate[2] (grāt), *v.*, **grated, grating.** —*v.i.* **1.** to have an irritating or unpleasant effect on the feelings. **2.** to make a sound as of rough scraping. **3.** to sound harshly; jar: *to grate on the ear.* **4.** to scrape or rub with rough or noisy friction, as one thing on or against another. —*v.t.* **5.** to rub together with a harsh, jarring sound: *to grate the teeth.* **6.** to reduce to small particles by rubbing against a rough surface or a surface with many sharp-edged openings: *to grate a nutmeg.* **7.** *Archaic.* to wear down or away by rough friction. [ME, t. OF: m. *grater*; of Gmc. orig. (cf. G *kratzen* scratch)] —**grat′er**, *n.* —**grat′ing**, *adj.* —**grat′ing·ly**, *adv.*

grate·ful (grāt′fəl), *adj.* **1.** warmly or deeply appreciative of kindness or benefits received; thankful: *I am grateful to you for your kindness.* **2.** actuated by or betokening gratitude: *a grateful letter, speech.* **3.** pleasing to the mind or senses; agreeable or welcome; refreshing: *grateful slumber.* [f. obs. *grate* pleasing, thankful (t. L: m.s. *grātus*) + -FUL] —**grate′ful·ly**, *adv.* —**grate′ful·ness**, *n.*

—**Syn. 1.** GRATEFUL, THANKFUL describe an appreciative attitude for what one has received. GRATEFUL indicates a warm or deep appreciation of personal kindness as shown to one: *grateful for favors, grateful to one's neighbors for help in time of trouble.* THANKFUL indicates a disposition to express gratitude by giving thanks, as to a benefactor or to a merciful Providence: there is often a sense of deliverance as well as of appreciation: *thankful that one's life was spared in an accident, thankful for the comfort of one's general situation.*

Gra·ti·an (grā′shĭ ən, -shən), *n.* (*Flavius Gratianus*) A.D. 359–383, Roman emperor, A.D. 375–383.

grat·i·fi·ca·tion (grăt′ə fə kā′shən), *n.* **1.** state of being gratified; great satisfaction. **2.** something that gratifies; source of pleasure or satisfaction. **3.** act of gratifying. **4.** *Archaic.* a reward, recompense, or gratuity.

grat·i·fy (grăt′ə fī′), *v.t.*, **-fied, -fying.** **1.** to give pleasure to (persons) by satisfying desires or humoring inclinations or feelings. **2.** to satisfy; indulge; humor: *to gratify desires or appetites.* **3.** *Obs.* to reward; remuner-

ate. [t. F: m. s. *gratifier*, t. L: m. *grātificārī* do a favor to, oblige, gratify] —**grat′i·fi′er**, *n.* —**Syn. 2.** See **humor**.

gra·ti·fy·ing (grăt′əfĭ′ĭng), *adj.* that gratifies; pleasing, satisfying. —**grat′i·fy′ing·ly**, *adv.* —**Syn.** See **interesting**.

grat·in (grăt′ăn; *Fr.* grȧ tăn′), *n.* See **au gratin**. [F, der. *gratter*, earlier *grater* scrape. See GRATE[2]]

grat·ing (grā′tĭng), *n.* **1.** a partition or frame of parallel or crossing bars; open latticework of wood or metal serving as a cover or guard, but admitting light, air, etc. **2.** *Physics.* a diffraction grating.

gra·tis (grā′tĭs, grăt′ĭs), *adv.* **1.** for nothing; gratuitously. —*adj.* **2.** free of cost; gratuitous. [t. L]

grat·i·tude (grăt′ə tūd′, -tōōd′), *n.* quality or feeling of being grateful or thankful. [t. LL: m.s. *grātitūdo*, der. L *grātus* pleasing, thankful]

Grat·tan (grăt′ən), *n.* **Henry,** 1746–1820, Irish statesman and orator.

grat·toir (grä twär′; *Fr.* grȧ twȧr′), *n.* *Archaeol.* a chipped stone implement used for working wood or leather; scraper. [ĭ. F, der. *gratter* scrape]

gra·tu·i·tous (grə tū′ə təs, -tōō′-), *adj.* **1.** freely bestowed or obtained; free. **2.** being without reason, cause, or justification: *a gratuitous insult.* **3.** *Law.* given without receiving any return value. [t. L: m. *grātuītus* free, spontaneous] —**gra·tu′i·tous·ly**, *adv.* —**gra·tu′i·tous·ness**, *n.*

gra·tu·i·ty (grə tū′ə tĭ′, -tōō′-), *n., pl.* **-ties.** **1.** a gift of money, over and above payment due for service; tip. **2.** that which is given without claim or demand. **3.** *Chiefly Brit.* a bounty given to soldiers.

grat·u·late (grăch′ə lāt′), *v.*, **-lated, -lating.** *Obs.* or *Archaic.* —*v.t.* **1.** to hail with joy; express joy at. **2.** to congratulate. —*v.i.* **3.** to express joy. [t. L: m.s. *grātulātus*, pp., having expressed joy, congratulated, or thanked] —**grat·u·la·to·ry** (grăch′ə lə tōr′ĭ), *adj.*

grat·u·la·tion (grăch′ə lā′shən), *n.* *Archaic.* **1.** a feeling of joy. **2.** the expression of joy.

Grau·bün·den (grau′bỹn′dən), *n.* German name of Grisons.

grau·pel (grou′pəl), *n.* a snow pellet. [t. G]

gra·va·men (grə vā′mĕn), *n., pl.* **-vamina** (-văm′ĭ nə). *Law.* **1.** that part of an accusation which weighs most heavily against the accused; the burden or substantial part of a charge or complaint. **2.** a grievance. [t. LL, der. L *gravāre* load, weigh down. Cf. GRIEVE]

grave[1] (grāv), *n.* **1.** an excavation made in the earth to receive a dead body in burial. **2.** any place of interment; a tomb or sepulcher. **3.** any place that becomes the receptacle of what is dead, lost, or past: *the grave of dead reputations.* **4.** death: *O grave, where is thy victory?* [ME; OE *græf*, c. G *grab*. See GRAVE[3]]

grave[2] (grāv), *adj.*, **graver, gravest**, *n.* —*adj.* **1.** dignified; sedate; serious; earnest; solemn: *a grave person, grave thoughts, grave ceremonies.* **2.** weighty, momentous, or important: *grave responsibilities.* **3.** important or critical; involving serious issues: *a grave situation.* **4.** *Phonet.* **a.** unaccented. **b.** spoken on a low pitch or falling pitch because of musical accent. **c.** noting or having a particular accent (`) indicating orig. a comparatively low pitch (as in ancient Greek); later, quality of sound (as in the French *père*), distinct syllabic value (as in *belovèd*), etc. **5.** *Rare.* (of colors) dull; somber. —*n.* **6.** the grave accent. [t. F, t. L: m.s. *gravis* heavy] —**grave′ly**, *adv.* —**grave′ness**, *n.*

—**Syn. 1.** GRAVE, SOBER, SOLEMN refer to the condition of being serious in demeanor or appearance. GRAVE indicates a weighty dignity, or the character, aspect, demeanor, speech, etc. of one conscious of heavy responsibilities or cares, or of threatening possibilities: *the jury looked grave while studying the evidence.* SOBER (from its original sense of freedom from intoxication, and hence temperate, staid, sedate) has come to indicate absence of levity, gaiety, or mirth, and thus to be akin to serious and grave: *as sober as a judge, a sober expression on one's face.* SOLEMN implies an impressive seriousness and deep earnestness: *the minister's voice was solemn as he announced the text.* —**Ant. 1.** gay, frivolous.

grave[3] (grāv), *v.t.*, **graved, graved** or **graven, graving.** **1.** to incise or engrave. **2.** to impress deeply: *graven on the mind.* [ME *grave(n)*, OE *grafan*, c. G *graben*. Cf. GRAVE, GROOVE, and GRAVURE] —**grav′er**, *n.*

grave[4] (grāv), *v.t.*, **graved, graving.** *Naut.* to clean (a ship's bottom or a ship) by burning or scraping off accretions and paving it over with pitch. [orig. obscure]

gra·ve[5] (grä′vě), *Music.* —*adj.* **1.** slow; solemn. —*adv.* **2.** slowly; solemnly. [It., g. L *gravis* GRAVE[2]]

grave-clothes (grāv′klōz′, -klōthz′), *n.pl.* the clothes in which a dead body is interred; cerements.

grav·el (grăv′əl), *n., v.*, **-eled, -eling** or (*esp. Brit.*) **-elled, -elling.** —*n.* **1.** small stones and pebbles, or a mixture of these with sand. **2.** *Pathol.* **a.** multiple small calculi formed in the kidneys. **b.** the disease characterized by such concretions. —*v.t.* **3.** to cover with gravel. **4.** to bring to a standstill from perplexity; puzzle. **5.** *U.S. Colloq.* to be a cause of irritation to. **6.** *Obs.* to run (a vessel) aground, as on a beach. [ME, t. OF: m. *gravele*, dim. of *grave* sandy shore; of Celtic orig.]

grav·el-blind (grăv′əl blīnd′), *adj.* more blind or dim-sighted than sand-blind and less than stone-blind.

grav·el·ly (grăv′ə lĭ), *adj.* **1.** abounding in gravel. **2.** consisting of or resembling gravel.

gra·ve·men·te (grä′vě měn′tě), *adv.* *Italian.* gravely.

grav·en (grā′vən), *v.* **1.** pp. of grave[3]. —*adj.* **2.** deeply impressed; firmly fixed. **3.** *Archaic.* carved; engraved.

Gra·ven·ha·ge (sкнrä′vənhä′кнə), *n.* **'s,** Dutch name of **The Hague.**

graven image, an idol.

Gra·ven·stein (grā′vənstīn′, gräv′ənstēn′), *n.* a large yellowish-red apple maturing in the autumn. [named after *Gravenstein* in Holstein, Germany]

grav·er (grā′vər), *n.* **1.** any of various tools for chasing, engraving, etc., as a burin. **2.** *Archaic.* an engraver.

Graves (grävz), *n.* **Robert Ranke** (räng′kə), born 1895, British poet, novelist, and critic.

Graves (grävz, grävz; *Fr.* gràv), *n.pl.* a class of red and white Bordeaux wines, esp. the white.

Graves' disease (grävz), *Pathol.* a disease characterized by an enlarged thyroid, rapid pulse, and increased basal metabolism due to excessive thyroid secretion. [named after R. J. *Graves*, 1796–1853, Irish physician]

Graves·end (grävz′ĕnd′), *n.* a seaport in SE England, in Kent, on the Thames. 41,230 (est. 1946).

grave·stone (grāv′stōn′), *n.* a stone marking a grave.

grave·yard (grāv′yärd′), *n.* cemetery; burial ground.

grav·id (grăv′ĭd), *adj.* pregnant. [t. L: s. *gravidus*] —**gra·vid′i·ty,** *n.*

grav·i·met·ric (grăv′ə mĕt′rĭk), *adj.* **1.** of or pertaining to measurement by weight. **2.** *Chem.* denoting a method of analyzing compound bodies by finding the weight of their elements (opposed to *volumetric*). Also, **grav′i·met′ri·cal.** —**grav′i·met′ri·cal·ly,** *adv.*

grav·im·e·try (grə vĭm′ə trĭ), *n.* the measurement of weight or density. [f. L *gravi*(s) heavy + -METRY]

grav·ing dock (grā′vĭng), a dry dock.

grav·i·tate (grăv′ə tāt′), *v.i.*, **-tated, -tating. 1.** to move or tend to move under the influence of gravitational force. **2.** to tend toward the lowest level; sink; fall. **3.** to have a natural tendency or be strongly attracted (fol. by *to* or *toward*). [t. NL: s. *gravitātus*, pp., der. L *gravis* heavy]

grav·i·ta·tion (grăv′ə tā′shən), *n.* **1.** *Physics.* **a.** that force of attraction between all particles or bodies, or that acceleration of one toward another, of which the fall of bodies to the earth is an instance. **b.** an act or process caused by this force. **2.** a sinking or falling. **3.** natural tendency toward some point or object of influence: *the gravitation of people toward suburbs.* —**grav′i·ta′tion·al,** *adj.* —**grav′i·ta′tion·al·ly,** *adv.*

grav·i·ta·tive (grăv′ə tā′tĭv), *adj.* **1.** of or pertaining to gravitation. **2.** tending or causing to gravitate.

grav·i·ty (grăv′ə tĭ), *n., pl.* **-ties. 1.** the force of attraction by which terrestrial bodies tend to fall toward the center of the earth. **2.** heaviness or weight: *the center of gravity, specific gravity.* **3.** gravitation in general. **4.** seriousness; dignity; solemnity: *to preserve one's gravity.* **5.** serious or critical character: *the gravity of the situation.* **6.** lowness in pitch, as of sounds. [t. L: m.s. *gravitas* heaviness]

gravity fault, *Geol.* a fault along an inclined plane in which the upper side or hanging wall appears to have moved downward with respect to the lower side or footwall (opposed to *thrust fault*).

gra·vure (grə vyŏŏr′, grā′vyər), *n.* **1.** a process of photomechanical printing, such as photogravure or rotogravure. **2.** a plate or print produced by gravure. **3.** the metal or wooden plate used in photogravure. [t. F: engraving, der. *graver* engrave, t. Gmc.; cf. GRAVE³]

gra·vy (grā′vĭ), *n., pl.* **-vies.** the fat and juices that drip from cooking meat, often made into a dressing for meat, etc. [ME *grave*, t. OF: kind of dressing]

gravy boat, a small boat-shaped (or other) vessel for serving gravy or sauce.

gray (grā), *adj.* **1.** of a color between white and black, having no definite hue; ash-colored; technically, an achromatic color. **2.** dark, dismal, or gloomy. **3.** gray-haired. **4.** pertaining to old age; mature. **5.** old or ancient. —*n.* **6.** any achromatic color; any color with zero chroma from white to black. **7.** something of this color. **8.** gray material or clothing: *to dress in gray.* **9.** an unbleached and undyed condition. —*v.t., v.i.* **10.** to make or become gray. Also, *esp. Brit.*, **grey.** [ME; OE grǣg, c. G *grau*] —**gray′ly,** *adv.* —**gray′ness,** *n.*

Gray (grā), *n.* **1. Asa** (ā′sə), 1810–88, U.S. botanist. **2. Thomas,** 1716–71, British poet.

gray·back (grā′băk′), *n.* **1.** any of various animals, as a bird, the knot *Tringa canutus*, and a whale, *Rhachianectes glaucus*, of the northern Pacific. **2.** *U.S. Colloq.* a Confederate soldier. Also, *Brit.*, **grey′back.**

gray·beard (grā′bĭrd′), *n.* a man whose beard is gray; old man; sage. Also, *Brit.*, **grey′beard′.**

gray duck, any of several ducks in which certain immature or female plumages are predominantly gray, as the gadwell, *Anas strepera*, and the pintail, *A. acuta.* Also, *Brit.*, **grey duck.**

gray·fish (grā′fĭsh′), *n., pl.* **-fishes,** (*esp. collectively*) **-fish.** a market name for several American sharks, esp. the dogfish (genus *Squalus*) and fishes of the genera *Cynias, Mustelus,* and related genera, often sold for food.

Gray Friar, a Franciscan friar.

gray-head·ed (grā′hĕd′ĭd), *adj.* **1.** having gray hair. **2.** of or pertaining to old age or old men. **3.** old. Also, *Brit.*, **grey′-head′ed.**

gray·hound (grā′hound′), *n.* greyhound.

gray·ish (grā′ĭsh), *adj.* having a tinge of gray: *the sky was full of dark grayish clouds.* Also, *esp. Brit.*, **greyish.**

gray·lag (grā′lăg′), *n.* the common gray wild goose, *Anser anser,* of Europe. Also, *Brit.*, **grey′lag′.**

gray·ling (grā′lĭng), *n.* **1.** any of the fresh-water fishes constituting the genus *Thymallus,* allied to the trout, but having a longer and higher dorsal fin or resplendent color. **2.** any of certain somber gray moths of the family *Satyridae.*

gray matter, 1. *Anat.* nervous tissue, esp of the brain and spinal cord, containing both fibers and nerve cells, and of a dark reddish-gray color. **2.** *Colloq.* brains or intellect.

gray plover, a large plover, *Squatarola squatarola,* of both the New and the Old World, called "gray plover" in Europe because it is gray in winter plumage, "black-bellied plover" in America because of the strikingly black under parts of the breeding plumage.

Gray's Inn (grāz), *Brit.* See **Inns of Court.**

Gray·son (grā′sən), *n.* **David,** pen name of **Ray Stannard Baker.**

gray squirrel, a gray American squirrel, *Sciurus carolinensis,* common in city parks.

gray·wacke (grā′wăk′, -wăk′ə), *n.* *Geol.* a dark-colored sandstone or grit, containing fragments of various rocks such as slate and schist. Also, *Brit.*, **grey′-wacke′.** [half trans., half adoption of G *grauwacke.* See WACKE]

Graz (gräts), *n.* a city in SE Austria. 208,016 (1939).

graze¹ (grāz), *v.*, **grazed, grazing.** —*v.i.* **1.** to feed on growing herbage, as cattle, sheep, etc., do. —*v.t.* **2.** to feed on (growing grass). **3.** to put cattle, sheep, etc., to feed on (grass, lands, etc.). **4.** to tend (cattle, sheep, etc.) while at pasture. [ME *grase*(n), OE *grasian,* der. *grǣs* GRASS] —**graz′er,** *n.*

graze² (grāz), *v.*, **grazed, grazing,** *n.* —*v.t.* **1.** to touch or rub lightly in passing. **2.** to scrape the skin from; abrade. —*v.i.* **3.** to touch or rub something lightly, or so as to produce slight abrasion, in passing. —*n.* **4.** a grazing; a touching or rubbing lightly in passing. **5.** a slight scratch in passing; abrasion. [orig. uncert.]

gra·zier (grā′zhər), *n.* *Chiefly Brit.* one who grazes cattle for the market.

graz·ing (grā′zĭng), *n.* pasture land; a pasture.

Gr. Br., Great Britain. Also, **Gr. Brit.**

grease (*n.* grēs; *v.* grēs, grēz), *n., v.,* **greased, greasing.** —*n.* **1.** the melted or rendered fat of animals, esp. when in a soft state. **2.** fatty or oily matter in general; lubricant. **3.** Also, **grease wool.** wool, as shorn, before being cleansed of the oily matter. **4.** *Vet. Sci.* inflammation of a horse's skin in the fetlock region, attended with an oily secretion. —*v.t.* **5.** to put grease on; lubricate: *he greased the axle but it did no good.* **6.** to smear with grease. **7.** to cause to run easily. **8.** *Slang.* to bribe. [ME *grese,* t. OF: m. *graisse,* g. L *crassus* fat] —**grease′-less,** *adj.* —**greas′er,** *n.*

grease paint, 1. a mixture of tallow or hard grease and a pigment, used by actors for painting their faces. **2.** theatrical make-up.

grease·wood (grēs′wŏŏd′), *n.* **1.** a chenopodiaceous shrub, *Sarcobatus vermiculatus,* of the alkaline regions of the western U.S., containing a small amount of oil and used for fuel. **2.** any of various similar shrubs. Also, **grease·bush** (grēs′bŏŏsh′).

greas·y (grē′sĭ, -zĭ), *adj.*, **greasier, greasiest. 1.** smeared or soiled with grease. **2.** composed of or containing grease; oily: *greasy food.* **3.** greaselike in appearance or to the touch; slippery. **4.** *Vet. Sci.* affected with grease. —**greas′i·ly,** *adv.* —**greas′i·ness,** *n.*

great (grāt), *adj.* **1.** unusually or comparatively large in size or dimensions: *a great house, lake, or fire.* **2.** large in number; numerous: *a great many, in great detail.* **3.** unusual or considerable in degree: *great pain.* **4.** notable or remarkable: *a great occasion.* **5.** distinguished; famous: *Alexander the Great.* **6.** of much consequence; important: *great issues.* **7.** chief or principal: *the great seal.* **8.** of high rank, official position, or social standing: *a great noble.* **9.** of noble or lofty character: *great thoughts.* **10.** much in use or favor: "*humor*" *was a great word with the old physiologists.* **11.** being such in an extreme degree: *great friends, a great talker.* **12.** of extraordinary powers; having unusual merit; very admirable: *a great statesman.* **13.** *Colloq.* much addicted; skillful or expert (fol. by *to* or *at*). **14.** *Colloq.* first-rate; very good; fine: *we had a great time.* **15.** *Genealogy.* more remote in direct ascent or descent than a specified relationship: *great-grandfather.* **16.** *Archaic.* pregnant. [ME *greet,* OE *grēat,* c. D *groot,* G *gross*] —**great′ness,** *n.*
—**Syn. 1.** immense, enormous, gigantic. GREAT, BIG, LARGE refer to size, extent, and degree. In reference to the size and extent of concrete objects, BIG is the most general and most colloquial word, LARGE is somewhat more formal, and GREAT is highly formal and even poetic, suggesting also that the object is notable or imposing: *a big tree, a large tree. a great oak; a big field, a large field, great plains.* When the reference is to degree or a quality, GREAT is the usual word: *great beauty, great mistake, great surprise,* though BIG sometimes alternates with it in colloquial style: *a big mistake, a big surprise;* LARGE is not used in reference to degree, but may be used in a quantitative reference: *a large number* (*great number*). **5.** eminent, renowned, illustrious. **6.** weighty, serious, momentous. —**Ant. 1.** little, small.

great auk, a large, flightless seabird, *Pinguinis impennis,* of the North Atlantic, now extinct.

great-aunt (grāt′ănt′, -änt′), *n.* a father's or mother's aunt; a grandaunt.

Great Australian Bight, a wide, open bay in S Australia.

Great Barrier Reef, a coral reef parallel to the coast of Queensland, in NE Australia. ab. 1250 mi. long.

Great Basin, a region without drainage to the ocean, in the W United States, including most of Nevada and parts of Utah, California, Oregon, and Idaho. ab. 210,-000 sq. mi.

Great Bear, *Astron.* Ursa Major.

Great Bear Lake, a large lake in NW Canada, in the Northwest Territories. ab. 11,800 sq. mi.

Great Britain, an island of NW Europe, separated from the mainland by the English Channel and the North Sea: since 1707 the name has applied politically to England, Scotland, and Wales. 45,890,200 pop. (est. 1946); 88,139 sq. mi. See **United Kingdom.**

great circle, 1. a circle on a sphere the plane of which passes through the center of the sphere. Cf. **small circle.** 2. the line of shortest distance between two points on the surface of the earth.

great-circle sailing, navigation along a great circle of the earth, usually by a series of rhumb lines.

great·coat (grāt′kōt′), *n.* Chiefly Brit. a heavy overcoat.

Great Dane, one of a breed of large, powerful, short-haired dogs, somewhat resembling the mastiff.

Great Dane
(30 in. or more high at the shoulder)

Great Divide, 1. the continental divide of North America: the Rocky Mountains. 2. any similar continental divide. 3. separation between life and death: *across the Great Divide.* 4. a crucial stage; crisis.

Great Dog. See **dog** (def. 7).

great·en (grā′tən), *Archaic.* —*v.t.* 1. to make greater; enlarge; increase. —*v.i.* 2. to become greater.

Greater Antilles. See **Antilles.**

greater yellowlegs, a large American shore bird, *Totanus melanoleucus,* with bright yellow legs and feet.

greatest common divisor. See **common divisor.**

Great Falls, a city in central Montana, on the Missouri. 39,214 (1950).

great-grand·child (grāt′grănd′chīld′), *n., pl.* **-children.** a grandchild of one's son or daughter.

great-grand·daugh·ter (grāt′grănd′dô′tər), *n.* a granddaughter of one's son or daughter.

great-grand·fa·ther (grāt′grănd′fä′ᵗħər), *n.* a parent's grandfather.

great-grand·moth·er (grāt′grănd′mŭᵗħ′ər), *n.* a parent's grandmother.

great-grand·par·ent (grāt′grănd′pâr′ənt), *n.* a grandfather or grandmother of one's father or mother.

great-grand·son (grāt′grănd′sŭn′), *n.* a son's or daughter's grandson.

great-heart·ed (grāt′här′tĭd), *adj.* 1. having or showing a generous heart; magnanimous. 2. highspirited; courageous; fearless. —**great′-heart′ed·ness,** *n.*

great horned owl, a large, rapacious, American owl, *Bubo virginianus,* found from the tree limit in the north southward into South America.

Great Lakes, a series of five large lakes between the United States and Canada, connected with the Atlantic by the St. Lawrence: Lakes Erie, Huron, Michigan, Ontario, and Superior.

great·ly (grāt′lĭ), *adv.* 1. in or to a great degree; much. 2. in a great manner.

Great Mogul, 1. an emperor of the Mongol or Mogul empire of India, which flourished 1526 to 1761 and continued nominally until 1857. 2. (*l.c.*) an important or distinguished person.

great-neph·ew (grāt′nĕf′ū, -nĕv′ū), *n.* a grandnephew; nephew's or niece's son.

great-niece (grāt′nēs′), *n.* a grandniece; nephew's or niece's daughter.

Great Plains, a semiarid region E of the Rocky Mountains in the United States and Canada.

great rhododendron, the tall pink- or whiteflowering rhododendron, *Rhododendron maximum,* common in the eastern U.S. Also, **great rosebay.**

Great Russians, the main stock of the Russian people, dwelling chiefly in the northern and central parts of the Soviet Union in Europe.

greats (grāts), *n.pl. Brit. Colloq.* 1. the course in classics or *Literae Humaniores* at Oxford University. 2. the final examination for the B.A. in this subject.

Great Salt Lake, a shallow salt lake in NW Utah. ab. 2300 sq. mi.; ab. 80 mi. long; maximum depth, 60 ft.

great seal, 1. the principal seal of a government or state. 2. (*caps.*) Brit. the keeper of the great seal, the Lord Chancellor.

Great Slave Lake, a large lake in NW Canada, in the Northwest Territories. ab. 10,700 sq. mi.

Great Smoky Mountains, a mountain range in North Carolina and Tennessee: a part of the Appalachian

system. Highest peak, Clingman's Dome, 6642 ft. Also, **Smoky Mountains** or **Great Smokies.**

great-un·cle (grāt′ŭng′kəl), *n.* a granduncle.

Great Wall of China, a system of walls constructed as a defense for China against the nomads of the regions that are now Mongolia and Manchuria: completed in the third century B.C., but later repeatedly modified and rebuilt. ab. 1400 mi. long.

Great War, World War I.

Great Week, *Eastern Ch.* Holy Week.

great white heron, 1. a large white heron, *Ardea occidentalis,* of Florida and the Florida Keys. 2. a large white egret, *Casmerodius albus,* of southeastern Europe, tropical Africa, Asia, New Zealand, and America.

great white trillium, a trillium, *Trillium grandiflorum,* of the eastern and central U.S., the flowers having large white petals that turn rose color.

Great White Way, the theater district along Broadway, near Times Square in New York City, brilliantly lighted at night.

great willow herb, the willow herb.

Great Yar·mouth (yär′məth), a seaport in E England, in Norfolk. 44,950 (est. 1946).

greave (grēv), *n.* armor for the leg from knee to ankle, usually of front and back plates. [ME *greves* (pl.), t. OF; orig. obscure]

greaves (grēvz), *n.pl.* the sediment of melted tallow or animal fat, used as dog food, fish bait, etc.

grebe (grēb), *n.* any of several diving birds of the order *Colymbiformes,* related to the loons, but having lobate rather than webbed toes and a rudimentary tail, as the **great crested grebe,** *Colymbus cristatus,* of Europe, and the **pied-billed grebe,** *Podilymbus podiceps,* of America. [t. F, orig. uncert.]

Horned grebe, *Colymbus auritus*
(14 in. long)

Gre·cian (grē′shən), *adj.* 1. Greek. —*n.* 2. a Greek. 3. an expert in the Greek language or literature.

Gre·cism (grē′sĭzəm), *n.* 1. the spirit of Greek thought, art, etc. 2. adoption or imitation of this. 3. an idiom or peculiarity of Greek. Also, *esp. Brit.,* **Graecism.**

Gre·cize (grē′sīz), *v.,* **-cized, -cizing.** —*v.t.* 1. to impart Greek characteristics to. 2. to translate into Greek. —*v.i.* 3. to conform to what is Greek; adopt Greek speech, customs, etc. Also, *esp. Brit.,* **Graecize.** [t. L m.s. *Graecizāre,* der. *Graecus* Greek. See -IZE]

Gre·co (grĕk′ō; *It.* grě′kō), *n.* El (ĕl). See **El Greco.**

Greco-, a word element meaning "Greek." Also, *esp. Brit.,* **Graeco-.** [t. L: m. *Graeco-,* comb. form of *Graecus*]

gree¹ (grē), *n. Archaic and Scot.* 1. superiority, mastery, or victory. 2. the prize for victory. [ME *gre,* t. OF, g. L *gradus* step]

gree² (grē), *n. Obs. or Archaic.* 1. favor; good will. 2. satisfaction, as for an injury. [ME *gre,* t. OF, g. L *grātum,* adj. neut., pleasing, grateful]

gree³ (grē), *v.t., v.i.* greed, greeing. *Scot. and Brit. Dial.* to bring or come into accord. [aphetic var. of AGREE. Cf. F *grēer*]

Greece (grēs), *n.* a kingdom in S Europe at the S end of the Balkan Peninsula. 7,108,814 pop. (est. 1938); 50,147 sq. mi. *Cap.:* Athens. Ancient Greek, **Hellas.**

greed (grēd), *n.* inordinate or rapacious desire, esp for wealth. [OE *grǣd* (only in dat. pl.), c. Icel. *grādhr* hunger, greed, Goth. *grēdus* hunger] —**greed′less,** *adj.* —**Syn.** avidity, avarice, cupidity, covetousness. GREED, GREEDINESS denote an excessive, extreme desire for something, often more than one's proper share. GREED means avid desire for gain or wealth (unless some other application is indicated) and is definitely uncomplimentary in implications: *his greed drove him to exploit his workers.* GREEDINESS, when unqualified, suggests a craving for food; it may, however, be applied to all avid desires, and need not be always uncomplimentary: *greediness for knowledge, fame, praise.*

greed·y (grē′dĭ), *adj.,* **greedier, greediest.** 1. very eager for wealth; avaricious. 2. greatly desiring food or drink. 3. keenly desirous; eager (often fol. by *of*): *greedy of praise.* [ME *gredy,* d. OE *grēdig,* r. OE *grǣdig.* See GREED] —**greed′i·ly,** *adv.* —**greed′i·ness,** *n.* —**Syn.** 1. grasping, rapacious. 2. ravenous, voracious, gluttonous.

gree-gree (grē′grē), *n.* grigri.

Greek (grēk), *adj.* 1. of or pertaining to Greece, the Greeks, or their language. 2. pertaining to the Greek Church. [adj. use of *n.*] —*n.* 3. a native inhabitant of Greece. 4. the language of the ancient Greeks and any of the languages which have developed from it, such as Hellenistic Greek, Biblical Greek, the Koine, and Modern Greek. 5. anything unintelligible, as speech, etc.: *it's Greek to me.* 6. a member of the Greek Church. 7. the group of Indo-European languages to which Greek belongs; Hellenic. [ME *Grekes* (pl.), OE *Grēcas,* learned var. of *Crēcas* (pl.), ult. t. L: m. *Graecī,* pl. of *Graecus* a Greek, t. Gk.: m. *Graikós,* orig. adj.]

Greek Catholic, 1. a communicant of any Greek Orthodox Church. 2. a Greek or Byzantine acknowledging allegiance to the Pope and to the faith of the

---

Western Church but disagreeing in forms of liturgy and ritual; a Uniat.

Greek cross, a cross consisting of an upright crossed in the middle by a horizontal piece of the same length. See illus. under **cross.**

Greek fire, an incendiary used by the Byzantine Greeks to set fire to enemy ships, etc.

Greek Orthodox Church, 1. the Christian church of the countries in communion or doctrinal agreement with the patriarch of Constantinople, comprising the former Eastern (Roman) Empire and countries evangelized from it, as Russia. **2.** Also, **Greek Church.** that part of this church which constitutes the established church in Greece.

Gree·ley (grē′lǐ), *n.* **1. Horace,** 1811–72, U.S. journalist and politician; a founder of the Republican Party. **2.** a city in N Colorado. 20,354 (1950).

Gree·ly (grē′lǐ), *n.* **Adolphus Washington,** 1844–1935, U.S. general, Arctic explorer, and meteorologist.

green (grēn), *adj.* **1.** of the color of growing foliage, between yellow and blue in the spectrum. **2.** covered with herbage or foliage; verdant: *green fields.* **3.** characterized by the presence of verdure. **4.** full of life and vigor. **5.** unseasoned; not dried or cured: *green timber.* **6.** not fully developed or perfected in growth or condition; unripe; not properly aged. **7.** immature in age or judgment; untrained; inexperienced: *a green hand.* **8.** simple; gullible; easily fooled. **9.** fresh, recent, or new: *a green wound.* **10.** pale; sickly; wan: *green with fear.* **11.** freshly killed: *green meat.* **12.** not fired, as bricks or pottery. **13.** *Metall.* (in molding) the moist condition of the sand used in founding. —*n.* **14.** green color. **15.** green coloring matter, paint, etc. **16.** green material or clothing. **17.** grassy land; a plot of grassy ground. **18.** *Golf.* **a.** the whole course or links on which golf is played. **b.** a putting green alone. **19.** a piece of grassy ground constituting a town or village common. **20.** (*pl.*) **a.** fresh leaves or branches of trees, shrubs, etc., used for decoration; wreaths. **b.** the leaves and stems of plants, as spinach (or esp. in England, cabbage), used for food. —*v.i., v.t.* **21.** to become or make green. [ME and OE *grēne,* c. G *grün;* akin to GROW, GRASS] —**green′ness,** *n.*

Green (grēn), *n.* **1. John Richard,** 1837–83, British historian. **2. William,** born 1873, U.S. labor leader; president of the AFL since 1924.

green algae, *Bot.* algae belonging to the class *Chlorophyceae,* grass-green in color.

green·back (grēn′bǎk′), *n.* a United States legaltender note, usually printed in green on the back, originally issued against the credit of the country and not against gold or silver on deposit.

Greenback party, *U.S. Hist.* a former political party, organized in 1874, opposed to the retirement or reduction of greenbacks and favoring their increase as the only paper currency. —**Green′back′er,** *n.*

Green Bay, 1. an arm of Lake Michigan, in NE Wisconsin. ab. 90 mi. long. **2.** a port in E Wisconsin at the S end of this bay. 52,735 (1950).

green belt, an area of parks and unoccupied ground surrounding a town.

green·bri·er (grēn′brī′ər), *n.* **1.** a climbing liliaceous plant, *Smilax rotundifolia,* of the eastern U.S., with prickly stem and thick leaves. **2.** any plant of this genus.

green corn, sweet corn (def. 2).

green dragon, an American araceous herb, *Arisaema Dracontium,* with a greenish or whitish spathe.

Greene (grēn), *n.* **1. Nathanael,** 1742–86, American Revolutionary general. **2. Robert,** c1560–92, British dramatic poet and pamphleteer.

green·er·y (grē′nər′ĭ), *n., pl.* **-eries. 1.** green foliage or vegetation; verdure. **2.** a place where green plants are reared or kept.

green-eyed (grēn′īd′), *adj.* jealous.

green·finch (grēn′fĭnch′), *n.* a European finch, *Chloris chloris,* with green and yellow plumage.

green·gage (grēn′gāj′), *n.* one of several varieties of light-green plums. [f. GREEN + *Gage,* named after Sir Wm. *Gage,* who introduced it into England c1725]

green gland, *Zool.* one of the pair of excretory organs in the head region of decapod crustaceans.

green·gro·cer (grēn′grō′sər), *n. Brit.* a retailer of fresh vegetables and fruit. —**green′gro′cer·y,** *n.*

green·head (grēn′hěd′), *n.* a male mallard.

green·heart (grēn′härt′), *n.* **1.** a South American lauraceous tree, *Ocotea* (or *nectandra*) *Rodiaei,* whose hard durable wood is often used for wharves, bridges, and in shipbuilding, and whose bark yields bebeerine; bebeeru. **2.** any of certain other timber trees of tropical America. **3.** their valuable greenish wood.

green heron, a small American heron, *Butorides virescens,* with glossy green wings.

green·horn (grēn′hôrn′), *n. Colloq.* **1.** a raw, inexperienced person. **2.** a person easily imposed upon. [orig. applied to an ox with green or young horns]

green·house (grēn′hous′), *n.* a glasshouse for the cultivation or protection of tender plants.

green·ing (grē′nǐng), *n.* any of several varieties of apple the skin of which is green even when ripe. [f. GREEN, adj. + -ING[1]]

green·ish (grē′nǐsh), *adj.* somewhat green; having a tinge of green.

Green·land (grēn′lənd), *n.* a Danish colony NE of North America: the largest island in the world. 18,431 pop. (est. 1938); ab. 840,000 sq. mi. (over 700,000 sq. mi. ice-capped).

green·let (grēn′lǐt), *n.* vireo.

green light, a green lamp, used as a traffic signal to mean "go."

green·ling (grēn′lǐng), *n.* any of the acanthopterygian fishes constituting the genus *Hexagrammos,* found about rocks and kelp in the north Pacific Ocean.

green manure, *Agric.* **1.** a green crop, esp. clover and other nitrogen-fixing plants, plowed under for fertilizer. **2.** manure which has not undergone decay.

green monkey, a monkey, *Cercopithecus aethiops sabaeus,* of West Africa, with a greenish-gray back and yellow tail.

Green Mountains, a mountain range in Vermont: a part of the Appalachian system. Highest peak, Mt. Mansfield, 4393 ft.

Green·ock (grē′nək, grěn′ək), *n.* a seaport in SW Scotland, on the Firth of Clyde. 78,863 (1939).

Green·ough (grē′nō), *n. Horatio,* 1805–52, U.S. sculptor.

green pepper, 1. the fruit of the bell or sweet pepper, *Capsicum frutescens* var. *grossum.* **2.** the mild, unripe fruit of any of the garden peppers, *Capsicum frutescens,* used as a green vegetable.

green plover, lapwing.

Green River, a river flowing from W Wyoming S through E Utah to the Colorado. 730 mi.

green·room (grēn′rōōm′, -rŏŏm′), *n.* a retiring room in a theater, for the use of the actors and actresses when not required on the stage.

green·sand (grēn′sǎnd′), *n.* a sandstone containing much glauconite, which gives it a greenish hue.

Greens·bor·o (grēnz′bûr′ō), *n.* a city in N North Carolina. 74,389 (1950).

green·shank (grēn′shǎngk′), *n.* a common European shore bird, *Glottis nebularia,* with green legs.

green·sick·ness (grēn′sǐk′nǐs), *n.* chlorosis (def. 2).

green soap, a soap made chiefly from potassium hydroxide and linseed oil, used in treating skin diseases.

green·stone (grēn′stōn′), *n.* any of various altered basaltic rocks having a dark-green color caused by the presence of chlorite, epidote, etc.

green·sward (grēn′swôrd′), *n.* turf green with grass.

green tea, a tea which has been subjected to a heating process without previous special withering and fermenting.

green vegetables, vegetables useful for the part grown above the ground; leafy vegetables.

Green·ville (grēn′vǐl), *n.* **1.** a city in NW South Carolina. 58,101 (1950). **2.** a city in W Mississippi, on the Mississippi river. 29,936 (1950).

green vitriol, ferrous sulfate, FeSO4·7H2O, in the form of bluish-green crystals; copperas.

Green·wich (grǐn′ǐj, grěn′-, -ǐch), *n.* a SE borough of London, England: Royal Observatory; the prime meridian passes through here. 79,070 (est. 1946).

Greenwich Time, the standard of time as designated at the Observatory in Greenwich, England. Used in England and as a basis of calculation elsewhere.

Green·wich Village (grěn′ǐch), a section of New York City in Manhattan: artists' and writers' center.

green-winged teal, a small fresh-water duck of America, *Anas carolinense,* and Europe, *A. crecca,* having a shining green speculum in the wing.

green·wood (grēn′wŏŏd′), *n.* a wood or forest when green, as in summer.

greet[1] (grēt), *v.t.* **1.** to address with some form of salutation; welcome. **2.** to receive with demonstrations of welcome or expression of pleasure. **3.** to manifest itself to: *music greets the ear.* —*v.i.* **4.** to give salutations on meeting. [ME *grete(n),* OE *grētan,* c. G *grüssen*] —**greet′er,** *n.* —Syn. **1.** hail, accost.

greet[2] (grēt), *Archaic, Scot. and N. Eng.* —*v.i.* **1.** to weep; lament; grieve. —*v.t.* **2.** to lament; bewail. [ME *grete,* OE *grētan,* north. var. of *grǣtan,* c. Icel. *grāta*]

greet·ing (grē′tǐng), *n.* **1.** act or words of one who greets. **2.** (*usually pl.*) a friendly message: *to send greetings.*

greg·a·rine (grěg′ə·rīn′, -rǐn), *n.* **1.** a type of sporozoan parasite that inhabits the digestive and other cavities of various invertebrates and produces cysts filled with spores. —*adj.* **2.** having the characteristics of or pertaining to a gregarine or gregarines. [t. NL: m.s. *Gregarīna,* der. L *gregārius* GREGARIOUS]

gre·gar·i·ous (grǐ·gâr′ĭ·əs), *adj.* **1.** living in flocks or herds, as animals. **2.** *Bot.* growing in open clusters; not matted together. **3.** fond of company; sociable. **4.** pertaining to a flock or crowd. [t. L: m. *gregārius*] —**gre·gar′i·ous·ly,** *adv.* —**gre·gar′i·ous·ness,** *n.*

gre·go (grē′gō, grā′-), *n., pl.* **-gos.** a short coarse jacket or cloak with a hood, worn by the Greeks and the Levantines. [ult. t. L: m. *Graecus* Greek, adj.]

Gre·go·ri·an (grǐ·gō′rǐ·ən), *adj.* of or pertaining to any of the popes named Gregory.

Gregorian calendar, the reformed Julian calendar now in use, according to which the ordinary year consists of 365 days, and a leap year of 366 days occurs in every year whose number is exactly divisible by 4 except centenary years whose numbers are not exactly divisible by 400, as 1700, 1800, and 1900.

Gregorian chant, 1. the plain song or cantus firmus used in the ritual of the Roman Catholic Church (named after Pope Gregory I). 2. a melody in this style.

Gregorian telescope, a telescope similar to the Cassegrainian telescope, but less common.

Greg·o·ry (grĕg′ərĭ), *n.* **Lady Augusta,** (*Augusta Persse*) 1852–1932, Irish dramatist, poet, and writer.

Greg·o·ry I (grĕg′ərĭ), Saint, ("*Gregory the Great*") A.D. c540–604, Italian cleric; pope, A.D. 590–604.

Gregory VII, Saint, (*Hildebrand*) c1020–1085, Italian ecclesiastic; pope, 1073–85.

Gregory XIII, (*Ugo Buoncompagni*) 1502–85, Italian ecclesiastic; pope, 1572–85. His revised calendar is the one now used.

Gregory of Nys·sa (nĭs′ə), Saint, A.D. c335–c395, Christian bishop and theologian of Asia Minor.

Gregory of Tours, Saint, A.D. 538?–594, Frankish bishop and historian.

grei·sen (grī′zən), *n.* an altered rock of granitic texture composed chiefly of quartz and mica, common in the tin mines of Saxony. [t. G]

gre·mi·al (grē′mĭ′əl), *n.* a cloth placed on a bishop's lap when he sits in celebrating mass or in conferring orders. [t. LL: s. *gremiālis* (as n., ML *gremiāle*) der. L *gremium* lap, bosom]

grem·lin (grĕm′lĭn), *n.* a mischievous invisible being, said by airplane pilots to cause engine trouble and mechanical difficulties. **—Syn.** See **goblin.**

Gre·na·da (grĭ·nā′də), *n.* a British colony in the Windward Islands of the West Indies, consisting of the island of Grenada and the S part of the Grenadines. 90,000 pop. (est. 1939); 133 sq. mi. *Cap.*: St. George's.

gre·nade (grĭ·nād′), *n.* 1. a small explosive shell thrown by hand or fired from a rifle. 2. a glass missile for scattering chemicals. [t. F, t. Sp.: m. *granada* pomegranate, der. *granado* having grains, g. L *grānātus*]

gren·a·dier (grĕn′ə·dĭr′), *n.* 1. (in the British army) a member of the first regiment of household infantry (**Grenadier Guards**). 2. a tall foot soldier. 3. (formerly) a soldier who threw grenades. 4. a fish, *Coryphaenoides fabricii* or *C. rupestris*, of the deep water of the North Atlantic, the tail part of which ends in a sharp point. 5. any other fish of the family *Coryphaenoididae* (*Macrouridae*). [t. F, der. *grenade* GRENADE]

gren·a·dine¹ (grĕn′ə·dēn′, grĕn′ə·dēn′), *n.* a thin dress fabric of leno weave in silk, rayon, or wool. [t. F, ? named after *Granada,* in Spain]

gren·a·dine² (grĕn′ə·dēn′, grĕn′ə·dēn′), *n.* a syrup made from pomegranate juice. [t. F, dim. of *grenade* pomegranate. See GRENADE]

Gren·a·dines (grĕn′ə·dēnz′, grĕn′ə·dēnz′), *n.pl.* a chain of ab. 600 islands, forming a part of the Windward Islands in the British West Indies.

Gren·fell (grĕn′fĕl), *n.* **Sir Wilfred Thomason,** 1865–1940, British physician and missionary in Labrador and Newfoundland.

Gre·no·ble (grə·nō′bəl; *Fr.* grə·nô′bl), *n.* a city in SE France, on the Isère river. 102,161 (1946).

Gren·ville (grĕn′vĭl), *n.* 1. **George,** 1712–70, British statesman. 2. **Sir Richard,** c1541–91, British naval commander.

Gresh·am (grĕsh′əm), *n.* **Sir Thomas,** 1519?–1579, British merchant and financier.

Gresham's law, *Econ.* the tendency of the inferior of two forms of currency to circulate more freely than, or to the exclusion of, the superior, because of the hoarding of the latter. [named after T. GRESHAM]

gres·so·ri·al (grĕ·sōr′ĭ·əl), *adj.* *Zool.* adapted for walking, as the feet of some birds.

Gret·na Green (grĕt′nə), a village in S Scotland, near the English border, to which many runaway English couples formerly eloped.

Greuze (grœz), *n.* **Jean Baptiste** (zhän bȧ·tēst′), 1725–1805, French painter.

Grev·ille (grĕv′ĭl), *n.* **Fulke.** See **Brooke, 1st Baron.**

grew (grōō), *v.* pt. of **grow.**

Grew (grōō), *n.* **Joseph Clark,** born 1880, U.S. diplomat.

grew·some (grōō′səm), *adj.* gruesome.

grey (grā), *adj., n., v.* Chiefly Brit. gray. **—grey′ly,** *adv.* **—grey′ness,** *n.*

Grey (grā), *n.* 1. **Charles,** (*2nd Earl Grey*) 1764–1845, British statesman; prime minister, 1830–34. 2. **Sir Edward,** (*Viscount Fallodon*) 1862–1933, British statesman. 3. **Lady Jane,** (*Lady Jane Dudley*) 1537–54, descendant of Henry VII of England; executed as usurper of the crown.

grey·hound (grā′hound′), *n.* 1. one of a breed of tall, slender dogs, notable for keen sight and for fleetness. 2. a swift ship, esp. a fast ocean liner. Also, **grayhound.** [ME *gre(i)hound,* appar. t. Scand.; cf. Icel. *greyhundr,* f. *grey* dog, bitch + *hundr* HOUND¹; r. OE *grīghund*]

Greyn·ville (grĕn′vĭl), *n.* **Sir Richard.** See **Grenville.**

grib·ble (grĭb′əl), *n.* a small marine isopod crustacean, *Limnoria,* which destroys submerged timber by boring into it. [? akin to GRUB]

Greyhound
(28 in. high at the shoulder)

grid (grĭd), *n.* 1. a grating of crossed bars; gridiron. 2. *Elect.* a metallic framework employed in a storage cell or battery for conducting the electric current and supporting the active material. 3. *Brit.* the system of electrical distribution (esp. the high tension wires) throughout a country. 4. *Electronics.* the electrode in an electron tube, usually made of parallel wires, a helix or coil of wire or a screen, which controls the electron flow between the other electrodes. See **vacuum tube.** [back formation from GRIDIRON]

grid circuit, *Electronics.* that part of a circuit which contains the cathode and the grid of an electron tube.

grid condenser, *Electronics.* a condenser arranged in series with the grid circuit.

grid current, *Electronics.* the current which moves within the electron tube from the grid to the cathode.

grid·dle (grĭd′əl), *n., v.,* **-dled, -dling.** **—n.** 1. a handled frying pan with only a slight ledge at the edge, for cooking pancakes, etc. over direct heat. **—v.t.** 2. to cook on a griddle. [ME *gredil,* t. OF: *gridiron.* See GRILL¹]

grid·dle·cake (grĭd′əl·kāk′), *n.* a thin cake of batter cooked on a griddle; flapjack; pancake.

gride (grīd), *v.,* **grided, griding,** *n.* **—v.i.** 1. to grate; grind; scrape harshly; make a grating sound. **—v.t.** 2. to pierce or cut. **—n.** 3. a griding or grating sound. [metathetic var. of GIRD²]

grid·i·ron (grĭd′ī′ərn), *n.* 1. a utensil consisting of metal parallel bars to broil meat, etc. on. 2. any framework or network resembling a gridiron. 3. *Football.* the field of play, so called on account of the transverse white lines crossing it every five yards. 4. a structure above the stage of a theater, from which hung scenery, etc. is manipulated. [ME *gredirne,* etc., r. ME *gredire,* assimilated var. of *gredile* GRIDDLE; variants in *-irne, -iron* show pop. etymological assoc. with ME *ire, irne* iron]

grid leak, *Electronics.* a high-resistance device which permits excessive charges on the grid to leak off or escape.

grief (grēf), *n.* 1. keen mental suffering or distress over affliction or loss; sharp sorrow; painful regret. 2. **come to grief,** to come to a bad end; turn out badly. 3. a cause or occasion of keen distress or sorrow. [ME, t. OF, der. *grever* GRIEVE] **—grief′less,** *adj.* **—Syn.** 1. anguish, heartache, woe; sadness. See **sorrow.**

grief-strick·en (grēf′strĭk′ən), *adj.* stricken or smitten with grief or sorrow; afflicted.

Grieg (grēg; *Norw.* grĭg), *n.* **Edvard** (ĕd′värt), 1843–1907, Norwegian composer.

griev·ance (grē′vəns), *n.* 1. a wrong, real or fancied, considered as grounds for complaint: *a popular grievance.* 2. resentment or complaint, or the grounds for complaint, against an unjust act: *to have a grievance against someone.* **—Syn.** 1. injustice, injury.

grieve (grēv), *v.,* **grieved, grieving.** **—v.i.** 1. to feel grief; sorrow. **—v.t.** 2. to distress mentally; cause to feel grief or sorrow. 3. *Obs.* to oppress or wrong. [ME *greve(n),* t. OF: m. *grever,* ult. der. L *gravāre* weigh down] **—griev′er,** *n.* **—griev′ing·ly,** *adv.* **—Syn.** 1. lament, weep. GRIEVE, MOURN imply showing suffering caused by sorrow. GRIEVE is the stronger word, implying deep mental suffering often endured alone and in silence but revealed by one's aspect: *to grieve over the loss (or death) of a friend.* MOURN usually refers to manifesting sorrow outwardly, either with or without sincerity: *to mourn publicly and wear black.*

griev·ous (grē′vəs), *adj.* 1. causing grief or sorrow: *grievous news.* 2. flagrant; atrocious: *a grievous fault.* 3. full of or expressing grief; sorrowful: *a grievous cry.* 4. *Archaic.* burdensome or oppressive. [ME *grevous,* t. OF, der. *grever* GRIEVE] **—griev′ous·ly,** *adv.* **—griev′ous·ness,** *n.* **—Syn.** 2. deplorable, lamentable, calamitous, heinous.

griffe¹ (grĭf), *n.* *U.S. Dial.* 1. the offspring of a Negro and a mulatto. 2. a person of mixed Negro and American Indian blood. 3. a mulatto, esp. a woman. [t. F. Cf. Sp. *grifo* a griffin]

griffe² (grĭf), *n.* *Archit.* an ornament at the base of a column, projecting from the torus toward a corner of the plinth. [t. F: claw; of Gmc. orig.]

Griffe²

grif·fin¹ (grĭf′ĭn), *n.* *Gk. Myth.* a fabulous monster, usually having the head and wings of an eagle and the body of a lion. Also, **griffon, gryphon.** [ME *griffon,* t. OF: m. *grifon,* der. L *grȳphus,* var. of *grȳps,* t. Gk.]

grif·fin² (grĭf′ĭn), *n.* (in India and the East) a newcomer. [orig. uncert.]

Grif·fith (grĭf′ĭth), *n.* **David Wark,** 1880–1948, U.S. motion-picture director and producer.

Griffin

grif·fon¹ (grĭf′ən), *n.* a vulture of the genus *Gyps,* esp. *G. fulvus* of southern Europe. [t. F. See GRIFFIN¹]

grif·fon² (grĭf′ən), *n.* 1. a small, wiry-haired pet dog of Belgian origin. 2. one of a breed of coarse-haired hunting dogs combining the qualities of the pointer and the setter. [t. F; akin to GRIFFIN¹]

grif·fon³ (grĭf′ən), *n.* griffin¹.

grift·er (grĭf′tər), *n.* one who manages a side show at a circus, fair, etc.

grig (grĭg), *n.* *Dial.* 1. a cricket or grasshopper. 2. a small or young eel. 3. a lively person. [orig. uncert.]

b., blend of, blended; c., cognate with; d., dialect, dialectal; der., derived from; f., formed from; g., going back to; m., modification of; r., replacing; s., stem of; t., taken from; ?, perhaps. See the full key on inside cover.

gri·gri (grē′grē), *n.*, *pl.* **-gris.** an African charm, amulet, or fetish. Also, **greegree.**

grill[1] (grĭl), *n.* **1.** a grated utensil for broiling meat, etc., over a fire; gridiron. **2.** a dish of grilled meat, etc. **3.** grillroom. **4.** *Philately.* a series of small pyramidal impressions in parallel rows impressed or embossed on the stamp. —*v.t.* **5.** to broil on a gridiron or other apparatus over or before a fire. **6.** to torment with heat. **7.** to mark with a series of parallel bars like those of a grill. **8.** *U.S. Colloq.* to subject to severe and persistent cross-examination or questioning. —*v.i.* **9.** to undergo broiling. [t. F: m. *gril* gridiron, ult. der. L *crāticulum,* dim. of *crātis* wickerwork, hurdle. Cf. GRILLE] —**grill′er,** *n.*

grill[2] (grĭl), *n.* grille.

gril·lage (grĭl′ĭj), *n.* a framework of crossing beams used for spreading heavy loads over large areas. [t. F, der. *grille.* See GRILL[1]]

grille (grĭl), *n.* **1.** a grating or openwork barrier, as for a gate, usually of metal and often of decorative design. **2.** *Court Tennis.* a square-shaped opening in the far corner of the court, on the side of the hazard. Also, **grill.** [t. F: grating. See GRILL[1]] —**grilled,** *adj.*

Grill·par·zer (grĭl′pär′tsər), *n.* **Franz** (fränts), 1791–1872, Austrian poet and dramatist.

grill·room (grĭl′rōōm′, -rŏŏm′), *n.* a room or restaurant where meats, etc. are grilled and served.

grilse (grĭls), *n.*, *pl.* **grilse.** a salmon which has ceased to be a smolt and is ready to return, or has returned from the sea to the river for the first time. [ME; orig. unknown]

grim (grĭm), *adj.*, **grimmer, grimmest. 1.** stern; unrelenting; merciless; uncompromising: *grim necessity.* **2.** of a sinister or ghastly character; repellent: *a grim joke.* **3.** of a fierce or forbidding aspect: *a grim countenance.* **4.** fierce, savage, or cruel: *grim warrior.* [ME and OE, c. OS, OHG *grim,* Icel. *grimmr*] —**grim′·ly,** *adv.* —**grim′ness,** *n.* —Syn. **1.** harsh, unyielding. **3.** severe, stern, harsh, hard. —Ant. **3.** gentle.

gri·mace (grĭ mās′, grĭ′məs), *n.*, *v.*, **-maced, -macing.** —*n.* **1.** a wry face; facial contortion; ugly facial expression. —*v.i.* **2.** to make grimaces. [t. F, t. Sp.: m. *grimazo* panic, fear, der. *grima* fright, t. Goth.] —**gri·mac′er,** *n.*

Gri·mal·di (grĭ mäl′dĭ), *n.* **Joseph,** 1779–1837, British mimic and clown.

gri·mal·kin (grĭ mäl′kĭn, -môl′-), *n.* **1.** a cat. **2.** an old female cat. **3.** an ill-tempered old woman. [appar. f. m. GRAY + *malkin,* dim. of *Maud,* proper name]

grime (grīm), *n.*, *v.*, **grimed, griming.** —*n.* **1.** dirt or foul matter, esp. on or ingrained in a surface. —*v.t.* **2.** to cover with dirt; soil; make very dirty. [appar. special use of OE *grīma* mask, to denote layer of dust, etc., that forms on the face and elsewhere. Cf. Flem. *grym*]

Grimes Golden (grīmz), a yellow eating apple maturing in late autumn. [named after Thomas P. *Grimes* of W. Va.]

Grimm (grĭm), *n.* **Jakob Ludwig Karl** (yä′kôp lōōt′vĭKH kärl), 1785–1863, or his brother, **Wilhelm Karl** (vĭl′hĕlm kärl), 1786–1859, German philologists and collectors of fairy tales.

Grimm's law (grĭmz), *Ling.* the statement of a system of consonant changes from primitive Indo-European into the Germanic languages, especially as differently reflected in Low and High German, formulated by Jakob Grimm (1820–22) and independently recognized by Rasmus Rask (1818).

Grims·by (grĭmz′bĭ), *n.* a seaport in E England at the mouth of the Humber estuary. 87,970 (est. 1946).

grim·y (grī′mĭ), *adj.*, **grimier, grimiest.** covered with grime; dirty. —**grim′i·ly,** *adv.* —**grim′i·ness,** *n.*

grin (grĭn), *v.*, **grinned, grinning,** *n.* —*v.i.* **1.** to smile broadly, or with a wide distention of the mouth. **2.** to draw back the lips so as to show the teeth, as a snarling dog or a person in pain. —*v.t.* **3.** to express or produce by grinning. —*n.* **4.** act of grinning; broad smile. **5.** act of withdrawing the lips and showing the teeth. [ME *grin(en),* OE *grennian*] —**grin′ner,** *n.* —**grin′ning·ly,** *adv.* —Syn. **1.** See **laugh.**

grind (grīnd), *v.*, **ground** or (*Rare*) **grinded, grinding,** *n.* —*v.t.* **1.** to wear, smooth, or sharpen by friction; whet: *to grind a lens, an ax, etc.* **2.** to reduce to fine particles, as by pounding or crushing; bray, triturate, or pulverize. **3.** to oppress or torment. **4.** to rub harshly or gratingly; grate together; grit: *to grind one's teeth.* **5.** to operate by turning a crank: *to grind a hand organ.* **6.** to produce by pulverizing, turning a crank, etc.: *to grind flour.* —*v.i.* **7.** to perform the operation of reducing to fine particles. **8.** to rub harshly; grate. **9.** to be or become ground. **10.** to be polished or sharpened by friction. **11.** *Colloq.* to work or study laboriously. —*n.* **12.** act of grinding. **13.** a grinding sound. **14.** *Colloq.* laborious work; close or laborious study. **15.** *College Slang.* a student who works hard at his studies. [ME *grind(en),* OE *grindan.* Cf. L *frendere* gnash the teeth, grind to pieces] —**grind′ing·ly,** *adv.* —Syn. **2.** crush, powder, comminute. **3.** harass, persecute.

grin·de·li·a (grĭn dē′lĭ ə), *n.* **1.** any of the coarse, yellow-flowered asteraceous herbs constituting the genus *Grindelia.* **2.** the dried leaves and tops of certain species of this plant, used in medicine. [NL; named after D. H. *Grindel* (1777–1836), Russian scientist]

grind·er (grīn′dər), *n.* **1.** one who or that which grinds. **2.** a sharpener of tools. **3.** a molar tooth.

grind·stone (grīnd′stōn′), *n.* **1.** a rotating solid stone wheel used for sharpening, shaping, etc. **2.** a millstone.

grin·go (grĭng′gō), *n.*, *pl.* **-gos.** (among Spanish Americans) a foreigner, esp. an Anglo-Saxon. [Mex. Sp. use of Sp. *gringo* gibberish]

grip (grĭp), *n.*, *v.*, **gripped** or **gript, gripping.** —*n.* **1.** act of grasping; a seizing and holding fast; firm grasp: *the grip of a vise.* **2.** the power of gripping. **3.** a grasp, hold, or control. **4.** *U.S.* a small suitcase. **5.** mental or intellectual hold. **6.** a special mode of clasping hands. **7.** something which seizes and holds, as a clutching device on a cable car. **8.** a handle or hilt. **9.** a sudden, sharp pain; spasm of pain. **10.** grippe. **11.** *Theat. Slang.* a stagehand, esp. one who works on the stage floor. —*v.t.* **12.** to grasp or seize firmly; hold fast. **13.** to take hold on; hold the interest of: *to grip the mind.* **14.** to attach by a grip or clutch. —*v.i.* **15.** to take firm hold; hold fast. **16.** to take hold on the mind. [ME and OE *gripe* grasp, c. G *griff,* OE *gripa* handful, sheaf. See GRIPE, v.] —**grip′per,** *n.* —**grip′ping·ly,** *adv.*

gripe (grīp), *v.*, **griped, griping,** *n.* —*v.t.* **1.** to seize and hold firmly; grip; grasp; clutch. **2.** to distress or oppress. **3.** to produce pain in the bowels as if by constriction. —*v.i.* **4.** to grasp or clutch, as a miser at gain. **5.** to suffer pain in the bowels. **6.** *U.S. Colloq.* to complain constantly; grumble. **7.** *Naut.* to tend to come up into the wind. —*n.* **8.** act of griping, grasping, or clutching. **9.** a firm hold; clutch. **10.** a grasp; hold; control. **11.** that which grips or clutches; a claw or grip. **12.** (*pl.*) *Naut.* lashing by which a boat is secured on the deck or on the davits of a ship. **13.** a handle, hilt, etc. **14.** (*usually pl.*) *Pathol.* an intermittent spasmodic pain in the bowels. [ME *gripe(n),* OE *grīpan,* c. D *grijpen,* G *greifen* gripe, seize. Cf. GRIP, GROPE] —**grip′er,** *n.*

grippe (grĭp), *n.* influenza. [t. F, der. *gripper* seize, b. with Russ. *khrip* hoarseness] —**grippe′like′,** *adj.*

grip·sack (grĭp′săk′), *n.* *U.S.* a traveling bag; grip.

gript (grĭpt), *v.* pt. and pp. of **grip.**

Gri·qua (grē′kwə, grĭk′wə), *n.* a South African half-breed.

gri·saille (grĭ zāl′; *Fr.* grē zä′y), *n.* **1.** monochromatic painting in shades of gray, usually simulating sculpture. **2.** a painting, a stained-glass window, etc., executed in this way. [t. F, der. *gris* gray. See GRIZZLE]

Gri·sel·da (grĭ zĕl′də), *n.* a woman of exemplary meekness and patience. [a character in Boccaccio, Chaucer, and elsewhere]

gris·e·ous (grĭs′ē əs, grĭz′-), *adj.* gray; pearl-gray. [t. ML: m. *griseus*]

gri·sette (grĭ zĕt′), *n.* a French working girl or shop-girl. [t. F: orig., a common gray fabric worn by working girls, der. *gris* gray. See GRIZZLE]

gris·ly (grĭz′lĭ), *adj.*, **-lier, -liest. 1.** such as to cause a shuddering horror; gruesome: *a grisly monster.* **2.** formidable; grim: *a grisly countenance.* [ME; late OE *grislic* horrible. Cf. OE *āgrīsan* shudder] —**gris′li·ness,** *n.*

gri·son (grī′sən, grĭz′ən), *n.* a musteline carnivore, *Grison vittata,* of South and Central America, having the upper surface of the body grayish-white and the lower dark-brown. [t. F, der. *gris* gray]

Gri·sons (grē zôN′), *n.* a canton in E Switzerland. 130,500 pop. (est. 1944); 2747 sq. mi. *Cap.*: Chur. German, **Graubünden.**

grist (grĭst), *n.* **1.** grain to be ground. **2.** ground grain; meal produced from grinding. **3.** a quantity of grain for grinding at one time; the amount of meal from one grinding. **4.** *U.S. Colloq.* a quantity or lot. [ME; OE *grist,* der. *grindan* GRIND]

gris·tle (grĭs′əl), *n.* cartilage. [ME and OE; c. OFris. and MLG *gristel.* Cf. OE *grost* cartilage]

gris·tly (grĭs′lĭ), *adj.* of the nature of, containing, or pertaining to gristle; cartilaginous.

grist·mill (grĭst′mĭl′), *n.* a mill for grinding grain, esp. the customer's own grain.

grit (grĭt), *n.*, *v.*, **gritted, gritting.** —*n.* **1.** fine, stony, or hard particles such as are deposited like dust from the air or occur as impurities in food, etc. **2.** a coarse-grained siliceous rock, usually with sharp, angular grains. **3.** *U.S.* firmness of character; indomitable spirit; pluck. —*v.t.* **4.** to grate or grind: *to grit the teeth.* —*v.i.* **5.** to give forth a grating sound, as of sand under the feet; grate. [ME *gre(e)t,* OE *grēot,* c. G *greiss.* Cf. GRITS] —**grit′less,** *adj.* —Syn. **2.** sand, gravel. **3.** resolution, fortitude, courage.

grits (grĭts) *n.pl.* **1.** grain, hulled and often coarsely ground. **2.** *U.S.* coarsely ground hominy. [ME *gryttes,* OE *gryttan* (pl.), c. G *grütze*]

grit·ty (grĭt′ĭ), *adj.*, **-tier, -tiest. 1.** consisting of, containing, or resembling grit; sandy. **2.** *U.S.* resolute and courageous; plucky. —**grit′ti·ly,** *adv.* —**grit′ti·ness,** *n.*

griv·et (grĭv′ĭt), *n.* a small Abyssinian monkey, *Cercopithecus aethiops,* with a grayish back, gray tail, black face, and dark extremities. [orig. unknown]

griz·zle (grĭz′əl), *v.*, **-zled, -zling,** *adj.*, *n.* —*v.i.*, *v.t.* **1.** to become or make gray. —*adj.* **2.** gray; devoid of hue. —*n.* **3.** gray hair. **4.** a gray wig. [ME *grisel,* t. OF, der. *gris* gray; (cf. G *greis* gray, hoary)]

griz·zled (grĭz′əld), *adj.* **1.** gray-haired. **2.** gray.

griz·zly (grĭz′lĭ), *adj.*, **-zlier, -zliest,** *n.*, *pl.* **-zlies.** —*adj.* **1.** somewhat gray; grayish. **2.** gray-haired. —*n.* **3.** a grizzly bear.

---

grizzly bear, a large, ferocious bear, *Ursus horribilis,* of western North America, varying in color from grayish to brownish.

gro., gross; 144 articles.

groan (grōn), *n.* **1.** a low, mournful sound uttered in pain or grief. **2.** a deep murmur uttered in derision or disapproval. —*v.i.* **3.** to utter a deep inarticulate sound expressive of grief or pain; moan. **4.** to make a sound resembling a groan; resound harshly. **5.** to be overburdened or overloaded. **6.** to suffer lamentably (fol. by *beneath, under, with*). —*v.t.* **7.** to utter or salute with groans. [ME *grone(n),* OE *grānian,* akin to G *greinen* whine] —**groan′er,** *n.* —**groan′ing,** *n., adj.* —**groan′ing·ly,** *adv.*

Grizzly bear,
Ursus horribilis
(6 to 8½ ft long, 3 to 3½ ft. high at the shoulder)

—**Syn. 1.** GROAN, MOAN refer to sounds indicating deep suffering. A GROAN is a brief, strong, deep-throated sound emitted involuntarily under pressure of pain or suffering: *the wounded man groaned when they lifted him.* A MOAN is a prolonged, more or less continuous, low, inarticulate sound indicative of suffering, either physical or mental: *she was moaning after the operation, she did not weep but moaned softly.*

groat (grōt), *n.* an English silver coin, issued 1351–1662, worth fourpence. [ME *groot,* t. MD: lit., thick (coin)]

groats (grōts), *n.pl.* **1.** hulled and crushed (or whole) grain, as wheat. **2.** the parts of oat kernels used as food. [ME *grotes,* OE *grotan* coarse meal. Cf. OE *grot* particle]

gro·cer (grō′sər), *n.* a dealer in general supplies for the table, as flour, sugar, coffee, etc., and in other articles of household use. [ME *grosser,* t. OF: m. *grossier,* ult. der. LL *grossus* gross]

gro·cer·y (grō′sər·ĭ), *n., pl.* **-ceries. 1.** *U.S.* a grocer's store. **2.** (*usually pl.*) a commodity sold by grocers. **3.** the business of a grocer.

Grod·no (grôd′nô), *n.* a city in the W Soviet Union, on the Niemen river: formerly in Poland. 49,700 (1931).

grog (grŏg), *n.* **1.** a mixture of alcoholic liquor and water. **2.** strong drink. [said to be from "Old Grog," nickname of the British Admiral Vernon (with allusion to his *grogram* cloak), who in 1740 ordered the mixture to be served, instead of pure spirits, to sailors]

grog·ger·y (grŏg′ər·ĭ), *n., pl.* **-geries.** *U.S. Slang.* a saloon.

grog·gy (grŏg′ĭ), *adj.,* **-gier, -giest.** *Colloq.* **1.** staggering, as from exhaustion or blows. **2.** drunk; intoxicated. —**grog′gi·ly,** *adv.* —**grog′gi·ness,** *n.*

grog·ram (grŏg′rəm), *n.* a coarse fabric of silk, of silk and mohair or wool, or of wool, formerly in use. [t. F: m. *gros grain.* See GROSGRAIN]

grog·shop (grŏg′shŏp′), *n. Brit.* (in contemptuous use) a saloon.

groin (groin), *n.* **1.** *Anat.* the fold or hollow on either side of the body where the thigh joins the abdomen. **2.** *Archit.* the curved line or edge formed by the intersection of two vaults. —*v.t.* **3.** *Archit.* to form with groins. [earlier *gryne,* ME *grynde.* Cf. OE *grynde* abyss, akin to *grund* bottom, GROUND]

A. A. Groins,
in early 12th century vaulting

Gro·li·er (grō′lĭ′ər; *Fr.* grô·lyĕ′), *adj. Bookbinding.* **1.** referring to **Grolier design,** decorative bookbinding consisting of bands interlaced in geometrical forms. **2.** of or pertaining to **Jean Grolier de Servières** (1479–1565), French bibliophile noted for his decorative leather bindings.

grom·met (grŏm′ĭt), *n.* **1.** *Mach.* a ring or eyelet of metal, etc. **2.** *Naut.* an eyelet of rope, metal, or the like, as on the edge of a sail. Also, **grummet.** [t. F: m. *gromette* (obs.) curb of bridle, ult. der. LL *grumus* throat]

grom·well (grŏm′wəl), *n.* any plant of the boraginaceous genus *Lithospermum,* comprising hairy herbs with varicolored flowers and smooth, stony nutlets. [ME *gromyl,* t. OF: m. *gromil,* g. L *gruinum milium* crane millet]

Gro·my·ko (grō·mē′kō; *Russ.* grō·mī′kō), *n.* **Andrei Andreievich** (än·drā′ än·drā′yə·vĭch), born 1909, Russian diplomat.

Gro·ning·en (grō′nĭng·ən; *Du.* ᴋʜrō′-), *n.* a city in NE Netherlands. 129,372 (est. 1946).

groom (grōōm, grŏŏm), *n.* **1.** a man or boy in charge of horses or the stable. **2.** a man newly married, or about to be married; bridegroom. **3.** any of several officers of the English royal household. **4.** *Archaic.* a manservant. —*v.t.* **5.** to tend carefully as to person and dress; make neat or tidy. **6.** to tend (horses). **7.** *U.S.* to prepare for a position, election, etc.: *groom a political candidate.* [ME *grom(e)* boy, man, groom; cf. D *grom* offspring; appar. akin to GROW]

groom's cake, a fruit cake in layers of graduated sizes, served at a wedding.

grooms·man (grōōmz′mən, grŏŏmz′-), *n., pl.* **-men.** a best man at a wedding.

Groot (grōt), *n.* **Gerhard** (gĕr′härt), (*Gerhardus Magnus*) 1340–84, Dutch religious reformer and founder of a monastic order ("Brothers of the Common Life").

groove (grōōv), *n., v.,* **grooved, grooving.** —*n.* **1.** a

---

furrow or channel cut by a tool. **2.** a rut, furrow, or channel formed by any agency. **3.** a fixed routine: *to get into a groove.* **4.** *Print.* the furrow at the bottom of a piece of type. See diag. under **type. 5. in the groove,** *Jazz.* played in such a way as to arouse enthusiasm in the listener. —*v.t.* **6.** to cut a groove in; furrow. **7.** to fix in a groove. [ME *grofe, groof* mining shaft, OE *grōf* ditch, sewer, c. G *grube* ditch, pit; akin to GRAVE[1], GRAVE[3]] —**groove′less,** *adj.* —**groove′like′,** *adj.*

grope (grōp), *v.,* **groped, groping.** —*v.i.* **1.** to feel about with the hands; feel one's way. **2.** to search blindly or uncertainly. —*v.t.* **3.** to seek by or as by feeling. [ME *grop(i)en,* OE *grāpian,* der. *grāp,* n., grasp; akin to GRIPE, v.] —**grop′er,** *n.* —**grop′ing·ly,** *adv.*

Gro·pi·us (grō′pǐ·əs; *Ger.* -pē·ōōs′), *n.* **Walter** (wôl′tər; *Ger.* väl′-), born 1883, German architect, now in U.S.

Gros (grō), *n.* **Antoine Jean** (äɴ·twän′ zhäɴ), **Baron,** 1771–1835, French painter.

gros·beak (grōs′bēk′), *n.* any of various finches having a large, stout conical bill, as the pine grosbeak, *Pinicola enucleator.* [t. F: m. *grosbec* large beak]

gro·schen (grō′shən), *n., pl.* **-schen. 1.** a former small German silver coin. **2.** *Colloq.* the 10-pfennig German nickel coin. **3.** (in Austria) a bronze coin valued at one hundredth of a schilling. [t. G, f. MHG *grosse,* lit., thick (coin) + -*chen* dim. suffix. See GROSS]

gros de Lon·dres (grō′ də lôɴ′dr), *French.* a cross-ribbed, silk dress fabric with ribs alternating in color or in coarse and fine yarn.

gros·grain (grō′grān′), *n.* heavy, corded, silk or rayon ribbon or cloth. [t. F: m. *gros grain* large grain. Cf. GROGRAM]

gross (grōs), *adj., n., pl.* **grosses** for 6, **gross** for 8, 9; *v.* —*adj.* **1.** whole, entire, or total, esp. without having been subjected to deduction, as for charges, loss, etc.: *gross profits.* **2.** glaring or flagrant: *gross injustice.* **3.** morally coarse; indelicate, or indecent: *gross tastes.* **4.** large, big, or bulky. **5.** thick; dense; heavy: *gross vegetation.* —*n.* **6.** the main body, bulk, or mass. **7. in the gross, a.** taken as a whole; in bulk. **b.** wholesale. **8.** a unit consisting of twelve dozen, or 144. **9. a great gross,** twelve gross, or 144 dozen. —*v.t.* **10.** to make a gross profit of; earn a total of. [ME *gros,* t. OF: m. *gros* large (as n., *grosse* twelve dozen), g. LL *grossus* thick] —**gross′ly,** *adv.* —**gross′ness,** *n.* —**Syn. 2.** shameful, outrageous, heinous. **3.** low, animal, sensual.

gross ton, 2,240 lbs.

gross·su·lar·ite (grŏs′yə·lə·rīt′), *n.* a mineral, calcium-aluminum garnet, $Ca_3Al_2Si_3O_{12}$, occurring in crystals. [f. s. NL *grossulāria* gooseberry + -ITE]

Gross·war·dein (grŏs′vär·dīn′), *n.* German name of Oradea.

gross weight, total weight without deduction for tare, tret, or waste.

Grosz (grōs), *n.* **George,** born 1893, German painter, in U.S. since 1932.

Italian grotesque work.
16th century

grot (grŏt), *n. Poetic.* a grotto. [t. F: m. *grotte,* t. It.: m. *grotta.* See GROTTO]

Grote (grōt), *n.* **George,** 1794–1871, British historian.

gro·tesque (grō·tĕsk′), *adj.* **1.** fantastic in the shaping and combination of forms, as in decorative work combining incongruous human and animal figures with scrolls, foliage, etc. **2.** odd or unnatural in shape, appearance, or character; fantastically ugly or absurd; bizarre. —*n.* **3.** any grotesque object or thing. [t. F, t. It.: m. *grottesco* (as n., *grottesca* grotesque decoration, such appar. as was found in ancient excavated dwellings) der. *grotta.* See GROTTO] —**gro·tesque′ly,** *adv.* —**gro·tesque′ness,** *n.*

gro·tes·quer·y (grō·tĕs′kər·ĭ), *n., pl.* **-queries. 1.** grotesque character. **2.** something grotesque. **3.** grotesque work. Also, **gro·tes′quer·ie.**

Gro·ti·us (grō′shǐ·əs), *n.* **Hugo,** (*Huig De Groot*) 1583–1645, Dutch jurist, statesman, and writer.

grot·to (grŏt′ō), *n., pl.* **-toes, -tos. 1.** a cave or cavern. **2.** an artificial cavernlike recess or structure. [t. It.: m. *grotta,* g. VL *crupta,* in L *crypta* subterranean passage or chamber, crypt, t. Gk.: m. *krýptē* vault]

grouch (grouch), *n. U.S. Colloq.* —*v.i.* **1.** to be sulky or morose; show discontent; complain. —*n.* **2.** a sulky or morose person. **3.** a sulky or morose mood. [var. of obs. *grutch,* t. OF: m. *groucher* grumble]

grouch·y (grou′chǐ), *adj.,* **grouchier, grouchiest.** *U.S. Colloq.* sullenly discontented; sulky; morose; ill-tempered. —**grouch′i·ly,** *adv.* —**grouch′i·ness,** *n.*

Grou·chy (grōō·shē′), *n.* **Emmanuel** (ĕ·må·ny·ĕl′), **Marquis de,** 1766–1847, French general.

ground[1] (ground), *n.* **1.** the earth's solid surface; firm or dry land: *fall to the ground.* **2.** earth or soil: *stony ground.* **3.** land having a special character: *rising ground.* **4.** (*often pl.*) a tract of land occupied, or appropriated to a special use: *baseball grounds.* **5.** (*often pl.*) the foundation or basis on which a theory or action rests; motive; reason: *grounds for a statement.* **6.** the underlying or main surface, or background, in painting, decorative work, lace, etc. **7.** (*pl.*) dregs or sediment: *coffee grounds.* **8.** *Elect.* **a.** a conducting connection between an electric circuit or equipment and the earth or some similarly conducting body. **b.** the terminal to which the grounding lead is attached. **9.** *Music.* a ground bass. **10.** *Naut.* the solid bottom under water. **11.** *Com.* groundage. **12.** Some special noun phrases are: **break ground, 1.** to plow. **2.** to begin the construction of a building. **3.** to begin the execution of any ˉ lan. **cover ground, 1.** to go across a certain area. **2.** to go from place to place. **3.** to make a certain amount of progress in a piece of work, etc. **from the ground up,** thoroughly. **gain ground, 1.** to advance; make progress. **2.** to gain acceptance. **give ground,** to give up some of one's position; give way. **hold** or **stand one's ground,** to maintain one's position; not yield or give way. **lose ground, 1.** to lose what one has gained; retreat; give way. **2.** to become less well-known or accepted. **shift one's ground,** to take another position or defense in an argument or situation. —*adj.* **13.** situated on or at, or adjacent to, the surface of the earth: *the ground floor.* **14.** pertaining to the ground. —*v.t.* **15.** to lay or set on the ground. **16.** to place on a foundation; found; fix firmly; settle or establish. **17.** to instruct in elements or first principles. **18.** to furnish with a ground or background on decorative work, etc. **19.** *Elect.* to establish a ground for (a circuit, device, etc.). **20.** *Naut.* to run aground. —*v.i.* **21.** to come to or strike the ground. [ME and OE *grund*, c. D *grond*, G *grund* bottom, ground] **—Syn. 2.** land, mold, loam, dirt. **5.** premise.

ground[2] (ground), *v.* **1.** pt. and pp. of **grind.** —*adj.* **2.** reduced to fine particles or dust by grinding. **3.** having the surface abraded or roughened by or as by grinding: *ground glass.* [see GRIND]

ground·age (groun'dĭj), *n. Brit.* a tax levied on vessels stopping at a port.

ground alert, *Mil.* state of waiting for orders in or near combat airplanes ready to take to the air at once.

ground bait, bait dropped to the bottom of the water.

ground bass (bās), *Music.* a short fundamental bass part continually repeated throughout a whole movement.

ground beetle, any of the numerous beetles of the family *Carabidae,* most of which are terrestrial.

ground cherry, an American plant of the genus *Physalis,* as *P. peruviana,* the edible Cape gooseberry.

ground connection, *Elect.* the conductor used to establish a ground.

ground crew, *Mil.* ground personnel connected with air operations, as maintenance technicians.

ground·er (groun'dər), *n. Baseball, etc.* a ball knocked or thrown along the ground and not rising into the air.

ground floor, *U.S. Colloq.* the most advantageous position or relationship in a business matter or deal.

ground glass, glass whose polished surface has been removed by grinding, as to diffuse light.

ground hog, woodchuck.

ground-hog day (ground'hŏg', -hôg'), Candlemas, Feb. 2, from the legend that the ground hog first emerges after hibernation on that day, and, if he sees his shadow, retires for six more weeks of winter.

ground ivy, a trailing labiate herb, *Glecoma hederacea,* bearing blue flowers.

ground·less (ground'lĭs), *adj.* without basis or reason: *groundless fears.* **—ground'less·ly,** *adv.* **—ground'-less·ness,** *n.*

ground·ling (ground'lĭng), *n.* **1.** a plant or animal that lives on or close to the ground. **2.** any of various fishes that live at the bottom of the water. **3.** a spectator, reader, or other person of crude or uncultivated tastes; an uncritical or uncultured person. **4.** *Obs.* a spectator in the pit of a theater which formerly was literally on the ground, having neither floor nor benches.

ground loop, *Aviation.* a sharp horizontal loop performed, usually involuntarily, while touching the ground.

ground·mass (ground'măs'), *n.* the crystalline, granular, or glassy base or matrix of a porphyry, in which the more prominent crystals are embedded.

ground·nut (ground'nŭt'), *n.* **1.** any of various plants with edible underground portions, as the peanut, *Arachis hypogaea,* and the American climbing leguminous vine, *Apios tuberosa,* which has an edible tuberous root. **2.** its edible tuber, pod, or the like.

ground owl, burrowing owl.

ground pine, 1. a European labiate herb, *Ajuga Chamaepitys,* having a resinous odor. **2.** any of several species of club moss, particularly *Lycopodium obscurum* and *L. complanatum.*

ground pink, 1. an annual herb, *Gilia dianthoides,* of southern California. **2.** the moss pink.

ground plan, 1. the plan of a floor of a building. **2.** first or fundamental plan.

ground plate, 1. *Elect.* a metal plate used for making a ground connection to earth. **2.** a groundsill.

ground plum, 1. a leguminous plant, *Astragalus caryocarpus,* of the American prairie regions. **2.** its plum-shaped fruit.

ground rent, *Chiefly Brit.* the rent at which land is let to a tenant for a long term or perpetually.

ground robin, the towhee or chewink, *Pipilo erythrophthalmus,* of North America.

ground·sel[1] (ground'səl), *n. Chiefly Brit.* any plant of the genus *Senecio* of the aster family, as *S. vulgaris,* a weed bearing small yellow flowers. [ME *grundeswilie,* etc., OE g(r)*undeswelge,* etc., appar. f. *gund* pus + *swelgan* swallow (from its use in medicine); or f. *grund* ground + *swelgan* (from its speed in spreading)]

ground·sel[2] (ground'səl), *n.* groundsill.

ground·sill (ground'sĭl'), *n.* the lowest horizontal timber of a frame or building lying next to the ground. [ME *gronsel,* etc., f. GROUND[1], n. + SILL]

ground speed, the speed of an aircraft in reference to the ground (in contrast to *air speed*).

ground squirrel, any of various terrestrial rodents of the squirrel family, as of the genus *Tamias* (chipmunks) and of the genus *Citellus* (or *Spermophilus*).

ground swell, a broad, deep swell or rolling of the sea, due to a distant storm or gale.

ground water, the water beneath the surface of the ground, consisting largely of surface water that has seeped down; the source of water in springs and wells.

ground wire, a lead from electrical apparatus to the ground or to a grounded connection.

ground·work (ground'wûrk'), *n.* the foundation, base, or basis.

group (grōōp), *n.* **1.** any assemblage of persons or things; cluster; aggregation. **2.** a number of persons or things ranged or considered together as being related in some way. **3.** *Ethnol.* a classification more limited than a branch. **4.** *Chem.* a number of atoms in a molecule connected or arranged together in some special manner; a radical: *the hydroxyl group,* =OH. **5.** *Linguistics.* **a.** a subdivision of a family, usually the greatest. **b.** any grouping of languages, whether geographically, on the basis of relationship, or otherwise. **6.** *Geol.* a division of stratified rocks comprising two or more formations. **7.** *U.S. Army.* **a.** a military unit of supporting troops, such as artillery or engineers, consisting of two or more battalions and a headquarters and headquarters troops. **b.** an administrative and tactical unit of the Army Air Forces, smaller than a wing and composed of two or more squadrons. **8.** *Music.* a section of an orchestra, comprising the instruments of the same class. **9.** *Art.* a number of figures or objects arranged together. —*v.t.* **10.** to place in a group, as with others. **11.** to arrange in or form into a group or groups. —*v.i.* **12.** to form a group. **13.** to be part of a group. [t. F: m. *groupe,* t. It: m. *gruppo;* ult. of Gmc. orig.]

group·er (grōō'pər), *n., pl.* **-ers,** (*esp. collectively*) **-er.** any of various serranoid fishes, esp. of the genus *Epinephelus,* as *E. morio* (**red grouper**), an important food fish of the southern Atlantic coast of the U.S., West Indies, etc. [t. Pg.: m. *garupa,* appar. repr. some S Amer. name]

group insurance, life, accident, or sickness insurance written on groups of lives, without medical examination.

group marriage, a form of marriage in which a group of males are united with a group of females to form a single conjugal unit.

group representation, *Govt.* representation in a governing body on the basis of interests rather than by geographical location.

grouse[1] (grous), *n., pl.* **grouse.** any of numerous gallinaceous birds of the family *Tetraonidae,* including such important game species as the **red grouse** (*Lagopus scoticus*) of Great Britain, **black grouse** (*Lyrurus tetrix*) and **capercaillie** or **wood grouse** (*Tetrao urogallus*) of Europe, and **spruce grouse** (*Canachites canadensis*) and **ruffed grouse** (*Bonasa umbellus*) of North America. [orig. uncert.] **—grouse'like',** *adj.*

Ruffed grouse, *Bonasa umbellus* (16½ in. long)

grouse[2] (grous), *v.,* **groused, grousing,** *n. Slang.* —*v.i.* **1.** to grumble; complain. —*n.* **2.** a complaint. [orig. unknown. Cf. GROUCH] **—grous'er,** *n.*

grout (grout), *n.* **1.** a thin coarse mortar poured into the joints of masonry and brickwork. **2.** a finishing or setting coat of plaster for walls and ceilings. **3.** (*usually pl.*) lees or grounds. **4.** coarse meal or porridge. **5.** (*pl.*) groats. —*v.t.* **6.** to fill up, form, or finish the spaces between stones with grout. **7.** to use as grout. [OE *grūt;* akin to GRITS, GROATS, and GRIT]

grove (grōv), *n.* a small wood or plantation of trees. [ME; OE *grāf*] **—Syn.** See **forest.**

grov·el (grŭv'əl, grŏv'-), *v.i.,* **-eled, -eling** or (*esp. Brit.*) **-elled, -elling. 1.** to humble oneself or act in an abject manner, as in fear or in mean servility. **2.** to lie or move with the face downward and the body prostrate, esp. in abject humility, fear, etc. **3.** to take pleasure in mean or base things. [back formation from *groveling,* adv. (f. obs. *grufe* face down (t. Scand.) + -LING[2]), taken for ppr.] **—grov'el·er;** *esp. Brit.,* **grov'el·ler,** *n.* **—grov'el·ing·ly;** *esp. Brit.,* **grov'el·ling·ly,** *adv.*

grow (grō), *v.,* **grew, grown, growing.** —*v.i.* **1.** to increase by natural development, as any living organism or part by assimilation of nutriment; increase in size or substance. **2.** to arise or issue as from a germ, stock, or originating source. **3.** to increase gradually; become greater. **4.** to increase in influence or effect (fol. by *on* or *upon*): *a habit that grows on one.* **5.** to become gradually attached or united by or as by growth. **6.** to come to be, or become, by degrees: *to grow old.* **7. grow up, a.** to increase in growth; attain maturity. **b.** to spring up; arise. —*v.t.* **8.** to cause to grow: *he grows corn.* **9.** to allow to grow: *to grow a beard.* **10.** to cover with a growth (used in the passive): *a field grown with corn.* [ME *growe(n)*, OE *grōwan*, akin to D *groeien*, OHG *gruwan*, Icel. *grōa.* Cf. GRASS, GREEN]

grow·er (grō'ər), *n.* **1.** one who grows anything. **2.** a plant that grows in a certain way: *a quick grower.*

growing pains, 1. dull, indefinite pains in the limbs during childhood and adolescence, often popularly associated with the process of growing. **2.** difficulties attending any new project.

growing season, the period between the last killing frost in spring and the first killing frost in fall.

growl (groul), *v.i.* **1.** to utter a deep guttural sound of anger or hostility: *a dog growls.* **2.** to murmur or complain angrily; grumble. **3.** to rumble: *the thunder growled.* —*v.t.* **4.** to express by growling. —*n.* **5.** act or sound of growling. [ME *groule* rumble (said of the bowels), c. G *grollen* rumble] —**growl'ing·ly,** *adv.* —**Syn. 2.** See **complain.**

growl·er (grou'lər), *n.* **1.** one who or that which growls. **2.** *U.S. Slang.* a pitcher, pail, or other vessel brought by a customer for beer. **3.** *Brit. Slang.* a four-wheeled hansom cab.

grown (grōn), *adj.* **1.** advanced in growth: *a grown boy.* **2.** arrived at full growth or maturity; adult: *a grown man.* —*v.* **3.** pp. of **grow.**

grown-up (grōn'ŭp'), *n.* a grown-up person; an adult.

grown-up (grōn'ŭp'), *adj.* **1.** having reached the age of maturity. **2.** characteristic of or suitable for adults.

growth (grōth), *n.* **1.** act, process, or manner of growing; development; gradual increase. **2.** something that has grown, or developed by or as by a natural process; a product: *a growth of weeds.* **3.** *Pathol.* a morbid mass of tissue, as a tumor. **4.** source; production: *a story of English growth.* —**Syn. 1.** augmentation, expansion.

Groz·ny (grôz'nĭ), *n.* a city in the S Soviet Union in Europe, in Caucasia. 172,468 (1939).

grub (grŭb), *n.*, *v.*, **grubbed, grubbing.** —*n.* **1.** the bulky larva of certain insects, esp. of scarabaeid and other beetles. **2.** a dull, plodding person; drudge. **3.** *Slang.* food or victuals. —*v.t.* **4.** to dig; clear of roots, etc. **5.** to dig up by the roots; uproot (often fol. by *up* or *out*). **6.** *Slang.* to supply with food. —*v.i.* **7.** to dig; search by or as by digging. **8.** to lead a laborious or groveling life; drudge. **9.** to make laborious research; study closely. **10.** *Slang.* to take "grub" or food. [ME *grubbe(n)* dig. Cf. G *grübeln* grub, rake, rack (the brains), Icel. *gryfja* hole, pit; prob. akin to GRAVE¹] —**grub'ber,** *n.*

grub·by (grŭb'ĭ), *adj.*, **-bier, -biest. 1.** dirty; slovenly. **2.** infested with or affected by grubs or larvae. [f. GRUB, n. + -Y¹] —**grub'bi·ly,** *adv.* —**grub'bi·ness,** *n.*

grub hoe, a heavy hoe for grubbing up roots, etc.

grub·stake (grŭb'stāk'), *n.*, *v.*, **-staked, -staking.** *U.S.* —*n.* **1.** provisions, outfit, etc., furnished to a prospector on condition of participating in the profits of his discoveries. —*v.t.* **2.** to furnish with a grubstake.

Grub Street, 1. a London street (now Milton Street) much inhabited by needy, inferior writers. **2.** petty and needy authors, or literary hacks, collectively.

grub-street (grŭb'strēt'), *adj.* **1.** hack; poor: *grub-street book.* —*n.* **2.** Grub Street (def. 2).

grudge (grŭj), *n.*, *v.*, **grudged, grudging.** —*n.* **1.** a feeling of ill will or resentment excited by some special cause, as a personal injury or insult, etc. —*v.t.* **2.** to give or permit with reluctance; submit to unwillingly. **3.** to be dissatisfied at seeing the good fortune of (another). —*v.i.* **4.** to feel dissatisfaction or ill will. [earlier *grutch*, ME *gruche(n)*, t. OF: m. *gruchier*, *groucier* murmur, grumble; orig. uncert. Cf. GROUCH] —**grudge'less,** *adj.* —**grudg'er,** *n.* —**grudg'ing·ly,** *adv.*

—**Syn. 1.** GRUDGE, MALICE, SPITE refer to ill will held against another or others. A GRUDGE is a feeling of resentment harbored because of some real or fancied wrong: *to hold a grudge because of jealousy, she has a grudge against him.* MALICE is the state of mind which delights in doing harm, or seeing harm done, to others, whether expressing itself in an attempt seriously to injure or merely in sardonic humor: *malice in watching someone's embarrassment, to tell lies about someone out of malice.* SPITE is petty, and often sudden, resentment that manifests itself usually in trifling retaliations: *to reveal a secret out of spite, to build a high fence between properties out of spite.* **3.** begrudge, envy.

gru·el (grōo'əl), *n.*, *v.*, **-eled, -eling** or (*esp. Brit.*) **-elled, -elling.** —*n.* **1.** a light, usually thin, cooked cereal made by boiling meal, esp. oatmeal, in water or milk. **2.** any similar substance. —*v.t.* **3.** to punish or use severely; exhaust; disable. [ME, t. OF: meal, g. dim. of ML *grūtum*, t. Gmc. Cf. GROUT]

gru·el·ing (grōo'əl ĭng, grōol'-), *adj.* **1.** exhausting; very tiring; severe. —*n.* **2.** any trying or exhausting procedure or experience. Also, *esp. Brit.*, **gru'el·ling.**

grue·some (grōo'səm), *adj.* such as to make one shudder; inspiring horror; revolting. Also, **grewsome.** [f. *grue*, v., shudder (c. G *grauen*, Dan. *grue*) + -SOME¹. Cf. G *grausam* horrible] —**grue'some·ly,** *adv.* —**grue'some·ness,** *n.*

gruff (grŭf), *adj.* **1.** low and harsh; hoarse: *a gruff voice.* **2.** rough; surly: *a gruff manner.* [earlier *grof*, t. D, f. ge- prefix (c. OE ge-) + *rof*, akin to OE *hrēof* rough]

—**gruff'ly,** *adv.* —**gruff'ness,** *n.* —**Syn. 1.** harsh. **2.** grumpy, brusque. —**Ant. 1.** pleasant. **2.** courteous.

grum·ble (grŭm'bəl), *v.*, **-bled, -bling,** *n.* —*v.i.* **1.** to murmur in discontent; complain ill-humoredly. **2.** to utter low, indistinct sounds; growl. **3.** to rumble: *the thunder grumbled.* —*v.t.* **4.** to express or utter with murmuring or complaining. —*n.* **5.** an ill-humored complaining; murmur; growl. **6.** (*pl.*) a grumbling, discontented mood. **7.** a rumble. [? freq. of OE *grymman* wail, mourn. Cf. OE *grymettan* grunt, roar, rage, G *grummeln* rumble, F *grommeler* mutter] —**grum'bler,** *n.* —**grum'bling·ly,** *adv.* —**Syn. 1.** See **complain.**

grum·met (grŭm'ət), *n.* grommet.

gru·mous (grōo'məs), *adj. Bot.* formed of clustered grains, granules, etc., as certain roots. Also, **gru·mose** (grōo'mōs). [f. *grume* (t. L: m. s. *grūmus* little heap, hillock) + -OUS]

grump·y (grŭm'pĭ), *adj.*, **grumpier, grumpiest.** surly; ill-tempered. [f. *grump* the sulks (b. GRUNT and DUMP) + -Y¹] —**grump'i·ly,** *adv.* —**grump'i·ness,** *n.*

Grun·dy (grŭn'dĭ), *n.* **Mrs.,** society in regard to its censorship of personal conduct. [a character in Thomas Morton's play *Speed the Plough* (1798)]

grun·ion (grōon'yən), *n.* a small slender food fish, *Leuresthes tenuis*, of southern California.

grunt (grŭnt), *v.i.* **1.** to utter the deep guttural sound characteristic of a hog. **2.** to utter a similar sound. **3.** to grumble, as in discontent. —*v.t.* **4.** to express with a grunt. —*n.* **5.** the sound of grunting. **6.** any of various marine fishes of the genus *Haemulon* and allied genera, which can emit a grunting sound. [ME *grunten*, OE *grunnettan*, freq. of *grunian* grunt. Cf. G *grunzen*, L *grunnīre*] —**grunt'ing·ly,** *adv.*

grunt·er (grŭn'tər), *n.* **1.** a hog. **2.** any animal or person that grunts. **3.** a grunt (def. 6).

grutch (grŭch), *n.*, *v.t.*, *v.i. Brit. Dial.* grudge.

Gru·yère cheese (grĭ yâr', grōo-; *Fr.* grÿ yěr'), a firm, pale-yellow variety of French and Swiss cheese containing many holes. [named after *Gruyère*, district in Switzerland]

gryph·on (grĭf'ən), *n.* griffin.

gt., 1. great. **2.** (*pl.* **gtt.**) gutta.

Gt. Br., Great Britain. Also, **Gt. Brit.**

g.t.c., 1. good till canceled. **2.** good till countermanded.

gtd., guaranteed.

gua·cha·ro (gwä'chä rō'), *n.*, *pl.* **-ros.** a nocturnal fruit-eating South American bird, *Steatornis caripensis*, valued by the natives for the oil produced from the fat of the young. [Sp., t. Araucanian: m. *uachar* cave]

gua·co (gwä'kō), *n.*, *pl.* **-cos. 1.** a climbing asteraceous plant, *Mikania Guaco*, of tropical America. **2.** its medicinal leaves, or a substance obtained from them, used as an antidote for snake bites. **3.** a tropical American plant, *Aristolochia maxima*, also used for snake bites. [t. Sp.; from native name]

Gua·da·la·ja·ra (gwä'dä lä hä'rä), *n.* a city in W Mexico: the capital of Jalisco. 227,631 (1940).

Gua·dal·ca·nal (gwä'dəl kə näl', -däl kä näl'), *n.* one of the Solomon Islands, in the S Pacific: U.S. victory over the Japanese, 1942–43. 14,300 pop. (1931); ab. 2500 sq. mi.

Gua·dal·qui·vir (gwä'däl kē věr'), *n.* a river in S Spain, flowing W to the Gulf of Cádiz. 374 mi.

Gua·da·lupe Hi·dal·go (gwä'də lōop' hǐ däl'gō; *Sp.* gwä'dä lōo'pě ē däl'gō), a city in the Federal District of Mexico: famous shrine; peace treaty, 1848. 25,929 (1940). Official name, **Gustavo A. Madero.**

Gua·de·loupe (gwä'də lōop'), *n.* two islands separated by a narrow channel in the Leeward Islands of the West Indies: together with five dependencies they form a department of France. 304,000 pop. (1936); 687 sq. mi. *Cap.:* Basse-Terre.

Gua·di·a·na (gwä'dē ä'nä), *n.* a river flowing from central Spain S through SE Portugal to the Gulf of Cádiz. 515 mi.

guai·a·col (gwī'ə kōl', -kôl'), *n. Chem.* a colorless liquid, $CH_3OC_6H_4OH$, resembling creosote, obtained by distillation from guaiacum resin, and in other ways: used to treat phthisis, bronchitis, etc. [f. GUAIAC(UM) + -OL²]

guai·a·cum (gwī'ə kəm), *n.* **1.** any of the hard-wooded tropical American trees and shrubs constituting the zygophyllaceous genus *Guaiacum*, esp. *G. officinale* of the West Indies and South America, and *G. sanctum* of the West Indies and Florida. **2.** the hard, heavy wood of such a tree. See **lignum vitae** (def. 1). **3.** a greenish-brown resin obtained from such a tree, used as a stimulant and alterative, and as a remedy for rheumatism, cutaneous eruptions, etc. Also, **guai'o·cum, gui·ac** (gwī'ăk). [NL, der. Sp. *guayaco*; from Haitian]

Guai·ra (gwī'rä), *n.* La (lä). See **La Guaira.**

Guam (gwäm), *n.* an island belonging to the U.S. in the N Pacific, E of the Philippine Islands: the largest of the Marianas group; U.S. naval station. 59,498 pop. (1950); 206 sq. mi. *Cap.:* Agaña.

guan (gwän), *n.* any of various large gallinaceous birds constituting the subfamily *Penelopinae* (family *Cracidae*), chiefly of Central and South America, allied to the curassows. [? of W. Ind. orig.]

gua·na·co (gwä nä/kō), *n.*, *pl.* **-cos.** a wild South American ruminant, *Lama guanicoe*, of which the llama and alpaca are thought to be domesticated varieties, related to the camels. [t. Sp., t. Kechua: m. *huanacu*]

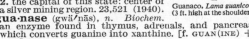
Guanaco, *Lama guanicoe* (3 ft. high at the shoulder)

Gua·na·jua·to (gwä/nä hwä/tō), *n.* 1. a state in central Mexico. 1,046,-490 pop. (1940); 11,805 sq. mi. 2. the capital of this state: center of a silver mining region. 23,521 (1940).

gua·nase (gwä/nās), *n. Biochem.* an enzyme found in thymus, adrenals, and pancreas which converts guanine into xanthine. [f. GUAN(INE) + -ASE]

guan·i·dine (gwăn/ə dēn/, -dĭn, gwä/nə-), *n.* a strongly caustic substance, C(NH)(NH₂)₂, forming crystalline salts and a wide variety of organic derivatives: used in the manufacture of plastics, resins, rubber accelerators, explosives, etc. Also, **guan·i·din** (gwăn/ə dĭn, gwä/nə-). [der. GUANINE with infixed -ID³]

gua·nine (gwä/nēn, gwä/nĭn), *n. Chem.* a white crystalline substance, C₅H₅N₅O, found in guano, in the liver and pancreas of animals, in the scales of fishes, etc., and as a decomposition product of nucleic acids. Also, **gua·nin** (gwä/nĭn, gōō/ə-). [f. GUAN(O) + -INE²]

gua·no (gwä/nō), *n.*, *pl.* **-nos.** 1. a natural manure composed chiefly of the excrement of sea birds, found esp. on islands near the Peruvian coast. 2. any similar substance, as an artificial fertilizer made from fish. [t. Sp., t. Kechua: m. *huanu* dung]

Guan·tá·na·mo (gwän tä/nä mō/), *n.* a city in SE Cuba. 42,445 (1943).

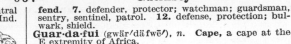

Guantánamo Bay, a bay on the SE coast of Cuba: U.S. naval station.

Gua·po·ré (gwä/-pô rĕ/), *n.* a river forming part of the boundary between Brazil and Bolivia, flowing NW to the Mamoré river. ab. 900 mi.

Gua·ra·ni (gwä/rä nē/), *n.*, *pl.* **-ni** (-nē/), **-nis** (-nēz/). 1. an important central South American tribe of Tupian family and affiliation. 2. a member of this tribe. 3. the Tupian language of the Guarani tribe.

guar·an·tee (găr/ən tē/), *n.*, *v.*, **-teed, -teeing.** —*n.* 1. a warrant, pledge, or formal assurance given by way of security. 2. one who warrants, or gives a formal assurance or guaranty, as for the fulfillment of obligations. 3. one to whom a guarantee is made. 4. that which is taken or presented as security. 5. something that has the force or effect of a guaranty: *wealth is no guarantee of happiness.* —*v.t.* 6. to secure, as by giving or taking security. 7. to make oneself answerable for in behalf of one primarily responsible: *to guarantee the carrying out of a contract.* 8. to undertake to secure to another, as rights or possessions. 9. to serve as a warrant or guaranty for. 10. to engage (to do something). 11. to engage to protect or indemnify (fol. by *from, against,* or *in*): *to guarantee one against loss.* [appar. for GUARANTY]—**Syn. 1.** guaranty, surety. 11. See **warrant.**

guar·an·tor (găr/ən tôr/, -tər), *n.* one who makes or gives a guarantee.

guar·an·ty (găr/ən tĭ), *n.*, *pl.* **-ties,** *v.*, **-tied, -tying.** —*n.* 1. a warrant, pledge, or promise given by way of security. 2. act of giving security. 3. one who acts as a guarantee. —*v.t.* 4. to guarantee. [t. AF: m. *guarantie,* der. *guarant, warant* WARRANT]

guard (gärd), *v.t.* 1. to keep safe from harm; protect; watch over. 2. to keep under close watch in order to prevent escape, outbreaks, etc.: *to guard a prisoner.* 3. to keep in check, from caution or prudence: *to guard the tongue.* 4. to provide with some safeguard or protective appliance, etc. —*v.i.* 5. to take precautions (fol. by *against*): *to guard against errors.* 6. to give protection; keep watch; be watchful. —*n.* 7. one who guards, protects, or keeps protecting or restraining watch. 8. one who keeps watch over prisoners or others under restraint. 9. a body of men, esp. soldiers, charged with guarding a place from disturbance, theft, fire, etc. 10. restraining watch, as over a prisoner or other person under restraint: *to be kept under close guard.* 11. a contrivance, appliance, or attachment designed for guarding against injury, loss, etc. 12. something intended or serving to guard or protect; a safeguard. 13. a posture of defense or readiness, as in fencing, boxing, bayonet drill, etc. 14. *Football.* either of two players holding a position of defense at the right and the left of the center, in the forward line. 15. *Basketball.* one of the defensive players on a team. 16. **off one's guard,** unprepared to meet a sudden attack; unwary. 17. **on one's guard,** watchful or vigilant against attack; cautious; wary. 18. *Brit.* the conductor of a railroad train, etc. 19. (*cap., pl.*) the name of certain bodies of troops in the British army. [ME *garde,* t. F, of Gmc. orig.; see WARD²]—**guard/er,** *n.* —**Syn. 1.** shield, safeguard, preserve, save. See **de-**

fend. 7. defender, protector; watchman; guardsman, sentry, sentinel, patrol. 12. defense, protection; bulwark, shield.

Guar·da·fui (gwär/dä fwē/), *n.* **Cape,** a cape at the E extremity of Africa.

guard cell, *Bot.* either of two specialized epidermal cells which flank the pore of a stoma and usually cause it to open and close.

guard·ed (gär/dĭd), *adj.* 1. cautious; careful: *to be guarded in one's speech.* 2. protected or watched, as by a guard. —**guard/ed·ly,** *adv.* —**guard/ed·ness,** *n.*

guard duty, military duties equivalent in general to those of civilian police, but including the watching over of military prisoners at work.

guard·house (gärd/hous/), *n.* 1. a military jail in which soldiers are confined for misconduct, or while awaiting trial for serious offenses. 2. the headquarters and quarters of the guard.

guard·i·an (gär/dĭ ən), *n.* 1. one who guards, protects, or preserves. 2. *Law.* one who is entrusted by law with the care of the person or property, or both, of another, as of a minor or of some other person legally incapable of managing his own affairs. —*adj.* 3. guarding; protecting: *a guardian angel.* [ME *gardein,* t. AF, der. *g(u)arde* GUARD, n.] —**guard/i·an·ship/,** *n.* —**Syn. 1.** protector, defender. 2. trustee, warden, keeper.

guards·man (gärdz/mən), *n.*, *pl.* **-men.** 1. a man who acts as a guard. 2. *Chiefly Brit.* a member of any body of troops called "Guards." 3. *U.S.* a member of the National Guard.

Guar·ne·ri (gwär nĕ/rē), *n.* **Giuseppe Antonio** (jōō-zĕp/pĕ än tô/nyô), (*Joseph Guarnerius*) 1683–1745, Italian violinmaker.

Guar·ne·ri·us (gwär när/Yəs), *n.* a violin made by Guarneri or by a member of his family.

Guat., Guatemala.

Gua·te·ma·la (gwä/tə mä/lə; *Sp.* -tĕ mä/lä), *n.* 1. a republic in Central America. 3,283,209 pop. (1940); 42,042 sq. mi. 2. Also, **Guatemala City.** the capital of this republic. 163,826 (1940). —**Gua/te·ma/lan,** *adj., n.*

gua·va (gwä/və), *n.* 1. any of various trees or shrubs of the myrtaceous genus *Psidium,* esp. *P. Guajava,* natives of tropical or subtropical America, with a fruit used for jelly, etc. 2. the fruit, used for making jam, jelly, etc. [t. Sp.: m. *guayaba*; from S Amer. name]

Guay·a·quil (gwä/yä kēl/), *n.* a seaport in W Ecuador, on the **Gulf of Guayaquil,** an arm of the Pacific. 172,948 (est. 1944).

gua·yu·le (gwä yōō/lĕ), *n.* 1. a rubber-yielding bushlike composite plant, *Parthenium argentatum,* of northern Mexico, etc. 2. the rubber obtained from this plant. [t. Sp.; from native name]

gu·ber·na·to·ri·al (gū/bər nə tōr/Yəl), *adj. Chiefly U.S.* pertaining to a governor. [f. L *gubernātor* steersman, governor + -IAL]

gu·ber·ni·ya (gŏō bĕr/nĭ yä/), *n.* 1. (in the Soviet Union) an administrative division of the volosts, smaller than a district. 2. (in Russia before 1917) an administrative division equivalent to the province.

gude (gyd), *adj., adv., n. Scot. and Brit. Dial.* good.

Gude (gyd), *n. Scot. and Brit. Dial.* God.

gudg·eon (gŭj/ən), *n.* 1. a small European freshwater fish, *Gobio gobio,* of the minnow family, with a threadlike barbel at the corner of the mouth: easily caught, and much used for bait. 2. any of certain related fish. 3. one who is easily duped or cheated. 4. a bait or allurement. —*v.t.* 5. to dupe; cheat. [ME *gogen,* t. OF: m. *goujon,* g. s. L. *gōbio,* var. of *gōbius* GOBY]

Gud·run (gŏōd/rōōn), *n.* 1. (in the Volsunga saga) daughter of the king of the Nibelungs; wife of Sigurd and later of Atli. 2. the heroine of the important Middle High German epic poem called by her name. Also, **Kudrun.**

guel·der-rose (gĕl/dər rōz/), *n.* the European snowball, a cultivated variety of the European high-bush cranberry, *Viburnum Opulus* var. *roseum.* [named after *Geldern,* German town, or *Gelder(land),* Dutch province of which Geldern was formerly capital]

Guel·ders (gĕl/dərz), *n.* Gelderland.

Guelph (gwĕlf), *n.* 1. a member of the papal and popular party in medieval Italy, opposed to the Ghibellines. 2. a member of a secret society in Italy in the early 19th century, opposed to foreign rulers and reactionary ideas. Also, **Guelf.** [t. It.: m. *Guelfo,* t. G: m. *Welf,* name of founder of a princely German family] —**Guelph/ic,** *adj.*

gue·non (gə nôn/), *n.* any of the agile, long-tailed African monkeys, of the genus *Cercopithecus,* with their hairs many-banded, giving a speckled coloration. [t. F]

guer·don (gûr/dən), *Poetic.* —*n.* 1. a reward, recompense, or requital. —*v.t.* 2. to give a guerdon to; reward. [ME, t. OF, var. of *werdoun,* t. ML: m. s. *widerdonum,* alter. (prob. by assoc. with L *dōnum* gift), of OHG *widarlōn,* f. *widar* again, back + *lōn* reward, c. OE *witherlēan*]

Guern·sey (gûrn/zĭ), *n.* **Isle of,** one of the Channel Islands, in the English Channel. 38,283 pop. (1931); 24½ sq. mi.

Guern·sey (gûrn/zĭ), *n.*, *pl.* **-seys.** 1. one of a breed of dairy cattle of average size, originating on Isle of Guernsey in the English Channel, giving a good supply of rich, golden-colored milk. 2. (*l.c.*) a close-fitting knitted woolen shirt much worn by seamen.

ăct, āble, dâre, ärt; ĕbb, ēqual; Yf, īce; hŏt, ōver, ôrder, oil, bŏŏk, ōoze, out; ŭp, ūse, ûrge; ə = a in alone; ch, chief; g, give; ng, ring; sh, shoe; th, thin; ŧħ, that; zh, vision. See the full key on inside cover.

guer·ril·la (gərῐl′ə), *n.* **1.** a member of a small independent band of soldiers which harasses the enemy by surprise raids, attacks on communication and supply lines, etc. —*adj.* **2.** pertaining to such fighters or their warfare. Also, **gue·ril′la** [t. Sp., dim. of *guerra* WAR]

Guesde (gĕd), *n.* **Jules** (zhyl), (*Mathieu Basile*) 1845–1922, French socialist leader, editor, and writer.

guess (gĕs), *v.t.* **1.** to form an opinion of at random or from evidence admittedly uncertain: *to guess the age of a woman.* **2.** to estimate or conjecture correctly: *to guess a riddle.* **3.** to think, believe, or suppose: *I guess I can get there in time.* —*v.i.* **4.** to form an estimate or conjecture (often fol. by *at*): *to guess at the height of a building.* **5.** to estimate or conjecture correctly. —*n.* **6.** a notion, judgment, or conclusion gathered from mere probability or imperfect information; conjecture; surmise. [ME *gessen*, prob. t. Scand.; cf. MDan. *getze, gitse* (Dan. *gisse*) f. *get-* guess + *-s*, suffix, c. MD *gessen*, MLG *gissen*] —**guess′er**, *n.* —**guess′ing·ly**, *adv.*
—**Syn. 1, 2, 4.** suppose. GUESS, GUESS AT, CONJECTURE, SURMISE imply attempting to form an opinion as to the probable. To GUESS is to risk an opinion regarding something one does not know about; or, wholly or partly by chance, to arrive at the correct answer to a question: *to guess the outcome of a game.* GUESS AT implies more haphazard or random guessing: *to guess at the solution of a crime.* To CONJECTURE is to make inferences in the absence of sufficient evidence to establish certainty: *to conjecture the circumstances of the crime.* SURMISE implies making an intuitive conjecture which may or may not be correct: *to surmise the motives which led to it.* —**Ant. 3.** know.

guess-rope (gĕs′rōp′), *n.* guest-rope.

guess·work (gĕs′wûrk′), *n.* work or procedure based on or consisting in guessing; conjecture.

guest (gĕst), *n.* **1.** a person entertained at the house or table of another. **2.** one who receives the hospitality of a club, a city, or the like. **3.** a person who pays for lodging, and sometimes food, at a hotel, etc. **4.** *Zool.* a commensal (chiefly of insects living in other insects' nests). —*v.t.* **5.** *Rare.* to entertain as a guest. —*v.i.* **6.** *Rare.* to be a guest. [ME *gest(e)*, t. Scand.; cf. Icel. *gestr*; r. OE *g(i)est*, c. D and G *gast*; akin to L *hostis* stranger, enemy] —**guest′less**, *adj.* —**Syn. 1, 2.** See **visitor.**

Guest (gĕst), *n.* **Edgar Albert,** born 1881, U.S. poet.

guest room, a room for the lodging of guests.

guest-rope (gĕst′rōp′), *n.* **1.** a line along a ship's side or from a boom for boats to make fast alongside. **2.** a line, in addition to the towrope, to steady a boat in tow. Also, **guess-rope.**

guf·faw (gŭf·ô′), *n.* **1.** a loud, coarse burst of laughter. —*v.i.* **2.** to laugh loudly and boisterously.

Gui., Guiana.

Gui·an·a (gē·ăn′ə, -ä′nə; *Sp.* gyä′nä), *n.* **1.** a vast tropical region in NE South America, bounded by the Orinoco, Río Negro, Amazon, and the Atlantic. ab. 690,000 sq. mi. **2.** a coastal portion of this region, including British Guiana, French Guiana, and Surinam. 556,000 pop. (est. 1939); ab. 185,000 sq. mi.

Guiana (def. 2)

guid·ance (gī′dəns), *n.* **1.** act of guiding; leadership; direction. **2.** something that guides.

guide (gīd), *v.*, **guided, guiding,** *n.* —*v.t.* **1.** to lead or conduct on the way, as to a place or through a region; show the way to. **2.** to direct the movement or course of: *to guide a horse.* **3.** to lead or direct in any course or action. —*n.* **4.** one who guides, esp. one employed to guide travelers, tourists, hunters, etc. **5.** a mark or the like to direct the eye. **6.** guidebook. **7.** guidepost. **8.** a contrivance for regulating progressive motion or action: *a sewing-machine guide.* **9.** a spirit said to direct the utterances of a medium. [ME *guide(n)*, t. OF: m. *guider*, t. Gmc.; cf. OE *wītan* look after] —**guid′-a·ble,** *adj.* —**guide′less,** *adj.* —**guid′er,** *n.*
—**Syn. 1.** pilot, steer. GUIDE, CONDUCT, DIRECT, LEAD imply showing the way or pointing out or determining the course to be taken. GUIDE implies continuous presence or agency in showing or indicating a course: *to guide a traveler.* To CONDUCT is to precede or escort to a place, sometimes with a degree of ceremony: *to conduct a guest to his room.* To DIRECT is to give information for guidance, or instructions or orders for a course of procedure: *to direct someone to the station.* To LEAD is to bring onward in a course, guiding by contact or by going in advance; hence, fig. to influence or induce to some course of conduct: *to lead a procession, to lead astray.* —**Ant. 3.** follow.

guide·board (gīd′bōrd′), *n.* a board on a guidepost containing directions to travelers.

guide·book (gīd′bŏŏk′), *n.* a book of directions and information for travelers, tourists, etc.

guided missile, an aerial missile, such as a rocket, steered during its flight by radio signals, clockwork controls, etc.

guide·post (gīd′pōst′), *n.* a post, usually mounted on the roadside or the intersection of two or more roads, bearing a sign for the guidance of travelers.

guide rope, 1. *Aeron.* a long rope hung downward from a balloon and trailing along the ground, used to regulate the altitude automatically and to act as a brake. **2.** rope fastened, usually at an angle, to a hoisting or towing line, to guide the object being moved.

Gui·do d'A·rez·zo (gwē′dō dä·rĕt′tsô), A.D. c990–c1050, Italian or French monk, reformer of musical notation, who added lines to the staff and wrote notes on both spaces and lines.

gui·don (gī′dən), *n. Mil.* **1.** a small flag or streamer carried as a guide, for marking or signaling, or for identification. **2.** the soldier carrying it. [t. F, t. It.: m. *guidone*, b. *guidare* GUIDE and *gonfalone* GONFALON]

Gui·do Re·ni (gwē′dō rĕ′nē), 1575–1642, an Italian painter.

Gui·enne (gwē·yĕn′), *n.* a former province in SW France. Also, **Guyenne.**

guild (gῐld), *n.* **1.** an organization of persons with common professional or cultural interests formed for mutual aid and protection. **2.** *Hist.* one of the associations, numerous in the middle ages, formed for mutual aid and protection or for a common purpose: most frequently persons associated in trade or industry. **3.** *Bot.* all of the plants, such as parasites, having a similar habit of growth and nutrition. Also, **gild.** [ME *gild(e)*, t. Scand. (cf. Icel. *gildi* guild, payment); r. OE *gegyld* guild; akin to G *geld* money, Goth. *gild* tribute]

guil·der (gῐl′dər), *n.* gulden. Also, **gilder.** [early mod. E *gildren*, var. of ME *guldren*, both t. D: m. (with intrusive *-r-*) *gulden*]

guild·hall (gῐld′hôl′), *n.* **1.** *Brit.* the hall built or used by a guild or corporation for its assemblies; town hall. **2.** *Hist.* a guild assembly hall. Also, **gildhall.**

guilds·man (gῐldz′mən), *n., pl.* **-men.** a member of a guild. Also, **gildsman.**

guild socialism, a kind of English socialism by which workers' guilds manage and control government-owned industry.

guile (gīl), *n.* insidious cunning; treachery. [ME, t. OF; of Gmc. orig., and akin to WILE] —**Syn.** See **deceit.**

guile·ful (gīl′fəl), *adj.* full of guile; wily; deceitful; treacherous. —**guile′ful·ly,** *adv.* —**guile′ful·ness,** *n.*

guile·less (gīl′lῐs), *adj.* free from guile; sincere; honest; frank. —**guile′less·ly,** *adv.* —**guile′less·ness,** *n.*

guil·le·mot (gῐl′ə·mŏt′), *n.* any of several relatively narrow-billed northern oceanic birds of the genera *Cepphus* and *Uria*, as the **black guillemot,** *Cepphus grylle,* and **common guillemot,** *Uria aalge.* [t. F, appar. dim. of *Guillaume* William]

guil·loche (gῐ·lōsh′), *n.* an ornamental band or field with paired ribbons or lines flowing in interlaced curves. [t. F: graining tool, der. MF *goie* a kind of sickle, d. var. of F *gouge* GOUGE, n.]

Ionic guilloche

guil·lo·tine (n. gῐl′ə·tēn′; v. gῐl′ə·tēn′), *n., v.,* **-tined, -tining.** —*n.* **1.** a machine for beheading persons by means of a heavy blade falling in two grooved posts. **2.** an instrument for cutting the tonsils. —*v.t.* **3.** to behead by the guillotine. [t. F; named after J. I. Guillotin (1738–1814), French physician, who urged its use] —**guil′lo·tin′er,** *n.*

guilt (gῐlt), *n.* **1.** fact or state of having committed an offense or crime; grave culpability, as for some conscious violation of moral or penal law. **2.** guilty conduct. [ME *gilt,* OE *gylt* offense] —**Syn. 1.** guiltiness. **2.** criminality. —**Ant. 1.** innocence.

Guillotine

A, Knife; B, Cord, which releases knife; C, Board, to which victim is tied; D, Hole, for head of victim; E, Basket

guilt·less (gῐlt′lῐs), *adj.* **1.** free from guilt; innocent. **2.** having no knowledge or experience (fol. by *of*). **3.** destitute or devoid (fol. by *of*). —**guilt′less·ly,** *adv.* —**guilt′less·ness,** *n.* —**Syn. 1.** See **innocent.**

guilt·y (gῐl′tῐ), *adj.,* **guiltier, guiltiest. 1.** having incurred guilt or grave culpability, as by committing an offense or crime; justly chargeable with guilt (often fol. by *of*): *guilty of murder.* **2.** characterized by, connected with, or involving guilt: *guilty intent.* **3.** affected with or showing a sense of guilt: *a guilty conscience.* [ME *gilti,* OE *gyltig*] —**guilt′i·ly,** *adv.* —**guilt′i·ness,** *n.*

guimpe (gῐmp, gămp), *n.* a kind of chemisette or yoke of lace, embroidery, or other material, worn with a dress cut out at the neck. [t. F: wimple]

Guin., Guinea.

Guin·ea (gῐn′ῐ), *n.* **1.** a coastal region in W Africa, of indefinite extent, but generally considered as extending from the Gambia river to the Gabon estuary. **2.** Gulf of, a large open bay in the angle of W Africa. **3.** (*l.c.*) a British gold coin issued from 1663 to 1813, at first of a nominal value of 20 shillings, but having since 1717 a fixed value of 21 shillings. **4.** *Colloq.* guinea fowl.

Guinea corn, durra.

guinea fowl, any member of an African gallinaceous bird family, the *Numididae,* which has (usually) dark-gray plumage with small white spots, one species of which is now domesticated throughout the world and valued for its flesh and eggs.

Common guinea fowl
Numida meleagris
(25 in. long)

guinea hen, 1. the female of the guinea fowl. **2.** any guinea fowl.

Guinea pepper, pepper pods, esp. of *Capsicum frutescens* var. *longum,* from which cayenne is ground.

guinea pig, a short-eared, short-tailed rodent of the genus *Cavia*, usually white, black, and tawny, much used in scientific experiments, commonly regarded as the domesticated form of one of the South American wild species of cavy. [f. GUINEA + PIG; reason for associating animal with Guinea unknown]

Guinea pig. *Cavia porcellus* (9 to 10 in. long)

Guinea worm, a long, slender, nematode worm, *Dracunculus medinensis*, parasitic under the skin of man and other animals, common in parts of India and Africa.

Guin·e·vere (gwĭn/ə vĭr/), *n. Arthurian Romance.* wife of King Arthur, and mistress of Lancelot. Also, **Guin·e·ver** (gwĭn/ə vər).

gui·pure (gĭ pyŏŏr/; *Fr.* gē̇ pyr/), *n.* **1.** any of various laces, often heavy, made of linen, silk, etc., with the pattern connected by brides (rather than by a net ground). **2.** any of various laces or trimmings formerly in use, made with cords or heavy threads, metal, etc. [t. F, der. *guiper* cover or whip with silk, etc., t. Gmc.; cf. WIPE, WHIP]

Guis·card (gēs kär/), *n.* **Robert** (rŏ/bẽr/), *(Robert de Hauteville)* c1015–85, Norman conqueror in Italy.

guise (gīz), *n., v.,* **guised, guising.** —*n.* **1.** external appearance in general; aspect or semblance: *an old principle in a new guise.* **2.** assumed appearance or mere semblance: *under the guise of friendship.* **3.** *Archaic.* style of dress: *in the guise of a shepherdess.* **4.** *Obs.* manner; mode. —*v.t.* **5.** *Archaic.* to dress; attire. —*v.i.* **6.** *Scot. and N. Eng.* to go in disguise. [ME, t. OF, t. Gmc.; cf. WISE²] —Syn. **1.** See **appearance.**

Guise (gēz), *n.* **1. François de Lorraine** (frän swä/ də lō rĕn/), **2nd Duc de,** 1519–63, French general and statesman. **2. Henri I de Lorraine** (än rē/), **Duc de,** 1550–88, French general and leader of opposition to the Huguenots.

gui·tar (gĭ tär/), *n.* a musical stringed instrument with a long fretted neck and a flat, somewhat violinlike, body. The strings, usually six in number, are plucked or twanged with the fingers. [t. Sp.: m. *guitarra*, t. Gk.: m. *kithára* cithara] —**gui·tar/ist,** *n.* —**gui·tar/like/,** *adj.*

Man playing a guitar

gui·tar·fish (gĭ tär/fĭsh/), *n., pl.* **-fishes** (*esp. collectively*) **-fish.** a sharklike ray of the family *Rhinobatidae* inhabiting warm seas; specif., *Rhinobatus productus.*

Gui·try (gē trē/), *n.* **Sacha** (sà shà/), born 1885, French actor and dramatist, born in Russia.

Gui·zot (gē zō/), *n.* **François Pierre Guillaume** (frän swä/ pyĕr gē yōm/), 1787–1874, French historian and statesman.

Gu·ja·rat (gŏŏj/ə rät/), *n.* a level region in W India, N of the Narbada river: formerly a kingdom.

Gu·ja·ra·ti (gŏŏj/ə rä/tĭ), *n.* an Indic language of western India.

gulch (gŭlch), *n. U.S.* a deep, narrow ravine, esp. one marking the course of a stream or torrent. [orig. uncert.]

gul·den (gŏŏl/dən), *n., pl.* **-dens, -den. 1.** the gold monetary unit of the Netherlands, equal to 26.3 U.S. cents. **2.** a Dutch silver coin of this value (also called *florin*). **3.** the Austrian florin. **4.** one of several gold coins formerly current in Germany from the 14th century, and in the Low Countries from the 15th century. Also, **guilder, gilder.** [t. D and G: lit., golden]

Gü·lek Bo·gaz (gȳ lĕk/ bō gäz/), Turkish name of the Cilician Gates.

gules (gūlz), *n. Her.* red. [ME *goules*, t. OF: m. *gueules* red fur neckpiece, ult. der. *gole* throat, g. L *gula*]

gulf (gŭlf), *n.* **1.** a portion of an ocean or sea partly enclosed by land. **2.** a deep hollow; chasm or abyss. **3.** any wide separation, as in station, education, etc. **4.** something that engulfs or swallows up. —*v.t.* **5.** to swallow like a gulf, or as in a gulf; engulf. [ME *goulf*, t. OF: m. *golfe*, t. It.: m. *golfo*, t. LGk.: m. *kólphos*, Gk. *kólpos* bosom, gulf] —**gulf/like/,** *adj.*

Gulf States, those States of the U.S. bordering on the Gulf of Mexico: Florida, Alabama, Mississippi, Louisiana, and Texas.

Gulf Stream, a warm oceanic current issuing from the Gulf of Mexico, flowing northward along the U.S. coast and thence northeasterly toward the British Isles.

gulf·weed (gŭlf/wēd/), *n.* **1.** a coarse olive-brown seaweed, *Sargassum bacciferum*, found in the Gulf Stream and elsewhere, characterized by numerous berrylike air vessels. **2.** any seaweed related to it.

gull¹ (gŭl), *n.* any of numerous long-winged, web-footed, aquatic birds constituting the subfamily *Larinae* (family *Laridae*), esp. of the genus *Larus*, usually white with gray back and wings. [ME *gull(e)*, ? repr. OE word (unrecorded) akin to OE *giellan* yell]

gull² (gŭl), *v.t.* **1.** to deceive; trick; cheat. —*n.* **2.** one easily deceived or cheated; a dupe. [? akin to obs. *gull*, v., swallow, guzzle]

Herring gull. *Larus argentatus-smithsonianus* (22 to 25 in. long)

Gul·lah (gŭl/ə), *n.* **1.** a member of a Negro people settled as slaves on the sea islands and coastal region of Georgia and South Carolina. **2.** their English dialect.

gul·let (gŭl/ĭt), *n.* **1.** the esophagus, or tube by which food and drink swallowed pass to the stomach. **2.** the throat or pharynx. **3.** something like the gullet. **4.** a channel for water. **5.** a gully or ravine. **6.** a preparatory cut in excavations. [ME *golet*, t. OF: m. *goulet*, ult. der. L *gula* throat]

gul·li·ble (gŭl/ə bəl), *adj.* easily deceived or cheated. —**gul/li·bil/i·ty,** *n.* —**gul/li·bly,** *adv.*

Gul·li·ver's Travels (gŭl/ə vẽrz), a social and political satire (1726) by Swift, narrating the voyages of Lemuel Gulliver to four imaginary regions: Lilliput, Brobdingnag, Laputa, and the land of the Houyhnhnms.

gul·ly (gŭl/ĭ), *n., pl.* **-lies,** *v.,* **-lied, -lying.** —*n.* **1.** a small valley or canyon cut by running water. **2.** a ditch or gutter. —*v.t.* **3.** to make gullies in. **4.** to form (channels) by the action of water. [appar. var. of GULLET, with substitution of -Y³ for F -*et*]

gulp (gŭlp), *v.i.* **1.** to gasp or choke as when taking large drafts of liquids. —*v.t.* **2.** to swallow eagerly, or in large drafts or pieces (usually fol. by *down*). **3.** to take in, as by swallowing eagerly; choke back: *to gulp down a sob.* —*n.* **4.** act of gulping. **5.** the amount swallowed at one time; mouthful. [ME *gulpe(n)*. Cf. D *gulpen* gulp, Norw. *glupa* swallow] —**gulp/er,** *n.*

gum¹ (gŭm), *n., v.,* **gummed, gumming.** —*n.* **1.** any of various viscid, amorphous exudations from plants, hardening on exposure to air, and soluble in, or forming a viscid mass with, water. **2.** any of various similar exudations, as resin, gum resin, or the like. **3.** a preparation of such a substance, as for use in the arts, etc. **4.** chewing gum. **5.** mucilage; glue. **6.** rubber. **7.** a gum tree. **8.** *Philately.* See **original gum. 9.** (*usually pl.*) *U.S. Local.* a rubber overshoe. —*v.t.* **10.** to smear, stiffen, or stick together with gum. **11.** to clog with or as with some gummy substance. —*v.i.* **12.** to exude or form gum. **13.** to become gummy; become clogged with some gummy substance. [ME *gomme*, t. OF, g. var. of L *gummi*, t. Gk.: m. *kómmi*] —**gum/like/,** *adj.*

gum² (gŭm), *n.* (*often pl.*) the firm, fleshy tissue covering the alveolar parts of either jaw and enveloping the necks of the teeth. [ME *gome*, OE *gōma* palate, inside of the mouth; akin to Icel. *gōmr*, G *gaumen* palate]

gum ammoniac, a medicinal gum resin from the umbelliferous plant, *Dorema ammoniacum*, of Persia, India, etc.

gum arabic, a gum obtained from *Acacia Senegal* and other species of acacia: used in calico printing, in making mucilage, ink, and the like, in medicine, etc.

gum benzoin, a resin obtained from *Styrax Benzoin* in Siam, containing benzoic acid, vanillin, and essential oils, used in the perfume and cosmetic industries.

gum·bo (gŭm/bō), *n., pl.* **-bos. 1.** the okra plant. **2.** its mucilaginous pods. **3.** a soup, usually chicken, thickened with okra pods. **4.** a kind of silty soil in the southern and western U.S., becoming very sticky when wet. Also, **gombo.** [from Angola name]

gum boil (gŭm/boil/), *n.* a small abscess on the gum.

gum·bo·til (gŭm/bə tĭl/), *n. Geol.* a sticky clay formed by the thorough weathering of glacial drift, the thickness of the clay furnishing means for comparing relative lengths of interglacial ages.

gum·drop (gŭm/drŏp/), *n. U.S.* a droplike confection of gum arabic, gelatin, or the like, sweetened and flavored.

gum elastic, rubber.

gum·ma (gŭm/ə), *n., pl.* **gummata** (gŭm/ə tə), **gummas.** *Pathol.* the rubbery, tumorlike lesion of tertiary syphilis. [NL, der. L *gummi* GUM¹]

gum·ma·tous (gŭm/ə təs), *adj.* **1.** of the nature of or resembling a gumma. **2.** pertaining to a gumma.

gum·mite (gŭm/īt), *n.* a yellow to red alteration product of pitchblende, having a greasy luster, and occurring in gumlike masses, a minor ore of uranium.

gum·mo·sis (gŭ mō/sĭs), *n. Bot.* an abnormal condition of certain plants such as the cherry, plum, sugar cane, cotton, etc., which causes the excessive formation of gum. [NL, f. L *gumm*(i) + -OSIS. See GUM¹]

gum·my (gŭm/ĭ), *adj.,* **-mier, -miest. 1.** of the nature of gum; viscid. **2.** covered with or clogged by gum or sticky matter. **3.** exuding gum. —**gum/mi·ness,** *n.*

gum plant, a plant of the composite genus *Grindelia*, of the western U.S., covered with a viscid secretion.

gump·tion (gŭmp/shən), *n. Colloq.* **1.** initiative; resourcefulness. **2.** shrewd, practical sense. [orig. Scot.]

gum·shoe (gŭm/shōō/), *n., v.,* **-shoed, -shoeing.** —*n.* **1.** a shoe made of gum elastic or India rubber; rubber overshoe. **2.** (*pl.*) sneakers. **3.** *U.S. Slang.* **a.** one who goes about softly, as if wearing rubber shoes. **b.** a policeman or detective. —*v.i.* **4.** *U.S. Slang.* to go softly as if wearing rubber shoes; move or act stealthily.

gum tree, 1. any tree that exudes gum, as a eucalyptus, the sour gum, the sweet gum, etc. **2.** any of various other gum-yielding trees, as the tupelo, or the sapodilla.

gum·wood (gŭm/wŏŏd/), *n.* the wood of a gum tree, esp. the wood of the eucalyptus of Australia, or a gum tree of western U.S.

gun¹ (gŭn), *n., v.,* **gunned, gunning.** —*n.* **1.** a metallic tube, with its stock or carriage and attachments, from which heavy missiles are thrown by the force of gunpowder, etc.; a piece of ordnance. **2.** any portable firearm except a pistol or revolver, as a rifle. **3.** a long-barreled cannon, having a flat trajectory. **4.** *U.S. Colloq.* a pistol or revolver. **5.** any similar device for projecting something: *an air gun, cement gun.* **6.** *Brit.* a member of a shooting party. —*v.i.* **7.** to hunt with a gun. **8.** to shoot with a gun. **9.** to seek with intent to kill (fol. by *for*). **10.** to seek; try to obtain (fol. by *for*): *to gun for support.* —*v.t.* **11.** *U.S. Colloq.* to shoot with a gun. **12.** *Aviation Slang.* to cause to increase in speed very quickly. **13.** to feed gas to, suddenly and quickly: *to gun an engine.* [ME *gunne, gonne,* appar. short for *Gunilda* (L), *gonnyld* (ME), name for engine of war, ult. t. Scand.; cf. Icel. *Gunna,* short for *Gunnhildr,* woman's name] —**gun'less,** *adj.*

gun² (gŭn), *v.* *Archaic and Poetic.* pp. of **gin³.**

gun·boat (gŭn'bōt/), *n.* **1.** a small vessel carrying mounted guns. **2.** a small, armed war vessel of light draft, used for visiting shallow-water ports, etc.

gun carriage, the carriage or structure on which a gun is mounted or moved, and on which it is fired.

gun·cot·ton (gŭn'kŏt/ən), *n.* a highly explosive cellulose nitrate, made by digesting clean cotton in a mixture of 1 part nitric acid and 3 parts sulfuric acid.

gun dog, a trained dog which accompanies hunters when they shoot game, esp. game birds.

gun·fire (gŭn'fīr/), *n.* **1.** the firing of a gun or guns. **2.** *Mil.* the tactical use of firearms, esp. cannon, as distinguished from other weapons, as bayonets or torpedoes, and from shock or charge tactics.

gun·flint (gŭn'flĭnt/), *n.* the flint in a flintlock.

gung ho (gŭng'hō/), *Chinese.* work together (a U.S. Marine slogan of World War II).

gun·lock (gŭn'lŏk/), *n.* the mechanism of a firearm by which the charge is exploded.

gun·man (gŭn'mən), *n.,* *pl.* **-men.** **1.** *U.S.* a man armed with, or expert with, a gun, esp. one ready to use a gun unlawfully for hire. **2.** one who makes guns.

gun metal, 1. any of various alloys or metallic substances with a dark-gray or blackish color or finish, used for chains, belt buckles, etc. **2.** a dark gray with bluish or purplish tinge. **3.** a bronze formerly much employed for cannon. —**gun'-met/al,** *adj.*

Gun·nar (gŏōn'när), *n.* brother of Gudrun and husband of Brynhild in the *Völsunga Saga.* [Icel.]

gun·nel¹ (gŭn'əl), *n.* any of certain elongate blennies (fishes), esp. the butterfish, *Pholis gunnellus,* which is found in the northern Atlantic. [orig. uncert.]

gun·nel² (gŭn'əl), *n.* gunwale.

gun·ner (gŭn'ər), *n.* **1.** one who works a gun or cannon. **2.** *U.S. Army.* a rating in the artillery. **3.** *U.S. Navy.* a warrant officer having charge of the ordnance, etc., on a ship, or engaged in other duties. **4.** *Brit.* a man assigned to the artillery. **5.** a hunter with a gun.

gun·ner·y (gŭn'ər·ĭ), *n.* **1.** the art and science of constructing and managing guns, esp. large guns. **2.** the firing of guns. **3.** guns collectively.

gun·ning (gŭn'ĭng), *n.* **1.** act, practice, or art of shooting with guns. **2.** hunting of game with guns.

gun·ny (gŭn'ĭ), *n.,* *pl.* **-nies.** **1.** a strong, coarse material made commonly from jute, used for bagging, etc. **2.** Also, **gunny bag** or **sack.** a bag or sack made of this material. [t. Hind.: m. *gōni*]

gun·pa·per (gŭn'pā/pər), *n.* *Mil.* a type of paper treated with nitric acid so that it has a composition similar to that of guncotton.

gun·pow·der (gŭn'pou/dər), *n.* **1.** an explosive mixture of saltpeter (potassium nitrate), sulfur, and charcoal, used esp. in gunnery. **2.** a fine variety of green China tea, each leaf of which is rolled into a little ball.

Gunpowder Plot, *Eng. Hist.* an unsuccessful plot to blow up King James I, the Lords, and the Commons assembled in Parliament on Nov. 5, 1605 in revenge for the laws against Roman Catholics.

gun room, 1. a room in which guns are kept. **2.** *Brit.* a room for the use of junior naval officers.

gun·run·ning (gŭn'rŭn/ĭng), *n.* the smuggling of guns, etc., into a country. —**gun'run/ner,** *n.*

gun·shot (gŭn'shŏt/), *n.* **1.** a shot fired from a gun. **2.** the range of a gun: *out of gunshot.* **3.** the shooting of a gun. —*adj.* **4.** made by a gunshot.

gun-shy (gŭn'shī/), *adj.* frightened at gunshot.

gun·smith (gŭn'smĭth/), *n.* one who makes or repairs firearms.

gun·stock (gŭn'stŏk/), *n.* the stock or support in which the barrel of a shoulder weapon is fixed.

Gun·ter (gŭn'tər), *n.* **Edmund,** 1581–1626, British mathematician and inventor of the sector and scale.

Gun·ter's chain (gŭn'tərz), a surveyor's chain.

Gun·ther (gŏōn'tər), *n.* (in the Nibelungen epic) a Burgundian king, brother of Kriemhild and husband of Brunhild.

gun·wale (gŭn'əl), *n.* *Naut.* **1.** the upper edge of a vessel's or boat's side. **2.** the uppermost wale of a ship, next below the bulwarks. Also, **gunnel.** [f. GUN + *wale* a plank; so called because guns were set upon it]

gup·py (gŭp'ĭ), *n.,* *pl.* **-pies.** a live-bearing top minnow, *Lebistes reticulatus,* of the family Poeciliidae, commonly kept in household aquaria.

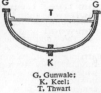

G. Gunwale;
K. Keel;
T. Thwart

gur·gi·ta·tion (gûr/jə·tā'shən), *n.* surging rise and fall; ebullient motion, as of water. [f. s. LL *gurgitātus,* pp., engulfed + -ION]

gur·gle (gûr'gəl), *v.,* **-gled, -gling,** *n.* —*v.i.* **1.** to flow in a broken, irregular, noisy current: *water gurgles from a bottle.* **2.** to make a sound as of water doing this (often used of birds or of human beings). —*v.t.* **3.** to utter with a gurgling sound. —*n.* **4.** act or noise of gurgling. [? imit. Cf. G *gurgeln* GARGLE] —**gur'gling·ly,** *adv.*

Gur·kha (gŏōr'kä), *n.* a member of a warlike Rajput people, Hindu in religion, living in Nepal.

gur·nard (gûr'nərd), *n.,* *pl.* **-nards,** (*esp. collectively*) **-nard.** **1.** any of various marine acanthopterygian fishes, esp. of the genus *Trigla* of Europe and the genus *Prionotus* of America, having a spiny head with mailed cheeks, and three pairs of free, fingerlike pectoral rays. **2.** See **flying gurnard.** any of various similar fishes. [ME, t. OF: m. *gornard,* prob. lit., grunter, der. Pr. *gourgna* grunt, ult. der. L *grunnīre* grunt]

gush (gŭsh), *v.i.* **1.** to issue with force, as a fluid from confinement; flow suddenly and copiously. **2.** *Colloq.* to express oneself extravagantly or emotionally; talk effusively. **3.** to have a copious flow of something, as of blood, tears, etc. —*v.t.* **4.** to emit suddenly, forcibly, or copiously. —*n.* **5.** a sudden and violent emission of a fluid. **6.** the fluid emitted. **7.** *Colloq.* gushing or effusive language. [ME *gusche,* ? ult. f. *gus-* (see GUST) + -*k,* suffix. Cf. Icel. *gusa*] —**gush'ing·ly,** *adv.* —**Syn. 1.** pour, stream, spurt, spout. See **flow.**

gush·er (gŭsh'ər), *n.* **1.** *Chiefly U.S.* a flowing oil well, usually of large capacity. **2.** a person who gushes.

gush·y (gŭsh'ĭ), *adj.,* **gushier, gushiest.** given to or marked by gush or effusiveness. —**gush'i·ness,** *n.*

gus·set (gŭs'ĭt), *n.* **1.** an angular piece of material inserted in a shirt, etc., usually under the armhole. **2.** a metallic plate used for connections, as in a steel truss connecting the members framing into a joint. **3.** *Armor.* **a.** mail strips in the armpit region sewn to cloth sleeves. **b.** a narrow articulated plate of breastplate adjacent to the arm. [ME, t. OF: m. *gousset,* der. *gousse* pod, husk]

gust (gŭst), *n.* **1.** a sudden, strong blast of wind. **2.** a sudden rush or burst of water, fire, smoke, sound, etc. **3.** an outburst of passionate feeling. [t. Scand.; cf. Icel. *gustr* a gust, blast, f. *gus-* (akin to *gjōsa, gusa* gush) + -*t,* suffix] —**Syn. 1.** See **wind¹.**

gus·ta·to·ry (gŭs'tə·tōr/ĭ), *adj.* of taste or tasting.

Gus·ta·vo A. Ma·de·ro (gŏōs·tä'vō, mä·dĕ'rō), official name of Guadalupe Hidalgo.

Gus·ta·vus I (gŭs·tā'vəs), (*Gustavus Vasa*) 1496–1560, king of Sweden, 1523–60.

Gustavus V, 1858–1950, king of Sweden, 1907–50.

Gustavus VI, born 1882, king of Sweden since 1950.

Gustavus A·dol·phus (ə·dŏl'fəs), 1594–1632, king of Sweden, 1611–32. Also, **Gustavus II.**

gus·to (gŭs'tō), *n.,* *pl.* **-tos.** **1.** keen relish or hearty enjoyment, as in eating, drinking, or in action or speech generally: *to tell a story with gusto.* **2.** individual taste or liking. [t. It., g. L *gustus* taste, relish]

gust·y (gŭs'tĭ), *adj.,* **gustier, gustiest.** **1.** blowing or coming in gusts, as wind, rain, storms, etc. **2.** affected or marked by gusts of wind, etc.: *gusty day.* **3.** occurring or characterized by sudden bursts or outbursts, as sound, laughter, etc. —**gust'i·ly,** *adv.* —**gust'i·ness,** *n.*

gut (gŭt), *n., v.,* **gutted, gutting.** —*n.* **1.** the alimentary canal between the pylorus and the anus, or some portion of it. **2.** (*pl.*) the bowels or entrails. **3.** (*pl.*) *Slang.* courage; stamina; endurance: *to have guts.* **4.** the substance forming the case of the intestine; intestinal tissue or fiber: *sheep's gut.* **5.** a preparation of the intestines of an animal used for various purposes, as for violin strings, tennis rackets, fishing lines, etc. **6.** the silken substance taken from a silkworm killed when about to spin its cocoon, used in making snells for fishhooks. **7.** a narrow passage, as a channel of water or a defile between hills. —*v.t.* **8.** to take out the guts or entrails of; disembowel. **9.** to plunder of contents. **10.** to destroy the interior of: *fire gutted the building.* [ME; OE *guttas,* pl., akin to *gēotan* pour] —**Syn. 3.** pluck.

gut·buck·et (gŭt'bŭk/ĭt), *adj.* *Jazz.* in a low-down, primitive style.

Gu·ten·berg (gŏō'tən·bûrg/; *Ger.* -bĕrкн), *n.* **Johannes** (yō·hän'ĕs), (*Johann Gensfleisch*) c1398–1468, German printer.

Gutenberg Bible, an edition of the Vulgate printed at Mainz before 1456, ascribed to Gutenberg and others: prob. the first large book printed with movable type.

Guth·rie (gŭth'rĭ), *n.* a city in central Oklahoma: the former state capital. 10,113 (1950).

gut·ta (gŭt'ə), *n., pl.* **guttae** (gŭt'ē). **1.** a drop, or something resembling one. **2.** *Archit.* one of a series of pendent ornaments, generally in the form of a frustum of a cone, attached to the under side of the mutules, etc. of the Doric entablature. [t. L: a drop]

gut·ta-per·cha (gŭt'ə·pûr'chə), *n.* the concrete milky juice, nearly white when pure, of various Malaysian sapotaceous trees, esp. *Palaquium Gutta,* variously used in the arts, medicine, and manufactures, as for insulating electric wires. [f. Malay: m. *getah* gum, balsam + *percha* kind of tree producing the substance]

gut·ter (gŭt'ər), *n.* **1.** a channel at the side (or in the middle) of a road or street, for leading off surface water. **2.** any channel, trough, or the like for carrying off fluid. **3.** a channel at the eaves or on the roof of a building, for carrying off rain water. **4.** a furrow or channel made by running water. **5.** the abode or resort of the lowest class of persons in the community: *the language of the gutter.* —*v.i.* **6.** to flow in streams: *the candles guttered down.* **7.** to form gutters, as water does. —*v.t.* **8.** to make gutters in; channel. **9.** to furnish with a gutter or gutters: *to gutter a house or shed.* [ME *goter*, t. OF: m. *goutiere*, ult. der. L *gutta* a drop] —**gut′ter·like′**, *adj.* —**gut′ter·y**, *adj.*

gut·ter·snipe (gŭt′ər·snīp′), *n.* *Colloq.* a street child of the lowest class; street Arab; gamin.

gut·tur·al (gŭt′ər·əl), *adj.* **1.** pertaining to the throat. **2.** harsh; throaty. **3.** *Phonet.* pertaining to sounds articulated in the back of the mouth, esp. the velars. —*n.* **4.** a guttural sound. [t. NL: s. *gutturālis*, der. L *guttur* throat] —**gut′tur·al·ly**, *adv.* —**gut′tur·al·ness**, *n.*

guy[1] (gī), *n.*, *v.*, **guyed, guying.** —*n.* **1.** *Slang.* a fellow or person: *he's a nice guy.* **2.** *Brit.* a person of grotesque appearance; a fright. **3.** a grotesque effigy of Guy Fawkes, the leader of the Gunpowder Plot, carried about and burned on Guy Fawkes Day. —*v.t.* **4.** *Slang.* to jeer at or make fun of; ridicule. [from *Guy Fawkes*]

guy[2] (gī), *n.*, *v.*, **guyed, guying.** —*n.* **1.** a rope or appliance used to guide and steady a thing being hoisted or lowered, or to secure anything liable to shift its position. —*v.t.* **2.** to guide, steady, or secure with a guy or guys. [ME *gye*, t. OF: m. *guie* a guide, der. *guier* GUIDE]

Guy·enne (gwē·yĕn′), *n.* Guienne.

Guy Fawkes Day (gī′ fôks′), *Brit.* Nov. 5, celebrated by fireworks, etc. See **Gunpowder Plot.**

guz·zle (gŭz′əl), *v.i.*, *v.t.*, **-zled, -zling.** to drink frequently and greedily. —**guz′zler**, *n.*

Gwa·li·or (gwä′lĭ·ôr′), *n.* **1.** a state in central India. 4,006,000 pop. (1941); 26,008 sq. mi. *Cap.:* Lashkar. **2.** a former town in the N part of this state, now a part of Lashkar: famous fort.

Gwyn (gwĭn), *n.* **Nell,** 1650–87, British actress and mistress of Charles II.

gybe (jīb), *v.i.*, *v.t.*, *n.* *Naut.* jibe[1].

gym (jĭm), *n.* gymnasium.

gym·kha·na (jĭm·kä′nə), *n.* *Chiefly Brit.* **1.** a series of athletic contests, esp. in racing. **2.** the place where this is held. [t. Hind.: m. *gendkhāna*, lit., ball house]

gym·na·si·a (jĭm·nā′zĭ·ə), *n.* pl. of gymnasium.

gym·na·si·arch (jĭm·nā′zĭ·ärk′), *n.* a magistrate who superintended the gymnasia and certain public games in ancient Athens. [t. L: s. *gymnasiarchus*, t. Gk.: m. *gymnasiarchos*]

gym·na·si·um (jĭm·nā′zĭ·əm), *n.*, *pl.* **-siums, -sia** (-zĭ·ə). **1.** a building or room designed and equipped for physical education activities. **2.** a place where Greek youths met for exercise and discussion. [t. L, t. Gk.: m. *gymnāsion* (see def. 2)]

Gym·na·si·um (jĭm·nā′zĭ·əm; *Ger.* gĭm·nä′zĭ·ŏŏm′, gĭm-), *n.* (in continental Europe, esp. Germany) a classical school preparatory to the universities. [G, t. L. See GYMNASIUM]

gym·nast (jĭm′năst), *n.* one trained and skilled in, or a teacher of, gymnastics. [t. Gk.: s. *gymnastēs* trainer of athletes]

gym·nas·tic (jĭm·năs′tĭk), *adj.* pertaining to exercises which develop flexibility, strength, and agility. —**gym·nas′ti·cal·ly**, *adv.*

gym·nas·tics (jĭm·năs′tĭks), *n.* **1.** (*construed as pl.*) gymnastic exercises. **2.** (*construed as sing.*) the practice or art of gymnastic exercises.

gym·no·sperm (jĭm′nə·spûrm′), *n.* *Bot.* a plant having its seeds exposed or naked, not enclosed in an ovary (opposed to *angiosperm*). [t. NL: s. *gymnospermus*, t. Gk.: m. *gymnóspermos*]

gym·no·sper·mous (jĭm′nə·spûr′məs), *adj.* *Bot.* of the gymnosperm class; having naked seeds.

gyn-, var. of gyno-, occurring before vowels, as in *gynarchy.*

gy·nae·ce·um (jĭ·nə·sē′əm, jĭn′ə-), *n.*, *pl.* **-cea** (-sē′ə). **1.** *Bot.* gynoecium. **2.** (among the Greeks) that part of a dwelling used by women. Also, **gy·nae·ci·um** (jĭ·nə·sī′əm, jĭn′ə-).

gy·nae·co·mor·phous (jĭ·nē′kō·môr′fəs, jĭn′ə·kō-), *adj.* gynecomorphous.

gy·nan·drous (jĭ·năn′drəs, jĭ-), *adj.* *Bot.* having the stamens borne on the pistil and united in a column, as in orchids. [t. Gk.: m. *gýnandros* of doubtful sex]

gy·nar·chy (jī′när·kĭ, jĭn′ər-), *n.*, *pl.* **-chies.** government by a woman or women.

gy·ne·ci·um (jĭ·nē′sĭ·əm, jĭ-), *n.*, *pl.* **-cia** (-sĭ′ə). gynoecium.

gy·ne·coc·ra·cy (jĭ·nə·kŏk′rə·sĭ, jĭn′ə-), *n.*, *pl.* **-cies.** government by a woman or women. Also, **gy′nae·coc′ra·cy.** [t. Gk.: m.s. *gynaikokratía*]

gy·ne·col·o·gy (gī′nə·kŏl′ə·jĭ, jĭ′nə-, jĭn′ə-), *n.* that department of medical science which deals with the functions and diseases peculiar to women. Also, **gy′nae·col′o·gy.** [f. m. Gk. *gynaiko-* (comb. form of *gynē* woman) + -LOGY] —**gy·ne·co·log·i·cal** (gī′nə·kə·lŏj′ə·kəl, jĭ′nə-, jĭn′ə-), *adj.* —**gy·ne·col′o·gist**, *n.*

gy·ne·co·mor·phous (jĭ·nē′kō·môr′fəs, jĭ-), *adj.* *Biol.* having the form, appearance, or attributes of a female. Also, **gynaecomorphous.** [t. Gk.: m. *gynai·kómorphos* in the shape of a woman]

gy·ne·pho·bi·a (jī′nə·fō′bĭ·ə, jĭn′ə-), *n.* a neurotic fear of women. [f. Gk. *gynē* woman + -PHOBIA]

gy·ni·at·rics (jĭ′nĭ·ăt′rĭks, jĭn′ĭ-), *n.* the treatment of diseases peculiar to women. [f. Gk. *gyn(ē)* woman + -IATRIC(S)]

gyno-, a word element meaning "woman," "female," as in *gynogenic.* Also, **gyn-.** [t. Gk., comb. form of *gynē* woman]

gy·noe·ci·um (jĭ·nē′sĭ·əm, jĭ-), *n.*, *pl.* **-cia** (-sĭ′ə). *Bot.* the pistil, or the pistils collectively, of a flower. Also, **gynaeceum, gynaecium, gynecium.** [t. NL, f. *gyn-* GYN- + m. Gk. *oikíon* house]

gy·no·gen·ic (jĭ′nə·jĕn′ĭk, jĭn′ə-), *adj.* *Embryol.* female-producing or feminizing (opposite to *androgenic*).

gy·no·phore (jĭ′nə·fōr′, jĭn′ə-), *n.* *Bot.* the elongated pedicel or stalk bearing the pistil in some flowers.

-gynous, 1. an adjective combining form referring to the female sex, as in *androgynous.* **2.** a suffix meaning "woman." [t. Gk.: m. *-gynos*, der. *gynē* woman]

gyp[1] (jĭp), *v.*, **gypped, gypping**, *n.* *U.S. Slang.* —*v.t.* **1.** to swindle; cheat; defraud or rob by some sharp practice. **2.** to obtain by swindling or cheating; steal. —*n.* **3.** a swindle. **4.** a swindler or cheat. Also, **gip.** [orig. uncert.] —**gyp′per**, *n.*

gyp[2] (jĭp), *n.* *Brit. Colloq.* a male college servant, as at Cambridge, England. [? short for GYPSY]

gyp·soph·i·la (jĭp·sŏf′ə·lə), *n.* any of the genus *Gypsophila* of slender, graceful herbs, chiefly Mediterranean, allied to the pinks and having small panicled flowers. [NL, f. Gk.: *gýpso(s)* chalk + *phíla*, neut. pl. of *phílos*, adj., fond of]

gyp·sum (jĭp′səm), *n.* a very common mineral, hydrated calcium sulfate, $CaSO_4 \cdot H_2O$, occurring in crystals and in masses, soft enough to be scratched by the fingernail: used to make plaster of Paris, as an ornamental material, as a fertilizer, etc. [t. L, t. Gk.: m. *gýpsos* chalk, gypsum]

Gyp·sy (jĭp′sĭ), *n.*, *pl.* **-sies. 1.** one of a nomadic Caucasian minority race of Hindu origin. **2.** Romany; the language of the Gypsies. **3.** (*l.c.*) a person who resembles or lives like a Gypsy. **4.** (*l.c.*) a gypsy winch. —*adj.* **5.** (*l.c.*) pertaining to the gypsies. Also, *esp. Brit.,* **Gipsy.** [back formation from *gipcyan*, aphetic var. of *Egyptian*] —**gyp′sy·like′**, *adj.*

gypsy moth, a moth, *Lymantria dispar*, introduced from Europe, whose caterpillar is destructive to trees.

gypsy winch, *Naut.* a small winch or crab.

gy·rate (*adj.* jī′rāt; *v.* jī′rāt, jī·rāt′), *v.*, **-rated, -rating,** *adj.* —*v.i.* **1.** to move in a circle or spiral, or around a fixed point; whirl. —*adj.* **2.** *Zool.* having convolutions. [t. L: m. s. *gyrātus*, pp., wheeled round, turned]

gy·ra·tion (jī·rā′shən), *n.* act of gyrating; circular or spiral motion; revolution; rotation; whirling.

gy·ra·to·ry (jī′rə·tōr′ĭ), *adj.* moving in a circle or spiral; gyrating.

gyre (jīr), *n.* *Poetic.* **1.** a ring or circle. **2.** a circular course or motion.

gyr·fal·con (jûr′fôl′kən, -fô′kən), *n.* gerfalcon.

gy·ro (jī′rō), *n.*, *pl.* **-ros. 1.** gyrocompass. **2.** gyroscope. [short for GYROCOMPASS, GYROSCOPE]

gyro-, a word element meaning: **1.** "ring"; "circle." **2.** "spiral." [t. Gk., comb. form of *gŷros* ring, circle]

gy·ro·com·pass (jī′rō·kŭm′pəs), *n.* a device used like the ordinary compass for determining directions, but employing a continuously driven gyroscope instead of a magnetized needle or bar, the gyroscope being so mounted that its axis constantly maintains its position with reference to the geographical north, thus dealing with true geographical meridians used in navigation instead of magnetic meridians.

gy·ro·plane (jī′rō·plān′), *n.* an airplane having lifting airfoils arranged in vanes rotated by the forward motion of the craft.

gy·ro·scope (jī′rə·skōp′), *n.* an apparatus consisting of a rotating wheel so mounted that its axis can turn freely in certain or all directions, and capable of maintaining the same absolute direction in space in spite of movements of the mountings and surrounding parts. It is based on the principle that a body rotating steadily about an axis will tend to resist changes in the direction of the axis, and is used to maintain equilibrium, as in an airplane or ship, to determine direction, etc. [t. F. See GYRO-, -SCOPE] —**gy·ro·scop·ic** (jī′rə·skŏp′ĭk), *adj.*

Gyroscope

gy·ro·sta·bi·liz·er (jī′rō·stā′bə·lī′zər), *n.* a device for stabilizing a seagoing vessel by counteracting its rolling motion from side to side, consisting essentially of a rotating gyroscope weighing about 1 per cent of the displacement of the vessel.

gy·ro·stat (jī′rə·stăt′), *n.* a modification of the gyroscope, consisting of a rotating wheel pivoted within a rigid case.

gy·ro·stat·ic (jī′rə·stăt′ĭk), *adj.* pertaining to the gyrostat or to gyrostatics. —**gy·ro·stat′i·cal·ly**, *adv.*

gy·ro·stat·ics (jī′rə·stăt′ĭks), *n.* *Mech.* the science which deals with the laws of rotating bodies.

gy·rus (jī′rəs), *n.*, *pl.* **gyri** (jī′rī). *Anat.* a convolution, esp. of the brain. [t. L, t. Gk.: m. *gŷros* ring, circle]

gyve (jīv), *n.*, *v.*, **gyved, gyving.** —*n.* **1.** (*usually pl.*) a shackle, esp. for the leg; fetter. —*v.t.* **2.** to shackle. [ME *gives, gyves* (pl.); orig. uncert.]

H

H, h (āch), n., pl. **H's** or **Hs, h's** or **hs. 1.** a consonant, the 8th letter of the English alphabet. **2.** (as a symbol) the eighth in a series. **3.** Med. Roman Numerals. 200.

H, 1. Elect. henry. **2.** Chem. hydrogen. **3.** Physics. intensity of magnetic field.

h., 1. harbor. **2.** hard. **3.** hardness. **4.** height. **5.** high. **6.** Baseball. hits. **7.** hour. **8.** husband.

ha (hä), interj. an exclamation of surprise, interrogation, suspicion, triumph, etc. Also, **hah.**

ha., hectare.

h. a., (L hoc anno) in this year.

Haa·kon VII (hô′kŏŏn), born 1872, king of Norway since 1905; exiled in England, 1940–45.

Haar·lem (här′ləm), n. a city in W Netherlands, W of Amsterdam. 150,773 (est. 1946).

Hab., Habakkuk.

Ha·bak·kuk (hə băk′ək, hăb′ə kŭk′), n. **1.** a Hebrew prophet and poet. **2.** his book of prophecies, the eighth of the minor prophets of the Old Testament.

Ha·ba·na (ä bä′nä), n. Spanish name of Havana.

ha·be·as cor·pus (hā′bĭ əs kôr′pəs), Law. a writ requiring the body of a person to be brought before a judge or court, esp. for investigation of a restraint of the person's liberty. [t. L: you may have the body]

hab·er·dash·er (hăb′ər dăsh′ər), n. **1.** U.S. a dealer in men's furnishings, as shirts, ties, gloves, etc. **2.** Chiefly Brit. a dealer in small wares, as buttons, needles, etc. [orig. obscure. Cf. Anglo-F hapertas kind of fabric]

hab·er·dash·er·y (hăb′ər dăsh′ər ĭ), n., pl. **-eries. 1.** a haberdasher's shop. **2.** the goods sold there.

hab·er·geon (hăb′ər jən), n. **1.** a short hauberk. **2.** any hauberk. Also, **haubergeon.** [ME haubergeon, t. OF, dim. of hauberc HAUBERK]

hab·ile (hăb′ĭl), adj. skillful; dexterous. [t. F, t. L: m. habilis fit, apt]

ha·bil·i·ment (hə bĭl′ə mənt), n. **1.** (pl.) clothes or garments. **2.** dress; attire. [ME habylement, t. OF: m. habillement, der. habiller dress, der. habile (see HABILE)] —**ha·bil′i·ment′ed,** adj.

ha·bil·i·tate (hə bĭl′ə tāt′), v.t., **-tated, -tating. 1.** Western U.S. to furnish money or means to work (a mine). **2.** Rare. to clothe or dress. [t. ML: m.s. habilitātus, pp. of habilitāre, der. L habilitas ability]

hab·it (hăb′ĭt), n. **1.** a disposition or tendency, constantly shown, to act in a certain way. **2.** such a disposition acquired by frequent repetition of an act. **3.** a particular practice, custom, or usage: the habit of smoking. **4.** customary practice or use: to act from force of habit. **5.** the mental character or disposition: habit of mind. **6.** characteristic bodily or physical condition: habit of body. **7.** the characteristic form, aspect, mode of growth, etc., of an animal or plant: a twining habit. **8.** garb of a particular rank, profession, religious order, etc.: monk's habit. **9.** a woman's riding dress. —v.t. **10.** to clothe; array. **11.** Obs. to dwell in. —v.i. **12.** Obs. to dwell. [t. L: s. habitus condition, appearance, dress; r. ME abit, t. OF] —**Syn. 2.** See custom.

hab·it·a·ble (hăb′ə tə bəl), adj. capable of being inhabited. —**hab′it·a·bil′i·ty, hab′it·a·ble·ness,** n. —**hab′it·a·bly,** adv.

hab·it·ant (hăb′ə tənt; for 2 also Fr. à bē tän′), n. **1.** an inhabitant. **2.** a French settler in Canada or Louisiana, or a descendant of one, esp. one of the farming class. [late ME, t. F, t. L: s. habitans, ppr., dwelling]

hab·i·tat (hăb′ə tăt′), n. **1.** the kind of place where a given animal or plant naturally lives or grows, as warm seas, mountain tops, fresh waters, etc. **2.** place of abode; habitation. [t. L: it inhabits]

hab·i·ta·tion (hăb′ə tā′shən), n. **1.** a place of abode; dwelling. **2.** act of inhabiting; occupancy by inhabitants. —**Syn. 1.** residence, domicile, quarters.

ha·bit·u·al (hə bĭch′ŏŏ əl), adj. **1.** of the nature of a habit, or fixed by or resulting from habit: habitual courtesy. **2.** being such by habit: a habitual drunkard. **3.** commonly used (by a given person): she took her habitual place at the table. [t. LL: s. habituālis] —**ha·bit′u·al·ly,** adv. —**ha·bit′u·al·ness,** n. —**Syn. 2.** confirmed, inveterate. **3.** See usual. —**Ant. 2.** occasional. **3.** unaccustomed.

ha·bit·u·ate (hə bĭch′ŏŏ āt′), v.t., **-ated, -ating. 1.** to accustom (a person, the mind, etc.), as to something; make used (to). **2.** U.S. Colloq. to frequent. [t. LL: m.s. habituātus, pp. of habituāre bring into a condition, der. L habitus HABIT] —**ha·bit′u·a′tion,** n. —**Syn. 1.** familiarize; inure, harden, acclimatize, acclimate.

hab·i·tude (hăb′ə tūd′, -tŏŏd′), n. **1.** customary condition, character, or habit. **2.** Rare. a habit or custom. **3.** Obs. relationship. [t. F, t. L: m. habitūdo condition]

ha·bit·u·é (hə bĭch′ŏŏ ā′; Fr. à bē twē′), n. a habitual frequenter of a place. [ME, pp. of habituer HABITUATE]

Habs·burg (hăps′bûrg; Ger. häps′bŏŏrкн), n. Hapsburg.

ha·chure (n. hă shŏŏr′, hăsh′ŏŏr; v. hă shŏŏr′), n., v., **-chured, -churing.** —n. **1.** (in drawing, engraving, etc.) hatching. **2.** (on a map) shading used to indicate relief features, consisting of lines drawn parallel to the slopes and varying in width with the degree of slope. —v.t. **3.** to mark or shade with, or indicate by, hachures. [t. F, der. hacher HATCH³]

ha·ci·en·da (hä′sĭ ĕn′də; Sp. ä syĕn′dä), n. Spanish American. **1.** a landed estate; country house. **2.** a stock-raising, mining, or manufacturing establishment in the country. [t. Sp.: landed property, estate, g. L facienda things to be done, neut. pl. ger. of facere do]

hack¹ (hăk), v.t. **1.** to cut, notch, or chop irregularly, as with heavy blows. **2.** to break up the surface of (the ground). **3.** Basketball. to strike the arm of (a player). **4.** to kick the shins of intentionally, as in Rugby football. —v.i. **5.** to make rough cuts or notches; deal cutting blows. **6.** to emit short, frequently repeated coughs. **7.** to kick an opponent's shins intentionally, as in Rugby football. —n. **8.** a cut, gash, or notch. **9.** a tool, as an ax, hoe, pick, etc., for hacking. **10.** an act of hacking; a cutting blow. **11.** a short, broken cough. **12.** a hesitation in speech. **13.** Basketball. a personal foul. **14.** Brit. a gash in the skin produced by a kick, as in Rugby football. [ME hacke(n), OE (tō)hac̄ian hack to pieces, c. D hakken, G hacken] —**hack′er,** n. —**Syn. 1.** See cut.

hack² (hăk), n. **1.** Brit. a horse kept for common hire, or adapted for general work, esp. ordinary riding. **2.** Brit. a saddle horse for the road. **3.** an old or worn-out horse; a jade. **4.** a person who hires himself out for general work, esp. literary work. **5.** U.S. a coach or carriage kept for hire; a hackney. **6.** Colloq. a taxi. —v.t. **7.** to make a hack of; let out for hire. **8.** to make trite or stale by frequent use; hackney. —v.i. **9.** Brit. to ride on the road at an ordinary pace, as distinguished from cross-country or military riding. **10.** Colloq. to drive a taxi. —adj. **11.** hired; of a hired sort: hack work. **12.** hackneyed; trite. [short for HACKNEY]

hack·a·more (hăk′ə mōr′), n. **1.** a coil of rope which passes through the horse's mouth and about his neck, used to break a horse. **2.** Western U.S. any of several forms of halter used esp. for breaking horses.

hack·ber·ry (hăk′bĕr′ĭ), n., pl. **-ries. 1.** the small, edible, cherrylike fruit of American trees of the ulmaceous genus Celtis. **2.** a tree bearing this fruit. **3.** its wood. [var. of HAGBERRY]

hack·but (hăk′bŭt), n. harquebus. [t. MF: m. haquebute, b. buter to butt and MF haquebusche (t. MD: m. hakebus, lit., a hook gun)]

Hack·en·sack (hăk′ən săk′), n. a city in NE New Jersey, near New York City. 29,219 (1950).

hack hammer, an adzlike tool for dressing stone.

hack·le¹ (hăk′əl), n., v., **-led, -ling.** —n. **1.** one of the long, slender feathers on the neck or saddle of certain birds, as the domestic rooster, much used in making artificial flies for anglers. **2.** the whole neck plumage of the domestic rooster, etc. **3.** Angling. **a.** an artificial fly's legs made with hackles (def. 1). **b.** a hackle fly. **4.** a comb for dressing flax or hemp. —v.t. **5.** Angling. to supply with a hackle. **6.** to comb, as flax or hemp. [ME hakell. See HECKLE] —**hack′ler,** n.

hack·le² (hăk′əl), v.t., **-led, -ling.** to cut roughly; hack; mangle. [freq. of HACK¹, c. MD hakkelen]

hack·le·back (hăk′əl băk′), n. the shovel-nosed sturgeon, Scaphirhynchus platorynchus, of the Mississippi Valley.

hackle fly, an artificial fly made with hackles, usually without wings.

hack·ly (hăk′lĭ), adj. rough or jagged. [f. HACKLE² + -Y¹]

hack·man (hăk′mən, -măn′), n., pl. **-men** (-mən, -mĕn′). U.S. the driver of a hack.

hack·ma·tack (hăk′mə tăk′), n. **1.** the tamarack, Larix laricina, an American larch. **2.** its wood. [t. N Amer. Ind.]

hack·ney (hăk′nĭ), n., pl. **-neys,** adj., v., **-neyed, -neying.** —n. **1.** a horse for ordinary riding or driving. **2.** a horse kept for hire. **3.** a carriage kept for hire. —adj. **4.** let out, employed, or done for hire. —v.t.

5. to make common, stale, or trite by frequent use. **6.** to use as a hackney. [ME *hakeney;* orig. uncert.]

hack·neyed (hăk′nĭd), *adj.* **1.** made commonplace or trite; stale. **2.** habituated. —**Syn. 1.** See **commonplace.**

hack·saw (hăk′sô′), *n.* a saw used for cutting metal, consisting typically of a narrow, fine-toothed blade fixed in a frame.

Hacksaw

had (hăd), *v.* pt. and pp. of **have.**

Had·ding·ton (hăd′ĭng tən), *n.* former name of **East Lothian.**

had·dock (hăd′ək), *n., pl.* **-docks,** (*esp. collectively*) **-dock. 1.** a food fish, *Melanogrammus aeglefinus,* of the northern Atlantic, related to but smaller than the cod. **2.** the rosefish. [ME *haddoc;* orig. unknown]

hade (hād), *n., v.,* **haded, hading.** *Geol.* —*n.* **1.** the angle between a fault plane and a vertical plane striking parallel to the fault. —*v.i.* **2.** to incline from a vertical position. [orig. uncert.]

Ha·des (hā′dēz), *n.* **1.** *Gk. Myth.* **a.** the gloomy subterranean abode of departed spirits or shades over which Pluto ruled. **b.** Pluto; the lord of the underworld. **2.** (in the Revised Version of the New Testament) the abode or state of the dead. **3.** (*l.c.*) *Colloq.* hell. [t. Gk.: m. *Haídēs* (orig. *aídēs*)] —**Ha·de·an** (hā dē′ən, hā′dĭ ən), *adj.*

Had·field (hăd′fēld′), *n.* **Sir Robert Abbott,** 1858–1940, British scientist and metallurgist.

Ha·dhra·maut (hä′drä môt′), *n.* a region along the S coast of the Arabian peninsula, in the Aden protectorate. Also, **Ha′dra·maut′.**

hadj (hăj), *n.* hajj.

hadj·i (hăj′ĭ), *n., pl.* **hadjis.** hajji.

Had·ley (hăd′lĭ), *n.* **Henry Kimball,** 1871–1937, U.S. composer.

Ha·dri·an (hā′drĭ ən), *n.* A.D. 76–138, Roman emperor, A.D. 117–138. Also, **Adrian.**

Hadrian's Wall, a wall of defense for the Roman province of Britain, constructed by Hadrian between Solway Firth and the mouth of the Tyne.

hae (hā, hă), *v.t. Scot.* have.

Haeck·el (hĕk′əl), *n.* **Ernest Heinrich** (ĕrnst hīn′-rĭKH), 1834–1919, German biologist and philosopher.

Hadrian's Wall in A.D. 410

haem-, *var.* of **hem-.** For words beginning in **haem-, haema-, haemo-,** see preferred spelling under **hem-, hema-, hemo-.**

hae·ma·tox·y·lin (hē′ma tŏk′sə lən, hĕm′ə-), *n.* **1.** a leguminous plant of a genus *Haematoxylon,* of which only one species, *H. campechianum,* the logwood tree, is known. **2.** the wood of the logwood. **3.** the dyestuff, hematoxylin. [f. s. NL *haematoxylum* logwood (f. Gk.: *haimato-* HEMATO- + m. *xŷlon* wood) + -IN²]

-haemia, *var.* of **-emia.**

haemo-, *var.* of **hemo-.** Also, **haem-.** For words beginning in **haemo-,** see preferred spelling under **hemo-.**

hae·res (hĭr′ēz), *n., pl.* **haeredes** (hĭ rē′dēz). heres.

ha·fiz (hä′fĭz), *n.* a title of a Mohammedan who knows the Koran by heart. [t. Ar.: *ḥāfiz* a guard, one who keeps (in memory)]

Ha·fiz (hä fĭz′), *n.* died c1389, Persian poet.

haf·ni·um (hăf′nĭ əm, häf′-), *n. Chem.* a metallic element with a valence of four, found in zirconium ores. *Symbol:* Hf; *at. wt.:* 178.6; *at. no.:* 72; *sp. gr.:* 12.1. [f. *Hafn(ia),* L name of Copenhagen + -IUM]

haft (hăft, häft), *n.* **1.** a handle, esp. of a knife, sword, dagger, etc. —*v.t.* **2.** to furnish with a haft or handle; set in a haft. [ME; OE *hæft,* c. D and G *heft*]

haf·ta·rah (häf′tä rä′, häf tôr′ä), *n.* haphtarah.

hag¹ (hăg), *n.* **1.** a repulsive, often vicious or malicious, old woman. **2.** a witch. **3.** a hagfish. [ME *hagge, hegge;* appar. a familiar short form (with hypocoristic gemination) of OE *hægtesse* fury, witch; akin to G *hexe* witch] —**hag′like′,** *adj.*

hag² (hăg, häg), *n. Scot. and Dial.* **1.** a soft spot in boggy land. **2.** a firm spot in a bog. [ME *hag* chasm, t. Scand.; cf. Icel. *högg* a cut, ravine]

Hag., *var.* of **Haggai.**

Ha·gar (hā′gär, -gər), *n. Bible.* Egyptian concubine of Abraham, mother of Ishmael. Gen. 16.

hag·ber·ry (hăg′bĕr′ĭ), *n., pl.* **-ries.** the American hackberry. [t. Scand.; cf. Dan. *hæggebær*]

hag·but (hăg′bŭt), *n.* harquebus.

hag·don (hăg′dən), *n.* any of various oceanic birds along the North Atlantic coasts of Europe and America, esp. the greater shearwater, *Puffinus gravis.*

Ha·gen (hä′gən), *n.* (in the Nibelungenlied) the slayer of Siegfried. [G, c. OE *Hagena*]

Ha·gers·town (hā′gərz toun′), *n.* a city in NW Maryland. 36,260 (1950).

hag·fish (hăg′fĭsh′), *n., pl.* **-fishes,** (*esp. collectively*) **-fish.** any of the eellike marine cyclostomes constituting the group or order *Hyperotreta,* notable esp. for their circular suctorial mouth and their habit of boring into the bodies of fishes.

Hag·ga·da (hə gä′də), *n., pl.* **-doth** (-dōth). Haggadah.

Hag·ga·dah (hə gä′də), *n., pl.* **-doth** (-dōth). *Jewish Lit.* **1.** the nonlegal part of Jewish traditional literature. **2.** the free exposition or illustration, chiefly homiletic, of the scripture. **3.** the ritual used on the first two nights of Passover. **4.** a book containing it. [t. Heb.: (m.) *haggādāh* narrative, der. *higgīd* tell] —**hag·gad·ic** (hə găd′ĭk, -gä′dĭk), **hag·gad′i·cal,** *adj.*

hag·ga·dist (hə gä′dĭst), *n.* **1.** a writer of Haggadoth. **2.** a student of the Haggadah. —**hag·ga·dis·tic** (hăg′ə dĭs′tĭk), *adj.*

Atlantic hagfish *Myxine glutinosa* (1½ ft. long)

Hag·ga·i (hăg′ī ′, hăg′ī), *n.* **1.** fl. B.C. 520, the tenth of the minor prophets of Israel. **2.** his book in the Old Testament.

hag·gard (hăg′ərd), *adj.* **1.** wild-looking, as from prolonged suffering, anxiety, exertion, want, etc.; careworn; gaunt. **2.** *Falconry.* wild or untamed, esp. of a hawk caught after it has assumed adult plumage. [orig. uncert. Cf. F *hagard* (? t. E)] —**hag′gard·ly,** *adv.* —**hag′gard·ness,** *n.* —**Syn. 1.** emaciated, drawn; hollow-eyed. —**Ant. 1.** unstrained.

Hag·gard (hăg′ərd), *n.* **Henry Rider,** 1856–1925, British novelist.

hagged (hăgd, hăg′ĭd), *adj. Dial.* **1.** haglike. **2.** haggard.

hag·gis (hăg′ĭs), *n. Chiefly Scot.* a dish made of the heart, liver, etc., of a sheep, etc., minced with suet and oatmeal, seasoned, and boiled in the stomach of the animal. [? f. *hag* chop + *es,* OE *æs* food, meat]

hag·gish (hăg′ĭsh), *adj.* of or like a hag; old and ugly. —**hag′gish·ly,** *adv.* —**hag′gish·ness,** *n.*

hag·gle (hăg′əl), *v.,* **-gled, -gling,** *n.* —*v.i.* **1.** to bargain in a petty and tedious manner. **2.** to wrangle, dispute, or cavil. —*v.t.* **3.** to harass with wrangling or haggling. **4.** to mangle in cutting; hack. —*n.* **5.** act of haggling; wrangle or dispute over terms. [freq. of d. *hag,* v., cut, hew, hack, t. Scand.; cf. Icel. *höggva* strike, hack, c. OE *hēawan* hew] —**hag′gler,** *n.* —**Syn. 1.** chaffer, higgle; negotiate.

hagio-, a word element meaning "saint." Also, **hagi-.** [t. Gk., comb. form of *hágios* sacred, holy]

hag·i·oc·ra·cy (hăg′ĭ ŏk′rə sĭ, hā′jĭ-), *n., pl.* **-cies.** government by a body of persons esteemed as holy.

Hag·i·og·ra·pha (hăg′ĭ ŏg′rə fə, hā′jĭ-), *n. pl.* the third of the three Jewish divisions of the Old Testament, variously arranged, but usually comprising the Psalms, Proverbs, Job, Canticles, Ruth, Lamentations, Ecclesiastes, Esther, Daniel, Ezra, Nehemiah, and Chronicles. [t. LL, f., Gk.: *hagio-* HAGIO- + *grapha* (for *gráphia*) writings]

hag·i·og·ra·pher (hăg′ĭ ŏg′rə fər, hā′jĭ-), *n.* **1.** one of the writers of the Hagiographa. **2.** a writer of lives of the saints; a hagiologist. Also, **hag′i·og′ra·phist.**

hag·i·og·ra·phy (hăg′ĭ ŏg′rə fĭ, hā′jĭ-), *n., pl.* **-phies.** the writing and critical study of the lives of the saints; hagiology. —**hag·i·o·graph·ic** (hăg′ĭ ə grăf′ĭk, hā′jĭ-), **hag·i·o·graph′i·cal,** *adj.*

hag·i·ol·a·try (hăg′ĭ ŏl′ə trĭ, hā′jĭ-), *n.* the veneration of saints. [f. HAGIO- + -*latry* (see LATRIA)] —**hag′-i·ol′a·ter,** *n.* —**hag′i·ol′a·trous,** *adj.*

hag·i·ol·o·gy (hăg′ĭ ŏl′ə jĭ, hā′jĭ-), *n., pl.* **-gies. 1.** that branch of literature which deals with the lives and legends of the saints. **2.** a work on these. **3.** a collection of such lives or legends. —**hag·i·o·log·ic** (hăg′ĭ ə lŏj′ĭk, hā′jĭ-), **hag′i·o·log′i·cal,** *adj.* —**hag′i·ol′o·gist,** *n.*

hag·rid·den (hăg′rĭd′ən), *adj.* worried or tormented, as by a witch.

Hague (hāg), *n.* **The,** a city in W Netherlands, near the North Sea: seat of the government, royal residence, and Permanent Court of International Justice. 482,840 (est. 1946). Dutch, **'s Graven-hage.**

Hague Tribunal, The, the permanent court of arbitration for the peaceful settlement of international disputes, established at The Hague by the international peace conference of 1899, whose panel of jurists nominate a list of persons from which members of the United Nations International Court of Justice are elected.

hah (hä), *interj.* ha.

ha-ha¹ (hä′hä′), *interj., n.* an imitation of the sound of laughter.

ha-ha² (hä′hä′), *n.* a barrier consisting of a trench or ditch; a sunk fence. [t. F: m. *haha*]

Hahn (hän), *n.* **Otto** (ŏt′ō), born 1879, German physicist.

Hah·ne·mann (hä′nə mən; *Ger.* -män′), *n.* **Samuel** (săm′yŏŏ əl; *Ger.* zä′mŏŏ ĕl′), (*Christian Fredrich Samuel*) 1755–1843, German physician: founder of homeopathy. —**Hah·ne·mann·i·an** (hä′nə män′ĭən, -mä′nĭ-), *adj.* —**Hah′ne·mann·ism,** *n.*

Hai·da (hī′də), *n.* **1.** an American Indian language of southeastern Alaska. 2. a linguistic stock of the Na-Dene phylum, including Haida.

Hai·dar A·li (hī′dər ä′lē, ä′lē′), Hyder Ali.

Hai·duk (hī′dŏŏk), n. 1. one of a class of mercenary soldiers in 16th century Hungary. 2. a patriotic brigand in the Slav portions of the Balkan Peninsula. 3. a male servant or attendant dressed in Hungarian semimilitary costume. Also, **Heyduck, Heyduke, Heyduc, Heiduc, Heiduk.** [repr. Hung. *hajduk* (pl. of *hajdu*) kind of foot soldiers, and Polish *hajduk* retainers, ult. t. Turk.: m. *haidud* marauder, brigand]

Hai·fa (hī′fə), n. a seaport in NW Israel. 128,800 (est. 1944).

Haig (hāg), n. **Douglas, 1st Earl,** 1861–1928, British field marshal: commander in chief of the British forces in France from 1915–18.

haik (hīk, hāk), n. an oblong cloth used as an outer garment by the Arabs. [t. Ar.: m. *hayk,* der. *hāk* weave]

hai·kwan (hī′kwän′), n. maritime customs in China. [t. Chinese (Mandarin): f. *hai* sea + *kuan* gateway]

haikwan tael (tāl), 1. the customs unit in China, which is the basis for other local taels, equal to 1.20666 troy ounces of fine silver. 2. a liang.

hail[1] (hāl), v.t. 1. to salute or greet; welcome. 2. to salute or name as: *to hail one victor.* 3. to call out to, in order to attract attention: *to hail a person.* —v.i. 4. to call out in order to greet, attract attention, etc. 5. **hail from,** to belong to as the place of residence, point of departure, etc. —n. 6. a shout or call to attract attention. 7. act of hailing. 8. a salutation or greeting. 9. **within hail,** within reach of the voice. —interj. 10. *Poetic and Literary.* an exclamation of salutation or greeting. [ME *haile(n),* der. obs. *hail,* n. and adj.; health(y), t. Scand.; cf. Icel. *heill* health, healthy, c. OE *hǣl* (n.), *hāl* (adj.). Cf. WASSAIL] —**hail′er,** n.

hail[2] (hāl), n. 1. pellets or small, usually rounded, masses of ice falling from the clouds in a shower. 2. a shower or storm of such masses. 3. a shower of anything: *a hail of bullets.* —v.i. 4. to pour down hail; fall as hail. —v.t. 5. to pour down as or like hail. [ME *hail(e),* OE *hægl,* c. D and G *hagel*]

Hai·le Se·las·sie (hī′lĭ′ səläs′ĭ, -läs′ĭ), born 1890, emperor of Ethiopia, 1930–36 and since 1941; exiled in England, 1936–41.

hail fellow, on familiar terms: often in the form *hail fellow well met.*

Hail Mary, Ave Maria.

hail·stone (hāl′stōn′), n. a pellet of hail. [ME, f. HAIL[2] + STONE; r. ME *hawelstone,* OE *hagolstān*]

hail·storm (hāl′stôrm′), n. a storm with hail.

Hai·nan (hī′nän′), n. an island in the South China Sea, separated from the mainland of S China by **Hainan Strait** (15 mi. wide): a part of Kwangtung province. ab. 2,500,000 pop.; ab. 13,200 sq. mi.

Hai·naut (ĕnō′), n. a medieval county in territory now in SW Belgium and N France.

hain't (hānt), contraction of *have not* or *has not* (not regarded as good usage).

Hai·phong (hī′fŏng′), n. a seaport in NE French Indo-China, in Viet Nam, near the Gulf of Tonkin. 70,000 (1936).

hair (hâr), n. 1. the natural covering of the human head. 2. the aggregate of hairs which grow on an animal. 3. one of the numerous fine, usually cylindrical filaments growing from the skin and forming the coat of most mammals. 4. a similar fine, filamentous outgrowth from the body of insects, etc. 5. *Bot.* a filamentous outgrowth of the epidermis. 6. cloth made of hair from such animals as camel and alpaca. 7. a very small magnitude, measure, degree, etc.: *he lost the race by a hair.* 8. **split hairs,** to make fine or unnecessary distinctions. [ME *ha(i)re,* t. Scand. (cf. Icel. *hār*); r. ME *her*(e), OE *hǣr,* c. D and G *haar*] —**hair′like′,** adj.

Section of skin, showing the roots of two hairs (highly magnified): A. Cuticle; B, Deeper root parts of skin; C, A hair; D, Erecting muscle; E, Sebaceous glands

Hairs (highly magnified) Longitudinal section: A, Man; B, Sable; C, Mouse. External view: D, Mouse; E, Indian bat

hair·breadth (hâr′brĕdth′), n., adj. hair's-breadth.

hair·brush (hâr′brŭsh′), n. a brush for dressing the hair.

hair·cloth (hâr′klôth′, -klŏth′), n. cloth woven of hair from horses' tails and manes with cotton warp for interlinings of clothes, etc.

hair·cut (hâr′kŭt′), n. act or style of cutting the hair.

hair·do (hâr′dōō′), n., pl. **-dos.** 1. any method of arranging a woman's hair. 2. hair so dressed.

hair·dress·er (hâr′drĕs′ər), n. one who arranges or cuts hair, esp. women's hair. —**hair′dress′ing,** n., adj.

hair follicle, *Anat.* a small cavity from which a hair develops.

hair·less (hâr′lĭs), adj. without hair; bald. —**hair′-less·ness,** n.

hair·line (hâr′līn′), n. 1. a very slender line. 2. worsted fabric woven with very fine lines or stripes. 3. *Print.* a. a very thin line on the face of a type. b. a style of type consisting entirely of such lines.

hair·pin (hâr′pĭn′), n. 1. a slender U-shaped piece of wire, shell, etc. used by women to fasten up the hair or hold a headdress. —adj. 2. (of a road, track, etc.) doubling back in a U-shape.

hair·rais·ing (hâr′rā′zĭng), adj. terrifying.

hair's-breadth (hârz′brĕdth′), n. 1. a very small space or distance. —adj. 2. extremely narrow or close. Also, **hairs′breadth′, hairbreadth.**

hair seal, any of various seals with coarse hair and no soft underlying fur (distinguished from *fur seal*).

hair shirt, a garment of coarse haircloth, worn next the skin by ascetics and penitents.

hair space, *Print.* the thinnest metal space used to separate words, etc.

hair·split·ter (hâr′splĭt′ər), n. one who makes fine or unnecessary distinctions. —**hair′split′ting,** n., adj.

hair·spring (hâr′sprĭng′), n. a fine, spiraled spring in a timepiece for regulating the motion of the balance.

hair·streak (hâr′strēk′), n. any of certain small dark butterflies of the family *Lycaenidae,* distinguished by one or two thin tails on each of the hind wings.

hair stroke, a fine line in writing or printing.

hair trigger, a trigger that allows the firing mechanism of a firearm to be operated by very slight pressure.

hair·worm (hâr′wûrm′), n. any of a number of small, slender worms of the family *Trichostrongylidae,* parasitic in the alimentary canals of various animals.

hair·y (hâr′ĭ), adj., **hairier, hairiest.** 1. covered with hair; having much hair. 2. consisting of or resembling hair. —**hair′i·ness,** n.

Hai·ti (hā′tĭ), n. 1. a republic in the West Indies, occupying the W part of the island of Hispaniola. 3,000,000 pop. (est. 1944); 10,714 sq. mi. *Cap.:* Port-au-Prince. 2. former name of Hispaniola. —**Hai·ti·an** (hā′tĭ·ən, -shən), adj., n.

hajj (hăj), n. the pilgrimage to Mecca, which every good Mohammedan is supposed to make at least once in his lifetime. Also, **hadj.** [t. Ar.: m. *hajj* pilgrimage]

haj·ji (hăj′ĭ), n., pl. **-jis.** 1. a Mohammedan who has performed his hajj to Mecca. 2. a Greek or Armenian who has visited the Holy Sepulcher at Jerusalem. Also, **hadji.** [t. Turk.: m. *hājjī,* t. Ar.: m. *hājj* pilgrim]

hake (hāk), n., pl. **hakes,** (esp. collectively) **hake.** 1. any of several marine gadoid fishes of the genus *Merluccius,* related to the cod, as *M. bilinearis* (**silver hake**) of the New England coast. 2. any of various related marine fishes, esp. of the genus *Urophycis,* or allied genera as *U. tenius* (**white hake**) of the New England coast. [ME; orig. uncert.]

ha·kim[1] (hä′kēm′), n. (in Mohammedan countries) 1. a wise or learned man. 2. a physician. Also, **ha·keem** (hä·kēm′). [t. Ar.: m. *ḥakim* wise, wise man]

ha·kim[2] (hä′kēm), n. (in Mohammedan countries) a ruler; governor; judge. [t. Ar.: m. *ḥākim* governor]

Hak·luyt (hăk′lōōt, -lĭt), n. **Richard,** 1552?–1616, British geographer and editor of explorers' narratives.

Ha·ko·da·te (hä′kō dä′tĕ), n. a seaport in N Japan at the S end of Hokkaido island. 187,367 (1946).

hal-, var. of **halo-** before vowels, as in **halite.**

Hal, *Chem.* halogen.

Ha·la·kah (hä′lä KHä′, hä lä′KHä), n. the legal part of Jewish traditional literature. Also, **Ha·la·cha** (hä′lä-KHä′, hä lä′KHä). [t. Heb.: m. *halākāh* rule to go by]

ha·la·tion (hā lā′shən, hä-), n. *Photog.* the blurring in a negative or print of very light areas (as a window in an interior view) caused by the reflection of light from the back of the support on which the emulsion is coated. [contracted formation, f. HAL(O) + -ATION]

hal·berd (hăl′bərd; *formerly* hôl′-, hō′-), n. a shafted weapon with an axlike cutting blade, beak, and apical spike, used esp. in the 15th and 16th centuries. Also, **hal·bert** (hăl′bərt; *formerly* hôl′-, -hō′-). [late ME; t. OF: m. *hallebarde,* t. MHG: m. *helmbarde*]

hal·berd·ier (hăl′bər dĭr′), n. a soldier, guard, or attendant armed with a halberd.

hal·cy·on (hăl′sĭ′ən), n. 1. a bird, usually identified with the kingfisher, fabled by the ancients to breed about the time of the winter solstice, in a nest floating on the sea and to have the power of charming winds and waves into calmness. 2. any of various kingfishers, esp. of the genus *Halcyon.* 3. calm, tranquil, or peaceful. 4. of or pertaining to the halcyon or kingfisher. [t. L. pseudo-etymological var. of *alcyon,* t. Gk.: m. *alkyōn* kingfisher]

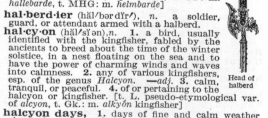

Head of halberd

halcyon days, 1. days of fine and calm weather about the winter solstice, when the halcyon was anciently believed to brood; esp. the seven days before and as many after the winter solstice. 2. days of peace and tranquility.

Hal·dane (hôl′dān), n. 1. **John Burdon Sanderson,** born 1892, British biologist and writer on science. 2. his father, **John Scott,** 1860–1936, British physiologist and writer on science. 3. **Richard Burdon,** (*Viscount*

Haldane of Cloan) 1856–1928, British statesman and jurist (brother of John Scott Haldane).

hale[1] (hāl), *adj.*, **haler, halest. 1.** free from disease or infirmity; robust; vigorous. **2.** *Scot. and N. Eng.* free from injury or defect. [ME; OE *hāl*, c. Icel. *heill* hale, whole] **—hale/ness,** *n.* **—Syn. 1.** sound, healthy, hearty. See **strong. —Ant. 1.** sickly.

hale[2] (hāl), *v.t.*, **haled, haling. 1.** to haul, pull, or draw with force. **2.** to drag, or bring as by dragging: *to hale a man into court.* [ME *hale(n),* t. OF: m. *haler* hale, haul, t. Gmc.; cf. OHG *halōn,* G *holen* fetch] **—hal/er,** *n.*

Hale (hāl), *n.* **1. Edward Everett,** 1822–1909, U.S. clergyman and author. **2. Sir Matthew,** 1609–76, British jurist: Lord Chief Justice, 1671–76. **3. Nathan,** 1755–76, American soldier hanged as spy by British.

Ha·le·a·ka·la (hä/lē ä/kä lä/), *n.* an extinct volcano in the Hawaiian Islands, on the island of Maui. Crater, 19 sq. mi.; ab. 2000 ft. deep; 10,032 ft. high.

Ha·lé·vy (à lē vē/), *n.* **1. Jacques François Fromental Elie** (zhàk frän swä/ frō män tàl/ ē lē/), 1799–1862, French composer and teacher of music. **2. Ludovic** (lȳ-dô vēk/), 1834–1908, French dramatist and novelist.

half (häf, häf), *n., pl.* **halves** (hävz, hävz), *adj., adv.* **—n. 1.** one of the two equal (or approximately equal) parts into which anything is or may be divided. **2.** *Sports.* either of the two periods of a game. **3.** *Football.* a halfback. **4.** *Golf.* an equal score (with the opponent) either on a hole or a round. **—adj. 5.** being one of the two equal (or approximately equal) parts into which anything is or may be divided. **6.** being equal to only about half of the full measure: *half speed.* **7.** partial or incomplete. **—adv. 8.** to the extent or measure of half: *a bucket half full of water.* **9.** in part; partly. **10.** to some extent. [ME and OE, c. MD and MLG *halve* side, half]

half-and-half (häf/ənd häf/, häf/ənd häf/), *adj.* **1.** half one thing and half another. **—adv. 2.** in two equal portions. **—n. 3.** a mixture of two things. **4.** *Chiefly Brit.* a mixture of two malt liquors, esp. porter and ale.

half·back (häf/bàk/, häf/-), *n. Football, etc.* one of the players behind the forward line.

half·baked (häf/bākt/, häf/-), *adj.* **1.** insufficiently cooked. **2.** not completed: *a half-baked scheme.* **3.** lacking mature judgment or experience: *half-baked theorists.*

half·beak (häf/bēk/, häf/-), *n.* any of certain marine fishes constituting the genus *Hemirhamphus* and allied genera, having a long protruding lower jaw.

half binding, a book having a leather binding on the back and corners, and paper or cloth sides.

half blood, the relation between persons having only one of their parents in common.

half-blood (häf/blŭd/, häf/-), *n.* **1.** a half-breed. **2.** a person related by half blood.

half-blood·ed (häf/blŭd/ĭd, häf/-), *adj.* having parents of different breeds.

half boot, a boot reaching about halfway to the knee.

half-bound (häf/bound/, häf/-), *adj.* bound in half binding.

half-breed (häf/brēd/, häf/-), *n.* **1.** the offspring of parents of different races; one who is half-blooded. **2.** the offspring of a white person and an American Indian.

half brother, a brother by one parent only.

half cadence, *Music.* a cadence ending with dominant harmony.

half-caste (häf/kàst/, häf/käst/), *n.* **1.** a person of mixed race. **2.** one of mixed European and Hindu or Mohammedan parentage.

half cock, 1. the position of the hammer of a firearm when held halfway by mechanism so that it will not operate. **2. go off at half cock,** to act prematurely.

half crown, an English silver coin worth 2*s.*6*d.*

half dollar, a silver coin of the United States worth 50 cents, weighing 385.8 grains to the dollar, 0.900 fine.

half eagle, a gold coin of the United States worth $5.

half gainer, *Swimming.* a type of dive in which the diver takes off facing forward and performs a back dive either with or without a jackknife.

half-heart·ed (häf/här/tĭd, häf/-), *adj.* having or showing little enthusiasm. **—half/-heart/ed·ly,** *adv.* **—half/-heart/ed·ness,** *n.* **—Syn.** indifferent, perfunctory. **—Ant.** enthusiastic.

half hitch, a hitch formed by passing the end of a rope round its standing part and bringing it up through the bight. See illus. under **knot.**

half hose, short hose; socks.

half-hour (häf/our/, häf/-), *n.* **1.** a period of thirty minutes. **2.** the mid point between the hours.

half-hour·ly (häf/our/lĭ, häf/-), *adj.* **1.** of or lasting a half-hour. **2.** occurring once every half-hour. **—adv. 3.** during a half-hour.

half leather, *Bookbinding.* half binding.

half-length (häf/length/, häf/-), *n.* **1.** a portrait showing only the upper part of the body, including the hands. **—adj. 2.** of or denoting such a portrait.

half life, *Physics, etc.* (of a radioactive substance) the time required for one half the atoms of a sample of the substance to disintegrate.

half-mast (häf/mäst/, häf/mäst/), *n.* **1.** a position approximately halfway below the top of a mast, staff, etc. **—v.t. 2.** to place (a flag) at half-mast (as a mark of respect for the dead, or as a signal of distress).

half moon, 1. See **moon** (def. 2b). **2.** something of the shape of a half moon or crescent.

half mourning, 1. a mourning garb less somber than full mourning. **2.** the period during which it is worn.

half nelson, *Wrestling.* a method of attack, usually from behind, in which the wrestler pushes his arm under his opponent's arm and places the hand on the nape of his opponent's neck.

half note, *Music.* a note, formerly the shortest in use, but now equivalent in time value to one half of a semibreve. See illus. under **note.**

half pay, 1. half the full wages or salary. **2.** a reduced allowance paid to a British army or navy officer when not in actual service or after retirement.

half·pen·ny (hā/pə nĭ, hāp/nĭ), *n., pl.* **halfpennies** (hā/pə nĭz, hāp/nĭz) for 1; **halfpence** (hā/pəns) for 2; *adj.* **—n. 1.** a British bronze coin of half the value of a penny. **2.** the sum of half a penny. **—adj. 3.** of the price or value of a halfpenny. **4.** of trifling value.

half sister, a sister by one parent only.

half sole, that part of the sole of a boot or shoe which extends from the shank to the end of the toe.

half-sole (häf/sōl/, häf/-), *v.t.,* **-soled, -soling.** to repair by putting on a new half sole.

half sovereign, a British gold coin worth 10 shillings and weighing about 61.6372 grains troy.

half step, 1. *Music.* a semitone. **2.** *Mil.* a step fifteen inches long in quick time and eighteen inches long in double time.

half tide, the state of the tide when halfway between high water and low water.

half-tim·bered (häf/tĭm/bərd, häf/-), *adj.* (of a house or building) having the frame and principal supports of timber, but with the interstices filled in with masonry, plaster, or the like.

half title, 1. the short title of a book at the head of the first page of the text. **2.** the title of any subdivision of a book that immediately precedes that subdivision, when printed on a full page and in one line.

half-tone (häf/tōn/, häf/-), *n.* **1.** *Painting, Photog., etc.* a value intermediate between high light and deep shade. **2.** *Photoengraving.* **a.** a process in which gradation of tone is obtained by a system of minute dots produced by a screen, placed in the camera a short distance in front of the sensitized plate. **b.** the metal plate made by photoengraving for reproduction by letterpress printing. **c.** a print from it. **—adj. 3.** pertaining to, using, or used in, the half-tone process.

half tone, *Music.* a semitone.

half-track (häf/tràk/, häf/-), *n.* a motor vehicle with its driving wheels on caterpillar treads.

half-truth (häf/trooth/, häf/-), *n.* a proposition or statement only partly true.

half volley, *Tennis, Cricket, etc.* a "ball" or its return, hit the moment after it bounces from the ground.

half-vol·ley (häf/vŏl/ĭ, häf/-), *v.t., v.i.,* **-leyed, -leying.** to hit or play (a half volley).

half·way (häf/wā/, häf/-), *adv.* **1.** half over the way: *to go halfway to a place.* **2.** to or at half the distance: *the rope reaches only halfway.* **—adj. 3.** midway, as between two places or points. **4.** going to or covering only half the full extent; partial: *halfway measures.*

half-wit (häf/wĭt/, häf/-), *n.* one who is feebleminded.

half-wit·ted (häf/wĭt/ĭd, häf/-), *adj.* feeble-minded. **—half/-wit/ted·ly,** *adv.* **—half/-wit/ted·ness,** *n.*

hal·i·but (hàl/ə bət, hŏl/-), *n., pl.* **-buts,** (*esp. collectively*) **-but. 1.** either of two species of large flatfishes, *Hippoglossus hippoglossus* of the North Atlantic and *H. stenolepis* of the North Pacific; the largest of the flatfishes and widely used for food. **2.** any of various other similar flatfishes. Also, **holibut.** [ME *halybutte,* appar. f. *haly* (OE *hālig* holy) + *butte* kind of fish. Cf. LG *heilbutt;* so called because eaten on holy days]

Hal·i·car·nas·sus (hàl/ə kär näs/əs), *n.* an ancient city of Caria, in SW Asia Minor: site of the Mausoleum, one of the seven wonders of the ancient world.

hal·ide (hàl/ĭd, hā/līd), *Chem.* **—n. 1.** a compound, usually of two elements only, one of which is a halogen. **—adj. 2.** of the nature of, or pertaining to, a halide; haloid. Also, **hal·id** (hàl/ĭd, hā/lĭd). [f. HAL(OGEN) + -IDE]

Hal·i·fax (hàl/ə fàks/), *n.* **1.** a seaport in SE Canada: the capital of Nova Scotia. 70,488 (1941). **2.** a city in central England, in SW Yorkshire. 94,360 (est. 1946).

Hal·i·fax (hàl/ə fàks/), *n.* **Earl of,** (*Edward Frederick Lindley Wood*) born 1881, British statesman.

hal·ite (hàl/īt, hā/līt), *n.* rock salt. [f. HAL- + -ITE[1]]

hal·i·to·sis (hàl/ə tō/sĭs), *n.* bad or offensive breath. [NL: f. s. L *hālitus* breath + -ōsis -OSIS]

hal·i·tus (hàl/ə təs), *n.* the breath. [t. L: breath]

hall (hôl), *n.* **1.** *U.S.* a corridor or passageway in a building. **2.** the entrance room or vestibule of a house or building. **3.** a large and impressive room of public nature. **4.** a large building for residence, instruction, or other purposes, as in a university or college. **5.** the occupants of such a building. **6.** (in English colleges) **a.** a large room in which the members and students dine. **b.** dinner in such a room. **7.** *Chiefly Brit.* the proprietor's residence on a large landed estate. **8.** the chief room in a medieval castle or similar structure, used for eating, sleeping, and entertaining. **9.** the house of a medieval chieftain or noble. [ME and OE, c. OHG *halla,* akin to OE *helan* cover, hide, L *cēlāre* hide, Gk. *kalýptein* cover]

Hall (hôl), *n.* **1. Charles Francis,** 1821–1871, U.S. Arctic explorer. **2. Charles Martin,** 1863–1914, U.S. chemist and inventor. **3. Granville Stanley,** 1846–1924, U.S. psychologist and educator.

Hal·lam (hăl′əm), *n.* **1. Arthur Henry,** 1811–33, British poet and essayist: subject of Tennyson's *In Memoriam.* **2. Henry,** 1777–1859, British historian.

Hal·le (häl′ə), *n.* a city in central Germany. 220,092 (1939).

Hal·leck (hăl′ĭk, -ək), *n.* **1. Fitz-Greene,** 1790–1867, U.S. poet. **2. Henry Wager,** 1815–72, Union general in the U.S. Civil War and writer on military subjects.

hal·lel (hə lāl′, hăl′ĕl), *n. Jewish Rel.* a hymn of praise consisting of Psalms 113–118 or of Psalm 136. [t. Heb.: m. *hallēl* praise]

hal·le·lu·jah (hăl′ə lōō′yə), *interj.* **1.** Praise ye the Lord! —*n.* **2.** an exclamation of "hallelujah!" **3.** a musical composition wholly or principally based upon the word *hallelujah.* Also, **hal′le·lu′iah.** [t. Heb.: m. *hallelūyah* praise ye Jehovah]

Hal·ley (hăl′ĭ), *n.* **Edmund,** 1656–1742, British astronomer: first to predict the return of the comet now known as **Halley's Comet.**

hal·liard (hăl′yərd), *n.* halyard.

hall·mark (hôl′märk′), *n.* **1.** an official mark or stamp indicating a standard of purity, used in marking gold and silver articles assayed by the Goldsmith's Company of London. **2.** any mark or special indication of genuineness, good quality, etc. [from Goldsmiths' *Hall* (in London), the seat of the Goldsmiths' Company]

hal·lo (hə lō′), *interj., n., v.* hollo. Also, **hal·loa** (hə lō′).

Hall of Fame, a colonnade at New York University having tablets and busts in honor of famous Americans.

hal·loo (hə lōō′), *interj., n., v., pl.* **-loos,** *v.* —*interj.* **1.** an exclamation used to attract attention, to incite the dogs in hunting, etc. —*n.* **2.** the cry "halloo!" —*v.i.* **3.** to call with a loud voice; shout; cry, as after dogs. —*v.t.* **4.** to incite or chase with shouts and cries of "halloo!" **5.** to cry aloud to. **6.** to utter with shouts.

hal·low¹ (hăl′ō), *v.t.* **1.** to make holy; sanctify; consecrate. **2.** to honor as holy. [ME *halow*(*e*), OE *hālgian* der. *hālig* holy]

hal·low² (hə lō′), *interj., n., v.* halloo. [var. of HALLOO]

hal·lowed (hăl′ōd; *in liturgical use frequently* hăl′ō ĭd), *adj.* **1.** made holy; sacred; consecrated. **2.** honored or observed as holy. —**hal′lowed·ness,** *n.* —**Syn. 1.** See holy.

Hal·low·een (hăl′ō ēn′, hŏl′-), *n.* the evening of Oct. 31; the eve of All Saints' Day. Also, **Hal′low·e′en′.** [f. *hallow* saint + *een,* var. of *even* EVE]

Hal·low·mas (hăl′ō məs, -măs′), *n. Archaic.* the feast of Allhallows or All Saints' Day, on Nov. 1.

Hall·stat·ti·an (hăl stăt′ĭ ən), *adj.* pertaining to a variously dated pre-Christian stage of culture in central Europe, characterized by the use of bronze, the introduction of iron, artistic work in pottery, jewelry, etc., as shown by the contents of a burial ground of the period found near Hallstatt, a village in central Austria.

hal·lu·cal (hăl′yə kəl), *adj. Anat.* referring to the great toe. [f. s. NL *hallux* (see HALLUX) + -AL¹]

hal·lu·ci·nate (hə lōō′sə nāt′), *v.t.* **-nated, -nating.** to affect with hallucination. [t. L: m.s. *hallūcinātus,* pp. of (*h*)*allūcinārī* wander in mind, dream]

hal·lu·ci·na·tion (hə lōō′sə nā′shən), *n.* **1.** an apparent perception, as by sight or hearing, for which there is no real external cause. **2.** a suffering from illusion or false notions. —**Syn.** See illusion.

hal·lu·ci·na·to·ry (hə lōō′sə nə tōr′ĭ), *adj.* pertaining to or characterized by hallucination.

hal·lu·ci·no·sis (hə lōō′sə nō′sĭs), *n. Psychiatry.* a psychosis or state characterized and produced by hallucinations. [f. HALLUCIN(ATION) + -OSIS]

hal·lux (hăl′əks), *n., pl.* **-luces** (-yə sēz′). *Anat., Zool.* the innermost of the five digits normally present in the hind foot of air-breathing vertebrates, as: **a.** (in man) the great toe. **b.** (in birds) the hind toe. [NL, m. L (*h*)*allex* great toe, with -*u*- by contam. with (*h*)*allus* thumb]

hall·way (hôl′wā′), *n. U.S.* **1.** a corridor, as in a building. **2.** an entrance hall.

halm (hôm), *n. Brit.* haulm.

Hal·ma·he·ra (hăl′mä hĕ′rä), *n.* an island in the U.S. of Indonesia: the largest of the Moluccas. 83,700 pop. (1930); 7565 sq. mi. Also, **Jilolo.**

ha·lo (hā′lō), *n., pl.* **-los, -loes,** *v.,* **-loed, -loing.** —*n.* **1.** a radiance surrounding the head in the representation of a sacred personage. **2.** an ideal glory investing an object viewed with feeling or sentiment: *the halo around Shakespeare's plays.* **3.** *Meteorol.* a circle of light appearing around the sun or moon, caused by the refraction of light in suspended ice crystals. —*v.t.* **4.** to surround with a halo. —*v.i.* **5.** to form a halo. [t. L: m. *halōs,* t. Gk.: disk, halo, threshing floor (on which the oxen trod out a circular path)] —**ha′lo·like′,** *adj.*

halo-, a word element meaning "salt," as in halogen. [t. Gk., comb. form of *hāls*]

hal·o·gen (hăl′ə jən, hā′lə-), *n. Chem.* any of the negative elements fluorine, chlorine, iodine, and bromine, which form binary salts by direct union with metals.

hal·o·gen·a·tion (hăl′ə jən ā′shən, hā′lə-), *n.* the introduction of a halogen into an organic compound.

hal·oid (hăl′oid, hā′loid), *adj.* **1.** denoting any halogen derivative. —*n.* **2.** a haloid salt or derivative.

hal·o·phyte (hăl′ə fīt′), *n.* a plant which grows in salty or alkaline soil. —**hal·o·phyt·ic** (hăl′ə fĭt′ĭk), *adj.*

Hals (häls), *n.* **Frans** (fräns), 1580?–1666, Dutch portrait painter.

Hal·sey (hôl′zĭ), *n.* **William Frederick,** born 1882, U.S. admiral.

Häl·sing·borg (hĕl′sĭng bôr′y), *n.* a seaport in SW Sweden, opposite Helsingör. 65,357 (est. 1944).

halt¹ (hôlt), *v.i.* **1.** to make a temporary stop, as in marching, etc. —*v.t.* **2.** to cause to halt. —*n.* **3.** temporary stop. [t. G: stoppage] —**Syn. 2.** See stop.

halt² (hôlt), *v.i.* **1.** to proceed in a faulty way, as in speech, reasoning, etc. **2.** to be in doubt; waver; hesitate. **3.** *Archaic.* to be lame; walk lamely; limp. —*adj.* **4.** *Archaic.* lame; limping. —*n.* **5.** *Archaic.* lameness; a limp. [ME; OE *h*(*e*)*alt,* c. OHG *halz*] —**halt′ing,** *adj.* —**halt′ing·ly,** *adv.* —**halt′ing·ness,** *n.*

hal·ter¹ (hôl′tər), *n.* **1.** a rope or strap with a noose or headstall, for leading or fastening horses or cattle. **2.** a rope with a noose for hanging criminals. **3.** death by hanging. **4.** a woman's sports waist, tied behind the neck and across the back, leaving the arms and back bare. —*v.t.* **5.** to put a halter on; restrain as by a halter. **6.** to hang (a person). [ME; OE *hælftre,* c. G *halfter*] —**hal′ter·like′,** *adj.*

hal·ter² (hăl′tər), *n., pl.* **halteres** (hăl tĭr′ēz). one of a pair of slender, club-shaped appendages attached to the body of a fly (order *Diptera*) near the wings, used for balancing in flight; balancer. [t. L, t. Gk.: usually pl. (*haltēres*) leaping weights]

halt·er³ (hôl′tər), *n.* one who halts or hesitates. [f. HALT² + -ER¹]

halt·er⁴ (hôl′tər), *n.* one who halts or stops. [f. HALT¹ + -ER¹]

halve (hăv, häv), *v.t.,* **halved, halving. 1.** to divide in halves; share equally. **2.** to reduce to half. **3.** *Golf.* to play (a hole, match, etc.) in the same number of strokes, as two opponents. [ME *halven,* der. HALF]

halves (hăvz, hävz), *n.* **1.** pl. of **half.** **2.** by halves, *a.* incompletely. *b.* half-heartedly.

hal·yard (hăl′yərd), *n.* a rope or tackle used to hoist or lower a sail, yard, flag, etc. Also, **halliard.** [ME *halier, hallyer* that which hales or hauls (f. HALE² + -IER); influenced by YARD¹]

ham (hăm), *n., v.,* **hammed, hamming.** —*n.* **1.** one of the rear quarters of a hog, esp. the heavy-muscled part, between hip and hock. **2.** the meat of this part. **3.** the part of the leg back of the knee. **4.** (*often pl.*) the back of the thigh, or the thigh and the buttock together. **5.** *Theat. Slang.* **a.** an actor who overacts. **b.** overacting. **6.** *Slang.* an amateur: *a radio ham.* —*v.i.* **7.** *Theat. Slang.* to act with exaggerated expression of emotion; overact. [ME *hamme,* OE *hamm,* c. OHG *hamma* angle of the knee. Cf. LL *camba* bend of leg]

Ham (hăm), *n. Bible.* second son of Noah. Gen. 10:1.

Ham·a·dan (hăm′ə dän′; *Persian* häm′ə dän′), *n.* a city in W Iran. ab. 104,000. See Ecbatana.

ham·a·dry·ad (hăm′ə drī′əd, -ăd), *n., pl.* **-ads, -ades** (-ə dēz′). *Class. Myth.* a wood nymph fabled to live and die with the tree which she inhabited. [t. L: s. *Hamādryas,* t. Gk.: f. *hāma* together + *dryás* wood nymph]

Ha·ma·mat·su (hä′mä mä′tsōō), *n.* a city in central Japan, on Honshu island. 101,818 (1946).

ham·a·me·li·da·ceous (hăm′ə mē′lə dā′shəs, -mĕl′ə-), *adj.* belonging to the *Hamamelidaceae,* a family of shrubs and trees including the witch hazel, etc. [f. s. NL *hamamēlis* (t. Gk.: a kind of medlar) + -ACEOUS]

Ha·man (hā′mən), *n. Bible.* (in the Book of Esther) an enemy of the Jews who was hanged when his plot for their destruction was exposed.

ha·mate (hā′māt), *adj. Anat.* **1.** hook-shaped. **2.** having a hooklike process. [t. L: m. *hāmātus*]

Ham·ble·to·ni·an (hăm′bəl tō′nĭ ən), *n.* **1.** a superior strain of American trotting horses descended from Hambletonian (foaled 1849, died 1876). **2.** the principal annual harness race for three-year old trotters, held at Goshen, N. Y.

Ham·born (hăm′bôrn), *n.* See **Duisburg-Hamborn.**

ham·burg (hăm′bûrg), *n.* hamburger.

Ham·burg (hăm′bûrg; *Ger.* häm′bŏŏrkн), *n.* **1.** a state in N Germany. 288 sq. mi. **2.** the capital of this state, on the Elbe: the largest seaport in continental Europe. 1,711,877 (1939).

ham·burg·er (hăm′bûr′gər), *n.* **1.** Hamburg steak. **2.** ground beef from which Hamburg steaks are made. **3.** a roll or bun containing such meat, often with relish.

Ham·burg steak (hăm′bûrg), (*sometimes l.c.*) chopped beef, seasoned, and fried or broiled in cakes.

hame (hām), *n.* either of two curved pieces lying upon the collar in the harness of an animal, to which the traces are fastened. See illus. under **harness.** [ME; akin to G *hamen* fishhook, dragnet, OE *hamele* rowlock]

Ha·meln (hä′məln), *n.* a city in NW Germany, on the Weser river: scene of the legend of the Pied Piper of Hamelin. 31,797 (1939). Also, **Ham·e·lin** (hăm′ə lĭn).

Ha·mil·car Bar·ca (hə mĭl′kär bär′kə, hăm′əl kär′), died 228? B.C., Carthaginian general: Hannibal's father.

Ham·il·ton (hăm′əl tən), *n.* **1. Alexander,** 1757–1804, American statesman and writer on government. **2. Lady Emma,** (*Amy,* or *Emily, Lyon*) 1765?–1815, mistress of Viscount Nelson. **3. Sir Ian Standish Monteith** (ē′ən *or* ī′ən, mŏn tēth′), 1853–1947, British general.

4. Sir William, 1788–1856, Scottish philosopher. **5. Sir William Rowan,** 1805–65, British mathematician and astronomer. **6.** a city in SE Canada: a port near the W end of Lake Ontario. 166,337; with suburbs, 176,110 (1941). **7.** a city in SW Ohio. 57,951 (1950). **8.** a city in S Scotland, SE of Glasgow. 38,355 (1939). **9.** the capital of Bermuda. 1863 (est. 1944). **10.** Also, **Grand River.** a river flowing ab. 600 mi. through S Labrador into Hamilton Inlet, an arm (ab. 150 mi. long) of the Atlantic. See **Grand Falls. 11. Mount,** a mountain of the Coast Range in W California, near San Francisco: the site of Lick Observatory. 4209 ft.

Ham·il·to·ni·an (hăm′əl tō′nĭ ən), *adj.* pertaining to or holding the political doctrines of Alexander Hamilton (strong central government, protective tariff, etc.).

Ham·ite (hăm′īt), *n.* **1.** a descendant of Ham. Gen. 10: 1, 6–20. **2.** a member of any of various nations of Africa, as the ancient Egyptians and modern Berbers. **3.** any population speaking a Hamitic language.

Ham·it·ic (hă mĭt′ĭk, hə-), *adj.* **1.** of or pertaining to the Hamites or their speech. —*n.* **2.** a family of languages related to the Semitic, spoken in North Africa, including ancient Egyptian and modern Berber.

ham·let (hăm′lĭt), *n.* **1.** a small village. **2.** a little cluster of houses in the country. **3.** *Brit.* a village without a church of its own, but belonging to the parish of another village or a town. [ME *hamelet*, t. OF, dim. of *hamel* hamlet, dim. of *ham*, t. Gmc.; cf. OE *hamm* enclosed land] —**Syn. 1.** See **community.**

Ham·let (hăm′lĭt), *n.* **1.** a tragedy (first printed, 1603) by Shakespeare. **2.** its hero.

Ham·lin (hăm′lĭn), *n.* **Hannibal,** 1809–1901, U.S. statesman: vice-president of the U.S., 1861–65.

ham·mer (hăm′ər), *n.* **1.** an instrument consisting of a solid head, usually of metal, set crosswise on a handle, used for beating metals, driving nails, etc. **2.** any of various instruments or devices resembling a hammer in form, action, or use. **3.** *Firearms.* that part of the lock which by its fall or action causes the discharge, as by exploding the percussion cap; the cock. **4.** one of the padded levers by which the strings of a piano are struck. **5.** *Athletics.* a metal ball attached to a long, flexible handle, used in certain throwing contests. **6.** *Anat.* the malleus. **7. come** or **go under the hammer,** to be sold at auction. —*v.t.* **8.** to beat or drive with or as with a hammer. **9.** to form with a hammer (often fol. by *out*). **10.** to fasten by or as by using a hammer. **11.** to contrive or work out laboriously (often fol. by *out*). —*v.i.* **12.** to strike blows with or as with a hammer. **13.** to make persistent or laborious attempts. [ME *hamer*, OE *hamor*, c. G *hammer*] —**ham′mer·er,** *n.* —**ham′mer·like′,** *adj.*

Types of hammers (def. 1) A. Nail hammer; B. Engineer's hammer; C. Machinist's hammer; D. Shoemaker's hammer; E. Carpenter's hammer

hammer and tongs, *Colloq.* with great noise, vigor, or violence.

hammered work, metalwork formed by the hammers, anvils, punches, etc., of craftsmen.

Ham·mer·fest (hăm′ər fĕst′), *n.* a seaport on an island in N Norway: the northernmost town in Europe. 3649 (1930).

ham·mer·head (hăm′ər hĕd′), *n.* any of the sharks constituting the genus *Sphyrna*, characterized by a head expanded laterally so as to resemble a double-headed hammer, esp. *S. zygaena*, a widely distributed species.

Hammerhead, *Sphyrna zygaena* (15 ft. long)

ham·mer·less (hăm′ər lĭs), *adj.* (of firearms) having no hammer or no visible hammer.

hammer lock, *Wrestling.* a hold whereby the opponent's arm is twisted and pushed behind his back.

Ham·mer·stein (hăm′ər stīn′), *n.* **Oscar,** 1847?–1919, U.S. theatrical manager, born in Germany.

ham·mock (hăm′ək), *n.* a kind of hanging bed or couch made of canvas, netted cord, or the like. [t. Sp.: m. *hamaca*; of W Ind. orig.] —**ham′mock·like′,** *adj.*

Ham·mond (hăm′ənd), *n.* a city in NW Indiana, near Chicago. 87,594 (1950).

Hammond organ, 1. a musical instrument, resembling in shape an upright piano, with two keyboards, electronic tone generation, and a great variety of tone colors. **2.** (*cap.*) a trademark for this instrument.

Ham·mu·ra·bi (hä′mŏŏ rä′bĭ, hăm′ŏŏ-), *n.* fl. c2100 B.C., king of Babylonia: famous code of laws made in his reign.

Hamp·den (hămp′dən, hăm′dən), *n.* **1. John,** 1594–1643, British statesman who defended the rights of the House of Commons against Charles I. **2. Walter,** (*Walter Hampden Dougherty*) born 1879, U.S. actor.

ham·per[1] (hăm′pər), *v.t.* **1.** to impede; hinder; hold back. —*n.* **2.** *Naut.* articles which, while necessary to a ship's equipment, are often in the way. [ME *hampren*, orig. uncert.] —**Syn. 1.** obstruct, encumber, trammel. See **prevent.** —**Ant. 1.** assist.

ham·per[2] (hăm′pər), *n.* a large basket or wickerwork receptacle, usually with a cover. [ME *hampere*; syncopated var. of HANAPER]

Hamp·shire (hămp′shĭr, -shər), *n.* **1.** Also, **Hants.** a county in S England, including the administrative counties of Southampton and Isle of Wight. **2.** an English breed of sheep of the mutton type, noted for the rapid growth of its lambs, popular in the U.S.

Hamp·stead (hămp′stĭd), *n.* a NW borough of London: residences of artists and writers. 91,860 (est. 1946).

Hamp·ton (hămp′tən), *n.* **Wade,** 1818–1902, Confederate general: U.S. senator, 1879–91.

Hampton Roads, a channel in SE Virginia between the mouth of the James river and Chesapeake Bay: battle between the Monitor and the Merrimac, 1862.

ham·ster (hăm′stər), *n.* **1.** any of a number of short-tailed, stout-bodied, burrowing rodents, as *Cricetus cricetus*, which have large cheek pouches, and which inhabit parts of Europe and Asia. **2.** the fur. [t. G]

Hamster, *Cricetus cricetus* (Ab. 10 in. long)

ham·string (hăm′strĭng), *n., v.,* **-strung** or (*Rare*) **-stringed; -stringing.** —*n.* **1.** (in man) any of the tendons which bound the ham, or hollow of the knee. **2.** (in quadrupeds) the great tendon at the back of the hock. —*v.t.* **3.** to cut the hamstring or hamstrings of and thus disable. **4.** to cripple or disable.

Ham·sun (häm′sŏŏn), *n.* **Knut** (knŏŏt), 1859–1952, Norwegian novelist.

Ham·tramck (hăm trăm′ĭk), *n.* a city in SE Michigan, within the city limits of Detroit. 43,355 (1950).

ham·u·lus (hăm′yə ləs), *n., pl.* **-li** (-lī′). *Anat., Zool., Bot., etc.* a small hook or hooklike process. [t. L, dim. of *hāmus* a hook]

Han (hän), *n.* **1.** Chinese dynasty, 206 B.C.–A.D. 220, with an interregnum, A.D. 9–25, known as the **Earlier** or **Western Han** before the interregnum and as the **Later** or **Eastern Han** afterwards. The Han was distinguished for the revival of letters and the beginnings of Buddhism; its bureaucracy became a model for later dynasties. **2.** a river flowing from central China into the Yangtze at Hankow. ab. 900 mi.

han·a·per (hăn′ə pər), *n.* a wicker receptacle for documents. [ME *hanypere*, t. OF: m. *hanapier* case for holding a cup, der. *hanap* cup, t. Gmc.; cf. OS *hnapp* cup]

hance (häns, hăns), *n.* **1.** *Naut.* a curved rise to a higher part, as of the bulwarks from the waist to the quarter-deck. **2.** *Archit.* **a.** the sharply curving portion nearest the impost at either side of an elliptical or similar arch. **b.** the haunch of an arch. [n. use of *hance*, v., raise (now obs.), aphetic var. of ENHANCE]

Han Cities (hän), Wuhan.

Han·cock (hăn′kŏk), *n.* **1. John,** 1737–93, American statesman: first signer of the Declaration of Independence. **2. Winfield Scott,** 1824–86, Union general in the U.S. Civil War.

hand (hănd), *n.* **1.** (in man) the terminal, prehensile part of the arm, consisting of the palm and five digits. **2.** the corresponding part of the forelimb in any of the higher vertebrates. **3.** the terminal part of any limb when prehensile, as the hind foot of a monkey, the chela of a crustacean, or (in falconry) the foot of a hawk. **4.** something resembling a hand in shape or function: *the hands of a clock.* **5.** a sign used in writing or printing to draw attention to something. **6.** a person employed in manual labor; worker; laborer: *a factory hand.* **7.** a person who does a specified thing: *a book by several hands.* **8.** the persons of any company or number: *all hands gave assistance, all hands on deck.* **9.** (*often pl.*) possession or power; control, custody, or care: *to have someone's fate in one's hands.* **10.** agency; active coöperation in doing something: *a helping hand.* **11.** side: *on every hand.* **12.** a side of a subject, question, etc.: *on the other hand.* **13.** a person considered as a source, as of information or of supply: *at first hand.* **14.** style of handwriting. **15.** a person's signature. **16.** skill; execution; touch: *a painting that shows a master's hand.* **17.** a person, with reference to action, ability, or skill: *a poor hand at writing letters.* **18.** a round or outburst of applause for a performer: *to get a hand.* **19.** a pledge of marriage. **20.** a lineal measure used in giving the height of horses, etc., equal to four inches. **21.** *Cards.* **a.** the cards dealt to or held by each player at one time. **b.** the person holding the cards. **c.** a single part of a game, in which all the cards dealt at one time are played. **22.** *Rom. Law.* the husband's control over the wife. **23.** skill or knack at manipulating the reins. **24.** a bundle of tobacco leaves tied together. **25.** Some special noun phrases are: **a heavy hand,** severity or oppression. **a high hand,** dictatorial manner or arbitrary conduct. **at hand, 1.** within reach; near by. **2.** near in time. **3.** ready for use. **at the hand** or **hands of,** from the action or agency of. **by hand,** by the use of the hands (as opposed to any other means): *to make pottery by hand.* **come to hand,** to be received; come within one's reach. **from hand to hand,** from one person to another. **from hand to mouth, 1.** by eating at once whatever one gets. **2.** with attention to immediate wants only; precariously.

hand and glove or **hand in glove**, very intimate.
hand in hand, 1. with hands mutually clasped. **2.** conjointly or concurrently.
hands off, keep off; refrain from blows or touching.
hand to hand, in close combat; at close quarters.
have a hand in, to have a part or concern in doing.
have one's hands full, to be fully occupied.
in hand, 1. under control. **2.** in immediate possession: *cash in hand.* **3.** in process: *keep to the matter in hand.*
off one's hands, out of one's responsible charge or care.
on hand, 1. in immediate possession: *cash on hand.* **2.** before one for attention. **3.** *U.S.* in attendance; present: *to be on hand early.*
on or **upon one's hands**, under one's care, management, or responsibility.
out of hand, 1. beyond control: *to let one's temper get out of hand.* **2.** at once; without delay. **3.** no longer in process; over and done with.
to hand, 1. within reach; at hand. **2.** into one's immediate possession.
wash one's hands of, to have nothing more to do with.
—*v.t.* **26.** to deliver or pass with the hand. **27.** to help or conduct with the hand. **28.** *Naut.* to furl, as a sail. **29.** to pass on; transmit (fol. by *on*). **30. hand down, a.** to deliver the decision of a court. **b.** to transmit from the higher to the lower, in space or time: *to hand down to posterity.* **31. hand over, a.** to deliver into another's keeping. **b.** to give up or yield control of. —*adj.* **32.** of or belonging to the hand. **33.** done or made by hand. **34.** that may be carried in, or worn on, the hand. **35.** operated by hand. [ME and OE, c. G *hand*] —**hand'less**, *adj.* —**hand'like'**, *adj.*
hand·bag (hănd'băg'), *n.* a bag for carrying in the hand, as a small valise or a woman's bag for carrying money, small purchases, toilet articles, etc.
hand·ball (hănd'bôl'), *n.* **1.** a game in which a small ball is batted against a wall with the (usually gloved) hand. **2.** the kind of ball used in this game.
hand·bar·row (hănd'băr'ō), *n.* **1.** a frame with handles at each end by which it is carried. **2.** a handcart.
hand·bill (hănd'bĭl'), *n.* a small printed bill or announcement, usually for distribution by hand.
hand·book (hănd'bŏŏk'), *n.* **1.** a small book or treatise, serving for guidance, as in an occupation or study: *handbook of radio.* **2.** a guidebook for travelers.
hand brake, a brake operated by a hand lever.
hand·breadth (hănd'brĕdth'), *n.* a unit of linear measure from 2½ to 4 inches. Also, **hand's-breadth**.
hand·car (hănd'kär'), *n.* *U.S.* a light car propelled by a mechanism worked by hand, used on some railroads for inspecting tracks and transporting workmen.
hand·cart (hănd'kärt'), *n.* a small cart drawn or pushed by hand.
hand·cuff (hănd'kŭf'), *n.* **1.** (*usually pl.*) a ring-shaped shackle for the wrist, usually one of a pair connected by a short chain or linked bar. —*v.t.* **2.** to put handcuffs on.
hand·ed (hănd'ĭd), *adj.* **1.** having a hand or hands. **2.** having a hand characterized in some specified manner: *right-handed.* **3.** done by hand in a specified way: *open-handed rowing.* **4.** done by a specified number of hands: *a double-handed game.*
Han·del (hăn'dəl), *n.* **George Frederick**, (*Georg Friedrich Händel*) 1685–1759, German composer.
hand·ful (hănd'fŏŏl'), *n., pl.* **-fuls. 1.** as much or as many as the hand can grasp or contain. **2.** a small quantity or number: *a handful of men.* **3.** *Colloq.* a thing or a person that is as much as one can manage.
hand glass, 1. a small mirror with a handle. **2.** a magnifying glass for holding in the hand.
hand grenade, 1. a grenade or explosive shell which is thrown by hand and exploded either by impact or by means of a fuse. **2.** a grenade or glass missile containing a chemical, for extinguishing fire.
hand·grip (hănd'grĭp'), *n.* **1.** a grasping with the hand; a grip, as in greeting. **2.** (*pl.*) hand-to-hand combat. **3.** a handle. [ME; OE *handgripe*]
hand·i·cap (hăn'dĭkăp'), *n., v.,* **-capped, -capping.** —*n.* **1.** a race or other contest in which certain disadvantages or advantages of weight, distance, time, etc., are placed upon competitors to equalize their chances of winning. **2.** the disadvantage or advantage itself. **3.** any encumbrance or disadvantage that makes success more difficult. —*v.t.* **4.** to serve as a handicap or disadvantage to: *his age handicaps him.* **5.** to subject to a disadvantageous handicap, as a competitor of recognized superiority. **6.** to assign handicaps to (competitors). [orig. *hand i' cap* (with *i'* for *in* before a consonant); reason for this name uncert.] —**hand'i·cap'per**, *n.*
hand·i·craft (hăn'dĭkrăft', -kräft'), *n.* **1.** manual skill. **2.** a manual art or occupation. [alter. of earlier *handcraft*, OE *handcræft*, modeled on HANDIWORK]
hand·i·crafts·man (hăn'dĭkrăfts'mən, -kräfts'-), *n., pl.* **-men.** a person skilled in a handicraft; craftsman.
hand·i·ly (hăn'dəlĭ), *adv.* **1.** dexterously; expertly. **2.** conveniently.
hand·i·ness (hăn'dĭnĭs), *n.* **1.** state or character of being handy or expert. **2.** quality of being easily handled; convenience.
hand·i·work (hăn'dĭwûrk'), *n.* **1.** work done or a thing or things made by the hands. **2.** the labor or

action of a particular doer or maker: *the handiwork of man.* **3.** the result of one's action or agency. [ME *handiwerk*, OE *handgeweorc*]
hand·ker·chief (hăng'kərchĭf', -chēf'), *n.* **1.** a small piece of linen, silk, or other fabric, usually square, carried about the person for wiping the face, nose, etc. **2.** a neckerchief or a kerchief. [f. HAND + KERCHIEF]
han·dle (hăn'dəl), *n., v.,* **-dled, -dling.** —*n.* **1.** a part of a thing which is intended to be grasped by the hand in using or moving it. **2.** that by which anything may be held. **3.** something that may be taken advantage of in effecting a purpose. —*v.t.* **4.** to touch or feel with the hand; use the hands on, as in picking up. **5.** to manage in use with the hands; manipulate. **6.** to wield, employ, or use: *to handle one's fists well in a fight.* **7.** to manage, direct, or control: *to handle troops.* **8.** to deal with or treat, as a matter or subject. **9.** to deal with or treat in a particular way: *to handle a person with tact.* **10.** to deal or trade in (goods, etc.). [ME *handlen*, OE *handlian* (c. G *handeln*), der. *hand* HAND] —**han'dled**, *adj.* —**han'dle·less**, *adj.*
handle bar, (*often pl.*) the curved steering bar of a bicycle, etc. in front of the rider.
han·dler (hănd'lər), *n.* **1.** a person or thing that handles. **2.** *Boxing.* a person who assists in the training of a fighter or is his second during the fight. **3.** the individual who manages and arouses a dog, etc. in a contest.
han·dling (hănd'lĭng), *n.* **1.** a touching, grasping, or using with the hands. **2.** management; treatment.
hand·made (hănd'mād'), *adj.* made by hand, rather than by machine.
hand·maid (hănd'mād'), *n.* a female servant or personal attendant. Also, **hand'maid'en.**
hand-me-down (hănd'mĭ'doun'), *adj., n. Now U.S. Colloq.* **1.** an article of clothing handed down or acquired at second hand. **2.** a cheap, ready-made garment.
hand organ, a portable barrel organ played by means of a crank turned by hand.
hand·out (hănd'out'), *n. U.S. Slang.* a portion of food or the like given to a beggar.
hand-pick (hănd'pĭk'), *v.t.* **1.** to pick by hand **2.** to select carefully. **3.** to select for ulterior purposes: *to hand-pick a candidate for office.* —**hand'-picked'**, *adj.*
hand·rail (hănd'rāl'), *n.* a rail serving as a support or guard at the side of a stairway, platform, etc.
hand·saw (hănd'sô'), *n.* a saw used with one hand.
hand's-breadth (hăndz'brĕdth'), *n.* handbreadth.
hand·sel (hăn'səl), *n., v.,* **-seled, -seling** or (*esp. Brit.*) **-selled, -selling.** —*n.* **1.** a gift or token for good luck or as an expression of good wishes, as at the beginning of the new year, at entering upon a new condition, situation, or enterprise. **2.** a first installment of payment. **3.** the first use or experience of anything; foretaste. —*v.t.* **4.** to give a handsel to. **5.** to inaugurate auspiciously. **6.** to use, try, or experience for the first time. Also, **hansel.** [ME *handselne*, OE *handselen*, lit., hand gift; akin to Icel. *handsal* the binding of a bargain by joining hands]
hand·set (hănd'sĕt'), *n.* a part of a telephone combining both the receiver and the transmitter in one structure which can be held to the face of the speaker.
hand·some (hăn'səm), *adj.,* **-somer, -somest. 1.** of fine or admirable appearance; comely; tastefully or elegantly fine: *a handsome person.* **2.** considerable, ample, or liberal in amount: *a handsome fortune.* **3.** gracious; generous: *a handsome gift.* **4.** *U.S. Colloq.* dexterous; graceful: *a handsome speech.* [ME *handsom*, f. HAND + -SOME[1]; orig., easy to handle] —**hand'some·ly**, *adv.* —**hand'some·ness**, *n.* —**Syn. 1.** See **beautiful.**
hand·spike (hănd'spīk'), *n.* a bar used as a lever. [t. D: m. *handspeck* hand bar, assimilated to *spike*]
hand·spring (hănd'sprĭng'), *n.* a kind of somersault in which the body is supported upon one or both hands while turning in the air.
hand-to-hand, *adj.* in close combat; at close quarters.
hand-to-mouth (hănd'tə mouth'), *adj.* precarious; unsettled.
hand·work (hănd'wûrk'), *n.* work done by hand, as distinguished from that done by machine.
hand·writ·ing (hănd'rī'tĭng), *n.* **1.** writing done with the hand. **2.** a kind or style of writing.
hand·y (hăn'dĭ), *adj.,* **handier, handiest. 1.** ready to hand; conveniently accessible: *to have aspirins handy.* **2.** ready or skillful with the hands; deft; dexterous. **3.** convenient to handle; easily manipulated or maneuvered: *a handy ship.* **4.** convenient or useful: *a handy tool.*
handy man, a man hired to do various kinds of work.
hang (hăng), *v.,* **hung** or (*esp. for capital punishment and suicide*) **hanged; hanging;** *n.* —*v.t.* **1.** to fasten or attach (a thing) so that it is supported only from above; suspend. **2.** to suspend so as to allow free movement, as on a hinge. **3.** to fasten or suspend (a person) on a cross, gallows, or the like, as a mode of capital punishment; to suspend by the neck until dead. **4.** to let droop or bend downward: *to hang one's head in shame.* **5.** to furnish or decorate with something suspended: *to hang a room with pictures.* **6.** to fasten into position; fix at a proper angle: *to hang a scythe.* **7.** to attach (paper, etc.) to walls. **8.** (used in maledictions and

emphatic expressions): *I'll be hanged if I do.* **9.** to keep (a jury) from rendering a verdict, as one juror by refusing to agree with the others. —*v.i.* **10.** to be suspended; dangle. **11.** to swing freely, as on a hinge. **12.** to be suspended from a cross or gallows; suffer death in this way as punishment. **13.** to bend forward or downward; lean over; incline downward. **14.** to be conditioned or contingent; be dependent. **15.** to hold fast, cling, or adhere; rest for support (fol. by *on* or *upon*). **16.** to be doubtful or undecided; waver or hesitate; remain unfinished. **17.** to loiter or linger: *to hang about a place.* **18.** to rest, float, or hover in the air. **19.** to impend; be imminent. **20.** to remain in attention or consideration: *to hang upon a person's words.* **21.** to fail to agree, as a jury. **22.** Some special verb phrases are:
hang back, to resist advance; be reluctant to proceed.
hang in the balance, to be in doubt or suspense: *for days his life hung in the balance.*
hang out, 1. to lean through an opening. **2.** *Slang.* to live at or frequent a particular place. **3.** to suspend in open view; display: *to hang out a banner.*
hang together, 1. to hold together; remain united. **2.** to be consistent: *his statements do not hang together.*
hang up, 1. to suspend on a hook or peg. **2.** to put into or hold in abeyance; keep back; delay. **3.** to break off telephonic communication: *only courtesy kept him from hanging up.*
—*n.* **23.** the way in which a thing hangs: *the hang of a drape.* **24.** *U.S. Colloq.* the precise manner of doing, using, etc. something: *to get the hang of a tool.* **25.** *U.S. Colloq.* meaning or force: *to get the hang of a subject.* **26.** in the least degree (in mild expletives): *not to give a hang.*
[fusion of three verbs: (1) ME and OE *hōn* (orig., v.t., now obs.; (2) ME *hang(i)en,* OE *hangian* (orig., v.i.); (3) ME *heng(e), hing,* t. Scand. (cf. Icel. *hengja* cause to hang)]
—**Syn. 3.** HANG, LYNCH through a widespread misconception have been thought of as synonyms. They do have in common the meaning of "to put to death," but lynching is not always by hanging. HANG, in the sense of "execute," is in accordance with a legal sentence, the method of execution being to suspend by the neck until dead. To LYNCH, however, implies the summary putting to death, by any method, of someone charged with a flagrant offense (though guilt may not have been proved). Lynching is done by private persons, usually a mob, without legal authority.
hang·ar (hăng′ər), *n.* **1.** a shed or shelter. **2.** a shed for airplanes or airships. [t. F, ? t. Gmc.]
hang·bird (hăng′bûrd′), *n.* a bird that builds a hanging nest, esp. the Baltimore oriole.
Hang·chow (hăng′chou′; *Chin.* häng′jō′), *n.* a seaport in and the capital of Chekiang province in E China, on **Hangchow Bay,** a funnel-shaped bay of the East China Sea. 600,023 (est. 1937).
hang·dog (hăng′dôg′, -dŏg′), *adj.* **1.** (of persons) having a mean or sneaking appearance. **2.** mean; sneaking: *a hangdog look.* —*n.* **3.** a degraded, contemptible person.
hang·er (hăng′ər), *n.* **1.** a contrivance that hangs things. **2.** a shaped support for a coat or other garment when not in use. **3.** something by which a thing is hung, as a loop on a garment. **4.** *Auto.* a double-hinged device linking the chassis with each of the springs. **5.** a light sabre of the 17th and 18th centuries, often worn at sea. **6.** one who hangs something.
hang·er-on (hăng′ər ŏn′), *n., pl.* **hangers-on.** one who clings to a service, place, or connection; follower.
hang·ing (hăng′ĭng), *n.* **1.** capital punishment by suspension with strangulation on a gallows. **2.** (*often pl.*) something that hangs or is hung on the walls of a room, as a drapery, tapestry, etc. **3.** act of one who or that which hangs; suspension. —*adj.* **4.** deserving punishment by hanging. **5.** punishable by, or inclined to inflict, death by hanging: *a hanging crime.* **6.** that hangs; pendent; overhanging. **7.** situated on a steep slope or at a height: *a hanging garden.* **8.** directed downward: *a hanging look.* **9.** made for hanging an object on: *the hanging post of a door.*
hanging indention, *Print., etc.* an indentation of uniform amount at the beginning of each line except the first, which is of full width.
hang·man (hăng′mən), *n., pl.* **-men.** one who hangs persons condemned to death; public executioner.
hang·nail (hăng′nāl′), *n.* a small piece of partly detached skin at the side or base of the nail. [aspirated var. of *angnail,* OE *angnægl;* the aspirated form became standard by popular etymology (assoc. with *hang*)]
hang·out (hăng′out′), *n.* *Slang.* a place where one lives or frequently visits.
hang·o·ver (hăng′ō′vər), *n.* *U.S. Colloq.* **1.** something remaining behind from a former period or state of affairs. **2.** the effect on a person after excessive indulgence in alcoholic liquor.
hank (hăngk), *n.* **1.** a skein, as of thread or yarn. **2.** a definite length of thread or yarn: *a hank of cotton yarn measures 840 yards.* **3.** a coil, knot, or loop: *a hank of hair.* **4.** *Naut.* a ring, as of iron or wood, round a stay, to which a sail is attached. [ME, t. Scand.; cf. Icel. *hönk* hank, coil, skein]
han·ker (hăng′kər), *v.i.* to have a restless or incessant longing (often fol. by *after, for,* or an infinitive). —**han′·ker·er,** *n.*
han·ker·ing (hăng′kər ĭng), *n.* a restless or incessant longing.

Han·kow (hăn′kou′; *Chin.* hän′kō′), *n.* a city in E China, in Hupeh province: a port at the head of ocean navigation on Yangtze. 725,185 (est. 1938). See **Wuhan.**
han·ky-pan·ky (hăng′kĭ păng′kĭ), *n.* *Brit. Slang.* **1.** trickery. **2.** jugglery or legerdemain.
Han·na (hăn′ə), *n.* **Marcus Alonzo,** 1837–1904, U.S. politician and senator, 1897–1904.
Han·ni·bal (hăn′ə bəl), *n.* **1.** 247–183? B.C., Carthaginian general who crossed the Alps and invaded Italy. **2.** a city in NE Missouri: a port on the Mississippi; Mark Twain's boyhood home. 20,444 (1950).
Han·no·ver (hä nō′vər), *n.* German name of **Hanover** (defs. 1, 2).
Ha·noi (hä′noi′), *n.* a city in NE French Indo-China, on the Songka river: the capital of Viet Nam. 149,000 (1936).
Ha·no·taux (à nô tō′), *n.* **Gabriel Albert Auguste** (gà brē ĕl′ àl bĕr′ ō gyst′), 1853–1944, French statesman and historian.
Han·o·ver (hăn′ō vər), *n.* **1.** German, **Hannover.** a province in NW Germany. 3,457,477 pop. (1939); 14,944 sq. mi. **2.** German, **Hannover.** the capital of this province. 470,950 (1939). **3.** the name of the English royal family from 1714 to 1901. **4.** a college town in W New Hampshire, on the Connecticut river. 4999 (1950).
Han·o·ve·ri·an (hăn′ō vĭr′ĭ ən), *adj.* **1.** of or pertaining to the former ruling house of Hanover. —*n.* **2.** *Brit. Pol.* a supporter of the house of Hanover.
Han·sard (hăn′sərd), *n.* the official stenographic reports of British Parliamentary debates, so called after a family of former compilers.
hanse (hăns), *n.* **1.** a company or guild of merchants. **2.** a fee paid to a medieval trading guild. **3.** Also, **Hanse Towns.** (*cap.*) Hanseatic League. [ME, t. OF, t. MHG: company (of merchants)]

CENTERS OF THE HANSEATIC LEAGUE

Han·se·at·ic League (hăn′sĭ ăt′ĭk), a medieval league of towns of northern Germany and adjacent countries for the promotion and protection of commerce. See the map just above.
han·sel (hăn′səl), *n., v.t.,* **-seled, -seling** or (*esp. Brit.*) **-selled, -selling.** handsel.
han·som (hăn′səm), *n.* a low-hung, two-wheeled, covered vehicle drawn by one horse, for two passengers, the driver being mounted on an elevated seat behind, and the reins running over the roof. [named after J. A. *Hansom,* British patentee (1834)]
Han·son (hăn′sən), *n.* **Howard (Harold),** born 1896, U.S. composer.
Hants (hănts), *n.* Hampshire (def. 1).
Ha·nuk·kah (hä′nŏŏ kä′; *Heb.* KHÄ′-), *n.* the Feast of the Dedication, a Jewish festival in commemoration of the victory of the Maccabees, lasting eight days (mostly in December). [t. Heb.: m. *ḥanukkāh* dedication]

Hansom

Han·u·man (hŭn′ŏŏ män′), *n.* *Hindu Myth.* a monkey chief who is a conspicuous figure in the Ramayana. [t. Hind.: lit., the one with a jaw, the jawed one]
Han·yang (hän′yäng′), *n.* a city in E China at the junction of the Han and Yangtze rivers. 495,476 (1931). See **Wuhan.**
hap (hăp), *n., v.,* **happed, happing.** *Archaic.* —*n.* **1.** one's luck or lot. **2.** an occurrence, happening, or accident. —*v.i.* **3.** to happen: *if it so hap.* [ME, t. Scand.; cf. Icel. *happ* hap, chance, good luck. Cf. OE *gehæp,* adj., fit, convenient]
hap·haz·ard (*adj., adv.* hăp′hăz′ərd; *n.* hăp′hăz′ərd), *adj.* **1.** determined by or dependent on mere chance: *a haphazard remark.* —*adv.* **2.** in a haphazard manner; at random; by chance. —*n.* **3.** mere chance; accident: *to proceed at haphazard.* [f. HAP + HAZARD] —**hap′·haz′·ard·ly,** *adv.* —**hap′·haz′·ard·ness,** *n.*
haph·ta·rah (häf′tä rä′, häf tôr′ä), *n., pl.* **-roth** (-rōth′, -rōth). a portion of the Prophets read immediately after a portion of the Pentateuch in the Jewish synagogue on Sabbaths and festivals. Also, **haftarah.** [t. Heb.: conclusion]
hap·less (hăp′lĭs), *adj.* luckless; unfortunate; unlucky. —**hap′·less·ly,** *adv.* —**hap′·less·ness,** *n.*
hap·lite (hăp′līt), *n.* *Geol.* aplite.

haplo-, a word element meaning "single," "simple." [t. Gk., comb. form of *haplóos*]

hap·loid (hăp′loid), *adj.* Also, **hap·loi′dic.** 1. single; simple. 2. *Biol.* pertaining to a single set of chromosomes. —*n.* 3. *Biol.* an organism or cell having only one complete set of chromosomes, ordinarily half the normal diploid number.

hap·lo·sis (hăp lō′sĭs), *n.* *Biol.* the production of haploid chromosome groups during meiosis.

hap·ly (hăp′lĭ), *adv.* *Archaic.* perhaps; by chance.

hap·pen (hăp′ən), *v.i.* 1. to come to pass, take place, or occur. 2. to come to pass by chance; occur without apparent reason or design; chance. 3. to have the fortune or lot (to do or be as specified): *I happened to see him.* 4. to befall, as to a person or thing. 5. to come by chance (fol. by *on* or *upon*): *to happen on a clue to a mystery.* 6. to be, come, or go (as specified) by chance: *to happen in to see a friend.* [ME *happene(n)*, *ha′men*; f. HAP, n. + -EN¹]
—**Syn.** 1. HAPPEN, CHANCE, OCCUR refer to the taking place of an event. HAPPEN, which originally denoted the taking place by hap or chance, is now the most general word for coming to pass: *an accident has happened.* CHANCE suggests the fortuitousness of an event: *it chanced to rain that day.* OCCUR is often interchangeable with HAPPEN, but is more formal, and is usually more specific as to time and event: *his death occurred the following year.*

hap·pen·ing (hăp′ən ĭng, hăp′nĭng), *n.* an occurrence; event.

hap·pi·ly (hăp′ə lĭ), *adv.* 1. in a happy manner; with pleasure. 2. luckily. 3. with skill; aptly; appropriately.

hap·pi·ness (hăp′ĭ nĭs), *n.* 1. quality or state of being happy. 2. good fortune; pleasure, content, or gladness. 3. aptness or felicity, as of expression.
—**Syn.** 1. beatitude, blessedness, contentedness. HAPPINESS, BLISS, CONTENTMENT, FELICITY imply an active or passive state of pleasure or pleasurable satisfaction. HAPPINESS results from the possession or attainment of what one considers good: *the happiness of visiting one's family.* BLISS is unalloyed happiness or supreme delight: *the bliss of perfect companionship.* CONTENTMENT is a peaceful kind of happiness in which one rests without desires, even though every wish may not have been gratified: *contentment in one's surroundings.* FELICITY is a formal word for happiness of an especially fortunate or intense kind: *to wish a young couple felicity in life.* —**Ant.** 1. wretchedness.

hap·py (hăp′ĭ), *adj.,* **-pier, -piest.** 1. characterized by or indicative of pleasure, content, or gladness: *a happy mood.* 2. delighted, pleased, or glad, as over a particular thing: *to be happy to see a person.* 3. favored by fortune; fortunate or lucky: *a happy event.* 4. apt or felicitous, as actions, utterances, ideas, etc. [ME; f. HAP¹, n. + -Y¹] —**Syn.** 1. joyous, joyful, glad, blithe, cheerful. 3. favorable, propitious. See **fortunate.** 4. appropriate, fitting. —**Ant.** 1. depressed. 3. unlucky.

hap·py-go-luck·y (hăp′ĭ gō lŭk′ĭ), *adj.* 1. trusting cheerfully to luck. —*adv.* 2. haphazard; by mere chance.

Haps·burg (hăps′bûrg), *Ger.* häps′bŏŏrkʜ), *n.* a German princely family, prominent since the 11th century, which has furnished sovereigns to the Holy Roman Empire, Austria, Spain, etc. Also, **Habsburg.** [var. of *Habsburg,* shortening of *Habichtsburg* (hawk's castle) name of a castle in Aargau, Switzerland]

ha·ra-ki·ri (hä′rə kĭr′ĭ), *n.* suicide by ripping open the abdomen with a dagger or knife: the national form of honorable suicide in Japan, formerly practiced by the higher classes when in disgrace or under sentence of death. Also, **ha·ra·ka·ri** (hä′rə kä′rĭ), **hari-kari.** [t. Jap.: belly cut]

ha·rangue (hə răng′), *n., v.,* **-rangued, -ranguing.** —*n.* 1. a passionate, vehement speech; noisy and intemperate address. 2. any long, declamatory or pompous speech. —*v.t.* 3. to address in a harangue. —*v.i.* 4. to deliver a harangue. [t. F, t. Gmc.; cf. OE and OHG *hring* RING¹] —**ha·rangu′er,** *n.* —**Syn.** 1. See **speech.**

Ha·rar (hä′rər), *n.* a city in E Ethiopia. ab. 40,000.

har·ass (hăr′əs, hə răs′), *v.t.* 1. to trouble by repeated attacks, incursions, etc., as in war or hostilities; harry; raid. 2. to disturb persistently; torment, as with troubles, cares, etc. [t. F: s. *harasser,* der. OF *harer* set a dog on] —**har′ass·er,** *n.* —**har′ass·ing·ly,** *adv.* —**Syn.** 2. badger, vex, pester, plague. See **worry.**

har·ass·ment (hăr′əs mənt, hə răs′mənt), *n.* 1. act of harassing. 2. state of being harassed; worry. 3. something that harasses.

Har·bin (här′bĭn′, -bĭn), *n.* a city in NE China, in central Manchuria. 637,573 (est. 1941).

har·bin·ger (här′bĭn jər), *n.* 1. one who goes before and makes known the approach of another. 2. *Obs.* one sent in advance of troops, a royal train, etc., to provide or secure lodgings and other accommodations. —*v.t.* 3. to act as harbinger to; herald the coming of. [ME *herbergere,* t. OF: m. *herbergeor,* der. *herbergier* provide lodging for, der. *herberge* lodging, t. OG: m. *heriberga*]

har·bor (här′bər), *n.* 1. a portion of a body of water along the shore deep enough for ships, and so situated with respect to coastal features, whether natural or artificial, as to provide protection from winds, waves, and currents. 2. any place of shelter or refuge. —*v.t.* 3. to give shelter to: *to harbor fugitives.* 4. to conceal; give a place to hide: *to harbor smuggled goods.* 5. to entertain in the mind; indulge (usually unfavorable or evil feelings): *to harbor suspicion.* 6. to shelter (a ship) in a harbor or haven. —*v.i.* 7. (of a ship, etc.) to take

shelter in a harbor. 8. *Obs.* to take or have shelter or lodging. Also, *Brit.,* **harbour.** [ME *herber(we), hereberge,* OE *herebeorg* lodgings, quarters, f. *here* army + (ge)*beorg* refuge; c. G *herberge*] —**har′bor·er,** *n.* —**har′bor·less,** *adj.*
—**Syn.** 1. HARBOR, HAVEN, PORT indicate a shelter for ships. A HARBOR may be natural or artificially constructed or improved: *a fine harbor on the eastern coast.* A HAVEN is usually a natural harbor which can be utilized by ships as a place of safety; the word is common in poetic use: *a haven in time of storm, a haven of refuge.* A PORT is a harbor viewed esp. in its commercial relations, though it is frequently applied in the meaning of harbor or haven, also: *a thriving port, any old port in a storm.* 5. See **cherish.**

har·bor·age (här′bər ĭj), *n.* 1. shelter for ships, as in a harbor. 2. shelter or lodging. 3. a place of shelter. Also, *Brit.,* **har′bour·age.**

harbor master, an officer in charge of the mooring and berthing of ships and other harbor regulations.

harbor seal. See **seal** (def. 1).

har·bour (här′bər), *n., v.t., v.i.* *Brit.* harbor.

hard (härd), *adj.* 1. solid and firm to the touch; not soft. 2. firmly formed; tight: *a hard knot.* 3. difficult to do or accomplish; fatiguing; troublesome: *a hard task.* 4. difficult or troublesome with respect to an action specified: *hard to please.* 5. difficult to deal with, manage, control, overcome, or understand: *a hard problem.* 6. carried on or performed with great exertion, energy, or persistence: *hard work.* 7. carrying on work in this manner: *a hard worker.* 8. vigorous or violent; severe: *a hard rain.* 9. oppressive; harsh; rough: *hard treatment.* 10. harsh or severe in dealing with others: *a hard master.* 11. incapable of being denied or explained away: *hard facts.* 12. harsh or unfriendly; not easily moved: *hard feelings.* 13. harsh or unpleasant to the eye, ear, or aesthetic sense. 14. severe or rigorous in terms: *a hard bargain.* 15. not swayed by sentiment or sophistry; shrewd: *to have a hard head.* 16. *Colloq.* incorrigible; disreputable: *a hard character.* 17. *Chiefly Dial.* niggardly; stingy. 18. in coin rather than in paper currency, or as distinguished from other property: *hard cash.* 19. *U.S.* strong; spirituous or intoxicating: *hard liquors.* 20. (of water) containing mineral salts which interfere with the action of the soap. 21. *Agric.* noting wheats with high gluten content, milled for a bread flour as contrasted with pastry flour. 22. *Phonet.* **a.** (of consonants) fortis. **b.** (of *c* and *g*) pronounced as in *come* and *go.* **c.** (of consonants in Slavic languages) not palatalized. 23. **hard of hearing,** partly deaf. 24. **hard up,** *Colloq.* urgently in need of money. —*adv.* 25. with great exertion; with vigor or violence: *to work hard.* 26. earnestly or intently: *to look hard at a thing.* 27. harshly or severely; gallingly: *it goes hard.* 28. so as to be solid or firm: *frozen hard.* 29. **hard put to it,** in great perplexity or difficulty. 30. *Naut.* closely, fully, or to the extreme limit: *hard aport.* [ME; OE *heard,* c. G *hart*]
—**Syn.** 1. inflexible, rigid, unyielding, resisting, adamantine, flinty, impenetrable. See **firm¹.** 3. toilsome, burdensome, wearisome, exhausting. HARD, DIFFICULT both describe something resistant to one's efforts or one's endurance. HARD is the general word: *hard times, it was hard to endure the severe weather.* DIFFICULT means not easy, and particularly denotes that which requires special effort or skill: *a difficult task.* 5. perplexing, puzzling, intricate, knotty, tough. 6. arduous, onerous, laborious. 9. severe, rigorous, grinding, cruel, merciless, unsparing. 10. stern, austere, strict, exacting. HARD, CALLOUS, UNFEELING, UNSYMPATHETIC imply a lack of interest in, feeling for, or sympathy with others. HARD implies insensibility, either natural or acquired, so that the plight of others makes no impression on one: *a hard taskmaster.* CALLOUS may mean the same, or that one is himself insensitive to hurt, as the result of continued repression and indifference: *a callous answer, callous to criticism.* UNFEELING implies natural inability to feel with and for others: *an unfeeling and thoughtless remark.* UNSYMPATHETIC implies an indifference or coldness which makes no attempt to pity, sympathize, etc.: *unsympathetic toward distress.*

hard and fast, 1. strongly binding; not to be set aside or violated: *hard and fast rules.* 2. firmly and securely: *bound hard and fast.*

hard-bit·ten (härd′bĭt′ən), *adj.* tough; stubborn.

hard-boiled (härd′boild′), *adj.* 1. boiled until hard, as an egg. 2. *Colloq.* hardened by experience: *a hard-boiled person.* 3. *Slang.* rough or tough.

hard cider, cider which has fermented.

hard coal, anthracite.

Har·de·ca·nute (här′də kə nūt′, -nōōt′), *n.* c1019–42. king of Denmark, 1035–42, and king of England, 1040–42.

hard·en (här′dən), *v.t.* 1. to make hard or harder. 2. to make obdurate or unyielding; make unfeeling or pitiless: *to harden one's heart.* 3. to strengthen or confirm with respect to any element of character; toughen. 4. to make hardy, robust, or capable of endurance. —*v.i.* 5. to become hard or harder. 6. to become obdurate, unfeeling, or pitiless. 7. to become inured or toughened. 8. *Com.* (of prices, the market, etc.) **a.** to become higher; rise. **b.** to cease to fluctuate. —**Syn.** 1. solidify, indurate; petrify, ossify. 3. fortify, steel, brace, nerve. 4. inure, discipline, toughen, season, temper. —**Ant.** 1. soften. 3. weaken. 4. debilitate.

Har·den·berg (fre′drĭkʜ fən), ("Novalis") 1772–1801, German author. **Friedrich von**

hard·ened (här′dənd), *adj.* 1. made hard; indurated; inured. 2. obdurate; unfeeling.

hard·en·er (härʹdən ər), n. 1. a person or thing that hardens. 2. one who hardens a specified thing. 3. a substance mixed with paint or other protective covering to make the finish harder or more durable.

hard·en·ing (härʹdən ĭng), n. a material which hardens another, as water used as a bath in making steel.

hard·fa·vored (härd/fāʹvərd), adj. having a hard, unpleasant countenance.

hard·fea·tured (härd/fēʹchərd), adj. having hard or harsh features.

hard·fist·ed (härd/fĭsʹtĭd), adj. 1. niggardly; stingy. 2. having hard or strong hands, as a laborer.

hard·hack (härd/hăkʹ), n. a woolly-leaved rosaceous shrub, Spiraea tomentosa, of North America, having terminal panicles of rose-colored or white flowers.

hard·hand·ed (härd/hănʹdĭd), adj. 1. having hands hardened by toil. 2. ruling with a strong or cruel hand. —hard/·hand/ed·ness, n.

hard·head (härd/hĕdʹ), n. 1. a shrewd, practical person. 2. a blockhead.

hard·head·ed (härd/hĕdʹĭd), adj. 1. not easily moved or deceived; practical; shrewd. 2. obstinate; stubborn; willful. —hard/·head/ed·ly, adv. —hard/head/ed·ness, n.

hard·heart·ed (härd/härʹtĭd), adj. unfeeling; unmerciful; pitiless. —hard/·heart/ed·ly, adv. —hard/heart/ed·ness, n.

har·di·hood (härʹdĭ hŏŏd/), n. hardy spirit or character; boldness or daring.

har·di·ly (härʹdəlĭ), adv. in a hardy manner.

har·di·ness (härʹdĭ nĭs), n. 1. robustness; capability of endurance; strength. 2. hardihood; audacity.

Har·ding (härʹdĭng), n. Warren Gamaliel (gə mā/lĭ·əl), 1865–1923, 29th president of the U.S., 1921–23.

hard·ly (härd/lĭ), adv. 1. barely; almost not at all: hardly any, hardly ever. 2. not quite: that is hardly true. 3. with little likelihood: he will hardly come now. 4. with trouble or difficulty. 5. harshly or severely.
—Syn. 1. HARDLY, BARELY, SCARCELY imply a narrow margin by which performance was, is, or will be achieved. HARDLY, though often interchangeable with SCARCELY and BARELY, usually emphasizes the idea of the difficulty involved: we could hardly endure the winter. BARELY emphasizes the narrowness of the margin of safety, "only just and no more": we barely succeeded. SCARCELY implies a very narrow margin, below satisfactory performance: we can scarcely read.

hard maple, U.S. the sugar maple, Acer saccharum.

hard·ness (härd/nĭs), n. 1. state or quality of being hard. 2. an instance of this quality. 3. that quality in impure water which is imparted by the presence of dissolved salts, especially calcium sulfate. 4. Mineral. the comparative capacity of a substance to scratch another or be scratched by another. See **Mohs scale**.

hard·pan (härd/pănʹ), n. Chiefly U.S. 1. any layer of firm detrital matter, as of clay, underlying soft soil. 2. hard, unbroken ground. 3. solid foundation; hard underlying reality. 4. the lowest level.

hard rubber, rubber vulcanized with a large amount of sulfur, usually 25–35%, to render it stiff and comparatively inflexible.

hards (härdz), n.pl. the refuse or coarser parts of flax or hemp, separated in hackling. Also, **hurds**. [ME herdes, OE heordan]

hard sauce, a creamed mixture of butter and confectioners' sugar, often with flavoring and cream, used on warm puddings, pies, etc.

hard·set (härd/sĕtʹ), adj. 1. in a difficult position; 2. firmly or rigidly set. 3. determined; obstinate.

hard·shell (härd/shĕlʹ), adj. 1. having a firm, hard shell, as a crab in its normal state, not having recently molted. 2. U.S. Colloq. rigid or uncompromising.

hard·ship (härd/shĭp), n. 1. a condition that bears hard upon one; severe toil, trial, oppression, or need. 2. an instance of this; something hard to bear.
—Syn. 1. HARDSHIP, PRIVATION, AUSTERITY are terms for something hard to endure. HARDSHIP applies to a circumstance in which excessive and painful effort of some kind is required, as enduring acute discomfort from cold, battling over rough terrain, and the like. PRIVATION has particular reference to lack of food, clothing, and other necessities or comforts. AUSTERITY, which became established as a general term in England during World War II, not only includes the ideas of privations and hardships but also carries connotations of deliberate control of emotional reactions to these. —Ant. 1. ease.

hard·spun (härd/spŭnʹ), adj. (of yarn) compactly twisted in spinning.

hard·tack (härd/tăkʹ), n. a kind of hard biscuit much used by sailors and soldiers. [f. HARD + tack taste]

hard·ware (härd/wârʹ), n. metalware, as tools, locks, hinges, cutlery, etc.

hard·wood (härd/wŏŏdʹ), n. 1. the hard, compact wood or timber of various trees, as the oak, cherry, maple, mahogany, etc. 2. a tree yielding such wood.

har·dy¹ (härʹdĭ), adj., -di·er, -di·est. 1. fitted for enduring fatigue, hardship, exposure, etc.: hardy animals. 2. (of plants) able to withstand the cold of winter in the open air. 3. requiring great physical endurance: the hardiest sports. 4. bold or daring; courageous, as persons, actions, etc. 5. unduly bold; presumptuous; foolhardy. [ME hardi, t. OF. hardi, pp. of hardir harden, t. Gmc.; akin to HARD] —Syn. 1. vigorous, sturdy, robust, hale. 4. intrepid, resolute. —Ant. 1. weakly. 4. timid.

har·dy² (härʹdĭ), n., pl. -dies. a chisel or fuller with a square shank for insertion into a square hole (**hardy hole**) in a blacksmith's anvil. [appar. der. HARD]

Har·dy (härʹdĭ), n. Thomas, 1840–1928, British novelist and poet.

hare (hâr), n., pl. hares, (esp. collectively) hare, v., hared, haring. —n. 1. any rodentlike mammal of the genus Lepus (family Leporidae), with long ears, divided upper lip, short tail, and lengthened hind limbs adapted for leaping. 2. any of the larger species of this genus, as distinguished from certain of the smaller ones known as rabbits. 3. any of various similar animals of the same family. 4. the person chased or pursued in the game of hare and hounds. —v.i. 5. Chiefly Brit. to run fast. [ME; OE hara, c. Dan. hare; akin to G hase. Cf. OE hasu gray] —hare/like/, adj.

hare and hounds, an outdoor sport in which certain players (**hares**) start off in advance on a long run, scattering small pieces of paper (**scent**), the other players (**hounds**) following the trail so marked in an effort to catch the hares before they reach home.

hare·bell (hâr/bĕlʹ), n. 1. a low campanulaceous herb, the bluebell of Scotland, Campanula rotundifolia, with blue, bell-shaped flowers. 2. a liliaceous plant, Scilla nonscripta, with bell-shaped flowers.

hare·brained (hâr/brāndʹ), adj. giddy; reckless.

hare·lip (hâr/lĭpʹ), n. 1. a congenitally deformed lip, usually the upper one, in which there is a vertical fissure causing it to resemble the cleft lip of a hare. 2. the deformity itself. —hare/lipped/, adj.

har·em (hâr/əm, hăr/-), n. 1. that part of an Oriental palace or house reserved for the residence of women. 2. the women in an Oriental household: mother, sisters, wives, concubines, daughters, entertainers, servants, etc. [t. Ar.: m. harīm, lit., (something) forbidden]

Har·greaves (här/grēvz), n. James, died 1778, British inventor (of spinning machinery).

har·i·cot (här/ə kō/), n. Chiefly Brit. 1. a plant of the genus Phaseolus, esp. P. vulgaris, the common kidney bean. 2. its seed. [t. F, identical with haricot ragout]

ha·ri·ka·ri (hä/rĭ kä/rĭ), n. hara-kiri.

hark (härk), v.i. 1. to listen; harken (used chiefly in the imperative). 2. hark back, a. to return to a previous point or subject. as in discourse or thought; revert. b. (of hounds) to return along the course in order to regain a lost scent. —v.t. 3. Archaic. to listen to; hear. —n. 4. a hunter's cry to hounds. [ME herk(i)en, c. OFris. herkia. Cf. HEARKEN]

hark·ee (här/kē), interj., hark ye.

hark·en (här/kən), v.i. Poetic. 1. to listen; to give heed or attend to what is said. —v.t. 2. Archaic. to listen to; hear. Also, **hearken**. [ME herken, OE he(o)rcnian; akin to HARK] —hark/en·er, n.

Har·lem (här/ləm), n. 1. the chief Negro section of New York City, in the NE part of Manhattan. 2. a tidal river in New York City, separating the boroughs of Manhattan and the Bronx and (with Spuyten Duyvil creek) connecting the Hudson and East rivers, 8 mi.

Har·le·quin (här/lə kwĭn, -kĭn), n. 1. (sometimes l.c.) a droll character in comedy (orig. the early Italian) and pantomime, usually masked, dressed in particolored spangled tights, and bearing a wooden sword or magic wand. 2. (l.c.) a buffoon. 3. (l.c.) any one of various small, handsomely marked snakes. —adj. 4. (l.c.) fancifully varied in color, decoration, etc. 5. (of a piece of furniture, esp. of the 18th century) combining or concealing parts or articles for various uses. [t. F: OF Harlequin, Herlequin, t. ME: m. Herle King King Herla (mythical figure); modern meaning from It. arlecchino, t. F: m. Harlequin]

har·le·quin·ade (här/lə kwĭ nād/, -kĭ-), n. 1. a pantomime or similar play in which the harlequin plays the principal part. 2. buffoonery. [t. m. arlequinade]

harlequin cabbage bug, the calicoback.

harlequin duck, a small North American diving duck, Histrionicus histrionicus, in which the male is bluish-gray, marked with black, white, and chestnut.

har·le·quin·esque (här/lə kwĭn ĕsk/), adj. in the style or manner of a harlequin.

Har·ley (här/lĭ), n. Robert. See Oxford, 1st Earl of.

Harley Street, a street in London, England, noted for the doctors who have offices there.

har·lot (här/lət), n. 1. a lewd woman; prostitute; strumpet. —adj. 2. pertaining to or like a harlot; low. [ME, t. OF: rogue, knave; orig. uncert.]

har·lot·ry (här/lə trĭ), n., pl. -ries. 1. the practice or trade of prostitution. 2. a harlot.

harm (härm), n. 1. injury; damage; hurt: to do him bodily harm. 2. moral injury; evil; wrong. —v.t. 3. to do harm to; injure; damage; hurt. [ME; OE hearm, c. G harm. Cf. Russ. sram shame] —harm/er, n. —Syn. 1, 2. See **damage**.

har·mat·tan (här/mə tăn/), n. a dry, parching land wind, charged with dust, on the west coast of Africa. [t. W. African (Fanti or Tshi)]

harm·ful (härm/fəl), adj. fraught with or doing harm. —harm/ful·ly, adv. —harm/ful·ness, n. —Syn. injurious, hurtful, detrimental; deleterious, noxious, pernicious. —Ant. beneficial.

harm·less (härm/lĭs), adj. 1. without power or tendency to harm: harmless play. 2. Rare. unharmed. —harm/less·ly, adv. —harm/less·ness, n.

har·mon·ic (härmŏn′ Yk), *adj.* **1.** pertaining to harmony, as distinguished from melody and rhythm. **2.** marked by harmony; in harmony; concordant; consonant. **3.** *Physics.* denoting an integral multiple of a given frequency, thus 256, 512, 768, cycles per second are the *first, second,* and *third harmonics* of 256 cycles per second. **4.** *Math.* having relations resembling those of musical concords: *a harmonic progression is a series of numbers the reciprocals of which are in arithmetical progression.* —*n.* **5.** an overtone. [t. L: s. *harmonicus*, t. Gk.: m. *harmonikós* skilled in music] —**har·mon′i·cal·ly,** *adv.*

har·mon·i·ca (härmŏn′ə kə), *n.* **1.** a musical instrument having a set of small metallic reeds mounted in a case and played by the breath; a mouth organ. **2.** any of various percussion instruments which use graduated bars of metal or other hard material as sounding elements. [t. L, *n.* use of fem. of *harmonicus* HARMONIC]

harmonic mean, *Statistics.* the mean of *n* positive numbers obtained by taking the reciprocal of the average of the reciprocals of the numbers.

harmonic minor, *Music.* the minor scale from which chords are formed, having the sixth degree a semitone above the dominant and the seventh degree a semitone below the tonic.

har·mon·i·con (härmŏn′ə kən), *n.* any of various musical instruments, as a harmonica or an orchestrion. [t. Gk.: m. *harmonikón* (neut.) harmonic]

har·mon·ics (härmŏn′ Yks), *n. Music.* **1.** the science of musical sounds. **2.** (*construed as pl.*) the partials or overtones of a fundamental. Cf. **harmonic** (def. 2). **3.** (*construed as pl.*) the flageoletlike tones of a string (as a violin string) made to vibrate so as to bring out an overtone. [pl. of HARMONIC. See -ICS]

harmonic tone, *Music.* a tone produced by suppressing the fundamental tone and bringing into prominence one of its overtones.

har·mo·ni·ous (härmō′nY əs), *adj.* **1.** marked by agreement in feeling or action: *a harmonious group.* **2.** forming a pleasingly consistent whole; congruous. **3.** agreeable to the ear; tuneful; melodious. —**harmo′ni·ous·ly,** *adv.* —**har·mo′ni·ous·ness,** *n.* —**Syn. 1.** amicable, congenial; sympathetic. **2.** concordant, congruent, consonant, consistent. —**Ant. 1, 3.** discordant.

har·mo·nist (här′mə nYst), *n.* **1.** one skilled in harmony. **2.** one who makes a harmony, as of the Gospels.

har·mo·nis·tic (här′mə nYs′tYk), *adj.* **1.** pertaining to a harmonist or harmony. **2.** pertaining to the collation and harmonizing of parallel passages, as of the Gospels. —**har′mo·nis′ti·cal·ly,** *adv.*

har·mo·ni·um (härmō′nY əm), *n.* a reed organ, esp. one in which the air is forced outward through the reeds. [t. F, der. *harmonie,* t. L: m. *harmonia* HARMONY]

har·mo·nize (här′mə nīz′), *v.,* **-nized, -nizing.** —*v.t.* **1.** to bring into harmony, accord, or agreement: *to harmonize the views.* **2.** *Music.* to accompany with appropriate harmony. —*v.i.* **3.** to be in agreement in action, sense, or feeling. **4.** *Colloq.* to sing in harmony. Also, *esp. Brit.,* **har′mo·nise′.** —**har′mo·ni·za′tion,** *n.* —**har′mo·niz′er,** *n.*

har·mo·ny (här′mə nY), *n., pl.* **-nies. 1.** agreement; accord; harmonious relations. **2.** a consistent, orderly, or pleasing arrangement of parts; congruity. **3.** *Music.* **a.** any simultaneous combination of tones. **b.** the simultaneous combination of tones; chordal structure, as distinguished from melody and rhythm. **c.** the science of the structure, relations, and practical combination of chords. **4.** an arrangement of the contents of the Gospels (either of all four or of the first three) designed to show their parallelism, mutual relations, and differences. [ME *harmonie,* t. F, t. L: m. *harmonia,* t. Gk.: a joining, concord, music]

—**Syn. 1.** concord, unity, peace, amity, friendship. **2.** consonance, conformity, correspondence, consistency. **3.** HARMONY, MELODY in music suggest a combination of sounds from voices or musical instruments. HARMONY is the blending of simultaneous sounds of different pitch or quality, making chords: *harmony in part singing, harmony between violins and horns.* MELODY is the rhythmical combination of successive sounds of various pitch, making up the tune or air: *a tuneful melody to accompany cheerful words.* —**Ant. 1.** discord. **3.** dissonance.

har·ness (här′nYs), *n.* **1.** the combination of straps, bands, and other parts forming the working gear of a horse or other draft animal (except the ox). See the illus. in the next column. **2.** routine of work: *to die in harness.* **3.** *Archaic.* armor for men or horses (or other animals), or a suit of armor. —*v.t.* **4.** to put harness on (a horse, etc.); attach by a harness, as to a vehicle. **5.** to bring under conditions for working: *to harness water power.* **6.** *Archaic.* to array in armor or equipments of war. [ME, t. OF: m. *harneis,* ? t. OHG; cf. OE *herenet* corselet] —**har′ness·er,** *n.* —**har′ness·less,** *adj.* —**har′ness·like′,** *adj.*

harness hitch, *Naut.* a knot of various uses which forms an eye in the bight of a line.

Har·ney Peak (här′nY), the highest peak in the Black Hills, in SW South Dakota. 7242 ft.

Har·old I (här′əld), (surnamed *Harefoot*) died 1040, king of England, 1035–40 (son of Canute).

Harold II, c1022–1066, king of England in 1066 (successor of Edward the Confessor and son of Earl Godwin); defeated by William the Conqueror in Battle of Hastings.

harp (härp), *n.* **1.** a musical instrument consisting of a triangular frame (comprising a soundboard, a pillar, and a curved neck) and strings stretched between soundboard and neck and plucked with the fingers. —*v.i.* **2.** to play on a harp. **3.** to dwell persistently or tediously in speaking or writing (fol. by *on* or *upon*). —*v.t.* **4.** *Poetic.* to bring, put, etc., by playing on a harp. **5.** *Archaic.* to give voice or utterance to. [ME *harp(e),* OE *hearpe,* c. D *harp,* G *harfe,* Icel. *harpa*] —**harp′er,** *n.* —**harp′like′,** *adj.*

Har·pers Ferry (här′pərz), a town in NE West Virginia at the confluence of the Shenandoah and Potomac rivers: John Brown's raid, 1859. Also, **Harper's Ferry.**

harp·ings (här′pYngz), *n.pl. Naut.* the stout wales about the bow of a ship. Also, **harp·ins** (här′pYnz).

harp·ist (här′pYst), *n.* one who plays on the harp, esp. professionally.

har·poon (härpoon′), *n.* **1.** a barbed, spearlike missile attached to a rope, and thrown by hand or shot from a gun, used in capturing whales and large fish. —*v.t.* **2.** to strike, catch, or kill with or as with a harpoon. [t. D: m. *harpoen,* t. F: m. *harpon,* der. *harper* grapple, of Gmc. orig.] —**har·poon′er,** *n.* —**har·poon′like′,** *adj.*

harp·si·chord (härp′sY kôrd′), *n.* a keyboard instrument, precursor of the piano, in common use from the 16th to the 18th century, and revived in the 20th, in which the strings are plucked by leather or quill points connected with the keys. [t. F. (obs.): m. *harpechorde,* f. *harpe* (of Gmc. orig.) harp + *chorde* string (see CHORD[1])]

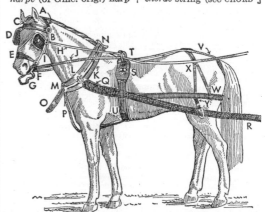

Harness of a horse: A, Crown; B, Cheekpiece; C, Front; D, Blinds; E, Noseband; F, Bit; G, Curb; H, Checkrein; I, Throatlatch; J, Rein; K, Collar; L, Hame; M, Hame link; N, Hame strap; O, Pole strap; P, Martingale; Q, Trace tug; R, Trace; S, Saddle; T, Terret; U, Bellyband; V, Crupper; W, Breeching; X, Hip strap; Y, Tracebearer

Modern harp
A, Pedestal; B, Pedals;
C, Back; D, Soundboard; E, Neck;
F, Pillar

Har·py (här′pY), *n., pl.* **-pies. 1.** *Gk. Myth.* a ravenous, filthy monster having a woman's head and a bird's body. **2.** (*l.c.*) a rapacious, grasping person. [t. L: m. s. *harpyia,* t. Gk.: lit., snatcher]

harpy eagle, a large, powerful, crested bird of prey, *Thrasaetus harpyia,* of tropical America.

har·que·bus (här′kwə bəs), *n.* a light hand gun with matchlock or wheel-lock mechanism. Also, **arquebus.** [t. F: m. (*h*)*arquebuse,* t. It. (obs.): m. *arcobuso,* t. D: m. *haakbus*]

har·que·bus·ier (här′kwə bə sYr′), *n.* a soldier armed with a harquebus.

har·ri·dan (här′ə dən), *n.* a disreputable violent woman; vicious old hag. [cf. F *haridelle* sorry horse, jade]

har·ri·er[1] (här′Y ər), *n.* **1.** one who or that which harries. **2.** any of several hawks of the genus *Circus* (family *Falconidae*), all of which course back and forth over meadowlands searching for the small birds and mammals on which they feed. [f. HARRY, v., + -ER[1]]

har·ri·er[2] (här′Y ər), *n.* **1.** a breed of small hounds employed in hunting the hare. **2.** a cross-country runner. [special use of HARRIER[1], by assoc. with HARE]

Har·ri·man (här′ə mən), *n.* William Averell, born 1891, U.S. diplomat.

Har·ris (här′Ys), *n.* **1.** Joel Chandler (jō′əl), 1848–1908, U.S. author: creator of Uncle Remus. **2.** Roy, born 1898, U.S. composer.

Har·ris·burg (här′Ys bûrg′), *n.* capital of Pennsylvania, in the S part, on the Susquehanna. 89,544 (1950).

Har·ri·son (här′ə sən), *n.* **1.** Benjamin, 1833–1901, 23rd president of the U.S. 1889–93. **2.** his grandfather, William Henry, 1773–1841, U.S. general: 9th president of the U.S., in 1841.

Har·ro·vi·an (hərō′vY ən), *adj.* of or pertaining to Harrow. See **Harrow-on-the-Hill.**

b., blend of, blended; c., cognate with; d., dialect, dialectal; der., derived from; f., formed from; g., going back to; m., modification of; r., replacing; s., stem of; t., taken from; ?, perhaps. See the full key on inside cover.

har·row (hăr'ō), *n.* **1.** a wheelless agricultural implement set with teeth, upright disks, etc., usually of iron, drawn over plowed land to level it, break clods, etc. —*v.t.* **2.** to draw a harrow over (land, etc.); break or tear with a harrow. **3.** to disturb keenly or painfully; distress the mind, feelings, etc. —*v.i.* **4.** to be broken up by harrowing, as soil, etc. [ME *haru, harwe.* Cf. Icel. *herfi* harrow, MLG *harke* rake] —**har'row·er,** *n.* —**har'row·ing,** *adj.* —**har'row·ing·ly,** *adv.*

Har·row-on-the-Hill (hăr'ō·ŏn·thə·hĭl'), an urban district in SE England, near London: the seat of **Harrow,** a famous boys' school (founded 1571). 211,550 (est. 1946).

har·ry (hăr'ĭ), *v.,* **-ried, -rying.** —*v.t.* **1.** to harass by forced exactions, rapacious demands, etc.; torment; worry. **2.** to ravage, as in war; devastate. —*v.i.* **3.** to make harassing incursions. [ME *herien,* OE *her(g)ian* ravage (der. *here* army), c. G *(ver)heeren* harry, lay waste] —**Syn. 2.** plunder, strip, rob.

harsh (härsh), *adj.* **1.** rough to the touch or to any of the senses: *a harsh surface, a harsh voice.* **2.** ungentle and unpleasant in action or effect: *harsh treatment.* **3.** jarring upon the esthetic sense; inartistic: *his painting was full of harsh lines and clashing colors.* [unexplained doublet of ME *harsk.* Cf. Dan. *harsk* rancid, G *harsch* harsh, rough, hard] —**harsh'ly,** *adv.* —**harsh'ness,** *n.* —**Syn. 2.** severe, austere; brusque, rough; hard, rigorous, unfeeling, unkind, brutal. See **stern[1].** **3.** discordant, dissonant, inharmonious. —**Ant. 2.** mild. **3.** pleasing.

hart (härt), *n., pl.* **harts,** (*esp. collectively*) **hart.** a male of the deer, commonly the red deer, *Cervus elaphus,* esp. after its fifth year. [ME *hert,* OE *heort,* c. G *hirsch;* akin to L *cervus* stag]

Hart (härt), *n.* **Moss,** born 1904, U.S. dramatist and writer of librettos.

har·tal (här'täl'), *n.* (in India) a day of mourning: a form of passive resistance including the closing of shops. [t. Hind.: m. *hathtal* market-stoppage]

Harte (härt), *n.* (**Francis**) **Bret,** 1839–1902, U.S. author, esp. of short stories.

har·te·beest (här'tə·bēst', härt'-bēst'), *n.* **1.** a large South African antelope of the genus *Alcephalus,* as *A. caama,* of a red color, having a long face with naked muzzle. **2.** any of various allied African antelopes, as some species of the genus *Damaliscus.* [t. S Afr. D: hart beast]

Hartebeest.
Alcephalu sbuselaphus (4 to 4½ ft. high at the shoulder)

Hart·ford (härt'fərd), *n.* the capital of Connecticut, in the central part: a port on the Connecticut river. 177,397 (1950).

Hart·ley (härt'lĭ), *n.* **David,** 1705–57, British physician and philosopher.

harts·horn (härts'hôrn'), *n.* **1.** the antler of the hart, formerly much used as a source of ammonia. **3.** *Old Chem., Pharm.* ammonium carbonate; sal volatile. [var. of *hart's horn*]

hart's-tongue (härts'tŭng'), *n.* a fern, *Phyllitis Scolopendrium,* which has long simple fronds. Also, **harts'tongue'.**

har·um-scar·um (hăr'əm·skâr'əm), *adj.* **1.** reckless; rash. —*adv.* **2.** recklessly; wildly. —*n.* **3.** a reckless person. **4.** reckless conduct. [? var. of *hare 'em scare 'em* (with obs. *hare* harry, scare)]

Ha·run-al-Ra·shid (hä·rōōn'äl·rä·shēd'; *Arab.* är'rä-shēd'), *n.* A.D. 763?–809, caliph of Bagdad, A.D. 786–809: hero in many of the stories in the *Arabian Nights.*

ha·rus·pex (hə·rŭs'pĕks, hăr'ə·spĕks'), *n., pl.* **harus·pices** (hə·rŭs'pə·sēz'). (in ancient Rome) one of a class of minor priests who practiced divination, esp. from the entrails of animals killed in sacrifice. [t. L]

Har·vard (här'vərd), *n.* **John,** 1607–38, British nonconformist minister who settled in America and was the principal founder of Harvard College.

har·vest (här'vĭst), *n.* **1.** the gathering of crops. **2.** the season of gathering ripened crops, esp. of grain. **3.** a crop or yield, as of grain. **4.** a supply of anything gathered at maturity and stored up: *a harvest of nuts.* **5.** the product or result of any labor or process. —*v.t.* **6.** to gather, as a crop. **7.** to gather the crop from: *to harvest the fields.* —*v.i.* **8.** to gather a crop; reap. [ME; OE *hærfest,* c. G *herbst* autumn] —**har'vest·ing,** *n.* —**har'vest·less,** *adj.* —**Syn. 3.** See **crop.**

har·vest·er (här'vĭs·tər), *n.* **1.** one who harvests; a reaper. **2.** any of various machines for harvesting or gathering field crops, such as grain, flax, potatoes, etc.

harvest fly, any of certain cicadas, as *Tibicen linnei,* noted for its shrill, noisy song in late summer.

harvest home, 1. the bringing home of the harvest. **2.** the time of doing it. **3.** an English festival celebrated at the close of the harvest.

har·vest·man (här'vĭst·mən), *n., pl.* **-men. 1.** a man engaged in harvesting. **2.** any of the arachnids of the order *Opiliones* (or *Phalangida*), comprising spiderlike creatures with small rounded body and usually very long legs; daddy-longlegs.

harvest moon, the moon at and about the period of fullness which is nearest to the autumn equinox.

harvest tick, any of various acarids in an immature stage, common in late summer and autumn, which attach themselves to the skin of man and animals.

Har·vey (här'vĭ), *n.* **William,** 1578–1657, British physician, discoverer of the circulation of the blood.

Harz Mountains (härts), a range of low mountains in central Germany between the Elbe and Weser rivers. Highest peak, Brocken, 3745 ft.

Harvest ticks (magnified)
A. *"Leptus" irritans;*
B, *Trombidium americanum*

has (hăz), *v.* 3rd pers. sing. pres. indic. of **have.**

Ha·sa (hä'sə), *n.* a region in E Saudi Arabia, on the Persian Gulf. Also, **El Hasa.**

Ha·san (hä'sən), *n.* a son of Ali by Fatima, daughter of Mohammed.

has-been (hăz'bĭn'), *n. Colloq.* a person or thing that is no longer effective, successful, popular, etc.

Has·dru·bal (hăz'drōō·bəl, hăz·drōō'-), *n.* **1.** died 207 B.C., Carthaginian general (brother of Hannibal). **2.** died 221 B.C., Carthaginian general (brother-in-law of Hannibal).

hash (hăsh), *n.* **1.** a dish of chopped meat and potatoes, usually sautéed in a frying pan. **2.** a mess, jumble, or muddle. **3.** any preparation of old material worked over. —*v.t.* **4.** to chop into small pieces; mince; make into a hash. [t. F: m.s. *hacher,* der. *hache* ax. See HATCHET, and cf. HATCH[3]]

Hash·e·mite Kingdom of Jordan (hăsh'ə·mīt), official name of Trans-Jordan.

hash·ish (hăsh'ēsh, -ĭsh), *n.* **1.** the flowering tops, leaves, etc., of Indian hemp, smoked, chewed, or otherwise used in the Orient as a narcotic and intoxicant. **2.** any of certain preparations made from this plant.

has·let (hăs'lĭt, hāz'-), *n.* the heart, liver, etc., of a hog or other animal, as used for food. [ME *hastelet,* t. OF: roasted bit of meat, der. *haste* spit, g. L *hasta* spear]

has·n't (hăz'ənt), contraction of *has not.*

hasp (hăsp, häsp), *n.* **1.** a clasp for a door, lid, etc., esp. one passing over a staple and fastened by a pin or a padlock. —*v.t.* **2.** to fasten with or as with a hasp. [ME *hasp(e),* OE *hæsp, hæpse,* c. G *haspe;* akin to Icel. *hespa*]

Has·sam (hăs'əm), *n.* **Childe,** 1859–1935, U.S. artist.

has·sle (hăs'əl), *n. U.S. Slang.* quarrel; squabble.

has·sock (hăs'ək), *n.* **1.** a thick, firm cushion used as a footstool or for kneeling. **2.** a rank tuft of coarse grass or sedge, as in a bog. [ME; OE *hassuc* coarse grass]

hast (hăst), *v. Poetic* or *Solemn.* 2nd pers. sing. pres. indic. of **have.**

has·tate (hăs'tāt), *adj. Bot.* (of a leaf) triangular or shaped like a halberd, with two spreading lobes at the base. [t. L: m. s. *hastatus* armed with a spear]

haste (hāst), *n., v.,* **hasted, hasting.** —*n.* **1.** energetic speed in motion or action. **2.** need, or sense of need, of speed: *to be in great haste.* **3. make haste, a.** to exert oneself to do something quickly. **b.** (with adjunct) to go with haste. **4.** thoughtless or rash speed: *haste makes waste.* —*v.t., v.i.* **5.** *Poetic.* to hasten. [ME, t. OF, t. Gmc.; cf. OE *hæst* violence] —**Syn. 1.** swiftness, celerity, quickness; rapidity. **2.** hurry, flurry, bustle.

Hastate leaf

has·ten (hā'sən), *v.i.* **1.** to move or act with haste; proceed with haste; hurry: *to hasten to a place.* —*v.t.* **2.** to cause to hasten; accelerate. —**has'ten·er,** *n.* —**Syn. 2.** urge, press; expedite, quicken, precipitate. —**Ant. 1.** lag. **2.** delay.

Has·tings (hās'tĭngz), *n.* **1. Warren,** 1732–1818, British statesman: first governor-general of India, 1773–85. **2.** a seaport in SE England, in Sussex: William the Conqueror defeated the Saxons near here (on Senlac Hill), 1066. 59,720 (est. 1946). **3.** a city in S Nebraska. 20,211 (1950).

Hastings, A.D. 1066

hast·y (hās'tĭ), *adj.,* **hastier, hastiest. 1.** moving or acting with haste; speedy; quick; hurried. **2.** made or done with haste or speed: *a hasty visit.* **3.** unduly quick in movement or action; precipitate; rash: *hasty temper.* **4.** done with or characterized by thoughtless or angry haste: *hasty words.* **5.** easily excited to anger; quick-tempered; irascible. [ME, t. OF: m. *hastif,* der. *haste* HASTE] —**hast'i·ly,** *adv.* —**hast'i·ness,** *n.* —**Syn. 1.** swift; rapid, fast. **3.** foolhardy, reckless. —**Ant. 1.** slow. **3.** deliberate.

hasty pudding, 1. a dish made of flour or oatmeal stirred into seasoned boiling water or milk and quickly cooked. **2.** *U.S.* corn-meal mush.

hat (hăt), *n., v.,* **hatted, hatting.** —*n.* **1.** a shaped covering for the head, usually with a crown and a brim, worn outdoors. **2. pass (round) the hat, a.** to present a hat to receive contributions, as at a public meeting. **b.** to ask for money for charitable use or some purpose of common interest. **3.** *Rom. Cath. Ch.* **a.** the distinctive red head covering of a cardinal. **b.** the office or dignity of cardinal. —*v.t.* **4.** to provide with a hat; put a hat on. [ME; OE *hæt* head covering, c. Icel. *höttr* hood; akin to HOOD] —**hat′less**, *adj.* —**hat′like′**, *adj.*

hat·a·ble (hā′tə bəl), *adj.* capable or worthy of being hated. Also, **hateable.**

hat·band (hăt′bănd′), *n.* **1.** a band or ribbon placed about the crown of a hat, just above the brim. **2.** a black band similarly worn as a sign of mourning.

hat·box (hăt′bŏks′), *n.* a case or box for a hat.

hatch[1] (hăch), *v.t.* **1.** to bring forth (young) from the egg. **2.** to cause young to emerge from (the egg). **3.** to contrive; devise; concoct: *to hatch a plot.* —*v.i.* **4.** to be hatched. —*n.* **5.** act of hatching. **6.** that which is hatched, as a brood. [ME *hacche*, akin to G *hecken*] —**hatch′er**, *n.* —**Syn. 1.** incubate, brood.

hatch[2] (hăch), *n.* **1.** a cover for an opening in a ship's deck, a floor, a roof, or the like. **2.** (*often pl.*) a hatchway. **3.** a ship's deck: *under hatches.* **4.** an opening in the floor or roof of a building. **5.** the cover over such an opening. **6.** the lower half of a divided door. [ME *hacche*, OE *hæc* grating, hatch]

hatch[3] (hăch), *v.t.* **1.** to mark with lines, esp. closely set parallel lines, as for shading in drawing or engraving. —*n.* **2.** a shading line in drawing or engraving. [t. F: m. *hacher* chop, hash, hatch. See HASH]

Hatch Acts, two Congressional acts, passed 1939 and 1940, regulating expenditures, contributions, and procedures in political campaigns.

hatch·el (hăch′əl), *n., v.,* **-eled, -eling** or (*esp. Brit.*) **-elled, -elling.** —*n.* **1.** an instrument for cleaning flax; heckle. —*v.t.* **2.** to heckle. [phonetic doublet of HACKLE[1]. Cf. HECKLE] —**hatch′el·er,** *esp. Brit.* **hatch′el·ler,** *n.*

hatch·er·y (hăch′ər ĭ), *n., pl.* **-eries.** a place for hatching eggs of hens, fish, etc.

hatch·et (hăch′ĭt), *n.* **1.** a small, short-handled ax for use with one hand. **2.** a tomahawk. **3. bury the hatchet,** to make peace. **4. dig up the hatchet,** to prepare for war. [ME, t. F: m. *hachette*, dim. of *hache* ax, t. Gmc.; cf. HACK[1]] —**hatch′et·like′,** *adj.*

hatchet face, a sharp, narrow face. —**hatch′et-faced′,** *adj.*

hatch·ing (hăch′ĭng), *n.* a series of lines, generally parallel, used in shading or modeling. [f. HATCH[3] + -ING[1]]

hatch·ment (hăch′mənt), *n.* *Chiefly Brit.* a square tablet, set diagonally, bearing the arms of a deceased person. [aspirated var. of *atch(e)ment*, syncopated form of ACHIEVEMENT]

hatch·way (hăch′wā′), *n.* **1.** an opening (covered by a hatch) in a ship's deck, for passage to parts below. **2.** the opening of any trap door, as in a floor, ceiling, or roof.

Hatchment of an esquire

hate (hāt), *v.,* **hated, hating,** *n.* —*v.t.* **1.** to regard with a strong or passionate dislike; detest. **2.** to dislike; be unwilling: *I hate to do it.* —*v.i.* **3.** to feel hatred. —*n.* **4.** hatred; strong dislike. **5.** the object of hatred. [ME *hat(i)en*, OE *hatian*, c. G *hassen*] —**hat′er,** *n.*

—**Syn. 1.** loathe, execrate; despise. HATE, ABHOR, DETEST, ABOMINATE imply feeling intense dislike or aversion toward something. HATE, the simple and general word suggests passionate dislike and a feeling of enmity: *to hate autocracy.* ABHOR expresses a deeprooted horror, and a sense of repugnance: *to abhor cruelty.* DETEST implies intense, even vehement, dislike and antipathy, besides a sense of disdain: *to detest a combination of ignorance and arrogance.* ABOMINATE expresses a strong feeling of disgust and repulsion toward something thought of as unworthy, unlucky, and the like: *to abominate treachery.*

hate·a·ble (hā′tə bəl), *adj.* hatable.

hate·ful (hāt′fəl), *adj.* **1.** exciting hate; detestable; odious. **2.** *Archaic.* full of hate; malignant; malevolent. —**hate′ful·ly,** *adv.* —**hate′ful·ness,** *n.*

Syn. 1. abominable, execrable, abhorrent, repugnant; invidious, loathsome. HATEFUL, OBNOXIOUS, ODIOUS, OFFENSIVE refer to that which causes strong dislike or annoyance. HATEFUL implies actually causing hatred or extremely strong dislike: *the sight of him is hateful to me.* OBNOXIOUS emphasizes causing annoyance or discomfort by objectionable qualities: *his persistence made him seem obnoxious, his piggish manners made him obnoxious to his companions.* ODIOUS emphasizes the disagreeable or displeasing: *an odious little man, odious servility.* OFFENSIVE emphasizes the distaste and resentment caused by something which may be either displeasing or insulting: *an offensive odor, remark.* —**Ant. 1.** likable, pleasant, agreeable.

hath (hăth), *v.* *Archaic.* 3rd pers. sing. pres. indic. of **have.**

Hath·a·way (hăth′ə wā′), *n.* **Anne,** 1557–1623, the wife of William Shakespeare.

Hath·or (hăth′ôr), *n.* *Egypt. Myth.* the goddess of love and joy, often represented with the head, horns, or ears of a cow. [t. Egyptian: the castle of Hor]

Ha·thor·ic (hə thŏr′ĭk, -thôr′-), *adj.* **1.** of or pertaining to Hathor. **2.** *Archit.* decorated with a face or head assumed to represent this goddess, as the capital of a column.

ha·tred (hā′trĭd), *n.* the feeling of one who hates; intense dislike; detestation. [ME *hatered(en)*, f. *hate* hate + *-reden*, OE *-ræden* suffix making abstract nouns] —**Syn.** aversion, animosity.

hat·ter (hăt′ər), *n.* a maker or seller of hats.

Hat·ter·as (hăt′ər əs), *n.* **Cape,** a promontory on an island off the E coast of North Carolina: dangerous to shipping.

Hat·ties·burg (hăt′ĭz bûrg′), *n.* a city in SE Mississippi. 29,474 (1950).

hat tree, a stand with spreading arms or pegs on which hats, coats, etc., may be hung. Also, **hat rack.**

hau·ber·geon (hô′bər jən), *n.* habergeon.

hau·berk (hô′bûrk), *n.* a piece of armor originally intended for the protection of the neck and shoulders, but early developed into a long coat of mail reaching below the knees. [ME, t. OF: m. *hauberc*, t. Gmc.; cf. OHG *halsberg* neck protection]

haugh·ty (hô′tĭ), *adj.,* **-tier, -tiest. 1.** disdainfully proud; arrogant; supercilious. **2.** *Archaic.* exalted; lofty, or noble. [extended form of *haught*, orig. *haut*, t. F: high, in OF *halt*, g. L *altus*, b. with OG *hauh* (later *hōh*) high] —**haugh′ti·ly,** *adv.* —**haugh′ti·ness,** *n.* **1.** lordly, disdainful, contemptuous. See **proud.** —**Ant. 1.** humble, unpretentious, unassuming.

Hauberk, 12th and 13th centuries

haul (hôl), *v.t.* **1.** to pull or draw with force; move or transport by drawing. **2. haul up,** *Colloq.* **a.** to bring up, as before a superior, for reprimand; call to account. **b.** to change the course of (a ship), esp. so as to sail closer to the wind. —*v.i.* **3.** to pull or tug. **4.** to change one's course of procedure or action; go in a given direction. **5.** *Naut.* to sail, as in a particular direction. **6.** (of the wind) to change direction, shift, or veer (often fol. by *round* or *to*). **7. haul off, a.** *Naut.* to change the course of a ship so as to get further off from an object. **b.** to draw off or away. **c.** to draw back the arm in preparation for a blow. —*n.* **8.** act of hauling; a strong pull or tug. **9.** that which is hauled. **10.** the distance through which anything is hauled. **11.** *Fishing.* **a.** the quantity of fish taken at one draft of the net. **b.** the draft of a fishing net. **c.** the place where a seine is hauled. **12.** *Colloq.* the taking or acquisition of anything, or that which is taken. [earlier *hall*, phonetic var. of HALE[2]] —**haul′er,** *n.* —**Syn. 1.** See **draw.**

haul·age (hô′lĭj), *n.* **1.** act or labor of hauling. **2.** the amount of force expended in hauling. **3.** a charge made by a railroad for hauling cars, equipment, or commodities.

haulm (hôm), *n.* *Brit.* **1.** stems or stalks collectively, as of grain or of peas, beans, hops, etc., esp. as used for litter or thatching. **2.** a single stem or stalk. Also, **halm.** [ME *halm*, OE *healm*, c. D and G *halm*]

haunch (hônch, hänch), *n.* **1.** the hip. **2.** the fleshy part of the body about the hip. **3.** a hind quarter of an animal. **4.** the leg and loin of an animal, as used for food. **5.** *Archit.* **a.** either side of an arch, extending from the vertex or crown to the impost. **b.** the part of a beam projecting below a floor or roof slab. [ME *hanche*, t. OF, t. Gmc.; cf. MD *hancke*]

haunch bone, the ilium or hipbone.

haunt (hônt; hänt; *for 9 sometimes also* hănt), *v.t.* **1.** to reappear frequently to after death; visit habitually as a supposed spirit or ghost. **2.** to intrude upon continually; recur to persistently: *memories that haunt one.* **3.** to resort to much; visit frequently. **4.** to frequent the company of; be often with. —*v.i.* **5.** to reappear continually, as a disembodied spirit. **6.** to resort habitually. **7.** to associate, as with a person. —*n.* **8.** (*often pl.*) a place of frequent resort: *to revisit one's old haunts.* **9.** *Dial.* a ghost. [ME *haunten*, t. OF: m. *hanter* haunt, dwell, t. OE: m. *hāmettan* shelter, der. *hām* home] —**haunt′er,** *n.* —**haunt′ing·ly,** *adv.*

haunt·ed (hôn′tĭd, hän′-), *adj.* **1.** frequented or visited by ghosts: *a haunted house.* **2.** much resorted to.

Haupt·mann (houpt′män), *n.* **Gerhart** (gĕr′härt), 1862–1946, German dramatist, novelist, and poet.

Hau·sa (hou′sä), *n.* **1.** a prominent Negro stock in northern Nigeria and the Sudan. **2.** their language, used widely as a language of commerce.

Haus·frau (hous′frou′), *n.* a housewife.

haus·tel·lum (hô stĕl′əm), *n., pl.* **haustella** (hô stĕl′ə). (in certain crustaceans and insects) an organ or part of the proboscis adapted for sucking blood or plant juices. [NL, dim. of L *haustrum* machine for drawing water]

haus·to·ri·um (hô stōr′ĭ əm), *n., pl.* **haustoria** (hô stōr′ĭ ə). *Bot.* an intracellular feeding organ of a parasite which does not kill the host cells but lives with them. [NL, der. *haustor* drinker]

haut·boy (hō′boi, ō′boi), *n.* oboe. [t. F: m. *hautbois*, f. *haut* high + *bois* wood; named with reference to its high notes]

hau·teur (hō tûr′; *Fr.* ō tœr′), *n.* haughty manner or spirit; haughtiness. [t. F, der. *haut* high. See HAUGHTY]

haut monde (ō mônd′), *French.* high society.

Ha·van·a (hə văn′ə), *n.* **1.** Spanish, **Habana,** a seaport in and the capital of Cuba, on the NW coast. 676,376 (1943). **2.** a cigar made in Cuba or of Cuban tobacco.

have (hăv), *v., pres.* **1 have, 2 have** or **hast, 3 has** or **hath,** *pl.* **have;** *pt. and past part.* **had;** *pres. part.* **having.** —*v.t.* **1.** to possess; own; to hold for use; contain: *to have property, the work has an index.* **2.** to hold or possess in some other relation, as of kindred, relative position, etc.: *to have one's opponent down.* **3.** to get, receive, or take: *to have no news.* **4.** to be required, compelled, or under obligation (fol. by an infinitive): *I*

b., blend of, blended; c., cognate with; d., dialect, dialectal; der., derived from; f., formed from; g., going back to; m., modification of; r., replacing; s., stem of; t., taken from; ?, perhaps. See the full key on inside cover.

have to stop now. **5.** to experience, enjoy, or suffer: *to have a pleasant time.* **6.** to hold in mind, sight, etc.: *to have doubts.* **7.** to require or cause (to do something, be done, or as specified): *have him come here at five.* **8.** to show or exhibit in action: *to have a care.* **9.** to engage in or perform: *to have a talk.* **10.** to permit or allow: *I will not have it.* **11.** to assert or maintain: *rumor has it so.* **12.** to know or understand: *to have neither Latin nor Greek.* **13.** to give birth to: *to have a baby.* **14.** to wear (fol. by *on*). **15.** *Colloq.* to hold at a disadvantage: *he has you there.* **16.** *Chiefly Brit. Slang.* to outwit, deceive, or cheat: *a person not easily had.* **17. have it in for,** to hold a grudge against. **18. have it out,** to come to a final understanding by discussion. **19. have rather,** to consider as preferable: *I had much rather he go.* —*aux. v.* **20.** (used with the past participle of a verb to form a compound or perfect tense): *they have gone* [ME *have(n)*, OE *habban*, c. D *hebben*, G *haben*, Icel. *hafa*, Goth. *haban*; akin to L *capere* take] —**Syn. 1.** HAVE, HOLD, OCCUPY, OWN mean to be, in varying degrees, in the possession of something. HAVE, being the most general word, admits of the widest range of application: *to have money, rights, discretion, a disease, a glimpse, an idea; to have a friend's umbrella.* To HOLD is to have in one's grasp or one's control, but not necessarily as one's own: *to hold stakes.* To OCCUPY is to hold and use, but not necessarily by any right of ownership: *to occupy a chair, a house, a position.* To OWN is to have the full rights of property in a thing, which, however, another may be holding or enjoying: *to own a house which is rented to tenants.* —**Ant. 1.** lack.

have·lock (hăv′lŏk), *n.* a cap cover with a flap hanging over the back of the neck, for protection from the sun. [named after H. *Havelock* (1795–1857),Brit. general]

ha·ven (hā′vən), *n.* **1.** a harbor or port. **2.** any place of shelter and safety. —*v.t.* **3.** to shelter as in a haven. [ME; OE *hæfen*, c. G *hafen*] —**ha′ven·less,** *adj.* —**Syn.** See **harbor.**

have·n't (hăv′ənt), contraction of *have not.*

Hav·er·ford (hăv′ərfôrd), *n.* a township in SE Pennsylvania, near Philadelphia. 39,641 (1950).

Ha·ver·hill (hā′vər·ĭl, -rĭl), *n.* a city in NE Massachusetts, on the Merrimack river. 47,280 (1950).

hav·er·sack (hăv′ərsăk′), *n.* **1.** a soldier's bag for rations. **2.** any bag used for provisions. [t. F: m. *havresac*, t. LG: m. *habersack*, lit., oat sack]

Ha·ver·sian canal (həvûr′shən), a microscopic channel in bone, through which a blood vessel runs. [named after C. *Havers*, British anatomist, 1650–1702]

hav·oc (hăv′ək), *n., v.,* **-ocked, -ocking.** —*n.* **1.** devastation; ruinous damage. **2. play havoc with,** to ruin; destroy. **3.** *Archaic.* a word used as the signal for pillage in warfare: *to cry havoc.* —*v.t.* **4.** to work havoc upon. —*v.i.* **5.** to work havoc. [ME *havok,* t. AF, var. of OF *havot,* used esp. in phrase *crier havot* cry havoc, give the call for pillaging; prob. from Gmc.] —**hav′ock·er,** *n.* —**Syn. 1.** See **ruin.**

Ha·vre (hä′vər), *n.* See **Le Havre.**

haw[1] (hô), *n.* the fruit of the Old World hawthorn, *Crataegus Oxyacantha,* or of other species of the same genus. [ME; OE *haga,* c. D *haag*]

haw[2] (hô), *interj.* **1.** an utterance marking hesitation in speech. —*n.* **2.** the utterance "haw." —*v.i.* **3.** to use "haw," as in hesitation. [imit.]

haw[3] (hô), *interj.* **1.** a word of command to horses, etc., usually directing them to turn to the left. —*v.t., v.i.* **3.** to turn to the left (said of horses and cattle). [appar. orig. the same as *haw,* impv., look!, ME *hawen,*OE *hāwian*]

haw[4] (hô), *n.* the nictitating membrane of a horse, dog, etc., formerly only when inflamed. [orig. uncert.]

Ha·wai·i (həwī′ē, -wä′yə), *n.* **1.** Hawaiian Islands. **2.** the largest of the Hawaiian Islands. 67,683 pop. (prelim. 1950); 4021 sq. mi.

Ha·wai·ian (həwī′yən, -wä′-), *adj.* **1.** of or pertaining to Hawaii. —*n.* **2.** a native or inhabitant of Hawaii or the Hawaiian Islands. **3.** the aboriginal language of Hawaii, a Polynesian language.

Hawaiian Islands, a group of islands belonging to the United States, in the N Pacific, 2090 mi. SW of San Francisco, forming (with the Midway Islands) the **Territory of Hawaii** (*abbrev.* T.H.). 499,794 pop. (1950); 6454 sq. mi. *Cap.:* Honolulu. Also, **Hawaii.** Formerly, **Sandwich Islands.**

Hawaii National Park, a large park that includes the active volcanoes Kilauea and Mauna Loa on the island of Hawaii and the extinct crater Haleakala on Maui. 343 sq. mi.

haw·finch (hô′fĭnch′), *n.* a European grosbeak, *Coccothraustes coccothraustes.*

haw-haw (hô′hô′), *n.* **1.** a word representing the sound of a loud, boisterous laugh. **2.** a guffaw.

hawk[1] (hôk), *n.* **1.** any of numerous diurnal birds of prey of the family *Falconidae,* as the falcons, buzzards, kites, harriers, etc., esp. the short-winged, long-tailed accipiters, as the goshawk. **2.** any of certain nonfalconiform birds, as the nighthawk. **3.** a person who preys on others, as a sharper. —*v.i.* **4.** to fly, or hunt on the wing, like a hawk. **5.** to hunt with hawks trained to pursue game. [ME *hauk(e),* OE *hafoc,* c. G *habicht*] —**hawk′ish,** *adj.*

Red-tailed hawk, *Buteo borealis* (19 to 22½ in. long)

hawk[2] (hôk), *v.t.* **1.** to offer for sale by outcry in a street or from door to door. —*v.i.* **2.** to carry wares about; peddle. [back formation from HAWKER[2]]

hawk[3] (hôk), *v.i.* **1.** to make an effort to raise phlegm from the throat; clear the throat noisily. —*v.t.* **2.** to raise by hawking: *to hawk up phlegm.* —*n.* **3.** a noisy effort to clear the throat. [imit.]

hawk[4] (hôk), *n.* a small square board with a handle underneath, used by plasterers to hold small quantities of mortar. [orig. uncert.]

hawk·bill (hôk′bĭl′), *n.* hawksbill.

hawk·er[1] (hô′kər), *n.* a falconer. [f. HAWK[1], v. + -ER[1]]

hawk·er[2] (hô′kər), *n.* one who offers goods for sale by outcry in the streets; peddler. [appar. t. MLG: m. *hoker.* Cf. G *höker,* D *heuker* retail dealer. See HUCKSTER]

hawk-eyed (hôk′īd′), *adj.* having keen eyes, like those of a hawk.

hawk·ing (hô′kĭng), *n.* falconry.

Haw·kins (hô′kĭnz), *n.* **Sir John,** 1532–95, British slave trader and rear admiral. Also, **Hawkyns.**

hawk moth, any of certain moths of the family *Sphingidae,* noted for their very swift flight and ability to hover while sipping nectar from flowers.

hawk-nose (hôk′nōz′), *n.* a nose curved like the beak of a hawk. —**hawk′-nosed′,** *adj.*

hawk owl, a strikingly barred gray and white owl, *Surnia ulula,* of northern parts of the northern hemisphere, so named because it is diurnal.

hawk's-beard (hôks′bîrd′), *n.* any herb of the composite genus *Crepis,* having yellow or orange flowers.

hawks·bill (hôks′bĭl′), *n.* a marine turtle, *Eretmochelys imbricata,* yielding tortoise shell and having a mouth shaped like the bill of a hawk. Also, **hawk′s-bill′, hawkbill, hawksbill turtle.**

hawk's-eye (hôks′ī′), *n.* a dark-green chatoyant quartz formed like tiger's-eye by the silicification of an asbestos and used for ornamental purposes.

hawk·shaw (hôk′shô′), *n.* a detective.

hawk·weed (hôk′wēd′), *n.* **1.** any herb of the composite genus *Hieracium,* with yellow, orange, or red flowers. **2.** any of various related plants.

Haw·kyns (hô′kĭnz), *n.* Hawkins.

hawse (hôz, hôs), *n.* **1.** the part of a ship's bow having holes for the cables to pass through. **2.** a hawsehole. **3.** the space between a ship at anchor and her anchors. **4.** the situation of a ship's cables when she is moored with both bow anchors: *a clear hawse.* [ME *halse,* prob. t. Scand.; cf. Icel. *hāls* part of ship's bow, front sheet of sail, lit., neck, c. OE *hals* neck]

hawse·hole (hôz′hōl′, hôs′-), *n.* a hole in the bow of a ship, through which a cable is passed.

haw·ser (hô′zər, -sər), *n.* *Naut.* a small cable or large rope used in warping, mooring, towing, etc. [ME *haucer,* der. OF *haucier* raise, ult. der. L *altus* high]

hawser bend, a knot uniting the ends of two lines.

haw·ser-laid (hô′zər lād′, -sər-), *adj.* **1.** made of three small ropes laid up into one. **2.** cable-laid.

haw·thorn (hô′thôrn′), *n.* **1.** any species of the rosaceous genus *Crataegus,* usually small trees with stiff thorns, cultivated in hedges for their white or pink blossoms and bright-colored fruits. **2.** a thorny shrub *Crataegus Oxyacantha,* native in the Old World, but introduced in the U.S. [ME; OE *haguthorn.* See HAW[1]]

Haw·thorne (hô′thôrn′), *n.* **Nathaniel,** 1804–64, U.S. novelist and short-story writer.

hay[1] (hā), *n.* **1.** grass cut and dried for use as fodder. **2.** grass mowed or intended for mowing. **3. make hay, a.** to cut and cure grass for fodder. **b.** to scatter everything in disorder. —*v.t.* **4.** to convert (grass) into hay. **5.** to furnish (horses, etc.) with hay. [ME; OE *hēg, hīeg,* c. G *heu*]

hay[2] (hā), *n.* a kind of old country dance with winding movements. [t. F (15th cent.): m. *haye* kind of dance]

Hay (hā), *n.* **John Milton,** 1838–1905, U.S. statesman and author.

hay·cock (hā′kŏk′), *n.* *Chiefly Brit.* a small conical pile of hay thrown up in a hayfield, while the hay is awaiting removal to a barn.

Hay·dn (hā′dən; *Ger.* hī′dən), *n.* **Franz Joseph** (fränts yō′zĕf), 1732–1809, Austrian composer.

ăct, āble, dâre, ärt; ĕbb, ēqual; ĭf, īce; hŏt, ōver, ôrder, oil, bŏŏk, ōōze, out; ŭp, ūse, ûrge; ə = a in alone; ch, chief; g, give; ng, ring; sh, shoe; th, thin; ŧh, that; zh, vision. See the full key on inside cover.

Hayes (hāz), *n.* **1. Helen,** born 1900, U.S. actress. **2. Rutherford Birchard** (bûr′chərd), 1822–93, 19th president of the U.S., 1877–81.

hay fever, a catarrhal affection of the mucous membranes of the eyes and respiratory tract, attacking susceptible persons (usually) during the summer, and due to the action of the pollen of certain plants.

hay·field (hā′fēld′), *n.* a field in which grass is grown for making into hay, or from which hay is being cut.

hay·fork (hā′fôrk′), *n.* a fork used for turning or lifting hay, operated either by hand or machine.

hay·loft (hā′lôft′, -lŏft′), *n.* a loft in a stable or barn, for the storage of hay.

hay·mak·er (hā′mā′kər), *n.* **1.** one who makes hay. **2.** one who tosses and spreads hay to dry after it has been mowed. **3.** *Boxing.* a swinging, knockout blow.

Hay·mar·ket (hā′mär′kĭt), *n.* a famous London market (1644–1830), now the theatrical center.

hay·mow (hā′mou′), *n.* **1.** a mow or mass of hay stored in a barn. **2.** the place in a barn where hay is stored. **3.** a rick or stack of hay.

hay·rack (hā′răk′), *n.* **1.** a rack for holding hay for feeding horses or cattle. **2.** a rack or framework mounted on a wagon, for use in carrying hay, straw, etc. **3.** the wagon and rack together.

hay·seed (hā′sēd′), *n.* **1.** grass seed, esp. that shaken out of hay. **2.** small bits of the chaff, etc., of hay. **3.** *U.S. Slang.* a countryman or rustic.

hay·stack (hā′stăk′), *n.* a stack of hay with a conical or ridged top, built up in the open air for preservation, and sometimes thatched or covered. Also, *esp. Brit.,* **hay·rick** (hā′rĭk′).

hay·ward (hā′wôrd′), *n.* *Obs.* an officer having charge of hedges and fences, esp. to keep cattle from breaking through, and to impound strays. [ME *heiward.* See HAY¹, WARD²]

hay·wire (hā′wīr′), *n.* **1.** wire used to bind bales of hay. —*adj.* **2.** *Slang.* in disorder; out of order. **3.** *Slang.* out of control; crazy: *to go haywire.*

haz·ard (hăz′ərd), *n.* **1.** exposure to danger or harm; risk; peril: *at all hazards.* **2.** chance, or a chance. **3.** *Golf.* an obstacle as a bunker, road, bush, water, or the like on the course. **4.** the uncertainty of the result in throwing a die. **5.** a game played with two dice; an earlier and more complicated form of modern craps. **6.** something risked or staked. **7.** *Court Tennis.* **a.** any of certain openings in the walls of the court, the striking of a ball into which scores the striker a point. **b.** that side of the court into which the ball is served (**hazard side**). **8.** *English Billiards.* a stroke by which the player pockets the object ball (**winning hazard**), or his own ball after contact with another ball (**losing hazard**). —*v.t.* **9.** to venture to offer (a statement, conjecture, etc.). **10.** to put to the risk of being lost; to expose to risk. **11.** to take or run the risk of (a misfortune, penalty, etc.). **12.** to venture upon (anything of doubtful issue). [ME *hasard,* t. OF, t. Ar.: m. *az-zahr* the die] —**haz′ard·a·ble,** *adj.* —**haz′ard·er,** *n.* —**haz′ard·less,** *adj.* —**Syn. 1.** jeopardy. See **danger. 10.** stake, venture, endanger, peril, imperil. —**Ant. 1.** safety.

haz·ard·ous (hăz′ər dəs), *adj.* **1.** full of risk; perilous; risky. **2.** dependent on chance: *a hazardous contract.* —**haz′ard·ous·ly,** *adv.* —**haz′ard·ous·ness,** *n.*

haze¹ (hāz), *n.* **1.** an aggregation of minute suspended particles of vapor, dust, etc., near the surface of the earth, causing an appearance of thin mist in the atmosphere. **2.** obscurity or vagueness of the mind. [orig. obscure] —**Syn. 2.** See **cloud.**

haze² (hāz), *v.t.,* **hazed, hazing. 1.** to subject (freshmen in a college or newcomers generally) to abusive or ridiculous tricks. **2.** *Chiefly Naut.* to harass with unnecessary or disagreeable tasks. [cf. OF *haser* irritate, annoy] —**haz′er,** *n.*

ha·zel (hā′zəl), *n.* **1.** any of the shrubs or small trees of the betulaceous genus *Corylus,* which bear edible nuts, as *C. Avellana* of Europe or *C. americana* and *C. cornuta* of America. **2.** any of certain other shrubs or trees (as *Pomaderris apetala,* a rhamnaceous shrub of Australia, etc.), or their wood. **3.** the hazelnut or filbert. **4.** the wood of a hazel. **5.** light reddish brown of a hazelnut. —*adj.* **6.** of or pertaining to the hazel. **7.** made of the wood of the hazel. **8.** having a hazel color. [ME *hasel*(l), OE *hæs*(e)*l,* c. G *hasel;* akin to L *corylus* hazel shrub]

ha·zel·nut (hā′zəl nŭt′), *n.* the nut of the hazel.

haz·ing (hā′zĭng), *n.* act or practice of one who hazes.

Ha·zle·ton (hā′zəl tən), *n.* a city in E Pennsylvania. 35,491 (1950).

Haz·litt (hăz′lĭt), *n.* **William,** 1778–1830, British critic and essayist.

ha·zy (hā′zĭ), *adj.,* **-zier, -ziest. 1.** characterized by the presence of haze; misty: *hazy weather.* **2.** lacking distinctness; vague; confused: *a hazy proposition.* —**ha′zi·ly,** *adv.* —**ha′zi·ness,** *n.*

haz·zan (hä zän′, hä′zän), *n.* chazzan.

H.B.M., His (or Her) Britannic Majesty.

H-bomb, hydrogen bomb.

H.C., House of Commons.

H.C.F., highest common factor. Also, **h.c.f.**

h.c.l., *Colloq.* high cost of living.

hd., **1.** hand. **2.** head.

hdqrs., headquarters.

he (hē; *unstressed* ē, ĭ), *pron., nom.,* **he;** *gen.,* **his,** *of* **him,** *of* **his;** *dat. and acc.,* **him;** *pl. nom.,* **they;** *gen.,* **theirs, their,** *of* **them,** *of* **theirs;** *acc.,* **them;** *n., pl.* **hes. 1.** the male being in question or last mentioned. **2.** anyone; that person: *he who hesitates is lost.* —*n.* **3.** a man or any male person (correlative to *she*). **4.** a male, esp. of an animal. [ME *he,* OE *hē* (gen. *his,* dat. *him,* acc. *hine*), c. OS *he, hi,* OFris. *hi, he.* Cf. SHE, HER, IT, HENCE, HERE; HITHER]

He, *Chem.* helium.

H.E. 1. His Eminence. **2.** His Excellency.

head (hĕd), *n.* **1.** the upper part of the human body, joined to the trunk by the neck. **2.** the corresponding part of an animal's body. **3.** the head considered as the seat of thought, memory, understanding, etc.: *to have a head for mathematics.* **4.** the position of leadership; chief command; greatest authority. **5.** one to whom others are subordinate; a leader or chief. **6.** that part of anything which forms or is regarded as forming the top, summit, or upper end: *head of a pin, head of a page.* **7.** the foremost part or end of anything; a projecting part: *head of a procession, head of a rock.* **8.** a person considered with reference to his mind, disposition, attributes, etc.: *wise heads, crowned heads.* **9.** a person or animal considered merely as one of a number (often with *pl.* **head**): *ten head of cattle, to charge so much a head.* **10.** culmination or crisis; conclusion: *to bring matters to a head.* **11.** the hair covering the head: *to comb someone's head.* **12.** something resembling a head in form: *a head of lettuce.* **13.** a rounded or compact part of a plant, usually at the top of the stem, as of leaves (as in the cabbage or lettuce), leafstalks (as in the celery), flower buds (as in the cauliflower), sessile florets, etc. **14.** the maturated part of an abscess, boil, etc. **15.** a projecting point of a coast, esp. when high, as a cape, headland, or promontory. **16.** the obverse of a coin, as bearing a head or other principal figure (opposed to *tail*). **17.** one of the chief points or divisions of a discourse; topic. **18.** strength or force gradually attained; progress. **19.** the source of a river or stream. **20.** froth or foam. **21.** the headline or group of headlines at the top of a newspaper article. **22.** *Naut.* **a.** the forepart of a ship, etc. **b.** the upper edge (or corner) of a sail. **23.** *Gram.* **a.** that member of an endocentric construction which belongs to the same form class and may play the same grammatical role as the construction itself. **b.** the member upon which another depends and to which it is subordinate, e.g., in *the first president, first president* is head and *the* is attribute, and in *first president,* the head is *president* and the attribute is *first.* **24.** the stretched membrane covering the end of a drum or similar instrument. **25.** *Coal Mining.* a level or road driven into the solid coal for proving or working a mine. **26.** the height of the free surface of a liquid above a given level. **27.** *Mach.* a device on turning and boring machines, esp. lathes, holding one or more cutting tools to the work. **28.** the pressure of a confined body of steam, etc., per unit of area. **29.** the height of a column of fluid required for a certain pressure. **30.** Some special noun phrases are:
by, or **down by, the head,** *Naut.* so loaded as to draw more water forward than aft.
go to one's head, 1. to make one confused or dizzy. **2.** to make one conceited.
lay heads together, to come together to scheme.
make head or **tail of,** to understand; figure out.
out of one's head or **mind,** *Chiefly U.S.* demented; delirious.
over one's head, 1. passing over one having a prior claim or a superior position. **2.** beyond one's comprehension.
—*adj.* **31.** situated at the head, top, or front: *the head division of a parade.* **32.** being in the position of leadership or superiority. **33.** coming from in front: *a head wind.*
—*v.t.* **34.** to go at the head of or in front; lead, precede: *to head a list.* **35.** to outdo or excel. **36.** to be the head or chief of. **37.** to turn the head or front of in a specified direction: *to head one's boat for the shore.* **38.** to go round the head of (a stream, etc.). **39.** to furnish or fit with a head. **40.** to take the head of (an animal) off. **41.** to poll (a tree). —*v.i.* **42.** to move forward toward a point specified; direct one's course; go in a certain direction. **43.** to come or grow to a head; form a head. **44.** *Chiefly U.S.* (of a river or stream) to have the head or source where specified. [ME *he*(*v*)*ed,* OE *hēafod,* c. D *hoofd,* G *haupt,* Icel. *höfudh,* Goth. *haubith*] —**head′like′,** *adj.* —**Syn. 5.** commander, director. **32.** cardinal, foremost, first. —**Ant. 32.** subordinate.

-head, a suffix denoting state, condition, character, etc.: *godhead,* and other words, now mostly archaic or obsolete, many being superseded by forms in **-hood.** [ME *-hede, -hed,* der. *hede* rank, condition, character; akin to OE *hād,* whence the suffix -HOOD]

head·ache (hĕd′āk′), *n.* a pain located in the head.

head·band (hĕd′bănd′), *n.* **1.** a band worn around the head; a fillet. **2.** *Print.* a band for decorative effect at the head of a chapter or of a page in a book. **3.** a band sewn to the head and tail of the back of the book to protect and strengthen the binding.

head·board (hĕd′bôrd′), *n.* a board forming the head of anything, esp. of a bed.

head·cheese (hĕd/chēz/), *n.* a preparation of parts of the head and feet of hogs cut up, cooked, and seasoned, and forming when cold a jellied mass or loaf.

head·dress (hĕd/drĕs/), *n.* **1.** a covering or decoration for the head. **2.** an arrangement of the hair.

head·ed (hĕd/ĭd), *adj.* **1.** having a heading. **2.** shaped or grown into a head.

-headed, a suffix meaning: **1.** having a specified kind of head: *long-headed, wrong-headed.* **2.** having a specified number of heads: *two-headed.*

head·er (hĕd/ər), *n.* **1.** one who or an apparatus which removes or puts a head on something. **2.** a form of reaping machine which cuts off and gathers only the heads of the grain. **3.** a chamber to which the ends of a number of tubes are connected so that water or steam may pass freely from one tube to the other. **4.** *Building.* **a.** a brick or stone laid with its length across the thickness of a wall. **b.** a timber or beam in the framing about an opening in a floor or roof, placed so as to fit between two long beams and support the ends of short ones. **5.** *Colloq.* a plunge or dive headforemost, as into water.

head·first (hĕd/fûrst/), *adv.* **1.** with the head in front or bent forward; headlong. **2.** rashly; precipitately. Also, **head·fore·most** (hĕd/fōr/mōst/, -məst).

head gate, 1. a control gate at the upstream end of a canal or lock. **2.** a floodgate of a race, sluice, etc.

head·gear (hĕd/gîr/), *n.* **1.** any covering for the head. **2.** the parts of a harness about the animal's head.

head·hunt·ing (hĕd/hŭn/tĭng), *n.* (among certain savage tribes) the practice of making incursions for procuring human heads as trophies or for use in religious ceremonies. **—head/-hunt/er,** *n.*

head·ing (hĕd/ĭng), *n.* **1.** something that serves as a head, top, or front. **2.** a title or caption of a page, chapter, etc. **3.** a section of a subject of discourse; a topic. **4.** a horizontal passage in the earth, as for an intended tunnel, for working a mine, for ventilation or drainage, etc.; a drift. **5.** the end of such a passage. **6.** *Aeron.* the compass point towards which a craft is flying.

head·land (hĕd/lənd *for 1;* hĕd/lănd/ *for 2), n.* **1.** a promontory extending into a large body of water, such as a sea or lake. **2.** a strip of unplowed land at the ends of furrows or near a fence or border.

head·less (hĕd/lĭs), *adj.* **1.** having no head; deprived of the head. **2.** without a leader or chief. **3.** foolish; stupid. [ME *he(ve)dles,* OE *hēafodlēas.* See -LESS]

head·light (hĕd/līt/), *n.* a lamp equipped with a reflector, on the front of an automobile, locomotive, etc.

head·line (hĕd/līn/), *n., v.,* **-lined, -lining.** *—n.* **1.** a display line over an article, etc., as in a newspaper. **2.** the line at the top of a page, containing the title, pagination, etc. *—v.t.* **3.** to furnish with a headline.

head·lin·er (hĕd/lī/nər), *n.* **1.** *Theat. Slang.* a performer whose name appears at the head of a bill, or in larger letters than other names on the bill. **2.** *Journalism.* one who writes headlines.

head·lock (hĕd/lŏk/), *n.* *Wrestling.* a hold in which a wrestler locks his arm around his opponent's head.

head·long (hĕd/lông/, -lŏng/), *adv.* **1.** headforemost: *to plunge headlong.* **2.** hastily. **3.** rashly; without deliberation. *—adj.* **4.** done or going with the head foremost. **5.** hasty. **6.** rash; impetuous. **7.** steep; precipitous. [late ME *hedlong,* f. *hed* HEAD + *long,* adv. suffix; r. *headling,* ME *hedlyng.* See -LING²]

head·man (hĕd/mən), *n., pl.* **-men.** a chief man; a chief or leader. [ME *hevedman,* OE *hēafodman]*

head·mas·ter (hĕd/măs/tər, -mäs/tər), *n.* *Chiefly Brit.* the principal master of a school or seminary. Also, **head master.** **—head/mas/ter·ship/,** *n.* **—head·mis·tress** (hĕd/mĭs/trĭs), *n. fem.*

head money, 1. a tax of so much per head or person. **2.** a reward paid for each person captured or brought in. **3.** a reward for the head of an outlaw or enemy.

head·most (hĕd/mōst/), *adj.* foremost; most advanced.

head-on (hĕd/ŏn/, -ôn/), *adj.* with the head foremost: *a head-on collision.*

head·phone (hĕd/fōn/), *n.* (*often pl.*) a headset.

head·piece (hĕd/pēs/), *n.* **1.** armor for the head: a helmet. **2.** any covering for the head. **3.** a headset. **4.** the head as the seat of the intellect; judgment. **5.** the top piece or part of any of various things. **6.** *Print.* a decorative piece at the head of a page, chapter, etc.

head pin, *Tenpins.* the kingpin.

head·quar·ters (hĕd/kwôr/tərz), *n.pl. or sing.* **1.** any center from which official orders are issued: *police headquarters.* **2.** any center of operations. **3.** the offices of a military commander, the place where a commander customarily issues his orders. **4.** a military unit consisting of the commander, his staff, and other assistants. **5.** the building occupied by a headquarters.

head·race (hĕd/rās/), *n.* the race, flume, or channel leading to a water wheel or the like.

head resistance, *Aeron.* the drag inherent in the shape of an airplane and not due to a component of the aerodynamic lift.

head·rest (hĕd/rĕst/), *n.* a rest or support of any kind for the head.

head·sails (hĕd/sālz/; *Naut.* -səlz), *n.pl.* *Naut.* sails set forward of the foremast.

head·set (hĕd/sĕt/), *n.* *Radio, Teleph., etc.* a device consisting of one or two telephone receivers, with attachments for holding them over the ears.

head·ship (hĕd/shĭp), *n.* the position of head or chief; chief authority; leadership; supremacy.

heads·man (hĕdz/mən), *n., pl.* **-men.** one who beheads condemned persons; a public executioner.

head·spring (hĕd/sprĭng/), *n.* **1.** the fountainhead or source of a stream. **2.** the source of anything.

head·stall (hĕd/stôl/), *n.* that part of a bridle or halter which encompasses the head.

head·stock (hĕd/stŏk/), *n.* the part of a machine containing the working members, as the assembly supporting and driving the live spindle in a lathe.

head·stone (hĕd/stōn/), *n.* a stone set at the head of a grave.

head·strong (hĕd/strông/, -strŏng/), *adj.* **1.** bent on having one's own way; willful. **2.** proceeding from willfulness: *a headstrong course.* **—head/strong/ness,** *n.* **—Syn. 1.** perverse, froward, stubborn, unruly, obstinate; ungovernable, intractable, heady. See **willful.**

head tone, *Music.* a vocal tone so produced as to bring the cavities of the nose and head into sympathetic vibration.

head·wa·ters (hĕd/wô/tərz, -wŏt/ərz), *n.pl.* the upper tributaries of a river.

head·way (hĕd/wā/), *n.* **1.** motion forward or ahead; advance. **2.** progress in general. **3.** rate of progress. **4.** the interval between two trains, etc., traveling in the same direction over the same route. **5.** clear space in height, as in a doorway or under an arch.

head·work (hĕd/wûrk/), *n.* mental labor; thought. **—head/work/er,** *n.*

head·y (hĕd/ĭ), *adj.,* **headier, headiest. 1.** rashly impetuous. **2.** intoxicating. [ME *he(ve)di.* See HEAD, *n.,* -Y¹] **—head/i·ly,** *adv.* **—head/i·ness,** *n.*

heal (hēl), *v.t.* **1.** to make whole or sound; restore to health; free from ailment. **2.** to free from anything evil or distressing; amend: *to heal a quarrel.* **3.** to cleanse or purify. *—v.i.* **4.** to effect a cure. **5.** to become whole or sound; get well (often fol. by *up* or *over*). [ME *hele(n),* OE *hǣlan,* der. *hāl* hale, WHOLE] **—heal/er,** *n.* **—heal/ing,** *n.* **—heal/ing·ly,** *adv.* **—Syn. 1.** See **cure.**

heal·ing (hē/lĭng), *adj.* **1.** that heals; curing; curative. **2.** growing sound; getting well.

health (hĕlth), *n.* **1.** soundness of body; freedom from disease or ailment. **2.** the general condition of the body or mind with reference to soundness and vigor: *good health.* **3.** a polite or complimentary wish for a person's health, happiness, etc., esp. as a toast. [ME *helthe,* OE *hǣlth,* der. *hāl* hale, whole. See WHOLE, -TH¹]

health·ful (hĕlth/fəl), *adj.* **1.** conducive to health; wholesome, or salutary: *healthful diet.* **2.** healthy. **—health/ful·ly,** *adv.* **—health/ful·ness,** *n.* **—Syn. 2.** See **healthy.**

health insurance, insurance which indemnifies the insured against loss of time occasioned by illness.

health·y (hĕl/thĭ), *adj.,* **healthier, healthiest. 1.** possessing or enjoying health: *healthy body or mind.* **2.** pertaining to or characteristic of health: *a healthy appearance.* **3.** conducive to health, or healthful: *healthy recreations.* **—health/i·ly,** *adv.* **—health/i·ness,** *n.* **—Syn. 1.** hale, hearty, robust, vigorous, strong, sound, well. **3.** nutritious, nourishing; hygienic, salubrious; invigorating, bracing. HEALTHY, HEALTHFUL, SALUTARY, WHOLESOME refer to that which promotes health. HEALTHY, while applied esp. to what possesses health, is also used of what is conducive to health: *a healthy climate, not a healthy place to be.* HEALTHFUL is applied chiefly to what is conducive to health: *healthful diet or exercise.* SALUTARY is applied to that which is conducive to well-being generally, as well as beneficial in preserving or in restoring health: *salutary effects, to take salutary measures.* It is used also of what s morally beneficial: *to have a salutary fear of consequences.* WHOLESOME has connotations of attractive freshness and purity; it applies to what is good for one, physically, morally, or both: *wholesome food or air, wholesome influences or advice.* **—Ant. 1.** sick, ill. **3.** injurious.

heap (hēp), *n.* **1.** an assemblage of things lying one on another; a pile: *a heap of stones.* **2.** *Colloq.* a great quantity or number; a multitude. *—v.t.* **3.** to gather, put, or cast in a heap; pile (often fol. by *up, on, together,* etc.). **4.** to accumulate or amass (often fol. by *up*): *to heap up riches.* **5.** to cast or bestow in great quantity: *to heap blessings or insults upon a person.* **6.** to load or supply abundantly with something: *to heap a person with favors.* *—v.i.* **7.** to become heaped or piled, as sand snow, etc.; rise in a heap or heaps. [ME *heep,* OE *hēap* heap, multitude, troop, c. LG *hōp;* akin to G *haufe*] **—heap/er,** *n.* **—Syn. 1.** mass, stack; cumulation; accumulation.

hear (hîr), *v.,* **heard** (hûrd), **hearing.** *—v.t.* **1.** to perceive by the ear. **2.** to listen to: *to refuse to hear a person.* **3.** to learn by the ear or by being told; be informed of: *to hear news.* **4.** to be among the audience at or of: *to hear an opera.* **5.** to give a formal, official, or judicial hearing to, as a sovereign, a teacher, an assembly, or a judge does. **6.** to listen to with favor, assent, or compliance. *—v.i.* **7.** to have perception of sound by the ear; have the sense of hearing. **8.** to listen or take heed (in imperative, "hear! hear!"), used, chiefly in Britain, to applaud or endorse a speaker). **9.** to receive information by the ear or otherwise: *to hear from a friend.* **10.** to listen with favor or assent; *he would not hear of it.* [ME *here(n),* OE *hēran,* c. G *hören*] **—hear/er,** *n.* **—Syn. 1. 2.** HEAR, LISTEN apply to the perception of sound. To HEAR is to have such perception by means of the auditory sense: *to hear distant bells.* To LISTEN is to give attention in order to hear and understand the meaning of a sound or sounds: *to listen to what is being said, to listen for a well-known footstep.* —Ant. 6. disregard.

hear·ing (hĭr′ĭng), *n.* **1.** the faculty or sense by which sound is perceived. **2.** act of perceiving sound. **3.** opportunity to be heard: *to grant a hearing.* **4.** *Law.* a presentation of testimony and arguments, as in a suit at law. **5.** earshot: *their conversation was beyond my hearing.*

heark·en (här′kən), *v.i., v.t.* harken. —**heark′en·er,** *n.*

Hearn (hûrn), *n.* **Lafcadio** (lăf·kăd′ĭ·ō′), 1850–1904, U.S. author who became a Japanese citizen.

hear·say (hĭr′sā′), *n.* gossip; rumor.

hearsay rule, *Law.* the rule which excludes out-of-court statements, oral or written, when offered as evidence (**hearsay evidence**). There are many exceptions to the rule, as for dying declarations, book entries, etc.

hearse (hûrs), *n.* **1.** a funeral vehicle for conveying a dead person to the place of burial. **2.** a triangular frame for holding candles, used at the service of Tenebrae in Holy Week. [ME *herse,* t. OF: m. *herce* harrow, frame, ult. g. L *hirpex, irpex* large rake used as harrow]

Hearst (hûrst), *n.* **William Randolph,** 1863–1951, U.S. editor and publisher.

heart (härt), *n.* **1.** a hollow muscular organ which by rhythmic contractions and relaxations keeps the blood in circulation throughout the body. **2.** this organ considered as the seat of life or vital powers, or of thought, feeling, or emotion: *to die of a broken heart.* **3.** the seat of emotions and affections (often in contrast to the *head* as the seat of the intellect): *to win a person's heart.* **4.** feeling; sensibility; capacity for sympathy: *to have no heart.* **5.** spirit, courage, or enthusiasm: *to take heart.* **6.** the innermost or middle part of anything. **7.** the vital or essential part; core: *the very heart of the matter.* **8.** the breast or bosom: *to clasp a person to one's heart.* **9.** a person, esp. in expressions of praise or affection: *dear heart.* **10.** a figure or object with rounded sides meeting in an obtuse point at the bottom and curving inward to a cusp at the top. **11.** *Cards.* **a.** a playing card of a suit marked with heart-shaped figures in red. **b.** the suit of cards bearing this symbol. **c.** (*pl. construed as sing.*) a game in which the players try to avoid taking tricks containing hearts. **12.** *Bot.* the core of a tree; the solid central part without sap or albumen. **13.** good condition for production, growth, etc., as of land or crops. **14.** Some special noun phrases are:

Section of human heart A. Vena cava; B. Right auricle; C. Right ventricle; D. Aorta; E. Pulmonary artery; F. Left auricle; G. Left ventricle

Heart (def. 10)

at heart, in one's heart, thoughts, or feelings; inwardly; in reality.
break the heart of, 1. to disappoint grievously in love. **2.** to crush with sorrow or grief.
from one's heart, sincerely.
have at heart, to have as an object, aim, etc.
have the heart, 1. to have enough courage. **2.** (in negative sentences) to be unfeeling enough.
heart and soul, completely; wholly.
take to heart, 1. to think seriously about. **2.** to be deeply affected by; grieve over.
with all one's heart, with all willingness; heartily.
—*v.t. Archaic.* **15.** to encourage. **16.** to fix in the heart. [ME *herte,* OE *heorte,* c. G *herz*]

heart·ache (härt′āk′), *n.* mental anguish; sorrow.

heart·beat (härt′bēt′), *n. Physiol.* a pulsation of the heart, including one complete systole and diastole.

heart·break (härt′brāk′), *n.* sorrow or grief that breaks the heart.

heart·break·ing (härt′brā′kĭng), *adj.* causing heart-break. —**heart′break′er,** *n.*

heart·bro·ken (härt′brō′kən), *adj.* crushed with sorrow or grief. —**heart′bro′ken·ly,** *adv.* —**heart′bro′ken·ness,** *n.*

heart·burn (härt′bûrn′), *n.* **1.** an uneasy, burning sensation in the stomach, often extending toward the esophagus; cardialgia. **2.** envy; bitter jealousy.

heart·burn·ing (härt′bûr′nĭng), *n.* rankling discontent, esp. from envy or jealousy; a grudge.

heart cherry, a heart-shaped kind of cherry with soft, sweet flesh.

heart disease, any condition of the heart which impairs its functioning.

heart·ed (här′tĭd), *adj.* having a specified kind of heart: *hard-hearted, sad-hearted.*

heart·en (här′tən), *v.t.* to give courage to; cheer.

heart·felt (härt′fĕlt′), *adj.* deeply or sincerely felt; earnest; sincere: *heartfelt joy or words.*

heart-free (härt′frē′), *adj.* not in love.

hearth (härth), *n.* **1.** that part of the floor of a room on which the fire is made or above which is a stove, fire-place, furnace, etc. **2.** the fireside; home. **3.** *Metall.* **a.** the lower part of a blast furnace, cupola, etc., in which the molten metal collects and from which it is tapped out. **b.** the part of an open hearth, reverberatory furnace, etc., upon which the charge is placed and melted down or refined. **4.** *Soldering.* a brazier, chafing dish,

or box for charcoal. [ME *herth(e),* OE *he(o)rth,* c. G *herd;* akin to L *carbo* charcoal]

hearth·stone (härth′stōn′), *n.* **1.** a stone forming a hearth. **2.** the fireside; home. **3.** a soft stone, or a preparation of powdered stone and clay, used to whiten or scour hearths, steps, floors, etc.

heart·i·ly (här′tə·lĭ), *adv.* **1.** in a hearty manner; sincerely; cordially. **2.** eagerly; enthusiastically. **3.** with a hearty appetite. **4.** thoroughly; completely.

heart·less (härt′lĭs), *adj.* **1.** without heart or feeling; unfeeling; cruel: *heartless words.* **2.** without courage or enthusiasm: *a heartless mood.* —**heart′less·ly,** *adv.* —**heart′less·ness,** *n.*

heart point, the mid point of an escutcheon. See diag. under **escutcheon.**

heart·rend·ing (härt′rĕn′dĭng), *adj.* causing acute mental anguish. —**heart′-rend′ing·ly,** *adv.*

hearts (härts), *n.* See **heart** (def. 11c).

hearts·ease (härts′ēz′), *n.* **1.** peace of mind. **2.** the pansy, or some other plant of the genus *Viola.* **3.** (in some parts of the U.S.) the common persicary. Also, **heart's′-ease′.** [ME *hertes ese.* See HEART, EASE]

heart-shaped (härt′shāpt′), *adj.* having the shape of a heart; cordate.

heart·sick (härt′sĭk′), *adj.* **1.** sick at heart; grievously depressed or unhappy. **2.** characterized by or showing grievous depression. —**heart′sick′ness,** *n.*

heart·sore (härt′sōr′), *adj.* **1.** sore at heart; grieved. **2.** showing grief.

heart·strick·en (härt′strĭk′ən), *adj.* stricken to the heart: *heart-stricken with grief.* Also, **heart-struck** (härt′strŭk′).

heart·strings (härt′strĭngz′), *n.pl.* the deepest feelings; the strongest affections: *to pull at one's heartstrings.*

heart·throb (härt′thrŏb′), *n.* a passionate or senti-mental emotion.

heart-to-heart (härt′tə·härt′), *adj.* frank; sincere.

heart-whole (härt′hōl′), *adj.* **1.** having the heart untouched by love. **2.** wholehearted; sincere.

heart·wood (härt′wŏŏd′), *n.* the hard central wood of the trunk of an exogenous tree; the duramen.

heart·worm (härt′wûrm′), *n.* a filarial worm living in the heart and pulmonary arteries of dogs.

heart·y (här′tĭ), *adj.,* **heartier, heartiest,** *n., pl.* **hearties.** —*adj.* **1.** warm-hearted; affectionate; cordial; friendly: *a hearty welcome.* **2.** heartfelt; genuine; sincere: *hearty approval or dislike.* **3.** enthusiastic or zealous; vigorous: *a hearty laugh.* **4.** physically vigorous; strong and well: *hale and hearty.* **5.** substantial or satisfying: *a hearty meal.* **6.** enjoying or requiring abundant food: *a hearty appetite.* **7.** (of soil) fertile. —*n.* **8.** a brave or good fellow. **9.** a sailor. —**heart′i·ness,** *n.* —**Syn.** 1. warm, genial. 4. healthy, hale. —**Ant.** 1. cool, aloof, reserved. 4. ailing.

heat (hēt), *n.* **1.** the quality or condition of being hot. **2.** degree of hotness; temperature. **3.** the sensation of hotness or warmth; heated bodily condition. **4.** *Psychol.* a blended sensation, caused by stimulating the warmth and cold receptors on the skin. **5.** a form of energy resident in the random motion of molecules, which will raise the temperature of a body to which it is added. **6.** hot condition of the atmosphere or physical environment; hot season or weather. **7.** warmth or intensity of feeling: *the heat of an argument.* **8.** a fit of passion. **9.** the height or greatest intensity of any action: *to do a thing at white heat.* **10.** a single intense effort. **11.** a single course in or division of a race or other contest. **12.** a single operation of heating, as of metal in a furnace, in the heat treating and melting of metals. **13.** *Zool.* **a.** sexual excitement in female animals. **b.** the period or duration of such excitement. —*v.t.* **14.** to make hot or warm. **15.** to excite in mind or feeling; inflame with passion. —*v.i.* **16.** to become hot or warm. **17.** to become excited in mind or feeling. [ME *hete,* OE *hǣtu;* akin to G *hitze*] —**heat′less,** *adj.* —**Syn.** 1. hotness, warmth, caloric. 6. caloricity. 7. ardor, fervor; vehemence, rage. —**Ant.** 1. cold. 7. indifference.

heat·ed (hē′tĭd), *adj.* inflamed; vehement; angry. —**heat′ed·ly,** *adv.*

heat engine, an engine which transforms heat energy into mechanical energy.

heat·er (hē′tər), *n.* **1.** an apparatus for heating, as a furnace. **2.** *Electronics.* that element of an electron tube which carries the current for heating a cathode.

heath (hēth), *n.* **1.** *Brit.* a tract of open and unculti-vated land; waste land overgrown with shrubs. **2.** any of various low evergreen ericaceous shrubs common on waste land, as *Calluna vulgaris,* the common heather of England and Scotland with small pinkish-purple flowers. **3.** any plant of the genus *Erica,* or of the family *Ericaceae.* See **ericaceous.** **4.** any of several heathlike but not ericaceous shrubs, as *Frankenia lævis* (**sea heath**) of the European coasts. [ME; OE *hǣth,* c. D and G *heide*] —**heath′like′,** *adj.*

heath aster, a pasture weed, *Aster ericoides,* with small white heads, very abundant in the eastern U.S.

heath·ber·ry (hēth′bĕr′ĭ), *n., pl.* **-ries. 1.** crowberry. **2.** any berry found on heaths, esp. the bilberry.

heath·bird (hēth′bûrd′), *n.* the black grouse.

heath cock, the male heathbird.

hea·then (hē′thən), *n., pl.* **-thens, -then,** *adj.* —*n.* **1.** an unconverted individual of a people which does not acknowledge the God of the Bible; a Gentile or

pagan. **2.** an irreligious or unenlightened person. —*adj.* **3.** pagan; pertaining to the heathen. **4.** irreligious or unenlightened. [ME *hethen*, OE *hǣthen*, n., adj., c. D *heiden*, n., G *heide*, n., Icel. *heidhinn*, adj.; commonly explained as meaning orig. heath dweller. See HEATH[1], and cf. PAGAN] —**hea′then·ness**, *n.*
—**Syn. 4.** HEATHEN, PAGAN are both applied to peoples who are not Christian, Jewish, or Moslem. HEATHEN is often distinctively applied to unenlightened or barbaric idolaters, such as the tribes of Africa: *heathen rites, idols.* PAGAN, though applying to any of the more civilized peoples not worshiping according to the three religions mentioned above, is almost exclusively used in speaking of the ancient Greeks and Romans: *a pagan poem, a pagan civilization.*

hea·then·dom (hē′*th*ən dəm), *n.* **1.** heathenism; heathen worship or customs. **2.** heathen lands or people.

hea·then·ish (hē′*th*ən ĭsh), *adj.* **1.** pertaining to the heathen. **2.** like or befitting the heathen; barbarous. —**hea′then·ish·ly**, *adv.*, —**hea′then·ish·ness**, *n.*

hea·then·ism (hē′*th*ə nĭz′əm), *n.* **1.** the condition, belief, or practice of heathen. **2.** pagan worship; irreligion. **3.** barbaric morals or behavior; barbarism.

hea·then·ize (hē′*th*ə nīz′), *v.*, **-ized, -izing.** —*v.t.* **1.** to make heathen or heathenish. —*v.i.* **2.** to become heathen or heathenish. **3.** to practice heathenism.

hea·then·ry (hē′*th*ən rĭ), *n.* **1.** heathenism. **2.** heathen people; the heathen.

heath·er (hĕ*th*′ər), *n.* any of various heaths, esp. *Calluna vulgaris* (**Scotch heather**). See **heath** (def. 2). [b. HEATH and obs. *hadder* heather (orig. uncert.)]

heath·er·y (hĕ*th*′ər ĭ), *adj.* **1.** of or like heather. **2.** abounding in heather. Also, **heath·y** (hē′*th*ĭ).

heath grass, a European grass, *Sieglingia decumbens,* growing in spongy, wet, cold soils. Also, **heather grass.**

heath hen, 1. an extinct American bird, *Tympanuchus cupido cupido,* closely related to the prairie chicken (*T. c. pinnatus*). **2.** the female black grouse.

heat lightning, flashes of light near the horizon on summer evenings, reflections of more distant lightning.

heat of fusion, the heat required just to melt a unit mass of a solid, already at the melting temperature.

heat of vaporization, the heat required to convert one gram of liquid into a vapor, without a rise in temperature.

heat·stroke (hēt′strōk′), *n.* collapse or fever caused by exposure to excessive heat.

heat wave, 1. an air mass of high temperature, covering an extended area and moving relatively slowly. **2.** a prolonged period of excessively warm weather.

heaume (hōm), *n.* a large supplemental medieval headpiece reaching to the shoulders and worn over an inner helmet. [t. F. See HELMET]

heave (hēv), *v.,* **heaved** or (*esp. Naut.*) **hove; heaving;** *n.* —*v.t.* **1.** to raise or lift with effort or force; hoist. **2.** to lift and throw, often with effort or force: *to heave an anchor overboard.* **3.** *Naut.* to haul, draw, or pull, as by a cable. **4.** to utter laboriously or painfully: *to heave a sigh.* **5.** to cause to rise and fall with or as with a swelling motion. **6.** to raise or force up in a swelling movement; force to bulge. **7.** *Geol.* to cause a horizontal displacement in (a stratum, vein, etc.). See **heave** (def. 18). **8. heave to,** to stop the headway of (a vessel), esp. by bringing the head to the wind and trimming the sails so that they act against one another. —*v.i.* **9.** to rise and fall with or as with a swelling motion. **10.** to breathe with effort; pant. **11.** to vomit; retch. **12.** to rise as if thrust up, as a hill; swell or bulge. **13.** *Naut.* **a.** to haul or pull, as at a cable; to push, as at the bar of a capstan. **b.** to move a ship, or move as a ship does, by such action. **c.** to move or go (fol. by *about, ahead,* etc.). **14. heave in sight,** to rise into view as from below the horizon, as a ship. **15. heave to,** *Naut.* to heave a vessel to. —*interj.* **16. heave ho!,** an exclamation used by sailors when heaving the anchor up, etc. —*n.* **17.** act of heaving. **18.** *Geol.* the horizontal component of the apparent displacement resulting from a fault, measured in a vertical plane perpendicular to its strike. **19.** (*pl. construed as sing.*) a disease of horses, similar to asthma in man, characterized by difficult breathing; broken wind. [ME *heve(n)*, OE *hebban* (pret. *hōf, hefde,* pp. *hafen*), c. G *heben;* akin to L *capere* take] —**Syn. 1.** See **raise.**

heav·en (hĕv′ən), *n.* **1.** the abode of God, the angels, and the spirits of the righteous after death; the place or state of existence of the blessed after the mortal life. **2.** (*cap., often pl.*) the celestial powers; God. **3.** a euphemistic term for God in various emphatic expressions: *for heaven's sake.* **4.** (*chiefly pl.*) the sky or firmament, or expanse of space surrounding the earth. **5.** a place or state of supreme bliss: *a heaven on earth.* **6.** See **seventh heaven.** [ME *heven,* OE *hefen, heofon* (c. MLG *heven*), appar. akin to Goth. *himins,* Icel. *himinn*]

heav·en·born (hĕv′ən bôrn′), *adj.* **1.** heaven-sent; born with a special aptitude. **2.** of heavenly birth.

heav·en·ly (hĕv′ən lĭ), *adj.* **1.** resembling or befitting heaven; blissful; beautiful: *a heavenly spot.* **2.** of or in the heavens: *the heavenly bodies.* **3.** of, belonging to, or coming from the heaven of God, the angels, etc. **4.** celestial or divine: *heavenly peace.* —**heav′en·li·ness**, *n.* —**Syn. 4.** supernal, sublime; blessed, beatific. —**Ant.** **4.** infernal, hellish.

heav·en·ward (hĕv′ən wərd), *adv.* **1.** Also, **heav′en·wards.** toward heaven. —*adj.* **2.** directed toward heaven.

heav·er (hē′vər), *n.* **1.** one who or that which heaves. **2.** *Naut.* a staff, generally from two to three feet long, used for twisting or heaving tight rope or strap.

heaves (hēvz), *n.* See **heave** (def. 19).

heav·i·er-than-air (hĕv′ĭ ər *th*ən âr′), *adj.* *Aeron.* **1.** of greater specific gravity than the air, as airplanes. **2.** of or pertaining to such aircraft.

heav·i·ly (hĕv′ə lĭ), *adv.* **1.** with great weight or burden: *a heavily loaded wagon.* **2.** in an oppressive manner: *cares weigh heavily upon him.* **3.** severely; intensely: *to suffer heavily.* **4.** densely; thickly: *heavily wooded.* **5.** laboriously; sluggishly: *he walked heavily across the room to the fireplace.*

heav·i·ness (hĕv′ĭ nĭs), *n.* state or quality of being heavy; weight; burden; gravity.

Heav·i·side (hĕv′ĭ sīd′), *n.* **Oliver,** 1850–1925, British physicist.

Heaviside layer, the lower region, or regions, of the ionosphere chiefly responsible for the reflection of radio waves of certain frequencies, thus making long-distance short wave radio communication possible; Kennelly-Heaviside layer. [named after Oliver HEAVISIDE]

heav·y (hĕv′ĭ), *adj.,* **heavier, heaviest,** *n., pl.* **heavies.** *adv.* —*adj.* **1.** of great weight; hard to lift or carry: *a heavy load.* **2.** of great amount, force, intensity, etc.: *a heavy vote.* **3.** bearing hard upon; burdensome; harsh; distressing: *heavy taxes.* **4.** having much weight in proportion to bulk; being of high specific gravity: *a heavy metal.* **5.** broad, thick, or coarse; not delicate: *heavy lines.* **6.** of more than the usual, average, or specified weight: *heavy freight.* **7.** *Mil.* **a.** heavily armed or equipped. **b.** of the larger sizes: *heavy weapons.* **8.** serious; intense: *a heavy offense.* **9.** hard to deal with; trying; difficult: *a heavy task.* **10.** being such in an unusual degree: *a heavy buyer.* **11.** weighted or laden: *air heavy with moisture.* **12.** depressed with trouble or sorrow; showing sorrow: *a heavy heart.* **13.** overcast or cloudy: *heavy sky.* **14.** clumsy; slow in movement or action. **15.** without vivacity or interest; ponderous; dull: *a heavy style.* **16.** loud and deep: *a heavy sound.* **17.** exceptionally dense in substance; insufficiently raised or leavened; thick: *heavy bread.* **18.** not easily digested: *heavy food.* **19.** pregnant. **20.** *Theat.* sober, serious, or somber: *a heavy part.* **21.** *Chem.* referring to that isotope of greater atomic weight: *heavy hydrogen.* —*n.* **22.** *Theat.* **a.** a villainous part or character. **b.** an actor who plays villainous parts or characters. **23.** *Mil.* a gun of great weight or large caliber. —*adv.* **24.** heavily. [ME *hevi,* OE *hefig,* der. *hefe* weight; akin to HEAVE,v.]
—**Syn. 1.** ponderous, massive. **3.** onerous, oppressive; trying, difficult, severe; hard, harsh. **8.** HEAVY, MOMENTOUS, WEIGHTY refer to anything having a considerable amount of figurative weight. HEAVY suggests the carrying of a figurative burden: *words heavy with menace.* MOMENTOUS emphasizes the idea of great and usually serious consequences: *a momentous occasion, statement.* WEIGHTY, seldom used literally, refers to something heavy with importance, often concerned with public affairs, which may require deliberation and careful judgment: *a weighty matter, problem.* **12.** serious, grave; gloomy, sad. **14.** sluggish, lumbering. —**Ant. 1.** light. **12.** cheerful. **14.** nimble.

heav·y-armed (hĕv′ärmd′), *adj.* (formerly) equipped with heavy arms or armor, as troops.

heav·y-du·ty (hĕv′ĭ dū′tĭ, -dōō′-), *adj.* **1.** sturdy; durable. **2.** having a high import or export tax rate.

heavy earth, baryta.

heav·y-hand·ed (hĕv′ĭ hăn′dĭd), *adj.* **1.** oppressive; harsh. **2.** clumsy. —**heav′y-hand′ed·ness**, *n.*

heav·y-heart·ed (hĕv′ĭ här′tĭd), *adj.* sorrowful; melancholy; dejected. —**heav′y-heart′ed·ness**, *n.*

heavy hydrogen, *Chem.* **1.** any of the heavy isotopes of hydrogen. **2.** deuterium, one of these isotopes, occurring in minute quantities in ordinary water. *Symbol:* D or H[2]; *at. no.:* 1; *at. wt.:* 2.014; *sp. gr.:* 1.1056.

heav·y-lad·en (hĕv′ĭ lā′dən), *adj.* **1.** laden with a heavy burden. **2.** very weary or troubled.

heavy spar, barite.

heavy water, water in which hydrogen atoms have been replaced by deuterium, used mainly as a source of deuterons for experiments in nuclear physics. *Symbol:* D_2O; *at. wt.:* 2; *sp. gr.:* 1.1056.

heav·y·weight (hĕv′ĭ wāt′), *n.* **1.** one of more than average weight. **2.** a boxer or other contestant in the heaviest group; a fighter of more than 175 pounds. **3.** *Colloq.* a very intelligent or influential person.

Heb., 1. Hebrew. **2.** Hebrews.

heb·do·mad (hĕb′də măd′), *n.* **1.** the number seven. **2.** seven days; a week. [t. L: s. *hebdomas,* t. Gk.]

heb·dom·a·dal (hĕb dŏm′ə dəl), *adj.* weekly. Also, **heb·dom·a·dar·y** (hĕb dŏm′ə dĕr′ĭ). [t. LL: s. *hebdomadālis*] —**heb·dom′a·dal·ly**, *adv.*

He·be (hē′bĭ), *n.* *Gk. Myth.* the goddess of youth and spring, cupbearer (before Ganymede) of Olympus, and wife of Hercules. [t. L, t. Gk.: youth, youthful prime]

he·be·phre·ni·a (hē′bə frē′nĭ ə), *n.* *Psychiatry.* a form of dementia praecox incident to the age of puberty, characterized by childish behavior, hallucinations, and emotional deterioration. [f. Gk.: *hēbē* youth + *phrēn* mind + *-ia* -IA]

He·ber (hē′bər), *n.* **Reginald,** 1783–1826, British bishop and hymn writer.

heb·e·tate (hĕb′ə tāt′), v. -tated, -tating, adj. —v.t., v.i. 1. to make or become blunt. —adj. 2. Bot. having a blunt, soft point, as awns. [t. L: m.s. hebetātus, pp., blunted, dulled] —**heb·e·ta′tion,** n.

he·bet·ic (hǐ bĕt′ǐk), adj. Physiol. pertaining to or occurring during puberty. [t. Gk.: s. hēbētikós youthful]

heb·e·tude (hĕb′ə tūd′, -tōōd′), n. state of being dull; lethargy. [t. LL: m. hebetūdo, der. L hebes dull]

He·bra·ic (hǐ brā′ǐk), adj. Hebrew. [t. LL: s. Hebraicus, t. Gk.: m. Hebraikós; r. OE Ebrēisc] —**He·bra′i·cal·ly,** adv.

He·bra·ism (hē′brā ǐz′əm, -brǐ-), n. 1. a Hebrew idiom. 2. Hebrew character, spirit, thought, or practice.

He·bra·ist (hē′brāǐst, -brǐ-), n. 1. one versed in Hebrew learning. 2. a specialist in Hebrew philology. 3. one imbued with the Hebrew spirit.

He·bra·is·tic (hē′brā ǐs′tǐk, -brǐ-), adj. pertaining to Hebraists or Hebraism. Also, **He′bra·is′ti·cal.**

He·bra·ize (hē′brā īz′, -brǐ-), v. -ized, -izing. —v.t. 1. to make Hebrew. —v.i. 2. to become Hebrew. 3. to conform to the Hebrew usage or type. 4. to use a Hebrew idiom or manner of speech. [t. Gk.: s. hebraïzein speak Hebrew]

He·brew (hē′brōō), n. 1. a member of that branch of the Semitic race descended from the line of Abraham; an Israelite; a Jew. 2. a Semitic language, the language of the ancient Hebrews, which although not a vernacular after 100 B.C. was retained as the scholarly and liturgical language of Jews and now is used as the language of Palestinian Jews. —adj. 3. of or pertaining to the Hebrews or their language. [ME Ebreu, t. OF, t. ML: m.s. Ebreus, L Hebraeus, t. Gk.: m. Erebraîos t. Aram.: m. 'Ebhrāyā, t. Heb.: m. 'Ibhrī, said to mean "one from beyond"; r. OE Ebrēas (pl.), t. ML: m. Ebrēī]

He·brews (hē′brōōz), n. a New Testament epistle, preserved among the Epistles of Paul.

Heb·ri·des (hĕb′rə dēz′), n.pl. a group of islands off the W coast of and belonging to Scotland. 61,800 pop. (1931); ab. 2900 sq. mi. Also, **Western Islands.** —**Heb/ri·de′an,** adj.

He·bron (hē′brən), n. a city in Palestine. 24,560 (est. 1944).

Hec·a·te (hĕk′ə tǐ; in Shak. hĕk′ǐt), n. Gk. Myth. a goddess of the moon, earth, and infernal regions, also associated with magic and witchcraft. Also, **Hekate.** [t. L, t. Gk.: m. Hekátē, prop. fem. of hékatos far-darting (epithet of Apollo)]

hec·a·tomb (hĕk′ə tōm′, -tōōm′), n. 1. a great public sacrifice, orig. of a hundred oxen, as to the Greek gods. 2. any great slaughter. [t. L: m. hecatombē, t. Gk.: m. hekatómbē]

Hecht (hĕkt), n. **Ben,** born 1894, U.S. writer.

heck·le (hĕk′əl), v. -led, -ling, n. —v.t. 1. Also, **hatchel.** to badger or torment; harass, esp. a public speaker, with questions and jibes. 2. to cut (flax or hemp) with a hatchel. [der. HECKLE, n.] —n. 3. hatchel. [late ME hekele, n., phonetic var. of ME hechele; akin to HACKLE[1], HATCHEL] —**heck′ler,** n. —**heck′ling,** n.

hec·tare (hĕk′târ), n. a surface measure, the common unit of land measure in the metric system, equal to 100 ares, or 10,000 square meters, equivalent to 2.471 acres. Also, **hektare.** [t. F. See HECTO-, ARE[2]]

hec·tic (hĕk′tǐk), adj. 1. characterized by great excitement, passions, etc.: hectic pleasures. 2. marking a particular habit or condition of body, as the fever of phthisis (**hectic fever**) when this is attended by flushed cheeks (**hectic flush**), hot skin, and emaciation. 3. pertaining to or affected with such fever; consumptive. —n. 4. a hectic fever. 5. a hectic flush. 6. a consumptive person. [t. LL: s. hecticus, t. Gk.: m. hektikós habitual, hectic] —**hec′ti·cal·ly,** adv.

hecto-, a word element meaning "hundred," used in the metric system to indicate the multiplication of the unit by 100. [comb. form representing Greek hekatón]

hec·to·cot·y·lus (hĕk′tə kŏt′ə ləs), n., pl. -li (-lī′). Zool. a modified arm of the male of certain cephalopods which is used to transfer sperm into the female. [NL, f. hecto- HECTO- + m. Gk. kotýlē cup]

hec·to·gram (hĕk′tə grăm′), n. Metric System. a unit of 100 grams, equivalent to 3.527 ounces avoirdupois. Also, **hektogram;** esp. Brit., **hec′to·gramme′.**

hec·to·graph (hĕk′tə gräf′, -gräf′), n. 1. a process for making copies of a writing, etc., from a prepared gelatin surface to which the original writing has been transferred. 2. the apparatus used. —v.t. 3. to copy with the hectograph.

hec·to·li·ter (hĕk′tə lē′tər), n. Metric System. a unit of capacity of 100 liters, equivalent to 2.8378 bushels, or 26.418 U.S. gallons. Also, **hektoliter;** esp. Brit., **hec′to·li′tre.**

hec·to·me·ter (hĕk′tə mē′tər), n. Metric System. a measure of length equal to 100 meters, or 328.08 ft. Also, esp. Brit., **hec′to·me′tre.**

Hec·tor (hĕk′tər), n. 1. the eldest son of Priam and husband of Andromache, the noblest of Homer's heroes, slain by Achilles. 2. (l.c.) a blustering, domineering fellow; a swashbuckler; a bully. —v.t. 3. (l.c.) to treat with insolence; bully; torment. —v.i. 4. (l.c.) to act in a blustering, domineering way; be a bully.

Hec·u·ba (hĕk′yŏŏ bə), n. Gk. Legend. the wife of Priam.

he′d (hēd; unstressed ēd, ǐd), contraction of: 1. he had. 2. he would.

hed·dle (hĕd′əl), n. (in a loom) one of the sets of vertical cords or wires, forming the principal part of the harness which guides the warp threads. [metathetic var. of heald, OE hefeld thread (for weaving)]

hedge (hĕj), n., v., hedged, hedging. —n. 1. a row of bushes or small trees planted close together, esp. when forming a fence or boundary. 2. any barrier or boundary. 3. an act or a means of hedging a bet or the like. —v.t. 4. to enclose with or separate by a hedge (often fol. by in, off, about, etc.): to hedge a garden. 5. to surround, as with a hedge; hem in (often fol. by in). 6. to surround so as to prevent escape or hinder free movement; obstruct (often fol. by in or up): to be hedged by difficulties. 7. to protect (a bet, etc.) by taking some offsetting risk. —v.i. 8. to turn aside; swerve; avoid an open or decisive course. 9. to protect a bet, speculation, etc., by taking some offsetting risk. 10. Finance. to enter transactions that will protect against loss through a compensatory price movement. 11. to hide as in a hedge; skulk. [ME hegge, OE hegge (oblique case), c. G hecke. Cf. HAW[1], HAY[1]]

hedge garlic, an erect cruciferous herb, Sisymbrium officinale, with a garliclike odor.

hedge·hog (hĕj′hŏg′, -hôg′), n. 1. an insectivorous mammal frequenting hedges and gardens, esp. in Europe, having spiny hairs on the back and sides, not found in America; not to be confused with the porcupine. 2. U.S. the porcupine.

Hedgehog,
Erinaceus europaeus
(10 to 11 in. long)

hedge·hop (hĕj′hŏp′), v.i. to fly an airplane at a very low altitude, as for spraying crops, bombing in warfare, etc. —**hedge′hop′per,** n. —**hedge′hop′ping,** n., adj.

hedge hyssop, 1. any of the low herbs constituting the scrophulariaceous genus Gratiola, as G. officinalis, a medicinal species of Europe. 2. any of certain similar plants, as Scutellaria minor, an English skullcap.

hedg·er (hĕj′ər), n. Brit. 1. one who makes or repairs hedges. 2. one who hedges in betting, etc.

hedge·row (hĕj′rō′), n. a row of bushes or trees forming a hedge.

hedge sparrow, a small European passerine bird, Prunella modularis, which frequents hedges.

hedg·y (hĕj′ǐ), adj. abounding in hedges.

He·din (hĕ dēn′), n. **Sven Anders** (svĕn än′dərs), born 1865, Swedish explorer in Asia.

He·djaz (hē jăz′; Arab. hĕ zhăz′), n. Hejaz.

he·don·ic (hē dŏn′ǐk), adj. 1. pertaining to or consisting in pleasure. 2. pertaining to hedonism or hedonics. [t. Gk.: m.s. hēdonikós pleasurable] —**he·don′i·cal·ly,** adv.

he·don·ics (hē dŏn′ǐks), n. Psychol. the study of pleasurable and painful states of consciousness.

he·don·ism (hē′də nǐz′əm), n. 1. the doctrine that pleasure or happiness is the highest good. 2. devotion to pleasure. —**he′don·ist,** n., adj. —**he′do·nis′tic,** adj. —**he′do·nis′ti·cal·ly,** adv.

-hedron, a combining form denoting geometrical solid figures having a certain number of faces, as in polyhedron. [t. Gk.: etymological m. -edron, neut. of -edros, adj., having bases, -sided, der. hédra seat, base]

heed (hēd), v.t. 1. to give attention to; regard; notice. —v.i. 2. to give attention; have regard. —n. 3. careful attention; notice; observation (usually with give or take). [ME hede(n), OE hēdan, c. G hüten attend to, mind; akin to HOOD, n.] —**heed′er,** n. —**Syn.** 1. note, observe, consider. 3. consideration, care.

heed·ful (hēd′fəl), adj. attentive; mindful: heedful of others. —**heed′ful·ly,** adv. —**heed′ful·ness,** n.

heed·less (hēd′lǐs), adj. careless; thoughtless; unmindful. —**heed′less·ly,** adv. —**heed′less·ness,** n.

hee·haw (hē′hô′), n. 1. the braying sound made by an ass. 2. rude laughter. —v.i. 3. to bray. [imit.]

heel[1] (hēl), n. 1. (in man) the back part of the foot, below and behind the ankle. 2. an analogous part in other vertebrates. 3. either hind foot or hoof of some animals, as the horse. 4. the foot as a whole: small fauns with cloven heel. 5. the part of a stocking, shoe, or the like, covering the heel. 6. a solid part of wood, rubber, etc., attached to the sole of a shoe, under the heel. 7. something resembling the human heel in position, shape, etc.: heel of bread. 8. the latter or concluding part of anything: heel of a session. 9. Naut. a. the after end of a ship's keel. b. the lower part of a mast, a boom, a sternpost, a rafter, etc. 10. the crook in the head of a golf club. 11. Some special noun phrases are: **at one's heels,** close behind one. **down at the heels,** 1. having the shoe heels worn down. 2. shabby. 3. slipshod or slovenly. **take to one's heels,** to run off or away. **to heel,** 1. close behind: the dog followed the hunter to heel. 2. subservient. —v.t. 12. to follow at the heels of; chase closely. 13. to furnish with heels, as shoes. 14. to perform (a dance) with the heels. 15. Golf. to strike the (ball) with the heel of the club. 16. to arm (a gamecock) with spurs. —v.i. 17. to follow at one's heels. 18. to use the heels, as in dancing. [ME; OE hēl(a), appar. der. hōh HOCK. Cf. D hiel, Icel. hæll] —**heel′less,** adj.

heel² (hēl), *v.i.* **1.** (of a ship, etc.) to lean to one side; cant; tilt. *—v.t.* **2.** to cause to lean or cant. *—n.* **3.** a heeling movement; a cant. [earlier *heeld*, ME *helde*(*n*), OE *h*(*i*)*eldan* bend, incline, der. *heald*, adj., sloping]

heel³ (hēl), *n.* *Colloq.* a cad; a low character. [special use of HEEL¹. See HEELER]

heel-and-toe (hēl′ən tō′), *adj.* noting a pace, as in walking contests, in which the heel of the front foot touches the ground before the toes of the rear one leave it.

heel·er (hē′lər), *n.* **1.** one who heels. **2.** *U.S. Slang.* a servile follower or hanger-on of a political boss: *ward heeler.* [see HEEL¹, sec. 11: TO HEEL, def. 2]

heel·piece (hēl′pēs′), *n.* **1.** a piece serving as or fitted to a heel of a shoe or stocking. **2.** a terminal piece or part of anything.

heel·post (hēl′pōst′), *n.* a post made to withstand strain, forming or fitted to the heel or end of something, as the post on which a gate or door is hinged.

heel·tap (hēl′tăp′), *n.* **1.** a layer of leather or the like in a shoe heel; a lift. **2.** a small portion of liquor left in a glass after drinking.

heft (hĕft), *n.* **1.** *U.S. and Brit. Dial.* weight; heaviness. **2.** *U.S. Colloq.* the bulk or main part. *—v.t.* **3.** to try the weight of by lifting. **4.** *U.S. Colloq. and Brit. Dial.* to heave or lift. [der. HEAVE]

heft·y (hĕf′tĭ), *adj.*, **heftier, heftiest.** *Colloq.* **1.** heavy; weighty. **2.** big and strong; powerful; muscular.

He·gel (hā′gəl), *n.* **Georg Wilhelm Friedrich** (gā ôrkH′ vĭl′hĕlm frā′drĭкH), 1770–1831, German philosopher.

He·ge·li·an (hā gā′lĬ ən, hĬ jē′–), *adj.* **1.** of or pertaining to Hegel or to Hegelianism. *—n.* **2.** one who accepts the philosophical opinions of Hegel.

He·ge·li·an·ism (hā gā′lĬ ə nĬz′əm, hĬ jē′–), *n.* the philosophical system of Hegel, which during the second quarter of the 19th century was the leading system of metaphysical thought in Germany. It is characterized by the **Hegelian dialectic,** the scheme of which is *thesis, antithesis, synthesis* (i.e., an original tendency, its opposing tendency, and their unification in a new movement).

he·gem·o·ny (hĬ jĕm′ə nĬ, hĕj′ə mō′nĬ), *n.*, *pl.* **-nies. 1.** leadership or predominant influence exercised by one state over others, as in a confederation. **2.** leadership; predominance. [t. Gk.: m.s. *hēgemonía*]

He·gi·ra (hĬ jī′rə, hĕj′ərə), *n.* **1.** the flight of Mohammed from persecutions in Mecca to his successes in Medina. The date, A.D. 622, is the starting point in the Mohammedan calendar. **2.** the Mohammedan era itself. **3.** (*l.c.*) a flight similar to Mohammed's. Also, **Hejira.** [t. ML, t. Ar.: m. *hijra* departure, migration]

he·gu·men (hĬ gū′mən), *n.* *Gk. Orth. Ch.* the head of a monastery. Also, **he·gu·me·nos** (hĬ gū′mə nŏs′), [t. ML; s. *hēgúmenus*, t. Gk.: m. *hēgoúmenos*, prop. ppr. of *hēgeĩsthai* lead]

Hei·del·berg (hī′dəl bûrg′; *Ger.* hī′dəl bĕrкH′), *n.* a city in SW Germany, in Baden. 80,407 (1939).

Heidelberg jaw, *Anthropol.* a lower jaw supposed to belong to a very early human species, found in 1907 near Heidelberg, Germany.

Heidelberg man, the primitive man reconstructed from the Heidelberg jaw.

Hei·duc (hī′dŏŏk), *n.* Haiduk. Also, **Hei′dku.**

heif·er (hĕf′ər), *n.* a cow that has not produced a calf and is under three years of age. [ME *hayfre*, OE *hēa*(*h*)*f*(*o*)*re*, *hēahfora*, f. *hēah* HIGH (i.e. grown) + *-fore*, fem. equivalent of *fearr* bull. Cf. Gk. *póris* young cow]

Hei·fetz (hī′fĬts), *n.* **Jascha** (yä′shə), born 1901, a Russian-born violinist in the U.S.

heigh (hā, hī), *interj.* an exclamation used to call attention, give encouragement, etc.

heigh-ho (hī′hō′, hā′–), *interj.* an exclamation of surprise, exultation, melancholy, or weariness.

height (hīt), *n.* **1.** state of being high. **2.** extent upward; altitude; stature; distance upward; elevation: *height of an object above the ground.* **3.** considerable or great altitude or elevation. **4.** a high place or level; a hill or mountain. **5.** the highest part; the top; apex. **6.** the highest or culminating point; utmost degree: *the height of the season.* **7.** high degree, as of a quality. [ME; OE *hīehtho, hē*(*a*)*hthu.* See HIGH, -TH¹]
—Syn. 1. HEIGHT, ALTITUDE, ELEVATION refer to distance above a level. HEIGHT denotes extent upward (as from foot to head) as well as any measurable distance above a given level: *the tree has a height of 10 feet; they climbed to a great height.* ALTITUDE usually refers to the distance, determined by instruments, above a given level: *altitude of an airplane.* ELEVATION implies a distance to which something has been raised or uplifted above a level: *a hill's elevation above sea level.* **5.** summit. **6.** zenith, culmination. **—Ant. 2.** depth.

height·en (hī′tən), *v.t.* **1.** to increase the height of; make higher. **2.** to increase the intensity of, as in a drawing: *to heighten a picture with highlights of Chinese white. —v.i.* **3.** to become higher. **4.** to increase; augment. **—height′en·er,** *n.* **—Syn. 1.** See **elevate.**

height-to-pa·per (hīt′tə pā′pər), *n.* *Print.* the standard height of type, in the U.S. 0.9186 of an inch.

heil (hīl), *interj.* *German.* hail! (a greeting).

Heil·bronn (hīl′brŏn), *n.* a city in SW Germany, in Württemberg. 77,569 (1939).

Hei·lung·kiang (hā′lŏŏng′jyäng′), *n.* a province in NE China, in Manchuria. 2,714,700 pop. (est. 1946); 76,562 sq. mi.

Heim·dall (hām′däl), *n.* *Scand. Myth.* a god of light, the guardian against the giants of the bridge of the gods; the slayer of Loki. [t. Icel.: s. *Heimdallr*]

Hei·ne (hī′nə), *n.* **Heinrich** (hīn′rĬKH), 1797–1856, German lyric and satiric poet, journalist, and critic.

hei·nous (hā′nəs), *adj.* hateful; odious; gravely reprehensible: *a heinous offense.* [ME *heynous,* t. OF: m. *hainos,* der. *haine* hatred, der. *haïr* hate; of Gmc. orig. and akin to HATE] **—hei′nous·ly,** *adv.* **—hei′nous·ness,** *n.* **—Syn.** wicked, infamous. **—Ant.** trivial.

heir (âr), *n.* **1.** *Anglo-American Law.* one who inherits, or has a right of inheritance in the (real) property of an intestate person. **2.** *Civil Law.* one who inherits the property of a deceased person, testate or intestate, and is liable for the payments of the debts of the deceased and of the legacies. **3.** one to whom something falls or is due. *—v.t.* **4.** to inherit; succeed to. [ME, t. OF, g. L *hēres*] **—heir′less,** *adj.*

heir apparent, *pl.* **heirs apparent.** an heir whose right is indefeasible, provided he survives the ancestor.

heir·dom (âr′dəm), *n.* heirship; inheritance.

heir·ess (âr′Ĭs), *n.* **1.** a female heir. **2.** a woman inheriting or expected to inherit considerable wealth.

heir·loom (âr′lŏŏm′), *n.* **1.** any family possession transmitted from generation to generation. **2.** *Law.* a chattel that because of its close connection with the mansion house descends to the heir, as a portrait of an ancestor, etc. [f. HEIR + LOOM¹, orig. tool or implement]

heir presumptive, an heir whose expectation may be defeated by the birth of a nearer heir.

heir·ship (âr′shĬp), *n.* the position or rights of an heir; right of inheritance; inheritance.

He·jaz (hē jăz′; *Arab.* hĕ zhäz′), *n.* a former independent kingdom in W Arabia, bordering on the Red Sea, now forming a part of Saudi Arabia: the holy cities of Islam, Mecca and Medina, are in Hejaz. ab. 1,500,000 pop.; ab. 150,000 sq. mi. *Cap.:* Mecca. Also, **Hedjaz.**

He·ji·ra (hĬ jī′rə, hĕj′ərə), *n.* Hegira.

Hek·a·te (hĕk′ə tĬ; *in Shak.* hĕk′Ĭt), *n.* Hecate.

hek·tare (hĕk′târ), *n.* hectare.

hek·to·gram (hĕk′tə grăm′), *n.* hectogram.

hek·to·li·ter (hĕk′tə lē′tər), *n.* hectoliter.

Hel (hĕl), *n.* *Scand. Myth.* the goddess of Niflheim, the realm of the dead: the daughter of Loki. [t. Icel.]

held (hĕld), *v.* pt. and pp. of **hold.**

Hel·en (hĕl′ən), *n.* the beautiful daughter of Zeus and Leda, and wife of Menelaus of Sparta. Her abduction by Paris caused the Trojan war. See **apple of discord.**

Hel·e·na (hĕl′ə nə), *n.* the capital of Montana, in the W part. 17,581 (1950).

Hel·go·land (hĕl′gō länt′), *n.* a German island in the North Sea. Its heavy fortifications were destroyed, 1947; British naval victory in nearby Helgoland Bight, 1914. 4460 pop. (1939); ¼ sq. mi. Also, **Heligoland.**

heli-, var. of **helio-,** before vowels, as in *helianthus.*

he·li·a·cal (hĬ lī′ə kəl), *adj.* *Astron.* pertaining to or occurring near the sun, esp. applied to such risings and settings of a star as are most nearly coincident with those of the sun while yet being visible. Also, **he·li·ac** (hē′lĬ ăk′). [f. s. LL *hēliacus* (t. Gk.: m. *hēliakós* of the sun) + -AL¹] **—he·li′a·cal·ly,** *adv.*

he·li·an·thus (hē′lĬ ăn′thəs), *n.* a sunflower. [NL, f. Gk.: s. *hélios* sun + m. *ánthos* flower]

hel·i·cal (hĕl′ə kəl), *adj.* pertaining to or having the form of a helix. [f. s. L *helix* HELIX + -AL¹] **—hel′i·cal·ly,** *adv.*

hel·i·ces (hĕl′ə sēz′), *n.* pl. of helix.

hel·i·coid (hĕl′ə koid′; *Aeronaut. often* hē′lə–), *adj.* **1.** coiled or curving like a helix; spiral. *—n.* **2.** *Geom.* a warped surface generated by a straight line so moving as always to cut or touch a fixed helix. [t. Gk.: m.s. *helikoeidēs* of spiral form] **—hel′i·coi′dal,** *adj.* **—hel′i·coi′dal·ly,** *adv.*

Hel·i·con (hĕl′ə kŏn′, -kən), *n.* **1.** a mountain in S Greece, in Boeotia. 5738 ft. **2.** *Gk. Myth.* this mountain regarded as the source of poetry and poetic inspiration. From it flowed the fountains of Aganippe and Hippocrene, associated with the Muses. **3.** (*l.c.*) a tuba in coiled form to be carried over the shoulder in cavalry bands. **—Hel·i·co·ni·an** (hĕl′ə kō′nĬ ən), *adj.*

hel·i·cop·ter (hĕl′ə kŏp′tər; *Aeronaut. often* hē′lə–), *n.* any of a class of heavier-than-air craft which are lifted and sustained in the air by helicoid surfaces or propellers turning on vertical axes by virtue of power supplied from an engine. [t. F: m. *hélicoptère*, f. *hélico-* (comb. form. See HELIX) + m.s. Gk., *pterón* wing]

Hel·i·go·land (hĕl′ə gō länd′), *n.* Helgoland.

helio-, a word element meaning "sun," as in *heliocentric.* Also, **heli-.** [t. Gk., comb. form of *hélios*]

he·li·o·cen·tric (hē′lĬ ō sĕn′trĬk), *adj.* *Astron.* **1.** as viewed or measured from the center of the sun. **2.** having or representing the sun as a center.

heliocentric parallax. See **parallax** (def. 3).

He·li·o·gab·a·lus (hē′lĬ ə găb′ə ləs), *n.* Elagabalus.

he·li·o·gram (hē′lĬ ə grăm′), *n.* a heliographic message. [b. HELIO(GRAPH) and (TELE)GRAM]

he·li·o·graph (hē′lĬ ə grăf′, -gräf′), *n.* **1.** a device for signaling by means of a movable mirror which flashes beams of light to a distance. **2.** an apparatus for photographing the sun. *—v.t., v.i.* **3.** to communicate by heliograph. **—he·li·og·ra·pher** (hē′lĬ ŏg′rə fər), *n.* **—he′li·o·graph′ic,** *adj.* **—he·li·og·ra·phy,** *n.*

He·li·op·o·lis (hē′lĭ ŏp′ə lĭs), n. **1.** Biblical, **On.** an ancient ruined city in N Egypt, on the Nile delta. **2.** ancient Greek name of **Baalbek.**

He·li·os (hē′lĭ ŏs′), n. Gk. Myth. the sun god, son of Hyperion, represented as driving a chariot across the heavens. [t. Gk.: the sun, the sun god]

he·li·o·stat (hē′lĭ ə stăt′), n. an instrument consisting of a mirror moved by clockwork, for reflecting the sun's rays in a fixed direction.

he·li·o·tax·is (hē′lĭ ə tăk′sĭs), n. a phototaxis in response to sunlight. —**he·li·o·tac·tic** (hē′lĭ ə tăk′tĭk), adj.

he·li·o·ther·a·py (hē′lĭ ə thĕr′ə pĭ), n. treatment of disease by means of sunlight.

he·li·o·trope (hē′lĭ ə trōp′, hēl′yə- or, esp. Brit., hĕl′-yə-), n. **1.** Bot. any plant that turns toward the sun. **2.** any herb or shrub of the boraginaceous genus Heliotropium, esp. H. arborescens (peruvianum), a garden plant with small, fragrant purple flowers. **3.** the medicinal valerian (Valeriana officinalis). **4.** light tint of purple; reddish lavender. **5.** bloodstone. [t. F, t. L: m.s. hēliotropium, t. Gk.: m. hēliotrópion sundial, plant, bloodstone]

he·li·o·trop·ic (hē′lĭ ə trŏp′ĭk, -trō′pĭk), adj. Bot. growing towards the light. —**he·li·o·trop·i·cal·ly**, adv.

he·li·ot·ro·pism (hē′lĭ ŏt′rə pĭz′əm), n. heliotropic habit of growth.

he·li·o·type (hē′lĭ ə tīp′), n., v., -**typed**, -**typing**. —n. **1.** a picture or print produced by a photomechanical process in which the impression in ink is taken directly from a prepared gelatin film which has been exposed under a negative. **2.** Also, **he·li·o·typ·y** (hē′lĭ ə tī′pĭ). the process itself. —v.t. **3.** to make a heliotype of. —**he·li·o·typ·ic** (hē′lĭ ə tĭp′ĭk), adj.

he·li·o·zo·an (hē′lĭ ə zō′ən), n. one of the Heliozoa, an order of protozoans, distinguished by a spherical body and radiating pseudopods.

he·li·um (hē′lĭ əm), n. Chem. an inert gaseous element present in the sun's atmosphere, certain minerals, natural gas, etc., and also occurring as a radioactive decomposition product, used as a substitute for inflammable gases in dirigible balloons. Symbol: He; at. wt.: 4.003; at. no.: 2; density: 0.1785 at 0°C. and 760 mm. pressure. [NL, der. Gk. hēlios sun]

he·lix (hē′lĭks), n., pl. **helices** (hĕl′ə sēz′), **helixes. 1.** any spiral. **2.** a spiral object or part. **3.** Archit. **a.** a spiral ornament. **b.** a volute under the abacus of the Corinthian capital. **4.** Geom. the curve assumed by a straight line drawn on a plane when that plane is wrapped round a cylindrical surface of any kind, especially a right circular cylinder, as the curve of a screw thread. **5.** Anat. the curved fold forming most of the rim of the external ear. See diag. under **ear.** [t. L, t. Gk.: anything of spiral shape]

H. Helix, in a Corinthian capital (def. 3b)

hell (hĕl), n. **1.** the place or state of punishment of the wicked after death; the abode of evil and condemned spirits; Gehenna or Tartarus. **2.** any place or state of torment or misery: a hell on earth. **3.** the powers of evil. **4.** anything that causes torment. **5.** the abode of the dead; Sheol or Hades. **6.** a gambling house. **7.** a receptacle into which a tailor throws his shreds or a printer his type. [ME helle, OE hel(l), c. G hölle. Cf. HALL] —**Syn. 2.** inferno, Abaddon, pandemonium, Avernus. —**Ant. 2.** paradise.

he'll (hēl; unstressed hĭl, ĭl), contraction of: **1.** he will. **2.** he shall.

Hel·las (hĕl′əs), n. ancient and modern Greek name of **Greece.**

hell·bend·er (hĕl′bĕn′-dər), n. a large aquatic salamander, Cryptobranchus alleganiensis, of the Ohio and certain other American rivers.

Hellbender, Cryptobranchus alleganiensis (Ab. 18 in. long)

hell·broth (hĕl′brôth′, -brŏth′), n. a magical broth prepared for an infernal purpose.

hell·cat (hĕl′kăt′), n. **1.** an evil-tempered, unmanageable woman. **2.** a hag or witch.

hell·div·er (hĕl′dī′vər), n. a grebe, esp. the American pied-billed grebe.

hel·le·bore (hĕl′ə bōr′), n. **1.** any plant of the ranunculaceous genus Helleborus, esp. H. niger (**black hellebore**), a European herb with showy flowers. **2.** any of the coarse herbs constituting the melanthiaceous genus Veratrum, as V. album (**European white hellebore**) and V. viride (**American white hellebore**). **3.** the powdered root of American white hellebore used to kill lice and caterpillars. [t. Gk.: m.s. hellēboros; r. earlier ellebor(e), ME el(l)bre, etc., t. L: m. elleborus]

Hel·len (hĕl′ən), n. Gk. Legend. a king of Phthia (in Thessaly), eponymous ancestor of the Hellenes.

Hel·lene (hĕl′ēn), n. a Greek. [t. Gk.: m. Héllēn]

Hel·len·ic (hĕ lĕn′ĭk, -lē′nĭk), adj. **1.** pertaining to the Greeks. —n. **2.** a group of Indo-European languages, including Greek. **3.** Greek, especially Modern Greek.

Hel·len·ism (hĕl′ə nĭz′əm), n. **1.** ancient Greek culture or ideals. **2.** the character or spirit of the Greeks. **3.** adoption of Greek speech, ideas, or customs.

Hel·len·ist (hĕl′ən ĭst), n. **1.** one who adopts the Greek speech, ideas, or customs. **2.** one who admires or studies Greek civilization. [t. Gk.: s. Hellēnistḗs]

Hel·len·is·tic (hĕl′ən ĭs′tĭk), adj. **1.** pertaining to Hellenists. **2.** following or resembling Greek usage. **3.** pertaining to the Greeks or their language, culture, etc., after the time of Alexander the Great when Greek characteristics were modified by foreign elements.

Hel·len·ize (hĕl′ə nīz′), v., -**ized**, -**izing.** —v.t. **1.** to make Greek in character. —v.i. **2.** to adopt Greek ideas or customs. [t. Gk.: m.s. Hellēnizein] —**Hel·len·i·za·tion**, n. —**Hel′len·iz′er**, n.

hel·ler (hĕl′ər), n., pl. **heller. 1.** a small German coin formerly current, generally worth half a pfennig. **2.** a copper Austrian coin equal to one hundredth of a krone. **3.** Czechoslovakian money of account equal to one hundredth of a koruna. [G]

Hel·les (hĕl′ĭs), n. **Cape,** a cape in European Turkey at the S end of Gallipoli Peninsula.

Hel·les·pont (hĕl′ə spŏnt′), n. ancient name of the **Dardanelles.** [t. Gk.: m. Hellḗspontos sea of HELLE]

hell·fire (hĕl′fīr′), n. **1.** the fire of hell. **2.** punishment in hell.

Hell Gate, a narrow channel in the East River, in New York City.

BULGARIA | Black Sea | Istanbul (Constantinople) | HELLESPONT | K E Y

hell·gram·mite (hĕl′grə mīt′), n. the aquatic larva of the dobson, used as a bait by anglers.

hell·hound (hĕl′hound′), n. **1.** a hound of hell; a demon. **2.** a fiendish person. [ME hellehound, OE hellehund hell's hound]

hell·ion (hĕl′yən), n. Colloq. a troublesome, mischief-making person.

hell·ish (hĕl′ĭsh), adj. of, like, or befitting hell; infernal; wicked. —**hell′ish·ly**, adv. —**hell′ish·ness**, n.

hel·lo (hĕ lō′, hə-, hĕl′ō), interj., n., pl. -**los**, v., -**loed**, -**loing.** —interj. **1.** an exclamation to attract attention or express greeting. **2.** an exclamation of surprise, etc. —n. **3.** the call "hello". —v.i. **4.** to call "hello," so to attract attention or in greeting. Also, **hullo.** [var. of HALLO]

helm[1] (hĕlm), n. **1.** the tiller or wheel by which the rudder of a vessel is controlled. **2.** the entire steering apparatus. **3.** a moving of the helm. **4.** the place or post of control: the helm of affairs. —v.t. **5.** to steer; direct. [ME helme, OE helma; akin to MHG helm handle, Icel. hjalm rudder] —**helm′less**, adj.

helm[2] (hĕlm), n. **1.** Archaic. a helmet. —v.t. **2.** to furnish or cover with a helmet. [ME and OE, c. D and G helm. See HELMET]

Hel·mand (hĕl′mənd), n. a river flowing from E Afghanistan SW to a lake in E Iran. ab. 650 mi.

hel·met (hĕl′mĭt), n. **1.** a defensive covering for the head: **a.** any of various forms of protective head covering worn by soldiers, firemen, divers, etc. **b.** medieval armor for the head. **c.** Fencing, Singlestick, etc. a protective device for the head and face consisting of reinforced wire mesh. **2.** anything resembling a helmet in form or position. [ME, t. OF, dim. of helme helm, helmet, t. Gmc. See HELM[2]] —**hel′met·ed,** adj.

Helmets
A, Medieval, 15th century;
B, Modern, World War II

Helm·holtz (hĕlm′hōlts), n. **Hermann Ludwig Ferdinand von** (hĕr′män lōōt′vĭkh fĕr′dĭ nänt′ fən), 1821–94, German physiologist and physicist.

hel·minth (hĕl′mĭnth), n. a worm, especially a parasitic worm. [t. Gk.: s. hélmins]

hel·min·thi·a·sis (hĕl′mĭn thī′ə sĭs), n. Pathol. a condition characterized by worms in the body. [NL, f. s. Gk. helminthiân suffer from worms + -(i)āsis -(I)ASIS]

hel·min·thic (hĕl mĭn′thĭk), adj. **1.** pertaining to worms. **2.** expelling intestinal worms.

hel·min·thol·o·gy (hĕl′mĭn thŏl′ə jĭ), n. the science of worms, especially of parasitic worms.

helms·man (hĕlmz′mən), n., pl. -**men.** the man at the helm who steers a ship; a steersman.

Hé·lo·ïse (ĕl′ō ēz′), n. pupil, mistress, and wife of Abélard, later an abbess. See **Abélard.**

hel·ot (hĕl′ət, hē′lət), n. **1.** one of the serfs in ancient Sparta, owned by the state and under allotment to landowners. **2.** (l.c.) a serf or slave; a bondman.

hel·ot·ism (hĕl′ə tĭz′əm, hē′lə-), n. serfdom.

hel·ot·ry (hĕl′ət rĭ, hē′lət-), n. **1.** serfdom; slavery. **2.** helots collectively.

help (hĕlp), v., **helped** or (Archaic) **holp; helped** or (Archaic) **holpen; helping**; n. —v.t. **1.** to coöperate effectively with a person; aid; assist: to help a man in his work. **2.** to furnish aid to; contribute strength or means to; assist in doing: remedies that help digestion. **3.** to succor; save. **4.** to relieve (someone) in need, sickness, pain, or distress. **5.** to refrain from; avoid (with can or cannot): he can't help doing it. **6.** to remedy, stop, or prevent: nothing will help now. **7.** to serve food to at table (fol. by to): to help her to a salad. **8. help oneself to,** to take or appropriate at will. —v.i. **9.** to give aid;

be of service or advantage: *every little bit helps.* **—n.**
10. act of helping; aid or assistance; relief or succor.
11. a person or thing that helps. **12.** a hired helper.
13. a body of such helpers. **14.** *U.S.* a domestic servant or a farm laborer. **15.** means of remedying, stopping, or preventing: *the thing is done, and there is no help
for it now.* **16.** *Rare or Dial.* a helping (def. 2). [ME
helpe(n), OE *helpan*, c. G *helfen*] **—help'a·ble**, *adj.*
—Syn. 1. encourage, befriend; support, second, uphold,
back, abet. HELP, AID, ASSIST, SUCCOR agree in the idea of
furnishing another with something needed, especially when
the need comes at a particular time. HELP implies furnishing
anything that furthers his efforts or relieves his wants or
necessities. AID and ASSIST, somewhat more formal, imply
especially a furthering or seconding of another's efforts.
AID implies a more active helping; ASSIST implies less need
and less help. To SUCCOR is to give timely help and relief
in difficulty or distress. **2.** facilitate, further, promote,
foster. **4.** ameliorate, alleviate, remedy, cure heal. **10.**
support, backing. **—Ant. 1.** hinder. **4.** afflict.
help·er (hĕl'pər), *n.* a person or thing that helps.
—Syn. aid, assistant; supporter, backer, auxiliary, ally;
associate, colleague, coadjutor, collaborator; abetter,
accessory.
help·ful (hĕlp'fəl), *adj.* giving or affording help; useful.
—help'ful·ly, *adv.* **—help'ful·ness**, *n.* **—Syn.** useful,
convenient; beneficial, advantageous.
help·ing (hĕl'pĭng), *n.* **1.** act of one who or that which
helps. **2.** a portion served to a person at one time.
—help'ing·ly, *adv.*
help·less (hĕlp'lĭs), *adj.* **1.** unable to help oneself;
weak or dependent: *a helpless invalid.* **2.** without help,
aid, or succor. **3.** incapable, inefficient, or shiftless.
4. *Rare.* affording no help. **—help'less·ly**, *adv.*
—help'less·ness, *n.*
help·mate (hĕlp'māt'), *n.* **1.** a companion and helper.
2. a wife or husband. [f. HELP + MATE. Cf. HELPMEET]
help·meet (hĕlp'mēt'), *n.* helpmate. [erroneously
from Gen. 2:18, 20, "an help meet for him"]
Hel·sing·ör (hĕl'sĭng œr'), *n.* a seaport in NE Denmark, on Zealand island: the scene of Shakespeare's
Hamlet. 17,965 (1940). Also, **Elsinore.**
Hel·sin·ki (hĕl'sĭng kē), *n.* a seaport in and the capital
of Finland, on the S coast. 319,939 (1940). Swedish, **Hel-
sing·fors** (hĕl'sĭng fôrz', -fôrs').
hel·ter-skel·ter (hĕl'tər skĕl'tər), *adv.* **1.** in headlong, disorderly haste: *to run helter-skelter.* **—n. 2.** tumultuous haste or disorder. **3.** a helter-skelter flight,
course, or performance. **—adj. 4.** confused; disorderly;
carelessly hurried. [imit.]
helve (hĕlv), *n., v.,* **helved, helving.** *Chiefly Brit.* **—n.**
1. the handle of an ax, hatchet, hammer, or the like.
—v.t. 2. to furnish with a helve. [ME; OE *h(i)elfe*]
Hel·vel·lyn (hĕl vĕl'ĭn), *n.* a mountain in NW England. 3118 ft.
Hel·ve·tia (hĕl vē'shə), *n.* **1.** an Alpine region in Roman times, corresponding to the W and N parts of
modern Switzerland. **2.** *Poetic.* Switzerland.
Hel·ve·tian (hĕl vē'shən), *adj.* **1.** of or pertaining to
Helvetia or the Helvetii. **2.** Swiss. **—n. 3.** one of the
Helvetii. **4.** a Swiss. [f. s. L *Helvetius* + -AN]
Hel·vet·ic (hĕl vĕt'ĭk), *n.* **1.** a Swiss Protestant; a
Zwinglian. **—adj. 2.** Helvetian.
Hel·ve·ti·i (hĕl vē'shĭ ī'), *n.pl.* the ancient inhabitants
of Helvetia in the time of Julius Caesar. [L]
Hel·ve·tius (hĕl vē'shəs; *Fr.* ĕl vē syys'), **Claude Adri-
en** (klōd ȧd rē ăN'), 1715–71, French philosopher.
hem[1] (hĕm), *v.,* **hemmed, hemming,** *n.* **—v.t. 1.** to enclose or confine (fol. by *in, around,* or *about*): *hemmed in
by enemies.* **2.** to fold back and sew down the edge of
(cloth, a garment, etc.). **3.** to form an edge or border
to or about. **—n. 4.** the edge made by folding back the
margin of cloth and sewing it down. **5.** the edge or
border of a garment, etc. **6.** the edge, border, or margin
of anything. [ME *hemm(e)*, OE *hem*, prob. akin to
hamm enclosure]
hem[2] (hĕm), *interj., n., v.,* **hemmed, hemming.** **—interj.**
1. an utterance resembling a slight clearing of the throat,
used to attract attention, express doubt, etc. **—n. 2.** the
utterance or sound of "hem." **—v.i. 3.** to utter the
sound "hem." **4.** to hesitate in speaking. [imit.]
hem-, var. of hemo-, before vowels, as in *hemal.* Also,
haem-. Cf. **haemat-.**
hema-, var. of hemo-.
he·ma·chrome (hē'mə krōm', hĕm'ə-), *n.* the red
coloring matter of the blood. Also, **haemachrome.**
he·mal (hē'məl), *adj.* **1.** of or pertaining to the blood
or blood vessels. **2.** *Zool.* noting, pertaining to, or on
the side of the body ventral to the spinal axis, containing the heart and great blood vessels. Also, **haemal.**
Hem·ans (hĕm'ənz, hē'mənz), *n.* **Mrs.** (*Felicia Dorothea Browne*) 1793–1835, British poet.
hemat-, a prefix equivalent to hemo-, as in *hematin.*
Also, **hemato-.**
he·mat·ic (hē măt'ĭk), *adj.* **1.** of or pertaining to
blood; hemic. **2.** acting on the blood, as a medicine.
—n. 3. a hematic medicine. Also, **haematic.** [t. Gk.: m.s.
haimatikós of the blood]
hem·a·tin (hĕm'ə tĭn, hē'mə-), *n.* a pigment containing iron, produced in the decomposition of hemoglobin.
Also, **haematin, hem·a·tine** (hĕm'ə tĭn, -tĭn', hē'mə-).
hem·a·tin·ic (hĕm'ə tĭn'ĭk, hē'mə-), *n.* **1.** a medicine,
as a compound of iron, which tends to increase the

amount of hematin or hemoglobin in the blood. **—adj.**
2. of or obtained from hematin. Also, **haematinic.**
hem·a·tite (hĕm'ə tīt', hē'mə-), *n.* a very common
mineral, iron oxide, Fe_2O_3, occurring in steel-gray to
black crystals and in red earthy masses, the principal
ore of iron. Also, **haematite.** [t. L: m.s. *haematites*
hematite, t. Gk.: m. *haimatitēs* bloodlike] **—hem·a·tit-
ic** (hĕm'ə tĭt'ĭk, hē'mə-), *adj.*
hemato-, a prefix equivalent to hemo-, as in *hemato-
genesis.* Also, **hemat-, haemato-.**
hem·a·to·cele (hĕm'ə tō sēl', hē'mə-), *n.* *Pathol.* (usually) a hemorrhage imprisoned in membranous tissue.
Also, **haematocele.**
hem·a·toc·ry·al (hĕm'ə tŏk'rĭ əl, -tō krī'əl, hē'mə-),
adj. cold-blooded. Also, **haematocryal.**
hem·a·to·gen·e·sis (hĕm'ə tō jĕn'ə sĭs, hē'mə-), *n.*
the formation of blood. Also, **haematogenesis.**
hem·a·tog·e·nous (hĕm'ə tŏj'ə nəs, hē'mə-), *adj.* **1.**
originating in the blood. **2.** blood-producing. Also,
haematogenous.
he·ma·toid (hē'mə toid', hĕm'ə-), *adj.* bloodlike. Also,
haematoid. [t. Gk.: m.s. *haimatoeidēs* bloodlike]
he·ma·to·ma (hē'mə tō'mə, hĕm'ə-), *n., pl.* **-mata**
(-mə tə), **-mas.** *Pathol.* a swelling filled with extravasated blood. Also, **haematoma.**
hem·a·to·poi·e·sis (hĕm'ə tō poi ē'sĭs, hē'mə-), *n.* the
formation of blood. Also, **haematopoiesis.** [t. NL: m.
haematopoiēsis, f. Gk.: m. *haimato-* HEMATO- + *poiēsis* a
making] **—hem·a·to·poi·et·ic** (hĕm'ə tō poi ĕt'ĭk, hē'-
mə-), *adj.*
he·ma·to·sis (hē'mə tō'sĭs, hĕm'ə-), *n.* **1.** the formation of blood. **2.** *Physiol.* the conversion of venous into
arterial blood; oxygenation in the lungs. Also, **haematosis.** [t. NL: m. *haematosis*, t. Gk.: m. *haimátosis*, der.
haimatoûn make into blood]
hem·a·to·ther·mal (hĕm'ə tō thûr'məl, hē'mə-), *adj.*
warm-blooded. Also, **haematothermal.**
he·ma·tox·y·lin (hē'mə tŏk'sə lĭn, hĕm'ə-), *n.* a
colorless or pale-yellow crystalline compound, $C_{16}H_{14}O_6\cdot
3H_2O$, the coloring material of logwood, used as a mor-
dant dye and as an indicator. **2.** haematoxylin.
hem·a·to·zo·ön (hĕm'ə tō zō'ŏn, -ən, hē'mə-), *n., pl.*
-zoa (-zō'ə). an animal parasite, usually protozoan,
living in the blood. Also, **haematozoön.** [t. NL: m.
haematozoön. See HEMATO-, -ZOON] **—hem'a·to·zo'ic,**
adj.
hem·el·y·tron (hĕ mĕl'ə trŏn'), *n., pl.* **-tra** (-trə).
Entomol. one of the forewings of hemipterous and especially heteropterous insects, coriaceous at the base
and membranous at the tip. Also, **hemielytron.** [var. of
hemielytron, f. HEMI- + ELYTRON]
hem·er·a·lo·pi·a (hĕm'ər ə lō'pĭ ə), *n.* day blindness.
hemi-, a prefix meaning "half," as in *hemialgia.* Cf.
semi-. [t. Gk.]
-hemia, var. of **-emia.**
hem·i·al·gi·a (hĕm'ĭ ăl'jĭ ə), *n.* *Pathol.* pain or neuralgia involving only one side of the body or head.
he·mic (hē'mĭk, hĕm'ĭk), *adj.* hematic. Also, **haemic.**
hem·i·cel·lu·lose (hĕm'ĭ sĕl'yə lōs'), *n.* *Chem.* any of
a group of gummy polysaccharides, intermediate in
complexity between sugar and cellulose, which hydrolyze to monosaccharides more readily than cellulose.
Hem·i·chor·da·ta (hĕm'ĭ kôr dā'tə), *n.pl.* a chordate
subphylum that comprises a large number of small,
widely distributed marine animals.
hem·i·chor·date (hĕm'ĭ kôr'dāt), *adj.* denoting or
pertaining to the *Hemichordata.*
hem·i·cra·ni·a (hĕm'ĭ krā'nĭ ə), *n.* *Pathol.* migraine.
[t. LL, t. Gk.: m. *hēmikranía* a pain on one side of the
head]
hem·i·cy·cle (hĕm'ĭ sī'kəl), *n.* **1.** a semicircle. **2.** a
semicircular structure. [t. F, t. L: m.s. *hēmicyclium*, t.
Gk.: m. *hēmikýklion*]
hem·i·dem·i·sem·i·qua·ver (hĕm'ĭ dĕm'ĭ sĕm'-
ĭ kwā'vər), *n. Chiefly Brit. Music.* a sixty-fourth note.
See illus. under **note.**
hem·i·el·y·tron (hĕm'ĭ ĕl'ə trŏn'), *n., pl.* **-tra** (-trə).
hemelytron.
hem·i·he·dral (hĕm'ĭ hē'drəl), *adj.* (of a crystal)
having only half the planes or faces required by the
maximum symmetry of the system to which it belongs.
[f. HEMI- + s. Gk. *hédra* seat, base + -AL[1]]
hem·i·hy·drate (hĕm'ĭ hī'drāt), *n.* *Chem.* a hydrate
in which there are two molecules of the compound for
each molecule of water.
hem·i·mor·phic (hĕm'ĭ môr'fĭk), *adj.* (of a crystal)
having the two ends of an axis unlike in their planes or
modifications; lacking a center of symmetry.
hem·i·mor·phite (hĕm'ĭ môr'fīt), *n.* *Brit.* calamine.
he·min (hē'mĭn), *n.* the typical, reddish-brown crystals, of microscopic size, resulting when a sodium chloride crystal, a drop of glacial acetic acid, and some blood
are heated on a slide: used to identify the blood of different species. [f. HEM- + -IN[2]]
Hem·ing·way (hĕm'ĭng wā'), *n.* **Ernest,** born 1898,
U.S. novelist and short-story writer.
hem·i·ple·gi·a (hĕm'ĭ plē'jĭ ə), *n.* *Pathol.* paralysis of
one side of the body, resulting from a disease of the brain
or of the spinal cord.
he·mip·ter·ous (hĭ mĭp'tər əs), *adj.* belonging or pertaining to insects of the order *Hemiptera,* including the
true bugs (*Heteroptera*), whose forewings are in part

ăct, āble, dâre, ärt; ĕbb, ēqual; ĭf, īce; hŏt, ōver, ôrder, oil, bŏŏk, ōōze, out; ŭp, ūse, ûrge; ə = a in alone;
ch, chief; g, give; ng, ring; sh, shoe; th, thin; ŧħ, that; zh, vision. See the full key on inside cover.

thickened and leathery, and the cicadas, leaf hoppers, aphids, etc. (*Homoptera*), whose wings are entirely membranous. [f. HEMI- + s. Gk. *pterón* wing + -OUS]

hem·i·sphere (hĕm'ə sfĭr'), *n.* **1.** half of the terrestrial globe or celestial sphere. **2.** a map or projection of either of these. **3.** the half of a sphere. **4.** *Anat.* either of the lateral halves of the cerebrum. [t. L: m.s. *hēmisphaerium*, t. Gk.: m. *hēmisphaîrion*; r. ME *emysperie*, t. OF: m. *emispere*]

hem·i·spher·i·cal (hĕm'ə sfĕr'ə kəl), *adj.* **1.** of or pertaining to a hemisphere. **2.** in the form of a hemisphere. Also, **hem/i·spher/ic.** —**hem/i·spher/i·cal·ly,** *adv.*

hem·i·spher·oid (hĕm'ə sfĭr'oid), *n.* half of a spheroid. —**hem/i·spher·oi/dal,** *adj.*

hem·i·stich (hĕm'ə stĭk'), *n. Pros.* **1.** the exact or approximate half of a stich, or poetic verse or line, esp. as divided by a caesura or the like. **2.** an incomplete line, or a line of less than the usual length. [t. L: m.s. *hemistichium*, t. Gk.: m. *hemistíchion*]

hem·i·ter·pene (hĕm'ĭ tûr'pēn), *n.* one of a group of hydrocarbon isomers of the general formula C_5H_8, related to, and half the molecular weight of, the terpenes.

hem·i·trope (hĕm'ə trōp'), *adj., n. Crystall.* twin. [t. F. See HEMI-, -TROPE] —**hem·i·trop·ic** (hĕm'ə trŏp'-ĭk), *adj.*

hem·lock (hĕm'lŏk), *n.* **1.** *Chiefly Brit.* a poisonous umbelliferous herb, *Conicum maculatum*, with spotted stems, finely divided leaves, and small white flowers, used medicinally as a powerful sedative. **2.** a poisonous drink made from this herb. **3.** any of various other apiaceous herbs, esp. species of the genus *Cicuta* (**water hemlock**). **4.** *U.S.* **a.** the hemlock spruce. **b.** its wood. [ME *hemeluc*, OE *hemlic, hym(e)lic(e)*, ? f. *hymele* hop plant + -*k* suffix (see -OCK). Note that hemlock and hops agree in having a sedative effect]

hemlock spruce, any of the trees of the coniferous genus *Tsuga*, esp. a tree of eastern North America, *T. canadensis*, whose bark is used in tanning.

hem·mer (hĕm'ər), *n.* **1.** one who or that which hems. **2.** a sewing-machine attachment for hemming edges.

hemo-, a word element meaning "blood," as in *hemolysis.* Also, **hem-, haem-, haemo-.** Cf. **hema-, haema-, haemat-, haemato-.** [t. Gk.: m. *haimo-*, comb. form of *haîma*]

he·mo·glo·bin (hē'mə glō'bĭn, hĕm'ə-), *n.* the protein coloring matter of the red blood corpuscles, which serves to convey oxygen to the tissues: occurring in reduced form (**reduced hemoglobin**) in venous blood, and in combination with oxygen (**oxyhemoglobin**) in arterial blood. Also, **haemoglobin.** [short for *hematoglobulin*, f. *hemato-* (for HEMATIN) + GLOBULIN]

he·moid (hē'moid), *adj.* bloodlike. Also, **haemoid.**

he·mo·leu·co·cyte (hē'mə loo'kə sīt', hĕm'ə-), *n. Anat.* any white blood cell that circulates in the blood. Also, **haemoleucocyte,** **he/mo·leu/ko·cyte/.**

he·mo·ly·sin (hē'mə lī'sĭn, hĕm'ə-, hī' mŏl'ə-), *n. Immunol.* an antibody which, in coöperation with a material in fresh blood, causes dissolution of the red blood corpuscles. Also, **haemolysin.**

he·mol·y·sis (hĭ mŏl'ə sĭs), *n. Immunol.* the breaking down of the red blood cells with liberation of hemoglobin. Also, **haemolysis.** —**he·mo·lyt·ic** (hē'mə lĭt'ĭk, hĕm'ə-), *adj.*

Hé·mon (ĕ môN'), *n.* **Louis** (lwē), 1880–1913, French-Canadian novelist.

he·mo·phil·i·a (hē'mə fĭl'ĭ ə, hĕm'ə-), *n. Pathol.* a morbid condition, usually congenital, characterized by a tendency to bleed immoderately, as from an insignificant wound, caused by improper coagulation of the blood. Also, **haemophilia.** [NL: m. *haemophilia,* f. Gk.: m. *haimo-* HEMO- + *philía* affection, fondness]

he·mo·phil·i·ac (hē'mə fĭl'ĭ ăk', hĕm'ə-), *n.* a person or organism which has hemophilia. Also, **haemophiliac.**

he·mo·phil·ic (hē'mə fĭl'ĭk, hĕm'ə-), *adj.* **1.** affected by hemophilia. **2.** *Biol.* (of bacteria) developing best in a culture containing blood, or in blood itself. Also, **haemophilic.**

he·mop·ty·sis (hĭ mŏp'tə sĭs), *n. Pathol.* the expectoration of blood or bloody mucus. [t. NL: m. *haemoptysis,* f. Gk.: m. *haimo-* HEMO- + *ptýsis* spitting]

hem·or·rhage (hĕm'ər ĭj, hĕm'rĭj), *n.* a discharge of blood, as from a ruptured blood vessel. Also, **haemorrhage.** [t. L: m.s. *haemorrhagia,* t. Gk.: m. *haimor-rhagía* a violent bleeding] —**hem·or·rhag·ic** (hĕm'ə-răj'ĭk), *adj.*

hemorrhagic septicemia, *Vet. Sci.* an acute infectious disease of animals, marked by fever, catarrhal symptoms, pneumonia, and general blood infection.

hem·or·rhoid (hĕm'ə roid', hĕm'roid), *n. Pathol.* a dilation of the veins under the skin of the anus; a pile. Also, **haemorrhoid.** [t. L: m.s. *haemorrhoida* piles, t. Gk.: m.s. *haimorrhoîs*] —**hem·or·rhoi/dal,** *adj.*

hem·or·rhoid·ec·to·my (hĕm'ə roi dĕk'tə mĭ), *n., pl.* -**mies.** *Surg.* the operation for removal of hemorrhoids.

he·mo·stat (hē'mə stăt', hĕm'ə-), *n.* an instrument or agent used to compress or treat bleeding vessels in order to arrest hemorrhage. Also, **haemostat.**

he·mo·stat·ic (hē'mə stăt'ĭk, hĕm'ə-), *adj.* **1.** arresting hemorrhage, as a drug; styptic. **2.** pertaining to stagnation of the blood. —*n.* **3.** a hemostatic agent or substance. Also, **haemostatic.**

hemp (hĕmp), *n.* **1.** a tall, annual moraceous herb, *Cannabis sativa*, native in Asia, but cultivated in many

parts of the world. **2.** the tough fiber of this plant, used for making coarse fabrics, ropes, etc. **3.** an East Indian variety, *Cannabis sativa indica* (or *Cannabis indica*), of common hemp, yielding hashish, bhang, cannabin, etc. **4.** any of various plants resembling hemp. **5.** any of various fibers similar to hemp. **6.** a narcotic drug obtained from Indian hemp. [ME; OE *henep, hænep,* c. G *hanf,* Gk. *kánnabis*]

hemp agrimony, a European composite herb, *Eupatorium cannabinum,* with dull purplish flowers.

hemp·en (hĕm'pən), *adj.* **1.** made of hemp. **2.** of or pertaining to hemp. **3.** resembling hemp.

hemp nettle, **1.** a coarse labiate weed, *Galeopsis Tetrahit,* likened to the hemp from its general appearance, and to the nettle from its bristly hairs. **2.** any plant of the same genus.

hemp·seed (hĕmp'sēd'), *n.* the seed of hemp, used as a food for cage birds.

Hemp·stead (hĕmp'stĕd), *n.* a village in SE New York, on Long Island. 29,135 (1950).

hem·stitch (hĕm'stĭch'), *v.t.* **1.** to hem along a line from which threads have been drawn out, stitching the cross threads into a series of little groups. —*n.* **2.** the stitch used or the needlework done in hemstitching. [f. HEM, *n.* + STITCH[1], *v.*]

hen (hĕn), *n.* **1.** the female of the domestic fowl. **2.** the female of any bird, esp. of a gallinaceous bird. [ME and OE *hen(n)* (der. OE *hana* cock), c. G *henne*]

hen-and-chick·ens (hĕn'ə n chĭk'ənz), *n.* **1.** any of several herbs, esp. those having offshoot or runner plants growing around the parent. **2.** a species of houseleek, *Sempervivum globiferum,* native of Europe. **3.** the ground ivy, *Glecoma hederacea.*

hen·bane (hĕn'bān'), *n.* a solanaceous Old World herb, *Hyoscyamus niger,* bearing sticky, hairy foliage of a disagreeable odor, and yellowish-brown flowers, and possessing narcotic and poisonous properties: esp. destructive to domestic fowls. [ME. See HEN, BANE]

hen·bit (hĕn'bĭt'), *n.* a labiate weed, *Lamium amplexicaule,* with small purplish flowers.

hence (hĕns), *adv.* **1.** as an inference from this fact; for this reason; therefore: *of the best quality and hence satisfactory.* **2.** from this time onward; henceforth. **3.** at the end of a given period: *a month hence.* **4.** from this source or origin. **5.** from this place; away from here. —*interj.* **6.** depart! [ME *hen(ne)s,* f. *hen* hence (OE *heona, heonan*) + -(*e*)*s,* adv. suffix]

hence·forth (hĕns'fôrth'), *adv.* from this time forth; from now on. Also, **hence·for·ward** (hĕns'fôr'wərd).

hench·man (hĕnch'mən), *n., pl.* -**men.** **1.** a trusty attendant or follower. **2.** a servile and unscrupulous follower. **3.** *Obs.* a squire or page. [ME *henchemanne, henxtman,* prob. orig. meaning groom, and appar. f. OE *hengest* stallion + *mann* man]

hen·dec·a·gon (hĕn dĕk'ə gŏn'), *n.* a polygon having eleven angles and eleven sides. [f. m. Gk. *héndeka* eleven + -GON] —**hen·dec·ag·o·nal** (hĕn'də kăg'ə nəl), *adj.*

hen·dec·a·syl·la·ble (hĕn'dĕk ə sĭl'ə bəl), *n. Pros.* a metrical line of eleven syllables. [t. L: m. *hendecasyllabus* (conformed to *syllable*), t. Gk.: m. *hendekasýllabos*] —**hen·dec·a·syl·lab·ic** (hĕn'dĕk ə sĭ lăb'ĭk), *adj., n.*

hen·di·a·dys (hĕn dī'ə dĭs), *n. Rhet.* a figure in which a complex idea is expressed by two words connected by a copulative conjunction: "to look with eyes and envy" instead of "with envious eyes." [t. LL, der. Gk. phrase *hèn dià dyoîn* one through two]

Hen·don (hĕn'dən), *n.* a city in SE England, in Middlesex, near London. 154,110 (est. 1946).

hen·e·quen (hĕn'ə kĭn), *n.* the fiber of an agave, *Agave fourcroydes,* of Yucatan, used for making ropes, coarse fabrics, etc. Also, **hen/e·quin.** [t. Sp.: m. *jeniquén;* from native name]

Hen·gist (hĕng'gĭst, hĕn'jĭst), *n.* died A.D. 488, chief of the Jutes; joint founder with his brother Horsa of the English kingdom of Kent.

Hen·ley (hĕn'lĭ), *n.* **William Ernest,** 1849–1903, British poet, critic, and editor.

Hen·ley-on-Thames (hĕn'lĭ ŏn tĕmz'), *n.* a city in S England, on the Thames: annual regatta. 8868 (1939).

hen·na (hĕn'ə), *n.* **1.** a shrub or small tree, *Lawsonia inermis,* of Asia and the Levant. **2.** a reddish-orange dye or cosmetic made from the leaves of this plant. **3.** reddish or orangeish brown. —*v.t.* **4.** to tint or dye with henna. [t. Ar.: m. *ḥinnā*']

Hen·ne·pin (hĕn'ə pĭn; *Fr.* ĕn păN'), *n.* **Louis** (lwē), 1640–d. sometime after 1701, Belgian Catholic missionary in America.

hen·ner·y (hĕn'ər ĭ), *n., pl.* -**neries.** a place where fowls are kept.

hen·o·the·ism (hĕn'ə thē'ĭz'əm). *n.* **1.** the worship of some one particular divinity among others existent, in contrast with monotheism which teaches that there exists only one God. **2.** ascription of supreme divine attributes to whichever one of several gods is at the time addressed. [f. *heno-* (comb. form repr. Gk. neut. *hén* one) + THEISM] —**hen/o·the/ist,** *n.* —**hen/o·the·is/tic,** *adj.*

hen·peck (hĕn'pĕk'), *v.t.* (of a wife) to domineer over (her husband). —**hen/pecked/,** *adj.*

hen·ry (hĕn'rĭ), *n., pl.* -**ries,** -**rys.** *Elect.* the practical unit of inductance, equivalent to the inductance of a circuit in which an electromotive force of one volt is pro-

---

b., blend of, blended; c., cognate with; d., dialect, dialectal; der., derived from; f., formed from; g., going back to; m., modification of; r., replacing; s., stem of; t., taken from; ?, perhaps. See the full key on inside cover.

duced by a current in the circuit which varies at the rate of one ampere per second. [named after Joseph Henry]

Hen·ry (hĕn′rĭ), *n.* **1. Joseph,** 1797–1878, U.S. physicist. **2. O.,** (*William Sidney Porter*) 1862–1910, U.S. short-story writer. **3. Patrick,** 1736–99, American patriot, orator, and statesman. **4. Cape,** a cape in SE Virginia at the mouth of Chesapeake Bay. **5. Fort,** a fort in NW Tennessee, on the Tennessee river: Union victory, 1862.

Henry I, 1. 1068–1135, king of England, 1100–35 (brother of William II). **2.** 1008?–1060, king of France, 1031–60.

Henry II, 1. (*of Anjou*) 1133–89, king of England, 1154–89 (successor of Stephen and 1st king of Plantagenet line). **2.** 1519–59, king of France, 1547–59.

Henry III, 1. (*of Winchester*) 1207–72, king of England, 1216–72 (son of John). **2.** 1551–89, king of France, 1574–89.

Henry IV, 1. 1050–1106, emperor of Holy Roman Empire, 1056–1106. **2.** (*of Bolingbroke*) 1367–1413, king of England, 1399–1414 (successor of Richard II, son of John of Gaunt, and 1st king of house of Lancaster). **3.** (*of Navarre*) 1553–1610, king of France, 1589–1610.

Henry V, (*of Monmouth*) 1387–1422, king of England, 1413–22 (son of Henry IV).

Henry VI, (*of Windsor*) 1421–71, king of England, 1422–61 and 1470–71 (son of Henry V).

Henry VII, 1457–1509, king of England, 1485–1509 (successor of Richard III and 1st king of house of Tudor).

Henry VIII, 1491–1547, king of England, 1509–47, and of Ireland, 1541–47 (son of Henry VII).

Henry of Portugal, (*"the Navigator"*) 1394–1460, prince of Portugal, promoter of geographic exploration.

Hens·lowe (hĕnz′lō), *n.* **Philip,** died 1616, British theater manager.

Hen·ty (hĕn′tĭ), *n.* **George Alfred,** 1832–1902, British author of boys' stories.

hep (hĕp), *adj. U.S. Slang.* having inside knowledge, or being informed (fol. by *to*): *to be hep to swing music.*

hep·a·rin (hĕp′ə·rĭn), *n.* a glucoside produced in the liver which prevents the coagulation of the blood, and is used in the treatment of thrombosis.

he·pat·ic (hĭ·păt′ĭk), *adj.* **1.** of or pertaining to the liver. **2.** acting on the liver, as a medicine. **3.** liver-colored; dark reddish-brown. **4.** *Bot.* belonging or pertaining to the liverworts. —*n.* **5.** a medicine acting on the liver. **6.** a liverwort. [t. L: s. *hēpaticus*, t. Gk.: m. *hēpatikós* of the liver]

he·pat·i·ca (hĭ·păt′ə·kə), *n., pl.* **-cas, -cae** (-sē′). any of the ranunculaceous herbs, with three-lobed leaves and delicate purplish, pink, or white flowers constituting the genus *Hepatica.* [NL, prop. fem. of L *hēpaticus* HEPATIC]

hep·a·ti·tis (hĕp′ə·tī′tĭs), *n. Pathol.* inflammation of the liver. [NL, f. s. Gk. *hēpar* liver + *-ītis* -ITIS]

hep·a·tize (hĕp′ə·tīz′), *v.t.,* **-tized, -tizing.** *Pathol.* to convert (a lung, etc.) into liverlike tissue by engorgement. —**hep′a·ti·za′tion,** *n.*

hep·cat (hĕp′kăt′), *n. Jazz Slang.* an expert performer, or a knowing admirer, of jazz.

He·phaes·tus (hĕ·fĕs′təs), *n. Gk. Myth.* the god of fire and metalworking. [t. Gk.: m. *Hēphaistos*]

Hep·ple·white (hĕp′əl·hwīt′), *n.* **1. George,** died 1786, British furniture designer and cabinetmaker. —*adj.* **2.** in the style of Hepplewhite.

hepta-, a prefix meaning "seven." Also, before vowels, **hept-.** [t. Gk., comb. form of *heptá*]

hep·tad (hĕp′tăd), *n.* **1.** the number seven. **2.** a group of seven. **3.** *Chem.* an element, atom, or radical having a valence of seven. [t. LL: s. *heptas*, t. Gk.: the number seven]

hep·ta·gon (hĕp′tə·gŏn′), *n.* a polygon having seven angles and seven sides. [t. Gk.: s. *heptágōnos* seven-cornered] —**hep·tag·o·nal** (hĕp·tăg′ə·nəl), *adj.*

hep·ta·he·dron (hĕp′tə·hē′drən), *n., pl.* **-drons, -dra** (-drə). a solid figure having seven faces. —**hep′ta·he′dral,** *adj.*

Regular   Irregular

Heptagons

hep·tam·er·ous (hĕp·tăm′ər·əs), *adj.* **1.** consisting of or divided into seven parts. **2.** *Bot.* (of flowers) having seven members in each whorl.

hep·tam·e·ter (hĕp·tăm′ə·tər), *n. Pros.* a verse of seven metrical feet. [t. LL: m. *heptametrum*, t. Gk.: m. *heptámetron*] —**hep·ta·met·ri·cal** (hĕp′tə·mĕt′rə·kəl), *adj.*

hep·tane (hĕp′tān), *n.* any of nine isomeric hydrocarbons, C_7H_{16}, of the methane series, some of which are obtained from petroleum: used in fuels, as solvents, and as chemical intermediates.

hep·tan·gu·lar (hĕp·tăng′yə·lər), *adj.* having seven angles.

hep·tar·chy (hĕp′tär·kĭ), *n., pl.* **-chies. 1.** a government by seven persons. **2.** a group of seven states or kingdoms, each under its own ruler. **3.** (*often cap.*) the seven principal concurrent early English kingdoms. [f. HEPT- + -ARCHY] —**hep′tarch,** *n.* —**hep·tar′chic,** *adj.*

hep·ta·stich (hĕp′tə·stĭk′), *n. Pros.* a strophe, stanza, or poem consisting of seven lines or verses. [f. HEPTA- + s. Gk. *stíchos* row, line]

Hep·ta·teuch (hĕp′tə·tūk′, -tōōk′), *n.* the first seven books of the Old Testament. [t. LL: s. *Heptateuchos*, t. Gk.: seven-volume (work)]

her (hûr; *unstressed* hər), *pron.* **1.** the objective case of *she.* —*adj.* **2.** the possessive form of *she,* used before a noun (cf. **hers**). **3.** of, belonging to, or having to do with a female person or personified thing. [ME *her*(*e*), OE *hire,* gen. and dat. of *hēo* she (fem. of *hē* he)]

her., **1.** heraldic. **2.** heraldry.

He·ra (hĭr′ə), *n. Gk. Myth.* a goddess, wife and sister of Zeus and queen of heaven. Also, **Here.** [t. L, t. Gk.]

Her·a·cle·a (hĕr′ə·klē′ə), *n.* an ancient city in S Italy, near the Gulf of Taranto: Roman defeat, 280 B.C.

Her·a·cles (hĕr′ə·klēz′), *n.* Greek name of **Hercules.** Also, **Her′a·kles′.** —**Her′a·cle′an,** *adj.*

Her·a·clid (hĕr′ə·klĭd), *n., pl.* **Her·a·cli·dae** (hĕr′ə·klī′dī). a descendant of Hercules, esp. one of the Dorian aristocracy of Sparta, who claimed descent from him. Also, **Her′a·klid.** —**Her·a·cli·dan** (hĕr′ə·klī′dən), *adj.*

Her·a·cli·tus (hĕr′ə·klī′təs), *n.* (*"the Weeping Philosopher"*) c535–c475 B.C., Greek philosopher.

Her·a·cli·us (hĕr′ə·klī′əs, hĭ·răk′lĭ·əs), *n.* A.D. c575–641, Byzantine emperor, A.D. 610–641.

He·ra·klei·on (ē·rä′klē·ŏn′), *n.* Greek name of **Candia.**

her·ald (hĕr′əld), *n.* **1.** a messenger; forerunner or harbinger. **2.** one who proclaims or announces (often used as the name of a newspaper). **3.** a royal or official proclaimer or messenger. **4.** an officer who arranged tournaments and other medieval functions, announced challenges, marshaled combatants, etc., later employed also to arrange tourneys, processions, funerals, etc., and to regulate the use of armorial bearings. —*v.t.* **5.** to give tidings of; proclaim. **6.** to usher in. [t. ME: s. *heraldus* (of Gmc. orig.); r. ME *heraud,* t. OF: m. *herau*(*l*)*t*]

he·ral·dic (hē·răl′dĭk), *adj.* of or pertaining to heralds or heraldry. —**he·ral′di·cal·ly,** *adv.*

her·ald·ry (hĕr′əl·drĭ), *n., pl.* **-ries. 1.** the science of armorial bearings. **2.** the art of blazoning armorial bearings, of settling the right of persons to bear arms or to use certain bearings, of tracing and recording genealogies, of recording honors, and of deciding questions of precedence. **3.** the office or duty of a herald. **4.** a heraldic device, or a collection of such devices. **5.** a coat of arms; armorial bearings. **6.** heraldic symbolism. **7.** *Poetic.* heraldic pomp or ceremony.

Heralds' College, a royal corporation in England, instituted in 1483, occupied chiefly with armorial bearings, genealogies, honors, and precedence.

He·rat (hĕ·rät′), *n.* a city in NW Afghanistan. ab. 50,000.

herb (ûrb, hûrb), *n.* **1.** a flowering plant whose stem above ground does not become woody and persistent. **2.** such a plant when valued for its medicinal properties, flavor, scent, or the like. **3.** *Rare.* herbage. [ME (*h*)*erbe,* t. F, g. L *herba* vegetation, grass, herb] —**herb′less,** *adj.* —**herb′like′,** *adj.*

her·ba·ceous (hûr·bā′shəs), *adj.* **1.** of, pertaining to, or of the nature of a herb; herblike. **2.** (of plants or plant parts) not woody. **3.** (of flowers, sepals, etc.) having the texture, color, etc., of an ordinary foliage leaf.

herb·age (ûr′bĭj, hûr′-), *n.* **1.** nonwoody vegetation. **2.** the succulent parts (leaves and stems) of herbaceous plants. **3.** *Brit.* vegetation grazed by animals; pasturage. [ME, t. F, der. *herbe* grass. See HERB]

herb·al (hûr′bəl, ûr′-), *adj.* **1.** of, pertaining to, or consisting of herbs. —*n.* **2.** a treatise on herbs or plants. **3.** a herbarium.

herb·al·ist (hûr′bəl·ĭst, ûr′-), *n.* **1.** one who collects or deals in herbs, esp. medicinal herbs. **2.** (formerly) an expert in herbs or plants.

her·bar·i·um (hûr·bâr′ĭ·əm), *n., pl.* **-bariums, -baria** (-bâr′ĭ·ə). **1.** a collection of dried plants systematically arranged. **2.** a room or building in which an herbarium is kept. [t. LL, der. L *herba* HERB. Cf. ARBOR¹]

Her·bart (hĕr′bärt), *n.* **Johann Friedrich** (yō′hän frē′drĭкн), 1776–1841, German philosopher.

Her·bar·ti·an (hûr·bär′tĭ·ən), *adj.* **1.** of or pertaining to Herbart's system of philosophy. —*n.* **2.** one who accepts the doctrines of Herbart. —**Her·bar′ti·an·ism,** *n.*

herb bennet, a European perennial rosaceous herb, *Geum urbanum,* having yellow flowers and an aromatic, tonic, and astringent root.

Her·bert (hûr′bərt), *n.* **1. George,** 1593–1633, British poet. **2. Victor,** 1859–1924, U.S. composer and orchestra conductor, born in Ireland.

her·biv·o·rous (hûr·bĭv′ər·əs), *adj.* feeding on plants. [t. NL: m. *herbivorus* herb-eating. See HERB, -VOROUS]

herb Paris, a European liliaceous herb, *Paris quadrifolia,* formerly used in medicine.

herb Robert, a species of geranium, *Geranium Robertianum,* with reddish-purple flowers.

herb·y (ûr′bĭ, hûr′-), *adj.* **1.** abounding in herbs or grass. **2.** pertaining to or like herbs.

Her·ce·go·vi·na (hĕr′tsĕ·gô′vĭ·nä), *n.* Serbian name of Herzegovina.

Her·cu·la·ne·um (hûr′kyə·lā′nĭ·əm), *n.* a buried city at the foot of Mt. Vesuvius, in SW Italy: destroyed along with Pompeii by an eruption, A.D. 79.

her·cu·le·an (hûr·kū′lĭ·ən, hûr′kyə·lē′ən), *adj.* **1.** requiring the strength of a Hercules; very hard to perform: *a herculean task.* **2.** prodigious in strength, courage, or size: *a herculean athlete.* **3.** (*cap.*) of or relating to Hercules.

Her·cu·les (hûr′kyə·lēz′), *n.* **1.** Also, *Greek,* **Heracles, Herakles.** *Class. Myth.* a celebrated hero of great strength and courage who performed twelve extra-ordinary tasks: also known as Alcides. **2.** a northern constellation, between Lyra and Corona Borealis. [t. L, t. Gk.: m. *Hēraklēs*, lit., having the glory of Hera]

Her·cu·les'-club (hûr'kyə lēz'klŭb'), *n.* **1.** a prickly rutaceous tree, *Zanthoxylum Clava-Herculis*, with a me-dicinal bark and berries. **2.** a prickly araliaceous shrub, *Aralia spinosa*, with medicinal bark and root.

herd¹ (hûrd), *n.* **1.** a number of animals, kept, feeding, or traveling together; drove; flock. **2.** a large company of people (now in a disparaging sense). **3. the herd**, the common people; the rabble. —*v.i.* **4.** to unite or go in a herd; to assemble or associate as a herd. —*v.t.* **5.** to form into or as if into a herd. [ME; OE *heord*, c. G *herde*] —**Syn. 1.** See **flock¹**.

herd² (hûrd), *n.* **1.** a herdsman (usually in composi-tion): *cowherd*. —*v.t.* **2.** to tend, drive, or lead a herd of cattle, sheep, etc. [ME; OE *heorde*, c. G *hirte*; der. Gmc. stem represented by **HERD¹**]

herd·er (hûr'dər), *n.* **1.** a herdsman. **2.** *Chiefly U.S.* a person in charge of a herd of cattle or a flock of sheep.

Her·der (hĕr'dər), *n.* **Johann Gottfried von** (yō'hän gôt'frēt fən), 1744–1803, German philosopher and poet.

her·dic (hûr'dĭk), *n.* a low-hung carriage with two or four wheels, having the entrance at the back and the seats at the side. [named after P. *Herdic*, the inventor]

herd's-grass (hûrdz'gräs', -gräs'), *n.* any of certain grasses used for pasture or hay, as timothy or redtop.

herds·man (hûrdz'mən), *n., pl.* **-men. 1.** *Chiefly Brit.* the keeper of a herd. **2.** (*cap.*) *Astron.* the northern constellation Boötes.

here (hĭr), *adv.* **1.** in this place; in this spot or locality (opposed to *there*): *put it here.* **2.** to or toward this place; hither: *come here.* **3.** at this point; at this juncture: *here the speaker paused.* **4.** (often used in pointing out or em-phasizing some person or thing present): *my friend here knows the circumstances.* **5.** present (used in answer to roll call, etc.). **6.** in the present life or state. **7.** Some special adverb phrases are:
here and there, **1.** in this place and in that; in various places; at intervals. **2.** hither and thither; to and fro.
here goes! an exclamation to show one's resolution on the beginning of some bold or unpleasant act.
here's to, a formula in offering a toast: *here's to you!*
here we (or **you**) **are,** *Colloq.* here is what we (or you) want, or are looking for.
neither here nor there, 1. irrelevant; unimportant. **2.** neither in this place nor in that.
—*n.* **8.** this place. **9.** this world; this life.
[ME; OE *hēr*, c. D and G *hier*, Icel. and Goth. *hēr*; from the demonstrative stem represented by **HE**]

He·re (hĭr'ē), *n.* Hera.

here-, a word element meaning "this (place)," "this (time)," etc., used in combination with certain adverbs and prepositions. [special use of **HERE**]

here·a·bout (hĭr'ə bout'), *adv.* about this place; in this neighborhood. Also, **here'a·bouts'.**

here·af·ter (hĭr ăf'tər, -äf'-), *adv.* **1.** after this in time or in order; at some future time; farther along. **2.** in the world to come. —*n.* **3.** a future life; the world to come. **4.** time to come; the future. [ME *hereafter*, OE *hēræfter* f. *hēr* **HERE** + *æfter* **AFTER**]

here·at (hĭr ăt'), *adv.* **1.** at this time; when this hap-pened. **2.** by reason of this; because of this.

here·by (hĭr bī'), *adv.* **1.** by this; by means of this; as a result of this. **2.** *Archaic.* near by.

her·e·di·ta·ble (hĭ rĕd'ə tə bəl), *adj.* heritable. [t. F (obs.), der. LL *hērēditāre* inherit, der. L *hēres* heir] —**he·red'i·ta·bil'i·ty,** *n.* —**he·red'i·ta·bly,** *adv.*

her·e·dit·a·ment (hĕr'ə dĭt'ə mənt), *n.* *Law.* any inheritable estate or interest in property. [t. ML: s. *hērēditāmentum*, der. LL *hērēditāre.* See **HEREDITABLE**]

he·red·i·tar·y (hĭ rĕd'ə tĕr'ĭ), *adj.* **1.** passing, or capable of passing, naturally from parents to offspring: *hereditary traits.* **2.** pertaining to inheritance or hered-ity: *hereditary descent.* **3.** being such through feelings, etc., derived from predecessors: *a hereditary enemy.* **4.** *Law.* **a.** descending by inheritance. **b.** transmitted or transmissible in the line of descent by force of law. **c.** holding a title, etc., by inheritance: *a hereditary pro-prietor.* [t. L: m.s. *hērēditārius* of an inheritance] —**he·red'i·tar'i·ly,** *adv.* —**he·red'i·tar'i·ness,** *n.*

he·red·i·tist (hĭ rĕd'ə tĭst), *n.* one who maintains that the whole personality is determined by heredity.

he·red·i·ty (hĭ rĕd'ə tĭ), *n., pl.* **-ties. 1.** *Biol.* the transmission of genetic characters from parents to prog-eny; the protoplasmic or biochemical fixation of genetic units (genes) as the result of continuous selection in na-ture or by man. **2.** the genetic characteristics trans-mitted to an individual by its parents. [t. L: m.s. *hērēditas* heirship, inheritance]

Her·e·ford (hĕr'ə fərd, hûr'fərd), *n.* **1.** one of a breed of beef cattle originating in Herefordshire, characterized by a red body, white face, and other white markings. **2.** a city in W England: cathedral. 29,203 (1939).

Her·e·ford·shire (hĕr'ə fərd shĭr', -shər), *n.* a county in W England. 120,000 pop. (est. 1946); 842 sq. mi. *Co. seat:* Hereford. Also, **Hereford.**

here·in (hĭr ĭn'), *adv.* **1.** in or into this place. **2.** in this fact, circumstance, etc.; in view of this. [ME and OE *hērinne*, f. *hēr* **HERE** + *inne* **IN**, adv.]

here·in·af·ter (hĭr'ĭn ăf'tər, -äf'-), *adv.* afterward in this document, statement, etc.

here·in·be·fore (hĭr'ĭn bĭ fôr'), *adv.* before in this document, statement, etc.

here·in·to (hĭr ĭn'tōō), *adv.* **1.** into this place. **2.** into this matter or affair.

here·of (hĭr ŏv'), *adv.* **1.** of this: *upon the receipt hereof.* **2.** concerning this: *more hereof later.*

here·on (hĭr ŏn', -ôn'), *adv.* hereupon.

he·res (hĭr'ēz), *n., pl.* **heredes** (hĭ rē'dēz). *Civil Law.* an heir. Also, **haeres.** [L]

he·re·si·arch (hĭ rē'sĭ ärk', hĕr'ə-), *n.* a leader in heresy; the chief of a heretical sect. [t. LL: m.s. *haere-siarcha*, t. Gk.: m. *hairesiárches* leader of a school]

her·e·sy (hĕr'ə sĭ), *n., pl.* **-sies. 1.** opinion or doctrine at variance with the orthodox or accepted doctrine, esp. of a church or religious system. **2.** the maintaining of such an opinion or belief. [ME (*h*)*eresie*, t. OF, der. L *haeresis*, t. Gk.: m. *hairesis* a taking, choice]

her·e·tic (hĕr'ə tĭk), *n.* **1.** a professed believer who maintains religious opinions contrary to those accepted by his church or rejects doctrines prescribed by his church. —*adj.* **2.** heretical. [ME *heretyke*, t. F: m. *hērētique*, t. LL: m.s. *haereticus*, adj., n., t. Gk.: m. *hairetikós* heretical, able to choose]

he·ret·i·cal (hə rĕt'ə kəl), *adj.* of, pertaining to, or like heretics or heresy. —**he·ret'i·cal·ly,** *adv.*

here·to (hĭr tōō'), *adv.* to this place, thing, document, circumstance, proposition, etc.: *attached hereto.* Also, **here·un·to** (hĭr ŭn'tōō', hĭr'ŭn tōō').

here·to·fore (hĭr'tə fôr'), *adv.* before this time.

here·un·der (hĭr ŭn'dər), *adv.* **1.** under this; subse-quently set down. **2.** under authority of this.

here·up·on (hĭr'ə pŏn', -pôn'), *adv.* upon this; fol-lowing immediately upon this.

here·with (hĭr wĭth', -wĭ̄th'), *adv.* **1.** along with this. **2.** by means of this.

Her·ges·hei·mer (hûr'gəs hī'mər), *n.* **Joseph,** born 1880, U.S. novelist.

He·ring (hā'rĭng), *n.* **Ewald** (ā'vält), 1834–1918, Ger-man physiologist and psychologist.

her·i·ot (hĕr'ĭ ət), *n.* *Eng. Law.* a feudal service or tribute, orig. of military equipment, etc., due to the lord on the death of a tenant. [ME; OE *heregeatwa* war gear, f. *here* army + *geatwa*, pl., equipment]

her·it·a·ble (hĕr'ə tə bəl), *adj.* **1.** capable of being in-herited; inheritable; hereditary. **2.** capable of inherit-ing. [t. OF, der. *heriter.* See **HERITAGE**] —**her'it·a·bil'i·ty,** *n.* —**her'it·a·bly,** *adv.*

her·it·age (hĕr'ə tĭj), *n.* **1.** that which comes or be-longs to one by reason of birth; an inherited lot or por-tion. **2.** something reserved for one: *the heritage of the righteous.* **3.** *Law.* **a.** that which has been or may be inherited by legal descent or succession. **b.** any prop-erty, esp. land, that devolves by right of inheritance. **4.** *Bible.* God's chosen people; the Israelites. **5.** the Christian church. [ME (*h*)*eritage*, t. OF, der. *heriter* inherit, g. LL *hērēditāre*] —**Syn. 1.** See **inheritance.**

her·it·ance (hĕr'ə təns), *n.* *Archaic.* inheritance.

her·i·tor (hĕr'ə tər), *n.* inheritor. [ME *heriter*, t. AF, g. L *hērēditārius* **HEREDITARY**] —**her'i·tress** (hĕr'ə trĭs), *n. fem.*

Her·ki·mer (hûr'kə mər), *n.* **Nicholas,** 1715?–77, American Revolutionary general.

herl (hûrl), *n.* **1.** a barb, or the barbs, of a feather, much used in dressing anglers' flies. **2.** a fly so dressed.

her·ma (hûr'mə), *n., pl.* **-mae** (-mē), **-mai** (-mī). *Gk. Antiq.* a kind of monument or statue, common in an-cient Athens, consisting of a head, usually that of the god Hermes, sup-ported on a quadrangular pillar cor-responding roughly in mass to the absent body. Also, **herm, hermes.** [t. L, also *Hermēs*, t. Gk.]

her·maph·ro·dite (hûr măf'rə dīt'), *n.* **1.** an animal or a flower having normally both the male and the female organs of generation. **2.** a person or thing in which two oppo-site qualities are combined. —*adj.* **3.** of or like a hermaphrodite. **4.** combining two opposite qualities. **5.** *Bot.* monoclinous. [ME, t. L: m.s. *hermaphrodītus*, t. Gk.: m. *herma-phródītos.* As proper name, son of Hermes and Aphrodite, who became united in body with the nymph Salmacis while bathing in her fountain] —**her·maph·ro·dit·ic** (hûr măf'rə dĭt'ĭk), *adj.* —**her·maph'ro·dit'i·cal·ly,** *adv.*

Upper part of a double herma

hermaphrodite brig, *Naut.* a two-masted vessel square-rigged on the foremast and schooner-rigged on the mainmast.

her·maph·ro·dit·ism (hûr măf'rə dī tĭz'əm), *n.* the condition of a hermaphrodite.

her·me·neu·tic (hûr'mə nū'tĭk, -nōō'-), *adj.* inter-pretative; explanatory. [t. Gk.: m.s. *hermēneutikós* of interpreting] —**her'me·neu'ti·cal·ly,** *adv.*

her·me·neu·tics (hûr'mə nū'tĭks, -nōō'-), *n.* **1.** the science of interpretation, esp. of the Scriptures. **2.** that branch of theology which treats of the principles of Biblical exegesis.

Her·mes (hûr'mēz), *n.* **1.** *Gk. Myth.* a deity, herald and messenger of the gods, and god of roads, commerce, invention, cunning, and theft. **2.** (*l.c.*) *Gk. Antiq.* herma.

---

b., blend of, blended; c., cognate with; d., dialect, dialectal; der., derived from; f., formed from; g., going back to; m., modification of; r., replacing; s., stem of; t., taken from; ?, perhaps. See the full key on inside cover.

Hermes Tris·me·gis·tus (trĭs′mə jĭs′təs), a name given by Neoplatonists and others to the Egyptian god Thoth, who was to some extent identified with the Grecian Hermes, and to whom were attributed various works embodying mystical, theosophical, astrological, and alchemical doctrines. [t. Gk.: m. *Hermēs trismégistos* thrice greatest Hermes]

her·met·ic (hûr mĕt′ĭk), *adj.* **1.** made airtight by fusion or sealing. **2.** pertaining to occult science, esp. alchemy. **3.** (*cap.*) of or pertaining to Hermes Trismegistus or the writings, etc., ascribed to him. Also, **her·met′i·cal.** [t. ML: s. *hermēticus,* der. L *Hermēs,* t. Gk.]

her·met·i·cal·ly (hûr mĕt′ĭk lĭ), *adv.* so as to be airtight: *hermetically sealed.*

Her·mi·o·ne (hûr mī′ə nĭ), *n.* the daughter of Menelaus and Helen: wife of Orestes.

her·mit (hûr′mĭt), *n.* **1.** one who has retired to a solitary place for a life of religious seclusion. **2.** any person living in seclusion. **3.** *Zool.* an animal of solitary habits. **4.** a spiced molasses cooky, often containing raisins and sometimes nuts. **5.** *Obs.* a beadsman. [ME (*h*)*ermite,* t. OF, t. LL: m. *erēmīta,* t. Gk.: m. *erēmītēs* a hermit, prop. adj., of the desert] —**her·mit′ic, her·mit′i·cal,** *adj.* —**her·mit′i·cal·ly,** *adv.* —**her′mit·like′,** *adj.*

her·mit·age (hûr′mə tĭj), *n.* **1.** the habitation of a hermit. **2.** any secluded habitation. **3.** (*cap.*) a full-bodied wine produced in SE France.

hermit crab, any of numerous decapod crustaceans of the genera *Pagurus, Eupagurus,* etc., which protect their soft uncovered rear by occupying the castoff shell of a univalve mollusk.

hermit thrush, a North American thrush, *Turdus aonalaschkae* (or *Hylocichla guttata*).

Her·mon (hûr′mŏn), *n.* **Mount,** a mountain in SW Syria, in the Anti-Lebanon range: ab. 9200 ft.

hern (hûrn), *n. Archaic.* or *Dial.* heron.

her·ni·a (hûr′nĭ ə), *n., pl.* **-nias, -niae** (-nĭ ē′). *Pathol.* the protrusion of an organ or tissue through an opening in its surrounding walls, esp. in the abdominal region. [ME, t. L] —**her′ni·al,** *adj.*

her·ni·or·rha·phy (hûr′nĭ ôr′ə fĭ, -ŏr′-), *n., pl.* **-phies.** *Surg.* the operation for repair of a hernia.

he·ro (hĭr′ō), *n., pl.* **heroes. 1.** a man of distinguished valor or performance, admired for his noble qualities. **2.** one invested with heroic qualities in the opinion of others. **3.** the principal male character in a story, play, etc. **4.** (in early mythological antiquity) a being of godlike prowess and beneficence, often a "culture hero," who came to be honored as a divinity. **5.** (in the Homeric period) a warrior chieftain of special strength, courage, or ability. **6.** (in later periods of antiquity) an immortal being intermediate in nature between gods and men. [back formation from ME *heroes,* pl., t. L, t. Gk.]

Hero and Le·an·der (lĭ ăn′dər), *Gk. Legend.* two lovers in a late Greek poem. Leander, a youth of Abydos, swam the Hellespont nightly to visit Hero. On a stormy night the guiding lamp in her tower at Sestos was extinguished and he was drowned. Hero, finding his body, hurled herself to the rocks beside it.

Her·od (hĕr′əd), *n.* (*the Great*) died 4 B.C., king of the Jews from 37 to 4 B.C.

Herod A·grip·pa (ə grĭp′ə), 10 B.C.–A.D. 44, king of Judea, A.D. 41–44.

Herod An·ti·pas (ăn′tĭ păs′), died after A.D. 39, ruler of Galilee, A.D. 4–39; executed John the Baptist and presided at the trial of Jesus.

He·ro·di·an (hĭ rō′dĭ ən), *adj.* pertaining to Herod the Great, his family, or its partizans.

He·ro·di·as (hĭ rō′dĭ əs), *n. Bible.* the wife of Herod Antipas and mother of Salome. She was responsible for the death of John the Baptist. See **Salome.**

He·rod·o·tus (hĭ rŏd′ə təs), *n.* 484?–425? B.C., Greek historian.

he·ro·ic (hĭ rō′ĭk), *adj.* Also, **he·ro′i·cal. 1.** of or pertaining to heroes. **2.** suitable to the character of a hero; daring; noble. **3.** having or displaying the character or attributes of a hero; intrepid; determined: *a heroic explorer.* **4.** having or involving recourse to bold, daring, or extreme measures. **5.** dealing with or applicable to heroes, as in literature. **6.** of or pertaining to the heroes of antiquity: *the heroic age.* **7.** used in heroic poetry. See **heroic verse. 8.** resembling heroic poetry in language or style; magniloquent; grand. **9.** (of style or language) high-flown; extravagant; bombastic. **10.** *Arts.* of a size larger than life and (usually) less than colossal. —*n.* **11.** (*usually pl.*) heroic verse. **12.** (*pl.*) extravagant language or sentiment; bombast. —**he·ro′i·cal·ly,** *adv.* —**he·ro′i·cal·ness, he·ro′ic·ness,** *n.* —**Syn. 1.** intrepid, valiant, dauntless, gallant. —**Ant. 1.** cowardly.

heroic age, the time when the heroes of Greek antiquity are supposed to have lived.

heroic verse, a form of verse adapted to the treatment of heroic or exalted themes: in classical poetry, the hexameter; in English, German, and Italian, the iambic of ten syllables; and in French, the Alexandrine (which see). The following is an example of English heroic verse: *Achilles' wrath, to Greece the direful spring*
Of woes unnumbered, heavenly goddess, sing!

her·o·in (hĕr′ō ĭn), *n. Pharm.* **1.** a derivative of morphine, $C_{21}H_{23}NO_5$, used (usually in the form of a hydrochloride) as a sedative, etc., and constituting a dangerous habit-forming drug. **2.** (*cap.*) a trademark for this drug. [t. G, f. Gk. *hḗrō*(*s*) HERO + *-in* -IN²]

her·o·ine (hĕr′ō ĭn), *n.* **1.** a woman of heroic character; a female hero. **2.** the principal female character in a story, play, etc. [t. L, t. Gk., der. *hḗrōs* hero]

her·o·ism (hĕr′ō ĭz′əm), *n.* **1.** the qualities of a hero or heroine: *a heroic trait.* **2.** heroic conduct; valor. —**Syn. 1.** intrepidity, valor, prowess, gallantry. —**Ant. 2.** timidity.

her·on (hĕr′ən), *n.* **1.** any of numerous long-legged, long-necked, long-billed wading birds constituting the subfamily *Ardeinae* (**true herons**), as the **gray heron** (*Ardea cinerae*) of Europe or **great blue heron** (*A. herodias*) of America. **2.** any bird of the family *Ardeidae,* as the egret, bittern, or boatbill. [ME *heiroun,* t. OF: m. *hairon,* ult. t. Gmc.; cf. OHG *heiger*]

He·ron (hĭr′ŏn), *n.* fl. A.D. 1st cent. or earlier, Greek mathematician and mechanician, of Alexandria.

her·on·ry (hĕr′ən rĭ), *n., pl.* **-ries.** a place where a colony of herons breeds.

Great blue heron,
Ardea herodias
(38 in. long)

hero worship, **1.** profound reverence for great men or their memory. **2.** the worship of deified heroes, as practiced by the ancients. —**hero worshipper.**

herp., herpetology. Also, **herpet.**

her·pes (hûr′pēz), *n. Pathol.* any of certain inflammatory infections of the skin or mucous membrane, characterized by clusters of vesicles which tend to spread. [t. L, t. Gk.: lit., a creeping] —**her·pet·ic** (hər pĕt′ĭk), *adj.*

herpes fa·ci·a·lis (fā′shĭ ā′lĭs), *Pathol.* cold sore. Also, **herpes la·bi·a·lis** (lā′bĭ ā′lĭs). [L]

herpes sim·plex (sĭm′plĕks), *n. Pathol.* cold sore.

herpes zos·ter (zŏs′tər), *Pathol.* shingles.

her·pe·tol·o·gy (hûr′pə tŏl′ə jĭ), *n.* the branch of zoölogy that treats of reptiles and amphibians. [f. Gk. *herpetó*(*n*) reptile + -LOGY] —**her·pe·to·log·i·cal** (hûr′-pə tə lŏj′ə kəl), *adj.* —**her′pe·tol′o·gist,** *n.*

Herr (hĕr), *n., pl.* **Herren** (hĕr′ən). *German.* Mr.

Her·ren·volk (hĕr′ən fôlk′), *n. German.* the master race.

Her·re·ra (ĕr rĕ′rä), *n.* **Francisco de** (frän thĕs′kô dĕ), 1576–1656, Spanish painter.

Her·rick (hĕr′ĭk), *n.* **Robert,** 1591–1674, British poet.

her·ring (hĕr′ĭng), *n., pl.* **-rings,** (*esp. collectively*) **-ring. 1.** an important food fish, *Clupea harengus,* of the north Atlantic, occurring in enormous shoals in the North Sea and on the northern American coast. **2.** the north Pacific representative, *Clupea pallasii,* of the Atlantic herring, of similar appearance, size, and habits. **3.** any fish of the family *Clupeidae,* which includes the herring, shad, sardine, etc. [ME *hering,* OE *hǣring,* c. G *häring*]

her·ring·bone (hĕr′ĭng bōn′), *n.* **1.** a pattern of parallel lines, set obliquely, with each successive line slanting away from the other: used of masonry, textiles, embroidery, etc. **2.** an embroidery stitch resembling cross-stitch. —*adj.* **3.** having or resembling a herringbone pattern.

Herringbone pattern

herring gull, a common large gull, *Larus argentatus,* virtually world-wide in distribution.

Her·ri·ot (ĕryō′), *n.* **Édouard** (ĕdwår′), born 1872, French statesman, political leader, and author.

hers (hûrz), *pron.* **1.** form of the possessive *her,* used predicatively or without a noun following: *hers was the fault.* **2.** the person(s) or thing(s) belonging to her: *herself and hers, a friend of hers.*

Her·schel (hûr′shəl), *n.* **1. Sir John Frederick William,** 1792–1871, British astronomer and philosopher. **2.** his father, **Sir William** (*Friedrich Wilhelm Herschel*) 1738–1822, German-born British astronomer.

her·self (hər sĕlf′), *pron.* **1.** an emphatic form of *her* or *she.* **2.** a reflexive form of *her.*

Hert·ford·shire (här′fərd shĭr′, -shər, härt′-), *n.* a county in SE England. 559,000 pop. (est. 1946); 632 sq. mi. *Co. seat:* Hertford. Also, **Hert′ford, Herts.**

Her·to·gen·bosch (sĕr′tō кнän bôs′), *n.* **'s.** See **'s Hertogenbosch.**

Hertz (hĕrts), *n.* **Heinrich Rudolph** (hīn′rĭ нк rōō′-dôlf), 1857–94, German physicist. —**Hertz·i·an** (hĕrt′-sĭ ən), *adj.*

hertzian wave, an electromagnetic wave, artificially produced as a means of transmission in radio telegraphy: first fully investigated by Hertz.

Her·tzog (hĕr′tsôкн), *n.* **James Barry Munnik** (mœn′ək), 1866–1942, South African statesman and general: prime minister, 1924–39.

Her·ze·go·vi·na (hĕr′tsə gō vē′nə), *n.* a former Turkish province in S Europe: a part of Austria-Hungary, 1878–1914; now a part of Bosnia and Herzegovina. Serbian, **Hercegovina.** —**Her′ze·go·vi′ni·an,** *adj., n.*

he's (hēz; *unstressed* hĭz), contraction of *he is.*

Hesh·van (hĕsh′văn), *n.* (in the Jewish calendar) the second month of the year. Also, **Hesh′wan.**

He·si·od (hē′sĭ əd, hĕs′ĭ-), *n.* fl. 8th? cent. B.C., Greek poet. —**He·si·od·ic** (hē′sĭ ŏd′ĭk, hĕs′ĭ-), *adj.*

ăct, āble, dâre, ärt; ĕbb, ēqual; ĭf, īce; hŏt, ōver, ôrder, oil, bŏŏk, ōōze, out; ŭp, ūse, ûrge; ə = a in alone; ch, chief; g, give; ng, ring; sh, shoe; th, thin; ᵺ, that; zh, vision. See the full key on inside cover.

He·si·o·ne (hĭˈsīˌə nēˈ), n. Gk. Legend. daughter of Laomedon, King of Troy, rescued from a sea monster by Hercules.

hes·i·tan·cy (hĕzˈə tən sĭ), n., pl. -cies. hesitation; indecision. Also, **hes·i·tance**. [t. L: m.s. haesitantia stammering]

hes·i·tant (hĕzˈə tənt), adj. 1. hesitatingₐ; undecided. 2. lacking readiness of speech. —**hesˈi·tant·ly**, adv.

hes·i·tate (hĕzˈə tātˈ), v.i., -tated, -tating. 1. to hold back in doubt or indecision: to hesitate to believe. 2. to have scrupulous doubts; be unwilling. 3. to pause. 4. to falter in speech; stammer. [t. L: m.s. haesitātus, pp., stuck fast] —**hesˈi·tatˈer, hesˈi·taˌtor**, n. —**hesˈi·tatˈing**, adj. —**hesˈi·tatˈing·ly**, adv. —**Syn.** 1. waver, vacillate, falter. 3. demur, delay. —**Ant.** 1. decide. 3. hasten.

hes·i·ta·tion (hĕzˈə tāˈshən), n. 1. act of hesitating; a delay from uncertainty of mind: to be lost by hesitation. 2. a state of doubt. 3. a halting or faltering in speech. —**Syn.** 1. hesitancy, indecision, irresolution, vacillation.

hes·i·ta·tive (hĕzˈə tāˈtĭv), adj. characterized by hesitation; hesitating. —**hesˈi·taˌtive·ly**, adv.

Hes·pe·ri·an (hĕs pĭrˈĭ ən), adj. western. [f. s. L Hesperius (t. Gk.: m. hespérios at evening, western) + -AN]

Hes·per·i·des (hĕs pĕrˈə dēzˈ), n.pl. Gk. Myth. certain nymphs, variously given as from three to seven, fabled to guard, with the aid of a fierce serpent, a garden at the western extremity of the world in which grew golden apples, the wedding gift of Gaea to Hera. [t. L, pl., prop. pl. of hesperís western] —**Hes·per·idˈi·an** (hĕsˈpə rĭdˈĭ ən), adj.

hes·per·i·din (hĕs pĕrˈə dĭn), n. a crystallizable glycoside found in the spongy envelope of oranges and lemons. [f. s. Gk. Hesperídes, a class of plants including the orange + -IN²]

hes·per·id·i·um (hĕsˈpə rĭdˈĭ əm), n., pl. -peridia (-pə rĭdˈĭ ə). Bot. the fruit of a citrus plant, as an orange.

Hes·per·us (hĕsˈpər əs), n. the evening star, esp. Venus. [t. L, t. Gk.: m. Hésperos the evening star, orig. adj., of or at evening, western]

Hesse (hĕs), n. a state in W Germany. 1,469,215 (1939); 2970 sq. mi. Cap.: Darmstadt. German, **Hes·sen** (hĕsˈən).

Hesse-Nas·sau (hĕsˈnäsˈô), n. a province in W Germany. 2,675,111 pop. (1939); ab. 6504 sq. mi. Cap.: Kassel. German, **Hes·sen-Nas·sau** (hĕsˈən näsˈou).

Hes·sian (hĕshˈən), adj. 1. of or pertaining to Hesse or its inhabitants. —n. 2. a native or inhabitant of Hesse. 3. U.S. a Hessian mercenary used by England during the American Revolution. 4. a hireling or ruffian.

Hessian boots, high tasseled boots fashionable in England during the early 19th century.

Hessian fly, a small dipterous insect, Phytophaga destructor, whose larva is one of the most destructive pests of wheat.

hes·so·nite (hĕsˈə nītˈ), n. a yellowish or brownish variety of garnet, sometimes used in jewelry. [f. Gk. hḗsson less, inferior + -ITE¹]

hest (hĕst), n. Archaic. behest. [ME hest(e), OE hǣs, akin to hātan bid]

Hessian fly, Phytophaga destructor A, Larva; B, Pupa; C, Adult

Hes·ti·a (hĕsˈtĭ ə), n. Gk. Myth. goddess of the hearth and hearth fire.

Hes·ton and I·sle·worth (hĕsˈtən, īˈzəl wûrthˈ), a municipal borough in SE England, in Middlesex, near London. 104,490 (est. 1946).

Hes·y·chast (hĕsˈə kăstˈ), n. one of a sect of mystics which originated in the 14th century among the monks on Mt. Athos, Greece. [t. Gk.: s. hēsychastḗs a recluse] —**Hesˈy·chastˈic**, adj.

he·tae·ra (hĭ tĭrˈə), n., pl. -taerae (-tĭrˈē). a female paramour, or concubine, esp. in ancient Greece. [t. Gk.: m. hetaíra, fem. of hetaíros companion]

he·tai·ra (hĭ tīˈrə), n., pl. -tairai (-tīˈrī). hetaera.

hetero-, a word element meaning "other" or "different," as in heterocercal. Also, before vowels, **heter-**. [t. Gk., comb. form of héteros]

het·er·o·cer·cal (hĕtˈər ə sûrˈkəl), adj. Ichthyol. 1. having an unequally divided tail or caudal fin, the backbone usually running into a much larger upper lobe. 2. denoting such a tail or caudal fin (contrasted with homocercal). [f. HETERO- + m.s. Gk. kérkos tail + -AL¹]

Heterocercal tail

het·er·o·chro·mat·ic (hĕtˈər ə krōˈmătˈĭk), adj. 1. of, having, or pertaining to more than one color. 2. having a pattern of mixed colors.

het·er·o·chro·ma·tin (hĕtˈər ə krōˈmə tĭn), n. Biol. chromatin which remains compact during mitosis. Sex chromosomes may consist entirely of heterochromatin.

het·er·o·chro·mo·some (hĕtˈər ə krōˈmə sōmˈ), n. Biol. a sex chromosome.

het·er·o·chro·mous (hĕtˈər ə krōˈməs), adj. of different colors. [t. Gk.: m. heteróchrōmos]

het·er·o·clite (hĕtˈər ə klītˈ), adj. 1. exceptional or anomalous. 2. Gram. irregular in inflection. —n. 3. a person or thing that deviates from the ordinary rule or form. 4. Gram. a heteroclite word. [t. F, t. LL: m.s. heteroclitus, t. Gk.: m. heteróklitos irregularly inflected]

het·er·o·cy·clic (hĕtˈər ə sīˈklĭk, -sĭkˈlĭk), adj. Chem. 1. referring to organic chemistry as dealing with ring compounds with both carbon atoms and atoms of other elements in the ring. 2. denoting such compounds.

het·er·o·dox (hĕtˈər ə dŏksˈ), adj. 1. not in accordance with established or accepted doctrines or opinions, esp. in theology. 2. holding unorthodox doctrines or opinions. [t. Gk.: s. heteródoxos of another opinion]

het·er·o·dox·y (hĕtˈər ə dŏkˈsĭ), n., pl. -doxies. 1. heterodox state or quality. 2. a heterodox opinion, etc.

het·er·o·dyne (hĕtˈər ə dīnˈ), adj., v., -dyned, -dyning. Radio. —adj. 1. denoting or pertaining to a method of receiving continuous-wave radiotelegraph signals by impressing upon the continuous radio-frequency oscillations another set of radio-frequency oscillations of a slightly different frequency, the interference resulting in fluctuations or beats of audio frequency. —v.i. 2. to produce a heterodyne effect.

het·er·oe·cious (hĕtˈə rēˈshəs), adj. Biol. pertaining to or characterized by heteroecism. [f. HETER- + m.s. Gk. oikía house + -OUS]

het·er·oe·cism (hĕtˈə rēˈsĭzəm), n. Biol. the development of different stages of a parasitic species on different host plants, as in fungi.

het·er·o·ga·mete (hĕtˈər ə gə mētˈ), n. Biol. a gamete of different character from one of the opposite sex (opposed to isogamete).

het·er·og·a·mous (hĕtˈə rŏgˈə məs), adj. 1. Biol. having unlike gametes, or reproducing by the union of such gametes (opposed to isogamous). 2. Bot. having flowers or florets of two sexually different kinds (opposed to homogamous).

het·er·og·a·my (hĕtˈə rŏgˈə mĭ), n. heterogamous state.

het·er·o·ge·ne·i·ty (hĕtˈər ə jə nēˈə tĭ), n., pl. -ties. the character or state of being heterogeneous; composition from dissimilar parts; disparateness.

het·er·o·ge·ne·ous (hĕtˈər ə jēˈnĭ əs), adj. 1. different in kind; unlike; incongruous. 2. composed of parts of different kinds; having widely unlike elements or constituents; not homogeneous. [t. ML: m. heterogeneus, t. Gk.: m. heterogenḗs of different kinds] —**het·er·o·geˈne·ous·ly**, adv. —**het·er·o·geˈne·ous·ness**, n.

het·er·og·e·nous (hĕtˈə rŏjˈə nəs), adj. Biol., Pathol. having its source or origin outside the organism; having a foreign origin.

het·er·og·o·nous (hĕtˈə rŏgˈə nəs), adj. 1. Bot. noting or pertaining to monoclinous flowers of two or more kinds occurring on different individuals of the same species, the kinds differing in the relative length of stamens and pistils (opposed to homogonous). 2. Zool. heterogynous.

het·er·og·o·ny (hĕtˈə rŏgˈə nĭ), n. Biol. a. the alteration of dioecious and hermaphrodite individuals in successive generations, as in certain nematodes. b. (in more recent usage) the alternation of parthenogenetic and sexual generations.

het·er·og·ra·phy (hĕtˈə rŏgˈrə fĭ), n. spelling different from that in current use. —**het·er·o·graph·ic** (hĕtˈər ə grăfˈĭk), adj.

het·er·og·y·nous (hĕtˈə rŏjˈə nəs), adj. Zool. having females of two different kinds, one sexual and the other abortive or neuter, as ants.

het·er·ol·o·gous (hĕtˈə rŏlˈə gəs), adj. 1. having a different relation; not corresponding. 2. Pathol. consisting of tissue unlike the normal tissue, as a tumor.

het·er·ol·o·gy (hĕtˈə rŏlˈə jĭ), n. 1. Biol. the lack of correspondence of organic structures as the result of unlike origins of constituent parts. 2. Pathol. abnormality; structural difference from a type or normal standard.

het·er·ol·y·sis (hĕtˈə rŏlˈə sĭs), n. Biochem. dissolution of the cells of one organism by the lysins of another.

het·er·om·er·ous (hĕtˈə rŏmˈər əs), adj. having or consisting of parts which differ in quality, number of elements, or the like: a heteromerous flower.

het·er·o·mor·phic (hĕtˈər ə môrˈfĭk), adj. 1. Biol. dissimilar in shape, structure, or magnitude. 2. Entomol. undergoing complete metamorphosis; possessing varying forms. —**het·er·o·morˈphism**, n.

het·er·on·o·mous (hĕtˈə rŏnˈə məs), adj. 1. subject to or involving different laws. 2. pertaining to, or characterized by, heteronomy. 3. Biol. characterizing an organism which is metameric, or segmented, most or all of whose segments are specialized in different ways. [f. HETERO- + s. Gk. nómos law + -OUS]

het·er·on·o·my (hĕtˈə rŏnˈə mĭ), n. condition of being under the rule of another (opposed to autonomy).

het·er·o·nym (hĕtˈər ə nĭmˈ), n. a word having a different sound and meaning from another, but the same spelling, as lead (to conduct) and lead (a metal).

het·er·on·y·mous (hĕtˈə rŏnˈə məs), adj. 1. pertaining to or of the nature of a heteronym. 2. having different names, as a pair of correlatives. 3. Optics. denoting or pertaining to the images formed in a kind of double vision in which the image seen by the right eye is on the left side and vice versa. [t. Gk.: m. heterónymos having a different name]

b., blend of, blended; c., cognate with; d., dialect, dialectal; der., derived from; f., formed from; g., going back to; m., modification of; r., replacing; s., stem of; t., taken from; ?, perhaps. See the full key on inside cover.

Het·er·o·öu·si·an (hĕt/ər ō ōō/sĭ ən, -ou/sĭ ən), *n.* **1.** *Eccles.* one who believes the Father and Son to be unlike in substance or essence; an Arian (opposed to *Homoöusian*). —*adj.* **2.** of or pertaining to the Heteroöusians or their doctrine. [f. s. LGk. *heteroöusios* of different nature + -AN]

het·er·o·phyl·lous (hĕt/ər ə fĭl/əs), *adj. Bot.* having different kinds of leaves on the same plant. [f. HETERO- + s. Gk. *phýllon* leaf + -OUS] —**het/er·o·phyl/ly,** *n.*

het·er·o·plas·ty (hĕt/ər ə plăs/tĭ), *n. Surg.* the repair of lesions with tissue from another individual.

het·er·op·ter·ous (hĕt/ə rŏp/tər əs), *adj.* pertaining to the true bugs, *Heteroptera*, which constitute a suborder of the order *Hemiptera*. [f. s. NL *Heteroptera*, class name (f. *hetero-* HETERO- + Gk. *pterá* wings) + -OUS]

het·er·o·sex·u·al (hĕt/ər ə sĕk/shŏŏ əl), *adj.* **1.** *Biol.* pertaining to the other sex or to both sexes. **2.** pertaining to or exhibiting heterosexuality.

het·er·o·sex·u·al·i·ty (hĕt/ər ə sĕk/shŏŏ ăl/ə tĭ), *n.* sexual feeling for a person (or persons) of opposite sex.

het·er·o·sis (hĕt/ə rō/sĭs), *n. Genetics.* the increase in growth, size, fecundity, function, yield, or other characters in hybrids over those of the parents. [t. LGk.: alteration]

het·er·os·po·rous (hĕt/ə rŏs/pər əs, hĕt/ə rə spôr/əs), *adj. Bot.* having more than one kind of spores.

het·er·os·po·ry (hĕt/ə rŏs/pər ĭ), *n. Bot.* the production of both male spores and female spores.

het·er·o·tax·is (hĕt/ə rə tăk/sĭs), *n.* abnormal or irregular arrangement, as of parts of the body, geological strata, etc. (opposite of *homotaxis*). Also, **het/er·o·tax/y.** —**het/er·o·tax/ic,** *adj.*

het·er·o·thal·lic (hĕt/ə rə thăl/ĭk), *adj. Bot.* having mycelia of two unlike types both of which must participate in the sexual process (opposite of *homothallic*). [f. HETERO- + s. Gk. *thallós* shoot, sprout + -IC]

het·er·o·to·pi·a (hĕt/ər ō tō/pĭ ə), *n. Pathol.* **1.** misplacement or displacement, as of an organ. **2.** the formation of tissue in a part where it is abnormal. Also, **het·er·ot·o·py** (hĕt/ə rŏt/ə pĭ). [NL, f. Gk.: *hetero-* HETERO- + *-topia* (der. *tópos* place)] —**het·er·o·top·ic** (hĕt/ər ə tŏp/ĭk), **het·er·o·t·o·pous** (hĕt/ə rŏt/ə pəs), *adj.*

het·er·o·troph·ic (hĕt/ər ə trŏf/ĭk), *adj. Biol.* incapable of synthesizing proteins and carbohydrates, as animals and dependent plants (opposite of *autotrophic*).

het·er·o·typ·ic (hĕt/ər ə tĭp/ĭk), *adj. Biol.* applying meiotic division which reduces the chromosome number during the development of the reproductive cells. Also, **het/er·o·typ/i·cal.**

het·er·o·zy·gote (hĕt/ər ə zī/gōt, -zĭg/ōt), *n. Genetics.* a hybrid containing genes for two unlike characteristics; an organism which will not breed true to type. —**het·er·o·zy·gous** (hĕt/ər ə zī/gəs), *adj.*

het·man (hĕt/mən), *n., pl.* **-mans.** a Cossack chief. [t. Pol., said to be t. G: m. *hauptmann* captain]

heu·ris·tic (hyōō rĭs/tĭk), *adj.* **1.** serving to find out; furthering investigation. **2.** (of a teaching method) encouraging the student to discover for himself. [appar. f. Gk. *hourís(kein)* find and obs. *(heure)tic* inventive (t. Gk.: m.s. *heuretikós*)] —**heu·ris/ti·cal·ly,** *adv.*

Heus·sler alloys (hūs/lər; *Ger.* hois/-), alloys of manganese and other nonferromagnetic metals which exhibit ferromagnetism.

he·ve·a (hē/vĭ ə), *n.* Pará rubber.

hew (hū), *v.,* **hewed, hewed** or **hewn, hewing.** —*v.t.* **1.** to strike forcibly with an ax, sword, or the like; chop; hack. **2.** to make or shape with cutting blows: *to hew a passage.* **3.** to sever (a part from a whole) by means of cutting leaves (fol. by *away, off, out, from,* etc.) **4.** to cut down; fell: *to hew down trees.* —*v.i.* **5.** to deal cutting blows; to cut: *hew to the line, let the chips fall where they may.* [ME *hewe(n),* OE *hēawan,* c. G *hauen*] —**hew/er,** *n.* —**Syn. 1.** See cut.

hewers of wood and drawers of water, menial workers. Joshua 9:21.

Hew·lett (hū/lĭt), *n.* **Maurice,** 1861–1923, British author.

hex (hĕks), *v.t. U.S. Colloq.* or *Dial.* **1.** to bewitch; practice witchcraft on. [v. use of n.] —*n.* **2.** a witch. **3.** a spell. [t. G: m. *hexe* witch. See HAG[1]]

hexa-, a prefix meaning "six," as in *hexagon.* Also, before vowels, **hex-.** [t. Gk., comb. form of *héx*]

hex·a·chord (hĕk/sə kôrd/), *n. Music.* a diatonic series of six tones, having (in medieval music) a half step between the third and fourth tones and whole steps between the others. [t. LGk.: s. *hexáchordos*]

hex·ad (hĕk/săd), *n.* **1.** the number six. **2.** a group or series of six. [t. LL: s. *hexas,* t. Gk.: six] —**hex·ad/ic,** *adj.*

hex·a·gon (hĕk/sə gŏn/, -gən), *n.* a polygon having six angles and six sides.

hex·ag·o·nal (hĕk săg/ə nəl), *adj.* **1.** of, pertaining to, or having the form of a hexagon. **2.** having a hexagon as a base or cross section. **3.** divided into hexagons, as a surface. **4.** *Crystall.* noting or pertaining to the hexagonal system. —**hex·ag/o·nal·ly,** *adv.*

Regular hexagon

hexagonal system, *Crystall.* a system of crystallization characterized by three equal lateral axes intersecting at angles of 60° and a vertical axis of hexagonal symmetry and of different length at right angles to them.

hex·a·gram (hĕk/sə grăm/), *n.* **1.** a six-pointed star-like figure formed of two equilateral triangles placed concentrically with their sides parallel, and on opposite sides of the center. **2.** *Geom.* a figure of six lines.

Hexagram (def. 1)

hex·a·he·dron (hĕk/sə hē/drən), *n., pl.* **-drons, -dra** (-drə). a solid figure having six faces. —**hex/a·he/dral,** *adj.*

hex·am·er·ous (hĕks ăm/ər əs), *adj.* **1.** consisting of or divided into six parts. **2.** *Zool.* having a radially symmetrical arrangement of organs in six groups. **3.** *Bot.* having six members in each whorl.

hex·am·e·ter (hĕks ăm/ə tər), *n.* **1.** *Pros.* the dactylic verse of six feet, of Greek and Latin epic and other poetry (**dactylic hexameter**), in which the first four feet are dactyls or spondees, the fifth is ordinarily a dactyl, and the last is a trochee or spondee with a caesura usually following the long syllable in the third foot. It is imitated in the line "Strongly it bears us along in swelling and limitless billows." **2.** any hexameter verse. —*adj.* **3.** consisting of six metrical feet. [t. L, t. Gk.: m. *hexámetros* of six measures] —**hex·a·met·ric** (hĕk/sə mĕt/rĭk), **hex/a·met/ri·cal,** *adj.*

hex·a·meth·yl·ene·tet·ra·mine (hĕk/sə mĕth/ə lēn tĕt/rə mēn/), *n. Chem.* a colorless crystalline compound, $C_6H_{12}N_4$, used as a urinary antiseptic, an accelerator, an absorbent in gas masks, and in the manufacture of synthetic resins and of RDX. Also, **hex/a·meth/yl·ene·tet/ra·min** (-tĕt/rə mĭn).

hex·ane (hĕk/sān), *n. Chem.* any of the five isomeric saturated hydrocarbons, C_6H_{14}, derived from the fractional distillation of petroleum. [f. Gk. *héx* six (with reference to the atoms of carbon) + -ANE]

hex·an·gu·lar (hĕks ăng/gyə lər), *adj.* having six angles.

hex·a·pla (hĕk/sə plə), *n.* an edition of the Old Testament containing six versions in parallel columns, as one compiled by Origen. [t. Gk., prop. neut. pl. of *hexaplóos* sixfold] —**hex/a·plar,** *adj.*

hex·a·pod (hĕk/sə pŏd/), *n.* **1.** one of the *Hexapoda* (or *Insecta*); an insect. —*adj.* **2.** having six feet. [t. Gk.: s. *hexápous* six-footed] —**hex·ap·o·dous** (hĕks-ăp/ə dəs), *adj.*

hex·ap·o·dy (hĕks ăp/ə dĭ), *n., pl.* **-dies.** *Pros.* a line or verse consisting of six metrical feet.

hex·ar·chy (hĕk/sär kĭ), *n., pl.* **-chies.** a group of six states or kingdoms, each under its own ruler.

hex·a·stich (hĕk/sə stĭk), *n. Pros.* a strophe, stanza, or poem consisting of six lines or verses. Also, **hex·as·ti·chon** (hĕks ăs/tə kŏn/). [t. Gk.: s. *hexástichos* of six rows or lines]

Hex·a·teuch (hĕk/sə tūk/, -tōōk/), *n.* the first six books of the Old Testament. [f. HEXA- + s. Gk. *teûchos* book] —**Hex/a·teuch/al,** *adj.*

hex·one (hĕk/sōn), *n. Chem.* any of various organic ketones which contain six atoms of carbon in the molecule. [f. Gk. *héx* six + -ONE, after G *hexon*]

hex·o·san (hĕk/ōō săn/), *n.* any of a group of hemicelluloses which hydrolyse to hexoses. [f. HEXOS(E) + -AN]

hex·ose (hĕk/sōs), *n. Chem.* any of a class of sugars containing six atoms of carbon, including glucose and fructose.

hex·yl (hĕk/sĭl), *n. Chem.* the univalent radical, C_6H_{13}, derived from hexane.

hex·yl·res·or·cin·ol (hĕk/sĭl rə zôr/sə nôl/, -nŏl/), *n.* a colorless, crystalline antiseptic, $C_{12}H_{18}O_2$, which is less toxic and more powerful than phenol.

hey (hā), *interj.* an exclamation to express pleasure, surprise, bewilderment, etc., or to call attention.

hey·day (hā/dā/), *n.* **1.** the stage or period of highest vigor or fullest strength. **2.** high spirits. —*interj.* **3.** an exclamation of cheerfulness, surprise, wonder, etc.

Hey·duck (hī/dŏŏk), *n.* Haiduk. Also, **Hey/duke, Hey/duc.**

Hey·se (hī/zə), *n.* **Paul Johann Ludwig von** (poul yō/hän lōōt/vĭкн fən), 1830–1914, German writer.

Hey·ward (hā/wərd), *n.* **DuBose** (də bōz/), 1885–1940, U.S. author and dramatist.

Hey·wood (hā/wŏŏd), *n.* **1. John,** 1497?–1580?, British dramatist and epigrammatist. **2. Thomas,** died c1650, British dramatist, actor, and poet.

Hez·e·ki·ah (hĕz/ə kī/ə), *n.* a king of Judah of the 8th–7th centuries B.C. II Kings 18, etc.

Hf, *Chem.* hafnium.

HG, 1. High German. **2.** *Brit.* Home Guard.

Hg, (L *hydrargyrum*) *Chem.* mercury.

hg., hectogram.

H.G., 1. His, or Her, Grace. **2.** High German.

H.H., 1. His, or Her, Highness. **2.** His Holiness.

hhd., hogshead.

H-hour (āch/our/), *n. Mil.* the time set for an attack.

hi (hī), *interj.* an exclamation, esp. of greeting.

H.I., Hawaiian Islands.

hi·a·tus (hī ā/təs), *n., pl.* **-tuses, -tus. 1.** a break, with a part missing; an interruption; lacuna: *a hiatus in a manuscript.* **2.** a gap or opening. **3.** *Gram. and Pros.* a break or slight pause due to the coming together without contraction of two vowels in successive words or syllables. **4.** *Anat.* a natural fissure, cleft, or foramen in a bone or other structure. [t. L: gap]

Hi·a·wath·a (hī′ə wŏth′ə, -wô′thə, hē′ə-), *n.* the central figure of *The Song of Hiawatha* (1855), a poem by Longfellow.

hi·ber·nac·u·lum (hī′bər năk′yə ləm), *n.*, *pl.* **-la** (-lə). **1.** a protective case or covering for winter, as of an animal or a plant bud. **2.** Also, **hi·ber·nac·le** (hī′bər-năk/əl). winter quarters, as of a hibernating animal. [t. L: winter residence]

hi·ber·nal (hī bûr′nəl), *adj.* of or pertaining to winter; wintry. [t. LL: s. *hībernālis* wintry]

hi·ber·nate (hī′bər nāt′), *v.i.*, **-nated, -nating. 1.** to spend the winter in close quarters in a dormant condition, as certain animals. **2.** to remain in seclusion. [t. L: m.s. *hībernātus*, pp., wintered] **—hi·ber·na′tion,** *n.*

Hi·ber·ni·a (hī bûr′nī ə), *n.* Latin or literary name of Ireland. [t. L]

Hi·ber·ni·an (hī bûr′nī ən), *adj.* **1.** Irish. **—***n.* **2.** a native of Ireland. [s. L *Hibernia* Ireland + -AN]

Hi·ber·ni·cism (hī bûr′nə sĭz′əm), *n.* **1.** an idiom peculiar to Irish English. **2.** an Irish characteristic. Also, **Hi·ber·ni·an·ism** (hī bûr′nī ə nĭz′əm).

hi·bis·cus (hī bĭs′kəs, hī-), *n.* any of the herbs, shrubs, or trees of the malvaceous genus *Hibiscus,* many of which, as the shrub althea, *H. syriacus,* have large showy flowers. [t. L, t. Gk.: m. *ibískos* mallow]

hic·cup (hĭk′ŭp, -əp), *n.* **1.** a quick, involuntary inspiration suddenly checked by closure of the glottis, producing a characteristic sound. **2.** (*usually pl.*) the condition of having such spasms: *to have the hiccups.* **—***v.i.* **3.** to make the sound of a hiccup. **4.** to have the hiccups. Also, **hic·cough** (hĭk′ŭp, -əp). [earlier *hickock,* f. *hick* (imit.) + -OCK. Cf. LG *hick* hiccup]

hic ja·cet (hĭk jā′sĕt), *Latin.* here lies (often used to begin epitaphs on tombstones).

hick (hĭk), *Slang.* **—***n.* **1.** an unsophisticated person. **2.** a farmer. **—***adj.* **3.** pertaining to or characteristic of hicks. [familiar form of *Richard,* man's name]

hick·ey (hĭk′ī), *n.*, *pl.* **-eys. 1.** any device. **2.** *Elect.* a fitting used to mount a lighting fixture in an outlet box or on a pipe or stud.

Hick·ok (hĭk′ŏk), *n.* **James Butler,** ("*Wild Bill*") 1837–76, U.S. frontiersman.

hick·o·ry (hĭk′ə rĭ), *n.*, *pl.* **-ries. 1.** any of the North American trees constituting the juglandaceous genus *Carya,* certain of which, as the pecan, *C. illinoensis* (*C. Pecan*), bear sweet, edible nuts (**hickory nuts**), and others, as the shagbark, *C. ovata,* yield valuable hard wood and edible nuts. **2.** the wood of such a tree. **3.** a switch, stick, etc., of this wood. [t. Amer. Ind. (Va.). Cf. Algonquian *pawcohiccoro* walnut kernel mush]

hick·wall (hĭk′wôl′), *n.* any of certain European woodpeckers, esp. the green woodpecker, *Gecinus viridis.*

hid (hĭd), *v.* pt. and pp. of **hide.**

hi·dal·go (hĭ dăl′gō; *Sp.* ē däl′gō), *n.*, *pl.* **-gos** (-gōz; *Sp.* -gôs). (in Spain) a man of the lower nobility. [t. Sp., contr. of *hijo de algo* son of somebody (important)]

Hi·dal·go (hĭ dăl′gō; *Sp.* ē däl′gō), *n.* state in central Mexico. 771,818 pop. (1940); 8057 sq. mi. *Cap.*: Pachuca.

Hi·dat·sa (hē dät′sä), *n.* a Siouan language, and tribe dwelling on the Missouri river.

hid·den (hĭd′ən), *adj.* **1.** concealed; obscure; latent. **—***v.* **2.** pp. of **hide. —Syn.** secret, covert; occult.

hid·den·ite (hĭd′ə nīt′), *n.* a rare, transparent emerald-green or yellowish-green variety of spodumene, a valuable gemstone. [named after W. E. *Hidden,* who discovered it (1879). See -ITE[1]]

hide[1] (hīd), *v.*, **hid, hidden** or **hid, hiding. —***v.t.* **1.** to conceal from sight; prevent from being seen or discovered. **2.** to obstruct the view of; cover up: *the sun was hidden by clouds.* **3.** to conceal from knowledge; keep secret: *to hide one's feelings.* **—***v.i.* **4.** to conceal oneself; lie concealed. **—***n.* **5.** *Brit.* a covered place to hide in while shooting. Cf. *U.S.* **blind** (def. 19). [ME *hide*(n), OE *hȳdan,* c. MLG *hüden*] **—hid′er,** *n.* **—Syn. 1.** screen, mask, cloak, veil, shroud, disguise. HIDE, CONCEAL, SECRETE mean to put out of sight or in a secret place. HIDE is the general word: *to hide or conceal one's money or purpose, a dog hides a bone.* CONCEAL, somewhat more formal, is to cover from sight: *a rock hid or concealed them from view.* SECRETE means to hide carefully, in order to keep secret: *the banker secretes important papers* **3.** dissemble, suppress. **—Ant. 1.** reveal, display.

hide[2] (hīd), *n.*, *v.*, **hided, hiding. —***n.* **1.** the skin of an animal, raw or dressed: *the hide of a calf.* **2.** *Slang.* the human skin. **—***v.t.* **3.** *Colloq.* to flog or thrash. [ME; OE *hȳd,* c. G *haut*] **—Syn. 1.** See **skin.**

hide[3] (hīd), *n.* an old English measure of land, usually 120 acres, considered adequate for one free family and its dependents. [ME; OE *hīd*(*e*), *hīg*(*i*)*d,* f. *hīg*(*an*) family, household + -*id,* suffix of appurtenance]

hide-and-seek (hīd′-ən sēk′), *n.* a children's game in which some hide and others seek them.

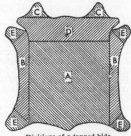

Divisions of a tanned hide
A, Butt; B, Belly; C, Cheek;
D, Shoulder; E, Shank

hide·bound (hīd′bound′), *adj.* **1.** narrow and rigid in opinion: *a hidebound pedant.* **2.** (of a horse, etc.) having the back and ribs bound tightly by the hide. [f. HIDE[2] + BOUND]

hid·e·ous (hĭd′ĭ əs), *adj.* **1.** horrible or frightful to the senses; very ugly: *a hideous monster.* **2.** shocking or revolting to the moral sense: *a hideous crime.* [ME *hidous,* t. AF, der. *hi*(*s*)*de* horror, fear; orig. uncert.] **—hid′e·ous·ly,** *adv.* **—hid′e·ous·ness,** *n.* **—Syn. 1, 2.** grisly, grim; repulsive, detestable, odious. **—Ant. 1.** attractive, pleasing.

hide-out (hīd′out′), *n.* a safe place for hiding (usually from the law).

hid·ing[1] (hī′dĭng), *n.* **1.** act of concealing; concealment: *to remain in hiding.* **2.** a place or means of concealment. [f. HIDE[1] + -ING[1]]

hid·ing[2] (hī′dĭng), *n.* *Colloq.* a flogging or thrashing. [f. HIDE[2] + -ING[1]]

bi·dro·sis (hĭ drō′sĭs), *n.* *Pathol.* **1.** excessive perspiration due to drugs, disease, or the like. **2.** any of certain diseases characterized by sweating. [NL, special use of Gk. *hídrosis* perspiration] **—hi·drot·ic** (hĭ drŏt′-ĭk), *adj.*

hie (hī), *v.i.*, **hied, hieing** or **hying.** to hasten; speed; go in haste. [ME; OE *hīgian* strive. Cf. D *hijgen* pant]

hi·er·arch (hī′ə rärk′), *n.* **1.** one who rules or has authority in sacred things. **2.** a chief priest. **3.** one of a body of officials or minor priests in some ancient Greek temples. [t. ML: s. *hierarcha,* t. Gk.: m. *hierárchēs* steward of sacred rites] **—hi·er·ar′chal,** *adj.*

hi·er·ar·chi·cal (hī′ə rär′kə kəl), *adj.* of or belonging to a hierarchy. Also, **hi′er·ar′chic. —hi·er·ar′chi·cal·ly,** *adv.*

hi·er·ar·chism (hī′ə rär′kĭz əm), *n.* hierarchical principles, rule, or influence.

hi·er·ar·chy (hī′ə rär′kĭ), *n.*, *pl.* **-chies. 1.** any system of persons or things in a graded order, etc. **2.** *Science.* a series of successive terms of different rank. The terms *phylum, class, order, family, genus,* and *species* constitute a hierarchy in zoölogy. **3.** government by ecclesiastical rulers. **4.** the power or dominion of a hierarch. **5.** an organized body of ecclesiastical officials in successive ranks or orders: *the Roman Catholic hierarchy.* **6.** one of the three divisions of the angels, each made up of three orders, conceived as constituting a graded body. **7.** the collective body of angels (**celestial hierarchy**).

hi·er·at·ic (hī′ə răt′ĭk), *adj.* **1.** pertaining to priests or to the priesthood; priestly. **2.** noting or pertaining to a form of ancient Egyptian writing consisting of abridged forms of hieroglyphics, used by the priests in their records. **3.** noting or pertaining to certain styles in art whose types or methods are fixed by or as by religious tradition. Also, **hi·er·at′i·cal.** [t. L: s. *hierāticus,* t. Gk.: m. *hierātikós* priestly, sacerdotal] **—hi·er·at′i·cal·ly,** *adv.*

hiero-, a word element meaning "sacred," as in *hierocracy.* [t. Gk., comb. form of *hierós* holy]

hi·er·oc·ra·cy (hī′ə rŏk′rə sĭ), *n.*, *pl.* **-cies.** rule or government by priests or ecclesiastics. **—hi·er·o·crat·ic** (hī′ər ə krăt′ĭk), *adj.*

hi·er·o·dule (hī′ər ə dūl′, -dool′), *n.* a slave in an ancient Greek temple, dedicated to the service of a deity. [t. Gk.: m.s. *hieródoulos* temple slave]

hi·er·o·glyph·ic (hī′ər ə glĭf′ĭk, hī′rə-), *adj.* Also, **hi·er·o·glyph′i·cal. 1.** designating or pertaining to a writing system, particularly that of the ancient Egyptians, in which many of the symbols are conventionalized pictures of the thing named by the words for which the symbols stand. **2.** inscribed with hieroglyphic symbols. **3.** hard to decipher; hard to read. **—***n.* **4.** Also, **hi·er·o·glyph′.** a hieroglyphic symbol. **5.** (*usually pl.*) hieroglyphic writing. **6.** a figure or symbol with a hidden meaning. **7.** (*pl.*) writing difficult to decipher. [t. LL: s. *hieroglyphicus,* t. Gk: m. *hieroglyphikós*] **—hi·er·o·glyph′i·cal·ly,** *adv.*

hi·er·ol·o·gy (hī′ə rŏl′ə jĭ), *n.* literature or learning regarding sacred things.

Hi·er·on·y·mite (hī′ə rŏn′ə mīt′), *n.* a member of the "Congregation of Hermits of St. Jerome."

Hi·er·on·y·mus (hī′ə rŏn′ə məs), *n.* Jerome (Saint). **—Hi·er·o·nym·i·an** (hī′ər ə nĭm′ĭ ən), **Hi′er·o·nym′ic,** *adj.*

hi·er·o·phant (hī′ər ə fănt′, hī′ĕr ə-), *n.* **1.** (in ancient Greece, etc.) an official expounder of rites of worship and sacrifice. **2.** any interpreter of sacred mysteries or esoteric principles. [t. LL: s. *hierophantēs,* t. Gk.] **—hi·er·o·phan·tic** (hī′ər ə făn′tĭk, hī′ĕr′ə-), *adj.*

hi·fa·lu·tin (hī′fə loo′tən), *adj.* *Colloq.* highfalutin.

Hig·gin·son (hĭg′ĭn sən), *n.* **Thomas Wentworth,** 1823–1911, U.S. author, soldier, and social reformer.

hig·gle (hĭg′əl), *v.i.*, **-gled, -gling.** to bargain, esp. in a petty way; haggle. [appar. var. of HAGGLE]

hig·gle·dy-pig·gle·dy (hĭg′əl dĭ pĭg′əl dĭ), *Colloq. adv.* **1.** in a jumbled confusion. **—***adj.* **2.** confused; jumbled. **—***n.* **3.** confusion; a disorderly jumble.

hig·gler (hĭg′lər), *n.* a huckster or peddler.

high (hī), *adj.* **1.** having a great or considerable reach or extent upward; lofty; tall. **2.** having a specified extent upward. **3.** situated above the ground or some base; elevated. **4.** intensified; exceeding the common degree or measure; strong; intense, energetic: *high speed.* **5.** expensive, costly, or dear. **6.** exalted in rank, station, estimation, etc.; of exalted character or quality: *a high official.* **7.** *Music.* **a.** acute in pitch. **b.** a little sharp, or above the desired pitch. **8.** produced by relatively rapid vibrations; shrill: *high sounds.* **9.** extending to or from an elevation: *a high dive.* **10.** of great amount, degree, force, etc.: *a high temperature.* **11.** chief; principal; main: *the high altar of a church.* **12.** of great consequence; important; grave; serious: *high treason.* **13.** lofty; haughty; arrogant: *he spoke in a high and mighty manner.* **14.** advanced to the utmost extent, or to the culmination: *high noon.* **15.** elated; merry or hilarious: *high spirits.* **16.** *Colloq.* excited with drink. **17.** remote: *high latitude, high antiquity.* **18.** extreme in opinion or doctrine, esp. religious or political. **19.** designating or pertaining to highland or inland regions: *the High Germans.* **20.** *Biol.* having a relatively complex structure: *the higher mammals.* **21.** *Auto.* operating at or pertaining to the highest transmission gear ratio. **22.** *Phonet.* pronounced with the tongue relatively close to the roof of the mouth: *"feed" and "food" have high vowels.* **23.** (of meat, esp. game) tending toward a desirable amount of decomposition; slightly tainted. **24. high relief.** See **relief** (defs. 9, 10) and **alto-relievo.** **25. on high, a.** at or to a height; above. **b.** in heaven. —*adv.* **26.** at or to a high point, place, or level, or a high rank or estimate, a high amount or price, or a high degree. **27.** *Naut.* close to the wind (said of a ship when sailing by the wind, with reference to the smallest angle with the wind at which the sails will remain full and the ship make headway). **28. high and low,** everywhere. —*n.* **29.** *Auto.* a transmission gear providing the highest forward speed ratio, usually turning the drive shaft at the same rate as the engine crankshaft. **30.** *U.S. Colloq.* high school. **31.** *Meteorol.* a pressure system characterized by relatively high pressure at its center; an anticyclone. **32.** *Cards.* the ace or highest trump out, esp. in games of the seven-up family. [ME *heigh,* etc., OE *hēah,* c. G *hoch*] —**Syn. 1.** HIGH, LOFTY, TALL, TOWERING refer to that which has considerable height. HIGH is a general term, and denotes either extension upward or position at a considerable height: *six feet high, a high shelf.* LOFTY denotes imposing or even inspiring height: *lofty crags.* TALL is applied either to that which is high in proportion to its breadth, or to anything higher than the average of its kind: *a tall tree, building.* TOWERING is applied to that which rises to a great or conspicuous height as compared with something else: *a towering mountain, cliff.* **6.** elevated, eminent. —**Ant. 1.** low.

high·ball (hī′bôl′), *n.* *U.S.* a drink of whiskey or other liquor diluted with water, seltzer, or ginger ale, and served with ice in a tall glass.

high·bin·der (hī′bīn′dər), *n.* *U.S. Slang.* **1.** a member of a secret Chinese band or society employed for blackmail, assassination, etc. **2.** a ruffian or rowdy.

high·born (hī′bôrn′), *adj.* of high rank by birth.

high·boy (hī′boi′), *n.* a tall chest of drawers supported on legs. Cf. **lowboy.**

high·bred (hī′brĕd′), *adj.* **1.** of superior breed. **2.** characteristic of superior breeding: *highbred manners.*

high·brow (hī′brou′), *n.* *Colloq.* **1.** a person of intellectual tastes. Cf. **lowbrow.** —*adj.* **2.** of or pertaining to highbrows. **3.** being a highbrow.

High Church, a party in the Anglican Church which lays great stress on church authority and jurisdiction, ritual, etc. (opposed to *Low Church* and *Broad Church*). —**High′-Church′,** *adj.* —**High Churchman.**

high-col·ored (hī′kŭl′ərd), *adj.* **1.** deep in color. **2.** florid or red: *a high-colored complexion.*

high comedy, comedy dealing with polite society, depending largely on the witty dialogue. Cf. **low comedy.**

high day, 1. a holy or festal day. **2.** heyday.

higher criticism, the study of literature, esp. the Bible, by scientific and historical techniques.

higher education, education beyond secondary education.

higher mathematics, the more scientifically treated and advanced portions of mathematics customarily embracing all beyond ordinary arithmetic, geometry, algebra, and trigonometry.

high·er-up (hī′ər ŭp′), *n.* *U.S. Colloq.* one occupying a superior position.

high explosive, a class of explosive, as TNT, in which the reaction is so rapid as to be practically instantaneous, used for bursting charges in shells and bombs.

high·fa·lu·tin (hī′fə lōō′tən), *adj.* *Colloq.* pompous; haughty; pretentious. Also, **hifalutin, high′fa·lu′ting.**

high-fi·del·i·ty (hī′fī dĕl′ə tī), *adj.* *Electronics.* (of an amplifier, radio receiver, etc.) reproducing the full audio range of the original signal of sounds with relatively little distortion.

high·fli·er (hī′flī′ər), *n.* **1.** one who or that which flies high. **2.** one who is extravagant or goes to extremes in aims, pretensions, opinions, etc. Also, **high′fly′er.**

high-flown (hī′flōn′), *adj.* **1.** extravagant in aims, pretensions, etc. **2.** pretentiously lofty; bombastic.

high-fly·ing (hī′flī′ĭng), *adj.* **1.** that flies high, as a bird. **2.** extravagant or extreme in aims, opinions, etc.

high-fre·quen·cy (hī′frē′kwən sī), *adj.* noting or pertaining to frequencies above the upper limit of the audible range, esp. as used in radio.

High German, 1. any form of the German of central and southern Germany, Switzerland, and Austria, including Old High German and Middle High German. **2.** standard German.

high-hand·ed (hī′hăn′dĭd), *adj.* overbearing; arbitrary: *high-handed oppression.* —**high′-hand′ed·ly,** *adv.* —**high′-hand′ed·ness,** *n.*

high hat, a top hat.

high-hat (v. hī′hăt′; *adj.* hī′hăt′), *v.,* -**hatted,** -**hatting,** *adj.* *U.S. Slang.* —*v.t.* **1.** to snub or treat condescendingly. —*adj.* **2.** snobbish. **3.** fashionable.

high·hole (hī′hōl′), *n.* *U.S. Dial.* flicker[2]. Also, **high·hold·er** (hī′hōl′dər).

high·jack (hī′jăk′), *v.t., v.i.* *U.S. Slang.* hijack.

high jump, *Athletics.* **1.** a vertical jump in which one attempts to go as high as possible. **2.** a contest for the highest such jump.

high·land (hī′lənd), *n.* **1.** an elevated region; a plateau: *a jutting highland.* **2.** (*pl.*) a mountainous region or elevated part of a country. —*adj.* **3.** of, pertaining to, or characteristic of highlands.

High·land·er (hī′lən dər), *n.* **1.** a member of the Gaelic race of the Highlands. **2.** a soldier of a Highland regiment. **3.** (*l.c.*) an inhabitant of high land.

Highland fling, a vigorous Scotch country dance, a form of the reel.

High·land Park (hī′lənd), *n.* a city in SE Michigan, within the city limits of Detroit. 46,393 (1950).

High·lands (hī′ləndz), *n.pl.* a mountainous region in Scotland, N of the Grampians.

high·light (hī′līt′), *v.,* -**lighted, -lighting,** *n.* —*v.t.* **1.** to emphasize or make prominent. **2.** *Art.* to emphasize (the areas of greatest brightness) with paint or by exposing lighter areas. —*n.* **3.** Also, **high light.** a conspicuous or striking part: *the highlight of his talk.* **4.** an important event, scene, etc. **5.** *Art.* the point of most intense light in a picture or form.

high-low-jack (hī′lō′jăk′), *n.* *Cards.* any game of the seven-up family.

high·ly (hī′lī), *adv.* **1.** in or to a high degree: *highly amusing.* **2.** with high appreciation or praise: *to speak highly of a person.* **3.** at or to a high price.

High Mass, *Rom. Cath. Ch.* a Mass celebrated according to the complete rite by a priest or prelate attended by a deacon and subdeacon, parts of the Mass being chanted or sung by the ministers and parts by the choir. During a High Mass incense is burned before the oblations, the altar, the ministers, and the people.

high-mind·ed (hī′mīn′dĭd), *adj.* **1.** having or showing high, exalted principles or feelings: *a high-minded ruler.* **2.** proud or arrogant. —**high′-mind′ed·ly,** *adv.* —**high′-mind′ed·ness,** *n.* —**Syn. 1.** See **noble.**

high-necked (hī′nĕkt′), *adj.* (of a garment) high at the neck.

high·ness (hī′nĭs), *n.* **1.** state of being high; loftiness; dignity. **2.** (*cap.*) a title of honor given to royal or princely personages (prec. by *His, Your,* etc.).

high-oc·tane gasoline (hī′ŏk′tān), gasoline with a relatively high octane number, used when efficiency and anti-knock qualities are desirable. See **octane number.**

high place, (in Semitic religions) a place of worship, usually on a hilltop.

High Point, a city in central North Carolina. 39,973 (1950).

high-pres·sure (hī′prĕsh′ər), *adj.* **1.** having or involving a pressure above the normal: *high-pressure steam.* **2.** vigorous; persistent: *high-pressure salesmanship.*

high-priced (hī′prīst′), *adj.* expensive. —**Syn.** See **expensive.**

high priest, chief priest.

high-proof (hī′prōōf′), *adj.* containing a high percentage of alcohol: *high-proof spirits.*

high·road (hī′rōd′), *n.* **1.** a main road; a highway. **2.** an easy or certain course: *the highroad to success.*

high school, 1. a school following the ordinary grammar school and corresponding to grades 9 through 12. **2.** either of two schools, one (**junior high school**) corresponding to the upper grades or grade of the ordinary grammar school together with one or more years of the ordinary high school, and another (**senior high school**) corresponding to the remainder of the ordinary high school.

high sea, 1. sea or ocean beyond the three-mile limit. **2.** (*usually pl.*) the open, unenclosed waters of any sea or ocean, common highway. **3.** (*usually pl.*) the area within which transactions are subject to court of admiralty jurisdiction.

high-sound·ing (hī′soun′dĭng), *adj.* having an imposing or pretentious sound: *high-sounding titles.*

high-spir·it·ed (hī′spĭr′ə tĭd), *adj.* having a high, proud, or bold spirit; mettlesome.

high-strung (hī′strŭng′), *adj.* at great tension; highly nervous: *high-strung nerves, high-strung persons.*

hight (hīt), *adj.* *Archaic.* called or named: *Childe Harold was he hight.* [ME; OE *heht,* reduplicated preterit of *hātan* name, call, promise, command, c. G *heissen*; current meaning taken from OE *hātte,* passive of *hātan*]

high tea, *Brit.* an evening meal, commonly supper.

high-ten·sion (hī′tĕn′shən), *adj.* *Elect.* (of a device, circuit, circuit component, etc.) subjected to, or capable of operating under, a relatively high voltage, usually 1000 volts or more.

high-test (hī′tĕst′), *adj.* (of gasoline) boiling at a comparatively low temperature.

high tide, 1. the tide at high water. 2. the time of high water. 3. the culminating point.

high time, 1. the right time; the time just before it is too late: *it's high time that was done.* 2. *Slang.* an enjoyable and gay time: *a high old time at the party.*

high-toned (hī′tōnd′), *adj.* 1. high in tone or pitch. 2. having high principles; dignified. 3. *U.S. Colloq.* fashionable or stylish.

high treason, treason against the sovereign or state. See **treason** (def. 1a).

high-ty-tigh-ty (hī′tĭ tī′tĭ), *interj., adj.* hoity-toity.

high water, 1. high tide. 2. water at its greatest elevation, as in a river.

high-wa-ter mark (hī′wô′tər, -wŏt′ər), 1. a mark showing the highest level reached by a body of water. 2. the highest point of anything.

high-way (hī′wā′), *n.* 1. a main road, as one between towns. 2. any public passage, either a road or waterway. 3. any main or ordinary route, track, or course.

high-way-man (hī′wā′mən), *n., pl.* **-men.** a robber on the highway, esp. one on horseback.

high-wrought (hī′rôt′), *adj.* 1. wrought with a high degree of skill; ornate. 2. highly agitated.

H.I.H., His, or Her, Imperial Highness.

Hii-u-maa (hē′ōō mä′), *n.* an island in the Baltic, E of and belonging to the Estonian Republic of the Soviet Union. 373 sq. mi. Danish, **Dagö.**

hi-jack (hī′jăk′), *U.S. Slang.* —*v.t.* 1. to steal (liquor or other goods) from bootleggers or smugglers while it is in transit. —*v.i.* 2. to engage in such stealing. Also, **highjack.** [back formation from HIJACKER]

hi-jack-er (hī′jăk′ər), *n.* one who hijacks. [f. HIGH + *jacker,* appar. der. *jack,* v., hunt by night with aid of a jack light]

hike (hīk), *v.,* **hiked, hiking,** *n.* —*v.i.* 1. to march or tramp, as soldiers or pleasure seekers. —*v.t.* 2. to move, draw, or raise with a jerk. —*n.* 3. a march or tramp. [? akin to HITCH] —**hik′er,** *n.*

hi-lar-i-ous (hĭ lâr′Ĭ əs, hī-), *adj.* 1. boisterously gay. 2. cheerful. [f. HILARI(TY) + -OUS] —**hi-lar′i-ous-ly,** *adv.* —**hi-lar′i-ous-ness,** *n.*

hi-lar-i-ty (hĭ lăr′ə tĭ, hī-), *n.* 1. boisterous gaiety. 2. cheerfulness. [t. L: m.s. *hilaritas*] —**Syn.** 1. See **mirth.**

Hil-a-ry of Poitiers (hĭl′ərĭ), **Saint,** A.D. 353?–368, French bishop and theologian. French, **Hi-laire** (ē lĕr′).

Hil-de-brand (hĭl′də brănd′), *n.* See **Gregory VII.**

Hil-des-heim (hĭl′dĕs hīm′), *n.* a city in central Germany. 72,101 (1939).

hill (hĭl), *n.* 1. a conspicuous natural elevation of the earth's surface, smaller than a mountain. 2. an artificial heap or pile: *anthill.* 3. a little heap of earth raised about a cultivated plant or a cluster of such plants. 4. the plant or plants so surrounded. —*v.t.* 5. to surround with hills: *to hill potatoes.* 6. to form into a hill or heap. [ME; OE *hyll,* c. MD *hille;* akin to L *collis* hill, *columen* top, *columna* COLUMN] —**hill′er,** *n.* —**Syn.** 1. eminence; mound, knoll, hillock; foothill. —**Ant.** 1. hollow.

Hill (hĭl), *n.* 1. **Ambrose Powell,** 1825–65, Confederate general in the U.S. Civil War. 2. **James Jerome,** 1838–1916, U.S. railroad builder and financier, born in Canada.

hill-bil-ly (hĭl′bĭl′Ĭ), *n., pl.* **-lies.** *U.S. Colloq.* a person, usually uncouth or ignorant, living in the backwoods or mountains of the South. [f. HILL- + BILLY²]

Hill-man (hĭl′mən), *n.* **Sidney,** 1887–1946, U.S. labor leader, born in Lithuania.

hill myna, any of the Asiatic birds constituting the genus *Eulabes* (of the starling family, *Sturnidae*), esp. *E. religiosa,* easily tamed and taught to speak.

hill-ock (hĭl′ək), *n.* a little hill or mound. —**hill′-ock-y,** *adj.*

hill-side (hĭl′sīd′), *n.* the side or slope of a hill.

hill-site (hĭl′sīt′), *n.* situation on a hill; an elevated site.

hill-top (hĭl′tŏp′), *n.* the top or summit of a hill.

hill-y (hĭl′Ĭ), *adj.,* **hillier, hilliest.** 1. abounding in hills: *hilly country.* 2. elevated; steep. —**hill′i-ness,** *n.*

Hi-lo (hē′lō), *n.* a seaport in the Hawaiian Islands, on the island of Hawaii. 27,019 (prelim. 1950).

hilt (hĭlt), *n.* 1. the handle of a sword or dagger. 2. the handle of any weapon or tool. 3. **to the hilt,** fully; completely: *armed to the hilt.* —*v.t.* 4. to furnish with a hilt. [ME *hylt,* OE *hilt, hilte,* c. MD *hilt, hilte;* of obscure orig.] —**hilt′ed,** *adj.*

Hil-ton (hĭl′tən), *n.* **James,** born 1900, British novelist.

hi-lum (hī′ləm), *n., pl.* **-la** (-lə). 1. *Bot.* **a.** the mark or scar on a seed produced by separation from its funicle or placenta. See diag. under **seed.** **b.** the nucleus of a granule of starch. 2. *Anat.* the region at which the vessels, nerves, etc., enter or emerge from a part. [t. L: little thing, trifle]

him (hĭm), *pron.* objective case of *he.* [ME and OE; dat. of *hē* HE]

H.I.M., His, or Her, Imperial Majesty.

Hi-ma-la-yas (hĭ măl′yəz, hĭm′ə lā′əz), *n.pl.* **The,** a lofty mountain system extending ab. 1500 mi. along the border between India and Tibet. Highest peak (in the world), Mt. Everest, 29,141 ft. Also, **The Himalaya** or **Himalaya Mountains.** [t. Skt.: lit., snow dwelling] —**Hi-ma-la-yan** (hĭ măl′yən, hĭm′ə lā′ən), *adj.*

hi-mat-i-on (hĭ măt′Ĭ ŏn′), *n., pl.* **-matia** (-măt′Ĭ ə). *Gk. Antiq.* a garment consisting of a rectangular piece of cloth thrown over the left shoulder and wrapped about the body. [t. Gk.]

Hi-me-ji (hē′mĕ jē), *n.* a city in S Japan, on Honshu island, W of Kobe. 175,734 (1946).

Himm-ler (hĭm′lər), *n.* **Heinrich** (hīn′rĭKH), 1900–45, high Nazi party leader in Germany and head of the Gestapo.

him-self (hĭm sĕlf′; *medially often* Ĭm-), *pron.* 1. a reflexive form of *him: he cut himself.* 2. an emphatic form of *him* or *he* used: **a.** as object: *he used it for himself.* **b.** in apposition to a subject or object: *he himself did it.* 3. his proper or normal self; his usual state of mind (used after *be, become* or *came*): *he is himself again.*

Him-yar-ite (hĭm′yə rīt′), *n.* 1. one of an ancient people of southern Arabia, of an advanced civilization, speaking an Arabic dialect closely akin to Ethiopic. 2. a descendant of these people. —*adj.* 3. Himyaritic. [f. Ar. *Himyar* (name of a tribe and an old dynasty of Yemen) + -ITE¹]

Him-yar-it-ic (hĭm′yə rĭt′Ĭk), *adj.* 1. pertaining to the Himyarites and to the remains of their civilization. —*n.* 2. a Semitic language anciently spoken in southern Arabia, surviving in a small area of the southern coast.

hind¹ (hīnd), *adj.,* **hinder, hindmost** or **hindermost.** situated in the rear or at the back; posterior: *the hind legs of an animal.* [? short for BEHIND, but cf. OE *hindan,* adv., from behind, G *hinten,* adv.] —**Syn.** See **back¹.**

hind² (hīnd), *n. Zool.* the female of the deer, chiefly the red deer, esp. in and after the third year. [ME and OE; c. Icel. *hind.* Cf. D and G *hinde*]

hind³ (hīnd), *n. Archaic.* 1. a peasant or rustic. 2. a farm laborer. [ME *hine,* sing., earlier ME and OE *hīne,* pl., der. *hī(g)na,* gen. pl. of *hīgan* members of a household, domestics. See HIDE³]

Hind., 1. Hindustan. 2. Hindustani.

hind-brain (hīnd′brān′), *n. Anat.* 1. the cerebellum, pons, and medulla oblongata or the embryonic nervous tissue from which they develop; the entire rhombencephalon or some part of it. 2. the metencephalon.

Hin-de-mith (hĭn′də mĭt), *n.* **Paul** (poul), born 1895, German composer, now in the U.S.

Hin-den-burg (hĭn′dən bûrg′; *Ger.* -dŏōrKH′), *n.* 1. **Paul von** (poul fən), (*Paul von Beneckendorff und von Hindenburg*) 1847–1934, German field marshal; 2nd president of Germany, 1925–34. 2. German name of **Zabrze.**

Hindenburg line, a line of elaborate fortification established by the German army in World War I, near the French-Belgian border, extending from Lille SE to Metz.

hin-der¹ (hĭn′dər), *v.t.* 1. to interrupt; check; retard: *to be hindered by storms.* 2. to prevent from acting or taking place; stop: *to hinder a man from committing a crime.* —*v.i.* 3. to be an obstacle or impediment. [ME *hindre(n),* OE *hindrian* (c. G. *hindern,* etc.), der. *hinder* behind, back] —**hin′der-er,** *n.* —**hin′der-ing-ly,** *adv.* —**Syn.** 1. impede, encumber, delay, hamper, obstruct, trammel. 2. block, thwart. See **prevent.** —**Ant.** 1. expedite. 2. aid.

hind-er² (hīn′dər), *adj.* situated at the rear or back; posterior: *the hinder part of the ship.* [ME, appar. repr. OE *hinder,* adv., behind, c. G *hinter,* prep.]

hind-gut (hīnd′gŭt′), *n. Embryol., Zool.* the lower portion of the embryonic digestive canal from which the colon and rectum develop.

Hin-di (hĭn′dē), *n.* 1. one of the modern Indic languages of northern India, usually divided into Eastern and Western Hindi. 2. a literary language derived from Hindustani, used by Hindus. [t. Hind., der. *Hind* India]

hind-most (hīnd′mōst′), *adj.* furthest behind; nearest the rear; last. Also, **hind-er-most** (hīn′dər mōst′).

Hin-doo (hĭn′dōō), *n., pl.* **-doos,** *adj.* Hindu.

Hin-doo-ism (hĭn′dōō Ĭz′əm), *n.* Hinduism.

Hin-doo-sta-ni (hĭn′dōō stä′nĭ, -stän′Ĭ), *adj., n.* Hindustani. Also, **Hin-do-sta-ni** (hĭn′dō stä′nĭ, -stän′Ĭ).

hind-quar-ter (hīnd′kwôr′tər), *n.* the posterior end of a halved carcass of beef, lamb, etc., sectioned usually between the twelfth and thirteenth ribs.

hin-drance (hĭn′drəns), *n.* 1. an impeding, stopping, or preventing. 2. a means or cause of hindering. —**Syn.** 2. impediment, encumbrance, obstruction, check; restraint. See **obstacle.** —**Ant.** 2. aid.

hind-sight (hīnd′sīt′), *n.* perception of the nature and exigencies of a case after the event: *hindsight is easier than foresight.*

Hin-du (hĭn′dōō), *n.* 1. one of the Hindu or Indian race. 2. (in Anglo-Indian usage) any native of India who adheres to a form of the ancient national religion, which recognizes the primacy of the Brahman caste, and therefore excludes Mohammedans, Sikhs, Parsis, Buddhists, etc. 3. any native of Hindustan or India. —*adj.* 4. of or pertaining to the people of Hindustan generally. 5. of or pertaining to natives of India accepting the Brahmanic religion. Also, **Hindoo.** [t. Hind., Pers., der. *Hind* India]

Hin-du-ism (hĭn′dōō Ĭz′əm), *n.* the religious and social doctrines and rites of the Hindus, characterized by faith in one supreme deity and by its system of divinely ordained caste. Also, **Hindooism.**

Hin·du Kush (hĭn′dŏŏ kŏŏsh′), a lofty mountain system largely in NE Afghanistan, extending W from the Himalayas. Highest peak, Tirach Mir, 25,420 ft. Also, **Hindu Kush Mountains.**

Hin·du·stan (hĭn′dŏŏ stän′, -stăn′), n. **1.** Persian name of India, esp. the part N of the Deccan. **2.** the predominantly Hindu areas of the peninsula of India as contrasted to Pakistan, the predominantly Moslem areas. See **India.**

Hin·du·sta·ni (hĭn′dŏŏ stä′nĭ, -stän′ĭ), n. **1.** a standard language or lingua franca of northern India based on a dialect of Western Hindi spoken about Delhi. —*adj.* **2.** of or pertaining to Hindustan, its people, or their languages. Also, **Hindoostani, Hindostani.** [t. Hind., Pers., der. *Hindustan* (f. *hindu* Hindu + *stan* country)]

hind·ward (hīnd′wərd), *adv., adj.,* backward.

hinge (hĭnj), *n., v.,* **hinged, hinging.** —*n.* **1.** the movable joint or device on which a door, gate, shutter, lid, or the like, turns or moves. **2.** a natural anatomic joint at which motion occurs about a transverse axis, as that of the knee or a bivalve shell. **3.** that on which something turns or depends; principle; central rule. —*v.i.* **4.** to depend or turn on, or as if on, a hinge: *everything hinges on his decision.* —*v.t.* **5.** to furnish with or attach by a hinge or hinges. **6.** to attach as by a hinge. **7.** to cause to depend: *to hinge action upon future sales.* [ME *heng, hing,* OE *hencg.* See HANG, v.] —**hinged,** *adj.*

hin·ny (hĭn′ĭ), *n., pl.* **-nies.** the offspring of a stallion and she-donkey. See **mule**[1] (defs. 1, 2). [t. L: m.s. *hinnus*]

hint (hĭnt), *n.* **1.** an indirect or covert suggestion or implication; an intimation. **2.** *Obs.* an occasion or opportunity. —*v.t.* **3.** to give a hint of. —*v.i.* **4.** to make indirect suggestion or allusion (usually fol. by *at*). [var. of *hent,* n., der. HENT, v., seize] —**hint′er,** *n.*

—**Syn. 1.** allusion, insinuation, innuendo; memorandum, reminder; inkling. **3.** imply. HINT, INTIMATE, INSINUATE, SUGGEST denote the conveying of an idea to the mind indirectly or without full or explicit statement. To HINT is to convey an idea covertly or indirectly, but intelligibly: *to hint that one would like a certain present, to hint that hints of gossip might be true.* To INTIMATE is to give a barely perceptible hint, often with the purpose of influencing action: *to intimate that something may be possible.* To INSINUATE is to hint artfully, often what one would not dare to say directly: *to insinuate something against someone's reputation.* SUGGEST denotes particularly recalling something to the mind or starting a new train of thought by means of association of ideas: *the name doesn't suggest anything to me.* —**Ant. 3.** express, declare.

hin·ter·land (hĭn′tər lănd′; *Ger.* -länt′), *n.* **1.** the area on the landward side of a port that it serves in the export and import of commodities. **2.** the land lying behind a coast district. **3.** an area or sphere of influence in the unoccupied interior claimed by the state possessing the coast. [t. G: lit., hinder land, i.e. land behind]

hip[1] (hĭp), *n., v.* **hipped, hipping.** —*n.* **1.** the projecting part of each side of the body formed by the side of the pelvis and the upper part of the femur, with the flesh covering them; the haunch. **2.** the hip joint. **3.** *have someone on* (or *upon*) *the hip,* to have someone at a disadvantage. **4.** *Archit.* the inclined projecting angle formed by the junction of a sloping side and a sloping end, or of two adjacent sloping sides, of a roof. See illus. under **hip roof.** —*v.t.* **5.** to injure or dislocate the hip of. **6.** *Archit.* to form (a roof) with a hip or hips. [ME; OE *hype,* c. G *hüfte*] —**hip′less,** *adj.* —**hip′like′,** *adj.*

hip[2] (hĭp), *n.* the ripe fruit of a rose, esp. of a wild rose. [ME *hepe,* OE *hēope* hip, briar, c. OHG *hiufo* bramble]

hip[3] (hĭp), *interj.* an exclamation used in cheers or in signaling for cheers: *hip, hip, hurrah!* [orig. unknown]

hip·bone (hĭp′bōn′), *n.* **1.** the innominate bone. **2.** the ilium. **3.** the neck of the femur.

hip joint, the joint between the hip and the thigh.

hip·parch (hĭp′ärk), *n. Gk. Antiq.* a commander of cavalry. [t. Gk.: s. *hipparchos*]

Hip·par·chus (hĭ pär′kəs), *n.* **1.** died 514 B.C., tyrant of Athens. **2.** fl. 146–126 B.C., Greek astronomer, mathematician, and geographer.

hipped[1] (hĭpt), *adj.* **1.** having hips. **2.** having the hip injured or dislocated. **3.** *Archit.* formed with a hip or hips, as a roof. [f. HIP[1] + -ED[3]]

hipped[2] (hĭpt), *adj.* **1.** *U.S. Slang.* having an obsession: *he's hipped on playing a tuba.* **2.** Also, **hip′pish.** *Chiefly Brit.* melancholy. **3.** vexed. [earlier *hypped,* der. *hyp,* n., short for HYPOCHONDRIA]

hip·po (hĭp′ō), *n., pl.* **-pos.** *Colloq.* hippopotamus.

Hip·po (hĭp′ō), *n.* Hippo Regius.

hip·po·cam·pus (hĭp′ə kăm′pəs), *n., pl.* **-pos, -pi** (-pī). **1.** *Class. Myth.* a sea horse with two forefeet, and a body ending in the tail of a dolphin or fish. **2.** *Anat.* an enfolding of cerebral cortex into the cavity of a cerebral hemisphere having the shape in cross section of a sea horse. [t. L: a sea monster, t. Gk.: m. *hippokámpos*]

hip·po·cras (hĭp′ə krăs′), *n.* an old medicinal cordial made of wine mixed with spices, etc. [ME *ypocras,* t. OF; from the name of *Hippocrates*]

Hip·poc·ra·tes (hĭ pŏk′rə tēz′), *n.* 460?–357 B.C., Greek physician, known as the father of medicine. —**Hip·po·crat·ic** (hĭp′ə krăt′ĭk), *adj.*

Hippocratic oath, an oath embodying the duties and obligations of physicians, usually taken by those about to enter upon the practice of medicine.

Hip·po·crene (hĭp′ə krēn′, hĭp′ə krē′nĭ), *n.* a spring on Mount Helicon, sacred to the Muses and regarded as a source of poetic inspiration. [t. L, t. Gk.: m. *Hippokrēnē,* for *Hippou krēnē* horse's fountain']

hip·po·drome (hĭp′ə drōm′), *n.* **1.** an arena or structure for equestrian and other spectacles. **2.** (in ancient Greece and Rome) a course or circus for horse races and chariot races. [t. L: m.s. *hippodromos* a race course, t. Gk.]

hip·po·griff (hĭp′ə grĭf′), *n.* a fabulous creature resembling a griffin but having the body and hind parts of a horse. Also, **hip′po·gryph′.** [t. F: m. *hippogriffe,* t. It.: m. *ippogrifo,* f. *ippo-* (t. Gk.: m. *híppos* horse) + *grifo* GRIFFIN[1]]

Hip·pol·y·te (hĭ pŏl′ə tē′), *n. Gk. Legend.* a queen of the Amazons, slain by Hercules.

Hip·pol·y·tus (hĭ pŏl′ə təs), *n. Gk. Legend.* the son of Theseus by Hippolyte, who was falsely accused by his stepmother Phaedra of ravishing her. Theseus called upon Poseidon for vengeance, and the god sent a sea monster which so terrified Hippolytus' horses that they dragged him to death.

Hip·pom·e·nes (hĭ pŏm′ə nēz′), *n.* (in some stories) the successful suitor of Atalanta.

hip·po·pot·a·mus (hĭp′əpŏt′ə məs), *n., pl.* **-muses, -mi** (-mī′). a large herbivorous mammal, *Hippopotamus amphibius,* having a thick hairless body, short legs, and large head and muzzle, found in and near

Hippopotamus, *Hippopotamus amphibius* (13 ft. long, 4½ ft. or more high at the shoulder)

the rivers, lakes, etc., of Africa, and able to remain under water for a considerable time. [t. L, t. Gk.: lit., river horse; r. ME *ypotame,* t. OF, t. ML: m. *ypotamus*]

Hip·po Re·gi·us (hĭp′ō rē′jĭ əs), a seaport of ancient Numidia: St. Augustine was bishop here; the site of modern Bône, Algeria. Also, **Hippo.**

Hip·po Za·ry·tus (hĭp′ō zə rī′təs), an ancient city in N Africa: the site of modern Bizerte, Tunisia.

hip roof, *Archit.* a roof with sloping ends and sides; a hipped roof.

hip·shot (hĭp′shŏt′), *adj.* **1.** having the hip dislocated. **2.** lame; awkward. [f. HIP[1], n. + SHOT[2], pp.]

Hi·ram (hī′rəm), *n.* tenth century B.C., king of Tyre. I Kings 5.

H. Hip on hip roof

hir·cine (hûr′sīn, -sĭn), *adj.* **1.** of, pertaining to, or resembling a goat. **2.** having a goatish odor. **3.** lustful. [t. L: m.s. *hircinus* of a goat]

hire (hīr), *v.,* **hired, hiring,** *n.* —*v.t.* **1.** to engage the services of for hire: *to hire a clerk.* **2.** to engage the temporary use of for hire. *to hire a car.* **3.** to grant the temporary use of, or the services of, for a compensation (often fol. by *out*). **4.** to pay for the desired action or conduct of; bribe; reward. —*v.i.* **5.** *U.S.* to engage oneself for a compensation (usually fol. by *out*). [ME; OE *hýr(i)an,* c. G *heuern*]

—*n.* **6.** the price or compensation paid, or contracted to be paid, for the temporary use of something or for personal services or labor; pay. **7.** act of hiring. **8.** the fact of being hired. [ME; OE *hýr,* c. G *heuer*] —**hir′able,** *adj.* —**hir′er,** *n.*

—**Syn. 1, 2.** let, lease. HIRE, CHARTER, RENT refer to paying money for the use of something. HIRE is a general word, most commonly applied to paying money for labor or services, but is also used in reference to paying for the temporary use of teams, trucks, halls, etc.; in New England, it is used in speaking of borrowing money on which interest is to be paid (to distinguish from borrowing from a friend, who would not accept any interest): *to hire a gardener, a delivery truck, a hall for a convention.* CHARTER formerly meant to pay for the use of a vessel, but is now applied with increasing frequency to hiring any conveyance for the use of a group: *to charter a boat, a bus.* RENT is used in the latter sense, also, but is usually applied to paying a set sum once or at regular intervals for the use of a dwelling, room, personal effects, etc: *to rent a business building, a house, a garage, an evening dress.*

hire·ling (hīr′lĭng), *n.* **1.** one serving for hire (now usually in contempt). **2.** a mercenary. —*adj.* **3.** serving for hire (now usually in contempt). **4.** venal; mercenary.

Hir·o·hi·to (hĭr′ōhē′tō; *Jap.* hē′rō hē′tō), *n.* born 1901, emperor of Japan since 1926.

Hir·o·shi·ma (hĭr′əshē′mə; *Jap.* hē′rōshē′mä), *n.* a seaport in SW Japan, on Honshu island: the first military use of the atomic bomb, Aug. 6, 1945. 171,902 (1946); 343,968 (1940).

hir·sute (hûr′sōōt), *adj.* **1.** hairy. **2.** *Bot., Zool.* covered with long, rather stiff hairs. **3.** of, pertaining to, or of the nature of hair. [t. L: m.s. *hirsutus* rough, hairy] —**hir′sute·ness,** *n.*

Hir·u·din·e·a (hĭr′ŏŏ dĭn′ĭ ə), *n.pl.* a class of annelid worms comprising the leeches. [NL, der. L *hirūdo* leech]

ăct, āble, dâre, ärt; ĕbb, ēqual; ĭf, īce; hŏt, ōver, ôrder, oil, bŏŏk, ōōze, out; ŭp, ūse, ûrge; ə = a in alone; ch, chief; g, give; ng, ring; sh, shoe; th, thin; ŧℏ, that; zh, vision. See the full key on inside cover.

hi·run·dine (hĭrŭn'dĭn, -dīn), adj. of, pertaining to, or resembling the swallow. [t. LL: s. hirundineus]

his (hĭz), pron. **1.** the possessive form of he: this book is his. **2.** the person(s) or thing(s) belonging to him: himself and his, a friend of his. —adj. **3.** belonging to, pertaining to, or owned by him; made, done, experienced, etc., by him. [ME and OE; gen. of masc. hē HE, also of neut. hit IT]

His·pa·ni·a (hĭspā'nĭə, -nyə), n. Poetic. Spain. [t. L the Spanish peninsula (with Portugal)]

His·pan·ic (hĭspăn'ĭk), adj. Spanish.

His·pan·i·cism (hĭspăn'əsĭz'əm), n. a Spanish idiom.

His·pan·io·la (hĭs'pən yō'lə; Sp. ēs'pän yō'lä). n. an island in the West Indies, including the republic of Haiti and the Dominican Republic. ab. 5,060,000 pop.; 29,843 sq. mi. Formerly, **Haiti.**

his·pid (hĭs'pĭd), adj. Bot., Zool. rough with stiff hairs, bristles, or minute spines. [t. L: s. hispidus] —**his·pid'·i·ty,** n.

hiss (hĭs), v.i. **1.** to make or emit a sharp sound like that of the letter s prolonged, as a goose or a serpent does, or as steam does rushing through a small opening. **2.** to express disapproval or contempt by making this sound. —v.t. **3.** to express disapproval of by hissing. **4.** to force or drive by hissing (fol. by away, down, etc.). **5.** to utter with a hiss. —n. **6.** a hissing sound, esp. in disapproval. [unexplained var. of d. E hish, ME hisshe(n) hiss, OE hyscan jeer at, rail] —**hiss'er,** n.

hiss·ing (hĭs'ĭng), n. **1.** act of hissing. **2.** the sound of a hiss. **3.** Archaic. an occasion or object of scorn.

hist (hĭst), interj. **1.** a sibilant exclamation used to attract attention, command silence, etc. —v.t. **2.** to use the exclamation "hist" to.

hist., **1.** histology. **2.** historical. **3.** history.

his·tam·i·nase (hĭs tăm'ə nās'), n. an enzyme capable of making histamine inactive, used in treating allergies.

his·ta·mine (hĭs'tə mēn', -mĭn), n. an amine, $C_5H_9N_3$, obtained from histidine and found in ergot. It is released by the tissues in allergic reactions, is a powerful uterine stimulant, and lowers the blood pressure. —**his·ta·min·ic** (hĭs'tə mĭn'ĭk), adj.

his·ti·dine (hĭs'tə dēn', -dĭn), n. an amino acid, $C_6H_9N_3O_2$, derived from fish protamines or from ptomaines when acted upon by sulfuric acid, converted by putrefactive organisms into histamine. [f. HIST- + -ID³ + -INE². Cf. G histidin]

histo-, a word element meaning "tissue," as in histogen. Also, before vowels, **hist-.** [t. Gk., comb form of histós web, tissue; also used as comb. form of Gk. histân check]

his·to·gen (hĭs'tə jĕn), n. Bot. the regions in a plant in which tissues undergo differentiation.

his·to·gen·e·sis (hĭs'tə jĕn'ə sĭs), n. Biol. the formation and differentiation of a tissue.

his·to·gram (hĭs'tə grăm'), n. Statistics. a graph of a frequency distribution in which equal intervals of values are marked on a horizontal axis and the frequency corresponding to each interval is indicated by the height of a rectangle having the interval as its base.

his·toid (hĭs'toid), adj. Pathol. denoting a tumor composed of connective tissue or its equivalent.

his·tol·o·gy (hĭs tŏl'ə jĭ), n. **1.** the science that treats of organic tissues. **2.** the study of the structure, esp. the microscopic structure, of organic tissues. —**his·to·log·i·cal** (hĭs'tə lŏj'ə kəl), **his'to·log'ic,** adj. —**his·tol'o·gist,** n.

his·tol·y·sis (hĭs tŏl'ə sĭs), n. Biol. disintegration or dissolution of organic tissues.

his·tone (hĭs'tōn), n. Biochem. any of a class of protein substances, as globin, having marked basic properties. Also, **his·ton** (hĭs'tŏn). [f. HIST- + -ONE. Cf. G histon]

his·to·ri·an (hĭs tŏr'ĭ ən), n. **1.** a writer of history. **2.** an expert in history; an authority on history.

his·tor·ic (hĭs tŏr'ĭk, -tŏr'-), adj. **1.** well-known or important in history: historic scenes. **2.** historical.

his·tor·i·cal (hĭs tŏr'ə kəl, -tŏr'-), adj. **1.** relating to or concerned with history or historical events. **2.** dealing with or treating of history or historical events. **3.** pertaining to or of the nature of history: historical evidence. **4.** pertaining to or of the nature of history as opposed to legend or fiction: the historical King Arthur. **5.** narrated or mentioned in history; belonging to the past. **6.** historic. **7.** Gram. used in the statement of past facts or the narration of past events. [f. L historicus (t. Gk.: m. historikós) + -AL¹] —**his·tor'i·cal·ly,** adv. —**his·tor'i·cal·ness,** n.

historical geography, **1.** the study of the geography of a past period or periods. **2.** geographic history.

historical method, the development of general principles by the study of the historical facts.

historical present, Gram. the present tense used in narrating a past event as if it were happening at the time of narration. Also, **historic present.**

historical school, **1.** a group of economists who adhere to the so-called historical method, as compared with the method of theoretical analysis. **2.** Law. the school of jurists who maintain that law is not to be regarded as made by commands of the sovereign, but is the result of its historical and social circumstances.

his·to·ric·i·ty (hĭs'tə rĭs'ə tĭ), n. historical authenticity.

his·to·ri·og·ra·pher (hĭs tŏr'ĭ ŏg'rə fər), n. **1.** a historian. **2.** an official historian, as of a court, an institution, etc. [f. s. LL historiographus (t. Gk.: m. historiográphos) + -ER¹] —**his·to·ri·og'ra·phy,** n.

his·to·ry (hĭs'tə rĭ), n., pl. -ries. **1.** the branch of knowledge dealing with past events. **2.** the record of past events, esp. in connection with the human race. **3.** a continuous, systematic written narrative, in order of time, of past events as relating to a particular people, country, period, person, etc. **4.** the aggregate of past events. **5.** a past worthy of record or out of the ordinary: a ship with a history. **6.** a systematic account of any set of natural phenomena, without reference to time. **7.** a drama representing historical events. [ME, t. L: m.s. historia, t. Gk.: a learning or knowing by inquiry, information, narrative, history] —**Syn.** 2. account, record, chronicle; annals. See **narrative.**

his·tri·on·ic (hĭs'trĭ ŏn'ĭk), adj. **1.** of or pertaining to actors or acting. **2.** artificial; affected. Also, **his'tri·on'i·cal.** [t. LL: s. histrionicus] —**his'tri·on'i·cal·ly,** adv.

his·tri·on·ics (hĭs'trĭ ŏn'ĭks), n.pl. **1.** dramatic representation; theatricals; acting. **2.** artificial behavior, speech, etc., for effect.

hit¹ (hĭt), v., **hit, hit·ting,** n. —v.t. **1.** to deal a blow or stroke; bring forcibly into collision: to hit a child. **2.** to come against with an impact or collision, as a missile, a flying fragment, a falling body, or the like does. **3.** to reach with a missile, a weapon, a blow, or the like (intentionally or otherwise), as one throwing, shooting, or striking. **4.** to succeed in striking: to hit the mark. **5.** to drive or propel by a stroke. **6.** to touch effectively; affect severely. **7.** to assail effectively and sharply: to be hit by satire. —v.i. **8.** to strike with a missile, a weapon, or the like; deal a blow or blows. **9.** to drive the piston in the cylinder of an internal-combustion engine by the combustion of fuel. **10.** hit or miss, whether one hits or misses; at haphazard. —n. **11.** an impact or collision, as of one thing against another. **12.** a stroke that reaches an object; a blow. **13.** a stroke of satire, censure, etc. **14.** Baseball. a ball so hit that even when fielded without error it enables the batter to reach base safely and without forcing out another baserunner. **15.** Backgammon. **a.** a game won by a player after his opponent has thrown off one or more men from the board. **b.** any winning game. [ME hitte, hutte, hete, of unknown orig.] —**hit'ter,** n. —**Syn.** 1. See **strike, beat.**

hit² (hĭt), v., **hit, hit·ting,** n. —v.t. **1.** to come or light upon; meet with; find: to hit the right road. **2.** to agree with; suit exactly: this hits my fancy. **3.** to guess correctly. **4.** to succeed in representing or producing exactly: to hit a likeness in a portrait. **5.** U.S. Colloq. to arrive at: to hit town. **6.** U.S. Colloq. to go to or upon: to hit the trail. **7. hit it off,** Colloq. to agree; get on, as with a person, or with each other. **8. hit off, a.** to represent, reproduce, or describe aptly. **b.** to produce readily or offhand. —v.i. **9.** to come into collision (often fol. by against, on, or upon). **10.** to come or light (fol. by upon or on): to hit on a new way. —n. **11.** a successful stroke, performance, or production; success: the play is a hit. **12.** an effective or telling expression or saying. [ME hitte(n), OE hittan, t. Scand.; cf. Icel. hitta come upon (by chance), meet]

hitch (hĭch), v.t. **1.** to make fast, esp. temporarily, by means of a hook, rope, strap, etc.; tether. **2.** to harness (an animal) to a vehicle (often fol. by up). **3.** to raise with jerks (usually fol. by up): to hitch up one's trousers. **4.** to move or draw (something) with a jerk. —v.i. **5.** to harness an animal to a vehicle (fol. by up). **6.** to become fastened or caught, as on something. **7.** to stick, as when caught. **8.** to fasten oneself or itself to something (often fol. by on). **9.** to move jerkily: to hitch along. **10.** Colloq. to get on together; agree. **11.** to hobble or limp. —n. **12.** a making fast, as to something, esp. temporarily. **13.** Naut., etc. any of various forms of knot or fastening made with rope or the like. **14.** a halt; an obstruction: a hitch in the proceedings. **15.** a hitching movement; a jerk or pull. **16.** a hitching gait; a hobble or limp. **17.** a fastening that joins a movable tool to the mechanism that pulls it. [ME hytche(n); orig. uncert.] —**hitch'er,** n. —**Syn.** 1. fasten, attach, tie, tether. **2.** yoke. —**Ant.** 1. loosen.

hitch·hike (hĭch'hīk'), v.i., -hiked, -hiking. Colloq. to travel by walking, with occasional rides in passing automobiles. —**hitch'hik'er,** n.

hitching post, a post to which horses, etc., are tied.

hith·er (hĭŧħ'ər), adv. **1.** to or toward this place: to come hither. —adj. **2.** on or toward this side; nearer: the hither side of the hill. **3.** earlier; more remote. [ME and OE hider, c. Icel. hedhra; der. demonstrative stem represented by HE]

hith·er·most (hĭŧħ'ər mōst'), adj. nearest in this direction.

hith·er·to (hĭŧħ'ər tōō'), adv. **1.** up to this time; until now: a fact hitherto unknown. **2.** Archaic. to here.

hith·er·ward (hĭŧħ'ər wərd), adv. hither. Also, **hith'er·wards.**

Hit·ler (hĭt'lər), n. Adolf (äd'ŏlf, ä'dŏlf; Ger. ä'dōlf), ("der Führer") 1889–1945?, Nazi leader and dictator of Germany, born in Austria: German Chancellor, 1933–45; president, 1934–45.

Hit·tite (hĭt'īt), n. **1.** one of a powerful, civilized ancient people who flourished in Asia Minor and adjoining regions (1900–1200 B.C.). **2.** records in cuneiform inscriptions of an ancient language of Asia Minor, derived from the same stock as the primitive Indo-European. **3.** records, in hieroglyphics, of a language ascribed to the Hittites, perhaps unrelated to the preceding. —*adj.* **4.** having to do with the Hittites or their langauge. [f. Heb. *Hitt(īm)*; cf. Hittite *Khatti* + -ITE[1], r. earlier *Hethite* (cf. Vulgate *Hethaeī*)]

hive (hīv), *n., v.,* **hived, hiving.** —*n.* **1.** an artificial shelter for honeybees; a beehive. **2.** the bees inhabiting a hive. **3.** something resembling a beehive in structure or use. **4.** a place swarming with busy occupants: *a hive of industry.* **5.** a swarming or teeming multitude. —*v.t.* **6.** to gather into or cause to enter a hive. **7.** to shelter as in a hive. **8.** to store up in a hive. **9.** to lay up for future use or enjoyment. —*v.i.* **10.** to enter a hive. **11.** to live together in a hive. [ME; OE *hyf.* Cf. Icel. *hūfr* ship's hull] —**hive′less,** *adj.* —**hive′like′,** *adj.*

hives (hīvz), *n.* any of various eruptive diseases of the skin, as the wheals of urticaria. [orig. Scot.]

H.J., (L *hic jacet*) here lies.

H.J.S., (L *hic jacet sepultus*) here lies buried.

hl., hectoliter.

hm., hectometer.

H.M., His (or Her) Majesty.

H.M.S., **1.** His, or Her, Majesty's Service. **2.** His, or Her, Majesty's Ship.

H.M.S. Pinafore, an operetta (1878) by Gilbert and Sullivan.

ho (hō), *interj.* **1.** an exclamation of surprise, exultation, etc., or, when repeated, derisive laughter. **2.** a call to attract attention (sometimes specially used after a word denoting a destination): *westward ho!* [ME; c. Icel. *hō*]

Ho, *Chem.* holmium.

ho·ac·tzin (hō ăk′tsĭn), *n.* hoatzin.

Hoang-ho (hwäng′hō′; *Chin.* -hü′), *n.* Hwang Ho.

hoar (hōr), *adj.* **1.** gray or white with age. **2.** gray-haired with age; old. **3.** gray or white, as with frost. —*n.* **4.** hoariness. **5.** a hoary coating or appearance. **6.** hoarfrost. [ME *hor*, OE *hār*, c. G *hehr* august, sublime]

hoard (hōrd), *n.* **1.** an accumulation of something for preservation or future use: *a hoard of money.* —*v.t.* **2.** to accumulate for preservation or future use. —*v.i.* **3.** to accumulate money, food, or the like. [ME *hord(e),* OE *hord,* c. OHG *hort* treasure] —**hoard′er,** *n.* —**Syn. 2.** accumulate, lay up, collect; store, save. —**Ant. 2.** scatter, disperse.

hoard·ing[1] (hōr′dĭng), *n.* **1.** act of one who hoards. **2.** (*pl.*) that which is hoarded. [f. HOARD + -ING[1]]

hoard·ing[2] (hōr′dĭng), *n. Brit.* **1.** a temporary fence enclosing a building during erection. **2.** a billboard. [der. obs. *hoard,* n., appar. t. MD: m. *horde* hurdle. Cf. obs. F *hourd* scaffolding]

Hoare (hōr), *n.* **Sir Samuel John Gurney** (gûr′nĭ), born 1880, British statesman.

hoar·frost (hōr′frôst′, -frŏst′), *n.* frost (def. 3).

hoar·hound (hōr′hound′), *n.* horehound.

hoarse (hōrs), *adj.,* **hoarser, hoarsest. 1.** having a vocal tone characterized by weakness of intensity and excessive breathiness; husky. **2.** having a raucous voice. **3.** making a harsh, low sound. [ME *hoors,* appar. t. Scand.; cf. Icel. *hāss;* r. ME *hoos,* OE *hās,* c. LG *hēs*] —**hoarse′ly,** *adv.* —**hoarse′ness,** *n.* —**Syn. 1.** gruff, harsh, grating.

hoar·y (hōr′ĭ), *adj.,* **hoarier, hoariest. 1.** gray or white with age. **2.** ancient or venerable. **3.** gray or white. —**hoar′i·ness,** *n.*

ho·at·zin (hō ăt′sĭn), *n.* a South American crested bird, *Opisthocomus hoazin,* remarkable for claws on its wings. Also, **hoactzin.** [native name]

hoax (hōks), *n.* **1.** a humorous or mischievous deception, esp. a practical joke. —*v.t.* **2.** to deceive by a hoax. [appar. contr. of *hocus*] —**hoax′er,** *n.*

hob[1] (hŏb), *n.* **1.** a projection or shelf at the back or side of a fireplace. **2.** a rounded peg or pin used as a target in certain games, as quoits. **3.** any of these games. [var. of obs. *hub* hob (in a fireplace); ? same as HUB]

hob[2] (hŏb), *n.* **1.** a hobgoblin or elf. **2.** *Colloq.* mischief: *to play hob.* [ME *Hob,* for Robert, or Robin, man's name]

Ho·bart (hō′bärt, -bərt), *n.* a seaport in and the capital of Tasmania, in the S part. 67,900 (est. 1941).

Hob·be·ma (hŏb′ə mä), *n.* **Meindert** (mīn′dərt), c1638–1709, Dutch landscape painter.

Hobbes (hŏbz), *n.* **Thomas,** 1588–1679, British philosopher.

Hob·bism (hŏb′ĭz əm), *n.* the doctrines of Hobbes, who advocated unreserved submission on the part of the subject to the will of the sovereign in all things.

hob·ble (hŏb′əl), *v.,* **-bled, -bling,** *n.* —*v.i.* **1.** to walk lamely; limp. **2.** to proceed irregularly and haltingly: *hobbling verse.* —*v.t.* **3.** to cause to limp. **4.** to fasten together the legs of (a horse, etc.) so as to prevent free motion. **5.** to embarrass; impede; perplex. —*n.* **6.** act of hobbling; an uneven, halting gait; a limp. **7.** a rope, strap, etc., used to hobble an animal. **8.** *Dial.* or *Colloq.* an awkward or difficult situation. [ME *hobelen;* appar. akin to *hob* protuberance, uneven ground. Cf. d. HG *hoppeln* jolt] —**hob′bler,** *n.* —**hob′bling,** *adj.* —**hob′bling·ly,** *adv.*

hob·ble·bush (hŏb′əl boosh′), *n.* a caprifoliaceous shrub, *Viburnum alnifolium,* with white flowers and berrylike fruit.

hob·ble·de·hoy (hŏb′əl dĭ hoi′), *n.* **1.** an adolescent boy. **2.** an awkward, clumsy boy. [orig. uncert.]

hobble skirt, a woman's skirt which is so narrow at the bottom that it restricts her ability to walk naturally.

hob·by[1] (hŏb′ĭ), *n., pl.* **-bies. 1.** a favorite occupation, topic, etc., pursued for amusement. **2.** *Dial.* a small or medium-sized horse. **3.** a child's hobbyhorse. [ME *hoby, hobyn,* prob. for *Robin,* or *Robert,* man's name. Cf. DOBBIN, HOB[2]. Def. 2 was original meaning, whence def. 3 and *hobbyhorse.* Def. 1 is short for *hobbyhorse*]

hob·by[2] (hŏb′ĭ), *n., pl.* **-bies.** a small Old World falcon, *Falco subbuteo,* formerly flown at such small game as larks. [ME, t. OF: m. *hobet,* dim. of *hobe* hobby (falcon), prob. ult. der. L *albus* white (as applied to a special kind of falcon), ? also b. with OF *hober* hop]

hob·by·horse (hŏb′ĭ hôrs′), *n.* **1.** a stick with a horse's head, or a rocking horse, ridden by children. **2.** a figure of a horse, attached to the waist of a performer in a morris dance, pantomime, etc.

hob·gob·lin (hŏb′gŏb′lĭn), *n.* **1.** anything causing superstitious fear; a bogy. **2.** a mischievous goblin. **3.** (*cap.*) Puck; Robin Goodfellow. [f. HOB[2] + GOBLIN]

hob·nail (hŏb′nāl′), *n.* a short, large-headed nail for protecting the soles of heavy boots and shoes. [f. HOB[1] + NAIL]

hob·nailed (hŏb′nāld′), *adj.* **1.** furnished with hobnails. **2.** rustic or clownish.

hob·nob (hŏb′nŏb′), *v.i.,* **-nobbed, -nobbing. 1.** to associate on very friendly terms. **2.** to drink together. [earlier *hab* or *nab* alternately, lit., have or have not]

ho·bo (hō′bō), *n., pl.* **-bos, -boes.** *U.S.* **1.** a tramp or vagrant. **2.** a wandering worker. [rhyming formation, ? based on *beau* fop, used as (sarcastic) word of greeting, e.g. in *hey, bo!*] —**ho′bo·ism,** *n.*

Ho·bo·ken (hō′bō kən), *n.* a seaport in NE New Jersey, opposite New York City. 50,676 (1950).

Hob·son's choice (hŏb′sənz), the choice of taking either the thing offered or nothing. [after Thomas *Hobson,* about 1544–1631, of Cambridge, England, who rented horses, and obliged each customer to take in his turn the horse nearest the stable door or none at all]

Hoch·hei·mer (hōkh′hī′mər; *Ger.* hōкн′-), *n.* a Rhine wine produced at Hochheim, near Mainz, Germany.

hock[1] (hŏk), *n.* **1.** the joint in the hind leg of the horse, etc., above the fetlock joint, corresponding to the ankle in man but raised from the ground and protruding backward when bent. See illus. under **horse. 2.** a corresponding joint in a fowl. —*v.t.* **3.** to hamstring. [ME *hoch, hogh, howh,* OE *hōh* hock, heel. Cf. HEEL[1]]

hock[2] (hŏk), *n. Chiefly Brit.* any white Rhine wine. [short for *Hockamore* HOCHHEIMER]

hock[3] (hŏk), *v.t., n. U.S. Slang.* pawn. [t. D: m. *hok* hovel, prison, debt]

hock·ey (hŏk′ĭ), *n.* **1.** a game in which opposing sides seek with clubs curved at one end to drive a ball or disk into their opponent's goal. **2.** the club so used (**hockey stick**). [der. *hock* stick with hook at end, var. of HOOK]

ho·cus (hō′kəs), *v.t.,* **-cused, -cusing,** or (*esp. Brit.*) **-cussed, -cussing. 1.** to play a trick on; hoax; cheat. **2.** to stupefy with drugged liquor. **3.** to drug (liquor).

ho·cus-po·cus (hō′kəs pō′kəs), *n., v.,* **-cused, -cusing,** or (*esp. Brit.*) **-cussed, -cussing.** —*n.* **1.** a formula used in conjuring or incantation. **2.** a juggler's trick; sleight of hand. **3.** trickery or deception. —*v.t.* **4.** to play tricks on or with. —*v.i.* **5.** to perform tricks. [orig. jugglers' jargon, simulating Latin]

hod (hŏd), *n.* **1.** a portable trough for carrying mortar, bricks, etc., fixed crosswise on top of a pole and carried on the shoulder. **2.** a coal scuttle. [cf. MD *hodde* basket, c. HG *hotte,* OF *hotte* (t. G), d. E *hot* (t. OF) pannier]

hod carrier, a laborer who uses a hod.

Ho·dei·da (hō dě′ĭ dä), *n.* the chief seaport of Yemen, in SW Arabia, on the Red Sea. ab. 50,000.

Hodg·en·ville (hŏj′en vĭl), *n.* a town in central Kentucky: birthplace of Abraham Lincoln. 1695 (1950).

hodge·podge (hŏj′pŏj′), *n.* a heterogenous mixture; a jumble. [var. of HOTCHPOTCH]

hod·man (hŏd′mən), *n., pl.* **-men.** hod carrier.

hoe (hō), *n., v.,* **hoed, hoeing.** —*n.* **1.** a long-handled implement with a thin, flat blade usually set transversely, used to break up the surface of the ground, destroy weeds, etc. —*v.t.* **2.** to dig, scrape, weed, cultivate, etc., with a hoe. —*v.i.* **3.** to use a hoe. [ME *howe,* t. OF: m. *houe,* t. Gmc.; cf. G *haue*] —**ho′er,** *n.* —**hoe′like′,** *adj.*

hoe·cake (hō′kāk′), *n. Southern U.S.* a cake made with corn meal, originally baked on a hoe.

Hoek van Hol·land (hōōk vän hŏl′änt), Dutch name of **Hook of Holland.**

Ho·fer (hō′fər), *n.* **Andreas** (än drā′äs), 1767–1810, Tyrolese patriot.

Hoff·mann (hôf′män), *n.* **Ernst Theodor Wilhelm** (ěrnst tā′ō dōr′ vĭl′hělm), 1776–1822, German writer, musician, painter, and jurist.

A, B, Dutch hoes; C, Warren hoe; D, Hoe and rake combination; E, Common garden hoe; F, Weeding hoe

Hoes

Hof·mann (hŏf′mən; *Pol.* hôf′män), *n.* **Josef** (jō′zəf), born 1876, U.S. pianist and composer, born in Poland.

hog (hŏg, hôg), *n.*, *v.*, **hogged, hogging.** —*n.* **1.** an omnivorous nonruminant mammal of the family *Suidae*, suborder *Artiodactyla*, and order *Ungulata*; a pig, sow, or boar; a swine. **2.** a domesticated swine weighing more than 120 pounds, raised for market. **3.** *Colloq.* a selfish, gluttonous, or filthy person. —*v.t.* **4.** *Slang.* to appropriate selfishly; take more than one's share of. **5.** to arch (the back) upward like that of a hog. **6.** to cut (a horse's mane) short. —*v.i.* **7.** to droop at both ends, as a ship. [ME; OE *hogg*, t. OBritish; cf. Welsh *hwch* sow] —**hog′like′,** *adj.*

ho·gan (hō′gŏn), *n.* a Navaho Indian dwelling, a structure of posts and branches covered with earth.

Ho·garth (hō′gärth), *n.* **William,** 1697–1764, British painter and engraver. —**Ho·garth′i·an,** *adj.*

hog·back (hŏg′băk′, hôg′-), *n. Geol.* a long, sharply crested ridge, generally formed of steeply inclined strata that are especially resistant to erosion.

hog cholera, a specific, acute, highly fatal, highly contagious disease of swine caused by a filterable virus.

hog·fish (hŏg′fĭsh′, hôg′-), *n.*, *pl.* **-fishes,** (*esp. collectively*) **-fish.** any of various fishes, as *Lachnolaemus maximus*, a labroid food fish of the Florida coast and the West Indies, or *Percina caprodes*, a darter of American lakes and streams, or *Orthopristis chrysopterus*, one of the grunts of the southern coasts of the U.S.

Hogg (hŏg), *n.* **James,** ("the Ettrick Shepherd") 1770–1835, Scottish poet.

hog·gish (hŏg′ĭsh, hôg′ĭsh), *adj.* **1.** like or befitting a hog. **2.** selfish; gluttonous; filthy. —**hog′gish·ly,** *adv.* —**hog′gish·ness,** *n.*

hog·nose snake (hŏg′nōz′, hôg′-), any of the harmless American snakes constituting the genus *Heterodon*, notable for their hoglike snouts and their curious actions and contortions when disturbed.

hog·nut (hŏg′nŭt′, hôg′-), *n.* **1.** the nut of the brown hickory, *Carya glabra*. **2.** the tree itself. **3.** the pignut. **4.** the earthnut of Europe, *Conopodium denudatum*.

hog peanut, a twining fabaceous plant, *Amphicarpa bracteata*, with pods which ripen in or on the ground.

hogs·head (hŏgz′hĕd′, hôgz′-), *n.* **1.** a large cask of varying capacities depending on locality or purpose, esp. one containing from 63 to 140 gallons. **2.** a varying unit of liquid measure, esp. one containing 63 wine gallons. [ME *hoggeshed*, lit., hog's head; unexplained]

hog-tie (hŏg′tī′, hôg′-), *v.t.*, **-tied, -tying.** to tie as a hog is tied, with all four feet together.

Hogue (ōg), *n.* **La** (là). See **La Hogue.**

hog·wash (hŏg′wŏsh′, -wôsh′, hôg′-), *n.* **1.** refuse given to hogs; swill. **2.** any worthless stuff.

Hoh·en·lin·den (hō′ən lĭn′dən), *n.* a village in S Germany, in Bavaria, near Munich: French victory over the Austrians, 1800.

Hoh·en·lo·he (hō′ən lō′ə), *n.* a German princely family, fl. 12–19th centuries.

Hoh·en·stau·fen (hō′ən shtou′fən), *n.* a German princely family, founded in the 11th century, which ruled Germany 1138–1208 and 1215–54, and Sicily 1194–1266.

Hoh·en·zol·lern (hō′ən zŏl′ərn; *Ger.* hō′ən tsŏl′ərn), *n.* a German princely family which attained prominence after 1415 as rulers of Brandenburg, Prussia, which became the kingdom of Prussia in 1701: rulers of the German Empire, 1871–1918, and of Rumania, 1866–1947.

hoicks (hoiks), *interj.* a cry used to incite hounds in hunting. Also, **hoick** (hoik).

hoi·den (hoi′dən), *n.*, *adj.* hoyden.

hoi pol·loi (hoi′ pəloi′), *Greek.* the common people; the masses (sometimes preceded pleonastically by *the*).

hoist (hoist), *v.t.* **1.** to raise or lift, esp. by some mechanical appliance: *to hoist sail.* —*n.* **2.** an apparatus for hoisting, as an elevator. **3.** (esp. in England) a freight elevator. **4.** act of hoisting; a lift. **5.** *Naut.* **a.** the vertical length of any sail other than a course. **b.** the perpendicular height of a sail or flag. [later form of *hoise*; cf. G *hissen*] —**hoist′er,** *n.* —**Syn. 1.** See **raise.**

hoi·ty-toi·ty (hoi′tĭ toi′tĭ), *interj.* **1.** an exclamation denoting somewhat contemptuous surprise. —*adj.* **2.** giddy; flighty. **3.** assuming; haughty. —*n.* **4.** giddy behavior. **5.** haughtiness. Also, **highty-tighty** for 1–3. [redupl. deriv. of obs. *hoit*, v., to romp, riot]

ho·key-po·key (hō′kĭ pō′kĭ), *n.* **1.** hocus-pocus; trickery. **2.** ice cream sold by street vendors.

Ho·kiang (hŭ′jyäng′), *n.* a province in NE China, in Manchuria. 1,604,600 pop. (1946); 47,730 sq. mi.

Hok·kai·do (hŏk′kī dô′), *n.* a large island in N Japan. 3,488,013 pop. (1946); 30,333 sq. mi. Formerly, *Yezo.*

Ho·ko·da·te (hō′kō dä′tĕ), *n.* a seaport in N Japan, on Hokkaido island. 187,367 (1946).

ho·kum (hō′kəm), *n. Slang.* **1.** nonsense; bunk. **2.** elements of low comedy introduced into a play or the like for the laughs they may bring. **3.** sentimental or pathetic matter of an elementary or stereotyped kind introduced into a play or the like. [b. HOCUS-POCUS and BUNKUM]

Ho·ku·sai (hō′kŏo sī′), *n.* **Katsushika** (kä′tsŏo shē′kä), 1760–1849, Japanese painter and illustrator.

Hol·bein (hŏl′bīn; *Ger.* hôl′-), *n.* **1. Hans** (häns), ("the elder") c1460–1524, German painter. **2.** his son, **Hans,** ("the younger") 1497?–1543, German painter.

HOLC, Home Owners' Loan Corporation.

hold[1] (hōld), *v.*, **held; held** or (*Archaic*) **holden; holding;** *n.* —*v.t.* **1.** to have or keep in the hand; keep fast; retain: *to be held until called for.* **2.** to bear, sustain, or support with the hand, arms, etc., or by any means. **3.** to keep in a specified state, relation, etc.: *to hold the enemy in check.* **4.** to engage in; preside over; carry on; pursue; observe or celebrate: *to hold a meeting.* **5.** to keep back from action; hinder or restrain. **6.** to have the ownership or use of; keep as one's own; occupy: *to hold office.* **7.** to contain or be capable of containing: *this basket holds two bushels.* **8.** to have or keep in the mind; think or believe; entertain: *to hold a belief.* **9.** to regard or consider: *to hold a person responsible.* **10.** to decide legally. **11.** to regard with affection: *to hold one dear.* **12.** to keep forcibly, as against an adversary. —*v.i.* **13.** to remain or continue in a specified state, relation, etc.: *to hold still.* **14.** to remain fast; adhere; cling: *the anchor holds.* **15.** to keep or maintain a grasp on something. **16.** to maintain one's position against opposition; continue in resistance. **17.** to hold property by some tenure; derive title (fol. by *from* or *of*). **18.** to remain attached, faithful, or steadfast: *to hold to one's purpose.* **19.** to remain valid; be in force: *the rule does not hold.* **20.** to keep going on; proceed. **21.** to refrain or forbear (usually in the imperative). **22.** Some special verb phrases are:

hold or **keep back, 1.** to restrain or check. **2.** to cancel.

hold forth, 1. to put forward to view; propose. **2.** to harangue.

hold in, 1. to restrain, check, or curb. **2.** to restrain or contain oneself.

hold off, 1. to keep aloof or at a distance. **2.** to refrain from action.

hold on, 1. to keep fast hold on something. **2.** to continue; keep going. **3.** *Colloq.* to stop or halt (chiefly in the imperative).

hold one's own, to maintain one's position or condition.

hold one's tongue or **one's peace,** to keep silent; cease or refrain from speaking.

hold out, 1. to offer or present. **2.** to extend or stretch forth. **3.** to keep out; keep back. **4.** to continue to endure or resist; last. **5.** to refuse to yield or submit. **6.** *U.S. Slang.* to keep back something expected or due.

hold over, 1. to keep for future consideration or action; postpone. **2.** *Music.* to prolong (a tone) from one measure to the next. **3.** to remain in possession or in office beyond the regular term.

hold up, 1. to keep in an erect position. **2.** to present to notice; exhibit; display. **3.** to stop. **4.** to stop by force in order to rob. **5.** to support or uphold: *gold holds up its price.* **6.** to keep up; maintain one's position, condition, etc.; endure. **7.** to stop; cease.

hold water, 1. to retain water; not let water run through. **2.** to prove sound, tenable, or valid.

—*n.* **23.** act of holding fast by a grasp of the hand or by some other physical means; grasp; grip: *take hold.* **24.** something to hold a thing by, as a handle; something to grasp for support. **25.** a thing that holds fast or supports something else. **26.** a controlling force, or dominating influence: *to have a hold on a person.* **27.** *Music.* a pause (symbol). **28.** a prison or prison cell. **29.** a receptacle for something. **30.** *Archaic.* a fortified place, or stronghold. [ME *holden*, OE *h(e)aldan*, c. G *halten*] —**Syn. 6.** possess, own. See **have. 7.** See **contain. 9.** deem, esteem.

hold[2] (hōld), *n. Naut.* the interior of a ship below the deck, esp. where the cargo is stowed. [var. of HOLE, c. D *hol* hole, hold]

hold·all (hōld′ôl′), *n.* **1.** *Chiefly Brit.* a portable case or bag for miscellaneous articles, used by soldiers, travelers, etc. **2.** a container of odds and ends.

hold·back (hōld′băk′), *n.* **1.** the iron or strap on the shaft of a vehicle to which the breeching of the harness is attached, enabling the horse to hold back or to back the vehicle. **2.** a restraint; check.

hold·er (hōl′dər), *n.* **1.** something to hold a thing with. **2.** one who has the ownership, possession, or use of something; an owner; a tenant. **3.** *Law.* one who has the legal right to enforce a negotiable instrument.

hold·fast (hōld′făst′, -fäst′), *n.* something used to hold or secure a thing in place; a catch, hook, or clamp.

hold·ing (hōl′dĭng), *n.* **1.** act of one who or that which holds. **2.** land, or a piece of land, held, esp. of a superior. **3.** (*often pl.*) property owned, esp. stocks, bonds, and real estate.

holding company, *Finance.* **1.** a company controlling, or able to control, other companies by virtue of stock ownership in these companies. **2.** a company which owns stocks or securities of other companies, deriving income from them.

hold·o·ver (hōld′ō′vər), *n. U.S. Colloq.* something which remains behind from a former period.

hold·up (hōld′ŭp′), *n. U.S. Colloq.* **1.** a forcible stopping and robbing of a person. **2.** anything like this.

hole (hōl), *n.*, *v.*, **holed, holing.** —*n.* **1.** an opening through anything; an aperture. **2.** a hollow place in a solid body or mass; a cavity: *a hole in the ground.* **3.** the excavated habitation of an animal; a burrow. **4.** a small, dingy, or mean abode. **5.** a dungeon. **6.** *Colloq.* an embarrassing position or predicament: *to find oneself in a hole.* **7.** *U.S.* a cove or small harbor. **8.** *Colloq.* a fault or flaw: *to pick holes in a plan.* **9.** a deep, still place in a stream: *a swimming hole.* **10.** *Sports.*

a. a small cavity, into which a marble, ball, or the like is to be played. **b.** a score made by so playing. —*v.t.* **11.** to make a hole or holes in. **12.** to put or drive into a hole. **13.** *Golf.* to drive the ball into (a hole). **14.** to bore (a tunnel, etc.). —*v.i.* **15.** to make a hole or holes. **16.** *Golf.* to drive the ball into a hole (often fol. by *out*). **17.** to go into a hole; retire for the winter, as a hibernating animal (usually fol. by *up*). [ME; OE *hol* hole, cave, den, orig. neut. of *hol*, adj., c. G *hohl* hollow] —**hole′less**, adj. —**hole′y**, adj.

—**Syn. 1, 2.** HOLE, CAVITY, EXCAVATION refer to a hollow place in anything. HOLE is the common word for this idea: *a hole in turf.* CAVITY is a more formal or scientific term for a hollow within the body or in a substance, whether with or without a passage outward: *a cavity in a tooth, the cranial cavity.* An EXCAVATION is an extended hole made by digging out or removing material: *an excavation before the construction of a building.*

hol·i·but (hŏl′ə bət), n., pl. **-buts,** (esp. collectively) **-but.** halibut.

hol·i·day (hŏl′ə dā′), n. **1.** a day fixed by law or custom on which ordinary business is suspended in commemoration of some event or in honor of some person, etc. **2.** any day of exemption from labor. **3.** (often pl.) *Chiefly Brit.* a period of cessation from work, or of recreation; a vacation. **4.** *Archaic.* holy day. —adj. **5.** pertaining to a festival; joyous: *a holiday mood.* **6.** suited only to a holiday. —*v.i.* **7.** *Brit.* to vacation: *they are holidaying at the seaside.* [ME; OE *hāligdæg* holy day]

ho·li·ly (hō′lə lĭ), adv. **1.** piously or devoutly. **2.** sacredly. [ME; OE *hāliglīce*, f. *hālig* HOLY + -*līce* -LY]

ho·li·ness (hō′lĭ nĭs), n. **1.** state or character of being holy; sanctity. **2.** (cap.) a title of the Pope, and formerly also of other high ecclesiastical dignitaries, etc. (prec. by *his* or *your*). [ME *holynesse*, OE *hālignes*] —**Syn. 1.** godliness, saintliness; piety; sacredness.

Hol·ins·hed (hŏl′ĭnz hĕd′, hŏl′ĭn shĕd′), n. **Raphael,** died c1580, British chronicler.

Hol·land (hŏl′ənd), n. **1.** a medieval county and province on the North Sea, now included in North and South Holland provinces of the Netherlands. **2.** the Netherlands.

hol·lan·daise sauce (hŏl′ən dāz′), a yellow sauce of eggs, lemon juice or vinegar, butter, and seasonings.

Hol·land·er (hŏl′ən dər), n. a native of the Netherlands; a Dutchman.

Hol·lands gin (hŏl′əndz), gin originally made in Holland, distinguished from other gins by the juniper being mixed in the mash.

hol·ler (hŏl′ər), Dial. —*v.i.* **1.** to cry aloud; shout. —*v.t.* **2.** to shout (something). —n. **3.** a loud cry of pain, surprise, to attract attention, etc. [var. of HOLLO]

hol·lo (hŏl′ō, hə lō′), interj., n., pl. **-los,** v., **-loed, -loing.** —interj. **1.** an exclamation to call attention or in answer to one who hails. —n. **2.** a cry of "hollo"; a shout. **3.** a shout of exultation. —*v.i.* **4.** to cry "hollo"; shout. —*v.t.* **5.** to shout (something). **6.** to cry "hollo" to. Also, **hallo, halloa, hollo′a, hul′loa, hullo.**

hol·low (hŏl′ō), adj. **1.** having a hole or cavity within; not solid; empty: *a hollow ball.* **2.** having a depression or concavity: *a hollow surface.* **3.** sunken, as the cheeks or eyes. **4.** (of sound) not resonant; dull, muffled, or deep: *a hollow voice.* **5.** without substantial or real worth; vain: *a hollow victory.* **6.** insincere or false: *hollow compliments.* **7.** hungry. —n. **8.** an empty space within anything; a hole; a depression or cavity. **9.** a valley: *Sleepy Hollow.* —*v.t.* **10.** to make hollow; form by making hollow (often fol. by *out*). —*v.i.* **11.** to become hollow. —adv. **12.** in a hollow manner. **13.** *Colloq.* utterly (often prec. by *all* for emphasis): *to beat someone all hollow.* [ME *hol(o)u, holw(e)*, n., adj., OE *holh* hollow (place)] —**hol′low·ly**, adv. —**hol′low·ness**, n.

hol·low-eyed (hŏl′ō īd′), adj. having sunken eyes.

hol·low·ware (hŏl′ō wâr′), n. silver dishes, as serving dishes, tea service, etc., having some depth (distinguished from *flatware*).

hol·ly (hŏl′ĭ), n., pl. **-lies. 1.** any of the trees or shrubs of the genus *Ilex*, esp. those species having glossy, spiny-edged leaves and small, whitish flowers succeeded by bright-red berries. **2.** the foliage and berries, much used for decoration, esp. during the Christmas season. [ME *holig, holi*, OE *holegn* (with loss of -*n*); akin to D and G *hulst*, F *houx*]

hol·ly·hock (hŏl′ĭ hŏk′, -hôk′), n. **1.** a tall malvaceous plant, common in cultivation, *Althaea rosea*, having showy flowers of various colors. **2.** the flower itself. [ME *holihoc*, f. *holi* HOLY + *hoc* mallow, OE *hocc*]

holly oak, the holm oak.

Hol·ly·wood (hŏl′ĭ wŏŏd′), n. a part of Los Angeles, California: center of American motion-picture industry.

holm[1] (hōm), n. *Chiefly Brit. Dial. and Scot.* **1.** a low, flat tract of land beside a river or stream. **2.** a small island, esp. one in a river or lake. [ME and OE, t. Scand.; cf. Icel. *holmr* islet]

holm[2] (hōm), n. **1.** the holm oak. **2.** *Brit. Dial.* the holly. [ME; dissimilated var. of *holn*, OE *holen* holly (dental + dental became dental + labial)]

Hol·man-Hunt (hōl′mən hŭnt′), n. **William,** 1827–1910, British painter.

Holmes (hōmz), n. **1. John Haynes,** born 1879, U.S. clergyman. **2. Oliver Wendell,** 1809–94, U.S. author and physician. **3.** his son, **Oliver Wendell,** 1841–1935,

associate justice of the U.S. Supreme Court, 1902–32. **4. Sherlock,** a detective in many mystery stories by Sir Arthur Conan Doyle.

hol·mic (hōl′mĭk), adj. *Chem.* of or containing holmium (Ho+3).

hol·mi·um (hōl′mĭ əm), n. *Chem.* a rare-earth element found in gadolinite. *Symbol:* Ho; *at. wt.:* 164.94; *at. no.:* 67. [NL; named after *Stockholm*, in Sweden]

holm oak, an evergreen oak, *Quercus ilex*, of southern Europe, with foliage resembling that of the holly.

holo-, a word element meaning "whole" or "entire," as in *holocaust.* [t. Gk., comb. form of *hólos*]

hol·o·blas·tic (hŏl′ə blăs′tĭk), adj. *Embryol.* (of eggs which undergo total cleavage) wholly germinal (opposed to *meroblastic*).

hol·o·caine (hŏl′ə kān′), n. **1.** *Chem.* a colorless crystalline basic compound, $C_{18}H_{22}N_2O_2$, used as a local anesthetic. **2.** *Pharm.* a local anesthetic resembling cocaine in its action, used chiefly for the eye.

hol·o·caust (hŏl′ə kôst′), n. **1.** great or wholesale destruction of life, esp. by fire. **2.** an offering or sacrifice devoted wholly to burning; a burnt offering. [t. LL: s. *holocaustum*, t. Gk.: m. *holókauston* a burnt offering, prop. neut. of *holókaustos* burnt whole] —**hol′o·caus′tic,** adj.

hol·o·cene (hŏl′ə sēn′), adj. *Geol.* designating or pertaining to the Human or Recent era. [f. HOLO- + -CENE]

Hol·o·fer·nes (hŏl′ə fûr′nēz), n. *Bible.* a general of Nebuchadnezzar killed by Judith in the apocryphal Book of Judith.

hol·o·graph (hŏl′ə gräf′, -gräf′), adj. **1.** wholly written by the person in whose name it appears: *a holograph letter.* —n. **2.** a holograph writing. [t. LL: s. *holographus*, t. Gk.: m. *hológraphos*]

hol·o·graph·ic (hŏl′ə gräf′ĭk), adj. *Law.* (of wills) totally in the handwriting of the testator and therefore not requiring attestation of witnesses.

hol·o·he·dral (hŏl′ə hē′drəl), adj. (of a crystal) having all the planes or faces required by the maximum symmetry of the system to which it belongs. [f. HOLO- + s. Gk. *hédra* seat, base + -AL[1]]

hol·o·phote (hŏl′ə fōt′), n. an apparatus by which practically all the light from a lighthouse lamp, etc., is made available for illumination by reflection or refraction or both. [f. HOLO- + m.s. Gk. *phôs* light] —**hol′-o·pho′tal,** adj.

hol·o·phras·tic (hŏl′ə frăs′tĭk), adj. expressing a whole phrase or sentence in a single word. [f. HOLO- + m.s. Gk. *phrastikós* suited for expressing]

hol·o·thu·ri·an (hŏl′ə thŏŏr′ĭ ən), n. any of the *Holothuroidea.* [f. s. NL *Holothūria* genus name (t. L, t. Gk.: m. *holothoúria*) + -AN]

Hol·o·thu·roi·de·a (hŏl′ə thŏŏ roi′dĭ ə), n.pl. a class of echinoderms known as sea cucumbers, having a long leathery body and tentacles around the anterior end.

holp (hōlp), v. *Archaic.* pt. of **help.**

hol·pen (hōl′pən), v. *Archaic.* pp. of **help.**

Hol·stein (hōl′stīn, -stēn for 1; hōl′stīn; *Ger.* hôl′shtīn for 2), n. **1.** one of a breed of large, black-and-white dairy cattle, originating in North Holland and Friesland. Also, **Hol·stein-Frie·sian** (hōl′stīn frē′zhən, -stēn-). **2.** a district in N Germany at the base of the peninsula of Jutland: a former duchy. See **Schleswig-Holstein.**

hol·ster (hōl′stər), n. a leather case for a pistol, attached to a belt or a saddle. [var. of *hulster*, t. Sw.: m. *hôlster*, whence also D *holster*; akin to OE *heolstor* cover] —**hol′stered,** adj.

Holstein, *Bos taurus*
(4 ft. high at the shoulder)

holt (hōlt), n. *Chiefly Poetic.* **1.** a wood or grove. **2.** a wooded hill. [ME *holte*, OE *holt*, c. G *holz* wood]

ho·lus-bo·lus (hō′ləs bō′ləs), adv. *Colloq.* all at once.

ho·ly (hō′lĭ), adj., **-lier, -liest,** n., pl. **-lies.** —adj. **1.** specially recognized or declared sacred by religious use or authority; consecrated: *a holy day.* **2.** dedicated or devoted to the service of God, the church, or religion: *a holy man.* **3.** saintly or godly; pious or devout. **4.** of religious purity, exaltation, solemnity, etc.: *a holy love.* **5.** entitled to worship or profound religious reverence because of divine character or origin, or connection with God or divinity: *holy Bible.* **6.** religious: *holy rites.* —n. **7.** a place of worship; a sacred place. **8.** that which is holy. [ME *holi*, OE *hālig, hāleg*, c. D and G *heilig*, akin to HALE[2] and HEAL]

—**Syn. 1.** blessed. HOLY, SACRED, CONSECRATED, HALLOWED imply possession of a sanctity which is the object of religious veneration. HOLY refers to the divine, that which has its sanctity directly from God or as connected with Him: *Remember the Sabbath day to keep it holy.* That which is SACRED, while sometimes accepted as entitled to religious veneration, may have its sanctity from human authority: *a sacred oath.* That which is CONSECRATED is specially or formally dedicated to some religious use: *a life consecrated to service.* That which is HALLOWED has been made holy by being worshiped: *a hallowed shrine.*

Holy Alliance, a league formed by the principal sovereigns of Europe (without the Pope and Sultan) in 1815 after the fall of Napoleon, with the professed object of Christian brotherhood, but the practical object of repressing revolution.

Holy Bible, Bible (def. 1).

Holy City, a city regarded as particularly sacred by the adherents of a religious faith, as Jerusalem by Jews and Christians, Mecca and Medina by Mohammedans, Benares by Hindus, Rome by Roman Catholics, etc.

Holy Communion. See communion (def. 5b).

Holy Cross, Mountain of the, a peak in central Colorado, in the Sawatch Range: snow-filled cross-shaped crevasses; a national monument (2 sq. mi.). 13,798 ft.

holy day, a consecrated day or religious festival, esp. one other than Sunday.

Holy Father, a title of the Pope.

Holy Ghost, the third person of the Trinity.

Holy Grail, grail.

Holy Innocents' Day, Dec. 28, a day of religious observance commemorating the slaughter of the children of Bethlehem by Herod's order; Childermas. Matt. 2:16.

Holy Land, Palestine.

Holy Office, a congregation of the Roman Catholic Church entrusted with matters pertaining to the faith and doctrine of the Church. Cf. **inquisition** (def. 6).

holy of holies, 1. a place of special sacredness. 2. the inner and smaller chamber of the Jewish tabernacle and temple entered only by the high priest only once a year.

Hol·yoke (hōl′yōk), n. a city in S Massachusetts, on the Connecticut river. 54,661 (1950).

holy orders, 1. the rite or sacrament of ordination. 2. the rank or status of an ordained Christian minister. 3. the major degrees or grades of the Christian ministry.

Holy Roman Empire, the empire in western and central Europe which began with the coronation of Otto the Great, king of Germany, as Roman emperor A.D. 962, and ended with the renunciation of the Roman imperial title by Francis II in 1806, regarded theoretically as the continuation of the Western Empire and as the temporal form of a universal dominion whose spiritual head was the Pope. It is sometimes regarded as originating with Charlemagne, who was crowned Roman emperor A.D. 800.

Holy Roman Empire, A.D. 1200

Holy Rood, 1. the cross on which Jesus died. 2. (l.c.) a crucifix, esp. one above a rood screen.

Holy Saturday, the Saturday in Holy Week.

Holy Scripture, scripture (def. 1).

Holy See, Rom. Cath. Ch. 1. the see of Rome; the office or jurisdiction of the Pope. 2. the papal court.

Holy Sepulcher, the sepulcher in which the body of Jesus lay between His burial and His resurrection.

Holy Spirit, the Holy Ghost.

ho·ly·stone (hō′lĭ stōn′), n., v., -stoned, -stoning. —n. 1. a soft sandstone used for scrubbing the decks of a ship. —v.t. 2. to scrub with a holystone.

Holy Thursday, 1. Ascension Day. 2. Rom. Cath. Ch. the Thursday in Holy Week; Maundy Thursday.

ho·ly·tide (hō′lĭ tīd′), n. Archaic. a holy season.

Holy Trinity, trinity (def. 1).

holy water, water blessed by a priest.

Holy Week, the week preceding Easter Sunday.

Holy Writ, the Scriptures.

hom·age (hŏm′ĭj, ŏm′-), n. 1. respect or reverence paid or rendered. 2. the formal acknowledgment by which a feudal tenant or vassal declared himself to be the man of his lord, owing him fealty and service. 3. the relation thus established of a vassal to his lord. 4. something done or given in acknowledgment or consideration of vassalage. [ME, t. OF, ult. der. LL homo vassal, L man] —Syn. 1. deference, obeisance; honor, tribute, praise. 2. allegiance, fealty.

hom·bre (ŏm′brĕ), n. Spanish. man.

hom·burg (hŏm′bûrg), n. a felt hat with a soft crown dented lengthwise and a partially rolled brim.

home (hōm), n., adj., adv., v., homed, homing. —n. 1. a house, apartment, or other shelter that is the fixed residence of a person, a family, or a household. 2. the place of one's domestic affections. 3. an institution for the homeless, sick, etc. 4. the dwelling place or retreat of an animal. 5. the place or region where something is native or most common. 6. any place of existence or refuge: a heavenly home. 7. one's native place or own country. 8. the goal. 9. Baseball. the plate at which the batter stands and which he must return to and touch after running around the bases, in order to score a run. 10. at home. a. in one's own house or country. b. in a situation familiar to one; at ease. c. prepared to receive social visits. —adj. 11. of, pertaining to, or connected with one's home or country; domestic. 12. that strikes home, or to the mark aimed at; to the point: a home thrust. —adv. 13. to, toward, or at home: to go home. 14. deep; to the heart; effectively and completely. 15. to the mark or point aimed at: to strike home. 16. Naut. all the way; as far as possible: to heave the hawser home. —v.i. 17. to go or return home. 18. to

have the home where specified. —v.t. 19. to bring or send home. 20. to provide with a home. [ME; OE hām home, dwelling, c. G heim] —Syn. 1. abode, dwelling, habitation; domicile, residence. See **house.**

home·bred (hōm′brĕd′), adj. 1. bred at home; native; indigenous; domestic. 2. unpolished; unsophisticated.

home-brew (hōm′broō′), n. beer or other beverage brewed at home, as for home consumption.

home economics, 1. the art and science of homemaking, including the purchase, preparation, and service of food for nutritionally balanced meals, the selection and construction of clothing, the choice and use of equipment and furnishings, the care and training of children, etc. 2. the teaching or study of homemaking, etc.

home·land (hōm′lănd′), n. one's native land.

home·less (hōm′lĭs), adj. 1. having no home. 2. affording no home: the homeless sea. —**home′less·ly,** adv. —**home′less·ness,** n.

home·like (hōm′līk′), adj. like or suggestive of home; familiar; comfortable. —**home′like′ness,** n. —Syn. See **simple.**

home·ly (hōm′lĭ), adj., -lier, -liest. 1. proper or suited to the home or to ordinary domestic life; plain; unpretentious: homely fare. 2. U.S. not good-looking; ugly. 3. not having elegance, refinement, or cultivation. —**home′li·ness,** n. —Syn. 1. See **simple.**

home·made (hōm′mād′), adj. made at home.

homeo-, a word element meaning "similar" or "like," as in homeomorphism. Also, **homoeo-, homoio-.** [t. Gk.: m. homoio-, comb. form of hómoios like]

Home Office, the department of the English government that manages internal affairs, roughly corresponding to the U.S. Dept. of the Interior.

ho·me·o·mor·phism (hō′mĭ ə môr′fĭz əm), n. similarity in crystalline form, but not necessarily in chemical composition. Also, **homoeomorphism.** [f. m.s. Gk. homoiómorphos of like form + -ISM] —**ho′me·o·mor′phous,** adj.

ho·me·o·path·ic (hō′mĭ ə păth′ĭk), adj. 1. of, pertaining to, or according to the principles of homeopathy. 2. practicing or advocating homeopathy. Also, **homoeopathic.** —**ho′me·o·path′i·cal·ly,** adv.

ho·me·op·a·thist (hō′mĭ ŏp′ə thĭst), n. one who practices or favors homeopathy. Also, **homoeopathist, ho·me·o·path** (hō′mĭ ə păth′).

ho·me·op·a·thy (hō′mĭ ŏp′ə thĭ), n. the method of treating disease by drugs, given in minute doses, which would produce in a healthy person symptoms similar to those of the disease (opposed to allopathy). Also, **homoeopathy.**

Ho·mer (hō′mər), n. 1. c10th cent. B.C., Greek epic poet, reputed author of the Iliad and Odyssey. 2. Winslow, 1836–1910, U.S. painter.

hom·er[1] (hō′mər), n. Colloq. 1. Baseball. a home run. 2. a homing pigeon. [f. HOME + -ER[1]]

ho·mer[2] (hō′mər), n. a Hebrew unit of capacity in liquid or dry measure equal to 10 baths or 10 ephahs; kor. [t. Heb.: m. khomer, lit., heap]

Ho·mer·ic (hō mĕr′ĭk), adj. of, pertaining to, or suggestive of Homer or his poetry. —**Ho·mer′i·cal·ly,** adv.

Homeric laughter, loud, hearty laughter.

home rule, self-government in local matters by city, province, state, or other component part of a country.

home ruler, an advocate of home rule.

home run, Baseball. a run made on a hit which enables the batter, without aid from fielding errors of the opponents, to make a nonstop circuit of the bases.

home·sick (hōm′sĭk′), adj. ill or depressed from a longing for home. —**home′sick′ness,** n.

home·spun (hōm′spŭn′), adj. 1. spun or made at home: homespun cloth. 2. made of such cloth. 3. plain; unpolished; simple. —n. 4. cloth made at home, or of homespun yarn. 5. cloth of similar appearance to that hand-spun and hand-woven. 6. Obs. a rustic person.

home·stead (hōm′stĕd, -stĭd), n. 1. U.S. a dwelling with its land and buildings, occupied by the owner as a home, and exempted by law (**homestead law**) from seizure or sale for debt. 2. any dwelling with its land and buildings. [OE hāmstede, f. hām HOME + stede place]

Home·stead (hōm′stĕd, -stĭd), n. a borough in SW Pennsylvania, near Pittsburgh. 10,046 (1950).

Homestead Act, a special act of Congress of 1862 which made homesteads available to the people.

home·stead·er (hōm′stĕd′ər), n. 1. one who holds a homestead. 2. U.S. a settler under the Homestead Act.

home stretch, the straight part of a race track leading to the finish line, after the last turn.

home·ward (hōm′wərd), adv. Also, **home′wards.** 1. toward home. —adj. 2. directed toward home.

home·work (hōm′wûrk′), n. 1. the part of a lesson or lessons prepared at home. 2. any work done at home, esp. work on contract for manufacturers or middlemen.

home·y (hō′mĭ), adj., homier, homiest. Colloq. homelike. Also, **homy.** —Syn. See **simple.**

hom·i·cid·al (hŏm′ə sī′dəl), adj. 1. pertaining to homicide. 2. having a tendency to homicide. —**hom′i·cid′al·ly,** adv.

hom·i·cide[1] (hŏm′ə sīd′), n. the killing of one human being by another. [ME, t. OF, t. L: m.s. homicīdium]

hom·i·cide[2] (hŏm′ə sīd′), n. a murderer. [ME, t. OF, t. L: m. homicīda manslayer]

hom·i·let·ic (hŏm′ə lĕt′ĭk), *adj.* **1.** pertaining to preaching or to homilies. **2.** of the nature of a homily. **3.** of or pertaining to homiletics. Also, **hom′i·let′i·cal.** [t. Gk.: m.s. *homilētikós* affable] —**hom′i·let′i·cal·ly,** *adv.*

hom·i·let·ics (hŏm′ə lĕt′ĭks), *n.* the art of preaching; the branch of practical theology that treats of homilies or sermons. [pl. of HOMILETIC. See -ICS]

hom·i·list (hŏm′ə lĭst), *n.* one who writes or delivers homilies.

hom·i·ly (hŏm′ə lĭ), *n., pl.* **-lies. 1.** a religious discourse addressed to a congregation; a sermon. **2.** an admonitory or moralizing discourse. [t. ML: m.s. *homīlia,* t. Gk.: discourse; r. ME *omelie,* t. OF]

homing pigeon, a pigeon trained to fly home from a distance, employed to carry messages.

hom·i·ny (hŏm′ə nĭ), *n.* white corn hulled and crushed or coarsely ground: prepared for use as food by boiling in water or milk. [t. Algonquian (New England or Va.); cf. *tackhummin* grind corn (der. *ahäm* he beats, he pounds + *min* berry, fruit)]

Ho·mo (hō′mō), *n., pl.* **Homines** (hŏm′ə nēz′). the primate genus that includes modern man, *Homo sapiens,* and a number of closely related extinct species, as the Neanderthal man. [L: man]

homo-, a combining form meaning "the same" (opposed to *hetero-*), as in *homocercal.* [t. Gk., comb. form of *homós* same]

ho·mo·cer·cal (hō′mə sûr′kəl, hŏm′ə-), *adj. Ichthyol.* **1.** having the tail or the caudal fin symmetrical as to its upper and under halves. **2.** denoting such a tail or caudal fin. [f. HOMO- + m.s. Gk. *kérkos* tail + -AL[1]]

ho·mo·chro·mat·ic (hō′mə krō- măt′ĭk, hŏm′ə-), *adj.* pertaining to or of one hue; monochromatic. —**ho·mo·chro·ma·tism** (hō′mə krō′mə tĭz′əm, hŏm′ə-), *n.*

Homocercal tail

ho·mo·chro·mous (hō′mə krō′məs, hŏm′ə-), *adj. Bot., Zool.* being all of one color as a composite flower or flower head. [t. Gk.: m. *homóchrōmos*]

homoeo-, var. of homeo-.

ho·moe·o·mor·phism (hō′mĭ ə môr′fĭz əm), *n.* homeomorphism. —**ho′moe·o·mor′phous,** *adj.*

ho·moe·op·a·thy (hō′mĭ ŏp′ə thĭ), *n.* homeopathy. —**ho′moe·o·path′ic,** *adj.* —**ho′moe·o·path′i·cal·ly,** *adv.* —**ho·moe·op·a·thist** (hō′mĭ ŏp′ə thĭst), **ho·moe·o·path** (hō′mĭ ə păth′), *n.*

ho·mog·a·mous (hō mŏg′ə məs), *adj. Bot.* **1.** having flowers or florets which do not differ sexually (opposed to *heterogamous*). **2.** having the stamens and pistils maturing simultaneously (opposed to *dichogamous*). [t. Gk.: m. *homógamos* married to the same wife]

ho·mog·a·my (hō mŏg′ə mĭ), *n.* **1.** *Bot.* state of being homogamous. **2.** *Biol.* interbreeding of individuals of like characteristics.

ho·mo·ge·ne·i·ty (hō′mə jə nē′ə tĭ, hŏm′ə-), *n.* composition from like parts; congruity of constitution.

ho·mo·ge·ne·ous (hō′mə jē′nĭ əs, hŏm′ə-), *adj.* **1.** composed of parts all of the same kind; not heterogeneous. **2.** of the same kind or nature; essentially alike. **3.** *Math.* **a.** having a common property. **b.** denoting a sum of terms all of the same degree. [t. ML: m. *homogeneus,* t. Gk.: m. *homogenēs* of the same kind] —**ho′mo·ge′ne·ous·ly,** *adv.* —**ho′mo·ge′ne·ous·ness,** *n.*

ho·mog·e·nize (hō mŏj′ə nīz′, hō′mə jə-), *v.t.,* **-nized, -nizing.** to make homogeneous; form by mixing and emulsifying: *homogenized milk.* —**ho·mog·e·ni·za·tion** (hō mŏj′ə nə zā′shən, hō′mə jē′nə-), *n.* —**ho·mog·e·niz·er** (hō mŏj′ə nī′zər, hō′mə jə-), *n.*

ho·mog·e·nous (hō mŏj′ə nəs), *adj. Biol.* (of organs or the like) corresponding in structure because of a common origin.

ho·mog·e·ny (hō mŏj′ə nĭ), *n. Biol.* correspondence of structure and embryological development. [t. Gk.: m. *homogéneia* community of origin]

ho·mog·o·nous (hō mŏg′ə nəs), *adj. Bot.* pertaining to monoclinous flowers which do not differ in the relative length of stamens and pistils. —**ho·mog′o·nous·ly,** *adv.*

ho·mog·o·ny (hō mŏg′ə nĭ), *n. Bot.* state of being homogonous. [f. HOMO- + s. Gk. *gónos* offspring + -Y[3]]

hom·o·graph (hŏm′ə grăf′, -gräf′), *n.* a word of the same written form as another, but of different origin and signification, as *homer*[1] (a home run) and *homer*[2] (a unit of measure). —**hom′o·graph′ic,** *adj.*

homoio-, var. of homeo-.

Ho·moi·ou·si·an (hō′moi ōō′sĭ ən, -ou′sĭ ən), *n.* **1.** one of a 4th century church party which maintained that the essence of the Son is similar to, but not the same with, that of the Father. —*adj.* **2.** relating to the Homoiousians or their belief. [f. s. LGk. *homoioúsios* of like substance + -AN]

ho·mol·o·gate (hō mŏl′ə gāt′), *v.t.,* **-gated, -gating.** to approve; ratify. [t. ML: m.s. *homologātus,* pp. of *homologāre,* t. Gk.: m. *homologeín* agree to, allow] —**ho·mol′o·ga′tion,** *n.*

ho·mo·log·i·cal (hō′mə lŏj′ə kəl), *adj.* homologous. Also, **ho′mo·log′ic.** —**ho′mo·log′i·cal·ly,** *adv.*

ho·mol·o·gize (hō mŏl′ə jīz′), *v.,* **-gized, -gizing.** —*v.t.* **1.** to make or show to be homologous. —*v.i.* **2.** to be homologous; correspond.

ho·mol·o·gous (hō mŏl′ə gəs), *adj.* **1.** having the same

or a similar relation; corresponding, as in relative position, structure, etc. **2.** *Biol.* corresponding in type of structure and in origin, but not necessarily in function: *the wing of a bird and the foreleg of a horse are homologous.* **3.** *Chem.* of the same chemical type, but differing by a fixed increment in certain constituents. **4.** *Immunol., Med., etc.* pertaining to the relation between bacterium and the immune serum prepared from it. [t. ML: m. *homologus,* or t. Gk.: m. *homólogos* agreeing, of one mind]

homologous chromosomes, *Biol.* pairs of similar chromosomes, one of maternal, the other of paternal origin, which synapse or pair at the reduction divisions. They carry the Mendelian pairs of alleles or genes.

hom·o·logue (hŏm′ə lŏg′, -lôg′), *n.* **1.** something homologous. **2.** *Biol.,* a homologous organ or part.

ho·mol·o·gy (hō mŏl′ə jĭ), *n., pl.* **-gies. 1.** state of being homologous; homologous relation or correspondence. **2.** *Biol.* **a.** a fundamental similarity due to community of descent. **b.** a structural similarity of two segments of one animal based on a common developmental origin. **3.** *Chem.* the similarity of organic compounds of a series in which each member differs from its adjacent compounds by a single group. [t. LL: m.s. *homologia,* t. Gk.: agreement, assent, conformity]

ho·mo·mor·phism (hō′mə môr′fĭz əm, hŏm′ə-), *n.* **1.** *Biol.* correspondence in form or external appearance but not in type of structure and in origin. **2.** *Bot.* possession of perfect flowers of only one kind. **3.** *Zool.* resemblance between the young and the adult. Also, **ho′mo·mor′phy.** —**ho′mo·mor′phic, ho′mo·mor′phous,** *adj.*

hom·o·nym (hŏm′ə nĭm), *n.* **1.** a word like another in sound and perhaps in spelling, but different in meaning, as *meat* and *meet.* **2.** a homophone. **3.** a homograph. **4.** a namesake. **5.** *Biol.* a name given to a species or genus, which has been used at an earlier date for a different species or genus, and which is therefore rejected. [t. L: s. *homōnymus* having the same name, t. Gk.: m. *homōnymos*] —**hom′o·nym′ic,** *adj.*

ho·mon·y·mous (hō mŏn′ə məs), *adj.* **1.** of the nature of homonyms; having the same name. **2.** *Optics.* denoting or pertaining to the images formed in a kind of double vision in which the image seen by the right eye is on the right side and vice versa.

ho·mon·y·my (hō mŏn′ə mĭ), *n.* homonymous state.

Ho·mo·öu·si·an (hō′mō ōō′sĭ ən, -ou′sĭ ən, hŏm′ō-), *n.* **1.** one of a 4th century church party which maintained that the essence or substance of the Father and the Son is the same. —*adj.* **2.** (*l.c.*) pertaining to the Homoöusians or their doctrines. [f. s. LGk. *homooúsios* of the same substance + -AN]

hom·o·phone (hŏm′ə fōn′), *n.* **1.** *Phonet.* a word pronounced the same as another, whether spelled the same or not: *heir, air* (atmosphere), and *air* (melody), are homophones. **2.** (in a system of writing) an element which represents the same spoken unit as another, as (usually) English *ks* and *x.*

hom·o·phon·ic (hŏm′ə fŏn′ĭk), *adj.* **1.** having the same sound. **2.** having one part or melody predominating (opposed to *polyphonic*). [f. s. Gk. *homóphōnos* of the same sound + -IC]

ho·moph·o·nous (hō mŏf′ə nəs), *adj.* identical in pronunciation.

ho·moph·o·ny (hō mŏf′ə nĭ), *n.* **1.** the quality of being homophonic. **2.** homophonic music.

ho·mop·ter·ous (hō mŏp′tər əs), *adj.* pertaining or belonging to the *Homoptera,* a suborder of hemipterous insects having wings of the same texture throughout, comprising the aphids, cicadas, etc. [t. Gk.: m. *homópteros* with the same plumage]

Ho·mo sa·pi·ens (hō′mō sā′pĭ ĕnz′), modern man, the single surviving species of the genus *Homo* and of the primate family, *Hominidae,* to which it belongs. [L]

ho·mo·sex·u·al (hō′mə sĕk′shōō əl, hŏm′ə-), *adj.* **1.** pertaining to or exhibiting homosexuality. —*n.* **2.** a homosexual person.

ho·mo·sex·u·al·i·ty (hō′mə sĕk′shōō ăl′ə tĭ, hŏm′ə-), *n.* sexual feeling for a person of the same sex, with an impulse towards genital expression.

ho·mos·po·rous (hō mŏs′pər əs, hō′mə spōr′əs), *adj. Bot.* having spores of one kind only.

ho·mos·po·ry (hō mŏs′pər ĭ), *n.* the production of a single kind of spore, neither microspore nor megaspore.

ho·mo·tax·is (hō′mə tăk′sĭs, hŏm′ə-), *n.* similarity of arrangement, as of geological strata, which though not necessarily contemporaneous, have the same relative position. —**ho′mo·tax′ic,** *adj.*

ho·mo·thal·lic (hō′mə thăl′ĭk, hŏm′ə-), *adj. Bot.* having all mycelia alike, the opposite sexual functions being performed by different cells of a single mycelium. [f. HOMO- + s. Gk. *thallós* sprout + -IC]

ho·mo·zy·go·sis (hō′mə zī gō′sĭs, -zĭ′-, hŏm′ə-), *n. Biol.* the union of like gametes, resulting in a homozygote. [f. HOMO- + Gk. *zýgōsis* joining]

ho·mo·zy·gote (hō′mə zī′gōt, -zĭ′gŏt, hŏm′ə-), *n. Biol.* an organism with identical pairs of genes with respect to any given pair of hereditary characters, and hence breeding true for those characteristics. —**ho·mo·zy·gous** (hō′mə zī′gəs, hŏm′ə-), *adj.*

Homs (hōms), *n.* a city in W Syria. 64,940 (est. 1942).

ho·mun·cu·lus (hō mŭng′kyə ləs), *n., pl.* **-li** (-lī′). **1.** a little man; a dwarf. **2.** a spermatozoön. [t. L, dim. of *homo* man]

hom·y (hō′mĭ), *adj.*, **-mier, -miest.** homey.
Hon., Honorable.
hon., 1. honorably. 2. *Chiefly Brit.* honorary.
Ho·nan (hō′nän′; *Chin.* hŭ′nän′), *n.* a province in E China. 31,805,600 pop. (est. 1944); 64,545 sq. mi. *Cap.:* Kaifeng.
Hond., Honduras.
Hon·do (hŏn′dō), *n.* Honshu.
Hon·du·ras (hŏn dŏŏr′əs, -dyŏŏr′-), *n.* 1. a republic in Central America. 1,173,032 pop. (est. 1943); 59,161 sq. mi. *Cap.:* Tegucigalpa. 2. See **British Honduras.** —**Hon·du′ran,** *adj., n.*
hone (hōn), *n., v.,* **honed, honing.** —*n.* 1. a whetstone of fine, compact texture, esp. one for sharpening razors. —*v.t.* 2. to sharpen on or as on a hone: *to hone a razor.* [ME; OE *hān* stone, rock, c. Icel. *hein* hone]
hon·est (ŏn′ĭst), *adj.* 1. honorable in principles, intentions, and actions; upright: *an honest person.* 2. showing uprightness and fairness; gained fairly: *honest methods.* 3. open; sincere: *an honest face.* 4. genuine or unadulterated: *honest commodities.* 5. chaste or virtuous. [ME *honeste,* t. OF, t. L: m. *honestus* honorable, worthy, virtuous] —**hon′est·ly,** *adv.* —**Syn.** 1. fair, just, incorruptible, trusty, trustworthy; truthful. 3. straightforward, frank, candid. —**Ant.** 1. corrupt.
hon·es·ty (ŏn′ĭs tĭ), *n.* 1. the quality or fact of being honest; uprightness, probity, or integrity. 2. truthfulness, sincerity, or frankness. 3. freedom from deceit or fraud. 4. *Bot.* a cruciferous herb, *Lunaria annua,* with purple flowers and semitransparent satiny pods. 5. *Archaic.* chastity. —**Syn.** 1. fairness, justice; rectitude. 2. candor. See **honor.** —**Ant.** 1. crookedness.
hone·wort (hōn′wûrt′), *n.* any of several umbelliferous plants, esp. a kind of parsley.
hon·ey (hŭn′ĭ), *n., pl.* **honeys,** *adj. v.,* **honeyed** or **honied, honeying.** —*n.* 1. a sweet, viscid fluid produced by bees from the nectar collected from flowers, and stored in their nests or hives as food. 2. the nectar of flowers. 3. any of various similar products produced by insects or in other ways. 4. something sweet, delicious, or delightful: *the honey of flattery.* 5. sweet one; darling (a term of endearment). 6. of or like honey; sweet; dear. —*v.i.* 7. *Archaic* or *U.S.* to talk sweetly; use endearments. [ME *huny,* OE *hunig,* c. D and G *honig*] —**hon′ey·like′,** *adj.*
hon·ey·bee (hŭn′ĭ bē′), *n.* a bee that collects and stores honey, specif. *Apis mellifera.*
hon·ey·comb (hŭn′ĭ kōm′), *n.* 1. a structure of wax containing rows of hexagonal cells, formed by bees for the reception of honey and pollen and of their eggs. 2. any substance, as a casting of iron, etc., having cells like those of a honeycomb. 3. the reticulum of a ruminant. —*adj.* 4. having the structure or appearance of a honeycomb: *honeycomb weave.* —*v.t.* 5. to reduce to a honeycomb; pierce with many holes or cavities: *a rock honeycombed with passages.* 6. to penetrate in all parts: *a city honeycombed with vice.* [ME *hunycomb,* OE *hunigcamb*]
honey creeper, any of the small, usually brightly colored, somewhat scansorial, tropical or semitropical American birds of the family *Coerebidae.*
hon·ey·dew (hŭn′ĭ dū′, -dōō′), *n.* 1. the sweet material which exudes from the leaves of certain plants in hot weather. 2. a sugary material secreted by plant lice, leaf hoppers, etc.
honeydew melon, a sweet-flavored, white-fleshed muskmelon with a smooth, pale-green rind.
honey eater, any of the numerous oscine birds constituting the family *Meliphagidae,* chiefly of Australasia, with a bill and tongue adapted for extracting the nectar from flowers.
hon·eyed (hŭn′ĭd), *adj.* 1. dulcet or mellifluous; ingratiating: *honeyed words.* 2. containing, consisting of, or resembling honey: *honeyed drinks.* Also, **honied.**
honey guide, any of various small, dull-colored nonpasserine birds (genus *Indicator, Prodotiscus, Melichneutes,* etc.), of Africa, Asia, and the East Indies, some of which are said to guide men or animals to places where honey may be found.
honey locust, a thorny North American tree, *Gleditsia triacanthos,* bearing pods with a sweet pulp and small compound leaves.
hon·ey·moon (hŭn′ĭ mōōn′), *n.* 1. a holiday spent by a newly married couple in traveling or visiting. 2. the first month, more or less, after marriage. —*v.i.* 3. to spend one's honeymoon (usually fol. by *in* or *at*). —**hon′ey·moon′er,** *n.*
honey plant, any plant especially useful in furnishing nectar to bees, as the cleome or figwort.
hon·ey·suck·er (hŭn′ĭ sŭk′ər), *n.* 1. a bird that eats the nectar of flowers. 2. a honey eater.
hon·ey·suck·le (hŭn′ĭ sŭk′əl), *n.* 1. any of the upright or climbing shrubs constituting the caprifoliaceous genus *Lonicera,* some species of which are cultivated for their fragrant white, yellow, or red tubular flowers. 2. any of various other fragrant or ornamental plants. [ME *honiesoukel,* f. *honisouke* (OE *hunisūce*) lit., honey-suck + *-el,* dim. suffix] —**hon′ey·suck′led,** *adj.*
hon·ey·sweet (hŭn′ĭ swēt′), *adj.* sweet as honey.
hong (hŏng), *n.* 1. (in China) a group of rooms or buildings forming a warehouse, factory, etc. 2. one of the foreign factories formerly maintained at Canton. [t. Chinese (Cantonese): row, rank (Mandarin *hang*)]

Hong Kong (hŏng′ kŏng′), 1. a British crown colony in SE China, comprising the island of Hong Kong (32 sq. mi.) and the adjacent mainland. 980,000 pop. (est. 1942); 390 sq. mi. *Cap.:* Victoria. 2. Victoria. Also, **Hongkong.**
hon·ied (hŭn′ĭd), *adj.* honeyed.
ho·ni soit qui mal y pense (ô nē′ swä′ kē mål ē päns′), *French.* shamed be the one who thinks evil of it (motto of the Order of the Garter).
honk (hŏngk, hôngk), *n.* 1. the cry of the wild goose. 2. any similar sound, as of an automobile horn. —*v.i.* 3. to emit a honk. [imit.] —**honk′er,** *n.*
honk·y-tonk (hŏng′kĭ tŏngk′, hông′kĭ tôngk′), *n.* *U.S. Slang.* a cheap, sordid saloon, cabaret, etc. [orig. uncert.]
Hon·o·lu·lu (hŏn′ə lōō′lōō), *n.* a seaport in the Hawaiian Islands, on the island of Oahu: capital of the Territory of Hawaii. 245,612 (prelim. 1950).
hon·or (ŏn′ər), *n.* 1. high public esteem; fame; glory: *a roll of honor.* 2. credit or reputation for behavior that is becoming or worthy. 3. a source of credit or distinction: *to be an honor to one's family.* 4. high respect, as for worth, merit, or rank: *to be held in honor.* 5. such respect manifested: *to be received with honor.* 6. a special privilege or favor: *I have the honor to acknowledge your letter.* 7. (usually *pl.*) high rank, dignity, or distinction: *political honors.* 8. a deferential title, esp. of judges and mayors (prec. by *his, your,* etc.). 9. highminded character or principles; fine sense of one's obligations: *a man of honor.* 10. (usually *pl.*) special rank or distinction conferred by a university, college, or school upon a student for eminence in scholarship or success in some particular subject. 11. chastity or purity in a woman. 12. *Bridge, etc.* any one of the five highest trump cards. 13. *Golf.* the preference of teeing off before the other players or side, given after the first hole to the player or players who won the previous hole. 14. **do honor to, a.** to show respect to. **b.** to be a credit to. —*v.t.* 15. to hold in honor or high respect; revere. 16. to treat with honor. 17. to confer honor or distinction upon. 18. to worship (the Supreme Being). 19. to show a courteous regard for: *to honor an invitation.* 20. *Com.* to accept and pay (a draft, etc.) when due. Also, *Brit.,* **honour.** [ME *onur, honour, honor,* t. OF: (m.) *onur,* g. L *honor* honor, repute] —**hon′or·er,** *n.* —**hon′or·less,** *adj.*
—**Syn.** 4. respect, deference, homage; reverence, veneration. HONOR, CONSIDERATION, DISTINCTION refer to the regard in which one is held by his fellows. HONOR suggests a combination of liking and respect: *his townsmen held him in great honor.* CONSIDERATION suggests honor because of proved worth: *a man worthy of the highest consideration.* DISTINCTION suggests particular honor because of qualities or accomplishments: *he achieved distinction at an early age as a violinist.* 9. probity, uprightness. HONOR, HONESTY, INTEGRITY, SINCERITY refer to one who is characterized by possession of the highest moral principles and the absence of deceit or fraud. HONOR denotes a fine sense of, and a strict conformity to, what is considered morally right or due: *a high sense of honor, worthy of honor.* HONESTY denotes the presence of probity and particularly the absence of deceit or fraud, esp. in business dealings: *uncompromising honesty and trustworthiness.* INTEGRITY indicates a soundness of moral principle which no power or influence can impair: *a man of unquestioned integrity and dependability.* SINCERITY implies absence of dissimulation or deceit, and a strong adherence to truth: *his sincerity was evident in every word.* 15. esteem, venerate. —**Ant.** 9. dishonesty, deceitfulness.
hon·or·a·ble (ŏn′ər ə bəl), *adj.* 1. in accordance with principles of honor; upright: *an honorable man.* 2. of high rank, dignity, or distinction; noble, illustrious, or distinguished. 3. entitling to honor or distinction: prefixed to the names of certain officials and others, esp. in England as a title of the younger children of peers, from earls to barons. *Abbr.:* Hon. 4. (of persons or things) worthy of honor and high respect. 5. bringing honor or credit; consistent with honor: *an honorable peace.* Also, *Brit.,* **honourable.** —**hon′or·a·ble·ness,** *n.* —**hon′or·a·bly,** *adv.* —**Syn.** 1. honest, noble, highminded. 4. estimable. —**Ant.** 1. untrustworthy.
hon·o·rar·i·um (ŏn′ə râr′ĭ əm), *n., pl.* **-rariums, -raria** (-râr′ĭ ə). 1. an honorary reward, as in recognition of professional services on which no price may be set. 2. a fee for services rendered by a professional person. [t. L, prop. neut. of *honōrārius* HONORARY]
hon·or·ar·y (ŏn′ə rĕr′ĭ), *adj.* 1. given for honor only, without the usual duties, privileges, emoluments, etc.: *an honorary title.* 2. holding a title or position conferred for honor only: *an honorary president.* 3. (of an obligation) depending on one's honor for fulfillment. 4. given, made, or serving as a token of honor: *an honorary gift.* [t. L: m.s. *honōrārius* relating to honor]
hon·or·if·ic (ŏn′ə rĭf′ĭk), *adj.* Also, **hon′or·if′i·cal.** 1. doing or conferring honor. 2. having the quality of an honorific. —*n.* 3. (in certain languages, as Chinese and Japanese) a class of forms used to show respect, especially in direct address. 4. titles or terms of respect. *Examples: Doctor, Professor, Rt. Hon.* [t. L: s. *honōrificus.* See HONOR, n., -(I)FIC] —**hon′or·if′i·cal·ly,** *adv.*
Ho·no·ri·us (hō nōr′ĭ əs), *n.* 1. Flavius (flā′vĭ əs), A.D. 384–423, Roman emperor of the Western Empire, A.D. 395–423. 2. the name of four popes.
honor man, one who takes honors on graduation from a college or university.

honor point, *Her.* a point midway between the heart point and top of an escutcheon. See diag. under **escutcheon.**

honors of war, *Mil.* privileges granted to a capitulating force, as of marching out of their camp or entrenchments with all their arms and with colors flying.

honor system, a system of management, as in schools, penal institutions, etc., whereby obedience to rules is sought by putting persons upon their honor, rather than by using special guards and constraints.

hon·our (ŏn′ər), *n., v.t. Brit.* honor. —**hon′our·a·ble,** *adj.*

Hon·shu (hŏn′shōō), *n.* the chief island of Japan. 55,194,449 pop. (1946); 88,851 sq. mi. Also, **Hondo.**

hooch (hōōch), *n. U.S. Slang.* **1.** alcoholic beverages. **2.** liquor illicitly distilled and distributed. [short for *hoochinoo*, alter. of *Hutanuwu*, name of Alaskan Indian tribe who made liquor]

hood (hŏŏd), *n.* **1.** a soft or flexible covering for the head and neck, either separate or attached to a cloak or the like. **2.** something resembling or suggesting this, as a hood-shaped petal or sepal, etc. **3.** the cover over an automobile engine. **4.** *Brit.* the top of an automobile. **5.** *Falconry.* a cover for the entire head of a hawk, used when it is not in pursuit of game. **6.** *Slang.* a hoodlum. —*v.t.* **7.** to furnish with a hood. **8.** to cover with, or as with, a hood. [ME *hode*, OE *hōd*, c. G *hut* hat] —**hood′-less,** *adj.* —**hood′like′,** *adj.*

Hood (hŏŏd), *n.* **1. Mount,** a volcanic peak in N Oregon, in the Cascade Range. 11,253 ft. **2. John Bell,** 1831–79, Confederate general in the U.S. Civil War. **3. Thomas,** 1799–1845, British poet and humorist. **4. Robin.** See **Robin Hood.**

-hood, a suffix denoting state, condition, character, nature, etc., or a body of persons of a particular character or class: *childhood, likelihood, priesthood, sisterhood.* [ME *-hode, -hod*, OE *-hād*, c. G *-heit*; orig. separate word, OE *hād* condition, state, etc.]

hood·ed (hŏŏd′ĭd), *adj.* **1.** having, or covered with, a hood. **2.** hood-shaped. **3.** *Zool.* having on the head a hoodlike formation, crest, arrangement of colors, or the like. **4.** *Bot.* cucullate.

hooded seal, *Zool.* bladdernose.

hood·ie (hŏŏd′ĭ; *Scot.* hōō′dĭ), *n. Scot.* the hooded crow, *Corvus cornix.* Also, **hoodie crow.**

hood·lum (hōōd′ləm), *n. U.S.* a petty gangster; ruffian. [orig. uncert.] —**hood′lum·ism,** *n.*

hood·man-blind (hŏŏd′mən blīnd′), *n. Archaic.* blindman's buff.

hoo·doo (hōō′dōō), *n., pl.* **-doos,** *v.,* **-dooed, -dooing.** —*n.* **1.** voodoo. **2.** *Colloq.* a person or thing that brings bad luck. **3.** *Colloq.* bad luck. —*v.t.* **4.** *Colloq.* to bring or cause bad luck to. [appar. var. of VOODOO]

hood·wink (hŏŏd′wĭngk′), *v.t.* **1.** to deceive; humbug. **2.** to blindfold. **3.** to cover or hide. —**hood′wink′er,** *n*

hoo·ey (hōō′ĭ), *U.S. Slang.* —*interj.* **1.** an exclamation of disapproval. —*n.* **2.** silly or worthless stuff; nonsense.

hoof (hŏŏf, hōōf), *n., pl.* **hoofs,** *(Rare)* **hooves;** *v.* —*n.* **1.** the horny covering protecting the ends of the digits or incasing the foot in certain animals, as the ox, horse, etc. **2.** the entire foot of a horse, donkey, etc. **3.** a hoofed animal; one of a herd. **4.** (in humorous use) the human foot. **5. on the hoof,** (of livestock) alive; not butchered. —*v.i.* **6.** *Colloq.* to walk. **7.** *Colloq.* to dance. [ME; OE *hōf*, c. G *huf*] —**hoof′like′,** *adj.*

hoof·bound (hŏŏf′bound′, hōōf′-), *adj.* (of horses) having the heels of the hoofs dry and contracted, causing lameness.

hoofed (hŏŏft, hōōft), *adj.* having hoofs; ungulate.

hoof·er (hŏŏf′ər, hōōf′ər), *n.* one who makes dancing an occupation, as a chorus girl.

Hoogh·ly (hōōg′lē), *n.* a river in NE India, in W Bengal: the westernmost channel by which the Ganges enters the Bay of Bengal. ab. 120 mi. Also, **Hugli.**

hook (hŏŏk), *n.* **1.** a curved or angular piece of metal or other firm substance catching, pulling, or sustaining something. **2.** a fishhook. **3.** that which catches; a snare; a trap. **4.** something curved or bent like a hook, as a mark or symbol, etc. **5.** a sharp curve or angle in the length or course of anything. **6.** a curved spit of land: *Sandy Hook.* **7.** a recurved and pointed organ or appendage of an animal or plant. **8.** *Golf.* a drive or other stroke which curves to the left of the player striking the ball. **9.** *Baseball.* a curve. **10.** *Cricket.* act of pulling. **11.** *Boxing.* a swinging stroke or blow. **12.** *Music.* a stroke or line attached to the stem of eighth notes, sixteenth notes, etc. **13. by hook or by crook,** by any means, fair or foul. **14. on one's own hook,** *Slang.* on one's own responsibility. —*v.t.* **15.** to seize, fasten, or catch hold of and draw, with or as with a hook. **16.** to catch (fish) with a fishhook. **17.** *Slang.* to seize by stealth, pilfer, or steal. **18.** to catch by artifice. **19.** to catch on the horns, or attack with the horns. **20.** to catch hold of and draw (loops of yarn) through cloth with or as with a hook. **21.** *Sports.* to strike with a hook or so as to result in a hook. **22.** to make hook-shaped; crook. **23. hook up, a.** to fasten with a hook or hooks. **b.** to put together (mechanical apparatus) and connect it to the source of power. **24. hook it,** *Slang.* to depart. —*v.i.* **25.** to become attached or fastened by or as by a hook; join on. **26.** to curve or bend like a hook. **27.**

Slang. to depart. [ME *hoke,* OE *hōc,* c. D *hoek* hook, angle, corner, point of land] —**hook′less,** *adj.* —**hook′like′,** *adj.*

hook·ah (hŏŏk′ə), *n.* a tobacco pipe with a long, flexible tube by which the smoke is drawn through a vase of water and thus cooled. Also, **hook′a.** [t. Ar.: m. *ḥuqqa* box, vase, pipe for smoking]

hook-and-lad·der truck (hŏŏk′-ən lăd′ər), a fire engine with ladders, axes, etc., whose crew is used in making rescues.

hooked (hŏŏkt), *adj.* **1.** bent like a hook; hook-shaped. **2.** having a hook or hooks. **3.** made with a hook. —**hook·ed·ness** (hŏŏk′ĭd nĭs), *n.*

Hookah

hooked rug, *U.S.* a rug made by drawing loops of yarn or cloth through a foundation of burlap, or the like, to form a pattern.

hook·er (hŏŏk′ər), *n.* **1.** *Colloq.* a kind of small fishing smack. **2.** any old-fashioned or clumsy vessel. [t. D: m. *hoeker,* der. *hoek* HOOK]

Hook·er (hŏŏk′ər), *n.* **1. Joseph,** 1814–79, Union general in the U.S. Civil War. **2. Richard,** 1554?–1600, British author and clergyman. **3. Thomas,** 1586?–1647, British Puritan clergyman: one of the founders of the colony of Connecticut.

Hook of Holland (hŏŏk), a cape and harbor in SW Netherlands. Dutch, **Hoek van Holland.**

hook·up (hŏŏk′ŭp′), *n.* **1.** *Radio.* **a.** a diagram of radio apparatus, showing the connection of the different elements. **b.** the elements as set up for operation. **2.** combination; connection.

hook·worm (hŏŏk′wûrm′), *n.* **1.** any of certain bloodsucking nematode worms, as *Ancylostoma duodenale* and *Necator americanus,* parasitic in the intestine of man and other animals. **2.** hookworm disease.

hookworm disease, a disease characterized by severe anemia, caused by hookworms.

hook·y¹ (hŏŏk′ĭ), *adj.* **1.** full of hooks. **2.** hook-shaped. [f. HOOK- + -Y¹]

hook·y² (hŏŏk′ĭ), *n.* in phrase **play hooky,** to be unjustifiably absent from school. [f. HOOK (defs. 25, 26) + -Y³]

hoo·li·gan (hōō′lə gən), *Slang. n.* **1.** a hoodlum. —*adj.* **2.** of or like hooligans. [var. of *Houlihan,* Irish surname which came to be assoc. with rowdies] —**hoo′li·gan·ism,** *n.*

hoop (hŏŏp, hōōp), *n.* **1.** a circular band or ring of metal, wood, or other stiff material. **2.** such a band to hold together the staves of a cask, tub, etc. **3.** a large ring of iron or wood for a child to roll along the ground. **4.** something resembling a hoop. **5.** that part of a finger ring which surrounds the finger. **6.** *Chiefly Brit.* one of the iron arches used in croquet. **7.** a circular band of stiff material used to expand a woman's skirt. **8.** a hoop skirt. —*v.t.* **9.** to bind or fasten with a hoop or hoops. **10.** to encircle; embrace. [ME *hop(e),* late OE *hōp,* c. D *hoep*] —**hooped,** *adj.* —**hoop′like′,** *adj.*

hoo·poe (hōō′pōō), *n.* any of the Old World nonpasserine birds constituting the family *Upupidae,* esp. *Upupa epops,* a European species with an erectile fanlike crest. [earlier *hoop,* t. F: m. *huppe,* g. VL *ūpupa,* var. of *upupa;* so called from its cry]

hoop skirt, 1. a woman's skirt, made to stand out from the waist by an undergarment of flexible hoops connected by tapes. **2.** the framework for such a skirt.

hoop snake, a harmless snake, *Abastor erythrogrammus,* believed to take its tail in its mouth and roll along like a hoop.

hoo·ray (hŏŏ rā′), *interj., v.i., n. Chiefly Brit.* hurrah

hoose·gow (hōōs′gou), *n. U.S. Slang.* a jail. Also **hoos′gow.** [t. Sp.: m. *juzga(d)o,* court of justice (in Mex. Sp.) jail]

Hoo·sier (hōō′zhər), *n. U.S.* an inhabitant of Indiana. [orig. uncert.]

hoot (hōōt), *v.i.* **1.** to cry out or shout, esp. in disapproval or derision. **2.** (of an owl) to utter its cry. **3.** to utter a similar sound. **4.** *Brit.* to blow a horn or whistle; honk. —*v.t.* **5.** to assail with shouts of disapproval or derision. **6.** to drive (out, away, off, etc.) by hooting. **7.** to express in hoots. —*n.* **8.** the cry of an owl. **9.** any similar sound, as an inarticulate shout. **10.** a cry or shout, esp. of disapproval or derision. **11.** *Brit.* a honk or factory whistle. **12.** a thing of no value: *I don't give a hoot.* [ME *huten;* prob. imit.] —**hoot′er,** *n.*

Hoo·ton (hōō′tən), *n.* **Earnest Albert** (ûr′nĭst), born 1887, U.S. anthropologist and writer.

hoot owl, an owl that hoots (distinguished from *screech owl*).

Hoo·ver (hōō′vər), *n.* **Herbert Clark,** born 1874, 31st president of the U.S., 1929–33.

Hoover Dam, official name of **Boulder Dam.**

Hoo·ver·ville (hōō′vər vĭl′), *n.* a collection of huts and shacks, as at the edge of a city, housing the unemployed during the 1930's. [named after Herbert HOOVER]

hooves (hŏŏvz, hōōvz), *n. Rare.* pl. of **hoof.**

hop¹ (hŏp), *v.,* **hopped, hopping,** *n.* —*v.i.* **1.** to leap; move by leaping with all feet off the ground. **2.** to spring or leap on one foot. **3.** to make a flight or trip.

4. *Colloq.* (of an airplane, etc.) to leave the ground in beginning a flight (often fol. by *off*). 5. *Colloq.* to dance. 6. to limp. —*v.t.* 7. *Colloq.* to hop about (a place), off (something elevated), or over (a fence, ditch, etc.). 8. *Colloq.* to jump onto: *to hop a train.* 9. *Colloq.* (of an airplane, etc.) to cross by a flight. —*n.* 10. an act of hopping; short leap. 11. a leap on one foot. 12. *Colloq.* a flight of an airplane. 13. *Colloq.* a dance, or dancing party. 14. *Slang.* opium. [ME *hoppen,* OE *hoppian,* c. G *hopfen*]

hop² (hŏp), *n., v.,* **hopped, hopping.** —*n.* 1. one of the twining plants of three species of the genus *Humulus,* the male flowers of which grow in panicled racemes and the female in conelike forms. 2. (*pl.*) the dried ripe cones of the female flowers of the hop plant, used in brewing, medicine, etc. —*v.t.* 3. to treat or flavor with hops. [ME *hoppe,* t. MD, c. G *hopfen*]

hop clover, a trefoil, *Trifolium procumbens,* whose withered yellow flowers resemble the strobiles of hop.

hope (hōp), *n., v.,* **hoped, hoping.** —*n.* 1. expectation of something desired; desire accompanied by expectation. 2. a particular instance of such expectation or desire: *a hope of success.* 3. confidence in a future event; ground for expecting something: *there is no hope of his recovery.* 4. a person or thing that expectations are centered in: *the hope of the family.* —*v.t.* 5. to look forward to with desire and more or less confidence. 6. to trust in the truth of a matter (with a clause): *I hope that you are satisfied.* —*v.i.* 7. to have an expectation of something desired: *we hope to see you, to hope for his pardon.* 8. *Archaic.* to trust or rely. [ME; OE *hopa,* c. G *hoffe*] —**Syn.** 7. See **expect.**

Hope (hōp), *n.* **Anthony,** (*Sir Anthony Hope Hawkins*) 1863–1933, British novelist.

hope chest, a chest or the like in which a young unmarried woman collects articles toward furnishing a home of her own in the event of her future marriage.

hope·ful (hōp′fəl), *adj.* 1. full of hope; expressing hope: *hopeful words.* 2. exciting hope; promising advantage or success: *a hopeful prospect.* —*n.* 3. a promising young person. —**hope′ful·ly,** *adv.* **hope′ful·ness,** *n.* —**Syn.** 1. expectant, sanguine; optimistic, confident.

Ho·peh (hō′pā′; *Chin.* hŭ′bä′), *n.* a province in NE China. 28,644,000 pop. (est. 1944); 54,154 sq. mi. *Cap.:* Peiping. Also, **Ho′pei′.** Formerly, **Chihli.**

hope·less (hōp′lĭs), *adj.* 1. affording no hope; desperate: *a hopeless case.* 2. without hope; despairing: *hopeless grief.* —**hope′less·ly,** *adv.* —**hope′less·ness,** *n.* —**Syn.** 2. HOPELESS, DESPAIRING, DESPONDENT, DESPERATE all describe an absence of hope. HOPELESS is used of a feeling of hopelessness and passive abandonment of oneself to fate: *hopeless and grim, he still clung to the cliff.* DESPAIRING refers to the loss of hope in regard to a particular situation whether important or trivial; it suggests an intellectual judgment concerning probabilities: *despairing of victory, despairing of finding his gloves.* DESPONDENT always suggests melancholy and depression; it refers to an emotional state rather than to an intellectual judgment: *despondent over ill health, she became more and more despondent and suspicious.* DESPERATE conveys a suggestion of recklessness resulting from loss of hope: *as the time grew shorter, he became desperate.* DESPERATE may apply either to feelings or to situations: *the case seems hopeless but is not yet desperate; hopeless confusion; a desperate remedy.* DESPAIRING and DESPONDENT may apply only to feelings.

Ho·pi (hō′pī), *n., pl.* **-pis.** 1. a Pueblo tribe of Shoshonean speech affiliation inhabiting seven (now nine) stone-built towns in northern Arizona. 2. their language.

Hop·kins (hŏp′kĭnz), *n.* 1. **Sir Frederick Gowland,** 1861–1947, British biochemist. 2. **Gerard Manley,** 1844–89, British poet. 3. **Harry Lloyd,** 1890–1946, U.S. political official: special assistant to President Roosevelt, 1942. 4. **Johns,** 1795–1873, U.S. financier and philanthropist. 5. **Mark,** 1802–87, U.S. clergyman and educator.

Hop·kin·son (hŏp′kĭn sən), *n.* **Francis,** 1731–91, American patriot and writer.

hop·lite (hŏp′līt), *n.* a heavy-armed foot soldier of ancient Greece. [t. Gk.: m.s. *hoplītēs*]

hop-o′-my-thumb (hŏp′ə mī thŭm′), *n.* a tiny person.

hopped up, *U.S. Slang.* very aroused; excited.

hop·per (hŏp′ər), *n.* 1. one who or that which hops. 2. any one of various jumping insects, as grasshoppers, leaf hoppers, cheese maggots, etc. 3. a funnel-shaped chamber in which materials are stored temporarily and later discharged through the bottom.

hopper car, *Railroads.* a car for coal, sand, etc., with devices by which the contents can be speedily dumped.

hop·ple (hŏp′əl), *v.t.,* **-pled, -pling.** to hobble; tether.

hop·scotch (hŏp′skŏch′), *n.* a children's game in which the player hops from one compartment to another of an oblong figure traced on the ground, without resting on a line. [f. HOP¹ + SCOTCH (def. 2)]

hor., 1. horizon. 2. horizontal. 3. horology.

Hor·ace (hôr′ĭs, hŏr′-), *n.* (*Quintus Horatius Flaccus*) 65–8 B.C., Roman lyric poet and satirist.

Ho·rae (hōr′ē), *n.pl. Gk. Myth.* goddesses of the seasons and of the hours, and hence of regularity and orderliness.

ho·ral (hōr′əl), *adj.* pertaining to an hour or hours; hourly. [t. LL: s. *hōrālis,* der. L *hōra* HOUR]

ho·ra·ry (hōr′ə rĭ), *adj.* 1. pertaining to an hour; indicating the hours: *the horary circle.* 2. occurring every hour; hourly. 3. lasting an hour. [t. ML: m.s. *hōrārius,* der. L *hōra* HOUR]

Ho·ra·tian (hə rā′shən, hō-), *adj.* 1. of or pertaining to Horace. 2. resembling the poetry or style of Horace.

Horatian ode. See **ode** (def. 5).

Ho·ra·tius (hə rā′shəs, hō-), *n. Rom. Legend.* a hero celebrated for his defense of the bridge over the Tiber against the Etruscans.

horde (hōrd), *n., v.,* **horded, hording.** —*n.* 1. a great company or multitude (often in disparagement). 2. a tribe or troop of Asiatic nomads. 3. any nomadic group. —*v.i.* 4. to gather in a horde. [t. F, ult. t. Turk.: m. *urdū* camp. See URDU]

Ho·reb (hōr′ĕb), *n. Bible.* (apparently) Mount Sinai.

hore·hound (hōr′hound′), *n.* 1. a perennial herb, *Marrubium vulgare,* a native in the Old World, with downy leaves and small whitish flowers and containing a bitter medicinal juice. 2. any of various plants of the mint family. 3. a brittle candy flavored with the extract of the herb. Also, **hoarhound.** [ME *horehune,* OE *hārhūne,* f. *hār* grey + *hūne* horehound]

ho·ri·zon (hə rī′zən), *n.* 1. the line or circle which forms the apparent boundary between earth and sky (**apparent** or **visible horizon**). 2. *Astron.* **a.** the plane which is tangent to the earth at the place of the observer and extends to the celestial sphere (**sensible horizon**). **b.** the great circle of the celestial sphere whose plane is parallel to the sensible horizon of a particular place and passes through the center of the earth, or the plane itself (**astronomical** or **celestial horizon**). 3. the limit or range of perception, knowledge, or the like. 4. *Geol.* a plane in rock strata characterized by particular features, as occurrence of distinctive fossil species. 5. one of the series of distinctive layers found in a vertical cross section of any well-developed soil. [t. L, t. Gk.: bounding circle, horizon, prop. ppr., bounding; r. ME *orizonte,* t. OF] —**ho·ri′zon·less,** *adj.*

hor·i·zon·tal (hôr′ə zŏn′təl, hŏr′-), *adj.* 1. at right angles to the vertical: *a horizontal position.* 2. near, on, or parallel to the horizon. 3. of or pertaining to the horizon. 4. measured or contained in a plane parallel to the horizon: *a horizontal distance.* —*n.* 5. a horizontal line, plane, position, etc. —**hor′i·zon·tal′i·ty, hor′-i·zon·tal·ness,** *n.* —**hor′i·zon·tal·ly,** *adv.*

horizontal bar, *Gymnastics.* a bar for swinging, chinning, and other gymnastic exercises.

horizontal union, a labor union organized by skills or trades of its members rather than by industries.

hor·mone (hôr′mōn), *n. Physiol.* any of various substances which are formed in endocrine organs and which activate specifically receptive organs when transported to them by the body fluids. The internal secretions of the thyroid gland, insulin, etc., are hormones. [t. Gk.: m. *hormōn,* ppr., setting in motion]

Hor·muz (hôr′mŭz), *n.* **Strait of,** a strait between Iran and Trucial Oman, connecting the Persian Gulf and the Gulf of Oman. Also, **Ormuz.**

horn (hôrn), *n.* 1. a hard, projected, often curved and pointed, hollow and permanent growth (usually one of a pair, a right and a left) on the head of certain mammals, as cattle, sheep, goats, antelopes, etc. (**true horn**). 2. each of the pair of solid, deciduous, usually branched, bony growths, or antlers, on the head of a deer. 3. some similar growth, as the tusk of a narwhal. 4. a process projecting from the head of an animal and suggestive of a horn, as a feeler, tentacle, crest, etc. 5. the substance of which true horns are composed. 6. any similar substance, as that of hoofs, nails, corns, etc. 7. an article made of horn, as a thimble, a spoon, or a shoehorn. 8. any hornlike projection or extremity. 9. something formed from or resembling the hollow horn of an animal: *a drinking horn.* 10. a part like a horn of an animal attributed to deities, demons, etc.: *the devil's horn.* 11. *Obs.* the imaginary projection on the brow of a cuckold. 12. *Music.* a wind inment, orig. formed from the hollow horn of an animal but now usually made of brass or other metal or material. 13. *Slang.* a trumpet. 14. an instrument for sounding a warning signal: *automobile horn.* 15. *Aeron.* any of certain short, armlike levers on an airplane. 16. *Radio.* a tube of varying cross section used in some loud-speakers to couple the diaphragm to the sound transmitting space. 17. the high protuberant part at the front and top of a saddle; the pommel. 18. one of the extremities of the crescent moon. 19. a symbol of power, as in the Bible: *an horn of salvation.* 20. *Logic.* each of the alternatives of a dilemma. —*v.t.* 21. to butt or gore with the horns. 22. to furnish with horns. 23. to give the shape of a horn to. —*v.i.* 24. **horn in,** *U.S. Slang.* to thrust oneself forward obtrusively. —*adj.* 25. made of horn.

Horns
A, French or orchestral horn; B, C, Military bugles, with and without keys; D, Hunting horn; E, Coaching horn

b., blend of, blended; c., cognate with; d., dialect, dialectal; der., derived from; f., formed from; g., going back to; m., modification of; r., replacing; s., stem of; t., taken from; ?, perhaps. See the full key on inside cover.

[ME *horn(e)*, OE *horn*, c. G *horn*; akin to L *cornu*, Gk. *kēras* horn] **—horned**, *adj.* **—horn′less**, *adj.* **—horn′-like′**, *adj.*

Horn (hôrn), *n.* **Cape**, a headland on a small island at the S extremity of South America.

horn·beam (hôrn′bēm′), *n.* any of the shrubs or small trees constituting the betulaceous genus *Carpinus*, with a heavy, hard wood, as the American species *C. caroliniana* (**American hornbeam**).

horn·bill (hôrn′bĭl′), *n.* any of the large nonpasserine, tropical Old World birds constituting the family *Bucerotidae*, characterized by a very large bill surmounted by a horny protuberance, sometimes of enormous size.

horn·blende (hôrn′blĕnd′), *n.* any of the common black or dark-colored aluminous varieties of amphibole. [t. G] **—horn·blen′dic,** *adj.*

hornblende schist, *Petrog.* a variety of schist containing needles of hornblende which lie in parallel planes in the rock.

horn·book (hôrn′bŏŏk′), *n.* **1.** a leaf or page containing the alphabet, religious materials, etc., covered with a sheet of transparent horn and fixed in a frame with a handle, formerly used in teaching children to read. **2.** a primer, or book of rudiments.

horned pout, a large-headed fresh-water catfish, *Ameiurus nebulosus*, one of the bullheads, with conspicuous barbels.

horned toad, any of various small, harmless lizards, genus *Phrynosoma*, of western North America, with flattened body and hornlike spines on the head and body.

horned viper. See viper (def. 4).

hor·net (hôr′nĭt), *n.* any large, strong, social wasp of the family *Vespidae* having an exceptionally severe sting, as the **giant hornet** of Europe, *Vespa crabo*, now occurring in the U.S., and the **bald-faced hornet**, *Dolichovespula maculata*, of North America. [ME *harnete*, OE *hyrnet(u)*, c. G *hornisse*]

American hornet, *Vespa maculata* (Ab. 1 in. long)

hor·ni·to (hōr nē′tô; *Sp.* ôr nē′tô), *n.*, *pl.* **-tos** (-tōz; *Sp.* -tôs). *Geol.* a low oven-shaped mound, common in the volcanic districts of South America, etc., usually emitting hot smoke and vapors from its sides and summit. [t. Sp., dim. of *horno*, g. L *furnus* oven]

horn-mad (hôrn′măd′), *adj.* **1.** enraged enough to gore with the horns, as a bull. **2.** raging mad; furious.

horn of plenty, the cornucopia.

horn·pipe (hôrn′pīp′), *n.* **1.** an English folk clarinet with an oxhorn to conceal the reed and another one to form the bell. **2.** a lively dance (orig. to hornpipe music) usually by a single person, popular among sailors. **3.** a piece of music for or in the style of such a dance.

horn silver, cerargyrite.

horn·stone (hôrn′stōn′), *n.* **1.** a variety of quartz resembling flint. **2.** an argillaceous rock baked and partly recrystallized by the heat of an igneous intrusion.

horn·swog·gle (hôrn′swŏg′ol), *v.t.*, **-gled, -gling.** *Slang.* to swindle, cheat, or hoax.

horn·tail (hôrn′tāl′), *n.* any of various wasplike insects of the family *Siricidae*, the females of which have a hornlike spine at the end of the abdomen.

horn·worm (hôrn′wûrm′), *n.* any of various caterpillars of sphinx moths and hawk moths, as the tobacco worm, characterized by a hornlike caudal projection.

horn·wort (hôrn′wûrt′), *n.* any plant of the genus *Ceratophyllum*, comprising aquatic herbs common in ponds and slow streams.

horn·y (hôr′nĭ), *adj.*, **hornier, horniest. 1.** hornlike through hardening; callous: *horny hands.* **2.** consisting of a horn or a hornlike substance; corneous. **3.** more or less translucent, like horn. **4.** having a horn or horns or hornlike projections. **—horn′i·ness,** *n.*

horol., horology.

hor·o·loge (hôr′ə lōj′, -lŏj′, hŏr′-), *n.* any instrument for indicating the time. [t. L: m.s. *hōrologium*, t. Gk.: m. *hōrológion* an instrument for telling the hour; r. ME *orloge*, t. OF]

hor·o·log·ic (hôr′ə lŏj′ĭk, hŏr′-), *adj.* pertaining to a horologe or to horology. Also, **hor′o·log′i·cal.**

ho·rol·o·gist (hō rŏl′ə jĭst), *n.* an expert in horology. Also, **ho·rol′o·ger.**

ho·rol·o·gy (hō rŏl′ə jĭ), *n.* the art or science of making timepieces or of measuring time.

hor·o·scope (hôr′ə skōp′, hŏr′-), *n.* **1.** a diagram of the heavens for use in calculating nativities, etc. **2.** the art or practice of foretelling future events by observation of the stars and planets. [ME and OE *horoscopus*, t. L, t. Gk.: m. *hōroskópos* nativity, horoscope]

ho·ros·co·py (hō rŏs′kə pĭ), *n.* **1.** the casting or taking of horoscopes. **2.** the aspects of the heavens at a given moment, esp. that of a person's birth.

Hor·o·witz (hôr′ə wĭts, hŏr′-; *Russ.* hô′rô vĭts), *n.* **Vladimir** (vlăd′ə mĭr′; *Russ.* vlä dē′mĭr′), born 1904, Russian pianist, now in U.S.

hor·ren·dous (hô rĕn′dəs, hŏ-), *adj.* dreadful; horrible. [t. L: m. *horrendus*, ger. of *horrēre* bristle, shudder] **—hor·ren′dous·ly,** *adv.*

hor·rent (hôr′ənt, hŏr′-), *adj.* bristling; standing erect like bristles. [t. L: s. *horrens*, ppr., standing on end. Cf. HORRID]

hor·ri·ble (hôr′ə bəl, hŏr′-), *adj.* **1.** causing or tending to cause horror; dreadful: *a horrible sight.* **2.** extremely unpleasant; deplorable; excessive: *horrible conditions.* [ME, t. OF, t. L: m. *horribilis* terrible, fearful] **—hor′ri·ble·ness,** *n.* **—hor′ri·bly,** *adv.* **—Syn. 1.** terrible, awful, appalling, frightful; hideous, grim, ghastly, shocking, revolting, repulsive, horrid. **—Ant. 1.** attractive.

hor·rid (hôr′ĭd, hŏr′-), *adj.* **1.** such as to cause horror; dreadful; abominable. **2.** *Colloq.* extremely unpleasant or disagreeable: *horrid weather.* [t. L: s. *horridus* bristling, rough] **—hor′rid·ly,** *adv.* **—hor′rid·ness,** *n.*

hor·rif·ic (hô rĭf′ĭk, hŏ-), *adj.* causing horror. [t. L: s. *horrificus*]

hor·ri·fy (hôr′ə fī′, hŏr′-), *v.t.*, **-fied, -fying.** to cause to feel horror; strike with horror; shock intensely. [t. L: m. *horrificāre* cause horror] **—hor′ri·fi·ca′tion,** *n.*

hor·rip·i·la·tion (hô rĭp′ə lā′shən, hŏ-), *n.* a bristling of the hair on the skin from cold, fear, etc.; goose flesh. [t. LL: s. *horripilātio*, der. L *horripilāre* bristle with hairs]

hor·ror (hôr′ər, hŏr′-), *n.* **1.** a shuddering fear or abhorrence; a painful emotion excited by something frightful or shocking: *to shrink back in horror.* **2.** anything that excites such a feeling: *the horrors of war.* **3.** a character, look, appearance, etc., such as to excite a shuddering fear: *a scene of horror.* **4.** *Colloq.* something considered atrocious or bad: *that hat is a horror.* **5.** a painful or intense aversion or repugnance: *a horror of publicity.* **6.** *Obs.* a bristling. [t. L; r. ME *orrour*, t. OF] **—Syn. 1.** See **terror.**

Hor·sa (hôr′sə), *n.* died A.D. 455, chief of the Jutes; brother of Hengist. Cf. **Hengist.**

hors de com·bat (ôr də kôN bȧ′), *French.* out of the fight; disabled; no longer able to fight.

hors d'oeu·vre (ôr dœ′vr), *pl.* **d'oeuvres** (dœ′vr). a relish such as olives or radishes, served before or between the regular courses of a meal. [t. F: aside from (the main body of the) work]

horse (hôrs), *n.*, *pl.* **horses,** (esp. *collectively*) **horse,** *v.*, **horsed, horsing,** *adj.* **—n. 1.** a large, solid-hoofed quadruped, *Equus caballus*, domesticated since prehistoric times, and employed as a beast of draft and burden and for carrying a rider. **2.** the male horse, in distinction from the female or mare; a stallion or gelding. **3.** any animal of the family *Equidae* (**horse family**), which includes the ass, zebra, etc. **4.** soldiers serving on horseback; cavalry: *a thousand horse.* **5.** something on which a person rides, sits, or exercises, as if on a horse's back: *rocking horse.* **6.** a leather-covered block having two pommels, used for vaulting and other gymnastic exercises. **7.** a frame, block, etc. with legs on which something is mounted or supported. **8.** (in opprobrious or playful use) a man; fellow. **9.** *U.S. School Slang.* a crib, translation, or other illicit aid to study. **10.** *Mining.* a mass of rock enclosed within a lode or vein. **11.** *Chess. Colloq.* a knight. **—v.t. 12.** to provide with a horse or horses. **13.** to set on horseback. **14.** to set or carry on a person's back or on one's own back. **15.** to place on a person's back or on a wooden horse or the like to be flogged. **16.** to flog. **17.** *Colloq.* to drive or urge (a person) at work, esp. unfairly or tyrannically. **18.** *Slang.* to make (a person) the target of boisterous jokes. **19.** *Slang.* to perform boisterously, as a part or a scene in a play. **—v.i. 20.** to mount or go on a horse. **—adj. 21.** unusually large for one of its kind. [ME and OE *hors*, c. OS and OHG *hros*, G *ross*, Icel. *hross*]

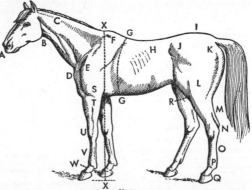

Horse
A, Muzzle; B, Gullet; C, Crest; D, Chest; E, Shoulder; F, Withers; GG, Girth; H, Loin; I, Croup; J, Hip; K, Haunch; L, Thigh; M, Hamstring; N, Hock; O, Cannon; P, Fetlock; Q, Hoof; R, Stifle; S, Elbow; T, Arm; U, Knee; V, Shank; W, Pastern, XX, Height

horse·back (hôrs′băk′), *n.* **1.** the back of a horse: *on horseback.* **2.** *U.S.* a low ridge of sand, gravel, or rock. Cf. **hogback. —adv. 3.** on horseback: *to ride horseback.*

horse·car (hôrs′kär′), *n.* **1.** *U.S.* a streetcar drawn by a horse or horses. **2.** a car fitted for the transportation of horses, either by railroad or by autotruck.

horse chestnut, 1. the shiny, brown nutlike seed of several species of *Aesculus*, ornamental trees bearing large digitate leaves and upright clusters of showy white,

---

red, or yellow flowers, principally *A. Hippocastanum* (**common horse chestnut**) and *A. glabra* (Ohio buckeye). **2.** the tree itself.

horse·cloth (hôrs/klôth/, -klŏth/), *n.* a cloth used to cover a horse, or as part of its trappings.

horse·flesh (hôrs/flĕsh/), *n.* **1.** the flesh of a horse. **2.** horses collectively, esp. for riding, racing, etc.

horse·fly (hôrs/flī/), *n., pl.* **-flies.** any of certain flies of the family *Tabanidae* that bite horses; gadfly.

Horse Guards, 1. a body of cavalry serving as a guard. **2.** the guard, a brigade of cavalry, of the British royal family.

horse·hair (hôrs/hâr/), *n.* **1.** a hair, or the hair, of a horse, esp. from the mane or tail. **2.** a sturdy, glossy fabric woven of horsehair.

horse·hide (hôrs/hīd/), *n.* **1.** the hide of a horse. **2.** leather made from the hide of a horse.

horse latitudes, *Naut.* belts of northern and southern latitudes lying between the region of westerly winds and the region of the trade winds, marked by light baffling winds and occasional calms.

horse·laugh (hôrs/läf/, -läf/), *n.* a loud, coarse laugh.

horse·leech (hôrs/lēch/), *n.* a large leech, as *Haemopsis sanguisorba*, said to attack the mouths of horses while they are drinking.

horse·less (hôrs/lĭs), *adj.* **1.** without a horse. **2.** self-propelled: *a horseless carriage.*

horse mackerel, 1. the common tunny, *Thunnus thynnus*. **2.** a carangoid fish, *Trachurus symmetricus*, of the Pacific coast of the U.S.

horse·man (hôrs/mən), *n., pl.* **-men. 1.** a rider on horseback. **2.** one who attends to horses or is skilled in managing them.

horse·man·ship (hôrs/mən shĭp/), *n.* **1.** the management of horses. **2.** equestrian skill.

horse marine, 1. a member of an imaginary corps of mounted marine soldiers. **2.** (formerly) a marine mounted on horseback, or a cavalryman doing duty on shipboard. **3.** a person out of his element.

horse·mint (hôrs/mĭnt/), *n.* **1.** a wild mint, *Mentha longifolia*, orig. a native of Europe but now found in America. **2.** any of various other menthaceous plants, as *Monarda punctata*, an erect odorous herb of America.

horse nettle, a prickly North American solanaceous weed, *Solanum carolinense.*

horse pistol, a kind of large pistol formerly carried by horsemen.

horse·play (hôrs/plā/), *n.* rough or boisterous play.

horse·pow·er (hôrs/pou/ər), *n.* a unit for measuring power, or rate of work, equivalent to 550 foot-pounds per second.

horse·rad·ish (hôrs/răd/ĭsh), *n.* **1.** a cultivated cruciferous plant, *Armoracia rusticana.* **2.** its pungent root, ground and used as a condiment and in medicine.

horse rake, a large, wheeled rake drawn by a horse.

horse sense, *Colloq.* plain, practical, common sense.

horse·shoe (hôrs/shoo/), *n., v.,* **-shoed, -shoeing. —n. 1.** a U-shaped iron plate nailed to a horse's hoof to protect it. **2.** something shaped like a horseshoe. **3.** (*pl. construed as sing.*) a game using horseshoes or similar pieces, the object being to throw the piece so as to encircle an iron stake 30 or 40 feet away. **—v.t. 4.** to put horseshoes on; to shoe.

Horseshoes
A. Shoe for forefoot;
B. Shoe for hindfoot;
T. Toe calk; H. Heel calk

horseshoe crab, any of various marine arthropods, esp. of the genus *Limulus*, with a carapace shaped somewhat like a horseshoe; king crab.

horse·tail (hôrs/tāl/), *n.* **1.** any of the perennial, herbaceous pteridophytic plants constituting the widely distributed genus *Equisetum*, characterized by hollow, jointed stems. **2.** a horse's tail formerly used as a Turkish military standard or as an ensign of a pasha, the number of horsetails increasing with rank.

horse·weed (hôrs/wēd/), *n.* **1.** a troublesome asteraceous weed, *Erigeron canadense.* **2.** any of various other plants, as *Lactuca canadensis*, an herb of the lettuce genus.

Horseshoe crab
Limulus polyphemus
(Ab. 2 ft. long)

horse·whip (hôrs/hwĭp/), *n., v.,* **-whipped, -whipping. —n. 1.** a whip for controlling horses. **—v.t. 2.** to beat with a horsewhip.

horse·wom·an (hôrs/wŏŏm/ən), *n., pl.* **-women. 1.** a woman who rides on horseback. **2.** a woman who is skillful in managing or riding horses.

hors·y (hôr/sĭ), *adj.,* **horsier, horsiest. 1.** pertaining to, characteristic of, or of the nature of a horse or horses: *horsy talk.* **2.** dealing with, interested in, or devoted to horses, horse racing, etc. **3.** *Slang.* gross in size, appearance, etc. **—hors/i·ness,** *n.*

hort., **1.** horticultural. **2.** horticulture.

hor·ta·tive (hôr/tə tĭv), *adj.* hortatory. [t. L: m.s. *hortātīvus*] **—hor/ta·tive·ly,** *adv.*

hor·ta·to·ry (hôr/tə tōr/ĭ), *adj.* encouraging; inciting;

exhorting; urging to some course of conduct or action: *a hortatory address.* [t. LL: m.s. *hortātōrius* encouraging]

Hor·tense (ôr täns/), *n.* (*Eugénie Hortense de Beauharnais*) 1783–1837, queen of Holland (mother of Louis Napoleon).

Hor·thy (hôr/tĭ), *n.* **Miklós von** (mĭk/lōsh fôn), born 1868, Hungarian admiral; regent of Hungary, 1920–45.

hor·ti·cul·ture (hôr/tə kŭl/chər), *n.* **1.** the cultivation of a garden. **2.** the science and art of cultivating garden plants. [f. *horti-* (comb. form of L *hortus* garden) + CULTURE] **—hor/ti·cul/tur·al,** *adj.* **—hor/ti·cul/tur·ist,** *n.*

hor·tus sic·cus (hôr/təs sĭk/əs), a collection of dried plants; a herbarium. [t. L: dry garden]

Ho·rus (hōr/əs), *n.* *Egyptian Myth.* a solar deity, the son of Osiris and Isis. [t. LL, t. Gk.: m. *Hōros*, t. Egyptian: m. *Hur*, lit., hawk]

Hos., Hosea.

ho·san·na (hō zăn/ə), *interj.* **1.** an exclamation, orig. an appeal to God for deliverance, used in praise of God or Christ. **—n. 2.** a cry of "hosanna." **3.** a shout of praise or adoration; an acclamation. [t. LL, t. Gk., t. Heb.: m. *hosh(i)'āhnnā* save, pray!]

hose (hōz), *n., pl.* **hose,** (*Archaic*) **hosen,** *v.,* **hosed, hosing. —n. 1.** an article of clothing for the foot and lower part of the leg; a stocking. **2.** a garment for the legs and thighs, as tights or breeches, formerly worn by men. **3.** a flexible tube for conveying water, etc., to a desired point: *a garden hose.* **4.** a sheath, or sheathing part, as that enclosing the kernel of grain. **—v.t. 5.** to water, wash, or drench by means of a hose. [ME and OE, c. D *hoos*, G *hose*, Icel. *hosa*]

Ho·se·a (hō zē/ə, -zā/ə), *n.* **1.** a Hebrew prophet of the 8th century B.C. **2.** the first of the books of the minor prophets in the Old Testament. [t. Heb.: m. *Hōshēa'*, with *s* from *Osēe* (Vulgate and Septuagint)]

ho·sier (hō/zhər), *n.* one who makes or deals in hose or stockings, or goods knitted or woven like hose.

ho·sier·y (hō/zhə rĭ), *n.* **1.** hose or stockings of any kind. **2.** the business of a hosier.

hosp., hospital.

hos·pice (hŏs/pĭs), *n.* a house of shelter or rest for pilgrims, strangers, etc., esp. one kept by a religious order. [t. F, t. L: m.s. *hospitium* hospitality]

hos·pi·ta·ble (hŏs/pĭ tə bəl *or, esp. Brit.,* hŏs pĭt/ə bəl), *adj.* **1.** affording a generous welcome to guests or strangers: *a hospitable city.* **2.** inclined to or characterized by hospitality: *a hospitable reception.* **3.** favorably receptive or open (fol. by to): *hospitable to new ideas.* [t. F (obs.), f. s. LL *hospitāre* receive as a guest + -ABLE] **—hos/pi·ta·ble·ness,** *n.* **—hos/pi·ta·bly,** *adv.*

hos·pi·tal (hŏs/pĭ tal), *n.* **1.** an institution in which sick or injured persons are given medical or surgical treatment. **2.** a similar establishment for the care of animals. **3.** *Brit.* an old people's home. [ME, t. OF, t. LL: s. *hospitāle* inn, prop. neut. of L *hospitālis* pertaining to guests, hospitable] **—Syn. 1.** retreat. HOSPITAL, ASYLUM, SANATORIUM, SANITARIUM are names of institutions for persons needing some sort of care. A HOSPITAL is an institution in which sick or injured persons are given medical or surgical treatment, ray therapy, etc.: *the woman was in the hospital awaiting an operation.* An ASYLUM is an institution (usually owned by the state), for the care of particularly afflicted or dependent persons; though it originally meant a place of refuge, the word has acquired unpleasant connotations, so that HOSPITAL is now the preferred term for that type of institution, also: *an asylum for the deaf (insane, blind); an orphan asylum.* The terms SANATORIUM and SANITARIUM are sometimes used interchangeably. However, the former, stressing curative and healing measures, often means a health resort for persons needing mainly rest and recuperation in pleasant surroundings: *nature therapy and raw foods are specialties of this sanatorium.* SANITARIUM stresses hygienic conditions, and usually has patients needing special treatment: *the sanitarium for tubercular patients.*

Hos·pi·tal·er (hŏs/pĭ təl ər), *n.* **1.** a member of a religious and military order (**Knights Hospitalers**) taking its origin about the time of the first Crusade (1096–99) from a hospital at Jerusalem. **2.** (*l.c.*) a person, esp. a member of a religious order, devoted to the care of the sick or needy in hospitals. **3.** (*l.c.*) (in some London hospitals) the chief resident official. Also, **Hos/pi·tal·ler.** [ME, t. OF: m. *hospitalier*, der. *hospital* HOSPITAL]

hos·pi·tal·i·ty (hŏs/pə tăl/ə tĭ), *n., pl.* **-ties.** the reception and entertainment of guests or strangers with liberality and kindness.

hos·pi·tal·ize (hŏs/pĭ tə līz/), *v.t.,* **-ized, -izing.** to place for care in a hospital. **—hos/pi·tal·i·za/tion,** *n.*

hos·po·dar (hŏs/pə där/), *n.* a former title of governors or princes of Walachia and Moldavia. [Rumanian]

host¹ (hōst), *n.* **1.** one who entertains guests in his own home or elsewhere: *the host at a theater party.* **2.** the landlord of an inn. **3.** an animal or plant from which a parasite obtains nutrition. [ME (h)*oste*, t. OF, g. L *hospes* host, guest, stranger. Cf. GUEST, HOST²]

host² (hōst), *n.* **1.** a multitude or great number of persons or things: *a host of details.* **2.** *Archaic.* an army. [ME, t. OF, g. L *hostis* stranger, enemy, ML army. Cf. GUEST, HOST¹]

Host (hōst), *n.* *Eccles.* the bread consecrated in the celebration of the Eucharist; a consecrated wafer. [ME *hoste*, t. OF: m. (h)*oiste*, g. L *hostia* animal sacrificed]

hos·tage (hŏs′tĭj), *n.* **1.** a person given or held as a security for the performance of certain actions. **2.** the condition of a hostage. **3.** a security or pledge. [ME *(h)ostage*, t. OF, der. *oste* guest, g. s. L *hospes* and ? b. with s. L *obses* hostage] **—hos′tage·ship′**, *n.*

hos·tel (hŏs′təl), *n.* **1.** a supervised lodging place for young people traveling by bicycle or walking. **2.** *Brit.* a residence hall at a university. **3.** *Archaic.* an inn. [ME *(h)ostel*, t. OF, der. *oste* guest]

hos·tel·ry (hŏs′təl·rĭ), *n.*, *pl.* **-ries.** *Archaic.* a hostel or inn. [ME *(h)ostelerie*, t. OF, der. *hostel.* See HOSTEL]

host·ess (hŏs′tĭs), *n.* **1.** a female host; a woman who entertains guests. **2.** a woman employed in a restaurant or place of amusement to seat the guests, etc. **3.** a paid dancing partner. **4.** a female innkeeper.

hos·tile (hŏs′təl; *Brit.* -tīl), *adj.* **1.** opposed in feeling, action, or character; unfriendly; antagonistic: *hostile criticism.* **2.** of or characteristic of an enemy: *hostile ground.* [late ME, t. L *hostīlis*, der. *hostis* enemy. See HOST²] **—hos′tile·ly**, *adv.*

Syn. 1. warlike; adverse, averse, opposed. HOSTILE, INIMICAL indicate that which characterizes an enemy or something injurious to one's interests. HOSTILE applies to the spirit, attitude, or action of an enemy: *they showed a hostile and menacing attitude.* INIMICAL applies to an antagonistic or injurious tendency or influence: *their remarks were inimical to his reputation, the climate was inimical to her health.* **—Ant. 2.** amicable.

hos·til·i·ty (hŏs·tĭl′ə·tĭ), *n.*, *pl.* **-ties. 1.** hostile state; enmity; antagonism. **2.** a hostile act. **3.** *(pl.)* acts of warfare. **—Syn. 1.** animosity, ill will, unfriendliness; opposition. **3.** war, warfare, fighting.

hos·tler (hŏs′lər, ŏs′lər), *n.* *Archaic.* one who takes care of horses, esp. at an inn. [var. of OSTLER]

hot (hŏt), *adj.*, **hotter, hottest,** *adv.*, *v.*, **hotted, hotting.** *—adj.* **1.** having or communicating heat; having a high temperature: *a hot stove.* **2.** actively conducting current: *a hot wire.* **3.** having a sensation of great bodily heat; attended with or producing such a sensation. **4.** having an effect as of burning on the tongue, skin, etc., as pepper, mustard, a blister, etc. **5.** having or showing intense feeling; ardent or fervent; vehement; excited: *hot temper.* **6.** lustful. **7.** violent, furious, or intense: *the hottest battle.* **8.** strong or fresh, as a scent or trail. **9.** new: *hot from the press.* **10.** following very closely; close: *to be hot on one's heels.* **11.** *Games.* close to the sought-for object or answer. **12.** *Slang.* fashionable and exciting. **13.** *Jazz.* **a.** (of a musician) performing in an enthusiastic manner, with improvisatory or decorative additions to the original melody. **b.** (of music) marked by such improvisation. **c.** arousing, or capable of arousing, enthusiasm and admiration. **14.** *Slang.* recently stolen or otherwise illegally obtained. **15.** radioactive, esp. to a degree injurious to health. **16. in hot water,** *Colloq.* in trouble. **17. make** (it, etc.) **hot for,** *Colloq.* to make (a place or a situation) unpleasant for. *—adv.* **18.** in a hot manner; hotly. *—v.t.* **19.** *Brit.* to heat. [ME *ho(o)t,* OE *hāt,* c. G *heiss*] **—hot′ly,** *adv.* **—hot′ness,** *n.* **—Syn. 1.** heated; burning, scorching; scalding; boiling; torrid, sultry. **4.** pungent, biting, peppery. **5.** fervid; fiery, passionate; angry. **—Ant. 1.** cold.

hot air, *Slang.* empty, pretentious talk or writing.

hot·bed (hŏt′bĕd′), *n.* **1.** a bed of earth, heated by fermenting manure, etc., and usually covered with glass, for growing plants out of season. **2.** a place favoring rapid growth, esp. of something bad: *a hotbed of vice.*

hot-blood·ed (hŏt′blŭd′ĭd), *adj.* having hot blood; excitable; impetuous.

hot·box (hŏt′bŏks′), *n.* an overheated journal box, in a railroad car or locomotive, caused by the friction of a rapidly revolving axle.

hotch·pot (hŏch′pŏt′), *n.* *Law.* the bringing together of shares or properties in order to divide them equally, esp. when they are to be divided among the children of a parent dying intestate. [ME *hochepot,* t. OF: ragout, f. *hocher* shake + *pot* pot]

hotch·potch (hŏch′pŏch′), *n.* *Brit.* **1.** hodgepodge. **2.** *Law.* hotchpot. [riming var. of HOTCHPOT]

hot cockles, a children's game in which someone covers his eyes and attempts to guess who has hit him.

hot cross bun, a bun with a cross of frosting on it, eaten chiefly during Lent.

hot dog, *Colloq.* a hot frankfurter or wiener (sausage), esp. as served in a split roll.

ho·tel (hō·tĕl′; *Brit. also* ō·tĕl′), *n.* a public house offering lodging, food, etc. for travelers, etc. (commonly preceded in England by *an* rather than *a*). [t. F: (earlier *hostel*) HOSTEL]

—Syn. HOTEL, HOUSE, INN, TAVERN refer to establishments for the lodging or entertainment of travelers and others. HOTEL is the common word, suggesting a more or less commodious establishment with up-to-date appointments though this is not necessarily true: *Grand Hotel, the best hotel in the city.* The word HOUSE is often used in the name of a particular hotel, the connotation being wealth and luxury: *the Parker House, the Palmer House.* INN suggests a place of homelike comfort and old-time appearance or ways; it is used for quaint or archaic effect in the names of some public houses and hotels in the U.S.: *The Pickwick Inn, The Wayside Inn.* A TAVERN, like the English PUBLIC HOUSE, is a house where liquors are sold for drinking on the premises; until recently it was archaic or dialectal in the U.S., but has been revived to substitute for *saloon,* which had unfavorable connotations: *taverns are required to close by two o'clock in the morning.* The word has also been used in the

sense of INN, esp. in New England, ever since Colonial days: *The Old Ship Tavern, King's Tavern* (Boston).

Hô·tel des In·va·lides (ō tĕl′ dĕ zăn và lēd′), the site in Paris of Napoleon's tomb: orig. a hospital for invalided veterans.

hô·tel de ville (ō tĕl′ də vēl′), *French.* a city hall.

hô·tel Dieu (ō tĕl′ dyœ′), *French.* a hospital.

hot·foot (hŏt′fŏŏt′), *adv.* **1.** with great speed in going; in hot haste. *—v.i.* **2.** to go in great haste: *to hotfoot it.*

hot·head (hŏt′hĕd′), *n.* a hot-headed person.

hot-head·ed (hŏt′hĕd′ĭd), *adj.* hot or fiery in spirit or temper; impetuous; rash. **—hot′-head′ed·ly,** *adv.* **—hot′-head′ed·ness,** *n.*

hot·house (hŏt′hous′), *n.* an artificially heated glasshouse for the cultivation of tender plants.

hothouse lamb, a lamb born in the fall or early winter, usually reared indoors, specially fed, and marketed when from 9 to 16 weeks of age.

hot plate, 1. a portable appliance for cooking, heated formerly by a gas burner beneath, now chiefly by an electrical unit in the appliance. **2.** a dish of warm food.

hot pot, *Chiefly Brit.* mutton or beef cooked with potatoes, etc., in a covered pot.

hot-press (hŏt′prĕs′), *n.* **1.** a machine applying heat in conjunction with mechanical pressure, as for producing a smooth surface on paper, for expressing oil, etc. *—v.t.* **2.** to subject to treatment in a hot-press. **—hot′-press′er,** *n.*

Hot Springs, a city (29,307 in 1950) in central Arkansas, adjoining **Hot Springs National Park,** a tourist area in which there are over forty thermal mineral springs.

hot·spur (hŏt′spûr′), *n.* an impetuous person; a hothead. [first applied to Sir Henry PERCY].

Hot·ten·tot (hŏt′ən tŏt′), *n.* **1.** a member of a native South African yellowish-brown race of low stature, probably of mixed Bushman and Bantu (Negro) origin. **2.** the language of the Hottentots, having no certain affinity. [t. D, orig. phrase *hot en tot* "hot and tot" (words supposedly frequent in Hottentot speech)]

Hou·dan (hōō′dăn), *n.* a breed of the domestic fowl of French origin, having a heavy, globular crest and evenly mottled black-and-white plumage. [named after *Houdan,* town in France, near Paris]

Hou·di·ni (hōō dē′nĭ), *n.* **Harry,** (*Erich Weiss*) 1874–1926, U.S. magician and writer.

Hou·don (ōō dôN′), *n.* **Jean Antoine** (zhän än twän′), 1741–1828, French sculptor.

Hou·ma·yun (hōō mä′yōōn), *n.* Humayun.

hound¹ (hound), *n.* **1.** a dog of any of various breeds used in the chase and commonly hunting by scent. **2.** any dog. **3.** *Slang.* a mean, despicable fellow. **4.** *Slang.* an addict: *a movie hound.* **5.** a player in hare and hounds. *—v.t.* **6.** to hunt or track with hounds, or as a hound does; pursue. **7.** to incite (a hound, etc.) to pursuit or attack; urge on. [ME; OE *hund,* c. G *hund.* Cf. L *canis,* Gk. *kýon* dog]

hound² (hound), *n.* **1.** *Naut.* a projection at a masthead, serving to support rigging or trestletrees. **2.** a bar usually used in pairs to strengthen various portions of the running gear of a vehicle. [ME *hūn,* t. Scand.; cf. Icel. *hūnn* knob at the masthead]

hound's-tongue (houndz′tŭng′), *n.* **1.** a troublesome boraginaceous weed, *Cynoglossum officinale,* with prickly nutlets and tonguelike leaves. **2.** any other plant of the genus *Cynoglossum.* [ME and OE *hundestunge,* trans. of L *cynoglossum,* t. Gk. m. *kynōglōsson* dog-tongued]

hour (our), *n.* **1.** a space of time equal to one 24th part of a mean solar day or civil day; 60 minutes. **2.** a short or limited period of time. **3.** a particular or appointed time: *the hour of death.* **4.** the present time: *the man of the hour.* **5.** any definite time of day, or the time indicated by a timepiece: *what is the hour?* **6.** *(pl.)* time spent for work, study, etc.: *after hours.* **7.** *(pl.)* customary time of going to bed and getting up: *to keep late hours.* **8.** distance normally covered in an hour's traveling. **9.** *Astron.* **a.** a unit of measure of right ascension, etc., representing 15 degrees, or the 24th part of a great circle. **b.** See **sidereal hour. 10.** *Educ.* **a.** a single period of class instruction. **b.** one unit of academic credit, usually representing attendance at one scheduled period of instruction per week throughout a semester, quarter, or term. **11.** *(pl.) Eccles.* **a.** the seven stated times of the day set apart for prayer and devotion. **b.** the offices or services prescribed for these times. **c.** a book containing them. **12. the Hours,** *Class. Myth.* the Horae. [ME *ure, ore, hore,* t. OF, g. L *hōra* time, season, hour, t. Gk.; akin to YEAR]

hour circle, *Astron.* any great circle in the celestial sphere passing through the celestial poles.

hour·glass (our′glăs′, -gläs′), *n.* an instrument for measuring time, consisting of two bulbs of glass joined by a narrow passage through which a quantity of sand (or mercury) runs in just an hour.

hour hand, the hand that indicates the hours on a clock or watch.

hou·ri (hōōr′ĭ, hour′ĭ), *n.*, *pl.* **-ris.** one of the beautiful virgins provided in Paradise to all faithful Mohammedans. [t. F, t. Pers.: m. *ḥūrī,* der. Ar. *ḥūr,* pl. of *aḥwar* black-eyed, orig. applied to gazelles]

hour·ly (our′lY), *adj.* **1.** of, pertaining to, occurring, or done each successive hour. **2.** frequent; continual. —*adv.* **3.** every hour; hour by hour. **4.** frequently.

house (*n.* hous; *v.* houz), *n., pl.* **houses** (hou′zYz), *v.,* **housed, housing.** —*n.* **1.** a building for human habitation. **2.** a place of lodgment, rest, etc., as of an animal. **3.** a household. **4.** a building for any purpose: *a house of worship.* **5.** a place of entertainment; a theater. **6.** the audience of a theater, etc. **7.** a family regarded as consisting of ancestors and descendants: *the house of Hapsburg.* **8.** the building in which a legislative or deliberative body meets. **9.** the body itself: *the House of Representatives.* **10.** a quorum of such a body. **11.** a firm or commercial establishment: *the house of Rothschild.* **12.** an advisory or deliberative group, esp. in church or college affairs. **13.** a college in English-style universities. **14.** a residential hall for students, esp. in colleges. **15.** the members or residents of any such house. **16. put** or **set one's house in order,** to put one's affairs into good condition. **17. bring down the house,** to be well received or applauded. **18. on the house,** free; as a gift from the management. —*v.t.* **19.** to put or receive into a house; provide with a house. **20.** to give shelter to; harbor; lodge. **21.** to remove from exposure; put in a safe place. **22.** *Naut.* to place in a secure or protected position. **23.** *Carp.* to fix in a socket or the like. —*v.i.* **24.** to take shelter; dwell. [ME *hous,* OE *hūs,* c. D *huis,* G *haus,* Icel. and Goth. *hūs*] —**house′less,** *adj.*

—**Syn. 1.** domicile. HOUSE, DWELLING, RESIDENCE, HOME are terms applied to a place to live in. DWELLING is now chiefly poetic, or in legal use, as in a lease. RESIDENCE implies size and elegance of structure and surroundings. These two terms and HOUSE have always had reference to the structure to be lived in. HOME has recently taken on this meaning and become practically equivalent to HOUSE, the new meaning tending to crowd out the older connotations of family ties and domestic comfort. See **hotel.**

House (hous), *n.* **Col. Edward Mandell,** 1858–1938, U.S. diplomatic agent and political adviser.

house agent, *Brit.* real-estate agent.

house·boat (hous′bōt′), *n.* a boat fitted up for use as a floating dwelling but not suited to rough water.

house·break·er (hous′brā′kər), *n.* **1.** one who breaks into and enters a house with a felonious intent. **2.** *Brit.* one who dismantles houses. —**house′break′ing,** *n.*

house·bro·ken (hous′brō′kən), *adj.* trained to live indoors, as a dog.

house·carl (hous′kärl′), *n.* a member of the household troops or bodyguard of a Danish or early English king or noble. [modernization of OE *hūscarl,* t. Scand.; cf. Icel. *hūskarl* houseman]

house coat, a long, tailored, dresslike garment of one piece, worn about the house.

house·dress (hous′drĕs′), *n.* a dress worn in the house, esp. while doing housework.

Housefly.
Musca domestica
(¼ in. long)

house·fly (hous′flī′), *n., pl.* **-flies.** a common dipterous insect, *Musca domestica,* found in nearly all parts of the world.

house·hold (hous′hōld′, -ōld′), *n.* **1.** the people of a house collectively; a family, including servants, etc.; a domestic establishment. —*adj.* **2.** of or pertaining to a household; domestic: *household furniture.*

household arts, *Educ.* instruction concerned with homemaking, family living, and allied skills.

house·hold·er (hous′hōl′dər), *n.* **1.** one who holds or occupies a house. **2.** the head of a family.

house·keep·er (hous′kē′pər), *n.* a woman who does or directs the work of a household.

house·keep·ing (hous′kē′pYng), *n.* **1.** the maintaining of a house or domestic establishment. **2.** the management of household affairs.

hou·sel (hou′zəl), *n.* *Archaic.* the Eucharist. [ME; OE *hūsl,* c. Goth. *hūnsl* sacrifice]

house·leek (hous′lēk′), *n.* **1.** a crassulaceous Old World herb, *Sempervivum tectorum,* with pink flowers and thick, succulent leaves, found growing on the roofs and walls of houses. **2.** any plant of the genus *Sempervivum.*

house·line (hous′lYn′), *n.* *Naut.* a small line of three strands, used for seizings, etc.

house·maid (hous′mād′), *n.* a female servant employed in general work in a household.

housemaid's knee, *Pathol.* inflammation of the bursa over the anterior region of the kneepan.

house·mas·ter (hous′măs′tər, -mäs′tər), *n.* (in English boys' schools) a teacher who is in charge of a residence.

house·moth·er (hous′mŭth′ər), *n.* a woman who is head of a group, esp. of students, living together.

House of Burgesses, the assembly of representatives in colonial Virginia.

House of Commons, the elective house of the British parliament.

house of correction, a place for the confinement and reform of persons convicted of minor offenses and not regarded as confirmed criminals.

House of Delegates, the lower house of the General Assembly in Virginia, West Virginia, and Maryland.

House of Lords, the nonelective house of the Parliament of Great Britain and Northern Ireland.

House of Peers, the upper house of the Imperial Diet, the Japanese legislature.

House of Representatives, the lower legislative branch in national and state governing bodies, as in the United States, Australia, Mexico, etc.

house organ, a periodical issued by a business house, etc., presenting news of its activities, etc.

house party, **1.** an entertainment of guests for some days at a host's house, esp. in the country. **2.** the guests.

house physician, a resident physician in a hospital, hotel, or other public institution.

house·top (hous′tŏp′), *n.* the top or roof of a house.

house·warm·ing (hous′wôr′mYng), *n.* a party to celebrate beginning one's occupancy of a new house.

house·wife (hous′wif′ or usually hŭz′Yf for 2), *n., pl.* **-wives** (-wīvz′). **1.** the woman in charge of a household. **2.** *Chiefly Brit.* a small case for needles, thread, etc.

house·wife·ly (hous′wif′lY), *adj.* of, like, or befitting a housewife. —**house′wife′li·ness,** *n.*

house·wif·er·y (hous′wi′fə rY, -wif′rY, hŭz′Yf rY), *n.* the function or work of a housewife; housekeeping.

house·work (hous′wûrk′), *n.* the work of cleaning, cooking, etc., to be done in housekeeping.

hous·ing[1] (hou′zYng), *n.* **1.** something serving as a shelter, covering, or the like; a shelter; lodging. **2.** houses collectively. **3.** act of one who houses or puts under shelter. **4.** the providing of houses for the community: *the housing of veterans.* **5.** *Mach.* a frame, plate, or the like, that supports a part of a machine, etc. **6.** *Carp.* the space made in one piece of wood, or the like, for the insertion of another. **7.** *Naut.* **a.** the inboard end of a bowsprit. **b.** the part of a mast which is below deck. **8.** a niche for a statue. [f. HOUSE, v. + -ING[1]]

hous·ing[2] (hou′zYng), *n.* **1.** a covering of cloth for the back and flanks of a horse or other animal, for protection or ornament. **2.** a covering of cloth or the like. **3.** (*often pl.*) a caparison or trapping. [f. *house* (ME, t. OF: m. *houce*) covering of cloth + -ING[1]]

Hous·man (hous′mən), *n.* **Alfred Edward,** 1859–1936, British poet and classical scholar.

Hous·ton (hū′stən), *n.* **1. Sam,** 1793–1863, U.S. frontier hero and soldier: president of Texas, 1836–38. **2.** a city in SE Texas: a port on a ship canal, ab. 50 mi. from the Gulf of Mexico. 596,163 (1950).

hous·to·ni·a (hōō stō′nY ə), *n.* any herb of the North American rubiaceous genus *Houstonia,* as *H. caerulea,* the common bluet or innocence. [NL; named after Dr. W. *Houston* (d. 1733), British botanist. See -IA]

Hou·yhn·hnm (hōō Yn′əm, hwYn′əm), *n.* (in Swift's *Gulliver's Travels*) one of a race of horses endowed with reason, who rule the Yahoos, a race of degraded, brutish creatures having the form of man.

hove (hōv), *v.* pt. and pp. of **heave.**

hov·el (hŭv′əl, hŏv′-), *n., v.,* **-eled, -eling,** or (*esp. Brit.*) **-elled, -elling.** —*n.* **1.** a small, mean dwelling house; a wretched hut. **2.** an open shed, as for sheltering cattle, tools, etc. —*v.t.* **3.** to shelter or lodge as in a hovel. [ME *hovel, hovyl;* orig. uncert.]

hov·er (hŭv′ər, hŏv′-), *v.i.* **1.** to hang fluttering or suspended in the air: *a hovering bird.* **2.** to keep lingering about; wait near at hand. **3.** to remain in an uncertain or irresolute state; waver: *hovering between life and death.* —*n.* **4.** act of hovering. **5.** state of hovering. [ME *hoveren,* freq. of *hoven* hover; orig. uncert.] —**hov′er·er,** *n.* —**hov′er·ing·ly,** *adv.* —**Syn. 1.** See **fly**[1].

Hov·ey (hŭv′Y), *n.* **Richard,** 1864–1900, U.S. poet.

how (hou), *adv.* **1.** in what way or manner; by what means: *how did it happen?* **2.** to what extent, degree, etc.: *how much?* **3.** at what price: *how do you sell these apples?* **4.** in what state or condition: *how are you?* **5.** for what reason; why. **6.** to what effect or with what meaning: *how do you mean?* **7.** what? —*n.* **8.** a question beginning with "how." **9.** way or manner of doing: *to consider all the hows and wherefores.* [ME *hou, how,* OE *hū,* c. D *hoe;* akin to WHO]

How·ard (hou′ərd), *n.* **1. Catherine,** died 1542, fifth wife of Henry VIII. **2. Henry.** See **Surrey,** Earl of.

how·be·it (hou bē′Yt), *adv.* **1.** nevertheless. —*conj.* **2.** *Obs.* although. [ME *how be hit* however it may be. Cf. ALBEIT]

how·dah (hou′də), *n.* (in the East Indies) a seat, commonly with a railing and a canopy, placed on the back of an elephant. [t. Hind.: m. *haudah,* t. Ar.: m. *haudaj*]

Howe (hou), *n.* **1. Elias,** 1819–67, U.S. inventor (of the sewing machine). **2. Julia Ward,** 1819–1910, U.S. author. **3. Richard,** 1725–99, British admiral. **4. William,** (*5th Viscount Howe*) 1729–1814, British general: commander in chief of the British forces, 1775–78, in the American Revolutionary War.

how·e'er (hou âr′), *conj., adv.* however.

How·ells (hou′əlz), *n.* **William Dean,** 1837–1920, U.S. novelist and editor.

how·ev·er (hou ĕv′ər), *conj.* **1.** nevertheless; yet; in spite of that. —*adv.* **2.** to whatever extent or degree; no matter how (far, much, etc.). **3.** in whatever manner. **4.** *Brit.* (interrogatively) how under any circumstances: *however did you manage?* [ME] —**Syn. 1.** See **but**[1].

how·itz·er (hou′Yt sər), *n.* a comparatively short-barreled cannon, used esp. for curved fire, as in reaching troops behind cover. [earlier *hauwitzer,* appar. t. D: m. *houwitser,* der. *houwits(e)* catapult. Cf. G *haubitze,* earlier *haufnitz,* t. Czech: m. *houfnice* catapult]

howl (houl) *v.i.* **1.** to utter a loud, prolonged, mournful cry, as that of a dog or wolf. **2.** to utter a similar cry in distress, pain, rage, etc.; wail. **3.** to make a sound like an animal howling: *the wind is howling.* —*v.t.* **4.** to utter with howls. **5.** to drive or force by howls. —*n.* **6.** the cry of a dog, wolf, etc. **7.** a cry or wail, as of pain or rage. **8.** a sound like wailing: *the howl of the wind.* **9.** a loud scornful laugh or yell. [ME *houle.* Cf. G *heulen;* imit.]

How·land Island (hou′lənd),   a small island in the central Pacific, near the equator: U.S. aerological station and airfield. 1 sq. mi.

howl·er (hou′lər), *n.* **1.** one who or that which howls. **2.** Also, **howling monkey.** any of the large, prehensile-tailed tropical American monkeys of the genus *Alouatta,* the males of which make a howling noise. **3.** *Colloq.* an especially ludicrous blunder, as in a school recitation.

How·rah (hou′rä), *n.* a city in NE India, on the Hooghly river opposite Calcutta. 379,292 (1941).

how·so·ev·er (hou′sō·ĕv′ər), *adv.* **1.** to whatsoever extent or degree. **2.** in whatsoever manner.

hoy·den (hoi′dən), *n.* **1.** a rude or ill-bred girl; tomboy. —*adj.* **2.** hoydenish; boisterous. Also, **hoiden.** [orig. uncert.] —**hoy′den·ish,** *adj.* —**hoy′den·ish·ness,** *n.*

Hoyle (hoil), *n.* **Edmund** or **Edmond,** 1672–1769, British writer on card games.

HP, 1. Also, **H.P.** *Elect.* high power. **2.** Also, **H.P., h.p.** high pressure. **3.** Also, **hp, H.P., h.p.** horsepower.

H.Q., headquarters. Also, **h.q.**

Hr., (Ger. *Herr*) equivalent of **Mr.**

hr., *pl.* **hrs.** hour; hours.

H.R., House of Representatives.

Hr·dlič·ka (hûr′dlĭch kä), *n.* **Aleš** (ä′lĕsh), 1869–1943, U.S. anthropologist, born in Bohemia.

H.R.H., His, or Her, Royal Highness.

H.R.I.P., (L *hic requiescit in pace*) here rests in peace.

Hrolf (hrŏlf), *n.* See **Rollo.**

H.S., 1. High School. **2.** *Brit.* Home Secretary.

h.s., (L *hoc sensu*) in this sense.

H.S.H., His, or Her, Serene Highness.

Hsing·an (shĭng′än′), *n.* a province in NE China, in Manchuria. 1,292,500 pop. (est. 1945); 103,918 sq. mi.

Hsin·king (shĭn′jĭng′), *n.* Changchun.

H.S.M., His, or Her, Serene Majesty.

ht., height.

H.T., Hawaiian Territory.

Huás·car (wäs′kär), *n.* c1495–1533, Inca ruler of Peru.

Huas·ca·rán (wäs′kä rän′), *n.* a mountain in W Peru, in the Andes. 22,205 ft.

hub (hŭb), *n.* **1.** the central part of a wheel, as that part into which the spokes are inserted. **2.** the part in central position around which all else revolves: *the hub of the universe.* **3. the Hub,** Boston, Mass. **4.** the peg or hob used as a target in quoits, etc. **5.** *Coining.* a de sign of hardened steel in relief used as a punch in making a die. [cf. HOB¹]

hub·ba hub·ba (hŭb′ə hŭb′ə), *U.S. Slang.* an exclamation of liking or approval. Also, **hub′a hub′a.**

Hub·bard (hŭb′ərd), *n.* **Elbert,** 1856–1915, U.S. author.

hub·bub (hŭb′ŭb), *n.* **1.** a loud, confused noise, as of many voices. **2.** tumult; uproar. —**Syn. 1.** See **noise.**

huck·a·back (hŭk′ə bǎk′), *n.* toweling of linen or cotton, of a distinctive weave. Also, **huck.**

huck·le·ber·ry (hŭk′əl bĕr′ĭ), *n., pl.* **-ries. 1.** the dark-blue or black edible berry of any of various shrubs of the ericaceous genus *Gaylussacia.* **2.** a shrub yielding such a berry. **3.** blueberry (def. 1). [var. of *hurtleberry* WHORTLEBERRY]

Huckleberry Finn (fĭn), **The Adventures of,** a novel (1884) by Mark Twain.

huck·le·bone (hŭk′əl bōn′), *n. Anat.* **1.** the hipbone. **2.** the anklebone, astragalus, or talus.

huck·ster (hŭk′stər), *n.* Also, **huck′ster·er. 1.** a retailer of small articles; a hawker. **2.** a street peddler in fruits and vegetables. **3.** a cheaply mercenary person. **4.** *U.S. Slang.* an advertising man. —*v.i.* **5.** to deal in small articles or make petty bargains. [ME *huccster,* *hokester.* Cf. G *höken* to retail goods]

Hud·ders·field (hŭd′ərz fēld′), *n.* a city in central England, in SW Yorkshire. 121,920 (est. 1946).

hud·dle (hŭd′əl), *v.,* **-dled, -dling,** *n.* —*v.t.* **1.** to heap or crowd together confusedly. **2.** to draw (oneself) closely together; nestle (often fol. by *up*). **3.** to do hastily and carelessly (often fol. by *up, over,* or *together*). **4.** to put on (clothes) with careless haste (often fol. by *on*). —*v.i.* **5.** to gather or crowd together in a confused mass. **6.** *Football.* to get together in a huddle to determine the next play. —*n.* **7.** a confused heap, mass, or crowd; a jumble. **8.** confusion or disorder. **9.** *Colloq.* a conference held in secret. **10.** *Football.* a gathering of the team behind the scrimmage line for instructions, signals, etc. [cf. ME *hodre,* c. LG *hudren*] —**hud′dler,** *n.*

Hu·di·bras·tic (hū′də brăs′tĭk), *adj.* **1.** of or pertaining to, or resembling the style of, Samuel Butler's **Hudibras** (published 1663–78), a mock-heroic satirical poem directed against the Puritans, written in tetrameter couplets with many comical rhymes; mock-heroic. **2.** of a playful burlesque style.

Hud·son (hŭd′sən), *n.* **1. Henry,** died 1611?, British navigator and explorer in North America. **2. William Henry,** 1841–1922, British naturalist and author. **3.** a river in E New York, flowing S to New York Bay. 306 mi.

Hudson Bay, a large inland sea in N Canada. ab. 850 mi. long; ab. 600 mi. wide; ab. 400,000 sq. mi.

Hudson seal, muskrat fur which has been plucked and dyed to give the appearance of seal.

Hudson Strait, a strait connecting Hudson Bay and the Atlantic. ab. 450 mi. long; ab. 100 mi. wide.

hue¹ (hū), *n.* **1.** that property of color by which the various regions of the spectrum are distinguished, as red, blue, etc. **2.** variety of a color; a tint: *pale hues.* **3.** color: *all the hues of the rainbow.* **4.** *Obs.* form or appearance. **5.** *Obs.* complexion. [ME *hewe,* OE *hīw* form, appearance, color]

hue² (hū), *n.* outcry, as of pursuers; clamor. [ME *hu,* t. OF, der. *heur* cry out, shout; prob. imit.]

Hué (hwĕ), *n.* a seaport in E French Indo-China, in Viet Nam: the former capital of Annam. 40,000 (1936).

hue and cry, 1. *Law.* the pursuit of a felon or an offender with loud outcries or clamor to give an alarm. **2.** any public clamor against or over something.

hued (hūd), *adj.* having a hue or color: *golden-hued.*

Huel·va (wĕl′vä), *n.* a seaport in SW Spain, near the Gulf of Cádiz. 56,427 (1940).

Huer·ta (wĕr′tä), *n.* **Victoriano** (vēk′tō ryä′nō), 1854–1916, Mexican general: president of Mexico, 1913–14.

huff (hŭf), *n.* **1.** a sudden swell of anger; a fit of resentment: *to leave in a huff.* —*v.t.* **2.** to give offense to; make angry. **3.** to treat with arrogance or contempt; bluster at; hector or bully. **4.** *Checkers.* to remove (a piece) from the board as penalty for failing to make a compulsory capture. —*v.i.* **5.** to take offense. **6.** *Archaic.* to swell with pride or arrogance; swagger or bluster. **7.** *Brit. Dial.* to puff or blow. [imit.]

huff·ish (hŭf′ĭsh), *adj.* **1.** petulant. **2.** swaggering; hectoring. —**huff′ish·ly,** *adv.* —**huff′ish·ness,** *n.*

huff·y (hŭf′ĭ), *adj.,* **huffier, huffiest. 1.** easily offended or touchy. **2.** offended; sulky. *u huffy mood.* —**huff′i·ly,** *adv.* —**huff′i·ness,** *n.*

hug (hŭg), *v.,* **hugged, hugging,** *n.* —*v.t.* **1** to clasp tightly in the arms, esp. with affection; embrace. **2.** to cling firmly or fondly to: *to hug an opinion.* **3.** to keep close to, as in sailing or going along: *to hug the shore.* —*v.i.* **4.** to cling together; lie close. —*n.* **5.** a tight clasp with the arms; a warm embrace. [cf. Icel. *hugga* console]

huge (hūj), *adj.,* **huger, hugest.** extraordinarily large in bulk, quantity, or extent: *a huge mountain.* [ME *huge, hoge;* ? aphetic var. of OF *ahuge* great, large, high; orig. uncert.] —**huge′ly,** *adv.* —**huge′ness,** *n.*

—**Syn.** mammoth, gigantic, colossal; vast; stupendous; bulky. HUGE, ENORMOUS, IMMENSE, TREMENDOUS imply great magnitude. HUGE, when used of concrete objects, usually adds the idea of massiveness, bulkiness, or even shapelessness: *a huge mass of rock, a huge collection of antiques.* ENORMOUS, lit. out of the norm, applies to what exceeds in extent, magnitude, or degree, a norm or standard: *an enormous iceberg, enormous curiosity.* TREMENDOUS applies to anything so huge as to be astonishing or to inspire awe: *a tremendous amount of equipment.* IMMENSE, lit. not measurable, is particularly applicable to what is exceedingly great, without reference to a standard: *immense buildings.* All are used figuratively: *a huge success, enormous curiosity, tremendous effort, immense joy.* —**Ant.** small, tiny, diminutive.

hug·ger-mug·ger (hŭg′ər mŭg′ər), *n.* **1.** disorder or confusion; a muddle. **2.** *Archaic.* secrecy or concealment: *in hugger-mugger.* —*adj.* **3.** secret or clandestine. **4.** disorderly or confused. —*v.t.* **5.** to keep secret or concealed. —*v.i.* **6.** to act secretly; take secret counsel.

Hugh Ca·pet (hū kā′pĭt, kăp′ĭt; *Fr.* kà pĕ′). See **Capet.**

Hughes (hūz), *n.* **1. Charles Evans,** 1862–1948, U.S. statesman: chief justice of the United States Supreme Court, 1930–41. **2. Langston** (lăng′stən), born 1902, U.S. writer. **3. Thomas,** 1822–96, British author.

Hug·li (hōōg′lē), *n.* Hooghly.

hug-me-tight (hŭg′mē tīt′), *n.* *U.S.* a tight, sometimes sleeveless, knitted jacket.

Hu·go (hū′gō; *Fr.* y gō′), *n.* **Victor Marie** (vĭk′tər mə rē′; *Fr.* vĕk tôr′ mà rē′), **Viscount,** 1802–85, French poet, novelist, and dramatist.

Hu·gue·not (hū′gə nŏt′), *n.* a member of the Reformed or Calvinistic communion of France in the 16th and 17th centuries; a French Protestant. [t. F, earlier *eiguenot,* t. Swiss G: m. *eidgenosse* confederate, f. *eid* oath + *genoss* companion, associate, influenced by name *Hugues* Hugh]

hu·la-hu·la (hōō′lə hōō′lə), *n.* a kind of native Hawaiian dance with intricate arm movements which tell a story in pantomime. Also, **hu′la.** [t. Hawaiian]

hulk (hŭlk), *n.* **1.** the body of an old or dismantled ship. **2.** a dismasted wreck. **3.** a vessel specially built to serve as a storehouse, prison, etc., and not for sea service. **4.** a bulky or unwieldy person or mass of anything. **5.** *Archaic.* a heavy, unwieldy vessel. —*v.i.* **6.** to loom in bulky form; be bulky (often fol. by *up*). **7.** *Dial.* to lounge or slouch in a heavy, loutish manner. [ME *hulke,* OE *hulc,* prob. t. ML: s. *hulcus,* t. Gk.: m. *holkás* trading vessel]

hulk·ing (hŭl′kĭng), *adj.* bulky; heavy and clumsy. Also, **hulk′y.**

hull¹ (hŭl), *n.* **1.** the husk, shell, or outer covering of a seed or fruit. **2.** the calyx of certain fruits, as the strawberry and raspberry. **3.** any covering or envelope. —*v.t.* **4.** to remove the hull of. [ME; OE *hulu* husk, pod; akin to *helan* cover, hide. Cf. HALL, HELL, HOLE] —**hull′er,** *n.*

ăct, āble, dâre, ärt; ĕbb, ēqual; ĭf, īce; hŏt, ōver, ôrder, oil, bŏŏk, ōōze, out; ŭp, ūse, ûrge; ə = a in alone; ch, chief; g, give; ng, ring; sh, shoe; th, thin; ŧh, that; zh, vision.   See the full key on inside cover.

hull[2] (hŭl), *n.* **1.** the frame or body of a ship, exclusive of masts, yards, sails, and rigging. **2.** *Aeron.* **a.** the boatlike fuselage of a flying boat on which the plane lands or takes off. **b.** the cigar-shaped arrangement of girders enclosing the gasbag of a rigid dirigible. —*v.t.* **3.** to strike or pierce the hull of (a ship), as with a torpedo. [orig. uncert. Cf. HULL[1], HOLD[2], HOLE]

Hull (hŭl), *n.* **1. Cordell,** born 1871, U.S. statesman: Secretary of State, 1933–44. **2. William,** 1753–1825, American general. **3.** Official name, **Kingston-upon-Hull.** a seaport in E England, on the Humber estuary. 279,600 (est. 1946). **4.** a city in SE Canada, on the Ottawa river opposite Ottawa. 32,947 (1941).

hul·la·ba·loo (hŭl′ə bə lōō′), *n.* a clamorous noise or disturbance; an uproar.

hul·lo (hə lō′), *interj., n., v.* **1.** hollo. **2.** hello.

hum (hŭm), *v.,* **hummed, humming,** *n., interj.* —*v.i.* **1.** to make a low, continuous, droning sound. **2.** to give forth an indistinct sound of mingled voices or noises. **3.** to utter an indistinct sound in hesitation, embarrassment, dissatisfaction, etc.; hem. **4.** to sing with closed lips, without articulating words. **5.** *Colloq.* to be in a state of busy activity: *to make things hum.* —*v.t.* **6.** to sound, sing, or utter by humming. **7.** to bring, put, etc., by humming: *to hum a child to sleep.* —*n.* **8.** act or sound of humming; an inarticulate or indistinct murmur; a hem. —*interj.* **9.** an inarticulate sound uttered in hesitation, dissatisfaction, etc. [ME *humme,* c. G *hummen* hum; imit. Cf. HUMBLEBEE] —**hum′mer,** *n.*

hu·man (hū′mən), *adj.* **1.** of, pertaining to, or characteristic of man: *human nature.* **2.** having the nature of man; being a man: *the human race.* **3.** of or pertaining to mankind generally: *human affairs.* —*n.* **4.** *Colloq. or Humorous.* a human being. [t. L: s. *hūmānus* of a man; r. ME *humain,* t. OF] —**hu′man·ness,** *n.*
—**Syn. 1.** HUMAN, HUMANE may refer to that which is, or should be, characteristic of human beings. In thus describing characteristics, HUMAN may refer to good and bad traits of mankind alike (*human kindness, human weakness*), with, perhaps, more emphasis upon the latter, HUMAN being seen then in contrast to DIVINE: *to err is human, to forgive divine; he was only human.* HUMANE (the original spelling of HUMAN, and since 1700 restricted in meaning) takes into account only the nobler aspects of man: a HUMANE person is, specifically, one actuated by benevolence in his treatment of his fellows, or of helpless animals; the word once had also connotations of courtesy and refinement (hence, the application of HUMANE to those branches of learning intended to refine the mind). —**Ant. 3.** animal.

hu·mane (hū mān′), *adj.* **1.** characterized by tenderness and compassion for the suffering or distressed: *humane feelings.* **2.** (of branches of learning or literature) tending to refine; polite: *humane studies.* [var. of HUMAN. Cf. GERMANE, GERMAN] —**hu·mane′ly,** *adv.* —**hu·mane′ness,** *n.* —**Syn. 1.** merciful, kind, kindhearted, tender. See **human.** —**Ant. 1.** brutal.

hu·man·ism (hū′mə nĭz′əm), *n.* **1.** any system or mode of thought or action in which human interests predominate. **2.** devotion to or study of the humanities; polite learning; literary culture. **3.** (*sometimes cap.*) the studies, principles, or culture of the Humanists (def. 4).

hu·man·ist (hū′mən ĭst), *n.* **1.** a student of human nature or affairs. **2.** one devoted to or versed in the humanities. **3.** a classical scholar. **4.** (*sometimes cap.*) one of the scholars of the Renaissance who pursued and disseminated the study and understanding of the cultures of ancient Rome and Greece. —**hu′man·is′tic,** *adj.*

hu·man·i·tar·i·an (hū măn′ə târ′Ĭ ən), *adj.* **1.** having regard to the interests of all mankind; broadly philanthropic. **2.** pertaining to ethical or theological humanitarianism. —*n.* **3.** one who professes ethical or theological humanitarianism. **4.** a philanthropist.

hu·man·i·tar·i·an·ism (hū măn′ə târ′Ĭ ə nĭz′əm), *n.* **1.** humanitarian principles or practices; comprehensive philanthropy. **2.** *Ethics.* **a.** the doctrine that man's obligations are concerned wholly with the welfare of the human race. **b.** the doctrine that mankind may become perfect without divine aid. **3.** *Theol.* the doctrine that Jesus Christ possessed a human nature only.

hu·man·i·ty (hū măn′ə tĭ), *n., pl.* **-ties. 1.** the human race; mankind. **2.** the condition or quality of being human; human nature. **3.** the quality of being humane; kindness; benevolence. **4.** polite learning in its various branches, as grammar, rhetoric, poetry, etc. **5. the humanities, a.** the study of the Latin and Greek classics. **b.** the study of literature, philosophy, art, etc., as distinguished from the social and physical sciences. [ME *humanitee,* t. F: m. *humanité,* t. L: m.s. *hūmānitas*]

hu·man·ize (hū′mə nīz′), *v.,* **-ized, -izing.** —*v.t.* **1.** to make humane, kind, or gentle. **2.** to make human. —*v.i.* **3.** to become human or humane. —**hu′man·i·za′tion,** *n.* —**hu′man·iz′er,** *n.*

hu·man·kind (hū′mən kīnd′), *n.* the human race.

hu·man·ly (hū′mən lĭ), *adv.* **1.** in a human manner; by human means. **2.** according to human knowledge.

human nature, 1. the quality inherent in all persons by virtue of their common humanity. **2.** *Sociol.* the make-up of conduct of human beings that distinguishes them from other animal forms, generally regarded as produced by living in primary groups.

hu·ma·num est er·ra·re (hū mā′nəm ĕst ĕr ār′Ĭ), *Latin.* to err is human.

Hu·ma·yun (hŏō mä′yōōn), *n.* 1508–56, Mogul emperor of Hindustan. Also, **Houmayun.**

Hum·ber (hŭm′bər), *n.* the estuary of the Ouse and Trent rivers in E England. 37 mi. long.

Hum·bert I (hŭm′bərt), (*Umberto I*) 1844–1900, king of Italy, 1878–1900.

hum·ble (hŭm′bəl, ŭm′-), *adj.,* **-bler, -blest,** *v.,* **-bled, -bling.** —*adj.* **1.** low in station, grade of importance, etc.; lowly: *humble origin.* **2.** modest; meek; without pride. **3.** courteously respectful: *in my humble opinion.* **4.** low in height, level, etc. —*v.t.* **5.** to lower in condition, importance, or dignity; abase. **6.** to make meek: *to humble one's heart.* [ME, t. OF, g. L *humilis* low, humble] —**hum′ble·ness,** *n.* —**hum′bler,** *n.* —**hum′bling,** *adj.* —**hum′bling·ly,** *adv.* —**hum′bly,** *adv.*
—**Syn. 1.** unassuming, plain, common, poor. **2.** submissive. **5.** HUMBLE, DEGRADE, HUMILIATE suggest lowering or causing to seem lower. To HUMBLE is to bring down the pride of another (often righteously) or to reduce him to a state of abasement: *to humble an arrogant enemy.* To DEGRADE is to demote in rank or standing, or to reduce to a low level in condition, manners, or morals: *to degrade an officer, one's dependents.* To HUMILIATE is to make others feel or appear inadequate or unworthy; esp. in some public setting: *to humiliate a sensitive person.* —**Ant. 1.** noble, illustrious. **2.** self-assertive. **3.** insolent; proud. **5.** elevate. **6.** exalt.

hum·ble·bee (hŭm′bəl bē′), *n. Chiefly Brit.* bumblebee.

humble pie, 1. *Obs.* a pie made of the umbles (inward, less delectable parts) of deer, etc. **2. eat humble pie,** to be humiliated; be forced to apologize humbly.

Hum·boldt (hŭm′bōlt; *Ger.* hŏŏm′bŏlt), *n.* **1. Friedrich Heinrich Alexander** (frē′drĬkH hīn′rĬkH ä′lĕksän′dər), **Baron von,** 1769–1859, German scientist and writer. **2. Karl Wilhelm** (kärl vĬl′hĕlm), **Baron von,** 1767–1835, German philologist and statesman.

hum·bug (hŭm′bŭg), *n., v.,* **-bugged, -bugging.** —*n.* **1.** a deluding trick; a hoax; a fraud. **2.** quality of falseness or deception. **3.** one who seeks to impose deceitfully upon others; a cheat; an impostor. —*v.t.* **4.** to impose upon by humbug or false pretense; delude. —*v.i.* **5.** to practice humbug. [orig. unknown] —**hum′bug′ger,** *n.* —**Syn. 1.** imposture, deception. **2.** pretense, sham. **3.** pretender, deceiver, charlatan.

hum·bug·ger·y (hŭm′bŭg′ər Ĭ), *n.* pretense; sham.

hum·ding·er (hŭm dĬng′ər), *n. Slang.* a person or thing remarkable of its kind.

hum·drum (hŭm′drŭm′), *adj.* **1.** lacking variety; dull: *a humdrum existence.* —*n.* **2.** humdrum character or routine; monotony. **3.** monotonous or tedious talk. **4.** a dull boring fellow. [varied redupl. of HUM]

Hume (hūm), *n.* **David,** 1711–76, Scottish philosopher and historian.

hu·mer·al (hū′mər əl), *adj.* **1.** of the shoulder. **2.** *Anat., Zool.* of or related to the humerus or brachium. [f. s. L *humerus* shoulder + -AL[1]]

hu·mer·us (hū′mər əs), *n., pl.* **-meri** (-mə rī′). *Anat., Zool.* **1.** (in man) the single long bone in the arm which extends from the shoulder to the elbow. See diag. under **shoulder.** **2.** the brachium. **3.** a corresponding bone in the forelimb of other animals or in the wings of birds. [t. L, prop. *umerus* shoulder]

hu·mic (hū′mĬk), *adj. Chem.* of or denoting something (as an acid) derived from humus. [f. s. L *humus* ground, mould + -IC]

hu·mid (hū′mĬd), *adj.* moist or damp, with liquid or vapor: *humid air.* [t. L: s. (*h*)*ūmidus* moist] —**hu′mid·ly,** *adv.* —**hu′mid·ness,** *n.* —**Syn.** See **damp.**

hu·mid·i·fy (hū mĬd′ə fī′), *v.t.,* **-fied, -fying.** to make humid. —**hu·mid′i·fi·ca′tion,** *n.* —**hu·mid′i·fi′er,** *n.*

hu·mid·i·ty (hū mĬd′ə tĬ), *n.* **1.** humid condition; dampness. **2.** *Meteorol.* the ratio (percentage) of the water vapor in the atmosphere to the amount required to saturate it at the same temperature (called specifically **relative humidity**).

hu·mi·dor (hū′mə dôr′), *n.* a container or storage room for cigars or other preparations of tobacco, fitted with means for keeping the tobacco suitably moist.

hu·mil·i·ate (hū mĬl′Ĭ āt′), *v.t.,* **-ated, -ating.** to lower the pride or self-respect of; cause a painful loss of dignity to; mortify. [t. LL: m.s. *humiliātus,* pp., humbled] —**Syn.** degrade, abase, debase; dishonor, disgrace, shame. See **humble.** See also **ashamed.** —**hu·mil′i·at′ing,** *adj.* —**hu·mil′i·at·ing·ly,** *adv.* —**Ant.** exalt, honor.

hu·mil·i·a·tion (hū mĬl′Ĭ ā′shən), *n.* **1.** act of humiliating. **2.** state or feeling of being humiliated; mortification. —**Syn. 2.** See **shame.**

hu·mil·i·ty (hū mĬl′ə tĬ), *n., pl.* **-ties.** quality of being humble; modest sense of one's own significance. [ME *humilite,* t. F, t. L: m.s. *humilitas*] —**Syn.** lowliness, meekness. —**Ant.** pride.

hum·ming (hŭm′Ĭng), *adj.* **1.** that hums; buzzing. **2.** *Colloq.* extraordinarily active, intense, great, or big. **3.** *Colloq.* foaming, strong, or heady: *humming ale.*

hum·ming·bird (hŭm′Ĭng bûrd′), *n.* any of numerous very small American birds constituting the family *Trochilidae,* characterized by narrow wings whose rapid vibration produces a hum, by slender bill, and usually by brilliant plumage.

Ruby-throated hummingbird, *Archilochus colubris* (Ab. 3 in. long)

hummingbird moth, any of the hawk moths.

---

b., blend of, blended; c., cognate with; d., dialect, dialectal; der., derived from; f., formed from; g., going back to; m., modification of; r., replacing; s., stem of; t., taken from; ?. perhaps. See the full key on inside cover.

hum·mock (hŭm′ək), *n.* **1.** an elevated tract rising above the general level of a marshy region; a hammock. **2.** a knoll or hillock. **3.** a ridge in an ice field.

hum·mock·y (hŭm′ək·ĭ), *adj;* **1.** abounding in hummocks. **2.** like a hummock.

hu·mor (hū′mər, ū′-), *n.* **1.** the quality of being funny: *the humor of a situation.* **2.** the faculty of perceiving what is amusing or comical: *sense of humor.* **3.** the faculty of expressing the amusing or comical. **4.** speech or writing showing this faculty. **5.** (*pl.*) amusing or comical features: *humors of the occasion.* **6.** mental disposition or tendency; frame of mind. **7.** capricious or freakish inclination; whim or caprice; odd traits. **8.** *Old Physiol.* one of the four chief bodily fluids, blood, choler or yellow bile, phlegm, and melancholy or black bile (**cardinal humors**), regarded as determining, by their relative proportions in the system, a person's physical and mental constitution. **9.** *Biol.* any animal or plant fluid, whether natural or morbid, such as the blood or lymph. **10. out of humor,** displeased or dissatisfied; cross. —*v.t.* **11.** to comply with the humor of; indulge: *to humor a child.* **12.** to accommodate oneself to. Also, *Brit.*, **humour**. [ME *humour*, t. AF, g. L (*h*)*ūmor* moisture, liquid] —**hu′mor·less,** *adj.*

—**Syn. 3.** HUMOR, WIT are contrasting terms which agree in referring to an ability to express a sense of the clever or amusing. HUMOR consists in the bringing together of certain incongruities which arise naturally from situation or character, frequently so as to illustrate some fundamental absurdity in human nature or conduct; it is a more kindly trait than wit: *a genial and mellow type of humor.* WIT is a purely intellectual, often spontaneous, manifestation of cleverness and quickness of apprehension in discovering analogies between things really unlike, and expressing them in brief, diverting, and sometimes sharp observations or remarks: *humor produces a smile, but wit produces sudden laughter.* **6.** temperament, mood. **11.** HUMOR, GRATIFY, INDULGE imply attempting to satisfy the wishes or whims of (oneself or) others. To HUMOR is to comply with the mood, fancy, or caprice of another, as in order to satisfy, soothe, or manage: *to humor an invalid, a child.* To GRATIFY is to please by satisfying the likings or desires: *to gratify someone by praising him.* INDULGE suggests a yielding to wishes by way of favor or complaisance, and may imply a habitual or excessive yielding to whims: *to indulge an unreasonable demand, to indulge an irresponsible son.* —**Ant. 11.** discipline, restrain.

hu·mor·esque (hū′mə·rĕsk′), *n.* a musical composition of humorous or capricious character. [t. G: m. *humoreske*, f. L *hūmor* HUMOR + -*eske* -ESQUE]

hu·mor·ist (hū′mər·ĭst, ū′-), *n.* **1.** one who exercises the faculty of humor. **2.** a professional writer, actor, etc., whose work is humorous. —**hu′mor·is′tic,** *adj.*

hu·mor·ous (hū′mər·əs, ū′-), *adj.* **1.** characterized by humor; amusing; funny: *the humorous side of things.* **2.** having or showing the faculty of humor; droll; facetious: *a humorous person.* **3.** *Obs.* pertaining or due to the bodily humors. **4.** *Obs.* moist. —**hu′mor·ous·ly,** *adv.* —**hu′mor·ous·ness,** *n.*

—**Syn. 2.** waggish, jocose, jocular, comic, comical. HUMOROUS, WITTY, FACETIOUS, WAGGISH imply that which arises from cleverness or a sense of fun. HUMOROUS implies a genuine sense of fun and the comic, impersonal or gently personal: *a humorous account, a humorous view of life.* WITTY implies quickness to perceive the amusing, striking, or unusual and to express it cleverly and entertainingly; it sometimes becomes rather sharp and unkind, particularly in quick repartee of a personal nature: *a witty and interesting companion, witty at someone else's expense.* FACETIOUS suggests a desire or attempt to be jocular or witty, often unsuccessful or inappropriate or trifling: *a facetious treatment of a serious subject.* WAGGISH suggests the spirit of sly mischief and roguery of the constant joker (making jokes, not playing them), with no harm intended: *a waggish good humor.* —**Ant. 1.** solemn, sober, serious.

hu·mour (hū′mər, ū′-), *n., v.t. Brit.* humor.

hump (hŭmp), *n.* **1.** a rounded protuberance, esp. on the back, as that due to abnormal curvature of the spine in man, or that normally present in certain animals such as the camel and bison. **2.** a low, rounded rise of ground; hummock. **3. the hump, a.** *Brit. Slang.* a fit of bad humor: *to get the hump.* **b.** (*cap.*) (in World War II) the Himalayas. —*v.t.* **4.** to raise (the back, etc.) in a hump. **5.** *U.S. Slang.* to exert (oneself) in a great effort. **6.** *Australian Slang.* **a.** to place or bear on the back or shoulder. **b.** to carry. —*v.i.* **7.** to rise in a hump. **8.** *U.S. Slang.* to exert oneself. [back formation from HUMPBACKED] —**humped,** *adj.* —**hump′less,** *adj.*

hump·back (hŭmp′băk′), *n.* **1.** a back with a hump. **2.** one who has such a back. **3.** a whale of the genus *Megaptera*, with a humplike back.

hump·backed (hŭmp′băkt′), *adj.* having a hump on the back. [b. *crumpbacked* and *huckbacked* (or *hunchbacked*)]

Hum·per·dinck (hŏŏm′pər·dĭngk′), *n.* **Engelbert** (ĕng′əlbĕrt′), 1854–1921, German composer.

humph (hŭmf), *interj.* an expression indicating disbelief, dissatisfaction, contempt, etc.

Hum·phrey (hŭm′frĭ), *n.* (*Duke of Gloucester*) 1391–1447, English soldier and statesman (youngest son of Henry IV).

Hump·ty Dump·ty (hŭmp′tĭ dŭmp′tĭ), the subject of a nursery riddle; he (an egg) fell from a wall and could not be put together again.

hump·y (hŭm′pĭ), *adj.,* **humpier, humpiest. 1.** full of humps. **2.** humplike.

hu·mus (hū′məs), *n.* the dark organic material in soils, produced by the decomposition of vegetable or animal matter, essential to fertility and favorable moisture supply. [t. L: earth, ground]

Hun (hŭn), *n.* **1.** a member of a warlike Asiatic people who devastated Europe in the 4th and 5th centuries. **2.** a barbarous, destructive person. [sing. of *Huns*, OE *Hūnas,* Icel. *Hunar.* Cf. LL *Hunni,* Chinese *Han;* all from native name of people]

Hu·nan (hōō′nän′), *n.* a province in S China. ab. 28,166,000 pop. (est. 1944); 78,378 sq. mi. *Cap.:* Changsha.

hunch (hŭnch), *v.t.* **1.** to thrust out or up in a hump: *to hunch one's back.* —*v.i.* **2.** to thrust oneself forward jerkily; lunge forward. —*n.* **3.** a hump. **4.** *U.S. Colloq.* a premonition or suspicion. **5.** a lump or thick piece. [appar. back formation from HUNCHBACKED]

hunch·back (hŭnch′băk′), *n.* humpback (def. 2).

hunch·backed (hŭnch′băkt′), *adj.* humpbacked. [b. *huckbacked* and *bunchbacked*]

hun·dred (hŭn′drəd), *n., pl.* **-dreds,** (*as after a numeral*) **-dred. 1.** a cardinal number, ten times ten. **2.** a symbol for this number, as 100 or C. **3.** a set of a hundred persons or things. *a hundred of the men.* **4.** a historical administrative division of an English county. **5.** a similar division in colonial Pennsylvania, Delaware, and Virginia; still surviving in Delaware. —*adj.* **6.** amounting to one hundred in number. [ME *hondred,* OE *hundred,* c. G *hundert*]

hun·dred·fold (hŭn′drəd·fōld′), *adj.* **1.** comprising a hundred parts or members. **2.** a hundred times as great or as much. —*adv.* **3.** in a hundredfold measure.

hun·dred-per·cent·er (hŭn′drəd pər·sĕn′tər), *n.* a patriotic, or sometimes jingoistic, person.

hun·dredth (hŭn′drədth), *adj.* **1.** next after the ninety-ninth. **2.** being one of a hundred equal parts. —*n.* **3.** a hundredth part, esp. of one ($1/100$). **4.** the hundredth member of a series.

hun·dred·weight (hŭn′drəd·wāt′), *n., pl.* **-weights,** (*as after a numeral*) **-weight.** a unit of avoirdupois weight commonly equivalent to 100 pounds in the U.S. and 112 pounds in England.

Hun·e·ker (hŭn′ə·kər). *n.* **James Gibbons,** 1860–1921, U.S. author.

hung (hŭng), *v.* pt. and pp. of **hang.**

Hung., 1. Hungarian. **2.** Hungary.

Hun·gar·i·an (hŭng·gâr′ĭ·ən), *adj.* **1.** of or pertaining to Hungary or its people. —*n.* **2.** a native or inhabitant of Hungary; a Magyar. **3.** the language of Hungary, of the Ugric group; Magyar. [f. HUNGARY + -AN]

Hun·ga·ry (hŭng′gə·rĭ), *n.* a republic in central Europe. (as of 1947 boundaries) 9,467,000 pop. (est. 1943); 35,926 sq. mi. *Cap.:* Budapest. Hungarian, **Magyar-ország.**

hun·ger (hŭng′gər), *n.* **1.** the painful sensation or state of exhaustion caused by need of food: *to collapse from hunger.* **2.** a craving appetite; need for food. **3.** strong or eager desire: *hunger for praise.* —*v.i.* **4.** to feel hunger; be hungry. **5.** to have a strong desire. —*v.t.* **6.** to subject to hunger; starve. [ME, OE *hungor,* c. G *hunger*]

hunger strike, a persistent refusal to eat, as a protest against imprisonment, restraint, compulsion, etc.

hun·gry (hŭng′grĭ), *adj.,* **-grier, -griest. 1.** craving food; having a keen appetite. **2.** indicating, characteristic of, or characterized by hunger: *a lean and hungry look.* **3.** strongly or eagerly desirous. **4.** lacking needful or desirable elements; not fertile; poor: *hungry land.* **5.** *Rare.* marked by scarcity of food. [ME; OE *hungrig.* See -Y¹] —**hun′gri·ly,** *adv.* —**hun′gri·ness,** *n.*

—**Syn. 1.** ravenous, famishing. HUNGRY, FAMISHED, STARVED describe a condition resulting from a lack of food. HUNGRY is a general word, expressing various degrees of eagerness or craving for food: *hungry between meals, desperately hungry after a long fast, hungry as a bear.* FAMISHED denotes the condition of one reduced to actual suffering from want of food but sometimes is used lightly or in an exaggerated statement: *famished after being lost in a wilderness, simply famished* (hungry). STARVED denotes a condition resulting from long-continued lack or insufficiency of food, and implies enfeeblement, emaciation, or death (originally death from any cause, but now death from lack of food): *to look thin and starved; by the end of the terrible winter, thousands had starved* (to death). It is also used humorously: *I'm simply starved* (hungry). —**Ant. 1.** satiated, surfeited.

hunk (hŭngk), *n.* *Colloq.* a large piece or lump; a chunk.

hunks (hŭngks), *n. sing. and pl.* **1.** a crabbed, disagreeable person. **2.** a covetous, sordid man; a miser.

hunk·y¹ (hŭngk′ĭ), *adj. U.S. Slang.* **1.** Also, **hunk·y-do·ry** (hŭngk′ĭ dōr′ĭ). satisfactory; well; right. **2.** even; leaving no balance. [orig. unknown]

hunk·y² (hŭngk′ĭ), *n., pl.* **hunkies.** *U.S. Slang and Derogatory.* an unskilled or semiskilled workman of foreign birth, esp. a Hungarian. [? der. HUNGARIAN]

hunt (hŭnt), *v.t.* **1.** to chase (game or other wild animals) for the purpose of catching or killing. **2.** to scour (a region) in pursuit of game. **3.** to use or manage (a horse, etc.) in the chase. **4.** to pursue with force, hostility, etc.: *he was hunted from the village.* **5.** to search for; seek; endeavor to obtain or find. **6.** to search (a place) thoroughly. **7.** *Bell Ringing.* to alter the place of (a bell) in a hunt. —*v.i.* **8.** to engage in the chase. **9.** to make a search or quest (often fol. by *for* or *after*). **10.** *Bell Ringing.* to alter the place of a bell in its set according to certain rules. —*n.* **11.** act of hunting game or other wild animals; the chase. **12.** a body of persons associated for the purpose of hunting; an association of huntsmen. **13.** a pack of hounds engaged in the chase. **14.** a district hunted with hounds. **15.** pursuit. **16.** a search. **17.** *Bell Ringing.* a regularly varying order of permutations in the ringing of a group of from five to twelve bells. [ME *hunte*(*n*), OE *huntian*, der. *hunta* hunter. Cf. OE *hentan* pursue] **—Syn. 1.** pursue, track.

Hunt (hŭnt), *n.* **1.** (James Henry) **Leigh** (lē), 1784–1859, British essayist and poet. **2. William Holman,** 1827–1910, British painter.

hunt·er (hŭn′tər), *n.* **1.** one who hunts game or other wild animals; a huntsman. **2.** one who searches or seeks for something: *a fortune hunter.* **3.** an animal that hunts game or prey, esp. a dog or horse used in hunting.

hunt·ing (hŭn′tĭng), *n.* **1.** act of one who or that which hunts. **2.** *Elect.* the periodic oscillating of a rotating electromechanical system about a mean space position, as in a synchronous motor. *—adj.* **3.** of, for, or engaged in hunting: *a hunting cap.*

hunting case, a watchcase with a hinged cover to protect the crystal, orig. against accidents in hunting.

Hunt·ing·don·shire (hŭn′tĭng dən shĭr′, -shər), *n.* a county in E England. 61,000 pop. (est. 1946); 366 sq. mi. *Co. seat:* Huntingdon. Also, **Hun′ting·don, Hunts** (hŭnts).

hunting knife, a knife sometimes used to kill the game, but more commonly to skin and cut it up.

Hun·ting·ton (hŭn′tĭng tən), *n.* a city in W West Virginia, on the Ohio river. 86,353 (1950).

Huntington Park, a city in SW California, near Los Angeles. 29,450 (1950).

hunt·ress (hŭn′trĭs), *n.* **1.** a woman who hunts. **2.** a mare employed in hunting.

hunts·man (hŭnts′mən), *n., pl.* **-men.** *Chiefly Brit.* **1.** a hunter. **2.** the manager of a hunt.

hunts·man's-cup (hŭnts′mənz kŭp′), *n.* a plant of the genus *Sarracentia,* particularly *S. purpurea,* the pitcher plant of bogs.

Hu·nya·di (hōō′nyŏ dǐ), *n.* **János** (yä′nôsh), (*Johannes Corvinus Huniades*) c1387–1456, Hungarian patriot.

Hu·on pine (hū′ŏn), a large taxaceous tree, *Dacrydium Franklinii,* of Tasmania. [named after the river *Huon,* in Tasmania]

Hu·pa (hōō′pə), *n.* an Athabascan language of northwestern California.

Hu·peh (hōō′pä′; *Chin.* hōō′bĕ′), *n.* a province in central China. 24,659,000 pop. (est. 1944); 71,955 sq. mi. *Cap.:* Wuchang.

hur·dle (hûr′dəl), *n., v.,* **-dled, -dling.** *—n.* **1.** a barrier in a racecourse, to be leaped by the contestants. **2.** the **hurdles,** a race in which such barriers are leaped. **3.** a difficult problem to be overcome; obstacle. **4.** *Chiefly Brit.* a movable rectangular frame of interlaced twigs, crossed bars, or the like, as for a temporary fence. **5.** a frame or sledge on which criminals were formerly drawn to the place of execution. *—v.t.* **6.** to leap over (a hurdle, etc.) as in a race. **7.** to master (a difficulty, problem, etc.). **8.** to construct with hurdles; enclose with hurdles. *—v.i.* **9.** to leap over a hurdle or other barrier. [ME *hirdel, hurdel,* OE *hyrdel,* f. *hyrd-* (c. G *hürde* hurdle) + *-l* suffix; akin to L *crātis* wickerwork, Gk. *kyrtos* basket, cage] **—hur′dler,** *n.*

hurds (hûrdz), *n.pl.* hards.

hur·dy-gur·dy (hûr′dĭ gûr′dĭ), *n., pl.* **-dies. 1.** a barrel organ or similar instrument played by turning a crank. **2.** a lute or guitar-shaped stringed musical instrument sounded by the revolution. against the strings, of a rosined wheel turned by a crank. [appar. imit.]

hurl (hûrl), *v.t.* **1.** to drive or throw with great force. **2.** to throw down; overthrow. **3.** to utter with vehemence. *—v.i.* **4.** to throw a missile. **5.** *Baseball.* to pitch a ball. *—n.* **6.** a forcible or violent throw; a fling. [ME *hurlen;* early assoc. with HURTLE, but prop. freq. of obs. *hurr* (imit.) make a vibrating sound. Cf. obs. *hurling,* n., roll of thunder, d. G *hurlen* roll, rumble (said of thunder)] **—hurl′er,** *n.*

hurl·y (hûr′lĭ), *n., pl.* **hurlies.** commotion; hurly-burly.

hurl·y-burl·y (hûr′lĭ bûr′lĭ), *n., pl.* **-burlies,** *adj. —n.* **1.** commotion; tumult. *—adj.* **2.** full of commotion; tumultuous. [m. *hurling and burling*]

Hu·ron (hyŏŏr′ən), *n.* **1. Lake,** a lake between Lakes Michigan and Erie: second in area of the Great Lakes. ab. 23,000 sq. mi. **2.** one of an Indian tribe, the northwestern member of the Iroquoian family, living west to Lake Huron. [t. F: unkempt person, bristly savage; applied to Indians about 1600]

hur·rah (hə rä′, -rô′), *interj.* **1.** an exclamation of joy, exultation, applause, or the like. *—v.i.* **2.** to shout "hurrah." *—n.* **3.** the exclamation "hurrah." Also, **hur·ray** (hə rā′); *esp. Brit.,* **hooray.**

hur·ri·cane (hûr′ĭ kān′), *n.* **1.** a violent tropical cyclonic storm. **2.** a storm of the intensest severity. **3.** anything suggesting a violent storm. [t. Sp.: m. *huracán,* t. Carib]

hurricane deck, a light upper deck on passenger steamers, etc.

hurricane lamp, 1. a candlestick with a chimney. **2.** *Chiefly Brit.* a kerosene lantern.

hur·ried (hûr′ĭd), *adj.* **1.** driven or impelled to hurry, as a person. **2.** characterized by or done with hurry; hasty. **—hur′ried·ly,** *adv.* **—hur′ried·ness,** *n.*

hur·ry (hûr′ĭ). *v.,* **-ried, -rying,** *n., pl.* **-ries.** *—v.i.* **1.** to move, proceed, or act with haste, often undue haste. *—v.t.* **2.** to drive or move (someone or something) with speed, often with confused haste. **3.** to hasten; urge forward (often fol. by *up*). **4.** to impel with undue haste to thoughtless action: *to be hurried into a decision. —n.* **5.** need or desire for haste: *to be in a hurry to begin.* **6.** hurried movement or action; haste. [orig. obscure; ? imit.] **—hur′ry·ing·ly,** *adv.* **—Syn. 1.** See **rush¹. 3.** accelerate, quicken; expedite; hustle. **6.** bustle; celerity; expedition, dispatch. **—Ant. 3.** delay.

hur·ry-scur·ry (hûr′ĭ skûr′ĭ), *n., pl.* **-ries,** *adv., adj., v.,* **-ried, -rying.** *—n.* **1.** headlong, disorderly haste; hurry and confusion. *—adv.* **2.** with hurrying and scurrying. **3.** confusedly; in a bustle. *—adj.* **4.** characterized by headlong, disorderly flight or haste. *—v.i.* **5.** to rush or go hurry-scurry. Also, **hur′ry-skur′ry.** [var. reduplication of HURRY]

hurt (hûrt), *v.,* **hurt, hurting,** *n. —v.t.* **1.** to cause bodily injury to (with or without consequent pain). **2.** to cause bodily pain to or in: *the wound still hurts him.* **3.** to damage (a material object, etc.) by striking, rough use, or otherwise: *to hurt furniture.* **4.** to affect adversely; harm: *to hurt one's reputation.* **5.** to cause mental pain to; grieve: *to hurt one's feelings. —v.i.* **6.** to cause pain (bodily or mental): *my finger still hurts.* **7.** to cause injury, damage, or harm. *—n.* **8.** a blow that inflicts a wound; bodily injury. **9.** injury; damage or harm. **10.** an injury that gives mental pain, as an insult. [ME *hurte*(*n*), prob. t. OF: m. *hurter* strike against, der. *hurt* a blow] **—Syn. 8.** See **injury.**

hurt·er (hûr′tər), *n.* **1.** a supporting or strengthening part. **2.** (in a vehicle) a butting piece on the shoulder of an axle against which the hub strikes. [ME *hurtour,* f. HURT, v. + *-our* -OR². Cf. F *hurtoir* (a knocker)]

hurt·ful (hûrt′fəl), *adj.* such as to cause hurt or injury; injurious; harmful. **—hurt′ful·ly,** *adv.* **—hurt′ful·ness,** *n.* **—Syn.** destructive, pernicious; noxious, baneful, deleterious, unwholesome.

hur·tle (hûr′təl), *v.,* **-tled, -tling,** *n. —v.i.* **1.** to strike together or against something. **2.** to rush violently and noisily. **3.** to resound, as in collision or rapid motion. *—v.t.* **4.** to drive violently; fling; dash. **5.** to dash against; collide with. *—n.* **6.** clash; collision; shock; clatter. [ME; freq. of HURT]

Hus (hŭs; *Ger., Czech.* hŏŏs), *n.* Huss.

hus·band (hŭz′bənd), *n.* **1.** the man of a married pair (correlative of *wife*). *—v.t.* **2.** to manage, esp. with prudent economy; economize: *to husband one's resources.* **3.** to provide with a husband. **4.** *Rare.* to act as a husband to; marry. **5.** *Obs.* to till; cultivate. [ME *husbond*(*e*), OE *hūsbōnda,* f. *hūs* house + *bōnda* householder. See BOND] **—hus′band·less,** *adj.*

hus·band·man (hŭz′bənd mən), *n., pl.* **-men.** a farmer.

hus·band·ry (hŭz′bən drĭ), *n.* **1.** the business of a farmer; agriculture; farming. **2.** careful or thrifty management; frugality; thrift. **3.** the management of domestic affairs, or of resources generally.

Hu·sein ibn-A·li (hŏŏ sīn′ ĭb′ən ä lē′, -ä′lē; hŏŏ-sän′), 1856–1931, king of Hejaz, 1916–24.

hush (hŭsh), *interj.* **1.** a command to be silent or quiet. *—v.i.* **2.** to become or be silent or quiet. *—v.t.* **3.** to make silent; silence. **4.** to suppress mention of; keep concealed. **5.** to calm or allay: *to hush someone's fears. —n.* **6.** silence or quiet, esp. after noise. *—adj.* **7.** *Archaic.* silent; quiet. [appar. back formation from ME *hussht,* also *husht, huyst,* adj. (orig. interj.), taken as pp. Cf. WHIST¹] **—Syn. 3.** See **still¹.**

hush money, a bribe to keep silent about something.

husk (hŭsk), *n.* **1.** the dry external covering of certain fruits or seeds, esp. (*U.S.*) of an ear of corn. **2.** the enveloping or outer part of anything, esp. when dry or worthless. *—v.t.* **3.** to remove the husk from. [ME *huske;* f. *hus-* (cf. OE *hosu* pod, husk) + *-k* suffix. See -OCK] **—husk′er,** *n.* **—husk′like′,** *adj.*

husk·ing (hŭs′kĭng), *n.* **1.** act of removing husks, esp. (*U.S.*) those of corn. **2.** a husking bee.

husking bee, *U.S.* a gathering of persons to assist in husking corn, usually a kind of merrymaking.

husk·y (hŭs′kĭ), *adj.,* **huskier, huskiest,** *n.pl.* **huskies. —adj. 1.** *U.S. Colloq.* burly; big and strong. **2.** having a semiwhispered vocal tone; somewhat hoarse. **3.** abounding in husks. **4.** like husks. *—n.* **5.** *U.S. Colloq.* a big and strong person. [f. HUSK, n. + -Y¹] **—husk′i·ly,** *adv.* **—husk′i·ness,** *n.*

Husk·y (hŭs′kĭ), *n., pl.* **Huskies.** an Eskimo dog. Also, **hus′ky.** [? a shortened var. of ESKIMO]

Huss (hŭs; *Ger., Czech.* hŏŏs), *n.* **John,** 1369?–1415, Bohemian religious reformer and martyr. Also, **Hus.**

hus·sar (hŏŏ zär′), *n.* **1.** (orig.) one of a body of light Hungarian cavalry formed during the 15th century. **2.** one of a class of similar troops, usually with striking or showy uniforms, in European armies. [t. Hung.: m. *huszár,* orig. freebooter, t. OSerbian: m. *husar,* var. of *kursar,* t. It.: m. *corsaro* CORSAIR]

Hus·serl (hŏŏs′ĕrl), *n.* **Edmund** (ĕt′mŏŏnt), 1859–1938, German philosopher.

Huss·ite (hŭs′īt), *n.* a follower of John Huss.

hus·sy (hŭs′ĭ, hŭz′ĭ), *n., pl.* **-sies. 1.** an ill-behaved girl. **2.** a worthless woman. [familiar var. of HOUSE-WIFE (ME *huswif*)]

---

b., blend of, blended; c., cognate with; d., dialect, dialectal; der., derived from; f., formed from; g., going back to; m., modification of; r., replacing; s., stem of; t., taken from; ?, perhaps. See the full key on inside cover.

hus·tings (hŭs′tĭngz), *n. pl. or sing.* *Brit.* **1.** the temporary platform from which candidates for Parliament were (before 1872) nominated and addressed the electors. **2.** any electioneering platform. **3.** election proceedings. [ME *husting*, t. Scand.; cf. Icel. *hūsthing* house assembly, council summoned by king or leader]

hus·tle (hŭs′əl). *v.*, **-tled, -tling,** *n.* —*v.i.* **1.** *Colloq.* to proceed or work rapidly or energetically. **2.** to push or force one's way. —*v.t.* **3.** to force roughly or hurriedly: *they hustled him out of the city.* **4.** to shake, push, or shove roughly. —*n.* **5.** *Colloq.* energetic activity, as in work. **6.** discourteous shoving, pushing, or jostling. [var. sp. of *hussell, hus(s)le*, t. D: s. *husselen*, assimilated var. of *hutselen*, freq. of *hutsen* shake, jog] —**hus′tler,** *n.*

hut (hŭt), *n., v.*, **hutted, hutting.** —*n.* **1.** a small, rude, or humble dwelling. **2.** *Mil.* a wooden or metal structure for the temporary housing of troops. —*v.t.* **3.** to place in or furnish with a hut. —*v.i.* **4.** to lodge or take shelter in a hut. [t. F: m. *hutte*, t. G: m. *hütte*; prob. akin to HIDE³] —**hut′like′,** *adj.* —**Syn. 1.** See **cottage.**

hutch (hŭch), *n.* **1.** a pen for confining small animals: *rabbit hutch.* **2.** a hut or cabin. **3.** *U.S. Dial.* a fisherman's shanty. **4.** a chest, box, or trough: *a grain hutch.* **5.** a baker's kneading trough. —*v.t.* **6.** to put away in or as in a hutch; hoard. [ME *huche*, t. OF, t. ML: m.s. *hūtica* chest; ? of Gmc. orig.]

Hutch·ins (hŭch′ĭnz), *n.* **Robert Maynard** (mā′nərd), born 1899, U.S. educator.

Hutch·in·son (hŭch′ĭn sən), *n.* **1.** a city in central Kansas, on the Arkansas river. 33,575 (1950). **2. Mrs. Anne Marbury,** 1590?–1643, British religious enthusiast in New England. **3. Thomas,** 1711–80, British colonial governor of Massachusetts, 1769–74.

hut·ment (hŭt′mənt), *n.* an encampment of huts.

Hux·ley (hŭks′lĭ), *n.* **1. Aldous Leonard** (ôl′dəs), born 1894, British novelist and essayist. **2.** his brother, **Julian Sorrell,** born 1887, British biologist and writer. **3.** their grandfather, **Thomas Henry,** 1825–95, British biologist and writer.

Huy·ghens (hī′gənz; *Du.* hoi′gĕns), *n.* **Christian** (krĭs′tĭ än′), 1629–95, Dutch mathematician, physicist, and astronomer.

Huys·mans (*Du.* hois′mäns; *Fr.* wēs mäns′), *n.* **Joris Karl** (yō′rĭs kärl), 1848–1907, French novelist.

huz·za (hə zä′), *interj., n., pl.* **-zas,** *v.* **-zaed, -zaing.** —*interj.* **1.** an exclamation of exultation, applause, or the like. —*n.* **2.** the exclamation "huzza." —*v.i.* **3.** to shout "huzza." —*v.t.* **4.** to salute with huzzas: *crowds huzzaed the triumphant hero.*

Hwang Hai (hwäng′ hī′), Chinese name of the **Yellow Sea.**

Hwang Ho (hwäng′ hō′; *Chin.* hü′), a river flowing from W China into the Yellow Sea. ab. 2700 mi. Also, **Hoangho, Yellow River.** See map under **Yangtze.**

hy·a·cinth (hī′ə sĭnth), *n.* **1.** any of the bulbous liliaceous plants constituting the genus *Hyacinthus,* esp. *H. orientalis,* widely cultivated for its spikes of fragrant, white or colored, bell-shaped flowers. **2.** a hyacinth bulb or flower. **3.** (among the ancients) a plant supposed to spring from the blood of Hyacinthus and variously identified as iris, gladiolus, larkspur, etc. **4.** a reddish-orange zircon; the jacinth. **5.** (among the ancients) an uncertain gem, possibly our amethyst or sapphire. [t. L: s. *hyacinthus,* t. Gk.: m. *hyákinthos* kind of flower, also a gem. Cf. JACINTH]

hy·a·cin·thine (hī′ə sĭn′thĭn, -thĭn), *adj.* **1.** of or like the hyacinth. **2.** adorned with hyacinths.

Hy·a·cin·thus (hī′ə sĭn′thəs), *n. Gk. Myth.* a beautiful youth (loved by Apollo but killed out of jealousy by Zephyrus) from whose blood sprang a flower marked with the letters of an exclamation of grief, "AI AI."

Hy·a·des (hī′ə dēz′), *n.pl.* **1.** *Astron.* a group of stars comprising a moving cluster in the constellation Taurus, supposed by the ancients to indicate the approach of rain when they rose with the sun. **2.** *Gk. Myth.* a group of nymphs, sisters of the Pleiades.

hy·ae·na (hī ē′nə), *n.* hyena.

hy·a·line (hī′ə lĕn′, -lĭn for 1, 2; hī′ə lĭn, -lĭn′ for 3, 4), *n.* **1.** Also, **hy·a·lin** (hī′ə lĭn). *Biochem.* a horny substance found in hydatid cysts, closely resembling chitin. **2.** *Anat.* the hyaloid membrane. **3.** something glassy or transparent. —*adj.* **4.** glassy; crystalline; transparent. [t. LL: m.s. *hyalinus,* t. Gk.: m. *hyálinos* of glass]

hyaline cartilage, *Anat.* the typical translucent form of cartilage, containing little fibrous tissue.

hy·a·lite (hī′ə līt′), *n.* a colorless variety of opal, sometimes transparent like glass, and sometimes whitish and translucent. [f. HYAL(O)- + -ITE¹]

hyalo-, a word element meaning "glass." Also, before vowels, **hyal-.** [t. Gk., comb. form of *hýalos*]

hy·a·loid (hī′ə loid′), *n.* **1.** *Anat.* the hyaloid membrane of the eye. —*adj.* **2.** glassy; hyaline. [t. Gk.; m.s. *hyaloeidēs* like glass. See HYALO-, -OID]

hyaloid membrane, *Anat.* the capsule of the vitreous humor of the eye, a delicate, pellucid, and nearly structureless membrane.

hy·a·lo·plasm (hī′ə lō plăz′əm), *n. Biol.* the pellucid portion of the protoplasm of a cell, as distinguished from the granular and reticular portions.

hy·brid (hī′brĭd), *n.* **1.** the offspring of two animals or plants of different races, breeds, varieties, species, or genera. **2.** a half-breed; a mongrel. **3.** anything derived from heterogeneous sources, or composed of elements of different or incongruous kinds. —*adj.* **4.** bred from two distinct races, breeds, varieties, species, or genera. **5.** composed of elements originally drawn from different languages, as a word. [t. L: s. *hybrida,* var. of *hibrida* offspring of a tame sow and wild boar, a mongrel] —**Syn. 4.** HYBRID, MONGREL refer to animals or plants of mixed origin. HYBRID is the scientific term: *hybrid corn, a hybrid variety of sheep.* MONGREL, used originally of dogs to denote especially the offspring of repeated crossings of different breeds, is now extended to other animals and to plants; it is usually depreciatory, as denoting mixed, nondescript, or degenerate breed or character: *a mongrel pup.* —**Ant. 4.** purebred, thoroughbred.

hy·brid·ism (hī′brə dĭz′əm), *n.* **1.** Also, **hy·brid·i·ty** (hī brĭd′ə tĭ). hybrid character. **2.** the production of hybrids.

hy·brid·ize (hī′brə dīz′), *v.*, **-ized, -izing.** —*v.t.* **1.** to cause to produce hybrids; cross. **2.** to form in a hybrid manner: *to hybridize plants.* —*v.i.* **3.** to cause the production of hybrids by crossing different species, etc. Also, *esp. Brit.,* **hy′brid·ise′.** —**hy′brid·i·za′tion,** *n.* —**hy′brid·iz′er,** *n.*

hy·dan·to·in (hī dăn′tō ĭn), *n.* a colorless, needlelike, crystalline compound, $C_3H_4N_2O_2$, used in the synthesis of pharmaceutical substances and resins. [irreg. f. Gk. *hýd(ōr)* water + (all)*antoin* (f. ALLANTO(IS) + -IN²)]

hy·da·tid (hī′də tĭd), *n.* **1.** a cyst with watery contents, produced in man and animals by a tapeworm in the larval state. **2.** the encysted larva of a tapeworm; a cysticercus. [t. Gk.: s. *hydatis* watery vesicle]

Hyde (hīd), *n.* **1. Douglas,** 1860?–1949, Irish author and statesman: president of Eire, 1938–45. **2. Edward.** See **Clarendon,** 1st Earl of. **3. Mr.,** the criminal side of the leading character in Stevenson's *Dr. Jekyll and Mr. Hyde.* See **Jekyll.**

Hyde Park, 1. a park in London, England. **2.** a village in SE New York, on the Hudson: site of the estate and burial place of Franklin D. Roosevelt.

Hy·der·a·bad (hī′dər ə bäd′, -bäd′, hī′drə-), *n.* **1.** a state in S India; incorporated into the republic of India, Sept. 1948. 16,338,500 pop. (1941); 82,313 sq. mi. **2.** the capital of this state, in the central part. 739,159 (1941). **3.** a city in Pakistan, in Sind province, on the Indus river. 127,521 (1941).

Hy·der A·li (hī′dər ä′lē, ä lē′), died 1782, a Mohammedan ruler of Mysore and military leader against the British in India. Also, **Haidar Ali.**

hyd·no·car·pate (hĭd′nō kär′pāt), *n. Chem.* a salt or ester of hydnocarpic acid. [f. s. NL *Hydnocarpus* (f. Gk.; *hýdno(n)* truffle + m. *karpós* fruit) + -ATE²]

hyd·no·car·pic acid (hĭd′nō kär′pĭk), *Chem.* a white crystalline acid, C_5H_7-$(CH_2)_{10}$-COOH, obtained from chaulmoogra oil, used to treat leprosy.

hydr-¹, var. of **hydro-¹,** before vowels, as in *hydrangea.*

hydr-², var. of **hydro-²,** before vowels, as in *hydrazine.*

hy·dra (hī′drə), *n., pl.* **-dras, -drae** (-drē). **1.** (*cap.* or *l.c.*) *Gk. Myth.* a monstrous serpent, slain by Hercules, represented as having nine heads, each of which was replaced by two after being cut off, unless the wound was cauterized. **2.** *Zool.* any of the fresh-water polyps constituting the genus *Hydra.* **3.** any persistent evil arising from many sources or difficult to overcome. **4.** (*cap.*) *Astron.* a southern constellation, representing a sea serpent. [t. L, t. Gk.: water serpent; r. ME *ydre,* t. OF]

hy·drac·id (hī drăs′ĭd), *n. Chem.* an acid which contains no oxygen.

hy·dran·gea (hī drăn′jə, -drăn′jĭ ə), *n.* any shrub of the genus *Hydrangea,* species of which are cultivated for their large showy white, pink, or blue flower clusters. [t. NL, f. *hydr-* HYDR-¹ + m. Gk. *angeî(on)* vessel + *-a* (ending); so called from cup-shaped seed capsule]

hy·drant (hī′drənt), *n.* an upright pipe with a spout, nozzle, or other outlet, usually in the street, for drawing water from a main or service pipe.

hy·dranth (hī′drănth), *n.* the terminal part of a hydroid polyp that bears the mouth and tentacles and contains the stomach region. [f. HYDR(A) (def. 2) + s. Gk. *ánthos* flower]

hy·drar·gy·ri·a·sis (hī′drär jĭ rī′ə sĭs), *n. Pathol.* mercurial poisoning; mercurialism.

hy·drar·gy·rum (hī drär′jĭ rəm), *n. Chem.* mercury. [NL, der. L *hydrargyrus,* t. Gk.: m. *hydrárgyros*]

hy·dras·tine (hī drăs′tēn, -tĭn), *n.* **1.** a yellow medicine from goldenseal, formerly used as a stomachic. **2.** an alkaloid found in the root of goldenseal. [f. HYDRAST(IS) + -INE²]

hy·dras·tis (hī drăs′tĭs), *n.* goldenseal (def. 2).

hy·drate (hī′drāt), *n., v.*, **-drated, -drating.** *Chem.* —*n.* **1.** any of a class of compounds containing chemically combined water. In some hydrates the bonds may be weak covalence linkages, as in washing soda, Na_2CO_3. $10 H_2O$, which loses its water of hydration on standing in the air; in others, they may be primary valence bonds, as in sulfuric acid, H_2SO_4, a monohydrate of SO_3. —*v.t.* **2.** to combine chemically with water. —**hy·dra′tion,** *n.* —**hy′dra·tor,** *n.*

hy·drat·ed (hī′drā tĭd), *adj.* chemically combined with water in its molecular form.

hydraul., hydraulics.

hy·drau·lic (hī drô′lĭk), *adj.* **1.** operated by or employing water or other liquid. **2.** pertaining to water or other liquid, or to hydraulics. **3.** hardening under water, as a cement. [t. L: s. *hydraulicus*, t. Gk.: m. *hydraulikós* pertaining to the water organ] —**hy·drau′li·cal·ly,** *adv.*

hydraulic brake, a brake operated by fluid pressures in cylinders and connecting tubular lines.

hydraulic machinery, mechanical devices such as pumps, turbines, couplings, etc.. in which the flow of a liquid either produces or is produced by their operation.

hydraulic press, a machine permitting a small force applied to a small piston to produce through fluid pressure a large force on a large piston.

hydraulic ram, a device by which the energy of descending water is utilized to raise a part of the water to a height greater than that of the source.

hy·drau·lics (hī drô′lĭks), *n.* the science treating of the laws governing water or other liquids in motion and their applications in engineering; practical or applied hydrodynamics. [pl. of HYDRAULIC. See -ICS]

hy·dra·zine (hī′drə zēn′, -zĭn), *n. Chem.* **1.** a compound, N_2H_4, which is a weak base in solution and forms a large number of salts resembling ammonium salts, used as a reducing agent and as a jet-propulsion fuel. **2.** a class of substances derived by replacing one or more hydrogen atoms in hydrazine by an organic radical. [f. HYDR-[2] + AZ(O)- + -INE[2]]

hy·dra·zo·ic (hī′drə zō′ĭk), *adj.* denoting or pertaining to hydrazoic acid; triazoic.

hy·dra·zo·ic acid (hī′drə zō′ĭk), *Chem.* an acid composed of hydrogen and nitrogen, HN_3, occurring as a very explosive, colorless liquid with a penetrating odor.

hy·dride (hī′drĭd, -drĭd), *n. Chem.* **1.** a compound of hydrogen with another element or a radical. **2.** (formerly) a hydroxide. Also, **hy·drid** (hī′drĭd).

hy·dri·od·ic acid (hī′drī ŏd′ĭk), **1.** a colorless gas, HI, with a suffocating odor. **2.** an aqueous solution of this gas. [f. HYDR-[2] + IOD(INE) + -IC]

hydro-[1], a word element meaning "water," as in *hydrogen.* Also, **hydr-.** [t. Gk., comb. form of *hýdōr* water]

hydro-[2], *Chem.* a word element often indicating combination of hydrogen with some negative element or radical, as in *hydrobromic.* Also, **hydr-.** [comb. form of HYDROGEN]

hy·dro·air·plane (hī′drō âr′plān′), *n.* a hydroplane.

hy·dro·bro·mic acid (hī′drə brō′mĭk), *Chem.* **1.** a colorless gas, HBr, with a pungent odor. **2.** an aqueous solution of this gas.

hy·dro·car·bon (hī′drə kär′bən), *n. Chem.* any of a class of compounds containing only hydrogen and carbon, such as methane, CH_4, ethylene, C_2H_4, acetylene, C_2H_2, and benzene, C_6H_6. [f. HYDRO-[2] + CARBON]

hy·dro·cele (hī′drə sēl′), *n. Pathol.* an accumulation of serous fluid, usually about the testis. [t. L, t. Gk.]

hy·dro·ceph·a·lus (hī′drə sĕf′ə ləs), *n. Pathol.* an accumulation of serous fluid within the cranium, esp. in infancy, often causing great enlargement of the head. [NL, der. Gk. *hydroképhalon* water in the head] —**hy′·dro·ceph′a·lous,** *adj.*

hy·dro·chlo·ric acid (hī′drə klôr′ĭk), a colorless gas, HCl, or an aqueous solution of it, which is extensively used in chemical and industrial processes; muriatic acid. [f. HYDRO-[1] + CHLORIC]

hy·dro·chlo·ride (hī′drə klôr′īd, -ĭd), *n. Chem.* a salt formed by the direct union of hydrochloric acid with an organic base, rendering the latter more soluble.

hy·dro·cy·an·ic acid (hī′drō sī ăn′ĭk), a colorless, poisonous liquid, HCN, with an odor like that of bitter almonds; prussic acid. [f. HYDRO-[2] + CYANIC]

hy·dro·dy·nam·ic (hī′drō dī năm′ĭk, -dĭ-), *adj.* **1.** pertaining to forces in or motions of fluids. **2.** pertaining to hydrodynamics.

hy·dro·dy·nam·ics (hī′drō dī năm′ĭks, -dĭ-), *n.* **1.** the science of the mechanics of fluids, generally liquids, including hydrostatics and hydrokinetics. **2.** hydrokinetics.

hy·dro·e·lec·tric (hī′drō ĭ lĕk′trĭk), *adj.* pertaining to the generation and distribution of electric energy derived from the energy of falling water or any other hydraulic source. —**hy·dro·e·lec·tric·i·ty** (hī′drō ĭ lĕk′trĭs′ə tĭ′), *n.*

hy·dro·flu·or·ic acid (hī′drō floō ôr′ĭk, -ŏr′-), a colorless, corrosive, volatile liquid, HF, used for etching glass and as a condensing agent in chemical syntheses, such as alkylation. [f. HYDRO-[2] + FLUORIC]

hy·dro·gen (hī′drə jən), *n. Chem.* a colorless, odorless, inflammable gas, which combines chemically with oxygen to form water: the lightest of the known elements. *Symbol:* H; *at. wt.:* 1.008; *at. no.:* 1; *weight of one liter at 760 mm. pressure and 0° C.:* .08987 g. [t. F: m. *hydrogène,* f. *hydro-* HYDRO-[1] + -*gène* -GEN]

hy·dro·gen·ate (hī′drə jə nāt′), *v.t.,* -**ated, -ating.** to combine or treat with hydrogen. —**hy′dro·gen·a′tion,** *n.*

hydrogen bomb, a bomb whose potency is based on the release of nuclear energy resulting from the fusion of hydrogen isotopes in the formation of helium. It will, reputedly, be many times more powerful than the atom bomb.

hydrogen ion, *Chem.* ionized hydrogen of the form H+, found in all acids.

hy·dro·gen·ize (hī′drə jə nīz′, hī drŏj′ə-), *v.t.,* -**ized, -izing.** hydrogenate.

hy·drog·e·nous (hī drŏj′ə nəs), *adj.* **1.** of or containing hydrogen. **2.** formed or produced by water.

hydrogen peroxide, a colorless, unstable, oily liquid, H_2O_2, the aqueous solution of which is used as an antiseptic and a bleaching agent.

hydrogen sulfide, a colorless, inflammable, cumulatively poisonous gas, H_2S, smelling like rotten eggs.

hy·drog·ra·phy (hī drŏg′rə fĭ), *n.* **1.** the science of the measurement, description, and mapping of the surface waters of the earth, with special reference to their use for navigation. **2.** those parts of a map, collectively, that represent surface waters. —**hy·drog′ra·pher,** *n.* —**hy·dro·graph·ic** (hī′drə grăf′ĭk), **hy·dro·graph′i·cal,** *adj.* —**hy′dro·graph′i·cal·ly,** *adv.*

hy·droid (hī′droid), *adj.* **1.** denoting or pertaining to that form of hydrozoan which is asexual and grows into branching colonies by budding. —*n.* **2.** that phase of a hydrozoan coelenterate that consists of polyp forms usually growing as an attached colony. [f. HYDR(A) (def. 2) + -OID]

hy·dro·ki·net·ic (hī′drō kĭ nĕt′ĭk, -kĭ-), *adj.* **1.** pertaining to the motion of fluids. **2.** pertaining to hydrokinetics. Also, **hy′dro·ki·net′i·cal.**

hy·dro·ki·net·ics (hī′drō kĭ nĕt′ĭks, -kĭ-), *n.* the branch of hydromechanics that treats of the laws governing liquids or gases in motion.

hy·drol·o·gy (hī drŏl′ə jĭ), *n.* the science dealing with water on the land, its properties, laws, geographical distribution, etc. —**hy·dro·log·ic** (hī′drə lŏj′ĭk), **hy′dro·log′i·cal,** *adj.* —**hy·drol′o·gist,** *n.*

hy·drol·y·sis (hī drŏl′ə sĭs), *n., pl.* -**ses** (-sēz′). chemical decomposition by which a compound is resolved into other compounds by taking up the elements of water.

hy·dro·lyt·ic (hī′drə lĭt′ĭk), *adj.* producing hydrolysis, or related to the process or results of hydrolysis.

hy·dro·lyze (hī′drə līz′), *v.t., v.i.,* -**lyzed, -lyzing.** to subject or be subjected to hydrolysis. Also, *esp. Brit.,* **hy′dro·lyse′.** —**hy′dro·lyz′a·ble,** *adj.*

hy·dro·man·cy (hī′drə măn′sĭ), *n.* divination by means of water. [t. F: m. *hydromancie,* t. LL: m.s. *hy·dromantia,* f. Gk.: *hydro-* HYDRO-[1] + m. *manteía* divination] —**hy′dro·man′tic,** *adj.*

hy·dro·me·chan·ics (hī′drō mə kăn′ĭks), *n.* hydrodynamics (def. 1). —**hy′dro·me·chan′i·cal,** *adj.*

hy·dro·me·du·sa (hī′drō mĭ dū′sə, -dōō′-), *n., pl.* -**sae** (-sē). the medusa form of a hydrozoan coelenterate. [NL. See HYDRO-[1], MEDUSA] —**hy′dro·me·du′san,** *adj.*

hy·dro·mel (hī′drə mĕl′), *n.* a liquor consisting of honey and water: when fermented, known also as mead. [t. L: m. *hydromeli,* t. Gk.: honey water]

hy·dro·met·al·lur·gy (hī′drə mĕt′ə lûr′jĭ), *n.* the practice of extracting metals from ores by leaching with solutions such as mercury, cyanides, acids, brines, etc. —**hy′dro·met′al·lur′gi·cal,** *adj.*

hy·dro·me·te·or (hī′drə mē′tĭ ər), *n. Meterol.* state or effect of water, water vapor, or ice in the atmosphere, as rain, ice crystals, hail, fog, and clouds.

hy·drom·e·ter (hī drŏm′ə tər), *n.* a sealed cylinder with weighted bulb and graduated stem for determining the specific gravity of liquids by reading the level of the liquid on the emerging stem. —**hy·dro·met·ric** (hī′drə mĕt′rĭk), **hy′dro·met′ri·cal,** *adj.* —**hy·drom′e·try,** *n.*

hy·drop·a·thy (hī drŏp′ə thĭ), *n.* the treatment of disease by the use of water; hydrotherapy. [f. HYDRO-[1] + -PATHY] —**hy·dro·path·ic** (hī′drə păth′ĭk), **hy′dro·path′i·cal,** *adj.* —**hy·drop′a·thist, hy′dro·path′,** *n.*

hy·dro·phane (hī′drə fān′), *n.* a partly translucent variety of opal, which becomes more translucent or transparent when immersed in water. —**hy·droph·a·nous** (hī drŏf′ə nəs), *adj.*

hy·dro·pho·bi·a (hī′drə fō′bĭ ə), *n. Pathol.* **1.** rabies. **2.** a morbid dread of water, as in rabies; any morbid or unnatural dread of water. [t. LL, t. Gk.: horror of water] —**hy·dro·pho·bic** (hī′drə fō′bĭk, -fŏb′ĭk), *adj.*

hy·dro·phone (hī′drə fōn′), *n.* **1.** an instrument employing the principles of the microphone, used to detect the flow of water through a pipe. **2.** a device for locating sources of sound under water, as for detecting submarines by the noise of their engines, etc. **3.** *Med.* an instrument used in auscultation, whereby sounds are intensified through a column of water.

hy·dro·phyl·la·ceous (hī′drō fĭ lā′shəs), *adj.* of or belonging to the widespread family *Hydrophyllaceae,* mostly consisting of herbaceous plants.

hy·dro·phyte (hī′drə fīt′), *n.* a plant growing in water or very moist ground. —**hy·dro·phyt·ic** (hī′drə fīt′ĭk), *adj.*

hy·drop·ic (hī drŏp′ĭk), *adj.* dropsical. Also, **hy·drop′i·cal.** [t. L: s. *hydropicus,* t. Gk.: m. *hydrōpikós;* r. ME *ydropik,* t. OF]

hy·dro·plane (hī′drə plān′), *n., v.,* -**planed, -planing.** —*n.* **1.** an airplane provided with floats, or with a boatlike underpart, enabling it to light upon or ascend from water. **2.** an attachment to an airplane enabling it to glide on the water. **3.** a light, high-powered boat, usually with one or more steps in the bottom, designed to plane along the surface of the water at very high speeds. **4.** a horizontal rudder for submerging or elevating a submarine boat. —*v.i.* **5.** to skim over water in the manner of a hydroplane. **6.** to travel in a hydroplane (boat).

hy·dro·pon·ics (hī′drə pŏn′ĭks), *n.* the cultivation of plants by placing the roots in liquid nutrient solutions rather than in soil; soilless growth of plants. [f. HYDRO¹- + s. L. *ponere* place + -ICS] —**hy′dro·pon′ic,** *adj.*

hy·dro·qui·none (hī′drə kwĭ′nōn′,-kwĭn′ōn),*n. Chem.* a white, crystalline compound, $C_6H_4(OH)_2$, formed by the reduction of quinone, used to inhibit autoxidation reactions. Also, **hy·dro·quin·ol** (hī′drə kwĭn′ōl, -ŏl).

hydros., hydrostatics.

hy·dro·scope (hī′drə skōp′), *n.* an optical apparatus which enables the observer to view objects below the surface of the sea. —**hy·dro·scop·ic** (hī′drə skŏp′ĭk), *adj.*

hy·dro·sol (hī′drə sŏl′, -sōl′), *n. Phys. Chem.* a colloidal suspension in water. Also, **hy·dro·sole** (hī′drə sōl′). [f. HYDRO- + SOL(UTION)]

hy·dro·some (hī′drə sōm′), *n. Zool.* the entire body of a compound hydrozoan. Also, **hy·dro·so·ma** (hī′drə sō′mə).

hy·dro·sphere (hī′drə sfĭr′), *n.* the water on the surface of the globe; the water of the oceans.

hy·dro·stat (hī′drə stăt′), *n.* 1. an electrical device for detecting the presence of water, as from overflow or leakage. 2. any of various devices for preventing injury to a steam boiler from low water.

hy·dro·stat·ic (hī′drə stăt′ĭk), *adj.* of or pertaining to hydrostatics. Also, **hy/dro·stat/i·cal.** —**hy/dro·stat/i·cal·ly,** *adv.*

hy·dro·stat·ics (hī′drə stăt′ĭks), *n.* the statics of fluids, a branch of science usually confined to the equilibrium and pressure of liquids.

hy·dro·sul·fate (hī′drə sŭl′fāt), *n. Chem.* a compound between sulfuric acid and an organic base, esp. with alkaloids. Also, **hy/dro·sul/phate.**

hy·dro·sul·fide (hī′drə sŭl′fīd, -fĭd), *n. Chem.* 1. a compound containing the HS- radical. 2. (loosely) a sulfide. Also, **hy·dro·sul·fid** (hī′drə sŭl′fĭd), **hy/dro·sul/phide.**

hy·dro·sul·fite (hī′drə sŭl′fīt), *n.* sodium hyposulfite, $Na_2S_2O_4$, used as a bleach. Also, **hy/dro·sul/phite.**

hy·dro·sul·fu·rous (hī′drō′ sŭl fyōō′ r′əs, -sŭl′fə rəs), *adj.* hyposulfurous. Also, **hy/dro·sul·phur/ous.**

hy·dro·tax·is (hī′drō tăk′sĭs), *n.* a movement of organisms toward or away from water.

hy·dro·ther·a·peu·tics (hī′drō thĕr′ə pū′tĭks), *n.* that branch of therapeutics which deals with the curative use of water. —**hy/dro·ther/a·peu/tic,** *adj.*

hy·dro·ther·a·py (hī′drə thĕr′ə pĭ), *n.* treatment of disease by means of water. —**hy·dro·the·rap·ic** (hī′drō-thə răp′ĭk), *adj.*

hy·dro·ther·mal (hī′drə thûr′məl), *adj. Geol.* 1. denoting or pertaining to the action of hot, aqueous solutions or gases within or on the surface of the earth. 2. designating the results of such action.

hy·dro·tho·rax (hī′drə thôr′ăks), *n. Pathol.* the presence of serous fluid in one or both pleural cavities. —**hy·dro·tho·rac·ic** (hī′drō thə răs′ĭk), *adj.*

hy·dro·trop·ic (hī′drə trŏp′ĭk), *adj. Bot.* 1. turning or tending toward moisture, as growing organs. 2. taking a particular direction with reference to moisture.

hy·drot·ro·pism (hī drŏt′rə pĭz′əm), *n. Bot., Zool.* 1. a tropism in response to water. 2. hydrotropic tendency or growth.

hy·drous (hī′drəs), *adj.* 1. containing water. 2. *Chem.* containing water or its elements in some kind of union, as in hydrates or in hydroxides.

hy·drox·ide (hī drŏk′sīd, -sĭd), *n. Chem.* a compound containing the hydroxyl (OH) group. Also, **hy·drox·id** (hī drŏk′sĭd).

hy·drox·y acid (hī drŏk′sĭ), 1. organic acid containing both a carboxyl and a hydroxyl group. 2. one of a class of organic acids containing a hydroxyl group and showing properties of both an alcohol and acid.

hy·drox·yl radical or **group** (hī drŏk′sĭl), *Chem.* a univalent radical or group, OH, containing hydrogen and oxygen.

hy·drox·yl·a·mine (hī drŏk′sĭl ə mēn′, -ăm′ĭn), *n. Chem.* an unstable, weakly basic, crystalline compound, NH_2OH, used as a reducing agent, analytical reagent, and chemical intermediate.

Hy·dro·zo·a (hī′drə zō′ə), *n.pl.* a class of coelenterates that comprises solitary or colonial polyps and free-swimming medusae.

hy·dro·zo·an (hī′drə zō′ən), *adj.* 1. pertaining to the *Hydrozoa.* —*n.* 2. a member of the *Hydrozoa.* [f. s. NL *Hydrozöön* (f. *hydro-,* comb. form of *hydra* (def. 2) + m. Gk. *zöion* animal) + -AN]

hy·e·na (hī ē′nə), *n.* any of the nocturnal carnivores of the family *Hyaenidae,* feeding chiefly on carrion, as *Hyaena hyaena,* the **striped laughing hyena,** an African and Asiatic species about the size of a large dog, *H. brunnea,* the **brown hyena** of South Africa, and *Crocuta crocuta,* the **spotted hyena** of Africa south of the Sahara. Also, **hyaena.** [t. L: m. *hyaena,* t. Gk.: m. *hýaina,* der. *hŷs* hog; r. ME *hiene,* t. OF]

Striped hyena, *Hyaena hyaena*
(Total length 4½ ft., tail 1½ ft.)

Hy·ge·ia (hī jē′ə), *n. Class. Myth.* the goddess of health,

daughter of Aesculapius. [t. Gk., late var. of *Hygīeia,* personification of *hygieia* health]

hy·giene (hī′jēn, -jĭ ēn′), *n.* the science which deals with the preservation of health. Also, **hy·gi·en·ics** (hī′jĭ ĕn′ĭks, -jē′nĭks). [t. F, t. Gk.: m.s. *hygieinós* healthful, sanitary]

hy·gi·en·ic (hī′jĭ ĕn′ĭk, -jē′nĭk), *adj.* 1. sanitary. 2. pertaining to hygiene. —**hy/gi·en/i·cal·ly,** *adv.* —Syn. 1. See **sanitary.**

hy·gi·en·ist (hī′jĭ ĕn ĭst), *n.* an expert in hygiene. Also, **hy·ge·ist** (hī′jē ĭst), **hy/gie·ist.**

hygro-, a word element meaning "wet," "moist." Also, before vowels, **hygr-.** [t. Gk., comb. form of *hygrós*]

hy·gro·graph (hī′grə grăf′, -gräf′), *n.* a self-recording hygrometer.

hy·grom·e·ter (hī grŏm′ə tər), *n.* an instrument for determining the humidity of the atmosphere.

hy·gro·met·ric (hī′grə mĕt′rĭk), *adj.* pertaining to the hygrometer or hygrometry.

hy·grom·e·try (hī grŏm′ə trĭ), *n.* the branch of physics that treats of the determination of the humidity of air and gases.

hy·gro·scope (hī′grə skōp′), *n.* an instrument which indicates the approximate humidity of the air.

hy·gro·scop·ic (hī′grə skŏp′ĭk), *adj.* absorbing or attracting moisture from the air.

hy·ing (hī′ĭng), *v.* pres. part. of **hie.**

Hyk·sos (hĭk′sŏs, -sōs), *n.pl.* a succession of foreign rulers of Egypt between the 13th and 18th dynasties, c2000 B.C.

hy·la (hī′lə), *n.* a tree toad. [NL, t. Gk.: m. *hýlē* wood]

hylo-, a word element meaning "wood," "matter." [t. Gk., comb. form of *hýlē*]

hy·lo·zo·ism (hī′lə zō′ĭz əm), *n.* the doctrine that matter is inseparable from life, which is a property of matter. [f. HYLO- + s. Gk. *zöē* life + -ISM] **hy/lo·zo/ist,** *n.* —**hy/lo·zo·is/tic,** *adj.* —**hy/lo·zo·is/ti·cal·ly,** *adv.*

hy·men (hī′mən), *n. Anat.* a fold of mucous membrane partially closing the external orifice of the vagina in a virgin. [t. Gk.: thin skin, membrane]

Hy·men (hī′mən), *n. Gk. Myth.* the god of marriage, represented as a young man bearing a bridal torch.

hy·me·ne·al (hī′mə nē′əl), *adj.* 1. pertaining to marriage. —*n.* 2. marriage song.

hy·me·nop·ter (hī′mə nŏp′tər), *n., pl.* **-tera** (-tər ə) hymenopteron. —**hy/me·nop/ter·an,** *adj., n.*

hy·me·nop·ter·on (hī′mə nŏp′tər ən), *n.* a hymenopterous insect.

hy·me·nop·ter·ous (hī′mə nŏp′tər əs), *adj.* belonging or pertaining to the *Hymenoptera,* an order of insects having (when winged) four membranous wings, and including the wasps, bees, ants, etc. [t. Gk.: m. *hymenópteros* membrane-winged]

Hy·met·tus (hī mĕt′əs), *n.* a mountain in SE Greece, near Athens: famous for honey produced there. 3370 ft.

hymn (hĭm), *n.* 1. a song or ode in praise or honor of God, a deity, a nation, etc. —*v.t.* 2. to praise or celebrate in a hymn; express in a hymn. —*v.i.* 3. to sing hymns. [t. LL: m. *hymnus,* t. Gk.: m. *hýmnos;* r. ME *ymne* (t. OF) and ME *ymyn,* OE *ym(e)n,* t. LL (Eccl.): (m.) s. *ymnus*] —**hymn/like/,** *adj.*

hym·nal (hĭm′nəl), *n.* 1. Also, **hymn′book/.** a book of hymns for use in divine worship. —*adj.* 2. of or pertaining to hymns.

hym·nist (hĭm′nĭst), *n.* a composer of hymns.

hym·no·dy (hĭm′nə dĭ), *n.* 1. the singing or the composition of hymns or sacred songs. 2. hymns collectively. [t. ML: m.s. *hymnōdia,* t. Gk.: m. *hymnōidía* the singing of a hymn] —**hym/no·dist,** *n.*

hym·nol·o·gy (hĭm nŏl′ə jĭ), *n.* 1. the study of hymns, their history, classification, etc. 2. the composition of hymns. 3. hymns collectively. —**hym·no·log·ic** (hĭm′nə lŏj′ĭk), **hym/no·log/i·cal,** *adj.* —**hym·nol/o·gist,** *n.*

hy·oid (hī′oid), *Anat.* —*adj.* 1. denoting or pertaining to a U-shaped bone at the root of the tongue in man, or a corresponding bone or collection of bones in animals. See diag. under **mouth.** —*n.* 2. the hyoid bone, cartilage, arch. ligament, etc. [t. NL: m.s. *hyoīdēs,* t. Gk.: m. *hyoeidēs* shaped like the letter upsilon]

hy·os·cine (hī′ə sēn′, -sĭn), *n.* 1. *Chem.* an alkaloid chemically identical with scopolamine, used as a mydriatic, etc. 2. *(cap.)* a trademark for this substance. [syncopated var. of HYOSCYAMINE]

hy·os·cy·a·mine (hī′ə sī′ə mēn′, -mĭn), *n. Chem.* a poisonous alkaloid, $C_{17}H_{23}NO_3$, obtained from henbane and other solanaceous plants, used as a sedative, mydriatic, etc. [f. s. L *hyoscyamus* (t. Gk.: m. *hyoskýamos* henbane, lit., hog's bean) + -INE²]

hyp., 1. hypotenuse. 2. hypothesis. 3. hypothetical.

hyp-, var. of **hypo-,** before most vowels, as in *hypethial.*

hyp·a·byss·al (hĭp′ə bĭs′əl), *adj. Geol.* intermediate in texture, as some igneous rocks, between coarse-grained forms and extrusive lava.

hyp·aes·the·sia (hĭp′əs thē′zhə, -zhĭ ə), *n.* hypesthesia. —**hyp/aes·the/sic,** *adj.*

hy·pae·thral (hĭ pē′thrəl, hī-), *adj.* hypethral.

Hy·pa·tia (hī pā′shə), *n.* died A.D. 415, a wise and beautiful woman of Alexandria, Egypt.

hyper-, **1.** a prefix meaning "over," and usually implying excess or exaggeration. **2.** *Chem.* the same as **super-,** indicating the highest of a series of compounds: *hyperchloric acid.* The prefix *per-* is now generally used for *hyper-: perchloric, permanganic, etc.* [t. Gk., repr. *hypér,* prep., over, above, beyond, as adv. overmuch, beyond measure; akin to SUPER, OVER]

hy·per·a·cid·i·ty (hī'pər ə sĭd'ə tĭ), *n.* excessive acidity as of the gastric juice. **—hy·per·ac·id** (hī'pər ăs'ĭd), *adj.*

hy·per·a·cu·sis (hī'pər ə kū'sĭs), *n.* *Pathol.* excessive acuteness of the sense of hearing. [NL, f. Gk.: *hyper-* HYPER- + m. *ákousis* hearing]

hy·per·ae·mi·a (hī'pər ē'mĭ ə), *n.* hyperemia. **—hy'per·ae'mic,** *adj.*

hy·per·aes·the·sia (hī'pər əs thē'zhə, -zhĭ ə), *n.* hyperesthesia. **—hy·per·aes·thet·ic** (hī'pər əs thĕt'ĭk), *adj.*

hy·per·al·ge·si·a (hī'pər ăl jē'zĭ ə, -sĭ ə), *n.* I *athol.* an exaggerated feeling or sense of pain. [NL, f. Gk.: *hyper-* HYPER- + s. *álgēsis* sense of pain + *-ia* -IA] **—hy'per·al·ge'sic,** *adj.*

hy·per·bo·la (hī pûr'bə lə), *n.,* *pl.* **-las.** *Geom.* a curve consisting of two distinct and similar branches, formed by the intersection of a plane with a right circular cone when the plane makes a greater angle with the base than does the generator of the cone. [NL, t. Gk.: m. *hyperbolē,* lit., a throwing beyond. See HYPERBOLE]

Hyperbola
DBE, GAH, Opposite branches of a hyperbola; F, F, Foci; C, Center; AB, Transverse axis; A', B', Conjugate axis; NCP, A diameter

hy·per·bo·le (hī pûr'bə lē', -lĭ), *n.* *Rhet.* obvious exaggeration, for effect; an extravagant statement not intended to be understood literally. [t. L, t. Gk.: a throwing beyond, excess, hyperbole, also a hyperbola]

hy·per·bol·ic (hī'pər bŏl'ĭk), *adj.* **1.** having the nature of hyperbole; exaggerated. **2.** using hyperbole, or exaggerating. **3.** of or pertaining to the hyperbola. Also, **hy'per·bol'i·cal. —hy'per·bol'i·cal·ly,** *adv.*

hy·per·bo·lism (hī pûr'bə lĭz'əm), *n.* the use of hyperbole.

hy·per·bo·lize (hī pûr'bə līz'), *v.,* **-lized, -li·zing. —v.i. 1.** to use hyperbole; exaggerate. **—v.t. 2.** to represent or express with hyperbole or exaggeration.

Hy·per·bo·re·an (hī'pər bōr'ĭ ən), *n.* **1.** *Gk. Legend.* one of a people supposed to live in a land of perpetual sunshine and plenty beyond the north wind. **—adj. 2.** of or pertaining to the Hyperboreans. **3.** of the far north; arctic; frigid: *hyperborean regions.* [t. LL: s. *Hyperboreānus,* in L *Hyperboreus,* t. Gk.: m. *Hyperbóreos* beyond the north wind. See BOREAS]

hy·per·crit·ic (hī'pər krĭt'ĭk), *n.* one who is excessively or captiously critical.

hy·per·crit·i·cal (hī'pər krĭt'ə kəl), *adj.* excessively critical; overcritical. **—hy'per·crit'i·cal·ly,** *adv.*

hy·per·du·li·a (hī'pər dyōō lī'ə, -dŏŏ-), *n.* *Rom. Cath. Theol.* the veneration offered to the Virgin Mary as the most exalted of mere creatures. [t. ML. See HYPER-, DULIA]

hy·per·e·mi·a (hī'pər ē'mĭ ə), *n.* *Pathol.* an increase in the blood in any part of the body. Also, **hyperaemia.** [NL. See HYPER-, -EMIA] **—hy'per·e'mic,** *adj.*

hy·per·es·the·sia (hī'pər əs thē'zhə, -zhĭ ə), *n.* *Pathol.* increased sense of pain, heat, cold, or touch. Also, **hyperaesthesia. —hy·per·es·thet·ic** (hī'pər əs thĕt'ĭk), *adj.*

hy·per·eu·tec·tic (hī'pər yōō tĕk'tĭk), *adj.* noting or pertaining to iron whose combined carbon content is over 4.3%, the amount in the eutectic alloy of carbon and iron.

hy·per·ex·ten·sion (hī'pər ĭk stĕn'shən), *n.* *Physiol.* **1.** the extension of a part beyond the plane of the body, as when the arm is drawn back to its maximum extent. **2.** the state of being so drawn.

Hy·pe·ri·on (hī pĭr'ĭ ən), *n.* *Gk. Myth.* **1.** a Titan, a son of Uranus and Gaea: the father of Helios, Selene, and Eos. **2.** (later) Apollo. [t. L, t. Gk.]

hy·per·ir·ri·ta·bil·i·ty (hī'pər ĭr'ə tə bĭl'ə tĭ), *n.* *Med.* increased irritability.

hy·per·ki·ne·sia (hī'pər kĭ nē'zhə, -zhĭ ə, -kĭ-), *n.* *Pathol.* abnormal amount of muscular action; spasm. [NL, f. Gk.: *hyper-* HYPER- + s. *kīnēsis* movement + *-ia* -IA] **—hy·per·ki·net·ic** (hī'pər kĭ nĕt'ĭk, -kĭ-), *adj.*

hy·per·me·ter (hī pûr'mə tər), *n.* *Pros.* a verse or line having one or more syllables at the end in addition to those proper to the meter.

hy·per·met·ric (hī'pər mĕt'rĭk), *adj.* *Pros.* of more than regular metrical length. Also, **hy'per·met'ri·cal.**

hy·per·me·tro·pi·a (hī'pər mə trō'pĭ ə), *n.* *Pathol.* a condition of the eye in which parallel rays are focused behind the retina. distant objects being seen more distinctly than near ones; far-sightedness. [NL, f. Gk.: s. *hypérmetros* beyond measure + *-opia* -OPIA]

hy·per·me·trop·ic (hī'pər mə trŏp'ĭk), *adj.* pertaining to or affected with hypermetropia; far-sighted.

Hy·perm·nes·tra (hī'pərm nĕs'trə), *n.* *Gk. Legend.* the one daughter of Danaüs who refused to kill her husband as commanded by her father.

hy·per·o·pi·a (hī'pər ō'pĭ ə), *n.* hypermetropia. **—hy·per·op·ic** (hī'pər ŏp'ĭk), *adj.*

hy·per·os·to·sis (hī'pər ŏs tō'sĭs), *n.,* *pl.* **-ses** (-sēz). *Anat., Pathol.* **1.** an increase or outgrowth of bony tissue. **2.** an overgrowth of bone.

hy·per·phys·i·cal (hī'pər fĭz'ə kəl), *adj.* above or beyond the physical; immaterial; supernatural.

hy·per·pi·e·sia (hī'pər pī ē'zhə, -zhĭ ə), *n.* *Pathol.* unusually high blood pressure. [NL, f. Gk.: *hyper-* HYPER- + s. *píesis* pressure + *-ia* -IA]

hy·per·pi·tu·i·ta·rism (hī'pər pĭ tū'ə rĭz'əm, -tōō'-), *n.* *Pathol.* **1.** overactivity of the pituitary gland. **2.** the resultant condition, i.e., giantism or acromegaly.

hy·per·pla·sia (hī'pər plā'zhə, -zhĭ ə), *n.* **1.** *Pathol., Bot.* abnormal multiplication of cells. **2.** *Pathol.* enlargement of a part due to numerical increase of its cells. **—hy·per·plas·ic** (hī'pər plăs'ĭk), **hy·per·plas·tic,** *adj.*

hy·per·ploid (hī'pər ploid'), *adj.* *Biol.* pertaining to a chromosome number in excess of the diploid but not a multiple of it. [f. HYPER- + (DI)PLOID]

hy·per·pne·a (hī'pərp nē'ə, hī'pər nē'ə), *n.* *Pathol.* energetic or labored respiration. Also, **hy'per·pne'a.** [NL, f. Gk.: *hyper-* HYPER- + m. *pnoiē* breathing]

hy·per·py·rex·i·a (hī'pər pī rĕk'sĭ ə), *n.* *Pathol.* an abnormally high fever. **—hy·per·py·rex·i·al,** *adj.*

hy·per·sen·si·tive (hī'pər sĕn'sə tĭv), *adj.* **1.** excessively sensitive. **2.** *Pathol.* allergic to a substance to which a normal individual does not react. **—hy'per·sen'si·tive·ness, hy·per·sen·si·tiv·i·ty,** *n.*

hy·per·sthene (hī'pər sthēn'), *n.* a common mineral of the pyroxene group, iron magnesium silicate, occurring in green to black masses as an important constituent of basic igneous rocks. [f. HYPER- + m.s. Gk. *sthénos* strength (with reference to frangibility)] **—hy·per·sthen·ic** (hī'pər sthĕn'ĭk), *adj.*

hy·per·ten·sion (hī'pər tĕn'shən), *n.* *Pathol.* **1.** elevation of the blood pressure, especially the diastolic pressure. **2.** an arterial disease of which this is the outstanding sign.

hy·per·thy·roid·ism (hī'pər thī'roi dĭz'əm), *n.* **1.** *Pathol.* overactivity of the thyroid gland. **2.** a pathological condition, consisting of a complex of symptoms, produced by this. **—hy'per·thy'roid,** *n.*

hy·per·ton·ic (hī'pər tŏn'ĭk), *adj.* **1.** *Physiol.* possessing too much tone. **2.** *Chem.* denoting a solution of higher osmotic pressure than another solution with which it is compared.

hy·per·tro·phy (hī pûr'trə fĭ), *n.,* *pl.* **-phies,** *v.,* **-phied, -phying. 1.** *Pathol., Bot.* enlargement of a part or organ; excessive growth. **2.** excessive growth or accumulation of any kind. **—v.t., v.i. 3.** to affect with or undergo hypertrophy. **—hy·per·troph·ic** (hī'pər trŏf'ĭk), *adj.*

hyp·es·the·sia (hĭp'əs thē'zhə, -zhĭ ə), *n.* *Pathol.* diminished sense of pain, heat, cold, or touch. Also, **hyp·aesthesia. —hyp·es·the·sic** (hĭp'əs thē'sĭk), *adj.*

hy·pe·thral (hĭ pē'thrəl, hī-), *adj.* open to the sky or having no roof, as a building (used esp. of classical architecture). Also, **hypaethral.** [f. s. L *hypaethrus* (t. Gk.: m. *hýpaithros* under the sky) + -AL¹]

hy·pha (hī'fə), *n.,* *pl.* **-phae** (-fē). *Bot.* (in fungi) one of the threadlike elements of the mycelium. [NL, t. Gk.: m. *hyphē* web] **—hy'phal,** *adj.*

hy·phen (hī'fən), *n.* **1.** a short line (-) used to connect the parts of a compound word or the parts of a word divided for any purpose, as for syllabication. **—v.t. 2.** hyphenate. [t. LL, t. Gk.: name of sign, special use of *hyphén,* adv., prop. phrase *hyph'hén* under one, together]

hy·phen·ate (hī'fə nāt'), *v.,* **-ated, -ating,** *adj.,* *n.* **—v.t. 1.** to join by a hyphen. **2.** to write with a hyphen. **—adj. 3.** hyphenated. **—hy'phen·a'tion,** *n.*

hy·phen·ize (hī'fə nīz'), *v.t.,* **-ized, -izing.** hyphenate. **—hy'phen·i·za'tion,** *n.*

hypno-, a word element meaning "sleep" or "hypnosis," as in *hypnology.* Also, before vowels (usually), **hypn-.** [t. Gk., comb. form of *hýpnos* sleep]

hyp·no·a·nal·y·sis (hĭp'nō ə năl'ə sĭs), *n.* *Psychoanal.* a method employed by some psychoanalysts who attempt to secure analytic data, free associations, and early emotional reactions under hypnosis.

hyp·noi·dal (hĭp noi'dəl), *adj.* *Psychol.* in a state which resembles that of mild hypnosis but is (usually) not induced hypnotically. Also, **hyp'noid.**

hyp·nol·o·gy (hĭp nŏl'ə jĭ), *n.* the science dealing with the phenomena of sleep. **—hyp·no·log·ic** (hĭp'nə lŏj'ĭk), **hyp'no·log'i·cal. —hyp·nol'o·gist,** *n.*

hyp·no·sis (hĭp nō'sĭs), *n.,* *pl.* **-ses** (-sēz). **1.** *Psychol.* a condition or state, allied to normal sleep, which can be artificially produced and is characterized by marked susceptibility to suggestion, loss of will power, more or less loss of sensation, etc. **2.** the production of sleep. **3.** a sleepy condition. **4.** hypnotism. [NL, der. Gk. *hypnoûn* put to sleep]

hyp·no·ther·a·py (hĭp'nō thĕr'ə pĭ), *n.* treatment of disease by means of hypnotism.

hyp·not·ic (hĭp nŏt'ĭk), *adj.* **1.** pertaining to hypnosis or hypnotism. **2.** susceptible to hypnotism, as a person. **3.** hypnotized. **4.** inducing sleep. **—n. 5.** an agent or drug that produces sleep; a sedative. **6.** one subject to hypnotic influence. **7.** a person under the influence of

b., blend of, blended; c., cognate with; d., dialect, dialectal; der., derived from; f., formed from; g., going back to; m., modification of; r., replacing; s., stem of; t., taken from; ?, perhaps. See the full key on inside cover.

hypnotism. [t. LL: s. *hypnōticus*, t. Gk.: m. *hypnōtikós* inclined to sleep] **—hyp·not/i·cal·ly,** *adv.*

hyp·no·tism (hĭp/nə tĭz/əm), *n.* **1.** the science dealing with the induction of hypnosis. **2.** the induction of hypnosis. **3.** hypnosis.

hyp·no·tist (hĭp/nə tĭst), *n.* one who hypnotizes.

hyp·no·tize (hĭp/nə tīz/), *v.t.*, **-tized, -tizing.** to put in the hypnotic state. Also, *esp. Brit.*, **hyp/no·tise/.** **—hyp/no·tiz/a·ble,** *adj.* **—hyp/no·ti·za/tion,** *n.* **—hyp/no·tiz/er,** *n.*

hy·po¹ (hī/pō), *n. Chem.* sodium thiosulfate, $Na_2S_2O_3$·$5H_2O$, a photographic fixing agent. [short for HYPO-SULFITE]

hy·po² (hī/pō), *n. Slang.* a hypodermic needle or injection. [short for HYPODERMIC]

hypo-, **1.** a prefix meaning "under," either in place or in degree ("less," "less than"). **2.** *Chem.* a prefix applied to the inorganic acids (as *hypochlorous acid*) and to their salts (as *potassium hypochlorite*) to indicate a low valence state for the designated element. Also, **hyp-.** [t. Gk., repr. *hypó*, prep. and adv., under; akin to SUB-]

hy·po·a·cid·i·ty (hī/pō ə sĭd/ə tĭ), *n.* acidity in a lesser degree than is usual or normal, as of the gastric juice.

hy·po·blast (hī/pə blăst/, hĭp/ə-), *n. Embryol.* the inner layer of a gastrula, consisting of endoblast, or endoblast and mesoblast. **—hy/po·blas/tic,** *adj.*

hyp·o·caust (hĭp/ə kôst/, hī/pə-), *n.* a hollow space or system of flues in the floor or walls of a Roman building or room, which received and distributed the heat from a furnace. [t. L: s. *hypocaustum*, t. Gk.: m. *hypó-kauston* room heated from below]

hy·po·chlo·rous acid (hī/pə klôr/əs, hĭp/ə-), *Chem.* an acid, HClO, whose solutions have strong bleaching properties.

hy·po·chon·dri·a (hī/pə kŏn/drĭ ə, hĭp/ə-), *n.* **1.** *Psychiatry.* a morbid condition characterized by depressed spirits and fancies of ill health, referable to the physical condition of the body or one of its parts. **2.** (*orig. as pl.*) the parts of the body under the cartilage of the breastbone and above the navel. [t. LL; pl., the abdomen, t. Gk.: m. *hypochóndria* (neut. pl.) def. 2; orig. thought to be the seat of melancholy]

hy·po·chon·dri·ac (hī/pə kŏn/drĭ ăk/, hĭp/ə-), *adj.* Also, **hy·po·chon·dri·a·cal** (hī/pō kŏn drī/ə kəl, hĭp/ō-). **1.** pertaining to or suffering from hypochondria or morbid depression. **2.** of or pertaining to the hypochondria (def. 2): *the hypochondriac regions.* **—n. 3.** a person suffering from or subject to hypochondria. **—hy/po·chon-dri/a·cal·ly,** *adv.*

hy·po·chon·dri·um (hī/pə kŏn/drĭ əm, hĭp/ə-), *n., pl.* **-dria** (-drĭ ə). *Anat., Zool.* **1.** either of two regions of the human abdomen, situated on opposite sides (left and right) of the epigastrium, above the lumbar regions. **2.** a corresponding region in lower animals. [NL]

hyp·o·co·ris·tic (hĭp/ə kō rĭs/tĭk, hī/pə-), *adj.* endearing, as a pet name; diminutive; euphemistic. [t. Gk.: m.s. *hypokoristikós*]

hy·po·cot·yl (hī/pə kŏt/əl, hĭp/ə-), *n. Bot.* (in the embryo of a plant) that part of the stem below cotyledons. [HYPO- + COTYL-(EDON)] **—hy/po·cot/y·lous,** *adj.*

hy·poc·ri·sy (hĭ pŏk/rə sĭ), *n., pl.* **-sies.** **1.** act of pretending to have a character or beliefs, principles, etc., that one does not possess. **2.** pretense of virtue or piety; false goodness. [ME *ypocrisie*, t. OF, t. LL: m.s. *hypocrisis*, t. Gk.: m. *hypókrisis* acting of a part, pretense] **—Syn. 1.** See **deceit.**

hyp·o·crite (hĭp/ə krĭt), *n.* one given to hypocrisy; one who feigns virtue or piety; a pretender. [ME *ypocrite*, t. OF, t. LL: m.s. *hypocrita*, t. Gk.: m. *hypokritēs* actor, pretender, hypocrite] **—hyp/o·crit/i·cal,** *adj.* **—hyp/o·crit/i·cal·ly,** *adv.*

hy·po·cy·cloid (hī/pə sī/kloid, hĭp/ə-), *n. Geom.* a curve generated by the motion of a point on the circumference of a circle which rolls internally, without slipping, on a given circle. **—hy/po·cy·cloi/dal,** *adj.*

H. Hypocyc oid traced by point P; C' Center of moving circle; C Center of fixed circle

hy·po·derm (hī/pə dûrm/), *n.* **1.** the epidermis of an arthropod. **2.** *Bot.* hypodermis. **—hy/po·der/mal,** *adj.*

hy·po·der·mic (hī/pə dûr/mĭk), *adj.* **1.** characterized by the introduction of medical remedies under the skin: *hypodermic injection.* **2.** introduced under the skin: *a hypodermic syringe.* **3.** pertaining to parts under the skin. **4.** lying under the skin, as tissue. **—n. 5.** a hypodermic remedy. **6.** a hypodermic injection. **7.** the administration of drugs into subcutaneous body tissues. **8.** a hypodermic syringe. **—hy/po·der/mi·cal·ly,** *adv.*

hypodermic needle, a hollow needle used to inject solutions subcutaneously.

hypodermic syringe, a small glass piston or barrel syringe having a detachable hollow needle used to inject solutions subcutaneously.

hy·po·der·mis (hī/pə dûr/mĭs, hĭp/ə-), *n. Zool.* **1.** the surface epithelium of an invertebrate when covered over by the noncellular secretion that it produces. **2.** *Bot.* a tissue or layer of cells beneath the epidermis. [NL]

hy·po·eu·tec·tic (hī/pō yōō tĕk/tĭk, hĭp/ō-), *adj. Metall.* noting or pertaining to iron whose combined carbon content in under 4.3%, the amount in the eutectic alloy of carbon and iron.

hy·po·gas·tric (hī/pə găs/trĭk, hĭp/ə-), *adj. Anat.* **1.** situated below the stomach. **2.** of or pertaining to the hypogastrium.

hy·po·gas·tri·um (hī/pə găs/trĭ əm, hĭp/ə-), *n., pl.* **-tria** (-trĭ ə). *Anat.* **1.** the lower part of the abdomen. **2.** the region between the right and left iliac regions. [NL, t. Gk.: m. *hypogástrion*, prop. neut. of *hypogástrios* abdominal]

hy·po·ge·al (hī/pə jē/əl, hĭp/ə-), *adj.* underground; subterranean. [f. s. L *hypogēus* t. Gk.: m. *hypógeios* underground) + -AL¹]

hyp·o·gene (hĭp/ə jēn/, hī/pə-), *adj. Geol.* formed beneath the earth's surface, as granite (opposed to *epigene*). [f. HYPO- + -*gene* (var. of -GEN)]

hy·pog·e·nous (hī pŏj/ə nəs, hī-), *adj. Bot.* growing beneath, or on the under surface, as fungi on leaves.

hy·po·ge·ous (hī/pə jē/əs, hĭp/ə-), *adj.* **1.** underground; subterranean. **2.** *Bot.* growing or remaining underground. [t. L: m. *hypogēus*, t. Gk.: m. *hypógeios*]

hyp·o·ge·um (hĭp/ə jē/əm, hī/pə-), *n., pl.* **-gea** (-jē/ə). *Anc. Archit.* **1.** the underground part of a building. **2.** an underground structure; an artificial cave. [t. L, t. Gk.: m. *hypógeion*, neut. of *hypógeios* underground]

hy·po·glos·sal (hī/pə glŏs/əl, hĭp/ə-), *Anat., Zool.* **—adj. 1.** situated under the tongue wholly or in part. **—n. 2.** a hypoglossal nerve. [f. HYPO- + s. Gk. *glōssa* tongue + -AL¹]

hypoglossal nerve, either of the last pair of cranial nerves which gives rise to the movements of the tongue.

hy·pog·y·nous (hī pŏj/ə nəs, hī-), *adj. Bot.* **1.** situated on the receptacle beneath the pistil, as stamens, etc. **2.** having stamens, etc., so arranged. **—hy·pog/y·ny,** *n.*

hy·po·nas·ty (hī/pə năs/tĭ, hĭp/ə-), *n. Bot.* increased growth along the lower surface of an organ or part, causing it to bend upward. [f. HYPO- + s. Gk. *nastós* pressed close, compact + -Y³] **—hy/po·nas/tic,** *adj.*

hy·po·ni·trous acid (hī/pə nī/trəs), *Chem.* an unstable crystalline acid, $H_2N_2O_2$.

hy·po·phos·phite (hī/pə fŏs/fīt), *n. Chem.* a salt of hypophosphorus acid, containing the radical H_2PO_2-¹.

hy·po·phos·phor·ic acid (hī/pō fŏs fôr/ĭk, -fôr/-), *Chem.* a tetrabasic acid, $H_4P_2O_6$, produced by the slow oxidation of phosphorus in moist air.

hy·po·phos·pho·rous (hī/pə fŏs/fə rəs), *adj. Chem.* a monobasic acid of phosphorus, H_3PO_2, having salts which are used in medicine.

hy·poph·y·sis (hī pŏf/ə sĭs, hī-), *n., pl.* **-ses** (-sēz/). *Anat.* the pituitary gland of the brain. [NL, t. Gk.: undergrowth, process]

hy·po·pi·tu·i·ta·rism (hī/pō pĭ tū/ə tə rĭz/əm, -tōō/-, hĭp/ō-), *n. Pathol.* **1.** abnormally diminished activity of the pituitary gland. **2.** the pathological condition produced by this, resulting in obesity, retention of adolescent traits, and, in extreme cases, dwarfism.

hy·po·pla·sia (hī/pə plā/zhə, -zhĭ ə, hĭp/ə-), *n.* **1.** *Pathol., Bot.* abnormal deficiency of cells or structural elements. **2.** *Pathol.* an underdeveloped condition in which an organ or structure remains immature or subnormal in size. [f. HYPO- + -PLASIA]

hy·po·py·on (hī pō/pĭ ŏn/, hī-), *n. Pathol.* an effusion of pus into the anterior chamber of the eye, or that cavity which contains the aqueous humor. [NL, t. Gk.: ulcer, prop. neut. of *hypópyos* tending to suppuration]

hy·pos·ta·sis (hī pŏs/tə sĭs, hī-), *n., pl.* **-ses** (-sēz/). **1.** *Metaphys.* **a.** that which stands under and supports; foundation. **b.** the underlying or essential part of anything as distinguished from attributes; substance, essence, or essential principle. **2.** *Theol.* **a.** one of the three real and distinct subsistences in the one undivided substance or essence of God. **b.** a person of the Trinity. **c.** the one personality of Christ in which His two natures, human and divine, are united. **3.** *Med.* the accumulation of blood or solids of gravity due to poor circulation or standing. [t. LL, t. Gk.: substance, nature, essence, also sediment]

hy·po·stat·ic (hī/pə stăt/ĭk, hĭp/ə-), *adj.* **1.** of or pertaining to a hypostasis; elementary. **2.** *Theol.* pertaining to or constituting a distinct personal being or subsistence. **3.** *Med.* arising from downward pressure: *hypostatic congestion.* **4.** *Genetics.* (of nonallelic genes) recessive. Also, **hy/po·stat/i·cal.** [t. Gk.: m.s. *hypostatikós* pertaining to substance] **—hy/po·stat/i·cal·ly,** *adv.*

hy·pos·ta·tize (hī pŏs/tə tīz/, hī-), *v.t.*, **-tized, -tizing.** to treat or regard as a distinct substance or reality. Also, *esp. Brit.*, **hy·pos/ta·tise/.** **—hy·pos/ta·ti·za/tion,** *n.*

hyp·o·style (hĭp/ə stīl/, hī/pə-), *Archit.* **—adj. 1.** having many columns carrying the roof or ceiling: *a hypostyle hall.* **—n. 2.** a hypostyle structure. [t. Gk.: m.s. *hypóstȳlos* resting on pillars]

hy·po·sul·fite (hī/pə sŭl/fīt), *n. Chem.* **1.** a salt of hyposulfurous acid. **2.** sodium thiosulfate, antichlor, or hypo ($Na_2S_2O_3$), a bleach and photographic fixing agent. Also, **hy/po·sul/phite.**

hy·po·sul·fu·rous acid (hī/pō sŭl fyŏŏr/əs, -sŭl/fə rəs), an acid, $H_2S_2O_4$, next in a series below sulfurous acid.

hy·po·tax·is (hī′pə tăk′sĭs, hĭp′ə-), *n. Gram.* dependent relation or construction, as of clauses. [NL, t. Gk.: subjection] —**hy′po·tac′tic**, *adj.*

hy·pot·e·nuse (hī pŏt′ə nūs′, -nōōs′), *n. Geom.* the side of a right triangle opposite the right angle. Also, **hypothenuse**. [t. LL: m.s. *hypotēnūsa*, t. Gk.: m. *hypoteînousa*, ppr. fem., subtending]

hy·po·thal·a·mus (hī′pə thăl′ə məs, hĭp′ə-), *n. Anat.* the portion of the diencephalon concerned with emotional expression and visceral responses.

hy·poth·ec (hī pŏth′ĭk, hĭ-), *n. Rom. and Civil Law.* a lien held by a creditor on the property of his debtor without possession of it. It may be created either by agreement or by operation of law. [t. LL: s. *hypothēca*, t. Gk.: m. *hypothēkē* deposit, pledge]

hy·poth·e·car·y (hī pŏth′ə kĕr′ĭ, hĭ-), *adj.* **1.** of or pertaining to a hypothec. **2.** created or secured by a hypothec.

hy·poth·e·cate (hī pŏth′ə kāt′, hĭ-), *v.t.,* **-cated, -cating. 1.** to pledge to a creditor as security without delivering over; mortgage. **2.** to put in pledge by delivery, as stocks given as security for a loan. [t. ML: m.s. *hypothēcātus*, pp., of *hypothēcāre*, der. LL *hypothēca* HYPOTHEC] —**hy·poth′e·ca′tion**, *n.* —**hy·poth′e·ca′tor**, *n.*

hy·poth·e·nuse (hī pŏth′ə nūs′, -nōōs′, hĭ-), *n.* hypotenuse.

hy·poth·e·sis (hī pŏth′ə sĭs, hĭ-), *n.,* *pl.* **-ses** (-sēz′). **1.** a proposition (or set of propositions) proposed as an explanation for the occurrence of some specified group of phenomena, either asserted merely as a provisional conjecture to guide investigation (a **working hypothesis**), or accepted as highly probable in the light of established facts. **2.** a proposition assumed as a premise in an argument. **3.** the antecedent of a conditional proposition. **4.** a mere assumption or guess. [NL, t. Gk.: supposition, postulate] —**Syn. 1.** See **theory.**

hy·poth·e·size (hī pŏth′ə sīz′, hĭ-), *v.,* **-sized, -sizing** —*v.i.* **1.** to form a hypothesis. —*v.t.* **2.** to assume by hypothesis. Also, *esp. Brit.,* **hy·poth′e·sise′.**

hy·po·thet·i·cal (hī′pə thĕt′ə kəl), *adj.* **1.** assumed by hypothesis; supposed: *a hypothetical case.* **2.** pertaining to, involving, or of the nature of hypothesis: *hypothetical reasoning.* **3.** given to making hypotheses: *a hypothetical person.* **4.** *Logic.* **a.** conditional; characterizing propositions having the form *if A, then B.* **b.** (of a syllogism) having a premise which is a hypothetical proposition. **c.** (of a proposition) not well supported by evidence, whose status is therefore highly conjectural. Also, **hy′po·thet′ic.** [f. *hypothetic* (t. Gk.: m.s. *hypothetikós* supposed) + -AL[1]] —**hy′po·thet′i·cal·ly,** *adv.*

hy·po·thy·roid·ism (hī′pō thī′roi dĭz′əm, hĭp′ō-), *n. Pathol.* **1.** abnormally diminished activity of the thyroid gland. **2.** the condition produced by a deficiency of thyroid secretion, resulting in goiter, myxedema, and, in children, cretinism.

hy·po·ton·ic (hī′pə tŏn′ĭk, hĭp′ə-), *adj. Physiol.* under the normal tone.

hy·po·xan·thine (hī′pə zăn′thēn, -thĭn), *n. Chem.* a crystalline alkaloid, $C_5H_4N_4O$, related to xanthine and found in animal and vegetable tissues. —**hy′po·xan′thic,** *adj.*

hyp·som·e·ter (hĭp sŏm′ə tər), *n.* **1.** an instrument for measuring altitude by determining the boiling point of a liquid at the given height. **2.** (sometimes) the boiler of a hypsometer. [f. Gk. *hýpso(s)* height + -METER]

hyp·som·e·try (hĭp sŏm′ə trĭ), *n.* vertical control in mapping; the establishment of elevations or altitudes. —**hyp′so·met′ric** (hĭp′sə mĕt′rĭk), **hyp′so·met′ri·cal,** *adj.* —**hyp′so·met′ri·cal·ly,** *adv.*

hy·ra·coid (hī′rə koid′), *adj.* belonging or pertaining to the order *Hyracoidea,* that comprises the hyraxes. [f.

s. NL *hyrax* HYRAX + -OID] —**hy·ra·coi·de·an** (hī′rə koi′dĭ ən), *adj., n.*

hy·rax (hī′răks), *n.,* *pl.* **hyraxes, hyraces** (hī′rə sēz′). any of a number of small, timid mammals of Asia and Africa, superficially resembling the ground hog but having tiny hoofs and other distinctive characteristics. They constitute a separate order, the *Hyracoidae,* the **rock hyrax,** genus *Procavia* (or *Hyrax*), living mostly in rocky places, the closely similar **tree hyrax** of Africa, genus *Dendrohyrax,* being arboreal. [NL, t. Gk.: shrewmouse]

Hyr·ca·ni·a (hərkā′nĭ ə), *n.* an ancient province of the Persian empire, SE of the Caspian Sea. —**Hyr·ca′·ni·an,** *adj.*

hy·son (hī′sən), *n.* a Chinese green tea, the early crop and the inferior leaves being called **young hyson** and **hyson skin** respectively. [t. Chinese (Cantonese): m. *hei-ch'un,* lit., blooming spring (Mandarin *hsi-ch'un*)]

hys·sop (hĭs′əp), *n.* **1.** an aromatic labiate herb, *Hyssopus officinalis,* with blue flowers. **2.** (in the Bible and derived use) a plant, perhaps the caper, whose twigs were used in ceremonial sprinkling. [t. L: s. *hyssōpus,* t. Gk.: m. *hýssōpos* kind of plant; r. OE *ysope*]

hyster-, var. of **hystero-,** before vowels, as in *hysterectomy.*

hys·ter·ec·to·my (hĭs′tə rĕk′tə mĭ), *n.,* *pl.* **-mies.** *Surg.* the excision of the uterus.

hys·ter·e·sis (hĭs′tə rē′sĭs), *n. Physics.* any of several effects resembling a sort of internal friction suffered by a body subjected to a varying stress or intensity, as of magnetism, electricity, or physical strain. They are accompanied by heat losses. [NL, t. Gk.: deficiency] —**hys·ter·et·ic** (hĭs′tə rĕt′ĭk), *adj.*

hysteresis loop, loop (def. 6b).

hys·te·ri·a (hĭs tĭr′ĭ ə, -tĕr′-), *n.* **1.** morbid or senseless emotionalism; emotional frenzy. **2.** a psychoneurotic disorder characterized by violent emotional outbreaks, perversion of sensory and motor functions, and various morbid effects due to autosuggestion. [f. HYSTER- + -IA]

hys·ter·ic (hĭs tĕr′ĭk), *n.* **1.** (*usually pl.*) a fit of hysteria; hysteria. **2.** a person subject to hysteria. —*adj.* **3.** hysterical.

hys·ter·i·cal (hĭs tĕr′ə kəl), *adj.* **1.** resembling or suggesting hysteria; emotionally disordered. **2.** of, pertaining to, or characteristic of hysteria: *a hysterical fit.* **3.** suffering from or subject to hysteria. [f. s. L *hystericus* (t. Gk.: m. *hysterikós* suffering in the uterus) + -AL[1]] —**hys·ter′i·cal·ly,** *adv.*

hysterical fever, an increase in temperature without obvious cause other than hysteria.

hystero-, a word element meaning "uterus," as in *hysterotomy.* Also, **hyster-.** [t. Gk.: comb. form of *hystéra*]

hys·ter·oid (hĭs′tə roid′), *adj.* resembling hysteria. Also, **hys′ter·oi′dal.** [f. HYSTER- + -OID]

hys·ter·on prot·er·on (hĭs′tə rŏn′ prŏt′ə rŏn′). **1.** *Logic.* an attempted proof of a proposition which is based on premises that can be established only with the help of that proposition. This involves a fallacy, since it inverts the true order of logical dependence. **2.** *Rhet.* a figure of speech in which the logical order of two elements in discourse is reversed. [t. LL, t. Gk.: *hýsteron* (neut. of *hýsteros* latter), *próteron* (neut. of *próteros* being before, sooner)]

hys·ter·ot·o·my (hĭs′tə rŏt′ə mĭ), *n.,* *pl.* **-mies.** *Surg.* the operation of cutting into the uterus, as used in Caesarean section.

hys·tri·co·mor·phic (hĭs′trə kō môr′fĭk), *adj.* belonging or pertaining to the *Hystricomorpha,* the suborder of rodents that includes the porcupines, chinchilla, agouti, coypu, guinea pig, etc. [f. *hystrico-* (comb. form of L *hystrix* porcupine, t. Gk.) + -MORPHIC]

hy·zone (hī′zōn), *n. Chem.* triatomic hydrogen, H_3.

I

I[1], i (ī), *n.,* *pl.* **I's** or **Is, i's** or **is. 1.** the 9th letter of the English alphabet. **2.** the letter I. **3.** any sound represented by the letter I. **4.** an I-shaped object. **5.** Roman numeral for 1.

I[2] (ī), *pron., n., nom.* **I,** *poss.* **my** or **mine,** *obj.* **me;** *pl.nom.* **we,** *poss.* **ours** or **our,** *obj.* **us;** *pl.* **I's.** —*pron.* **1.** the subject form of the singular pronoun of the first person, used by a speaker of himself. —*n.* **2.** the pronoun *I* used as a noun: *the "I" in this novel is John.* **3.** *Metaphys.* the ego. [ME *ik, ich, i,* OE *ic, ih,* c. G *ich;* akin to L *ego,* Gk. *egō*]

I, *Chem.* iodine.

I., 1. Independent. **2.** Island; Islands. **3.** Isle; Isles.

i., 1. intransitive. **2.** island.

-i-, an ending for the first element of many compounds, originally found in the combining form of many Latin and Greek words, but often used in English as a connective irrespective of etymology, as in *cuneiform, Frenchify,* etc.

-ia, a suffix of nouns, esp. having restricted application in various fields, thus, in medicine (disease: *malaria*), in geography (countries: *Rumania,* in botany (genera: *Wistaria*), in names of Roman feasts (*Lupercalia*), in Latin or Latinizing plurals (*Reptilia, bacteria*), and in collectives (*insignia, militia*). [t. L or Gk., both f. *-i-* orig. or connective vowel + *-a* (fem. sing. nom. ending) or *-a* (neut. pl. nom. ending)]

Ia., Iowa.

I·a·go (ĭ·ä′gō), n. the villain in Shakespeare's *Othello*.

-ial, var. of **-al**, as in *judicial, imperial.* [t. L: s. *-iālis, -iāle*, adj. suffix, f. *-i-*, orig. or connective vowel + *-ālis, -āle* -AL¹]

i·amb (ī′ămb), n. *Pros.* a metrical foot of two syllables, a short followed by a long, or an unaccented by an accented (˘ —), as in Come live | with me | and be | my love. [t. L: s. *iambus* an iambic verse or poem, t. Gk.: m. *iambos*]

i·am·bic (ī·ăm′bĭk), adj. **1.** *Pros.* **a.** pertaining to the iamb. **b.** consisting of or employing an iamb or iambs. **2.** *Gk. Lit.* of or pertaining to a kind of satirical poetry written in iambs. —n. **3.** *Pros.* **a.** an iamb. **b.** (*usually pl.*) a verse or poem consisting of iambs. **4.** a satirical poem in this meter.

i·am·bus (ī·ăm′bəs), n., pl. **-bi** (-bī), **-buses.** iamb.

-ian, var. of **-an**, as in *amphibian, Grecian.* [t. L: s. *-iānus*, f. *-i-* orig. or connective vowel + *-ānus* -AN]

-iana. See **-ian, -ana.**

Ia·şi (yäsh), n. Rumanian name of **Jassy.**

-iasis, a suffix of nouns denoting state or condition, esp. a morbid condition or a form of disease, as in *psoriasis.* [NL, t. Gk.: f. *-i-* orig. or connective vowel (see -I) + *-āsis* -ASIS]

i·at·ric (ī·ăt′rĭk), adj. pertaining to a physician or to medicine. Also, **i·at′ri·cal.** [t. Gk.: s. *iātrikós*]

-iatry, a combining form meaning "medical care," as in *psychiatry.* [t. Gk.: m.s. *iātreía* healing]

ib., ibidem.

I·ba·dan (ē·bä′dän), n. a city in SW Nigeria, in British West Africa. With environs, 387,133 (1931).

I·bá·ñez (ē·bän′yĕth), n. See **Blasco Ibáñez.**

I-beam (ī′bēm′), n. a beam in the shape of the capital I.

I·be·ri·a (ī·bĭr′ĭə), n. **1.** Also, **Iberian Peninsula.** a peninsula in SW Europe, comprising Spain and Portugal. **2.** an ancient region S of the Caucasus Mountains, corresponding to modern Georgia. [t. L, t. Gk., ancient Greek name of Spain]

I·be·ri·an (ī·bĭr′ĭən), adj. **1.** of or pertaining to Iberia in Europe or its inhabitants. **2.** *Ethnol.* denoting or pertaining to a dark dolichocephalic race inhabiting parts of southern Europe and northern Africa, comprising the ancient Iberians, some of the ancient Britons, and other peoples, and their descendants. **3.** of or pertaining to ancient Iberia in Asia or its inhabitants. —n. **4.** one of the ancient inhabitants of Iberia in Europe, from whom the Basques are supposed to be descended. **5.** the language of the ancient Iberians of Europe, from which Basque developed. **6.** one of the ancient inhabitants of Iberia in Asia.

I·ber·ville (dē·bĕr′vēl′), n. **Pierre le Moyne** (pyĕr lə mwăn′), **Sieur d′,** 1661–1706, French naval officer, born in Canada: founder of first Louisiana settlement (1699).

i·bex (ī′bĕks), n., pl. **ibexes, ibices** (ĭb′ə·sēz′, ī′bə-), (*esp. collectively*) **ibex,** any of various Old World wild goats with large recurved horns, esp. *Capra ibex,* of the Alps and Apennines. [t. L]

Asiatic ibex. *Capra sibirica* (Ab. 3½ ft. high at the shoulder)

ibid., ibidem.

i·bi·dem (ĭ·bī′dĕm), adv. Latin. in the same book, chapter, page, etc.

i·bis (ī′bĭs), n., pl. **ibises** (ī′bĭs·ĭz), (*esp. collectively*) **ibis. 1.** any of various large wading birds of warm regions, allied to the herons and storks, forming the family *Threskiornithidae.* **2.** the **sacred ibis,** *Threskiornis aethiopica* of Egypt and other parts of Africa, with white-and-black plumage, venerated by the (ancient) Egyptians. [t. L, t. Gk.; of Egyptian orig.]

-ible, var. of **-able**, occurring in words taken from the Latin, as in *credible, horrible, legible, visible,* or modeled on the Latin type as *addible* (for *addable*), *reducible.* [ME *-ible*, t. OF, t. L: m.s. *-ibilis,* var. of *-bilis* after consonant stems. See -BLE]

ibn-Rushd (ĭb′ən·rōōsht′), n. Arabic name of **Averroës.**

Wood ibis. *Mycteria americana* (4 ft. long, bill 8½ in. long)

ibn-Sa·ud (ĭb′ən·sä·ōōd′), n. **Abdul-Aziz** (äb·dōōl′ä·zēz′), born 1880, ruler of Nejd, 1901–32, king of Saudi Arabia since 1932.

ibn-Si·na (ĭb′ən·sē′nä), n. Arabic name of **Avicenna.**

Ib·ra·him Pa·sha (ĭb′rä·hēm′ pä′shä), 1789–1848, Egyptian general, governor of Syria.

Ib·sen (ĭb′sən; *Nor.* ĭp′sən), n. **Henrik** (hĕn′rĭk), 1828–1906, Norwegian dramatist and poet.

-ic, 1. a suffix forming adjectives from nouns or stems not used as words themselves, meaning "pertaining or belonging to" (*poetic, metallic, Homeric*), found extensively in adjective nouns of a similar type (*public, magic*), and in nouns the adjectives of which end in *-ical* (*music, critic*). **2.** *Chem.* a suffix showing that an element is present in a compound at a high valence, at least higher than when the suffix *-ous* is used. [repr. in part s. Gk. *-ikos;* often s. L *-icus;* sometimes F *-ique*]

I·ça (ē′sä), n. Brazilian name of **Putumayo.**

-ical, a compound suffix forming adjectives from nouns (*rhetorical*), providing synonyms to words ending

in *-ic* (*poetical*), and providing an adjective with additional meanings to those in the *-ic* form (*economical*). [f. *-ic* + *-al¹*; in some cases repr. LL *-icālis,* f. adj. endings *-ic(us)* -ic + *-ālis* -AL¹]

I·car·i·an (ī·kâr′ĭ·ən, ĭ-), adj. of or like Icarus.

Ic·a·rus (ĭk′ə·rəs, ī′kə-), n. *Gk. Legend.* the son of Daedalus. Together they escaped from Crete using wax wings, but Icarus, flying so high that the sun melted his wings, drowned in the Aegean.

I.C.C., Interstate Commerce Commission. Also, **ICC**

ice (īs), n., v., **iced, icing,** adj. —n. **1.** the solid form of water, produced by freezing; frozen water. **2.** the frozen surface of a body of water. **3.** any substance resembling this: *camphor ice.* **4.** *U.S.* a frozen dessert made of sweetened water and fruit juice. **5.** *Brit.* ice cream. **6.** icing. **7.** reserve; formality: *to break the ice.* **8.** *Slang.* a diamond or diamonds. **9. on thin ice,** in a risky or delicate situation. **10. cut no ice,** *U.S. Colloq.* to have no importance. —v.t. **11.** to cover with ice. **12.** to change into ice; freeze. **13.** to cool with ice, as a drink. **14.** to refrigerate with ice, as air. **15.** to make cold as if with ice. **16.** to cover (cakes, etc.) with icing; frost. —v.i. **17.** to freeze. —adj. **18.** of or pertaining to ice. [ME *is(e),* OE *īs,* c. G *eis*] —**ice′less,** adj. —**ice′like′,** adj.

-ice, a suffix used in many nouns to indicate state or quality, as in *service, justice.* [ME *-is(e),* *-ys(e),* etc., t. OF: m. *-ice, -ise,* g. L *-itius, -itia, -itium*]

ice age, *Geol.* the glacial epoch.

ice bag, a bag containing ice, applied to the head.

ice·berg (īs′bûrg′), n. a large floating mass of ice, detached from a glacier and carried out to sea. [half Anglicization, half adoption of D *ijsberg* ice mountain, c. G *eisberg,* Sw. *isberg*]

ice·blink (īs′blĭngk′), n. a luminous appearance near the horizon, due to the reflection of light from ice.

ice·boat (īs′bōt′), n. **1.** a triangular frame with runners, sails, etc., for sailing on ice. **2.** icebreaker (def. 1).

ice·bound (īs′bound′), adj. **1.** held fast or hemmed in by ice; frozen in: *an icebound ship.* **2.** obstructed or shut off by ice: *an icebound harbor.*

ice·box (īs′bŏks′), n. a box or chest to hold ice for keeping food, etc., cool.

ice·break·er (īs′brā′kər), n. **1.** a strong ship for breaking channels through ice. **2.** a tool or machine for chopping ice into small pieces. **3.** a structure of masonry or timber for protection against moving ice.

ice·cap (īs′kăp′), n. a cap of ice over an area (sometimes vast), sloping in all directions from the center.

ice-cold (īs′kōld′), adj. cold as ice.

ice cream, 1. a frozen food made of cream, sweetened and variously flavored. **2.** (in commercial use) a food made in imitation of this, and containing milk, egg whites, custard, cornstarch, etc.

iced (īst), adj. **1.** covered with ice. **2.** cooled by means of ice. **3.** *Cooking.* covered with icing.

ice field, a large ice floe.

ice floe, a large sheet of floating ice.

ice foot, a belt of ice along the shore in polar regions, formed where snow on the land meets the sea water.

ice·house (īs′hous′), n. a building for storing ice.

Icel., 1. Iceland. **2.** Icelandic.

Ice·land (īs′lənd), n. a large island in the N Atlantic between Greenland and Denmark: formerly Danish, it has been an independent republic since 1944. 130,356 pop. (est. 1945); 39,698 sq. mi. *Cap.:* Reykjavik. —**Ice·land·er** (īs′lăn′dər, -lən′dər), n.

Ice·lan·dic (īs·lăn′dĭk), adj. **1.** pertaining to Iceland, its inhabitants, or their language. —n. **2.** the language of Iceland, a Scandinavian language.

Iceland moss, an edible lichen, *Cetraria islandica,* of arctic regions, used to some extent in medicine.

Iceland spar, a transparent variety of calcite that is double-refracting and is used for polarizing light.

ice·man (īs′măn′), n., pl. **-men** (-mĕn′). *U.S.* a man engaged in gathering, storing, selling, or delivering ice.

ice needles, *Meteorol.* a form of precipitation consisting of very small ice crystals that seem to float in the air.

I·ce·ni (ī·sē′nī), n.pl. an ancient Celtic tribe of Eastern England, whose queen, Boudicca, headed the insurrection of A.D. 61 against the Romans. [t. L]

ice pack, a large area of floating ice, as in arctic seas.

ice pick, a pick or other tool for breaking ice.

ice plant, one of the figworts, *Mesembryanthemum crystallinum,* a succulent, low shrub, orig. of the Old World, with leaves covered by glistening vesicles.

ice-scoured area (īs′skourd′), *Phys. Geog.* an area having surface features resulting from scouring by an advancing ice sheet during glaciation.

ice sheet, 1. a broad, thick sheet of ice covering an extensive area for a long period of time. **2.** a glacier covering a large fraction of a continent.

ice skate, (*usually pl.*) **1.** a thin metal runner attached to the shoe, for skating on ice. **2.** a shoe fitted with such a runner.

ice-skate (īs′skāt′), v.i., **-skated, -skating.** to skate on ice.

I·chang (ē′chăng′), n. a city in central China, in Hupeh province: a port on the Yangtze river. 108,000 (est. 1930).

ăct, āble, dâre, ärt; ĕbb, ēqual; ĭf, īce; hŏt, ōver, ôrder, oil, bŏŏk, ōōze, out; ŭp, ūse, ûrge; ə = a in alone; ch, chief; g, give; ng, ring; sh, shoe; th, thin; ŧħ, that; zh, vision. See the full key on inside cover.

ich dien (Ῠκн dēn'), *German.* I serve (motto of the Prince of Wales).

ich·neu·mon (Ῠk nū'mən, -nōō'-), *n.* **1.** a slender carnivorous mammal, *Herpestes ichneumon*, of Egypt, resembling the weasel in form and habits, but the size of a cat: said to devour crocodiles' eggs. **2.** an ichneumon fly. [t. L, s. Gk.: lit., tracker]

ichneumon fly, any insect belonging to the large hymenopterous family *Ichneumonidae*, whose larvae parasitize and destroy caterpillars and other larvae.

ich·nite (Ῠk'nīt), *n.* *Paleontol.* a fossil footprint. [f. s. Gk. *íchnos* track + -ITE[1]]

ich·nog·ra·phy (Ῠk nŏg'rə fῐ), *n., pl.* **-phies.** **1.** the drawing of ground plans. **2.** a ground plan. [t. L: m.s. *ichnographia*, t. Gk.: a tracing out. See -GRAPHY] —**ich·no·graph·ic** (Ῠk'nə grăf'Ῠk), **ich·no·graph/i·cal,** *adj.*

i·chor[1] (ī'kôr, ī'kər), *n.* *Class. Myth.* an ethereal fluid supposed to flow in the veins of the gods. [t. Gk.]

i·chor[2] (ī'kôr, ī'kər), *n.* *Pathol.* an acrid watery discharge, as from an ulcer or wound. [NL, t. Gk.] —**i·chor·ous** (ī'kər əs), *adj.*

ichth., ichthyology. Also, **ichthyol.**

ich·thy·ic (Ῠk'thῐ Ῠk), *adj.* piscine. [t. Gk.: m. s. *ichthyïkós* fishy]

ichthyo-, a word element meaning "fish," as in *ichthyology*. Also, before vowels, **ichthy-.** [t. Gk., comb. form of *ichthŷs*]

ich·thy·oid (Ῠk'thῐ oid'), *adj.* **1.** Also, **ich'thy·oi'dal.** fishlike. —*n.* **2.** any fishlike vertebrate. [t. Gk.: m.s. *ichthyoeidḗs* fishlike. See -OID]

ich·thy·ol (Ῠk'thῐ ōl', -ŏl'), *n.* *Pharm.* **1.** a dark-brown to black syrupy compound, $C_{28}H_{36}O_6S_3(NH_3)_2.2H_2O$, used as an astringent, antiseptic, and alterative, esp. for skin diseases. **2.** (*cap.*) a trademark for this drug. [f. ICHTHY- + -OL[2]; so called because obtained from rocks containing fossilized fishes]

ich·thy·ol·o·gy (Ῠk'thῐ ŏl'ə jῐ), *n.* the branch of zoölogy that treats of fishes. —**ich·thy·o·log·ic** (Ῠk'thῐ ə lŏj'Ῠk), **ich·thy·o·log'i·cal,** *adj.* —**ich·thy·ol'o·gist,** *n.*

ich·thy·or·nis (Ῠk'thῐ ôr'nῐs), *n.* any of an extinct genus of toothed birds, *Ichthyornis*, with vertebrae resembling those of fishes. [NL, f. Gk.: *ichthy-* ICHTHY- + *órnis* bird]

ich·thy·o·saur (Ῠk'thῐ ə sôr'), *n.* any of an extinct order, *Ichthyosauria*, of marine reptiles, fishlike in form, ranging from 4 to 40 feet in length, with a round tapering body, a large head, four paddle-like flippers, and a vertical caudal fin. [t. NL: s. *ichthyosaurus*, f. Gk.: *ichthyo-* ICHTHYO- + m. *saûros* lizard]

ich·thy·o·sau·rus (Ῠk'thῐ ə sôr'əs), *n., pl.* **-sauri** (-sôr'ī). ichthyosaur.

Ichthyosaur, *Stenopterygius quadriscissus* (4 ft. long)

ich·thy·o·sis (Ῠk'thῐ ō'sῐs), *n.* *Pathol.* a congenital disease in which the epidermis continually flakes off in large scales or plates. —**ich·thy·ot·ic** (Ῠk'thῐ ŏt'Ῠk), *adj.*

-ician, a compound suffix especially applied to an expert in a field, as in *geometrician*. [f. -IC + -IAN; r. ME *-icien*, t. OF]

i·ci·cle (ī'sῐ kəl), *n.* a pendent tapering mass of ice formed by the freezing of dripping water. [ME *isykle*, OE *īsgicel*, f. *īs* ice + *gicel* icicle. Cf. Icel. *jökull* mass of ice, glacier] —**i'ci·cled,** *adj.*

i·ci·ly (ī'sə lῐ), *adv.* in an icy manner.

i·ci·ness (ī'sῐ nῐs), *n.* the state of being icy or very cold.

ic·ing (ī'sῐng), *n.* a preparation of sugar, often made with egg whites, for covering cakes, etc.; frosting.

icing sugar, *Brit.* powdered sugar.

i·ci on parle fran·çais (ē sē' ŏn pȧrl frän sě'), *French.* French spoken here.

ick·er (Ῠk'ər), *n.* *Scot.* the fruit-bearing spike of any cereal plant. [d. var. of EAR[2], g. O Northumbrian *eher*, *æhher*]

Ick·es (Ῠk'ēz), *n.* **Harold LeClair,** 1874–1952, U.S. political official.

i·con (ī'kŏn), *n., pl.* **icons, icones** (ī'kə nēz'), **1.** a picture, image, or other representation. **2.** *Eastern Ch.* a representation in painting, enamel, etc., of some sacred personage, as Christ or a saint or angel, itself venerated as sacred. **3.** *Logic.* a sign or representation which stands for its object by virtue of a resemblance or analogy to it. Also, **eikon, ikon.** [t. L, t. Gk.: m. *eikṓn* likeness, image] —**Syn. 1.** See **image.**

i·con·ic (ī kŏn'Ῠk), *adj.* **1.** pertaining to or of the nature of an icon, portrait, or image. **2.** *Art.* (of statues, portraits, etc.) executed according to a convention or tradition. Also, **i·con'i·cal.** [t. L: s. *íconicus*, t. Gk.: m. *eikonikós* representing a figure, copied]

icono-, a word element meaning "likeness" or "image", as in *iconography*. [t. Gk., comb. form of *eikṓn*]

i·con·o·clasm (ī kŏn'ə klăz'əm), *n.* the action or spirit of iconoclasts.

i·con·o·clast (ī kŏn'ə klăst'), *n.* **1.** a breaker or destroyer of images, esp. those set up for religious veneration. **2.** one who attacks cherished beliefs as based on error or superstition. [t. LL: s. *íconoclastēs*, t. LGk.: m. *eikonoklástēs*, f. *eikono-* ICONO- + *klástēs* breaker] —**i·con'o·clas'tic,** *adj.* —**i·con'o·clas'ti·cal·ly,** *adv.*

i·con·o·graph·ic (ī kŏn'ə grăf'Ῠk), *adj.* of or pertaining to icons. Also, **i·con'o·graph/i·cal.**

i·co·nog·ra·phy (ī'kə nŏg'rə fῐ), *n., pl.* **-phies.** **1.** the making of an icon; representation by means of drawing, painting, or carving figures, etc. **2.** the subject matter of an icon, image, or representation, or of groups of them. **3.** the description or analysis of icons. [t. ML: m.s. *iconographia*, t. Gk.: m. *eikonographía*. See ICONO-, -GRAPHY]

i·co·nol·a·try (ī'kə nŏl'ə trῐ), *n.* the worship or adoration of icons. —**i·co·nol'a·ter,** *n.*

i·co·nol·o·gy (ī'kə nŏl'ə jῐ), *n.* **1.** the branch of knowledge concerned with pictorial or sculptural representations. **2.** such representations collectively. **3.** symbolical representation. **4.** a description or interpretation of statues, pictures, etc. —**i·con·o·log·i·cal** (ī kŏn'ə lŏj'ə kəl), *adj.* —**i'co·nol'o·gist,** *n.*

i·con·o·scope (ī kŏn'ə skōp'), *n.* *Television.* **1.** the cathode-ray tube which focuses the optical image which the cathode-ray beam scans. **2.** (*cap.*) a trademark for this tube.

i·con·o·sta·sis (ī'kə nŏs'tə sῐs), *n., pl.* **-ses** (-sēz'). *Eastern Ch.* a partition or screen on which icons are placed, separating the sanctuary from the main part of the church. Also, **i·con·o·stas** (ī kŏn'ə stăs'). [NL, t. NGk.: m. *eikonóstasis*, f. Gk.: *eikono-* ICONO- + *stásis* a standing, station]

i·co·sa·he·dron (ī'kō sə hē'drən), *n., pl.* **-drons, -dra** (-drə). a solid figure having twenty faces. [t. Gk.: m. *eikosáedron*] —**i'co·sa·he'dral,** *adj.*

ics, a suffix of nouns, originally plural as denoting things pertaining to a particular subject, but now mostly used as singular as denoting the body of matters, facts, knowledge, principles, etc., pertaining to a subject, and hence a science or art, as in *ethics, physics, politics, tactics.* [pl. of -IC; orig. repr. Gk. *-iká* (in L *-ica*), prop. neut. pl. adj. suffix meaning (things) pertaining to]

Regular Icosahedron

ic·ter·ic (Ῠk tĕr'Ῠk), *adj.* *Pathol.* pertaining to or affected with icterus; jaundiced. Also, **ic·ter/i·cal.** [t. L: s. *íctericus*, t. Gk.: m. *íkterikós*]

ic·ter·us (Ῠk'tər əs), *n.* *Pathol.* jaundice. [NL, t. Gk.: m. *íkteros*]

ic·tus (Ῠk'təs), *n., pl.* **-tuses, -tus.** **1.** *Pros.* rhythmical or metrical stress. **2.** *Pathol.* **a.** a fit. **b.** a stroke, as sunstroke. [t. L: blow, stroke]

i·cy (ī'sῐ), *adj.,* **icier, iciest. 1.** made of or covered with ice. **2.** resembling ice. **3.** cold: *icy wind.* **4.** slippery: *icy road.* **5.** without warmth of feeling; frigid: *an icy stare.* [late ME *isy*, OE *īsig*. See ICE, -Y[1]]

id (Ῠd), *n.* *Psychoanal.* the part of the psyche residing in the unconscious which is the source of instinctive energy. Its impulses, which seek satisfaction in accordance with the pleasure principle, are modified by the ego and the superego before they are given overt expression. [special use of L *id* it, as trans. of G *es*]

I'd (Ῠd), contraction of *I would, I should,* or *I had.*

-id[1], **1.** a noun suffix meaning "daughter of," as in *Nereid,* and used also (*Astron.*) to form names of meteors appearing to radiate in showers from particular constellations, etc., as in *Andromedid.* **2.** a suffix used in naming epics, as in *Aeneid.* [t. L: *-id-* (nom. *-is*), fem. patronymic suffix, t. Gk.]

-id[2], a suffix of nouns and adjectives indicating members of a zoölogical family, as in *cichlid,* or of some other group or division, as in *acarid, arachnid.* [t. NL: s. *-idae,* in zoölogical family names pl. of L *-idēs* (masc. patronymic suffix), t. Gk.; sometimes, t. NL: s. *-ida,* in group names, taken as neut. pl. of L *-idēs.* Cf. F *-ide*]

-id[3], var. of **-ide,** as in *parotid.*

-id[4], a quasi suffix common in adjectives, esp. of states which appeal to the senses, as in *torrid, acid.* [t. L: s. *-idus*]

id., idem.

I·da (ī'də), *n.* **Mount,** **1.** a peak in NW Asia Minor, overlooking the site of ancient Troy and the Aegean. 5750 ft. **2.** Modern name, **Mount Psiloriti.** the highest mountain of Crete.

Ida., Idaho.

-idae, *Zool.* a suffix of the names of families, as in *Canidae.* [(N)L, t. Gk.: m. *-idai,* pl. of *-idēs,* patronymic suffix]

I·da·ho (ī'də hō'), *n.* a State in the NW United States. 588,637 pop. (1950); 83,557 sq. mi. *Cap.:* Boise. *Abbr.:* Id., Ida. —**I'da·ho'an,** *n., adj.*

-ide, a noun suffix in names of chemical compounds, as in *bromide.* Also, **-id**[3]. [abstracted from OXIDE]

i·de·a (ī dē'ə), *n.* **1.** any conception existing in the mind as the result of mental apprehension or activity. **2.** a thought, conception, or notion: *what an idea!* **3.** an impression: *a general idea of what it's like.* **4.** an opinion, view, or belief. **5.** a plan of action; an intention: *the idea of becoming an engineer.* **6.** a fantasy. **7.** *Philos.* **a.** a concept developed by the mind (if empirical, in close connection with sense perception). **b.** a conception of what is desirable, or what ought to be; a governing conception or principle; ideal. **c.** (in Platonic philosophy) an archetype or pattern of which the individual objects in any natural class are imperfect copies and from which

---

b., blend of, blended; c., cognate with; d., dialect, dialectal; der., derived from; f., formed from; g., going back to; m., modification of; r., replacing; s., stem of; t., taken from; ?, perhaps. See the full key on inside cover.

they derive their being. 8. *Music*. a theme, phrase, or figure. 9. *Obs.* a likeness. 10. *Obs.* a mental image. [t. L, t. Gk., der. *idein* see; orig. in def. 7c.] —**i·de·a'·less**, *adj*.

i·de·al (ī dē'/əl, ī dēl'), *n*. 1. a conception of something in its highest perfection. 2. a standard of perfection or excellence. 3. a person or thing regarded as realizing such a conception or conforming to such a standard, and taken as a model for imitation. 4. an ultimate object or aim of endeavor, esp. one of high or noble character. 5. that which exists only in idea. —*adj*. 6. conceived as constituting a standard of perfection or excellence: *ideal beauty*. 7. regarded as perfect in its kind: *an ideal spot for a home*. 8. existing only in idea. 9. not real or practical; visionary. 10. based upon an ideal or ideals: *the ideal school in art*. 11. *Philos*. **a.** existing as an archetype or Platonic idea. **b.** pertaining to a possible state of affairs considered as highly desirable. **c.** pertaining to or of the nature of idealism. [t. LL: s. *idealis*. der. L *idea* IDEA] —**i·de'al·ness**, *n*.

—**Syn.** 1, 2. IDEAL, EXAMPLE, MODEL refer to something considered as a standard to strive toward or something considered worthy of imitation. An IDEAL is a concept or standard of perfection, existing merely as an image in the mind, or based upon a person or upon conduct: *the high ideals of a religious person, Sir Philip Sidney was considered the ideal in gentlemanly conduct*. An EXAMPLE is a person or his conduct or achievements regarded as worthy of being followed or imitated in a general way; or sometimes, as properly to be avoided: *an example of courage; a bad example to one's children*. A MODEL is primarily a physical shape to be closely copied, but is also a pattern for exact imitation in conduct or character: *they took their leader as a model*.

i·de·al·ise (ī dē'/ə līz'), *v.t., v.i.*, **-ised, -ising**. *Chiefly Brit*. idealize.

i·de·al·ism (ī dē'/ə līz'/əm), *n*. 1. the cherishing or pursuing of ideals, as for attainment. 2. the practice of idealizing. 3. something idealized; an ideal representation. 4. the imaginative treatment of subjects in art or literature, usually on a high ethical plane and devoid of accidental details (opposed to *realism*). 5. *Philos*. **a.** any system or theory which maintains that the real is of the nature of thought, or that the object of external perception consists of ideas. **b.** the tendency to represent things in an ideal form, or as they might be rather than as they are, with emphasis on values.

i·de·al·ist (ī dē'/əl ĭst), *n*. 1. one who cherishes or pursues ideals, as for attainment. 2. a visionary or unpractical person. 3. one who represents things as they might be rather than as they are. 4. a writer or artist who treats subjects imaginatively. 5. one who accepts the doctrines of idealism. Also, *adj*. 6. idealistic.

i·de·al·is·tic (ī dē'/ə līs'/tĭk), *adj*. pertaining to idealism or to idealists. —**i·de·al·is·ti·cal·ly**, *adv*.

i·de·al·i·ty (ī'/dī ǎl'/ə tī'), *n., pl*. **-ties**. 1. ideal quality or character. 2. capacity to idealize. 3. *Philos*. state of existing only in idea and not in actuality.

i·de·al·ize (ī dē'/ə līz'), *v*., **-ized, -izing**. —*v.t.* 1. to make ideal; represent in an ideal form or character; exalt to an ideal perfection or excellence. —*v.i.* 2. to represent something in an ideal form; imagine or form an ideal or ideas. Also, *esp. Brit*., **idealise**. —**i·de'al·i·za'tion**, *n*. —**i·de'al·iz'er**, *n*.

i·de·al·ly (ī dē'/əl ī), *adv*. 1. in accordance with an ideal; perfectly. 2. in idea, thought, or imagination.

ideal type, *Sociol*. an imaginary construction of what an object would be if it were allowed to develop without any interference from accidental or irrelevant factors.

i·de·ate (*v*. ī dē'/āt; *n*. ī dē'/ĭt, -āt), *v*., **-ated, -ating**, *n*. —*v.t.* 1. to form in idea, thought, or imagination. —*v.i.* 2. to form ideas; think. —*n*. 3. *Philos*. the external object of which an idea is formed. —**i·de·a'tion**, *n*. —**i·de·a'tion·al**, *adj*. —**i·de·a'tion·al·ly**, *adv*.

i·dée fixe (ē dē' fēks'), *French*. a fixed idea; obsession.

i·dem (ī'/dĕm, ĭd'/ĕm), *pron., adj*. *Latin*. the same as previously given or mentioned.

i·den·tic (ī dĕn'/tĭk), *adj*. 1. identical. 2. *Diplomacy*. (of action, notes, etc.) identical in form, as when two or more governments deal simultaneously with another government. [t. ML: s. *identicus*]

i·den·ti·cal (ī dĕn'/tə kəl), *adj*. 1. agreeing exactly. 2. the same or being the same one. [f. IDENTIC + -AL[1]. See IDENTITY] —**i·den'ti·cal·ly**, *adv*. —**i·den'·ti·cal·ness**, *n*.

identical classes, *Logic*. classes denoted by two terms whose extensions contain the same individuals as members.

identical proposition, a proposition, expressed by two sentences having the same meaning.

identical twin, one of a pair of twins of the same sex which develop from one fertilized ovum.

i·den·ti·fi·ca·tion (ī dĕn'/tə fə kā'/shən), *n*. 1. act of identifying. 2. state of being identified. 3. something that identifies one: *have you any identification?*

i·den·ti·fy (ī dĕn'/tə fī'), *v.t.*, **-fied, -fying**. 1. to recognize or establish as being a particular person or thing; attest or prove to be as purported or asserted: *to identify handwriting, identify the bearer of a check*. 2. *Biol*. to determine to what group (a given specimen) belongs. 3. to make, represent to be, or regard or treat as the same or identical. 4. to associate in feeling, interest, action, etc. (fol. by *with*). 5. *Psychol*. to make (oneself) one with another person by putting oneself in his place. 6. to serve as a means of identification for. —**i·den'ti·fi·a·ble**, *adj*. —**i·den'ti·fi'er**, *n*.

i·den·ti·ty (ī dĕn'/tə tī'), *n., pl*. **-ties**. 1. state or fact of remaining the same one, as under varying aspects or conditions. 2. the condition of being oneself or itself, and not another: *he doubted his own identity*. 3. condition or character as to who a person or what a thing is: *a case of mistaken identity*. 4. state or fact of being the same one. 5. exact likeness in nature or qualities. 6. an instance or point of sameness or likeness. [t. LL: m.s. *identitas*, appar. f. L *identi-* (as in *identidem* repeatedly), for *idem* the same + *-tas* -TY[2]]

ideo-, a word element meaning "idea," as in *ideograph*. [t. Gk., comb. form of *idéa* idea]

id·e·o·graph (ĭd'/ī ə grăf', -gräf', ī'/dī-), *n*. a written symbol which represents something in the nonsymbolic world directly instead of standing for a sound of a word in the language of its users. Also, **id·e·o·gram** (ĭd'/ī ə grăm', ī'/dī-). —**id/e·o·graph'ic, id/e·o·graph/i·cal**, *adj*. —**id/e·o·graph/i·cal·ly**, *adv*.

id·e·og·ra·phy (ĭd'/ī ŏg'/rə fī', ī'/dī-), *n*. the use of ideographs.

i·de·o·log·ic (ī'/dī ə lŏj'/ĭk, ĭd'/ī-), *adj*. 1. pertaining to ideology. 2. speculative; visionary. Also, **i'/de·o·log/i·cal**. —**i/de·o·log/i·cal·ly**, *adv*.

i·de·ol·o·gist (ī'/dī ŏl'/ə jĭst, ĭd'/ī-), *n*. 1. an expert in ideology. 2. one who deals with systems of ideas. 3. a visionary.

i·de·ol·o·gy (ī'/dī ŏl'/ə jī', ĭd'/ī-), *n., pl*. **-gies**. 1. the body of doctrine, myth, and symbols of a social movement, institution, class, or large group. 2. such a body of doctrine, etc. with reference to some political and cultural plan, as that of fascism, along with the devices for putting it into operation. 3. *Philos*. **a.** the science of ideas. **b.** a system which derives ideas exclusively from sensation. 4. theorizing of a visionary or unpractical nature.

ides (īdz), *n.pl*. (in the ancient Roman calendar) the 15th day of March, May, July, or October, and the 13th day of the other months. [t. F, t. L: m. *īdūs*, pl.]

id est (ĭd ĕst'), *Latin*. that is.

idio-, a word element meaning "peculiar" or "proper to one," as in *idiosyncrasy*. [t. Gk., comb. form of *idios* own, private, peculiar]

id·i·o·blast (ĭd'/ī ə blăst'), *n*. *Bot*. a cell which differs greatly from the surrounding cells or tissue.

id·i·o·cy (ĭd'/ī ə sī'), *n., pl*. **-cies**. 1. the condition of being an idiot; extreme degree of mental deficiency. 2. senseless folly. [? t. Gk.: m.s. *idiōteia* uncouthness, defenseless condition; or der. IDIOT, on model of *prophecy* from *prophet*]

id·i·o·graph·ic (ĭd'/ī ə grăf'/ĭk), *adj*. *Psychol*. pertaining to the intensive study of an individual case, as a personality or social situation (opposed to *nomothetic*).

id·i·om (ĭd'/ī əm), *n*. 1. a form of expression peculiar to a language. 2. a variety or form of a language; a dialect. 3. the language peculiar to a people. 4. the peculiar character or genius of a language. 5. a distinct style or character, as in music, art, etc.: *the idiom of Bach*. [t. LL: m. *idiōma*, t. Gk.: a peculiarity]

id·i·o·mat·ic (ĭd'/ī ə măt'/ĭk), *adj*. 1. peculiar to or characteristic of a particular language. 2. exhibiting the characteristic modes of expression of a language. Also, **id/i·o·mat/i·cal**. [t. Gk.: m.s. *idiōmatikós*] —**id/·i·o·mat/i·cal·ly**, *adv*. —**id/i·o·mat/i·cal·ness**, *n*.

id·i·o·mor·phic (ĭd'/ī ə môr'/fĭk), *adj*. 1. noting or pertaining to a mineral constituent of a rock, which has its own characteristic outward crystalline form, and not one forced upon it by the other constituents of the rock. 2. having its own form. —**id/i·o·mor/phi·cal·ly**, *adv*.

id·i·o·path·ic (ĭd'/ī ə păth'/ĭk), *adj*. *Pathol*. of unknown cause, as a disease.

id·i·op·a·thy (ĭd'/ī ŏp'/ə thī'), *n., pl*. **-thies**. *Pathol*. a disease not preceded or occasioned by any other. [t. Gk.: m.s. *idiopátheia*. See IDIO-, -PATHY]

id·i·o·phone (ĭd'/ī ə fōn'), *n*. *Music*. an instrument made of some solid, naturally sonorous material, as cymbals, xylophones, glass harmonicas.

id·i·o·plasm (ĭd'/ī ə plăz'/əm), *n*. *Biol*. germ plasm. —**id/i·o·plas'mic, id·i·o·plas·mat·ic** (ĭd'/ī ə plăz măt'/ĭk), *adj*.

id·i·o·syn·cra·sy (ĭd'/ī ə sĭng'/krə sī', -sĭn'-), *n., pl*. **-sies**. 1. any tendency, characteristic, mode of expression, or the like, peculiar to an individual. 2. the physical constitution peculiar to an individual. 3. a peculiarity of the physical or the mental constitution, esp. susceptibility toward drugs, food, etc. See **allergy** (def. 1). [t. Gk.: m.s. *idiosynkrāsía*] —**id·i·o·syn·crat·ic** (ĭd'/ī ə sĭn krăt'/ĭk), *adj*. —**id/i·o·syn·crat/i·cal·ly**, *adv*.

id·i·ot (ĭd'/ī ət), *n*. 1. an utterly foolish or senseless person. 2. one hopelessly deficient, esp. from birth, in the ordinary mental powers; one lacking the capacity to develop beyond the mental level of three or four years. [ME, t. L: s. *idiōta*, t. Gk.: m. *idiōtēs* a private, non-professional, or ignorant person]

id·i·ot·ic (ĭd'/ī ŏt'/ĭk), *adj*. of or like an idiot; senselessly foolish. Also, **id/i·ot/i·cal**. [t. LL: s. *idiōticus*, t. Gk.: m. *idiōtikós* private, unskillful] —**id/i·ot/i·cal·ly**, *adv*. —**Syn.** half-witted, stupid. —**Ant.** intelligent.

id·i·ot·ism (ĭd'/ī ə tĭz'/əm), *n*. 1. idiotic conduct or action. 2. idiocy. 3. *Obs*. an idiom. [f. IDIOT + ISM; in def. 3. t. F: m. *idiotisme*, t. LL: m.s. *idiōtismus* a common way of speaking. t. Gk.: m. *idiōtismós* common manners]

-idium, a diminutive suffix (Latinization of Greek *-idion*) used in zoölogical, biological, botanical, anatomical, and chemical terms.

i·dle (ī'dəl), *adj.*, idler, idlest, *v.*, idled, idling. —*adj.*
1. unemployed, or doing nothing: *idle workmen.* 2. unoccupied, as time: *idle hours.* 3. not kept busy or in use or operation: *idle machinery.* 4. habitually doing nothing or avoiding work. 5. of no real worth, importance, or significance: *idle talk.* 6. baseless or groundless: *idle fears.* 7. frivolous or vain: *idle pleasures.* 8. futile or ineffective: *idle threats.* 9. useless: *idle rage.* —*v.i.* 10. to pass time in idleness. 11. to move, loiter, or saunter idly. 12. *Mach.* to operate, usually at minimum speed, while the transmission is disengaged. —*v.t.* 13. to pass (time) in idleness. 14. to cause (a person) to be idle. [ME and OE *īdel*, c. G *eitel*] **—i'dle·ness,** *n.* **—i'dly,** *adv.*
—Syn. 1. IDLE, INDOLENT, LAZY, SLOTHFUL apply to one who is not active. To be IDLE is to be inactive or not working at a job. The word may be derogatory, but not necessarily so, since one may be relaxing temporarily or may be idle through necessity: *pleasantly idle on a vacation, to be idle because one is unemployed or because supplies are lacking.* The INDOLENT person is naturally disposed to avoid exertion: *indolent and slow in movement, an indolent and contented fisherman.* The LAZY person is averse to exertion or work, and esp. to continued application; the word is usually derogatory: *too lazy to earn a living; incurably lazy.* SLOTHFUL denotes a reprehensible unwillingness to do such work as is demanded of man: *so slothful as to be a burden on others.* **11.** See **loiter.** **—Ant. 1.** busy, industrious.

idle pulley, *Mach.* a loose pulley made to press or rest on a belt in order to tighten or guide it.

i·dler (ī'dlər), *n.* **1.** one who idles. **2.** *Mach.* an idle pulley or wheel. **3.** *Railroads.* an empty car.

i·dlesse (ī'dlĕs), *n.* *Poetic.* idleness.

idle wheel, *Mach.* **1.** a cogwheel placed between two other cogwheels in order to transfer the motion of one to the other without changing the direction of rotation. **2.** an idle pulley.

I·do (ē'dō), *n.* a revised and simplified form of Esperanto, put forth in 1907.

I Idle wheel; C. Cogwheel

i·do·crase (ī'də krās', ĭd'ə-), *n.* the mineral vesuvianite. [t. F, f. Gk.: m. *eîdos* form + m. *krâsis* mixture]

i·dol (ī'dəl), *n.* **1.** an image or other material object representing a deity to which religious worship is addressed. **2.** *Bible.* a false god, as of a heathen people. **3.** any person or thing blindly adored or revered: *a matinee idol.* **4.** a mere image or semblance of something, visible but without substance, as a phantom. **5.** a figment of the mind. **6.** a false conception or notion; fallacy. [ME, t. OF: m. *idole*, t. L: m. *īdōlum*, t. Gk.: m. *eídōlon* image, phantom, idol] **—Syn. 1.** See **image.**

i·dol·a·ter (ī dŏl'ə tər), *n.* **1.** a worshiper of idols. **2.** an adorer or devotee. Also, **i·dol·ist** (ī'dəl ĭst). [ME *idolatrer,* t. OF: m. *idolatre,* g. LL *īdōlolatrēs,* t. Gk.: m. *eidōlolátrēs* idol worshiper] **—i·dol·a·tress** (ī dŏl'ə trĭs), *n. fem.*

i·dol·a·trize (ī dŏl'ə trīz'), *v.,* **-trized, -trizing.** —*v.t.* **1.** to idolize. —*v.i.* **2.** to worship idols.

i·dol·a·trous (ī dŏl'ə trəs), *adj.* **1.** pertaining to or of the nature of idolatry. **2.** worshiping idols. **3.** used in or designed for idolatry. **4.** blindly adoring. **—i·dol'a·trous·ly,** *adv.* **—i·dol'a·trous·ness,** *n.*

i·dol·a·try (ī dŏl'ə trĭ), *n., pl.* **-tries.** **1.** the worship of idols. **2.** blind adoration, reverence, or devotion. [ME *idolatrie,* t. OF, g. LL *īdōlolatrīa,* t. Gk.: m. *eidōlolatreía*]

i·dol·ism (ī'dəl ĭz'əm), *n.* **1.** idolatry. **2.** idolizing.

i·dol·ize (ī'dəl īz'), *v.t.,* **-ized, -izing.** to worship as an idol; regard with blind adoration, reverence, or devotion. Also, *esp. Brit.,* **i'dol·ise'.** **—i·dol·i·za'tion,** *n.* **—i'dol·iz'er,** *n.*

I·dom·e·neus (ī dŏm'ə nūs', -nōōs'), *n.* *Gk. Legend.* a Cretan king and important chief of the Greek army in the Trojan War.

i·do·ne·ous (ī dō'nĭ əs), *adj.* fit. [t. L: m. *idōneus*]

Id·u·mae·a (ĭd'yŏō mē'ə, ī'dyŏō-), *n.* Greek name of Edom. Also, **Id·u·me'a.** **—Id·u·mae'an,** *adj., n.*

I·dun (ē'dŏōn), *n.* *Scand. Myth.* Ithunn.

i·dyl (ī'dəl), *n.* **1.** a poem or prose composition consisting of a "little picture," usually describing pastoral scenes or events or any charmingly simple episode, appealing incident, or the like. **2.** a simple descriptive or narrative piece in verse or prose. **3.** material suitable for an idyl. **4.** an episode or scene of idyllic simplicity or charm. **5.** *Music.* a composition, usually instrumental, of a pastoral or sentimental character. Also, **i/dyll.** [t. L: m.s. *īdyllium,* t. Gk.: m. *eidýllion,* dim. of *eídos* form]

i·dyl·ist (ī'dəl ĭst), *n.* a writer of idyls. Also, *esp. Brit.,* **i/dyll·ist.**

i·dyl·lic (ī dĭl'ĭk), *adj.* **1.** suitable for or suggestive of an idyl; charmingly simple or poetic. **2.** of, pertaining to, or of the nature of an idyl. **—i·dyl'li·cal·ly,** *adv.*

-ie, a hypocoristic suffix of nouns, same as **-y²,** as in *dearie, laddie, Willie.*

IE, Indo-European. Also, **I.E.**

i.e., id est.

-ier, var. of **-eer,** as in *brigadier, halberdier,* etc. [t. F, g. L *-ārius*]

if (ĭf), *conj.* **1.** in case that; granting or supposing that; on condition that. **2.** even though. **3.** whether. —*n.* **4.** a condition; a supposition. [ME; OE *gif,* c. Icel. *if,* later *ef* if (also used as n., *ef* doubt)]
—Syn. 1. IF, PROVIDED both imply a condition on which something else depends. IF is much more general. It may be used to indicate suppositions or hypothetical conditions (often involving doubt or uncertainty): *if you like, we can go straight home; if I had known, I wouldn't have gone.* IF may mean "even though": *if I am wrong, you are not right.* It may mean "whenever": *if I do not understand, I ask questions.* PROVIDED always indicates some stipulation: *I will subscribe ten dollars provided that you do, too; provided he goes, we can go along.* (PROVIDING means "just in case some certain thing should happen": *providing he should come, we must have extra supplies ready.*)

if·fy (ĭf'ĭ), *adj.* *Colloq.* indefinite; doubtful.

If·ni (ēf'nē), *n.* a Spanish colony on the NW coast of Africa. ab. 20,000 pop.; 965 sq. mi.

I.F.S., Irish Free State.

-ify, var. of **-fy,** used when preceding stem or word element ends in a consonant, as in *intensify.* [f. **-i-** + **-FY**]

I.G., **1.** Indo-Germanic. **2.** Inspector General.

Ig·dra·sil (ĭg'drə sĭl), *n.* *Scand. Myth.* Ygdrasil.

ig·loo (ĭg'lōō), *n., pl.* **-loos.** **1.** an Eskimo hut, domeshaped, built of blocks of hard snow. **2.** an excavation made by a seal in the snow over its breathing hole in the ice. Also, **ig'lu.** [t. Eskimo: house]

Ig·na·tius (ĭg nā'shəs), *n.* Saint, (*Ignatius Theophorus*) died A.D. c107?, bishop of Antioch; Christian martyr.

Ignatius of Loy·o·la (loi ō'lə), Saint, (*Iñigo López de Recalde*) 1491–1556, Spanish soldier and priest: founder of the Jesuit order.

ig·ne·ous (ĭg'nĭ əs), *adj.* **1.** *Geol.* produced under conditions involving intense heat, as rocks of volcanic origin or rocks crystallized from molten magma. **2.** pertaining to or of the nature of fire. [t. L: m. *igneus* of fire]

igneous rock. See **rock** (def. 2a).

ig·nes·cent (ĭg nĕs'ənt), *adj.* **1.** emitting sparks of fire, as certain stones when struck with steel. **2.** bursting into flame. —*n.* **3.** an ignescent substance. [t. L: s. *ignescens,* ppr., taking fire]

ig·nis fat·u·us (ĭg'nĭs făch'ŏō əs), *pl.* **ignes fatui** (ĭg'nēz făch'ŏō ī'). **1.** a flitting phosphorescent light seen at night, chiefly over marshy ground, and supposed to be due to spontaneous combustion of gas from decomposed organic matter; a will-o'-the-wisp. **2.** something deluding or misleading. [NL: foolish fire]

ig·nite (ĭg nīt'), *v.,* **-nited, -niting.** —*v.t.* **1.** to set on fire; kindle. **2.** *Chem.* to heat intensely; roast. —*v.i.* **3.** to take fire; begin to burn. [t. L: m.s. *ignītus,* pp.] **—ig·nit'a·ble, ig·nit'i·ble,** *adj.* **—ig·nit'a·bil'i·ty, ig·nit'i·bil'i·ty,** *n.* **—Syn. 1.** See **kindle.**

ig·nit·er (ĭg nī'tər), *n.* **1.** one who or that which ignites. **2.** *Electronics.* the carborundum rod used to initiate the discharge in an ignitron tube.

ig·ni·tion (ĭg nĭsh'ən), *n.* **1.** act of igniting. **2.** state of being ignited. **3.** (in an internal-combustion engine) the process which ignites the fuel in the cylinder. **4.** a means or device for igniting.

ig·ni·tron (ĭg'nə trŏn'), *n.* *Electronics.* **1.** a mercury-pool cathode-arc rectifier with a carborundum rod projecting into the mercury pool. The tube conducts current when the anode is positive. **2.** (*cap.*) a trade name for this rectifier.

ig·no·ble (ĭg nō'bəl), *adj.* **1.** of low character, aims, etc.; mean; base. **2.** of low grade or quality; inferior. **3.** not noble; of humble birth or station. **4.** *Falconry.* denoting short-winged hawks which chase or rake after the quarry (opposite to *noble*). [t. L: m.s. *ignōbilis* unknown, low-born] **—ig'no·bil'i·ty, ig·no'ble·ness,** *n.* **—ig·no'bly,** *adv.* **—Syn. 1.** degraded, dishonorable, contemptible, vulgar. **3.** lowly, obscure, plebeian.

ig·no·min·i·ous (ĭg'nə mĭn'ĭ əs), *adj.* **1.** marked by or attended with ignominy; discreditable; humiliating: *an ignominious retreat.* **2.** covered with or deserving ignominy; contemptible. **3.** base. [t. L: m.s. *ignōminiōsus*] **—ig'no·min'i·ous·ly,** *adv.* **—ig'no·min'i·ous·ness,** *n.*

ig·no·min·y (ĭg'nə mĭn'ĭ), *n., pl.* **-minies.** **1.** disgrace; dishonor; public contempt. **2.** base quality or conduct; a cause of disgrace. [t. L: m.s. *ignōminia* disgrace, dishonor] **—Syn. 1.** See **disgrace.**

ig·no·ra·mus (ĭg'nə rā'məs), *n., pl.* **-muses.** an ignorant person. [t. L: we do not know, we disregard]

ig·no·rance (ĭg'nə rəns), *n.* state or fact of being ignorant; lack of knowledge, learning, or information.

ig·no·rant (ĭg'nə rənt), *adj.* **1.** destitute of knowledge; unlearned. **2.** lacking knowledge or information as to a particular subject or fact. **3.** uninformed; unaware. **4.** due to or showing lack of knowledge: *an ignorant statement.* [ME, t. L: s. *ignōrans,* ppr., not knowing] **—ig'no·rant·ly,** *adv.*
—Syn. 1. IGNORANT, ILLITERATE, UNLETTERED, UNEDUCATED mean lacking in knowledge or in training. IGNORANT may mean knowing little or nothing, or it may mean uninformed about a particular subject: *an ignorant person can be dangerous; to be ignorant of mathematics.* ILLITERATE originally meant lacking a knowledge of literature or similar learning, but is specifically applied to one unable to read or write: *the illiterate voter; necessary training for illiterate soldiers.* UNLETTERED is a translation of the word ILLITERATE, but emphasizes the idea of being without knowledge of or love of literature: *unlettered though highly trained in*

---

b., blend of, blended; c., cognate with; d., dialect, dialectal; der., derived from; f., formed from; g., going back to; m., modification of; r., replacing; s., stem of; t., taken from; ?., perhaps. See the full key on inside cover.

science. **Uneducated** refers especially to lack of schooling or to lack of access to a body of knowledge equivalent to that learned in schools: *uneducated but highly intelligent.* —**Ant. 2.** learned.

ig·nore (ĭg nōr′), *v.t.,* **-nored, -noring. 1.** to refrain from noticing or recognizing: *ignore his remarks.* **2.** *Law.* (of the grand jury) to reject (a bill of indictment) as without sufficient evidence. [t. L: m.s. *ignōrāre* not to know, disregard] —**ig·nor′er,** *n.* —**Syn. 1.** overlook; slight, disregard.

Ig·o·rot (ĭg′ə rōt′, ē′gə-), *n., pl.* **-rot, -rots. 1.** a member of a people of the Malay stock in northern Luzon, Philippine Islands, comprising various tribes, some noted as head-hunters. **2.** their language, of the Indonesian group. Also, **Ig·or·ro·te** (ē′gôr rō′tĕ). [t. Sp.: m. *igorrote,* from native name]

I·graine (ĭ grān′), *n. Arthurian Romance.* the mother of King Arthur. Also, **Ygerne.**

i·gua·na (ĭ gwä′nə), *n.* **1.** any lizard of the genus *Iguana* of tropical America, esp. *I. iguana,* a large, arboreal, herbivorous species 5 feet or more in length, esteemed as food. **2.** some lizard of a related genus. [t. Sp.; from Carib name] —**i·gua·ni·an** (ĭ gwä′nĭ ən), *adj., n.*

i·guan·o·don (ĭ gwän′ə dŏn′), *n.* any member of the extinct bipedal dinosaurian genus *Iguanodon,* found fossil in Europe, comprising reptiles from 15 to 30 feet long, with denticulate teeth like those of the iguana. [f. iguan(a) + m.s. Gk. *odoús* tooth]

I·guas·sú (ē′gwä sōō′), *n.* a river in S Brazil, flowing W to the Paraná river. 380 mi.

Iguassú Falls, falls of great volume on the Iguassú river, on the boundary between Brazil and Argentina. 210 ft. high. Also, **Victoria Falls.**

ih·ram (ē räm′), *n.* the dress worn by Mohammedan pilgrims to Mecca, consisting of two white cotton cloths, one round the waist, the other over the left shoulder. [t. Ar., der. *ḥarama* forbid]

IHS, shortening of Greek ΙΗΣΟΤΣ Jesus, sometimes taken as representing: **1.** (L *Iesus Hominum Salvator*) Jesus, Saviour of Men. **2.** (L *In Hoc Signo Vinces*) in this sign (the cross) shalt thou conquer. **3.** (L *In Hoc Salus*) in this (cross) is salvation.

Ijs·sel (ī′səl), *n.* a branch of the Rhine in central Netherlands, flowing N to Ijssel Lake. 70 mi.

Ijssel Lake, a lake in NW Netherlands: created by diking of the Zuider Zee. 465 sq. mi. Dutch, **Ijsselmeer.**

Ikh·na·ton (ĭk nä′tən), *n.* See **Amenhotep IV.**

i·kon (ī′kŏn), *n.* icon.

il-¹, var. of in-², (by assimilation) before *l,* as in *illation.*

il-², var. of in-³, (by assimilation) before *l,* as in *illogical.*

-il, var. of **-ile,** as in *civil.*

Il, *Chem.* illinium.

i·lang-i·lang (ē′läng ē′läng), *n.* ylang-ylang.

-ile, a suffix of adjectives expressing capability, susceptibility, liability, aptitude, etc., as in *agile, docile, ductile, fragile, prehensile, tensile, volatile.* Also, **-il.** [t. L: m.s. *-ilis;* also used to repr. L *-īlis*]

il·e·ac (ĭl′ĭ ăk′), *adj.* of or pertaining to the ileum.

Ile de France (ēl də fräns′), **1.** a former province in N France, including Paris and the region around it. **2.** former name of **Mauritius.**

Ile du Dia·ble (ēl dy dyä′bl), French name of **Dev·il's Island.**

ileo-, a word element meaning "ileum," as in *ileostomy.* [t. L, comb. form of *ileum* groin, flank]

il·e·os·to·my (ĭl′ĭ ŏs′tə mĭ), *n., pl.* **-mies.** *Surg.* the formation of an artificial opening into the ileum.

il·e·um (ĭl′ĭ əm), *n.* **1.** *Anat.* the third and lowest division of the small intestine, continuous with the jejunum and ending at the caecum. See diag. under **intestine. 2.** *Entomol.* a narrower part of the intestine of an insect, following the stomach. [NL, in LL groin, flank, in L (usually pl.) *ilia* flanks, entrails]

il·e·us (ĭl′ĭ əs), *n. Pathol.* severe colic attended with vomiting, etc., due to intestinal obstruction. [t. L, t. Gk.: m. *ileós,* var. of *eileós* colic]

i·lex (ī′lĕks), *n.* **1.** the holm oak. **2.** any tree or shrub of the genus *Ilex.* **3.** holly. [NL: the holly genus, L the holm oak]

Il·ford (ĭl′fərd), *n.* a city in SE England, in Essex, near London. 174,550 (est. 1946).

il·i·ac (ĭl′ĭ ăk′), *adj.* of or pertaining to the ilium. [t. LL: s. *īliacus* pertaining to the flank, der. L *īlium*]

Il·i·ad (ĭl′ĭ əd), *n.* **1.** Greek epic poem describing the siege of Troy, ascribed to Homer. **2.** any similar poem; a long narrative. **3.** a long series of woes, etc. [t. L: s. *Ilias,* t. Gk., der. *Ilion* Ilium, Troy] —**Il′i·ad′ic,** *adj.*

Il·i·on (ĭl′ĭ ən), *n.* Greek name of ancient **Troy.**

-ility, a compound suffix making abstract nouns from adjectives by replacing the adj. suffixes: *-il(e), -le,* as in *civility, sterility, ability.* [t. F: m. *-ilité,* t. L: m. *-ilitas*]

Il·i·um (ĭl′ĭ əm), *n.* Latin name of ancient **Troy.**

il·i·um (ĭl′ĭ əm), *n., pl.* **ilia** (ĭl′ĭ ə). *Anat.* the broad upper portion of either innominate bone. See diag. under **pelvis.** [NL, special use of L *īlium* flank]

ilk (ĭlk), *adj.* **1.** same. **2.** *Scot. and N. Eng.* each; every. —*n.* **3.** family, class, or kind: *he and all his ilk.* [ME *ilk,* OE *elc, ylc,* var. of *ǣlc* each]

il·ka (ĭl′kə), *adj. Scot. and N. Eng.* ilk. [f. ilk + a¹ (indef. art.)]

---

ill (ĭl), *adj.* **worse, worst,** *n., adv.* —*adj.* **1.** physically disordered, as the health; unwell, sick, or indisposed. **2.** evil, wicked, or bad: *ill repute.* **3.** objectionable, unsatisfactory, poor, or faulty: *ill manners.* **4.** hostile or unkindly: *ill feeling.* **5.** unfavorable or adverse: *ill luck.* **6.** unskillful; inexpert. —*n.* **7.** evil. **8.** harm or injury. **9.** a disease or ailment. **10.** trouble or misfortune. **11.** *Archaic.* wickedness or sin. —*adv.* **12.** in an ill manner; wickedly. **13.** unsatisfactorily or poorly: *ill at ease.* **14.** in a hostile or unfriendly manner. **15.** unfavorably or unfortunately. **16.** with displeasure or offense. **17.** faultily or improperly. **18.** with trouble, difficulty, or inconvenience: *an expense we can ill afford.* [ME *ill,* t. Scand.; cf. Icel. *illr* ill, bad] —**Syn. 1.** ILL, SICK mean being in bad health, not being well. ILL is the more formal word. In the U.S. the two words are used practically interchangeably except that SICK is always used when the word modifies the following noun or is used as a collective noun: *he is very sick (ill) of a fever; he looks sick (ill); a sick person; a home for the sick.* There are certain phrases, also, in which SICK is used: *sick at heart; sick for home; it makes me sick.* In England, SICK is not interchangeable with ILL, but usually has the connotation of nausea; SICK is however used before nouns, in the collective, and in set phrases, just as in the U.S.: *he is ill, she felt ill, he looks ill; a sick man, to care for the sick,* and the like. **2.** See **bad¹.** —**Ant. 1.** well, healthy.

I'll (ĭl), contraction of *I will* or *I shall.*

Ill., Illinois.

ill., 1. illustrated. **2.** illustration.

ill-ad·vised (ĭl′əd vīzd′), *adj.* acting or done without due consideration; imprudent. —**ill-ad·vis·ed·ly** (ĭl′-əd vī′zĭd lĭ), *adv.*

Il·lam·pu (ē yäm′pōō), *n.* a mountain peak in W Bolivia, in the Andes, near Lake Titicaca. ab. 21,500 ft. Also, **Mount Sorata.**

il·la·tion (ĭ lā′shən), *n.* **1.** act of inferring. **2.** an inference or conclusion. [t. LL: s. *illātio* a carrying in]

il·la·tive (ĭl′ə tĭv, ĭ lā′tĭv), *adj.* pertaining to or expressing illation; inferential: *an illative word such as "therefore."* [t. L: m.s. *illātīvus*] —**il′la·tive·ly,** *adv.*

il·laud·a·ble (ĭ lô′də bəl), *adj.* not laudable. —**il·laud′a·bly,** *adv.*

ill-bod·ing (ĭl′bō′dĭng), *adj.* foreboding evil; inauspicious; unlucky: *ill-boding stars.*

ill-bred (ĭl′brĕd′), *adj.* showing or due to lack of proper breeding; unmannerly; rude: *he remained serene in a houseful of ill-bred children.*

il·le·gal (ĭ lē′gəl), *adj.* not legal; unauthorized. [t. ML: s. *illēgālis,* f. L: *il-* IL- + *lēgālis* LEGAL] —**il·le′gal·ly,** *adv.* —**il·le′gal·ness,** *n.* —**Syn.** unlawful, illegitimate; illicit; unlicensed.

il·le·gal·i·ty (ĭl′ē găl′ə tĭ), *n., pl.* **-ties. 1.** illegal condition or quality; unlawfulness. **2.** an illegal act.

il·le·gal·ize (ĭ lē′gə līz′), *v.t.* to make illegal: *they even wanted to illegalize smoking*

il·leg·i·ble (ĭ lĕj′ə bəl), *adj.* not legible; impossible or hard to read or decipher. —**il·leg·i·bil′i·ty, il·leg′i·ble·ness,** *n.* —**il·leg′i·bly,** *adv.*

il·le·git·i·ma·cy (ĭl′ĭ jĭt′ə mə sĭ), *n., pl.* **-cies.** state or quality of being illegitimate.

il·le·git·i·mate (ĭl′ĭ jĭt′ə mĭt), *adj.* **1.** not legitimate; unlawful: *an illegitimate act.* **2.** born out of wedlock: *an illegitimate child.* **3.** irregular; not in good usage. **4.** *Logic.* not in accordance with the principle of inference. —**il·le·git′i·mate·ly,** *adv.*

ill-fat·ed (ĭl′fā′tĭd), *adj.* **1.** destined to an unhappy fate: *an ill-fated person.* **2.** bringing bad fortune.

ill-fa·vored (ĭl′fā′vərd), *adj.* **1.** not pleasant in appearance; ugly: *an ill-favored child.* **2.** offensive; unpleasant; objectionable. —**ill′-fa′vored·ly,** *adv.* —**ill′-fa′vored·ness,** *n.*

ill-found·ed (ĭl′foun′dĭd), *adj.* on a weak or illogical basis: *an ill-founded plea for mercy.*

ill-got·ten (ĭl′gŏt′ən), *adj.* acquired by evil means: *ill-gotten gains.*

ill humor, a disagreeable mood. —**ill′-hu′mored,** *adj.* —**ill′-hu′mored·ly,** *adv.*

il·lib·er·al (ĭ lĭb′ər əl), *adj.* **1.** not generous in giving; niggardly. **2.** narrow-minded; bigoted. **3.** without culture; unscholarly; vulgar. [t. L: s. *illīberālis* mean, sordid] —**il·lib·er·al′i·ty, il·lib·er·al·ness,** *n.* —**il·lib′er·al·ly,** *adv.*

il·lic·it (ĭ lĭs′ĭt), *adj.* not permitted or authorized; unlicensed; unlawful. [t. L: s. *illicitus* forbidden] —**il·lic′it·ly,** *adv.* —**il·lic′it·ness,** *n.*

Il·li·ma·ni (ē′yē mä′nē), *n.* a mountain in W Bolivia, in the Andes, near La Paz. 21,188 ft.

il·lim·it·a·ble (ĭ lĭm′ĭt ə bəl), *adj.* not limitable; limitless; boundless. —**il·lim·it·a·bil′i·ty, il·lim·it·a·ble·ness,** *n.* —**il·lim′it·a·bly,** *adv.*

il·lin·i·um (ĭ lĭn′ĭ əm), *n. Chem.* a rare-earth element found spectroscopically (at the Univ. of Illinois) in 1926 but not yet isolated. *Symbol:* Il; *at. no.:* 61. [f. Illin(ois) + -ium]

Il·li·nois (ĭl′ə noi′, -noiz′), *n.* **1.** a State in the central United States: a part of the Midwest. 8,712,176 pop. (1950); 56,400 sq. mi. *Cap.:* Springfield. *Abbr.:* Ill. **2.** a river flowing from NE Illinois SW to the Mississippi, connected by a canal with Lake Michigan. 273 mi. [t.F., t. Illinois Indian, c. Shawnee *hileni,* Fox *ineniwa* man g., Proto-Algonquian *elenyiwa*] —**Il′li·nois′an,** *n., adj.*

Il·li·nois (Ĭl'ə noi', -noiz'), *n.*, *pl.* **-nois** (-noi', -noiz').
1. (*pl.*) a confederacy of North American Indians of
Algonquian stock, formerly occupying Illinois and adjoining regions westward. **2.** an Indian of this confederacy.

il·lit·er·a·cy (Ĭ lĭt'ər ə sĭ), *n.*, *pl.* **-cies.** **1.** lack of ability to read and write. **2.** state of being illiterate; lack of
education. **3.** *Rare.* a literal or a literary error.

il·lit·er·ate (Ĭ lĭt'ər Ĭt), *adj.* **1.** unable to read and
write: *an illiterate tribe.* **2.** lacking education. **3.** showing lack of culture. —*n.* **4.** an illiterate person. [t. L:
m.s. *illiterātus* unlettered] —**il·lit'er·ate·ly**, *adv.* —**il-
lit'er·ate·ness**, *n.* —**Syn. 1.** See **ignorant.**

ill-judged (Ĭl'jŭjd'), *adj.* injudicious; unwise.

ill-look·ing (Ĭl'lŏŏk'Ĭng), *adj.* **1.** ugly. **2.** sinister.

ill-man·nered (Ĭl'măn'ərd), *adj.* having bad manners; impolite; rude. —**ill'-man'nered·ly**, *adv.*

ill nature, unkindly or unpleasant disposition.

ill-na·tured (Ĭl'nā'chərd), *adj.* having or showing
an unkindly or unpleasant disposition. —**ill'-na'tured·
ly**, *adv.* —**ill'-na'tured·ness**, *n.* —**Syn.** See **cross.**

ill·ness (Ĭl'nĭs), *n.* **1.** a state of bad health; sickness.
2. an attack of sickness. **3.** *Obs.* wickedness.

il·log·i·cal (Ĭ lŏj'ə kəl), *adj.* not logical; contrary to or
disregardful of the rules of logic; unreasonable. —**il-
log'i·cal·i·ty, il·log'i·cal·ness**, *n.* —**il·log'i·cal·ly**,
adv.

ill-o·mened (Ĭl'ō'mənd), *adj.* having or attended by
bad omens; ill-starred.

ill-starred (Ĭl'stärd'), *adj.* **1.** under the influence of
an evil star; ill-fated; unlucky. **2.** disastrous.

ill temper, bad disposition. —**ill'-tem'pered**, *adj.*
—**ill'-tem'pered·ly**, *adv.* —**ill'-tem'pered·ness**, *n.*

ill-timed (Ĭl'tīmd'), *adj.* badly timed; inopportune.

ill-treat (Ĭl'trēt'), *v.t.* to treat badly; maltreat.
—**ill'-treat'ment**, *n.*

il·lume (Ĭ lōōm'), *v.t.*, **-lumed, -luming.** *Poetic.* to
illuminate.

il·lu·mi·nant (Ĭ lōō'mə nənt), *n.* an illuminating agent
or material.

il·lu·mi·nate (*v.* Ĭ lōō'mə nāt'; *adj., n.* Ĭ lōō'mə nĭt,
-nāt'), *v.* **-nated, -nating,** *adj., n.* —*v.t.* **1.** to supply
with light; light up. **2.** to throw light on (a subject);
make lucid or clear. **3.** *Chiefly Brit.* to decorate with
lights, as in celebration. **4.** to enlighten, as with knowledge. **5.** to make resplendent or illustrious. **6.** to
decorate (a letter, a page, a manuscript, etc.) with color,
gold, or the like. —*v.i.* **7.** to display lights, as in celebration. **8.** to become illuminated. —*adj.* **9.** *Archaic.*
illuminated. **10.** *Obs.* enlightened. —*n.* **11.** *Archaic.*
one who is or affects to be specially enlightened. [t. L:
m.s. *illūminātus*, pp.] —**il·lu'mi·nat'ing**, *adj.* —**il-
lu'mi·nat'ing·ly**, *adv.*

il·lu·mi·na·ti (Ĭ lōō'mə nā'tĭ, -nä'tē), *n.pl.*, *sing.* **-to**
(-tō). **1.** persons possessing or claiming to possess
superior enlightenment. **2.** (*cap.*) a name given to different religious societies or sects because of their claim
to enlightenment. [t. L, pl. of *illūminātus* enlightened]

il·lu·mi·na·tion (Ĭ lōō'mə nā'shən), *n.* **1.** act of illuminating. **2.** fact or condition of being illuminated.
3. *Chiefly Brit.* a decoration consisting of lights. **4.** intellectual or spiritual enlightenment. **5.** the intensity of
light falling at a given place on a lighted surface; the
luminus flux per unit area at a given point on an intercepting surface. **6.** a supply of light. **7.** decoration, as
of a letter, page, or manuscript, with a painted design
in color, gold, etc.

il·lu·mi·na·tive (Ĭ lōō'mə nā'tĭv), *adj.* illuminating.

il·lu·mi·na·tor (Ĭ lōō'mə nā'tər), *n.* **1.** one who or that
which illuminates. **2.** a device for illuminating, such as a
light source with lens or a mirror for concentrating light.
3. one who paints manuscripts, books, etc., with designs
in color, gold, or the like.

il·lu·mine (Ĭ lōō'mĭn), *v.t.*, *v.i.*, **-mined, -mining.** to
illuminate or be illuminated. [ME *illumyne(n)*, t. F:
m. *illuminer*, t. L: m. *illūmināre* light up] —**il·lu'-
mi·na·ble**, *adj.*

il·lu·mi·nism (Ĭ lōō'mə nĭz'əm),
n. **1.** the doctrines or claims of Il-
luminati. **2.** a doctrine advocating
enlightenment. —**il·lu'mi·nist**, *n.*

illus., **1.** illustrated. **2.** illustration.

ill-use (*v.* Ĭl'ūz'; *n.* Ĭl'ūs'), *v.*,
-used, -using, *n.* —*v.t.* **1.** to treat
badly, unjustly, or cruelly. —*n.*
2. Also, **ill-us·age** (Ĭl'ŭs'Ĭj, -zĬj).
bad, unjust, or cruel treatment.

il·lu·sion (Ĭ lōō'zhən), *n.* **1.** something that deceives by producing a
false impression. **2.** act of deceiving; deception; delusion; mockery.
3. state of being deceived, or an instance of this; a false impression or
belief. **4.** *Psychol.* a perception of a thing which misrepresents it, or gives it qualities not present in reality.
5. a very thin, delicate kind of tulle. [ME, t. L: s. *illūsio*
mocking, illusion]
—**Syn. 1.** ILLUSION, DELUSION, HALLUCINATION refer to
mental deceptions which arise from various causes. An
ILLUSION is a false mental image or conception which may

Optical illusion.
The parallel verticals
seem to diverge under
the influence of the
oblique crosspiece.

be a misinterpretation of a real appearance or may be
something imagined. It may be pleasing, harmless, or even
useful: *a mirage is an illusion, he had an illusion that the
doorman was a general.* A DELUSION is a fixed mistaken conception of something which really exists, and is not capable
of correction or removal by examination or reasoning.
DELUSIONS are often mischievous or harmful, as those of
a fanatic or a lunatic: *the delusion that all food is poisoned.*
A HALLUCINATION is a completely groundless false conception, belief, or opinion, caused by a disordered imagination; it is particularly frequent today in the pathological
sense, according to which it denotes hearing or seeing something that does not exist: *hallucinations caused by nervous
disorders.* —**Ant. 1.** reality.

il·lu·sion·al (Ĭ lōō'zhən əl), *adj.* pertaining to or characterized by illusions.

il·lu·sion·ism (Ĭ lōō'zhə nĭz'əm), *n.* a theory or doctrine that the material world is an illusion.

il·lu·sion·ist (Ĭ lōō'zhən Ĭst), *n.* **1.** one subject to illusions. **2.** a conjurer. **3.** an adherent of illusionism.

il·lu·sive (Ĭ lōō'sĬv), *adj.* illusory. —**il·lu'sive·ly**,
adv. —**il·lu'sive·ness**, *n.*

il·lu·so·ry (Ĭ lōō'sər Ĭ), *adj.* causing illusion; deceptive;
of the nature of an illusion; unreal. —**il·lu'so·ri·ly**,
adv. —**il·lu'so·ri·ness**, *n.*

illust., **1.** illustrated. **2.** illustration.

il·lus·trate (Ĭl'ə strāt', Ĭ lŭs'trāt), *v.t.*, **-trated, -trat-
ing.** **1.** to make clear or intelligible, as by examples;
exemplify. **2.** to furnish (a book, etc.) with drawings or
pictorial representations intended for elucidation or
adornment. **3.** *Archaic.* to enlighten. [t. L: m.s. *illus-
trātus*, pp., illuminated]

il·lus·tra·tion (Ĭl'ə strā'shən), *n.* **1.** that which illustrates, as a picture in a book, etc. **2.** a comparison or an
example intended for explanation or corroboration.
3. act of rendering clear; explanation; elucidation. **4.**
illustriousness; distinction. —**Syn. 2.** See **case**[1].

il·lus·tra·tive (Ĭ lŭs'trə tĬv, Ĭl'ə strā'tĬv), *adj.* serving
to illustrate. —**il·lus'tra·tive·ly**, *adv.*

il·lus·tra·tor (Ĭl'ə strā'tər, Ĭ lŭs'trā tər), *n.* **1.** an
artist who makes illustrations. **2.** one who or that
which illustrates.

il·lus·tri·ous (Ĭ lŭs'trĬ əs), *adj.* **1.** highly distinguished;
renowned; famous. **2.** glorious, as deeds, etc. **3.** *Obs.*
luminous; bright. [f. L *illustri(s)* lighted up, bright +
-OUS] —**il·lus'tri·ous·ly**, *adv.* —**il·lus'tri·ous·ness**, *n.*

ill will, hostile or unfriendly feeling. —**ill-willed**
(Ĭl'wĬld'), *adj.*

il·ly (Ĭl'Ĭ, Ĭl'lĬ), *adv.* ill.

Il·lyr·i·a (Ĭ lĬr'Ĭ ə), *n.* an ancient country along the E
coast of the Adriatic.

Il·lyr·i·an (Ĭ lĬr'Ĭ ən), *adj.* **1.** pertaining to Illyria.
—*n.* **2.** a native or inhabitant of Illyria. **3.** an extinct
Indo-European language probably allied with Albanian.
4. a group of Indo-European languages including Albanian.

il·men·ite (Ĭl'mə nīt'), *n.* a very common black mineral, iron titanate, FeTiO$_3$, occurring in crystals but
more commonly massive. [f. *Ilmen* (name of mountain
range in the Urals) + -ITE[1]]

I.L.O., International Labor Organization.

I·lo·i·lo (ē'lō ē'lō), *n.* a seaport in the Philippine
Islands, on Panay. 90,480 (1939).

I·lo·ka·no (ē'lō kä'nō), *n.*, *pl.* **-nos** (-nōz). **1.** an Indonesian language of Luzon. **2.** (in the Philippines) a
Christian Malay. [t. Sp.: m. *Ilocano*, der *Ilocos* the
name of two provinces, lit. river run, from Tagalog *ilog*
river]

Il Tro·va·to·re (ēl trō'vä tō'rĕ), an opera (1853) by
Verdi.

I'm (īm), contraction of *I am.*

im-[1], var. of **in-**[2] used before *b*, *m*, and *p*, as in *imbrute,
immingle.*

im-[2], var. of **in-**[3] used before *b*, *m*, and *p*, as in *immoral,
imparity, imperishable.*

im-[3], var. of **in-**[1], before *b*, *m*, and *p*, as in *imbed, impearl.*

I.M., Isle of Man.

im·age (Ĭm'Ĭj), *n.*, *v.*, **-aged, -aging.** —*n.* **1.** a likeness
or similitude of a person, animal, or thing. **2.** an optical
counterpart or appearance of an object, such as is produced by reflection from a mirror, refraction by a lens,
or the passage of luminous rays through a small aperture.
3. a mental picture or representation; an idea or conception. **4.** *Psychol.* the reliving of a sensation in the
absence of the original stimulus. **5.** form, appearance,
or semblance. **6.** a counterpart or copy: *the child is the
image of its mother.* **7.** a symbol or emblem. **8.** a type or
embodiment. **9.** a description of something in speech or
writing. **10.** *Rhet.* a figure of speech, esp. a metaphor or
a simile. **11.** *Archaic.* an illusion or apparition. —*v.t.*
12. to picture or represent in the mind; imagine; conceive. **13.** to make an image of. **14.** to set forth in
speech or writing; describe. **15.** to reflect the likeness
of; mirror. **16.** to symbolize or typify. **17.** *Rare.* to
resemble. [ME, t. F, t. L: m. *imāgo* copy, image]
—**Syn. 1.** IMAGE, ICON, IDOL refer to material representations of persons or things. An IMAGE is a representation as in
a statue or effigy, and is sometimes regarded as an object of
worship: *to set up an image of Apollo, an image of a saint,
graven images.* An ICON, in the Greek or Orthodox Eastern
Church, is a representation of Christ, an angel, or a saint, in
painting, relief, mosaic, or the like: *at least two icons are*

---

b., blend of, blended; c., cognate with; d., dialect, dialectal; der., derived from; f., formed from; g., going back to;
m., modification of; r., replacing; s., stem of; t., taken from; ?, perhaps. See the full key on inside cover.

found in each church. Small icons are also carried by the peasants; these are folded tablets of wood or metal, with representations of sacred subjects in enamel or in designs of black and white or silver: *an icon is honored by offerings of incense and lights.* An IDOL is an image, statue, or the like, representing a deity and worshiped as such: *a wooden idol. the heathen worship idols;* fig., *to make an idol of wealth.*

im·age·ry (Ĭm′ĭj·rĭ, Ĭm′ĭj·ə·rĭ), *n., pl.* **-ries. 1.** the formation of images, figures, or likenesses of things, or such images collectively: *a dream's dim imagery.* **2.** *Psychol.* a person's tendencies to form images. **3.** images or statues. **4.** the use of rhetorical images. **5.** figurative description or illustration; rhetorical images collectively. —**im·age·ri·al** (Ĭm′ə·jĭr′Ĭ·əl), *adj.*

im·ag·i·na·ble (Ĭ·măj′ə·nə·bəl), *adj.* capable of being imagined or conceived. —**im·ag′i·na·ble·ness,** *n.* —**im·ag′i·na·bly,** *adv.*

im·ag·i·nal (Ĭ·măj′ə·nəl), *adj. Entomol.* **1.** of or pertaining to an imago. **2.** in the form of an imago.

im·ag·i·nar·y (Ĭ·măj′ə·nĕr′Ĭ), *adj., n., pl.* **-naries.** —*adj.* **1.** existing only in the imagination or fancy; not real; fancied: *an imaginary illness.* **2.** *Math.* noting or pertaining to a quantity or expression involving the square root of a negative quantity. —*n.* **3.** *Math.* an imaginary expression or quantity. —**im·ag′i·nar′i·ly,** *adv.* —**i·mag′i·nar′i·ness,** *n.* —**Syn. 1.** visionary, shadowy, chimerical; baseless, unreal.

im·ag·i·na·tion (Ĭ·măj′ə·nā′shən), *n.* **1.** the action of imagining, or of forming mental images or concepts of what is not actually present to the senses. **2.** the faculty of forming such images or concepts. **3.** the power of reproducing images stored in the memory under the suggestion of associated images (**reproductive imagination**), or of recombining former experiences in the creation of new images different from any known by experience (**productive or creative imagination**). **4.** the faculty of producing ideal creations consistent with reality, as in literature (distinguished from *fancy*). **5.** the product of imagining; a conception or mental creation, often a baseless or fanciful one. **6.** *Archaic.* a plan, scheme, or plot. [ME, t. L: s. *imāginātiō*] —**im·ag′i·na′tion·al,** *adj.* —**Syn. 4.** See **fancy.**

im·ag·i·na·tive (Ĭ·măj′ə·nā′tĭv, -nə·tĭv), *adj.* **1.** characterized by or bearing evidence of imagination: *an imaginative tale.* **2.** pertaining to or concerned with imagination: *the imaginative faculty.* **3.** given to imagining, as persons. **4.** having exceptional powers of imagination. **5.** fanciful. —**im·ag′i·na′tive·ly,** *adv.* —**im·ag′·i·na′tive·ness,** *n.*

im·ag·ine (Ĭ·măj′Ĭn), *v.,* **-ined, -ining.** —*v.t.* **1.** to form a mental image of (something not actually present to the senses). **2.** to think, believe, or fancy. **3.** to assume or suppose. **4.** to conjecture or guess: *I cannot imagine whom you mean.* **5.** *Archaic.* to plan, scheme, or plot. —*v.i.* **6.** to form mental images of things not present to the senses; use the imagination. **7.** to suppose; think; conjecture. [ME *imagine(n),* t. F: m. *imaginer,* t. L: m. *imāginārī* picture to oneself, fancy] —**im·ag′in·er,** *n.* —**Syn. 1.** IMAGINE, CONCEIVE, CONCEIVE OF, REALIZE refer to bringing something before the mind. To IMAGINE is, literally, to form a mental image of something: *imagine yourself in London.* To CONCEIVE is to relate ideas or feelings to one another in a pattern: *how has the author conceived the first act of his play?* To CONCEIVE OF is to comprehend through the intellect something not perceived through the senses: *Wilson conceived of a world free from war.* To REALIZE is to make an imagined thing real or concrete to oneself, to grasp fully its implications: *to realize the extent of one's folly.*

im·ag·ism (Ĭm′ə·jĭz′əm), *n.* a method or movement in poetic composition, originating about 1912, which aimed particularly at "images" or clear pictures of what the poet has in mind without vagueness or symbolism, and used rhythm or cadence rather than the conventional metrical forms. See **free verse.** —**im′ag·ist,** *n., adj.* —**im′ag·is′tic,** *adj.*

i·ma·go (Ĭ·mā′gō), *n., pl.* **imagoes, imagines** (Ĭ·măj′ə·nēz′). **1.** *Entomol.* an adult insect. **2.** *Psychoanal.* an idealized concept of a loved one, formed in childhood and retained uncorrected in adult life. [NL, special use of L *imāgō* image]

i·mam (Ĭ·mäm′), *n.* **1.** the officiating priest of a mosque. **2.** the title for a Mohammedan religious leader or chief. **3.** one of a succession of seven or twelve religious leaders, believed to be divinely inspired, of the Shiites. Also, **i·maum** (Ĭ·mäm′, Ĭ·môm′). [t. Ar.: m. *imām* leader, guide]

i·mam·ate (Ĭ·mä′māt), *n.* **1.** the office of an imam. **2.** the region or territory governed by an imam.

i·ma·ret (Ĭ·mä′rĕt), *n.* (among the Turks) a hospice for pilgrims, etc. [Turk., t. Ar.: m. *'imāra(t)* building, dwelling place]

im·bal·ance (Ĭm·băl′əns), *n.* **1.** the state or condition of lacking balance. **2.** faulty muscular or glandular coördination.

im·balm (Ĭm·bäm′), *v.t. Obs.* embalm.

im·be·cile (Ĭm′bə·sĬl), *n.* **1.** a person of defective mentality above the grade of idiocy. —*adj.* **2.** mentally feeble. **3.** showing mental feebleness or incapacity. **4.** silly; absurd. **5.** *Rare.* weak or feeble. [t. F, t. L: m.s. *imbēcillus* weak, feeble] —**im′be·cile·ly,** *adv.*

im·be·cil·i·ty (Ĭm′bə·sĬl′ə·tĬ), *n., pl.* **-ties. 1.** feebleness of mind; mental weakness that falls short of absolute idiocy. **2.** an instance or point of weakness or feebleness. **3.** silliness or absurdity. **4.** an instance of it.

im·bed (Ĭm·bĕd′), *v.t.,* **-bedded, -bedding.** embed.

---

im·bibe (Ĭm·bīb′), *v.,* **-bibed, -bibing.** —*v.t.* **1.** to drink in, or drink. **2.** to absorb or take in as if by drinking. **3.** to take or receive into the mind, as knowledge, ideas, etc. —*v.i.* **4.** to drink; absorb liquid or moisture. **5.** *Obs.* to soak or saturate; imbue. [ME, t. L: m. *imbibere* drink in] —**im·bib′er,** *n.* —**Syn. 1.** See **drink.**

im·bi·bi·tion (Ĭm′bĬ·bĬsh′ən), *n.* act of imbibing.

im·bri·cate (*adj.* Ĭm′brə·kĬt, -kāt′; *v.* Ĭm′brə·kāt′), *adj., v.,* **-cated, -cating.** —*adj.* Also, **im′bri·cat′-ed. 1.** bent and hollowed like a roof tile. **2.** of, like, or decorated with lines or curves resembling overlapping tiles. **3.** *Biol.* overlapping like tiles, as scales, leaves, etc. **4.** characterized by, or as by, overlapping scales. —*v.t., v.i.* **5.** to overlap like tiles or shingles. [t. L: m.s. *imbricātus,* pp., covered with tiles] —**im′bri·cate·ly,** *adv.* —**im′bri·ca′tive,** *adj.*

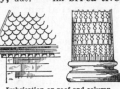

A. Imbricate flowerbud; B. Imbricate scale of cone

im·bri·ca·tion (Ĭm′brə·kā′shən), *n.* **1.** an overlapping, as of tiles or shingles. **2.** a decorative pattern imitating this.

im·bro·glio (Ĭm·brōl′yō), *n., pl.* **-glios. 1.** an intricate and perplexing state of affairs; a complicated or difficult situation. **2.** a misunderstanding or disagreement of a complicated nature, as between persons or nations. **3.** a confused heap. [t. It.: confusion, der. *imbrogliare* confuse, embroil]

Imbrication on roof and column

im·brue (Ĭm·brōō′), *v.t.,* **-brued, -bruing. 1.** to wet in or with something that stains, now esp. blood. **2.** (of blood, etc.) to wet or stain. [ME *enbrewe(n),* t. OF: m. *embreuver* give to drink, ult der. L *bibere* drink] —**im·brue′ment,** *n.*

im·brute (Ĭm·brōōt′), *v.t., v.i.,* **-bruted, -bruting.** to degrade or sink to the level of a brute. Also, **embrute.** [f. IM-¹ + BRUTE, *n.*] —**im·brute′ment,** *n.*

im·buc (Ĭm·bū′), *v.t.,* **-bued, -buing. 1.** to impregnate or inspire, as with feelings, opinions, etc. **2.** to saturate with moisture, impregnate with color, etc. **3.** to imbrue. [t. L: m.s. *imbuere*] —**im·bue′ment,** *n.*

im·id·az·ole (Ĭm′ə·dăz′ōl, -ĭd·ə·zōl′), *n. Chem.* an organic heterocyclic compound, $C_3H_4N_2$; glyoxalin. [f. IMID(E) + AZ(O)- + -OLE]

im·ide (Ĭm′īd, Ĭm′Ĭd), *n. Chem.* a compound derived from ammonia by replacement of two hydrogen atoms by acidic radicals, characterized by the NH group. Also, **im·id** (Ĭm′Ĭd). [arbitrary alter. of AMIDE]

imido-, *Chem.* a combining form indicating an imide.

i·mine (Ĭ·mēn′, Ĭm′Ĭn), *n. Chem.* a compound containing the NH group united with a nonacid radical. [alter. of AMINE modeled on IMIDE]

imino-, a combining form indicating an imine.

imit., **1.** imitation. **2.** imitative.

im·i·ta·ble (Ĭm′ə·tə·bəl), *adj.* that may be imitated. —**im′i·ta·bil′i·ty,** *n.*

im·i·tate (Ĭm′ə·tāt′), *v.t.,* **-tated, -tating. 1.** to follow or endeavor to follow in action or manner. **2.** to mimic or counterfeit. **3.** to make a copy of; reproduce closely. **4.** to have or assume the appearance of; simulate. [t. L: m.s. *imitātus,* pp., having copied] —**im′i·ta′tor,** *n.* —**Syn. 3.** IMITATE, COPY, DUPLICATE, REPRODUCE all mean to follow or try to follow an example or pattern. IMITATE is the general word for the idea: *to imitate someone's handwriting, behavior.* To COPY is to make a fairly exact imitation of an original creation: *to copy a sentence, a dress, a picture.* To DUPLICATE is to produce something which exactly resembles or corresponds to something else; both may be originals: *to duplicate the terms of two contracts.* To REPRODUCE is to make a likeness or reconstruction of an original: *to reproduce a 16th century theater.*

im·i·ta·tion (Ĭm′ə·tā′shən), *n.* **1.** a result or product of imitating. **2.** act of imitating. **3.** *Sociol.* the copying of patterns of activity and thought of other groups or individuals. **4.** *Biol.* close external resemblance of an organism to some other organism or to objects in its environment. **5.** *Psychol.* a response or state of mind which in some respects resembles the activating stimulus-situation. **6.** a counterfeit. **7.** a literary composition that imitates the manner or subject of another author or work. **8.** (in the arts) the imaginative representation of the actions, motives, or natures of men or of their environments; mimesis. **9.** *Music.* the repetition of a melodic phrase at a different pitch or key from the original, or in a different voice part. —*adj.* **10.** made to imitate a genuine or superior article or thing: *imitation pearls.* [t. L: s. *imitātiō*] —**im′i·ta′tion·al,** *adj.*

im·i·ta·tive (Ĭm′ə·tā′tĭv), *adj.* **1.** imitating or copying, or given to imitating. **2.** characterized by or involving imitation or copying. **3.** *Biol.* mimetic. **4.** made in imitation of something. **5.** onomatopoeic. —**im′i·ta′tive·ly,** *adv.* —**im′i·ta′tive·ness,** *n.*

im·mac·u·late (Ĭ·măk′yə·lĬt), *adj.* **1.** free from spot or stain; spotlessly clean, as linen. **2.** free from moral blemish or impurity; pure, or undefiled. **3.** free from fault or flaw; free from errors, as a text. **4.** *Zool., Bot.*

---

without spots or colored marks; unicolor. [late ME, t. L: m.s. *immaculātus* unspotted] —**im·mac′u·la·cy**, **im·mac′u·late·ness**, *n.* —**im·mac′u·late·ly**, *adv.*

Im·mac·u·late Con·cep·tion, *Rom. Cath. Ch.* the unique privilege by which the Virgin Mary was conceived in her mother's womb without the stain of original sin, through the anticipated merits of Jesus Christ.

im·ma·nent (ĭm′ə nənt), *adj.* 1. remaining within; indwelling; inherent. 2. (of a mental act) taking place within the mind of the subject, and having no effect outside of it. [t. LL: s. *immanens*, ppr., remaining in] —**im′ma·nence**, **im′ma·nen·cy**, *n.* —**im′ma·nent·ly**, *adv.*

Im·man·u·el (ĭ măn′yŏŏ əl), *n.* a name to be given to Christ (Matt. 1:23) as the son of a virgin (Isa. 7:14). Also, **Emmanuel**. [t. Heb.: m. '*Immānū′ēl*, lit., God with us]

im·ma·te·ri·al (ĭm′ə tĭr′ĭ əl), *adj.* 1. of no essential consequence; unimportant. 2. not material; incorporeal; spiritual. [t. ML: s. *immātēriālis*, f. LL: *im-* IM-² + *māteriālis* MATERIAL; r. ME *immaterielle*, t. F] —**im′ma·te′ri·al·ly**, *adv.* —**im′ma·te′ri·al·ness**, *n.*

im·ma·te·ri·al·ism (ĭm′ə tĭr′ĭ əl ĭz′əm), *n.* 1. the doctrine that there is no material world, but that all things exist only in and for minds. Cf. **idealism** (def. 5). 2. the doctrine that only immaterial substances or spiritual beings exist (opposed to *materialism*). —**im′ma·te′ri·al·ist**, *n.*

im·ma·te·ri·al·i·ty (ĭm′ə tĭr′ĭ ăl′ə tĭ), *n.*, *pl.* **-ties.** 1. state or character of being immaterial. 2. something immaterial.

im·ma·te·ri·al·ize (ĭm′ə tĭr′ĭ əl īz′), *v.t.*, **-ized, -izing.** to make immaterial.

im·ma·ture (ĭm′ə tyŏŏr′, -tŏŏr′), *adj.* 1. not mature, ripe, developed, or perfected. 2. *Phys. Geog.* youthful. 3. *Archaic.* premature. [t. L: m.s. *immātūrus* unripe] —**im′ma·ture′ly**, *adv.* —**im′ma·tu′ri·ty**, **im′ma·ture′ness**, *n.*

im·meas·ur·a·ble (ĭ mĕzh′ər ə bəl), *adj.* incapable of being measured; limitless. —**im·meas′ur·a·bil′i·ty**, **im·meas′ur·a·ble·ness**, *n.* —**im·meas′ur·a·bly**, *adv.*

im·me·di·a·cy (ĭ mē′dĭ ə sĭ), *n.* 1. the character of being immediate. 2. *Philos.* **a.** direct presence; spontaneous existence, not mediated by anything, not represented and not inferred. **b.** the direct content of the mind as distinguished from representation or cognition.

im·me·di·ate (ĭ mē′dĭ ĭt), *adj.* 1. occurring or accomplished without delay; instant: *an immediate reply.* 2. pertaining to the present time or moment: *our immediate plans.* 3. having no time intervening; present or next adjacent: *the immediate future.* 4. having no object or space intervening; nearest or next: *in the immediate vicinity.* 5. without intervening medium or agent; direct: *an immediate cause.* 6. having a direct bearing: *immediate consideration.* 7. *Metaphys.* indemonstrable; intuitive. [t. ML: m.s. *immediātus* not mediate] —**me′di·ate·ness**, *n.* —**Syn.** 5. See **direct**.

im·me·di·ate·ly (ĭ mē′dĭ ĭt lĭ), *adv.* 1. without lapse of time, or without delay; instantly; at once. 2. without intervening medium or agent; concerning or affecting directly. 3. with no object or space intervening. 4. closely: *immediately in the vicinity.* —*conj.* 5. *Chiefly Brit.* immediately that; the moment that; as soon as. —**Syn.** 1. IMMEDIATELY, DIRECTLY, INSTANTLY, PRESENTLY, were originally close synonyms denoting complete absence of delay or of any lapse of time. INSTANTLY is the only one retaining the meaning of action or occurrence on the instant: *he replied instantly to the accusation;* it is never used with the future tense (which must suggest a slight delay). IMMEDIATELY may have the same force: *he immediately got up;* more often, a slight delay: *the game will begin immediately.* DIRECTLY and PRESENTLY, now archaic or dialectal have weakened greatly in meaning and at present imply an appreciable lapse of time, so that they are equivalent to *soon*, or *in a little while: You go ahead; we'll be there presently (directly).* The expressions which have supplanted them are *right away* (which, in its turn, is also weakening) and *at once* (which is still usually equivalent to immediately): *he will come right away, I want to see him at once.*

im·med·i·ca·ble (ĭ mĕd′ə bəl), *adj.* incurable.

Im·mel·mann turn (ĭm′əl män′, -mən), a maneuver in which an airplane makes a half loop, then resumes its normal level position by making a half-roll: used to gain altitude while changing to the opposite direction.

im·me·mo·ri·al (ĭm′ə mōr′ĭ əl), *adj.* extending back beyond memory, record, or knowledge: *from time immemorial.* [t. ML: s. *immemoriālis*, f. L: *im-* IM-² + *memoriālis* MEMORIAL] —**im′me·mo′ri·al·ly**, *adv.*

im·mense (ĭ mĕns′), *adv.* 1. vast; huge; very great: *an immense territory.* 2. immeasurable; boundless. 3. *Slang.* very good or fine. [t. L: m.s. *immensus* boundless, unmeasured] —**im·mense′ly**, *adv.* —**im·mense′ness**, *n.* —**Syn.** 1. See **huge**.

im·men·si·ty (ĭ mĕn′sə tĭ), *n.*, *pl.* **-ties.** 1. vastness; hugeness; enormous extent: *the immensity of the Roman empire.* 2. state of being immense; boundless extent; infinity. 3. a vast expanse; an immense quantity.

im·men·su·ra·ble (ĭ mĕn′shŏŏ rə bəl, -sə rə-), *adj.* immeasurable. [t. LL: m.s. *immensurābilis*]

im·merge (ĭ mûrj′), *v.*, **-merged, -merging.** —*v.t.* 1. to immerse. —*v.i.* 2. to plunge, as into a fluid. 3. to disappear as by plunging. [t. L: m.s. *immergere*] —**im·mer′gence**, *n.*

im·merse (ĭ mûrs′), *v.t.*, **-mersed, -mersing.** 1. to plunge into or place under a liquid; dip; sink. 2. to bap-

tize by immersion. 3. to embed; bury. 4. to involve deeply; absorb. [t. L: m.s. *immersus*, pp., dipped] —**Syn.** 1. See **dip**.

im·mersed (ĭ mûrst′), *adj.* 1. plunged or sunk in or as in a liquid. 2. *Biol.* somewhat or wholly sunk in the surrounding parts, as an organ. 3. baptized.

im·mer·sion (ĭ mûr′shən), *n.* 1. act of immersing. 2. state of being immersed. 3. baptism by plunging the whole person into water. 4. state of being deeply engaged; absorption. 5. *Astron.* the disappearance of a celestial body by passing either behind another or into its shadow. Cf. **emersion**.

im·mer·sion·ism (ĭ mûr′shə nĭz′əm), *n.* 1. the doctrine that immersion is essential to Christian baptism. 2. the practice of baptism by immersion. —**im·mer′sion·ist**, *n.*

im·mesh (ĭ mĕsh′), *v.t.* enmesh.

im·me·thod·i·cal (ĭm′mə thŏd′ə kəl), *adj.* not methodical; without method. —**im′me·thod′i·cal·ly**, *adv.*

im·mi·grant (ĭm′ə grənt), *n.* 1. one who or that which immigrates. 2. a person who migrates into a country for permanent residence. —*adj.* 3. immigrating.

im·mi·grate (ĭm′ə grāt′), *v.*, **-grated, -grating.** —*v.i.* 1. to pass or come into a new habitat or place of residence. 2. to come into a country of which one is not a native for the purpose of permanent residence. —*v.t.* 3. to introduce as settlers. [t. L: m.s. *immigrātus*, pp.] —**im′mi·gra′tor**, *n.* —**Syn.** 1. See **migrate**.

im·mi·gra·tion (ĭm′ə grā′shən), *n.* 1. act of immigrating. 2. immigrants.

im·mi·nence (ĭm′ə nəns), *n.* 1. state or fact of being imminent or impending: *imminence of war.* 2. that which is imminent; impending evil or danger.

im·mi·nent (ĭm′ə nənt), *adj.* 1. likely to occur at any moment; impending: *war is imminent.* 2. projecting or leaning forward; overhanging. [t. L: s. *imminens*, ppr., projecting over] —**im′mi·nent·ly**, *adv.* —**Syn.** 1. IMMINENT, IMPENDING, THREATENING apply to that which menaces or portends misfortune or disaster. IMMINENT is applied usually to danger or evil that hangs, as it were, over one's head, ready to fall at any moment: *because of recent heavy rains, a flood was imminent.* IMPENDING is similarly used, but with less suggestion of immediateness: *a reform has been impending for some time.* THREATENING is applied loosely to that which indicates coming evil, or conveys some ominous or unfavorable suggestion: *threatening weather, sky, a threatening frown.* —**Ant.** 1. distant, remote.

im·min·gle (ĭ mĭng′gəl), *v.t.*, *v.i.*, **-gled, -gling.** to mingle in; intermingle.

im·mis·ci·ble (ĭ mĭs′ə bəl), *adj.* not miscible; incapable of being mixed. —**im·mis′ci·bil′i·ty**, *n.* —**im·mis′ci·bly**, *adv.*

im·mit·i·ga·ble (ĭ mĭt′əgə bəl), *adj.* not mitigable; not to be mitigated. [t. LL: m.s. *immītigābilis*] —**im·mit′i·ga·bil′i·ty**, *n.* —**im·mit′i·ga·bly**, *adv.*

im·mix (ĭ mĭks′), *v.t.* to mix in; mingle. [back formation from ME *immixt*, pp. (t. L: s. *immixtus*, pp., intermingled), appar. taken as pp. of E formation]

im·mix·ture (ĭ mĭks′chər), *n.* 1. act of inmixing. 2. state of being inmixed; involvement.

im·mo·bile (ĭ mō′bĭl, -bēl), *adj.* 1. not mobile; immovable. 2. that does not move; motionless. [t. L: m.s. *immōbilis*; r. ME *inmobill*, f. IN-³ + MOBIL(E)]

im·mo·bil·i·ty (ĭm′ō bĭl′ə tĭ), *n.* the character or condition of being immobile or irremovable.

im·mo·bi·lize (ĭ mō′bə līz′), *v.t.*, **-lized, -lizing.** 1. to make immobile; fix so as to be or become immovable. 2. *Finance.* to establish a monetary reserve by withdrawing (specie) from circulation; create fixed capital in place of (circulating capital). 3. to deprive of the capacity for mobilization. Also, *esp. Brit.*, **im·mo′bi·lise′.** —**im·mo′bi·li·za′tion**, *n.*

im·mod·er·ate (ĭ mŏd′ərĭt), *adj.* 1. not moderate; exceeding just or reasonable limits; excessive; extreme. 2. *Obs.* intemperate. 3. *Obs.* without bounds. [t. L: m.s. *immoderātus* without measure] —**im·mod′er·ate·ly**, *adv.* —**im·mod′er·ate·ness**, *n.* —**Syn.** 1. exorbitant, unreasonable; inordinate; extravagant.

im·mod·er·a·tion (ĭ mŏd′ə rā′shən), *n.* lack of moderation.

im·mod·est (ĭ mŏd′ĭst), *adj.* 1. not modest in conduct, utterance, etc.; indecent; shameless. 2. not modest in assertion or pretension; forward; impudent. —**im·mod′est·ly**, *adv.* —**im·mod′es·ty**, *n.*

im·mo·late (ĭm′ə lāt′), *v.t.*, **-lated, -lating.** 1. to sacrifice. 2. to kill as a sacrificial victim; offer in sacrifice. [t. L: m.s. *immolātus*, pp., sacrificed, orig. sprinkled with sacrificial meal] —**im′mo·la′tor**, *n.*

im·mo·la·tion (ĭm′ə lā′shən), *n.* 1. act of immolating. 2. state of being immolated. 3. a sacrifice.

im·mor·al (ĭ môr′əl, ĭ mŏr′-), *adj.* not moral; not conforming to the moral law. —**im·mor′al·ly**, *adv.* —**Syn.** IMMORAL, ABANDONED, DEPRAVED describe one who makes no attempt to curb self-indulgence. IMMORAL (the weakest of these words), referring to conduct, applies to one who does not obey or conform to standards of morality, but is licentious and perhaps dissipated. ABANDONED, referring to condition, applies to one hopelessly, and usually passively, sunk in wickedness and unrestrained appetites. DEPRAVED, referring to character, applies to one who voluntarily seeks evil and viciousness.

im·mo·ral·i·ty (ĭm′ə răl′ə tĭ), *n.*, *pl.* **-ties.** 1. immoral quality, character, or conduct; wickedness; vice. 2. sexual impurity; unchastity. 3. an immoral act.

im·mor·tal (ĭ môr'təl), *adj.* **1.** not mortal; not liable or subject to death; undying. **2.** remembered or celebrated through all time. **3.** not liable to perish or decay; imperishable; everlasting. **4.** perpetual, lasting, or constant: *an immortal enemy.* **5.** pertaining to immortal beings or immortality. —*n.* **6.** an immortal being. **7.** a person, esp. an author, of enduring fame. **8.** (*usually pl.*) one of the gods of classical mythology. [ME, t. L: s. *immortālis* undying] —**im·mor'tal·ly**, *adv.*

im·mor·tal·i·ty (ĭm'ôr tăl'ə tĭ), *n.* **1.** immortal condition or quality; unending life. **2.** enduring fame.

im·mor·tal·ize (ĭ môr'tə līz'), *v.t.*, **-ized, -izing. 1.** to make immortal; endow with immortality. **2.** to bestow unending fame upon; perpetuate. Also, *esp. Brit.*, **im·mor'tal·ise'.** —**im·mor·tal·i·za·tion**, *n.* —**im·mor'tal·iz'er**, *n.*

im·mor·telle (ĭm'ôr tĕl'), *n.* an everlasting (plant or flower) esp. *Xeranthemum annuum.* [t. F, prop. fem. of *immortel*, t. L: m.s. *immortālis* IMMORTAL]

im·mo·tile (ĭ mō'təl), *adj.* not motile.

im·mov·a·ble (ĭ mōō'və bəl), *adj.* **1.** incapable of being moved; fixed; stationary. **2.** not moving; motionless. **3.** not subject to change; unalterable. **4.** incapable of being affected with feeling; emotionless: *an immovable heart or face.* **5.** incapable of being moved from one's purpose, opinion, etc.; steadfast; unyielding. **6.** not changing from one date to another in different years: *an immovable feast.* **7.** *Law.* **a.** not liable to be removed, or permanent in place. **b.** (of property) real, as distinguished from personal. —*n.* **8.** something immovable. **9.** (*pl.*) *Law.* lands and the appurtenances thereof, as trees, buildings, etc. —**im·mov'a·bil'i·ty, im·mov'a·ble·ness,** *n.* —**im·mov'a·bly,** *adv.*

im·mune (ĭ mūn'), *adj.* **1.** protected from a disease or the like, as by inoculation. **2.** exempt. —*n.* **3.** one who is immune. [ME, t. L: m.s. *immūnis* exempt]

im·mu·ni·ty (ĭ mū'nə tĭ), *n., pl.* **-ties. 1.** state of being immune from or insusceptible to a particular disease or the like. **2.** exemption from any natural or usual liability. **3.** exemption from obligation, service, duty, or liability to taxation, jurisdiction, etc. **4.** special privilege. **5.** *Eccles.* **a.** the exemption of ecclesiastical persons and things from secular or civil liabilities, duties, and burdens. **b.** a particular exemption of this kind. [ME, t. L: m.s. *immūnitas* exemption, ML *sanctuary*] —**Syn. 1.** See **exemption.**

im·mu·nize (ĭm'yə nīz', ĭ mū'nīz), *v.t.,* **-nized, -nizing.** to make immune. —**im'mu·ni·za'tion,** *n.*

immunol., immunology.

im·mu·nol·o·gy (ĭm'yə nŏl'ə jĭ), *n.* that branch of medical science which deals with immunity from disease and the production of such immunity. —**im·mu·no·log·ic** (ĭ mū'nə lŏj'ĭk), **im·mu·no·log'i·cal,** *adj.* —**im'mu·nol'o·gist,** *n.*

im·mu·no·re·ac·tion (ĭ mū'nō rĭ ăk'shən), *n. Immunol.* an antigen-antibody reaction.

im·mure (ĭ myŏŏr'), *v.t.,* **-mured, -muring. 1.** to enclose within walls. **2.** to shut in; confine. **3.** to imprison. **4.** to build into or entomb in a wall. **5.** *Obs.* to surround with walls; fortify. [t. ML: m.s. *immurāre,* der. L *im-* IM-[1] + *murus* wall] —**im·mure'ment,** *n.*

im·mu·si·cal (ĭ mū'zə kəl), *adj.* unmusical.

im·mu·ta·ble (ĭ mū'tə bəl), *adj.* not mutable; unchangeable; unalterable; changeless. —**im·mu'ta·bil'i·ty, im·mu'ta·ble·ness,** *n.* —**im·mu'ta·bly,** *adv.*

imp (ĭmp), *n.* **1.** a little devil or demon; an evil spirit. **2.** a mischievous child. **3.** *Archaic.* a scion or offshoot. **4.** *Archaic.* an offspring. —*v.t.* **5.** *Falconry.* **a.** to graft (feathers) into a wing. **b.** to furnish (a wing, etc.) with feathers as to make good losses or deficiencies and improve powers of flight. **6.** to add a piece to; mend or repair. [ME and OE *impe* a shoot, a graft]

Imp., 1. (L *Imperator*) Emperor. **2.** (L *Imperatrix*) Empress.

imp., 1. imperative. **2.** imperfect. **3.** imperial. **4.** impersonal. **5.** import. **6.** importer. **7.** imprimatur.

im·pact (n. ĭm'păkt; v. ĭm păkt'), *n.* **1.** the striking of one body against another. **2.** an impinging: *the impact of light on the eye.* **3.** an impacting; forcible impinging: *the tremendous impact of the shot.* [n. use of v.] —*v.t.* **4.** to drive or press closely or firmly into something; pack in. [t. L: s. *impactus*, pp., driven in]

im·pact·ed (ĭm păk'tĭd), *adj.* **1.** wedged in. **2.** *Dentistry.* denoting a tooth incapable of growing out or erupting and remaining within the jawbone. **3.** driven together; tightly packed.

im·pac·tion (ĭm păk'shən), *n.* **1.** act of impacting. **2.** state of being impacted; close fixation. **3.** *Dentistry.* a tooth which has not erupted that is embedded in the jawbone.

im·pair (ĭm pâr'), *v.t., v.i.* **1.** to make or become worse; diminish in value, excellence, etc.; weaken. —*n.* **2.** *Archaic.* impairment. [ME *empeire(n)*, t. OF: m. *empeirer*, ult. der. L *in-* IN-[1] + *pējor* worse] —**im·pair'er,** *n.* —**im·pair'ment,** *n.* —**Syn. 1.** See **injure.**

im·pale (ĭm pāl'), *v.t.,* **-paled, -paling. 1.** to fix upon a sharpened stake or the like. **2.** to pierce with a sharpened stake thrust up through the body, as for torture or punishment. **3.** to fix upon, or pierce through with, anything pointed. **4.** to make helpless as if pierced through. **5.** to enclose with or as with pales or stakes; fence in; hem in. Also, **empale.** [t. ML: m.s. *impālāre,* der. L *im-* IM-[1] + *pālus* stake] —**im·pale'ment,** *n.*

im·pal·pa·ble (ĭm păl'pə bəl), *adj.* **1.** not palpable; incapable of being perceived by the sense of touch; intangible. **2.** incapable of being readily grasped by the mind: *impalpable distinctions.* **3.** (of powder) so fine that when rubbed between the fingers no grit is felt. —**im·pal'pa·bil'i·ty,** *n.* —**im·pal'pa·bly,** *adv.*

im·pa·na·tion (ĭm'pə nā'shən), *n. Theol.* the doctrine that the body and blood of Christ are in the bread and wine after consecration. [t. ML: s. *impānātio,* der. *impānāre* embody in bread, der. L *im-* IM-[1] + *pānis* bread

im·pan·el (ĭm păn'əl), *v.t.,* **-eled, -eling** or (*esp. Brit.*) **-elled, -elling. 1.** to enter on a panel or list for jury duty. **2.** to select (a jury) from the panel. **3.** to make a list of. Also, **empanel.** —**im·pan'el·ment,** *n.*

im·par·a·dise (ĭm păr'ə dīs'), *v.t.,* **-dised, -dising.** to put in or as in paradise; make supremely happy.

im·par·i·ty (ĭm păr'ə tĭ), *n., pl.* **-ties.** lack of parity or equality; disparity; an inequality.

im·park (ĭm pärk'), *v.t.* **1.** to shut up as in a park. **2.** to enclose as a park. [t. AF: m.s. *enparker.* See IM-[1], PARK] —**im·par·ka'tion,** *n.*

im·part (ĭm pärt'), *v.t.* **1.** to make known, tell, or relate: *to impart a secret.* **2.** to give, bestow, or communicate. **3.** to grant a part or share of. —*v.i.* **4.** *Archaic.* to grant a part or share; give. [ME, t. L: m. *impartīre* share] —**im'par·ta'tion, im·part'ment,** *n.* —**im·part'er,** *n.* —**Syn. 1.** See **communicate.**

im·par·tial (ĭm pär'shəl), *adj.* not partial; unbiased; just. —**im·par·ti·al·i·ty** (ĭm'pär shĭ ăl'ə tĭ), **im·par'tial·ness,** *n.* —**im·par'tial·ly,** *adv.* —**Syn.** See **fair**[1].

im·part·i·ble (ĭm pär'tə bəl), *adj.* not partible; indivisible. [t. LL: m.s. *impartibilis*] —**im·part'i·bil'i·ty,** *n.* —**im·part'i·bly,** *adv.*

im·pass·a·ble (ĭm păs'ə bəl, -päs'-), *adj.* not passable; that cannot be passed over, through, or along: *muddy, impassable roads.* —**im·pass'a·bil'i·ty, im·pass'a·ble·ness,** *n.* —**im·pass'a·bly,** *adv.*

im·passe (ĭm păs', ĭm'păs; *Fr.* ăn päs'), *n.* **1.** a position from which there is no escape. **2.** a road or way that has no outlet. [t. F]

im·pas·si·ble (ĭm păs'ə bəl), *adj.* **1.** incapable of suffering pain. **2.** incapable of suffering harm. **3.** incapable of emotion; impassive. [t. LL: m.s. *impassibilis.* See IM-[2], PASSIBLE] —**im·pas'si·bil'i·ty, im·pas'si·ble·ness,** *n.* —**im·pas'si·bly,** *adv.*

im·pas·sion (ĭm păsh'ən), *v.t.* to fill, or affect strongly, with passion. [t. It.: s. *impassionare,* der. *im-* IM-[1] + *passione* PASSION]

im·pas·sion·ate (ĭm păsh'ən ĭt), *adj. Now Rare.* free from passion; dispassionate. [t. It.: m. *impassionato,* pp., der. *im-* IM-[2] + *passione* PASSION]

im·pas·sioned (ĭm păsh'ənd), *adj.* filled with passion; passionate; ardent. —**im·pas'sioned·ly,** *adv.* —**im·pas'sioned·ness,** *n.*

im·pas·sive (ĭm păs'ĭv), *adj.* **1.** without emotion; apathetic; unmoved. **2.** calm; serene. **3.** unconscious. **4.** not subject to suffering. —**im·pas'sive·ly,** *adv.* —**im·pas'sive·ness, im·pas·siv·i·ty** (ĭm'pă sĭv'ə tĭ), *n.*

im·paste (ĭm pāst'), *v.t.,* **-pasted, -pasting. 1.** to cover with or enclose in a paste. **2.** to form into a paste. **3.** to lay on thickly, as paste. [t. It.: m.s. *impastare,* der. *im-* IM-[1] + *pasta* (g. LL *pasta* PASTE)] —**im·pas·ta'tion** (ĭm'păs tā'shən), *n.*

im·pas·to (ĭm päs'tō, -päs'-), *n. Painting.* **1.** the laying on of colors thickly. **2.** color so laid on. [t. It., der. *impastare.* See IMPASTE]

im·pa·tience (ĭm pā'shəns), *n.* **1.** lack of patience. **2.** eager desire for relief or change; restlessness. **3.** intolerance of anything that thwarts or hinders.

im·pa·ti·ens (ĭm pā'shĭ ĕnz'), *n.* any of a genus, *Impatiens,* of annual balsaminaceous plants having irregular flowers, in which the calyx and corolla are not clearly distinguishable. [NL, n. use of L ppr. See IMPATIENT]

im·pa·tient (ĭm pā'shənt), *adj.* **1.** not patient; not bearing pain, opposition, etc., with composure. **2.** indicating lack of patience: *an impatient answer.* **3.** intolerant (fol. by *of*): *impatient of any interruptions.* **4.** restless in desire or expectation; eagerly desirous (to do something). [ME *impacient,* t. L: m.s. *impatiens* not bearing or enduring] —**im·pa'tient·ly,** *adv.*

im·pav·id (ĭm păv'ĭd), *adj.* fearless. [t. L: s. *impavidus*] —**im·pav'id·ly,** *adv.*

im·pawn (ĭm pôn'), *v.t.* to put in pawn; pledge.

im·peach (ĭm pēch'), *v.t.* **1.** to accuse (a public official) before a competent tribunal of misconduct in office. **2.** to challenge the credibility of: *to impeach a witness.* **3.** to bring an accusation against. **4.** to call in question; cast an imputation upon: *to impeach one's motives.* **5.** to call to account. —*n.* **6.** *Obs.* impeachment. [ME *impeche(n),* t. OF: m. *empechier* hinder, g. LL *impedicāre* catch, entangle, der. L *in-* IN-[2] + *pedica* fetter] —**im·peach'er,** *n.*

im·peach·a·ble (ĭm pē'chə bəl), *adj.* **1.** liable to be impeached. **2.** making one liable to impeachment, as an offense. —**im·peach'a·bil'i·ty,** *n.*

im·peach·ment (ĭm pēch'mənt), *n.* **1.** the impeaching of a public official before a competent tribunal. **2.** (in Congress or a State legislature) the presentation of formal charges against a public official by the lower house, trial to be before the upper house. **3.** the demonstration that a witness is less worthy of belief. **4.** act of impeaching. **5.** state of being impeached.

ăct, āble, dâre, ärt; ĕbb, ēqual; ĭf, īce; hŏt, ōver, ôrder, oil, bŏŏk, ōōze, out; ŭp, ūse, ûrge; ə = a in alone; ch, chief; g, give; ng, ring; sh, shoe; th, thin; ŧħ, that; zh, vision. See the full key on inside cover.

im·pearl (Ĭm pûrl′), *v.t.* **1.** to form into pearllike drops. **2.** to make pearllike or pearly. **3.** *Poetic.* to adorn with pearls or pearllike drops.

im·pec·ca·ble (Ĭm pĕk′ə bəl), *adj.* **1.** faultless or irreproachable: *impeccable manners.* **2.** not liable to sin; exempt from the possibility of doing wrong. —*n.* **3.** an impeccable person. [t. LL: m.s. *impeccābilis,* Cf. PECCABLE] —**im·pec′ca·bil′i·ty,** *n.* —**im·pec′ca·bly,** *adv.*

im·pec·cant (Ĭm pĕk′ənt), *adj.* not sinning; sinless. —**im·pec′can·cy,** *n.*

im·pe·cu·ni·ous (Ĭm′pə kū′nĭ əs), *adj.* having no money; penniless; poor. —**im′pe·cu′ni·ous·ly,** *adv.* —**im′pe·cu′ni·ous·ness, im·pe·cu·ni·os·i·ty** (Ĭm′pə kū′nĭ ŏs′ə tĭ), *n.* —**Syn.** See poor.

im·ped·ance (Ĭm pē′dəns), *n.* **1.** *Elect.* the apparent resistance, or total opposition to current of an alternating-current circuit, consisting of two components, reactance and true or ohmic resistance. **2.** *Physics.* the ratio of pressure to particle velocity at a given point in a sound wave. [f. IMPEDE + -ANCE]

im·pede (Ĭm pēd′), *v.t.,* **-ped·ed, -ped·ing.** to retard in movement or progress by means of obstacles or hindrances; obstruct; hinder. [t. L: m.s. *impedīre* entangle, hamper (orig., as to the feet)] —**im·ped′er,** *n.* —**im·ped′ing·ly,** *adv.* —**Syn.** See prevent.

im·pe·di·ent (Ĭm pē′dĭ ənt), *adj.* **1.** impeding. —*n.* **2.** that which impedes. [t. L: s. *impediens,* ppr.]

im·ped·i·ment (Ĭm pĕd′ə mənt), *n.* **1.** some physical defect, esp. a speech disorder: *an impediment in speech.* **2.** obstruction or hindrance; obstacle. **3.** (*usually pl.*) impedimenta. **4.** *Law.* (esp. *Eccles.*) **a.** a bar, usually of blood or affinity, to marriage: *a diriment impediment.* **b.** a restraint on marriage, preventing a completely lawful union: *a minor impediment.* [ME, t. L: s. *impedimentum* hindrance] —**im·ped′i·men′tal, im·ped′i·men·ta·ry** (Ĭm pĕd′ə mĕn′tə rĭ), *adj.* —**Syn. 2.** See obstacle.

im·ped·i·men·ta (Ĭm pĕd′ə mĕn′tə), *n.pl.* **1.** supplies carried with an army. **2.** *Law.* impediments. [t. L]

im·ped·i·tive (Ĭm pĕd′ə tĭv), *adj.* tending to impede.

im·pel (Ĭm pĕl′), *v.t.,* **-pelled, -pel·ling. 1.** to drive or urge forward; press on; incite or constrain to action in any way. **2.** to drive, or cause to move, onward; propel; impart motion to. [t. L: m.s. *impellere*] —**im·pel′ler,** *n.* —**Syn. 1.** See compel.

im·pel·lent (Ĭm pĕl′ənt), *adj.* **1.** impelling. —*n.* **2.** an impelling agency or force.

im·pend (Ĭm pĕnd′), *v.i.* **1.** to be imminent; be near at hand. **2.** to hang or be suspended; overhang (fol. by *over*). [t. L: s. *impendēre* hang over]

im·pend·ent (Ĭm pĕn′dənt), *adj.* impending. —**im·pend′ence, im·pend′en·cy,** *n.*

im·pend·ing (Ĭm pĕn′dĭng), *adj.* **1.** about to happen; imminent. **2.** overhanging. —**Syn. 1.** See imminent.

im·pen·e·tra·bil·i·ty (Ĭm pĕn′ə trə bĭl′ə tĭ, Ĭm′pĕn-), *n.* **1.** impenetrable quality. **2.** *Physics.* that property of matter in virtue of which two bodies cannot occupy the same space simultaneously.

im·pen·e·tra·ble (Ĭm pĕn′ə trə bəl), *adj.* **1.** not penetrable; that cannot be penetrated, pierced, or entered. **2.** inaccessible to ideas, influences, etc. **3.** incapable of being comprehended; unfathomable: *an impenetrable mystery.* **4.** *Physics.* excluding all other bodies from the space occupied. —**im·pen′e·tra·ble·ness,** *n.* —**im·pen′e·tra·bly,** *adv.*

im·pen·i·tent (Ĭm pĕn′ə tənt), *adj.* not penitent; obdurate. —**im·pen′i·tence, im·pen′i·ten·cy, im·pen′i·tent·ness,** *n.* —**im·pen′i·tent·ly,** *adv.*

im·pen·nate (Ĭm pĕn′āt), *adj.* featherless or wingless.

imper., imperative.

im·per·a·tive (Ĭm pĕr′ə tĭv), *adj.* **1.** not to be avoided or evaded: *an imperative duty.* **2.** of the nature of or expressing a command; commanding. **3.** *Gram.* designating or pertaining to the verb mode specialized for use in command, requests, and the like, or a verb inflected for this mode, as *listen! go! run!* etc. —*n.* **4.** a command. **5.** *Gram.* **a.** the imperative mode. **b.** a verb therein. [t. L: m.s. *imperātīvus* of a command] —**im·per·a·ti·val** (Ĭm pĕr′ə tī′vəl), *adj.* —**im·per′a·tive·ly,** *adv.* —**im·per′a·tive·ness,** *n.*

im·pe·ra·tor (Ĭm′pə rā′tər), *n.* **1.** an absolute or supreme ruler. **2.** a title of the Roman emperors. **3.** a temporary title accorded a victorious Roman general. [t. L. Cf. EMPEROR] —**im·per·a·to·ri·al** (Ĭm pĕr′ə tōr′ĭ əl), *adj.* —**im·per′a·to′ri·al·ly,** *adv.*

im·per·cep·ti·ble (Ĭm′pər sĕp′tə bəl), *adj.* **1.** very slight, gradual, or subtle: *imperceptible gradations.* **2.** not perceptible; not affecting the perceptive faculties. —**im′per·cep′ti·bil′i·ty, im′per·cep′ti·ble·ness,** *n.* —**im′per·cep′ti·bly,** *adv.*

im·per·cep·tion (Ĭm′pər sĕp′shən), *n.* lack of perception.

im·per·cep·tive (Ĭm′pər sĕp′tĭv), *adj.* not perceptive; lacking perception. —**im·per·cep·tiv·i·ty** (Ĭm′pər sĕp tĭv′ə tĭ), **im′per·cep′tive·ness,** *n.*

imperf., imperfect.

im·per·fect (Ĭm pûr′fĭkt), *adj.* **1.** characterized by or subject to defects. **2.** not perfect; lacking completeness: *imperfect vision.* **3.** *Bot.* (of a flower) lacking certain parts; esp., diclinous. **4.** *Gram.* **a.** denoting action or state still in process at some temporal point of reference, particularly in the past. **b.** In English, action in process is expressed in six tense forms of the verb called

the progressive tenses: present progressive, *he is carrying;* past progressive, *he was carrying;* past perfect progressive, *he had been carrying.* **5.** *Law.* without legal effect or support; unenforceable. **6.** *Music.* noting the consonances of third and sixth. Cf. **perfect** (def. 12 a). —*n.* **7.** *Gram.* **a.** the imperfect tense. **b.** another verb formation or construction with imperfect meaning. **c.** a form therein. For example: Latin *portabam,* "I was carrying" or English *was doing* in *he was doing it when I came.* [t. L: s. *imperfectus* unfinished; r. ME *imparfit,* t. F: m. *imparfait*] —**im·per′fect·ly,** *adv.* —**im·per′fect·ness,** *n.*

—**Syn. 2.** IMPERFECT, RUDIMENTARY, UNDEVELOPED mean not complete or fully developed. That which is IMPERFECT is not complete or is defective in some respect; it may have met with some mishap while it was still developing: *an imperfect specimen of butterfly, knowledge of a subject.* That which is RUDIMENTARY is still in an early stage of development or in an embryonic stage; or it may be a vestige of something the development of which has been arrested: *rudimentary buds, the rudimentary facts, rudimentary organs.* That which is UNDEVELOPED is not fully grown, or not grown to normal size or extent: *an undeveloped adolescent, an undeveloped talent.* —**Ant. 1.** complete, perfect, developed.

im·per·fec·tion (Ĭm′pər fĕk′shən), *n.* **1.** an imperfect detail: *a law full of imperfections.* **2.** the character or condition of being imperfect.

im·per·fec·tive (Ĭm′pər fĕk′tĭv), *adj.* **1.** *Gram.* denoting an aspect of the verb, as in Russian, which indicates incompleteness of the action or state at a temporal point of reference. —*n.* **2.** *Gram.* **a.** the imperfective aspect. **b.** a verb therein.

im·per·fo·rate (Ĭm pûr′fə rĭt, -rāt′), *adj.* **1.** Also, **im·per′fo·rat′ed.** not perforate; having no perforation. **2.** *Philately.* having no perforations or cuts to separate the individual stamps readily. —*n.* **3.** an imperforate stamp. —**im·per′fo·ra′tion,** *n.*

im·pe·ri·al (Ĭm pĭr′ĭ əl), *adj.* **1.** of or pertaining to an empire. **2.** of or pertaining to an emperor or empress. **3.** characterizing the rule or authority of a sovereign state over its dependencies. **4.** of the nature or rank of an emperor or supreme ruler. **5.** of a commanding quality, manner, or aspect. **6.** domineering; imperious. **7.** befitting an emperor or empress; very fine or grand; magnificent. **8.** of special size or quality, as various products, commodities, etc. **9.** (of weights and measures) conforming to the standards legally established in Great Britan. —*n.* **10.** *Chiefly Brit.* a small part of the beard left growing beneath the under lip. **11.** a size of paper, 23 x 31 inches in America, 22 x 30 inches in England. **12.** a Russian gold coin originally worth 10 rubles, and from 1897–1917 worth 15 rubles. **13.** the top of a carriage, esp. of a diligence. **14.** a case for luggage carried there. **15.** a member of an imperial party or of imperial troops. **16.** an emperor or empress. **17.** any of various articles of special size or quality. [ME, t. L: s. *imperiālis* of the empire or emperor] —**im·pe′ri·al·ly,** *adv.* —**im·pe′ri·al·ness,** *n.*

im·pe·ri·al·ism (Ĭm pĭr′ĭ ə lĭz′əm), *n.* **1.** the policy of extending the rule or authority of an empire or nation over foreign countries, or of acquiring and holding colonies and dependencies. **2.** advocacy of imperial interests. **3.** (in British use) the policy of so uniting the separate parts of an empire with separate governments as to secure for certain purposes a single state. **4.** imperial government. **5.** an imperial system of government. —**im·pe′ri·al·ist,** *n., adj.* —**im·pe′ri·al·is′tic,** *adj.* —**im·pe′ri·al·is′ti·cal·ly,** *adv.*

Imperial Valley, an irrigated agricultural region in SE California and adjacent Mexico: formerly a part of the Colorado Desert, it is largely below sea level and contains the Salton Sink.

im·per·il (Ĭm pĕr′əl), *v.t.,* **-iled, -iling** or (*esp. Brit.*) **-illed, -illing.** to put in peril; endanger. —**im·per′il·ment,** *n.*

im·pe·ri·ous (Ĭm pĭr′ĭ əs), *adj.* **1.** domineering, dictatorial, or overbearing: *an imperious tyrant, imperious temper.* **2.** urgent; imperative: *imperious need.* [t. L: m.s. *imperiōsus* commanding] —**im·pe′ri·ous·ly,** *adv.* —**im·pe′ri·ous·ness,** *n.*

im·per·ish·a·ble (Ĭm pĕr′ĭsh ə bəl), *adj.* not perishable; indestructible; enduring. —**im·per′ish·a·bil′i·ty, im·per′ish·a·ble·ness,** *n.* —**im·per′ish·a·bly,** *adv.*

im·pe·ri·um (Ĭm pĭr′ĭ əm), *n., pl.* **-peria** (-pĭr′ĭ ə). **1.** command; supreme power. **2.** *Law.* the right to command the force of the state in order to enforce the law. [t. L. Cf. EMPIRE]

im·per·ma·nent (Ĭm pûr′mə nənt), *adj.* not permanent. —**im·per′ma·nence, im·per′ma·nen·cy,** *n.*

im·per·me·a·ble (Ĭm pûr′mĭ ə bəl), *adj.* **1.** not permeable; impassable. **2.** (of substances) not permitting the passage of a fluid through the pores, interstices, etc. —**im·per′me·a·bil′i·ty, im·per′me·a·ble·ness,** *n.* —**im·per′me·a·bly,** *adv.*

impers., impersonal.

im·per·son·al (Ĭm pûr′sən əl), *adj.* **1.** not personal; without personal reference or connection: *an impersonal remark.* **2.** having no personality: *an impersonal deity.* **3.** *Gram.* **a.** (of a verb) having only third person singular forms, rarely if ever accompanied by an expressed subject, as Latin *pluit* (it's raining), or accompanied regularly by an empty subject word, as English *it's raining.* **b.** (of a pronoun) indefinite, as French *on* (one). —*n.* **4.** *Gram.* an impersonal verb or pronoun. —**im·per′son·al′i·ty,** *n.* —**im·per′son·al·ly,** *adv.*

im·per·son·ate (Ĭm·pûr'sə·nāt'), v., -ated, -ating, adj. —v.t. 1. to assume the character of; pretend to be. 2. to represent in personal or bodily form; personify; typify. 3. to personate, esp. on the stage. —adj. 4. embodied in a person; invested with personality. —im·per'son·a'·tion, n. —im·per'son·a'tor, n.

im·per·ti·nence (Ĭm·pûr'tə·nəns), n. 1. unmannerly intrusion or presumption; insolence. 2. impertinent quality or action; irrelevance. 3. inappropriateness or incongruity. 4. triviality or absurdity. 5. something impertinent.

im·per·ti·nen·cy (Ĭm·pûr'tə·nən·sĭ), n., pl. -cies. impertinence.

im·per·ti·nent (Ĭm·pûr'tə·nənt), adj. 1. intrusive or presumptuous, as persons or their actions: an impertinent boy. 2. not pertinent or relevant; irrelevant: any impertinent detail. 3. inappropriate or incongruous. 4. trivial, silly, or absurd. [ME, t. LL: s. impertinens not belonging] —im·per'ti·nent·ly, adv.
—Syn. 1. IMPERTINENT, IMPUDENT, INSOLENT refer to bold, rude, and arrogant behavior. IMPERTINENT, from its primary meaning of not pertinent and hence inappropriate or out of place, has come to imply often an unseemly intrusion into what does not concern one, or a presumptuous rudeness toward one entitled to deference or respect: an impertinent interruption, question, manner toward a teacher. IMPUDENT suggests a bold and shameless impertinence: an impudent speech, young rascal. INSOLENT suggests insulting or arrogantly contemptuous behavior: unbearably insolent toward those in authority. —Ant. 1. polite, civil, deferential.

im·per·turb·a·ble (Ĭm'pər·tûr'bə·bəl), adj. incapable of being perturbed or agitated; not easily excited; calm: imperturbable composure. —im'per·turb'a·bil'i·ty, im'per·turb'a·ble·ness, n. —im'per·turb'a·bly, adv.

im·per·tur·ba·tion (Ĭm'pər·tər·bā'shən), n. freedom from perturbation; tranquillity; calmness.

im·per·vi·ous (Ĭm·pûr'vĭ·əs), adj. 1. not pervious; impermeable: impervious to water. 2. impenetrable: impervious to reason. Also, **im·per'vi·a·ble.** —im·per'vi·ous·ly, adv. —im·per'vi·ous·ness, n.

im·pe·ti·go (Ĭm'pə·tī'gō), n. Pathol. a contagious skin disease, esp. of children, marked by a superficial pustular eruption, particularly on the face. [t. L, der. impetere attack] —im·pe·tig·i·nous (Ĭm'pə·tĭj'ə·nəs), adj.

im·pe·trate (Ĭm'pə·trāt'), v.t., -trated, -trating. 1. to obtain by entreaty. 2. to entreat, or ask urgently for. [t. L: m.s. impetrātus, pp., obtained by request] —im'·pe·tra'tion, n. —im'pe·tra'tive, adj. —im'pe·tra'tor, n.

im·pet·u·os·i·ty (Ĭm·pĕch'ŏŏ·ŏs'ə·tĭ, Ĭm'pĕch-), n., pl. -ties. 1. impetuous quality. 2. an impetuous action.

im·pet·u·ous (Ĭm·pĕch'ŏŏ·əs), adj. 1. acting with or characterized by sudden or rash energy: an impetuous girl. 2. having great impetus; moving with great force; violent: the impetuous winds. [ME, t. LL: m.s. impetuōsus, der. L impetus an attack] —im·pet'u·ous·ly, adv. —im·pet'u·ous·ness, n.
—Syn. 1. IMPETUOUS, IMPULSIVE both refer to persons who are hasty and precipitate in action, or to actions not preceded by thought. IMPETUOUS suggests eagerness, violence, rashness: impetuous vivacity, impetuous desire, impetuous words. IMPULSIVE emphasizes spontaneity and lack of reflection: an impulsive act of generosity. —Ant. 1. cautious, deliberate.

im·pe·tus (Ĭm'pə·təs), n. 1. moving force; impulse; stimulus: a fresh impetus. 2. the force with which a moving body tends to maintain its velocity and overcome resistance; energy of motion. [t. L: onset, attack]

impf., imperfect.

im·pi (Ĭm'pĭ), n., pl. -pies. a band of Kaffir warriors. [Zulu]

im·pi·e·ty (Ĭm·pī'ə·tĭ), n., pl. -ties. 1. lack of piety; lack of reverence for God; ungodliness. 2. lack of dutifulness or respect. 3. an impious act, practice, etc.

im·pinge (Ĭm·pĭnj'), v.i., -pinged, -pinging. 1. to strike or dash; collide (fol. by on, upon, or against): rays of light impinging on the eye. 2. to encroach or infringe (fol. by on or upon). 3. Obs. to come into violent contact with. [t. L: m.s. impingere drive in or at, strike against] —im·pinge'ment, n.

im·pi·ous (Ĭm'pĭ·əs), adj. 1. not pious; lacking reverence for God; ungodly. 2. Rare. not reverent toward parents. [t. L: m. impius] —im'pi·ous·ly, adv. —im'·pi·ous·ness, n.

imp·ish (Ĭmp'ĭsh), adj. of or like an imp; mischievous. —imp'ish·ly, adv. —imp'ish·ness, n.

im·pla·ca·ble (Ĭm·plā'kə·bəl, -plăk'ə-), adj. not placable; not to be appeased or pacified; inexorable: an implacable enemy. —im·pla'ca·bil'i·ty, im·pla'ca·ble·ness, n. —im·pla'ca·bly, adv. —Syn. See inflexible.

im·pla·cen·tal (Ĭm'plə·sĕn'təl), adj. Zool. having no placenta, as a monotreme or marsupial.

im·plant (v. Ĭm·plănt', -plänt'; n. Ĭm'plănt', -plänt'), v.t. 1. to instill or inculcate: implant sound principles. 2. to plant in something; infix: implant living tissue. 3. to plant: implant the seeds. —n. 4. Med. **a.** tissue implanted into the body by grafting. **b.** a small tube containing a radioactive substance, as radium, surgically implanted in tissue for the treatment of tumors, cancer, etc. [f. IM-¹ + PLANT, v.] —im·plant'er, n.

im·plan·ta·tion (Ĭm'plăn·tā'shən), n. 1. act of implanting. 2. state of being implanted. 3. Pathol. **a.** the movement of cells to a new region. **b.** metastasis, when spontaneous. 4. Med. the application of solid medicine underneath the skin.

im·plau·si·ble (Ĭm·plô'zə·bəl), adj. not plausible; not having the appearance of truth or credibility. —im·plau'si·bly, adv.

im·plead (Ĭm·plēd'), v.t. 1. to sue in a court of justice. 2. to accuse; impeach. 3. Rare. to plead (a suit, etc.). [ME emplede(n), t. AF: m. empleder, var. of OF emplaidier, f. em- IM-¹ + plaidier PLEAD]

im·ple·ment (n. Ĭm'plə·mənt; v. -mĕnt'), n. 1. an instrument, tool, or utensil: agricultural implements. 2. an article of equipment or outfit, as household furniture or utensils, ecclesiastical vessels or vestments, etc. 3. a means; agent. —v.t. 4. to provide with implements. 5. to execute, as a piece of work. 6. to satisfy, as requirements or conditions. 7. to fill out or supplement. [late ME, t. LL: s. implementum a filling up (hence, prob., a thing that completes a want), der. L implēre fill up] —im'ple·men'tal, adj. —Syn. 1. See tool.

im·ple·tion (Ĭm·plē'shən), n. 1. act of filling. 2. state of being filled. 3. that which fills up; a filling. [t. LL: s. implētio, der. L implēre fill up]

im·pli·cate (Ĭm'plə·kāt'), v.t., -cated, -cating. 1. to involve as being concerned in a matter, affair, condition, etc.: to be implicated in a crime. 2. to imply as a necessary circumstance, or as something to be inferred or understood. 3. to fold or twist together; intertwine; interlace: implicated leaves. [t. L: m.s. implicātus, pp., entangled, involved] —Syn. 1. See involve.

im·pli·ca·tion (Ĭm'plə·kā'shən), n. 1. act of implying. 2. state of being implied. 3. something implied or suggested as naturally to be inferred without being expressly stated. 4. Logic. the relation which holds between two propositions (or classes of propositions) in virtue of which one is logically deducible from the other. 5. act of involving. 6. state of being involved in some matter: implication in a conspiracy. 7. act of intertwining or entangling. 8. the resulting condition.

im·pli·ca·tive (Ĭm'plə·kā'tĭv), adj. tending to implicate or imply; characterized by or involving implication. —im'pli·ca'tive·ly, adv.

im·plic·it (Ĭm·plĭs'ĭt), adj. 1. (of belief, confidence, obedience, etc.) unquestioning, unreserved, or absolute. 2. implied, rather than expressly stated: an implicit consent. 3. virtually contained (fol. by in). 4. Obs. entangled. [t. L: s. implicitus, var. of implicātus, pp., entangled, involved] —im·plic'it·ly, adv. —im·plic'it·ness, n.

im·plied (Ĭm·plīd'), adj. involved, indicated, or suggested by implying; tacitly understood: an implied rebuke.

im·pli·ed·ly (Ĭm·plī'ĭd·lĭ), adv. by implication.

im·plode (Ĭm·plōd'), v., -ploded, -ploding. —v.i. 1. to burst inward (opposed to explode). —v.t. 2. Phonet. to pronounce by implosion. [f. IM-¹ + -plode, modeled on EXPLODE]

im·plore (Ĭm·plōr'), v., -plored, -ploring. —v.t. 1. to call upon in urgent or piteous supplication, as for aid or mercy; beseech; entreat: they implored him to go. 2. to make urgent supplication for (aid, mercy, pardon, etc.): implore forgiveness. —v.i. 3. to make urgent or piteous supplication. [t. L: m.s. implōrāre invoke with tears] —im'plo·ra'tion, n. —im·plor·a·to·ry (Ĭm·plōr'ə·tōr'ĭ), adj. —im·plor'er, n. —im·plor'ing·ly, adv. —im·plor'ing·ness, n. —Syn. 2. crave, beg. —Ant. 2. spurn, reject.

im·plo·sion (Ĭm·plō'zhən), n. 1. a bursting inward (opposed to explosion). 2. Phonet. (of stops) **a.** a beginning marked by abrupt interruption of the breath stream, as for p, t, k. **b.** an ending marked by abrupt intake of air. [f. IM-¹ + -plosion, modeled on EXPLOSION]

im·plo·sive (Ĭm·plō'sĭv), Phonet. —adj. 1. characterized by a partial vacuum behind the point of closure. —n. 2. an implosive stop.

im·ply (Ĭm·plī'), v.t., -plied, -plying. 1. to involve as a necessary circumstance: speech implies a speaker. 2. (of words) to signify or mean. 3. to indicate or suggest, as something naturally to be inferred, without express statement. 4. Obs. to enfold. [ME implie(n), t. OF: m. emplier, g. L implicāre enfold, entangle, involve]

im·pol·i·cy (Ĭm·pŏl'ə·sĭ), n. bad policy; inexpediency.

im·po·lite (Ĭm'pə·līt'), adj. not polite or courteous; uncivil; rude. —im'po·lite'ly, adv. —im'po·lite'·ness, n. —Syn. discourteous, disrespectful; insolent.

im·pol·i·tic (Ĭm·pŏl'ə·tĭk), adj. inexpedient; injudicious. —im·pol'i·tic·ly, adv. —im·pol'i·tic·ness, n.

im·pon·der·a·ble (Ĭm·pŏn'dər·ə·bəl), adj. 1. not ponderable; that cannot be weighed. —n. 2. an imponderable thing, force, or agency. —im·pon'der·a·bil'i·ty, im·pon'der·a·ble·ness, n. —im·pon'der·a·bly, adv.

im·port (v. Ĭm·pōrt'; n. Ĭm'pōrt'), v.t. 1. to bring in from a foreign country, as merchandise or commodities, for sale, use, processing, or reëxport. 2. to bring or introduce from one use, connection, or relation into another. 3. to convey as a meaning or implication, as words, statements, actions, etc., do; to make known or express. 4. to be of consequence or importance to; concern. 5. to be incumbent on; be the duty of. —v.i. 6. to be of consequence or importance; matter. —n. 7. that which is imported from abroad; an imported commodity or article. 8. act of importing or bringing in; importation, as of goods from abroad. 9. meaning; implication; purport. 10. consequence or importance: matters of great import. [ME, t. L: s. importāre bring in,

bring about] —im·port′a·ble, adj. —im·port′a-
bil′i·ty, n. —im·port′er, n.

im·por·tance (ĭm pôr′təns), n. 1. the quality or fact
of being important. 2. important position or standing;
personal or social consequence. 3. consequential air or
manner. 4. Obs. an important matter. 5. Obs. im-
portunity. 6. Obs. import or meaning.
—Syn. 1. IMPORTANCE, CONSEQUENCE refer to a quality,
character, or standing such as to entitle to attention or
consideration. IMPORTANCE, referring originally to the
bringing or involving of noteworthy results, is the general
term. CONSEQUENCE, though of the same general sense, is
a weaker word, less suggestive of seriousness, dignity, or
extensiveness: fair weather is a matter of consequence to the
tourist, but of real importance to the farmer.

im·por·tant (ĭm pôr′tənt), adj. 1. of much significance
or consequence: an important event. 2. mattering much
(fol. by to): details important to a fair decision. 3. of
more than ordinary title to consideration or notice: an
important example. 4. prominent: an important part.
5. of considerable influence or authority, as a person,
position, etc. 6. of social consequence or distinction,
as a person, family, etc. 7. pompous. 8. Obs. importunate. [t. F, t. ML: s. importans, ppr., of importāre be
of consequence, L bring in, cause] —im·por′tant·ly, adv.

im·por·ta·tion (ĭm′pôr tā′shən), n. 1. the bringing
in of merchandise from foreign countries, for sale, use,
processing, or reëxport. 2. something imported.

im·por·tu·na·cy (ĭm pôr′chə nə sĭ), n. quality of being importunate.

im·por·tu·nate (ĭm pôr′chə nĭt), adj. 1. urgent or
persistent in solicitation. 2. pertinacious, as solicitations or demands. 3. troublesome. —im·por′tu-
nate·ly, adv. —im·por′tu·nate·ness, n.

im·por·tune (ĭm′pôr tūn′, -tōōn′, ĭm pôr′chən), v.,
-tuned, -tuning, adj. —v.t. 1. to beset with solicitations; beg urgently or persistently. 2. to beg for (something) urgently or persistently. 3. Obs. to annoy.
4. Obs. to press; impel. —v.i. 5. to make urgent or
persistent solicitations. —adj. 6. Rare. importunate.
[ME, t. MF: m. importun, t. L: s. importūnus unfit, inconvenient, troublesome] —im′por·tune′ly, adv.
—im′por·tun′er, n.

im·por·tu·ni·ty (ĭm′pôr tū′nə tĭ, -tōō′-), n., pl. -ties.
1. state of being importunate; persistence in solicitation. 2. (pl.) importunate solicitations or demands.

im·pose (ĭm pōz′), v., -posed, -posing. —v.t. 1. to lay
on or set as something to be borne, endured, obeyed, ful-
filled, etc.: to impose taxes. 2. to put or set by, or as by,
authority: to impose an arbitrary meaning upon words.
3. to obtrude or thrust (oneself, one's company, etc.)
upon others. 4. to pass or palm off fraudulently or deceptively. 5. to lay on (the hands) ceremonially, as in
confirmation or ordination. 6. Print. to lay (type
pages, etc.) in proper order on an imposing stone or the
like and secure in a chase for printing. 7. to subject
to some penalty, etc. 8. Archaic. to put or place on
something, or in a particular place. —v.i. 9. to make
an impression on the mind; to impose one's or its authority or influence. 10. to obtrude oneself or one's requirements, as upon others. 11. to presume, as upon
patience, good nature, etc. 12. (of something fraudulent) to produce a false impression or act with a delusive
effect (fol. by upon or on). [t. F: m.s. imposer, f. im-
IM-¹ + poser put (see POSE²)] —im·pos′a·ble, adj.
—im·pos′er, n.

im·pos·ing (ĭm pō′zĭng), adj. making an impression
on the mind, as by great size, stately appearance,
etc. —im·pos′ing·ly, adv. —im·pos′ing·ness, n.

imposing stone, Print. a slab resting upon a frame,
on which pages of type or plates are imposed and on
which type correcting in the page is done. Also, imposing table.

im·po·si·tion (ĭm′pə zĭsh′ən), n. 1. the laying on of
something as a burden, obligation, etc. 2. something
imposed, as a burden, etc; an unusual or extraordinarily
burdensome requirement or task. 3. act of imposing by
or as by authority. 4. an imposing upon a person as by
taking undue advantage of his good nature, or something
that has the effect of doing this. 5. act of imposing
fraudulently or deceptively on others; imposture.
6. the ceremonial laying on of hands, as in confirmation.
7. Print. the arrangement of pages in proper order in a
chase for printing. 8. Rare. act of putting, placing, or
laying on.

im·pos·si·bil·i·ty (ĭm pŏs′ə bĭl′ə tĭ, ĭm′pŏs-), n., pl.
-ties. 1. the quality of being impossible. 2. something
impossible.

im·pos·si·ble (ĭm pŏs′ə bəl), adj. 1. not possible; that
cannot be, exist, or happen. 2. that cannot be done or
effected. 3. that cannot be true, as a rumor. 4. not to
be done, endured, etc., with any degree of reason or
propriety: an impossible situation. 5. utterly impracticable. 6. hopelessly unsuitable, undesirable, or objectionable: an impossible person. [ME, t. L: m.s. im-
possibilis] —im·pos′si·bly, adv.

im·post¹ (ĭm′pōst), n. 1. a tax, tribute, or duty. 2. a
customs duty. 3. Racing. the weight (including that of
the jockey) assigned to a horse in a race. —v.t. 4. to determine customs duties on, according to the kind of imports. [t. ML: s. impostus a tax, L impositus laid on]

im·post² (ĭm′pōst), n. Archit. 1. the point where an
arch rests on a wall or column. See diag. under arch.
2. the condition of such resting or meeting. [t. F: m.

imposte, t. It.: m. imposta architectural impost, der.
impostare set upon, der. L. positus, pp., placed]

im·pos·tor (ĭm pŏs′tər), n. 1. one who imposes fraudulently upon others. 2. one who practices deception under an assumed character or name. [t. LL, der. L impōnere impose] —Syn. 1. pretender, deceiver, cheat.

im·pos·tume (ĭm pŏs′chōōm, -tūm), n. Now Rare. an
abscess. Also, im·pos′thume. [ME empostume, t. OF,
var. of apostume, t. LL: m. apostūma, var. of apostēma,
t. Gk.: lit., separation (of pus)]

im·pos·ture (ĭm pŏs′chər), n. 1. the action or practice of imposing fraudulently upon others. 2. deception
practiced under an assumed character or name, as by an
impostor. 3. an instance or piece of fraudulent imposition. [t. LL: m.s. impostūra, der. L impōnere impose]
—im·pos′tur·ous, adj.

im·po·sure (ĭm pō′zhər), n. imposition.

im·po·tence (ĭm′pə təns), n. 1. the condition or quality of being impotent; weakness. 2. complete failure of
sexual power, esp. in the male. 3. Obs. lack of self-
restraint. Also, im′po·ten·cy.

im·po·tent (ĭm′pə tənt), adj. 1. not potent; lacking
power or ability. 2. utterly unable (to do something).
3. without force or effectiveness. 4. lacking bodily
strength, or physically helpless, as an aged person or a
cripple. 5. wholly lacking in sexual power. 6. Obs.
without restraint. —im′po·tent·ly, adv.

im·pound (ĭm pound′), v.t. 1. to shut up in a pound,
as a stray animal. 2. to confine within an enclosure or
within limits: water impounded in a reservoir. 3. to
seize, take, or appropriate summarily. 4. to seize and
retain in custody of the law, as a document for evidence.
—im·pound·age (ĭm poun′dĭj), n. —im·pound′er, n.

im·pov·er·ish (ĭm pŏv′ər ĭsh, -pŏv′rĭsh), v.t. 1. to reduce to poverty: a country impoverished by war. 2. to
make poor in quality, productiveness, etc.; exhaust the
strength or richness of: to impoverish the soil. Also, em-
poverish. [ME empoveris(en), t. OF: m. empoveriss-, s.
empoverir, der. em- EM-¹ + povre POOR] —im·pov′er-
ish·er, n. —im·pov′er·ish·ment, n.

im·pov·er·ished (ĭm pŏv′ər ĭsht, -pŏv′rĭsht), adj. reduced to poverty. —Syn. See poor.

im·prac·ti·ca·ble (ĭm prăk′tə kə bəl), adj. 1. not
practicable; that cannot be put into practice with the
available means: an impracticable plan. 2. unsuitable
for practical use or purposes, as a device, material, etc.
3. (of ground, places, etc.) impassable. 4. (of persons,
etc.) hard to deal with because of stubbornness, stupidity, etc. —im·prac′ti·ca·bil′i·ty, im·prac′ti·ca-
ble·ness, n. —im·prac′ti·ca·bly, adv.

im·prac·ti·cal (ĭm prăk′tə kəl), adj. not practical.

im·pre·cate (ĭm′prə kāt′), v.t., -cated, -cating. to
call down or invoke (esp. evil or curses), as upon a person. [t. L: m.s. imprecātus, pp., having invoked]
—im′pre·ca′tor, n. —im·pre·ca·to·ry (ĭm′prə kə-
tōr′ĭ), adj.

im·pre·ca·tion (ĭm′prə kā′shən), n. 1. the act of im-
precating; cursing. 2. a curse or malediction.

im·preg·na·ble¹ (ĭm prĕg′nə bəl), adj. 1. strong
enough to resist attack; not to be taken by force: an
impregnable fort. 2. not to be overcome or overthrown:
an impregnable argument. [ME imprenable, t. F: f. im-
IM-¹ + prenable PREGNABLE] —im·preg′na·bil′i·ty, n.
—im·preg′na·bly, adv. —Syn. 1. See invincible.

im·preg·na·ble² (ĭm prĕg′nə bəl), adj. susceptible of
impregnation, as an egg. [f. IMPREGN(ATE) + -ABLE]

im·preg·nate (v. ĭm prĕg′nāt; adj. ĭm prĕg′nĭt, -nāt),
v., -nated, -nating, adj. —v.t. Also, Obs. or Poetic, im-
pregn (ĭm prēn′). 1. to make pregnant; get with child
or young. 2. to fertilize. 3. to charge with something
infused or permeating throughout; saturate. 4. to fill
interstices with a substance. 5. to furnish with some
actuating or modifying element infused or introduced;
imbue, infect, or tincture. —adj. 6. impregnated. [t.
LL: m. s. impraegnātus, pp., made pregnant] —im′-
preg·na′tion, n. —im·preg′na·tor, n.

im·pre·sa (ĭm prā′zə; It. ēm prĕ′zä), n. Obs. except
Hist. 1. a device or emblem. 2. a motto. Also, im-
prese (ĭm prēz′). [t. It.: impresa]

im·pre·sa·ri·o (ĭm′prə sär′ĭ ō′; It. ēm′prĕ sä′ryō), n.,
pl. -sarios, It. -sari (-sä′rē). 1. the organizer or
manager of an opera or concert company. 2. a personal
manager, teacher, or trainer of concert artists. [t. It., der.
impresa enterprise] —im·pre·sa·ri·o·ship, n.

im·pre·scrip·ti·ble (ĭm′prĭ skrĭp′tə bəl), adj. Law.
not subject to prescription. —im·pre·scrip′ti·bly, adv.

im·press¹ (v. ĭm prĕs′; n. ĭm′prĕs), v., -pressed or
(Archaic) -prest; -pressing; n. —v.t. 1. to affect
deeply or strongly in mind or feelings; influence in
opinion. 2. to fix deeply or firmly on the mind or
memory, as ideas, facts, etc. 3. to urge, as something
to be remembered or done. 4. to press (a thing) into
or on something. 5. to produce (a mark, figure, etc.) by
pressure; stamp; imprint. 6. to apply with pressure, so
as to leave a mark. 7. to subject to, or mark by, pressure with something. 8. to furnish with a mark, figure,
etc., by or as by stamping. 9. Elect. to produce (a
voltage), or cause (a voltage) to appear or be produced on
a conductor, circuit, etc. —n. 10. act of impressing.
11. a mark made by or as by pressure; stamp; imprint.
12. a distinctive character or effect imparted. [ME im-
presse(n), t. L: m.s. impressus, pp., pressed upon]
—im·press′er, n.

b., blend of, blended; c., cognate with; d., dialect, dialectal; der., derived from; f., formed from; g., going back to;
m., modification of; r., replacing; s., stem of; t., taken from; ?, perhaps. See the full key on inside cover.

im·press[2] (v. Ĭm prĕs′; n. Ĭm′prĕs), v., **-pressed** or (*Archaic*) **-prest; -pressing;** n. —v.t. **1.** to press or force into public service, as seamen. **2.** to seize or take for public use. —n. **3.** impressment. [f. IM-[1] + PRESS[2]]

im·press·i·ble (Ĭm prĕs′ə bəl), adj. capable of being impressed; impressionable. —**im·press′i·bil′i·ty,** n.

im·pres·sion (Ĭm prĕsh′ən), n. **1.** a strong effect produced on the intellect, feelings, or conscience. **2.** the first and immediate effect upon the mind in outward or inward perception; sensation. **3.** the effect produced by an agency or influence. **4.** a notion, remembrance, or belief, often one that is vague or indistinct. **5.** a mark, indentation, figure, etc., produced by pressure. **6.** *Print., etc.* **a.** the process or result of printing from type, plates, etc. **b.** a printed copy from type, a plate, an engraved block, etc. **c.** one of a number of printings made at different times from the same set of type, without alteration (as distinguished from an *edition*). **d.** the total number of copies of a book, etc., printed at one time from the one setting of type. **7.** *Dentistry.* a mold taken in plastic materials or plaster of Paris of teeth and the surrounding tissues. **8.** an image in the mind caused by something external to it. **9.** act of impressing. **10.** state of being impressed. [ME, t. L: s. *impressio.* See IMPRESS[1]]

im·pres·sion·a·ble (Ĭm prĕsh′ən ə bəl, -prĕsh′nə-), adj. **1.** easily impressed or influenced; susceptible. **2.** capable of being impressed. —**im·pres′sion·a·bil′i·ty, im·pres′sion·a·ble·ness,** n.

im·pres·sion·ism (Ĭm prĕsh′ə nĬz′əm), n. **1.** a way of painting (developed 1865–75) with informal subject matter and effects of light noted directly as they impress the artist, and developed as a method of expressing luminosity with juxtaposed touches of pure color. **2.** a theory and practice in literature which emphasizes immediate aspects of objects or actions without attention to details. **3.** a late 19th and early 20th century method of musical composition, marked by the use of unorthodox means to express impressions or emotions (as in the work of Debussy). —**im·pres′sion·ist,** n., adj. —**im·pres′sion·is′tic,** adj.

im·pres·sive (Ĭm prĕs′Ĭv), adj. such as to impress the mind; arousing solemn feelings: *an impressive ceremony.* —**im·pres′sive·ly,** adv. —**im·pres′sive·ness,** n.

im·press·ment (Ĭm prĕs′mənt), n. the impressing of men, property, etc., as for public service or use. [f. IMPRESS[2] + -MENT]

im·pres·sure (Ĭm prĕsh′ər), n. *Archaic.* impression.

im·prest[1] (Ĭm′prĕst), n. **1.** an advance of money, esp. for some public business. **2.** *Brit.* (formerly) an advance payment made to a soldier or sailor at enlistment. [f. IM-[1] + prest (t. OF: s. *prester* lend, g. L. *praestāre* stand for). Cf. It. *imprestare* lend]

im·prest[2] (Ĭm prĕst′), v. *Archaic.* pt. and pp. of impress.

im·pri·ma·tur (Ĭm′prĭ mā′tər, -prī-), n. **1.** an official license to print or publish a book, etc. **2.** license; sanction; approval. [NL: let it be printed]

im·pri·mis (Ĭm prī′mĭs), adv. *Latin.* in the first place.

im·print (n. Ĭm′prĭnt; v. Ĭm prĭnt′), n. **1.** a mark made by pressure; a figure impressed or printed on something. **2.** any impression or impressed effect. **3.** *Bibliog.* information printed at the foot of the title page of a book indicating the name of the publisher, usually supplemented with the place and date of publication. **4.** the printer's name and address as indicated on any printed matter. —v.t. **5.** to impress (a quality, character, or distinguishing mark). **6.** to produce (a mark, etc.) on something by pressure. **7.** to bestow (a kiss). **8.** to fix firmly on the mind, memory, etc. **9.** to make an imprint upon. [ME *empreynte(n),* t. OF: m. *empreinter,* der. *empreinte* a stamp, ult. der. L *imprimere* impress, imprint] —**im·print′er,** n.

im·pris·on (Ĭm prĬz′ən), v.t. **1.** to put into or confine in a prison; detain in custody. **2.** to shut up as if in a prison; hold in restraint. —**im·pris′on·ment,** n.

im·prob·a·bil·i·ty (Ĭm prŏb′ə bĬl′ə tĬ, Ĭm′prŏb-), n., pl. **-ties. 1.** the quality or fact of being improbable; unlikelihood. **2.** something improbable or unlikely.

im·prob·a·ble (Ĭm prŏb′ə bəl), adj. not probable; unlikely to be true or to happen. —**im·prob′a·bly,** adv.

im·pro·bi·ty (Ĭm prō′bə tĬ, -prŏb′ə tĬ), n. the reverse of probity; dishonesty; wickedness. [ME *improbite,* t. L: m.s. *improbitas* wickedness]

im·promp·tu (Ĭm prŏmp′tū, -tōō), adj. **1.** made or done without previous preparation: *an impromptu address.* **2.** suddenly or hastily prepared, made, etc.: *an impromptu dinner.* **3.** improvised, or having the character of an improvisation, as music. —adv. **4.** without preparation: *verses written impromptu.* —n. **5.** something impromptu; an impromptu speech, musical composition, performance, etc. [t. L: m. *in promptū* in readiness] —**Syn. 1.** See extemporaneous.

im·prop·er (Ĭm prŏp′ər), adj. **1.** not proper; not strictly belonging, applicable, or right: *an improper use for a thing.* **2.** not in accordance with propriety of behavior, manners, etc.: *improper conduct.* **3.** unsuitable or inappropriate, as for the purpose or occasion: *improper tools.* **4.** abnormal or irregular. —**im·prop′er·ly,** adv. —**im·prop′er·ness,** n.
—**Syn. 1-3.** IMPROPER, INDECENT, UNBECOMING, UNSEEMLY are applied to that which is unfitting or not in accordance with propriety. IMPROPER has a wide range, being applied to whatever is not suitable or fitting, and often specifically to what does not conform to the standards of conventional morality: *improper diet, improper behavior in church, improper language.* INDECENT, a strong word, is applied to what is offensively contrary to standards of propriety and esp. of modesty: *indecent behavior, literature.* UNBECOMING is applied to what is especially unfitting in the person concerned: *conduct unbecoming a minister.* UNSEEMLY is applied to whatever is unfitting or improper under the circumstances: *unseemly mirth.* —**Ant. 1.** fitting. **2.** modest. **3.** suitable.

improper fraction, a fraction having the numerator greater than the denominator.

im·pro·pri·ate (adj. Ĭm prō′prĬ Ĭt, -āt′; v. Ĭm prō′prĬ āt′), adj., v., **-ated, -ating.** —adj. **1.** *Brit. Eccles. Law.* devolved into the hands of a layman. **2.** *Obs.* appropriated to private use. —v.t. **3.** *Brit. Eccles. Law.* to place (ecclesiastical property) in lay hands. **4.** *Obs.* to appropriate. [t. ML: m.s. *impropriātus,* pp. of *impropriāre,* der. L *im-* IM-[1] + *proprius* one's own, PROPER] —**im·pro′pri·a′tion,** n.

im·pro·pri·a·tor (Ĭm prō′prĬ ā′tər), n. a layman in possession of church property or revenues.

im·pro·pri·e·ty (Ĭm′prə prī′ə tĬ), n., pl. **-ties. 1.** quality of being improper; incorrectness. **2.** inappropriateness. **3.** unseemliness. **4.** an erroneous or unsuitable expression, act, etc. **5.** an improper use of a word.

im·prove (Ĭm prōōv′), v., **-proved, -proving.** —v.t. **1.** to bring into a more desirable or excellent condition: *to improve one's health.* **2.** to make (land) more profitable or valuable by enclosure, cultivation, etc.; increase the value of (real property) by betterments, as buildings. **3.** to turn to account; make good use of: *to improve an opportunity.* —v.i. **4.** to increase in value, excellence, etc.; become better: *the situation is improving.* **5.** to make improvements (fol. by *on* or *upon*): *to improve on one's earlier work.* [t. AF: m. *emprower,* der. OF *em-* IM-[1] + *prou* profit] —**im·prov′a·ble,** adj. —**im·prov′-a·bil′i·ty, im·prov′a·ble·ness,** n. —**im·prov′a·bly,** adv. —**im·prov′er,** n. —**im·prov′ing·ly,** adv.
—**Syn. 1.** IMPROVE, AMELIORATE, BETTER imply bringing to a more desirable state. IMPROVE usually implies remedying a lack or a felt need: *to improve a process, oneself (gain additional knowledge, etc.).* AMELIORATE, a formal word, implies improving oppressive, unjust, or difficult conditions: *to ameliorate working conditions.* To BETTER is to improve conditions which, though not bad, are unsatisfying: *to better an attempt, oneself (gain a higher salary).* —**Ant. 1.** worsen.

im·prove·ment (Ĭm prōōv′mənt), n. **1.** the act of improving. **2.** the state of being improved. **3.** a change or addition whereby a thing is improved. **4.** some thing or person that represents an advance on another in excellence or achievement. **5.** a bringing into a more valuable or desirable condition, as of land or real property; a making or becoming better; a betterment. **6.** something done or added to real property which increases its value. **7.** profitable use: *the improvement of one's time.*

im·prov·i·dent (Ĭm prŏv′ə dənt), adj. **1.** not provident; lacking foresight; incautious or unwary. **2.** neglecting to provide for future needs. —**im·prov′i·dence,** n. **im·prov′i·dent·ly,** adv. —**Syn. 1.** thoughtless, careless, heedless. **2.** shiftless, thriftless, unthrifty; wasteful, prodigal. —**Ant. 1.** prudent. **2.** economical.

im·pro·vi·sa·tion (Ĭm′prə vĭ zā′shən, Ĭm′prŏv ə-), n. **1.** act of improvising. **2.** something improvised.

im·prov·i·sa·tor (Ĭm prŏv′ə zā′tər, Ĭm′prə vī-), n. one who improvises.

im·pro·vi·sa·to·ry (Ĭm′prə vī′zə tōr′Ĭ, -vĬz′ə-), adj. of or pertaining to an improvisator or improvisation. —**im·prov·i·sa·to·ri·al** (Ĭm prŏv′Ĭ zə tōr′Ĭ əl), adj. —**im·prov′i·sa·to′ri·al·ly,** adv.

im·pro·vise (Ĭm′prə vīz′), v., **-vised, -vising.** —v.t. **1.** to prepare or provide offhand or hastily; extemporize. **2.** to compose (verse, music, etc.) on the spur of the moment. **3.** to recite, sing, etc., extemporaneously. —v.i. **4.** to compose, utter, or execute anything extemporaneously: *he improvised in rhyme.* [t. F: m.s. *improviser,* t. It.: m. *improvvisare,* der. *improvviso* extempore, g. L *imprōvīsus* unforeseen, unexpected] —**im′pro·vis′er,** n.

im·pro·vised (Ĭm′prə vīzd′), adj. made or said without previous preparation. —**Syn.** See extemporaneous.

im·pro·vi·sa·to·re (ēm′prōv vē′zä tô′rĕ), n., pl. **-ri** (-rē). *Italian.* an improvisator.

im·pru·dent (Ĭm prōōd′dənt), adj. not prudent; lacking prudence or discretion. [t. L: s. *imprūdens*] —**im·pru′dence,** n. —**im·pru′dent·ly,** adv.

im·pu·dence (Ĭm′pyə dəns), n. **1.** the quality or fact of being impudent; effrontery; insolence. **2.** impudent conduct or language. **3.** *Obs.* lack of modesty; shamelessness. Also, **im′pu·den·cy.** —**Syn. 1.** impertinence, rudeness; brazenness, face. —**Ant. 1.** courtesy.

im·pu·dent (Ĭm′pyə dənt), adj. **1.** characterized by a shameless boldness, assurance, or effrontery: *impudent behavior.* **2.** *Obs.* shameless or brazenly immodest. [t. L: s. *impudens* shameless] —**im′pu·dent·ly,** adv. —**Syn. 1.** insolent, rude; saucy, pert; brazen. See impertinent. —**Ant. 1.** polite.

im·pu·dic·i·ty (Ĭm′pyōō dĬs′ə tĬ), n. immodesty.

im·pugn (Ĭm pūn′), v.t. **1.** to assail by words or arguments, as statements, motives, veracity, etc.; call in question; challenge as false. **2.** *Rare.* to assail a person for his statements or actions. [ME *impugne(n),* t. OF: m. *impugner,* t. L: m. *impugnāre* attack] —**im·pugn′-a·ble,** adj. —**im·pug·na·tion** (Ĭm′pəg nā′shən), **im·pugn·ment** (Ĭm pūn′mənt), n. —**im·pugn′er,** n.

im·pu·is·sant (ĭm·pū'ə·sənt), *adj.* impotent; feeble; weak. [t. F. See IM-², PUISSANT] —**im·pu'is·sance,** *n.*

im·pulse (ĭm'pŭls). *n.* **1.** the inciting influence of a particular feeling, mental state, etc.: *to act under the impulse of pity.* **2.** sudden, involuntary inclination prompting to action, or a particular instance of it: *to be swayed by impulse.* **3.** an impelling action or force, driving onward or inducing motion. **4.** the effect of an impelling force; motion induced; impetus given. **5.** *Physiol.* a stimulus conveyed by the nervous system, muscle fibers, etc., either exciting or limiting organic functioning. **6.** *Mech.* the product of a force and the time during which it acts (sometimes restricted to cases in which the force is great and the time short, as in the blows of a hammer). **7.** *Elect.* a single, usually sudden, flow of current in one direction. [t. L: m.s. *impulsus* a push against]

im·pul·sion (ĭm·pŭl'shən), *n.* **1.** the act of impelling, driving onward, or pushing. **2.** the resulting state or effect; impulse; impetus. **3.** the inciting influence of some feeling or motive; mental impulse. **4.** constraining or inciting action on the mind or conduct: *divine impulsion.* [ME, t. L: s. *impulsio* influence, instigation]

im·pul·sive (ĭm·pŭl'sĭv), *adj.* **1.** actuated or swayed by emotional or involuntary impulses: *an impulsive child.* **2.** having the power or effect of impelling; characterized by impulsion: *impulsive forces.* **3.** inciting to action: *an impulsive influence on humanity.* **4.** *Mech.* (of forces) acting momentarily; not continuous. —**im·pul'sive·ly,** *adv.* —**im·pul'sive·ness,** *n.* —Syn. **1.** See **impetuous.**

im·pu·ni·ty (ĭm·pū'nə·tĭ), *n.* exemption from punishment. [t. L: m.s *impūnitas* omission of punishment] —Syn. See **exemption.**

im·pure (ĭm·pyŏŏr'), *adj.* **1.** not pure; mixed with extraneous matter, esp. of an inferior or contaminating kind: *impure water.* **2.** modified by admixture, as color. **3.** mixed or combined with something else: *an impure style of architecture.* **4.** ceremonially unclean, as things, animals, etc. **5.** not morally pure; unchaste: *impure language.* **6.** marked by foreign and unsuitable or objectionable elements or characteristics, as a style of art or of literary expression. [t. L: m.s. *impūrus* not pure] —**im·pure'ly,** *adv.* —**im·pure'ness,** *n.*

im·pu·ri·ty (ĭm·pyŏŏr'ə·tĭ), *n., pl.* **-ties. 1.** the quality or state of being impure. **2.** (*often pl.*) that which is or makes impure: *impurities in drinking water.*

im·put·a·ble (ĭm·pū'tə·bəl), *adj.* that may be imputed; attributable. —**im·put'a·bil'i·ty, im·put'a·ble·ness,** *n.* —**im·put'a·bly,** *adv.*

im·pu·ta·tion (ĭm·pyŏŏ·tā'shən), *n.* **1.** the act of imputing. **2.** an attribution, esp. of fault, crime, etc.

im·pute (ĭm·pūt'), *v.t.,* **-puted, -puting. 1.** to attribute something discreditable to a person. **2.** to attribute or ascribe. **3.** *Law.* to charge. **4.** *Theol.* to attribute (righteousness, guilt, etc.) vicariously; ascribe as derived from another. **5.** *Obs.* to charge (a person) with fault. [ME, t. L: m.s. *imputāre* bring into the reckoning] —**im·put·a·tive** (ĭm·pū'tə·tĭv), *adj.* —**im·put'a·tive·ly,** *adv.* —**im·put'a·tive·ness,** *n.* —**im·put'er,** *n.* —Syn. **2.** See **attribute.**

impv., imperative.

in (ĭn), *prep.* **1.** a particle expressing inclusion, situation, presence, existence, action, etc., within limits, as of place, time, circumstances, etc., used to express: **a.** inclusion within space or limits, a whole, material or immaterial surroundings, etc.: *in the city, in the army, dressed in white, in politics.* **b.** inclusion within, or occurrence during the course of or at the expiration of, a period or limit of time: *in ancient times, to do a task in an hour, return in ten minutes.* **c.** situation, condition, occupation, action, manner, relation, means, etc.: *in darkness, in sickness, in service, in crossing the street, in confidence, in French.* **d.** object or purpose: *in honor of the event.* **e.** motion or direction from without to a point within (now usually into), or transition from one state to another: *to put in operation, break in two.* —*adv.* **2.** in or into some place, position, state, relation, etc. **3.** on the inside, or within. **4.** in one's house or office. **5.** in office or power. **6.** in possession or occupancy. **7.** having the turn to play, in a game. —*adj.* **8.** that is or gets in; internal; inward; incoming; inbound. —*n.* **9.** (*pl.*) those who are in, as the political party in power. **10. ins and outs, a.** nooks or recesses; windings and turnings. **b.** intricacies: *to know the ins and outs of a business.* [ME and OE, c. D and G *in,* Icel. ī, Goth. *in;* akin to L *in,* Gk. *en*]

in-¹, a prefix representing English *in,* as in *income, indwelling, inland,* but used also as a verb-formative with transitive, intensive, or sometimes little apparent force, as in *intrust, inweave,* etc. It often assumes the same phases as **in-²,** as **en-, em-,** and **im-³.** [ME and OE; repr. IN, adv.]

in-², a prefix of Latin origin meaning primarily "in," but used also as a verb-formative with the same force as **in-¹,** as in *incarcerate, incantation.* Also **-il¹, im-¹, ir-².** Cf. **em-, en-.** [t. L, repr. *in,* prep. (in F *en*), c. IN, prep.]

in-³, a prefix of Latin origin corresponding to English *un-,* having a negative or privative force, freely used as an English formative, esp. of adjectives and their derivatives and of nouns, as in *inattention, indefensible inexpensive, inorganic, invariable.* This prefix assumes the same phonetic phases as **in-²,** as in *impartial, immeasurable, illiterate, irregular,* etc. In French it became *en-* and thus occurs unfelt in such words as enemy (French *ennemi,* Latin *inimicus,* lit., not friendly). Also, **il-², im-², ir-².** [t. L; akin to Gk. *an-, a-,* A-⁶, and UN-²] —Syn. The prefixes IN- and UN- may both have, among other uses, a negative force IN- is the form from the classical languages (Greek and Latin) and is therefore used in learned words or in words derived from those languages: *inaccessible, inaccuracy, inadequate,* etc. UN- is the native form going back to Old English, used in words of native origin, and sometimes used in combination with words of other origins, if these words are in common use: *unloving, unmanly, unfeeling, unnecessary, unsafe.* Occasionally the prefix UN- is used with a frequently used word in a common meaning, as in *unsanitary* (not clean), and IN- with the same word in a more technical sense, as *insanitary* (likely to cause disease). In England the prefix IN- is more commonly used than in the United States.

-in¹, a suffix used in adjectives of Greek or Latin origin meaning "pertaining to" and (in nouns thence derived) also imitated in English, as in *coffin, cousin, lupin* (*lupine*), etc.; and occurring unfelt in abstract nouns formed as nouns in Latin, as *ruin.* [ME -*in,* -*ine,* t. OF, t. L: m. -*inus,* -*ina,* -*inum,* t. Gk.: m. -*inos,* -*inē,* -*inon*]

-in², a noun suffix used in a special manner in chemical and mineralogical nomenclature, as in *glycerin, acetin,* etc. In spelling usage wavers between -*in* and -*ine.* In chemistry a certain distinction of use is attempted, basic substances having the termination -*ine* rather than -*in,* as *aconitine, aniline,* etc., and -*in* being restricted to certain neutral compounds, glycerides, glucosides, and proteids, as *albumin, palmitin,* etc., but this distinction is not always observed. [t. NL: s. -*ina.* See -INE²]

In, *Chem.* indium.

in., inch; inches.

in·a·bil·i·ty (ĭn'ə·bĭl'ə·tĭ), *n.* lack of ability; lack of power, capacity, or means. —Syn. See **disability.**

in ab·sen·ti·a (ĭn ăb·sĕn'shĭ·ə), *Latin.* in or during (one's) absence.

in·ac·ces·si·ble (ĭn'ăk·sĕs'ə·bəl), *adj.* not accessible; inapproachable. —**in'ac·ces'si·bil'i·ty, in/ac·ces/si·ble·ness,** *n.* —**in'ac·ces'si·bly,** *adv.*

in·ac·cu·ra·cy (ĭn·ăk'yə·rə·sĭ), *n., pl.* **-cies. 1.** the quality of being inaccurate. **2.** that which is inaccurate. —Syn. **2.** error, mistake, blunder, slip.

in·ac·cu·rate (ĭn·ăk'yə·rĭt), *adj.* not accurate. —**in·ac'cu·rate·ly,** *adv.* —**in·ac'cu·rate·ness,** *n.* —Syn. inexact, loose; incorrect, erroneous, wrong, faulty.

In·a·chus (ĭn'ə·kəs), *n.* Gk. Myth. a river god who became the first king of Argos; father of Io.

in·ac·tion (ĭn·ăk'shən), *n.* absence of action; idleness.

in·ac·ti·vate (ĭn·ăk'tə·vāt'), *v.t.,* **-vated, -vating. 1.** to make inactive. **2.** *Immunol.* to stop the activity of (certain biological substances).

in·ac·tive (ĭn·ăk'tĭv), *adj.* **1.** not active; inert. **2.** indolent; sluggish; passive. **3.** *Mil.* not on active duty or status. **4.** *Phys. Chem.* denoting a compound which does not rotate the plane of vibration of polarized light. —**in·ac·ti·va·tion** (ĭn·ăk'tə·vā'shən, ĭn·ăk'-), *n.* —**in·ac'tive·ly,** *adv.* —**in'ac·tiv'i·ty, in·ac'tive·ness,** *n.* —Syn. **1, 2.** INACTIVE, DORMANT, INERT, SLUGGISH, TORPID suggest lack of activity. INACTIVE indicates absence of action, indisposition to activity, or cessation of activity: *an inactive compound, life, file of papers.* DORMANT suggests the quiescence or inactivity of that which sleeps but may be roused to action: *a dormant volcano.* INERT suggests the condition of dead matter, with no inherent power of motion or action; it may also mean unable to move, or heavy and hard to move: *an inert mass, inert from hunger.* SLUGGISH expresses slowness of natural activity or of that which does not move readily or vigorously: *a sluggish stream, brain.* TORPID suggests a state of suspended physical powers, a condition particularly of animals which hibernate: *snakes are torpid in cold weather.* —Ant. **1.** lively.

in·a·dapt·a·ble (ĭn'ə·dăp'tə·bəl), *adj.* not adaptable; incapable of being adapted. —**in'a·dapt'a·bil'i·ty,** *n.*

in·ad·e·quate (ĭn·ăd'ə·kwĭt), *adj.* not adequate. —**in·ad'e·qua·cy, in·ad'e·quate·ness,** *n.* —**in·ad'e·quate·ly,** *adv.* —Syn. inapt, incompetent; insufficient, incommensurate; defective, imperfect, incomplete.

in·ad·mis·si·ble (ĭn'əd·mĭs'ə·bəl), *adj.* not admissible: *inadmissible evidence.* —**in'ad·mis'si·bil'i·ty,** *n.* —**in'ad·mis'si·bly,** *adv.*

in·ad·vert·ence (ĭn'əd·vûr'təns), *n.* **1.** quality of being inadvertent; heedlessness. **2.** an act or effect of inattention; an oversight. [t. ML: m.s. *inadvertentia*]

in·ad·vert·en·cy (ĭn'əd·vûr'tən·sĭ), *n., pl.* **-cies.** inadvertence.

in·ad·vert·ent (ĭn'əd·vûr'tənt), *adj.* **1.** not attentive; heedless. **2.** characterized by lack of attention, as actions, etc. **3.** unintentional: *an inadvertent insult.* —**in'ad·vert'ent·ly,** *adv.*

in·ad·vis·a·ble (ĭn'əd·vī'zə·bəl), *adj.* not advisable; inexpedient. —**in'ad·vis'a·bil'i·ty,** *n.* —**in'ad·vis'a·bly,** *adv.*

-inae, *Zool.* a suffix of the names of subfamilies. [t. L, fem. pl. of adjectives ending in -*inus.* See -INE¹]

in ae·ter·num (ĭn ē·tûr'nəm), *Latin.* forever.

in·al·ien·a·ble (ĭn·āl'yən·ə·bəl), *adj.* not alienable; that cannot be transferred to another: *inalienable rights.* —**in·al'ien·a·bil'i·ty,** *n.* —**in·al'ien·a·bly,** *adv.*

in·al·ter·a·ble (ĭn·ôl'tər·ə·bəl), *adj.* not alterable. —**in·al'ter·a·bil'i·ty,** *n.* —**in·al'ter·a·bly,** *adv.*

in·am·o·ra·ta (ĭn ăm′/ə rä′/tə, ĭn/ăm-), *n.*, *pl.* -tas. a female lover; a woman who loves or is loved. [t. It.: m. *inamorata* sweetheart (fem.), der. *amore* love, g. L *amor*]

in·am·o·ra·to (ĭn ăm′/ə rä′/tō, ĭn/ăm-), *n.* a male lover. [see INAMORATA]

in-and-in (ĭn′/ənd ĭn′/), *adv.* repeatedly within the same family, strain, etc.: *to breed stock in-and-in.*

in·ane (ĭn ān′/), *adj.* **1.** lacking sense or ideas; silly: *inane questions.* **2.** empty; void. —*n.* **3.** that which is inane or void; the void of infinite space. [t. L: m. s. *inānis* empty, vain] —**in·ane′/ly,** *adv.*

in·an·i·mate (ĭn ăn′/ə mĭt), *adj.* **1.** not animate; lifeless. **2.** spiritless; sluggish; dull. —**in·an′/i·mate·ly,** *adv.* —**in·an′/i·mate·ness,** *n.*

in·a·ni·tion (ĭn′/ə nĭsh′/ən), *n.* **1.** exhaustion from lack of nourishment; starvation. **2.** emptiness. [ME, t. LL: s. *inānitio*, der. L *inānīre* make empty]

in·an·i·ty (ĭn ăn′/ə tĭ), *n.*, *pl.* -ties. **1.** lack of sense or ideas; silliness. **2.** an inane remark, etc. **3.** emptiness.

in·ap·peas·a·ble (ĭn′/ə pēz′/zə bəl), *adj.* not appeasable; not to be appeased: *inappeasable anger.*

in·ap·pe·tence (ĭn ăp′/ə təns), *n.* lack of appetence or appetite. Also, **in·ap′/pe·ten·cy.**

in·ap·pli·ca·ble (ĭn ăp′/lə kə bəl), *adj.* not applicable; unsuitable. —**in·ap′/pli·ca·bil′/i·ty, in·ap′/pli·ca·ble·ness,** *n.* —**in·ap′/pli·ca·bly,** *adv.*

in·ap·po·site (ĭn ăp′/ə zĭt), *adj.* not pertinent. —**in·ap′/po·site·ly,** *adv.*

in·ap·pre·ci·a·ble (ĭn′/ə prē′/shĭ ə bəl), *adj.* imperceptible; insignificant: *an inappreciable difference.* —**in′/ap·pre′/ci·a·bly,** *adv.*

in·ap·pre·ci·a·tive (ĭn′/ə prē′/shĭ ā′/tĭv), *adj.* not appreciative; lacking in appreciation. —**in′/ap·pre′/ci·a′/tive·ly,** *adv.* —**in′/ap·pre′/ci·a′/tive·ness,** *n.*

in·ap·pre·hen·si·ble (ĭn′/ăp rĭ hĕn′/sə bəl), *adj.* not to be grasped by the senses or intellect.

in·ap·pre·hen·sion (ĭn′/ăp rĭ hĕn′/shən), *n.* lack of apprehension.

in·ap·pre·hen·sive (ĭn′/ăp rĭ hĕn′/sĭv), *adj.* **1.** not apprehensive (often fol. by *of*). **2.** without apprehension.

in·ap·proach·a·ble (ĭn′/ə prō′/chə bəl), *adj.* **1.** not approachable. **2.** without rival. —**in′/ap·proach′/a·bil′/i·ty,** *n.* —**in′/ap·proach′/a·bly,** *adv.*

in·ap·pro·pri·ate (ĭn′/ə prō′/prĭ ĭt), *adj.* not appropriate. —**in′/ap·pro′/pri·ate·ly,** *adv.* —**in′/ap·pro′/pri·ate·ness,** *n.*

in·apt (ĭn ăpt′/), *adj.* **1.** not apt or fitted. **2.** without aptitude or capacity. —**in·apt′/ly,** *adv.* —**in·apt′/ness,** *n.* —**Syn. 1.** unsuited, unsuitable, inappropriate.

in·apt·i·tude (ĭn ăp′/tə tūd′/, -tōōd′/), *n.* **1.** lack of aptitude; unfitness. **2.** unskillfulness.

in·arch (ĭn ärch′/), *v.t. Bot.* to graft by uniting a growing branch to a stock without separating the branch from its parent stock. [f. IN-² + ARCH¹]

in·arm (ĭn ärm′/), *v.t.* to hold in, or as in, the arms.

in·ar·tic·u·late (ĭn′/är tĭk′/yə lĭt), *adj.* **1.** not articulate; not uttered or emitted with expressive or intelligible modulations: *inarticulate sounds.* **2.** unable to use articulate speech: *inarticulate with rage.* **3.** *Anat., Zool.* not jointed; having no articulation or joint. [t. LL: m.s. *inarticulātus* not distinct. See IN-³, ARTICULATE] —**in′/ar·tic′/u·late·ly,** *adv.* —**in′/ar·tic′/u·late·ness,** *n.*

Inarching

in·ar·ti·fi·cial (ĭn′/är′/tə fĭsh′/əl), *adj.* **1.** not artificial; natural; artless; plain or simple. **2.** inartistic. —**in·ar′/ti·fi′/ci·al′/i·ty,** *n.* —**in·ar′/ti·fi′/cial·ly,** *adv.*

in·ar·tis·tic (ĭn′/är tĭs′/tĭk), *adj.* **1.** not artistic; aesthetically poor. **2.** lacking in artistic sense. Also, **in′/ar·tis′/ti·cal.** —**in′/ar·tis′/ti·cal·ly,** *adv.*

in·as·much as (ĭn′/əz mŭch′/), **1.** in view of the fact that; seeing that; since. **2.** in so far as; to such a degree as. —**Syn. 1.** See **because.**

in·at·ten·tion (ĭn′/ə tĕn′/shən), *n.* **1.** lack of attention; negligence. **2.** an act of neglect.

in·at·ten·tive (ĭn′/ə tĕn′/tĭv), *adj.* not attentive. —**in′/at·ten′/tive·ly,** *adv.* —**in′/at·ten′/tive·ness,** *n.*

in·au·di·ble (ĭn ô′/də bəl), *adj.* incapable of being heard. —**in·au′/di·bil′/i·ty,** *n.* —**in·au′/di·bly,** *adv.*

in·au·gu·ral (ĭn ô′/gyə rəl, -gə rəl), *adj.* **1.** of or pertaining to an inauguration. —*n.* **2.** an address, as of a president, at the beginning of a term of office. [t. F, der. *inaugurer*, t. L: m. *inaugurāre* INAUGURATE]

in·au·gu·rate (ĭn ô′/gyə rāt′/, -gə-), *v.t.*, -rated, -rating. **1.** to make a formal beginning of; initiate; commence; begin. **2.** to induct into office with formal ceremonies; install. **3.** to introduce into public use by some formal ceremony. [t. L: m.s. *inaugurātus,* pp., consecrated or installed with augural ceremonies] —**in·au′/gu·ra′/tion,** *n.* —**in·au′/gu·ra′/tor,** *n.*

Inauguration Day, *U.S.* the day on which the president is inaugurated, being Jan. 20 of every year next after a year whose number is divisible by four. Prior to the Twentieth Amendment to the Constitution (ratified Feb. 6, 1933), it was March 4.

in·aus·pi·cious (ĭn′/ô spĭsh′/əs), *adj.* not auspicious. —**in′/aus·pi′/cious·ly,** *adv.* —**in′/aus·pi′/cious·ness,** *n.*

in·be·ing (ĭn′/bē′/ĭng), *n.* **1.** the condition of existing in something else; immanence. **2.** inward nature.

in·board (ĭn′/bōrd′/), *adv., adj. Naut.* within the hull or interior, or toward the center, of a ship.

in·born (ĭn′/bôrn′/), *adj.* implanted by nature; innate. —**Syn.** inbred, inherent, natural, native. —**Ant.** acquired.

in·bound (ĭn′/bound′/), *adj.* inward bound: *inbound ships.*

in·breathe (ĭn brēth′/), *v.t.*, -breathed, -breathing. **1.** to breathe in; infuse. **2.** to inspire.

in·bred (ĭn′/brĕd′/), *adj.* **1.** bred within; innate; native. **2.** resulting from or involved in inbreeding.

in·breed (ĭn brēd′/), *v.t.*, -bred, -breeding. **1.** to breed (animals) in-and-in. **2.** to breed within; engender.

in·breed·ing (ĭn′/brē′/dĭng), *n. Biol.* the mating of related individuals such as cousins, sire-daughter, brother-sister, or self-fertilized plants. Inbreeding automatically fixes the genes, making them homozygous.

in·burst (ĭn′/bûrst′/), *n.* a bursting in; irruption.

inc., **1.** inclosure. **2.** included. **3.** including. **4.** inclusive. **5.** (*also cap.*) incorporated. **6.** increase.

In·ca (ĭng′/kə), *n.* **1.** one of the dominant groups of South American Indians who occupied Peru prior to the Spanish conquest. **2.** the chief ruler of the race. [t. Sp., Pg., t. Peruvian] —**In′/can,** *n., adj.*

in·cage (ĭn kāj′/), *v.t.*, -caged, -caging. encage.

in·cal·cu·la·ble (ĭn kăl′/kyə lə bəl), *adj.* **1.** that cannot be calculated; beyond calculation. **2.** that cannot be forecast. **3.** uncertain. —**in·cal′/cu·la·bil′/i·ty, in·cal′/cu·la·ble·ness,** *n.* —**in·cal′/cu·la·bly,** *adv.*

in·ca·les·cent (ĭn′/kə lĕs′/ənt), *adj.* increasing in heat. [t. L: s. *incalescens,* ppr.] —**in′/ca·les′/cence,** *n.*

in·can·desce (ĭn′/kən dĕs′/), *v.i., v.t.*, -desced, -descing. to glow or cause to glow with heat. [t. L: m.s. *incandescere* grow hot, glow]

in·can·des·cence (ĭn′/kən dĕs′/əns), *n.* the state of a body caused by approximately white heat, when it may be used as a source of artificial light. Also, **in′/can·des′/cen·cy.**

in·can·des·cent (ĭn′/kən dĕs′/ənt), *adj.* **1.** (of light, etc.) produced by incandescence. **2.** glowing or white with heat. **3.** intensely bright; brilliant. [t. L: s. *incandescens,* ppr., growing hot] —**in′/can·des′/cent·ly,** *adv.*

incandescent lamp, a lamp whose light is due to the glowing of some material, as the common electric lamp which contains a filament rendered luminous by the passage of current through it.

in·can·ta·tion (ĭn′/kăn tā′/shən), *n.* **1.** the chanting or uttering of words purporting to have magical power. **2.** the formula employed; a spell or charm. **3.** magical ceremonies. **4.** magic; sorcery. [ME *incantacion,* t. LL: m.s. *incantātio* enchantment]

in·ca·pa·ble (ĭn kā′/pə bəl), *adj.* **1.** not capable. **2.** not having the capacity or power for a specified act or function (fol. by *of*). **3.** not open to the influence; not susceptible or admitting (fol. by *of*): *incapable of exact measurement.* **4.** without ordinary capability or ability; incompetent: *incapable workers.* **5.** without qualification, esp. legal qualification (often fol. by *of*): *incapable of holding public office.* —*n.* **6.** a thoroughly incompetent person. [t. LL: m.s. *incapābilis.* See IN-³, CAPABLE] —**in·ca′/pa·bil′/i·ty, in·ca′/pa·ble·ness,** *n.* —**in·ca′/pa·bly,** *adv.*

—**Syn. 1.** INCAPABLE, INCOMPETENT, INEFFICIENT, UNABLE are applied to one who or that which is lacking in ability, preparation, or power for whatever is to be done. INCAPABLE usually means inherently lacking in ability or power: *incapable of appreciating music; a bridge incapable of carrying heavy loads.* INCOMPETENT, generally used only of persons, means unfit or unqualified for a particular task: *incompetent as an administrator.* INEFFICIENT means wasteful in the use of effort or power: *an inefficient manager, inefficient methods.* UNABLE usually refers to a temporary condition of inability to do some specific thing: *unable to relax, to go to a concert.*

in·ca·pa·cious (ĭn′/kə pā′/shəs), *adj.* **1.** not capacious; lacking capacity; narrow; limited. **2.** mentally incapable. [f. INCAPACI(TY) + -OUS] —**in′/ca·pa′/cious·ness,** *n.*

in·ca·pac·i·tate (ĭn′/kə păs′/ə tāt′/), *v.t.*, -tated, -tating. **1.** to deprive of capacity; make incapable or unfit; disqualify. **2.** *Law.* to deprive of power to perform acts with legal consequences. —**in′/ca·pac′/i·ta′/tion,** *n.*

in·ca·pac·i·ty (ĭn′/kə păs′/ə tĭ), *n., pl.* -ties. **1.** lack of capacity; incapability. **2.** legal disqualification. [t. ML: m. *incapācitas*]

in·car·cer·ate (*v.* ĭn kär′/sə rāt′/; *adj.* ĭn kär′/sər ĭt, -sə rāt′/), *v.*, -ated, -ating, *adj.* —*v.t.* **1.** to imprison; confine. **2.** to enclose; constrict closely. —*adj.* **3.** imprisoned. [t. ML: m.s. *incarcerātus,* pp. of *incarcerāre,* der. L in- IN-² + *carcer* prison] —**in·car′/cer·a′/tion,** *n.* —**in·car′/cer·a′/tor,** *n.*

in·car·di·nate (ĭn kär′/də nāt′/), *v.t.*, -nated, -nating. **1.** to institute as a cardinal. **2.** to institute as chief presbyter, priest, etc., in a particular church or place. [t. ML: m.s. *incardinātus,* pp. See CARDINAL] —**in·car′/di·na′/tion,** *n.*

in·car·na·dine (ĭn kär′/nə dīn′/, -dĭn), *adj., n., v.,* -dined, -dining. —*adj.* **1.** flesh-colored; pale red. **2.** crimson. —*n.* **3.** an incarnadine color. —*v.t.* **4.** to make incarnadine. [t. F: m. *incarnadin,* t. d. It.: m. *incarnadino,* ult. der. LL *incarnātus.* See INCARNATE]

in·car·nate (*adj.* ĭn kär′nĭt, -nāt; *v.* ĭn kär′nāt), *adj.*, *v.*, **-nated, -nating.** —*adj.* **1.** embodied in flesh; invested with a bodily, esp. a human, form: *a devil incarnate.* **2.** personified or typified, as a quality or idea: *chivalry incarnate.* **3.** flesh-colored or crimson. —*v.t.* **4.** to put into or represent in a concrete form, as an idea. **5.** to be the embodiment or type of. **6.** to embody in flesh; invest with a bodily, esp. a human, form. [ME, t. LL: m.s. *incarnātus*, pp., made flesh]

in·car·na·tion (ĭn′kär nā′shən), *n.* **1.** an incarnate being or form. **2.** a living being embodying a deity or spirit. **3.** assumption of human form or nature, as by a divine being: *the incarnation of God in Christ.* **4.** a person or thing representing or exhibiting some quality, idea, etc., in typical form. **5.** act of incarnating. **6.** state of being incarnated. [ME, t. LL: s. *incarnātio*]

in·case (ĭn kās′), *v.t.*, **-cased, -casing.** to enclose in or as in a case. Also, **encase.** [f. IN-² + CASE²] —**in·case′-ment,** *n.*

in·cau·tion (ĭn kô′shən), *n.* lack of caution; heedlessness; carelessness. [f. IN-³ + CAUTION]

in·cau·tious (ĭn kô′shəs), *adj.* not cautious. —**in·cau′tious·ly,** *adv.* —**in·cau′tious·ness,** *n.*

in·cen·di·a·rism (ĭn sĕn′dĭ ə rĭz′əm), *n.* act or practice of an incendiary; malicious burning.

in·cen·di·a·ry (ĭn sĕn′dĭ ĕr′ĭ), *adj.*, *n.*, *pl.* **-aries.** —*adj.* **1.** used or adapted for setting property on fire: *incendiary bombs.* **2.** of or pertaining to the criminal setting on fire of property. **3.** tending to arouse strife, sedition, etc.; inflammatory: *incendiary speeches.* —*n.* **4.** one who maliciously sets fire to buildings or other property. **5.** *Mil.* a shell containing phosphorus or similar material producing great heat. **6.** one who stirs up strife, sedition, etc.; an agitator. [t. L: m.s. *incendiārius* causing fire]

in·cense¹ (ĭn′sĕns), *n.*, *v.*, **-censed, -censing.** —*n.* **1.** an aromatic gum or other substance producing a sweet odor when burned, used esp. in religious ceremonies. **2.** the perfume or smoke arising from such a substance when burned. **3.** any pleasant perfume or fragrance. **4.** homage or adulation. —*v.t.* **5.** to perfume with incense. **6.** to burn incense for. —*v.i.* **7.** to burn or offer incense. [t. LL: m.s. *incensum* incense, prop. pp. neut. of L *incendere* set on fire; r. ME *encens*, t. OF] —**in′cense·less,** *adj.*

in·cense² (ĭn sĕns′), *v.t.*, **-censed, -censing.** to inflame with wrath; make angry; enrage. [ME *incence*(n), t. L: m.s. *incensus*, pp., set on fire, kindled] —**in·cense′-ment,** *n.* —**Syn.** See **enrage.**

in·cen·tive (ĭn sĕn′tĭv), *n.* **1.** that which incites to action, etc. —*adj.* **2.** inciting, as to action; stimulating; provocative. [ME, t. L: *incentivus* inciting, setting the tune] —**in·cen′tive·ly,** *adv.* —**Syn. 1.** stimulus, spur, incitement; inducement. See **motive.**

in·cept (ĭn sĕpt′), *v.i.* **1.** *Brit.* to complete the taking of a degree of master or doctor in a university, esp. Cambridge. —*v.t.* **2.** to take in; intussuscept. [t. L: s. *inceptus*, pp., begun, commenced] —**in·cep′tion,** *n.* —**in·cep′tor,** *n.*

in·cep·tive (ĭn sĕp′tĭv), *adj.* **1.** *Gram.* (of a derived verb, or of an aspect in verb inflection) expressing the beginning of the action indicated by the underlying verb. For example: Latin verbs in *-sco* generally have inceptive force, as *calescō* "become or begin to be hot" from *caleō* "be hot." **2.** beginning; initial. —*n.* **3.** *Gram.* **a.** the inceptive aspect. **b.** a verb therein. —**in·cep′tive·ly,** *adv.*

in·cer·ti·tude (ĭn sûr′tə tūd′, -tōōd′), *n.* **1.** uncertainty; doubtfulness. **2.** insecurity. [f. IN-³ + CERTITUDE]

in·ces·sant (ĭn sĕs′ənt), *adj.* continuing without interruption: *an incessant noise.* [t. LL: s. *incessans* unceasing] —**in·ces′san·cy, in·ces′sant·ness,** *n.* —**in·ces′sant·ly,** *adv.* —**Syn.** ceaseless, unceasing, continual, continuous, constant. —**Ant.** intermittent.

in·cest (ĭn′sĕst), *n.* **1.** the crime of sexual intercourse between persons related by blood or marriage within the degrees in which marriage is prohibited. **2.** spiritual incest, *Eccles.* sexual intercourse between persons who have been baptized or confirmed together. [ME, t. L: s. *incestus*, or *incestum* (neut.) unchaste]

in·ces·tu·ous (ĭn sĕs′chŏŏ əs), *adj.* **1.** guilty of incest. **2.** involving incest. —**in·ces′tu·ous·ly,** *adv.* —**in·ces′-tu·ous·ness,** *n.*

inch¹ (ĭnch), *n.* **1.** a unit of length, ¹/₁₂ foot, equivalent to 2.54 centimeters. In the U.S., it is defined by law in terms of the meter, 39.37 in. being exactly equal to one meter. **2.** a very small amount of anything: *flogged within an inch of his life.* **3. by inches,** or **inch by inch,** very gradually. **4. every inch,** in every respect: *every inch a king.* —*v.i.*, *v.t.* **5.** to move by inches or small degrees. [ME; OE *ynce,* t. L: m.s. *uncia* twelfth part, inch, ounce. Cf. OUNCE¹]

inch² (ĭnch), *n. Scot.* an island. [ME, t. Gaelic: m. *innse*, gen. of *innis* island]

inch·meal (ĭnch′mēl′), *adv.* by inches; inch by inch; little by little (often prec. by *by*).

in·cho·ate (ĭn kō′ĭt), *adj.* **1.** just begun; incipient. **2.** rudimentary. [t. L: m.s. *inchoātus, incohātus,* pp., begun] —**in·cho′ate·ly,** *adv.* —**in·cho′ate·ness,** *n.*

in·cho·a·tion (ĭn′kō ā′shən), *n.* beginning; origin.

in·cho·a·tive (ĭn kō′ə tĭv), *adj.* **1.** *Gram.* inceptive. **2.** *Rare.* inchoate. —*n.* **3.** *Gram.* an inceptive.

inch·worm (ĭnch′wûrm′), *n.* measuring worm.

in·ci·dence (ĭn′sə dəns), *n.* **1.** the range of occurrence or influence of a thing, or the extent of its effects: *the incidence of a disease.* **2.** the falling, or direction or manner of falling, of a ray of light, etc., on a surface. **3.** a falling upon, affecting, or befalling. **4.** the fact or the manner of being incident. **5.** *Geom.* partial coincidence of two figures, as of a line and a plane containing it.

in·ci·dent (ĭn′sə dənt), *n.* **1.** an occurrence or event. **2.** a distinct piece of action, or an episode, as in a story, play, etc. **3.** something that occurs casually in connection with something else. **4.** something appertaining or attaching to something else. **5.** (in England as a euphemism in World War II) a case of bombing. —*adj.* **6.** likely or apt to happen (fol. by *to*). **7.** naturally appertaining: *hardships incident to the life of an explorer.* **8.** conjoined or attaching, esp. as subordinate to a principal thing. **9.** falling or striking on something. [ME, t. L: s. *incidens*, ppr., befalling] —**Syn. 1.** See **event.**

in·ci·den·tal (ĭn′sə dĕn′təl), *adj.* **1.** happening or likely to happen in fortuitous or subordinate conjunction with something else. **2.** liable to happen or naturally appertaining (fol. by *to*.) **3.** incurred casually and in addition to the regular or main amount: *incidental expenses.* —*n.* **4.** something incidental, as a circumstance. **5.** (*pl.*) minor expenses. —**Syn. 1.** casual, chance, fortuitous; contingent. —**Ant. 1.** fundamental.

in·ci·den·tal·ly (ĭn′sə dĕn′tə lĭ), *adv.* **1.** in an incidental manner. **2.** by the way.

in·cin·er·ate (ĭn sĭn′ə rāt′), *v.t.*, *v.i.*, **-ated, -ating.** to burn or reduce to ashes; cremate. [t. ML: m.s. *incinerātus*, pp., of *incinerāre*, der. L *in-* IN-² + *cinis* ashes] —**in·cin′er·a′tion,** *n.*

in·cin·er·a·tor (ĭn sĭn′ə rā′tər), *n.* a furnace or apparatus for incinerating.

in·cip·i·ent (ĭn sĭp′ĭ ənt), *adj.* beginning to exist or appear; in an initial stage. [t. L: s. *incipiens*, ppr.] —**in·cip′i·ence, in·cip′i·en·cy,** *n.* —**in·cip′i·ent·ly,** *adv.*

in·ci·pit (ĭn′sĭ pĭt), *Latin.* (here) begins.

in·cise (ĭn sīz′), *v.t.*, **-cised, -cising.** **1.** to cut into; cut marks, etc. upon. **2.** to make (marks, etc.) by cutting; engrave; carve. [t. F: m.s. *inciser*, ult. der. L *incīsus*, pp., cut into]

in·cised (ĭn sīzd′), *adj.* **1.** cut into: *the incised gums.* **2.** made by cutting: *an incised wound.*

in·ci·sion (ĭn sĭzh′ən), *n.* **1.** a cut, gash, or notch. **2.** act of incising. **3.** a cutting into, esp. for surgical purposes. **4.** incisiveness; keenness. [ME, t. L: s. *incīsio*]

in·ci·sive (ĭn sī′sĭv), *adj.* **1.** penetrating, trenchant, or biting: *an incisive tone of voice.* **2.** sharp; keen; acute. **3.** adapted for cutting: *the incisive teeth.* —**in·ci′sive·ly,** *adv.* —**in·ci′sive·ness,** *n.*

in·ci·sor (ĭn sī′zər), *n.* a tooth in the anterior part of the jaw adapted for cutting. [t. NL]

in·ci·so·ry (ĭn sī′sər ĭ), *adj.* adapted for cutting, as the incisor teeth.

in·ci·sure (ĭn sī′zhər), *n. Anat.* a notch, as in a bone or other structure. —**in·cis′ur·al,** *adj.*

in·cite (ĭn sīt′), *v.t.*, **-cited, -citing.** to urge on; stimulate or prompt to action. [late ME, t. L: m.s. *incitāre* set in motion] —**in·ci·ta·tion** (ĭn′sī tā′shən, -sĭ-), *n.* —**in·cit′er,** *n.* —**in·cit′ing·ly,** *adv.* —**Syn.** encourage; instigate, provoke, goad, spur, arouse, fire; induce.

in·cite·ment (ĭn sīt′mənt), *n.* **1.** act of inciting. **2.** that which incites; motive; incentive.

in·ci·vil·i·ty (ĭn′sə vĭl′ə tĭ), *n.*, *pl.* **-ties.** **1.** the quality or fact of being uncivil; uncivil behavior or treatment. **2.** an uncivil act.

incl. **1.** inclosure. **2.** including. **3.** inclusive.

in·clasp (ĭn klăsp′, -kläsp′), *v.t.* enclasp.

in·clem·ent (ĭn klĕm′ənt), *adj.* (of the weather, etc.) not clement; severe or harsh. [t. L: s. *inclēmens* harsh] —**in·clem′en·cy,** *n.* —**in·clem′ent·ly,** *adv.*

in·clin·a·ble (ĭn klī′nə bəl), *adj.* **1.** having a mental bent or tendency in a certain direction; inclined. **2.** favorable. **3.** capable of being inclined.

in·cli·na·tion (ĭn′klə nā′shən), *n.* **1.** a set or bent (esp. of the mind or will); a liking or preference: *much against his inclination.* **2.** that to which one is inclined. **3.** act of inclining. **4.** state of being inclined. **5.** deviation or amount of deviation from a normal, esp. horizontal or vertical, direction or position. **6.** an inclined surface. **7.** *Math.* the difference in direction of two lines or two planes as measured by the angle. **8.** *Astron.* **a.** one of the elements of an orbit of a planet, etc. **b.** the angle between the orbital plane and the ecliptic or other suitably chosen plane. [late ME, t. L: s. *inclīnātio* a leaning] —**in′cli·na′tion·al,** *adj.* —**Syn. 1.** tendency; propensity, proclivity, proneness, predilection. —**Ant. 1** distaste.

in·cli·na·to·ry (ĭn klī′nə tōr′ĭ), *adj.* related to or characterized by inclination.

in·cline (*v.* ĭn klīn′; *n.* ĭn′klīn, ĭn klīn′), *v.*, **-clined, -clining,** *n.* —*v.i.* **1.** to have a mental tendency; be disposed. **2.** to deviate from the vertical or horizontal; slant. **3.** to tend, in a physical sense; approximate: *the leaves incline toward a blue.* **4.** to tend in course or character. **5.** to lean; bend. —*v.t.* **6.** to dispose (a person) in mind, habit, etc. (fol. by *to*). **7.** to bow (the head, etc.). **8.** to cause to lean or bend in a particular direction. **9.** to turn toward (to listen favorably): *incline one's ear.* —*n.* **10.** an inclined surface; a slope. [t. L: m. s. *inclīnāre* incline; r. ME *enclyne*, t. OF: m. *encliner*] —**in·clin′er,** *n.*

---

b., blend of, blended; c., cognate with; d., dialect, dialectal; der., derived from; f., formed from; g., going back to; m., modification of; r., replacing; s., stem of; t., taken from; ?, perhaps.   See the full key on inside cover.

in·clined (ĭn·klīnd′), *adj.* **1.** disposed, esp. favorably (fol. by *to*): *inclined to stay.* **2.** having a (physical) tendency. **3.** deviating in direction from the horizontal or vertical; sloping. **4.** in a direction making an angle with anything else.

inclined plane, a plane surface inclined to the horizon, or forming with a horizontal plane any angle but a right angle.

AC, Inclined plane;
CB, Height of AC; BA, Base;
BAC, Angle of inclination

in·cli·nom·e·ter (ĭn′klə·nŏm′ə·tər), *n.* **1.** *Aeron.* an instrument for measuring the angle an aircraft makes with the horizontal. **2.** an instrument for determining the inclination or dip of the earth's magnetic force by the dip of a magnetic needle. [f. INCLINE + -O- + -METER]

in·close (ĭn·klōz′), *v.t.,* **-closed, -closing.** enclose. **—in·clos′er,** *n.*

in·clo·sure (ĭn·klō′zhər), *n.* enclosure.

in·clude (ĭn·klōōd′), *v.t.,* **-cluded, -cluding. 1.** to contain, embrace, or comprise, as a whole does parts or any part or element. **2.** to place in an aggregate, class, category, or the like. **3.** to contain as a subordinate element; involve as a factor. [ME *include(n),* t. L: m. *inclūdere* shut in] **—in·clud′i·ble, in·clud′a·ble,** *adj.*
—Syn. 1. INCLUDE, COMPREHEND, COMPRISE, EMBRACE imply containing parts of a whole. To INCLUDE is to contain as a part or member, or among the parts and members, of a whole: *the list includes many new names*. To COMPREHEND is to have within the limits, scope, or range of references, as either a part or the whole number of items concerned: *the plan comprehends several projects.* To COMPRISE is to consist of, as the various parts serving to make up the whole: *this genus comprises fifty species.* EMBRACE emphasizes the extent or assortment of that which is included: *the report embraces a great variety of subjects.* **—Ant. 1.** exclude.

in·clud·ed (ĭn·klōō′dĭd), *adj.* **1.** enclosed; embraced; comprised. **2.** *Bot.* not projecting beyond the mouth of the corolla, as stamens or a style.

in·clu·sion (ĭn·klōō′zhən), *n.* **1.** the act of including. **2.** the state of being included. **3.** that which is included. **4.** *Biol.* a body suspended in the cytoplasm, as a granule, etc. **5.** *Mineral.* a solid body or a body of gas or liquid enclosed within the mass of a mineral. [t. L: s. *inclūsio*]

inclusion body, *Pathol.* a particle which takes a characteristic stain, found in a virus-infected cell.

in·clu·sive (ĭn·klōō′sĭv), *adj.* **1.** including in consideration or account, as the stated limit or extremes: *from six to ten inclusive.* **2.** including a great deal, or including everything concerned; comprehensive. **3.** that includes; enclosing; embracing. **4. inclusive of,** including. **—in·clu′sive·ly,** *adv.* **—in·clu′sive·ness,** *n.*

in·co·er·ci·ble (ĭn′kō·ûr′sə·bəl), *adj.* **1.** not coercible. **2.** *Physics.* incapable of being reduced to a liquid form by any amount of pressure.

in·cog (ĭn·kŏg′), *adj., adv., n. Colloq.* incognita or incognito.

in·cog·i·ta·ble (ĭn·kŏj′ə·tə·bəl), *adj.* unthinkable. [t LL: m.s. *incogitābilis*] **—in·cog′i·ta·bil′i·ty,** *n.*

in·cog·i·tant (ĭn·kŏj′ə·tənt), *adj.* **1.** thoughtless; inconsiderate. **2.** not having the faculty of thinking.

in·cog·ni·ta (ĭn·kŏg′nə·tə), *adj.* **1.** (of a woman or girl) having the real name or identity concealed. **—n. 2.** a woman or girl who is incognita. [fem. of INCOGNITO]

in·cog·ni·to (ĭn·kŏg′nə·tō′), *adj., adv., n., pl.* **-tos.** **—adj. 1.** having one's identity concealed, as under an assumed name (esp. to avoid notice or formal attentions). **—adv. 2.** with the real identity concealed: *to travel incognito.* **—n. 3.** one who is incognito. **4.** the state of being incognito. [t. It., t. L: m. *incognitus* unknown]

in·cog·ni·zant (ĭn·kŏg′nə·zənt), *adj.* not cognizant; without knowledge; unaware (fol. by *of*). **—in·cog′·ni·zance,** *n.*

in·co·her·ence (ĭn′kō·hĭr′əns), *n.* **1.** the state of being incoherent. **2.** something incoherent; an incoherent statement, etc.

in·co·her·en·cy (ĭn′kō·hĭr′ən·sĭ), *n., pl.* **-cies.** incoherence.

in·co·her·ent (ĭn′kō·hĭr′ənt), *adj.* **1.** without logical connection; disjointed; rambling: *an incoherent sentence.* **2.** characterized by such thought or language, as a person: *incoherent with rage.* **3.** not coherent or cohering: *an incoherent mixture.* **4.** without physical cohesion; loose: *incoherent dust.* **5.** without unity or harmony of elements: *an incoherent public.* **6.** without congruity of parts; uncoördinated. **7.** naturally different, or incompatible, as things. **—in·co·her′ent·ly,** *adv.*

in·com·bus·ti·ble (ĭn′kəm·bŭs′tə·bəl), *adj.* **1.** not combustible; incapable of being burned. **—n. 2.** an incombustible substance. **—in′com·bus′ti·bil′i·ty, in′·com·bus′ti·ble·ness,** *n.* **—in′com·bus′ti·bly,** *adv.*

in·come (ĭn′kŭm), *n.* **1.** the returns that come in periodically, esp. annually, from property, business, labor, etc.; revenue; receipts. **2.** something that comes in. **3.** *Rare.* a coming in. **—Syn. 1.** interest, salary, wages, annuity, gain, return, earnings. **—Ant. 1.** outgo, expenditure.

in·com·er (ĭn′kŭm′ər), *n.* **1.** one who comes in. **2.** an immigrant. **3.** an intruder. **4.** a successor.

income tax, a tax levied on incomes; an annual government tax on personal incomes, usually graduated and with certain deductions and exemptions.

in·com·ing (ĭn′kŭm′ĭng), *adj.* **1.** coming in: *the incoming tide.* **2.** succeeding: *the incoming mayor.* **3.** immigrant. **4.** accruing, as profit. **5.** entering, as a tenant or an officeholder. **6.** *Scot.* ensuing. **—n. 7.** a coming in: *the incoming of spring.* **8.** (*usually pl.*) that which comes in, esp. revenue.

in·com·men·su·ra·ble (ĭn′kə·mĕn′shə·rə·bəl, -sə·rə-), *adj.* **1.** not commensurable; having no common measure or standard of comparison. **2.** utterly disproportionate. **3.** *Math.* (of two or more quantities) having no common measure. **—n. 4.** that which is incommensurable. **5.** *Math.* one of two or more incommensurable quantities. **—in′com·men′su·ra·bil′i·ty, in′com·men′su·ra·ble·ness,** *n.* **—in′com·men′su·ra·bly,** *adv.*

in·com·men·su·rate (ĭn′kə·mĕn′shə·rĭt, -sə·rĭt), *adj.* **1.** not commensurate; disproportionate; inadequate: *means incommensurate to our wants.* **2.** incommensurable. **—in′com·men′su·rate·ly,** *adv.* **—in′com·men′su·rate·ness,** *n.*

in·com·mode (ĭn′kə·mōd′), *v.t.,* **-moded, -moding. 1.** to inconvenience or discomfort. **2.** to impede; hinder. [t. L: m.s. *incommodāre*]

in·com·mo·di·ous (ĭn′kə·mō′dĭ·əs), *adj.* **1.** not affording sufficient room. **2.** inconvenient. **—in′com·mo′·di·ous·ly,** *adv.* **—in′com·mo′di·ous·ness,** *n.*

in·com·mod·i·ty (ĭn′kə·mŏd′ə·tĭ), *n., pl.* **-ties. 1.** inconvenience. **2.** something inconvenient.

in·com·mu·ni·ca·ble (ĭn′kə·mū′nə·kə·bəl), *adj.* **1.** incapable of being communicated, imparted, or told to others. **2.** incommunicative. **—in′com·mu′ni·ca·bil′i·ty, in′com·mu′ni·ca·ble·ness,** *n.* **—in′com·mu′ni·ca·bly,** *adv.*

in·com·mu·ni·ca·do (ĭn′kə·mū′nə·kä′dō), *adj.* (esp. of a prisoner) deprived of communication with others. [t. Sp.: m. *incomunicado,* der. *comunicar* COMMUNICATE]

in·com·mu·ni·ca·tive (ĭn′kə·mū′nə·kā′tĭv), *adj.* not communicative; reserved. **—in′com·mu′ni·ca′tive·ly,** *adv.* **—in′com·mu′ni·ca′tive·ness,** *n.*

in·com·mut·a·ble (ĭn′kə·mū′tə·bəl), *adj.* **1.** not exchangeable. **2.** unchangeable. **—in′com·mut′a·bil′i·ty, in′com·mut′a·ble·ness,** *n.* **—in′com·mut′a·bly,** *adv.*

in·com·pact (ĭn′kəm·păkt′), *adj.* not compact; loose. **—in′com·pact′ly,** *adv.* **—in′com·pact′ness,** *n.*

in·com·pa·ra·ble (ĭn·kŏm′pə·rə·bəl, -prə·bəl), *adj.* **1.** matchless or unequaled: *incomparable beauty.* **2.** not comparable. **—in·com′pa·ra·bil′i·ty, in·com′pa·ra·ble·ness,** *n.* **—in·com′pa·ra·bly,** *adv.*

in·com·pat·i·ble (ĭn′kəm·păt′ə·bəl), *adj.* **1.** not compatible; incapable of existing together in harmony. **2.** contrary or opposed in character; discordant. **3.** that cannot coexist or be conjoined. **4.** *Logic.* (of two or more propositions) that cannot be true simultaneously. **5.** (of positions, ranks, etc.) unable to be held simultaneously by one person. **6.** *Pharm., Med.* pertaining to drugs or the like which interfere with one another chemically or physiologically and therefore can not be prescribed together. **—n. 7.** (*usually pl.*) an incompatible person or thing. **8.** an incompatible drug or the like. **9.** (*pl.*) *Logic.* two or more attributes which cannot simultaneously belong to the same object. **—in′com·pat′i·bil′i·ty, in′com·pat′i·ble·ness,** *n.* **—in′com·pat′i·bly,** *adv.* **—Syn. 1.** See **inconsistent.**

in·com·pe·tence (ĭn·kŏm′pə·təns), *n.* **1.** the character or condition of being incompetent; inability. **2.** *Law.* the condition of lacking the power to act with legal effectiveness. Also, **in·com′pe·ten·cy.**

in·com·pe·tent (ĭn·kŏm′pə·tənt), *adj.* **1.** not competent; lacking qualification or ability: *an incompetent candidate.* **2.** characterized by or showing incompetence. **3.** *Law.* not legally qualified; inadmissible, as evidence. **—n. 4.** an incompetent person. **5.** *Law.* a person lacking power to act with legal effectiveness. [t. LL: s. *incompetens* insufficient] **—in·com′pe·tent·ly,** *adv.* **—Syn. 1.** See **incapable.**

in·com·plete (ĭn′kəm·plēt′), *adj.* not complete; lacking some part. [ME, t. LL: m.s. *incomplētus*] **—in′com·plete′ly,** *adv.* **—in′com·plete′ness, in′com·ple′tion,** *n.*

in·com·pli·ant (ĭn′kəm·plī′ənt), *adj.* **1.** not compliant; unyielding. **2.** not pliant. **—in′com·pli′ance, in′com·pli′an·cy,** *n.* **—in′com·pli′ant·ly,** *adv.*

in·com·pre·hen·si·ble (ĭn′kŏm·prĭ·hĕn′sə·bəl, ĭn·kŏm′-), *adj.* not comprehensible; not understandable; unintelligible. **—in′com·pre·hen′si·bil′i·ty, in′com·pre·hen′si·ble·ness,** *n.* **—in′com·pre·hen′si·bly,** *adv.*

in·com·pre·hen·sive (ĭn′kŏm·prĭ·hĕn′sĭv, ĭn·kŏm′-), *adj.* not comprehensive. **—in′com·pre·hen′sive·ly,** *adv.* **—in′com·pre·hen′sive·ness,** *n.*

in·com·press·i·ble (ĭn′kŏm·prĕs′ə·bəl), *adj.* not compressible. **—in′com·press′i·bil′i·ty,** *n.*

in·com·put·a·ble (ĭn′kəm·pū′tə·bəl), *adj.* incalculable.

in·con·ceiv·a·ble (ĭn′kən·sē′və·bəl), *adj.* not conceivable; unimaginable; unthinkable; incredible. **—in′·con·ceiv′a·bil′i·ty, in′con·ceiv′a·ble·ness,** *n.* **—in′·con·ceiv′a·bly,** *adv.*

in·con·clu·sive (ĭn′kən·klōō′sĭv), *adj.* **1.** not conclusive; not such as to settle a question: *inconclusive evidence.* **2.** without final results: *inconclusive experiments.* **—in′con·clu′sive·ly,** *adv.* **—in′con·clu′sive·ness,** *n.*

ăct, āble, dâre, ärt; ĕbb, ēqual; ĭf, īce; hŏt, ōver, ôrder, oil, bŏŏk, ōōze, out; ŭp, ūse, ûrge; ə = a in alone; ch, chief; g, give; ng, ring; sh, shoe; th, thin; ŧɦ, that; zh, vision. See the full key on inside cover.

in·con·den·sa·ble (ĭn/kən dĕn/sə bəl), *adj.* not condensable; incapable of being condensed. Also, **in/con·den/si·ble.** —**in/con·den/sa·bil/i·ty,** *n.*

in·con·dite (ĭn kŏn/dīt), *adj.* 1. ill-constructed. 2. crude. [t. L: m.s. *inconditus* disordered]

in·con·form·i·ty (ĭn/kən fôr/mə tĭ), *n.* lack of conformity; failure or refusal to conform.

in·con·gru·ent (ĭn kŏng/grōō ənt), *adj.* not congruent; incongruous. —**in·con/gru·ence,** *n.* —**in·con/·gru·ent·ly,** *adv.*

in·con·gru·i·ty (ĭn/kŏng grōō/ə tĭ), *n., pl.* **-ties.** 1. the quality of being incongruous. 2. something incongruous.

in·con·gru·ous (ĭn kŏng/grōō əs), *adj.* 1. out of keeping or place; inappropriate; unbecoming: *an incongruous effect.* 2. not harmonious in character; inconsonant; lacking harmony of parts: *incongruous mixtures.* 3. inconsistent: *acts incongruous with their principles.* [t. L: m. *incongruus*] —**in·con/gru·ous·ly,** *adv.* —**in·con/gru·ous·ness,** *n.* —Syn. 3. See **inconsistent.**

in·con·sec·u·tive (ĭn/kən sĕk/yə tĭv), *adj.* not consecutive. —**in/con·sec/u·tive·ly,** *adj.* —**in/con·sec/u·tive·ness,** *n.*

in·con·se·quent (ĭn kŏn/sə kwĕnt/, -kwənt), *adj.* 1. characterized by lack of sequence in thought, speech, or action. 2. not following from the premises: *an inconsequent deduction.* 3. characterized by lack of logical sequence: *inconsequent reasoning.* 4. irrelevant: *an inconsequent remark.* 5. not in keeping with the general character or design: *inconsequent ornamentation.* [t. L: s. *inconsequens* without connection] —**in·con/se·quence/,** *n.* —**in/con·se·quent/ly,** *adv.*

in·con·se·quen·tial (ĭn/kŏn sə kwĕn/shəl, ĭn kŏn/-), *adj.* 1. of no consequence; trivial. 2. inconsequent; illogical; irrelevant. —**in/con·se·quen/ti·al/i·ty,** *n.* —**in/con·se·quen/tial·ly,** *adv.*

in·con·sid·er·a·ble (ĭn/kən sĭd/ər ə bəl), *adj.* 1. small, as in value, amount, size, etc. 2. not worthy of consideration or notice; trivial. —**in/con·sid/er·a·ble·ness,** *n.* —**in/con·sid/er·a·bly,** *adv.*

in·con·sid·er·ate (ĭn/kən sĭd/ər ĭt), *adj.* 1. without due regard for the rights or feelings of others: *it was inconsiderate of him to forget.* 2. done or acting without consideration; thoughtless. —**in/con·sid/er·ate·ly,** *adv.* —**in/con·sid/er·ate·ness,** *n.* —**in/con·sid/er·a/tion,** *n.*

in·con·sist·en·cy (ĭn/kən sĭs/tən sĭ), *n., pl.* **-cies.** 1. the quality of being inconsistent. 2. something inconsistent. Also, **in/con·sist/ence.**

in·con·sist·ent (ĭn/kən sĭs/tənt), *adj.* 1. lacking in harmony between the different parts or elements; self-contradictory. 2. lacking agreement, as one thing with another, or two or more things in relation to each other; at variance. 3. not consistent in principles, conduct, etc. 4. acting at variance with professed principles. 5. *Logic.* incompatible. —**in/con·sist/ent·ly,** *adv.*
—Syn. 2. INCONSISTENT, INCOMPATIBLE, INCONGRUOUS refer to things which are out of keeping with each other. That which is INCONSISTENT involves variance, discrepancy, or even contradiction, esp. from the point of view of truth, reason, or logic: *his actions are inconsistent with his statements.* INCOMPATIBLE implies incapability of close association or harmonious relationship, as from differences of nature, character, temperament, and the like: *actions incompatible with honesty of purpose, qualities which make two people incompatible.* That which is INCONGRUOUS is inappropriate or out of keeping, often to the point of being ridiculous or absurd: *incongruous characters or situations frequently provide a basis for comedy.* —Ant. 1. harmonious.

in·con·sol·a·ble (ĭn/kən sō/lə bəl), *adj.* not consolable: *inconsolable grief.* —**in/con·sol/a·bil/i·ty,** **in/·con·sol/a·ble·ness,** *n.* —**in/con·sol/a·bly,** *adv.*

in·con·so·nant (ĭn kŏn/sə nənt), *adj.* not consonant or in accord. —**in·con/so·nance,** *n.* —**in·con/so·nant·ly,** *adv.*

in·con·spic·u·ous (ĭn/kən spĭk/yōō əs), *adj.* not conspicuous, noticeable, or prominent. —**in/con·spic/u·ous·ly,** *adv.* —**in/con·spic/u·ous·ness,** *n.*

in·con·stant (ĭn kŏn/stənt), *adj.* not constant; changeable; fickle; variable: *inconstant winds.* —**in·con/·stan·cy,** *n.* —**in·con/stant·ly,** *adv.*

in·con·sum·a·ble (ĭn/kən sōō/mə bəl), *adj.* not consumable; incapable of being consumed.

in·con·test·a·ble (ĭn/kən tĕs/tə bəl), *adj.* not contestable; not admitting of dispute; incontrovertible: *incontestable proof.* —**in/con·test/a·bil/i·ty,** **in/con·test/a·ble·ness,** *n.* —**in/con·test/a·bly,** *adv.*

in·con·ti·nent[1] (ĭn kŏn/tə nənt), *adj.* 1. not continent; not holding or held in; unceasing or unrestrained: *an incontinent flow of talk.* 2. lacking in restraint, esp. over the sexual appetite. 3. unable to contain or retain (usually fol. by *of*). 4. *Pathol.* unable to restrain natural discharges or evacuations. [ME, t. L: s. *incontinens* not holding back] —**in·con/ti·nence, in·con/ti·nen·cy,** *n.* —**in·con/ti·nent·ly,** *adv.*

in·con·ti·nent[2] (ĭn kŏn/tə nənt), *adv. Archaic.* immediately; at once; straightway. Also, **in·con/ti·nent·ly.** [ME, t. F, t. LL: m. *in continentī (tempore)* in continuous (time), without pause]

in·con·trol·la·ble (ĭn/kən trō/lə bəl), *adj.* not controllable; uncontrollable: *an incontrollable desire.*

in·con·tro·vert·i·ble (ĭn/kŏn trə vûr/tə bəl, ĭn kŏn/-), *adj.* not controvertible; indisputable: *absolute and incontrovertible truth.* —**in/con·tro·vert/i·bil/i·ty,** **in/·con·tro·vert/i·ble·ness,** *n.* —**in/con·tro·vert/i·bly,** *adv.*

in·con·ven·ience (ĭn/kən vēn/yəns), *n., v.,* **-ienced, -iencing.** —*n.* 1. the quality or state of being inconvenient. 2. an inconvenient circumstance or thing; something that causes discomfort, trouble, etc. —*v.t.* 3. to put to inconvenience; incommode.

in·con·ven·ien·cy (ĭn/kən vēn/yən sĭ), *n., pl.* **-cies.** inconvenience.

in·con·ven·ient (ĭn/kən vēn/yənt), *adj.* arranged or happening in such a way as to be awkward, inopportune, disadvantageous, or troublesome: *an inconvenient time for a visit.* [ME, t. L: s. *inconveniens* not consonant] —**in/con·ven/ient·ly,** *adv.* —Syn. untimely; annoying.

in·con·vert·i·ble (ĭn/kən vûr/tə bəl), *adj.* 1. (of paper money) not capable of being converted into specie. 2. not interchangeable. —**in/con·vert/i·bil/i·ty,** **in/·con·vert/i·ble·ness,** *n.* —**in/con·vert/i·bly,** *adv.*

in·con·vin·ci·ble (ĭn/kən vĭn/sə bəl), *adj.* not convincible; incapable of being convinced. —**in/con·vin/·ci·bil/i·ty,** —**in/con·vin/ci·bly,** *adv.*

in·co·ör·di·nate (ĭn/kō ôr/də nĭt), *adj.* not coördinate; not coördinated.

in·co·ör·di·na·tion (ĭn/kō ôr/də nā/shən), *n.* lack of coördination.

incor., 1. Also, **incorp.** incorporated. 2. incorrect.

in·cor·po·rate[1] (*v.* ĭn kôr/pə rāt/; *adj.* ĭn kôr/pə rĭt, -prĭt), *v.,* **-rated, -rating,** *adj.* —*v.t.* 1. to create or form a corporation. 2. to form into a society or organization. 3. to put or introduce into a body or mass as an integral part or parts. 4. to take in or include as a part or parts, as the body or mass does. 5. to form or combine into one body or uniform substance, as ingredients. 6. *Rare.* to embody. —*v.i.* 7. to unite or combine so as to form one body. 8. to form a corporation. —*adj.* 9. incorporated, as a company. 10. *Rare.* combined into one body, mass, or substance. 11. *Obs.* embodied. [ME, t. LL: m.s. *incorporātus,* pp., embodied. See IN-[2]] —**in·cor/po·ra/tion,** *n.* —**in·cor/po·ra/tive,** *adj.*

in·cor·po·rate[2] (ĭn kôr/pə rĭt, -prĭt), *adj.* not embodied; incorporeal. [t. LL: m.s. *incorporātus.* See IN-[3]]

in·cor·po·rat·ed (ĭn kôr/pə rā/tĭd), *adj.* 1. formed or constituted as a corporation. 2. combined in one body; made part of.

in·cor·po·ra·tor (ĭn kôr/pə rā/tər), *n.* 1. one of the signers of the articles or certificate of incorporation. 2. one of the persons to whom the charter is granted in a corporation created by special act of the legislature. 3. one who incorporates.

in·cor·po·re·al (ĭn/kôr pōr/ĭ əl), *adj.* 1. not corporeal; immaterial. 2. pertaining to immaterial beings. 3. *Law.* without material existence, but existing in contemplation of law, as a franchise. —**in/cor·po/re·al·ly,** *adv.*

in·cor·po·re·i·ty (ĭn kôr/pə rē/ə tĭ, ĭn/kôr-), *n., pl.* **-ties.** the quality of being incorporeal; disembodied existence or entity. Also, **in/cor·po/re·al/i·ty.**

in·cor·rect (ĭn/kə rĕkt/), *adj.* 1. not correct as to fact: *an incorrect statement.* 2. improper: *incorrect behavior.* 3. not correct in form or manner: *an incorrect copy.* —**in/cor·rect/ly,** *adv.* —**in/cor·rect/ness,** *n.* —Syn. 1. erroneous, inaccurate, inexact; untrue, wrong. 2. faulty, improper.

in·cor·ri·gi·ble (ĭn kôr/ĭ jə bəl, -kŏr/-), *adj.* 1. not corrigible; bad beyond correction or reform: *an incorrigible liar.* 2. impervious to punishment; willful; uncontrollable: *an incorrigible child.* 3. firmly fixed: *an incorrigible habit.* —*n.* 4. one who is incorrigible. —**in/cor·ri·gi·bil/i·ty,** **in·cor/ri·gi·ble·ness,** *n.* —**in·cor/ri·gi·bly,** *adv.*

in·cor·rupt (ĭn/kə rŭpt/), *adj.* 1. not corrupt; not debased or perverted; morally upright. 2. not to be bribed. 3. free from decomposition or putrefaction. 4. not vitiated by errors or alterations. Also, **in/cor·rupt/ed.** —**in/cor·rupt/ly,** *adv.* —**in/cor·rupt/ness,** *n.*

in·cor·rupt·i·ble (ĭn/kə rŭp/tə bəl), *adj.* 1. not corruptible; incapable of corruption: *a man of incorruptible integrity.* 2. that cannot be perverted or bribed: *incorruptible by money.* —**in/cor·rupt/i·bil/i·ty,** **in/·cor·rupt/i·ble·ness,** *n.* —**in/cor·rupt/i·bly,** *adv.*

in·cor·rup·tion (ĭn/kə rŭp/shən), *n. Archaic.* incorrupt condition.

incr., 1. increased. 2. increasing.

in·cras·sate (*v.* ĭn krăs/āt; *adj.* ĭn krăs/ĭt, -āt), *v.,* **-sated, -sating,** *adj.* —*v.t.* 1. to thicken. 2. *Pharm.* to make (a liquid) thicker by addition of another substance or by evaporation. —*v.i.* 3. to become thick or thicker. —*adj.* 4. Also, **in·cras/sat·ed.** *Bot., Entomol.* thickened or swollen. [t. LL: m.s. *incrassātus,* pp.] —**in/cras·sa/tion,** *n.*

in·crease (*v.* ĭn krēs/; *n.* ĭn/krēs), *v.,* **-creased, -creasing,** *n.* —*v.t.* 1. to make greater in any respect; augment; add to. 2. to make more numerous. —*v.i.* 3. to become greater or more numerous: *sales increased.* 4. to multiply by propagation. 5. *Poetic.* to wax, as the moon. —*n.* 6. growth or augmentation in numbers: *the increase of crime.* 7. multiplication by propagation; production of offspring. 8. offspring or progeny. 9. act or process of increasing. 10. that by which something is increased. 11. the result of increasing. 12. produce of the earth. 13. product; profit; interest. [ME *encrese(n),* t. AF: m. *encres(s)-,* var. of OF *encreis(s)-,* s. *encreistre,* g. L *increscere*] —**in/creas/a·ble,** *adj.* —**in·creas/er,** *n.* —**in·creas/ing·ly,** *adv.*
—Syn. 1. INCREASE, AUGMENT, ENLARGE may all mean to

make larger. To INCREASE means to make greater, as in quantity, extent, degree: *to increase someone's salary, to increase the velocity, increase the (degree of) concentration.* ENLARGE means to increase in size, extent, or range: *to enlarge a building, a business, one's conceptions.* AUGMENT, a more formal word, means to increase or enlarge especially by addition from the outside: *to augment one's income (by doing extra work).*

in·cre·ate (ĭn'krĭ āt', ĭn'krĭ āt'), *adj.* **1.** not created; uncreated. **2.** existing without having been created.

in·cred·i·ble (ĭn krĕd'ə bəl), *adj.* **1.** seeming too extraordinary to be possible: *an incredible story.* **2.** not credible; that cannot be believed. **—in·cred'i·bil'i·ty, in·cred'i·ble·ness,** *n.* **—in·cred'i·bly,** *adv.*

in·cre·du·li·ty (ĭn'krə dōo'lə tĭ, -dōō'-), *n.* the quality of being incredulous; a refusal of belief.

in·cred·u·lous (ĭn krĕj'ə ləs), *adj.* **1.** not credulous; indisposed to believe; skeptical. **2.** indicating unbelief: *an incredulous smile.* **—in·cred'u·lous·ly,** *adv.* **—in·cred'u·lous·ness,** *n.* **—Syn. 1.** See doubtful.

in·cre·ment (ĭn'krə mənt, ĭng'-), *n.* **1.** something added or gained; an addition or increase. **2.** profit. **3.** act or process of increasing; growth. **4.** *Math.* **a.** the difference between two values of a variable; an increase (positive, negative, or zero) in an independent variable. **b.** the increase of a function due to this. [ME, t. L: s. *incrementum* an increase] **—in'cre·men'tal,** *adj.*

in·cres·cent (ĭn krĕs'ənt), *adj.* increasing or waxing, as the moon. [t. L: s. *increscens,* ppr.]

in·cre·tion (ĭn krē'shən), *n.* **1.** a substance, as an autacoid, secreted internally. **2.** the process of such secretion. [back formation from *incretionary,* f. IN-² + *-cretion-ary,* modeled on *concretionary*]

in·crim·i·nate (ĭn krĭm'ə nāt'), *v.t.,* **-nated, -nating. 1.** to charge with a crime or fault. **2.** to involve in an accusation. [t. ML: m.s. *incriminātus,* pp., accused of a crime. See IN-², CRIMINATE] **—in·crim'i·na'tor,** *n.* **—in·crim'i·na·to·ry** (ĭn krĭm'ə nə tōr'ĭ), *adj.*

in·crust (ĭn krŭst'), *v.t.* **1.** to cover or line with a crust or hard coating. **2.** to form into a crust. **3.** to deposit as a crust. Also, **encrust.** [t. L: s. *incrustāre*]

in·crus·ta·tion (ĭn'krŭs tā'shən), *n.* **1.** an incrusting or being incrusted. **2.** a crust or coat of anything on the surface of a body; a covering, coating, or scale. **3.** the inlaying or addition of enriching materials to a surface. **4.** the inlaid or added enriching materials to a surface or an object. Also, **encrustation.**

in·cu·bate (ĭn'kyə bāt', ĭng'-), *v.,* **-bated, -bating.** **—v.t. 1.** to sit upon (eggs) for the purpose of hatching. **2.** to hatch (eggs), as by sitting upon them or by artificial heat. **3.** to maintain (bacterial cultures, etc.) at the most favorable temperature for development. **4.** to keep at even temperature, as immature infants. **5.** to produce as if by hatching. **—v.i. 6.** to sit upon eggs. **7.** to undergo incubation. **8.** to brood upon. [t. L: m.s. *incubātus,* pp., hatched, sat on] **—in'cu·ba'tive,** *adj.*

in·cu·ba·tion (ĭn'kyə bā'shən, ĭng'-), *n.* **1.** the act or process of incubating. **2.** the condition or quality of being incubated. **—in'cu·ba'tion·al,** *adj.*

incubation period, *Pathol.* the period between infection and the appearance of signs of a disease.

in·cu·ba·tor (ĭn'kyə bā'tər, ĭng'-), *n.* **1.** an apparatus for hatching eggs artificially, consisting essentially of a case heated by a lamp or the like. **2.** a boxlike apparatus in which prematurely born infants are kept at a constant and suitable temperature. **3.** a device in which bacterial cultures, etc. are developed at a constant suitable temperature. **4.** one who or that which incubates. [t. L]

in·cu·bus (ĭn'kyə bəs, ĭng'-), *n., pl.* **-bi** (-bī'), **-buses. 1.** an imaginary demon or evil spirit supposed to descend upon sleeping persons. **2.** something that weighs upon or oppresses one like a nightmare. **3.** a nightmare. [ME, t. LL: nightmare, ML a demon, der. L *incubāre* lie on]

in·cu·des (ĭn kū'dēz), *n., pl.* of **incus.**

in·cul·cate (ĭn kŭl'kāt, ĭn'kŭl kāt'), *v.t.,* **-cated, -cating.** to impress by repeated statement or admonition; teach persistently and earnestly (usually fol. by *upon* or *in*). [t. L: m.s. *inculcātus,* pp., stamped in, impressed upon] **—in·cul·ca'tion,** *n.* **—in·cul'ca·tor,** *n.*

in·cul·pa·ble (ĭn kŭl'pə bəl), *adj.* not culpable; blameless. **—in·cul'pa·bly,** *adv.*

in·cul·pate (ĭn kŭl'pāt, ĭn'kŭl pāt'), *v.t.,* **-pated, -pating. 1.** to charge with fault; blame; accuse. **2.** to involve in a charge; incriminate. [t. ML: m.s. *inculpātus,* pp. of *inculpāre,* f. in- IN-² + *culpāre* blame] **—in'cul·pa'tion,** *n.*

in·cul·pa·to·ry (ĭn kŭl'pə tōr'ĭ), *adj.* tending to inculpate; imputing blame; incriminating.

in·cult (ĭn kŭlt'), *adj. Archaic.* **1.** uncultivated; untilled. **2.** wild; rude; unrefined. [t. L: s. *incultus*]

in·cum·ben·cy (ĭn kŭm'bən sĭ), *n., pl.* **-cies. 1.** the state of being incumbent. **2.** that which is incumbent. **3.** an incumbent weight or mass. **4.** the position or term of an incumbent. **5.** *Now Rare.* a duty or obligation.

in·cum·bent (ĭn kŭm'bənt), *adj.* **1.** resting on one; obligatory: *a duty incumbent upon me.* **2.** lying, leaning, or pressing on something: *incumbent posture.* **—n. 3.** the holder of an office. **4.** *Brit.* one who holds an ecclesiastical benefice. [ME, t. L: s. *incumbens,* ppr., leaning upon] **—in·cum'bent·ly,** *adv.*

in·cum·ber (ĭn kŭm'bər), *v.t.* encumber.

in·cum·brance (ĭn kŭm'brəns), *n.* encumbrance.

in·cu·nab·u·la (ĭn'kyōō năb'yə lə), *n.pl., sing.* **-lum** (-ləm). **1.** books produced in the infancy of printing (before 1500) from movable type. **2.** the earliest stages or first traces of anything. [t. L: cradle, beginning, swaddling clothes] **—in'cu·nab'u·lar,** *adj.*

in·cur (ĭn kûr'), *v.t.,* **-curred, -curring. 1.** to run or fall into (some consequence, usually undesirable or injurious). **2.** to become liable or subject to through one's own action; bring upon oneself: *to incur his displeasure.* [ME, t. L: m.s. *incurrere* run into, or against]

in·cur·a·ble (ĭn kyŏŏr'ə bəl), *adj.* **1.** not curable. **—n. 2.** one suffering from an incurable disease. **—in·cur'a·bil'i·ty, in·cur'a·ble·ness,** *n.* **—in·cur'a·bly,** *adv.*

in·cu·ri·ous (ĭn kyŏŏr'ĭ əs), *adj.* **1.** not curious; inattentive or unobservant. **2.** indifferent. **3.** deficient in interest or novelty. **—in·cu·ri·os·i·ty** (ĭn kyŏŏr'ĭ ŏs'ə tĭ), **in·cu'ri·ous·ness,** *n.* **—in·cu'ri·ous·ly,** *adv.*

in·cur·rence (ĭn kûr'əns), *n.* the act of incurring, bringing on, or subjecting oneself to something.

in·cur·rent (ĭn kûr'ənt), *adj.* carrying, or relating to, an inward current. [t. L: s. *incurrens,* ppr., running into]

in·cur·sion (ĭn kûr'zhən, -shən), *n.* **1.** a hostile entrance into or invasion of a place or territory, esp. one of sudden character. **2.** a harmful inroad. **3.** a running in: *the incursion of sea water.* [ME, t. L: s. *incursio* onset]

in·cur·sive (ĭn kûr'sĭv), *adj.* making incursions.

in·cur·vate (*adj.* ĭn kûr'vĭt, -vāt; *v.* ĭn kûr'vāt), *adj., v.,* **-vated, -vating. —adj. 1.** curved, esp. inward. **—v.t. 2.** to make curved; turn from a straight line or course; curve, esp. inward. [t. L: m.s. *incurvātus,* pp., bent in] **—in·cur·va'tion,** *n.*

in·curve (*v.* ĭn kûrv'; *n.* ĭn'kûrv'), *v.,* **-curved, -curving,** *n. Baseball.* **—v.t. 1.** to curve inward. **—n. 2.** an inward-curving ball, i.e. toward the batter. [t. L: m.s. *incurvāre* bend in]

in·cus (ĭng'kəs), *n., pl.* **incudes** (ĭn kū'dēz). *Anat.* the middle one of a chain of three small bones in the middle ear of man and other mammals. See **malleus** and **stapes.** See diag. under **ear.** [t. L: anvil]

in·cuse (ĭn kūz'), *adj.* **1.** hammered or stamped in, as a figure on a coin. **—n. 2.** an incuse figure or impression. [t. L: m.s. *incūsus,* pp., forged with a hammer]

Ind (ĭnd), *n.* **1.** *Now Poetic.* India. **2.** *Obs.* the Indies.

ind-, var. of **indo-** before vowels, as in *indene.*

Ind., 1. India. **2.** Indian. **3.** Indiana. **4.** Indies.

ind., 1. independent. **2.** index. **3.** indicative.

in·da·ba (ĭn dä'bä), *n.* a conference or consultation between or with South African natives. [Zulu]

in·da·mine (ĭn'də mēn', -mĭn), *n. Chem.* any of a certain series of basic organic compounds which form bluish and greenish salts: used in the manufacture of dyes. Also, **in·da·min** (ĭn'də mĭn). [f. IND(IGO) + AMINE]

in·debt (ĭn dĕt'), *v.t.* to place under obligation for benefits, favors, assistance, etc., received (used chiefly in *indebted,* pp.). [first used in pp., ME *endetted,* after OF *endetter,* der. *en-* EN-¹ + *dette* DEBT] **—in·debt'ed,** *adj.*

in·debt·ed·ness (ĭn dĕt'ĭd nĭs), *n.* **1.** state of being indebted. **2.** an amount owed. **3.** debts collectively.

in·de·cen·cy (ĭn dē'sən sĭ), *n., pl.* **-cies. 1.** the quality of being indecent. **2.** impropriety; indelicacy or immodesty. **3.** obscenity. **4.** an indecent act, remark, etc.

in·de·cent (ĭn dē'sənt), *adj.* **1.** offending against recognized standards of propriety or good taste; vulgar: *indecent language.* **2.** not decent; unbecoming or unseemly: *indecent conduct.* **—in·de'cent·ly,** *adv.* **—Syn. 2.** See **improper.**

in·de·cid·u·ate (ĭn'dĭ sĭj'ŏŏ ĭt, -āt'), *adj.* **1.** *Zool.* not deciduate. **2.** *Bot.* having permanent leaves.

in·de·cid·u·ous (ĭn'dĭ sĭj'ŏŏ əs), *adj. Bot.* **1.** not deciduous, as leaves. **2.** (of trees) evergreen.

in·de·ci·pher·a·ble (ĭn'dĭ sī'fər ə bəl), *adj.* not decipherable. **—in'de·ci'pher·a·bil'i·ty,** *n.*

in·de·ci·sion (ĭn'dĭ sĭzh'ən), *n.* inability to decide.

in·de·ci·sive (ĭn'dĭ sī'sĭv), *adj.* **1.** not decisive or conclusive: *a severe but indecisive battle.* **2.** characterized by indecision, as persons; irresolute; undecided. **—in'de·ci'sive·ly,** *adv.* **—in'de·ci'sive·ness,** *n.*

indecl., indeclinable.

in·de·clin·a·ble (ĭn'dĭ klī'nə bəl), *adj. Gram.* not declined, especially of a word belonging to a form class most of whose members are declined, as the Latin adjective *decem* (ten). **—in'de·clin'a·bly,** *adv.*

in·de·com·pos·a·ble (ĭn'dē kəm pō'zə bəl), *adj.* not decomposable.

in·de·co·rous (ĭn dĕk'ə rəs, ĭn'dĭ kōr'əs), *adj.* not decorous; violating propriety; unseemly. [t. L: m. *indecōrus*] **—in·dec'o·rous·ly,** *adv.* **—in·dec'o·rous·ness,** *n.*

in·de·co·rum (ĭn'dĭ kōr'əm), *n.* **1.** indecorous behavior or character. **2.** something indecorous. [t. L, prop. neut. of *indecōrus* indecorous]

in·deed (ĭn dēd'), *adv.* **1.** in fact; in reality; in truth; truly (used for emphasis, to confirm and amplify a previous statement, to indicate a concession or admission, or, interrogatively, to obtain confirmation). **—interj. 2.** an expression of surprise, incredulity, irony, etc. [ME *in dede.* See IN, prep., DEED, n.]

indef., indefinite.

in·de·fat·i·ga·ble (ĭn'dĭ făt'ə gə bəl), *adj.* incapable of being tired out; not yielding to fatigue. [t. L: m.s. *indēfatīgābilis*] **—in'de·fat'i·ga·bil'i·ty, in'de·fat'i·ga·ble·ness,** *n.* **—in'de·fat'i·ga·bly,** *adv.*

ăct, āble, dâre, ärt; ĕbb, ēqual; ĭf, īce; hŏt, ōver, ôrder, oil, bŏŏk, ōōze, out; ŭp, ūse, ûrge; ə = a in alone; ch, chief; g, give; ng, ring; sh, shoe; th, thin; ŧħ, that; zh, vision. See the full key on inside cover.

in·de·fea·si·ble (ĭn'dĭ fē'zə bəl), *adj.* not defeasible; not to be annulled or made void; not forfeitable. **—in·de·fea'si·bil'i·ty,** *n.* **—in'de·fea'si·bly,** *adv.*

in·de·fect·i·ble (ĭn'dĭ fĕk'tə bəl), *adj.* **1.** not defectible; not liable to defect or failure; unfailing. **2.** not liable to fault or imperfection; faultless. **—in'de·fect'·i·bil'i·ty,** *n.* **—in'de·fect'i·bly,** *adv.*

in·de·fec·tive (ĭn'dĭ fĕk'tĭv), *adj.* not defective.

in·de·fen·si·ble (ĭn'dĭ fĕn'sə bəl), *adj.* **1.** that cannot be justified; inexcusable: *an indefensible remark.* **2.** that cannot be defended by force of arms: *an indefensible frontier.* **—in'de·fen'si·bil'i·ty, in'de·fen'si·ble·ness,** *n.* **—in'de·fen'si·bly,** *adv.*

in·de·fin·a·ble (ĭn'dĭ fī'nə bəl), *adj.* not definable. **—in'de·fin'a·ble·ness,** *n.* **—in'de·fin'a·bly,** *adv.*

in·def·i·nite (ĭn dĕf'ə nĭt), *adj.* **1.** not definite; without fixed or specified limit; unlimited: *an indefinite number.* **2.** not clearly defined or determined; not precise. **3.** *Gram.* not specifying precisely, as the indefinite pronoun *some.* **4.** *Bot.* **a.** very numerous or not easily counted, as stamens. **b.** (of an inflorescence) indeterminate. [t. L: m.s. *indefīnītus*] **—in·def'i·nite·ly,** *adv.* **—in·def'i·nite·ness,** *n.* **—Syn. 2.** vague, obscure.

indefinite article, the article (as *a, an*) which classes as "single and unidentified" the noun it modifies.

in·de·his·cent (ĭn'dĭ hĭs'ənt), *adj. Bot.* not dehiscent; not opening at maturity. **—in'de·his'cence,** *n.*

in·del·i·ble (ĭn dĕl'ə bəl), *adj.* **1.** incapable of being deleted or obliterated: *an indelible impression.* **2.** making indelible marks: *an indelible pencil.* [t. L: m.s. *indēlēbilis* that cannot be destroyed] **—in·del'i·bil'i·ty, in·del'i·ble·ness,** *n.* **—in·del'i·bly,** *adv.*

in·del·i·ca·cy (ĭn dĕl'ə kə sĭ), *n., pl.* **-cies. 1.** the quality of being indelicate. **2.** something indelicate.

in·del·i·cate (ĭn dĕl'ə kĭt), *adj.* **1.** not delicate; lacking delicacy. **2.** offensive to a sense of propriety, or modesty; unrefined. **—in·del'i·cate·ly,** *adv.*

in·dem·ni·fi·ca·tion (ĭn dĕm'nə fə kā'shən), *n.* **1.** the act of indemnifying. **2.** the state of being indemnified. **3.** that which serves to indemnify; compensation.

in·dem·ni·fy (ĭn dĕm'nə fī'), *v.t.,* **-fied, -fy·ing. 1.** to compensate for damage or loss sustained, expense incurred, etc. **2.** to engage to make good or secure against anticipated loss; give security against (future damage or liability). **—in·dem'ni·fi'er,** *n.*

in·dem·ni·tee (ĭn dĕm'nə tē'), *n.* one who receives indemnity.

in·dem·ni·tor (ĭn dĕm'nə tər), *n.* one who gives indemnity.

in·dem·ni·ty (ĭn dĕm'nə tĭ), *n., pl.* **-ties. 1.** protection or security against damage or loss. **2.** compensation for damage or loss sustained. **3.** something paid by way of such compensation. **4.** legal exemption from liabilities or penalties incurred by one's actions. **5.** legal exemption from penalties attaching to unconstitutional or illegal actions, granted to public officers and other persons. [late ME, t. LL: m.s. *indemnitas,* der. L *indemnis* unharmed]

in·de·mon·stra·ble (ĭn'dĭ mŏn'strə bəl, ĭn dĕm'ən-), *adj.* not demonstrable; incapable of being demonstrated or proved. **—in'de·mon'stra·bil'i·ty,** *n.* **—in'de·mon'stra·bly,** *adv.*

in·dene (ĭn'dēn), *n. Chem.* a colorless liquid hydrocarbon, C_9H_8, obtained from coal tar by fractional distillation. [f. IND- + -ENE]

in·dent[1] (*v.* ĭn dĕnt'; *n.* ĭn'dĕnt, ĭn dĕnt'), *v.t.* **1.** to form deep recesses in: *the sea indents the coast.* **2.** to set in or back from the margin, as the first line of a paragraph. **3.** to sever (a document drawn up in duplicate) along an irregular line as a means of identification. **4.** to cut or tear the edge of (copies of a document) in an irregular way. **5.** to make toothlike notches in; notch. **6.** to indenture, as an apprentice. **7.** to draw an order upon. **8.** to order, as commodities. **—v.i. 9.** to form a recess. **10.** to enter into an agreement by indenture; make a compact. **11.** to make out an order or requisition in duplicate. **12.** *Brit. Mil.* to make a requisition. **13.** *Obs.* to draw upon a person or thing for something. **—n. 14.** a toothlike notch or deep recess; an indentation. **15.** an indention. **16.** *Brit.* an official requisition for stores. **17.** an order for goods. **18.** an indenture. **19.** a certificate issued by the U.S. government at the close of the Revolutionary War, for the principal or interest due on the public debt. [ME *endente(n),* t. OF: m. *endenter,* der. *en-* EN-[1] + *dent* tooth] **—in·dent'er,** *n.*

Indented molding

in·dent[2] (*v.* ĭn dĕnt'; *n.* ĭn'dĕnt, ĭn dĕnt'), *v.t.* **1.** to dent or press in so as to form a dent. **2.** to make a dent in. **—n. 3.** a dent. [ME, f. IN-[2] + DENT[1]]

in·den·ta·tion (ĭn'dĕn tā'shən), *n.* **1.** a cut, notch, or deep recess: *various bays and indentations.* **2.** a series of incisions or notches. **3.** a notching or being notched. **4.** an indention. [f. INDENT[1] + -ATION]

in·den·tion (ĭn dĕn'shən), *n.* **1.** an indenting. **2.** an indentation. **3.** an indenting of a line or lines, and leaving of blank space. **4.** the blank space so left.

in·den·ture (ĭn dĕn'chər), *n., v.,* **-tured, -tur·ing. —n. 1.** a deed and agreement executed in two or more copies with edges correspondingly indented as a means of identification. **2.** any deed or sealed agreement. **3** a contract by which a person, as an apprentice, is bound to service. **4.** any official or formal list, certificate, etc., authenticated for use as a voucher or the like. **5.** the formal agreement between a group of bondholders and the debtor as to the terms of the debt. **6.** indentation. **—v.t. 7.** to bind by indenture, as an apprentice. **8.** *Obs.* to indent; wrinkle; furrow. [ME *endenture,* t. OF: m. *endenteure* indentation]

in·de·pend·ence ((ĭn'dĭ pĕn'dəns), *n.* **1.** the state or quality of being independent. **2.** freedom from subjection, or from the influence of others. **3.** exemption from external control or support. **4.** a competency. **—Syn. 1.** See freedom.

In·de·pend·ence (ĭn'dĭ pĕn'dəns), *n.* a city in W Missouri: starting point of the Santa Fe and Oregon trails. 36,963 (1950).

Independence Day, *U.S.* July 4, a holiday commemorating the adoption of the Declaration of Independence on July 4, 1776.

in·de·pend·en·cy (ĭn'dĭ pĕn'dən sĭ), *n., pl.* **-cies. 1.** independence. **2.** a territory not under the control of any other power. **3.** (*cap.*) *Eccles.* **a.** the principle that the individual congregation or church is an autonomous and equalitarian society free from any external ecclesiastical control. **b.** the polity based on this principle.

in·de·pend·ent (ĭn'dĭ pĕn'dənt), *adj.* **1.** not influenced by others in matters of opinion, conduct, etc.; thinking or acting for oneself: *an independent person.* **2.** not subject to another's authority or jurisdiction; autonomous; free. **3.** not influenced by the thought or action of others: *independent research.* **4.** not dependent; not depending or contingent on something else for existence, operation, etc. **5.** (adverbially) independently. **6.** not relying on another or others for aid or support. **7.** declining others' aid or support; refusing to be under obligations to others. **8.** possessing a competency. **9.** sufficient for a competency. **10.** expressive of a spirit of independence; self-confident; unconstrained. **11.** free from party commitments in voting. **12.** *Math.* (of a quantity or function) not depending upon another for value. **13.** (*cap.*) *Eccles.* of or pertaining to the Independents. **—n. 14.** an independent person or thing. **15.** *Pol.* one who votes without blind loyalty to any organized party. **16.** (*cap.*) *Eccles.* an adherent of an Independency. **17.** *Brit.* a Congregationalist. **—in'de·pend'ent·ly,** *adv.*

independent clause, *Gram.* main clause.

in·de·scrib·a·ble (ĭn'dĭ skrī'bə bəl), *adj.* not describable. **—in'de·scrib'a·bil'i·ty, in'de·scrib'a·ble·ness,** *n.* **—in'de·scrib'a·bly,** *adv.*

in·de·struct·i·ble (ĭn'dĭ strŭk'tə bəl), *adj.* not destructible. **—in'de·struct'i·bil'i·ty, in'de·struct'i·ble·ness,** *n.* **—in'de·struct'i·bly,** *adv.*

in·de·ter·mi·na·ble (ĭn'dĭ tûr'mə nə bəl), *adj.* **1.** not determinable; incapable of being ascertained. **2.** incapable of being decided or settled. **3.** *Rare.* interminable. **—n. 4.** that which is indeterminable. **—in'de·ter'mi·na·bly,** *adv.*

in·de·ter·mi·nate (ĭn'dĭ tûr'mə nĭt), *adj.* **1.** not determinate; not fixed in extent; indefinite; uncertain. **2.** not clear; vague: *a cloudy and indeterminate meaning.* **3.** not established. **4.** not settled or decided. **5.** *Bot.* (of an inflorescence) having the axis or axes not ending in a flower or bud, thus allowing further elongation. **—in'de·ter'mi·nate·ly,** *adv.* **—in'de·ter'mi·nate·ness,** *n.*

indeterminate sentence, *Penol.* a penalty imposed by a court which has relatively wide limits or no limits, as imprisonment for one to ten years.

in·de·ter·mi·na·tion (ĭn'dĭ tûr'mə nā'shən), *n.* **1.** condition or quality of being indeterminate. **2.** an unsettled state, as of the mind.

in·de·ter·min·ism (ĭn'dĭ tûr'mə nĭz'əm), *n. Philos.* **1.** the doctrine that human actions, though somewhat influenced by preëxisting psychological and other conditions, are not entirely governed by them, but contain a certain freedom and spontaneity. **2.** the theory that the will is to some extent independent of the strength of motives, or may itself modify their strength in choice. **—in'de·ter'min·ist,** *n., adj.*

in·dex (ĭn'dĕks), *n., pl.* **-dex·es, -di·ces** (-də sēz'), *v.* **—n. 1.** a detailed alphabetical key to names, places, and topics in a book with reference to their page location in the book. **2.** something used or serving to point out; a sign, token, or indication: *a true index of his character.* **3.** something that serves to direct attention to some fact, condition, etc.; a guiding principle. **4.** a pointer or indicator in a scientific instrument. **5.** a piece of wood, metal, or the like, serving as a pointer or indicator. **6.** *Print., etc.* a sign (☞) used to point out a particular note, paragraph, etc. **7.** the index finger; the forefinger. **8.** *Science.* a number or formula expressing some property, ratio, etc., of a thing indicated.

9. *Alg.* **a.** an exponent. **b.** the integer n in a radical $\sqrt[n]{\ }$ defining the n-th root: $\sqrt[3]{7}$ *is a radical having index three.*

10. (*cap.*) a list of books which Roman Catholics are forbidden by Church authority to read without special permission, or which are not to be read unless expurgated or corrected (L *Index Librorum Prohibitorum,* **Index of Prohibited Books**), or a list of books of the latter class only, with specification of objectionable passages (L *Index Expurgatorius,* **Expurgatory Index**). **11.** *Obs.* a table of contents. **12.** *Obs.* a preface. **—v.t. 13.** to provide with an index, as a book. **14.** to enter in an index, as a word. **15.** to serve to indicate. [ME, t. L:

---

b., blend of, blended;   c., cognate with;   d., dialect, dialectal;   der., derived from;   f., formed from;   g., going back to; m., modification of;   r., replacing;   s., stem of;   t., taken from;   ?, perhaps.   See the full key on inside cover.

index, forefinger, sign] —**in′dex·er,** *n.* —**in·dex·i·cal** (ĭn·dĕk′sə kəl), *adj.* —**in′dex·less,** *adj.*

index finger, the forefinger.

index number, *Statistics.* a series of numbers which shows relative changes in prices, immigration, etc.

In·di·a (ĭn′dĭ·ə), *n.* a large peninsula in southern Asia, S of the Himalayas and projecting into the Indian Ocean. Politically, India is divided into the two states of **India** (ab. 337,-110,000 pop., est. 1948; 1,246,880 sq. mi. *Cap.:* New Delhi) and **Pakistan** (ab. 80,260,000 pop., est. 1948; 360,780 sq. mi. *Cap.:* Karachi), and the smaller areas of French India and Portuguese India. The state of India became an independent republic on Jan. 26, 1950. Pakistan has dominion status in the British Commonwealth of Nations, [t. L, t. Gk., der. *Indós* river Indus (t. Pers.: m. *Hind,* c. Skt. *Sindhu* river Indus, orig. river)]

India, February, 1950

India ink, 1. a black pigment, made chiefly in China and Japan, consisting of lampblack mixed with a binding material and molded into sticks or cakes. 2. a liquid ink from this.

In·di·a·man (ĭn′dĭ·ə mən), *n., pl.* **-men.** a ship in the India trade, esp. a large one of the East India Company.

In·di·an (ĭn′dĭ·ən), *n.* 1. a member of the aboriginal race of America or of any of the aboriginal North and South American stocks, often excepting the Eskimos (**American Indian**). 2. *Colloq.* any of the American Indian languages. 3. a member of any of the native races of India or the East Indies (**East Indian**). 4. a European, esp. an Englishman, who resides or has resided in India or the East Indies. —*adj.* 5. denoting, belonging to, or pertaining to the race embracing the aborigines of America. 6. of or pertaining to India or the East Indies (often **East Indian**). 7. made of Indian corn: *Indian meal.* [ME, f. INDIA + -AN]

In·di·an·a (ĭn′dĭ·ăn′ə), *n.* a State in the central United States: a part of the Midwest. 3,934,224 pop. (1950); 36,291 sq. mi. *Cap.:* Indianapolis. *Abbr.:* Ind. —**In·di·an·i·an** (ĭn′dĭ ăn′ĭ ən), *adj., n.*

Indian agency, headquarters of an Indian agent.

Indian agent, 1. one serving as an agent among the Indians. 2. (in later use) an official representing the United States in dealing with an Indian tribe or tribes.

In·di·an·ap·o·lis (ĭn′dĭ ə năp′ə lĭs), *n.* the capital of Indiana, in the central part. 427,173 (1950).

Indian club, a gymnasium hand apparatus made of wood or metal, bottle-shaped, usually used in pairs.

Indian corn, *Chiefly Brit.* maize.

Indian Empire, (prior to recent political developments in India) British India, and the Indian states ruled by native princes but under indirect British control.

Indian file, single file, as of persons traveling.

Indian giver, *U.S. Colloq.* one who takes back a gift.

Indian hemp, 1. a plant, genus *Apocynum,* native to America, whose root has laxative and emotic properties. 2. an East Indian variety of hemp, *Cannabis sativa* or *indica.* Cf. **cannabis.**

Indian licorice, a fabaceous woody shrub, *Abrus precatorius,* of India, etc., whose seeds are used for beads, and whose root is employed as a substitute for licorice.

Indian mallow, 1. a malvaceous plant, *Abutilon Theophrasti,* with yellow flowers and velvety leaves, introduced into America, etc., from southern Asia. 2. any of certain related species.

Indian meal, *Chiefly Brit.* corn meal.

Indian millet, durra.

Indian Ocean, an ocean S of Asia, E of Africa, and W of Australia. ab. 28,350,000 sq. mi.

Indian paintbrush, any of several showy species of the scrophulariaceous genus *Castilleja,* as *C. linariaefolia* of southwestern U.S. (the State flower of Wyoming).

Indian pipe, a leafless saprophytic plant, *Monotropa uniflora,* of North America and Asia, having a solitary flower, and resembling a tobacco pipe.

Indian pudding, a sweet pudding made of corn meal.

Indian red, 1. earth of a yellowish-red color, found esp. in the Persian Gulf, which serves as a pigment and as a polish for gold and silver objects. 2. a pigment of that color prepared by oxidizing the salts of iron.

Indian rice, a graminaceous plant of marshes of the central and southeastern U.S., *Zizania aquatica.*

Indian summer, a period of mild, dry weather, usually accompanied by a hazy atmosphere, occurring in the U.S. and Canada in late autumn or early winter.

Indian Territory, a former territory of the United States: now in E Oklahoma. ab. 31,000 sq. mi.

Indian tobacco, a common American herb, *Lobelia inflata,* with small blue flowers and inflated capsules.

Indian turnip, 1. the jack-in-the-pulpit. 2. its root.

India paper, 1. a fine, thin but opaque paper made in the Orient, used chiefly in the production of thin-

paper editions and for impressions of engravings. 2. a thin, tough, rag paper used in printing Bibles, prayerbooks, large reference works, etc.

India print, a cotton fabric block-printed in India.

India rubber, 1. a highly elastic substance obtained from the milky juice of numerous tropical plants, used for rubbing out pencil marks, and variously in the arts and manufactures; caoutchouc; gum elastic; rubber. 2. *U.S. Obs.* a rubber overshoe. Also, **india rubber.**

In·dic (ĭn′dĭk), *adj.* 1. of or pertaining to India; Indian. 2. of or pertaining to a subgroup of the Indo-Iranian languages, associated with India ancient and modern. [t. L: s. *Indicus,* t. Gk.: m. *Indikós*]

indic., 1. indicating. 2. Also, **ind.** indicative.

in·di·can (ĭn′də kən), *n.* 1. *Chem.* a glucoside, $C_{14}H_{17}$-NO_6, which occurs in plants yielding indigo, and from which indigo is obtained. 2. *Biochem.* a component of urine, indoxyl potassium sulfate, $C_8H_6O_4SK$. [f. s. L *indicum* indigo + -AN]

in·di·cant (ĭn′də kənt), *adj.* 1. indicating. 2. indicative. —*n.* 3. that which indicates.

in·di·cate (ĭn′də kāt′), *v.t.,* **-cated, -cating.** 1. to be a sign of; betoken; imply: *his hesitation indicates unwillingness.* 2. to point out or point to; direct attention to: *to indicate a place on a map.* 3. to show, or make known: *the thermometer indicates temperature.* 4. to state or express, esp. briefly or in a general way: *to indicate one's intentions.* 5. *Med.* **a.** (of symptoms, etc.) to point out (a particular remedy, treatment, etc.) as suitable or necessary. **b.** to show the presence of (a disease, etc.). [t. L: m.s. *indicātus,* pp.]

in·di·ca·tion (ĭn′də kā′shən), *n.* 1. anything serving to indicate or point out, as a sign, token, etc. 2. *Med.* a special symptom or the like which points out a suitable remedy or treatment or shows the presence of a disease. 3. the act of indicating. 4. the degree marked by an instrument.

in·dic·a·tive (ĭn dĭk′ə tĭv), *adj.* 1. that indicates; pointing out; suggestive (fol. by *of*). 2. *Gram.* designating or pertaining to the verb mode of ordinary statements, questions, etc., in contrast to hypothetical statements or those made without reference to a specific actor or time of action. For example: in the sentence *John plays football,* the verb *plays* is in the indicative mode. —*n.* 3. *Gram.* **a.** the indicative mode. **b.** a verb therein. —**in·dic′a·tive·ly,** *adv.*

in·di·ca·tor (ĭn′də kā′tər), *n.* 1. one who or that which indicates. 2. a pointing or directing device, as a pointer on an instrument. 3. an instrument which indicates the condition of a machine, etc. 4. a pressure gage; an apparatus for recording the variations of pressure or vacuum in the cylinder of an engine. 5. *Chem.* a substance used (esp. in volumetric analysis) to indicate (as by a change in color) the condition of a solution, the point at which a certain reaction ends and another begins, etc.

in·di·ca·to·ry (ĭn′də kə tōr′ĭ), *adj.* serving to indicate.

in·di·ces (ĭn′də sēz′), *n.* pl. of **index.**

in·di·ci·a (ĭn dĭsh′ĭ ə), *n.pl., sing.* **-dicium** (-dĭsh′ĭ əm). 1. envelope markings substituted for stamps or other regular cancellations in a large shipment of mail. 2. *Rare.* indications. [t. L, pl. of *indicium* sign, mark] —**in·di·cial** (ĭn dĭsh′əl), *adj.*

in·dict (ĭn dīt′), *v.t.* 1. to charge with an offense or crime; accuse. 2. (of a grand jury) to bring a formal accusation against, as a means of bringing to trial. [ME *endite*(n), t. AF: m. *enditer* accuse, indict. Cf. OF *enditer* INDITE] —**in·dict′er, in·dict′or,** *n.*

in·dict·a·ble (ĭn dī′tə bəl), *adj.* 1. liable to be indicted, as a person. 2. making one liable to be indicted, as an offense.

in·dic·tion (ĭn dĭk′shən), *n.* 1. a proclamation made every 15 years in the later Roman Empire, fixing the valuation of property to be used as a basis for taxation. 2. a tax based on such valuation. 3. the recurring fiscal period of 15 years in the Roman Empire, long used for dating ordinary events. 4. a specified year in this period. 5. the number indicating it. 6. *Rare.* authoritative proclamation. [ME, t. L: s. *indictio*]

in·dict·ment (ĭn dīt′mənt), *n.* 1. the act of indicting. 2. *Law.* a formal accusation presented by a grand jury, usually required for felonies and other serious crimes. 3. an accusation. 4. the state of being indicted.

In·dies (ĭn′dēz), *n.pl.* 1. the West Indies. 2. a region in and near S and SE Asia: India, Indo-China and the East Indies. 3. the East Indies.

in·dif·fer·ence (ĭn dĭf′ər əns), *n.* 1. lack of interest or concern. 2. unimportance. 3. the quality or fact of being indifferent. 4. mediocre quality. Also, **in·dif′fer·en·cy.**

—**Syn.** 1. INDIFFERENCE, UNCONCERN, LISTLESSNESS, APATHY, INSENSIBILITY all imply lack of feeling. INDIFFERENCE denotes an absence of concern or interest; UNCONCERN, an absence of concern or solicitude, a calm or cool indifference in the face of what might be expected to cause uneasiness or apprehension; LISTLESSNESS, an absence of inclination or interest, a languid indifference to what is going on about one; APATHY, profound indifference suggestive of mental faculties either naturally sluggish or dulled by sickness and grief. INSENSIBILITY denotes an absence of capacity for feeling, or of susceptibility to emotional influences. —**Ant.** 1. eagerness, responsiveness.

in·dif·fer·ent (ĭn dĭf′ər ənt), *adj.* 1. without interest or concern; not caring; apathetic. 2. having no feeling favorable or unfavorable to some thing or person;

impartial. **3.** neutral in character or quality; neither good nor bad: *an indifferent specimen.* **4.** falling short of any standard of excellence; not very good: *indifferent success.* **5.** of only moderate amount, extent, etc. **6.** not making a difference, or mattering, either way, as to a person. **7.** immaterial or unimportant. **8.** not essential or obligatory, as an observance. **9.** making no difference or distinction, as between persons or things: *indifferent justice.* **10.** neutral in chemical, electrical, or magnetic quality. **11.** *Biol.* not differentiated or specialized, as cells or tissues. [ME, t. L: s. *indifferens* (def. 3)] **—in·dif′fer·ent·ly,** *adv.*

in·dif·fer·ent·ism (ĭn·dĭf′ər·ən·tĭz′əm), *n.* **1.** systematic indifference. **2.** adiaphorism. **3.** the principle that differences of religious belief are essentially unimportant. **—in·dif′fer·ent·ist,** *n.*

in·di·gence (ĭn′də·jəns), *n.* indigent state; poverty.

in·di·gene (ĭn′də·jēn′), *n.* one who or that which is indigenous or native; a native; an autochthon. Also, **in·di·gen** (ĭn′də·jən). [t. F, t. L: m. *indigena*]

in·dig·e·nous (ĭn·dĭj′ə·nəs), *adj.* **1.** originating in and characterizing a particular region or country; native (fol. by *to*): *the plants indigenous to Canada.* **2.** innate; inherent; natural (fol. by *to*). [t. LL: m. *indigenus,* der. L *indigena* native] **—in·dig′e·nous·ly,** *adv.* **—in·dig′e·nous·ness, in·di·gen·i·ty** (ĭn′də·jĕn′ə·tĭ), *n.*

in·di·gent (ĭn′də·jənt), *adj.* **1.** lacking the necessaries of life; needy; poor. **2.** destitute (fol. by *of*). **3.** *Archaic.* deficient in what is requisite. [ME, t. L: s. *indigens,* ppr.] **—in′di·gent·ly,** *adv.*

in·di·gest·ed (ĭn′də·jĕs′tĭd, -dī-), *adj.* **1.** without arrangement or order. **2.** unformed or shapeless. **3.** not digested; undigested. **4.** not duly considered.

in·di·gest·i·ble (ĭn′də·jĕs′tə·bəl, -dī-), *adj.* not digestible; not easily digested. **—in′di·gest·i·bil′i·ty, in′di·gest′i·ble·ness,** *n.* **—in′di·gest′i·bly,** *adv.*

in·di·ges·tion (ĭn′də·jĕs′chən, -dī-), *n.* incapability of, or difficulty in, digesting food; dyspepsia.

in·di·ges·tive (ĭn′də·jĕs′tĭv, -dī-), *adj.* attended with or suffering from indigestion; dyspeptic.

in·dign (ĭn·dīn′), *adj.* **1.** *Archaic.* unworthy. **2.** *Archaic.* unbecoming or disgraceful. **3.** *Now Poetic.* undeserved. [ME *indigne,* t. F, t. L: m.s. *indignus*]

in·dig·nant (ĭn·dĭg′nənt), *adj.* affected with or characterized by indignation. [t. L: s. *indignans,* ppr., deeming unworthy] **—in·dig′nant·ly,** *adv.*

in·dig·na·tion (ĭn′dĭg·nā′shən), *n.* displeasure at something deemed unworthy, unjust, or base; righteous anger. **—Syn.** See **anger.**

in·dig·ni·ty (ĭn·dĭg′nə·tĭ), *n., pl.* **-ties. 1.** injury to dignity; slighting or contemptuous treatment; a humiliating affront, insult, or injury. **2.** *Obs.* unworthiness. **3.** *Obs.* disgrace or disgraceful action. [t. L: m.s. *indignitas* unworthiness] **—Syn. 1.** See **insult.**

in·di·go (ĭn′də·gō′), *n., pl.* **-gos, -goes. 1.** a blue dye obtained from various plants, esp. of the genus *Indigofera.* **2.** indigo blue or indigotin, the coloring principle of this dye. **3.** a plant of the leguminous genus *Indigofera.* **4.** deep violet blue, between violet and blue in the spectrum. [t. Sp. or Pg., t. L: m.s. *indicum* indigo, lit., Indian (dye), t. Gk.: m. *indikŏn*] **—in·di·got·ic** (ĭn′də·gŏt′ĭk), *adj.*

indigo blue, 1. the color indigo. **2.** the essential coloring principle (a chemical compound, $C_{16}H_{10}N_2O_2$), which is contained, along with other substances, in the dye indigo, and which can also be prepared artificially. **—in′di·go-blue′,** *adj.*

indigo bunting, a North American fringilline songbird, *Passerina cyanea,* the male of which is indigo blue. Also, **indigo bird, indigo finch.**

in·di·goid (ĭn′də·goid′), *adj.* **1.** of or pertaining to that group of vat dyes which have a molecular structure like that of indigo. **—n. 2.** an indigoid substance. [f. INDIG(O) + -OID]

in·di·go·tin (ĭn′dĭg′ə·tĭn, ĭn′də·gō′tĭn), *n.* indigo blue.

in·di·rect (ĭn′də·rĕkt′, -dī-), *adj.* **1.** not direct in space; deviating from a straight line: *an indirect course in sailing.* **2.** coming or resulting otherwise than directly or immediately, as effects, consequences, etc.: *an indirect advantage.* **3.** not direct in action or procedure; not straightforward; crooked: *indirect methods.* **4.** not descending in a direct line of succession, as a title or inheritance. **5.** not direct in bearing, application, force, etc.: *indirect evidence.* **6.** *Gram.* not consisting exactly of the words originally used, as in *He said he was hungry* instead of the direct *He said, 'I am hungry.'* **—in′di·rect′ly,** *adv.* **—in′di·rect′ness,** *n.*

indirect initiative, a procedure in which a statute or amendment, proposed by popular petition, must receive legislative consideration before submission to the voters.

in·di·rec·tion (ĭn′də·rĕk′shən, -dī-), *n.* **1.** indirect action or procedure. **2.** a roundabout course or method. **3.** deceitful or crooked dealing.

indirect lighting, reflected or diffused light, used in interiors to avoid glare, shadows, etc.

indirect object, (in English and some other languages) the object with reference to which (for whose benefit, in whose interest, etc.) the action of a verb is performed, in English distinguished from the direct object by its position in the sentence or by the use of a preposition (*to* or *for*), e.g. *the boy* in *he gave the boy a book* or *he gave a book to the boy.*

indirect tax, a tax demanded from persons who reimburse themselves at the expense of others, the tax being levied on commodities before they reach the consumer and paid ultimately as part of their market price.

in·dis·cern·i·ble (ĭn′dĭ·zûr′nə·bəl, -sûr′-), *adj.* not discernible; imperceptible. **—in′dis·cern′i·ble·ness,** *n.* **—in′dis·cern′i·bly,** *adv.*

in·dis·cerp·ti·ble (ĭn′dĭ·sûrp′tə·bəl), *adj.* not discerptible; indivisible. **—in′dis·cerp′ti·bil′i·ty,** *n.*

in·dis·cov·er·a·ble (ĭn′dĭs·kŭv′ər·ə·bəl), *adj.* not discoverable; undiscoverable.

in·dis·creet (ĭn′dĭs·krēt′), *adj.* not discreet; lacking prudence; lacking sound judgment: *indiscreet praise.* **—in′dis·creet′ly,** *adv.* **—in′dis·creet′ness,** *n.*

in·dis·crete (ĭn′dĭs·krēt′, ĭn′dĭs·krēt′), *adj.* not discrete. [t. L: m.s. *indiscrētus* not separated]

in·dis·cre·tion (ĭn′dĭs·krĕsh′ən), *n.* **1.** lack of discretion; imprudence. **2.** an indiscreet act or step.

in·dis·crim·i·nate (ĭn′dĭs·krĭm′ə·nĭt), *adj.* **1.** not discriminating: *indiscriminate in one's friendships.* **2.** not discriminate; confused: *indiscriminate slaughter.* **—in′dis·crim′i·nate·ly,** *adv.* **—in′dis·crim′i·nate·ness,** *n.* **—Syn. 1.** See **miscellaneous.**

in·dis·crim·i·nat·ing (ĭn′dĭs·krĭm′ə·nā′tĭng), *adj.* not discriminating. **—in′dis·crim′i·nat′ing·ly,** *adv.*

in·dis·crim·i·na·tion (ĭn′dĭs·krĭm′ə·nā′shən), *n.* **1.** the fact of not discriminating. **2.** the condition of not being discriminated. **3.** lack of discrimination. **—in′dis·crim′i·na′tive,** *adj.*

in·dis·pen·sa·ble (ĭn′dĭs·pĕn′sə·bəl), *adj.* **1.** not dispensable; absolutely necessary or requisite: *an indispensable man.* **2.** that cannot be disregarded or neglected: *an indispensable obligation.* **—n. 3.** one who or that which is indispensable. **—in′dis·pen′sa·bil′i·ty, in′dis·pen′sa·ble·ness,** *n.* **—in′dis·pen′sa·bly,** *adv.* **—Syn. 1.** See **necessary.**

in·dis·pose (ĭn′dĭs·pōz′), *v.t.* **-posed, -posing. 1.** to put out of the proper condition (for something); make unfit; disqualify. **2.** to make ill, esp. slightly. **3.** to disincline; render averse or unwilling.

in·dis·posed (ĭn′dĭs·pōzd′), *adj.* **1.** sick or ill, esp. slightly: *indisposed with a cold.* **2.** disinclined or unwilling. **—Syn. 1.** See **sick.**

in·dis·po·si·tion (ĭn′dĭs·pə·zĭsh′ən), *n.* **1.** state of being indisposed; a slight illness. **2.** disinclination.

in·dis·put·a·ble (ĭn′dĭs·pū′tə·bəl, ĭn′dĭs·pyə-), *adj.* not disputable. **—in′dis·put′a·bil′i·ty, in′dis·put′a·ble·ness,** *n.* **—in′dis·put′a·bly,** *adv.*

in·dis·sol·u·ble (ĭn′dĭ·sŏl′yə·bəl, ĭn′dĭs·′ə·lyə·bəl), *adj.* **1.** not dissoluble; incapable of being dissolved, decomposed, undone, or destroyed. **2.** firm or stable. **3.** perpetually binding or obligatory. **—in′dis·sol′u·bil′i·ty, in′dis·sol′u·ble·ness,** *n.* **—in′dis·sol′u·bly,** *adv.*

in·dis·tinct (ĭn′dĭs·tĭngkt′), *adj.* **1.** not distinct; not clearly marked off or defined. **2.** not clearly distinguishable or perceptible, as to the eye, ear, or mind. **3.** not distinguishing clearly. [t. L: s. *indistinctus*] **—in′dis·tinct′ly,** *adv.* **—in′dis·tinct′ness,** *n.*

in·dis·tinc·tive (ĭn′dĭs·tĭngk′tĭv), *adj.* **1.** without distinctive characteristics. **2.** not capable of making distinction. **—in′dis·tinc′tive·ly,** *adv.* **—in′dis·tinc′tive·ness,** *n.*

in·dis·tin·guish·a·ble (ĭn′dĭs·tĭng′gwĭsh·ə·bəl), *adj.* **1.** not distinguishable. **2.** indiscernible. **—in′dis·tin′guish·a·ble·ness,** *n.* **—in′dis·tin′guish·a·bly,** *adv.*

in·dite (ĭn·dīt′), *v.t.* **-dited, -diting. 1.** to compose or write, as a speech, poem, etc. **2.** *Archaic.* to treat in a literary composition. **3.** *Obs.* to dictate. **4.** *Obs.* to prescribe. [ME *endite*(n), t. OF: m. *enditer* dictate, write, g. L *in-* IN-² + *dictāre* pronounce. Cf. INDICT] **—in·dite′ment,** *n.* **—in·dit′er,** *n.*

in·di·um (ĭn′dĭ·əm), *n. Chem.* a rare metallic element, soft, white, malleable and easily fusible, found combined in various ores, esp. sphalerite: so called from the two indigo-blue lines in its spectrum. *Symbol:* In; *at. wt.:* 114.76; *at. no.:* 49; *sp. gr.:* 7.3 at 20°C. [f. IND(O)- + -IUM]

in·di·vert·i·ble (ĭn′də·vûr′tə·bəl, -dī-), *adj.* not divertible; not to be turned aside. **—in′di·vert′i·bly,** *adv.*

individ., individual.

in·di·vid·u·al (ĭn′də·vĭj′ŏŏ·əl), *adj.* **1.** single; particular; separate. **2.** existing as a distinct, indivisible entity, or considered as such: *individual members.* **3.** pertaining or peculiar to a single person or thing: *individual tastes.* **4.** intended for the use of one person only: *individual portions.* **5.** distinguished by peculiar and marked characteristics; exhibiting individuality: *a highly individual style.* **6.** of which each is different or of a different design from the others: *a set of individual coffee cups.* **—n. 7.** a single human being, as distinguished from a group. **8.** a person: *a strange individual.* **9.** a distinct, indivisible entity; a single thing, being, instance, or item. **10.** a group considered as a unit. **11.** *Biol.* **a.** a single or simple organism capable of independent existence. **b.** a member of a compound organism or colony, as one of the distinct elements or zoöids which make up a compound hydrozoan, or sometimes (when a whole plant or tree is regarded as a colony or compound organism) a single shoot or bud. [ME, t. ML: m.s. *individuālis,* der. L *indīviduus* indivisible] **—Syn. 7.** See **person.**

in·di·vid·u·al·ism (ĭn′də·vĭj′ŏŏ·əl·ĭz′əm), *n.* **1.** a social theory advocating the liberty, rights, or independent action of the individual. **2.** the principle or

---

habit of independent thought or action. **3.** the pursuit of individual rather than common or collective interests; egoism. **4.** individual character; individuality. **5.** an individual peculiarity. **6.** *Philos.* **a.** the doctrine of pure egoism, or that nothing exists but the individual self. **b.** the doctrine that nothing is real but individual things. **c.** the principle that all actions are determined by, or at least exist for, the benefit of the individual and not the mass of men.

in·di·vid·u·al·ist (ĭn′də vĭj′ŏŏ əl ĭst), *n.* **1.** one characterized by individualism in thought or action. **2.** an advocate of individualism. —**in·di·vid·u·al·is′tic,** *adj.*

in·di·vid·u·al·i·ty (ĭn′də vĭj′ŏŏ ăl′ə tĭ), *n., pl.* **-ties.** **1.** the particular character, or aggregate of qualities, which distinguishes one person or thing from others: *a person of marked individuality.* **2.** (*pl.*) individual characteristics. **3.** a person or thing of individual or distinctive character. **4.** the state or quality of being individual; existence as a distinct individual. **5.** the interests of the individual as distinguished from the interests of the community. **6.** *Archaic.* state or quality of being indivisible or inseparable. —**Syn. 1.** See **character.**

in·di·vid·u·al·ize (ĭn′də vĭj′ŏŏ ə līz′), *v.t.,* **-ized, -iz-ing. 1.** to make individual; give an individual or distinctive character to. **2.** to mention, indicate, or consider individually; specify; particularize. —*v.i.* **3.** to become individual; specialize. **4.** to mention or consider individuals; particularize. —**in·di·vid′u·al·i·za′tion,** *n.* —**in·di·vid′u·al·iz′er,** *n.*

in·di·vid·u·al·ly (ĭn′də vĭj′ŏŏ ə lĭ), *adv.* **1.** in an individual manner. **2.** separately. **3.** personally.

in·di·vid·u·ate (ĭn′də vĭj′ŏŏ āt′), *v.t.,* **-ated, -ating. 1.** to form into an individual or distinct entity. **2.** to give an individual or distinctive character to; individualize. [t. ML: m.s. *indivīduātus,* pp. of *indivīduāre,* der. L *indivīduus.* See INDIVIDUAL]

in·di·vid·u·a·tion (ĭn′də vĭj′ŏŏ ā′shən), *n.* **1.** act of individuating. **2.** state of being individuated; individual existence; individuality. **3.** *Philos.* the determination or contraction of a general nature to an individual mode of existence; development of the individual from the general.

in·di·vis·i·ble (ĭn′də vĭz′ə bəl), *adj.* **1.** not divisible; incapable of being divided: *one nation indivisible.* —*n.* **2.** something indivisible. —**in′di·vis′i·bil′i·ty, in′di·vis′i·ble·ness,** *n.* —**in′di·vis′i·bly,** *adv.*

Indo-, a word element meaning "of or in India" as in *Indo-African* (of India and Africa), or "Indian" as in *Indo-British* (British in India). [t. L, t. Gk., comb. form of L *Indus,* Gk. *Indós*]

indo-, a combining form of indigo. Also, **ind-.**

In·do-Chi·na (ĭn′dō chī′nə), *n.* **1.** Also, **Farther India.** a peninsula in SE Asia between the Bay of Bengal and the South China Sea, comprising French Indo-China, Siam, the Malay Peninsula, and Burma. **2.** See **French Indo-China.**

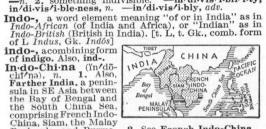

In·do-Chi·nese (ĭn′dō chī nēz′, -nēs′), *adj., n., pl.* **-nese.** —*adj.* **1.** of or pertaining to Indo-China. **2.** of or pertaining to the Mongoloid peoples of Indo-China or their languages. —*n.* **3.** Sino-Tibetan.

in·doc·ile (ĭn dŏs′ĭl), *adj.* not docile; not amenable to teaching. —**in·do·cil·i·ty** (ĭn′dō sĭl′ə tĭ), *n.*

in·doc·tri·nate (ĭn dŏk′trĭ nāt′), *v.t.,* **-nated, -nating. 1.** to instruct (in a doctrine, etc.). **2.** to teach or inculcate. **3.** to imbue (a person, etc.) with learning. [f. IN-² + s. L *doctrīna* teaching, DOCTRINE + -ATE¹] —**in·doc′tri·na′tion,** *n.* —**in·doc′tri·na′tor,** *n.*

In·do-Eu·ro·pe·an (ĭn′dō yŏŏr′ə pē′ən), *adj.* **1.** of or pertaining to a major family of languages that includes most of the languages of Europe (now spread to other parts of the world), of Asia, and a few scattered others. —*n.* **2.** this family of languages. **3.** a member of one of the races speaking the Indo-European languages. Also, **In·do-Ger·man·ic** (ĭn′dō jər măn′ĭk) for 1, 2.

In·do-Hit·tite (ĭn′dō hĭt′īt), *n.* a linguistic stock comprising Indo-European and the Anatolian languages.

In·do-I·ra·ni·an (ĭn′dō ĭ rā′nĭ ən, -ĭ rā′nĭ ən), *n.* one of the principal groups within the Indo-European family of languages, including Persian and the Indo-European languages of India.

in·dole (ĭn′dōl), *n.* a colorless, low-melting solid, C_8H_7N, with a fecal odor, found in the oil of jasmine and clove and as a putrefaction product from animals' intestines, used in perfumery and as a reagent. Also, **in·dol** (ĭn′dōl, -dŏl). [f. IND- + -OLE]

in·do·lence (ĭn′də ləns), *n.* the state of being indolent. [t. L: m.s. *indolentia* freedom from pain]

in·do·lent (ĭn′də lənt), *adj.* **1.** having or showing a disposition to avoid exertion: *an indolent person.* **2.** *Pathol.* causing little or no pain. [t. LL: s. *indolens* not suffering] —**in′do·lent·ly,** *adv.* —**Syn. 1.** See **idle.**

in·dom·i·ta·ble (ĭn dŏm′ə tə bəl), *adj.* that cannot be subdued or overcome, as persons, pride, courage, etc. [t. LL: m.s. *indomitābilis,* der. L *in-* IN-³ + s. *domitāre* (freq. of *domāre* tame)] —**in·dom′i·ta·ble·ness,** *n.* —**in·dom′i·ta·bly,** *adv.* —**Syn.** See **invincible.**

In·do·ne·sia (ĭn′dō nē′shə, -zhə), *n.* **1.** the East Indies. **2.** Republic of, a republic, proclaimed Aug. 1950,

of former states in the Malay Archipelago, including Sumatra, Java, Celebes, parts of Borneo and Timor, the Moluccas, and other islands: officially a Dutch-Indonesian union under the Crown. *Cap.:* Jakarta. Formerly, **Dutch East Indies.**

In·do·ne·sian (ĭn′dō nē′shən, -zhən), *n.* **1.** a member of the ethnic group consisting of the natives of the U.S. of Indonesia, the Filipinos, and the Malays of Malaya; Malaysian. **2.** a member of a light-colored race supposed to have been dominant in the Malay Archipelago before the Malays, and believed to constitute one element of the present mixed population of Malaysia and perhaps Polynesia. **3.** a group of Austronesian languages, including those of Formosa, the Philippines, Madagascar, and U.S. of Indonesia, as well as Malay; Malayan. —*adj.* **4.** of or pertaining to the Malay Archipelago. **5.** pertaining to the Indonesians or their languages. **6.** of the U.S. of Indonesia. [f. INDO- + s. Gk. *nêsos* island + -IAN]

in·door (ĭn′dôr′), *adj.* occurring, used, etc., in a house or building, rather than out of doors: *indoor games.*

in·doors (ĭn′dôrz′), *adv.* in or into a house or building.

in·do·phe·nol (ĭn′dō fē′nŏl, -nŏl), *n.* **1.** a coal-tar dye resembling indigo and giving indigo-blue shades. **2.** any of various related dyes. [f. INDO- + PHENOL]

In·dore (ĭn dôr′), *n.* **1.** a state in central India. 1,514,000 pop. (1941); 9934 sq. mi. **2.** the capital of this state. 203,695 (1941).

in·dorse (ĭn dôrs′), *v.t.,* **-dorsed, -dorsing.** endorse. [var. of *endorse,* conformed to ML *indorsāre* put on the back. See IN-², DORSUM] —**in·dors′a·ble,** *adj.* —**in·dor·see** (ĭn′dôr sē′, ĭn dôr sē′), *n.* —**in·dorse′ment,** *n.* —**in·dors′er, in·dor′sor,** *n.*

in·dox·yl (ĭn dŏk′sĭl), *n. Chem.* a crystalline compound, C_8H_7NO, which is formed by the hydrolysis of indican and is readily oxidized to furnish indigo.

In·dra (ĭn′drə), *n. Hinduism.* the Vedic god who presides over the deities of the middle realm (the air).

in·draft (ĭn′drăft′, -dräft′), *n.* **1.** a draft or drawing inward. **2.** an inward flow or current. Also, *esp. Brit.,* **in′draught′.**

in·drawn (ĭn′drôn′), *adj.* drawn in; introspective.

in·dri (ĭn′drĭ), *n., pl.* **-dris.** a short-tailed lemur, *Indri indri,* of Madagascar, about two feet in length. [t. Malagasy, said to be an exclamation, "lo! see!", erroneously taken as the name of the animal]

in·du·bi·ta·ble (ĭn dū′bə tə bəl, -dōō′-), *adj.* that cannot be doubted; unquestionable; certain. —**in·du′bi·ta·ble·ness,** *n.* —**in·du′bi·ta·bly,** *adv.*

in·duce (ĭn dūs′, -dōōs′), *v.t.,* **-duced. -ducing. 1.** to lead or move by persuasion or influence, as to some action, state of mind, etc.: *to induce a person to go.* **2.** to bring about, produce, or cause: *opium induces sleep.* **3.** *Physics.* to produce (an electric current, etc.) by induction. **4.** *Logic.* to assert or establish (a proposition about a class of phenomena) on the basis of observations on a number of particular facts. [ME *induce(n),* t. L: m. *indūcere* lead in, bring in, persuade] —**in·duc′er,** *n.* —**in·duc′i·ble,** *adj.* —**Syn. 1.** See **persuade.**

in·duce·ment (ĭn dūs′mənt, -dōōs′-), *n.* **1.** the act of inducing. **2.** something that induces or persuades; an incentive. —**Syn. 2.** See **motive.**

in·duct (ĭn dŭkt′), *v.t.* **1.** to lead or bring in; introduce, esp. formally, as into a place, office, etc. **2.** to introduce in knowledge or experience (fol. by *to*). **3.** *U.S.* to bring into military service. [ME, t. L: s. *inductus,* pp.]

in·duct·ance (ĭn dŭk′təns), *n. Elect.* **1.** that property of a circuit by virtue of which electromagnetic induction takes place. **2.** a piece of equipment providing inductance in a circuit or other system; inductor.

in·duc·tee (ĭn′dŭk tē′), *n.* a person inducted into military service.

in·duc·tile (ĭn dŭk′tĭl), *adj.* not ductile; not pliable. —**in′duc·til′i·ty,** *n.*

in·duc·tion (ĭn dŭk′shən), *n.* **1.** *Elect., Magnetism.* **a.** the process by which a body having electrical or magnetic properties calls forth similar properties in a neighboring body without direct contact, as (1) the process by which the relative motion of a wire and magnetic field produces an e.m.f. in the wire; (2) the process by which a changing current in a circuit produces an e.m.f. in the same or a neighboring circuit. **b.** a tendency of electric currents to resist change. **2.** *Logic.* **a.** the process of discovering explanations for a set of particular facts, by estimating the weight of observational evidence in favor of a proposition which (usually) asserts something about that entire class of facts. **b.** a conclusion reached by this process. **3.** a bringing forward or adducing, as of facts, evidence, etc. **4.** the act of inducing, bringing about or causing: *induction of the hypnotic state.* **5.** *Physiol.* the process whereby a tissue stimulates or alters other adjacent tissues. **6.** the act of inducting; introduction or initiation. **7.** formal introduction into an office or benefice; installation. **8.** an introductory unit in a literary work; a prelude or scene, independent of the main performance but related to it. **9.** *Archaic.* a preface. [ME, t. L: s. *inductio*]

induction coil, *Elect.* a transformer designed as two concentric coils with a common soft iron core, with the inner coil (primary) of few turns and the outer coil (secondary) of a great number of turns. When the primary is excited by rapidly interrupted or variable current high voltage is induced in the secondary.

in·duc·tive (ĭn dŭk′tĭv), *adj.* **1.** pertaining to or involving electrical or magnetic induction. **2.** operating by induction: *an inductive machine.* **3.** pertaining to or employing logical induction. **4.** *Physiol.* eliciting some reaction within an organism. **5.** serving to induce; leading or influencing (fol. by *to*). **6.** introductory. —**in·duc′tive·ly,** *adv.* —**in·duc′tive·ness,** *n.* —**Syn. 3.** See **deductive.**

in·duc·tiv·i·ty (ĭn′dŭk tĭv′ə tĭ), *n., pl.* **-ties. 1.** an inductive property. **2.** capacity of producing induction. **3.** inductance.

in·duc·tor (ĭn dŭk′tər), *n.* **1.** *Elect.* a device, the primary purpose of which is to introduce inductance into an electric circuit. **2.** one who inducts, as into office.

in·due (ĭn dū′, -dōō′), *v.t.,* **-dued, -duing.** endue.

in·dulge (ĭn dŭlj′), *v.,* **-dulged, -dulging.** —*v.i.* **1.** to indulge oneself; yield to an inclination (fol. by *in*): *to indulge in apple pie.* —*v.t.* **2.** to yield to, satisfy, or gratify (desires, feelings, etc.). **3.** to yield to the wishes or whims of: *to indulge a child.* **4.** to allow (oneself) to follow one's will (fol. by *in*). **5.** *Com.* to grant an extension of time, for payment or performance, to (a person, etc.) or on (a bill, etc.). **6.** *Now Rare.* to grant (something) by favor. [t. L: m.s. *indulgēre* be kind, yield, grant] —**in·dulg′er,** *n.* —**in·dulg′ing·ly,** *adv.* —**Syn. 3.** See **humor.**

in·dul·gence (ĭn dŭl′jəns), *n., v.,* **-genced, -gencing.** —*n.* **1.** the act or practice of indulging; gratification of desire. **2.** indulgent allowance or tolerance. **3.** humoring. **4.** something granted or taken in gratification of desire. **5.** *Rom. Cath. Ch.* a remission of the temporal punishment still due to sin after it has been forgiven. **6.** *Eng. and Scot. Hist.* (in the reigns of Charles II and James II) a grant by the king to Protestant Dissenters and Roman Catholics to be free from certain penalties imposed upon them by legislation on account of their religion. **7.** *Com.* an extension, through favor, of time for payment or performance. —*v.t.* **8.** *Rom. Cath. Ch.* to furnish with an indulgence.

in·dul·gen·cy (ĭn dul′jən sĭ), *n., pl.* **-cies.** indulgence.

in·dul·gent (ĭn dŭl′jənt), *adj.* characterized by or showing indulgence: *an indulgent parent.* [t. L: s. *indulgens,* ppr.] —**in·dul′gent·ly,** *adv.*

in·du·line (ĭn′dyə lēn′, -lĭn), *n.* any of a large class of dyes yielding colors similar to indigo. [f. IND- + *ul*- (t. L: s. *-ulum,* dim. suffix) + -INE²]

in·dult (ĭn dŭlt′), *n. Rom. Cath. Ch.* a general faculty granted for a specific time or a specific number of cases by the Holy See to bishops and others, of doing something not permitted; a grant, privilege, favor. [t. LL: s. *indultum* indulgence, prop. pp. neut.]

in·du·pli·cate (ĭn dū′plə kāt, -kāt′, -dōō′-), *adj. Bot.* folded or rolled inward (said of the parts of the calyx or corolla in estivation when the edges are bent abruptly toward the axis, or of leaves in vernation when the edges are rolled inward and then arranged about the axis without overlapping). Also, **in·du′pli·ca′tive.** [f. IN-² + DUPLICATE (def. 2)] —**in·du′pli·ca′tion,** *n.*

in·du·rate (ĭn′dyŏŏ rāt′, -dōō-; *adj.* ĭn′dyŏŏ rĭt, -dōō-), *v.,* **-rated, -rating,** *adj.* —*v.t., v.i.* **1.** to make or become hard; harden; inure. —*adj.* **2.** hardened; callous; inured. [ME, t. L: m.s. *indūrātus,* pp.] —**in·du·ra′tion,** *n.* —**in′du·ra′tive,** *adj.*

In·dus (ĭn′dəs), *n.* a river flowing from W Tibet through Kashmir and SW through Pakistan to the Arabian Sea. ab. 2000 mi.

in·du·si·um (ĭn dū′zĭ əm, -zhĭ əm, -dōō′-), *n., pl.* **-sia** (-zĭ ə, -zhĭ ə). **1.** *Bot.* a membranous outgrowth covering the sori in ferns. **2.** *Anat., Zool.* an enveloping layer or membrane. [t. L: tunic] —**in·du′si·al,** *adj.*

in·dus·tri·al (ĭn dŭs′trĭ əl), *adj.* **1.** of or pertaining to, of the nature of, or resulting from industry or productive labor: *the industrial arts.* **2.** having highly developed industries: *an industrial nation.* **3.** engaged in an industry or industries: *industrial workers.* **4.** pertaining to the workers in industries: *industrial training.* **5.** noting or pertaining to a form of life insurance for the working classes, with policies for comparatively low sums and with premiums payable weekly. —*n.* **6.** a worker in some industry, esp. a manufacturing industry. **7.** one who conducts or owns an industrial enterprise. **8.** (*pl.*) stocks or bonds of industrial enterprises. [f. m. INDUSTRY + -AL¹. Cf. F *industriel*] —**in·dus′tri·al·ly,** *adv.*

in·dus·tri·al·ism (ĭn dŭs′trĭ ə lĭz′əm), *n.* **1.** an economic organization of society built largely on mechanized industry rather than agriculture, craftsmanship, or commerce. **2.** the industrial branch of work or labor.

in·dus·tri·al·ist (ĭn dŭs′trĭ ə lĭst), *n.* **1.** one who conducts or owns an industrial enterprise. **2.** a person employed in or concerned with some branch of industry.

in·dus·tri·al·ize (ĭn dŭs′trĭ ə līz′), *v.t.,* **-ized, -izing. 1.** to introduce industry into (an area) on a large scale. **2.** to imbue with the spirit of industrialism. Also, *esp. Brit.,* **in·dus′tri·al·ise′.** —**in·dus′tri·al·i·za′tion,** *n.*

industrial revolution, the term applied to the social and economic changes in England from the mid 18th to the mid 19th centuries during the beginnings and growth of modern industrialism.

industrial school, 1. a school for teaching one or more branches of industry. **2.** a school for educating neglected children committed to its care and training them to some form of industry.

Industrial Workers of the World, an international industrial union, organized in Chicago in 1905. It disintegrated after World War I.

in·dus·tri·ous (ĭn dŭs′trĭ əs), *adj.* **1.** hard-working; diligent: *an industrious person.* **2.** *Obs.* skillful. [t. L: m.s. *industriōsus* diligent] —**in·dus′tri·ous·ly,** *adv.* —**in·dus′tri·ous·ness,** *n.* —**Syn. 1.** See **busy.**

in·dus·try (ĭn′dəs trĭ), *n., pl.* **-tries. 1.** a trade or manufacture: *the steel industry.* **2.** the ownership and management of companies, factories, etc.: *friction between labor and industry.* **3.** systematic work or labor. **4.** assiduous activity at any work or task. [ME *industrie,* t. L: m. *industria* diligence]

in·dwell (ĭn′dwĕl′), *v.,* **-dwelt, -dwelling.** —*v.t.* **1.** to inhabit. —*v.i.* **2.** to dwell (fol. by *in*). —**in′dwell′er,** *n.*

In·dy (dăN dē′), *n.* **Vincent d'** (väN säN′), 1851–1931, French composer.

-ine¹, an adjective suffix meaning "of or pertaining to," "of the nature of," "made of," "like," as in *asinine, crystalline, equine, marine.* [t. L: m. *-īnus;* also m. *-inus,* t. Gk.: m. *-inos*]

-ine², 1. a noun suffix denoting some action, procedure, art, place, etc., as in *discipline, doctrine, medicine, latrine.* **2.** a suffix occurring in many nouns of later formation and various meanings, as in *famine, routine, grenadine, vaseline.* **3.** a noun suffix used particularly in chemical terms, as *bromine, chlorine,* and esp. names of basic substances, as *amine, aniline, caffeine, quinine, quinoline.* Cf. *-in².* [t. F, g. L *-ina,* orig. fem. of *-inus;* also used to repr. Gk. *-inē,* fem. n. suffix, as in *heroine*]

in·earth (ĭn ûrth′), *v.t. Chiefly Poetic.* to bury; inter.

in·e·bri·ant (ĭn ē′brĭ ənt), *adj.* **1.** inebriating; intoxicating. —*n.* **2.** an intoxicant. [t. L: s. *inēbrians,* ppr.]

in·e·bri·ate (*v.* ĭn ē′brĭ āt′; *n., adj.* ĭn ē′brĭ ĭt), *v.,* **-ated, -ating,** *n., adj.* —*v.t.* **1.** to make drunk; intoxicate. **2.** to intoxicate mentally or emotionally; exhilarate. —*n.* **3.** an intoxicated person. **4.** a habitual drunkard. —*adj.* **5.** Also, **in·e′bri·at′ed.** drunk; intoxicated. [t. L: m.s. *inēbriātus,* pp.] —**in·e′bri·a′tion,** *n.* —**Syn. 4.** See **drunkard.**

in·e·bri·e·ty (ĭn′ĭ brī′ə tĭ), *n.* drunkenness.

in·ed·i·ble (ĭn ĕd′ə bəl), *adj.* not edible; unfit to be eaten. —**in·ed′i·bil′i·ty,** *n.*

in·ed·it·ed (ĭn ĕd′ĭt ĭd), *adj.* **1.** unpublished. **2.** not edited.

in·ef·fa·ble (ĭn ĕf′ə bəl), *adj.* **1.** that cannot be uttered or expressed; inexpressible; unspeakable: *ineffable joy.* **2.** that must not be uttered: *the ineffable name.* [ME, t. L: m.s. *ineffābilis*] —**in·ef′fa·bil′i·ty, in·ef′fa·ble·ness,** *n.* —**in·ef′fa·bly,** *adv.*

in·ef·face·a·ble (ĭn′ĭ fā′sə bəl), *adj.* not effaceable; indelible: *an ineffaceable impression.* —**in′ef·face′a·bil′i·ty,** *n.* —**in′ef·face′a·bly,** *adv.*

in·ef·fec·tive (ĭn′ĭ fĕk′tĭv), *adj.* **1.** not effective; ineffectual, as efforts. **2.** inefficient, as a person. **3.** lacking in artistic effect, as a design or work. —**in′ef·fec′tive·ly,** *adv.* —**in′ef·fec′tive·ness,** *n.*

in·ef·fec·tu·al (ĭn′ĭ fĕk′chŏŏ əl), *adj.* **1.** not effectual; without satisfactory or decisive effect: *an ineffectual remedy.* **2.** unavailing; futile: *his efforts were ineffectual.* **3.** powerless or impotent. —**in′ef·fec′tu·al·i·ty, in′ef·fec′tu·al·ness,** *n.* —**in′ef·fec′tu·al·ly,** *adv.* —**Syn. 2.** See **useless.**

in·ef·fi·ca·cious (ĭn′ĕf ə kā′shəs), *adj.* not able to produce the desired effect. —**in′ef·fi·ca′cious·ly,** *adv.* —**in′ef·fi·ca′cious·ness, in·ef·fi·cac·i·ty** (ĭn′ĕf ə kăs′ə tĭ), *n.*

in·ef·fi·ca·cy (ĭn ĕf′ə kə sĭ), *n.* lack of efficacy or power to produce the desired effect.

in·ef·fi·cien·cy (ĭn′ĭ fĭsh′ən sĭ), *n.* the condition or quality of being inefficient; lack of efficiency.

in·ef·fi·cient (ĭn′ĭ fĭsh′ənt), *adj.* not efficient; unable to effect or accomplish in a capable, economical way. —**in′ef·fi′cient·ly,** *adv.* —**Syn.** See **incapable.**

in·e·las·tic (ĭn′ĭ lăs′tĭk), *adj.* not elastic; lacking elasticity; unyielding. —**in·e·las·tic·i·ty** (ĭn′ĭ lăs tĭs′ə tĭ), *n.*

in·el·e·gance (ĭn ĕl′ə gəns), *n.* **1.** the state or character of being inelegant; lack of elegance. **2.** that which is inelegant or ungraceful.

in·el·e·gan·cy (ĭn ĕl′ə gən sĭ), *n., pl.* **-cies.** inelegance.

in·el·e·gant (ĭn ĕl′ə gənt), *adj.* not elegant; not nice or refined; vulgar. —**in·el′e·gant·ly,** *adv.*

in·el·i·gi·ble (ĭn ĕl′ĭ jə bəl), *adj.* **1.** not eligible; not proper or suitable for choice. **2.** legally disqualified to hold an office. **3.** legally disqualified to function as a juror, voter, witness, or to become the recipient of a privilege. —*n.* **4.** one who is ineligible, esp. as a suitor, husband, or member of an athletic team. —**in·el′i·gi·bil′i·ty,** *n.* —**in·el′i·gi·bly,** *adv.*

in·el·o·quent (ĭn ĕl′ə kwənt), *adj.* not eloquent. —**in·el′o·quence,** *n.* —**in·el′o·quent·ly,** *adv.*

in·e·luc·ta·ble (ĭn′ĭ lŭk′tə bəl), *adj.* that cannot be escaped from, as a fate. [t. L: m.s. *inēluctābilis*] —**in′e·luc′ta·bil′i·ty,** *n.* —**in′e·luc′ta·bly,** *adv.*

in·e·lud·i·ble (ĭn′ĭ lōō′də bəl), *adj.* not eludible; inescapable. —**in′e·lud′i·bly,** *adv.*

in·ept (ĭn ĕpt′), *adj.* **1.** not apt, fitted, or suitable; unsuitable. **2.** inappropriate; out of place. **3.** absurd or foolish, as a proceeding, remark, etc. [t. L: s. *ineptus*] —**in·ept′ly,** *adv.* —**in·ept′ness,** *n.*

in·ept·i·tude (ĭn ĕp′tə tūd′, -tōōd′), *n.* **1.** the quality of being inept. **2.** an inept act or remark.

b., blend of, blended; c., cognate with; d., dialect, dialectal; der., derived from; f., formed from; g., going back to; m., modification of; r., replacing; s., stem of; t., taken from; ?, perhaps. See the full key on inside cover.

in·e·qual·i·ty (ĭn′ĭ kwŏl′ə tĭ), *n.*, *pl.* **-ties.** **1.** the condition of being unequal; lack of equality; disparity: *inequality of treatment.* **2.** social disparity: *the inequality between the rich and the poor.* **3.** inadequacy. **4.** injustice; partiality. **5.** unevenness, as of surface. **6.** an instance of unevenness. **7.** variableness, as of climate. **8.** *Astron.* **a.** any component part of the departure from uniformity in astronomical phenomena, esp. in orbital motion. **b.** the amount of such a departure. **9.** *Math.* an expression of two unequal quantities connected by the sign > or <, as, *a* > *b*, "*a* is greater than *b*"; *a* < *b*, "*a* is less than *b*." [late ME, t. ML: m.s. *inaequālitas* unevenness]

inequi-, a word element meaning "unequal" or "unequally," as in *inequidistant.* [f. IN-³ + EQUI-]

in·e·qui·lat·er·al (ĭn′ē kwə lăt′ər əl), *adj.* not equilateral. **—in·e·qui·lat·er·al·ly,** *adv.*

in·eq·ui·ta·ble (ĭn ĕk′wə tə bəl), *adj.* not equitable; unfair. **—in·eq′ui·ta·bly,** *adv.*

in·eq·ui·ty (ĭn ĕk′wə tĭ), *n.*, *pl.* **-ties.** **1.** lack of equity; unfairness. **2.** an unfair circumstance or proceeding.

in·e·rad·i·ca·ble (ĭn′ĭ răd′ə kə bəl), *adj.* not eradicable; that cannot be eradicated, rooted out, or removed utterly. **—in·e·rad′i·ca·bly,** *adv.*

in·e·ras·a·ble (ĭn′ĭ rā′sə bəl), *adj.* not erasable; not to be erased or effaced. **—in·e·ras′a·bly,** *adv.*

in·er·ra·ble (ĭn ĕr′ə bəl, -ûr′-), *adj.* incapable of erring; infallible. [t. LL: m.s. *inerrābilis*] **—in·er′ra·bil′i·ty, in·er′ra·ble·ness,** *n.* **—in·er′ra·bly,** *adv.*

in·er·rant (ĭn ĕr′ənt, -ûr′-), *adj.* free from error. [t. L: s. *inerrans,* ppr., not wandering] **—in·er′ran·cy,** *n.*

in·er·rat·ic (ĭn′ĕ răt′ĭk), *adj.* not erratic or wandering; fixed, as a so-called "fixed" star.

in·ert (ĭn ûrt′), *adj.* **1.** having no inherent power of action, motion, or resistance: *inert matter.* **2.** without active properties, as a drug. **3.** of an inactive or sluggish habit or nature. [t. L: s. *iners* unskilled, idle] **—in·ert′ly,** *adv.* **—in·ert′ness,** *n.* **—Syn. 3.** See **inactive.**

in·er·tia (in ûr′shə), *n.* **1.** inert condition; inactivity; sluggishness. **2.** *Physics.* **a.** that property of matter by which it retains its state of rest or of uniform rectilinear motion so long as it is not acted upon by an external force. **b.** an analogous property of a force: *electric inertia.* [t. L: lack of skill, inactivity] **—in·er′tial,** *adj.*

in·es·cap·a·ble (ĭn′ĕs kā′pə bəl), *adj.* that cannot be escaped.

in es·se (ĭn ĕs′ĭ), *Latin.* in being; in actuality; actually existing (contrasted with *in posse*).

in·es·sen·tial (ĭn′ĭ sĕn′shəl), *adj.* **1.** not essential; not necessary; nonessential. **2.** *Rare.* without essence; insubstantial. **—n. 3.** that which is not essential. **—in′es·sen′ti·al·i·ty,** *n.*

in·es·ti·ma·ble (ĭn ĕs′tə mə bəl), *adj.* **1.** that cannot be estimated, or too great to be estimated. **2.** of incalculable value. [ME, t. F, t. L: m.s. *inaestimābilis.* See IN-³, ESTIMABLE] **—in·es′ti·ma·bly,** *adv.*

in·ev·i·ta·ble (in ĕv′ə tə bəl), *adj.* **1.** that cannot be avoided, evaded, or escaped; certain or necessary: *an inevitable conclusion.* **2.** sure to befall, happen, or come, by the very nature of things: *one's inevitable fate.* **—n. 3.** that which is unavoidable. [ME, t. L: m.s. *inēvitābilis.* See IN-³, EVITABLE] **—in·ev′i·ta·bil′i·ty, in·ev′i·ta·ble·ness,** *n.* **—in·ev′i·ta·bly,** *adv.*

in·ex·act (ĭn′ĭg zăkt′), *adj.* not exact; not strictly accurate. **—in′ex·act′ly,** *adv.* **—in′ex·act′ness,** *n.*

in·ex·act·i·tude (ĭn′ĭg zăk′tə tūd′, -tōōd′), *n.* state or character of being inexact or inaccurate; inexactness. [f. IN-³ + EXACTITUDE]

in·ex·cus·a·ble (ĭn′ĭk skū′zə bəl), *adj.* not excusable; incapable of being justified. **—in′ex·cus′a·bil′i·ty, in′ex·cus′a·ble·ness,** *n.* **—in′ex·cus′a·bly,** *adv.*

in·ex·e·cu·tion (ĭn ĕk′sə kū′shən), *n.* lack or neglect of execution.

in·ex·er·tion (ĭn′ĭg zûr′shən), *n.* lack of exertion.

in·ex·haust·i·ble (ĭn′ĭg zôs′tə bəl), *adj.* **1.** not exhaustible; incapable of being exhausted: *an inexhaustible supply.* **2.** unfailing; tireless. **—in′ex·haust′i·bil′i·ty, in′ex·haust′i·ble·ness,** *n.* **—in′ex·haust′i·bly,** *adv.*

in·ex·ist·ent (ĭn′ĭg zĭs′tənt), *adj.* **1.** not existent; having no existence. **2.** existing within; inherent. **—in′ex·ist′ence, in′ex·ist′en·cy,** *n.*

in·ex·o·ra·ble (ĭn ĕk′sə rə bəl), *adj.* **1.** unyielding or unalterable: *inexorable facts.* **2.** not to be persuaded, moved, or affected by prayers or entreaties. [t. L: m. s. *inexōrābilis.* See IN-³, EXORABLE] **—in·ex′o·ra·bil′i·ty, in·ex′o·ra·ble·ness,** *n.* **—in·ex′o·ra·bly,** *adv.* **—Syn. 2.** relentless, unrelenting, implacable. See **inflexible.**

in·ex·pe·di·ent (ĭn′ĭk spē′dĭ ənt), *adj.* not expedient; not suitable, judicious, or advisable. **—in′ex·pe′di·ence, in′ex·pe′di·en·cy,** *n.* **—in′ex·pe′di·ent·ly,** *adv.*

in·ex·pen·sive (ĭn′ĭk spĕn′sĭv), *adj.* not expensive; costing little. **—in′ex·pen′sive·ly,** *adv.* **—in′ex·pen′sive·ness,** *n.* **—Syn.** See **cheap.**

in·ex·pe·ri·ence (ĭn′ĭk spĭr′ĭ əns), *n.* lack of experience, or of knowledge or skill gained from experience.

in·ex·pe·ri·enced (ĭn′ĭk spĭr′ĭ ənst), *adj.* not experienced; without knowledge or skill gained from experience. **—Syn.** untrained, unskilled, inexpert; raw, green.

in·ex·pert (ĭn′ĭk spûrt′), *adj.* not expert; unskilled. **—in′ex·pert′ly,** *adv.* **—in′ex·pert′ness,** *n.*

in·ex·pi·a·ble (ĭn ĕk′spĭ′ə bəl), *adj.* **1.** not to be expiated; admitting of no expiation or atonement: *an inexpiable crime.* **2.** not to be appeased by expiation; im-

placable: *inexpiable hate.* [t. L: m.s. *inexpiābilis*] **—in·ex′pi·a·ble·ness,** *n.* **—in·ex′pi·a·bly,** *adv.*

in·ex·plain·a·ble (ĭn′ĭk splā′nə bəl), *adj.* not explainable; incapable of being explained; inexplicable.

in·ex·pli·ca·ble (ĭn ĕks′plə kə bəl or, *esp. Brit.* ĭn′ĭk splĭk′ə bəl), *adj.* not explicable; incapable of being explained. [late ME, t. L: m.s. *inexplicābilis* that cannot be unfolded] **—in·ex′pli·ca·bil′i·ty, in·ex′pli·ca·ble·ness,** *n.* **—in·ex′pli·ca·bly,** *adv.*

in·ex·plic·it (ĭn′ĭk splĭs′ĭt), *adj.* not explicit or clear; not clearly stated. [t. L: s. *inexplicitus*] **—in′ex·plic′it·ly,** *adv.* **—in′ex·plic′it·ness,** *n.*

in·ex·press·i·ble (ĭn′ĭk sprĕs′ə bəl), *adj.* **1.** not expressible; that cannot be uttered or represented in words: *inexpressible grief.* **—n. 2.** *(pl.) Humorous and Archaic.* breeches or trousers. **—in′ex·press′i·bil′i·ty, in′ex·press′i·ble·ness,** *n.* **—in′ex·press′i·bly,** *adv.*

in·ex·pres·sive (ĭn′ĭk sprĕs′ĭv), *adj.* **1.** not expressive; lacking in expression. **2.** *Archaic.* inexpressible. **—in′ex·pres′sive·ly,** *adv.* **—in′ex·pres′sive·ness,** *n.*

in·ex·pug·na·ble (ĭn′ĭk spŭg′nə bəl), *adj.* that cannot be taken by force; impregnable; unconquerable: *an inexpugnable fort.* [t. L: m.s. *inexpugnābilis*] **—in′ex·pug′na·bil′i·ty, in′ex·pug′na·ble·ness,** *n.* **—in′ex·pug′na·bly,** *adv.*

in·ex·ten·si·ble (ĭn′ĭk stĕn′sə bəl), *adj.* not extensible. **—in′ex·ten′si·bil′i·ty,** *n.*

in ex·ten·so (ĭn ĭk stĕn′sō), *Latin.* at full length.

in·ex·tin·guish·a·ble (ĭn′ĭk stĭng′gwĭsh ə bəl), *adj.* not extinguishable; not to be extinguished, quenched, suppressed, or brought to an end: *inextinguishable fire, inextinguishable rage.* **—in′ex·tin′guish·a·bly,** *adv.*

in·ex·tir·pa·ble (ĭn′ĭk stûr′pə bəl), *adj.* incapable of being extirpated: *an inextirpable disease.*

in ex·tre·mis (ĭn ĭk strē′mĭs), *Latin.* **1.** in extremity. **2.** near death.

in·ex·tri·ca·ble (ĭn ĕks′trə kə bəl), *adj.* **1.** from which one cannot extricate oneself: *an inextricable maze.* **2.** that cannot be disentangled, undone, or loosed, as a tangle, knot, grasp, etc. **3.** hopelessly intricate, involved, or perplexing: *inextricable confusion.* [late ME, t. L: m.s. *inextrīcābilis*] **—in·ex′tri·ca·bil′i·ty, in·ex′tri·ca·ble·ness,** *n.* **—in·ex′tri·ca·bly,** *adv.*

inf., **1.** *(also cap.)* infantry. **2.** infinitive. **3.** information. **4.** (L *infra*) below; after.

in·fal·li·ble (ĭn făl′ə bəl), *adj.* **1.** not fallible; exempt from liability to error, as persons, their judgment, pronouncements, etc. **2.** absolutely trustworthy or sure: *an infallible rule.* **3.** unfailing in operation; certain: *an infallible remedy.* **4.** *Rom. Cath. Ch.* immune from fallacy or liability to error in expounding matters of faith or morals in virtue of the promise made by Christ to the Church. **—n. 5.** an infallible person or thing. [late ME, t. ML: m.s. *infallibilis.* See IN-³, FALLIBLE] **—in·fal′li·bil′i·ty, in·fal′li·ble·ness,** *n.* **—in·fal′li·bly,** *adv.* **—Syn. 2, 3.** See **reliable.**

in·fa·mous (ĭn′fə məs), *adj.* **1.** of evil fame or repute: *an infamous city.* **2.** such as to deserve or to cause evil repute; detestable; shamefully bad: *infamous conduct.* **3.** *Law.* **a.** deprived of credit and of certain rights as a citizen, in consequence of conviction of certain offenses. **b.** (of offenses, etc.) involving such deprivation. [ME, t. ML: m.s. *infāmōsus* (in L *infāmis*)] **—in·fa·mous·ly,** *adv.* **—in·fa·mous·ness,** *n.* **—Syn. 1.** disreputable, notorious. **2.** disgraceful, scandalous; nefarious, odious, wicked. **—Ant. 1.** honored. **2.** praiseworthy.

in·fa·my (ĭn′fə mĭ), *n.*, *pl.* **-mies.** **1.** evil fame, shameful notoriety, or public reproach. **2.** infamous character or conduct. **3.** an infamous act or circumstance. **4.** *Law.* the loss of credit and rights incurred by conviction of an infamous offense. [late ME, t. L: m.s. *infāmia*] **—Syn. 1.** See **disgrace.**

in·fan·cy (ĭn′fən sĭ), *n.*, *pl.* **-cies.** **1.** the state or period of being an infant; babyhood; early childhood. **2.** the corresponding period in the existence of anything: *the infancy of the world.* **3.** infants collectively. **4.** *Law.* the period of life to the age of majority (in the common law, to the end of the twenty-first year); minority; nonage. [t. L: m.s. *infantia,* lit., inability to speak]

in·fant (ĭn′fənt), *n.* **1.** a child during the earliest period of its life, or a baby. **2.** *Law.* a person who is not of full age, esp. one who has not attained the age of twenty-one years. **3.** a beginner, as in learning. **4.** anything in the first period of existence or the first stage of progress. **—adj. 5.** of or pertaining to infants or infancy: *infant years.* **6.** being in infancy: *an infant child.* **7.** being in the earliest stage: *an infant industry.* **8.** of or pertaining to the legal state of infancy; minor. [t. L: s. *infans* young child, prop. adj., not speaking; r. ME *enfaunt,* t. OF] **—in′fant·hood′,** *n.*

in·fan·ta (ĭn făn′tə), *n.* **1.** a daughter of the king of Spain or of Portugal. **2.** an infante's wife. [t. Sp. and Pg. See INFANTE]

in·fan·te (ĭn făn′tā), *n.* a son of the king of Spain or of Portugal, not heir to the throne. [t. Sp. and Pg., g. L *infans* INFANT]

in·fan·ti·cide¹ (ĭn făn′tə sīd′), *n.* the killing of an infant. [t. LL: m.s. *infanticīdium*] **—in·fan′ti·cid′al,** *adj.*

in·fan·ti·cide² (ĭn făn′tə sīd′), *n.* one who kills an infant. [t. LL: m.s. *infanticīda*]

in·fan·tile (ĭn′fən tīl, -tĭl), *adj.* **1.** characteristic of or befitting an infant; babyish; childish: *infantile behavior.* **2.** of or pertaining to infants: *infantile diseases.* **3.** being in the earliest stage. [t. LL: m.s. *infantilis*] —**Syn.** 1. See **childish.**

in·fan·tile spinal paralysis, *Pathol.* an acute disease, most common in infants but often attacking older children and even adults, characterized by inflammation of the nerve cells, mainly of the anterior horns of the spinal cord, resulting in a motor paralysis, followed by muscular atrophy, etc., and often by permanent deformities if not treated. Also, **infantile paralysis.**

in·fan·ti·lism (Ĭn făn′tə lĬz′əm), *n.* 1. a pattern of speech characterized by those deviations from normal articulation or voice that are typical of very young children. 2. *Psychol.* the persistence in an adult of markedly childish anatomical, physiological, or psychological characteristics.

in·fan·tine (Ĭn′fən tĬn′, -tĬn), *adj.* infantile.

in·fan·try (Ĭn′fən trĬ), *n.* soldiers or military units that fight on foot, with bayonets, rifles, machine guns, grenades, mortars, etc. [t. F: m. *infanterie* t. It.: m. *infanteria,* der. *infante* youth, foot soldier. See INFANT]

in·fan·try·man (Ĭn′fən trĬ mən), *n., pl.* -**men.** a soldier of the infantry.

infants′ school, *Brit.* a primary school for children from about five to seven years of age. Also, **infant school.**

in·farct (Ĭn färkt′), *n. Pathol.* a circumscribed portion of tissue which has been suddenly deprived of its blood supply by embolism or thrombosis and which, as a result, is undergoing death (necrosis), to be replaced by scar tissue. [t. L: s. *infar(c)tus,* pp., stuffed in]

in·farc·tion (Ĭn färk′shən), *n. Pathol.* 1. the formation of an infarct. 2. an infarct.

in·fat·u·ate (*v.* Ĭn fäch′ŏŏ āt′; *adj., n.* Ĭn fäch′ŏŏ Ĭt, -āt′), *v.,* -**ated,** -**ating,** *adj.* —*v.t.* 1. to affect with folly; make fatuous. 2. to inspire or possess with a foolish or unreasoning passion, as of love. —*adj.* 3. infatuated. —*n.* 4. a person who is infatuated. [t. L: m.s. *infatuātus,* pp., made foolish]

in·fat·u·at·ed (Ĭn fäch′ŏŏ ā′tĬd), *adj.* made foolish by love; blindly in love. —**in·fat′u·at′ed·ly,** *adv.*

in·fat·u·a·tion (Ĭn fäch′ŏŏ ā′shən), *n.* 1. the act of infatuating. 2. the state of being infatuated. 3. foolish or all-absorbing passion.

in·fea·si·ble (Ĭn fē′zə bəl), *adj.* not feasible; impracticable. —**in·fea′si·bil′i·ty,** *n.*

in·fect (Ĭn fĕkt′), *v.t.* 1. to impregnate (a person, organ, wound, etc.) with disease-producing germs. 2. to affect with disease. 3. to impregnate with something that affects quality, character, or condition, esp. unfavorably: *to infect the air with poison gas.* 4. to taint, contaminate, or affect morally: *infected with greediness.* 5. to imbue with some pernicious belief, opinion, etc. 6. to affect so as to influence feeling or action: *his courage infected the others.* 7. *Law.* to taint with illegality, or expose to penalty, forfeiture, etc. —*adj.* 8. *Archaic.* infected. [ME *infect(en),* t. L: (m.) s. *infectus,* pp., put in, dyed, imbued, infected] —**in·fec′tor,** *n.*

in·fec·tion (Ĭn fĕk′shən), *n.* 1. the action of infecting. 2. an infecting with germs of disease, as through the medium of infected insects, air, water, clothing, etc. 3. an infecting agency or influence. 4. state of being infected. 5. an infectious disease. 6. the condition of suffering an infection. 7. an influence or impulse passing from one to another and affecting feeling or action. 8. *Gram.* (in Celtic languages) assimilation in which a vowel is influenced by a following vowel. 9. *Rare.* (in humorous use) affection.

in·fec·tious (Ĭn fĕk′shəs), *adj.* 1. communicable by infection, as diseases. 2. causing or communicating infection. 3. tending to spread from one to another: *laughter is infectious.* 4. *Law.* capable of contaminating with illegality; exposing to seizure or forfeiture. 5. *Obs.* diseased. —**in·fec′tious·ly,** *adv.* —**in·fec′tious·ness,** *n.* —**Syn.** 3. See **contagious.**

infectious disease, 1. a disease caused by germs, as bacteria or filterable viruses. 2. any disease, produced by the action of a microörganism in the body, which may or may not be contagious.

infectious mon·o·nu·cle·o·sis (mŏn′ō nū′klĬ ō′sĬs, -nŏŏ′-), glandular fever.

infectious myx·o·ma (mĬk sō′mə), a highly fatal, rapidly spreading virus disease of rabbits.

in·fec·tive (Ĭn fĕk′tĬv), *adj.* infectious. —**in·fec′tive·ness,** *in·fec′tiv′i·ty,** *n.*

in·fe·cund (Ĭn fē′kənd, -fĕk′ənd), *adj.* not fecund; unfruitful; barren. —**in·fe·cun·di·ty** (Ĭn′fĬ kŭn′də tĬ), *n.*

in·fe·lic·i·tous (Ĭn′fə lĬs′ə təs), *adj.* 1. not felicitous, happy, or fortunate; unhappy. 2. inapt or inappropriate: *an infelicitous remark.* —**in·fe·lic′i·tous·ly,** *adv.*

in·fe·lic·i·ty (Ĭn′fə lĬs′ə tĬ), *n., pl.* -**ties.** 1. the state of being unhappy; unhappiness. 2. ill fortune. 3. an unfortunate circumstance; a misfortune. 4. inaptness or inappropriateness as of action or expression. 5. something inapt or infelicitous: *infelicities of style.*

in·felt (Ĭn′fĕlt′), *adj.* felt within; heartfelt.

in·fer (Ĭn fûr′), *v.,* -**ferred,** -**ferring.** —*v.t.* 1. to derive by reasoning; conclude or judge from premises or evidence. 2. (of facts, circumstances, statements, etc.) to indicate or involve as a conclusion; imply. 3. to imply or hint. —*v.i.* 4. to draw a conclusion, as by reasoning. [t. L: s. *inferre* bring in or on, infer] —**in·fer·a·ble** (Ĭn fûr′ə bəl, Ĭn′fər-), *adj.* —**in·fer′a·bly,** *adv.*

in·fer·ence (Ĭn′fər əns), *n.* 1. the act or process of inferring. 2. that which is inferred: *to make rash inferences.*

3. *Logic.* **a.** the process of deriving the strict logical consequences of assumed premises. **b.** the process of arriving at some conclusion which, though it is not logically derivable from the assumed premises, possesses some degree of probability relative to the premises. **c.** a proposition reached by a process of inference.

in·fer·en·tial (Ĭn′fə rĕn′shəl), *adj.* pertaining to or depending on inference. —**in·fer·en′tial·ly,** *adv.*

in·fe·ri·or (Ĭn fĬr′Ĭ ər), *adj.* 1. lower in station, rank, degree, or grade (fol. by *to*). 2. of comparatively low grade; poor in quality: *an inferior brand.* 3. less important, valuable, or excellent: *an inferior workman.* 4. lower in place or position (now chiefly in scientific or technical use): *the inferior maxillary bone.* 5. *Bot.* **a.** situated below some other organ. **b.** (of a calyx) inserted below the ovary. **c.** (of an ovary) having a superior calyx. 6. *Astron.* **a.** (of a planet) having an orbit within that of the earth: applied to the planets Mercury and Venus. **b.** (of a conjunction of an inferior planet) taking place between the sun and the earth. **c.** lying below the horizon: *the inferior part of a meridian.* 7. *Print.* lower than the main line of type, as the figures in chemical formulas. —*n.* 8. one inferior to another or others, as in rank or merit. 9. *Print.* an inferior letter or figure. [ME, t. L, compar. of *inferus* being below, under, nether. Cf. UNDER] —**in·fe·ri·or·i·ty** (Ĭn fĬr′Ĭ ôr′ə tĬ, -ŏr′-), *n.* —**in·fe′ri·or·ly,** *adv.*

inferiority complex, feelings arising from one's real or imagined inferiorities. Also, **inferiority feelings.**

in·fer·nal (Ĭn fûr′nəl), *adj.* 1. of or pertaining to the lower world of classical mythology: *the infernal regions.* 2. of, inhabiting, or befitting hell. 3. hellish; fiendish; diabolical: *an infernal plot.* 4. *Colloq.* outrageous: *an infernal nuisance.* [ME, t. LL: s. *infernālis* of the lower regions] —**in·fer·nal′i·ty,** *n.* —**in·fer′nal·ly,** *adv.*

infernal machine, an explosive mechanical apparatus intended to destroy life or property.

in·fer·no (Ĭn fûr′nō), *n., pl.* -**nos.** 1. hell; the infernal regions. 2. an infernal or hell-like region. 3. **The Inferno,** the title of a part of Dante's *Divine Comedy.* [t. It.: hell; g. L *infernus* underground]

in·fer·tile (Ĭn fûr′tĬl), *adj.* not fertile; unfruitful; unproductive; barren: *infertile soil.* —**in·fer·til′i·ty,** *n.*

in·fest (Ĭn fĕst′), *v.t.* 1. to haunt or overrun in a troublesome manner, as predatory bands, destructive animals, vermin, etc., do. 2. to be numerous in, as anything troublesome: *the cares that infest the day.* 3. *Now Rare.* to harass. —*v.i.* 4. to become confirmed in evil; become habitually vicious. [late ME, t. L: s. *infestāre* assail, molest] —**in·fest′er,** *n.*

in·fes·ta·tion (Ĭn′fĕs tā′shən), *n.* 1. the act of infesting. 2. the state of being infested. 3. a harassing or troublesome invasion.

in·feu·da·tion (Ĭn′fyŏŏ dā′shən), *n. Eng. Law.* 1. the grant of an estate in fee. 2. the relation of lord and vassal established by the grant and acceptance of such an estate. [t. ML: s. *infeudātio,* der. *infeudāre* enfeoff]

in·fi·del (Ĭn′fə dəl), *n.* 1. an unbeliever. 2. one who does not accept a particular faith, esp. Christianity (formerly applied by Christians esp. to a Mohammedan). 3. (in Mohammedan use) one who does not accept the Mohammedan faith. —*adj.* 4. without religious faith. 5. due to or manifesting unbelief. 6. not accepting a particular faith, esp. Christianity or Mohammedanism; heathen. 7. rejecting the Christian religion while accepting no other; not believing in the Bible or any divine revelation: used especially of persons belonging to Christian communities. 8. of or pertaining to unbelievers or infidels. [late ME, t. L: s. *infidēlis* unfaithful, LL unbelieving] —**Syn.** 2, 3. See **atheist.**

in·fi·del·i·ty (Ĭn′fə dĕl′ə tĬ), *n., pl.* -**ties.** 1. unfaithfulness. 2. adultery. 3. lack of religious faith, esp. Christian. 4. a breach of trust.

in·field (Ĭn′fēld′), *n.* 1. *Baseball.* **a.** the diamond. **b.** the three basemen and the shortstop. 2. that part of farmlands nearest to the buildings.

in·field·er (Ĭn′fēl′dər), *n. Baseball.* an infield player.

in·fil·trate (Ĭn fĬl′trāt), *v.,* -**trated,** -**trating,** *n.* —*v.t.* 1. to filter into or through; permeate. 2. to cause to pass in by, or as by, filtering: *the troops infiltrated the enemy lines.* —*v.i.* 3. to pass in or through a substance, etc., by or as by filtering. —*n.* 4. that which infiltrates. 5. *Pathol.* cells or a substance which pass into the tissues and form a morbid accumulation. —**in·fil′tra·tive,** *adj.*

in·fil·tra·tion (Ĭn′fĬl trā′shən), *n.* 1. the act or process of infiltrating. 2. the state of being infiltrated. 3. that which infiltrates; an infiltrate. 4. *Mil.* a method of attack in which small bodies of soldiers or individual soldiers penetrate into the enemy's line at weak or unguarded points, in order to bring fire eventually upon the enemy's flanks or rear.

infin., infinitive.

in·fi·nite (Ĭn′fə nĬt), *adj.* 1. immeasurably great: *a truth of infinite importance.* 2. indefinitely or exceedingly great: *infinite sums of money.* 3. unbounded or unlimited; perfect: *the infinite wisdom of God.* 4. endless or innumerable; inexhaustible. 5. *Math.* **a.** not finite. **b.** (of an assemblage) having the same number of elements as some proper part of itself. —*n.* 6. that which is infinite. 7. **the Infinite** or **the Infinite Being,** God. 8. *Math.* an infinite quantity or magnitude. 9. the boundless regions of space. [ME, t. L: m.s. *infīnītus*] —**in′fi·nite·ly,** *adv.* —**in′fi·nite·ness,** *n.*

in·fin·i·tes·i·mal (ĭn/fĭn ə tĕs/ə məl), *adj.* **1.** indefinitely or exceedingly small; minute: *the infinitesimal vessels of the nervous system.* **2.** immeasurably small; less than an assignable quantity: *to an infinitesimal degree.* **3.** pertaining to or involving infinitesimals. —*n.* **4.** an infinitesimal quantity. **5.** *Math.* a variable having zero as a limit. —**in/fin·i·tes/i·mal·ly,** *adv.*

infinitesimal calculus, the differential calculus and the integral calculus, considered together.

in·fin·i·ti·val (ĭn/fĭn ə tī/vəl), *adj. Gram.* of or pertaining to the infinitive mode.

in·fin·i·tive (ĭn fĭn/ə tĭv), *Gram. n.* **1.** (in many languages) a noun form derived from verbs, which names the action or state without specifying the subject, as Latin *esse* to be, *fuisse* to have been. **2.** (in English) the simple form of the verb (*come, take, eat*) used after certain other verbs (I didn't *come*), or this simple form preceded by *to* (the **marked infinitive,** I wanted *to come*). —*adj.* **3.** of or pertaining to the infinitive or its meaning. [late ME, t. LL: m.s. *infinītīvus* unlimited, indefinite] —**in·fin/i·tive·ly,** *adv.*

in·fin·i·tude (ĭn fĭn/ə tūd/, -tōōd/), *n.* **1.** infinity: *divine infinitude.* **2.** an infinite extent, amount, or number.

in·fin·i·ty (ĭn fĭn/ə tĭ), *n., pl.* **-ties. 1.** the state of being infinite: *the infinity of God.* **2.** that which is infinite. **3.** infinite space, time, or quantity: *any time short of infinity.* **4.** an infinite extent, amount, or number. **5.** an indefinitely great amount or number. **6.** *Math.* **a.** the concept of increasing without bound. **b.** infinite distance, or an infinitely distant part of space. [ME *infinite,* t. L: m.s. *infīnitas*]

in·firm (ĭn fûrm/), *adj.* **1.** feeble in body or health. **2.** not steadfast, unfaltering, or resolute, as persons, the mind, etc.: *infirm of purpose.* **3.** not firm, solid, or strong: *an infirm support.* **4.** unsound or invalid, as an argument, a title, etc. —*v.t.* **5.** *Rare.* to invalidate. [ME, t. L: s. *infirmus*] —**in·firm/ly,** *adv.* —**in·firm/ness,** *n.*

in·fir·ma·ry (ĭn fûr/mə rĭ), *n., pl.* **-ries. 1.** a place for the care of the infirm, sick, or injured; a hospital. **2.** a dispensary. [t. ML: m.s. *infirmāria,* der. L *infirmus* infirm]

in·fir·mi·ty (ĭn fûr/mə tĭ), *n., pl.* **-ties. 1.** a physical weakness or ailment: *the infirmities of age.* **2.** the state of being infirm; lack of strength. **3.** a moral weakness or failing. [ME *infirmyte,* t. L: m.s. *infirmitas*]

in·fix (*v.* ĭn fĭks/; *n.* ĭn/fĭks/), *v.t.* **1.** to fix, fasten, or drive in: *he infixed the fatal spear.* **2.** to implant: *the habits they infixed.* **3.** to fix in the mind or memory, as a fact or idea; impress. **4.** *Gram.* to add as an infix. —*v.i.* **5.** *Gram.* (of a linguistic form) to admit an infix. —*n.* **6.** *Gram.* an affix which is inserted within the body of the element to which it is added, as Latin *m* in *accumbō* I lie down, as compared with *accubuī* I lay down. [t. L: s. *infixus,* pp., fastened in] —**in·fix/ion,** *n.*

in fla·gran·te de·lic·to (ĭn flə grăn/tĭ dĭ lĭk/tō), *Latin.* in the very act of committing the offense.

in·flame (ĭn flām/), *v.,* **-flamed, -flaming.** —*v.t.* **1.** to set aflame or afire. **2.** to light or redden with or as with flames: *the setting sun inflames the sky.* **3.** to kindle or excite (passions, desires, etc.). **4.** to arouse to a high degree of passion or feeling. **5.** to affect in appearance by passion, etc. **6.** to make more violent. **7.** to excite inflammation in: *her eyes were inflamed with crying.* **8.** to raise (the blood, bodily tissue, etc.) to a morbid or feverish heat. —*v.i.* **9.** to burst into flame; take fire. **10.** to be kindled, as passion. **11.** to become hot with passion, as the heart. **12.** to become morbidly affected with inflammation. [ME *enflame(n),* t. OF: m. *enflamer,* g. L *inflammāre* set on fire] —**in·flam/er,** *n.* —**in·flam/ing·ly,** *adv.* —**Syn. 1.** See **kindle.**

in·flam·ma·ble (ĭn flăm/ə bəl), *adj.* **1.** capable of being set on fire; combustible. **2.** easily roused to passion; excitable. —*n.* **3.** something inflammable. —**in·flam/ma·bil/i·ty, in·flam/ma·ble·ness,** *n.* —**in·flam/ma·bly,** *adv.*

in·flam·ma·tion (ĭn/flə mā/shən), *n.* **1.** the act of inflaming. **2.** the state of being inflamed. **3.** *Pathol.* a reaction of the body to injurious agents, commonly characterized by heat, redness, swelling, pain, etc., and disturbed function.

in·flam·ma·to·ry (ĭn flăm/ə tōr/ĭ), *adj.* **1.** tending to inflame; kindling passion, anger, etc.: *inflammatory speeches.* **2.** *Pathol.* pertaining to or attended with inflammation. —**in·flam/ma·to/ri·ly,** *adv.*

in·flate (ĭn flāt/), *v.,* **-flated, -flating.** —*v.t.* **1.** to distend; swell or puff out; dilate. **2.** to distend with gas: *inflate a balloon.* **3.** to puff up with pride, satisfaction, etc. **4.** to elate. **5.** to expand (currency, prices, etc.) unduly; raise above the previous or proper amount or value. —*v.i.* **6.** to cause inflation. **7.** to become inflated. [t. L: m.s. *inflātus,* pp., puffed up] —**in·flat/a·ble,** *adj.* —**in·flat/er, in·fla/tor,** *n.* —**Syn. 1.** See **expand.**

in·flat·ed (ĭn flā/tĭd), *adj.* **1.** distended with air or gas; swollen. **2.** puffed up, as with pride. **3.** turgid or bombastic, as language. **4.** resulting from inflation: *inflated values of land.* **5.** unduly expanded, as currency. **6.** *Bot.* hollow or swelled out with air: *inflated perianth.* —**in·flat/ed·ness,** *d.*

in·fla·tion (ĭn flā/shən), *n.* **1.** undue expansion or increase of the currency of a country, esp. by the issuing of paper money not redeemable in specie. **2.** a substantial rise of prices caused by an undue expansion in paper money or bank credit. **3.** the act of inflating. **4.** the state of being inflated.

in·fla·tion·ar·y (ĭn flā/shə nĕr/ĭ), *adj.* of or causing inflation: *inflationary legislation.*

in·fla·tion·ism (ĭn flā/shə nĭz/əm), *n.* the policy or practice of inflation through expansion of currency or bank deposits.

in·fla·tion·ist (ĭn flā/shən ĭst), *n.* an advocate of inflation through expansion of currency or bank deposits.

in·flect (ĭn flĕkt/), *v.t.* **1.** to bend; turn from a direct line or course. **2.** to modulate (the voice). **3.** *Gram.* **a.** to apply inflection to (a word). **b.** to recite or display all, or a distinct set of, the inflections of (a word), in a fixed order: *to inflect Latin "amō" as "amō, amās, amat," etc. or "nauta" as "nauta, nautae, nautae, nautam, nautā,"* etc. **4.** *Bot.* to bend in. —*v.i.* **5.** *Gram.* to be characterized by inflection. [ME *inflecte(n),* t. L: m. *inflectere* bend] —**in·flec/tive,** *adj.* —**in·flec/tor,** *n.*

in·flec·tion (ĭn flĕk/shən), *n.* **1.** modulation of the voice; change in pitch or tone of voice. **2.** *Gram.* **a.** the existence in a language of sets of forms built normally on a single stem, having different syntactic functions and meanings, but all those of a single stem being members of the same fundamental part of speech and constituting forms of the same "word." **b.** the set of forms of a single word, or a recital or display thereof in a fixed order. **c.** a single pattern of formation of such sets, as *noun inflection, verb inflection.* **d.** a change in the form of a word, generally by affixation by means of which a change of meaning or relationship to some other word or group of words is indicated. **e.** the affix added to the stem to produce this change. For example: the *-s* in *dogs* and *-ed* in *played* are inflections. **4.** a bend or angle. **5.** *Math.* a change of curvature from convex to concave or vice versa. Also, *esp. Brit.,* **inflexion.** —**in·flec/tion·al,** *adj.* —**in·flec/tion·al·ly,** *adv.* —**in·flec/tion·less,** *adj.*

inflection point, *Math.* a point of inflection on a curve.

in·flexed (ĭn flĕkst/), *adj. Bot., Zool.* inflected; bent or folded downward or inward: *an inflexed leaf.*

in·flex·i·ble (ĭn flĕk/sə bəl), *adj.* **1.** not flexible; rigid: *an inflexible rod.* **2.** unyielding in temper or purpose: *inflexible to threats.* **3.** unalterable; not permitting variation: *the law is inflexible.* [ME, t. L: m.s. *inflexibilis.* See IN-[3], FLEXIBLE] —**in·flex/i·bil/i·ty, in·flex/i·ble·ness,** *n.* —**in·flex/i·bly,** *adv.*

—**Syn. 2.** INFLEXIBLE, RELENTLESS, IMPLACABLE, INEXORABLE imply having the quality of not being turned from a purpose. INFLEXIBLE means unbending, adhering undeviatingly to a set plan, purpose, or the like: *inflexible in interpretation of rules, an inflexible will.* RELENTLESS suggests such a pitiless and unremitting following of purpose as to convey a sense of inevitableness: *as relentless as the passing of time.* IMPLACABLE means incapable of being placated or appeased: *implacable in wrath.* INEXORABLE means stern, rigorous, and unmoved by prayer or entreaty: *inexorable in demanding payment.* —**Ant. 2.** pliant.

in·flex·ion (ĭn flĕk/shən), *n. Chiefly Brit.* inflection. —**in·flex/ion·al,** *adj.* —**in·flex/ion·al·ly,** *adv.*

in·flict (ĭn flĭkt/), *v.t.* **1.** to lay on: *to inflict a dozen lashes.* **2.** to impose as something that must be borne or suffered: *to inflict punishment.* **3.** to impose (anything unwelcome). [t. L: s. *inflictus,* pp., struck against] —**in·flict/er, in·flic/tor,** *n.* —**in·flic/tive,** *adj.*

in·flic·tion (ĭn flĭk/shən), *n.* **1.** the act of inflicting. **2.** something inflicted, as punishment, suffering, etc.

in·flo·res·cence (ĭn/flō rĕs/əns,), *n.* **1.** a flowering or blossoming. **2.** *Bot.* **a.** the arrangement of flowers on the axis. See the illus. on the next page. **b.** the flowering part of a plant. **c.** a flower cluster. **d.** flowers collectively. **e.** a single flower. [t. NL: m.s. *inflōrescentia,* der. LL *inflōrescens,* ppr., coming into flower] —**in/flo·res/cent,** *adj.*

in·flow (ĭn/flō/), *n.* that which flows in; influx.

in·flu·ence (ĭn/flōō əns), *n., v.,* **-enced, -encing.** —*n.* **1.** invisible or insensible action exerted by one thing or person on another. **2.** power of producing effects by invisible or insensible means: *spheres of influence.* **3.** a thing or person that exerts action by invisible or insensible means: *beneficial influences.* **4.** electrostatic induction. **5.** *Astrol.* **a.** the supposed radiation of an ethereal fluid from the stars, regarded in astrology as affecting human actions and destinies, etc. **b.** the exercise of occult power by the stars, or such power as exercised. **6.** *Poetic.* the exercise of similar power by human beings. **7.** *Obs.* influx. —*v.t.* **8.** to exercise influence on; modify, affect, or sway: *to influence a person by bribery.* **9.** to move or impel to, or to do, something. [ME, t. ML: m.s. *influentia,* lit., a flowing in, der. L *influens* influent] —**in/flu·enc·er,** *n.* —**Syn. 1.** ascendancy, mastery; control, power. **2.** prestige; sway, rule. See **authority. 9.** incite; stir, induce, persuade.

in·flu·ent (ĭn/flōō ənt), *adj.* **1.** flowing in. —*n.* **2.** a tributary. [ME, t. L: s. *influens,* ppr., flowing in]

in·flu·en·tial (ĭn/flōō ĕn/shəl), *adj.* having or exerting influence, esp. great influence. [f. s. ML *influentia* INFLUENCE + -AL[1]] —**in/flu·en/tial·ly,** *adv.*

in·flu·en·za (ĭn/flōō ĕn/zə), *n.* **1.** *Pathol.* an acute, extremely contagious, commonly epidemic disease characterized by general prostration, and occurring in several forms with varying symptoms, usually with nasal catarrh and bronchial inflammation, and due to a specific microörganism; grippe. **2.** *Vet. Sci.* an acute, contagious disease occurring in horses and swine, manifested by fever, depression, and catarrhal inflammations of the eyes, nasal passages, and bronchi. [t. It.: influx of disease, epidemic, influenza. See INFLUENCE] **—in/-flu·en'zal,** *adj.* **—in/flu·en'za·like/,** *adj.*

in·flux (ĭn'flŭks'), *n.* **1.** the act of flowing in; an inflow. **2.** the place or point at which one stream flows into another or into the sea. **3.** the mouth of a stream. [t. LL: s. *influxus,* der. L *influere* flow in]

in·fold (ĭn fōld'), *v.t.* **1.** to wrap up; envelop: *infolded in a magic mantle.* **2.** to clasp; embrace. **3.** to imply or involve. **4.** to form into a fold or folds: *a cambium layer deeply infolded where it extends downwards.* **5.** to fold in or inward. Also, **enfold.** **—in·fold'er,** *n.* **—in·fold'ment,** *n.*

in·form[1] (ĭn fôrm'), *v.t.* **1.** to impart knowledge of a fact or circumstance to: *he informed him of his arrival.* **2.** to supply (oneself) with knowledge of a matter or subject: *he informed himself of all the pertinent facts.* **3.** to give character to; pervade with determining effect on the character. **4.** to animate or inspire. **5.** *Now Rare.* to train or instruct. **6.** *Obs.* to make known; disclose. **7.** *Obs.* to impart form to. **—v.i. 8.** to give information, esp. to furnish incriminating evidence to a prosecuting officer. [t. L: s. *informāre;* r. ME *enforme,* t. OF] **—in·form'er,** *n.* **—in·form'ing·ly,** *adv.* **—Syn. 1.** apprise; notify, advise, tell. **2.** acquaint.

in·form[2] (ĭn fôrm'), *adj.* without form; formless. [t. L: s. *informis* shapeless. See IN-[3]]

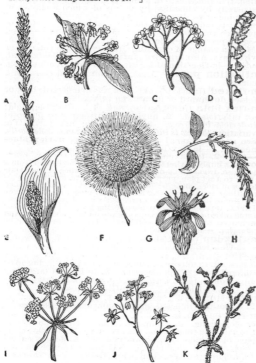

Forms of inflorescence

A, Spike of plantain, *Plantago major*; B, Simple umbel of milkweed, *Asclepias syriaca*; C, Corymb of red chokeberry, *Aronia arbutifolia*; D, Raceme of lily of the valley, *Convallaria maialis*; E, Spadix within the spathe of calla, *Calla palustris*; F, Flower head of buttonbush, *Cephalanthus occidentalis*; G, Anthodium of goldenrod, genus *Solidago*; H, Female catkin of willow, genus *Salix*; I, Compound umbel of water parsnip, *Sium cicutaefolium*; J, Panicle of blue cohosh, *Caulophyllum thalictroides*; K, Cyme of chickweed, genus *Cerastium*

in·for·mal (ĭn fôr'məl), *adj.* **1.** not according to prescribed or customary forms; irregular: *informal proceedings.* **2.** without formality; unceremonious: *an informal visit.* **3.** denoting speech characterized by colloquial usage, having the flexibility of grammar, syntax, and pronunciation allowable in conversation. **4.** characterizing the second singular pronominal or verbal form, or its use, in certain languages: *the informal "tu" in French.* **—in·for'mal·ly,** *adv.* **—Syn. 3.** See **colloquial.**

in·for·mal·i·ty (ĭn'fôr măl'ə tĭ), *n., pl.* **-ties. 1.** state of being informal; absence of formality. **2.** an informal act.

in·form·ant (ĭn fôr'mənt), *n.* **1.** one who gives information. **2.** one who supplies linguistic forms for analysis.

in·for·ma·tion (ĭn'fər mā'shən), *n.* **1.** knowledge communicated or received concerning some fact or circumstance; news. **2.** knowledge on various subjects, however acquired. **3.** the act of informing. **4.** the state of being informed. **5.** *Law.* **a.** an official criminal charge presented, usually by the prosecuting officers of the state, without the interposition of a grand jury. **b.** a criminal charge made under oath, before a justice of the peace, of an offense punishable summarily. **—in/for·ma'tion·al,** *adj.*

—Syn. 2. INFORMATION, KNOWLEDGE, WISDOM are terms for human acquirements through reading, study, and practical

experience. INFORMATION applies to facts told, read, communicated, which may be unorganized and even unrelated: *to pick up useful information.* KNOWLEDGE is an organized body of information, or the comprehension and understanding consequent on having acquired and organized a body of facts: *a knowledge of chemistry.* WISDOM is a knowledge of people, life, and conduct, with the facts so thoroughly assimilated as to have produced sagacity, judgment, and insight: *to use wisdom in handling people.* **—Ant. 2.** ignorance.

in·form·a·tive (ĭn fôr'mə tĭv), *adj.* affording information; instructive: *an informative book.*

in·for·tune (ĭn fôr'chən), *n.* **1.** *Astrol.* a planet or aspect of evil influence, esp. Saturn or Mars. **2.** *Obs.* misfortune. [ME, t. F. See IN-[3], FORTUNE]

in·fra (ĭn'frə), *adv. Latin.* below (in a text). Cf. **supra.**

infra-, a prefix meaning "below" or "beneath," as in *infra-axillary* (below the axilla). [t. L, repr. *infrā,* adv. and prep., below, beneath]

in·fra·cos·tal (ĭn'frə kŏs'təl, -kôs'-), *adj.* below the ribs.

in·fract (ĭn frăkt'), *v.t.* to break; violate or infringe [t. L: s. *infractus,* pp., broken off] **—in·frac'tor,** *n.*

in·frac·tion (ĭn frăk'shən), *n.* breach; violation; infringement: *an infraction of a treaty or law.*

in·fra dig (ĭn'frə dĭg'), *Chiefly Brit. Colloq.* infra dignitatem.

in·fra dig·ni·ta·tem (ĭn'frə dĭg'nə tā'təm), *Latin.* beneath (one's) dignity.

in·fra·lap·sar·i·an (ĭn'frə lăp sâr'ĭ ən), *n.* **1.** one who believes in infralapsarianism. **—adj. 2.** pertaining to infralapsarianism or those who hold it. [f. INFRA- + s. L *lapsus* a fall + -ARIAN]

in·fra·lap·sar·i·an·ism (ĭn'frə lăp sâr'ĭ ə nĭz'əm), *n. Theol.* the doctrine, held by Augustinians and by many Calvinists, that God planned the creation, permitted the fall, elected a chosen number, planned their redemption, and suffered the remainder to be eternally punished.

in·fran·gi·ble (ĭn frăn'jə bəl), *adj.* **1.** unbreakable. **2.** inviolable. **—in·fran/gi·bil/i·ty, in·fran/gi·ble·ness,** *n.* **—in·fran/gi·bly,** *adv.*

in·fra·red (ĭn'frə rĕd'), *n.* **1.** the part of the invisible spectrum contiguous to the red end of the visible spectrum, comprising radiation of greater wave length than that of red light. **—adj. 2.** denoting or pertaining to the infrared or its component rays.

in·fre·quen·cy (ĭn frē'kwən sĭ), *n.* the state of being infrequent. Also, **in·fre'quence.**

in·fre·quent (ĭn frē'kwənt), *adj.* **1.** happening or occurring at long intervals or not often: *infrequent visits.* **2.** not constant, habitual, or regular: *an infrequent visitor.* **3.** not plentiful. **—in·fre'quent·ly,** *adv.*

in·fringe (ĭn frĭnj'), *v.,* **-fringed, -fringing. —v.t. 1.** to commit a breach or infraction of; violate or transgress. **—v.i. 2.** to encroach or trespass (fol. by *on* or *upon*): *don't infringe on his privacy.* [t. L: m.s. *infringere* break off] **—in·fring'er,** *n.* **—Syn. 2.** See **trespass.**

in·fringe·ment (ĭn frĭnj'mənt), *n.* **1.** a breach or infraction, as of a law, right, or obligation; violation; transgression. **2.** act of infringing.

in·fun·dib·u·li·form (ĭn'fŭn dĭb'yə lə fôrm'), *adj. Bot.* funnel-shaped.

in·fun·dib·u·lum (ĭn'fŭn dĭb'yə ləm), *n., pl.* **-la** (-lə). **1.** a funnel-shaped organ or part. **2.** *Anat.* **a.** a funnel-shaped extension of the cerebrum connecting the pituitary body to the base of the brain. **b.** a space in the right auricle at the root of the pulmonary artery. [t. L: funnel] **—in·fun·dib·u·lar** (ĭn'fŭn dĭb'yə lər), **in·fun·dib·u·late** (ĭn'fŭn dĭb'yə lāt'), *adj.*

in·fu·ri·ate (*v.* ĭn fyoor'ĭ āt'; *adj.* ĭn fyoor'ĭ ĭt), *v.,* **-ated, -ating,** *adj.* **—v.t. 1.** to make furious; enrage. **—adj. 2.** infuriated. [t. ML: m.s. *infuriātus,* pp., enraged] **—in·fu'ri·ate·ly,** *adv.* **—in·fu'ri·at'ing·ly,** *adv.* **—in·fu'ri·a'tion,** *n.* **—Syn. 1.** See **enrage.**

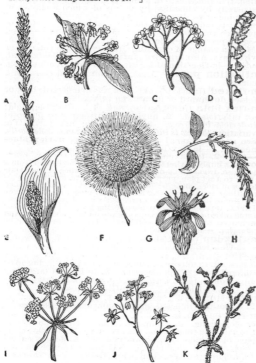
Infundibuliform
corolla

in·fus·cate (ĭn fŭs'kāt), *adj. Entomol.* darkened with a fuscous or brownish shade. Also, **in·fus'cat·ed.** [t. L: m.s. *infuscātus,* pp., darkened]

in·fuse (ĭn fūz'), *v.t.,* **-fused, -fusing. 1.** to introduce as by pouring; cause to penetrate; instil (fol. by *into*). **2.** to imbue or inspire (*with*). **3.** to pour in. **4.** to steep or soak (a plant, etc.) in a liquid so as to extract its soluble properties or ingredients. [ME, t. L: m.s. *infūsus,* pp., poured in or on] **—in·fus'er,** *n.*

in·fu·si·ble[1] (ĭn fū'zə bəl), *adj.* not fusible; incapable of being fused or melted. [f. IN-[3] + FUSIBLE] **—in·fu'si·bil'i·ty, in·fu'si·ble·ness,** *n.*

in·fu·si·ble[2] (ĭn fū'zə bəl), *adj.* capable of being infused. [f. INFUSE, v. + -IBLE]

in·fu·sion (ĭn fū'zhən), *n.* **1.** act of infusing. **2.** that which is infused. **3.** a liquid extract obtained from a substance by steeping or soaking it in water. **4.** *Med.* the introduction of a saline or other solution into a vein.

in·fu·sion·ism (ĭn fū'zhə nĭz'əm), *n. Theol.* the doctrine that the soul existed in a previous state and is infused into the body at conception or birth. **—in·fu'sion·ist,** *n.*

in·fu·sive (ĭn fū'sĭv), *adj.* infusing.

In·fu·so·ri·a (ĭn'fyoŏ sōr'ĭ ə), *n.pl.* **1.** *Zool.* protozoans of the class *Infusoria,* mostly microscopic and aquatic, having vibratile cilia. **2.** *Obs.* any of a miscellaneous variety of minute or microscopic animal and vegetable organisms (constituting the old group *Infusoria*) frequently developed in infusions of decaying organic matter. [t. NL, der. L *infūsus*, pp., poured in. See -ORY]

in·fu·so·ri·al (Yn/fyŏŏ sōr/Y əl), *adj.* containing or consisting of infusorians: *infusorial earth*.

in·fu·so·ri·an (Yn/fyŏŏ sōr/Y ən), *n.* any of the *Infusoria*.

in fu·tu·ro (Yn fyŏŏ tyŏŏr/ō, -tŏŏr/-), *Latin.* in the future.

-ing[1], a suffix of nouns formed from verbs, expressing the action of the verb or its result, product, material, etc., as in *the art of building, a new building, cotton wadding*. It is also used to form nouns from other words than verbs, as in *offing, shirting*. Verbal nouns ending in *-ing* are often used attributively, as in *the printing trade*, and in composition, as in *drinking song*. In some compounds, as *sewing machine*, the first element might reasonably be regarded as the participial adjective (see **-ing**[2]), the compound thus meaning "a machine that sews"; but it is commonly taken as a verbal noun, the compound being explained as "a machine for sewing." [ME *-ing*, OE *-ing, -ung*]

-ing[2], a suffix forming the present participle of verbs, such participles being often used as adjectives (participial adjectives), as in *warring factions*. Cf. **-ing**[1]. [ME *-ing, -inge*; r. ME *-inde, -ende*, OE *-ende*]

in·gath·er (Yn gáth/ər), *v.t.* to gather in; collect; bring in, as a harvest. —**in·gath/er·er,** *n.*

Inge (Yng), *n.* **William,** born 1860, British clergyman and author; ex-dean of St. Paul's Cathedral, London.

In·ge·low (Yn/jə lō/), *n.* **Jean,** 1820–97, British author.

in·gem·i·nate (Yn jĕm/ə nāt/), *v.t.,* **-nated, -nating.** to repeat; reiterate. [t. L: m.s. *ingemĭnātus*, pp., redoubled] —**in·gem/i·na/tion,** *n.*

in·gen·er·ate[1] (Yn jĕn/ər Yt), *adj.* not generated; self-existent. [t. LL: m.s. *ingenerātus*. See IN-[3]]

in·gen·er·ate[2] (*v.* Yn jĕn/ə rāt/; *adj.* Yn jĕn/ər Yt), *v.,* **-ated, -ating,** *adj. Now Rare.* —*v.t.* **1.** to generate within; engender. —*adj.* **2.** inborn; innate. [t. L: m.s. *ingenerātus*, pp., generated within. See IN-[2]] —**in·gen/er·a/tion,** *n.*

in·gen·ious (Yn jĕn/yəs), *adj.* **1.** (of things, actions, etc.) showing cleverness of invention or construction: *an ingenious machine.* **2.** having inventive faculty; skillful in contriving or constructing: *an ingenious mechanic.* [late Me, t. L: m.s. *ingeniōsus* of good natural talents] —**in·gen/ious·ly,** *adv.* —**in·gen/ious·ness,** *n.*

—**Syn. 2.** INGENIOUS, INGENUOUS are now distinct from each other and should not be confused or thought of as synonyms. INGENIOUS means clever, inventive, resourceful in contriving new explanations or methods, and the like: *an ingenious executive.* INGENUOUS means frank, candid, free from guile or deceit: *an ingenuous and sincere statement.*

in·gé·nue (ăN zhēN/), *n., pl.* **-nues** (-nyz/; *Fr.* -NY/). **1.** the part of an ingenuous girl, esp. as represented on the stage. **2.** the actress who plays such a part. [t. F, fem. of *ingénu* ingenuous, t. L: s. *ingenuus*]

in·ge·nu·i·ty (Yn/jə nū/ə tY, -nŏŏ/-), *n., pl.* **-ties. 1.** the quality of being ingenious; inventive talent. **2.** skillfulness of contrivance or design, as of things, actions, etc. **3.** an ingenious contrivance. **4.** *Obs.* ingenuousness. [t. L: m.s. *ingenuitas* frankness. Cf. INGENUOUS]

in·gen·u·ous (Yn jĕn/yŏŏəs), *adj.* **1.** free from reserve, restraint, or dissimulation. **2.** artless; innocent. [t. L: m. *ingenuus* native, innate, freeborn, noble, frank] —**in·gen/u·ous·ly,** *adv.* —**in·gen/u·ous·ness,** *n.* —**Syn. 1.** frank, candid. See **ingenious. 2.** naïve, guileless.

In·ger·soll (Yng/gər sôl/, -sōl/, -səl), *n.* **Robert Green,** 1833–99, U.S. lawyer, agnostic, and writer.

in·gest (Yn jĕst/), *v.t. Physiol.* to put or take (food, etc.) into the body. [t. L: s. *ingestus*, pp., carried, or poured in] —**in·ges/tion,** *n.* —**in·ges/tive,** *adj.*

in·ges·ta (Yn jĕs/tə), *n.pl.* substances ingested. [t. L]

in·gle (Yng/gəl), *n. Scot.* a household fire or fireplace.

in·gle·nook (Yng/gəl nŏŏk/), *n. Chiefly Brit.* a corner by the fire.

in·gle·side (Yng/gəl sīd/), *n. Scot.* a fireside.

In·gle·wood (Yng/gəl wŏŏd/), *n.* a city in SW California, near Los Angeles. 46,185 (1950).

in·glo·ri·ous (Yn glôr/Yəs), *adj.* **1.** shameful; disgraceful: *inglorious flight.* **2.** *Now Rare.* not famous. —**in·glo/ri·ous·ly,** *adv.* —**in·glo/ri·ous·ness,** *n.*

in·go·ing (Yn/gō/Yng), *adj.* going in; entering.

in·got (Yng/gət), *n.* **1.** the casting obtained when melted metal is poured into a mold (**ingot mold**) with the expectation that it be further processed. **2.** a cast metal mass, formed by rolling, etc., or by smelting and casting to shape. —*v.t.* **3.** to make ingots of; shape into ingots. [ME: mold for metal. Cf. OE *ingyte* pouring in]

in·graft (Yn gräft/, -gräft/), *v.t.* engraft. —**in·graft/ment,** *n.*

in·grain (*v.* Yn grān/; *adj., n.* Yn/grān/), *v.t.* **1.** to fix deeply and firmly, as in the nature or mind. —*adj.* **2.** ingrained; firmly fixed. **3.** (of carpets) made of yarn dyed before weaving, and so woven as to show the pattern on both sides. **4.** dyed in grain, or through the fiber. **5.** dyed in the yarn, or in a raw state, before manufacture. —*n.* **6.** yarn, wool, etc., dyed before manufacture. **7.** an ingrain carpet. Also, **engrain** for 1, 2.

in·grained (Yn grānd/, Yn/grānd/), *adj.* **1.** fixed firmly; deep-rooted: *ingrained habits.* **2.** inveterate; thorough.

in·grate (Yn/grāt), *n.* an ungrateful person. —*adj.*

2. *Archaic.* ungrateful. [ME, t. L: m.s. *ingrātus* unpleasing, not grateful]

in·gra·ti·ate (Yn grā/shY āt/), *v.t.,* **-ated, -ating.** to establish (oneself) in the favor or good graces of others. [f. IN-[2] + s. L *grātia* favor, grace + -ATE[1]] —**in·gra/ti·at/ing·ly,** *adv.* —**in·gra/ti·a/tion,** *n.*

in·gra·ti·a·to·ry (Yn grā/shY ə tōr/Y), *adj.* serving or intended to ingratiate.

in·grat·i·tude (Yn grăt/ə tūd/, -tŏŏd/), *n.* the state of being ungrateful; unthankfulness.

in·gra·ves·cent (Yn/grə vĕs/ənt), *adj. Pathol.* increasing in severity, as a disease. [t. L: s. *ingravescens,* ppr., growing heavier] —**in/gra·ves/cence,** *n.*

in·gre·di·ent (Yn grē/dY ənt), *n.* **1.** something that enters as an element into a mixture: *the ingredients of a cake.* **2.** a constituent element of anything. [late ME, t. L: s. *ingrediens,* ppr., entering] —**Syn. 1.** See **element.**

In·gres (ăN/gr), *n.* **Jean Auguste Dominique** (zhäN ō gyst/ dô mē nēk/), *n.* 1780–1867, French painter.

in·gress (Yn/grĕs), *n.* **1.** act of going in or entering. **2.** the right of going in. **3.** a means or place of going in; an entrance. [ME. t. L: s. *ingressus* entrance] —**in·gres/sion,** *n.* —**in·gres/sive,** *adj.* —**in·gres/sive·ness,** *n.*

in-group (Yn/grŏŏp/), *n. Sociol.* a group reserving favorable treatment and acceptance to its own members and denying them to members of other groups.

in·grow·ing (Yn/grō/Yng), *adj.* **1.** growing into the flesh: *an ingrowing nail.* **2.** growing within or inward.

in·grown (Yn/grōn/), *adj.* **1.** having grown into the flesh: *an ingrown toenail.* **2.** grown within or inward.

in·growth (Yn/grōth/), *n.* **1.** growth inward. **2.** something formed by growth inward.

in·gui·nal (Yng/gwə nəl), *adj.* of, pertaining to, or situated in the groin. [t. L: s. *inguinālis*]

in·gulf (Yn gŭlf/), *v.t.* engulf.

in·gur·gi·tate (Yn gûr/jə tāt/), *v.,* **-tated, -tating.** —*v.t.* **1.** to swallow greedily or in great quantity, as food. **2.** to engulf. —*v.i.* **3.** to drink largely; swill. [t. L: m.s. *ingurgitātus,* pp., poured in] —**in·gur/gi·ta/tion,** *n.*

in·hab·it (Yn hăb/Yt), *v.t.* **1.** to live or dwell in (a place), as persons or animals. **2.** to have its seat, or exist, in. —*v.i.* **3.** to live, dwell, or abide, as in a place; [t. L: m. *inhabitāre;* r. ME *inhabite,* t. F] —**in·hab/it·a·ble,** *adj.* —**in·hab/it·a·bil/i·ty,** —**in·hab/i·ta/tion,** *n.*

in·hab·it·an·cy (Yn hăb/ə tənsY), *n., pl.* **-cies.** residence as an inhabitant. Also, **in·hab/it·ance.**

in·hab·it·ant (Yn hăb/ə tənt), *n.* a person or an animal that inhabits a place; a permanent resident. Also, **in·hab/it·er.** [late ME, t. L: s. *inhabitans,* ppr., dwelling in]

in·hal·ant (Yn hā/lənt), *adj.* **1.** serving for inhalation. —*n.* **2.** an apparatus or medicine used for inhaling.

in·ha·la·tion (Yn/hə lā/shən), *n.* **1.** act of inhaling. **2.** a medicinal preparation to be inhaled.

in·ha·la·tor (Yn/hə lā/tər), *n.* an apparatus to help one inhale air, anesthetic, medicinal vapors, etc.

in·hale (Yn hāl/), *v.,* **-haled, -haling.** —*v.t.* **1.** to breathe in; draw in by, or as by, breathing: *to inhale air.* —*v.i.* **2.** to inhale, esp. smoke of cigarettes, cigars, etc.: *do you inhale?* [t. L: m.s. *inhālāre*]

in·hal·er (Yn hā/lər), *n.* **1.** an apparatus used in inhaling medicinal vapors, anesthetics, etc. **2.** a respirator. **3.** one who inhales.

In·ham·ba·ne (Yn/yəm bä/nə), *n.* a seaport in SE Mozambique. Municipal district, 46,899 (1940).

in·har·mon·ic (Yn/här mŏn/Yk), *adj.* not harmonic.

in·har·mo·ni·ous (Yn/här mō/nYəs), *adj.* not harmonious; discordant. [f. IN-[3] + HARMONIOUS] —**in/har·mo/ni·ous·ly,** *adv.* —**in/har·mo/ni·ous·ness,** *n.*

in·haul (Yn/hôl/), *n. Naut.* a rope for hauling in a sail or spar. Also, **in/haul/er.**

in·here (Yn hYr/), *v.i.,* **-hered, -hering.** to exist permanently and inseparably (in), as a quality, attribute, or element; belong intrinsically; be inherent. [t. L: m.s. *inhaerēre* stick in or to]

in·her·ence (Yn hYr/əns), *n.* **1.** the state or fact of inhering or being inherent. **2.** *Philos.* the relation of an attribute to its subject.

in·her·en·cy (Yn hYr/ənsY), *n., pl.* **-cies. 1.** inherence. **2.** something inherent.

in·her·ent (Yn hYr/ənt), *adj.* **1.** existing in something as a permanent and inseparable element, quality, or attribute. **2.** *Gram.* standing before a noun. **3.** *Rare.* inhering; infixed. [t. L: m.s. *inhaerens,* ppr., sticking in or to] —**in·her/ent·ly,** *adv.* —**Syn. 1.** See **essential.**

in·her·it (Yn hĕr/Yt), *v.t.* **1.** to take or receive (property, a right, a title, etc.) as the heir of the former owner. **2.** to succeed (a person) as heir. **3.** to receive (anything) as by succession from predecessors. **4.** to receive as one's portion. **5.** *Obs.* to make (one) heir (fol. by *of*). —*v.i.* **6.** to take or receive property, etc., as being heir to it. **7.** to have succession as heir. **8.** to receive qualities, powers, duties, etc., as by inheritance (fol. by *from*). [ME *enherite(n),* t. OF: m. *enheriter,* f. en- EN-[1] + *heriter* (g. L *hērēditāre* inherit)]

in·her·it·a·ble (Yn hĕr/ə tə bəl), *adj.* **1.** capable of being inherited. **2.** capable of inheriting; qualified to inherit. —**in·her/it·a·bil/i·ty, in·her/it·a·ble·ness,** *n.*

in·her·it·ance (Yn hĕr/ə təns), *n.* **1.** that which is or may be inherited; any property passing at the owner's death to the heir or those entitled to succeed. **2.** anything received from progenitors or predecessors as if by succession: *an inheritance of family pride.* **3.** portion, peculiar possession, or heritage: *the inheritance of the saints.* **4.** act or fact of inheriting: *to receive property by inheritance.* **5.** the right of inheriting.

—Syn. 1. INHERITANCE, HERITAGE denote something inherited. INHERITANCE is the common term for property or any possession that comes to an heir: *an inheritance from one's parents, a farm came to him by inheritance.* HERITAGE, a dignified or literary word, indicates whatever is bequeathed to a subsequent generation by an individual or by society: *our heritage from Greece and Rome.*

inheritance tax, a tax on those acquiring property by inheritance or bequest.

in·her·it·ed (ĭn hĕr′ə tĭd), *adj.* **1.** received by inheritance. **2.** *Gram.* found also in an earlier stage of the same language, esp. in the earliest reconstructed stage.

in·her·i·tor (ĭn hĕr′ə tər), *n.* one who inherits; heir. **—in·her·i·tress** (ĭn hĕr′ə trĭs), *n.fem.*

in·her·i·trix (ĭn hĕr′ə trĭks), *n., pl.* **inheritrices** (ĭn-hĕr′ə trī′sēz). a female inheritor.

in·he·sion (ĭn hē′zhən), *n.* state or fact of inhering; inherence. [t. LL: m.s. *inhaesio*]

in·hib·it (ĭn hĭb′ĭt), *v.t.* **1.** to restrain, hinder, arrest, or check (an action, impulse, etc.). **2.** to prohibit; forbid. [late ME, t. L: s. *inhibitus*, pp., held back, restrained] **—in·hib′it·er, in·hib′i·tor,** *n.* **—Syn. 2.** See **forbid.**

in·hi·bi·tion (ĭn′ĭ bĭsh′ən, ĭn′hĭ-), *n.* **1.** act of inhibiting. **2.** state of being inhibited. **3.** *Psychol.* the blocking of any psychological process by another psychological process. **4.** *Physiol.* a restraining, arresting, or checking, as of action: **a.** the reduction of a reflex or other activity as the result of an antagonistic stimulation. **b.** a state created at synapses making them less excitable to other sources of stimulation.

in·hib·i·to·ry (ĭn hĭb′ə tōr′ĭ), *adj.* serving or tending to inhibit. Also, **in·hib′i·tive.**

in hoc sig·no vin·ces (ĭn hŏk sĭg′nō vĭn′sēz), *Latin.* in this sign shalt thou conquer (motto used by Constantine the Great, from his vision of a cross with these words before battle).

in·hos·pi·ta·ble (ĭn hŏs′pĭ tə bəl; *less often* ĭn′hŏs pĭt′-ə bəl), *adj.* **1.** not inclined to or characterized by hospitality, as persons, actions, etc. **2.** (of a region, climate, etc.) not offering shelter, favorable conditions, etc. **—in·hos′pi·ta·ble·ness,** *n.* **—in·hos′pi·ta·bly,** *adv.*

in·hos·pi·tal·i·ty (ĭn′hŏs pə tăl′ə tĭ, ĭn hŏs′-), *n.* lack of hospitality; inhospitable attitude toward visitors, etc.

in·hu·man (ĭn hū′mən), *adj.* **1.** lacking natural human feeling or sympathy for others; brutal. **2.** not human; not of the ordinary type or kind. [late ME, t. L: s. *inhūmānus.* See IN-[3]] **—in·hu′man·ly,** *adv.* **—in·hu′man·ness,** *n.*

in·hu·mane (ĭn′hū mān′), *adj.* not humane; lacking humanity or kindness. **—in′hu·mane′ly,** *adv.*

in·hu·man·i·ty (ĭn′hū măn′ə tĭ), *n., pl.* **-ties. 1.** state or quality of being inhuman or inhumane; cruelty: *man's inhumanity to man.* **2.** an inhuman or inhumane act.

in·hu·ma·tion (ĭn′hū mā′shən), *n.* act of inhuming, especially as opposed to incremation; interment.

in·hume (ĭn hūm′), *v.t.,* **-humed, -huming.** to deposit in the earth, as a dead body; bury; inter. [t. L: m.s. *inhumāre* bury in the ground]

in·im·i·cal (ĭn ĭm′ə kəl), *adj.* **1.** adverse in tendency or effect: *a climate inimical to health.* **2.** unfriendly or hostile: *inimical opinions.* [t. LL: s. *inimīcālis*, der. L *inimīcus* unfriendly, an enemy] **—in·im′i·cal′i·ty,** *n.* **—in·im′i·cal·ly,** *adv.* **—Syn. 1.** See **hostile.**

in·im·i·ta·ble (ĭn ĭm′ə tə bəl), *adj.* incapable of being imitated; surpassing imitation. **—in·im′i·ta·bil′i·ty, in·im′i·ta·ble·ness,** *n.* **—in·im′i·ta·bly,** *adv.*

in·i·on (ĭn′ĭ ən), *n.* *Craniol.* a point at the external occipital protuberance of the skull. [t. NL, t. Gk.: back of the head]

in·iq·ui·tous (ĭ nĭk′wə təs), *adj.* characterized by iniquity. **—in·iq′ui·tous·ly,** *adv.* **—in·iq′ui·tous·ness,** *n.*

in·iq·ui·ty (ĭ nĭk′wə tĭ), *n., pl.* **-ties. 1.** gross injustice; wickedness. **2.** a violation of right or duty; an unjust or wicked action; a sin. [ME *iniquite*, t. L: m.s. *iniquitas* injustice]

init., initial.

in·i·tial (ĭ nĭsh′əl), *adj., n., v.,* **-tialed, -tialing** or (*esp. Brit.*) **-tialled, -tialling. —***adj.* **1.** of or pertaining to the beginning; incipient: *the initial step in a process.* **2.** at the beginning of a word or syllable. **—***n.* **3.** an initial letter, as of a word. **4.** the first letter of a proper name. **5.** a letter of extra size or ornamental character used at the beginning of a chapter or other division of a book, etc. **—***v.t.* **6.** to mark or sign with an initial or initials. [t. L: s. *initiālis* of the beginning] **—in·i′tial·ly,** *adv.*

in·i·ti·ate (*v.* ĭ nĭsh′ĭ āt′; *adj., n.* ĭ nĭsh′ĭ ĭt, -āt′), *v.,* **-ated, -ating,** *adj., n.* **—***v.t.* **1.** to begin, set going, or originate: *to initiate reforms.* **2.** to introduce into the knowledge of some art or subject. **3.** to admit with formal rites into secret knowledge, a society, etc. **4.** to propose (a measure) by initiative procedure: *to initiate a constitutional amendment.* **—***adj.* **5.** initiated; begun. **6.** admitted into a society, etc., or into the knowledge of a subject. **—***n.* **7.** one who has been initiated. [t. L: m.s. *initiātus*, pp., begun, initiated] **—in·i′ti·a′tor,** *n.* **—in·i·ti·a·tress** (ĭ nĭsh′ĭ ā′trĭs), **in·i·ti·a·trix** (ĭ nĭsh′ĭ-ā′trĭks), *n. fem.* **—Syn. 1.** commence; introduce, inaugurate. See **begin. —Ant. 1.** discontinue.

in·i·ti·a·tion (ĭ nĭsh′ĭ ā′shən), *n.* **1.** formal admission into a society, etc. **2.** the ceremonies of admission. **3.** act of initiating. **4.** fact of being initiated.

in·i·ti·a·tive (ĭ nĭsh′ĭ ə tĭv, -ĭ ā′tĭv), *n.* **1.** an introductory act or step; leading action: *to take the initiative.* **2.** readiness and ability in initiating action; enterprise: *to lack initiative.* **3.** *Govt.* **a.** procedure by which a specified number of voters may propose a statute, constitutional amendment, or ordinance, and compel a popular vote on its adoption. **b.** the general right or ability to present a new bill or measure, as in a legislature. **—***adj.* **4.** serving to initiate; pertaining to initiation. **—in·i′ti·a·tive·ly,** *adv.*

in·i·ti·a·to·ry (ĭ nĭsh′ĭ ə tōr′ĭ), *adj.* **1.** introductory; initial: *an initiatory step.* **2.** serving to initiate or admit into a society, etc. **—in·i′ti·a·to′ri·ly,** *adv.*

in·ject (ĭn jĕkt′), *v.t.* **1.** to force (a fluid, etc.) into a passage, cavity, or tissue. **2.** to introduce (something new or different) into a thing: *to inject comedy into a situation.* **3.** to introduce arbitrarily or inappropriately. **4.** to interject (a remark, suggestion, etc.), as into conversation. [t. L: s. *injectus*, pp., thrown or put in]

in·jec·tion (ĭn jĕk′shən), *n.* **1.** act of injecting. **2.** that which is injected. **3.** a liquid injected into the body, esp. for medicinal purposes, as a hypodermic or an enema. **4.** state of being hyperemic or bloodshot.

in·jec·tor (ĭn jĕk′tər), *n.* **1.** one who or that which injects. **2.** a device for forcing water into a steam boiler.

in·ju·di·cious (ĭn′jōō dĭsh′əs), *adj.* not judicious; showing lack of judgment; unwise; imprudent. **—in′ju·di′cious·ly,** *adv.* **—in′ju·di′cious·ness,** *n.*

in·junc·tion (ĭn jŭngk′shən), *n.* **1.** *Law.* a judicial process or order requiring the person or persons to whom it is directed to do or (more commonly) not to do a particular thing. **2.** act of enjoining. **3.** that which is enjoined; a command, order or admonition. [late ME, t. LL: s. *injunctio* command] **—in·junc′tive,** *adj.*

in·jure (ĭn′jər), *v.t.,* **-jured, -juring. 1.** to do or cause harm of any kind to; damage; hurt; impair: *to injure the hand.* **2.** to do wrong or injustice to. [back formation from INJURY, n., r. earlier *injury,* v.] **—in′jur·er,** *n.*

—Syn. 1. INJURE, IMPAIR mean to harm or damage something. INJURE is a general term referring to any kind or degree of damage: *to injure one's spine, to injure one's reputation.* To IMPAIR is to make imperfect in any way, often with a suggestion of progressive deterioration and of permanency in the result: *one's health is impaired by overwork.* **—Ant. 1.** benefit.

in·jured (ĭn′jərd), *adj.* **1.** harmed, damaged, or hurt. **2.** offended; wronged: *an injured look.*

in·ju·ri·ous (ĭn jŏŏr′ĭ əs), *adj.* **1.** harmful, hurtful, or detrimental, as in effect: *injurious habits.* **2.** doing or involving injury or wrong, as to another. **3.** insulting or abusive, as speech. [ME, t. L: m.s. *injūriōsus*, wrongful] **—in·ju′ri·ous·ly,** *adv.* **—in·ju′ri·ous·ness,** *n.* **—Syn. 1.** deleterious, pernicious; baneful, destructive, ruinous. **2.** unjust, wrongful, prejudicial. **3.** offensive; derogatory, defamatory, slanderous. **—Ant. 1.** beneficial.

in·ju·ry (ĭn′jə rĭ), *n., pl.* **-juries. 1.** harm of any kind done or sustained: *to escape without injury.* **2.** a particular form or instance of harm: *severe bodily injuries.* **3.** wrong or injustice done or suffered. **4.** *Law.* a wrong or detriment caused by the deliberate or negligent act of another and actionable in a court of law. **5.** *Obs.* injurious speech; calumny. [ME *injurie*, t. L: m. *injūria* wrong, harm, insult]

—Syn. 1-3. INJURY, HURT, WOUND refer to material or moral impairments or wrongs. INJURY, originally denoting a wrong done or suffered, is hence used for any kind of evil, impairment, or loss, caused or sustained: *physical injury, injury to one's reputation.* HURT suggests esp. physical injury, often bodily injury attended with pain: *a bad hurt from a fall.* A WOUND is usually a physical hurt caused by cutting, shooting, etc., or an emotional hurt: *a serious wound in the shoulder, to inflict a wound by betraying someone's trust.* **—Ant. 1.** benefit.

in·jus·tice (ĭn jŭs′tĭs), *n.* **1.** quality or fact of being unjust. **2.** unjust action or treatment; violation of another's rights. **3.** an unjust act or circumstance. [ME, t. F, t. L: m.s. *injustitia*]

ink (ĭngk), *n.* **1.** a fluid or viscous substance used for writing or printing. **2.** a dark protective fluid ejected by the cuttlefish and other cephalopods. **—***v.t.* **3.** to mark, stain, cover, or smear with ink. [ME *inke, enke*, t. OF: m. *enque*, g. LL *encaustum*, t. Gk.: m. *énkauston* kind of ink] **—ink′er,** *n.* **—ink′less,** *adj.* **—ink′-like′,** *adj.*

ink·ber·ry (ĭngk′bĕr′ĭ), *n., pl.* **-ries. 1.** a shrub, *Ilex glabra*, with leathery evergreen leaves and black berries. **2.** the pokeweed. **3.** the berry of either plant.

Ink·er·man (ĭng′kər măn′), *n.* a locality in the SW Soviet Union, in the Crimea: Russian defeat, 1854.

ink·horn (ĭngk′hôrn′), *n.* a small container of horn or other material, formerly used to hold writing ink.

in·kle (ĭng′kəl), *n.* **1.** a kind of linen tape. **2.** the linen thread or yarn from which this tape is made.

ink·ling (ĭngk′lĭng), *n.* **1.** a hint, intimation, or slight suggestion. **2.** a vague idea or notion. [f. *inkle*, v., hint (ME *incle*) + -ING[1]. Cf. OE *inca* suspicion]

ink·stand (ĭngk′stănd′), *n.* **1.** a stand for holding ink, pens, etc. **2.** a cuplike container for ink.

ink·well (ĭngk′wĕl′), *n.* a container for ink. Also, *Brit.,* **ink·pot** (ĭngk′pŏt′).

ink·wood (ĭngk′wŏŏd′), *n.* a sapindaceous tree,

b., blend of, blended; c., cognate with; d., dialect, dialectal; der., derived from; f., formed from; g., going back to; m., modification of; r., replacing; s., stem of; t., taken from; ?, perhaps. See the full key on inside cover.

Exothea paniculata, of the West Indies and Florida, with hard reddish-brown wood.

ink·y (ĭngk′ĭ), *adj.*, **inkier, inkiest. 1.** black as ink: *inky shadows.* **2.** resembling ink. **3.** stained with ink: *inky fingers.* **4.** of or pertaining to ink. **5.** consisting of or containing ink. **6.** written with ink. —**ink′i·ness,** *n.*

inky cap, any species of mushroom (genus *Coprinus*) whose gills disintegrate into blackish liquid after the spores mature, esp. *C. atramentarius.*

in·laid (ĭn′lād′, ĭn lād′), *adj.* **1.** set in the surface of a thing: *an inlaid design in wood.* **2.** decorated or made with a design set in the surface: *an inlaid table.*

in·land (*adj.* ĭn′lənd; *adv., n.* ĭn′lănd′, -lənd), *adj.* **1.** pertaining to or situated in the interior part of a country or region: *inland cities.* **2.** carried on within a country; domestic; not foreign: *inland trade;* (*Brit.*) *inland revenue* (*U.S.* "internal revenue"); (*Brit.*) *inland mails* (*U.S.* "domestic mails"). **3.** confined to a country; drawn and payable in the same country. —*adv.* **4.** in or toward the interior of a country. —*n.* **5.** the interior part of a country, away from the border. [ME and OE; f. IN-¹ + LAND]

in·land·er (ĭn′lən dər), *n.* a person living inland.

Inland Sea, a sea in SW Japan, enclosed by the islands of Honshu, Shikoku, and Kyushu. ab. 240 mi. long.

in·law (ĭn′lô′), *n. Colloq.* a relative by marriage.

in·lay (*v.* ĭn lā′; *n.* ĭn′lā′), *v.,* **-laid, -laying,** *n.* —*v.t.* **1.** to decorate (an object) with veneers of fine materials set in its surface. **2.** to insert, or apply (layers of fine materials) in a surface of an object. **3.** *Hort.* to place (a fitted scion) into a prepared stock, as in an inlay graft. —*n.* **4.** inlaid work. **5.** veneer of fine material inserted in something else, esp. for ornament. **6.** a design or decoration made by inlaying. **7.** *Dentistry,* a filling of metal, porcelain, or plastic which is fitted and fastened into a tooth as a solid mass. **8.** *Hort.* an inlay graft. **9.** the act or process of inlaying. —**in′lay′er,** *n.*

inlay graft, *Hort.* a graft in which the scion is matched into a place in the stock from which a piece of corresponding bark has been removed.

in·let (*n.* ĭn′lĕt; *v.* ĭn lĕt′), *n., v.,* **-let, -letting.** —*n.* **1.** an indentation of a shore line, usually long and narrow, or a narrow passage between islands. **2.** a place of admission; an entrance. **3.** something put in or inserted. —*v.t.* **4.** to put in; insert.

in·li·er (ĭn′lī′ər), *n. Geol.* outcrop of a formation completely surrounded by another of later date.

in loc. cit., (L *in loco citato*) in the place cited.

in lo·co (ĭn lō′kō), *Latin.* in place; in the proper place.

in lo·co pa·ren·tis (ĭn lō′kō pə rĕn′tĭs), *Latin.* in the place of a parent; replacing a parent.

in·ly (ĭn′lĭ), *adv. Now Poetic.* **1.** inwardly. **2.** intimately; deeply. —*adj.* **3.** *Obs.* inward. [ME *inliche,* OE *inlīce,* der. *inlic* inward]

in·mate (ĭn′māt′), *n.* **1.** one who dwells with another or others in the same house. **2.** one of those confined in a hospital, prison, etc. [f. IN-¹ + MATE¹]

in me·di·as res (ĭn me′dĭ ăs′ rēz′), *Latin.* in the middle of things: *Homer began his story in medias res.*

in mem., in memoriam.

in me·mo·ri·am (ĭn mə mōr′ĭ ăm′), in memory (of); to the memory (of); as a memorial (to). [t. L]

In Memoriam A.H.H., a long elegiac poem (1850) by Tennyson, on his friend Arthur Henry Hallam.

in·mesh (ĭn mĕsh′), *v.t.* enmesh.

in·most (ĭn′mōst′, -məst), *adj.* **1.** situated furthest within: *the inmost recesses of the forest.* **2.** most intimate: *one's inmost thoughts.* [ME; OE *innemest,* a double superl., f. *inne* within + *-m-* + *-est* (superl. suffix). See IN-¹, -MOST]

inn (ĭn), *n.* **1.** a public house that provides lodging, food, etc., for travelers and others; a small hotel: *a wayside inn.* **2.** a tavern. **3.** *Brit.* **a.** a house or place of residence for students (now only in names of buildings derived from such use): *the Inns of Court.* **b.** a legal society occupying such a house. [ME *inne,* OE *inn* house] —**inn′less,** *adj.* —**Syn. 1.** See **hotel.**

in·nate (ĭ nāt′, ĭn′āt), *adj.* **1.** inborn; existing or as if existing in one from birth: *innate modesty.* **2.** arising from the constitution of the mind, rather than acquired from experience: *innate ideas.* [ME, t. L: m. s. *innātus,* pp., inborn] —**in·nate′ly,** *adv.* —**in·nate′ness,** *n.*

in·ner (ĭn′ər), *adj.* **1.** situated farther within; interior: *an inner door.* **2.** more intimate, private, or secret: *the inner circle of his friends.* **3.** mental or spiritual: *the inner life.* **4.** not obvious; esoteric: *an inner meaning.* [ME; OE *innera,* compar. of *inne* within. Cf. INMOST] —**in′ner·ness,** *n.*

Inner Light, (as used by the Society of Friends) the light of Christ in the soul.

Inner Mongolia. See **Mongolia** (def. 2).

in·ner·most (ĭn′ər mōst′, -məst), *adj.* **1.** farthest inward; inmost. —*n.* **2.** innermost part. [ME, f. INNER + -MOST]

Inner Temple. See **Inns of Court.**

in·ner·vate (ĭ nûr′vāt, ĭn′ər vāt′), *v.t.,* **-vated, -vating. 1.** to communicate nervous energy to; stimulate through nerves. **2.** to grow nerves into. [f. IN-² + NERVE + -ATE¹]

in·ner·va·tion (ĭn′ər vā′shən), *n.* **1.** act of innervating. **2.** state of being innervated. **3.** *Anat.* the disposition of nerves in a body or some part of it.

in·nerve (ĭ nûrv′), *v.t.,* **-nerved, -nerving.** to supply with nervous energy; invigorate; animate.

In·ness (ĭn′ĭs), *n.* **1.** George, 1825–94, U.S. painter. **2.** his son George, 1854–1926, U.S. painter.

in·ning (ĭn′ĭng), *n.* **1.** *Baseball.* a round in which both teams bat, with each side getting three outs. **2.** (in other games) a similar opportunity to score. **3.** an opportunity for activity; a turn: *now the opposition will have its inning.* **4.** reclaiming, as of marsh or flooded land. **5.** land reclaimed from the sea, etc. **6.** enclosure, as of waste land. **7.** harvesting, as of crops. [ME *inninge,* OE *innung* a putting in]

in·nings (ĭn′ĭngz), *n.pl.* (construed as *sing.*) *Chiefly Brit.* inning (defs. 1, 2, 3).

inn·keep·er (ĭn′kē′pər), *n.* the keeper of an inn. Also, *now Rare,* **inn·hold·er** (ĭn′hōl′dər).

in·no·cence (ĭn′ə səns), *n.* **1.** state or fact of being innocent; freedom from sin or moral wrong. **2.** freedom from legal or specific wrong; guiltlessness: *the prisoner proved his innocence.* **3.** simplicity or guilelessness. **4.** lack of knowledge or sense. **5.** harmlessness or innocuousness. **6.** an innocent person or thing. **7.** the common North American bluet. **8.** a scrophulariaceous herb, *Collinsia verna,* with a blue-and-white flower. **9.** an allied and widely distributed California herb, *C. bicolor.*

in·no·cen·cy (ĭn′ə sən sĭ), *n.* innocence (defs. 1–6).

in·no·cent (ĭn′ə sənt), *adj.* **1.** free from any moral wrong; not tainted with sin; pure: *innocent children.* **2.** free from legal or specific wrong; guiltless: *to be innocent of crime.* **3.** not involving evil intent or motive: *an innocent misrepresentation.* **4.** free from any quality that can cause physical or moral injury; harmless: *innocent fun.* **5.** devoid (fol. by *of*): *a law innocent of merit.* **6.** having or showing the simplicity or naïveté of an unworldly person: *she looks so innocent.* —*n.* **7.** an innocent person. **8.** a young child. **9.** a guileless person. **10.** a simpleton or idiot. **11.** (*pl.*) *U.S.* the common bluet. [ME, t. L: s. *innocens* harmless] —**in′no·cent·ly,** *adv.*

—**Syn. 1.** sinless, virtuous; faultless, impeccable. **2.** INNOCENT, BLAMELESS, GUILTLESS imply freedom from the responsibility of having done wrong. INNOCENT may imply having done no wrong at any time, and having not even a knowledge of evil: *an innocent victim.* BLAMELESS denotes freedom from blame, esp. moral blame: *a blameless life.* GUILTLESS denotes freedom from guilt or responsibility for wrongdoing, usually in a particular instance: *guiltless of a crime.* **6.** simple, naïve, unsophisticated, artless, guileless, ingenuous. —**Ant. 1.** guilty.

In·no·cent (ĭn′ə sənt), *n.* the name of 13 popes.

Innocent II, (*Gregorio Papareschi*) died 1143, Italian ecclesiastic; pope, 1130–43.

Innocent III, (*Giovanni Lotario de' Conti*) 1161?–1216, Italian ecclesiastic; pope, 1198–1216.

Innocent IV, (*Sinibaldo de Fieschi*) died 1254, Italian ecclesiastic; pope, 1243–54.

Innocent XI, (*Benedetto Odescalchi*) 1611–89, Italian ecclesiastic; pope, 1676–89.

in·noc·u·ous (ĭ nŏk′yŏŏ əs), *adj.* not harmful or injurious; harmless. [t. L: m. *innocuus*] —**in·noc′u·ous·ly,** *adv.* —**in·noc′u·ous·ness,** *n.*

in·nom·i·nate (ĭ nŏm′ə nĭt), *adj.* having no name; anonymous. [t. LL: m.s. *innominātus* unnamed]

innominate bone, *Anat.* either of the two bones forming the sides of the pelvis, each consisting of three consolidated bones, known as ilium, ischium, and pubis. See diag. under **pelvis.**

in·no·vate (ĭn′ə vāt′), *v.,* **-vated, -vating.** —*v.i.* **1.** to bring in something new; make changes in anything established (fol. by *on* or *in*). —*v.t.* **2.** to bring in (something new) for the first time. **3.** *Obs.* to alter. [t. L: m.s. *innovātus,* pp., renewed, altered] —**in′no·va′tive,** *adj.* —**in′no·va′tor,** *n.*

in·no·va·tion (ĭn′ə vā′shən), *n.* **1.** something new or different introduced. **2.** act of innovating; introduction of new things or methods. —**in′no·va′tion·ist,** *n.*

in·nox·ious (ĭ nŏk′shəs), *adj.* harmless; innocuous. —**in·nox′ious·ly,** *adv.* —**in·nox′ious·ness,** *n.*

Inn River (ĭn), a river flowing from E Switzerland through Austria and Germany into the Danube. 320 mi.

Inns·bruck (ĭnz′brŏŏk; *Ger.* ĭns′brŏŏk), *n.* a city in W Austria, on the Inn river. 81,710 (1939).

Inns of Court, 1. the four voluntary legal societies in England (**Lincoln's Inn,** the **Inner Temple,** the **Middle Temple,** and **Gray's Inn**), which have the exclusive privilege of calling candidates to the English bar, after they have received such instruction and taken such examinations as the Inns provide. **2.** the buildings owned and used by the Inns.

in·nu·en·do (ĭn′yŏŏ ĕn′dō), *n., pl.* **-does. 1.** an indirect intimation about a person or thing, esp. of a derogatory nature. **2.** *Law.* **a.** a parenthetic explanation or specification in a pleading. **b.** (in an action for slander or libel) the explanation and elucidation of the words alleged to be defamatory. **c.** the word or expression thus explained. [t. L: intimation, abl. ger. of *innuere* give a nod, intimate]

in·nu·mer·a·ble (ĭ nū′mər ə bəl, -nŏŏ′-), *adj.* **1.** very numerous. **2.** incapable of being numbered or counted. Also, **in·nu′mer·ous.** —**in·nu·mer·a·ble·ness,** *n.* —**in·nu′mer·a·bly,** *adv.* —**Syn. 1.** See **many.**

in·nu·tri·tion (ĭn′yŏŏ trĭsh′ən, -nŏŏ′-), *n.* lack of nutrition. —**in′nu·tri′tious,** *adj.*

ăct, āble, dâre, ärt; ĕbb, ēqual; ĭf, īce; hŏt, ōver, ôrder, oil, bŏŏk, ōoze, out; ŭp, ūse, ûrge; ə = a in alone; ch, chief; g, give; ng, ring; sh, shoe; th, thin; ᵺ, that; zh, vision. See the full key on inside cover.

in·ob·serv·ance (ĭn/əb zûr/vəns), *n.* **1.** lack of observance or noticing; inattention: *drowsy inobservance.* **2.** nonobservance **—in/ob·serv/ant,** *adj.*

in·oc·u·la·ble (ĭ nŏk/yə lə bəl), *adj.* capable of being inoculated. **—in·oc/u·la·bil/i·ty,** *n.*

in·oc·u·lant (ĭ nŏk/yə lənt), *n.* an inoculating substance.

in·oc·u·late (ĭ nŏk/yə lāt/), *v.,* **-lated, -lating,** *n.* **—v.t.** **1.** to implant (a disease) in a person or animal by the introduction of germs or virus, as through a puncture, in order to produce a mild form of the disease and thus secure immunity. **2.** to impregnate (a person or animal) thus. **3.** to introduce (microörganisms) into surroundings suited to their growth, esp. into the body. **4.** to imbue (a person, etc.), as with ideas. **—v.i.** **5.** to perform inoculation **—n.** **6.** a substance to be inoculated. [ME, t. L: m.s. *inoculātus,* pp., grafted, implanted] **—in·oc/u·la·tive,** *adj.* **—in·oc/u·la/tor,** *n.*

in·oc·u·la·tion (ĭ nŏk/yə lā/shən), *n.* act of inoculating.

in·oc·u·lum (ĭ nŏk/yə ləm), *n.* the substance used to make an inoculation. [NL]

in·o·dor·ous (ĭn ō/dər əs), *adj.* not odorous; odorless. **—in·o/dor·ous·ness,** *n.*

in·of·fen·sive (ĭn/ə fĕn/sĭv), *adj.* **1.** doing no harm; harmless; unoffending: *a mild, inoffensive man.* **2.** not objectionable, or not being a cause of offense. **—in/of·fen/sive·ly,** *adv.* **—in/of·fen/sive·ness,** *n.*

in·of·fi·cious (ĭn/ə fĭsh/əs), *adj.* **1.** *Law.* not in accordance with moral duty: *an inofficious testament or will* (one disposing of property contrary to the dictates of natural affection or to just expectations). **2.** disobliging. [t. L: m.s. *inofficiōsus.* See IN-³, OFFICIOUS]

I·nö·nü (ĭ nœ nў/), *n.* Ismet (ĭs mĕt/), born 1884, president of Turkey since 1938.

in·op·er·a·ble (ĭn ŏp/ər ə bəl), *adj.* **1.** not operable. **2.** not admitting of a surgical operation without undue risk.

in·op·er·a·tive (ĭn ŏp/ə rā/tĭv, -ŏp/rə-), *adj.* **1.** not operative; not in operation. **2.** without effect: *inoperative remedies.* **—in·op/er·a/tive·ness,** *n.*

in·op·por·tune (ĭn ŏp/ər tūn/, -tōōn/), *adj.* not opportune; inappropriate; (with regard to time) unseasonable: *an inopportune visit.* **—in·op/por·tune/ly,** *adv.* **—in·op/por·tune/ness,** *n.*

in·or·di·nate (ĭn ôr/də nĭt), *adj.* **1.** not within proper limits; excessive: *inordinate demands.* **2.** disorderly. **3.** unrestrained in conduct, etc. **4.** irregular: *inordinate hours.* [ME, t. L: m.s. *inordinātus* disordered] **—in·or·di·na·cy** (ĭn ôr/də nə sĭ), **in·or/di·nate·ness,** *n.* **—in·or/di·nate·ly,** *adv.*

inorg., inorganic.

in·or·gan·ic (ĭn/ôr găn/ĭk), *adj.* **1.** not having the organization which characterizes living bodies. **2.** not characterized by vital processes. **3.** *Chem.* noting or pertaining to compounds not containing carbon, excepting cyanides and carbonates. Cf. **organic** (def. 1). **4.** not fundamental; extraneous. **—in/or·gan/i·cal·ly.** *adv.*

inorganic chemistry, the branch of chemistry which treats of inorganic substances.

in·os·cu·late (ĭn ŏs/kyə lāt/), *v.i., v.t.,* **-lated, -lating.** **1.** to unite by openings, as arteries in anastomosis. **2.** to connect or join so as to become or make continuous, as fibers. **3.** to unite intimately. [f. IN-² + m.s. LL *osculātus,* pp., supplied with a mouth or outlet] **—in·os/cu·la/tion,** *n.*

in·o·si·tol (ĭ nō/sə tōl/, -tŏl/), *n. Chem.* a sweet crystalline substance, $C_6H_6(OH)_6$, first found in heart muscle, but widely distributed in plants and seeds as phytin, and also occurring in animal tissue and in urine. Also, **in·o·site** (ĭn/ə sīt/). [f. *inosit(e)* (f. *in-*, comb. form repr. Gk. *ís* fiber, + -os(e)² + -ITE¹) + -OL²]

in·pa·tient (ĭn/pā/shənt), *n.* a patient who is lodged and fed as well as treated in a hospital.

in per·pe·tu·um (ĭn pər pĕt/yŏŏ əm), *Latin.* forever.

in per·so·nam (ĭn pər sō/năm), *Latin.* against a person, as a legal proceeding.

in pet·to (ĭn pĕt/ō; *It.* ēn pĕt/tô), *Italian.* not disclosed (of cardinals whom the Pope appoints but does not name in consistory).

in·phase (ĭn/fāz/), *adj. Elect.* in synchronism.

in pos·se (ĭn pŏs/ē), *Latin.* in possibility, rather than in actual existence (distinguished from *in esse*).

in·put (ĭn/pŏŏt/), *n.* **1.** that which is put in. **2.** the power supplied to a machine. **3.** *Scot.* a contribution.

in·quest (ĭn/kwĕst), *n.* **1.** a legal or judicial inquiry, esp. before a jury. **2.** one made by a coroner (**coroner's inquest**). **3.** the body of men appointed to hold such an inquiry, esp. a coroner's jury. **4.** their decision or finding. [ME *enqueste,* t. OF, g. L *inquīsīta* (*rēs*)(a thing) inquired into, prop. pp. fem.]ǁ

in·qui·e·tude (ĭn kwī/ə tūd/, -tōōd/), *n.* **1.** restlessness; uneasiness. **2.** (*pl.*) disquieting thoughts.

in·qui·line (ĭn/kwə līn/, -lĭn), *n. Zool.* an animal that lives in an abode properly belonging to another; a guest. [t. L: m.s. *inquilīnus*] **—in·qui·lin·i·ty** (ĭn/kwə lĭn/ə tĭ), *n.* **—in·qui·li·nous** (ĭn/kwə lī/nəs), *adj.*

in·quire (ĭn kwīr/), *v.,* **-quired, -quiring.** **—v.t.** **1.** to seek to learn by asking: *to inquire a person's name.* **2.** *Obs.* to seek. **3.** *Obs.* to question (a person). **—v.i.** **4.** to seek information by questioning; ask: *to inquire*

after a person. **5.** to make investigation (fol. by *into*). Also, **enquire.** [t. L: m.s. *inquīrere;* r. ME *enquere,* t. OF] **—in·quir/er,** *n.* **—in·quir/ing·ly,** *adv.* **—Syn. 1.** INQUIRE, ASK, QUESTION imply that a person (or persons) addresses another (or others) to obtain information. ASK is the general word: *ask what time it is.* INQUIRE is more formal and always implies asking about something specific: *inquire about a rumor.* To QUESTION implies repetition and persistence in asking; it often applies to legal examination or investigation: *question the survivor of an accident.* **—Ant. 1.** tell

in·quir·y (ĭn kwīr/ĭ, ĭn/kwə rĭ), *n., pl.* **-quiries. 1.** a seeking for truth, information, or knowledge. **2.** an investigation, as into a matter. **3.** act of inquiring, or seeking information by questioning; interrogation. **4.** a question or query. Also, **enquiry. —Syn. 2.** See **investigation.**

in·qui·si·tion (ĭn/kwə zĭsh/ən), *n.* **1.** act of inquiring; inquiry; research. **2.** an investigation, or process of inquiry. **3.** an inquiry conducted by judicial officers or such nonjudicial officers as a coroner. **4.** the finding of such an inquiry. **5.** the document embodying the result of such inquiry. **6.** (*cap.*) *Rom. Cath. Ch.* a special tribunal (officially, the **Holy Office**) for the defense of Catholic teaching in faith and morals, the judgment of heresy, the application of canonical punishment, and the judgment of mixed marriages and the Pauline privileges. [ME *inquisicion,* t. L: m.s. *inquīsītio* a searching into] **—in/qui·si/tion·al,** *adj.*

in·qui·si·tion·ist (ĭn/kwə zĭsh/ən ĭst), *n.* an inquisitor.

in·quis·i·tive (ĭn kwĭz/ə tĭv), *adj.* **1.** given to inquiry or research; desirous of or eager for knowledge; curious: *inquisitive attention.* **2.** unduly curious; prying. **—n.** **3.** an inquisitive person. **—in·quis/i·tive·ly,** *adv.* **—in·quis/i·tive·ness,** *n.* **—Syn. 2.** See **curious.**

in·quis·i·tor (ĭn kwĭz/ə tər), *n.* **1.** one who makes inquisition. **2.** a questioner, esp. an inquisitive one. **3.** one who investigates by virtue of his office. **4.** a member of the Inquisition. **—in·quis·i·tress** (ĭn kwĭz/ə trĭs), *n. fem.*

in·quis·i·to·ri·al (ĭn kwĭz/ə tōr/ĭ əl), *adj.* **1.** pertaining to an inquisitor or inquisitors, or to inquisition. **2.** exercising the office of an inquisitor. **3.** *Law.* pertaining to a trial with one person or group acting as prosecutor and judge, or to secret criminal prosecutions. **4.** resembling an inquisitor. **5.** inquisitive. **—in·quis/i·to/ri·al·ly,** *adv.* **—in·quis/i·to/ri·al·ness,** *n.*

in re (ĭn rē/), *Latin.* in the matter of.

in rem (ĭn rĕm/), *Latin.* against a thing, as a legal proceeding for its recovery.

in re·rum na·tu·ra (ĭn rĭr/əm nə tyŏŏr/ə, -tōŏr/ə), *Latin.* in the nature of things.

I.N.R.I., (L *Iesus Nazarenus, Rex Iudaeorum*) Jesus of Nazareth, King of the Jews.

in·road (ĭn/rōd/), *n.* **1.** forcible or serious encroachment: *inroads on our savings.* **2.** a hostile or predatory incursion; a raid; a foray.

in·rush (ĭn/rŭsh/), *n.* a rushing in; an influx. **—in/rush·ing** *n., adj.*

ins., **1.** inches. **2.** inspector. **3.** insulated. **4.** insurance.

I.N.S., International News Service, a news-gathering agency.

in·sal·i·vate (ĭn săl/ə vāt/), *v.t.,* **-vated, -vating.** to mix with saliva, as food. **—in·sal/i·va/tion,** *n.*

in·sa·lu·bri·ous (ĭn/sə lōō/brĭ əs), *adj.* unfavorable to health. **—in·sa·lu/bri·ous·ly,** *adv.* **—in·sa·lu·bri·ty** (ĭn/sə lōō/brə tĭ), *n.*

in·sane (ĭn sān/), *adj.* **1.** not sane; not of sound mind; mentally deranged. **2.** characteristic of one mentally deranged. **3.** set apart for the use of mentally deranged persons: *an insane asylum.* **4.** utterly senseless: *an almost insane attempt.* **—in·sane/ly,** *adv.* **—in·sane/ness,** *n.* **—Syn. 1.** demented; lunatic, crazed, crazy; maniacal. See **mad.** **2.** foolish, senseless.

in·san·i·tar·y (ĭn săn/ə tĕr/ĭ), *adj.* not sanitary; unhealthful: *insanitary houses.* **—in·san/i·tar/i·ness,** *n.*

in·san·i·ta·tion (ĭn săn/ə tā/shən), *n.* lack of sanitation or sanitary regulation; insanitary condition.

in·san·i·ty (ĭn săn/ə tĭ), *n., pl.* **-ties. 1.** condition of being insane; more or less permanent derangement of one or more psychical functions, due to disease of the mind. **2.** *Law.* such unsoundness of mind as affects legal responsibility or capacity. **3.** extreme folly. **—Syn. 1.** derangement, dementia; lunacy, craziness, madness.

in·sa·tia·ble (ĭn sā/shə bəl, -shĭ ə-), *adj.* not satiable; incapable of being satisfied: *insatiable desire.* **—in·sa/tia·bil/i·ty, in·sa/tia·ble·ness,** *n.* **—in·sa/tia·bly,** *adv.*

in·sa·ti·ate (ĭn sā/shĭ ĭt), *adj.* insatiable: *insatiate greed.* **—in·sa/ti·ate·ly,** *adv.* **—in·sa/ti·ate·ness,** *n.*

in·scribe (ĭn skrīb/), *v.t.,* **-scribed, -scribing. 1.** to write or engrave (words, characters, etc.). **2.** to mark (a surface) with words, characters, etc., esp. in a durable or conspicuous way. **3.** to address or dedicate (a book, photograph, etc.) informally, esp. by a handwritten note. **4.** to enroll, as on an official list. **5.** *Brit.* to record or register the names of purchasers of (stocks, etc.). **6.** *Geom.* to draw or delineate (one figure) within another figure so that the inner lies in the boundary of the outer at as many points as possible. [t. L: m.s. *inscrībere* write in or upon] **—in·scrib/a·ble,** *adj.* **—in·scrib/er,** *n.*

in·scrip·tion (ĭn skrĭp/shən), *n.* **1.** something inscribed. **2.** a brief, more or less informal dedication, as of a book or a work of art. 3. *Bibliog.* a note inscribed in a book, usually signed. 4. *Archaeol.* a historical, religious, or other record cut, impressed, painted, or written on stone, brick, metal, or other hard surface. 5. act of inscribing. 6. *Brit.* **a.** an inscribing of issued securities. **b.** such inscribed securities. [ME, t. L: s. *inscriptio*] —**in·scrip′tion·al,** *adj.* —**in·scrip′tion·less,** *adj.*

in·scrip·tive (ĭn skrĭp′tĭv), *adj.* pertaining to or of the nature of an inscription. —**in·scrip′tive·ly,** *adv.*

in·scroll (ĭn skrōl′), *v.t.* to write on a scroll.

in·scru·ta·ble (ĭn skrōō′tə bəl), *adj.* 1. incapable of being searched into or scrutinized; impenetrable to investigation. 2. impenetrable or unfathomable physically. [ME, t. LL: m.s. *inscrūtābilis*] —**in·scru′ta·bil′i·ty, in·scru′ta·ble·ness,** *n.* —**in·scru′ta·bly,** *adv.* —**Syn. 1.** See **mysterious.**

in·sculp (ĭn skŭlp′), *v.t.* *Now Rare.* to carve in or on something; engrave. [t. L: s. *insculpere*]

in·sect (ĭn′sĕkt), *n.* 1. *Zool.* any animal of the subphylum or class *Insecta*, a group of small, air-breathing arthropods characterized by a body clearly divided into three parts: head, thorax, and abdomen, and by having only three pairs of legs, and usually having two pairs of wings. 2. any small, air-breathing arthropod, such as a spider, tick, or centipede, having superficial, general similarity to the *Insecta*. 3. a contemptible person. —*adj.* 4. like an insect; contemptible. [t. L: s. *insectum* (so called from the segmented form), prop. neut. of *insectus*, pp., cut in or up] —**in′sect·like′,** *adj.*

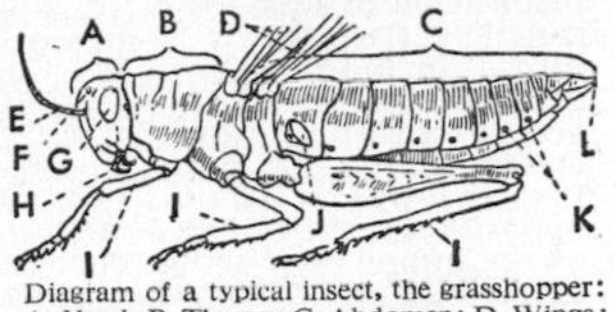

Diagram of a typical insect, the grasshopper: A, Head; B, Thorax; C, Abdomen; D, Wings; E, Antenna; F, Simple eye; G, Compound eye; H, Palpus; I, Legs; J, Ear; K, Spiracle; L, Ovipositor

in·sec·tar·i·um (ĭn′sĕk târ′ĭ əm), *n., pl.,* **-tariums, -taria** (-târ′ĭ ə). a place in which a collection of living insects is kept, as in a zoo. [NL]

in·sec·tar·y (ĭn′sĕk tĕr′ĭ), *n., pl.* **-taries.** a laboratory for the study of live insects, their life histories, effects on plants, reaction to insecticides, etc.

in·sec·ti·cide[1] (ĭn sĕk′tə sīd′), *n.* a substance or preparation used for killing insects. [f. s. L *insectum* an insect + -(I)CIDE[1]] —**in·sec′ti·cid′al,** *adj.*

in·sec·ti·cide[2] (ĭn sĕk′tə sīd′), *n.* the killing of insects. [f. s. L *insectum* insect + -(I)CIDE[2]]

in·sec·ti·vore (ĭn sĕk′tə vōr′), *n.* 1. an insectivorous animal or plant. 2. any of the *Insectivora*, the mammalian order that includes the moles, the shrews, and the Old World hedgehogs. [t. NL: m. *insectivorus*, f. L: s. *insectum* insect + *-i-* + *-vorus* devouring]

in·sec·tiv·o·rous (ĭn′sĕk tĭv′ə rəs), *adj.* adapted to feeding on insects, as shrews, moles, hedgehogs, etc.

in·se·cure (ĭn′sĭ kyŏŏr′), *adj.* 1. exposed to danger; unsafe. 2. not firm or safe: *insecure foundations.* 3. not free from fear, doubt, etc. —**in′se·cure′ly,** *adv.* —**Syn. 3.** See **uncertain.**

in·se·cu·ri·ty (ĭn′sĭ kyŏŏr′ə tĭ), *n., pl.* **-ties.** 1. unsafe condition; lack of assurance or sureness; uncertainty; instability. 2. something insecure.

in·sem·i·nate (ĭn sĕm′ə nāt′), *v.t.,* **-nated, -nating.** 1. to sow; inject seed into. 2. to impregnate. 3. to sow as seed in something; implant. [t. L: m.s. *insēminātus*, pp., sowed, planted in] —**in·sem′i·na′tion,** *n.*

in·sen·sate (ĭn sĕn′sāt, -sĭt), *adj.* 1. not endowed with sensation: *insensate stone.* 2. without feeling; unfeeling. 3. without sense, understanding, or judgment. —**in·sen′sate·ly,** *adv.* —**in·sen′sate·ness,** *n.*

in·sen·si·ble (ĭn sĕn′sə bəl), *adj.* 1. incapable of feeling or perceiving; deprived of sensation; unconscious, as a person after a violent blow. 2. without, or not subject to, a particular feeling: *insensible to shame.* 3. unconscious, unaware, or inappreciative: *we are not insensible of your kindness.* 4. not perceptible by the senses: *insensible transitions.* 5. unresponsive in feeling. 6. not susceptible of emotion or passion; void of feeling for. 7. *Now Rare.* not endowed with feeling or sensation, as matter. —**in·sen′si·bly,** *adv.*

in·sen·si·bil·i·ty (ĭn sĕn′sə bĭl′ə tĭ), *n., pl.* **-ties.** 1. lack of physical sensibility; absence of feeling or sensation. 2. lack of moral sensibility or susceptibility of emotion. —**Syn. 2.** See **indifference.**

in·sen·si·tive (ĭn sĕn′sə tĭv), *adj.* 1. not sensitive: *an insensitive skin.* 2. not susceptible to agencies or influences: *insensitive to light.* 3. deficient in sensibility or acuteness of feeling: *an insensitive nature.* —**in·sen′si·tive·ness, in·sen′si·tiv′i·ty,** *n.*

in·sen·ti·ent (ĭn sĕn′shĭ ənt, -shənt), *adj.* without sensation or feeling; inanimate. —**in·sen′ti·ence,** *n.*

in·sep·a·ra·ble (ĭn sĕp′ə rə bəl), *adj.* 1. incapable of being separated, parted, or disjoined: *inseparable companions.* —*n.* (*usually pl.*) 2. something inseparable. 3. an inseparable companion or friend. —**in·sep′a·ra·bil′i·ty, in·sep′a·ra·ble·ness,** *n.* —**in·sep′a·ra·bly,** *adv.*

in·sert (*v.* ĭn sûrt′; *n.* ĭn′sûrt), *v.t.* 1. to put or set in: *to insert a key in a lock.* 2. to introduce into the body of something: *to insert an ad in a newspaper.* —*n.* 3. something inserted, or to be inserted. 4. an extra leaf printed independently of the sheets comprising the book but included when the book is bound. 5. (in the postal service) a paper, circular, etc. placed within the folds of a newspaper or the leaves of a book, periodical, etc. [t. L: s. *insertus*, pp., put in] —**in·sert′er,** *n.*

in·sert·ed (ĭn sûr′tĭd), *adj.* 1. *Bot.* (esp. of the parts of a flower) attached to or growing out of some part. 2. *Anat.* having an insertion, as a muscle, tendon, or ligament; attached, as the more movable end of a muscle.

in·ser·tion (ĭn sûr′shən), *n.* 1. act of inserting: *each insertion of an ad.* 2. something inserted: *an insertion into a text.* 3. *Bot., Zool., etc.* **a.** the manner or place of attachment, as of an organ. **b.** attachment of a part or organ, with special reference to the site or manner of such attachment. 4. lace, embroidery, or the like, to be sewed at each edge between parts of other material.

in·ses·so·ri·al (ĭn′sĕ sōr′ĭ əl), *adj.* 1. adapted for perching, as a bird's foot. 2. habitually perching, as a bird. 3. of or pertaining to birds that perch. [f. s. NL *Insessorēs* the perching birds (considered as an order), pl. of *insessor* (f. *in* on + *sessor* sitter) + -IAL]

in·set (*n.* ĭn′sĕt′; *v.* ĭn sĕt′), *n., v.,* **-set, -setting.** —*n.* 1. something inserted; an insert. 2. a smaller picture, map, etc., inserted within the border of a larger one. 3. influx. 4. act of setting in. —*v.t.* 5. to set in; insert. 6. to insert an inset. 7. to insert an inset in.

in·sheathe (ĭn shēth′), *v.t.,* **-sheathed, -sheathing.** to enclose in or as in a sheath; sheathe.

in·shore (ĭn′shōr′), *adj.* 1. close to the shore: *the ship lay inshore.* 2. lying near the shore; operating close to the shore: *inshore fishing.* —*adv.* 3. toward the shore: *they went closer inshore.* 4. **inshore of,** closer to the shore (than): *inshore of the reef is a lagoon.*

in·shrine (ĭn shrīn′), *v.t.,* **-shrined, -shrining.** enshrine.

in·side (*prep., adv.* ĭn′sīd′; *n., adj.* ĭn′sīd′), *prep.* 1. inside of; within: *inside the circle.* —*adv.* 2. in or into the inner part: *to be inside.* 3. within the space or period (fol. by *of*): *to break down inside of a mile.* 4. on the inside: *he walks inside.* —*n.* 5. the inner part; interior: *the inside of the house.* 6. the inner side or surface: *the inside of the hand.* 7. (*often pl.*) *Colloq.* the inward parts of the body, esp. the stomach and intestines. 8. the inward nature. 9. an inside passenger or place in a coach, etc. 10. (*pl.*) internal thoughts or feelings, etc. —*adj.* 11. situated or being on or in the inside; interior; internal: *an inside seat.* 12. acting, employed, done, or originating within a building or place: *the robbery was an inside job.* 13. derived from the inner circle of those concerned in and having private knowledge of a case: *inside information.* 14. **inside track,** *Colloq.* advantage. —**Syn. 5.** INSIDE, INTERIOR both refer to the inner part or space within something. INSIDE is a common word, and is used with reference to things of any size, small or large: *the inside of a pocket.* INTERIOR, somewhat more formal, denotes the inner part or the space or the regions within; it usually suggests considerable size or extent, and sometimes a richness of decoration: *the interior of a country, of the earth; interior of a cathedral.* —**Ant. 5.** outside, exterior.

in·sid·er (ĭn′sī′dər), *n.* 1. one who is inside some place, society, etc. 2. *Colloq.* one who is within a limited circle of persons who understand the actual facts in a case. 3. *Colloq.* one who has some special advantage.

in·sid·i·ous (ĭn sĭd′ĭ əs), *adj.* 1. intended to entrap or beguile: *an insidious design.* 2. stealthily treacherous or deceitful: *an insidious enemy.* 3. operating or proceeding inconspicuously but with grave effect: *an insidious disease.* [t. L: m.s. *insidiōsus* cunning, artful] —**in·sid′i·ous·ly,** *adv.* —**in·sid′i·ous·ness,** *n.*

in·sight (ĭn′sīt′), *n.* 1. a sight had or given into something: *this little insight into the life of the village.* 2. penetrating mental vision or discernment; faculty of seeing into inner character or underlying truth: *a man of great insight.* 3. *Psychol.* **a.** the sudden grasping of a solution; configurational learning. **b.** the ability to see oneself as others see one; self-knowledge. **c.** (in psychiatry) the capacity of a mental patient to know that he is suffering from mental disorder. [ME; f. IN-[1] + SIGHT]

in·sig·ni·a (ĭn sĭg′nĭ ə), *n. pl., sing.* **insigne** (-nē). 1. badges or distinguishing marks of office of honor: *military insignia.* 2. distinguishing marks or signs of anything: *insignia of mourning.* [t. L, pl. of *insigne* mark, badge, prop. neut. of *insignis* distinguished by a mark]

in·sig·nif·i·cance (ĭn′sĭg nĭf′ə kəns), *n.* quality or condition of being insignificant; lack of significance.

in·sig·nif·i·can·cy (ĭn′sĭg nĭf′ə kən sĭ), *n., pl.* **-cies.** 1. insignificance. 2. an insignificant person or thing.

in·sig·nif·i·cant (ĭn′sĭg nĭf′ə kənt), *adj.* 1. unimportant, trifling, or petty, as things, matters, details, etc. 2. too small to be important: *an insignificant sum.* 3. of no consequence, influence, or distinction, as persons. 4. without weight of character; contemptible: *an insignificant fellow.* 5. without meaning; meaningless, as terms. —*n.* 6. a word, thing, or person without significance. —**in′sig·nif′i·cant·ly,** *adv.*

in·sin·cere (ĭn′sĭn sĭr′), *adj.* not sincere; not honest in the expression of actual feeling. —**in′sin·cere′ly,** *adv.*

in·sin·cer·i·ty (ĭn′sĭn sĕr′ə tĭ), *n., pl.* **-ties.** quality of being insincere; lack of sincerity; deceitfulness.

in·sin·u·ate (ĭn sĭn′yŏŏ āt′), *v.,* **-ated, -ating.** —*v.t.* 1. to suggest or hint slyly. 2. to instill or infuse subtly or artfully into the mind: *to insinuate doubt.* 3. to bring or introduce into a position or relation by indirect or artful methods: *to insinuate oneself into the favor of another.* —*v.i.* 4. to make insinuations. [t. L: m.s. *in-*

sinuātus, pp., brought in by windings or turnings]
—**in·sin'u·at'ing·ly,** *adv.* —**in·sin'u·a'tive,** *adj.*
—**in·sin'u·a'tor,** *n.* —**Syn.** 1. See **hint.**

in·sin·u·a·tion (ĭn sĭn'ū̇ō͞o ā'shən), *n.* 1. covert or artful suggestion or hinting, as of something not plainly stated. 2. a suggestion or hint of this kind. 3. subtle or artful instillment into the mind. 4. act of insinuating; a winding, worming, or stealing in. 5. ingratiation: *he made his way by flattery and insinuation.* 6. the art or power of stealing into the affections and pleasing. 7. an ingratiating act or speech.

in·sip·id (ĭn sĭp'ĭd), *adj.* 1. without distinctive, interesting, or attractive qualities: *an insipid tale.* 2. without sufficient taste to be pleasing, as food or drink: *a rather insipid fruit.* [t. LL: s. *insipidus* tasteless] —**in'-si·pid'i·ty, in·sip'id·ness,** *n.* —**in·sip'id·ly,** *adv.*

in·sip·i·ence (ĭn sĭp'ĭ əns), *n.* lack of wisdom; folly. [ME, t. L: m.s. *insipientia*] —**in·sip'i·ent,** *adj.*

in·sist (ĭn sĭst'), *v.i.* 1. to be emphatic, firm, or pertinacious on some matter of desire, demand, intention, etc.: *he insisted on that privilege.* 2. to lay emphasis in assertion: *to insist on the justice of a claim.* 3. to assert or maintain positively. 4. to dwell with earnestness or emphasis (fol. by *on* or *upon*): *to insist on a point in a discourse.* [t. L: s. *insistere* insist, stand or press upon] —**in·sist'er,** *n.*

in·sist·ence (ĭn sĭs'təns), *n.* 1. act or fact of insisting. 2. quality of being insistent.

in·sist·en·cy (ĭn sĭs'tən sĭ), *n., pl.* -**cies.** 1. quality of being insistent; insistence. 2. that which is insistent.

in·sist·ent (ĭn sĭs'tənt), *adj.* 1. insisting; earnest or emphatic in dwelling upon, maintaining, or demanding something; persistent. 2. compelling attention or notice: *an insistent tone.* —**in·sist'ent·ly,** *adv.*

in si·tu (ĭn sī'tū̇), *Latin.* in its original place.

in·snare (ĭn snâr'), *v.t.* -**snared,** -**snaring.** ensnare.

in·so·bri·e·ty (ĭn'sə brī'ə tĭ), *n.* lack of sobriety.

in·so·cia·ble (ĭn sō'shə bəl), *adj. Rare.* unsociable. —**in·so'cia·bil'i·ty,** *n.* —**in·so'cia·bly,** *adv.*

in·so·far (ĭn'sə fär'), *adv.* to such an extent (usually fol. by *as*). Also, **in so far.**

in·so·late (ĭn'sō lāt'), *v.t.,* -**lated,** -**lating.** to expose to the sun's rays; treat by exposure to the sun's rays. [t. L: m.s. *insōlātus,* pp., placed in the sun]

in·so·la·tion (ĭn'sō lā'shən), *n.* 1. exposure to the sun's rays, specif. as a process of treatment. 2. sunstroke. 3. *Meteorol.* solar radiation received on a given body or over a given area. [t. LL: s. *insōlātiō*]

in·sole (ĭn'sōl'), *n.* 1. the inner sole of a shoe or boot. 2. a thickness of warm or waterproof material laid as an inner sole within a shoe.

in·so·lence (ĭn'sə ləns), *n.* 1. insolent behavior or speech. 2. the quality of being insolent.

in·so·lent (ĭn'sə lənt), *adj.* 1. boldly rude or disrespectful; contemptuously impertinent; insulting: *an insolent reply.* —*n.* 2. an insolent person. [ME, t. L: s. *insolens* unaccustomed, unusual, excessive, arrogant] —**in·so·lent·ly,** *adv.* —**Syn.** 1. See **impertinent.**

in·sol·u·ble (ĭn sŏl'yə bəl), *adj.* 1. incapable of being dissolved: *insoluble salts.* 2. that cannot be solved: *an insoluble problem.* [ME, t. L: s. *insolūbilis*] —**in·sol'-u·bil'i·ty, in·sol'u·ble·ness,** *n.* —**in·sol'u·bly,** *adv.*

in·solv·a·ble (ĭn sŏl'və bəl), *adj.* incapable of being solved or explained: *an insolvable problem.*

in·sol·ven·cy (ĭn sŏl'vən sĭ), *n.* the condition of being insolvent; bankruptcy.

in·sol·vent (ĭn sŏl'vənt), *Law.* —*adj.* 1. not solvent; unable to satisfy creditors or discharge liabilities, either because liabilities exceed assets or because of inability to pay debts as they mature. 2. pertaining to bankrupt persons or bankruptcy. —*n.* 3. one who is insolvent.

in·som·ni·a (ĭn sŏm'nĭ ə), *n.* inability to sleep, esp. when chronic; sleeplessness. [t. L] —**in·som'ni·ous,** *adj.*

in·som·ni·ac (ĭn sŏm'nĭ ăk'), *n.* one who suffers from insomnia.

in·so·much (ĭn'sō mŭch'), *adv.* 1. to such an extent or degree (*that*); so (*that*). 2. inasmuch (*as*).

in·sou·ci·ance (ĭn sō͞o'sĭ əns; *Fr.* ăN sō͞o syäNs'), *n.* the quality of being insouciant. [t. F, der. *insouciant* INSOUCIANT]

in·sou·ci·ant (ĭn sō͞o'sĭ ənt; *Fr.* ăN sō͞o syäN'), *adj.* free from concern; without anxiety; carefree. [t. F, der. *soucier* care, g. L *sollicitāre*] —**in·sou'ci·ant·ly,** *adv.*

in·soul (ĭn sōl'), *v.t.* ensoul.

in·span (ĭn spăn'), *v.t.,* -**spanned,** -**spanning.** *South Africa.* to yoke or harness. [t. D: m. *inspannen*]

in·spect (ĭn spĕkt'), *v.t.* 1. to look carefully at or over; view closely and critically: *to inspect every part.* 2. to view or examine formally or officially: *to inspect troops.* [t. L: s. *inspectus,* pp.]

in·spec·tion (ĭn spĕk'shən), *n.* 1. inspecting or careful or critical inspecting or viewing. 2. formal or official viewing or examination: *an inspection of the troops.* 3. a district under an inspector. [ME, t. L: s. *inspectiō*] —**in·spec'tion·al,** *adj.* —**Syn.** 2. See **examination.**

in·spec·tive (ĭn spĕk'tĭv), *adj.* 1. given to making inspection. 2. pertaining to inspection.

in·spec·tor (ĭn spĕk'tər), *n.* 1. one who inspects. 2. an officer appointed to inspect. 3. an officer of police, usually ranking next below a superintendent. [t. L] —**in·spec'to·ral, in·spec·to·ri·al** (ĭn'spĕk tōr'ĭ əl), *adj.* —**in·spec'tor·ship',** *n.*

in·spec·tor·ate (ĭn spĕk'tər ĭt), *n.* 1. the office or function of an inspector. 2. a body of inspectors. 3. a district under an inspector.

in·sphere (ĭn sfîr'), *v.t.,* -**sphered,** -**sphering.** ensphere.

in·spir·a·ble (ĭn spîr'ə bəl), *adj.* capable of being inspired.

in·spi·ra·tion (ĭn'spə rā'shən), *n.* 1. an inspiring or animating action or influence : *I cannot write without inspiration.* 2. something inspired, as a thought. 3. a result of inspired activity. 4. a thing or person that inspires. 5. *Theol.* **a.** a divine influence directly and immediately exerted upon the mind or soul of a man. **b.** the divine quality of the writings or words of men so influenced. 6. the drawing of air into the lungs; inhalation. 7. act of inspiring. 8. state of being inspired.

in·spi·ra·tion·al (ĭn'spə rā'shən əl), *adj.* 1. imparting inspiration. 2. under the influence of inspiration; inspired. 3. of or pertaining to inspiration. —**in·spi·ra'tion·al·ly,** *adv.*

in·spir·a·to·ry (ĭn spîr'ə tōr'ĭ), *adj.* pertaining to inspiration or inhalation.

in·spire (ĭn spīr'), *v.,* -**spired,** -**spiring.** —*v.t.* 1. to infuse an animating, quickening, or exalting influence into: *his courage inspired his followers.* 2. to produce or arouse (a feeling, thought, etc.): *to inspire confidence in others.* 3. to affect with a specified feeling, thought, etc.: *inspire a person with distrust.* 4. to influence or impel: *opposition inspired him to a greater effort.* 5. to animate, as an influence, feeling, thought, or the like does: *inspired by a belief in a better future.* 6. to communicate or suggest by a divine or supernatural influence: *writings inspired by God.* 7. to guide or control by divine influence. 8. to prompt or instigate (utterances, etc.) by influence without avowal of responsibility. 9. to give rise to, occasion, or cause. 10. to take (air, gases, etc.) into the lungs in breathing; inhale. 11. *Archaic.* to infuse (breath, life, etc. *into*) by breathing. 12. *Archaic.* to breathe into or upon. —*v.i.* 13. to give inspiration. 14. to inhale. [ME *inspiren,* t. L: m. *inspīrāre* breathe into] —**in·spir'er,** *n.* —**in·spir'ing·ly,** *adv.*

in·spir·it (ĭn spĭr'ĭt), *v.t.* to infuse (new) spirit or life into. —**in·spir'it·ing·ly,** *adv.*

in·spis·sate (ĭn spĭs'āt), *v.t., v.i.,* -**sated,** -**sating.** to thicken, as by evaporation; make or become dense. [t. LL: m.s. *inspissātus,* pp.] —**in'spis·sa'tion,** *n.*

inst., 1. instant. See **instant** (def. 5). 2. (*also cap.*) institute. 3. (*also cap.*) institution. 4. instrumental.

in·sta·bil·i·ty (ĭn'stə bĭl'ə tĭ), *n.* state of being instable; lack of stability or firmness.

in·sta·ble (ĭn stā'bəl), *adj.* not stable; unstable.

in·stall (ĭn stôl'), *v.t.* 1. to place in position for service or use, as a system of electric lighting, etc. 2. to establish in any office, position, or place. 3. to induct into an office, etc., with ceremonies or formalities as by seating in a stall or official seat. [late ME, t. ML: s. *installāre.* See IN-², STALL¹] —**in·stall'er,** *n.*

in·stal·la·tion (ĭn'stə lā'shən), *n.* 1. something installed. 2. a system of machinery or apparatus placed in position for use. 3. act of installing. 4. fact of being installed. 5. *Mil.* any large supporting unit requiring much equipment, buildings, etc. [t. ML: s. *installātiō*]

in·stall·ment¹ (ĭn stôl'mənt), *n.* 1. any of several parts into which a debt or other sum payable is divided for payment at successive fixed times: *to pay for furniture by installments.* 2. a single portion of something furnished or issued by parts at successive times: *a serial in six installments.* Also, **in·stal'ment.** [f. IN-² + obs. *stalment* installment (der. STALL¹, v., arrange payment)]

in·stall·ment² (ĭn stôl'mənt), *n.* 1. act of installing. 2. fact of being installed; installation. Also, **in·stal'-ment.** [f. INSTALL, v. + -MENT]

installment plan, *Chiefly U.S.* a system for paying a debt in fixed amounts at specified intervals.

in·stance (ĭn'stəns), *n., v.,* -**stanced,** -**stancing.** —*n.* 1. a case of anything: *fresh instances of oppression.* 2. an example put forth in proof or illustration: *an instance of carelessness.* 3. **for instance,** for example; as an example. 4. *Archaic.* urgency in speech or action. 5. **at the instance of,** at the urgency, solicitation, instigation, or suggestion of. 6. legal process (now chiefly in certain expressions): *a court of last instance.* 7. *Archaic.* urgency. 8. *Obs.* an impelling motive. —*v.t.* 9. to cite as an instance or example. 10. *Now Rare.* to exemplify by an instance. —*v.i.* 11. *Now Rare.* to cite an instance. [ME, t. OF, t. L: m.s. *instantia* presence, urgency] —**Syn.** 2. See **case¹.**

in·stan·cy (ĭn'stən sĭ), *n.* 1. quality of being instant; urgency; pressing nature. 2. *Rare.* immediateness.

in·stant (ĭn'stənt), *n.* 1. an infinitesimal or very short space of time; a moment: *not an instant too soon.* 2. the point of time now present, or present with reference to some action or event. 3. a particular moment: *at the instant of contact.* —*adj.* 4. succeeding without any interval of time; immediate: *instant relief.* 5. present; current (now used elliptically): *the 10th instant* (the tenth day of the present month). 6. pressing or urgent: *instant need.* —*adv.* 7. *Poetic.* instantly. [ME, t. L: s. *instans,* ppr., standing upon, insisting, being at hand] —**Syn.** 1. See **minute².**

in·stan·ta·ne·ous (ĭn'stən tā'nĭ əs), *adj.* 1. occurring, done, or completed in an instant: *an instantaneous explosion.* 2. existing at or pertaining to a particular

---

b., blend of, blended; c., cognate with; d., dialect, dialectal; der., derived from; f., formed from; g., going back to; m., modification of; r., replacing; s., stem of; t., taken from; ?, perhaps. See the full key on inside cover.

instant: *the instantaneous position of something.* —in'stan·ta'ne·ous·ly, *adv.* —in'stan·ta'ne·ous·ness, *n.*

in·stan·ter (ĭn stăn'tər), *adv.* instantly. [t. L: urgently]

in·stant·ly (ĭn'stənt lĭ), *adv.* 1. immediately; at once. 2. *Archaic.* urgently. —Syn. 1. See immediately.

in·star[1] (ĭn'stär), *n.* an insect in any one of its periods of postembryonic growth between molts. [t. L: form, likeness]

in·star[2] (ĭn stär'), *v.t.*, -starred, -starring. 1. to place as a star. 2. to make a star of. 3. to set with or as with stars. [f. IN-[1] + STAR]

in·state (ĭn stāt'), *v.t.*, -stated, -stating. 1. to put into a certain state, condition, or position; install. 2. *Obs.* to endow with something. —in·state'ment, *n.*

in sta·tu quo (ĭn stā'tū kwō', stăch'ōō), *Latin.* in the state in which (anything was or is).

in·stau·ra·tion (ĭn'stô rā'shən), *n.* renewal; restoration; renovation; repair. [t. L: s. *instaurātio*]

in·stead (ĭn stĕd'), *adv.* 1. in the stead or place; in lieu (fol. by *of*): *come by plane instead of by train.* 2. in one's (its, their, etc.) stead: *she sent the boy instead.* [orig. two words, *in stead* in place]

in·step (ĭn'stĕp'), *n.* 1. the arched upper surface of the human foot between the toes and the ankle. 2. the part of a shoe, stocking, etc., over the instep. 3. the front of the hind leg of a horse, etc., between the hock and the pastern joint; cannon. [appar. f. IN-[1] + STEP, but with orig. notion uncert.]

in·sti·gate (ĭn'stə gāt'), *v.t.*, -gated, -gating. 1. to spur on, set on, or incite to some action or course: *to instigate someone to commit a crime.* 2. to bring about by incitement; foment: *to instigate a quarrel.* [t. L: m.s. *instīgātus*, pp.] —in'sti·ga'tive, *adj.* —in'sti·ga'tor, *n.*

in·sti·ga·tion (ĭn'stə gā'shən), *n.* 1. act of instigating; incitement, esp. to wrongdoing. 2. an incentive. [ME, t. L: s. *instīgātio*]

in·stil (ĭn stĭl'), *v.t.*, -stilled, -stilling. instill. —in·stil'ment, *n.*

in·still (ĭn stĭl'), *v.t.* 1. to infuse slowly or by degrees into the mind or feelings; insinuate; inject: *courtesy must be instilled in childhood.* 2. to put in drop by drop. [t. L: s. *instillāre* pour in by drops] —in·still'er, *n.* —in·still'ment, *n.*

in·stil·la·tion (ĭn'stə lā'shən), *n.* 1. act of instilling. 2. something instilled.

in·stinct[1] (ĭn'stĭngkt), *n.* 1. *Sociol., Psychol., etc.* an inborn pattern of activity and response common to a given biological stock. 2. innate impulse or natural inclination, or a particular natural inclination or tendency. 3. a natural aptitude or gift for something: *an instinct for art.* 4. natural intuitive power. [ME, t. L: s. *instinctus*, n., instigation, impulse]

in·stinct[2] (ĭn stĭngkt'), *adj.* urged or animated from within; infused or filled with some active principle (fol. by *with*). [t. L: s. *instinctus*, pp., instigated, impelled]

in·stinc·tive (ĭn stĭngk'tĭv), *adj.* 1. pertaining to or of the nature of instinct. 2. prompted by or resulting from instinct. —in·stinc'tive·ly, *adv.*

in·sti·tute (ĭn'stə tūt', -tōōt'), *v.*, -tuted, -tuting, *n.* —*v.t.* 1. to set up or establish: *institute a government.* 2. to set on foot; inaugurate; initiate: *institute a new course.* 3. to set in operation: *institute a suit.* 4. to bring into use or practice: *to institute laws.* 5. to establish in an office or position. 6. *Eccles.* to assign to or invest with a spiritual charge. —*n.* 7. a society or organization for carrying on a particular work, as of literary, scientific, or educational character. 8. the building occupied by such a society. 9. *Educ.* a. an institution, generally beyond the secondary school level, devoted to instruction in technical subjects, usually separate but sometimes organized as a part of a university. b. a unit within a university organized for advanced instruction and research in a relatively narrow field of subject matter. c. a short instructional program set up for a special group interested in some specialized type of activity. 10. an established principle, law, custom, or organization. 11. (*pl.*) an elementary textbook of law designed for beginners. 12. something instituted. [ME, t. L: m.s. *institūtus*, pp., set up, established]

in·sti·tut·er (ĭn'stə tū'tər, -tōō'-), *n.* instituter.

in·sti·tu·tion (ĭn'stə tū'shən, -tōō'-), *n.* 1. an organization or establishment for the promotion of a particular object, usually one for some public, educational, charitable, or similar purpose. 2. the building devoted to such work. 3. a concern engaged in some activity, as a retail store, broker, or insurance company. 4. *Sociol.* an organized pattern of group behavior, well-established and accepted as a fundamental part of a culture, such as slavery. 5. any established law, custom, etc. 6. *Colloq.* any familiar practice or object. 7. act of instituting or setting up; establishment: *the institution of laws.* 8. *Eccles.* a. the origination of the Eucharist, and enactment of its observance, by Christ. b. the investment of a clergyman with a spiritual charge.

in·sti·tu·tion·al (ĭn'stə tū'shən əl, -tōō'-), *adj.* 1. of, pertaining to, or established by institution. 2. pertaining to organized societies or to the buildings devoted to their work. 3. of the nature of an institution. 4. *Advertising.* having good will and a wider reputation as the primary object rather than the securing of present purchasers. 5. pertaining to institutes or principles, esp. of jurisprudence. —in'sti·tu'tion·al·ly, *adv.*

in·sti·tu·tion·al·ism (ĭn'stə tū'shən ə lĭz'əm, -tōō'-), *n.* 1. the system of institutions or organized societies for public, charitable, or similar purposes. 2. strong attachment to established institutions, as of religion.

in·sti·tu·tion·al·ize (ĭn'stə tū'shən ə līz', -tōō'-), *v.t.*, -ized, -izing. 1. to make institutional. 2. to make into or treat as an institution.

in·sti·tu·tion·ar·y (ĭn'stə tū'shə nĕr'ĭ, -tōō'-), *adj.* 1. of or relating to an institution or to institutions; institutional. 2. of or pertaining to institution, esp. ecclesiastical institution.

in·sti·tu·tive (ĭn'stə tū'tĭv, -tōō'-), *adj.* tending or intended to institute or establish. —in'sti·tu'tive·ly, *adv.*

in·sti·tu·tor (ĭn'stə tū'tər, -tōō'-), *n.* 1. one who inst, stitutes or founds. 2. *Prot. Episc. Ch.* one who institutes a minister into a parish or church. Also, instituter.

instr., 1. instructor. 2. instrument. 3. instrumental.

in·struct (ĭn strŭkt'), *v.t.* 1. to direct or command; furnish with orders or directions: *the doctor instructed me to diet.* 2. to furnish with knowledge, esp. by a systematic method; teach; train; educate. 3. to furnish with information; inform or apprise. 4. *Law.* (of a judge) to outline or explain the legal principles involved in a case, for the guidance of (the jury). [ME *instructe(n)*, t. L: m.s. *instructus*, pp., built, prepared, furnished, instructed] —Syn. 2. tutor, coach; drill, discipline; indoctrinate; school.

in·struc·tion (ĭn strŭk'shən), *n.* 1. act or practice of instructing or teaching; education. 2. knowledge or information imparted. 3. an item of such knowledge or information. 4. (*usually pl.*) an order or direction. 5. act of furnishing with authoritative directions. [ME, t. L: s. *instructio*] —in·struc'tion·al, *adj.* —Syn. 1. tutoring, coaching; training, drill; indoctrination; schooling. 5. command, mandate.

in·struc·tive (ĭn strŭk'tĭv), *adj.* serving to instruct or inform; conveying instruction, knowledge, or information. —in·struc'tive·ly, *adv.* —in·struc'tive·ness, *n.*

in·struc·tor (ĭn strŭk'tər), *n.* 1. one who instructs; a teacher. 2. the academic rank given in American colleges to a teacher inferior in grade to the lowest grade of professor. [late ME, t. ML: teacher, L preparer] —in·struc'tor·less, *adj.* —in·struc'tor·ship', *n.* —in·struc·tress (ĭn strŭk'trĭs), *n. fem.* —Syn. 1. tutor, schoolmaster, preceptor, pedagogue.

in·stru·ment (ĭn'strə mənt), *n.* 1. a mechanical device or contrivance; a tool; an implement: *a surgeon's instruments.* 2. a contrivance for producing musical sounds: *a stringed instrument.* 3. a thing with or by which something is effected; a means; an agency: *an instrument of government.* 4. a formal legal document, as a contract, promissory note, deed, grant, etc. 5. one who is used by another. 6. a device for measuring the present value of the quantity under observation. [ME, t. L: m.s. *instrūmentum*] —Syn. 1. See tool.

in·stru·men·tal (ĭn'strə mĕn'təl), *adj.* 1. serving as an instrument or means. 2. of or pertaining to an instrument. 3. helpful; useful. 4. performed on or written for a musical instrument or musical instruments: *instrumental music.* 5. *Gram.* a. (in some inflected languages) denoting a case, having as chief function the indication of means or agency. For example: Old English *beseah blīthe andweitan* "looked with a happy countenance." b. denoting the affix or other element characteristic of this case, or a word containing such an element. c. similar to such a case form in function or meaning, as the Latin *instrumental ablative*, *gladiō* "by means of a sword." —*n.* 6. *Gram.* a. the instrumental case. b. a word in that case. c. a construction of similar meaning. [ME, t. ML: s. *instrūmentālis*]

in·stru·men·tal·ism (ĭn'strə mĕn'tə lĭz'əm), *n. Philos.* the theory that the function of thought is to be instrumental to control of the environment, or that ideas have value according to their function in human experience or progress.

in·stru·men·tal·ist (ĭn'strə mĕn'tə lĭst), *n.* 1. one who performs on a musical instrument. 2. an advocate of instrumentalism. —in·stru·men'tal·is'tic, *adj.*

in·stru·men·tal·i·ty (ĭn'strə mĕn tăl'ə tĭ), *n.*, *pl.* -ties. 1. the quality of being instrumental. 2. the fact or function of serving some purpose. 3. a means or agency. 4. helpfulness; usefulness.

in·stru·men·tal·ly (ĭn'strə mĕn'tə lĭ), *adv.* 1. by the use of an instrument. 2. with or on an instrument.

in·stru·men·ta·tion (ĭn'strə mĕn tā'shən), *n.* 1. the arranging of music for instruments, esp. for an orchestra. 2. the use of, or work done by, instruments. 3. instrumental agency; instrumentality.

in·sub·or·di·nate (ĭn'sə bôr'də nĭt), *adj.* 1. not submitting to authority; disobedient: *insubordinate crew.* 2. not lower. —*n.* 3. one who is insubordinate. —in'sub·or'di·nate·ly, *adv.* —in'sub·or'di·na'tion, *n.*

in·sub·stan·tial (ĭn'səb stăn'shəl), *adj.* 1. not substantial; slight. 2. without reality; unreal: *this insubstantial pageant.* —in'sub·stan'ti·al'i·ty, *n.*

in·suf·fer·a·ble (ĭn sŭf'ər ə bəl), *adj.* not to be endured; intolerable; unbearable: *insufferable insolence.* —in·suf'fer·a·ble·ness, *n.* —in·suf'fer·a·bly, *adv.*

in·suf·fi·cien·cy (ĭn'sə fĭsh'ən sĭ), *n.* deficiency in amount, force, or fitness; inadequateness: *insufficiency of supplies.* Also, in'suf·fi'cience.

in·suf·fi·cient (ĭn'sə fĭsh'ənt), *adj.* 1. not sufficient; lacking in what is necessary or required: *an insufficient answer.* **2.** deficient in force, quality, or amount; inadequate: *insufficient protection.* —in'suf·fi'cient·ly, *adv.*

in·suf·flate (ĭn'sŭf'lāt, ĭn'sə flāt'), *v.t.*, **-flated, -flating. 1.** to blow or breathe (something) in. **2.** *Med.* to blow (air or a medicinal substance) into some opening or upon some part of the body. **3.** *Eccles.* to breathe upon, especially upon one being baptized or the water of baptism. [t. LL: m.s. *insufflātus*, pp., breathed into] —in'suf·fla'tion, *n.* —in·suf·fla·tor (ĭn'sə flā'tər), *n.*

in·su·lar (ĭn'sə lər), *adj.* **1.** of or pertaining to an island or islands: *insular possessions.* **2.** dwelling or situated on an island. **3.** forming an island: *insular rocks.* **4.** detached; standing alone. **5.** characteristic or suggestive of inhabitants of an island. **6.** narrow or illiberal: *insular prejudices.* **7.** *Pathol.* occurring in or characterized by one or more isolated spots, patches, or the like. **8.** *Anat.* pertaining to existing tissue, as an island (def. 6), esp. to Langerhans Islets. —*n.* **9.** an inhabitant of an island. [t. LL: s. *insulāris* of an island] —in·su·lar·i·ty (ĭn'sə lăr'ə tУ), —in'su·lar·ism, *n.* —in'su·lar·ly, *adv.*

in·su·late (ĭn'sə lāt'), *v.t.*, **-lated, -lating. 1.** to cover or surround (an electric wire, etc.) with nonconducting material. **2.** *Physics, etc.* to separate by the interposition of a nonconductor, in order to prevent or reduce the transfer of electricity, heat, or sound. **3.** to place in an isolated situation or condition; segregate. [t. L: m.s. *insulātus* made into an island]

in·su·la·tion (ĭn'sə lā'shən), *n.* **1.** material used for insulating. **2.** act of insulating. **3.** resulting state.

in·su·la·tor (ĭn'sə lā'tər), *n.* **1.** *Elect.* **a.** a material of such low conductivity that the flow of current through it can usually be neglected. **b.** insulating material, often glass or porcelain, in a unit form so designed as to support a charged conductor and electrically isolate it. **2.** one who or that which insulates.

in·su·lin (ĭn'sə lĭn), *n.* **1.** *Med.* an extract obtained from the pancreas of animals (which apparently contains the hormone of this organ, furnished by its islands), used in the treatment of diabetes, and causing a reduction of sugar in the blood and urine. **2.** (*cap.*) a trademark for this extract. [f. s. L *insula* island (with reference to the islands of the pancreas) + -IN²]

in·su·lin·ize (ĭn'sə lə nīz'), *v.t.*, **-ized, -izing.** to apply insulin therapy to.

in·sult (*v.* ĭn sŭlt'; *n.* ĭn'sŭlt), *v.t.* **1.** to treat insolently or with contemptuous rudeness; affront. **2.** *Rare.* to attack; assault. —*v.i.* **3.** *Archaic.* to behave with insolent triumph; exult contemptuously (fol. by *on*, *upon*, or *over*). —*n.* **4.** an insolent or contemptuously rude action or speech; affront. **5.** something having the effect of an affront. **6.** *Archaic.* an attack or assault. [t. L: s. *insultāre* leap on or at, insult] —in·sult'er, *n.* —in·sult'ing, *adj.* —in·sult'ing·ly, *adv.*

—Syn. **4.** INSULT, INDIGNITY, AFFRONT, SLIGHT imply an act which ·njures another's honor, self-respect, etc. INSULT implies such insolence of speech or manner as deeply humiliates or wounds one's feelings and arouses to anger. INDIGNITY is especially used of inconsiderate, contemptuous treatment towards one entitled to respect. AFFRONT implies open disrespect or offense, shown as it were, to the face; SLIGHT, perhaps only inadvertent, indifference or disregard, but may indicate ill-concealed contempt.

in·su·per·a·ble (ĭn sōō'pər ə bəl), *adj.* incapable of being passed over, overcome, or surmounted: *an insuperable barrier.* —in·su·per·a·bil'i·ty, in·su'per·a·ble·ness, *n.* —in·su'per·a·bly, *adv.*

in·sup·port·a·ble (ĭn'sə pōr'tə bəl), *adj.* not endurable; insufferable. —in'sup·port'a·ble·ness, *n.* —in'·sup·port'a·bly, *adv.*

in·sup·press·i·ble (ĭn'sə prĕs'ə bəl), *adj.* that cannot be suppressed. —in'sup·press'i·bly, *adv.*

in·sur·a·ble (ĭn shŏŏr'ə bəl), *adj.* **1.** capable of being insured, as against risk of loss or harm. **2.** proper to be insured. —in·sur'a·bil'i·ty, *n.*

in·sur·ance (ĭn shŏŏr'əns), *n.* **1.** the act, system, or business of insuring property, life, the person, etc., against loss or harm arising in specified contingencies, as fire, accident, death, disablement, or the like, in consideration of a payment proportioned to the risk involved. **2.** the contract thus made, set forth in a written or printed agreement (policy). **3.** the amount for which anything is insured. **4.** the premium paid for insuring a thing.

in·sur·ant (ĭn shŏŏr'ənt), *n.* the person who takes out an insurance policy.

in·sure (ĭn shŏŏr'), *v.,* **-sured, -suring.** —*v.t.* **1.** to make sure, secure, or certain: *to insure one's safety.* **2.** to guarantee against risk of loss or harm. **3.** to secure indemnity to or on, in case of loss, damage, or death. **4.** to issue or procure an insurance policy on. —*v.i.* **5.** to issue or procure an insurance policy. [var. of ENSURE]

in·sured (ĭn shŏŏrd'), *n.* a person covered by an insurance policy.

in·sur·er (ĭn shŏŏr'ər), *n.* **1.** one who contracts to indemnify against losses, etc.; an underwriter. **2.** one who or that which insures.

in·sur·gence (ĭn sûr'jəns), *n.* an act of insurgency.

in·sur·gen·cy (ĭn sûr'jən sУ), *n.* **1.** state or condition of being insurgent. **2.** *Internat. Law.* a condition of insurrection against an existing government by a group not recognized as a belligerent.

in·sur·gent (ĭn sûr'jənt), *n.* **1.** one who rises in forcible opposition to lawful authority; one who engages in armed resistance to a government or to the execution of

laws. **2.** *U.S. Pol.* a member of a section of a political party that revolts against the methods or policies of the party. —*adj.* **3.** rising in revolt; rebellious. [t. L: s. *insurgens,* ppr., rising on or up]

in·sur·mount·a·ble (ĭn'sər moun'tə bəl), *adj.* incapable of being surmounted, passed over, or overcome: *an insurmountable obstacle.* —in'sur·mount'a·bly, *adv.*

in·sur·rec·tion (ĭn'sə rĕk'shən), *n.* **1.** act of rising in arms or open resistance against civil or established authority. **2.** an instance of this; a revolt. [late ME.,t. LL: s. *insurrectio,* der. L *insurgere* rise up] —in'sur·rec'tion·al, *adj.* —in'sur·rec'tion·al·ly, *adv.* —in'sur·rec'tion·ism, *n.* —in'sur·rec'tion·ist, *n.* —Syn. **2.** See revolt.

in·sur·rec·tion·ar·y (ĭn'sə rĕk'shə nĕr'У), *adj., n., pl.* **-aries.** —*adj.* **1.** pertaining to or of the nature of insurrection. **2.** given to insurrection. —*n.* **3.** one who engages in insurrection; an insurgent.

in·sus·cep·ti·ble (ĭn'sə sĕp'tə bəl), *adj.* **1.** not admitting (fol. by *of*): *insusceptible of flattery.* **2.** not accessible or sensitive (fol. by *to*): *insusceptible to infection.* **3.** unsusceptible. —in'sus·cep'ti·bil'i·ty, *n.*

in·swathe (ĭn swā*th*'), *v.t.,* **-swathed, -swathing.** to enswathe.

in·swept (ĭn'swĕpt'), *adj.* tapering at the front or tip, as an airplane wing.

int., 1. interest. **2.** interior. **3.** interjection. **4.** internal. **5.** international. **6.** interpreter. **7.** intransitive.

in·tact (ĭn tăkt'), *adj.* remaining uninjured, unaltered, sound, or whole; unimpaired. [late ME, t. L: s. *intactus*] —in·tact'ness, *n.* —Syn. See complete.

in·tagl·io (ĭn tăl'yō. -täl'-; *It.* ēn tä'lyō), *n., pl.* **intagl·ios, intagli** (ēn tä'lyē). **1.** a gem, seal, piece of jewelry, or the like cut with an incised or sunken design. **2.** incised carving, as opposed to carving in relief. **3.** ornamentation with a figure or design sunk below the surface. **4.** an incised or countersunk die. **5.** a figure or design so produced. **6.** *Engraving.* any printmaking process by which the printing ink is transferred to paper, etc. from areas sunk below the surface. [t. It., der. *intagliare* cut in, engrave]

in·take (ĭn'tāk'), *n.* **1.** the point at which a fluid is taken into a channel, pipe, etc. **2.** act of taking in. **3.** that which is taken in. **4.** quantity taken in: *the intake of oxygen.* **5.** a narrowing or contraction.

in·tan·gi·ble (ĭn tăn'jə bəl), *adj.* **1.** incapable of being perceived by the sense of touch, as incorporeal or immaterial things. **2.** not definite or clear to the mind: *intangible arguments.* **3.** (of an asset) existing only in connection with something else, as the good will of a business. —*n.* **4.** something intangible. —in·tan'gi·bil'i·ty, in·tan'gi·ble·ness, *n.* —in·tan'gi·bly, *adv.*

in·tar·si·a (ĭn tär'sУ ə), *n.* a highly developed form of inlay or marquetry in wood practiced in Italy during the Renaissance period. [t. It., der. *intarsiare* inlay]

in·te·ger (ĭn'tə jər), *n.* **1.** one of the numbers 0, 1, 2, 3, 4, etc.; a whole number, as distinguished from a fraction or a mixed number. **2.** a complete entity. [t. L: untouched, whole, entire]

in·te·ger vi·tae (ĭn'tə jər vī'tē), *Latin.* blameless in life; innocent. (Horace, *Odes,* I.)

in·te·gra·ble (ĭn'tə grə bəl), *adj. Math.* capable of being integrated, as a mathematical function or differential equation.

in·te·gral (ĭn'tə grəl), *adj.* **1.** of or pertaining to a whole; belonging as a part of the whole; constituent or component: *the integral parts of the human body.* **2.** necessary to the completeness of the whole. **3.** made up of parts which together constitute a whole. **4.** entire or complete: *his integral love.* **5.** *Arith.* pertaining to or being an integer; not fractional. **6.** *Math.* pertaining to or involving integrals. —*n.* **7.** an integral whole. **8.** *Math.* the result of the operation inverse to differentiation (see **integration,** def. 4); an expression from which a given function, equation, or system of equations is derived by differentiation. [t. LL: s. *integrālis*] —in·te·gral·i·ty (ĭn'tə grăl'ə tУ), *n.* —in'te·gral·ly, *adv.*

integral calculus, the branch of mathematics dealing with the finding and properties of integrals.

in·te·grand (ĭn'tə grănd'), *n. Math.* the expression to be integrated. [t. L: s. *integrandus,* ger. of *integrāre* make whole]

in·te·grant (ĭn'tə grənt), *adj.* **1.** making up, or belonging as a part to, a whole; constituent. —*n.* **2.** an integrant part. [t. L: s. *integrans,* ppr., making whole]

in·te·grate (ĭn'tə grāt'), *v.t.,* **-grated, -grating. 1.** to bring together (parts) into a whole. **2.** to make up or complete as a whole, as parts do. **3.** to indicate the total amount or the mean value of. **4.** *Math.* to find the integral of. [t. L: m.s. *integrātus,* pp., made whole] —in'·te·gra'tive, *adj.*

in·te·gra·tion (ĭn'tə grā'shən), *n.* **1.** act of integrating; combination into an integral whole. **2.** behavior, as of the individual, in harmony with the environment. **3.** *Psychol.* the organization of personality traits into a hierarchy of functions. **4.** *Math.* the operation of finding the integral of a function or equation (the inverse of *differentiation*). [t. L: s. *integrātio* renewal, restoration]

in·te·gra·tor (ĭn'tə grā'tər), *n.* **1.** one who or that which integrates. **2.** an instrument for performing numerical integrations.

in·teg·ri·ty (ĭn tĕg'rə tУ), *n.* **1.** soundness of moral principle and character; uprightness; honesty. **2.** state

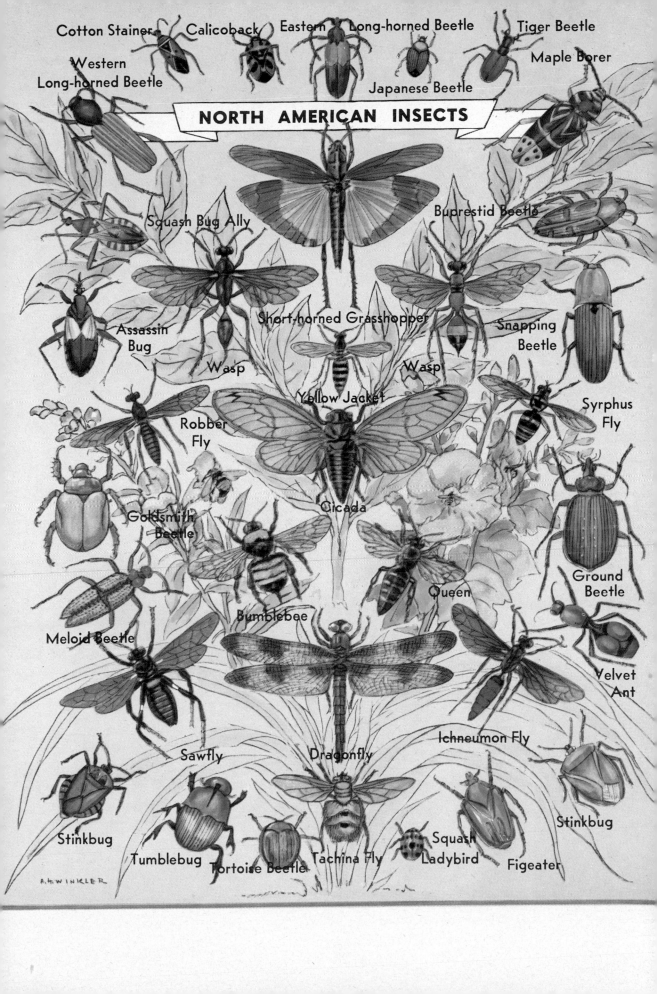

NORTH AMERICAN INSECTS

Cotton Stainer
Calicoback
Eastern Long-horned Beetle
Tiger Beetle
Maple Borer
Western Long-horned Beetle
Japanese Beetle
Squash Bug Ally
Buprestid Beetle
Assassin Bug
Short-horned Grasshopper
Snapping Beetle
Wasp
Wasp
Yellow Jacket
Robber Fly
Syrphus Fly
Goldsmith Beetle
Cicada
Ground Beetle
Meloid Beetle
Bumblebee
Queen
Velvet Ant
Sawfly
Dragonfly
Ichneumon Fly
Stinkbug
Tumblebug
Tortoise Beetle
Tachina Fly
Squash Ladybird
Stinkbug
Figeater

A.H.WINKLER

Red Admiral

Tortoise-Shell

Achemon
Sphinx Moth

Spicebush Swallowtail

Hydrangea
Sphinx Moth

Butterflies and Moths

Underwing Moth

Io Moth

Luna Moth

Tiger
Moth

Tiger Moth

Purple
Hairstreak

Imperial Moth

Cecropia
Moth

Cloudless
Sulphur

Tiger
Swallowtail

Grayling

Mourning
Cloak

Monarch

Buckeye

of being whole, entire, or undiminished: *to preserve the integrity of the empire.* **3.** sound, unimpaired, or perfect condition: *the integrity of the text.* [late ME, t. L: m.s. *integritas*] **—Syn. 1.** See **honor.**

in·teg·u·ment (ĭn tĕg′yə mənt), *n.* **1.** *Zool., Bot.* a skin, shell, rind, or the like. **2.** a covering. [t. L: s. *integumentum*]

in·teg·u·men·ta·ry (ĭn tĕg′yə mĕn′tə rĭ), *adj.* of, pertaining to, or like an integument.

in·tel·lect (ĭn′tə lĕkt′), *n.* **1.** the power or faculty of the mind by which one knows or understands, in distinction from that by which one feels and that by which one wills; the understanding. **2.** understanding or mental capacity, esp. of a high order. **3.** a particular mind or intelligence, esp. of a high order. **4.** the person possessing it. **5.** minds collectively, as of a number of persons, or the persons themselves. [ME, t. L: s. *intellectus* a discerning, perceiving] **—Syn. 1.** See **mind.**

in·tel·lec·tion (ĭn′tə lĕk′shən), *n.* **1.** the action or process of understanding; the exercise of the intellect. **2.** a particular act of the intellect. **3.** a conception or idea as the result of such an act.

in·tel·lec·tive (ĭn′tə lĕk′tĭv), *adj.* **1.** having power to understand; intelligent. **2.** of or pertaining to the intellect. **—in′tel·lec′tive·ly,** *adv.*

in·tel·lec·tu·al (ĭn′tə lĕk′chŏŏ əl), *adj.* **1.** appealing to or engaging the intellect: *intellectual pursuits.* **2.** of or pertaining to the intellect: *intellectual powers.* **3.** directed or inclined toward things that involve the intellect: *intellectual tastes.* **4.** possessing or showing intellect or mental capacity, esp. to a high degree: *an intellectual writer.* **5.** characterized by or suggesting a predominance of intellect: *an intellectual face.* **—n. 6.** an intellectual being or person. **7.** (*often pl.*) a member of a class or group professing, or supposed to possess, enlightened judgment and opinions with respect to public or political questions. **8.** (*pl.*) *Rare.* things pertaining to the intellect. **9.** (*pl.*) *Archaic.* the mental faculties. [ME, t. L: s. *intellectuālis*] **—in′tel·lec′tu·al·ly,** *adv.* **—in′tel·lec′tu·al·ness,** *n.* **—Syn. 4.** See **intelligent.**

in·tel·lec·tu·al·ism (ĭn′tə lĕk′chŏŏ ə lĭz′əm), *n.* **1.** the exercise of the intellect; devotion to intellectual pursuits. **2.** *Philos.* **a.** the doctrine that knowledge is wholly or chiefly derived from pure reason. **b.** the belief that reason is the final principle of reality. **—in′tel·lec′tu·al·ist,** *n.* **—in′tel·lec′tu·al·is′tic,** *adj.*

in·tel·lec·tu·al·i·ty (ĭn′tə lĕk′chŏŏ ăl′ə tĭ), *n., pl.* **-ties. 1.** quality of being intellectual. **2.** intellectual character or power.

in·tel·lec·tu·al·ize (ĭn′tə lĕk′chŏŏ ə līz′), *v.t., v.i., -ized, -izing.* to make or become intellectual. **—in′tel·lec′tu·al·i·za′tion,** *n.*

in·tel·li·gence (ĭn tĕl′ə jəns), *n.* **1.** capacity for understanding and for other forms of adaptive behavior; aptitude in grasping truths, facts, meaning. **2.** good mental capacity: *a task requiring intelligence.* **3.** the faculty of understanding. **4.** (*often cap.*) an intelligent being, esp. an incorporeal one. **5.** knowledge of an event, circumstance, etc., received or imparted; news; information. **6.** the gathering or distribution of information, esp. secret information. **7.** a staff of persons engaged in obtaining such information; secret service. **8.** *Rare.* interchange of information, thoughts, etc., or communication. **—Syn. 1.** See **mind.**

intelligence bureau, a governmental department charged with obtaining information, esp. for the use of the army or navy. Also, **intelligence department.**

intelligence office, 1. an intelligence bureau. **2.** *U.S. Obs.* an employment office, esp. for servants.

intelligence quotient, the mental age divided by the actual age. A child with a mental age of 12 years and an actual age of 10 years has an intelligence quotient, or IQ, of 1.2 (usually expressed as 120). In the computation of the IQ, age above 15 or 16 is commonly ignored.

in·tel·li·genc·er (ĭn tĕl′ə jən sər), *n.* **1.** one who or that which conveys information. **2.** an informer; a spy.

intelligence test, any of several psychological tests, either verbal or nonverbal, which attempt to measure the mental development of an individual.

in·tel·li·gent (ĭn tĕl′ə jənt), *adj.* **1.** having a good understanding or mental capacity; quick to understand, as persons or animals: *intelligent statesmen.* **2.** showing quickness of understanding, as actions, utterances, etc.: *an intelligent answer.* **3.** having the faculty of understanding: *an intelligent being.* **4.** *Rare.* having understanding or knowledge (fol. by *of*). [t. L: s. *intelligens,* var. of *intellegens,* ppr.] **—in·tel′li·gent·ly,** *adv.* **—Syn. 1.** INTELLIGENT, INTELLECTUAL describe distinctive mental capacity. INTELLIGENT often suggests a natural quickness of understanding: *an intelligent reader.* INTELLECTUAL implies not only having a high degree of understanding, but also a capacity and taste for the higher forms of knowledge: *intellectual interests.* **2.** See **sharp.** **—Ant. 1, 2.** stupid.

in·tel·li·gen·tial (ĭn tĕl′ə jĕn′shəl), *adj.* **1.** of or pertaining to the intelligence or understanding. **2.** endowed with intelligence. **3.** conveying information.

in·tel·li·gent·si·a (ĭn tĕl′ə jĕnt′sĭ ə, -gĕnt′sĭ ə), *n.pl.* a class or group of persons having or claiming special enlightenment in views or principles; the intellectuals. [t. Russ., t. L: m. *intelligentia* intelligence]

in·tel·li·gi·bil·i·ty (ĭn tĕl′ə jə bĭl′ə tĭ), *n., pl.* **-ties. 1.** quality or character of being intelligible; capability of being understood. **2.** something intelligible.

in·tel·li·gi·ble (ĭn tĕl′ə jə bəl), *adj.* **1.** capable of being understood; comprehensible: *an intelligible reason.* **2.** *Philos.* apprehensible by the mind. [ME, t. L: m.s. *intelligibilis,* var. of *intellegibilis*] **—in·tel′li·gi·ble·ness,** *n.* **—in·tel′li·gi·bly,** *adv.*

in·tem·er·ate (ĭn tĕm′ər ĭt), *adj. Now Rare.* inviolate; undefiled; unsullied; pure. [t. L: m.s. *intemerātus*]

in·tem·per·ance (ĭn tĕm′pər əns, -prəns), *n.* **1.** immoderate indulgence in alcoholic liquors. **2.** excessive indulgence of a natural appetite or passion. **3.** lack of moderation or due restraint, as in action or speech.

in·tem·per·ate (ĭn tĕm′pər ĭt, -prĭt), *adj.* **1.** given to or characterized by immoderate indulgence in intoxicating drink. **2.** immoderate as regards indulgence of appetite or passion. **3.** not temperate; unrestrained or unbridled. **4.** extreme in temperature, as climate, etc. **—in·tem′per·ate·ly,** *adv.* **—in·tem′per·ate·ness,** *n.*

in·tend (ĭn tĕnd′), *v.t.* **1.** to have in mind as something to be done or brought about: *he intends to enlist.* **2.** to design or mean for a particular purpose, use, recipient, etc.: *a book intended for reference.* **3.** to design to express or indicate. **4.** *Obs.* (of words, etc.) to signify. **5.** *Archaic.* to direct (the eyes, mind, etc.). **—v.i. 6.** to have a purpose or design: *he may intend otherwise.* **7.** *Obs.* to set out on one's course. [ME *intende(n),* t. L: m. *intendere* extend, intend; r. ME *entenden,* t. OF: m. *entendre*] **—in·tend′er,** *n.* **—Syn. 1.** INTEND, MEAN, DESIGN, PROPOSE imply knowing what one wishes to do and setting this as a goal. To INTEND is to have in mind something willed to be done or brought about: *no offense was intended.* MEAN is a simpler word for the same idea as INTEND, but suggests perhaps less definite thought or conscious choice: *he means to go away.* DESIGN implies planning to effect a particular result; the things to be done have a definite relationship to one another: *to design a plan for Christmas decorations.* PROPOSE suggests setting up a program before oneself for accomplishment, or offering it for consideration: *we propose to beautify our city.*

in·tend·ance (ĭn tĕn′dəns), *n.* **1.** a department of the public service, as in France, or the officials in charge of it. **2.** the official quarters of an intendant. **3.** the function of an intendant; superintendence; intendancy.

in·tend·an·cy (ĭn tĕn′dən sĭ), *n., pl.* **-cies. 1.** the office or function of an intendant. **2.** a body of intendants. **3.** a district under the charge of an intendant. [t. Sp.: m. *intendencia*]

in·tend·ant (ĭn tĕn′dənt), *n.* **1.** one who has the direction or management of some public business, the affairs of an establishment, etc.; a superintendent. **2.** the title of various public officials in France and elsewhere. [t. F, t. L: m.s. *intendens,* ppr., extending, attending]

in·tend·ed (ĭn tĕn′dĭd), *adj.* **1.** purposed or designed: *to produce the intended effect.* **2.** prospective: *one's intended wife.* **—n. 3.** *Colloq.* an intended husband or wife.

in·tend·ment (ĭn tĕnd′mənt), *n.* **1.** *Law.* the manner of understanding, construing, or viewing something. **2.** *Obs.* intention; design; purpose.

in·ten·er·ate (ĭn tĕn′ə rāt′), *v.t., -ated, -ating. Now Rare.* to make soft or tender; soften. [f. IN-² + L *tener* TENDER¹ + -ATE¹] **—in·ten′er·a′tion,** *n.*

intens., intensive.

in·tense (ĭn tĕns′), *adj.* **1.** existing or occurring in a high or extreme degree: *intense heat.* **2.** acute, strong, or vehement, as sensations, feelings, or emotions: *intense anxiety.* **3.** of an extreme kind; very great, strong, keen, severe, etc.: *an intense gale.* **4.** *Photog.* strong: *intense light.* **5.** having the characteristic qualities in a high degree: *the intense vault of heaven.* **6.** strenuous or earnest, as activity, exertion, diligence, thought, etc.: *an intense life.* **7.** exhibiting a high degree of some quality or action. **8.** having or showing great strength or vehemence of feeling, as a person, the face, language, etc. **9.** susceptible to strong emotion; emotional: *an intense person.* [ME, t. L: m.s. *intensus,* pp., stretched tight, intense] **—in·tense′ly,** *adv.* **—in·tense′ness,** *n.*

in·ten·si·fy (ĭn tĕn′sə fī′), *v., -fied, -fying. —v.t. 1.** to make intense or more intense. **2.** *Photog.* to make more dense or opaque, as a negative or print. **—v.i. 3.** to become intense or more intense. **—in·ten′si·fi·ca′tion,** *n.* **—in·ten′si·fi′er,** *n.* **—Syn. 1.** See **aggravate.**

in·ten·sion (ĭn tĕn′shən), *n.* **1.** intensification; increase in degree. **2.** intensity; high degree. **3.** relative intensity; degree. **4.** exertion of the mind; determination. **5.** *Logic.* the sum of the attributes contained in a concept or connoted by a term. Cf. **extension** (def. 10). [t. L: s. *intensio*]

in·ten·si·ty (ĭn tĕn′sə tĭ), *n., pl.* **-ties. 1.** quality or condition of being intense. **2.** great energy, strength, vehemence, etc., as of activity, thought, or feeling. **3.** high or extreme degree, as of cold. **4.** the degree or extent to which something is intense. **5.** *Speech.* **a.** loudness or softness of vocal tone. **b.** carrying power of voice. **6.** the strength or sharpness of a color due especially to its degree of freedom from admixture with its complementary color. **7.** *Photog.* strength, as of light. **8.** *Physics.* **a.** the strength of an electric current in amperes. **b.** potential difference; voltage. **c.** the strength of an electrical or magnetic field. **d.** the magnitude, as of a force, per unit of area, volume, etc.

in·ten·sive (ĭn tĕn′sĭv), *adj.* **1.** of, pertaining to, or characterized by intensity: *intensive fire from machine guns.* **2.** intensifying. **3.** *Med.* **a.** increasing in intensity or degree. **b.** instituting treatment to the limit of safety. **4.** *Econ.* of or denoting methods designed to increase effectiveness, as (in *Agric.*) a more thorough tillage, the application of fertilizers, etc., to secure the most from each acre (opposed to *extensive*). **5.** *Gram.* indicating increased emphasis or force. For example: *certainly*, *tremendously* are intensive adverbs. —*n.* **6.** something that intensifies. **7.** *Gram.* an intensive element or formation, as *-self* in *himself*, or Latin *-tō* in *iac-tō*, 'I hurl' compared with *iaciō*, 'I throw.' [late ME, t. ML: m.s. *intensīvus*] **—in·ten'sive·ly,** *adv.* **—in·ten'sive·ness,** *n.*

in·tent¹ (ĭn·tĕnt'), *n.* **1.** an intending or purposing, as to commit some act: *criminal intent.* **2.** that which is intended; purpose; aim; design; intention: *my intent was to buy.* **3.** *Law.* the state of a person's mind which directs his actions toward a specific object. **4. to all intents and purposes, a.** for all practical purposes; practically. **b.** for all the ends and purposes in view. **5.** the end or object intended. **6.** *Obs.* meaning. [partly ME *intent*, *entent*, t. OF: *entent* intention, g. L *intentus* a stretching out; partly ME *intente*, *entente*, t. OF: purpose, ult. der. L *intendere* stretch out] **—Syn. 1.** See **intention.**

in·tent² (ĭn·tĕnt'), *adj.* **1.** firmly or steadfastly fixed or directed (upon something): *an intent gaze.* **2.** having the gaze or thoughts earnestly fixed on something: *intent on one's job.* **3.** bent, as on some purpose: *intent on revenge.* **5.** earnest: *an intent person.* [t. L: s. *intentus*, pp., stretched, intent] **—in·tent'ly,** *adv.* **—in·tent'ness,** *n.*

in·ten·tion (ĭn·tĕn'shən), *n.* **1.** act of determining mentally upon some action or result; a purpose or design. **2.** the end or object intended. **3.** *Colloq.* (*pl.*) purposes with respect to a proposal of marriage. **4.** act or fact of intending or purposing. **5.** *Logic.* **a.** a general concept. **b. first intention,** a general conception obtained by abstraction from the ideas or images of sensible objects. **c. second intention,** a general conception obtained by reflection and abstraction applied to first intentions as objects. **6.** *Surg., Med.* a manner or process of healing, as in the healing of a lesion or fracture without granulation (**healing by first intention**) or the healing of a wound by granulation after suppuration (**healing by second intention**). **7.** *Rare.* intentness. **8.** meaning. [ME, t. L: s. *intentio*] **—Syn. 2.** INTENTION, INTENT, PURPOSE all refer to a wish which one means to carry out. INTENTION is the general word: *his intentions are good.* INTENT is chiefly legal or poetical: *intent to kill.* PURPOSE implies having a goal or a settled determination to achieve something: *there was no purpose in his actions.*

in·ten·tion·al (ĭn·tĕn'shən·əl), *adj.* **1.** done with intention or on purpose: *an intentional insult.* **2.** of or pertaining to intention or purpose. **3.** *Metaphys.* **a.** pertaining to an appearance, phenomenon, or representation in the mind; phenomenal; representational; referential. **b.** pertaining to the capacity of mind to refer to objects of all sorts. **—in·ten'tion·al·ly,** *adv.* **—Syn. 1.** See **deliberate.**

in·ter (ĭn·tûr'), *v.t.*, **-terred, -terring. 1.** to deposit (a dead body, etc.) in a grave or tomb; bury, esp. with ceremonies. **2.** *Obs.* to put into the earth. [ME *entere(n)*, t. OF: m. *enterrer*, der. *en-* EN-¹ + *terre* earth (g. L *terra*)]

inter-, a prefix meaning "between," "among," "mutually," "reciprocally," "together," as in *intercellular*, *intercity*, *intermarry*, *interweave.* [t. L, comb. form of *inter*, adv. and prep., between, among, during]

in·ter·act (ĭn'tər·ăkt'), *v.i.* to act on each other. **—in'ter·ac'tive,** *adj.*

in·ter·ac·tion (ĭn'tər·ăk'shən), *n.* action on each other; reciprocal action.

in·ter a·li·a (ĭn'tər ā'lĭ·ə), *Latin.* among other things.

in·ter a·li·os (ĭn'tər ā'lĭ·ōs'), *Latin.* among others.

in·ter-Al·lied (ĭn'tər·ə·līd', -ăl'īd), *adj.* between or among allied nations, esp. the Allies of World War I.

in·ter·blend (ĭn'tər·blĕnd'), *v.t.*, *v.i.*, **-blended** or **-blent, -blending.** to blend. one with another.

in·ter·bor·ough (ĭn'tər·bûr'ō), *adj.* between boroughs.

in·ter·brain (ĭn'tər·brān'), *n.* *Anat.* the diencephalon.

in·ter·breed (ĭn'tər·brēd'), *v.t.*, *v.i.*, **-bred, -breeding.** to breed by the crossing of different animal or plant species, breeds, varieties, or individuals.

in·ter·ca·lar·y (ĭn·tûr'kə·lĕr'ĭ), *adj.* **1.** interpolated; interposed; intervening. **2.** inserted or interpolated in the calendar, as an extra day, month, etc. **3.** having such an inserted day, month, etc., as a particular year. [t. L: m.s. *intercalārius*]

in·ter·ca·late (ĭn·tûr'kə·lāt'), *v.t.*, **-lated, -lating. 1.** to interpolate; interpose. **2.** to insert (an extra day, month, etc.) in the calendar. [t. L: m.s. *intercalātus*, pp.] **—in·ter'ca·la'tive,** *adj.*

in·ter·ca·la·tion (ĭn·tûr'kə·lā'shən), *n.* **1.** act of intercalating; insertion or interpolation, as in a series. **2.** that which is intercalated; an interpolation.

in·ter·cede (ĭn'tər·sēd'), *v.i.*, **-ceded, -ceding. 1.** to interpose in behalf of one in difficulty or trouble, as by pleading or petition: *to intercede with the governor for a condemned man.* **2.** *Rom. Hist.* (of a tribune or other magistrate) to interpose a veto. [t. L: m.s. *intercēdere* intervene] **—in'ter·ced'er,** *n.*

in·ter·cel·lu·lar (ĭn'tər·sĕl'yə·lər), *adj.* situated between or among cells or cellules.

in·ter·cept (*v.* ĭn'tər·sĕpt'; *n.* ĭn'tər·sĕpt'), *v.t.* **1.** to take or seize on the way from one place to another; cut off from the intended destination: *to intercept a*

messenger. **2.** to stop the natural course of (light, water, etc.). **3.** to stop or check (passage, etc.). **4.** to prevent or cut off the operation or effect of: *to intercept the view.* **5.** to cut off from access, sight, etc. **6.** *Chiefly Math.* to mark off or include, as between two points or lines. —*n.* **7.** an interception. **8.** *Math.* an intercepted part of a line. [t. L: s. *interceptus*, pp.] **—in'ter·cep'tive,** *adj.*

in·ter·cep·tion (ĭn'tər·sĕp'shən), *n.* **1.** act of intercepting. **2.** state or fact of being intercepted. **3.** *Mil.* engaging an enemy force in an attempt to hinder or prevent it from carrying out its mission.

Arc of circle intercepted by line between points X and Y

in·ter·cep·tor (ĭn'tər·sĕp'tər), *n.* **1.** one who or that which intercepts. **2.** *Mil.* a type of fighter airplane with a high rate of climb and speed, used chiefly for the interception of enemy aircraft. Also, **in'ter·cept'er.**

in·ter·ces·sion (ĭn'tər·sĕsh'ən), *n.* **1.** act of interceding. **2.** an interposing or pleading in behalf of one in difficulty or trouble. **3.** *Relig.* **a.** an interposing or pleading with God in behalf of another or others, as that of Christ (see Heb. 7:25) or that of the saints in behalf of men. **b.** a pleading against others (See Rom. 11:2). **4.** *Rom. Hist.* the interposing of a veto, as by a tribune. [t. L: s. *intercessio*] **—in'ter·ces'sion·al,** *adj.*

in·ter·ces·sor (ĭn'tər·sĕs'ər, ĭn'tər·sĕs'ər), *n.* one who intercedes.

in·ter·ces·so·ry (ĭn'tər·sĕs'ər·ĭ), *adj.* making intercession: *the Lord's Prayer has an intercessory petition.*

in·ter·change (*v.* ĭn'tər·chānj'; *n.* ĭn'tər·chānj'), *v.*, **-changed, -changing,** *n.* —*v.t.* **1.** to put each of (two things) in the place of the other. **2.** to cause (one thing) to change places with another; transpose. **3.** to give and receive (things) reciprocally; exchange: *they interchanged gifts.* **4.** to cause to follow one another alternately: *to interchange cares with pleasures.* —*v.i.* **5.** to occur by turns, in succession; alternate. **6.** to change places, as two persons or things, or as one with another. —*n.* **7.** act of interchanging; reciprocal exchange: *the interchange of commodities.* **8.** a changing of places, as between two persons or things, or of one with another. **9.** alternation; alternate succession. [f. INTER- + CHANGE; r. ME *enterchaunge*, t. OF: m. *entrechangier*(v.), *entrechange*(n.)] **—in'ter·chang'er,** *n.*

in·ter·change·a·ble (ĭn'tər·chān'jə·bəl), *adj.* **1.** capable of being put or used in the place of each other, as two things: *interchangeable words.* **2.** (of one thing) that may be put in the place of, or may change places with, something else. **—in'ter·change'a·bil'i·ty, in'ter·change'a·ble·ness,** *n.* **—in'ter·change'a·bly,** *adv.* **—Syn. 2.** See **exchangeable.**

in·ter·clav·i·cle (ĭn'tər·klăv'ə·kəl), *n.* *Zool., Anat.* a median membrane bone developed between the collarbones, or in front of the breastbone, in many *Vertebrata.* **—in·ter·cla·vic·u·lar** (ĭn'tər·klə·vĭk'yə·lər), *adj.*

in·ter·col·le·gi·ate (ĭn'tər·kə·lē'jĭ·ĭt, -jĭt), *adj.* between colleges, or representative of different colleges.

in·ter·co·lo·ni·al (ĭn'tər·kə·lō'nĭ·əl), *adj.* between colonies, as of one country. **—in'ter·co·lo'ni·al·ly,** *adv.*

in·ter·co·lum·nar (ĭn'tər·kə·lŭm'nər), *adj.* between columns.

in·ter·co·lum·ni·a·tion (ĭn'tər·kə·lŭm'nĭ·ā'shən), *n.* *Archit.* **1.** the space between two adjacent columns, usually the clear space between the lower parts of the shafts. **2.** the system of spacing between columns. [f. s. L *intercolumnium* space between columns + -ATION]

in·ter·com (ĭn'tər·kŏm'), *n.* *Mil. Slang.* an intercommunication system, as of an airplane or a tank.

in·ter·com·mon (ĭn'tər·kŏm'ən), *v.i.* *Eng. Law.* to share in the use of a common. [ME *entercomen*, t. AF: m. *entrecomuner*, f. *entre-* INTER- + *comuner* share]

in·ter·com·mu·ni·cate (ĭn'tər·kə·mū'nə·kāt'), *v.t., v.i.*, **-cated, -cating.** to communicate mutually, as people or rooms. **—in'ter·com·mu'ni·ca'tion,** *n.* **—in'ter·com·mu'ni·ca'tive,** *adj.*

in·ter·com·mun·ion (ĭn'tər·kə·mūn'yən), *n.* mutual communion, association, or relations.

in·ter·com·mu·ni·ty (ĭn'tər·kə·mū'nə·tĭ), *n., pl.* **-ties.** common ownership, use, participation, etc.

in·ter·con·nect (ĭn'tər·kə·nĕkt'), *v.t.* to connect, one with another. **—in'ter·con·nec'tion,** *n.*

in·ter·con·ti·nen·tal (ĭn'tər·kŏn'tə·nĕn'təl), *adj.* between continents: *intercontinental trade.*

in·ter·cos·tal (ĭn'tər·kŏs'təl, -kôs'təl), *adj.* **1.** pertaining to muscles, parts, or intervals between the ribs. **2.** situated between the ribs. —*n.* **3.** an intercostal muscle, part, or space. [t. NL: s. *intercostālis.* See INTER-, COSTA, -AL¹] **—in'ter·cos'tal·ly,** *adv.*

in·ter·course (ĭn'tər·kōrs'), *n.* **1.** dealings or communication between individuals. **2.** interchange of thoughts, feelings, etc. **3.** sexual relations. [f. INTER- + COURSE; r. ME *entercourse*, t. OF: m. *entrecors*, g. L *intercursus* a running between]

in·ter·crop (ĭn'tər·krŏp'), *v.t., v.i.*, **-cropped, -cropping.** *Agric.* to use (the space) between the rows of an orchard, vineyard, or field for the simultaneous production of a different cultivated crop.

in·ter·cross (ĭn'tər·krôs', -krŏs'), *v.t.* **1.** to cross (things), one with another. **2.** to cross (each other), as streets do. **3.** to cross in interbreeding. —*v.i.* **4.** to cross each other. **5.** to interbreed. —*n.* **6.** an instance of cross-fertilization.

in·ter·cur·rent (ĭn'tər kûr'ənt), *adj.* **1.** intervening, as of time or events. **2.** *Pathol.* (of a disease) occurring while another disease is in progress. [t. L: s. *intercurrens*, ppr., running between, intervening] **—in'ter·cur'·rence,** *n.*

in·ter·de·nom·i·na·tion·al (ĭn'tər dĭ nŏm'ə nā'shən-əl), *adj.* between (religious) denominations.

in·ter·den·tal (ĭn'tər dĕn'təl), *adj.* **1.** between teeth. **2.** *Phonet.* with the tip of the tongue between the upper and lower front teeth.

in·ter·de·pend·ent (ĭn'tər dĭ pĕn'dənt), *adj.* mutually dependent; dependent on each other. **—in'ter·de·pend'ence, in'ter·de·pend'en·cy,** *n.* **—in'ter·de·pend'ent·ly,** *adv.*

in·ter·dict (*n.* ĭn'tər dĭkt'; *v.* ĭn'tər dĭkt'), *n.* **1.** *Rom. Law.* a general or special order of the Roman praetor forbidding or commanding an act; the procedure by which an interdict was sought. **2.** *Civil Law.* any prohibitory act or decree of a court or an administrative officer. **3.** *Rom. Cath. Ch.* a punishment by which the faithful, remaining in communion with the Church, are prohibited from participation in certain sacred acts. **—v.t. 4.** *Eccles.* to cut off authoritatively from certain ecclesiastical functions and privileges. **5.** to forbid; prohibit. [t. L: s. *interdictus*, pp.; r. ME *entredite*(n), t. OF: m. *entredit*, pp. of *entredire*] **—in'ter·dic'tive,** *adj.* **—in'ter·dic'tor,** *n.*

in·ter·dic·tion (ĭn'tər dĭk'shən), *n.* **1.** act of interdicting. **2.** state of being interdicted. **3.** an interdict.

in·ter·dic·to·ry (ĭn'tər dĭk'tə rĭ), *adj.* interdicting.

in·ter·est (ĭn'tər ĭst, -trĭst), *n.* **1.** the feeling of one whose attention or curiosity is particularly engaged by something: *to have little interest in a subject.* **2.** a particular feeling of this kind: *a man of varied intellectual interests.* **3.** the power of exciting such feeling; interesting quality: *questions of great interest.* **4.** concernment, importance, or moment: *a matter of primary interest.* **5.** a business, cause, or the like, in which a number of persons are interested. **6.** a share in the ownership of property, in a commercial or financial undertaking, or the like. **7.** any right of ownership in property, commercial undertakings, etc. **8.** a number or group of persons, or a party, having a common interest: *the banking interest.* **9.** (*pl.*) the group of persons or organizations having extensive financial or business interests. **10.** something in which one has an interest, as of ownership, advantage, attention, etc. **11.** the relation of being affected by something in respect of advantage or detriment: *an arbitrator having no interest in the outcome.* **12.** benefit or advantage: *to have one's own interest in mind.* **13.** regard for one's own advantage or profit; self-interest: *rival interests.* **14.** influence from personal importance or capability; power of influencing the action of others. **15. in the interest** (or **interests**) **of,** on the side of what is advantageous to; in behalf of: *in the interest of good government.* **16.** *Com.* **a.** payment, or a sum paid, for the use of money borrowed (the *principal*), or for the forbearance of a debt. **b.** the rate percent per unit of time represented by such payment. **17.** something added or thrown in above an exact equivalent. **—v.t. 18.** to engage or excite the attention or curiosity of: *a story which interested him greatly.* **19.** to concern (a person, etc.) in something; involve: *every citizen is interested in this law.* **20.** to cause to take a personal concern or share; induce to participate: *to interest a person in an enterprise.* **21.** *Rare.* to concern, relate to, or affect. [late ME, n. use of L *interest* it concerns; r. ME *interesse*, t. ML: compensation for loss, n. use of L *inf.*]

in·ter·est·ed (ĭn'tər ĭs tĭd, -trĭs tĭd, -tə rĕs'tĭd), *adj.* **1.** having an interest in something; concerned: *those interested should apply in person.* **2.** participating; having an interest or share; having money involved: *one interested in the funds.* **3.** having the attention or curiosity engaged: *an interested spectator.* **4.** characterized by a feeling of interest. **5.** influenced by personal or selfish motives: *an interested witness.* **—in'ter·est·ed·ly,** *adv.* **—in'ter·est·ed·ness,** *n.*

in·ter·est·ing (ĭn'tər ĭs tĭng, -trĭs tĭng, -tə rĕs'tĭng), *adj.* **1.** arousing a feeling of interest: *an interesting face.* **2.** engaging or exciting and holding the attention or curiosity: *an interesting book.* **—in'ter·est·ing·ly,** *adv.* **—in'ter·est·ing·ness,** *n.*
—Syn. 2. INTERESTING, PLEASING, GRATIFYING mean satisfying to the mind. That which is INTERESTING occupies the mind with no connotation of pleasure or displeasure: *an interesting account of a battle.* That which is PLEASING engages the mind favorably: *a pleasing account of the wedding.* That which is GRATIFYING fulfils expectations, requirements, etc.: *a gratifying account of his whereabouts, a book gratifying in its detail.*

in·ter·face (ĭn'tər fās'), *n.* a surface regarded as the common boundary of two bodies or spaces.

in·ter·fa·cial (ĭn'tər fā'shəl), *adj.* **1.** included between two faces. **2.** pertaining to an interface.

in·ter·fere (ĭn'tər fîr'), *v.i.,* **-fered, -fering. 1.** to clash; come in collision; be in opposition: *the claims of two nations may interfere.* **2.** to come into opposition, as one thing with another, esp. with the effect of hampering action or procedure: *these interruptions interfere with the work.* **3.** to interpose or intervene for a particular purpose. **4.** to take a part in the affairs of others; meddle: *to interfere with others' disputes.* **5.** (of things) to strike against each other, or one against another, so as to hamper or hinder action; come into physical collision.

6. to strike one foot or leg against the opposite foot or leg in going, as a horse. **7.** *Football, etc.* to obstruct the action of an opposing player in a way barred by the rules. **8.** *Physics.* to cause interference. [t. OF: m. *entreferir* strike each other, f. *entre-* INTER- + *ferir* (g. L *ferīre* strike)] **—in'ter·fer'er,** *n.* **—in'ter·fer'ing·ly,** *adv.*

in·ter·fer·ence (ĭn'tər fîr'əns), *n.* **1.** act or fact of interfering. **2.** *Physics.* the reciprocal action of waves (as of light, sound, etc.), when meeting, by which they reinforce or cancel each other. **3.** *Radio.* **a.** the jumbling of radio signals because signals other than the desired ones are being received. **b.** the signals which produce the incoherence.

interference drag, the additional drag due to interaction of two aerodynamic bodies.

in·ter·fe·ren·tial (ĭn'tər fə rĕn'shəl), *adj.* of or pertaining to interference.

in·ter·fer·om·e·ter (ĭn'tər fə rŏm'ə tər), *n.* *Physics.* an instrument for measuring small lengths or distances by means of the interference of two rays of light.

in·ter·flow (*v.* ĭn'tər flō'; *n.* ĭn'tər flō'), *v.i.* **1.** to flow into each other; intermingle. **—n. 2.** an interflowing.

in·ter·flu·ent (ĭn'tər floo'ənt), *adj.* interflowing.

in·ter·fluve (ĭn'tər floov'), *n.* the higher land separating adjacent stream valleys.

in·ter·fold (ĭn'tər fōld'), *v.t.* to fold, one within another; fold together.

in·ter·fuse (ĭn'tər fūz'), *v.,* **-fused, -fusing. —v.t. 1.** to pour (something) between or through; diffuse throughout. **2.** to intersperse, intermingle, or permeate with something. **3.** to blend or fuse, one with another. **—v.i. 4.** to become blended or fused, one with another. [t. L: m. s. *interfūsus*, pp.] **—in'ter·fu'sion,** *n.*

in·ter·gla·cial (ĭn'tər glā'shəl), *adj.* *Geol.* occurring or formed between times of glacial action.

in·ter·grade (*n.* ĭn'tər grād'; *v.* ĭn'tər grād'), *n., v.,* **-graded, -grading. —n. 1.** an intermediate grade. **—v.i. 2.** to pass gradually, one into another, as different species. **—in'ter·gra·da'tion,** *n.* **—in·ter·gra·di·ent** (ĭn'tər grā'dĭ ənt), *adj.*

in·ter·growth (ĭn'tər grōth'), *n.* growth or growing together, as of one thing with another.

in·ter·im (ĭn'tər ĭm), *n.* **1.** an intervening time; the meantime: *in the interim.* **2.** a temporary or provisional arrangement. **3.** (*cap.*) *Eccles. Hist.* any of three provisional arrangements for the settlement of religious differences between German Protestants and Roman Catholics during the Reformation. **—adj. 4.** belonging to or connected with an intervening period of time; temporary: *an interim order.* **—adv. 5.** *Now Rare.* meantime. [t. L: in the meantime]

in·te·ri·or (ĭn tîr'ĭ ər), *adj.* **1.** being within; inside of anything; internal; further toward a center: *the interior parts of a house.* **2.** of or pertaining to that which is within; inside: *an interior view.* **3.** situated inside of and at a distance from the coast or border: *the interior parts of a country.* **4.** pertaining to the inland. **5.** domestic: *the interior trade.* **6.** inner, private, or secret: *an interior cabinet.* **7.** mental or spiritual. **8.** *Geom.* (of an angle) inner, as an angle formed between two parallel lines when cut by a third line, or an angle formed by two adjacent sides of a closed polygon. **—n. 9.** the internal part; the inside. **10.** *Art.* **a.** the inside part of a building, considered as a whole from the point of view of artistic design or general effect, convenience, etc., or a single room or apartment so considered. **b.** a pictorial representation of the inside of a building, room, etc. **11.** the inland parts of a region, country, etc.: *the interior of Africa.* **12.** the domestic affairs of a country as distinguished from its foreign affairs: *the Department of the Interior.* **13.** the inner or inward nature or character of anything. [t. L: inner] **—in·te·ri·or·i·ty** (ĭn tîr'ĭ ŏr'ə tĭ, -ŏr'-), *n.* **—in·te'ri·or·ly,** *adv.* **—Syn. 9.** See inside.

A. Interior angle; B, Exterior angle

interior decorator, a person whose occupation is planning the decoration, furnishings, draperies, etc., of homes, rooms, or offices.

interior drainage, a drainage system whose waters do not continue to the ocean either on the surface or underground, but evaporate within the land area.

interj., interjection.

in·ter·ject (ĭn'tər jĕkt'), *v.t.* **1.** to throw in abruptly between other things. **2.** to interpolate; interpose: *to interject a careless remark.* **3.** *Rare.* to come between. [t. L: s. *interjectus*, pp.] **—in'ter·jec'tor,** *n.*

in·ter·jec·tion (ĭn'tər jĕk'shən), *n.* **1.** act of throwing between; an interjecting. **2.** the utterance of ejaculations expressive of emotion; an ejaculation or exclamation. **3.** something, as a remark, interjected. **4.** *Gram.* **a.** (in many languages) a form class, or "part of speech," comprising words which constitute utterances or clauses in themselves, without grammatical connection. **b.** such a word, as English *tut-tut!* Such words often include speech sounds not otherwise found in the language. **c.** any word or construction similarly used, as English *goodness me!* **—in'ter·jec'tion·al,** *adj.* **—in'ter·jec'-tion·al·ly,** *adv.*

in·ter·jec·to·ry (ĭn'tər jĕk'tə rĭ), *adj.* **1.** interjectional. **2.** interjected. **—in'ter·jec'to·ri·ly,** *adv.*

---

in·ter·knit (Ĭn′tər nĭt′), *v.t.*, **-knitted** or **-knit**, **-knitting**. to knit together, one with another; intertwine.

in·ter·lace (Ĭn′tər lās′), *v.*, **-laced**, **-lacing**. —*v.i.* **1.** to cross one another as if woven together; intertwine; blend intricately: *interlacing boughs*. **2.** *Rare*. to become intermingled. —*v.t.* **3.** to dispose (threads, strips, parts, branches, etc.) so as to intercross one another, passing alternately over and under. **4.** to mingle; blend. **5.** to diversify as with threads woven in. **6.** to intersperse or intermingle. —**in′ter·lace′ment**, *n.*

In·ter·la·ken (Ĭn′tər lä′kən, Ĭn′tər lä′kən), *n.* a town in central Switzerland between the lakes of Brienz and Thun: a famous tourist center. 3,771 (1930).

in·ter·lam·i·nate (Ĭn′tər lăm′ə nāt′), *v.t.*, **-nated**, **-nating**. to interlay or lay between laminae; interstratify. —**in′ter·lam′i·na′tion**, *n.*

in·ter·lard (Ĭn′tər lärd′), *v.t.* **1.** to diversify with something intermixed or interjected; intersperse (fol. by *with*): *to interlard one's speech with oaths*. **2.** (of things) to be intermixed in. **3.** *Obs*. to mix, as fat with lean. [t. F: m.s. *entrelarder*, f. *entre-* INTER- + *larder* LARD, v.] —**in′ter·lard′ment**, *n.*

in·ter·lay (Ĭn′tər lā′), *v.t.*, **-laid**, **-laying**. **1.** to lay between; interpose. **2.** to diversify with something laid between or inserted: *silver interlaid with gold*.

in·ter·leaf (Ĭn′tər lēf′), *n.*, *pl.* **-leaves** (-lēvz′). an additional leaf, usually blank, inserted between or bound with, the regular printed leaves of a book.

in·ter·leave (Ĭn′tər lēv′), *v.t.*, **-leaved**, **-leaving**. **1.** to provide blank leaves in (a book) for notes or written comments. **2.** to insert blank leaves between (the regular printed leaves).

in·ter·li·brar·y loan (Ĭn′tər lī′brĕr′Ĭ, -brər Ĭ, -brĭ), a system by which one library borrows a publication from another library. **2.** a loan made in this way.

in·ter·line[1] (Ĭn′tər lĭn′), *v.t.*, **-lined**, **-lining**. **1.** to write or insert (words, etc.) between the lines of writing or print. **2.** to mark or inscribe (a document, book, etc.), between the lines. [ME, t. ML: s. *interlineāre*]

in·ter·line[2] (Ĭn′tər lĭn′), *v.t.*, **-lined**, **-lining**. to provide (a garment) with an inner lining, between the ordinary lining and the outer fabric. [f. INTER- + LINE[2]]

in·ter·lin·e·al (Ĭn′tər lĭn′Ĭ əl), *adj.* **1.** interlinear. **2.** *Rare*. alternating in lines. —**in′ter·lin′e·al·ly**, *adv.*

in·ter·lin·e·ar (Ĭn′tər lĭn′Ĭ ər), *adj.* **1.** situated between the lines; inserted between lines. **2.** having interpolated lines; interlined: *an interlinear translation*. **3.** having the same text in various languages set in alternate lines: *the interlinear Bible*.

in·ter·lin·e·ate (Ĭn′tər lĭn′Ĭ āt′), *v.t.*, **-ated**, **-ating**. to interline[1]. —**in′ter·lin′e·a′tion**, *n.*

in·ter·lin·ing[1] (Ĭn′tər lī′nĬng), *n.* **1.** an inner lining placed between the ordinary lining and the outer fabric of a garment. **2.** material used for this purpose. [f. INTERLINE[2] + -ING[1]]

in·ter·lin·ing[2] (Ĭn′tər lī′nĬng), *n.* interlineation.

in·ter·link (*v.* Ĭn′tər lĬngk′; *n.* Ĭn′tər lĬngk′), *v.t.* **1.** to link, one with another. —*n.* **2.** a connecting link.

in·ter·lock (Ĭn′tər lŏk′), *v.i.* **1.** to engage with each other: *interlocking branches*. **2.** to fit into each other, as parts of machinery, so that all action is simultaneous. **3.** (of railroad switches, signals, etc.) to arrange and operate in an interlocking system. —*v.t.* **4.** to lock one with another. **5.** to fit the parts of together so that all must move together, or in the same way. **6.** *Railroads*. to arrange (controls of switches, signals, etc.) so that their positions are not independent of one another and their movements succeed each other in prearranged order. —**in′ter·lock′er**, *n.*

in·ter·lo·cu·tion (Ĭn′tər lə kū′shən), *n.* interchange of speech; conversation; dialogue. [t. L: s. *interlocūtio* a speaking between]

in·ter·loc·u·tor (Ĭn′tər lŏk′yə tər), *n.* **1.** the man in the middle of the line of performers of a minstrel troupe, who carries on a conversation with the end men. **2.** one who takes parts in a conversation or dialogue. **3.** one who enters into conversation with, or questions, another. —**in·ter·loc·u·tress** (Ĭn′tər lŏk′yə trĬs), **in′ter·loc·u·trice**, **in·ter·loc·u·trix** (Ĭn′tər lŏk′yə trĬks), *n. fem.*

in·ter·loc·u·to·ry (Ĭn′tər lŏk′yə tōr′Ĭ), *adj.* **1.** of the nature of, pertaining to, or occurring in conversation: *interlocutory instruction*. **2.** interjected into the main course of speech. **3.** *Law*. **a.** pronounced during the course of an action, as a decision; not finally decisive of a case. **b.** pertaining to a provisional decision.

in·ter·lope (Ĭn′tər lōp′), *v.i.*, **-loped**, **-loping**. **1.** to intrude into some region or field or trade without a proper license. **2.** to thrust oneself into the affairs of others; intrude. [f. INTER- + LOPE, v.] —**in′ter·lop′er**, *n.*

in·ter·lude (Ĭn′tər lōōd′), *n.* **1.** an intervening episode, period, space, etc. **2.** a form of short dramatic piece, esp. of a light or farcical character, formerly introduced between the parts of miracle plays and moralities or given as part of other entertainments. **3.** one of the early English farces or comedies (such as those by John Heywood) which grew out of such pieces. **4.** an intermediate performance or entertainment, as between the acts of a play. **5.** an instrumental passage or a piece of music rendered between the parts of a song, church service, drama, etc. [ME, t. ML: m.s. *interlūdium*, f. *inter-* INTER- + *-lūdium*, der. L *lūdus* play]

in·ter·lu·nar (Ĭn′tər lōō′nər), *adj.* pertaining to the moon's monthly period of invisibility between the old moon and the new.

in·ter·lu·na·tion (Ĭn′tər lōō nā′shən), *n.* the interlunar period.

in·ter·mar·riage (Ĭn′tər măr′Ĭj), *n.* act or fact of intermarrying.

in·ter·mar·ry (Ĭn′tər măr′Ĭ), *v.i.*, **-ried**, **-rying**. **1.** to become connected by marriage, as two families, tribes, or castes. **2.** to marry within the limits of the family or of near relationship. **3.** to marry, one with another.

in·ter·max·il·lar·y (Ĭn′tər măk′sə lĕr′Ĭ), *adj.* **1.** situated between the maxillary or upper jawbones. **2.** of or pertaining to the back and middle of the upper jaw: *intermaxillary teeth*. **3.** (in *Crustacea*) situated between those somites of the head which bear the maxillae.

in·ter·med·dle (Ĭn′tər mĕd′dl), *v.i.*, **-dled**, **-dling**. to take part in a matter, esp. officiously; interfere; meddle. —**in′ter·med′dler**, *n.*

in·ter·me·di·a·cy (Ĭn′tər mē′dĬ ə sĬ), *n.* state of being intermediate, or of acting intermediately.

in·ter·me·di·ar·y (Ĭn′tər mē′dĬ ĕr′Ĭ), *adj.*, *n.*, *pl.* **-aries**. —*adj.* **1.** being between; intermediate. **2.** acting between persons, parties, etc.; serving as an intermediate agent or agency: *an intermediary power*. —*n.* **3.** an intermediate agent or agency; a go-between. **4.** a medium or means. **5.** an intermediate form or stage.

in·ter·me·di·ate[1] (Ĭn′tər mē′dĬ Ĭt), *adj.* **1.** being, situated, or acting between two points, stages, things, persons, etc.: *the intermediate links*. —*n.* **2.** something intermediate. **3.** *Chem.* a derivative of the initial material formed before the desired product of a chemical process. **4.** *Rare*. an intermediary. [t. ML: m. s. *intermediātus*, der. L *intermedius* between] —**in′ter·me′di·ate·ly**, *adv.* —**in′ter·me′di·ate·ness**, *n.*

in·ter·me·di·ate[2] (Ĭn′tər mē′dĬ āt′), *v.i.*, **-ated**, **-ating**. to act as an intermediary; intervene; mediate. [f. INTER- + MEDIATE, v.] —**in′ter·me′di·a′tion**, *n.* —**in′ter·me′di·a′tor**, *n.*

intermediate frequency *Radio*. the middle frequency in a superheterodyne receiver, at which most of the amplification takes place.

in·ter·ment (Ĭn tûr′mənt), *n.* act of interring; burial.

in·ter·mez·zo (Ĭn′tər mĕt′sō, -mĕd′zō; *It.* ēn′tĕr mĕd′dzō), *n.*, *pl.* **-zos**, **-zi** (-sē, -zē; *It.* -dzē). **1.** a short dramatic, musical, or other entertainment of light character introduced between the acts of a drama or opera. **2.** a short musical composition between main divisions of an extended musical work. **3.** an independent musical composition of similar character. [t. It., g. L *intermedius* between]

in·ter·mi·gra·tion (Ĭn′tər mĭ grā′shən), *n.* reciprocal migration; interchange of habitat by migrating bodies.

in·ter·mi·na·ble (Ĭn tûr′mə nə bəl), *adj.* **1.** that cannot be terminated; unending; endless: *interminable talk*. **2.** without termination; endless; having no limits or limitation: *interminable sufferings*. [ME, t. LL: m.s. *interminābilis*] —**in·ter′mi·na·bly**, *adv.*

in·ter·min·gle (Ĭn′tər mĬng′gəl), *v.t.*, *v.i.*, **-gled**, **-gling**. to mingle, one with another. —**in′ter·min′gle·ment**, *n.*

in·ter·mis·sion (Ĭn′tər mĬsh′ən), *n.* **1.** a period during which action temporarily ceases; an interval between periods of action or activity: *we smoked in the lobby during the intermission*. **2.** act of intermitting. **3.** state of being intermitted. [late ME, t. L: s. *intermissio*]

in·ter·mis·sive (Ĭn′tər mĬs′Ĭv), *adj.* **1.** characterized by intermission. **2.** intermittent.

in·ter·mit (Ĭn′tər mĬt′), *v.*, **-mitted**, **-mitting**. —*v.t.* **1.** to discontinue temporarily; suspend. —*v.i.* **2.** to stop or pause at intervals, or be intermittent. **3.** to cease or stop, or break off operations, for a time. [t. L: m.s. *intermittere* leave off, omit, leave an interval] —**in′ter·mit′ting·ly**, *adv.*

in·ter·mit·tent (Ĭn′tər mĬt′ənt), *adj.* **1.** that intermits, or ceases for a time: *an intermittent process*. **2.** alternately ceasing and beginning again: *an intermittent fever*. **3.** (of streams, lakes, or springs) recurrent; showing water only part of the time. —**in′ter·mit′tence**, **in′ter·mit′ten·cy**, *n.* —**in′ter·mit′tent·ly**, *adv.*

intermittent fever, a malarial fever in which feverish periods lasting a few hours alternate with periods in which the temperature is normal.

in·ter·mix (Ĭn′tər mĬks′), *v.t.*, *v.i.* to intermingle.

in·ter·mix·ture (Ĭn′tər mĬks′chər), *n.* **1.** act of intermixing. **2.** a mass of ingredients mixed together. **3.** something added by intermixing.

in·ter·mo·lec·u·lar (Ĭn′tər mə lĕk′yə lər, -mō-), *adj.* between molecules.

in·ter·mun·dane (Ĭn′tər mŭn′dān), *adj.* **1.** between worlds. **2.** between heavenly bodies.

in·tern[1] (*v.* Ĭn tûrn′; *n.* Ĭn′tûrn), *v.t.* **1.** to oblige to reside within prescribed limits under prohibition to leave them, as prisoners of war or enemy aliens, or as combatant troops who take refuge in a neutral country. **2.** to hold within a country until the termination of a war, as a vessel of a belligerent which has put into a neutral port and remained beyond a limited period allowed. —*n.* **3.** someone interned. [t. F: s. *interner*, ult. der. L *internus* internal]

in·tern[2] (Ĭn′tûrn), *n.* Also, **interne**. **1.** a resident member of the medical staff of a hospital, commonly a recent medical graduate acting as assistant. **2.** an inmate. —*v.i.* **3.** to be or perform the duties of an intern.

---

b., blend of, blended; c., cognate with; d., dialect, dialectal; der., derived from; f., formed from; g., going back to; m., modification of; r., replacing; s., stem of; t., taken from; ?, perhaps. See the full key on inside cover.

[t. F: m. *interne*, t. L: m. *internus* internal] —**in'-tern·ship'**, *n.*

in·tern³ (ĭn tûrn'), *adj.*, *n. Archaic.* internal. [t. L: s. *internus*]

in·ter·nal (ĭn tûr'nəl), *adj.* **1.** situated or existing in the interior of something; interior: *internal organs.* **2.** of or pertaining to the inside or inner part. **3.** to be taken inwardly: *internal stimulants.* **4.** existing, occurring, or found within the limits or scope of something. **5.** existing or occurring within a country; domestic: *internal affair.* **6.** pertaining to the domestic affairs of a country. **7.** *Brit. Educ.* pertaining to students in residence as distinguished from those who study by themselves and take examinations. **8.** being within or pertaining to the mind or soul; mental or spiritual; subjective. **9.** *Anat., Zool.* inner; not superficial; deepest; away from the surface or next to the axis of the body or of a part: *the internal carotid artery.* —*n.* **10.** (*pl.*) entrails. **11.** inner or intrinsic attribute. [t. ML: s. *internālis*, der. L *internus* inward] —**in·ter·nal/i·ty**, *n.* —**in·ter/nal·ly**, *adv.*

in·ter·nal-com·bus·tion (ĭn tûr'nəl kəm bŭs'chən), *adj.* of or pertaining to an internal-combustion engine.

internal-combustion engine, an engine of one or more working cylinders in which the process of combustion takes place within the cylinder.

internal medicine, the branch of medicine concerned with the diagnosis and cure of internal disorders.

internat., international.

in·ter·na·tion·al (ĭn'tər năsh'ən əl), *adj.* **1.** between or among nations: *an international armament race.* **2.** of or pertaining to different nations or their citizens: *a matter of international concern.* **3.** pertaining to the relations between nations: *international law.* **4.** (*cap.*) of or pertaining to any association known as an International. —*n.* **5.** (*cap.*) a socialistic association (in full, **International Workingmen's Association**) intended to unite the working classes of all countries in promoting their own interests and social and industrial reforms, by political means, formed in London in 1864, and dissolved in Philadelphia in 1876 (**First International**). **6.** (*cap.*) an international socialistic association formed in 1889, uniting socialistic groups or political parties of various countries, and holding international congresses from time to time (**Second International**). **7.** (*cap.*) an ultraradical and communistic association formed in Moscow, under Bolshevist auspices, in 1919 (dissolved, 1943), uniting communist groups of various countries and advocating the attainment of its ends by revolutionary or violent measures (**Third or Communist International**). **8.** (*cap.*) the Socialist organization formed in 1921 (**Vienna International,** often called the **Two-and-a-half International**). **9.** (*cap.*) the socialistic association formed in 1923 by the uniting of the Second International and the Vienna International at Hamburg and called in full the **Labor and Socialist International**. **10.** a loose federation of small ultraradical groups formed in 1936 (orig. under the leadership of Leon Trotsky), and hostile to the Soviet Union (sometimes called the **Fourth or Trotskyist International**). —**in'-ter·na/tion·al·i·ty**, *n.* —**in'·ter·na/tion·al·ly**, *adv.*

international candle. See **candle** (def. 3c).

international date line, date line (def. 2).

In·ter·na·tio·nale (ăɴ tĕr nä syô näl'), *n.* a revolutionary song, first sung in France in 1871 and since popular as a song of workers and Communists.

in·ter·na·tion·al·ism (ĭn'tər năsh'ən ə lĭz'əm), *n.* **1.** the principle of coöperation among nations, to promote their common good, sometimes as contrasted with nationalism, or devotion to the interests of a particular nation. **2.** international character, relations, coöperation, or control. **3.** (*cap.*) the principles or methods advocated by any association known as an International.

in·ter·na·tion·al·ist (ĭn'tər năsh'ən əl ĭst), *n.* **1.** an advocate of internationalism. **2.** one versed in international law and relations. **3.** (*cap.*) a member or adherent of an International.

in·ter·na·tion·al·ize (ĭn'tər năsh'ən ə līz'), *v.t.*, **-ized, -izing.** to make international; bring under international control. —**in'ter·na/tion·al·i·za/tion**, *n.*

International Labor Office, an organization formed in 1919, devoted to standardizing international labor practices and including representatives of government, management, and labor.

international law, the body of rules which civilized nations recognize as binding them in their conduct towards one another.

international nautical mile. See **mile** (def. 1c). Also, **international air mile.**

in·terne (ĭn'tûrn), *n.* intern².

in·ter·ne·cine (ĭn'tər nē'sīn, -sĭn), *adj.* **1.** mutually destructive: *an internecine duel.* **2.** characterized by great slaughter: *internecine war.* [t. L: m. s. *internecīnus*, der. *internecium* slaughter]

in·tern·ee (ĭn'tûr nē'), *n.* one who is or has been interned, as a prisoner of war.

in·tern·ment (ĭn tûrn'mənt), *n.* **1.** act of interning. **2.** state or condition of being interned; confinement, as of prisoners of war.

internment camp, (during wartime) a military camp for the confinement of enemy aliens, prisoners of war, etc.

in·ter·node (ĭn'tər nōd'), *n.* a part or space between two nodes, knots, or joints, as the portion of a plant stem between two nodes. —**in'ter·nod/al**, *adj.*

in·ter nos (ĭn'tər nōs'), *Latin.* between or among ourselves.

in·ter·nun·cial (ĭn'tər nŭn'shəl), *adj. Anat.* (of a nerve cell or a chain of nerve cells) linking the incoming and outgoing nerve fibers of the nervous system.

in·ter·nun·ci·o (ĭn'tər nŭn'shĭ ō'), *n., pl.* **-cios.** a papal ambassador ranking next below a nuncio. [t. It., t. L: m. *internuntius*]

in·ter·o·ce·an·ic (ĭn'tər ō'shĭ ăn'ĭk), *adj.* between oceans: *an interoceanic canal.*

in·ter·o·cep·tive (ĭn'tər ō sĕp'tĭv), *adj. Physiol.* pertaining to interoceptors, the stimuli impinging upon them, and the nerve impulses initiated by them.

in·ter·o·cep·tor (ĭn'tər ō sĕp'tər), *n.* a nerve ending or sense organ responding to stimuli originating from within the body. [f. *intero-* inside (NL comb. form modeled on *extero-* outside) + *-ceptor.* See RECEPTOR]

in·ter·os·cu·late (ĭn'tər ŏs'kyə lāt'), *v.i.*, **-lated, -lating. 1.** to inosculate one with another; interpenetrate. **2.** to form a connecting link between objects, species, or the like. —**in'ter·os/cu·la/tion**, *n.*

in·ter·pel·lant (ĭn'tər pĕl'ənt), *n.* one who interpellates. [t. F, ppr. of *interpeller*, t. L: m. *interpellāre* interrupt in speaking]

in·ter·pel·late (ĭn'tər pĕl'āt, ĭn tûr'pə lāt'), *v.t.*, **-lated, -lating.** to call formally upon (a minister or member of the government) in interpellation. [t. L: m. s. *interpellātus*, pp., interrupted in speaking] —**in·ter·pel·la·tor** (ĭn'tər pəlā'tər, ĭn tûr'pəlā'tər), *n.*

in·ter·pel·la·tion (ĭn'tər pə lā'shən, ĭn tûr'pə-), *n.* a procedure in some legislative bodies (as in France) of calling upon a member of the government to explain some official act or policy, usually leading in parliamentary government to a vote of confidence. [t. L: s. *interpellātio* interruption]

in·ter·pen·e·trate (ĭn'tər pĕn'ə trāt'), *v.*, **-trated, -trating.** —*v.t.* **1.** to penetrate thoroughly; permeate. **2.** to penetrate reciprocally. —*v.i.* **3.** to penetrate between things or parts. **4.** to penetrate each other. —**in'-ter·pen'e·tra/tion**, *n.* —**in·ter·pen'e·tra/tive**, *adj.*

in·ter·phone (ĭn'tər fōn'), *n.* a telephone connecting offices, stations, departments, etc., as in a building or ship.

in·ter·plan·e·tar·y (ĭn'tər plăn'ə tĕr'ĭ), *adj. Astron.* situated within the solar system, but not within the atmosphere of the sun or any planet.

in·ter·play (*n.* ĭn'tər plā'; *v.* ĭn'tər plā'), *n.* **1.** reciprocal play, action, or influence: *the interplay of plot and character.* —*v.i.* **2.** to exert influence on each other.

in·ter·plead (ĭn'tər plēd'), *v.i. Law.* to litigate with each other in order to determine which is the rightful claimant against a third party.

in·ter·plead·er (ĭn'tər plē'dər), *n. Law.* **1.** a proceeding by which two parties making the same claim against a third party determine judicially which is the rightful claimant. **2.** a party who interpleads.

in·ter·po·late (ĭn tûr'pə lāt'), *v.*, **-lated, -lating.** —*v.t.* **1.** to alter (a text, etc.) by the insertion of new matter, esp. deceptively or without authorization. **2.** to insert (new or spurious matter) thus. **3.** to introduce (something additional or extraneous) between other things or parts; interject; interpose; intercalate. **4.** *Math.* to insert or find intermediate terms in (a sequence). —*v.i.* **5.** to make interpolations. [t. L: m.s. *interpolātus*, pp. furbished, altered, falsified] —**in·ter/po·lat/er, in·ter/po·la/tor**, *n.* —**in·ter/po·la/tive**, *adj.*

in·ter·po·la·tion (ĭn tûr'pə lā'shən), *n.* **1.** act of interpolating. **2.** the fact of being interpolated. **3.** something interpolated, as a passage introduced into a text.

in·ter·pose (ĭn'tər pōz'), *v.*, **-posed, -posing.** —*v.t.* **1.** to place between; cause to intervene: *to interpose an opaque body between a light and the eye.* **2.** to put (a barrier, obstacle, etc.) between, or in the way. **3.** to bring (influence, action, etc.) to bear between parties, or in behalf of a party or person. **4.** to put in (a remark, etc.) in the midst of a conversation, discourse, or the like. —*v.i.* **5.** to come between other things; assume an intervening position or relation. **6.** to step in between parties at variance; mediate. **7.** to put in or make a remark by way of interruption. [t. F: m.s. *interposer.* See INTER-, POSE¹] —**in·ter/pos/er**, *n.* —**in'ter·pos/ing·ly**, *adv.* —**in·ter·po·si·tion** (ĭn'tər pə zĭsh'ən), **in/·ter·pos'al**, *n.*

in·ter·pret (ĭn tûr'prĭt), *v.t.* **1.** to set forth the meaning of; explain or elucidate: *to interpret omens.* **2.** to explain, construe, or understand in a particular way: *to interpret a reply as favorable.* **3.** to bring out the meaning of (a dramatic work, music, etc.) by performance or execution. **4.** to translate. —*v.i.* **5.** to translate what is said in a foreign language. **6.** to give an explanation. [ME *interprete*(*n*), t. L: m. *interpretārī* explain] —**in·ter/pret·a·ble**, *adj.* —**in·ter/pret·a·bil/i·ty**, *n.* —**in·ter/pret·er**, *n.* —**in·ter/pre·tive, -pre·tive**, *adj.* —**in·ter/pre·tive·ly**, *adv.* —**Syn. 1.** See **explain**.

in·ter·pre·ta·tion (ĭn tûr/prə tā'shən), *n.* **1.** act of interpreting; elucidation: *the interpretation of nature.* **2.** an explanation given: *to put a wrong interpretation on a passage.* **3.** a construction placed upon something: *a charitable interpretation.* **4.** a way of interpreting. **5.** the rendering of a dramatic part, music, etc., so as to bring out the meaning, or to indicate one's particular conception of it. **6.** translation. [ME, t. L: s. *interpretātio*] —**in·ter/pre·ta/tion·al**, *adj.*

in·ter·pre·ta·tive (ĭn tûr′prə tā′tĭv), *adj.* **1.** serving to interpret; explanatory. **2.** deduced by interpretation. —**in·ter′pre·ta·tive·ly**, *adv.*

in·ter·ra·cial (ĭn′tər rā′shəl), *adj.* **1.** existing or taking place between races, or members of different races. **2.** of, for, or pertaining to persons of different races: *interracial camps for children.*

in·ter·ra·di·al (ĭn′tər rā′dĭ əl), *adj.* situated between the radii or rays: *the interradial petals in an echinoderm.*

in·ter·reg·num (ĭn′tər rĕg′nəm), *n., pl.* **-nums, -na** (-nə). **1.** an interval of time between the close of a sovereign's reign and the accession of his normal or legitimate successor. **2.** any period during which a state has no ruler or only a temporary executive. **3.** any pause or interruption in continuity. [t. L, f. *inter-* INTER- + *regnum* REIGN] —**in′ter·reg′nal,** *adj.*

in·ter·re·late (ĭn′tər rĭ lāt′), *v.t.,* **-lated, -lating.** to bring into reciprocal relation.

in·ter·re·lat·ed (ĭn′tər rĭ lā′tĭd), *adj.* reciprocally related: *the interrelated sets of wires.*

in·ter·re·la·tion (ĭn′tər rĭ lā′shən), *n.* reciprocal relation. —**in′ter·re·la′tion·ship′,** *n.*

in·ter·rex (ĭn′tər rĕks′), *n., pl.* **interreges** (ĭn′tər rē′jēz). a person holding supreme authority in a state during an interregnum. [t. L, f. *inter-* INTER- + *rex* king]

interrog., **1.** interrogation. **2.** interrogative.

in·ter·ro·gate (ĭn tĕr′ə gāt′), *v.,* **-gated, -gating.** —*v.t.* **1.** to ask a question or a series of questions of (a person). **2.** to examine by questions; question: *they were interrogated by the police.* —*v.i.* **3.** to ask questions. [late ME, t. L: m. s. *interrogātus,* pp.] —**in·ter′ro·gat′·ing·ly,** *adv.* —**in·ter′ro·ga′tor,** *n.*

in·ter·ro·ga·tion (ĭn tĕr′ə gā′shən), *n.* **1.** act of interrogating; questioning. **2.** a question. **3.** an interrogation point. —**in·ter′ro·ga′tion·al,** *adj.*

interrogation point, question mark. Also, **interrogation mark.**

in·ter·rog·a·tive (ĭn′tə rŏg′ə tĭv), *adj.* **1.** pertaining to or conveying a question. **2.** *Gram.* (of an element or construction) forming or constituting a question: *an interrogative pronoun, an interrogative sentence.* —*n.* **3.** *Gram.* an interrogative word, element, or construction, as "*who?*" and "*what?*" —**in′ter·rog′a·tive·ly,** *adv.*

in·ter·rog·a·to·ry (ĭn′tə rŏg′ə tôr′ĭ), *adj., n., pl.* **-tories.** —*adj.* **1.** interrogative; questioning. —*n.* **2.** a question or inquiry. **3.** *Law.* a formal or written question. —**in′ter·rog′a·to′ri·ly,** *adv.*

in ter·ro·rem clause (ĭn tĕ rôr′ĕm), *Law.* a clause in a will stating that a beneficiary who starts a will contest shall lose his legacy.

in·ter·rupt (ĭn′tə rŭpt′), *v.t.* **1.** to make a break in (an otherwise continuous extent, course, process, condition, etc.). **2.** to break off or cause to cease, as in the midst or course: *he interrupted his work to answer the bell.* **3.** to stop (a person) in the midst of doing or saying something, esp. as by an interjected remark: *I don't want to be interrupted.* —*v.i.* **4.** to cause a break or discontinuance; interrupt action or speech: *please don't interrupt.* [ME *interrupte(n),* t. L: m. s. *interruptus,* pp., broken apart] —**in′ter·rup′tive,** *adj.* —**Syn. 1, 3.** INTERRUPT, DISCONTINUE, SUSPEND imply breaking off something temporarily or permanently. INTERRUPT may have either meaning: *to interrupt a meeting.* To DISCONTINUE is to stop or leave off, often permanently: *to discontinue a building program.* To SUSPEND is to break off relations, operations, proceedings, privileges, etc. for a longer or shorter period, usually intending to resume at a stated time: *to suspend operations during a strike.*

interrupted screw, a screw with a discontinuous helix, as in a cannon breech, formed by cutting away part or parts of the thread, sometimes with part of the shaft beneath, used with a lock nut having corresponding male sections.

in·ter·rupt·er (ĭn′tə rŭp′tər), *n.* **1.** one who or that which interrupts. **2.** *Elect.* a device for interrupting or periodically making and breaking a circuit. Also, **in′ter·rup′tor.**

in·ter·rup·tion (ĭn′tə rŭp′shən), *n.* **1.** act of interrupting. **2.** state of being interrupted: *serious interruption of trading.* **3.** something that interrupts. **4.** cessation; intermission.

in·ter·scap·u·lar (ĭn′tər skăp′yə lər), *adj. Anat., Zool.* between the scapulae or shoulder blades.

in·ter·scho·las·tic (ĭn′tər skə lăs′tĭk), *adj.* between elementary or secondary schools: *interscholastic football.*

in·ter se (ĭn′tər sē′), *Latin.* **1.** among or between themselves. **2.** (in livestock breeding) mating animals similarly bred to each other.

in·ter·sect (ĭn′tər sĕkt′), *v.t.* **1.** to cut or divide by passing through or lying across: *one road intersects another.* —*v.i.* **2.** to cross, as lines. **3.** *Geom.* to have, as two geometrical loci, one or more points in common: *intersecting lines.* [t. L: s. *intersectus,* pp., cut off]

in·ter·sec·tion (ĭn′tər sĕk′shən), *n.* act, fact, or place of intersecting. —**in′ter·sec′tion·al,** *adj.*

in·ter·sep·tal (ĭn′tər sĕp′təl), *adj.* between septa.

in·ter·sex (ĭn′tər sĕks′), *n. Biol.* an individual displaying characteristics of both the male and female sexes of the species.

in·ter·si·de·re·al (ĭn′tər sī dĭr′ĭ əl), *adj.* interstellar.

in·ter·space (*n.* ĭn′tər spās′; *v.* ĭn′tər spās′), *n., v.,* **-spaced, -spacing.** —*n.* **1.** a space between things. **2.** an intervening interval of time. —*v.t.* **3.** to put a

space between. **4.** to occupy or fill the space between. —**in′ter·spa′tial,** *adj.*

in·ter·sperse (ĭn′tər spûrs′), *v.t.,* **-spersed, -spersing. 1.** to scatter here and there among other things: *to intersperse flowers among shrubs.* **2.** to diversify with something scattered or introduced here and there: *his speech was interspersed with long and boring quotations from the poets.* [t. L: m.s. *interspersus* strewn] —**in·ter·sper·sion** (ĭn′tər spûr′shən, -zhən), *n.*

in·ter·state (ĭn′tər stāt′), *adj.* between or jointly involving states: *interstate commerce.* Cf. **intrastate.**

in·ter·stel·lar (ĭn′tər stĕl′ər), *adj.* among the stars; intersidereal: *interstellar space.*

in·ter·stice (ĭn tûr′stĭs), *n.* **1.** an intervening space. **2.** a small or narrow space between things or parts; small chink, crevice, or opening. **3.** *Rare.* an interval of time. [t. L: m. s. *interstitium* space between]

in·ter·sti·tial (ĭn′tər stĭsh′əl), *adj.* **1.** pertaining to, situated in, or forming interstices. **2.** *Anat.* situated between the cellular elements of a structure or part: *interstitial tissue.* —**in·ter·sti′tial·ly,** *adv.*

in·ter·strat·i·fy (ĭn′tər străt′ə fī′), *v.,* **-fied, -fying.** —*v.i.* **1.** to lie in interposed or alternate strata. —*v.t.* **2.** to interlay with or interpose between other strata. **3.** to arrange in alternate strata. —**in′ter·strat′i·fi·ca′tion,** *n.*

in·ter·tex·ture (ĭn′tər tĕks′chər), *n.* **1.** act of interweaving. **2.** the condition of being interwoven. **3.** something formed by interweaving.

in·ter·trib·al (ĭn′tər trī′bəl), *adj.* between tribes: *intertribal warfare.*

in·ter·trop·i·cal (ĭn′tər trŏp′ə kəl), *adj. Geog.* between the tropics (of Cancer and Capricorn).

in·ter·twine (ĭn′tər twīn′), *v.t., v.i.,* **-twined, -twining.** to twine together. —**in′ter·twine′ment,** *n.* —**in′ter·twin′ing·ly,** *adv.*

in·ter·twist (ĭn′tər twĭst′), *v.t., v.i.* to twist together. —**in′ter·twist′ing·ly,** *adv.*

in·ter·ur·ban (ĭn′tər ûr′bən), *adj.* **1.** between cities. —*n.* **2.** an interurban train or car.

in·ter·val (ĭn′tər vəl), *n.* **1.** an intervening period of time: *an interval of fifty years.* **2.** a period of cessation; a pause: *intervals between attacks.* **3.** *Brit. Theat.* an intermission. **4.** a space intervening between things, points, limits, qualities, etc.: *an interval of ten feet between columns.* **5. at intervals,** at particular times or places with gaps in between. **6.** the space between soldiers or units in military formation. **7.** *Music.* the difference in pitch between two tones, as, **a. harmonic interval,** an interval between two tones sounded simultaneously. **b. melodic interval,** an interval between two tones sounded successively. **8.** *U.S. and Canada.* intervale. [ME *intervall,* t. L: s. *intervallum*]

in·ter·vale (ĭn′tər vāl′), *n. U.S. and Canada.* a low-lying tract of land, as along a river, between hills, etc. [var. of INTERVAL, assoc. with VALE¹]

in·ter·vene (ĭn′tər vēn′), *v.i.,* **-vened, -vening. 1.** to come between in action; intercede: *to intervene in a dispute.* **2.** to come or be between, as in place, time, or a series. **3.** to fall or happen between other events or periods: *nothing interesting has intervened.* **4.** (of things) to occur incidentally so as to modify a result. **5.** to come in, as something not belonging. **6.** *Law.* to interpose and become a party to a suit pending between other parties. [t. L: m. s. *intervenīre* come between] —**in′ter·ven′er,** *n.*

in·ter·ven·ient (ĭn′tər vēn′yənt), *adj.* **1.** intervening, as in place, time, order, or action. **2.** incidental.

in·ter·ven·tion (ĭn′tər vĕn′shən), *n.* **1.** act or fact of intervening. **2.** the interposition or interference of one state in the affairs of another: *intervention in the domestic policies of smaller nations.* —**in′ter·ven′tion·al,** *adj.*

in·ter·ven·tion·ist (ĭn′tər vĕn′shən ĭst), *n.* one who favors intervention, as in the affairs of another state.

in·ter·view (ĭn′tər vū′), *n.* **1.** the conversation of a writer or reporter with a person or persons from whom material for a news or feature story or other writing is sought. **2.** the report of such conversation. **3.** a meeting of persons face to face, esp. for formal conference. —*v.t.* **4.** to have an interview with: *to interview the president.* [t. F: m. *intervue,* for. *entrevoir,* refl., see (each other), f. *entre-* INTER- + *voir* (g. L *vidēre*) see] —**in′ter·view′er,** *n.*

in·ter·volve (ĭn′tər vŏlv′), *v.t., v.i.,* **-volved, -volving.** to roll, wind, or involve, one within another. [f. INTER- + m.s. L *volvere* roll]

in·ter·weave (ĭn′tər wēv′), *v.,* **-wove or -weaved; -woven or -wove or -weaved; -weaving.** —*v.t.* **1.** to weave together, one with another, as threads, strands, branches, roots, etc. **2.** to intermingle or combine as if by weaving: *to interweave truth with fiction.* —*v.i.* **3.** to become woven together, interlaced, or intermingled. —**in′ter·weave′ment,** *n.* —**in′ter·weav′er,** *n.*

in·tes·ta·cy (ĭn tĕs′tə sĭ), *n.* state or fact of being intestate at death.

in·tes·tate (ĭn tĕs′tāt, -tĭt), *adj.* **1.** dying without having made a will. **2.** not disposed of by will; not legally devised or bequeathed. —*n.* **3.** one who dies intestate. [ME, t. L: m. s. *intestātus* having made no will]

in·tes·ti·nal (ĭn tĕs′tə nəl; *Brit.* ĭn′tĕs tī′nəl), *adj.* **1.** of or pertaining to the intestine. **2.** occurring or found in the intestine. [t. ML: s. *intestīnālis*] —**in·tes′ti·nal·ly,** *adv.*

in·tes·tine (ĭntĕs′tĭn), *n. Anat.* **1.** the lower part of the alimentary canal, extending from the pylorus to the anus. **2.** a definite portion of this part. The **small intestine** comprises the duodenum, jejunum, and ileum; the **large intestine** comprises the caecum, colon, and rectum. —*adj.* **3.** internal; domestic; civil: *intestine strife.* [t. L: m. s. *intestīna*, pl., entrails]

in·thral(ĭnthrôl′),*v.t.*,-**thralled**, -**thralling.** inthrall.

in·thrall (ĭn thrôl′), *v.t.* enthrall.

in·throne (ĭn thrōn′), *v.t.*, -**throned**, -**throning.** enthrone.

in·ti·ma (ĭn′tə mə), *n., pl.* -**mae** (-mē′). *Anat.* the innermost membrane or lining of some organ or part, esp. that of an artery, vein, or lymphatic. [t. NL, prop. fem. of L *intimus* inmost]

in·ti·ma·cy (ĭn′tə mə sĭ), *n., pl.* -**cies. 1.** state of being intimate; intimate association or friendship. **2.** an instance of this. **3.** illicit sexual relations.

in·ti·mate[1] (ĭn′tə mĭt), *adj.* **1.** associated in close personal relations: *an intimate friend.* **2.** characterized by or involving personally close or familiar association: *an intimate gathering.* **3.** private; closely personal: *one's intimate affairs.* **4.** maintaining illicit sexual relations. **5.** (of acquaintance, knowledge, etc.) arising from close personal connection or familiar experience. **6.** detailed; deep: *a more intimate analysis.* **7.** close union or combination of particles or elements: *an intimate mixture.* **8.** inmost; deep within. **9.** pertaining to the inmost or essential nature; intrinsic: *the intimate structure of an organism.* **10.** pertaining to or existing in the inmost mind: *intimate beliefs.* —*n.* **11.** an intimate friend or associate. [in form t. LL: m. s. *intimātus*, pp., put or pressed into, but with sense of L *intimus* inmost] —**in′ti·mate·ly**, *adv.* —**in′ti·mate·ness**, *n.* —**Syn. 1.** See familiar.

in·ti·mate[2] (ĭn′tə māt′), *v.t.*, -**mated**, -**mating. 1.** to make known indirectly; hint; suggest. **2.** *Rare.* to make known, esp. formally; announce. [t. LL: m.s. *intimātus*, pp., put or pressed into, announced] —**in′ti·ma′tion**, *n.* —**Syn. 1.** See hint.

in·tim·i·date (ĭn tĭm′ə dāt′), *v.t.*, -**dated**, -**dating. 1.** to make timid, or inspire with fear; overawe; cow. **2.** to force into or deter from some action by inducing fear: *to intimidate a voter.* [t. ML: m. s. *intimidatus*, pp., made afraid. See TIMID] —**in·tim′i·da′tion**, *n.* —**in·tim′i·da′tor**, *n.* —**Syn. 2.** See discourage.

in·tinc·tion (ĭn tĭngk′shən), *n.* (in the Eucharistic service) act of steeping the bread in the wine, to enable the communicants to receive the two conjointly. [t. LL: s. *intinctio*, der. L *intingere* dip in]

in·ti·tle (ĭn tī′təl), *v.t.*, -**tled**, -**tling.** entitle.

in·tit·ule (ĭn tĭt′ūl), *v.t.*, -**uled**, -**uling.** *Archaic.* to give a title to; entitle. [t. LL: m.s. *intitulāre*, der. L *in-* IN-[2] + *titulus* TITLE] —**in·tit′u·la′tion**, *n.*

in·to (ĭn′tōō; *unstressed* ĭn′tŏŏ, -tə), *prep.* **1.** in to; in and to (expressing motion or direction toward the inner part of a place or thing, and hence entrance or inclusion within limits, or change to new circumstances, relations, condition, form, etc.). **2.** *Math.* by: with *divide* (formerly, sometimes, *multiply*) implied. [ME *in to*]

in·toed (ĭn′tōd′), *adj.* having inwardly turned toes.

in·tol·er·a·ble (ĭn tŏl′ər ə bəl), *adj.* **1.** not tolerable; unendurable; insufferable: *intolerable agony.* —*adv.* **2.** *Obs.* exceedingly. —**in·tol′er·a·bil′i·ty, in·tol′er·a·ble·ness**, *n.* —**in·tol′er·a·bly**, *adv.* —**Syn. 1.** unbearable.

in·tol·er·ance (ĭn tŏl′ər əns), *n.* **1.** lack of toleration; indisposition to tolerate contrary opinions or beliefs. **2.** incapacity or indisposition to bear or endure: *intolerance of heat.* **3.** an intolerant act.

in·tol·er·ant (ĭn tŏl′ər ənt), *adj.* **1.** not tolerating contrary opinions, esp. in religious matters; bigoted: *an intolerant zealot.* **2.** unable or indisposed to tolerate or endure (fol. by *of*): *intolerant of excesses.* —*n.* **3.** one who does not favor toleration. —**in·tol′er·ant·ly**, *adv.*

—**Syn. 1.** INTOLERANT, FANATICAL, BIGOTED refer to strongly illiberal attitudes. INTOLERANT implies active (often violent) refusal to allow others to have or put into practice beliefs different from one's own: *intolerant in politics.* To be BIGOTED is to be so strongly attached to one's own belief as to be hostile to all others: *a bigoted person.* FANATICAL applies to unreasonable, often violent, action in maintaining one's beliefs and (often religious) practices: *a fanatical religious sect.* —**Ant.** liberal.

in·tomb (ĭn tōōm′), *v.t.* entomb. —**in·tomb′ment**, *n.*

in·to·nate (ĭn′tō nāt′), *v.t.*, -**nated**, -**nating. 1.** to utter with a particular tone or modulation of voice. **2.** to intone or chant. [t. ML: m.s. *intonātus*, pp.]

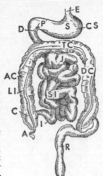

Human intestines
E, End of esophagus; CS, Cardiac end of stomach; S, Stomach; P, Pylorus; D, Duodenum; J, Jejunum: SI, Small intestine; I, Ileum; LI, Large intestine; C, Caecum; A, Vermiform appendix; AC, Ascending colon; TC, Transverse colon; DC, Descending colon, R; Rectum

in·to·na·tion (ĭn′tō nā′shən), *n.* **1.** the pattern or melody of pitch changes revealed in connected speech; esp., the pitch pattern of a sentence, which distinguishes kinds of sentences and speakers of different nationalities. **2.** act of intonating. **3.** the manner of producing musical tones, specifically the relation in pitch of tones to their key or harmony. **4.** the opening phrase in a Gregorian chant, usually sung by but one or two voices.

in·tone (ĭn tōn′), *v.*, -**toned**, -**toning.** —*v.t.* **1.** to utter with a particular tone; intonate. **2.** to give tone or variety of tone to; vocalize. **3.** to utter in a singing voice (the first tones of a section in a liturgical service). **4.** to recite in monotone. —*v.i.* **5.** to speak or recite in a singing voice, esp. in monotone. **6.** *Music.* to produce a tone, or a particular series of tones, like a scale, esp. with the voice; sing or chant. [late ME, t. ML: m.s. *intonāre.* Cf. INTONATE] —**in·ton′er**, *n.*

in·tor·sion (ĭn tôr′shən), *n.* a twisting or winding, as of the stem of a plant.

in·tort (ĭn tôrt′), *v.t.* to twist inward, curl, or wind: *intorted horns.* [t. L: s. *intortus*, pp.]

in to·to (ĭn tō′tō), *Latin.* in all; in the whole; wholly.

in·tox·i·cant (ĭn tŏk′sə kənt), *adj.* **1.** intoxicating. —*n.* **2.** an intoxicating agent, as liquor or certain drugs.

in·tox·i·cate (*v.* ĭn tŏk′sə kāt′; *adj.* ĭn tŏk′sə kĭt, -kāt′), *v.*, -**cated**, -**cating**, *adj.* —*v.t.* **1.** to affect temporarily with loss of control over the physical and mental powers, by means of alcoholic liquor, a drug, or other substance. **2.** to excite mentally beyond self-control or reason. **3.** *Obs.* to poison. —*v.i.* **4.** to cause or produce intoxication: *an intoxicating liquor.* —*adj.* **5.** *Archaic.* intoxicated. [ME, t. ML: m. s. *intoxicātus*, pp., poisoned. See TOXIC] —**in·tox′i·cat′ing·ly**, *adv.* —**in·tox′i·ca′tive**, *adj.*

in·tox·i·cat·ed (ĭn tŏk′sə kā′tĭd), *adj.* **1.** drunk. **2.** excited mentally beyond reason or self-control.

in·tox·i·ca·tion (ĭn tŏk′sə kā′shən), *n.* **1.** inebriation; drunkenness. **2.** *Pathol.* poisoning. **3.** act of intoxicating. **4.** overpowering action or effect upon the mind.

intr., intransitive.

intra-, a prefix meaning "within," freely used as an English formative, esp. in scientific terms, sometimes in opposition to *extra-*. Cf. **intro-**. [t. L, repr. *intrā*, adv. and prep., within, akin to *interior* inner, and *inter* between]

in·tra·car·di·ac (ĭn′trə kär′dĭ ăk′), *adj.* endocardial.

in·tra·cel·lu·lar (ĭn′trə sĕl′yə lər), *adj.* within a cell or cells.

in·tra·cra·ni·al (ĭn′trə krā′nĭ əl), *adj.* within the cranium or skull.

in·trac·ta·ble (ĭn trăk′tə bəl), *adj.* **1.** not docile; stubborn: *an intractable disposition.* **2.** (of things) hard to deal with; unmanageable. —**in·trac′ta·bil′i·ty, in·trac′ta·ble·ness**, *n.* —**in·trac′ta·bly**, *adv.*

in·tra·dos (ĭn trā′dŏs), *n. Archit.* the interior curve or surface of an arch or vault. Cf. **extrados.** See diag. under **arch.** [t. F, f. L *intra-* INTRA- + F *dos* (g. L *dorsum* back)]

in·tra·mo·lec·u·lar (ĭn′trə mə lĕk′yə lər, -mō-), *adj.* within the molecule or molecules.

in·tra·mu·ral (ĭn′trə myŏŏr′əl), *adj.* **1.** engaged in or pertaining to a single college, or its students: *intramural athletics.* **2.** within the walls or enclosing limits, as of a city or a building. **3.** *Anat.* within the substance of a wall, as of an organ.

in·tra mu·ros (ĭn′trə myŏŏr′ōs), *Latin.* within the walls, as of a city.

in·tra·mus·cu·lar (ĭn′trə mŭs′kyə lər), *adj.* located or occurring within a muscle.

intrans., intransitive.

in·tran·si·gent (ĭn trăn′sə jənt), *adj.* **1.** uncompromising, esp. in politics; irreconcilable. —*n.* **2.** one who is irreconcilable, esp. in politics. Also, *French,* **in·tran·si·geant** (ăn trän zē zhän′). [t. F: m. *intransigeant*, t. Sp., der. (los) *intransigentes* revolutionary party refusing compromise, f. L: *in-* IN-[3] + *transigentēs*, ppr. pl. coming to an agreement] —**in·tran′si·gence, in·tran′si·gen·cy**, *n.* —**in·tran′si·gent·ly**, *adv.*

in·tran·si·tive (ĭn trăn′sə tĭv), *adj.* **1.** having the quality of an intransitive verb. —*n.* **2.** an intransitive verb. —**in·tran′si·tive·ly**, *adv.*

intransitive verb, a verb that is never accompanied by a direct object, as *come, sit, lie,* etc.

in tran·si·tu (ĭn trăn′sə tū′, -tōō′), *Latin.* in transit; on the way.

in·trant (ĭn′trənt), *n.* one who enters (esp. a college, association, etc.); entrant. [t. L: s. *intrans*, ppr., entering]

in·tra·state (ĭn′trə stāt′), *adj.* within a state, esp. one of the United States: *intrastate commerce.*

in·tra·tel·lu·ric (ĭn′trə tə lŏŏr′ĭk), *adj.* **1.** *Geol.* located in, taking place in, or resulting from action, beneath the lithosphere. **2.** *Petrog.* designating the period of crystallization of an eruptive rock which precedes its extrusion on the surface or the crystals in a porphyritic lava formed prior to its extrusion.

in·tra·ve·nous (ĭn′trə vē′nəs), *adj.* **1.** within a vein or the veins. **2.** noting or pertaining to an injection into a vein. —**in′tra·ve′nous·ly**, *adv.*

in·treat (ĭn trēt′), *v.t.*, *v.i.* entreat.

in·trench (ĭn trĕnch′), *v.t.*, *v.i.* entrench. —**in·trench′er**, *n.* —**in·trench′ment**, *n.*

in·trep·id (Ĭn trĕp′ĭd), *adj.* fearless; dauntless: *intrepid courage.* [t. L: s. *intrepidus* not alarmed] —**in′-trep·id′i·ty**, *n.* —**in·trep′id·ly**, *adv.*

in·tri·ca·cy (Ĭn′trə kə sĭ), *n.., pl.* **-cies.** 1. intricate character or state. 2. an intricate part, action, etc.

in·tri·cate (Ĭn′trə kĭt), *adj.* 1. perplexingly entangled or involved: *a maze of intricate paths.* 2. confusingly complex; complicated; hard to understand: *an intricate machine.* [late ME, t. L: m. s. *intrīcātus*, pp., entangled] —**in′tri·cate·ly**, *adv.* —**in′tri·cate·ness**, *n.*

in·tri·gant (Ĭn′trə gənt; *Fr.* ăn trē gän′), *n., pl.* **-gants** (-gənts; *Fr.* -gän′). ore who carries on intrigue. Also, **in′tri·guant.** [t. F, t. It.: m. *intrigante*, ppr. of *intrigare.* See INTRIGUE, v.]

in·tri·gante (Ĭn′trə gänt′, -gänt′; *Fr.* ăn trē gänt′), *n., pl.* **-gantes** (-gänts′, -gänts′; *Fr.* gänt′). a woman intrigant.

in·trigue (*v.* Ĭn trēg′; *n.* Ĭn trēg′, Ĭn′trēg), *v.*, **-trigued**, **-triguing**, *n.* —*v.t.* 1. to excite the curiosity or interest of by puzzling, novel, or otherwise arresting qualities. 2. to take the fancy of: *her hat intrigued me.* 3. to beguile by appeal to the curiosity, interest, or fancy (fol. by *into*). 4. to puzzle: *I am intrigued by this event.* 5. to bring or force by underhand machinations. 6. *Now Rare.* to entangle. 7. *Obs.* to trick or cheat. 8. *Obs.* to plot for. —*v.i.* 9. to use underhand machinations; plot craftily. 10. to carry on a clandestine or illicit love affair. —*n.* 11. the use of underhand machinations to accomplish designs. 12. a plot or crafty dealing: *political intrigues.* 13. a clandestine or illicit love affair. 14. the series of complications forming the plot of a play. [t. F: s. *intriguer*, t. It.: m. *intrigare*, g. L *intrīcāre* entangle, perplex] —**in·tri′guer**, *n.* —**in·tri′-guing·ly**, *adv.*

in·trin·sic (Ĭn trĭn′sĭk), *adj.* 1. belonging to a thing by its very nature: *intrinsic merit.* 2. *Anat.* (of certain muscles, nerves, etc.) belonging to or lying within a given part. Also, **in·trin′si·cal.** [t. ML: m.s. *intrinsecus* inward (L inwardly)] —**in·trin′si·cal·ly**, *adv.* —**Syn.** 1. See **essential.** —**Ant.** 1, accidental.

intro-, a prefix meaning "inwardly," "within," occasionally used as an English formative. Cf. **intra-**. [t. L, repr. *intro*, adv., inwardly, within]

intro., 1. introduction. 2. introductory. Also, **introd.**

in·tro·duce (Ĭn′trə dūs′, -dōōs′), *v.t.*, **-duced**, **-ducing.** 1. to bring into notice, knowledge, use, vogue, etc.: *to introduce a fashion.* 2. to bring forward for consideration, as a proposed legislative bill, etc. 3. to bring forward with preliminary or preparatory matter: *to introduce a subject with a long preface.* 4. to bring (a person) to the knowledge or experience of something (fol. by *to*): *to introduce a person to chess.* 5. to lead, bring, or put into a place, position, surroundings, relations, etc.: *to introduce a figure into a design.* 6. to bring (a person) into the acquaintance of another: *he introduced his sister to us.* 7. to present formally, as to a person, an audience, or society: *she was introduced at court.* [late ME, t. L: m.s. *intrōdūcere* lead in] —**in′tro·duc′er**, *n.* —**in′tro·duc′i·ble**, *adj.*

—**Syn.** 6, 7. INTRODUCE, PRESENT mean to bring persons into personal acquaintance with each other, as by announcement of names, and the like. INTRODUCE is the ordinary term, referring to making persons acquainted who are ostensibly equals: *to introduce a friend to one's sister.* PRESENT, a more formal term, suggests a degree of ceremony in the process, and implies (if only as a matter of compliment) superior dignity, rank, or importance in the person to whom another is presented: *to present a visitor to the president.*

in·tro·duc·tion (Ĭn′trə dŭk′shən), *n.* 1. act of introducing. 2. a formal presentation of one person to another or others. 3. something introduced. 4. a preliminary part, as of a book, musical composition or the like, leading up to the main part. 5. an elementary treatise: *an introduction to botany.* [ME, t. L: s. *intrōductio*]

—**Syn.** 4. INTRODUCTION, FOREWORD, PREFACE refer to material given at the front of a book to explain or introduce it to the reader. An INTRODUCTION is a formal preliminary statement or guide to the book: *his purpose is stated in the introduction.* A FOREWORD is often an informal statement made to the reader. It is the same as PREFACE, but FOREWORD was substituted for it during the vogue for restoring native terms: *an unusual foreword, a short preface.*

in·tro·duc·to·ry (Ĭn′trə dŭk′tə rĭ), *adj.* serving to introduce; preliminary; prefatory. Also, **in′tro·duc′tive.** —**in′tro·duc′to·ri·ly**, *adv.* —**Syn.** See **preliminary.**

in·tro·it (Ĭntrō′ĭt), *n.* 1. *Rom. Cath. Ch.* part of a psalm with an antiphon recited by the celebrant of Mass at the foot of the altar and, at High Mass, sung by the choir when the priest begins the Mass. 2. *Anglican Ch.* psalm or anthem sung as the celebrant of the holy communion is entering the sanctuary. 3. (esp. in the Anglican Ch.) a musical composition at the beginning of the service. [late ME, t. L: s. *introitus* entrance]

in·tro·jec·tion (Ĭn′trə jĕk′shən), *n.* *Psychoanal.* a primitive and early unconscious psychic process by which an external object or individual is represented by an image which in turn is incorporated into the psychic apparatus of someone else. [f. INTRO- + s. L *-jectio* a throwing]

in·tro·mit (Ĭn′trə mĭt′), *v.t.*, **-mitted**, **-mitting.** *Now Rare.* to send, put, or let in; introduce; admit. [ME *intromitte(n)*, t. L: m. *intrōmittere* send in] —**in·tro·mis·sion** (Ĭn′trə mĭsh′ən), *n.* —**in′tro·mit′tent**, *adj.*

in·trorse (Ĭn trôrs′), *adj.* *Bot.* turned or facing inward, as anthers which open toward the gynoecium. [t. L: m. s. *introrsus*] —**in·trorse′ly**, *adv.*

in·tro·spect (Ĭn′trə spĕkt′), *v.i.* 1. to practice introspection; consider one's own internal state or feelings. —*v.t.* 2. to look into; examine. [t. L: s. *intrōspectus*, pp., looked into] —**in′tro·spec′tive**, *adj.* —**in′tro·spec′-tive·ly**, *adv.* —**in′tro·spec′tive·ness**, *n.*

in·tro·spec·tion (Ĭn′trə spĕk′shən), *n.* 1. observation or examination of one's own mental states or processes. 2. **sympathetic introspection**, *Sociol.* a study of human conduct by imagining oneself as engaged in that conduct.

in·tro·ver·sion (Ĭn′trə vûr′shən, -zhən), *n.* 1. act of introverting. 2. introverted state. 3. *Psychol.* interest directed inward or upon the self. Cf. **extroversion.** —**in·tro·ver·sive** (Ĭn′trə vûr′sĭv), *adj.*

in·tro·vert (*n., adj.* Ĭn′trə vûrt′; *v.* Ĭn′trə vûrt′), *n.* 1. *Psychol.* one characterized by introversion; a person concerned chiefly with his own thoughts. Cf. **extrovert.** 2. *Zool.*, etc. a part that is or can be introverted. —*adj.* 3. marked by introversion. —*v.t.* 4. to turn inward. 5. to direct (the mind, etc.) inward or upon the self. 6. *Zool.*, etc. to insheathe a part of, within another part; invaginate. [f. INTRO- + s. L *vertere* turn]

in·trude (Ĭn trōōd′), *v.*, **-truded**, **-truding.** —*v.t.* 1. to thrust or bring in without reason, permission, or welcome. 2. *Geol.* to thrust or force in. —*v.i.* 3. to thrust oneself in; come uninvited: *to intrude upon his privacy.* [t. L: m.s. *intrūdere* thrust in] —**in·trud′er**, *n.* —**in·trud′ing·ly**, *adv.* —**Syn.** 3. See **trespass.**

in·tru·sion (Ĭn trōō′zhən), *n.* 1. act of intruding: *an unwarranted intrusion.* 2. *Law.* a wrongful entry after the determination of a particular estate, made before the remainderman or reversioner has entered. 3. *Geol.* a. the forcing of extraneous matter, as molten rock, into some other formation. b. the matter forced in.

in·tru·sive (Ĭn trōō′sĭv), *adj.* 1. intruding. 2. characterized by or involving intrusion. 3. apt to intrude; coming unbidden or without welcome. 4. *Geol.* a. (of rocks) having been forced, while molten or plastic, into fissures or other openings or between layers of other rocks. b. noting or pertaining to plutonic rocks. 5. *Phonet.* inserted without grammatical or historical justification. —**in·tru′sive·ly**, *adv.* —**in·tru′sive·ness**, *n.*

in·trust (Ĭn trŭst′), *v.t.* entrust.

in·tu·bate (Ĭn′tyə bāt′), *v.t.*, **-bated**, **-bating.** *Med.* 1. to insert a tube into. 2. to treat by inserting a tube, as into the larynx. —**in′tu·ba′tion**, *n.*

in·tu·it (Ĭn′tyōō ĭt, -tōō-; Ĭn tū′ĭt, -tōō′-), *v.t., v.i.*, **-ited**, **-iting.** to know, or receive knowledge, by intuition. [t. L: s. *intuitus*, pp.]

in·tu·i·tion (Ĭn′tyōō ĭsh′ən, -tōō-), *n.* 1. direct perception of truths, facts, etc., independently of any reasoning process. 2. *Philos.* a. an immediate cognition of an object not inferred or determined by a previous cognition of the same object. b. any object or truth so discerned. c. pure, untaught, noninferential knowledge. [t. ML: s. *intuitio*, der. L *intuērī* look at, consider]

in·tu·i·tion·al (Ĭn′tyōō ĭsh′ən əl, -tōō-), *adj.* 1. pertaining to or of the nature of intuition. 2. characterized by intuition; having intuition. 3. based on intuition as a principle. —**in′tu·i′tion·al·ly**, *adv.*

in·tu·i·tion·al·ism (Ĭn′tyōō ĭsh′ən ə lĭz′əm, -tōō-), *n.* intuitionism. —**in′tu·i′tion·al·ist**, *n.*

in·tu·i·tion·ism (Ĭn′tyōō ĭsh′ən ĭz′əm, -tōō-), *n.* 1. *Ethics.* the doctrine that moral values and duties can be discerned directly. 2. *Metaphys.* a. the doctrine that in perception external objects are given immediately, without the intervention of a representative idea. b. the doctrine that knowledge rests upon axiomatic truths discerned directly. —**in′tu·i′tion·ist**, *n., adj.*

in·tu·i·tive (Ĭn tū′ə tĭv, -tōō′-), *adj.* 1. perceiving by intuition, as a person, the mind, etc. 2. perceived by, resulting from, or involving intuition: *intuitive knowledge.* 3. of the nature of intuition. —**in·tu′i·tive·ly**, *adv.* —**in·tu′i·tive·ness**, *n.*

in·tu·i·tiv·ism (Ĭn tū′ə tĭ vĭz′əm, -tōō′-), *n.* 1. ethical intuitionism. 2. intuitive perception; insight. —**in·tu′i·tiv·ist**, *n.*

in·tu·mesce (Ĭn′tyōō mĕs′, -tōō-), *v.i.*, **-mesced**, **-mescing.** 1. to swell up, as with heat; become tumid. 2. to bubble up. [t. L: s. *intumescere* swell up]

in·tu·mes·cence (Ĭn′tyōō mĕs′əns, -tōō-), *n.* 1. a swelling up as with congestion. 2. swollen state. 3. a swollen mass. —**in′tu·mes′cent**, *adj.*

in·turn (Ĭn′tûrn′), *n.* an inward turn, as of the toes.

in·tus·sus·cept (Ĭn′təs sə sĕpt′), *v.t.* to take within, as one part of the intestine into an adjacent part; invaginate. [back formation from INTUSSUSCEPTION] —**in′-tus·sus·cep′tive**, *adj.*

in·tus·sus·cep·tion (Ĭn′təs sə sĕp′shən), *n.* 1. a taking within. 2. *Physiol.* the conversion into protoplasm of foreign matter taken in by a living organism. 3. *Pathol.* the slipping of one part within another; invagination. [f. L: *intus* within + s. *susceptio* a taking up]

in·twine (Ĭn twīn′), *v.t., v.i.*, **-twined**, **-twining.** entwine.

in·twist (Ĭn twĭst′), *v.t.* entwist.

in·u·lase (Ĭn′yə lās′), *n.* *Biochem.* an enzyme which converts inulin into levulose. [f. INUL(IN) + -ASE]

in·u·lin (Ĭn′yə lĭn), *n.* *Chem.* a polysaccharide obtained from the roots of certain plants, esp. elecampane, dahlia,

---

b., blend of, blended; c., cognate with; d., dialect, dialectal; der., derived from; f., formed from; g., going back to; m., modification of; r., replacing; s., stem of; t., taken from; ?, perhaps. See the full key on inside cover.

and Jerusalem artichoke, which undergoes hydrolysis to the dextrorotatory form of fructose. [f. s. L *inula* elecampane + -IN²]

in·unc·tion (ĭn ŭngk′shən), *n.* **1.** act of anointing. **2.** *Med.* the rubbing in of an oil or ointment. **3.** an unguent. [late ME, t. L: s. *inunctio* an anointing]

in·un·dant (ĭn ŭn′dənt), *adj.* *Poetic.* inundating.

in·un·date (ĭn′ən dāt′, -ŭn-, ĭn ŭn′dāt), *v.t.*, **-dated, -dating.** **1.** to overspread with a flood; overflow; flood; deluge. **2.** to overspread as with or in a flood; overwhelm. [t. L: m. s. *inundātus*, pp., overflowed] **—in′un·da′tion,** *n.* **—in′un·da′tor,** *n.* **—Syn. 1.** See **flood.**

in·ur·bane (ĭn′ûr bān′), *adj.* not urbane; lacking in courtesy or suavity. **—in·ur·ban·i·ty** (ĭn′ûr băn′ə tĭ), *n.*

in·ure (ĭn yŏŏr′), *v.*, **-ured, -uring.** **—***v.t.* **1.** to toughen or harden by exercise; accustom; habituate (fol. by *to*): *to inure a person to danger.* **—***v.i.* **2.** to come into use; take or have effect. Also, **enure.** [late ME, v. use of obs. phrase *in ure* in use, f. IN, prep., + obs. *ure* use, work (t. AF, g. L *opera*)] **—in·ure′ment,** *n.*

in·urn (ĭn ûrn′), *v.t.* **1.** to put into an urn, esp. a funeral urn. **2.** to bury; inter. **—in·urn′ment,** *n.*

in·u·tile (ĭn ū′tĭl), *adj.* useless; of no use or service; unprofitable. [late ME, t. L: m. s. *inūtilis*]

in·u·til·i·ty (ĭn′yŏŏ tĭl′ə tĭ), *n.*, *pl.* **-ties.** **1.** uselessness. **2.** a useless thing or person.

inv., **1.** invented. **2.** inventor. **3.** invoice.

in va·cu·o (ĭn văk′yŏŏ ō′), *Latin.* in a vacuum.

in·vade (ĭn vād′), *v.*, **-vaded, -vading.** **—***v.t.* **1.** to enter as an enemy; go into with hostile intent: *Caesar invaded Britain.* **2.** to enter like an enemy: *locusts invaded the fields.* **3.** to enter as if to take possession: *to invade a friend's quarters.* **4.** to intrude upon: *to invade the privacy of a family.* **5.** to encroach or infringe upon: *to invade the rights of citizens.* **—***v.i.* **6.** to make an invasion. [t. L: m.s. *invādere* go into, attack] **—in·vad′er,** *n.*

in·vag·i·na·ble (ĭn văj′ə nə bəl), *adj.* capable of being invaginated; susceptible of invagination.

in·vag·i·nate (*v.* ĭn văj′ə nāt′; *adj.* ĭn văj′ə nĭt, -nāt′), *v.*, **-nated, -nating,** *adj.* **—***v.t.* **1.** to insert or receive as into a sheath; sheathe. **2.** to fold or draw (a tubular organ, etc.) back within itself; introvert; intussuscept. **—***v.i.* **3.** to become invaginated; undergo invagination. **4.** to form a pocket by turning in. **—***adj.* **5.** invaginated. [f. IN-² + s. L *vāgīna* sheath + -ATE¹]

in·vag·i·na·tion (ĭn văj′ə nā′shən), *n.* **1.** act or process of invaginating. **2.** *Embryol.* the inward movement of a portion of the wall of a blastula in the formation of a gastrula. **3.** *Pathol.* intussusception.

in·va·lid¹ (ĭn′və lĭd; *Brit.* -lēd′), *n.* **1.** an infirm or sickly person: *a hopeless invalid.* **2.** a soldier or sailor disabled for active service. **—***adj.* **3.** deficient in health; weak; sick: *his invalid sister.* **4.** of or for invalids: *invalid diets.* **—***v.t.* **5.** to affect with disease; make an invalid: *invalided for life.* **6.** to class, or remove from active service, as an invalid. **—***v.i.* **7.** to become an invalid. **8.** (of a soldier or a sailor) to retire from active service because of illness or injury. [t. L: s. *invalidus* infirm, not strong]

in·val·id² (ĭn văl′ĭd), *adj.* **1.** not valid; of no force, weight, or cogency; weak: *invalid arguments.* **2.** without legal force, or void, as a contract. [f. IN-³ + VALID] **—in·val′id·ly,** *adv.*

in·val·i·date (ĭn văl′ə dāt′), *v.t.*, **-dated, -dating.** **1.** to render invalid. **2.** to deprive of legal force or efficacy. **—in·val′i·da′tion,** *n.* **—in·val′i·da′tor,** *n.*

in·va·lid·ism (ĭn′və lĭd ĭz′əm), *n.* prolonged ill health.

in·va·lid·i·ty (ĭn′və lĭd′ə tĭ), *n.* lack of validity.

in·val·u·a·ble (ĭn văl′yŏŏ ə bəl), *adj.* that cannot be valued or appraised; of inestimable value. **—in·val′u·a·ble·ness,** *n.* **—in·val′u·a·bly,** *adv.* **—Syn.** priceless, precious. **—Ant.** worthless.

in·var (ĭn vär′), *n.* **1.** an iron alloy, containing 35.5% nickel, having a very low coefficient of expansion at atmospheric temperatures. **2.** (*cap.*) a trademark for this alloy. [short for INVARIABLE]

in·var·i·a·ble (ĭn vâr′ĭ ə bəl), *adj.* not variable or not capable of being varied; not changing or not capable of being changed; always the same. **—in·var′i·a·bil′i·ty, in·var′i·a·ble·ness,** *n.* **—in·var′i·a·bly,** *adv.* **—Syn.** unalterable, unchanging, uniform, constant.

in·var·i·ant (ĭn vâr′ĭ ənt), *adj.* **1.** unvarying; invariable; constant. **—***n.* **2.** *Math.* an invariable quantity.

in·va·sion (ĭn vā′zhən), *n.* **1.** act of invading or entering as an enemy. **2.** the entrance or advent of anything troublesome or harmful, as disease. **3.** entrance as if to take possession or overrun. **4.** infringement by intrusion. [t. LL: s. *invāsio* an attack]

in·va·sive (ĭn vā′sĭv), *adj.* **1.** characterized by or involving invasion; offensive: *invasive war.* **2.** invading, or tending to invade; intrusive.

in·vec·tive (ĭn vĕk′tĭv), *n.* **1.** vehement denunciation; an utterance of violent censure or reproach. **2.** a railing accusation; vituperation. **—***adj.* **3.** censoriously abusive; vituperative; denunciatory. [ME, t. LL: m.s. *invectīvus* abusive] **—in·vec′tive·ly,** *adv.* **—in·vec′tive·ness,** *n.* **—Syn. 1.** See **abuse.**

in·veigh (ĭn vā′), *v.i.* to attack vehemently in words; rail: *to inveigh against democracy.* [ME *inveh*, t. L: s. *invehere* carry or bear into, assail] **—in·veigh′er,** *n.*

in·vei·gle (ĭn vē′gəl, -vā′gəl), *v.t.*, **-gled, -gling.** **1.** to draw by beguiling or artful inducements (fol. by *into*, sometimes *from*, *away*, etc.): *to inveigle a person into playing bridge.* **2.** to allure, win, or seduce by beguiling. [earlier *enve(u)gle*, t. F: m.s. *aveugler* blind, delude] **—in·vei′gle·ment,** *n.* **—in·vei′gler,** *n.*

in·vent (ĭn vĕnt′), *v.t.* **1.** to originate as a product of one's own contrivance: *to invent a machine.* **2.** to produce or create with the imagination: *to invent a story.* **3.** to make up or fabricate as something merely fictitious or false: *to invent excuses.* **4.** *Obs.* to come upon; find. **—***v.i.* **5.** to devise something new, as by ingenuity. [ME *invent(en)*, t. L: m. s. *inventus*, pp. discovered, found out] **—in·vent′i·ble,** *adj.* **—Syn. 1.** See **discover.**

in·vent·er (ĭn vĕn′tər), *n.* inventor.

in·ven·tion (ĭn vĕn′shən), *n.* **1.** act of inventing. **2.** *Patent Law.* the conception of an idea and the means or apparatus by which the result is obtained. **3.** anything invented or devised. **4.** the exercise of imaginative or creative power in literature or art. **5.** act of producing or creating by exercise of the imagination. **6.** the power or faculty of inventing, devising, or originating. **7.** something fabricated, as a false statement. **8.** *Sociol.* the creation of a new culture trait, pattern, etc. **9.** *Music.* a short piece, contrapuntal in nature, generally based on one subject. **10.** *Speech.* (classically) one of the five steps in speech preparation, the process of choosing ideas appropriate to the subject, audience, and occasion. **11.** *Archaic.* act of finding. [ME, t. L: s. *inventio*]

in·ven·tive (ĭn vĕn′tĭv), *adj.* **1.** apt at inventing, devising, or contriving. **2.** having the function of inventing. **3.** pertaining to, involving, or showing invention. **—in·ven′tive·ly,** *adv.* **—in·ven′tive·ness,** *n.*

in·ven·tor (ĭn vĕn′tər), *n.* one who invents, esp. one who devises some new process, appliance, machine, or article; one who makes inventions. Also, **inventer.**

in·ven·to·ry (ĭn′vən tōr′ĭ), *n.*, *pl.* **-tories,** *v.*, **-toried, -torying.** **—***n.* **1.** a detailed descriptive list of articles, with number, quantity, and value of each. **2.** a formal list of movables, as of a merchant's stock of goods. **3.** a complete listing of work in progress, raw materials, finished goods on hand, etc., made each year by a business concern. **4.** items in such a list. **5.** the value of a stock of goods. **—***v.t.* **6.** to make an inventory of; enter in an inventory. [late ME, t. ML: m. s. *inventōrium*, L *inventārium* list] **—in′ven·to′ri·al,** *adj.* **—in′ven·to′ri·al·ly,** *adv.* **—Syn. 1.** See **list¹.**

in·ve·rac·i·ty (ĭn′və răs′ə tĭ), *n.*, *pl.* **-ties.** **1.** untruthfulness. **2.** an untruth.

In·ver·ness (ĭn′vər nĕs′), *n.* **1.** Also, **In·ver·ness-shire** (ĭn′vər nĕs′shĭr, -shər), a county in NW Scotland. 81,000 pop. (est. 1946); 4211 sq. mi. **2.** its county seat: a seaport. 25,100 (est. 1946). **3.** an overcoat with a long, removable cape (**Inverness cape**).

in·verse (*adj.*, *n.* ĭn vûrs′, ĭn′vûrs; *v.* ĭn vûrs′), *adj.*, *n.*, *v.*, **-versed, -versing.** **—***adj.* **1.** reversed in position, direction, or tendency: *inverse order.* **2.** opposite to in nature or effect, as a mathematical relation or operation: *subtraction is the inverse operation to addition.* **3.** inverted, or turned upside down. **—***n.* **4.** an inverted state or condition. **5.** that which is inverse; the direct opposite. **—***v.t.* **6.** *Now Rare.* to invert. [t. L: m.s. *inversus*, pp., turned about] **—in·verse′ly,** *adv.*

in·ver·sion (ĭn vûr′zhən, -shən), *n.* **1.** act of inverting. **2.** an inverted state. **3.** *Rhet.* reversal of the usual or natural order of words; anastrophe. **4.** *Anat.* the turning inward of a part, as the foot (opposed to *eversion*). **5.** *Chem.* a hydrolysis of certain carbohydrates, as cane sugar, which results in a reversal of direction of the rotatory power of the carbohydrate solution, the plane of polarized light being bent from right to left or vice versa. **6.** *Music.* **a.** the process, or result, of transposing the tones of an interval or chord so that the original bass becomes an upper voice. **b.** (in counterpoint) the transposition of the upper voice part below the lower, and vice versa. **c.** presentation of a melody in contrary motion to its original form. **7.** *Psychiatry.* assumption of the sexual role of the opposite sex; homosexuality. **8.** *Phonet.* retroflexion. **9.** *Meteorol.* a reversal in the normal temperature lapse rate, in which the temperature rises with increased elevation, instead of falling. **10.** something inverted. [t. L: s. *inversio*]

in·ver·sive (ĭn vûr′sĭv), *adj.* characterized by inversion.

in·vert (*v.* ĭn vûrt′; *adj.*, *n.* ĭn′vûrt), *v.t.* **1.** to turn upside down. **2.** to reverse in position, direction, or order. **3.** to turn or change to the opposite or contrary, as in nature, bearing, or effect: *to invert a process.* **4.** *Chem.* to subject to inversion. See **inversion** (def. 5). **5.** *Phonet.* to articulate, as a retroflex vowel. **—***adj.* **6.** *Chem.* inverted. **—***n.* **7.** one who or that which is inverted. **8.** a homosexual. [t. L: s. *invertere* turn about, upset] **—in·vert′er,** *n.* **—in·vert′i·ble,** *adj.* **—Syn. 2.** See **reverse.**

in·vert·ase (ĭn vûr′tās), *n.* *Biochem.* an enzyme which causes the inversion of cane sugar, thus changing it into invert sugar. It is found in yeast and in the digestive juices of animals. [INVERT + -ASE]

in·ver·te·brate (ĭn vûr′tə brĭt, -brāt′), *adj.* **1.** *Zool.* not vertebrate; without a backbone. **2.** without strength of character. **—***n.* **3.** an invertebrate animal. **4.** one who lacks strength of character. **—in·ver·te·bra·cy** (ĭn vûr′tə brə sĭ), **in·ver′te·brate·ness,** *n.*

inverted commas, *Brit.* quotation marks.

inverted mordent, *Music.* a pralltriller.

ăct, āble, dâre, ärt; ĕbb, ēqual; ĭf, īce; hŏt, ōver, ôrder, oil, bŏŏk, ōōze, out; ŭp, ūse, ûrge; ə = a in alone; ch, chief; g, give; ng, ring; sh, shoe; th, thin; th, that; zh, vision. See the full key on inside cover.

in·ver·tor (ĭn vûr′tər), *n. Elect.* a converter.

invert soap, an emulsifiable salt whose action is responsible for soapy qualities.

invert sugar, a mixture of the dextrorotatory forms of glucose and fructose formed naturally in fruits and produced artificially in syrups or fondants by treating cane sugar with acids.

in·vest (ĭn vĕst′), *v.t.* **1.** to put (money) to use, by purchase or expenditure, in something offering profitable returns, esp. interest or income. **2.** to spend: *to invest large sums in books.* **3.** to clothe. **4.** to cover or adorn as an article of attire does. **5.** *Rare.* to put on (a garment, etc.). **6.** to cover or surround as if with a garment, or like a garment: *spring invests the trees with leaves.* **7.** to surround (a place) with military forces or works so as to prevent approach or escape; besiege. **8.** to indue or endow: *to invest a friend with every virtue.* **9.** to belong to, as a quality or character does. **10.** to settle or vest (a power, right, etc.), as in a person. **11.** to clothe in or with the insignia of office. **12.** to install in an office or position; furnish with power, authority, rank, etc. —*v.i.* **13.** to invest money; make an investment. [late ME, t. L: s. *investīre* clothe] —**in·ves′tor**, *n.*

in·ves·ti·ga·ble (ĭn vĕs′tə gə bəl), *adj.* capable of being investigated.

in·ves·ti·gate (ĭn vĕs′tə gāt′), *v.,* **-gated, -gating.** —*v.t.* **1.** to search or inquire into; search or examine into the particulars of; examine in detail: *to investigate a murder.* —*v.i.* **2.** to make inquiry, examination, or investigation. [t. L: m.s. *investīgātus*, pp., tracked, traced out] —**in·ves′ti·ga′tive, in·ves·ti·ga·to·ry** (ĭn vĕs′tə gə tōr′ĭ), *adj.* —**in·ves′ti·ga′tor**, *n.*

in·ves·ti·ga·tion (ĭn vĕs′tə gā′shən), *n.* act or process of investigating; a searching inquiry in order to ascertain facts; a detailed or careful examination.
—**Syn.** INVESTIGATION, EXAMINATION, INQUIRY, RESEARCH express the idea of an active effort to find out something. An INVESTIGATION is a systematic, minute, and thorough attempt to learn the facts about something complex or hidden; it is often formal and official: *an investigation of a bank failure.* An EXAMINATION is an orderly attempt to obtain information about or to make a test of something, often something open to observation: *a physical examination.* An INQUIRY is an investigation made by asking questions rather than by inspection, or fig., by study of available evidence: *an inquiry into a proposed bond issue.* RESEARCH is careful and sustained investigation usually into a subject covering a wide range, or into remote recesses of knowledge: *chemical research.*

in·ves·ti·tive (ĭn vĕs′tə tĭv), *adj.* **1.** serving to invest: *an investitive act.* **2.** pertaining to investiture.

in·ves·ti·ture (ĭn vĕs′tə chər), *n.* **1.** act of investing. **2.** *Brit.* formal bestowal or presentation of a possessory or prescriptive right, as to a fief, usually involving the giving of insignia. **3.** state of being invested, as with a garment, quality, etc. **4.** *Archaic.* that which invests. [ME, t. ML: m. *investītūra*]

in·vest·ment (ĭn vĕst′mənt), *n.* **1.** the investing of money or capital in order to secure profitable returns, esp. interest or income. **2.** a particular instance or mode of investing. **3.** a thing invested in. **4.** that which is invested. **5.** act of investing or state of being invested, as with a garment. **6.** *Biol.* any covering, coating, outer layer, or integument, as of an animal or vegetable body. **7.** *Archaic.* a garment or vestment. **8.** an investing with a quality, attribute, etc. **9.** investiture with an office, dignity, or right. **10.** the surrounding of a place with military forces or works, as in besieging.

in·vet·er·a·cy (ĭn vĕt′ər ə sĭ), *n.* state of being inveterate: *the inveteracy of people's prejudices.*

in·vet·er·ate (ĭn vĕt′ər ĭt), *adj.* **1.** confirmed in a habit, practice, feeling, or the like: *an inveterate gambler.* **2.** firmly established by long continuance, as a disease or sore, a habit or practice (often bad), or a feeling (often hostile); chronic. [late ME, t. L: m.s. *inveterātus*, pp., rendered old] —**in·vet′er·ate·ly**, *adv.* —**in·vet′er·ate·ness**, *n.*

in·vid·i·ous (ĭn vĭd′ĭ əs), *adj.* **1.** such as to bring odium, unpopularity, or envious dislike: *an invidious honor.* **2.** calculated to excite ill will or resentment or give offense: *invidious remarks.* **3.** offensively or unfairly discriminating: *invidious comparisons.* **4.** *Obs.* envious. [t. L: m.s. *invidiōsus* envious] —**in·vid′i·ous·ly**, *adv.* —**in·vid′i·ous·ness**, *n.*

in·vig·i·late (ĭn vĭj′ə lāt′), *v.i.,* **-lated, -lating.** **1.** *Brit.* to keep watch over students at an examination. **2.** *Obs.* to keep watch. [t. L: m.s. *invigilātus*, pp., watched over] —**in·vig′i·la′tion**, *n.* —**in·vig′i·la′tor**, *n.*

in·vig·or·ant (ĭn vĭg′ər ənt), *n.* a tonic.

in·vig·or·ate (ĭn vĭg′ə rāt′), *v.t.,* **-ated, -ating.** to give vigor to; fill with life and energy: *to invigorate the body.* [f. IN-² + VIGOR + -ATE¹] —**in·vig′or·at′ing·ly**, *adv.* —**in·vig′or·a′tion**, *n.* —**in·vig′or·a′tive**, *adj.* —**in·vig′or·a′tive·ly**, *adv.* —**in·vig′or·a′tor**, *n.* —**Syn.** See animate.

in·vin·ci·ble (ĭn vĭn′sə bəl), *adj.* **1.** that cannot be conquered or vanquished: *the Invincible Armada.* **2.** insuperable; insurmountable: *invincible difficulties.* [ME, t. L: m.s *invincibilis.* See IN-³, VINCIBLE] —**in·vin′ci·bil′i·ty, in·vin′ci·ble·ness**, *n.* —**in·vin′ci·bly**, *adv.*
—**Syn.** **1.** INVINCIBLE, IMPREGNABLE, INDOMITABLE suggest that which cannot be overcome or mastered. INVINCIBLE is applied to that which cannot be conquered in combat or war, or overcome or subdued in any manner: *an invincible army, invincible courage.* IMPREGNABLE is applied to a place

or position that cannot be taken by assault or siege, and hence to whatever is proof against attack: *an impregnable fortress, impregnable virtue.* INDOMITABLE implies having an unyielding spirit, or stubborn persistence in the face of opposition or difficulty: *indomitable will.* —**Ant.** **1.** conquerable.

Invincible Armada, Armada (def. 1).

in·vi·o·la·ble (ĭn vī′ə lə bəl), *adj.* **1.** that must not be violated; that is to be kept free from violence or violation of any kind, or treated as if sacred: *an inviolable sanctuary.* **2.** that cannot be violated, subjected to violence, or injured. —**in·vi′o·la·bil′i·ty, in·vi′o·la·ble·ness**, *n.* —**in·vi′o·la·bly**, *adv.*

in·vi·o·late (ĭn vī′ə lĭt, -lāt′), *adj.* **1.** free from violation, injury, desecration, or outrage. **2.** undisturbed. **3.** unbroken. **4.** not infringed. —**in·vi′o·la·cy** (ĭn vī′ə lə sĭ), **in·vi′o·late·ness**, *n.* —**in·vi′o·late·ly**, *adv.*

in·vis·i·ble (ĭn vĭz′ə bəl), *adj.* **1.** not visible; not perceptible by the eye: *invisible ink.* **2.** withdrawn from or out of sight. **3.** not perceptible or discernible by the mind: *invisible differences.* **4.** (of colors) of a very deep shade, or a scarcely distinguishable hue: *invisible green.* **5.** not ordinarily found in financial statements: *good will is an invisible asset.* **6.** concealed from public knowledge. —*n.* **7.** an invisible thing or being. **8.** (prec. by *the*) **a.** the unseen or spiritual world. **b.** (*cap.*) God. —**in·vis′i·bil′i·ty, in·vis′i·ble·ness**, *n.* —**in·vis′i·bly**, *adv.*

in·vi·ta·tion (ĭn′və tā′shən), *n.* **1.** act of inviting. **2.** the written or spoken form with which a person is invited. **3.** attraction or allurement. [t. L: s. *invītātio*]

in·vi·ta·to·ry (ĭn vī′tə tōr′ĭ), *adj.* serving to invite; conveying an invitation.

in·vite (*v.* ĭn vīt′; *n.* ĭn′vīt), *v.,* **-vited, -viting,** *n.* —*v.t.* **1.** to ask in a kindly, courteous, or complimentary way, to come or go to some place, gathering, entertainment, etc., or to do something: *to invite friends to dinner.* **2.** to request politely or formally: *to invite donations.* **3.** to act so as to bring on or render probable: *to invite danger.* **4.** to give occasion for. **5.** to attract, allure, or tempt. —*v.i.* **6.** to give invitation; offer attractions or allurements. —*n.* **7.** *Slang.* an invitation. [t. L: m.s. *invītāre*] —**in·vit′er**, *n.* —**Syn.** **1.** See call.

in·vit·ing (ĭn vī′tĭng), *adj.* that invites; esp., attractive, alluring, or tempting: *an inviting offer.* —**in·vit′ing·ly**, *adv.* —**in·vit′ing·ness**, *n.*

in·vo·cate (ĭn′və kāt′), *v.t.,* **-cated, -cating.** *Now Rare.* invoke. [t. L: m.s. *invocātus*, pp.] —**in·voc·a·tive** (ĭn vŏk′ə tĭv, ĭn′və kā′tĭv), *adj.* —**in′vo·ca′tor**, *n.*

in·vo·ca·tion (ĭn′və kā′shən), *n.* **1.** act of invoking; calling upon a deity, etc., for aid, protection, inspiration, etc. **2.** a form of words used in invoking, esp. as part of a public religious service. **3.** an entreaty for aid and guidance from a Muse, deity, etc., at the beginning of an epic or epiclike poem. **4.** a calling upon a spirit by incantation, or the incantation or magical formula used.

in·voc·a·to·ry (ĭn vŏk′ə tōr′ĭ), *adj.* pertaining to or of the nature of invocation.

in·voice (ĭn′vois), *n., v.,* **-voiced, -voicing.** —*n.* **1.** a written list of merchandise, with prices, delivered or sent to a buyer. **2.** an itemized bill containing the prices which comprise the total charge. **3.** the merchandise or shipment itself. —*v.t.* **4.** to make an invoice of. **5.** to enter in an invoice. [m. *invoyes*, pl. of (obs.) *invoy* invoice, t. F: m. *envoy* sending, thing sent. See ENVOY¹]

in·voke (ĭn vōk′), *v.t.,* **-voked, -voking.** **1.** to call for with earnest desire: make supplication or prayer for: *to invoke God's mercy.* **2.** to call on (a divine being, etc.), as in prayer. **3.** to appeal to, as for confirmation. **4.** to call on to come or to do something. **5.** to call forth or upon (a spirit) by incantation; conjure. [late ME, t. L: m. *invocāre*] —**in·vok′er**, *n.*

in·vo·lu·cel (ĭn vŏl′yə sĕl′), *n. Bot.* a secondary involucre, as in a compound cluster of flowers. [t. NL: m.s. *involucellum*, dim. of L *involūcrum* cover]

in·vo·lu·crate (ĭn′və lōō′krĭt, -krāt), *adj.* having an involucre.

A. Involucel; B, Involucre

in·vo·lu·cre (ĭn′və lōō′kər), *n.* **1.** *Bot.* a collection or rosette of bracts subtending a flower cluster, umbel, or the like. **2.** a covering, esp. a membranous one. [t. F, t. L: m. *involūcrum* wrapper, covering] —**in′vo·lu′cral**, *adj.*

in·vo·lu·crum (ĭn′və lōō′krəm), *n., pl.* **-cra** (-krə). involucre.

in·vol·un·tar·y (ĭn vŏl′ən tĕr′ĭ), *adj.* **1.** not voluntary; acting, or done or made, without one's own volition, or otherwise than by one's own will or choice: *an involuntary listener.* **2.** unintentional. **3.** *Physiol.* acting independently of, or done or occurring without, conscious control: *involuntary muscles.* —**in·vol′un·tar′i·ly**, *adv.* —**in·vol′un·tar′i·ness**, *n.* —**Syn.** **1, 3.** See automatic.

in·vo·lute (ĭn′və lōōt′), *adj.* **1.** involved or intricate. **2.** *Bot.*

A. Involute leaves of branch of poplar; B, Transverse section rolled inward from the edge, as a leaf. **3.** *Zool.* (of shells) having the whorls closely wound. —*n.* **4.** *Geom.* any curve of which a given curve is the evolute. [t. L: m.s. *involūtus*, pp., rolled up] —**in·vo·lut′ed·ly,** *adv.*

in·vo·lu·tion (ĭn′və-lōō′shən), *n.* **1.** act of involving. **2.** state of being involved. **3.** something complicated. **4.** *Bot., etc.* **a.** a rolling up or folding in upon itself. **b.** a part formed by this. **5.** *Biol.* retrograde development; degeneration. **6.** *Physiol.* bodily changes involving a lessening of activity, esp. of the sex organs, occurring in late middle age. **7.** *Gram.* complicated construction; the separation of the subject from its predicate by the interjection of matter that should follow the verb or be placed in another sentence. **8.** *Math.* the raising of a quantity or expression to any given power. [t. LL: s. *involūtio* a rolling up]

Involute of a circle

in·volve (ĭn·vŏlv′), *v.t.,* **-volved, -volving. 1.** to include as a necessary circumstance, condition, or consequence; imply; entail. **2.** to affect, as something within the scope of operation. **3.** to include, contain, or comprehend within itself or its scope. **4.** to bring into an intricate or complicated form or condition. **5.** to bring into difficulties (fol. by *with*): *a plot to involve one government with another.* **6.** to cause to be inextricably associated or concerned, as in something embarrassing or unfavorable. **7.** to combine inextricably (fol. by *with*). **8.** to implicate, as in guilt or crime, or in any matter or affair. **9.** to be highly or excessively interested in. **10.** to roll, wrap, or shroud, as in something that surrounds. **11.** to envelop or infold, as the surrounding thing does. **12.** to swallow up, engulf, or overwhelm. **13.** to roll up on itself; wind spirally, coil, or wreathe. **14.** *Math.* to raise to a given power. [ME, t. L: m.s. *involvere* roll in or on, enwrap, involve] —**in·volve′-ment,** *n.* —**in·volv′er,** *n.*

—**Syn. 6.** INVOLVE, ENTANGLE, IMPLICATE imply getting a person connected or bound up with something from which it is difficult for him to extricate himself. To INVOLVE is to bring more or less deeply into something, esp. of a complicated, embarrassing, or troublesome nature: *to involve someone in debt.* To ENTANGLE (usually pass. or reflex.) is to involve so deeply in a tangle as to confuse and make helpless: *to entangle oneself in a mass of contradictory statements.* To IMPLICATE is to connect a person with something discreditable or wrong: *implicated in a plot.* —**Ant. 6.** extricate.

in·vul·ner·a·ble (ĭn·vŭl′nər·ə·bəl), *adj.* **1.** incapable of being wounded, hurt, or damaged. **2.** proof against attack: *invulnerable arguments.* —**in·vul′ner·a·bil′i·ty, in·vul′ner·a·ble·ness,** *n.* —**in·vul′ner·a·bly,** *adv.*

in·wall (ĭn·wôl′), *v.t.* to enclose with a wall.

in·ward (ĭn′wərd), *adv.* Also, **inwards. 1.** toward the inside or interior, as of a place, a space, or a body. **2.** into the mind or soul. **3.** in the mind or soul, or mentally or spiritually; inwardly. **4.** *Rare.* in the inside or interior. —*adj.* **5.** proceeding or directed toward the inside or interior. **6.** situated within; interior; internal: *an inward room.* **7.** pertaining to the inside or inner part. **8.** located within the body: *the inward parts.* **9.** pertaining to the inside of the body: *inward convulsions.* **10.** inland: *inward passage.* **11.** intrinsic; inherent; essential: *the inward nature of a thing.* **12.** inner, mental, or spiritual: *inward peace.* **13.** muffled or indistinct, as the voice. **14.** *Archaic.* domestic. **15.** *Obs.* closely personal; intimate; familiar. **16.** *Obs.* private or secret. —*n.* **17.** the inward or internal part; the inside. **18.** (*pl.*) the inward parts of the body. [ME *in(ne)ward,* OE *in(ne)weard,* f. *in(ne)* IN, adv. + -*weard* -WARD]

in·ward·ly (ĭn′wərd·lĭ), *adv.* **1.** in or on, or with reference to, the inside or inner part. **2.** privately, secretly: *laughing inwardly.* **3.** in low tones; not aloud. **4.** *Now Rare.* toward the inside, interior, or center.

in·ward·ness (ĭn′wərd·nĭs), *n.* **1.** the state of being inward or internal. **2.** depth of thought or feeling; earnestness. **3.** occupation with what concerns man's inner nature; spirituality. **4.** the inward or intrinsic character of a thing. **5.** inward meaning. **6.** *Obs.* intimacy.

in·wards (ĭn′wərdz), *adv.* **1.** inward. —*n.pl.* **2.** inward (def. 18).

in·weave (ĭn·wēv′), *v.t.,* **-wove** or **-weaved; -woven** or **-wove** or **-weaved; -weaving. 1.** to weave in or together. **2.** to introduce into or as into a fabric in weaving. **3.** to combine or diversify with something woven in. Also, **enweave.**

in·wind (ĭn·wīnd′), *v.t.,* **-wound, -winding.** enwind.

in·wrap (ĭn·răp′), *v.t.,* **-wrapped, -wrapping.** enwrap.

in·wreathe (ĭn·rēth′), *v.t.,* **-wreathed, -wreathing.** enwreathe.

in·wrought (ĭn·rôt′), *adj.* **1.** wrought or worked with something by way of decoration. **2.** wrought or worked in, as a decorative pattern. **3.** worked in or closely combined with something.

I·o (ī′ō), *n. Gk. Legend.* the daughter of Inachus of Argos, loved by Zeus and changed by jealous Hera into a white heifer. See **Argus** (def. 1).

I·o (ī′ō), *n., pl.* **Ios.** Io moth.

Io, *Chem.* ionium.

Io·an·ni·na (yỏ ä′nē nä′, yä′nē nä′), *n.* a city in NW Greece. 21,877 (1940). Serbian, **Janina** or **Yanina.**

iod-, var. of **iodo-,** usually before vowels, as in *iodic.*

i·o·date (ī′ə·dāt′), *n., v.,* **-dated, -dating.** —*n.* **1.** *Chem.* a salt of iodic acid, as *sodium iodate,* $NaIO_3$. —*v.t.* **2.** to iodize. —**i′o·da′tion,** *n.*

i·od·ic (ī·ŏd′ĭk), *adj. Chem.* containing iodine, esp. in the pentavalent state ($I+5$). [f. IOD- + -IC]

i·o·dide (ī′ə·dīd′, -dĭd), *n. Chem.* a compound usually of two elements only, one of which is iodine; a salt of hydriodic acid. Also, **i·o·did** (ī′ə·dĭd).

i·o·dim·e·try (ī′ə·dĭm′ə·trĭ), *n. Chem.* iodometry.

i·o·dine (ī′ə·dīn′, -dĭn; *in Chem.* -dēn′), *n. Chem.* a nonmetallic element occurring, at ordinary temperatures, as a grayish-black crystalline solid, which sublimes to a dense violet vapor when heated: used in medicine as an antiseptic, and in the arts. Symbol: I; *at.wt.:* 126.92; *at.no.:* 53; *sp. gr.:* (solid) 4.93 at 20°C. Also, **i·o·din** (ī′ə·dĭn). [f. F *iode* iodine (t. Gk.: m. *iṓdēs,* prop., rust-colored, but taken to mean violetlike) + -INE[2]]

i·o·dism (ī′ə·dĭz′əm), *n. Pathol.* a morbid condition due to the use of iodine or its compounds.

i·o·dize (ī′ə·dīz′), *v.t.,* **-dized, -dizing.** to treat, impregnate, or affect with iodine. —**i′o·diz′er,** *n.*

iodo-, a word element meaning "iodine," as in *iodometry.* Also, **iod-.** [comb. form repr. NL *iōdum*]

i·o·do·form (ī·ō′də·fôrm′, ĭ·ŏd′ə-), *n. Chem.* a yellowish crystalline compound, CHI_3, analogous to chloroform: used as an antiseptic. [f. IODO- + FORM(YL)]

i·o·dol (ī′ə·dōl′, -dŏl), *n. Chem.* a crystalline compound C_4HI_4N: used as a substitute for iodoform.

i·o·dom·e·try (ī′ə·dŏm′ə·trĭ), *n. Chem.* a volumetric analytical procedure for determining iodine, or materials which will liberate iodine or react with iodine. Also **iodimetry.** —**i·o·do·met·ric** (ī′ə·dō mĕt′rĭk), *adj.*

i·o·dous (ī·ō′dəs, ī′ō·dəs), *adj.* **1.** *Chem.* containing iodine, esp. in the divalent state ($I+2$). **2.** like iodine.

I.O.F., Independent Order of Foresters.

I·o·lan·the (ī′ə·lăn′thĭ), *n.* an operetta (1882) by Gilbert and Sullivan.

i·o·lite (ī′ə·līt′), *n.* cordierite. [f. Gk. *ío(n)* violet + -LITE]

i·o moth (ī′ō), a showy and beautiful moth of North America, *Automeris io,* of yellow coloration, with prominent pink and bluish eyespots on the hinder wings.

i·on (ī′ən, ī′ŏn), *n. Physics, Chem.* **1.** an electrically charged atom, radical, or molecule, formed by the loss or gain of one or more electrons. **Positive ions,** created by electron loss, are called *cations* and are attracted to the cathode in electrolysis. **Negative ions,** created by electron gain, are called *anions* and are attracted to the anode. The valence of an ion is equal to the number of electrons lost or gained and is indicated by a plus sign for cations and minus for anions, thus: $Na+$, $Cl-$, $Ca++$, $S=$. **2.** one of the electrically charged particles formed in a gas by the action of an electric discharge, etc. [t. Gk., ppr. neut. of *iénai* go] —**i·on·ic** (ī·ŏn′ĭk), *adj.*

-ion, a suffix of nouns denoting action or process, state or condition, or sometimes things or persons, as in *allusion, communion, flexion, fusion, legion, opinion, suspicion, union.* Also, **-tion** and **-ation.** Cf. **-cion, -xion.** [t. L: s. -*io;* suffix forming nouns, esp. from verbs]

I·o·na (ī·ō′nə), *n.* a small island in the Hebrides, off W coast of Scotland; center of early Celtic Christianity.

I·o·ni·a (ī·ō′nĭ ə), *n.* an ancient region on the W coast of Asia Minor and adjacent islands: colonized by the ancient Greeks.

I·o·ni·an (ī·ō′nĭ ən), *adj.* **1.** pertaining to Ionia. **2.** pertaining to a branch of the Greek race named from Ion, the legendary founder. —*n.* **3.** an Ionian Greek.

Ionian Islands, the islands along the W coast of Greece, including Corfu, Levkas, Ithaca, Cephalonia, and Zante, and Cerigo off the S coast.

Ionian Sea, an arm of the Mediterranean between S Italy, E Sicily, and Greece.

I·on·ic (ī·ŏn′ĭk), *adj.* **1.** *Archit.* noting or pertaining to one of the three Greek orders, distinguished by its slender proportions, the volutes on the capitals, and the continuous (often figured) frieze. See illus. under **order. 2.** *Pros.* noting or employing one of two feet consisting of two long and two short syllables: **the greater Ionic,** two long and two short syllables, – – ᵕ ᵕ **the lesser Ionic,** two short and two long syllables, ᵕ ᵕ – – **3.** pertaining to the Ionians. —*n.* **4.** *Pros.* an Ionic foot, verse, or meter. **5.** (*also l.c.*) *Print.* a style of type. **6.** a dialect of ancient Greek, including Attic and the language of Homer. [t. L: s. *Ionicus,* t. Gk.: m. *Iōnikós*]

i·o·ni·um (ī·ō′nĭ əm), *n. Chem.* a radioactive element formed in the decay of uranium. Symbol: Io; *at. no.:* 90; *at.wt.:* about 230. [t. NL. See ION]

i·on·ize (ī′ə·nīz′), *v.,* **-ized, -izing.** —*v.t.* **1.** to separate or change into ions. **2.** to produce ions in. —*v.i.* **3.** to become changed into the form of ions, as by dissolving. Also, *esp. Brit.,* **i′on·ise′.** —**i·on·i·za·tion** (ī′ə nə zā′-shən), *n.* —**i′on·iz′er,** *n.*

i·o·none (ī′ə·nōn′), *n.* either one or a mixture of two unsaturated ketones, $C_{13}H_{20}O$, used in perfumery.

i·on·o·sphere (ī·ŏn′ə·sfĭr′), *n.* **1.** the succession of ionized layers that constitute the outer regions of the earth's atmosphere beyond the stratosphere, considered as beginning with the Heaviside layer at about 60 miles, and extending several hundred miles up. **2.** *Obsolesc.* the Heaviside layer.

I.O.O.F., Independent Order of Odd Fellows.

I.O.R.M., Improved Order of Red Men.

i·o·ta (ī·ō′tə), *n.* **1.** the ninth letter (I, ι = English I, i) of the Greek alphabet (the smallest letter). **2.** a very small quantity; a tittle; a jot.

ăct, āble, dâre, ärt; ĕbb, ēqual; ĭf, īce; hŏt, ōver, ôrder, oil, bŏŏk, ōōze, out; ŭp, ūse, ûrge; ə = a in alone; ch, chief; g, give; ng, ring; sh, shoe; th, thin; t͟h, that; zh, vision. See the full key on inside cover.

i·o·ta·cism (ī·ō′tə·sĭz′əm), *n.* conversion of other vowel sounds into that of iota (English ē). [t. L: s. *iōtacismus*, t. Gk. m. *iōtakismós*]

I O U (ī′ō′ū′), a written acknowledgment of a debt, containing the expression *I OU* (I owe you). Also, **I.O.U.**

-ious, a termination consisting of the suffix *-ous* with a preceding original or euphonic vowel *i.* Cf. **-eous.**

I·o·wa (ī′ə·wə; *locally* ī′ə·wä′), *n.* 1. a State in the central United States: a part of the Midwest. 2,621,073 pop. (1950); 56,280 sq. mi. *Cap.:* Des Moines. *Abbr.:* Ia. 2. a river flowing from N Iowa SE to the Mississippi. 291 mi. 3. a Siouan language. **—I·o·wan** (ī′ə·wən), *adj., n.*

Iowa City, a city in SE Iowa. 27,212 (1950).

ip·e·cac (ĭp′ə·kăk′), *n.* 1. the dried root of two small, shrubby South American rubiaceous plants *Cephaelis Ipecacuanha,* and *C. acuminata,* used as an emetic, purgative, etc. 2. a drug consisting of the roots of these plants. 3. the plants themselves. Also, **ip·e·cac·u·an·ha** (ĭp′ə·kăk′yŏŏ·ăn′ə). [t. Pg., t. Tupi: m. *ipe-kaa-guêne,* f. *ipeh* low + *kaá* leaves + *guêne* vomit]

Iph·i·ge·ni·a (ĭf′ə·jĭ·nī′ə), *n. Gk. Legend.* the daughter of Agamemnon and Clytemnestra. She became a priestess of Artemis after the goddess saved her from sacrifice by Agamemnon. She saved her brother Orestes' life. According to the Aeschylean version she was sacrificed by her father at Aulis.

ip·o·moe·a (ĭp′ə·mē′ə, ī′pə-), *n.* 1. any plant of the genus *Ipomoea,* of the morning-glory family, containing many species with ornamental flowers. 2. the dried root of the convolvulaceous plant, *Ipomoea orizabensis,* yielding a resin which is a cathartic. [t. NL, f. Gk.: s. *íps* kind of worm + m. *hómoios* like]

ip·se dix·it (ĭp′sī dĭk′sĭt), *Latin.* 1. he himself said it. 2. an assertion without proof.

ip·so fac·to (ĭp′sō făk′tō), *Latin.* by the fact itself; by that very fact: *it is condemned ipso facto.*

Ip·sus (ĭp′səs), *n.* an ancient village in central Asia Minor, in Phrygia: the scene of a battle between the successors of Alexander the Great, 301 B.C.

Ips·wich (ĭps′wĭch), *n.* a seaport in E England, in Suffolk. 98,020 (est. 1946).

IQ, intelligence quotient. Also, **I.Q.**

i.q., (L *idem quod*) the same as.

I·qui·que (ē·kē′kě), *n.* a seaport in N Chile. 38,094 (1940).

ir-¹, var. of in-², before *r,* as in *irradiate.*

ir-², var. of in-³, before *r,* as in *irreducible.*

Ir, *Chem.* iridium.

Ir., 1. Ireland. 2. Irish.

i·ra·cund (ī′rə·kŭnd′), *adj.* prone to anger; irascible. [t. L: s. *īrācundus* angry] **—i′ra·cun′di·ty,** *n.*

i·ra·de (ĭ·rä′dě), *n.* a decree of the Sultan of Turkey. [Turk., t. Ar.: m. *irāda* will, desire]

I·rak (ĭ·räk′; *Pers.* ē·räk′), *n.* Iraq.

I·ran (ĭ·rän′, ī-; *Pers.* ē·rän′), *n.* 1. former official name (until 1935), **Persia.** a kingdom in SW Asia. ab. 15,-000,000 pop.; ab. 635.000 sq. mi. *Cap.:* Teheran. 2. **Plateau of,** a plateau covering most of Iran and Afghanistan, from E of the Tigris to W of the Indus. [t. Pers.]

I·ra·ni·an (ĭ·rā′nĭ·ən), *adj.* 1. pertaining to Iran (or Persia). 2. pertaining to Iranian (def. 3). **—n.** 3. a subgroup of Indo-European languages including Persian and Pushtu. 4. Persian (the language). 5. an inhabitant of Iran; a Persian. 6. an Iranian Aryan.

I·raq (ĭ·räk′; *Pers.* ē·räk′),*n.* a kingdom in SW Asia, N of Saudi Arabia and W of Iran, centering in the Tigris-Euphrates basin of Mesopotamia. 4,150,000 pop. (est. 1946); 116,600 sq. mi. *Cap.:* Bagdad. Also, **Irak.** Cf. **Mesopotamia.**

I·ra·qi (ē·rä′kē), *n., pl.* -qis, *adj.* **—n.** 1. a native of Iraq. 2. Also, **Iraqi Arabic,** the dialect of Arabic spoken in Iraq. **—adj.** 3. of Iraq or its inhabitants.

i·ras·ci·ble (ĭ·răs′ə·bəl, ī·răs′-), *adj.* 1. easily provoked to anger: *an irascible old man.* 2. characterized by, excited by, or arising from anger: *an irascible nature.* [ME, t. LL: m.s. *irascibilis*] **—i·ras′ci·bil′i·ty, i·ras′ci·ble·ness,** *n.* **—i·ras′ci·bly,** *adv.*

i·rate (ī′rāt, ī·rāt′), *adj.* angry; enraged: *the irate colonel.* [t. L: m.s. *īrātus,* pp.] **—i′rate·ly,** *adv.*

ire (īr), *n.* anger; wrath. [ME, t. OF, t. L: m. *īra*] **—ire′less,** *adj.*

Ire., Ireland.

ire·ful (īr′fəl), *adj.* 1. full of ire; wrathful: *an ireful look.* 2. irascible. **—ire′ful·ly,** *adv.* **—ire′ful·ness,** *n.*

Ire·land (īr′lənd), *n.* 1. a large western island of the British Isles, comprising Eire and Northern Ireland. ab. 4,277,000 pop.; 32,375 sq. mi. Latin, **Hibernia.** 2. **Republic of,** See **Eire.**

I·re·ne (ī·rē′nē), *n. Gk. Myth.* the daughter of Themis by Zeus. She became the goddess of peace.

i·ren·ic (ī·rěn′ĭk, ī·rē′nĭk), *adj.* peaceful; tending to promote peace, esp. with reference to ecclesiastical difference. Also, **i·ren′i·cal.** [t. Gk.: m.s. *eirēnikós*]

i·ren·ics (ī·rěn′ĭks, ī·rē′nĭks), *n.* irenic theology.

i·ri·da·ceous (ī′rə·dā′shəs, ĭr′ə-), *adj.* 1. belonging to the *Iridaceae,* or iris family of plants, which includes,

besides various flags, the crocus, gladiolus, and freesia. 2. resembling or pertaining to plants of the genus *Iris.* [f. s. NL *Iris* the iris genus (see IRIS) + -ACEOUS]

ir·i·des·cence (ĭr′ə·děs′əns), *n.* iridescent quality; a play of lustrous, changing colors.

ir·i·des·cent (ĭr′ə·děs′ənt), *adj.* displaying colors like those of the rainbow. [f. s. L *īris* rainbow + -ESCENT] **—ir′i·des′cent·ly,** *adv.*

i·rid·ic (ĭ·rĭd′ĭk, ī·rĭd′-), *adj. Chem.* of or containing iridium, esp. in the tetravalent state (Ir+4).

i·rid·i·um (ĭ·rĭd′ĭ·əm, ī·rĭd′-), *n. Chem.* a precious metallic element resembling platinum: used in platinum alloys and for the points of gold pens. *Symbol:* Ir; *at.wt.:* 193.1; *at.no.:* 77; *sp.gr.:* 22.4. at 20°C. [t. NL, der. L *īris* rainbow; named from its iridescence in solution]

ir·i·dize (ĭr′ə·dīz′, ī′rə-), *v.t.,* **-dized, -dizing.** to cover with iridium. **—ir′i·di·za′tion,** *n.*

ir·i·dos·mine (ĭr′ə·dŏz′mĭn, -dŏs′-, ī′rə-), *n.* a native alloy of iridium and osmium, usually containing some rhodium, ruthenium, platinum, etc., used esp. for the points of gold pens. Also, **ir·i·dos·mi·um** (ĭr′ə·dŏz′mĭ-əm, -dŏs′-, ī′rə-). [f. IRID(IUM) + OSM(IUM) + -INE³]

ir·i·dous (ĭr′ə·dəs, ī′rə-) *adj. Chem.* containing trivalent iridium (Ir+3).

i·ris (ī′rĭs), *n., pl.* **irises, irides** (ĭr′ə·dēz′, ī′rə-). 1. *Anat.* the contractile circular diaphragm forming the colored portion of the eye and containing a circular opening (the pupil) in its center. See diag. under eye. 2. *Bot.* **a.** a family of plants, *Iridaceae.* **b.** any plant of the genus *Iris,* including various perennial herbs with handsome flowers and sword-shaped leaves; the fleur-de-lis or flag. **c.** the flower of any such plant. **d.** orrisroot. 3. (*cap.*) *Gk. Myth.* a messenger of the gods, regarded as the goddess of the rainbow. 4. a rainbow. 5. any appearance resembling a rainbow. [ME, t. L, t. Gk.]

iris diaphragm, *Optics, Photog.* a composite diaphragm with a central aperture readily adjustable for size, used to regulate the amount of light admitted to a lens or optical system.

I·rish (ī′rĭsh), *adj., n., pl.* **Irish. —adj.** 1. of, pertaining to, or characteristic of Ireland or its people. **—n.** 2. the inhabitants of Ireland and their immediate descendants elsewhere. 3. the aboriginal Celtic-speaking population of Ireland. 4. the Celtic language of Ireland in its historical (Old Irish, Middle Irish) or modern form. 5. Irish English. [ME *Irisc, Iris(c)h,* der. OE *Iras,* pl., inhabitants of Ireland (c. Icel. *Irar*)]

Irish English, 1. the English dialects spoken in Ireland. 2. the standard English of Ireland.

Irish Free State, former name of **Eire** (1922–37)

I·rish·ism (ī′rĭsh·ĭz′əm), *n.* an Irish idiom, custom, etc.

I·rish·man (ī′rĭsh·mən), *n., pl.* **-men.** a man born in Ireland or of Irish ancestry. **—I′rish·wom′an,** *n. fem.*

Irish moss, 1. a purplish-brown, cartilaginous seaweed, *Chondrus crispus,* of the Atlantic coasts of Europe and North America; carrageen. 2. this seaweed, dried and bleached, used to keep solids in suspension as in hand lotions, and for making soup and blancmange.

Irish Pale. See **pale** (def. 1).

Irish potato, the common white potato.

Irish Sea, a part of the Atlantic between Ireland and England.

Irish setter
(24 in. high at the shoulder)

Irish setter, a dark mahogany-red variety of setter.

Irish stew, a stew usually made of mutton, lamb, or beef, with potatoes, onions, etc.

Irish terrier, one of a breed of small, active, intelligent dogs with wiry hair, usually of a reddish tinge.

Irish wolfhound, a shaggy-coated breed of wolfhound, the tallest known dog, developed in Ireland as early as the third century A.D. See illus. below.

i·ri·tis (ī·rī′tĭs), *n. Pathol.* inflammation of the iris of the eye. [t. NL; f. IR(IS) + -ITIS] **—i·rit·ic** (ī·rĭt′ĭk), *adj.*

Irish terrier
(18 in. high at the shoulder)

irk (ûrk), *v.t.* to weary, annoy, or trouble: *it irked him to wait.* [ME *irke, yrk(e).* Cf. MHG *erken* disgust]

irk·some (ûrk′səm), *adj.* 1. causing weariness, disgust, or annoyance: *irksome restrictions.* 2. *Obs.* distressing. **—irk′some·ly,** *adv.* **—irk′some·ness,** *n.* **—Syn.** 1. See **tedious.**

Ir·kutsk (ĭr·kŏŏtsk′), *n.* a city in the S Soviet Union in Asia, W of Lake Baikal. 243,-380 (1939).

i·ron (ī′ərn), *n.* 1. *Chem.* a ductile, malleable, silver-white metallic element, scarcely known in a pure condition, but abundantly used in its crude or impure forms containing carbon (**pig iron, cast iron, steel,** and **wrought**

Irish wolfhound
(31 in. high at the shoulder)

iron: see these entries) for making tools, implements, machinery, etc. *Symbol:* Fe (Lat. *ferrum*); *at. wt.:* 55.85; *at. no.:* 26; *sp. gr.:* 7.86 at 20°C. **2.** something hard, strong, rigid, unyielding, or the like: *hearts of iron.* **3.** an instrument, utensil, weapon, etc., made of iron. **4.** an iron implement used heated for smoothing or pressing cloth, etc. **5.** an iron-headed golf club intermediate between a cleek and a mashie: *a driving iron.* **6.** a branding iron. **7.** *Slang.* a pistol. **8.** *Archaic.* a sword. **9.** a harpoon. **10.** *Med.* a preparation of iron, or containing iron, used as a tonic, etc. **11.** (*pl.*) an iron shackle or fetter. **12. in irons,** *Naut.* lying head to the wind and lacking steerageway to cast off on either tack. **13. too many irons in the fire,** too many undertakings. —*adj.* **14.** made of iron. **15.** resembling iron in color, firmness, etc.: *an iron will.* **16.** stern, harsh, or cruel. **17.** not to be broken. **18.** degenerate, debased, or wicked. **19.** pertaining to the iron age. —*v.t.* **20.** to smooth or press with a heated iron, as clothes, etc. —*v.i.* **21.** to press clothes, etc., with a heated iron. **22.** to furnish, mount, or arm with iron. **23.** to shackle or fetter with irons. [ME *iren, ysen,* OE *īren, īsen, īsern,* c. G *eisen*] —**i/ron·less,** *adj.* —**i/ron·like/,** *adj.*

Iron Age, 1. *Archaeol.* the age of the history of Old World mankind (subsequent to the stone and bronze ages) marked by the use of iron implements. **2.** (*l.c.*) *Class. Myth.* the last and worst age of the world. **3.** (*l.c.*) any age or period of degeneracy or wickedness.

i·ron·bark (ī/ərn bärk/), *n.* any of the various Australian eucalyptuses with a hard, solid bark, as *Eucalyptus resinifera,* a tall tree yielding a valuable timber, and a gum.

i·ron·bound (ī/ərn bound/), *adj.* **1.** bound with iron. **2.** rock-bound; rugged. **3.** hard, rigid, or unyielding.

i·ron·clad (ī/ərn klăd/), *adj.* **1.** covered or cased with iron plates, as a vessel for naval warfare; armor-plated. **2.** very rigid or strict: *an ironclad agreement.* —*n.* **3.** one of the first naval ships fitted with armor.

iron curtain, a state of rigid censorship and secrecy. [coined by Winston Churchill in 1946 to describe the line of demarcation between western Europe and the Russian zone of influence]

Iron Duke, The, nickname of the first Duke of Wellington.

i·rone (ī rōn/, ī/rōn), *n.* a colorless liquid, $C_{14}H_{22}O$, obtained from the orrisroot, and used in perfumery.

i·ron·er (ī/ər nər), *n.* one who or that which irons.

Iron Gate, a gorge cut by the Danube through the Carpathian Mountains, between Yugoslavia and SW Rumania. 2 mi. long. Also, **Iron Gates.**

i·ron·gray (ī/ərn grā/), *adj.* of a gray like that of freshly broken iron.

Iron Guard, a Rumanian anti-Semitic fascist party, eliminated after World War II.

iron horse, 1. a locomotive. **2.** a bicycle or tricycle.

i·ron·i·cal (ī rŏn/ə kəl), *adj.* **1.** pertaining to, of the nature of, or characterized by irony: *an ironical compliment.* **2.** using, or addicted to irony: *an ironical speaker.* Also, **i·ron/ic.** [f. s. L *ironicus* (t. Gk.: m. *eirōnikós* dissembling, feigning ignorance) + -AL¹] —**i·ron/i·cal·ly,** *adv.* —**i·ron/i·cal·ness,** *n.*

iron lung, a chamber in which alternate pulsations of high and low pressure can be used to force normal lung movements, used esp. in some cases of infantile paralysis.

i·ron·mas·ter (ī/ərn măs/tər, -mäs/tər), *n. Chiefly Brit.* a manufacturer of iron; the master of ironworks.

i·ron·mon·ger (ī/ərn mŭng/gər), *n. Chiefly Brit.* a dealer in hardware.

i·ron·mon·ger·y (ī/ərn mŭng/gə rĭ), *n., pl.* **-geries.** *Chiefly Brit.* the goods, shop, or business of an ironmonger.

iron pyrites, 1. pyrite, or ordinary pyrites; fool's gold. **2.** marcasite. **3.** pyrrhotite.

i·ron·side (ī/ərn sīd/), *n.* **1.** a person with great power of endurance or resistance. **2.** (*cap., usually pl.*) **a.** Edmund II of England. **b.** Oliver Cromwell. **c.** one of Cromwell's troopers. **3.** (*pl.*) an ironclad.

i·ron·smith (ī/ərn smĭth/), *n.* a worker in iron; a blacksmith.

i·ron·stone (ī/ərn stōn/), *n.* any ore of iron (commonly a carbonate of iron) with clayey or siliceous impurities.

i·ron·ware (ī/ərn wâr/), *n.* articles of iron, as pots, kettles, tools, etc.; hardware.

i·ron·weed (ī/ərn wēd/), *n.* any of certain North American plants of the composite genus *Vernonia,* bearing tubular flowers, chiefly purple or red.

i·ron·wood (ī/ərn wŏŏd/), *n.* **1.** any of various trees with hard, heavy wood, as *Carpinus caroliniana,* an American species of hornbeam, or *Lyonothamnus floribundus,* found on the islands off the coast of southern California. **2.** the wood.

i·ron·work (ī/ərn wûrk/), *n.* **1.** work in iron. **2.** parts or articles made of iron: *ornamental ironwork.*

i·ron·work·er (ī/ərn wûr/kər), *n.* **1.** a worker in iron. **2.** one employed in the erection of steel bridges, etc.

i·ron·works (ī/ərn wûrks/), *n.pl. or sing.* an establishment where iron is smelted or where it is cast or wrought.

i·ron·y¹ (ī/rə nĭ), *n., pl.* **-nies. 1.** a figure of speech in which the literal meaning of a locution is the opposite of that intended, esp., as in the Greek sense, when the locution understates the effect intended: employed in ridicule or merely playfully. **2.** an ironical utterance or expression. **3.** simulated ignorance in discussion (**Socratic irony**). **4.** (in tragedy) the quality or effect of speeches understood by the audience but not grasped by the speakers on the stage (**tragic irony**). **5.** an outcome of events contrary to what was, or what might have been, expected. **6.** an ironical quality. [t. L: m. s. *īrōnīa,* t. Gk.: m. *eirōneía* dissimulation, understatement]

—**Syn. 1.** IRONY, SARCASM, SATIRE agree in indicating derision of something or someone. In IRONY the essential feature is the contradiction between the literal and the intended meaning, since one thing is said and another is implied; it attacks or derides, or, often, is merely playful: *"Beautiful weather, isn't it?"* (the weather is perfectly detestable). *"If you try hard, you may be able to do worse"* (what you have done is quite bad enough). In SARCASM the characteristic feature is the harsh or cutting quality; it may be ironical or may state directly what is meant: *"A fine musician you've turned out to be! You couldn't play one piece correctly if you had two assistants."* SATIRE, originally applied to a literary composition which attacks by means of irony or sarcasm, denotes also the use of such means formally in writing or speaking, for some serious purpose (as the exposing or denouncing of abuses) or in a malicious or merely playful spirit: *Swift's satires; a speech of satire against the wasteful city administration.*

i·ron·y² (ī/ər nĭ), *adj.* consisting of, containing, or resembling iron. [ME *yrony;* f. IRON + -Y¹]

Ir·o·quoi·an (ĭr/ə kwoi/ən), *adj.* belonging to or constituting a linguistic family of the Iroquoian-Caddoan stock of North American Indians, of Canada and the eastern U.S., including the Iroquois confederacy, the Cherokees, Wyandots or Hurons, Erie, and others.

Ir·o·quoi·an-Cad·do·an (ĭr/ə kwoi/ən kăd/ō ən), *n.* an American Indian linguistic stock combining the Iroquoian and Caddoan families and perhaps related to the Siouan-Muskogean stock.

Ir·o·quois (ĭr/ə kwoi/, -kwoiz/), *n.sing. and pl.* **1.** a member of the Indian confederacy, the Five Nations, comprising the Mohawks, Oneidas, Onondagas, Cayugas, and Senecas, with, later, the Tuscaroras. —*adj.* **2.** belonging or relating to the Iroquois or their tribes. [t. F, f. m. Algonquian *irinakhoiw* real adders + F suffix *-ois*]

ir·ra·di·ant (ĭ rā/dĭ ənt), *adj.* irradiating; radiant; shining. —**ir·ra/di·ance, ir·ra/di·an·cy,** *n.*

ir·ra·di·ate (*v.* ĭ rā/dĭ āt/; *adj.* ĭ rā/dĭ ĭt, -āt/), *v.,* **-ated, -ating,** *adj.* —*v.t.* **1.** to shed rays of light upon; illuminate. **2.** to illumine intellectually or spiritually. **3.** to brighten as if with light. **4.** to radiate (light, etc.). **5.** to heat with radiant energy. **6.** to cure by being exposed to radiation, as of ultraviolet light. **7.** to expose to radiation. —*v.i.* **8.** to emit rays; shine. **9.** to become radiant. —*adj.* **10.** irradiated; bright. [t. L: m.s. *irradiatus,* pp., illumined] —**ir·ra/di·a·tive,** *adj.* —**ir·ra/di·a·tor,** *n.*

ir·ra·di·a·tion (ĭ rā/dĭ ā/shən), *n.* **1.** act of irradiating. **2.** state of being irradiated. **3.** intellectual or spiritual enlightenment. **4.** a ray of light; a beam. **5.** *Optics.* the apparent enlargement of a bright object when seen against a dark ground. **6.** the use of x-rays or other radiations for the treatment of disease, etc. **7.** the process of exposure to radiation. **8.** the intensity of radiation falling on a given point; radiant energy received per unit of time per unit area of irradiated surface.

ir·ra·tion·al (ĭ răsh/ən əl), *adj.* **1.** without the faculty of, or not endowed with, reason: *irrational animals.* **2.** without, or deprived of, sound judgment. **3.** not in accordance with reason; utterly illogical: *irrational fear.* **4.** *Arith.* not capable of being exactly expressed by a ratio of two integers. **5.** *Math.* (of functions) not expressible as the ratio of two polynomials. **6.** *Gk. and Lat. Pros.* **a.** of or pertaining to a substitution in the normal metrical pattern, esp. a long syllable for a short syllable. **b.** noting a foot containing such a substitution. [late ME, t. L: s. *irrationālis*] —**ir·ra/tion·al·ly,** *adv.* —**ir·ra/tion·al·ness,** *n.*

ir·ra·tion·al·ism (ĭ răsh/ən ə lĭz/əm), *n.* irrationality in thought or action.

ir·ra·tion·al·i·ty (ĭ răsh/ə năl/ə tĭ), *n., pl.* **-ties. 1.** the quality of being irrational. **2.** an irrational, illogical, or absurd action, thought, etc.

Ir·ra·wad·dy (ĭr/ə wŏd/ĭ), *n.* a river flowing S through Burma to the Bay of Bengal. ab. 1250 mi.

ir·re·claim·a·ble (ĭr/ĭ klā/mə bəl), *adj.* not reclaimable; incapable of being reclaimed. —**ir/re·claim/a·bil/i·ty, ir/re·claim/a·ble·ness,** *n.* —**ir/re·claim/a·bly,** *adv.*

ir·rec·on·cil·a·ble (ĭ rĕk/ən sī/lə bəl, for emphasis often ĭ rĕk/ən sī/-), *adj.* **1.** that cannot be harmonized or adjusted; incompatible: *two irreconcilable statements.* **2.** that cannot be brought to acquiescence or content; implacably opposed: *irreconcilable enemies.* —*n.* **3.** one who or that which is irreconcilable. **4.** one who remains opposed to agreement or compromise. —**ir·rec/on·cil·a·bil/i·ty, ir·rec/on·cil/a·ble·ness,** *n.* —**ir·rec/on·cil/a·bly,** *adv.*

Irrawaddy River

ir·re·cov·er·a·ble (ĭr′ĭ kŭv′ər ə bəl), *adj.* **1.** that cannot be regained: *an irrecoverable debt.* **2.** that cannot be remedied or rectified: *irrecoverable sorrow.* —**ir′·re·cov′er·a·ble·ness,** *n.* —**ir′re·cov′er·a·bly,** *adv.*

ir·re·cu·sa·ble (ĭr′ĭ kū′zə bəl), *adj.* not to be objected to or rejected. [t. LL: m. s. *irrecūsābilis* not to be refused] —**ir′re·cu′sa·bly,** *adv.*

ir·re·deem·a·ble (ĭr′ĭ dē′mə bəl), *adj.* **1.** not redeemable; incapable of being bought back or paid off. **2.** not convertible into specie, as paper money. **3.** beyond redemption; irreclaimable. **4.** irremediable, irreparable, or hopeless. —**ir′re·deem′a·bly,** *adv.*

ir·re·den·tist (ĭr′ĭ děn′tĭst), *n.* **1.** (*usually cap.*) a member of an Italian association which became prominent in 1878, advocating the redemption, or the incorporation into Italy, of certain neighboring regions (**Italia irredenta**) having a primarily Italian population. **2.** a member of a party in any country advocating the acquiring of some region, actually included in another country, but claimed as properly belonging to the former country by reason of racial or other ties. —*adj.* **3.** pertaining to or advocating irredentism. [t. It.: s. *irredentista,* der. (*Italia*) *irredenta* (Italy) unredeemed, fem. of *irredento,* f. L: *in-* IN-³ + m. *redemptus,* pp., redeemed] —**Ir′re·den′tism,** *n.*

ir·re·duc·i·ble (ĭr′ĭ dū′sə bəl, -dōō′-), *adj.* **1.** not reducible; incapable of being reduced or diminished: *the irreducible minimum.* **2.** incapable of being brought into a different condition or form. —**ir′re·duc′i·bil′i·ty, ir′re·duc′i·ble·ness,** *n.* —**ir′re·duc′i·bly,** *adv.*

ir·re·frag·a·ble (ĭr ĕf′rə gə bəl), *adj.* not to be refuted; undeniable. [t. LL: m.s. *irrefragābilis*] —**ir·ref′ra·ga·bil′i·ty,** *n.* —**ir·ref′ra·ga·bly,** *adv.*

ir·re·fran·gi·ble (ĭr′ĭ frăn′jə bəl), *adj.* **1.** not to be broken or violated; inviolable: *an irrefrangible rule of etiquette.* **2.** incapable of being refracted: *x-rays are irrefrangible.* —**ir′re·fran′gi·bly,** *adv.*

ir·ref·u·ta·ble (ĭr ĕf′yə tə bəl, ĭr′ĭ fū′tə bəl), *adj.* not refutable; incontrovertible: *irrefutable logic.* —**ir·ref′·u·ta·bil′i·ty,** *n.* —**ir·ref′u·ta·bly,** *adv.*

irreg., **1.** irregular. **2.** irregularly.

ir·re·gard·less (ĭr′ĭ gärd′lĭs), *adj. Colloq.* regardless (not generally regarded as good usage).

ir·reg·u·lar (ĭ rěg′yə lər), *adj.* **1.** without symmetry, even shape, formal arrangement, etc.: *an irregular pattern.* **2.** not characterized by any fixed principle, method, or rate: *irregular intervals.* **3.** not according to rule, or to the accepted principle, method, course, order, etc. **4.** not conformed or conforming to rules of justice or morality, as conduct, transactions, mode of life, etc., or persons. **5.** *Bot.* not uniform, (of a flower) having the members of some or all of its floral circles or whorls differing from one another in size or shape, or extent of union. **6.** *Gram.* not conforming to the most prevalent pattern of formation, inflection, construction, etc.: *the verbs "keep" and "see" are irregular in their inflection.* **7.** *Mil.* (formerly, of troops) not belonging to the established forces. —*n.* **8.** one who or that which is irregular. **9.** *Mil.* a soldier not of a regular military force. [t. ML: s. *irregulāris;* r. ME *irreguler,* t. OF. See IR-², REGULAR] —**ir·reg′u·lar·ly,** *adv.*

—**Syn.** **1.** unsymmetrical, uneven. **2.** unmethodical, unsystematic; disorderly, capricious, erratic, eccentric, lawless. **3.** anomalous, unusual. IRREGULAR, ABNORMAL, EXCEPTIONAL imply a deviation from the regular, the normal, the ordinary, or the usual. IRREGULAR, not according to rule, refers to any deviation, as in form, arrangement, action, and the like; it may imply such deviation as a mere fact, or as regrettable, or even censurable. ABNORMAL implies a deviation from the common rule, resulting in a nontypical form or nature of a thing: *a two-headed calf is abnormal, abnormal lack of emotion.* EXCEPTIONAL means out of the ordinary or unusual; it may refer merely to the rarity of occurrence, or to the superiority of quality: *an exceptional case, an exceptional mind.*

ir·reg·u·lar·i·ty (ĭ rěg′yə lăr′ə tĭ), *n., pl.* **-ties.** **1.** state or fact of being irregular. **2.** something irregular.

ir·rel·a·tive (ĭ rěl′ə tĭv), *adj.* **1.** not relative; without relation (fol. by *to*). **2.** irrelevant. —**ir·rel′a·tive·ly,** *adv.* —**ir·rel′a·tive·ness,** *n.*

ir·rel·e·vance (ĭ rěl′ə vəns), *n.* **1.** the quality of being irrelevant: *the irrelevance of his arguments.* **2.** an irrelevant thing, act, etc.

ir·rel·e·van·cy (ĭ rěl′ə vən sĭ), *n., pl.* **-cies.** irrelevance.

ir·rel·e·vant (ĭ rěl′ə vənt), *adj.* **1.** not relevant; not applicable or pertinent: *irrelevant remarks.* **2.** *Law.* (of evidence) having no probative value upon any issue in the case. —**ir·rel′e·vant·ly,** *adv.*

ir·re·liev·a·ble (ĭr′ĭ lēv′və bəl), *adj.* not relievable.

ir·re·li·gion (ĭr′ĭ lĭj′ən), *n.* **1.** lack of religion. **2.** hostility to or disregard of religion; impiety. —**ir′·re·li′gion·ist,** *n.*

ir·re·li·gious (ĭr′ĭ lĭj′əs), *adj.* **1.** not religious; impious; ungodly. **2.** showing disregard for or hostility to religion. [t. LL: m.s. *irreligiōsus*] —**ir′re·li′gious·ly,** *adv.* —**ir′re·li′gious·ness,** *n.*

ir·rem·e·a·ble (ĭ rěm′ĭ ə bəl, ĭ rē′mĭ-), *adj. Now Poetic.* from which one cannot return. [t. L: m.s. *irremeābilis*] —**ir·rem′e·a·bly,** *adv.*

ir·re·me·di·a·ble (ĭr′ĭ mē′dĭ ə bəl), *adj.* not remediable; irreparable: *irremediable disease.* —**ir′re·me′di·a·ble·ness,** *n.* —**ir′re·me′di·a·bly,** *adv.*

ir·re·mis·si·ble (ĭr′ĭ mĭs′ə bəl), *adj.* **1.** not remissible; unpardonable, as a sin. **2.** that cannot be remitted, as a

duty. —**ir′re·mis′si·bil′i·ty, ir′re·mis′si·ble·ness,** *n.* —**ir′re·mis′si·bly,** *adv.*

ir·re·mov·a·ble (ĭr′ĭ mōō′və bəl), *adj.* not removable. —**ir′re·mov′a·bil′i·ty,** *n.* —**ir′re·mov′a·bly,** *adv.*

ir·rep·a·ra·ble (ĭ rěp′ə rə bəl), *adj.* not reparable; incapable of being rectified, remedied, or made good: *an irreparable loss.* —**ir·rep′a·ra·bil′i·ty, ir·rep′a·ra·ble·ness,** *n.* —**ir·rep′a·ra·bly,** *adv.*

ir·re·peal·a·ble (ĭr′ĭ pē′lə bəl), *adj.* not repealable.

ir·re·place·a·ble (ĭr′ĭ plā′sə bəl), *adj.* that cannot be replaced: *an irreplaceable souvenir.*

ir·re·plev·i·sa·ble (ĭr′ĭ plěv′ə sə bəl), *adj. Law.* not replevisable or repleviable: that cannot be replevied. Also, **ir·re·plev·i·a·ble** (ĭr′ĭ plěv′ĭ ə bəl).

ir·re·press·i·ble (ĭr′ĭ prěs′ə bəl), *adj.* not repressible. —**ir′re·press′i·bil′i·ty, ir′re·press′i·ble·ness,** *n.* —**ir′re·press′i·bly,** *adv.*

ir·re·proach·a·ble (ĭr′ĭ prō′chə bəl), *adj.* not reproachable; free from blame. —**ir′re·proach′a·ble·ness,** *n.* —**ir′re·proach′a·bly,** *adv.*

ir·re·sist·i·ble (ĭr′ĭ zĭs′tə bəl), *adj.* not resistible; that cannot be resisted or withstood: *an irresistible impulse.* —**ir′re·sist′i·bil′i·ty, ir′re·sist′i·ble·ness,** *n.* —**ir′re·sist′i·bly,** *adv.*

ir·res·o·lute (ĭ rěz′ə lōōt′), *adj.* not resolute; doubtful or undecided; infirm of purpose; vacillating. —**ir·res′o·lute′ly,** *adv.* —**ir·res′o·lute′ness,** *n.*

ir·res·o·lu·tion (ĭ rěz′ə lōō′shən), *n.* lack of resolution; lack of decision or purpose; vacillation.

ir·re·solv·a·ble (ĭr′ĭ zŏl′və bəl), *adj.* not resolvable; incapable of being resolved; not analyzable; not solvable.

ir·re·spec·tive (ĭr′ĭ spěk′tĭv), *adj.* without regard to something else, esp. something specified; independent (fol. by *of*): *irrespective of all rights.* —**ir′re·spec′tive·ly,** *adv.*

ir·re·spir·a·ble (ĭr′ĭ spīr′ə bəl, ĭ rěs′pĭr ə bəl), *adj.* not respirable; unfit for respiration.

ir·re·spon·si·ble (ĭr′ĭ spŏn′sə bəl), *adj.* **1.** not responsible; not answerable or accountable: *an irresponsible ruler.* **2.** not capable of responsibility; done without a sense of responsibility: *mentally irresponsible.* —*n.* **3.** an irresponsible person. —**ir′re·spon′si·bil′i·ty, ir′re·spon′si·ble·ness,** *n.* —**ir′re·spon′si·bly,** *adv.*

ir·re·spon·sive (ĭr′ĭ spŏn′sĭv), *adj.* not responsive; not responding, or not responding readily, as in speech, action, or feeling. —**ir′re·spon′sive·ness,** *n.*

ir·re·ten·tive (ĭr′ĭ těn′tĭv), *adj.* not retentive; lacking power to retain, esp. mentally. —**ir′re·ten′tive·ness,** *n.*

ir·re·trace·a·ble (ĭr′ĭ trā′sə bəl), *adj.* not retraceable; that cannot be retraced: *an irretraceable step.*

ir·re·triev·a·ble (ĭr′ĭ trē′və bəl), *adj.* not retrievable; irrecoverable; irreparable. —**ir′re·triev′a·bil′i·ty, ir′re·triev′a·ble·ness,** *n.* —**ir′re·triev′a·bly,** *adv.*

ir·rev·er·ence (ĭ rěv′ər əns), *n.* **1.** the quality of being irreverent; lack of reverence or respect. **2.** the condition of not being reverenced: *to be held in irreverence.*

ir·rev·er·ent (ĭ rěv′ər ənt), *adj.* not reverent; manifesting or characterized by irreverence; deficient in veneration or respect: *an irreverent reply.* [t. L: s. *irreverens*] —**ir·rev′er·ent·ly,** *adv.*

ir·re·vers·i·ble (ĭr′ĭ vûr′sə bəl), *adj.* not reversible; that cannot be reversed. —**ir′re·vers′i·bil′i·ty, ir′re·vers′i·ble·ness,** *n.* —**ir′re·vers′i·bly,** *adv.*

ir·rev·o·ca·ble (ĭ rěv′ə kə bəl), *adj.* not to be revoked or recalled; that cannot be repealed or annulled: *an irrevocable decree.* —**ir·rev′o·ca·bil′i·ty, ir·rev′o·ca·ble·ness,** *n.* —**ir·rev′o·ca·bly,** *adv.*

ir·ri·ga·ble (ĭr′ĭ gə bəl), *adj.* that may be irrigated.

ir·ri·gate (ĭr′ə gāt′), *v.t.* **-gated, -gating.** **1.** to supply (land) with water by means of streams passing through it, esp. artificial streams provided to promote vegetation. **2.** *Med.* to supply (a wound, etc.) with a constant flow of some liquid. **3.** *Now Rare.* to moisten; wet. [t. L: m.s. *irrigātus,* pp.] —**ir′ri·ga′tor,** *n.*

ir·ri·ga·tion (ĭr′ə gā′shən), *n.* **1.** the supplying of land with water from artificial channels to promote vegetation. **2.** *Med.* the covering or washing out of anything with water or other liquid for the purpose of making or keeping it moist, as in local medical treatment. **3.** state of being irrigated. —**ir′ri·ga′tion·al,** *adj.*

ir·ri·ga·tive (ĭr′ə gā′tĭv), *adj.* serving for or pertaining to irrigation.

ir·rig·u·ous (ĭ rĭg′yōō əs), *adj. Now Rare.* well-watered, as land. [t. L: m. *irriguus*]

ir·ri·ta·bil·i·ty (ĭr′ə tə bĭl′ə tĭ), *n., pl.* **-ties.** **1.** the quality of being irritable. **2.** an irritable state or condition. **3.** *Physiol., Biol.* the ability to be excited to a characteristic action or function by the application of some stimulus: *protoplasm displays irritability by responding to heat, etc.* [t. L: m.s. *irritābilitas*]

ir·ri·ta·ble (ĭr′ə tə bəl), *adj.* **1.** easily irritated; readily excited to impatience or anger. **2.** *Physiol., Biol.* displaying irritability (def. 3). **3.** *Pathol.* susceptible to physical irritation; liable to shrink, become inflamed, etc., when stimulated: *an irritable wound.* [t. L: m.s. *irritābilis*] —**ir′ri·ta·ble·ness,** *n.* —**ir′ri·ta·bly,** *adv.*

ir·ri·tant (ĭr′ə tənt), *adj.* **1.** irritating. —*n.* **2.** anything that irritates. **3.** *Pathol., Med.* something, as a poison or a therapeutic agent, producing irritation. [t. L: s. *irritans.* ppr.] —**ir′ri·tan·cy,** *n.*

ir·ri·tate (ĭr/ə tāt/), *v.t.*, **-tated, -tating. 1.** to excite to impatience or anger. **2.** *Physiol., Biol.* to excite (a living system) to some characteristic action or function. **3.** *Pathol.* to bring (a bodily part, etc.) to an abnormally excited or sensitive condition. [t. L: m.s. *irrītātus*, pp.] —**ir/ri·ta/tor**, *n.*
—**Syn. 1.** vex, chafe, fret, gall; nettle, ruffle, pique; incense, anger, enrage, infuriate. IRRITATE, EXASPERATE, PROVOKE mean to annoy or stir to anger. To IRRITATE is to excite to impatience or angry feeling, often of no great depth or duration: *to irritate by refusing to explain an action.* To EXASPERATE is to irritate to a point where self-control is threatened or lost: *to exasperate by continual delays and excuses.* To PROVOKE is to stir to a sudden, strong feeling of resentful anger as by unwarrantable acts or wanton annoyance: *to tease and provoke an animal until it attacks one.* —**Ant. 1.** appease, pacify.

ir·ri·tat·ing (ĭr/ə tā/tĭng), *adj.* causing irritation; provoking: *an irritating reply.* —**ir/ri·tat/ing·ly**, *adv.*

ir·ri·ta·tion (ĭr/ə tā/shən), *n.* **1.** act of irritating. **2.** state of being irritated. **3.** *Physiol., Pathol.* **a.** the bringing of a bodily part or organ to an abnormally excited or sensitive condition. **b.** the condition itself.

ir·ri·ta·tive (ĭr/ə tā/tĭv), *adj.* **1.** serving or tending to irritate. **2.** *Pathol.* characterized or produced by irritation of some bodily part, etc.: *an irritative fever.*

ir·rup·tion (ĭ rŭp/shən), *n.* a breaking or bursting in; a violent incursion or invasion. [t. L: s. *irruptio*]

ir·rup·tive (ĭ rŭp/tĭv), *adj.* **1.** characterized by or pertaining to irruption. **2.** *Petrol.* intrusive.

Ir·tish (ĭr tĭsh/), *n.* a river flowing from the Altai Mountains N W through the W Soviet Union in Asia to the Ob river. ab. 2300 mi. Also, **Ir·tysh/.**

Ir·ving (ûr/vĭng), *n.* **1. Sir Henry,** (*John Henry Brodribb*) 1838–1905, British actor. **2. Washington,** 1783–1859, U.S. essayist, story writer, and historian.

Ir·ving·ton (ûr/vĭng tən), *n.* a town in NE New Jersey, near Newark. 59,201 (1950).

is (ĭz), *v.* 3rd pers. sing. pres. indic. of **be.** [OE *is*, c. Icel. *es, er;* akin to G *ist,* Goth. *ist,* L *est,* Gk. *estí,* Skt. *astí.* See BE]

is-, var. of **iso-,** before some vowels, as in *isallobar.*

Is., 1. Also, **Isa.** Isaiah. **2.** Also, **is.** Island. **3.** Isle.

I·saac (ī/zək), *n.* a patriarch, son of Abraham and Sarah, and father of Jacob. Gen. 17:19. [t. L (Vulgate), t. Gk. (Septuagint), t. Heb.: m. *Yitshāq,* lit., laughs]

I·saacs (ī/zəks), *n.* **Sir Isaac Alfred,** 1855–1948, Australian jurist: governor general of Australia, 1931–36.

Is·a·bel·la I (ĭz/ə bĕl/ə), (*the Catholic*) 1451–1504, joint ruler, 1474–1504, of Castile and León, with her husband Ferdinand V, and patron of Columbus. Also, *Spanish,* **I·sa·bel** (ē/sä bĕl/).

i·sa·gog·ic (ī/sə gŏj/ĭk), *adj.* **1.** introductory, esp. to the interpretation of the Bible. —*n.* **2.** (*usually pl.*) **a.** introductory studies. **b.** the department of theology which is introductory to exegesis and the literary history of the Bible. [t. L: m.s. *īsagōgicus* introductory, t. Gk.: m. *eisagōgikós,* lit., leading into]

I·sa·iah (ī zā/ə, ī zī/ə), *n.* **1.** a great Hebrew prophet of the eighth century B.C. **2.** a long book of the Old Testament, belonging to the second division of the Hebrew canon and the first book of the major prophets. [ult. t. Heb.: m. *Yesha'yāh,* lit., Jehovah's salvation]

i·sal·lo·bar (ī săl/ə bär/), *n. Meteorol.* a line on a weather map connecting planes having equal pressure changes. [f. IS- + ALLO- + -BAR. See ISOBAR]

I·sar (ē/zär), *n.* a river flowing from W Austria NE through S Germany to the Danube. 215 mi.

i·sa·rithm (ī/sə rĭth/əm), *n.* isopleth.

Is·car·i·ot (ĭs kăr/ī ət), *n.* **1.** the surname of Judas, the betrayer of Jesus. Mark 3:19, 14:10–11. **2.** one who betrays another; a traitor. [t. L: s. *Iscariōta,* t. Gk.: m. *Iskariōtēs,* t. Heb.: m. *īsh-qerīyōth* man of *Kerioth* (a place in Palestine)]

is·che·mi·a (ĭs kē/mī ə), *n. Pathol.* local anemia produced by local obstacles to the arterial flow. Also, **is·chae/mi·a.** [t. NL, f. s. Gk. *ischein* check + -(a)*emia* -EMIA] —**is·che·mic** (ĭs kē/mĭk, -kĕm/ĭk), *adj.*

Is·chia (ē/skyä), *n.* **1.** an island off the SW coast of Italy, near Naples: destructive earthquake, 1883. 29,-288 pop. (1936); 18 sq. mi. **2.** a seaport on this island. 2858 (1936).

is·chi·ad·ic (ĭs/kĭ ăd/ĭk), *adj.* pertaining to the schium; sciatic. Also, **is·chi·at·ic** (ĭs/kĭ ăt/ĭk).

is·chi·um (ĭs/kĭ əm), *n., pl.* **-chia** (-kĭ ə). *Anat.* **1.** the lowermost of the three parts composing either innominate bone. See diag. under **pelvis. 2.** either of the bones on which the body rests when sitting. [t. NL, t. Gk.: m. *ischíon* hip joint, haunch, ischium] —**is/chi·al,** *adj.*

-ise¹, var. of **-ize,** as in *exercise.*

-ise², a noun suffix indicating quality, condition, or function, as in *merchandise, franchise.*

I·sère (ē zěr/), *n.* a river in SE France, flowing from the Alps to the Rhone river. ab. 150 mi.

I·seult (ĭ sōōlt/), *n. Arthurian Romance.* **1.** the daughter of Angus, king of Ireland, and wife of Mark, king of Cornwall, loved by Tristram (Tristan). **2.** daughter of the king of Brittany, and wife of Tristram. Also, **Isolde, Isolt.**

Is·fa·han (ĭs/fə hän/), *n.* a city in central Iran: the capital of Persia from the 16th into the 18th centuries. 205,000 (1940). Also, **Ispahan.**

-ish¹, 1. a suffix used to form adjectives from nouns, with the sense of: **a.** "belonging to" (a people, country, etc.), as in *British, Danish, English, Spanish.* **b.** "after the manner of," "having the characteristics of," "like," as in *babyish, girlish, mulish* (such words being now often depreciatory). **c.** "addicted to," "inclined or tending to," as in *bookish, freakish.* **2.** a suffix used to form adjectives from other adjectives, with the sense of "somewhat," "rather," as in *oldish, reddish, sweetish.* [ME; OE *-isc,* c. G *-isch,* Gk. *-iskos;* akin to -ESQUE] —**Syn. 1.** The suffixes -ISH, -LIKE, -LY, agree in indicating that something resembles something else. One of the common meanings of -ISH is derogatory; that is, it indicates that something has the bad qualities of something else, or that it has qualities similar which are not suitable to it: *childish, mannish* (of a woman). The suffix -LIKE, in the formation of adjectives, is usually complimentary: *childlike innocence, godlike serenity.* In an adverbial function, it may be slightly disparaging: *manlike, he wanted to run the show.* The suffix -LY, when it means having the nature or character of, is distinctly complimentary: *kingly, manly, motherly.*

**-ish², a suffix forming simple verbs. [t. F: m. *-iss-,* extended stem of verbs in *-ir,* g. L *-isc-,* in inceptive verbs]

Ish·ma·el (ĭsh/mā əl), *n.* **1.** the outcast son of Abraham and Hagar. See Gen. 16:11, 12. **2.** any outcast. [t. Heb.: m. *Yishmā'ēl,* lit., God will hear]

Ish·ma·el·ite (ĭsh/mā əl īt/), *n.* **1.** a descendant of Ishmael (from whom the Arabs claim descent). **2.** a wanderer; an outcast. —**Ish/ma·el·it/ish,** *adj.*

Ish·tar (ĭsh/tär), *n.* the chief goddess of the Babylonians and Assyrians. Cf. **Astarte.** [t. Akkadian]

Is·i·dore of Seville (ĭz/ə dōr/), (*Isidorus Hispalensis*) A.D. c560–636, Spanish archbishop and Latin encyclopedist.

i·sin·glass (ī/zĭng glăs/, -gläs/), *n.* **1.** a pure, transparent or translucent form of gelatin, esp. that derived from the air bladders of certain fishes. **2.** mica. [t. MD: pop. m. (by assoc. with GLASS) of *hysenblas,* c. G *hausenblase* isinglass, lit., sturgeon bladder. See HAUSEN]

I·sis (ī/sĭs), *n.* an Egyptian goddess, sister and wife of Osiris, usually distinguished by the solar disk and cow's horns on her head. [t. L, t. Gk., t. Egyptian: m. *Ese*]

Is·ken·de·run (ĭs kĕn/də rōōn/), *n.* Turkish name of **Alexandretta.**

isl., 1. (*pl.* **isls.**) island. **2.** isle.

Is·lam (ĭs/ləm, ĭs/läm/), *n.* **1.** the religious system of the Almighty Potentate Allah according to Mohammed; Mohammedanism. **2.** the whole body of Mohammedan believers, their civilization, and their lands. [t. Ar.: submission (to the will of God)] —**Is·lam·ic** (ĭs-läm/ĭk, -lä/mĭk), **Is·lam·it·ic** (ĭs/lə mĭt/ĭk), *adj.*

Is·lam·ism (ĭs/lə mĭz/əm), *n.* Mohammedanism.

Is·lam·ite (ĭs/lə mīt/), *n.* a Mohammedan.

is·land (ī/lənd), *n.* **1.** a tract of land completely surrounded by water, and not large enough to be called a continent. **2.** a clump of woodland in a prairie. **3.** an isolated hill. **4.** something resembling an island. **5.** a platform in the middle of a street, at a crossing, for the safety of pedestrians. **6.** *Physiol., Anat.* an isolated portion of tissue or aggregation of cells. —*v.t.* **7.** to make into or as into an island. **8.** to dot with or as with islands. **9.** to place on or as on an island; isolate. [ME *iland, yland,* OE *īland, īgland,* f. *īg, īeg* island + *land* land; -*s* inserted through erroneous assoc. with ISLE] —**is/land·less,** *adj.* —**is/land·like/,** *adj.*

is·land·er (ī/lən dər), *n.* a native or inhabitant of an island.

Islands of the Blessed, *Gk. Myth.* imaginary islands said to lie in the remote western part of the ocean whither after death the souls of heroes and good men were supposed to be transported.

island universe, *Astron.* a galaxy.

isle (īl), *n., v.,* **isled, isling.** —*n.* **1.** a small island: *the British Isles.* **2.** *Now Chiefly Poetic.* an island. —*v.t.* **3.** to make into or as into an isle. **4.** to place on or as on an isle. —*v.i.* **5.** to dwell or remain on an isle. [ME *isle, ile,* t. OF, g. L *insula*]

Isle of Pines. See **Pines, Isle of.**

Isle of Wight. See **Wight, Isle of.**

Isle Roy·ale (īl/ roi/əl), a large island in Lake Superior: a part of Michigan; now a national park. 208 sq. mi.

is·let (ī/lĭt), *n.* a small island. [t.F: m. *islette* (now *īlette*), dim. of *isle* ISLE]

Is·ling·ton (ĭz/lĭng tən), *n.* a N borough of London, England. 232,180 (est. 1946).

isls., islands.

ism (ĭz/əm), *n.* a distinctive doctrine, theory, system, or practice: *this is the age of isms.* [n. use of -ISM]

-ism, a suffix of nouns denoting action or practice, state or condition, principles, doctrines, a usage or characteristic, etc., as in *baptism, barbarism, criticism, Darwinism, plagiarism, realism.* Cf. **-ist** and **-ize.** [ult. (often directly) t. Gk.: s. *-ismos, -isma,* noun suffix. See -IZE]

Is·ma·il·i·an (ĭs/mä ĭl/ī ən), *n.* a member of a sect of Shiite Mohammedans whose doctrines vary widely from those of orthodox Mohammedans.

Is·ma·il Pa·sha (ĭs/mä ēl/ pä shä/), 1830–95, viceroy and khedive of Egypt, 1863–79.

is·n't (ĭz/ənt), contraction of *is not.*

iso-, 1. a prefix meaning "equal." **2.** *Chem.* a prefix added to the name of one compound to denote another isomeric with it. Also, **is-.** [t. Gk., comb. form of *īsos* equal]

ăct, āble, dâre, ärt; ĕbb, ēqual; ĭf, īce; hŏt, ōver, ôrder, oil, bŏŏk, ōōze, out; ŭp, ūse, ûrge; ə = a in alone; ch, chief; g, give; ng, ring; sh, shoe; th, thin; ŧℏ, that; zh, vision. See the full key on inside cover.

i·so·ag·glu·ti·na·tion (ī′sō ə gloō′tə nā′shən), n. Med. the clumping of the red blood cells of an animal by a tranfusion from another animal of the same species.

i·so·ag·glu·ti·nin (ī′sō ə gloō′tə nĭn), n. an agglutinin which can effect isoagglutination.

i·so·bar (ī′sə bär′), n. **1.** Meteorol., etc. a line drawn on a weather map, etc., connecting all points having the same barometric pressure (reduced to sea level) at a specified time or over a certain period. **2.** Physics., Chem. one of the two atoms of different atomic number, but having the same atomic weight. [t. Gk.: s. isobarēs of equal weight]

Isobars (def. 1)

i·so·bar·ic (ī′sə bär′ĭk), adj. **1.** having or showing equal barometric pressure. **2.** of or pertaining to isobars.

i·so·car·pic (ī′sə kär′pĭk), adj. Bot. having carpels equal in number to the other floral parts.

i·so·cheim (ī′sə kīm′), n. Climatology. a line on a map connecting places which have the same mean winter temperature. Also, **i′so·chime′**. [f. iso- + m.s. Gk. cheîma winter] —**i′so·chei′mal**, adj.

i·so·chor (ī′sə kôr′), n. Physics. a line representing the variation in pressure with temperature, under a constant volume. Also, **i′so·chore′**. [f. iso- + s. Gk. chōra place] —**i·so·chor·ic** (ī′sə kôr′ĭk, -kôr′-), adj.

i·so·chro·mat·ic (ī′sō krō măt′ĭk), adj. **1.** Optics. having the same color or tint. **2.** Physics. involving radiation of constant wave length or frequency. **3.** Photog. orthochromatic.

i·so·chron (ī′sə krŏn′), n. a mathematical function representing one percent of maturation time and used in the sciences of development. Also, **i·so·chrone** (ī′sə krŏn′).

i·soch·ro·nal (ī sŏk′rə nəl), adj. **1.** equal or uniform in time. **2.** performed in equal intervals of time. **3.** characterized by motions or vibrations of equal duration. [f. s. Gk. isóchronos equal in age or time + -AL¹] —**i·soch′ro·nal·ly**, adv.

i·soch·ro·nism (ī sŏk′rə nĭz′əm), n. isochronal character or action.

i·soch·ro·nize (ī sŏk′rə nīz′), v.t., -nized, -nizing. to make isochronal.

i·soch·ro·nous (ī sŏk′rə nəs), adj. isochronal. —**i·soch′ro·nous·ly**, adv.

i·soch·ro·öus (ī sŏk′rō əs), adj. having the same color throughout.

i·so·cli·nal (ī′sə klī′nəl), adj. **1.** of or pertaining to equal inclination; inclining or dipping in the same direction. **2.** denoting or pertaining to a line on the earth's surface connecting points of equal dip or inclination of the earth's magnetic field. **3.** Geol. noting or pertaining to a fold of strata which is of the nature of an iscoline. —n. **4.** an isoclinal line. Also, **i·so·clin·ic** (ī′sə klĭn′ĭk). [f. s. Gk. isoklīnḗs equally balanced + -AL¹]

Isoclinal lines (def. 2)

i·so·cline (ī′sə klīn′), n. Geol. a fold of strata so tightly compressed that the parts on each side dip in the same direction. [t. Gk.: m.s. isoklīnḗs equally balanced]

i·soc·ra·cy (ī sŏk′rə sĭ), n., pl. -cies. a government in which all have equal political power. [t. Gk.: m.s. isokratía. See iso-, -CRACY] —**i·so·crat·ic** (ī′sə krăt′ĭk), adj.

I·soc·ra·tes (ī sŏk′rə tēz′), n. 436–338 B.C., an Athenian orator and teacher of oratory.

i·so·cy·a·nine (ī′sə sī′ə nĭn, -nĭn), n. Chem. a member of the cyanines. See **cyanine**.

i·so·di·a·met·ric (ī′sə dī′ə mĕt′rĭk), adj. **1.** having equal diameters or axes. **2.** Bot. having the diameter similar throughout, as a cell. **3.** (of crystals) having two, or three, equal horizontal axes and a third, or fourth, unequal axis at right angles thereto.

i·so·di·mor·phism (ī′sō dī môr′fĭz əm), n. Crystall. isomorphism between the forms of two dimorphous substances. —**i·so·di·mor′phous**, adj.

i·so·dy·nam·ic (ī′sō dī năm′ĭk, -dī′-), adj. **1.** pertaining to or characterized by equality of force, intensity, or the like. **2.** denoting or pertaining to a line on the earth's surface connecting points of equal horizontal intensity of the earth's magnetic field. Also, **i·so·dy·nam′i·cal**.

i·so·e·lec·tric point (ī′sō ĭ lĕk′trĭk), Chem. the pH at which a substance is electrically neutral or at which it is at its minimum ionization.

i·so·ga·mete (ī′sō gə mēt′), n. Biol. one of a pair of conjugating gametes, exhibiting no sexual or morphological differentiation.

i·sog·a·mous (ī sŏg′ə məs), adj. Biol. having two similar gametes in which no differentiation can be distinguished, or reproducing by the union of such gametes (opposed to heterogamous).

i·sog·a·my (ī sŏg′ə mĭ), n. Biol. the fusion of two gametes of similar form, as in certain algae.

i·sog·e·nous (ī sŏj′ə nəs), adj. Biol. of the same or similar origin, as parts derived from the same or corresponding tissues of the embryo. [f. iso- + -GENOUS] —**i·sog′e·ny**, n.

i·so·ge·o·therm (ī′sə jē′ə thûrm′), n. Phys. Geog. an imaginary line or surface passing through points in the interior of the earth which have the same mean temperature. [f. iso- + GEO- + s. Gk. thérmē heat] —**i·so·ge′o·ther′mal, i′so·ge·o·ther′mic**, adj.

i·so·gloss (ī′sə glôs′, -glŏs′), n. an imaginary line separating two localities which differ in some feature of their speech. [f. iso- + s. Gk. glôssa word, speech, tongue]

i·sog·o·nal (ī sŏg′ə nəl), adj. **1.** equiangular; isogonic. —n. **2.** an isogonic line.

isogonal line, a line on the earth's surface connecting points of equal declination of the earth's magnetic field.

i·so·gon·ic (ī′sə gŏn′ĭk), adj. **1.** having or pertaining to equal angles. **2.** denoting or pertaining to an isogonal line. —n. **3.** an isogonal line. [f. m.s. Gk. isogónios having equal angles + -IC]

i·so·gram (ī′sə grăm′), n. Meteorol., Geog. a line representing equality with respect to a given variable, used to relate places on maps, charts, etc.

i·so·graph (ī′sə grăf′, -gräf′), n. a line drawn on a map to indicate areas having common linguistic characteristics. —**i·so·graph·ic** (ī′sə grăf′ĭk), adj.

i·so·hel (ī′sə hĕl′), n. a line on a map, etc., connecting places which receive equal amounts of sunshine.

i·so·hy·et (ī′sə hī′ət), n. a line drawn on a map connecting points having equal rainfall at a certain time or for a stated period. [f. iso- + s. Gk. hyetós rain]

i·so·la·ble (ī′sə lə bəl, ĭs′ə-), adj. that can be isolated.

i·so·late (ī′sə lāt′, ĭs′ə-), v.t., -lated, -lating. **1.** to set or place apart; detach or separate so as to be alone. **2.** Med. to keep (an infected person) from contact with noninfected ones. **3.** Chem. to obtain (a substance) in an uncombined or pure state. **4.** Elect. to insulate. [back formation from isolated, ppl. adj., f. s. It. isolato (g. L insulātus; see INSULATE) + -ED²] —**i·so·la′tor**, n.

isolating language, a language which uses few or no bound forms.

i·so·la·tion (ī′sə lā′shən, ĭs′ə-), n. **1.** act of isolating. **2.** state of being isolated. **3.** the complete separation from others of a person suffering from contagious or infectious disease. **4.** the separation of a nation from other nations by a policy of nonparticipation in international affairs. **5.** Sociol. See **social isolation.** —Syn. **2.** See **solitude.**

i·so·la·tion·ist (ī′sə lā′shən ĭst, ĭs′ə-), n. one who favors a policy of nonparticipation in international affairs. —**i′so·la′tion·ism**, n.

I·solde (ĭ sōld′, ĭ sōl′də; Ger. ē zōl′də), n. Iseult. Also, **I·solt** (ĭ sōlt′).

i·so·leu·cine (ī′sə loō′sēn, -sĭn), n. an amino acid, $C_2H_5CH(CH_3)CH(NH_2)COOH$, occurring in casein.

i·so·mag·net·ic (ī′sō măg nĕt′ĭk), adj. **1.** denoting or pertaining to an imaginary line on the earth's surface, or a corresponding line on a map or the like, connecting places which have the same magnetic elements. —n. **2.** an isomagnetic line.

i·so·mer (ī′sə mər), n. Chem. a compound which is isomeric with one or more other compounds.

i·so·mer·ic (ī′sə mĕr′ĭk), adj. Chem. (of compounds) composed of the same kinds and numbers of atoms which differ from each other in the arrangement of the atoms and, therefore, in one or more properties. [f. s. Gk. isomerḗs having equal parts + -IC]

i·som·er·ism (ī sŏm′ə rĭz′əm), n. state or condition of being isomeric.

i·som·er·ous (ī sŏm′ər əs), adj. **1.** having an equal number of parts, markings, etc. **2.** Bot. (of a flower) having the same number of members in each whorl.

i·so·met·ric (ī′sə mĕt′rĭk), adj. **1.** pertaining to or having equality of measure. **2.** Crystall. noting or pertaining to that system of crystallization which is characterized by three equal axes at right angles to one another. **3.** Pros. of equal measure; made up of regular feet. Also, **i′so·met′ri·cal**. [f. s. Gk. isómetros of equal measure + -IC] —**i′so·met′ri·cal·ly**, adv.

i·so·me·tro·pi·a (ī′sō mə trō′pĭ′ə), n. a condition in which the refraction is the same in the two eyes. [f. iso- + s. Gk. métron measure + -OPIA]

i·som·e·try (ī sŏm′ə trĭ), n. **1.** equality of measure. **2.** Geog. equality with respect to height above sea level.

i·so·morph (ī′sə môrf′), n. **1.** an organism which is isomorphic with another or others. **2.** an isomorphous substance.

i·so·mor·phic (ī′sə môr′fĭk), adj. **1.** Biol. being the same or of like form; different in ancestry, but alike in appearance. **2.** Crystall. isomorphous.

i·so·mor·phism (ī′sə môr′fĭz əm), n. state or property of being isomorphous or isomorphic.

i·so·mor·phous (ī′sə môr′fəs), adj. Chem., Crystall. (of a substance) undergoing a more or less extended, continuous variation in chemical composition, with accompanying variations in physical and chemical properties, but maintaining the same crystal structure.

i·son·o·my (ĭsŏn/əmĭ), *n.* equality of political rights. [t. Gk.: m.s. *isonomía*] —**i·so·nom·ic** (ī/sə nŏm/ĭk), *adj.*

I·son·zo (ē zŏn/tsō), *n.* a river forming a part of the boundary between Italy and Yugoslavia, flowing from the Julian Alps S to the Gulf of Trieste. 75 mi.

i·so·oc·tane (ī/sō ŏk/tān), *n.* an isomer of octane used to determine the knocking qualities of a gasoline.

i·so·pi·es·tic (ī/sō pī ĕs/tĭk), *adj.* 1. isobaric; denoting equal pressure. —*n.* 2. an isobar (def. 1). [f. ISO- + s. Gk. *piestós*, vbl. adj. of *piézein* press + -IC]

i·so·pleth (ī/sə plĕth/), *n.* a line drawn on a map through all points having the same numerical value of any element, or of the ratio of values of two elements. [t. Gk.: s. *isoplēthēs* equal in number]

i·so·pod (ī/sə pŏd/), *n.* 1. any of the *Isopoda*, an order of suborder of crustaceans (fresh-water, marine, and terrestrial) with seven pairs of legs, and body flattened dorso-ventrally. —*adj.* 2. pertaining to the *Isopoda*. 3. having the feet all alike, or similar in character. [t. NL: s. *Isopoda*, pl., genus type. See ISO-, -POD] —**i·sop·o·dan** (ī sŏp/ə dən), *adj.* —**i·sop/o·dous**, *adj.*

i·so·prene (ī/sə prēn/), *n.* *Chem.* a colorless liquid hydrocarbon, C_5H_8, of the terpene class, produced from rubber or from oil of turpentine by pyrolysis and convertible into rubber by polymerization. [? f. ISO- + PR(OPYL) + -ENE]

i·so·pro·pyl (ī/sə prō/pĭl), *n.* *Chem.* the univalent radical, $(CH_3)_2CH$.

isopropyl ether, a colorless liquid, $(C_3H_7)_2O$, used as a solvent for waxes, fats, etc.

i·sos·ce·les (ī sŏs/ə lēz/), *adj.* (of a triangle) having two sides equal. See illus. under **triangle.** [t. LL, t. Gk.: m. *isoskelēs* with equal legs]

i·so·seis·mic (ī/sə sīz/mĭk, -sīs/-), *adj.* 1. pertaining to equal intensity of earthquake shock. 2. noting or pertaining to an imaginary line on the earth's surface connecting points characterized by such intensity. —*n.* 3. an isoseismic line. Also, **i·so·seis/mal.**

i·sos·ta·sy (ī sŏs/tə sĭ), *n.* 1. *Geol.* the equilibrium of the earth's crust, a condition in which the forces tending to elevate balance those tending to depress. 2. equilibrium when there is pressure from all sides; hydrostatic equilibrium. [f. ISO- + m. Gk. *stásis* a standing]

i·so·stat·ic (ī/sə stăt/ĭk), *adj.* pertaining to or characterized by isostasy.

i·so·there (ī/sə thĭr/), *n.* *Climatology.* a line connecting places on the earth's surface which have the same mean summer temperature. [f. ISO- + m.s. Gk. *théros* summer] —**i·soth·er·al** (ī sŏth/ər əl), *adj.*

i·so·therm (ī/sə thûrm/), *n.* *Climatology.* a line connecting points on the earth's surface having the same (mean) temperature. 2. *Physics, Chem.* an isothermal line. [f. ISO- + s. Gk. *thérme* heat]

i·so·ther·mal (ī/sə thûr/məl), *adj.* 1. *Physics, Chem.* pertaining to or indicating equality of temperature. 2. *Climatology.* pertaining to an isotherm. —*n.* 3. *Climatology.* an isotherm. —**i/so·ther/mal·ly,** *adv.*

isothermal line, *Physics, Chem.* a line or graph showing relations of variables under conditions of uniform temperature.

isothermal process, *Meteorol.* a process which takes place without change in temperature.

i·so·ton·ic (ī/sə tŏn/ĭk), *adj.* 1. pertaining to solutions characterized by equal osmotic pressure. 2. *Physiol.* **a.** noting or pertaining to a solution containing just enough salt to prevent the destruction of the red blood corpuscles when added to the blood. **b.** noting or pertaining to a contraction of a muscle when under a constant tension. 3. *Music.* pertaining to or characterized by equal tones. [f. s. Gk. *isótonos* having equal accent or tone + -IC]

i·so·tope (ī/sə tōp/), *n.* *Chem.* any of two or more forms of a chemical element, occupying the same place in the periodic table and nearly identical in properties, but differing by one or more units in atomic weight. Most of the elements are mixtures of isotopes. [f. ISO- + m.s. Gk. *tópos* place] —**i·so·top·ic** (ī/sə tŏp/ĭk), *adj.*

i·sot·o·py (ī sŏt/ə pĭ), *n.* isotopic character.

i·so·trop·ic (ī/sə trŏp/ĭk, -trō/pĭk), *adj.* 1. *Physics.* having one or more properties that are the same in all directions. 2. *Zool.* lacking axes which are predetermined, as in some eggs. Also, **i·sot·ro·pous** (ī sŏt/rə pəs). [f. ISO- + s. Gk. *trópos* turn, way + -IC]

i·sot·ro·py (ī sŏt/rə pĭ), *n.* state or property of being isotropic.

Is·pa·han (ĭs/pə hän/), *n.* Isfahan.

Is·ra·el (ĭz/rĭ əl), *n.* 1. a name given to Jacob after he had wrestled with the angel. Gen. 32:28. 2. the people traditionally descended from Israel or Jacob; the Hebrew or Jewish people. 3. God's chosen people; the elect. 4. a republic comprising a part of Palestine: formed as a Jewish state May, 1948. 1,200,000 pop. (est. 1950); ab. 7200 sq. mi. *Cap.:* Tel Aviv. See map of **Palestine.** 5. the northern kingdom of the Hebrews, including the ten tribes, sometimes called by the name of the chief tribe, Ephraim. *Cap.:* Samaria. 6. the northern and southern kingdoms of the Hebrews. 7. the Christian church. Gal. 6:16. [ult. t. Heb.: m. *Yisrā'ēl* (appar.) he who striveth with God]

Is·rae·li (ĭz rā/lĭ), *n., pl.* **-lis,** *adj.* —*n.* 1. a native or

inhabitant of Israel (def. 4). —*adj.* 2. of or pertaining to Israel (def. 4).

Is·ra·el·ite (ĭz/rĭ əlīt/), *n.* 1. a descendant of Israel or Jacob; a Hebrew; a Jew. 2. one of God's chosen people. —*adj.* 3. pertaining to Israel; Jewish.

Is·ra·el·it·ish (ĭz/rĭ əlī/tĭsh), *adj.* of the Israelites; Hebrew. Also, **Is·ra·el·it·ic** (ĭz/rĭ əlĭt/ĭk).

Is·ra·fil (ĭz/rəfēl/), *n.* (in Koran) the angel of music.

Is·sei (ēs/sā/), *n., pl.* **-sei.** a person of Japanese ancestry, born in Japan, who has come to the United States to live, but retains his allegiance to Japan. [t. Jap: first born, first generation]

is·su·a·ble (ĭsh/ŏŏ ə bəl), *adj.* 1. that may be issued or may issue. 2. forthcoming, as rents. 3. *Law.* that admits of issue being taken. [f. ISSU(E) + -ABLE] —**is/su·a·bly,** *adv.*

is·su·ance (ĭsh/ŏŏ əns), *n.* 1. act of issuing. 2. issue.

is·su·ant (ĭsh/ŏŏ ənt), *adj.* 1. emerging. 2. *Her.* (of a beast) having only the upper half seen.

is·sue (ĭsh/ŏŏ or, *esp. Brit.,* ĭs/ū), *n., v.,* **-sued, -suing.** —*n.* 1. act of sending, or promulgation; delivery; emission. 2. that which is issued. 3. a quantity issued at one time: *the daily issues of a newspaper.* 4. *Bibliog.* the printing of copies of a work from the original setting of type, but with some slight changes in the preliminary or appended matter. 5. a point in question or dispute, as between contending parties in an action at law. 6. a point or matter the decision of which is of special or public importance: *the political issues.* 7. a point the decision of which determines a matter: *the real issue.* 8. a point at which a matter is ready for decision: *to bring a case to an issue.* 9. something proceeding from any source, as a product, effect, result, or consequence. 10. the ultimate result, event, or outcome of a proceeding, affair, etc.: *the issue of a contest.* 11. a distribution of food (rations), clothing, equipment, or ammunition to a number of officers or enlisted men, or to a military unit. 12. offspring or progeny: *to die without issue.* 13. a going, coming, passing, or flowing out: *free issue and entry.* 14. a place or means of egress; an outlet or vent. 15. that which comes out, as an outflowing stream. 16. *Pathol.* **a.** a discharge of blood, pus, or the like. **b.** an incision, ulcer, or the like emitting such a discharge. 17. *Now Law.* the yield or profit from land or other property. 18. *Obs.* a proceeding or action. 19. at issue, **a.** in controversy: *a point at issue.* **b.** in disagreement. **c.** inconsistent; inharmonious (fol. by *with*). 20. join issue, **a.** to join in controversy. **b.** to submit an issue jointly for legal decision. 21. take issue, to disagree. —*v.t.* 22. to send out; deliver for use; deliver authoritatively; put into circulation. 23. to print (a publication) for sale or distribution. 24. to distribute (food, clothing, etc.) to one or more officers or enlisted men or to a military unit. 25. to send out; discharge; emit. —*v.i.* 26. to go, pass, or flow out; come forth; emerge: *to issue forth to battle.* 27. to be sent or put forth authoritatively or publicly, as a writ, money, etc. 28. to be published, as a book. 29. to come or proceed from any source. 30. to arise as a result or consequence; result. 31. *Now Chiefly Law.* to proceed as offspring, or be born or descended. 32. *Chiefly Law.* to come as a yield or profit, as from land. 33. to have the specified outcome. 34. to result (often fol. by *in*). 35. to terminate. [ME, t. OF, der. pp. of *issir, eissir,* g. L *exīre* go out] —**is/sue·less,** *adj.* —**is/su·er,** *n.* —**Syn.** 26. See **emerge.** —**Ant.** 26. return.

Is·sus (ĭs/əs), *n.* an ancient town of Cilicia, in Asia Minor, near modern Alexandretta: victory of Alexander over Darius III, 333 B.C.

Is·syk-Kul (ĭs/ĭk kŏŏl/), *n.* a large mountain lake in the SW Soviet Union in Asia. ab.2240 sq. mi.

-ist, a suffix of nouns, often accompanying verbs ending in *-ize* or nouns ending in *-ism,* denoting one who does, practices, or is concerned with something, or holds certain principles, doctrines, etc., as in *apologist, dramatist, machinist, plagiarist, realist, socialist, theorist.* [ult. (often directly) t. Gk.: s. *-istēs* noun suffix. See -IZE, -ISM]

Is·tan·bul (ĭs/tăn bŏŏl/, -tän-; *Turk.* ĭs täm/bŏŏl). *n.* a city in European Turkey, on the Bosporus. 793,949 (1940). Formerly, **Constantinople.** Ancient, **Byzantium.** [Turk. alter. of MGk. *eis tēn pólin* in(to) the city]

Isth., isthmus. Also, **isth.**

isth·mi·an (ĭs/mĭ'an), *adj.* 1. of or pertaining to an isthmus. 2. (*cap.*) of the Isthmus of Corinth or of Panama. —*n.* 3. a native or inhabitant of an isthmus.

Isthmian games, one of the great national festivals of ancient Greece, held every two years on the Isthmus of Corinth.

isth·mus (ĭs/məs), *n., pl.* **-muses, -mi** (-mī). 1. a narrow strip of land, bordered on both sides by water, connecting two larger bodies of land. 2. (*cap.*) the Isthmus of Suez. 3. (*cap.*) the Isthmus of Panama. 4. *Anat., etc.* a connecting part, organ, or passage, esp. when narrow or joining structures or cavities larger than itself. [t. L, t. Gk.: m. *isthmós* narrow passage, neck, isthmus]

-istic, a suffix of adjectives (and in the plural of nouns from adjectives) formed from nouns in *-ist,* and having reference to such nouns, or to associated nouns in *-ism,* as in *deistic, euphuistic, puristic.* etc. In nouns it has usually a plural form, as in *linguistics.* [f. -IST + -IC]

-istical. See -istic, -al[1].

-istics. See -istic, -ics.

is·tle (Ĭst′lĕ, -lĭ′), *n.* a fiber from various tropical American trees of the species *Agave* or *Yucca*, used in making bagging, carpets, etc. Also, **ixtle**, **ixtle**. [t. Mex.: m. *ixtli*]

Is·tri·a (Ĭs′trĭ·ə; *It.* ēs′tryä), *n.* a peninsula at the N end of the Adriatic, in NE Italy and NW Yugoslavia. —**Is′tri·an**, *adj.*, *n.*

it (Ĭt), *pron.*, *nom.* **it**, *poss.* **its** or (*Obs.* or *Dial.*) **it**, *obj.* **it**; *pl. nom.* **they**, *poss.* **their** or **theirs**, *obj.* **them**; *n.* —*pron.* **1.** a personal pronoun of the third person and neuter gender, corresponding to *he* and *she*, used (**a**) as a substitute for a neuter noun or a noun representing something possessing sex when sex is not particularized or considered: *the baby lost its rattle;* (**b**) to refer to some matter expressed or understood, or some thing or notion not definitely conceived: *how goes it?* (**c**) to refer to the subject of inquiry or attention, whether impersonal or personal, in sentences asking or stating what or who this is: *who is it? it is I;* (**d**) as the grammatical subject of a clause of which the logical subject is a phrase or clause, generally following, regarded as in apposition with it: *it is hard to believe that;* (**e**) in impersonal constructions: *it snows;* and (**f**) without definite force after an intransitive verb: *to foot it* (go on foot). —*n.* **2.** (in children's games) the player called upon to perform some task, as in tag the one who must catch the other players. [ME and OE *hit* (gen. *his*, dat. *him*, acc. *hit*), neut. of *hē* HE]

it·a·col·u·mite (Ĭt′ə·kŏl′yə·mīt′), *n.* a sandstone consisting of interlocking quartz grains and mica scales, found in Brazil, North Carolina, etc., and remarkable for its flexibility when in thin slabs. [f. *Itacolumi*, mountain in Brazil + -ITE¹]

Ital., **1.** Italian. **2.** Italy. Also, **It.**

ital., italic (type).

I·ta·lia (ē tä′lyä), *n.* Italian name of **Italy.**

Italia ir·re·den·ta (ēr′rē dĕn′tä). See **irredentist.**

I·tal·ian (Ĭ tăl′yən), *adj.* **1.** of or pertaining to Italy, its people, or their language. —*n.* **2.** a native or inhabitant of Italy. **3.** a Romance language, the language of Italy; official also in Switzerland. [ME, t. L: s. *Italianūs*]

I·tal·ian·ate (*adj.* Ĭ tăl′yə nāt′, -yən Ĭt; *v.* Ĭ tăl′yə nāt′), *adj.*, *v.*, **-ated**, **-ating.** —*adj.* **1.** Italianized; conformed to the Italian type or style. —*v.t.* **2.** to Italianize.

Italian East Africa, a former Italian territory in E Africa, formed in 1936 by the merging of Eritrea and Italian Somaliland with newly conquered Ethiopia: taken by British Imperial forces, 1941. *Cap.:* Addis Ababa.

I·tal·ian·ism (Ĭ tăl′yə nĭz′əm), *n.* **1.** an Italian practice, trait, or idiom. **2.** Italian quality, spirit, or principles. **3.** attachment to Italian ideas or principles.

I·tal·ian·ize (Ĭ tăl′yə nīz′), *v.*, **-ized**, **-izing.** —*v.i.* **1.** to become Italian in manner, etc.; speak Italian. —*v.t.* **2.** to make Italian. —**I·tal′ian·i·za′tion**, *n.*

Italian Somaliland, a former Italian colony in E Africa. 1,140,000, pop. (est. 1946); ab. 194,000 sq. mi. (1935). *Cap.:* Mogadiscio. See **Italian East Africa.**

Italian sonnet, a form of sonnet, popularized by Petrarch. It is divided into two definite parts: the first 8 lines rhyme *abbaabba;* the last six lines rhyme by twos or threes in various combinations (*cdecde, cddcd,* etc.).

i·tal·ic (Ĭ tăl′Ĭk), *adj.* **1.** designating or pertaining to a style of printing types in which the letters usually slope to the right (thus, *italic*), patterned upon a compact manuscript hand, and used for emphasis, etc. **2.** (*cap.*) of or pertaining to Italy, esp. ancient Italy or its tribes. —*n.* **3.** (*often pl.*) italic type. **4.** (*cap.*) a principal group of Indo-European languages, including Latin and other languages of ancient Italy, notably Oscan and Umbrian, and closely related to Celtic. [t. L: s. *Italicus*]

I·tal·i·cism (Ĭ tăl′ə sĭz′əm), *n.* Italianism.

i·tal·i·cize (Ĭ tăl′ə sīz′), *v.*, **-cized**, **-cizing.** —*v.t.* **1.** to print in italic type. **2.** to underscore with a single line, as in indicating titles. —*v.i.* **3.** to use italics.

It·a·ly (Ĭt′ə lĭ′), *n.* a republic in S Europe, comprising a peninsula S of the Alps, and the islands of Sicily, Sardinia, Elba, etc.: a kingdom, 1870–1946. 45,527,000 pop. (est. 1942); 119,772 sq. mi. (1945). *Cap.:* Rome. Italian, **Italia.**

I·tas·ca (Ĭ tăs′kə), *n.* **Lake,** a small lake in N Minnesota: one of the sources of the Mississippi river.

itch (Ĭch), *v.i.* **1.** to have or feel a peculiar irritation of the skin which causes a desire to scratch the part affected. **2.** to have a desire to do or to get something: *itch after honor.* **3. an itching palm,** a grasping disposition; greed. —*n.* **4.** the sensation of itching. **5. the itch,** a contagious disease caused by the itch mite which burrows into the skin; scabies. **6.** an uneasy or restless desire or longing: *an itch for authorship.* [ME (y)*icchen*, OE *gicc(e)an,* c. D *jeuken,* G *jucken*]

itch mite, a parasitic mite, *Sarcoptes scabiei,* causing itch or scabies in man and a form of mange in animals.

itch·y (Ĭch′Ĭ), *adj.*, **itchier**, **itchiest.** **1.** having an itching sensation. **2.** of the nature of itching. —**itch′i·ness**, *n.*

-ite¹, a suffix of nouns denoting esp. (**a**) persons associated with a place, tribe, leader, doctrine, system, etc., as in *Campbellite, Israelite, laborite;* (**b**) minerals and fossils, as in *ammonite, anthracite;* (**c**) explosives, as in *cordite, dynamite;* (**d**) chemical compounds, esp. salts of acids whose names end in *-ous,* as in *phosphite, sulfites;* (**e**) pharmaceutical and commercial products, as in *vulcanite;* (**f**) a member or component of a part of the body, as in *somite.* [ult. (often directly) t. Gk.: m. *-ĭtēs* (fem. *-ĭtis*), noun and adj. suffix. Cf. -TTIS]

-ite², a suffix forming adjectives and nouns from adjectives, and some verbs, as in *apposite, composite, opposite, exquisite, requisite, erudite, recondite,* etc. [t. L: m. *-itus, -ītus,* pp. ending]

i·tem (*n., v.* ī′təm; *adv.* ī′tĕm), *n.* **1.** a separate article or particular: *fifty items on the list.* **2.** a separate piece of information or news, as in a newspaper. **3.** *Obs.* an admonition or warning. **4.** *Obs.* an intimation or hint. —*v.t.* **5.** to set down or enter as an item, or by or in items. **6.** to make a note or memorandum of. —*adv.* **7.** *Obs.* or *Archaic.* likewise. [ME, t. L: (adv.) just so, likewise]

i·tem·ize (ī′tə mīz′), *v.t.*, **-ized**, **-izing.** to state by items; give the particulars of: *to itemize an account.* —**i′tem·i·za′tion**, *n.* —**i′tem·iz′er**, *n.*

it·er·ance (Ĭt′ər əns), *n.* *Rare.* iteration.

it·er·ant (Ĭt′ər ənt), *adj.* repeating. [t. L: s. *iterans,* ppr.]

it·er·ate (Ĭt′ə rāt′), *v.t.*, **-ated**, **-ating.** **1.** to utter again or repeatedly. **2.** to do (something) over again or repeatedly. [t. L: m. s. *iterātus,* pp.] —**it′er·a′tion**, *n.*

it·er·a·tive (Ĭt′ə rā′tĬv), *adj.* **1.** repeating; making repetition; repetitious. **2.** *Gram.* frequentative.

Ith·a·ca (Ĭth′ə kə), *n.* **1.** one of the Ionian Islands, off the W coast of Greece: the legendary home of Ulysses. 9313 pop. (1940); 37 sq. mi. **2.** a city in S New York at the S end of Cayuga Lake. 29,257 (1950).

I·thunn (ē′thōōn), *n.* *Scand. Myth.* the goddess, wife of Bragi, who guarded in Asgard the apples eaten by the gods to preserve their youth. Also, **I′thun**, **Idun.**

ith·y·phal·lic (Ĭth′ə făl′Ĭk), *adj.* **1.** pertaining to the phallus, as carried in ancient festivals of Bacchus. **2.** grossly indecent; obscene. **3.** *Anc. Pros.* noting or pertaining to any of several meters employed in hymns sung in Bacchic processions. —*n.* **4.** a poem in ithyphallic meter. **5.** an indecent poem. [t. L: s. *ĭthyphallicus,* t. Gk.: m. *ĭthyphallikós,* der. *ithýphallos* erect phallus]

i·tin·er·an·cy (Ĭ tĬn′ər ən sĬ, Ĭ tĬn′-), *n.* **1.** act of traveling from place to place. **2.** a going about from place to place in the discharge of duty or the prosecution of business. **3.** a body of itinerants. **4.** state of being itinerant. **5.** the system of rotation governing the ministry of the Methodist Church. Also, **i·tin′er·a·cy.**

i·tin·er·ant (ī tĬn′ər ənt, Ĭ tĬn′-), *adj.* **1.** itinerating; journeying; traveling from place to place, or on a circuit, as a preacher, judge, or peddler. —*n.* **2.** one who travels from place to place, esp. for duty or business. [t. LL: s. *itinerans,* ppr.] —**i·tin′er·ant·ly**, *adv.*

i·tin·er·ar·y (ī tĬn′ə rĕr′Ĭ, Ĭ tĬn′-), *n.*, *pl.* **-aries**, *adj.* —*n.* **1.** a line of travel; a route. **2.** an account of a journey; a record of travel. **3.** a book describing a route or routes of travel, with information for travelers. **4.** a plan of travel. —*adj.* **5.** pertaining to traveling or travel routes. **6.** itinerant.

i·tin·er·ate (ī tĬn′ə rāt′, Ĭ tĬn′-), *v.i.*, **-ated**, **-ating.** to go from place to place, esp. in a regular circuit, as to preach. [t. LL: m. s. *itinerātus,* pp.] —**i·tin′er·a′tion**, *n.*

-ition, a noun suffix, as in *expedition, extradition,* etc., being *-tion* with a preceding original or formative vowel, or, in other words, *-ite¹* + *-ion.* [t. L: s. *-itio, -ītio.* Cf. F *-ition,* G *-ition*]

-itious, an adjective suffix occurring in adjectives associated with nouns in *-tion,* as *expeditious,* etc. [t. L: m. *-icius, -īcius*]

-itis, a noun suffix used in pathological terms denoting inflammation of some part or organ, as in *bronchitis, gastritis, neuritis.* [t. Gk. See -ITE¹]

-itive, a suffix, of adjectives and nouns of adjectival orig., as in *definitive, infinitive, fugitive.* [t. L: m.s. *-itīvus, -ītīvus*]

I·to (ē′tō′), *n.* **Prince Ito Hirobumi** (hē′rô bōō′mō), 1841–1909, Japanese statesman.

I·to (ē′tō), *n.* Jewish Territorial Organization: an agency for the advancement of Jewish national aims. [f. (*J)ewish* (*T)erritorial* (*O)rganization,* with *j* written as *i*]

-itol, *Chem.* a suffix used in names of alcohols containing more than one hydroxyl group. [f. -ITE¹ + -OL¹]

its (Ĭts), *adj.* possessive form of **it.** [poss. case of IT, formerly written *it′s*]

it′s (Ĭts), contraction of *it is.*

it·self (Ĭt sĕlf′), *pron.* emphatic or reflexive form of **it.**

-ity, a suffix forming abstract nouns of condition, characteristics, etc., as in *jollity, civility, Latinity.* [ME *-ite,* t. F: m. *-itē,* g. L *-itāt-,* s. *-itas*]

-ium, a suffix representing Latin neuter suffix, used esp. to form names of metallic elements.

I·van III (ī′vən; *Russ.* Ĭ vän′), (*the Great*) 1440–1505, grand duke of Muscovy. 1462–1505.

Ivan IV, (*the Terrible*) 1530–84, grand duke of Muscovy, 1533–47, and first czar of Russia, 1547–84.

I·van·hoe (ī′vən hō′), *n.* a novel (1819) by Sir Walter Scott about England in the twelfth century.

I·va·no·vo (Ĭ vä′nô vô), *n.* a city in the central Soviet Union, NE of Moscow. 285,069 (1939). Formerly, **I·va·no·vo-Voz·ne·sensk** (Ĭ vä′nô vô vôz nĕ sĕnsk′).

-ive, a suffix of adjectives (and nouns of adjectival origin) expressing tendency, disposition, function, connection, etc., as in *active, corrective, destructive, detective, passive, sportive.* Cf. **-ative.** [t. L: m.s. *-īvus;* also repr. F *-if* (masc.), *-ive* (fem.), g. L]

I've (īv), contraction of *I have*.

Ives (īvz), *n.* **1.** **Charles,** born 1874, U.S. composer. **2.** **Frederick Eugene,** 1856–1937, U.S. inventor. **3.** **James Merritt,** 1824–95, U.S. lithographer. See **Currier.**

i·vied (ī′vĭd), *adj.* covered or overgrown with ivy: *ivied walls.*

i·vo·ry (ī′və rĭ, ī′vrĭ), *n., pl.* **-ries,** *adj.* —*n.* **1.** the hard white substance, a variety of dentine, composing the main part of the tusks of the elephant, walrus, etc., used for carvings, billiard balls, etc. **2.** a tusk, as of an elephant. **3.** dentine of any kind. **4.** some substance resembling ivory. **5.** *Slang.* a tooth, or the teeth. **6.** an article made of ivory, as a carving or a billiard ball. **7.** (*pl.*) *Slang.* **a.** the keys of a piano, accordion, etc. **b.** dice. **8.** the hard endosperm (**vegetable ivory**) of the ivory nut, used for ornamental purposes, buttons, etc. **9.** creamy or yellowish white. —*adj.* **10.** consisting or made of ivory. **11.** of the color ivory. [ME *yvory,* etc., t. OF: m. *yvoire,* g. L *eboreus* made of ivory] —**i′vo·ry·like′,** *adj.*

ivory black, a fine black pigment made by calcining ivory.

Ivory Coast, a colony in French West Africa. 4,014,-000 pop. (1940); 184,222 sq. mi. *Cap.:* Abidjan.

ivory gull, a white arctic gull, *Pagophila eburnea.*

ivory nut, **1.** the seed of a low-growing South American palm, *Phytelephas macrocarpa,* forming the source of vegetable ivory. **2.** a similar seed from other palms.

ivory palm, the palm yielding the common ivory nut.

ivory tower, **1.** a place withdrawn from the real world and worldly acts and attitudes. **2.** an attitude of aloofness. [trans. of F *tour d'ivoire,* first used by Sainte-Beuve]

i·vy (ī′vĭ), *n., pl.* **ivies. 1.** a climbing vine, *Hedera helix,* with smooth, shiny, evergreen leaves, yellowish inconspicuous flowers, and black berries, widely grown as an ornamental (**English ivy**). **2.** any of various other climbing or trailing plants, as *Parthenocissus tricuspidata* (**Japanese ivy**), *Glecoma hederacea* (**ground ivy**), etc. [ME; OE *īfig;* akin to G *efeu*] —**i′vy·like′,** *adj.*

English ivy, *Hedera helix*

ivy vine, a vinelike plant, *Ampelopsis cordata,* of the U.S., differing from the grape vine esp. in having a corolla of wholly separate petals.

I.W., Isle of Wight.

i·wis (ĭ wĭs′), *adv. Obs.* certainly. Also, **ywis.** [ME adv. use of neut. of OE adj. *gewis* certain, c. D *gewis,* G *gewiss* certain, certainly; akin to **WIT,** v., know]

I·wo Ji·ma (ē′wə jē′mə; *Jap.* ē′wô jē′mä), one of the Volcano Islands, in the N Pacific, S of Japan: taken by U.S. forces in a costly campaign, Feb.-Mar., 1945.

I.W.W., Industrial Workers of the World.

Ix·elles (ēk sĕl′), *n.* a city in central Belgium, near Brussels. 88,237 (est. 1941).

ix·i·a (ĭk′sĭ ə), *n.* any plant of the iridaceous genus *Ixia,* comprising South African plants with sword-shaped leaves and showy ornamental flowers. [t. NL (named with ref. to the juice), t. Gk.: birdlime]

Ix·i·on (ĭk sī′ən), *n. Gk. Legend.* a king of the Lapithae, who was punished by Zeus for his love for Hera by being bound on an eternally revolving wheel in Tartarus.

Ix·tac·ci·huatl (ēs′tä sē′wä təl), *n.* an extinct volcano in S central Mexico, SE of Mexico City. 17,342 ft. Also, **Iztaccihuatl.**

ix·tle (ĭks′tlĕ, -tlĭ, ĭs′-), *n.* istle.

I·ye·ya·su (ē′yĕ yä′sōō), *n.* **Tokugawa** (tô′kōō gä′-wä), 1542–1616, Japanese general and statesman.

Iy·yar (ē′yär), *n.* (in the Jewish calendar) the eighth month of the year. Also, **I′yar.** [t. Heb., ult. from Akkadian]

iz·ard (ĭz′ərd), *n.* the chamois which inhabits the Pyrenees. [t. F: m. *isard*]

-ization, a suffix combination of **-ize** with **-ation.**

-ize, a suffix of verbs having the sense (a) intransitively, of following some one line of action, practice, policy, etc., as in *Atticize, apologize, economize, theorize, tyrannize,* or of becoming (as indicated), as *crystallize* and *oxidize* (intr.), and (b) transitively, of acting toward or upon, treating, or affecting in a particular way, as in *baptize, colonize, patronize, stigmatize,* or of making or rendering (as indicated), as in *civilize, legalize, mobilize, realize.* Also, **-ise**[1]. Cf. **-ism** and **-ist.** [ult. (often directly) t. Gk.: m. s. *-izein.* Cf. F *-iser,* G *-isieren,* etc.]

I·zhevsk (ĭ zhĕfsk′), *n.* a city in the E Soviet Union in Europe. 175,740 (1939).

Iz·mir (ĭz′mĭr), *n.* Turkish name of **Smyrna.**

Iz·tac·ci·huatl (ēs′täk sē′wä təl), *n.* Ixtaccihuatl.

iz·zard (ĭz′ərd), *n. Colloq.* **1.** the letter Z. **2. from A to izzard,** from beginning to end; completely. [unexplained var. of **ZED**]

J

J, j (jā), *n., pl.* **J's** or **Js, j's** or **js. 1.** a consonant, the 10th letter of the English alphabet. **2.** Roman numeral for 1.

J, *Physics.* joule.

J., **1.** Journal. **2.** Judge. **3.** Justice.

Ja., January.

J.A., Judge Advocate.

jab (jăb), *v.,* **jabbed, jabbing,** *n.* —*v.t., v.i.* **1.** to poke, or thrust smartly or sharply, as with the end or point of something. —*n.* **2.** a poke with the end or point of something; a smart or sharp thrust. Also, **job.** [var. (orig. Scot.) of **JOB**[2]]

jab·ber (jăb′ər), *v.i., v.t.* **1.** to talk or utter rapidly, indistinctly, imperfectly, or nonsensically; chatter. —*n.* **2.** jabbering talk or utterance; gibberish. [appar. imit.] —**jab′ber·er,** *n.* —**jab′ber·ing·ly,** *adv.*

jab·i·ru (jăb′ə rōō′), *n.* a large wading bird, *Jabiru mycteria,* of the stork family, inhabiting the warmer parts of America. [t. Tupi-Guarani]

jab·o·ran·di (jăb′ə răn′dĭ), *n., pl.* **-dis. 1.** any of certain South American shrubs of the rutaceous genus *Pilocarpus.* **2.** the dried leaflets of *Pilocarpus jaborandi* and other species containing the alkaloid, pilocarpine, used as a sudorific and sialagogue. [t. Tupi-Guarani]

ja·bot (zhă bō′ or, *esp. Brit.,* zhăb′ō), *n.* a falling ruffle, cascade, or other arrangement of lace, embroidery, or the like, worn at the neck or front of waist by women and formerly by men. [t. F: lit., bird's crop]

J.A.C., Junior Association of Commerce.

jac·a·mar (jăk′ə mär′), *n.* any bird of the tropical American family *Galbulidae,* usually bright-green above, with long bills. [t. Tupi: m. *jacamá-ciri*]

ja·ça·na (zhä′sə nä′), *n.* any of several tropical, plover-like, aquatic birds of the family *Jacanidae,* most of them having extremely long toes and claws for walking on floating water plants. [t. Pg., t. Tupi: m. *jasaná*]

jac·a·ran·da (jăk′ə răn′də), *n.* **1.** any of the tall tropical American trees constituting the bignoniaceous genus *Jacaranda.* **2.** their fragrant ornamental wood. **3.** any of various related or similar trees. **4.** their wood.

ja·cinth (jā′sĭnth, jăs′ĭnth), *n.* hyacinth (def. 4). [ME *iacynt,* t. OF: m. *jacinte,* g. L *hyacinthus* **HYACINTH**]

jack[1] (jăk), *n.* **1.** (*cap.*) a nickname for the name **John.** **2.** a man or fellow. **3.** (*cap. or l.c.*) a sailor. **4.** any of various mechanical contrivances or devices, as a contrivance for raising great weights small distances. **5.** a device for turning a spit, etc. **6.** *U.S.* any of the four knaves in playing cards. **7.** jackstone. **8.** *Brit.* a small bowl used as a mark for the players to aim at, in the game of bowls. **9.** a small union or ensign used by a ship or vessel as a signal, etc., and flown from the jack staff as an indication of nationality. **10.** jackass. **11.** jack rabbit. **12.** *Elect.* a connecting device to which the wires of a circuit may be attached and which is arranged for the insertion of a plug. **13.** *Naut.* a horizontal bar or crosstree of iron at the topgallant masthead, to spread the royal shrouds. **14. every man jack,** every one without exception. —*v.t.* **15.** to lift or move with or as with a jack, or contrivance for raising (usually fol. by *up*). **16.** *Colloq.* to raise (prices, wages, etc.) (usually fol. by *up*). **17.** *U.S.* to seek (game or fish) with a jack light. [orig. proper name *Jack,* earlier *Jacken,* dissimilated var. of *Jankin,* f. *Jan* John + **-KIN**]

Ratchet type jack (def. 4)
A. Lifting foot;
B. Handle

jack[2] (jăk), *n.* **1.** a Polynesian moraceous tree, *Artocarpus Leterophyllus,* with a fruit resembling breadfruit. **2.** the fruit itself, one of the largest known (up to 60 lbs.). [t. Pg.: m. *jaca,* t. Malayalam: m. *chakka*]

jack[3] (jăk), *n.* **1.** a defensive coat, usually of leather, formerly worn by foot soldiers and others. **2.** *Archaic.* a container for liquor, orig. of waxed leather coated with tar. [ME *iacke,* t. OF: m. *jaque, jaques,* t. Sp.: m. *jaco,* ? t. Ar.: m. *shakk*]

jack-a-dan·dy (jăk'ə dăn'dĭ), *n., pl.* **-dies.** dandy¹ (def. 1).

jack·al (jăk'ôl, -əl), *n.* **1.** any of several races of wild dog of the genus *Canis*, esp. *Canis sureus*, of Asia and Africa, which hunt in packs at night and which were formerly supposed to hunt prey for the lion. **2.** one who does drudgery for another, or who meanly serves the purpose of another. [t. Turk.: m. *chakāl*, t. Pers.: m. *shag(h)āl*]

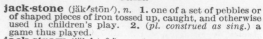

Black-backed jackal, *Canis mesomelas* (Total length 43 in., tail 11 in.)

jack·a·napes (jăk'ə nāps'), *n.* **1.** a pert, presuming man; whippersnapper. **2.** *Archaic.* an ape or monkey. [var. of ME *Jack Napes*, nickname of William, Duke of Suffolk, whose badge was an ape's clog and chain; prob. orig. used as name for tame ape or monkey]

jack·ass (jăk'ăs'), *n.* **1.** a male donkey. **2.** a very stupid or foolish person. [f. JACK¹ + ASS]

jack·boot (jăk'boot'), *n.* a large leather boot reaching up over the knee, orig. one serving as armor.

jack crosstree, jack (def. 13).

jack·daw (jăk'dô'), *n.* **1.** a glossy black European bird, *Coloeus monedula*, of the crow family, frequenting steeples, ruins, etc. **2.** the great-tailed grackle, *Cassidix Mexicanus*, a large glossy blackbird of the southern U.S. and Mexico. [f. JACK¹ + DAW, n.]

jack·et (jăk'ĭt), *n.* **1.** *Chiefly Brit.* a short coat, in various forms, worn by both sexes. **2.** something designed to be fastened about the body for other purpose than clothing: *a strait jacket.* **3.** an outer covering: *a book jacket.* **4.** a metal casing, as the steel covering of a cannon, the steel cover around the core of a bullet, or the water jacket on certain types of machine guns. **5.** *U.S.* a folded paper or open envelope containing an official document. —*v.t.* **6.** to cover with a jacket. [ME *iaquet*, t. OF: m. *jaquete*, dim. of *jaque* JACK³] —**jack'-et·ed,** *adj.* —**jack'et·less,** *adj.* —**jack'et·like',** *adj.*

Jack Frost, frost or freezing cold personified.

jack-in-the-box (jăk'ĭn thə bŏks'), *n.* a toy consisting of a figure, enclosed in a box, which springs out when the lid is unfastened. Also, **jack'-in-a-box'.**

jack-in-the-pul·pit (jăk'ĭn thə pŏŏl'pĭt), *n.* an araceous herb, *Arisaema atro rubens* (*A. triphyllum*), of North America, having an upright spadix arched over by a spathe; Indian turnip.

Jack Ketch (kĕch), *Brit.* a public executioner or hangman. [from a British executioner, *Jack* (or *John*) *Ketch* (d. 1686)]

jack·knife (jăk'nīf'), *n., pl.* **-knives.** *U.S.* **1.** a large pocketknife. **2.** a type of dive in which the diver assumes a folded position of the body while moving through the air, and straightens out before entering the water.

jack ladder, Jacob's ladder (def. 2).

jack light, *U.S.* a portable cresset, oil-burning lantern, or electric light used in hunting or fishing at night.

jack-of-all-trades (jăk'əv ôl'trādz'), *n.* one who can do any kind of work or business.

jack-o'-lan·tern (jăk'ə lăn'tərn), *n.* a lantern made of a rind, as a pumpkin shell, with holes cut to represent human eyes, nose, mouth, etc.

jack pine, a slender pine, *Pinus Banksiana*, covering tracts of barren land in Canada and the northern U.S.

jack pot, *Poker.* a pot that accumulates until a player opens the betting with a pair of jacks or better.

jack rabbit, any of various large hares of western North America, having very long limbs and ears.

Black-tailed jack rabbit, *Lepus alleni* (2 ft. long)

jack·screw (jăk'skroo'), *n.* a jack for raising weights, operated by a screw.

jack·snipe (jăk'snīp'), *n.* **1.** a small, relatively short-billed snipe, *Limnocryptes minima*, of Europe and Asia. **2.** any of several related snipes. **3.** the pectoral sandpiper. [f. JACK¹ + SNIPE]

Jack·son (jăk'sən), *n.* **1. Andrew,** 1767–1845, U.S. general, 7th president of the U.S., 1829–37. **2. Helen Hunt,** (*Helen Maria Fiske*) 1831–85, U.S. novelist and poet. **3. Robert Houghwout** (hou'ət), born 1892, U.S. jurist: associate justice of U.S. Supreme Court since 1941. **4. Thomas Jonathan,** (*"Stonewall Jackson"*) 1824–63, Confederate general in the U.S. Civil War. **5.** the capital of Mississippi, in the central part. 98,271 (1950). **6.** a city in S Michigan. 51,088 (1950). **7.** a city in W Tennessee. 30,207 (1950).

Jackson Day, *U.S.* Jan. 8, celebrated by Democratic party dinners in commemoration of Jackson's victory at New Orleans, 1815.

Jack·so·ni·an (jăk sō'nĭ ən), *adj.* **1.** of or pertaining to Andrew Jackson. —*n.* **2.** a follower of Jackson.

Jack·son·ville (jăk'sən vĭl'), *n.* a seaport in NE Florida, on the St. Johns river. 204,517 (1950).

jack·stay (jăk'stā'), *n.* *Naut.* **1.** a rope, rod, or the like, on a yard or gaff, for bending a sail to. **2.** a rod or rope running up and down on the forward side of a mast, for a yard to travel on; a traveler.

jack·stone (jăk'stōn'), *n.* **1.** one of a set of pebbles or of shaped pieces of iron tossed up, caught, and otherwise used in children's play. **2.** (*pl.* construed as *sing.*) a game thus played.

jack·straw (jăk'strô'), *n.* **1.** a straw-stuffed figure of a man. **2.** an insignificant person. **3.** one of a number of straws, or strips of wood, bone, etc., used in a game in which they are thrown on a table in confusion and are to be picked up singly without disturbing the others. **4.** (*pl.* construed as *sing.*) the game itself.

Jack Tar, a sailor. Also, **jack tar.**

jack towel, a long towel with the ends sewed together, for hanging on a roller.

Jack·y (jăk'ĭ), *n.* **1.** (*often l.c.*) a sailor. **2.** (*l.c.*) *Slang or Brit. Dial.* gin.

Ja·cob (jā'kəb), *n.* the second son of Isaac, the twin brother of Esau, and father of the 12 patriarchs. Gen. 25:24–34. [t. LL: s. *Jacōbus*, t. Gk.: m. *Iákōbos* Jacob, James, t. Heb.: m. *Ya'aqōb* Jacob, explained as one who takes by the heel, a supplanter. See Gen. 25:26, 27:36]

Jac·o·be·an (jăk'ə bē'ən), *adj.* **1.** of or pertaining to James I of England or his times. —*n.* **2.** a Jacobean writer, personage, etc. [f. m.s. NL *Jacōbaeus,* der. LL *Jacōbus* James (see JACOB) + -AN]

Jacobean architecture, late English Gothic architecture, showing Italian influence.

Jac·o·bin (jăk'ə bĭn), *n.* **1.** a member of a famous club or society of French revolutionists organized in 1789, so called from the convent in Paris in which they met. They developed clubs throughout France and worked for the success of the Mountain (def. 4) and the Reign of Terror. **2.** an extreme radical, esp. in politics. **3.** a Dominican friar. **4.** (*l.c.*) an artificial variety of the domestic pigeon, whose neck feathers form a hood. [ME, t. ML: s. *Jacōbīnus,* der. LL *Jacōbus* James (see JACOB)] —**Jac'o·bin'ic, Jac'o·bin'i·cal,** *adj.* —**Jac'o·bin'i·cal·ly,** *adv.*

Jac·o·bin·ism (jăk'ə bĭ nĭz'əm), *n.* **1.** the principles of the Jacobins. **2.** extreme radicalism, esp. in politics. **3.** a concept or characteristic like that of the Jacobins.

Jac·o·bin·ize (jăk'ə bĭ nīz'), *v.t.*, **-ized, -izing.** to imbue with Jacobinism.

Jac·o·bite (jăk'ə bīt'), *n.* a partisan or adherent of James II of England, after his overthrow (1688), or of his descendants. [t. ML: m. *Jacōbīta,* der. LL *Jacōbus* James (see JACOB)] —**Jac·o·bit·ic** (jăk'ə bĭt'ĭk), **Jac'o·bit'i·cal,** *adj.*

Jac·o·bit·ism (jăk'ə bīt'ĭz əm), *n.* the principles of the Jacobites.

Jacob's ladder, 1. a ladder leading up to heaven which Jacob saw in his dream. Gen. 28:12. **2.** *Naut.* a rope ladder with wooden steps.

Ja·cob's-lad·der (jā'kəbz lăd'ər), *n.* **1.** a garden plant, *Polemonium caeruleum,* whose leaves have a ladderlike arrangement. **2.** any of certain related species.

ja·co·bus (jə kō'bəs), *n.* an English gold coin struck in the reign of James I. [t. LL. See JACOB]

Jac·quard loom (jə kärd'; *Fr.* zhà kár'), a pattern loom for weaving elaborate designs. [named after J. M. *Jacquard* (1752–1834), French inventor]

Jacque·mi·not (jăk'mĭ nō'; *Fr.* zhàk mē nō'), *n.* a deep-red variety of the rose. [named after J. F. *Jacqueminot* (1787–1865), French general]

Jacque·rie (zhàk rē'), *n.* **1.** the revolt of the peasants of northern France against the nobles in 1358. **2.** (*l.c.*) any revolt of peasants. [F: (in OF *Jaquerie*) peasants; der. *Jaques* (see JACK¹) taken as a name for a peasant]

jac·ta·tion (jăk tā'shən), *n.* **1.** boasting. **2.** *Pathol.* a restless tossing of the body. [t. L: s. *jactātio* a throwing]

jac·ti·ta·tion (jăk'tə tā'shən), *n.* **1.** *Law.* the assertion of a false claim, to the injury of another. **2.** *Pathol.* jactation (def. 2). [t. ML: s. *jactitātio,* der. L *jactitāre* bring forward in public, utter]

jade¹ (jād), *n.* **1.** either of two minerals, jadeite or nephrite, sometimes green, highly esteemed as an ornamental stone for carvings, jewelry, etc. **2.** Also, **jade green.** green, varying from bluish green to yellowish green. [t. F., t. Sp.: m. (*piedra de*) *ijada,* lit., stone for colic (Sp. *ijada* pain in the side, colic, der. L *ilia* flanks. See ILEUM)] —**jade'like',** *adj.*

jade² (jād), *n., v.,* **jaded, jading.** —*n.* **1.** a horse, esp. one of inferior breed, or worn-out, or vicious. **2.** (in opprobrious use) a woman. —*v.t., v.i.* **3.** to make or become exhausted by working hard; to weary or fatigue; tire. [ME, orig. uncert. Cf. Icel. *jalda* mare] —**jad'ish,** *adj.* —**jad'ish·ly,** *adv.* —**jad'ish·ness,** *n.*

jad·ed (jā'dĭd), *adj.* **1.** worn out. **2.** sated: *a jaded appetite.* —**jad'ed·ly,** *adv.* —**jad'ed·ness,** *n.*

jade-green (jād'grēn'), *adj.* of the color of jade.

jade·ite (jā'dīt), *n.* a mineral, essentially sodium aluminum silicate, NaAlSi₂O₆, occurring in tough masses, whitish to dark green. See **jade¹** (def. 1).

jae·ger (yā'gər; *for 1 also* jā'-), *n.* **1.** any of the rapacious sea birds constituting the family *Stercorariidae* which pursue weaker birds in order to make them disgorge their prey; a skua. **2.** a hunter. **3.** a member of any certain groups of sharpshooters in the German or Austrian army. Also, **jäger, yager.** [t. G: hunter, der. *jagen* hunt]

Ja·én (hä ĕn'), *n.* a city in S Spain. 54,631 (1940).

Jaf·fa (jăf'ə; *locally* yä'fä), *n.* a seaport in W Israel. 94,310 (est. 1944). Ancient, **Joppa.**

Jaff·na (jäf/nə), *n.* a seaport in N Ceylon. 49,400 (est. 1941).

jag[1] (jäg), *n., v.* **jagged, jagging.** —*n.* **1.** a sharp projection on an edge or surface. —*v.t.* **2.** to cut or slash, esp. in points or pendants along the edge; form notches, teeth, or ragged points in. [ME *jaggen;* ? imit.]

jag[2] (jäg), *n.* **1.** *Dial.* a load, as of hay or wood. **2.** *U.S. Slang.* as much liquor as one can carry. **3.** *U.S. Slang.* a fit of intoxication: *to have a jag on.* [? orig. a load of broom or furze. Cf. OE *ceacga* broom, furze]

Jag·an·nath (jŭg/ə nät/, -nŏt/), *n.* Juggernaut. Also, **Jag·an·na·tha** (jŭg/ə nät/hə).

jä·ger (yä/gər), *n.* jaeger.

jag·ged (jäg/ĭd), *adj.* having notches, teeth, or ragged edges. —**jag/ged·ly,** *adv.* —**jag/ged·ness,** *n.*

jag·gy (jäg/ĭ), *adj.,* **-gier, -giest.** jagged; notched.

jag·uar (jäg/wär), *n.* a large, ferocious, spotted feline, *Panthera onca,* of tropical America. [t. Tupi-Guarani: m. *jaguara*]

ja·gua·run·di (jä/gwə rŭn/dĭ), *n., pl.* **-dis.** a short-legged, long-bodied South American cat, *Felis eyra.*

Jah·veh (yä/vĕ), *n.* Yahweh. Also, **Jah/ve, Jah** (yä).

Jaguar, *Panthera onca* (Total length ab. 7 ft., tail 2 ft.)

jai a·lai (hī ä lī/), a game resembling handball, esp. popular in Cuba, played on an indoor court with basketlike racquets.

jail (jāl), *n.* **1.** a prison, esp. one for the detention of persons awaiting trial or convicted of minor offenses; gaol. —*v.t.* **2.** to take into or hold in custody. Also, *Brit.,* **gaol.** [ME *jaiole,* t. OF: prison, cage; ult. der. L *cavea* cavity, enclosure, cage. See GAOL] —**jail/less,** *adj.* —**jail/like/,** *adj.*

jail·bird (jāl/bûrd/), *n.* one who is or has been confined in jail; a criminal.

jail delivery, 1. a deliverance of imprisoned persons, esp. by force. **2.** act of clearing a jail of prisoners by bringing them to trial, as at the assizes in England.

jail·er (jā/lər), *n.* the keeper of a jail. Also, **jail/or;** *Brit.,* **gaoler.**

Jain (jīn), *n.* **1.** an adherent of Jainism. —*adj.* **2.** of or pertaining to the Jains or their religion. [t. Hind.: m. *jaina,* g. Skt. *jaina,* der. *jina,* lit., conqueror]

Jain·ism (jī/nĭzəm), *n.* a dualistic, ascetic religion founded in the 6th century B.C. by a Hindu reformer as a revolt against the caste system and the vague world spirit of Hinduism. —**Jain/ist,** *n.*

Jai·pur (jī/pŏŏr), *n.* **1.** a state in N India, in Rajputana. 3,040,900 pop. (1941); 15,610 sq. mi. **2.** the capital of this state. 175,810 (1941).

Ja·kar·ta (jə kär/tə), *n.* official name of Batavia.

jal·ap (jäl/əp), *n.* **1.** a purgative drug obtained from the tuberous root of a plant, *Ipomoeapurga Exogonium Jalapa,* of Mexico, or of any of various other convolvulaceous plants. **2.** any of these plants. [t. Sp.: m. *jalapa;* named after the city. See JALAPA] —**ja·lap·ic** (jä lăp/ĭk), *adj.*

Ja·la·pa (hä lä/pä), *n.* a city in E Mexico: the capital of Vera Cruz state. 39,530 (1940).

jal·a·pin (jăl/ə pĭn), *n.* a resin which is one of the purgative principles of jalap. [f. JALAP + -IN[2]]

Ja·lis·co (hä lēs/kô), *n.* a state in W Mexico. 1,418,310 pop. (1940); 31,152 sq. mi. *Cap.:* Guadalajara.

ja·lop·y (jə lŏp/ĭ), *n., pl.* **-lopies.** *Colloq.* an old, decrepit, or unpretentious automobile.

jal·ou·sie (zhăl/ŏŏ zē/ or, esp. *Brit.,* zhăl/ŏŏ zē/), *n.* a kind of blind or shutter made with slats fixed at an angle. [t. F: lit., jealousy]

jam[1] (jăm), *v.,* **jammed, jamming.** —*v.t.* **1.** to press or squeeze tightly between bodies or surfaces, so that motion or extrication is made difficult or impossible. **2.** to bruise or crush by squeezing. **3.** to press, push, or thrust violently, as into a confined space or against some object. **4.** to fill or block up by crowding: *crowds jam the doors.* **5.** to cause to become wedged, caught, or displaced, so that it cannot work, as a machine, part, etc. **6.** *Radio.* **a.** to interfere with (signals, etc.) by sending out others of approximately the same frequency. **b.** (of signals, etc.) to interfere with (other signals, etc.). —*v.i.* **7.** to become wedged or fixed; stick fast. **8.** to press or push violently, as into a confined space or against one another. **9.** (of a machine, etc.) to become unworkable as through the wedging or displacement of a part. **10.** *Jazz Slang.* to enliven a composition by impromptu variations and improvisations. —*n.* **11.** act of jamming. **12.** state of being jammed. **13.** mass of objects jammed together, esp. in logging, the accumulation of timber blocking a river. Also, **jamb** for 1–9, 11–13. [appar. imit. Cf. CHAMP[1]] —**Syn.** **1.** wedge, pack, crowd; ram, force.

jam[2] (jăm), *n.* a preserve of whole fruit, slightly crushed, boiled with sugar. [appar. der. JAM[1]] —**jam/like/,** *adj.*

Jam., Jamaica.

Ja·mai·ca (jə mā/kə), *n.* an island in the West Indies, S of Cuba: with dependencies it forms a British colony. 1,237,000 pop. (1943); 4540 sq. mi. *Cap.:* Kingston.

Ja·mai·can (jə mā/kən), *adj.* **1.** of, pertaining to, or obtained from the island of Jamaica. —*n.* **2.** a native or an inhabitant of Jamaica.

jamb[1] (jăm), *n.* **1.** the side of an opening; a vertical piece forming the side of a doorway, window, or the like. **2.** jambeau. Also, **jambe.** [ME *jambe,* t. F: leg, jamb, g. LL *gamba* hoof]

jamb[2] (jăm), *v.t., v.i., n.* jam[1] (defs. 1–9, 11–13).

jam·beau (jăm/bō), *n., pl.* **-beaux** (-bōz). armor for the leg; a greave.

jam·bo·ree (jăm/bə rē/), *n.* **1.** *U.S. Slang.* a carousal; any noisy merrymaking. **2.** a large gathering or rally of boy scouts, usually international or interregional. [appar. b. JABBER and F *soirée,* with *-m-* from JAM[1] crowd]

J, Jamb

James (jāmz), *n.* **1.** an apostle, son of Zebedee and brother of the apostle John. (Matt. 4:21). **2.** ("*James the Lord's brother*") the reputed author of the Epistle of James. Gal. 1:19, Mark, 6:3. **3.** Also, **James the Less.** ("*James the son of Alphaeus*") an apostle. Matt. 10:3. **4.** the General Epistle of James, in the New Testament. **5.** the name of six kings of Scotland. **6. Henry,** 1811–82, U.S. writer on religious and social problems (father of Henry and William James). **7. Henry,** 1843–1916, U.S. novelist in England (brother of William James). **8. Jesse,** 1847–82, U.S. outlaw and bandit. **9. William,** 1842–1910, U.S. psychologist and philosopher (brother of Henry James).

James I, 1566–1625, king of England, 1603–25; as **James VI,** king of Scotland from 1567.

James II, 1633–1701, king of England, 1685–88.

James Bay, a S arm of Hudson Bay, in E Canada between Ontario and Quebec provinces, ab. 300 mi. long.

Jame·son (jām/sən), *n.* **Sir Leander Starr,** 1853–1917, British physician and colonial administrator.

James River, 1. a river flowing from the W part of Virginia E to Chesapeake Bay. 340 mi. **2.** a river flowing from central North Dakota S through South Dakota to the Missouri river. 710 mi.

James·town (jāmz/toun/), *n.* **1.** a ruined village in E Virginia: the first permanent English settlement in North America, 1607. **2.** a city in SW New York. 43,354 (1950).

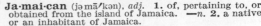

Jam·mu and Kash·mir (jŭm/ŏŏ; kăsh mĭr/), official name of Kashmir (including feudatories).

jam session, a meeting of musicians for a spontaneous and improvisatory performance of swing music without scores, for their own enjoyment.

Jam·shed·pur (jäm shĕd pŏŏr/), *n.* a city in NE India, in Bihar Province. 148,711 (1941).

Jam·shid (jäm shēd/), *n.* *Persian Myth.* the king of the Peris who, given a human form as punishment for his boast of immortality, became a powerful and wonderworking Persian king. Also, **Jam·shyd/.**

Jan., January.

Ja·ná·ček (yä/nä chĕk/), *n.* **Leoš** (lĕ/ôsh), 1854–1928, Czech composer.

Jane Eyre (jān âr/), novel (1847) by Charlotte Brontë.

Janes·ville (jānz/vĭl), *n.* a city in S Wisconsin. 24,899 (1950).

Ja·net (zhå nĕ/), **Pierre Marie Félix** (pyĕr må rē/ fĕ lēks/), 1859–1947, French psychologist and neurologist.

jan·gle (jăng/gəl), *v.,* **-gled, -gling,** *n.* —*v.i.* **1.** to sound harshly or discordantly: *a jangling noise.* **2.** to speak angrily; wrangle. —*v.t.* **3.** to cause to sound harshly or discordantly. —*n.* **4.** a harsh or discordant sound. **5.** an altercation; quarrel. [ME *jangle(n),* t. OF: m. *jangler* chatter, tattle; ? of Gmc. orig.] —**jan/gler,** *n.*

Ja·nic·u·lum (jə nĭk/yə ləm), *n.* a ridge near the Tiber in Rome.

Ja·ni·na (yä/nē nä/), *n.* Serbian name of Ioannina.

jan·i·tor (jăn/ə tər), *n.* **1.** a person employed to take care of a building, offices, etc. **2.** a doorkeeper or porter. [t. L: doorkeeper. See JANUS] —**jan·i·to·ri·al** (jăn/ə tōr/ĭ əl), *adj.* —**jan·i·tress** (jăn/ə trĭs), *n. fem.*

Jan·i·zar·y (jăn/ə zâr/ĭ), *n., pl.* **-zaries. 1.** an infantryman in the Turkish sovereign's personal standing army existing from the 14th century until 1826. **2.** any Turkish soldier. Also, **Jan/i·zar/y, Jan·is·sar·y** (jăn/ə sĕr/ĭ). [t. F: m. *janissaire,* t. Turk.: m. *yeñicheri* new soldiery]

Jan May·en (yän mī/ĕn), a volcanic island in the Arctic Ocean between Greenland and Norway: a possession of Norway. 144 sq. mi.

Jan·sen (jăn/sən; *Du.* yän/sən), *n.* **Cornelis** (kôr nā/lĭs), (*Cornelius Jansenius*) 1585–1638, Dutch theologian.

Jan·sen·ism (jăn/sə nĭz/əm), *n.* the doctrinal system of Cornelis Jansen, Roman Catholic bishop of Ypres, and his followers, which maintained the radical corruption of human nature and the inability of the will to do good, and that Christ died for the predestined and not for all men. —**Jan/sen·ist,** *n.* —**Jan/sen·is/tic,** *adj.*

Jan·u·ar·y (jăn/yŏŏ ĕr/ĭ, -ə rĭ), *n., pl.* **-aries.** the first month of the year, containing 31 days. [t. L: m.s.

Jānuārius the month of *Janus* (see JANUS); r. ME *Jenever*, t. ONF]

Ja·nus (jā′nəs), *n.* an ancient Italian (perhaps solar) deity, regarded by the Romans as presiding over doors and gates and over beginnings and endings, commonly represented with two faces in opposite directions. [L]

Ja·nus-faced (jā′nəs fāst′), *adj.* deceitful.

Jap (jăp), *adj.*, *n.* *Colloq. and Derogatory.* Japanese.

Jap., Japanese.

Ja·pan (jə păn′), *n.* **1.** Japanese, **Nippon.** an empire on a chain of islands off the E coast of Asia: main islands, Hokkaido, Honshu, Kyushu, and Shikoku. 73,110,995 pop. (1946); 142,267 sq. mi. (1946). *Cap.*: Tokyo. **2.** Sea of, an arm of the Pacific between Honshu and Hokkaido islands and the mainland of Asia. ab. 405,000 sq. mi.

ja·pan (jə păn′), *n.*, *adj.*, *v.*, **-panned, -panning.** —*n.* **1.** any of various hard, durable, black varnishes (orig. from Japan) for coating wood, metal, etc. **2.** work varnished and figured in the Japanese manner. —*adj.* **3.** of or pertaining to japan. —*v.t.* **4.** to varnish with japan; lacquer. **5.** to coat with any material which gives a hard, black gloss.

Japan clover, a drought-resistant perennial leguminous plant, *Lespedeza striata*, introduced to the southern Atlantic states from Asia, having numerous tiny trifoliate leaves valued for pasturage and hay.

Japan current, a warm current of the western North Pacific, starting off southeastern China, flowing past Japan, and continuing into the open Pacific.

Jap·a·nese (jăp′ə nēz′, -nēs′), *adj.*, *n.*, *pl.* **-nese.** —*adj.* **1.** of or pertaining to Japan, its people, or their language. —*n.* **2.** a native of Japan, or a descendant of one. **3.** the language of Japan (no known congeners).

Japanese beetle, a scarabaeid beetle, *Popillia japonica*, introduced into the eastern U.S. from Japan about 1916. It is very injurious to the foliage of fruit and other trees, and its larvae destroy lawns.

Japanese ivy, a woody, oriental, climbing shrub, *Parthenocissus tricuspidata*.

Japanese persimmon, **1.** the soft edible fruit of *Diospyrus Kaki*, orange or reddish in color, often 3 inches in diameter. **2.** the tree.

Japanese river fever, a group of infectious diseases occurring in Japan, the East Indies, and probably elsewhere, transmitted by the bites of mites.

jape (jāp), *v.*, **japed, japing,** *n.* —*v.i.* **1.** *Archaic.* to jest; joke; gibe. —*n.* **2.** a joke; jest; gibe. [ME; orig. uncert.] —**jap′er,** *n.*

Ja·pheth (jā′fĭth), *n.* *Bible.* the third son of Noah. [ult. t. Heb.: m. *Yepheth*]

Ja·phet·ic (jə fĕt′ĭk), *adj.* **1.** of or pertaining to Japheth. **2.** *Obs.* Indo-European.

ja·pon·i·ca (jə pŏn′ə kə), *n.* **1.** the camellia, *Camellia japonica.* **2.** the Japanese quince, *Chaenomeles lagenaria*, an Asiatic shrub with clusters of scarlet flowers and yellowish fruit. [t. NL, fem. of *Japonicus* of Japan]

Ja·pu·rá (zhä′pŏŏ rä′), *n.* a river flowing from the Andes in SW Colombia E through NW Brazil to the Amazon. ab. 1500 mi. Also, **Yapurá.**

Ja·ques (jā′kwēz, -kwĭz, jāks), *n.* a disillusioned and satiric observer of life, in Shakespeare's *As You Like It.*

jar¹ (jär), *n.* **1.** a broad-mouthed earthen or glass vessel, commonly cylindrical in form. **2.** the quantity contained in it. [t. F: m. *jarre*, t. Pr.: m. *jarro*, or Sp.: m. *jarra*, t. Ar.: m. *jarrah* earthen vessel]

jar² (jär), *v.*, **jarred, jarring,** *n.* —*v.i.* **1.** to produce a harsh, grating sound; sound discordantly. **2.** to have a harshly unpleasant effect upon the nerves, feelings, etc., or upon the person. **3.** to vibrate audibly; rattle. **4.** to vibrate or shake (without reference to sound). **5.** to be at variance; conflict; clash. —*v.t.* **6.** to cause to sound harshly or discordantly. **7.** to cause to rattle or shake. **8.** to have a harshly unpleasant effect upon (the feelings, nerves, etc., or the person). —*n.* **9.** a harsh, grating sound. **10.** a discordant sound or combination of sounds. **11.** a vibrating movement, as from concussion. **12.** a harshly unpleasant effect upon the mind or feelings due to physical or other shock. **13.** a quarrel; conflict, as of opinions, etc. [OE *ceorran* creak]

jar³ (jär), *n.* **1.** a turn or turning. **2. on the jar,** ajar. [var. of CHAR³, CHARE. Cf. AJAR]

jar·di·niere (jär′də nĭr′; *Fr.* zhàr dē nyĕr′), *n.* an ornamental receptacle or stand for holding plants, flowers, etc. [t. F, fem. of *jardinier* gardener, der. *jardin* GARDEN]

jar·gon¹ (jär′gən, -gŏn), *n.* **1.** unintelligible or meaningless talk or writing; gibberish. **2.** (in contempt) any talk or writing which one does not understand. **3.** the language peculiar to a trade, profession, or other group: *medical jargon.* **4.** a conventionalized form of a language which has been greatly simplified by its speakers to make it more intelligible to foreigners, especially servants or employees, as Pidgin English. **5.** a kind of speech abounding in uncommon or unfamiliar words. **6.** a lingua franca. —*v.i.* **7.** to utter or talk jargon or a jargon. [ME, t. OF, ult. der. *garg-* throat] —Syn. **3.** See **language.**

jar·gon² (jär′gŏn), *n.* a colorless to smoky variety of the mineral zircon. [t. F, t. It.: m. *giargone*, ? ult. t. Pers.: m. *zargūn* gold-colored. Cf. ZIRCON]

jar·gon·ize (jär′gə nīz′), *v.*, **-ized, -izing.** —*v.i.* **1.** to talk jargon or a jargon. —*v.t.* **2.** to translate into jargon.

jarl (yärl), *n.* *Scand. Hist.* a chieftain; an earl. [t. Scand.; cf. Icel. *jarl.* See EARL]

jar·o·site (jär′ə sīt′, jə rō′sīt′), *n.* a yellowish or brownish mineral, $K_2Fe_6(SO_4)_4(OH)_{12}$, occurring in crystals or massive. [named after Barranco *Jaroso*, in Almeria, southeastern Spain. See -ITE¹]

Jar·row (jär′ō), *n.* a seaport in NE England at the mouth of the Tyne river. 27,390 (est. 1946).

Jas., James.

jas·mine (jăs′mĭn, jăz′-), *n.* **1.** any of the fragrant-flowered shrubs constituting the oleaceous genus *Jasminum.* **2.** any of various plants of other genera, as *Gelsemium sempervirens* (**yellow jasmine**), *Gardenia jasminoides* (**Cape jasmine**) and *Plumeria rubra* (**red jasmine**, the frangipani). Also, **jessamine.** [t. F: m. *jasmin*, t. Ar.: m. *yāsmīn*, t. Pers.] —**jas′mine-like′,** *adj.*

Ja·son (jā′sən), *n.* *Gk. Legend.* the leader of the Argonautic expedition in quest of the Golden Fleece. He was the son of Aeson and Polymede, and the husband of Medea. See **Golden Fleece** and **Medea.**

jas·per (jăs′pər), *n.* a compact, opaque, often highly colored, cryptocrystalline variety of quartz, commonly used in decorative carvings. [ME *jaspre*, t. OF, var. of *jaspe*, t. L: *ias iaspis*, t. Gk.; of Eastern orig.]

Jas·per Park (jăs′pər), a national park in the Canadian Rockies in SW Canada, in W Alberta. 4400 sq. mi.

Jas·sy (yäs′ē), *n.* a city in NE Rumania. 108,812 (est. 1943). Rumanian, **Iasi.**

Jat (jät, jŏt), *n.* a member of an important Indo-Aryan people living mainly in northwestern India. In early times they offered vigorous resistance to the Moslem invaders of India. [t. Hind.]

jaun·dice (jôn′dĭs, jän′-), *n.*, *v.*, **-diced, -dicing.** —*n.* **1.** *Pathol.* a morbid bodily condition due to the presence of bile pigments in the blood, characterized by yellowness of the skin, the whites of the eyes, etc., by lassitude, and by loss of appetite. **2.** state of feeling in which views are colored or judgment is distorted. —*v.t.* **3.** to affect with jaundice. **4.** to affect with envy, jealousy, etc. [ME *jaunes, jaundis*, t. OF: m. *jaunisse*, der. *jaune* yellow, g. *galbinus* greenish-yellow]

jaunt (jônt, jänt), *v.i.* **1.** to make a short journey, esp. for pleasure. —*n.* **2.** such a journey. [? nasalized var. of *jot* jog, jolt] —Syn. **2.** See **excursion.**

jaunting car, a light two-wheeled vehicle, popular in Ireland, having seats on each side set back to back and a perch in front for the driver.

Jaunting car

jaun·ty (jôn′tĭ, jän′-), *adj.*, **-tier, -tiest. 1.** easy and sprightly in manner or bearing. **2.** smartly trim or effective, as dress. [earlier *janty*, t. F: m. *gentil.* See GENTLE, GENTEEL] —**jaun′ti·ly,** *adv.* —**jaun′ti·ness,** *n.*

Jau·rès (zhō rĕs′), *n.* **Jean Léon** (zhän lĕ ôn′), 1859–1914, French socialist and author.

Jav., Javanese.

Ja·va (jä′və), *n.* **1.** an island in the U.S. of Indonesia. 39,755,902 pop. (1930); 48,920 sq. mi. **2.** a kind of coffee obtained from the U.S. of Indonesia. **3.** *U.S. Slang.* any coffee.

Java man, Pithecanthropus (def. 1).

Jav·a·nese (jăv′ə nēz′, -nēs′), *adj.*, *n.*, *pl.* **-nese.** —*adj.* **1.** of or pertaining to the island of Java, its people, or their language. —*n.* **2.** a member of the native Malayan race of Java, esp. of that branch of it in the central part of the island. **3.** the language of central Java, of the Austronesian family.

Ja·va·ry (zhä′vä rē′), *n.* a river forming part of the boundary between Peru and Brazil, flowing NE in the upper Amazon. ab. 450 mi. Also, **Ja′va·ri′.**

Java Sea, a sea between Java and Borneo: naval engagement, 1942.

Java sparrow, a finchlike bird, *Munia oryzivora*, of the East Indies and Malaya; a common cage bird.

jave·lin (jăv′lĭn, jăv′ə lĭn), *n.* **1.** a spear to be thrown by hand. **2.** *Sports.* a wooden spear about 8½ feet long, hurled for distance. —*v.t.* **3.** to strike or pierce with or as with a javelin. [t. F: m. *javeline*; prob. from Celtic]

Ja·vel water (zhə vĕl′), sodium hypochlorite, NaOCl, dissolved in water, used as a bleach, antiseptic, etc. Also, **Javelle water.**

jaw (jô), *n.* **1.** one of the two bones or structures (upper and lower) which form the framework of the mouth. **2.** *Dentistry.* either jawbone containing its complement of teeth and covered by the soft tissues. **3.** the mouth parts collectively, or the mouth. **4.** anything likened to this: *the jaws of a gorge, of death,* etc. **5.** one of two or more parts, as of a machine, which grasp or hold something: *the jaws of a vise.* **6.** *Slang.* offensive talk. —*v.i.* **7.** *Slang.* to talk; gossip. **8.** *Slang.* to scold or use abusive language. —*v.t.* **9.** *Slang.* to scold. [ME *jawe, jowe*, t. OF: m. *jo(u)e* cheek, jaw] —**jaw′less,** *adj.*

jaw·bone (jô/bōn/), *n.* **1.** any bone of the jaws; a maxilla or mandible. **2.** the bone of the lower jaw.

jaw·break·er (jô/brā/kər), *n.* **1.** *Colloq.* a word hard to pronounce. **2.** Also, **jaw crusher.** a machine to break up ore, consisting of a fixed plate and a hinged jaw moved by a toggle joint. —**jaw/break/ing,** *adj.*

Jax·ar·tes (jăk sär/tēz), *n.* ancient name of Syr Darya.

jay (jā), *n.* **1.** any of several crested or uncrested birds of the corvine subfamily *Garrulinae,* all of them robust, noisy, and mischievous, as the **common jay,** *Garrulus glandarius,* of Europe, the **blue jay,** *Cyanocitta cristata,* of America, and the plain gray **Canada jay,** *Perisoreus canadensis.* **2.** *Slang.* a simple-minded or gullible person; a simpleton. [ME, t. OF. Cf. ML *gaius;* ? t. Gmc.]

Jay (jā), *n.* **John,** 1745–1829, American statesman and jurist; first chief justice of the U.S. Supreme Court, 1789–95.

Jay·hawk·er (jā/hô/kər), *n.* **1.** a native of Kansas. **2.** (*l.c.*) *U.S. Slang.* a plundering marauder; esp., one of the freebooting guerillas in Kansas, Missouri, and other States before and during the Civil War.

jay·walk (jā/wôk/), *v.i. Colloq.* to cross a street otherwise than by a regular crossing or in a heedless manner, as against traffic lights. [f. JAY (see def. 2) + WALK] —**jay/walk/er,** *n.* —**jay/walk/ing,** *n.*

jazz (jăz), *n.* **1.** dance music, usually of a "hot" improvisatory nature, with syncopated rhythms, such as is played by a jazz band. **2.** a piece of such music. **3.** dancing or a dance performed to such music, as with violent bodily motions and gestures. **4.** lively comedy elements introduced into a play, poem, etc. **5.** *Slang.* liveliness; spirit. —*adj.* **6.** of the nature of or pertaining to jazz. —*v.t.* **7.** to play (music) in the manner of jazz. **8.** *Slang.* to put vigor or liveliness into (often fol. by *up*). —*v.i.* **9.** to dance to such music. **10.** *Slang.* to act or proceed with great energy or liveliness. [orig. obscure; said to have been long used by Negroes of the southern U.S., esp. those of Louisiana]

jazz band, a band adapted for or devoted to the playing of jazz, which uses melodic instruments such as the trumpet, trombone, clarinet, and saxophone, and rhythmic instruments such as drums, piano, and guitar, producing novel tonal effects often adopted from vocal style, such as vibrato and sliding from tone to tone.

jazz·y (jăz/ĭ), *adj.,* **jazzier, jazziest.** *Slang.* pertaining to or suggestive of jazz music; wildly active or lively.

J. C., **1.** Jesus Christ. **2.** Julius Caesar. **3.** jurisconsult.

J. C. B., (L *Juris Civilis Baccalaureus*) Bachelor of Civil Law.

J. C. D., (L *Juris Civilis Doctor*) Doctor of Civil Law.

jct., junction. Also, **jctn.**

J. D., **1.** (L *Juris Doctor*) Doctor of Law. **2.** (L *Jurum Doctor*) Doctor of Laws. **3.** (L *Juris Doctor*) Doctor of Jurisprudence.

Je., June.

jeal·ous (jĕl/əs), *adj.* **1.** feeling envious resentment against a successful rival or at success, advantages, etc., (fol. by *of*): *to be jealous of a victor.* **2.** characterized by or proceeding from suspicious fears or envious resentment: *jealous intrigues.* **3.** inclined to or troubled by suspicions or fears of rivalry, as in love or aims: *a jealous husband.* **4.** solicitous or vigilant in maintaining or guarding something. **5.** (in Biblical use) intolerant of unfaithfulness or rivalry: *the Lord is a jealous God.* **6.** *Obs.* zealous. [ME *gelos, jalous,* t. OF, g. LL *zēlōsus,* der. L *zēlus,* t. Gk.: m. *zēlos* zeal] —**jeal/ous·ly,** *adv.* —**jeal/ous·ness,** *n.*

jeal·ous·y (jĕl/ə sĭ), *n., pl.* **-ousies. 1.** envious resentment against a successful rival or the possessor of any coveted advantage. **2.** mental uneasiness from suspicion or fear of rivalry, as in love or aims. **3.** state or feeling of being jealous. **4.** an instance of jealous feeling.

jean (jēn, jăn), *n.* **1.** a stout twilled cotton fabric. **2.** (*pl.*) clothes of this material; trousers; overalls. [prob. t. F: m. *Gênes* Genoa]

Jeanne d'Arc (zhän därk/), French name of **Joan of Arc.**

Jeans (jēnz), *n.* **Sir James Hopwood,** 1877–1946, British mathematician, physicist, and astronomer.

Jebb (jĕb), *n.* **Sir Richard Claverhouse** (klăv/ər hous/), 1841–1905, British classical scholar.

jeb·el (jĕb/əl), *n. Arabic.* mountain.

Jeb·el Mu·sa (jĕb/əl mōo/sä), a mountain in NW Spanish Morocco, opposite Gibraltar: one of the pillars of Hercules. ab. 2750 ft.

Jed·burgh (jĕd/bûr/ō, -bə rə), *n.* a border town in SE Scotland: ruins of a famous abbey. 3448 (est. 1944).

Jed·da (jĕd/də), *n.* Jidda.

jeep (jēp), *n.* a small (usually ¼ ton capacity) military motor vehicle. [? special use of *jeep* name of fabulous animal in comic strip "Popeye," or alter. of G.P. (for General Purpose Vehicle)]

jeer[1] (jĭr), *v.i.* **1.** to speak or shout derisively; gibe or scoff rudely. —*v.t.* **2.** to treat with scoffs or derision; make a mock of. **3.** to drive (*out, off,* etc.) by jeers. —*n.* **4.** a jeering utterance; a derisive or rude gibe. [? OE *cēir* clamor, der. *cēgan* call out] —**jeer/er,** *n.* —**jeer/ing·ly,** *adv.* —**Syn. 1.** See **scoff.**

jeer[2] (jĭr), *n.* (*usually pl.*) *Naut.* tackle for hoisting or lowering heavy yards. [? lit., mover, der. GEE, interj.]

je·fe (hĕ/fĕ), *n. Spanish.* leader; commanding officer. [Sp, t. OF: m. *chief,* g. L *caput* head]

Jef·fers (jĕf/ərz), *n.* **Robinson,** born 1887, U.S. poet.

Jef·fer·son (jĕf/ər sən), *n.* **1. Joseph,** 1829–1905, U.S. actor. **2. Thomas,** 1743–1826, American statesman, writer, and 3rd president of the U.S., 1801–09; important in framing the Declaration of Independence. **3. Mount,** a peak in NW Oregon, in the Cascade Range. 10,200 ft.

Jefferson City, the capital of Missouri, in the central part, on the Missouri river. 25,099 (1950).

Jefferson Day, April 13, Jefferson's birthday, sometimes celebrated with Democratic Party dinners.

Jef·fer·so·ni·an (jĕf/ər sō/nĭ ən), *adj.* **1.** of or pertaining to Thomas Jefferson or his political theories. —*n.* **2.** an adherent of Jefferson.

Jef·frey (jĕf/rĭ), *n.* **Francis,** (*Lord Jeffrey*) 1773–1850, Scottish jurist, editor, and critic.

Jef·freys (jĕf/rĭz), *n.* **George,** (*1st baron Jeffreys*) 1648–1689, British judge, notorious for his unjudicial conduct.

je·had (jĭ/hăd/), *n.* jihad.

Je·hol (jə hōl/, rĕ/hō/; *native* rŭ/hŭ/), *n.* **1.** a province in NE China: incorporated into Manchukuo by the Japanese, 1935. 2,083,700 pop. (est. 1944); 74,297 sq. mi. *Cap.:* Chengteh. **2.** Chengteh.

Je·hosh·a·phat (jĭ hŏsh/ə făt/, -hŏs/-), *n.* a king of Judah, son of Asa, who reigned in the 9th century B.C. 1 Kings 22:41–50.

Je·ho·vah (jĭ hō/və), *n.* **1.** a name of God in the Old Testament, an erroneous rendering of the ineffable name, JHVH, in the Hebrew Scriptures. **2.** (in modern Christian use) God.

Jehovah's Witnesses, a sect of Christians who are pacifists and do not recognize the authority of the state when in conflict with religious principles.

Je·ho·vist (jĭ hō/vĭst), *n.* **1.** the author of the earliest major source of the Pentateuch in which God is characteristically referred to as Yahweh (erroneously Jehovah). See **Yahwist. 2.** one who maintains that the vowel points annexed to the word *Jehovah* in Hebrew are the proper vowels of the word, and express the true pronunciation. —*adj.* **3.** characterized by the use of the name Jehovah for God (applied to part of the Pentateuch). —**Je·ho/vism,** *n.*

Je·ho·vis·tic (jē/hō vĭs/tĭk), *adj.* pertaining to or written by a Jehovist. Also, **Yahwistic.**

Je·hu (jē/hū), *n.* **1.** son of Hanani, a prophet of Judah under Jehoshaphat in the 9th century B.C. 1 Kings 16. **2.** (*l.c.*) a fast driver. **3.** (*l.c.*) *Slang.* any driver.

je·june (jĭ jōon/), *adj.* **1.** deficient in nourishing or substantial qualities. **2.** unsatisfying to the mind. [t. L: m.s. *jējūnus* fasting, empty, dry, poor] —**je·june/ly,** *adv.* —**je·june/ness, je·ju·ni·ty** (jĭ jōo/nə tĭ), *n.*

je·ju·num (jĭ jōo/nəm), *n. Anat.* the middle portion of the small intestine, between the duodenum and the ileum. See diag. under **intestine.** [t. NL, prop. neut. of L *jējūnus* empty]

Je·kyll (jē/kəl, jĕk/əl), *n.* **Dr.,** the central figure, who at times becomes a vicious being, in Stevenson's *Dr. Jekyll and Mr. Hyde* (1886).

jell (jĕl), *v.i. Colloq.* to form a jelly.

Jel·li·coe (jĕl/ĭ kō/), *n.* **John Rushworth,** (*1st Earl Jellicoe*) 1859–1935, British admiral.

jel·lied (jĕl/ĭd), *adj.* **1.** brought to the consistence of jelly. **2.** containing or spread over with jelly.

jel·li·fy (jĕl/ə fī/), *v.,* **-fied, -fying.** —*v.t.* **1.** to make into a jelly; reduce to a gelatinous state. —*v.i.* **2.** to become gelatinous; turn into jelly. —**jel/li·fi·ca/tion,** *n.*

jel·ly (jĕl/ĭ), *n., pl.* **-lies,** *v.,* **-lied, -lying.** —*n.* **1.** a food preparation of a soft, elastic consistency due to the presence of gelatin, pectin, etc., as fruit juice boiled down with sugar. **2.** anything of the consistency of jelly. —*v.t., v.i.* **3.** to bring or come to the consistency of jelly. [ME *gele,* t. OF: m. *gelee* frost, jelly, g. L *gelāta,* prop. pp. fem., frozen] —**jel/ly·like/,** *adj.*

jel·ly·fish (jĕl/ĭ fĭsh/), *n., pl.* **-fishes,** (*esp. collectively*) **-fish.** any of various marine coelenterates of a soft, gelatinous structure, esp. one with an umbrellalike body and long, trailing tentacles; a medusa.

Jellyfish, genus *Cephea* A, Disk or umbrella; B, Ramifications of brachia; C, Tentacles; D, Pillar supporting disk; E, Short tentacles

jem·a·dar (jĕm/ə där/), *n. India.* **1.** any of various government officials. **2.** the chief of a body of servants. **3.** a native officer in a sepoy regiment, corresponding in rank to a lieutenant. [t. Hind., t. Pers.: m. *jama'dār,* lit., holder or leader of an aggregation (of men)]

Je·mappes (zhə măp/), *n.* a town in SW Belgium, near Mons: French victory over the Austrians, 1792. 12,722 (est. 1944).

jem·my (jĕm/ĭ), *n., pl.* **-mies,** *v.t.,* **-mied, -mying.** *Brit.* jimmy.

Je·na (yā/nä), *n.* a city in central Germany, in Thuringia: Napoleon decisively defeated the Prussians near here, 1806. 70,573 (1939).

je ne sais quoi (zhən sĕ kwä/), *French.* I know not what; an indefinable something.

Jen·ghis Khan (jĕn/gĭz kän/, jĕng/-), Genghis Khan. Also, **Jen/ghiz Khan/.**

Jen·ner (jĕn/ər), n. **1. Edward,** 1749–1823, British physician, discoverer of smallpox vaccine. **2. Sir William,** 1815–98, British physician.

jen·net (jĕn/ĭt), n. **1.** a small Spanish horse. **2.** a female donkey; jenny ass. Also, **genet.** [ME genett, t. OF: m. genet, t. Sp.: m. jinete mounted soldier, horse, t. Ar.: m. Zenāta, name of a Berber tribe noted for its cavalry]

jen·ny (jĕn/ĭ), n., pl. **-nies. 1.** a spinning jenny. **2.** the female of certain animals: jenny wren. [prop. woman's name]

jeop·ard·ize (jĕp/ərdīz/), v.t., **-ized, -izing.** to put in jeopardy; hazard; risk; imperil. Also, **jeop/ard.**

jeop·ard·y (jĕp/ərdĭ), n. **1.** hazard or risk of loss or harm. **2.** peril or danger: for a moment his life was in jeopardy. **3.** Law. the hazard of being found guilty, and consequent punishment, undergone by criminal defendants upon trial. [ME iuparti, etc., t. OF: m. jeu parti, lit., divided game, even game or chance] **—Syn. 1, 2.** See **danger.**

Jeph·thah (jĕf/thə), n. a judge of Israel. Judges 11–14.

je·quir·i·ty (jəkwĭr/ətĭ), n., pl. **-ties. 1.** the Indian licorice plant, Abrus precatorius, of India and Brazil, whose seed (**jequirity bean**) is used as a bead and in medicine. **2.** the seeds collectively. [t. F: m. jéquirity, t. Tupi-Guarani: m. jekiriti]

Jer., 1. Jeremiah. **2.** Jersey. **3.** Jerusalem.

jer·bo·a (jərbō/ə), n. any of various mouselike rodents of North Africa and Asia, as of the genera Jaculus, Dipus, etc., with long hind legs used for jumping. [t. NL, t. Ar.: m. yarbū']

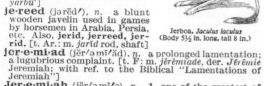

je·reed (jərēd/), n. a blunt wooden javelin used in games by horsemen in Arabia, Persia, etc. Also, **jerid, jerreed, jer-rid.** [t. Ar.: m. jarīd rod, shaft]

Jerboa, Jaculus Iaculus
(Body 5½ in. long, tail 8 in.)

jer·e·mi·ad (jĕr/əmī/ăd), n. a prolonged lamentation; a lugubrious complaint. [t. F: m. jérémiade, der. Jérémie Jeremiah; with ref. to the Biblical "Lamentations of Jeremiah"]

Jer·e·mi·ah (jĕr/əmī/ə), n. **1.** one of the greatest of the Hebrew prophets, whose career extended from about 650 to 585 B.C. **2.** a book of the Old Testament. [ult. t. Heb.: m. Yirmeyāh]

Je·rez (hĕrĕth/, -rĕs/), n. a city in SW Spain: noted for its sherry wine. 89,525 (1940). Also **Jerez de la Fron·te·ra** (dĕlä frônt ĕ/rä). Formerly, **Xeres.**

Jer·i·cho (jĕr/əkō/), n. an ancient city of Palestine, N of the Dead Sea.

je·rid (jərēd/), n. jereed.

Je·ri·tza (yĕ/rētsä/), n. **Ma·ria** (märē/ä), born 1887, Austrian operatic soprano.

jerk[1] (jûrk), n. **1.** a quick, sharp thrust, pull, throw, or the like; a sudden start. **2.** Physiol. a sudden movement of an organ or a part. **3. the jerks,** Western and Southern U.S. the paroxysms or violent spasmodic muscular movements sometimes resulting from excitement in connection with religious services. **4.** (pl.) Brit. physical exercises. **5.** Slang. an unknowing, unsophisticated, or unconventional person. **—v.t. 6.** to give a sudden thrust, pull, or twist to. **7.** to move or throw with a quick, suddenly arrested motion. **8.** to utter in a broken, spasmodic way. **—v.i. 9.** to give a jerk or jerks. **10.** to move with a quick, sharp motion; move spasmodically. **11.** to talk in a broken, spasmodic way. [appar. imit.]

jerk[2] (jûrk), v.t. **1.** to preserve meat, esp. beef (**jerked beef**) by cutting in strips and curing by drying in the sun. **—n. 2.** jerked meat, esp. beef. [t. Amer. Sp.: m. charquear, der. charque, charqui jerked meat, charqui, t. Peruvian Ind.]

jer·kin (jûr/kĭn), n. a close-fitting jacket or short coat, as one of leather worn in the 16th and 17th centuries.

jerk·wa·ter (jûrk/wô/tər, -wŏt/ər), n. U.S. Colloq. **1.** a train not running on the main line. **—adj. 2.** off the main line. **3.** of minor importance. [appar. f. JERK[1], v. + WATER]

jerk·y (jûr/kĭ), adj., **jerkier, jerkiest.** characterized by jerks or sudden starts; spasmodic. **—jerk/i·ly,** adv. **—jerk/i·ness,** n.

Jerkin

Jer·o·bo·am (jĕr/əbō/əm), n. the first king of Israel.

Je·rome (jərōm/, jĕr/əm), n. **Saint,** (Eusebius Sophronius Hieronymus) A.D. c340–420, monk and scholar of the Latin Church, maker of the Latin version of the Bible known as the Vulgate.

jer·reed (jərēd/), n. jereed. Also, **jer·rid/.**

Jer·ry (jĕr/ĭ), n., pl. **-ries.** Chiefly Brit. Colloq. **1.** nickname for a German. **2.** (collectively) Germans.

jer·ry-build (jĕr/ĭbĭld/), v.t., **-built, -building.** to build cheaply and flimsily. **—jer/ry-build/er,** n.

Jer·sey (jûr/zĭ), n. **1.** a British island in the English Channel: the largest of the Channel Islands. 50,462 pop. (1931); 45 sq. mi. Cap.: St. Helier. **2.** New Jersey.

Jer·sey (jûr/zĭ), n., pl. **-seys.** one of a breed of dairy cattle smaller than the Guernsey, originating on the island of Jersey. Their milk contains the highest percentage of butterfat of the milk of any dairy breed.

jer·sey (jûr/zĭ), n., pl. **-seys. 1.** a close-fitting knitted woolen jacket or shirt worn by seamen, athletes, and others. **2.** a similar garment of knitted material of wool, silk, etc. worn by women. **3.** jersey cloth.

Jersey City, a seaport in NE New Jersey, opposite New York City. 299,017 (1950).

jersey cloth, a machine-knitted fabric of wool, silk, or rayon, used for making garments, etc.

Je·ru·sa·lem (jĭrōō/sələm), n. the principal city of Palestine, in the central part: an ancient holy city and place of pilgrimage for Jews, Christians, and Moslems. 157,080 (est. 1940). [ult. t. Heb.: m. Yĕrushālam] **—Je·ru/sa·lem·ite/,** adj., n.

Jerusalem artichoke, 1. a species of sunflower, Helianthus tuberosus, having edible tuberous underground stems or rootstocks. **2.** the tuber itself. [t. It.: alter. (by pop. etymology) of girasole sunflower, f. s. of girare turn + sole sun]

Jerusalem cross, a cross whose four arms are each capped with a crossbar.

Jes·per·sen (yĕs/pərsən), n. **Jens Otto Harry** (yĕns ŏt/ō härˈē), 1860–1943, Danish linguist.

jess (jĕs), Falconry. **—n. 1.** a short strap fastened round the leg of a hawk and attached to the leash. **—v.t. 2.** to put jesses on (a hawk). [ME ges, t. OF, der. jeter throw, g. LL jectāre, r. L jactāre] **—jessed** (jĕst), adj.

jes·sa·mine (jĕs/əmĭn), n. jasmine.

jes·sant (jĕs/ənt), adj. Her. **1.** shooting up, as a plant. **2.** coming forth; issuant. **3.** lying across.

Jes·se (jĕs/ĭ), n. father of David. I Sam. 16.

jest (jĕst), n. **1.** a witticism, joke, or pleasantry. **2.** a piece of raillery or banter. **3.** sport or fun: to speak half in jest, half in earnest. **4.** the object of laughter, sport, or mockery; a laughingstock. **5.** Obs. an exploit. See gest. **—v.i. 6.** to speak in a playful, humorous, or facetious way; joke. **7.** to speak or act in mere sport, rather than in earnest; trifle (with). **8.** to utter derisive speeches; gibe or scoff. **—v.t. 9.** to jest at; deride; banter. [var. of GEST[1]] **—Syn. 1.** See **joke.**

jest·er (jĕs/tər), n. **1.** one who is given to witticisms, jokes, and pranks. **2.** a professional fool or clown, kept by a prince or noble, esp. during the Middle Ages.

jest·ing (jĕs/tĭng), adj. **1.** given to jesting; playful. **2.** fit for joking; unimportant; trivial: no jesting matter. **—n. 3.** pleasantry; triviality. **—jest/ing·ly,** adv.

Je·su (jē/zōō, -sōō), n. Poetic. Jesus. [t. L, oblique (usually voc.) case form of Jesus JESUS]

Jes·u·it (jĕzh/ōŏ ĭt, jĕz/yŏŏ-), n. **1.** a member of a Roman Catholic religious order (**Society of Jesus**) founded by Ignatius Loyola in 1534. **2.** a crafty, intriguing, or equivocating person (in allusion to the methods ascribed to the order by its opponents). [t. NL: s. Jesuīta, f. L. See Jesu, -ɪᴛ(ᴇ)[1]] **—Jes/u·it/ic, Jes/u·it/i·cal,** adj. **—Jes/u·it/i·cal·ly,** adv.

Jes·u·it·ism (jĕzh/ōŏ ĭ tĭz/əm, jĕz/yŏŏ-), n. **1.** the system, principles, or practices of the Jesuits. **2.** (usually l.c.) a principle or practice such as casuistry ascribed to the Jesuits by their opponents. Also, **Jes/u·it·ry.**

Jes·u·it·ize (jĕzh/ōŏ ĭ tīz/, jĕz/yŏŏ-), v.t., v.i., **-ized, -izing.** to make or be Jesuitical.

Je·sus (jē/zəs), n. the founder of the Christian religion. Also, **Jesus Christ.** [ME, t. LL, t. Gk.: m. Iēsoûs, t. Heb.: m. Yeshūa', earlier Yehōshūa', lit., Jehovah is salvation]

jet[1] (jĕt), n., v., **jetted, jetting. —n. 1.** a free or submerged stream of fluid produced by efflux from a nozzle, orifice, etc. **2.** that which so issues or spurts, as water or gas. **3.** the spout used: gas jet. **—v.i., v.t. 4.** to shoot forth in a stream; spout. [t. F, der. jeter, v.]

jet[2] (jĕt), n. **1.** a compact black coal, susceptible of a high polish, used for making beads, jewelry, buttons, etc. **2.** a deep, glossy black. **3.** Obs. black marble. **—adj. 4.** consisting or made of jet. **5.** of the color jet; black as jet. [ME gete, iete, t. OF: m. jaiet, g. L gagātēs, t. Gk, der. Gagai, town in Lycia, Asia Minor]

jet-black (jĕt/blăk/), adj. deep-black: jet-black hair.

jet plane, an airplane whose engine is operated by jet propulsion.

jet propulsion, a method of producing a propelling force upon an air or water craft through the reaction of a high-velocity jet, usually of heated gases, discharged toward the rear. **—jet/-pro·pelled/,** adj.

jet·sam (jĕt/səm), n. **1.** goods thrown overboard to lighten a vessel in distress. **2.** such goods when washed ashore. See **flotsam.** [var. of jetson, syncopated form of jettison; final -m as in FLOTSAM, etc.]

jet·ti·son (jĕt/əsən, -zən), n. **1.** act of casting overboard. **2.** jetsam. **—v.t. 3.** to throw (cargo, etc.) overboard, esp. to lighten a vessel in distress. **4.** to throw off, as an obstacle or burden. [t. AF: m. getteson, var. of OF getaison, der. geter throw]

jet·ton (jĕt/ən), n. an inscribed counter or token. [t. F: m. jeton, der. jeter throw. cast, cast up (accounts, etc.)]

Jericho, c1200 B.C.

---

b., blend of, blended; c., cognate with; d., dialect, dialectal; der., derived from; f., formed from; g., going back to; m., modification of; r., replacing; s., stem of; t., taken from; ?, perhaps. See the full key on inside cover.

jet·ty[1] (jĕt′ĭ), n., pl. **-ties.** **1.** a pier or structure of stones, piles, or the like, projecting into the sea or other body of water so as to protect a harbor, deflect the current, etc. **2.** a wharf or landing pier. **3.** the piles or wooden structure protecting a pier. [ME *gette*, t. OF: m. *jetee*, n. use of fem. pp. of *jeter* throw]

jet·ty[2] (jĕt′ĭ), adj. **1.** made of jet. **2.** resembling jet; black as jet, or of the color jet. [f. JET[2] + -Y[1]]

jeu de mots (zhœ də mō′), *French.* a pun.

jeu d'es·prit (zhœ dĕs prē′), *French.* a witticism.

Jev·ons (jĕv′ənz), n. **William Stanley,** 1835–82, British economist and logician.

Jew (jōō), n. **1.** one of the Hebrew or Jewish people; a Hebrew; an Israelite. —adj. **2.** of or pertaining to Jews; Jewish. —v.t. **3.** (*l.c.*) *U.S. Colloq. and Offensive.* to bargain with overkeenly; beat (*down*) in price. [ME *Jeu, Giu,* t. OF: m. *Juieu,* g. L *Jūdaeus,* t. Gk.: m. *Ioudaîos,* prop. one of the tribe of Judah, ult. der. Heb. *Yĕhūdāh* Judah]

Jew-bait·ing (jōō′bā′tĭng), n. active anti-Semitism. —**Jew′-bait′er,** n.

jew·el (jōō′əl), n., v., **-eled, -eling** or (*esp. Brit.*) **-elled, -elling.** —n. **1.** a cut and polished stone; a gem. **2.** a fashioned ornament for personal adornment, usually set with gems. **3.** a precious possession. **4.** a thing or person of great worth or rare excellence. **5.** a precious stone (or some substitute) used as a bearing of great durability in a watch or delicate instrument. **6.** an ornamental boss of glass, sometimes cut with facets, in stained-glass work. **7.** something resembling a gem in appearance, ornamental effect, etc., as a star, a berry, etc. —v.t. **8.** to set or adorn with jewels. [ME *iuel,* t. AF, ult. der. L *jocus* jest, sport] —**jew′el·like′,** adj.

jew·el·er (jōō′əl ər), n. one who makes, or deals in, jewels or jewelry. Also, *esp. Brit.,* **jew′el·ler.**

jew·el·fish (jōō′əl fĭsh′), n., pl. **-fishes,** (*esp. collectively*) **-fish.** a brilliantly colored aquarium fish, *Hemichromis bimaculatus.*

jew·el·ry (jōō′əl rĭ), n. jewels; articles made of gold, silver, precious stones, etc., for personal adornment. Also, *esp. Brit.,* **jew′el·ler·y.**

jew·el·weed (jōō′əl wēd′), n. an American touch-me-not, as *Impatiens biflora,* with orange-yellow flowers spotted with brown, or *I. pallida.*

Jew·ess (jōō′ĭs), n. a Jewish girl or woman.

Jew·ett (jōō′ĭt), n. **Sarah Orne** (ôrn), 1849–1909, U.S. short-story writer and novelist.

jew·fish (jōō′fĭsh′), n., pl. **-fishes,** (*esp. collectively*) **-fish.** any of several large marine fishes, *family Serranidae,* frequenting southern waters, such as the **spotted jewfish** (*Promicropsi taiara*) and the **black jewfish** (*Epinephelus nigritus*) of the south coast of the U.S., West Indies, etc., and the **California jewfish** (*Stereolepsi gigas*), all reaching a weight of several hundred pounds. [appar. f. JEW + FISH]

Jew·ish (jōō′ĭsh), adj. **1.** of, pertaining to, or characteristic of the Jews; Hebrew. —n. **2.** Yiddish.

Jewish calendar, the lunisolar calendar in use among the Jews, reckoning from the Creation (dated traditionally during the year 3761 B.C.), the year containing 12 or (in intercalary years) 13 months, of 29 or 30 days each, which, beginning during September or October, are as follows: Tishri, Heshvan, Kislev, Tebet, Shebat, Adar, Veadar (occurring only on intercalary years), Nisan, Iyyar, Sivan, Tammuz, Ab, and Elul.

Jew·ry (jōō′rĭ), n., pl. **-ries. 1.** the Jewish people. **2.** a district inhabited by Jews; a ghetto. **3.** *Archaic.* Judea. [ME *Jewerie,* t. AF: m. *juerie,* var. of OF *juierie*]

jew's-harp (jōōz′härp′), n. a steel tongue within an iron frame, held between the jaws and plucked while the varying position of the mouth changes the tone. Also, **jews′-harp′.** [appar. jocular in orig., as it is not a harp and has no connection with the Jews]

Jew's pitch, asphalt or maltha. Also, **Jews' pitch.**

Jew's-harp

Jez·e·bel (jĕz′ə bəl), n. **1.** the wife of Ahab, king of Israel, notorious for her conduct. I Kings 16:31, 21:25, II Kings, 9:30–37. **2.** a shameless, abandoned woman.

Jez·re·el (jĕz′rĭ əl, jĕz rēl′), n. **Plain of,** Esdraelon.

jg, junior grade. Also, **j.g.**

Jhan·si (jän′sē), n. a city in central India, in the SW United Provinces. 103,254 (1941).

Jhe·lum (jā′ləm), n. a river flowing from S Kashmir into the Chenab river in Pakistan. ab. 450 mi.

jib[1] (jĭb), n. *Naut.* **1.** a triangular sail (or either of two triangular sails, **inner jib** and **outer jib**) set in front of the forward (or single) mast. See illus. under **sail.** **2.** any of certain similar sails set beyond the jib proper, as a **flying jib.** [? akin to GIBBET]

jib[2] (jĭb), v.i., v.t., **jibbed, jibbing.** jibe[1].

jib[3] (jĭb), v.i., **jibbed, jibbing.** —v.i. **1.** *Chiefly Brit.* to move restively sidewise or backward instead of forward, as an animal in harness; balk. **2.** *Brit.* to hold back or balk at doing something. —n. **3.** a horse or other animal that jibs. [orig. uncert.; ? special use of JIB[2]] —**jib′ber,** n.

jib[4] (jĭb), n. the projecting arm of a crane; the boom of a derrick. [appar. short for GIBBET]

jib boom, *Naut.* a spar forming a continuation of a bowsprit. See illus. under **bowsprit.**

jibe[1] (jīb), v., **jibed, jibing,** n. *Naut.* —v.i. **1.** to shift from one side to the other when running before the wind, as a fore-and-aft sail or its boom. **2.** to alter the course so that the sail shifts in this manner. —v.t. **3.** to cause (a sail, etc.) to jibe. —n. **4.** act of jibing. Also, **gybe.** [var. of gybe, t. D: m. *gijben*]

jibe[2] (jīb), v.t., v.i., **jibed, jibing,** n. gibe. —**jib′er,** n.

jibe[3] (jīb), v.i., **jibed, jibing.** *U.S. Colloq.* to agree; be in harmony or accord. [orig. uncert.]

Ji·bu·ti (jē bōō′tē), n. Djibouti.

Jid·da (jĭd′də), n. the seaport of Mecca in Saudi Arabia, on the Red Sea. ab. 40,000. Also, **Jedda.**

jif·fy (jĭf′ĭ), n., pl. **-fies.** *Colloq.* a very short time: *to do something in a jiffy.* Also, **jiff.** [orig. unknown]

jig[1] (jĭg), n., v., **jigged, jigging.** —n. **1.** a device for holding the work in a machine tool, esp. one for accurately guiding a drill or group of drills so as to insure uniformity in successive pieces machined. **2.** a device used in fishing, esp. a hook or collection of hooks loaded with metal or having a spoon-shaped piece of bone or other material attached, for drawing through the water. **3.** an apparatus for separating ore from gangue, etc., by shaking in or treating with water. —v.t. **4.** to treat, cut, or produce by using any of the mechanical contrivances called jigs. —v.i. **5.** to use a jig (mechanical contrivance). [var. of GAUGE. Cf. E *jeg* kind of gauge]

jig[2] (jĭg), n., v., **jigged, jigging.** —n. **1.** a rapid, lively, springy, irregular dance for one or more persons, usually in triple rhythm. **2.** a piece of music for, or in the rhythm of, such a dance. **3.** *Dial. and Slang.* a piece of sport, a prank, or a trick. **4. the jig is up,** the game is up; there is no further chance. —v.t. **5.** to dance (a jig or any lively dance). **6.** to sing or play in the time or rhythm of a jig. **7.** to move with a jerky or bobbing motion; jerk up and down or to and fro. —v.i. **8.** to dance or play a jig. **9.** to move with a quick, jerky motion; hop; bob. [appar. var. of JOG, v.] —**jig′like′,** adj.

jig·ger[1] (jĭg′ər), n. **1.** one who or that which jigs. **2.** *Naut.* **a.** a small sail set in the stern of a canoe, yawl, etc. **b.** the mast or sail nearest the stern of a vessel with five masts, or the fifth, from forward, if she has more than five. **c.** a light tackle used about the deck of a ship. **3.** any of various mechanical devices, many of which have a jerky or jolting motion. **4.** *Colloq.* some contrivance, article, or part that one cannot name more precisely: *What is that little jigger on the pistol?* **5.** a jig for separating ore or for fishing. **6.** *Golf.* an ironheaded club, a cross between a mashie and a midiron, used in making an approach. **7.** *Billiards.* a bridge. **8.** *U.S.* a 1½ oz. measure used in cocktail recipes. [f. JIG[1] + -ER[1]]

jig·ger[2] (jĭg′ər), n. a chigoe.

jig·gered (jĭg′ord), adj. a word used as a vague substitute for a profane word: *I'm jiggered if I know.*

jig·gle (jĭg′əl), v., **-gled, -gling.** —v.t., v.i. **1.** to move up and down or to and fro with short, quick jerks. —n. **2.** a jiggling movement. [freq. of JIG[2]]

jig saw, a narrow saw mounted vertically in a frame, used for cutting curves, etc.

jig·saw puzzle (jĭg′sô′), a picture sawed or cut up into small irregular pieces to form a puzzle.

ji·had (jĭ häd′), n. **1.** a war of Mohammedans upon others, with a religious object. **2.** any crusade, as against some belief. Also, **jehad.** [t. Ar.: effort, strife]

Ji·lo·lo (jĭ lô′lō), n. Halmahera.

jilt (jĭlt), v.t. **1.** to cast off (a lover or sweetheart) after encouragement or engagement. —n. **2.** a woman who jilts a lover. [orig. uncert.] —**jilt′er,** n.

Jim Crow (jĭm krō′), *U.S. Slang.* **1.** (in contemptuous use) Negro. **2.** a practice or policy of segregating Negroes, as in public places, public vehicles, etc. —**Jim-Crow, jim-crow,** adj.

Ji·mé·nez de Cis·ne·ros (hē mě′něth dě sēs ně′rôs), **Francisco** (frän thēs′kô), 1436–1517, Spanish cardinal and statesman. Also, **Ximenes, Ximenez.**

jim·my (jĭm′ĭ), n., pl. **-mies,** v., **-mied, -mying.** —n. **1.** a short crowbar used by burglars. —v.t. **2.** to force open by a jimmy, as a door or window. Also, *Brit.,* **jemmy.** [appar. a special use of *Jimmy,* familiar form of *James*]

jim·son weed (jĭm′sən), a datura, *Datura Stramonium,* a coarse, ill-smelling weed with white flowers and poisonous leaves. Also, **Jimson weed,** *jimsontown weed;* named after Jamestown, Va.]

jin·gal (jĭn′gəl), n. a large musket fired from a rest, often mounted on a carriage; formerly used by natives in India, China, etc. Also, **gingal, gingall.**

jin·gle (jĭng′gəl), v., **-gled, -gling,** n. —v.i. **1.** to make clinking or tinkling sounds, as coins, keys, etc., when struck together. **2.** to move or proceed with such sounds. **3.** to sound in a manner suggestive of this, as verse or any sequence of words: *a jingling ballad.* **4.** to make rhymes. —v.t. **5.** to cause to jingle. —n. **6.** a clinking or tinkling sound, as of small bells or of small pieces of metal struck together. **7.** something that makes such a sound, as a small bell or a metal pendant. **8.** a musical succession of like sounds, as in rhyme or alliteration, without particular regard for sense; jingling verse. **9.** a piece of such verse. **10.** *Ireland and Australia.* a covered two-wheeled car. [ME *gynglen,* appar.

imit.; but cf. D *jengelen*] —**jin′gling·ly**, *adv.* —**jin′-gly**, *adj.*

Jingling Johnny, *Music.* a crescent (def. 6).

jin·go (jĭng′gō), *n., pl.* **-goes,** *adj.* —*n.* **1.** one who boasts of his country's preparedness for war, or who favors a bellicose or blustering foreign policy; a chauvinist. **2.** (orig.) a Conservative supporter of Disraeli's New Eastern policy (1877–78). **3.** *Colloq.* a word used in vehement asseveration in the phrase "by jingo!" —*adj.* **4.** of or pertaining to jingoes. **5.** characterized by jingoism. [orig. uncert.; first used in conjurer's jargon]

jin·go·ism (jĭng′gōĭz/əm), *n.* the spirit, policy, or practices of jingoes. —**jin′go·ist,** *n., adj.* —**jin′go·is′-tic,** *adj.*

jinks (jĭngks), *n.pl. Colloq.* romping games or play; boisterous, unrestrained merrymaking, esp. in the phrase *high jinks.*

jinn (jĭn), *n.pl., sing.* **jinni. 1.** *Mohammedan Myth.* a class of spirits lower than the angels, capable of appearing in human and animal forms, and influencing mankind for good and evil. **2.** (*construed as sing. with pl.* **jinns**) a spirit of this class. [t. Ar., pl. of *jinnī* a demon. Cf. **genie**]

Jin·nah (jĭn′ə), *n.* **Mohammed Ali** (mō hăm′ĭd ä′lē), 1876–1948, Moslem leader in India: governor general of Pakistan, 1947.

jin·rik·i·sha (jĭn rĭk′shô, -shä), *n.* a small two-wheeled hooded vehicle drawn by one or more men, used in Japan and elsewhere. Also, **jin·rick′sha.** [t. Jap.: lit. manpower carriage]

Jinrikisha

Jin·sen (jĭn′sĕn′), *n.* Japanese name of **Chemulpo.**

jinx (jĭngks), *n. Colloq.* a person, thing, or influence supposed to bring bad luck. [var. of *jynx,* t. L: m. *iynx,* t. Gk.: bird used in witchcraft, hence, a spell]

ji·pi·ja·pa (hē′pē hä′pä), *n.* **1.** a tropical American palmlike plant (*Carludovica palmata,* family *Cyclanthaceae*). **2.** a panama hat made from the young leaves of this plant. [named after a town in Ecuador]

jit·ney (jĭt′nĭ), *n., pl.* **-neys,** *v.,* **-neyed, -neying.** —*n.* **1.** *U.S. Colloq.* an automobile which carries passengers, orig. each for a fare of five cents. **2.** *U.S. Slang.* a five-cent piece. —*v.t., v.i.* **3.** to carry or ride in a jitney.

jit·ter (jĭt′ər), *U.S. Slang.* —*n.* **1.** (*pl.*) nervousness; nerves. —*v.i.* **2.** to behave nervously. [var. of *chitter* shiver. Cf. CHATTER]

jit·ter·bug (jĭt′ər bŭg/), *n., v.,* **-bugged, -bugging.** —*n.* **1.** one whose enthusiastic responses to the rhythms of swing music take the form of violent and unpredictable dance motions. —*v.i.* **2.** to dance in such a manner.

jit·ter·y (jĭt′ər ĭ), *adj. U.S. Slang.* nervous; jumpy.

jiu·jit·su (joō jĭt′soō), *n.* jujitsu. Also, **jiu·jut′su.**

jive (jīv), *n. Slang.* **1.** the talk of swing enthusiasts. **2.** swing music.

JJ., **1.** Judges. **2.** Justices.

Jno., John.

jo (jō), *n., pl.* **joes.** *Scot.* sweetheart. Also, **joe.** [var. of JOY]

Jo·a·chim (yō′ä κHĭm, yō ä′-), *n.* **Joseph** (yō′zĕf), 1831–1907, German violinist and composer.

Joan (jōn), *n.* **1.** mythical female pope about A.D. 855–858. **2.** ("Fair Maid of Kent") 1328–85, wife of Edward, the Black Prince, and mother of Richard II.

jo·an·nes (jō ăn′ēz), *n., pl.* **-nes.** johannes.

Joan of Arc, 1412–31, French heroine, called "the Maid of Orléans," who aroused the spirit of nationality in France against the English and was burned by them as a witch. In 1920 she was canonized. Also, *French,* **Jeanne d'Arc.**

job[1] (jŏb), *n., v.,* **jobbed, jobbing,** *adj.* —*n.* **1.** a piece of work; an individual piece of work done in the routine of one's occupation or trade. **2.** a piece of work of defined character undertaken for a fixed price. **3.** anything one has to do. **4.** *U.S.* a situation, or post of employment. **5.** *Colloq.* an affair, matter, occurrence, or state of affairs: *to make the best of a bad job.* **6.** the unit or material being worked upon. **7.** the product or result. **8.** a piece of public or official business carried through with a view to improper private gain. **9.** *Slang.* a theft or robbery, or any criminal deed. —*v.i.* **10.** to work at jobs, or odd pieces of work; work by the piece. **11.** to do business as a jobber. **12.** to turn public business, etc., improperly to private gain. —*v.t.* **13.** to buy in large quantities and sell to dealers in smaller lots. **14.** to let out (work) in separate portions, as among different contractors or workmen. —*adj.* **15.** of or for a particular job or transaction. **16.** bought or sold together; lumped together: used chiefly in the phrase *job lot.* [orig. uncert.] —**job′less,** *adj.* —**job′less·ness,** *n.* —Syn. **4.** See **position.**

job[2] (jŏb), *v., v.i.,* **jobbed, jobbing,** *n.* jab. [ME *jobbe(n);* ? imit. Cf. JAB]

Job (jōb), *n.* **1.** the much-afflicted hero of a dramatic Old Testament book of wisdom. **2.** the book itself. [ult. t. Heb.: m. *Iyyōbh*]

job·ber (jŏb′ər), *n.* **1.** a wholesale merchant, esp. one selling to retailers. **2.** (formerly) a merchant who dealt

in special, odd, or job lots. **3.** one who perpetrates corrupt public or official jobs. **4.** a pieceworker.

job·ber·y (jŏb′ər ĭ), *n.* **1.** the practice of making improper private gains from a public business or trust. **2.** the perpetration of corrupt public or official jobs.

job lot, **1.** any large lot of goods handled by a jobber. **2.** a sundry amount, usually of poor quality.

job printer, a printer who does miscellaneous work, as the printing of cards, posters, etc. —**job printing.**

Job's comforter, one who depresses and discourages under the appearance or with the purpose of consoling.

Job's-tears (jōbz′tĭrz/), *n.pl.* **1.** the hard, nearly globular involucres which surround the female flowers in a species of grass, *Coix Lacryma-Jobi,* and which when ripe are used as beads. **2.** (*construed as sing., l.c.*) the grass itself, native in Asia but cultivated elsewhere.

job work, **1.** miscellaneous printing work, as cards, circulars, posters, etc. **2.** work done by the job.

Jo·cas·ta (jō kăs′tə), *n. Gk. Legend.* the wife of Laius, and the mother, and later the wife, of Oedipus.

Jock (jŏk), *n.* nickname for a Scot.

jock·ey (jŏk′ĭ), *n., pl.* **-eys,** *v.,* **-eyed, -eying.** —*n.* **1.** one who professionally rides horses in races. —*v.t.* **2.** to ride (a horse) as a jockey. **3.** to bring, put, etc., by skillful maneuvering. **4.** to trick or cheat. **5.** to manipulate trickily. —*v.i.* **6.** to aim at an advantage by skillful maneuvering. **7.** to act trickily; seek an advantage by trickery. [dim. of *Jock,* Scot. var. of *Jack*] —**jock′ey·ship/,** *n.*

jock·o (jŏk′ō), *n., pl.* **jockos. 1.** the chimpanzee. **2.** (*cap.*) a familiar name for any monkey. [t. F, from W Afr. name of the chimpanzee, recorded as *engeco, ncheko*]

jock·strap (jŏk′străp/), *n.* an athletic supporter worn by men.

jo·cose (jō kōs′), *adj.* given to or characterized by joking; jesting; humorous; playful. [t. L: m.s. *jocōsus*] —**jo·cose′ly,** *adv.* —**jo·cose′ness,** *n.* —Syn. See **jovial.**

jo·cos·i·ty (jō kŏs′ə tĭ), *n., pl.* **-ties. 1.** state or quality of being jocose. **2.** a joke or jest. **3.** a joke or jest.

joc·u·lar (jŏk′yə lər), *adj.* given to, characterized by, intended for, or suited to joking or jesting; waggish; facetious. [t. L: s. *joculāris*] —**joc′u·lar·ly,** *adv.* —Syn. See **jovial.**

joc·u·lar·i·ty (jŏk′yə lăr′ə tĭ), *n., pl.* **-ties. 1.** state or quality of being jocular. **2.** jocular speech or behavior. **3.** a jocular remark or act.

joc·und (jŏk′ənd, jō′kənd), *adj.* cheerful; merry; gay; blithe; glad. [ME, t. LL: s. *jocundus* pleasant] —**joc′-und·ly,** *adv.* —Syn. See **jovial.**

jo·cun·di·ty (jō kŭn′də tĭ), *n., pl.* **-ties. 1.** state cf being jocund; gaiety. **2.** a jocund remark or act.

Jodh·pur (jōd′pŏŏr), *n.* **1.** Also, **Marwar.** a state in NW India, in Rajputana. 2,555,900 pop. (1941); 36,120 sq. mi. **2.** the capital of this state. 126,842 (1941).

jodh·purs (jōd′pərz, jōd′-), *n.pl.* riding breeches reaching to the ankle, and fitting closely from the knee down, worn also in sports, etc. [named after JODHPUR]

Joe (jō), *n. U.S. Colloq.* G. I. Joe.

joe (jō), *n.* jo.

Jo·el (jō′əl), *n.* a Hebrew prophet of the postexilian period, second among the "minor prophets" in the prophetic canon. [ult. t. Heb.: m. *Yō′ēl*]

joe-pye weed (jō′pī/), **1.** a tall composite weed, *Eupatorium purpureum,* of North America, with clusters of pinkish or purple flowers. **2.** a related species, *E. maculatum,* with similar flowers, and stems that are often spotted with purple (**spotted joe-pye weed**).

jo·ey (jō′ĭ), *n., pl.* **-eys.** *Australia.* **1.** any young animal, esp. a kangaroo. **2.** a young child. [t. native Australian: m. *joë*]

Jof·fre (zhôf′r), *n.* **Joseph Jacques Césaire** (zhō zĕf′ zhäk sĕ zĕr′), 1852–1931, French general in World War I.

jog[1] (jŏg), *v.,* **jogged, jogging,** *n.* —*v.t.* **1.** to move or shake with a push or jerk. **2.** to give a slight push to, as to arouse the attention; nudge. **3.** to stir up by hint or reminder: *to jog a person's memory.* **4.** *Print.* to straighten (sheets of paper) by jolting them into alignment. —*v.i.* **5.** to move with a jolt or jerk. **6.** to go or travel with a jolting pace or motion. **7.** to go in a steady or humdrum fashion (fol. by *on* or *along*). —*n.* **8.** a shake; a slight push; a nudge. **9.** a slow, steady walk, trot, etc. **10.** act of jogging. [b. *jot* jolt and *shog* shake (both now d.)] —**jog′ger,** *n.*

jog[2] (jŏg), *n. Chiefly U.S.* an irregularity of line or surface; a projection; a notch. [var. of JAG[1]]

jog·gle (jŏg′əl), *v.,* **-gled, -gling,** *n.* —*v.t.* **1.** to shake slightly; move to and fro as by repeated jerks. **2.** to join or fasten by a joggle or joggles. **3.** to fit or fasten with dowels. —*v.i.* **4.** to move irregularly; have a jogging or jolting motion; shake. —*n.* **5.** act of joggling. **6.** a slight shake; a jolt. **7.** a moving with jolts or jerks. **8.** a projection on one of two joining surfaces, or a notch on the other, to prevent slipping. **9.** a key or dowel between two surfaces, as for joining two blocks of masonry. **10.** a joint formed in either way. [freq. of JOG[1]]

joggle post, *Bldg. Trades,* a post having shoulders or notches for receiving the lower ends or feet of struts.

Jog·ja·kar·ta (jŏg′yä kär′tä), *n.* a city in the U.S. of Indonesia, in S Java. 136,649 (1930). Also, **Jokyakarta.** Dutch, **Djokjakarta.**

jog trot, **1.** a slow, regular, jolting pace, as of a horse. **2.** a routine or humdrum mode of procedure.

---

b., blend of, blended; c., cognate with; d., dialect, dialectal; der., derived from; f., formed from; g., going back to; m., modification of; r., replacing; s., stem of; t., taken from; ?, perhaps. See the full key on inside cover.

jo·han·nes (jō·hăn′ēz), *n., pl.* **-nes.** a Portuguese gold coin formerly current, worth about $9, and named from King John (João) V (who reigned 1706–50), by whom it was first issued. Also, **joannes.** [t. NL and ML, var. of LL *Jōannes.* See JOHN]

Jo·han·nes·burg (jō·hăn′ĭs·bûrg′, yō·hän′əs·bœrкн′), *n.* a city in the N part of the Union of South Africa, in Transvaal: gold mines. With suburbs, 727,943 (1946).

John (jŏn), *n.* **1.** the Apostle John, to whom is attributed the authorship of the fourth Gospel, three Epistles, and the Book of Revelation. **2.** the fourth Gospel, in the New Testament. **3.** one of the three Epistles of John, referred to as 1, 2, and 3 John. **4.** John the Baptist. Mark 1:4, etc. **5.** any of several characters with this name in the Bible. **6.** name of twenty-three popes. **7.** (*John Lackland*) 1167?–1216, king of England, 1199–1216, who signed the Magna Charta in 1215. **8. Augustus Edwyn,** born 1879, British painter and etcher. [ME *Iohan, John,* t. ML: m. *Jōhannes,* LL *Jōannes,* t. Gk.: m. *Iōánnēs,* t. Heb.: m. *Yōhānān,* lit., Jehovah hath been gracious]

John I, (*"the Great"*) 1357–1433, king of Portugal, 1385–1433.

John III, (*John Sobieski*) 1624–96, king of Poland, 1674–96.

John Bull, 1. the English people. **2.** the typical Englishman.

John Doe, a fictitious personage in legal proceedings.

John Do·ry (dōr′ĭ), a thin, deep-bodied marine fish, *Zeus faber,* with spiny plates along the base of the dorsal and anal fins. Also, **John Do′ree.** [f. JOHN + DORY² (*doree*), the name of the fish]

Joh·ne's disease (yō′nəz), *Vet. Sci.* a chronic diarrheal disease of cattle and sheep caused by infection with an organism related to the tubercle bacillus.

John Hancock, *U.S. Colloq.* one's signature. [from the first signer of the Declaration of Independence]

john·ny·cake (jŏn′ĭ·kāk′), *n.* *U.S.* a kind of cake or bread made of corn meal, water or milk, and often eggs, etc.; corn bread. [orig. obscure. The first element may be from obs. *jonakin, jonikin* (appar. of Indian origin) a form of thin griddle cake]

John·ny-jump-up (jŏn′ĭ·jŭmp′ŭp′), *n.* *U.S.* **1.** any of certain violets, esp. *Viola Kitaibeliana* var. *Rafinesqii.* **2.** a small form of the pansy, *Viola tricolor.*

Johnny on the spot, *Colloq.* one who is on hand to perform a duty, seize an opportunity, etc.

John of Austria, Don, 1547?–1578, Spanish naval commander and general.

John of Gaunt (gônt, gänt). See **Gaunt.**

John o'Groat's House (ə grōts′, ə grŏts′), a place at the northern tip of Scotland, often appearing in the phrase *from Land's End to John o'Groats.*

John of Ley·den (lī′dən), 1509?–30, Dutch Anabaptist.

John·son (jŏn′sən), *n.* **1. Andrew,** 1808–75, 17th president of the U. S., 1865–69. **2. Charles Spurgeon** (spûr′jən), born 1893, U.S. educator and sociologist. **3. James Weldon,** 1871–1938, U.S. author. **4. Samuel,** 1709–84, British author and lexicographer. **5. Sir William,** 1715–74, American colonial administrator and soldier, born in Ireland.

Johnson City, a city in NE Tennessee. 27,864 (1950).

John·son·ese (jŏn′sə·nēz′, -nēs′), *n.* a literary style characterized by pompous phraseology and the use of many words of Latin origin (so-called from that of Dr. Samuel Johnson).

John·so·ni·an (jŏn·sō′nĭ·ən), *adj.* having the quality of Johnsonese.

John·ston (jŏn′stən, -sən), *n.* **1. Albert Sidney,** 1803–62, Confederate general in the U. S. Civil War. **2. Joseph Eggleston** (ĕg′əl·stən), 1807–91, Confederate general in the U. S. Civil War.

Johns·town (jŏnz′toun′), *n.* a city in SW Pennsylvania: disastrous flood, 1889. 63,232 (1950).

John the Baptist, *Bible.* the forerunner of Jesus. Mat. 3.

Jo·hore (jə·hōr′), *n.* a native state in the Federation of Malaya: formerly one of the Unfederated Malay States. 605,416 pop. (est. 1937); 7330 sq. mi. *Cap.:* Johore.

joie de vi·vre (zhwà də vē′vr), *French.* joy of living.

join (join), *v.t.* **1.** to bring or put together, in contact or connection. **2.** to come into contact, connection, or union with: *the brook joins the river.* **3.** to bring together in relation, purpose, action, coexistence, etc.: *to join forces.* **4.** to become a member of (a society, regiment, party, etc.). **5.** to come into the company of: *I'll join you later.* **6.** to unite in marriage. **7.** to meet or engage in (battle, conflict, etc.). **8.** to adjoin: *his land joins mine.* **9.** *Geom.* to draw a curve or straight line between. —*v.i.* **10.** to come into or be in contact or connection, or form a junction. **11.** to become united, associated, or combined; associate or ally oneself (fol. by *with*). **12.** to take part with others (often fol. by *in*). **13.** to be contiguous or close; lie or come together; form a junction. **14.** to enlist in a branch of the armed forces. **15.** *Obs.* to meet in battle or conflict. —*n.* **16.** joining. **17.** a place or line of joining; a seam. [ME *join(en),* t. OF: m. *joindre,* g. L *jungere* join, yoke]

—**Syn. 1.** link, couple, fasten, attach; conjoin, combine; associate; consolidate, amalgamate. JOIN, CONNECT, UNITE all imply bringing two or more things together more or less closely. JOIN may refer to a connection or association

of any degree of closeness, but often implies direct contact: *one joins the corners of a mortise together.* CONNECT implies a joining as by a tie, link, wire, etc.: *one connects two batteries.* UNITE implies a close joining of two or more things so as to form one: *one unites layers of veneer sheets to form plywood.* —**Ant. 1.** separate.

join·der (join′dər), *n.* **1.** act of joining. **2.** *Law.* **a.** the joining of causes of action in a suit. **b.** the joining of parties in a suit. **c.** the acceptance by a party to an action of an issue tendered. [t. F: m. *joindre* JOIN]

join·er (joi′nər), *n.* **1.** one who or that which joins. **2.** a carpenter, esp. one who constructs doors, windows, and other fittings of houses, ships, etc. Much used in England where Americans say simply *carpenter.*

join·er·y (joi′nə·rĭ), *n.* **1.** the art or trade of a joiner **2.** a joiner's work or his product.

joint (joint), *n.* **1.** the place or part in which two things, or parts of one thing, are joined or united, either rigidly or so as to admit of motion; an articulation. **2.** (in an animal body) **a.** the movable place or part where two bones or two segments join. **b.** the hingelike or other arrangement of such a part. **3. out of joint, a.** dislocated. **b.** out of order; in a bad state. **4.** *Biol.* **a.** a portion, esp. of an animal or plant body, connected with another portion by an articulation, node, or the like. **b.** a portion between two articulations, nodes, or the like. **5.** *Bot.* the part of a stem from which a branch or a leaf grows; a node. **6.** one of the portions into which a carcass is divided by a butcher. **7.** *Geol.* a fracture plane in rocks, generally at right angles to the bedding of sedimentary rocks and variously oriented in igneous and metamorphic rocks, commonly arranged in two or more sets of parallel intersecting systems. **8.** *U.S. Slang.* **a.** a cheap, sordid place, as for opium smoking or the illicit sale of liquor. **b.** any resort or abode. [ME *iointe,* t. OF: m. *joint, jointe* (n. use of pp. of *joindre* JOIN) g. L *junctus, juncta,* prop. pp. of *jungere*] —*adj.* **9.** shared by or common to two or more. **10.** sharing or acting in common. **11.** joined or associated, as in relation, interest, or action: *joint owners.* **12.** held, done, etc., by two or more in conjunction or in common: *joint ownership.* **13.** *Law.* joined together in obligation or ownership. **14.** *Parl. Proc.* of or pertaining to both legislative branches. **15.** (of diplomatic action) in which two or more governments are formally united. —*v.t.* **16.** to unite by a joint or joints. **17.** to form or provide with a joint or joints. **18.** to divide at a joint, or separate into pieces. **19.** to prepare (a board, etc.) for fitting in a joint. [ME, t. OF, pp. of *joindre* JOIN]

joint account, a bank account kept in the names of two or more persons or parties and subject to withdrawals by any one of them.

joint·ed (join′tĭd), *adj.* provided with joints; formed with knots or nodes.

joint·er (join′tər), *n.* **1.** one who or that which joints. **2.** an implement or machine used in making joints. **3.** *Agric.* an instrument with a triangular head, used with a plow to bury trash.

joint ill, *Vet. Sci.* a disease of young foals (horses) characterized by swollen inflamed joints, high fever, and, usually, by death a few days after birth.

joint·ly (joint′lĭ), *adv.* together; in common.

joint resolution, a resolution adopted by both branches of a legislative assembly and requiring the signature of the chief executive to become law.

joint stock, 1. stock or capital divided into a number of shares. **2.** a pool of stock held in common; stock representing a common capital fund.

joint-stock company (joint′stŏk′), **1.** *U.S. Law.* an unincorporated business partnership or association of individuals, of which the capital is represented by transferable shares of stock. **2.** *Brit. Law.* any incorporated business with transferable shares of stock.

joint-stock corporation, a corporation whose ownership is divided into transferable shares, the object usually being the division of profits among the members in proportion to the number of shares held by each.

join·ture (join′chər), *n.* *Law.* **1.** an estate or property settled on a woman in consideration of marriage, and to be enjoyed by her after her husband's decease. **2.** *Obs.* a joint tenancy or holding in favor of a man and his wife. [ME, t. F, g. L *junctūra* a joining]

joint·weed (joint′wēd′), *n.* an American polygonaceous herb, *Polygonella articulata,* with many-jointed spikelike racemes of small white or rose-colored flowers.

joint·worm (joint′wûrm′), *n.* the larva of certain hymenopterous insects of the family *Eurytomidae,* very injurious to grain, esp. at the joints of the stalk.

Join·ville (zhwăn vēl′), *n.* **Jean de** (zhän də), c1224–c1319, French chronicler.

joist (joist), *n.* **1.** one of the pieces of timber to which are fastened the boards of a floor, the laths of a ceiling, or the like. —*v.t.* **2.** to furnish with or fix on joists. [ME *giste,* t. OF, der. *gesir* lie, rest, g. L *jacēre* lie; akin to GIST] —**joist′·less,** *adj.*

A. Joist; B. Floor boards

Jo·kai (yō′koi), *n.* **Maurus** (mou′rŏŏs) or **Mór** (mōr), 1825–1904, Hungarian author.

joke (jōk), *n., v.,* **joked, joking.** —*n.* **1.** something said or done to excite laughter or amusement; a playful or mischievous trick or remark. **2.** an amusing or ridic-

ulous circumstance. **3.** an object of joking or jesting; a thing or person laughed at rather than taken seriously. **4.** a matter for joking about; trifling matter: *the loss was no joke.* **5.** joking or jesting. —*v.i.* **6.** to speak or act in a playful or merry way. **7.** to say something in mere sport, rather than in earnest. —*v.t.* **8.** to subject to jokes; banter, rally, or chaff. [t. L: m.s. *jocus* jest, sport] —**joke′less,** *adj.* —**jok′ing·ly,** *adv.*
—**Syn. 1.** witticism, jape; quip; quirk, sally. JOKE, JEST refer to something said (or done) in sport, or to cause amusement. A JOKE is something said or done for the sake of exciting laughter; it may be raillery, a witty remark, or a prank or trick: *to tell a joke.* JEST, today a more formal word, nearly always refers to joking language and is more suggestive of scoffing or ridicule than is JOKE: *to speak in jest.*

jok·er (jō′kər), *n.* **1.** one who jokes. **2.** an extra playing card in a pack, used in some games, often counting as the highest card or to represent a card of any denomination or suit the holder wishes. **3.** *U.S.* a clause or expression inserted in a legislative bill with the unavowed object of defeating the ostensible purpose of the bill if passed. **4.** a hidden clause in any paper, document, etc., which largely changes its apparent nature. **5.** any device or expedient for getting the better of another.

Jok·ya·kar·ta (jōk′yä kär′tä), *n.* Jogjakarta.

Jo·li·et (jō′lǐ ět′, jō′lǐ ět′; *Fr.* zhô lyě′ *for 1 also*), *n.* **1.** Also, **Jol′li·et′. Louis,** 1645–1700, French explorer of the Mississippi. **2.** a city in NE Illinois. 51,601 (1950).

jol·li·fi·ca·tion (jōl′ə fə kā′shən), *n.* jolly merrymaking; a jolly festivity. [f. JOLLY, adj. + -FICATION]

jol·li·fy (jōl′ə fī′), *v.t., v.i.,* **-fied, -fying.** *Colloq.* to make or be jolly or merry.

jol·li·ty (jōl′ə tǐ), *n., pl.* **-ties. 1.** jolly state, mood, or proceedings. **2.** (*pl.*) jolly festivities.

jol·ly (jōl′ǐ), *adj.,* **-lier, -liest,** *v.,* **-lied, -lying,** *n., pl.* **-lies,** *adv.* —*adj.* **1.** in good spirits, gay: *in a moment he was as jolly as ever.* **2.** cheerfully festive or convivial. **3.** *Chiefly Brit. Colloq.* fine; pleasing. **4.** *Brit. Colloq.* big or great: *a jolly fool.* **5.** joyous, glad, or gay. —*v.t.* **6.** *Colloq.* to talk or act agreeably to (a person) in order to keep him in good humor; banter pleasantly. **7.** *Colloq.* to make fun of. —*v.i.* **8.** *Colloq.* to jolly a person. —*n.* **9.** *Colloq.* a bit of agreeable talk or action intended to put or keep a person in good humor, often in order to secure some end. —*adv.* **10.** *Brit. Colloq.* extremely; very: *jolly well.* [ME *joli*(*f*), t. OF, ? ult. of Gmc. orig.; cf. Icel. *jōl* YULE] —**jol′li·ly,** *adv.* —**jol′li·ness,** *n.* —**Syn. 1, 2.** merry, sportive, playful, frolicsome; hilarious. See **gay.** —**Ant. 1.** gloomy. **2.** melancholy.

jolly boat, a ship's work boat, smaller than a cutter, hoisted at the stern of a sailing vessel for handy use.

Jolly Rog·er (rŏj′ər), the pirates' flag.

Jo·lo (hô lô′), *n.* **1.** one of the Philippine Islands, in the SW part: the main island of the Sulu Archipelago. 130,870 pop. (1939); 345 sq. mi. **2.** a seaport on this island. 12,571 (1939).

jolt (jōlt), *v.t., v.i.* **1.** to jar or shake as by a sudden rough thrust; shake up roughly, as in passing over an uneven road. —*n.* **2.** a jolting shock or movement. [b. *jot* jolt and obs. *joll* knock about] —**jolt′er,** *n.*

jolt·y (jōl′tǐ), *adj.* jolting.

Jo·nah (jō′nə), *n.* **1.** a Hebrew prophet who for his impiety was thrown overboard from his ship to allay a tempest. He was swallowed by a large fish and lived in its belly for three days before he was vomited up. Jonah, 1,2. **2.** a short book of the Old Testament bearing his name. **3.** any person regarded as bringing bad luck. Also, **Jo·nas** (jō′nəs).

Jon·a·than (jŏn′ə thən), *n.* **1.** son of Saul, and friend of David. 1 Sam. 13, etc. **2.** *Hort.* a variety of red apple that matures in early fall. **3.** *Obsolesc.* a generic nickname for Americans, or, esp., New Englanders (often prefaced by *Brother*). [ult. t. Heb.: m. *Yonāthān*]

Jones (jōnz), *n.* **1. Casey** (kā′sǐ), (*John Luther Jones*), ?–1900, U.S. railroad engineer whose heroic death in train wreck inspired popular song about him. **2. Daniel,** born 1881, British phonetician. **3. Henry Arthur,** 1851–1929, British dramatist. **4. Inigo** (ǐn′ǐ gō′), 1573–1652, British architect. **5. John Paul,** 1747–92, American naval commander in the Revolutionary War, born in Scotland.

jon·gleur (jŏng′glər; *Fr.* zhôn glœr′), *n.* (in medieval France and Norman England) an itinerant minstrel or entertainer who sang songs (sometimes of his own composition), told stories, and otherwise entertained people. [t. F, b. OF *jogleor* and *jangler* JANGLE. See JUGGLER]

jon·quil (jŏng′kwǐl, jŏn′-), *n.* **1.** a species of narcissus, *Narcissus Jonquilla*, with long, narrow, rushlike leaves and fragrant yellow or white flowers. **2.** a jonquil bulb or flower. [t. F: m. *jonquille*, t. Sp.: m. *junquillo*, dim. of *junco*, g. L *juncus* a rush]

Jon·son (jŏn′sən), *n.* **Ben,** 1573?–1637, British dramatist and poet.

Jop·lin (jŏp′lǐn), *n.* city in SW Missouri. 38,711 (1950).

Jop·pa (jŏp′ə), *n.* ancient name of **Jaffa.**

Jor·dan (jôr′dən), *n.* **1.** a river flowing from S Lebanon through the Sea of Galilee and S along the boundary between Palestine and Trans-Jordan into the Dead Sea. ab. 200 mi. **2. David Starr,** 1851–1931, U. S. biologist and educator.

Jordan almond, a large, hard-shelled, high-quality type of Spanish almond. [ME *jardyne* (t. F: m. *jardin* garden) *almaunde*, i.e. garden almond. See ALMOND]

jo·rum (jōr′əm), *n.* a large bowl or vessel for holding drink, or its contents: *a jorum of punch.* [said to be named after *Joram*, who brought to David vessels of silver, gold, and brass. See 2 Sam. 8:10]

Jo·seph (jō′zəf), *n.* **1.** a Hebrew patriarch, the first son of Jacob by Rachel. His brothers sold him into slavery in Egypt. Gen. 30:22–24, Gen. 37. **2.** the husband of Mary, the mother of Jesus. Matt. 1:16–25. **3.** (*l.c.*) a long cloak with a cape, worn chiefly in the 18th century, esp. by women, as when riding. [ult. t. Heb.: m. *Yōsēph*]

Joseph II, 1741–90, emperor of the Holy Roman Empire, 1765–90.

Jo·se·phine (jō′zə fēn′), *n.* 1763–1814, first wife of Napoleon Bonaparte.

Joseph of Ar·i·ma·thae·a (ăr′ə mə thē′ə), a rich Israelite who believed in Christ and who laid the body of Jesus in the tomb. Matt. 27:57–60.

Jo·se·phus (jō sē′fəs), *n.* **Flavius** (flā′vǐ əs), A.D. 37?–95, Jewish historian, writing in Aramaic and Greek.

josh (jŏsh), *U.S. Slang.* —*v.t., v.i.* **1.** to chaff; banter in a teasing way. —*n.* **2.** a chaffing remark; a piece of banter. [b. JOKE and BOSH] —**josh′er,** *n.*

Josh·u·a (jŏsh′ōō ə), *n.* **1.** the successor of Moses as leader of the Israelites. Exodus 17:9–14. **2.** a book of the Old Testament. [ult. t. Heb.: m. *Yehōshūa*]

Joshua tree, a tree, *Yucca brevifolia,* growing in arid or desert regions of the southwestern U. S. See **yucca.**

joss (jŏs), *n.* a Chinese deity or idol. [Pidgin-English, t. Pg.: m. *deos,* g. L *deus* god]

joss house, a Chinese temple for idol worship.

joss stick, a slender stick of a dried fragrant paste, burned by the Chinese as incense, etc.

jos·tle (jŏs′əl), *v.,* **-tled, -tling,** *n.* —*v.t.* **1.** to strike or push roughly or rudely against; elbow roughly; hustle. **2.** to drive or force by or as by pushing or shoving. —*v.i.* **3.** to collide (fol. by *with*) or strike or push (fol. by *against*) as in passing or in a crowd; push or elbow one's way rudely. **4.** to strive as with collisions, rough pushing, etc., for room, place, or any advantage. —*n.* **5.** a collision, shock, or push, as in jostling. Also, **justle.** [ME *justil,* freq. of *just* JOUST] —**jos′tle·ment,** *n.* —**jos′tler,** *n.*

jot (jŏt), *n., v.,* **jotted, jotting.** —*n.* **1.** the least part of something; a little bit: *I don't care a jot.* —*v.t.* **2.** to write or mark down briefly (usually fol. by *down*). [t. L: m. *iōta* IOTA] —**jot′ter,** *n.*

jot·ting (jŏt′ǐng), *n.* **1.** act of one who jots. **2.** something jotted down; a brief note or memorandum.

Jo·tun (yô′tŏōn), *n. Scand. Myth.* one of a supernatural race of giants. Also, **Jo′tunn, Jö·tunn** (yœ′-tŏōn). [Icel., prop. *jötunn,* c. OE *eoten* giant]

Jo·tun·heim (yô′tŏōn hām′), *n. Scand. Myth.* the outer world, or realm of giants; Utgard. Also, **Jo′tunn·heim′, Jö·tunn·heim** (yœ′tŏōn hām′). [Icel.]

Jou·bert (zhōō bĕr′), *n.* **Joseph** (zhô zěf′), 1754–1824, French moralist and essayist.

joule (joul, jōōl), *n. Physics.* a unit of work or energy equal to 10⁷ ergs; one watt-second (approximately 0.74 foot-pounds). [named after J. P. JOULE]

Joule (joul), *n.* **James Prescott,** 1818–89, British physicist.

jounce (jouns), *v.,* **jounced, jouncing,** *n.* —*v.i., v.t.* **1.** to move violently up and down; bounce. —*n.* **2.** a jouncing movement. [? b. obs. *joll* knock about and BOUNCE]

jour., journal.

Jour·dan (zhōōr dän′), *n.* **Jean Baptiste** (zhän bä tēst′), Count, 1762–1833, French marshal.

jour·nal (jûr′nəl), *n.* **1.** a daily record, as of occurrences, experiences, or observations. **2.** a register of the daily transactions of a public or legislative body. **3.** a periodical, as the weekly diurnals of the 17th century, esp. the serials devoted to learned societies and professions. **4.** a newspaper, magazine, or the like. **5.** *Bookkeeping.* **a.** a daybook. **b.** (in double entry) a book in which all transactions are entered (from the daybook or blotter) in systematic form, to facilitate posting into the ledger. **6.** *Naut.* a log or logbook. **7.** *Mach.* that part of a shaft or axle in actual contact with a bearing. [ME, t. OF, g. LL *diurnālis* DIURNAL]

journal box, *Mach.* a bearing or box which contains a journal (def. 7).

jour·nal·ese (jûr′nə lēz′, -lēs′), *n.* the style of writing or expression (less considered than that of conventional literary work) supposed to characterize newspapers.

jour·nal·ism (jûr′nə lǐz′əm), *n.* **1.** the occupation of writing for, editing, and conducting newspapers and other periodicals. **2.** newspapers collectively.

jour·nal·ist (jûr′nəl ǐst), *n.* one engaged in journalism (used more widely in England than U.S.).

jour·nal·is·tic (jûr′nə lǐs′tǐk), *adj.* of, pertaining to, or characteristic of journalists or journalism. —**jour′nal·is′ti·cal·ly,** *adv.*

jour·nal·ize (jûr′nə līz′), *v.,* **-ized, -izing.** —*v.t.* **1.** to enter or record in a journal. **2.** to tell or relate, as done in a journal. **3.** (in double-entry bookkeeping) to systematize and enter in a journal, preparatory to posting to the ledger. —*v.i.* **4.** to keep or make entries in a journal. **5.** to engage in journalism. Also, *esp. Brit.,* **jour′nal·ise′.**

jour·ney (jûr′nǐ), *n., pl.* **-neys,** *v.,* **-neyed, -neying.** —*n.* **1.** a course of travel from one place to another, esp.

by land. **2.** a distance traveled, or suitable for traveling, in a specified time: *a day's journey.* —*v.i.* **3.** to make a journey; travel. [ME *jorney*, t. OF: m. *jornee* a day's time, ult. der L *diurnus* of the day, daily] —**jour′-ney·er,** *n.* —**Syn. 1.** excursion, jaunt; tour; expedition; pilgrimage. See **trip.**

jour·ney·man (jûr′nĭ mən), *n., pl.* **-men. 1.** one who has served his apprenticeship at a trade or handicraft, and who works at it for another. **2.** *Obs.* one hired to do work for another usually for a day. [f. *journey* a day's work (obs.) + MAN]

jour·ney·work (jûr′nĭ wûrk′), *n.* the work of a journeyman.

joust (just, joust), *n.* **1.** a combat in which two armored knights or men-at-arms on horseback opposed each other with lances. **2.** (*pl.*) a tournament. —*v.i.* **3.** to contend in a joust or tournament. Also, **just.** [ME *j(o)uste(n),* t. OF: m. *j(o)uster,* ult. der. *juxtā* near] —**joust′er,** *n.*

Jove (jōv), *n.* **1.** Jupiter. **2.** *Poetic.* the planet Jupiter. **3. by Jove,** a mild oath, esp. common in England. [t. L: m.s. *Jovis.* See JUPITER]

jo·vi·al (jō′vĭ əl), *adj.* **1.** endowed with or characterized by a hearty, joyous humor or a spirit of good-fellowship. **2.** (*cap.*) of or pertaining to the god Jove or Jupiter. [t. L: s. *Joviālis* of Jupiter (in astrology the planet is regarded as exerting a happy influence)] —**jo′vi·al·ly,** *adv.* —**jo′vi·al·ness,** *n.*
—**Syn. 1.** merry, jolly, convivial, gay. JOVIAL, JOCOSE, JOCULAR, JOCUND agree in referring to someone who is in a good humor JOVIAL suggests a hearty, joyous humor: *a jovial person.* JOCOSE refers to that which causes laughter; it suggests someone who is playful and given to jesting: *with jocose and comical airs.* JOCULAR means humorous, facetious, mirthful, and waggish: *jocular enough to keep up the spirits of all around him.* JOCUND, now a literary word, suggests a cheerful, light-hearted, and sprightly gaiety: *glad and jocund company.* —**Ant. 1.** saturnine, morose, gloomy, staid.

jo·vi·al·i·ty (jō′vĭ ăl′ə tĭ), *n.* state or quality of being jovial; merriment; jollity.

Jo·vi·an (jō′vĭ ən), *adj.* **1.** pertaining to the god Jupiter. **2.** pertaining to the planet Jupiter. **3.** (*Flavius Claudius Jovianus*) A.D. c332–364, Roman emperor, A.D. 363–364.

Jow·ett (jou′ĭt), *n.* **Benjamin,** 1817–93, British educator, Greek scholar, translator, and theologian.

jowl[1] (joul, jōl), *n.* **1.** a jaw, esp. the under jaw. **2.** the cheek. [ME *chawl, chavel,* OE *ceafl* jaw; akin to D *kevel* gum, d. G *kiefel* jaw, chap, Icel. *kjaptr* mouth, jaw]

jowl[2] (joul, jōl), *n.* **1.** a fold of flesh hanging from the jaw, as of a fat person. **2.** the dewlap of cattle. **3.** the wattle of fowls. [ME *cholle,* appar. der. OE *ceole* throat]

joy (joi), *n.* **1.** an emotion of keen or lively pleasure arising from present or expected good; exultant satisfaction; great gladness; delight. **2.** a source or cause of gladness or delight: *a thing of beauty is a joy forever.* **3.** a state of happiness or felicity. **4.** the manifestation of glad feeling; outward rejoicing; festive gaiety. —*v.i.* **5.** to feel joy; be glad; rejoice. —*v.t.* **6** *Obs.* to gladden. [ME *joie,* t. OF, g. L *gaudia,* pl. of *gaudium* joy, gladness] —**Syn. 1.** rapture. **3.** bliss. See **pleasure.**

joy·ance (joi′əns), *n. Archaic.* joyous feeling; gladness.

Joyce (jois), *n.* **James,** 1882–1941, Irish author.

joy·ful (joi′fəl), *adj.* **1.** full of joy, as a person, the heart, etc.; glad; delighted. **2.** showing or expressing joy, as looks, actions, speech, etc. **3.** causing or bringing joy, as an event, a sight, news, etc.; delightful. —**joy′-ful·ly,** *adv.* —**joy′ful·ness,** *n.* —**Syn. 1.** joyous, happy, blithe; buoyant, elated, jubilant. See **gay.**

joy·less (joi′lĭs), *adj.* **1.** destitute of joy or gladness. **2.** causing no joy or pleasure. —**joy′less·ly,** *adv.* —**joy′-less·ness,** *n.* —**Syn. 1.** sad, cheerless; gloomy, dismal.

joy·ous (joi′əs), *adj.* joyful. —**joy′ous·ly,** *adv.* —**joy′ous·ness,** *n.*

joy ride, *Colloq.* a pleasure ride in an automobile, esp. when the car is driven recklessly or used without the owner's permission. —**joy rider.** —**joy riding.**

joy stick, the control stick of an airplane.

JP, jet propulsion.

J.P., Justice of the Peace.

Jr., Junior. Also, **jr.**

Ju·an de Fu·ca (jōō′ən dĭ fū′kə; *Sp.* hwän′dĕ fōō′-kä) a strait between Vancouver island and NW Washington. ab. 100 mi. long; 15–20 mi. wide.

Ju·an Fer·nán·dez (jōō′ən fər nän′dĕz; *Sp.* hwän′-fĕr nän′dĕth), a group of three islands in the S Pacific, ab. 400 miles W of and belonging to Chile: Alexander Selkirk, the supposed prototype of "Robinson Crusoe," was marooned here, 1704.

Juá·rez (hwä′rĕs), *n.* **1. Benito Pablo** (bĕ nē′tô pä′blô), 1806–72, president of Mexico, 1853–63, and 1867–72. **2. Ciudad.** See **Ciudad Juárez.**

Ju·bal (jōō′bəl), *n.* son of Lamech by Adah, and purported inventor of musical instruments. Gen. 4:21.

Ju·ba (jōō′bä), *n.* a river flowing from S Ethiopia S through Italian Somaliland to the Indian Ocean. ab. 1000 mi. Italian, **Giuba.**

ju·ba (jōō′bə), *n.* a lively dance developed by plantation Negroes of the U.S.

jub·bah (jŏŏb′bə), *n.* a kind of long outer garment with sleeves, worn in Mohammedan countries. [t. Ar.]

Jub·bul·pore (jŭb′əl pōr′), *n.* a city in central India, in the Central Provinces. 178,339 (1941).

ju·be (jōō′bē), *n. Archit.* **1.** a screen with an upper platform, separating the choir of a church from the nave and often supporting a rood. **2.** a rood loft. [t. L: bid thou, the first word of a formula spoken from the gallery above the rood screen]

ju·bi·lant (jōō′bə lənt), *adj.* **1.** jubilating; rejoicing; exultant. **2.** expressing or exciting joy; manifesting or denoting exultation or gladness. [t. L: s. *jūbilans,* ppr.] —**ju′bi·lance, ju′bi·lan·cy,** *n.* —**ju′bi·lant·ly,** *adv.*

ju·bi·late (jōō′bə lāt′), *v.i.,* **-lated, -lating. 1.** to manifest or feel great joy; rejoice; exult. **2.** to celebrate a jubilee or joyful occasion. [t. L: m.s. *jūbilātus,* pp. of *jūbilāre* shout for joy] —**ju·bi·la·to·ry** (jōō′bə lə tōr′ĭ), *adj.*

Ju·bi·la·te (jōō′bə lā′tĭ, -lä′tĭ), *n.* **1.** the 100th Psalm (99th in the Vulgate), used as a canticle in the Anglican liturgy. **2.** the third Sunday (**Jubilate Sunday**) after Easter (when the 66th psalm, 65th in the Vulgate, is used as the introit). **3.** a musical setting of this psalm. [t. L: shout ye, the first word of both psalms in the Vulgate]

ju·bi·la·tion (jōō′bə lā′shən), *n.* **1.** act of jubilating; rejoicing; exultation. **2.** a joyful or festive celebration.

ju·bi·lee (jōō′bə lē′), *n.* **1.** the celebration of any of certain anniversaries, as the 25th (**silver jubilee**), 50th (**golden jubilee**), or 60th or 75th (**diamond jubilee**). **2.** the completion of the 50th year of any continuous course or period, as of existence or activity, or its celebration. **3.** *Rom. Cath. Ch.* an appointed year (or other period) now ordinarily every 25th year, in which remission from the penal consequences of sin is granted upon repentance and the performance of certain religious acts. **4.** (among the ancient Hebrews) a year to be observed every 50th year (see Lev. 25), and to be announced by the blowing of trumpets, during which the fields were to be left untilled, alienated lands to be restored, and Hebrew bondmen to be set free. **5.** any season or occasion of rejoicing or festivity. **6.** rejoicing or jubilation. [ME *jubile,* t. F, t. LL: m.s. *jūbilaeus,* t. Gk.: m. *iōbēlaios,* der. Heb. *yōbēl* ram, ram's horn (used as a trumpet; cf. Lev. 25:9)]

Jud., 1. Judges. **2.** Judith (Apocrypha).

Ju·dae·a (jōō dē′ə), *n.* Judea. —**Ju·dae′an,** *adj., n.*

Ju·dah (jōō′də), *n.* **1.** the fourth son of Jacob and Leah. Gen. 29:35, etc. **2.** the powerful tribe of his descendants. **3.** an ancient kingdom in S Palestine, including the tribes of Judah and Benjamin. *Cap.:* Jerusalem. See **Israel.** [ult. t. Heb.: m. *Yehūdāh*]

Ju·da·ic (jōō dā′ĭk), *adj.* of or pertaining to the Jews; Jewish.

Ju·da·ism (jōō′dĭ ĭz′əm), *n.* the religious system and polity of the Jews.

Ju·da·ist (jōō′dĭ ĭst), *n.* **1.** an adherent of Judaism. **2.** a Jewish Christian in the early church who followed or advocated Jewish rites or practices. —**Ju·da·is′tic,** *adj.*

Ju·da·ize (jōō′dĭ īz′), *v.,* **-ized, -izing.** —*v.i.* **1.** to conform to Judaism in any respect; adopt or affect the manners or customs of the Jews. —*v.t.* **2.** to bring into conformity with Judaism. —**Ju′da·i·za′tion,** *n.* —**Ju′-da·iz′er,** *n.*

Ju·das (jōō′dəs), *n.* **1.** Judas Iscariot, the disciple who betrayed Jesus. Mark 3:19. **2.** one treacherous enough to betray a friend. **3.** one of the twelve apostles (not Judas Iscariot). Luke 6:16; Acts 1:13; John 14:22. —**Ju′das·like′,** *adj.*

Judas Maccabaeus. See **Maccabaeus.**

Judas tree, 1. a purple-flowered leguminous European and Asiatic tree, *Cercis Siliquastrum,* supposed to be the kind upon which Judas hanged himself. **2.** any of various other trees of the same genus, as the redbud.

Jude (jōōd), *n.* a short book of the New Testament, written by a "brother of James" (and possibly of Jesus).

Ju·de·a (jōō dē′ə), *n.* the S part of Palestine under the Romans. Also, **Judaea.**

Ju·de·an (jōō dē′ən), *adj.* **1.** relating to Judea. **2.** of or pertaining to the Jews. —*n.* **3.** a native or inhabitant of Judea. **4.** a Jew. Also, **Judaean.** [f. m.s. L *Jūdaeus* (see JEW) + -AN]

Jude the Obscure, a novel (1895) by Thomas Hardy.

Judg., Judges.

judge (jŭj), *n., v.,* **judged, judging.** —*n.* **1.** a public officer authorized to hear and determine causes in a court of law; a magistrate charged with the administering of justice. **2.** a person appointed to decide in any competition or contest; an authorized arbiter. **3.** one qualified to pass a critical judgment: *a judge of horses.* **4.** an administrative officer at the head of the Hebrew nation in the period between Joshua and the kings. —*v.t.* **5.** to try (a person or a case) as a judge does; pass sentence on or in. **6.** to form a judgment or opinion of or upon; decide upon critically; estimate. **7.** to decide or decree judicially or authoritatively. **8.** to infer, think, or hold as an opinion. **9.** (of the Hebrew judges) to govern. —*v.i.* **10.** to act as a judge; pass judgment. **11.** to form an opinion or estimate. **12.** to make a mental judgment. [ME *juge,* t. OF, g. L *jūdex*] —**judg′-er,** *n.* —**judge′less,** *adj.* —**judge′like′,** *adj.* —**judge′ship,** *n.*
—**Syn. 1.** justice. **2.** arbitrator. JUDGE, REFEREE, UMPIRE refer to one who is entrusted with decisions affecting others. JUDGE, in its egal and other uses, implies particularly that

one has qualifications and authority for giving decisions in matters at issue: *a judge appointed to the Supreme Court.* A REFEREE usually examines and reports on the merits of a case as an aid to a court. An UMPIRE gives the final ruling when arbitrators of a case disagree. 3. connoisseur, critic, 8. conclude; consider, deem, regard. See **think**[1]. 10. adjudge, adjudicate.

judge advocate, *Mil., Naval.* the officer appointed to present the army or navy case before a court-martial, and assist in seeing that justice is done.

Judg·es (jŭj′ĭz), *n.* a book of the Old Testament, containing the history of Israel under the leaders (judges) from Deborah to Samuel.

judg·ment (jŭj′mənt), *n.* **1.** act of judging. **2.** *Law.* **a.** the judicial decision of a cause in court. **b.** the obligation, esp. a debt, arising from a judicial decision. **c.** the certificate embodying such a decision. **3.** ability to judge justly or wisely, esp. in matters affecting action; good sense; discretion. **4.** the forming of an opinion, estimate, notion, or conclusion, as from circumstances presented to the mind. **5.** the opinion formed. **6.** a misfortune regarded as inflicted by divine sentence, as for sin. **7.** the final trial of all mankind, both the living and the dead, at the end of the world (often, **Last Judgment**). Also, *esp. Brit.*, **judge′ment.** —**Syn. 2.** a verdict, decree. **3.** understanding; discrimination, discernment, perspicacity; sagacity.

judgment day, the day of God's final judgment of mankind at the end of the world; doomsday.

ju·di·ca·ble (jōō′də kə bəl), *adj.* **1.** capable of being judged or tried. **2.** liable to be judged or tried.

ju·di·ca·tive (jōō′də kā′tĭv), *adj.* having ability to judge; judging: *the judicative faculty.*

ju·di·ca·tor (jōō′də kā′tər) *n.* one who acts as judge or sits in judgment. [t. LL]

ju·di·ca·to·ry (jōō′də kə tôr′ĭ), *adj., n., pl.* **-tories.** —*adj.* **1.** of or pertaining to judgment or the administration of justice: *judicatory power.* [t. LL: m.s. *jūdicātōrius*] —*n.* **2.** a court of justice; a tribunal. **3.** the administration of justice. [t. LL: m.s. *jūdicātōrium*, prop. neut. of *jūdicātōrius* of a judge]

ju·di·ca·ture (jōō′də kə chər), *n.* **1.** the administration of justice, as by judges or courts. **2.** the office, function, or authority of a judge. **3.** the extent of jurisdiction of a judge or court. **4.** a body of judges. **5.** the power of administering justice by legal trial and determination. [t. ML: m.s. *jūdicātūra*, der. *jūdicātus*, pp., judged]

ju·di·ci·a·ble (jōō dĭsh′ĭ ə bəl), *adj.* capable of being judged or tried.

ju·di·cial (jōō dĭsh′əl), *adj.* **1.** pertaining to judgment in courts of justice or to the administration of justice: *judicial proceedings.* **2.** pertaining to courts of law or to judges: *judicial functions.* **3.** of or pertaining to a judge; proper to the character of a judge; judgelike. **4.** inclined to make or give judgments; critical; discriminating. **5.** decreed, sanctioned, or enforced by a court: *a judicial separation.* **6.** pertaining to judgment or decision in a dispute or contest: *a judicial duel.* **7.** inflicted by God as a judgment or punishment. [ME, t. L: s. *jūdiciālis* of a court of justice] —ju·di′cial·ly, *adv.* —**Syn. 4.** See **judicious.**

ju·di·ci·ar·y (jōō dĭsh′ĭ ĕr′ĭ, -dĭsh′ə rĭ), *adj., n., pl.* **-aries.** —*adj.* **1.** pertaining to judgment in courts of justice, or to courts or judges; judicial. —*n.* **2.** the judicial branch of government. **3.** the system of courts of justice in a country. **4.** the judges collectively.

ju·di·cious (jōō dĭsh′əs), *adj.* **1.** using or showing judgment as to action or practical expediency; discreet, prudent, or politic. **2.** having, exercising, or showing good judgment; wise, sensible, or well-advised: *a judicious selection.* [t. F: m. *judicieux*, der. L *jūdicium* judgment] —ju·di′cious·ly, *adv.* —ju·di′cious·ness, *n.* —**Syn. 1.** See **practical. 2.** JUDICIOUS, JUDICIAL both refer to a balanced and wise judgment. JUDICIOUS implies the possession and use of discerning and discriminating judgment: *a judicious use of one's time.* JUDICIAL has connotations of judgments made in a courtroom, and refers to a fair and impartial kind of judgment: *cool and judicial in examining the facts.* —**Ant. 1.** unwise.

Ju·dith (jōō′dĭth), *n.* **1.** an apocryphal book of the Old Testament. **2.** its heroine, who delivers her people by entering the camp of Holofernes and slaying him in his sleep. [ult. t. Heb.: m. *yehūdhīth* the Jewess]

ju·do (jōō′dō), *n.* jujitsu.

Ju·dy (jōō′dĭ), *n.* the wife of Punch in the puppet show called *Punch and Judy.* [a familiar var. of *Judith*, woman's name]

jug (jŭg), *n., v.,* **jugged, jugging.** —*n.* **1.** a vessel in various forms for holding liquids, commonly having a handle, often a spout or lip, and sometimes a lid. **2.** the contents of any such vessel. **3.** *U.S.* a deep vessel, usually of earthenware, with a handle and a narrow neck stopped by a cork. **4.** *Slang.* a prison or jail. —*v.t.* **5.** to put into a jug. **6.** *Slang.* to commit to jail, or imprison. [? special use of *Jug*, hypocoristic var. of *Joan* or *Joanna*, woman's name]

ju·gal (jōō′gəl), *adj.* of or pertaining to the cheek or the cheekbone. [t. L: s. *jugālis*, der. *jugum* a yoke]

jugal bone, 1. (in man) the cheekbone, or principal bone of the cheek. **2.** a corresponding bone in animals.

ju·gate (jōō′gāt, -gĭt), *adj. Bot.* having the leaflets in pairs, as a pinnate leaf. [t. L: m.s. *jugātus*, pp., joined]

jugged hare (jŭgd), *Chiefly Brit.* hare prepared by seething in a jar.

Jug·ger·naut (jŭg′ər nôt′), *n.* **1.** (the Hindu divinity Krishna) **a.** the eighth incarnation of Vishnu. **b.** an idol of this deity, at Puri in Orissa, India, annually drawn on an enormous car under whose wheels devotees are said to have thrown themselves to be crushed. **2.** anything to which a person blindly devotes himself, or is cruelly sacrificed. Also, **Jagannath, Jagannatha.** [t. Hind.: m. *Jagannāth*, g. Skt. *Jagannātha* lord of the world]

jug·gle (jŭg′əl), *v.,* **-gled, -gling,** *n.* —*v.t.* **1.** to perform conjuring tricks with (balls, knives, etc.). **2.** to manipulate by artifice or trickery: *to juggle accounts.* —*v.i.* **3.** to perform feats of manual or bodily dexterity, such as tossing up and keeping in continuous motion a number of balls, plates, knives, etc. **4.** to use artifice or trickery. —*n.* **5.** act of juggling; a trick; a deception. [ME *jogel(en)*, t. OF: m. *jogler*, g. L *joculārī* jest]

jug·gler (jŭg′lər), *n.* **1.** one who performs juggling feats, as with balls, knives, etc. **2.** one who deceives by trickery; a trickster. [ME *jugelour, jogeler*, t. OF: m. *jogleor*, g. L *joculātor* jester]

jug·gler·y (jŭg′lə rĭ), *n., pl.* **-gleries. 1.** the art or practice of a juggler. **2.** the performance of juggling feats. **3.** any trickery or deception.

ju·glan·da·ceous (jōō′glăn dā′shəs), *adj.* belonging to the *Juglandaceae*, or walnut family of trees. [f. s. L *jūglans* walnut + -ACEOUS]

Ju·go·slav (ū′gō släv′, -släv′), *n., adj.* Yugoslav. Also, **Ju/go-Slav′, Ju′go·slav′ic,** *adj.*

Ju·go·sla·vi·a (ū′gō slä′vĭ ə), *n.* Yugoslavia. —Ju′-go·sla′vi·an, *adj., n.*

jug·u·lar (jŭg′yə lər, jōō′gyə-), *adj.* **1.** *Anat.* **a.** of or pertaining to the throat or neck. **b.** noting or pertaining to any of certain large veins of the neck, esp. one (**external jugular vein**) collecting blood from the superficial parts of the head, or one (**internal jugular vein**) receiving blood from within the skull. **2.** (of a fish) having the ventral fins at the throat, in advance of the pectoral fins. —*n.* **3.** *Anat.* a jugular vein. [t. NL: m. *jugulāris*, der. L *jugulum* collarbone, throat, dim. of *jugum* a yoke]

ju·gu·late (jōō′gyə lāt′), *v.t.,* **-lated, -lating. 1.** to check or suppress (disease, etc.) by extreme measures. **2.** *Rare.* to cut the throat of; kill. [t. L: m.s. *jugulātus*, pp., slain] —ju/gu·la′tion, *n.*

Ju·gur·tha (jōō gûr′thə), *n.* died 104 B.C., king of Numidia, 112?–104 B.C.

juice (jōōs), *n.* **1.** the liquid part of plant or animal substance. **2.** any extracted liquid. **3.** *U.S. Slang.* **a.** electric power. **b.** gasoline, fuel oil, etc. used to run an engine. [ME *jus*, t. OF, g. L: broth] —juice′less, *adj.*

juic·y (jōō′sĭ), *adj.,* **juicier, juiciest. 1.** full of juice; succulent. **2.** interesting; vivacious; colorful. —juic′i·ly, *adv.* —juic′i·ness, *n.*

ju·jit·su (jōō jĭt′sōō), *n.* a Japanese method of offense and defense without weapons in personal encounter, which employs the strength and weight of the opponent to his disadvantage or undoing. Also, **jiujitsu, jiujutsu, ju·jut′su.** [t. Jap.: soft (or pliant) art]

ju·ju (jōō′jōō), *n.* (among native tribes of western Africa) **1.** some object venerated superstitiously and used as a fetish or amulet. **2.** the magical power attributed to such an object. **3.** a ban or interdiction effected by it. [t. West Afr.]

ju·jube (jōō′jōōb), *n.* **1.** the edible plumlike fruit of any of certain Old World trees of the genus *Zizyphus.* **2.** any tree producing this fruit. [t. F, t. ML: m. *jujuba*, t.LL: m. *zizyphum*, t. Gk.: m. *zizyphon*]

juke box, *U.S. Slang.* a coin-operated phonograph permitting selection of the record to be played.

Jukes (jōōks), *n.* the fictitious name of an actual New York family whose history over several generations showed a high incidence of disease, delinquency, and poverty.

Jul., July.

ju·lep (jōō′lĭp), *n.* **1.** a sweet drink, variously prepared and sometimes medicated. **2.** mint julep. [ME, t. OF, t. Ar.: m. *julāb*, t. Pers.: m. *gulāb* rose water, julep]

Jul·ian (jōōl′yən), *n.* ("the Apostate," *Flavius Claudius Julianus*), A.D. 331–363, Roman emperor, A.D. 361–363, who opposed Christianity.

Ju·li·an·a Lou·i·se Em·ma Ma·rie Wil·hel·mi·na (jōō′lĭ än′ə; *Du.* yΫ′lĭ ä′nä; lōō ē′sə ĕm′ä mä rē′ vΫl′hĕl mē′nä), born 1909, Queen of the Netherlands since 1948.

Julian Alps, a mountain range in NW Yugoslavia. Highest peak, Mt. Triglav, 9394 ft.

Julian calendar, the calendar established by Julius Caesar in 46 B.C. which fixed the length of the year at 365 days, with 366 days in every fourth year (leap year), and months similar to the present day calendar.

ju·li·enne (jōō′lĭ ĕn′; *Fr.* zhΫ lyĕn′), *adj.* **1.** (of vegetables) cut into thin strips or small pieces. —*n.* **2.** a clear soup containing vegetables cut into thin strips or small pieces. [t. F, special use of *Julienne*, woman's name]

Ju·li·et (jōō′lĭ ət, jōō′lĭ ĕt′), *n.* the heroine of Shakespeare's *Romeo and Juliet.*

Jul·ius Cae·sar (jōōl′yəs sē′zər), **1.** See **Caesar** (def. 1). **2.** historical tragedy (ab. 1600) by Shakespeare.

Jul·lun·dur (jŭl′ən dər), *n.* a city in NW India, in E Punjab. 135,283 (1941).

b., blend of, blended; c., cognate with; d., dialect, dialectal; der., derived from; f., formed from; g., going back to; m., modification of; r., replacing; s., stem of; t., taken from; ?, perhaps. See the full key on inside cover.

Ju·ly (jŏŏ lī′), *n.*, *pl.* **-lies.** the seventh month of the year, containing 31 days. [ME *Julie*, OE *Julius*, t. L; named after *Julius* Caesar, who was born in this month]

jum·ble (jŭm′bəl), *v.*, **-bled, -bling,** *n.* —*v.t.* **1.** to mix in a confused mass; put or throw together without order. **2.** to muddle or confuse mentally. —*v.i.* **3.** to meet or come together confusedly; be mixed up. —*n.* **4.** a confused mixture; a medley. **5.** a state of confusion or disorder. **6.** a small, flat, sweet cake, now commonly round, with a small hole in the middle. [? b. JOIN and TUMBLE] —**jum′bler,** *n.* —**Syn. 5.** muddle, hodgepodge; farrago; mess; chaos. —**Ant. 5.** order.

jumble sale, *Brit.* a rummage sale.

jum·bo (jŭm′bō), *n.*, *pl.* **-bos,** *adj.* *Colloq.* —*n.* **1.** a big, clumsy person, animal, or thing. —*adj.* **2.** very large.

Jum·na (jŭm′nə), *n.* a river in N India, flowing from the Himalayas SE to the Ganges at Allahabad. 860 mi.

jump (jŭmp), *v.i.* **1.** to spring clear of the ground or other support by a sudden muscular effort; leap. **2.** to move or go suddenly or abruptly, as with a leap. **3.** *Checkers.* to jump, and thus capture, an opponent's piece. **4.** to rise suddenly in amount, price, etc. **5.** to pass abruptly as if by a leap: *to jump to a conclusion.* **6.** *Motion Pictures.* to fail to line up properly with the preceding or following shots, due to mechanical fault in camera or projector. **7.** *Contract Bridge.* to bid exceptionally and unnecessarily high in order to indicate additional strength. —*v.t.* **8.** to pass over by a leap: *to jump a stream.* **9.** to cause to jump or leap. **10.** to skip or pass over. **11.** *Checkers.* to capture (an opponent's man) by leaping over it to an unoccupied square. **12.** *Bridge.* to raise (the bid) by more than the necessary overcall. **13.** to abscond from, or evade by absconding: *to jump one's bail.* **14.** to seize (a mining claim, etc.), as on the ground of some flaw in the holder's title. **15.** to spring off or leave (the track), as trains do. **16.** *U.S.* to get on or off (a train, etc.) by jumping. —*n.* **17.** act of jumping; a leap. **18.** a space or obstacle or apparatus cleared in a leap. **19.** a sudden rise in amount, price, etc. **20.** a sudden upward or other movement of an inanimate object. **21.** an abrupt transition from one point or thing to another, with omission of what intervenes. **22.** *U.S. Colloq.* a head start in time or space; advantageous beginning. **23.** *Sports.* any of several athletic games which feature a leap or jump. **24.** *Motion Pictures.* a break in the continuity of action due to a failure to match action between a long shot and a closer shot of the same scene. **25.** a sudden start, as from nervous excitement. **26.** (*pl.*) a physical condition characterized by such starts. [appar. imit.] —**Syn. 1.** spring, bound; skip, hop. JUMP, LEAP, VAULT imply propelling oneself by a muscular effort of the legs, either into the air or from one position or place to another. JUMP and LEAP are often used interchangeably, but JUMP indicates more particularly the springing movement of the feet in leaving the ground or support: *to jump up and down.* LEAP (which formerly also meant to run) indicates the passage, by a springing movement, from one point or position to another: *to leap across a brook.* VAULT implies leaping over or upon something: *to vault (over) a fence.*

jump ball, *Basketball.* a ball tossed between two opposing players by the referee.

jump bid, *Bridge.* any bid which is higher than that needed to increase the bid made previously.

jump·er[1] (jŭmp′ər), *n.* **1.** one who or that which jumps. **2.** a boring tool or device worked with a jumping motion. **3.** *Elect.* a short length of conductor used to make a connection, usually temporary, between terminals, around a break in a circuit, or around an instrument. **4.** a kind of sled. [f. JUMP, v. + -ER[1]]

jump·er[2] (jŭmp′ər), *n.* **1.** a one-piece, sleeveless dress worn with blouse or guimpe by women and children. **2.** *Chiefly Brit.* a loose jacket worn by women over a blouse. **3.** a loose outer jacket worn esp. by workmen and sailors. **4.** (*pl.*) rompers. [der. *jump*, nasalized var. of *jup* short coat (t. F: m. *juppe*). See -ER[2]]

jumping bean, the seed of any of certain Mexican euphorbiaceous plants (genus *Sebastiania*, etc.), which is inhabited by the larva of a small moth whose movements cause the seed to move about or jump.

jumping jack, a toy consisting of a jointed figure of a man which is made to jump, or go through various contortions, as by pulling a string attached to its limbs.

jump·ing-off place (jŭmp′ĭng ôf′, -ŏf′), *U.S.* an out-of-the-way place; the farthest limit of anything settled or civilized.

jump·y (jŭmp′ĭ), *adj.*, **jumpier, jumpiest. 1.** characterized by or inclined to sudden, involuntary starts, esp. from nervousness, fear, excitement, etc. **2.** causing to jump or start. —**jump′i·ness,** *n.*

Jun., **1.** June. **2.** Junior.

Junc., Junction.

jun·ca·ceous (jŭng kā′shəs), *adj.* pertaining or belonging to, or resembling, the *Juncaceae*, or rush family of plants. [f. s. L *juncus* a rush + -ACEOUS]

jun·co (jŭng′kō), *n.*, *pl.* **-cos.** any of several small finches of the North American genus *Junco*, all with white on the outer tail feathers; snowbird. [t. Sp., t. L: m. *juncus* a rush]

junc·tion (jŭngk′shən), *n.* **1.** act of joining; combination. **2.** state of being joined; union. **3.** a place or station where railroad lines meet or cross. **4.** a place of joining or meeting. [t. L: s. *junctio* a joining] —**Syn. 4.** JUNCTION, JUNCTURE refer to a place, line, or point at which two or more things join. A JUNCTION is a place where things come together: *the junction of two rivers.* A JUNCTURE is a line or point at which two bodies are joined, or a point of exigency or crisis in time: *the juncture of the head and neck, a critical juncture in a struggle.*

junc·ture (jŭngk′chər), *n.* **1.** a point of time, esp. one made critical or important by a concurrence of circumstances. **2.** a critical state of affairs; a crisis; a critical moment. **3.** the line or point at which two bodies are joined; a joint or articulation; a seam. **4.** act of joining. **5.** state of being joined; junction. **6.** something by which two things are joined. [ME, t. L: m. *junctūra* joining, joint] —**Syn. 3.** See **junction.**

June (jōōn), *n.* the sixth month of year, containing 30 days. [ME; OE *Iuni,* t. L: s. *Jūnius*; named after the *Jūnius* gens of Rome]

Ju·neau (jōō′nō), *n.* a seaport in and the capital of Alaska, in the SE part. 5818 (prelim. 1950).

June·ber·ry (jōōn′bĕr′ĭ), *n.*, *pl.* **-ries.** the American serviceberry, *Amelanchier canadensis.*

June bug, 1. (in the northern U.S.) any of the large, brown scarabaeid beetles of the genus *Phyllophaga* (*Lachnosterna*), which appear about June. **2.** (in the southern U.S.) a large, greenish scarabaeid beetle, *Cotinis nitida*; the figeater. Also, **June beetle.**

Jung (yŏŏng), *n.* **Carl Gustav** (kärl gŏŏs′täf), born 1875, Swiss psychiatrist and psychologist.

Northern June bug. *Phyllophaga fusca* (1 in. long)

Jung·frau (yŏŏng′frou′), *n.* a peak in the Bernese Alps, in S Switzerland. 13,668 ft.

jun·gle (jŭng′gəl), *n.* **1.** wild land overgrown with dense, rank vegetation, often nearly impenetrable, as in parts of India. **2.** a tract of such land. **3.** a wilderness of dense overgrowth; a piece of swampy thick-set forest land. **4.** *U.S. Slang.* a camp for hoboes or tramps. [t. Hind.: m. *jangal* desert, forest, g. Skt. *jangala* dry, desert]

jungle fever, a severe variety of malarial fever occurring in the East Indies and other tropical regions.

jungle hen, any of various East Indian gallinaceous birds of the genus *Gallus*, certain species of which are supposed to have given rise to the domestic fowl.

jun·ior (jōōn′yər), *adj.* **1.** younger (often used, esp. as abbreviated *Jr.* or *Jun.*, after the name of a person who is the younger of two persons bearing the name, as a son having the same name as his father). **2.** of more recent appointment or admission, as to an office or status; of lower rank or standing. **3.** (in American universities, colleges, and schools) noting or pertaining to the class or year next below that of the senior. **4.** *Law.* subordinate to preferred creditors, lienors, mortgagees, etc. **5.** of later date; subsequent to. —*n.* **6.** a person who is younger than another. **7.** one who is of more recent entrance into, or of lower standing in, an office, class, profession, etc.; one employed as the subordinate of another. **8.** a student who is in the next to the final year of a course of study. [t. L, contr. of *juvenior,* compar. of *juvenis* young]

junior college, a collegiate institution extending through the first one or two years of college instruction, and granting a certificate of title instead of a degree.

junior high school. See high school (def. 2).

jun·ior·i·ty (jōōn yôr′ə tĭ, -yŏr′-), *n.* state or fact of being junior in age, standing, etc.

ju·ni·per (jōō′nə pər), *n.* **1.** any of the coniferous evergreen shrubs or trees constituting the genus *Juniperus,* esp. *J. communis,* whose cones form purple berries used in making gin and in medicine as a diuretic, or *J. virginiana,* a North American species. **2.** a tree mentioned in the Bible. 1 Kings, 19:4. [ME *junipere,* t. L: m. *jūniperus.* See GENEVA and GIN[1]]

Ju·ni·us (jōōn′yəs), *n.* the pen name of the unknown author of public political letters (1768-72) against the British ministry.

junk[1] (jŭngk), *n.* **1.** any old or discarded material, as metal, paper, rags, etc. **2.** *Colloq.* anything that is regarded as worthless or mere trash. **3.** old cable or cordage used when untwisted for making gaskets, swabs, oakum, etc. **4.** hard salt meat used for food on shipboard. —*v.t.* **5.** *Colloq.* to cast aside as junk; discard as no longer of use. [orig. uncert.]

junk[2] (jŭngk), *n.* a kind of seagoing ship used in Chinese and other waters, having square sails spread by battens, a high stern, and usually a flat bottom. [t. Pg.: m. *junco,* t. Malay: m. *jong, ajong,* appar. t. Javanese: (m.) *jong*]

Canton trading junk

Jun·ker (yŏŏng′kər), *n.* **1.** a member of a class of aristocratic landholders, esp. in East Prussia, strongly devoted to maintaining the social and political privileges of their group. **2.** a narrow-minded, haughty, overbearing member of the aristocracy of Prussia, etc. [t. G, in MHG *junc herre* young gentleman]

Jun·ker·dom (yŏŏng′kər dəm), *n.* **1.** the body of Junkers. **2.** (*sometimes l.c.*) **a.** the condition or character of a Junker. **b.** the spirit or policy of the Junkers.

Jun·ker·ism (yŏŏng′kə rĭz′əm), *n.* (*sometimes l.c.*) the spirit or policy of the Junkers.

jun·ket (jŭng′kĭt), *n.* **1.** a sweet custardlike food of flavored milk curded with rennet. **2.** (*cap.*) a trademark for this food. **3.** a trip by a legislative committee ostensibly to obtain information. **4.** a feast or merrymaking; a picnic; a pleasure excursion. —*v.i.* **5.** to feast; picnic; go on a junket or pleasure excursion, esp. at public expense. —*v.t.* **6.** to entertain; feast; regale: *to junket her neighbors.* [ME *jonket* basket made of rushes, *joncate* curded food made in a vessel of rushes, t. OF: m. *jonquette*, der. *jonc* a rush, g. L *juncus*] —**jun′-ket·er,** *n.* —Syn. **3.** See **excursion.**

junk·man (jŭngk′măn′), *n.*, *pl.* **-men.** a dealer in junk, or old metal, paper, rags, etc.

Ju·no (jōō′nō), *n.* **1.** *Rom. Myth.* an ancient Roman goddess, the wife of Jupiter, presiding over marriage and women. Cf. **Hera.** **2.** a woman of imposing figure or appearance.

Ju·no·esque (jōō′nō ĕsk′), *adj.* (of a woman) stately.

Ju·not (zhy nō′), *n.* Andoche (äN dôsh′), (*Duc d'Abrantès*) 1771–1813, French marshal.

jun·ta (jŭn′tə), *n.* **1.** a meeting; a council. **2.** a deliberative or administrative council, esp. in Spain. **3.** a junto. [t. Sp., g. L *juncta,* fem. pp., joined]

jun·to (jŭn′tō), *n.*, *pl.* **-tos.** a self-appointed committee, esp. with political aims; cabal. [erron. var. of JUNTA]

Ju·pi·ter (jōō′pə tər), *n.* **1.** the supreme deity of the ancient Romans, the god of the heavens, manifesting himself esp. in atmospheric phenomena; Jove (Cf. **Zeus**). **2.** the largest planet, fifth in order from the sun. Its period of revolution is 11.86 years, its mean distance from the sun about 483,000,000 miles. Its diameter is about one tenth that of the sun (11 times that of the earth). It has 11 satellites. Symbol: ♃. [t. L, var. of *Jūppiter,* contr. of *Jovis pater* father Jove]

Jupiter Symphony, forty-first symphony (1788) by Mozart.

ju·pon (jōō′pŏn, jōō pŏn′), *n.* a close-fitting tunic, usually padded and bearing heraldic arms, worn over armor. [ME *jupone,* t. F: m. *jupon,* der. *jupe* jacket, t. Ar.: m. *jubbah*]

ju·ral (jŏŏr′əl), *adj.* **1.** pertaining to law; legal. **2.** pertaining to rights and obligations. [f. s. L *jūs* right, law + -AL¹] —**ju′ral·ly,** *adv.*

Ju·ra Mountains (jŏŏr′ə; *Fr.* zhy rä′), a mountain range between France and Switzerland, extending from the Rhine to the Rhone. Highest peak, Crêt de la Niege, 5654 ft.

Ju·ras·sic (jŏŏ răs′ĭk), *Stratig.* —*adj.* **1.** pertaining to a mid-Mesozoic geological period or system of rocks named from the Jura Mountains. —*n.* **2.** a period or system following the Triassic and preceding the Cretaceous. [t. F: m. *jurassique*]

ju·rat (jŏŏr′ăt), *n.* **1.** *Law.* a certificate on an affidavit, by the officer, showing by whom, when, and before whom it was sworn to. **2.** a sworn officer; a magistrate; a member of a permanent jury. [t. ML: s. *jūrātus,* lit., one sworn, *jūrātum,* neut., that which is sworn, prop. pp. of L *jūrāre* swear]

Jur. D., (L *Juris Doctor*) Doctor of Law.

ju·rel (hŏŏ rĕl′), *n.* any of certain carangoid food fishes of the genus *Caranx* as *C. latus,* a species of the West Indies, etc. [t. Sp., ult. der. Gk. *saûros* a sea fish]

ju·rid·i·cal (jŏŏ rĭd′ə kəl), *adj.* **1.** of or pertaining to the administration of justice. **2.** of or pertaining to law or jurisprudence; legal. Also, **ju·rid′ic.** [f. s. L *jūridicus* relating to justice + -AL¹] —**ju·rid′i·cal·ly,** *adv.*

juridical days, days in court on which law is administered; days on which the court can lawfully sit.

ju·ris·con·sult (jŏŏr′ĭs kən sŭlt′, -kŏn′sŭlt), *n.* **1.** *Rom. and Civil Law.* one authorized to give legal advice. **2.** *Civil Law.* a master of the civil law. *Abbr.:* J. C. [t. L: s. *jūrisconsultus* one skilled in law]

ju·ris·dic·tion (jŏŏr′ĭs dĭk′shən), *n.* **1.** the right, power, or authority to administer justice by hearing and determining controversies. **2.** power; authority; control. **3.** the extent or range of judicial or other authority. **4.** the territory over which authority is exercised. [ME, t. L: s. *jūrisdictio* administration of the law, authority] —**ju·ris·dic′tion·al,** *adj.* —**ju·ris·dic′tion·al·ly,** *adv.*

ju·ris·pru·dence (jŏŏr′ĭs prōō′dəns), *n.* **1.** the science or philosophy of law. **2.** a body or system of laws. **3.** a department of law: *medical jurisprudence.* **4.** *Civil Law.* decisions of courts of appeal or other higher tribunals. [t. L: m.s. *jūrisprūdentia* the science of the law] —**ju·ris·pru·den′tial** (jŏŏr′ĭs prōō dĕn′shal), *adj.*

ju·ris·pru·dent (jŏŏr′ĭs prōō′dənt), *adj.* **1.** versed in jurisprudence. —*n.* **2.** one versed in jurisprudence.

ju·rist (jŏŏr′ĭst), *n.* **1.** one who professes the science of law. **2.** one versed in the law. **3.** one who writes on the subject of law. [t. ML: s. *jūrista,* der. L *jūs* right, law]

ju·ris·tic (jŏŏ rĭs′tĭk), *adj.* of or pertaining to a jurist or to jurisprudence; relating to law; juridical; legal. Also, **ju·ris′ti·cal.** —**ju·ris′ti·cal·ly,** *adv.*

juristic act, an act not involving the exercise of legal authority which changes, ends, or affects the basis of a legal right.

ju·ror (jŏŏr′ər), *n.* **1.** one of a body of persons sworn to deliver a verdict in a case submitted to them; a member of any jury. **2.** one of the panel from which a jury is selected. **3.** one who has taken an oath or sworn allegiance. [ME *jurour,* t. AF, g. L *jūrātor* swearer]

Ju·ru·á (zhōō′rōŏ ä′), *n.* a river flowing from E Peru NE through W Brazil to the Amazon. ab. 1200 mi.

ju·ry¹ (jŏŏr′Y), *n.*, *pl.* **juries. 1.** a body of persons sworn to render a verdict or true answer on a question or questions officially submitted to them. **2.** such a body selected according to law and sworn to inquire into or determine the facts concerning a cause or an accusation submitted to them and to render a verdict. See **grand jury** and **petty jury. 3.** a body of persons chosen to adjudge prizes, etc., as in a competition. [ME *juree,* t. AF, der. *jure* one sworn, ult. der. L *jūrāre* swear] —**ju′ry·less,** *adj.*

ju·ry² (jŏŏr′Y), *adj.* *Naut.* makeshift, temporary, as for an emergency. [first found in *jury mast,* prob. t. OF: m. *ajurie* relief, help, der. L *adjūtāre* help]

ju·ry·man (jŏŏr′Y mən), *n.*, *pl.* **-men.** a juror.

jury mast, *Naut.* a temporary mast replacing one that has been broken or carried away. [see JURY²]

jur·y·rigged (jŏŏr′Y rĭgd′), *adj.* *Naut.* temporarily rigged. [see JURY²]

jus¹ (zhy), *n.* *French.* juice; gravy. [F, t. L]

jus² (jŭs), *n.*, *pl.* **jura** (jŏŏr′ə). *Law.* **1.** a right. **2.** law as a system or in the abstract. [t. L: law, right]

jus ca·no·ni·cum (jŭs kə nŏn′Y kəm), canon law.

jus ci·vi·le (jŭs sĭ vī′lY), *Rom. Law.* the rules and principles of law derived from the customs and legislation of Rome, as opposed to those derived from the customs of all nations (**jus gentium**) or from fundamental ideas of right and wrong implicit in the human mind (**jus naturale**).

jus di·vi·num (jŭs dĭ vī′nəm), *Latin.* divine law.

jus gen·ti·um (jŭs jĕn′shY əm). See **jus civile.**

jus na·tu·ra·le (jŭs năt′yŏŏ rā′lY). See **jus civile.**

Jus·se·rand (zhys räN′), *n.* Jean Jules (zhäN zhyl), 1855–1932, French diplomat and author.

jus·sive (jŭs′ĭv), *Gram.* **1.** expressing a mild command. The jussive mood occurs in the Semitic languages. —*n.* **2.** a jussive form or construction. [f. s. L *jussus,* pp., commanded + -IVE]

just¹ (jŭst), *adj.* **1.** actuated by truth, justice, and lack of bias: *to be just in one's dealings.* **2.** in accordance with true principles; equitable; evenhanded: *a just award.* **3.** based on right; rightful; lawful: *a just claim.* **4.** agreeable to truth or fact; true; correct: *a just statement.* **5.** given or awarded rightly, or deserved, as a sentence, punishment, reward, etc. **6.** in accordance with standards, or requirements; proper, or right: *just proportions.* **7.** righteous (esp. in Biblical use). **8.** actual, real, or true. —*adv.* **9.** within a brief preceding time, or but a moment before: *they have just gone.* **10.** exactly or precisely: *that is just the point.* **11.** by a narrow margin; barely: *it just missed the mark.* **12.** only or merely: *he is just an ordinary man.* **13.** *Colloq.* actually; truly; positively: *the weather is just glorious.* [ME, t. L: s. *justus* righteous] —Syn. **1.** upright; equitable, fair, impartial. **4.** accurate, exact; honest. **5.** rightful, legitimate, deserved, merited, condign. —Ant. **1.** biased. **4.** untrue. **5.** unjustified.

just² (jŭst), *n.*, *v.i.* joust. —**just′er,** *n.*

jus·tice (jŭs′tĭs), *n.* **1.** the quality of being just; righteousness, equitableness, or moral rightness: *to uphold the justice of a cause.* **2.** rightfulness or lawfulness, as of a claim or title; justness of ground or reason: *to complain with justice.* **3.** the moral principle determining just conduct. **4.** conformity to this principle as manifested in conduct; just conduct, dealing, or treatment. **5.** the requital of desert as by punishment or reward. **6.** the maintenance or administration of law, as by judicial or other proceedings: *a court of justice.* **7.** judgment of persons or causes by judicial process: *to administer justice in a community.* **8.** a judicial officer; a judge or magistrate. **9. do justice to, a.** to render or concede what is due to (a person or thing, merits, good intentions, etc.); treat or judge fairly. **b.** to exhibit (oneself) in a just light, as in doing something: *the speaker hardly did justice to himself this evening.* **c.** to show just appreciation of (something) by action: *to do justice to a good dinner by eating heartily.* [ME *justise,* t. OF, t. L: m.s. *justitia*]

justice of the peace, a local officer having jurisdiction to try and determine minor civil and criminal cases and to hold preliminary examinations of persons accused of more serious crimes, and having authority to administer oaths, solemnize marriages, etc.

jus·tice·ship (jŭs′tĭs shĭp′), *n.* the office of a justice.

jus·ti·ci·ar·y (jŭs tĭsh′Y ĕr′Y), *adj.*, *n.*, *pl.* **-aries.** —*adj.* **1.** of or pertaining to the administration of justice. —*n.* **2.** Also, **jus·ti·ci·ar** (jŭs tĭsh′Y ər). *Brit. Hist.* the chief administrator of justice and government from the time of William I to that of Henry III. [t. ML: m.s. *justitiārius* judge, der. L *justitia* justice]

jus·ti·fi·a·ble (jŭs′tə fī′ə bəl), *adj.* capable of being justified; that can be shown to be, or can be defended as being, just or right; defensible. —**jus′ti·fi·a·bil′i·ty, jus′ti·fi′a·ble·ness,** *n.* —**jus′ti·fi′a·bly,** *adv.*

jus·ti·fi·ca·tion (jŭs′tə fə kā′shən), *n.* **1.** something that justifies; a defensive plea; an excuse; a justifying fact or circumstance. **2.** act of justifying. **3.** state of being justified. **4.** *Theol.* the act of God whereby man is made or accounted just, or freed from the guilt or penalty of sin. **5.** *Print.* arrangement, as of type, by adjusting the spaces so that it fills a line precisely, or holds a cut in place.

jus·tif·i·ca·to·ry (jŭs'tĭf'ə kə tōr'ĭ, jŭs'tə fə kā'tə rĭ), *adj.* serving to justify; affording justification. Also, **jus-ti·fi·ca·tive** (jŭs'tə fə kā'tĭv).

jus·ti·fi·er (jŭs'tə fī'ər), *n.* one who or that which justifies.

jus·ti·fy (jŭs'tə fī'), *v.*, **-fied, -fy·ing.** —*v.t.* **1.** to show (an act, claim, statement, etc.) to be just, right, or warranted: *the end justifies the means.* **2.** to defend or uphold as blameless, just, or right. **3.** declare guiltless; absolve; acquit. **4.** *Print.* to adjust exactly; make (lines) of the proper length by spacing. —*v.i.* **5.** *Law.* **a.** to show a satisfactory reason or excuse for something done. **b.** to qualify as bail or surety. **6.** *Print.* to conform or fit exactly, as lines of type. [ME *justifie(n)*, t. OF: m. *justifier*, t. LL: m. *justificāre* act justly towards] —**Syn. 2.** vindicate; exonerate, exculpate. —**Ant. 2.** accuse, condemn.

Jus·tin·i·an I (jŭs tĭn'ĭ ən), ("*the Great*," *Flavius Anicius Justinianus*) A.D. 483–565, Byzantine emperor, A.D. 527–565, whose leading jurists formulated a code of laws called the **Justinian Code.**

Jus·tin Mar·tyr (jŭs'tĭn mär'tər), **Saint,** A.D. c100–c165, Christian saint, philosopher, and martyr, born in Syria.

jus·ti·ti·a om·ni·bus (jŭs tĭsh'ĭ ə ŏm'nə bəs), *Latin.* justice to all (motto of the District of Columbia).

jus·tle (jŭs'əl), *v.t., v.i.,* **-tled, -tling,** *n.* jostle.

just·ly (jŭst'lĭ), *adv.* **1.** in a just manner; honestly; fairly. **2.** in conformity to fact or rule; accurately.

just·ness (jŭst'nĭs), *n.* **1.** quality or state of being just, equitable, or right; lawfulness. **2.** conformity to fact or rule; correctness; exactness; accuracy.

jut (jŭt), *v.,* **jutted, jutting,** *n.* —*v.i.* **1.** to extend beyond the main body or line; project; protrude (often fol. by *out*). —*n.* **2.** something that juts out; a projection or protruding point. [var. of JET, v.]

jute (jōōt), *n.* **1.** a strong fiber used for making fabrics, cordage, etc., obtained from two tiliaceous East Indian plants, *Corchorus capsularis* and *C. olitorius.* **2.** either

of these plants. **3.** any plant of the same genus. **4.** a coarse fabric obtained from jute plant and woven into burlap or gunny. [t. Bengali: m. *jhōto,* g. Skt. *jūta* braid of hair] —**jute'like',** *adj.*

Jute (jōōt), *n.* a member of a Germanic tribe which invaded Britain from the continent and settled there in the 5th century. —**Jut'ish,** *adj.*

Jut·land (jŭt'lənd), *n.* a peninsula comprising the continental portion of Denmark: a major naval engagement between the British and German fleets was fought W of this peninsula, 1916. 1,723,000 pop. (1940); 11,411 sq. mi. Danish, **Jylland.**

Ju·tur·na (jōō tûr'nə), *n.* Gk. Myth. a fountain nymph said to have been beloved by Jupiter.

Ju·ve·nal (jōō'və nəl), *n.* (*Decimus Junius Juvenalis*) A.D. c60–c140, Roman satirical poet.

ju·ve·nal (jōō'və nəl), *n.* *Ornithol.* the plumage stage of an altricial bird when it leaves the nest. [t. L: s. *juvenālis,* var. of *juvenīlis* young, pertaining to youth]

ju·ve·nes·cent (jōō'və nĕs'ənt), *adj.* becoming youthful; growing young again; youthful. [t. L: s. *juvenescens,* ppr., reaching the age of youth] —**ju've·nes'cence,** *n.*

ju·ve·nile (jōō'və nəl, -nĭl, -nīl'), *adj.* **1.** pertaining to, suitable for, or intended for young persons: *juvenile behavior, juvenile books, a juvenile court.* **2.** young. —*n.* **3.** a young person; a youth. **4.** *Theat.* **a.** a youthful male role. **b.** an actor who plays such parts. **5.** *Ornithol.* a young bird in the stage when it has fledged, if altricial, or has replaced down of hatching, if precocial. **6.** a book for young people. [t. L: m.s. *juvenīlis* of youth] —**ju've·nile·ly,** *adv.* —**ju've·nile·ness,** *n.*

ju·ve·ni·li·a (jōō'və nĭl'ĭ'ə), *n.pl.* works, esp. writings, produced in youth.

ju·ve·nil·i·ty (jōō'və nĭl'ə tĭ), *n., pl.* **-ties. 1.** juvenile state, character, or manner. **2.** (*pl.*) youthful qualities or performances. **3.** young persons collectively.

juxta-, a word element meaning "near," "close to," "beside." [comb. form repr. L *juxtā,* prep., adv.]

jux·ta·pose (jŭks'tə pōz'), *v.t.,* **-posed, -posing.** to place in close proximity or side by side.

jux·ta·po·si·tion (jŭks'tə pə zĭsh'ən), *n.* **1.** a placing close together. **2.** position side by side. [t. F, f. L: *juxtā* JUXTA- + s. *positio* a placing, position]

Jy., July.

Jyl·land (yŭl'län), *n.* Danish name of **Jutland.**

K

K, k (kā), *n., pl.* **K's** or **Ks, k's** or **ks.** a consonant, the 11th letter of the English alphabet.

K, *Chem.* potassium.

K., **1.** *Chess.* King. **2.** Knight.

k., **1.** *Elect.* capacity. **2.** karat or carat. **3.** kilogram. **4.** *Chess.* king. **5.** knight. **6.** knot. **7.** kopeck.

K2, *n.* a mountain peak in N W India, in the Karakoram range in N Kashmir: second loftiest peak in the world. 28,250 ft. Also, **Godwin Austen.**

ka (kä), *n.* *Egypt. Relig.* a presiding or second spirit supposed to be present in a man or statue. [t. Egyptian]

Kaa·ba (kä'bə, kä'ə bə), *n.* a small cube-shaped building in the Great Mosque at Mecca, containing a sacred stone said to have been turned black by the tears of repentant pilgrims or, according to another tradition, by the sins of those who have touched it: the most sacred shrine of the Mohammedans. Also, **Caaba.** [t. Ar.: m. *ka'ba* a square building, der. *ka'b* cube]

kab (käb), *n.* cab².

kab·a·la (käb'ə lə, kə bä'lə), *n.* cabala. Also, **kab'ba·la.**

ka·bob (kə bŏb'), *n.* **1.** (*pl.*) an oriental dish consisting of small pieces of meat seasoned and roasted on a skewer. **2.** *Anglo-Indian.* roast meat in general. Also, **cabob.** [t. Ar.: m. *kabab*]

Ka·bul (kä'bŏŏl), *n.* **1.** the capital of Afghanistan, in the NE part. ab. 120,000. **2.** a river flowing from NE Afghanistan E to the Indus in Pakistan. ab. 360 mi.

Ka·byle (kə bīl'), *n.* **1.** one of a branch of the Berber race dwelling in Algeria and Tunisia. **2.** their language, a Berber dialect. [t. Ar.: m. *qabīla* tribe]

Ka·desh (kā'dĕsh), an ancient city in W Syria.

ka·di (kä'dĭ, kā'dĭ), *n., pl.* **-dis.** cadi.

Kaf·fir (käf'ər, kä'fər), *n.* **1.** a member of a South African Negroid race inhabiting parts of the Cape of Good Hope, Natal, etc. **2.** a Bantu language. **3.** (*l.c.*) any of certain grain sorghums, varieties of *Sorghum vulgare,* with stout, short-jointed, leafy stalks, cultivated in South Africa and introduced into the U.S. [t. Ar.: m. *kāfir* unbeliever]

Kaf·frar·i·a (kə frâr'ĭ'ə), *n.* a region in S part of the Union of South Africa: inhabited mostly by Kaffirs.

Kaf·ir (käf'ər, kä'fər), *n.* **1.** a member of a nationality, of Indo-European speech, in Kafiristan. **2.** Kaffir.

Ka·fi·ri·stan (kä'fĭ rĭ stän'), *n.* a mountainous region in NE Afghanistan. ab. 5000 sq. mi.

Kaf·ka (käf'kä), *n.* **Franz** (fränts), Bohemian novelist, 1883–1924.

kaf·tan (käf'tən, käf tän'), *n.* caftan.

Ka·ga·no·vich (kä'gä nō'vĭch), *n.* **Lazar Moiseevich** (lä'zär moi sē'ə vĭch), born 1893, Soviet statesman.

Ka·ga·wa (kä'gä wä'), *n.* **Toyohiko** (tô'yô hē'kô), born 1888, Japanese reformer and social worker.

Ka·ge·ra (kä gē'rä), *n.* a river in equatorial Africa, flowing into Lake Victoria from the west: the most remote headstream of the Nile. ab. 430 mi.

Ka·go·shi·ma (kä'gô shē'mä), *n.* a seaport in SW Japan, on Kyushu island. 123,533 (1946).

kai·ak (kī'ăk), *n.* kayak.

Kai·e·teur (kī'ĕ tōŏr'), *n.* a waterfall in central British Guiana, on a tributary of the Essequibo river. ab. 760 ft. high.

kaif (kīf), *n.* kef.

Kai·feng (kī'fŭng'), *n.* a city in E China: the capital of Honan province. 245,000 (est. 1938).

kail (kāl), *n.* kale.

Kair·ouan (kĕr wän'), *n.* a city in NE Tunisia: a holy city of Islam. 23,000 (est. 1930). Also, **Kair·wan** (kĭr wän').

Kai·ser (kī'zər), *n.* **1.** a German emperor. **2.** an Austrian emperor. **3.** *Hist.* a ruler of the Holy Roman Empire. **4.** (*l.c.*) an emperor; a Caesar. [t. G, r. ME *caiser(e), keiser(e),* t. Scand. (cf. Icel *keisari*); r. ME and OE *cāsere,* ult. t. L: m. *Caesar*] —**kai'ser·ship',** *n.*

Kai·ser (kī'zər), **Henry J.,** born 1882, U.S. industrialist.

Kai·sers·lau·tern (kī'zərs lou'tərn), *n.* a city in SW Germany, in the Palatinate. 70,713 (1939).

Ka·jar (kä jär'), *n.* Persian or Iranian dynasty which ruled 1794–1925.

ka·ka (kä'kə), *n.* any of certain New Zealand parrots of the genus *Nestor,* esp. *N. meridionalis,* a species about the size of a crow with a mostly greenish, olive-brown coloration. [t. Maori]

ka·ka·po (kä′kä pō′), *n., pl.* **-pos** (-pōz′). a large, almost flightless, nocturnal parrot, *Strigops habroptilus*, of New Zealand. [t. Maori: f. *kaka* parrot + *po* night]

ka·ke·mo·no (kä′kě mō′nō), *n., pl.* **-nos.** an upright Japanese wall picture, usually long and narrow, painted on silk, paper or other material, and mounted on a roller. [t. Jap.: f. *kake* hang + *mono* thing]

ka·ki (kä′kē), *n., pl.* **-kis.** 1. the Japanese persimmon tree. 2. its fruit. [t. Jap.]

kal., kalends.

Ka·la·ha·ri (kä′lä hä′rē), *n.* a desert region in SW Africa, largely in Bechuanaland. ab. 350,000 sq. mi.

Kal·a·ma·zoo (kăl′ə mə zōō′), *n.* a city in SW Michigan. 57,704 (1950).

Ka·lat (kə lät′), *n.* a state in W Pakistan, in the province of Baluchistan. 253,300 pop. (1941); 53,995 sq. mi. *Cap.:* Kalat. Also, **Khelat.**

kale (kāl), *n.* 1. a plant of the mustard family, *Brassica oleracea*, var. *acephala*, with leaves not forming a head, used as a potherb. 2. *Scot.* cabbage or greens. 3. *U.S. Slang.* money. Also, **kail.** [ME *cale*, northern var. of COLE]

ka·lei·do·scope (kə lī′də skōp′), *n.* an optical instrument in which bits of colored glass, etc., in a rotating tube are shown by reflection in continually changing symmetrical forms. [f. s. Gk. *kalós* beautiful + Gk. *eîdo(s)* form + -SCOPE] —**ka·lei·do·scop·ic** (kə lī′də skŏp′ĭk), **ka·lei·do·scop′i·cal,** *adj.* —**ka·lei·do·scop′i·cal·ly,** *adv.*

kal·ends (kăl′əndz), *n.pl.* calends.

Ka·le·va·la (kä′lĭ vä′lə), *n.* the national epic of Finland. [t. Finnish: lit., house of a hero]

kale·yard (kāl′yärd′), *n. Scot.* a kitchen garden.

kaleyard school, school of writers describing homely life in Scotland, with much use of Scottish dialect: in vogue toward the close of the 19th century, when books by J. M. Barrie and others were appearing.

Kal·gan (kăl′gän′), *n.* a city in NE China: the capital of Chahar province. ab. 70,000.

kal·i (kăl′ī, kā′lī), *n., pl.* **kalis.** glasswort. [t. Ar.: m. *qalī* (*qila*). See ALKALI]

kal·ian (kăl yän′), *n.* an Eastern tobacco pipe in which the smoke is drawn through water. [t. Pers.]

Ka·li·da·sa (kä′lĭ dä′sə), *n.* Hindu dramatist and poet of the 6th century or earlier.

Ka·li·nin (kä lē′nĭn), *n.* 1. **Mikhail Ivanovich** (mĭ hä ēl′ Ĭ vä′nō vĭch), 1875–1946, president of the Praesidium of the Supreme Council of the Soviet Union, 1938–1946. 2. Formerly, **Tver.** a city in the central Soviet Union in Europe, on the Volga. 216,131 (1939).

Ka·li·nin·grad (kä lē′nĭn gräd′), *n.* Russian name of Königsberg.

ka·liph (kā′lĭf, kăl′ĭf), *n.* caliph.

Ka·lisz (kä′lĭsh), *n.* a city in central Poland. 50,427 (1946). German, **Kalisch** (kä′lĭsh).

Kal·li·kaks (kăl′ə kăks′), *n.pl.* **The,** the fictitious name of an actual New Jersey family whose history over several generations showed a high incidence of disease, delinquency, and poverty.

Kal·mar (kăl′mär), *n.* a seaport in SE Sweden, on **Kalmar Sound,** a strait between Oland and the mainland. 23,834 (est. 1944).

kal·mi·a (kăl′mĭ ə), *n.* any plant of the North American ericaceous genus *Kalmia*, comprising evergreen shrubs with showy flowers, as *K. latifolia*, the mountain laurel. [t. NL, named after P. *Kalm* (1715–79), Swedish botanist]

Kal·muck (kăl′mŭk), *n.* 1. a member of any of a group of Buddhistic Mongol tribes of a region extending from western China to the valley of the lower Volga river. 2. their language, a member of the Mongolian family. Also, **Kal′muk.** [ult. t. Tatar: lit., deserter]

ka·long (kä′lŏng), *n.* any of the large fruit bats or flying foxes, belonging to the genus *Pteropus*. [t. Malay]

kal·so·mine (kăl′sə mĭn′, -mĭn), *n., v.t.,* **-mined, -mining.** calcimine. [orig. obscure]

Ka·lu·ga (kä lōō′gä), *n.* a city in the central Soviet Union in Europe, SW of Moscow. 89,484 (1939).

Ka·ma (kä′mä), *n.* a river flowing from the Ural area in the Soviet Union into the Volga S of Kazan. ab. 1100 mi.

Ka·ma·ku·ra (kä′mä kōō′rä), *n.* a town in central Japan, on Honshu island: great statue of Buddha.

ka·ma·la (kə mä′lə, kăm′ə-lə), *n.* a powder from the capsules of an East Indian euphorbiaceous tree, *Mallotus philippinensis*, used as a yellow dye and in medicine as an anthelmintic. [t. Skt.]

Kam·chat·ka (kăm chăt′-kə; *Russ.* käm chät′kä), *n.* a peninsula in the E Soviet Union in Asia, extending S between the Bering Sea and the Sea of Okhotsk. ab. 750 mi. long; ab. 104,000 sq. mi.

kame (kām), *n.* 1. *Phys. Geog.* a ridge or mound of detrital material, esp. of stratified sand and gravel left by a retreating ice sheet. 2. *Scot.* comb. [var. of COMB¹]

Ka·me·rad (kä′mə rät′), *n. German.* comrade (used as a shout of surrender).

Ka·me·run (kä′mə rōōn′), *n.* German name of Cameroons (def. 1).

Ka·mi·ka·ze (kä′mĭ kä′zě), *n.pl. Japanese.* suicide pilots. [Jap.: divine wind]

kam·seen (kăm sēn′), *n.* khamsin. Also, **kam·sin** (kăm′sĭn).

Kan., Kansas.

Ka·nak·a (kə näk′ə, kăn′ə kə), *n.* 1. a native Hawaiian. 2. a South Sea islander. [t. Hawaiian: lit., man]

Ka·na·rese (kä′nə rēz′, -rēs′), *adj., n., pl.* **-rese.** —*adj.* 1. of or pertaining to Kanara, a part of the Bombay province of India. —*n.* 2. one of a Dravidian people of the districts of North and South Kanara, in southwestern India. 3. a Dravidian language of southern India in any of its historical, standard, or dialect forms.

Ka·na·za·wa (kä′nä zä′wä), *n.* a seaport in central Japan, on Honshu island. 207,287 (1946).

Kan·chen·jun·ga (kän′chən jŏong′gə), *n.* a peak of the E Himalayas, on the boundary between Nepal and Sikkim: third loftiest peak in the world. 28,146 ft. Also, **Kan·chan·jan·ga** (kän′chən jäng′gə), or **Kinchinjunga.**

Kan·da·har (kŭn′də här′), *n.* a city in S Afghanistan. ab. 60,000.

Kan·dy (kän′dĭ; *native* kän′-dē), *n.* a city in central Ceylon: famous Buddhist temples. 42,600 (est. 1941).

kan·ga·roo (kăng′gə rōō′), *n., pl.* **-roos,** (*esp. collectively*) **-roo.** any of a family, *Macropodidae*, of herbivorous marsupials of the Australian region with powerful hind legs developed for leaping, a sturdy tail serving as a support and balance, a small head, and very short forelimbs. [? t. native Australian] —**kan′ga·roo′like′,** *adj.*

Kangaroo, *Macropus rufus*
(Total length 8½ ft., tail 3½ ft.)

kangaroo court, *Colloq.* an unauthorized or irregular court conducted with disregard for or perversion of legal procedure, as a mock court by prisoners in a jail, or an irregularly conducted court in a frontier district.

kangaroo rat, 1. any of various small jumping rodents of the family *Heteromyidae*, of Mexico and the western U.S., such as those of the genus *Dipodomys*. 2. an Australian rodent of the genus *Notomys*, found in arid areas.

Kang Te (käng′ tě′). See **Pu-Yi.**

Kan·ka·kee (kăng′kə kē′), *n.* a city in NE Illinois. 25,856 (1950).

Kan·nap·o·lis (kə năp′ə lĭs), *n.* a city in W North Carolina. 28,448 (1950).

Ka·no (kä′nō), *n.* a city in N Nigeria. 97,031 (1931).

Kans., Kansas.

Kan·sas (kăn′zəs), *n.* 1. a State in the central United States: a part of the Midwest. 1,905,299 pop. (1950); 82,276 sq. mi. *Cap.:* Topeka. *Abbr.:* Kans. or Kan. 2. a river in NE Kansas, flowing E to the Missouri river. 169 mi. —**Kan′san,** *adj., n.*

Kansas City, 1. a city in W Missouri at the confluence of the Kansas and the Missouri rivers. 456,622 (1950). 2. a city in NE Kansas, adjacent to Kansas City, Missouri. 129,553 (1950).

Kan·su (kän′sōō′; *Chin.* gän′sōō′), *n.* a province in NW China. 6,554,500 pop. (est. 1944); 151,160 sq. mi. *Cap.:* Lanchow.

Kant (känt; *Ger.* känt), *n.* **Immanuel** (ĭ män′yōō əl; *Ger.* ĭ mä′nōō ěl′), 1724–1804, German philosopher.

kan·tar (kän tär′), *n.* (in Mohammedan countries) a unit of weight corresponding to the hundredweight, but varying in different localities. [t. Ar.: m. *qintar*, ult. der. L. *centenārium* one hundred (lbs.) weight. See QUINTAL]

Kant·i·an (kän′tĭ ən), *adj.* 1. of or pertaining to Immanuel Kant. —*n.* 2. a follower of Kant.

Kant·i·an·ism (kän′tĭ ə nĭz′əm), *n.* the doctrine of Immanuel Kant that every attribute is merely a mode in which the mind is affected, and has no application to a thing in itself. A thing in itself is unthinkable, and ideas are of two kinds only: those presented in sensation, and those introduced in the process of thinking. Religious and strict moral ideas are, however, admitted as regulative principles.

ka·o·li·ang (kä′ō lĭ äng′), *n.* one of the varieties of grain sorghums, *Sorghum vulgare*. [t. Chinese (Mandarin): f. *kao* tall + *liang* millet]

ka·o·lin (kā′ə lĭn), *n.* a fine white clay used in the manufacture of porcelain. Also, **ka′o·line.** [t. F, t. Chinese: m. *Kao-ling* high hill, name of a mountain in China which yielded the first kaolin sent to Europe]

ka·o·lin·ite (kā′ə lĭ nīt′), *n.* hydrated aluminum disilicate, $Al_2Si_2O_5(OH)_4$, a very common mineral, the commonest constituent of kaolin.

Ka·pell·meis·ter (kä pěl′mīs′tər), *n., pl.* **-ter.** 1. choir leader. 2. a conductor of an orchestra. 3. bandmaster. [G: f. *kapelle* chapel (choir) + *meister* master]

ka·pok (kā′pŏk, kăp′ək), *n.* the silky down which invests the seeds of a silk-cotton tree (**kapok tree**), *Ceiba pentandra*, of the East Indies, Africa, and tropical America: used for stuffing pillows, etc. and for sound insulation. [t. Malay: m. *kāpoq*]

kap·pa (kăp′ə), *n.* the tenth letter of the Greek alphabet (Κ, κ).

ka·put (kä pŏŏt′), *adj.* smashed; ruined; done for. [G]

b., blend of, blended; c., cognate with; d., dialect, dialectal; der., derived from; f., formed from; g., going back to; m., modification of; r., replacing; s., stem of; t., taken from; ?, perhaps. See the full key on inside cover.

Ka·ra·chi (kə rä′chĭ), *n.* a seaport in and the capital of Pakistan, in Sind province, near the Indus delta. 359,492 (1940).

Ka·ra·fu·to (kä′rä foo′tô), *n.* Japanese name of the S part of Sakhalin.

Ka·ra·gan·da (kä′rä gän′dä), *n.* a city in the SW Soviet Union in Asia. 165,937 (1939).

Kar·a·ite (kâr′ə ĭt′), *n.* one of a Jewish sect which arose in the 8th century in opposition to the Talmud.

Ka·ra·ko·ram (kä′rä kôr′əm), *n.* **1.** a lofty mountain range in NW India, in N Kashmir. Highest peak, K2, 28,250 ft. **2.** a pass traversing this range, on the route from India to Sinkiang province, China. 18,317 ft.

Ka·ra·ko·rum (kä′räkôr′əm), *n.* See **Mongol Empire.**

kar·a·kul (kär′ə kəl), *n.* **1.** an Asiatic breed of sheep used primarily for the production of lambskin fur. Black is the prevailing color of the lambs, but the fleeces of the old sheep turn to various shades of brown and gray. **2.** caracul (the fur). [orig. place name, widely used in Turkestan, esp. in naming lakes]

Ka·ra Kum (kä rä′ koom′), a desert in the SW Soviet Union in Asia, S of the Aral Sea and largely in the Turkmen Republic. ab. 110,000 sq. mi.

Ka·ra Sea (kä′rä), an arm of the Arctic Ocean between Novaya Zemlya and the N Soviet Union.

kar·at (kär′ət), *n.* a twenty-fourth part (used in expressing the fineness of gold, pure gold being 24 karats fine). [t. F, t. It.: m. *carato*, t. Ar.: m. *qīrāṭ* a light weight, t. Gk.: m. *kerátion* carob bean, carat, dim. of *kéras* horn]

Ka·re·lia (kə rēl′yə; *Rus.* kä rĕ′lǐ ä′), *n.* a former autonomous republic in the NW Soviet Union.

Ka·re·lo-Fin·nish Soviet Socialist Republic (kə rē′lô fĭn′ĭsh), a constituent republic of the Soviet Union, in the NW part: formed from Karelia and territory ceded by Finland, 1940. 600,000 pop. (est. 1947); 68,900 sq. mi. (1946). *Cap.:* Petrozavodsk.

Kar·lo·vy Va·ry (kär′lô vǐ vä′rǐ), Czech name of **Carlsbad.**

Karls·bad (kärlz′bäd; *Ger.* kärls′bät), *n.* German name of Carlsbad.

Karls·ruh·e (kärls′roo′ə), *n.* a city in SW Germany: capital of the state of Baden. 190,081 (1939).

kar·ma (kär′mə), *n.* **1.** *Hinduism and Buddhism.* the cosmic operation of retributive justice, according to which a person's status in life is determined by his own deeds in a previous incarnation. **2.** *Theos.* the doctrine of inevitable consequence. **3.** fate; destiny. [t. Skt.: deed, action]

Kar·nak (kär′näk), *n.* a village in Upper Egypt, on the Nile: the N part of the ruins of ancient Thebes.

Kar·roo (kə roo′), *n., pl.* (for def. 2) **-roos.** **1.** a vast plateau in the S part of the Union of South Africa, in Cape of Good Hope province. ab. 100,000 sq. mi.; 3000 4000 ft. high. **2.** (*l.c.*) one of the arid tablelands, with red clay soil, in South Africa. Also, **ka·roo′.** [later var. of *Karo*, appar. mishearing of Hottentot *torô* karroo or *garo* desert]

karyo-, a word element meaning "nucleus of a cell." [t. Gk., comb. form of *káryon* nut, kernel]

kar·y·o·ki·ne·sis (kär′ĭ ō kǐ nē′sǐs, -kī-), *n.* *Biol.* **1.** mitosis. **2.** the series of active changes which take place in the nucleus of a living cell in the process of division. [f. KARYO- + Gk. *kínēsis* movement] —**kar·y·o·ki·net·ic** (kär′ĭ ō kǐ nĕt′ĭk, -kī-), *adj.*

kar·y·o·lymph (kär′ə lǐmf′), *n.* *Bot.* the transparent or translucent fluid in a nucleus.

kar·y·om·i·tome (kär′ĭ ŏm′ə tōm′), *n.* *Biol.* the network or reticulum in the nucleus of a cell. [f. KARYO- + s. Gk. *mítos* thread + -*ome*, var. of -OMA]

kar·y·o·plasm (kär′ə plăz′əm), *n.* *Biol.* the substance of the nucleus of a cell. —**kar′y·o·plas′mic,** *adj.*

kar·y·o·some (kär′ĭ ə sōm′), *n.* *Biol.* **1.** any of certain irregular or spherical bodies observed in and supposed to be in a portion of the netlike structure in the nucleus of a cell. See diag. under **cell.** **2.** the nucleus of a cell. **3.** a chromosome. [f. KARYO- + -SOME³]

kar·y·o·tin (kär′ĭ ō′tǐn), *n.* *Biol.* nuclear material; chromatin. [f. s. Gk. *karyōtós* nutlike + -IN²]

Kas·bah (käs′bä), *n.* the older, native quarter of Algiers. Also, **Casbah.**

ka·sher (kä′shər), *adj., n.* kosher.

Kash·gar (käsh′gär′), *n.* a city in extreme W China, in Sinkiang province. 80,000. Also, **Shufu.**

Kash·mir (kăsh mǐr′), *n.* a state adjacent to the republic of India, the dominion of Pakistan, Sinkiang province, China, and Tibet. Including feudatories, 4,021,- 600 pop. (1941); 82,258 sq. mi. *Cap.:* Srinagar. Also, **Cashmere.** Official name, **Jammu and Kashmir.** —**Kash·mir·i·an** (käsh mǐr′ĭ ən), *adj.*

kash·mir (käsh′mǐr), *n.* cashmere.

Kashmir rug, an Oriental hand made rug, woven flat without pile, and having the patterns which entirely cover its surface embroidered of colored yarns.

Kas·sa (kôsh′shŏ), *n.* Hungarian name of **Košice.**

Kas·sa·la (kä′sä lä′), *n.* a city in the E Anglo-Egyptian Sudan, near Eritrea: taken by the Italians, 1894. 30,026 (est. 1940).

Kas·sel (käs′əl), *n.* a city in central Germany. 216,141 (1939). Also, **Cassel.**

Kas·tro (käs′trô), *n.* Mytilene (def. 2).

ka·tab·o·lism (kə tăb′ə lǐz′əm), *n.* catabolism.

Ka·tah·din (kə tä′dǐn), *n.* **Mount,** the highest peak in Maine, in the central part. 5273 ft.

Ka·thi·a·war (kä′tēä wär′), *n.* a peninsula on the W coast of India.

kath·ode (käth′ōd), *n.* cathode.

kat·i·on (kăt′ī′ən), *n.* cation.

Kat·mai (kăt′mī), *n.* **1. Mount,** an active volcano in SW Alaska: eruption, 1912. ab. 7500 ft. **2.** a national monument including Mt. Katmai and the Valley of Ten Thousand Smokes. ab. 1700 sq. mi.

Kat·man·du (kăt′măn doo′), *n.* the capital of Nepal. ab. 108,800.

Ka·to·wi·ce (kä′tô vē′tsĕ), *n.* a city in S Poland. 128,- 000 (1946). German, **Kat·to·witz** (kä′tô vǐts).

Kat·rine (kăt′rǐn), *n.* **Loch,** a beautiful lake in central Scotland: scene of Scott's *Lady of the Lake.* 8 mi. long.

Kat·te·gat (kăt′ə găt′), *n.* the strait between Jutland and Sweden. 40–70 mi. wide. Also, **Cattegat.**

ka·ty·did (kä′tǐ dǐd), *n.* any of the large, usually green, long-horned American grasshoppers of the family *Tettigoniidae,* known for the loud note of the males of some species, notably *Platyphyllum concavum.* [imit. of the sound made]

Katydid, *Platyphyllum concavum* (About 1¾ in. long)

Ka·u·a·i (kä′ōō ä′ē), *n.* one of the Hawaiian Islands, in the N W part of the group. 29,838 pop. (prelim. 1950); 511 sq. mi.

Kauf·man (kôf′mən), *n.* **George S.,** born 1889, U.S. dramatist.

Kau·nas (kou′näs), *n.* a city in the W Soviet Union, in the Lithuanian Republic. 108,198 (est. 1937). Russian, **Kovno.**

kau·ri (kour′ĭ), *n., pl.* **-ris. 1.** a tall coniferous tree, *Agathis australis,* of New Zealand, yielding a valuable timber and a resin. **2.** its wood. **3.** kauri resin. **4.** any of various other trees of the genus *Agathis.* **5.** their wood. [t. Maori]

kauri resin, the resin, used in making varnish, which exudes from the thick bark of the kauri. Masses weighing as much as 100 pounds are found in soil where the trees have grown. Also, **kauri gum, kauri copal.**

kau·ry (kour′ĭ), *n., pl.* **-ries.** kauri.

ka·va (kä′və), *n.* **1.** a Polynesian shrub, *Piper methysticum,* of the pepper family. Its root has aromatic and pungent qualities. **2.** a fermented, intoxicating beverage made from the roots of the kava. [t. Polynesian]

Ka·ver·i (kô′vərǐ), *n.* Cauvery.

Ka·wa·gu·chi (kä′wä goo′chē), *n.* a city in central Japan, on Honshu island near Tokyo. 105,933 (1946).

Ka·wa·sa·ki (kä′wä sä′kē), *n.* a seaport in central Japan, on Honshu island, near Tokyo. 210,157 (1946).

Kay (kā), *n.* **Sir,** *Arthurian Romance.* the rude, boastful foster brother and seneschal of Arthur.

kay·ak (kī′ăk), *n.* an Eskimo hunting craft with a skin cover on a light framework, made watertight by flexible closure around the waist of the occupant. Also, **kaiak.** [t. Eskimo]

Kayak

Kaye-Smith (kā′smǐth′), *n.* **Sheila,** (*Mrs. Fry*) born 1887, British novelist.

Kay·se·ri (kī′sĕ rē′), *n.* a city in central Turkey. 52,467 (1940). Ancient, **Caesarea.**

Ka·zak Soviet Socialist Republic (kä zäk′), a constituent republic of the Soviet Union, E and N of the Caspian Sea. 6,145,937 pop. (1939); 1,055,900 sq. mi. *Cap.:* Alma-Ata. Also, **Ka·zakh′, Ka·zak·stan** (kä′zäk stän′).

Ka·zan (kä zän′y), *n.* a city in the E Soviet Union in Europe, near the Volga. 401,665 (1939).

K.B., 1. *Chess.* king's bishop. **2.** King's Bench. **3.** Knight Bachelor.

kc., kilocycle; kilocycles.

K.C., 1. King's Counsel. **2.** Knight Commander. **3.** Knights of Columbus.

K.C.B., Knight Commander of the Bath.

ke·a (kä′ə, kē′ə), *n.* a large, greenish New Zealand parrot, *Nestor notabilis.* [t. Maori]

Ke·a (kĕ′ä), *n.* Keos.

Kean (kēn), *n.* **Edmund,** 1787–1833, British tragedian.

Kear·ny (kär′nĭ), *n.* **1.** a city in NE New Jersey, near Newark. 39,952 (1950). **2. Philip,** 1815–62, U.S. general.

keat (kēt), *n.* the young of the guinea fowl.

Keats (kēts), *n.* **John,** 1795–1821, British poet.

Ke·ble (kē′bəl), *n.* **John,** 1792–1866, British clergyman and poet.

Kech·ua (kĕch′wə), *n.* **1.** a Kechua-speaking Indian of Peru, Bolivia, or Ecuador. **2.** the language spoken originally by the Indians of Cuzco, Peru, spread widely by the conquests of the Incas. Also, **Quechua.** [native name] —**Kech′uan,** *adj., n.*

keck (kĕk), *v.i.* **1.** to retch; be nauseated. **2.** to feel or show disgust or strong dislike. [cf. OE *cecil* choking]

Kecs·ke·mét (kĕch′kĕ māt′), *n.* a city in central Hungary. 87,269 (1941).

ked (kĕd), *n.* the sheep tick.

Ke·dah (kā′dä), *n.* a native state in the Federation of Malaya: formerly one of the Unfederated Malay States. 492,219 pop. (est. 1937); 3660 sq. mi. *Cap.:* Alor Star.

ked·dah (kĕd/ə), *n.* kheda.

kedge (kĕj), *v.*, **kedged, kedging,** *n.* —*v.t.* **1.** to warp or pull (a ship, etc.) along by means of a rope attached to an anchor. —*v.i.* **2.** to move by being pulled along with the aid of an anchor. —*n.* **3.** Also, **kedge anchor.** a small anchor used in kedging and otherwise.

Ke·dron (kē/drən), *n.* a ravine in central Palestine, E of Jerusalem: in ancient times a brook. Also, **Kidron.**

ke·ef (kĭ̄f/), *n.* kef (def. 2).

keel[1] (kēl), *n.* **1.** a longitudinal timber, or combination of timbers, iron plates, or the like, extending along the middle of the bottom of a vessel from stem to stern and supporting the whole frame. See diag. under **gunwale.** **2.** a ship. **3.** a part corresponding to a ship's keel in some other structure, as in a dirigible balloon. **4.** *Bot., Zool.* a longitudinal ridge, as on a leaf or bone; a carina. —*v.t., v.i.* **5.** to turn or upset so as to bring the wrong side or part uppermost. [ME *kele,* t. Scand.; cf. Icel. *kjölr*]

keel[2] (kēl), *n.* a fatal disease of domestic ducks. [special use of KEEL[1]]

keel·boat (kēl/bōt/), *n.* a shallow freight boat or barge, built with a keel and decked over, used on rivers of the western U.S.

keel·haul (kēl/hôl/), *v.t. Naut.* to haul (a person) under the keel of a vessel, as for punishment. [t. D.: m.s. *kielhalen,* f. *kiel* keel + *halen* haul]

Kee·ling Islands (kē/lĭng), Cocos Islands.

keel·son (kĕl/sən, kēl/-), *n. Naut.* a strengthening line of timbers or iron plates in a ship, above and parallel with the keel. Also, **kelson.** [der. KEEL[1]; formation obscure]

Kee·lung (kē/lŏŏng/), *n.* a seaport on the N coast of Formosa. 100,128 (1939).

keen[1] (kēn), *adj.* **1.** sharp, or so shaped as to cut or pierce substances readily: *a keen blade.* **2.** sharp, piercing, or biting: *a keen wind, keen satire.* **3.** characterized by strength and distinctness of perception, as the ear or hearing, the eye, sight, etc. **4.** having or showing great mental penetration or acumen: *keen reasoning.* **5.** animated by or showing strong feeling or desire: *keen competition.* **6.** intense, as feeling, desire, etc. **7.** ardent; eager (often fol. by *about, for,* etc., or an infinitive). [ME *kene,* OE *cēne,* c. G *kühn* bold] —**keen/ly,** *adv.* —**keen/ness,** *n.* —Syn. **1, 4.** See **sharp.**

keen[2] (kēn), *Irish.* —*n.* **1.** a wailing lament for the dead. —*v.i.* **2.** to wail in lamentation for the dead. [t. Irish: m *caoine,* der. *caoinim* I lament] —**keen/er,** *n.*

keep (kēp), *v.*, **kept, keeping,** *n.* —*v.t.* **1.** to maintain in one's action or conduct: *to keep watch, step, or silence.* **2.** to cause to continue in some place, position, state, course, or action specified: *to keep a light burning.* **3.** to maintain in condition or order, as by care and labor. **4.** to hold in custody or under guard, as a prisoner; detain; prevent from coming or going. **5.** to have habitually in stock or for sale. **6.** to maintain in one's service or for one's use or enjoyment. **7.** to have the charge or custody of. **8.** to withhold from the knowledge of others: *to keep a secret.* **9.** to withhold from use; reserve. **10.** to maintain by writing, entries, etc.: *to keep a diary.* **11.** to record (business transactions, etc.) regularly: *to keep records.* **12.** to observe; pay obedient regard to (a law, rule, promise, etc.). **13.** to conform to; follow; fulfill: *to keep one's word.* **14.** to observe (a season, festival, etc.) with formalities or rites: *to keep Christmas.* **15.** to maintain or carry on, as an establishment, business, etc.; manage: *to keep house.* **16.** to guard; protect. **17.** to maintain or support (a person, etc.). **18.** to take care of; tend: *to keep sheep.* **19.** to maintain in active existence, or hold, as an assembly, court, fair, etc. **20.** to remain in (a place, etc.). **21.** to maintain one's position in or on. **22.** to continue to follow (a path, track, course, etc.). **23.** to continue to hold or have: *to keep a thing in mind.* **24.** to save, hold, or retain in possession. —*v.i.* **25.** to continue in an action, course, position, state, etc.: *to keep in sight.* **26.** to remain, or continue to be, as specified: *to keep cool.* **27.** to remain or stay in a place: *to keep indoors.* **28.** to continue unimpaired or without spoiling: *the milk will keep on ice.* **29.** to admit of being reserved for a future occasion. **30.** to keep oneself or itself (fol. by *away, back, off, out,* etc.): *keep off the grass.* **31.** to restrain oneself: *try to keep from smiling.* **32.** Some special verb phrases are: **keep in with,** *Colloq.* to keep oneself in favor with. **keep time, 1.** to record time, as a watch or clock does. **2.** to beat, mark, or observe the rhythmic accents. **3.** to perform rhythmic movements in unison. **keep to, 1.** to adhere to (an agreement, plan, facts, etc.). **2.** to confine oneself to: *to keep to one's bed.* **keep to oneself,** to hold aloof from the society of others. **keep track of,** take on, to keep account (of). **keep up, 1.** to maintain an equal rate of speed, activity, or progress, as with another. **2.** to bear up; continue without breaking down, as under strain. —*n.* **33.** subsistence; board and lodging: *to work for one's keep.* **34.** the innermost and strongest structure or central tower of a medieval castle. **35.** (*pl.*) a game in which the winner has the right to keep his winnings. **36. for keeps,** *Colloq.* **a.** for keeping as one's own permanently: *to play for keeps.* **b.** permanently; altogether. [ME *kepen,* OE *cēpan* observe, heed, regard, await, take; akin to Icel. *kōpa* stare] —Syn. **2.** KEEP, RESERVE, RETAIN, WITHHOLD refer to having and holding in possession. KEEP (a common word) and RETAIN (a more formal one) agree in meaning to continue to have or hold, as opposed to losing, parting with, or giving up: *to keep a book for a week.* To RESERVE is to keep for some future use, occasion, or recipient, or to hold back for a time: *to reserve judgment.* To WITHHOLD is generally to hold back altogether: *to withhold help.* **4.** detain, hold, confine.

keep·er (kē/pər), *n.* **1.** one who keeps, guards, or watches. **2.** something that keeps, or serves to guard, hold in place, retain, etc. **3.** something that keeps or lasts well, as a fruit. **4.** a guard ring. —**keep/er·less,** *adj.* —Syn. **1.** guard, warden; custodian, guardian.

keep·ing (kē/pĭng), *n.* **1.** just conformity in things or elements associated together: *his deeds are not in keeping with his words.* **2.** act of one who or that which keeps; observance, custody, or care. **3.** maintenance or keep. **4.** holding, reserving, or retaining. —Syn. **1.** agreement, congruity, harmony. **2.** protection. See **custody.**

keep·sake (kēp/sāk/), *n.* anything kept, or given to be kept, for the sake of the giver.

Kee·wa·tin (kē wä/tĭn), *n.* a district in N Canada, in the Northwest Territories. 228,160 sq. mi.

kef (kāf), *n.* (among the Arabs) **1.** a state of drowsy contentment, as from the use of a narcotic. **2.** Also, **keef.** a substance, esp. a smoking preparation of hemp leaves, used to produce this state. Also, **kief, kaif.**

keg (kĕg), *n.* **1.** a small cask or barrel, usually holding from 5 to 10 gallons. **2.** a unit of weight, equal to 100 lbs., used for nails. [late ME *cag,* t. Scand.; cf. Icel. *kaggi*]

Kei·jo (kā/jō/, -rō/), *n.* Japanese name of Seoul.

keir (kĭr), *n.* kier.

Kei·tel (kī/təl), *n.* **Wilhelm** (vĭl/hĕlm), 1882–1946, German marshal: chief of Nazi High Command.

Keith (kēth), *n.* **Sir Arthur,** born 1866, British anthropologist.

Ke·lan·tan (kə län/tän/), *n.* a state in the Federation of Malaya: formerly one of Unfederated Malay States. 390,342 pop. (est. 1937); 5750 sq. mi. *Cap.:* Kota Bahru.

Kel·ler (kĕl/ər), *n.* **Helen Adams,** born 1880, U.S. author, blind and deaf, who learned to speak.

Kel·logg (kĕl/ôg, -ŏg, -əg), *n.* **Frank Billings,** 1856–1937, U.S. statesman.

ke·loid (kē/loid), *n. Pathol.* a kind of fibrous tumor forming hard, irregular, clawlike excrescences upon the skin. Also, **cheloid.** [*k-* var., f. Gk. *kēl(is)* stain + -OID; *ch-* var., f. Gk. *chēl(ē)* claw + -OID]

kelp (kĕlp), *n.* **1.** any of the large brown seaweeds belonging to the family *Laminariaceae.* **2.** the ash of such seaweeds. [ME *culp;* ult. orig. unknown]

kel·pie (kĕl/pĭ), *n.* **1.** *Scot.* a fabled water spirit, usually in the form of a horse, reputed to give warning of or to cause drowning. [orig. uncert.] **2.** *Australian.* a breed of sheep dogs.

kel·py (kĕl/pĭ), *n., pl.* **-pies.** kelpie.

kel·son (kĕl/sən), *n.* keelson.

Kelt (kĕlt), *n.* Celt. —**Kelt/ic,** *n., adj.*

kelt (kĕlt), *n.* a salmon that has spawned.

kel·ter (kĕl/tər), *n. Brit. Dial.* kilter.

Kel·vin (kĕl/vĭn), *n.* **William Thomson, 1st Baron,** 1824–1907, British physicist and mathematician.

Kelvin scale, *Physics.* an absolute scale of temperature (**Kelvin temperature**), based on thermodynamic principles, in which zero is equivalent to −459.4°F or −273°C.

Ke·mal A·ta·türk (kě mäl/ ä/tä tyrk/), (*Mustafa Kemal Pasha*) 1880–1938, president of Turkey, 1923–38.

Kem·ble (kĕm/bəl), *n.* **1. Frances Anne,** or **Fanny,** (*Mrs. Butler*) 1809–93, British actress and author. **2. John Philip,** 1757–1823, British tragedian.

Ke·me·ro·vo (kě/mĕ rŏ vŏ), *n.* a city in the S Soviet Union in Asia. 132,978 (1938).

Kem·pis (kĕm/pĭs), *n.* **Thomas à** (ə), 1380?–1471, German churchman and reputed author.

ken (kĕn), *n., v.,* **kenned** or **kent, kenning.** —*n.* **1.** range of sight or vision. **2.** knowledge or cognizance; mental perception. —*v.t.* **3.** *Archaic.* to see; descry; recognize. **4.** *Scot.* to have aquaintance with. **5.** *Scot. Law.* to acknowledge as heir; recognize by a judicial act. —*v.i.* **6.** *Archaic., Scot., or Brit. Dial.* to have knowledge of something. [ME *kennen,* OE *cennan,* c. Icel. *kenna* make known, know (cf.later E senses), G *kennen* know; orig. a causative of the verb represented by CAN[1]]

Ken., Kentucky.

Ken·dal green (kĕn/dəl), **1.** a green woolen cloth formerly in use. **2.** green produced by a dye extracted from the woodwaxen plant.

Ken·il·worth (kĕn/əl wûrth/), *n.* a town in central England, in Warwickshire: ruined castle. 9457 (1939).

Ken·ne·bec (kĕn/ə bĕk/), *n.* a river flowing through W Maine S to the Atlantic. 164 mi.

ken·nel (kĕn/əl), *n., v.,* **-neled, -neling** or (*esp. Brit.*) **-nelled, -nelling.** —*n.* **1.** a house for a dog or dogs. **2.** (*often pl.*) an establishment where dogs are bred. **3.** (*in contemptuous use*) a wretched abode. —*v.t.* **4.** to put into or keep in a kennel. —*v.i.* **5.** to take shelter or lodge in a kennel. [ME *kenel,* t. ONF, g. VL *canīle,* der. L *canis* dog]

Ken·nel·ly-Heav·i·side layer (kĕn/ə lĭ hĕv/ĭ sīd/), Heaviside layer.

ken·ning (kĕn/ĭng), *n.* a descriptive poetical name used for, or in addition to, the usual name of a person or thing. *Example:* "a wave traveler" for "a boat." [t. Icel.]

Ken·ny (kĕn′ĭ), *n.* **Elizabeth,** (*Sister Kenny*) born 1884?, Australian nurse: developed a method of treating infantile paralysis.

ke·no (kē′nō), *n.* a game of chance, adapted from lotto for gambling purposes.

ke·no·gen·e·sis (kē′nō jĕn′ə sĭs, kĕn′ō-), *n.* cenogenesis.

Ke·no·sha (kĭ nō′shə), *n.* a city in SE Wisconsin: a port on Lake Michigan. 54,368 (1950).

ke·no·sis (kĭ nō′sĭs), *n.* **1.** *Theol.* the renunciation of the divine nature or dignity in the incarnation (used of Christ, "who, being in the form of God . . . took upon himself the form of a servant, and was made in the likeness of men." Phil. 2:6, 7, R.V.). **2.** one of several doctrines or concepts about this. [t. NL, t. Gk.: an emptying] —**ke·not·ic** (kĭ nŏt′ĭk), *adj.*

Ken·sing·ton (kĕn′zĭng tən), *n.* a W borough of London, England. 154,150 (est. 1946).

Kent (kĕnt), *n.* **1.** a county in SE England. 1,412,000 pop. (est. 1946); 1525 sq. mi. *Cap.:* Maidstone. **2.** an ancient English kingdom in SE Britain. See map under Mercia. **3. James,** 1763–1847, U.S. jurist. **4. Rockwell,** born 1882, U.S. painter and writer.

Kent·ish (kĕn′tĭsh), *adj.* of or pertaining to Kent.

kent·ledge (kĕnt′lĭj), *n. Naut.* pig iron used as permanent ballast. [orig. obscure]

Ken·tuck·y (kən tŭk′ĭ), *n.* **1.** a State in the E central United States. 2,944,806 pop. (1950); 40,395 sq. mi. *Cap.:* Frankfort. *Abbr.:* Ky. or Ken. **2.** a river flowing from E Kentucky NW to the Ohio river. 259 mi. —**Ken·tuck′i·an,** *adj., n.*

Kentucky bluegrass, a common grass, *Poa pratensis,* esp. of the Mississippi valley, highly valued for pasturage and hay.

Kentucky coffee tree, a tall tree of North America, *Gymnocladus dioica,* whose seeds (**Kentucky coffee beans**) were formerly used as a substitute for coffee beans.

Ken·ya (kĕn′yə, kēn′-), *n.* **1.** a British crown colony and protectorate in E Africa. 3,724,000 pop. (est. 1943); 219,730 sq. mi. *Cap.:* Nairobi. **2. Mount,** volcanic mountain in central Kenya. 17,040 ft.

Ke·o·kuk (kē′ə kŭk′), *n.* a city in SE Iowa, on the Mississippi: large power dam. 16,144 (1950).

Ke·os (kē′ŏs), *n.* an island of the Cyclades, off the SE coast of Greece. 3854 pop. (1940); 56 sq. mi. Also, **Zea.**

Ke·phal·le·ni·a (kĕ′fä lē nē′ä), *n.* Greek name of **Cephalonia.**

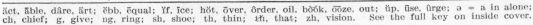

A. Stiff; B, Soft

Kepis

kep·i (kĕp′ĭ), *n., pl.* **kepis.** a French military cap with a flat circular top and a horizontal visor. [t. F, t. d. G: m. *käppi,* dim. of G *kappe* cap]

Kep·ler (kĕp′lər), *n.* **Johann** (yō′hän), 1571–1630, German astronomer.

kept (kĕpt), *v.* pt. and pp. of **keep.**

ke·ram·ic (kĭ răm′ĭk), *adj.* ceramic.

ker·a·tin (kĕr′ə tĭn), *n. Zool.* an albuminous substance, consisting of the dead outer corneal skin layer, and variously modified into horn, feathers, hair, hoofs. Also, **ceratin.** [f. s. Gk. *kéras* horn + -IN²]

ker·a·tog·e·nous (kĕr′ə tŏj′ə nəs), *adj.* producing horn or a horny substance. [f. *kerato-* (comb. form repr. Gk. *kéras* horn) + -GENOUS]

ker·a·toid (kĕr′ə toid′), *adj.* resembling horn; horny. [t. Gk.: m.s. *keratoeidēs*]

ker·a·tol (kĕr′ə tōl′, -tŏl′), *n.* **1.** a leatherlike waterproofed synthetic cloth. **2.** (*cap.*) a trademark for this cloth.

ker·a·to·plas·ty (kĕr′ə tō plăs′tĭ), *n., pl.* **-ties.** a plastic surgical operation upon the cornea; specif., a corneal transplantation.

kerb (kûrb), *n., v.t. Brit.* curb (defs. 4, 10).

kerb·stone (kûrb′stōn′), *n. Brit.* curbstone.

Kerch (kĕrch), *n.* a seaport in the SW Soviet Union, on **Kerch Strait,** a strait connecting the Sea of Azov and the Black Sea. 104,471 (1939).

ker·chief (kûr′chĭf), *n.* **1.** a cloth worn as a head covering, esp. by women. **2.** a cloth worn or carried on the person. [ME *curchef,* contr. of *coverchef,* t. OF: m. *couvrechief,* t. *covrir* COVER + *chief* head. Cf. CHIEF]

Ke·ren·ski (kĕ rĕn′skĭ), *n.* **Aleksandr Feodorovich** (ä′lĕksän′dər fē ô′dô rô′vĭch), born 1881, Russian revolutionist; premier, 1917. Also, **Ke·ren′sky.**

Ker·e·san (kĕr′ə sən), *n.* a linguistic stock of Pueblo tribes of the Rio Grande valley and neighboring areas.

kerf (kûrf), *n.* **1.** the cut or incision made by a saw or other instrument. **2.** that which is cut. [ME *kerf, kyrf,* OE *cyrf* a cutting, akin to *ceorfan,* v., cut, CARVE]

Ker·gue·len (kûr′gə lĕn′; *Fr.* kĕrg län′), *n.* a desolate island in the S Indian Ocean: a possession of France. ab. 1400 sq. mi.

Ker·ky·ra (kĕr′kē rä′), *n.* Greek name of **Corfu.**

Ker·man (kĕr män′), *n.* a city in SE Iran. ab. 50,000.

ker·mes (kûr′mēz), *n.* **1.** a red dye formerly prepared from the dried bodies of the females of a scale insect, *Kermes ilices,* which lives on certain oaks of the Mediterranean region. **2.** the small evergreen oak, *Puercus coccifera,* on which it is found. [t. Ar., Pers.: m. *qirmiz.* Cf. CARMINE, CRIMSON]

ker·mis (kûr′mĭs), *n.* **1.** (in the Low Countries) an annual fair or festival attended with sports and merrymaking. **2.** *U.S.* a similar entertainment, usually for charitable purposes. Also, **ker′mess, kirmess.** [t. D, var. of *kermisse, kerkmisse* church mass (on the anniversary of the dedication of a church)]

kern¹ (kûrn), *n. Archaic.* **1.** a band of light-armed foot soldiers of ancient Ireland. **2.** *Archaic.* (in Ireland or sometimes in the Scottish Highlands) a soldier. **3.** an Irish peasant. Also, **kerne.** [ME *kerne,* t. Irish: m. *ceithern* band of foot soldiers. See CATERAN]

kern² (kûrn), *Print.* —*n.* **1.** a part of the face of a type projecting beyond the body or shank, as in certain italic letters. —*v.t.* **2.** to form or furnish with a kern, as a type or letter. [t. F: m. *carne* point, g. s. L *cardo* hinge]

Kern (kûrn), *n.* **Jerome David,** 1885–1945, U.S. composer.

ker·nel (kûr′nəl), *n., v.,* **-neled, -neling** or (*esp. Brit.*) **-nelled, -nelling.** —*n.* **1.** the softer, usually edible, part contained in the shell of a nut or the stone of a fruit. **2.** the body of a seed within its husk or integuments. **3.** a grain, as of wheat. **4.** the central part of anything; the nucleus; the core. —*v.t.* **5.** to enclose as a kernel. [ME *kirnel, curnel,* OE *cyrnel,* dim. of *corn* seed, grain. See CORN¹] —**ker′nel·less,** *adj.*

kern·ite (kûr′nīt), *n.* a mineral, hydrated sodium borate, (Na₂B₄O₇·4H₂O), occurring in transparent colorless crystals: the principal source of boron compounds in the U.S.

ker·o·sene (kĕr′ə sēn′, kĕr′ə sēn′), *n.* an oil for lamps and heating, a mixture of hydrocarbons, distilled from petroleum, bituminous shale, coal, etc.; illuminating or burning oil. [f. Gk. *kērós* wax + -ENE]

Ker·ry (kĕr′ĭ), *n.* a county in SW Eire, in Munster. 136,072 pop. (est. 1943); 1815 sq. mi. *Cap.:* Tralee.

ker·ry (kĕr′ĭ), *n., pl.* **-ries.** one of a breed of small dairy cattle originating in Kerry.

ker·sey (kûr′zĭ), *n., pl.* **-seys.** **1.** a compact, wellfulled woolen cloth with a fine nap and smooth face. **2.** a coarse twilled woolen cloth with a cotton warp. [ME; ? named after *Kersey,* in Suffolk, England]

kes·trel (kĕs′trəl), *n.* a common small falcon, *Falco tinnunculus,* of northern parts of the Eastern Hemisphere, notable for hovering in the air with its head to the wind. [var. of earlier *castrel.* Cf. F *cresselle*]

ketch (kĕch), *n.* a fore-and-aft rigged vessel with a large mainmast and a smaller mast aft, but forward of the rudder post. [earlier *catch,* appar. der. CATCH, v.]

Ketch·i·kan (kĕch′ə kăn′), *n.* a seaport in SE Alaska. 5202 (prelim. 1950).

ketch·up (kĕch′əp), *n.* catchup. [appar. t. Chinese (Amoy d.): m. *kê-tsiap* brine of pickled fish. Cf. Malay *kechop* sauce (? t. Chinese)]

ke·tene (kē′tēn), *n. Chem.* **1.** a gas, H₂C = C = O, with a penetrating odor, obtained from acetic anhydride or acetone. **2.** a class of compounds having the type formulas, RHC=C=O and R₂C=C=O. [f. KET(ONE) + -ENE]

ke·to-e·nol tautomerism (kē′tō ē′nōl, -nŏl), *Chem.* a type of tautomerism in which the individual tautomers may be isolated as a keto form and an enol. —**ke′to-e′nol tau′to·mer′ic.**

ke·to form (kē′tō), *Chem.* (in a keto-enol tautomeric substance) the form with the characteristics of a ketone.

ke·tone (kē′tōn), *n. Chem.* any of a class of organic compounds, having the general formula, RCOR, containing the carbonyl group, CO, attached to two organic radicals, as acetone, CH₃COCH₃. [t. G: m. *keton,* with *-e* from *acetone,* of the G equivalent of which *keton* is a form apheticically der.] —**ke·ton·ic** (kĭ tŏn′ĭk), *adj.*

ke·tose (kē′tōs), *n. Chem.* any of the sugars which have a ketone group or its equivalent.

ke·to·sis (kĭ tō′sĭs), *n. Pathol.* condition of having too much of a ketone in the body, as in diabetes, acidosis, etc. [f. KET(ONE) + -OSIS]

ket·tle (kĕt′əl), *n.* **1.** a container for boiling liquids, cooking foods, etc.; a pot. **2.** teakettle. **3.** kettledrum. **4. kettle of fish,** a mess, muddle, or awkward state of things (often preceded ironically by *pretty, fine,* etc.). **5.** a kettle hole. [ME *ketel,* OE *cetel* (c. G *kessel*); t. L: m.s. *catillus,* dim. of *catīnus* bowl, pot]

ket·tle·drum (kĕt′əl drŭm′), *n.* a drum consisting of a hollow hemisphere of brass or copper with a skin stretched over it, which can be accurately tuned.

kettle hole, a kettle-shaped cavity in rock or detrital material, esp. in glacial drift.

Kettledrum

kev·el (kĕv′əl), *n. Naut.* a sturdy bit, bollard, etc., on which the heavier hawsers of a ship may be secured. [ME *kevile,* t. ONF: m. *keville* pin, g. L *clāvicula* little key]

Kew (kū), *n.* a part of Richmond, in SE England, near London: famous botanical gardens. 3101 (1931).

kew·pie (kū′pĭ), *n.* **1.** a small, very plump doll, usually made of plaster or celluloid. **2.** (*cap.*) a trademark for such a doll.

key¹ (kē), *n., pl.* **keys,** *adj., v.,* **keyed, keying.** —*n.* **1.** an instrument for fastening or opening a lock by moving its bolt. **2.** a means of attaining, understanding, solving, etc.: *the key to a problem.* **3.** a book or the like

containing the solutions or translations of material given elsewhere as exercises. **4.** a systematic explanation of abbreviations, symbols, etc., used in a dictionary, map, etc. **5.** something that secures or controls entrance to a place. **6.** a pin, bolt, wedge, or other piece inserted in a hole or space to lock or hold parts of a mechanism or structure together; a cotter. **7.** a contrivance for grasping and turning a bolt, nut, etc. **8.** one of a set of levers or parts pressed in operating a telegraph, typewriter, etc. **9.** *Music.* **a.** that part of the lever mechanism of piano, organ, or wood wind, which a finger operates. **b.** the keynote or tonic of a scale. **c.** the relationship perceived between all tones in a given unit of music to a single tone or a keynote; tonality. **d.** the principal tonality of a composition: *symphony in the key of C minor.* **10.** tone or pitch, as of voice: *to speak in a high key.* **11.** strain, or characteristic style, as of expression or thought. **12.** *Elect.* **a.** a device for opening and closing electrical contacts. **b.** a hand-operated switching device ordinarily formed of concealed spring contacts with an exposed handle or push button, capable of switching one or more parts of a circuit. **13.** *Bot., Zool.* a systematic tabular classification of the significant characteristics of the members of a group of organisms to facilitate identification and comparison. **14.** *Masonry.* a keystone. **15.** degree of intensity, as of feeling or action. **16.** *Bot.* a samara.
—*adj.* **17.** acting or operating like a key; controlling; of chief or critical importance; pivotal; fundamental: *the key industries of a nation.*
—*v.t.* **18.** to bring to a particular degree of intensity of feeling, excitement, energy, etc. (often fol. by *up*). **19.** to adjust (speech, etc.) as if to a particular key. **20.** *Music.* to regulate the key or pitch of. **21.** to fasten, secure, or adjust with a key, wedge, or the like, as parts of a mechanism. **22.** to provide with a key or keys. **23.** to lock with, or as with, a key. **24.** *Masonry.* to provide (a key) at a juncture of members.
[ME *key(e)*, *kay(e)*, OE *cǣg*, c. OFris. *kei*, *kai*]

key² (kē), *n.*, *pl.* **keys.** a reef or low island; cay. [t. Sp.: m. *cayo*, t. F: m. *quai*, older *cai*; of Celtic orig.]

Key (kē), *n.* **Francis Scott**, 1780–1843, U.S. lawyer: author of *The Star-Spangled Banner.*

key·board (kē′bôrd′), *n.* **1.** the row or set of keys in a piano, typewriter, etc. **2.** any of two or more sets of keys, as in large organs or harpsichords.

key fruit, *Bot.* a samara.

key·hole (kē′hōl′), *n.* a hole for a key to a lock.

Keynes (kānz), *n.* **John Maynard** (mā′nərd, -närd), **1st Baron,** 1883–1946, British economist and writer.

key·note (kē′nōt′), *n.*, *v.*, **-noted, -noting.** —*n.* **1.** *Music.* the note or tone on which a key (system of tones) is founded; the tonic. **2.** the determining principle governing the spirit of speech, thought, action, etc. **3.** the line of policy to be followed by a party in a political (or other) campaign, as set forth authoritatively in advance in a public speech or other formal announcement. —*v.t.* **4.** to announce the policy of (a political party, etc.). **5.** *Music.* to give the keynote of.

key·not·er (kē′nō′tər), *n.* one who gives the keynote, as of a political campaign or convention.

Key·ser·ling (kī′zər lǐng), *n.* **Hermann Alexander** (hĕr′män ä/lĕ ksän′dər), **Count,** 1880–1946, German writer and traveler.

key signature, *Music.* (in notation) the group of sharps or flats placed after the clef to indicate the tonality of the music following.

key·stone (kē′stōn′), *n.* **1.** the wedge-shaped piece at the summit of an arch, regarded as holding the other pieces in place. See diag. under **arch.** **2.** something on which associated things depend.

Key West, 1. an island in S Florida, in the Gulf of Mexico. **2.** a seaport on this island: the southernmost city in the U.S.; naval base. 26,433 (1950).

kg., 1. keg; kegs. **2.** kilogram; kilograms.

K.G., Knight of the Garter.

Kha·ba·rovsk (hä bä′rôfsk), *n.* **1.** Formerly, **Far Eastern Region.** a maritime territory in the E Soviet Union in Asia. 1,430,875 pop. (1939); ab. 993,000 sq. mi. **2.** the capital of this territory, in the SE part: a port on the Amur river. 199,364 (1939).

Khai·bar Pass (kī′bər), Khyber Pass.

khak·i (kăk′ĭ, kä′kĭ), *n.*, *pl.* **khakis. 1.** dull yellowish brown. **2.** stout twilled cotton uniform cloth of this color. **3.** a similar fabric of wool. —*adj.* **4.** of the color of khaki. **5.** made of khaki. [t. Hind.: dusty, der. *khāk* dust]

kha·lif (kā′lĭf, kăl′ĭf), *n.* caliph. Also, **kha·li·fa** (kə lē′fə).

Khal·ki·di·ke (häl′kē dē′kē), *n.* Greek name of **Chalcidice.**

kham·sin (kăm′sĭn, kăm sēn′), *n.* a hot southerly wind (varying from southeast to southwest) that blows regularly in Egypt for about 50 days, commencing about the middle of March. Also, **kamseen, kamsin.** [t. Ar.: m. *khamsīn*, lit., fifty]

khan¹ (kän, kăn), *n.* **1.** (in the Manchu-Mongol-Turkish-Tatar group of languages) the title borne by hereditary rulers, as **a.** hereditary chief of a tribal following; **b.** hereditary lord of a territorial domain. **2.** the supreme ruler of the Tatar tribes, as well as emperor of China, during the middle ages; a descendant of Genghis Khan. **3.** a title of respect in Iran, Afghanistan, India, etc. [ME, t. Turk. (whence Pers. and Ar.): lord, prince]

khan² (kän, kăn), *n.* an inn or caravansary. [t. Pers.]

khan·ate (kä′nāt, kăn′āt), *n.* the dominion or jurisdiction of a khan.

Kha·ni·a (kä nē′ə; *Gk.* hän yä′), *n.* Greek name of **Canea.**

Khar·kov (kär′kôf, -kŏv; *Rus.* här′kŏf), *n.* a city in the S Soviet Union in Europe: former capital of the Ukrainian Republic. 833,423 (1939).

Khar·toum (кнär tōōm′), *n.* the capital of the Anglo-Egyptian Sudan, at the junction of the White and Blue Nile rivers: besieged, 1895; retaken by the British, 1898. 44,950 (est. 1940). Also, **Khar·tum′.**

khed·a (kĕd′ə), *n.* (in India) an enclosure constructed to ensnare wild elephants. Also, **khed′ah, keddah.**

khe·dive (kə dēv′), *n.* title of the Turkish viceroys in Egypt, 1867–1914. [t. Turk.: m. *khedīv*, t. Pers.: m. *khidīv* lord, sovereign] —**khe·di′val, khe·di·vi·al** (kə dē′vΥəl), *adj.*

Khe·lat (kə lät′), *n.* Kalat.

Kher·son (hĕr sôn′), *n.* a city in the SW Soviet Union: a port on the Dnieper near the Black Sea. 97,186 (1939).

khid·mut·gar (kĭd′mət gär′), *n.* (in India) a waiter or subordinate butler.

Khi·os (kĭ′ŏs; *Gk.* hē′ŏs), *n.* Greek name of **Chios.**

Khi·va (hē′vä), *n.* a former Asiatic khanate along the Amu Darya river, S of the Aral Sea: now divided between the Uzbek and Turkman republics of the U.S.S.R.

Khmer (kmêr), *n.* **1.** a member of the Cambodian nation, of Mon-Khmer affiliation, which during the Middle Ages produced an important civilization in Indo-China. **2.** a language of Cambodia, of the Mon-Khmer family.

Kho·tan (кнō′tän′), *n.* **1.** an oasis in W China, in SW Sinkiang province. **2.** the chief city in this oasis. 158,200 (est. 1933).

Khu·fu (kōō′fōō), *n.* Cheops.

Khy·ber Pass (kī′bər), the chief mountain pass between India and Afghanistan, W of Peshawar in Pakistan. 33 mi. long; 6825 ft. high. Also, **Khaibar Pass.**

ki·a·boo·ca wood (kī′ə bōō′kə), Padouk wood.

ki·ang (kĭ′ăng′), *n.* onager (def. 1).

Kiang·ling (kyäng′lĭng′; *Chin.* jyäng′-), *n.* a city in central China, in Hupeh province, on the Yangtze. ab. 300,000. Also, **Kingchow.**

Kiang·si (kyäng′sē′; *Chin.* jyäng′sē′), *n.* a province in SE China. 13,761,100 pop. (est. 1944); 66,600 sq. mi. *Cap.:* Nanchang.

Kiang·su (kyäng′sōō′; *Chin.* jyäng′sōō′), *n.* a maritime province in E China. 36,469,300 pop. (est. 1944); 42,056 sq. mi. *Cap.:* Nanking.

Kiao·chow (kyou′chou′; *Chin.* jyou′jō′), *n.* a territory (ab. 200 sq. mi.) in E China, in the Shantung peninsula around **Kiachow Bay,** an inlet of the Yellow Sea: leased to Germany, 1898–1914. Chief city, Tsingtao.

kibe (kīb), *n.* a chapped or ulcerated chilblain, esp. on the heel. [ME; cf. Welsh *cibi*]

Ki·bei (kē′bā′), *n.*, *pl.* **-bei.** a person of Japanese descent, born in the U.S., who goes to Japan for an education. [t. Jap, m. Chinese: returned to America]

kib·itz (kĭb′Υts), *v.i. Colloq.* to act as a kibitzer.

kib·itz·er (kĭb′Υt sər), *n.* **1.** *Colloq.* a spectator at a card game who looks at the players' cards over their shoulders. **2.** a giver of unwanted advice. [t. Yiddish, f. colloq. G *kiebitz* kibitzer (orig. lapwing) + *-er* -ER¹]

kib·lah (kĭb′lä), *n.* **1.** the point (the Kaaba at Mecca) toward which Mohammedans turn at prayer. **2.** the "facing" towards Mecca, wherever orthodox Mohammedans pray. [t. Ar.: m. *qibla*]

ki·bosh (kī′bŏsh, kΥ bŏsh′), *n. Slang.* **1.** nonsense. **2. put the kibosh on,** to render definitely impossible or out of the question.

kick (kĭk), *v.t.* **1.** to give a blow or thrust to with the foot. **2.** to drive, force, make, etc., by or as by kicks. **3.** *Football.* to win (a goal) by a kick. **4.** to strike in recoiling. —*v.i.* **5.** to strike out with the foot. **6.** to have the habit of thus striking out, as a horse. **7.** *Colloq.* to resist, object, or complain. **8.** to recoil, as a firearm when fired. **9. kick off, a.** *Football.* to give the ball the first kick, which starts the play. **b.** *Slang.* to die. —*n.* **10.** act of kicking; a blow or thrust with the foot. **11.** power or disposition to kick. **12.** a recoil, as of a gun. **13.** *Slang.* an objection or complaint. **14.** *Slang.* any thrill or excitement that gives pleasure; any act that gives satisfaction. **15.** *Slang.* a stimulating or intoxicating quality in alcoholic drink. **16.** *Slang.* vigor, energy, or vim. **17.** *Football.* the right of or a turn at kicking the ball. [ME *kike.* Cf. Icel. *kikna* sink at the knees] —**kick′er,** *n.*

Kick·a·poo (kĭk′ə pōō′), *n.* an Algonquian language.

kick·back (kĭk′băk′), *n. Colloq.* **1.** a response, usually vigorous. **2.** the practice of an employer, foreman, or person in a supervisory position of taking back a portion of the wages due to workers.

kick·off (kĭk′ôf′, -ŏf′), n. *Football*. a place kick down the field from the 40-yard line of the side kicking, as at the beginning of the first and third periods.

kick·shaw (kĭk′shô′), n. 1. any fancy dish in cookery. 2. any dainty, unsubstantial, or paltry trifle. [t. F: alter. of *quelque chose* something]

kid[1] (kĭd), n., v., **kidded, kidding.** —n. 1. a young goat. 2. leather made from the skin of a kid or goat, used in making shoes and gloves. 3. (*pl.*) *Colloq.* gloves of this leather. 4. *Slang.* a child or young person. —v.i., v.t. 5. (of a goat) to give birth to (young). [ME, appar. t. Scand.; cf. Icel. *kidh*, Sw. and Dan. *kid*]

kid[2] (kĭd), v., **kidded, kidding,** n. *Slang.* —v.t. 1. to tease; banter; jest with. 2. to humbug or fool. —v.i. 3. to speak or act deceptively, in jest; jest. —n. 4. kidding; humbug; chaffing. [? special use of KID[1] (def. 4)] —**kid′der,** n.

kid[3] (kĭd) n. a tublike wooden vessel in which food is served to sailors. [? var. of KIT[1]]

Kidd (kĭd), n. **William,** ("*Captain Kidd*") c1645–1701, British navigator and privateer, hanged for piracy.

Kid·der·min·ster (kĭd′ər mĭn′stər), n. a kind of ingrain carpet.

kid·nap (kĭd′năp), v.t., **-naped, -naping** or (*esp. Brit.*) **-napped, -napping.** to steal or abduct (a child or other person) against his will by unlawful force or by fraud, often with a demand for ransom. [f. KID[1] (def. 4) + *nap*, v., seize] —**kid′nap·er;** *esp. Brit.,* **kid′nap·per,** n.

kid·ney (kĭd′nĭ), n., pl. **-neys.** 1. (in man) either of a pair of bean-shaped glandular organs, about 4 inches in length, in the back part of the abdominal cavity, which excrete urine. 2. a corresponding organ in other vertebrate animals, or an organ of like function in invertebrates. 3. the meat of an animal's kidney used as a food. 4. constitution or temperament. 5. kind, sort, or class. [ME *kidenei,* f. *kiden-* (orig. and meaning uncert.) + *ey* egg] —**kid′ney·like′,** adj.

kidney bean, 1. the common bean, *Phaseolus vulgaris.* 2. its kidney-shaped seed.

kid·ney-shaped (kĭd′nĭ shāpt′), adj. having the general shape of a long oval indented at one side.

Section of human kidney
A. Suprarenal gland;
B. Cortex; C. Tubular portion. consisting of cones; D. Papilla; E. Pelvis; F. Ureter

kidney vetch, an Old World leguminous herb, *Anthyllis vulneraria,* formerly used as a remedy for kidney diseases.

kidney worm, a nematode worm of the family *Strongylidae, Stephanurus dentatus,* parasitic in the kidneys of pigs.

Ki·dron (kē′drən), n. Kedron.

kief (kēf), n. kef.

Kief·fer (kē′fər), n. *Hort.* a hybrid variety of pear, grown in eastern U.S.

Kiel (kēl), n. a seaport in N Germany at the Baltic end of the **Kiel Canal,** a ship canal (61 mi. long) connecting the North and Baltic Seas. 273,735 (1939).

Kiel·ce (kyĕl′tsĕ), n. a city in S Poland. 49,554 (1946).

kier (kĭr), n. a large boiler or vat used in bleaching, etc. Also, **keir.** [t. Scand.; cf. Icel. *ker* tub]

Kier·ke·gaard (kĭr′kə gôr′), n. **Soren Aabye** (sœ′rən ô′by), 1813–55, Danish religious philosopher.

kie·sel·guhr (kē′zəl goor′), n. diatomaceous earth. [t. G: f. *kiesel* flint + *guhr* earthy deposit]

Ki·ev (kē′ĕf), n. a city in the SW Soviet Union, on the Dnieper. 846,293 (1939).

kil., kilometer; kilometers.

Ki·lau·e·a (kē′lou ä′ä), n. a crater on active Mauna Loa volcano in Hawaii. 2 mi. wide; 4040 ft. high.

Kil·dare (kĭl dâr′), n. a county in E Eire, in Leinster. 64,559 pop. (est. 1943); 654 sq. mi. *Co. seat:* Kildare.

kil·der·kin (kĭl′dər kĭn), n. 1. a unit of capacity, usually equal to half a barrel or two firkins. 2. *Obs.* an English unit of capacity, equal to 18 U.S. gallons. [ME, t. MD: m. (by dissimilation) *kyn(d)erkyn,* var. of *kinnekyn,* f. *kinne* (orig. uncert.) + *-kyn* -KIN]

Kil·i·man·ja·ro (kĭl′ĭ män jä′rō), n. a volcanic mountain in N Tanganyika: highest peak in Africa. 19,321 ft.

Kil·ken·ny (kĭl kĕn′ĭ), n. 1. a county in SE Eire, in Leinster. 68,006 pop. (est. 1943); 796 sq. mi. 2. its county seat. 11,192 pop. (est. 1943).

kill[1] (kĭl), v.t. 1. to deprive (any living creature or thing) of life in any manner; cause the death of; slay. 2. to destroy; do away with; extinguish: *kill hope.* 3. to destroy or neutralize the active qualities of. 4. to spoil the effect of. 5. to get rid of (time) by some method (usually easy) of spending it. 6. to overcome completely or with irresistible effect. 7. to cancel (a word, paragraph, item, etc.). 8. to defeat or veto (a legislative bill, etc.). 9. *Elect.* to render (a circuit) dead. 10. *Lawn Tennis.* to hit (a ball) with such force that its return is impossible. —v.i. 11. to inflict or cause death. 12. to commit murder. —n. 13. act of killing (game, etc.). 14. an animal killed. [ME *cullen, kyllen;* appar. der. OE *-colla* in *morgen-colla* morning slaughter(?)]

—**Syn.** 1. slaughter, massacre, butcher; hang, electrocute, behead, guillotine, strangle, garrote. KILL, EXECUTE, MURDER all mean to deprive of life. KILL is the general word, with no implication of the manner of killing, the

agent or cause or the nature of what is killed (whether human being, animal, or plant): *to kill a person.* EXECUTE is used of (any means of) putting to death in accordance with a legal sentence: *to execute a criminal.* MURDER is used of killing a human being unlawfully, esp. after premeditation: *he murdered him for his money.*

kill[2] (kĭl), n. *U.S. Dial.* a channel; a creek; a stream; a river. [t. D: m. *kil*]

Kil·lar·ney (kĭ lär′nĭ), n. 1. a town in SW Eire. 5790 (est. 1943). 2. **Lakes of,** three beautiful lakes nearby.

kill·deer (kĭl′dĭr′), n. the largest and commonest of the ring plovers of America, *Charadrius vociferus.* Also, **kill·dee** (kĭl′dē′). [imit. of its note]

killdeer plover. See plover (def. 1).

kill·er (kĭl′ər), n. 1. one who or that which kills. 2. any of various ravenous, gregarious cetaceans of the dolphin family, esp. of the genus *Orca* as *O. gladiator,* the common species of the northern Atlantic.

kil·lick (kĭl′ĭk), n. 1. a small anchor or weight for mooring a boat, sometimes consisting of a stone secured by pieces of wood. 2. any anchor. Also, **kil·lock** (kĭl′ək).

Kil·lie·cran·kie (kĭl′ĭ krăng′kĭ), n. a pass in the Grampians in central Scotland: battle, 1689.

kil·li·fish (kĭl′ĭ fĭsh′), n., pl. **-fishes,** (*esp. collectively*) **-fish.** any of various small fishes, esp. of the genus *Fundulus* (family *Cyprinodontidae*), which abound in shallow bays, channels, rivers, etc. of eastern North America and other regions.

kill·ing (kĭl′ĭng), n. 1. act of one who or that which kills. 2. the total game killed on a hunt. 3. *Colloq.* a stroke of extraordinary execution, as in a successful speculation in stocks. —adj. 4. that kills. 5. exhausting: *a killing pace.* 6. *Colloq.* irresistibly funny. —**kill′ing·ly,** adv.

kill-joy (kĭl′joi′), n. a person or thing that spoils the joy or enjoyment of others.

Kil·mar·nock (kĭl mär′nak), n. a city in SW Scotland, 8W of Glasgow. 40,417 (est. 1944).

Kil·mer (kĭl′mər), n. **Joyce,** 1886–1918, U.S. poet.

kiln (kĭl, kĭln), n. 1. a furnace or oven for burning, baking, or drying something, esp. one for calcining limestone or one for baking bricks. —v.t. 2. to burn, bake, or treat in a kiln. [ME *kylne,* OE *cyl(e)n,* ult. t. L: m. *culina* kitchen]

kiln-dry (kĭl′drī′, kĭln′-), v.t., **-dried, -drying.** to dry in a kiln.

kil·o (kĭl′ō, kē′lō), n., pl. **-los.** 1. kilogram. 2. kilometer.

kilo-, a prefix meaning "thousand," used in the nomenclature of the metric system and of other scientific systems of measurement. [t. F, repr. Gk. *chílioi*]

kil·o·am·pere (kĭl′ō ăm′pĭr), n. *Elect.* a unit of current equal to 1000 amperes.

kil·o·cal·o·rie (kĭl′ə kăl′ər ĭ), n. *Physics.* a large calorie. See **calorie** (def. 1b). Also, **kilogram calorie.**

kil·o·cy·cle (kĭl′ə sī′kəl), n. a unit equal to 1000 cycles: used esp. in radio as 1000 cycles per second for expressing the frequency of electromagnetic waves.

kil·o·gram (kĭl′ə grăm′), n. *Metric System.* a unit of mass and weight, equal to 1000 grams, and equivalent to 2.2046 pounds avoirdupois. Also, *esp. Brit.,* **kil′o·gramme′.** [t. F: m. *kilogramme.* See KILO-, -GRAM]

kil·o·gram-me·ter (kĭl′ə grăm′mē′tər), n. *Metric System.* a unit of work, being the work done by one kilogram of force when its point of appreciation moves a distance of one meter in the direction of the force. It is equivalent to about 7.2 foot pounds. Also, *esp. Brit.,* **kil′o·gram′-me′tre.**

kil·o·li·ter (kĭl′ə lē′tər), n. *Metric System.* 1000 liters; a cubic meter. Also, *esp. Brit.,* **kil′o·li′tre.** [t. F: m. *kilolitre.* See KILO-, LITER]

kilom., kilometer.

kil·o·me·ter (kĭl′ə mē′tər; *occas.* kĭ lŏm′ə tər), n. *Metric System.* a unit of length, the common measure of distances equal to 1000 meters, and equivalent to 3280.8 feet or 0.621 mile. Also, *esp. Brit.,* **kil′o·me′tre.** [t. F: m. *kilomètre.* See KILO-, -METER] —**kil·o·met·ric** (kĭl′ə mĕt′rĭk), **kil′o·met′ri·cal,** adj.

kil·o·volt (kĭl′ə vōlt′), n. *Elect.* a unit of electromotive force equal to 1000 volts.

kil·o·watt (kĭl′ə wŏt′), n. *Elect.* a unit of power, equal to 1000 watts. [f. KILO- + WATT]

kil·o·watt-hour (kĭl′ə wŏt′our′), n. *Elect.* a unit of energy equivalent to that transferred or expended in one hour by one kilowatt of power, approx. 1.34 horsepower hour.

Kil·pat·rick (kĭl păt′rĭk), n. **Hugh Judson** (jŭd′sən), 1836–81, Union general in the U.S. Civil War.

kilt (kĭlt), n. 1. any short, plaited skirt, esp. one worn by men in the Scottish highlands. [n. use of *kilt,* v.t.] —v.t. 2. to draw or tuck up (the skirt, etc.) about one. 3. to pleat (cloth, a skirt, etc.) in deep vertical folds. [ME *kylte,* prob. t. Scand.; cf. Dan. *kilte* tuck up] —**kilt′like′,** adj.

kilt·ed (kĭl′tĭd), adj. 1. wearing a kilt. 2. pleated.

kil·ter (kĭl′tər), n. *U.S. Dial.* good condition; order: *the engine was out of kilter.* Also, *Brit. Dial.,* **kelter.**

kilt·ing (kĭl′tĭng), n. an arrangement of flat plaits set close together, each hiding half of the last.

Kim·ber·ley (kĭm′bər lĭ), n. a city in the central part of the Union of South Africa, in Cape of Good Hope province: diamond mines. With suburbs, 55,545 (1946).

ki·mo·no (kə mō′nə, -nō), *n.*, *pl.* **-nos.** **1.** a wide-sleeved robe characteristic of Japanese costume. **2.** a woman's loose dressing gown. [t. Jap.]

kin (kĭn), *n.* **1.** one's relatives collectively, or kinsfolk. **2.** family relationship or kinship. **3.** of kin, of the same family; related; akin. **4.** *Archaic.* a group of persons descended from a common ancestor, or constituting a family, clan, tribe, or race. **5.** *Archaic.* a relative or kinsman. —*adj.* **6.** of kin; related; akin. **7.** of the same kind or nature; having affinity. [ME; OE *cynn*, c. OHG *chunni*, Icel. *kyn*, Goth. *kuni*; from Gmc. root equivalent to L *gen-*, Gk. *gen-*, Skt. *jan-* beget, produce] **—kin′-less,** *adj.*

-kin, a diminutive suffix, attached to nouns to signify a little object of the kind mentioned: *lambkin, catkin.* [ME; akin to D and LG *-ken,* G *-chen*]

kin·aes·the·sia (kĭn′əs thē′zhə), *n.* kinesthesia. Also, **kin′aes·the′sis.**

Kin·car·dine (kĭn kär′dĭn), *n.* a county in E Scotland. 27,700 pop. (est. 1946); 379 sq. mi. *Co. seat:* Stonehaven. Also, **Kin·car·dine·shire** (kĭn kär′dĭn shĭr′, -shər).

Kin·chin·jun·ga (kĭn′chĭn jŏŏn′gä), *n.* Kanchenjunga.

kind[1] (kīnd), *adj.* **1.** of a good or benevolent nature or disposition, as a person. **2.** having, showing, or proceeding from benevolence: *kind words.* **3.** indulgent, considerate, or helpful (often fol. by *to*): *to be kind to animals.* **4.** *Archaic.* affectionate or loving. **5.** adaptable; tractable. [ME *kinde,* OE *gecynde,* der. *gecynd* nature. See KIND[2]] **—Syn. 1.** KIND, GRACIOUS, KINDHEARTED, KINDLY imply a sympathetic attitude toward others, and a willingness to do good or give pleasure. KIND implies a deep-seated characteristic shown either habitually or on occasion by considerate behavior: *a kind father.* GRACIOUS applies to kindness from a superior or older person to a subordinate, an inferior, a child, etc.: *a gracious old lady.* KINDHEARTED implies an emotionally sympathetic nature, sometimes easily imposed upon: *a kindhearted old woman.* KINDLY, a mild word, refers usually to general disposition, appearance, manner, etc.: *a kindly face.* **—Ant. 1.** cruel.

kind[2] (kīnd), *n.* **1.** a class or group of individuals of the same nature or character, esp. a natural group of animals or plants. **2.** nature or character as determining likeness or difference between things: *things differing in degree rather than in kind.* **3.** a person or thing as being of a particular character or class: *he is a strange kind of hero.* **4.** a more or less adequate or inadequate example, or a sort, of something: *the vines formed a kind of roof.* **5. in kind, a.** in something of the same kind in the same way: *to retaliate in kind.* **b.** in the particular kind of thing, or in goods or natural produce, instead of money. **6. kind of** (used adverbially), *Colloq.* after a fashion; to some extent; somewhat; rather: *the room was kind of dark.* **7.** *Archaic.* the nature, or natural disposition or character: *after one's kind.* **8.** *Obs.* gender; sex. [ME *kinde,* OE *gecynd.* See KIN]

kin·der·gar·ten (kĭn′dər gär′tən), *n.* a school for furthering the mental, moral, and physical development of young children by means of games, occupations, etc., that make use of their natural tendency to express themselves in action. [t. G: children's garden]

kin·der·gart·ner (kĭn′dər gärt′nər), *n.* **1.** a child who attends a kindergarten. **2.** a kindergarten teacher. Also, **kin′der·gar′ten·er.**

kind·heart·ed (kīnd′här′tĭd), *adj.* having or showing a kind heart; kindly. **—kind′heart′ed·ly,** *adv.* **—kind′heart′ed·ness,** *n.* **—Syn.** See KIND[1].

kin·dle (kĭn′dəl), *v.,* **-dled, -dling.** —*v.t.* **1.** to set (a fire, flame, etc.) to burning or blazing. **2.** to set fire to, or ignite (fuel or any combustible matter). **3.** to excite; stir up or set going; to animate, rouse, or inflame. **4.** to light up, illuminate, or make bright. —*v.i.* **5.** to begin to burn, as combustible matter, a light, or a fire or flame. **6.** to become roused, ardent, or inflamed. **7.** to become lighted up, bright, or glowing, as the sky at dawn or the eyes with ardor. [ME *kindlen,* prob. t. Icel.: cf. Icel. *kynda* kindle, *kyndill* candle, torch] **—kin′dler,** *n.* **—Syn. 1-3.** KINDLE, IGNITE, INFLAME imply setting something on fire. To KINDLE is especially to cause something gradually to begin burning; it is often used figuratively: *to kindle someone's interest.* To IGNITE is to set something on fire with a sudden burst of flame: *to ignite dangerous hatreds.* INFLAME, a literary word meaning to set aflame, is now found chiefly in figurative uses, as referring to unnaturally hot, sore, or swollen conditions in the body, or to exciting the mind by strong emotion: *the wound was greatly inflamed.* **—Ant. 1.** quench, smother, extinguish.

kind·li·ness (kīnd′lĭ nĭs), *n.* **1.** state or quality of being kindly; benevolence. **2.** a kindly deed.

kin·dling (kĭn′dlĭng), *n.* **1.** material for starting a fire. **2.** act of one who kindles.

kind·ly (kīnd′lĭ), *adj.,* **-lier, -liest,** *adv.* —*adj.* **1.** having, showing, or proceeding from a benevolent disposition or spirit; kindhearted; good-natured; sympathetic: *kindly people.* **2.** gentle or mild, as rule or laws. **3.** pleasant, genial, or benign. **4.** favorable, as soil for crops. [ME *kyndly,* OE *gecyndelīc,* f. *gecynde* KIND[1] + -*līc* -LY] —*adv.* **5.** in a kindly or kind manner; with sympathetic or helpful kindness. **6.** cordially or heartily: *we thank you kindly.* **7.** with pleasure or liking; favorably: *to take kindly to an idea.* [ME; OE *gecyndelīce.* See -LY] **—Syn. 1.** See kind[1].

kind·ness (kīnd′nĭs), *n.* **1.** state or quality of being kind. **2.** a kind act: *his many kindnesses to me.* **3.** kind behavior: *I will never forget your kindness.* **4.** friendly feeling, or liking. **—Syn. 1, 3.** benignity, benevolence. **2.** service, favor.

kin·dred (kĭn′drĭd), *n.* **1.** a body of persons related to another, or a family, tribe, or race. **2.** one's relatives collectively; kinsfolk, or kin. **3.** relationship by birth or descent, or sometimes by marriage; kinship. **4.** natural relationship, or affinity. —*adj.* **5.** associated by origin, nature, qualities, etc.: *kindred languages.* **6.** related by birth or descent, or having kinship: *kindred tribes.* **7.** belonging to kin or relatives: *kindred blood.* [ME *kinrede(n).* See KIN, -RED]

kine (kīn), *n.pl.* *Archaic.* pl. of **cow.**

kin·e·mat·ics (kĭn′ə măt′ĭks), *n.* **1.** that branch of mechanics which treats of pure motion, without reference to mass or cause. **2.** the theory of mechanical contrivance for converting one kind of motion into another; applied kinematics. [f. s. Gk. *kī́nēma* motion + -ICS] **—kin·e·mat′ic, kin·e·mat′i·cal,** *adj.*

kin·e·mat·o·graph (kĭn′ə măt′ə gräf′, -gräf′), *n.,* *v.t.,* *v.i.* cinematograph.

kin·e·scope (kĭn′ə skōp′), *n.* *Television.* **1.** a cathode-ray tube with a screen on which the image is reproduced. **2.** (*cap.*) a trademark for this tube.

kin·es·the·sia (kĭn′əs thē′zhə), *n.* the sensation of movement or strain in muscles, tendons, joints. Also, **kinaesthesia, kin·es·the·sis** (kĭn′əs thē′sĭs). [NL, f. Gk.: s. *kī́nein* move + -*aisthēsia* perception] **—kin·es·thet·ic** (kĭn′əs thĕt′ĭk), *adj.*

ki·net·ic (kĭ nĕt′ĭk, kī-), *adj.* **1.** pertaining to motion. **2.** caused by motion. [t. Gk.: m.s. *kīnētikós*]

ki·net·ics (kĭ nĕt′ĭks, kī-), *n.* the branch of mechanics which treats of the action of forces in producing or changing the motion of masses.

kinetic theory of gases, a theory that the particles in a gas move freely and rapidly along straight lines but often collide, resulting in variations in their velocity and direction. Pressure is thus interpreted as the force due to the impacts of these particles, and other macroscopic variables are similarly treated.

kinetic theory of heat, a theory that a body's temperature is determined by the average kinetic energy of its particles and that an inflow of heat increases this energy.

kinetic theory of matter, the theory that matter is composed of small particles, all in random motion.

kin·folks (kĭn′fōks′), *n.pl.* *Colloq.* kinsfolk. Also, **kin′folk′.**

king (kĭng), *n.* **1.** a male sovereign or monarch; a man who holds by life tenure (and usually by hereditary right) the chief authority over a country and people. **2.** (*cap.*) God or Christ: *King of Kings, King of heaven.* **3.** a person or thing preëminent in its class: *the lion is the king of beasts, an oil king.* **4.** a playing card bearing a picture of a king. **5.** the chief piece in a game of chess, moving one square at a time in any direction. **6.** a piece that has moved entirely across the board in the game of checkers or draughts and has been crowned. [ME; OE *cyng, cynig, cyning,* c. D *koning,* G *könig,* Icel. *konungr,* Sw. *konung,* Dan. *konge*] **—king′less,** *adj.*

King (kĭng), *n.* **1.** Rufus (rōō′fəs), 1755–1827, American statesman. **2.** William Lyon Mackenzie (mə-kĕn′zĭ), 1874–1950, Canadian statesman; prime minister, 1921–1926, 1926–1930, and 1935–1948.

king·bird (kĭng′bûrd′), *n.* any of various flycatchers of the New World family *Tyrannidae,* esp. *Tyrannus tyrannus,* a pugnacious bird of the eastern U.S.

king·bolt (kĭng′bōlt′), *n.* a vertical bolt connecting the body of a horse-drawn vehicle with the fore axle, the body of a railroad car with a truck, etc.

King Charles spaniel, a small black and tan toy spaniel with a rounded head, short muzzle, full eyes, and well-fringed ears and feet.

King·chow (jĭng′jō′), *n.* Kiangling.

king cobra, a large cobra, *Naja hannah,* of southeastern Asia.

king crab, a horseshoe crab.

king·craft (kĭng′kräft′, -kräft′), *n.* the art of ruling as king; royal statesmanship.

king·cup (kĭng′kŭp′), *n.* **1.** any of various common buttercups, as *Ranunculus bulbosus.* **2.** *Chiefly Brit.* the marsh marigold.

king·dom (kĭng′dəm), *n.* **1.** a state or government having a king or queen as its head. **2.** anything conceived as constituting a realm or sphere of independent action or control: *the kingdom of thought.* **3.** a realm or province of nature, esp., one of the three great divisions of natural objects: *the animal, vegetable, and mineral kingdoms.* **4.** the spiritual sovereignty of God or Christ. **5.** the domain over which this extends, whether in heaven or on earth. [ME; OE *cyningdōm*] **—Syn. 1.** KINGDOM, MONARCHY, REALM refer to the state or domain ruled by a king or queen. A KINGDOM is a governmental unit ruled by a king or queen: *the kingdom of Norway.* A MONARCHY is primarily a form of government in which a single person is sovereign; it is also the type of powers exercised by the monarch: *this kingdom is not an absolute monarchy.* A REALM is the domain (including the subjects) over which the king has jurisdiction; fig., a sphere of power or influence: *the laws of the realm.*

king·fish (kĭng′fĭsh′), *n.,* *pl.* **-fishes,** (*esp. collectively*) **-fish. 1.** any of various fishes conspicuous for size or some other quality. **2.** a marine food fish. *Menticirrus*

---

b., blend of, blended; c., cognate with; d., dialect, dialectal; der., derived from; f., formed from; g., going back to; m., modification of; r., replacing; s., stem of: t.. taken from; ?, perhaps. See the full key on inside cover.

nebulosus, of the drumfish family, much esteemed for food in the northeastern U.S. **3.** a marine food fish, *Genyonemus lineatus*, of the California coast. **4.** the opah. **5.** the Spanish mackerel.

king·fish·er (kǐng′fǐsh′ər), *n.* any of numerous fish- or insect-eating birds of the almost cosmopolitan family *Alcedinidae*, all of which are stout-billed and small-footed, and many of which are crested or brilliantly colored. Those which eat fish capture them by diving.

king·hood (kǐng′hŏŏd), *n.* kingship.

King James Version. See **Authorized Version.**

King·lake (kǐng′lāk′), *n.* **Alexander William**, 1809–1891, British historian and traveler.

King Lear (lǐr), a tragedy (written 1605) by Shakespeare.

king·let (kǐng′lǐt), *n.* **1.** a king ruling over a small country or territory. **2.** any of the diminutive greenish birds constituting the genus *Regulus*, esp. the **ruby-crowned kinglet** (*R. calendula*) of America, the **fire-crest** (*R. ignicapillus*) of Europe, and the **goldcrest** or **golden-covered kinglet** (*R. regulus*) of both Europe and North America.

king·ly (kǐng′lǐ), *adj.,* **-lier, -liest,** *adv.* —*adj.* **1.** being a king. **2.** consisting of kings or of royal rank. **3.** resembling, suggesting, or befitting a king; kinglike: *he strode into the room with a kingly air.* **4.** pertaining or proper to a king or kings. —*adv.* **5.** in a kingly manner. —**king′li·ness,** *n.*
—**Syn. 3, 4.** princely, sovereign, majestic, august, magnificent, exalted, grand. KINGLY, REGAL, ROYAL refer to that which is closely associated with a king, or is suitable for one. What is KINGLY may either belong to a king, or be befitting, worthy of, or like a king: *a kingly presence, appearance, graciousness.* REGAL is especially applied to the office of kingship or the outward manifestations of grandeur and majesty: *regal authority, bearing, splendor, munificence.* ROYAL is applied especially to what pertains to or is associated with the person of a monarch: *the royal family, word, robes, salute; a royal residence.*

king·pin (kǐng′pǐn′), *n.* **1.** (in bowling games) **a.** the pin in the center when the pins are in place. **b.** the pin at the front apex. **2.** *Colloq.* the principal person in a company, etc. **3.** *Colloq.* the chief element of any system or the like. **4.** kingbolt.

king post, a vertical post between the apex of a triangular roof truss and the tie beam.

Kings (kǐngz), *n.pl.* certain books of the Bible which contain the history of the reigns of the kings of Israel and Judah (usually the 11th and 12th books of the Old Testament, called I Kings and II Kings).

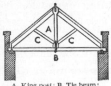
A, King post; B, Tie beam; C, Strut or brace

king salmon, chinook salmon.

King's Bench, *Brit. Law.* (formerly) the most important trial court, having primary jurisdiction in criminal matters affecting the king's peace and an acquired civil jurisdiction concurrent with the Court of Common Pleas, with appellate jurisdiction over the Court of Common Pleas. Also, **Queen's Bench.**

king's English, correct English usage.

king's evidence, *Brit. Law.* state's evidence. Also, **queen's evidence.**

king's evil, scrofula: orig. so called because it was supposed to be curable by the touch of the sovereign.

king·ship (kǐng′shǐp), *n.* **1.** kingly state, office, or dignity. **2.** kingly rule. **3.** aptitude for kingly duties. **4.** a title used in referring to a king (prec. by *his, your,* etc.).

king-size (kǐng′sīz′), *adj. Colloq.* larger than the usual size. Also, **king′-sized′.**

Kings·ley (kǐngz′lǐ), *n.* **1. Charles,** 1819–75, British clergyman, novelist, and poet. **2. Sidney,** born 1906, U.S. dramatist.

Kings Mountain (kǐngz), a ridge in N South Carolina: American victory over the British, 1780.

king snake, any of certain large harmless American snakes, esp. *Lampropeltis getulus*, which feeds on other snakes, including rattlesnakes.

King's speech, (in the English parliament) a speech reviewing domestic conditions and foreign relations, prepared by the ministry in the name of the sovereign, and read at the opening of the Parliament either by the sovereign in person or by commission.

Kings·ton (kǐngz′tən, kǐng′stən), *n.* **1.** a seaport in and the capital of Jamaica. 109,000 (1943). **2.** a city in SE Canada: a port at the E end of Lake Ontario. 30,126 (1941). **3.** a city in SE New York, on the Hudson. 28,817 (1950). **4.** a borough in E Pennsylvania, on the Susquehanna river opposite Wilkes-Barre. 21,096 (1950).

Kings·ton-up·on-Hull (kǐngz′tən ə pŏn′hŭl′), *n.* official name of Hull (def. 3).

King·teh·chen (jǐng′dŭ′jěn′), *n.* a city in E China, in Kiangsi province: fine porcelain. ab. 500,000.

king truss, a truss framed with a king post.

king·wood (kǐng′wŏŏd′), *n.* **1.** a Brazilian wood streaked with violet tints, used esp. in cabinet work. **2.** the tree, *Dalbergia cearensis*, which yields it.

kink (kǐngk), *n.* **1.** a twist or curl, as in a thread, rope, or hair, caused by its doubling or bending upon itself. **2.** a crick, as in the neck or back. **3.** a mental twist, an odd notion, or a whim or crotchet. —*v.i., v.t.* **4.** to form

or cause to form a kink or kinks, as a rope. [orig. nautical term, prob. t. D: twist, twirl. Cf. Icel. *kinka* nod archly]

kin·ka·jou (kǐng′kə jōō′), *n.* a pale-brown, soft-furred, arboreal, prehensile-tailed mammal, *Potos flavus*, of Central and South America, related to the raccoon. [t. Canadian F; orig. the same word as CARCAJOU]

kink·y (kǐngk′ǐ), *adj.,* **kinki-er, kinkiest.** full of kinks. —**kink′i·ness,** *n.*

Kinkajou, *Potos flavus* (Total length 33 in.; tail 17 in.)

ki·no gum (kē′nō), the reddish or black catechulike inspissated juice or gum of certain tropical trees, esp. that obtained from *Pterocarpus marsupium*, a tall fabaceous tree of India and Ceylon; used in medicine, tanning, etc. [appar. t. W Afr. (Gambia)]

Kin·ross (kǐn rôs′, -rŏs′), *n.* a county in E Scotland. 7600 pop. (est. 1946); 82 sq. mi. *Co. seat:* Kinross. Also, **Kin·ross·shire** (kǐn rôs′shǐr, -shər, -rŏs′-).

Kin·sey (kǐn′zǐ) *n.* **Alfred Charles,** born 1894, U.S. zoölogist: director of a survey of human sex behavior.

kins·folk (kǐnz′fōk′), *n.pl.* relatives or kindred. Also, *Colloq.,* **kinfolks, kinfolk.**

kin·ship (kǐn′shǐp), *n.* **1.** state or fact of being of kin; family relationship. **2.** relationship by nature, qualities, etc.; affinity. —**Syn. 1.** See **relationship.**

kins·man (kǐnz′mən), *n., pl.* **-men. 1.** a male blood relative. **2.** (sometimes) a relative by marriage. **3.** a person of the same race. —**kins′wom′an,** *n. fem.*

ki·osk (kǐ ŏsk′, kǐ′ŏsk), *n.* **1.** a kind of open pavilion or summerhouse common in Turkey and Iran. **2.** a similar structure used as a bandstand, as a newsstand, etc. [t. Turk.: m. *kiûshk* pavilion]

Kio·to (kyô′tô′), *n.* Kyoto.

Ki·o·wa (kī′ə wə), *n.* a linguistic stock of western Kansas and eastern Colorado, related to Uto-Aztecan.

kip[1] (kǐp), *n.* **1.** the hide of a young or small beast. **2.** a bundle or set of such hides, containing a definite number. [orig. unknown]

kip[2] (kǐp), *n.* a thousand pounds.

Kip·ling (kǐp′lǐng), *n.* **Rudyard** (rŭd′yərd), 1865–1936, British writer and poet.

kip·per (kǐp′ər), *n.* **1.** a kippered fish, esp. a herring. **2.** a method of curing fish by splitting, salting, drying, and smoking. —*v.t.* **3.** to cure (herring, salmon, etc.) by cleaning, salting, etc., and drying in the air or in smoke. [? special use of *kipper*, OE *cypera* spawning salmon]

Kirch·hoff (kǐrkh′hôf), *n.* **Gustav Robert** (gŏŏs′täf rō′běrt), 1824–87, German physicist.

Kir·ghiz (kǐr gēz′), *n., pl.* **-ghiz, -ghizes. 1.** a member of a widespread people of Mongolian physical type and Turkic speech, dwelling chiefly in west central Asia. **2.** their language.

Kirghiz Soviet Socialist Republic, a constituent republic of the Soviet Union, in the Asiatic part adjoining Sinkiang province, China. 1,459,301 (1939); ab. 77,800 sq. mi. *Cap.:* Frunze.

Kirghiz Steppe, a vast steppe in the SW Soviet Union in Asia, in Kazak Republic. Also, **The Steppes.**

Ki·rin (kē′rǐn′), *n.* **1.** a province in NE China, in Manchuria. 6,416,600 pop. (1946); ab. 33,700 sq. mi. **2.** the capital of this province: a port on the Sungari river. 225,153 (est. 1941).

kirk (kûrk), *n.* **1.** *Scot. and N. Eng.* a church. **2.** the **Kirk,** *Eng.* the Established Church of Scotland, as distinguished from that of England and from the Scottish Episcopal Church. [t. Scand.; cf. Icel. *kirkja*, c. CHURCH]

Kirk·cud·bright (kǐr kōō′brǐ), *n.* a county in SW Scotland. 29,700 pop. (est. 1946); 896 sq. mi. *Co. seat:* Kircudbright. Also, **Kirk·cud·bright·shire** (kər kōō′-brǐ′shǐr′, -shər).

kirk·man (kûrk′mən), *n., pl.* **-men. 1.** *Scot. and N. Eng.* a member or follower of the Kirk. **2.** *Scot.* a churchman.

Kir·man (kǐr män′), *n.* a Persian rug marked by ornate flowing designs and light, muted colors. [var. of *Kerman*, name of a town and province in Iran]

kir·mess (kûr′mǐs), *n.* kermis.

Ki·rov (kē′rôf), *n.* a city in the E Soviet Union in Europe. 143,181 (1939). Formerly, **Vyatka.**

Ki·ro·va·bad (kē′rō vä bät′), *n.* a city in the SW Soviet Union, in Azerbaijan Republic. 98,743 (1939). Formerly, **Elisavetpol** or **Gandzha.**

Ki·ro·vo·grad (kē′rō vō grät′), *n.* a city in the SW Soviet Union, in the Ukrainian Republic. 100,331 (1939). Formerly, **Elisavetgrad** or **Zinovievsk.**

kirsch·was·ser (kǐrsh′väs′ər), *n.* a colorless brandy distilled in Germany, Alsace, and Switzerland from wild black cherries. Also, **kirsch.** [t. G: cherry water]

Ki·shi·nev (kǐ shǐ nyôf′), *n.* a city in the SW Soviet Union: capital of the Moldavian Republic. 52,950 (est. 1943). Rumanian, **Chisinău.**

kir·tle (kûr′təl), *n.* **1.** a woman's gown or skirt. **2.** *Archaic or Dial.* a man's tunic or coat. [ME *kurtel*, OE *cyrtel*, c. Icel. *kyrtill* tunic, ult. der. L *curtus* cut short] —**kir′tled,** *adj.*

Kis·lev (kǐs′lěf), *n.* (in the Jewish calendar) the third month of the year. [t. Heb.]

kis·met (kǐz′mět, kǐs′-), *n.* fate; destiny. [t. Turk., t. Pers.: m. *qismat*, t. Ar., der. *qasama* divide]

kiss (kĭs), *v.t.* **1.** to touch or press with the lips, while compressing and then separating them, in token of greeting, affection, etc. **2.** to touch gently or lightly. **3.** to put, bring, take, etc., by, or as if by, kissing. —*v.i.* **4.** to kiss someone, something, or each other. —*n.* **5.** act of kissing. **6.** a slight touch or contact. **7.** a baked confection of egg whites and confectioner's sugar, served as a cooky. **8.** a piece of toffeelike confectionery, sometimes containing nuts, coconut, or the like. [ME *kyss*(*n*), OE *cyssan* (c. G *küssen*), der. *coss* a kiss, c. G *kuss*] —**kiss′a·ble,** *adj.* – **kiss′er,** *n.*

kissing bug, any of certain assassin bugs which have been known to pierce a person's lip.

Kist·na (kĭst′nə), *n.* a river in S India, flowing from the Western Ghats E to the Bay of Bengal. ab. 800 mi.

kit[1] (kĭt), *n.* **1.** a set or collection of tools, supplies, etc., for a special purpose. **2.** the case containing these, or this with its contents. **3.** *Colloq.* a set, lot, or collection of things or persons. **4.** a wooden tub, pail, etc., usually circular. [ME *kyt, kitt,* appar. t. MD: m. *kitte* kind of tub. Cf. Norw. *kitte* bin]

kit[2] (kĭt), *n.* a kind of small violin, used by the dancing masters from the 16th to the 18th century. [orig. uncert.]

kit[3] (kĭt), *n.* shortened form of *kitten.*

kitch·en (kĭch′ən), *n.* **1.** a room or place equipped for or appropriated to cooking. **2.** the culinary department; cuisine. [ME *kitchene,* OE *cycene,* ult. t. L: m. *coquina*]

kitchen cabinet, *U.S. Colloq.* a group of unofficial advisers to a president or governor.

kitch·en·er (kĭch′ən ər), *n.* **1.** one employed in, or in charge of, a kitchen. **2.** an elaborate kitchen stove.

Kitch·en·er (kĭch′ən ər), *n.* a city in SE Canada, in S Ontario. 35,657 (1941).

Kitchener of Khartoum, Horatio Herbert Kitchener, 1st Earl, 1850–1916, British field marshal.

kitch·en·ette (kĭch′ə nĕt′), *n.* a small kitchen.

kitchen garden, a garden in which vegetables and fruit for the table are grown. —**kitchen gardener.**

kitchen midden, *Anthropol.* a mound consisting of shells of edible mollusks and other refuse, marking the site of a prehistoric human habitation. [t. Dan.: m. *køkkenmødding*]

kitchen police, *Mil.* **1.** duty as assistant to the cooks. *Abbr.*: K.P. **2.** soldiers on kitchen duty.

kitch·en·ware (kĭch′ən wâr′), *n.* cooking equipment or utensils.

kite (kīt), *n., v.,* **kited, kiting.** —*n.* **1.** a light frame covered with some thin material, to be flown in the wind at the end of a long string. **2.** any of various falconiform birds of the genera *Milvus, Elanus, Elanoides,* etc., with long, pointed wings, which prey on small quarry, as *Elanus leucurus,* the **white-tailed kite** of North and South America. **3.** a person who preys on others; a sharper. **4.** *Naut.* any light sail that is usually spread in light winds, and furled in a strong breeze. **5.** *Com.* a fictitious negotiable instrument, not representing any actual transaction, used for raising money or sustaining credit. —*v.i.* **6.** *Colloq.* to fly or move with a rapid or easy motion like that of a kite. **7.** *Com.* to obtain money or credit through kites. —*v.t.* **8.** *Com.* to employ as a kite. [ME *kyte,* OE *cȳta;* akin to G *kauz* kind of owl]

kith (kĭth), *n.* one's acquaintances or friends (now chiefly Scot. and N Eng. except in *kith and kin* and often confused in meaning with *kin*). [ME *kitthe,* OE *cȳth, cȳththu* knowledge, acquaintance, native land, der. *cūth* known, pp. of *cunnan* CAN[1]]

kith and kin, acquaintances and kindred, or friends and relatives.

kith·a·ra (kĭth′ə rə), *n.* a musical instrument of ancient Greece; cithara. [t. Gk.]

kit·ten (kĭt′ən), *n.* **1.** a young cat. —*v.t., v.i.* **2.** to bring forth (kittens). [ME *kitoun, kyton,* t. d. OF; cf. OF *chitoun, chaton,* dim. of *chat* cat] —**kit′ten·like′,** *adj.*

kit·ten·ish (kĭt′ən ĭsh), *adj.* kittenlike; artlessly playful. —**kit′ten·ish·ly,** *adv.* —**kit′ten·ish·ness,** *n.*

kit·ti·wake (kĭt′ĭ wāk′), *n.* either of two gulls of the genus *Rissa,* having the hind toe very short or rudimentary. [imit. of its cry]

Kit·tredge (kĭt′rĭj), *n.* George Lyman (lī′mən), 1860–1941, U.S. philologist and educator.

kit·ty[1] (kĭt′ĭ), *n., pl.* **-ties. 1.** a kitten. **2.** a pet name for a cat. [f. KIT[3] + -Y[2]]

kit·ty[2] (kĭt′ĭ), *n., pl.* **-ties. 1.** a pool into which each player in a card game puts a certain amount of his winnings, for some special purpose, as to pay for refreshments, etc. **2.** any similar pool. **3.** the cards left over after a deal which may be used by the highest bidder. [appar. familiar der. of *kitcot,* phonetic var. of *kidcot* prison, f. KID[1] (in sense of slave or criminal) + COT[2]]

Kit·ty·hawk (kĭt′ĭ hôk′), *n.* a village in NE North Carolina: Wright brothers' airplane flight, 1903.

Kiung·chow (kyŏŏng′chō′, -chou′; *Chin.* jyŏŏng′jō′), *n.* a seaport in S China, on Hainan island. ab. 59,000. Also, **Kiungshan** (kyŏŏng′shän′; *Chin.* jyŏŏng′-).

Kiu·shu (kū′shŏŏ′), *n.* Kyushu.

ki·va (kē′və), *n.* a large chamber, often wholly or partly underground, in a Pueblo Indian village, used for religious ceremonies and other purposes. [t. N Amer. Ind. (Hopi)]

Ki·wa·nis (kĭ wä′nĭs), *n.* an organization, founded in 1915, comprising many clubs throughout the U.S. and Canada, aiming to provide leadership for the realization of higher ideals in business, industrial, and professional life. [coined word] —**Ki·wa·ni·an** (kĭ wä′nĭ ən), *n., adj.*

ki·wi (kē′wĭ), *n., pl.* **-wis** (-wĭz). **1.** an apteryx (flightless ratite bird of New Zealand). **2.** *Colloq.* a man in an aviation service who does not make flights. **3.** *Australian Colloq.* a New Zealander. [t. Maori]

Kiz·il Ir·mak (kĭz′ĭl ĭr mäk′), a river flowing through central Turkey N to the Black Sea. ab. 600 mi.

Kjö·len (chœ′lən), *n.* a mountain range between Norway and Sweden. Highest peak, Mt. Kebnekaise, 7005 ft.

K.K.K., Ku Klux Klan. Also, **KKK.**

K Kt, *Chess.* king's knight.

kl., kiloliter.

Kla·gen·furt (klä′gən fŏŏrt′), *n.* a city in S Austria. 56,701 (1939).

Klai·pe·da (klī′pĕ dä′), *n.* Lithuanian name of **Memel.**

Klam·ath (klăm′əth), *n.* a river flowing from SW Oregon through NW California into the Pacific. ab. 250 mi.

Klamath Falls, a city in SW Oregon. 15,875 (1950).

Klamath Lakes, two lakes draining into the Klamath river: **Upper Klamath Lake** in SW Oregon, **Lower Klamath Lake** in N California.

Klan (klăn), *n.* Ku Klux Klan.

Klans·man (klănz′mən), *n., pl.* **-men.** a member of the Ku Klux Klan.

Klau·sen·burg (klou′zən bŏŏrkн′), *n.* German name of Cluj.

Klebs-Löf·fler bacillus (klāps′lœf′lər), the bacillus *Corynebacterium diphtheriae,* which causes diphtheria.

Kleen·ex (klē′nĕks), *n.* **1.** a soft clothlike tissue, used esp. as a handkerchief. **2.** a trademark for this tissue.

Klein (klīn), *n.* Felix (fē′lĭks; *Ger.* fā′-), 1849–1925, German mathematician.

klepht (klĕft), *n.* a Greek or Albanian brigand, exalted in the war of Greek independence as a patriotic robber; guerilla. [t. mod. Gk.: s. *kléphtēs,* Gk. *kléptēs* thief]

klep·to·ma·ni·a (klĕp′tə mā′nĭ ə), *n.* an irresistible desire to steal, without regard to personal needs. Also, **cleptomania.** [t. NL, f. Gk.: m.s. *kléptēs* thief + *-mania* -MANIA]

klep·to·ma·ni·ac (klĕp′tə mā′nĭ ăk′), *n.* one affected with kleptomania. Also, **cleptomaniac.**

klieg eyes (klēg), inflammation and edema of the eyes as a result of prolonged exposure to arc lights, as the klieg lights of the motion picture industry.

klieg light, a floodlight with an arc-light source used in motion-picture studios to project a beam of high actinic power. [named after *Kliegl* brothers, the inventors]

Kling·sor (klĭng′zōr), *n.* an enchanter in Wagner's opera *Parsifal.*

klip·spring·er (klĭp′sprĭng′ər), *n.* a small, active African antelope, *Oreotragus oreotragus,* of mountainous regions from the Cape of Good Hope to Ethiopia. [t. S Afr. D: cliff springer]

Klon·dike (klŏn′dīk), *n.* **1.** a region of the Yukon territory in NW Canada: gold rush, 1897–98. **2.** a river in this region, flowing into the Yukon. **3.** (*l.c.*) a card game of solitaire.

Klop·stock (klŏp′shtok), *n.* Friedrich Gottlieb (frē′drĭкн gōt′lēp), 1724–1803, German poet.

Kluck (klŏŏk), *n.* Alexander H. R. von (ä′lĕ ksän′-dər fən), 1846–1934, German general.

klys·tron (klī′stron), *n.* **1.** a vacuum tube containing an electron gun, a **buncher resonator** which changes the velocity of the electron beam in accordance with a signal, a **drift tube** in which the electron velocity does not change, a **catcher resonator** which abstracts energy from the electron beam, and a **collector electrode** for the electrons. It has several ultra high frequency applications. **2.** (*cap.*) a trademark for this tube. Cf. **resonator** (def. 4). [appar. from Gk. *klystēr* syringe]

km., **1.** kilometer; kilometers. **2.** kingdom.

km/sec, kilometers per second.

kn., kronen.

knack (năk), *n.* **1.** a faculty or power of doing something with ease as from mere skill; aptitude. **2.** a habit or practice. [ME *knak;* ? akin to *knack,* v., strike (imit.)] —**Syn. 1.** aptness; facility; dexterity, adroitness, expertness. —**Ant. 1.** ineptitude.

knag·gy (năg′ĭ), *adj.* knotty; rough with knots. [f. *knag* (ME, m. G *knagge* knot, peg) + -Y[1]]

knap·sack (năp′săk′), *n.* a leather or canvas case for clothes and the like, carried on the back, esp. by soldiers. [t. LG: f. s. *knappen* bite, eat + *sack* SACK[1]]

knap·weed (năp′wēd′), *n.* a plant of the composite genus *Centaurea,* esp. *C. nigra,* a perennial weed with rose-purple flowers set on a dark-colored knoblike involucre. [ME *knopweed.* See KNOP, WEED[1]]

knar (när), *n.* a knot on a tree or in wood. [ME *knarre,* c. D *knar*] —**knarred,** *adj.*

knave (nāv), *n.* **1.** an unprincipled or dishonest fellow. **2.** *Cards.* a jack. **3.** *Archaic.* a male servant or man of humble position. [ME; OE *cnafa,* c. G *knabe* boy] —**Syn. 1.** KNAVE, RASCAL, ROGUE, SCOUNDREL are disparaging terms applied to persons considered base, dishonest, or worthless. KNAVE, formerly merely a boy or servant, in modern use emphasizes baseness of nature and intention: *a dishonest and swindling knave.* RASCAL suggests shrewdness and trickery in dishonesty: *a plausible rascal.* A ROGUE is a worthless fellow who sometimes preys extensively upon the community by fraud: *photographs of criminals in a rogues' gallery.* A SCOUNDREL is a blackguard and rogue of the worst sort: *a thorough scoundrel.* RASCAL and ROGUE are often used humorously (*an entertaining rascal, a saucy rogue*) but KNAVE and SCOUNDREL are not.

knav·er·y (nā'vər ǐ), *n., pl.* **-er·ies. 1.** action or practice characteristic of a knave. **2.** unprincipled or dishonest dealing; trickery. **3.** a knavish act or practice.

knav·ish (nā'vǐsh), *adj.* **1.** like or befitting a knave; dishonest. **2.** waggish; mischievous. **—knav'ish·ly,** *adv.* **—knav'ish·ness,** *n.*

knead (nēd), *v.t.* **1.** to work (dough, etc.) into a uniform mixture by pressing, folding and stretching. **2.** to manipulate by similar movements, as the body in massage. **3.** to make by kneading. [ME *kneden,* OE *cnedan,* c. G *kneten*] **—knead'er,** *n.*

knee (nē), *n., v.,* **kneed, knee·ing. —n. 1.** the joint or region in man between the thigh and the lower part of the leg. **2.** the joint or region of other vertebrates corresponding or homologous to the human knee, as in the leg of a bird, the hind limb of a horse, etc. **3.** a joint or region likened to this but not homologous with it, as the tarsal joint of a bird, or the carpal joint in the fore limb of the horse, cow, etc. **4.** the part of a garment covering the knee. **5.** something resembling a knee joint, esp. when bent, as a fabricated support or brace with a leg running at an angle to the main member. **—v.t. 6.** to strike or touch with the knee. **—v.i. 7.** *Obs.* or *Poetic.* to go down on the knees; kneel. [ME *know(e), kne(w),* OE *cnēo(w),* c. D and G *knie.* Cf. KNEEL]

knee action, *Auto.* a method of suspending the front wheels of a motor vehicle to the chassis by individual spindle and coil-spring mountings for each wheel.

knee breeches, breeches reaching to or just below the knee.

knee·cap (nē'kǎp'), *n.* **1.** the patella, the flat, movable bone at the front of the knee. **2.** a protective covering, usually knitted, for the knee.

knee-deep (nē'dēp'), *adj.* **1.** so deep as to reach the knees: *the snow lay knee-deep.* **2.** submerged or covered by something having such depth.

knee-high (nē'hī'), *adj.* as high as the knees.

knee jerk, a brisk reflex lifting of the leg induced by tapping the tendon below the kneecap; patellar reflex.

kneel (nēl), *v.,* **knelt** or **kneeled, kneel·ing,** *n.* **—v.i. 1.** to fall or rest on the knees or a knee, as in supplication or homage. **—n. 2.** the action or position of kneeling. [ME *knele(n), knewlen,* OE *cnēowlian* (c. D *knielen,* LG *knelen*), der. *cnēow* KNEE] **—kneel'er,** *n.*

knee·pad (nē'pǎd'), *n.* a pad to protect the knee section of stockings, etc., or to protect the knee.

knee·pan (nē'pǎn'), *n.* the kneecap or patella.

knee·piece (nē'pēs'), *n.* armor for the knee, of hardened leather or of steel.

knee-sprung (nē'sprŭng'), *adj. Vet. Sci.* (of a horse, mule, etc.) having a forward bowing of the knee caused by inflammatory shortening of the flexor tendons.

knell (nĕl), *n.* **1.** the sound made by a bell rung slowly for a death or a funeral. **2.** any sound announcing the death of a person or the extinction, failure, etc., of something. **3.** any mournful sound. **—v.i. 4.** to sound, as a bell, esp. as a funeral bell. **5.** to give forth a mournful, ominous, or warning sound. **—v.t. 6.** to proclaim or summon by, or as by, a bell. [ME *knelle, knylle,* OE *cnyllan* strike, ring (a bell), c. Icel. *knylla* beat, strike]

knelt (nĕlt), *v.* pt. and pp. of **kneel.**

knew (nū, nōō), *v.* pt. of **know.**

Knick·er·bock·er (nǐk'ər bŏk'ər), *n.* **1.** a descendant of the Dutch settlers of New York. **2.** any New Yorker.

knick·ers (nǐk'ərz), *n.pl.* **1.** loosely fitting short breeches gathered in at the knee. **2.** a bloomerlike undergarment worn by women. Also, **knick·er·bock·ers** (nǐk'ər bŏk'ərz). [der. KNICKERBOCKER]

knick-knack (nǐk'nǎk'), *n.* **1.** a pleasing trifle; a trinket or gimcrack. **2.** a bit of bric-à-brac. Also, **nicknack.** [dissimilated redupl. of KNACK]

knife (nīf), *n., pl.* **knives,** *v.,* **knifed, knif·ing. —n. 1.** a cutting instrument consisting essentially of a thin blade (usually of steel and with a sharp edge) attached to a handle. **2.** a knifelike weapon; a dagger; a short sword. **3.** any blade for cutting, as in a tool or machine. **—v.t. 4.** to apply a knife to; cut, stab, etc., with a knife. **5.** *U.S. Slang.* to endeavor to defeat in a secret or underhand way. [ME *knif,* OE *cnīf,* c. Icel. *knīfr*] **—knife'less,** *adj.* **—knife'like',** *adj.*

knife edge, 1. the edge of a knife. **2.** anything very sharp. **3.** a wedge, on the fine edge of which a scale beam, pendulum, or the like, oscillates.

knife-edged (nīf'ĕjd'), *adj.* having a thin, sharp edge.

knife switch, *Elect.* a form of air switch in which the moving element, usually a hinged blade, enters or embraces the contact clips.

knight (nīt), *n.* **1.** *Medieval Hist.* **a.** a mounted soldier serving under a feudal superior. **b.** a man, usually of noble birth, who after an apprenticeship as page and squire was raised to honorable military rank and bound to chivalrous conduct. **2.** any person of a rank similar to that of the medieval knight. **3.** a man upon whom a certain dignity, corresponding to that of the medieval knight, is conferred by a sovereign because of personal merit or for services rendered to the country. In the

British Empire he holds the rank next below that of a baronet, and the title *Sir* is prefixed to the Christian name, as in *Sir John Smith.* Neither the dignity nor the title is hereditary. **4.** *Chess.* a piece shaped like a horse's head, moving one square horizontally or vertically, and then one square obliquely. It captures only on the terminal square. **5.** a member of any order or association of men bearing the name of *Knights: Knights of Pythias.* **—v.t. 6.** *Hist.* to dub or create (one) a knight. [ME; OE *cniht* boy, manservant, c. D and G *knecht*] **—knight'less,** *adj.*

knight banneret, banneret[1] (def. 2).

knight-er·rant (nīt'ĕr'ənt), *n., pl.* **knights-errant.** *Hist.* a wandering knight; a knight who traveled in search of adventures, to exhibit military skill, etc.

knight-er·rant·ry (nīt'ĕr'ən trǐ), *n., pl.* **knight-errantries. 1.** conduct or a performance like that of a knight-errant. **2.** quixotic conduct or action.

knight·head (nīt'hĕd'), *n. Naut.* either of the two timbers rising from the keel or stem of a ship, one on each side, and supporting the inner end of the bowsprit.

knight·hood (nīt'hŏŏd'), *n.* **1.** the rank or dignity of a knight. **2.** the profession or vocation of a knight. **3.** knightly character or qualities. **4.** the body of knights.

knight·ly (nīt'lǐ), *adj.* **1.** of or belonging to a knight: *knightly deeds.* **2.** characteristic of a knight. **3.** being or resembling a knight. **4.** composed of knights. **—adv. 5.** in a manner befitting a knight. **—knight'li·ness,** *n.*

Knights Hospitalers. See Hospitaler (def. 1).

Knights of Columbus, a Roman Catholic fraternal organization, founded in 1882, aiming to associate men of the church for religious and civic usefulness.

Knights of Pythias, a secret fraternal order founded at Washington, D.C., in 1864.

Knights of St. John of Jerusalem, Knights Hospitaler. See Hospitaler (def. 1).

Knight Templar. See Templar (def. 2).

knit (nǐt), *v.,* **knitted** or **knit, knitting,** *n.* **—v.t. 1.** to form fabric, such as jersey cloth or hose, by interlacing loops of yarn with hand needles or a power machine. **2.** to join closely and firmly together, as members or parts. **3.** to contract into folds or wrinkles: *to knit the brow.* **—v.i. 4.** to become closely and firmly joined together; grow together, as broken bones do. **5.** to contract, as the brow does. **6.** to become closely or intimately united. **—n. 7.** fabric produced by interlooping of a yarn or yarns. [ME *knitte,* OE *cynttan* tie, der. *cnotta* KNOT[1]] **—knit'ter,** *n.*

knit·ting (nǐt'ǐng), *n.* **1.** act of a person or thing that knits. **2.** act of forming a fabric by looping a continuous yarn. **3.** knitted work.

knitting needle, an instrument for knitting; a straight, slender rod, usually steel, with rounded ends.

knives (nīvz), *n.* pl. of **knife.**

knob (nŏb), *n.* **1.** a rounded (or otherwise shaped) projecting part forming the handle of a door, drawer, or the like. **2.** a rounded lump or protuberance on the surface or at the end of something, as a knot on a tree trunk, a pimple on the skin, etc. **3.** *Archit.* an ornamental boss, as of carved work. **4.** a rounded hill or mountain, esp. an isolated one. [ME. Cf. G *knobbe*] **—knobbed,** *adj.* **—knob'like',** *adj.*

knob·by (nŏb'ǐ), *adj.,* **-bier, -biest. 1.** abounding in knobs. **2.** knoblike. **—knob'bi·ness,** *n.*

knob·ker·rie (nŏb'kĕr'ǐ), *n.* a short, heavy stick or club with a knob on one end, used for both striking and throwing by South African natives. [t. S Afr. D: m. *knopkiri,* f. *knop* knob + Hottentot *kiri* stick, club]

knock (nŏk), *v.i.* **1.** to strike a sounding blow with the fist, knuckles, or anything hard, esp. on a door, window, or the like, as in seeking admittance, calling attention, giving a signal, etc. **2.** to make a noise as of striking or pounding, as machinery. **3.** *U.S. Slang.* to make harsh or ill-natured criticisms. **4.** to strike in collision. **5.** *Colloq.* to wander in an aimless way (fol. by *about*). **—v.t. 6.** to give a sounding or forcible blow to; hit; strike; beat. **7.** to drive, force, or render by a blow or blows: *to knock a man senseless.* **8.** to strike (a thing) against something else. **9.** *U.S. Slang.* to criticize ill-naturedly or harshly. **10.** Some special verb phrases are: **knock off,** *Colloq.* **1.** to dispose of, or get rid of. **2.** to stop doing something, esp. work. **3.** to disable, overcome, or defeat completely.

knock down, 1. (in auctions) to signify the sale of (the thing bid for) by a blow with a hammer or mallet; assign as sold to the highest bidder. **2.** to take apart (an automobile, machine, etc.) in order to facilitate handling. **3.** *U.S. Colloq.* (of a car conductor or other employee) to embezzle (money) from passengers' fares or other sums passing through his hands.

knock out, to defeat (an opponent) in a pugilistic contest by striking him down with a blow after which he does not rise within a prescribed time.

knock out or **knock out of the box,** *Baseball.* to cause (a pitcher) to be removed by making too many hits. **—n. 11.** act or the sound of knocking. **12.** a rap, as at a door. **13.** a blow or thump. **14.** *U.S. Slang.* an ill-natured criticism or comment. **15.** the noise resulting from faulty combustion or from incorrect functioning of some part of an internal-combustion engine. [ME *knokke,* unexpl. var. of *knoke,* OE *cnocian,* c. Icel. *knoka;* ? imit. in orig.] **—Syn. 1.** See **strike.**

knock·a·bout (nŏk'ə bout'), *n.* 1. *Naut.* a small handy yacht with a jib and mainsail but no bowsprit. —*adj.* 2. suitable for rough use, as a garment. 3. characterized by knocking about; rough; boisterous.

knock-down (nŏk'doun'), *adj.* 1. such as to knock something down; overwhelming; irresistible: *a knock-down blow.* 2. constructed in separate parts, so as to be readily knocked down or taken apart, as a boat, a piece of furniture, etc. —*n.* 3. such an object. 4. act of knocking down, esp. by a blow. 5. that which fells or overwhelms.

knock·er (nŏk'ər), *n.* 1. one who or that which knocks. 2. a hinged knob, bar, etc., on a door, for use in knocking.

knock-knee (nŏk'nē'), *n.* 1. inward curvature of the legs, causing the knees to knock together in walking. 2. (*pl.*) such knees. —**knock'-kneed'**, *adj.*

knock·out (nŏk'out'), *n.* 1. act of knocking out. 2. state or fact of being knocked out. 3. a knockout blow. 4. *U.S. Slang.* a person or thing of overwhelming success or attractiveness. —*adj.* 5. that knocks out.

knoll[1] (nōl), *n.* a small, rounded hill or eminence; a hillock. [ME *knol,* OE *cnol(l)* c. Norw. *knoll* hillock]

knoll[2] (nōl), *v.t.* 1. to ring a knell for; announce by strokes of a bell or the like. 2. *Archaic or Dial.* to ring or toll (a bell). —*v.i.* 3. to sound, as a bell; ring. 4. to sound a knell. —*n.* 5. a stroke of a bell in ringing or tolling. [ME; akin to KNELL]

knop (nŏp), *n.* a small, rounded protuberance; a knob; a boss, stud, or the like, as for ornament. [ME and OE; c. G *knopf*]

Knos·sos (nŏs'əs), *n.* a ruined city in Crete: capital of the ancient Minoan civilization. Also, **Cnossus.**

knot[1] (nŏt), *n., v.,* **knotted, knotting.** —*n.* 1. an interlacement of a cord, rope, or the like, drawn tight into a lump or knob, as for fastening to something. 2. a piece of ribbon or similar material tied or folded upon itself and used or worn as an ornament. 3. a cluster of persons or things. 4. a protuberance in the tissue of a plant; an excrescence on a stem, branch, or root; a node or joint in a stem, esp. when of swollen form. 5. the hard, crossgrained mass of wood at the place where a branch joins the trunk of a tree. 6. a part of this mass showing in a piece of lumber, etc. 7. any of various diseases of trees characterized by the formation of an excrescence, knob, or gnarl. 8. *Naut.* a. one of a series of equal divisions on a log line, marked off by strings knotted through the strands, and made of such a length that the number running out in a certain time will indicate the ship's speed in nautical miles per hour. b. a unit of speed of one nautical mile an hour. c. nautical mile. 9. something involved or intricate; a difficulty; a knotty problem. 10. a bond or tie. —*v.t.* 11. to tie in a knot or knots; form a knot or knots in. 12. to secure by a knot. 13. to form protuberances, bosses, or knobs in; make knotty. —*v.i.* 14. to become tied or tangled in a knot or knots. 15. to form knots or joints. [ME *knot(te),* OE *cnotta,* c. D *knot*] —**knot'-less,** *adj.* —**Syn.** 3. group, company. 4. lump, knob, gnarl. 9. perplexity, puzzle.

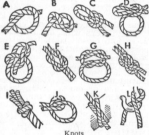

Knots
A. Overhand; B. Figure of eight; C. Slipknot; D. Bowknot; E. Bowline; F. Square knot; G. Granny's knot; H. Single carrick bend; I. Matthew Walker; J. Half hitch; K. Clove hitch; L. Blackwall hitch

knot[2] (nŏt), *n.* a wading bird, *Calidris canutus,* of the snipe family. [orig. unknown]

knot·grass (nŏt'gräs', -gräs'), *n.* 1. a common polygonaceous weed, *Polygonum aviculare,* with nodes in its stems. 2. any of certain other species of this genus.

knot·hole (nŏt'hōl'), *n.* a hole in a board or plank formed by the falling out of a knot or a portion of a knot.

knot·ted (nŏt'ĭd), *adj.* 1. knotty. 2. *Bot.* having many nodes or nodelike swellings; gnarled. 3. *Zool.* having one or more swellings; nodose.

knot·ty (nŏt'ĭ), *adj.,* **-tier, -tiest.** 1. characterized by knots; full of knots. 2. involved, intricate, or difficult: *a knotty problem.* —**knot'ti·ness,** *n.*

knot·weed (nŏt'wēd'), *n.* any of various knotty-stemmed plants of the polygonaceous genus *Polygonum,* as *P. maritimum* (seaside knotweed), a glaucous herb of sandy soils.

knout (nout), *n.* 1. a kind of whip or scourge formerly used in Russia for flogging criminals. —*v.t.* 2. to flog with the knout. [t. F, t. Russ.: m. *knut*]

know (nō), *v.,* **knew, known, knowing,** *n.* —*v.t.* 1. to perceive or understand as fact or truth, or apprehend with clearness and certainty. 2. to have fixed in the mind or memory: *to know a poem by heart.* 3. to be cognizant or aware of; to be acquainted with (a thing, place, person, etc.), as by sight, experience, or report. 4. to understand from experience or attainment (fol. by *how* before an infinitive): *to know how to make something.* 5. to be able to distinguish, as one from another. 6. **know the ropes, a.** to know the various ropes about a vessel, as a sailor does. **b.** *Colloq.* to understand the details or methods of any business or the like. —*v.i.* 7. to have knowledge, or clear and certain perception, as of fact or truth. 8. to be cognizant or aware as of some fact, circumstance, or occurrences; have information, as about something. —*n.* 9. the fact of knowing; knowledge: now chiefly in the colloquial phrase **in the know,** (in the circle of those who have inside knowledge). [ME *knowe(n), knawe(n),* OE *(ge)cnāwan,* c. OHG *-cnāan* know, Icel. *knā* (pres. ind.) know how, can; akin to L *(g)noscere,* Gk. *gignōskein*] —**know'er,** *n.* —**Syn.** 1. KNOW, COMPREHEND, UNDERSTAND imply being aware of meanings. To KNOW is to be aware of something as a fact or truth: *he knows the basic facts of the subjec ; I know that he agrees with me.* To COMPREHEND is to know something thoroughly and to perceive its relationships to certain other ideas, facts, etc. To UNDERSTAND is to be fully aware not only of the meaning of something but also its implications: *I could comprehend all he said, but did not understand that he was joking.*

know·a·ble (nō'ə bəl), *adj.* that may be known. —**know'a·ble·ness,** *n.*

know-how (nō'hou'), *n.* knowledge of how to do something; faculty or skill for a particular thing.

know·ing (nō'ĭng), *adj.* 1. shrewd, sharp, or astute; often, affecting or suggesting shrewd or secret understanding of matters: *a knowing glance.* 2. that knows; having knowledge or information; intelligent; wise. 3. conscious; intentional; deliberate. —**know'ing·ly,** *adv.* —**know'ing·ness,** *n.*

knowl·edge (nŏl'ĭj), *n.* 1. acquaintance with facts, truths, or principles, as from study or investigation; general erudition. 2. familiarity or conversance, as with a particular subject, branch of learning, etc. 3. acquaintance; familiarity gained by sight, experience, or report: *a knowledge of human nature.* 4. fact or state of knowing; perception of fact or truth; clear and certain mental apprehension. 5. state of being cognizant or aware, as of a fact or circumstance. 6. **to one's knowledge, a.** according to one's certain knowledge. **b.** (with a negative) so far as one knows: *I never saw him, to my knowledge.* 7. that which is known, or may be known. 8. the body of truths or facts accumulated by mankind in the course of time. 9. the sum of what is known. 10. cognizance of facts, or range cognizance: *this has happened twice within my knowledge.* [ME *knowleche,* der. KNOW] —**Syn.** 1. See **information.** 4. understanding. 8. learning, lore, erudition, scholarship; wisdom, science.

knowl·edge·a·ble (nŏl'ĭj ə bəl), *adj. Colloq.* possessing knowledge or understanding; intelligent.

known (nōn), *v.* pp. of **know.**

know-noth·ing (nō'nŭth'ĭng), *n.* 1. an ignoramus. 2. an agnostic. 3. (*cap.*) a member of a political party (the **American party,** orig. a secret society whose members professed ignorance concerning it), prominent from 1853 to 1856, whose aim was to keep the control of the government in the hands of native citizens. —*adj.* 4. grossly ignorant. 5. agnostic. 6. (*cap.*) of or pertaining to the Know-Nothings.

known quantity, *Math.* a quantity wh ose value is given: in algebra, etc., frequently represented by a letter from the first part of the alphabet, as *a, b,* or *c.*

Knox (nŏks), *n.* 1. **Henry,** 1750–1806, American general; first Secretary of War, 1789–94. 2. **John,** 1505?–1572, leader of the Protestant Reformation in Scotland; preacher, statesman, and historian.

Knox·ville (nŏks'vĭl), *n.* a city in E Tennessee, on the Tennessee river. 124,769 (1950).

Knt., Knight.

knuck·le (nŭk'əl), *n., v.,* **-led, -ling.** —*n.* 1. a joint of a finger, esp. one of the joints at the roots of the fingers. 2. the rounded prominence of such a joint when the finger is bent. 3. a joint of meat, consisting of the parts about the carpal or tarsal joint of a quadruped. 4. an angle between two members or surfaces of a vessel. 5. See **brass knuckles.** 6. a cylindrical projecting part on a hinge, through which an axis or pin passes; the joint of a hinge. —*v.i.* 7. to hold the knuckles close to the ground in playing marbles. 8. to apply oneself vigorously or earnestly, as to a task (fol. by *down*). 9. to yield or submit (often fol. by *down* or *under*). [ME *knokel;* akin to D *kneukel,* G *knöchel,* dim. of a word repr. by D *knok,* G *knochen* bone]

knuckle ball, *Baseball.* a slow pitched ball which curves in different directions before reaching the plate.

knuck·le·bone (nŭk'əl bōn'), *n.* 1. (in man) a bone forming a knuckle of a finger. 2. (in quadrupeds) a bone homologous with wrist, ankle, or finger bones of man, or its knobbed end.

knuck·le-dust·er (nŭk'əl dŭs'tər), *n.* brass knuckles.

knuckle joint, 1. a joint forming a knuckle. 2. *Mach.* a flexible hinged joint formed by two abutting links.

knurl (nûrl), *n.* 1. a small ridge or the like, esp. one of a series, as on the edge of a thumbscrew to assist in obtaining a firm grip. —*v.t.* 2. to make knurls or ridges on. [appar. der. *knur* lump, knot, ME *knurre*]

knurled (nûrld), *adj.* 1. having small ridges on the edge or surface; milled. 2. having knurls or knots; gnarled.

knurl·y (nûr'lĭ), *adj.,* **knurlier, knurliest.** having knurls or knots; gnarled.

Knut (kə nōōt', -nŭt'), *n.* Canute.

K.O., knockout. Also, **k.o.**

---

b., blend of, blended; c., cognate with; d., dialect, dialectal; der., derived from; f., formed from; g., going back to; m., modification of; r., replacing; s., stem of; t., taken from; ?, perhaps. See the full key on inside cover.

ko·a·la (kō·ä′lə), *n.* a sluggish, tailless, gray, furry, arboreal marsupial, *Phascolarctos cinereus,* of Australia, about 2 feet long. [t. native Australian]

Ko·be (kō′bĕ′), *n.* a seaport in S Japan, on S Honshu island. 443,344 (1946).

Kö·ben·havn (kœ′pən houn′), *n.* Danish name of **Copenhagen**.

Ko·blenz (kō′blĕnts), *n.* Coblenz.

ko·bold (kō′bŏld, -bōld), *n.* (in German folklore) **1.** a kind of spirit or goblin, often mischievous, that haunts houses. **2.** a kind of spirit that haunts mines or other underground places. [t. G]

Koala.
Phascolarctos cinereus
(28 to 32 in. long)

Koch (kôкн), *n.* **Robert** (rō′bĕrt), 1843–1910, German bacteriologist and physician.

Ko·chi (kō′chē′), *n.* a seaport in SW Japan, on Shikoku island. 125,993 (1946).

Ko·da·chrome (kō′dəkrōm′), *n.* a trademark for a photographic film which is sensitive to and reproduces color.

ko·dak (kō′dăk), *n., v.,* **-daked, -daking. —*n.* 1.** a kind of portable photographic camera, esp. adapted for instantaneous work, employing a continuous roll of sensitized film upon which successive negatives are made. **2.** (*cap.*) a trademark for this camera. **—*v.t., v.i.* 3.** to photograph with a kodak. [arbitrary word coined by George Eastman as a trademark] **—ko′dak·er,** *n.*

Ko·di·ak (kō′dĭ′ăk′), *n.* an island in the N Pacific, near the base of the Alaska Peninsula. ab. 100 mi. long.

Ko·dok (kō′dŏk), *n.* See **Fashoda.**

ko·el (kō′əl), *n.* a cuckoo of the genus *Eudynamys,* as the Indian koel, *E. orientalis.* [t. Hind.: m. *kōīl,* der. Skt. *kokila*]

K. of C., Knights of Columbus.

Koff·ka (kôf′kä), *n.* **Kurt** (koórt), 1886–1941, German psychologist in U.S.

K. of P., Knights of Pythias.

Koh·i·noor (kō′ə noŏr′), *n.* one of the world's large diamonds, 109 carats, first discovered in India and now part of the British crown jewels. [t. Pers.: m. *kŏh-i-nūr* mountain of light]

kohl (kōl), *n.* a powder, as finely powdered sulfide of antimony, used in the East to darken the eyelids, make eyebrows, etc. [t. Ar.: m. *kohl.* Cf. ALCOHOL]

Köh·ler (kœ′lər), *n.* **Wolfgang** (vôlf′gäng), born 1887, German psychologist.

kohl·ra·bi (kōl′rä′bĭ′), *n., pl.* **-bies.** a cultivated variety of *Brassica oleracea,* var. *gongylodes,* whose stem above ground swells into an edible bulblike formation. [t. G, b. G *kohl* cabbage and It. *cauli* (or *cavoli*) *rape,* pl. of *cavolo rapa* cabbage turnip. Cf. COLE, RAPE²]

Koi·ne (koi nā′), *n.* the standard Greek of Attic type which replaced other dialects and flourished under the Roman Empire. [Gk., short for *koinē dialektos* common dialect]

Ko·kand (kō känt′), *n.* a city in the SW Soviet Union in Asia, in Uzbek Republic: formerly the center of a powerful khanate. 84,663 (1939).

Ko·ko·mo (kō′kəmō′), *n.* a city in central Indiana. 38,672 (1950).

Ko·ko Nor (kō′kō′ nôr′), **1.** a lake in W China, in Chinghai province. ab. 2300 sq. mi. **2.** Chinghai.

Ko·ku·ra (kō′kōō rä′), *n.* a seaport in SW Japan, on Kyushu island. 149,047 (1946).

ko·la (kō′lə), *n.* **1.** the kola nut. **2.** an extract prepared from it. **3.** the tree producing it. Also, **cola.** [t. W Afr.]

Ko·la (kō′lä), *n.* a peninsula in the NW Soviet Union in Europe between the White and Barents seas.

ko·la nut (kō′lə), a brownish seed, about the size of a chestnut, produced by a sterculiaceous tree of western tropical Africa, the West Indies, and Brazil, *Cola nitida,* which contains both caffein and theobromine: used as a stimulant in soft drinks. Also, **cola nut.**

Ko·lar Gold Fields (kō′lär′), a city in S India, in Mysore state: rich mining district. 133,859 (1941).

kol·khoz (kŏl hôz′), *n.* U.S.S.R. a collective farm, the holding being common property of all.

ko·lin·sky (kə lĭn′skĭ), *n.* **1.** the chorok, red sable, or Siberian mink, *Putorius sibiricus,* about 15 inches long, with a bushy tail 8 or 10 inches long, the fur uniformly buff or tawny, somewhat paler below, varied with black and white on the head. **2.** the fur of such an animal. [t. Russ.: m. *Kolinski,* adj., pertaining to KOLA]

Köln (kœln), *n.* German name of **Cologne.**

Ko·lozs·vár (kō′lōzh vär′), *n.* Hungarian name of **Cluj.**

Ko·ly·ma (kŏ′lĭ′mä′), *n.* a river in the NE Soviet Union in Asia, flowing NE to the Arctic Ocean. ab. 1000 mi. Also, **Ko·li·ma′.**

Kom·in·tern (kŏm′ĭn tûrn′), *n.* Comintern.

Ko·mu·ra (kō′mōō rä′), *n.* **Marquis Jutaro** (jōō′tä·rō′), 1855–1911, Japanese statesman and diplomat.

Ko·na·kri (kō′nä krē′), *n.* Conakry.

Kö·nig·grätz (kœ′nĭкн grĕts′), *n.* a town in NW Czechoslovakia, on the Elbe in Bohemia: the Prussians defeated the Austrians near here in the Battle of Sadowa, 1866. ab. 18,000.

Kö·nigs·berg (kœ′nĭg bûrg′; *Ger.* kœ′nĭкнs bĕrкн), *n.* a seaport in the W Soviet Union: formerly the capital of East Prussia. 372,164 (1939). Russian, **Kaliningrad.**

Kö·nigs·hüt·te (kœ′nʏкнs hʏ′tə), *n.* German name of **Królewska Huta.**

Kon·stanz (kōn′shtänts), *n.* German name of **Constance.**

Ko·nya (kôn′yä), *n.* a city in S Turkey. 56,465 (1940). Also, **Ko′nia.**

Koo (kōō), *n.* **Wellington** (*Vi Kyuin Wellington Koo*), born 1888, Chinese statesman and diplomat.

koo·doo (kōō′dōō), *n., pl.* **-doos.** a large handsome African antelope, *Strepsiceros strepsiceros,* the males of which have large corkscrewlike horns. Also, **kudu.** [t. S Afr. (Hottentot)]

kook·a·bur·ra (kŏŏk′ə bûr′ə), *n. Australia.* the laughing jackass. [t. native Australian]

Greater koodoo.
Strepsiceros strepsiceros
(5 ft. high at the shoulder, total length 9 ft., horns 3 to 4 ft. long)

Koo·te·nay (kōō′tə nā′), *n.* a river flowing from SE British Columbia, through NW Montana and N Idaho, swinging back into Canada where it enters **Kootenay Lake** (75 mi. long) and empties into the Columbia river. ab. 400 mi. Spelled **Koo′te·nai′** in the U.S.

kop (kŏp), *n.* (in South Africa) a hill. [t. D: head]

ko·peck (kō′pĕk), *n.* a Russian monetary unit and copper coin, 1/100 of a ruble, equivalent to about 1/2 of a U.S. cent. Also, **ko′pek, copeck.** [t. Russ.: m. *kopeika*]

kop·je (kŏp′ĭ), *n. South African.* a small hill. [D, dim. of *kop* KOP]

kor (kôr), *n.* homer². [t. Heb.]

Ko·ran (kō rän′, -răn′), *n.* the sacred scripture of Islam, believed by orthodox Mohammedans to contain revelations made in Arabic by Allah directly to Mohammed. [t. Ar.: m *qur'ān* reading, recitation, der. *qara'a* read] **—Ko·ran·ic** (kō rän′ĭk), *adj.*

Kor·do·fan (kôr′dō fän′), *n.* a province in the central Anglo-Egyptian Sudan. 1,251,300 pop. (est. 1940); ab 147,100 sq. mi. *Cap.:* El Obeid.

Ko·re·a (kō rē′ə), *n.* a country in E Asia, on a peninsula SE of Manchuria and between the Sea of Japan and the Yellow Sea: under Japanese rule, 1910–45; currently divided at 38° N into **South Korea** (21,000,000 pop.; 36,600 sq. mi.; *Cap.:* Seoul) and **North Korea** (9,000,000 pop.; 50,000 sq. mi.; *Cap.:* Pyongyang). Outbreak of war (June 25, 1950) led to United Nations aid in defense of South Korea. Japanese, **Chosen.**

Korea

Ko·re·an (kō rē′an), *adj.* **1.** pertaining to Korea, its people, or language. **—*n.* 2.** a native or inhabitant of Korea. **3.** the language of Korea, of no known linguistic affinity.

Korea Strait, the strait between Korea and Japan, connecting the Sea of Japan and the East China Sea.

Kor·o·seal (kôr′ə sēl′, kŏr′-), *n.* a trademark for a plastic derived from vinyl chloride by polymerization.

ko·ru·na (kô′rōō′nä), *n., pl.* **koruny** (kô′rōō′nĭ), **korun** (kô′rōōn). the monetary unit of Czechoslovakia, stabilized in 1929 to equal $0.03 in the U.S., now worth about 2 cents. *Symbol:* Kcs. [t. Czech, t. L: m. *corona* crown]

kos (kōs), *n., pl.* **kos.** a unit of land distances in India, of various lengths from 1 to 3 mi. [t. Hind., g. Skt. *krōsa*]

Kos·ci·us·ko (kŏs′ĭ ŭs′kō), *n.* **1. Thaddeus** (thăd′ĭ əs), (*Tadeusz Kościuszko*) 1746–1817, Polish patriot and general who served as an officer in the American Revolutionary army. **2. Mount,** the highest mountain in Australia, in SE New South Wales. 7328 ft.

ko·sher (kō′shər), *adj.* **1.** fit, lawful, or ritually permitted, according to the Jewish law: used of food and vessels for food ritually proper for use, esp. of meat slaughtered in accordance with the law of Moses. **2.** U.S. *Slang.* genuine. **—*n.* 3.** *Colloq.* kosher food. Also, **kasher.** [t. Heb.: m. *kāshēr* fit, proper, lawful]

Ko·ši·ce (kô′shĭ′tsĕ), *n.* a city in SE Czechoslovakia, in Slovakia. 70,117 (1930). Hungarian, **Kassa.**

Kos·suth (kŏs′ōōth; *Hung.* kô′shōōt), *n.* **1. Francis** or **Ferencz** (fĕr′ĕnts), 1841–1914, Hungarian patriot, statesman, and writer. **2.** his father, **Louis** or **Lajos** (lŏ′yōsh), 1802–94, Hungarian patriot and orator.

Ko·stro·ma (kŏ strō mä′), *n.* a city in the central Soviet Union in Europe, on the Volga. 121,205 (1939).

ko·to (kō′tō; *Jap.* kô′tō′), *n., pl.* **-tos.** a Japanese musical instrument having numerous strings, stretched over a vaulted, wooden sounding board: plucked with the fingers. [t. Jap.]

ko·tow (kō′tou′), *v.i., n.* kowtow. **—ko′tow′er,** *n.*

Kot·ze·bue (kôt′sə bōō′), *n.* **August Friedrich Ferdinand von** (ou′gŏŏst frē′drʏкн fĕr′dʏ nänt fən), 1761–1819, German dramatist.

kou·mis (kōō′mĭs), *n.* kumiss. Also, **kou′miss, kou′myss.**

Kous·se·vitz·ky (kōō′sə vĭt′skĭ), *n.* **Serge** or **Sergei Alexandrovich** (sĕrzh *or* sĕr gā′ ä′lĕ ksän′drō vĭch), 1874–1951, Russian-born orchestra conductor in U.S.

Kov·no (kôv′nŏ), *n.* Russian name of **Kaunas.**

Ko·weit (kō wāt′), *n.* Kuwait.

Kow·loon (kou′loon′), *n.* **1.** a peninsula in SE China, opposite Hong Kong island: a part of Hong Kong Colony leased from China. 3 sq. mi. **2.** a seaport on this peninsula. 300,550 (1934).

kow·tow (kou′tou′, kō′-), *v.i.* **1.** to knock the forehead on the ground while kneeling, as an act of reverence, worship, apology, etc. **2.** to act in an obsequious manner; show servile deference. —*n.* **3.** act of kowtowing. Also, **kotow.** [t. Chinese (Mandarin): m. *k'o-t'ou*, lit., knock-head] —**kow′tow′er,** *n.*

KP, *Chess.* king's pawn.

K.P. 1. Kitchen Police. **2.** Knight of the Order of St. Patrick. **3.** Knights of Pythias.

KR, *Chess.* king's rook.

Kr, *Chem.* krypton.

kr., 1. kreutzer. **2.** krona; kronor. **3.** krone²; kronen. **4.** krone¹; kroner.

Kra (krä), *n.* **Isthmus of,** the narrowest part of the Malay peninsula, between the Bay of Bengal and the Gulf of Siam. ab. 35 mi. wide.

kraal (kräl), *n.* **1.** a village of South African natives, usually surrounded by a stockade or the like and often having a central space for cattle, etc. **2.** the kraal as a social unit. **3.** *South African.* an enclosure for cattle, etc. —*v.t.* **4.** to shut up in a kraal, as cattle. [t. S Afr. D, t. Pg.: m. *curral* enclosure. Cf. CORRAL]

Krafft-E·bing (kräft′ā′bĭng), *n.* **Richard** (rĭKH′ärt), **Baron von,** 1840–1902, German psychiatrist and physician.

krait (krīt), *n.* any of the extremely venomous snakes of the genus *Bungarus* of India and southeastern Asia. [t. Hind.: m. *karait*]

Kra·ka·tau (krä′kä tou′), *n.* a small volcanic island in the U.S. of Indonesia between Java and Sumatra: violent eruption, 1883. Also, **Kra·ka·to·a** (krä′kä tō′ä).

kra·ken (krä′kən, krä′-), *n.* a mythical sea monster said to appear at times off Norway. [t. Norw.]

Kra·ków (krä′kŏŏf), *n.* Polish name of **Cracow.**

kran (krän), *n.* a Persian monetary unit and silver coin, equal to about 8 U.S. cents.

Kras·no·dar (kräs′nŏ där′), *n.* a city in the S Soviet Union in Europe: a port near the Sea of Azov. 203,946 (1939). Formerly, **Ekaterinodar.**

Kras·no·yarsk (kräs′nŏ yärsk′), *n.* a city in the S Soviet Union in Asia, on the Yenisei. 189,999 (1939).

K-ra·tion (kā′răsh′ən, -rā′shən), *n. U.S. Army.* one of the emergency field rations used when other rations are not available.

Kre·feld (krā′fĕld; *Ger.* -fĕlt), *n.* a city in W Germany, in the Rhineland. 170,968 (1939). Also, **Crefeld.**

Kreis·ler (krīs′lər), *n.* **Fritz** (frĭts), born 1875, Austrian violinist, in the U.S.

Krem·en·chug (krĕm′ĕn chŏŏk′), *n.* a city in the SW Soviet Union, on the Dnieper river. 89,553 (1939).

krem·lin (krĕm′lĭn), *n.* **1.** the citadel of a Russian town or city. **2.** (*cap.*) that of Moscow, including within its walls the chief office of the Soviet government. [t. Russ.: m. *kreml* citadel]

kreut·zer (kroit′sər), *n.* **1.** a former German coin equivalent to about half a U. S. cent. **2.** an Austrian copper coin (no longer coined) and monetary unit, equal to one hundredth of a florin. [t. G: m. *kreuzer*, der. *kreuz* cross (orig. the device on the coin)]

Kreutzer Sonata, a sonata for violin and pianoforte (1803, Op. 47) by Beethoven.

Kreym·borg (krām′bôrg), *n.* **Alfred,** born 1883, U.S. poet and author.

krieg·spiel (krēg′spēl), *n.* a game designed to teach military science by means of blocks or the like, representing guns, etc., moved on maps or other surfaces.

Kriem·hild (krēm′hĭlt), *n.* the legendary heroine of the *Nibelungenlied,* wife of Siegfried and avenger of his death: the counterpart of the Scandinavian Gudrun.

krim·mer (krĭm′ər), *n.* a lambskin from the Crimean region, dressed as a fur, with wool in loose soft curls and usually whitish or pale gray. Also, **crimmer.** [t. G., der. *Krim* Crimea]

kris (krēs), *n.* creese.

Krish·na (krĭsh′nə), *n.* the most popular Hindu deity, as an incarnation of Vishnu; the famous teacher in the Bhagavad Gita. [t. Skt., special use of *krishna* black]

Kriss Krin·gle (krĭs′ krĭng′gəl), Santa Claus. [t. G: m. *Christkindl, -del* Christ child, Christmas gift]

Kri·voi Rog (krĭ voi′ rôg′), a city in the SW Soviet Union, in the Ukrainian Republic. 197,621 (1939).

Kró·lew·ska Hu·ta (krŏŏ lĕf′skä hŏŏ′tä), a city in S Poland. 103,417 (1946). Also, **Chorzów.** German, **Königshütte.**

kro·na (krō′nə; *Sw.* krŏŏ′nə), *n., pl.* **-nor** (-nôr). the monetary unit and a silver coin of Sweden and Iceland, roughly equivalent to the krone of Denmark and Norway. [t. Icel. and Sw. See KRONE¹]

kro·ne¹ (krō′nĕ), *n., pl.* **-ner** (-nĕr). the monetary unit and a silver coin of Denmark and of Norway, equal to about 14 U.S. cents. [t. Dan. and Norw., c. Icel. and Sw. *krona* CROWN]

kro·ne² (krō′nə), *n., pl.* **-nen** (-nən). **1.** a former German gold coin equal to 10 marks, or about $2.38. **2.** former monetary unit and a silver coin of Austria, equal to 100 heller, or about 20.3 U.S. cents. [t. G. See KRONE¹]

Kro·nos (krō′nŏs), *n.* Cronus.

Kron·stadt (krŏn shtät′ *for 1*; krŏn′shtät *for 2*), *n.* **1.** a seaport in the NW Soviet Union, on an island in the Gulf of Finland, W of Leningrad: naval base. 31,197 (1926). **2.** German name of **Brasov.**

kroon (kroon), *n., pl.* **kroons, krooni** (krōō′nĭ). the coin and monetary unit of Estonia equivalent to the Swedish krona. [t. Estonian: crown]

Kro·pot·kin (krŏ pŏt′kĭn; *Russ.* krŏ pôt′-), *n.* **Peter** (*Prince Pëtr Alekseevich*), 1842–1921, Russian anarchist, writer, and geographer, in England.

Kru·ger (krōō′gər; *Du.* krȳ′gər), *n.* **Stephanus Johannes Paulus** (stē fä′nŏŏs yō hän′əs pou′lŏŏs), (*"Oom Paul"*) 1825–1904, Boer statesman and president of the South African Republic, 1883–1900.

Kru·gers·dorp (krōō′gərz dôrp′; *Du.* krȳ′gərs-), *n.* a city in the NE Union of South Africa, in Transvaal, near Johannesburg. With suburbs, 71,631 (1946).

krul·ler (krŭl′ər), *n.* cruller.

Krupp (krŭp; *Ger.* krŏŏp), *n.* **Alfred** (äl′frät), 1812–87, German manufacturer of armaments.

Krup·ska·ya (krōōp′skä yä), *n.* **Nadezhda Konstantinovna** (nä dĕzh′dä kôn′stän tē′nŏv nä), 1869–1939, Russian social worker and wife of Nikolai Lenin.

kryp·ton (krĭp′tŏn), *n. Chem.* an inert monatomic gaseous element present in very small amounts in the atmosphere, of some use in high power, tungsten filament light bulbs. *Symbol:* Kr; *at. wt.:* 83.7; *at. no.:* 36; *weight of one liter at 0°C, and 760 mm. pressure:* 3.708. [t. NL, t. Gk., neut. of *kryptós* hidden. See CRYPT]

Kshat·ri·ya (kshăt′rĭ yə), *n.* a member of the military caste among the Hindus. [t. Skt., der. *kshatra* rule, n.]

Kt, *Chess.* knight.

Kt., Knight.

kt., 1. karat, carat. **2.** knot.

K.T., Knights Templars.

Kua·la Lum·pur (kwä′lə lŏŏm′pŏŏr′), a city in the SW Malay Peninsula: the capital of Selangor state and of the Federation of Malaya; formerly the capital of the Federated Malay States. 111,418 (1931).

Ku·blai Khan (kōō′blī kän′), 1216?–94, Mongol emperor, 1259–94, founder of the Mongol dynasty in China (grandson of Genghis Khan).

Ku·bla Khan (kōō′blə kän′), a poetic fragment (1816) by Coleridge.

ku·chen (kōō′KHən), *n.* a yeast-raised coffee cake, usually including fruit. [G]

ku·dos (kū′dŏs), *n.* glory; renown. [t. Gk.: m. *kŷdos*]

Kud·run (kŏŏd′rŏŏn, kŏŏth′-), *n.* Gudrun.

ku·du (kōō′dōō), *n.* koodoo.

Kuen·lun (kŏŏn′lŏŏn′), *n.* Kunlun.

Kui·by·shev (kwē′bə shĕf′; *Russ.* kōō′ĭ bwē shĕf′), *n.* a city in the E Soviet Union in Europe: a port on the Volga. 390,267 (1939). Formerly, **Samara.**

Ku Klux Klan (kū′ klŭks′ klän′), **1.** a secret organization in the southern U.S., active for several years after the Civil War, which aimed to suppress the newly acquired powers of the Negroes and to oppose carpetbaggers from the North, and was responsible for many lawless and violent proceedings. **2.** a secret organization (**Knights of the Klu Klux Klan**) inspired by the former, founded in 1915 and active in the southern and other parts of the U. S., admitting to membership none but native-born, white, Gentile, Protestant Americans, and professing Americanism as its object. Also, **Ku Klux.** [? f. m. Gk. *kŷklos* circle + m. CLAN]

ku·lak (kōō läk′), *n. Russia.* **1.** (before the revolution) a hardfisted merchant or a village usurer. **2.** (more recently) any peasant who employed hired labor or possessed any machinery. [t. Russ.: fist, tightfisted person]

Kul·tur (kŏŏl tōōr′), *n.* **1.** culture as a social force causing evolutionary development to higher forms of civilization. **2.** a civilization characteristic of a time or a people. [G, t. L: m.s. *cultūra* CULTURE]

Kul·tur·kampf (kŏŏl tōōr′kämpf′), *n.* the conflict between the German imperial government and the Roman Catholic Church from 1872 or 1873 until 1886, chiefly over the control of educational and ecclesiastical appointments. [G: civilization struggle]

Ku·ma·mo·to (kōō′mä mō′tŏ), *n.* a city in SW Japan, on Kyushu island. 206,016 (1946).

Ku·mas·i (kŏŏ mäs′ĭ), *n.* the capital of Ashanti, in the Gold Coast, British West Africa. 35,829 (1931).

ku·miss (kōō′mĭs), *n.* **1.** fermented mare's or camel's milk, used as a beverage by Asiatic nomads, etc. **2.** a similar drink prepared from other milk, esp. that of the cow, and used for dietetic and medicinal purposes. Also, **koumis, koumiss, koumyss.** [t. Russ.: m. *kumys*, t. Tatar: m. *kumiz*. Cf. F *koumis*, G *kumys*]

küm·mel (kĭm′əl; *Ger.* kȳm′əl), *n.* a colorless cordial or liqueur flavored with cumin, caraway seeds, etc., made esp. in regions bordering on the eastern coast of the Baltic Sea. [t. G: cumin, *kümmel*]

kum·mer·bund (kŭm′ər bŭnd′), *n.* cummerbund.

kum·quat (kŭm′kwŏt), *n.* **1.** a small, round or oblong citrus fruit with a sweet rind and acid pulp, used chiefly for preserves, being the fruit of *Fortunella japonica* and related species, rutaceous shrubs native in China and cultivated in Japan, Florida, California, etc. **2.** the plant itself. Also, **cumquat.** [t. Chinese, Cantonese pronunciation of Mandarin *kin ku*, lit., gold orange]

---

b., blend of, blended; c., cognate with; d., dialect, dialectal; der., derived from; f., formed from; g., going back to; m., modification of; r., replacing; s., stem of; t., taken from; ?, perhaps. See the full key on inside cover.

Kun (kŏŏn), *n.* **Béla** (bā′lŏ), born 1886, Hungarian Communist leader.

Kung-fu-tse (kŏŏng′fōō′dzŭ′), *n.* Chinese name of **Confucius.**

Kun-lun (kŏŏn′lŏŏn′), *n.* a lofty mountain system bordering to the N the Tibetan plateau and extending W across central China. Highest peak, over 20,000 ft. Also, **Kuenlun.**

Kun-ming (kŏŏn′mĭng′), *n.* a city in SW China: the capital of Yünnan province; an important transshipment point on the Burma Road in World War II. ab. 150,000. Also, **Yünnan.**

kunz-ite (kŏŏnts′īt), *n.* a transparent lilac variety of spodumene, used as a gem. [named after G. F. *Kunz*, American expert in precious stones. See -ITE¹]

Kuo-min-tang (kwō′mĭn′tăng′; *Chin.* gwō′mĭn′-däng′), *n.* a Chinese political party, deriving historically from earlier parties and political societies organized or led by Sun Yat-sen, formerly controlling a large part of China. The Kuomintang was first formed in 1912, after the foundation of the Chinese Republic, by the fusion of several political groups, and has, since 1927, claimed a monopoly in expounding and executing the ideas of Dr. Sun. Its director-general is Chiang Kaishek. [t. Chinese (Mandarin): f. *kuo* nation + *min* people + *tang* party]

Ku-ra (kŏŏ rä′), *n.* a river flowing from NE Turkey through the Georgian and Azerbaijan Republics of the Soviet Union SE to the Caspian Sea. ab. 810 mi.

Kurd (kûrd; *Pers.* kŏŏrd), *n.* a member of a pastoral and warlike people speaking an Iranian language and dwelling chiefly in Kurdistan. —**Kurd′ish,** *adj.*

Kur-di-stan (kûr′də stän′; *Pers.* kŏŏr′dĭ stän′), *n.* **1.** a mountain and plateau region in SE Turkey, NW Iran, and N Iraq, peopled largely by Kurds. ab. 74,000 sq. mi. **2.** any of several rugs woven by the Kurds of Turkey or Iran.

Ku-re (kŏŏ′rĕ′) *n.* a seaport in SW Japan, on Honshu island. 170,285 (1946).

Kurg (kŏŏrg), *n.* Coorg.

Ku-rile Islands (kŏŏr′Yl, kŏŏ rēl′), a chain of small islands off the NE coast of Asia, extending from N Japan to the S tip of Kamchatka: ceded to the Soviet Union by Japan, 1945. Also, **Kur′il Islands.** Japanese, **Chishima.**

Kur-land (kŏŏr′land), *n.* Courland.

Ku-ro-ki (kŏŏ′rô kē′), *n.* **Count Tamemoto** (tä′mĕmô′tô), 1844–1923, Japanese general.

Ku-ro-pat-kin (kŏŏ′rŏ pät′kĭn), *n.* **Aleksei Nikolaevich** (ä′lĕksĕ′ĭ nY′kŏ lä′yə vĭch), 1848–1925, Russian general.

Kursk (kŏŏrsk), *n.* a city in the central Soviet Union in Europe, N of Kharkov. 119,972 (1939)

Ku-tu-zov (kŏŏ tōō′zôf), *n.* **Mikhail Ilarionovich** (mY′ hä ēl′ Ylä′rĭ ŏ nô′vĭch), 1745–1813, Russian general.

Ku-wait (kŏŏ wīt′), *n.* **1.** a sheikdom in NE Arabia, on the NW coast of the Persian Gulf: a British protectorate. 100,000 pop. (est. 1946); ab. 1950 sq. mi. **2.** a seaport in and the capital of this shiekdom. ab. 70,000. Also, **Koweit.**

Kuyp (koip), *n.* Cuyp.

Kuz-netsk Basin (kŏŏz nĕtsk′), an industrial region in the S Soviet Union in Asia: coal fields.

Kv-a., Kilovolt ampere.

kvass (kväs), *n.* quass.

kw., kilowatt.

Kwa-ki-u-tl (kwä′kY̆ōō′təl), *n.* a group of American Indians of Wakashan linguistic stock in Vancouver Island and British Columbia, Canada, the two great divisions of which are Nootka and Kwakiutl, the latter meaning "beach at north side of river," or in native folk etymology, "smoke of the world."

Kwang-chow (gwäng′jō′), *n.* Canton.

Kwang-cho-wan (gwäng′jō′wän′), *n.* a territory in S China, on the SW coast of Kwangtung province: leased to France, 1898–1945. ab. 250,000 pop.; ab. 190 sq. mi.

Kwang-si (kwäng′sē′; *Chin.* gwäng′-), *n.* a province in S China. 14,927,400 pop. (est. 1944); 85,452 sq. mi. *Cap.*: Nanning.

Kwang-tung (kwäng′tŏŏng′; *Chin.* gwäng′dŏŏng′), *n.* a province in SE China. 31,819,500 pop. (est. 1944); 85,447 sq. mi. *Cap.*: Canton.

Kwan-tung (kwän′tŏŏng′; *Chin.* gwän′dŏŏng′), *n.* a territory in NE China at the tip of Liotang Peninsula, Manchuria: leased to Japan, 1905–45. 1,493,400 pop. (est. 1941); 1337 sq. mi. Also, **Kwangtung.**

Kwei-chow (kwä′chou′; *Chin.* gwä′jō′), *n.* **1.** a province in S China. 10,755,500 pop. (est. 1944); 68,139 sq. mi. *Cap.*: Kweiyang. **2.** a city in central China, on the Yangtze in Szechwan province. ab. 250,000.

Kwei-lin (gwä′lYn′), *n.* a city in S China: the former capital of Kwangsi province. 107,400 (est. 1940).

Kwei-sui (gwä′swä′), *n.* a city in N China, in Inner Mongolia: the capital of Suiyüan province. ab. 75,000. Formerly, **Kwei-hwa-ting** (gwä′hwä′tYng′).

Kwei-yang (gwä′yäng′), *n.* a city in S China: the capital of Kweichow province. 127,400 (est. 1940).

K.W.H., kilowatt-hour. Also, **kw-h, kw-hr, kw.-hr.**

Ky., Kentucky.

ky-ack (kī′ăk), *n.* *Western U.S.* a type of knapsack which can hang from either side of a pack animal.

ky-a-nite (kī′ə nīt′), *n.* cyanite.

Kyd (kYd), *n.* **Thomas,** 1558–94, British dramatist.

ky-lix (kī′lYks, kYl′Yks), *n., pl.* **kylikes** (kYl′ə kēz′). cylix.

ky-mo-graph (kī′mə grăf′, -gräf′), *n.* **1.** an instrument by which variations of fluid pressure, as the waves of the pulse, can be measured and graphically recorded. **2.** an instrument measuring the angular oscillations of an airplane in flight with respect to axes fixed in space. Also, **cymograph.** [f. *kymo-* (comb. form of Gk. *kŷma* wave) + -GRAPH] —**ky′mo-graph′ic,** *adj.*

Kym-ric (kY̆m′rY̆k), *adj., n.* Cymric.

Kym-ry (kY̆m′rY̆), *n.pl.* Cymry.

Kyo-to (kyô′tô′), *n.* a city in central Japan, on S Honshu island: the capital of Japan, A.D. 784–1868. 914,655 (1946). Also, **Kioto.**

ky-pho-sis (kī fō′sY̆s), *n.* *Pathol.* a curvature of the spine, convex backward. [t. NL, t. Gk.: hunched state]

Kyr-i-e e-le-i-son (kY̆r′Y̆ ĕ′ ə lā′ə sŏn′), **1.** "Lord, have mercy," a brief petition used in various offices of the Eastern and Roman churches. **2.** a response or petition in the Anglican service, beginning with the words, "Lord, have mercy upon us." **3.** a musical setting of either of these. [t. Gk.: m. *Kŷrie elḗēson*]

Ky-the-ra (kē′thē rä′), *n.* Greek name of **Cerigo.**

Kyu-shu (kū′shōō′), *n.* a large island in SW Japan. 10,548,861 pop. (1946); 15,750 sq. mi. Also, **Kiushu.**

L

L¹, l (ĕl), *n., pl.* **L's** or **Ls, l's** or **ls. 1.** a consonant, the 12th letter of the English alphabet. **2.** the Roman numeral for 50.

L², ** *pl.* **L's. 1. something having a shape like that of the letter L. **2.** ell. **3.** *Elect.* Also, **l.** coefficient of inductance. **4.** elevated railroad. **5.** Latin. **6.** *Physics.* length. **7.** (L *libra*) pound. **8.** *Geog.* (terrestrial) longitude.

L., 1. Lake. **2.** Latin. **3.** latitude. **4.** law. **5.** left. **6.** (L *liber*) book. **7.** Liberal. **8.** Low.

l., 1. latitude. **2.** law. **3.** leaf. **4.** league. **5.** left. **6.** length. **7.** (*pl.* **ll.**) line. **8.** link. **9.** lira; liras. **10.** liter.

l-, *Chem.* levo-. Also, **l**

la¹ (lä), *n.* *Music.* the syllable used for the sixth tone of a scale, and sometimes for the tone A. See **sol-fa.** [See GAMUT]

la² (lô, lä), *interj.* an exclamation of wonder, surprise, etc. [ME and OE; weak var. of OE *lā* LO]

La, *Chem.* lanthanum.

La., Louisiana.

laa-ger (lä′gər), *South African.* —*n.* **1.** a camp or encampment, esp. within circle of wagons. —*v.t., v.i.* **2.** to arrange or encamp in a laager. Also, **lager.** [t. S Afr. D, var. of *lager*, c. G *lager* camp. Cf. LAIR]

Laa-land (lô′län), *n.* an island of SE Denmark, S of Zealand. 87,150 pop. (1945); 479 sq. mi. Also, **Lolland.**

lab (lăb), *n.* *U.S. Colloq.* laboratory.

Lab., 1. Labrador. **2.** Laborite.

La-ban (lā′bən), *n.* *Bible.* the Syrian father-in-law of Jacob. Gen. 24:29–60.

lab-a-rum (lăb′ə rəm), *n., pl.* **-ra** (-rə). **1.** an ecclesiastical standard or banner, as for carrying in procession. **2.** the military standard of Constantine the Great and later Christian emperors of Rome, bearing Christian symbols. [t. L, corresp. to Gk. *lábaron*; ult. orig. unknown]

lab-da-num (lăb′də nəm), *n.* a resinous juice that exudes from various rockroses of the genus *Cistus*, and used in perfumery, fumigating substances, medicinal plasters, etc. Also, **ladanum.** [t. ML, g. L *ládanum,* t. Gk.: m. *ládanon* mastic. Cf. Pers. *lādan* shrub]

ăct, āble, dâre, ärt; ĕbb, ēqual; Yf, īce; hŏt, ōver, ôrder, oil, bŏŏk, ōoze, out; ŭp, ūse, ûrge; ə = a in alone; ch, chief; g, give; ng, ring; sh, shoe; th, thin; ŧh, that; zh, vision. See the full key on inside cover.

lab·e·fac·tion (lăb′ə făk′shən), *n.* a shaking or weakening; overthrow; downfall. Also, *esp. Brit.,* **lab·e·fac·ta·tion** (lăb′ə făk tā′shən). [f. s. L *labefactus,* pp., weakened + -ION]

la·bel (lā′bəl), *n., v.,* **-beled, -beling** or (*esp. Brit.*) **-belled, -belling.** —*n.* **1.** a slip of paper or other material, marked or inscribed, for affixing to something to indicate its nature, ownership, destination, etc. **2.** a short word or phrase of description for a person, group, movement, etc. **3.** a strip or narrow piece of anything. **4.** *Archit.* a molding or dripstone over a door or window, esp. one which extends horizontally across the top of the opening and vertically downward for a certain distance at the sides. —*v.t.* **5.** to affix a label to; mark with a label. **6.** to designate or describe by or on a label: *the bottle was labeled poison.* **7.** to put in a certain class; to describe by a verbal label. [ME, t. OF, ult. der. L root *lamb-* lick] —**la′bel·er**; *esp. Brit.,* **la′bel·ler**, *n.*

La Belle Dame Sans Mer·ci (là bĕl dàm sän mĕr sē′), a ballad (1819) by Keats.

la·bel·lum (lə bĕl′əm), *n., pl.* **-bella** (-bĕl′ə). *Bot.* that division of the corolla of an orchidaceous plant which differs more or less markedly from the other divisions, often forming the most conspicuous part. [t. L, dim. of *labrum* lip]

la·bi·a (lā′bĭ ə), *n.* pl. of **labium.**

la·bi·al (lā′bĭ əl), *adj.* **1.** pertaining to or of the nature of a labium. **2.** *Music.* giving forth tones produced by the impact of a stream of air upon the sharp edge of a lip, as a flute or the flue pipes of an organ. **3.** of or pertaining to the lips. **4.** *Phonet.* involving lip articulation, as *p, v, m, w,* or a rounded vowel. [t. ML: s. *labiālis,* der. L *labium* lip] —**la′bi·al·ly,** *adv.*

L. Labellum, lady's-slipper. *Cypripedium hirsutum*

la·bi·al·ize (lā′bĭ ə līz′), *v.t.,* **-ized, -izing.** *Phonet.* to give a labial character to (a sound); e.g. to round (a vowel). —**la′bi·al·i·za′tion,** *n.*

la·bi·ate (lā′bĭ āt′, -ĭt), *adj.* **1.** lipped; having parts which are shaped or arranged like lips. **2.** *Bot.* **a.** belonging to the *Labiatae* (or *Menthaceae,* formerly *Lamiaceae*), the mint family of plants, most of which have bilabiate corollas. **b.** (usually) two-lipped; bilabiate: said of a gamopetalous corolla or gamosepalous calyx. —*n.* **3.** a labiate plant.

La·biche (là bēsh′), *n.* **Eugène Marin** (œ zhĕn′ mà răn′), 1815–88, French dramatist.

Labiate corolla of selfheal, *Prunella vulgaris*
A, Seen from the side; B, Laid open, front view

la·bile (lā′bĭl), *adj.* **1.** apt to lapse or change; unstable; lapsable. **2.** *Med.* noting or pertaining to a mode of application of electricity in which the active electrode is moved over the part to be acted upon. [late ME *labyl,* t. LL: m.s. *lābilis,* der. L *lābī* fall, slide. Cf. LAPSE] —**la·bil′i·ty,** *n.*

la·bi·o·den·tal (lā′bĭ ō dĕn′təl), *Phonet.* —*adj.* **1.** with the lower lip close to the upper front teeth, as in *f* or *v.* —*n.* **2.** a labiodental sound.

la·bi·o·ve·lar (lā′bĭ ō vē′lər), *Phonet.* —*adj.* **1.** with simultaneous bilabial and velar articulations. —*n.* **2.** a labiovelar sound.

la·bi·um (lā′bĭ əm), *n., pl.* **-bia** (-bĭ ə). **1.** a lip or liplike part. **2.** *Anat.* **a.** either lip, upper or under, of the mouth, respectively called **labium superiore** and **labium inferiore. b.** one of the four "lips" guarding the orifice of the vulva, including the two outer cutaneous folds (**labia majora**) and the two inner membranous folds (**labia minora**). **3.** *Bot.* the lower lip of a bilabiate corolla. **4.** *Entomol.* the posterior unpaired member of the mouth parts of an insect, formed by the united second maxillae. [t. L: lip]

La Bo·hème (là bō ĕm′), an opera (1896) by Puccini.

la·bor (lā′bər), *n.* **1.** bodily toil for the sake of gain or economic production. **2.** those engaged in such toil considered as a class: *the rights of labor.* **3.** work, esp. of a hard or fatiguing kind. **4.** a work or task done or to be done: *the twelve labors of Hercules.* **5.** the pangs and efforts of childbirth; travail. —*v.i.* **6.** to perform labor; exert one's powers of body or mind; work; toil. **7.** to work (*for*); strive, as toward a goal. **8.** to be burdened, troubled, or distressed: *you are laboring under a misapprehension.* **9.** to be in travail or childbirth. **10.** to roll or pitch heavily, as a ship, —*v.t.* **11.** to work hard and long at; elaborate: *don't labor the point.* **12.** *Archaic or Poetic.* to work or till (soil, etc.). Also, *Brit.,* **labour.** [ME *labour,* t. OF, t. L: m. *labor* toil, distress] —**la′bor·ing·ly,** *adv.* —**Syn. 3.** toil, exertion. See **work.** —**Ant. 3.** leisure. **6.** rest.

lab·o·ra·to·ry (lăb′rə tōr′ĭ, lăb′ə rə-; *Brit.* lə bŏr′ə tə-rĭ), *n., pl.* **-ries,** *adj.* —*n.* **1.** a building or part of a building fitted with apparatus for conducting scientific investigations, experiments, tests, etc., or for manufacturing chemicals, medicines, etc. **2.** any place where or in which similar processes are carried on by natural forces. —*adj.* **3.** serving a function in a laboratory. **4.** relating to techniques of work in a laboratory. [t. ML: m.s. *labōrātōrium* workshop] —**lab′o·ra·to′ri·al,** *adj.*

Labor Day, (in most States of the U.S.) a legal holiday, commonly the first Monday in September, in honor of the laboring class.

la·bored (lā′bərd), *adj.* **1.** laboriously formed; made or done with laborious pains or care. **2.** not easy, natural, or spontaneous: *a labored style.* Also, *Brit.* **laboured.** —**Syn. 1.** See **elaborate.**

la·bor·er (lā′bər ər), *n.* **1.** one engaged in work which requires bodily strength rather than skill or training: *a day laborer.* **2.** one who labors. Also, *Brit.* **labourer.**

la·bo·ri·ous (lā bōr′ĭ əs), *adj.* **1.** requiring much labor, exertion, or perseverance: *a laborious undertaking.* **2.** requiring labor in construction or execution. **3.** given to or diligent in labor. [ME, t. L: m.s. *labōriōsus*] —**la·bo′ri·ous·ly,** *adv.* —**la·bo′ri·ous·ness,** *n.* —**Syn. 1.** toilsome, arduous, onerous. **3.** hard-working, industrious, assiduous. —**Ant. 1.** easy. **3.** lazy.

La·bor·ite (lā′bər īt′), *n.* a member of a party advocating labor interests, as in British politics.

labor market, the available supply of labor considered with reference to the demand for it.

la·bor om·ni·a vin·cit (lā′bôr ŏm′nĭ ə vĭn′sĭt), *Latin.* toil conquers all things (motto of Oklahoma).

la·bor-sav·ing (lā′bər sā′vĭng), *adj.* saving, or effecting economy in, labor: *a labor-saving device.*

labor union, an organization of wage earners or salaried employees for mutual aid and protection, and for dealing collectively with employers; a trade union.

la·bour (lā′bər), *n., v.i., v.t. Brit.* labor.

Labour Party, the British political party representing socialist groups, trade unions, and labor in general. It was formed in the latter part of the 19th century, but did not exert political influence until the 1920's.

Lab·ra·dor (lăb′rə dôr′), *n.* **1.** a peninsula in NE North America between Hudson Bay, the Atlantic, and the Gulf of St. Lawrence, containing the Canadian provinces of Newfoundland and Labrador. ab. 500,000 sq. mi. **2.** the portion of Newfoundland in the E part of this peninsula. 4716 pop. (1935); ab. 120,000 sq. mi.

lab·ra·dor·ite (lăb′rə dôr īt′, lăb′rə dôr′īt), *n.* a mineral of the plagioclase feldspar group, often characterized by a brilliant change of colors with blue and green most common. [f. *Labrador,* where it was discovered + -ITE¹]

la·bret (lā′brĕt), *n.* a lip ornament worn by primitive tribes, in a pierced hole. [f. s. L *labrum* lip + -ET]

lab·roid (lăb′roid), *adj.* **1.** belonging to or resembling the *Labridae,* a family of thick-lipped marine fishes including the tautog, cunners, etc. —*n.* **2.** a labroid fish. [f. s. L *lābrus* kind of fish + -OID]

la·brum (lā′brəm, lăb′rəm), *n., pl.* **labra** (lā′brə, lăb′-rə). **1.** a lip or liplike part. **2.** *Zool.* **a.** the anterior unpaired member of the mouth parts of an arthropod, projecting in front of the mouth. **b.** the outer margin of the aperture of a gastropod's shell. **3.** *Anat.* a ring of cartilage about the edge of a joint surface of a bone. [t. L: lip]

La Bru·yère (là br y ĕr′), **Jean de** (zhän də), 1645–1696, French moralist and author.

La·bu·an (lā′bōō än′), *n.* an island off the coast of British North Borneo, now forming part of that colony: formerly one of the Straits Settlements. 8111 pop. (est. 1937); 35 sq. mi. *Cap.:* Victoria.

la·bur·num (lə bûr′nəm), *n.* any of several small leguminous trees, having pendulous racemes of yellow flowers, somewhat similar as to those of wisteria. *Laburnum anagyroides* of Europe is most common. [t. L]

lab·y·rinth (lăb′ə rĭnth), *n.* **1.** an intricate combination of passages in which it is difficult to find one's way or to reach the exit. **2.** a maze of paths bordered by high hedges, as in a park or garden. **3.** a complicated or tortuous arrangement, as of streets, buildings, etc. **4.** any confusingly intricate state of things or events; an entanglement. **5.** (*cap.*) *Gk. Myth.* the Cretan labyrinth, constructed by Daedalus, the abode of the fabled Minotaur. **6.** *Anat.* **a.** the internal ear, a complex structure including a bony portion (**osseous labyrinth**) and a membranous portion (**membranous labyrinth**) contained in it. **b.** the aggregate of air chambers in the ethmoid bone, between the eye and the upper part of the nose. [t. L: s. *labyrinthus,* t. Gk.: m. *labýrinthos*]

lab·y·rin·thine (lăb′ə rĭn′thĭn, -thēn), *adj.* **1.** pertaining to or forming a labyrinth. **2.** mazy; intricate. Also, **lab·y·rin·thi·an** (lăb′ə rĭn′thĭ ən), **lab′y·rin′thic.**

lac¹ (lăk), *n.* a resinous substance deposited on the twigs of various trees in southern Asia by the lac insect, and used in the manufacture of varnishes, sealing wax, etc., and in the production of a red coloring matter. See **shellac.** [t. Hind.: m. *lākh,* g. Skt. *lākshā*]

lac² (lăk), *n. India.* **1.** the sum of 100,000, esp. of rupees. The usual pointing for sums of Indian money above a lac is with a comma after the number of lacs: Rs. 30,52,000 (i.e. thirty lacs: and fifty-two thousand) instead of 3,052,000. **2.** an indefinitely large number. Also, **lakh.** [t. Hind.: m. *lākh,* g. Skt. *laksha* mark, hundred thousand]

Lac·ca·dive Islands (lăk′ə dīv′), a group of small islands and coral reefs in the Arabian Sea, off the SW coast of India: a part of Madras province. 18,393 pop. (1941); ab. 80 sq. mi.

lac·co·lith (lăk′ə lĭth), *n. Geol.* a mass of igneous rock formed from lava which when rising from below did not find its way to the surface, but spread out laterally into

b., blend of, blended; c., cognate with; d., dialect, dialectal; der., derived from; f., formed from; g., going back to; m., modification of; r., replacing; s., stem of; t., taken from; ?, perhaps. See the full key on inside cover.

a lenticular body, thereby causing the overlying strata to bulge upward. Also, **lac·co·lite** (lăk′ə lĭt′). [f. m. Gk. *lákko(s)* pond + -LITH] —**lac′co·lith′ic, lac·co·lit·ic** (lăk′ə lĭt′ĭk), *adj.*

lace (lās), *n., v.,* **laced, lacing.** —*n.* **1.** openwork, ornamental texture made of threads by hand or machine. **2.** a cord or string for holding or drawing together, as when passed through holes in opposite edges: *shoe laces.* **3.** ornamental cord or braid, as on uniforms. **4.** spirits added to coffee or other beverage. —*v.t.* **5.** to fasten, draw together, or compress by means of a lace. **6.** to pass (a cord, etc.) as a lace, as through holes. **7.** to adorn or trim with lace. **8.** to compress the waist of (a person) by drawing tight the laces of a corset, etc. **9.** to interlace or intertwine. **10.** *Colloq.* to lash, beat, or thrash. **11.** to mark or streak, as with color. **12.** to intermix, as coffee with spirits. —*v.i.* **13.** to be fastened with a lace. [ME *las,* t. OF: m. *laz* noose, string, g. L *laqueus* noose, snare. Cf. LASSO] —**lace′-like′,** *adj.*

Lac·e·dae·mon (lăs′ə dē′mən), *n.* ancient Sparta. —**Lac·e·dae·mo·ni·an** (lăs′ə dĭ mō′nĭ ən), *adj., n.*

lace·mak·ing (lās′mā′kĭng), *n.* the art, act, or process of making lace.

lac·er·ate (*v.* lăs′ə rāt′; *adj.* lăs′ə rāt′, -ər ĭt), *v.,* **-ated, -ating,** *adj.* —*v.t.* **1.** to tear roughly; mangle: *to lacerate the flesh.* **2.** to hurt: *to lacerate a person's feelings.* —*adj.* **3.** lacerated. [t. L: m.s. *lacerātus,* pp.] —**Syn. 1.** See **maim.**

lac·er·at·ed (lăs′ə rā′tĭd), *adj.* **1.** mangled; jagged. **2.** *Bot., Zool.* having the edge variously cut as if torn into irregular segments, as a leaf.

lac·er·a·tion (lăs′ə rā′shən), *n.* **1.** act of lacerating. **2.** the result of lacerating; rough, jagged tear.

lac·er·til·i·an (lăs′ər tĭl′ĭ ən), *adj.* **1.** of or pertaining to the *Lacertilia,* an order (or suborder) of reptiles comprising the common lizards and their allies. See **saurian** (def. 1). —*n.* **2.** a lacertilian reptile. [f. s. NL *Lacertilia,* pl. (dcr. L *lacerta* lizard) + -AN]

lace·wing (lās′wĭng′), *n.* any of various neuropterous insects of the family *chrysopidae,* with delicate lacelike wings, whose larvae prey chiefly on aphids.

La Chaise (lä shĕz′), **Père François d'Aix de** (pĕr frän swä′ dĕks də), 1624–1709. French Roman Catholic priest, confessor to Louis XIV.

lach·es (lăch′ĭz), *n. Law.* neglect to do a thing at the proper time, esp. such delay as will bar a party from bringing a legal proceeding. [ME *lachesse,* t. AF, var. of *Laschesse,* der. *lasche* loose, g. L *laxus* lax]

Lach·e·sis (lăk′ə sĭs), *n. Class. Myth.* that one of the three Fates whose duty it was to determine the length of each individual's life, or, sometimes, to decide his fate during life. [t. L, t. Gk.: lit., lot, destiny]

lach·ry·mal (lăk′rə məl), *adj.* **1.** of or pertaining to tears; producing tears. **2.** characterized by tears; indicative of weeping. **3.** *Anat., etc.* denoting, pertaining to, or situated near the glands, ducts, or the like, concerned in the secretion or conveyance of tears. —*n.* **4.** (*pl.*) *Anat.* tear-secreting glands. **5.** a lachrymatory. Also, **lacrimal, lacrymal.** [t. ML: s. *lachrymālis, lacrimālis,* der. L *lacrima* tear]

Section of human eye showing A, lachrymal duct, and B, lachrymal gland

lach·ry·ma·to·ry (lăk′rə mə tōr′ĭ), *adj., n., pl.* **-ries.** —*adj.* **1.** of, pertaining to, or causing the shedding of tears. —*n.* **2.** a small, narrow-necked vase found in ancient Roman tombs, formerly thought to have been used for containing the tears of bereaved friends.

lach·ry·mose (lăk′rə mōs′), *adj.* **1.** given to shedding tears; tearful. **2.** suggestive of or tending to cause tears; mournful. [t. L: m.s. *lac(h)rimōsus,* der *lac(h)rima* tear] —**lach′ry·mose′ly,** *adv.*

lac·ing (lā′sĭng), *n.* **1.** act of one who or that which laces. **2.** a laced fastening, or a lace for such use. **3.** a trimming of lace or braid. **4.** a thrashing.

la·cin·i·ate (lə sĭn′ĭ āt′, -ĭt), *adj. Bot., Zool.* cut into narrow, irregular lobes; slashed; jagged. [f. s. L *lacinia* lappet + -ATE¹]

lac insect (lăk), a homopterous Indian insect, *Lacciier lacca,* the females of which produce lac.

Laciniate leaf

lack (lăk), *n.* **1.** deficiency or absence of something requisite, desirable, or customary: *lack of money or skill.* **2.** something lacking or wanting: *skilled labor was the chief lack.* —*v.t.* **3.** to be deficient in, destitute of, or without: *to lack strength.* **4.** to fall short in respect of: *the vote lacks three of being a majority.* —*v.i.* **5.** to be absent, as something requisite or desirable. [ME *lak,* t. MLG or MD: deficiency. Cf. Icel. *lakr* deficient] —**Syn. 1.** want, need, dearth, scarcity, paucity. —**Ant. 1.** surplus.

lack·a·dai·si·cal (lăk′ə dā′zə kəl), *adj.* sentimentally or affectedly languishing; weakly sentimental; listless. [f. *lackadaisy,* var. of LACKADAY (see ALACK) + -ICAL] —**lack′a·dai′si·cal·ly,** *adv.* —**lack′a·dai′si·cal·ness,** *n.*

lack·a·day (lăk′ə dā′), *interj. Archaic.* alack.

Lack·a·wan·na (lăk′ə wŏn′ə), *n.* a city in W New York, on Lake Erie, near Buffalo. 27,658 (1950).

lack·er (lăk′ər), *n., v.t.* lacquer. —**lack′er·er,** *n.*

lack·ey (lăk′ĭ), *n., pl.* **-eys,** *v.,* **-eyed, -eying.** —*n.* **1.** a footman or liveried manservant. **2.** a servile follower. —*v.t.* **3.** to attend as a lackey does. Also, **lacquey.** [t. F: m. *laquais,* t. Sp.: m. *lacayo* foot soldier]

lack·lus·ter (lăk′lŭs′tər), *adj.* **1.** lacking luster or brightness; dull. —*n.* **2.** a lack of luster; that which lacks brightness. Also, *esp. Brit.,* **lack′lus′tre.**

La·co·ni·a (lə kō′nĭ ə), *n.* an ancient country in the S part of Greece. *Cap.:* Sparta. —**La·co′ni·an,** *adj., n.*

la·con·ic (lə kŏn′ĭk), *adj.* using few words; expressing much in few words; concise. Also, **la·con′i·cal.** [t. L: s. *lacōnicus,* t. Gk.: m. *lakōnikós* Laconian] —**la·con′i·cal·ly,** *adv.*

lac·o·nism (lăk′ə nĭz′əm), *n.* **1.** laconic brevity. **2.** a laconic utterance or sentence. Also, **la·con·i·cism** (lə kŏn′ə sĭz′əm). [t. Gk.: m.s. *lakōnismōs* imitation of Lacedaemonians, who were noted for brief, pithy speech]

La Co·ru·ña (lä kô rōō′nyä), a seaport in NW Spain. 104,220 (1940). Also, **Coruña.**

lac·quer (lăk′ər), *n.* **1.** a protective coating consisting of a resin and/or a cellulose ester dissolved in a volatile solvent, sometimes with pigment added. **2.** any of various resinous varnishes, esp. a natural varnish obtained from a Japanese tree, *Rhus verniciflua,* used to produce a highly polished, lustrous surface on wood, etc. **3.** ware coated with a lacquer varnish, and often inlaid. —*v.t.* **4.** to coat with or as with lacquer. Also, **lacker.** [t. F (obs.): m. *lacre* sealing wax, ult. t. Ar.: m. *lakk,* t. Pers.: m. *lāk*] —**lac′quer·er,** *n.*

lac·quey (lăk′ĭ), *n., pl.* **-queys,** *v.t.,* **-queyed, -queying.** lackey.

lac·ri·mal (lăk′rə məl), *adj., n.* lachrymal. Also, **lac′ry·mal.**

la·crosse (lə krôs′, -krŏs′), *n.* a game of ball, of American Indian origin, played by two teams of 12 players each, who strive to send a ball through a goal by means of long-handled racquets. [t. F: m. *la crosse* the crook (the racquet used in the game). See CROSSE]

La Crosse (lə krôs′, krŏs′), a city in W Wisconsin, on the Mississippi. 47,535 (1950).

lact-, a word element meaning "milk." Also, **lacto-.** [t. L: m. *lacti-,* comb. form of *lac*]

lac·tam (lăk′tăm), *n. Biochem.* an organic compound formed from an amino acid by elimination of water from the amino and carboxyl groups. [f. LACT- + AM(MONIA)]

lac·tase (lăk′tās), *n. Chem.* an enzyme capable of hydrolyzing lactose into glucose and galactose.

lac·tate (lăk′tāt), *n., v.,* **-tated, -tating.** —*n.* **1.** *Chem.* an ester or salt of lactic acid. —*v.i.* **2.** to produce milk.

lac·ta·tion (lăk tā′shən), *n.* **1.** the secretion or formation of milk. **2.** the period of milk production.

lac·te·al (lăk′tĭ əl), *adj.* **1.** pertaining to, consisting of, or resembling milk; milky. **2.** *Anat.* conveying or containing chyle. —*n.* **3.** *Anat.* any of the minute lymphatic vessels which convey chyle from the small intestine to the thoracic duct. [f. s. L *lacteus* milky + -AL¹] —**lac′te·al·ly,** *adv.*

lac·te·ous (lăk′tĭ əs), *adj.* milky; of the color of milk.

lac·tes·cent (lăk tĕs′ənt), *adj.* **1.** becoming or being milky. **2.** *Bot.* forming a milky juice. **3.** *Entomol.* secreting a milky fluid. [t. L: s. *lactescens,* ppr.] —**lac·tes′cence,** *n.*

lac·tic (lăk′tĭk), *adj.* pertaining to or obtained from milk.

lactic acid, *Chem.* an acid, $CH_3CHOHCOOH$, found in sour milk.

lac·tif·er·ous (lăk tĭf′ə rəs), *adj.* **1.** producing milk; concerned with the secretion of milk. **2.** conveying milk or a milky fluid. [f. LL *lactifer* milk-bearing + -OUS]

lacto-, var. of lact-, before consonants.

lac·to·ba·cil·lus (lăk′tō bə sĭl′əs), *n., pl.* **-cilli** (-sĭl′ī). any bacterium of the genus *Lactobacillus,* a group of aerobic, long, slender rods which produce large amounts of lactic acid in the fermentation of carbohydrates, esp. in milk. The species most important to man is *Lactobacillus acidophilus.* See **acidophilus milk.**

lac·to·fla·vin (lăk′tō flā′vĭn), *n.* riboflavin.

lac·tom·e·ter (lăk tŏm′ə tər), *n.* an instrument for determining the specific gravity of milk.

lac·tone (lăk′tōn), *n. Chem.* one of a class of internal esters derived from hydroxy acids. —**lac·ton·ic** (lăk tŏn′ĭk), *adj.*

lac·to·pro·te·in (lăk′tō prō′tē ĭn, -prō′tēn), *n.* any protein existing in milk.

lac·tose (lăk′tōs), *n. Chem.* a crystalline disaccharide, $C_{12}H_{22}O_{11}$, present in milk, used as a food and in medicine; sugar of milk. [f. LACT- + -OSE²]

la·cu·na (lə kū′nə), *n., pl.* **-nae** (-nē), **-nas.** **1.** a pit or cavity; an interstitial or intercellular space as in plant or animal tissue. **2.** *Anat.* one of the numerous minute cavities in the substance of bone, supposed to contain nucleated cells. **3.** *Bot.* an air space lying in the midst of the cellular tissue of plants. **4.** a gap or hiatus, as in a manuscript. [t. L: gap]

la·cu·nal (lə kū′nəl), *adj.* **1.** of or pertaining to a lacuna. **2.** having lacunae. Also, **lac·u·nar·y** (lăk′yŏŏ-nĕr′ĭ, lə kū′nə rĭ).

la·cu·nar (lə kū′nər), *adj., n., pl.* **lacunars, lacunaria** (lăk′yŏŏ nâr′ĭ ə). —*adj.* **1.** lacunal. —*n.* **2.** *Archit.* **a.** a ceiling, or an undersurface, as of a cornice, formed of sunken compartments. **b.** one of the compartments. [t. L, der. *lacūna* pit, hollow]

la·cu·nose (ləkū′nōs), *adj.* full of or having lacunae.

la·cus·trine (ləkŭs′trĭn), *adj.* **1.** of or pertaining to a lake. **2.** living or occurring on or in lakes, as various animals and plants. **3.** formed at the bottom or along the shore of lakes, as geological strata. [f. s. L **lacustris* (der. *lacus* lake, modeled on *palustris* of a swamp) +-INE¹]

lac·y (lā′sĭ), *adj.*, **lacier, laciest.** resembling lace; lacelike. —**lac′i·ly,** *adv.* —**lac′i·ness,** *n.*

lad (lăd), *n.* **1.** a boy or youth (in common use in England but literary in U.S.). **2.** *Colloq.* (in familiar use) any male. [ME *ladde* attendant, OE *Ladda* (nickname), of obscure orig. Cf. Norw. *askeladd* male Cinderella]

lad·a·num (lăd′ənəm), *n.* labdanum.

lad·der (lăd′ər), *n.* **1.** a structure of wood, metal, or rope, commonly consisting of two sidepieces between which a series of bars or rungs are set at suitable distances, forming a means of ascent or descent. **2.** something resembling or suggesting a ladder. **3.** a means of rising, as to eminence: *ladder of success.* [ME; OE *hlǣder,* c. G *leiter*]

ladder stitch, an embroidery stitch in which cross bars at equal distances are produced between two solid ridges of raised work.

lad·die (lăd′ĭ), *n.* *Chiefly Scot.* a young lad; a boy.

lade (lād), *v.*, **laded, laden** or **laded, lading.** —*v.t.* **1.** to put (something) on or in as a burden, load, or cargo; load. **2.** to load oppressively; burden: *laden with responsibilities.* **3.** to fill abundantly: *trees laden with fruit.* **4.** to lift or throw in or out, as a fluid, with a ladle or other utensil. —*v.i.* **5.** to take on a load. **6.** to lade a liquid. [ME *lade(n),* OE *hladan* load, draw (water), c. D *laden;* akin to G *laden* load. Cf. LADLE.]

La·din (lədēn′), *n.* **1.** a Rhaeto-Romanic language of the southern Tyrol. **2.** Romansh. **3.** a person who speaks Ladin. [t. Romansh, g. L *Latinus* Latin]

lad·ing (lā′dĭng), *n.* **1.** act of lading. **2.** that with which something is laden; load; freight; cargo.

La·di·no (lädē′nō), *n.* **1.** a mixed Spanish and Hebrew dialect spoken by Jews of Spanish extraction now living in Turkey and elsewhere. **2.** (in Spanish America) a Spanish-speaking half-breed; a mestizo. [t. Sp., g. L *Latinus* Latin]

Lad·is·laus (lăd′ĭslôs), *n.* **Saint,** 1040–95, king of Hungary, 1077–95. Also, **Lad·is·las** (lăd′ĭsləs, -läs′).

la·dle (lā′dəl), *n.*, *v.*, **-dled, -dling.** —*n.* **1.** a long-handled utensil with a dish-shaped or cup-shaped bowl for dipping or conveying liquids. —*v.t.* **2.** to dip or convey with or as with a ladle. [ME *ladel,* OE *hlædel,* der. *hladan* LADE] —**la′dle·ful′,** *n.* —**la′dler,** *n.*

La·do·ga (lä′dōgä), *n.* a lake in the NW Soviet Union, NE of Leningrad: largest lake in Europe. ab. 7000 sq. mi.

La·drone Islands (lədrōn′), former name of **Marianas Islands.** Also, **La·drones** (lədrōnz′; *Sp.* lä drō′nĕs).

la·dy (lā′dĭ), *n.*, *pl.* **-dies,** *adj.* —*n.* **1.** a woman of good family or social position, or of good breeding, refinement, etc. (correlative of *gentleman*). **2.** a polite term for any woman. **3.** (*cap.*) in Great Britain, the proper title of any woman whose husband is higher in rank than baronet or knight, or who is the daughter of a nobleman not lower than an earl, though the title is given by courtesy also to the wives of baronets, and knights. **4.** a woman who has proprietary rights or authority, as over a manor (correlative of *lord*). **5.** (*cap.*) the Virgin Mary (usually, **Our Lady**). **6.** the mistress of a household: *the lady of the house.* **7.** a woman who is the object of chivalrous devotion. —*adj.* **8.** being a lady: *a lady reporter.* **9.** of a lady; ladylike. [ME *lavedi, levedi,* OE *hlǣfdige,* ? orig. meaning loaf-kneader, f. *hlāf* LOAF¹ +-*dige,* akin to *dāh* DOUGH. Cf. LORD] —**Syn. 1.** See **woman.**

la·dy·bird (lā′dĭbûrd′), *n.* ladybug. [f. LADY (uninflected poss. case) Virgin Mary + BIRD; i.e., (our) Lady's bird]

la·dy·bug (lā′dĭbŭg′), *n.* a beetle of the family *Coccinellidae,* of graceful form and delicate coloration. The larvae feed upon plant lice and small insects. Also, **lady beetle.**

Ladybug, *Epilachna borealis*

Lady Chapel, a chapel dedicated to the Virgin Mary, attached to a church, and generally behind the high altar at the extremity of the apse.

Lady Day, 1. the feast of the Annunciation, March 25. **2.** one of various days celebrated in honor of the Virgin Mary. **3.** *Brit.* the spring quarter day, when quarterly rents and accounts are due.

la·dy·fin·ger (lā′dĭfĭng′gər), *n.* a small, finger-shaped sponge cake.

la·dy·fish (lā′dĭfĭsh′), *n.*, *pl.* **-fishes,** (*esp. collectively*) **-fish.** a small game fish, *Albula vulpes,* of tropical waters.

lady in waiting, a lady who is in attendance upon a queen or princess.

la·dy·kill·er (lā′dĭkĭl′ər), *n.* *Slang.* a man supposed to be dangerously fascinating to ladies. —**la′dy·kill′ing,** *n.*, *adj.*

la·dy·like (lā′dĭlīk′), *adj.* **1.** like a lady. **2.** befitting a lady: *ladylike manners.* —**la′dy·like′ness,** *n.*

la·dy·love (lā′dĭlŭv′), *n.* a beloved lady; sweetheart.

Lady of the Lake, The, 1. a romance in verse (1810) by Scott. **2.** Vivian.

la·dy·ship (lā′dĭshĭp′), *n.* **1.** (*often cap.*) the form used in speaking of or to a woman having the title of *Lady* (prec. by *her, your,* etc.). **2.** the condition or rank of a lady.

lady's maid, a maid who is a lady's personal attendant in dressing, etc.

La·dy·smith (lā′dĭsmĭth′), *n.* a city in the E part of the Union of the South Africa, in Natal: besieged by Boers, 1899–1900. 9702 (1936).

la·dy's-slip·per (lā′dĭzslĭp′ər), *n.* **1.** any plant of the genus *Cypripedium,* comprising orchids whose flowers have a protruding labellum somewhat resembling a slipper. **2.** any plant of several other genera of the orchid family whose flowers resemble *Cypripedium,* as *Paphiopedilum, Phragmipedium,* and *Selenipedium.* Also, **la′dy-slip′per.**

la·dy's-smock (lā′dĭz smŏk′), *n.* a cruciferous plant, *Cardamine pratensis,* with white or purple flowers.

la·dy's-tress·es (lā′dĭz trĕs′ĭz), *n.* any orchid of the genus *Spiranthes.*

La·er·tes (lāûr′tēz), *n.* *Gk. Legend.* the father of Odysseus.

Lae·tar·e Sunday (lētâr′ĭ), *Rom. Cath. Ch.* the fourth Sunday of Lent when the Introit begins with "Laetare Jerusalem." Isaiah 66:10.

laevo-, var. of levo.

lae·vo·ro·ta·tion (lē′vōrōtā′shən), *n.* levorotation.

lae·vo·ro·ta·to·ry (lē′vōrō′tətōr′ĭ), *adj.* levorotatory.

La Farge (lə färzh′, färj′), **John,** 1835–1910, U.S. painter, artist in stained glass, and author.

La·fa·yette (lăf′ĭyĕt′, lä′fĭy-; *Fr.* lȧ fȧ yĕt′ *for 1;* lăf′ĭyĕt′ *for 2*), *n.* **1. Marie Joseph Paul Yves Roch Gilbert du Motier** (mȧ rē′ zhōzĕf′ pōl ēv rôk zhēlbĕr′ dy mōtyē′), **Marquis de,** 1757–1834, French soldier, statesman, and liberal leader, who served in the American Revolutionary Army and took a leading part in the French Revolutions of 1789 and 1830. **2.** a city in W Indiana, on the Wabash. 35,568 (1950). **3.** a city in S Louisiana. 33,541 (1950).

La Fol·lette (lə fŏl′ĭt), **Robert Marion,** 1855–1925, U.S. political leader: U.S. senator, 1906–25.

La Fon·taine (lȧ fôN tĕn′), **Jean de** (zhäN də), 1621–1695, French poet and writer of fables.

lag¹ (lăg), *v.*, **lagged, lagging,** *n.* —*v.i.* **1.** to move slowly; fall behind; hang back (often fol. by *behind*). **2.** *Marbles.* to throw one's shooting marble toward a line on the ground in order to decide on the order of play. **3.** *Billiards.* (in deciding the order of play) to drive the cue ball to the end cushion and return, the winner being the one who comes nearest to the head rail. —*n.* **4.** a lagging or falling behind; retardation. **5.** *Mech.* the amount of retardation of some movement. **6.** *Marbles, Billiards.* act of lagging. [t. Scand.; cf. Norw. *lagga* go slowly] —**Syn. 1.** loiter, linger. —**Ant. 1.** hasten.

lag² (lăg), *v.*, **lagged, lagging,** *n.* *Slang.* —*v.t.* **1.** to send to penal servitude. —*n.* **2.** a convict. **3.** a term of penal servitude. [orig. unknown]

lag³ (lăg), *n.*, *v.*, **lagged, lagging.** —*n.* **1.** one of the staves or strips which form the periphery of a wooden drum, the casing of a steam cylinder, or the like. —*v.t.* **2.** to cover, as a steam boiler, to prevent radiation of heat. [t. Scand.; cf. Sw. *lagg* stave]

lag·an (lăg′ən), *n.* *Law.* anything sunk in the sea, but attached to a buoy, etc., so that it may be recovered. Also, **ligan.** [t. OF; of Scand. orig. and akin to LIE², LAY¹]

Lag b'O·mer (läg bō′mər), a Jewish holiday, the thirty-third day from the second day of Passover. [t. Heb.: *lag* thirty-third (day) in the 'omer count of forty-nine days from Passover to the Feast of the Pentecost]

la·ger¹ (lä′gər, lô′-), *n.* a beer stored from 6 weeks to 6 months before use. Also, **lager beer.** [short for *lager beer,* half adoption, half trans. of G *lagerbier*]

la·ger² (lä′gər), *n.*, *v.t.*, *v.i.* *South African.* laager.

La·ger·löf (lä′gərloef′), **Selma** (sĕl′mä), 1858–1940, Swedish author.

lag·gard (lăg′ərd), *adj.* **1.** lagging; backward; slow. —*n.* **2.** one who lags; lingerer. —**lag′gard·ly,** *adv.* —**lag′gard·ness,** *n.*

lag·ger (lăg′ər), *n.* one who lags; a laggard.

lag·ging (lăg′ĭng), *n.* **1.** act of lagging behind. **2.** act of covering a boiler, etc., with heat-insulating material. **3.** the covering formed. **4.** the material used.

La Gio·con·da (lä jōkôn′dä). See **Mona Lisa.**

la·gniappe (lăn yăp′, lăn′yăp), *n.* something given with a purchase to a customer, by way of compliment or for good measure. Also, **la·gnappe′.** [t. Louisiana F, t. Amer. Sp.: m. *la ñapa* the gift]

lag·o·morph (lăg′əmôrf′), *n.* any of the *Lagomorpha,* an order of mammals resembling the rodents but having two pairs of upper incisors, and including the hares, rabbits, and pikas, formerly classified as a suborder of rodents. [f. Gk. *lagō(s)* hare + -MORPH]

la·goon (ləgōōn′), *n.* **1.** an area of shallow water separated from the sea by low banks. **2.** any small, pondlike body of water, esp. one communicating with a larger body of water. Also, **la·gune′.** [t. It., Sp.: m. *laguna,* g. L *lacūna* pool, pond]

Lagoon Islands, Ellice Islands.

La·gos (lā′gŏs, lä′gŏs), *n.* a seaport in and the capital of Nigeria, in the SW part. Municipal area, 155,900 pop. (est. 1937); 24 sq. mi.

La Grange (lȧ gränzh′ *for 1;* lə gränj′ *for 2*), **1. Joseph Louis** (zhō zĕf′ lwē), **Count,** 1736–1813, French mathematician and astronomer, born in Italy. **2.** a city in W Georgia. 25,025 (1950).

Lag·thing (lăg′tĭng′), n. See **Storthing**.

La Guai·ra (lä gwī′rä), a seaport in N Venezuela: the port of Caracas. 9717 (1941).

La Guar·di·a (lə gwär′dĭ̍ə), **Fiorello Henry** (fē′ə-rĕl′ō), 1882–1947, U.S. political leader.

La Hogue (lä ôg′), a roadstead off the NW coast of France: naval battle, 1692. Also, **La Hougue** (lä ōōg′).

La·hore (lə hōr′), n. a city in Pakistan, in W Punjab. 671,659 (1941).

Lai·bach (lī′bäкн), n. German name of Ljubljana.

la·ic (lā′ĭk), adj. 1. Also, **la′i·cal**. lay; secular. —n. 2. layman. [t. ⁖L: s. lāicus, t. Gk.: m. lāïkós, der. lāós people] —**la′i·cal·ly**, adv.

la·i·cize (lā′ə sīz′), v.t., **-cized, -cizing**. to deprive of clerical character. —**la′i·ci·za′tion**, n.

laid (lād), v. pt. and pp. of **lay**.

laid paper, paper with fine parallel and cross lines produced in manufacturing. Cf. **wove paper**.

lain (lān), v. pp. of **lie²**.

lair (lâr), n. 1. the den or resting place of a wild beast. 2. a place in which to lie or rest; a bed. —v.t. 3. to place in a lair. 4. to serve as a lair for. —v.i. 5. to go to, lie in, or have a lair. [ME leir, OE leger, c. D and OHG leger bed, camp; akin to **LIE²**]

laird (lârd), n. Scot. a landed proprietor. [var. of **LORD**] —**laird′ship**, n.

lais·ser-al·ier (lĕ sĕ ȧ lē′), n. French. unrestraint.

lais·sez faire (lĕs′ā fâr′; Fr. lĕ sĕ fĕr′), the theory or system of government that upholds the autonomous character of the economic order, believing that government should intervene as little as possible in the direction of economic affairs. Also, **lais′ser faire′**. [t. F: lit., allow to act]

la·i·ty (lā′ə tĭ), n. 1. laymen, as distinguished from clergymen. 2. the people outside of a particular profession, as distinguished from those belonging to it. [f. **LAY³** + **-TY²**]

La·ius (lā′əs, lā′ĭ̍əs), n. Gk. Legend. a king of Thebes, killed unwittingly by his son, Oedipus.

lake¹ (lāk), n. 1. a body of water (fresh or salt) of considerable size, surrounded by land. 2. some similar body of water, or other liquid. [ME; OE lacu stream, pool, pond; r. ME lac, t. OF, t. L: s. lacus lake, tank]

lake² (lāk), n. 1. any of various pigments prepared from animal, vegetable, or coal-tar coloring matters by union (chemical or other) with metallic compounds. 2. a red pigment prepared from lac or cochineal by combination with a metallic compound. [t. F: m. laque, t. Pers.: m. lăk. See **LAC¹**]

Lake (lāk), n. **Simon**, 1866–1945, U.S. engineer and naval architect.

Lake Charles, a city in SW Louisiana. 41,272 (1950).

Lake District, a picturesque mountainous region abounding in lakes, in NW England.

lake dweller, an inhabitant of a lake dwelling.

lake dwelling, a dwelling, esp. of prehistoric times, built on piles or other support over the water of a lake.

lake herring, a cisco (whitefish), Leucichthys artedi, of the Great Lakes and small glacial lakes of eastern North America.

Lake·hurst (lāk′hûrst), n. a borough in central New Jersey: naval air station; dirigible hangar. 1518 (1950).

Lake·land (lāk′lənd), n. a city in central Florida. 30,851 (1950).

Lake of the Woods, a lake between N Minnesota and Ontario and Manitoba provinces, Canada: summer resort region. ab. 90 mi. long; 1851 sq. mi.

Lake poets, the poets Wordsworth, Coleridge, and Southey (from their residence in the Lake District).

lake trout, a large, fork-tailed char, Cristivomer namaycush, common in the Great Lakes and to the northward, a fish of commercial importance. Cf. **brook trout**.

Lake·wood (lāk′wo͝od′), n. a city in NE Ohio, on Lake Erie, near Cleveland. 68,071 (1950).

lakh (lăk), n. lac².

lak·y¹ (lā′kĭ), adj. of or like a lake. [f. **LAKE¹** + **-Y¹**]

lak·y² (lā′kĭ), adj. of the color of a lake pigment. [f. **LAKE²** + **-Y¹**]

lall (lăl), v.i. Phonet. to make imperfect l or r sounds, or both, often by substituting w for r and y for l. [imit. See **LALLATION**]

Lal·lan (lăl′ən), Scot. —adj. 1. belonging to the Lowlands of Scotland. —n. 2. the Lowland Scottish dialect.

lal·la·tion (lă lā′shan), n. Phonet. a speech defect consisting in pronouncing an l sound instead of r. [f. s. L lallāre sing lullaby + **-ATION**]

Lam., Lamentations.

lam¹ (lăm), v.t., **lammed, lamming**. Slang. to beat; thrash. [t. Scand.; cf. Icel. lamda, past tense of lemja beat; akin to **LAME¹**]

lam² (lăm) n., v., **lammed, lamming**. Slang. —n. 1. precipitate escape. 2. **on the lam**, escaping or fleeing. 3. **take it on the lam**, to flee or escape in great haste. —v.i. 4. to run quickly; run off or away. [special use of **LAM¹**. Cf. beat it be off]

la·ma (lä′mə), n. a priest or monk of the form of Buddhism prevailing in Tibet, Mongolia, etc. [t. Tibetan: m. blama (b- is silent)]

La·ma·ism (lä′mə ĭz′əm), n. the form of Buddhism in Tibet and Mongolia which has developed an organized hierarchy and a host of deities and saints. —**La′ma·ist**, n.

La Man·cha (lä män′chä), a barren plateau region in central Spain: the home of Cervantes' Don Quixote.

La·marck (lə märk′; Fr. lȧ mȧrk′), n. **Jean Baptiste Pierre Antoine de Monet de** (zhän bȧ tēst′ pyĕr än twän′ də mô nĕ′ də), 1744–1829, French biologist.

La·marck·i·an (lə mär′kĭ̍ən), adj. 1. of or pertaining to Jean de Lamarck or his theory of organic evolution. —n. 2. one who holds this theory.

La·marck·ism (lə mär′kĭzəm), n. Biol. the theory that characters acquired by habits, use, disuse, or adaptations to changes in environment may be inherited.

La·mar·tine (lä mȧr tēn′), n. **Alphonse Marie Louis de** (ȧl fôns′ mȧ rē′ lwē də), 1790–1869, French poet, historian, and statesman.

la·ma·ser·y (lä′mə sĕr′ĭ), n., pl. **-series**. (in Tibet, Mongolia, etc.) a monastery of lamas.

lamb (lăm), n. 1. a young sheep. 2. the meat of a young sheep. 3. one who is young, gentle, meek, innocent, etc. 4. **the Lamb**, Christ. 5. one who is easily cheated, esp. an inexperienced speculator. —v.i. 6. to give birth to a lamb. [ME and OE, c. G lamm]

Lamb (lăm), n. **Charles**, ("Elia") 1775–1834, British essayist and critic.

lam·baste (lăm bāst′), v.t., **-basted, -basting**. Slang. 1. to beat severely. 2. (in sailors' use) to beat with a rope's end. [appar. f. **LAM¹** + **BASTE³**]

lamb·da (lăm′də), n. the eleventh letter of the Greek alphabet (Λ, λ).

lamb·doid (lăm′doid), adj. having the shape of the Greek capital lambda (Λ). Also, **lamb·doi′dal**. [t. NL: s. lambdoīdēs, t. Gk.: m. lambdoeidḗs. See **LAMBDA**, **-OID**]

lambdoidal suture, Anat. the suture between the occipital and the two parietal bones of the skull, continued forward between the parietal bones. See diag. under **cranium**.

lam·ben·cy (lăm′bən sĭ), n., pl. **-cies**. 1. the quality of being lambent. 2. that which is lambent.

lam·bent (lăm′bənt), adj. 1. running or moving lightly over a surface: lambent tongues of flame. 2. playing lightly and brilliantly over a subject: lambent wit. 3. softly bright: a steady, lambent light. [t. L: s. lambens, ppr., licking] —**lam′bent·ly**, adv.

lam·bert (lăm′bərt), n. the cgs unit of brightness; the brightness of a perfectly diffusing surface emitting or reflecting one lumen per square centimeter. [named after J. H. Lambert, German physicist, (d. 1777)]

Lam·beth (lăm′bĭth), n. a S borough of London, England. 217,120 (est. 1946).

Lambeth Palace, the London residence of the Archbishop of Canterbury, near the Thames in S London.

Lambeth walk, Brit. a type of dance popular in the late 1930's.

lamb·kin (lăm′kĭn), n. 1. a little lamb. 2. any young and tender creature.

lamb·like (lăm′līk′), adj. like a lamb; gentle; meek.

Lamb of God, Christ.

lam·bre·quin (lăm′brə kĭn, lăm′bər-), n. 1. a textile fabric worn over a helmet in medieval times to protect it from heat, rust, and sword blows. 2. a hanging or drapery covering the upper part of an opening, as a door or window, or suspended from a shelf. [t. F, t. Flemish: m. lamperkin, dim of lamper veil]

lamb·skin (lăm′skĭn′), n. 1. the skin of a lamb, esp. when dressed with the wool on. 2. leather made from such skin. 3. parchment made from such skin.

lame¹ (lām), adj., **lamer, lamest**, v., **lamed, laming**. —adj. 1. crippled or physically disabled, as a person or animal, esp. in the foot or leg so as to limp or walk with difficulty. 2. impaired or disabled through defect or injury, as a limb. 3. defective in quality or quantity; insufficient: a lame excuse. —v.t. 4. to make lame or defective. [ME; OE lama, c. G lahm] —**lame′ly**, adv. —**lame′ness**, n.

lame² (lām; Fr. lȧm), n. one of numerous overlapping plates used in building corselets of flexible armor. [t. F, g. L lāmina thin piece or plate]

la·mé (lä mā′; Fr. lȧ mĕ′), n. an ornamental fabric in which metallic threads are woven with silk, wool, rayon, or cotton. [t. F: lit., laminated, der. lame gold or silver thread or wire]

lame duck (lām), 1. U.S. Colloq. a Congressman who has failed of reëlection and is serving at the last session of his term. 2. Colloq. a person or thing that is disabled, helpless, ineffective, or inefficient.

la·mel·la (lə mĕl′ə), n., pl. **-mellae** (-mĕl′ē), **-mellas**. 1. a thin plate, scale, membrane, or layer, as of bone, tissue, cell walls, etc. 2. Bot. **a**. an erect scale or blade inserted at the junction of the claw and limb in some corollas, and forming a part of their corona or crown. **b**. a gill, one of the radiating vertical plates on the under side of the pileus of an agaric. **c**. (in mosses) a thin sheet of cells standing up along the midrib of a leaf. [t. L, dim. of lāmina **LAMINA**]

la·mel·lar (lə mĕl′ər, lăm′ə lər), adj. 1. referring to a lamella or lamellae. 2. lamellate.

lam·el·late (lăm′ə lāt′, -lĭt; lə mĕl′āt, -ĭt), adj. 1. composed of or having lamellae. 2. flat; platelike. Also, **lam′el·lat′ed**.

la·mel·li·branch (lə mĕl′ə brăngk′), n. Zool. any of the Lamellibranchiata. [t. NL: m. Lāmellibranchia, pl., f. L lāmelli- thin plate + Gk. bránchia gills] —**la·mel·li·bran·chi·ate** (lə mĕl′ə brăng′kĭ̍ āt′, -ĭt), adj., n.

La·mel·li·bran·chi·a·ta (lə mĕl/ə brăng/kĭ ā/tə), *n.pl.* a class of mollusks comprising the oysters, clams, mussels, scallops, etc., characterized by a bivalve shell enclosing the headless body and lamelate gills.

la·mel·li·corn (lə mĕl/ə kôrn/), *adj. Entomol.* **1.** having antennae with lamellate and leaflike terminal segments, as beetles of the group *Lamellicornia*, which includes the scarabaeids and stag beetles. **2.** (of antennae) having leaflike terminal segments. —*n.* **3.** a lamellicorn beetle. [t. NL: s. *lāmellicornis*, f. L: *lāmelli-* thin plate + *-cornis* horned]

la·mel·li·ros·tral (lə mĕl/ə rŏs/trəl), *adj. Ornith.* having a beak equipped with thin plates or lamellae for straining water and mud from food, as the ducks, geese, swans, and flamingoes. Also, **la·mel·li·ros·trate** (lə mĕl/ə rŏs/trāt). [f. L *lāmelli-* thin plate + ROSTRAL]

la·mel·lose (lə mĕl/ōs, lăm/ə lōs/), *adj.* lamellate.

la·ment (lə mĕnt/), *v.t.* **1.** to feel or express sorrow or regret for; mourn for or over: *lament his absence, one's folly.* —*v.i.* **2.** to feel, show, or express grief, sorrow, or sad regret. —*n.* **3.** an expression of grief or sorrow. **4.** a formal expression of sorrow or mourning, esp. in verse or song; an elegy or dirge. [t. L: s. *lāmentārī* wail, weep] —**la·ment/er,** *n.* —**la·ment/ing,** *adj.* —**la·ment/ing·ly,** *adv.* —**Ant. 2.** rejoice.

lam·en·ta·ble (lăm/ən tə bəl), *adj.* **1.** that is to be lamented: *a lamentable occurrence.* **2.** *Now Rare.* mournful. —**lam/en·ta·ble·ness,** *n.* —**lam/en·ta·bly,** *adv.*

lam·en·ta·tion (lăm/ən tā/shən), *n.* **1.** act of lamenting. **2.** a lament. **3.** **Lamentations,** book of the Old Testament, ascribed by tradition to Jeremiah.

la·ment·ed (lə mĕn/tĭd), *adj.* **1.** mourned for, as one who is dead: *the late lamented Grady.* **2.** regretted.

la·mi·a (lā/mĭ ə), *n., pl.* **-mias, -miae** (-mĭ ē/). **1.** *Class. Myth.* one of a class of fabulous monsters, commonly represented with the head and breast of a woman and the body of a serpent, said to allure youths and children in order to suck their blood. **2.** a vampire; a female demon. [ME, t. L, t. Gk.]

la·mi·a·ccous (lā/mĭ ā/shəs), *adj. Bot.* belonging or pertaining to the mint family (*Lamiaceae, Menthaceue*, or, more commonly, *Labiatae*) including species valued as aromatic and in medicine. See **labiate** (def. 2a). [f. s. NL *Lamiāceae* (der. L *lāmium* dead nettle) + -ous]

lam·i·na (lăm/ə nə), *n., pl.* **-nae** (-nē/), **-nas.** **1.** a thin plate, scale, or layer. **2.** a layer or coat lying over another: applied to the plates of minerals, bones, etc. **3.** *Bot.* the blade or expanded portion of a leaf. [t. L: thin plate, leaf, layer. Cf. LAMELLA]

lam·i·na·ble (lăm/ə nə bəl), *adj.* capable of being laminated.

lam·i·nar (lăm/ə nər), *adj.* composed of, or arranged in, laminae.

laminar flow, *Hydraulics.* a flow of a viscous fluid in which neighboring "layers" are not mixed.

lam·i·nate (*v.* lăm/ə nāt/; *adj.* lăm/ə nāt/, -nĭt), *v.*, **-nated, -nating,** *adj.* —*v.t.* **1.** to separate or split into thin layers. **2.** to form (metal) into a lamina, as by beating or rolling. **3.** to construct by placing layer upon layer. **4.** to cover or overlay with laminae. —*v.i.* **5.** to split into thin layers. —*adj.* **6.** composed of, or having, a lamina or laminae.

lam·i·nat·ed (lăm/ə nā/tĭd), *adj.* formed of, or set in, thin layers or laminae.

lam·i·na·tion (lăm/ə nā/shən), *n.* **1.** act or process of laminating. **2.** state of being laminated. **3.** laminated structure; arrangement in thin layers. **4.** a lamina.

lam·i·ni·tis (lăm/ə nī/tĭs), *n. Vet. Science.* inflammation of sensitive laminae in the hoof of a horse, caused by overwork, overfeeding, etc. [t. NL]

lam·i·nose (lăm/ə nōs/), *adj.* laminate; laminar.

Lam·mas (lăm/əs), *n.* **1.** *Rom. Cath. Ch.* a church festival observed on August 1 in memory of St. Peter's imprisonment and miraculous deliverance. **2.** (*orig.*) a harvest festival formerly held in England on August 1 (**Lammas Day**). [ME *Lammasse*, OE *hlāfmæsse* loaf mass. See -MAS]

Lam·mas·tide (lăm/əs tīd/), *n.* the season of Lammas.

lam·mer·gei·er (lăm/ər gī/ər), *n.* the bearded vulture, *Gypaëtus barbatus*, the largest European bird of prey, ranging in the mountains from southern Europe to China. Also, **lam/mer·geir, lam/mer·gey/er.** [t. G: m. *lämmergeier*, lit., lambs' vulture (from its preying on lambs)]

lamp (lămp), *n.* **1.** any of various devices for using an illuminant, as gas or electricity, or for heating, as by burning alcohol. **2.** a vessel for containing an inflammable liquid, as oil, which is burned at a wick as a means of illumination. **3.** *Poetic.* a torch. **4.** *Poetic.* a celestial body, as the moon. **5.** a source of intellectual or spiritual light. **6.** (*pl.*) *Slang.* the eyes. [ME *lampe*, t. OF, g. L *lampas*, t. Gk.: torch, light, lamp]

lamp·black (lămp/blăk/), *n.* a fine black pigment consisting of almost pure carbon collected as soot from the smoke of burning oil, gas, etc.

Lam·pe·du·sa (lăm/pě dōō/zä), *n.* a small Italian island in the Mediterranean between Tunisia and Malta.

lam·per eel (lăm/pər), lamprey.

lam·pi·on (lăm/pĭ ən), *n.* a kind of lamp, often of colored glass. [t. F, t. It.: m. *lampione* carriage or street lamp, der. *lampa* LAMP]

lamp·light (lămp/līt/), *n.* the light shed by a lamp.

lamp·light·er (lămp/lī/tər), *n.* **1.** one who lights street lamps. **2.** a contrivance for lighting lamps.

lam·poon (lăm pōōn/), *n.* **1.** a malicious or virulent satire upon a person, in either prose or verse. —*v.t.* **2.** to assail in a lampoon. [t. F: m. *lampon*, said to be m. *lampons* let us drink (used in songs or verses), impv. of *lamper*] —**lam·poon/er, lam·poon/ist,** *n.*

lamp·post (lămp/pōst/), *n.* a post, usually iron, used to support a lamp which lights a street, park, etc.

lam·prey (lăm/prĭ), *n., pl.* **-preys.** any of the eellike cyclostome fishes constituting the group *Hypercoartia*. Some species attach themselves to fishes and rasp a hole in the flesh with their horny teeth so that they can suck the blood of the victim. [ME, t. OF: m. *lampreie*, g. LL *lampreda*]

Spotted sea lamprey, *Petromyzon marinus* (Ab. 3 ft. long)

lamp shell, a brachiopod.

la·na·i (lä nä/ē), *n., pl.* **-nais.** *Hawaiian.* a veranda.

La·na·i (lä nä/ē), *n.* one of the Hawaiian Islands, in the central part of the group. 3131 pop. (prelim. 1950); 141 sq. mi.

Lan·ark (lăn/ərk), *n.* a county in S Scotland. 1,572,600 pop. (est. 1946); 888 sq. mi. *Co. seat:* Lanark. Also, **Lan·ark·shire** (lăn/ərk shĭr/, -shər).

la·nate (lā/nāt), *adj.* wooly; covered with something resembling wool. [t. L: m.s. *lānātus*]

Lan·ca·shire (lăng/kə shĭr/, -shər), *n.* a county in NW England. 4,869,000 pop. (est. 1946); 1878 sq. mi. *Co. seat:* Lancaster. Also, **Lancaster.**

Lan·cas·ter (lăng/kəstər; *for 1 also* lăng/kăs/tər), *n.* **1.** a city in SE Pennsylvania. 63,774 (1950). **2.** a city in NW England. 50,530 (est. 1946). **3.** Lancashire.

Lan·cas·tri·an (lăng kăs/trĭ ən), *adj.* **1.** of or pertaining to the English royal house of Lancaster, descended from John of Gaunt (Duke of Lancaster), including Henry IV, Henry V, and Henry VI, who reigned from 1399 to 1461. —*n.* **2.** an adherent or member of the house of Lancaster, esp. in the Wars of the Roses. **3.** a native or resident of Lancashire. Also, **Lancaster.**

lance (lăns, läns), *n., v.,* **lanced, lancing.** —*n.* **1.** a long, shafted weapon with a metal head, used by mounted soldiers in charging. **2.** a soldier armed with this weapon. **3.** an implement resembling the weapon, as a spear for killing a harpooned whale. **4.** a lancet. —*v.t.* **5.** to open with, or as if with, a lancet: *to lance an abscess.* [ME, t. F, g. L *lancea*]

lance corporal, *Brit. Mil.* a private appointed to act as corporal, without increase in pay; an acting corporal.

lance·let (lăns/lĭt, läns/-), *n.* a small fishlike animal, of the genus *Branchiostoma* (*Amphioxus*), found in sand in shallow waters, related to the vertebrates. [f. LANCE, n. + -LET]

Lancelet, *Branchiostoma pulchellum* (Ab. 2½ in. long)

Lan·ce·lot (lăn/sə lət, -lŏt/, län/-), *n. Arthurian Romance.* the greatest of Arthur's knights, and the lover of Queen Guinevere.

lan·ce·o·late (lăn/sĭ ə lāt/, -lĭt), *adj.* **1.** shaped like the head of a lance. **2.** (of leaves, etc.) narrow, and tapering toward the apex or (sometimes) each end. [t. L: m.s. *lanceolātus*, der. *lanceola*, dim. of *lancea* lance]

lanc·er (lăn/sər, län/-), *n.* a mounted soldier armed with a lance.

lance rest, (in medieval armor) a support, bolted to the breastplate, upon which the lance rested when couched for use.

lanc·ers (lăn/sərz, län/-), *n.pl.* **1.** a form of quadrille (dance). **2.** music for such a set of dances.

lance sergeant, *Brit. Mil.* a corporal appointed to act as sergeant, without increase in pay; an acting sergeant.

lan·cet (lăn/sĭt, län/-), *n.* **1.** a small surgical instrument, usually sharp-pointed and two-edged, for letting blood, opening abscesses, etc. **2.** *Archit.* **a.** a lancet arch. **b.** a lancet window. [ME *lawnset*, t. OF: m. *lancette*, dim. of *lance* LANCE]

lancet arch, *Archit.* an arch the head of which is acutely pointed.

lan·cet·ed (lăn/sə tĭd, län/-), *adj.* having a lancet arch or lancet windows.

lancet fish, a large marine fish of the genus *Alepisaurus*, with enormous daggerlike teeth.

lancet window, *Archit.* a high, narrow window terminating in a lancet arch.

lance·wood (lăns/wŏŏd/, läns/-), *n.* **1.** the tough, elastic wood of any of various trees, as *Oxandra lanceolata*, of tropical America, used for carriage shafts, cabinetwork, etc. **2.** a tree which yields it.

Lan·chow (län/jō/), *n.* a city in N China, on the Hwang Ho: capital of Kansu province. 102,700 (est. 1937).

lan·ci·nate (lăn/sə nāt/), *v.t.,* **-nated, -nating.** to tear or rend; stab or pierce. [t. L: m.s. *lancinātus*, pp.] —**lan/ci·na/tion,** *n.*

land (lănd), *n.* **1.** the solid substance of the earth's surface. **2.** the exposed part of the earth's surface, as distinguished from the submerged part: *to travel by land.*

Lanceolate leaf

3. ground, esp. with reference to quality, character, or use: *forest land.* **4.** *Law.* **a.** any part of the earth's surface which can be owned as property, and everything annexed to it, whether by nature or by the hand of man. **b.** any hereditament, tenement, or other interest held in land. **5.** *Econ.* natural resources as a factor of production. **6.** a part of the earth's surface marked off by natural or political boundaries or the like; a region or country. **7.** the people of a country; a nation. **8.** a realm or domain: *the land of the living.* **9.** a surface between furrows, as on a millstone or on the interior of a rifle barrel. —*v.t.* **10.** to bring to or put on land or shore: *to land passengers or goods from a vessel.* **11.** to bring into, or cause to arrive in, any place, position, or condition. **12.** *Colloq.* to catch or capture; gain. **13.** *Angling.* to bring (a fish) to land, or into a boat, etc., as with a hook or a net. —*v.i.* **14.** to come to land or shore: *the boat lands at Cherbourg.* **15.** to go or come ashore from a ship or boat. **16.** to alight upon the ground, as from an airplane, a train, or after a jump or the like. **17.** to come to rest or arrive in any place, position, or condition. [ME and OE, c. G *land*]

Landau

lan·dau (lăn′dô, -dou), *n.* **1.** a four-wheeled, two-seated vehicle with a top made in two parts, which may be let down or folded back. **2.** a sedan-type automobile with a short convertible back. [named after *Landau*, town in Germany]

lan·dau·let (lăn′dô lĕt′), *n.* an automobile having a convertible top for the back seat, with the front seat either roofed or open. Also, **lan′dau·lette′.**

land bank, a banking association which issues its notes in exchange for mortgages on land or other real property transactions.

land·ed (lăn′dĭd), *adj.* **1.** owning land: *a landed proprietor.* **2.** consisting of land: *landed property.*

land·fall (lănd′fôl′), *n.* **1.** an approach to or sighting of land. **2.** the land sighted or reached.

land grant, a tract of land given by the government, as for colleges, railroads, etc.

land-grant college or **university,** *U.S.* a college or university entitled to support from the Federal government under the provisions of the Morrill Acts (1862, 1890).

land·grave (lănd′grāv′), *n.* **1.** the title of certain princes. **2.** (orig.) a German count having jurisdiction over a considerable territory. [t. G: m. *landgraf*]

land·gra·vi·ate (lănd grā′vĭ ĭt, -āt′), *n.* the office, jurisdiction, or territory of a landgrave.

land·gra·vine (lănd′grə vēn′), *n.* **1.** the wife of a landgrave. **2.** a woman of the rank of a landgrave. [t. G: m. *landgräfin*]

land·hold·er (lănd′hōl′dər), *n.* a holder, owner, or occupant of land. —**land′hold′ing,** *adj.*

land·ing (lăn′dĭng), *n.* **1.** act of one who or that which lands. **2.** a place where persons or goods are landed, as from a ship. **3.** *Archit.* **a.** the floor at the head or foot of a flight of stairs. **b.** a platform between flights of stairs.

landing gear, the wheels, floats, etc. of an aircraft, upon which it moves on ground or water.

land·la·dy (lănd′lā′dĭ), *n., pl.* **-dies.** **1.** a woman who owns and leases land, buildings, etc. **2.** a woman who owns or runs an inn, lodging house, or boarding house.

land·less (lănd′lĭs), *adj.* without land; owning no land.

land·locked (lănd′lŏkt′), *adj.* **1.** shut in more or less completely by land. **2.** living in waters shut off from the sea, as some fish: *a landlocked salmon.*

landlocked salmon. See **salmon** (def. 2).

land·lord (lănd′lôrd′), *n.* **1.** one who owns and leases land, buildings, etc. to another. **2.** the master of an inn, lodging house, etc. **3.** a landowner.

land·lord·ism (lănd′lôr dĭz′əm), *n.* the practice under which ownership is had by one and land is occupied by such owner's tenants.

land·lub·ber (lănd′lŭb′ər), *n. Naut.* a landsman or raw seaman. [f. LAND + LUBBER]

land·mark (lănd′märk′), *n.* **1.** a conspicuous object on land that serves as a guide, as to vessels at sea. **2.** a prominent or distinguishing feature, part, event, etc.: *the landmarks of human progress.* **3.** something used to mark the boundary of land.

land mine, a large ground-concealed explosive bomb.

land office, a government office for the transaction of business relating to public lands.

land-office business, *U.S. Colloq.* a rushing business.

Land of Promise, Canaan, the land promised by God to Abraham. Gen. 12.

Lan·dor (lăn′dər, -dôr), *n.* **Walter Savage,** 1775–1864, British author.

land·own·er (lănd′ō′nər), *n.* an owner or proprietor of land. —**land′own′er·ship,** *n.* —**land′own′ing,** *n., adj.*

land-poor (lănd′pŏŏr′), *adj.* in need of ready money while owning much unremunerative land.

land power, **1.** a nation having an important and powerful army. **2.** military power on land.

land·scape (lănd′skāp′), *n., v.,* **-scaped, -scaping.** —*n.* **1.** a view or prospect of rural scenery, more or less extensive, such as is comprehended within the scope or range of vision from a single point of view. **2.** a piece of such scenery. **3.** a picture representing natural inland or coastal scenery. **4.** such pictures as a category. —*v.t.* **5.** to improve the landscape. —*v.i.* **6.** to do landscape gardening as a profession. [earlier *landskip, landscap,* t. D: m. *landschap,* c. OE *landsceap, landscipe,* G *landschaft* region. See LAND, -SHIP]

landscape architecture, the art of arranging or modifying the features of a landscape, the streets, buildings, etc., to secure beautiful or advantageous effects. —**landscape architect.**

landscape gardening, the art of arranging trees, shrubbery, paths, fountains, etc., to produce picturesque effects. —**landscape gardener.**

Land·seer (lănd′sĭr, -sēr), *n.* **Sir Edwin Henry,** 1802–73, British painter, esp. of animals.

Land's End, the SW tip of England.

lands·knecht (länts′knĕK͟t′), *n.* lansquenet.

land·slide (lănd′slīd′), *n.* **1.** the sliding down of a mass of soil, detritus, or rock on a steep slope. **2.** the mass itself. **3.** an election in which a particular candidate or party receives an overwhelming mass or majority of votes. **4.** any overwhelming victory. Also, *esp. Brit.,* **land·slip** (lănd′slĭp′) for 1, 2.

lands·man (lăndz′mən), *n., pl.* **-men.** **1.** one who lives, or engages in an occupation, on land (opposed to *seaman*). **2.** *Naut.* **a.** a sailor on his first voyage. **b.** an inexperienced seaman, rated below an ordinary seaman.

Lands·ting (läns′tĭng), *n.* the upper house of the Danish Rigsdag or parliament. Also, **Lands·thing** (läns′tĭng′). [Dan., f. *lands,* poss. of *land* land + *t(h)ing* parliament]

Land·sturm (länt′shtŏŏrm′), *n.* (in Germany, Switzerland, etc.) **1.** a general levy of the people in time of war. **2.** the force so called out or subject to such call, consisting of all men capable of bearing arms and not in the army, navy, or Landwehr. [G: land storm]

land·ward (lănd′wərd), *adv.* **1.** Also, **land′wards.** toward the land or interior. —*adj.* **2.** lying, facing, or tending toward the land or away from the coast: *a landward breeze.* **3.** being in the direction of the land.

Land·wehr (länt′vār′), *n.* (in Germany, Austria, etc.) that part of the organized military forces of the nation which has completed a certain amount of compulsory training and of which continuous service is required only in time of war. [G: land defense]

lane (lān), *n.* **1.** a narrow way or passage between hedges, fences, walls, or houses. **2.** any narrow or well-defined passage, track, channel, or course. **3.** a fixed route pursued by ocean steamers or airplanes. **4.** a part of a highway for traffic moving in one line. **5.** (in sprint races) each of the spaces between the cords or chalked lines which mark the courses of the competitors. [ME and OE, c. D *laan*] —**Syn.** 1. See **path.**

Lang (lăng), *n.* **1. Andrew,** 1844–1912, British writer. **2. Cosmo Gordon** (kŏz′mō), 1864–1945, British clergyman: archbishop of Canterbury, 1928–1942.

lang., language.

Lang·er·hans (läng′ər häns), *n.* See **pancreas.**

Lang·land (lăng′lənd), *n.* **William,** c1330–c1400, British poet.

Lang·ley (lăng′lĭ), *n.* **1. Edmund of.** See **York,** 1st Duke of. **2. Samuel Pierpont,** 1834–1906, U.S. astronomer, physicist, and pioneer in aeronautics. **3. William.** See **Langland.**

Lang·muir (lăng′myŏŏr), *n.* **Irving,** born 1881, U.S. chemist.

Lan·go·bard (lăng′gə bärd′), *n.* a member of an ancient Germanic tribe which finally settled in N Italy. [t. LL: s. *Langobardī,* pl., of Gmc. orig.]

Lan·go·bar·dic (lăng′gə bär′dĭk), *adj.* **1.** pertaining to the Langobards. —*n.* **2.** the language of the Langobards, a dialect of High German.

lan·grage (lăng′grĭj), *n.* a kind of shot consisting of bolts, nails, etc., fastened together or enclosed in a case, formerly used for damaging sails and rigging in battles at sea. Also, **lan′gridge.** [orig. unknown]

lang·syne (lăng′sīn′, -zīn′; *Scot.* lăng′sīn′), *Scot.* —*adv.* **1.** long since; long ago. —*n.* **2.** time long past. [f. *lang* long + *syne,* contr. of ME *sithen,* OE *siththan* since]

Lang·ton (lăng′tən), *n.* **Stephen,** died 1228, British cardinal and archbishop of Canterbury.

lan·guage (lăng′gwĭj), *n.* **1.** communication by voice in the distinctively human manner, using arbitrary, auditory symbols in conventional ways with conventional meanings. **2.** any set or system of such symbols as used in a more or less uniform fashion by a number of people, who are thus enabled to communicate intelligibly with one another. **3.** the nonlinguistic means of communication of animals: *the language of birds.* **4.** communication of meaning in any way: *the language of flowers.* **5.** linguistics. **6.** instruction in one or more languages: *language study.* **7.** the speech or phraseology peculiar to a class, profession, etc. **8.** form or manner of expression: *in his own language.* **9.** speech or expression of a particular character: *flowery language.* **10.** diction or style of writing. [ME, t. OF: m. *langage,* der. *langue* tongue, g. L *lingua*]

—**Syn.** 1. See **speech.** 2. LANGUAGE, DIALECT, JARGON, VERNACULAR refer to patterns of vocabulary, syntax, and usage characteristic of communities of various sizes and types. LANGUAGE is applied to the general pattern of a people or race: *the English language*. DIALECT is applied to certain forms or varieties of a language, often those which provincial communities or special groups retain (or develop) even after a standard has been established: *Scottish dialect*. A JARGON is an artificial pattern used by a particular (usually occupational) group within a community; or a special pattern created for communication in business or trade between members of the groups speaking different languages: *the jargon of the theater, the Chinook jargon*. A VERNACULAR is the authentic natural pattern of speech, now usually on the colloquial level, used by persons indigenous to a certain community, large or small: *to speak in a local vernacular*.

Langue·doc (läng̍dŏk′), *n.* a former province in S France. *Cap.*: Toulouse.

langue d'oc (läng dŏk′), **1.** the Romance language of medieval southern France. **2.** Provençal. [OF: "*oc*" language, i.e. the language in which *oc* yes was used. See LANGUE D'OIL]

langue d'o·ïl (läng dô ēl′, dô′ĭ), the French of medieval northern France. [OF: "*oïl*" language (OF *oïl* yes). See LANGUE D'OC]

lan·guet (läng′gwĕt), *n.* any of various small tongue-shaped parts, processes, or projections. [ME, t. F: m. *languette*, dim. of *langue*, g. L *lingua* tongue]

lan·guette (läng′gwĕt), *n. Music.* a thin plate fastened to the mouth of certain organ pipes.

lan·guid (läng′gwĭd), *adj.* **1.** drooping or flagging from weakness or fatigue; faint. **2.** lacking in spirit or interest; indifferent. **3.** lacking in vigor or activity; slack; dull: *a languid market*. [t. L: s. *languidus*] —**lan′guid·ly**, *adv.* —**lan′guid·ness**, *n.* —**Syn. 1.** weak, feeble, weary, exhausted. **3.** listless, spiritless, lifeless, apathetic. —**Ant. 1.** vigorous. **3.** energetic.

lan·guish (läng′gwĭsh), *v.i.* **1.** to become or be weak or feeble; droop or fade. **2.** to lose activity and vigor. **3.** to pine or suffer under any unfavorable conditions: *to languish ten years in a dungeon*. **4.** to pine with desire or longing for. **5.** to assume an expression of tender, sentimental melancholy. —*n.* **6.** act of languishing. **7.** a languishing expression. [ME *languish(en)*, t. F: m. *languiss-*, s. *languir*, der. L *languēre*] —**lan′guish·er**, *n.*

lan·guish·ing (läng′gwĭsh ĭng), *adj.* **1.** becoming languid, in any way. **2.** lingering: *a languishing death*. **3.** expressive of languor; indicating tender, sentimental melancholy: *a languishing sigh*. —**lan′guish·ing·ly**, *adv.*

lan·guish·ment (läng′gwĭsh mənt), *n.* **1.** act of languishing. **2.** languishing condition. **3.** a languishing expression.

lan·guor (läng′gər), *n.* **1.** physical weakness or faintness. **2.** lack of bodily energy; indolence. **3.** emotional softness or tenderness. **4.** lack of spirit or vigorous activity. **5.** soothing or oppressive stillness. [t. L; r. ME *langur*, t. OF]

lan·guor·ous (läng′gər əs), *adj.* **1.** characterized by languor; languid. **2.** inducing languor: *languorous fragrance.* —**lan′guor·ous·ly**, *adv.*

lan·gur (lŭng göor′), *n.* any of certain large, slender, long-limbed, long-tailed Asiatic monkeys of the subfamily *Colobinae*, as the entellus (the sacred monkey of India). [t. Hind. Cf. Skt. *lāngūlin* having a tail]

lan·iard (län′yərd), *n.* lanyard.

La·nier (lə nĭr′), *n.* **Sidney**, 1842–81, U.S. poet and musician.

lan·i·tal (län′ə tăl′), *n.* a casein derivative which is chemically and functionally similar to wool. [f. s. L *lāna* wool + -ITE[1] + -AL[3]]

lank (längk), *adj.* **1.** meagerly slim; lean; gaunt: *a tall, lank man.* **2.** (of plants, etc.) unduly long and slender. **3.** (of a purse, etc.) only partially filled. **4.** (of hair) straight and flat. [OE *hlanc*, akin to OHG *hlanca* loin, side. Cf. FLANK] —**lank′ly**, *adv.* —**lank′ness**, *n.*

Lan·kes·ter (läng′kə stər, -kĕs′tər), *n.* **Sir Edwin Ray**, 1847–1929, British zoölogist.

lank·y (längk′ĭ), *adj.*, **lankier, lankiest. somewhat lank; ungracefully tall and thin. —**lank′i·ly**, *adv.* —**lank′i·ness**, *n.*

lan·ner (län′ər), *n.* **1.** a falcon, *Falco biarmicus*, of southern Europe, northern Africa, and southern Asia. **2.** Falconry. the female of this bird. Cf. **lanneret**. [ME *lanere*, t. OF: m. *lanier* cowardly (bird)]

lan·ner·et (län′ə rĕt′), *n.* Falconry. the male lanner, which is smaller than the female. [ME *lanret*, t. OF, F: m. *laneret*, der. *lanier* LANNER]

lan·o·lin (län′ə lĭn), *n.* a fatty substance, extracted from wool, used in ointments. Also, **lan·o·line** (län′ə lĭn, -lēn′). [f. s. L *lāna* wool + -OL[2] + -IN[2]]

Lan·sing (län′sĭng), *n.* **1.** the capital of Michigan, in the S part. 92,129 (1950). **2. Robert,** 1864–1928, U.S. lawyer and statesman; secretary of state, 1915–20.

lans·que·net (läns′kə nĕt′), *n.* mercenary foot soldier, commonly armed with a pike or lance, formerly used in the German and other Continental armies. Also, **landsknecht.** [t. F, d. G: m. *landsknecht*, f. *lands* land's + *knecht* manservant. See KNIGHT]

lan·ta·na (län tä′nə, -tā′-), *n.* any plant of the verbenaceous, mostly tropical genus *Lantana*, including species much cultivated for their aromatic yellow or orange flowers, *L. camara*. [NL]

lan·tern (län′tərn), *n.* **1.** a transparent or translucent case for enclosing a light and protecting it from the wind, rain, etc. **2.** a magic lantern. **3.** a street lamp on which the French Revolutionaries hanged aristocrats. **4.** the chamber at the top of a lighthouse, surrounding the light. **5.** *Archit.* **a.** a more or less open construction on the top of a tower or crowning a dome. **b.** any light decorative structure of relatively small size crowning a roof. **c.** a raised construction on the roof of a building, designed to admit light. **d.** an open-sided structure on a roof to let out smoke or to assist ventilation. [ME *lanterne*, t. F, t. L: m. *lanterna*, t. Gk.: m.s. *lamptḗr* a light, torch, b. with L *lucerna* a lamp]

lantern fish, any small marine fish of the family *Myctophidae*, with rows of luminescent spots, living in the open sea and coming to the surface at night.

lantern fly, any of certain tropical homopterous insects (of the family *Fulgoridae*), formerly supposed to emit light.

lantern jaws, long, thin jaws (with sunken cheeks). —**lan′tern-jawed′**, *adj.*

lantern slide, slide (def. 12).

lantern wheel, a wheel used like a pinion consisting essentially of two parallel disks or heads whose peripheries are connected by a series of bars which engage with the teeth of another wheel. Also, **lantern pinion.**

Lantern wheel (at left)

lan·tha·num (län′thə nəm), *n. Chem.* a rare-earth, trivalent, metallic element, allied to aluminum, found in certain rare minerals, as monazite. *Symbol:* La; *at. wt.*: 138.92; *at. no.*: 57; *sp. gr.*: 6.15 at 20°C. [t. NL, der. Gk. *lanthánein* escape notice]

lant·horn (länt′hôrn′, länt′tərn), *n. Obs.* lantern.

Lan·tsang (län′tsäng′), *n.* Chinese name of **Mekong.**

la·nu·gi·nose (lə nū′jə nōs′, -nōō′-), *adj.* **1.** covered with lanugo, or soft, downy hairs. **2.** of the nature of down; downy. Also, **la·nu·gi·nous** (lə nū′jə nəs, -nōō′-). [t. L: m.s. *lānūginōsus* woolly]

la·nu·go (lə nū′gō, -nōō′-), *n. Biol.* a coat of delicate, downy hairs, esp. that with which the human fetus or a newborn infant is covered. [t. L: woolly substance]

lan·yard (län′yərd), *n.* **1.** *Naut.* **a.** a short rope or cord for securing or holding something, esp. a rope rove through deadeyes to secure and tighten rigging. **b.** knife lanyard, a cord to which a knife is attached, worn by seamen around the neck. **2.** *Mil.* a cord with a small hook at one end, used in firing certain kinds of cannon. Also, **laniard.** [b. ME *lanyer* (t. F: m. *lanière* rope) and YARD[1]]

La·oag (lä wäg′), *n.* a seaport in the Philippine Islands, on NW Luzon. 41,842 (1939).

La·oc·o·ön (lā ŏk′ə wän′, -ō ŏn′), *n. Gk. Legend.* a priest of Apollo at Troy who warned against the Trojan Horse and, with his two sons, was killed by serpents sent by Athene or Apollo.

La·od·i·ce·a (lā ŏd′ə sē′ə, lā′ə də sē′ə), *n.* an ancient seaport of Syria, on the site of modern Latakia.

La·od·i·ce·an (lā ŏd′ə sē′ən, lā′ə də sē′ən), *adj.* **1.** lukewarm; indifferent, esp. in religion (like the early Christians of Laodicea). —*n.* **2.** one who is lukewarm or indifferent, esp. in religion.

La·om·e·don (lā ŏm′ə dŏn′), *n. Gk. Legend.* father of Priam, and founder and king of Troy.

La·os (lā′ŏs; *Fr.* là ôs′), *n.* a state in central and NW French Indo-China. 1,012,000 pop. (1936); 89,340 sq. mi. *Cap.*: Vientiane.

Lao-tse (lou′dzŭ′), *n.* born c604 B.C., Chinese philosopher, the supposed founder of Taoism. Also, **Lao′tsze′, Lao′-tzu′.**

lap[1] (läp), *n.* **1.** the part of the clothing that lies on the front portion of the body from the waist to the knees when one sits. **2.** this portion of the body, esp. as the place in or on which something is held or a child is nursed, cherished, etc. **3.** that in which anything rests or reposes, or is nurtured or fostered. **4.** a laplike or hollow place, as a hollow among hills. **5.** the front part of a skirt, etc. as held up to contain something. **6.** a loose border or fold. **7.** a part of a garment which projects or extends over another, as the front lap of a coat. [ME *lappe*, OE *læppa*, c. D *lap*; akin to G *lappen* lap]

lap[2] (läp), *v.*, **lapped, lapping,** *n.* —*v.t.* **1.** to fold over or about something; wrap or wind round something. **2.** to enwrap in something; wrap up; clothe. **3.** to enfold or hold in or as in the lap; nurse, fondle, or cherish. **4.** to lay (something) partly over something underneath; lay (things) together, one partly over another. **5.** to lie partly over (something underneath). **6.** to get a lap or more ahead of (a competitor) in racing. **7.** to cut or polish (a gem, etc.) with a lap. **8.** to join, as by scarfing, to form a single piece with the same dimensions throughout. —*v.i.* **9.** to be folded over; fold or wind round something. **10.** to lie partly over or alongside of something else; lie together, one partly over or beside another. **11.** to lie upon and extend beyond a thing. **12.** to extend beyond a limit. —*n.* **13.** act of lapping. **14.** the amount of a material required to go round a thing once. **15.** a single round or circuit of the course in racing. **16.** act of overlapping. **17.** state of overlapping. **18.** the point or place of overlapping. **19.** an overlapping part. **20.** the extent or amount of overlapping. **21.** a rotating wheel or disk holding an abrasive or polishing powder on its surface, used for gems, cutlery, etc. [ME *lappe(n)*; appar. der. LAP[1]] —**lap′per,** *n.*

lap³ (lăp), v., **lapped, lapping,** n. —v.t. **1.** (of water) to wash against or beat upon (something) with a lapping sound. **2.** to take up (liquid) with the tongue; lick up. —v.i. **3.** (of water) to wash with a sound as of licking up a liquid. **4.** to take up liquid with the tongue; lick up a liquid. —n. **5.** act of lapping liquid. **6.** the lapping of water against something. **7.** the sound of this. **8.** something lapped up, as liquid food for dogs. [ME *lappe,* unexplained var. of *lape,* OE *lapian,* c. MLG *lapen;* akin to L *lambere,* Gk. *láptein* lick, lap] —**lap/per,** n.

La Paz (lä päs/), a city in W Bolivia: seat of the government (Sucre is the nominal capital). 301,000 pop. (est. 1942); ab. 12,000 ft. high.

lap·board (lăp/bôrd/), n. a thin, flat board to be held on the lap for use as a table.

lap dog, a small pet dog.

la·pel (lə pĕl/), n. a part of a garment folded back on the breast, esp. a continuation of a coat collar. [dim. of LAP¹]

La Pe·rouse (lá pĕ rōōz/), **Jean François de Galaup** (zhäṅ fräṅ swä/ də gá lō/), **Count de,** 1741–88?, French naval officer and explorer.

lap·ful (lăp/fŏŏl/), n., pl. **-fuls.** as much as the lap can hold.

lap·i·dar·y (lăp/ə dĕr/ĭ), n., pl. **-daries,** adj. —n. **1.** a workman who cuts, polishes, and engraves precious stones. **2.** an old book on the lore of gems. —adj. **3.** pertaining to the cutting or engraving of precious stones. **4.** of or pertaining to inscriptions cut in stone, or to any formal inscriptions. **5.** characteristic of or suitable for monumental inscriptions. [ME *lapidarie,* t. L: m. *lapidārius* of stones or stone (as n., a stone-cutter)]

lap·i·date (lăp/ə dāt/), v.t., **-dated, -dating. 1.** to pelt with stones. **2.** to stone to death. [t. L: m.s. *lapidātus,* pp.] —**lap/i·da/tion,** n.

la·pid·i·fy (lə pĭd/ə fī/), v.t., v.i., **-fied, -fying.** to turn to stone; petrify. —**la·pid/i·fi·ca/tion,** n.

la·pil·li (lə pĭl/ī), n.pl., sing. **-pillus** (-pĭl/əs). stony particles or fragments ejected from volcanoes, technically those of rounded shape and less than an inch in diameter. [L, dim. of *lapis* a stone]

lap·in (lăp/ĭn; Fr. là päN/), n. **1.** a rabbit. **2.** its fur. [t. F]

la·pis (lā/pĭs, lăp/ĭs), n., pl. **lapides** (lăp/ə dēz/). Latin. a stone (used in Latin phrases).

lap·is laz·u·li (lăp/ĭs lăz/yŏŏ lī/, -lĭ), **1.** a deep-blue stone containing sodium, aluminum, calcium, sulfur, and silicon, and consisting of a mixture of several minerals, used chiefly for ornamental purposes. **2.** sky-blue; azure. [t. ML: f. L *lapis* stone + ML *lazulī,* gen. of *lazulum* lapis lazuli (see AZURE)]

Lap·i·thae (lăp/ə thō/), n.pl. Gk. Legend. a mythical people of Thessaly, who defeated the centaurs in a war which arose at the wedding of Pirithous.

lap joint, a joint used where two boards intersect and one or both are cut out to allow for the intersection.

La·place (lá pläs/), n. **Pierre Simon** (pyĕr ɛ̄ môN/), **Marquis de,** 1749–1827, French astronomer and mathematician.

Lap·land (lăp/lănd/), n. a region inhabited by Lapps in N Norway, N Sweden, N Finland, and the Kola peninsula of the NW Soviet Union.

La Pla·ta (lä plä/tä), **1.** a seaport in E Argentina. 256,378 (est. 1944). **2.** See **Plata, Rio de la.**

Lapp (lăp), n. **1.** Also, **Lap·land·er** (lăp/lăn/dər). one of a Finnic people of northern Norway, Sweden, and Finland, and adjacent regions, characterized by dwarfish stature and short, broad heads. **2.** Also, **Lap/pish.** any of the languages of the Lapps, closely related to Finnish. [t. Sw.]

lap·pet (lăp/ĭt), n. **1.** a small lap, flap, or loosely hanging part, esp. of a garment or headdress. **2.** a loose fold of flesh or the like. **3.** a lobe of the ear, etc. **4.** Ornith. a wattle or other fleshy process on a bird's head. [dim. of LAP¹]

lap robe, a fur robe, blanket, etc., to cover the lap and legs when riding in an automobile, etc.

laps·a·ble (lăp/sə bəl), adj. liable to lapse.

lapse (lăps), n., v., **lapsed, lapsing.** —n. **1.** a slip or slight error: *a lapse of memory.* **2.** a failure or miscarriage through some fault, slip, or negligence: *a lapse of justice.* **3.** a gliding or passing away, as of time. **4.** act of falling, slipping, sliding, etc., slowly or as by degrees. **5.** Law. the termination of a right or privilege through neglect to exercise it or through failure of some contingency. **6.** a falling, or sinking to a lower grade, condition, or degree: *a lapse into savagery.* **7.** a moral fall, as from rectitude. **8.** a falling into disuse. —v.i. **9.** to pass slowly, silently, or by degrees. **10.** Law. **a.** to pass from one to another by lapse. **b.** to become void, as a legacy to one who predeceases the testator. **11.** to fall or sink to a lower grade or condition. **12.** to fall, slip, or glide, esp. downward. **13.** to deviate from principles, accuracy, etc.; make a slip or error. **14.** to

pass away, as time. [late ME, t. L: m.s. *lapsus,* n., a fall, slip] —**laps/er,** n.

lapse rate, Meteorol. the rate of decrease of atmospheric temperature with increase of elevation vertically above a given location.

lap·streak (lăp/strēk/), adj. **1.** (of a boat) built with each plank overlapping the one below it; clinker-built. —n. **2.** a lapstreak boat. [f. LAP², n. + STREAK]

lap·sus ca·la·mi (lăp/səs kăl/ə mī/). Latin. a slip of the pen.

lap·sus lin·guae (lăp/səs lĭng/gwē), Latin. a slip of the tongue.

Lap·tev Sea (lăp/tĕf), Nordenskjöld Sea.

La·pu·ta (lə pū/tə), n. an imaginary flying island described in Swift's *Gulliver's Travels,* whose inhabitants were engaged in all sorts of ridiculous projects.

lap·wing (lăp/wĭng/), n. a large Old World plover, *Vanellus vanellus,* with strikingly upcurved slender crest, erratic courtship flight, and shrill cries; pewit; green plover. [ME *lapwinge,* OE *hlēapewince,* f. *hlēapan* leap + -*wince* (akin to OHG *winkan* waver, totter, and OE *wincian* wink)]

lar (lär), n., pl. **lares** (lâr/ēz, lā/rēz), **lars** (lärz). See **lares.**

Lar·a·mie (lăr/ə mĭ), n. **1.** a city in SE Wyoming. 15,581 (1950). **2. Fort,** a former U.S. fort in SE Wyoming: an important post on the Oregon Trail.

lar·board (lär/bôrd/; Naut. -bərd), Naut. —n. **1.** the side of a ship to the left of a person looking from the stern toward the bow; port (opposed to *starboard*). —adj. **2.** on, or pertaining to, the larboard. [early mod. E *larborde* (assimilated to STARBOARD); r. ME *laddeborde,* f. *ladde* (orig. unknown) + *borde,* OE *bord* ship's side]

lar·ce·nous (lär/sə nəs), adj. **1.** of, like, or of the nature of larceny. **2.** guilty of larceny. —**lar/ce·nous·ly,** adv.

lar·ce·ny (lär/sə nĭ), n., pl. **-nies.** Law. the wrongful taking and carrying away of the personal goods of another from his possession with intent to convert them to the taker's own use: distinguished as **grand larceny** and **petty** (or **petit**) **larceny,** depending on the value of the property taken. [late ME, appar. f. m. AF *larcin* (g. L *latrōcinium* robbery) + -Y³]

larch (lärch), n. **1.** any of the coniferous trees constituting the pinaceous genus *Larix,* characterized by a tough, durable wood. **2.** the wood of such a tree. [t. G: m. *lärche,* ult. t. L: m.s. *larix*]

lard (lärd), n. **1.** the rendered fat of hogs, esp. the internal fat of the abdomen. —v.t. **2.** to apply lard or grease to. **3.** to prepare or enrich (lean meat, etc.) with pork or bacon, esp. with lardons. **4.** to intersperse with something for improvement or ornamentation. [ME, t. OF: fat of pork, bacon, g. L *lār(t)dum* fat of pork] —**lard/like/,** adj.

lar·da·ceous (lär dā/shəs), adj. lardlike; fatty.

lard·er (lär/dər), n. a room or place where food is kept; a pantry. [ME, t. OF: m. *lardier,* der. *lard* LARD]

Lard·ner (lärd/nər), n. **Ring,** (Ringgold Wilmer Lardner) 1885–1933, U.S. writer of short stories.

lar·don (lär/dən), n. a piece of pork or bacon used in larding, esp. drawn through the substance of meat, etc., with a kind of needle or pin. Also, **lar·doon** (lär dōōn/). [late ME, t. F, der. *lard* LARD, n.]

lard·y (lär/dĭ), adj. abounding in or resembling lard.

La·re·do (lə rā/dō), n. a city in S Texas, on the Rio Grande. 51,910 (1950).

lar·es (lâr/ēz, lā/rēz), n. pl., sing. **lar.** Rom. Myth. household or other tutelary gods or spirits. [L]

lares and pe·na·tes (pə nā/tēz), **1.** household gods. See **lares, penates. 2.** the cherished possessions of a family or household.

large (lärj), adj., **larger, largest,** n., adv. —adj. **1.** being of more than common size, amount, or number. **2.** of great scope or range; extensive or broad: *large powers.* **3.** on a great scale: *a large producer.* **4.** grand or pompous. **5.** Obs. generous. **6.** Obs. unrestrained by decorum. **7.** Obs. (of the wind) free; fair. —n. **8.** freedom; unrestraint: Obs. except in **at large, a.** at liberty; free from restraint or confinement: *the murderer is at large.* **b.** at length; to a considerable length: *to discourse at large on a subject.* **c.** as a whole; in general: *the country at large.* **d.** representing the whole of a state, district, or body, not one division or part of it: *a Congressman at large.* **9. in large,** or **in the large,** on a large scale: *viewed in the large.* —adv. **10.** Naut. before the wind; with the wind free or on the quarter, or in such a direction that studding sails will draw. [ME, t. OF, g. L *larga,* fem. of *largus* abundant, liberal] —**large/ness,** n. —**Syn. 1.** big, huge, enormous, immense, gigantic, colossal; massive; vast. See **great.** —**Ant. 1.** small.

large calorie. See **calorie** (def. 1b).

large-heart·ed (lärj/här/tĭd), adj. having or showing generosity. —**large/-heart/ed·ness,** n.

large·ly (lärj/lĭ), adv. **1.** to a great extent; in great part. **2.** in great quantity; much.

large-mind·ed (lärj/mīn/dĭd), adj. having or showing tolerant views or liberal ideas. —**large/-mind/ed·ness,** n.

large-scale (lärj/skāl/), adj. **1.** very extensive; of great scope. **2.** made to a large scale: *a large-scale map.*

lar·gess (lär/jĭs), n. **1.** generous bestowal of gifts.

2. the gifts or a gift (as of money) so bestowed. 3. *Archaic.* generosity. Also, **lar′gesse**. [ME *larges*, t. OF: m. *largesse*, der. *large* LARGE]

lar·ghet·to (lär gĕt′ō), *adj., n., pl.* **-ghettos**. *Music.* —*adj.* 1. somewhat slow; not so slow as largo, but usually slower than andante. —*n.* 2. a larghetto movement. [t. It., dim. of *largo* LARGO]

larg·ish (lär′jĭsh), *adj.* rather large.

lar·go (lär′gō), *adj., n., pl.* **-gos**. *Music.* —*adj.* 1. slow; in a broad, dignified style. —*n.* 2. a largo movement. [t. It., g. L *largus* large]

lar·i·at (lăr′ĭ ət), *n. U.S.* 1. a long, noosed rope for catching horses, cattle, etc.; a lasso. 2. a rope or cord for picketing horses or mules while grazing. [t. Sp.: m. *la reata* the rope]

lar·ine (lär′ĭn), *adj.* 1. of the nature of or resembling a gull. 2. of or pertaining to the suborder *Lari*, family *Laridae*, or subfamily *Larinae*, containing the gulls. [t. NL: m.s. *Larinae*, der. LL *larus*, t. Gk.: m. *láros* kind of sea bird]

La·ris·sa (lə rĭs′ə; *Gk.* lä′rē sä′), *n.* a city in E Greece, in Thessaly. 27,694 (1940). Also, **La·ri·sa′**.

lark¹ (lärk), *n.* 1. any of numerous oscine singing birds, mostly of the Old World, of the family *Alaudidae*, characterized by an unusually long, straight hind claw, esp. the skylark, *Alauda arvensis.* 2. any of various similar birds of other families, as the meadow lark (*Icteridae*) of America, and the titlark (*Motacillidae*) of both America and Europe. [ME *larke*, OE *lāwerce*, c. G *lerche*]

lark² (lärk), *Colloq.* —*n.* 1. a merry or hilarious adventure; prank. —*v.i.* 2. to play pranks; have fun. [orig. uncert.] —**lark′er,** *n.* —**lark·some** (lärk′səm), *adj.*

lark·spur (lärk′spûr′), *n. Bot.* any plant of the genus *Delphinium*, so-called from the spur-shaped formation of the calyx and petals. [f. LARK¹ + SPUR]

La Roche·fou·cauld (lȧ rôsh fōō kō′), **François de** (frän swä′ də), (*Prince de Marcillac*) 1613–80, French writer.

La Ro·chelle (lȧ rô shĕl′), a seaport in W France: besieged as a Huguenot stronghold, 1627–28. 48,-923 (1946).

Flower of field larkspur, *Delphinium consolida,* cut longitudinally

La·rousse (lȧ rōōs′), *n.* **Pierre Athanase** (pyĕr ȧ tȧ näz′),1817–75, French grammarian, lexicographer, and encyclopedist.

lar·ri·kin (lăr′ə kĭn), *n. Chiefly Australian Slang.* —*n.* 1. a street rowdy; a hoodlum. —*adj.* 2. disorderly; rowdy. [?f. *Larry* (hypocoristic var. of *Lawrence*) +-KIN]

lar·rup (lăr′əp), *v.t.,* **-ruped, -ruping.** *Colloq.* to beat; thrash. —**lar′rup·er,** *n.*

lar·um (lăr′əm), *n. Archaic.* alarum.

lar·va (lär′və), *n., pl.* **-vae** (-vē). 1. *Entomol.* the young of any insect which undergoes metamorphosis. 2. any animal in an analogous immature form. 3. the young of any invertebrate animal. [t. NL, special use of L *larva* ghost, specter, skeleton, mask]

lar·val (lär′vəl), *adj.* 1. of or in the form of a larva. 2. *Pathol.* (of disease) masked, not clearly defined.

lar·vi·cide (lär′və sīd′), *n.* an agent for killing larvae.

la·ryn·ge·al (lə rĭn′jĭ əl), *adj.* of or pertaining to the larynx. Also, **la·ryn·gal** (lə rĭng′gəl). [f. s. NL *laryngeus* (der. *larynges,* pl. of *larynx* LARYNX) + -AL¹]

lar·yn·gi·tis (lăr′ən jī′tĭs), *n. Pathol.* inflammation of the larynx. [t. NL; f. LARYNG- + -ITIS] —**lar·yn·git·ic** (lăr′ən jĭt′ĭk), *adj.*

laryngo-, a combining form of **larynx.** Also, be°ore vowels, **laryng-.**

la·ryn·go·scope (lə rĭng′gə skōp′), *n. Med.* an apparatus for examining the larynx. —**la·ryn·go·scop·ic** (lə rĭng′gə skŏp′ĭk), *adj.*

lar·ynx (lăr′ĭngks), *n., pl.* **larynges** (lə rĭn′jēz), **larynxes.** 1. *Anat.* the cavity at the upper end of the human trachea or windpipe, containing the vocal cords and acting as the organ of voice. 2. *Zool.* **a.** a similar vocal organ in other mammals, etc. **b.** a corresponding structure in other animals. [t. NL, t. Gk.]

La Salle (lə sȧl′; *Fr.* lȧ sȧl′), **René Robert** (rə nĕ′ rô bĕr′), **Cavelier de,** 1643–87, French explorer of the Mississippi.

las·car (lăs′kər), *n.* an East Indian sailor. [t. Pg.: m. *laschar*, short for *lasquarin* soldier, t. Hind. (Pers.): m. *lashkarī*, adj., military (as n., soldier), der. *lashkar* army, camp]

Las Ca·sas (läs kä′säs), **Bartolomé de** (bär tô′lō mĕ′ dĕ), 1474–1566, Spanish missionary in the Americas.

las·civ·i·ous (lə sĭv′ĭ əs), *adj.* 1. inclined to lust; wanton or lewd. 2. inciting to lust or wantonness. [t. LL: m.s. *lascivīōsus,* der. L *lascivia* wantonness] —**las·civ′i·ous·ly,** *adv.* —**las·civ′i·ous·ness,** *n.*

lash¹ (lăsh), *n.* 1. the flexible part of a whip; the piece of cord or the like forming the extremity of a whip. 2. a swift stroke or blow, with a whip, etc., as a punishment:

Section of human larynx
A, Larynx; B, Epiglottis; C, Trachea; D, Esophagus

sentenced *to fifty lashes.* 3. a sharp stroke given to the feelings, etc., as of censure or satire. 4. a swift dashing or sweeping movement; a switch: *a lash of an animal's tail.* 5. a violent beating or impact, as of waves, rain, etc., against something. 6. an eyelash. —*v.t.* 7. to strike or beat, now usually with a whip or something slender and flexible. 8. to beat violently or sharply against. 9. to drive by strokes of a whip or the like. 10. to move or switch sharply through the air. 11. to dash, fling, or toss suddenly and swiftly. 12. to assail severely with words as by censure or satire. —*v.i.* 13. to strike vigorously at, as with a weapon, whip, or the like (often fol. by *out*). 14. to move suddenly and swiftly, rush, dash, or flash. 15. to burst into violent action or speech (fol. by *out*). [ME *lassh*; orig. obscure] —**lash′er,** *n.*

lash² (lăsh), *v.t.* to bind or fasten with a rope, cord, or the like. [special use of LASH¹] —**lash′er,** *n.*

lashed (lăsht), *adj.* having lashes, or eyelashes.

lash·ing¹ (lăsh′ĭng), *n.* 1. the act of one who or that which lashes. 2. a whipping. 3. a severe scolding. [f. LASH¹ + -ING¹]

lash·ing² (lăsh′ĭng), *n.* 1. a binding or fastening with a rope or the like. 2. the rope or the like used. [f. LASH² + -ING¹]

Lash·io (lăsh′yō), *n.* a town in Upper Burma, in the Northern Shan States: the SW terminus of the Burma Road. 4638 (1931).

Lash·kar (lŭsh′kər), *n.* a city in N India, in N Gwalior state. 182,492 (1941).

Las·ki (lăs′kĭ), *n.* **Harold Joseph,** 1893–1950, British Socialist leader and author.

Las Pal·mas (läs päl′mäs), a seaport in the Canary Islands, on Gran Canaria. 119,595 (1940).

La Spe·zia (lä spĕ′tsyä), a seaport in NW Italy, on the Ligurian Sea: naval base. 119,395 (est. 1946).

lass (lăs), *n.* 1. a girl or young woman. 2. any woman. 3. a female sweetheart. [ME *lasse*; orig. uncert.]

Las·sa (lä′sə, -sä), *n.* Lhasa.

Las·salle (lə säl′; *Ger.* lä säl′), *n.* **Ferdinand** (fĕr′dĭ nänt′), 1825–64, German socialist and writer.

Las·sen Volcanic National Park (lăs′ən), a national park in the Sierra Nevada Mountains, including **Lassen Peak** (10,465 ft.), the only active volcano in the U.S. proper. 163 sq. mi.

las·sie (lăs′ĭ), *n.* a little lass.

las·si·tude (lăs′ə tūd′, -tōōd′), *n.* weariness of body or mind from strain, oppressive climate, etc.; languor. [t. L: m. *lassitūdo* weariness]

las·so (lăs′ō; *older* lä sōō′), *n., pl.* **-sos, -soes,** *v.,* **-soed, -soing.** —*n.* 1. a long rope or line of hide or other material, with a running noose at one end, used for catching horses, cattle, etc. —*v.t.* 2. to catch with a lasso. [t. Sp.: m. *lazo,* g. L *laqueus* noose, snare. Cf. LACE] —**las′so·er,** *n.*

last¹ (lăst, läst), *adj.* 1. occurring or coming latest, or after all others, as in time, order, or place: *the last line on the page.* 2. latest; next before the present; most recent: *last week.* 3. being the only remaining: *one's last dollar.* 4. final: *in his last hours.* 5. conclusive: *the last word in an argument.* 6. utmost; extreme. 7. coming after all others in importance. 8. coming after all others in suitability or likelihood. 9. *Eccles.* extreme or final, as to a dying person (applied to the sacraments of penance, viaticum, and extreme unction collectively). —*adv.* 10. after all others. 11. on the most recent occasion. 12. in the end; finally; in conclusion. —*n.* 13. that which is last. 14. *Colloq.* the final mention or appearance: *to see the last of that woman.* 15. the end or conclusion. 16. **at long last,** after much has intervened. [ME *last, latst,* syncopated var. of *latest,* OE *latost, lætest,* superl. of *læt* late]

—**Syn.** 1. LAST, FINAL, ULTIMATE refer to what comes as an ending. That which is LAST comes or stands after all others in a stated series or succession; LAST may refer to objects or activities: *a seat in the last row.* That which is FINAL comes at the end, or serves to end or terminate, admitting of nothing further; FINAL is rarely used of objects: *to make a final attempt.* That which is ULTIMATE (literally, most remote) is the last that can be reached, as in progression or regression, experience, or a course of investigation: *ultimate truths.*

last² (lăst, läst), *v.i.* 1. to go on, or continue in progress, existence or life; endure: *so long as the world lasts.* 2. to continue unexpended or unexhausted; be enough (*for*): *while our money lasts.* 3. to continue in force, vigor, effectiveness, etc.: *to last in a race.* [ME *lasten,* OE *lǣstan* follow, perform, continue, last (der. *lǣst* track), c. OHG *leisten* follow. See LAST³] —**last′er,** *n.* —**Syn.** 1. See **continue.**

last³ (lăst, läst), *n.* 1. a model of the human foot, of wood or other material, on which boots or shoes are shaped, as in the making. —*v.t.* 2. to shape on or fit to a last. [ME; OE *lǣste* (der. *lǣst* sole of foot, track), c. G *leisten* last] —**last′er,** *n.*

last⁴ (lăst, läst), *n.* any of various large units of weight or capacity, varying in amount in different localities and for different commodities, often equivalent to 4000 pounds. [ME; OE *klæst,* c. G *last* load; akin to LADE]

Las·tex (lăs′tĕks), *n.* a trademark for a yarn made from a core of latex rubber covered with fabric strands.

last·ing (lăs′tĭng, läs′-), *adj.* 1. that lasts; enduring; permanent; durable. —*n.* 2. a strong, durable, closely woven fabric, used for the uppers of shoes, for covering buttons, etc. —**last′ing·ly,** *adv.* —**last′ing·ness,** *n.*

---

b., blend of, blended; c., cognate with; d., dialect, dialectal; der., derived from; f., formed from; g., going back to; m., modification of; r., replacing; s., stem of; t., taken from; ?, perhaps. See the full key on inside cover.

Last Judgment. See **judgment** (def. 7).

last·ly (lăst′lĭ, läst′-), *adv.* finally, in conclusion, or in the last place.

Last Supper, the supper of Jesus and His apostles on the eve of His crucifixion, at which He instituted the sacrament of the Lord's Supper.

Las Ve·gas (läs vā′gəs), a city in SE Nevada. 24,624 (1950).

lat (lăt), *n., pl.* **lats** (läts), **latu** (lä′tōō). **1.** the Latvian monetary unit, equal to 0.29+ gram of gold. **2.** a Latvian coin equal to $0.1930 in U.S. [abstracted from *Lat(vija)* Latvia]

Lat., Latin.

lat., latitude.

Lat·a·ki·a (lăt′ə kē′ə or, *esp. for 1,* lä′tä kē′ä), *n.* **1.** a seaport in NW Syria. 38,500 (est. 1942). Ancient, *Laodicea.* **2.** a variety of Turkish tobacco.

latch (lăch), *n.* **1.** a device for holding a door, gate, or the like closed, consisting basically of a bar falling or sliding into a catch, groove, hole, etc. —*v.t.* **2.** to close or fasten with a latch. **3. latch on to,** *Slang.* to fasten or attach (oneself) to [ME. *lacche,* OE *læccan* take hold of, catch, take]

latch·et (lăch′ĭt), *n. Archaic.* a strap or lace for fastening a shoe. [ME *lachet,* t. OF. d. var. of *lacet,* dim. of *laz* LACE]

latch·key (lăch′kē′), *n.* a key for drawing back or releasing a latch, esp. on an outer door.

latch·string (lăch′strĭng′), *n.* a string passed through a hole in a door, for raising the latch from the outside: *their latchstring was always out to strangers.*

late (lāt), *adj.,* **later** or **latter, latest** or **last,** *adv.,* **later, latest.** —*adj.* **1.** occurring, coming, or being after the usual or proper time: *late frosts.* **2.** continued until after the usual time or hour; protracted: *a late session.* **3.** far advanced in time: *a late hour.* **4.** belonging to time just before the present: *the latest fashions.* **5.** immediately preceding that which now exists: *his late residence.* **6.** recently deceased: *the late president.* **7.** occurring at an advanced stage in life: *a late marriage.* **8.** belonging to an advanced period or stage in the history or development of something: *Late Latin.* **9.** of late, recently. —*adv.* **10.** after the usual or proper time, or after delay: *to come late.* **11.** until after the usual time or hour; until a late hour at night: *to work late.* **12.** at or to an advanced time, period, or stage. **13.** recently but no longer. [ME; OE *læt* slow, late, c. G *lass* slothful] —**late′ness,** *n.* —**Syn. 1.** tardy; slow, dilatory; delayed, belated. **4.** See **modern.** —**Ant. 1.** early.

lat·ed (lā′tĭd), *adj. Poetic.* belated.

la·teen (lă tēn′, lə-), *adj.* pertaining to or having a lateen sail or sails. [t. F: m. *(voile) latine* Latin (sail)]

la·teen-rigged (lă tēn′rĭgd′, lə-), *adj.* having lateen sails.

lateen sail, a triangular sail extended by a long tapering yard, slung at about one quarter the distance from the lower end, which is brought down at the tack: used in xebecs, feluccas, etc., on the Mediterranean.

Late Greek, the Greek of the early Byzantine Empire and of the patristic literature, from about A.D. 300 to 700.

Lateen sail

Late Latin, the Latin of the late Western Roman Empire and of patristic literature, from about A.D. 300 to 700.

late·ly (lāt′lĭ), *adv.* of late; recently; not long since: *he had lately gone to the country.*

la·ten·cy (lā′tən sĭ), *n.* state of being latent.

latency period, *Psychoanal.* the stage of personality development, extending from about 4 or 5 years of age to the beginning of puberty, during which sexual urges often appear to lie dormant.

la·tent (lā′tənt), *adj.* **1.** hidden; concealed; present, but not visible or apparent: *latent ability.* **2.** *Pathol.* (of an infectious agent) remaining in a resting or hidden phase; dormant. **3.** *Psychol.* below the surface, but potentially able to achieve expression. **4.** *Bot.* (of buds which are not externally manifest) dormant or undeveloped. [t. L: s. *latens,* ppr., lying hid] —**la′tent·ly,** *adv.* —**Syn. 1.** LATENT, POTENTIAL refer to powers or possibilities existing but hidden or not yet actualized. LATENT emphasizes the hidden character or the dormancy of what is named: *latent qualities, defects, diseases.* That which is POTENTIAL exists in an as yet undeveloped state, but is thought of as capable of coming into full being or activity at some future time: *potential genius, tragedy.* POTENTIAL may be applied also to tangibles: *high tension wires are a potential source of danger.* —**Ant. 1.** actual, active, effectual.

latent period, 1. *Pathol.* the period that elapses before the presence of a disease is manifested by symptoms. **2.** *Physiol.* the lag between stimulus and reaction.

lat·er·al (lăt′ər əl), *adj.* **1.** of or pertaining to the side; situated at, proceeding from or directed to a side: *a lateral view.* **2.** *Phonet.* with the voice or breath passing beside the tongue: *"l" is a lateral sound.* —*n.* **3.** a lateral part or extension, as a branch or shoot. **4.** *Mining.* a small drift off to the side of a principal one. **5.** *Phonet.* a lateral sound. **6.** *Football.* a lateral pass. [t. L: s. *lateralis,* der. *latus* side] —**lat′er·al·ly,** *adv.*

lateral line, *Ichthyol.* the line of mucous pores, with sensory function, along the sides of fishes.

lateral pass, *Football.* a pass in which the ball is thrown in a direction almost parallel with the goal line.

Lat·er·an (lăt′ər ən), *n.* **1.** a complex of papal buildings in Rome, the residence of the popes throughout the Middle Ages. It contains the Church of St. John in the Lateran (ranking highest of all Roman Catholic churches), a papal palace, rebuilt 1586, and several other buildings. —*adj.* **2.** pertaining to the general church councils held there. [t. L: s. *Lateranus,* Roman family name]

lat·er·ite (lăt′ə rīt′), *n. Geol.* **1.** a reddish ferruginous soil formed in tropical regions by the decomposition of the underlying rocks. **2.** a similar soil formed of materials transported by water. **3.** any soil produced by the decomposition of the rocks beneath it. [f. L *later* brick + -ITE[1]] —**lat·er·it·ic** (lăt′ə rĭt′ĭk), *adj.*

la·tes·cent (lə tĕs′ənt), *adj.* becoming latent. [t. L: s. *latescens,* ppr., hiding oneself] —**la·tes′cence,** *n.*

la·tex (lā′tĕks), *n., pl.* **latices** (lăt′ə sēz′), **latexes** (lā′tĕk sĭz). *Bot.* a milky liquid in certain plants, as milkweeds, euphorbias, poppies, the plants yielding india rubber, etc., which coagulates on exposure to the air. [t. L: liquid]

lath (lăth, läth), *n., pl.* **laths** (lăthz, läths, läⁿhz, läths), *v.* —*n.* **1.** a thin, narrow strip of wood used with others like it to form a groundwork for supporting the slates or other covering of a roof or the plastering of a wall or ceiling, to construct latticework, and for other purposes. **2.** such strips collectively. **3.** work consisting of such strips. **4.** wire cloth or the like used in place of laths, as in plastering. **5.** a thin, narrow, flat piece of wood used for any purpose. —*v.t.* **6.** to cover or line with laths. [ME *la(th)the,* r. ME *latt,* OE. *lætt,* c. D *lat*] —**lath′like′,** *adj.*

lathe (lāⁿh), *n., v.,* **lathed, lathing.** —*n.* **1.** a machine for use in working metal, wood, etc., which holds the material and rotates it about a horizontal axis against a tool that shapes it. —*v.t.* **2.** to cut, shape, or otherwise treat on a lathe. [ME *lath* stand, t. Scand.; cf. Dan. *-lad* stand, lathe, c. OE *hlæd* heap, mound]

lath·er[1] (lăth′ər), *n.* **1.** foam or froth made from soap moistened with water, as by a brush for shaving. **2.** foam or froth formed in profuse sweating, as of a horse. —*v.i.* **3.** to form a lather, as soap. **4.** to become covered with lather, as a horse. —*v.t.* **5.** to apply lather to; cover with lather. **6.** *Colloq.* to beat or flog. [OE *lēathor,* c. Icel. *laudhr* washing soda, foam] —**lath′er·er,** *n.*

lath·er[2] (lăth′ər, läth′ər), *n.* a workman who puts up laths. [f. LATH, v. + -ER[1]]

lath·er·y (lăth′ər ĭ), *adj.* consisting of, covered with, or capable of producing lather.

lath·ing (lăth′ĭng, läth′ĭng), *n.* **1.** act or process of applying laths to a wall or the like. **2.** work consisting of laths; laths collectively. Also, **lath·work** (lăth′wûrk′, läth′-).

lath·y (lăth′ĭ, läth′ĭ), *adj.* lathlike; long and thin.

lat·i·ces (lăt′ə sēz′), *n.* pl. of **latex.**

la·tic·if·er·ous (lăt′ə sĭf′ər əs), *adj. Bot.* bearing or containing latex. [f. s. L *latex* a liquid + -(I)FEROUS]

lat·i·fun·di·um (lăt′ə fŭn′dĭ əm), *n., pl.* **-dia** (-dĭə). *Rom. Hist.* a great estate. [t. L: f. *latus* (comb. form of *latus* broad) + s. *fundus* estate + -*ium* -IUM]

Lat·i·mer (lăt′ə mər), *n.* **Hugh,** c1490–1555, British Protestant Reformation bishop, reformer, and martyr.

Lat·in (lăt′ən, -ĭn), *n.* **1.** the Italic language spoken in ancient Rome, fixed in 2d-1st century B.C., becoming the official language of the Empire. **2.** one of the forms of literary Latin, as Medieval Latin, Late Latin, Biblical Latin, Liturgical Latin, or of nonclassical Latin, as Vulgar Latin. **3.** Romance. **4.** a native or inhabitant of ancient Latium; an ancient Roman. **5.** a member of any Latin race. —*adj.* **6.** denoting or pertaining to those peoples (the Italians, French, Spanish, Portuguese, Rumanians, etc.) using languages derived from that of ancient Rome. **7.** noting or pertaining to the Western Church (which from early times down to the Reformation everywhere used Latin as its official language) or the Roman Catholic Church. **8.** of or pertaining to Latium or its inhabitants. [ME, t. L: s. *Latinus*]

Latin America, part of the American continents south of the United States, in which Romance languages are officially spoken. —**Lat′in-A·mer′i·can,** *adj., n.*

Latin Church, the Roman Catholic Church.

Latin cross, an upright bar crossed near the top by a shorter transverse piece. See illus. under **cross.**

Lat·in·ism (lăt′ə nĭz′əm), *n.* a mode of expression imitating Latin.

La·tin·ist (lăt′ə nĭst), *n.* a specialist in Latin.

La·tin·i·ty (lə tĭn′ə tĭ), *n.* **1.** use of the Latin language. **2.** Latin style or idiom.

La·tin·ize (lăt′ə nīz′), *v.,* **-ized, -izing.** —*v.t.* **1.** to cause to conform to the customs, etc., of the Latins or Latin Church. **2.** to intermix with Latin elements. **3.** to translate into Latin. —*v.i.* **4.** to use words and phrases from Latin: *he Latinizes frequently in his poetry.* —**Lat′in·i·za′tion,** *n.*

Latin Quarter, the quarter of Paris on the south side of the Seine, frequented for centuries by students and artists. [t. F: trans. of *Quartier Latin*]

Latin school, *U.S.* (esp. formerly) a preparatory school in which Latin is taught.

lat·ish (lā′tĭsh), *adj.* somewhat late.

lat·i·tude (lăt′ə tūd′, -tōōd′), *n.* **1.** *Geog.* **a.** the angular distance north or south from the equator of a point on the earth's surface, measured on the meridian of the point. **b.** a place or region as marked by its latitude. **2.** freedom from narrow restrictions; permitted freedom of action, opinion, etc. **3.** *Astron.* the angular distance of a heavenly body from the ecliptic (**celestial latitude**), or from the galactic plane (**galactic latitude**). **4.** *Photog.* the range of exposures over which proportional representation of subject brightness is obtained. [ME, t. L: m. *lātitūdo* breadth] —**Syn. 2.** See **range**.

LATITUDE AND PARALLEL
LONGITUDE AND MERIDIAN

lat·i·tu·di·nal (lăt′ə tū′də nəl, -tōō′-), *adj.* pertaining to latitude. —**lat′i·tu′di·nal·ly,** *adv.*

lat·i·tu·di·nar·i·an (lăt′ə tū′də när′ĭ ən, -tōō′-), *adj.* **1.** allowing, or characterized by, latitude in opinion or conduct, esp. in religious views. —*n.* **2.** one who is latitudinarian in opinion or conduct. **3.** *Anglican Ch.* one of those divines in the 17th century who maintained the wisdom of the episcopal form of government and ritual, but denied that they possess divine origin and authority. —**lat′i·tu′di·nar′i·an·ism,** *n.*

La·ti·um (lā′shĭ əm), *n.* an ancient country in Italy, SE of Rome.

La·to·na (lə tō′nə), *n.* *Class. Myth.* the Roman name of the Greek goddess Leto, mother of Apollo and Diana.

La Trappe (lá trảp′), an abbey in Normandy, France, at which the Trappist order was founded.

la·tri·a (lə trī′ə), *n.* *Rom. Cath. Theol.* that supreme worship which may be offered to God only. Cf. **dulia** and **hyperdulia**. [t. LL, t. Gk.: m. *latreía* service, worship]

la·trine (lə trēn′), *n.* a privy, esp. in a camp, barracks, a factory, or the like. [t. F, t. L: m. *lātrīna*]

lat·ten (lăt′ən), *n.* **1.** a brasslike alloy, commonly made in thin sheets, formerly much used for church utensils. **2.** tin plate. **3.** any metal in thin sheets. [ME *latoun*, t. OF: m. *laton*, der. *latte*. See LATTICE]

lat·ter (lăt′ər), *adj.* **1.** being the second mentioned of two (opposed to *former*): *I prefer the latter proposition to the former.* **2.** more advanced in time; later: *in these latter days of human progress.* **3.** nearer, or comparatively near, to the end or close: *the latter years of one's life.* **4.** *Poetic.* being the concluding part of. [ME *latt(e)re,* OE *lætra,* compar. of *læt* late]

lat·ter-day (lăt′ər dā′), *adj.* **1.** of a latter or more advanced day or period, or modern: *latter-day problems.* **2.** of the concluding or final days of the world.

Latter-day Saint, a Mormon.

lat·ter·ly (lăt′ər lĭ), *adv.* **1.** of late; lately. **2.** in the latter or concluding part of a period.

lat·ter·most (lăt′ər mōst′, -məst), *adj.* latest; last.

lat·tice (lăt′ĭs), *n., v.,* **-ticed, -ticing.** —*n.* **1.** a structure of crossed wooden or metal strips with open spaces between, used as a screen, etc. **2.** a window, gate, or the like, so constructed. —*v.t.* **3.** to furnish with a lattice or latticework. **4.** to form into or arrange like latticework. [ME *latis,* t. OF: m. *lattis,* der. *latte* lath, t. Gmc.; cf. OE *lætt* lath]

lat·tice·work (lăt′ĭs wûrk′), *n.* **1.** work consisting of crossed strips with openings between. **2.** a lattice.

lat·tic·ing (lăt′ĭs ĭng), *n.* **1.** act or process of furnishing with or making latticework. **2.** latticework.

Lat·vi·a (lăt′vĭ ə), *n.* a constituent republic of the Soviet Union, in the W part, on the Baltic: an independent state, 1918–40. 1,950,502 pop. (1935); 25,395 sq. mi. *Cap.:* Riga. Lettish, **Lat·vi·ja** (lăt′vĭ yä′). Official name, **Latvian Soviet Socialist Republic.**

Lat·vi·an (lăt′vĭ ən), *adj.* **1.** of or pertaining to Latvia. —*n.* **2.** a native or inhabitant of Latvia. **3.** the Lettish language.

laud (lôd), *v.t.* **1.** to praise; extol. —*n.* **2.** music or a song in praise or honor of anyone. **3.** (*pl.*) *Eccles.* a canonical hour, characterized esp. by psalms of praise (**laudes**) which follows, and is usually recited with, matins. [ME *laude,* back formation from *laudes,* pl., t. L: praises] —**laud′er,** *n.*

Laud (lôd), *n.* **William,** 1573–1645, archbishop of Canterbury and opponent of Puritanism, executed for treason.

laud·a·ble (lô′də bəl), *adj.* **1.** praiseworthy or commendable: *a laudable idea.* **2.** *Med. Obs.* healthy, wholesome, or not noxious. —**laud′a·bil′i·ty, laud′a·ble·ness,** *n.* —**laud′a·bly,** *adv.*

lau·da·num (lô′də nəm, lôd′nəm), *n.* **1.** the tincture of opium. **2.** (formerly) any preparation in which opium was the chief ingredient. [orig. ML var. of LADANUM; arbitrarily used by Paracelsus to name a remedy based on opium]

lau·da·tion (lô dā′shən), *n.* act of lauding; praise.

laud·a·to·ry (lô′də tōr′ĭ), *adj.* containing or expressing praise: *overwhelmed by the speaker's laudatory remarks.* Also, **laud′a·tive.**

Lau·der (lô′dər), *n.* **Sir Harry MacLennan** (mə klĕn′ən), 1870–1950, Scottish ballad singer and comedian.

laugh (lăf, läf), *v.i.* **1.** to express mirth, amusement, derision, etc., by an explosive, inarticulate sound of the voice, facial expressions, etc. **2.** to experience the emotion so expressed. **3.** to utter a cry or sound resembling the laughing of human beings, as some animals do. **4. laugh at,** to make fun of; deride; ridicule. **5. laugh in one's sleeve,** to laugh inwardly at something. **6.** to drive, put, bring, etc., by or with laughter. **7.** to utter with laughter: *he laughed his consent.* —*n.* **8.** act or sound of laughing, or laughter. **9.** an expression of mirth, derision, etc., by laughing. [ME *laugh(en),* d. OE *hlæhhan,* OE *hliehhan,* c. Icel. *hlæja,* Goth *hlahjan;* akin to G *lachen*] —**laugh′er,** *n.*

—**Syn. 1.** chortle; cackle, cachinnate, hawhaw, guffaw, roar; giggle, snicker, snigger, titter. **8.** LAUGH, CHUCKLE, GRIN, SMILE, refer to methods of expressing mirth, appreciation of humor, etc. A LAUGH may be a sudden, voiceless exhalation, but is usually an audible sound, either soft or loud: *a hearty laugh.* CHUCKLE suggests a barely audible series of sounds expressing private amusement or satisfaction: *a delighted chuckle.* A SMILE is a (usually pleasant) lighting up of the face and an upward curving of the corners of the lips (which may or may not be open); it may express amusement or mere recognition, friendliness, etc.: *a courteous smile.* A GRIN, in which the teeth are usually visible, is like an exaggerated smile, less controlled in expressing the feelings: *a friendly grin.*

laugh·a·ble (lăf′ə bəl, läf′ə-), *adj.* such as to excite laughter; funny; amusing; ludicrous. —**laugh′a·ble·ness,** *n.* —**laugh′a·bly,** *adv.* —**Syn.** See **funny**.

laugh·ing (lăf′ĭng, läf′ĭng), *n.* **1.** laughter. —*adj.* **2.** that laughs; giving vent to laughter, as persons. **3.** no laughing matter, a serious matter. **4.** uttering sounds like human laughter, as some birds. **5.** suggesting laughter by brightness, etc. —**laugh′ing·ly,** *adv.*

laughing gas, nitrous oxide, N_2O, which when inhaled sometimes produces exhilarating effects, used as an anesthetic in dentistry, etc.

laughing jackass, a harsh-voiced Australian bird, *Dacelo gigas* (a kind of kingfisher).

laugh·ing·stock (lăf′ĭng stŏk′, läf′ĭng-), *n.* a butt for laughter; an object of ridicule.

laugh·ter (lăf′tər, läf′-), *n.* **1.** the action or sound of laughing. **2.** an experiencing of the emotion expressed by laughing: *inward laughter.* **3.** an expression or appearance of merriment or amusement. **4.** a subject or matter for laughing. [ME; OE *hleahtor*]

launce (läns, läns), *n.* sand launce.

Laun·ces·ton (lôn′sĕs′tən, län′-), *n.* a city in N Tasmania. With suburbs, 32,833 (1933).

launch[1] (lônch, länch), *n.* **1.** a heavy open boat. **2.** the largest boat carried by a warship. [t. Sp., Pg.: m. *lancha*]

launch[2] (lônch, länch), *v.t.* **1.** to set (a boat) afloat; lower into the water. **2.** to cause (a newly built ship) to move or slide from the stocks into the water. **3.** to start on a course, career, etc. **4.** to set going: *to launch a scheme.* **5.** to send forth; start off (forcefully): *the plane was launched from the deck of the carrier.* **6.** to throw or hurl: *to launch a spear.* —*v.i.* **7.** to burst out or plunge boldly into action, speech, etc. **8.** to start out or forth; push out or put forth on the water. —*n.* **9.** the sliding or movement of a boat or vessel from the land or dock into the water. [ME *launche(n),* t. ONF: m. *lancher,* var. of central OF *lancier* LANCE, v.] —**launch′er,** *n.*

laun·der (lôn′dər, län′-), *v.t.* **1.** to wash and iron (clothes, etc.). —*v.i.* **2.** to do or wash laundry. —*n.* **3.** (in ore dressing) a passage carrying products of intermediate grade, and residue, which are in water suspension. [ME *launder* one who washes, contr. of *lavender,* t. OF: m. *lavandier* a washer, t. LL: m.s. *lavandārius,* der. L *lavandus,* ger. of *lavāre* wash] —**laun′der·er,** *n.*

laun·dress (lôn′drĭs, län′-), *n.* a woman whose occupation is the washing and ironing of clothes, etc.

laun·dry (lôn′drĭ, län′-), *n., pl.* **-dries. 1.** articles of clothes, etc. to be washed. **2.** a place or establishment where clothes, etc. are laundered. **3.** act of laundering.

laun·dry·man (lôn′drĭ mən, län′-), *n., pl.* **-men. 1.** a man who works in or conducts a laundry. **2.** a man who collects and delivers laundry.

laun·dry·wom·an (lôn′drĭ wŏŏm′ən, län′-), *n., pl.* **-women.** a laundress.

lau·ra·ceous (lô rā′shəs), *adj.* belonging to the *Lauraceae,* or laurel family of plants. [f. s. L *laurus* laurel + -ACEOUS]

lau·re·ate (lôr′ĭ ĭt), *adj.* **1.** crowned or decked with laurel as a mark of honor. **2.** specially recognized or distinguished, or deserving of distinction, esp. for poetic merit: *poet laureate.* **3.** consisting of laurel. —*n.* **4.** one crowned with laurel. **5.** a poet laureate. [ME *laureat,* t. L: s. *laureātus* (def. 1)] —**lau′re·ate·ship,** *n.*

lau·rel (lôr′əl, lŏr′əl), *n., v.t.* **-reled, -reling** or (*esp. Brit.*) **-relled, -relling.** —*n.* **1.** a small lauraceous evergreen tree, *Laurus nobilis,* of Europe (the **true laurel**). **2.** any tree of the same genus (*Laurus*). **3.** any of various trees or shrubs similar to the true laurel, as *Kalmia latifolia,* a large ericaceous shrub with glossy leaves and showy flowers (the American, or **mountain laurel**) or *Rhododendron maximum,* the great rhododendron (or **great laurel**). **4.** the foliage of the true laurel as an emblem of victory or distinction. **5.** a branch or wreath of it. **6.** (*usually pl.*) honor won, as by achievement. —*v.t.* **7.** to adorn or wreathe with laurel. **8.** to honor with marks of distinction. [ME *laurer, laureal,* t. F: m. *laurier, lorier,* der. OF *lor,* g. L *laurus*]

---

b., blend of, blended; c., cognate with; d., dialect, dialectal; der., derived from; f., formed from; g., going back to; m., modification of; r., replacing; s., stem of; t., taken from; ?, perhaps. See the full key on inside cover.

Lau·rel (lôr′əl, lŏr′əl), *n.* a city in SE Mississippi. 25,038 (1950).

Lau·ren·tian (lô rĕn′shən), *adj.* **1.** of or pertaining to the St. Lawrence river. **2.** *Geol.* noting or pertaining to a series of rocks of the Archean system, occurring in Canada near the St. Lawrence river and the Great Lakes.

Laurentian Mountains, a range of low mountains in E Canada between the St. Lawrence and Hudson Bay.

Lau·ren·tides Park (lôr′ən tīdz′; *Fr.* lō rän tēd′), a national park in SE Canada, in Quebec province between the St. Lawrence and Lake St. John.

Lau·ri·er (lôr′ĭ ā′; *Fr.* lō ryĕ′), *n.* **Sir Wilfrid,** 1841–1919, prime minister of Canada, 1896–1911.

lau·rus·ti·nus (lôr′ə stī′nəs), *n.* a caprifoliaceous evergreen garden shrub, *Viburnum tinus,* native in southern Europe, with white or pinkish flowers. [t. NL: f. L *laurus* laurel + *tīnus* kind of plant]

Lau·sanne (lō zän′; *Fr.* lō zän′), *n.* a city in W Switzerland, on the Lake of Geneva. 97,800 (est. 1944).

laus De·o (lôs dē′ō, lous dā′ō), *Latin.* praise (be) to God.

Lau·trec (lō trĕk′), *n.* See **Toulouse-Lautrec.**

lau·wine (lô′wĭn; *Ger.* lou vē′nə), *n.* lawine.

la·va (lä′və, lăv′ə), *n.* **1.** the molten or fluid rock which issues from a volcano or volcanic vent. **2.** the substance formed when this solidifies, occurring in many varieties differing greatly in structure and constitution. [t. It. (Neapolitan): orig., stream, der. *lavare* wash, g. L]

la·va·bo (lə vā′bō), *n., pl.* **-boes.** *Eccles.* **1.** the ritual washing of the celebrant's hands after the offertory in the Mass, accompanied in the Roman rite by the recitation of Psalms 26:6–12, or, in the Douay Version, Psalms 25:6–12 (so called from the first word of this passage in the Latin version). **2.** the passage recited. **3.** the small towel or the basin used. **4.** (in many medieval monasteries) a large stone basin from which the water issued by a number of small orifices around the edge, for the performance of ablutions. [t. L: I will wash]

lav·age (lăv′ĭj; *Fr.* là vàzh′), *n.* **1.** a washing. **2.** *Med.* **a.** cleansing by injection or the like. **b.** the washing out of the stomach. [t. F, der. *laver* LAVE]

La·val (là vàl′), *n.* **Pierre** (pyĕr′), 1883–1945, premier of France, 1931–32, 1935–36; premier of Vichy France, 1942–44; convicted of treason and executed.

lav·a·liere (lăv′ə lîr′), *n.* an ornamental, usually jeweled, pendant on a small chain, worn by women about the neck. Also, **lav′a·lier′;** *French,* **la·val·lière** (là và lyĕr′). [named after the Duchesse de *La Vallière* (1644–1710), mistress of Louis XIV of France]

la·va·tion (lă vā′shən), *n.* the process of washing. —**la·va′tion·al,** *adj.*

lav·a·to·ry (lăv′ə tōr′ĭ), *n., pl.* **-ries. 1.** a room fitted up with means for washing the hands and face, and often with other toilet conveniences. **2.** a bowl or basin for washing or bathing purposes. **3.** any place where washing is done. [ME *lavatorie,* t. LL: m. *lavātōrium*]

lave (lāv), *v.,* **laved, laving.** —*v.t.* **1.** *Poetic.* to wash; bathe. **2.** *Poetic.* (of a river, the sea, etc.) to wash or flow against. —*v.i.* **3.** to bathe. **4.** to wash or flow as against something. [ME; OE *lafian* pour water on, wash. Cf. F *laver,* L *lavāre*]

lav·en·der (lăv′ən dər), *n.* **1.** pale, bluish purple. **2.** a plant of the menthaceous genus *Lavandula,* esp. *L officinalis,* a small Old World shrub with spikes of fragrant pale-purple flowers, yielding an oil **(oil of lavender)** used in medicine and perfumery. **3.** the dried flowers or other parts of this plant used to place among linen, etc., for scent or as a preservative. [ME *lavendre,* t. AF, t. ML: m.s. *lavandula, livendula;* ? der. L *lavāre* wash or L *livēre* be livid or bluish]

la·ver¹ (lā′vər), *n.* **1.** *Poetic.* a basin, bowl, or cistern to wash in. **2.** *Poetic.* any bowl or pan for water. **3.** *Old Testament.* a large basin upon a foot or pedestal in the court of the Jewish tabernacle, and subsequently in the temple, containing water for the ablutions of the priests, and for the washing of the sacrifices in the temple service. **4.** *Eccles.* the font or the water of baptism. **5.** any spiritually cleansing agency. [ME, t. OF: m. *laveoir,* g. LL *lavātōrium* lavatory]

la·ver² (lā′vər), *n.* any of several edible seaweeds, esp. of the genus *Porphyra.* [t. L: kind of water plant]

La Vé·ren·drye (là vĕ rän drē′), **Pierre Gaultier de Varennes** (pyĕr′ gō tyĕ′ də và rĕn′), Sieur de, 1685–1749, French-Canadian explorer of North America.

lav·ish (lăv′ĭsh), *adj.* **1.** using or bestowing in great abundance or without stint (often fol. by *of*): *lavish of time.* **2.** expended, bestowed, or occurring in profusion: *lavish gifts, lavish spending.* [late ME, adj. use of obs. *lavish* profusion, t. OF: m. *lavache* deluge] —*v.t.* **3.** to expend or bestow in great abundance or without stint: *to lavish favors on a person.* [v. use of adj.] —**lav′ish·er,** *n.* —**lav′ish·ly,** *adv.* —**lav′ish·ness,** *n.* —**Syn. 1, 2.** unstinted, extravagant, excessive. LAVISH, PRODIGAL, PROFUSE refer to that which exists in abundance and is poured out copiously. LAVISH suggests (sometimes excessive) generosity and openhandedness: *lavish hospitality, much too lavish.* PRODIGAL suggests wastefulness, improvidence, and reckless impatience of restraint: *a prodigal extravagance.* PROFUSE emphasizes abundance, but may suggest over-emotionalism, exaggeration, and the like: *profuse thanks, compliments, apologies.* —**Ant. 2.** limited.

La·voi·sier (là vwä zyĕ′), *n.* **Antoine Laurent** (än twàn′ lō rän′), 1743–94, French chemist.

law (lô), *n.* **1.** the principles and regulations emanating from a government and applicable to a people, whether in the form of legislation or of custom and policies recognized and enforced by judicial decision. **2.** any written or positive rule, or collection of rules, prescribed under the authority of the state or nation, whether by the people in its constitution, as the **organic law,** or by the legislature in its **statute law,** or by the treaty-making power, or by municipalities in their ordinances or **bylaws. 3.** the controlling influence of such rules; the condition of society brought about by their observance: *to maintain law and order.* **4.** a system or collection of such rules. **5.** the department of knowledge concerned with these rules; jurisprudence: *to study law.* **6.** the body of such rules concerned with a particular subject or derived from a particular source: *commercial law.* **7.** an act of the supreme legislative body of a state or nation, as distinguished from the constitution. **8.** the principles applied in the courts of common law, as distinguished from equity. **9.** the profession which deals with law and legal procedure: *to practice law.* **10.** legal action; litigation: *to go to law.* **11.** any rules or injunctions that must be obeyed: *to lay down the law.* **12.** (in philosophical and scientific use) **a.** a statement of a relation or sequence of phenomena invariable under the same conditions. **b.** a mathematical rule. **13.** a commandment or a revelation from God. **14.** (*often cap.*) a divinely appointed order or system. **15. the Law,** the Mosaic law (often in contrast to *the gospel*). **16.** the five books of Moses (the Pentateuch) containing this system and forming the first of the three Jewish divisions of the Old Testament. **17.** the preceptive part of the Bible, esp. of the New Testament, in contradistinction to its promises: *the law of Christ.* **18.** *Chiefly Brit. Sports.* an allowance given a weaker competitor. [ME *law, lagh,* OE *lagu,* t. Scand.; cf. Icel. *lag* layer, pl. *lög* law, lit. that which is laid down; akin to LAY¹, LIE²]

Law (lô), *n.* **John,** 1671–1729, Scottish financier.

law·a·bid·ing (lô′ə bī′dĭng), *adj.* abiding by or keeping the law; obedient to law: *law-abiding citizens.*

law·break·er (lô′brā′kər), *n.* one who breaks or violates the law. —**law′break′ing,** *n., adj.*

Lawes (lôz), *n.* **Harry,** 1596–1662, British song writer.

law·ful (lô′fəl), *adj.* **1.** allowed or permitted by law; not contrary to law. **2.** legally qualified or entitled: *lawful king.* **3.** recognized or sanctioned by law. **4.** valid; legitimate: *a lawful marriage.* —**law′ful·ly,** *adv.* —**law′ful·ness,** *n.* —**Syn. 1.** legal. **3.** licit.

law·giv·er (lô′gĭv′ər), *n.* one who gives or promulgates a law or a code of laws. —**law′giv′ing,** *n., adj.*

la·wine (lô′wĭn; *Ger.* lä vē′nə), *n.* an avalanche. Also, **lauwine.** [t. G. Cf. L *lābī* fall down, slip, slide]

law·less (lô′lĭs), *adj.* **1.** regardless of or contrary to law: *lawless violence.* **2.** uncontrolled by law; unbridled: *lawless passions.* **3.** without law; not regulated by law. —**law′less·ly,** *adv.* —**law′less·ness,** *n.*

law·mak·er (lô′mā′kər), *n.* one who makes or enacts law; a legislator. —**law′mak′ing,** *n., adj.*

law merchant, the principles and rules, drawn chiefly from custom, determining the rights and obligations of commercial transactions; commercial law.

lawn¹ (lôn), *n.* **1.** a stretch of grass-covered land, esp. one closely mowed, as near a house, etc. **2.** *Archaic or Dial.* a glade. [earlier *laund,* t. OF: m. *la(u)nde* wooded ground; of Celtic orig.] —**lawn′y,** *adj.*

lawn² (lôn), *n.* a thin or sheer linen or cotton fabric, either plain or printed. [ME *laun(e), laund(e);* prob. named after *Laon,* city in northern France, where much linen was made] —**lawn′y,** *adj.*

lawn mower, a machine for cutting grass.

lawn sleeves, 1. the sleeves of lawn of an Anglican bishop. **2.** the office of a bishop. **3.** a bishop or bishops.

lawn tennis, a form of tennis, played on an unenclosed rectangular plot on a lawn or other level surface.

law of contradiction, *Logic.* the law which asserts that a proposition cannot be both true and false, or alternatively that a thing cannot both have and not have a given property.

Law of Moses, the Pentateuch or Torah.

law of nations, 1. international law. **2.** (in Roman use) the body of rules common to the law of all nations.

Law·rence (lôr′əns, lŏr′-), *n.* **1. D(avid) H(erbert),** 1885–1930, British novelist and poet. **2. Ernest Orlando,** born 1901, U.S. physicist: inventor of cyclotron. **3. James,** 1781–1813, U.S. naval officer in the War of 1812. **4. Sir Thomas,** 1769–1830, British portrait painter. **5. Thomas Edward,** (after 1927, *Thomas Edward Shaw,* "Lawrence of Arabia") 1888–1935, British soldier, archaeologist, and writer. **6.** a city in NE Massachusetts, on the Merrimack river. 80,536 (1950).

law·suit (lô′sōōt′), *n.* a suit at law; a prosecution of a claim in a law court.

Law·ton (lô′tən), *n.* a city in SW Oklahoma. 34,757 (1950).

law·yer (lô′yər), *n.* **1.** one whose profession it is to conduct suits in court or to give legal advice and aid. **2.** *New Testament.* an interpreter of the Mosaic law. **3.** a burbot (fresh-water cod): from the beardlike barbel.

lax (lăks), *adj.* **1.** lacking in strictness or severity; careless or negligent: *lax morals.* **2.** not rigidly exact or precise; vague: *lax ideas of a subject.* **3.** loose or slack; not tense, rigid, or firm: *a lax cord.* **4.** open or not retentive, as the bowels. **5.** having the bowels unduly open, as a person. **6.** loosely cohering; open or not compact, as a panicle of a plant. **7.** *Phonet.* pronounced with relatively relaxed muscles. [ME, t. L: s. *laxus* loose, slack] —**lax′-ly,** *adv.* —**lax′ness,** *n.*

lax·a·tion (lăk sā′shən), *n.* **1.** a loosening or relaxing. **2.** state of being loosened or relaxed. **3.** a laxative. [ME *laxacion*, t. L: s. *laxātio* a widening]

lax·a·tive (lăk′sə tĭv), *n.* **1.** *Med.* a laxative medicine or agent. —*adj.* **2.** *Med.* mildly purgative. **3.** *Pathol.* **a.** (of the bowels) subject to looseness. **b.** (of a disease) characterized by looseness of the bowels. [t. L: m.s. *laxā-tīvus* loosening; r. ME *laxatif*, t. F]

lax·i·ty (lăk′sə tĭ), *n.* state or quality of being lax or loose. [t. F: m. *laxitê*, t. L: m.s. *laxitas*]

lay¹ (lā), *v.,* **laid, laying,** *n.* —*v.t.* **1.** to put or place in a position of rest or recumbency: *to lay a book on a desk.* **2.** to bring, throw, or beat down, as from an erect position: *to lay a person low.* **3.** to cause to subside: *to lay the dust.* **4.** to allay, appease, or suppress: *to lay a person's doubts.* **5.** to smooth down or make even: *to lay the nap of cloth.* **6.** to bury. **7.** to bring forth and deposit (an egg or eggs). **8.** to deposit as a wager; stake; bet: *I'll lay you ten to one.* **9.** to put away for future use (fol. by *by*). **10.** to place, set, or cause to be in a particular situation, state, or condition: *to lay hands on a thing.* **11.** to place before a person, or bring to a person's notice or consideration: *he laid his case before the commission.* **12.** to put to; place in contiguity; apply: *to lay a hand on a child.* **13.** to set (a trap, etc.). **14.** to place or locate (a scene): *the scene is laid in France.* **15.** to present, bring forward, or prefer, as a claim, charge, etc. **16.** to impute, attribute, or ascribe. **17.** to impose as a burden, duty, penalty, or the like: *to lay an embargo on shipments of oil.* **18.** to bring down (a stick, etc.), as on a person, in inflicting punishment. **19.** to dispose or place in proper position or in an orderly fashion: *to lay bricks.* **20.** to set (a table). **21.** to form by twisting strands together, as a rope. **22.** to place on or over a surface, as paint; cover or spread with something else. **23.** to devise or arrange, as a plan. **24.** *Naut.* to head a ship toward (an object or compass point) esp. on the closest course she will make to the wind. **25.** to move a cannon in vertical plane for elevation. **26.** to put (dogs) on a scent. **27.** Some special phrases are: **lay hold of** or **on,** to grasp; seize; catch.
lay off, 1. to put aside. **2.** to dismiss, esp. temporarily, as a workman. **3.** to mark or plot off.
lay on the table, (in parliamentary use) to table.
lay out, 1. to extend at length. **2.** to spread out to the sight, air, etc.; spread out in order. **3.** to stretch out and prepare (a body) for burial. **4.** *Slang.* to expend (money) for a particular purpose. **5.** to exert (oneself) to effect a purpose, produce a good effect, etc. **6.** to plot or plan out.
lay siege to, to besiege.
lay to, *Naut.* **1.** to check the motion of (a ship). **2.** to put (a ship, etc.) in a dock or other place of safety.
lay up, 1. to put away, as for future use; store up. **2.** to cause to remain in bed or indoors through illness.
—*v.i.* **28.** to lay eggs. **29.** to wager or bet. **30.** to deal or aim blows (fol. by *on, at, about,* etc.). **31.** to apply oneself vigorously. **32.** *Colloq.* to lie in wait (fol. by *for*). **33.** *Colloq.* or *Dial.* to plan or scheme (often fol. by *out*). **34.** *Naut.* to take a specified position. **35.** (in substandard use) to lie.
—*n.* **36.** the way or position which a thing is laid or lies. **37.** *Ropemaking.* the quality of a fiber rope characterized by the degree of twist, the angles formed by the strands and by the fibers in the strands. **38.** a share of the profits or the catch of a whaling or fishing voyage, distributed to officers and crew.
[ME *lay(en), legge(n),* OE *lecgan* (causative of *ligcan* LIE²), c. D *leggen,* G *legen,* Icel. *leggja,* Goth. *lagjan*] —**Syn. 1.** place; deposit, set. See **put, lie²**.

lay² (lā), *v.* pt. of **lie²**.

lay³ (lā), *adj.* **1.** belonging to, pertaining to, or performed by the people or laity, as distinguished from the clergy: *a lay sermon.* **2.** not belonging to, connected with, or proceeding from a profession, esp. the law or medicine. [ME *laye,* t. OF: m. *lai,* g. LL *lāicus* LAIC]

lay⁴ (lā), *n.* **1.** a short narrative or other poem, esp. one to be sung. **2.** a song. [ME *lai,* t. OF, ? t. Celtic; cf. OIrish *laid*]

Lay·a·mon (lā′ə mən, lä′yə-), *n.* fl. c1200, British chronicler in verse. [modern misspelling of early ME *Laghamon,* ME *Laweman.* See LAW, MAN]

Lay·ard (lârd, lā′ərd), *n.* **Sir Austen Henry,** 1817–94, British archaeologist, writer, and diplomat.

lay brother, a man who has taken religious vows and habit, but is employed chiefly in manual labor.

lay day, 1. *Com.* one of a certain number of days allowed by a charter party for loading or unloading a vessel without demurrage. **2.** *Naut.* a day in which a vessel is delayed in port.

lay·er (lā′ər), *n.* **1.** a thickness of some material laid on or spread over a surface; a stratum. **2.** something which is laid. **3.** one who or that which lays. **4.** *Hort.* **a.** a shoot or twig placed partly under ground while still attached to the living stock, for the purpose of propagation. **b.** a plant which has been

Layer (def. 4)

propagated by layerage. —*v.t.* **5.** to make a layer of. **6.** *Hort.* to propagate by layers. [ME, f. LAY¹ + -ER¹]

lay·er·age (lā′ər ĭj), *n.* *Hort.* a method of propagating plants by causing their shoots to take root while still attached to the mother plant.

layer cake, a cake made in layers with a cream, jelly, or other filling between layers.

lay·ette (lā ĕt′), *n.* an outfit of clothing, toilet articles, etc., for a newborn child. [t. F: box, drawer, layette, dim. of *laie* chest, trough; t. Flemish: m. *laeye*]

lay figure, 1. a jointed model of the human body, usually of wood, from which artists work in the absence of a living model. **2.** a similar figure used in shops to display costumes. **3.** a mere puppet or nonentity; a person of no importance. [r. obs. *layman* (t. D: m. *leeman,* f. *lee* joint, limb (c. E *lith,* now d.) + *man* MAN), with *figure* substituted for *man,* to avoid confusion with eccl. term]

lay·man (lā′mən), *n., pl.* **-men.** one of the laity; one not a clergyman or not a member of some particular profession. [f. LAY³ + MAN]

lay·off (lā′ôf′, -ŏf′), *n.* **1.** act of laying off. **2.** an interval of enforced unemployment.

lay·out (lā′out′), *n.* **1.** a laying or spreading out. **2.** an arrangement or plan. **3.** the plan or sketch of a page or advertisement indicating the arrangement of materials. **4.** *Slang.* a display; a spread. **5.** a collection or set of tools, implements, or the like.

lay·o·ver (lā′ō′vər), *n.* stopover.

lay·wom·an (lā′wŏom′ən), *n., pl.* **-women.** a female member of the laity.

laz·ar (lăz′ər; *more correctly* lā′zər), *n.* *Archaic.* **1.** a person, esp. a beggar or poor person, infected with a loathsome disease. **2.** a leper. [ME, t.ML: s. *lazarus,* special use of LAZARUS] —**laz′ar·like′,** *adj.*

laz·a·ret·to (lăz′ərĕt′ō), *n., pl.* **-tos.** **1.** a hospital for those affected with contagious or loathsome diseases. **2.** a building or a ship set apart for quarantine purposes. **3.** *Naut.* a place in some merchant ships, usually near the stern, in which provisions and stores are kept. Also, **laz·a·ret** (lăz′ə rĕt′), **laz′a·rette′.** [t. It.: m. *lazzaretto,* var. of Venetian *luzureto,* b. *nazareto* (abbr. from name of leper hospital *Santa Maria di Nazaret* and *lazaro*) *lazar, leper*]

Laz·a·rus (lăz′ə rəs), *n.* **1.** the beggar, "full of sores," of the parable in Luke 16:19–31. **2.** the brother of Mary and Martha, and friend of Jesus, who raised him from the dead. John 11:1–44; 12:1–18. **3. Emma,** 1849–87, U.S. poet. [t. LL, t. Gk.: m. *Lázaros,* t. Heb.: m. *El'āzār* Eleazar]

laze (lāz), *v.,* **lazed, lazing.** —*v.i.* **1.** to be lazy; idle or lounge lazily. —*v.t.* **2.** to pass (time etc.) lazily (fol. by *away*). [back formation from LAZY]

laz·u·lite (lăz′yə līt′), *n.* an azure-blue mineral, hydrous magnesium iron aluminum phosphate, (Fe Mg) $Al_2P_2O_8(OH)_2$. [f. s. ML *lāzulum* lapis lazuli + -ITE¹]

laz·u·rite (lăz′yə rīt′), *n.* a mineral, sodium aluminum silicate and sulfide, $Na_5Al_3Si_3O_{12}S_3$, occurring in deep-blue crystals and used for ornamental purposes. [f. ML *lāzur* AZURE + -ITE¹]

la·zy (lā′zĭ), *adj.,* **lazier, laziest. 1.** disinclined to exertion or work; idle. **2.** slow-moving; sluggish; *a lazy stream.* **3.** noting a kind of livestock brand which is placed on its side instead of upright. [orig. uncert.] —**la′zi·ly,** *adv.* —**la′zi·ness,** *n.* —**Syn. 1.** indolent, slothful. See **idle.** —**Ant. 1.** industrious; active.

la·zy·bones (lā′zĭ bōnz′), *n.* *Colloq.* a lazy person.

lazy Su·san (sōō′zən), a large revolving tray for food, placed at the center of the table.

lazy tongs, a kind of extensible tongs for grasping objects at a distance consisting of a series of pairs of crossing pieces, each pair pivoted together in the middle and connected with the next pair at the extremities.

lb., *pl.* **lbs., lb.** (L *libra, pl. librae*) pound (weight).

Lazy tongs

L.C., Library of Congress.

l.c., 1. left center. **2.** letter of credit. **3.** (L *loco citato*) in the place cited. **4.** *Print.* lower case.

L/C, letter of credit. Also, l/c.

l.c.d., lowest common denominator.

L.C.L., less than carload lot. Also, **l.c.l.**

L.C.M., least common multiple. Also, **l.c.m.**

LD, Low Dutch. Also, **L.D.**

Ld., 1. Limited. **2.** Lord.

l.e., *Football.* left end.

lea¹ (lē), *n.* *Poetic.* a tract of open ground, esp. grassland; a meadow. [ME *ley,* OE *lēa(h),* c. OHG *lōh,* L *lūcus* grove]

lea² (lē), *n.* a measure of yarn of varying quantity, for wool usually 80 yards, cotton and silk 120 yards, linen 300 yards. [ME, ? akin to F *lier* tie]

lea., 1. league. **2.** leather.

leach (lēch), *v.t.* **1.** to cause (water, etc.) to percolate through something. **2.** to remove soluble constituents from (ashes, etc.) by percolation. —*v.i.* **3.** (of ashes, etc.) to undergo the action of percolating water. **4.** to percolate, as water. —*n.* **5.** a leaching. **6.** the material leached. **7.** a vessel for use in leaching. [unexplained var. of *letch,* v. (whence d. *letch,* n., bog, etc.), OE *leccan* moisten, wet, causative of LEAK]

leach·y (lē′chĭ), *adj.* porous.
Lea·cock (lē′kŏk), *n.* Stephen Butler, 1869–1944, Canadian humorist and economist.
lead[1] (lēd), *v.*, **led, leading,** *n.* —*v.t.* **1.** to take or conduct on the way; go before or with to show the way. **2.** to conduct by holding and guiding: *to lead a horse by a rope.* **3. lead the way,** to go in advance of others, esp. as a guide. **4.** to guide in direction, course, action, opinion, etc.; to influence or induce: *too easily led.* **5.** to conduct or bring (water, wire, etc.) in a particular course. **6.** (of a road, passage, etc.) to serve to bring (a person, etc.) to a place through a region, etc. **7.** to take or bring: *the prisoners were led in.* **8.** to be at the head of, command, or direct (an army, organization, etc.). **9.** to go at the head of or in advance of (a procession, list, body, etc.); to be first in or go before. **10.** to have the directing or principal part in (a movement, proceedings, etc.). **11.** to begin or open, as a dance, discussion, etc. **12.** to act as leader of (an orchestra, etc.). **13.** to go through or pass (life, etc.): *to lead a dreary existence.* **14.** *Cards.* to begin a round, etc., with (a card or suit specified). **15.** to aim and fire a firearm or cannon ahead of (a moving target) in order to allow for the travel of the target while the bullet or shell is reaching it. —*v.i.* **16.** to act as a guide; show the way. **17.** to be led, or submit to being led, as an animal. **18.** to afford passage to a place, etc., as a road, stairway, or the like does. **19.** to go first; be in advance. **20.** to take the directing or principal part. **21.** to take the initiative (often fol. by *off*). **22.** *Boxing.* to take the offensive by jabbing an opponent. **23.** *Cards.* to make the first play. —*n.* **24.** the first or foremost place; position in advance of others. **25.** the extent of advance. **26.** something that leads. **27.** a guiding indication. **28.** precedence. **29.** *Theat.* **a.** the principal part in a play. **b.** the person who plays it. **30.** *Cards.* **a.** the act or right of playing first, as in a round. **b.** the card, suit, etc., so played. **31.** *Journalism.* a short summary serving as an introduction to a news story or article. **32.** *Elect.* **a.** a single conductor, often flexible and insulated, used in connections between pieces of electrical apparatus. **b.** an antenna lead-in wire. **33.** *Boxing.* act of taking the offensive by jabbing an opponent. **34.** *Naut.* the course of a rope. **35.** an open channel through a field of ice. **36.** *Mining.* **a.** a lode. **b.** an auriferous deposit in an old river bed. **37.** act of aiming a gun ahead of a target moving across the line of fire. [ME *leden,* OE *lǣdan* (causative of *līthan* go, travel), c. D *leiden,* G *leiten,* Icl. *leidha*] —**Syn. 1.** See **guide.**
lead[2] (lĕd), *n.* **1.** *Chem.* a heavy, comparatively soft, malleable bluish-gray metal, sometimes found native, but usually combined as sulfide, in galena. *Symbol:* Pb; *at. no.:* 82; *at. wt.:* 207.21; *sp. gr.:* 11.34 at 20°C. **2.** something made of this metal or one of its alloys. **3.** a plummet or mass of lead suspended by a line, as for taking soundings. **4.** bullets; shot. **5.** black lead or graphite. **6.** a small stick of it as used in pencils. **7.** *Print.* Also, **leading.** a thin strip of type metal or brass, less than type high, for increasing the space between lines of type. **8.** frames of lead in which panes are fixed, as in windows of stained glass. **9.** (*pl.*) sheets or strips of lead used for covering roofs. **10.** white lead. —*v.t.* **11.** to cover, line, weight, treat, or impregnate with lead or one of its compounds. **12.** *Print.* to insert leads between the lines of. **13.** to fix (window glass) in position with leads. [ME *lede,* OE *lēad,* c. D *lood,* G *lot* plummet]
lead arsenate (lĕd), *Chem.* plumbous arsenate, Pb₃(AsO₄)₂, a very poisonous crystalline compound, used as an insecticide.
lead·en (lĕd′ən), *adj.* **1.** consisting or made of lead. **2.** inertly heavy, or hard to lift or move, as weight, the limbs, etc. **3.** oppressive, as the air. **4.** sluggish, as the pace. **5.** dull, spiritless, or gloomy, as the mood, thoughts, etc. **6.** of a dull gray: *leaden skies.* —**lead′·en·ly,** *adv.* —**lead′en·ness,** *n.*
lead·er (lē′dər), *n.* **1.** one who or that which leads. **2.** a guiding or directing head, as of an army, movement, etc. **3.** *Music.* **a.** a conductor or director, as of an orchestra, band, or chorus. **b.** the player at the head of the first violins in an orchestra, the principal cornetist in a band, or the principal soprano in a chorus, to whom any incidental solos are usually assigned. **4.** a horse harnessed at the front of a team. **5.** a principal or important editorial article, as in a newspaper. **6.** a featured article of trade, esp. one offered at a low price to attract customers. **7.** a pipe for conveying rainwater, etc. **8.** *Naut.* a piece of metal or wood having apertures for lines to lead them to their proper places. **9.** (*pl.*) *Print.* a row of dots or short lines to lead the eye across a space. **10.** *Fishing.* **a.** a length of silkworm gut or the like, to which the fly or baited hook is attached. **b.** the net used to direct fish into a weir, pound, etc. —**lead′er·less,** *adj.*
lead·er·ship (lē′dər shĭp′), *n.* **1.** the position, function, or guidance of a leader. **2.** ability to lead.
lead·ing[1] (lē′dĭng), *n.* **1.** act of one who or that which leads; guidance; direction; lead. —*adj.* **2.** directing; guiding. **3.** chief; principal; most important; foremost. [f. LEAD[1] + -ING[1]]
lead·ing[2] (lĕd′ĭng), *n.* **1.** a covering or framing of lead. **2.** *Print.* lead[2] (def. 7). [f. LEAD[2] + -ING[1]]
lead·ing article (lē′dĭng), a principal editorial article in a newspaper; a leader.

lead·ing edge (lē′dĭng), *Aeron.* the edge of an airfoil or propeller blade facing the direction of motion.
lead·ing question (lē′dĭng), a question so worded as to suggest the proper or desired answer.
lead·ing string (lē′dĭng), **1.** a string for leading and supporting a child when learning to walk. **2.** excessively restraining guidance.
lead·ing tone (lē′dĭng), *Music.* the seventh degree of the scale.
lead-in wire (lĕd′ĭn′), *Radio.* that portion of the antenna connected to the receiving set.
lead line (lĕd), *Naut.* a line used in taking soundings.
lead-off (lĕd′ôf′, -ŏf′), *n.* **1.** an act which starts something; start; beginning. —*adj.* **2.** *Baseball.* the player who is first in the batting order.
lead pencil (lĕd), an implement for writing or drawing made of graphite in a wooden or metal holder.
lead·plant (lĕd′plănt′, -plänt′), *n.* a North American shrub of the family *Leguminosae, Amorpha canescens,* so called on account of the gray cast of its twigs and leaves.
lead poisoning (lĕd), *Pathol.* a diseased condition due to the introduction of lead into the system, common among workers in lead or its compounds; plumbism.
leads·man (lĕdz′mən), *n., pl.* **-men.** *Naut.* a man who heaves the lead in taking soundings.
lead·y (lĕd′ĭ), *adj.* like lead; leaden.
leaf (lēf), *n., pl.* **leaves** (lēvz), *v.* —*n.* **1.** one of the expanded, usually green, organs, borne by the stem of a plant. **2.** any similar or corresponding lateral outgrowth of a stem. **3.** a petal: *a rose leaf.* **4.** foliage or leafage. **5. in leaf,** covered with foliage or leaves. **6.** *Bibliog.* a unit generally comprising two printed pages of a book, one on each side, but also applied to blank or illustrated pages. **7.** a thin sheet of metal, etc. **8.** a lamina or layer. **9.** a sliding, hinged, or detachable flat part, as of a door, table top, etc. **10.** a single strip of metal in a composite, or leaf, spring. **11.** a layer of fat, esp. that about the kidneys of a hog. —*v.i.* **12.** to put forth leaves. —*v.t.* **13.** *U.S.* to thumb through the pages of; turn leaves: *to leaf (through) a book.* [ME *leef,* OE *lēaf,* c. G *laub*] —**leaf′like′,** *adj.*
leaf·age (lē′fĭj), *n.* foliage.
leaf hopper, any of the leaping homopterous insects of the family *Cicadellidae,* including many crop pests.
leaf lard, lard prepared from the leaf of the hog.
leaf·less (lēf′lĭs), *adj.* without leaves. —**leaf′less·ness,** *n.*
leaf·let (lēf′lĭt), *n.* **1.** one of the separate blades or divisions of a compound leaf. **2.** a small leaflike part or structure. **3.** a small or young leaf. **4.** a small flat or folded sheet of printed matter, as for distribution.
leaf spring, a long, narrow, multiple spring composed of several layers of spring metal bracketed together. See illus. under **spring.**
leaf·stalk (lēf′stôk′), *n.* petiole (def. 1).
leaf·y (lē′fĭ), *adj.,* **leafier, leafiest. 1.** abounding in, covered with, or consisting of leaves or foliage: *the leafy woods.* **2.** leaflike; foliaceous. —**leaf′i·ness,** *n.*
league[1] (lēg), *n., v.,* **leagued, leaguing.** —*n.* **1.** a covenant or compact made between persons, parties, states, etc., for the maintenance or promotion of common interests or for mutual assistance or service. **2.** the aggregation of persons, parties, states, etc., associated in such a covenant; a confederacy. **3. in league,** united by or having a compact or agreement; allied (often fol. by *with*). —*v.t.* **4.** to unite in a league; combine. [ME *ligg,* t. OF: m. *ligue,* t. It.: m. *liga, lega,* der. *legare,* g. L *ligāre* bind] —**Syn. 1.** See **alliance.**
league[2] (lēg), *n.* **1.** a unit of distance, varying at different periods and in different countries, in English-speaking countries usually estimated roughly at 3 miles. **2.** a square league, as a unit of land measure. [ME *le(u)ge,* t. LL: m. *leuga, leuca,* said to be of Gallic orig.]
League of Nations, the organization of nations of the world to promote world peace and coöperation which was created by the Treaty of Versailles (1919) and dissolved, April, 1946, by action of its 21st Assembly.
lea·guer[1] (lē′gər), *n., v.t. Archaic.* —*v.t.* **1.** to besiege; beleaguer. —*n.* **2.** a siege. **3.** a military camp, esp. of a besieging army. [t. D: m. *leger* bed, camp. See LAIR, LAAGER]
lea·guer[2] (lē′gər), *n.* a member of a league. [f. LEAGUE[1] + -ER[1]]
Le·ah (lē′ə), *n.* the first wife of Jacob.
Lea·hy (lā′hĭ), *n.* William David, born 1875, U.S. admiral and diplomat.
leak (lēk), *n.* **1.** an unintended hole, crack, or the like by which water, etc., enters or escapes. **2.** any avenue or means of unintended entrance or escape, or the entrance or escape itself. **3.** *Elect.* a point where current escapes from a conductor, as because of poor insulation. **4.** act of leaking. —*v.i.* **5.** to let water, etc., enter or escape, as through an unintended hole, crack, permeable material, or the like: *the roof is leaking.* **6.** to pass in or out in this manner, as water, etc.: *gas leaking from a pipe.* **7.** to transpire or become known undesignedly

Leaf of pansy,
Viola tricolor
B. Blade; P. Petiole; S. Stipule

(fol. by *out*). —*v.t.* 8. to let (water, etc.) leak in or out. [ME *leke*, t. Scand.; cf. Icel. *leka* drip, leak, c. MD *leken*]

leak·age (lē′kĭj), *n.* 1. act of leaking; leak. 2. that which leaks in or out. 3. the amount that leaks in or out. 4. *Com.* an allowance for loss by leaking.

leakage current, *Elect.* a relatively small current flowing through or across the surface of an insulator when a voltage is impressed upon it.

leak·y (lē′kĭ), *adj.*, **leakier, leakiest.** 1. allowing water, etc., to leak in or out. 2. apt to disclose secrets, as a person. —**leak′i·ness**, *n.*

leal (lēl), *adj. Archaic or Scot.* loyal. [ME *lele*, t. OF: m. *leial*. See LOYAL] —**leal′ly**, *adv.*

lean[1] (lēn), *v.*, **leaned** or (*esp. Brit.*) **leant, leaning,** *n.* —*v.i.* 1. to incline or bend from a vertical position or in a particular direction. 2. to incline in feeling, opinion, action, etc.: *to lean toward socialism.* 3. to rest against or on something for support: *lean against a wall.* 4. to depend or rely: *to lean on empty promises.* —*v.t.* 5. to incline or bend: *he leaned his head forward.* 6. to cause to lean or rest (fol. by *against, on, upon,* etc.): *lean your arm against the railing.* —*n.* 7. act of leaning; inclination. [ME *lene(n)*, OE *hleonian*, c. G *lehnen*; akin to L -*clīnāre* incline]

lean[2] (lēn), *adj.* 1. (of persons or animals) scant of flesh; not plump or fat: *lean cattle.* 2. (of meat) containing little or no fat. 3. lacking in richness, fullness, quantity, etc.: *a lean diet, lean years.* —*n.* 4. that part of flesh which consists of muscle rather than fat. 5. the lean part of anything. [ME *lene*, OE *hlǣne*] —**lean′ly**, *adv.* —**lean′ness**, *n.* —**Syn.** 1. spare, skinny, lank, lanky. See **thin.**

Le·an·der (lĭ·ăn′dər), *n.* See **Hero and Leander.**

lean·ing (lē′nĭng), *n.* inclination; tendency: *strong literary leanings.*

leant (lĕnt), *v. Chiefly Brit.* pt. and pp. of **lean**[1].

lean-to (lēn′tōō′), *n., pl.* **-tos.** 1. a shack or shed supported at one side by trees or posts and with an inclined roof. 2. a roof of single pitch, the higher end abutting a wall or larger building. 3. a structure with such a roof.

leap (lēp), *v.*, **leaped** or **leapt, leaping,** *n.* —*v.i.* 1. to spring through the air from one point or position to another: *to leap over a ditch.* 2. to move quickly and lightly: *to leap aside.* 3. to pass, come, rise, etc., as if with a bound: *to leap to a conclusion.* —*v.t.* 4. to jump over: *to leap a wall.* 5. to pass over as if by a leap. 6. to cause to leap. —*n.* 7. a spring, jump, or bound; a light springing movement. 8. the space cleared in a leap. 9. a place leaped, or to be leaped, over or from. 10. an abrupt transition. [ME *lepe(n)*, OE *hlēapan* leap, run, c. G *laufen* run. Cf. LOPE] —**leap′er**, *n.* —**Syn.** 1. See **jump.**

leap·frog (lēp′frŏg′, -frôg′), *n.* a game in which one player leaps over another who is in a stooping posture.

leapt (lĕpt, lēpt), *v.* pt. and pp. of **leap.**

leap year, a year containing 366 days, or one day (Feb. 29) more than the ordinary year, to offset the difference in length between the ordinary year and the astronomical year (being, in practice, every year whose number is exactly divisible by 4, as 1948, except centenary years not exactly divisible by 400, as 1900).

Lear (lĭr), *n.* 1. See **King Lear.** 2. Edward, 1812–88, British humorist and painter.

learn (lûrn), *v.*, **learned** (lûrnd) or **learnt, learning.** —*v.t.* 1. to acquire knowledge of or skill in by study, instruction, or experience: *to learn French.* 2. to memorize. 3. to become informed of or acquainted with; ascertain: *to learn the truth.* —*v.i.* 4. to acquire knowledge or skill: *to learn rapidly.* 5. to become informed (fol. by *of*): *to learn of an accident.* [ME *lernen*, OE *leornian*, c. G *lernen*; akin to OE *gelǣran* teach] —**learn′er**, *n.*

—**Syn.** 1. LEARN, ASCERTAIN, DETECT, DISCOVER imply adding to one's store of facts. To LEARN is to add to one's knowledge or information: *to learn a language.* To ASCERTAIN is to verify facts by inquiry or analysis: *to ascertain the truth about an event.* To DETECT implies becoming aware of something which had been obscure, secret, or concealed: *to detect a flaw in reasoning.* To DISCOVER is also used with obj. clauses as a synonym of LEARN in order to suggest that the new information acquired is surprising to the learner: *I discovered that she had been married before.*

learn·ed (lûr′nĭd), *adj.* 1. having much knowledge; scholarly: *a group of learned men.* 2. pertaining to or showing learning. —**learn′ed·ly**, *adv.* —**learn′ed·ness**, *n.*

learn·ing (lûr′nĭng), *n.* 1. knowledge acquired by systematic study in any field or fields of scholarly application. 2. the act or process of acquiring knowledge or skill. 3. *Psychol.* the modification of behavior through interaction with the environment.

—**Syn.** 1. LEARNING, ERUDITION, LORE, SCHOLARSHIP refer to knowledge existing or acquired. LEARNING is knowledge acquired by systematic study, as of literature, history, or science: *a body of learning; fond of literary learning.* ERUDITION suggests a thorough, formal, and profound sort of knowledge obtained by extensive research; it is esp. applied to knowledge in fields other than those of mathematics and physical sciences: *a man of vast erudition in languages.* LORE is accumulated knowledge in a particular field, esp. of a curious, anecdotal, or traditional nature; the word is now somewhat poetic: *gypsy lore.* SCHOLARSHIP is the formalized learning which is taught in schools, esp. as actively employed by one trying to master some field of knowledge or extend its bounds: *high standards of scholarship in history.*

lease (lēs), *n., v.,* **leased, leasing.** —*n.* 1. an instrument conveying property to another for a definite period, or at will, usually in consideration of rent or other periodical compensation. 2. the property leased. 3. the period of time for which it is made. 4. an allotted period or term. [ME *lese*, t. AF: m. *les* a letting, der. OF *laissier* let]

—*v.t.* 5. to grant the temporary possession or use of (lands, tenements, etc.) to another, usually for compensation at a fixed rate; let. 6. to take or to hold by a lease, as lands. [ME *lese(n)*, t. AF: m. *lesser* let go, let, g. L *laxāre* loosen] —**leas′er**, *n.*

lease·hold (lēs′hōld′), *n.* 1. a land interest acquired under a lease. —*adj.* 2. held by lease.

lease·hold·er (lēs′hōl′dər), *n.* a tenant under a lease.

leash (lēsh), *n.* 1. a thong or line for holding a dog or other animal in check. 2. *Sports.* a brace and a half, as of hounds. 3. a set of three. —*v.t.* 4. to secure or hold in or as in a leash. [ME *lees, lese*, t. OF: m. *laisse*, g. L *laxa*, fem. of L *laxus* loose, lax.]

least (lēst), *adj.* 1. little beyond all others in size, amount, degree, etc.; smallest; slightest: *the least distance.* 2. lowest in consideration or dignity. —*n.* 3. that which is least; the least amount, quantity, degree, etc. 4. **at least, a.** at the least or lowest estimate. **b.** at any rate; in any case. 5. **in the least,** in the smallest degree, as a thing not in the least likely. —*adv.* 6. to the least extent, amount, or degree. [ME *leest(e)*, OE *lǣst*, superl. of *lǣs(sa)* LESS]

least common multiple. See **common multiple.**

least flycatcher, a small flycatcher, *Empidonax minimus,* of eastern North America; the chebec.

least sandpiper, a small American shorebird or peep, *Erolia minutilla,* related to the several stints of Europe, and known in England as the American stint.

least squares, *Statistics.* a method of determining constants from observations, by minimizing squares of residuals between observations and their theoretical expected values.

least·wise (lēst′wīz′), *adv. Colloq.* at least; at any rate. Also, **least·ways** (lēst′wāz′).

leath·er (lĕth′ər), *n.* 1. the skin of animals prepared for use by tanning or a similar process. 2. some article or appliance made of this material. —*v.t.* 3. to cover or furnish with leather. 4. *Colloq.* to beat with a leather strap. [ME *lether*, OE *lether* (in compounds), c. D and G *leder*, Icel. *ledhr*]

leath·er·back (lĕth′ər·băk′), *n.* a large marine turtle, *Dermochelys coriacea,* with a longitudinally ridged flexible carapace formed of a mosaic of small bony plates embedded in a leathery skin.

leath·ern (lĕth′ərn), *adj.* 1. made of leather. 2. resembling leather. [ME and OE *lether(e)n.* See -EN[2]]

leath·er·neck (lĕth′ər·nĕk′), *n. Slang.* a U.S. marine.

leath·er·oid (lĕth′ər·oid′), *n.* a substitute for leather used in making bags, suitcases, etc., consisting mostly of vegetable fiber, as paper stock, variously treated.

leath·er·wood (lĕth′ər·wŏŏd′), *n.* an American shrub, *Dirca palustris,* with a tough bark.

leath·er·y (lĕth′ər·ĭ), *adj.* like leather; tough and flexible.

leave[1] (lēv), *v.*, **left, leaving.** —*v.t.* 1. to go away from, depart from, or quit, as a place, a person, or a thing. 2. to let stay or be as specified: *to leave a door unlocked.* 3. to desist from, stop, or abandon (fol. by *off*). 4. to let (a person, etc.) remain in a position to do something without interference: *leave him alone.* 5. to let (a thing) remain for action or decision. 6. to omit (fol. by *out*). 7. to allow to remain in the same place, condition, etc.: *there is plenty of work left.* 8. to let remain, or have remaining behind, after going, disappearing, ceasing, etc.: *the wound left a scar.* 9. to have remaining after death: *he leaves a widow.* 10. to give in charge; give for use after one's death or departure. 11. to have as a remainder after subtraction: *2 from 4 leaves 2.* —*v.i.* 12. to go away, depart or set out: *we leave for Europe tomorrow.* [ME *leve(n)*, OE *lǣfan* (der. *lāf* remainder), c. OHG *leiben*, Icel. *leifa*, Goth. *-laibjan*] —**leav′er**, *n.* —**Syn.** 1. vacate; abandon, forsake, desert. 4. See **let**[1]. 10. bequeath, will; devise, transmit.

leave[2] (lēv), *n.* 1. permission to do something. 2. permission to be absent, as from duty: *to be on leave.* 3. the time this permission lasts: *30 day's leave.* 4. a farewell: *to take leave of someone.* [ME *leve*, OE *lēaf.* Cf. D (*oor*)*lof*, G (*ur*)*laub*, (*ver*)*laub*]

leave[3] (lēv), *v.i.,* **leaved, leaving.** to put forth leaves; leaf. [var. of LEAF, v.i.]

leaved (lēvd), *adj.* having leaves; leafed.

leav·en (lĕv′ən), *n.* 1. a mass of fermenting dough reserved for producing fermentation in a new batch of dough. 2. an agency which works in a thing to produce a gradual change or modification. —*v.t.* 3. to produce bubbles of gas in (dough or batter) by means of any of a variety of leavening agents. 4. to permeate with an altering or transforming influence. [ME *levain*, t. OF, g. L *levāmen* that which raises] —**leav′en·ing**, *n.*

Leav·en·worth (lĕv′ən·wûrth′, -wərth), *n.* 1. a city in NE Kansas. 20,579 (1950). 2. a Federal prison there.

leaves (lēvz), *n.* pl. of **leaf.**

Leaves of Grass, a book of poems (first version, 1855; final (9th) edition, 1891–92) by Whitman.

leave-tak·ing (lēv′tā′kĭng), *n.* the saying of farewell.

leav·ing (lē'vǐng), *n.* **1.** that which is left; residue. **2.** (*pl.*) remains; refuse.

leav·y (lē'vǐ), *adj.,* **leavier, leaviest.** *Poetic.* leafy.

Leb·a·nese (lĕb'ə nēz', -nēs'), *adj.* **1.** of or pertaining to Lebanon. —*n.* **2.** a native of Lebanon.

Leb·a·non (lĕb'ə nən), *n.* **1.** a republic at the E end of the Mediterranean, N of Palestine. 1,022,- 000 pop. (est. 1942); 3927 sq. mi. *Cap.:* Beirut. **2.** a city in SE Pennsylvania. 28,156 (1950).

Lebanon Mountains, a mountain range extending the length of Lebanon in the central part. Highest peak, 10,049 ft.

Le·bens·raum (lā'bəns roum'), *n.* additional territory desired by a nation for expansion of trade, etc. [G: room for living]

Le·brun (lə brœN'), *n.* **1.** Albert (ál bĕr'), 1871–1950, president of France, 1932–40. **2.** Also, **Le Brun, Charles** (shárl), 1619–90, French painter. **3.** **Marie Anne Elisabeth Vigée** (má rē' án ē lē zá bĕt' vē zhĕ'), (*Madame Vigée-Lebrun*) 1755–1842, French painter.

lech·er (lĕch'ər), *n.* a man immoderately given to sexual indulgence; a lewd man. [ME *lechur,* t. OF: m *lecheor* gourmand, sensualist, der. *lechier* lick, live in sensuality, t. Gmc.; cf. LICK]

lech·er·ous (lĕch'ər əs), *adj.* **1.** given to or characterized by lechery. **2.** inciting to lechery. —**lech'er·ous·ly,** *adv.* —**lech'er·ous·ness,** *n.*

lecher wires, *Electronics.* parallel wires of such length and terminations that the system will resonate (i.e. standing waves will appear) if the frequency of the excitation is correct.

lech·er·y (lĕch'ər ǐ), *n.* free indulgence of lust; lewdness.

lec·i·thin (lĕs'ə thǐn), *n.* *Biochem.* one of a group of yellow-brown fatty substances, found in animal and plant tissues and egg yolk, composed of units of choline, phosphoric acid, fatty acids, and glycerol. [f. m.s. Gk. *lēkithos* egg yolk + -IN²]

Leck·y (lĕk'ǐ), *n.* **William Edward Hartpole,** 1838– 1903, British historian and writer, born in Ireland.

Le·conte de Lisle (lə kônt' də lēl'), **Charles Marie** (shárl' má rē'), 1818–94, French poet.

Le Cor·bu·sier (lə kôr by zyē'), (*Charles Édouard Jeanneret*) born 1887, Swiss modern architect in France.

Le Creu·sot (lə krœ zō'), a city in E France. 24,104 (1946).

lect., **1.** lecture. **2.** lecturer.

lec·tern (lĕk'tərn), *n.* a reading desk in a church, esp. that from which the lessons are read. [earlier *lecturn,* Latinized and metathetic var. of ME *lettrun,* t. OF, t. ML: m. *lectrum,* der. L *legere* read]

lec·tion (lĕk'shən), *n.* **1.** a reading or version of a passage in a particular copy of a text. **2.** a lesson, or portion of sacred writing, read in divine service. [ME, t. L: s. *lectio* a reading]

lec·tion·ar·y (lĕk'shə nĕr'ǐ), *n., pl.* **-aries.** a book, or a list, of lections for reading in divine service.

lec·tor (lĕk'tər), *n.* a reader, as of lectures in a college or university or of scriptural lessons. [late ME, t. L]

lec·ture (lĕk'chər), *n., v.,* **-tured, -turing.** —*n.* **1.** a discourse read or delivered before an audience, esp. for instruction or to set forth some subject: *a lecture on Picasso.* **2.** a speech of warning or reproof as to conduct; a long, tedious reprimand. —*v.i.* **3.** to give a lecture. —*v.t.* **4.** to deliver a lecture to or before; instruct by lectures. **5.** to rebuke or reprimand at some length: *he lectured her for two hours on good manners.* [ME, t. LL: m. *lectura,* der. L *legere* read]

lec·tur·er (lĕk'chər ər), *n.* **1.** one who lectures. **2.** a temporary appointee who performs instructional duties in a college or university, usually on a part-time basis.

lec·ture·ship (lĕk'chər shǐp'), *n.* the office of lecturer.

led (lĕd), *v.* pt. and pp. of **lead.**

Le·da (lē'də), *n.* *Gk. Myth.* the mother by Zeus of Helen, Clytemnestra, Castor, and Pollux.

ledge (lĕj), *n.* **1.** any relatively narrow, horizontal projecting part, or any part affording a horizontal shelf-like surface. **2.** a more or less flat shelf of rock protruding from a cliff or slope. **3.** a reef, ridge, or line of rocks in the sea or other water bodies. **4.** *Mining.* **a.** a layer or mass of rock underground. **b.** a lode or vein. [ME *legge* transverse bar, OE *lecg* (exact meaning not clear), der. *lecgan* LAY¹] —**ledged,** *adj.*

ledg·er (lĕj'ər), *n.* **1.** *Bookkeeping.* an account book of final entry, containing all the accounts. **2.** a horizontal timber fastened to the vertical uprights of a scaffold, to support the putlogs. **3.** a flat slab of stone laid over a grave or tomb. [ME *legger* (book), der. *leggen* LAY¹ (see LEDGE)]

ledger board, the horizontal member along the top of a fence, rail, etc.

ledger line, *Music.* leger line.

ledger tackle, *Angling.* fishing apparatus set up so that the lead lies on the bottom.

lee¹ (lē), *n.* **1.** shelter. **2.** the side or part that is sheltered or turned away from the wind. **3.** *Chiefly Naut.* the quarter or region toward which the wind blows.

—*adj.* **4.** *Chiefly Naut.* pertaining to, situated in, or moving toward the quarter or region toward which the wind blows (opposed to *weather*). [ME; OE *hlēo* shelter, c. Icel. *hlē* (naut.) lee]

lee² (lē), *n.* (*usually pl.*) that which settles from a liquid, esp. from wine; sediment; dregs. [ME *lie,* t. OF, g. LL *lia,* of Gallic orig.]

Lee (lē), *n.* **1.** **Charles,** 1731–82, American Revolutionary general, born in England. **2.** **Fitzhugh** (fǐts'- hū'), 1835–1905, U.S. general. **3.** **Francis Lightfoot,** 1734–97, American patriot. **4.** **Henry,** ("*Light-Horse Harry*") 1756–1818, American Revolutionary general (father of Robert E. Lee). **5.** **Richard Henry,** 1732–94, American patriot and statesman. **6.** **Robert E.,** 1807– 1870, Confederate general in the U.S. Civil War. **7.** **Sir Sidney,** 1859–1926, British biographer and critic.

lee·board (lē'bōrd'), *n.* a flat board let down vertically into the water on the lee side of a ship or boat to prevent leeward motion.

leech¹ (lēch), *n.* **1.** any of the blood-sucking or carnivorous, usually aquatic, worms constituting the class *Hirudinea,* certain fresh-water species of which were formerly much used by physicians for bloodletting. **2.** an instrument used for drawing blood. **3.** a person who clings to another with a view to gain. **4.** *Archaic.* a physician. —*v.t.* **5.** to apply leeches to so as to bleed. **6.** *Archaic.* to cure; heal. [ME *leche,* OE *lǣce* (by confusion with *lǣce* physician); r. ME *liche,* OE *lȳce,* der. *lūcan* draw out, burst out] —**leech'like',** *adj.*

leech² (lēch), *n.* *Naut.* **1.** either of the perpendicular or sloping edges of a square sail. **2.** the after edge of a fore-and-aft sail. [ME *lek, leche,* appar. c. G *liek* bolt rope, leech rope; akin to G *leik* leech line]

Leeds (lēdz), *n.* a city in N England, in Yorkshire. 483,560 (est. 1946).

leek (lēk), *n.* **1.** a plant of the lily family, *Allium Porrum,* allied to the onion but having a cylindrical bulb, and used in cookery. **2.** any of various allied species. [ME; OE *lēac,* c. G *lauch*]

leek-green (lēk'grēn'), *adj.* dull bluish-green.

leer (lǐr), *n.* **1.** a side glance, esp. of sly or insulting suggestion or malicious significance. —*v.i.* **2.** to look with a leer. [? special use of obs. *leer* cheek, OE *hlēor*] —**leer'ing·ly,** *adv.*

leer·y (lǐr'ǐ), *adj.* *Slang.* **1.** wary; suspicious. **2.** knowing.

lees (lēz), *n.* pl. of **lee².**

lee shore, a shore toward which the wind blows.

leet (lēt), *n.* *Brit., Archaic.* **1.** a special type of manorial court or its jurisdiction. **2.** its meeting day.

lee tide, a tidal current running in the direction toward which the wind is blowing. Also, **leeward tide.**

Leeu·wen·hoek (lā'vən hŏŏk'), *n.* **Anton van** (än'- tôn vän), 1632–1723, Dutch naturalist and maker of microscopes.

lee·ward (lē'wərd; *Naut.* lōō'ərd), *adj.* **1.** pertaining to, situated in, or moving toward the quarter toward which the wind blows; opposed to windward. —*n.* **2.** the lee side; the point or quarter toward which the wind blows. —*adv.* **3.** toward the lee.

Lee·ward Islands (lē'wərd), **1.** a group of islands in the N Lesser Antilles of the West Indies, extending from Puerto Rico SE to Martinique. **2.** a British colony in this group. 98,135 pop. (est. 1942); 421½ sq. mi. *Cap.:* St. John.

lee·way (lē'wā'), *n.* **1.** the lateral movement of a ship to leeward, or the resulting deviation from her true course. **2.** *Aeron.* the amount a plane is blown off its normal course by cross winds. **3.** *Colloq.* extra space, time, money, etc.

left¹ (lĕft), *adj.* **1.** belonging or pertaining to the side of a person or thing which is turned toward the west when facing north (opposed to *right*). —*n.* **2.** the left side, or what is on the left side. **3.** (in continental Europe) that part of a legislative assembly which sits on the left side of the chamber as viewed by the president, a position customarily assigned to representatives holding socialistic or radical views. **4.** (*often cap.*) a party holding such views. [ME; special use of d. OE *left* (OE *lyft*) weak, infirm. Cf. MD and MLG *lucht*]

left² (lĕft), *v.* pt. and pp. of **leave¹.**

left-hand (lĕft'hănd'), *adj.* **1.** on or to the left. **2.** of, for, or with the left hand.

left-hand·ed (lĕft'hăn'dǐd), *adj.* **1.** having the left hand more serviceable than the right; preferably using the left hand. **2.** adapted to or performed by the left hand. **3.** situated on the side of the left hand. **4.** moving or rotating from right to left. **5.** ambiguous or doubtful: *a left-handed compliment.* **6.** clumsy or awkward. **7.** morganatic (from the bridegroom's giving the bride his left hand instead of his right as was customary at morganatic weddings). —**left'-hand'ed·ly,** *adv.* —**left'-hand'ed·ness,** *n.*

left·ist (lĕf'tǐst), *n.* **1.** a member of a socialistic or radical party or a person sympathizing with their views. —*adj.* **2.** having socialistic or radical political ideas. [f. LEFT¹ (def. 3) + -IST]

left·o·ver (lĕft'ō'vər), *n.* **1.** something left over or remaining. **2.** a remnant of food, as from a meal.

left·ward (lĕft'wərd), *adv.* **1.** Also, **left'wards.** toward or on the left. —*adj.* **2.** situated on the left. **3.** directed toward the left.

left wing, 1. members of a socialistic or radical political party, or those favoring extensive political reform. 2. such a political party or group of such parties. —**left′wing′,** adj.

leg (lĕg), n., v., **legged, legging.** —n. 1. one of the members or limbs which support and move the human or animal body. 2. that part of the limb between the knee and the ankle. 3. something resembling or suggesting a leg in use, position, or appearance. 4. that part of a garment, such as a stocking, trousers, or the like, which covers the leg. 5. one of the supports of a piece of furniture. 6. one of the sides of a pair of dividers or compasses. 7. one of the sides of a triangle other than the base or hypotenuse. 8. a timber, bar, etc. serving to prop or shore up a structure. 9. one of the distinct portions of any course: *the last leg of a trip.* 10. *Naut.* **a.** one of the series of straight runs which make up the zigzag course of a sailing ship. **b.** one straight or nearly straight part of a multiple-sided course in a sailing race. 11. *Sports.* the first part of a contest successfully completed, when a second or third part is required to determine the winner. 12. *Cricket.* **a.** the part of the field to the left of and behind the batsman as he faces the bowler (or to the right of and behind him if he is left-handed). **b.** the fielder occupying this part of the field. 13. **have not a leg to stand on,** not to have any good reason at all. 14. **pull (someone's) leg,** to make fun of (someone). 15. **shake a leg,** *Slang.* to hurry up. 16. **leg it,** *Colloq.* to walk or run. [ME, t. Scand.; cf. Icel. *leggr*] —**leg′less,** adj.

leg., 1. legal. 2. legate. 3. legato. 4. legislative. 5. legislature.

leg·a·cy (lĕg′ə sĭ), n., pl. **-cies.** 1. *Law.* a gift of property, esp. personal property, as money, by will; a bequest. 2. anything handed down by an ancestor or predecessor. [ME *legacie,* t. OF: legateship; t. ML: m.s. *lēgātia,* der. L *lēgātus* LEGATE]

le·gal (lē′gəl), adj. 1. appointed, established, or authorized by law; deriving authority from law. 2. of or pertaining to law; connected with the law or its administration: *the legal profession.* 3. permitted by law, or lawful: *such acts are not legal.* 4. recognized by law rather than by equity. 5. characteristic of the profession of the law: *a legal mind.* 6. *Theol.* **a.** of or pertaining to the Mosaic law. **b.** of or pertaining to the doctrine of salvation by good works rather than through free grace. —n. 7. (pl.) legally authorized investments which may be made by fiduciaries as savings banks, trustees, etc. [t. L: s. *lēgālis* pertaining to law] —**le′gal·ly,** adv.

legal cap, *U.S.* ruled writing paper made in long sheets, with the fold at the top, for lawyers' use.

le·gal·ism (lē′gə lĭz′əm), n. 1. strict adherence, or the principle of strict adherence, to law or prescription. 2. *Theol.* the doctrine of salvation by good works. —**le′gal·ist,** n. —**le′gal·is′tic,** adj.

le·gal·i·ty (lĭ găl′ə tĭ), n., pl. **-ties.** 1. state or quality of being in conformity with the law; lawfulness. 2. attachment to or observance of law. 3. *Theol.* reliance on good works for salvation, rather than on free grace.

le·gal·ize (lē′gə līz′), v.t., **-ized, -izing.** to make legal; authorize; sanction. —**le′gal·i·za′tion,** n.

Le Gal·lienne (lə găl yĕn′, găl′yən), 1. **Eva,** born 1899, U.S. actress and director. 2. **Richard,** 1866-1947, British poet and writer.

legal reserve, *Banking.* cash assets of Federal Reserve banks, member banks, savings banks, etc., held in accordance with provisions established in law.

legal separation, *Law.* a judicial act effecting a limited divorce.

legal tender, *Law.* currency which may be lawfully tendered or offered in payment of money debts and which may not be refused by creditors.

Le·gas·pi (lĕ gäs′pĭ), n. a seaport in the Philippine Islands, on SE Luzon. 41,468 (1939). Formerly, **Albay.**

leg·ate (lĕg′ĭt), n. 1. an ecclesiastic delegated by the Pope as his representative. 2. *Rom. Hist.* **a.** an assistant to a general or to a consul or magistrate, in the government of any army or a province; a commander of a legion. **b.** a provincial governor of senatorial rank appointed by the emperor. 3. an envoy. [ME *legat,* t. L: s. *lēgātus* deputy, prop. pp., deputed] —**leg′ate·ship′,** n.

leg·a·tee (lĕg′ə tē′), n. one to whom a legacy is bequeathed.

le·ga·tion (lĭ gā′shən), n. 1. a diplomatic minister and his staff when the minister is not of the highest (or ambassadorial) rank. 2. the official residence or place of business of a minister. 3. the office or position of a legate. [ME, t. L: s. *lēgātio* embassy] —**le·ga·tion·ar·y** (lĭ gā′shə nĕr′ĭ), adj.

le·ga·to (lĭ gä′tō; *It.* lĕ gä′tô), adj. *Music.* smooth and connected, without breaks between the successive tones (opposed to *staccato*). [t. It., pp. of *legare,* g. L *ligāre* bind]

le·ga·tor (lĭ gā′tər, lĕg′ə tôr′), n. one who bequeaths; a testator. —**leg·a·to·ri·al** (lĕg′ə tōr′ĭ əl), adj.

leg·end (lĕj′ənd), n. 1. a nonhistorical or unverifiable story handed down by tradition from earlier times and popularly accepted as historical. 2. matter of this kind. 3. an inscription, esp. on a coin, a coat of arms, a monument, or under a picture, or the like. 4. a story of the life of a saint. 5. *Obs. except Hist.* a collection of such stories. 6. a collection of stories of any admirable person. [ME *legende,* t. OF, t. ML: m. *legenda,* lit., things to be read, orig. neut. pl. gerundive of L *legere* read]

—**Syn.** 1. LEGEND, FABLE, MYTH refer to fictitious stories, usually handed down by tradition (though some fables are modern). LEGEND, originally denoting a story concerning the life of a saint, is applied to any fictitious story, sometimes involving the supernatural, and usually concerned with a real person, place, or other subject: *the legend of St. Andrew.* A FABLE is specifically a fictitious story (often with animals or inanimate things as speakers or actors) designed to teach a moral: *a fable about industrious bees.* A MYTH is one of a class of stories, usually concerning gods, heroes, imaginary animals, etc., current since primitive times, the purpose of which is to attempt to explain some belief or natural phenomenon: *the Greek myth about Demeter.* —**Ant.** 1. history, fact.

leg·end·ar·y (lĕj′ən dĕr′ĭ), adj., n., pl. **-aries.** —adj. 1. pertaining to or of the nature of a legend or legends. 2. celebrated or described in legend. —n. 3. a collection of legends.

Le·gen·dre (lə zhän′dr), n. **Adrien Marie** (à drē än′ mà rē′), 1752–1833, French mathematician.

leg·end·ry (lĕj′ən drĭ), n. legends collectively.

leg·er·de·main (lĕj′ər də mān′), n. 1. sleight of hand. 2. trickery; deception. 3. any artful trick. [ME, t. F: m. *léger de main* light(ness) of hand]

leg·er line (lĕj′ər), *Music.* a short line added when necessary above or below the lines of a staff to increase the range of the staff. Also, **ledger line.** [var. of *ledger line,* f. LEDGER (special use) + LINE[1]]

L. Leger lines

le·ges (lē′jēz), n. pl. of lex.

leg·ged (lĕg′ĭd, lĕgd), adj. having a specified number or kind of legs: *one-legged, long-legged.*

leg·ging (lĕg′ĭng), n. (usually pl.) an extra outer covering for the leg, usually extending from the ankle to the knee, but sometimes higher.

leg·gy (lĕg′ĭ), adj. having awkwardly long legs.

Leg·horn (lĕg′hôrn′ *for 1–3;* lĕg′ərn, -hôrn′ *for 4*), n. 1. Italian, **Livorno.** a seaport in W Italy, on the Ligurian sea. 133,521 (est. 1946). 2. a fine, smooth, plaited straw. 3. (l.c.) a hat, etc., made of it. 4. a Mediterranean breed of the domestic fowl, characterized by prolific laying of white-shelled eggs.

leg·i·ble (lĕj′ə bəl), adj. 1. that may be read or deciphered, esp. with ease, as writing or printing. 2. that may be discerned or distinguished. [ME, t. LL: m.s. *legibilis,* der. L *legere* read] —**leg′i·bil′i·ty, leg′i·ble·ness,** n. —**leg′i·bly,** adv.

le·gion (lē′jən), n. 1. an infantry brigade in the army of ancient Rome, numbering from 3000 to 6000 men, and usually combined with from 300 to 700 cavalry. 2. a military or semi-military unit. 3. **the Legion, a.** the American Legion. **b.** the French Foreign Legion. 4. any large body of armed men. 5. any great host or multitude, whether of persons or of things. [ME, t. OF, t. L: s. *legio*]

le·gion·ar·y (lē′jə nĕr′ĭ), adj., n., pl. **-aries.** —adj. 1. pertaining or belonging to a legion. 2. constituting a legion or legions. —n. 3. *Hist.* a soldier of a legion. 4. *Brit.* a member of the British Legion (corresponding to the U.S. *legionnaire*).

legionary ant, 1. an army ant. 2. any driver ant.

le·gion·naire (lē′jə nâr′), n. 1. (often cap.) a member of the American Legion. 2. legionary. [t. F]

Legion of Honor, a French order of distinction, instituted in 1802 by Napoleon, membership being granted for meritorious civil or military services.

Legis., Legislature.

leg·is·late (lĕj′ĭs lāt′), v., **-lated, -lating.** —v.i. 1. to exercise the function of legislation; make or enact laws. —v.t. 2. to effect, bring (into), put (out), etc., by legislation. [back formation from LEGISLATION or LEGISLATOR]

leg·is·la·tion (lĕj′ĭs lā′shən), n. 1. act of making or enacting laws. 2. a law or a body of laws enacted. [t. LL: s. *lēgislātio,* L *lēgis lātio* the proposing of a law]

leg·is·la·tive (lĕj′ĭs lā′tĭv), adj. 1. having the function of making laws: *a legislative body.* 2. of or pertaining to legislation: *legislative proceedings.* 3. ordained by legislation: *a legislative penalty.* 4. pertaining to a legislature: *a legislative recess.* —n. 5. the legislature. —**leg′is·la′tive·ly,** adv.

leg·is·la·tor (lĕj′ĭs lā′tər), n. 1. one who gives or makes laws. 2. a member of a legislative body. [t. L: *legis lātor* bringer of a law] —**leg·is·la·tress** (lĕj′ĭs lā′trĭs), n. fem.

leg·is·la·to·ri·al (lĕj′ĭs lə tōr′ĭ əl), adj. of or pertaining to legislators or legislations.

leg·is·la·ture (lĕj′ĭs lā′chər), n. the legislative body of a country or state, esp. (in the U.S.) of a State.

le·gist (lē′jĭst), n. one versed in law.

le·git (lə jĭt′), *Slang.* —adj. 1. legitimate; truthful. —n. 2. the legitimate theater or stage employing actors in person, as opposed to motion pictures.

leg·i·tim (lĕj′ə tĭm), n. *Civil Law.* that part of a decedent's estate which must be left to his wife, children, or other relative(s). [t. L: s. *lēgitima* (pars) lawful (part)]

le·git·i·ma·cy (lĭ jĭt′ə mə sĭ), n. state or fact of being legitimate.

le·git·i·mate (adj. lĭ jĭt′ə mĭt; v. lĭ jĭt′ə māt′), adj., v., **-mated, -mating.** —adj. 1. according to law; lawful.

2. in accordance with established rules, principles, or standards. **3.** of the normal or regular type or kind. **4.** in accordance with the laws of reasoning; logically inferable; logical: *a legitimate conclusion.* **5.** born in wedlock, or of parents legally married. **6.** resting on or ruling by the principle of hereditary right: *a legitimate sovereign.* **7.** genuine; not spurious. —*v.t.* **8.** to make or pronounce lawful. **9.** to establish as lawfully born. **10.** to show or declare to be legitimate or proper. **11.** to authorize; justify. [t. ML: m. s. *lēgitimātus*, pp. of *lēgit-imāre* make lawful, der. L *lēgitimus* lawful] —**le·git/i·mate·ly,** *adv.* —**le·git/i·mate·ness,** *n.* —**le·git/i-ma/tion,** *n.*

legitimate drama, 1. drama for production on the stage (as opposed to motion pictures). **2.** drama as literature (as distinct from farce and melodrama).

le·git·i·ma·tize (lǐ jǐt/ə mə tīz/), *v.t.,* **-tized, -tizing.** to legitimate.

le·git·i·mist (lǐ jǐt/ə mǐst), *n.* a supporter of legitimate authority, esp. of a claim to a throne based on direct descent. —**le·git/i·mism,** *n.* —**le·git/i·mis/tic,** *adj.*

le·git·i·mize (lǐ jǐt/ə mīz/), *v.t.,* **-mized, -mizing.** to legitimate. —**le·git/i·mi·za/tion,** *n.*

leg-of-mut·ton (lĕg/ə mŭt/ən, -əv-), *adj.* having the triangular shape of a leg of mutton, as a sail, sleeve, etc.

Le·gree (lǐ grē/), *n.* **Simon, 1.** the brutal slave dealer in *Uncle Tom's Cabin* by Harriet Beecher Stowe. **2.** a harsh and brutal master.

leg·ume (lĕg/ūm, lǐ gūm/), *n.* **1.** any plant of the family *Leguminosae,* esp. those used for feed, food, or soil-improving crop. **2.** the pod or seed vessel of such a plant, which is usually dehiscent by both sutures, thus dividing into two parts or valves. **3.** any table vegetable of the family *Leguminosae.* [t. F, t. L: m. *legūmen* legume, pulse, lit., something gathered (or picked)]

le·gu·min (lǐ gū/mən), *n.* *Biochem.* a proteid resembling casein, obtained from the seeds of leguminous and other plants. [f. LEGUME + -IN²]

le·gu·mi·nous (lǐ gū/mə nəs), *adj.* **1.** pertaining to, of the nature of, or bearing legumes. **2.** belonging or pertaining to the *Leguminosae,* an order or family regarded as comprising the legume-bearing plants, and sometimes subdivided into the bean, senna, and mimosa families. [f. s. L *legūmen* LEGUME + -OUS]

Le·hár (lě/här), *n.* **Franz** (fränts), 1870–1948, Hungarian composer of operettas.

Le Ha·vre (lə hä/vrə; *Fr.* lə á/vr), a seaport in N France at the mouth of the Seine. 106,934 (1946). Also, **Havre.**

Le·high (lē/hī), *n.* a river in E Pennsylvania, flowing into the Delaware river. ab. 120 mi.

Leh·man (lē/mən, lā/-), *n.* **Herbert Henry,** born 1878, U.S. banker and statesman.

le·hu·a (lě hōō/ä), *n.* **1.** a red-flowered tree, *Metrosideros polymorpha,* common in the Pacific Islands and having a hard wood. **2.** the bright red corymbose flower of this tree, the territorial flower of Hawaii. [t. Hawaiian]

le·i¹ (lā/ē, lā), *n.,* *pl.* **leis.** (in the Hawaiian Islands) a wreath of flowers, leaves, etc., for the neck or head. [t. Hawaiian]

lei² (lā), *n.* pl. of **leu.**

Leib·nitz (līb/nǐts; *Ger.* līp/nǐts), *n.* **Gottfried Wilhelm von** (gôt/frēt vǐl/hělm fən), 1646–1716, German philosopher, writer, and mathematician. Also, **Leib/niz.** —**Leib·nitz·i·an** (līb nǐt/sǐ ən), *adj., n.*

Leices·ter (lěs/tər), *n.* **1. Robert Dudley, Earl of,** 1532?–88, British statesman: favorite of Queen Elizabeth. **2.** a city in central England: county seat of Leicestershire. 269,890 (est. 1946). **3.** Leicestershire. **4.** a large English variety of early maturing sheep with coarse, long wool and a heavy mutton yield.

Leices·ter·shire (lěs/tər shǐr/, -shər), *n.* a county in central England. 590,000 pop. (est. 1946); 832 sq. mi. *Co. seat:* Leicester. Also, **Leicester.**

Lei·den (lī/dən), *n.* a city in W Netherlands. 83,836 (est. 1946). Also, **Leyden.**

Leigh·ton (lā/tən), *n.* **Frederic, Baron,** 1830–96, British painter and sculptor.

Lein·ster (lěn/stər), *n.* a province in E Eire. 1,259,790 pop. (est. 1943); 7643 sq. mi.

lei·o·my·o·ma (lī/ō mī ō/mə), *n.,* *pl.* **-omata** (-ō/mə tə), **-omas.** a tumor made up of nonstriated muscular tissue. Cf. **rhabdomyoma.** [f. *leio-* (t. Gk., comb. form of *leîos* smooth) + MYOMA]

Leip·zig (līp/sǐg, -sǐk; *Ger.* līp/tsǐkн), *n.* a city in central Germany, in Saxony. 707,365 (1939). Also, **Leip·sic** (līp/sǐk).

leis·ter (lēs/stər), *n.* **1.** a spear having three or more prongs used to strike a fish. —*v.t.* **2.** to strike (a fish) with a leister. [t. Scand.; cf. Icel. *liōstr,* der. *liōsta* strike]

lei·sure (lē/zhər, lězh/ər), *n.* **1.** the condition of having one's time free from the demands of work or duty; ease: *enjoying a life of leisure.* **2.** free or unoccupied time. **3. at leisure, a.** with free or unrestricted time. **b.** without haste. **c.** unoccupied; disengaged. **4. at one's leisure,** when one has leisure. —*adj.* **5.** free or unoccupied: *leisure hours.* **6.** having leisure: *the leisure class.* [ME *leiser,* t. OF: m. *leisir* (inf.), g. L *licēre* be permitted]

lei·sure·ly (lē/zhər lǐ, lězh/ər-), *adj.* Also, **lei·sured** (lē/zhərd, lězh/ərd). **1.** acting, proceeding, or done without haste; deliberate: *a leisurely speech.* **2.** showing or suggesting ample leisure; unhurried: *a leisurely manner.* —*adv.* **3.** in a leisurely manner; without haste. —**lei/sure·li·ness,** *n.* —**Syn. 1.** See **slow.** —**Ant. 1.** hurried.

Leith (lēth), *n.* a seaport in SE Scotland, on the Firth of Forth: now a part of Edinburgh. ab. 81,618 (1931).

leit·mo·tif (līt/mō tēf/), *n.* (in a music drama) a motif or theme associated throughout the work with a particular person, situation, or idea. Also, **leit/mo·tiv/.** [t. G: (m.) *leitmotiv* leading motive]

Lek (lěk), *n.* See **Rhine.**

Le·ly (lē/lǐ; *Du.* lā/lǐ), *n.* **Sir Peter** (pē/tər; *Du.* pā/-), *(Pieter van der Faes)* 1618–80, Dutch portrait painter in England.

Le·maî·tre (lə mě/tr), *n.* **François Élie Jules** (frän-swä/ ě lē/ zhyl), 1853–1915, French critic and writer.

lem·an (lěm/ən, lē/mən), *n.* *Archaic.* **1.** a sweetheart. **2.** a mistress. [ME *lemman,* earlier *leofmon,* f. *leof* dear (see LIEF) + *mon* MAN]

Le·man (lē/mən), *n.* **Lake.** See **Geneva, Lake of.**

Le Mans (lə män/), a city in NW France. 100,455 (1946).

Lem·berg (lěm/bûrg; *Ger.* lěm/běrкн), *n.* German name of **Lwów.**

lem·ma¹ (lěm/ə), *n., pl.* **lemmas, lemmata** (lěm/ə tə). **1.** a subsidiary proposition introduced in proving some other proposition; a helping theorem. **2.** an argument, theme, or subject. **3.** heading of a written entry. [t. L, t. Gk.: m. *lêmma* premise]

lem·ma² (lěm/ə), *n., pl.* **lemmas, lemmata** (lěm/ə tə). *Bot.* a bract in a grass spikelet just below the pistil and stamens. [t. Gk.: m. *lêmma* shell, husk]

lem·ming (lěm/ǐng), *n.* any of various small, mouselike rodents of the genera *Lemmus, Myopus,* and *Dicrostonyx,* of far northern regions, as *L. lemmus,* of Norway, Sweden, etc. [t. Norw.]

Lemming, *Lemmus lemmus* (6 in. long)

Lem·nos (lěm/nŏs; *Gk.* lěm/nŏs), *n.* a Greek island in the NE Aegean. 26,497 pop. (1940); 186 sq. mi. *Cap.:* Kastro. —**Lem·ni·an** (lěm/nǐ ən), *adj., n.*

lem·on (lěm/ən), *n.* **1.** the yellowish acid fruit of the subtropical rutaceous tree, *Citrus Limon.* **2.** the tree itself. **3.** clear, light yellow color. **4.** *Slang.* something distasteful, disappointing, or unpleasant. —*adj.* **5.** having a clear, light yellow color. [ME *lymon,* t. OF: m. *limon,* t. Ar., Pers.: m. *līmūn*]

lem·on·ade (lěm/ə nād/), *n.* **1.** a beverage consisting of lemon juice mixed with water and sweetened. **2.** *Brit.* lemon soda, usually in bottles. Also, *Brit.,* **lemon squash.** [t. F: m. *limonade,* der. *limon* LEMON]

lemon geranium, *Bot.* a hybrid plant, *Pelargonium Limoneum,* whose leaves give off a lemon fragrance.

lemon verbena, a verbenaceous garden shrub, *Lippia citriodora,* with long, slender leaves, having a lemonlike fragrance.

lem·pi·ra (lěm pē/rä), *n.* the monetary unit and gold coin of Honduras stabilized in 1926 as equal to 50 cents in the U.S. [t. Amer. Sp.; named after a native chief]

le·mur (lē/mər), *n.* any of various small, arboreal, chiefly nocturnal mammals, esp. of the genus *Lemur,* allied to the monkeys, usually having a foxlike face and woolly fur, and found chiefly in Madagascar. [t. NL, der. L *lemures,* pl., ghosts, specters; so called because of nocturnal habits. Cf. LEMURES] —**le/mur·like/,** *adj.*

Lemur, *Lemur catta* (ab. 3½ ft. long)

lem·u·res (lěm/yə rēz/), *n.pl.* (among the ancient Romans) the spirits of the departed. [t. L. Cf. LEMUR]

lem·u·roid (lěm/yə roid/), *adj.* **1.** lemurlike; of the lemur kind. —*n.* **2.** a lemur.

Le·na (lē/nə; *Russ.* lǐ/nä), *n.* a river flowing from near Lake Baikal, in the S Soviet Union in Asia, through the Yakut Republic into the Arctic Ocean. ab. 2800 mi.

lend (lěnd), *v.,* **lent, lending.** —*v.t.* **1.** to give the temporary use of (money, etc.) for a consideration. **2.** to grant the use of (something) with the understanding that it (or its equivalent in kind) shall be returned. **3.** to furnish or impart: *distance lends enchantment to the view.* **4.** to give or contribute obligingly or helpfully: *to lend one's aid to a cause.* **5.** to accommodate or adapt oneself (or itself) to something. —*v.i.* **6.** to make a loan or loans. [ME *lende;* r. ME *lene(n),* OE *lǣnan,* der. *lǣn* loan] —**lend/er,** *n.*

Lend-Lease Act (lěnd/lēs/), an act (Mar. 11, 1941) enabling the U.S. government to furnish material aid to nations at war with Germany and Italy.

L'En·fant (län fän/), *n.* **Pierre Charles** (pyěr shàrl), 1754–1825, French engineer who planned Washington, D.C.

length (lěngkth, lěngth), *n.* **1.** the linear magnitude of anything as measured from end to end: *the length of a river.* **2.** extent from beginning to end of a series, enumeration, account, book, etc. **3.** extent in time; duration: *the length of a battle.* **4.** a distance determined by the length of something specified: *to hold a thing at arm's length.* **5.** a piece or portion of a certain or a known length: *a length of rope.* **6.** a stretch or extent of something, esp. a long stretch. **7.** the extent, or an extent, of going, proceeding, etc. **8.** the quality or fact of being long rather than short: *a journey remarkable for its length.* **9.** the measure from end to end of a horse, boat, etc. as a unit of distance in racing: *a horse wins by two lengths.* **10.** *Pros. and Phonet.* **a.** (of a vowel or syllable) quantity (whether long or short). **b.** the quality of vowels. **11. at length, a.** to or in the full extent. **b.** after a time; in the end. [ME and OE, der. *lang* LONG[1]. See -TH[1]]

length·en (lĕngk′thən, lĕng′-), *v.t.* **1.** to make greater in length. —*v.i.* **2.** to become greater in length. —**Syn. 1.** LENGTHEN, EXTEND, STRETCH, PROLONG, PROTRACT agree in the idea of making longer. To LENGTHEN is to make longer, either in a material or an immaterial sense: *to lengthen a dress.* To EXTEND is to lengthen beyond some original point or so as to reach a certain point: *to extend a railway line by a hundred miles.* To STRETCH is primarily to lengthen by drawing or tension: *to stretch a rubber band.* Both PROLONG and PROTRACT mean esp. to lengthen in time, and therefore apply to intangibles. To PROLONG is to continue beyond the desired, estimated, or allotted time: *to prolong an interview.* To PROTRACT is to draw out to undue length or to be slow in coming to a conclusion: *to protract a discussion.* —**Ant. 1.** shorten.

length·ways (lĕngkth′wāz′, lĕngth′-), *adv.* lengthwise.

length·wise (lĕngkth′wīz′, lĕngth′-), *adv., adj.* in the direction of the length.

length·y (lĕngk′thĭ, lĕng′-), *adj.*, **lengthier, lengthiest.** having, or being of great length, esp. speeches, writings, etc. —**length′i·ly,** *adv.* —**length′i·ness,** *n.*

le·ni·en·cy (lē′nĭ ən sĭ, lēn′yən-), *n.* the quality of being lenient. Also, **le′ni·ence.**

le·ni·ent (lē′nĭ ənt, lēn′yənt), *adj.* **1.** mild, clement, or merciful, as in treatment, spirit, or tendency; gentle. **2.** *Archaic.* softening, soothing, or alleviative. [t. L: s. *lēniens,* ppr., softening] —**le′ni·ent·ly,** *adv.*

Len·in (lĕn′ĭn), *n.* **Nikolai** (nĭ′kŏ lī′), (*Vladimir Ilich Ulyanov*) 1870–1924. Russian revolutionary leader and writer. He was the chief leader of the 1917 Revolution, and head of the Soviet government from 1917 to 1924.

Le·ni·na·kan (lĕ′nĭ nä kän′), *n.* a city in the SW Soviet Union, in the Armenian Republic. 67,707 (1939). Formerly, **Aleksandropol.**

Len·in·grad (lĕn′ĭn grăd′; *Rus.* lĕ′nĭn grät′), *n.* a seaport in the NW Soviet Union: capital of the Russian Empire, 1703–1917. 3,191,304 (1939). Formerly, **St. Petersburg** or **Petrograd.**

Len·in·ism (lĕn′ĭn ĭz′əm), *n.* Russian communism as taught by Nikolai Lenin, with emphasis on the "dictatorship of the proletariat."

le·nis (lē′nĭs), *adj., n., pl.* **lenes** (lē′nēz). *Phonet.* —*adj.* **1.** pronounced with relatively weak muscular tension and breath pressure, resulting in weak sound effect: thus, in *potato* the second *t* is lenis; the first, fortis. —*n.* **2.** a lenis consonant. [t. L: gentle]

le·ni·tion (lĭ nĭsh′ən), *n.* *Phonet.* a weakening of the articulation of a consonant, often leading to radical sound-changes and even to loss of the sound. [f. LENI(S) + -TION]

len·i·tive (lĕn′ə tĭv), *adj.* **1.** softening, soothing, or mitigating, as medicines or applications. **2.** mildly laxative. —*n.* **3.** a lenitive medicine or application; a mild laxative. **4.** *Rare.* anything that softens or soothes.

len·i·ty (lĕn′ə tĭ), *n., pl.* **-ties.** **1.** the quality or fact of being mild or gentle, as toward others. **2.** a lenient act. [t. L: m.s. *lēnitas*]

le·no (lē′nō), *adj.* (of a weave) having the warp yarns woven in twisted pairs between the filling yarns, usually in a light, gauzy fabric.

lens (lĕnz), *n., pl.* **lenses.** **1.** a piece of transparent substance, usually glass, having two (or two main) opposite surfaces, either both curved or one curved and one plane, used for changing the convergence of light rays, as in magnifying, or in correcting errors of vision. **2.** a combination of such pieces. **3.** some analogous device, as for affecting sound waves, electromagnetic radiation or streams of electrons. **4.** *Anat.* a part of the eye, a crystalline lens. [t. L: a lentil (which is shaped like a convexo-convex lens)]

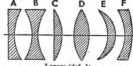

Lenses (def. 1)
A, Plano-concave; B, Biconcave (concavo-concave); C, Plano-convex; D, Biconvex (convexo-convex); E, The meniscus (converging concavo-convex, converging meniscus); F, Concavo-convex

lent (lĕnt), *v.* pt. and pp. of **lend.**

Lent (lĕnt), *n.* **1.** an annual season of fasting and penitence in preparation for Easter beginning on Ash Wednesday and including the forty weekdays next before Easter, observed by the Roman Catholic, Anglican, and other churches. **2.** (in the Middle Ages) a period from Martinmas (Nov. 11) to Christmas, known as St. Martin's Lent. [ME *lente(n),* OE *len(c)ten* spring, Lent; akin to D *lente* spring, G *lenz*]

len·ta·men·te (lĕn′tä mĕn′tĕ), *adv.* *Music.* slowly. [It., der. *lento* LENTO]

len·tan·do (lĕn tän′dō), *adj.* *Music.* becoming slower. [It. ger. of *lentare* slacken, der. L *lentus* slow]

Lent·en (lĕn′tən), *adj.* (*often l.c.*) of, pertaining to, or suitable for Lent. [f. LENT + -EN[2]]

len·ti·cel (lĕn′tə sĕl′), *n.* *Bot.* a body of cells formed in the periderm of a stem, appearing on the surface of the plant as a lens-shaped spot, and serving as a pore. [t. NL: m.s. *lenticella,* var. of L *lenticula* LENTIL]

len·tic·u·lar (lĕn tĭk′yə lər), *adj.* **1.** of or pertaining to a lens. **2.** convexo-convex. **3.** resembling a lentil (seed) in form. [t. L: s. *lenticulāris* lentil-shaped]

len·ti·go (lĕn tī′gō), *n., pl.* **-tigines** (-tĭj′ə nēz′). *Med.* a freckle. [t. L, der. *lens* a lentil]

len·til (lĕn′tĭl), *n.* **1.** an annual plant, *Lens culinaris,* having flattened, convexo-convex seeds which constitute a food similar to peas and beans. **2.** the seed. [ME *lentille,* t. F, g. L *lenticula,* dim. of *lens* a lentil]

len·tis·si·mo (lĕn tĭs′ə mō′; *It.* lĕn tēs′sē mô′), *Music.* —*adj.* **1.** very slow. —*adv.* **2.** very slowly. [It., der. *lento* LENTO]

len·to (lĕn′tō), *Music.* —*adj.* **1.** slow. —*adv.* **2.** slowly. [It., g. L *lentus*]

l'en·voi (lĕn′voi, lĕn voi′; *Fr.* län vwä′), the envoy of a poetical or prose composition. Also, **l'en′voy.** [t. OF: (m.) *l'envoy,* lit., the sending. See ENVOY[1]]

Le·o (lē′ō), *n., gen.* **Leonis** (lĭ ō′nĭs). **1.** a zodiacal constellation; the Lion. **2.** the fifth sign of the zodiac. See diag. under **zodiac.** [t. L. See LION]

Le·o I (lē′ō; *It.* lā′ō), **Saint,** ("*Leo the Great*") died A.D. 461, Italian cleric; pope, A.D. 440–461.

Leo III, **Saint,** died A.D. 816, Italian ecclesiastic; pope, A.D. 795–816.

Leo X, (*Giovanni de'Medici*) 1475–1521, Italian ecclesiastic; pope, 1513–21.

Leo XIII, (*Gioacchino Pecci*) 1810–1903, Italian ecclesiastic; pope, 1878–1903.

Leom·in·ster (lĕm′ĭn stər), *n.* a city in N Massachusetts. 24,075 (1950).

Le·ón (lē ōn′), *n.* **1.** a region in NW Spain: formerly a kingdom. 1,732,082 pop. (1940); 21,024 sq. mi. **2.** a city in NW Spain. 33,269 (est. 1943). **3.** a city in central Mexico, in Guanajuato state. 74,155 (1940). **4.** a city in W Nicaragua: the former capital. 31,779 (est. 1941).

Le·o·nar·desque (lē′ə när dĕsk′), *adj.* resembling the manner of Leonardo da Vinci.

Le·on·ca·val·lo (lē ōn′kä väl′lō), *n.* **Ruggiero** (rōōd-jĕ′rō), 1858–1919, Italian operatic composer.

Le·o·nid (lē′ə nĭd), *n., pl.* **Leonids, Leonides** (lĭ ŏn′ə dēz′). *Astron.* any of a shower of meteors occurring about Nov. 15 and appearing to radiate from Leo. [back formation from *Leonides,* pl., t. L. See LEO, -ID[1]]

Le·on·i·das (lĭ ŏn′ə dəs), *n.* died 480 B.C., Spartan king, 491?–480 B.C., slain in the battle of Thermopylae.

le·o·nine (lē′ə nīn′), *adj.* **1.** of or pertaining to the lion. **2.** lionlike. [ME *leonyne,* t. L: m.s. *leōnīnus*]

leop·ard (lĕp′ərd), *n.* **1.** a large, ferocious, spotted Asiatic or African carnivore, *Panthera pardus,* of the cat family, usually tawny, with black markings; the Old World panther. **2.** any of various related animals, as the jaguar (**American leopard**), the cheetah (**hunting leopard**), and the ounce (**snow leopard**). **3.** *Her.* a lion pictured as walking with his head turned toward the spectator, one front paw usually raised. [ME, t. OF, t. LL: s. *leopardus,* t. LGk.: m. *leópardos.* See LION, PARD[1]] —**leop·ard·ess** (lĕp′ər dĭs), *n. fem.*

Leopard and leopardess, *Panthera pardus* (Total length 7 ft., tail 1½ ft.)

Le·o·par·di (lē′ō pär′dē), *n.* **Count Giacomo** (jä′kō-mō′), 1798–1837, Italian poet.

Le·o·pold I (lē′ə pōld′), **1.** 1640–1705, emperor of the Holy Roman Empire, 1658–1705. **2.** 1790–1865, king of Belgium, 1831–65.

Leopold II, 1. 1747–92, emperor of the Holy Roman Empire, 1790–92. **2.** 1835–1909, king of Belgium, 1865–1909.

Leopold III, born 1901, king of Belgium, 1934–1951.

Le·o·pold·ville (lē′ə pōld vĭl′; *Fr.* lā ô pōld vēl′), *n.* the capital of the Belgian Congo, in the W part: a port on the Congo river. 102,760 (1943).

le·o·tard (lē′ə tärd′), *n.* a close-fitting, sleeveless garment with a low neck and tights, worn by acrobats, dancers, etc.

Le·pan·to (lĭ păn′tō; *It.* lĕ′pän tô′), *n.* **1.** a seaport in W Greece, on the **Strait of Lepanto,** a strait opening into the Gulf of Corinth: Turkish seapower was destroyed here in a famous naval battle, 1571. **2. Gulf of.** See **Corinth, Gulf of.**

lep·er (lĕp′ər), *n.* a person affected with leprosy. [ME *lepre,* t. OF: leprosy, t. L: m. *lepra,* t. Gk., prop. fem. of *leprós* scaly]

leper house, a hospital or asylum for lepers.

lepido-, a word element meaning "scale" used esp. in scientific terms. [t. Gk., comb. form of *lepis* scale]

le·pid·o·lite (lĭ pĭd′ə līt′, lĕp′ə də līt′), *n.* a mineral of the mica group, potassium lithium aluminum silicate, commonly occurring in lilac, rose-colored, or grayish-white scaly masses. [f. LEPIDO- + -LITE]

lep·i·dop·ter·on (lĕp′ə dŏp′tər ən), n., pl. **-tera** (-tər ə). any lepidopterous insect.

lep·i·dop·ter·ous (lĕp′ə dŏp′tər əs), adj. belonging or pertaining to the Lepidoptera, an order of insects, comprising the butterflies, moths, and skippers, which in the adult state have four membranous wings more or less covered with small scales. Also, **lep′i·dop′ter·al**. [f. s. NL Lepidoptera, pl., having wings + -ous. See LEPIDO-, -PTEROUS] —**lep′i·dop′ter·an**, adj., n.

lep·i·do·si·ren (lĕp′ə dō sī′rən), n. a lungfish, Lepidosiren paradoxa, of the Amazon River, South America, having an eel-shaped body. [t. NL, f. Gk.: lepidoLEPIDO- + m. seirēn siren]

lep·i·dote (lĕp′ə dōt′), adj. Bot. covered with scurfy scales or scaly spots. [t. Gk.: m.s. lepidōtós scaly]

Lep·i·dus (lĕp′ə dəs), n. **Marcus Aemilius** (mär′kəs ē mĭl′ĭ əs), died 13 B.C., Roman politician. Octavian, Antony, and Lepidus formed the second triumvirate.

Le·pon·tine Alps (lĭ pŏn′tīn), a central range of the Alps in S Switzerland and N Italy. Highest peak, Mt. Leone, 11,684.

lep·o·rine (lĕp′ə rīn′, -rĭn), adj. Zool. of, pertaining to, or resembling the hare. [t. L: m.s. leporīnus]

lep·re·chaun (lĕp′rə kôn′), n. Irish Folklore. a pygmy, sprite, or goblin. [earlier lubrican, t. Irish: m. lupracān, metathetic var. of luchorpān a pigmy sprite, f. lu little + corpān, dim. of corp body (t. L: m. corpus)]

lep·ro·sy (lĕp′rə sĭ), n. a mildly infectious disease due to a microörganism, Bacillus leprae, and variously characterized by ulcerations, tubercular nodules, spots of pigmentary excess or deficit, loss of fingers and toes, anaesthesia in certain nerve regions, etc. [f. s. L leprōsus leprous + -y³]

lep·rous (lĕp′rəs), adj. **1.** affected with leprosy. **2.** of or like leprosy. [ME, t. LL: m.s. leprōsus. der. L lepra leprosy. See LEPER] —**lep′rous·ly**, adv.

lepto-, a combining form meaning "fine," "small," "thin," often occurring in terms of zoölogy and botany. [t. Gk., comb. form of leptós]

lep·ton (lĕp′tŏn), n., pl. **-ta** (-tə). a minor modern Greek coin equal to one hundredth of a drachma. [t. Gk., prop. neut. of leptós small]

lep·to·phyl·lous (lĕp′tō fĭl′əs), adj. having long, slender leaves. [f. LEPTO- + -PHYLLOUS]

lep·tor·rhine (lĕp′tə rīn), adj. Anthropol. having a narrow and a high-bridged nose. [f. LEPTO- + m.s. Gk. rhís nose]

Ler·mon·tov (lĕr′mŏn tôf′), n. **Mikhail Yurievich** (mĭ hä ēl′ yōor′yə vĭch), 1814–41, Russian poet and novelist.

Ler·ner (lûr′nər), n. **Max,** born 1902, U.S. editor and author.

le roi est mort, vive le roi (lə rwä ĕ môr′, vēv lə rwä′), French. the king is dead, long live the king!

Le Sage (lə säzh′), **Alain René** (á lăn′ rə nĕ′), 1668–1747, French novelist and dramatist.

Les·bi·an (lĕz′bĭ ən), adj. **1.** of or pertaining to Lesbos. **2.** erotic (from the reputed character of the ancient inhabitants of Lesbos and the tone of their poetry). —n. **3.** an inhabitant of Lesbos. **4.** (l.c.) one addicted to Lesbianism.

Les·bi·an·ism (lĕz′bĭ ən ĭz′əm), n. homosexual relations between women.

Les·bos (lĕz′bŏs; Gk. lĕz′vôs), n. ancient and modern name of Mytilene (def. 1).

lese maj·es·ty (lēz′ măj′ĭs tĭ), Law. any crime or offense against the sovereign power in a state. [t. F: m. lèse-majesté, t. L: m. laesa mājestas injured sovereignty]

le·sion (lē′zhən), n. **1.** an injury; a hurt; a wound. **2.** Pathol. any localized, morbid structural change in the body. [late ME, t. ML: s. lēsio, L laesio an injury]

Les Mi·sé·ra·bles (lĕ mē zĕ rá′bl), a novel (1862) by Victor Hugo.

less (lĕs), adv. **1.** to a smaller extent, amount, or degree: less exact. —adj. **2.** smaller in size, amount, degree, etc.; not so large, great, or much: less speed. **3.** lower in consideration, dignity, or importance: no less a person than the manager. —n. **4.** a smaller amount or quantity. —prep. **5.** lacking; minus; without: a year less two days. [ME; OE lǣs(sa), c. OFris. lēs(sa) less; a compar. form (positive lacking, superl. least)] —**Syn. 2.** See **less, fewer.**

-less, a suffix of adjectives meaning "without," "destitute of," as in childless, peerless. In adjectives derived from verbs, it indicates failure or inability to perform or be performed, e.g., resistless, countless. [ME -les, OE -lēas, repr. lēas, adj., free from, without, c. Icel. lauss free, LOOSE]

les·see (lĕ sē′), n. one to whom a lease is granted. —**les·see′ship,** n.

less·en (lĕs′ən), v.i. **1.** to become less. —v.t. **2.** to make less. **3.** to represent as less; depreciate; disparage. —**Syn. 1.** decrease, diminish. **3.** reduce.

Les·seps (lĕs′əps; Fr. lĕsĕps′), n. **Viscount Ferdinand de** (fĕr dē näx′ də), 1805–94, French diplomat, promoter of the construction of the Suez Canal.

less·er (lĕs′ər), adj. **1.** less; smaller, as in size, amount, importance, etc.: a lesser evil. **2.** being the smaller or less important of two. [late ME, f. LESS + -ER⁴]

Lesser Antilles. See **Antilles.**

Lesser Bear, Astron. Ursa Minor.

Lesser Dog, Astron. Canis Minor.

Les·sing (lĕs′ĭng), n. **Gotthold Ephraim** (gôt′hôlt ā′frä ĭm), 1729–81, German critic and dramatist.

les·son (lĕs′ən), n. **1.** something to be learned or studied: a music lesson. **2.** a part of a book or the like assigned to a pupil for study: the lesson for today is on page 22. **3.** a useful or salutary piece of practical wisdom imparted or learned: this experience taught me a lesson. **4.** something from which one learns or should learn, as an instructive or warning example: this experience was a lesson to me. **5.** a reproof or punishment intended to teach one better ways. **6.** a portion of Scripture or other sacred writing read, or appointed to be read, at divine service. —v.t. **7.** to admonish or reprove. [ME, t. OF: m. leçon, g. L lectio a reading]

les·sor (lĕs′ôr, lĕ sôr′), n. one who grants a lease.

lest (lĕst), conj. **1.** for fear that; that ... not; so that ... not. **2.** (after words expressing fear, danger, etc.) that: there was danger lest the plan become known. [ME leste, late OE the lǣste, earlier thȳ lǣs the lest (lit., whereby less that; the is the relative particle)]

let¹ (lĕt), v., let, letting, n. —v.t. **1.** to allow or permit. **2.** to allow to pass, go, or come. **3.** to cause or allow to escape. **4.** to grant the occupancy or use of (land, buildings, rooms, space, etc., or movable property) for rent or hire (occasionally fol. by out). **5.** to contract for performance: to let work to a carpenter. **6.** to cause or make: to let one know. **7.** (as an auxiliary) used to propose or order: let me see. **8.** to disappoint; fail (fol. by down). **9. let on, a.** to allow to be known. **b.** Colloq. to pretend. —v.i. **10.** to be rented or leased. **11.** Colloq. to be dismissed or ended, as school (fol. by out). **12.** Colloq. to cease; stop (fol. by up). —n. **13.** Brit. to lease. [ME leten, OE lǣtan, c. D laten, G lassen; akin to LATE] —**Syn. 1.** LET, LEAVE, though not synonyms, are often confused, LEAVE being the one used more frequently in both meanings. A further confusion of the verb LEAVE with the noun LEAVE may have helped to perpetuate the misuse. (The noun LEAVE, meaning "permission," might readily be associated with LET, whose most common meaning is "permit" or "allow." The verb LEAVE, however, does not have a meaning of "permit" or "allow"; its most common meaning is "to go away from.") In the constructions in which the confusion arises, it should be noted that, although either verb can take a noun object, only LET can take the infinitive (with to not expressed). In certain idiomatic expressions, the two verbs are used in parallel constructions, but the meanings differ widely: LET it out means "allow it to escape" (as the breath), but LEAVE it out means "omit it" (as a sentence). LET him alone means "allow him to be without interference" (don't bother him), but LEAVE him alone means "go away, so that he will be alone." See **allow.**

let² (lĕt), n., v., letted or let, letting. Archaic. —n. **1.** hindrance or obstruction; an impediment or obstacle: without let or hindrance. **2.** Tennis, etc. an interference with the course of the ball (of some kind specified in the rules) on account of which the stroke or point must be played over again. —v.t. **3.** to hinder; prevent; stand in the way of. [ME letten, OE lettan, (der. lǣt slow, tardy, LATE), c. Icel. letja hinder]

-let, a diminutive suffix, e.g., kinglet, used often for little objects, e.g., frontlet, bracelet. [t. OF: m. -elet, f. -el (sometimes g. L -ellus, dim. suffix, sometimes g. L -āle, neut. See -AL¹) + -et -ET]

l'é·tat, c'est moi (lā tä′, sĕ mwä′), French. I am the state (supposed to have been said by Louis XIV).

let·down (lĕt′doun′), n. **1.** a decrease in some exertion of force or energy: a letdown in sales. **2.** disillusion or disappointment. **3.** a humbling or deflating.

le·thal (lē′thəl), adj. of, pertaining to, or such as to cause death; deadly. [t. L: s. lēt(h)ālis]

le·thar·gic (lĭ thär′jĭk), adj. **1.** pertaining to or affected with lethargy; drowsy; sluggish. **2.** producing lethargy. Also, **le·thar′gi·cal.** —**le·thar′gi·cal·ly,** adv.

leth·ar·gy (lĕth′ər jĭ), n., pl. **-gies. 1.** a state of drowsy dullness or suspension of the faculties and energies; apathetic or sluggish inactivity. **2.** Pathol. a morbid state or a disorder characterized by overpowering drowsiness or sleep. [t. L: m.s. lēthargia, t. Gk.: forgetfulness; r. ME litargie, t. ML: m. litaigia]

Le·the (lē′thĭ), n. **1.** Gk. Myth. a river in Hades, whose water caused forgetfulness of the past in those who drank of it. **2.** forgetfulness; oblivion. [t. L, t. Gk.: lit., forgetfulness] —**Le·the·an** (lĭ thē′ən), adj.

Le·to (lē′tō), n. Gk. Myth. the mother by Zeus of Apollo and Artemis.

l'é·toile du nord (lĕ twäl′ dʏ nôr′), French. the north star (motto of Minnesota).

Lett (lĕt), n. **1.** one of a people living on and near the eastern coast of the Baltic Sea, closely related to the Lithuanians. **2.** the Lettish language.

let·ter (lĕt′ər), n. **1.** a communication in writing or printing addressed to a person or a number of persons. **2.** one of the marks or signs conventionally used in writing and printing to represent speech sounds; an alphabetic character. **3.** a printing-type bearing such a mark or character. **4.** a particular style of type. **5.** such types collectively. **6.** actual terms or wording, as distinct from general meaning or intent. **7.** (pl.) literature in general; belles-lettres. **8.** (pl.) the profession of literature, or authorship: a man of letters. **9. to the letter,** with close adherence to the actual wording or the literal meaning. **b.** to the fullest extent. —*v.t.* **10.** to mark or write with letters. [ME, t. OF: m. *lettre*, g. L *littera*, *lītera*, alphabetical character, pl. epistle, literature] —**let′ter·er**, *n.* —**Syn. 7.** See **literature.**

letter box, *Chiefly Brit.* mail box.

letter carrier, *U.S.* postman.

let·tered (lĕt′ərd), *adj.* **1.** educated or learned. **2.** pertaining to or characterized by polite learning or literary culture. **3.** marked with or as with letters.

let·ter·gram (lĕt′ərgrăm′), *n.* night letter.

let·ter·head (lĕt′ərhĕd′), *n.* **1.** a printed heading on letter paper, esp. one giving the name and address of a business concern, an institution, etc. **2.** a sheet of paper with such a heading.

let·ter·ing (lĕt′ərĭng), *n.* **1.** act or process of inscribing with or making letters. **2.** the letters themselves.

letter of advice, 1. a document, esp. in commercial shipments, giving specific information as to the consignor's agent in the consignee's territory, his bank, warehouse, etc. **2.** *Com.* a drawer document, usually forwarded ahead of the bill of lading and other papers giving title to goods shipped by the drawer, that a bill has been issued against the drawee.

letter of credit, 1. an order issued by a banker, allowing a person named to draw money to a specified amount from correspondents of the issuer. **2.** an instrument issued by a banker, authorizing a person named to make drafts upon the issuer up to an amount specified.

letter of marque, license or commission granted by a state to a private citizen to capture and confiscate the merchant ships of another nation. Also, **letter of marque and reprisal.**

let·ter-per·fect (lĕt′ər pûr′fĭkt), *adj.* knowing one's part, lesson, or the like, to the letter, or perfectly.

let·ter·press (lĕt′ərprĕs′), *n.* **1.** matter printed from letters or type, rather than from engraved plates. **2.** printed text or reading matter, as distinguished from illustrations, etc.

letters of administration, *Law.* an instrument issued by a court or public official authorizing an administrator to take control of and dispose of the estate of a decedent.

letters of credence, papers formally authorizing a nation's diplomatic agents, issued by the appointing state.

letters patent, *Law.* a written or printed instrument issued by the sovereign power, conferring upon a patentee for a limited time the exclusive right to make, use, and sell his invention.

letters testamentary, *Law.* an instrument issued by a court or public official authorizing an executor to take control of and dispose of the estate of a decedent.

Let·tic (lĕt′ĭk), *adj.* **1.** pertaining or related to the Letts. —*n.* **2.** Lettish. **3.** *Obs.* the Baltic group of languages.

Let·tish (lĕt′ĭsh), *adj.* **1.** pertaining to the Letts or their language. —*n.* **2.** the language of Latvia.

let·tre de ca·chet (lĕt′r də kȧ shĕ′), *French Hist.* a letter under the seal of the sovereign, esp. one ordering imprisonment, frequently without trial.

let·tre de change (lĕt′r də shänzh′), *French.* a letter or bill of exchange.

let·tuce (lĕt′ĭs), *n.* **1.** an important salad plant, *Lactuca sativa*, in many varieties, having large, succulent leaves which are much used for salad. **2.** any species of *Lactuca.* [ME *letuse*, t. OF: m. *laitues*, pl., g. L *lactūca*]

let·up (lĕt′ŭp′), *n.* *Colloq.* cessation; pause.

le·u (lĕ′ŏŏ), *n.*, *pl.* **lei** (lā). the Rumanian monetary unit equal to 100 bani and worth about one U.S. cent.

Leu·cas (lōō′kəs), *n.* Levkas. Also, **Leu′kas.**

leu·ce·mi·a (lōō sē′mĭ ə), *n.* leukemia.

leu·cine (lōō′sēn, -sĭn), *n.* *Biochem.* a white crystal-line amino acid, $C_6H_{13}NO_2$, a constituent of proteins and also synthesized. Also, **leu·cin** (lōō′sĭn). [f. LEUC(O)- + -INE[2]]

leu·cite (lōō′sīt), *n.* a whitish or grayish mineral, potassium aluminum silicate, $KAlSi_2O_6$, found in certain volcanic rocks. [t. G: m. *leucit*, f. *leuc-* LEUC(O) + *-it* -ITE[1]] —**leu·cit·ic** (lōō sĭt′ĭk), *adj.*

leuco-, a word element meaning "white." Also, before vowels, **leuc-.** [t. Gk.: m. *leuko-*, comb. form of *leukós*]

leu·co base (lōō′kō), *Chem.* a noncolored or slightly colored compound made by reducing a dye and which is readily oxidized to regenerate the dye.

leu·co·crat·ic (lōō′kə krăt′ĭk), *adj.* *Geol.* composed predominantly of light-colored minerals. [f. LEUCO- + -CRAT + -IC]

leu·co·cyte (lōō′kə sīt′), *n.* *Physiol.* one of the white or colorless corpuscles of the blood, concerned in the destruction of disease-producing microörganisms, etc.

leu·co·cy·the·mi·a (lōō′kō sī thē′mĭ ə), *n.* *Pathol.* leukemia. Also, **leu′co·cy·thae′mi·a.** [NL. See LEUCO-, -CYTE, -HEMIA]

leu·co·cyt·ic (lōō′kə sĭt′ĭk), *adj.* **1.** pertaining to leucocytes. **2.** characterized by an excess of leucocytes.

leu·co·cy·to·sis (lōō′kō sī tō′sĭs), *n.* *Physiol.*, *Pathol.* the presence of an increased number of leucocytes in the blood, esp. when temporary, as in infection, and not due to leukemia. [NL. See LEUCOCYTE, -OSIS] —**leu·co·cy·tot·ic** (lōō′kō sī tŏt′ĭk), *adj.*

leu·co·ma·ine (lōō kō′mə ēn′, -ĭn), *n.* *Biochem.* any of a class of poisonous nitrogenous substances normally produced in a living animal body through metabolism. [f. LEUCO- + (PTO)MAINE]

leu·co·pe·ni·a (lōō′kə pē′nĭ ə), *n.* *Physiol.* a decrease in the number of white cells in the blood.

leu·co·plast (lōō′kə plăst′), *n.* *Bot.* one of the colorless bodies found within the protoplasm of vegetable cells, and serving as points around which starch forms.

leu·co·poi·e·sis (lōō′kō poi ē′sĭs), *n.* *Physiol.* the formation and development of the white blood cells.

leu·cor·rhe·a (lōō′kə rē′ə), *n.* *Pathol.* a whitish discharge from the female genital organs. Also, **leu′cor·rhoe′a.** [NL. See LEUCO-, -RRHEA]

leu·co·stic·te (lōō′kō stĭk′tĭ), *n.* any of several montane finches of the genus *Leucosticte*, commonly called rosy finches, as the Aleutian rosy finch (*L. tephrocotis griseonucha*).

Leuc·tra (lōōk′trə), *n.* a town in ancient Greece, in Boeotia: Thebans defeated Spartans here, 371 B.C.

leu·ke·mi·a (lōō kē′mĭ ə), *n.* *Pathol.* a somewhat rare, almost uniformly fatal disease, characterized by excessive production of white blood cells, which are usually found in greatly increased numbers in the blood. There is an accompanying anemia, often severe, and the spleen and lymphatic glands are usually enlarged and in a state of great activity. Also, **leu·kae′mi·a, leucemia.** [t. NL, f. s. Gk. *leukós* white + *-emia* -EMIA]

lev (lĕf), *n.*, *pl.* **leva** (lĕ′və). the monetary unit and a gold coin of Bulgaria equal to 100 stotinki and stabilized in 1928 to equal approx. one cent in the U.S.

Lev., Leviticus.

Le Val·lois-Per·ret (lə vȧl wȧ′ pĕ rĕ′), a city in N France, on the Seine, near Paris. 61,681 (1946).

Le·vant (lĭ vănt′), *n.* **1.** lands bordering the E shore of the Mediterranean and the Aegean, esp. Syria, Lebanon, and Palestine. **2.** (*l.c.*) a superior grade of morocco having a large and prominent grain, orig. made in the Levant; Levant morocco. [t. F, prop. ppr. of (*se*) *lever* rise (with reference to the rising sun). See LEVER]

Levant dollar, a silver coin used for trade purposes, originally minted in Austria, and circulating in Ethiopia, Eritrea, Aden, etc.; Maria Theresa thaler. Its value changes with the price of silver and economic conditions of countries where it is used.

Le·van·tine (lĭ văn′tĭn, lĕv′ən tīn′, -tēn′), *adj.* **1.** of or pertaining to the Levant. —*n.* **2.** a native or a vessel of the Levant. [f. LEVANT + -INE[1]. Cf. F *levantin*]

Levant morocco, levant (def. 2).

le·va·tor (lĭ vā′tər, -tôr), *n.*, *pl.* **levatores** (lĕv′ə tōr′ēz). **1.** that which raises or elevates. **2.** *Anat.* a muscle that raises some part of the body. **3.** *Surg.* an instrument used to raise a depressed part of the skull. [t. L: a lifter]

lev·ee[1] (lĕv′ĭ), *n.* **1.** *Southern U.S.* an embankment for preventing the overflowing of a river. **2.** *Agric.* one of the small continuous ridges surrounding fields that are to be irrigated. **3.** *Hist.* a landing place for vessels; a quay. [t. F: m. *levée*, der. *lever* raise. See LEVER]

lev·ee[2] (lĕv′ĭ, lĕ vē′), *n.* **1.** (in Great Britain) a public court assembly, held in the early afternoon, at which men only are received. **2.** a reception: *a presidential levee at the White House.* **3.** *Hist.* a reception of visitors held on rising from bed, as formerly by a royal or other personage. [t. F: m. *levé, lever* a rising. See LEVER]

lev·el (lĕv′əl), *adj., n., v.,* **-eled, -eling** or (*esp. Brit.*) **-elled, -elling,** *adv.* —*adj.* **1.** having no part higher than another; having an even surface. **2.** being in a plane parallel to the plane of the horizon; horizontal. **3.** on an equality, as one thing with another, or two or more things with one another. **4.** even, equable, or uniform. **5.** mentally well-balanced: *a level head.* **6. one's level best,** *Colloq.* one's very best; one's utmost.
—*n.* **7.** a device used for determining, or adjusting something to, a horizontal surface. **8.** such a device consisting of a glass tube containing alcohol or ether with a movable bubble which when in the center indicates horizontalness. **9.** a surveying instrument combining such a device with a mounted telescope. **10.** a measuring of differences in elevation with such an instrument. **11.** an imaginary line or surface everywhere perpendicular to the plumb line. **12.** the horizontal line or plane in which anything is situated, with regard to its elevation. **13.** level position or condition. **14.** a level tract of land, or an extent of country approximately horizontal and unbroken by irregularities. **15.** a level or flat surface. **16.** one of various positions with respect to height; a height (*of*): *the water rose to a level of thirty feet.* **17.** a position or plane, high or low: *acting on the level of amateurs.*
—*v.t.* **18.** to make (a surface) level or even: *to level ground before building.* **19.** to raise or lower to a particular level, or position. **20.** to bring (something) to the level of the ground; knock down, as a person: *the city was leveled by one atomic bomb.* **21.** to bring (two or more things) to an equality of status, condition, etc. **22.** to make even or uniform, as coloring. **23.** to aim or point at a mark, as a weapon, etc. **24.** to turn (looks, etc.) in a particular direction. **25.** *Survey.* to find the relative elevation of different points in (land) as with a level.
—*v.i.* **26.** to bring things or persons to a common level. **27.** to aim a weapon, etc. **28.** to direct the mind,

purpose, etc., at something. **29.** *Survey.* to take levels; use a level. **30.** *Aeron.* to fly parallel to the ground, usually just before landing (fol. by *off*).
—*adv.* **31.** in a level, direct or even way or line. [ME *livel,* t. OF., ult. g. L *lībella,* dim. of *lībra* a balance, level] —lev′el·er; *esp. Brit.,* lev′el·ler, *n.* —lev′el·ly, *adv.* —lev′el·ness, *n.*
—**Syn.** 1, 2. LEVEL, EVEN, FLAT, SMOOTH suggest a uniform surface without marked unevenness. That which is LEVEL is parallel to the horizon: *a level surface; a billiard table must be level.* FLAT is applied to any plane surface free from marked irregularities: *a flat roof.* With reference to land or country, FLAT connotes lowness or unattractiveness; LEVEL does not suggest anything derogatory. That which is EVEN is free from irregularities, though not necessarily level or plane: *an even land surface with no hills.* SMOOTH suggests a high degree of evenness in any surface, esp. to the touch and sometimes to the sight: *as smooth as silk.*

lev·el-head·ed (lĕv′əl·hĕd′ĭd), *adj.* having common sense and sound judgment.

leveling rod, *Survey.* a graduated rod used for measuring heights in connection with a surveyor's level.

Le·ven (lē′vən), *n.* **Loch,** a lake in E Scotland: ruins of a castle in which Mary Queen of Scots was imprisoned.

lev·er (lĕv′ər, lē′vər), *n.* **1.** a bar or rigid piece acted upon at different points by two forces, as a voluntarily applied force (the *power*) and a resisting force (the *weight*), which generally tend to rotate it in opposite directions about a fixed axis or support (the *fulcrum*). **2.** any of various mechanical devices operating on this principle, as a crow bar. —*v.t., v.i.* **3.** to move with or apply a lever. [ME *levere,* t. OF.: m. *leveor,* lit., raiser, der. *lever* raise, (refl.) rise, g. L *levāre* lighten, lift, raise] —lev′er·like′, *adj.*

Le·ver (lē′vər), *n.* **Charles James,** 1806–72, Irish novelist.

lev·er·age (lĕv′ər·ĭj, lē′vər·ij), *n.* **1.** the action of a lever. **2.** the mechanical advantage or power gained by using a lever. **3.** increased power of action.

lev·er·et (lĕv′ər·ĭt), *n.* a young hare. [ME, t. OF: m. *levrete,* dim. of *levre,* g. L *lepus* hare]

Le·ver·rier (lə·vĕ·ryē′), *n.* **Urbain** (yr·băn′), 1811–77, French astronomer.

Le·vi (lē′vī), *n.* *Bible.* a son of Jacob and Leah: ancestor of the Levites. Gen. 29:34, etc. [t. Heb.: m. *Lēwī*]

lev·i·a·ble (lĕv′ĭə·bəl), *adj.* **1.** that may be levied. **2.** liable or subject to a levy.

le·vi·a·than (lĭ·vī′ə·thən), *n.* **1.** a sea monster mentioned in the Old Testament. Job 41. **2.** any huge marine animal, as the whale. **3.** anything, esp. a ship, of huge size. [ME, t. LL, t. Heb.: m. *liwyāthān,* prob. meaning the coiling up (snake)]

lev·i·gate (lĕv′ə·gāt′), *v.t.* -gated, -gating. **1.** to rub, grind, or reduce to a fine powder, as in a mortar, with or without the addition of a liquid. **2.** *Chem.* to make a homogeneous mixture of, as gels. [t. L: m.s. *lēvigātus,* pp., made smooth] —lev′i·ga′tion, *n.*

lev·in (lĕv′ĭn), *n. Archaic.* lightning. [ME *leven(e),* presumably repr. OE **lēamne* or the like, c. Goth. *lauhmuni* lightning]

lev·i·rate (lĕv′ər·ĭt, -rāt′, lē′və-), *n.* a custom, as among the ancient Hebrews, requiring a man under certain circumstances to marry the widow of his brother or nearest kinsman. [f. L *lēvir* husband's brother + -ATE¹] —lev·i·rat·ic (lĕv′ə·răt′ĭk, lē′vĭ-), lev·i·rat′i·cal, *adj.*

Le·vis (lē′vĭz), *n.pl. Trademark.* heavy blue denim trousers reinforced with copper rivets at the strain points. [pl. of *Levi* (Strauss), name of manufacturer]

Levit., Leviticus.

lev·i·tate (lĕv′ə·tāt′), *v.,* -tated, -tating. —*v.i.* **1.** to rise or float in the air by reason of lightness, or, now usually, through some alleged supernormal power that overcomes gravity. —*v.t.* **2.** to cause to rise or float in the air. [f. LEVIT(Y) + -ATE¹; modeled on GRAVITATE] —lev′i·ta′tor, *n.*

lev·i·ta·tion (lĕv′ə·tā′shən), *n.* **1.** act or phenomenon of levitating. **2.** (among spiritualists) the alleged phenomenon of bodies heavier than air being by spiritual means rendered buoyant in the atmosphere. **3.** an illusory object floating about in the air, esp. in dreams.

Le·vite (lē′vīt), *n.* **1.** a descendant of Levi; one of the tribe of Levi. **2.** one of those who assisted the priests in the tabernacle and temple. [ME, t. L: m.s. *levīta, levītes,* t. Gk.: (m.) *levītēs,* der. *Leuī* Levite, t. Heb.]

Le·vit·i·cal (lĭ·vĭt′ə·kəl), *adj.* of or pertaining to the Levites, the book of Leviticus, or the law (**Levitical law**) contained in the book of Leviticus.

Le·vit·i·cus (lĭ·vĭt′ə·kəs), *n.* the third book of the Old Testament, containing laws relating to the priests and Levites and to the forms of Jewish ceremonial observance. [t. LL, t. Gk.: m. *Leuītikós,* der. *Leutēs* LEVITE]

lev·i·ty (lĕv′ə·tĭ), *n., pl.* -ties. **1.** lightness of mind, character, or behavior; lack of proper seriousness or earnestness. **2.** an instance or exhibition of this. **3.** fickleness. **4.** lightness in weight. [t. L: m.s. *levitas*]

Lev·kas (lĕf′käs), *n.* an island in the Ionian group, off the W coast of Greece. 26,691 pop. (1928); 114 sq. mi. Also, **Leucas.** Italian, **Santa Maura.**

levo-, *Chem.* denoting a substance which rotates the plane of polarized light to the left. *Abbr.:* l-, l. [comb. form repr. L *laevus* left]

le·vo·glu·cose (lē′vō·glōō′kōs), *n. Chem.* the levorotatory form of glucose.

le·vo·ro·ta·tion (lē′vō·rō·tā′shən), *n. Optics, Chem.. etc.* the rotation of the plane of polarization of light to the left. Also, **laevorotation.**

le·vo·ro·ta·to·ry (lē′vō·rō′tə·tôr′ĭ), *adj. Optics, Chem., etc.* turning the plane of polarization of light to the left, as certain crystals. Also, **laevorotatory.**

lev·u·lin (lĕv′yə·lĭn), *n. Chem.* an amorphous substance from which levulose can be formed, occurring in the tubers of certain species of helianthus, etc.

lev·u·lin·ic acid (lĕv′yə·lĭn′ĭk), a hygroscopic acid, $CH_3COCH_2CH_2COOH$, derived from the nucleic acid of the thymus. It is industrially obtained from sugar by reaction with hydrochloric acid, and used to clean metals, such as milk cans, to guard against bacterial infection.

lev·u·lose (lĕv′yə·lōs′), *n. Chem.* fructose; fruit sugar. [f. m.s. L *laevus* left + -ULE + -OSE²]

lev·y (lĕv′ĭ), *n., pl.* levies, *v.,* levied, levying. —*n.* **1.** a raising or collecting, as of money or troops, by authority or force. **2.** that which is raised, as a tax assessment or a body of troops. —*v.t.* **3.** to make a levy of; collect (taxes, contributions, etc.). **4.** to impose as an assessment (*on*). **5.** to raise or enlist (troops, etc.) for service. **6.** to set going, start, or make (war, etc.). —*v.i.* **7.** to make a levy. **8.** *Law.* to seize or attach property by judicial order. [ME, t. F: m. *levée,* der. *lever* raise. See LEVER] —lev′i·er (lĕv′ĭ′ər), *n.*

lev·y en masse (lĕv′ĭ ĕn mäs′, än mäs′), a preparation for defense by a country threatened with invasion, by organized groups of civilians. [t. F: m. *levée en masse*]

lewd (lōōd), *adj.* **1.** inclined to, characterized by, or inciting to lust or lechery. **2.** obscene or indecent, as language, songs, etc. **3.** *Obs.* base or vile. [ME *leud, lewede,* OE *lǣw(e)de* lay, *adj.;* orig. uncert.] —lewd′ly, *adv.* —lewd′ness, *n.*

Lew·es (lōō′ĭs), *n.* **1. George Henry,** 1817–78, British philosophical writer and critic. **2.** a city in SE England, in Sussex: battle, 1264. 13,312 (1939).

Lew·is (lōō′ĭs), *n.* **1. John Llewellyn** (lōō ĕl′ĭn), born 1880, U.S. labor leader. **2. Matthew Gregory,** (*Monk Lewis*) 1775–1818, British novelist and dramatist. **3. Meriwether** (mĕr′ĭ·wĕth′ər), 1774–1809, U.S. explorer: leader of the Lewis and Clark expedition. **4. Sinclair,** 1885–1951, U.S. novelist.

lew·is·ite (lōō′ə·sīt′), *n.* a chemical warfare agent, $C_2H_2AsCl_3$, characterized by its vesicant action. [named after W. Lee *Lewis,* Am. chemist. See -ITE¹]

Lew·is·ton (lōō′ĭs·tən), *n.* a city in SW Maine, on the Androscoggin river. 40,974 (1950).

Lewis with Har·ris (hăr′ĭs), the northernmost island of the Hebrides, in NW Scotland. 33,654 pop. (1931); 825 sq. mi.

lex (lĕks), *n., pl.* **leges** (lē′jēz). law. [L: the law]

lex·i·cal (lĕk′sə·kəl), *adj.* **1.** pertaining to words or to a vocabulary, as that of an author or a language. **2.** pertaining to or of the nature of a lexicon. [f. LEXIC(ON) + -AL¹]

lexical meaning, *Gram.* that part of the meaning of a linguistic form which does not depend on its membership in a particular form class, esp. (of inflected words) the meaning common to all the members of an inflectional paradigm, e.g., the meaning common to *eat, eats, ate, eaten, eating,* despite their differences in form.

lexicog., 1. lexicographical. 2. lexicography.

lex·i·cog·ra·pher (lĕk′sə·kŏg′rə·fər), *n.* a writer or compiler of a dictionary. [f. m.s. LGk. *lexikográphos* (f. *lexikó(n)* wordbook + *-gráphos* writer) + -ER¹]

lex·i·cog·ra·phy (lĕk′sə·kŏg′rə·fĭ), *n.* the writing or compiling of dictionaries. —lex·i·co·graph·ic (lĕk′sə·kō·grăf′ĭk), lex·i·co·graph′i·cal, *adj.* —lex·i·co·graph′i·cal·ly, *adv.*

lex·i·con (lĕk′sə·kən), *n.* **1.** a wordbook or dictionary, esp. of Greek, Latin, or Hebrew. **2.** the list or vocabulary of words belonging to a particular subject, field, or class. [? t. NL (much used in Latin titles of dictionaries), t. Gk.: m. *lexikón,* neut. of *lexikós* of or for words]

Lex·ing·ton (lĕk′sĭng·tən), *n.* **1.** a town in E Massachussetts, N W of Boston: the first battle of the American Revolution was fought here, April 19, 1775. 17,335 (1950). **2.** a city in N Kentucky. 55,534 (1950).

lex lo·ci (lĕks lō′sī), *Latin.* the law of a place.

lex non scrip·ta (lĕks nŏn skrĭp′tə), *Latin.* unwritten law; common law.

lex scrip·ta (lĕks skrĭp′tə), *Latin.* written law; statute law.

lex ta·li·o·nis (lĕks tăl′ĭ·ō′nĭs), *Latin.* the law of retaliation.

Ley·den (lī′dən), *n.* Leiden.

Leyden Jar, *Elect.* a device for storing electric charge, consisting essentially of a glass jar lined inside and outside, for about two thirds of its height, with tinfoil. [named after *Leyden* (*Leiden*), city in Holland]

Ley·te (lā′tā; *Sp.* -tĕ), *n.* one of the Philippine Islands, in central part of group: focal point of the U.S. invasion of the Philippines, 1944. 835,532 pop. (1939); 3085 sq. mi.

Ley·ton (lā′tən), *n.* a city in SE England, in Essex, near London. 102,400 (est. 1946).

lf., *Baseball.* left fielder.

L.F., low-frequency.

LG, Low German. Also, **L.G.**

l.g., *Football.* left guard.

LGk., Late Greek. Also, **L.Gk.**

l.h., *Music.* left hand.

Lha·sa (lä′so, -sä), *n.* the capital of Tibet, in the SE part: sacred city of Lamaism. ab. 50,000 pop.; ab. 12,000 ft. high. Also, **Lassa.**

l.h.b., *Football.* left half-back.

L.H.D., (L *Litterarum Humaniorum Doctor*) Doctor of the More Humane Letters; Doctor of the Humanities.

L-head engine (ĕl′hĕd′), an internal-combustion engine in which both valves are located in a pocket at one side of the piston.

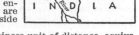

li (lē), *n., pl.* **li** (lē). a Chinese unit of distance, equivalent to about one third of a mile.

Li, *Chem.* lithium.

li·a·bil·i·ty (lī′ə bĭl′ə tĭ), *n., pl.* **-ties.** 1. an obligation, esp. for payment; debt or pecuniary obligations (opposed to *asset*). 2. something disadvantageous. 3. state or fact of being liable: *liability to jury duty, liability to disease.*

liability insurance, employers liability insurance.

li·a·ble (lī′ə bəl), *adj.* 1. subject, exposed, or open to something possible or likely; something undesirable. 2. under legal obligation; responsible or answerable. [late ME, f. s. F *lier* bind (g. L *ligāre*) + -ABLE] —**li·a·ble·ness,** *n.* —**Syn.** 1. See likely.

li·ai·son (lē′ā zŏn′, lē′ə zŏn′, -zən; lǐ ā′zən; *Fr.* lyĕ-zōn′), *n.* 1. *Mil., etc.* the contact maintained between units, in order to ensure concerted action. 2. a similar connection or relation to be maintained between nonmilitary units, bodies, etc. 3. an illicit intimacy between a man and a woman. 4. *Cookery.* a thickening, as of beaten eggs and cream, for sauces, soups, etc. 5. *Phonet.* a type of sandhi in which the final written consonant of one word is pronounced in syllable with a following initial vowel (used especially of French, as where the pre-consonantal form of the word shows no consonant corresponding to the consonant joined by liaison). [t. F, g. L *ligātio* a binding]

Li·a·kou·ra (lyä′kōō rä′), *n.* See **Parnassus, Mount.**

li·a·na (lǐ ä′nə, lǐ ăn′ə), *n.* a climbing plant or vine. Also, **li·ane** (lǐ än′). [t. F: m. *liane*, earlier *lierne*, b. with *viorne* (g. L *viburnum* viburnum) and *lier* bind (g. L *ligāre*)]

liang (lyäng), *n., pl.* **liang.** a Chinese unit of weight, equal to ¹/₁₆ catty, and equivalent to about 1¹/₃ ounce; a haikwan tael.

Liao (lyou), *n.* a river in NE China, flowing through S Manchuria into the Gulf of Liaotung. ab. 600 mi.

Liao·ning (lyou′nǐng′), *n.* a province in NE China, in Manchuria. 10,059,900 pop. (1946); 25,969 sq. mi. Formerly, **Fengtien.**

Liao·peh (lyou′bä′), *n.* a province in NE China, in Manchuria. 4,634,700 pop. (1946); 47,612 sq. mi.

Liao·tung (lyou′dŏong′), *n.* 1. a peninsula in NE China, in Manchuria, extending S into the Yellow Sea. 2. Gulf of, a gulf W of this peninsula.

Liao·yang (lyou′yäng′), *n.* a city in NE China, in Manchuria, S of Mukden. 102,478 (est. 1941).

li·ar (lī′ər), *n.* one who lies, or tells lies.

Li·ard (lǐ är′, -ärd′), *n.* a river in W Canada, flowing from S Yukon through N British Columbia and the Northwest Territories into the Mackenzie river. 550 mi.

Li·as (lī′əs), *n. Stratig.* the lowermost main part of the European Jurassic. [ME, t. OF: m. *liois* kind of limestone, of Gmc. orig.] —**Li·as·sic** (lī ăs′ĭk), *adj.*

Lib., Liberal.

lib., 1. (L *liber*) book. 2. librarian. 3. library.

li·ba·tion (lī bā′shən), *n.* 1. a pouring out of wine or other liquid in honor of a deity. 2. the liquid poured out. [ME, t. L: s. *lībātio*]

Li·bau (lē′bou), *n.* German name of **Liepāja.**

Li·ba·va (lǐ bä′vä), *n.* Russian name of **Liepāja.**

li·bel (lī′bəl), *n., v.,* **-beled, -beling,** (*esp. Brit.*) **-belled, -belling.** —*n.* 1. *Law.* **a.** defamation by written or printed words, pictures, or in any form other than by spoken words or gestures. **b.** the crime of publishing it. 2. anything defamatory, or that maliciously or damagingly misrepresents. 3. *Law.* a formal written declaration or statement, as one containing the allegations of a plaintiff or the ground of a charge. —*v.t.* 4. to publish a malicious libel against. 5. to misrepresent damagingly. 6. to institute suit against by a libel, as in an admiralty court. [ME, t. L: m.s. *libellus*, dim. of *liber* book]

li·bel·ant (lī′bəl ənt), *n. Law.* one who libels, or institutes suit. Also, *esp. Brit.,* **li′bel·lant.**

li·bel·ee (lī′bə lē′), *n. Law.* one against whom a libel instituting a suit has been filed; the respondent. Also, *esp. Brit.,* **li′bel·lee′.**

li·bel·er (lī′bəl ər). *n.* one who libels; one who publishes a libel assailing another. Also, *esp. Brit.,* **li′bel·ler.**

li·bel·ous (lī′bəl əs), *adj.* containing, constituting, or involving a libel; maliciously defamatory. Also, *esp. Brit.,* **li′bel·lous.** —**li′bel·ous·ly,** *adv.*

li·ber (lī′bər), *n. Bot.* phloëm. [t. L]

lib·er·al (lĭb′ər əl, lĭb′rəl), *adj.* 1. favorable to progress or reform, as in religious or political affairs. 2. (*often cap.*) noting or pertaining to a political party advocating measures of progressive political reform: *the Liberal party.* 3. favorable to or in accord with the policy of leaving the individual as unrestricted as possible in the opportunities for self-expression or self-fulfillment. 4. of representative forms of government rather than aristocracies and monarchies. 5. free from prejudice or bigotry; tolerant. 6. giving freely or in ample measure: *a liberal donor.* 7. given freely or abundantly: *a liberal donation.* 8. not strict or rigorous: *a liberal interpretation of a rule.* 9. befitting a freeman, a gentleman, or a nonprofessional person. —*n.* 10. a person of liberal principles or views, esp. in religion or politics. 11. (*often cap.*) a member of a liberal party in politics, esp. of the Liberal Party in Great Britain. [ME, t. L: s. *līberālis* pertaining to a free man] —**lib′er·al·ly,** *adv.* —**lib′er·al·ness,** *n.* —**Syn.** 7. See ample.

liberal arts, the course of instruction at a modern college granting an academic (as distinguished from an engineering or other technical) degree, comprising the arts, natural sciences, social sciences, and humanities. [Anglicization of L *artēs līberālēs* arts of freemen]

lib·er·al·ism (lĭb′ər ə lĭz′əm, lĭb′rə-), *n.* 1. liberal principles, as in religion or politics. 2. (*sometimes cap.*) the principles and practices of a liberal party in politics. 3. a movement in modern Protestantism which emphasizes freedom from tradition and authority, the adjustment of religious beliefs to scientific conceptions, and the spiritual capacities of men. —**lib′er·al·ist,** *n., adj.* —**lib′er·al·is′tic,** *adj.*

lib·er·al·i·ty (lĭb′ə răl′ə tĭ), *n., pl.* **-ties.** 1. the quality of being liberal in giving; generosity; bounty. 2. a liberal gift. 3. breadth of mind. 4. liberalism.

lib·er·al·ize (lĭb′ər ə līz′, lĭb′rə-), *v.t., v.i.,* **-ized, -izing.** to make or become liberal. —**lib′er·al·i·za′tion,** *n.* —**lib′er·al·iz′er,** *n.*

Liberal Party, the British political party, a fusion of Whigs and Radicals, formed in the 1830's, and one of the principal political parties in Great Britain until World War I.

lib·er·ate (lĭb′ə rāt′), *v.t.,* **-ated, -ating.** 1. to set free, as from bondage; release. 2. to disengage; set free from combination, as a gas. [t. L: m.s. *līberātus*, pp.] —**lib′er·a′tion,** *n.* —**lib′er·a′tor,** *n.* —**lib·er·a·tress** (lĭb′ə rā′trĭs), *n. fem.*

Li·be·ri·a (lī bĭr′ĭ ə), *n.* a republic in W Africa: founded by freed American slaves, 1847. 2,500,000 pop. (est. 1939); ab. 46,000 sq. mi. *Cap.:* Monrovia. —**Li·be′ri·an,** *adj., n.*

lib·er·tar·i·an (lĭb′ər târ′ĭ ən), *n.* 1. one who advocates liberty, esp. with regard to thought or conduct. 2. one who maintains the doctrine of the freedom of the will. [f. LIBERT(Y) + -ARIAN] —**lib′er·tar′i·an·ism,** *n.*

li·ber·ti·cide[1] (lī bûr′tə sīd′), *n.* a destroyer of liberty. [f. LIBERTY + -CIDE[1]]

li·ber·ti·cide[2] (lī bûr′tə sīd′), *n.* destruction of liberty. [f. LIBERTY + -CIDE[2]] —**li·ber′ti·cid′al,** *adj.*

lib·er·tine (lĭb′ər tēn′), *n.* 1. one free from restraint or control. 2. one free from moral restraints. 3. a dissolute man. —*adj.* 4. characteristic of a libertine. 5. free from moral restraints; dissolute; licentious. [ME, t. L: m.s. *lībertīnus* freedman]

lib·er·tin·ism (lĭb′ər tēn ĭz′əm, -tĭn-), *n.* libertine practices or habits of life; licentiousness.

lib·er·ty (lĭb′ər tĭ), *n., pl.* **-ties.** 1. freedom from arbitrary or despotic government, or, often, from other rule or law than that of a self-governing community. 2. freedom from external or foreign rule, or independence. 3. freedom from control, interference, obligation, restriction, hampering conditions, etc.; power or right of doing, thinking, speaking, etc., according to choice. 4. freedom from captivity, confinement, or physical restraint: *the prisoner soon regained his liberty.* 5. leave granted to a sailor, esp. in the navy, to go ashore. 6. the freedom of, or right of frequenting or using a place, etc. 7. unwarranted or impertinent freedom in action or speech, or a form or instance of it. 8. at liberty, **a.** free from bondage, captivity, confinement, or restraint. **b.** unoccupied or disengaged. **c.** free, permitted, or privileged to do or be as specified. [ME *libertie*, t. OF: m. *liberte*, t. L: m.s. *lībertas*] —**Syn.** 4. See **freedom.**

liberty cap, a Phrygian cap used as a symbol of liberty (from the cap of this kind given to a freedman in ancient Rome at his manumission).

Liberty Ship, a U. S. merchant ship built in large numbers during World War II, carrying about 10,000 gross tons.

Li·bia (lē′byä), *n.* Italian name of **Libya** (def. 2).

li·bid·i·nous (lǐ bǐd′ə nəs), *adj.* full of lust; lustful; lewd. [ME *lybydynous*, t. L: m.s. *lībīdinōsus*] —**li·bid′i·nous·ly,** *adv.* —**li·bid′i·nous·ness,** *n.*

li·bi·do (lǐ bī′dō, -bē′dō), *n.* 1. *Psychoanal.* all of the instinctual energies and desires which are derived from the Id. 2. the innate actuating or impelling force in living beings; the vital impulse or "urge." [t. L: pleasure, longing] —**li·bid·i·nal** (lǐ bǐd′ə nəl), *adj.*

li·bra (lī′brə for 1; lē′brä for 2), n., pl. **-brae** (-brē) for 1, **-bras** (-bräs) for 2. **1.** the ancient Roman pound (containing 5053 grains). **2.** a Peruvian gold coin, now called a sol. [(def. 1) t. L; (def. 2) t. Sp., g. L]

Li·bra (lī′brə), n., gen. **-brae** (-brē). **1.** Astron. the Balance, a zodiacal constellation. **2.** the seventh sign of the zodiac. See diag. under **zodiac**. [t. L: pound, balance, level]

li·brar·i·an (lī brâr′ī ən), n. **1.** a person trained in library science and engaged in library service. **2.** an officer in charge of a library.

li·brar·i·an·ship (lī brâr′ī ən shĭp′), n. **1.** a profession concerned with organizing collections of books and related materials in libraries and servicing these resources to readers and others. **2.** the office or work of a librarian.

li·brar·y (lī′brĕr′ĭ, -brə rĭ, -brĭ), n., pl. **-braries. 1.** a place set apart to contain books and other literary material for reading, study, or reference, as a room, set of rooms, or building where books may be read or borrowed. **2.** a public body organizing and maintaining such an establishment: *the Library of Congress.* **3.** a commercial establishment lending books for a fixed charge. **4.** a collection of manuscripts, publications, and other materials for reading, study, or reference. **5.** a series of books of similar character, or alike in size, binding, etc., issued by a single publishing house. **6.** Brit. a ticket agency for theaters, etc. [ME *librarie*, t. L: m. *librārium* place to keep books]

library science, the body of knowledge and techniques utilized for well-organized library service.

li·bra·tion (lī brā′shən), n. Astron. a real or apparent oscillatory motion, esp. of the moon. [t. L: s. *librātio* balance, a moving from side to side]

li·bra·to·ry (lī′brə tōr′ĭ), adj. oscillatory.

li·bret·tist (lĭ brĕt′ĭst), n. the writer of a libretto.

li·bret·to (lĭ brĕt′ō; It. lē brĕt′tō), n., pl. **-tos, -ti** (-tē). **1.** the text or words of an opera or other extended musical composition. **2.** a book or booklet containing such a text. [t. It., dim. of *libro* book, g. L *liber*]

li·bri·form (lī′brə fôrm′), adj. Bot. having the form of or resembling liber. [f. LIB(E)R + -(I)FORM]

Lib·y·a (lĭb′ī ə). **1.** Ancient Geog. the part of N Africa W of Egypt. **2.** Italian, **Libia.** a territory in N Africa between Tunisia and Egypt: annexed by Italy, 1912. 817,376 pop. (1936); 679,400 sq. mi. Cap.: Tripoli.

Lib·y·an (lĭb′ī ən), adj. **1.** of or pertaining to Libya. —n. **2.** a native or inhabitant of Libya. **3.** Berber, esp. in its ancient form.

Libyan Desert, a part of the Sahara W of the Nile, in E Libya, W Egypt, and NW Anglo-Egyptian Sudan.

lice (līs), n. pl. of **louse.**

li·cence (lī′səns), n., v., **-cenced, -cencing.** license. — **li′cenc·er,** n.

li·cense (lī′səns), n., v., **-censed, -censing.** —n. **1.** formal permission or leave to do or not to do something. **2.** formal permission from a constituted authority to do something, as to carry on some business or profession, etc. **3.** a certificate of such permission; an official permit. **4.** freedom of action, speech, thought, etc., permitted or conceded. **5.** intentional deviation from rule, convention, or fact, as for the sake of literary or artistic effect: *poetic license.* **6.** excessive or undue freedom or liberty. **7.** licentiousness. —v.t. **8.** to grant authoritative permission or license to. [ME *licence*, t. OF, t. L: m.s. *licentia*] —**li′cens·a·ble,** adj. —**li′cens·er,** (in Law) **li′cen·sor,** n.

li·cen·see (lī′sən sē′), n. one to whom a license is granted. Also, **li′cen·cee′.**

li·cen·ti·ate (lī sĕn′shĭ ĭt, -āt′), n. **1.** one who has received a license, as from a university, to practice an art or profession. **2.** the holder of a certain university degree intermediate between that of bachelor and that of doctor, now confined chiefly to certain continental European universities. —**li·cen′ti·ate·ship′,** n.

li·cen·tious (lī sĕn′shəs), adj. **1.** sensually unbridled; libertine; lewd. **2.** unrestrained by law or morality; lawless; immoral. **3.** going beyond customary or proper bounds or limits. [t. L: m.s. *licentiōsus*] —**li·cen′tious·ly,** adv. —**li·cen′tious·ness,** n.

li·chee (lē′chē′), n. litchi.

li·chen (lī′kən), n. **1.** any one of the group, *Lichenes,* of the *Thallophyta,* compound plants (fungi in symbiotic union with algae) having a vegetative body (thallus) growing in greenish, gray, yellow, brown or blackish crustlike patches or bushlike forms on rocks, trees, etc. **2.** Pathol. any of various eruptive skin diseases. [t. L, t. Gk.: m. *leichēn*] —**li′chen·like′,** adj. —**li′chen·ous,** adj.

li·chen·in (lī′kən ĭn), n. Chem. a polysaccharide starch, $C_6H_{10}O_5$, a white gelatinous substance derived from certain mosses. [f. LICHEN + -IN²]

li·chen·oid (lī′kə noid′), adj. lichenlike.

li·chen·ol·o·gy (lī′kə nŏl′ə jĭ), n. the branch of botany that treats of lichens.

Lich·field (lĭch′fēld′), n. a town in central England, in Staffordshire: birthplace of Samuel Johnson. 9183 (1939).

lich gate (lĭch), (in England and elsewhere) a roofed gate to a churchyard, under which a bier is set down to await the coming of the clergyman. Also, **lych gate.** [f. *lich* (OE *līc,* c. D *lijk*) body, corpse + GATE]

li·chi (lē′chē′), n., pl. **-chis.** litchi.

lic·it (lĭs′ĭt), adj. permitted; lawful. [late ME, t. L: s. *licitus,* pp.] —**lic′it·ly,** adv.

lick (lĭk), v.t. **1.** to pass the tongue over the surface of (often fol. by *up, off, from,* etc.). **2.** to make by strokes of the tongue: *to lick the plate clean.* **3.** to pass or play lightly over, as waves or flames do. **4.** Colloq. to beat, thrash, or whip, as for punishment. **5.** Colloq. to overcome in a fight, war, etc.; defeat. **6.** Colloq. to outdo; surpass. —n. **7.** a stroke of the tongue over something. **8.** a small quantity. **9.** a place to which wild animals resort to lick salt occurring naturally there. **10.** Colloq. a blow. **11.** Colloq. a brief or brisk stroke of activity or endeavor. **12.** Colloq. speed. [ME *licke(n),* OE *liccian,* c. D *likken,* G *lecken;* akin to L *lingere*] —**lick′er,** n.

lick·er·ish (lĭk′ər ĭsh), adj. Archaic. **1.** eager for choice food. **2.** greedy. **3.** lustful. Also, **liquorish.** [earlier *lickerous* (influenced by *lick* and *liquor,* with substitution of suffix -ISH¹ for -OUS), ME *likerous,* repr. an AF var. of OF *lecheros,* der. *lecheor* gourmand, sensualist. See LECHER]

lick·ing (lĭk′ĭng), n. **1.** Colloq. a beating or thrashing. **2.** act of one who or that which licks.

lick·spit·tle (lĭk′spĭt′əl), n. an abject toady.

lic·o·rice (lĭk′ə rĭs, lĭk′rĭsh), n. **1.** a leguminous plant, *Glycyrrhiza glabra,* of Europe and Asia. **2.** the sweet-tasting dried root of this plant, or an extract made from it, used in medicine, confectionery, etc. **3.** any of various related or similar plants. Also, **liquorice, liquorish.** [ME *lycorys,* t. AF, t. LL: m.s. *liquiritia,* L *glycyrrhīza,* t. Gk.: m. *glykyrrhīza;* influenced by L *liquor* liquor]

lic·tor (lĭk′tər), n. (in ancient Rome) one of a body of attendants on certain magistrates, who preceded them carrying the fasces. [ME, t. L]

lid (lĭd), n. **1.** a movable piece, whether separate or hinged, for closing the opening of a vessel, box, etc.; a movable cover. **2.** an eyelid. **3.** (in mosses) a. the cover of the capsule; operculum. **b.** the upper section of a pyxidium. **4.** Slang. a hat. [ME; OE *hlid,* c. D and G *lid*] —**lid′ded,** adj.

Lid·dell Hart (lĭd′əl härt′), **Basil Henry,** born 1895, British writer on military science and affairs.

lid·less (lĭd′lĭs), adj. **1.** having no lid. **2.** (of eyes) having no lids. **3.** Poetic. vigilant.

Li·do (lē′dō; It. -dô), n. a chain of sandy islands in NE Italy, lying between the Lagoon of Venice and the Adriatic: fashionable beach resort.

lie¹ (lī), n., v., **lied, lying.** —n. **1.** a false statement made with intent to deceive; an intentional untruth; a falsehood. **2.** something intended or serving to convey a false impression. **3.** the charge or accusation of lying, a flat contradiction. **4. give the lie (to), a.** to charge with lying; contradict flatly. **b.** to imply or show to be false; belie. [ME; OE *lyge,* Icel. *lygi*] —v.i. **5.** to speak falsely or utter untruth knowingly, as with intent to deceive. **6.** to express what is false, or convey a false impression. **7.** to get (*out*) as of a difficulty, by lies. —v.t. **8.** to bring, put, etc., by lying: *to lie oneself out of a difficulty.* [ME *lien,* OE *lēogan,* c. Goth. *liugan*] —**Syn. 1.** See *falsehood.*

lie² (lī), v., **lay, lain, lying,** n. —v.i. **1.** to be in a recumbent or prostrate position, as on a bed or the ground; recline. **2.** to assume such a position (fol. by *down*): *to lie down on the ground.* **3.** to be buried (in a particular spot). **4.** to rest in a horizontal position; be stretched out or extended: *a book lying on the table.* **5.** to be or remain in a position or state of inactivity, subjection, restraint, concealment, etc.: *to lie in ambush.* **6.** to rest, press, or weigh (fol. by *on* or *upon*); *these things lie upon my mind.* **7.** to depend (fol. by *on* or *upon*). **8.** to be found, occur, or be (where specified): *the fault lies here.* **9.** to be placed or situated: *land lying along the coast.* **10.** to consist or be grounded (fol. by *in*): *the real remedy lies in education.* **11.** to be in or have a specified direction: *the trail from here lies to the west.* **12.** Law. to be sustainable or admissible, as an action or appeal. **13.** Archaic. to lodge; sojourn. **14.** lie in, to be confined in childbed. **15. lie to,** Naut. (of a ship) to lie comparatively stationary, usually with the head as near the wind as possible. —n. **16.** manner of lying; the relative position or direction in which something lies (the English say *lie of the land* where Americans say *lay of the land*). **17.** the place where a bird, beast, or fish is accustomed to lie or lurk. **18.** Golf. the ground position of the golf ball. [ME *lie(n), liggen,* OE *licgan,* c. D *liggen,* G *liegen,* Icel. *liggja,* Goth. *ligan*] —**Syn. 1.** LIE, LAY, often confused, are not synonyms. LIE, meaning "to recline or rest," does not require an object. Its principal parts, too, are irregular, and are therefore distinctive. LAY (originally *to cause to lie*), with its forms *laid, have laid, laying,* etc., means "to put or place." If "put" or "place" can be substituted in a contemplated sentence, the verb to use is LAY. Moreover, since one must always "put" or "place" *something,* the verb LAY is used only when there is a grammatical object to complete the sense. (It should be noticed, however, that the past tense of LIE is also spelled LAY.)

Lie (lē), n. **1. Jonas,** 1880–1940, U.S. painter, born in Norway. **2. Trygve Halvdan** (trĭg′və hälv′dän; Nor. trȳg′və), born 1896, Norwegian statesman: secretary general of United Nations since 1946.

Lie·big (lē′bĭkн; It. **Justus** (yŏŏs′tŏŏs), **Baron von** (fən), 1803–73, German chemist.

Lieb·knecht (lēp′knĕкнt), n. **Wilhelm** (vĭl′hĕlm), 1826–1900, German journalist and political leader.

ăct, āble, dâre, ärt; ĕbb, ēqual; ĭf, īce; hŏt, ōver, ôrder, oil, bŏŏk, ōōze, out; ŭp, ūse, ûrge; ə = a in alone; ch, chief; g, give; ng, ring; sh, shoe; th, thin; ᵺ, that; zh, vision.   See the full key on inside cover.

Liech·ten·stein (lĭk/tən stīn'; *Ger.* lēкн/tən shtīn'), *n.* a small principality in central Europe between Austria and Switzerland. 11,138 pop. (1941); 65 sq. mi. *Cap.:* Vaduz.

lied (lēd; *Ger.* lēt), *n.*, *pl.* **lieder** (lē/dər). *German.* a German song, lyric, or ballad. [G]

lie·der·kranz (lē/dər kränts/), *n.* **1. a.** a cheese mellower than Camembert but not as strong as Limburger. **b.** (*cap.*) a trademark for this cheese. **2.** a German choral society or singing club, esp. of men. [G: garland of songs]

lief (lēf), *adv.* **1.** Also, **lieve.** gladly; willingly. —*adj.* *Archaic.* **2.** willing. **3.** dear. [ME *leef*, OE *lēof*, c. G *lieb*]

liege (lēj), *n.* **1.** a lord entitled to allegiance and service. **2.** a vassal or subject, as of a ruler. —*adj.* **3.** entitled to, or owing, allegiance and service. **4.** pertaining to the relation between vassal and lord. **5.** loyal; faithful. [ME *lige*, t. OF: liege, free, exempt, g. LL *leticus*, der. *letus* free man, of Gmc. orig.]

Li·ège (lĭ äzh/; *Fr.* lyězh), *n.* a city in E Belgium, on the Meuse river: one of the first cities attacked in World War I. 157,880 (est. 1941).

liege·man (lēj/mən), *n.*, *pl.* **-men. 1.** a vassal; a subject. **2.** a faithful follower.

Lieg·nitz (lēg/nĭts), *n.* a city in SW Poland: formerly in Germany. 24,437 (1946). Polish, **Lignica.**

lien (lēn, lē/ən), *n.* a legal right to hold property or to have it sold or applied for payment of a claim. [t. F, g. L *ligāmen* band, tie]

li·en·ter·y (lī/ən tĕr/ĭ), *n.* *Pathol.* a form of diarrhea in which the food is discharged undigested or only partly digested. [t. ML: m.s. *lienteria*, t. Gk.: m. *leienteria*] —**li/en·ter/ic,** *adj.*

Li·e·pā·ja (lē/ĕ/pä yä), *n.* a seaport in the W Soviet Union, in the Latvian Republic, on the Baltic. 57,098 (1935). Russian, **Libava.** German, **Libau.**

li·er (lī/ər), *n.* one who lies (down, etc.).

li·erne (lĭ ûrn/), *n.* *Archit.* a short connecting rib in vaulting. [late ME, t. F, var. of *liorne.* See LIANA]

Lie·tu·va (lĭ/ĕ tōō/vä), *n.* Lithuanian name of **Lithuania.**

lieu (lōō), *n.* **1.** place; stead. **2. in lieu of,** instead of. [ME *liue*, t. F: m. *lieu*, g. L *locus* place]

Lieut., lieutenant.

lieu·ten·an·cy (lōō tĕn/ən sĭ), *n.*, *pl.* **-cies. 1.** the office, authority, incumbency, or jurisdiction of a lieutenant. **2.** lieutenants collectively.

lieu·ten·ant (lōō tĕn/ənt; *in Brit. use, except in the navy,* lĕf tĕn/ənt), *n.* **1.** *Mil.* a commissioned officer ranking next below a captain. **a. first lieutenant,** an officer ranking between a second lieutenant and a captain. **b. second lieutenant,** the commissioned officer of the lowest rank, ranking below a first lieutenant. **2.** *Nav.* a commissioned officer ranking next below a lieutenant commander. **a. lieutenant junior grade,** a commissioned officer ranking between an ensign and a lieutenant senior grade. **b. lieutenant senior grade,** an officer ranking between lieutenant junior grade and lieutenant commander. **3.** one who holds an office, civil or military, in subordination to a superior, for whom he acts. [ME *levetenant*, t. F: m. *lieutenant*, f. *lieu* (g. L *locus*) place + *tenant*, ppr. of *tenir* (g. L *tenēre*) hold]

lieutenant colonel, *Mil.* a commissioned officer ranking next below a colonel and next above a major.

lieutenant commander, *Nav.* an officer next in rank below a commander and next above a lieutenant, senior grade.

lieutenant general, *Mil.* an officer ranking next below a general and next above a major general.

lieutenant governor, 1. *U.S.* a State officer next in rank to the governor, whose place he takes in case of the latter's absence, disability, or death. **2.** *Brit.* a deputy governor.

lieve (lēv), *adv.* lief.

life (līf), *n.*, *pl.* **lives. 1.** the condition which distinguishes animals and plants from inorganic objects and dead organisms. The distinguishing manifestations of life are: growth through metabolism, reproduction, and the power of adaptation to environment through changes originating internally. **2.** (collectively) the distinguishing phenomena (esp. metabolism, growth, reproduction, and spontaneous adaptation to environment) of plants and animals, arising out of the energy relationships with protoplasm. **3.** the animate existence, or the term of animate existence, of an individual: *to risk one's life.* **4.** a corresponding state, existence, or principle of existence conceived as belonging to the soul: *eternal life.* **5.** the term of existence, activity, or effectiveness of something inanimate, as a machine or a lease. **6.** a living being: *several lives were lost.* **7.** living things collectively, whether animals or plants: *insect life.* **8.** course or mode of existence: *married life.* **9.** a biography: *a life of Churchill.* **10.** animation, liveliness: *a speech full of life.* **11.** that which makes or keeps alive; the vivifying or quickening principle. **12.** existence in the world of affairs, society, etc. **13.** one who or that which enlivens: *the life of the party.* **14.** effervescence or sparkle, as of wines. **15.** pungency or strong, sharp flavor, as of substances when fresh or in good condition. **16.** the living form or model as the subject or representation in art. [ME; OE *līf*, c. D *liff* body, G *leib*, Icel. *líf* life, body] —Syn. **10.** vivacity, sprightliness; spirit. —Ant. **10.** inertness, dullness.

life assurance, life insurance.

life belt, a beltlike life preserver.

life·blood (līf/blŭd/), *n.* **1.** the blood necessary to life. **2.** the element that vivifies or animates anything.

life·boat (līf/bōt/), *n.* a boat, provisioned and equipped for abandoning ship, carried in davits so it may be lowered quickly.

life buoy, a buoyant device (in various forms) for throwing, as from a vessel, to persons in the water, to enable them to keep afloat until rescued.

life cycle, the course of development from the fertilization of the egg to the production of a new generation of germ cells.

life expectancy, the probable life span of an individual or class of persons, determined statistically, and affected by such factors as heredity, physical condition, nutrition, occupation, etc.

life·guard (līf/gärd/), *n.* *U.S.* a man employed on a bathing beach to aid in case of accident to bathers.

life history, 1. *Biol.* the series of living phenomena exhibited by an organism in the course of its development from the egg to its adult state. **2.** a life cycle.

life insurance, a contract insuring payment of a specific sum of money to a named beneficiary, or to the insured's estate, upon the death of the assured or which provides for payment to the policyholder should he survive a specified period of time. Also, **life assurance.**

life·less (līf/lĭs), *adj.* **1.** not endowed with life: *lifeless matter.* **2.** destitute of living things: *a lifeless planet.* **3.** deprived of life, or dead: *lifeless bodies.* **4.** without animation, liveliness, or spirit: *lifeless performance.* **5.** insensible, as one in a faint. —**life/less·ly,** *adv.* —**life/less·ness,** *n.* —Syn. **1.** inanimate, inorganic. **3.** See dead. **4.** dull; inactive, inert, passive; sluggish, torpid; spiritless. —Ant. **1, 3.** living. **4.** lively.

life·like (līf/līk/), *adj.* resembling or simulating real life: *a lifelike picture.* —**life/like/ness,** *n.*

life line, 1. a line fired across a vessel by which a hawser for a breeches buoy may be hauled aboard. **2.** a line or rope for saving life, as one attached to a life boat. **3.** the line by which a diver is lowered and raised. **4.** any of several lines, which are anchored and used by bathers for support. **5.** a route over which supplies can be sent to an area otherwise isolated.

life·long (līf/lông/, -lŏng/), *adj.* lasting or continuing through life: *lifelong regret.*

life net, a strong net or the like held by firemen or others to catch persons jumping from a burning building.

life preserver, 1. a buoyant jacket, belt, or other like device for saving persons in the water from sinking and drowning. **2.** *Brit.* a weapon, esp. a short stick with a loaded head, used for self-defense; a blackjack.

lif·er (līf/fər), *n.* *Slang.* one sentenced to jail for life.

life·sav·er (līf/sā/vər), *n.* **1.** a person who rescues another from danger of death, esp. from drowning. **2.** a life guard. **3.** *Slang.* someone or something which saves one from trouble, embarrassment, etc. —**life/sav/ing,** *adj., n.*

life-size (līf/sīz/), *adj.* of the size of life or the living original: *life-size picture or statue.*

life span, the longest period over which the life of any plant or animal organism or species may extend, according to the available biological knowledge concerning it. Cf. **life expectancy.**

life·time (līf/tīm/), *n.* the time that one's life continues; one's term of life: *peace within our lifetime.*

life·work (līf/wûrk/), *n.* the work, labor, or task of a lifetime.

lift (līft), *v.t.* **1.** to move or bring (something) upward from the ground or other support to some higher position; hoist. **2.** to raise or direct upward: *to lift the hand, head, or eyes.* **3.** to hold up or display on high. **4.** to raise in rank, condition, estimation, etc.; elevate or exalt. **5.** to send up audibly or loudly by utterance: *to lift the voice.* **6.** *Colloq.* to steal; plagiarize. **7.** *U.S.* to pay off a mortgage, etc. **8.** *Golf.* to pick or take up. —*v.i.* **9.** to go up; give to upward pressure: *the lid won't lift.* **10.** to pull or strain in the effort to lift something: *to lift at a heavy weight.* **11.** to move upward or rise; rise and disperse, as clouds, fog, etc. **12.** to rise to view above the horizon when approached, as land seen from the sea. —*n.* **13.** act of lifting, raising, or rising: *the lift of a hand.* **14.** extent of rise, or distance through which anything is raised. **15.** lifting or raising force. **16.** the weight or load lifted. **17.** a helping upward or onward. **18.** a ride in a vehicle, given to help along a traveler on foot. **19.** exaltation or uplift, as in feeling. **20.** a device or apparatus for lifting. **21.** *Chiefly Brit.* an elevator, a dumbwaiter, or the like, in a building. **22.** a rise or elevation of ground. **23.** *Aeron.* the component of the force exerted by the air on an airfoil having a direction opposite to the force of gravity, and causing an aircraft to stay aloft. **24.** one of the layers of leather forming the heel of a boot or shoe. **25.** *Mining.* a slice or thickness (of ore) mined in one operation. [ME *lifte(n)*, t. Scand.; cf. Icel. *lypta* lift, der. *lopt* air, sky] —**lift/er,** *n.* —Syn. **1.** See raise.

lift pump, any pump which merely lifts or raises a liquid (distinguished from *force pump*).

lig·a·ment (līg/ə mənt), *n.*, *pl.* **ligaments, ligamenta** (līg/ə mĕn/tə). **1.** *Anat.* a band of tissue, usually white and fibrous, serving to connect bones, hold organs in

---

b., blend of, blended; c., cognate with; d., dialect, dialectal; der., derived from; f., formed from; g., going back to; m., modification of; r., replacing; s., stem of; t., taken from; ?, perhaps. See the full key on inside cover.

place, etc. **2.** a connecting tie; bond. [ME, t. L: s. *ligamentum* a tie, band]

lig·a·men·tous (lĭg′ə mĕn′təs), *adj.* pertaining to, of the nature of, or forming a ligament. Also, **lig·a·men·ta·ry** (lĭg′ə mĕn′tə rĭ).

li·gan (lī′gən), *n. Law.* lagan.

li·gate (lī′gāt), *v.t.*, **-gated, -gating.** to bind, as with a ligature; tie up, as a bleeding artery. [t. L: m.s. *ligātus*, pp.] —**li·ga′tion,** *n.*

lig·a·ture (lĭg′ə choor′, -chər), *n.*, *v.*, **-tured, -turing.** —*n.* **1.** act of binding or tying up. **2.** anything that serves for binding or tying up, as a band, bandage, or cord. **3.** a tie or bond. **4.** *Print. and Writing.* a stroke or bar connecting two letters. **5.** *Print.* a character or type combining two or more letters, as *fi, ffl.* **6.** *Music.* **a.** a slur. **b.** a group of notes connected by a slur. **7.** *Surg.* a thread or wire for constriction of blood vessels, etc., or for removing tumors by strangulation. —*v.t.* **8.** to bind with a ligature; tie up; ligate. [ME, t. LL: m.s. *ligātūra*, der. L *ligāre* bind]

light¹ (līt), *n.*, *adj.*, *v.*, **lighted** or **lit, lighting.** —*n.* **1.** that which makes things visible, or affords illumination: *all colors depend on light.* **2.** *Physics.* **a.** electromagnetic radiation to which the organs of sight react, ranging in wave length from about 4000 to 7700 angstrom units and propagated at a speed of about 186,300 miles per second. It is considered variously as a wave, corpuscular, or quantum phenomenon. Also called *luminous* or *radiant energy.* **b.** the sensation produced by it on the organs of sight. **c.** a similar form of radiant energy which does not affect the retina, as ultraviolet or infrared rays. **3.** an illuminating agent or source, as the sun, a lamp, or a beacon. **4.** the light, radiance, or illumination from a particular source: *the light of a candle.* **5.** the illumination from the sun, or daylight. **6.** daybreak or dawn. **7.** daytime. **8.** measure or supply of light; illumination: *the wall cuts off our light.* **9.** a particular light or illumination in which an object seen takes on a certain appearance: *viewing the portrait in various lights.* **10.** *Art.* **a.** the effect of light falling on an object or scene as represented in a picture. **b.** one of the brightest parts of a picture. **11.** the aspect in which a thing appears or is regarded: *this shows up in a favorable light.* **12.** a gleam or sparkle, as in the eyes. **13.** a means of igniting, as a spark, flame, match, or the like: *could you give me a light?* **14.** state of being visible, exposed to view, or revealed to public notice or knowledge: *to come to light.* **15.** a window, or a pane or compartment of a window. **16.** mental or spiritual illumination or enlightenment: *to throw light on a mystery.* **17.** (*pl.*) information, ideas, or mental capacities possessed: *to act according to one's lights.* **18.** a person who is an illuminating or shining example; a luminary. **19.** a lighthouse. **20.** *Archaic.* the eyesight. **21. see the light, a.** to come into existence. **b.** to be made public, or published, as a book. **c.** to accept or understand an idea. —*adj.* **22.** having light or illumination, rather than dark: *the lightest room in the entire house.* **23.** pale, whitish, or not deep or dark in color: *a light red.* —*v.t.* **24.** to set burning (a candle, lamp, pipe, for smoking, etc.); kindle (a fire); ignite (fuel, a match, etc.). **25.** to give light to; illuminate. **26.** to furnish with light or illumination. **27.** to make bright as with light or color (usually with *up*): *a huge room lighted up with candles.* **28.** to brighten (the face, etc.): *a smile lighted up her face.* **29.** to conduct with a light: *a candle to light you to bed.* —*v.i.* **30.** to take fire or become kindled. **31.** to become bright as with light or color: *the sky lights up at sunset.* **32.** to brighten with animation or joy, as the face, eyes, etc. (often fol. by *up*). [ME; OE *lēoht*, c. D and G *licht*; akin to Icel. *ljōs*, Goth. *liuhath*, also to L *lux* light, Gk. *leukós* light, bright]

light² (līt), *adj.* **1.** of little weight; not heavy: *a light load.* **2.** of little weight in proportion to bulk; of low specific gravity: *a light metal.* **3.** of less than the usual or average weight: *light clothing.* **4.** weighing less than the proper or standard amount: *to use light weights in trade.* **5.** of small amount, force, intensity, etc.: *a light vote, a light rain, light sleep.* **6.** easy to endure, deal with, or perform: *light taxes.* **7.** not profound, serious, or heavy: *light reading.* **8.** of little moment or importance; trivial: *the loss was no light matter.* **9.** easily digested, as food. **10.** not heavy or strong, as wine, etc. **11.** spongy or well leavened, as bread. **12.** porous or friable, as soil. **13.** slender or delicate in form or appearance: *a light, graceful figure.* **14.** airy or buoyant in movement: *light as air.* **15.** nimble or agile: *light fingers.* **16.** free from any burden of sorrow or care: *a light heart.* **17.** cheerful; gay: *a light laugh.* **18.** characterized by lack of proper seriousness; frivolous: *light conduct.* **19.** wanton. **20.** easily swayed or changing; volatile: *to be light of love.* **21.** dizzy; slightly delirious: *his head is light.* **22.** *Mil.* lightly armed or equipped: *light infantry.* **23.** laden or encumbered but slightly or not at all: *a ship sailing light.* **24.** adapted by small weight or slight build for small loads or swift movement: *light vessels.* **25.** (of wind) having a velocity up to 7 mi. per hour; having a Beaufort scale number of 1 (**light air**: 1–3 mi. per hour) or 2 (**light breeze**: 4–7 mi. per hour). **26.** *Phonet.* **a.** having a less than normally strong pronunciation, as of a vowel or syllable. **b.** (of *l* sounds) resembling a front vowel in quality: *French l is lighter than English l.* —*adv.* **27.** lightly. [ME; OE *lēoht, līht,* c. D *licht,* G *leicht*]

light³ (līt), *v.i.*, **lighted** or **lit, lighting.** **1.** to get down or descend as from a horse or a vehicle. **2.** to come to rest, as on a spot or thing; land. **3.** to come by chance, happen, or hit (fol. by *on* or *upon*): *to light on a clue.* **4.** to fall, as a stroke, weapon, vengeance, choice, etc., on a place or person. **5.** *Slang.* to jump on or attack (fol. by *into*). [ME *liht(en), light(en),* OE *līhtan* alight, orig. make light, relieve of a weight, der. *līht* LIGHT², adj.]

light·en¹ (lī′tən), *v.i.* **1.** to become lighter or less dark; brighten. **2.** to shine, gleam, or be bright. **3.** to flash as or like lightning. **4.** to reveal by light. **5.** to brighten (the face, eyes, etc.). **6.** to give light to; illuminate. —*v.t.* **7.** to flash (something) like lightning. [ME, f. LIGHT¹, adj. + -EN¹] —**light′en·er,** *n.*

light·en² (lī′tən), *v.t.* **1.** to make lighter; lessen the weight of (a load, etc.); reduce the load of (a ship, etc.). **2.** to make less burdensome; mitigate: *to lighten taxes.* **3.** to cheer or gladden. [ME, f. LIGHT², adj. + -EN¹]

light·er¹ (lī′tər), *n.* one who or that which lights. [ME; f. LIGHT¹, v. + -ER¹]

light·er² (lī′tər), *n.* **1.** a vessel, commonly a flat-bottomed unpowered barge, used in lightening or unloading and also in loading ships, or in transporting goods for short distances. —*v.t.* **2.** to convey in or as in a lighter. [ME, f. LIGHT², v. + -ER¹, or t. D: m. *lichter*]

light·er·age (lī′tər ĭj), *n.* **1.** the use of lighters. **2.** a fee paid for lighter service.

light·er-than-air (lī′tər thən âr′), *adj.* **1.** *Aeron.* of less specific gravity than the air. **2.** of or pertaining to such aircraft.

light·face (līt′fās′), *n. Print.* a type characterized by thin lines.

light·fin·gered (līt′fĭng′gərd). *adj.* having nimble fingers, esp. in picking pockets; thievish.

light-foot·ed (līt′fŏŏt′ĭd), *adj.* stepping lightly or nimbly. Also, *Poetic,* **light′-foot′.** —**light′-foot′ed·ly,** *adv.* —**light′-foot′ed·ness,** *n.*

light-head·ed (līt′hĕd′ĭd), *adj.* **1.** having or showing a frivolous or volatile disposition: *light-headed persons.* **2.** giddy, dizzy, or delirious. —**light′-head′ed·ly,** *adv.* —**light′-head′ed·ness,** *n.*

light-heart·ed (līt′här′tĭd), *adj.* carefree; cheerful; gay: *a light-hearted laugh.* —**light′-heart′ed·ly,** *adv.* —**light′-heart′ed·ness,** *n.*

light heavyweight, *Boxing.* a fighter whose weight is between 160 and 175 pounds.

light-horse·man (līt′hôrs′mən), *n.,* *pl.* **-men.** a light-armed cavalry soldier.

light·house (līt′hous′), *n.* a tower or other structure displaying a light or lights for the guidance of mariners.

light·ing (lī′tĭng), *n.* **1.** act of igniting or illuminating. **2.** arrangement or method of lights. **3.** the way light falls upon a face, object, etc., esp. in a picture.

light·ish (lī′tĭsh), *adj.* rather light, as in color.

light·less (līt′lĭs), *adj.* **1.** without light; receiving no light; dark. **2.** giving no light.

light·ly (līt′lĭ), *adv.* **1.** with little weight, force, intensity, etc.: *to press lightly on a bell.* **2.** to but a small amount or degree. **3.** easily; without trouble or effort: *lightly come, lightly go.* **4.** cheerfully: *to take bad news lightly.* **5.** frivolously: *to behave lightly.* **6.** without due consideration or reason (often with a negative): *an offer not lightly to be refused.* **7.** nimbly: *to leap lightly aside.* **8.** indifferently or slightingly: *to think lightly of one's achievements.* **9.** airily; buoyantly: *flags floating lig'tly.*

light-mind·ed (līt′mĭn′dĭd), *adj.* having or showing a light mind; characterized by levity; frivolous. —**light′-mind′ed·ly,** *adv.* —**light′-mind′ed·ness,** *n.*

light·ness¹ (līt′nĭs), *n.* **1.** state of being light, illuminated, or whitish. **2.** thin or pale coloration. [ME *lightnesse,* OE *līhtnes,* f. *līht* light, bright + *-nes* -NESS]

light·ness² (līt′nĭs), *n.* **1.** state or quality of being light in weight. **2.** light as to specific gravity: *the lightness of cork.* **3.** the quality of being agile, nimble, or graceful. **4.** lack of pressure or burdensomeness. **5.** gayness; cheerfulness. **6.** levity in actions, thought, or speech. [f. LIGHT², adj. + -NESS]

light·ning (līt′nĭng), *n.* **1.** a flashing of light, or a sudden illumination of the heavens, caused by the discharge of atmospheric electricity. [var. of *lightening,* f. LIGHT-EN¹, v. + -ING¹]

lightning arrester, a device preventing damage to radio, telephonic, or other electrical equipment from lightning or other high voltage currents, reducing the voltage of a surge applied to its terminals, interrupting follow current if present, and restoring itself to its original operating condition.

lightning bug, *U.S.* a firefly.

lightning rod, a rodlike conductor installed to divert atmospheric electricity away from a structure and protect the structure from lightning by providing a path to earth.

light-o′-love (līt′ə lŭv′), *n.* a wanton coquette.

light quantum, *Physics.* a photon.

lights (līts), *n.pl.* the lungs, esp. of sheep, pigs, etc.

light·ship (līt′shĭp′), *n.* a ship anchored in a specific location and displaying a light or lights for the guidance of mariners.

light·some¹ (līt′səm), *adj.* **1.** light, esp. in form, appearance, or movement; airy; buoyant; nimble. **2.** cheerful; gay. **3.** frivolous. [f. LIGHT² + -SOME¹] —**light′some·ly,** *adv.* —**light′some·ness,** *n.*

---

light·some[2] (līt/səm), *adj.* **1.** luminous. **2.** well-lighted or illuminated. [f. LIGHT[1] + -SOME[1]] —**light/-some·ness,** *n.*

lights out, *Chiefly Mil.* a signal that all or certain lights are to be extinguished.

light-struck (līt/strŭk/), *adj.* *Photog.* (of film, etc.) injured or fogged by accidental exposure to light.

light·weight (līt/wāt/), *adj.* **1.** light in weight. —*n.* **2.** one of less than average weight. **3.** *Colloq.* a person of little mental force or of slight influence or importance. **4.** a boxer or other contestant who weighs between 127 and 135 pounds.

light·wood (līt/wŏŏd/), *n.* **1.** wood used in lighting a fire. **2.** (in the southern U.S.) resinous pine wood.

light-year (līt/yĭr/), *n.* *Astron.* the distance traversed by light in one year (about 5,880,000,000,000 miles): used as a unit in measuring stellar distances.

lig·ne·ous (lĭg/nĭ əs), *adj.* of the nature of or resembling wood; woody. [t. L: m. *ligneus* wooden]

ligni-, var. of **ligno-.**

Lig·ni·ca (lĕg nĭ/tsä), *n.* Polish name of **Liegnitz.**

lig·ni·form (lĭg/nə fôrm/), *adj.* having the form of wood; resembling wood, as a variety of asbestos.

lig·ni·fy (lĭg/nə fī/), *v.,* **-fied, -fying.** —*v.t.* **1.** to convert into wood. —*v.i.* **2.** to become wood. —**lig/ni·fi·ca/tion,** *n.*

lig·nin (lĭg/nĭn), *n.* *Bot.* an organic substance which, with cellulose, forms the chief part of woody tissue.

lig·nite (lĭg/nīt), *n.* an imperfectly formed coal, usually dark-brown, and often having a distinct woody texture; brown coal. [t. F, der. L *lignum* wood. See -ITE[1]] —**lig·nit·ic** (lĭg nĭt/ĭk), *adj.*

ligno-, a word element meaning "wood." [comb. form repr. L *lignum*]

lig·no·cel·lu·lose (lĭg/nō sĕl/yə lōs/), *n.* any of various compounds of lignin and cellulose found in wood and other fibers.

lig·nose (lĭg/nōs), *n.* one of the constituents of lignin. [t. L: m.s. *lignōsus* woody]

lig·num vi·tae (lĭg/nəm vī/tē), **1.** the hard, extremely heavy wood of either of two species of guaiacum, *Guaiacum officinale* and *G. sanctum,* used for making pulleys, rulers, etc., and formerly thought to have great medicinal powers. **2.** either tree. **3.** any of various other trees with a similar hard wood. [NL: wood of life]

lig·ro·in (lĭg/rō ĭn), *n.* *Chem.* a petroleum ether. Also, **lig/ro·ine.**

lig·u·la (lĭg/yə lə), *n., pl.* **-lae** (-lē/), **-las. 1.** *Bot., Zool.* a tonguelike or strap-shaped part or organ. **2.** *Bot.* **a.** the membranous appendage projecting from the summit of the leaf sheath in many grasses. **b.** the blade formed by the gamopetalous corolla in the ray flowers, of numerous composite plants. Also, **lig·ule** (lĭg/ūl). [t. L: strap, var. of *lingula,* dim. of *lingua* tongue] —**lig/u·lar,** *adj.*

A. Ligula; B. Leaf blade; C. Leaf sheath; D. Stem

lig·u·late (lĭg/yə lĭt, -lāt/), *adj.* **1.** having or forming a ligula. **2.** strap-shaped.

lig·ure (lĭg/yŏŏr), *n.* an unidentified precious stone mentioned in the Bible. See Ex. 28:19. [ME *ligury,* t. LL: m.s. *ligūrius,* t. Gk.: m. *ligýrion* (used to render Heb. *leshem*)]

Li·gu·ri·a (lĭ gyŏŏr/ĭ ə), *n.* a department in NW Italy. 1,533,100 pop. (est. 1942); 2099 sq. mi. —**Li·gu/ri·an,** *adj., n.*

Ligurian Sea, a part of the Mediterranean between Corsica and the NW coast of Italy.

Li Hung-chang (lē/ hŏŏng/jäng/), 1823–1901, Chinese statesman.

lik·a·ble (lī/kə bəl), *adj.* such as to be liked; pleasing. Also, **likeable.** —**lik/a·ble·ness,** *adj.*

like[1] (līk), *adj.* (*Poetic.* **liker, likest**), *prep., adv., conj., n.* —*adj.* **1.** resembling (followed by a noun or pronoun): *he is just like his father.* **2.** characteristic of: *it would be like him to come without notice.* **3.** of the same form, appearance, kind, character, amount, etc.: *a like instance.* **4.** corresponding or agreeing in general or in some noticeable respect; similar; analogous: *drawing, painting, and other like arts.* **5.** bearing resemblance. **6.** giving promise or indication of: *it looks like rain.* **7.** disposed or inclined to (after *feel*): *to feel like going to bed.* **8.** *Archaic* or *Dial.* probable or likely. **9.** *Archaic, Dial.* or *Colloq.* likely to (do, be, etc). **10.** *Now Dial.* or *Colloq.* about to (to do, etc.). —*prep.* **11.** in like manner with; similarly to; in the manner characteristic of: *to work like a beaver.* —*adv.* **12.** *Colloq.* likely or probably: *like enough.* **13.** *Dial.* or *Slang.* as it were: *of a sudden like.* **14. in like manner,** *Archaic.* to a like extent or degree; equally, or alike. —*conj.* **15.** *Colloq.* like as, just as, or as. **16.** *Colloq.* as if: *he acted like he was afraid.* —*n.* **17.** something of a similar nature (prec. by *the*): *oranges, lemons, and the like.* **18.** a like person or thing, or like persons or things, a counterpart, match, or equal: *no one has seen his like in a long time.* [ME; OE *gelīc,* c. D *gelijk,* G *gleich,* Icel. *glīkr,* Goth. *galeiks* like, lit. of the same body, or form]

like[2] (līk), *v.,* **liked, liking,** *n.* —*v.t.* **1.** to take pleasure in, find agreeable to one's taste. **2.** to regard with favor, or have a kindly or friendly feeling for (a person, etc.). —*v.i.* **3.** to feel inclined, or wish: *come whenever you like.*

4. *Dial.* or *Colloq.* to come near (doing something). **5.** *Obs.* or *Archaic.* to suit the tastes or wishes. —*n.* **6.** (*usually pl.*) a favorable feeling; preference: *likes and dislikes.* [ME *like(n),* OE *līcian,* c. D *lijken,* Icel. *līka*]

-like, suffixal use of **like**[1], *adj.,* e.g., *childlike, lifelike, horselike,* sometimes hyphenated. —**Syn.** Cf. **-ish**[1].

like·a·ble (lī/kə bəl), *adj.* likable. —**like/a·ble·ness,** *n.*

like·li·hood (līk/lĭ hŏŏd/), *n.* **1.** state of being likely or probable; probability. **2.** a probability or chance of something: *there is a strong likelihood of his succeeding.* **3.** *Obs.* or *Archaic.* promising character, or promise. Also, **like/li·ness.**

like·ly (līk/lĭ), *adj.,* **-lier, -liest,** *adv.* —*adj.* **1.** probably or apparently going or destined (to do, be, etc.): *not likely to happen.* **2.** seeming like truth, fact, or certainty, or reasonably, to be believed or expected; probable; *a likely story.* **3.** apparently suitable: *a likely spot to build on.* **4.** promising: *a fine likely boy.* —*adv.* **5.** probably. [ME, t. Scand.; cf. Icel. *līkligr,* f. *līkr* LIKE[1], adj. + *-ligr* -LY]

—**Syn. 1.** LIKELY, APT, LIABLE are not alike in indicating probability; though APT is used colloquially, and LIABLE, mistakenly, in this sense. LIKELY is the only one of these words which means "probable" or "to be expected": *it is likely to rain today.* APT refers to a natural bent or inclination; if something is natural and easy, it is often probable; hence APT comes to be associated with LIKELY and to be used informally as a substitute for it: *he is apt at drawing, he is apt to do well at drawing.* LIABLE should not be used to mean "probable." When used with an infinitive, it may remind one of LIKELY: *he is liable to be arrested.* But the true meaning, susceptibility to something unpleasant, or exposure to risk, becomes evident when it is used with a prepositional phrase: *he is liable to arrest, liable to error.*

like-mind·ed (līk/mīn/dĭd), *adj.* having a like opinion, or purpose. —**like/-mind/ed·ness,** *n.*

lik·en (lī/kən), *v.t.* to represent as like; compare.

like·ness (līk/nĭs), *n.* **1.** a representation, picture, or image, esp. a portrait. **2.** the semblance or appearance of something: *to assume the likeness of a swan.* **3.** state or fact of being like.

like·wise (līk/wīz/), *adv.* **1.** moreover; also; too. **2.** in like manner. [abbr. of *in like wise.* See LIKE[1],-WISE, n.]

li·kin (lē/kĕn/), *n.* a Chinese provincial duty imposed on articles of trade in transit. [t. Chinese: f. *li* 1/1000 of an ounce + *kin* money]

lik·ing (lī/kĭng), *n.* **1.** preference, inclination, or favor. **2.** pleasure or taste: *much to his liking.* **3.** the state or feeling of one who likes. [ME; OE *līcung,* der. *līcian* please]

li·lac (lī/lək), *n.* **1.** any of the oleaceous shrubs constituting the genus *Syringa,* as *S. vulgaris,* the common garden lilac, with large clusters of fragrant purple or white flowers. **2.** pale reddish purple. [t. F (obs.), or t. Sp., t. Ar.: m. *līlak,* t. Pers., var. of *nīlak* bluish, der. *nīl* blue, indigo (Skt. *nīla* dark-blue). Cf. ANIL]

li·la·ceous (lī lā/shəs), *adj.* of or approaching the color lilac.

lil·i·a·ceous (lĭl/ĭ ā/shəs), *adj.* **1.** of or like the lily. **2.** belonging to the *Liliaceae,* or lily family of plants, sometimes subdivided in smaller units such as the *Melanthiaceae, Alliaceae, Convallariaceae, Smilacaceae, Trilliaceae,* etc. [t. LL: m. *liliāceus,* der. L *līlium* LILY]

lil·ied (lĭl/ĭd), *adj.* **1.** lilylike; white. **2.** abounding in lilies.

Lil·i·en·thal (lĭl/ĭ ən thôl/ *for 1;* lē/lē ən täl/ *for 2*), *n.* **1. David Ely,** born 1899, U.S. public administrator: chairman, U.S. Atomic Energy Commission 1947–1950. **2. Otto** (ôt/ō), 1848–96, German aeronautical engineer and inventor.

Lil·ith (lĭl/ĭth), *n.* **1.** *Bible and Talmudic Lit.* a female demon that dwells in deserted places and assaults children. **2.** *Jewish Legend.* Adam's first wife. [t. Heb., ult. from Akkadian]

Li·li·u·o·ka·la·ni (lē lē/ŏŏ ō kä lä/nē), *n.* **Lydia Kamekeha** (kä/mē kě/hä), 1838–1917, last queen of the Hawaiian Islands, 1891–93.

Lille (lēl), *n.* a city in N France. 188,871 (1946). Formerly, **Lisle.**

lil·li·bul·le·ro (lĭl/ĭ bə lĭr/ō), *n.* **1.** a part of the refrain to a song deriding the Irish Roman Catholics, popular in England during and after the Revolution of 1688. **2.** the song, or the tune to which it was sung.

Lil·li·put (lĭl/ĭ pŭt/, -pət), *n.* the imaginary country of Lilliput, inhabited by tiny people, described in Swift's *Gulliver's Travels.*

Lil·li·pu·tian (lĭl/ĭ pū/shən), *adj.* **1.** tiny; diminutive. —*n.* **2.** an inhabitant of Lilliput. **3.** a tiny being. **4.** a person of small intellect or importance.

lilt (lĭlt), *n.* **1.** rhythmic swing or cadence. **2.** a lilting song or tune. —*v.i., v.t.* **3.** to sing or play in a light, tripping, or rhythmic manner. [ME *lulte;* orig. obscure]

lil·y (lĭl/ĭ), *n., pl.* **lilies.** —*n.* **1.** any plant of the genus *Lilium,* comprising scaly-bulbed herbs with showy funnel-shaped or bell-shaped flowers of various colors, as *L. candidum* (**Madonna lily**), *L. longiflorum eximium* or *L. Harrisii* (once the common **Easter lily**), or *L. philadelphicum* (**Orangecup lily**). **2.** the flower or the bulb of such a plant. **3.** any of various related or similar plants or their flowers, as the Mariposa lily or the calla lily. **4.** fleur-de-lis. —*adj.* **5.** white as a lily. **6.** delicately fair. **7.** pure; unsullied. **8.** pale. [ME and OE *lilie,* t. L: m. *līlium,* t. Gk.: m. *leirion*] —**lil/y·like/,** *adj.*

lily iron, a harpoon whose head may be detached.

lil·y-liv·ered (lĭl'ĭ lĭv'ərd), *adj.* cowardly.

lily of the valley, *pl.* **lilies of the valley.** a stemless convallariaceous herb, *Convallaria majalis*, with a raceme of drooping, bell-shaped, fragrant white flowers.

lily pad, the large, floating leaf of a water lily.

Li·ma (lē'mə *for 1*; lī'mə *for 2*) *n.* 1. the capital of Peru, in the W part, near the Pacific coast. 533,645 (1940). 2. a city in NW Ohio. 50,246 (1950).

Li·ma bean (lī'mə), 1. a kind of bean, including several varieties of *Phaseolus limensis*, with a broad, flat edible seed. 2. the seed, much used for food.

lim·a·cine (lĭm'ə sīn', -sĭn, lī'mə-), *adj.* pertaining to, or having the characteristics of, the slugs. [f. s. L *līmax* slug, snail + -INE[1]]

limb[1] (lĭm), *n.* 1. a part or member of an animal body distinct from the head and trunk, as a leg, arm, or wing. 2. a large or main branch of a tree. 3. a projecting part or member: *the four limbs of a cross.* 4. a person or thing regarded as a part, member, branch, offshoot, or scion of something. 5. *Colloq.* an imp, young scamp, or mischievous child. 6. **out on a limb.** *U.S. Colloq.* at a great disadvantage. [ME and OE *lim*, c. Icel. *limr*] —**limbed** (lĭmd), *adj.* —**limb'less,** *adj.* —**Syn.** 1. See **member.** 2. See **branch.**

limb[2] (lĭm), *n.* 1. the edge of the disk of the sun, moon, or planet. 2. the graduated edge of a quadrant or similar instrument. 3. *Bot.* the upper spreading part of a gamopetalous corolla; the expanded portion of a petal, sepal, or leaf. 4. *Archery.* the upper or lower portion of a bow. [t. L: s. *limbus* border. Cf. LIMBUS and LIMBO]

lim·bate (lĭm'bāt), *adj.* *Bot., Zool.* bordered, as a flower in which one color is surrounded by an edging of another. [t. LL: m.s. *limbātus*, der. L *limbus* LIMB[2]]

lim·ber[1] (lĭm'bər), *adj.* 1. bending readily; flexible; pliant. 2. characterized by ease in bending the body; supple; lithe. —*v.i.* 3. to make oneself limber (fol. by *up*). —*v.t.* 4. to make limber. [see LIMP[2]] —**lim'ber·ly,** *adv.* —**lim'ber·ness,** *n.* —**Syn.** 1. See **flexible.**

lim·ber[2] (lĭm'bər), *Mil.* —*n.* 1. the detachable forepart of the carriage of a field gun, consisting of two wheels, an axle, a pole, etc. —*v.t., v.i.* 2. to attach the limber to (a gun), in preparation for moving away (usually fol. by *up*). [late ME, ? t. F: m. *limonière*]

lim·ber[3] (lĭm'bər), *n.* (*usually pl.*) *Naut.* one of a series of holes or channels for the passage of water to the pump well. [? t. F: alter. of *lumière* hole, lit. light]

lim·bic (lĭm'bĭk), *adj.* pertaining to or of the nature of a limbus or border; marginal.

lim·bo (lĭm'bō), *n.* 1. (*often cap.*) a supposed region on the border of hell or heaven, the abode after death of unbaptized infants (**limbo of infants**), or one serving as the temporary abode of the righteous who died before the coming of Christ (**limbo of the fathers or patriarchs**). 2. a place to which persons or things are regarded as being relegated when cast aside, forgotten, past, or out of date. 3. prison, jail, or confinement. [ME, t. L. abl. of *limbus* border, edge, ML limbo]

Lim·bourg (lăn boor'), *n.* See **Limburg.**

Lim·burg (lĭm'bûrg; *Du.* lĭm'bœrkн), *n.* medieval duchy in W Europe: now divided into provinces of **Limburg** in SE Netherlands and **Limbourg** in NE Belgium.

Lim·burg·er (lĭm'bûrg'ər), *n.* a soft variety of cheese of strong odor and flavor. Also, **Limburg cheese.**

lim·bus (lĭm'bəs), *n.*, *pl.* **-bi** (-bī). 1. limbo. 2. (in scientific or technical use) a border, edge, or limb. [t.L]

lime[1] (līm), *n.*, *v.*, **limed, liming.** —*n.* 1. the oxide of calcium, CaO, a white caustic solid (**quicklime** or **unslaked lime**) prepared by calcining limestone, etc., used in making mortar and cement. When treated with water it produces calcium hydroxide, $Ca(OH)_2$, or **slaked lime.** 2. any calcium compounds for improving crops on lime deficient soils. 3. birdlime. —*v.t.* 4. to treat (soil, etc.) with lime or compounds of calcium. 5. to smear (twigs, etc.) with birdlime. 6. to catch with, or as with, birdlime. [ME; OE *lim*, c. D *lijm*, G *leim*, L *līmus* slime; akin to LOAM]

lime[2] (līm), *n.* 1. the small, greenish-yellow, acid fruit of a tropical tree, *Citrus aurantifolia*, allied to the lemon. 2. the tree. [t. F, t. Sp.: m. *lima*; akin to LEMON]

lime[3] (līm), *n.* linden. [unexplained var. of obs. *line*, *lind*, ME and OE *lind*. See LINDEN]

lime burner, one who makes lime by burning or calcining limestone, etc.

Lime·house (līm'hous'), *n.* a district in the East End of London, noted for its squalor.

lime-kiln (līm'kĭl', -kĭln'), *n.* a kiln or furnace for making lime by calcining limestone or shells.

lime·light (līm'līt'), *n.* 1. a strong light thrown upon the stage to illuminate particular persons or objects. 2. the glare of public observation or notoriety.

li·men (lī'mĕn), *n.*, *pl.* **limens, limina** (lĭm'ə nə). *Psychol.* threshold (def. 4). [t. L]

lim·er·ick (lĭm'ər ĭk), *n.* a kind of humorous verse of five lines, in which the first and second lines rhyme with the fifth line, and the shorter third line rhymes with the shorter fourth. [named after *Limerick*, Ireland; orig., a song with refrain, "Will you come up to Limerick?"]

Lim·er·ick (lĭm'ər ĭk), *n.* 1. a county in SW Eire, in Munster. 142,211 pop. (est. 1943); 1037 sq. mi. 2. its county seat: a seaport at the head of the Shannon estuary. 42,070 (est. 1943).

Li·mes (lī'mēz; *Ger.* lē'mĕs), *n.* the Siegfried Line. [t. L: boundary]

lime·stone (līm'stōn'), *n.* a rock consisting wholly or chiefly of calcium carbonate, originating principally from the calcareous remains of organisms, and when heated yielding quick lime.

lime tree, (in the Old World) the linden or basswood.

lime twig, 1. a twig smeared with birdlime to catch birds. 2. a snare.

lime-wa·ter (līm'wô'tər, -wŏt'ər), *n.* 1. an aqueous solution of slaked lime, used medicinally and otherwise. 2. water containing naturally an unusual amount of calcium carbonate or calcium sulfate.

lim·ey (lī'mĭ), *n.*, *pl.* **-eys.** *Colloq.* a British sailor or ship (from the prescribed use of lime juice against scurvy).

li·mic·o·line (lī mĭk'ə lĭn', -lĭn), *adj.* shore-inhabiting; of or pertaining to numerous birds of the families *Charadriidae* (plovers) and *Scolopacidae* (sandpipers). [f. s. LL *līmicola* dweller in mud + -INE[1]]

lim·i·nal (lĭm'ə nəl, lī'mə-), *adj.* *Psychol.* of or pertaining to the limen. [f. s. L *līmen* threshold + -AL[1]]

lim·it (lĭm'ĭt), *n.* 1. the final or furthest bound or point as to extent, amount, continuance, procedure, etc.: *the limit of vision.* 2. a boundary or bound, as of a country, tract, district, etc. 3. *Obs.* an area or region within boundaries. 4. *Math.* (of a function) a number such that the value of the function can be made arbitrarily close to this number by restricting its argument to be sufficiently near the point at which the limit is to be taken. 5. *Games.* the maximum sum by which a bet may be raised at any one time. —*v.t.* 6. to restrict by or as by fixing limits (fol. by *to*): *to limit questions to 25 words.* 7. to confine or keep within limits: *to limit expenditures.* 8. *Obs. exc. Law.* to fix or assign definitely or specifically. [ME *lymyte*, t. OF: m. *limite*, t. L.: m.s. *līmes* boundary] —**lim'it·a·ble,** *adj.* —**lim'it·er,** *n.*

lim·i·tar·y (lĭm'ə tĕr'ĭ), *adj.* 1. of, pertaining to, or serving as a limit. 2. subject to limits; limited.

lim·i·ta·tion (lĭm'ə tā'shən), *n.* 1. that which limits; a limit or bound; a limiting condition or circumstance; restriction. 2. act of limiting. 3. state of being limited. 4. *Law.* the assignment, as by statute, of a period of time within which an action must be brought, or the period of time assigned: *a statute of limitations.*

lim·i·ta·tive (lĭm'ə tā'tĭv), *adj.* limiting; restrictive.

lim·it·ed (lĭm'ĭt ĭd), *adj.* 1. confined within limits; restricted, circumscribed, or narrow: *a limited space.* 2. restricted with reference to governing powers by limitations prescribed in a constitution: *a limited monarchy.* 3. *Chiefly Brit.* restricted as to amount of liability: *a limited company.* 4. (of railroad trains, buses, etc.) restricted as to number or class of passengers, time occupied in transit, etc. —*n.* 5. *U.S.* a limited train, bus, etc. —**lim'it·ed·ly,** *adv.* —**lim'it·ed·ness,** *n.*

limited edition, an edition of a book of which there is an announced limited number of copies available.

limited payment insurance, life insurance where increased premiums for a stipulated period of years cause the insurance to become full paid at an age short of the maturity date of the policy.

limited policy, *Insurance.* a policy which covers only certain types of losses within an area of risks.

lim·it·ing (lĭm'ĭt ĭng), *adj.* *Gram.* of the nature of a limiting adjective or a restrictive clause.

limiting adjective, *Gram.* (in English and some other languages) one of a small group of adjectives, which modifies the noun to which it is applied by restricting rather than describing or qualifying. *This*, *some*, *certain*, are limiting adjectives.

lim·it·less (lĭm'ĭt lĭs), *adj.* without limit; boundless.

limn (lĭm), *v.t.* 1. to represent in drawing or painting. 2. *Archaic.* to portray in words. [ME *lymne(n)*, var. of *lumine* illuminate, t. OF: m. *luminer*, ult. der. L *lūmen* light]

lim·nol·o·gy (lĭm nŏl'ə jĭ), *n.* the scientific study of bodies of fresh water, as lakes and ponds, with reference to their physical, geographical, biological, and other features. [f. s. Gk. *limnē* lake + -(o)LOGY]

Li·moges (lĭ mōzh'; *Fr.* lē môzh'), *n.* 1. a city in central France. 107,874 (1946). 2. Also, **Limoges ware.** a type of porcelain manufactured at Limoges.

lim·o·nene (lĭm'ə nēn'), *n.* *Chem.* a liquid terpene, $C_{10}H_{16}$, occurring in two optically different forms, the dextrorotatory form being present in the essential oils of lemon, orange, etc., and the levorotatory in Douglas fir needle oil. [f. s. NL *limonum* lemon + -ENE]

li·mo·nite (lī'mə nīt'), *n.* an important iron ore, a hydrated ferric oxide, $2Fe_2O_3·3H_2O$, varying in color from dark brown to yellow. [f. m. Gk. *leimōn* meadow + -ITE[1]] —**li·mo·nit·ic** (lī'mə nĭt'ĭk), *adj.*

Li·mou·sin (lē mōō zăn'), *n.* a former province in central France. *Cap.*: Limoges.

lim·ou·sine (lĭm'ə zēn', lĭm'ə zēn'), *n.* an automobile having a permanently enclosed compartment for from three to five persons, the roof of which projects forward over the driver's seat in front. [t. F, der. *Limousin*]

limp[1] (lĭmp), *v.i.* 1. to walk with a labored, jerky movement, as when lame. 2. to proceed in a lame or faulty manner: *his verse limps.* —*n.* 3. a lame movement or gait. [ME; cf. MHG *limphin* and OE *lemphealt* lame] —**limp'er,** *n.*

limp[2] (lĭmp), *adj.* **1.** lacking stiffness or firmness, as of substance, fiber, structure, or bodily frame: *a limp body.* **2.** without proper firmness, force, energy, etc., as of character. [akin to Icel. *limpa* indisposition] —**limp′ly**, *adv.* —**limp′ness**, *n.*

lim·pet (lĭm′pĭt), *n. Zool.* any of various marine gastropods with a low conical shell open beneath, found adhering to rocks, used for bait and sometimes for food. [ME *lempet*, OE *lempedu*, t. LL: m. *lamprēda* limpet, LAMPREY]

lim·pid (lĭm′pĭd), *adj.* **1.** clear, transparent, or pellucid, as water, crystal, air, etc. **2.** free from obscurity; lucid: *a limpid style.* [t. L: s. *limpidus*] —**lim·pid′i·ty**, **lim′pid·ness**, *n.* —**lim′pid·ly**, *adv.*

limp·kin (lĭmp′kĭn), *n.* a large, loud-voiced, wading bird, *Aramus guarauna*, intermediate in size and character between the cranes and the rails, which inhabits Florida, Central America, and the West Indies.

Lim·po·po (lĭm pō′pō), *n.* a river flowing from the Union of South Africa through S Mozambique into the Indian Ocean. ab. 1000 mi. Also, **Crocodile River.**

lim·u·loid (lĭm′yə loid′), *Zool.* —*adj.* **1.** resembling or pertaining to the horseshoe crabs, esp. to *Limulus.* —*n.* **2.** a horseshoe crab. [f. LIM-UL(US) + -OID]

lim·u·lus (lĭm′yə ləs), *n., pl.* **-li** (-lī′). a crab of the genus *Limulus;* a horseshoe crab. [t. NL, t. L: somewhat askew, dim. of *līmus* sidelong]

lim·y (lī′mĭ), *adj.*, **limier, limiest. 1.** consisting of, containing, or like lime. **2.** smeared with bird lime.

lin., 1. lineal. 2. linear.

lin·age (lī′nĭj), *n.* **1.** alignment. **2.** number of lines of written or printed matter covered. Also, **lineage.**

lin·al·o·öl (lĭ năl′ō ōl′, -ŏl′, lĭn′ə lōōl′), *n. Chem.* a colorless, liquid, unsaturated alcohol, $C_{10}H_{17}OH$, related to the terpenes, found in several essential oils. [f. Sp. *linalo(e)* fragrant Mexican wood + -OL[1]]

linch·pin (lĭnch′pĭn′), *n.* a pin inserted through the end of an axletree to keep the wheel on. [f. *linch*-, OE *lynis* linchpin + PIN]

Lin·coln (lĭng′kən), *n.* **1. Abraham,** 1809–65, 16th president of the U.S., 1861–65. **2. Benjamin,** 1733–1810, American Revolutionary general. **3.** the capital of Nebraska, in the SE part. 98,884 (1950). **4.** a city in E England. 66,090 (est. 1946). **5.** Lincolnshire. **6.** a large English variety of mutton sheep, with a heavy fleece of coarse, long wool.

Lincoln Park, a city in SE Michigan. 29,310 (1950).

Lin·coln·shire (lĭng′kən shĭr′, -shər), *n.* a county in E England. 645,000 pop. (est. 1946); 2663 sq. mi. *Co. seat:* Lincoln. Also, **Lincoln.**

Lin·coln's Inn (lĭng′kənz). See Inns of Court.

Lind (lĭnd), *n.* **Jenny** (jĕn′ĭ), (*Mrs. Otto Goldschmidt*) 1820–87, Swedish soprano singer.

Lind·bergh (lĭnd′bûrg, lĭn′-), *n.* **Charles Augustus,** born 1902, U.S. aviator who made the first nonstop solo flight from New York to Paris in 1927.

lin·den (lĭn′dən), *n.* any of the trees of the genus *Tilia,* which have yellowish or cream-colored flowers and more or less heart-shaped leaves, as *T. europaea,* a common European species, and *T. americana,* a large American species often cultivated as a shade tree. [n. use of obs. ME and OE adj. *linden* pertaining to a lime tree, f. *lind* lime tree (c. G *linde*) + -EN[2]]

Lin·den (lĭn′dən), *n.* a city in NE New Jersey, near Newark. 30,644 (1950).

Lind·es·nes (lĭn′dəs nĕs′), *n.* a cape at the S tip of Norway, on the North Sea. Also, **The Naze.**

Lind·say (lĭnd′zĭ, lĭn′-), *n.* **1. Howard,** born 1889, U.S. dramatist and actor. **2. (Nicholas) Vachel** (vā′chəl), 1879–1931, U.S. poet.

Lind·sey (lĭnd′sĭ), *n.* **Benjamin Barr,** 1869–1943, U.S. jurist and authority on juvenile delinquency.

line[1] (līn), *n., v.,* **lined, lining.** —*n.* **1.** a mark or stroke long in proportion to its breadth, made with a pen, pencil, tool, etc., on a surface. **2.** something resembling a traced line, as a band of color, a seam, a furrow, etc.: *lines of stratification in rock.* **3.** a furrow or wrinkle on the face, etc. **4.** something arranged along a line, esp. a straight line; a row or series: *a line of trees.* **5.** a row of written or printed letters, words, etc.: *a page of thirty lines.* **6.** a verse of poetry. **7.** (*pl.*) the spoken words of a drama, etc., or of an actor's part: *the hero forgot his lines.* **8.** a short written message: *a line from a friend.* **9.** an indication of demarcation; boundary; limit: *to draw a line between right and wrong.* **10.** a course of action, procedure, thought, etc.: *the Communist party line.* **11.** a course of direction; route: *the line of march.* **12.** a continuous series of persons in chronological succession, esp. in family descent: *a line of great kings.* **13.** (*pl.*) outline or contour: *a ship of fine lines.* **14.** (*pl.*) plan of construction, action, or procedure: *two books written on the same lines.* **15.** (*pl.*) *Colloq.* a certificate of marriage. **16.** (*pl.*) one's lot or portion. **17.** a department of activity; a kind of occupation or business. **18.** any transportation company or system. **19.** a system of public conveyances, as buses, steamers, etc.,

plying regularly between places. **20.** a strip of railroad track, a railroad, or a railroad system. **21.** *Elect.* a wire circuit connecting two or more pieces of electrical apparatus, esp. **a.** the wire or wires connecting points or stations in a telegraph or telephone system. **b.** the system itself. **22.** *Television.* one scanning line. **23.** *Fine Arts.* a mark from a crayon, pencil, brush, etc., in a work of graphic art, which defines the limits of the forms employed and is used either independently or in combination with modeling by means of shading. **24.** *Math.* a continuous extent of length, straight or curved, without breadth or thickness; the trace of a moving point. **25.** a straight line drawn from an observed object to the fovea of the eye. **26.** a circle of the terrestrial or of the celestial sphere: *the equinoctial line.* **27.** *Geog.* the equator (prec. by *the*). **28.** a supply of commercial goods of the same general class. **29.** *Law.* a limit defining one estate from another; the outline or boundary of a piece of real estate. **30.** *Bridge.* the line drawn between points counting towards game (**below the line**) and bonus, sometimes known as honor points (**above the line**). **31.** *Music.* one of the straight, horizontal, parallel strokes of the staff, or placed above or below it. **32.** *Mil.* **a.** a trench or rampart. **b.** a series of military fieldworks: *the Maginot line.* **33.** (*pl.*) a distribution of troops, sentries, etc., for the defense of a position or for an attack: *within the enemy's lines.* **34.** the line of arrangement of an army or of the ships of a fleet as drawn up ready for battle: *line of battle.* **35.** a body or formation of troops or ships drawn up abreast. **36.** the combatant forces of an army, as distinguished from the supply services, etc. **37.** the class of officers in charge of the fighting operations and the operating of warships. **38.** (formerly) the regular forces of an army or navy. **39.** a thread, string, cord, rope, or the like. **40.** a strong cord or slender rope. **41.** a cord, wire, or the like used for measuring or as a guide. **42.** *Naut.* **a.** a length of rope for any purpose. **b.** a pipe or hose: *a steam line.* **43.** a cord bearing a hook or hooks, used in fishing. **44.** *Football.* the players lined up even with the ball before a down begins, as distinguished from the backs. —*v.i.* **45.** to take a position in a line; range. —*v.t.* **46.** to bring into a line, or into line with others. **47.** to trace by or as by a line or lines; delineate: *to line streets.* **48.** to mark with a line or lines: *to line paper for writing.* **49.** to sketch verbally or in writing; outline. **50.** to arrange a line along: *to line a coast with colonies.* **51.** to form a line along: *people lined the streets.* **52.** to measure or test with a line. [ME *lyne, line,* OE *līne* line, row, rule (c. G *leine* cord, Icel. *lína* line, rope), t. L: m. *linea* thread, string, der. *līnum* flax] —**line′like′,** *adj.*

line[2] (līn), *v.t.,* **lined, lining. 1.** to cover or fit on the inner side with something: *walls lined with bookcases.* **2.** to provide with a layer of material applied to the inner side: *to line a coat with silk.* **3.** to furnish or fill: *to line one's pocket with money.* **4.** to reinforce the back of a book with glued fabric, paper, vellum, etc. [ME *lyne(n),* der. *line, n.,* flax, linen, OE *līn,* t. L: s. *līnum*]

lin·e·age[1] (lĭn′ĭj), *n.* **1.** lineal descent from an ancestor; ancestry or extraction. **2.** the line of descendants of a particular ancestor; family; race. [f. LINE(AL) + -AGE; r. ME *linage,* t. OF: m. *lignage,* der. *ligne* LINE[1]]

lin·e·age[2] (lī′nĭj), *n.* lineage.

lin·e·al (lĭn′ĭ əl), *adj.* **1.** being in the direct line, as a descendant, ancestor, etc., or descent, etc. **2.** of or transmitted by lineal descent. **3.** linear. [ME, t. LL: s. *lineālis,* der. L *linea* line] —**lin′e·al·ly,** *adv.*

lin·e·a·ment (lĭn′ĭ ə mənt), *n.* **1.** a feature or detail of a face, body or figure, considered with respect to its outline or contour. **2.** a distinctive characteristic. [ME, t. L: s. *lineāmentum*]

lin·e·ar (lĭn′ĭ ər), *adj.* **1.** extended in a line: *a linear series.* **2.** involving measurement in one dimension only; pertaining to length: *linear measure.* **3.** of or pertaining to a line or lines: *linear perspective.* **4.** consisting of or involving lines: *linear design.* **5.** looking like a line: *linear nebulae.* **6.** *Math.* of the first degree, as an equation. **7.** resembling a thread; narrow and elongated: *a linear leaf.* [t. L: s. *lineāris,* der. *linea* LINE[1]] —**lin′e·ar·ly,** *adv.*

linear perspective, that branch of perspective which regards only the apparent positions, magnitudes, and forms of objects delineated.

lin·e·ate (lĭn′ĭ ĭt, -āt′), *adj.* marked with lines, esp. longitudinal and more or less parallel lines. Also, **lin′e·at·ed.** [t. L: m.s. *līneātus,* pp. lined]   **Lin-ear leaf**

lin·e·a·tion (lĭn′ĭ ā′shən), *n.* **1.** a marking with or tracing by lines. **2.** a division into lines. **3.** a line; an outline. **4.** an arrangement or group of lines.

line breeding, *Genetics.* a form of mild inbreeding directed toward keeping the offspring closely related to a highly admired ancestor.

line engraving, 1. style of engraving that flourished about 1600–1850 in which the burin makes curved regular furrows that markedly swell and taper. **2.** a plate so engraved. **3.** a print or picture made from it.

line·man (līn′mən), *n., pl.* **-men. 1.** one who sets up or keeps in repair telegraph, telephone, or other wires. **2.** one who gives sights on line in surveying, etc. **3.** *Football.* a player who plays on the forward line.

lin·en (lĭn′ən), *n.* **1.** fabric woven from flax yarns. **2.** clothes or other articles made of linen cloth or some substitute, as cotton. **3.** yarn made of flax fiber. **4.** thread made of flax yarns. —*adj.* **5.** made of linen. [ME *lin(n)en*, n. and adj., OE *linnen*, *linen*, adj., f. *lin* linen + -EN²]

linen draper, *Brit.* a drygoods merchant.

linen paper, paper made from pure linen or from substitutes which produce a similar paper finish.

line of credit, the amount of credit a customer is authorized to utilize.

line officer, *Mil.* a captain or a lieutenant.

line of force, *Physics.* a line in a field of force whose direction at any point is that of the force in the field at that point.

lin·e·o·late (lĭn′ē ə lāt′), *adj.* *Zool., Bot.* marked with minute lines; finely lineate. Also, **lin′e·o·lat′ed.** [f. s. L *līneola*, dim. of *linea* LINE¹ + -ATE¹]

lin·er¹ (lī′nər), *n.* **1.** one of a commercial line of steamships or airplanes. **2.** one who or that which traces by or marks with lines. **3.** *Baseball.* a ball batted with much force nearly parallel to the ground. [f. LINE¹ + -ER¹]

lin·er² (lī′nər), *n.* **1.** one who fits or provides linings. **2.** something serving as a lining. [f. LINE² + -ER¹]

lines·man (līnz′mən), *n., pl.* **-men. 1.** a lineman, as on a telegraph line, etc. **2.** (in certain games) an official employed to watch the lines which mark out the field, etc. **3.** *Football.* **a.** an official who marks the distances gained and lost in the progress of the play and otherwise assists the referee and field judge. **b.** a forward.

line squall, *Meteorol.* (on a map) a more or less continuous line of thunderstorms or clouds of severe turbulence marking the position of an advancing cold front.

line-up (līn′ŭp′), *n.* **1.** a particular order or disposition of persons or things as lined up or drawn up for action: *the line-up of players in a football game.* **2.** the persons or things themselves: *the police line-up.* **3.** *Games.* the arrangement of the players. **4.** an organization of people, companies, etc., for some common purpose. Also, **line′up′.**

line·y (lī′nĭ), *adj.,* **linier, liniest.** liny.

ling¹ (lĭng), *n., pl.* **ling, lings. 1.** an elongated marine ganoid food fish, *Molva molva,* of Greenland and northern Europe. **2.** either of the two species of burbot, freshwater food fishes of northeastern North America, *Lota maculosa,* and northern Eurasia, *Lota lota.* **3.** any of various other fishes. [ME *ling, lenge;* akin to LONG¹]

ling² (lĭng), *n.* the common heather, *Calluna vulgaris.* [ME *lyng,* t. Scand.; cf. Icel. *lyng,* Dan. *lyng,* Sw. *ljung*]

-ling¹, suffix found in some nouns, often pejorative, denoting one concerned with (*hireling, underling*); also diminutive (*princeling, duckling*). [ME and OE]

-ling², an adverbial suffix expressing direction, position, state, etc., as in *darkling, flatling, groveling, sideling.* [ME and OE]

lin·ga (lĭng′gə), *n.* **1.** *Sanskrit Gram.* the masculine gender. **2.** (in popular Hindu mythology) a phallus, symbol of Siva. Also, **lin·gam** (lĭng′gəm). [f. Skt.: *linga* (stem), neut. nom. *lingam*]

Lin·ga·yén Gulf (lĭng′gä yēn′), a gulf on the NW coast of Luzon, in the Philippine Islands: focal point of the Japanese invasion of Luzon, Dec., 1941; reinvaded by U.S. forces, Jan., 1945.

lin·ger (lĭng′gər), *v.i.* **1.** to remain or stay on in a place longer than is usual or expected, as if from reluctance to leave it. **2.** to remain alive; continue or persist, although tending to cease or disappear: *hope lingers.* **3.** to dwell in contemplation, thought, or enjoyment. **4.** to be tardy in action; delay; dawdle. **5.** to walk slowly; to saunter along. —*v.t.* **6.** to drag out or protract. **7.** to pass (time, life, etc.) in a leisurely or a tedious manner (fol. by *away* or *out*). [ME *lenger,* freq. of *lenge,* OE *lengan* delay, der. *lang* LONG¹] —**lin′ger·er,** *n.*

lin·ge·rie (län′zhə rā′, lăn′zhə rē′, -jə-; *Fr.* lăNzh rē′), *n.* **1.** underwear or other garments of linen, cotton, silk, rayon, lace, etc., worn by women. **2.** linen goods in general. [t. F, der. *linger* linen draper, der. *linge* linen, g. L *līnum* flax]

lin·go (lĭng′gō), *n., pl.* **-goes.** (in contemptuous or humorous use) **1.** language. **2.** peculiar or unintelligible language. **3.** language or terminology peculiar to a particular field, group, etc. [t. Lingua Franca, t. Pr.: m. *lengo,* b. with It. *lingua,* both g. L *lingua* tongue]

lin·gua (lĭng′gwə), *n., pl.* **-guae** (-gwē). the tongue or a part like a tongue. [t. L]

lin·gua fran·ca (lĭng′gwə frăng′kə), **1.** a jargon which is widely used as an international auxiliary language. **2.** (*cap.*) the Italian-Provençal jargon formerly widely used in eastern Mediterranean ports. [t. It.: Frankish tongue]

lin·gual (lĭng′gwəl), *adj.* **1.** of or pertaining to the tongue or some tonguelike part. **2.** pertaining to languages. **3.** *Phonet.* articulated with the tongue, esp. with the tip of the tongue. [t. ML: s. *linguālis,* der. L *lingua* tongue, language] —**lin′gual·ly,** *adv.*

lin·gui·form (lĭng′gwə fôrm′), *adj.* tongue-shaped. [f. s. L *lingua* tongue + -(I)FORM]

lin·guist (lĭng′gwĭst), *n.* **1.** a person who is skilled in foreign languages; polyglot. **2.** a person who investigates linguistic phenomena. [f. s. L *lingua* language + -IST]

lin·guis·tic (lĭng gwĭs′tĭk), *adj.* **1.** of or belonging to language: *linguistic change.* **2.** of or pertaining to linguistics. Also, **lin·guis′ti·cal.** —**lin·guis′ti·cal·ly,** *adv.*

linguistic form, any meaningful unit of speech, as a sentence, phrase, word, suffix, etc.

lin·guis·tics (lĭng gwĭs′tĭks), *n.* the science of language, including among its fields phonetics, phonemics, morphology, and syntax, and having as principal divisions **descriptive linguistics,** which treats the classification and arrangement of the features of language, and **comparative (or historical) linguistics,** which treats linguistic change, especially by the study of data taken from various languages.

linguistic stock, 1. a parent language and all its derived dialects and languages. **2.** the people speaking any of these dialects or languages.

lin·gu·late (lĭng′gyə lāt′), *adj.* formed like a tongue; ligulate. [f. L: m.s. *lingulātus*]

lin·i·ment (lĭn′ə mənt), *n.* a liquid preparation, usually oily, for rubbing on or applying to the skin, as for sprains, bruises, etc. [ME, t. LL: s. *linimentum*]

li·nin (lī′nĭn), *n.* *Biol.* the substance forming the netlike structure which connects the chromatin granules in the nucleus of a cell. [f. s. L *līnum* flax + -IN²]

lin·ing (lī′nĭng), *n.* **1.** that with which something is lined; a layer of material on the inner side of something. **2.** *Bookbinding.* the material used to strengthen the back of a book after the sheets have been folded, backed, and sewed. **3.** act of one who or that which lines something. [ME, f. LINE² + -ING¹]

link¹ (lĭngk), *n.* **1.** one of the rings or separate pieces of which a chain is composed. **2.** anything serving to connect one part or thing with another; a bond or tie. **3.** a ring, loop, or the like: *a link of hair.* **4.** one of a number of sausages in a chain. **5.** one of the 100 wire rods forming the divisions of a surveyor's chain of 66 feet. **6.** the net or effective length of one of these links, used as a measuring unit, equal to 7.92 in. **7.** *Chem.* bond. **8.** *Elect.* fuse link. **9.** *Mach.* a rigid movable piece or rod connected with other parts by means of pivots or the like, for the purpose of transmitting motion. —*v.t., v.i.* **10.** to join by or as by a link or links; unite. [ME *link(e),* t. Scand.; cf. Sw. *länk,* c. OE *hlence* corselet] —Syn. **2.** See **bond.**

link² (lĭngk), *n.* *Obs.* a torch of tow and pitch or the like. [? special use of LINK¹]

link·age (lĭngk′ĭj), *n.* **1.** act of linking. **2.** state or manner of being linked. **3.** a system of links. **4.** *Biol.* the association or correlation of two or more hereditary characters because their genes are located on the same pair of chromosomes. This results in the parental combinations occurring more frequently in the progeny than the non-parental. A group of such linked genes is termed a **linkage group. 5.** *Mech.* any of various mathematical or drawing devices consisting of a combination of bars or pieces pivoted together so as to turn about one another, usually in parallel planes. **6.** *Elect.* the product of the magnetic flux passing through an electric circuit by the number of turns in the circuit.

link·boy (lĭngk′boi′), *n.* a boy hired to carry a torch for a pedestrian on dark streets. Also, **link·man** (lĭngk′mən).

linked (lĭngkt), *n.* *Biol.* exhibiting linkage.

link motion, a mechanism for operating a valve in a steam engine, one feature of which is a slotted bar (the **link**) in which slides a block (the **link block**) which terminates the rod working the valve.

links (lĭngks), *n.pl.* a golf course. [ME *lynkys* slopes, OE *hlincas,* pl. of *hlinc* rising ground, der. *hlin* (cf. *hlinian* lean, recline)]

Link trainer (lĭngk), *Aeron.* a ground training device used in instrument flight training.

link·work (lĭngk′wûrk′), *n.* **1.** a thing composed of links, as a chain. **2.** a linkage. **3.** *Mach.* a mechanism or device in which motion is transmitted by links.

Lin·lith·gow (lĭn lĭth′gō), *n.* former name of **West Lothian.**

Lin·nae·us (lĭ nē′əs), *n.* **Carolus** (kăr′ə ləs), (**Carl von Linné**) 1707–78, Swedish botanist.

Lin·ne·an (lĭ nē′ən), *adj.* **1.** of or pertaining to Linnaeus, who established the binomial system of scientific nomenclature. **2.** noting or pertaining to, a system of botanical classification introduced by him and formerly used, which was based mainly on the number or characteristics of the stamens and pistils. Also, **Lin·nae′an.**

lin·net (lĭn′ĭt), *n.* **1.** a small Old World fringilline song bird, *Carduelis cannabina.* **2.** any of various related birds, as the house finch, *Carpodacus mexicanus,* of North America (**California linnet**). [ME *linet,* OE *līnete,* short for *līnetwige,* lit., flax-plucker]

lin·o·le·ic acid (lĭn′ə lē′ĭk, lĭ nō′lĭ ĭk), *Chem.* an unsaturated fatty acid, $C_{17}H_{31}COOH$, occurring as a glyceride in drying oils such as linseed oil.

li·no·le·um (lĭ nō′lĭ əm), *n.* a floor covering formed by coating burlap or canvas with linseed oil, powdered cork, and rosin. Pigments are added to create the desired colors and patterns. [f. L: s. *līnum* flax + *oleum* oil]

lin·o·type (lī′nə tīp′), *n.* **1.** a kind of typesetting

ăct, āble, dâre, ärt; ĕbb, ēqual; ĭf, īce; hŏt, ōver, ôrder, oil, bŏŏk, ōōze, out; ŭp, ūse, ûrge; ə = a in alone; ch, chief; g, give; ng, ring; sh, shoe; th, thin; ŧh, that; zh, vision. See the full key on inside cover.

machine, with keyboard, which casts solid lines of type. **2.** (*cap.*) a trademark for this machine. [orig. phrase, "*line o' type*" line of type]

lin·sang (lĭn′săng), *n.* a catlike, viverrine carnivore with retractile claws and a long tail of the genus *Prionodon* (or *Linsang*) of the East Indies, or *Poina* of Africa. [t. Javanese]

lin·seed (lĭn′sēd′), *n.* flaxseed. [ME *linsed*, OE *līnsǣd*, f. *līn* flax + *sǣd* seed]

linseed oil, a drying oil obtained by pressing linseed, used in making paints, printing inks, linoleum, etc.

lin·sey-wool·sey (lĭn′zĭ wŏŏl′zĭ), *n.*, *pl.* **-seys. 1.** a coarse fabric woven from linen warp and coarse wool filling. **2.** any poor or incongruous mixture. [ME *lynsy wolsye*, f. *lynsy* (f. OE *līn* flax + ME *-sey*, meaningless suffix) + *wolsye* (f. *wull* wool + ME *-sey*)]

lin·stock (lĭn′stŏk′), *n.* a staff with one end forked to hold a match, formerly used in firing cannon. [earlier *lyntstock*, t. D: m. *lontstok*, f. *lont* match + *stok* stick]

lint (lĭnt), *n.* **1.** a soft material for dressing wounds, etc., procured by scraping or otherwise treating linen cloth. **2.** bits of thread. [ME *lyn(e)t* flax, ? OE *linwyrt*, f. *līn* flax + *wyrt* WORT]

lin·tel (lĭn′təl), *n.* a horizontal supporting member above an opening such as a window or a door. [ME *lyntel*, t. OF: m. *lintel*, *linter*, g. VL *līmitāle*, dim. of L *līmes* boundary, LIMIT]

lint·er (lĭn′tər), *n.* **1.** (*pl.*) short cotton fibers which stick to seeds after a first ginning. **2.** a machine which removes lint from cloth.

lint·y (lĭn′tĭ), *adj.*, **lintier, lintiest. 1.** full of or covered with lint. **2.** like lint: *linty bits on his coat.*

lin·y (lī′nĭ), *adj.*, **linier, liniest. 1.** full of or marked with lines. **2.** linelike. Also, **liney.**

Lin Yu·tang (lĭn′ ū′täng), Chinese author.

Linz (lĭnts), *n.* a city in N Austria: a port on the Danube. 129,022 (1939).

li·on (lī′ən), *n.* **1.** a large, grayish-tan cat, *Panthera Leo*, native in Africa and southern Asia, the male of which usually has a mane. **2.** this animal as the national emblem of Great Britain. **3.** a man of great strength, courage, etc. **4.** a person of note or celebrity who is much sought after. **5.** an object of interest or note. **6.** (*cap.*) *Astron.* Leo. [ME, t. OF, g. s. L *leo*, t. Gk.: m. *léōn*. Cf. LEO]

li·on·ess (lī′ən ĭs), *n.* a female lion.

li·on-heart·ed (lī′ən här′tĭd), *adj.* courageous; brave.

Lion and lioness, *Panthera Leo*
(3 ft. high at the shoulder, total length 8 to 9 ft.)

li·on·ize (lī′ə nīz′), *v.*, **-ized, -izing.** —*v.t.* **1.** to treat (a person) as a celebrity. **2.** to visit or exhibit the objects of interest of (a place). —*v.i.* **3.** to visit the objects of interest of a place. —**li′on·i·za′tion,** *n.*

Li·ons (lī′ənz), *n.* Gulf of, a wide bay of the Mediterranean off the S coast of France. Also, **Gulf of the Lion.** French, **Golfe du Li·on** (gôlf dy lē ôN′).

lip (lĭp), *n.*, *adj.*, *v.*, **lipped, lipping.** —*n.* **1.** either of the two fleshy parts or folds forming the margins of the mouth and performing an important function in speech. **2.** (*pl.*) these parts as organs of speech. **3.** speech as passing between them: *to hang on a person's lips.* **4.** *Slang.* impudent talk. **5.** a liplike part or structure. **6.** *Bot.* either of the two parts (**upper** and **lower**) into which the corolla or calyx of certain plants (esp. the mint family) is divided. **7.** *Zool.* **a.** labium. **b.** the outer or the inner margin of the aperture of a gastropod's shell. **8.** *Music.* the position and arrangement of lips and tongue in playing a wind instrument. **9.** any edge or rim. **10.** the margin or edge of a container. **11.** a projecting edge as of a pitcher. **12.** the edge of an opening or cavity, as of a canyon or a wound. **13.** the rim of the lateral hole in a flue pipe. **14.** the blade at the end of an auger bit which cuts the chip after it has been circumscribed by the spur. —*adj.* **15.** of or pertaining to the lips or a lip. **16.** pertaining to, characterized by, or made with the lips. **17.** superficial or insincere: *pay lip service.* —*v.t.* **18.** to touch with the lips. **19.** *Golf.* to hit the ball over the rim of (the hole). **20.** to utter, esp. softly. **21.** *Obs.* to kiss. —*v.i.* **22.** to use the lips in playing a musical wind instrument. [ME *lip(pe)*, OE *lippa*, c. D *lip*, G *lippe*; akin to L *labium*, *labrum*]

lip-, var. of lipo-, before vowels, as in *lipectomy.*

Lip·a·ri Islands (lĭp′ə rē′; *It.* lē′pä rē′), a group of volcanic islands N of Sicily, belonging to Italy. 17,195 pop. (1936); 44 sq. mi.

li·pase (lī′pās, lĭp′ās), *n.* *Biochem.* one of the ferments produced by the liver, pancreas, and other organs of the digestive system which converts oils or fats into fatty acids and glycerol. [f. LIP(O)- + -ASE]

lip·ec·to·my (lĭp pĕk′tə mĭ), *n.*, *pl.* **-mies.** *Surg.* an operation for removal of superficial fat, usually a pendulous abdominal apron of fat, in obese persons.

li·pid (lī′pĭd, lĭp′ĭd), *n.* *Biochem.* any of a group of organic compounds which make up the fats and other

esters which have analogous properties. They have a greasy feeling and are insoluble in water, but soluble in alcohols, ethers, and other fat solvents. Also, **li·pide** (lī′pĭd, lĭp′īd). [f. LIP- + -ID³]

Li Po (lē′ pō′; *Chin.* lē′ bō′), A.D. c700–762, Chinese poet. Also, **Li Tai Po.**

lipo-, *Chem.* a word element connoting fat as in *lipochrome*, a fat-soluble pigment. Also, **lip-.** [t. Gk., comb. form of *lípos* fat]

lip·oid (lĭp′oid, lī′poid), *adj.* **1.** fatty; resembling fat. —*n.* **2.** one of a group of fats or fatlike substances such as lecithins, steroids, waxes. [f. LIP- + -OID]

li·pol·y·sis (lĭ pŏl′ə sĭs), *n.* *Chem.* the resolution of fats into fatty acids and glycerol, as by lipase. [f. LIPO- + -LYSIS] —**lip·o·lyt·ic** (lĭp′ə lĭt′ĭk), *adj.*

li·po·ma (lĭ pō′mə), *n.*, *pl.* **-mata** (-mə tə), **-mas.** *Pathol.* a tumor made up of fat tissue; a fatty tumor. [f. LIP- + -OMA]

Lip·pe (lĭp′ə), *n.* a state in NW Germany. 187,220 pop. (1939); 469 sq. mi. *Cap.:* Detmold.

lipped (lĭpt), *adj.* **1.** having lips or a lip. **2.** *Bot.* labiate.

Lip·pi (lēp′pē), *n.* **1.** Filippino (fē′lēp pē′nô), 1457?–c1505, Italian painter. **2.** his father, **Fra Filippo** (frä fē′lēp′pô) or **Fra Lippo** (frä lēp′pô), c1406–69, Italian painter.

Lipp·mann (lĭp′mən), *n.* **Walter,** born 1889, U.S. journalist and author.

lip reading, the reading or understanding, as by a deaf person, of the movements of another's lips when forming words. —**lip reader.**

lip service, service with words only; insincere profession of devotion or good will.

lip·stick (lĭp′stĭk′), *n.* a stick or elongated piece of cosmetic preparation for heightening the color of the lips.

liq., **1.** liquid. **2.** liquor.

li·quate (lī′kwāt), *v.t.*, **-quated, -quating.** *Metall.* **1.** to heat (a metal, etc.) sufficiently to melt the more fusible portion and so separate a metal from impurities or other metals. **2.** to separate by such a fusion (often fol. by *out*). [t. L: m.s. *liquatus*, pp., made liquid, melted] —**li·qua·tion** (lī kwā′shən), *n.*

liq·ue·fac·tion (lĭk′wə făk′shən), *n.* the process of liquefying or making liquid.

liq·ue·fy (lĭk′wə fī′), *v.t.*, *v.i.*, **-fied, -fying.** to make or become liquid. [late ME, t. L: m.s. *liquefacere* make liquid] —**liq′ue·fi′a·ble,** *adj.* —**liq′ue·fi′er,** *n.*

li·ques·cent (lĭ kwĕs′ənt), *adj.* **1.** becoming liquid; melting. **2.** tending toward a liquid state. [t. L: s. *liquescens*, ppr.] —**li·ques′cence, li·ques′cen·cy,** *n.*

li·queur (lĭ kûr′ or, esp. Brit., -kyŏŏr′; Fr. lē kœr′), *n.* any of a class of alcoholic liquors, usually strong, sweet, and highly flavored, as chartreuse, curaçao, etc.; a cordial. [t. F. See LIQUOR]

liq·uid (lĭk′wĭd), *adj.* **1.** composed of molecules which move freely among themselves but do not tend to separate like those of gases; neither gaseous nor solid. **2.** of or pertaining to liquids: *liquid measure.* **3.** such as to flow like water. **4.** clear, transparent, or bright: *liquid eyes.* **5.** sounding smoothly or agreeably: *liquid tones.* **6.** in cash or easily convertible into cash: *liquid assets.* **7.** *Phonet.* palatal or palatalized, esp. referring to Spanish palatal *ll* and *ñ* as compared to *l, n.* —*n.* **8.** a liquid substance. **9.** *Phonet.* either *r* or *l.* [ME, t. L: s. *liquidus*] —**liq′uid·ly,** *adv.* —**liq′uid·ness,** *n.* —**Syn. 8.** LIQUID, FLUID agree in referring to that which is not solid. LIQUID commonly refers to substances such as water, oil, alcohol, and the like, which are neither solids nor gaseous: *water ceases to be a liquid when it is frozen or turned to steam.* FLUID is applied to anything that flows, whether liquid or gaseous: *pipes can carry fluids from place to place.*

liquid air, air in its liquid state; an intensely cold, transparent liquid.

liq·uid·am·bar (lĭk′wĭd ăm′bər; for genus -bär), *n.* **1.** any tree of the genus *Liquidambar*, as *L. Styraciflua*, a large American tree having star-shaped leaves and, in warm regions, exuding a fragrant yellowish balsamic liquid used in medicine. **2.** this liquid. See **storax** (def. 2). [t. NL, f. s. L *liquidus* LIQUID + ML *ambar* AMBER]

liq·ui·date (lĭk′wə dāt′), *v.*, **-dated, -dating.** —*v.t.* **1.** to settle or pay (a debt, etc.): *to liquidate a claim.* **2.** to reduce (accounts) to order; determine the amount of (indebtedness or damages). **3.** to convert into cash. **4.** *Slang.* to murder (a person). **5.** to break up, abolish, or do away with. —*v.i.* **6.** to liquidate debts or accounts; go into liquidation. [t. ML: m.s. *liquidātus*, pp., der. L *liquidus* LIQUID]

liq·ui·da·tion (lĭk′wə dā′shən), *n.* **1.** the process of realizing upon assets and of discharging liabilities in winding up the affairs of a business, estate, etc. **2.** the process of converting securities or commodities into cash for the purpose of taking profits or preventing losses. **3.** liquidated state.

liq·ui·da·tor (lĭk′wə dā′tər), *n.* a court-appointed receiver who directs the liquidation of a business.

liquid crystal, a liquid having different optical properties in different directions and other crystalline characteristics.

liquid fire, flaming petroleum or the like as employed against the enemy in warfare.

liquid glass, water glass (def. 5).

---

li·quid·i·ty (lĭkwĭd′ə tĭ), *n.* liquid state or quality.

liquid measure, the system of units of capacity ordinarily used in measuring liquid commodities, such as milk, oil, etc.: 4 gills = 1 pint; 2 pints = 1 quart; 4 quarts = 1 gallon.

liq·uor (lĭk′ər), *n.* **1.** a distilled or spirituous beverage (as brandy or whisky) as distinguished from a fermented beverage (as wine or beer). **2.** any liquid substance. **3.** *Pharm.* a solution of a medicinal substance in water. **4.** a solution of a substance, esp. a concentrated one used in the industrial arts. —*v.t.*, *v.i.* **5.** *Slang.* to furnish with or imbibe liquor or drink (often fol. by *up*). [t. L: liquid (state), liquid; r. ME *licur, licour,* t. OF]

liq·uo·rice[1] (lĭk′ə rĭs, lĭk′rĭsh), *n.* licorice. Also, **liq·uor·ish** (lĭk′ər ĭsh).

liq·uo·rice[2] (lĭk′ə rĭs), *adj.* *Archaic.* lickerish.

li·ra (lē′rä), *n., pl.* **lire** (lē′rĕ), **liras. 1.** the monetary unit and a coin of Italy, equal to 100 centesimi, present value .44 cent. **2.** a monetary unit and a gold coin of Turkey, equal to 100 piasters, and equivalent to about $7.45; the Turkish pound. [t. It., d. var. of *lib(b)ra,* g. L *lībra* pound]

lir·i·o·den·dron (lĭr′ĭ ō dĕn′drən), *n., pl.* **-drons, -dra** (-drə). a tree of the magnoliaceous genus *Liriodendron,* of which the tulip tree, *L. Tulipifera,* is native in eastern North America, is the chief representative (see **tulip tree**). [t. NL, f. m.s. Gk. *leírion* lily + *-dendron* -DEN-DRON]

lir·i·pipe (lĭr′ĭ pīp′), *n.* **1.** *Hist.* the tail or pendent part at the back of a hood, as in 14th and 15th century French costume. **2.** a scarf or tippet; a hood. [t. ML: m.s. *liripipium;* orig. unknown]

Lis·bon (lĭz′bən), *n.* a seaport in and the capital of Portugal, on the Tagus estuary. 694,389 (1940). Portuguese, **Lis·bo·a** (lēzh bô′ə).

lisle (līl), *n.* **1.** knit goods, as gloves or hose, made of lisle thread. —*adj.* **2.** made of lisle thread.

Lisle (līl; *Fr,* lēl), *n.* former name of Lille.

Lisle (lēl), *n.* **de. 1.** See **Leconte de Lisle. 2.** See **Rouget de Lisle.** Also, **l'Isle.**

lisle thread (līl), a smooth, hard-twisted linen or cotton thread. [orig., LISLE thread]

lisp (lĭsp), *n.* **1.** a speech defect consisting in pronouncing *s* and *z* like or nearly like the *th* sounds of *thin* and *this,* respectively. **2.** the act, habit, or sound of lisping. —*v.t., v.i.* **3.** to pronounce or speak with a lisp. [ME *wlispe, lipse,* OE *-wlispian* (in *āwlyspian*), der. *wlisp* lisping. Cf. D *lispen,* G *lispeln*] —**lisp′er,** *n.* —**lisp′ing·ly,** *adv.*

lis pen·dens (lĭs pĕn′dĕnz), *Latin.* **1.** a pending suit listed on the court docket. **2.** the rule placing property involved in litigation under the court's jurisdiction.

lis·some (lĭs′əm), *adj.* **1.** lithesome or lithe, esp. of body; limber or supple. **2.** agile or active. Also, **lis′som.** [var. of LITHESOME] —**lis′some·ness,** *n.*

lis·sot·ri·chous (lĭ sŏt′rə kəs), *adj.* *Anthropol.* having straight hair. [f. Gk. *lissó(s)* smooth + s. Gk. *thríx* hair + -OUS]

list[1] (lĭst), *n.* **1.** a record consisting of a series of names, words, or the like; a number of names of persons or things set down one after another. —*v.t.* **2.** to set down together in a list; to make a list of. **3.** to enter in a list with others. **4.** to enlist. **5.** to register a security on a stock exchange so that it may be traded there. —*v.i.* **6.** to enlist. [special use of LIST[2]. Cf. F *liste* (t. G) in same sense]
—**Syn. 1.** LIST, CATALOGUE, INVENTORY, ROLL, SCHEDULE imply a definite arrangement of items. LIST denotes a series of names, items, or figures arranged in a row or rows: *a list of groceries.* CATALOGUE adds the idea of alphabetical or other orderly arrangement, and, often, descriptive particulars and details: *a library catalogue.* An INVENTORY is a detailed descriptive list of property, stock, goods, or the like made for legal or business purposes: *a store inventory.* A ROLL is a list of names of members of some defined group often used to ascertain their presence or absence: *a class roll.* A SCHEDULE is a methodical (esp. official) list, often indicating the time or sequence of certain events: *a train schedule.*

list[2] (lĭst), *n.* **1.** a border or bordering strip of anything (now chiefly of cloth) or only of cloth). **2.** a selvage. **3.** selvages collectively. **4.** a strip of cloth or other material. **5.** a strip or band of any kind. **6.** a stripe of color. **7.** a division of the hair or beard. **8.** one of the ridges or furrows of earth thrown up by a lister. —*adj.* **9.** made of selvages or strips of cloth. —*v.t.* **10.** to border or edge. **11.** to arrange in strips, bands, or stripes. **12.** to apply list or strips of cloth to. **13.** to produce furrows and ridges in (land) by means of a lister. **14.** (in cotton culture) to prepare (land) for the crop by making alternating ridges and furrows. **15.** to shape (a block, stave, etc.) roughly by chopping. [ME *lyst(e),* OE *līste,* c. D *lijst,* G *leiste*]

list[3] (lĭst), *n.* **1.** a careening, or leaning to one side, as of a ship. —*v.i.* **2.** (of a ship) to careen; incline to one side: *the ship listed to starboard.* —*v.t.* **3.** to cause (a ship) to lean to one side: *the weight of the misplaced cargo listed the ship to starboard.* [orig. obscure]

list[4] (lĭst), *Archaic.* —*v.t.* **1.** to be pleasing to; please. **2.** to like or desire. —*v.i.* **3.** to like; wish; choose. [ME *luste(n),* OE *lystan,* c. G *lüsten,* Icel. *lysta*]

list[5] (lĭst), *Archaic or Poetic.* —*v.i.* **1.** to listen. —*v.t.* **2.** to listen to. [ME *list(e),* OE *hlystan,* der. *hlyst* hearing (c. Icel. *hlust* ear); akin to LISTEN]

lis·tel (lĭs′təl), *n.* *Archit.* a narrow list or fillet. [t. F, t. It.: m. *listello,* dim. of *lista,* t. OHG]

lis·ten (lĭs′ən), *v.t., v.i.* **1.** to give attention with the ear; attend closely for the purpose of hearing; give ear. **2.** to give heed; yield to advice. [ME *lis(t)ne(n),* OE *hlysnan,* c. MHG *lüsenen;* akin to LIST[5]] —**lis′ten·er,** *n.*
—**Syn. 1.** See **hear.**

listening post, 1. *Mil.* a post or position, as in advance of a defensive line, established for the purpose of listening to detect the enemy's movements. **2.** any position maintained to obtain information.

Lis·ter (lĭs′tər), *n.* **Joseph, 1st Baron,** 1827–1912, British surgeon: the first to use antiseptics in surgery.

list·er (lĭs′tər), *n.* a plow with a double moldboard used to prepare the soil for planting by producing furrows and ridges, and often fitted with attachments for dropping and covering the seeds. Also, **lister plow.** [see LIST[2] (def. 8)]

Lis·ter·ism (lĭs′tə rĭz′əm), *n.* an antiseptic method introduced by Lister, involving the spraying of the parts under operation with a carbolic acid solution.

list·less (lĭst′lĭs), *adj.* **1.** feeling no inclination toward or interest in anything. **2.** characterized by or indicating such feeling: *a listless mood.* [late ME, f. LIST[4] + -LESS] —**list′less·ly,** *adv.*

list·less·ness (lĭst′lĭs nĭs), *n.* **1.** state of being listless. **2.** languid inattention. —**Syn. 2.** See **indifference.**

list price, *Com.* price given in a catalogue.

lists (lĭsts), *n.pl.* **1.** the barriers enclosing the field of combat at a tournament. **2.** the enclosed field. **3.** any place or scene of combat. **4. enter the lists,** to take part in a contest or competition. [ME *liste* boundary, limit (same word as LIST[2])]

Liszt (lĭst), *n.* **Franz** (fränts), 1811–86, Hungarian composer and pianist.

lit[1] (lĭt), *v.* pt. and pp. of **light**[1] and **light**[3].

lit[2] (lĭt), *n.* litas.

lit., **1.** liter. **2.** literal. **3.** literally. **4.** literary. **5.** literature.

Li Tai Po (lē′ tī′ bô′), Li Po.

lit·a·ny (lĭt′ə nĭ), *n., pl.* **-nies. 1.** a ceremonial or liturgical form of prayer consisting of a series of invocations or supplications with responses which are the same for a number in succession. **2.** Also, **The Litany.** the "general supplication" of this form in the Book of Common Prayer. [t. LL: m.s. *litania,* t. Gk.: m. *litaneía* litany, an entreating; r. ME *letanie,* t. OF]

li·tas (lē′täs), *n., pl.* **-tai** (-tā), **-tu** (-tōō). the monetary unit and a coin of Lithuania equal to 10 cents in the U.S.

Lit. B., (L *Lit(t)erarum Baccalaureus*) Bachelor of Letters; Bachelor of Literature.

li·tchi (lē′chē′; *Chin.* lē′dzü′), *n., pl.* **-tchis. 1.** the fruit of a Chinese sapindaceous tree, *Litchi chinensis,* consisting of a thin, brittle shell, enclosing a sweet, jellylike pulp and a single seed. **2.** the tree. Also, **lichee, lichi.**

litchi nut, the brownish, dried litchi fruit. [t. Chinese]

Lit. D., (L *Lit(t)erarum Doctor*) Doctor of Letters; Doctor of Literature.

lit de jus·tice (lē də zhys tēs′), *French.* **1.** the sofa upon which the king of France sat when holding formal sessions of the parliament. **2.** such a session.

-lite, a word element used in names of minerals, fossils: *chrysolite, aerolite.* [t. F, t. Gk.: m. *líthos* stone. Cf. G *-lit(h)*]

li·ter (lē′tər), *n.* *Metric System.* a unit of capacity equal to the volume of one kilogram of water at its maximum density, or very nearly one cubic decimeter, and equivalent to 1.0567 U.S. liquid quarts. Also, *esp. Brit.,* **litre.** [t. F: m. *litre,* der. *litron* old measure of capacity, der. LL *lītra* measure for liquids, t. Gk.: pound]

lit·er·a·cy (lĭt′ər ə sĭ), *n.* state of being literate; possession of education.

literacy test, an examination to determine whether a person meets the literacy requirement for voting.

lit·er·al (lĭt′ər əl), *adj.* **1.** following the letter, or exact words, of the original, as a translation. **2.** (of persons) tending to construe words in the strict sense or in an unimaginative way; matter-of-fact; prosaic. **3.** in accordance with, involving, or being the natural or strict meaning of the words or word; not figurative or metaphorical: *the literal meaning of a word.* **4.** true to fact; not exaggerated: *a literal statement of conditions.* **5.** being actually such, without exaggeration or inaccuracy: *the literal extermination of a city.* **6.** of or pertaining to the letters of the alphabet. **7.** of the nature of letters. **8.** expressed by letters. **9.** affecting a letter or letters: *a literal error.* [ME, t. LL: m.s. *litterālis,* der. *littera* LET-TER] —**lit′er·al·ness,** *n.*

lit·er·al·ism (lĭt′ər əl ĭz′əm), *n.* **1.** adherence to the exact letter or the literal sense, as in translation or interpretation. **2.** a peculiarity of expression resulting from this. **3.** exact representation or portrayal, without idealization, as in art or literature. —**lit′er·al·ist,** *n., adj.* —**lit′er·al·is′tic,** *adj.*

lit·er·al·i·ty (lĭt′ər ăl′ə tĭ), *n., pl.* **-ties. 1.** the quality of being literal. **2.** a literal interpretation.

lit·er·al·ize (lĭt′ər ə līz′), *v.t.* **-ized, -izing.** to make literal; interpret literally. —**lit′er·al·iz′er,** *n.*

lit·er·al·ly (lĭt′ər ə lĭ), *adv.* **1.** in a literal manner; word for word: *to translate literally.* **2.** in the literal sense. **3.** actually; without exaggeration or inaccuracy: *the city was literally destroyed.*

lit·er·ar·y (lĭt'ə·rĕr'ĭ), *adj.* **1.** pertaining to or of the nature of books and writings, esp. those classed as literature: *literary history.* **2.** versed in or acquainted with literature. **3.** engaged in writing books, etc. or in literature as a profession: *a literary man.* —**lit'er·ar'i·ly,** *adv.* —**lit'er·ar'i·ness,** *n.*

lit·er·ate (lĭt'ər·ĭt), *adj.* **1.** able to read and write. **2.** having an education; educated. **3.** literary. —*n.* **4.** one who can read and write. **5.** a learned person. [ME *litterate,* t. L: m. *litterātus, līterātus* lettered]

lit·e·ra·ti (lĭt'ə·rä'tĭ, -rä'tĭ), *n.pl.* men of learning; men of letters; scholarly or literary people. [t. L]

lit·e·ra·tim (lĭt'ə·rā'tĭm), *adv.* letter for letter; literally. [t. ML, der. L *littera* LETTER[2]]

lit·er·a·ture (lĭt'ər·ə·chər, -chŏor', lĭt'rə-), *n.* **1.** writings in which expression and form, in connection with ideas of permanent and universal interest, are characteristic or essential features, as poetry, romance, history, biography, essays, etc.; belles-lettres. **2.** the entire body of writings of a specific language, period, people, subject, etc.: *the literature of England.* **3.** the writings dealing with a particular subject. **4.** the profession of a writer or author. **5.** literary work or production. **6.** *Colloq.* printed matter of any kind, as circulars or advertising matter. **7.** *Rare.* polite learning or literary culture. [ME *litterature,* t. F, t. L: m. *litterātūra* learning] —**Syn. 1.** LITERATURE, BELLES-LETTRES, LETTERS refer to artistic writings worthy of being remembered. In the broadest sense, LITERATURE includes any type of writings on any subject: *the literature of medicine;* usually, however, it means the body of artistic writings of a country or period which are characterized by beauty of expression and form and by universality or intellectual and emotional appeal: *English literature of the sixteenth century.* BELLES-LETTRES is a more specific term for such writings: *his talent is not for scholarship but for belles-lettres.* LETTERS (rare today outside of certain fixed phrases) refers to literature as a domain of study or creation: *a man of letters.*

lith-, a combining form meaning "stone." Also, **litho-.** [t. Gk., comb. form of *lithos*]

-lith, a noun termination meaning "stone," as in *acrolith, coccolith, megalith, nephrolith, paleolith:* sometimes occurring in words, as *batholith, laccolith,* that are variants of forms in *-lite.* Cf. **-lite.** [see LITH-]

Lith., **1.** Lithuania. **2.** Lithuanian.

lith., **1.** lithograph. **2.** lithography.

lith·arge (lĭth'ärj, lĭ·thärj'), *n.* lead monoxide, a yellow earthy substance used in compounding glass and glasses. [ME *litarge,* t. OF, t. L: m.s. *lithargyrus,* t. Gk.: m. *lithárgyros* spume of silver]

lithe (līth), *adj.* bending readily; pliant; limber; supple. Also, **lithe·some** (līth'səm). [ME *lith(e),* OE *līthe,* c. G *lind* mild] —**lithe'ly,** *adv.* —**lithe'ness,** *n.*

lith·i·a (lĭth'ĭ·ə, -yə), *n.* a white oxide of lithium, Li_2O. [t. NL, der. Gk. *líthos* stone]

lithia water, a mineral water, natural or artificial, containing lithium salts.

lith·ic (lĭth'ĭk), *adj.* **1.** pertaining to or consisting of stone. **2.** *Pathol.* pertaining to stony concretions, or calculi, formed within the body, esp. in the bladder. **3.** *Chem.* of, pertaining to, or containing lithium. [t. Gk.: m.s. *lithikós* of stones]

-lithic, an adjective suffix identical with **lithic,** used especially in archeology, e.g., *paleolithic.*

lith·i·um (lĭth'ĭ·əm), *n. Chem.* a soft silver-white metallic element (the lightest of all metals) occurring combined in certain minerals. *Symbol:* Li; *at. wt.:* 6.94; *at. no.:* 3; *sp. gr.:* 0.53 at 20°C. [t. NL, f. s. Gk. *líthos* stone + *-ium* -IUM; so named because found in minerals]

litho-, var. of **lith-,** before consonants, as in *lithography.*

litho., **1.** lithograph. **2.** lithography.

lithog., **1.** lithograph. **2.** lithography.

lith·o·graph (lĭth'ə·grăf', -gräf'), *n.* **1.** a print produced by lithography. —*v.t.* **2.** to produce or copy by lithography.

li·thog·ra·pher (lĭ·thŏg'rə·fər), *n.* a person who works at lithography.

li·thog·ra·phy (lĭ·thŏg'rə·fĭ), *n.* **1.** the art or process of producing a picture, writing, or the like, on a flat, specially prepared stone, with some greasy or oily substance, and of taking ink impressions from this as in ordinary printing. **2.** a similar process in which a substance other than stone, as aluminum or zinc, is used. —**lith·o·graph·ic** (lĭth'ə·grăf'ĭk), **lith'o·graph'i·cal,** *adj.* —**lith'o·graph'i·cal·ly,** *adv.*

lith·oid (lĭth'oid), *adj.* stonelike; stony. Also, **li·thoi'·dal.** [t. Gk.: m.s. *lithoeidēs.* See LITH-, -OID]

lithol., lithology.

li·thol·o·gy (lĭ·thŏl'ə·jĭ), *n.* **1.** the science dealing with the minute mineral characters of rock specimens. **2.** *Med.* the science treating of calculi in the human body. —**lith·o·log·ic** (lĭth'ə·lŏj'ĭk), **lith'o·log'i·cal,** *adj.*

lith·o·marge (lĭth'ə·märj'), *n.* kaolin clay in compact, massive, usually impure form. [t. NL: m. *lithomarga,* f. LITHO- + L *marga* marl]

lith·o·phyte (lĭth'ə·fīt'), *n.* **1.** *Zool.* a polyp with a hard or stony structure, as a coral. **2.** *Bot.* any plant growing on the surface of rocks. —**lith·o·phyt·ic** (lĭth'ə·fĭt'ĭk), *adj.*

lith·o·pone (lĭth'ə·pōn'), *n.* a white pigment consisting of zinc sulfide and barium sulfate, used in the manufacture of linoleum and rubber articles. [f. LITHO- + *-pone* (orig. uncert.)]

lith·o·sphere (lĭth'ə·sfĭr'), *n.* the crust of the earth.

li·thot·o·my (lĭ·thŏt'ə·mĭ), *n., pl.* **-mies.** *Surg.* the operation or art of cutting for stone in the urinary bladder. [t. LL: m.s. *lithotomia,* t. Gk. See LITHO-, -TOMY] —**lith·o·tom·ic** (lĭth'ə·tŏm'ĭk), *adj.* —**li·thot'o·mist,** *n.*

lith·o·trite (lĭth'ə·trīt'), *n. Surg.* an instrument for performing lithotrity.

li·thot·ri·ty (lĭ·thŏt'rə·tĭ), *n., pl.* **-ties.** *Surg.* the operation of crushing stone in the urinary bladder into particles that may be voided. [f. LITHO- + s. L *trītus,* pp., rubbed + -Y[3]]

Lith·u·a·ni·a (lĭth'o͞o·ā'nĭ·ə), *n.* a constituent republic of the Soviet Union, in the W part, on the Baltic: an independent state, 1918–40. 2,550,000 pop. (est. 1937); 24,100 sq. mi. *Cap.:* Vilna. Official name, **Lithuanian Soviet Socialist Republic.** Lithuanian, **Lietuva.** —**Lith'u·a'ni·an,** *adj., n.*

lith·y (lĭ'thĭ), *adj. Archaic.* lithe.

lit·i·ga·ble (lĭt'ə·gə·bəl), *adj.* subject to litigation.

lit·i·gant (lĭt'ə·gənt), *n.* **1.** one engaged in a lawsuit. —*adj.* **2.** litigating; engaged in a lawsuit. [t. L: s. *lītigans,* ppr.]

lit·i·gate (lĭt'ə·gāt'), *v.,* **-gated, -gating.** —*v.t.* **1.** to make the subject of a lawsuit; to contest at law. **2.** to dispute (a point, etc.). —*v.i.* **3.** to carry on a lawsuit. [t. L: m.s. *lītigātus,* pp.] —**lit'i·ga'tor,** *n.*

lit·i·ga·tion (lĭt'ə·gā'shən), *n.* **1.** the process of litigating. **2.** a lawsuit.

li·ti·gious (lĭ·tĭj'əs), *adj.* **1.** of or pertaining to litigation. **2.** overly inclined to litigate: *a litigious person.* [ME, t. L: m.s. *lītigiōsus* disputatious] —**li·ti'gious·ly,** *adv.* —**li·ti'gious·ness,** *n.*

lit·mus (lĭt'məs), *n.* a blue coloring matter obtained from certain lichens, esp. *Roccella tinctoria.* In alkaline solution litmus turns blue, in acid solution red; hence it is widely used as an indicator, esp. in the form of strips of paper impregnated with a solution of the coloring matter (**litmus paper**). [t. AF: m. *lytemoise,* of doubtful orig. Cf. MD *lijcmoes* (D *lakmoes*) lac pulp]

lit·o·ral (lĭt'ə·rəl), *adj.* littoral.

li·to·tes (lī'tə·tēz', -tō-, lī't·ə-), *n. Rhet.* a figure in which an affirmative is expressed by the negative of its contrary, as in *not bad at all.* [t. NL, t. Gk.: diminution]

li·tre (lē'tər), *n. Chiefly Brit.* liter.

Litt. B., (L *Lit(t)erarum Baccalaureus*) Bachelor of Letters; Bachelor of Literature.

Litt. D., (L *Lit(t)erarum Doctor*) Doctor of Letters; Doctor of Literature.

lit·ter (lĭt'ər), *n.* **1.** things scattered about; scattered rubbish. **2.** a condition of disorder or untidiness. **3.** a number of young brought forth at one birth. **4.** a framework of canvas stretched between two parallel bars, for the transportation of the sick and the wounded. **5.** a vehicle carried by men or animals, consisting of a bed or couch, often covered and curtained, suspended between shafts. **6.** straw, hay, etc., used as bedding for animals, or as a protection for plants. **7.** the rubbish of dead leaves and twigs scattered upon the floor of the forest. —*v.t.* **8.** to strew (a place) with scattered objects. **9.** to scatter (objects) in disorder. **10.** to be strewed about (a place) in disorder (fol. by *up*). **11.** to give birth to (young): said chiefly of animals. **12.** to supply (an animal) with litter for a bed. **13.** to use (straw, hay, etc.) for litter. **14.** to cover (a floor, etc.) with litter, or straw, hay, etc. —*v.i.* **15.** to give birth to a litter. [ME *litere,* t. AF, der. *lit* bed, g. L *lectus*] —**Syn. 3.** See **brood.**

lit·ter·y (lĭt'ər·ĭ), *adj.* of or covered with litter; untidy.

lit·te·rae hu·ma·ni·o·res (lĭt'ə·rē' hū·măn'ĭ·ŏr'ēz), (at Oxford and Cambridge universities) the faculty and school of classical languages and literature.

lit·té·ra·teur (lĭt'ə·rə·tûr'; *Fr.* lē·tĕ·rä·tœr'), *n.* a writer of literary works. Also, **lit'te·ra·teur'.** [t. F, t. L: m. *litterātor*]

lit·tle (lĭt'əl), *adj., less* or *lesser, least;* or *littler, littlest; adv., less, least; n.* —*adj.* **1.** small in size; not big or large: *a little child.* **2.** small in extent or duration; short; brief: *a little while.* **3.** small in number: *a little army.* **4.** small in amount or degree; not much: *little hope.* **5.** being such on a small scale: *little farmers.* **6.** small in force; weak: *a little voice.* **7.** small in consideration, dignity, consequence, etc.: *little discomforts.* **8.** mean, narrow, or illiberal: *a little mind.* **9.** endearingly small or considered as such: *Bless your little heart!* **10.** amusingly small or so considered: *I understand his little ways.* —*adv.* **11.** not at all (before a verb): *he little knows what awaits him.* **12.** in only a small amount or degree; not much: *a zeal little tempered by humanity.* —*n.* **13.** that which is little; a small amount, quantity, or degree. **14.** a short distance: *please step back a little.* **15.** a short time: *stay here a little.* [ME and OE *lytel,* c. D *luttel,* d. G *lützel*] —**lit'tle·ness,** *n.* —**Syn. 1-4.** LITTLE, DIMINUTIVE, MINUTE, SMALL refer to that which is not large or significant. LITTLE (the opposite of *big*) is very general, covering size, extent, number, quantity, amount, duration, or degree: *a little boy, a little time.* SMALL (the opposite of *large* and of *great*) can many times be used interchangeably with LITTLE, but is especially applied to what is limited or below the average in size: *small oranges.* DIMINUTIVE denotes (usually physical) size that is much less than the average or ordinary; it may suggest delicacy: *the baby's diminutive fingers, diminutive in size but autocratic in manner.* MINUTE suggests that which is so tiny that it is

---

b., blend of, blended; **c.,** cognate with; **d.,** dialect, dialectal; **der.,** derived from; **f.,** formed from; **g.,** going back to; **m.,** modification of; **r.,** replacing; **s.,** stem of; **t.,** taken from; **?,** perhaps.   See the full key on inside cover.

difficult to discern, or that which implies attentiveness to the smallest details: *a minute quantity, examination.*

Little America, the base of the Antarctic expeditions of Adm. Richard E. Byrd, on the Bay of Whales, S of the Ross Sea.

Little Bear, *Astron.* Ursa Minor.

Little Dipper, the Dipper (def. 3b).

Little Dog. See **dog** (def. 7).

Little Englander, *Brit.* one who believes that the best interests of England are served by attention to England itself rather than the Empire.

Little Fox, *Astron.* Vulpecula.

little hours, *Rom. Cath. Ch.* the hours of prime, tierce, sext, and none, and sometimes also vespers and complin.

lit·tle·neck (lĭt/əl něk/), *n.* the hard or round clam, *Venus mercenaria,* when young and small, but of a size suitable for eating raw on the half shell.

little office, *Rom. Cath. Ch.* a service, resembling the Breviary but shorter, in honor of the Virgin Mary.

Little Rock, the capital of Arkansas, in the central part, on the Arkansas river. 102,213 (1950).

Little Russia, an indefinite region in the SW Soviet Union, consisting mainly of the Ukraine, but sometimes including adjacent areas.

Little Russian, a member of a division of the Russian people dwelling in southern and southwestern Soviet Union in Europe and in adjoining regions. Cf. Ruthenian.

little theater, 1. a small theater, producing plays whose effectiveness would be lost in larger houses. 2. plays that would not draw audiences sufficient to fill the ordinary theater, esp. as produced by a movement in the early 20th century, identified with various theatrical experiments and innovations. 3. amateur theatricals.

lit·to·ral (lĭt/ə rəl), *adj.* 1. pertaining to the shore of a lake, sea, or ocean. [t. L: s. *littōrālis*] —*n.* 2. a littoral region. [t. It.: m. *littorale,* t. L: m.s. *littōrālis*]

li·tu (lē/tōō), *n.* pl. of **litas.**

li·tur·gi·cal (lĭ tûr/jə kəl), *adj.* 1. of or pertaining to public worship. 2. having to do with liturgies or forms of public worship. 3. of or pertaining to the liturgy or eucharistic service. 4. of or pertaining to liturgics. Also, **li·tur/gic.** [f. m.s. Gk. *leitourgikós* ministering + -AL[1]] —**li·tur/gi·cal·ly,** *adv.*

Liturgical Latin, the Latin characteristic of the liturgies of the Western Church.

li·tur·gics (lĭ tûr/jĭks), *n.* 1. the science or art of conducting public worship. 2. the study of liturgies.

lit·ur·gist (lĭt/ər jĭst), *n.* 1. an authority on liturgies. 2. a compiler of a liturgy or liturgies. 3. one who uses, or favors the use of, a liturgy.

lit·ur·gy (lĭt/ər jĭ), *n., pl.* **-gies.** 1. a form of public worship; a ritual. 2. a collection of formularies for public worship. 3. a particular arrangement of services. 4. a particular form or type of the eucharistic service. 5. the service of the eucharist, esp. in the Eastern Church. [t. ML: m.s. *līturgia,* t. Gk.: m. *leitourgíā* public duty. public worship]

Lit·vi·nov (lĭt vē/nôf), *n.* **Maksim Maksimovich** (mäk sēm/ mäk/sĭ mô/vĭch), 1876–1951, Soviet statesman.

liv·a·ble (lĭv/ə bəl), *adj.* 1. suitable for living in; habitable. 2. that can be lived with; companionable. 3. worth living; endurable. Also, **liveable.** —**liv/a·ble·ness,** *n.*

live[1] (lĭv), *v.,* **lived, living.** —*v.i.* 1. to have life, as an animal or plant; be alive; be capable of vital functions. 2. to continue to live; remain alive: *to live long.* 3. to continue in existence, operation, memory, etc.; last: *looks which lived in my memory.* 4. to escape destruction or remain afloat, as at sea. 5. to maintain life; rely for maintenance: *to live on one's income.* 6. to feed or subsist (fol. by *on* or *upon*): *to live on rice.* 7. to dwell or reside: *to live in a cottage.* 8. to pass life (as specified): *they lived happily ever after.* 9. to direct or regulate one's life: *to live by the golden rule.* 10. to experience or enjoy life to the full. 11. **live in** (or **out**), to reside at (or away from) the place of one's work. —*v.t.* 12. to pass (life): *to live a life of ease.* 13. to carry out or exhibit in one's life. 14. **live down,** to live so as to cause (something) to lose force or be forgotten: *to live down a mistake.* [ME *liv(i)en,* OE *lifian, libban,* c. D *leven,* G *leben*]

live[2] (līv), *adj.* 1. being in life, living, or alive: *live animals.* 2. of or pertaining to life of living beings: *live weight* (the weight of an animal while living). 3. characterized by or indicating the presence of living creatures. 4. full of life, energy, or activity. 5. *Colloq.* alert; wide-awake; up-to-date. 6. *Chiefly U.S. Colloq.* of present interest, as a question or issue. 7. burning or glowing, as a coal. 8. vivid or bright, as color. 9. flowing freely, as water. 10. fresh, as air. 11. loaded or unexploded, as a cartridge or shell. 12. *Elect.* electrically connected to a source of potential difference, or electrically charged so as to have a potential different from

that of earth: *a live wire.* 13. moving, or imparting motion or power: *the live center on a lathe.* 14. still in use, or to be used, as type set up or copy for printing. [aphetic var. of ALIVE, used attributively]

live·a·ble (līv/ə bəl), *adj.* livable.

live·bear·er (līv/bâr/ər), *n.* any fish of the viviparous family *Poeciliidae,* esp. those kept in home aquariums.

live center (līv). See **center** (def. 10a).

lived (līvd), *adj.* having life or a life (as specified): *long-lived.*

live-for·ev·er (līv/fər ĕv/ər), *n.* the garden variety of orpine, *Sedum purpureum,* an Old World succulent.

live·li·hood (līv/lĭ hŏŏd/), *n.* means of maintaining life; maintenance: *to gain a livelihood.* [earlier *liveliod,* metathetic var. of ME *livelod,* OE *līf(ge)lād* life-support (cf. LIFE, LODE, LOAD); current form influenced by obs. *livelihood* liveliness] —**Syn.** See **living.**

live load (līv), a load that is applied temporarily, as the weight of a train passing over a bridge.

live·long (lĭv/lông/, -lŏng/), *adj.* 1. long to the full extent (used of time): *the livelong day.* 2. whole or entire. [alter. (by assoc. with LIVE[1]) of *leeve long,* ME *leve longe* dear long. Cf. LIEF, LONG[1]]

live·ly (līv/lĭ), *adj.,* **-lier, -liest,** *adv.* —*adj.* 1. full or suggestive of life or vital energy; active, vigorous, or brisk: *a lively discussion.* 2. animated, spirited, vivacious, or sprightly: *a lively tune.* 3. eventful, stirring, or exciting: *a lively time.* 4. strong, keen, or distinct: *a lively recollection.* 5. striking, telling, or effective, as an expression or instance. 6. vivid or bright, as color or light. 7. sparkling, as wines. 8. fresh, as air. 9. rebounding quickly, as a baseball. 10. riding the sea buoyantly, as a ship. —*adv.* 11. with activity, vigor, or animation; briskly. [ME; OE *līflīc*] —**live/li·ly,** *adv.* —**live/li·ness,** *n.*

liv·en (lī/vən), *v.t.* 1. to put life into; rouse; cheer (often fol. by *up*). —*v.i.* 2. to become more lively; brighten (usually fol. by *up*). —**liv/en·er,** *n.*

live oak (līv), 1. an evergreen species of oak, *Quercus virginiana,* of the southern U.S., with a hard wood used in shipbuilding, etc. 2. any of various related trees.

liv·er[1] (lĭv/ər), *n.* (in man) a large, reddish-brown glandular organ (divided by fissures into five lobes) in the upper right-hand side of the abdominal cavity, secreting bile and performing various metabolic functions, and formerly supposed to be the seat of love, desire, courage, etc. 2. an organ in other animals similar to the human liver, often used as food. [ME; OE *lifer,* c. D *lever,* G *leber,* Icel. *lifr*]

liv·er[2] (lĭv/ər), *n.* 1. one who lives. 2. one who leads a life (as specified): *an evil liver.* 3. a dweller. [f. LIVE[1] + -ER[1]]

liver extract, an extract of mammalian liver, used to treat anemia.

liv·er·ied (lĭv/ər ĭd, lĭv/rĭd), *adj.* clad in livery, as servants.

liv·er·ish (lĭv/ər ĭsh), *adj.* 1. having one's liver out of order. 2. disagreeable as to disposition.

Liv·er·pool (lĭv/ər pōōl/), *n.* a seaport in W England on the Mersey estuary. 739,000 (est. 1946).

liv·er·wort (lĭv/ər wûrt/), *n.* any of the cryptogamic plants which belong to the class *Hepaticae,* comprising mosslike or thalloid plants which grow mostly on damp ground, in water, on tree trunks.

liv·er·wurst (lĭv/ər wûrst/, -wŏŏrst/), *n.* a sausage made with a large percentage of liver. [half trans., half adoption of G *leberwurst*]

liv·er·y (lĭv/ə rĭ, lĭv/rĭ), *n., pl.* **-eries.** 1. a distinctive dress, badge, or cognizance provided for retainers, as of a feudal lord. 2. a kind of uniform worn by servants, now only menservants, of a person or household. 3. a distinctive dress worn by an official, a member of a company or guild, etc. 4. Also, **livery company.** the entire guild company entitled to wear such livery. 5. characteristic dress, garb, or outward appearance: *the green livery of summer.* 6. the keep, or feeding, stabling, etc., of horses for pay. 7. *U.S.* a livery stable. 8. *Law.* an ancient method of conveying a freehold by formal delivery of possession. [ME *livere, levere,* t. AF: m. *liverē,* pp. of *livrer* deliver, g. L *līberāre* liberate]

liv·er·y·man (lĭv/ə rĭ mən, lĭv/rĭ-), *n., pl.* **-men.** 1. a keeper or an employee in a livery stable. 2. *Brit.* a member of a livery company. 3. *Obs.* a person in livery.

livery stable, a stable where horses and vehicles are cared for or let out for pay.

lives (līvz), *n.* pl. of **life.**

live steam (līv), 1. steam fresh from the boiler and at full pressure. 2. steam which has performed no work or only part of its work (distinguished from *dead steam* or *exhaust steam*).

live·stock (līv/stŏk/), *n.* the horses, cattle, sheep and other useful animals kept or raised on a farm or ranch.

live wire (līv), *Slang.* an energetic, alert person.

liv·id (lĭv/ĭd), *adj.* 1. having the discolored bluish appearance due to a bruise, to congestion of blood vessels, etc., as the flesh, face, hands, or nails. 2. dull blue; dark grayish blue. [t. L: s. *līvidus*] —**liv/id·ly,** *adv.* —**liv/id·ness, li·vid/i·ty,** *n.*

liv·ing (lĭv/ĭng), *adj.* 1. that lives; alive, or not dead. 2. in actual existence or use: *living languages.* 3. active; strong: *a living faith.* 4. burning or glowing, as a coal. 5. flowing freely, as water. 6. lifelike, as a picture.

ăct, āble, dâre, ärt; ĕbb, ēqual; ĭf, īce; hŏt, ōver, ôrder, oil, bŏŏk, ōōze, out; ŭp, ūse, ûrge; ə = a in alone; ch, chief; g, give; ng, ring; sh, shoe; th, thin; ŧħ, that; zh, vision. See the full key on inside cover.

7. of or pertaining to living beings: *within living memory.* **8.** pertaining to or sufficient for living: *living conditions.* —*n.* **9.** the act or condition of one who or that which lives: *living is very expensive these days.* **10.** manner or course of life: *holy living.* **11.** means of maintaining life; livelihood: *to earn one's living.* **12.** *Brit.* an ecclesiastical office or cure, as a rectory, with revenues attached. —**liv·ing·ly,** *adv.* —**liv·ing·ness,** *n.*
—**Syn. 1.** live, quick. **3.** lively, vigorous. **11.** LIVING, LIVELIHOOD, MAINTENANCE, SUPPORT refer, directly or indirectly, to what is earned or spent for subsistence. LIVING and LIVELIHOOD (a somewhat more formal word), both refer to what one earns to keep (oneself) alive, but are seldom interchangeable within the same phrase: *to earn one's living, to seek one's livelihood.* "To make a living" suggests making just enough to keep alive, and is particularly frequent in the negative: *you cannot make a living out of that.* "To make a livelihood out of something" suggests rather making a business of it: *to make a livelihood out of trapping foxes.* MAINTENANCE and SUPPORT refer usually to what is spent for the living of another: *to provide for the maintenance or support of someone.* MAINTENANCE occasionally refers to the allowance itself provided for livelihood: *they are entitled to a maintenance from this estate.*

living room, *U.S.* a room for general use; parlor.

Liv·ing·ston (lĭv′ĭng stən), *n.* **Robert R.,** 1746–1813, U.S. statesman and jurist.

Liv·ing·stone (lĭv′ĭng stən), *n.* **1. David,** 1813–73, Scottish missionary and explorer in Africa. **2.** a town in Northern Rhodesia, on the Zambesi river, near Victoria Falls: the former capital. ab. 10,000.

living wage, a wage on which it is possible for a wage earner to live according to minimum customary standards.

Li·vo·ni·a (lĭ vō′nĭ ə), *n.* a former Russian province on the Baltic: now part of the Latvian and Estonian republics of the Soviet Union.

Li·vor·no (lē vôr′nô), *n.* Italian name of **Leghorn.**

li·vre (lē′vər; *Fr.* lē′vr), *n.* an old French money of account and coin, with gradual reductions in value. [t. F, g. L *lībra* pound]

Liv·y (lĭv′ĭ), *n.* (*Titus Livius*) 59 B.C.–A.D. 17, Roman historian.

lix·iv·i·ate (lĭk sĭv′ĭ āt′), *v.t.,* **-ated, -ating.** to treat with a solvent; leach. [f. LIXIVI(UM) + -ATE[1]] —**lix·iv′·i·a′tion,** *n.*

lix·iv·i·um (lĭk sĭv′ĭ əm), *n., pl.* **lixiviums, lixivia** (lĭk sĭv′ĭ ə). **1.** the solution, containing alkaline, salts, obtained by leaching wood ashes with water; lye. **2.** any solution obtained by leaching. [t. L, prop. neut. of *lixīvius* made into lye]

liz·ard (lĭz′ərd), *n.* **1.** any of the typical lizards of the Old World family *Lacertidae,* esp. of the genus *Lacerta.* **2.** any reptile of the order *Sauria,* including also larger forms, the monitors, geckos, chameleons, and various limbless forms. **3.** *Slang.* an idler or lounger in places of social enjoyment, public resort, etc. **4. The Lizard,** Lizard Head. [ME *lesard,* t. OF (masc.), also *lesarde,* fem., t. L: m. *lacertus,* masc., *lacerta,* fem.]

Common lizard (Total length 5 or 6 in.)

lizard fish, any of various large-mouthed fishes (family *Synodontidae*) with lizardlike heads, esp. *Synodus foetens* of the Atlantic coast of the United States and *Synodus lucioceps* of California.

Lizard Head, a promontory in SW England, in Cornwall: the southernmost point in England. Also, **The Lizard.**

Lju·blja·na (lū′blyä′nä), *n.* a city in NW Yugoslavia: capital of Slovenia. 59,768 (1931). German, **Laibach.**

ll., 1. lines. **2.** (L *loco laudato*) in the place cited.

LL, 1. Late Latin. **2.** Low Latin. Also, **L.L.**

lla·ma (lä′mə), *n.* **1.** a woolly-haired South American ruminant of the genus *Lama* (or *Auchenia*), probably a domesticated variety of the guanaco, used as a beast of burden. **2.** the fine, soft fleece of the llama, combined with the wool for coating. [t. Sp., t. Kechua]

Llama, *Lama glama* (Ab. 3½ ft. high at the shoulder)

Llan·el·ly (lăn ĕl′ĭ), *n.* a seaport in S Wales. 34,560 (est. 1946).

lla·no (lä′nō; *Sp.* lyä′nō, yä′-), *n., pl.* **-nos** (-nōz; *Sp.* -nōs). (in Spanish America) an extensive grassy plain with few trees. [t. Sp.: a plain, as adj., flat, level, g. L *plānus* PLAIN[2]]

Lla·no Es·ta·ca·do (lä′nō ĕs′tə kä′dō), a large plateau in W Texas and SE New Mexico: cattle-grazing region. 1000–5000 ft. high. Also, **Staked Plain.**

LL.B., (L *Legum Baccalaureus*) Bachelor of Laws.

LL.D., (L *Legum Doctor*) Doctor of Laws.

LL.M., (L *Legum Magister*) Master of Laws.

Lloyd George (loid jôrj′), **David,** 1863–1945, British statesman; prime minister, 1916–22.

Lloyd's (loidz), *n.* an association at the Royal Exchange, London, comprising underwriters, merchants, ship-owners, and brokers, for the furtherance of commerce, esp. marine insurance. It has published since 1716 Lloyd's List, a periodical of shipping intelligence.

L.M., Licentiate in Midwifery.

lo (lō), *interj.* look! see! behold! [ME; OE *lā*! lo! behold! c. Goth. *laian* revile, Icel. *lā* scold]

loach (lōch), *n.* any of various slender European and Asiatic fresh-water fishes of the family *Cobitidae,* with several barbels about a small mouth: related to the minnows. [ME *loch,* t. OF: m. *loche;* ? of Celtic orig.]

load (lōd), *n.* **1.** that which is laid on or placed in anything for conveyance. **2.** the quantity that can be or usually is carried, as in a cart; this quantity taken as a unit of measure or weight. **3.** anything upborne or sustained: *the load of fruit on a tree.* **4.** something that weighs down or oppresses like a burden. **5.** the charge of a firearm. **6.** (*pl.*) *Colloq.* a great quantity or number: *loads of people.* **7.** the weight supported by a structure or part. **8.** *Elect.* the power delivered by a generator, motor, power station, or transformer (often fol. by *on*). **9.** *Mech.* the external resistance overcome by an engine, dynamo, or the like, under a given condition, measured by the power required. **10.** *Slang.* a sufficient quantity of liquor drunk to intoxicate. —*v.t.* **11.** to put a load on or in: *to load a cart.* **12.** to supply abundantly or excessively with something: *to load a person with gifts.* **13.** to weigh down, burden, or oppress. **14.** to add to the weight of, often fraudulently. **15. load dice,** to make dice heavier on one side than on the others by fraudulent means so as to cause them to fall with a particular face upward. **16.** *Insurance.* to add to the net premium. See **loading** (def. 5). **17.** to take on as a load: *a vessel loading coal.* **18.** to charge a firearm. —*v.i.* **19.** to put on or take on a load. **20.** to load a firearm. **21.** to become loaded. [ME *lode;* orig. the same word as LODE (OE *lād* way, course, carrying), but now differentiated in spelling and sense and assoc. with LADE] —**load′er,** *n.*
—**Syn. 4.** LOAD, BURDEN referred originally to something placed on a person or animal or put into a vehicle for conveyance; LOAD has still retained this concrete meaning, BURDEN has lost it, except in such fixed phrases as: *beast of burden,* and a *ship of 1500 tons burden* (carrying capacity). Both words have come to be used figuratively to refer to duties, cares, etc., that are oppressively heavy and this is now the main meaning of BURDEN: *you have taken a load off my mind; some children are a burden.*

load displacement, *Naut.* the amount of water displaced by a ship when it is fully loaded.

load factor, *Elect.* the ratio of the average load over a designated period of time to the peak load occurring in that period.

load·ing (lō′dĭng), *n.* **1.** act of one who or that which loads. **2.** that with which something is loaded, a load; a burden, a charge. **3.** *Elect.* the process of adding inductances to a telephone circuit, radio antenna, etc. **4.** the ratio of the gross weight of an airplane to engine power (**power loading**), wing span (**span loading**), or wing area (**wing loading**). **5.** *Insurance.* an addition to the net mathematical premium, to cover expenses and contingencies and to allow for a margin of safety.

loading coil, *Elect.* an inductance coil used to improve the characteristics of a transmission line.

load line, *Naut.* one of several lines on the side of a ship established by statue and indicating the maximum legal draft for a certain set of conditions.

load·star (lōd′stär′), *n.* lodestar.

load·stone (lōd′stōn′), *n.* **1.** a variety of magnetite which possesses magnetic polarity and attracts iron. **2.** a piece of this serving as a magnet. **3.** something that attracts. Also, **lodestone.** [f. LOAD + STONE]

loaf[1] (lōf), *n., pl.* **loaves** (lōvz). **1.** a portion of bread or cake baked in a mass of definite form. **2.** a shaped or molded mass of food, as of sugar, chopped meat, etc.: *a veal loaf.* [ME *lo(o)f,* OE *hlāf* loaf, bread, c. G *laib*]

loaf[2] (lōf), *v.i.* **1.** to lounge or saunter lazily and idly. **2.** to idle away time. —*v.t.* **3.** to idle (*away*): *to loaf one's life away.* [orig. obscure] —**loaf′er,** *n.*

loaf·er (lō′fər), *n.* a casual, moccasinlike shoe.

loam (lōm), *n.* **1.** a loose soil composed of clay and sand, esp. a kind containing organic matter and of great fertility. **2.** a mixture of clay, sand, straw, etc., used in making molds for founding, and in plastering walls, stopping holes, etc. **3.** *Archaic.* earth. **4.** *Obs.* clay. —*v.t.* **5.** to cover or stop with loam. [ME *lome, lam(e),* OE *lām,* c. D *leem,* G *lehm* loam, clay] —**loam′y,** *adj.*

loan (lōn), *n.* **1.** act of lending; a grant of the use of something temporarily: *the loan of a book.* **2.** something lent or furnished on condition of being returned, esp. a sum of money lent at interest. —*v.t.* **3.** to make a loan of; lend. **4.** *Chiefly U.S.* to lend (money) at interest. —*v.i.* **5.** *Chiefly U.S.* to make a loan or loans. [ME *lon(e), lan(e),* OE *lān,* appar. t. Scand.; cf. Icel. *lān,* c. OE *lǣn* loan, grant] —**loan′er,** *n.*

Lo·an·da (lō än′də), *n.* a seaport in and the capital of Angola, in SW Africa. 61,028 (1940). Also, **Sao Pau·lo de Lo·an·da** (soun pou′lōō də lō än′də).

loan office, 1. an office for making loans. **2.** a pawnbroker's shop. **3.** a public office for receiving subscriptions to a government loan.

loan shark, *U.S. Colloq.* one who loans money at an excessive rate of interest.

loan word, a word of one language adopted into another at any period in history. Examples: *wine* (into Old English from Latin), *blitz* (into Modern English from German). [trans. of G *lehnwort*]

---

b., blend of, blended;   **c.,** cognate with;   **d.,** dialect, dialectal;   **der.,** derived from;   **f.,** formed from;   **g.,** going back to;   **m.,** modification of;   **r.,** replacing;   **s.,** stem of;   **t.,** taken from;   **?,** perhaps.   See the full key on inside cover.

loath (lōth), *adj.* reluctant, averse, or unwilling. Also, **loth**. [ME *lothe*, OE *lāth* hostile, hateful, c. Icel. *leidhr* loathed, D *leed*, G *leid* sorrow] —**Syn.** See **reluctant**.

loathe (lōth), *v.t.* 1. to feel hatred, disgust, or intense aversion for. 2. to feel a physical disgust for (food, etc.). [ME *lothien*, OE *lāthian* be hateful, der. *lāth* LOATH] —**loath′er**, *n.* —**Syn.** 1. abominate, detest.

loath·ing (lō′thĭng), *n.* 1. strong dislike mingled with disgust; intense aversion. 2. physical disgust, as for food. —**loath′ing·ly**, *adv.* —**Syn.** 1. See **aversion**.

loath·ly[1] (lōth′lĭ; *older* lōth′lĭ), *adv.* reluctantly; unwillingly. [f. LOATH + -LY]

loath·ly[2] (lōth′lĭ), *adj.* *Literary.* loathsome. [f. LOATHE + -LY]

loath·some (lōth′səm), *adj.* 1. such as to excite loathing; hateful; disgusting. 2. physically disgusting; sickening. —**loath′some·ly**, *adv.* —**loath′some·ness**, *n.*

loaves (lōvz), *n.* pl. of **loaf**[1].

lob[1] (lŏb), *n.*, *v.*, **lobbed**, **lobbing**. —*n.* 1. *Tennis.* a ball struck high to the back of the opponent's court. 2. *Cricket.* a slow underhand ball. —*v.t.* 3. *Tennis.* to strike (a ball) high into the air to the back of the opponent's court. 4. *Cricket.* to bowl with a slow movement. —*v.i.* 5. *Tennis.* to lob a ball. [ME *lobbe* pollack; later, bumpkin; as v., move clumsily. See LUBBER]

lob[2] (lŏb), *n.* lobworm.

lo·bar (lō′bər), *adj.* of or pertaining to a lobe, as o the lungs: *lobar pneumonia.*

lo·bate (lō′bāt), *adj.* 1. having a lobe or lobes; lobed. 2. having the form of a lobe. 3. *Ornithol.* noting or pertaining to a foot in which the individual toes have membranous flaps along the sides. Also, **lo′bat·ed**. [t. NL: m.s. *lobātus*, der. LL *lobus* LOBE] —**lo′bate·ly**, *adv.*

lo·ba·tion (lō bā′shən), *n.* 1. lobate formation. 2. a lobe.

lob·by (lŏb′ĭ), *n.*, pl. **-bies**, *v.*, **-bied**, **-bying**. —*n.* 1. a corridor, vestibule, or entrance hall, as in a public building, often serving as an anteroom. 2. *Chiefly U.S.* the persons who frequent a legislative lobby or chamber, esp. to influence the members. —*v.i.* 3. to frequent the lobby of a legislative chamber to influence the members. 4. to solicit the votes of members of a legislative body in the lobby or elsewhere. —*v.t.* 5. *Chiefly U.S.* to influence (legislators), or urge or procure the passage of (a bill), by lobbying. [t. ML: m.s. *lobia, lobium* covered walk; from Gmc. (cf. G *laube* an arbor). See LODGE]

lob·by·ism (lŏb′ĭz′əm), *n.* *U.S.* 1. the system of lobbying. 2. the practices of those who lobby. —**lob′by·ist**, *n.*

lobe (lōb), *n.* 1. a roundish projection of division, as of an organ, a leaf, etc. 2. *Anat.* the soft pendulous lower part of the external ear. See diag. under **ear**. [t. F, t. LL: m.s. *lobus*, t. Gk.: m. *lobós*]

lobed (lōbd), *adj.* 1. having a lobe or lobes; lobate. 2. *Bot.* (of a leaf) having lobes or divisions extending less than halfway to the middle of the base.

lo·bel·ia (lō bēl′yə), *n.* any of the herbaceous plants constituting the genus *Lobelia*, comprising many species, both wild and cultivated, with blue, red, yellow, or white flowers. [t. NL, named after M. de *Lobel* (1538–1616), Flemish botanist, physician to James I of England]

lob·lol·ly (lŏb′lŏl′ĭ), *n.*, pl. **-lies**. 1. a pine, *Pinus Taeda*, of the southern U.S. 2. the wood of this tree. Also, **loblolly pine**.

loblolly boy, *Obs.* the attendant of a ship's surgeon.

lo·bo (lō′bō), *n.*, pl. **-bos**. *Zool.* a large gray wolf of the western U.S. [t. Sp., g. L *lupus* wolf]

lo·bot·o·my (lō bŏt′ə mĭ), *n.* *Surgery.* the cutting into or across a lobe of the brain, usually of the cerebrum, to alter brain function, especially in the treatment of mental disorders.

lob·scouse (lŏb′skous), *n.* *Prov. Eng. and Naut.* a stew of meat, potatoes, onions, shipbiscuit, etc.

lob·ster (lŏb′stər), *n.* 1. any of various large, edible, marine, stalk-eyed, decapod crustaceans of the family *Homaridae*, esp. of the genus *Homarus*. 2. the spiny lobster or rock lobster. 3. any of various similar crustaceans, as certain crawfishes. [ME *lobster*, *lop(i)ster*, OE *loppestre*, der. *loppe* spider (both creatures having many projecting parts). See LOP[1], -STER]

lobster pot, a trap in which lobsters are caught.

Lobster. *Homarus americanus*

lob·ule (lŏb′ūl), *n.* 1. a small lobe. 2. a subdivision of a lobe. [t. NL: m.s. *lobulus*, dim. of LL *lobus* LOBE] —**lob′u·lar**, *adj.*

lob·worm (lŏb′wûrm′), *n.* the lugworm. Also, **lob**.

lo·cal (lō′kəl), *adj.* 1. pertaining to or characterized by place, or position in space: *local situation.* 2. pertaining to, characteristic of, or restricted to a particular place or particular places: *a local custom.* 3. pertaining to a town or a small district rather than the entire state or country. 4. pertaining to or affecting a particular part or particular parts, as of a system or object: *a local disease.* 5. stopping at all stations: *a local train.* —*n.* 6. a local train. 7. a newspaper item of local interest. 8. a local branch of a trade union, fraternity, etc. [ME, t. LL: s. *locālis*, der. L *locus* place]

local color, 1. distinctive characteristics or peculiarities of a place or period as represented in literature, drama, etc., or observed in reality. 2. the natural color of any particular object or part in a picture.

lo·cale (lō kāl′, -käl′), *n.* a place or locality, esp. with reference to events or circumstances connected with it. [t. F: m. *local*, n. use of adj. See LOCAL, adj.]

local government, the administration of the local affairs of a town or district by its inhabitants, rather than by the state or country at large.

lo·cal·ism (lō′kəlĭz′əm), *n.* 1. a manner of speaking, pronunciation, usage, or inflection that is peculiar to one locality. 2. a local custom. 3. attachment to a particular locality. 4. provincialism.

lo·cal·i·ty (lō kăl′ə tĭ), *n.*, pl. **-ties**. 1. a place, spot, or district, with or without reference to things or persons in it. 2. the place in which a thing is or occurs. 3. state or condition of being local or having place.

lo·cal·ize (lō′kə līz′), *v.t.*, **-ized, -izing**. to make local; fix in, or assign or restrict to, a particular place or locality. —**lo′cal·iz′a·ble**, *adj.* —**lo′cal·i·za′tion**, *n.*

lo·cal·ly (lō′kəlĭ), *adv.* 1. in a particular place, or places. 2. with regard to place. 3. in a local respect.

local option, a right of choice exercised by a minor political division, esp. as to allowing the sale of liquor.

Lo·car·no (lō kär′nō), *n.* a town in S Switzerland, on Lake Maggiore: Locarno Pact, 1925. 6575 (1930).

lo·cate (lō′kāt, lō kāt′), *v.*, **-cated, -cating**. —*v.t.* 1. to discover the place or location of: *to locate a leak in a pipe.* 2. *Chiefly U.S.* to set, fix, or establish in a place, situation or locality; place; settle: *to locate one's headquarters in Dallas.* 3. *U.S.* to enter a claim to (a tract of land); to take up (land). 4. to refer (something), as by opinion or statement, to a particular place: *locate the garden of Eden in Babylonia.* —*v.i.* 5. *U.S.* to establish oneself in a place; settle. [t. L: m.s. *locātus*, pp., placed]

lo·ca·tion (lō kā′shən), *n.* 1. a place of settlement or residence: *a good location for a doctor.* 2. a place or situation occupied: *a house in a fine location.* 3. a tract of land located, or of designated situation or limits: *a mining location.* 4. *Motion Pictures.* a place, outside of the studio, affording suitable environment for photographing particular plays, incidents, etc. 5. act of locating. 6. state of being located. 7. *Civil Law.* a letting or lease; from the point of view of the lesser.

loc·a·tive (lŏk′ə tĭv), *Gram.* —*adj.* 1. (in some inflected languages) denoting a case, having as chief function indication of place in or at which, as Latin *domī* "at home." —*n.* 2. the locative case. 3. a word in that case. [t. ML: m.s. *locātīvus*. See LOCATE, -IVE]

lo·ca·tor (lō′kā tər, lō kā′tər), *n.* *U.S.* one who fixes the boundaries of a land or mining claim. [t. L]

loc. cit., loco citato.

loch (lŏk, lŏкн), *n.* *Scot.* 1. a lake. 2. an arm of the sea, esp. when partially landlocked. [t. Gaelic. Cf. LOUGH]

lo·chi·a (lō′kĭ ə, lŏk′ĭ ə), *n.pl.* *Med.* the liquid discharge from the uterus after childbirth. [t. NL, t. Gk.: m. *lóchia*, neut. pl. of *lóchios* pertaining to childbirth] —**lo·chi·al** (lō′kĭ əl), *adj.*

lo·ci (lō′sī), *n.* pl. of **locus**.

lock[1] (lŏk), *n.* 1. a device for securing a door, gate, lid, drawer, or the like, in position when closed, consisting of a bolt or system of bolts propelled and withdrawn by a mechanism operated by a key, dial, etc. 2. a device to keep a wheel from rotating, as in descending a hill. 3. a contrivance for fastening or securing something. 4. the mechanism in a firearm by means of which it can be kept from operating. 5. an enclosed portion of a canal, river, etc., with gates at each end, for raising or lowering vessels from one level to another. 6. any of various grapples or holds in wrestling, esp. any hold in which an arm or leg of one wrestler is intertwined about the body of his opponent. —*v.t.* 7. to fasten or secure (a door, building, etc.) by the operation of a lock. 8. to shut in a place fastened by a lock or locks, as for security or restraining (fol. by *up, in,* etc.): *to lock a prisoner in a cell.* 9. to exclude by or as by a lock (usually fol. by *out*). 10. to make fast or immovable by or as by a lock: *to lock a wheel.* 11. to fasten or fix firmly, as by engaging parts (often fol. by *up*). 12. *Print.* to make (type, etc.) immovable in a chase by securing the quoins (fol. by *up*). 13. to join or unite firmly by interlinking or intertwining: *to lock arms.* 14. to move (a ship) by means of a lock or locks, as in a canal. 15. to furnish with locks, as a canal. 16. to enclose (a waterway) with a lock (fol. by *off*). —*v.i.* 17. to become locked: *this door locks with a key.* 18. to become fastened, fixed, or interlocked. 19. to go or pass by means of a lock or locks, as a vessel. 20. to construct locks in waterways. [ME; OE *loc* fastening; akin to OE *lūcan*, D *luiken*, Icel. *lūka*, Goth. *galūkan* shut, close]

lock[2] (lŏk), *n.* 1. a tress or portion of hair. 2. (*pl.*) the hair of the head. 3. a flock or small portion of wool, cotton, flax, etc. [ME *locke*, OE *locc* lock of hair, c. Icel. *lokkr*, D *lok* curl, G *locke*]

lock·age (lŏk′ĭj), *n.* 1. the construction, use, or operation of locks, as in a canal or stream. 2. passage through a lock or locks. 3. toll paid for such passage.

Locke (lŏk), *n.* **John**, 1632–1704, British philosopher.

lock·er (lŏk′ər), *n.* 1. a chest, drawer, compartment, closet, or the like, that may be locked. 2. *Naut.* a chest or compartment in which to stow things. 3. one who or that which locks.

Lock·er-Lamp·son (lŏk′ər lăm′sən), *n.* **Frederick,** 1821–95, British poet and author.

lock·et (lŏk′Ĭt), *n.* a small case for a miniature portrait, a lock of hair, or other keepsake, usually worn on a necklace. [ME, t. F: m. *loquet* latch, catch, dim. of OF *loc* lock, t. Gmc.; cf. LOCK¹]

lock·jaw (lŏk′jô′), *n. Pathol.* tetanus in which the jaws become firmly locked together.

lock nut, 1. a supplementary nut screwed down upon another to prevent it from shaking loose. **2.** a nut in which spontaneous motion is prevented by springs fitting between the threads, or by interlocking parts. Also, **lock′nut′.**

lock·out (lŏk′out′), *n.* **1.** the closing of a business or wholesale dismissal of employees by the employer because the employees refuse to accept his terms or because the employer refuses to operate on terms set by a union. —*v.t.* **2.** to conduct a lockout against (employees).

Lock·port (lŏk′pōrt′), *n.* a city in W New York, on the New York State Barge Canal. 25,133 (1950).

lock·smith (lŏk′smĭth′), *n.* one who makes or mends locks.

lock step, a mode of marching in very close file, in which the leg of each person moves with and closely behind the corresponding leg of the person ahead.

lock stitch, a sewing-machine stitch in which two threads are locked together at small intervals.

lock·up (lŏk′ŭp′), *n.* **1.** a jail. **2.** act of locking up.

Lock·yer (lŏk′yər), *n.* **Sir Joseph Norman,** 1836–1920, British astronomer.

lo·co (lō′kō), *n., pl.* **-cos,** *v.* **-coed, -coing,** *adj. U.S.* —*n.* **1.** locoweed. **2.** loco disease. —*v.t.* **3.** to poison with locoweed. **4.** to make crazy. —*adj.* **5.** *U.S. Slang.* insane; crazy. [t. Sp.: insane, g. L *glaucus* sparkling]

lo·co ci·ta·to (lō′kō sĭ tā′tō), *Latin.* in the place, or passage, already mentioned. *Abbr.:* loc. cit.

loco disease, a disease affecting the brain of animals, caused by eating locoweed.

Lo·co·fo·co (lō′kō fō′kō), *n.* the equal-rights or radical section of the Democratic party in the United States about 1835.

lo·co·mo·tion (lō′kə mō′shən), *n.* act or power of moving from place to place. [f. L *locō,* abl. of *locus* place + MOTION]

lo·co·mo·tive (lō′kə mō′tĭv), *n.* **1.** a self-propelled vehicle running on a railroad track, designed to pull railroad cars. **2.** any self-propelled vehicle. —*adj.* **3.** moving or traveling by means of its own mechanism or powers. **4.** serving to produce such movement, or adapted for or used in locomotion: *locomotive organs.* **5.** of or pertaining to movement from place to place. **6.** having the power of locomotion. [f. L *locō,* abl. of *locus* place + MOTIVE, *adj.*]

lo·co·mo·tor (lō′kə mō′tər), *adj.* **1.** of or pertaining to locomotion. —*n.* **2.** one who or that which has locomotive power.

locomotor a·tax·i·a (ə tăk′sĭ ə), *Pathol.* a degenerative disease of the spinal cord, marked by loss of control over the muscular movements, mainly in walking.

lo·co·weed (lō′kō wēd′), *n.* any of various fabaceous plants of the genera *Astragalus* and *Oxytropis* of the southwestern U.S., producing loco disease in sheep, horses, etc.

Lo·cris (lō′krĭs), *n.* either of two districts in the central part of ancient Greece. —**Lo·cri·an** (lō′krĭ ən), *n.*

loc·u·lar (lŏk′yə lər), *adj.* having one or more loculi, chambers, or cells. [t. LL: s. *loculāris* kept in boxes, der. L *loculus* box, cell]

loc·u·late (lŏk′yə lāt′, -lĬt), *adj. Bot.* having one or more locules. Also, **loc′u·lat′ed.** [t. L: m.s. *loculātus* furnished with compartments]

loc·u·lus (lŏk′yə ləs), *n., pl.* **-li** (-lī′). **1.** *Bot., Zool., Anat.* a small compartment or chamber; a cell. **2.** *Bot.* **a.** the cell of a carpel in which the seed is located. **b.** the cell of an anther in which the pollen is located. [t. L: a little place, box, dim. of *locus* place]

lo·cum te·nens (lō′kəm tē′nĕnz), *Chiefly Brit.* a temporary substitute, esp. for a clergyman or doctor. [ML]

lo·cus (lō′kəs), *n., pl.* **loci** (lō′sī). **1.** a place; a locality. **2.** *Math.* a curve or other figure considered as generated by a point, line, or surface, which moves or is placed according to a definite law. **3.** *Genetics.* the chromosomal position of a gene as determined by its linear order relative to the other genes on that chromosome. [t. L: place]

lo·cus clas·si·cus (lō′kəs klăs′ə kəs), *Latin.* a passage commonly cited to illustrate or explain a subject.

lo·cus si·gil·li (lō′kəs sĭ jĬl′ī), *Latin.* the place of the seal (on a document, etc.). *Abbr.:* L.S.

lo·cust (lō′kəst), *n.* **1.** any of the grasshoppers with short antennae which constitute the family *Locustidae,* including the notorious migratory species, such as *Locusta migratoria* of the Old World, and the Rocky Mountain locust, *Melanoplus spretus,* which swarm in immense numbers and strip the vegetation from large areas. **2.** any of various cicadas, as *Magicicada septendecim* (the **seventeen-year locust**). **3.** a thorny-branched, white-flowered American fabaceous

Migratory locust, *Locusta migratoria*
(2 in. long)

tree, *Robinia pseudoacacia.* **4.** its durable wood. **5.** any of various other trees, as the carob and the honey locust. [ME, t. L: s. *locusta* locust, lobster]

lo·cus·ta (lō kŭs′tə), *n., pl.* **-tae** (-tē). *Bot.* the spikelet of grasses. [t. NL, special use of L *locusta* LOCUST]

lo·cu·tion (lō kū′shən), *n.* **1.** a particular form of expression; a phrase or expression. **2.** style of speech or verbal expression; phraseology. [ME, t. L: s. *locūtio*]

lode (lōd), *n.* **1.** a veinlike deposit, usually metalliferous. **2.** any body of ore set off from adjacent rock formations. [ME; OE *lād* way, course, carrying (see LOAD), c. OHG *leita* procession, Icel. *leidh* way, course]

lode·star (lōd′stär′), *n.* **1.** a star that shows the way. **2.** Polaris. **3.** something that serves as a guide or on which the attention is fixed. Also, **loadstar.** [ME *loode sterre.* See LOAD, LODE, STAR, n.]

lode·stone (lōd′stōn′), *n.* loadstone.

lodge (lŏj), *n., v.,* **lodged, lodging.** —*n.* **1.** a small, slight or rude shelter or habitation, as of boughs, poles, skins, earth, rough boards, or the like; cabin or hut. **2.** a house used as a temporary abode, as in the hunting season. **3.** a summer cottage. **4.** a house or cottage, as in a park or on an estate, occupied by a gatekeeper, caretaker, gardener, or the like. **5.** a place of abode or sojourn. **6.** the meeting place of a branch of a secret society. **7.** the members composing the branch. **8.** the home of a college head or master at Cambridge University, England. **9.** *U.S.* an Indian habitation. **10.** den or habitation of an animal or animals, esp. beavers. —*v.i.* **11.** to have a habitation or quarters, esp. temporarily, as in a place or house. **12.** to live in hired quarters in another's house. **13.** to be fixed or implanted, or be caught in a place or position. —*v.t.* **14.** to furnish with a habitation or quarters, esp. temporarily. **15.** to furnish with a room or rooms in one's house for payment, or have as a lodger. **16.** to serve as a habitation or shelter for, as a house does; shelter; harbor. **17.** to put or deposit, as in a place, for storage or keeping. **18.** to bring or send into a particular place or position: *to lodge a bullet in one's heart.* **19.** to vest (power, etc.). **20.** to lay (information, a complaint, etc.) before a court or the like. **21.** to beat down or lay flat, as vegetation in a storm. **22.** to track (a deer) to its lair. [ME *loge,* t. OF: hut, orig. leafy shelter, t. Gmc. (cf. OHG *laube* arbor)] —**Syn. 1.** See **cottage.**

Lodge (lŏj), *n.* **1. Henry Cabot** (kăb′ət), 1850–1924, U.S. political leader; senator, 1893–1924. **2. Sir Oliver Joseph,** 1851–1940, British physicist and writer. **3. Thomas,** c1558–1625, British dramatist and writer.

lodg·er (lŏj′ər), *n.* one who lives in hired quarters in another's house.

lodg·ing (lŏj′ĭng), *n.* **1.** accommodation in a house, esp. in rooms for hire: *to furnish board and lodging.* **2.** a place of abode, esp. a temporary one. **3.** (*pl.*) a room or rooms hired for residence in another's house.

lodging house, a house in which lodgings are let, esp. a house other than an inn or hotel.

lodg·ment (lŏj′mənt), *n.* **1.** act of lodging. **2.** state of being lodged. **3.** something lodged or deposited. **4.** *Mil.* a position or foothold gained from an enemy, or an intrenchment made upon it. **5.** a lodging place; lodgings. Also, *esp. Brit.,* **lodge′ment.**

Lo·di (lō′dē), *n.* a town in N Italy, in Lombardy: Napoleon defeated the Austrians near here, 1796. 23,053 (1936).

Łódz (lŏŏj), *n.* a city in central Poland. 496,861 (1946). Russian, **Lodz** (lôdz).

Loeb (lōb; *Ger.* lœb), *n.* **Jacques** (zhäk), 1859–1924, German physiologist and experimental biologist in U.S.

lo·ess (lō′ĭs; *Ger.* lœs), *n.* a loamy deposit formed by wind, usually yellowish and calcareous, common in the Mississippi valley and in Europe and Asia. [t. G]

Lo·fo·ten Islands (lō′fōōt′ən), a group of islands NW of and belonging to Norway: rich fishing grounds. 24,884 pop. (1930); 474 sq. mi.

loft (lôft, lŏft), *n.* **1.** the space between the under side of a roof and the ceiling of a room beneath it. **2.** a gallery or upper level in a church, hall, etc., designed for a special purpose: *a choir loft.* **3.** a hay loft. **4.** *U.S.* any upper story of a warehouse, mercantile building, or factory, esp. of buildings designed for small, light industries. **5.** *U.S.* a building consisting of such lofts. **6.** *Golf.* **a.** the slope of the face of a club backward from the vertical, tending to drive the ball upward. **b.** act of lofting. **c.** a lofting stroke. —*v.t.* **7.** *Golf.* **a.** to slant the face of (a club). **b.** to hit (a ball) into the air or over an obstacle. **c.** to clear (an obstacle) thus. **8.** to provide (a house, etc.) with a loft. —*v.i.* **9.** *Golf.* to loft the ball. [ME *lofte,* late OE *loft,* t. Scand.; cf. Icel. *lopt* the air, sky, an upper room; akin to LIFT¹, LIFT²]

loft·ing iron (lôf′tĭng, lŏf′-), *Golf.* an iron-headed club used in lofting the ball. Also, **loft′er.**

loft·y (lôf′tĭ, lŏf′-), *adj.,* **loftier, loftiest. 1.** extending high in the air; of imposing height: *lofty mountains.* **2.** exalted in rank, dignity, or character. **3.** elevated in style or sentiment, as writings, etc. **4.** haughty; proud. —**loft′i·ly,** *adv.* —**loft′i·ness,** *n.* —**Syn. 1.** See **high.**

log (lôg, lŏg), *n., v.,* **logged, logging.** —*n.* **1.** an unhewn portion or length of the trunk or a large limb of a felled tree. **2.** something inert or heavy. **3.** *Naut.* **a.** a device for determining the speed of and distance covered by a ship. **b. chip log,** a chip (**log chip**) attached to the end of a line (**log line**) thrown over the stern to measure the speed of a ship. **c. patent log,** a screw-shaped implement on the end of a line trailing astern which indicates speed and distance. **4.** the official record of a ship's voyage; logbook. **5.** a listing of navigational, meteorological and other significant data concerning an air journey. **6.** the register of the operation of a machine. **7.** a record kept of development during the drilling of a well, esp. of the geological formations penetrated. —*v.t.* **8.** to cut (trees) into logs. **9.** to cut down the trees or timber on (land). **10.** *Naut.* **a.** to enter in a ship's log. **b.** to travel (a distance) according to the indication of a log. —*v.i.* **11.** to cut down trees and get out logs from the forest for timber. [ME *logge*; appar. var. of LUG, n.]

log., logarithm.

Lo·gan (lō′gən), *n.* **Mount,** a mountain in W Canada, in SW Yukon Territory: the second highest peak in North America. 19,850 ft.

lo·gan·ber·ry (lō′gən ber′Ĭ), *n., pl.* **-ries.** the large, dark-red acid fruit, *Rubus loganobaccus,* with long prostrate canes, of California origin. [named after J. H. *Logan,* of California, by whom it was first grown]

lo·ga·ni·a·ceous (lō gā′nĬ ā′shəs), *adj.* belonging to the *Loganiaceae,* a family of herbs, shrubs, and trees of tropical and subtropical regions, including the nux vomica tree and other plants with poisonous properties. [f. s. NL *Logania,* the typical genus (named after James *Logan* 1674–1751, of Philadelphia) + -ACEOUS]

Lo·gans·port (lō′gənz pōrt′), *n.* a city in N Indiana, on the Wabash. 21,031 (1950).

log·a·oe·dic (lŏg′ə ē′dĬk, lŏg′ə-), *Pros.* —*adj.* **1.** composed of dactyls and trochees or of anapaests and iambi, producing a movement somewhat suggestive of prose. —*n.* **2.** a logaoedic verse. [t. LL.: s. *logaoedicus,* t. Gk.: m. *logaoidikós,* f. s. *lógos* prose + s. *aoidé* song + *-ikos -ic*]

log·a·rithm (lŏg′ə rĬth′əm, -rĬth′əm, lŏg′ə-), *n. Math.* the exponent of that power to which a fixed number (called the base) must be raised in order to produce a given number (called the *antilogarithm*): *3 is the logarithm of 8 to the base 2.* [t. NL: s. *logarithmus,* f. Gk.: s. *lógos* proportion + m. *arithmós* number]

log·a·rith·mic (lŏg′ə rĬth′mĬk, -rĬth′mĬk, lŏg′ə-), *adj.* pertaining to a logarithm or logarithms. Also, **log′a·rith′mi·cal.** —**log′a·rith′mi·cal·ly,** *adv.*

log·book (lŏg′bŏŏk′, lŏg′-), *n. Naut.* **1.** a book in which are officially recorded the indications of the log, as well as the weather and other important particulars of a ship's voyage. **2.** the record itself.

loge (lōzh; *Fr.* lōzh), *n.* a box in a theater or opera house. [t. F. See LODGE]

log·ger (lŏg′ər, lŏg′ər), *n.* **1.** the person who cuts trees into suitable lengths after the trees have been felled. **2.** a tractor used in logging. **3.** a machine for loading logs.

log·ger·head (lŏg′ər hĕd′, lŏg′ər-), *n.* **1.** a thick-headed or stupid person; a blockhead. **2.** Also, **logger-head turtle.** a large-headed marine turtle, *Caretta caretta,* of all oceans. **3.** Also, **loggerhead shrike.** a common North American butcherbird, *Lanius ludovicianus,* gray above, white below, with black and white wings and tail and black facial mask. **4.** a ball or bulb of iron with a long handle, used, after being heated, to melt tar, heat liquids, etc. **5.** a rounded post in the stern of a whale-boat, around which the harpoon line is passed. **6. at loggerheads,** engaged in dispute. [back formation from *loggerheaded,* var. of obs. *log-headed* stupid]

log·gia (lŏj′ə, lŏj′Ĭə; *It.* lōd′jä), *n., pl.* **-gias;** *It.* **-gie** (-jĕ). **1.** a gallery or arcade open to the air on at least one side. **2.** a space within the body of a building but open to the air on one side, serving as an open-air room or as an entrance porch. [t. It. See LODGE, n.]

log·ging (lŏg′Ĭng, lŏg′Ĭng), *n.* the process, work, or business of cutting down trees and getting out logs from the forest for timber.

log·i·a (lŏg′Ĭə), *n. pl.* of **logion.**

log·ic (lŏj′Ĭk), *n.* **1.** the science which investigates the principles governing correct or reliable inference. **2.** reasoning or argumentation, or an instance of it. **3.** the system or principles of reasoning applicable to any branch of knowledge or study. **4.** reasons or sound sense, as in utterances or actions. **5.** convincing force: *the irresistible logic of facts.* [ME *logik,* t. ML: m.s. *logica,* t. Gk.: m. *logiké,* prop. fem. of *logikós* pertaining to reason]

log·i·cal (lŏj′ə kəl), *adj.* **1.** according to the principles of logic: *a logical inference.* **2.** reasoning in accordance with the principles of logic, as a person, the mind, etc. **3.** reasonable; reasonably to be expected: *war was the logical consequence of such threats.* **4.** of or pertaining to logic. —**log′i·cal′i·ty, log′i·cal·ness,** *n.* —**log′i·cal·ly,** *adv.*

logical positivism, a philosophy stressing the logical and linguistic analysis of science.

lo·gi·cian (lō jĬsh′ən), *n.* one skilled in logic.

log·i·on (lŏg′Ĭ ŏn′), *n., pl.* **logia** (lŏg′Ĭə). **1.** a traditional saying or maxim, as of a religious teacher. **2.** *(often cap.)* a saying of Jesus (used esp. with reference to sayings of Jesus contained in collections supposed to have been among the sources of the present Gospels, or to sayings ascribed to Jesus but not recorded in the Gospels. [t. Gk.: announcement, oracle]

lo·gis·tic (lō jĬs′tĬk), *adj.* pertaining to military logistics. Also, **lo·gis′ti·cal.** [see LOGISTICS]

lo·gis·tics (lō jĬs′tĬks), *n.* the branch of military science concerned with the mathematics of transportation

and supply, and the movement of bodies of troops. [t. F.: m. *logistique,* der. *loger* lodge, or *logis* lodging. See -ICS]

logo-, a word element denoting speech. [t. Gk., comb. form of *lógos* word, speech]

log·o·gram (lŏg′ə grăm′, lŏg′ə-), *n.* a conventional abbreviated symbol for a frequently recurring word or phrase. Also, **log·o·graph** (lŏg′ə gräf′, -grăf′, lŏg′ə-). —**log·o·gram·mat·ic** (lŏg′ə grə măt′Ĭk, lŏg′ə-), *adj.*

log·o·graph·ic (lŏg′ə grăf′Ĭk, lŏg′ə-), *adj.* **1.** consisting of logographs: *logographic writing.* **2.** of or pertaining to logography. Also, **log′o·graph′i·cal.**

lo·gog·ra·phy (lō gŏg′rə fĬ), *n.* **1.** printing with logotypes. **2.** a method of longhand reporting, each of several reporters in succession taking down a few words. [t. Gk.: m.s. *logographia* a writing of speeches]

log·o·griph (lŏg′ə grĬf, lŏg′ə-), *n.* **1.** an anagram, or a puzzle involving anagrams. **2.** a puzzle in which a certain word, and other words formed from any or all of its letters, must be guessed from indications given in a set of verse. [t. F: m. *logogriphe,* f. Gk.: *lógos-* LOGO- + m. *gríphos* fishing-basket, riddle] —**log′o·griph′ic,** *adj.*

lo·gom·a·chy (lō gŏm′ə kĬ), *n., pl.* **-chies. 1.** contention about words, or in words merely. **2.** a game played with cards, each bearing one letter, with which words are formed. [t. Gk.: m.s. *logomachía.* See LOGO-, -MACHY] —**lo·gom′a·chist,** *n.*

log·os (lŏg′ŏs), *n.* **1.** *(often cap.) Philos.* the rational principle that governs and develops the universe. **2.** *(cap.) Theol.* Jesus Christ, the Divine Word (see John, 1:1, 14), the second person of the Trinity. [t. Gk.: word, speech, reason, account, reckoning, proportion]

log·o·type (lŏg′ə tĬp′, lŏg′ə-), *n. Print.* a single type bearing two or more distinct (not combined) letters, or a syllable or word. Cf. **ligature.** —**log′o·typ′y,** *n.*

log·roll (lŏg′rōl′, lŏg′-), *v.t.* **1.** to procure the passage of (a bill) by logrolling. —*v.i.* **2.** to engage in political logrolling. —**log′roll′er,** *n.*

log·roll·ing (lŏg′rō′lĬng, lŏg′-), *n.* **1.** *Chiefly U.S.* (used esp. with reference to legislators) the combining of two or more persons to assist one of them, in consideration of like combined assistance in the interest of each of the others in return. **2.** the action of rolling logs to a particular place. **3.** birling.

log·wood (lŏg′wŏŏd′, lŏg′-), *n.* **1.** the heavy brownish-red heartwood of a West Indian and Central American caesalpiniaceous tree, *Haematoxylon campechianum,* much used in dyeing. **2.** the tree itself.

lo·gy (lō′gĬ), *adj.,* **-gier, -giest.** *U.S.* heavy; sluggish; dull. [orig. uncert. Cf. D *log* heavy, dull]

-logy, 1. a combining form naming sciences or bodies of knowledge, e.g., *paleontology, theology.* **2.** a termination of many nouns referring to writing, collections, e.g., *trilogy, martyrology.* [t. Gk.: m.s. *-logia,* der. *log-* speak, *lógos* discourse; r. earlier *-logie,* t. F. Cf. G *-logie*]

Lo·hen·grin (lō′ən grĬn, -grēn′), *n.* **1.** *German Legend.* the knight of the swan, the son of Parzival, and a knight of the Holy Grail. **2.** a romantic opera (composed, 1846–48; premiere, 1850) by Wagner.

loin (loin), *n.* **1.** *(usually pl.)* the part or parts of the body of man or of a quadruped animal on either side of the vertebral column, between the false ribs and hipbone. **2.** a cut of meat from this region of an animal, esp. a portion including the vertebrae of such parts. **3.** *Biblical and Poetic.* the part of the body which should be clothed or girded, or which is regarded as the seat of physical strength and generative power. [ME *loyne,* t. OF: m. *loigne,* der. L *lumbus*]

loin·cloth (loin′klôth′, -klŏth′), *n.* a piece of cloth worn about the loins or hips.

Loire (lwär), *n.* a river flowing from S France into the Bay of Biscay: the longest river in France. ab. 625 mi.

loi·ter (loi′tər), *v.i.* **1.** to linger idly or aimlessly in or about a place. **2.** to move or go in a slow or lagging manner: *to loiter along.* **3.** to waste time or dawdle over work, etc. —*v.t.* **4.** to pass (time, etc.) in an idle or aimless manner (fol. by *away*). [ME *lotere,* appar. freq. of obs. *lote* lurk, ME *lotie(n), lutie(n), loyt.* Cf. OE *lūtian* lurk] —**loi′ter·er,** *n.* —**loi′ter·ing·ly,** *adv.*

—**Syn. 1.** LOITER, DALLY, DAWDLE, IDLE imply moving or acting slowly, stopping for unimportant reasons, and in general wasting time. To LOITER is to linger aimlessly: *to loiter until late.* To DALLY is to loiter indecisively or to delay sportively as if free from care or responsibility: *to dally on the way home.* To DAWDLE is to saunter, stopping often, and taking a great deal of time, or to fritter away time working in a half-hearted way: *to dawdle over a task.* To IDLE is to move slowly and aimlessly, or to spend a great deal of time doing nothing: *to idle away the hours.*

Lo·ki (lō′kĬ), *n. Scand. Myth.* the god of destruction, and father of Hel and the serpent of Midgard. [t. Icel.]

loll (lŏl), *v.i.* **1.** to recline or lean in a relaxed or indolent manner; lounge: *to loll on a sofa.* **2.** to hang loosely or droopingly. —*v.t.* **3.** to allow to hang or droop. —*n.* **4.** act of lolling. **5.** one who or that which lolls. [ME *lolle, lulle.* Cf. MD *lollen* sleep] —**loll′er,** *n.*

Lol·land (lō′län), *n.* Laaland.

Lol·lard (lŏl′ərd), *n.* an English or Scottish follower of the religious teaching of John Wycliffe from the 14th century to the 16th. [ME, t. MD.: m. *lollaerd* mumbler, der. *lollen* mumble, hum]

lol·li·pop (lŏl′Ĭ pŏp′), *n.* a kind of taffy or other candy, often a piece on the end of a stick.

Lom·bard (lŏm′bərd, -bärd, lŭm′-), *n.* **1.** a native or inhabitant of Lombardy. **2.** a Langobard. —*adj.* **3.** Also, **Lom·bar′dic.** **4.** pertaining to the Lombards or Lombardy. [ME, t. OF, t. It.: m. *lombardo*, g. LL *Longobardus*, L *Langobardus*, t. Gmc. See LANGOBARD]

Lom·bard (lŏm′bərd, -bärd, lŭm′-; *Fr.* lôn bär′), *n.* **Pe·ter,** (*Petrus Lombardus*) c1100–1160 or 1164, Italian theologian; bishop of Paris.

Lombard Street, a street in London, England, famous as a financial center.

Lom·bard·y (lŏm′bər dY, lŭm′-), *n.* a department in N Italy: a former kingdom. 6,176,300 pop. (est. 1942); 9190 sq. mi.

Lombardy poplar. See **poplar** (def. 1).

Lom·bok (lŏm bŏk′), *n.* an island in the U.S. of Indonesia, E of Java. 701,290 pop. (1930); 1826 sq. mi.

Lom·bro·si·an school (lŏm brō′zY ən), a school of criminology, holding the theories and employing the methods developed by Lombroso.

Lom·bro·so (lŏm brō′sô), *n.* **Cesare** (chĕ′zä rĕ′), 1836–1909, Italian physician and criminologist.

lo·ment (lō′mĕnt), *n.* *Bot.* a legume which is contracted in the spaces between the seeds, and breaks at maturity into one-seeded indehiscent joints. [ME *lomente*, t. L: s. *lōmentum* bean meal] —**lo′ment·like′,** *adj.*

lo·men·ta·ceous (lō′mən tā′shəs), *adj.* *Bot.* of the nature of a loment; lomentlike.

lo·men·tum (lō mĕn′təm), *n., pl.* **-ta** (-tə). *Bot.* loment. [t. L]

Lo·mond (lō′mənd), *n.* **Loch,** a lake in W Scotland. 23 mi. long; 27 sq. mi.

Lon·don (lŭn′dən), *n.* **1.** a metropolis in SE England, on the Thames: capital of the United Kingdom and the British Empire. **2.** **City of,** an old city in the central part of London county: the ancient nucleus of the metropolis. 4990 pop. (est. 1946); 1 sq. mi. **3.** **County of,** an administrative county comprising the City of London and the 28 metropolitan boroughs. 3,132,000 pop. (est. 1946); 117 sq. mi. **4.** **Greater,** an urban area comprising the City of London, London and Middlesex counties, and parts of Essex, Kent, Surrey, and Hertfordshire. 7,877,590 pop. (est. 1946); 693 sq. mi. **5.** a city in SE Canada, in S Ontario. 78,264 (1941). **6. Jack,** 1876–1916, U.S. short-story writer and novelist.

Lon·don·der·ry (lŭn′dən dĕr′Y), *n.* **1.** a county in Northern Ireland. 149,800 pop. (est. 1946); 804 sq. mi. **2.** its county seat: a seaport. 49,500 (est. 1946). Also, **Derry.**

Lon·don·er (lŭn′dən ər), *n.* a native or inhabitant of London.

lone (lōn), *adj.* **1.** being alone; unaccompanied; solitary: *a lone traveler.* **2.** standing apart, or isolated, as a house. **3.** *Poetic.* lonely. **4.** lonesome. **5.** unmarried or widowed. [aphetic var. of ALONE, used attributively] **Syn. 1.** See **alone.**

lone·ly (lōn′lY), *adj.,* **-lier, -liest. 1.** lone; solitary; without company. **2.** destitute of sympathetic or friendly companionship or relationships: *a lonely exile.* **3.** remote from men or from places of human habitation or resort: *a lonely road.* **4.** standing apart; isolated: *a lonely tower.* **5.** affected with, characterized by, or causing a depressing feeling of being alone; lonesome: *a lonely heart.* —**lone′li·ly,** *adv.* —**lone′li·ness,** *n.* —**Syn. 1.** See **alone.**

lone·some (lōn′səm), *adj.* **1.** lonely in feeling; depressed by solitude or by a sense of being alone: *to feel lonesome.* **2.** attended with or causing such a state of feeling: *a lonesome journey.* **3.** depressingly lonely in situation: *a lonesome road.* —**lone′some·ly,** *adv.* —**lone′some·ness,** *n.* —**Syn.** See **alone.**

Lone Star State, Texas (a nickname).

long[1] (lông, lŏng), *adj.,* **longer,** (lông′gər, lŏng′-), **longest** (lông′gYst, lŏng′-), *n., adv.* —*adj.* **1.** having considerable or great extent from end to end; not short: *a long distance.* **2.** having considerable or great extent in duration: *a nice long visit.* **3.** having considerable or great extension from beginning to end, as a series, enumeration, account, book, etc.; not brief. **4.** having a specified extension in space, duration, etc.: *ten feet long.* **5.** continuing too long: *a long speech.* **6.** beyond the normal extension in space, duration, quantity, etc.: *a long dozen* (thirteen). **7.** extending to a great distance in space or time: *a long memory.* **8.** having a long time to run, as a promissory note. **9.** *Chiefly Law.* distant or remote in time: *a long date.* **10.** relatively much extended: *a long arm.* **11.** tall. **12.** (of the head or skull) of more than ordinary length from front to back. **13.** *Phonet.* **a.** lasting a relatively long time: *"feed" has a longer vowel than "feet" or "fit."* **b.** belonging to a class of sounds considered as usually longer in duration than another class, such as the vowel of *bought* as compared to *hot*: conventionally, the vowels of *mate, meet, mite, mote, moot* and *mute.* **14.** *Com.* **a.** owning some commodity or stock. **b.** depending for profit on a rise in prices. **15.** (in gambling) **a.** of an exceptionally large difference in proportional amounts on an event: *long odds.* **b.** of or pertaining to the larger number in the odds in betting. **16.** in the long run, after a long course of experience; in the final result. —*n.* **17.** a long time: *before long.* **18.** something that is long. —*adv.* **19.** for or through a great extent of space or, esp., time: *a reform long advocated.* **20.** for or throughout a specified extent, esp. of time: *how long did he stay?* **21.** (in elliptical expressions) gone, occupying, delaying, etc., a long or a specified time: *don't be long.* **22.** (for emphasis, after nouns denoting a period of time) throughout the whole length: *all summer long.* **23.** at a point of time far distant from the time indicated: *long before.* **24. so** (or **as**) **long as,** provided that. [ME *longe*, OE *lang, long,* c. D and G *lang*]

long[2] (lông, lŏng), *v.i.* **1.** to have a prolonged or unceasing desire, as for something not immediately (if ever) attainable. **2.** to have an earnest or strong desire. [ME *longen,* OE *langian* lengthen (impersonal), yearn, der. *lang* LONG[1]]

long., longitude.

lon·gan (lông′gən), *n.* **1.** the small, one-seeded, greenish-brown, pleasant-tasting fruit of the large evergreen, Sapindaceous tree, *Euphoria Longan,* native in China and allied to the litchi. **2.** the tree. Also, **lungan.** [t. NL: s. *longanum,* t. Chinese: m. *lung-yen* dragon's eye]

Long Beach, a city in SW California, S of Los Angeles: a seaside resort. 250,767 (1950).

long·boat (lông′bōt′, lŏng′-), *n.* *Naut.* the largest and strongest boat belonging to a sailing ship.

long·bow (lông′bō′, lŏng′-), *n.* **1.** the bow drawn by hand and discharging a long feathered arrow. **2. draw the longbow,** to tell exaggerated stories.

long·cloth (lông′klôth′, lŏng′klôth′), *n.* a kind of muslin, light and soft in texture.

long distance, *U.S.* telephone service between distant points. —**long′-dis′tance,** *adj.*

long-drawn (lông′drôn′, lŏng′-), *adj.* **1.** drawn out; prolonged: *a long-drawn narrative.* **2.** long.

lon·ge·ron (lŏn′jə rən; *Fr.* lônzh rôn′), *n.* *Aeron.* a main longitudinal brace or support on an airplane. [t. F, der. *long* LONG]

lon·gev·i·ty (lŏn jĕv′ə tY), *n.* **1.** length or duration of life. **2.** long life; great duration of life.

lon·ge·vous (lŏn jē′vəs), *adj.* long-lived; living to a great age. [t. L: m. *longaevus* aged]

Long·fel·low (lông′fĕl′ō, lŏng′-), *n.* **Henry Wadsworth** (wŏdz′wərth), 1807–82, U.S. poet.

long green, *U.S. Slang.* paper currency.

long·hand (lông′hănd′, lŏng′-), *n.* writing of the ordinary kind, in which the words are written out in full (distinguished from *shorthand*).

long·head (lông′hĕd′, lŏng′-), *n.* **1.** a dolichocephalic person. **2.** a head with a cephalic index of 76 and under.

long·head·ed (lông′hĕd′Yd, lŏng′-), *adj.* **1.** dolichocephalic. **2.** of great discernment or foresight; far-seeing or shrewd. —**long′-head′ed·ness,** *n.*

long·horn (lông′hôrn′, lŏng′-), *n.* one of a kind of cattle predominating on the ranges of northern Mexico and the Great Plains of the U.S. in the early 19th century, developed from Spanish cattle introduced at Vera Cruz about 1521, characterized by long horns and rangy conformation.

long house, 1. a house of great length, particularly a communal dwelling of the Iroquois and of other North American tribes. **2.** (*caps.*) the League of the Iroquois.

lon·gi·corn (lŏn′jə kôrn′), *adj.* **1.** having long antennae, as beetles of the group *Longicornia* (family *Cerambycidae*). **2.** belonging to this group. —*n.* **3.** a longicorn or long-horned beetle. [t. NL: s. *longicornis,* f. L: *longi-* long + *-cornis* horned]

long·ing (lông′Yng, lŏng′-), *n.* **1.** prolonged, unceasing, or earnest desire. **2.** an instance of it. —*adj.* **3.** having a prolonged or earnest desire. **4.** characterized by or showing such desire: *a longing look.* —**long′ing·ly,** *adv.* —**Syn. 1.** See **desire.**

Lon·gi·nus (lŏn jī′nəs), *n.* **Dionysius Cassius** (dī′ə nYsh′əs kăsh′əs), A.D. c213–273, Greek rhetorician and philosophical critic.

long·ish (lông′Ysh, lŏng′-), *adj.* somewhat long.

Long Island, an island in SE New York: the boroughs of Brooklyn and Queens of New York City are located at its W end. 118 mi. long; 12–20 mi. wide; 1682 sq. mi.

Long Island Sound, an arm of the Atlantic between Connecticut and Long Island. ab. 110 mi. long.

lon·gi·tude (lŏn′jə tūd′, -tōōd′), *n.* **1.** *Geog.* angular distance east or west on the earth's surface, measured by the angle contained between the meridian of a particular place and some prime meridian, as that of Greenwich, England, or by the corresponding difference in time. **2.** *Astron.* the arc of the ecliptic measured eastward from the vernal equinox to the foot of the great circle passing through the poles of the ecliptic and the point on the celestial sphere in question (**celestial longitude**). [ME, t. L: m. *longitūdo* length]

lon·gi·tu·di·nal (lŏn′jə tū′də nəl, -tōō′-), *adj.* **1.** of or pertaining to longitude or length: *longitudinal distance.* **2.** *Zool.* pertaining to or extending along the long axis of the body, or the direction from front to back, or head to

---

b., blend of, blended; c., cognate with; d., dialect, dialectal; der., derived from; f., formed from; g., going back to; m., modification of; r., replacing; s., stem of; t., taken from; ?, perhaps. See the full key on inside cover.

tail. **3.** extending in the direction of the length of a thing; running lengthwise. See diag. under **section.** —lon/gi·tu/di·nal·ly, *adv.*

long jump, *Athletics.* broad jump.

long·leaf pine (lông′lēf′, lŏng′-), **1.** an important American pine, *Pinus palustris*, valued as a source of turpentine and for its timber. **2.** the wood of this tree.

long measure, linear measure.

long moss, Florida moss.

Lon·go·bard (lŏng′gō bärd′), *n.* Langobard.

Long Parliament, *Eng. Hist.* the Parliament which assembled Nov. 3, 1640, was expelled by Cromwell in 1653, reconvened in 1659, and was dissolved in 1660.

long pig, *Maori and Polynesian.* human meat eaten by cannibals.

long·shore (lông′shōr′, lŏng′-), *adj.* existing, found, or employed along the shore: *longshore fisheries.*

long·shore·man (lông′shōr′man, lŏng′-), *n.,* *pl.* **-men.** a man employed on the wharves of a port, as in loading and unloading vessels. [f. *longshore*, aphetic var. of *alongshore* + -MAN]

long·sight·ed (lông′sī′tĭd, lŏng′-), *adj.* **1.** far-sighted; hypermetropic. **2.** having great foresight; foreseeing remote results. —**long′-sight′ed·ness,** *n.*

Longs Peak (lôngz, lŏngz), a peak in the Rocky Mountain National Park, in N Colorado. 14,255 ft.

long·spur (lông′spûr′, lŏng′-), *n.* any of various fringilline birds of the genera *Calcarius* and *Rhynchophanes* inhabiting treeless northern regions and characterized by a long, spurlike hind claw.

long·stand·ing (lông′stăn′dĭng, lŏng′-), *adj.* existing or occurring for a long time: *a longstanding feud.*

Long·street (lông′strēt′, lŏng′-), *n.* **James,** 1821-1904, Confederate general in the U.S. Civil War.

long·suf·fer·ing (lông′sŭf′ər·ĭng, lŏng′-), *adj.* **1.** enduring injury or provocation long and patiently. —*n.* **2.** long and patient endurance of injury or provocation.

long-term bond (lông′tûrm′, lŏng′-), a bond not maturing for several years or more.

long tom (tŏm), **1.** *Army Slang.* cannon. **2.** long heavy cannon formerly carried by small naval vessels.

long ton, a ton of 2,240 pounds.

long-wind·ed (lông′wĭn′dĭd, lŏng′-), *adj.* **1.** talking or writing at tedious length, as persons. **2.** continued to a tedious length in speech or writing: *another of his long-winded election speeches.* —**long′-wind′ed·ly,** *adv.* —**long′-wind′ed·ness,** *n.*

long·wise (lông′wīz′, lŏng′-), *adv.* lengthwise. Also, **long·ways** (lông′wāz′, lŏng′-).

loo (lōō), *n., pl.* **loos,** *v.,* **looed, looing.** —*n.* **1.** a game at cards in which forfeits are paid into a pool. **2.** the forfeit or sum paid into the pool. **3.** the fact of being looed. —*v.t.* **4.** to subject to a forfeit at loo.

look (lōōk), *v.i.* **1.** to fix the eyes upon something or in some direction in order to see. **2.** to glance or gaze, in a manner specified: *to look questioningly at a person.* **3.** to use the sight in seeking, searching, examining, watching, etc.: *to look through the papers.* **4.** to tend, as in bearing or significance: *conditions look toward war.* **5.** to appear or seem (as specified) to the eye: *to look pale.* **6.** to seem to the mind: *the case looks promising.* **7.** to direct the mental regard or attention: *to look at the facts.* **8.** to direct the expectations or hopes (esp. fol by *for* or *to*). **9.** to have an outlook or afford a view: *the window looks upon the street.* **10.** to face or front: *the house looks to the east.* **11.** Some special phrases are: **look after, 1.** to follow with the eye, as a person or thing moving away. **2.** to seek, as something desired. **3.** to take care of: *to look after a child.* **look for, 1.** to seek, as a person or thing. **2.** to anticipate; expect. **look in, 1.** to take a look into a place. **2.** to come in for a brief visit. **look on,** to be a mere spectator. **look out, 1.** to look forth, as from a window or a place of observation. **2.** to be on guard: *look out for trouble.* **3.** to take watchful care (fol. by *for*): *to look out for oneself.* **look to, 1.** to direct the glance or gaze to. **2.** to give attention to. **3.** to direct the expectations or hopes to, as for something desired. **4.** to look forward expectantly to. **look up, 1.** to direct the eyes upward. **2.** *Colloq.* to rise in amount or value; improve. **3.** *U.S.* to search for: *to look up the date.* —*v.t.* **12.** to try to find; seek: *to look a name up in a directory.* **13.** to express or suggest by looks: *to look daggers at a person.* **14.** to bring, put, etc., by looks. **15.** *Obs.* to view, inspect, or examine. —*n.* **16.** act of looking: *a look of inquiry.* **17.** a visual search or examination. **18.** way of looking or appearing to the eye or to the mind; aspect: *the look of an honest man.* **19.** (*pl.*) general aspect; appearance: *to like the looks of a place, good looks.* [ME *lōke(n)*, OE *lōcian.* Cf. d. G *lugen* look out, spy] —Syn. **1.** See **watch. 6.** See **seem.**

look·er (lōōk′ər), *n.* **1.** one who looks. **2.** *U.S. Slang.* an unusually handsome person.

look·er-on (lōōk′ər ŏn′), *n., pl.* **lookers-on.** one who looks on; a spectator.

looking glass, 1. a mirror made of glass with a metallic or amalgam backing. **2.** such glass as a material.

look·out (lōōk′out′), *n.* **1.** act of looking out. **2.** a watch kept, as for something that may come or happen. **3.** a person or group stationed or employed to keep such a watch. **4.** a station or place from which a watch is kept. **5.** view; prospect; outlook. **6.** *Colloq.* the proper object of one's watchful care or concern.

Lookout Mountain, a mountain ridge in Georgia, Tennessee, and Alabama: a battle of the Civil War was fought on this ridge near Chattanooga, Tennessee, 1863. Highest point, 2126 ft.

loom¹ (lōōm), *n.* **1.** a machine or apparatus for weaving yarn or thread into a fabric. **2.** the art or the process of weaving. **3.** the part of an oar between the blade and the handle. —*v.t.* **4.** to weave on a loom. [ME *lome*, OE *gelōma* tool, implement. Cf. HEIRLOOM]

loom² (lōōm), *v.i.* **1.** to appear indistinctly, or come into view in indistinct and enlarged form. **2.** to rise before the vision with an appearance of great or portentous size. —*n.* **3.** a looming appearance, as of something seen indistinctly at a distance or through a fog. [cf. d. Sw. *loma* move slowly]

loom³ (lōōm), *n.* **1.** loon¹. **2.** a guillemot or murre. [t. Scand.; cf. Icel. *lōmr*, Sw. *lom*. See LOON¹]

L.O.O.M., Loyal Order of Moose.

loon¹ (lōōn), *n.* any of several large, short-tailed webfooted, fish-eating diving birds of the northern hemisphere, constituting the genus *Gavia*, as the common loon or great northern diver, *Gavia immer*, of the New and Old Worlds. [var. of LOOM³]

loon² (lōōn), *n.* a worthless, sorry, lazy, or stupid fellow. [ME *lowen, loun.* Cf. Icel. *lūinn* exhausted]

loon·y (lōō′nĭ), *adj.,* **loonier, looniest,** *n., pl.* **loonies.** —*adj.* **1.** lunatic; crazy. **2.** *Slang.* extremely or senselessly foolish. —*n.* **3.** *Slang.* a lunatic. Also, **luny.** [var. of *luny*, familiar shortening of LUNATIC] —**loon′i·ness,** *n.*

loop¹ (lōōp), *n.* **1.** a folding or doubling of a portion of a cord, lace, ribbon, etc. upon itself, so as to leave an opening between the parts. **2.** anything shaped more or less like a loop, as a line drawn on paper, a part of a letter, a part of a path, a line of motion, etc. **3.** a curved piece or a ring of metal, wood, etc., used for the insertion of something, or as a handle, or otherwise. **4.** *Aeron.* a maneuver executed in such a manner that the airplane performs a closed curve in a vertical plane. **5.** *Physics.* the part of a vibrating string, column of air, or the like, between two adjacent nodes; antinode. **6.** *Elect.* **a.** a closed electric or magnetic circuit. **b.** a closed curve showing the relation between the magnetizing force and the induction in a ferromagnetic substance when the magnetizing field is carried through a complete cycle. —*v.t.* **7.** to form into a loop or loops. **8.** to make a loop or loops in. **9.** to enfold or encircle in or with something arranged in a loop. **10.** to fasten by forming into a loop, or by means of something formed into a loop. **11.** to fly (an airplane) in a loop or series of loops. **12.** to construct a closed electric or magnetic circuit. —*v.i.* **13.** to make or form a loop or loops. **14.** to move by forming loops, as a measuring worm. [ME *loupe.* Cf. Gaelic and Irish *lub* loop, bend]

loop² (lōōp), *n.* *Archaic.* a small or narrow opening, as in a wall; a loophole. [ME *loupe.* Cf. MD *lūpen* peer]

loop·er (lōō′pər), *n.* **1.** one who or that which loops something or forms loops. **2.** a measuring worm. **3.** the thread holder in a sewing machine using two threads.

loop·hole (lōōp′hōl′), *n., v.,* **-holed, -holing.** —*n.* **1.** a small or narrow opening, as in a wall, for looking through, or for admitting light and air, or particularly, in a fortification, for the discharge of missiles against an enemy outside. **2.** an opening or aperture. **3.** an outlet, or means of escape or evasion. —*v.t.* **4.** to furnish with loopholes. [f. LOOP² + HOLE, n.]

loop·y (lōō′pĭ), *adj.* full of loops.

loose (lōōs), *adj.,* **looser, loosest,** *adv., v.,* **loosed, loosing.** —*adj.* **1.** free from bonds, fetters, or restraint: *to get one's hand loose.* **2.** free or released from fastening or attachment: *a loose end.* **3.** uncombined, as a chemical element. **4.** not bound together, as papers or flowers. **5.** not put up in a package or other container: *loose mushrooms.* **6.** *Colloq.* unemployed or unappropriated: *loose funds.* **7.** wanting in retentiveness or power of restraint: *a loose tongue.* **8.** lax, as the bowels. **9.** free from moral restraint, or lax in principle or conduct. **10.** wanton or unchaste: *a loose woman.* **11.** not firm or rigid: *a loose tooth, a loose rein.* **12.** not fitting closely, as garments. **13.** not close or compact in structure or arrangement; having spaces between the parts, or open: *a loose weave.* **14.** (of earth, soil, etc.) not cohering: *loose sand.* **15.** not strict, exact, or precise: *loose thinking.* **16. at loose ends,** in an unsettled or disorderly condition. —*adv.* **17.** in a loose manner; loosely. —*v.t.* **18.** to let loose, or free from bonds or restraint. **19.** to release, as from constraint, obligation, penalty, etc. **20.** *Chiefly Naut.* to set free from fastening or attachment: *loose a boat from its moorings.* **21.** to unfasten, undo, or untie, as a bond, fetter, or knot. **22.** to shoot, or let fly. **23.** to make less tight; slacken or relax. **24.** *Archaic.* to render less firmly fixed, or loosen. —*v.i.* **25.** to loose something. **26.** to let go a hold. **27.** to weigh anchor. **28.** to shoot or let fly an arrow, etc. **29.** to become loose. [ME *los, loos,* t. Scand.; cf. Icel. *lauss* loose, free, empty. c. D and G *los* loose, free] —**loose′ly,** *adv.* —**loose′ness,** *n.*

---

loose-joint·ed (lōōs′join′tĭd), *adj.* **1.** having loose joints. **2.** loosely built or framed.

loos·en (lōō′sən), *v.t.* **1.** to unfasten or undo, as a bond or fetter. **2.** to make less tight; slacken or relax: *to loosen one's grasp.* **3.** to make less firmly fixed in place: *to loosen a clamp.* **4.** to let loose or set free from bonds, restraint, or constraint. **5.** to make less close or compact in structure or arrangement. **6.** to make less dense or coherent: *to loosen the soil.* **7.** to open, or relieve the costiveness of (the bowels). **8.** to relax in strictness or severity, as restraint or discipline. —*v.i.* **9.** to become loose or looser. —**loos′en·er,** *n.*

loose sentence, a sentence containing subordinate elements not necessary to its completeness.

loose·strife (lōōs′strīf′), *n.* **1.** any of various leafy-stemmed herbs of the primulaceous genus *Lysimachia,* as *L. vulgaris,* a common yellow-flowered species (**yellow loosestrife**), and *L. quadrifolia,* a species with leaves in whorls of four or five (**whorled loosestrife**). **2.** any of various herbaceous plants of the lythraceous genus *Lythrum,* as *L. Salicaria,* a purple-flowered species (**purple loosestrife**). [f. LOOSE, v., + STRIFE, erroneous trans. of L *lysimachia* (actually der. Gk. proper name *Lysimachos,* lit., the one loosing (i.e. ending) strife)]

loot (lōōt), *n.* **1.** spoils or plunder taken by pillaging, as in war. **2.** anything dishonestly and ruthlessly appropriated: *a burglar's loot.* **3.** act of looting or plundering: *the loot of a conquered city.* —*v.t.* **4.** to take, or carry off, as loot. **5.** to despoil by taking loot; plunder or pillage (a city, house, etc.), as in war. **6.** to rob, as by burglary, corrupt practice in public office, etc. —*v.i.* **7.** to take loot; plunder. [t. Hind.: m. *lūt*] —**loot′er,** *n.* —**Syn. 4.** sack, rifle.

lop[1] (lŏp), *v.,* **lopped, lopping,** *n.* —*v.t.* **1.** to cut off the branches, twigs, etc., of (a tree or other plant). **2.** to cut off the head, limbs, etc. of (a person) or parts of (a thing). **3.** to cut off (branches, twigs, etc.) from a tree or other plant. **4.** to cut off (the head, limbs, etc.) from a person. —*v.i.* **5.** to cut off branches, twigs, etc., as of a tree. **6.** to remove parts by or as by cutting. —*n.* **7.** parts or a part lopped off. **8.** the smaller branches and twigs of trees. [ME (def. 8), etymologically identical with obs. *lop* spider, both objects being marked by many projecting parts] —**lop′per,** *n.*

lop[2] (lŏp), *v.,* **lopped, lopping.** —*v.i.* **1.** to hang loosely or limply; droop. **2.** to sway, move, or go in a drooping or heavy, awkward way. —*v.t.* **3.** to let hang or droop. [der. obs. *lop,* n., lobe (var. of LAP[1] lobe); lit., to behave like a *lop,* i.e., to dangle, hang loosely]

lope (lōp), *v.,* **loped, loping,** *n.* —*v.i.* **1.** to move or run with bounding steps, as a quadruped, or with a long, easy stride, as a person. **2.** to canter leisurely with a rather long, easy stride, as a horse. —*v.t.* **3.** to cause to lope, as a horse. —*n.* **4.** the act or the gait of loping. **5.** a long, easy stride. [late ME, var. of obs. *loup* leap, t. Scand.; cf. Icel. *hlaupa*] —**lop′er,** *n.*

lop-eared (lŏp′ĭrd′), *adj.* having ears that lop or hang down.

lo·pho·branch (lō′fə brăngk′, lŏf′ə-), *n.* **1.** any of the *Lophobranchii,* an order or group of teleostean fishes having gills in tufts, as the sea horses, pipefishes, etc. —*adj.* **2.** belonging or pertaining to the *Lophobranchii.* [f. Gk.: *lópho(s)* crest + *m.s. bránchia* gills] —**lo·pho·bran·chi·ate** (lŏf′ə brăng′kĭ ĭt, -āt′, lō′fə-), *adj.,* *n.*

lop·py (lŏp′ĭ), *adj.* lopping; limp. [f. LOP[2] + -Y[1]]

lop·sid·ed (lŏp′sī′dĭd), *adj.* **1.** lopping or inclining to one side. **2.** heavier, larger, or more developed on one side than on the other; unsymmetrical. —**lop′sid′ed·ly,** *adv.* —**lop′sid′ed·ness,** *n.*

loq., loquitur.

lo·qua·cious (lō kwā′shəs), *adj.* **1.** talking or disposed to talk much or freely; talkative. **2.** characterized by or showing a disposition to talk much: *a loquacious mood.* [f. LOQUACI(TY) + -OUS] —**lo·qua′cious·ly,** *adv.* —**Syn. 1.** See talkative.

lo·quac·i·ty (lō kwăs′ə tĭ), *n.* **1.** state of being loquacious. **2.** loquacious flow of talk. [t. L: m.s. *loquācitas*]

lo·quat (lō′kwŏt, -kwät), *n.* **1.** a small, evergreen, malaceous tree, *Eriobotrya japonica,* native in China and Japan, but cultivated elsewhere for ornament and for its yellow, plumlike fruit; Japanese medlar. **2.** the fruit. [t. Chinese (Canton): m. *luh kwat* rush orange]

lo·qui·tur (lŏk′wə tər), *v.* Latin. he (or she) speaks.

Lo·rain (lō rān′), *n.* a city in N Ohio: a port on Lake Erie. 51,202 (1950).

lo·ran (lōr′ən), *n.* a device by which a navigator can locate his position by determining the time displacement between radio signals from two known stations. [short for *lo(ng) ra(nge) n(avigation)*]

Lor·ca (lôr′kä), *n.* a city in SE Spain. 24,127 (1940).

lord (lôrd), *n.* **1.** one who has dominion over others; a master, chief, or ruler. **2.** one who exercises authority from property rights; an owner or possessor of land, houses, etc. **3.** a feudal superior; the proprietor of a manor. **4.** a titled nobleman, or peer, or one whose ordinary appellation contains by courtesy the title *Lord* or some higher title. **5. Lords,** the temporal and spiritual members of the House of Lords. **6.** (*cap.*) Brit. **a.** the title (in collocation with some other word or words) of certain high officials: *Lord Mayor of London.* **b.** (in ceremonious use) the title of a bishop: *Lord Bishop of Durham.* **c.** the title substituted in less formal use for marquis, earl, viscount, etc.: *Lord Kitchener* for

Earl Kitchener. **7.** (*cap.*) the Supreme Being, Jehovah, or God. **8.** (*cap.*) the Savior, Jesus Christ. **9.** *Astrol.* a planet having dominating influence. —*interj.* **10.** (*often cap.*) the noun Lord (God) used as an exclamation of surprise, etc. —*v.i.* **11.** to play the lord; behave in a lordly manner; domineer (often with indefinite *it*): *to lord it over someone.* [ME *lord, loverd,* OE *hlāford,* f. *hlāf* LOAF[1] + *weard* keeper. Cf. LADY, WARD]

Lord Chancellor, the highest judicial officer of the British crown, law adviser of the ministry, keeper of the great seal, presiding officer in the House of Lords, etc.

Lord Chief Justice, the highest judicial officer of England.

lord·ling (lôrd′lĭng), *n.* a little or petty lord.

lord·ly (lôrd′lĭ), *adj.,* **-lier, -liest,** *adv.* —*adj.* **1.** suitable for a lord, as things; grand or magnificent. **2.** insolently imperious: *lordly contempt.* **3.** of or pertaining to a lord or lords. **4.** having the character or attributes of a lord, as a person. **5.** befitting a lord, as actions. —*adv.* **6.** in the manner of a lord. —**lord′li·ness,** *n.* —**Syn. 2.** haughty, arrogant. —**Ant. 2.** meek.

Lord of hosts, Jehovah, the Supreme Ruler.

Lord of Misrule, a person formerly chosen to direct revels and sports.

lor·do·sis (lôr dō′sĭs), *n.* *Pathol.* anterior curvature of the spine; i.e., convexity anterior or to the front. [t. NL, t. Gk.: a bending back] —**lor·dot·ic** (lôr dŏt′ĭk), *adj.*

Lord Protector, protector (def. 2b).

Lord Protector of the Commonwealth, protector (def. 2b).

Lord Provost, provost (def. 1a).

Lord's day, the, Sunday.

lord·ship (lôrd′shĭp), *n.* **1.** (*often cap.*) the form used in speaking of or to a man having the title of Lord, or of or to a judge, as in British use (prec. by *his, your,* etc.). **2.** the state or dignity of a lord. **3.** *Hist.* **a.** the authority or power of a lord. **b.** the domain of a lord.

Lord's Prayer, the, the prayer given by Jesus to his disciples. Mat. 6:9–13; Luke, 11:2–4.

Lord's Supper, the, 1. the last supper of Jesus and his disciples. **2.** the sacrament in commemoration of this; the eucharist; the communion; the mass.

Lord's table, the, the communion table or the altar.

lore[1] (lōr), *n.* **1.** the body of knowledge, esp. of a traditional, anecdotal, or popular nature, on a particular subject: *the lore of herbs.* **2.** learning, knowledge, or erudition. **3.** *Archaic.* **a.** teaching or instruction. **b.** that which is taught. [ME; OE *lār,* c. D *leer,* G *lehre* teaching. Cf. LEARN] —**Syn. 2.** See learning.

lore[2] (lōr), *n.* *Zool.* the space between the eye and the bill of a bird, or a corresponding space in other animals, as serpents. [t. L: m.s. *lōrum* thong]

Lor·e·lei (lōr′ə lī′; Ger. lō′rə-). *n.* German Legend. an enchantress who, by her singing, caused sailors to wreck their boats on her rock in the Rhine. [t. G]

Lo·rentz (lō′rĕnts), *n.* Hendrik Antoon (hĕn′drĭk än′tōn), 1853–1928, Dutch physicist.

lor·gnette (lôr nyĕt′), *n.* **1.** a pair of eyeglasses mounted on a long handle. **2.** an opera glass. [t. F, der. *lorgner* look sidelong at, eye, der. OF *lorgne* squinting]

lor·gnon (lôr nyôN′), *n.* **1.** an eyeglass, or a pair of eyeglasses. **2.** an opera glass. [F, der. *lorgner.* See LORGNETTE]

lo·ri·ca (lō rī′kə), *n.,* *pl.* **-cae** (-sē). **1.** *Zool.* a hard protective case or sheath, as the protective coverings secreted by certain infusorians. **2.** a cuirass or corselet, orig. of leather. [t. L: a corselet, a defense]

lor·i·cate (lôr′ə kāt′, lŏr′-), *adj.* covered with a lorica. Also, **lor′i·cat′ed.**

Lo·ri·ent (lô ryäN′), *n.* a seaport in NW France, in Brittany; shipbuilding; held by the Germans during World War II. 11,838 (1946).

lor·i·keet (lôr′ə kēt′, lôr′-, lôr′ə kēt′, lôr′-), *n.* any of various small lories. [f. LORY + (PARRA)KEET]

lo·ris (lōr′ĭs), *n.,* *pl.* **-ris.** **1.** a small, slender, tailless, large-eyed, nocturnal lemur, *Loris gracilis,* of Ceylon (**slender loris**). **2.** any lemur of the related genus *Nycticebus* (**slow loris**). [t. NL, t. D: m. *loeris* booby]

lorn (lôrn), *adj.* **1.** *Archaic.* forsaken, desolate, wretched or forlorn. **2.** *Obs.* lost, ruined, or undone. [ME *lorn,* OE *loren,* pp. of *-lēosan* LOSE (recorded in compounds)]

Lor·rain (lō rān′; Fr. lô räN′), *n.* Claude (klôd; Fr. klōd), (*Claude Gelée*) 1600–82, French landscape painter.

Lor·raine (lō rān′; Fr. lô rĕn′), *n.* **1.** a medieval kingdom in W Europe along the Moselle, Meuse, and Rhine rivers. **2.** a region in NE France, once included in this kingdom: a former province. See **Alsace-Lorraine.** **3. Cross of,** a cross having two horizontal arms, the upper one shorter than the other.

lor·ry (lôr′ĭ, lŏr′ĭ), *n.,* *pl.* **-ries. 1.** *Brit.* a motor truck, esp. for heavy work. **2.** any of various vehicles or cars running on rails, as for transporting material in a mine or factory. **3.** a long, low, horse-drawn wagon without sides, common in England. [cf. d. E *lurry* pull, drag, lug]

lo·ry (lōr′ĭ), *n.,* *pl.* **-ries.** any of various parrots, (subfamily *Loriinae*) of the Malay Archipelago, Australia, etc., mostly bright-colored, brush-tongued, and of small size. [t. Malay: m. *lūrī*]

los·a·ble (lōō′zə bəl), *adj.* that may be lost.

Los An·ge·les (lŏs ăng′gə ləs, ăn′jə ləs, -lēz′), a seaport in SW California. 1,970,358 pop.; with suburbs, 4,329,225 (1950): 452 sq. mi.

lose (lōōz), v., **lost, losing.** —v.t. **1.** to come to be without, by some chance, and not know the whereabouts of: *to lose a ring.* **2.** to suffer the loss or deprivation of: *to lose one's life.* **3.** to be bereaved of by death: *to lose a child.* **4.** to fail to keep, preserve, or maintain: *to lose one's balance.* **5.** to cease to have: *to lose all fear.* **6.** to bring to destruction or ruin (now chiefly in the passive): *ship and crew were lost.* **7.** to have slip from sight, hearing, attention, etc.: *to lose a face in a crowd.* **8.** to become separated from and ignorant of (the way, etc.). **9.** to leave far behind in a pursuit, race, etc. **10.** to use to no purpose, or waste: *to lose time in waiting.* **11.** to fail to have, get, catch, etc.; miss: *to lose a bargain.* **12.** to fail to win (a prize, stake, etc.). **13.** to be defeated in (a game, lawsuit, battle, etc.). **14.** to cause the loss of: *the delay lost the battle for them.* **15.** to let (oneself) go astray; become bewildered: *to be lost in a wood.* **16.** to absorb or engross in something to the exclusion of knowledge or consciousness of all else (usually used reflexively or in the passive): *to be lost in thought.* —v.i. **17.** to suffer loss: *to lose on a contract.* **18.** to lose ground, fall behind, or fail to hold one's own, as in a race or other contest. **19.** to fail to win, as in a contest; be defeated. [ME *lose(n),* OE *-lēosan;* r. ME *lese(n),* OE *-lēosan* (cf. *choose,* r. *chese*), c. G. *(ver)lieren.* See LOSS] —**los′er,** n.

los·ing (lōō′zĭng), adj. **1.** that loses. —n. **2.** (pl.) losses. —**los′ing·ly,** adv.

loss (lôs, lŏs), n. **1.** detriment or disadvantage from failure to keep, have, or get: *to bear the loss of a robbery.* **2.** that which is lost. **3.** amount or number lost. **4.** a being deprived of or coming to be without something that one has had: *loss of friends.* **5.** the accidental or inadvertent losing of something dropped, misplaced, or of unknown whereabouts: *to discover the loss of a document.* **6.** a losing by defeat, or failure to win: *the loss of a bet.* **7.** failure to make good use of something, as time; waste. **8.** failure to preserve or maintain: *loss of speed.* **9.** destruction or ruin. **10.** *Mil.* **a.** the losing of soldiers by death, capture, etc. **b.** *(often pl.)* the number of soldiers so lost. **11.** *Insurance.* **a.** occurrence of a risk, as death or damage to property, covered by a contract of insurance so as to result in insurer liability. **b.** that which causes such a loss. **c.** an example of such a loss. **12.** *Elect.* the difference between power input and power output of an electric circuit, device, machine, or system incident to the process of electric transmission or energy conversion. **13.** **at a loss, a.** in a state of bewilderment or uncertainty. **b.** in a state of embarrassment for lack of something: *to be at a loss for words.* [ME; OE *los* destruction, c. Icel. *los* breaking up; akin to LOSE]

loss leader, a popular article which is sold at a loss for the purpose of attracting trade to a retail store.

loss ratio, *Insurance.* the ratio of paid-in premiums to losses sustained during a certain period.

lost (lôst, lŏst), adj. **1.** no longer possessed or retained: *lost friends.* **2.** no longer to be found: *lost articles.* **3.** having gone astray or lost the way; bewildered as to place, direction, etc. **4.** not used to good purpose, as opportunities, time, labor, etc.; wasted. **5.** that one has failed to win: *a lost prize.* **6.** attended with defeat: *a lost battle.* **7.** destroyed or ruined: *lost ships.* **8. lost to, a.** no longer belonging to. **b.** no longer possible or open to: *the opportunity was lost to him.* **c.** insensible to: *to be lost to all sense of duty.* —v. **9.** pt. of **lose.**

lost cause, a cause for which defeat has occurred or is inevitable.

Lost Pleiad. See **Pleiades** (def. 1).

lot (lŏt), n., v., **lotted, lotting.** —n. **1.** one of a set of objects drawn from a receptacle, etc., to decide a question or choice by chance. **2.** the casting or drawing of such objects as a method of deciding something: *to choose a person by lot.* **3.** the decision or choice so made. **4.** allotted share or portion. **5.** the portion in life assigned by fate or Providence, or one's fate, fortune, or destiny. **6.** a distinct portion or piece of land. **7.** a piece of land forming a part of a district, city, or other community. **8.** *Motion Pictures.* the site of a motion picture being filmed, esp. a studio. **9.** a distinct portion or parcel of anything, as of merchandise. **10.** a number of things or persons collectively. **11.** *Colloq.* a person of a specified sort. **12.** *(often pl.)* *Colloq.* a great many or a great deal: *a lot of books.* **13.** *Chiefly Brit.* a tax or duty. —v.t. **14.** to cast or draw lots for. **15.** to divide or distribute by lot. **16.** to assign to one as his lot; allot. **17.** to divide into lots, as land. —v.i. **18.** to draw lots. [ME; OE *hlot,* akin to G *loos,* Icel. *hlutr,* Goth. *hlauts*]

Lot (lŏt), n. *Bible.* the nephew of Abraham. His wife was changed into a pillar of salt for looking back during their flight from Sodom. Gen. 13:1–12, 19. [t. Heb]

Lot (lŏt), n. a river in S France, flowing W to the Garonne. ab. 300 mi.

loth (lōth), adj. loath.

Lo·thair I (lō thâr′, -târ′), c795–855, emperor of the Holy Roman Empire, 843–855.

Lothair II, *("the Saxon")* c1070–1137, emperor of the Holy Roman Empire, 1125–37.

Lo·thaire (lō târ′), n. French name for **Lothair.**

Lo·thar (lō′tär, lō tär′), n. German name for **Lothair.**

Lo·thar·i·o (lō thâr′ĭō), n., pl. **-tharios.** a jaunty libertine; a rake.

Lo·thi·ans (lō′thĭənz, -thĭ-), n.pl. **The,** three counties in Scotland: East Lothian, Midlothian, West Lothian.

Lo·ti (lō tē′), n. **Pierre** (pyĕr′), *(Louis Marie Julien Viaud)* 1850–1923, French novelist.

lo·tion (lō′shən), n. *Pharm., etc.* a watery liquid containing insoluble medicinal matter applied externally to the skin without rubbing. [ME, t. L: s. *lōtio* a washing]

lot·ter·y (lŏt′ərĭ), n., pl. **-teries. 1.** a scheme or arrangement for raising money, as for some public, charitable, or private purpose, by the sale of a large number of tickets, certain among which, as determined by chance after the sale, entitle the holders to prizes. **2.** any scheme for the distribution of prizes by chance. **3.** any affair of chance. [t. It.: m. *lotteria,* der. *lotto* lot, t. F: m. *lot,* t. Gmc.; cf. LOT]

lot·to (lŏt′ō), n. a game played by drawing numbered disks from a bag or the like and covering corresponding numbers on cards. [t. It. See LOTTERY]

lo·tus (lō′təs), n. **1.** a plant, commonly identified with a species of jujube or of nettle tree, referred to in Greek legend as yielding a fruit which induced a state of dreamy and contented forgetfulness in those who ate it. **2.** the fruit itself. **3.** either of the two species of nelumbo, *Nelumbium Nelumbo* (**sacred lotus of India**) and *N. pentapetalum* (**water chinquapin**). **4.** any of various nymphaeaceous plants, as either of two Egyptian water lilies, *Nymphaea Lotus* and *N. caerulea.* **5.** a representation of such a plant, common in Egyptian and Hindu decorative art. **6.** any of the shrubbery herbs, with red, pink, or white flowers, constituting the leguminous genus *Lotus,* certain of which are valued as pasture plants. Also, **lo′tos.** [t. L, t. Gk.: m. *lōtós*]

lo·tus-eat·er (lō′təs ē′tər), n. **1.** an eater of the fruit which induced languor and forgetfulness of home. Homer's *Odyssey,* ix. **2.** one who leads a life of dreamy, indolent ease, indifferent to the busy world.

loud (loud), adj. **1.** striking strongly upon the organs of hearing, as sound, noise, the voice, etc.; strongly audible. **2.** making, emitting, or uttering strongly audible sounds: *loud knocking.* **3.** full of sound or noise, or resounding. **4.** clamorous, vociferous, or blatant. **5.** emphatic or insistent: *to be loud in one's praises.* **6.** *Colloq.* strong or offensive in smell. **7.** excessively striking to the eye, or offensively showy, as colors, dress or the wearer, etc. **8.** obtrusively vulgar, as manners, persons, etc. —adv. **9.** loudly, etc. [ME; OE *hlūd,* c. G *laut*] —**loud′ly,** adv. —**loud′ness,** n. —**Syn. 1.** resounding; deafening; stentorian. LOUD, NOISY describe a strongly audible sound or sounds. LOUD means characterized by a full, powerful sound or sounds, which make a strong impression on the organs of hearing: *a loud voice, laugh, report.* NOISY refers to a series of sounds, and suggests clamor and discordance, or persistence in making loud sounds which are disturbing and annoying. **7.** gaudy, flashy, showy. —**Ant. 1.** quiet.

loud·ish (lou′dĭsh), adj. somewhat loud.

loud-mouthed (loud′mouthd′, -mouth′), adj. loud of voice or utterance; vociferous; blatant.

loud-speak·er (loud′spē′kər), n. any of various devices by which speech, music, etc., can be made audible throughout a room, hall, or the like.

lough (lŏk, lŏKH), n. *Irish.* **1.** a lake. **2.** an arm of the sea. [ME, t. Irish: m. *loch.* Cf. LOCH]

lou·is (lōō′ĭ), n., pl. **louis** (lōō′ĭz). louis d'or.

Lou·is (lōō′ĭs), n. **Joe,** *(Joseph Louis Barrow)* born 1914, U.S. heavyweight boxing champion, 1937–1949.

Lou·is (lōō′ĭ, lōō′ĭs; Fr. lwē), n. name of 18 kings of France.

Louis I, *("le Débonnaire," "the Pious")* A.D. 778–840, king of France and emperor of the Holy Roman Empire, A.D. 814–840 (son of Charlemagne).

Louis II, *("the German")* A.D. 804?–876, king of all Germany E of Rhine by Treaty of Verdun (A.D. 843). German, **Ludwig II.**

Louis II de Bourbon. See **Condé.**

Louis IV, *("the Bavarian")* 1287?–1347, emperor of the Holy Roman Empire, 1314–47.

Louis V, *("le Fainéant")* A.D. 967?–987, king of France, A.D. 986–987; the last of the Carolingian family of rulers in France.

Louis IX, *(Saint Louis)* 1215–70, king of France, 1226–1270; canonized in 1297.

Louis XI, 1423–83, king of France, 1461–83.

Louis XII, *("the Father of the People")* 1462–1515, king of France, 1498–1515.

Louis XIII, 1601–43, king of France, 1610–43.

Louis XIV, *("the Great")* 1638–1715, king of France, 1643–1715.

Louis XV, 1710–74, king of France, 1715–74.

Louis XVI, 1754–93, king of France from 1774, deposed in 1792, guillotined in 1793.

Louis XVII, 1785–95, son of Louis XVI. He never reigned, but was called king of France, 1793–95, by the monarchists.

Louis XVIII, 1755–1824, king of France, 1814–24.

Lou·is·burg (lōō′ĭs bûrg′), n. a seaport in SE Canada, on Cape Breton Island, Nova Scotia: the important French fortress here was captured by the British, 1745, 1758. 1012 (1941).

lou·is d'or (lōō′ĭ dôr′; Fr. lwē), a French gold coin, issued 1640–1795, worth from about $4 to about $4.60. Also, **louis.** [F: gold louis]

Lou·ise (lōō ēz′), n. **Lake,** a glacial lake in the Canadian Rockies, in SW Alberta, Canada: resort. 5670 ft. high.

ăct, āble, dâre, ärt; ĕbb, ēqual; ĭf, īce; hŏt, ōver, ôrder, oil, bŏŏk, ōōze, out; ŭp, ūse, ûrge; ə = a in alone; ch, chief; g, give; ng, ring; sh, shoe; th, thin; th, that; zh, vision. See the full key on inside cover.

Lou·i·si·an·a (lŏŏ ē´zĭ ăn´ə, lŏŏ´ĭ zĭ-), *n.* a State in the S United States. 2,683,516 pop. (1950); 48,522 sq. mi. *Cap.:* Baton Rouge. *Abbrev.:* La. —**Lou·i·si·an´an,** **Lou·i·si·an·i·an** (lŏŏ ē´zĭ ăn´ī ən, lŏŏ´ĭ zĭ-), *adj., n.*

Louisiana Purchase, The, a huge territory which the United States purchased from France in 1803, extending from the Mississippi to the Rocky Mountains and from the Gulf of Mexico to British America.

Louis Napoleon, Napoleon III.

Louis Phi·lippe (fē lēp´), 1773–1850, king of France, 1830–48.

Louis Qua·torze (kə tôrz´; *Fr.* kȧ tôrz´), of the period of Louis XIV of France or the styles of architecture, decoration, etc., prevailing about that time (1650–1700), relying more upon classical models than those of the Louis Treize period, and richly ornamented. [t. F: Louis Fourteenth]

Louis Quinze (kănz), of the period of Louis XV of France or the styles of architecture, decoration, etc., (known as *rococo*) prevailing about that time (1700–1750), smaller in scale and more delicate in ornament than those of the Louis Quatorze period. [t. F: Louis Fifteenth]

Louis Seize (sĕz), of the period of Louis XVI of France or the styles of architecture, decoration, etc. prevailing about that time (1750–1790), characterized by a recurrence of classical models. [t. F: Louis Sixteenth]

Louis Treize (trĕz), of the period of Louis XIII of France or the styles of architecture, decoration, etc., prevailing about that time (1600–1650), less light and elegant than those of the earlier Renaissance, and employing forms and features based on the classical. [t. F: Louis Thirteenth]

Lou·is·ville (lŏŏ´ĭ vĭl´), *n.* a city in N Kentucky: a port on the Ohio river; Kentucky Derby. 369,129 (1950).

lounge (lounj), *v.,* **lounged, lounging,** *n.* —*v.i.* 1. to pass time idly and indolently. 2. to recline indolently; loll. 3. to move or go (*about, along, off,* etc.) in a leisurely, indolent manner. —*v.t.* 4. to pass (time, etc.) in lounging (fol. by *away* or *out*). —*n.* 5. a kind of sofa for reclining on, with or without a back, and with a headrest at one end. 6. a place for lounging, esp. a large room, as in a hotel, esp. in England, a high-class part of a public house. 7. the act or a spell of lounging. 8. a lounging gait. [? akin to obs. *lungis* laggard, t. OF: m. *longis* one who is long (i.e. slow)] —**loung´er,** *n.*

loup (lŏŏ), *n.* a cloth mask, often of silk, which covers only half the face. [F: lit., wolf, g. L *lupus*]

loup-ga·rou (lŏŏ gȧ rŏŏ´), *n., pl.* **loups-garous** (lŏŏ-gȧ rŏŏ´). French. a werewolf; a lycanthrope. [F: f. *loup* wolf (g. L *lupus*) + *garou* werewolf, of Gmc. orig.]

loup·ing ill (lou´pĭng, lŏ´-), an acute, virus-induced infectious disease of sheep, transmitted by a tick, which affects the nervous system and also attacks man.

lour (lour), *v.i., n.* lower².

Lourdes (lŏŏrd), *n.* a city in SW France: famous shrine. 9399 (1936).

Lou·ren·ço Mar·ques (lō rĕn´sō mär´kĕs; *Port.* lô-rĕn´sŏŏ mär´kēzh), a seaport in and the capital of Mozambique, on Delagoa Bay. 68,223 (1940).

louse (lous), *n., pl.* **lice** (līs). 1. any of the small, wingless, blood-sucking insects of the order *Anoplura,* including several species associated with man, as the **human louse,** *Pediculus humanus* (including the races known as **head louse,** *P. capitis,* and **body louse,** *P. corporis*), and the **crab louse,** *Phthirus pubis.* 2. any of various other insects parasitic on animals or plants, as those of the order *Mallophaga* (**biting bird lice**) or the homopterous family *Aphididae* (**plant lice**). [ME *lows(e),* *lous(e),* OE *lūs* (pl. *lȳs*), c. G *laus*]

louse·wort (lous´wûrt´), *n.* any of the scrophulariaceous herbs constituting the large genus *Pedicularis,* as *P. sylvatica* (**pasture lousewort**), an English species formerly supposed to breed lice in sheep, and *P. canadensis* (**wood betony**).

Head louse, Pediculus capitis

lous·y (lou´zĭ), *adj.,* **lousier, lousiest. 1.** infested with lice. **2.** *Slang.* mean, or contemptible. **3.** *Slang.* well supplied. —**lous´i·ly,** *adv.* —**lous´i·ness,** *n.*

lout (lout), *n.* an awkward, stupid person; a boor. [akin to archaic *lout* bow or obs. *lout* lurk]

lout·ish (lou´tĭsh), *adj.* like or characteristic of a lout; boorish. —**lout´ish·ly,** *adv.* —**lout´ish·ness,** *n.*

Lou·vain (lŏŏ văN´), *n.* a city in central Belgium. 35,926 (est. 1944).

lou·ver (lŏŏ´vər), *n.* **1.** a turret or lantern on the roof of a medieval building, to supply ventilation or light. **2.** an arrangement of louver boards or the like closing a window or other opening, or a single louver board. **3.** one of a series of slitlike openings in the hood or body of an automobile for the escape of heated air from within. [ME *lover,* t. OF; orig. obscure]

louver boards, one of a series of overlapping, sloping boards, slats, or the like, in an opening, so arranged as to admit air but exclude rain.

Lou·vre (lŏŏ´vr), *n.* a royal palace (begun 1541) in Paris, largely occupied since 1793 by a famous museum.

Louys (lwē), *n.* **Pierre** (pyĕr), 1870–1925, French author.

lov·a·ble (lŭv´ə bəl), *adj.* of such a nature as to attract love; amiable. Also, **loveable.** —**lov´a·bil´i·ty,** **lov´a·ble·ness,** *n.* —**lov´a·bly,** *adv.*

lov·age (lŭv´ĭj), *n.* a European apiaceous herb, *Levisticum officinale,* cultivated in old gardens and used as a domestic remedy. [ME *loveache,* t. OF: alter. of *levesche,* g. LL *levisticum,* appar. alter. of L *ligusticum,* prop. neut. of *Ligusticus* Ligurian]

love (lŭv), *n., v.,* **loved, loving.** —*n.* **1.** a strong or passionate affection for a person of the opposite sex. **2.** sexual passion or desire, or its gratification. **3.** an object of love or affection; a sweetheart. **4.** (*cap.*) a personification of sexual affection, as Eros or Cupid. **5.** a feeling of warm personal attachment or deep affection, as for a friend (or between friends), parent, child, etc. **6.** strong predilection or liking for anything: *love of books.* **7.** the benevolent affection of God for His creatures, or the reverent affection due from them to God. **8.** *Tennis, etc.* nothing; no score. **9. for love, a.** out of affection. **b.** for nothing; without compensation. **10. in love,** feeling deep affection or passion (often fol. by *with*). [ME; OE *lufu,* c. OHG *luba*] —*v.t.* **11.** to have love or affection for. **12.** to have a strong or passionate affection for (one of the opposite sex). **13.** to have a strong liking for; take great pleasure in: *to love music.* —*v.i.* **14.** to have love or affection, esp., to be or fall in love with one of the opposite sex. [ME; OE *lufian,* der. *lufu* LOVE, n.] —**Syn. 1, 5.** LOVE, AFFECTION, DEVOTION all mean a deep and enduring emotional regard, usually for another person. Love may apply to various kinds of regard: the charity of the Creator, reverent adoration toward God or toward a person, the relation of parent and child, the regard of friends for each other, romantic feelings for one of the opposite sex, etc. AFFECTION is a fondness for persons of either sex, that is enduring and tender, but calm. DEVOTION is an intense love and steadfast, enduring loyalty to a person; it may also imply consecration to a cause. —**Ant. 5.** hate.

love·a·ble (lŭv´ə bəl), *adj.* lovable.

love affair, a particular experience of being in love.

love apple, the tomato.

love·bird (lŭv´bûrd´), *n.* any of various small parrots, esp. of the genera *Agapornis,* of Africa, and *Psittacula,* of South America, remarkable for the fact that the members of each pair keep close together when perching.

love feast, 1. (among the early Christians) a meal eaten in token of brotherly love and charity. **2.** a rite practiced by a few denominations such as Mennonites and Dunkers; a fellowship meal. **3.** a banquet or gathering of persons to promote good feeling.

love-in-a-mist (lŭv´ĭn ə mĭst´), *n.* *Bot.* a ranunculaceous plant, *Nigella damascena,* with feathery dissected leaves and whitish or blue flowers.

love-in-i·dle·ness (lŭv´ĭn ī´dəl nĭs), *n.* the wild pansy, *Viola tricolor.*

love knot, a knot of ribbon as a token of love.

Love·lace (lŭv´lās), *n.* **Richard,** 1618–58, British poet.

love·less (lŭv´lĭs), *adj.* **1.** devoid of or unattended with love. **2.** feeling no love. **3.** receiving no love. —**love´less·ly,** *adv.* —**love´less·ness,** *n.*

love-lies-bleed·ing (lŭv´līz blē´dĭng), *n.* any of several species of amaranth, esp. *Amaranthus caudatus,* with spikes of crimson flowers.

love·lock (lŭv´lŏk´), *n.* **1.** any conspicuous lock of hair. **2.** (formerly) a long, flowing lock or curl, dressed separately from the rest of the hair, worn by courtiers.

love·lorn (lŭv´lôrn´), *adj.* forsaken by one's love; forlorn or pining from love. —**love´lorn´ness,** *n.*

love·ly (lŭv´lĭ), *adj.,* **-lier, -liest. 1.** charmingly or exquisitely beautiful: *a lovely flower.* **2.** having a beauty that appeals to the heart as well as to the eye, as a person, a face, etc. **3.** *Colloq.* delightful, or highly pleasing: *to have a lovely time.* **4.** of a great moral or spiritual beauty: *lovely character.* [ME *lovelich,* OE *luflic* amiable] —**love´li·ness,** *n.* —**Syn. 2.** See **beautiful.**

lov·er (lŭv´ər), *n.* **1.** one who is in love with a person of the opposite sex (now used almost exclusively of the man). **2.** (*pl.*) a man and woman in love with each other. **3.** one who has a strong predilection or liking for something: *a lover of music.* **4.** one who loves.

Lov·er (lŭv´ər), *n.* **Samuel,** 1797–1868, Irish novelist, artist, and composer.

love seat, a seat for two persons.

love·sick (lŭv´sĭk´), *adj.* **1.** sick or languishing with love. **2.** expressive of such languishing. —**love´sick´ness,** *n.*

lov·ing (lŭv´ĭng), *adj.* feeling or showing love; affectionate; fond: *loving glances.* —**lov´ing·ly,** *adv.* —**lov´ing·ness,** *n.*

loving cup, a large cup, as of silver, commonly with several handles, for passing among persons who drink from it in turn, as at the close of a banquet.

lov·ing-kind·ness (lŭv´ĭng kind´nĭs), *n.* kindness arising from love (used primarily of the Deity).

low¹ (lō), *adj.* **1.** situated or occurring not far above the ground, floor, or base: *a low shelf.* **2.** not far above the horizon, as a heavenly body. **3.** lying or being below the general level: *low ground.* **4.** (of a garment) low-necked. **5.** designating or pertaining to regions near the sea level or sea as opposed to highland or inland regions: *low Germans*. **6.** prostrate or dead: *to lay one low*. **7.** profound or deep, as a bow. **8.** of small extent upward, or not high or tall: *low walls*. **9.** rising but slightly from a surface: *low relief*. **10.** of less than average or normal height or depth, as a liquid, stream, etc. **11.** lacking in strength or vigor; feeble; weak. **12.** affording little strength or nourishment, as diet. **13.** small in amount, degree, force, etc.: *a low number*. **14.** denoted by a low number: *a low latitude* (one near the equator). **15.** assigning or attributing no great amount, value, or excellence: *a low estimate of something*. **16.** depressed or dejected: *low spirits*. **17.** far down in the scale of rank or estimation; humble: *low birth*. **18.** of inferior quality or character: *a low type of intellect*. **19.** lacking in dignity or elevation, as of thought or expression. **20.** groveling or abject; mean or base: *a low trick*. **21.** coarse or vulgar: *low company*. **22.** *Biol.* having a relatively simple structure; not complex in organization. **23.** *Music.* produced by relatively slow vibrations, as sounds; grave in pitch. **24.** not loud: *a low murmur*. **25.** relatively late or recent, as a date. **26.** *Chiefly Brit.* holding to Low Church principles and practices. **27.** *Phonet.* pronounced with the tongue held relatively low in the mouth: *"hot" has a low vowel*. **28.** *Auto.* of or pertaining to low transmission gear ratio. —*adv.* **29.** in or to a low position, point, degree, etc. **30.** near the ground, floor, or base, or not aloft. **31.** humbly; meanly. **32.** cheaply. **33.** at or to a low pitch. **34.** in a low tone; softly or quietly. **35.** far down in time, or late. —*n.* **36.** that which is low. **37.** *Auto.* a transmission gear ratio providing the least forward speed, usually used to start a motor vehicle, or for extra power; first. **38.** *Meteorol.* a pressure system characterized by relatively low pressure at the center. **39.** *Cards.* the lowest trump card, esp. in game of the seven up family. [ME *lowe, lohe*, earlier *lah*, t. Scand.; cf. Icel. *lāgr*, akin to LIE²] —**low′ness,** *n.* —**Syn. 17.** lowly, meek, obscure. **20.** ignoble, degraded, sordid. **21.** See **mean².** **23.** deep. **24.** subdued. —**Ant. 17.** lofty.

low² (lō), *v.i.* **1.** to utter the sound characteristic of cattle; moo. —*v.t.* **2.** to utter by or as by lowing. —*n.* **3.** the act or the sound of lowing. [ME *low*(*en*), OE *hlōwan*, c. D *loeien*]

Low (lō), *n.* **David,** born 1891, British cartoonist.

Low Archipelago (lō), Tuamoto Archipelago.

low area, *Meteorol.* a region where the atmospheric or barometric pressure is lower than that of the surrounding regions: *the low area in the central part of a cyclone*.

low·born (lō′bôrn′), *adj.* of humble birth.

low·boy (lō′boi′), *n.* a low chest of drawers supported on short legs.

low·bred (lō′brĕd′), *adj.* characterized by or characteristic of low or vulgar breeding.

low·brow (lō′brou′), *Slang.* —*n.* **1.** a person of low intellectual caliber or culture. —*adj.* **2.** being a lowbrow. **3.** pertaining or proper to lowbrows.

Low Church, a Low-Church party in the Anglican church.

Low-Church (lō′chûrch′), *adj.* laying little stress on sacraments and church authority, etc.; holding evangelical views (used of a party in the Anglican church and opposed to *High-Church*). —**Low′-Church′man,** *n.*

low comedy, comedy which depends on physical action and situation rather than on wit and dialogue.

Low Countries, the lowland region near the North Sea, forming the lower basin of the Rhine, Meuse, and Scheldt rivers, divided in the Middle Ages into numerous small states: corresponding to modern Netherlands, Belgium, and Luxemburg.

low-down (lō′doun′), *n.* **1.** *Slang.* the actual, unadorned facts or truth on some subject (prec. by *the*). —*adj.* **2.** *Chiefly U.S. Colloq.* low, esp. in the social or moral scale; degraded.

Low·ell (lō′əl), *n.* **1. Abbott Lawrence,** 1856–1943, U.S. educator; president of Harvard, 1909–33. **2.** his sister, **Amy Lawrence,** 1874–1925, U.S. poet and critic. **3. James Russell,** 1819–91, U.S. poet, essayist, and diplomat. **4. Percival,** 1855–1916, U.S. astronomer (brother of A. L. Lowell). **5.** a city in NE Massachusetts, on the Merrimack river. 97,249 (1950).

low·er¹ (lō′ər), *v.t.* **1.** to reduce in amount, price, degree, force, etc. **2.** to make less loud, as the voice. **3.** to bring down in rank or estimation, degrade, or humble; abase (oneself), as by some sacrifice of dignity. **4.** to cause to descend, or let down: *to lower a flag*. **5.** to make lower in height or level: *to lower the water in a canal*. **6.** *Music.* to make lower in pitch; flatten. —*v.i.* **7.** to become lower or less. **8.** to descend; sink. [v. use of *lower*, compar. of LOW¹, adj.] —**Syn. 1.** decrease, diminish. **3.** humiliate, dishonor. —**Ant. 1.** raise, increase.

low·er² (lou′ər), *v.i.* **1.** to be dark and threatening, as the sky or the weather. **2.** to frown, scowl, or look sullen. —*n.* **3.** a dark, threatening appearance, as of the sky, weather, etc. **4.** a frown or scowl. Also, **lour.** [ME *loure*(*n*) frown, lurk; cf. G *lauern* lurk]

Low·er Austria (lō′ər), a province in NE Austria. 1,492,846 pop. (est. 1946); 7452 sq. mi.

Lower California, a narrow peninsula in NW Mexico between the Gulf of California and the Pacific, forming two territories of Mexico. 130,378 pop. (1940);

55,634 sq. mi. *Capitals:* Mexicali (Northern Territory) and La Paz (Southern Territory). Spanish, **Baja California.**

Lower Canada, the name of Quebec province, 1791–1841.

lower case, *Print.* the lower half of a pair of cases, which contains the small letters of the alphabet.

low·er-case (lō′ər kās′), *adj., v.,* **-cased, -casing.** —*adj.* **1.** (of a letter) small (as opposed to capital). **2.** *Print.* pertaining to or belonging in the lower case. See **case** (def. 7). —*v.t.* **3.** to print or write with a lower-case letter or letters.

Lower Egypt. See Egypt.

Lower House, (*often l.c.*) one of two branches of a legislature, generally more representative and with more members than the upper branch.

low·er·ing (lou′ər ĭng), *adj.* **1.** dark and threatening, as the sky, clouds, weather, etc. **2.** frowning or sullen, as the face, gaze, etc. —**low′er·ing·ly,** *adv.*

low·er·most (lō′ər mōst′), *adj.* lowest.

lower world, 1. the regions of the dead, conceived by the ancients as lying beneath the earth's surface; Hades. **2.** the earth as distinguished from the heavenly bodies or from heaven.

lowest common multiple. See **common multiple.**

Lowes·toft (lōs′tôft; *locally* -təf), *n.* a seaport in E England, in Suffolk: famous for a type of China. 39,370 (est. 1946).

low explosive, a relatively slow-burning explosive, usually set off by heat or friction, and used for propelling charges in guns or for ordinary blasting.

Low German, 1. the Germanic speech of northern Germany and the Low Countries. **2.** Plattdeutsch.

low·land (lō′lənd), *n.* **1.** land low with respect to neighboring country. **2. the Lowlands,** a low, level region in S, central, and E Scotland. —*adj.* **3.** of, pertaining to, or characteristic of lowland or lowlands.

Low·land·er (lō′lən dər), *n.* **1.** a native of the Lowlands. **2.** (*l.c.*) an inhabitant of lowland or lowlands.

Low Latin, any form of nonclassical Latin, as Late Latin, Vulgar Latin, or medieval Latin.

low·ly (lō′lĭ), *adj.,* **-lier, -liest,** *adv.* —*adj.* **1.** humble in station, condition, or nature: *a lowly cottage*. **2.** low in growth or position. **3.** humble in spirit; meek. —*adv.* **4.** in a low position, manner, or degree. **5.** in a lowly manner; humbly. —**low′li·ness,** *n.* —**Syn.** modest, unassuming.

Low Mass, a Mass said, and not sung, by a priest, assisted by a server only.

low-mind·ed (lō′mīn′dĭd), *adj.* having or showing a low, coarse, or vulgar mind; mean. —**low′-mind′-ed·ly,** *adv.* —**low′-mind′ed·ness,** *n.*

low-necked (lō′nŏkt′), *adj.* (of a garment) cut low so as to leave the neck and shoulders exposed; décolleté.

low-pitched (lō′pĭcht′), *adj.* **1.** pitched in a low register or key. **2.** produced by slow vibrations; relatively grave in pitch or soft in sound. **3.** (of a roof) having a low proportion of vertical to lateral dimension.

low-pres·sure (lō′prĕsh′ər), *adj.* having or involving a pressure (as of steam, etc.) which is low or below normal.

low-spir·it·ed (lō′spĭr′ĭt ĭd), *adj.* having low spirits; depressed; dejected. —**low′-spir′it·ed·ly,** *adv.* —**low′-spir′it·ed·ness,** *n.*

Low Sunday, the Sunday next after Easter.

low-ten·sion (lō′tĕn′shən), *adj. Elect.* **1.** having or designed for use at low voltage, usually less than 750 volts. **2.** the winding of a transformer designed to operate at the lower voltage. Cf. **high-tension.**

low-test (lō′tĕst′), *adj.* (of gasoline) boiling at a comparatively high temperature.

low tide, 1. the tide at low water. **2.** the time of low water. **3.** the lowest point of decline of anything.

low-volt·age (lō′vōl′tĭj), *adj.* denoting an electric system with an operating voltage under 750 volts.

low water, water at its lowest level, as in a river.

lox·o·drom·ic (lŏk′sə drŏm′ĭk), *adj.* pertaining to oblique sailing or sailing on rhumbs (**loxodromic lines**). Also, **lox′o·drom′i·cal.** [f. Gk. *loxó*(*s*) oblique + s. Gk. *drómos* a running, course + -IC]

lox·o·drom·ics (lŏk′sə drŏm′ĭks), *n.* the art of oblique sailing. Also, **lox·od·ro·my** (lŏk sŏd′rə mĭ).

loy·al (loi′əl), *adj.* **1.** faithful to one's allegiance, as to the sovereign, government, or state: *a loyal subject*. **2.** faithful to one's oath, engagements or obligations: *to be loyal to a vow*. **3.** faithful to any leader, party, or cause, or to any person or thing conceived as imposing obligations: *a loyal friend*. **4.** characterized by or showing faithfulness to engagements, allegiance, obligations, etc.: *loyal conduct*. [t. F, g. L *lēgālis* LEGAL] —**loy′-al·ly,** *adv.* —**Syn. 2.** See **faithful.**

loy·al·ist (loi′əl ĭst), *n.* **1.** one who is loyal; a supporter of the sovereign or the existing government, esp. in time of revolt. **2.** (*sometimes cap.*) one who remained loyal to the British government during the American Revolutionary period. **3.** (*cap.*) an adherent of the Republic during the Spanish Civil War. —**loy′al·ism,** *n.*

loy·al·ty (loi′əl tĭ), *n., pl.* **-ties. 1.** state or quality of being loyal; faithfulness to engagements or obligations. **2.** faithful adherence to a sovereign or government, or to a leader, cause, or the like.

ăct, āble, dâre, ärt; ĕbb, ēqual; ĭf, īce; hŏt, ōver, ôrder, oil, bŏŏk, ōōze, out; ŭp, ūse, ûrge; ə = a in alone; ch, chief; g, give; ng, ring; sh, shoe; th, thin; ᵺ, that; zh, vision. See the full key on inside cover.

—**Syn. 2.** LOYALTY, ALLEGIANCE, FIDELITY, all imply a sense of duty or of devoted attachment to something or someone. LOYALTY connotes sentiment and the feeling of devotion which one holds for one's country, creed, family, friends, etc. ALLEGIANCE applies particularly to a citizen's duty to his country, or, by extension, one's obligation to support a party, cause, leader, etc. FIDELITY implies unwavering devotion and allegiance to a person, principle, etc.

Loy·o·la (loi ō′lə), *n.* **Ignatius** (ĭg nā′shəs), (*Iñigo Ló-pez de Recalde*) 1491–1556, Spanish soldier, priest, and saint, founder of the Jesuit order.

loz·enge (lŏz′ĭnj), *n.* **1.** a small flavored cake or confection of sugar, often medicated, orig., diamond shaped. **2.** *Math.* diamond. [ME *losenge*, t. OF, appar. der. Pr. *lausa* stone slab]

LP (ĕl′pē′), *adj.* **1.** denoting a phonograph record impressed with microgrooves that revolves at 33⅓ revolutions per minute. —*n.* **2.** such a record. **3.** a trademark for such a record. [initials of *long-playing*]

L.S.S., Lifesaving Service.

l.s.t., local standard time.

Lt., Lieutenant.

l.t., 1. *Football.* left tackle. **2.** local time. **3.** long ton.

Ltd., *Chiefly Brit.* limited. See **limited** (def. 3). Also, **ltd.**

Lu, *Chem.* lutecium.

Lu·a·la·ba (loo′ä lä′bä), *n.* a river in the SE Belgian Congo: a headstream of the Congo river.

lub·ber (lŭb′ər), *n.* **1.** a big, clumsy, stupid person. **2.** (among sailors) an awkward or unskilled seaman; landlubber. [ME *lober*, akin to Norw. *lubb(a)* short, stout person. See LOB]

lub·ber·ly (lŭb′ər lĭ), *adj.* **1.** like or of a lubber. —*adv.* **2.** in a lubberly manner. —**lub′ber·li·ness,** *n.*

lubber's hole, *Naut.* an open space in the platform at the head of a lower mast, through which a sailor may mount and descend without going outside the rim.

Lub·bock (lŭb′ək), *n.* **1.** a city in NW Texas. 71,747 (1950). **2. Sir John,** (*Baron Avebury*) 1834–1913, British statesman, scientist, and writer.

Lü·beck (ly′bĕk), *n.* a seaport in N Germany: important Baltic port in the medieval Hanseatic League. 154,811 (1930). See map under **Hanseatic Cities.**

Lu·blin (lyōō′blĭn), *n.* a city in E Poland. 98,000 (1946). Russian, **Lyublin.**

lu·bri·cant (loo′brə kənt), *n.* **1.** a lubricating material. —*adj.* **2.** lubricating.

lu·bri·cate (loo′brə kāt′), *v.t.,* **-cated, -cating. 1.** to apply some oily, greasy, or other substance to, in order to diminish friction; oil or grease, as parts of a mechanism. **2.** to make slippery or smooth. [t. L: m.s. *lūbricātus,* pp., made slippery] —**lu′bri·ca′tion,** *n.* —**lu′bri·ca′tive,** *adj.*

lu·bri·ca·tor (loo′brə kā′tər), *n.* a person or a device that lubricates or furnishes lubricant.

lu·bri·cious (loo brĭsh′əs), *adj.* wanton; lewd.

lu·bric·i·ty (loo brĭs′ə tĭ), *n., pl.* **-ties. 1.** slipperiness or oily smoothness of surface. **2.** capacity for lubrication. **3.** shiftiness. **4.** lewdness. [t. LL: m.s. *lūbricitas,* der. L *lūbricus* lubricous]

lu·bri·cous (loo′brə kəs), *adj.* **1.** slippery, as of surface; of an oily smoothness. **2.** unstable; uncertain; shifty. **3.** lewd. [t. L: m. *lūbricus*]

Lu·can (loo′kən), *n.* (*Marcus Annaeus Lucanus*) A.D. 39–65, Roman poet, born in Spain.

Lu·ca·ni·a (loo kā′nĭ ə), *n.* **1.** an ancient region in S Italy, NW of the Gulf of Taranto. **2.** a modern department in S Italy, comprising most of the ancient region. 531,674 pop. (1936); 3856 sq. mi.

Luc·ca (loo′kä), *n.* a city in NW Italy. 32,896 (1936).

lu·cent (loo′sənt), *adj. Archaic.* **1.** shining. **2.** transparent. [t. L: s. *lūcens,* ppr., shining] —**lu′cence, lu′cen·cy,** *n.*

lu·cerne (loo sûrn′), *n. Chiefly Brit.* alfalfa. [t. F: m. *luzerne,* t. Pr.: m. *luzerno,* ult. der. L *lux* light]

Lu·cerne (loo sûrn′; *Fr.* ly sĕrn′), *n.* **1.** a canton in central Switzerland. 211,800 pop. (est. 1944); 576 sq. mi. **2.** the capital of this canton, on the **Lake of Lucerne** (24 mi. long; 44 sq. mi.). German, **Luzern.**

lu·ces (loo′sēz), *n.* pl. of **lux.**

Lu·cian (loo′shən), *n.* A.D. c120–c180, Greek humorist and satirist.

lu·cid (loo′sĭd), *adj.* **1.** shining or bright. **2.** clear or transparent. **3.** clear to the mind; easily understood: *a lucid explanation.* **4.** characterized by clear perception or understanding; rational or sane: *a lucid interval.* [t. L: s. *lūcidus*] —**lu·cid′i·ty, lu·cid′ness,** *n.* —**lu′cid·ly,** *adv.*

Lu·ci·fer (loo′sə fər), *n.* **1.** a proud rebellious archangel, identified with Satan, who fell from heaven. **2.** the planet Venus when appearing as the morning star. **3.** (*l.c.*) a friction match. [t. L: the morning star, prop. adj., light-bringing]

lu·cif·er·ase (loo sĭf′ə rās′), *n. Biochem.* an enzyme which is present in the luminous organs of fireflies, etc., and which, acting upon luciferin, produces luminosity. [f. L *lūcifer* light-bringing + -ASE]

lu·cif·er·in (loo sĭf′ər ĭn), *n. Biochem.* a protein occurring in fireflies, etc. luminous when acted upon by luciferase. [f. L *lūcifer* light-bringing + -IN²]

lucifer match, lucifer (def. 3).

lu·cif·er·ous (loo sĭf′ər əs), *adj.* bringing or giving light. [f. L *lūcifer* light-bringing + -OUS]

Lu·ci·na (loo sī′nə), *n.* the Roman goddess of childbirth.

lu·cite (loo′sīt), *n.* **1.** a plastic compound, the acrylic resin polymethyl methacrylate, with unusual optical properties, used for reflectors, ornaments, airplane windows, etc. **2.** (*cap.*) a trademark for this plastic. [f. s. L *lux* light + -ITE¹]

luck (lŭk), *n.* **1.** that which happens to a person, as if by chance, in the course of events: *to have good luck.* **2.** good fortune; advantage or success considered as the result of chance: *to wish one luck.* **3.** some object on which good fortune is supposed to depend. [ME *lucke,* t. LG or D: m. *luk,* also *geluk,* c. G *glück*]

luck·i·ly (lŭk′ə lĭ), *adv.* by good luck, fortunately.

luck·less (lŭk′lĭs), *adj.* having no luck. —**luck′-less·ly,** *adv.* —**luck′less·ness,** *n.*

Luck·now (lŭk′nou), *n.* a city in N India, in the United Provinces: the British were besieged here for several months (1857–58) during the Sepoy Rebellion. 387,177 (1941).

luck·y (lŭk′ĭ), *adj.,* **luckier, luckiest. 1.** having or attended with good luck; fortunate. **2.** happening fortunately: *a lucky accident.* **3.** bringing or presaging good luck, or supposed to do so: *a lucky penny.* —**luck′i·ness,** *n.* —**Syn. 1.** See **fortunate.**

lu·cra·tive (loo′krə tĭv), *adj.* profitable; remunerative: *a lucrative business.* [ME, t. L: m.s. *lucrātīvus*] —**lu′-cra·tive·ly,** *adv.* —**lu′cra·tive·ness,** *n.*

lu·cre (loo′kər), *n.* gain or money as the object of sordid desire. [ME, t. L: m.s. *lucrum* gain]

Lu·cre·tius (loo krē′shəs), *n.* (*Titus Lucretius Carus*) c96–c55 B.C., Roman poet. —**Lu·cre′tian,** *adj.*

lu·cu·brate (loo′kyŏŏ brāt′), *v.i.,* **-brated, -brating. 1.** to work, write, study, etc., laboriously, esp. at night. **2.** to write learnedly. [t. L: m.s. *lūcubrātus,* pp.] —**lu′-cu·bra′tor,** *n.*

lu·cu·bra·tion (loo′kyŏŏ brā′shən), *n.* **1.** laborious work, study, etc., esp. at night. **2.** a learned or carefully written production. **3.** (*often pl.*) any literary effort.

lu·cu·lent (loo′kyŏŏ lənt), *adj.* **1.** clear or lucid, as explanations, etc. **2.** convincing. [ME, t. L: s. *lūculentus*] —**lu′cu·lent·ly,** *adv.*

Lu·cul·lus (loo kŭl′əs), *n.* **Lucius Licinius** (loo′shəs lǐ sĭn′ĭ əs), c110–57 ? B.C., Roman consul and general, famous for his great wealth and luxury. —**Lu·cul′lan, Lu·cul·le·an** (loo′kə lē′ən), **Lu·cul′li·an,** *adj.*

lu·cus a non lu·cen·do (loo′kəs ā nŏn loo sĕn′dō), *Latin.* a grove (so called) from not being light (used as a type of illogical or absurd derivation or reasoning).

Lud·dite (lŭd′īt), *n.* a member of any of various bands of workmen in England (1811–16) organized to destroy manufacturing machinery, under the belief that its use diminished employment.

Lu·den·dorff (loo′dən dôrf′), *n.* **Erich Friedrich Wilhelm von** (ā′rǐĸ frē′drǐĸ vǐl′hĕlm fən), 1865–1937, German general.

Lü·der·itz (ly′dər ĭts), *n.* a seaport in South-West Africa: diamond mining center. 2560 (1936).

Lu·dhi·a·na (loo′dǐ ä′nä), *n.* a city in NW India, in E Punjab. 111,639 (1941).

lu·di·crous (loo′də krəs), *adj.* such as to cause laughter or derision; ridiculous; amusingly absurd: *a ludicrous incident.* [t. L: m. *lūdicrus* sportive] —**lu′di·crous·ly,** *adv.* —**lu′di·crous·ness,** *n.* —**Syn.** laughable, comical. See **funny.** —**Ant.** solemn, impressive.

Lud·wig (loot′vǐĸĥ, lood′-), *n.* **Emil** (ā′mĕl), 1881–1948, German biographer.

Lud·wig II (loot′vǐĸĥ, lood′-), *n.* See **Louis II.**

Lud·wigs·ha·fen (loot′vǐĸĥs hä′fən, lood′-), *n.* a city in SW Germany, on the Rhine opposite Mannheim. 144,425 (1939).

lu·es (loo′ēz), *n.* syphilis. [t. L: plague]

luff (lŭf), *Naut.* —*n.* **1.** the forward edge of a fore-and-aft sail. —*v.i.* **2.** to bring the head of a sailing vessel closer to or directly into the wind, with sails shaking. [early ME *lof, loof,* appar. t. OF: m. *lof* a contrivance for altering a ship's course (later, as also D *loef,* the weather side), of Gmc. orig.]

Luft·waf·fe (lŏŏft′väf′ə), *n. German.* (under the Nazis) the German Air Force.

lug¹ (lŭg), *v.,* **lugged, lugging,** *n.* —*v.t.* **1.** to pull along or carry with force or effort. **2.** *Colloq.* to bring (in or into) unnaturally or irrelevantly: *to lug personal habits into a discussion.* **3.** (of a ship) to carry more sail in a strong breeze than is safe or desirable. —*v.i.* **4.** to pull; tug. —*n.* **5.** an act of lugging; a forcible pull; a haul. [ME *lugg(e),* t. Scand.; cf. Sw. *lugga* pull by the hair]

lug² (lŭg), *n.* **1.** a projecting piece by which anything is held or supported. **2.** a leather loop dependent from a saddle, through which a shaft is passed for support. [orig. uncert.]

lug³ (lŭg), *n.* lugsail. [see LUGSAIL]

lug⁴ (lŭg), *n.* lugworm. [cf. D *log* heavy, unwieldy]

Lu·gansk (loo gänsk′), *n.* former name of **Voroshilov-grad.**

lug·gage (lŭg′ĭj), *n. Chiefly Brit.* baggage. [f. LUG¹ + -AGE]

lug·ger (lŭg′ər), *n.* a vessel with lugsails. [der. LUGSAIL]

lug·sail (lŭg′sāl′; *Naut.* -səl), *n. Naut.* a quadrilateral sail bent upon a yard that crosses the mast obliquely. Also, **lug.** [f. *lug* pole (now d.) + SAIL]

---

b., blend of, blended; c., cognate with; d., dialect, dialectal; der., derived from; f., formed from; g., going back to; m., modification of; r., replacing; s., stem of; t., taken from; ?, perhaps. See the full key on inside cover.

lu·gu·bri·ous (lŏŏ·gū′brĭ·əs, -gŏŏ′-), *adj.* mournful; doleful; dismal: *lugubrious tones.* [f. L *lūgubri(s)* mournful + -OUS] **—lu·gu′bri·ous·ly,** *adv.* **—lu·gu′bri·ous·ness,** *n.*

lug·worm (lŭg′wûrm′), *n.* any annelid of the genus *Arenicola,* comprising marine worms with tufted gills, which burrow in the sand of the seashore and are much used for bait. Also, **lug.** [f. LUG⁴ + WORM]

Luke (lŏŏk), *n.* **1.** the Evangelist; an early Christian disciple, probably a gentile, a physician, and companion of St. Paul; traditionally, the author of the third Gospel. **2.** the third Gospel, in the New Testament. [t. L: m. *Lūcās,* t. Gk.: m. *Loukâs*]

luke·warm (lŏŏk′wôrm′), *adj.* **1.** moderately warm, tepid. **2.** having or showing little ardor or zeal; indifferent: *lukewarm applause.* [ME *lukewarme,* f. *luke* tepid (appar. der. *lew* tepid, OE *-hlēow*) + *warme* WARM] **—luke′warm·ly,** *adv.* **—luke′warm′ness,** *n.*

lull (lŭl), *v.t.* **1.** to put to sleep or rest by soothing means: *to lull a child by singing.* **2.** to soothe or quiet. *—v.i.* **3.** to become lulled, quieted, or stilled. *—n.* **4.** a lulled condition; a temporary quiet or stillness: *a lull in a storm.* **5.** a soothing sound: *the lull of falling waters.* [ME *lulle(n).* Cf. Sw. *lulla,* G *lullen,* also L *lallāre* sing lullaby]

lull·a·by (lŭl′ə·bī′), *n., pl.* **-bies,** *v.,* **-bied, -bying.** *—n.* **1.** the utterance "lullaby" or a song containing it; a cradlesong. **2.** any lulling song. *—v.t.* **3.** to lull with or as with a lullaby. [orig. interj., *lulla!* + *by!*]

Lul·ly (lŭl′ĭ; *for 1 also* Fr. ly lē′), *n.* **1. Jean Baptiste** (zhän bà tēst′), 1632–87, Italian composer in France. **2. Raymond,** c1235–1315, Spanish philosopher and missionary.

lum·ba·go (lŭm·bā′gō), *n.* *Pathol.* myalgia in the lumbar region; rheumatic pain in the muscles of the small of the back. [t. LL, der. L *lumbus* loin]

lum·bar (lŭm′bər), *adj.* **1.** of or pertaining to the loin or loins. *—n.* **2.** a lumbar vertebra, artery, or the like. [t. NL: s. *lumbāris,* der. L *lumbus* loin]

lum·ber¹ (lŭm′bər), *n.* **1.** *U.S. and Canada.* timber sawed or split into planks, boards, etc. **2.** miscellaneous useless articles that are stored away. *—v.i.* **3.** *U.S. and Canada.* to cut timber and prepare it for market. *—v.t.* **4.** to heap together in disorder. **5.** to fill up or obstruct with miscellaneous useless articles; encumber. [orig. uncert.] **—lum′ber·er,** *n.*

lum·ber² (lŭm′bər), *v.i.* **1.** to move clumsily or heavily, esp. from great or ponderous bulk. **2.** to make a rumbling noise. [ME *lomere(n).* Cf. d. Sw. *lomra* resound, *loma* walk heavily]

lum·ber·ing¹ (lŭm′bər·ĭng), *n.* *U.S. and Canada.* the trade or business of cutting and preparing timber. [f. LUMBER¹ + -ING¹]

lum·ber·ing² (lŭm′bər·ĭng), *adj.* **1.** moving clumsily or heavily; awkward. **2.** that rumbles. [f. LUMBER² + -ING²] **—lum′ber·ing·ly,** *adv.*

lum·ber·jack (lŭm′bər·jăk′), *n.* *U.S. and Canada.* one who works at lumbering.

lum·ber·man (lŭm′bər·mən), *n., pl.* **-men.** *U.S. and Canada.* **1.** one who cuts and prepares timber. **2.** one who deals in lumber.

lum·ber·yard (lŭm′bər·yärd′), *n.* *U.S. and Canada.* a yard where lumber is stored for sale.

lum·bri·cal (lŭm′brə·kəl), *n.* *Anat.* one of four wormlike muscles in the palm of the hand and in the sole of the foot. Also, **lum·bri·ca·lis** (lŭm′brə·kā′lĭs). [t. NL: s. *lumbricālis,* der. L *lumbricus* earthworm]

lum·bri·coid (lŭm′brə·koid′), *adj.* resembling an earthworm. [f. s. L *lumbricus* earthworm + -OID]

lu·men (lŏŏ′mən), *n., pl.* **-mina** (-mə·nə). **1.** the unit of luminous flux; the light emitted by a source of one international candle in a unit solid angle. **2.** *Anat.* the canal, duct, or cavity of a tubular organ. **3.** *Bot.* of **a** cell) the cavity which the cell walls enclose. [t. L: light, window]

Lu·mi·nal (lŏŏ′mə·nəl), *n.* a trademark for phenobarbital.

lu·mi·nar·y (lŏŏ′mə·nĕr′ĭ), *n., pl.* **-naries. 1.** a celestial body, as the sun or moon. **2.** a body or thing that gives light. **3.** a person who enlightens mankind or makes some subject clear. [late ME, t. ML: m.s. *lūminārium* a light, lamp, heavenly body]

lu·mi·nesce (lŏŏ′mə·nĕs′), *v.i.,* **-nesced, -nescing.** to exhibit luminescence.

lu·mi·nes·cence (lŏŏ′mə·nĕs′əns), *n.* an emission of light not due directly to incandescence and occurring at a temperature below that of incandescent bodies: a term including phosphorescence, fluorescence, etc.

lu·mi·nes·cent (lŏŏ′mə·nĕs′ənt), *adj.* characterized by or pertaining to luminescence. [f. s. L *lūmen* light + -ESCENT]

lu·mi·nif·er·ous (lŏŏ′mə·nĭf′ər·əs), *adj.* producing light. [f. s. L *lūmen* light + -(I)FEROUS]

lu·mi·nos·i·ty (lŏŏ′mə·nŏs′ə·tĭ), *n., pl.* **-ties. 1.** the quality of being luminous. **2.** something luminous.

lu·mi·nous (lŏŏ′mə·nəs), *adj.* **1.** radiating or reflecting light; shining. **2.** lighted up or illuminated; well lighted. **3.** brilliant intellectually; enlightening, as a writer or his writings. **4.** clear; readily intelligible. [ME *luminose,* t. L: m.s. *lūminōsus*] **—lu′mi·nous·ly,** *adv.* **—lu′mi·nous·ness,** *n.*

luminous energy, light.

luminous flux, rate of transmission of luminous energy; luminous power. Its unit is the lumen.

luminous intensity, *Photom.* (of a light source) the luminous flux emitted per unit solid angle. A source of 1 candle emits 4 lumens.

lum·mox (lŭm′əks), *n.* *U.S. Colloq.* a clumsy, stupid person.

lump¹ (lŭmp), *n.* **1.** a piece or mass of solid matter without regular shape, or of no particular shape. **2.** a protuberance or swelling: *a lump on the head.* **3.** an aggregation, collection, or mass: *in the lump.* **4.** *Colloq.* a stupid, clumsy person. *—adj.* **5.** in the form of a lump or lumps: *lump sugar.* **6.** including a number of items taken together or in the lump: *a lump sum.* *—v.t.* **7.** to unite into one aggregation, collection, or mass. **8.** to deal with in the lump or mass. **9.** to make into a lump or lumps. **10.** to raise into or cover with lumps. *—v.i.* **11.** to form or raise a lump or lumps. **12.** to move heavily. [ME *lumpe, lomp(e).* Cf. Dan. *lump(e)* lump, d. Norw. *lump* block]

lump² (lŭmp), *v.t.* *Colloq.* to endure or put up with (a disagreeable necessity): *if you don't like it, you can lump it.* [orig. uncert.]

lump·er (lŭmp′ər), *n.* a laborer employed to load and unload vessels in port.

lump·fish (lŭmp′fĭsh′), *n., pl.* **-fishes,** (*esp. collectively*) **-fish.** a clumsy-looking fish, *Cyclopterus lumpus,* with a high, ridged back, of the Northern Atlantic Ocean.

lump·ish (lŭmp′ĭsh), *adj.* **1.** like a lump. **2.** clumsy or stupid: *she called him a lumpish boor.* **—lump′ish·ly,** *adv.* **—lump′ish·ness,** *n.*

lump·suck·er (lŭmp′sŭk′ər), *n.* a lumpfish.

lump·y (lŭmp′ĭ), *adj.,* **lumpier, lumpiest. 1.** full of lumps: *lumpy gravy.* **2.** covered with lumps, as a surface. **3.** like a lump, as in being heavy or clumsy. **4.** (of water) rough or choppy. **—lump′i·ly,** *adv.* **—lump′i·ness,** *n.*

lumpy jaw, *Pathol.* actinomycosis of the jaw.

Lu·na (lŏŏ′nə), *n.* **1.** the moon, personified by the Romans as a goddess. **2.** *Alchemy.* silver. [t. L: moon]

lu·na·cy (lŏŏ′nə·sĭ), *n., pl.* **-cies. 1.** intermittent insanity. **2.** any form of insanity (usually, except idiocy). **3.** extreme foolishness or an instance of it: *her decision to resign was sheer lunacy.* **4.** *Law.* unsoundness of mind sufficient to incapacitate one for civil transactions. [f. LUN(ATIC) + -ACY]

luna moth, a large American moth, *Tropaea luna,* with light-green coloration, purple-brown markings, lunate spots, and long tails. Also, **Luna moth.**

lu·nar (lŏŏ′nər), *adj.* **1.** of or pertaining to the moon: *the lunar orbit.* **2.** measured by the moon's revolutions: *a lunar month.* **3.** resembling the moon; round or crescent-shaped. **4.** of or pertaining to silver. [t. L: s. *lūnāris* of the moon, crescent]

lunar caustic, *Med., Chem.* silver nitrate, AGNO₃, esp. in a sticklike mold, used to cauterize tissues.

lu·nar·i·an (lŏŏ·nâr′ĭ·ən), *n.* **1.** a supposed inhabitant of the moon. **2.** a selenographer.

lunar month. See **month** (def. 5).

lunar year. See **year** (def. 4).

lu·nate (lŏŏ′nāt), *adj.* crescent-shaped. Also, **lu′nat·ed.** [t. L: m.s. *lūnātus*]

lu·na·tic (lŏŏ′nə·tĭk), *n.* **1.** an insane person (except, usually, an idiot). *—adj.* Also, **lu·nat·i·cal** (lŏŏ·năt′ə·kəl). **2.** insane or mad; crazy. **3.** indicating lunacy; characteristic of a lunatic. **4.** designated for or used by the insane: *a lunatic asylum.* [ME *lunatik,* t. LL: m.s. *lūnāticus* mad, der. L *lūna* moon] **—lu·nat′i·cal·ly,** *adv.*

lu·na·tion (lŏŏ·nā′shən), *n.* the time from one new moon to the next (about 29½ days); a lunar month.

lunch (lŭnch), *n.* **1.** a light meal between breakfast and dinner; luncheon. **2.** a light meal. *—v.i.* **3.** to eat lunch: *we lunched quite late today.* *—v.t.* **4.** to provide lunch for: *they lunched us in regal fashion.* [short for LUNCHEON] **—lunch′er,** *n.*

lunch·eon (lŭn′chən), *n.* lunch. [b. LUMP¹ and d. *nuncheon* (ME *nonshench,* f. *non* noon + *shench* (OE *scenc*) a drink)]

lunch·eon·ette (lŭn′chə·nĕt′), *n.* a lunchroom or restaurant where lunches are served.

lunch·room (lŭnch′rŏŏm′, -rŏŏm′), *n.* a restaurant that specializes in serving light meals. Also, **lunch room.**

Lun·dy's Lane (lŭn′dĭz), a road near Niagara Falls, in Ontario, Canada: battle between the British and Americans, 1814.

lune¹ (lŏŏn), *n.* **1.** anything shaped like a crescent or a half-moon. **2.** a crescent-shaped plane figure bounded by two arcs of circles, either on a plane or a spherical surface. [t. F, g. L *lūna* moon]

lune² (lŏŏn), *n.* the line for holding a hawk. [ME; var. of *loigne,* t. OF, g. LL *longia,* der. L *longus* long]

lu·nette (lŏŏ·nĕt′), *n.* **1.** any of various objects or spaces of crescentlike or semicircular outline or section. **2.** an arched or rounded aperture or window, as in a vault. **3.** a painting, etc., filling an arched space, usually a semicircle or a flatter chord of a circle. **4.** *Fort.* a work consisting of a salient angle with two flanks and an open gorge. **5.** *Ordn.* a towing ring in the trail plate of a towed vehicle, as a gun carriage. Also, **lu·net** (lŏŏ′nĭt). [t. F, dim. of *lune* moon. See LUNE¹]

Lu·né·ville (ly nĕ vēl′), *n.* a city in NE France: treaty between France and Austria, 1801. 20,377 (1946).

---

lung (lŭng), n. 1. either of the two saclike respiratory organs in the thorax of man and the higher vertebrates. 2. an analogous organ in certain invertebrates, as arachnids, terrestrial gastropods, etc. [ME *lunge*(n), OE *lungen*, c. G *lunge*; akin to LIGHT². Cf. LIGHTS lungs]

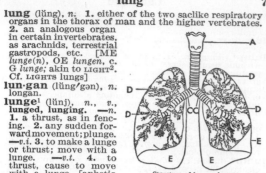

Structure of human lungs
A, Larynx; B, Trachea; C, Bronchi; D, Ramifications of bronchial tubes; E, Uncut smooth surface

lun·gan (lŭng′gən), n. longan.

lunge¹ (lŭnj), n., v., **lunged, lunging.** 1. a thrust, as in fencing. 2. any sudden forward movement; plunge. —v.i. 3. to make a lunge or thrust; move with a lunge. —v.t. 4. to thrust, cause to move with a lunge. [aphetic var. of *allonge* (obs.), t. F, der. *allonger* lengthen, extend, lunge, der. à to (g. L *ad*) + *long* long (g. L *longus*)]

lunge² (lŭnj), n., v., **lunged, lunging.** —n. 1. a long rope used to guide a horse during training or exercise. 2. a ring or circular track for such training or exercise. —v.t. 3. to train or exercise (a horse) by the use of a lunge or rope, or on a lunge or track. [t. F: m. *longe* halter, lunge, var. of OF *loigne*. See LUNE²]

lung·fish (lŭng′fĭsh′), n., pl. **-fishes,** (esp. collectively) **-fish.** a dipnoan.

Lung·ki (lōōng′kē′), n. Changchowfu.

lung·worm (lŭng′wûrm′), n. 1. any nematode worm of the superfamily *Metastrongylidae*, parasitic in lungs of various mammals. 2. a nematode worm of the genus *Rhabdias* parasitic in the lungs of reptiles and amphibians.

lung·wort (lŭng′wûrt′), n. 1. a European blue-flowered boraginaceous plant, *Pulmonaria officinalis.* 2. an American blue-flowered plant, *Mertensia virginica,* of the same family.

luni-, a word element meaning "moon." [comb. form repr. L *lūna*]

lu·ni·so·lar (lōō′nə sō′lər), adj. pertaining to or based upon the relations or joint action of the moon and sun: *the lunisolar cycle.*

lu·ni·tid·al (lōō′nə tī′dəl), adj. pertaining to that part of the tidal movement dependent on the moon.

lunitidal interval, the period of time between the moon's transit and the next high lunar tide.

lunk·head (lŭngk′hĕd′), n. U.S. Colloq. a thickheaded or stupid person; a blockhead.

Lunt (lŭnt), n. **Alfred,** born 1893, U.S. actor.

lu·nu·la (lōō′nyə lə), n., pl. **-lae** (-lē′). something shaped like a narrow crescent, as the small white area at the base of the human fingernail. Also, **lu·nule** (lōō′nūl). [t. L, dim. of *lūna* moon]

lu·nu·lar (lōō′nyə lər), adj. crescent-shaped: *lunular markings.*

lu·nu·late (lōō′nyə lāt′), adj. 1. having lunular markings. 2. crescent-shaped. Also, **lu′nu·lat′ed.**

lun·y (lōō′nĭ), adj., **lunier, luniest,** n., pl. **lunies.** loony.

Lu·per·ca·li·a (lōō′pər kā′lĭ ə), n.pl. an ancient Roman festival celebrated annually on Feb. 15 in honor of **Lupercus,** a rustic deity identified with the Roman Faunus and the Greek Pan. [t. L.]

lu·pine¹ (lōō′pĭn), n. any plant of the leguminous genus *Lupinus,* as *L. albus* (**white lupine**), a European herb with edible seeds cultivated from ancient times, or *L. perennis,* a wild species with blue, pink, or white flowers common in sandy soil in the eastern U. S. [ME, t. L: m.s. *lupīnus, lupinum.* See LUPINE²]

lu·pine² (lōō′pĭn), adj. 1. pertaining to or resembling the wolf. 2. allied to the wolf. 3. savage; ravenous. [t. L: m.s. *lupīnus* of a wolf]

lu·pu·lin (lōō′pyə lĭn), n. the glandular hairs of the hop, *Humulus lupulus,* used in medicine. [f. s. NL *lupulus* (dim. of L *lupus* hop) + -IN²]

lu·pus (lōō′pəs), n. Pathol. a cutaneous disease due to the tubercle bacillus. [t. L: wolf]

lurch¹ (lûrch), n. 1. sudden leaning or roll to one side, as of a ship or a staggering person. 2. a sudden swaying or staggering movement. —v.i. 3. to make a lurch; move with lurches; stagger: *the wounded man lurched across the room at his assailant.* [orig. obscure; first in nautical use]

lurch² (lûrch), n. 1. the position of one discomfited or in a helpless plight: *to leave someone in the lurch.* 2. a situation at the close of various games in which the loser scores nothing or is far behind his opponent. [t. F: m. *lourche* a game so called, as adj. discomfited; ? of Gmc. orig.]

lurch·er (lûr′chər), n. 1. one who lurks or prowls; a petty thief; a poacher. 2. a crossbred hunting dog.

lure (lōōr), n., v., **lured, luring.** —n. 1. anything that attracts, entices, or allures. 2. a decoy; a bait, esp. an artificial one, used in angling. 3. a feathered decoy, sometimes baited, on a long thong, used in falconry to recall the hawk. 4. a flap or tassel dangling from the

dorsal fin of pediculate fish. —v.t. 5. to decoy; entice; allure. 6. to draw as by a lure. [ME, t. OF: m. *leurre,* t. Gmc.; cf. G *luder* bait] —**lur′er,** n.

lu·rid (lōōr′ĭd), adj. 1. lighted up or shining with an unnatural or wild (esp. red or fiery) glare: *a lurid sky.* 2. glaringly vivid or sensational: *lurid tales.* 3. terrible in fiery intensity, fierce passion, or wild unrestraint: *lurid crimes.* 4. wan, pallid, or ghastly in hue. [t. L: s. *lūridus* pale-yellow, wan] —**lu′rid·ly,** adv. —**lu′rid·ness,** n.

lurk (lûrk), v.i. 1. to lie in concealment, as men in ambush; remain in or about a place secretly or furtively. 2. to go furtively; slink; steal. 3. to exist unperceived or unsuspected. [ME, freq. of LOWER. Cf. Norw. *lurka* sneak away] —**lurk′er,** n. —**lurk′ing·ly,** adv. —Syn. 1. LURK, SKULK, SNEAK, PROWL suggest avoiding observation, often because of a sinister purpose. To LURK is to lie in wait for someone, or to hide about a place, often without motion for periods of time. SKULK suggests cowardliness and stealth of movement. SNEAK emphasizes the attempt to avoid being seen. It has connotations of slinking and of an abject meanness of manner, whether the object is to avoid punishment for some misdeed or whether there is a sinister intent. PROWL implies the definite purpose of seeking for prey; it suggests continuous action in roaming or wandering, slowly and quietly but watchfully, as a cat that is hunting mice.

Lu·sa·ti·a (lōō sā′shǐ ə, -shə), n. a region between the Oder and the Elbe rivers, in E Germany and SW Poland.

Lu·sa·tian (lōō sā′shən), n. Sorbian.

lus·cious (lŭsh′əs), adj. 1. highly pleasing to the taste or smell: *luscious peaches.* 2. sweet to the senses or the mind. 3. sweet to excess, or cloying. [ME; ? aphetic var. of DELICIOUS] —**lus′cious·ly,** adv. —**lus′cious-ness,** n. —Syn. 2. See delicious.

lush¹ (lŭsh), adj. 1. tender and juicy, as plants or vegetation; succulent; luxuriant. 2. characterized by luxuriant vegetation. [ME *lusch,* prob. var. of *lasch,* t. OF: m. *lasche* loose, slack] —**lush′ly,** adv. —**lush′ness,** n.

lush² (lŭsh), Slang. —n. 1. intoxicating liquor. 2. a drunken person. —v.i. 3. to drink liquor. —v.t. 4. to drink (liquor). [orig. uncert.]

lush·y (lŭsh′ĭ), adj. Slang. drunk; tipsy.

Lu·si·ta·ni·a (lōō′sə tā′nĭ ə), n. 1. an ancient region and Roman province in the Iberian Peninsula, corresponding largely to modern Portugal. 2. a British steamship sunk by a German submarine in the North Atlantic on May 7, 1915: one of the events precipitating U.S. entry into World War I.

lust (lŭst), n. 1. passionate or overmastering desire (fol. by *for* or *of*): *lust for power.* 2. sexual desire or appetite. 3. unbridled or lawless sexual desire or appetite. 4. sensuous desire or appetite considered as sinful. 5. Obs. pleasure or delight. —v.i. 6. to have strong sexual desire. 7. to have a strong or inordinate desire (often fol. by *for* or *after*). [ME *luste,* OE *lust,* c. D and G *lust* pleasure, desire]

lus·ter¹ (lŭs′tər), n. 1. state or quality of shining by reflecting light; glitter, glisten, sheen, or gloss: *the luster of satin.* 2. some substance used to impart sheen or gloss. 3. radiant or luminous brightness; radiance. 4. radiance of beauty, excellence, merit, distinction, or glory: *achievements that add luster to one's name.* 5. a shining object. 6. a chandelier, or candleholder, usually ornamented with cut-glass pendants. 7. a fabric of wool and cotton with a lustrous surface. 8. Ceramics. a shiny, metallic, sometimes iridescent film produced on the surface of pottery or porcelain. 9. Mineral. the nature of the surface of a mineral with respect to its reflecting qualities: *greasy luster.* —v.t. 10. to finish with a luster or gloss. —v.i. 11. Rare. to shine with luster. Also, esp. Brit., **lustre.** [t. F: m. *lustre,* t. It.: m. *lustro,* der. *lustrare* to shine, g. L: illuminate] —Syn. 1. brightness, brilliance. See **polish.** —Ant.1. dullness.

lus·ter² (lŭs′tər), n. lustrum. Also, esp. Brit., **lus′tre.**

lus·tered (lŭs′tərd), adj. having a luster. Also, esp. Brit., **lust′red.**

lust·ful (lŭst′fəl), adj. 1. full of or imbued with lust; libidinous. 2. Archaic. lusty. —**lust′ful·ly,** adv. —**lust′ful·ness,** n.

lust·i·hood (lŭst′ĭ hŏŏd′), n. Archaic. lustiness.

lus·tral (lŭs′trəl), adj. 1. of, pertaining to, or employed in the lustrum or rite of purification. 2. occurring every five years. [t. L: s. *lustrālis*]

lus·trate (lŭs′trāt), v.t., **-trated, -trating.** to purify by a propitiatory offering or other ceremonial method. [t. L: pp. *lustrātus.*] —**lus·tra′tion,** n.

lus·tre (lŭs′tər), n., v.t., v.i., **-tred, -tring.** Chiefly Brit. luster.

lus·trous (lŭs′trəs), adj. 1. having luster; shining; glossy, as silk; bright, as eyes. 2. brilliant or splendid. —**lus′trous·ly,** adv. —**lus′trous·ness,** n.

lus·trum (lŭs′trəm), n., pl. **-trums, -tra** (-trə). 1. a period of five years. 2. a lustration or ceremonial purification of the ancient Roman people performed every five years, after the taking of the census. [t. L]

lust·y (lŭs′tĭ), adj., **lustier, lustiest.** 1. full of or characterized by healthy vigor. 2. hearty, as a meal or the like. [ME; f. LUST, n. + -Y¹] —**lust′i·ly,** adv. —**lust′i·ness,** n. —Syn. 1. robust, strong, sturdy. —Ant. 1. feeble.

lu·sus na·tu·rae (lōō′səs nə tyŏŏr′ē, -tŏŏr′ē). Latin. a deformed person or thing; a freak. [L: a jest of nature]

lu·ta·nist (lōō'tə nĭst), *n.* a player on the lute. Also, **lu'te·nist**. [t. ML: s. *lūtānista*, der. *lūtāna* lute]

lute (lōōt), *n., v.,* **luted, luting.** —*n.* 1. a stringed musical instrument formerly much used, having a long, fretted neck and a hollow, typically pear-shaped body with a vaulted back, the strings being plucked with the fingers of one hand (or struck with a plectrum) and stopped on the frets with those of the other. —*v.i.* 2. to play on a lute. [ME, t. OF: m. *lut,* t. Pr.: m. *laüt,* t. Ar.: m. *al-'ūd* the lute]

Man playing a lute

lu·te·ci·um (lōō tē'shĭ əm), *n. Chem.* a rare-earth, trivalent, metallic element. Symbol: Lu; at. wt.: 174.99; at. no.: 71. [NL, der. L *Lutetia* Paris]

lu·te·o·lin (lōō'tĭ ə lĭn), *n. Chem.* a yellow coloring matter obtained from the weed, *Reseda Luteola;* used in dyeing silk, etc., and formerly in medicine. [t. F: m. *lutéoline,* der. L *lūteolus* yellowish]

lu·te·ous (lōō'tĭ əs), *adj.* yellow, generally orangish or reddish. [t. L: m. *lūteus* golden-yellow]

Luth., Lutheran.

Lu·ther (lōō'thər; *Ger.* lōōt'ər), *n.* **Martin** (mär'tēn), 1483–1546, German leader of the Protestant Reformation; a theological writer, and translator of the Bible.

Lu·ther·an (lōō'thər ən), *adj.* 1. of or pertaining to Luther, adhering to his doctrines, or belonging to one of the Protestant churches which bears his name. —*n.* 2. a follower of Luther, or an adherent of his doctrines; a member of the Lutheran Church. —**Lu'ther·an·ism,** *n.*

lu·thern (lōō'thərn), *n.* a dormer window.

lut·ist (lōō'tĭst), *n.* 1. a lute player. 2. a maker of lutes.

Lüt·zen (lyt'sən), *n.* a town in central Germany, near Leipzig: noted for two battles, 1632, 1813. 4738 (1939).

lux (lŭks), *n., pl.* **luces** (lōō'sēz). the international unit of illumination, being the illumination received by a surface at distance of one meter from a light source whose intensity is taken as unity. It equals 0.0929 foot-candle, or 1 lumen per square meter. [t. L: light]

Lux., Luxemburg.

lux·ate (lŭk'sāt), *v.t.,* **-ated, -ating.** to put out of joint; dislocate. [t. L: s. *luxātus,* pp.] —**lux·a'tion,** *n.*

luxe (lōōks, lŭks; *Fr.* lyks), *n.* luxury; elegance: *articles de luxe.* [t. F, t. L: m. *luxus*]

Lux·em·bourg (lŭk'səm bûrg'; *Fr.* lyk săn bōōr'), *n.* a province in SE Belgium: formerly a part of the grand duchy of Luxemburg. 214,125 pop. (est. 1945); 1706 sq. mi. *Cap.:* Arlon. Also, **Luxemburg.**

Lux·em·burg (lŭk'səm bûrg'; *Ger.* lōōk'səm bōōrкн/), *n.* 1. a grand duchy between Germany, France, and Belgium. 301,367 pop. (est. 1938); 999 sq. mi. 2. the capital of this duchy. 60,980 (est. 1938). French, **Luxembourg.**

Lux·or (lŭk'sôr), *n.* a town in Upper Egypt, on the Nile: ruins of ancient Thebes. ab. 15,000.

lux·u·ri·ance (lŭg zhōōr'ĭ əns, lŭk shōōr'-), *n.* the condition of being luxuriant; luxuriant growth or productiveness; rich abundance. Also, **lux·u'ri·an·cy.**

lux·u·ri·ant (lŭg zhōōr'ĭ ənt, lŭk shōōr'-), *adj.* 1. abundant or exuberant in growth, as vegetation. 2. producing abundantly, as soil. 3. richly abundant, profuse, or superabundant. 4. florid, as imagery or ornamentation. [t. L: s. *luxurians,* ppr., growing rank] —**lux·u'ri·ant·ly,** *adv.*

lux·u·ri·ate (lŭg zhōōr'ĭ āt', lŭk shōōr'-), *v.i.,* **-ated, -ating.** 1. to indulge in luxury; revel; enjoy oneself without stint. 2. to take great delight. [t. L: m.s. *luxuriātus,* pp., grown exuberantly, indulged to excess] —**lux·u'ri·a'tion,** *n.*

lux·u·ri·ous (lŭg zhōōr'ĭ əs, lŭk shōōr'-), *adj.* 1. characterized by luxury; ministering or conducing to luxury: *a luxurious hotel.* 2. given or inclined to luxury. —**lux·u'ri·ous·ly,** *adv.* —**lux·u'ri·ous·ness,** *n.*

lux·u·ry (lŭk'shə rĭ), *n., pl.* **-ries.** 1. anything conducive to sumptuous living, usually a delicacy, elegance, or refinement of living rather than a necessity. 2. any form or means of enjoyment. 3. free indulgence in sumptuous living, costly food, clothing, comforts, etc. 4. the means of luxurious enjoyment or sumptuous living. [ME *luxurie* lust, t. L: m.s. *luxuria*]

Lu·zern (lōō tsĕrn'), *n.* German name of **Lucerne.**

Lu·zon (lōō zŏn'; *Sp.* lōō sôn'), *n.* the chief island of the Philippine Islands, in the N part of the group. 7,374,798 pop. (1939); 40,420 sq. mi. *Cap.:* Manila.

lv., 1. leave; leaves. 2. livre; livres.

Lwów (lvōōf), *n.* a city in the SW Soviet Union: formerly in Poland. 317,000 (est. 1937). German, **Lemberg.** Russian, **Lvov** (lvôf).

LXX, Septuagint.

-ly, 1. the normal adverbial suffix, added to almost any descriptive adjective, e.g., *gladly, gradually.* 2. the adverbial suffix applied to units of time meaning "per," e.g., *hourly, daily.* [ME *-li, -lich(e),* OE *-līce,* der. *-līc.* See def. 3] 3. adjective suffix meaning "like," e.g., *saintly, manly.* [ME *-li, -ly, lich(e),* OE *-līc,* c. G *-lich,* repr. a Gmc. noun (OE *līc,* etc.) meaning body. See LIKE[1]] —**Syn.** 3. See **-ish[1].**

ly·ard (lī'ərd), *adj. Brit. Dial.* of a streaked gray. Also, **ly·art** (lī'ərt). [ME, t. OF: m. *liart;* of obscure orig.]

Lyau·tey (lyō tě'), *n.* **Louis Hubert Gonzalve** (lwē y bĕr' gŏN zälv'), 1854–1934, marshal of France, administrator in Morocco.

ly·can·thrope (lī'kən thrōp', lī kăn'thrōp), *n.* 1. a person affected with lycanthropy. 2. a werewolf or alien spirit in the physical form of a bloodthirsty wolf. [t. Gk.: m.s. *lykánthropos,* lit., wolf-man]

ly·can·thro·py (lī kăn'thrə pĭ), *n.* 1. a kind of insanity in which the patient imagines himself to be a wolf or other wild beast. 2. the supposed or fabled assumption of the form of a wolf by a human being. —**ly·can·throp·ic** (lī'kən thrŏp'ĭk), *adj.*

Ly·ca·on (lī kā'ŏn), *n. Gk. Myth.* an Arcadian king who tested the divinity of the disguised Zeus by offering him a plate of human flesh. As punishment, Zeus turned him into a wolf.

Lyc·a·o·ni·a (lĭk'ĭ ō'nĭ ə), *n.* an ancient country in S Asia Minor: later a Roman province.

ly·cée (lē sě'), *n.* (in France) a secondary school maintained by the state. [F, t. L: m.s. *Lycēum* LYCEUM]

ly·ce·um (lī sē'əm), *n.* 1. U.S. an association for discussion and popular instruction by lectures and other means. 2. a building, hall, or the like, devoted to instruction by lectures; a library, etc. 3. (*cap.*) a public place with covered walks outside of ancient Athens, where Aristotle taught. 4. (*cap.*) the Aristotelian or Peripatetic school of philosophy. 5. lycée. [t. L, t. Gk.: m. *Lýkeion* the Lyceum at Athens (so named from the neighboring temple of Apollo), prop. neut. of *Lý-keios* an epithet of Apollo]

lych gate (lĭch), lich gate.

lych·nis (lĭk'nĭs), *n.* any of the showy-flowered plants constituting the caryophyllaceous genus *Lychnis,* as *L. chalcedonica* (**scarlet lychnis**), cultivated for its flowers, and *L. coronaria,* the rose campion. [t. L, t. Gk.]

Ly·ci·a (lĭsh'ĭ ə), *n.* an ancient country in SW Asia Minor: later a Roman province.

Ly·ci·an (lĭsh'ĭ ən), *adj.* 1. of or pertaining to Lycia. —*n.* 2. an inhabitant of Lycia. 3. the language of Lycia, probably related to the cuneiform Hittite.

Lyc·i·das (lĭs'ə dəs), *n.* an elegy (1637) by Milton in memory of his college mate, Edward King.

ly·co·po·di·um (lī'kə pō'dĭ əm), *n.* any plant of the genus *Lycopodium,* which comprises erect or creeping, usually mosslike, evergreen-leaved pteridophytic plants, as *L. clavatum,* the common club moss, and *L. obscurum,* the ground pine, both much used in Christmas decorations. Also, **ly·co·pod** (lī'kə pŏd'). [t. NL: f. m. Gk. *lýko(s)* wolf + *-podium* -PODIUM]

Ly·cur·gus (lī kûr'gəs), *n.* fl. 9th? century B.C., political reformer of Sparta, reputed founder of Spartan constitution.

lydd·ite (lĭd'īt), *n.* a high explosive consisting chiefly of picric acid. [named after *Lydd,* in Kent, England. See -ITE[1]]

Lyd·i·a (lĭd'ĭ ə), *n.* an ancient kingdom in W Asia Minor: under Croesus, a wealthy empire including most of Asia Minor.

Lyd·i·an (lĭd'ĭ ən), *adj.* 1. of or pertaining to Lydia. 2. (of music) softly or sensuously sweet; voluptuous. —*n.* 3. an inhabitant of Lydia. 4. the language of Lydia, probably Anatolian.

lye (lī), *n.* any solution resulting from leaching, percolation, or the like. [ME *lie, ley,* OE *lēag,* c. G *lauge*]

Ly·ell (lī'əl), *n.* **Sir Charles,** 1797–1875, British geologist.

ly·ing[1] (lī'ĭng), *n.* 1. the telling of lies; untruthfulness. —*adj.* 2. that lies; untruthful; false. [der. LIE[1]. See -ING[1], -ING[2]]

ly·ing[2] (lī'ĭng), *v.* pres. part. of **lie.**

ly·ing-in (lī'ĭng ĭn'), *n.* 1. confinement in childbed. —*adj.* 2. pertaining to childbirth: *a lying-in hospital.*

Ly·ly (lĭl'ĭ), *n.* **John,** 1554?–1606, British writer of romances and plays. See **euphuism.**

lymph (lĭmf), *n. Anat., Physiol.* a clear yellowish, slightly alkaline fluid (which may be regarded as dilute blood minus the red corpuscles) derived from the tissues of the body and conveyed to the blood stream by the lymphatic vessels. [t. L: s. *lympha* water]

lymph-, a combining form of **lymph,** as in *lymphoid.*

lym·phad (lĭm'făd), *n.* a galley with one mast and usually a yard upon it.

lym·phad·e·ni·tis (lĭm făd'ə nī'tĭs, lĭm'fə də-), *n. Pathol.* inflammation of a lymphatic gland. [f. LYMPH- + ADEN- + -ITIS]

lym·phan·gi·al (lĭm făn'jĭ əl), *adj.* relating to the lymphatic vessels.

lym·phan·gi·i·tis (lĭm făn'jĭ ī'tĭs), *n. Pathol.* inflammation of the lymphatic vessels. [f. *lymph-* LYMPH- + m. s. Gk. *angei(on)* vessel + -*itis* -ITIS]

lym·phat·ic (lĭm făt'ĭk), *adj.* 1. pertaining to, containing, or conveying lymph: *a lymphatic vessel.* 2. noting, pertaining to, or having a temperament characterized by sluggishness of thought and action, formerly supposed to be due to an excess of lymph in the system. —*n.* 3. a lymphatic vessel. [t. NL: s. *lymphāticus* pertaining to lymph. Cf. L *lymphātus* mad]

lymph cell, lymphocyte.

lymph gland, any of the glandlike bodies occurring in the lymphatic vessels and supposed to be a source of leucocytes. Also, **lymph node, lymphatic gland.**

lympho-, var. of **lymph-,** before consonants.

lym·pho·cyte (lĭm′fə sīt′), *n. Anat.* a leucocyte formed in lymphoid tissues, smaller than the granulocyte, with little cytoplasm and no cytoplasmic granules. Their numbers are increased in certain diseases such as tuberculosis and typhoid fever. Also, **lymph cell.**

lymph·oid (lĭm′foid), *adj.* 1. resembling, of the nature of, or pertaining to, lymph. 2. noting or pertaining to a tissue (**lymphoid tissue**) forming the greater part of the lymphatic glands. 3. pertaining to a lymphocyte.

Lyrate leaf

lyn·ce·an (lĭn sē′ən), *adj.* 1. lynxlike. 2. sharp-sighted.

lynch (lĭnch), *v.t.* to put (a person) to death (by hanging, burning, or otherwise) by some concerted action without authority or process of law, for some offense known or imputed. [see LYNCH LAW] —**lynch′er,** *n.* —**lynch′ing,** *n.* —**Syn.** See **hang.**

Lynch·burg (lĭnch′bûrg), *n.* a city in central Virginia. 47,727 (1950).

lynch law, the administration of summary punishment, esp. death, upon an offender (actual or reputed) by private persons acting in concert without authority of law. [orig. *Lynch's law;* named after the author, Captain William Lynch, 1742–1820, of Virginia]

Lynn (lĭn), *n.* a seaport in E Massachusetts, on Massachusetts Bay. 99,738 (1950).

Lyn·wood (lĭn′wŏŏd), *n.* a city in SW California. 25,823 (1950).

lynx (lĭngks), *n., pl.* **lynxes.** (*esp. collectively*) **lynx.** any of various wildcats of the genus *Lynx,* having long limbs and short tail, and usually with tufted ears, as *L. rufus,* the **bay lynx,** a common North American species, and *L. canadensis,* a large, densely furred species of Canada and the northern U.S. [ME, t. L, t. Gk.] —**lynx′like′,** *adj.*

Bay lynx, *Lynx rufus* (3 ft. long)

lynx-eyed (lĭngks′īd′), *adj.* sharp-sighted.

Ly·on (lī′ən), *n.* **Mary,** 1797–1849, U.S. leader in education for women: founder of Mount Holyoke College.

Ly·on·nais (lēô nĕ′), *n.* a former province in E France.

ly·on·naise (lī′ə nāz′; *Fr.* lēôɔ̂ nĕz′), *adj.* (of food, esp. fried potatoes) cooked with pieces of onion. [t. F]

Ly·on·nesse (lī′ə nĕs′), *n. Arthurian Romance.* the mythical region where Sir Tristram was born, located near Cornwall in SW England, and supposed to have been submerged by the sea. [t. OF: m. *Leonois*]

Ly·ons (lī′ənz), *n.* a city in E France at the confluence of the Rhone and Saône rivers. 460,748 (1946). French, **Lyon** (lyôn).

Ly·ra (lī′rə), *n. Astron.* a northern constellation, containing Vega, one of the brightest stars in the sky. [t. L, t. Gk.: lyre]

ly·rate (lī′rāt, -rĭt), *adj.* 1. *Bot.* (of a pinnate leaf) divided transversely into several lobes, the smallest at the base. See the illus. above. 2. *Zool.* lyre-shaped, as the tail of certain birds. Also, **ly′rat·ed.**

lyre (līr), *n.* 1. a musical instrument of ancient Greece, consisting of a sound box (usually a turtle shell), with two curving arms carrying a cross bar (yoke) from which strings are stretched to the body, used to accompany the voice in singing and recitation. 2. (*cap.*) *Astron.* Lyra. [ME *lire,* t. OF, t. L: m. *lyra,* t. Gk.]

Woman playing an ancient Greek lyre

lyre·bird (līr′bûrd′), *n.* an Australian passerine bird of the genus *Menura,* the male of which has a long tail which is lyrate when spread. See the illus. in the next column.

lyr·ic (lĭr′ĭk), *adj.* Also, **lyr′i·cal. 1.** (of poetry) having the form and musical quality of a song, and esp. the character of a songlike outpouring of the poet's own thoughts and feelings (as distinguished from *epic* and

dramatic poetry, with their more extended and set forms and their presentation of external subjects). **2.** pertaining to or writing such poetry: *a lyric poet.* **3.** characterized by or indulging in a spontaneous, ardent expression of feeling. **4.** pertaining to, rendered by, or employing singing. **5.** pertaining, adapted, or sung to the lyre, or composing poems to be sung to the lyre: *ancient Greek lyric odes.* **6.** (of a voice) relatively light of volume and modest in range (most suited for graceful, cantabile melody). —*n.* **7.** a lyric poem. **8.** *Colloq.* the words of a song. **Syn.** L: s. *lyricus,* t. Gk.: m. *lyrikós* of a lyre] —**lyr′i·cal·ly,** *adv.* —**lyr′i·cal·ness,** *n.*

Lyrebird, *Menura superba* (Total length ab. 3 ft., tail ab. 1½ ft.)

lyr·i·cism (lĭr′ə sĭz′əm), *n.* **1.** lyric character or style, as in poetry. **2.** lyric outpouring of feeling; emotionally expressed enthusiasm.

lyr·ism (lĭr′ĭz əm), *n.* **1.** lyricism, esp. of expression. **2.** lyric enthusiasm.

lyr·ist (līr′ĭst *for 1;* lĭr′ĭst *for 2*), *n.* **1.** one who plays on the lyre. **2.** a lyric poet.

Lys (lēs), *n.* a river flowing from N France through W Belgium into the Scheldt river at Ghent. ab. 100 mi.

Ly·san·der (lī săn′dər), *n.* died 395 B.C., Spartan naval commander and statesman.

lyse (līs), *v.,* **lysed, lysing.** *Immunol., Biochem.* —*v.t.* **1.** to cause dissolution or destruction of cells by lysins. —*v.i.* **2.** to undergo lysis. [back formation from LYSIN]

Lys·i·as (lĭs′ĭ əs), *n.* c450–c380 B.C., Athenian orator.

Ly·sim·a·chus (lī sĭm′ə kəs), *n.* c360–281 B.C., Macedonian general and king of Thrace, 306–281 B.C.

ly·sin[1] (lī′sĭn), *n. Immunol., Biochem.* an antibody which disintegrates either the bacterial cell (bacteriolysis) or the red blood cell (hemolysis). [special use of LYSIN(E)]

ly·sin[2] (lī′sĭn), *n.* lysine.

ly·sine (lī′sēn, -sĭn), *n. Biochem.* an amino acid essential for animal growth, $C_6H_{14}N_2O_2$, formed by hydrolyzing many of the proteins. Also, **lysin.** [f. s. Gk. *lýsis* a loosening + -IN[2]]

Ly·sip·pus (lī sĭp′əs), *n.* fl. c360–c316 B.C., Greek sculptor.

ly·sis (lī′sĭs), *n.* **1.** *Immunol., Biochem.* the dissolution or destruction of cells by lysins. **2.** *Med.* the gradual recession of a disease, as distinguished from the crisis, in which the change is abrupt. [NL, t. Gk.: a loosing]

-lysis, a word element, especially scientific, meaning breaking down, decomposition, as in *analysis, electrolysis.* [t. Gk. See LYSIS]

ly·sol (lī′sôl, -sŏl), *n.* **1.** a clear, brown, oily liquid, a solution of cresols in soap: used as a disinfectant and antiseptic. **2.** (*cap.*) a trademark for this substance. [f. s. Gk. *lýsis* solution + -OL[2]]

lys·so·pho·bi·a (lĭs′ə fō′bĭ ə), *n. Psychiatry.* an obsessive fear of losing the mind; dread of insanity. [f. s. Gk. *lýssa* rage, rabies + -(O)PHOBIA]

-lyte, a word element denoting something subjected to a certain process (indicated by a noun ending in -*lysis*), as in *electrolyte.* [t. Gk.: m. -*lytos* that may be or is loosed]

lyth·ra·ceous (lĭth rā′shəs, lī thrā′-), *adj.* belonging to the Lythraceae, or loosestrife family of plants.

lyt·ic (lĭt′ĭk), *adj.* pertaining to -*lyte* or -*lysis,* especially adapted in biochemistry to hydrolytic enzyme action. [independent use of -LYTIC]

-lytic, a termination of adjectives corresponding to nouns in -*lysis,* as in *analytic (analysis), paralytic (paralysis).* [t. Gk.: m.s. -*lytikós*]

lyt·ta (lĭt′ə), *n., pl.* **lyttas, lyttae** (lĭt′ē). a long, wormlike cartilage in the tongue of the dog and other carnivorous animals.

Lyt·ton (lĭt′ən), *n.* **1. Edward George Earle Lytton Bulwer-Lytton, 1st Baron,** 1803–73, British novelist, dramatist, and politician. **2.** his son, **Edward Robert Bulwer-Lytton, 1st Earl of,** (*Owen Meredith*) 1831–91, British diplomatist and poet.

Lyu·blin (lyŏŏ′blĭn), *n.* Russian name of **Lublin.**

-lyze, a word element making verbs of processes represented by nouns in -*lysis,* e.g., *catalyze.* [b. -LY(SIS) and -(I)ZE]

M

M (ĕm), *n., pl.* **M's** or **Ms, m's** or **ms. 1.** a consonant, the 13th letter of the English alphabet. **2.** the Roman numeral for 1000. **3.** *Print.* em.

M, 1. Medieval. **2.** Middle. Also **m.**

M., 1. Majesty. **2.** Manitoba. **3.** Manual. **4.** (L *meri-*

dies) noon. **5.** Monday. **6.** (*pl.* **MM.**) Monsieur. **7.** mountain.

m., 1. male. **2.** mark (German money). **3.** married. **4.** masculine. **5.** *Mech.* mass. **6.** medium. **7.** (L *meridies*) noon. **8.** meter. **9.** mile. **10.** minim. **11.** minute. **12.** modification of. **13.** month. **14.** moon. **15.** morning.

M'-, Mac.

m-, *Chem.* abridgment of meta- (def. 2).

ma (mä), *n. Colloq.* mamma; mother.

Ma, *Chem.* masurium.

M.A., **1.** (L *Magister Artium*) Master of Arts. **2.** Military Academy.

ma'am (măm, mäm; *unstressed* məm), *n.* **1.** *Colloq.* madam. **2.** *Brit.* the term of address used to the Queen or to a royal princess.

Maas (mäs), *n.* Dutch name for the part of the **Meuse** river in the Netherlands.

Maas·tricht (mäs′trĭкнт), *n.* a city in SE Netherlands, on the Maas river. 72,593 (est. 1946). Also, **Maestricht.**

Mab·i·no·gi·on (măb′ə·nō′gĭ·ən), *n.* **The,** a collection of medieval Welsh romances which were translated (1838–1849) by Lady Charlotte Guest.

Mac, prefix found in many family names of Irish or Scottish Gaelic origin. Also written **Mc-, Mᶜ-,** and **M'-.** [t. Irish and Gaelic: son]

ma·ca·bre (məkä′bər, -brə), *adj.* **1.** gruesome; horrible; grim; ghastly. **2.** pertaining to or suggestive of the allegorical dance of death (**danse macabre**) in which a skeleton Death leads people to the grave. Also, **ma·ca′ber.** [ME, t. F, ? ult. t. Ar.: m. *maqbara* graveyard]

mac·ad·am (məkăd′əm), *n.* **1.** a macadamized road or pavement. **2.** the broken stone used in making such a road. [named after J. L. *McAdam* (1756–1836), Scottish inventor]

mac·ad·am·ize (məkăd′ə·mīz′), *v.t.,* **-ized, -izing.** to construct (a road) by laying and rolling successive layers of broken stone. —**mac·ad′am·i·za′tion,** *n.*

Ma·cao (məkou′), *n.* **1.** a Portuguese colony in S China, on a peninsula of Macao island and two small adjacent islands at the mouth of the Chu-Kiang. 374,737 pop. (1940); 6 sq. mi. **2.** the seaport and capital of this colony. 148,456 (1940). Portuguese, **Ma·cá·u** (mə·kä′/ōō)

ma·caque (məkäk′), *n.* any monkey of the genus *Macaca,* chiefly found in Asia, characterized by cheek pouches and, generally, a short tail. [t. F, t. Pg.: m. *macaco,* t. Afr. (Congo)]

Pig-tailed macaque, *Macaca nemestrina* (Total length 2½ ft.; tail 7 to 9 in.)

mac·a·ro·ni (măk′ə·rō′nĭ), *n., pl.* **-nis, -nies.** **1.** a kind of paste of Italian origin, prepared from wheat flour, in the form of dried, hollow tubes, to be cooked for food. **2.** an English dandy of the 18th century who affected foreign ways. Also, **maccaroni.** [t. It.: m. *maccaroni,* now *maccheroni,* pl. of *maccarone,* now *mac cherone,* ult. der. LGk. *makaría* food of broth and pearl barley, orig. happiness]

mac·a·ron·ic (măk′ə·rŏn′ĭk), *adj.* Also, **mac·a·ron′i·cal.** **1.** characterized by a mixture of Latin words with words from another language, or with non-Latin words provided with Latin terminations, as a kind of burlesque verse. **2.** involving a mixture of languages. **3.** mixed; jumbled. —*n.* **4.** (*pl.*) macaronic verses. [t. ML: s. *mac·arōnicus,* der. It. *maccaroni* MACARONI] —**mac′a·ron′i·cal·ly,** *adv.*

mac·a·roon (măk′ə·rōōn′), *n.* a sweet drop cooky made of egg whites, sugar, little or no flour, and frequently almond paste, coconut, etc. [t. F: m. *macaron,* t. It.: m. *maccarone,* sing., MACARONI]

Mac·Ar·thur (məkär′thər), *n.* **Douglas,** born 1880, U.S. general.

Ma·cas·sar (məkăs′ər), *n.* **1.** a seaport in the U.S. of Indonesia, on SW Celebes island. 84,855 (1930). **2. Strait of,** a strait between Borneo and Celebes: naval engagement between the Allies and the Japanese, Jan., 1942. Dutch, **Makassar.**

Macassar oil, 1. (originally) an oil for the hair stated to be made from materials obtained from Macassar. **2.** a similar oil or preparation for the hair.

Ma·cau·lay (məkô′lĭ), *n.* **1. Rose,** born 1889?, British novelist and poet. **2. Thomas Babington Macaulay, Baron,** 1800–59, British essayist, historian, poet, and statesman.

ma·caw (məkô′), *n.* any of various large, long-tailed parrots, chiefly of the genus *Ara,* of tropical and subtropical America, noted for their brilliant plumage and harsh voice. [t. Pg.: m. *macao;* of Brazilian orig.]

Mac·beth (məkbĕth′, măk-), *n.* a tragedy (first played in 1606) by Shakespeare.

Mac·ca·bae·us (măk′ə·bē′əs), *n.* **Judas** (jōō′dəs), a Jewish patriot, a leader of the Maccabees.

Mac·ca·be·an (măk′ə·bē′ən), *adj.* of or pertaining to the Maccabees or to Judas Maccabaeus.

Mac·ca·bees (măk′ə·bēz′), *n. pl.* **1.** a family of heroes, deliverers of Judea during the Syrian persecutions of 175–164 B.C. **2.** the last two books of the Apocrypha, recording the struggle of the Maccabees.

mac·ca·boy (măk′ə·boi′), *n.* a kind of snuff, usually rose-scented. Also, **mac′co·boy′.** [m. *Macouba,* name of district in Martinique]

mac·ca·ro·ni (măk′ə·rō′nĭ), *n., pl.* **-nis, -nies.** macaroni.

Mac·don·ald (məkdŏn′əld), *n.* **1. George,** 1824–1905, Scottish novelist and poet. **2. Sir John Alexander,** 1815–91, Canadian statesman; prime minister, 1867–73, and 1878–91.

Mac·Don·ald (məkdŏn′əld), *n.* **James Ramsay,** 1866–1937, British labor leader and statesman; prime minister in 1924 and 1929–35.

Mac·Don·ough (məkdŏn′ə), *n.* **Thomas,** 1783–1825, U.S. naval officer: defeated British on Lake Champlain, 1814.

Mac·Dow·ell (məkdou′əl), *n.* **Edward Alexander,** 1861–1908, U.S. composer and pianist.

mace¹ (mās), *n.* **1.** *Hist.* a clublike weapon of war often with a flanged or spiked metal head. **2.** a staff borne before or by certain officials as a symbol of office. **3.** the bearer of such a staff. **4.** *Billiards.* a light stick with a flat head, formerly used at times instead of a cue. [ME, t. OF. Cf. L *mateola* mallet]

mace² (mās), *n.* a spice ground from the layer between a nutmeg shell and its outer husk, resembling nutmeg in flavor. [ME *macis,* t. OF, t. L: m. *mac(c)is* a spice]

mace·bear·er (mās′bâr′ər), *n.* macer.

Maced., Macedonia.

mac·é·doine (mäs′ĭ·dwän′; *Fr.* mȧ·sĕ·dwän′), *n.* **1.** a mixture of vegetables, served as a salad or otherwise. **2.** a jellied mixture of fruits. **3.** a medley. [t. F: lit., Macedonian]

Mac·e·don (măs′ə·dŏn′), *n.* Macedonia (def. 1).

Mac·e·do·ni·a (măs′ə·dō′nĭ·ə), *n.* **1.** an ancient country in the Balkan Peninsula, N of ancient Greece. **2.** a region in S Europe, including parts of Greece, Bulgaria, and Yugoslavia. —**Mac′e·do′ni·an,** *adj., n.*

Ma·cei·ó (mä′sā·ô′), *n.* a seaport in E Brazil. 85,949 (1940).

Macedonia (def. 2)

mac·er (mā′sər), *n.* one who bears a mace¹ (def. 2). [ME *masere,* t. OF: m. *maissier,* der. *masse* MACE¹]

mac·er·ate (măs′ə·rāt′), *v.,* **-ated, -ating.** —*v.t.* **1.** to soften, or separate the parts of (a substance) by steeping in a liquid, with or without heat. **2.** to soften or break up (food) by action of a solvent. **3.** to cause to grow thin. —*v.i.* **4.** to undergo maceration. **5.** to become thin; waste away. [t. L: m.s. *mācerātus,* pp.] —**mac′er·at′er, mac′er·a′tor,** *n.* —**mac′er·a′tion,** *n.*

mach., **1.** machine. **2.** machinery. **3.** machinist.

Ma·cha·do (mächä′dō), *n.* **Gerardo** (hĕrär′dō), (*Gerardo Machado y Morales*) 1871–1939, president of Cuba, 1925–33.

Mach·en (măk′ən), *n.* **Arthur,** born 1863, British novelist and essayist.

ma chère (mȧ shĕr′), *French.* my dear (fem.).

ma·che·te (mächā′tā, məshĕt′; *Sp.* mä·chĕ′tĕ), *n.* a large, heavy knife used esp. in Spanish-American countries as both a tool and a weapon. [t. Sp., ult. der. L *mactāre* slaughter]

Mach·i·a·vel·li (măk′ĭ·ə·vĕl′ĭ; *It.* mä′kyä·vĕl′lē), *n.* **Niccolò di Bernardo** (nē′kō·lô′ dē bĕr·när′dō), 1469–1527, Italian statesman and writer on government.

Mach·i·a·vel·li·an (măk′ĭ·ə·vĕl′ĭ·ən), *adj.* **1.** of, like, or befitting Machiavelli. **2.** being or acting in accordance with Machiavelli's political doctrines, which placed expediency above political morality, and countenanced the use of craft and deceit in order to maintain the authority and effect the purposes of the ruler. **3.** characterized by subtle or unscrupulous cunning; wily; astute. —*n.* **4.** a follower of Machiavelli or his doctrines. Also, **Mach′i·a·vel′i·an.** —**Mach′i·a·vel′li·an·ism, Mach′i·a·vel′lism,** *n.*

ma·chic·o·lat·ed (məchĭk′ə·lā′tĭd), *adj.* formed or furnished with machicolations. [f. s. ML *machicolātus,* pp., + -ED²]

ma·chic·o·la·tion (məchĭk′ə·lā′shən), *n. Archit.* **1.** an opening in the floor between the corbels of a projecting gallery or parapet, as on a wall or in the vault of a passage, through which missiles, molten lead, etc., might be cast upon an enemy beneath. **2.** a projecting gallery or parapet with such openings.

mach·i·nate (măk′ə·nāt′), *v.,* **-nated, -nating.** to contrive or devise, esp. artfully or with evil purpose. [t. L: m.s. *māchinātus,* pp.] —**mach′i·na′tor,** *n.*

mach·i·na·tion (măk′ə·nā′shən), *n.* **1.** the act or process of machinating. **2.** (*usually pl.*) a crafty scheme; evil design; plot.

A. Machicolation; B. Parapet; C. Corbels

ma·chine (məshēn′), *n., v.,* **-chined, -chining.** —*n.* **1.** an apparatus consisting of interrelated parts with separate functions, which is used in the performance of some kind of work: *a sewing*

machine. **2.** a mechanical apparatus or contrivance; a mechanism. **3.** something operated by a mechanical apparatus, as an automobile, a bicycle, or airplane. **4.** *Mech.* **a.** a device which transmits and modifies force or motion. **b.** See **simple machines.** the six (sometimes more) elementary mechanisms: the lever, wheel and axle, pulley, screw, wedge, and inclined plane. **5.** a contrivance, esp. in the ancient theater, for producing stage effects. **6.** some agency, personage, incident, or other feature introduced for effect into a literary composition. **7.** any complex agency or operating system: *the machine of government.* **8.** the body of persons conducting and controlling the activities of a political party or other organization. **9.** a person or agency acting like a mere mechanical apparatus. —*v.t.* **10.** to make, prepare, or finish with a machine. [t. F, t. L: m.s. *māchina*, t. d. Gk.: m. *māchinē*, Attic Gk. *mēchanē*]

machine gun, a small arm operated by a mechanism, able to deliver a rapid and continuous fire of bullets as long as the firer keeps pressure on the trigger.

ma·chine-gun (məshēn′gŭn′), *v.t.,* **-gunned, -gunning.** to shoot at, using a machine gun.

ma·chin·er·y (məshē′nərĭ), *n., pl.* **-eries.** **1.** machines or mechanical apparatus. **2.** the parts of a machine, collectively: *the machinery of a watch.* **3.** contrivances for producing stage effects. **4.** personages, incidents, etc., introduced into a literary composition, as in developing a story or plot. **5.** any system by which action is maintained: *the machinery of government.*

machine shop, a workshop in which metal and other substances are cut, shaped, etc., by machine tools.

machine tool, a power-operated machine, as a lathe, etc., used for general cutting and shaping operations.

ma·chin·ist (məshē′nĭst), *n.* **1.** a person who operates machinery, esp. a highly trained and skilled operator of machine tools. **2.** one who makes and repairs machines. **3.** *U.S. Navy.* a warrant officer whose duty is to assist the engineer officer in the engine room. **4.** a person who builds or operates machinery in a theater.

Mach number (mŏk), a number indicating the ratio between the air speed of an object and the speed of sound at a given altitude, etc.

-machy, a combining form meaning combat, as in *logomachy.* [t. Gk.: m. s. *-machia,* der. *-machos* fighting]

mac·in·tosh (măk′ĭntŏsh′), *n.* mackintosh.

Mack·en·sen (măk′ənzən), n. **August von** (ou′gōōst fən) 1849–1945, German field marshal.

Mac·ken·zie (məkĕn′zĭ), *n.* **1.** **Sir Alexander,** 1755?–1820, Scottish explorer in Canada. **2.** **William Lyon,** 1795–1861, Canadian political leader and journalist, born in Scotland. **3.** a river in NW Canada, flowing from the Great Slave Lake NW to the Arctic Ocean. ab. 900 mi.; with tributaries, ab. 2525 mi. **4.** a district in NW Canada, in the SW part of the Northwest Territories. 527,490 sq. mi.

mack·er·el (măk′ərəl), *n., pl.* **-el,** (*occasionally, esp. with reference to different species*) **-els.** **1.** an abundant food fish of the North Atlantic, *Scomber scombrus,* with wavy cross markings on the back and streamlined for swift swimming. **2.** Spanish mackerel. **3.** any of various other streamlined fishes, as the **Atka mackerel,** *Pleuropterygius monopterygius,* of the Aleutian Islands. [ME *makerel,* t. OF: m. *maquerel;* orig. unknown]

mackerel sky, a sky spotted with small white fleecy clouds; an extensive group of cirro-cumulus or alto-cumulus clouds, esp. when well-marked in their arrangement.

Mack·i·nac (măk′ənô′), *n.* **1. Strait of,** a strait joining Lakes Michigan and Huron. Least width, 4 mi. **2.** an island in Lake Huron at the entrance of this strait: Michigan state park; summer resort. 3 mi. long. **3.** a town on this island.

mack·i·naw (măk′ənô′), *n.* a Mackinaw coat. [shortened form of *Michilli-mackinaw,* name of an island near the strait connecting Lakes Michigan and Huron; said to mean turtle in Ojibwa; cf. *mičimakinak* big turtle]

Mackinaw blanket, a kind of thick blanket, often woven with bars of color, formerly much used in the northern and western U.S. by Indians, lumbermen, etc.

Mackinaw boat, a flat-bottomed boat with sharp prow and square stern, propelled by oars and sometimes sails, as used on the upper Great Lakes.

Mackinaw coat, a short coat of a thick, blanketlike, commonly plaid, woolen material.

Mackinaw trout, the lake trout.

mack·in·tosh (măk′ĭntŏsh′), *n.* **1.** a rain coat made of cloth rendered waterproof by India rubber. **2.** such cloth. **3.** any raincoat. Also, **macintosh.** [named after Charles *Mackintosh* (1766–1843), the inventor]

mack·le (măk′əl), *n., v.,* **-led, -ling.** —*n.* **1.** a blur in printing, as from a double impression. —*v.t., v.i.* **2.** to blur, as from a double impression in printing. Also, **macule.** [t. F: m. *macule,* t. L: m. *macula* spot]

Mac·lar·en (məklâr′ən), *n.* **Ian** (ē′ən, ī′ən), pen name of John Watson.

ma·cle (măk′əl), *n.* *Crystal.* a twin. [t. F, t. L: m.s. *macula* spot]

Mac·leish (məklēsh′), *n.* **Archibald,** born 1892, U.S. poet.

Mac·leod (məkloud′), *n.* **Fiona** (fĭō′nə), pen name of William Sharp.

Mac·Ma·hon (măk mä ôN′), *n.* **Marie Edme Patrice Maurice,** (märē′ ĕd′mə pä trēs′ mō rēs′), **Count de,** (*Duke of Magenta*) 1808–93, president of France, 1873–79.

Mac·Mil·lan (məkmĭl′ən), *n.* **Donald Baxter,** born 1874, U.S. arctic explorer.

Mac·Mon·nies (məkmŭn′ĭz), *n.* **Frederick William,** 1863–1937, U.S. sculptor and painter.

Ma·con (mā′kən), *n.* a city in central Georgia. 70,252 (1950).

Mac·pher·son (məkfûr′sən), *n.* **James,** 1736–96, Scottish author or translator of the poems of "Ossian."

Mac·quar·ie (məkwôr′ĭ, -kwŏr′ĭ), *n.* a river in SE Australia, in New South Wales, flowing NW to the Darling river. ab. 750 mi.

mac·ra·mé (măk′rəmā′), *n.* a kind of lace or ornamental work made by knotting thread or cord in patterns. [cf. Turk. *maqrama* towel, handkerchief, etc.]

Mac·rea·dy (məkrē′dĭ), *n.* **William Charles,** 1793–1873, British tragedian.

macro-, a word element meaning "long," "large," "great," "excessive," used esp. in biology and botany, contrasting with *micro-.* Also, before vowels, **macr-.** [t. Gk.: m. *makro-,* comb. form of *makrós*]

mac·ro·cosm (măk′rəkŏz′əm), *n.* the great world, or universe (opposed to *microcosm*). [t. F: m. *macrocosme.* t. ML: m.s. *macrocosmus,* f. *macro-* MACRO- + m. Gk. *kósmos* world] —**mac′ro·cos′mic,** *adj.*

mac·ro·cyst (măk′rəsĭst′), *n.* **1.** a cyst of large size, esp. the archicarp of certain *Discomycetes.* **2.** a multinuclear mass of protoplasm enclosed in a cyst.

mac·ro·cyte (măk′rəsīt′), *n.* *Pathol.* an abnormally large red blood cell. —**mac·ro·cyt·ic** (măk′rōsĭt′ĭk), *adj.*

mac·ro·cyt·ic anemia (măk′rəsĭt′ĭk), *Pathol.* an anemia characterized by predominance of macrocytes.

mac·ro·ga·mete (măk′rōgəmēt′), *n.* *Biol.* the female (and larger) of two conjugating gametes.

mac·ro·graph (măk′rəgrăf′, -grăf′), *n.* a photograph or other image equal to or somewhat larger than the original.

ma·cron (mā′krŏn, măk′rŏn), *n.* a short horizontal line used as a diacritic over a vowel to indicate that it is a "long" sound, as in *fāte.* [t. Gk.: m. *makrón,* neut., long]

mac·ro·phys·ics (măk′rəfĭz′ĭks), *n.* the part of physics that deals with physical objects large enough to be observed and treated directly.

mac·ro·scop·ic (măk′rəskŏp′ĭk), *adj.* visible to the naked eye (opposed to *microscopic*).

mac·ro·spore (măk′rəspôr′), *n.* *Bot.* megaspore.

ma·cru·ran (məkrŏŏr′ən), *adj.* **1.** belonging or pertaining to the *Macrura,* a group of stalk-eyed decapod crustaceans with long tails, including the lobsters, prawns, shrimps, etc. —*n.* **2.** a macruran crustacean. [f. s. NL *macrūra,* pl. (f. Gk.: s. *makrós* long + m. *ourá* tail) + -AN]

ma·cru·rous (məkrŏŏr′əs), *adj.* long-tailed, as the lobster (opposed to *brachyurous*).

mac·u·la (măk′yələ), *n., pl.* **-lae** (-lē′). a spot on the sun, in the skin, or the like. [ME, t. L] —**mac′u·lar,** *adj.*

mac·u·late (*v.* măk′yəlāt′; *adj.* măk′yəlĭt), *v.,* **-lated, -lating,** *adj.* —*v.t.* **1.** to mark with a spot or spots; stain. **2.** to sully or pollute. —*adj.* **3.** spotted; stained. **4.** defiled or impure. [ME, t. L: m.s. *maculātus,* pp.]

mac·u·la·tion (măk′yəlā′shən), *n.* **1.** act of spotting. **2.** a spotted condition. **3.** a marking of spots, as on an animal. **4.** a disfiguring spot or stain. **5.** defilement.

mac·ule (măk′ūl), *n., v.t., v.i.,* **-uled, -uling.** mackle.

mad (măd), *adj.,* **madder, maddest,** *v.,* **madded, madding.** —*adj.* **1.** disordered in intellect; insane. **2.** *Colloq.* moved by anger. **3.** (of wind, etc.) furious in violence. **4.** (of animals) **a.** abnormally furious: *a mad bull.* **b.** affected with rabies; rabid: *a mad dog.* **5.** wildly excited; frantic: *mad haste.* **6.** senselessly foolish or imprudent: *a mad scheme.* **7.** wild with eagerness or desire; infatuated: *to be mad about someone.* **8.** wildly gay or merry: *to have a mad time.* **9.** like mad, **a.** in the manner of a madman. **b.** with great haste, impetuosity, or enthusiasm. —*v.t.* **10.** *Archaic.* to make mad. —*v.i.* **11.** *Archaic.* to be, become, or act mad. [ME *mad, madd*(*e*), OE *gemǣd*(*d*), *gemǣded,* pp. of a verb der. from OE *gemǣd* mad, c. OHG *gameit* foolish]

—**Syn.** **1.** demented, lunatic, deranged, maniacal. **2.** furious, exasperated, angry. **6.** MAD, CRAZY, INSANE are used to characterize wildly impractical or foolish ideas, actions, etc. MAD suggests senselessness and excess: *the scheme of selling the bridge was absolutely mad.* CRAZY suggests recklessness and impracticality: *a crazy young couple.* INSANE is used with some opprobrium to express unsoundness and possible harmfulness: *the new traffic system is simply insane.* —**Ant.** **6.** sensible, practical; sound, safe.

Madag., Madagascar.

Mad·a·gas·car (măd′əgăs′kər), *n.* an island in the Indian Ocean, ab. 240 mi. off the SE coast of Africa: a French colony. 4,227,000 pop. (est. 1941); ab. 228,600 sq. mi. *Cap.:* Tananarive. —**Mad′a·gas′can,** *n., adj.*

mad·am (măd′əm), *n., pl.* **madams, mesdames** (mĕdăm′). **1.** a polite term of address orig. to a woman of rank or authority, but now used to any woman. **2.** the woman in charge of a brothel. [ME *madame,* t. OF, orig. *ma dame* my lady. See DAME]

mad·ame (măd′əm; *Fr.* mȧ dȧm′), *n.*, *pl.* **mesdames** (mē dȧm′). a conventional French title of respect, orig. for a woman of rank, used distinctively to or of a married woman, either separately or prefixed to the name. *Abbr.*: Mme., *pl.* Mmes. [t. F. See MADAM]

Madame Butterfly, an opera (1904) by Puccini.

Ma·da·ri·a·ga (mä′dä ryä′gä), *n.* **Salvador de** (säl′-vä dôr′ dĕ), born 1886, Spanish author and diplomat.

mad·cap (măd′kăp′), *adj.* **1.** wildly impulsive; lively: *a madcap girl.* —*n.* **2.** a madcap person, esp. a girl.

mad·den (măd′ən), *v.t.* **1.** to make mad or insane. **2.** to excite to frenzy; infuriate. —*v.i.* **3.** to become mad; act as if mad; rage.

mad·den·ing (măd′ən ĭng), *adj.* **1.** driving to madness or frenzy. **2.** infuriating; exasperating. **3.** raging; furious. —**mad′den·ing·ly,** *adv.*

mad·der (măd′ər), *n.* **1.** a plant of the rubiaceous genus *Rubia, R. tinctorum,* a European herbaceous climbing plant with panicles of small yellowish flowers. **2.** the root of this plant, used to some extent (esp. formerly) in medicine, and particularly for making dyes which give red and other colors. **3.** the dye or coloring matter itself. **4.** a color produced by such a dye. [ME *mad(d)er,* OE *mæd(e)re,* c. Icel. *madhra*]

Mad·dern (măd′ərn), *n.* **Minnie.** See **Fiske, Mrs.**

mad·ding (măd′ĭng), *adj.* **1.** mad; acting as if mad: *the madding crowd.* **2.** making mad.

made (mād), *v.* **1.** pt. and pp. of **make.** —*adj.* **2.** produced by making, preparing, etc. **3.** artificially produced. **4.** invented or made-up. **5.** assured of success or fortune: *a made man.*

Ma·dei·ra (mə dēr′ə; *Port.* mä dĕ′rə), *n.* **1.** a group of five islands off the NW coast of Africa, belonging to Portugal. 249,450 pop. (1940); 308 sq. mi. *Cap.*: Funchal. **2.** the chief island of this group. 247,423 pop. (1940); 286 sq. mi. **3.** (*often l.c.*) a rich strong white wine resembling sherry made there. **4.** a river flowing from W Brazil NE to the Amazon: the chief tributary of the Amazon. ab. 1100 mi. [t. Pg.: lit., wood, timber, g. L *materia;* so called because island was once a thick forest]

mad·e·moi·selle (măd′mwȧ zĕl′; *Fr.* mȧd mwȧ zĕl′), *n.*, *pl.* **mesdemoiselles** (*Fr.* mĕd mwȧ zĕl′). the conventional French title of respect for a girl or unmarried woman, either used separately or prefixed to the name. *Abbr.*: Mlle., *pl.* Mlles. [F., orig. *ma demoiselle* my demoiselle. See DEMOISELLE, DAMSEL]

Ma·de·ro (mä dĕ′rō), *n.* **Francisco Indalecio** (frän-sēs′kō ēn′dä lĕ′syō), 1873–1913, president of Mexico, 1911–13.

made-up (mād′ŭp′), *adj.* **1.** concocted; invented: *a made-up story.* **2.** artificial, as of the complexion. **3.** put together; finished.

mad·house (măd′hous′), *n.* **1.** an asylum for the insane. **2.** a place of commotion and confusion.

Mad·i·son (măd′ə sən), *n.* **1. James,** 1751–1836, 4th president of the U.S., 1809–17. **2. Mrs.,** (*Dolly Madison, Dorothy Payne*) 1768–1849, wife of James. **3.** the capital of Wisconsin, in the S part. 96,056 (1950).

mad·ly (măd′lĭ), *adv.* **1.** insanely. **2.** wildly; furiously: *they worked madly all night to repair the bombed bridge.* **3.** foolishly.

mad·man (măd′măn′, -mən), *n.*, *pl.* **-men.** an insane person.

mad·ness (măd′nĭs), *n.* **1.** state of being mad; insanity. **2.** rabies. **3.** senseless folly. **4.** frenzy; rage.

Ma·doe·ra (mä dōō′rä), *n.* Dutch name of **Madura.**

Ma·don·na (mə dŏn′ə), *n.* **1.** the Virgin Mary (usually prec. by *the*). **2.** a picture or statue representing the Virgin Mary. **3.** (*l.c.*) an Italian title of respect for a woman. [t. It.: my lady. See DONNA]

mad·ras (măd′rəs, mə drăs′, -dräs′), *n.* **1.** a light cotton fabric with cords set at intervals or with woven stripes or figures, often of another color, used for shirts, etc. **2.** a thin curtain fabric of a light, gauzelike weave with figures of heavier yarns. **3.** a large brightly colored kerchief, of either silk or cotton, often used for turbans. [named after MADRAS]

Ma·dras (mə drăs′, -dräs′), *n.* **1.** a large province in S India: formerly a presidency. 49,342,000 pop. (1941); 126,166 sq. mi. **2.** a seaport in and the capital of this province, on the Bay of Bengal. 777,481 (1941).

ma·dre (mä′drĕ), *n.* Spanish. mother. [Sp., g. L *mater*]

mad·re·pore (măd′rə pōr′), *n.* any of various corals (**madreporarians**) of the genus *Madrepora,* noted for reef building in tropical seas. [t. F, t. It.: m. *madrepora,* appar. f. *madre* mother (g. L *mater*) + m. *poro* (t. Gk.: m. *pôros* kind of stone)] —**mad·re·por·ic** (măd′rə pôr′ĭk, -pŏr′-), *adj.*

Ma·drid (mə drĭd′; *Sp.* mä drēd′), *n.* the capital of Spain, in the central part. 1,141,000 (est. 1945).

Madrepore

mad·ri·gal (măd′rĭ gəl), *n.* **1.** a lyric poem suitable for musical setting, usually short and often of amatory character (esp. in vogue in the 16th century and later in Italy, France, England, and elsewhere). **2.** a part song, without instrumental accompaniment, usually for five or six voices, making abundant use of contrapuntal imitation. **3.** any part song. **4.** any song. [t. It.: m. *madrigale,* g. L *matricale* simple, naïve, der. *matrix* womb]

mad·ri·gal·ist (măd′rĭ gəl ĭst), *n.* a composer or a singer of madrigals.

ma·dro·ña (mə drō′nyä), *n.* an ericaceous evergreen tree or shrub, *Arbutus Menziesii,* of western North America, having a hard wood and a smooth bark, and bearing a yellow, scarcely edible berry. [t. Sp.: the arbutus or strawberry tree, ult. der. L *maturus* ripe]

ma·dro·ño (mə drō′nyō), *n.*, *pl.* **-ños.** madroña.

Ma·du·ra (mä dōōr′ä for 1, mä′dōō rə for 2), *n.* **1.** Dutch, **Madoera.** an island in the U.S. of Indonesia, off the NE coast of Java. 1,962,462 pop. (1930); 2112 sq. mi. **2.** a city in S India, in Madras province. 239,144 (1941).

ma·du·ro (mə dōōr′ō), *adj.* (of cigars) strong and darkly colored. [t. Sp.: mature, g. L *maturus*]

mad·wom·an (măd′wŏŏm′ən), *n.*, *pl.* **-women.** a mad or insane woman.

mad·wort (măd′wûrt′), *n.* **1.** any of several plants, as an alyssum, gold-of-pleasure. **2.** a boraginaceous plant, *Asperugo procumbens.*

Mae·an·der (mē ăn′dər), *n.* ancient name of **Menderes** (def. 1).

Ma·e·ba·shi (mä′ĕ bä′shē), *n.* a city in central Japan, on Honshu island. 81,406 (1946).

Mae·ce·nas (mē sē′nəs), *n.* **1. Gaius Cilnius** (gā′əs sĭl′nĭ əs), between 73 and 63 B.C.–8 B.C., Roman statesman, friend and patron of Vergil and Horace. **2.** a generous patron, esp. of the arts.

Mael·strom (māl′strəm), *n.* **1.** a famous whirlpool off the NW coast of Norway. **2.** (*l.c.*) any great or violent whirlpool. **3.** (*l.c.*) a resistless confusion of affairs, influence, etc. [t. early mod. D: now spelled *maalstroom,* f. *malen* grind, whirl + *stroom* stream]

mae·nad (mē′năd), *n.* **1.** a female attendant of Bacchus; a bacchante. **2.** any frenzied or raging woman. Also, **menad.** [t. L: s. *Maenas,* t. Gk.: m. *mainás* a mad woman] —**mae·nad′ic,** *adj.*

ma·es·to·so (mä′ĕs tō′sō), *adj., adv. Music.* with majesty; stately. [It., der. *maestà* majesty, t. L: m. *majestas*]

Maes·tricht (mäs′trĭĸнt), *n.* Maastricht.

maes·tro (mīs′trō; *It.* mä′ĕs′trō), *n.*, *pl.* **-tri** (-trē). **1.** an eminent musical composer, teacher, or conductor. **2.** a master of any art. [It.: master]

Mae·ter·linck (mā′tər lĭngk′; *Fr.* mä tĕr lăn′; *Du.* mä′tər lĭngk′), *n.* **Maurice** (mō rēs′), 1862–1949, Belgian dramatist, essayist, and poet.

Mae West, an inflatable life-preserver vest for aviators who fall in the sea. [named after *Mae West,* U.S. stage and screen actress]

Maf·e·king (măf′ə kĭng′), *n.* a town in the N part of the Union of South Africa: administrative seat of the Bechuanaland protectorate; besieged for 217 days by the Boers, 1899–1900. 4666 (1936).

maf·fick (măf′ĭk), *v.i. Brit.* to celebrate with extravagant public demonstrations. [back formation from *Mafeking* (see MAFEKING); the relief of the city was celebrated in London with extravagant joy] —**maf′-fick·er,** *n.*

Ma·fi·a (mä′fĭ ä′), *n.* **1.** (in Sicily) **a.** (*l.c.*) a popular spirit of hostility to legal restraint and to the law, often manifesting itself in criminal acts. **b.** a 19th century secret society (similar to the Camorra in Naples) acting in this spirit. **2.** a criminal secret society of Sicilians or other Italians, at home or in foreign countries. Also, **Maf′fi·a′.** [t. It., Sicilian: boldness, bravery, der. *Maffio,* var. of *Maffeo,* t. It.: *Matthaeus* Matthew]

ma foi (mȧ fwȧ′), *French.* my faith! really!

mag., **1.** magazine. **2.** magnetism. **3.** magnitude.

Ma·gal·la·nes (mä gä yä′nĕs), *n.* Punta Arenas.

mag·a·zine (măg′ə zēn′, măg′ə zēn′), *n.* **1.** a periodical publication, usually bound and with a paper cover, containing miscellaneous articles or pieces, in prose or verse, often with illustrations. **2.** a room or place for keeping gunpowder and other explosives, as in a fort or on a warship. **3.** a building or place for keeping military stores, as arms, ammunition, provisions, etc. **4.** a collection of war munitions. **5.** a metal receptacle for a number of cartridges which is inserted into certain types of automatic weapons and which must be removed when empty and replaced by a full receptacle in order to continue firing. **6.** a supply chamber in a stove, a camera, etc. **7.** a storehouse; warehouse. [t. F: m. *magasin,* t. It.: m. *magazzino* storehouse, t. Ar.: m. *makhāzin,* pl. of *makhzan* storehouse]

mag·a·zin·ist (măg′ə zē′nĭst), *n.* one engaged in magazine work, esp. writing for magazines.

Mag·da·le·na (mäg′dä lĕ′nä), *n.* a river flowing from SW Colombia N to the Caribbean. ab. 1060 mi.

Magdalena Bay, a bay on the SW coast of Lower California, Mexico. ab. 40 mi. long.

Mag·da·lene (măg′də lēn′, măg′də lē′nē), *n.* **1. the,** Mary Magdalene. Mark 15:40, 16:9; John 20:1–18. **2.** (*l.c.*) a reformed prostitute. Also, **Mag·da·len** (măg′də lən).

Mag·da·le·ni·an (măg′də lē′nĭ ən), *adj.* denoting the period or culture stage in the Old World Stone Age (upper Paleolithic) in which Cro-Magnon man reached his highest level of industry and art. [from (La) *Madelaine,* France, where implements and art of this period were found]

ăct, ā le, dâre, ärt; ĕbb, ēqual; ĭf, īce; hŏt, ōver, ôrder, oil, bŏŏk, ōoze, out; ŭp, ūse, ûrge; ə = a in alone; ch, chief; g, give; ng, ring; sh, shoe; th, thin; ᴛн, that; zh, vision. See the full key on inside cover.

Magdalenian period, the most advanced culture of the European paleolithic period, named from discoveries in La Madeleine, France.

Mag·de·burg (măg′də bûrg′; *Ger.* mäg′də bŏŏrкн/), *n.* a city in central Germany: a port on the Elbe river. 336,838 (1939).

mage (māj), *n. Archaic.* a magician. [ME, t. F, t. L: m.s. *magus*]

Ma·gel·lan (mə jĕl′ən), *n.* **1.** Ferdinand, c1480–1521, Portuguese navigator, discoverer of the Strait of Magellan and the Philippine Islands. **2. Strait of, a** strait near the S tip of South America between the mainland of Chile and Tierra del Fuego and other islands, connecting the Atlantic and Pacific Oceans. ab. 360 mi. long; 2½–17 mi. wide.

Mag·el·lan·ic (măj′ə lăn′ĭk), *adj.* pertaining to or named after Ferdinand Magellan.

Magellanic cloud, *Astron.* either of two bright cloudlike patches of stars in the southern heavens.

ma·gen·ta (mə jĕn′tə), *n.* **1.** fuchsin. **2.** reddish purple. [named after MAGENTA; discovered year of battle.]

Ma·gen·ta (mə jĕn′tə), *n.* a town in N Italy, W of Milan: the French and Sardinians defeated the Austrians here, 1859. 10,470 (1936).

Mag·gio·re (mə jôr′Y; *It.* mäd jō′rĕ), *n.* **Lago** (lä′gô), a lake in N Italy and S Switzerland. 83 sq. mi.

mag·got (măg′ət), *n.* **1.** the legless larva of a fly, as of the housefly. **2.** a fly larva living in decaying matter. **3.** an odd fancy; whim. [ME *magot*; orig. uncert.]

mag·got·y (măg′ə tY), *adj.* **1.** infested with maggots, as food. **2.** having queer notions; full of whims.

Ma·gi (mā′jī), *n.pl., sing.* **-gus** (-gəs). **1.** (*also l.c.*) the three "wise men" who "came from the east" to Jerusalem to do homage to the infant Jesus. Matt. 2:1–12. **2.** the "Wise Men" or Zoroastrian priests of Ancient Media and Persia reputed to possess supernatural powers. [See MAGUS] —**Ma·gi·an** (mā′jY ən), *adj.* —**Ma′gi·an·ism,** *n.*

mag·ic (măj′Yk), *n.* **1.** the pretended art of producing effects beyond the natural human power by means of supernatural agencies or through command of occult forces in nature. **2.** the exercise of this art. **3.** the effects produced. **4.** power or influence exerted through this art. **5.** any extraordinary or irresistible influence: *the magic in a great name.* **6.** legerdemain; conjuring. —*adj.* Also, **mag′i·cal.** (Note: *magic* is generally not used predicatively, but *magical* is used both predicatively and attributively.) **7.** employed in magic: *magic spells.* **8.** mysteriously enchanting: *magic beauty.* **9.** of, pertaining to, or due to magic: *magic rites.* **10.** producing the effects of magic; like magic. [ME *magike*, t. LL: m. *magica*, in L *magicē*, t. Gk.: m. *magikē*, prop. fem. of *magikós* Magian, magic] —**mag′i·cal·ly,** *adv.* —**Syn. 1.** enchantment. MAGIC, NECROMANCY, SORCERY, WITCHCRAFT imply producing results through mysterious influences or unexplained powers. MAGIC may have glamorous and attractive connotations; the other terms suggest the harmful and sinister. MAGIC is an art of using some occult force of nature: *fifty years ago television would have seemed to be magic.* NECROMANCY is an art of prediction, supposedly because of communicating with the dead (it is called "the black art," because Greek *nekro,* dead, was confused with Latin *niger,* black): *necromancy led to violating graves.* SORCERY, originally divination by casting lots, came to mean supernatural knowledge gained through the aid of evil spirits, and often used for evil ends: *spells and charms used in sorcery.* WITCHCRAFT esp. suggests a malign kind of magic, often used by aged and half-crazed women against innocent victims: *in early New England, persons accused of witchcraft were executed.*

Magic Flute, The, an opera (1791) by Mozart.

ma·gi·cian (mə jYsh′ən), *n.* **1.** one skilled in magic arts. **2.** a juggler; conjurer. [ME *magicien,* t. OF, der. L *magicus* MAGIC] —**Syn. 1.** sorcerer, necromancer.

magic lantern, a lantern slide projector.

Magic Mountain, The, a novel (1924, Eng. trans. 1926) by Thomas Mann.

Ma·gi·not line (măzh′ə nō′; *Fr.* mȧ zhē nō′), a zone of French fortifications erected along the French-German border in the years preceding World War II.

mag·is·te·ri·al (măj′Ys tYr′Y əl), *adj.* **1.** of, pertaining to, or befitting a master; authoritative: *a magisterial pronouncement.* **2.** imperious; domineering. **3.** of, pertaining to, or befitting a magistrate or his office. **4.** of the rank of a magistrate. [t. ML: s. *magisteriālis,* der. LL *magisterius,* der. L *magister* MASTER] —**mag′is·te′ri·al·ly,** *adv.* —**mag′is·te′ri·al·ness,** *n.*

mag·is·tra·cy (măj′Ys trə sY), *n., pl.* **-cies. 1.** the office or function of a magistrate. **2.** a body of magistrates. **3.** the district under a magistrate. Also, **mag′is·tra·ture** (măj′Ys trā′chər).

mag·is·tral (măj′Ys trəl), *adj.* **1.** *Pharm.* prescribed or prepared for a particular occasion, as a remedy (opposed to *officinal*). **2.** *Fort.* principal. **3.** *Rare.* magisterial. —*n.* **4.** magistral line. [t. L: s. *magistrālis* of a master]

magistral line, *Fort.* the line from which the position of the other lines of field works is determined.

mag·is·trate (măj′Ys trāt′, -trYt), *n.* **1.** a civil officer charged with the administration of the law. **2.** a minor judicial officer, as a justice of the peace or a police justice, having jurisdiction to try minor criminal cases

and to conduct preliminary examinations of persons charged with serious crimes. [ME *magistrat,* t. L: s. *magistrātus* the office of a chief, a magistrate]

mag·ma (măg′mə), *n., pl.* **-mata** (-mə tə). **1.** any crude mixture of finely divided mineral or organic matters. **2.** *Geol.* molten material beneath the solid crust of the earth, from which igneous rock is formed. **3.** *Chem., Pharm.* a paste composed of solid and liquid matter. [t. L, t. Gk.: a salve] —**mag·mat·ic** (măg măt′Yk), *adj.*

Mag·na Char·ta (măg′nə kär′tə), **1.** the "great charter" of English liberties, forced from King John by the English barons at Runnymede, June 15, 1215. **2.** any fundamental constitution or law guaranteeing rights. Also, **Mag′na Car′ta.** [t. ML: great charter]

mag·na cum lau·de (măg′nə kŭm lô′dY, măg′nə kŏŏm lou′dĕ), *Latin.* with great praise (the second highest of the honors granted at graduation).

Mag·na Grae·ci·a (măg′nə grē′shY ə), ancient name of the colonial cities of Greece in S Italy.

mag·na·nim·i·ty (măg′nə nYm′ə tY), *n., pl.* **-ties. 1.** quality of being magnanimous. **2.** a magnanimous act.

mag·nan·i·mous (măg năn′ə məs), *adj.* **1.** generous in forgiving an insult or injury; free from petty resentfulness or vindictiveness. **2.** high-minded; noble. **3** proceeding from or revealing nobility of mind, etc. [t. L: m. *magnanimus* great-souled] —**mag·nan′i·mous·ly,** *adv.* —**mag·nan′i·mous·ness,** *n.* —**Syn. 2.** See noble.

mag·nate (măg′nāt), *n.* **1.** a great or dominant person in a district or, esp. in some field of business: *a railroad magnate.* **2.** a person of eminence or distinction in any field. **3.** a member of the upper house of certain European parliaments, as formerly in Hungary and Poland. [ME, t. LL: m.s. *magnas,* der. L *magnus* great]

mag·ne·sia (măg nē′shə, -zhə), *n.* magnesium oxide, a white tasteless substance used in medicine as an antacid and laxative. [ME, t. ML (in alchemy), t. Gk.: (*hē*) *Magnēsia* (*líthos*), (the) Magnesian (stone); i.e. stone from Magnesia in Thessaly] —**mag·ne′sian,** **mag·ne·sic** (măg nē′sYk), *adj.*

Mag·ne·si·a (măg nē′shY ə, -zhY ə), *n.* ancient name of Manisa.

mag·ne·site (măg′nY sīt′), *n.* a mineral, magnesium carbonate, $MgCO_3$, usually occurring in white masses.

mag·ne·si·um (măg nē′shY əm, -zhY əm, -zhəm), *n. Chem.* a light, ductile, silver-white metallic element which burns with a dazzling white light, used in lightweight alloys. Symbol: Mg; at. wt.: 24.32; at. no.: 12; sp. gr.: 1.74, at 20°C. [NL, der. *magnesia* MAGNESIA]

magnesium light, the strongly actinic white light produced when magnesium is burned, used in photography, signaling, pyrotechnics, etc.

mag·net (măg′nYt), *n.* **1.** a body (as a piece of iron or steel) which, like loadstone, possesses the property of attracting certain substances, esp. iron. **2.** loadstone. **3.** a thing or person that attracts, as by some inherent power or charm. [ME *magnete,* t. OF, t. L: m.s. *magnes* loadstone, magnet, t. Gk.: *Mágnēs* (*líthos*) (stone) of Magnesia (in Thessaly), loadstone. Cf. MAGNESIA]

mag·net·ic (măg nĕt′Yk), *adj.* **1.** of or pertaining to a magnet or magnetism. **2.** having the properties of a magnet. **3.** capable of being magnetized or attracted by a magnet. **4.** pertaining to the earth's magnetism: *the magnetic equator.* **5.** exerting a strong attractive power or charm: *a magnetic personality.* Also, **mag·net′i·cal.** —**mag·net′i·cal·ly,** *adv.*

magnetic equator, the aclinic line.

magnetic field, a condition of space in the vicinity of a magnet or electric current which manifests itself as a force on magnetic objects within that space.

magnetic flux, 1. the total magnetic induction through a given cross section. **2.** magnetomotive force divided by reluctance.

magnetic induction, a measure of the magnetic effect at a given point.

magnetic needle, a slender magnetized steel rod which, when adjusted to swing in a horizontal plane, as in a compass, indicates the direction of the earth's magnetic fields or the approximate north and south.

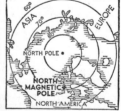

magnetic north, the direction in which the needle of a compass points, differing in most places from true north.

magnetic pole, 1. a pole of a magnet. **2.** either of the two points on the earth's surface where the dipping needle stands vertical, one in the arctic regions, and the other in the antarctic.

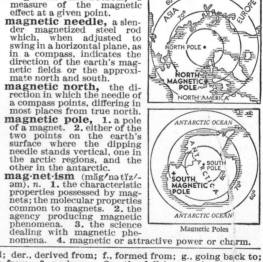

Magnetic Poles

mag·net·ism (măg′nə tYz′əm), *n.* **1.** the characteristic properties possessed by magnets; the molecular properties common to magnets. **2.** the agency producing magnetic phenomena. **3.** the science dealing with magnetic phenomena. **4.** magnetic or attractive power or charm.

---

b., blend of, blended; c., cognate with; d., dialect, dialectal; der., derived from; f., formed from; g., going back to; m., modification of; r., replacing; s., stem of; t., taken from; ?. perhaps. See the full key on inside cover.

mag·net·ite (măg′nə tīt′), *n.* a very common black iron oxide, Fe₃O₄, that is strongly attracted by a magnet; an important iron ore.

mag·net·ize (măg′nə tīz′), *v.t.* **-ized, -izing. 1.** to communicate magnetic properties to. **2.** to exert an attracting or compelling influence upon. **3.** *Obs.* to mesmerize. —**mag′net·i·za′tion,** *n.* —**mag′net·iz′er,** *n.*

mag·ne·to (măg nē′tō), *n., pl.* **-tos.** a small electric generator, the poles of which are permanent magnets, as a hand operated generator for telephone signaling, or the generator producing sparks in an internal-combustion engine.

magneto-, a combining form of **magnet** or **magnetic.**

mag·ne·to·chem·is·try (măg nē′tō kĕm′ĭs trĭ), *n.* the study of magnetic and chemical phenomena in their relation to one another. —**mag·ne′to·chem′i·cal,** *adj.*

mag·ne·to·e·lec·tric (măg nē′tō ĭ lĕk′trĭk), *adj.* pertaining to the induction of electric currents by means of magnets. Also, **mag·ne·to·e·lec′tri·cal.**

mag·ne·to·e·lec·tric·i·ty (măg nē′tō ĭ lĕk′trĭs′ə tĭ), *n.* electricity developed by the action of magnets.

mag·ne·to·gen·er·a·tor (măg nē′tō jĕn′ər ā′tər), *n.* a magnetoelectric generator.

mag·ne·tom·e·ter (măg nē tŏm′ə tər), *n.* an instrument for measuring magnetic forces. —**mag′ne·tom′e·try,** *n.*

mag·ne·to·mo·tive (măg nē′tō mō′tĭv), *adj.* producing magnetic effects, or pertaining to such production.

magnetomotive force, magnetic flux multiplied by reluctance, the force which gives rise to magnetic effects or magnetic flux.

mag·ne·ton (măg′nə tŏn′), *n. Physics.* a hypothetical ultimate magnetic particle.

mag·ne·tron (măg′nə trŏn′), *n. Electronics.* a two-element vacuum tube in which the flow of electrons is under the influence of an external magnetic field, used to generate extremely short radio waves. [f. MAGNE(T) + (ELEC)TRON]

magni-, **1.** a word element meaning "large," "great," as in *magnify.* **2.** *Zool.* a word element denoting length. [t. L, comb. form of *magnus* great]

mag·nif·ic (măg nĭf′ĭk), *adj. Archaic.* **1.** magnificent; imposing. **2.** grandiose; pompous. Also, **mag·nif′i·cal.** [t. L: s. *magnificus*] —**mag·nif′i·cal·ly,** *adv.*

Mag·nif·i·cat (măg nĭf′ə kăt′), *n.* **1.** the hymn of the Virgin Mary in Luke, 1:46-55, beginning "My soul doth magnify the Lord," used as a canticle at evensong or vespers. **2.** a musical setting of it. [ME, t. L: doth magnify, the first word of the hymn in the Vulgate]

mag·ni·fi·ca·tion (măg′nə fə kā′shən), *n.* **1.** act of magnifying. **2.** state of being magnified. **3.** the power to magnify. **4.** a magnified copy or reproduction.

mag·nif·i·cence (măg nĭf′ə səns), *n.* **1.** the quality or state of being magnificent; splendor; grandeur; impressiveness; sublimity. **2.** impressiveness of surroundings. [ME, t. OF, t. L: m.s. *magnificentia*] —**Syn. 1.** sumptuousness, pomp, state, majesty.

mag·nif·i·cent (măg nĭf′ə sənt), *adj.* **1.** making a splendid appearance or show: *a magnificent cathedral.* **2.** extraordinarily fine; superb: *a magnificent opportunity.* **3.** noble; sublime: *a magnificent poem.* **4.** great in deeds (now only as a title): *Lorenzo the Magnificent.* **5.** *Rare.* lavish. [t. OF, t. L: *magnificent-* (recorded in compar., superl., and other forms), for *magnificus.* See MAGNIFIC] —**mag·nif′i·cent·ly,** *adv.*
—**Syn. 1, 2.** august, stately, majestic, imposing; sumptuous, grand. MAGNIFICENT, GORGEOUS, SPLENDID, SUPERB are terms of high admiration and all are used colloquially in weak hyperbole. That which is MAGNIFICENT is beautiful, princely, grand, or ostentatious: *a magnificent display of paintings.* That which is GORGEOUS moves one to admiration by the richness and (often colorful) variety of its effects: *a gorgeous array of handsome gifts.* That which is SPLENDID is dazzling or impressive in its brilliance, radiance, or excellence: *splendid jewels, a splendid body of scholars.* That which is SUPERB is above others in, or is of the highest degree of, excellence or elegance (less often, today, of grandeur): *a superb rendition of a song, superb wines.* —**Ant. 1.** modest.

mag·nif·i·co (măg nĭf′ə kō′), *n., pl.* **-coes. 1.** a Venetian grandee. **2.** any grandee or great personage. [t. It., t. L: m. *magnificus* MAGNIFIC]

mag·ni·fy (măg′nə fī), *v.,* **-fied, -fying.** —*v.t.* **1.** to increase the apparent size of, as a lens does. **2.** to make greater in size; enlarge. **3.** to cause to seem greater or more important. **4.** *Archaic.* to extol; praise. —*v.i.* **5.** to increase or be able to increase the apparent size of an object, as a lens does. [ME *magnifie(n),* t. L: m. *magnificāre* make much of] —**mag′ni·fi′er,** *n.* —**Syn. 2.** augment, increase, amplify. **3.** exaggerate, overstate. —**Ant. 1, 2.** reduce. **3.** minimize.

mag·nil·o·quent (măg nĭl′ə kwənt), *adj.* speaking or expressed in a lofty or grandiose style. [L *magniloquus* + -ENT] —**mag·nil′o·quence,** *n.* —**mag·nil′o·quent·ly,** *adv.*

Mag·ni·to·gorsk (măg nĭ′tō gôrsk′), *n.* a city in the Soviet Union, on the Ural river near the boundary between Europe and Asia. 145,870 (1939).

mag·ni·tude (măg′nə tūd′, -tōōd′), *n.* **1.** size; extent: *to determine the magnitude of an angle.* **2.** great amount, importance, etc.: *affairs of magnitude.* **3.** greatness; great size: *the magnitude of the loss.* **4.** moral greatness: *magnitude of mind.* **5.** *Astron.* the brightness of a star expressed according to an arbitrary numerical system (the brightest degree being the **first magnitude,** and those less bright the **second, third,** or other **magnitude**). Stars brighter than the sixth magnitude are visible to the unaided eye. **6.** *Math.* a number characteristic of a quantity and forming a basis for comparison with similar quantities. [ME, t. L: m. *magnitūdo* greatness]

mag·no·li·a (măg nō′lĭ ə), *n.* **1.** any plant of the genus *Magnolia,* comprising shrubs and trees with large, usually fragrant flowers and an aromatic bark, much cultivated for ornament. **2.** the magnolia blossom. [NL; named from P. *Magnol* (1638–1715), a French botanist]

mag·no·li·a·ceous (măg nō′lĭ ā′shəs), *adj.* belonging to the *Magnoliaceae,* or magnolia family of plants, including the magnolias generally, the tulip trees, etc.

mag·num (măg′nəm), *n., pl.* **-nums** *for 1,* **-na** (-nə) *for 2.* **1.** a large bottle for wine or spirits, containing about two quarts. **2.** *Anat.* a bone of the carpus, at the base of the metacarpal bone of the middle finger. [t. L, neut. of *magnus* great]

magnum o·pus (ō′pəs), **1.** a great work. **2.** one's chief work, esp a literary or artistic work. [L]

mag·nus hitch (măg′nəs), a knot like a clove hitch but with one more turn, used to bend a line onto a spar, etc.

mag·pie (măg′pī′), *n.* **1.** any of various noisy, mischievous, corvine birds of the genus *Pica,* having a long, graduated tail and black-and-white plumage, as the **black-billed magpie,** *P. pica,* of Europe and North America, and the **yellow-billed magpie,** *P. nuttalli,* of California. **2.** a chattering person. [f. *Mag,* familiar var. of *Margaret,* woman's name + PIE²]

M.Agr., Master of Agriculture.

mag·uey (măg′wā; *Sp.* mä gĕ′ē), *n.* **1.** any of several species of the amaryllidaceous genus *Agave,* esp. *A. Cantala,* or the allied genus *Eurcraea.* **2.** the fiber from these plants. [t. Sp., prob. from Haitian]

Ma·gus (mā′gəs), *n., pl.* **-gi** (-jī). **1.** (*also l.c.*) See **Magi** (def. 1). **2.** (*l.c.*) an ancient astrologer or charlatan, esp. Simon Magus. Acts 8:9–24. [ME, t. L, t. Gk.: m. *Mágos,* t. OPers.: m. *magus*]

Mag·yar (măg′yär; *Hung.* mŏ′dyŏr), *n.* **1.** a member of the ethnic group, of the Finno-Ugric stock, which forms the predominant element of the population of Hungary. **2.** the Hungarian language. —*adj.* **3.** of or pertaining to the Magyars or their language; Hungarian. [t. Hung.]

Ma·gyar·or·szág (mŏ′dyŏr ŏr′säg), *n.* Hungarian name of Hungary.

Ma·ha·bha·ra·ta (mə hä′bä′rə tə), *n.* one of the two chief epics of ancient India. Its central subject is the war between the Kauravas and the Pandavas. Also, **Ma·ha·bha·ra·tam** (mə hä′bä′rə təm). [t. Skt.: f. *mahā-* great + *Bharata* descendant of a king or a tribe named *Bharata*]

Ma·han (mə hăn′), *n.* **Alfred Thayer** (thā′ər), 1840–1914, U.S. naval officer and writer on naval history.

ma·ha·ra·jah (mä′hə rä′jə; *Hind.* mə hä′rä′jə), *n.* the title of certain great Mohammedan ruling princes in India. Also, **ma·ha·ra·ja.** [t. Skt.: great raja]

ma·ha·ra·nee (mä′hə rä′nē; *Hind.* mə hä′rä′nē), *n. India.* **1.** the wife of a maharajah. **2.** a female sovereign in her own right. Also, **ma·ha·ra·ni.** [t. Hind.: great queen]

ma·hat·ma (mə hät′mə, -hät′-), *n.* **1.** an adept in Brahmanism. **2.** *Theosophy.* one of a class of reputed beings with preternatural powers. [t. Skt.: m. *mahātman* great-souled] —**ma·hat′ma·ism,** *n.*

Mah·di (mä′dē), *n., pl.* **-dis. 1.** (in Mohammedan usage) the title of an expected spiritual and temporal ruler destined to establish a reign of righteousness throughout the world. **2.** any of various claimants of this title, esp. Mohammed Ahmed (died 1885), who set up in the Egyptian Sudan an independent government which lasted until 1898. [t. Ar.: m. *mahdiy,* lit., the guided or directed one] —**Mah·dism** (mä′dĭz əm), *n.* —**Mah′dist,** *n.*

Ma·hi·can (mə hē′kən), *n.* **1.** a tribe or confederacy of North American Indians of Algonquian speech, centralized formerly in the upper Hudson valley. **2.** an Indian of this confederacy. **3.** a member of the Mohegan Indian tribe formerly in Connecticut. Also, **Mohican.** [t. Amer. Ind. (Algonquian): wolf]

mah-jongg (mä′jŏng′, -jŏng′), *n.* a game of Chinese origin, for four persons (or, sometimes, 3, 2, or 5), with 136 (or sometimes 144) dominolike pieces or tiles marked in suits, counters, and dice. Also, **mah′-jong′.** [t. Chinese (Mandarin): m. *ma-ch'iao* sparrow (lit., hemp-bird), pictured on the first tiles of one of the suits]

Mah·ler (mä′lər), *n.* **Gustav** (gŏŏs′täf), 1860–1911, Bohemian composer and conductor.

mahl·stick (mäl′stĭk′, môl′-), *n.* a painter's stick, held in one hand as a support for the hand which holds the brush. Also, **maulstick.** [t. D: m. *maalstok*]

Mah·mud II (mä mōōd′), 1785–1839, sultan of Turkey, 1809–39. Also, **Mah·moud′.**

ma·hog·a·ny (mə hŏg′ə nĭ), *n., pl.* **-nies,** *adj.* —*n.* **1.** any of certain tropical American meliaceous trees, esp. *Swietenia Mahagoni* and *S. macrophylla,* yielding a hard, reddish-brown wood highly esteemed for making fine furniture, etc. **2.** the wood itself. **3.** any of various related or similar trees, or their wood. **4.** a reddish-brown color. —*adj.* **5.** pertaining to or consisting of

mahogany. **6.** of the color mahogany. [? t. some non-Carib W. Indian tongue]

Ma·hom·et (məhŏm′ĭt), n. Mohammed. —**Ma·hom′-et·an,** adj., n.

Ma·hound (məhound′, -hōōnd′), n. **1.** the prophet Mohammed. **2.** Scot. the devil. [early ME Mahun, Mahum, t. OF, shortened form of Mahomet, b. with HOUND]

ma·hout (məhout′), n. (in the East Indies) the keeper and driver of an elephant. [t. Hind.: m. mahāut]

Mah·rat·ta (mərăt′ə), n. a member of a Hindu people inhabiting central and western India. Also, **Maratha.** [t. Hind.: m. Marhatā]

Mahratta Confederacy, a loose league of states in central and western India, broken up in 1818.

Mah·rat·ti (mərăt′ĭ), n. the language of the Mahrattas; an Indic language of western India. Also, **Marathi.**

Mäh·ren (mĕ′rən), n. German name of **Moravia.**

Mäh·risch-Os·trau (mĕ′rĭsh ŏs′trou), n. German name of **Moravská Ostrava.**

mah·zor (mäкH zōr′), n. a Hebrew prayer book containing the ritual for festivals. See **siddur.**

Ma·ia (mā′yə, mī′ə). n. Gk. Myth. the eldest of the Pleiades, mother by Zeus of Hermes.

maid (mād), n. **1.** a girl; young unmarried woman. **2.** a spinster (usually in the expression old maid). **3.** a female servant. **4. the Maid,** Joan of Arc. [apocopated var. of MAIDEN]

maid·en (mā′dən), n. **1.** a maid; girl; young unmarried woman. **2.** Also, **the Maiden.** an instrument resembling the guillotine, formerly used in Edinburgh for beheading criminals. **3.** Cricket. a maiden over. **4.** a maiden horse. **5.** a maiden race. —adj. **6.** of, pertaining to, or befitting a girl or unmarried woman. **7.** unmarried: a maiden lady. **8.** made, tried, appearing, etc., for the first time: maiden voyage. **9.** (of a horse, etc.) that never has won a race or a prize. **10.** (of a prize or a race) offered for or open to maiden horses, etc. **11.** untried, as a knight, soldier, or weapon. [ME; OE mægden, f. mægd- (Vernerian var. of mægth, c. G magd maid) + -en -EN⁶]

maid·en·hair (mā′dən hâr′), n. any of the ferns constituting the genus Adiantum. The cultivated species have fine, glossy stalks and delicate, finely divided fronds.

maid·en·head (mā′dən hĕd′), n. **1.** maidenhood; virginity. **2.** the hymen.

maid·en·hood (mā′dən hŏŏd′), n. the state or time of being a maiden; virginity.

maid·en·ly (mā′dən lĭ′), adj. **1.** pertaining to a maiden: maidenly years. **2.** characteristic of or befitting a maiden: maidenly behavior. —**maid′en·li·ness,** n.

maiden name, a woman's surname before marriage.

maiden over, Cricket. an over in which no runs are made.

Maid Marian, **1.** (orig.) Queen of the May, one of the characters in the old morris dance. **2.** a morris dance. **3.** Robin Hood's sweetheart.

maid of honor, **1.** the chief unmarried attendant of a bride. **2.** an unmarried woman, usually of noble birth, attendant on a queen or princess.

Maid of Orleans, Joan of Arc.

maid·serv·ant (mād′sûr′vənt), n. a female servant.

Maid·stone (mād′stōn′, -stən), n. a city in SE England: the county seat of Kent. 49,440 (est. 1946).

ma·ieu·tic (mā ū′tĭk), adj. (of the Socratic mode of inquiry) bringing out ideas latent in the mind. Also, **ma·ieu′ti·ca.** t. Gk.: m.s. maieutikós of midwifery]

mai·gre (mā′gər), adj. containing neither flesh nor its juices, as food permissible on days of religious abstinence. [t. F. See MEAGER]

mai·hem (mā′hĕm), n. mayhem.

mail¹ (māl), n. **1.** letters, packages, etc., arriving or sent by post. **2.** the system of transmission of letters, etc., by post. **3.** a train, boat, person, etc., by which postal matter is carried. —adj. **4.** of or pertaining to mail: a mail bag. —v.t. **5.** to send by mail; place in a postoffice or mailbox for transmission. [ME male, t. OF, t. Gmc.; cf. OHG malha wallet]

mail² (māl), n. **1.** flexible armor of interlinked rings, the ends riveted, butted, or soldered. **2.** defensive armor. —v.t. **3.** to clothe or arm with or as with mail. [ME maille, t. F, g. L macula spot, mesh of a net]

mail·box (māl′bŏks′), n. **1.** a public box for the mailing of letters. **2.** a private box for the delivery of mail.

Coat of mail and detail of same

mailed (māld), adj. clad or armed with mail: the mailed fist. [f. MAIL² + -ED²]

mailing machine, a machine which addresses, stamps, or otherwise handles letters, or the like.

mail·man (māl′măn′), n., pl. **-men.** one who delivers mail; postman.

mail-or·der house (māl′ôr′dər), a business house conducting a business by receiving orders (**mail orders**) and cash by mail and shipping goods to the buyers.

maim (mām). v.t. **1.** to deprive of the use of some bodily member; mutilate; cripple. **2.** to impair; make essentially defective. —n. **3.** Rare. an injury or defect. [var. of MAYHEM] —**maim′er,** n.

—**Syn. 1.** MAIM, LACERATE, MANGLE, MUTILATE indicate the infliction of painful and severe injuries on the body. To MAIM is to injure by giving a disabling wound, or by depriving a person of one or more members or their use: maimed in an accident. To LACERATE is to inflict severe cuts and tears on the flesh or skin: to wound and lacerate an arm. To MANGLE is to chop undiscriminatingly or to crush or rend by blows or pressure as if caught in machinery: bodies mangled in a train wreck. To MUTILATE is to injure the completeness or beauty of a body, esp. by cutting off an important member: to mutilate a statue, a tree, a person.

Mai·mon·i·des (mī mŏn′ə dēz′), n. (Moses ben Maimon) 1135–1204, Spanish-Jewish scholar and philosopher.

main¹ (mān), adj. **1.** chief; principal; leading: the main office. **2.** sheer; utmost, as strength, force, etc.: by main force. **3.** of or pertaining to a broad expanse: main sea. **4.** Gram. See **main clause.** **5.** Obs. strong or mighty. **6.** Obs. high-ranking; essential. **7.** Naut. pertaining to the mainmast or mainsail. —n. **8.** a principal pipe or duct in a system used to distribute water, gas, etc. **9.** strength; force; violent effort: with might and main. **10.** the chief or principal part or point. **11.** Poetic. the open ocean; high sea. **12.** the mainland. **13. in the main,** for the most part. [ME meyn, OE mægen strength, power, c. Icel. megin strength, main part] —**Syn. 1.** cardinal, prime, paramount.

main² (mān), n. a cockfighting match. [orig. obscure]

Main (mān; Ger. mīn), n. a river flowing from the Bohemian Forest in E Germany W to the Rhine at Mainz. 305 mi.

main clause, Gram. (in a complex sentence) the clause which may stand syntactically as a sentence by itself; independent clause. For example: in I was out when he came in, the main clause is I was out.

Maine (mān), n. **1.** a State in the NE United States, on the Atlantic coast. 913,774 pop. (1950); 33,215 sq. mi. Cap.: Augusta. Abbr.: Me. **2.** a former province in NW France. Cap.: Le Mans. **3.** a U.S. battleship blown up in Havana harbor, Cuba, Feb. 15, 1898: one of the events precipitating the Spanish-American War.

main·land (mān′lănd′, -lənd), n. the principal land, as distinguished from islands or peninsulas. —**main′-land′er,** n.

Main·land (mān′lănd′, -lənd), n. **1.** the largest of the Shetland Islands, NE of Scotland. ab. 13,000 pop.; ab. 200 sq. mi. **2.** Pomona.

main line, a through railroad route; a principal line of a railroad as contrasted with a branch or secondary line.

main·ly (mān′lĭ), adv. **1.** chiefly; principally; for the most part. **2.** Obs. greatly.

main·mast (mān′măst′, -mäst′; Naut. -məst), n. Naut. **1.** the principal mast in a ship or other vessel. **2.** (in a schooner, brig, bark, etc.), the second mast from the bow. **3.** (in a yawl or ketch) the mast nearer the bow.

main·sail (mān′sāl′; Naut. -səl), n. Naut. **1.** (in a square-rigged vessel) the sail bent to the main yard. See illus. under **sail.** **2.** (in a fore-and-aft rigged vessel) the large sail set abaft the mainmast.

main·sheet (mān′shēt′), n. Naut. a sheet of a mainsail.

main·spring (mān′sprĭng′), n. **1.** the principal spring in a mechanism, as in a watch. **2.** the chief motive power; the impelling cause.

main·stay (mān′stā′), n. **1.** Naut. the stay which secures the mainmast forward. **2.** a chief support.

Main Street, a novel (1920) by Sinclair Lewis.

main·tain (mān tān′), v.t. **1.** to keep in existence or continuance; preserve; retain: to maintain good relations with Canada. **2.** to keep in due condition, operation, or force; keep unimpaired: to maintain order, maintain public highways. **3.** to keep in a specified state, position, etc. **4.** to affirm; assert (with a clause, or with an object and infinitive). **5.** to assert to be true. **6.** to support in speech or argument, as a statement, etc. **7.** to keep or hold against attack: to maintain one's ground. **8.** to provide with the means of existence. [ME maintein(en), t. F: m. maintenir, g. L manū tenēre hold in the hand] —**main·tain′er,** n. —**Syn. 1.** keep up, continue. **5.** contend, claim. **8.** uphold, defend, vindicate. **8.** provide for. See **support.** —**Ant. 1.** break (off). **5.** deny. **6.** contradict.

main·te·nance (mān′tə nəns), n. **1.** act of maintaining. **2.** state of being maintained. **3.** means of provision for maintaining; means of subsistence. **4.** Law. an officious intermeddling in a suit in which the meddler has no interest, by assisting either party with means to prosecute or defend it. —**Syn. 3.** support, livelihood. See **living.**

maintenance of membership, an arrangement or agreement between an employer and a labor union by which employees who are members of the union at the time the agreement is made, or who subsequently join, must either remain members until the agreement expires, or be discharged.

Main·te·non (măNt nôN′), n. **Marquise de,** (Françoise d' Aubigné) 1635–1719, second wife of Louis XIV.

main·top (mān′tŏp′), n. Naut. a platform at the head of the lower mainmast.

---

b., blend of, blended; c., cognate with; d., dialect, dialectal; der., derived from; f., formed from; g., going back to; m., modification of; r., replacing; s., stem of; t., taken from; ?, perhaps. See the full key on inside cover.

main-top·gal·lant (mān′tə găl′ənt, -tŏp-), *n.* the main-topgallantmast, its sail, or yard. See illus. under **sail**.

main-top·gal·lant·mast (mān′tə găl′ənt măst′, -măst′, -məst; -tŏp-), *n. Naut.* the mast next above the main-topmast.

main-top·mast (mān′tŏp′məst), *n. Naut.* the mast next above the lower mainmast.

main-top·sail (mān′tŏp′səl), *n. Naut.* the sail set on the main-topmast. See illus. under **sail**.

main yard, *Naut.* the lower yard on the mainmast.

Mainz (mīnts), *n.* a city in W Germany: a port at the confluence of the Rhine and Main rivers. 158,533 (1939). French, **Mayence.**

mai·son de san·té (mĕ zôN′ də sän tĕ′), *French.* a private hospital for the sick or insane.

mai·son·ette (mā′zə nĕt′), *n. Brit.* a small apartment.

Mait·land (māt′lənd), *n.* **Frederic William,** 1850-1906, British legal historian and lawyer.

maî·tre d'hô·tel (mĕ′tr dō tĕl′), **1.** a steward or butler. **2.** a headwaiter. **3.** the owner or manager of a hotel. **4.** with maître d'hôtel sauce. [t. F: house master]

maize (māz), *n. Technical and Brit.* **1.** a widely cultivated cereal plant, *Zea Mays,* occurring in many varieties, bearing grain in large ears or spikes; corn; Indian corn. **2.** its grain. **3.** corn color; a pale yellow. [t. Sp.: m. *maíz,* t. Antillean: m. *maysi, mahiz,* t. Arawak: m. *marise*]

Maj., Major.

ma·jes·tic (mə jĕs′tĭk), *adj.* characterized by or possessing majesty; of lofty dignity or imposing aspect; stately; grand. Also, **ma·jes′ti·cal.** —**ma·jes′ti·cal·ly,** *adv.* —**Syn.** august, regal, imperial.

maj·es·ty (măj′ĭs tĭ), *n., pl.* **-ties.** **1.** regal, lofty, or stately dignity; imposing character; grandeur. **2.** supreme greatness or authority; sovereignty. **3.** a royal personage, or royal personages collectively. **4.** (*usually cap.*) a title used when speaking of or to a sovereign (prec. by *his your,* etc.). [ME *maieste,* t. F: m. *majesté,* t. L: m.s. *mājestas* greatness, grandeur, majesty]

ma·jol·i·ca (mə jŏl′ə kə, mə yŏl′-), *n.* **1.** a kind of Italian pottery coated with enamel and decorated, often in rich colors. **2.** a more or less similar pottery made elsewhere. [t. It.: m. *maiolica* MAJORICA]

ma·jor (mā′jər), *n.* **1.** *Mil.* a commissioned officer ranking next below a lieutenant colonel and next above a captain. **2.** one of superior rank in a specified class. **3.** *U.S.* a subject or field of study chosen by a student to represent his principal interest and upon which he concentrates a large share of his efforts. **4.** a person of full legal age. **5.** *Music.* a major interval, chord, scale, etc. —*adj.* **6.** greater, as in size, amount, extent, importance, rank, etc.: *the major part of the town.* **7.** greater, as in rank or importance: *a major question.* **8.** of or pertaining to the majority. **9.** *Logic.* broader or more extensive. The **major term** of a syllogism is the term that enters into the predicate of the conclusion; the **major premise** is that premise of a syllogism which contains the major term. **10.** of full legal age. **11.** *Music.* **a.** (of an interval) being between the tonic and the second, third, sixth, and seventh degrees of a major scale: *the major third, sixth, etc.* **b.** (of a chord) having a major third between the root and the note next above it. **12.** elder; senior: used after a name: *Cato Major.* In English public schools, used after a boy's name to distinguish him from a younger boy of the same name. **13.** *U.S.* noting or pertaining to educational majors: *a major field of study.* —*v.i.* **14.** *U.S.* to pursue a major or principal subject or course of study (fol. by *in*). [ME, t. L: greater, larger, superior, compar. of *magnus* great] —**Syn. 6.** See **capital**[1].

Ma·jor·ca (mə jôr′kə), *n.* a Spanish island in the W Mediterranean: the largest of the Balearic Islands. 327,120 pop. (1940); 1405 sq. mi. *Cap.:* Palma. Spanish, **Mallorca.**

ma·jor·do·mo (mā′jər dō′mō), *n., pl.* **-mos.** **1.** a man in charge of a great household, as that of a sovereign; a chief steward. **2.** a steward or butler. [t. Sp.: m. *mayordomo,* or t. It.: m. *maggiordomo,* t. ML: m. *mājor domūs* chief officer of the house]

major general, *Mil.* an officer ranking next below a lieutenant general and next above a bridagier general. —**ma′jor-gen′er·al·cy, ma′jor-gen′er·al·ship′,** *n.*

ma·jor·i·ty (mə jôr′ə tĭ, -jŏr′-), *n., pl.* **-ties.** **1.** the greater part or number: *the majority of mankind.* **2.** a number of voters or votes, jurors, or others in agreement, constituting more than half of the total number. **3.** the excess whereby the greater number, as of votes, surpasses the remainder. **4.** the party or faction with the majority vote. **5.** the state or time of being of full legal age: *to attain one's majority.* **6.** the military rank or office of a major. [t. F: m. *majorité,* t. ML: m.s. *mājoritas,* der. L *mājor* MAJOR]

major league, either of the two main professional baseball leagues in the U.S.: the American or National League.

major orders. See **orders** (def. 15).

Major Prophets. See **prophet** (def. 4b).

major scale, mode, or **key,** a scale, mode, or key whose third tone forms a major third with the fundamental tone. See illus. under **scale**.

major suit, *Bridge.* hearts or spades (because they have higher point values).

ma·jus·cule (mə jŭs′kūl), *adj.* **1.** large, as letters (whether capital or uncial). **2.** written in such letters (opposed to *minuscule*). —*n.* **3.** a majuscule letter. [t.

F, t. L: m.s. *mājusculus* somewhat greater or larger] —**ma·jus′cu·lar,** *adj.*

Ma·kas·sar (mə kăs′ər), *n.* Dutch name of **Macassar.**

make (māk), *v.,* **made, making,** *n.* —*v.t.* **1.** to bring into existence by shaping material, combining parts, etc.: *to make a dress.* **2.** to produce by any action or causative agency: *to make trouble.* **3.** to cause to be or become; render: *to make an old man young.* **4.** to constitute; appoint: *to make someone a judge.* **5.** to put into proper condition for use: *to make a bed.* **6.** to bring into a certain form or condition: *to make clay into bricks.* **7.** to cause, induce, or compel (to do something): *to make a horse go.* **8.** to give rise to; occasion. **9.** to produce, earn, or win for oneself: *to make a fortune.* **10.** to compose, as a poem. **11.** to draw up, as a legal document. **12.** to do; effect: *to make a bargain.* **13.** to fix; establish; enact: *to make laws.* **14.** to become by development; prove to be: *he will make a good lawyer.* **15.** to form in the mind, as a judgment, estimate, or plan. **16.** to entertain mentally, as doubt, scruple, etc. **17.** to judge or infer as to the truth, nature, meaning, etc.: *what do you make of it?* **18.** to estimate; reckon: *to make the distance ten miles.* **19.** (of material or parts) to compose; form: *two and two make four.* **20.** to bring to; bring up the total to: *to make an even dozen.* **21.** to serve for or as: *to make good reading.* **22.** to be sufficient to constitute; be essential to. **23.** to assure the success or fortune of. **24.** to put forth; deliver: *to make a speech.* **25.** to accomplish by traveling, etc.: *to make sixty miles an hour.* **26.** to arrive at or reach: *to make a port.* **27.** *Colloq.* to secure a place on, as a team. **28.** *Cards.* **a.** to name (the trump). **b.** to achieve a trick with (a card). **c.** *Bridge.* to achieve (a bid). **d.** to mix up or shuffle (the cards). **29.** *Sports and Games.* to earn as a score. **30.** to close (an electric circuit). —*v.i.* **31.** to act or start (to do, or as if to do, something). **32.** to cause oneself, or something understood, to be as specified: *to make sure.* **33.** to show oneself in action or behavior: *to make merry.* **34.** to direct or pursue the course; go: *to make for home.* **35.** to rise, as the tide, or as water in a ship, etc. **36.** to be of effect; operate (usually fol. by *for* or *against*). **37.** to go toward; approach, esp. hostilely (fol. by *for*). **38.** to go off or depart suddenly or hastily; run off (fol. by *off*). **39.** Some special verb phrases are:

make away with, 1. to get rid of. **2.** to kill or destroy.

make believe, 1. to pretend. **2.** to cause to believe.

make heavy weather, *Naut.* to roll and pitch in heavy seas.

make out, 1. to write out (a bill, a check, etc.). **2.** to prove; establish. **3.** to discern; discover; decipher. **4.** to finish or complete. **5.** *U.S. Colloq.* to get along; manage; succeed.

make over, 1. to make anew; alter: *to make over a dress.* **2.** to hand over into the possession or charge of another. **3.** to transfer the title of (property); convey.

make sternway, to move backwards; go astern.

make time, *Colloq.* to go fast.

make up, 1. (of parts) to constitute; form. **2.** to put together; construct; compile. **3.** to concoct; invent. **4.** to compensate for; make good. **5.** to complete. **6.** to prepare; put in order. **7.** to bring to a definite conclusion, as one's mind. **8.** to settle amicably, as differences. **9.** to become reconciled after a quarrel. **10.** *Print.* to arrange set type, etc., into columns or pages. **11.** to prepare for a part, as on the stage, by appropriate dress, cosmetics, etc. **12.** to adjust or balance, as accounts; to prepare, as statements. **13.** *Educ.* to repeat a course (or examination in which one has failed) or to take an (examination) from which one has been absent. **14.** to beautify artificially, as the face. **15.** to make (oneself) up by appropriate dress, etc., as for a part.

make up to, 1. *Colloq.* to try to be on friendly terms with; fawn on. **2.** to make advances; pay court to. —*n.* **40.** style or manner of being made; form; build. **41.** production with reference to the maker: *our own make.* **42.** disposition; character; nature. **43.** act or process of making. **44. on the make,** *Slang.* intent on gain or one's own advantage. **45.** quantity made; output. **46.** *Cards.* act of naming the trump, or the suit named as trump. **47.** *Elect.* the closing of an electric circuit (opp. to *break*).

[ME *make*(n), OE *macian,* c. LG and D *maken,* G *machen*]

—**Syn. 1.** form; build; produce; fabricate, create. MAKE, CONSTRUCT, MANUFACTURE mean to put into definite form, to produce, or to put parts together to make a whole. MAKE is the general term: *bees make wax.* CONSTRUCT, more formal, means to put parts together, usually according to a plan or design: *to construct a building.* MANUFACTURE refers to producing from raw materials, now almost entirely by means of machinery: *to manufacture automobiles.* The term is used contemptuously of producing imitations of works of art, etc. and is also used abstractly with the same idea of denying genuineness: *to manufacture an excuse.* **6.** convert; transform, change, turn. **9.** get, gain, acquire, obtain. **12.** perform, execute, accomplish. —**Ant. 1.** destroy. **9.** lose.

make and break, *Elect.* a device for alternately making and breaking an electric circuit.

make-be·lieve (māk′bə lēv′), *n.* **1.** pretense; feigning; sham. **2.** a pretender; one who pretends. —*adj.* **3.** pretended; feigned; sham.

make·fast (māk′făst′, -fäst′), *n. Naut.* any structure to which a vessel is tied up, as a bollard, buoy, etc.

ăct, āble, dâre, ärt; ĕbb, ēqual; ĭf, īce; hŏt, ōver, ôrder, oil, bŏŏk, ōōze, out; ŭp, ūse, ûrge; ə = a in alone; ch, chief; g, give; ng, ring; sh, shoe; th, thin; ŧh, that; zh, vision. See the full key on inside cover.

make-peace (māk′pēs′), *n.* *Rare.* a peacemaker.
mak·er (mā′kər), *n.* 1. one who makes. 2. (*cap.*) God. 3. *Law.* the party executing a legal instrument, esp. a promissory note. 4. *Bridge, Pinochle, etc.* the one who first designates the successful bid. 5. *Archaic.* a poet.
make-read·y (māk′rĕd′y), *n.* the process of preparing a form for printing by overlays or underlays to equalize the impression.
make-shift (māk′shĭft′), *n.* 1. a temporary expedient or substitute. —*adj.* 2. serving as or of the nature of a makeshift.
make-up (māk′ŭp′), *n.* 1. the way in which an actor or other person dresses himself, paints his face, etc., for a part. 2. the articles used for this purpose, esp., cosmetics, etc. 3. the manner of being made up or put together; composition. 4. physical or mental constitution. 5. *Print.* the arrangement of set type, cuts, etc., into columns or pages. 6. *Colloq.* a course or examination taken to make up a deficiency.
make-weight (māk′wāt′), *n.* 1. something put in a scale to complete a required weight. 2. anything added to supply a lack.
Ma·ke·ev·ka (mä kĕ′yĕf kä), *n.* a city in the SW Soviet Union. 240,145 (1939). Also, **Ma·ke′yev·ka.**
Ma·khach Ka·la (mä häch′ kä lä′), a seaport in the Soviet Union, on the Caspian Sea. 86,847 (1939).
mak·ing (mā′kĭng), *n.* 1. act of one who or that which makes. 2. **in the making,** being made; not yet finished. 3. structure; constitution; make-up. 4. means or cause of success or advancement: *to be the making of someone.* 5. (*often pl.*) material of which something may be made. 6. something made. 7. the quantity made.
mal-, a prefix having attributive relation to the second element, meaning "bad," "wrongful," "ill," as in *maladjustment, malpractice.* [t. F, repr. *mal,* adv. (g. L *male* badly, ill), or *mal,* adj. (g. L *malus*) bad]
Mal., 1. Malachi. 2. Malayan.
Mal·a·bar Coast (măl′ə bär′), 1. a coastal district in SW India, in Madras province. 3,929,000 pop. (1941); 5,790 sq. mi. *Cap.*: Calicut. 2. a region along the entire SW coast of India, extending from the Arabian Sea inland to the Western Ghats.
Ma·lac·ca (mə läk′ə), *n.* 1. a settlement in the SW Malay Peninsula: formerly a part of the British Straits Settlements; now in the Federation of Malaya. 212,282 pop. (est. 1937); 640 sq. mi. 2. a seaport in and the capital of this settlement. 38,042 (1931). 3. Strait of, a strait between Sumatra and the Malay Peninsula. 35–185 mi. wide.

Malacca cane, a cane or walking stick made of the brown, often mottled or clouded stem of an East Indian ratan palm, *Calamus scipionum.* [named after *Malacca*]
ma·la·ceous (mə lā′shəs), *adj.* belonging to the *Malaceae,* or apple family of plants, which includes the apple, pear, quince, medlar, loquat, hawthorn, etc. [f. s. L *mālus* apple tree + -ACEOUS]
Mal·a·chi (măl′ə kī′), *n.* Hebrew prophet of the 5th century B.C. and author of the last book of the "minor prophets" which bears his name.
mal·a·chite (măl′ə kīt′), *n.* a green mineral basic copper carbonate, $Cu_2CO_3(OH)_2$, an ore of copper, also used for making ornamental articles. [t. F, f. s. Gk. *maláchē* mallow + -ite -ITE[1]]
mal·a·col·o·gy (măl′ə kŏl′ə jĭ), *n.* the science that treats of mollusks. [f. m. Gk. *malakó(s)* soft (with ref. to the soft body of the mollusks) + -LOGY] —**mal′a·col′-o·gist,** *n.*
mal·a·cop·ter·yg·i·an (măl′ə kŏp′tə rĭj′ĭ ən), *adj. Zool.* of or pertaining to a division, *Malacopterygii,* of soft-finned teleost fishes. [f. m. Gk. *malakó(s)* soft + s. Gk. *ptéryx* wing, fin + -IAN]
mal·a·cos·tra·can (măl′ə kŏs′trə kən), *adj.* 1. Also, **mal′a·cos′tra·cous.** belonging to the *Malacostraca,* a subclass of crustaceans which have a comparatively complex organization, including the lobsters, shrimps, crabs, etc. 2. a malacostracan crustacean. [f. s. NL *Malacostraca* (t. Gk.: m. *malakóstraka* (neut. pl.) soft-shelled) + -AN]
mal·ad·just·ed (măl′ə jŭs′tĭd), *adj.* badly adjusted.
mal·ad·just·ment (măl′ə jŭst′mənt), *n.* a faulty adjustment.
mal·ad·min·is·ter (măl′əd mĭn′əs tər), *v.t.* to manage (esp. public affairs) badly or inefficiently. —**mal′ad·min′is·tra′tion,** *n.* —**mal′ad·min′is·tra′tor,** *n.*
mal·a·droit (măl′ə droit′), *adj.* lacking in adroitness; unskillful; awkward. [t. F. See MAL-, ADROIT] —**mal′-a·droit′ly,** *adv.* —**mal′a·droit′ness,** *n.*
mal·a·dy (măl′ə dĭ), *n., pl.* -dies. 1. any bodily disorder or disease, esp. one that is chronic or deep-seated. 2. any form of disorder: *social maladies.* [ME *maladie,* t. OF, der. *malade* sick, g. LL *male habitus,* lit., ill-conditioned] —**Syn.** 1. See **disease.**
ma·la fi·de (mā′lə fī′dĭ), *Latin.* in bad faith; not genuine (opposed to *bona fide*).
Mál·a·ga (măl′ə gə; *Sp.* mä′lä gä′), *n.* a seaport in S Spain, on the Mediterranean. 259,000 (est. 1945).
Mal·a·ga (măl′ə gə), *n.* 1. a sweet strong white wine with a pronounced muscat grape flavor, produced in the

province of Málaga, Spain. 2. any of the grapes grown in or exported from Málaga.
Mal·a·gas·y (măl′ə gäs′ĭ), *n., pl.* -gasy, -gasies. 1. a native of Madagascar. 2. an Austronesian language, the language of Madagascar.
ma·laise (mä lāz′; *Fr.* må lĕz′), *n.* a condition of indefinite bodily weakness or discomfort, often marking the onset of a disease. [t. F: f. *mal* ill + *aise* EASE]
mal·an·ders (măl′ən dərz), *n. pl.* a dry, scabby or scurfy eruption or scratch behind the knee in horses. [late ME, t. F: m. *malandres,* g. L *malandria* blisters on the neck]
mal·a·pert (măl′ə pûrt′), *Archaic.* —*adj.* 1. unbecomingly bold or saucy. —*n.* 2. a malapert person. [ME, t. OF: f. *mal* badly + *appert,* for *espert,* g. L *expertus* EXPERT] —**mal′a·pert′ly,** *adv.* —**mal′a·pert′ness,** *n.*
Mal·a·prop (măl′ə prŏp′), *n.* **Mrs.,** the "old weatherbeaten she-dragon" of Sheridan's *Rivals* (1775), noted for her misapplication of words.
mal·a·prop·ism (măl′ə prŏp′ĭz/əm), *n.* 1. act or habit of ridiculously misusing words. 2. a word so misused. [named after Mrs. MALAPROP. Cf. MALAPROPOS.]
mal·ap·ro·pos (măl′ăp rə pō′), *adj.* 1. inappropriate. —*adv.* 2. inappropriately. [t. F: *mal à propos* not to the point. See MAL-, APROPOS.]
ma·lar (mā′lər), *Anat.* —*adj.* 1. of or pertaining to the cheekbone or cheek. —*n.* 2. Also, **malar bone.** the cheekbone. [t. NL: s. *mālāris,* der. L *māla* cheekbone, cheek]
Mä·lar (mĕ′lär), *n.* a lake in S Sweden, extending ab. 80 mi. W from Stockholm: contains over 1200 islands. ab. 440 sq. mi.
ma·lar·i·a (mə lâr′ĭ ə), *n.* 1. a group of febrile diseases, usually intermittent or remittent, and characterized by attacks of chills, fever, and sweating, formerly supposed to be due to swamp exhalations, but now known to be caused by five or more species of parasitic protozoans which are transferred to the human blood by mosquitoes (genus *Anopheles*) and which occupy and destroy the red blood corpuscles. 2. unwholesome or poisonous air. [t. It.: contr. of *mala aria* bad air] —**ma·lar′i·al, ma·lar′i·an, ma·lar′i·ous,** *adj.*
mal·as·sim·i·la·tion (măl′ə sĭm′ə lā′shən), *n. Pathol.* imperfect assimilation or nutrition.
mal·ate (măl′āt, mā′lāt), *n. Chem.* a salt or ester of malic acid. [f. MAL(IC) + -ATE[2]]
Ma·lay (mā′lā, mə lā′), *adj.* 1. of or pertaining to the Malays or their country or language. 2. noting or pertaining to the so-called "brown" race, characterized by short stature, roundish skull, moderate prognathism, and straight black hair. —*n.* 3. a member of the dominant people of the Malay Peninsula and adjacent islands. 4. an Austronesian language, widespread in the East Indies as a language of commerce.
Ma·lay·a (mə lā′ə), *n.* 1. the Malay Peninsula. 2. **Federation of,** a British protectorate in the S Malay Peninsula, comprising nine semi-independent native states (the former Federated Malay States and Unfederated Malay States) and the British settlements of Penang and Malacca. ab. 4,652,000 pop.; 53,097 sq. mi. *Cap.*: Kuala Lumpur. Formerly (1946–48), **Malayan Union.**
Mal·a·ya·lam (măl′ə yä′ləm), *n.* a Dravidian language spoken in extreme southwestern India.
Ma·lay·an (mə lā′ən), *adj.* 1. Malay. —*n.* 2. a Malay. 3. Indonesian (def. 4).
Malayan Union, former name (1946–48) of the **Federation of Malaya.**
Malay Archipelago, an extensive archipelago in the Indian and Pacific Oceans, SE of Asia: the islands of the East Indies, including the Sunda Islands, the Moluccas, Borneo, and the Philippine Islands. Also, **Malaysia.**
Ma·lay·o-Pol·y·ne·sian (mə lā′ō pŏl′ə nē′shən,-zhən), *adj.* Austronesian.
Malay Peninsula, a peninsula in SE Asia, consisting of British Malaya and the S part of Siam. Also, **Malaya.**
Ma·lay·sia (mə lā′zhə, -shə), *n.* Malay Archipelago.
Ma·lay·sian (mə lā′zhən, -shən), *n.* 1. a native of Malaysia. 2. Indonesian (def. 1). 3. Malay (def. 3). —**Ma·lay′sian,** *adj.*
Malay States, a group of states in the Malay Peninsula, under British protection. ab. 4,079,000 pop.; 51,887 sq. mi. See **Malaya** (def. 2).
mal·con·tent (măl′kən tĕnt′), *adj.* 1. discontented; dissatisfied. 2. dissatisfied with the existing administration; inclined to rebellion. —*n.* 3. a malcontent person. [t. OF. See MAL-, CONTENT[2]]
mal de mer (mål də mĕr′), seasickness. [F]
Mal·den (môl′dən), *n.* a city in E Massachusetts, near Boston. 59,804 (1950).
Mal·dive Islands (măl′dīv), a group of coral atolls in the Indian Ocean, SW of India: a dependency of Ceylon. 88,000 pop. (est. 1941); 115 sq. mi.
mal du pa·ys (mål dy pĕ ē′), *French.* homesickness.
male (māl), *adj.* 1. belonging to the sex which begets young, or any division or group corresponding to it. 2. pertaining to or characteristic of this sex; masculine. 3. composed of males: *a male choir.* 4. *Bot.* **a.** designating or pertaining to any reproductive structure which produces or contains elements that bring about the fertilization of the female element. **b.** (of seed plants)

staminate. **5.** *Mach.* designating some part, etc., which fits into a corresponding part. **—n. 6.** a male human being; a man or boy. **7.** any animal of male sex. **8.** *Bot.* a staminate plant. [ME, t. OF, g. L *masculus*] **—Syn. 1.** MALE, MASCULINE, VIRILE are descriptive of one belonging to the paternal sex. MALE always refers to sex, whether of human beings, animals, or plants: *male animals are often larger than the females.* MASCULINE applies to the qualities that properly characterize the male sex: *a masculine love of sports.* The term may be applied to women, also, in either of two ways. It usually suggests some incongruity (as, *a masculine appearance*), but it may be used with complimentary implications: *she has a masculine mind.* VIRILE is a strong and comprehensive term, which formerly emphasized obvious maleness, but now usually implies the vigor, health, and force of mature manhood: *a virile opponent.*

Male·branche (mȧl brȧnsh′), *n.* **Nicolas de** (nē-kô lä′ də), 1638–1715, French philosopher.

mal·e·dict (măl′ə dĭkt), *adj. Obs.* accursed. [t. L]

mal·e·dic·tion (măl′ə dĭk′shən), *n.* **1.** a curse; the utterance of a curse. **2.** slander. [late ME, t. L: s. *maledictio* abuse] **—mal·e·dic·to·ry** (măl′ə dĭk′tər ĭ), *adj.*

mal·e·fac·tion (măl′ə făk′shən), *n.* an evil deed.

mal·e·fac·tor (măl′ə făk′tər), *n.* **1.** an offender against the law; a criminal. **2.** one who does evil. [late ME, t. L] **—mal·e·fac·tress** (măl′ə făk′trĭs), *n. fem.*

male fern, the rhizome and stipes of *Dryopteris Filix-Mas,* the oleoresin of which is used in medicine as a taeniafuge.

ma·lef·ic (mə lĕf′ĭk), *adj.* productive of evil; malign. [t. L: s. *maleficus* evil-doing]

ma·lef·i·cence (mə lĕf′ə səns), *n.* **1.** the doing of evil or harm. **2.** maleficent or harmful character.

ma·lef·i·cent (mə lĕf′ə sənt), *adj.* doing evil or harm; harmful. [t. L: back formation from *maleficientia* MALEFICENCE. Cf. BENEFICENT]

ma·le·ic acid (mə lē′ĭk), *Chem.* crystalline dibasic acid, $C_2H_2(COOH)_2$, an isomer of fumaric acid.

ma·lev·o·lence (mə lĕv′ə ləns), *n.* state or feeling of being malevolent; ill will. **—Syn.** MALEVOLENCE, MALIGNITY, RANCOR suggest the wishing of evil to others. MALEVOLENCE is a smoldering ill will: *a vindictive malevolence in his expression.* MALIGNITY is a deepseated and virulent disposition to injure; it is more dangerous than MALEVOLENCE, because it is not only more completely concealed but it often instigates harmful acts: *the malignity of his nature was shocking.* RANCOR is a lasting, corrosive, and implacable hatred and resentment: *rancor held for years against an unsuspecting person.*

ma·lev·o·lent (mə lĕv′ə lənt), *adj.* **1.** wishing evil to another or others; showing ill will. **2.** *Astrol.* evil or malign in influence. [t. L: s. *malevolens* wishing ill] **—ma·lev·o·lent·ly,** *adv.*

mal·fea·sance (măl fē′zəns), *n. Law.* the wrongful performance of an act which the actor has no right to perform. [t. F: m. *malfaisance* evil-doing, der. *malfaisant,* f. *mal* evil + *faisant,* ppr. of *faire* do, g. L *facere*] **—mal·fea·sant,** *adj.,* *n.*

mal·for·ma·tion (măl′fôr mā′shən), *n.* faulty or anomalous formation or structure, esp. in a living body.

mal·formed (măl fôrmd′), *adj.* faultily formed.

mal·gré (mȧl grā′), *prep. French.* despite.

Mal·herbe (mȧl ĕrb′), *n.* **François de** (frän swȧ′ də), 1555–1628, French poet and critic.

mal·ic (măl′ĭk, mā′lĭk), *adj.* pertaining to or derived from apples. [t. F: m. *malique,* der. L *malum* apple]

malic acid, *Chem.* a crystalline, dibasic hydroxy acid, $C_2H_3OH(COOH)_2$, occurring in apples and other fruits.

mal·ice (măl′ĭs), *n.* **1.** desire to inflict injury or suffering on another. **2.** *Law.* evil intent on the part of one who commits a wrongful act injurious to others. [ME, t. OF, g. L *malitia* badness, spite, malice] **—Syn. 1.** ill will, spite, spitefulness; animosity, enmity; malevolence. See **grudge. —Ant. 1.** benevolence; good will.

malice aforethought, *Law.* (in homicide) the distinguishing characteristic between common law murder and manslaughter, such as an intent to kill, or to do serious bodily harm, except when a killing is committed in the heat of passion from a reasonable provocation.

ma·li·cious (mə lĭsh′əs), *adj.* **1.** full of, characterized by, or showing malice; malevolent. **2.** *Law.* motivated by vicious, wanton, or mischievous purposes. **—ma·li·cious·ly,** *adv.* **—ma·li·cious·ness,** *n.*

ma·lign (mə līn′), *v.t.* **1.** to speak ill of; slander. **—adj. 2.** evil in effect; pernicious; baleful. **3.** having or showing an evil disposition; malevolent. [ME *maligne,* t. OF, t. L: m.s. *malignus* ill-disposed] **—ma·lign′er,** *n.* **—ma·lign·ly,** *adv.*

ma·lig·nant (mə lĭg′nənt), *adj.* **1.** disposed to inflict suffering or cause distress; malicious. **2.** threatening great danger; harmful in influence or effect. **3.** *Pathol.* deadly, or tending to produce death, as a disease, a tumor, etc. [t. LL: s. *malignans,* ppr., injuring maliciously] **—ma·lig′nance, ma·lig′nan·cy,** *n.* **—ma·lig′nant·ly,** *adv.*

ma·lig·ni·ty (mə lĭg′nə tĭ), *n., pl.* **-ties. 1.** state or character of being malign; malevolence. **2.** (*pl.*) malignant feelings, actions, etc. [late ME, t. L: m.s. *malignitas*] **—Syn. 1.** See **malevolence.**

Ma·lines (mə lēnz′; *Fr.* mȧ lēn′), *n.* French name of **Mechlin.**

ma·lines (mə lēn′; *Fr.* mȧ lēn′), *n.* **1.** Also, **ma·line′.** a delicate net resembling tulle, originally made by hand in the town of Malines, Belgium. **2.** Mechlin lace.

ma·lin·ger (mə lĭng′gər), *v.i.* to feign sickness or injury, esp. in order to avoid duty, work, etc. [t. F: m. *malingre* sickly, ailing, f. *mal* bad(ly) + OF *heingre* haggard, of Gmc. orig.] **—ma·lin′ger·er,** *n.*

Ma·li·now·ski (mä′lĭ nôf′skĭ), *n.* **Bronislaw Kaspar** (brô nē′släf käs′pər), 1884–1942, Polish anthropologist, in the U.S.

mal·i·son (măl′ə zən, -sən), *n. Archaic or Dial.* a curse. [ME, t. OF: m. *maleiçon,* g. L *maledictio* MALEDICTION]

mall (môl, măl), *n.* **1.** a shaded walk, usually public. **2.** the mallet used in the game of pall-mall. **3.** the game. **4.** the place or alley where it was played. [ME *malle,* t. OF: m. *ma(i)l,* g. L *malleus* hammer]

mal·lard (măl′ərd), *n., pl.* **-lards,** (*esp. collectively*) **-lard. 1.** a common, almost cosmopolitan wild duck, *Anas platyrhynchos,* from which the domestic ducks descended. **2.** a male of this species. [ME, t. OF: m. *malart,* prob. t. Gmc.: m. proper name *Madalhart,* given to animal in beast epic]

Mal·lar·mé (mȧ lȧr mē′), *n.* **Stéphane** (stĕ fȧn′), 1842–1898, French poet.

mal·le·a·ble (măl′ĭ ə bəl), *adj.* **1.** capable of being extended or shaped by hammering or by pressure with rollers. **2.** adaptable or tractable. [ME *malliable,* t. OF: m. *malleable,* der. L *malleāre* beat with a hammer. See **-ABLE**] **—mal·le·a·bil′i·ty, mal′le·a·ble·ness,** *n.*

malleable cast iron, white cast-iron castings given a special heat treatment to make them tough.

malleable iron, 1. malleable cast iron. **2.** the purest form of commercial iron, easily welded or forged.

mal·lee (măl′ē), *n.* **1.** any of various dwarf Australian species of *Eucalyptus,* as *Eucalyptus dumosa* and *E. oleosa,* which sometimes form large tracts of brushwood. **2.** such brushwood. [t. Australian]

mal·le·muck (măl′ə mŭk′), *n.* any of various oceanic birds, as the fulmar or albatross. [t. D: m. *mallemok,* f. m. *mal* foolish + *mok* gull]

mal·le·o·lar (mə lē′ə lər), *adj. Anat.* pertaining to a malleolus. [f. MALLEOL(US) + -AR¹]

mal·le·o·lus (mə lē′ə ləs), *n., pl.* **-li** (-lī′). *Anat.* either of two bony protuberances, one on each side of the ankle, situated in man at the lower end of the fibula and tibia respectively. [t. L, dim. of *malleus* hammer]

mal·let (măl′ĭt), *n.* **1.** a hammerlike tool with a head commonly of wood but occasionally of rawhide, plastic, etc., used for driving any tool with a wooden handle, as a chisel. **2.** the wooden implement used to strike the balls in croquet. **3.** the stick used to drive the ball in polo. [ME *maylet,* t. OF: m. *maillet,* dim. of *mail* MALL]

mal·le·us (măl′ĭ əs), *n., pl.* **-lei** (-lĭ ī′). *Anat.* the outermost of three small bones in the middle ear of man and other mammals. See diag. under **ear.** [t. L: hammer]

Mal·lor·ca (mȧ lyôr′kä), *n.* Spanish name of Majorca.

mal·low (măl′ō), *n.* **1.** any plant of the genus *Malva,* comprising herbs with leaves usually angularly lobed or dissected, and purple, pink, or white flowers, as *M. sylvestris,* common in Europe; and *M. neglecta* (*M. rotundifolia*), the dwarf mallow. **2.** any malvaceous plant, as the marshmallow. [ME *malue,* OE *mealwe,* t. L: m. *malva*]

malm (mäm), *n.* **1.** a kind of soft, friable limestone. **2.** a chalk-bearing soil of the southeastern part of England. [ME *malme,* OE *mealm,* c. Icel. *mālmr* ore]

Mal·mé·dy (mȧl mĕ dē′), *n.* See **Eupen and Malmédy.**

Malm·ö (măl′mō; *Sw.* mälm′œ′), *n.* a seaport in S Sweden, on the Sound opposite Copenhagen, Denmark. 171,158 (est. 1945).

malm·sey (mäm′zĭ), *n.* a strong, sweet wine of a high flavor, orig. made in Greece, but now in Madeira. [ME *malmesey,* t. ML: m.s. *malmasia,* t. NGk.: alter. of *Monemvasia* a seaport in southern Greece]

mal·nu·tri·tion (măl′nū trĭsh′ən, -nōō-), *n.* imperfect nutrition; lack of proper nutrition.

mal·oc·clu·sion (măl′ə klōō′zhən), *n.* faulty occlusion, closing, or meeting, as of opposing teeth in the upper and lower jaw.

mal·o·dor (măl ō′dər), *n.* a bad odor; a stench.

mal·o·dor·ous (măl ō′dər əs), *adj.* having a bad odor. **—mal·o′dor·ous·ly,** *adv.* **—mal·o′dor·ous·ness,** *n.*

Ma·lone (mə lōn′), *n.* **Edmond,** 1741–1812, Irish scholar and editor of Shakespeare.

ma·lo·nic acid (mə lō′nĭk, lŏn′ĭk), a dibasic acid, $CH_2(COOH)_2$, easily decomposed by heat. [t. F: m. *malonique,* alter. of *malique* MALIC]

malonic ester, *Chem.* a colorless fluid, $CH_2(COOC_2H_5)_2$, used in organic syntheses.

Mal·o·ry (măl′ə rĭ), *n.* **Sir Thomas,** fl. 1470, British translator and compiler of *Morte d'Arthur.*

Mal·pi·ghi (mäl pē′gē), *n.* **Marcello** (mär chĕl′lō), 1628–94, Italian anatomist. **—Mal·pigh·i·an** (mäl pĭg′ĭ ən), *adj.*

mal·pigh·i·a·ceous (măl pĭg′ĭ ā′shəs), *adj.* belonging or pertaining to the *Malpighiaceae,* a large family of tropical plants, certain of which are cultivated for ornamental purposes. [f. s. NL *Malpighia* the typical genus (named after MALPIGHI) + -ACEOUS]

Malpighian bodies, *Anat.* certain small round bodies occurring in the cortical substance of the kidney. Also, **Malpighian corpuscles.**

Malpighian layer, *Anat.* the layer of nonhorny cells in the epidermis.

Malpighian tubes, the excretory organs of insects, tubular outgrowths of the alimentary canal near the junction of the ventriculus and intestine. Also, **Malpighian vessels.**

mal·po·si·tion (măl′pə zĭsh′ən), n. Pathol. faulty or wrong position, esp. of a part or organ of the body or of a fetus in the uterus.

mal·prac·tice (măl prăk′tĭs), n. 1. improper professional action or treatment by a physician, as from reprehensible ignorance or neglect or with criminal intent. 2. any improper conduct. —**mal·prac·ti·tion·er** (măl′prăk tĭsh′ən ər), n.

Mal·raux (mål rō′), n. André (än drě′), born 1895, French novelist.

malt (môlt), n. 1. germinated grain (usually barley), used in brewing and distilling. 2. liquor produced from malt by fermentation, as beer or ale. —v.t. 3. to convert (grain) into malt. 4. to treat or mix with malt or malt product. 5. to make (liquor) with malt. —v.i. 6. to become malt. 7. to produce malt from grain. [ME; OE mealt, c. G malz; akin to MELT]

Mal·ta (môl′tə), n. 1. a British island in the Mediterranean between Sicily and Africa: naval station. 222,000 pop. (1938); 95 sq. mi. 2. a British colony consisting of this island and two small adjacent islands. 268,688 pop. (1938); 122 sq. mi. Cap.: Valletta.

Malta fever, undulant fever.

malt·ase (môl′tās), n. Biochem. an enzyme which converts maltose into dextrose, and which also causes similar cleavage of many other glucosides, as sucrose. [f. MALT + -ASE]

malted milk, 1. a soluble powder made of dehydrated milk and malted cereals. 2. a beverage made from this powder dissolved, usually, in milk.

Mal·tese (môl tēz′, -tēs′), adj., n., pl. **-tese.** —adj. 1. of or pertaining to Malta, its people, or their language. —n. 2. a native or inhabitant of Malta. 3. the Arabic dialect spoken in Malta.

Maltese cat, a bluish-gray variety of domestic cat.

Maltese cross, a cross having four equal arms that expand in width outward. See illus. under **cross.**

malt extract, a sweet gummy substance derived from an infusion of malt.

mal·tha (măl′thə), n. 1. any of various cements or mortars, bituminous or otherwise. 2. any of various natural mixtures of hydrocarbons, as ozocerite. 3. a viscous mineral liquid or semiliquid bitumen; a mineral tar. [late ME, t. L, t. Gk.: mixture of wax and pitch]

Mal·thus (măl′thəs), n. Thomas Robert, 1766–1834, British political economist.

Mal·thu·si·an (măl thoo′zĭ ən), adj. 1. of or pertaining to T. R. Malthus, who contended that population, tending to increase faster than the means of subsistence, should be checked by social and moral restraints. —n. 2. a follower of Malthus, or a believer in his doctrines. —**Mal·thu′si·an·ism,** n.

malt liquor, an alcoholic beverage, as beer, fermented from malt.

malt·ose (môl′tōs), n. Chem. a white crystalline sugar, $C_{12}H_{22}O_{11}H_2O$, formed by the action of diastase (as in malt) on starch. Also, **malt sugar.** [f. MALT + -OSE[2]]

mal·treat (măl trēt′), v.t. to treat ill; handle roughly or cruelly; abuse. [t. F: m. maltraiter. See MAL-, TREAT, v.] —**mal·treat′ment,** n.

malt·ster (môlt′stər), n. a maker of or dealer in malt.

malt·y ((môl′tĭ), adj. of, like, or containing malt.

mal·va·ceous (măl vā′shəs), adj. belonging to the Malvaceae, or mallow family of plants, which includes the abutilon, althea, hollyhock, okra, cotton plant, etc. [t. L: m. malvāceus of mallows]

mal·va·si·a (măl′və sē′ə), n. a sweet grape from which malmsey wine is made. [t. It. See MALMSEY]

Mal·vern (môl′vərn), n. an urban area in W England, in Worcestershire, comprising several small towns and villages on the E slope of the **Malvern Hills:** mineral springs; resort. 18,459 (1939).

Malvern Hill (măl′vərn), a plateau in E Virginia, SE of Richmond: battle, 1862.

mal·ver·sa·tion (măl′vər sā′shən), n. improper or corrupt behavior in office. [t. F, der. malverser, t. L: m. male versārī behave wrongly]

mal·voi·sie (măl′voi zĭ′, -və-), n. 1. malmsey wine. 2. malvasia grape. [late ME, t. F. See MALMSEY]

ma·ma (mä′mə, mə mä′), n. mother; mamma.

mam·ba (măm′bä), n. any of the long, slender, arboreal African snakes of the genus Dendroaspis, whose bite is almost certain death, and which is said to attack without provocation. [t. S Afr. (Kaffir): m. m'namba]

Mam·e·luke (măm′ə look′), n. 1. a member of an Egyptian military class, originally slaves, in power from 1250 to 1517, and influential under Turkish rule until destroyed by Mohammed Ali in 1811. 2. (l.c.) (in Mohammedan countries) a slave. [t. Ar.: m. mamlūk slave]

ma·mey (mä mā′, -mě′), n. mammee.

mam·ma[1] (mä′mə, mə mä′), n. (esp. in childish use) mother. [redupl. of a syllable common in natural infantile utterance. cf. F maman, L mamma, Gk. mámmē, Russ. and Lith. mama]

mam·ma[2] (măm′ə), n., pl. **mammae** (măm′ē). Comp. Anat. the organ, characteristic of mammals, which in the female secretes milk; a breast or udder. [OE, t. L: breast, pap]

mam·mal (măm′əl), n. a member of the Mammalia. —**mam′mal·like′,** adj.

Mam·ma·li·a (mă mā′lĭ ə), n.pl. a class of vertebrates whose young feed upon milk from the mother's breast. Most species (except cetaceans) are more or less hairy, all have a diaphragm, and all (except the monotremes) are viviparous. [NL, neut. pl. of LL mammālis of the breast] —**mam·ma′li·an,** n., adj.

mam·mal·o·gy (mă măl′ə jĭ), n. the science that treats of mammals. [f. MAMMA(LIA) + -LOGY]

mam·ma·ry (măm′ə rĭ), adj. Anat., etc. of or pertaining to the mamma or breast; mammalike.

mam·ma·to·cu·mu·lus (mă mā′tō kū′myə ləs), n., pl. **-li** (-lī′). Meteorol. a cloud formation whose lower surface forms pockets or festoons.

mam·mee (mă mā′, -mē′), n. 1. a tall, tropical American guttiferous tree, Mammea americana. 2. Also, **mammee apple.** its large, edible fruit. 3. sapodilla. 4. marmalade tree. Also, **mamey.** [t. Sp.: m. mamey; from Haitian]

mam·mif·er·ous (mă mĭf′ər əs), adj. having mammae; mammalian. [f. s. L mamma breast + -(I)FEROUS]

mam·mil·la (mă mĭl′ə), n., pl. **-millae** (-mĭl′ē). 1. Anat. the nipple of the mamma or breast. 2. any nipplelike process or protuberance. [t. L, dim. of mamma MAMMA[2]]

mam·mil·lar·y (măm′ə lěr′ĭ), adj. of, pertaining to, or resembling a mammilla.

mam·mil·late (măm′ə lāt′), adj. having a mammilla or mammillae. Also, **mam′mil·lat′ed.**

mam·mon (măm′ən), n. 1. New Testament. riches or material wealth. Mat. 6:24; Luke 16:9, 11, 13. 2. (cap.) a personification of riches as an evil spirit or deity. [t. LL: s. mammōna, t. Gk.: m. mamōnâs, t. Aram.: m. māmōn(ā) riches] —**mam′mon·ish,** adj.

mam·mon·ism (măm′ə nĭz′əm), n. the greedy pursuit of riches. —**mam′mon·ist, mam′mon·ite′,** n. —**mam′mon·is′tic,** adj.

Mammillary structure of malachite

mam·moth (măm′əth), n. 1. a large, extinct species of elephant, Mammuthus primigenius, the **northern woolly mammoth,** which resembled the present Indian elephant but had a hairy coat and long, curved tusks. 2. any of various related extinct species of elephant, as the **imperial mammoth,** Mammuthus imperator, the largest mammoth. —adj. 3. huge; gigantic: a mammoth enterprise. [t. Russ.: m. mammot', now mamant'] —Syn. 3. See **gigantic.**

Columbian mammoth, Mammuthus columbi (9 ft. high, 16 ft. long, tusks ab. 9 ft.)

Mammoth Cave, a large limestone cavern in central Kentucky: a national park.

mam·my (măm′ĭ), n., pl. **-mies.** 1. (in childish use) mother. 2. Southern U.S. a colored female nurse or old family servant.

Ma·mo·ré (mä′mô rě′), n. a river flowing generally N through Bolivia and joining the Beni on the Brazilian border to form the Madeira river. ab. 700 mi.

man (măn), n., pl. **men,** v., **manned, manning.** —n. 1. Anthropol. an individual (genus Homo, family Hominidae, class Mammalia) at the highest level of animal development, mainly characterized by his exceptional mentality. 2. the human creature or being as representing the species or as distinguished from other beings, animals, or things; the human race; mankind. 3. a human being; a person: to elect a new man. 4. the male human being, as distinguished from woman. 5. a husband: man and wife. 6. one; anyone (prec. by a): to give a man a chance. 7. a male follower, subordinate, or employee: officers and men of the army. 8. one having manly qualities or virtues. 9. Obs. manly character or courage. 10. a male servant; a valet. 11. a word of familiar address implying disparagement, impatience, etc. 12. one of the pieces used in playing certain games, as chess or checkers. 13. Hist. a liegeman; vassal. 14. to a man, all; to the last man. [ME and OE mann, man (pl. menn, men), c. Icel. madhr, D man, G mann] —v.t. 15. to furnish with men, as for service or defense. 16. to take one's place for service, as at a gun, post, etc. 17. to make manly; brace. 18. to accustom (a hawk) to the presence of men. [ME manne(n), OE mannian]

Man (măn), n. Isle of, an island in the Irish Sea: one of the British Isles. 48,485 pop. (est. 1938); 227 sq. mi. Cap.: Douglas.

Man., 1. Manila. 2. Manitoba.

ma·na (mä′nä), n. Anthropol. impersonal, supernatural force which may be concentrated in objects or persons.

man about town, a frequenter of theaters, clubs, etc.

Man·a·bo·zho (măn′ə·bō′zhō), *n.*, *pl.* **-zhos.** the trickster–culture hero of the Ottawa, Chippewa, Potawatomi, and other Central Algonquian tribes; referred to under a variety of names (Manabozho, Michabo, Nanabush, Nenabozho, etc.).

man·a·cle (măn′ə·kəl), *n.*, *v.*, **-cled, -cling.** —*n.* (*usually pl.*) 1. a shackle for the hand; handcuff. 2. a restraint. —*v.t.* 3. to handcuff; fetter. 4. to hamper; restrain. [ME *manicle*, t. OF: handcuff, t. L: m. *manicula*, dim. of *manus* hand]

man·age (măn′ĭj), *v.*, **-aged, -aging.** —*v.t.* 1. to bring about; succeed in accomplishing: *he managed to see the governor.* 2. to take charge or care of: *to manage an estate.* 3. to dominate or influence (a person) by tact, address, or artifice. 4. to handle, direct, govern, or control in action or use. 5. to wield (a weapon, tool, etc.). 6. to succeed in accomplishing a task, purpose, etc. 7. to contrive to get along. 8. to handle or train (a horse) in the exercises of the manège. 9. *Obs.* or *Archaic.* to use sparingly. —*v.i.* 10. to conduct affairs. [t. It.: m. *maneggiare* handle, train (horses), der. *mano* hand, g. L *manus*; sense influenced by F *manège* act of managing and *ménage* household] —**Syn.** 1. arrange, contrive. 4. guide, conduct, regulate, engineer. See **rule.** 5. handle, manipulate.

man·age·a·ble (măn′ĭj·ə·bəl), *adj.* that may be managed; governable; controllable; tractable. —**man′age·a·bil′i·ty, man′age·a·ble·ness,** *n.* —**man′age·a·bly,** *adv.*

managed currency, a monetary system governed by an administrative organization or according to some specially contrived set of rules (contrasted with the automatic gold standard).

man·age·ment (măn′ĭj·mənt), *n.* 1. act or manner of managing; handling, direction, or control. 2. skill in managing; executive ability. 3. the person or persons managing an institution, business, etc.: *conflicts between labor and management.* —**Syn.** 1. regulation, administration; superintendence, care, charge.

man·ag·er (măn′ĭj·ər), *n.* 1. one who manages. 2. one charged with the management or direction of an institution, a business, or the like. 3. one who manages resources and expenditures, as of a household. —**man′ag·er·ship′,** *n.* —**Syn.** 1. administrator, executive, superintendent, supervisor; boss.

man·ag·er·ess (măn′ĭj·ər·ĭs; *Brit.* măn′ə·jə·rĕs′), *n. Chiefly Brit.* a female manager.

man·a·ge·ri·al (măn′ə·jĭr′ĭ·əl), *adj.* pertaining to management or a manager: *managerial functions.* —**man′a·ge′ri·al·ly,** *adv.*

Ma·na·gua (mä·nä′gwä), *n.* the capital of Nicaragua, in the W part, on Lake Managua (38 mi. long): almost totally destroyed by an earthquake, 1931. 93,032 (est. 1943).

man·a·kin (măn′ə·kĭn), *n.* 1. any of various songless passerine birds, family *Piprldae*, of the warmer parts of America, mostly small and brilliantly colored. 2. manikin. [var. of MANIKIN]

ma·ña·na (mä·nyä′nä), *n.*, *adv. Spanish.* tomorrow; the indefinite future.

Ma·náos (mä·nous′), *n.* a city in N Brazil, on the Rio Negro near its confluence with the Amazon: a seaport ab. 900 mi. from the Atlantic. 67,866 (1940). Also, **Ma·naus′.**

Ma·nas·sas (mə·năs′əs), *n.* a town in NE Virginia: battles of Bull Run, 1861, 1862. 1804 (1950).

Ma·nas·seh (mə·năs′ə), *n.* 1. son of the patriarch Joseph. Gen. 41:51. 2. one of the ten tribes of Israel. 3. king of Judah, of the 7th century B.C. II Kings 21.

man-at-arms (măn′ət·ärmz′), *n.*, *pl.* **men-at-arms.** 1. a soldier. 2. a heavy-armed soldier on horseback.

man·a·tee (măn′ə·tē′), *n.* any of various herbivorous, gregarious sirenians constituting the genus *Trichechus*, having two flippers in front and a spoonshaped tail, of West Indian, Floridian, and Gulf coast waters. [t. Sp.: m. *manatí*; from Carib] —**man·a·toid** (măn′ə·toid′), *adj.*

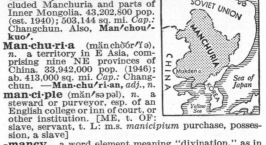

Florida manatee,
Trichechus manatus latirostris
(11 to 13 ft. long)

ma·nav·el·ins (mə·năv′əl·ĭnz), *n.pl. Naut. Slang.* miscellaneous pieces of gear and material. Also, **ma·nav′il·ins.**

Man·ches·ter (măn′chĕs′tər, -chĭs·tər), *n.* 1. a city in W England, in Lancashire: connected with the Mersey estuary by a ship canal (35½ mi. long). 671,500 (est. 1946). 2. a city in S New Hampshire. 82,732 (1950).

man·chi·neel (măn′chə·nēl′), *n.* a tropical American euphorbiaceous tree or shrub, *Hippomane Mancinella*, with a milky, highly caustic, poisonous sap. [t. F: m. *mancenille*, t. Sp.: m. *manzanilla*, dim. of *manzana* apple, g. L (*māla*) *Matiāna* (apples) of Matius (author of a cooking manual)]

Man·chu (măn·chōō′), *n.* 1. one of a Mongolian people inhabiting Manchuria, who conquered China in the 17th century. 2. a Tungusic language, spoken by the Manchus. —*adj.* 3. of or pertaining to the Manchus, their country, or their language.

Man·chu·kuo (măn′chōō·kwō′; *Chin.* män′jō′kwō′), *n.* a former country (1932–45) in E Asia, N of China, under Japanese control. It included Manchuria and parts of Inner Mongolia. 43,202,800 pop. (est. 1940); 503,144 sq. mi. *Cap.:* Changchun. Also, **Man′chou′-kuo′.**

Man·chu·ri·a (măn·chŏor′ĭ·ə), *n.* a territory in E Asia, comprising nine NE provinces of China. 33,942,000 pop. (1946); ab. 413,000 sq. mi. *Cap.:* Changchun. —**Man·chu′ri·an,** *adj., n.*

man·ci·ple (măn′sə·pəl), *n.* a steward or purveyor, esp. of an English college or inn of court, or other institution. [ME, t. OF: slave, servant, t. L: m.s. *manicipium* purchase, possession, a slave]

-mancy, a word element meaning "divination," as in necromancy. [ME *-manci(e)*, *-mancy(e)*, t. OF: (m.) *mancie*, g. LL *mantīa*, t. Gk.: m. *manteīa* divination].

Man·dae·an (măn·dē′ən), *n.* 1. a member of an ancient Gnostic sect still surviving in southern Mesopotamia. 2. the Aramaic language of the Mandaean sacred books. [f. m.s. Mandaean *mandayyā* (der. *mandā* knowledge) + -AN]

Man·da·lay (măn′də·lā′, măn′də·lā′), *n.* a city in central Burma, on the Irrawaddy river: the former capital of Upper Burma. 134,950 (1931).

man·da·mus (măn·dā′məs), *n.* 1. *Law.* a writ from a superior court to an inferior court, or to an officer, a corporation, etc., commanding a specified thing to be done. 2. (in early English law) any prerogative writ directing affirmative action. —*v.t.* 3. *Colloq.* to intimidate or serve with such writ. [t. L: we command]

Man·dan (măn′dăn), *n.* a Siouan language.

man·da·rin (măn′də·rĭn), *n.* 1. a member of any of the nine ranks of public officials in the Chinese Empire, each distinguished by a particular kind of button worn on the cap. 2. (*cap.*) standard Chinese. 3. (*cap.*) the north China language, esp. that of Peking. 4. a small, flattish citrus fruit of which the tangerine is one variety, native in southwestern Asia, of a characteristic sweet and spicy flavor. 5. the tree producing it, *Citrus reticulata*, and related species. [t. Chinese Pidgin E, t. Pg.: m. *mandarim*, der. *mundar* to command, b. with Malay and Hind. *mantrī*, g. Skt. *mantrin* counselor, der. *mantra* thought, counsel]

mandarin duck, a crested duck, *Aix galericulata*, with variegated plumage of purple, green, chestnut and white, native in China.

man·da·tar·y (măn′də·tĕr′ĭ), *n.*, *pl.* **-taries.** a person or nation holding a mandate. [t. L: m.s. *manddtārius*, der. L *mandātum* MANDATE]

man·date (*n.* măn′dāt, -dĭt; *v.* măn′dāt), *n.*, *v.*, **-dated, -dating.** —*n.* 1. a commission given to one nation (the mandatary) by an associated group of nations (such as the League of Nations) to administer the government and affairs of a people in a backward territory. 2. a mandated territory. 3. *Pol.* the instruction as to policy given or supposed to be given by the electors to a legislative body or to one or more of its members. 4. a command from a superior court or official to an inferior one. 5. a command; order. 6. an order issued by the pope, esp. one commanding the preferment of a certain person to a benefice. 7. *Roman and Civil Law.* a contract by which one engages gratuitously to perform services for another. 8. *Roman Law.* an order or decree by the emperor, esp. to governors of provinces. —*v.t.* 9. to consign (a territory, etc.) to the charge of a particular nation under a mandate. [t. L: m.s. *mandātum*, prop. pp. neut. of *mandāre* commit, enjoin, command]

man·da·tor (măn·dā′tər), *n.* one who gives a mandate.

man·da·to·ry (măn′də·tōr′ĭ), *adj.*, *n.*, *pl.* **-ries.** —*adj.* 1. pertaining to, of the nature of, or containing a mandate. 2. obligatory. 3. *Law.* permitting no option: *a mandatory clause.* 4. having received a mandate, as a nation. —*n.* 5. mandatary.

Man·de·ville (măn′də·vĭl), *n.* 1. Bernard, 1670?–1733, British philosopher and writer of satires, born in Holland. 2. Sir John, the ostensible (British) author of a 14th century book of travels.

man·di·ble (măn′də·bəl), *n.* 1. the bone of the lower jaw. 2. (in birds) a. the lower part of the beak: the lower jaw. b. (*pl.*) the upper and lower parts of the beak; the jaws. 3. (in arthropods) one of the first pair of mouth-part appendages, typically a jawlike biting organ, but styliform or setiform in piercing and sucking species. [t. LL: m.s. *mandibula, mandibulum* jaw]

Head of bee
M, Mandible(def. 3);
A, Antenna

man·dib·u·lar (măn·dĭb′yə·lər), *adj.* pertaining to or of the nature of a mandible.

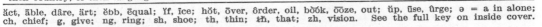

man·dib·u·late (măn dĭb′yə lĭt, -lāt′), *adj.* having mandibles.

Man·din·go (măn dĭng′gō), *n., pl.* **-gos, -goes,** *adj.* —*n.* **1.** a member of any of a number of Negro peoples forming an extensive linguistic group in western Africa. **2.** a principal language of West Africa, used widely as a lingua franca. —*adj.* **3.** pertaining to the Mandingos or their language.

man·do·lin (măn′də lĭn, măn′də lĭn′), *n.* a musical instrument with a pear-shaped wooden body (smaller than that of the lute) and a fretted neck, usually having metal strings plucked with a plectrum. [t. F: m. *mandoline,* t. It.: m. *mandolino,* dim. of *mandola, mandora,* var. of *pandora.* See PANDORA, BANDORE] —**man′do·lin′ist,** *n.*

man·drag·o·ra (măn drăg′ərə), *n.* **1.** mandrake. **2.** a mandrake root. [t. LL, in L *mandragoras,* t. Gk.]

man·drake (măn′drāk, -drĭk), *n.* **1.** a narcotic, short-stemmed European solanaceous herb, *Mandragora officinarum,* with a fleshy, often forked root fancied to resemble a human form. **2.** *U.S.* the May apple. [ME; popular etymological alter. of MANDRAGORA which was interpreted as MAN + DRAKE²]

Mandolin

man·drel (măn′drəl), *n. Mach.* a spindle, axle, bar or arbor, usually tapered, pressed into a hole in a piece of work to support the work during the machining process, as between the centers of a lathe. Also, **man′dril.** [t. F, dissimilated var. of *mandrin*]

man·drill (măn′drĭl), *n.* a large, ferocious-looking baboon, *Papio sphinx,* of western Africa, the male of which has the face marked with blue and scarlet and the muzzle ribbed. [f. MAN + DRILL⁴]

man·du·cate (măn′jŏŏ kāt′), *v.t.,* **-cated, -cating.** *Rare.* to chew; masticate; eat. [t. L: m.s. *manducātus,* pp.] —**man′du·ca′tion,** *n.* —**man·du·ca·to·ry** (măn′jŏŏ kə tōr′ĭ), *adj.*

mane (mān), *n.* the long hair growing on the back of or about the neck and neighboring parts of some animals, as the horse, lion, etc. [ME; OE *manu,* c. G *mähne*] —**maned** (mānd), *adj.*

Mandrill, *Papio sphinx*
(Ab. 3½ ft. long)

man·eat·er (măn′ē′tər), *n.* **1.** a cannibal. **2.** an animal, esp. a tiger, lion, or shark, that eats or is said to eat men. **3.** the great white shark, *Carcharodon carcharias,* reputedly the most dangerous shark to man.

maned wolf, the largest wild South American canid, *Chrysocyon jubatus,* a red-coated, large-eared, long-legged fox, found in Paraguay and Matto Grosso.

ma·nège (mă nězh′, -nāzh′), *n.* **1.** the art of training and riding horses. **2.** the action or movements of a trained horse. **3.** a school for training horses and teaching horsemanship. Also, **ma·nege′.** [t. F. See MANAGE]

ma·nes (mā′nēz), *n.pl.* **1.** (among the ancient Romans) the deified souls of the dead. **2.** the spirit or shade of a particular dead person. Also, **Ma′nes.** [L]

Ma·net (mă ně′), *n.* Édouard (ĕdwär′), 1832–83, French impressionist painter.

ma·neu·ver (mə nŏŏ′vər), *n., v.,* **-vered, -vering.** —*n.* **1.** a planned and regulated movement or evolution of troops, war vessels, etc. **2.** (*pl.*) a series of tactical exercises usually carried out in the field by large bodies of troops in imitation of war. **3.** an adroit move; artful proceeding, measure, etc. **4.** maneuvering; artful management. —*v.t.* **5.** to change the position of (troops, vessels, etc.) by a maneuver. **6.** to bring, put, drive, or make by maneuvers. **7.** to manipulate with skill or adroitness. —*v.i.* **8.** to perform a maneuver or maneuvers. **9.** to manage with address or art; scheme. Also, **manoeuvre.** [t. F: m. *manœuvre* manipulation, der. *manœuvrer* work, g. LL *manū operāre* work by hand] —**ma·neu′ver·a·ble,** *adj.* —**ma·neu′ver·a·bil′i·ty,** *n.* —**ma·neu′ver·er,** *n.*

man·ful (măn′fəl), *adj.* having or showing manly spirit; resolute. —**man′ful·ly,** *adv.* —**man′ful·ness,** *n.* —Syn. see **manly.**

man·ga·nate (măng′gə nāt′), *n. Chem.* a salt of manganic acid: *potassium manganate* K₂MnO₄.

man·ga·nese (măng′gə nēs′, -nēz′), *n. Chem.* a hard, brittle, grayish-white metallic element, whose oxide (**manganese oxide,** MnO₂) is a valuable oxidizing agent, used as alloying agent in steel to give it toughness. *Symbol:* Mn; *at. wt.:* 54.93; *at. no.:* 25; *sp. gr.:* 7.2 at 20°C. [t. F, t. It., t. ML: m. *magnēsia* MAGNESIA]

manganese steel, a steel alloy containing 10 to 14 per cent of manganese, used for railway switches and other devices involving heavy wear and strain.

man·gan·ic (măn găn′ĭk), *adj. Chem.* of or containing manganese, esp. in the trivalent state (Mn +³).

manganic acid, *Chem.* an acid, H₂MnO₄, not known in the free state.

man·ga·nite (măng′gə nīt′), *n.* **1.** a gray to black mineral, hydrous manganese oxide, MnO(OH), a minor ore of manganese. **2.** *Chem.* any of a series of salts containing tetravalent manganese, and derived from the acids H₄MnO₄ or H₂MnO₃. [f. MANGAN(ESE) + -ITE¹]

man·ga·nous (măng′gə nəs, măn găn′əs), *adj. Chem.* containing divalent manganese (Mn+²).

mange (mānj), *n.* any of various skin diseases due to parasitic mites affecting animals and sometimes man, characterized by loss of hair and scabby eruptions. [late ME *manjewe,* t. OF: m. *manjue* itch, der. *mangier* eat, g. L *mandūcāre* chew]

man·gel-wur·zel (măng′gəl wûr′zəl), *n. Chiefly Brit.* a coarse variety of the common beet, *Beta vulgaris,* extensively cultivated as food for cattle, etc. Also, **man′-gel.** [t. G, var. of *mangoldwurzel* beet root]

man·ger (măn′jər), *n.* a box or trough, as in a stable, from which horses or cattle eat. [ME, t. OF: m. *mangeoire,* der. L *mandūcāre* chew]

man·gle¹ (măng′gəl), *v.t.,* **-gled, -gling.** **1.** to cut, slash, or crush so as to disfigure: *a corpse mangled in battle.* **2.** to mar; spoil: *to mangle a text by poor typesetting.* [ME *mangel*(en), t. AF: m. *mangler,* ? freq. of OF *mahaignier* MAIM] —**man′gler,** *n.* —Syn. **1.** See **maim.**

man·gle² (măng′gəl), *n., v.,* **-gled, -gling.** —*n.* **1.** a machine for smoothing or pressing cloth, household linen, etc., by means of rollers. —*v.t.* **2.** to smooth with a mangle. [t. D: m. *mangel;* ult. akin to MANGONEL]

man·go (măng′gō), *n., pl.* **-goes, -gos.** **1.** the oblong, slightly acid fruit of a tropical anacardiaceous tree, *Mangifera indica,* which is eaten ripe, or preserved or pickled. **2.** the tree itself. [t. Pg.: m. *manga,* t. Malay: m. *manggā,* t. Tamil: m. *mānkāy*]

man·go·nel (măng′gə nĕl′), *n.* a large ancient military engine, or powerful crossbow, for throwing arrows, darts, or stones. [ME, t. OF, dim. der. LL *manganum,* t. Gk.: m. *mánganon* engine of war]

man·go·steen (măng′gə stēn′), *n.* **1.** the juicy edible fruit of an East Indian guttiferous tree, *Garcinia Mangostana.* **2.** the tree itself. [t. Malay: m. *mangustan*]

man·grove (măng′grōv, măn′-), *n.* **1.** any tree or shrub of the tropical genus *Rhizophora,* the species of which are mostly low trees remarkable for a copious development of interlacing adventitious roots above the ground. **2.** any of various similar plants, as the **white mangrove,** *Avicennia marina,* a valued source of tannin. [f. m. Sp. *mangle* (t. Malay: alter. of *manggi-manggi* mangrove) + GROVE]

man·gy (măn′jĭ), *adj.,* **-gier, -giest.** **1.** having, caused by, or like the mange. **2.** contemptible; mean. **3.** squalid; shabby. —**man′gi·ly,** *adv.* —**man′gi·ness,** *n.*

man·han·dle (măn′hăn′dəl, măn hăn′dəl), *v.t.,* **-dled, -dling.** **1.** to handle roughly. **2.** to move by force of men, without mechanical appliances.

Man·hat·tan (măn hăt′ən), *n.* **1.** an island in New York City between the Hudson, East, and Harlem rivers. 13½ mi. long; 2½ mi. greatest width; 22¼ sq. mi. **2.** a borough of New York City coextensive with Manhattan Island: chief business district. 1,960,101 pop. (1950). **3.** a cocktail of whiskey and sweet vermouth, often with a dash of bitters and a cherry.

Manhattan District, the large-scale project which developed the atomic bomb.

man·hole (măn′hōl′), *n.* a hole, usually with a cover, through which a man may enter a sewer, drain, steam boiler, etc., as to make repairs.

man·hood (măn′hŏŏd), *n.* **1.** state of being a man or adult male person. **2.** manly qualities. **3.** men collectively. **4.** state of being human.

man·hour (măn′our′), *n.* an hour of work by one man, used as an industrial time unit.

ma·ni·a (mā′nĭə), *n.* **1.** great excitement or enthusiasm; craze. **2.** *Psychiatry.* a form of insanity characterized by great excitement, with or without delusions, and in its acute stage by great violence. [late ME, t. L, t. Gk.: madness]

-mania, a combining form of **mania** (as in *megalomania*), extended to mean exaggerated desire or love for, as *Anglomania.*

ma·ni·ac (mā′nĭ ăk′), *n.* **1.** a raving lunatic; a madman. —*adj.* **2.** raving with madness; mad.

ma·ni·a·cal (mə nī′ə kəl), *adj.* of or pertaining to mania or a maniac. —**ma·ni′a·cal·ly,** *adv.*

ma·nic (mā′nĭk, măn′ĭk), *adj. Med.* pertaining to mania. [t. Gk.: m.s. *manikós* insane]

man·ic-de·pres·sive (măn′ĭk dĭ prĕs′ĭv), *Psychiatry.* —*adj.* **1.** having a mental disorder marked by cyclothymic manifestations of excitation and depression. —*n.* **2.** one who is suffering from this disorder.

Man·i·che·an (măn′ə kē′ən), *n.* **1.** an adherent of the religious system of the Persian teacher Mani or Manichaeus (A.D. 216?–276?), composed of Gnostic Christian, Buddhistic, Zoroastrian, and various other elements, the principal feature being a dualistic theology which represented a conflict between light and darkness and included belief in the inherent evil of matter. —*adj.* **2.** of or pertaining to Mani or the Manicheans. Also, **Man′i·chae′an.** [f. LL: (m.) s. *Manichaeus* (t. L Gk.: m. *Manichaîos;* from the name of the founder of the sect) + -AN] —**Man′i·che′an·ism, Man′i·che′ism,** *n.*

man·i·cure (măn′ə kyŏŏr′), *n., v.,* **-cured, -curing.** —*n.* **1.** professional care of the hands and fingernails. **2.** a manicurist. —*v.t., v.i.* **3.** to care for (the hands and fingernails). [t. F, f. L: m.s. *manus* hand + m. *cura* care]

man·i·cur·ist (măn′ə kyŏŏr′ĭst), *n.* a person who does manicuring.

man·i·fest (măn′ə fĕst′), *adj.* **1.** readily perceived by the eye or the understanding; evident; obvious; apparent; plain: *a manifest error.* **2.** *Psychoanal.* apparent or disguising (used of conscious feelings and ideas which conceal and yet incorporate unconscious ideas and impulses): *the manifest content of a dream as opposed to the latent content which it conceals.* —*v.t.* **3.** to make manifest to the eye or the understanding; show plainly. **4.** to prove; put beyond doubt or question. **5.** to record in a ship's manifest. —*n.* **6.** a list of a ship's cargo, signed by the master, for the information and use of customhouse officers. **7.** a list of goods transported by land. [ME, t. L: s. *manifestus* palpable, evident] —**man′i·fest′ly,** *adv.* —**man′i·fest′ness,** *n.* —**Syn. 1.** clear, distinct, unmistakable. **3.** reveal; disclose; evince. See **display.** —**Ant. 1.** obscure. **3.** conceal.

man·i·fes·ta·tion (măn′ə fĕs tā′shən), *n.* **1.** act of manifesting. **2.** state of being manifested. **3.** a means of manifesting; indication. **4.** a public demonstration, as for political effect. **5.** *Spiritualism,* a materialization.

man·i·fes·to (măn′ə fĕs′tō), *n., pl.* **-toes.** a public declaration, as of a sovereign or government, or of any person or body of persons taking important action, making known intentions, objects, motives, etc.; a proclamation. [t. It.: manifest, n.]

man·i·fold (măn′ə fōld′), *adj.* **1.** of many kinds, numerous and varied: *manifold duties.* **2.** having many different parts, elements, features, forms, etc. **3.** doing or operating several things at once. —*n.* **4.** something having many different parts or features. **5.** a copy or facsimile, as of writing, such as is made by manifolding. **6.** a pipe with a number of inlets or outlets. —*v.t.* **7.** to make copies of, as with carbon paper. [ME *monifald,* OE *manigfeald.* See MANY, -FOLD] —**man′i·fold′ly,** *adv.* —**man′i·fold′ness,** *n.* —**Syn. 1.** See **many.**

man·i·fold·er (măn′ə fōl′dər), *n.* a contrivance for making manifolds or copies, as of writing.

man·i·kin (măn′ə kĭn), *n.* **1.** a little man; a dwarf; pygmy. **2.** mannequin. **3.** a model of the human body for teaching anatomy, demonstrating surgical operations, etc. Also, **manakin, mannikin.** [t. D: m. *manneken,* dim. of *man* man. Cf. MANNEQUIN]

Ma·nil·a (mə nĭl′ə), *n.* **1.** a seaport in and the capital of the Philippine Islands, on W Luzon Island. 623,492 (1939). **2.** Manila hemp. **3.** Manila paper.

Manila Bay, a large bay in the Philippine Islands, in W Luzon Island: the American fleet under Admiral Dewey defeated the Spanish fleet here, 1898.

Manila hemp, a fibrous material obtained from the leaves of the abaca, *Musa textilis,* used for making ropes, fabrics, etc.

Manila paper, strong light-brown paper derived orig. from Manila hemp, but now also from wood pulp substitutes not of equal strength.

Manila rope, rope manufactured from Manila hemp.

ma·nil·la (mə nĭl′ə), *n.* **1.** Manila hemp. **2.** Manila paper.

man in the street, the average citizen.

man·i·oc (măn′ĭ ŏk′, mā′nĭ ŏk′), *n.* cassava. [repr. Sp., Pg. *mandioca,* Tupi *manioca,* Guarani *mandio*]

man·i·ple (măn′ə pəl), *n.* **1.** a subdivision of the Roman legion, consisting of 120 or 60 men. **2.** *Eccles.* one of the eucharistic vestments, consisting of an ornamental band or strip worn on the left arm near the wrist. See illus. under **chasuble.** [ME, t. OF, t. L: m.s. *manipulus* handful, company]

ma·nip·u·late (mə nĭp′yə lāt′), *v.t.,* **-lated, -lating. 1.** to handle, manage, or use, esp. with skill, in some process of treatment or performance. **2.** to manage or influence by artful skill: *to manipulate prices.* **3.** to adapt or change (accounts, figures, etc.) to suit one's purpose or advantage. [back formation from MANIPULATION] —**ma·nip′u·la′tive, ma·nip′u·la·to′ry,** *adj.* —**ma·nip′u·la′tor,** *n.*

ma·nip·u·la·tion (mə nĭp′yə lā′shən), *n.* **1.** skillful or artful management. **2.** act of manipulating. **3.** state or fact of being manipulated. [t. F, der. L *manipulus* handful]

Ma·ni·pur (mŭn′ĭ poor′), *n.* a state in NE India, in Assam. 512,069 pop. (1941); 8620 sq. mi. *Cap.:* Imphal.

Ma·ni·sa (mä′nĭ sä′), *n.* a city in W Turkey, near the Aegean: the Romans defeated Antiochus the Great here, 190 B.C. 37,623 (1940). Ancient, **Magnesia.**

man·i·to (măn′ə tō′), *n., pl.* **-tos.** (among the Algonquian Indians) a good or evil spirit; a being or object of supernatural power. Also, **man·i·tou** (măn′ə tōō′). [t. Algonquian (Mass. d.): m. *manitto* he is a god]

Man·i·to·ba (măn′ə tō′bə), *n.* **1.** a province in central Canada. 729,744 pop. (1941); 246,512 sq. mi. *Cap.:* Winnipeg. **2.** a lake in the S part of this province. 1817 sq. mi.; ab. 120 mi. long. —**Man′i·to′ban,** *adj., n.*

Man·i·tou·lin (măn′ə tōō′lĭn), *n.* a Canadian island in N Lake Huron. ab. 80 mi. long.

Man·i·to·woc (măn′ə tə wŏk′), *n.* a city in E Wisconsin: a port on Lake Michigan. 27,598 (1950).

Ma·ni·za·les (mä′nē sä′lĕs), *n.* a city in W Colombia. 104,110 (est. 1943).

man·kind (măn′kīnd′ *for 1;* măn′kīnd′ *for 2*), *n.* **1.** the human race; human beings collectively. **2.** men, as distinguished from women.

man·like (măn′līk′), *adj.* **1.** resembling a man. **2.** belonging or proper to a man; manly: *manlike fortitude.*

man·ly (măn′lĭ), *adj.,* **-lier, -liest,** *adv.* —*adj.* **1.** possessing qualities proper to a man; strong; brave; honorable. **2.** pertaining to or befitting a man: *manly sports.* —*adv.* **3.** *Archaic.* in a manly manner. —**man′li·ly,** *adv.* —**man′li·ness,** *n.* —**Syn. 1.** MANLY, MANFUL, MANNISH mean possessing the qualities of a man. MANLY implies possession of the noblest and most worthy qualities a man can have (as opposed to servility, insincerity, underhandedness, etc.): *a manly man is the noblest work of God.* MANFUL has particular reference to courage, strength, and industry: *manful resistance.* MANNISH applies to that which resembles man: *a boy with a mannish voice.* Applied to a woman, the term is derogatory, suggesting ostentatious imitation of man: *a mannish stride.*

Mann (măn *for 1, 3;* män *for 2*), *n.* **1.** Heinrich (hīn′rĭKH), 1871–1950, German writer in U.S. (brother of Thomas). **2.** Horace, 1796–1859, U.S. educational reformer: established first training school for teachers in the U.S. **3.** Thomas (tō′mäs), born 1875, German novelist, in U.S. since 1938.

man·na (măn′ə), *n.* **1.** the food miraculously supplied the children of Israel in the wilderness. Ex. 16:14–36. **2.** divine or spiritual food. **3.** anything likened to the manna of the Israelites. **4.** an exudate of the flowering ash, *Fraxinus Ornus,* of southern Europe, used in pharmacy. [OE, t. LL, t. Gk., t. Heb.: m. *mān*]

man·ne·quin (măn′ə kĭn), *n.* **1.** a person employed to wear clothing to exhibit to customers. **2.** a figure or model used by artists, tailors, etc. Also, **manikin.** [t. F, t. D: m. *manneken.* See MANIKIN]

man·ner (măn′ər), *n.* **1.** way of doing, being done, or happening; mode of action, occurrence, etc. **2.** characteristic or customary way of doing: *houses built in the Mexican manner.* **3.** (*pl.*) the prevailing customs, modes of living, etc., of a people, class, period, etc. **4.** a person's outward bearing; way of addressing and treating others. **5.** (*pl.*) ways of behaving, esp. with reference to polite standards: *bad manners.* **6.** good or polite ways of behaving: *have you no manners?* **7.** air of distinction: *he had quite a manner.* **8.** kind; sort: *all manner of things.* **9.** characteristic style in art, literature, or the like: *verses in the manner of Spenser.* **10.** mannered style; mannerism. **11.** *Obs.* or *Archaic.* nature; character; guise. **12. by all manner of means,** by all means; certainly. **13. in a manner,** after a fashion. [ME *manere,* t. AF: orig., way of handling, g. L *manuāria,* fem. of *manuārius* of or for the hand] —**Syn. 2.** mode, fashion, style; habit, custom. **4.** demeanor, deportment. MANNER, AIR, BEARING all refer to one's outward aspect or behavior. MANNER applies to a distinctive mode of behavior, or social attitude toward others, etc.: *a gracious manner.* AIR applies to outward appearance insofar as this is distinctive or indicative: *an air of martyrdom.* AIRS imply affectation: *airs and graces.* BEARING applies especially to carriage: *a noble bearing.*

man·nered (măn′ərd), *adj.* **1.** having (specified) manners: *ill-mannered.* **2.** having mannerisms; affected.

Man·ner·heim (män′ər hām′), *n.* Baron Carl Gustaf Emil von (kärl gōōs′täf ā′mēl fən), 1867–1951, Finnish soldier and statesman.

man·ner·ism (măn′ə rĭz′əm), *n.* **1.** marked or excessive adherence to an unusual manner, esp. in literary work. **2.** a habitual peculiarity of manner. —**man′ner·ist,** *n.* —**man′ner·is′tic,** *adj.*

man·ner·less (măn′ər lĭs), *adj.* without (good) manners.

man·ner·ly (măn′ər lĭ), *adj.* **1.** having or showing (good) manners; courteous; polite. —*adv.* **2.** with (good) manners; courteously; politely. —**man′ner·li·ness,** *n.*

Mann·heim (măn′hīm; *Ger.* män′hīm), *n.* a city in SW Germany, in Baden, on the Rhine. 284,957 (1939).

man·ni·kin (măn′ə kĭn), *n.* manikin.

Man·ning (măn′ĭng), *n.* Henry Edward, 1808–92. British Roman Catholic cardinal and writer.

man·nish (măn′ĭsh), *adj.* **1.** characteristic of or natural to a man. **2.** resembling a man. **3.** imitating a man. —**man′nish·ly,** *adv.* —**man′nish·ness,** *n.* —**Syn.** See **manly.**

man·ni·tol (măn′ə tōl′, -tŏl′), *n. Chem.* a white, sweetish crystalline carbohydrate alcohol, HOCH₂(CHOH)₄-CH₂OH, occurring in three optically different forms, the common one being found in the manna of the ash *Fraxinus Ornus,* and in other plants.

man·nose (măn′ōs), *n.* a hexose $C_6H_{12}O_6$ obtained from the hydrolysis of the ivory nut, and yielding mannitol on reduction. [f. MANN(A) + -OSE²]

ma·noeu·vre (mə nōō′vər), *n., v.t., v.i.,* **-vred, -vring.** maneuver.

man of God, **1.** a saint, prophet, etc. **2.** a clergyman.

Man of Sorrows, Jesus Christ. Cf. Isa. 53:3.

man of the world, a sophisticated man.

man-of-war (măn′əv wôr′), *n., pl.* **men-of-war.** a warship.

ma·nom·e·ter (mə nŏm′ə tər), *n.* an instrument for determining the pressure of gases, vapors, or liquids. [t. F: m. *manomètre,* f. Gk. *manó(s)* thin, rare + F *-mètre* METER] —**man·o·met·ric** (măn′ə mĕt′rĭk), *adj.*

Ma·non (má nôn′), *n.* an opera (1884) by Massenet.

man on horseback, a military leader who acquires such influence over the people as to threaten the existence of the government.

man·or (măn′ər), *n.* **1.** (in England) a landed estate or territorial unit, orig. of the nature of a feudal lordship, consisting of a lord's demesne and of lands within which he has the right to exercise certain privileges and exact certain fees, etc.   **2.** *Obs.* the mansion of a lord with the land pertaining to it. [ME *manere*, t. OF: m. *manoir*, n. use of *manoir*, inf., dwell, g. L *manēre* remain]   **ma·no·ri·al** (mə nōr′Y əl), *adj.*

manor house, the house or mansion of the lord of a manor.

man-o′-war bird, the frigate bird.

man power, 1. the power supplied by the physical exertions of a man or men.   **2.** a unit assumed to be equal to the rate at which a man can do mechanical work, commonly taken as ¹/₁₀ horsepower.   **3.** rate or work in terms of this unit.   **4.** power in terms of men available or required: *the man power of an army.*

man·rope (măn′rōp′), *n.* *Naut.* a rope placed at the side of a gangway, ladder, or the like, to serve as a rail.

man·sard (măn′särd), *n.*   **1.** Also, **mansard roof.** a form of curb roof the lower slope of which approaches the vertical and usually contains dormer windows, while the upper slope is nearly flat.   **2.** the story under such a roof. [named after F. *Mansarde,* French architect (1598–1666)]

Mansard roof

manse (măns), *n.*   **1.** the house and land occupied by a minister or parson.   **2.** (orig.) the dwelling of a landholder, with the land attached. [t. ML: m.s. *mansa* dwelling, orig. pp. fem. of L *manēre* remain]

man·serv·ant (măn′sûr′vənt), *n., pl.* **menservants.** a male servant.

Mans·field (mănz′fēld), *n.* **1. Katherine,** (*Kathleen Beauchamp, Mrs. John Middleton Murry*) 1888–1923, British short-story writer. **2. Richard,** 1857–1907, U.S. actor, born in England. **3.** a city in central England, in Nottinghamshire. 49,660 (est. 1946). **4.** a city in N Ohio. 43,564 (1950). **5. Mount,** a mountain in N Vermont: highest peak of the Green Mountains, 4393 ft.

man·sion (măn′shən), *n.* **1.** an imposing or stately residence. **2.** a manor house. **3.** (*often pl.*) *Brit.* an apartment house. **4.** *Archaic.* a place of abode. **5.** *Oriental and Medieval Astron.* each of twenty-eight divisions of the ecliptic occupied by the moon on successive days. [ME, t. OF, t. L: s. *mansio* a remaining, dwelling]

man·slaugh·ter (măn′slô′tər), *n.* **1.** the killing of a human being by a human being; homicide. **2.** *Law.* the killing of a human being unlawfully but without malice aforethought. See **malice aforethought.**

man·slay·er (măn′slā′ər), *n.* one who kills a human being; a homicide. —**man′slay′ing,** *n., adj.*

Man·sur (măn sŏŏr′), *n.* See **Al-Mansur.**

man·ta (măn′tə; *Sp.* män′tä), *n.* **1.** (in Spain and Spanish America) a cloak or wrap. **2.** (in South America) a kind of wrap worn by women. **3.** the type of blanket or cloth used on a horse or mule. **4.** *Mil.* a movable shelter formerly used to protect besiegers; a mantelet. **5.** a manta ray. [t. Sp., t. Pr.: blanket]

manta ray, a huge tropical ray, reaching a width of twenty feet, with earlike flaps on either side of the head.

man·teau (măn′tō; *Fr.* män tō′), *n., pl.* **-teaus** (-tōz), *Fr.* **-teaux** (-tō′). *Obs.* a mantle or cloak, esp. one worn by women. [t. F. See MANTLE]

Man·te·gna (män tĕ′nyä), *n.* **Andrea** (än drĕ′ä), 1431–1506, Italian painter and engraver.

man·tel (măn′təl), *n.* **1.** the more or less ornamental structure above and about a fireplace, usually having a shelf or projecting ledge. **2.** Also, **man′tel·piece′.** the shelf. [var. of MANTLE]

man·tel·et (măn′təl ĕt′, măn′tlĭt), *n.* **1.** a short mantle. **2.** Also, **mantlet.** *Mil.* **a.** manta (def. 4). **b.** any of various bulletproof shelters or screens. [ME, t. OF, dim. of *mantel* MANTLE]

Man·tell (măn tĕl′, măn′tĕl), *n.* **Robert Bruce,** 1854–1928, British actor in America and England.

man·tel·let·ta (măn′tə lĕt′ə), *n.* *Rom. Cath. Ch.* a sleeveless vestment of silk or woolen stuff reaching to the knees, worn by cardinals, bishops, abbots, etc. [t. It., dim. of *mantello,* der. L *mantellum* MANTLE]

man·tel·tree (măn′təl trē′), *n.* a wooden beam or arch forming the lintel of a fireplace; mantelpiece.

man·tic (măn′tĭk), *adj.* **1.** of or pertaining to divination. **2.** having the power of divination. [t. Gk.: m.s. *mantikós* prophetic, of a prophet] —**man′ti·cal·ly,** *adv.*

man·til·la (măn tĭl′ə), *n.* **1.** a silk or lace head scarf arranged over a high comb and falling over the back and shoulders, worn in Spain, Mexico, etc. **2.** a short mantle or light cape. [t. Sp., dim. of *manta.* See MANTA]

Man·ti·ne·a (măn′tĭ nē′ə), *n.* an ancient city of Arcadia, in S Greece: battles, 362 B.C., 207 B.C.

man·tis (măn′tĭs), *n., pl.* **-tises, -tes** (-tēz). any of the carnivorous orthopterous insects constituting the family *Mantidae,* which have a long prothorax and which are remarkable for their manner of holding the forelegs doubled up as if in prayer. [NL, t. Gk.: prophet, kind of insect]

Praying mantis, *Mantis religiosa* (Ab. 2½ in. long)

mantis crab, *Zool.* any of the stomatopod crustaceans with appendages resembling those of the mantis. Also, **mantis shrimp.**

man·tis·sa (măn tĭs′ə), *n.* *Math.* the decimal part of a logarithm. Cf. **characteristic** (def. 3). [t. L: an addition]

man·tle (măn′təl), *n., v.,* **-tled, -tling.** —*n.* **1.** a loose, sleeveless cloak. **2.** something that covers, envelops, or conceals. **3.** a single or paired outgrowth of the body wall that lines the inner surface of the valves of the shell in mollusks and brachiopods. **4.** a chemically prepared, incombustible network hood for a gas jet, which, when the jet is lighted, becomes incandescent and gives a brilliant light. **5.** *Ornith.* the back, scapular, and inner wing feathers taken together, esp. when these are all of the same color. **6.** the outer enveloping masonry of a blast furnace over the hearth. —*v.t.* **7.** to cover with or as with a mantle; envelop; conceal. —*v.i.* **8.** to spread like a mantle, as a blush over the face. **9.** to flush; blush. **10.** to spread out first one wing and then the other over the corresponding outstretched leg, as a hawk does by way of relief. **11.** (of a liquid) to be or become covered with a coating; foam. [ME *mantel,* OE *mæntel,* t. L: m.s. *mantellum, mantēlum* cloak]

mantle rock, *Phys. Geog.* the layer of disintegrated and decomposed rock fragments, including soil, just above the solid rock of the earth's crust; regolith.

mant·let (mănt′lĭt), *n.* *Mil.* mantelet (defs. 2a, 2b).

Man·tu·a (măn′chŏŏ ə), *n.* a city in N Italy, in Lombardy: birthplace of Vergil. 34,642 (1936). Italian, **Man·to·va** (män′tô vä). —**Man′tu·an,** *adj., n.*

man·tu·a (măn′chŏŏ ə), *n.* **1.** a kind of loose gown formerly worn by women. **2.** a mantle. [m. MANTEAU, due to assoc. with *Mantua,* in Italy]

Ma·nu·a Islands (mä nŏŏ′ä), a group of three small islands in the E part of American Samoa. 2817 (prelim. 1950).

man·u·al (măn′yŏŏ əl), *adj.* **1.** of or pertaining to the hand or hands; done by the hand or hands. **2.** of the nature of a manual or handy book. —*n.* **3.** a small book, esp. one giving information or instructions. **4.** *Mil.* prescribed exercises in the handling of the rifle: *the manual of the rifle.* **5.** *Music.* a keyboard played with the hands. [t. L: s. *manuālis* (as n., ML *manuāle*) of the hand; r. ME *manuel,* t. OF] —**man′u·al·ly,** *adv.*

manual training, the training of pupils in the various manual crafts and arts by actual practice (used esp. in U.S. schools to mean training in wood-working).

ma·nu·bri·um (mə nū′brĭ əm, -nōō′-), *n., pl.* **-bria** (-brĭ ə), **-briums. 1.** *Anat., Zool.* a segment, bone, cell, etc., resembling a handle. **2.** *Anat.* **a.** the uppermost of the three portions of the sternum. **b.** the long process of the malleus. [t. L: a handle]

manuf., 1. manufacture. **2.** manufacturer. **3.** manufacturing.

man·u·fac·to·ry (măn′yə făk′tə rY), *n., pl.* **-ries.** a factory.

man·u·fac·ture (măn′yə făk′chər), *n., v.,* **-tured, -turing.** —*n.* **1.** the making of goods or wares by manual labor or by machinery, esp. on a large scale. **2.** the making of anything. **3.** the thing or material manufactured. —*v.t.* **4.** to make or produce by hand or machinery, esp. on a large scale. **5.** to work up (material) into form for use. **6.** to produce artificially; invent fictitiously. **7.** to produce by mere mechanical industry. [t. F, f. L: *manū,* abl. of *manus* hand + m. *factūra* a making] —**man′u·fac′tur·ing,** *n.*

—**Syn. 4.** MANUFACTURE, ASSEMBLE, FABRICATE apply to processes in industry. MANUFACTURE, originally to make by hand, now means to make by machine or by industrial process: *to manufacture rubber tires* To ASSEMBLE is to fit together the manufactured parts of something mechanical: *to assemble an automobile.* To FABRICATE is to construct or build by fitting standardized parts together: *to fabricate houses.* See **make.**

man·u·fac·tur·er (măn′yə făk′chər ər), *n.* **1.** one who owns or runs a manufacturing plant. **2.** one who manufactures.

man·u·mis·sion (măn′yə mĭsh′ən), *n.* **1.** act of manumitting. **2.** state of being manumitted.

man·u·mit (măn′yə mĭt′), *v.t.,* **-mitted, -mitting.** to release from slavery or servitude. [t. L: m.s. *manūmittere*] —**man′u·mit′ter,** *n.*

ma·nure (mə nyŏŏr′, -nŏŏr′), *n., v.,* **-nured, -nuring.** —*n.* **1.** any natural or artificial substance for fertilizing the soil. **2.** dung or refuse of the stable, etc. —*v.t.* **3.** to treat (land) with fertilizing matter; apply manure to. [ME *maynour*(en), v., t. AF: m. *maynoverer* work by hand, der. OF *manuevre.* See MANEUVER, n.] —**ma·nur′er,** *n.*

ma·nus (mā′nəs), *n., pl.* **-nus. 1.** *Anat.* the distal segment of the forelimb of a vertebrate, including the carpus and the forefoot or hand. **2.** *Rom. Law.* power over persons, as that of the husband over the wife. [t. L: hand]

man·u·script (măn′yə skrĭpt′), *n.* **1.** a book, document, letter, etc., written by hand. **2.** an author's copy of his work written by hand or typewriter which is used as the basis for typesetting. **3.** writing, as distinguished from print. —*adj.* **4.** written or typed by hand (not printed). [t. ML: s. *manūscriptus,* lit., handwritten] —**man′u·script′al,** *adj.*

Ma·nu·ti·us (mə nū′shY əs, -nōō′-), *n.* **Aldus** (ôl′dəs, ăl′-), (*Aldo Manuzio*) 1450–1515, Italian printer.

---

b., blend of, blended; c., cognate with; d., dialect, dialectal; der., derived from; f., formed from; g., going back to; m., modification of; r., replacing; s., stem of; t., taken from; ?, perhaps.   See the full key on inside cover.

man·ward (măn′wərd), *adv.* 1. Also, **man′wards**. toward man. —*adj.* 2. directed toward man.

Manx (măngks), *adj.* 1. of or pertaining to the Isle of Man, its inhabitants, or their language. —*n.* 2. (*construed as pl.*) the inhabitants of the Isle of Man. 3. the Gaelic of the Isle of Man, virtually extinct. [metathetic and syncopated form of earlier *Maniske*]

manx cat, a tailless variety of the domestic cat.

Manx·man (măngks′mən), *n., pl.* **-men.** a native or inhabitant of the Isle of Man.

man·y (měn′ĭ), *adj.,* **more, most.** 1. constituting or forming a large number: *many people.* 2. relatively numerous (after *as, so, too,* or *how*): *six may be too many.* 3. being one of a large number (fol. by *a* or *an*): *many a day.* —*n.* 4. a great or considerable number (often followed by a noun with *of* expressed or understood): *a great many people.* 5. (as a collective plural) many persons or things. [ME *mani, manye,* etc., OE *manig,* c. G *manch*]
—**Syn.** 1. multifarious, multitudinous, myriad. MANY, INNUMERABLE, MANIFOLD, NUMEROUS imply the presence or succession of a large number of units. MANY is a popular and common word for this idea: *many times.* NUMEROUS, a more formal word, refers to a great number, or to containing very many units: *letters too numerous to mention.* INNUMERABLE denotes number that is beyond count, or, more loosely, what is extremely difficult to count: *the innumerable stars in the sky.* MANIFOLD implies not only that the number is large but also that there is variety or complexity. —**Ant.** 1. few, single.

man·y·plies (měn′ĭ plīz′), *n. Zool.* the omasum (so called from the many plies or folds of its membrane). [f. MANY + *plies,* pl. of PLY²]

man·y·sid·ed (měn′ĭ sī′dĭd), *adj.* 1. having many sides. 2. having many aspects, capabilities, etc.: *a manysided man.* —**man′y-sid′ed·ness,** *n.*

Man·za·nil·lo (măn′sä nē′yô), *n.* a seaport in SE Cuba. 35,730 (1943).

man·za·ni·ta (măn′zə nē′tə), *n.* 1. any of various shrubs of the ericaceous genus *Arctostaphylos,* of the western U.S. 2. the fruit of one of these shrubs. [t. Sp., dim. of *manzana* apple. See MANCHINEEL]

Man·zo·ni (mändzō′nē), *n.* **Alessandro** (ä′lĕssän′drō), 1785–1873, Italian novelist and poet.

Ma·o·ri (mä′ōrĭ, mou′rĭ, mä′rĭ), *n., pl.* **-ris.** 1. a member of the native brown race or Polynesians of New Zealand. 2. their language, of the Polynesian group of Austronesian.

Mao Tse-tung (mou′ dzŭ′dŏong′), born 1893, Chinese communist leader.

map (măp), *n., v.,* **mapped, mapping.** —*n.* 1. a representation, on a flat surface, of a part or the whole of the earth's surface, the heavens, or a heavenly body. 2. a maplike representation of anything. 3. **off the map,** out of existence, into oblivion: *whole cities were wiped off the map.* —*v.t.* 4. to represent or delineate in or as in a map. 5. to sketch or plan (often fol. by *out*): *to map out a new career.* [t. ML: m.s. *mappa (mundi)* map (of the world), in L *mappa* napkin.]
—**Syn.** 1. MAP, CHART, GRAPH refer to representations of surfaces, areas, or facts. MAP most commonly refers to a representation of the surface of the earth or a section of it, or an area of the sky: *a map of England.* A CHART may be an outline map with symbols conveying information superimposed on it, a map designed esp. for navigators on water or in the air, a diagram, or a table giving information in an orderly form: *a chart of the shoals off a coast.* A GRAPH may be a diagram representing a set of interrelated facts by means of dots or lines on a coördinate background; or it may use small figures (people, animals, machines, etc.) appropriate to the facts being represented, each figure standing for a specific number in statistics being given: *a graph of the rise in population from 1900–1940.*

Map (măp), *n.* **Walter,** died c1209, Welsh author and churchman. Also, **Mapes** (māps, mä′pēz).

ma·ple (mā′pəl), *n.* 1. any tree of the genus *Acer,* of the north temperate zone, species of which are valued for shade and ornament, for their wood, or for their sap, from which a syrup (**maple syrup**) and a sugar (**maple sugar**) are obtained. 2. the wood of any such tree. [ME *mapel,* OE *mapel-* in *mapeltrēow* maple tree]

Ma·quis (måkē′), *n. sing.* and *pl. French.* a member of one of the French underground groups resisting the Germans in World War II. [F, special use of *maquis, makis* wild, bushy land (Corsican d.)]

mar (mär), *v.t.,* **marred, marring.** 1. to damage; impair; ruin. 2. to disfigure; deface. [ME *marre,* OE *merran* hinder, waste, c. OHG *merrien* hinder]
—**Syn.** 1, 2. spoil, injure; blot. MAR, DEFACE, DISFIGURE, DEFORM agree in applying to some form of injury. MAR is general, but usually refers to an external or surface injury, if it is a physical one: *the table top was marred by dents and scratches.* DEFACE refers to a surface injury which may be temporary or easily repaired: *a table cloth defaced by penciled notations.* DISFIGURE applies to external injury of a more permanent and serious kind: *a birthmark disfigured one side of his face.* DEFORM suggests that something has been distorted or internally injured so severely as to change its normal form or qualities, or else that some fault has interfered with its proper development: *deformed by an accident which had crippled him, to deform feet by binding them.* —**Ant.** 2. enhance, adorn.

Mar., March.

mar., 1. maritime. 2. married.

mar·a·bou (măr′ə boo′), *n.* 1. any of three large storks,

Leptoptilos crumeniferus of Africa, and *L. dubius,* adjutant bird, and *L. javanicus* of the East Indies, having under the wings and tail soft, downy feathers that are used in millinery and for making a furlike trimming or material. 2. one of the feathers. 3. the trimming or material made of them. [t. F: m. *marabout,* orig. a Mohammedan hermit]

Mar·a·cai·bo (mär′ə kī′bō; *Sp.* mä′räkī′bô), *n.* 1. a seaport in NW Venezuela. 112,519 (1941). 2. **Gulf of,** a gulf on the NW coast of Venezuela. 3. **Lake,** a lake in NW Venezuela, connected with the gulf. ab. 100 mi. long; ab. 75 mi wide.

Ma·ra·jó (mä′räzhô′), *n.* an island at the mouth of the Amazon in N Brazil. ab. 20,000 sq. mi.

Ma·ra·ñón (mä′rä nyôn′), *n.* a river flowing from W Peru N and then E, joining the Ucayali to form the Amazon. ab. 1000 mi.

Marabou.
Leptoptilos crumeniferus
(Total length ab. 3½ ft.)

ma·ras·ca (mə räs′kə), *n.* a wild cherry, *Prunus Cerasus* var. *Marasca,* with small, acid, bitter fruit, from which maraschino is made.

mar·a·schi·no (măr′ə skē′nō), *n.* a cordial or liqueur distilled from marascas. [t. It., der. (*a*)*marasca* kind of cherry, der. *amaro* bitter, g. L *amārus*]

maraschino cherries, cherries cooked in colored syrup and flavored with imitation maraschino.

ma·ras·mus (mə räz′məs), *n. Pathol.* gradual loss of flesh and strength, as from malnutrition, old age, etc., rather than from actual disease. [NL, t. Gk.: m. *marasmós* a wasting] —**ma·ras′mic,** *adj.*

Ma·rat (mårå′), *n.* **Jean Paul** (zhän pôl), ("*The Friend of the People*") 1743–93, leader during the French Revolution, assassinated by Charlotte Corday.

Ma·ra·tha (mə rä′tə), *n.* Mahratta.

Ma·ra·thi (mə rä′tē, -rät′ē), *n.* Mahratti.

mar·a·thon (măr′ə thŏn′, -thən), *n.* 1. any long-distance race. 2. a foot race of about 26 miles. 3. any long contest with endurance as the primary factor: *a dance marathon.* 4. (*cap.*) a plain in Attica, ab. 20 mi. NE of Athens, Greece: the Athenians defeated the Persians there, 490 B.C. 5. (*cap.*) an ancient village near this plain. [defs. 1–3 from the messenger's running to Athens to carry news of the Greek victory over the Persians (see def. 4)] —**mar′a·thon′er,** *n.*

Marathon, 450 B.C.

Mar·a·tho·ni·an (măr′ə thō′nĭ ən), *adj.* 1. of or pertaining to Marathon. —*n.* 2. a native or inhabitant of Marathon.

ma·raud (mə rôd′), *v.i.* 1. to rove in quest of plunder; make a raid for booty. —*v.t.* 2. to raid for plunder. —*n.* 3. act of marauding. [t. F: s. *marauder,* der. *maraud* rogue, vagabond] —**ma·raud′er,** *n.* —**ma·raud′ing,** *adj.*

mar·a·ve·di (măr′ə vā′dĭ), *n., pl.* **-dis.** 1. a gold coin struck by the Moors in Spain. 2. an obsolete Spanish copper coin unit of low value. [t. Sp., t Ar.: m. *Murābitīn* name of the Moorish dynasty of the Almoravides (11th and 12th centuries), pl. of *murābiṭ* member of a religious order]

mar·ble (mär′bəl), *n., adj., v.,* **-bled, -bling.** —*n.* 1. limestone in a more or less crystalline state and capable of taking a polish, occurring in a wide range of colors and variegations, and much used in sculpture and architecture. 2. a variety of this stone. 3. a piece of this stone. 4. a work of art carved in marble. 5. a marbled appearance or pattern; marbling. 6. something resembling marble in hardness, coldness, smoothness, etc. 7. *Games.* **a.** a little ball of stone, baked clay, glass, etc., used in a children's game. **b.** (*pl. construed as sing.*) the game itself. —*adj.* 8. consisting of marble. 9. like marble, as being hard, cold, unfeeling, etc. 10. of variegated or mottled color. —*v.t.* 11. to color or stain like variegated marble. [ME *marbre,* t. OF, g. L *marmor*]

marble cake, a loaf cake given a marblelike appearance by the use of masses of dark and light batter.

Mar·ble·head (mär′bəl hĕd′, mär′bəl hĕd′), *n.* a resort in NE Massachusetts: yachting. 13,765 (1950).

mar·bling (mär′blĭng), *n.* 1. act, process, or art of coloring or staining in imitation of variegated marble. 2. an appearance like that of variegated marble. 3. *Bookbinding.* marblelike decoration on the paper edges, lining, or binding boards of a book.

mar·bly (mär′blĭ), *adj.* rigid, cold, etc., like marble.

Mar·burg (mär′bûrg; *Ger.* mär′bŏŏrкн), *n.* a city in W Germany. 27,920 (1939).

marc (märk; *Fr.* mär), *n.* 1. the grapes contained in the wine press, and the residue (skins and pips) remaining after the juice is expressed. 2. the brandy distilled from grape pomace. [t. F, der. *marcher* treat, press]

mar·ca·site (mär′kə sīt′), *n.* 1. a common mineral (white iron pyrites), iron disulfide (FeS₂), of the same composition as pyrite, but differing in crystal system. 2. (formerly) any of the crystallized forms of iron pyrites, much used in the 18th century for ornaments. **3.** a specimen or ornament of this substance. [t. ML: m.s. *marcasīta*, t. Ar.: m. *marqashīṭā*, from Aram.]

mar·cel (märsĕl′), *v.*, **-celled, -celling**, *n.* —*v.t.* **1.** to wave (the hair) by means of special irons, producing the effect of regular, continuous waves (**marcel waves**). —*n.* **2.** a marcelling. **3.** a marcelled condition. [from *Marcel*, a French hairdresser, the originator]

Mar·cel·lus (märsĕl′əs), *n.* **Marcus Claudius** (mär′kəs klô′dĭ əs), 268?–208 B.C., Roman general in the second Punic war.

mar·ces·cent (märsĕs′ənt), *adj. Bot.* withering but not falling off, as a part of a plant. [t. L: s. *marcescens*, ppr., withering] —**mar·ces′cence,** *n.*

march[1] (märch), *v.i.* **1.** to walk with regular and measured tread, as soldiers; advance in step in an organized body. **2.** to walk in a stately or deliberate manner. **3.** to proceed; advance. —*v.t.* **4.** to cause to march. —*n.* **5.** act or course of marching. **6.** the distance traversed in a single course of marching. **7.** advance; forward movement: *the march of progress.* **8.** a piece of music with a rhythm suited to accompany marching. **9. steal a march,** to gain an advantage secretly or slyly (often fol. by *on* or *upon*). [t. F: s. *marcher* walk, march, go, earlier *trample*, der. L *marcus* hammer]

march[2] (märch), *n.* **1.** a tract of land along a border of a country; frontier. **2.** (*pl.*) the border districts between England and Scotland, or England and Wales. —*v.i.* **3.** to touch at the border; border (fol. by *upon, with*, etc.). [ME *marche*, t. OF, t. Gmc.; cf. OHG *marcha*]

March (märch), *n.* the third month of the year, containing thirty-one days. [ME, t. AF: m. *marche*, c. OF *marz*, g. L *Martius*, lit., month of Mars]

March (märкн), *n.* German name of the **Morava** (def. 1).

March., Marchioness.

Mär·chen (mĕr′кнən), *n. German.* fairy story; folk tale.

march·er[1] (mär′chər), *n.* one who marches (on foot). [f. MARCH[1] + -ER[1]]

march·er[2] (mär′chər), *n. Hist.* an inhabitant of, or an officer or lord having jurisdiction over, marches or border territory. [f. MARCH[2] + -ER[1]]

March·es (mär′chĭz), *n.* **The,** a department in central Italy, on the Adriatic. 1,249,865 pop. (1936); 3743 sq. mi.

mar·che·sa (märkĕ′zä), *n., pl.* **-se** (-zĕ). *Italian.* marchioness. [It., fem. of *marchese*]

mar·che·se (märkĕ′zĕ), *n.,pl.* **-si** (-zĕ). *Italian.* marquis.

mar·chion·ess (mär′shənĭs, mär′shənĕs′), *n.* **1.** the wife or widow of a marquis. **2.** a lady holding in her own right the rank equal to that of a marquis. [t. ML: m.s. *marchiōnissa*, fem. of *marchio* MARQUIS]

march·pane (märch′pān′), *n.* marzipan. [t. F, d. var. of *massepain, marcepain*, t. It.: m. *marzapane*, orig. sugar-candy box, t. Ar.: m. *martabān* glazed vessel]

Mar·co·ni (märkō′nĭ; *It.* -kô′nē), *n.* **Guglielmo** (gōō-yĕl′mō), 1874–1937, Italian inventor of the first successful wireless telegraph.

Mar·co Po·lo (mär′kō pō′lō). See **Polo, Marco.**

Mar·cus Au·re·li·us (mär′kəs ô rē′lĭ əs, ô rēl′yəs), (*Marcus Aurelius Antoninus*) A.D. 121–180, emperor of Rome, A.D. 161–180: Stoic philosopher and writer.

Mar·cy (mär′sĭ), *n.* **Mount,** a mountain in NE New York: the highest peak of the Adirondack Mountains. 5344 ft.

Mar·di gras (mär′dĭ grä′), Shrove Tuesday; the last day of carnival: celebrated in Paris, New Orleans, etc., with special festivities. [t. F: meat-eating Tuesday]

Mar·duk (mär′dŏŏk), *n. Babylon. Relig.* the chief of the Babylonian deities. [t. Babylonian]

mare[1] (mâr), *n.* the female of the horse kind. [ME *mare, mere*, OE *mere, myre* (c. Icel. *merr*), fem. of *mearh* horse (c. OHG *marah*, Icel. *marr*). Cf. MARSHAL]

mare[2] (mâr), *n. Obs.* the evil spirit supposed to cause bad dreams. [ME and OE, c. Icel. *mara*]

ma·re clau·sum (mâr′ĭ klô′səm), *Latin.* a closed sea (within the jurisdiction of a particular nation).

Mare Island (mâr), an island in the N part of San Francisco Bay, California: U. S. navy yard.

ma·re li·be·rum (mâr′ĭ lĭb′ə rəm), *Latin.* an open sea (to which all countries have unrestricted access).

ma·rem·ma (mərĕm′ə), *n., pl.* **-remme** (-rĕm′ē). **1.** a marshy, unhealthy region near the seashore, as in Italy. **2.** the miasma associated with such a region. [t. It., g. L *maritima*, fem. of *maritimus* maritime]

Ma·ren·go (mərĕng′gō), *n.* a village in NW Italy, in Piedmont: Napolean defeated the Austrians here, 1800.

ma·re nos·trum (mâr′ĭ nŏs′trəm), *Latin.* our sea (esp. the Mediterranean to the Romans and Italians).

mare's-nest (mârz′nĕst′), *n.* something imagined to be an extraordinary discovery but proving to be a delusion or a hoax.

mare's-tail (mârz′tāl′), *n.* **1.** an erect aquatic Old World plant, *Hippuris vulgaris*, with crowded whorls of narrow, hairlike leaves. **2.** a cirrus cloud resembling a horse's tail.

Mar·ga·ret of Anjou (mär′gə rĭt, -grĭt), 1430–82, queen of England, wife of Henry VI.

Margaret of Navarre, 1492–1549, queen of Navarre, noted for her poems, short stories, and letters.

Margaret of Valois, 1553–1615, first queen of Henry IV of France.

mar·gar·ic acid (märgăr′ĭk, -gär′ĭk), *Chem.* a white, fatty acid, $C_{17}H_{34}O_2$, resembling stearic acid and obtained from lichens or synthetically. [f. s. Gk. *márgaron* pearl + -IC]

mar·ga·rine (mär′jərēn′; *less often* -gə-), *n.* a butter-like product made by emulsifying vegetable fats (**nut margarine**) or animal fats (**oleomargarine**) in ripened milk. Also, **mar·ga·rin** (mär′jə rĭn, -gə-). [t. F: f. s. Gk. *márgaron* white of pearl + -*ine* -INE[2]]

Mar·gate (mär′gāt), *n.* a seaside resort in SE England, in Kent. 37,970 (est. 1946).

mar·gay (mär′gā), *n.* a small tiger cat, *Gelis tigrina*, of tropical America.

marge[1] (märj), *n. Poetic.* margin.

marge[2] (märj), *n. Chiefly Brit. Colloq.* margarine.

mar·gin (mär′jĭn), *n.* Also, *Archaic*, **mar·gent** (mär′jənt). **1.** a border or edge. **2.** (*pl.*) the space bordering the printed or written matter on a page. **3.** a limit, or a condition, etc., beyond which something ceases to exist or be possible: *the margin of consciousness*. **4.** an amount allowed or available beyond what is actually necessary. **5.** *Finance.* **a.** security, as a percentage in money, deposited with a broker as a provision against loss on transactions on behalf of his principal. **b.** the amount representing the customer's investment or equity in a margin account. **6.** *Com.* the difference between the cost and the selling price. **7.** *Econ.* the point at which the return from economic activity barely covers the cost of production, and below which production is unprofitable. —*v.t.* **8.** to provide with a margin or border. **9.** to furnish with marginal notes, as a document. **10.** to enter in the margin, as of a book. **11.** *Finance.* to deposit a margin upon. [ME *margine*, t. L: m.s. *margo* border, edge] —**Syn. 1.** See **edge.**

mar·gin·al (mär′jə nəl), *adj.* **1.** pertaining to a margin. **2.** situated on the border or edge. **3.** written or printed in the margin of a page: *a marginal note.* **4.** *Econ.* **a.** supplying goods at a rate merely covering the cost of production. **b.** of or pertaining to goods produced and marketed at margin: *marginal profits*. [t. NL: s. *marginālis*, der. L *margo* MARGIN] —**mar′gin·al·ly,** *adv.*

mar·gi·na·li·a (mär′jə nā′lĭ ə, -nāl′yə), *n.pl.* marginal notes. [NL]

marginal man, *Sociol.* a person who lives on the margins of two cultural groups without feeling identified with either group.

mar·gin·ate (mär′jə nāt′), *adj., v.,* **-nated, -nating.** —*adj.* Also, **mar·gin·at·ed.** **1.** having a margin. **2.** *Entomol.* having the margin of a distinct color: *marginate with purple.* —*v.t.* **3.** to furnish with a margin; border. [t. L: m.s. *marginātus*, pp.] —**mar′gin·a′tion,** *n.*

mar·grave (mär′grāv), *n.* **1.** the hereditary title of the rulers of certain states. **2.** *Hist.* a hereditary German title, equivalent to *marquis*. **3.** (orig.) a German military governor of a mark, or border province. [t. MD: m. *markgrave* mark or border count]

mar·gra·vi·ate (märgrā′vĭ āt′, -ĭt), *n.* the province of a margrave.

mar·gra·vine (mär′grə vēn′), *n.* the wife of a margrave.

mar·gue·rite (mär′gə rēt′), *n.* **1.** the common European daisy. *Bellis perennis.* **2.** any of several flowers of the daisy kind, esp. *Chrysanthemum frutescens*, cultivated for its numerous white-rayed, yellow-centered flowers. [t. F: daisy, pearl, t. L: m. *margarita* pearl]

ma·ri·age de con·ve·nance (må ryäzh′ də kôn və näns′), *French.* a marriage of convenience or expediency, usually for money or position.

Mar·i·an (mâr′ĭ ən), *adj.* **1.** of or pertaining to the Virgin Mary. **2.** of or pertaining to some other Mary, as Mary, queen of England, or to Mary, queen of Scotland. —*n.* **3.** one who has a particular devotion to the Virgin Mary. **4.** an adherent or defender of Mary, Queen of Scots.

Ma·ri·a·na·o (mä′rē ä nä′ô), *n.* a city in NW Cuba, near Havana. 114,143 (1943).

Ma·ri·a·nas Islands (mä′rē ä′näs), *n.* group of 15 small islands in the Pacific, E of the Philippine Islands: formerly mandated to Japan (except Guam); now under U.S. trusteeship. ab. 66,000 pop.; 453 sq. mi. Also, **Ladrone Islands** or **Ladrones.**

Mar·i·anne (mâr′ĭ än′), *n.* a popular name for the French Republic personified.

Ma·ri·a The·re·sa (mə rē′ə tə rē′sə, -zə, mə rī′ə) 1717–80, archduchess of Austria, queen of Hungary and Bohemia, 1740–80. German, **Ma·ri·a The·re·si·a** (mä rē′ä tĕ rä′zĭ ä′).

Maria Theresa thaler, Levant dollar.

Ma·rie An·toi·nette (mə rē′ ăn′twə nĕt′; *Fr.* må rē′ än twä nĕt′), 1755–93, queen of France, 1774–93, and wife of Louis XVI, executed in the French Revolution.

Ma·rie Byrd Land (mə rē′ bûrd′), a part of Antarctica, SE of the Ross Sea: discovered and explored by Adm. Richard E. Byrd; claimed by the U.S.

Ma·rie Lou·ise (mə rē′ lŏŏ ēz′; *Fr.* må rē′ lwēz′), 1791–1847, empress of France, second wife of Napoleon I.

Ma·ri·en·bad (mä rē′ən bät′), *n.* a spa and resort town in W Czechoslovakia, in Bohemia. 11,919 (1939).

mar·i·gold (măr′ə gōld′), *n.* **1.** any of various chiefly golden-flowered plants esp. of the composite genus *Tagetes*, as *T. erecta*, with strong-scented foliage. See also **marsh marigold.** **2.** any of various other plants, esp. of the asteraceous genus *Calendula*, as *C. officinalis*, a common garden plant of some use in dyeing and medicine. [ME, f. MARY (the Virgin) + GOLD]

ma·ri·jua·na (mä′rə hwä′nə), *n.* **1.** the Indian hemp, *Cannabis sativa.* **2.** its dried leaves and flowers, used in cigarettes as a narcotic. Also, **ma′ri·hua′na.** [t. Amer. Sp.; ? native word, b. with name *Maria Juana* Mary Jane]

ma·rim·ba (mə rĭm′bə), *n.* a musical instrument, originating in Africa but popularized and perfected in Central America, formed of strips of wood of various sizes (often having resonators beneath to reinforce the sound), struck by hammers or sticks. [t. West Afr.]

Modern marimba

mar·i·nade (*n.* măr′ə nād′; *v.* măr′ə nād′), *n., v.,* **-naded, -nading.** —*n.* **1.** a pickling liquid, usually of vinegar or wine with oil, herbs, spices, etc., to steep meat, fish, vegetables, etc. in before cooking. **2.** meat or fish steeped in it. —*v.t.* **3.** to marinate. [t. F, der. *mariner* pickle in brine, der. *marin* MARINE]

mar·i·nate (măr′ə nāt′), *v.t.,* **-nated, -nating. 1.** to let stand in a seasoned vinegar-oil mixture; marinade. **2.** to apply French dressing to (a food) which will be used later in a salad with mayonnaise. [f. s. F *mariner* (see MARINADE) + -ATE[1]] —**mar′i·na′tion,** *n.*

Ma·rin·du·que (mä′rĭn dōō′kě), *n.* one of the Philippine Islands, between Luzon and Mindora islands. 79,781 pop. (1939); 347 sq. mi.

ma·rine (mə rēn′), *adj.* **1.** of or pertaining to the sea; existing in or produced by the sea. **2.** pertaining to navigation or shipping; nautical; naval; maritime. **3.** serving on shipboard, as soldiers. **4.** of or belonging to the marines. **5.** adapted for use at sea: *a marine barometer.* —*n.* **6.** seagoing vessels collectively, esp. with reference to nationality or class; shipping in general. **7.** one of a class of naval troops serving both on shipboard and on land. **8.** a member of the U. S. Marine Corps. **9.** a picture with a marine subject. **10.** naval affairs, or the department of a government (as in France) having to do with such affairs. [ME *maryne,* t. F: m. *marin* (fem. *marine*), g. L *marīnus* of the sea]

Marine Corps, a branch of the U.S. Navy, trained, organized, and equipped very much as land soldiers are, and usually employed as a landing force.

marine insurance, insurance covering loss or damage to maritime property occasioned by any of the numerous perils on and of the sea.

mar·i·ner (măr′ə nər), *n.* one who directs or assists in the navigation of a ship; seaman; sailor. [ME, t. AF, der. F *marin* MARINE] —Syn. See **sailor.**

Mar·i·ol·a·try (mâr′ĭ ŏl′ə trĭ), *n.* (in opprobious use) the religious veneration of the Virgin Mary. [f. MARY + (ID)OLATRY] —**Mar′i·ol′a·ter,** *n.* —**Mar′i·ol′a·trous,** *adj.*

Mar·i·on (măr′ĭ ən, mâr′-), *n.* **1.** Francis, 1732?-95, American Revolutionary general. **2.** a city in central Ohio. 33,817 (1950). **3.** a city in central Indiana. 30,081 (1950).

mar·i·o·nette (măr′ĭ ə nĕt′), *n.* a puppet moved by strings or the hands, as on a mimic stage. [t. F, der. *Marion*, dim. of *Marie* Mary]

Mar·i·po·sa lily (măr′ə pō′sə, -zə), any of the plants constituting the liliaceous genus *Calochortus*, of the western U. S. and Mexico, having tuliplike flowers of various colors. Also, **Mariposa tulip.** [t. Sp.: *mariposa* butterfly, ult. der. *posar* to rest, g. L *pausāre*]

mar·ish (măr′ĭsh), *Archaic or Poetic.* —*n.* **1.** a marsh. —*adj.* **2.** marshy. [ME *mareis,* t. OF. See MORASS]

Mar·ist (mâr′ĭst), *n. Rom. Cath. Ch.* a member of the "Society of Mary," founded in 1816.

Ma·ri·tain (mà rē tăN′), *n.* **Jacques** (zhăk), born 1882, French philosopher and diplomat.

mar·i·tal (măr′ə təl), *adj.* **1.** of or pertaining to marriage. **2.** of or pertaining to a husband. [t. L: s. *marītālis* pertaining to married people] —**mar′i·tal·ly,** *adv.*

mar·i·time (măr′ə tīm′), *adj.* **1.** connected with the sea in relation to navigation, shipping, etc.: *maritime law.* **2.** of or pertaining to the sea. **3.** bordering on the sea. **4.** living near the sea. **5.** characteristic of a seaman; nautical. [t. L: m.s. *maritimus* of the sea]

Maritime Alps, a range of the Alps in SE France and NW Italy.

Maritime Provinces, the Canadian provinces of Nova Scotia, New Brunswick, and Prince Edward Island.

Ma·ri·tsa (mä′rēt sä′), *n.* a river flowing from S Bulgaria along the boundary between Greece and European Turkey into the Aegean. ab. 300 mi.

mar·i·um (mâr′ĭ əm), *n.* one of the large, dark, fairly level plains on the moon, probably lava beds, which look like "seas." [t. NL, der. L *mare* sea]

Ma·ri·u·pol (mä′rĭ ōō′pôl′y), *n.* a seaport in the SW Soviet Union, on the Sea of Azov. 222,427 (1939).

Mar·i·us (mâr′ĭ əs), *n.* **Gaius** (gā′əs), c155–86 B.C., Roman general and consul: opponent of Sulla.

Ma·ri·vaux (mà rē vō′), *n.* **Pierre Carlet de Chamblain de** (pyěr kàr lě′ də shäN blăN′ də), 1688–1763, French novelist and dramatist.

mar·jo·ram (mär′jə rəm), *n.* any plant of the mint family of the genus *Origanum*, esp. the species *Marjorana hortensis* (**sweet marjoram**) which is used in cookery or *O. vulgare*, a wild species native in Europe and naturalized in North America. [ME *majorane*, t. OF, ult. der. L *amāracus*]

mark[1] (märk), *n.* **1.** a visible trace or impression upon anything, as a line, cut, dent, stain, bruise, etc.: *a birthmark.* **2.** a badge, brand, or other visible sign assumed or imposed. **3.** a symbol used in writing or printing: *a punctuation mark.* **4.** a sign, usually a cross, made by an illiterate person by way of signature. **5.** an affixed or impressed device, symbol, inscription, etc., serving to give information, identify, indicate origin or ownership, attest to character or comparative merit, or the like. **6.** a sign, token, or indication. **7.** a symbol used in rating conduct, proficiency, attainment, etc., as of pupils in a school. **8.** something serving as an indication of position: *bookmark.* **9.** a recognized standard: *to be below the mark.* **10.** note, importance, or distinction: *a man of mark.* **11.** a distinctive trait. **12.** an object aimed at, as a target. **13.** an object or end desired or striven for, as a goal. **14.** an object of derision, scorn, hostile schemes, swindling, or the like: *an easy mark.* **15.** *Track.* the starting point alloted to a contestant. **16.** *Boxing.* the middle of the stomach. **17.** *Bowls.* See **jack**[1] (def. 8). **18.** (on a nautical leadline) one of the measured indications of depth, consisting of a white, blue, or red rag, a bit of leather, or a knot of small line. **19.** *Brit. Mil.* model. **20.** a tract of land held in common by a medieval community of freemen. **21.** *Obs. except Hist. and Archaic.* a boundary; frontier. **22. beside the mark,** irrelevant. —*v.t.* **23.** to be a distinguishing feature of: *a day marked by rain.* **24.** to put a mark or marks on. **25.** to attach or affix to (something) figures or signs indicating price, identification, as a trademark, etc.: *to mark a book down to 49 cents.* **26.** to trace or form by or as by marks (often fol. by *out*). **27.** to indicate or designate by or as by marks. **28.** to single out; destine. **29.** to record, as a score. **30.** to make manifest. **31.** to give heed or attention to. **32.** to separate (fol. by *off*). **33.** to notice or observe. **34. mark time, a.** to suspend advance or progress, temporarily, as while awaiting development. **b.** *Mil.* to move the foot alternately as in marching, but without advancing. —*v.i.* **35.** to take notice; give attention; consider. [ME; OE *mearc* boundary, land mark, c. G *mark*; akin to L *margo* border] —Syn. **11.** characteristic, feature.

mark[2] (märk), *n.* **1.** the monetary unit and a silver coin of Germany, normally equivalent to about 23.8 U. S. cents. See **reichsmark. 2.** the monetary unit and a coin of Finland; markka. **3.** an obsolete silver coin of Scotland originally worth 13s.–4d. **4.** a former European unit of weight, esp. for gold and silver, generally equal to 8 ounces. [ME; OE *m(e)arc*, c. G *mark*]

Mark (märk), *n.* **1.** the evangelist John Mark, traditionally considered the author of the second Gospel. **2.** the second Gospel, in the New Testament. **3. King,** *Arthurian Romance.* ruler of Cornwall, husband of Iseult and uncle to Sir Tristram. [t. L; m. s. *Marcus*]

Mark An·to·ny (märk ăn′tə nĭ). See **Antony.**

mark·down (märk′doun′), *n.* a reduction in price.

marked (märkt), *adj.* **1.** strikingly noticeable; conspicuous: *with marked success.* **2.** watched as an object for suspicion or vengeance: *a marked man.* **3.** having a mark or marks. —**mark·ed·ly** (mär′kĭd lĭ), *adv.* —**mark′ed·ness,** *n.*

mark·er (mär′kər), *n.* **1.** one who or that which marks. **2.** something used as a mark or indication, as a bookmark, tombstone, etc. **3.** one who records a score, etc. **4.** a counter used in card playing.

mar·ket (mär′kĭt), *n.* **1.** a meeting of people for selling and buying. **2.** the assemblage of people at such a meeting. **3.** an open space or a covered building where such meetings are held, esp. for the sale of food, etc. **4.** a store for the sale of food: *a meat market.* **5.** trade or traffic, esp. as regards a particular commodity. **6.** a body of persons carrying on extensive transactions in a specified commodity: *the cotton market.* **7.** the field of trade or business: *the best shoes in the market.* **8.** demand for a commodity: *an unprecedented market for leather.* **9.** a region where anything is or may be sold: *the foreign market.* **10.** current price or value: *a rising market.* **11. at the market,** at the best obtainable price in the open market. —*v.i.* **12.** to deal (buy or sell) in a market. —*v.t.* **13.** to carry or send to market for disposal. **14.** to dispose of in a market; sell. [ME and late OE, t. VL: m.s. *marcātus,* L *mercātus* trading, traffic, market]

mar·ket·a·ble (mär′kĭt ə bəl), *adj.* **1.** readily salable. **2.** pertaining to selling or buying. —**mar′ket·a·bil′i·ty,** *n.*

market order, an order to purchase or sell at the current market price.

market place, a place, esp. an open space in a town, where a market is held.

market price, the price at which a commodity,

security, or service is selling in the open market. Also, market value.

market town, *Chiefly Brit.* a town where a market is held.

Mark·ham (mär/kəm), *n.* **1. Edwin**, 1852–1940. U. S. poet. **2. Mount**, a mountain in Antarctica, SW of the Ross Sea. ab. 15,100 ft.

mark·ing (mär/kĭng), *n.* **1.** a mark, or a number or pattern of marks. **2.** act of one who or that which marks.

mark·ka (märk/kä), *n., pl.* **-kaa** (-kä). mark[2] (def. 2). [t. Finn., t. Sw.: m. *mark*]

marks·man (märks/mən), *n., pl.* **-men. 1.** one skilled in shooting at a mark; one who shoots well. **2.** *U.S. Army.* the lowest qualification at target practice. —**marks/man·ship**, *n.*

mark·up (märk/ŭp/), *n.* the amount or percentage added to the cost of the article in fixing the selling price: *a 50% markup on cameras.*

marl[1] (märl), *n.* **1.** a soil or earthy deposit consisting of clay and calcium carbonate, used esp. as a fertilizer. **2.** *Poetic.* earth. —*v.t.* **3.** to fertilize with marl. [ME, t. OF., g. LL *margila* dim. of L *marga*] —**mar·la·ceous** (mär lā/shəs), **marl/y,** *adj.*

marl[2] (märl), *v.t. Naut.* to wind (a rope, etc.) with marline, every turn being secured by a hitch. [t. D: s *marlen,* appar. freq. of *marren* tie. Cf. MARLINESPIKE]

Marl·bor·ough (märl/bərə, -brə, môl/-), *n.* **John Churchill, 1st Duke of,** 1650–1722, British general who defeated the French at Blenheim in 1704.

mar·lin (mär/lĭn), *n.* any of a genus (*Makaira*) of large, powerful fishes with a spearlike snout, as *M. ampla,* of the warm waters of the Atlantic, a favorite big game fish. [short for MARLINE-SPIKE]

mar·line (mär/lĭn), *n. Naut.* small cord of two loosely twisted strands, used for seizing. [half adoption, half trans. of D *marlijn,* f. *marr(en)* tie + *lijn* LINE[1]]

mar·line·spike (mär/lĭn spīk/), *n. Naut.* a pointed iron implement used in marling, separating the strands of rope in splicing, etc. Also, **mar·lin·spike/, mar/ling·spike.** See MARL[2], SPIKE]

A, Marlinespike; B, Marlinespike separating strands of rope

Mar·lowe (mär/lō), *n.* **1. Christopher,** 1564–93, British dramatist and poet. **2. Julia,** (*Sarah Frances Frost, Mrs. E. H. Sothern*) 1866–1950, U. S. actress, born in England.

mar·ma·lade (mär/mə lād/, mär/mə lād/), *n.* a clear, jellylike preserve with fruit (usually citrus) suspended in small pieces. [late ME, t. F: m. *marmelade,* t. Pg.: m. *marmelada* der. *marmelo* quince, g. L *melimēlum,* t. Gk.: m. *melímēlon,* lit. honey apple]

marmalade tree, a sapotaceous tree, *Calocarpum Sapota,* of tropical America, with a durable wood resembling mahogany and a fruit used in preserving.

Mar·ma·ra (mär/mərə), *n.* **Sea of,** a sea between European and Asiatic Turkey, connected with the Black Sea by the Bosporus, and with the Aegean by the Dardanelles. ab. 170 mi. long; ab. 50 mi. wide; ab. 4500 sq. mi. Also, **Mar·mo·ra** (mär/mərə, mär mōr/ə).

Mar·mo·la·da (mär/mō lä/dä), *n.* a mountain in N Italy: highest peak in the Dolomite Alps. 11,020 ft.

mar·mo·re·al (mär mōr/ĭ əl), *adj.* of or like marble. Also, **mar·mo/re·an.** [f. s. L *marmoreus* of marble + -AL[1]]

mar·mo·set (mär/mə zĕt/), *n.* any of various small, squirrellike South and Central American monkeys, genera *Callithrix* and *Leontocebus,* and allied genera, with soft fur and a long, slightly furry, nonprehensile tail. [ME *marmusette,* t. OF: m. *marmouset* grotesque little figure, der. OF *merme* under age, g. L *minimus* least, b. with Gk. *mormōtós* frightful]

Ring-tailed marmoset, *Callithrix lacchus* (Total 22 in., tail 12 in.)

mar·mot (mär/mət), *n.* **1.** any of the bushy-tailed, thick-set rodents constituting the genus *Marmota,* as the common woodchuck. **2.** any of certain related animals, as the prairie dogs. [t. F: m. *marmotte,* back formation from *marmottaine;* g. L *mūsmontānus,* f. *mūs* mouse + *montānus* of the mountains]

Marne (märn; *Fr.* märn), *n.* a river in NE France, flowing W to the Seine near Paris; battles, 1914, 1918, 1944. 325 mi.

ma·roon[1] (mə rōōn/), *n., adj.* dark brownish-red. [t. F: m. *marron,* t. It.: m. *marrone* chestnut]

ma·roon[2] (mə rōōn/), *v.t.* **1.** to put ashore and leave on a desolate island or coast by way of punishment, as was done by buccaneers, etc. **2.** to isolate as if on a desolate island. —*n.* **3.** one of a class of Negroes, orig. fugitive slaves, living in the wilder parts of the West Indies and Dutch

Hoary marmot, *Marmota caligata* (Total length 27 to 28 in.)

Guiana. [t. F: m. *marron.* Cf. Sp. *cimarrón* wild, der. *cimarra* bushes]

Ma·ros (mŏ/rŏsh), *n.* Hungarian name of **Mures.**

mar·plot (mär/plŏt/), *n.* one who mars or defeats a plot, design, or project by officious interference.

Marq., 1. Marquess. **2.** Marquis.

Mar·quand (märkwŏnd/), *n.* **John Phillips,** born 1893, U.S. novelist.

marque (märk), *n.* seizure by way of reprisal. [t. F, t. Pr.: m. *marca,* der. *marcar* seize in reprisal, der. *marc* token of pledge, t. Gmc. See MARK[1]]

mar·quee (mär kē/), **1.** a rooflike shelter, as of glass, projecting above an outer door and over a sidewalk or a terrace. **2.** *Chiefly Brit.* a large tent or tentlike shelter with open sides, esp. one for temporary use in entertainments, receptions, etc. [assumed sing. of MARQUISE (def. 4) taken as pl.]

Marquee (def. 1)

Mar·que·sas Islands (mär kā/səs), a group of French islands in the S Pacific. 2400 pop. (1936). ab. 492 sq. mi.

mar·que·try (mär/kə trĭ), *n.* inlaid work of variously colored woods or other materials, esp. in furniture. Also, **mar·que·te·rie** (mär/kə trĭ). [t. F: m. *marqueterie,* der. *marqueter* mark, checker, inlay, ult. der. *marque* MARK[1]]

Mar·quette (mär kĕt/), *n.* **Jacques** (zhäk), (*Père Marquette*) 1637–1675, French Jesuit missionary and explorer.

mar·quis (mär/kwĭs; *Fr.* mär kē/), *n.* a nobleman ranking next below a duke and above an earl or count. Also, *Brit.,* **mar·quess** (mär/kwĭs). [t. F; r. ME *markis.* t. OF: m. *marchis,* der. *marche* MARCH[2]]

Mar·quis (mär/kwĭs), *n.* **Donald Robert Perry,** 1878–1937, U.S. humorist and writer.

mar·quis·ate (mär/kwĭz ĭt), *n.* **1.** the rank of a marquis. **2.** the territory ruled by a marquis or a margrave.

mar·quise (mär kēz/; *Fr.* mär kēz/), *n.* **1.** the wife or widow of a marquis. **2.** a lady holding the rank equal to that of a marquis. **3.** a common diamond shape, pointed oval, usually with normal brilliant facets. **4.** marquee. [t. F, fem. of *marquis*]

mar·qui·sette (mär/kĭ zĕt/, -kwĭ-), *n.* light weight open fabric of leno weave in cotton, rayon silk, or nylon. [t. F, dim. of *marquise*]

Mar·ra·kech (mär rä/kĕsh), *n.* a city in W Morocco, in the French zone: one of the capitals of the sultanate. 190,314 (1936). Also, **Mar·ra/kesh, Morocco.**

mar·riage (mär/ĭj), *n.* **1.** the legal union of a man with a woman for life; state or condition of being married; the legal relation of spouses to each other; wedlock. **2.** the formal declaration or contract by which act a man and a woman join in wedlock. **3.** any intimate union. [ME *mariage,* t. OF, der. *marier* MARRY[1]] —**Syn. 1.** MARRIAGE, WEDDING, NUPTIALS are terms for the ceremony uniting couples in wedlock. MARRIAGE is the simple and usual term, without implications as to circumstances and without emotional connotations: *to announce the marriage of a daughter.* WEDDING has strong emotional, even sentimental, connotations, and suggests the accompanying festivities, whether elaborate or simple: *a beautiful wedding, a reception after the wedding.* NUPTIALS is a formal and lofty word applied to the ceremony and attendant social events; it does not have emotional connotations but strongly implies surroundings characteristic of wealth, rank, pomp, and grandeur: *royal nuptials.*

mar·riage·a·ble (mär/ĭj ə bəl), *adj.* fit, esp. old enough, for marriage. —**mar/riage·a·bil/i·ty, mar/riage·a·ble·ness,** *n.*

Marriage of Fig·a·ro (fĭg/ə rō/; *Fr.* fē gá rō/), an opera (1786) by Mozart.

marriage portion, dowry.

mar·ried (mär/ĭd), *adj.* **1.** united in wedlock; wedded. **2.** pertaining to marriage or married persons.

mar·ron (mär/ən), *n.* a chestnut; esp. as used in cookery, or candied or preserved in syrup. [t. F. See MAROON[1]]

mar·rons gla·cés (mȧ rôN/ glȧ sĕ/), *French.* chestnuts glazed or coated with sugar.

mar·row (mär/ō), *n.* **1.** a soft, fatty, vascular tissue in the interior cavities of bones. **2.** the inmost or essential part. **3.** strength or vitality. **4.** rich and nutritious food. **5.** *Brit.* vegetable marrow. [ME *marowe, marw(e),* OE *mearg,* c. G *mark*]

mar·row·bone (mär/ō bōn/), *n.* **1.** a bone containing edible marrow. **2.** (*pl.*) (in humorous use) the knees. **3.** (*pl.*) crossbones.

mar·row·fat (mär/ō făt/), *n.* **1.** a tall variety of the pea with a large seed. **2.** the seed.

marrow squash, *U.S.* any variety of *Curbita Pepo* with a smooth surface, oblong shape, and hard rind.

mar·ry[1] (mär/ĭ), *v.,* **-ried, -rying.** —*v.t.* **1.** to take in marriage. **2.** to unite in wedlock. **3.** to give in marriage. **4.** to unite intimately. **5.** *Naut.* to join together, as two ropes, end to end without increasing the diameter. —*v.i.* **6.** to take a husband or wife; wed. [ME *marie(n),* t. F: m. *marier,* g. L *marītāre* wed] —**mar/ri·er,** *n.*

mar·ry[2] (mär/ĭ), *interj. Archaic.* an exclamation of surprise, etc. [euphemistic var. of MARY (the Virgin)]

Mar·ry·at (mär/ĭ ət), *n.* **Frederick,** 1792–1848, British novelist and naval officer.

Mars (märz), *n.* **1.** the ancient Roman god of war. **2.** *Astron.* the planet next outside the earth, fourth in

---

order from the sun. Its period of revolution is 686.9 days, its mean distance from the sun about 142,000,000 miles, and its diameter 4230 miles. It has two satellites.

Mar·sa·la (mär sä′lä), *n.* a seaport in W Sicily. 70,040 (est. 1946).

Mar·seil·laise (mär′sə lāz′; *Fr.* mår sĕ′yĕz′), *n.* the French national song, written in 1792 by Rouget de Lisle.

Mar·seilles (mär sā′; *older* -sālz′; *Fr.* -sĕ′y), *n.* a seaport in SE France. 635,939 (1946). Also, French, **Marseille′**.

mar·seilles (mär sālz′). *n.* a thick cotton fabric woven in figures or stripes, with an embossed effect.

marsh (märsh), *n.* a tract of low, wet land; a swamp. [ME *mershe*, OE *mersc*, syncopated var. of *merisc* (c. G. *marsch*), f. *mere* pool + *-isc* -ISH[1]. See MERE[2]]

Marsh (märsh), *n.* **Reginald**, born 1898, U.S. painter.

mar·shal (mär′shəl), *n., v.,* **-shaled, -shaling** or (*esp. Brit.*) **-shalled, -shalling.** —*n.* **1.** a military officer of high rank. In many countries the title is commonly modified by some other term: thus, in England, it has the form *field marshal* and in France, *marshal of France.* **2.** an administrative officer of a U. S. judicial district who performs duties similar to those of a sheriff. **3.** a court officer serving process, attending court, giving personal attention to the judges, etc. **4.** the police officer in some communities. **5.** a high officer of a royal household or court. **6.** a person charged with the arrangement or regulation of ceremonies, etc. —*v.t.* **7.** to arrange in due or proper order. **8.** to array for battle, etc. **9.** to usher or lead. [ME *mareschal*, t. OF, g. VL *mariscalcus* groom, t. Gmc.; cf. OE *mearh* horse, *scealc* servant] —**mar′shal·cy, mar′shal·ship′,** *n.* —**mar′shal·er;** *esp. Brit.,* **mar′shal·ler,** *n.* —Syn. **7.** See gather.

Mar·shall (mär′shəl), *n.* **1. George Catlett** (kăt′lĭt), born 1880, U.S. general and statesman: secretary of state 1947–1949; secretary of defense 1950–1951. **2. John,** 1755–1835, U. S. jurist and statesman: chief justice of the Supreme Court, 1801–35.

Marshall Islands, a group of 24 islands in the N Pacific: formerly mandated to Japan; now under U.S. trusteeship. 10,684 pop. (1939); 74 sq. mi.

Marshall Plan, former name of **European Recovery Program.**

Mar·shal·sea (mär′shəl sē′), *n. Brit. Hist.* **1.** the court of the marshal of the royal household. **2.** a prison in London, latterly a debtors' prison (abolished in 1849).

marsh elder, 1. *U.S.* any of various composite plants of the genus *Iva*, as *I. frutescens,* which grows in saltmarshes. **2.** the cranberry tree.

marsh gas, a gaseous decomposition product of organic matter, consisting largely of methane.

marsh harrier, a well-known hawk, *Circus aeruginosus,* of the Old World, having a cream-colored head and, in the male, gray secondary wing feathers and tail.

marsh hawk, a slender American hawk, *Circus cyaneus hudsonius,* which frequents marshes and meadows, feeding on frogs, snakes, etc.

marsh hen, any of various rails or raillike birds.

marsh·mal·low (märsh′măl′ō; *incorrectly often* -mĕl′ō), *n.* **1.** a sweetened paste or confection made from the mucilaginous root of the marsh mallow. **2.** a similar confection containing gum arabic or gelatin, sugar, corn syrup, and flavoring. [ME *marshmalve,* OE *merscmealwe.* See MARSH, MALLOW]

marsh mallow, an Old World mallow, *Althaea officinalis,* with pink flowers, found in marshy places.

marsh marigold, a yellow-flowered ranunculaceous plant, *Caltha palustris,* growing in marshes and meadows; cowslip.

marsh wren, either of two American species of marsh-inhabiting wrens, the long-billed (*Telmatodytes palustris*), or the short-billed (*Cistothorus platensis*).

marsh·y (mär′shĭ), *adj.,* **marshier, marshiest. 1.** like a marsh; soft and wet. **2.** pertaining to a marsh. **3.** consisting of or containing marsh. —**marsh′i·ness,** *n.*

mar·si·po·branch (mär′sĭ pō brăngk′), *adj.* **1.** belonging to the *Marsipobrachii* or *Cyclostomata,* a group or class of vertebrates comprising the cyclostomes (the lampreys and hagfishes), characterized by pouchlike gills. —*n.* **2.** a marsipobranch fish.

Mars·ton (mär′stən), *n.* **John,** c1575–1634, British dramatist and satirical poet.

Marston Moor, a former moor in NE England, W of York: Cromwell victory over the Royalists, 1644.

mar·su·pi·al (mär sōō′pĭ əl), *adj.* **1.** pertaining to, resembling, or having a marsupium. **2.** of or pertaining to the marsupials. —*n.* **3.** any of the *Marsupialia,* the order which includes all of the viviparous, but non-placental, mammals, such as the opossums, kangaroos, wombats, bandicoots, etc. Most members have a marsupium containing the mammary glands and serving as a receptacle for the young. [t. NL: s. *marsūpiālis,* der. L *marsūpium.* See MARSUPIUM]

mar·su·pi·um (mär sōō′pĭ əm), *n., pl.* **-pia** (-pĭ ə). the pouch or fold of skin on the abdomen of a female marsupial. [t. L: pouch, t. Gk.: m. *marsȳpion, marsȳpion,* dim. of *mársipos* bag, pouch]

mart (märt), *n.* **1.** market; trading center. **2.** *Archaic.* a fair. [t. D, spoken var. of *markt* MARKET]

Mar·tel. See **Charles Martel.**

Mar·tel·lo tower (mär tĕl′ō), *Fort.* a circular, towerlike fort with guns on the top. Also, **mar·tel′lo.**

mar·ten (mär′tən, -tĭn), *n., pl.* **-tens,** (*esp. collectively*) **-ten. 1.** any of various slender, fur-bearing carnivores of the subgenus *Martes* of the genus *Mustela,* as the American **pine marten,** *M. americana,* of the northern U.S. and Canada. **2.** the fur of such an animal. [ME *martren,* t. OF: m. *martrine,* prop. the fur, n. use of *martrin,* adj., der. *martre* marten; from Gmc.]

Marten, *Martes americana*
(Total length 2 ft., tail 7½ in.)

Mar·tha (mär′thə), *n. Bible.* the sister of Lazarus, whose house in Bethany Jesus often visited. Luke 10: 38–42; John 11:1–44.

Martha's Vineyard, an island off SE Massachusetts: summer resort. 5577 pop. (1950); 108¾ sq. mi.

mar·tial (mär′shəl), *adj.* **1.** inclined or disposed to war; warlike; brave. **2.** pertaining to or connected with the army and navy. **3.** pertaining to or appropriate for war: *martial music.* **4.** characteristic of or befitting a warrior: *a martial stride.* [ME, t. L: s. *martiālis* of Mars] —**mar′tial·ly,** *adv.* —**mar′tial·ness,** *n.*

Mar·tial (mär′shəl), *n.* (*Marcus Valerius Martialis*) A.D. c40–c102, Roman writer of epigrams, born in Spain.

martial law, the law imposed upon an area by state or national military forces when civil authority has broken down.

Mar·tian (mär′shən, -shĭ ən), *adj.* **1.** pertaining to the planet Mars. —*n.* **2.** a supposed inhabitant of the planet Mars. [f. s. L *Martius* of Mars + -AN]

mar·tin (mär′tən, -tĭn), *n.* any of various swallows, as *Chelidon urbica,* the common European **house martin,** which builds its nest about houses, or *Progne subis,* the American **purple martin,** one of the largest birds of the swallow family. [late ME, from *Martin,* man's name]

Mar·tin (mär′tən, -tĭn), *n.* **1.** Homer Dodge, 1836–97, U.S. landscape painter. **2. Joseph William,** born 1884, U.S. political leader. **3. Saint,** A.D. c316–397 or 400, French bishop.

Mar·ti·neau (mär′tĭ nō′), *n.* **Harriet,** 1802–76, British writer.

mar·ti·net (mär′tə nĕt′, mär′tə nĕt′), *n.* a rigid disciplinarian, esp. military or naval. [from General *Martinet,* French drillmaster of the reign of Louis XIV] —**mar′ti·net′ish,** *adj.* —**mar′ti·net′ism,** *n.*

mar·tin·gale (mär′tən gāl′), *n.* **1.** a strap of a horse's harness passing from the bit or headgear, between the forelegs, to the girth, for holding the head down. See illus. under **harness. 2.** *Naut.* a short, perpendicular spar under the bowsprit end, used for guying down the jib boom. **3.** a gambling system in which the stakes are doubled after each loss. [t. F, t. Pr.: m. *marte(n)-galo,* fem. of *marte(n)gan,* inhabitant of Martigue (supposedly noted for stinginess)]

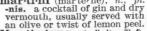

mar·ti·ni (mär tē′nē), *n., pl.* **-nis.** a cocktail of gin and dry vermouth, usually served with an olive or twist of lemon peel.

M, Martingale (def. 2); B, Bowsprit cap; J, Jib boom

Mar·ti·nique (mär′tə nēk′), *n.* an island in the West Indies, in the Lesser Antilles, forming a department of France. 261,595 pop. (1946); 425 sq. mi. *Cap.:* Fort-de-France.

Mar·tin·mas (mär′tĭn məs), *n.* a church festival, November 11, in honor of St. Martin. [f. *Martin* + -MAS]

mart·let (märt′lĭt), *n.* a European martin. [t. F: m. *martelet,* var. of *martinet,* dim. of *martin* MARTIN]

mar·tyr (mär′tər), *n.* **1.** one who willingly suffers death rather than renounce his religion. **2.** one who is put to death or endures great suffering on behalf of any belief, principle, or cause. **3.** one undergoing severe or constant suffering. —*v.t.* **4.** to put to death as a martyr. **5.** to make a martyr of. **6.** to torment or torture. [ME *marter,* OE *martyr,* t. L, t. Gk.: s. *mártys,* orig., witness]

mar·tyr·dom (mär′tər dəm), *n.* **1.** the condition, sufferings, or death of a martyr. **2.** extreme suffering.

mar·tyr·ize (mär′tə rīz′), *v.t.,* **-ized, -izing. 1.** to make a martyr of. **2.** to torment. —**mar′tyr·i·za′tion,** *n.*

mar·tyr·ol·o·gy (mär′tə rŏl′ə jĭ), *n., pl.* **-gies. 1.** the branch of knowledge dealing with the lives of martyrs. **2.** an account or history of martyrs. **3.** such histories collectively. **4.** a list of martyrs. —**mar·tyr·o·log·i·cal** (mär′tər ə lŏj′ə kəl), *adj.* —**mar′tyr·ol′o·gist,** *n.*

mar·tyr·y (mär′tər ĭ), *n., pl.* **-tyries.** a shrine, chapel, or the like, erected in honor of a martyr. [t. LL: m.s. *martyrium,* t. LGk.: m. *martýrion*]

mar·vel (mär′vəl), *n., v.,* **-veled, -veling** or (*esp. Brit.*) **-velled, -velling.** —*n.* **1.** a wonderful thing; a wonder or prodigy. **2.** *Archaic.* the feeling of wonder. —*v.t.* **3.** to wonder at (now fol. only by a clause as object). **4.** to wonder or be curious about (fol. by a clause). —*v.i.* **5.** to be affected with wonder, as at something surprising or extraordinary. [ME *merveille,* t. F, g. L *mīrābilia* wonderful things, prop. neut. pl. of *mīrābilis* wonderful]

Mar·vell (mär′vəl), *n.* Andrew, 1621–78, British poet.

mar·vel-of-Pe·ru (mär′vəl əv pə rōō′), *n.* the four-o'clock (plant).

mar·vel·ous (mär′vələs), *adj.* **1.** such as to excite wonder; surprising; extraordinary. **2.** improbable or incredible (often used absolutely in the phrase *the marvelous*). Also, *esp. Brit.*, **mar′vel·lous.** —**mar′vel·ous·ly,** *adv.* —**mar′vel·ous·ness,** *n.*

Mar·war (mär′wär), *n.* Jodhpur (def. 1).

Marx (märks), *n.* **Karl** (kärl), 1818–83, German founder of modern socialism and communism, and writer on economics and economic history.

Marx·i·an (märk′sĭ′ən), *adj.* of or pertaining to Karl Marx or his theories. —**Marx′i·an·ism,** *n.*

Marx·ism (märk′sĭzəm), *n.* the system of thought developed by Karl Marx, along with Engels, esp. the doctrine that the state throughout history has been a device for the exploitation of the masses by a dominant class, that class struggle has been the main agency of historical change, and that the capitalist state contained from the first the "seeds of its own decay" and will inevitably, after a transitional period known as "the dictatorship of the proletariat," be superseded by a socialist order and a classless society.

Marx·ist (märk′sĭst), *n.* **1.** an adherent of Karl Marx or his theories. —*adj.* **2.** pertaining to Karl Marx or his theories.

Mar·y (mâr′Ĭ), *n.* **1.** *New Testament.* **a.** the mother of Jesus. Matt. 1:18–25. Often called the **Virgin Mary** or **Saint Mary. b.** the sister of Lazarus and Martha. Luke 10:38–42; John 11:1–2. **2.** born 1867, queen of England, 1910–36, wife of George V. [ME *Marie,* OE *Maria,* t. L, t. Gk., t. Heb.: m. *Miryām*]

Mary I, ("*Bloody Mary*") 1516–58, queen of England, 1553–58, and wife of Philip II of Spain. Also, **Mary Tudor.**

Mary II, 1662–94, queen of England, 1689–94, joint ruler with her husband, William III.

Mar·y·land (mĕr′ələnd), *n.* a State in the E United States, on the Atlantic coast. 2,343,001 pop. (1950); 10,577 sq. mi. *Cap.*: Annapolis. *Abbr.*: Md.

Mary Magdalene, Mary of Magdala, mentioned in Luke 8:2, and traditionally identified with the repentant woman in Luke 7:37–50.

Mary Stu·art (stū′ərt, stōō′-), 1542–87, queen of Scotland, 1542–67, beheaded for plotting to assassinate her cousin, Queen Elizabeth of England. Also, **Mary, Queen of Scots.**

mar·zi·pan (mär′zəpăn′), *n.* a confection made of almonds reduced to a paste with sugar, etc., and molded into various forms, usually diminutive fruits and vegetables. Also, **marchpane.** [t. G. See MARCHPANE]

-mas, a final element in certain names of holidays and Christian feasts, e.g., *Michaelmas.* [comb. form of MASS[2]]

Ma·sa·ryk (mä′sär′Ĭk), *n.* **Tomáš Garrigue** (tô′mäsh gə rēg′), 1850–1937, Czech statesman; first president of Czechoslovakia, 1918–35.

Mas·ba·te (mäsbä′tĕ), *n.* one of the Philippine Islands, in the central part of the group. 145,065 pop. (1940); 1262 sq. mi.

masc., masculine.

Mas·ca·gni (mäskä′nyĕ), *n.* **Pietro** (pyĕ′trô), 1863–1945, Italian operatic composer.

mas·car·a (mäskăr′ə), *n.* a substance used to color the eyelashes. [t. Sp.: a mask]

mas·cle (măs′kəl), *n.* *Her.* a bearing in the form of a voided lozenge. [ME, prob. for OF *macle,* g. L *macula* spot, mesh of a net. Cf. MAIL[2]]

mas·cot (măs′kŏt, -kŏt), *n.* a person, animal, or thing supposed to bring good luck. [t. F: m. *mascotte,* dim. of Pr. *masco* witch; of Gmc. orig.]

mas·cu·line (măs′kyəlĭn), *adj.* **1.** having manlike qualities; strong; manly: *a masculine voice.* **2.** pertaining to or characteristic of a man or men: *masculine attire.* **3.** *Gram.* denoting or pertaining to one of the three genders of Latin, German, Greek, etc., or one of the two of French, Spanish, etc., so termed because most or all nouns denoting males belong to it. Not all masculine nouns, however, denote persons or things having to do with the male sex. Spanish *hombre* "man," *dedo* "finger," *sol* "sun" are all masculine. **4.** (of a woman) mannish. —*n.* **5.** *Gram.* the masculine gender. **6.** a noun of that gender. **7.** another element marking that gender. [ME *masculin,* t. L: s. *masculīnus* male] —**mas′cu·line·ly,** *adv.* —**mas′cu·lin′i·ty, mas′cu·line·ness,** *n.* —Syn. **1.** See male.

masculine rhyme, *Pros.* a rhyme of but a single stressed syllable; single rhyme: *disdain, complain.*

Mase·field (mās′fēld, māz′-), *n.* **John,** born 1878, British poet, dramatist, and novelist; poet laureate since 1930.

mash (măsh), *n.* **1.** a soft, pulpy mass. **2.** pulpy condition. **3.** a mess of boiled grain, bran, meal, etc., fed warm to horses and cattle. **4.** crushed malt or meal of grain mixed with hot water to form wort. —*v.t.* **5.** to crush. **6.** to reduce to a soft, pulpy mass, as by heating or pressure. **7.** to mix (crushed malt, etc.) with hot water to form wort. **8.** *Obsolesc. Slang.* to flirt with. [ME *masche,* OE *māsc-* (in compounds), c. G *maisch*] —**mash′er,** *n.*

Ma·shar·brum (mŭsh′ər brōōm′), *n.* a mountain in N India, in the Himalayas. ab. 25,700 ft.

mash·ie (măsh′Ĭ), *n.* *Golf.* a club having a short iron head with a sloping face for making lofting shots. [alter. of F *massue* club]

mash·y (măsh′Ĭ), *n., pl.* **mashies.** mashie.

Mas·i·nis·sa (măs′ə nĭs′ə), *n.* c238–149 B.C., king of Numidia who aided Scipio against Hannibal. Also, **Massinissa.**

mas·jid (mŭs′jĭd), *n.* mosque. Also, **musjid.** [t. Ar. See MOSQUE]

mask (măsk, mȧsk), *n.* **1.** a covering for the face, esp. one worn for disguise; a false face. **2.** a piece of cloth, silk, or plastic material, covering the face of an actor, to symbolize the character he represents: used in Greek and Roman drama and in some modern plays. **3.** anything that disguises or conceals; a disguise; a pretense. **4.** a person wearing a mask. **5.** a masquerade or revel. **6.** a masque (defs. 1, 2). **7.** a likeness of a face, as one molded in plaster after death. **8.** the face or head, as of a fox. **9.** *Archit., etc.* a representation of a face or head, generally grotesque, used as an ornament. **10.** a covering of wire, gauze, etc., to protect the face, as from splinters, dust, a hard pitched ball, etc. **11.** a gas mask. **12.** *Fort.* a screen, as of earth or brush, for concealing or protecting a battery or any military operation. —*v.t.* **13.** to disguise or conceal. **14.** to cover with a mask. **15.** *Fort.* to conceal (a battery or any military operation) from the enemy. **16.** to hinder (an army, etc.) from conducting an operation. —*v.i.* **17.** to put on a mask; disguise oneself. [t. F: m. *masque,* t. It.: m. *maschera,* der. LL *masca*]

mas·ka·longe (măs′kəlŏnj′), *n.* muskellunge.

masked ball, a ball at which masks are worn.

mask·er (măs′kər, mȧs′-), *n.* one who masks; one who takes part in a masque. Also, **masquer.**

mas·och·ism (măz′əkĭz′əm), *n.* *Psychiatry.* the condition in which sexual gratification depends on suffering, physical pain, and humiliation. [named after Leopold von Sacher *Masoch* (1836–95), Austrian novelist, who described it] —**mas′och·ist,** *n.* —**mas′och·is′tic,** *adj.*

ma·son (mā′sən), *n.* **1.** one who builds with brick, stone, or the like. **2.** one who molds cement, concrete, etc., in imitation of stonework. **3.** (*often cap.*) a Freemason. —*v.t.* **4.** to construct of or strengthen with masonry. [ME, t. OF: m. *maçon,* der. LL *maccāre* beat; of Gmc. orig.]

mason bee, any of certain bees of the family *Megachilidae,* which construct their nests of clay.

Ma·son City (mā′sən), a city in N Iowa. 27,980 (1950).

Ma·son-Dix·on line (mā′sən dĭk′sən), the boundary between Pennsylvania and Maryland, partly surveyed by Charles Mason and Jeremiah Dixon between 1763 and 1767, popularly considered before the extinction of slavery as a line of demarcation between free and slave States. Also, **Mason and Dixon's line.**

ma·son·ic (məsŏn′ĭk), *adj.* (*often cap.*) pertaining to or characteristic of Freemasons or Freemasonry.

ma·son·ite (mā′sənĭt′), *n.* **1.** a kind of wood fiber material, pressed in sheets and used for partitions, insulation, etc. **2.** (*cap.*) a trademark for this substance.

Mason jar, a glass jar with an airtight screw top, much used in home canning. [named after American patentee, John L. *Mason*]

ma·son·ry (mā′sənrĬ), *n., pl.* **-ries. 1.** the art or occupation of a mason. **2.** work constructed by a mason, esp., stonework. **3.** (*often cap.*) freemasonry.

Ma·so·ra (məsôr′ə), *n.* **1.** the Hebrew tradition, formed gradually through a succession of centuries, as to the correct form of the text of the Scriptures. **2.** the collection of critical notes in which it is embodied. Also, **Ma·so′rah, Massora.** [t. Heb.: (m.) *māsorāh* tradition]

Mas·o·rete (măs′ə rēt′), *n.* **1.** a Hebrew scholar versed in the Masora. **2.** one of the body of Jewish scholars who reduced the Masora to writing. Also, **Mas·o·rite** (măs′ə rīt′), **Massorete.**

Mas·o·ret·ic (măs′ə rĕt′Ĭk), *adj.* of or pertaining to the Masora, the Masoretes, or their system. Also, **Mas′o·ret′i·cal.**

Mas·pe·ro (măspərō′), *n.* **Sir Gaston Camille Charles** (gȧs tôn′ kȧ mē′y shȧrl′), 1846–1916, a French Egyptologist.

Mas·qat (mŭskăt′), *n.* Arabic name of **Muscat.**

masque (măsk, mȧsk), *n.* **1.** a form of aristocratic entertainment in 16th and 17th century England, orig. consisting of pantomime and dancing but later with dialogue and song, in elaborate productions given by amateur and professional actors. **2.** a dramatic composition for such entertainment. **3.** a masquerade; a revel. Also, **mask.** [see MASK]

mas·quer (măs′kər, mȧs′-), *n.* masker.

mas·quer·ade (măs′kərād′), *n., v.,* **-aded, -ading.** —*n.* **1.** an assembly of persons wearing masks and other disguises, and often rich or fantastic dress, for dancing, etc. **2.** disguise such as is worn at such an assembly. **3.** disguise, or false outward show. **4.** a going about under false pretenses. —*v.i.* **5.** to go about under false pretenses or a false character. **6.** to disguise oneself. **7.** to take part in a masquerade. [t. F: m. *mascarade,* t. It.: m. *mascherata,* der. *maschera* MASK] —**mas′quer·ad′er,** *n.*

mass (măs), *n.* **1.** a body of coherent matter, usually of indefinite shape and often of considerable size: *a mass of dough.* **2.** an aggregation of incoherent particles, parts, or objects regarded as forming one body: *a mass of troops.* **3.** a considerable assemblage, number, or quantity: *a mass of errors.* **4.** an expanse, as of color, light, or shade in a painting. **5.** the main body, bulk, or greater part of anything: *the great mass of American products.* **6.** bulk, size, or massiveness. **7.** *Physics.* that property of a body, commonly but inadequately defined as the measure of the quantity of matter in it, to which its inertia is ascribed: the quotient of the weight of the body and the acceleration due to gravity. **8.** *Pharm.* a preparation of thick, pasty consistency, from which pills are made. **9. the masses,** the great body of the common people; the working classes or lower social orders. —*v.i.* **10.** to come together in or form a mass or masses: *the clouds are massing in the west.* —*v.t.* **11.** to gather into or dispose in a mass or masses; assemble: *the houses are massed in blocks, to mass troops.* [ME *masse*, t. L: m. *massa* mass, lump] —**Syn. 2.** aggregate, aggregation, assemblage. **3.** collection, accumulation, pile, conglomeration. **6.** See size[1]. **11.** assemble; collect, gather. —**Ant. 11.** disperse.

Mass (măs), *n.* **1.** the celebration of the Eucharist. See **High Mass, Low Mass. 2.** a musical setting of certain parts of this service (now chiefly as celebrated in the Roman Catholic Church), as the Kyrie Eleison, Gloria, Credo, Sanctus and Benedictus, Agnus Dei. Also, **mass.** [ME *masse*, OE *mæsse*, t. VL: m. *messa*, L *missa*; orig. application of L term uncert.]

Mass., Massachusetts.

Mas·sa·chu·setts (măs′ə·chōō′sĭts), *n.* **1.** a State in the NE United States, on the Atlantic coast. 4,690,514 pop. (1950); 8257 sq. mi. *Cap.:* Boston. *Abbr.:* Mass. **2.** an Algonquian language.

Massachusetts Bay, a large, open bay off the E coast of Massachusetts.

mas·sa·cre (măs′ə·kər), *n., v.,* **-cred, -cring.** —*n.* **1.** the unnecessary, indiscriminate killing of a number of human beings, as in barbarous warfare or persecution, or for revenge or plunder. **2.** a general slaughter of human beings. —*v.t.* **3.** to kill indiscriminately or in a massacre. [t. F, der. OF *macecler* to butcher, der. *mache-col* butcher, f. s. *macher* smash (g. *maccāre* to strike; cf Gmc. orig.) + *col* neck (g. L *collum*); ? also influenced by *masselier* butcher, g. L *macellārius*] —**mas·sa·crer** (-krər), *n.* —**Syn. 3.** See **slaughter.**

mas·sage (mə·säzh′; *esp. Brit.* măs′äzh), *n., v.,* **-saged, -saging.** —*n.* **1.** act or art of treating the body by rubbing, kneading, or the like, to stimulate circulation, increase suppleness, etc. —*v.t.* **2.** to treat by massage. [t. F, der. *masser* knead, der. *masse* mass] —**mas·sag′er, mas·sag′ist,** *n.* —**mas·sa·geuse** (măs′ə·zhœz′), *n. fem.*

mas·sa·sau·ga (măs′ə·sô′gə), *n.* a small rattlesnake, *Sistrurus miliarius,* of the southern U.S.

Mas·sa·soit (măs′ə·soit′), *n.* c1580–1661, American Indian chief who was friendly with the Plymouth colony (father of King Philip).

Mas·sa·ua (mäs·sä′wä), *n.* a seaport in Eritrea, on the Red Sea. 17,169 (1939). Also, **Mas·sa·wa.**

mass defect, *Physics.* The difference between the mass of a nucleus and the total mass of its constituent particles, due to the equality of mass and energy.

mas·sé (mă·sā′; *esp. Brit.* măs′Y), *n.* *Billiards.* a stroke made by hitting the cue ball with the cue held almost or quite perpendicular to the table. Also, **massé shot.** [t. F, pp. of *masser* strike by a massé, der. *masse* kind of cue, MACE[1]]

Mas·sé·na (mă·sě·nä′), *n.* **André** (än·drě′), (*Prince d'Essling*) 1758–1817, French marshal under Napoleon I.

mass-en·er·gy equivalence (măs′ĕn′ər·jY), *Physics.* the theory that mass and energy are connected and equivalent. Equivalent to a given mass is an energy equal to the mass times the square of the velocity of light.

Mas·se·net (măs·ně′), *n.* **Jules Émile Frédéric** (zhYl ě·mēl′ frě·dě·rēk′), 1842–1912, French composer.

mas·se·ter (mă·sē′tər), *n.* *Anat.* an important masticatory muscle which serves to close the jaws by raising the mandible. [t. NL, t. Gk.: m. *masētēr* a chewer] —**mas·se·ter·ic** (măs′ə·těr′Yk), *adj.*

mas·seur (mă·sœr′), *n.* a man who practises massage. [t. F, der. *masser* to massage] —**mas·seuse** (mă·sœz′), *n. fem.*

Mas·sey (măs′Y), *n.* **Vincent,** born 1887, governor general of Canada since 1952.

mas·si·cot (măs′Y·kŏt′), *n.* monoxide of lead, PbO, in the form of a yellow powder, used as a pigment and drier. [t. F, t. Sp.: m. *mazacote* soda, t. Ar.: m. *shabb qubṭī* Egyptian alum]

mas·sif (măs′Yf; *Fr.* mă·sēf′), *n.* **1.** a compact portion of a mountain range, containing one or more summits. **2.** a band or zone of the earth's crust raised or depressed as a unit and bounded by faults. [t. F, n. use of *massif* MASSIVE]

Mas·sil·lon (măs′ə·lən), *n.* a city in NE Ohio. 29,594 (1950).

Mas·sine (mă·sēn′), *n.* **Léonide** (lě·ô·nēd′), born 1896, U.S. dancer and choreographer, born in Russia.

Mas·sin·ger (măs′ən·jər), *n.* **Philip,** 1583–1640, British dramatist.

Mas·si·nis·sa (măs′ə·nYs′ə), *n.* Masinissa.

mas·sive (măs′Yv), *adj.* **1.** consisting of or forming a large mass; bulky and heavy. **2.** large, as the head or forehead. **3.** solid or substantial; great or imposing. **4.** *Mineral.* without outward crystal form, although perhaps crystalline in internal structure. **5.** *Geol.* homogeneous. **6.** *Med.* affecting a large continuous mass of bodily tissue, as a disease. [ME *massiffe*, t. F: m. *massif*, der. *masse* MASS[1]] —**mas′sive·ly,** *adv.* —**mas′sive·ness,** *n.*

mass meeting, a large or general assembly of the people to discuss or hear discussed some matter of common interest.

Mass Observation, *Brit. Trademark.* research or poll on public opinion *Abbr.:* M.O.

Mas·so·ra (mə·sōr′ə), *n.* Masora.

Mas·so·rete (măs′ə·rēt′), *n.* Masorete.

mas·so·ther·a·py (măs′ō·thěr′ə·pY), *n.* *Med.* treatment by massage. [f. F *mass(er),* v., massage + -o- + THERAPY]

mass spectrograph, *Physics.* a device for separating atoms or molecules of different masses by utilizing the fact that the ions of such entities are deflected in a magnetic field by an amount which depends on the mass.

mass·y (măs′Y), *adj.,* **massier, massiest.** massive. —**mass′i·ness,** *n.*

mast[1] (măst, mäst), *n.* **1.** a tall spar rising more or less vertically from the keel or deck of a vessel, which supports the yards, sails, etc. **2. before the mast.** *Naut.* as an unlicensed seaman, from the living quarters of seamen forward of the foremast in the forecastle. **3.** any upright pole. —*v.t.* **4.** to provide with a mast or masts. [ME; OE *mæst,* c. G *mast*; akin to L *mālus*] —**mast′like,** *adj.*

mast[2] (măst, mäst), *n.* the fruit (acorns, chestnuts, beechnuts, etc. of certain forest trees, esp. as food for swine. [ME; OE *mæst,* c. G *mast*; akin to MEAT]

mast-, var. of **masto-,** before vowels, as in *mastectomy.*

mas·ta·ba (măs′tə·bə), *n.* an ancient Egyptian tomb, rectangular in plan, with sloping sides and a flat roof. Also, **mas′ta·bah.** [t. Ar. (Egypt. d.): bench]

mas·tec·to·my (măs·těk′tə·mY), *n., pl.* **-mies.** *Surg.* the operation of removing the breast or mamma. [f. MAST- + -ECTOMY]

mas·ter (măs′tər, mäs′-), *n.* **1.** one who has the power of controlling, using, or disposing of something at pleasure: *a master of several languages.* **2.** an employer of workmen or servants. **3.** the commander of a merchant vessel. **4.** the male head of a household. **5.** an owner of a slave, horse, dog, etc. **6.** a presiding officer. **7.** *Chiefly Brit.* a male teacher, tutor or schoolmaster. **8.** a person whose teachings one accepts or follows. **9.** (*cap.*) Christ (prec. by *the, our,* etc.). **10.** a victor. **11.** a workman qualified to teach apprentices and to carry on his trade independently. **12.** a man eminently skilled in something, as an occupation, art, or science. **13.** a painting or other work of art by such a man. **14. the old masters,** a title given collectively to the eminent painters of earlier periods. **15.** an officer of the court to whom some or all of the issues in a case may be referred for the purpose of taking testimony and making a report to the court. **16.** *Educ.* **a.** a person who has taken a certain advanced degree at a college or university, orig. conveying qualification to teach: *master of arts.* **b.** such a degree. **17.** a title of respect for a man or a boy (now *mister* in ordinary speech except when given to boys). **18.** a youth or boy; a young gentleman. —*adj.* **19.** being master, or exercising mastery. **20.** chief or principal; *the master bedroom.* **21.** directing or controlling. **22.** dominating or predominant. **23.** being a master carrying on his trade independently, rather than a workman employed by another. **24.** being a master of some occupation, art, etc.; eminently skilled. **25.** characteristic of a master; showing mastery. —*v.t.* **26.** to become the master of; conquer or subdue; reduce to subjection. **27.** to rule or direct as master. **28.** to make oneself master of; to become an adept in. [ME *maister,* OE *magister,* t. L] —**mas′ter·dom,** *n.* —**mas′ter·less,** *adj.*

mas·ter-at-arms (măs′tər·ət·ärmz′, mäs′-), *n., pl.* **masters-at-arms.** *Naval.* a petty officer who has various duties, such as keeping order on the ship, taking charge of prisoners, etc.

master builder, 1. a building contractor. **2.** an architect.

mas·ter·ful (măs′tər·fəl, mäs′-), *adj.* **1.** having or showing the qualities of a master; authoritative; domineering. **2.** showing mastery or skill; masterly. —**mas′ter·ful·ly,** *adv.* —**mas′ter·ful·ness,** *n.*

master hand, 1. an expert. **2.** great expertness.

master key, a key that will open a number of locks whose proper keys are not interchangeable.

mas·ter·ly (măs′tər·lY, mäs′-), *adj.* **1.** like or befitting a master, as in skill or art. —*adv.* **2.** in a masterly manner. —**mas′ter·li·ness,** *n.*

master mason, 1. a Freemason who has reached the third degree. **2.** an expert mason.

master mechanic, a mechanic in charge of other mechanics.

Master of Arts, 1. a master's degree, esp. in the liberal arts, granted by a college or other authorized body, usually based on at least one year of study beyond the bachelor's degree. **2.** one holding this degree.

ăct, āble, dâre, ärt; ĕbb, ēqual; Yf, īce; hŏt, ōver, ôrder, oil, bŏŏk, ōōze, out; ŭp, ūse, ûrge; ə = a in alone; ch, chief; g, give; ng, ring; sh, shoe; th, thin; ŧħ, that; zh, vision. See the full key on inside cover.

master of ceremonies, a person who directs the entertainment at a party, dinner, etc.

Master of Science, 1. an academic degree similar to the Master of Arts, but taken in the field of natural sciences or mathematics. **2.** one holding this degree.

mas·ter·piece (măs′tər pēs′, mäs′-), *n.* **1.** one's most excellent production, as in an art: *the masterpiece of a painter.* **2.** any production of masterly skill. **3.** a consummate example of skill or excellence of any kind.

Mas·ters (măs′tərz, mäs′-), *n.* **Edgar Lee,** 1869–1950 U.S. poet and novelist.

master sergeant, *U.S. Army.* a noncommissioned officer of the highest rank.

mas·ter·ship (măs′tər shĭp′, mäs′-) *n.* **1.** the office, function, or authority of a master. **2.** control. **3.** mastery, as of a subject. **4.** masterly skill or knowledge.

mas·ter·sing·er (măs′tər sĭng′ər, mäs′-), *n.* Meistersinger.

master stroke, a masterly action or achievement.

mas·ter·work (măs′tər wûrk′, mäs′-), *n.* a masterpiece.

master workman, 1. a workman in charge. **2.** one who is master of his craft.

mas·ter·y (măs′tə rĭ, mäs′-), *n., pl.* **-ter·ies. 1.** state of being master; power of command or control. **2.** command or grasp, as of a subject. **3.** victory. **4.** the action of mastering, as a subject, etc. **5.** expert skill or knowledge. [f. MASTER + -Y³; r. ME *maistrie,* t. OF, der. *maistre* MASTER]

mast·head (măst′hĕd′, mäst′-), *n.* **1.** the top or head of the mast of a ship or vessel; technically, the top or head of the lower mast, but by extension the highest point of the mast. **2.** a statement printed (usually on the editorial page) in all issues of a newspaper, magazine, etc., giving the name, owner, staff, etc. —*v.t.* **3.** *Naut.* to hoist to the top or head of a mast. **4.** to send to the masthead as a punishment.

mas·tic (măs′tĭk), *n.* **1.** an aromatic, astringent resin obtained from a small anacardiaceous evergreen tree, *Pistacia lentiscus,* native in the Mediterranean region: used in making varnish. **2.** a similar resin yielded by other trees of the same genus, or a resin likened to it. **3.** a tree yielding a mastic, esp. *Pistacia lentiscus.* **4.** a pasty form of cement used for filling holes in masonry or plastered walls. [ME *mastyk,* t. OF: m. *mastic,* t. L: m.s. *mastichum,* t. Gk.: m. *mastíchē*]

mas·ti·cate (măs′tə kāt′), *v.t., v.i.,* **-cat·ed, -cat·ing. 1.** to chew. **2.** to reduce to a pulp by crushing or kneading, as rubber. [t. LL: m.s. *masticātus,* pp., chewed] **—mas′ti·ca′tion,** *n.* **—mas′ti·ca′tor,** *n.*

mas·ti·ca·to·ry (măs′tə kə tōr′ĭ), *adj., n., pl.* **-tories.** —*adj.* **1.** of, pertaining to, or used in or for mastication. —*n.* **2.** a medicinal substance to be chewed, as to promote the secretion of saliva.

mas·tiff (măs′tĭf, mäs′-), *n.* one of a breed of powerful, stoutly built dogs with large head, drooping ears, and pendulous lips. [ME, t. OF, b. *mastin* mastiff and *mestif* mongrel]

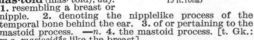

Mastiff
(30 in. or more high at the shoulder)

mas·ti·tis (măs tī′tĭs), *n.* **1.** *Pathol.* inflammation of the breast. **2.** *Vet. Sci.* garget. [t. NL; see MAST-, -ITIS]

masto-, a word element meaning the breast, mastoid. Also, **mast-.** [t. Gk., comb. form of *mastós* breast]

mas·to·don (măs′tə dŏn′), *n.* any of various species of large, extinct mammals (genus *Mammut,* etc.) of the elephant kind, characterized by nipplelike elevations on the molar teeth. [t. NL, f. Gk.: *mast-* MAST- + m.s. *odoús* tooth]

Mastodon. *Mammut americanum* (Ab. 9 ft. high at the shoulder, 15 ft. long)

mas·toid (măs′toid), *adj.* **1.** resembling a breast or nipple. **2.** denoting the nipplelike process of the temporal bone behind the ear. **3.** of or pertaining to the mastoid process. —*n.* **4.** the mastoid process. [t. Gk.: m.s. *mastoeidḗs* like the breast]

mas·toid·ec·to·my (măs′toi dĕk′tə mĭ), *n., pl.* **-mies.** *Surg.* the removal of part of a mastoid bone.

mas·toid·i·tis (măs′toi dī′tĭs), *n. Pathol.* inflammation of the mastoid process of the temporal bone of the skull. [f. MASTOID + -ITIS]

mas·tur·bate (măs′tər bāt′), *v.i.,* **-bated, -bating.** to practice masturbation. **—mas′tur·ba′tor,** *n.*

mas·tur·ba·tion (măs′tər bā′shən), *n.* sexual self-gratification; onanism (def. 2). [t. L: s. *masturbātio*]

Ma·su·ri·a (mə zŏŏr′ĭə), *n.* a region in NE Poland, formerly in East Prussia, containing the **Masurian Lakes,** near which the Germans defeated the Russians, 1914–15. German, **Ma·su·ren** (mä zōō′rən).

ma·su·ri·um (mə sŏŏr′ĭəm), *n. Chem.* a manganese family element discovered spectroscopically in 1925 but not isolated, present in small quantities in columbite,

gadolinite, zircon, etc. *Symbol:* Ma; *at. wt.:* about 98; *at. no.:* 43. [f. MASUR(IA) + -IUM]

mat¹ (măt), *n., v.,* **matted, matting.** —*n.* **1.** a piece of fabric made of plaited or woven rushes, straw, hemp, or other fiber, or a similar article made of some other material, used to cover a floor, to wipe the shoes on, etc. **2.** a smaller piece of material, often ornamental, set under a dish of food, a lamp, vase, etc. **3.** a thick covering, as of padded canvas, laid on a floor on which wrestlers contend, in order to protect them. **4.** a thickly growing or thick and tangled mass, as of hair or weeds. **5.** a sack made of matting, as for coffee or sugar. **6.** *Print.* **a.** the intaglio (usually of papier-maché), impressed from type or cut, from which a stereotype plate is cast. **b.** the brass die used in a linotype, each carrying a letter in intaglio. —*v.t.* **7.** to cover with or as with mats or matting. **8.** to form into a mat, as by interweaving. —*v.i.* **9.** to become entangled; form tangled masses. [ME *matte,* OE *meatt(e),* t. LL: m. *matta*]

mat² (măt), *n.* a more or less wide, framelike piece of pasteboard or other material placed in front of a picture. [t. F. See MAT¹, MAT³, adj.]

mat³ (măt), *adj., n., v.,* **matted, matting.** —*adj.* **1.** lusterless and dull in surface. —*n.* **2.** a dull or dead surface, without luster, produced on metals, as gold or silver, by some special operation. **3.** a tool for producing it. —*v.t.* **4.** to finish with a mat surface. [t. F, der. *matir* make dull or weak, der. *mat* mated (in chess), t. Ar.: m. *māt,* t. Pers.: (the king) died]

Mat·a·be·les (măt′ə bē′lĭz), *n.pl.* a Zulu people whom the Boers forced out of the Transvaal in 1837, now living in **Matabeleland,** a region in Southern Rhodesia.

mat·a·dor (măt′ə dôr′), *n.* **1.** the man who kills the bull in bullfights. **2.** one of the principal cards in skat and certain other games. [t. Sp., g. L *mactātor* slayer]

Mat·a·mo·ros (măt′ə môr′əs; *Sp.* mä′tä mô′rôs), *n.* a seaport in NE Mexico, on the Rio Grande opposite Brownsville, Texas. 15,699 (1940).

Mat·a·nus·ka (măt′ə nōōs′kə), *n.* a valley in S Alaska, NE of Anchorage: recently developed as an agricultural region by homesteaders.

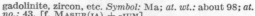

Ma·tan·zas (mə tän′zəs; *Sp.* mä tän′säs), *n.* a seaport on the NW coast of Cuba. 49,591 (1943).

Mat·a·pan (măt′ə păn′), *n.* **Cape,** a cape in S Greece: the S tip of the Peloponnesus.

match¹ (măch), *n.* **1.** a short, slender piece of wood or other material tipped with a chemical substance which produces fire when rubbed on a rough or chemically prepared surface. **2.** a wick, cord or the like, prepared to burn at an even rate, used to fire cannon, etc. [ME *matche,* t. OF: m. *meiche*; orig. uncert.]

match² (măch), *n.* **1.** a person or thing that equals or resembles another in some respect. **2.** a person or thing that is an exact counterpart of another. **3.** one able to cope with another as an equal: *to meet one's match.* **4.** a corresponding or suitably associated pair. **5.** *Chiefly Brit.* a contest or game. **6.** an engagement for a contest or game. **7.** a person considered with regard to suitability as a partner in marriage. **8.** a matrimonial compact or alliance. —*v.t.* **9.** to equal, or be equal to. **10.** to be the match or counterpart of: *the color of the skirt does not match that of the coat.* **11.** to adapt; make to correspond. **12.** to fit together, as two things. **13.** to procure or produce an equal to. **14.** to place in opposition or conflict. **15.** to provide with an adversary or competitor of equal power: *the teams were well matched.* **16.** to encounter as an adversary with equal power. **17.** to prove a match for. **18.** to unite in marriage; procure a matrimonial alliance for. —*v.i.* **19.** to be equal or suitable. **20.** to correspond; be of corresponding size, shape, color, pattern, etc. **21.** to ally oneself in marriage. [ME *macche,* OE *gemæcca* mate, fellow] **—match′a·ble,** *adj.* **—match′er,** *n.*

match·board (măch′bōrd′), *n.* a board which has a tongue cut along one edge and a groove in the opposite edge: used in making floors, etc., the tongue of one such board fitting into the groove of the next.

match·less (măch′lĭs), *adj.* having no equal; peerless: *matchless courage.* **—match′less·ly,** *adv.* **—match′less·ness,** *n.* **—Syn.** unrivaled, incomparable, inimitable.

match·lock (măch′lŏk′), *n.* **1.** an old form of gunlock in which the priming was ignited by a slow match. **2.** a handgun, usually a musket, with such a lock.

match·mak·er¹ (măch′mā′kər), *n.* **1.** one who makes, or seeks to bring about, matrimonial matches. **2.** one who makes or arranges matches for contests, etc. [f. MATCH² + MAKER] **—match′mak′ing,** *n., adj.*

match·mak·er² (măch′mā′kər), *n.* one who makes matches for burning. [f. MATCH¹ + MAKER] **—match′-mak′ing,** *n., adj.*

match play, *Golf.* play in which the score is reckoned by counting the holes won by each side.

match point, the final point required to win a contest.

match·wood (măch′wŏŏd′), *n.* **1.** wood suitable for matches. **2.** splinters.

---

b., blend of, blended; c., cognate with; d., dialect, dialectal; der., derived from; f., formed from; g., going back to; m., modification of; r., replacing; s., stem of; t., taken from; ?, perhaps. See the full key on inside cover.

mate[1] (māt), *n.*, *v.*, **mated, mating.** —*n.* **1.** one joined with another in any pair. **2.** a counterpart. **3.** husband or wife. **4.** one of a pair of mated animals. **5.** a habitual associate; comrade; partner. **6.** an officer of a merchant vessel who ranks below the captain or master (called **first mate, second mate**, etc., when there are more than one on a ship). **7.** an assistant to a warrant officer or other functionary on a ship. **8.** *Archaic.* a suitable associate. —*v.t.* **9.** to join as a mate or as mates. **10.** to match or marry. **11.** to pair, as animals. **12.** to join suitably, as two things. **13.** to treat as comparable, as one thing with another. —*v.i.* **14.** to associate as a mate or as mates. **15.** to marry. **16.** to pair. **17.** to consort; keep company. [ME, t. MLG, var. of *gemate*; akin to OE *gemetta* sharer of food, guest. See MEAT]

mate[2] (māt), *n.*, *v.t.*, *v.i.*, **mated, mating.** *Chess.* checkmate. [ME *mate(n)*, t. OF: m. *mater*, der. *mat* checkmated, overcome, t. Ar. See MAT[3], CHECKMATE]

ma·te[3] (mä′tā, mät′ā), *n.* maté.

ma·té (mä′tā, mät′ā), *n.* **1.** a tealike South American beverage made from the leaves of a species of holly, *Ilex paraguariensis*, native in Paraguay and Brazil. **2.** the plant itself. Also, **mate.** [t. Sp.: prop., a vessel, t. Peruvian: m. *mati* calabash]

ma·ter (mā′tər), *n. Brit. Colloq.* mother. [L]

ma·ter do·lo·ro·sa (mā′tər dō′lō rō′sə), *Latin.* **1.** the sorrowful mother. **2.** (*cap.*) the mother of Christ sorrowing for her son, esp. as represented in art.

ma·ter·fa·mil·i·as (mā′tər fə mĭl′ĭ ăs′), *n. Latin.* the mother of a family.

ma·te·ri·al (mə tĭr′ĭ əl), *n.* **1.** the substance or substances of which a thing is made or composed. **2.** any constituent element of a thing. **3.** anything serving as crude or raw matter for working upon or developing. **4.** a textile fabric. **5.** (*pl.*) articles of any kind requisite for making or doing something: *writing materials.* —*adj.* **6.** formed or consisting of matter, physical; corporeal: *the material world.* **7.** relating to, concerned with, or involving matter: *material force.* **8.** concerned or occupied unduly with corporeal things or interest. **9.** pertaining to the physical rather than the spiritual or intellectual aspect of things: *material civilization.* **10.** of substantial import, of much consequence, or important. **11.** pertinent or essential (fol. by *to*). **12.** *Law.* (of evidence, etc.) likely to influence the determination of a cause. **13.** *Philos.* of or pertaining to matter as distinguished from form. [ME, t. LL: s. *māteriālis*, der. *māteria* matter] —**ma·te′ri·al·ness,** *n.* —**Syn.** 1. See **matter.**

ma·te·ri·al·ism (mə tĭr′ĭ ə lĭz′əm), *n.* **1.** the philosophical theory which regards matter and its motions as constituting the universe, and all phenomena, including those of mind, as due to material agencies. **2.** *Ethics.* the doctrine that self-interest is and ought to be the first law of life. **3.** devotion to material rather than spiritual objects, needs, and considerations.

ma·te·ri·al·ist (mə tĭr′ĭ əl ĭst), *n.* **1.** an adherent of philosophical materialism. **2.** one absorbed in material interests; one who takes a material view of life. —**ma·te′ri·al·is′tic,** *adj.* —**ma·te′ri·al·is′ti·cal·ly,** *adv.*

ma·te·ri·al·i·ty (mə tĭr′ĭ ăl′ə tĭ), *n.*, *pl.* **-ties. 1.** material nature or quality. **2.** something material.

ma·te·ri·al·ize (mə tĭr′ĭ ə līz′), *v.*, **-ized, -izing.** —*v.t.* **1.** to give material form to. **2.** to invest with material attributes. **3.** to make physically perceptible. **4.** to render materialistic. —*v.i.* **5.** to assume material or bodily form. **6.** to come into perceptible existence; appear. —**ma·te′ri·al·i·za′tion,** *n.* —**ma·te′ri·al·iz′er,** *n.*

ma·te·ri·al·ly (mə tĭr′ĭ ə lĭ), *adv.* **1.** to an important degree; considerably. **2.** with reference to matter or material things; physically. **3.** *Philos.* with regard to matter or substance as distinguished from form.

ma·te·ri·a med·i·ca (mə tĭr′ĭ ə mĕd′ĭ kə), **1.** the remedial substances employed in medicine. **2.** the branch of medicine treating of these. [t. ML: medical material]

ma·té·ri·el (mə tĭr′ĭ ĕl′), *n.* **1.** the aggregate of things used or needed in any business, undertaking, or operation (distinguished from *personnel*). **2.** *Mil.* arms, ammunition, and equipment in general. [t. F. See MATERIAL]

ma·ter·nal (mə tûr′nəl), *adj.* **1.** of or pertaining to, befitting, having the qualities of, or being a mother. **2.** derived from a mother. **3.** related through a mother: *his maternal aunt.* [late ME, f. s. L *māternus* of a mother + -AL[1]] —**ma·ter′nal·ly,** *adv.*

ma·ter·ni·ty (mə tûr′nə tĭ), *n.* **1.** state of being a mother; motherhood. **2.** motherliness.

maternity hospital, a hospital for the care of women during confinement in childbirth.

mate·y (mā′tĭ), *Brit. Colloq.* —*adj.* **1.** comradely; cozy. —*n.* **2.** comrade; chum.

math., **1.** mathematical. **2.** mathematician. **3.** mathematics.

math·e·mat·i·cal (măth′ə măt′ĭ kəl), *adj.* **1.** of, pertaining to, or of the nature of mathematics. **2.** employed in the operations of mathematics. **3.** having the exactness or precision of mathematics. Also, **math′e·mat′ic.** [f. *mathematic* MATHEMATICS + -AL[1]] —**math′e·mat′i·cal·ly,** *adv.*

mathematical expectation, *Statistics.* the average of a set of possible values of a variable, the values being weighted by the probabilities associated with these values.

mathematical logic, a modern development of formal logic employing a special notation or symbolism

capable of manipulation in accordance with precise rules; symbolic logic.

math·e·ma·ti·cian (măth′ə mə tĭsh′ən), *n.* an expert in mathematics.

math·e·mat·ics (măth′ə măt′ĭks), *n.* the science that treats of the measurement, properties, and relations of quantities, including arithmetic, geometry, algebra, etc. [pl. of *mathematic*, t. L: s. *mathēmaticus*, t. Gk.: m. *mathēmatikós* pertaining to science. See -ICS]

Math·er (măth′ər, măth′-), *n.* **1.** Cotton, 1663–1728, American clergyman and author. **2.** his father, **Increase,** 1639–1723, American clergyman and author.

mat·in (măt′ĭn), *n.* **1.** (*pl.*) *Eccles.* **a.** the first of the seven canonical hours, or the service for it, properly beginning at midnight, sometimes at daybreak. **b.** the order for public morning prayer in the Anglican Church. **2.** *Poetic.* a morning song, esp. of a bird. —*adj.* **3.** Also, **mat′in·al.** pertaining to the morning or to matins. Also, **mattin.** [ME *matyn*, (pl. *matines*), t. OF: m. *matin* morning, g. L *mātūtīnus* of or in the morning]

mat·i·née (măt′ə nā′; *esp. Brit.* măt′ə nā′), *n.* an entertainment, esp. a dramatic or musical performance, held in the daytime, usually in the afternoon. Also, **mat′i·nee′.** [t. F, der. *matin* morning. See MATIN]

Ma·tisse (mà tēs′), *n.* Henri (äṇrē′), born 1869, French painter.

mat·rass (măt′rəs), *n. Chem.* **1.** glass vessel, etc. **2.** small glass closed at one end. Also, **mattrass.**

matri-, a word element meaning "mother." [t. L, comb. form of *māter*]

ma·tri·arch (mā′trĭ ärk′), *n.* a woman holding a position analogous to that of a patriarch, as in a family or tribe. [f. MATRI- + -ARCH; modeled on PATRIARCH] —**ma′tri·ar′chal, ma′tri·ar′chic,** *adj.* —**ma′tri·ar′chal·ism,** *n.*

ma·tri·ar·chate (mā′trĭ är′kĭt, -kāt), *n.* **1.** a matriarchal system or community. **2.** *Sociol.* a social order believed to have preceded patriarchal tribal society in the early period of human communal life, embodying rule by the mothers, or by all adult women.

ma·tri·ar·chy (mā′trĭ är′kĭ), *n.*, *pl.* **-chies.** the matriarchal system; a form of social organization, as in certain primitive tribes, in which the mother is head of the family, and in which descent is reckoned in the female line, the children belonging to the mother's clan.

ma·tri·ces (mā′trĭ sēz′, măt′rĭ-), *n.* pl. of **matrix.**

ma·tri·cide[1] (mā′trə sīd′, măt′rə-), *n.* one who kills his mother. [t. L: m. s. *mātricīda.* See MATRI-, -CIDE[1]] —**ma′tri·cid′al,** *adj.*

ma·tri·cide[2] (mā′trə sīd′, măt′rə-), *n.* act of killing one's mother. [t. L: m.s. *mātricīdium.* See MATRI-, -CIDE[2]]

ma·tric·u·lant (mə trĭk′yə lənt), *n.* one who matriculates; a candidate for matriculation.

ma·tric·u·late (*v.* mə trĭk′yə lāt′; *n.* mə trĭk′yə lĭt), *v.*, **-lated, -lating,** *n.* —*v.t.* **1.** to enroll or admit to membership and privileges by enrolling, esp. in a college or university. —*v.i.* **2.** to be matriculated. —*n.* **3.** one who has been matriculated. [f. s. LL *mātrīcula*, dim. of *mātrix* public register, roll + -ATE[1]] —**ma·tric′u·la′tion,** *n.* —**ma·tric′u·la′tor,** *n.*

mat·ri·mo·ni·al (măt′rə mō′nĭ əl), *adj.* of or pertaining to matrimony; nuptial; connubial. —**mat′ri·mo′ni·al·ly,** *adv.*

mat·ri·mo·ny (măt′rə mō′nĭ), *n.*, *pl.* **-nies.** the rite, ceremony, or sacrament of marriage. [ME *matrimonye*, t. L: m. *mātrimōnium* marriage]

matrimony vine, any of the plants constituting the solanaceous genus *Lycium*, species of which are cultivated for their foliage, flowers, and berries; boxthorn.

ma·trix (mā′trĭks, măt′rĭks), *n.*, *pl.* **matrices** (mā′trĭ sēz′, măt′rĭ-), **matrixes. 1.** that which gives origin or form to a thing, or which serves to enclose it. **2.** *Anat.* a formative part, as the corium beneath a nail. **3.** *Biol.* the intercellular substance of a tissue. **4.** the womb. **5.** the rock in which a crystallized mineral is embedded. **6.** *Mining.* gangue. **7.** *Print.* **a.** a mold for casting type faces. **b.** mat[1] (def. 6). **8.** (in a punching machine) a perforated block upon which the object to be punched is rested. [t. L: breeding animal, LL womb, source]

ma·tron (mā′trən), *n.* **1.** a married woman, esp. one of ripe years and staid character or established position. **2.** a woman in charge of the feminine or domestic affairs of an institution or the like. [ME *matrone*, t. OF, t. L: m. *mātrōna* married woman] —**ma·tron·al** (mā′trən əl, măt′rən-), *adj.*

ma·tron·age (mā′trən ĭj, măt′rən-), *n.* **1.** state of being a matron. **2.** guardianship by a matron. **3.** matrons collectively.

ma·tron·ly (mā′trən lĭ), *adj.* **1.** like a matron, or having the characteristics of a matron. **2.** characteristic of or suitable for a matron. —**ma′tron·li·ness,** *n.*

matron of honor, a married woman acting as the principal attendant of the bride at a wedding.

Ma·tsu·ya·ma (mä′tsŏŏ yä′mä), *n.* a seaport in SW Japan, on Shikoku island. 127,367 (1946).

Matt., Matthew.

matte (măt), *n. Metall.* an unfinished metallic product of the smelting of certain sulfide ores, esp. those of copper. [t. F. See MAT[1]]

mat·ted[1] (măt′ĭd), *adj.* **1.** covered with a dense growth or a tangled mass. **2.** covered with mats or matting.

3. formed into a mat; entangled in a thick mass: *matted hair.* 4. formed of mats, or of plaited or woven material. [f. MAT¹ + -ED²]

mat·ted² (măt′ĭd), *adj.* having a dull finish. [f. MAT³ + -ED²]

Mat·te·ot·ti (mät′tĕ ôt′tē), *n.* **Giacomo** (jä′kō mō′), 1885–1924, Italian socialist leader.

mat·ter (măt′ər), *n.* **1.** the substance or substances of which physical objects consist or are composed. **2.** physical or corporeal substance in general (whether solid, liquid, or gaseous), esp. as distinguished from incorporeal substance (as spirit or mind), or from qualities, actions, etc. **3.** whatever occupies space. **4.** a particular kind of substance: *coloring matter.* **5.** some substance excreted by a living body, esp. pus. **6.** the material or substance of a discourse, book, etc., often as distinguished from the form. **7.** things written or printed: *printed matter.* **8.** a thing, affair, or business: *a matter of life and death.* **9.** an amount or extent reckoned approximately: *a matter of ten miles.* **10.** something of consequence: *it is no matter.* **11.** importance or significance: *what matter?* **12.** the trouble or difficulty (prec. by *the*): *there is nothing the matter.* **13.** ground, reason, or cause. **14.** *Philos.* that stuff which by integrative organization forms chemical substances and living things. In Aristotelian tradition *matter* is to *form* as *potentiality* to *actuality.* **15.** *Law.* statement or allegation. **16.** *Print.* **a.** material for work; copy. **b.** type set up. —*v.i.* **17.** to be of importance; signify: *it matters little.* **18.** to suppurate. [ME *matere,* t. OF. t. L: m.s. *māteria* stuff, material]
—**Syn. 1.** MATTER, MATERIAL, STUFF, SUBSTANCE refer to that of which physical objects are composed (though all these terms are also used abstractly). MATTER, as distinct from mind and spirit, is a broad word which applies to anything perceived, or known to be occupying space: *solid matter, gaseous matter.* MATERIAL usually means some definite kind, quality, or quantity of matter, esp. as intended for use: *woolen material, a house built of good materials.* STUFF, a less technical word, with approximately the same meanings as MATERIAL, is characterized by being of colloquial level when it refers to physical objects (*dynamite is queer stuff*), and of literary or poetic application when it is used abstractly (*the stuff that dreams are made of*). SUBSTANCE is the matter that composes a thing, thought of in relation to its essential properties: *a sticky substance.*

Mat·ter·horn (măt′ər hôrn′), *n.* a peak in the Pennine Alps on the Swiss-Italian border. 14,780 ft. French, **Mont Cervin.**

mat·ter-of-course (măt′ər əv kôrs′), *adj.* occurring or proceeding as if in the natural course of things.

mat·ter-of-fact (măt′ər əv făkt′), *adj.* adhering to actual facts; not imaginative; prosaic; commonplace.

Mat·thew (măth′ū), *n.* **1.** a customs collector at Capernaum summoned to be one of the twelve apostles. Matt. 9:9–13. **2.** the first Gospel in the New Testament. [t. F: m. *Mathieu,* t. LL: m. *Matthaeus,* t. Gk.: m. *Matthaios,* t. Heb: m. *Mattĭthyāh*]

Matthew of Paris, c1200–59, British chronicler.

Mat·thews (măth′ūz), *n.* **James Brander,** 1852–1929, U.S. scholar and author.

Matthew Walker, a kind of knot. See illus. under **knot.**

Mat·thi·as (mə thī′əs), *n.* a disciple chosen to take the place of Judas Iscariot as one of the apostles. Acts 1:23–26. [see MATTHEW]

mat·tin (măt′ĭn), *n., adj.* matin.

mat·ting¹ (măt′ĭng), *n.* **1.** a coarse fabric of rushes, grass, straw, hemp, or the like, used for covering floors, as a material for wrapping articles, etc. **2.** material for mats. [f. MAT¹ + -ING¹]

mat·ting² (măt′ĭng), *n.* a dull, slightly roughened surface, free from polish, produced by the use of the mat. [f. MAT³ + -ING¹]

mat·tock (măt′ək), *n.* an instrument for loosening the soil in digging, shaped like a pickax, but having one end broad instead of pointed. [ME *mattok,* OE *mattuc*]

mat·toid (măt′oid), *n.* a person of abnormal mentality bordering on insanity. [t. It.: m. *mattoide,* der. *matto* mad, g. L *mattus* intoxicated]

mat·trass (măt′rəs), *n. Chem.* matrass.

mat·tress (măt′rĭs), *n.* **1.** a case filled with hair, straw, cotton, etc., usually quilted or fastened together at intervals, used as or on a bed. **2.** a mat woven of brush, poles, or similar material used to prevent erosion of the surface of dikes, jetties, embankments, dams, etc. [ME *materas,* t. OF. t. It.: m. *materasso,* t. Ar.: m. (*al*-)*maṭraḥ* (the) mat, cushion]

mat·u·rate (măch′ŏŏ rāt′, măt′yŏŏ-), *v.i.* **-rated, -rating. 1.** to suppurate. **2.** to mature. [t. L: m.s. *māturātus,* pp., ripened] —**mat·u·ra·tive** (mə chŏŏr′ə tĭv, măch′ŏŏ rā′tĭv, măt′yŏŏ-), *adj.*

mat·u·ra·tion (măch′ŏŏ rā′shən, măt′yŏŏ-), *n.* **1.** act or process of maturating. **2.** *Biol.* the second phase of gametogenesis resulting in the production of mature eggs and sperms from oögonia and spermatogonia.

ma·ture (mə tyŏŏr′, -tŏŏr′), *adj., v.,* **-tured, -turing.** —*adj.* **1.** complete in natural growth or development, as plant and animal forms, cheese, wine, etc. **2.** ripe, as fruit. **3.** fully developed in body or mind, as a person. **4.** pertaining to or characteristic of full development: *a mature appearance.* **5.** completed, perfected, or elaborated in full by the mind: *mature plans.* **6.** *Com.* having reached the limit of its time; having become payable or due, as a note. **7.** *Med.* in a state of perfect sup-

puration. **8.** *Phys. Geog.* (of topographical features) exhibiting the stage of maximum stream development, as in the process of erosion of a land surface. —*v.t.* **9.** to make mature, esp. to ripen. **10.** to bring to full development. **11.** to complete or perfect. —*v.i.* **12.** to become mature, esp. to ripen. **13.** to come to full development. **14.** *Com.* to become due, as a note. [t. L: m.s. *māturus* ripe, timely, early] —**ma·ture′ly,** *adv.* —**ma·ture′ness,** *n.* —**Syn. 2.** See ripe.

ma·tu·ri·ty (mə tyŏŏr′ə tĭ, -tŏŏr′-), *n.* **1.** state of being mature; ripeness. **2.** full development; perfected condition. **3.** *Physiol.* period following attainment of full development of bodily structure and reproductive faculty. **4.** *Com.* **a.** state of being due. **b.** the time when a note or bill of exchange becomes due.

ma·tu·ti·nal (mə tŭ′tə nəl, -tōō′-), *adj.* pertaining to or occurring in the morning; early in the day. [t. L: s. *mātūtinālis* of the morning] —**ma·tu′ti·nal·ly,** *adv.*

matz·o (mät′sō), *n., pl.* **matzoth** (mät′sōth), **matzos** (mät′sōs). a cake of unleavened bread, eaten by Jews during the Feast of Passover. [t. Heb.: m. *matstsāh* cake of unleavened bread]

Mau·beuge (mō bœzh′), *n.* a city in N France, on the Sambre river, near the Belgian border. 20,859 (1946).

maud (môd), *n.* **1.** a gray woolen plaid worn by shepherds and others in S Scotland. **2.** a rug or wrap of like material, used in traveling.

maud·lin (môd′lĭn), *adj.* **1.** tearfully or weakly emotional or sentimental. **2.** tearfully or emotionally silly from drink. [from *Maudlin,* familiar var. of *Magdalen* (Mary Magdalene), often represented in art as weeping] —**maud′lin·ly,** *adv.* —**maud′lin·ness,** *n.*

Maugham (môm), *n.* **William Somerset,** born 1874, British novelist, dramatist, and short-story writer.

mau·gre (mô′gər), *prep. Archaic.* in spite of; notwithstanding. Also, **mau′ger.** [ME *maugre,* t. OF: prop., ill will, spite. See MAL-, GREE²]

Ma·u·i (mä′ŏŏ ē′, mou′ē), *n.* one of the Hawaiian Islands, in the central part of the group. 40,317 pop. (prelim. 1950); 728 sq. mi.

maul (môl), *n.* **1.** a heavy hammer, as for driving piles. **2.** *Obs.* a heavy club or mace. —*v.t.* **3.** to handle or use roughly. **4.** *U.S.* to split with a maul and a wedge, as a rail. **5.** *Obs. except Archaic and Hist.* to beat with or as with a maul. [var. of MALL] —**maul′er,** *n.*

Maul·main (môl mān′, môl-), *n.* Moulmein.

maul·stick (môl′stĭk′), *n.* mahlstick.

Mau·na Ke·a (mou′nə kā′ə, mô′nə kē′ə), an extinct volcano on the island of Hawaii. 13,825 ft.

Mau·na Lo·a (mou′nə lō′ə, mô′nə lō′ə), an active volcano on the island of Hawaii. 13,675 ft.

maund (mônd), *n.* a unit of weight in India and other parts of Asia, varying greatly according to place: in India, from about 25 to 82.286 pounds (the latter being the government maund). [t. Hind., Pers.: m. *mān*]

maun·der (môn′dər), *v.i.* **1.** to talk in a rambling, foolish or imbecile way. **2.** to move, go, or act in an aimless, confused manner. —**maun′der·er,** *n.*

Maun·dy Thursday (môn′dĭ), the Thursday of Holy Week, commemorating Jesus′ last supper and His washing of the disciples′ feet upon that day. [ME *maunde,* t. OF: m. *mande,* t. L: m.s. *mandātum* a command, mandate. See John 13:5, 14, 34]

Mau·pas·sant (mō pȧ säN′), *n.* **(Henri René Albert) Guy de** (äN rē′ rə nā′ ȧl bĕr′ gē də), 1850–93, French short-story writer and novelist.

Mau·re·ta·ni·a (môr′ə tā′nĭ ə), *n.* an ancient kingdom in NW Africa: it included the territory that is modern Morocco and part of Algeria. Also, **Mauritania.**

Mau·rice (môr′ĭs, mŏr′ĭs), *n.* 1521–53, elector of Saxony.

Maurice of Nassau, 1567–1625, Dutch statesman.

Mau·ri·ta·ni·a (môr′ə tā′nĭ ə), *n.* a colony in the NW part of French West Africa. 347,000 pop. (1940); 322,390 sq. mi. **2.** Mauretania.

Mau·ri·tius (mô rĭsh′əs, -rĭsh′ĭ əs), *n.* **1.** an island in the Indian Ocean, E of Madagascar. 403,718 pop. (est. 1938); 720 sq. mi. **2.** a British colony consisting of this island and dependencies. 426,000 pop.; 809 sq. mi. *Cap.:* Port Louis.

Mau·rois (mō rwȧ′), *n.* **André** (äN drē′), (*Emile Herzog*) born 1885, French biographer and novelist.

mau·so·le·um (mô′sə lē′əm), *n., pl.* **-leums, -lea** (-lē′ə). **1.** a stately and magnificent tomb. **2.** (*cap.*) a magnificent tomb erected at Halicarnassus in Asia Minor in 350 B.C. See **Seven Wonders of the World.** [t. L, t. Gk.: m. *mausoleĭon* the tomb of Mausolus (king of Caria)] —**mau′so·le′an,** *adj.*

mauve (mōv), *n.* **1.** pale bluish-purple. **2.** a purple dye obtained from aniline discovered in 1856, the first of the coal-tar dyes. —*adj.* **3.** of the color of mauve: *a mauve dress.* [t. F: orig., mallow, g. L *malva* MALLOW]

mav·er·ick (măv′ər ĭk), *n. U.S.* **1.** (in cattle-raising regions) **a.** an animal found without an owner′s brand. **b.** a calf separated from its dam. **2.** a dissenter. [prob. named after Samuel *Maverick,* a Texas cattle raiser who neglected to brand his cattle]

ma·vis (mā′vĭs), *n.* the European throstle or song thrush, *Turdus philomelus.* [ME *mavys,* t. OF: m. *mauvis;* of Celtic orig.]

ma·vour·neen (mə vŏŏr′nēn, -vōr′-), *n. Irish.* my darling. Also, **ma·vour′nin.** [t. Irish: m. *mo mhuirnin*]

---

b., blend of, blended; c., cognate with; d., dialect, dialectal; der., derived from; f., formed from; g., going back to; m., modification of; r., replacing; s., stem of; t., taken from; ?, perhaps. See the full key on inside cover.

maw (mô), *n.* **1.** the mouth, throat, or gullet as concerned in devouring (now chiefly of animals or in figurative use). **2.** the crop or craw of a fowl. **3.** the stomach. [ME *mawe*, OE *maga*, c. G *magen*]

mawk·ish (mô′kĭsh), *adj.* **1.** sickish or slightly nauseating. **2.** characterized by sickly sentimentality. [f. *mawk* maggot (t. Scand.; cf. Icel. *madhkr*) + -ISH[1]] —**mawk′ish·ly**, *adv.* —**mawk′ish·ness**, *n.*

Maw·son (mô′sən), *n.* **Sir Douglas,** born 1882, Australian Antarctic explorer, born in England.

max., maximum.

max·il·la (măk sĭl′ə), *n.,* *pl.* -sillae (-sĭl′ē). **1.** a jaw or jawbone, esp. the upper. **2.** one of the paired appendages immediately behind the mandibles of arthropods. [t. L: jaw]

max·il·lar·y (măk′sə lĕr′ĭ, măk sĭl′ə rĭ), *adj.,* *n.,* *pl.* -laries. —*adj.* **1.** of or pertaining to a jaw, jawbone, or maxilla. —*n.* **2.** a maxilla or maxillary bone.

Inferior maxillary or lower jaw bone of man A. Symphisis; B. Ramus; C. Angle of jaw; D. Ascending ramus; E. Coronoid process; F. Condyle.

max·im (măk′sĭm), *n.* **1.** an expression, esp. an aphoristic or sententious one, of a general truth, esp. as to conduct. **2.** a principle of conduct. [ME *maxime*, t. OF, t. L: m. *maxima* (*prōpositio*), lit., greatest (proposition)] —**Syn. 1.** See **proverb.**

Max·im (măk′sĭm), *n.* **1. Sir Hiram Stevens,** 1840–1916, British inventor of a machine gun. **2.** his brother, **Hudson,** 1853–1927, U.S. inventor.

max·i·ma (măk′sə mə), *n.* pl. of **maximum.**

max·i·mal (măk′sə məl), *adj.* pertaining to or being a maximum; greatest possible; highest. —**max′i·mal·ly,** *adv.*

Max·i·mal·ist (măk′sə məl ĭst), *n.* a member of an extremist group or faction of socialists, as of a faction of the Russian Social Revolutionary party.

Max·i·mil·ian (măk′sə mĭl′yən), *n.* **1.** 1832–67, archduke of Austria and emperor of Mexico, 1804-67.

Maximilian I, 1459–1519, emperor of the Holy Roman Empire, 1493–1519.

Maximilian II, 1527–76, emperor of the Holy Roman Empire, 1564–76.

max·im·ite (măk′sə mīt′), *n.* a powerful explosive consisting largely of picric acid. [named after Hudson MAXIM (1853–1927), U.S. inventor. See -ITE[1]]

max·i·mize (măk′sə mīz′), *v.t.,* -mized, -mizing. to increase to the greatest possible amount or degree. [f. s. L *maximus* greatest + -IZE] —**max′i·mi·za′tion,** *n.* —**max′i·miz′er,** *n.*

max·i·mum (măk′sə məm), *n.,* *pl.* -ma (-mə), -mums, *adj.* —*n.* **1.** the greatest quantity or amount possible, assignable, allowable, etc.; the highest amount, value, or degree attained or recorded (opposed to *minimum*). **2.** *Math.* a value of a function at a certain point which is not exceeded in the immediate vicinity of that point. —*adj.* **3.** that is a maximum; greatest possible; highest. **4.** pertaining to a maximum or maximums. [t. L, neut. of *maximus* greatest]

maximum likelihood estimation, *Statistics.* a method of estimating population characteristics from a sample by choosing the values of the parameters which will maximize the probability of getting the particular sample actually obtained from the population.

Max Mul·ler (măks mŭl′ər; *Ger.* măks mY′lər), **Frie′drich.** See **Müller, Friedrich Max.**

Max·well (măks′wĕl), *n.* **James Clerk.** See **Clerk-Maxwell.**

max·well (măks′wĕl), *n.* *Elect.* a unit of magnetic flux, being the flux through a square centimeter in a field in air whose intensity is one gauss. [named after James C. *Maxwell*, 1831–1879, British physicist]

may (mā), *v.,* *pres.* **1.** may, **2.** (*Archaic*) **mayest** or **mayst, 3.** may, *pl.* may; *pret.* **might. 1.** used as an auxiliary to express: **a.** possibility, opportunity, or permission: *you may enter.* **b.** wish or prayer: *may you live long.* **c.** contingency, esp. in clauses expressing condition, concession, purpose, result, etc. **d.** *Archaic.* ability or power (more commonly *can*). **2.** *Law.* (in a statute) must (when used not to confer a favor, but to impose a duty). [OE *mæg*, 1st and 3rd pers. sing. pres. ind. of *magan*, c. G *mögen*] —**Syn. 1.** See **can[1].**

May (mā), *n.* **1.** the fifth month of the year, containing 31 days. **2.** the early part of springtime, as of life. **3.** the festivities of May Day. **4.** (*l.c.*) *Brit.* the hawthorn. **5. Cape,** a cape at the SE tip of New Jersey, on Delaware Bay. —*v.i.* **6.** to gather flowers in the spring: *to go a maying.* [ME; OE *Maius*, t. L]

Ma·ya (mä′yə), *n.* **1.** a member of an aboriginal people of Yucatán which had attained a relatively high civilization before the discovery of America. **2.** the historical and modern language of the Mayas, of Mayan stock.

Ma·ya·güez (mä′yä gwĕs′), *n.* a seaport in W Puerto Rico. 58,744 (prelim. 1950).

Ma·yan (mä′yən), *adj.* **1.** of or pertaining to the Mayas. —*n.* **2.** a member of the Mayan tribe. **3.** a linguistic stock of southern Mexico, Guatemala, and British Honduras, including Maya and Quiche, and probably related to Penutian.

May apple, 1. an American perennial herb, *Podophyllum peltatum*, bearing an edible, yellowish, egg-shaped fruit. **2.** the fruit.

may·be (mā′bĭ, -bē), *adv.* perhaps. [short for *it may be*]

May Day, the first day of May, long celebrated with various festivities, as the crowning of the May queen, dancing round the Maypole, etc., and, in recent years, often marked by labor parades, etc.

May·day (mā′dā′), *n.* (according to international radio regulations) the radio telephonic distress signal used by ships or aircraft. [t. F: alter. of *m'aidez* help me]

Ma·yence (mà yäns′), *n.* French name of **Mainz.**

May·fair (mā′fâr′), *n.* a fashionable locality in London, England, E of Hyde Park.

May·flow·er (mā′flou′ər), *n.* **1.** the ship in which the Pilgrim Fathers sailed from Southampton to the New World in 1620. **2.** any of various plants whose flowers blossom in May: **a.** (in the U.S.) chiefly the trailing arbutus, hepatica, and anemone. **b.** (in England) the hawthorn, cowslip, etc.

Mayflower compact, an agreement to establish a government, entered into by the Pilgrims in the cabin of the Mayflower, November 12, 1620.

May fly, 1. any of the *Ephemerida*, an order of delicate-winged insects having the fore wings much larger than the hind wings, the larvae being aquatic, and the winged adults being very short-lived; an ephemerid. **2.** an artificial fly made in imitation of this fly.

may·hap (mā′hăp′, mā′hăp), *adv.* *Archaic.* perhaps. [short for *it may hap*]

may·hem (mā′hĕm, mā′əm), *n.* *Law.* the crime of violently inflicting a bodily injury rendering a man less able to defend himself or to annoy his adversary (now often extended by statute to include any willful mutilation of another's body). Also, **maihem.** [ME *maheym*, t. AF, var. of OF *mahaigne* injury. See MAIM]

May·ing (mā′ĭng), *n.* the celebration of May Day.

May·o (mā′ō), *n.* **1. Charles Horace,** 1865–1939, U.S. surgeon. **2.** his brother, **William James,** 1861–1939, U.S. surgeon. **3.** a county in NW Eire, in Connaught province, 150,985 pop. (est. 1943); 2084 sq. mi. *Co. seat:* Castlebar.

Ma·yon (mä yôn′), *n.* an active volcano in the Philippine Islands, on SE Luzon island. ab. 8000 ft.

may·on·naise (mā′ə nāz′), *n.* a thick dressing of egg yolks, vinegar or lemon juice, seasonings, and oil, used for salads or vegetables. [t. F: earlier *magnonaise, mahonnaise*, ult. der. *Mahon*, a Pr. port]

may·or (mā′ər, mâr), *n.* the principal officer of a municipality; the chief magistrate of a city or borough. [ME *maire*, t. F, g. L *mājor* greater. Cf. MAJOR] —**may′-or·ship′,** *n.*

may·or·al·ty (mā′ər əl tĭ, mâr′əl-), *n.,* *pl.* -ties. **1.** the office of a mayor. **2.** his period of service.

may·or·ess (mā′ər ĭs, mâr′ĭs), *n.* **1.** *U.S.* a woman mayor. **2.** *Brit.* the wife of a mayor.

Ma·yotte (mà yōt′), *n.* one of the Comoro Islands, in the Indian Ocean, NW of Madagascar. 17,477 pop. (1936); 143 sq. mi.

May·pole (mā′pōl′), *n.* a high pole, decorated with flowers or ribbons, for the merrymakers to dance round at May Day (or May) festivities. Also, **may′pole′.**

may·pop (mā′pŏp′), *n.* **1.** the edible fruit of a passion flower, *Passiflora incarnata*, of the southern U.S. **2.** the plant itself. [? repr. a Virginia var. of Algonquian *maracock*]

May queen, a girl or young woman crowned with flowers and honored as queen in the sports of May Day.

mayst (māst), *v.* *Archaic.* 2nd pers. sing. indic. of **may.**

May·time (mā′tīm′), *n.* the month of May. Also, **May·tide** (mā′tīd′).

may tree, *Brit.* the hawthorn.

may·weed (mā′wēd′), *n.* a composite herb, *Anthemis Cotula*, native in Europe and Asia, and naturalized in America, having pungent, ill-scented foliage, and flower heads with a yellow disk and white rays. [f. obs. *mayth* mayweed (OE *mægtha*) + WEED[1], with loss of -*th*]

May·wood (mā′wŏŏd), *n.* a city in NE Illinois, near Chicago. 27,473 (1950).

Maz·a·rin (măz′ə rĭn, măz′ə rēn′; *Fr.* mà zà răn′), *n.* **Jules** (zhYl), (*Giulio Mazarini*) 1602–61, French cardinal and statesman, born in Italy; chief minister of Louis XIV, 1642–61.

Ma·zat·lán (mä′sät län′), *n.* a seaport in W Mexico, in Sinaloa state. 32,117 (1940).

Maz·da·ism (măz′də ĭz′əm), *n.* Zoroastrianism. Also, **Maz/de·ism.**

maze (māz), *n.,* *v.,* **mazed, mazing.** —*n.* **1.** a confusing network of intercommunicating paths or passages; a labyrinth. **2.** a state of bewilderment or confusion. **3.** a winding movement, as in dancing. [ME; der. MAZE, v.] —*v.t.* **4.** *Archaic or Dial.* to stupefy or daze. [ME *mase*(*n*); aphetic var. of AMAZE] —**maze′ment,** *n.* —**maze′like′,** *adj.*

ma·zur·ka (mə zûr′kə, -zŏŏr′-), *n.* **1.** a lively Polish dance in moderately quick triple rhythm. **2.** music for, or in the rhythm of, this dance. Also, **ma·zour′ka.** [t. Pol.: woman of Mazovia (district in Poland)]

ma·zy (mā′zĭ), *adj.,* -zier, -ziest. mazelike; full of intricate windings. —**ma′zi·ly,** *adv.* —**ma′zi·ness,** *n.*

maz·zard (măz′ərd), *n.* a wild sweet cherry, *Prunus Avium*, used as a rootstock for cultivated varieties of cherries. [earlier *mazer*. Cf. obs. *mazers* spots, measles]

ăct, āble, dâre, ärt; ĕbb, ēqual; Yf, īce; hŏt, ōver, ôrder, oil, bŏŏk, ōōze, out; ŭp, ūse, ûrge; ə = a in alone; ch, chief; g, give; ng, ring; sh, shoe; th, thin; ŧh, that; zh, vision. See the full key on inside cover.

Maz·zi·ni (mät tsē′nē, mäd dzē′-), *n.* **Giuseppe** (jōō-zĕp′pĕ), 1805–72, Italian patriot and revolutionist.
M.B., *Chiefly Brit.* (L *Medicinae Baccalaureus*) Bachelor of Medicine.
M.B.A., Master of Business Administration.
Mc-, Mac.
M.C., 1. Master ′Commandant. 2. Master of Ceremonies. 3. Member of Congress.
Mc·Clel·lan (mə klĕl′ən), *n.* **George Brinton,** 1826–85, Union general in the U.S. Civil War.
Mc·Cor·mack (mə kôr′mĭk), *n.* **John,** 1884–1945, Irish-American tenor singer.
Mc·Cor·mick (mə kôr′mĭk), *n.* 1. **Cyrus Hall,** 1809–1884, U.S. inventor (of harvesting machinery). 2. **Robert Rutherford,** born 1880, U.S. newspaper publisher.
Mc·Coy (mə koi′), *n.* **the real,** the best of its kind.
Mc·Dow·ell (mək dou′əl), *n.* **Irvin,** 1818–85, Union general in the U.S. Civil War.
Mc·Guf·fey (mə gŭf′ĭ), *n.* **William Holmes,** 1800–73, U.S. educator: editor of *McGuffey's Readers.*
Mc·Hen·ry (mək hĕn′rĭ), *n.* **Fort,** a former U.S. fort in N Maryland at the entrance to Baltimore harbor: unsuccessfully bombarded by the British, 1814, during which Key wrote *The Star Spangled Banner.*
Mc·In·tosh (măk′ĭn tŏsh′), *n. Hort.* a high quality, red eating apple that ripens in early autumn.
Mc·Kees·port (mə kēz′pōrt), *n.* a city in SW Pennsylvania, near Pittsburgh. 51,502 (1950).
Mc·Kin·ley (mə kĭn′lĭ), 1. **William,** 1843–1901, 25th president of the U.S., 1897–1901. 2. **Mount,** a mountain in central Alaska: the highest peak of North America. 20,300 ft.
Mc·Mas·ter (mək măs′tər, -mäs′tər), *n.* **John Bach,** 1852–1932, U.S. historian.
Mc·Nutt (mək nŭt′), *n.* **Paul Vories** (vōr′ēz), born 1891, U.S. public official.
Md., Maryland.
M.D., (L *Medicinae Doctor*) Doctor of Medicine.
M-day (ĕm′dā′), *n. Mil.* mobilization day; a day assumed by the War Department as the first day of mobilization, used by the military for planning purposes.
Mdme., *pl.* **Mdmes.** *Brit.* Madame. [F]
M.D.S., Master of Dental Surgery.
mdse., merchandise.
me (mē; *unstressed* mĭ), *pers.pron.* objective case of the pronoun I. [ME *me,* OE *mē mē,* dat. sing. (c. D *mig,* G *mir*): akin to L *mē* (acc.), etc.]
ME, Middle English. Also, **M.E.**
Me, *Chem.* methyl.
Me., Maine.
M.E., 1. Master of Engineering. 2. Mechanical Engineer. 3. Methodist Episcopal. 4. Middle English. 5. Mining Engineer.
mead[1] (mēd), *n. Poetic.* a meadow. [ME *mede,* OE *mǣd.* See MEADOW]
mead[2] (mēd), *n.* 1. an alcoholic liquor made by fermenting a mixture of honey and water. 2. any of various nonalcoholic beverages. [ME *mede,* OE *medu,* c. G *met*]
Mead (mēd), *n.* **Lake,** a lake made by Hoover Dam in the Colorado river, in NW Arizona and SE Nevada: largest artificial lake in world. 115 mi. long; 227 sq. mi.
Meade (mēd), *n.* **George Gordon,** 1815–72, Union general in the U.S. Civil War.
mead·ow (mĕd′ō), *n.* 1. a piece of grassland, whether used for the raising of hay or for pasture. 2. a low, level tract of uncultivated ground, as along a river, producing coarse grass. [ME *medwe,* OE *mǣdw-,* in inflectional forms of *mǣd* (cf. MEAD[1]); akin to G *matte*]
meadow grass, any grass of the genus *Poa,* esp. *P. pratensis,* the Kentucky bluegrass.
meadow lark, a common American songbird of the genus *Sturnella* (family *Icteridae*) esp. the **eastern meadow lark,** *S. magna,* and **western meadow lark,** *S. neglecta,* both of which are robust, yellow-breasted birds about the size of the American robin.
meadow rue, any plant of the ranunculaceous genus *Thalictrum,* having leaves resembling those of rue, esp. (in North America) *T. dioicum* (**early meadow rue**).
mead·ow·sweet (mĕd′ō swēt′), *n. Brit.* 1. any plant of the rosaceous genus *Spiraea,* esp. *S. latifolia,* a low shrub with white or pink flowers. 2. any plant of the closely related genus *Filipendula* (or *Ulmaria*).
mead·ow·y (mĕd′ō ĭ), *adj.* pertaining to, resembling, or consisting of meadow.
mea·ger (mē′gər), *adj.* 1. deficient in quantity or quality, or without fullness or richness. 2. having little flesh, lean, or thin. 3. maigre. Also, **mea′gre.** [ME *megre,* t. OF: m. *maigre,* g. L *macer* lean] —**mea′ger·ly,** *adv.* —**mea′ger·ness,** *n.* —Syn. 1. See **scanty.**
meal[1] (mēl), *n.* 1. one of the regular repasts of the day, as breakfast, dinner, or supper. 2. the food eaten or served for a repast. [ME; OE *mǣl* measure, fixed time, occasion, meal, c. G *mal* time, *mahl* meal]
meal[2] (mēl), *n.* 1. the edible part of any grain (now usually excluding wheat) ground into a (coarse) powder and unbolted. 2. *U.S.* coarse, unbolted grain, cornmeal, or Indian meal. 3. any ground or powdery substance, as of nuts or seeds, resembling this. [ME *mele,* OE *melu,* c. G *mehl*]
meal·time (mēl′tīm′), *n.* the usual time for a meal.

meal worm, the larva of the beetle, *Tenebrio molitor,* which infests granaries. It is raised in great numbers as food for birds and animals.
meal·y (mē′lĭ), *adj.,* **mealier, mealiest.** 1. having the qualities of meal; powdery; soft, dry, and crumbly: *mealy potatoes.* 2. of the nature of, or containing, meal; farinaceous. 3. covered with or as with meal or powder. 4. flecked as if with meal, or spotty. 5. pale, as the complexion. 6. mealy-mouthed. —**meal′i·ness,** *n.*
meal·y-mouthed (mē′lĭ mouťhd′, -moutħ′), *adj.* 1. avoiding the use of plain terms, as from timidity, excessive delicacy, or hypocrisy. 2. using soft words.
mean[1] (mēn), *v.,* **meant, meaning.** —*v.t.* 1. to have in the mind as in intention or purpose (often with an infinitive as object): *I mean to talk to him.* 2. to intend for a particular purpose, destination, etc.: *they were meant for each other.* 3. to intend to express or indicate: *By "liberal" I mean . . . .* 4. (of words, things, etc.) to have as the signification; signify. —*v.i.* 5. to be minded or disposed; have intentions: *he means well.* [ME *mene*(n), OE *mǣnan,* c. G *meinen*] —Syn. 1. purpose, contemplate. See **intend.** 4. import; denote, indicate.
mean[2] (mēn), *adj.* 1. inferior in grade, quality, or character. 2. low in station, rank, or dignity. 3. of little importance or consequence. 4. unimposing or shabby: *a mean abode.* 5. without moral dignity; small-minded or ignoble: *mean motives.* 6. penurious, stingy, or miserly: *a man who is mean about money.* 7. *U.S. Colloq.* pettily offensive or unaccommodating; nasty. 8. *U.S. Colloq.* small, humiliated, or ashamed: *to feel mean over some ungenerous action.* 9. *U.S. Colloq.* in poor physical condition. 10. *U.S. Colloq.* troublesome or vicious, as a horse. [ME *mene,* aphetic var. of *imene,* OE *gemǣne,* c. G *gemein* common]
—Syn. 2. common, humble. 3. insignificant, petty, paltry. 5. contemptible, despicable. MEAN, LOW, BASE, SORDID, and VILE all refer to ignoble characteristics worthy of dislike, contempt, or disgust. MEAN suggests pettiness and small-mindedness and vulgarity: *to take a mean advantage.* LOW suggests coarseness and vulgarity: *low company.* BASE suggests selfish cowardice or moral depravity: *base motives.* SORDID suggests a wretched uncleanness, or sometimes an avariciousness without dignity or moral scruples: *a sordid slum, sordid gain.* VILE suggests disgusting foulness or repulsiveness: *a vile insinuation, a vile creature.* 6. niggardly; close. —Ant. 1. noble, admirable. 2. lofty. 5. generous.
mean[3] (mēn), *n.* 1. (*usually pl.*) an agency, instrumentality, method, etc., used to attain an end: *there are no means that he will not resort to;* (often with sense and construction of *sing.*) *a means of communication.* 2. (*pl.*) disposable resources, esp. pecuniary resources: *to live beyond one's means.* 3. (*pl.*) considerable pecuniary resources: *a man of means.* 4. something intermediate; that which is midway between two extremes. 5. *Math.* a. a quantity having a value intermediate between the values of other quantities; an average, esp. the arithmetical mean. b. either the second or third term in a proportion of four terms. 6. *Logic.* the middle term in a syllogism. 7. **by all means, a.** at any cost; without fail. b. (in emphasis) certainly: *go, by all means.* 8. **by any means,** in any way; at all. 9. **by no means, a.** in no way; not at all: *a thing by no means certain.* b. on no account; certainly not: *a practice by no means to be recommended.* —*adj.* 10. occupying a middle position or an intermediate place. 11. intermediate in kind, quality, degree, time, etc. [ME *mene,* t. OF: m. *meien,* g. LL *mediānus* in the middle] —Syn. 10. middling; intermediate; average, medium, moderate.
me·an·der (mĭ ăn′dər), *v.i.* 1. to proceed by a winding course. 2. to wander aimlessly. —*n.* 3. (*usually pl.*) a turning or winding; a winding path or course. 4. a circuitous movement or journey. 5. an intricate variety of fret or fretwork. [t. L, t. Gk.: m. *maiandros* a winding, orig. the name of a winding river (now Mendere) in western Asia Minor] —**me·an′der·ing·ly,** *adv.* —Syn. 2. See **stroll.**
mean distance, the arithmetic mean of the greatest and least distances of a planet from the sun, called the semimajor axis, and used in stating the size of an orbit.
mean·ing (mē′nĭng), *n.* 1. that which is intended to be, or actually is, expressed or indicated; signification; import. —*adj.* 2. intending. 3. expressive or significant: *a meaning look.* —**mean′ing·ly,** *adv.*
—Syn. 1. tenor, gist, drift, trend. MEANING, PURPORT, SENSE, SIGNIFICANCE denote that which is expressed or indicated by something. MEANING is the general word denoting that which is intended to be or actually is expressed or indicated: *the meaning of a word or glance.* SENSE may be used to denote a particular meaning (among others) of a word or phrase: *the word has become obsolete in this sense.* SENSE may also be used loosely to refer to "intelligible meaning": *there's no sense in what he says.* SIGNIFICANCE refers particularly to a meaning that is implied rather than expressed (*the significance of her glance*); or to a meaning the importance of which may not be easy to perceive immediately: *the real significance of his words was not grasped at the time.* PURPORT is mainly limited to the meaning of a formal document, of a speech, of a particularly important conversation, etc., and refers to the gist, the general meaning of something fairly complicated: *the purport of his letter to the editor.* 3. See **expressive.**
mean·ing·ful (mē′nĭng fəl), *adj.* full of meaning; significant.
mean·ing·less (mē′nĭng lĭs), *adj.* without meaning or significance. —**mean′ing·less·ly,** *adv.* —**mean′ing·less·ness,** *n.*

mean·ly (mēn′lĭ), *adv.* in a mean manner; poorly; basely; stingily. [f. MEAN² + -LY]

mean·ness (mēn′nĭs), *n.* 1. state or quality of being mean. 2. a mean act.

mean noon, *Astron.* the moment when the mean sun's center crosses the meridian.

mean solar time, *Astron.* time measured by the hour angle of the mean sun. Also, **mean time.**

means test, *Brit.* an inquiry into the income of a person who receives unemployment relief.

mean sun, *Astron.* an imaginary and fictitious sun moving uniformly in the celestial equator and taking the same time to make its annual circuit as the true sun does in the ecliptic.

meant (měnt), *v.* pt. and pp. of **mean¹.**

mean·time (mēn′tīm′), *n.* 1. the intervening time. —*adv.* 2. in the intervening time; during the interval; at the same time. Also, **mean·while** (mēn′hwīl′).

mea·sled (mē′zəld), *adj.* affected with measles (def. 3).

mea·sles (mē′zəlz), *n.* 1. an acute infectious disease occurring mostly in children, characterized by catarrhal and febrile symptoms and an eruption of small red spots; rubeola. 2. any of certain other eruptive diseases, as rubella (**German measles**). 3. a disease in swine and other animals caused by the larvae of certain tapeworms of the genus *Taenia.* 4. (*pl.*) the larvae which cause measles. [partly ME *maseles*, c. D *mazelen*, akin to G *masern* measles, pl. of *maser* spot; partly ME *mesels*, pl. of *mesel*, akin to OHG *māsa* spot]

mea·sly (mē′zlĭ), *adj.*, **-slier, -sliest. 1.** infected with measles, as an animal or its flesh. **2.** pertaining to or resembling measles. **3.** *Slang.* wretchedly poor or unsatisfactory.

meas·ur·a·ble (mězh′ər ə bəl), *adj.* that may be measured. —**meas′ur·a·bil′i·ty, meas′ur·a·ble·ness,** *n.* —**meas′ur·a·bly,** *adv.*

meas·ure (mězh′ər), *n., v.,* **-ured, -uring.** —*n.* **1.** act or process of ascertaining the extent, dimensions, quantity, etc., of something, esp. by comparison with a standard. **2.** size, dimensions, quantity, etc., as thus ascertained. **3.** an instrument, as a graduated rod or a vessel of standard capacity, for measuring. **4.** a unit or standard of measurement. **5.** a definite or known quantity measured out. **6.** a system of measurement. **7.** any standard of comparison, estimation, or judgment. **8.** a quantity, degree, or proportion. **9.** a limit, or an extent or degree not to be exceeded: *to know no measure.* **10.** reasonable bounds or limits: *beyond measure.* **11.** a legislative bill or enactment. **12.** an action or procedure intended as a means to an end: *to take measures to avert suspicion.* **13.** a short rhythmical movement or arrangement, as in poetry or music. **14.** a particular kind of such arrangement. **15.** a metrical unit. **16.** *Poetic.* an air or melody. **17.** *Archaic.* a slow, stately dance or dance movement. **18.** *Music, etc.* the music contained between two bar lines; bar. **19.** (*pl.*) *Geol.* beds; strata. —*v.t.* **20.** to ascertain the extent, dimensions, quantity, capacity, etc., of, esp. by comparison with a standard.

M, Measure (def. 18)

21. to mark or lay off or out, or deal out, with reference to measure (often fol. by *off* or *out*). **22.** to estimate the relative amount, value, etc., of, by comparison with some standard. **23.** to judge of or appraise by comparison with something else. **24.** to serve as the measure of. **25.** to adjust or proportion. **26.** to bring into comparison or competition. **27.** to travel over or traverse. —*v.i.* **28.** to take measurements. **29.** to admit of measurement. **30.** to be of a specified measure. [ME *mesure(n)*, t. OF: m. *mesurer*, g. L *mensūrāre*] —**meas′ur·er,** *n.*

meas·ured (mězh′ərd), *adj.* **1.** ascertained or apportioned by measure. **2.** accurately regulated or proportioned. **3.** regular or uniform, as in movement; rhythmical. **4.** deliberate and restrained: *measured speech.* **5.** in the form of meter or verse; metrical. —**meas′ured·ly,** *adv.*

Measure for Measure, a comedy (1604) by Shakespeare.

meas·ure·less (mězh′ər lĭs), *adj.* without bounds; unlimited; immeasurable: *caverns measureless to man.* —**meas′ure·less·ly,** *adv.* —**meas′ure·less·ness,** *n.*

meas·ure·ment (mězh′ər mənt), *n.* **1.** act of measuring. **2.** an ascertained dimension. **3.** extent, size, etc., ascertained by measuring. **4.** a system of measuring or of measures.

measuring worm, the larva of any geometrid moth, which progresses by bringing the rear end of the body forward and then advancing the front end.

meat (mēt), *n.* **1.** the flesh of animals as used for food. **2.** food in general: *meat and drink.* **3.** the edible part of anything, as a fruit, nut, etc. **4.** the principal meal: *to say grace before meat.* [ME and OE *mete*, c. OHG *maz*] —**meat′less,** *adj.*

me·a·tus (mĭ ā′təs), *n., pl.* **-tuses, -tus.** *Anat.* an opening or foramen, esp. in a bone or bony structure, as the opening of the ear, nose, etc. See diag. under **ear.** [t. L: passage]

meat·y (mē′tĭ), *adj.,* **meatier, meatiest. 1.** of or like meat. **2.** abounding in meat. **3.** full of substance; pithy.

Mec·ca (měk′ə), *n.* **1.** a city in W Saudi Arabia: the capital of Hejaz; one of the two federal capitals; the birthplace of Mohammed, and spiritual center of Islam. **2.** any center or goal for many people. —**Mec′can,** *adj., n.*

mech., **1.** mechanical. **2.** mechanics. **3.** mechanism.

me·chan·ic (mə kăn′ĭk), *n.* **1.** a skilled worker with tools or machines. **2.** one who repairs machinery. [late ME, t. L: s. *mēchanicus*, t. Gk.: m. *mēchanikós* of machines]

me·chan·i·cal (mə kăn′ə kəl), *adj.* **1.** having to do with machinery. **2.** of the nature of a device or contrivance for controlling or utilizing material forces, or of a mechanism or machine. **3.** acting or operated by means of such a contrivance, or of a mechanism or machine. **4.** produced by such means. **5.** acting or performed without spontaneity, spirit, individuality, etc. **6.** belonging or pertaining to the subject matter of mechanics. **7.** pertaining to, or controlled or effected by, physical forces. **8.** explaining phenomena as due to mechanical action or the material forces of the universe, as philosophical theories or their advocates. **9.** subordinating the spiritual to the material; materialistic. **10.** involving the material objects or physical conditions: *hindered by mechanical difficulties.* **11.** pertaining to or concerned with the use of tools and the like, or the contrivance and construction of machines or mechanisms. **12.** pertaining to or concerned with manual labor or skill. **13.** exhibiting skill in the use of tools and the like, in the contrivance of machines, etc.: *a mechanical genius.* —**me·chan′i·cal·ly,** *adv.* —**me·chan′i·cal·ness,** *n.*

mechanical drawing, drawing, as of machinery, done with the aid of rulers, scales, compasses, etc.

mech·a·ni·cian (měk′ə nĭsh′ən), *n.* one skilled in constructing, working or repairing machines.

me·chan·ics (mə kăn′ĭks), *n.* **1.** the branch of knowledge concerned (both theoretically and practically) with machinery or mechanical appliances. **2.** the science dealing with the action of forces on bodies and with motion, and comprising kinetics, statics, and kinematics. **3.** (*construed as pl.*) the mechanical or technical part or aspect.

Me·chan·ics·ville (mə kăn′ĭks vĭl), *n.* a village in E Virginia, near Richmond: battle, 1862.

mech·an·ism (měk′ə nĭz′əm), *n.* **1.** a piece of machinery. **2.** the machinery, or the agencies or means, by which a particular effect is produced or a purpose is accomplished. **3.** machinery or mechanical appliances in general. **4.** the structure, or arrangement of parts, of a machine or similar device, or of anything analogous. **5.** such parts collectively. **6.** mechanical execution, as in painting or music; technique. **7.** the theory that everything in the universe is produced by matter in motion. **8.** *Philos., Biol.* a natural process interpreted as machinelike or as explicable in terms of Newtonian physics. **9.** *Psychoanal.* (used as an analogy drawn from mechanics) the operation and interaction of psychological forces. [t. NL: s. *mēchanismus*, f. Gk.: s. *mēchanḗ* machine + m. *-ismos* -ISM]

mech·a·nist (měk′ə nĭst), *n.* **1.** one who believes in mechanism. **2.** *Rare.* a mechanician.

mech·a·nis·tic (měk′ə nĭs′tĭk), *adj.* pertaining to mechanists or mechanism, or to mechanics (def. 1), or to mechanical theories in philosophy.

mech·a·nize (měk′ə nīz′), *v.t.,* **-nized, -nizing. 1.** to make mechanical. **2.** to operate or perform by or as if by machinery. **3.** to introduce machinery into (an industry, etc.). **4.** *Mil.* to equip with tanks and other armored motor vehicles. —**mech′a·ni·za′tion,** *n.*

mech·a·no·ther·a·py (měk′ə nō thěr′ə pĭ), *n.* curative treatment by mechanical means. [f. s. Gk. *mēchanḗ* machine + -o- + THERAPY]

Mech·lin (měk′lĭn), *n.* a city in N Belgium. 61,510 (est. 1941). French, **Malines.** Flemish, **Mech·e·len** (měкн′ə lən).

Mechlin lace, 1. (orig.) handmade bobbin lace with raised cord, made in Flanders. **2.** (now) a similar lace copied by machine.

Meck·len·burg (měk′lən bûrg′; *Ger.* -bōórкн′), *n.* a state in N Germany, formed in 1934 from the two states **Meck·len·burg-Schwe·rin** (měk′lən bōórкн′ shvä rēn′) and **Meck·len·burg-Stre·litz** (měk′lən bōórкн′ shtrā′lĭts). 900,417 pop. (1939); 6070 sq. mi. *Cap.:* Schwerin.

med., 1. medical. **2.** medicine. **3.** medieval. **4.** medium.

M.Ed., Master of Education.

med·al (měd′əl), *n., v.,* **-aled, -aling** or (*esp. Brit.*) **-alled, -alling.** —*n.* **1.** a flat piece of metal, circular in form, bearing an inscription, device, etc., issued to commemorate a person, action, or event, or given to serve as a reward for bravery, merit, or the like. —*v.t.* **2.** to decorate or honor with a medal. [t. F: m. *médaille*, t. It.: m. *medaglia*, ult. der. L *metallum* metal]

med·al·ist (měd′əl ĭst), *n.* **1.** a designer, engraver, or maker of medals. **2.** one to whom a medal has been awarded. Also, *esp. Brit.*, **med′al·list.**

ăct, āble, dâre, ärt; ĕbb, ēqual; ĭf, īce; hŏt, ōver, ôrder, oil, bŏŏk, ōoze, out; ŭp, ūse, ûrge; ə = a in alone; ch, chief; g, give; ng, ring; sh, shoe; th, thin; ŧħ, that; zh, vision.   See the full key on inside cover.

me·dal·lic (mə·dăl′ĭk), *adj.* pertaining to medals.
me·dal·lion (mə·dăl′yən), *n.* 1. a large medal. 2. *Archit.* a. a tablet, usually rounded, often bearing objects represented in relief. b. a member in a decorative design resembling a panel. [t. F: m. *médaillon*, t. It.: m. *medaglione*, aug. of *medaglia* MEDAL]
Medal of Honor, *U.S.* a medal awarded by Congress to soldiers, sailors, and marines who, in action involving actual conflict with an enemy, distinguish themselves conspicuously by gallantry and intrepidity at the risk of life above and beyond the call of duty.
medal play, *Golf.* play in which the score is reckoned by counting the strokes taken to complete the round.
Me·dan (mĕ·dän′), *n.* a city in the U.S. of Indonesia, in NE Sumatra. 76,584 (1930).
med·dle (mĕd′əl), *v.i.,* **-dled, -dling.** to concern or busy oneself with or in something without warrant or necessity; interfere. [ME *medle(n)*, t. OF: m. *medler*, ult. der. L *miscēre* mix] **—med′dler,** *n.*
med·dle·some (mĕd′əl səm), *adj.* given to meddling. **—med′dle·some·ly,** *adv.* **—med′dle·some·ness,** *n.* **—Syn.** See *curious*.
Mede (mēd), *n.* a native or inhabitant of Media, an ancient kingdom of Asia, south of the Caspian Sea.
Me·de·a (mĭ·dē′ə), *n.* 1. *Gk. Legend.* a sorceress, daughter of Aeëtes, king of Colchis, and wife of Jason, whom she assisted in obtaining the Golden Fleece. 2. a play (431 B.C.) by Euripides.
Me·del·lín (mĕ′dĕ·yēn′), *n.* a city in W Colombia. 207,450 (est. 1943).
Med·ford (mĕd′fərd), *n.* a city in E Massachusetts, near Boston. 66,113 (1950).
me·di·a[1] (mē′dĭ·ə), *n.* pl. of **medium.**
me·di·a[2] (mē′dĭ·ə), *n., pl.* **-diae** (-dĭ·ē′). 1. *Phonet., Gram.* a voiced stop: b, d, g. 2. *Anat.* the middle layer of an artery or lymphatic vessel. [t. L: middle (fem. adj.)]
Me·di·a (mē′dĭ·ə), *n.* an ancient country in W Asia, S of the Caspian Sea, corresponding generally to NW Iran. *Cap.:* Ecbatana.

Media, 500 B.C.

me·di·a·cy (mē′dĭ·ə·sĭ), *n.* state of being mediate.
me·di·ae·val (mē′dĭ·ē′vəl, mĕd′ĭ-), *adj.* medieval. **—me′di·ae′val·ism,** *n.* **—me′di·ae′val·ist,** *n.*
me·di·al (mē′dĭ·əl), *adj.* 1. situated in or pertaining to the middle; median; intermediate. 2. pertaining to a mean or average; average. 3. ordinary. 4. within a word or syllable; neither initial nor final. **—n.** 5. a medial linguistic element. 6. *Phonet.* media[2] (def. 1). [t. LL: s. *mediālis,* der. L *medius* middle] **—me′di·al·ly,** *adv.*
me·di·an (mē′dĭ·ən), *adj.* 1. noting or pertaining to a plane dividing something into two equal parts, esp. one dividing an animal into right and left halves. 2. situated in or pertaining to the middle; medial. **—n.** 3. the middle number in a given sequence of numbers: *4 is the median of 1, 3, 4, 8, 9.* 4. a line through a vertex of a triangle bisecting the opposite side. [t. L: s. *mediānus* in the middle] **—me′di·an·ly,** *adv.*
Me·di·an (mē′dĭ·ən), *adj.* 1. of or pertaining to Media or the Medes. **—n.** 2. a Mede.
me·di·as·ti·num (mē′dĭ·ăs·tī′nəm), *n., pl.* **-tina** (-tī′nə). *Anat.* 1. a median septum or partition between two parts of an organ, or paired cavities of the body. 2. the partition separating the right and left thoracic cavities, formed of the two inner pleural walls, and, in man, containing all the viscera of the thorax except the lungs. [t. ML, prop. neut. of ML *mediastīnus* in the middle, der. L *medius* middle] **—me′di·as·ti′nal,** *adj.*
me·di·ate (*v.* mē′dĭ·āt′; *adj.* mē′dĭ·ĭt), *v.,* **-ated, -ating,** *adj.* **—v.t.** 1. to bring about (an agreement, peace, etc.) between parties by acting as mediator. 2. to settle (disputes, etc.) by mediation; reconcile. 3. to effect (a result), convey (a gift), etc., as or by an intermediary or medium. **—v.i.** 4. to act between parties to effect an agreement, compromise, or reconciliation. 5. to occupy an intermediate place or position. **—adj.** 6. acting through, dependent on, or involving an intermediate agency; not direct or immediate. [late ME, t. LL: m.s. *mediātus,* pp., divided, situated in the middle] **—me′di·ate·ly,** *adv.*
me·di·a·tion (mē′dĭ·ā′shən), *n.* 1. action in mediating between parties, as to effect an agreement or reconciliation. 2. *Internat. Law.* an attempt to effect a peaceful settlement between disputing nations through the friendly good offices of another power.
me·di·a·tive (mē′dĭ·ā′tĭv), *adj.* mediating; mediatory.
me·di·a·tize (mē′dĭ·ə·tīz′), *v.t.,* **-tized, -tizing.** to annex (a principality) to another state (while allowing certain rights to its former sovereign). [t. F: m. *médiatiser,* or t. G: m. *mediatisieren,* der. LL *mediātus,* pp., divided] **—me′di·a·ti·za′tion,** *n.*
me·di·a·tor (mē′dĭ·ā′tər), *n.* 1. one who mediates. 2. one who mediates between parties at variance.
me·di·a·to·ry (mē′dĭ·ə·tōr′ĭ), *adj.* 1. pertaining to

mediation. 2. having the function of mediating. Also, **me′di·a·to′ri·al.**
med·ic (mĕd′ĭk), *n.* any plant of the fabaceous genus *Medicago,* as *M. sativa* (alfalfa), and *M. lupulina* (black medic), an herb with black pods. [t. L: s. *mēdica,* t. Gk.: m. *(póa) Mēdikē* Median (grass)]
med·i·ca·ble (mĕd′ə·kə·bəl), *adj.* susceptible of medical treatment; curable. [t. L: m.s. *medicābilis*]
med·i·cal (mĕd′ə·kəl), *adj.* 1. of or pertaining to the science or practice of medicine. 2. curative; medicinal; therapeutic: *the medical properties of a plant.* [t. F, t. LL: s. *medicālis,* der. L *medicus* of healing] **—med′i·cal·ly,** *adv.*
medical jurisprudence, the science which treats of the application of medical knowledge to questions of civil and criminal law; forensic (or legal) medicine.
me·dic·a·ment (mə·dĭk′ə·mənt, mĕd′ə·kə-), *n.* curative or healing substance. [t. L: s. *medicāmentum*] **—med·i·ca·men·tal** (mĕd′ə·kə mĕn′təl), **med′i·ca·men′ta·ry,** *adj.*
med·i·cate (mĕd′ə·kāt′), *v.t.,* **-cated, -cating.** 1. to treat with medicine or medicaments. 2. to impregnate with a medicine. [t. L: m.s. *medicātus,* pp., cured]
med·i·ca·tion (mĕd′ə·kā′shən), *n.* 1. the use or application of medicine. 2. a medicament; a medicinal agent.
med·i·ca·tive (mĕd′ə·kā′tĭv), *adj.* medicinal.
Med·i·ci (mĕd′ə·chĭ; *It.* mĕ′dē·chē′), *n.* 1. an Italian family of the city of Florence, rich and powerful in the 15th and 16th centuries. 2. **Catherine de′** (dĭ), (Fr. *Catherine de Médicis*) 1519–89, queen of Henry II of France, and mother of Francis II, Charles IX, and Henry III. 3. **Cosmo** (kŏz′mō) or **Cosimo de′** (kō′zē·mō′ dĕ), ("the Elder") 1389–1464, Italian banker, statesman, and patron of art and literature. 4. **Cosmo** or **Cosimo de′,** ("the Great") 1519–74, duke of Florence and first grand duke of Tuscany. 5. **Giovanni de′** (jō vän′nē dĕ). See **Leo X.** 6. **Giulio de′** (jōō′lyō dĕ), Clement VII. 7. **Lorenzo de′** (lō rĕn′tsō dĕ), ("Lorenzo the Magnificent"; *Lorenzo I*) 1449–1492, ruler of Florence, patron of art and literature, and poet. 8. **Marie de′** (mə rē′; Fr. mȧ rē′ də), (Maria de′) 1573–1642, queen of Henry IV of France, and regent of France, 1610–17. Also, *French,* **Médicis.**
me·dic·i·nal (mə·dĭs′ə·nəl), *adj.* pertaining to, or having the properties of, a medicine; curative; remedial: *medicinal properties, medicinal substances.* [ME, t. L: s. *medicīnālis* of medicine] **—me·dic′i·nal·ly,** *adv.*
med·i·cine (mĕd′ə·sən; *Brit.* mĕd′sĭn), *n., v.,* **-cined, -cining.** **—n.** 1. any substance or substances used in treating disease; a medicament; a remedy. 2. the art or science of restoring or preserving health or due physical condition, as by means of drugs, surgical operations or appliances, manipulations, etc. (often divided into medicine proper, surgery and obstetrics). 3. the art or science of treating disease with drugs or curative substances (distinguished from *surgery* and *obstetrics*). 4. the medical profession. 5. any object or practice regarded by savages as of magical efficacy. **—v.t.** 6. to administer medicine to. [ME, t. L: m. *medicīna*]
medicine ball, a large, solid, leather-covered ball, of considerable weight, thrown from one person to another for exercise.
medicine lodge, 1. a structure used for various ceremonials of the North American Indians. 2. *(caps.)* the most important religious society among the Central Algonquian tribes of North America.
medicine man, (among American Indians and other primitive peoples) a man supposed to possess mysterious or supernatural powers.
Mé·di·cis (mā·dē·sēs′), *n.* French name for **Medici.**
med·i·co (mĕd′ə·kō′), *n., pl.* **-cos.** *Slang.* a doctor. [t. It. and Sp., t. L: m. *medicus* a physician]
me·di·e·val (mē′dĭ·ē′vəl, mĕd′ĭ-), *adj.* of or pertaining to, characteristic of, or in the style of the Middle Ages: *medieval architecture.* See **Middle Ages.** Also, **mediaeval.** [f. m. NL *(medi(um) aev(um)* middle age + -AL[1]] **—me′di·e′val·ly,** *adv.*
Medieval Greek, the Greek language of the Middle Ages, usually dated A.D. 700–1500. Also, **Middle Greek.**
me·di·e·val·ism (mē′dĭ·ē′vĭz′əm, mĕd′ĭ-), *n.* 1. the spirit, practices, or methods of the Middle Ages. 2. devotion to or adoption of medieval ideals or practices. 3. a medieval belief, practice, or the like. Also, **mediaevalism.**
me·di·e·val·ist (mē′dĭ·ē′vəl ĭst, mĕd′ĭ-), *n.* 1. an expert in medieval history and affairs. 2. one in sympathy with the spirit and methods of the Middle Ages. Also, **mediaevalist.**
Medieval Latin, the Latin language of the literature of the Middle Ages (usually dated A.D. 700 to 1500), including many Latinized words from other languages.
Me·di·na (mĕ·dē′nä), *n.* a city in W Saudi Arabia, where Mohammed was first accepted as the supreme Prophet from Allah, and where his tomb is located. ab. 30,000.
me·di·o·cre (mē′dĭ·ō′kər, mē′dĭ·ō′kər), *adj.* of middling quality; of only moderate excellence; neither good nor bad; indifferent; ordinary: *a person of mediocre abilities.* [t. F, t. L: m.s. *mediocris* in a middle state] **—Syn.** medium, average, commonplace.
me·di·oc·ri·ty (mē′dĭ·ŏk′rə·tĭ), *n., pl.* **-ties,** 1. state or quality of being mediocre. 2. mediocre ability or accomplishment. 3. a person of but moderate ability.

Medit., Mediterranean.

med·i·tate (měd/ə tāt/), v., -tated, -tating. —v.t.
1. to consider in the mind as something to be done or effected; to intend or purpose. —v.i. **2.** to engage in thought or contemplation; reflect. [t. L: m.s. meditātus, pp.] —med/i·ta/tor, n. —Syn. **1.** contemplate, plan. **2.** ponder, muse, ruminate; cogitate, think.

med·i·ta·tion (měd/ə tā/shən), n. **1.** act of meditating. **2.** continued thought; reflection; contemplation.

med·i·ta·tive (měd/ə tā/tĭv), adj. given to, characterized by, or indicative of meditation. —med/i·ta/tive·ly, adv. —med/i·ta/tive·ness, n. —Syn. See pensive.

Med·i·ter·ra·ne·an (měd/ə tərā/nĭ·ən), n. **1.** the Mediterranean Sea. —adj. **2.** pertaining to, situated on or near, or dwelling about the Mediterranean Sea. [f. s. L mediterrāneus midland, inland + -AN]

Mediterranean fever, undulant fever.

Mediterranean race, a Caucasian race division inhabiting the area bordering the Mediterranean Sea, including the ancient Iberians, Ligurians, Minoans, and some Hamites, and most modern Mediterranean peoples except those in the Balkan and Anatolian peninsulas.

Mediterranean Sea, the sea between Africa, Europe, and Asia. ab. 1,145,000 sq. mi.; greatest known depth, 14,436 ft.

me·di·um (mē/dĭ·əm), n., pl. -diums, -dia (-dĭ·ə), adj. —n. **1.** a middle state or condition; a mean. **2.** something intermediate in nature or degree. **3.** an intervening substance, as air, etc., through which a force acts or an effect is produced. **4.** the element in which an organism has its natural habitat. **5.** one's environment; surrounding things, conditions, or influences. **6.** an agency, means, or instrument: newspapers as an advertising medium. **7.** Biol. the substance by which specimens are displayed or preserved. **8.** Bacteriol. a nutritive substance containing protein, carbohydrates, salts, water, etc., either liquid or solidified through the addition of gelatin or agar agar, in or upon which microorganisms are grown for study. **9.** Painting. a liquid with which pigments are mixed for application. **10.** a person serving or conceived as serving, as an instrument for the manifestation of another personality or of some alleged supernatural agency: a spiritualistic medium. —adj. **11.** intermediate in degree, quality, etc.: a man of medium size. [t. L: (neut. adj.) middle, intermediate]

me·di·um·is·tic (mē/dĭ·əmĭs/tĭk), adj. pertaining to a spiritualistic medium.

med·lar (měd/lər), n. **1.** a small malaceous tree, Mespilus germanica, the fruit of which resembles an open-topped crab apple and is not edible until in the early stages of decay. **2.** its fruit. **3.** any of certain other malaceous trees. **4.** the fruit of such a tree. [ME medler, t. OF, var. of meslier the medlar tree, der. mesle, the fruit, g. L mespilum, t. Gk.: m. méspilon]

med·ley (měd/lĭ), n., pl. -leys, adj. —n. **1.** a mixture, esp. of heterogeneous elements; a jumble. **2.** a piece of music combining airs or passages from various sources. —adj. **3.** mixed; mingled; motley. [ME medlee, t. OF, var. of meslee a mixing, orig. pp. fem. of mesler mix]

Mé·doc (mě dôk/), n. **1.** a district in SW France, NW of Bordeaux. **2.** a claret wine produced there.

me·dul·la (mĭ dŭl/ə), n., pl. -dullae (-dŭl/ē). **1.** Anat. **a.** the marrow of bones. **b.** the soft marrowlike center of an organ, such as the kidney, suprarenal, etc. **c.** the medulla oblongata. **2.** Bot. the pith of plants. See diag. under exogen. [t. L: marrow, pith]

medulla ob·lon·ga·ta (ŏb/lŏng gā/tə), Anat. the lowest or hindmost part of the brain, continuous with the spinal cord. [t. NL: prolonged medulla]

med·ul·lar·y (měd/ə lěr/ĭ, mĭ dŭl/ə rĭ), adj. pertaining to, consisting of, or resembling the medulla of an organ or the medulla oblongata.

medullary ray, Bot. (in the stems of exogenous plants) one of the vertical bands or plates of parenchymatous tissue which radiate between the pith and the bark. See diag. under exogen.

medullary sheath, **1.** Bot. a narrow zone made up of the innermost layer of woody tissue immediately surrounding the pith in plants. See diag. under exogen. **2.** myelin.

med·ul·lat·ed (měd/ə lā/tĭd, mĭ dŭl/ā tĭd), adj. Anat. covered by a medullary substance; possessing myelin sheaths.

Me·du·sa (mə dū/sə, -zə, -dōō/-), n., pl. -sas. Gk. Legend. that one of the three Gorgons who was slain by Perseus and whose head was afterward borne on the aegis or shield of Athena.

me·du·sa (mə dū/sə, -zə, -dōō/-), n., pl. -sas, -sae (-sē, -zē). Zool. a jellyfish. —me·du·soid (mə dū/soid, -dōō/-), adj.

me·du·san (mə dū/sən, -dōō/-), adj. **1.** pertaining to a medusa or jellyfish. —n. **2.** a medusa or jellyfish.

meed (mēd), n. Archaic. a reward or recompense for service or desert (good or bad). [ME mede, OE mēd, c. G miete hire]

meek (mēk), adj. **1.** humbly patient or submissive, as under provocation from others. **2.** unduly patient or submissive; spiritless; tame. **3.** Obs. gentle, kind. [ME meke, meoc, t. Scand.; cf. Icel. mjūkr soft, mild, meek] —meek/ly, adv. —meek/ness, n. —Syn. **1.** forbearing; yielding, docile; humble. See gentle. —Ant. **1.** aggressive.

Meer (mĭr; Du. mār), n. **Jan van der** (yän vän dər), ("Vermeer of Delft") 1632–1675, Dutch painter.

meer·schaum (mĭr/shəm, -shôm), n. **1.** a mineral, hydrous magnesium silicate, $H_4Mg_2Si_3O_{10}$, occurring in white, claylike masses, used for ornamental carvings, for pipe bowls, etc.; sepiolite. **2.** a tobacco pipe the bowl of which is made of this substance. [t. G: sea foam]

Mee·rut (mē/rət), n. a city in N India, in the United Provinces. 169,290 (1941).

meet¹ (mēt), v., met, meeting, n. —v.t. **1.** to come into contact, junction, or connection with. **2.** to come before or to (eye, gaze, ear, etc.). **3.** to come upon or encounter; to come face to face with or into the presence of. **4.** to go to the place of arrival of, as to welcome, speak with, accompany, etc.: to meet one's guests at the door. **5.** to come into the company of (a person, etc.) in intercourse, dealings, conference, etc. **6.** to come into personal acquaintance with, as by formal presentation: to meet the governor. **7.** to face, eye, etc., directly or without avoidance. **8.** to encounter in opposition or conflict. **9.** to oppose: to meet charges with countercharges. **10.** to cope or deal effectively with (an objection, difficulty, etc.). **11.** to satisfy (needs, obligations, demands, etc.). **12.** to come into conformity with (wishes, expectations, views, etc.). **13.** to encounter in experience: to meet hostility. —v.i. **14.** to come together, face to face, or into company: we met on the street. **15.** to assemble, as for action or conference as a committee, a legislature, a society, etc. **16.** to become personally acquainted. **17.** to come into contact or form a junction, as lines, planes, areas, etc. **18.** to be conjoined or united. **19.** to concur or agree. **20.** to come together in opposition or conflict, as adversaries, hostile forces, etc. **21.** to encounter; come across. **22.** to experience; undergo; receive (praise, blame, etc.). —n. **23.** a meeting, as of huntsmen for a hunt, of cyclists for a ride, etc. **24.** those assembled at such a meeting. **25.** the place of meeting. [ME mete(n), OE mētan, gemētan, der. mōt, gemōt meeting. See MOOT] —Syn. **1.** intersect, converge. **7.** confront, face. **11.** settle; discharge, fulfill. **15.** gather, congregate, convene. **22.** suffer. —Ant. **1.** diverge. **8.** greet. **11.** repudiate. **15.** adjourn. **22.** escape.

meet² (mēt), adj. suitable; fitting; proper. [ME mete, repr. d. OE form, r. OE gemǣte suitable, c. G gemäss conformable]

meet·ing (mē/tĭng), n. **1.** a coming together. **2.** an assembling, as of persons for some purpose. **3.** an assembly or gathering held. **4.** the persons present. **5.** a hostile encounter; a duel. **6.** an assembly for religious worship, esp. of Quakers. **7.** a coming into or being in contact, as of things; junction or union.

meeting house, **1.** a house or building for religious worship. **2.** a house of worship of Quakers.

meet·ly (mēt/lĭ), adv. suitably; fittingly; properly.

mega-, a word element meaning "great," and, in physics, 1,000,000 times a given unit, as in megohm, megacycle. Also, before vowels, **meg-.** [t. Gk., comb. form of mégas]

meg·a·ce·phal·ic (měg/ə sə făl/ĭk), adj. **1.** Craniom. having a skull with a large cranial capacity or one exceeding the mean. Cf. microcephalic. **2.** large-headed. Also, **meg·a·ceph·a·lous** (měg/ə sěf/ə ləs). [f. MEGA- + m.s. Gk. kephalē head + -IC]

meg·a·cy·cle (měg/ə sī/kəl), n. Physics. a million cycles, esp. a million cycles per second. See kilocycle.

Me·gae·ra (mə jē/rə), n. Gk. Myth. one of the Furies.

meg·a·ga·mete (měg/ə gə mēt/), n. a macrogamete.

meg·a·lith (měg/ə lĭth), n. Archaeol. a stone of great size, esp. in ancient constructive work (as the Cyclopean masonry) or in primitive monumental remains (as menhirs, dolmens, cromlechs, etc.). —meg/a·lith/ic, adj.

megalo-, a word element denoting bigness or exaggeration. [t. Gk., comb. form of mégas great]

meg·a·lo·ce·phal·ic (měg/ə lō sə făl/ĭk), adj. megacephalic. Also, **meg·a·lo·ceph·a·lous** (měg/ə lō sěf/ə ləs). —meg/a·lo·ceph/a·ly, n.

meg·a·lo·ma·ni·a (měg/ə lə mā/nĭ·ə), n. **1.** Psychiatry. a form of mental alienation marked by delusions of greatness, wealth, etc. **2.** a mania for big or great things. [t. NL. See MEGALO-, -MANIA]

meg·a·lo·ma·ni·ac (měg/ə lə mā/nĭ·ăk/), n. one who is afflicted with megalomania. —meg·a·lo·ma·ni·a·cal (měg/ə lō mə nī/ə kəl), adj.

meg·a·lo·saur (měg/ə lə sôr/), n. any of the gigantic carnivorous dinosaurs that constitute the extinct genus Megalosaurus. [t. NL: s. megalosaurus] —meg/a·lo·sau/ri·an, adj., n.

meg·a·phone (měg/ə fōn/), n. a device for magnifying sound, or for directing it in increased volume, as a large funnel-shaped instrument used in addressing a large audience out of doors or in calling to a distance. —meg·a·phon·ic (měg/ə fŏn/ĭk), adj.

meg·a·pod (měg/ə pŏd/), adj. having large feet.

meg·a·pode (měg/ə pōd/), n. any of the Megapodiidae, a family of large-footed Australian gallinaceous birds.

Meg·a·ra (měg/ə rə; Gk. mě/gä rä/), n. a city of ancient Greece: the capital of **Meg·a·ris** (měg/ə rĭs), a district between the gulfs of Corinth and Aegina.

meg·a·spo·ran·gi·um (měg/ə spō răn/jĭ·əm), n., pl. -gia (-jĭ·ə). Bot. a sporangium containing megaspores.

meg·a·spore (měg/ə spōr/), n. Bot. **1.** the larger of the two kinds of spores produced by some pteridophytes. **2.** the embryo sac of a flowering plant.

meg·a·spo·ro·phyll (mĕg′əspōr′əfĭl), *n. Bot.* a sporophyll producing megasporangia only.

meg·a·there (mĕg′əthĭr′), *n.* any of the huge sloth-like animals constituting the extinct genus *Megatherium*. [t. NL: m.s. *megathērium*, f. Gk.: *mega-* MEGA- + m. *thēríon* beast]

Me·gid·do (məgĭd′ō), *n.* an ancient city in N Israel, in the plain of Esdraelon: scene of many battles; probably the same as Armageddon in the Bible.

meg·ohm (mĕg′ōm′), *n. Elect.* a large unit of resistance, equal to a million ohms.

me·grim (mē′grĭm), *n.* **1.** (*pl.*) morbid low spirits. **2.** *Archaic.* a whim or caprice. **3.** migraine. [ME *migraine*, t. F, t. LL: m. *hemicrānia* HEMICRANIA]

Me·hem·et A·li (mĭhĕm′ĕt älē′, ä′lē), 1769–1849, pasha and viceroy of Egypt. Also, **Mohammed Ali.**

Meigs (mĕgz), *n.* **Fort,** a former U.S. fort in NW Ohio: unsuccessfully attacked by the British, 1813.

Mei·ji (mā′jē), *n. Jap. Hist.* the reign style of the Japanese Emperor Mutsuhito, 1868–1912. [Jap.: lit., enlightened peace]

Mei·lhac (mĕyàk′), *n.* **Henri** (änrē′), 1831–97, French dramatist, collaborator with Ludovic Halévy.

Mein Kampf (mīn kämpf′), the autobiography of Adolf Hitler, setting forth his political philosophy and his plan for the German conquest of Europe.

mei·o·sis (mīō′sĭs), *n. Biol.* the maturation process of gametes, consisting of chromosome conjugation and two cell divisions, in the course of which the diploid chromosome number becomes reduced to the haploid. [t. Gk.: a lessening] —**mei·ot·ic** (mīŏt′ĭk), *adj.*

Meis·sen (mī′sən), *n.* a city in E Germany, on the Elbe river: famous for the fine porcelain made there. 48,311 (1939).

Meis·so·nier (mĕsō̇nyĕ′), *n.* **Jean Louis Ernest** (zhän lwē ĕrnĕst′), 1815–91, French painter.

Meis·ter·sing·er (mīs′tərsĭng′ər, -zĭng′ər), *n., pl.* **-singer.** Also, **mastersinger.** **1.** a member of one of the guilds, chiefly of workingmen, established during the 14th, 15th, and 16th centuries in the principal cities of Germany, for the cultivation of poetry and music. **2. Die** (dē), an opera (1807) by Wagner.

Meit·ner (mīt′nər), *n.* **Lise** (lē′zə), born 1878, Austrian nuclear physicist.

Me·kong (mā′kŏng′; *Thai.* mäkŏng′), *n.* a river flowing from W China SE along most of the boundary between Siam and French Indo-China to the South China Sea. ab. 2600 mi. Chinese, **Lantsang.**

melan-, var. of **melano-,** as in *melancholy.*

mel·an·cho·li·a (mĕl′ənkō′lĭə), *n. Psychiatry.* mental disease characterized by great depression of spirits and gloomy forebodings. [t. LL. See MELANCHOLY]

mel·an·cho·li·ac (mĕl′ənkō′lĭ̇äk′), *adj.* **1.** affected with melancholia. —*n.* **2.** one affected with melancholia.

mel·an·chol·ic (mĕl′ənkŏl′ĭk), *adj.* **1.** disposed to or affected with melancholy; gloomy; melancholy. **2.** pertaining to melancholia. —**mel′an·chol′i·cal·ly,** *adv.*

mel·an·chol·y (mĕl′ənkŏl′ĭ), *n., pl.* **-cholies,** *adj.* —*n.* **1.** a gloomy state of mind, esp. when habitual or prolonged; depression. **2.** sober thoughtfulness; pensiveness. **3.** *Archaic.* **a.** condition of having too much black bile. **b.** the bile itself. —*adj.* **4.** affected with, characterized by, or showing melancholy: *a melancholy mood.* **5.** attended with or inducing melancholy or sadness: *a melancholy occasion.* **6.** soberly thoughtful; pensive. [ME *melancholie*, t. LL: m. *melancholia*, t. Gk.: black bile] —**Syn. 1.** dejection, despondency; gloominess; hypochondria. **4.** See **sad.** —**Ant. 5.** happy.

Me·lanch·thon (məlängk′thən; *Ger.* mälänкн′tôn), *n.* **Philipp** (fē′lĭp), 1497–1560, German Protestant reformer.

Mel·a·ne·sia (mĕl′ənē′shə, -zhə), *n.* one of the three principal divisions of Oceania, comprising the island groups in the S Pacific, NE of Australia. [f. Gk. *mélas* black + s. Gk. *nêsos* island + -IA; ? so named from black appearance of islands seen from sea]

Mel·a·ne·sian (mĕl′ənē′shən, -zhən), *adj.* **1.** of or pertaining to Melanesia, its inhabitants, or their languages. —*n.* **2.** a member of any of the dark-skinned, frizzy-haired peoples inhabiting Melanesia. **3.** any of the Austronesian languages of Melanesia.

mé·lange (mĕlänzh′), *n.* a mixture; medley. [t. F, der. *mêler* mix. See MEDDLE]

mel·a·nin (mĕl′ənĭn), *n. Biochem.* the dark pigment in the body of man and certain animals, as that occurring in the hair, epidermis, etc., of colored races, or one produced in certain diseases. [f. MELAN- + -IN[2]]

mel·a·nism (mĕl′əniz′əm), *n. Ethnol.* the condition of having a high amount of dark or black pigment granules in the skin, hair, and eyes of a human being.

mel·a·nite (mĕl′ənīt′), *n. Mineral.* a deep-black variety of garnet. [f. MELAN- + -ITE[1]]

melano-, a word element meaning "black." [t. Gk., comb. form of *mélas* black]

Mel·a·noch·ro·i (mĕl′ənŏk′rōī′), *n.pl.* light complexioned Caucasians with dark hair. [t. NL, repr. coined Gk. *melánŏchroi* (nom. pl.) black-pale] —**Mel·a·noch·roid** (mĕl′ənŏk′roid), *adj.*

mel·a·noid (mĕl′ənoid′), *adj.* **1.** characterized by or pertaining to melanosis. **2.** resembling the color of melanin.

mel·a·no·ma (mĕl′ənō′mə), *n., pl.* **-mata** (-mətə). *Med.* a dark-colored tumor. [t. NL. See MELAN-, -OMA]

mel·a·no·sis (mĕl′ənō′sĭs), *n. Pathol.* **1.** morbid deposition or development of black or dark pigment in the tissues, sometimes leading to the production of malignant pigmented tumors. **2.** a discoloration caused by this. [t. NL, t. Gk.: a blackening] —**mel·a·not·ic** (mĕl′ənŏt′ĭk), *adj.*

mel·an·tha·ceous (mĕl′ənthā′shəs), *adj.* belonging to the *Melanthaceae*, a family of monocotyledonous bulbless plants related to and sometimes classified in the lily family, including the bellwort, white hellebore, etc. [f. s. NL *Melanthăceae* the typical genus (f. Gk. *mĕl(as)* black + s. Gk. *ánthos* flower + L *-āceae*, suffix) + -OUS]

mel·a·phyre (mĕl′əfīr′), *n.* any of various dark-colored igneous rocks of porphyritic texture. [t. F: f. Gk. *mēla(s)* black + F (*por*)*phyre* porphyry]

Mel·ba (mĕl′bə), *n.* **Madame,** (*Mrs. Nellie Mitchell Armstrong*) 1861–1931, Australian operatic soprano.

Melba toast, narrow slices of thin toast.

Mel·bourne (mĕl′bərn), *n.* **1.** a seaport in SE Australia, in Victoria. With suburbs, 1,107,000 pop. (est. 1941). **2. William Lamb, 2nd Viscount,** 1779–1848, British statesman.

Mel·chers (mĕl′chərz), *n.* **Gari** (gär′ĭ), 1860–1932, U.S. painter.

Mel·chiz·e·dek (mĕlkĭz′ədĕk′), *n.* **1.** *Old Testament.* a priest-king of Salem. Gen. 14:18. **2.** the higher order of priesthood in the Mormon church. [t. LL (Vulgate): m. *Melchisedek*, t. Gk. (Septuagint), t. Heb.: m. *Malkīṣedeq*]

meld (mĕld), *Pinochle, etc.* —*v.t., v.i.* **1.** to announce and display (a counting combination of cards in the hand) for a score. —*n.* **2.** act of melding. **3.** any combination of cards to be melded. [t. G: s. *melden* announce]

Mel·e·a·ger (mĕl′ĭ ā′jər), *n. Gk. Legend.* the heroic son of Althea. He was an Argonaut, and the slayer of the Calydonian boar. It had been prophesied to his mother that as long as a certain brand remained unburnt Meleager would live; after he killed his uncles in argument over the boar, Althea threw the brand into the fire and so killed her son.

me·lee (mā′lā, mĕl′ā; *Fr.* mĕlē′), *n.* a confused, general hand-to-hand fight. Also, **mê·lée.** [t. F. See MEDLEY]

me·li·a·ceous (mē′lĭ ā′shəs), *adj.* belonging to the *Meliaceae*, a family of trees and shrubs including the azedarach, mahogany, Spanish cedar, etc. [f. s. NL *Melia* the typical genus (t. Gk.: ash tree) + -ACEOUS]

mel·ic (mĕl′ĭk), *adj.* **1.** intended to be sung. **2.** noting or pertaining to the more elaborate form of Greek lyric poetry, as distinguished from iambic and elegiac poetry. [t. Gk.: m.s. *melikós*, der. *mélos* song]

mel·i·lot (mĕl′əlŏt′), *n.* any of the cloverlike fabaceous herbs constituting the genus *Melilotus*. [ME *mellilot*, t. OF, t. L: m.s. *melilōtos*, t. Gk.: a kind of clover]

mel·i·nite (mĕl′ənīt′), *n.* a high explosive, containing picric acid. [f. s. Gk. *mēlinos* quince-yellow + -ITE[1]]

me·li·o·rate (mēl′yərāt′), *v.t., v.i.* **-rated, -rating.** to make or become better; improve; ameliorate. [t. LL: m.s. *meliōrātus*, pp.] —**mel′io·ra′tion,** *n.* —**mel′io·ra′tive,** *adj.* —**mel′io·ra′tor,** *n.*

me·li·o·rism (mēl′yərĭz′əm), *n.* the doctrine that the world tends to become better, or may be made better by human effort. [f. L *melior* better + -ISM] —**mel′io·rist,** *n., adj.* —**mel′io·ris′tic,** *adj.*

me·li·or·i·ty (mēl yôr′ətĭ, -yōr′-), *n.* superiority.

mel·lif·er·ous (məlĭf′ərəs), *adj.* yielding or producing honey. [f. L *mellifer* honey-bearing + -OUS]

mel·lif·lu·ent (məlĭf′lŏ̇ənt), *adj.* mellifluous. [t. LL: s. *mellifluens* flowing with honey] —**mel·lif′lu·ence,** *n.* —**mel·lif′lu·ent·ly,** *adv.*

mel·lif·lu·ous (məlĭf′lŏ̇əs), *adj.* **1.** sweetly or smoothly flowing: *mellifluous tones.* **2.** flowing with honey; sweetened with or as with honey. [late ME, t. LL: m. *mellifluus* flowing with honey] —**mel·lif′lu·ous·ly,** *adv.* —**mel·lif′lu·ous·ness,** *n.*

Mel·lon (mĕl′ən), *n.* **Andrew William,** 1855–1937, U.S. financier; secretary of the treasury, 1921–32.

mel·low (mĕl′ō), *adj.* **1.** soft and full-flavored from ripeness, as fruit. **2.** well-matured, as wines. **3.** softened, toned down, or improved as if by ripening. **4.** soft and rich, as sound, tones, color, light, etc. **5.** genial; jovial. **6.** friable or loamy, as soil. —*v.t., v.i.* **7.** to make or become mellow; soften by or as by ripening. [ME *mel(o)we*, OE *meru* tender, soft, with change of *r* to *l*, presumably by dissimilation in sequence *melowe fruit*] —**mel′low·ly,** *adv.* —**mel′low·ness,** *n.* —**Syn. 1.** See **ripe.**

me·lo·de·on (məlō′dĭ ən), *n.* **1.** a small reed organ. **2.** a kind of accordion. [pseudo-Gk. var. of *melodium* (der. MELODY). Cf. ACCORDION]

me·lo·di·a (məlō′dĭ ə), *n.* an 8-foot wooden flue-pipe stop organ resembling the clarabella in tone. [t. NL, special use of LL *melōdia* MELODY]

me·lod·ic (məlŏd′ĭk), *adj.* **1.** melodious. **2.** pertaining to melody as distinguished from harmony and rhythm. —**me·lod′i·cal·ly,** *adv.*

me·lod·ics (məlŏd′ĭks), *n.* that branch of musical science concerned with the pitch and succession of tones.

me·lo·di·ous (məlō′dĭ̇əs), *adj.* **1.** of the nature of or characterized by melody; tuneful. **2.** producing melody or sweet sound. —**me·lo/di·ous·ly**, adv. —**me·lo/di·ous·ness**, n.

mel·o·dist (měl/ə dĭst), n. a composer or a singer of melodies.

mel·o·dize (měl/ə dīz/), v., -dized, -dizing. —v.t. 1. to make melodious. —v.i. 2. to make melody. 3. to blend melodiously. —**mel/o·diz/er**, n.

mel·o·dra·ma (měl/ə drä/mə, -drăm/ə), n. 1. a play which does not observe the dramatic laws of cause and effect, which intensifies sentiment and exaggerates passion. 2. (in the 17th, 18th and early 19th centuries) a romantic dramatic composition with music interspersed. [t. F: m. *mélodrame*, t. It.: m. *melodramma* musical drama, f. Gk.: *mélo*(s) song, music + m. *dráma* DRAMA] —**mel·o·dram·a·tist** (měl/ə drăm/ə tĭst), n.

mel·o·dram·at·ic (měl/ə drə măt/ĭk), adj. 1. of, like, or befitting melodrama; sentimental and exaggerated. —n. 2. (pl.) melodramatic behavior. —**mel/o·dra·mat/i·cal·ly**, adv.

mel·o·dy (měl/ə dĭ), n., pl. -dies. 1. musical sounds in agreeable succession or arrangement. 2. *Music.* **a.** the succession of single tones in musical compositions, as distinguished from harmony and rhythm. **b.** the principal part in a harmonic composition; the air. **c.** a rhythmical succession of single tones producing a distinct musical phrase or idea. 3. a poem suitable for singing. [ME *melodie*, t. OF, t. LL: m. *melōdia*, t. Gk.: m. *melōidía* singing, choral song] —**Syn.** 1. See **harmony.**

mel·oid (měl/oid), n. a blister beetle. [t. NL: s. *Meloïdae* the typical genus, der. *meloë* beetle]

mel·on (měl/ən), n. 1. the fruit of any of various cucurbitaceous plants, as the muskmelon or watermelon. 2. deep pink; medium crimson. 3. **cut a melon**, *U.S. Slang.* to declare a large extra dividend to shareholders. [ME, t. OF, t. LL: s. *melo*, t. Gk.: short for *melōpépōn* applelike gourd]

Me·los (mē/lŏs), n. an island of the Cyclades group, in the Aegean, S of Greece: statue of Venus of Milo found here, 1820. 2607 pop. (1940); 61 sq. mi. Also, **Milo.**

Mel·pom·e·ne (měl pŏm/ə nĭ), n. the Muse of tragedy. [t. L, t. Gk., prop. ppr. fem. of *mélpesthai* sing]

Mel·rose (měl/rōz), n. 1. a city in E Massachusetts, near Boston. 26,988 (1950). 2. a village in SE Scotland, on the Tweed river: ruins of a famous abbey.

melt (mělt), v., **melted, melted** or **molten, melting**, n. —v.i. 1. to become liquefied by heat, as ice, snow, butter, metal, etc. 2. to become liquid; dissolve. 3. to pass, dwindle, or fade gradually. 4. to pass, change, or blend gradually (often fol. by *into*). 5. to become softened in feeling by pity, sympathy, love, or the like. 6. *Archaic.* to fail or faint, as the heart or soul, from fear, grief, etc. —v.t. 7. to reduce to a liquid state by heat; fuse. 8. to cause to pass or fade (*away*). 9. to cause to pass or blend gradually. 10. to soften in feeling, as a person, the heart, etc. —n. 11. act or process of melting. 12. the state of being melted. 13. that which is melted. 14. a quantity melted at one time. [ME *melte*(n), OE *meltan*, v.i., *m*(i)*eltan*, v.t.; akin to Icel. *melta* digest, Gk. *méldein* melt] —**melt/er**, n.

—**Syn.** 1. MELT, DISSOLVE, FUSE, THAW imply reducing a solid substance to a liquid state. To MELT is to bring a solid to a liquid condition by the agency of heat: *to melt butter.* DISSOLVE, though sometimes used interchangeably with melt, applies to a different process, depending upon the fact that certain solids, placed in certain liquids, distribute their particles throughout the liquids: *a greater number of solids can be dissolved in water and in alcohol than in any other liquids.* To FUSE is to subject the solid (usually a metal) to a very high temperature; it applies esp. to melting or blending metals together: *bell metal is made by fusing copper and tin.* To THAW is to reduce a frozen substance (whose ordinary condition is liquid) to a liquid or semiliquid by raising its temperature above the freezing point: *sunshine will thaw ice in a lake.* —**Ant.** 2. solidify.

melt·age (měl/tĭj), n. the amount melted or the result of melting.

melting point, the temperature at which a solid substance melts or fuses.

melting pot, 1. a pot in which metals or other substances are melted or fused. 2. a country in which immigrants of various races are united in citizenship.

mel·ton (měl/tən), n. a smooth, heavy woolen cloth, used for overcoats, hunting jackets, etc. [from *Melton* Mowbray, town in Leicestershire, England]

Mel·ville (měl/vĭl), n. **Herman,** 1819–91, U.S. author.

Melville Island, a Canadian island in the Arctic Ocean, N of Canada. ab. 200 mi. long; ab. 130 mi. wide.

Melville Peninsula, a peninsula in N Canada, SE of the Gulf of Boothia. ab. 250 mi. long.

mem., 1. member. 2. memoir. 3. memorandum. 4. memorial.

mem·ber (měm/bər), n. 1. each of the persons composing a society, party, community, or other body. 2. each of the persons included in the membership of a legislative body, as the U.S. Congress (chiefly the House of Representatives) or the British Parliament (chiefly the House of Commons). 3. a part or organ of an animal body, a limb, as a leg, arm, or wing. 4. a constituent part of any structural or composite whole, as a subordinate architectural feature of a building or the like. 5. either side of an algebraic equation. [ME *membre*, t. OF, t. L *membrum* limb, part]

—**Syn.** 3, 4. MEMBER, LIMB refer to an integral part of a larger body. MEMBER is the general term applied to any

integral part or vital organ of an organized animal body, or, more widely, to any integral or distinguishable constituent part of a whole which is considered as organic: *the nose, tongue, and arms are members of the body; a member of a family.* LIMB, which once, like MEMBER, referred to any organ of the body, is now restricted to the legs and arms (particularly of human beings); secondarily applied to the branches of a tree. It has such figurative uses as a *limb of Satan,* or a *limb of the law.* The Victorian "limb" as a prudish euphemism for "leg" stimulated further the use of the word in humorous contexts.

mem·ber·ship (měm/bər shĭp/), n. 1. state of being a member, as of a society or other body. 2. the status of a member. 3. the total number of members belonging to a body.

mem·brane (měm/brān), n. a thin, pliable sheet or layer of animal or vegetable tissue, serving to line an organ, connect parts, etc. [t. L: m.s. *membrāna* the skin that covers the several members of the body, parchment]

membrane bone, a bone which originates in membranous tissue (opposed to *cartilage bone*).

mem·bra·nous (měm/brə nəs), adj. 1. consisting of, of the nature of, or resembling membrane. 2. characterized by the formation of a membrane. Also, **mem·bra·na·ceous** (měm/brə nā/shəs).

Me·mel (mā/məl), n. 1. a seaport in the W Soviet Union, in the Lithuanian Republic. 41,297 (est. 1941). 2. a territory including this seaport: ceded to Germany by Lithuania, 1939; incorporated into the Soviet Union, 1945. 154,694 pop. (1939); 933 sq. mi. 3. name of the lower course of the Nieman river. Lithuanian (for defs. 1 and 2), **Klaipéda.**

Memel (def. 2)

me·men·to (mĭ měn/tō), n., pl. -tos, -toes. 1. something that serves as a reminder of what is past or gone. 2. anything serving as a reminder or warning. 3. (*cap.*) *Rom. Cath. Ch.* (in the canon of the Mass) either of two prayers beginning with the word "Memento" (remember), the first for persons living, and the second for persons deceased. [t. L, impv. of *meminisse* remember!]

me·men·to mo·ri (mĭ měn/tō mōr/ī), 1. *Latin.* remember that thou must die (lit., to die). 2. an object as a skull or the like, serving as a reminder of death

Mem·ling (měm/lĭng), n. **Hans** (häns), c1430–c94, Flemish painter. Also, **Mem·linc** (měm/lĭngk).

Mem·non (měm/nŏn), n. 1. a colossal statue near Egyptian Thebes which was said to produce musical sounds when struck by the rays of the morning sun. 2. *Gk. Legend.* an Oriental or Ethiopian hero slain by Achilles in the Trojan War. [t. L, t. Gk.]

mem·o (měm/ō), n., pl. memos. *Colloq.* memorandum.

mem·oir (měm/wär, -wôr), n. 1. (*pl.*) records of facts or events in connection with a particular subject, historical period, etc., as known to the writer or gathered from special sources. 2. (*pl.*) records of one's own life and experiences. 3. a biography. 4. (*pl.*) a collection of reports made to a scientific or other learned society. [t. F: m. *mémoire*, masc., memorandum, memorial, *mémoire*, fem., MEMORY]

mem·o·ra·bil·i·a (měm/ər ə bĭl/ĭ ə), n.pl., sing. -rabile (-răb/ə lĭ). memorable things; matters or events worthy to be remembered. [t. L, neut. pl. of *memorābilis* memorable]

mem·o·ra·ble (měm/ər ə bəl), adj. 1. worthy to be remembered; notable: *a memorable speech.* 2. easy to be remembered. [t. L: m.s. *memorābilis*] —**mem/o·ra·bil/i·ty, mem/o·ra·ble·ness,** n. —**mem/o·ra·bly,** adv.

mem·o·ran·dum (měm/ər ăn/dəm), n., pl. -dums, -da (-də). 1. a note made of something to be remembered, as in future action. 2. a record or written statement of something. 3. *Law.* a writing, usually informal, containing the terms of a transaction. 4. *Diplomacy.* a summary of the state of a question, the reasons for a decision agreed on, etc. 5. a document which includes the terms of a shipment of unsold goods and authorizes their return within a specified time. [t. L, neut. of *memorandus* (ger.) that is to be remembered]

me·mo·ri·al (mə mōr/ĭ əl), n. 1. something designed to preserve the memory of a person, event, etc., as a monument, a periodic observance, etc. 2. a written statement of facts presented to a sovereign, a legislative body, etc., as the ground of, or expressed in the form of, a petition or remonstrance. —adj. 3. preserving the memory of a person or thing; commemorative: *memorial services.* 4. of or pertaining to the memory. [ME, t. L: s. *memoriālis* of memory] —**me·mo/ri·al·ly,** adv.

Memorial Day, *U.S.* 1. a day, May 30, set apart in most States for observances in memory of dead soldiers and sailors; Decoration Day. 2. any of several days (April 26, May 10, or June 3) similarly observed in various Southern States.

me·mo·ri·al·ize (mə mōr/ĭ ə līz/), v.t., -ized, -izing. 1. to commemorate. 2. to present a memorial to. —**me·mo/ri·al·i·za/tion,** n. —**me·mo/ri·al·iz/er,** n.

mem·o·rize (měm/ə rīz/), v.t., -rized, -rizing. to commit to memory, or learn by heart: *Davy finally memorized the poem.* —**mem/o·riz/a·ble,** adj. —**mem/o·ri·za/tion,** n. —**mem/o·riz/er,** n.

mem·o·ry (mĕm′ərĭ), n., pl. **-ries. 1.** the mental capacity or faculty of retaining and reviving impressions, or of recalling or recognizing previous experiences. **2.** this faculty as possessed by a particular individual: *to have a good memory.* **3.** the act or fact of retaining mental impressions; remembrance; recollection: *to draw from memory.* **4.** the length of time over which recollection extends: *a time within the memory of living men.* **5.** a mental impression retained; a recollection: *one's earliest memories.* **6.** the reputation of a person or thing, esp. after death. **7.** the state or fact of being remembered. **8.** a person or thing remembered. **9.** commemorative remembrance; commemoration: *a monument in memory of Columbus.* **10.** *Speech.* the step in the classical preparation of a speech in which the wording is memorized. [ME *memorie*, t. L: m. *memoria*]

Mem·phis (mĕm′fĭs), n. **1.** a city in SW Tennessee: a port on the Mississippi. 396,000 (1950). **2.** a ruined city in Upper Egypt, on the Nile, S of Cairo: the ancient capital of Egypt. See map under **Media.**

Mem·phre·ma·gog (mĕm′frĭ mā′gŏg), n. **Lake,** a lake in N Vermont and S Quebec province, Canada. ab. 30 mi. long.

mem-sa·hib (mĕm′sä′ĭb, -sä′hĭb), n. (in India) a native's term of respect for a European lady. [t. Hind.: f. *mem* (t. E: m. *ma'am*) + *sāhib* master]

men (mĕn), n. pl. of **man.**

men·ace (mĕn′ĭs), n., v., **-aced, -acing. —**n. **1.** something that threatens to cause evil, harm, injury, etc.; a threat. **—**v.t. **2.** to utter or direct a threat against; threaten. **3.** to serve as a probable cause of evil, etc., to. [ME, t. OF, g. L *minācia* a threat] **—men′ac·er,** n. **—men′ac·ing·ly,** adv.

me·nad (mē′năd), n. maenad.

mé·nage (mā nàzh′; *Fr.* mĕ nàzh′), n. **1.** a household; a domestic establishment. **2.** housekeeping. Also, **menage′.** [t. F, ult. der. L *mansio* MANSION]

me·nag·er·ie (mə năj′ə rĭ, -năzh′-), n. **1.** a collection of wild or strange animals, esp. for exhibition. **2.** a place where they are kept or exhibited. [t. F: management of a household, menagerie, der. *ménage* MENAGE]

Men·ai Strait (mĕn′ī), a strait between Anglesey island and the mainland of NW Wales. 14 mi. long.

Me·nam (mă näm′), n. a river flowing from N Siam S to the Gulf of Siam. ab. 750 mi.

Me·nan·der (mĭ năn′dər), n. 342?–291 B.C. Greek writer of comedies.

Men·ci·us (mĕn′shĭ əs), n. (*Meng-tse*) 385 or 372–289 B.C., Chinese philosopher.

Menck·en (mĕngk′ən), n. **Henry Louis,** born 1880, U.S. author, editor, and critic.

mend (mĕnd), v.t. **1.** to make whole or sound by repairing, as something broken, worn, or otherwise damaged; repair: *to mend clothes,* (or in England) *to mend a road.* **2.** to remove or correct defects or errors in. **3.** to remove or correct (a defect, etc.). **4.** to set right; make better; improve: *to mend matters.* **—**v.i. **5.** to progress toward recovery, as a sick person. **6.** (of conditions) to improve. **—**n. **7.** act of mending; repair or improvement. **8.** a mended place. **9. on the mend, a.** recovering from sickness. **b.** improving in condition or state of affairs. [aphetic var. of AMEND] **—mend′able,** adj. **—mend′er,** n.

—Syn. 1. MEND, DARN, PATCH mean to repair something and thus renew its usefulness. MEND is an informal and general expression which emphasizes the idea of making whole something damaged: *to mend a broken dish, a tear in an apron.* DARN and PATCH are more specific, referring particularly to repairing holes or rents. To DARN is to repair by means of stitches interwoven with one another: *to darn stockings.* To PATCH is to cover a hole or rent (usually) with a piece or pieces of similar material and to secure the edges of these; it implies a more temporary or makeshift repair than the others: *to patch the knees of trousers, a rubber tire, a hole in a building.*

men·da·cious (mĕn dā′shəs), adj. **1.** false or untrue: *a mendacious report.* **2.** lying or untruthful. [f. MEN-DACI(TY) + -OUS] **—men·da′cious·ly,** adv. **—men·da′cious·ness,** n.

men·dac·i·ty (mĕn dăs′ə tĭ), n., pl. **-ties. 1.** quality of being mendacious. **2.** a falsehood; a lie. [t. LL: m.s. *mendācitas*]

Men·del (mĕn′dəl), n. **Gregor Johann** (grā′gōr yō′hän), 1822–84, Austrian biologist. **—Men·de·li·an** (mĕn dē′lĭ ən), adj.

Men·del·ism (mĕn′də lĭz′əm), n. the theories of heredity advanced by G. J. Mendel. Also, **Men·de·li·an·ism** (mĕn dē′lĭ ə nĭz′əm).

Mendel's laws, *Genetics.* the basic principles of heredity discovered by Gregor Mendel, showing that alternative hereditary factors of hybrids exhibit a clean-cut separation or segregation from one another, and that different pairs of hereditary traits are independently assorted from each other.

Men·dels·sohn (mĕn′dəl sən; *Ger.* mĕn′dəls zōn′), n. **1. Felix** (fā′lĭks), *Jacob Ludwig Felix Mendelssohn-Bartholdy* 1809–47, German composer of music. **2.** his grandfather, **Moses** (mō′zĕs), 1729–86, German philosopher.

Men·de·lye·ev (mĕn′də lā′əf; *Russ.* mĕn′dĕ lyĕ′ĕf), n. **Dmitri Ivanovich** (dmē′trĭ ĭ vä′nō vĭch), 1834–1907, Russian chemist: helped develop the periodic law.

Men·de·res (mĕn′dĕ rĕs′), n. **1.** Ancient, **Mæander.** a river in W Asia Minor, flowing into the Aegean near

Samos. ab. 240 mi. **2.** Ancient, **Scamander.** a river in NW Asia Minor, flowing across the Trojan plain into the Dardanelles. ab. 65 mi.

men·di·cant (mĕn′də kənt), adj. **1.** begging, practicing begging, or living on alms. **2.** pertaining to or characteristic of a beggar. **—**n. **3.** one who lives by begging; a beggar. **4.** a mendicant friar. [t. L: s. *mendīcans*, ppr., begging] **—men′di·can·cy,** n.

men·dic·i·ty (mĕn dĭs′ə tĭ), n. **1.** the practice of begging. **2.** the condition of life of a beggar. [ME *mendicite*, t. L: m.s. *mendīcitas* beggary]

Men·do·ci·no (mĕn′də sē′nō), n. **Cape,** a cape in NW California: the westernmost point in California.

Men·do·za (mĕn dō′sä), n. a city in W Argentina. 100,429 (est. 1944).

Men·do·za (mĕn dō′thä, -sä), n. **Pedro de** (pĕ′drô dĕ), 1487?–1537, Spanish soldier and explorer: founder of Buenos Aires (?1536).

Men·e·la·us (mĕn′ə lā′əs), n. *Gk. Legend.* a king of Sparta, brother of Agamemnon and husband of Helen; one of the leaders of the Greeks before Troy.

Men·e·lik II (mĕn′ə lĭk), 1844–1913, emperor of Ethiopia, 1889–1913.

Me·nén·dez de A·vi·lés (mĕ nĕn′dĕth dĕ ä′vē lĕs′), **Pedro** (pĕ′drô), 1519–74, Spanish admiral and colonizer; founder of St. Augustine, Florida, in 1565.

Me·nes (mē′nēz), n. fl. c4750? B.C., traditional first king of Egypt, founder of 1st dynasty.

Meng-tse (mŭng′dzŭ′), n. Gk. Chinese name of **Mencius.**

men·ha·den (mĕn hā′dən), n., pl. **-den.** any marine clupeoid fish of the genus *Brevoortia,* esp. *B. tyrannus,* having the appearance of a shad but with a more compressed body, common along the eastern coast of the U.S., and used for making oil and fertilizer. [t. N Amer. (Narragansett) Ind: they manure]

men·hir (mĕn′hĭr), n. *Archaeol.* an upright monumental stone, standing either alone or with others, as in a cromleck, found chiefly in Cornwall. [t. Breton: *men hir* long stone]

me·ni·al (mē′nĭ əl), adj. **1.** pertaining or proper to domestic servants. **2.** servile. **—**n. **3.** a domestic servant. **4.** a servile person. [ME, t. AF, der. *meiniee,* ult. der. L *mansio* household, MANSION] **—me′ni·al·ly,** adv. **—Syn. 2.** See servile.

me·nin·ges (mĭ nĭn′jēz), n.pl., sing. **meninx** (mē′nĭngks). *Anat.* the three membranes (dura mater, arachnoid, and pia mater) investing the brain and spinal cord. [t. NL, pl. of *mēninx,* t. Gk.: membrane, esp. of the brain] **—me·nin·ge·al** (mĭ nĭn′jĭ əl), adj.

men·in·gi·tis (mĕn′ĭn jī′tĭs), n. *Pathol.* inflammation of the meninges, esp. of the pia mater and arachnoid. [t. NL, f. Gk.: s. *mēninx* membrane + -*itis*-ITIS] **—men·in·git·ic** (mĕn′ĭn jĭt′ĭk), adj.

me·nis·cus (mĭ nĭs′kəs), n., pl. **-nisci** (-nĭs′ī), **-niscuses. 1.** a crescent or crescent-shaped body. **2.** a lens with a crescent-shaped section. See illus. under **lens. 3.** the convex or concave upper surface of a column of liquid, the curvature of which is caused by capillarity. **4.** a disc of cartilage between the articulating ends of the bones in a joint. [t. NL, t. Gk.: m. *mēnískos* crescent, dim. of *mēnē* moon] **—me·nis·coid** (mĭ nĭs′koid), adj.

Menisci (def. 3) A, Concave, containing water; B, Convex, containing mercury

men·i·sper·ma·ceous (mĕn′ĭ spər mā′shəs), adj. belonging to the *Menispermaceae,* a family of dicotyledonous plants, mostly woody climbers, having small, usually three-parted, dioecious flowers, some possessing medicinal properties. See **moonseed.** [f. s. NL *Menispermum* the typical genus, moonseed (f. Gk.: m. *mēnē* moon + m. *spérma* seed) + -ACEOUS]

Men·non·ite (mĕn′ə nīt′), n. a member of a Christian denomination opposed to infant baptism, the taking of oaths, the holding of public office, and military service.

me·no (mĕ′nō), adv. *Music.* less. [t. It., g. L *minus*]

meno-, a word element meaning "month." [t. Gk., comb. form of *mēn*]

me·nol·o·gy (mĭ nŏl′ə jĭ), n., pl. **-gies. 1.** a calendar of the months. **2.** a record or account, as of saints, arranged in the order of a calendar. [t. NL: m.s. *menologium,* t. LGk.: m. *mēnológion,* f. *mēno-* MENO- + *lógion* saying]

men·o·pause (mĕn′ə pôz′), n. *Physiol.* the period of irregular menstrual cycles prior to the final cessation of the menses, occurring normally between the ages of 45 and 50. [f. MENO- + PAUSE] **—men′o·pau′sic,** adj.

Me·nor·ca (mĕ nôr′kä), n. Spanish name of **Minorca.**

men·or·rha·gi·a (mĕn′ə rā′jĭ ə), n. *Pathol.* excessive menstrual discharge. [t. NL. See MENO-, -RRHAGIA]

men·sal¹ (mĕn′səl), adj. monthly. [f. s. L. *mēnsis* month + -AL¹]

men·sal² (mĕn′səl), adj. of, pertaining to, or used at the table. [ME, t. LL: s. *mensālis* of a table]

men·ses (mĕn′sēz), n.pl. *Physiol.* the (approximately) monthly discharge of blood and mucosal tissue from the uterus. [t. L, pl. of *mensis* month]

Men·she·vik (mĕn′shĕ vĭk), n., pl. **-viki** (-vĭkē′), **-viks.** *Russia.* **1.** (orig.) a member of the less radical faction (the *Mensheviki*) of the Social Democratic party. **2.** (after the revolution of Nov. 7, 1917) a member of a

---

b., blend of, blended; c., cognate with; d., dialect, dialectal; der., derived from; f., formed from; g., going back to; m., modification of; r., replacing; s., stem of; t., taken from; ?, perhaps. See the full key on inside cover.

less radical socialistic party or group succeeding the earlier Menshevik faction and opposing the Bolshevik government. [t. Russ.: one of smaller (group), der. *menshe* less] **—Men·she·vism** (měn'shə vĭz'əm), n. **—Men'she·vist**, *adj.*

mens sa·na in cor·po·re sa·no (měnz sā'nə ĭn kôr'pə rē' sā'nō), *Latin*. a sound mind in a sound body.

men·stru·al (měn'strŏŏ əl), *adj.* **1.** *Physiol.* of or pertaining to the menses. **2.** monthly. [t. L: s. *menstruālis* monthly]

men·stru·ate (měn'strŏŏ āt'), *v.i.*, **-ated, -ating.** to discharge the menses. **—men'stru·a'tion,** *n.*

men·stru·ous (měn'strŏŏ əs), *adj.* pertaining to menstruation. [t. L: m. *menstruus* monthly]

men·stru·um (měn'strŏŏ əm), *n., pl.* **-struums, -strua** (-strŏŏ ə). a solvent. [t. ML, prop. neut. of L *menstruus* monthly]

men·sur·a·ble (měn'shər ə bəl), *adj.* measurable. [t. LL: m.s. *mensūrābilis*] **—men'sur·a·bil'i·ty,** *n.*

men·su·ral (měn'shə rəl), *adj.* pertaining to measure.

men·su·ra·tion (měn'shə rā'shən), *n.* **1.** that branch of mathematics which deals with the determination of length, area, and volume. **2.** the act, art, or process of measuring. [t. LL: s. *mensūrātio*]

men·su·ra·tive (měn'shə rā'tĭv), *adj.* adapted for or concerned with measuring.

-ment, a suffix of nouns, often concrete, denoting an action or state resulting (*abridgment, refreshment*), a product (*fragment*), or means (*ornament*). [t. F, t. L: s. *-mentum,* suffix forming nouns, usually from verbs]

men·tal[1] (měn'təl), *adj.* **1.** of or pertaining to the mind. **2.** performed by or existing in the mind: *mental arithmetic.* **3.** pertaining to the intellect; intellectual. [late ME, t. LL: s. *mentālis*]

men·tal[2] (měn'təl), *adj.* of or pertaining to the chin. [f. s. L *mentum* chin + -AL[1]]

mental age, *Psychol.* the degree of mental development or intelligence of an individual in comparison with the average intelligence of normal children at different ages. It is determined by a graded series of tests, in the form of tasks or questions, designed to measure native ability rather than the result of education: *a child 10 years old with a mental age of 12.*

mental deficiency, *Psychol.* a condition characterized by subnormal intelligence so as to handicap the individual in his school or adult life: feeblemindedness. It embraces all types of idiocy, imbecility, and moronity.

mental healing, the healing of any ailment or disorder by mental concentration and suggestion.

men·tal·i·ty (měn tăl'ə tĭ), *n., pl.* **-ties.** mental capacity or endowment; intellectuality; mind: *she was of average mentality.*

men·tal·ly (měn'tə lĭ), *adv.* **1.** in or with the mind or intellect; intellectually. **2.** with regard to the mind.

men·tha·ceous (měn thā'shəs), *adj.* belonging to the *Menthaceae* (usually included in the *Labiatae*) or mint family of plants, including the horsemint, peppermint, pennyroyal, savory, etc. [f. s. L *mentha* MINT[1] + -ACEOUS]

men·thene (měn'thēn), *n. Chem.* a liquid cycloalkene, $C_{10}H_{18}$, synthetically obtainable from menthol. [t. G: m. *menthen,* f. s. L *mentha* MINT[1] + -*en* -ENE]

men·thol (měn'thôl, -thŏl), *n.* a colorless, crystalline alcohol, $C_{10}H_{20}O$, present in peppermint oil, used in perfume and confectionery, and for colds and nasal disorders because of its cooling effect on mucous membranes. [t. G: f. s. L *mentha* MINT[1] + -*ol* -OL[1]]

men·tho·lat·ed (měn'thə lā'tĭd), *adj.* **1.** covered or treated with menthol. **2.** saturated with or containing menthol.

men·tion (měn'shən), *v.t.* **1.** to refer briefly to; refer to by name incidentally; name, specify, or speak of. **2.** to say incidentally (with a clause). **—***n.* **3.** a speaking of or mentioning; a reference, direct or incidental. [t. L: s. *mentio* a calling to mind, mention; r. ME *mencioun,* t. OF] **—men'tion·a·ble,** *adj.* **—men'tion·er,** *n.*

Men·ton (měn tôn'; *Fr.* män tôn'), *n.* a city in SE France, on the Mediterranean: winter resort. 13,864 (1946). Italian, **Men·to·ne** (měn tô'ně).

Men·tor (měn'tər), *n.* **1.** the friend to whom Odysseus, when departing for Troy, gave the charge of his household. **2.** (*l.c.*) a wise and trusted counselor.

men·u (měn'ū, mā'nū; *Fr.* mə ny'), *n.* **1.** a list of the dishes served at a meal; a bill of fare. **2.** the dishes served. [t. F: detailed list, orig. adj., small, g. L *minūtus* MINUTE[2]]

Men·u·hin (měn'yŏŏ ĭn), *n.* **Yehudi** (yə hŏŏ'dĭ), born 1917, U.S. violinist.

me·ow (mĭ ou', myou), *n.* **1.** the sound a cat makes. **—***v.i.* **2.** to make such a sound. Also, **miaow, miaou, miaul.**

Meph·i·stoph·e·les (měf'ə stŏf'ə lēz'), *n. Medieval Demonology.* one of the seven chief devils. He is represented in Goethe's *Faust* as a crafty, sardonic, and scoffing fiend. **—Meph·is·to·phe·li·an** (měf'ĭs tŏ fē'lĭ ən), *adj.*

me·phit·ic (mĭ fĭt'ĭk), *adj.* **1.** offensive to the smell. **2.** noxious; pestilential; poisonous. **—me·phit'i·cal·ly,** *adv.*

me·phi·tis (mĭ fī'tĭs), *n.* **1.** a noxious or pestilential exhalation, esp. from the earth. **2.** a noisome or poisonous stench. [t. L]

mer·can·tile (mûr'kən tĭl, -tīl'), *adj.* **1.** of or pertaining to merchants or to trade; commercial. **2.** engaged in trade or commerce. **3.** *Econ.* of or pertaining to the mercantile system. [t. F, t. It., der. *mercante,* g. L *mercans,* ppr., trading] **—Syn. 1.** See **commercial.**

mercantile agency, a concern which obtains information concerning the financial standing, business reputation, and credit ratings of individuals, firms, and corporations for the benefit of its subscribers.

mercantile paper, negotiable commercial paper as promissory notes given by merchants for goods purchased, drafts drawn against purchasers, etc.

mercantile system, *Econ.* a system of political and economic policy, evolving with the modern national state, which sought to secure the political supremacy of a state in its rivalry with other states. According to this system, money was regarded as a store of wealth, and the great object of a state was the importation of the precious metals, by exporting the utmost possible quantity of its products and importing as little as possible, thus establishing a favorable balance of trade.

mer·can·til·ism (mûr'kən tĭl ĭz'əm, -tīl ĭz'əm), *n.* **1.** the mercantile spirit. **2.** the mercantile system. **—mer'can·til·ist,** *n.*

mer·cap·tan (mər kăp'tăn), *n. Chem.* any of a class of sulfur-containing compounds, with the type formula RSH, the low boiling members of which have an extremely offensive odor, esp. **ethyl mercaptan,** C_2H_5SH, a colorless liquid, with an offensive, garliclike odor. [t. G: arbitrary abbr. of L expression (*corpus*) *mer(curium) captan(s)* body catching mercury]

Mer·ca·tor (mər kā'tər; *Flem.* měr kä'tŏr), *n.* **Gerhard** (gĕr'härt), (*Gerhard Kremer*) 1512–94, Flemish cartographer and geographer.

Mercator's projection, a map projection with rectangular grid which is conformable and on which any rhumb line is represented as a straight line, particularly useful for navigation, though the scale varies notably with latitude and areal size and the shapes of large areas are greatly distorted.

Mercator's projection

mer·ce·nar·y (mûr'sə něr'ĭ), *adj., n., pl.* **-naries. —***adj.* **1.** working or acting merely for gain. **2.** hired (now only of soldiers serving in a foreign army). **—***n.* **3.** a professional soldier serving in a foreign army. **4.** any hireling. [t. L: m.s. *mercēnārius* hired for pay] **—mer'ce·nar'i·ly,** *adv.* **—mer'ce·nar'i·ness,** *n.* **—Syn. 1.** venal, grasping, sordid; acquisitive, avaricious. **—Ant. 1.** unworldly.

mer·cer (mûr'sər), *n. Brit.* a dealer in textile fabrics, esp. silks, etc. [ME, t. OF: m. *mercier,* der. OF *merz* goods, wares, g. L *merx*]

mer·cer·ize (mûr'sə rīz'), *v.t.,* **-ized, -izing.** to treat (cotton yarns or fabric) with caustic alkali under tension, increasing strength, luster and affinity for dye. [from J. *Mercer,* English calico-printer, the patentee (1850) of the process. See -IZE] **—mer'cer·i·za'tion,** *n.*

mer·cer·y (mûr'sə rĭ), *n., pl.* **-ceries.** *Brit.* **1.** a mercer's shop. **2.** mercers' wares. [ME *mercerie,* t. OF, der. *mercier* MERCER]

mer·chan·dise (*n.* mûr'chən dīz', -dīs'; *v.* mûr'chən dīz'), *n., v.,* **-dised, -dising. —***n.* **1.** goods; commodities; esp. manufactured goods. **—***v.i., v.t.* **2.** to trade; buy and sell. Also, **mer'chan·dize'.** [ME *marchandise,* t. OF, der. *marchand* MERCHANT] **—mer'chan·dis'er,** *n.*

mer·chant (mûr'chənt), *n.* **1.** one who buys and sells commodities for profit, in England chiefly a wholesaler. **2.** a storekeeper. **—***adj.* **3.** pertaining to trade or commerce: *a merchant ship.* **4.** pertaining to the merchant marine. [ME, t. OF: m. *marcheant,* ult. der. L *mercārī* trade]

mer·chant·a·ble (mûr'chən tə bəl), *adj.* marketable: *merchantable war-surplus goods.*

mer·chant·man (mûr'chənt mən), *n., pl.* **-men.** a trading vessel.

merchant marine, **1.** the vessels of a nation engaged in commerce. **2.** the officers and crews of merchant vessels.

Merchant of Venice, The, a comedy (about 1598) by Shakespeare.

mer·ci (měr sē'), *interj. French.* thank you.

Mer·ci·a (mûr'shĭ ə, -shə), *n.* an early English kingdom in central Britain. **—Mer'ci·an,** *adj., n.*

mer·ci beau·coup (měr sē' bō kŏŏ'), *French.* thank (you) very much.

Mer·cier (měr syě'), *n.* **Dé·siré Joseph** (dā zē rē' zhō zěf'), 1851–1926, Belgian cardinal and patriot.

Mercia, A.D. 800

mer·ci·ful (mûr'sĭ fəl), *adj.* full of mercy; exercising, or characterized by, mercy; compassionate. **—mer'ci·ful·ly,** *adv.* **—mer'ci·ful·ness,** *n.* **—Syn.** kind, clement, lenient. **—Ant.** hard-hearted.

mer·ci·less (mûr′sĭ lĭs), *adj.* without any mercy; pitiless. —**mer′ci·less·ly**, *adv.* —**mer′ci·less·ness**, *n.*

mer·cu·rate (mûr′kyə rāt′), *v.t.*, **-rated**, **-rating.** 1. to add mercury to (a compound). 2. *Obsolesc.* to expose to the action of mercury.

mer·cu·ri·al (mər kyŏŏr′Y əl), *adj.* 1. pertaining to, consisting of or containing, or caused by, the metal mercury. 2. (*cap.*) of or pertaining to the god Mercury or the planet Mercury. 3. sprightly; volatile. 4. flighty; fickle; changeable. —*n.* 5. a preparation of mercury used as a drug. [t. L: s. *mercuriālis* of Mercury] —**mer·cu′ri·al·ly**, *adv.* —**mer·cu′ri·al·ness**, *n.*

mer·cu·ri·al·ism (mər kyŏŏr′Y ə lĭz′əm), *n. Pathol.* a morbid condition caused by mercury.

mer·cu·ri·al·ize (mər kyŏŏr′Y ə līz′), *v.t.*, **-ized**, **-izing.** 1. to make mercurial. 2. to treat or impregnate with mercury or one of its compounds. —**mer·cu′ri·al·i·za′tion**, *n.*

mer·cu·ric (mər kyŏŏr′Yk), *adj. Chem.* of or containing mercury, esp. in the divalent state (Hg+2).

mercuric chloride, corrosive sublimate. Also, **mercury chloride.**

mer·cu·ro·chrome (mər kyŏŏr′ə krōm′), *n.* 1. an iridescent green powder which dissolves in water to furnish a red solution, used as an antiseptic and germicide. 2. a solution of this compound. 3. (*cap.*) a trademark for this substance or its solution. [f. *mercuro-* (comb. form of MERCURY) + CHROME]

mer·cu·rous (mər kyŏŏr′əs, mûr′kyə rəs), *adj. Chem.* containing monovalent mercury Hg+1 or Hg₂+2.

mer·cu·ry (mûr′kyə rY), *n., pl.* **-ries.** 1. *Chem.* a heavy, silver-white metallic element, remarkable for its fluidity at ordinary temperatures; quicksilver. *Symbol:* Hg (for **hydrargyrum**); *at. wt.:* 200.6; *at. no.:* 80; *sp. gr.:* 13.546 at 20° C.; *freezing point:* −38.9° C.; *boiling point:* 357° C. 2. a preparation of mercury (metal) used in medicine. 3. (*cap.*) *Astron.* the planet nearest the sun, having a mean distance from the sun of about 36,000,000 miles, and a period of revolution of 88.0 days. Its diameter is 3000 miles. 4. (*cap.*) a Roman deity, messenger of the gods, and god of commerce, dexterity, and eloquence (identified with *Hermes*). 5. a messenger, or carrier of news (sometimes used as the name of a newspaper or periodical). 6. any herb of the euphorbiaceous genus *Mercurialis*, as *M. perennis* (**dog's-mercury**), a poisonous weed. [ME, t. L: m.s. *Mercurius* (def. 3, 4; in ML def. 1)]

mercury chloride, mercuric chloride.

mercury fulminate, the mercury salt of fulminic acid, Hg(ONC)₂, which explodes as a result of very slight friction or shock when dry, used as a detonator.

mer·cu·ry-va·por lamp (mûr′kyə rY vā′pər), a lamp producing a light with a high actinic and ultraviolet content by means of an electric arc in mercury vapor.

mer·cy (mûr′sY), *n., pl.* **-cies.** 1. compassionate or kindly forbearance shown toward an offender, an enemy, or other person in one's power; compassion, pity, or benevolence. 2. disposition to be merciful: *an adversary wholly without mercy.* 3. discretionary power as to clemency or severity, pardon or punishment, or the like: *to be at the mercy of a conqueror.* 4. an act of forbearance, compassion, or favor, esp. of God toward his creatures. [ME, t. OF: m. *merci*, fem., favor, mercy; masc., thanks, g. L *merces* pay, ML mercy] —**Syn.** 1. forgiveness, indulgence; clemency, leniency. —**Ant.** 1. cruelty.

mercy killing, euthanasia.

mercy seat, 1. the gold covering on the ark of the covenant, regarded as the resting place of God (see Ex. 25:17–22). 2. the throne of God.

mere[1] (mYr), *adj., superl.* **merest.** 1. being nothing more nor better than what is specified; pure and simple. 2. *Chiefly Law.* belonging or pertaining to a single individual or group, or sole. 3. *Obs.* pure or unmixed. 4. *Obs.* absolute or unqualified. [late ME, t. L: m.s. *merus* pure, unmixed, mere]
—**Syn.** 1. MERE, BARE imply a scant sufficiency. They are often interchangeable, but MERE frequently means "no more than (enough)." BARE suggests "scarcely as much as (enough)." Thus *a mere livelihood* means enough to live on but no more; *a bare livelihood* means scarcely enough to live on. —**Ant.** 1. abundant.

mere[2] (mYr), *n. Poetic or Brit. Dial.* a lake; a pond. [ME and OE, c. G *meer*; akin to L *mare* sea]

-mere, a word element meaning "part," as in *blastomere*. [comb. form repr. Gk. *méros*]

Mer·e·dith (mĕr′ə dĭth), *n.* 1. George, 1828–1909, British novelist and poet. 2. Owen, pen name of Edward Robert Bulwer-Lytton. See Lytton (def. 2).

mere·ly (mYr′lY), *adv.* 1. only as specified, and nothing more; simply: *merely as a matter of form.* 2. *Obs.* purely. 3. *Obs.* absolutely or entirely.

mer·e·tri·cious (mĕr′ə trĭsh′əs), *adj.* 1. alluring by a show of false attractions; showily attractive; tawdry. 2. *Archaic.* of, pertaining to, or characteristic of a prostitute. [t. L: m. *meretrīcius* of prostitutes] —**mer′e·tri′cious·ly**, *adv.* —**mer′e·tri′cious·ness**, *n.*

mer·gan·ser (mər găn′sər), *n., pl.* **-sers**, (*esp. collectively*) **-ser.** any of several saw-billed, fish-eating, diving ducks of the subfamily *Merginae*, as the American **hooded merganser**, *Lophodytes cucullatus*, the male of which has a black-and-white, fanlike crest. [t. NL, f. s. L *mergus* diver (bird) + *anser* goose]

merge (mûrj), *v.*, **merged**, **merging.** —*v.t.* 1. to cause to be swallowed up or absorbed; to sink the identity of by combination (often fol. by *in* or *into*). —*v.i.* 2. to become swallowed up or absorbed; lose identity by absorption (often fol. by *in* or *into*). [t. L: m.s. *mergere* dip, plunge, sink] —**mer·gence** (mûr′jəns), *n.*

merg·er (mûr′jər), *n.* 1. a statutory combination of two or more corporations by the transfer of the properties to one, surviving corporation. 2. any combination of two or more business enterprises into a single enterprise. 3. act of merging.

Mé·ri·da (mĕ′rē dä′), *n.* a city in SE Mexico: the capital of Yucatán state. 98,852 (1940).

Mer·i·den (mĕr′ə dən), *n.* a city in central Connecticut. 44,088 (1950).

me·rid·i·an (mə rĭd′Y ən), *n.* 1. *Geog.* **a.** a great circle of the earth passing through the poles and any given point on the earth's surface. **b.** the half of such a circle included between the poles. 2. *Astron.* the great circle of the celestial sphere which passes through its poles and the observer's zenith. 3. a point or period of highest development, greatest prosperity, or the like. —*adj.* 4. of or pertaining to a meridian. 5. of or pertaining to midday or noon: *the meridian hour.* 6. pertaining to a period of greatest elevation, prosperity, splendor, etc.; culminating. [t. L: s. *merīdiānus* of midday, of the south; r. ME *meridien*, t. OF]

Me·rid·i·an (mə rĭd′Y ən), *n.* a city in E Mississippi. 41,893 (1950).

me·rid·i·o·nal (mə rĭd′Y ə nəl), *adj.* 1. of, pertaining to, or resembling a meridian. 2. characteristic of the south or people inhabiting the south, esp. of France. 3. southern; southerly. —*n.* 4. an inhabitant of the south, esp. of France. [ME, t. LL: s. *merīdiōnalis* of midday] —**me·rid′i·o·nal·ly**, *adv.*

Mé·ri·mée (mĕ rē mĕ′), *n.* **Prosper** (prôs pĕr′), 1803–1870, French short-story writer, novelist, and essayist.

me·ringue (mə răng′), *n.* 1. a mixture of sugar and beaten egg whites formed into small cakes and baked, or spread over pastry, puddings, etc. 2. a dish made with it. [t. F, t. G: m. *meringe*, lit., cookie of Mehringen]

me·ri·no (mə rē′nō), *n., pl.* **-nos**, *adj.* —*n.* 1. a variety of sheep which originated in Spain, valued for its fine wool. 2. wool from merino sheep. 3. a knitted fabric made of wool or wool and cotton. —*adj.* 4. made of merino wool, yarn, or cloth. [t. Sp., der. L (*lāna*) *mera* pure (wool)]

Merino, *Ovis aries*
(2 ft. high at the shoulder)

Mer·i·on·eth·shire (mĕr′Y ŏn′Yth shĭr′, -shər), *n.* a county in N Wales. 39,000 pop. (est. 1946); 660 sq. mi. *Co. Seat:* Dolgelly. Also, **Mer′i·on·eth.**

mer·i·stem (mĕr′ə stĕm′), *n. Bot.* embryonic tissue; undifferentiated, growing, actively dividing cells. [f. Gk.: s. *meristós* divided + *-ēm*(a), n. suffix]

mer·it (mĕr′Yt), *n.* 1. claim to commendation; excellence; worth. 2. something that entitles to reward or commendation; a commendable quality, act, etc.: *the merits of a book or a play.* 3. (*pl.*) the substantial right and wrong of a matter unobscured by technicalities: *the merits of a case.* 4. the state or fact of deserving well; good desert. 5. that which is deserved, whether good or bad. 6. (*sometimes pl.*) state or fact of deserving, or desert: *to treat a person according to his merits.* —*v.t.* 7. to be worthy of; deserve. —*v.i.* 8. *Chiefly Theol.* to acquire merit. [ME *merite*, t. F, t. L: m. *meritum*, prop. pp. neut., deserved, earned]
—**Syn.** 1. MERIT, DESERT, WORTH refer to the quality in a person, action, or thing which entitles to recognition, esp. favorable recognition. MERIT is usually the excellence which entitles to praise: *a man of great merit.* DESERT is the quality which entitles one to a just reward: *according to his deserts.* WORTH is always used in a favorable sense and signifies inherent value or goodness: *the worth of his contribution is incalculable.* —**Ant.** 1. worthlessness.

mer·it·ed (mĕr′Yt əd), *adj.* deserved. —**mer′it·ed·ly**, *adv.*

mer·i·to·ri·ous (mĕr′ə tôr′Y əs), *adj.* deserving of reward or commendation; possessing merit. [ME, t. ML: m. *meritōrius* meritorious, L serving to earn money] —**mer′i·to′ri·ous·ly**, *adv.* —**mer′i·to′ri·ous·ness**, *n.*

merle (mûrl), *n. Chiefly Scot. and Poetic.* the common European blackbird, *Turdus merula*. Also, **merl.** [t. F, g. L *merula, merulus*]

mer·lin (mûr′lYn), *n.* any of various bold small hawks of the genus *Falco*, esp. the **European merlin**, *F. columbarius aesalon*, and the closely related North American pigeon hawk, *F. c. columbarius.* [ME *merlion*, t. AF: m. *merilun*, der. OF *esmeril*, t. Gmc.; cf. OHG *smirl*]

Mer·lin (mûr′lYn), *n. Arthurian Romance.* a venerable magician and seer. [t. Welsh: unexplained m. *Myrddin*]

mer·lon (mûr′lən), *n.* (in a battlement) the solid part between two crenels. See illus. under **battlement.** [t. F, t. It.: m. *merlone*, ult. der. L *mergae* fork]

mer·maid (mûr′mād′), *n.* an imaginary female marine creature, typically having the head and trunk of a woman and the tail of a fish. [ME *mermayde.* See MERE[2], MAID]

b., blend of, blended; c., cognate with; d., dialect, dialectal; der., derived from; f., formed from; g., going back to; m., modification of; r., replacing; s., stem of; t., taken from; ?, perhaps. See the full key on inside cover.

mer·man (mûr′măn′), *n., pl.* **-men.** an imaginary man of the sea, corresponding to a mermaid.

mer·o·blas·tic (mĕr′ə blăs′tĭk), *adj. Embryol.* applied to large eggs that undergo partial cleavage (opposed to *holoblastic*). [f. Gk. *mĕro(s)* part + -BLAST + -IC]

Mer·o·ë (mĕr′ō ē), *n.* a ruined city in the Anglo-Egyptian Sudan, on the Nile, NE of Khartoum: a capital of ancient Ethiopia.

me·rog·o·ny (mə rŏg′ə nĭ), *Embryol.* the development of egg fragments. [f. Gk. *mĕro(s)* part + -GONY]

Mer·o·vin·gi·an (mĕr′ə vĭn′jĭ ən), *adj.* designating or pertaining to the Frankish dynasty which reigned in Gaul and Germany from about A.D. 500 to A.D. 751.

mer·o·zo·ite (mĕr′ə zō′īt), *n.* one of the products of reproduction in the asexual phase of parasitic protozoans of the class *Sporozoa*, as malaria parasites.

Mer·ri·mac (mĕr′ə măk′), *n.* the first ironclad warship: used by the Confederates in a battle against the *Monitor* (1862).

Mer·ri·mack (mĕr′ə măk′), *n.* a river flowing from central New Hampshire through NE Massachusetts into the Atlantic. 110 mi.

mer·ri·ment (mĕr′ĭ mənt), *n.* **1.** merry gaiety; mirth; hilarity; laughter. **2.** *Obs.* merrymaking. —**Syn. 1.** See **mirth.**

mer·ry (mĕr′ĭ), *adj.,* **mer·ri·er, mer·ri·est. 1.** full of cheer or gaiety; festive; joyous in disposition or spirit. **2.** laughingly gay; mirthful; hilarious. **3.** *Archaic.* pleasant or delightful: *merry England.* **4. make merry,** to be gay or festive. [ME *meri(e), myrie, murie,* OE *myr(i)ge, mer(i)ge* pleasant, delightful] —**mer′ri·ly,** *adv.* —**mer′ri·ness,** *n.* —**Syn. 1.** joyous. See **gay. 2.** jolly, jovial. —**Ant. 1.** sad. **2.** solemn.

mer·ry-an·drew (mĕr′ĭ ăn′drōō), *n.* a clown; buffoon.

mer·ry-go-round (mĕr′ĭ gō round′), *n.* **1.** a revolving machine, as a circular platform fitted with hobbyhorses, etc., on which persons, esp. children, ride for amusement. **2.** any whirl or rapid round.

mer·ry·mak·er (mĕr′ĭ mā′kər), *n.* one who is making merry.

mer·ry·mak·ing (mĕr′ĭ mā′kĭng), *adj.* **1.** the act of making merry. **2.** a merry festivity; a revel. —*adj.* **3.** producing mirth; gay; festive.

mer·ry·thought (mĕr′ĭ thôt′), *n. Chiefly Brit.* the wishbone of a bird. [from the custom of two persons pulling the bone until it breaks; the person holding the longer (sometimes shorter) piece will supposedly marry first or will be granted a wish made at the time]

Mer·sey (mûr′zĭ), *n.* a river in W England, flowing from Derbyshire W to the Irish Sea. ab. 70 mi.

Mer·thyr Tyd·fil (mûr′thər tĭd′vĭl; *Welsh* tŭd′vĭl), a city in SE Wales. 60,460 (est. 1946).

mes-, var. of **meso-,** sometimes used before vowels, as in *mesencephalon.*

me·sa (mā′sə; *Sp.* mě′sä), *n.* a land form having a relatively flat top and bounded wholly or in part with steep, rock walls, common in arid and semiarid parts of the southwestern U.S. [t. Sp.; g. L *mensa* table]

mé·sal·li·ance (mā zál′ĭ əns; *Fr.* mě zál yäns′), *n.* a marriage with a social inferior; a misalliance. [F: f. *més-* MIS- + *alliance* ALLIANCE[1]]

Me·sa Ver·de (mā′sə vûrd′; *Sp.* mě′sä věr′dě), a national park in SW Colorado: ruins of cliff dwellings. 80 sq. mi.

mes·cal (měs kăl′), *n.* **1.** either of two species of cactus, *Lophophora Williamsii* and *L. Lewinii*, of Texas and northern Mexico, whose buttonlike tops (**mescal buttons**) are dried and used as a stimulant, esp. by the Indians. **2.** an intoxicating spirit distilled from the fermented juice of certain species of agave. **3.** any agave yielding this spirit. [t. Sp.: m. *mezcal,* t. Aztec: m. *mexcalli metl* (maguey) liquor]

mes·dames (mē dăm′), *n.* pl. of **madame.**

mes·de·moi·selles (mēd mwá zěl′), *n.* pl. of **mademoiselle.** [t. F]

me·seems (mē sēmz′), *v.impers.; pt.* **meseemed.** *Archaic.* it seems to me.

mes·en·ceph·a·lon (měs′ěn sěf′ə lŏn′), *n., pl.* **-la** (-lə). *Anat.* the middle segment of the brain; the midbrain. [t. NL. See MES-, ENCEPHALON] —**mes·en·ce·phal·ic** (měs′ěn sə făl′ĭk), *adj.*

mes·en·chyme (měs′ěng kĭm), *n. Embryol.* the nonepithelial mesoderm. Also, **mes·en·chy·ma** (měs ěng′kə mə). [t. NL, f. Gk.: *mes-* MES- + m. *ěnchyma* infusion] —**mes·en·chy·mal** (měs ěng′kə məl), **mes·en·chym·a·tous** (měs ěng kĭm′ə təs), *adj.*

mes·en·ter·y (měs′ən těr′ĭ), *n., pl.* **-teries.** *Anat.* a fold or duplicature of peritoneum, investing and attaching to the posterior wall of the abdomen. [t. NL: m.s. *mesenterium,* t. Gk.: m. *mesentĕrion* the middle intestine] —**mes·en·ter′ic,** *adj.*

mesh (měsh), *n.* **1.** one of the open spaces of network of a net. **2.** (*pl.*) the threads that bound such spaces. **3.** (*pl.*) means of catching or holding fast: *caught in the meshes of the law.* **4.** a network or net. **5.** *Mach.* **a.** the engagement of gear teeth. **b. in mesh,** with gears engaged. —*v.t.* **6.** to catch or entangle in or as in the meshes of a net; enmesh. **7.** to form with meshes, as a net. **8.** *Mach.* to engage, as gear teeth. —*v.i.* **9.** to become enmeshed. **10.** *Mach.* to become or be engaged, as the teeth of one wheel with those of another. [cf. OE *mǣx* and *mǣscre* net]

Me·shach (mē′shăk). See **Shadrach.**

Mes·hed (měsh′hěd; *Per.* mäsh häd′), *n.* a city in NE Iran: a Mohammedan shrine. 176,471 (1940).

mesh·work (měsh′wûrk′), *n.* meshed work; network.

mesh·y (měsh′ĭ), *adj.* formed with meshes; meshed.

me·si·al (mē′zĭ əl, měs′ĭ əl), *adj.* medial. [f. MES- + -IAL] —**me′si·al·ly,** *adv.*

me·sit·y·lene (mĭ sĭt′ə lēn′, měs′ə tə lēn′), *n. Chem.* a colorless, liquid aromatic hydrocarbon, $C_6H_3(CH_3)_3$, found in coal tar but prepared from acetone. [f. *mesityl* (f. s. Gk. *mesĭtēs* go-between + -YL) + -ENE]

mes·mer·ic (měs měr′ĭk, měz-), *adj.* hypnotic. —**mes·mer′i·cal·ly,** *adv.*

mes·mer·ism (měs′mər ĭz′əm, měz′-), *n.* hypnotism. [named after F. A. *Mesmer* (1733–1815), German physician, who propounded the doctrine. See -ISM] —**mes′·mer·ist,** *n.*

mes·mer·ize (měs′mə rīz′, měz′-), *v.t., v.i.,* **-ized, -izing.** to hypnotize. —**mes′mer·i·za′tion,** *n.* —**mes′·mer·iz′er,** *n.*

mesn·al·ty (mē′nəl tĭ), *n. Law.* the estate of a mesne lord. [t. F: m. *mesnalte,* der. OF *mesne* MESNE]

mesne (mēn), *adj. Law.* intermediate or intervening. [t. F, altered sp. of AF *meen* MEAN[3]]

mesne lord, a feudal lord who held land of a superior.

meso-, a word element meaning "middle," used in combination, chiefly in scientific terms. Also, **mes-.** [t. Gk., comb. form of *mĕsos* middle]

mes·o·blast (měs′ə blăst′, mē′sə-), *n. Embryol.* the prospective mesoderm. —**mes·o·blas′tic,** *adj.*

mes·o·carp (měs′ə kärp′, mē′sə-), *n. Bot.* the middle layer of pericarp, as the fleshy part of certain fruits. See diag. under **endocarp.**

mes·o·ce·phal·ic (měs′ō sə făl′ĭk, mē′sō-), *adj. Cephalom.* having a head with a cephalic index between that of dolichocephaly and brachycephaly.

mes·o·cra·nic (měs′ō krā′nĭk, mē′so·), *adj. Craniom.* having a skull with a cranial index between that of dolichocrany and brachycrany.

mes·o·crat·ic (měs′ə krăt′ĭk, mē′sə-), *adj. Geol.* composed of light and dark minerals in nearly equal amounts. [f. MESO- + m. s. Gk. *krátos* rule + -IC]

mes·o·derm (měs′ə dûrm′, mē′sə-), *n. Embryol.* the middle germ layer of a metazoan embryo. —**mes′o·der′mal, mes′o·der′mic,** *adj.*

mes·o·gas·tri·um (měs′ə găs′trĭ əm, mē′sə-), *n. Anat.* the umbilical region of the abdomen, situated above the hypogastrium and below the epigastrium. [t. NL, f. *meso-* MESO- + Gk. *gastēr* belly + *-ium* -IUM] —**mes′·o·gas′tric,** *adj.*

me·sog·na·thous (mĭ sŏg′nə thəs), *adj. Anthropol.* **1.** having medium, slightly protruding jaws. **2.** having a moderate or intermediate gnathic index of from 98 to 103. —**me·sog′na·thism, me·sog′na·thy,** *n.*

Mes·o·lon·ghi (mě′sō lông′gē), *n.* Missolonghi.

me·son (měs′ŏn, mē′sŏn), *n. Physics.* a constituent particle of cosmic rays, having a mass of the order of 200 times that of an electron and a unit negative or positive charge.

mes·o·neph·ros (měs′ə něf′rŏs, mē′sə-), *n. Embryol.* the middle kidney, developing between the pronephros and the metanephros, in proximity with the sex glands. In males of the higher vertebrates, it becomes a part of the epididymis. [t. NL, f. Gk.: *meso-* MESO- + *nephrŏs* kidney] —**mes′o·neph′ric,** *adj.*

mes·o·phyll (měs′ə fĭl′, mē′sə-), *n. Bot.* the parenchyma which forms the interior parts of a leaf, usually containing chlorophyll.

mes·o·phyte (měs′ə fīt′, mē′sə-), *n. Ecol.* a plant growing under conditions of well balanced moisture supply. Cf. **hydrophyte** and **xerophyte.** —**mes·o·phyt·ic** (měs′ə fĭt′ĭk, mē′sə-), *adj.*

Mes·o·po·ta·mi·a (měs′ə pə tā′mĭ ə), *n.* **1.** an ancient country in Asia between the Tigris and Euphrates rivers: the modern kingdom of Iraq includes much of this ancient region. **2.** (loosely) Iraq. —**Mes′o·po·ta′mi·an,** *adj., n.*

mes·or·rhine (měs′ə rĭn′, -rĭn, mē′sə-), *adj. Anthropol.* having a moderately broad and high-bridged nose. [f. MESO- + m.s. Gk. *rhīs* nose]

mes·o·the·li·um (měs′ə thē′lĭ əm, mē′sə-), *n., pl.* **-lia** (-lĭ ə). *Anat., Embryol.* epithelium of mesodermal origin, which lines the body cavities. [f. MESO- + *-thelium* as in EPITHELIUM] —**mes′o·the′li·al,** *adj.*

mes·o·tho·rax (měs′ə thôr′ăks, mē′sə-), *n., pl.* **-tho·raxes, -thoraces** (-thôr′ə sēz′). the middle one of the three divisions of an insect's thorax, bearing the second pair of legs and the first pair of wings. —**mes·o·tho·rac·ic** (měs′ə thō rǎs′ĭk), *adj.*

mes·o·tho·ri·um (měs′ə thôr′ĭ əm, měz′ə-), *n. Chem.* an isotope of radium (though far more radioactive) formed from thorium minerals, and existing in two forms, **mesothorium I,** *at. no.:* 88; *at. wt.:* 228; *half-life:* 6.7 yrs.; **mesothorium II,** *at. no.:* 89; *at. wt.:* 228; *half-life:* 6.2 hrs.

mes·o·tron (měs′ə trŏn′, mē′sə-), *n. Physics.* meson.

Mes·o·zo·ic (měs′ə zō′ĭk, mē′sə-), *Stratig.* —*adj.* **1.** pertaining to the geological era or rocks intermediate between Paleozoic and Cenozoic; the era of "medieval life" or age of reptiles. —*n.* **2.** the era or rocks comprising the Triassic, Jurassic, and Cretaceous periods or systems. [f. MESO- + s. Gk. *zōē* life + -IC]

mes·quite (měs·kēt′, měs′kēt), *n.* **1.** a mimosaceous tree or shrub, *Prosopis glandulosa,* of the southwestern U.S., Mexico, etc., whose beanlike pods are rich in sugar and form a valuable fodder. **2.** any species of *Prosopis.* [t. Amer. Sp.: m. *mezquite,* from Aztec name]

mess (měs), *n.* **1.** a dirty or untidy condition: *the room was in a mess.* **2.** a state of embarrassing confusion: *his affairs are in a mess.* **3.** an unpleasant or difficult situation: *to get into a mess.* **4.** a dirty or untidy mass, litter, or jumble: *a mess of papers.* **5.** a group regularly taking meals together, as in the army. **6.** the meal so taken. **7.** a quantity of food sufficient for a dish or a single occasion. **8.** *Colloq. or Dial.* a quantity of food of indefinite amount. **9.** a sloppy or unappetizing preparation of food. **10.** a dish or quantity of soft or liquid food. —*v.t.* **11.** to make dirty or untidy (often fol. by *up*): *to mess up a room.* **12.** to make a mess of, or muddle (affairs, etc.). **13.** to supply with meals, as soldiers, etc. —*v.i.* **14.** to eat in company, esp. as a member of a mess. **15.** to make a dirty or untidy mess. **16.** to busy oneself in an untidy or confused way (often with *around*). **17. mess in,** to meddle officiously. [ME *mes,* t. OF: lit., put (on the table), g. L *missum,* pp. neut., sent, put]

mes·sage (měs′ĭj), *n.* **1.** a communication, as of information, advice, direction, or the like, transmitted through a messenger or other agency. **2.** an official communication, as from a chief executive to a legislative body: *the President's message to Congress.* **3.** an inspired communication of a prophet. [ME, t. OF, der. *mes* envoy, g. L *missus,* pp., sent]

Mes·sa·li·na (měs′ə·lī′nə), *n.* **Valeria** (və·lĭr′ĭ·ə), died A.D. 48, third wife of the Roman emperor Claudius, notorious for her immorality.

mes·sa·line (měs′ə·lēn′, měs′ə·lēn′), *n.* a thin, soft silk fabric with a twilled or a satin weave. [t. F]

Mes·se·ne (mě·sē′nē), *n.* a city of ancient Greece: the capital of **Mes·se·ni·a** (mě·sē·nē′ä), a district in the SW Peloponnesus.

mes·sen·ger (měs′ən·jər), *n.* **1.** one who bears a message or goes on an errand, esp. as a matter of duty or business. **2.** one employed to convey official despatches or to go on other official or special errands: *a bank messenger.* **3.** a herald or harbinger. **4.** anything regarded as sent on an errand. [ME *messanger, messager,* t. OF: m. *messager,* der. *message* MESSAGE] —**Syn. 1.** bearer, courier. **3.** forerunner, precursor.

mess hall, a place where a group eats regularly.

Mes·si·ah (mə·sī′ə), *n.* **1.** the title applied to an expected deliverer of the Jewish people, and hence to Jesus (see John 4:25, 26). **2.** any expected deliverer. **3.** an oratorio (1742) by Handel. Also, **Mes·si·as** (mə·sī′əs). [var. of L *Messīas* (Vulgate), t. Gk., Hellenized form of Heb. *māshīaḥ* anointed] —**Mes·si·ah·ship′,** *n.* —**Mes·si·an·ic** (měs′ĭ·an′ĭk), *adj.*

Mes·si·dor (měs·sē·dôr′), *n.* (in the calendar of the first French republic) the tenth month of the year, extending from June 19 to July 18. [F: f. L *messi*(s) harvest + s. Gk. *dôron* gift]

mes·sieurs (měs′ərz; *Fr.* mě·syœ′) *n.* pl. of **monsieur.**

Mes·si·na (mě·sē′nə), *n.* **1.** a seaport in NE Sicily: totally destroyed by an earthquake, 1908. 211,587 (est. 1946). **2. Strait of,** a strait between Sicily and Italy. 2½ mi. wide.

Mes·sines (mě·sēn′), *n.* a village in W Belgium, near Ypres: battles, 1914, 1917.

mess kit, a portable metal dish with eating utensils, esp. one carried by a soldier in the field.

mess·mate (měs′māt′), *n.* an associate in a mess, esp. in a ship's mess.

Messrs. messieurs (used as if a plural of *Mr.*).

mes·suage (měs′wĭj), *n. Law.* a dwelling house with its adjacent buildings and the lands appropriated to the use of the household. [ME *mesuage,* t. AF: (m.)*me*(s)-*suage,* prob. m. *mesnage.* See MENAGE]

mess·y (měs′ĭ), *adj.* **messier, messiest. 1.** of the nature of a mess: *a messy concoction.* **2.** being in a mess: *a messy table.* **3.** attended with or making a mess; dirty; untidy: *messy work.* —**mess′i·ness,** *n.*

mes·tee (měs·tē′), *n.* mustee.

mes·ti·zo (měs·tē′zō), *n., pl.* **-zos, -zoes. 1.** a person of mixed blood. **2.** (in Spanish America) one who has Spanish and American Indian blood. **3.** one of European and East Indian, Negro, or Malay blood. **4.** a Philippine Island native with Chinese blood. [t. Sp., g. LL *mixtīcius* of mixed race] —**mes·ti·za** (měs·tē′zə), *n. fem.*

Meš·tro·vić (měsh′trə·vĭch; *Yugosl.* měsh′trô·vět′y), *n.* **Ivan** (ē′vän), born 1883, Yugoslav sculptor.

met (mět), *v.* pt. and pp. of **meet.**

met. 1. metaphor. **2.** metaphysics. **3.** metropolitan.

meta-, 1. a prefix meaning "among," "along with," "after," "behind," and often denoting change, found chiefly in scientific words. **2.** *Chem.* **a.** a prefix meaning "containing least water," used of acids and salts, as in *meta-antimonic,* HSbO₃, *meta-antimonous,* HSbO₂. **b.** a prefix indicating an organic derivative of such an acid. [t. Gk., repr. *metá,* prep., with, after]

me·tab·o·lism (mə·tăb′ə·lĭz′əm), *n. Biol.* the sum of the processes or chemical changes in an organism or a single cell by which food is built up (*anabolism*) into living protoplasm and by which protoplasm is broken down (*catabolism*) into simpler compounds with the exchange of energy. [f. META- + s. Gk. *bolē* change + -ISM] —**met·a·bol·ic** (mět′ə·bŏl′ĭk), *adj.*

me·tab·o·lite (mə·tăb′ə·līt), *n.* a substance acted upon or produced in metabolism.

me·tab·o·lize (mə·tăb′ə·līz), *v.t.* **-lized, -lizing.** to subject to metabolism; change by metabolism.

met·a·car·pal (mět′ə·kär′pəl), *adj.* **1.** of or pertaining to the metacarpus. —*n.* **2.** a metacarpal bone.

met·a·car·pus (mět′ə·kär′pəs), *n., pl.* **-pi** (-pī). *Anat.* the part of a hand or fore limb (esp. of its bony structure) included between the wrist or carpus and the fingers or phalanges. See diag. under **shoulder.** [t. NL (see META-, CARPUS); r. *metacarpium,* t. Gk.: m. *metakārpion*]

met·a·cen·ter (mět′ə·sěn′tər), *n.* the point where the vertical line through the center of buoyancy of a floating body (as a ship) in equilibrium meets the vertical line through the new center of buoyancy when the body is in a slightly inclined position (less than one degree). The equilibrium of the body is stable when this point is above its center of gravity, and unstable when it is below. Also, *esp. Brit.,* **met′a·cen′tre.** [t. F: m. *métacentre,* f. Gk.: *meta-* META- + m.s. *kéntron* CENTER] —**met′a·cen′tric,** *adj.*

Metacenter of a boat M, Metacenter; G, Center of gravity; B, Center of buoyancy; B′, Center of buoyancy when boat is displaced

met·a·chro·ma·tism (mět′ə·krō′mə·tĭz′əm), *n.* change of color, esp. that due to variation in the temperature of a body. [f. META- + s. Gk. *chrōma* color + -ISM] —**met·a·chro·mat·ic** (mět′ə·krō·măt′ĭk), *adj.*

met·a·gal·ax·y (mět′ə·găl′ək·sĭ), *n., pl.* **-axies.** *Astron.* the complete system of external galaxies, or extragalactic nebulae.

met·age (mē′tĭj), *n.* **1.** the official measurement of contents or weight. **2.** the charge for it. [f. METE, v., + -AGE]

met·a·gen·e·sis (mět′ə·jěn′ə·sĭs), *n. Biol.* reproduction characterized by the alternation of a sexual generation and a generation which reproduces asexually by budding. —**met·a·ge·net·ic** (mět′ə·jə·nět′ĭk), *adj.*

me·tag·na·thous (mə·tăg′nə·thəs), *adj. Ornith.* having the tips of the mandibles crossed, as the crossbills. —**me·tag′na·thism,** *n.*

met·al (mět′əl), *n., v.,* **-aled, -aling** or (*esp. Brit.*) **-alled, -alling. 1.** any of a class of elementary substances, as gold, silver, copper, etc., all of which are crystalline when solid and many of which are characterized by opacity, ductility, conductivity, and a peculiar luster when freshly fractured. **2.** an alloy or mixture composed wholly or partly of such substances. **3.** *Chem.* **a.** a metal (def. 1) in its pure state, as distinguished from alloys. **b.** an element yielding positively charged ions in aqueous solutions of its salts. **4.** formative material; mettle. **5.** *Printing, etc.,* **a.** type metal. **b.** the state of being set up in type. **6.** *Brit.* broken stone used for roads or railroad track ballast. **7.** molten glass in the pot or melting tank. **8.** *Her.* either of the tinctures gold (*or*) and silver (*argent*). —*v.t.* **9.** to furnish or cover with metal. [ME, t. OF, g. L: m.s. *metallum* mine, mineral, metal, t. Gk.: m. *métallon* mine]

metal., 1. metallurgical. **2.** metallurgy.

met·al·ize (mět′ə·līz′), *v.t.,* **-lized, -lizing.** to make metallic; give the characteristics of metal to. Also, **met′al·lize′.** —**met′al·i·za′tion,** *n.*

metall., metallurgy.

me·tal·lic (mə·tăl′ĭk), *adj.* **1.** of, pertaining to, or consisting of metal. **2.** of the nature of metal: *metallic luster, metallic sounds.* **3.** *Chem.* **a.** (of a metal element) being in the free or uncombined state: *metallic iron.* **b.** containing or yielding metal. —**me·tal′li·cal·ly,** *adv.*

met·al·lif·er·ous (mět′ə·lĭf′ər·əs), *adj.* containing or yielding metal. [f. L *metallifer* yielding metals + -OUS]

met·al·line (mět′ə·lĭn, -līn′), *adj.* **1.** metallic. **2.** containing one or more metals or metallic salts.

met·al·log·ra·phy (mět′ə·lŏg′rə·fĭ), *n.* **1.** the microscopic study of the structure of metals and alloys. **2.** an art or process allied to lithography, in which metallic plates are substituted for stones. —**me·tal·lo·graph·ic** (mə·tăl′ə·grăf′ĭk), *adj.*

met·al·loid (mět′ə·loid′), *n.* **1.** a nonmetal. **2.** an element which is both metallic and nonmetallic, as arsenic, silicon, or bismuth. —*adj.* **3.** of or pertaining to a metalloid. **4.** resembling both a metal and nonmetal.

me·tal·lo·ther·a·py (mə·tăl′ō·thĕr′ə·pĭ), *n. Med.* therapy by the use of metals or their salts.

met·al·lur·gy (mět′ə·lûr·jĭ, mě·tăl′ər·jĭ), *n.* **1.** the art or science of separating metals from their ores. **2.** the art or science of making and compounding alloys. **3.** the art or science of working or heat treating metals so as to give them certain desired shapes or properties. [t. NL: m.s. *metallurgia,* f. s. Gk. *metallourgós* mineworker + -*ia* (suffix)] —**met′al·lur′gic, met′al·lur′gi·cal,** *adj.* —**met′al·lur′gi·cal·ly,** *adv.* —**met·al·lur·gist** (mět′ə·lûr′jĭst, mě·tăl′ər·jĭst), *n.*

met·al·work·ing (mět′əl·wûr′kĭng), *n.* act of making metal objects. —**met′al·work′,** *n.* —**met′al·work′er,** *n.*

met·a·mere (mět′ə·mĭr′), *n.* a somite. —**me·tam·er·al** (mə·tăm′ə·rəl), **met·a·mer·ic** (mět′ə·měr′ĭk), *adj.*

me·tam·er·ism (mə·tăm′ə·rĭz′əm), *n. Zool.* **1.** division into metameres, the developmental process of somite formation. **2.** the condition of consisting of metameres.

met·a·mor·phic (mĕt/ə·môr/fĭk), *adj.* **1.** pertaining to or characterized by change of form, or metamorphosis. **2.** *Geol.* pertaining to or exhibiting structural change, or metamorphism.

met·a·mor·phism (mĕt/ə·môr/fĭz·əm), *n.* **1.** metamorphosis. **2.** *Geol.* a change in the structure or constitution of a rock, due to natural agencies, as pressure and heat, esp. when the rock becomes harder and more completely crystalline.

met·a·mor·phose (mĕt/ə·môr/fōz, -fōs), *v.t.*, **-phosed, phosing. 1.** to transform. **2.** to subject to metamorphosis or metamorphism.

met·a·mor·pho·sis (mĕt/ə·môr/fə·sĭs), *n., pl.* **-ses** (-sēz/). **1.** change of form, structure, or substance, by transformation by magic or witchcraft. **2.** any complete change in appearance, character, circumstances, etc. **3.** a form resulting from any such change. **4.** a change of form during the post-embryonic or embryonic growth of an animal by which it is adapted temporarily to a special environment or way of living usually different from that of the preceding stage: *the metamorphosis of tadpoles into frogs.* **5.** *Pathol.* **a.** a type of alteration or degeneration in which tissues are changed: *fatty metamorphosis of the liver.* **b.** the resultant form. **6.** *Bot.* the structural or functional modification of a plant organ or structure during its development. [t. L, t. Gk.: transformation]

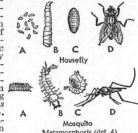

Housefly

Mosquito
Metamorphosis (def. 4)
A, Eggs; B, Larva; C, Pupa; D, Adult

met·a·mor·phous (mĕt/ə·môr/fəs), *adj.* metamorphic.

met·a·neph·ros (mĕt/ə·nĕf/rŏs), *n. Embryol.* the pelvic kidney, developing from the lowest portion of the nephric blastema cords. [t. NL, f. Gk.: *meta-* META- + *nephrós* kidney]

metaph., 1. metaphysical. **2.** metaphysics.

met·a·phase (mĕt/ə·fāz/), *n. Biol.* the middle stage in mitotic cell division in which the chromosomes in the equatorial plane of the cell split.

met·a·phor (mĕt/ə·fər, -fôr/), *n.* **1.** a figure of speech in which a term or phrase is applied to something to which it is not literally applicable, in order to suggest a resemblance, as *A mighty fortress is our God.* **2. mixed metaphor,** a figurative expression in which two or more metaphors are employed, producing an incongruous assemblage of ideas, as *The king put the ship of state on its feet.* [t. L: s. *metaphora,* t. Gk.: a transfer] **—met·a·phor·i·cal** (mĕt/ə·fôr/ə·kəl, -fŏr/-), **met/·a·phor/ic, adj. —met/a·phor/i·cal·ly, adv.**

met·a·phos·phor·ic acid (mĕt/ə·fŏs·fôr/ĭk, -fŏr/-), *Chem.* an acid, HPO₃, derived from phosphorous pentoxide, and containing the least water of the phosphoric acids. See **phosphoric acids.**

met·a·phrase (mĕt/ə·frāz/), *n., v.,* **-phrased, -phrasing. —n. 1.** a translation. **—v.t. 2.** to translate, esp. literally. **3.** to change the phrasing or literary form (of). [t. NL: s. *metaphrasis,* t. Gk.: a translation]

metaphys., metaphysics.

met·a·phys·i·cal (mĕt/ə·fĭz/ə·kəl), *adj.* **1.** pertaining to or of the nature of metaphysics. **2.** *Philos.* **a.** concerned with abstract thought or subjects, as existence, causality, truth, etc. **b.** concerned with first principles and ultimate grounds, as being, time, substance. **3.** highly abstract or abstruse. **4.** designating or pertaining esp. to that school of early 17th century English poets of whom John Donne was the chief, whose characteristic style is highly intellectual, philosophical, and crowded with ingenious conceits and turns of wit. **5.** *Archaic.* imaginary. **—met/a·phys/i·cal·ly, adv.**

met·a·phy·si·cian (mĕt/ə·fĭ·zĭsh/ən), *n.* one versed in metaphysics. Also, **met·a·phys·i·cist** (mĕt/ə·fĭz/ə·sĭst).

met·a·phys·ics (mĕt/ə·fĭz/ĭks), *n.* **1.** that branch of philosophy which treats of first principles, including the sciences of being (*ontology*) and of the origin and structure of the universe (*cosmology*). It is always intimately connected with a theory of knowledge (*epistemology*). **2.** philosophy, esp. in its more abstruse branches. [t. ML: m. *metaphysica,* t. MGk.: m. (*tà*) *metaphysiká* (neut. pl.), repr. *tà metà tà physiká* the (works) after the physics; with reference to the arrangement of Aristotle's writings]

met·a·plasm (mĕt/ə·plăz/əm), *n.* **1.** *Biol.* the lifeless matter or inclusions (as starch, pigment, etc.) in the protoplasm of a cell. **2.** *Obsolesc.* a change in the structure of a word by adding, removing, or transposing the sounds of which it is composed or their representation in spelling. **3.** the formation of oblique cases from a stem other than that of the nominative. **—met/a·plas/mic, adj.**

met·a·pro·te·in (mĕt/ə·prō/tē·ĭn, -tēn), *n.* a hydrolytic derivative of protein, insoluble in water, but soluble in dilute acids or alkalies.

met·a·so·ma·tism (mĕt/ə·sō/mə·tĭz·əm), *n. Geol.* **1.** the processes whereby minerals or rocks are replaced by others of different chemical composition as a result of the introduction of material, usually in very hot

aqueous solutions, from sources external to the formation undergoing change. **2.** replacement (def. 3). [f. META- + s. Gk. *sôma* body + -ISM]

me·tas·ta·sis (mə·tăs/tə·sĭs), *n., pl.* **-ses** (-sēz/). **1.** *Physiol., Pathol.* transference of a fluid, disease, or the like, from one part of the body to another. **2.** *Chiefly Pathol.* the translocation of cancerous cells to other parts of the body via the circulation, lymphatics, or membranous surfaces. **3.** a transformation. **4.** *Rhet.* a rapid transition, as from one subject to another. [t. LL, t. Gk.: removal] **—met·a·stat·ic** (mĕt/ə·stăt/ĭk), *adj.*

me·tas·ta·size (mə·tăs/tə·sīz/), *v.i.,* **-sized, -sizing.** *Pathol.* (esp. of cells of malignant tumors, or microörganisms) to spread to other regions by dissemination through the circulation, or other channels.

met·a·tar·sal (mĕt/ə·tär/səl), *adj.* **1.** of or pertaining to the metatarsus. **—n. 2.** a metatarsal bone.

met·a·tar·sus (mĕt/ə·tär/səs), *n., pl.* **-si** (-sī). *Anat., Zool.* **1.** the part of a foot or hind limb (esp. of its bony structure) included between the tarsus and the toes or phalanges. See diag. under **skeleton. 2.** (in birds) a bone composed of both tarsal and metatarsal elements, extending from the tibia to the phalanges. [NL. See META-, TARSUS]

me·tath·e·sis (mə·tăth/ə·sĭs), *n., pl.* **-ses** (-sēz/). **1.** the transposition of letters, syllables, or sounds in a word. **2.** *Chem.* a double decomposition, as when two compounds react with each other to form two other compounds. [t. LL, t. Gk.: transposition] **—met·a·thet·ic** (mĕt/ə·thĕt/ĭk), **met/a·thet/i·cal, adj.**

met·a·tho·rax (mĕt/ə·thōr/ăks), *n., pl.* **-thoraxes, -thoraces** (-thōr/ə·sēz/). the posterior division of an insect's thorax, bearing the third pair of legs and the second pair of wings. **—met·a·tho·rac·ic** (mĕt/ə·thō·răs/ĭk), *adj.*

met·a·xy·lem (mĕt/ə·zī/lĕm), *n. Bot.* the part of the primary xylem which is the last to be formed, usually having weblike or pitted surfaces.

Met·a·zo·a (mĕt/ə·zō/ə), *n.pl.* a large zoölogical division comprising all the animals above the protozoans, i.e., those organisms which, although originating from a single cell, are composed of many cells. See **Protozoa.** [t. NL, pl. of *metazöon,* f. Gk.: *meta-* META- + *zôion* animal] **—met/a·zo/an, adj., n. —met/a·zo/ic, adj.**

Metch·ni·koff (mĕch·nē·kôf/), *n.* Élie (ĕ·lē/). 1845–1916, Russian biologist and bacteriologist, in France.

mete¹ (mēt), *v.t.,* **meted, meting. 1.** to distribute or apportion by measure; allot (usually fol. by *out*). **2.** *Archaic.* to measure. [ME *mete*(n), OE *metan*]

mete² (mēt), *n.* **1.** a limiting mark. **2.** a limit. [ME, t. OF, t. L: m.s. *mēta* goalmark, turning post]

met·em·pir·ic (mĕt/ĕm·pĭr/ĭk), *n.* a supporter of the metempirical philosophy. [f. MET(A)- + EMPIRIC]

met·em·pir·i·cal (mĕt/ĕm·pĭr/ə·kəl), *adj.* **1.** beyond, or outside of, the field of experience. **2.** of or pertaining to metempirics.

met·em·pir·ics (mĕt/ĕm·pĭr/ĭks), *n.* the philosophy dealing with things transcending the field of experience, as regards their existence.

me·temp·sy·cho·sis (mə·tĕmp/sə·kō/sĭs, mĕt/əm·sī-), *n., pl.* **-ses** (-sēz). **1.** the passage of the soul from one body to another. **2.** the rebirth of the soul at death in another body either of human or animal form. [t. L, t. Gk.]

met·en·ceph·a·lon (mĕt/ĕn·sĕf/ə·lŏn/), *n., pl.* **-la** (-lə). *Anat.* the segment of the brain including the cerebellum and pons and the upper portion of the medulla oblongata; the hindbrain. [t. NL. See MET(A)-, ENCEPHALON] **—met·en·ce·phal·ic** (mĕt/ĕn·sə·făl/ĭk), *adj.*

me·te·or (mē/tĭ·ər), *n.* **1.** a transient fiery streak in the sky produced by a meteoroid passing through the earth's atmosphere; a bolide or shooting star. **2.** any meteoroid or meteorite. **3.** *Obs.* any atmospheric phenomenon, as hail, a typhoon, etc. [late ME, t. NL: s. *meteōrum,* t. Gk.: m. *metéōron* (pl. *metéōra* phenomena in the heavens), neut. adj.; raised, high in air]

meteor., 1. meteorological. **2.** meteorology.

me·te·or·ic (mē/tĭ·ôr/ĭk, -ŏr/ĭk), *adj.* **1.** pertaining to or like a meteor. **2.** consisting of meteors: *a meteoric shower.* **3.** flashing like a meteor; transiently brilliant: *a meteoric career.* **4.** swift or rapid. **5.** of the atmosphere; meteorological. **—me/te·or/i·cal·ly, adv.**

me·te·or·ite (mē/tĭ·ə·rīt/), *n.* **1.** a mass of stone or metal that has reached the earth from outer space; a fallen meteoroid. **2.** a meteor or a meteoroid. **—me·te·or·it·ic** (mē/tĭ·ə·rĭt/ĭk), *adj.*

me·te·or·o·graph (mē/tĭ·ər·ə·gräf/, -gräf/; mē/tĭ·ôr/ə-, -ŏr/ə-), *n.* an instrument for automatically recording various meteorological conditions, as of barometric pressure, temperature, etc., at the same time.

me·te·or·oid (mē/tĭ·ə·roid/), *n. Astron.* any of the small bodies, often remnants of comets, traveling through space, which, when encountering the earth's atmosphere, are heated to luminosity, thus becoming meteors.

meteorol., 1. meteorological. **2.** meteorology.

me·te·or·o·log·i·cal (mē/tĭ·ər·ə·lŏj/ə·kəl), *adj.* pertaining to meteorology, or to phenomena of the atmosphere or weather. Also, **me/te·or·o·log/ic. —me/te·or·o·log/i·cal·ly, adv.**

me·te·or·ol·o·gy (mē/tĭ·ə·rŏl/ə·jĭ), *n.* the science dealing with the atmosphere and its phenomena, esp. as relating to weather. [t. Gk.: m.s. *meteōrologiá.* See METEOR, -LOGY] **—me/te·or·ol·o·gist, n.**

me·ter[1] (mē′tər), *n.* the fundamental unit of length in the metric system, equivalent to 39.37 U.S. inches, originally intended to be, and being very nearly, equal to one ten-millionth of the distance from the equator to the pole measured on a meridian, but actually defined as the distance between two lines on a platinum-iridium bar (the "International Prototype Meter") preserved at the International Bureau of Weights and Measures, near Paris. Also, *esp. Brit.*, **metre.** [t. F.: m. *mètre*, t. Gk.: m. *métron* measure]

me·ter[2] (mē′tər), *n.* **1.** *Pros.* **a.** poetic measure; arrangement of words in regularly measured or patterned or rhythmic lines or verses. **b.** a particular form of such arrangement, depending on the kind and number of feet constituting the verse: *iambic trimeter.* **2.** *Music.* **a.** the rhythmic element as measured by division into parts of equal time-value. **b.** the unit of measurement, in terms of number of beats, adopted for a given piece of music. See **measure** (def. 18). Also, *esp. Brit.*, **metre.** [ME *metir*, *metur*, OE *mēter*, t. L: m.s. *metrum* poetic meter, verse. t. Gk.: m. *métron* measure; r. ME *metre*, t. F]

me·ter[3] (mē′tər), *n.* **1.** an instrument that measures. **2.** one that automatically measures and records the quantity of gas, water, electricity, or the like, passing through it or actuating it. —*v.t.* **3.** to measure by means of a meter. [ME; f. METE[1] + ER[1]]

-meter, a word element used in names of instruments for measuring quantity, extent, degree, etc.; e.g., *altimeter*, *barometer*. [t. NL: m. *-metrum*, t. Gk. (see METER[1]). Cf. METER[3]]

me·ter-kil·o·gram-sec·ond system (mē′tər kĭl′-ə gram′ sĕk′ənd), a system of units used in science, based on the meter, kilogram, and second as the fundamental units of length, mass, and time.

Meth., Methodist.

meth·ac·ry·late (mĕth ăk′rə lāt′), *n. Chem.* an ester or salt derived from methacrylic acid.

meth·a·cryl·ic acid (mĕth′ə krĭl′ĭk), a colorless liquid acid, $CH_2C(CH_3)COOH$, produced synthetically, the esters of which are used in making plastics.

meth·ane (mĕth′ān), *n. Chem.* a colorless, odorless, inflammable gas, CH_4, the main constituent of marsh gas and the firedamp of coal mines and obtained commercially from natural gas; the first member of the methane or paraffin series of hydrocarbons. [f. METH(YL) + -ANE]

methane series, *Chem.* a homologous series of saturated aliphatic hydrocarbons, with the general formula, $C_n H_{2n+2}$, as *methane* (CH_4), *ethane* (C_2H_6), *etc.*; paraffin series; alkanes.

meth·a·nol (mĕth′ə nōl′, -nŏl′), *n. Chem.* methyl alcohol, or wood alcohol. [f. METHAN(E) + -OL[1]]

met·he·mo·glo·bin (mĕt hē′mə glō′bĭn, -hĕm′ə-, mĕ-thē′mə-), *n. Biochem.* a brownish compound, a combination of oxygen and hemoglobin, formed in the blood, as by the use of certain drugs. [f. MET(A)- + HEMOGLOBIN]

meth·e·na·mine (mĕ thē′nə mēn′, -mĭn), *n. Pharm.* the U.S.P. designation for hexamethylenetetranine, ($CH_2)_6N_4$, a diuretic and urinary antiseptic.

me·thinks (mĭ thĭngks′), *v. impers.; pt.* **methought.** *Archaic and Poetic.* it seems to me. [ME *me thinketh*, OE *me thyncth* it seems to me]

me·thi·o·nine (mĕ thī′ə nēn′, -nĭn), *n. Biochem.* an amino acid, $CH_3SCH_2CH_2CH(NH_2)COOH$, found in such proteins as casein, wool, gelatin, etc.

meth·od (mĕth′əd), *n.* **1.** a mode of procedure, esp. an orderly or systematic mode: *a method of instruction.* **2.** a way of doing something, esp. in accordance with a definite plan. **3.** order or system in doing anything: *to work with method.* **4.** orderly or systematic arrangement. [t. L: s. *methodus* mode of procedure, method, t. Gk.: m. *méthodos* a following after, method] —**Syn. 1.** METHOD, MODE, WAY imply a manner in which a thing is done or in which it happens. METHOD refers to a settled kind of procedure, usually according to a definite, established, logical, or systematic plan: *the open-hearth method of making steel, method of solving a problem.* MODE is a more formal word which implies a customary or characteristic fashion of doing something: *kangaroos have a peculiar mode of carrying their young.* WAY, a word in popular use for the general idea, is equivalent to various more specific words: *a child's way* (manner) *of staring at people; the way* (method) *of rapid calculating; the way* (mode) *of holding a pen.*

me·thod·i·cal (mə thŏd′ə kəl), *adj.* performed, disposed, or acting in a systematic way; systematic; orderly: *a methodical man.* Also, **me·thod·ic.** —**me·thod′i·cal·ly,** *adv.* —**me·thod′i·cal·ness,** *n.* —**Syn.** See **orderly.**

Meth·od·ism (mĕth′ə dĭz′əm), *n.* the doctrines, polity, and worship of the Methodist Church.

Meth·od·ist (mĕth′əd ĭst), *n.* **1.** a member of one of the Christian denominations which grew out of the revival of religion led by John Wesley. —*adj.* **2.** of or pertaining to the Methodists or Methodism. —**Meth′od·is′tic,** *adj.*

meth·od·ize (mĕth′ə dīz′), *v.t.*, **-ized, -izing. 1.** to reduce to method. **2.** to arrange with method. —**meth′od·iz′er,** *n.*

meth·od·ol·o·gy (mĕth′ə dŏl′ə j), *n., pl.* **-gies.** the science of method, esp.: **a.** a branch of logic dealing with the logical principles underlying the organization of the various special sciences, and the conduct of scientific inquiry. **b.** *Educ.* a branch of pedagogics concerned with analysis and evaluation of subject matter and methods of teaching.

Me·thu·en (mĭ thū′ən), *n.* a town in NE Massachusetts, near Lawrence. 24,477 (1950).

Me·thu·se·lah (mĭ thōō′zə lə), *n.* a Biblical patriarch before the Flood who according to tradition lived 969 years. Gen. 5:27. [t. Heb.: *M'thūshelaḥ*]

meth·yl (mĕth′ĭl), *n. Chem.* a univalent hydrocarbon radical, CH_3, derived from methane. [t. F: m. *méthyle*, back formation from *méthylène* METHYLENE]

methyl acetate, *Chem.* a colorless, combustible, volatile liquid, CH_3COOCH_3, having a fragrant odor, used as a solvent; the methyl ester of acetic acid.

meth·yl·al (mĕth′ə lăl′, mĕth′ə lăl′), *n. Chem.* a liquid compound with a pleasant odor, $CH_2(OCH_3)_2$, used in medicine as a hypnotic. [f. METHYL + AL(COHOL)]

methyl alcohol, *Chem.* a colorless, inflammable, poisonous liquid, CH_3OH, of the alcohol class, formerly obtained by the distillation of wood, but now produced synthetically from carbon monoxide and hydrogen, used as a fuel, solvent, etc.; wood alcohol.

meth·yl·a·mine (mĕth′əl ə mēn′, -ăm′ĭn), *n. Chem.* any of three derivatives of ammonia in which one or all of the hydrogen atoms are replaced by methyl radicals, esp. a gas, CH_3NH_2, with an ammonialike odor, the simplest alkyl derivative of ammonia and, like the latter, forming a series of salts.

meth·yl·ate (mĕth′ə lāt′), *n., v.,* **-ated, -ating.** —*n.* **1.** *Chem.* a methyl alcohol derivative in which the hydrogen of the hydroxyl group has been replaced by a metal. —*v.t.* **2.** to combine with methyl. **3.** to mix with methyl alcohol as in the denaturation of ethyl alcohol: *methylated spirits.* [f. METHYL + -ATE[2]]

methylated spirits, denatured or wood alcohol.

meth·yl·a·tion (mĕth′ə lā′shən), *n. Chem.* the process of replacing a hydrogen atom with a methyl radical.

meth·yl·ene (mĕth′ə lēn′), *n. Chem.* a bivalent hydrocarbon radical, CH_2, derived from methane. [t. F: f. s. Gk. *méthy* wine + *-yl* -YL + *-ène* -ENE]

methylene blue, a thiazine dye, $C_{16}H_{18}ClN_3S·3H_2O$, also used as an antidote for cyanide poisoning.

methyl methacrylate, a transparent plastic, formed by polymerizing a methacrylate, which can be molded, and may replace glass in optical instruments.

meth·yl·naph·tha·lene (mĕth′əl năf′thə lēn′), *n. Chem.* a compound, $C_{11}H_{10}$, the alpha form of which, a colorless liquid, is used in determining cetane numbers. Cf. **cetane number.**

me·tic·u·lous (mə tĭk′yə ləs), *adj.* solicitous about minute details; minutely or finically careful. [t. L: m.s. *meticulōsus* fearful] —**me·tic·u·los·i·ty** (mə tĭk′yə lŏs′-ə tĭ), *n.* —**me·tic′u·lous·ly,** *adv.*

mé·tier (mē tyē′), *n.* trade; profession; line of work or activity. [t. F, g. L *ministerium* MINISTRY]

mé·tis (mē tēs′), *n.* **1.** any person of mixed ancestry. **2.** *U.S.* a person of one eighth Negro ancestry; an octoroon. **3.** *Canada.* a half-breed of white, esp. French, and Indian parentage. [t. F, g. LL *mixtīcius* of mixed blood] —**mé·tisse′,** *n. fem.*

me·tol (mē′tōl, -tŏl), *n.* a soluble white powder, $C_{14}H_{18}N_2O_2·H_2SO_4$, used as a developer.

Me·ton·ic cycle (mĭ tŏn′ĭk), a cycle of 19 years, after which the new moon recurs on the same day of the year as at the beginning of the cycle. [named after the discoverer, *Meton*, an Athenian astronomer. See -IC]

met·o·nym (mĕt′ə nĭm), *n.* a word used by metonymy.

met·o·nym·i·cal (mĕt′ə nĭm′ə kəl), *adj.* having the nature of metonymy. Also, **met′o·nym′ic.** —**met′o·nym′i·cal·ly,** *adv.*

me·ton·y·my (mĭ tŏn′ə mĭ), *n. Rhet.* the use of the name of one thing for that of another to which it has some logical relation, as "scepter" for "sovereignty," or "the bottle" for "strong drink." [t. LL: m.s. *metōnymia*, t. Gk.: a change of name]

met·o·pe (mĕt′ə pē′, -ōp), *n. Archit.* one of the square spaces, either decorated or plain, between triglyphs in the Doric frieze. [t. Gk.]

me·tral·gi·a (mĭ trăl′jĭ ə), *n. Pathol.* pain in the uterus. [t. NL, f. Gk.: s. *mētra* uterus + *-algia* -ALGIA]

met·ra·zol (mĕt′rə zōl′, -zŏl′), *n.* **1.** a drug, $C_6H_{10}N_4$, which increases the activity of the heart and lungs and is also used to induce a convulsive state for the treatment of certain mental diseases. **2.** (*cap.*) a trademark for this drug.

M. Metope; T. Triglyph

me·tre (mē′tər), *n. Chiefly Brit.* meter.

met·ric[1] (mĕt′rĭk), *adj.* pertaining to the meter, or to the system of measures and weights originally based upon it. [t. F: m. *métrique*, der. *mètre* METER[1]]

met·ric[2] (mĕt′rĭk), *adj.* metrical. [t. L: s. *metricus*, t. Gk.: m. *metrikós* pertaining to meter or measure]

met·ri·cal (mĕt′rə kəl), *adj.* **1.** pertaining to meter or poetic measure. **2.** composed in meter or verse. **3.** pertaining to measurement. Also, **metric.** —**met′-ri·cal·ly,** *adv.*

me·tri·cian (mē trĭsh′ən), *n.* a metrist.

met·rics (mĕt′rĭks), *n.* **1.** the science of meter. **2.** the art of metrical composition.

metric system, a decimal system of weights and measures, adopted first in France, but now widespread over the world; universally used in science, mandatory for use for all purposes in a large number of countries, and permitted for use in most (as in U.S. and Great Britain). The basic units are the meter (39.37 inches) for length, and the gram (15.432 grains) for mass or weight. Derived units are the liter (0.908 U.S. dry quart, or 1.0567 U.S. liquid quart) for capacity, being the volume of 1000 grams of water under specified conditions, the are (119.6 square yards) for area being the area of a square 10 meters on a side, and the stere (35.315 cubic feet) for volume, being the volume of a cube 1 meter on a side, the term stere being, however, usually restricted to measuring fire wood. Names for units larger and smaller than these are formed from the above names by the use of the following prefixes:

| kilo | 1000 | deka | 10 | centi | 0.01 |
| hecto | 100 | | | deci | 0.1 | milli | 0.001 |

To these are often added mega = 1,000,000, myria = 10,000, and micro = 0.000 001. Not all of the possible units are in common use. In many countries names of old units are applied to roughly similar metric units.

met·ric ton, a unit of 1000 kilograms, equivalent to 2204.62 avoirdupois pounds.

met·ri·fy (mĕt′rə fī′), *v.t.*, **-fied, -fying.** to put into meter; compose in verse. [t. OF: m. *metrifier*, t. ML: m.s. *metrificare* put in meter, f. *metri-* (comb. form of *metrum* meter) + *-ficāre* -FY] **—met′ri·fi′er,** *n.*

met·rist (mĕt′rĭst, mē′trĭst), *n.* one versed in the use of poetic meters. [t. ML: s. *metrista,* der. L *metrum* METER[2]]

me·tri·tis (mĭ trī′tĭs), *n.* *Pathol.* inflammation of the uterus. [t. NL, f. Gk.: s. *mētra* uterus + *-ītis* -ITIS]

me·trol·o·gy (mĭ trŏl′ə jĭ), *n., pl.* **-gies.** the science of measures and weights. [f. Gk. *metro(n)* measure + -LOGY] **—met·ro·log·i·cal** (mĕt′rə lŏj′ə kəl), *adj.* **—me·trol′o·gist,** *n.*

met·ro·nome (mĕt′rə nōm′), *n.* a mechanical contrivance for marking time, as for music. [f. Gk.: *metro(n)* measure + m.s. *nómos* law] **—met·ro·nom·ic** (mĕt′rə nŏm′ĭk), *adj.*

met·ro·nym·ic (mē′trə nĭm′ĭk, mĕt′rə-), *adj.* **1.** derived from the name of a mother or other female ancestor. **—n. 2.** a metronymic name. [t. Gk.: m. s. *mētrōnymikós* named after one's mother]

me·trop·o·lis (mə trŏp′ə lĭs), *n., pl.* **-lises** (-lĭs ĭz), **-leis** (līs′). **1.** the chief city (not necessarily the capital) of a country, state, or region. **2.** a central or principal point, as of some activity. **3.** the mother city or parent state of an ancient Greek (or other) colony. **4.** the chief see of an ecclesiastical province. [t. LL, t. Gk.: a mother state or city]

Metronome
(The dotted lines show the extent of vibration of the pendulum)

met·ro·pol·i·tan (mĕt′rə pŏl′ə tən), *adj.* **1.** characteristic of a metropolis or chief city, or of its inhabitants. **2.** pertaining to or constituting a mother country. **3.** pertaining to an ecclesiastical metropolis. **—n. 4.** an inhabitant of a metropolis or chief city. **5.** one having metropolitan manners, etc. **6.** the next highest rank to Patriarch in the Russian Orthodox Church. **7.** a citizen of the mother city or parent state of a colony.

me·tror·rha·gi·a (mē′trə rā′jĭ ə, mĕt′rə-), *n.* *Pathol.* non-menstrual discharge of blood from the uterus; uterine hemorrhage. [t. NL, f. Gk.: m.s. *mētra* uterus + *-rrhagia* -RRHAGIA]

-metry, a word element denoting the process of measuring, abstract for *-meter,* as in anthropometry, chronometry. [t. Gk.: m.s. *-metria,* der. *-metros* measuring]

Met·ter·nich (mĕt′ər nĭκH), *n.* **Klemens Wenzel Nepomuk Lothar** (klā′mĕns vĕn′tsəl nā′pô mŏŏk lō′tär), **Prince von,** 1773–1859, Austrian statesman.

met·tle (mĕt′əl), *n.* **1.** the characteristic disposition or temper: *to try a man's mettle.* **2.** spirit; courage. **3. on one's mettle,** incited to do one's best. [var. of METAL]

met·tle·some (mĕt′əl səm), *adj.* spirited; courageous. Also, **met·tled** (mĕt′əld).

Metz (mĕts; *Fr.* mĕs), *n.* a fortress city in NE France: battles, 1870, 1918, 1940, 1944. 70,105 (1946).

me·um et tu·um (mē′əm ĕt tū′əm, tōō′-), *Latin.* mine and thine.

Meuse (mūz; *Fr.* mœz), *n.* a river flowing from NE France through E Belgium and S Netherlands into the North Sea. 575 mi. Dutch, **Maas.**

mew[1] (mū), *n.* **1.** the sound a cat makes. **—v.i. 2.** to make this sound. [imit.]

mew[2] (mū), *n.* a seagull, esp. the common gull, *Larus canus,* of Europe. [OE, c. G *möwe*]

mew[3] (mū), *n.* **1.** a cage for hawks, esp. while molting. **2.** a place of retirement or concealment. **3.** (*usually pl.*) *Brit.* a set of stables about a court or alley. **—v.t. 4.** to shut up in or as in a mew; to confine; conceal (often fol. by *up*). [ME *mue,* t. OF, der. *muer* MEW[4]]

mew[4] (mū), *v.t., v.i.* to shed (feathers); to molt. [ME *mewe(n),* t. OF: m. *muer* molt, change, g. L *mūtāre*]

mewl (mūl), *v.i.* to cry as a young child. [imit.]

Mex., 1. Mexican. **2.** Mexico.

Mex·i·can (mĕk′sə kən), *adj.* **1.** of or pertaining to Mexico. **—n. 2.** a native or inhabitant of Mexico.

Mexican bean beetle, a species of ladybug, *Epilachna varivestris,* which eats the leaves of beans.

Mexican hairless, a very small dog which grows very little hair.

Mex·i·ca·no (mĕk′sə kä′nō), any Nahuatl language.

Mexican War, the war between the United States and Mexico, 1846–48.

Mex·i·co (mĕk′sə kō′; *Sp.* mĕ′hēkô′), *n.* **1.** a republic in S North America. 22,753,000 pop. (est. 1946); 760,373 sq. mi. *Cap.:* Mexico City. **2.** a state in central Mexico. 1,146,034 pop. (1940); 8268 sq. mi. *Cap.:* Toluca. **3. Gulf of,** an arm of the Atlantic between the U.S., Cuba, and Mexico. ab. 716,000 sq. mi.; greatest depth, 12,714 ft.

Mexico City, the capital of the republic of Mexico, in the central part. 1,448,422 pop. (1940); ab. 7400 ft. high. Official name, **México, D. F.**

Mey·er·beer (mī′ər bār′), *n.* **Giacomo** (jä′kô mô′), (*Jakob Meyer Beer*) 1791–1864, German composer.

Meyn·ell (mĕn′əl), *n.* **Alice,** (*Alice Christiana Thompson, Mrs. Wilfred Meynell*) 1850–1922, British poet and essayist.

me·ze·re·on (mĭ zĭr′ĭ ŏn′), *n.* an Old World thyme-laeaceous shrub, *Daphne Mezereum,* cultivated for its fragrant purplish pink flowers, which appear in early spring. [t. ML, t. Ar.: m. *māzariyūn* the camellia]

me·zu·zah (mĭ zŏŏ′zä), *n., pl.* **-zoth** (-zōth). *Jewish Rel.* a piece of parchment inscribed on one side with the passages Deut. 6:4–9 and 11:13–21, and on the other with the word "Shaddai" (a name applied to God), and so placed in a case that the divine name is visible from the outside, the case being attached to the doorpost of a house in fulfillment of the injunction in each of the passages. Also, **me·zu′za.** [t. Heb.: door-post (see Deut. 6:9, 11:20)]

mez·za·nine (mĕz′ə nēn′, -nĭn), *n.* a low story between two other stories of greater height, esp. when the low story and the one beneath it form part of one composition; an entresol. [t. F, t. It.: m. *mezzanino,* dim. of *mezzano* middle, g. L *mediānus* MEDIAN]

mez·zo (mĕt′sō, mĕz′ō; *It.* mĕd′dzō), *adj.* middle; medium; half. [t. It., g. L *medius* middle]

mez·zo-re·lie·vo (mĕt′sō rĭ lē′vō), *n., pl.* **-vos** (-vōz). middle relief, between alto-relievo and bas-relief. Also, *Italian,* **mez·zo-ri·lie·vo** (mĕd′zō rē lyĕ′vô). [t. It.]

mez·zo-so·pran·o (mĕt′sō sə prän′ō, -prä′nō, mĕz′ō-), *n., pl.* **-pranos, -prani** (-prä′nē). *Music.* **1.** a voice or voice part intermediate in compass between soprano and contralto. **2.** a person having such a voice. [t. It.]

mez·zo·tint (mĕt′sō tĭnt′, mĕz′ō-), *n.* **1.** a method of engraving on copper or steel by burnishing or scraping away a uniformly roughened surface. **2.** a print produced by this method. **—v.t. 3.** to engrave in mezzotint. [t. It.: m. *mezzotinto* half-tint]

MF, Middle French. Also, **M.F.**

mf., **1.** *Music.* (It. *mezzo forte*). moderately loud. **2.** microfarad.

mfg., manufacturing.

mfr., 1. manufacture. **2.** (*pl.* **mfrs.**) manufacturer.

Mg, *Chem.* magnesium.

mg., milligram; milligrams.

MGk., Medieval Greek.

mgr., 1. manager. **2.** Monseigneur. **3.** Monsignor.

MHG., Middle High German.

mho (mō), *n.* *Elect.* a unit of electrical conductivity, equal to the conductivity of a body whose resistance is one ohm; a reciprocal ohm. [coined by Lord Kelvin (1824–1907); reversed spelling of OHM]

M.H.R., Member of the House of Representatives.

mi (mē), *n.* *Music.* the syllable used for the third tone of a scale, and sometimes for the tone E. See **sol-fa** (def. 1). [See GAMUT]

mi., 1. mile; miles. **2.** mill; mills.

Mi·am·i (mī ăm′ĭ, -ə), *n.* **1.** a city in SE Florida: seaside winter resort. 249,276 (1950). **2.** a river flowing S through W Ohio into the Ohio river. ab. 160 mi.

Mi·am·i (mī ăm′ĭ, -ə), *n., pl.* **Miamis. 1.** (*pl.*) a North American Indian tribe of the Algonquian family, formerly located in N Indiana, S Michigan, perhaps Illinois; now extinct as a tribe. **2.** a member of this tribe.

Miami Beach, a city in SE Florida. 46,282 (1950).

mi·aow (mī ou′, myou), *n., v.i.* meow. Also **mi·aou′, mi·aul** (mī oul′, mī ôl′). [imit.]

mi·as·ma (mī ăz′mə, mĭ-), *n., pl.* **-mata** (-mə tə), **-mas.** noxious exhalations from putrescent organic matter; poisonous effluvia or germs infecting the atmosphere. [t. NL, t. Gk.: pollution] **—mi·as′mal, mi·as·mat·ic** (mī′ăz măt′ĭk), **mi·as·mat′i·cal, mi·as′mic,** *adj.*

mib (mĭb), *n.* *Dial.* **1.** one marble. **2.** (*pl.*) the game of marbles.

Mic., Micah.

mi·ca (mī′kə), *n.* any member of a group of minerals, hydrous disilicates of aluminum with other bases, chiefly potassium, magnesium, iron, and lithium, that separate readily into thin, tough, often transparent, and usually elastic laminae. [t. NL, special use of L *mica* crumb, grain, little bit]

mi·ca·ceous (mī kā′shəs), *adj.* **1.** consisting of, containing, or resembling mica. **2.** of or pertaining to mica.

Mi·cah (mī′kə), *n.* **1.** a Hebrew prophet of the 8th century B.C. **2.** the sixth book of the "minor prophets," in the Old Testament, which bears his name.

Mi·caw·ber (mĭ kô′bər), *n.* **Wilkins,** (in Dickens'

ăct, āble, dâre, ärt; ĕbb, ēqual; ĭf, īce; hŏt, ōver, ôrder, oil, bŏŏk, ōōze, out; ŭp, ūse, ûrge; ə = a in alone; ch, chief; g, give; ng, ring; sh, shoe; th, thin; ŧħ, that; zh, vision. See the full key on inside cover.

David Copperfield) the improvident, chronically unlucky, father of a family, who persists in his optimism.
mice (mīs), *n.* pl. of **mouse.**
mi·celle (mĭ sĕl′), *n.* *Phys. Chem.* a colloidal particle formed by the reversible aggregation of dissolved molecules. Electrically charged micelles form colloidal electrolytes, as soaps and detergents. [t. NL: m. *mĭcella,* dim. of L *mīca* crumb]
Mich., 1. Michaelmas. 2. Michigan.
Mi·chael (mī′kəl), *n.* a militant archangel. Dan. 10:13.
Michael I, (*Mihai*) born 1921, king of Rumania, 1927–30 and 1940–47.
Mich·ael·mas (mĭk′əl məs), *n.* *Chiefly Brit.* 1. a festival celebrated on Sept. 29, in honor of the archangel Michael. 2. Sept. 29 (**Michaelmas day**). [OE (*Sanct*) *Michaeles masse* St. Michael's mass]
Michaelmas daisy, *Brit.* an aster.
Mi·chel·an·ge·lo (mī′kel ăn′jə lō′, mĭk′əl-; *It.* mē′-kĕl än′jĕ lô′), *n.* (*Michelangolo, Michelangelo Buonarroti*) 1475–1564, Italian sculptor, painter, architect, and poet.
Mi·che·let (mēsh lĕ′), *n.* **Jules** (zhꞰl), 1798–1874, French historian.
Mi·chel·son (mī′kəl sən), *n.* **Albert Abraham,** 1852–1931, U.S. physicist, born in Germany.
Mich·i·gan (mĭsh′ə gən), *n.* 1. a State in the N central United States. 6,371,766 pop. (1950); 58,216 sq. mi. *Cap.:* Lansing. *Abbr.:* Mich. 2. **Lake,** a lake between Wisconsin and Michigan: one of the five Great Lakes. ab. 22,400 sq. mi.
Michigan City, a city in NW Indiana: a port on Lake Michigan. 28,395 (1950).
Mick·ey (mĭk′Ɪ), *n.,* pl. **-eys.** a drink to which a sleeping drug or knockout drops have been added. Also, **Mickey Finn** (fĭn).
Mic·kie·wicz (mĭts kyĕ′vĭch), *n.* **Adam** (ä′däm), 1798–1855, Polish poet.
mick·le (mĭk′əl), *adj.* *Archaic or Brit. Dial.* great; large; much. [ME *mikel,* OE *micul,* var. of *micel* MUCH]
Mic·mac (mĭk′măk), *n.* 1. a tribe of Algonquian Indians inhabiting the southern shores of the Gulf of St. Lawrence. 2. a member of this tribe.
mi·cra (mī′krə), *n.* pl. of **micron.**
mi·cri·fy (mī′krə fī′), *v.t.,* **-fied, -fying.** to make small or insignificant. [f. MICR(O)- + -IFY; modeled on MAGNIFY]
micro-, a word element meaning "very small," used to mean "enlarging" (*microphone*), as a combining form of **microscopic** (*microörganism*) and to represent the millionth part of a unit (*microgram*). Also, before vowels, **micr-.** [t. Gk.: m. *mīkro-,* comb. form of *mīkrós* small]
mi·cro·a·nal·y·sis (mī′krō ə năl′ə sĭs), *n.,* pl. **-ses** (-sēz′). *Chem.* the analysis of extremely small quantities. —**mi·cro·a·lyt·i·cal** (mī′krō ə lĭt′ə kəl), *adj.*
mi·cro·bar·o·graph (mī′krō băr′ə grăf′, -gräf′), *n.* *Meteorol.* a barograph for recording minute fluctuations of atmospheric pressure.
mi·crobe (mī′krōb), *n.* 1. a microörganism, usually one of vegetable nature; a germ. 2. a bacterium, esp. one causing disease. [t. F, f. Gk.: m. *mīkro-* MICRO- + m.s. *bíos* life] —**mi·cro·bi·al** (mī krō′bĭ əl), **mi·cro′bic,** *adj.*
mi·cro·ce·phal·ic (mī′krō sə făl′Ꞥk), *adj.* 1. *Craniom.* having a skull with a small cranial capacity. 2. *Pathol.* having an abnormally small skull. Also, **mi·cro·ceph·a·lous** (mī′krō sĕf′ə ləs). —**mi′cro·ceph′a·ly,** *n.*
mi·cro·chem·is·try (mī′krō kĕm′Ꞥs trꞮ), *n.* chemistry as concerned with minute or microscopic objects or quantities. —**mi′cro·chem′i·cal,** *adj.*
mi·cro·cli·ma·tol·o·gy (mī′krō klī′mə tŏl′ə jꞮ), *n.* a branch of climatology dealing with studies of small-scale climatic conditions, as local climatic changes induced by planting trees as a windbreak.
mi·cro·cline (mī′krə klīn′), *n.* a mineral of the feldspar group, potassium aluminum silicate, KASi₃O₈, identical in composition with orthoclase, but differing in crystal system, used in making porcelain. [t. G: m. *mikroklin,* f. Gk.: *mīkro-* MICRO- + s. *klīneín* incline]
mi·cro·coc·cus (mī′krə kŏk′əs), *n.,* pl. **-cocci** (-kŏk′sī). any member of the genus *Micrococcus,* comprising globular or oval bacterial organisms, of which certain species cause disease, and others produce fermentation, coloration, etc. [t. NL. See MICRO-, -COCCUS]
mi·cro·cop·y (mī′krə kŏp′Ꞥ), *n.,* pl. **-copies.** *Library Science.* a greatly reduced photographic copy of a newspaper or book page, etc., usually read by enlargement on a ground glass screen.
mi·cro·cosm (mī′krə kŏz′əm), *n.* 1. a little world. 2. anything regarded as a world in miniature. 3. man viewed as an epitome of the universe (opposed to *macrocosm*). [t. F: m. *microcosme,* t. LL: m.s. *microcosmus,* t. LGk.: m. *mīkrós kósmos* little world] —**mi′-cro·cos′mic, mi′cro·cos′mi·cal,** *adj.*
microcosmic salt, *Chem.* a phosphate, sodium ammonium, NaNH₄HPO₄4H₂O, orig. obtained from human urine, much used as a blowpipe flux in testing metallic oxides.
mi·cro·crys·tal·line (mī′krō krꞮs′tə lꞮn, -līn′), *adj.* minutely crystalline; composed of microscopic crystals.
mi·cro·cyte (mī′krə sīt′), *n.* 1. a minute cell or corpuscle. 2. *Pathol.* an abnormally small-sized red blood cell, usually deficient in hemoglobin.
mi·cro·de·tec·tor (mī′krō dĭ′ tĕk′tər), *n.* 1. an instrument measuring small quantities or changes. 2. *Elect.* a sensitive galvanometer.

mi·cro·dont (mī′krə dŏnt′), *adj.* 1. having small or short teeth. —*n.* 2. a small or short tooth. —**mi′cro·don′tous,** *adj.*
mi·cro·far·ad (mī′krō făr′əd, -ăd), *n.* *Elect.* a convenient unit of capacitance in common use, equal to one millionth of a farad.
mi·cro·film (mī′krə fĭlm′), *n.* 1. a narrow film, esp. of motion picture stock, on which microcopies are made. 2. microphotograph.
mi·cro·ga·mete (mī′krō gə mēt′), *n.* *Biol.* (in heterogamous reproduction) the smaller of the two gametes, usually the male cell.
mi·cro·gram (mī′krō grăm′), *n.* a small unit of mass or weight used in microchemistry, equal to a millionth part of a gram. *Abbr.:* μg or γ. Also, *esp. Brit.,* **mi′cro·gramme′.**
mi·cro·graph (mī′krō grăf′, -gräf′), *n.* 1. an instrument for executing extremely minute writing or engraving. 2. a photograph or a drawing of an object as seen through a microscope.
mi·crog·ra·phy (mī krŏg′rə fꞮ), *n.* 1. the description or delineation of microscopic objects. 2. examination or study with the microscope. 3. the art or practice of writing in very small characters. —**mi·cro·graph·ic** (mī′krō grăf′Ꞥk), *adj.*
mi·cro·groove (mī′krə groōv′), *n.* 1. (in a phonograph record) a needle groove about ⅓ the conventional width, permitting a greater number of grooves than is possible on conventional records. 2. a record impressed with such grooves. 3. (*cap.*) a trademark for such a groove or record.
mi·cro·inch (mī′krō Ꞥnch′), *n.* a unit of length equal to a millionth of an inch.
mi·cro·li·ter (mī′krō lē′tər), *n.* a unit of capacity equal to a millionth of a liter, used esp. in microchemistry. *Abbr.* μ l or λ. Also, *esp. Brit.,* **mi·cro·li′tre.**
mi·crol·o·gy (mī krŏl′ə jꞮ), *n.* excessive attention to petty details or distinctions. [t. Gk.: m.s. *mīkrología.* See MICRO-, LOGY]
mi·crom·e·ter (mī krŏm′ə tər), *n.* 1. any of various devices for measuring minute distances, angles, etc., as in connection with a telescope or microscope. 2. a micrometer caliper. [t. F: m. *micromètre,* f. *micro-* MICRO- + *-mètre* -METER]
micrometer caliper, an instrument for measuring thickness (as of wire or sheet metal) with precision.
micrometer screw, a screw with a very fine thread and a graduated head, used in micrometers, etc.
mi·crom·e·try (mī krŏm′ə trꞮ), *n.* the method or art of measuring with a micrometer.
mi·cro·mil·li·me·ter (mī′krō mĭl′ə mē′tər), *n.* the millionth part of a millimeter; a millimicron. Also, *esp. Brit.,* **mi′cro·mil′li·me′tre.**
mi·cro·mo·tion (mī′krō mō′shən), *n.* a motion, esp. a periodic one, of very short duration or length.
mi·cron (mī′krŏn), *n.,* pl. **-cra** (-krə), **-cras.** 1. the millionth part of a meter. *Symbol:* μ. 2. *Phys. chem.* a colloidal particle whose diameter is between .2 and 10 μ. Also, **mikron.** [t. NL, t. Gk.: m. *mīkrón* (neut. adj.,) small]
Mi·cro·ne·sia (mī′krə nē′zhə, -shə), *n.* groups of small Pacific islands, N of the equator, E of the Philippine Islands: the main groups included are the Marianas, the Caroline, and the Marshall islands. [f. MICRO- + s. Gk. *nêsos* island + -IA]
Mi·cro·ne·sian (mī′krə nē′zhən, -shən), *adj.* 1. of or pertaining to Micronesia, its inhabitants, or their languages. —*n.* 2. a native of Micronesia, which is inhabited by a mixture of peoples, chiefly Polynesian. 3. any of the Austronesian languages or dialects spoken in the Micronesian islands.
mi·cro·ör·gan·ism (mī′krō ôr′gə nꞮz′əm), *n.* a microscopic (animal or vegetable) organism.
mi·cro·par·a·site (mī′krō păr′ə sīt′), *n.* a parasitic microörganism. —**mi·cro·par·a·sit·ic** (mī′krō păr′ə-sĭt′Ꞥk), *adj.*
mi·cro·phone (mī′krə fōn′), *n.* an instrument which is capable of transforming the air pressure waves of sound into changes in electric currents or voltages. Qualifying adjectives, as *condenser, crystal, velocity,* etc., describe the method of developing the electric quantity. —**mi·cro·phon·ic** (mī′krə fŏn′Ꞥk), *adj.*
mi·cro·pho·to·graph (mī′krō fō′tə grăf′, -gräf′), *n.* 1. a small photograph requiring optical enlargement to render it visible in detail. 2. *Library Science.* a film reproduction of a large or bulky publication, as a file of newspapers, used to conserve space or to copy material which is difficult to obtain. 3. a photomicrograph. —**mi·cro·pho′to·graph′ic,** *adj.* —**mi·cro·pho·tog·ra·phy** (mī′krō fə tŏg′rə fꞮ), *n.*
mi·cro·print (mī′krō prꞮnt′), *n.* a microphotograph reproduced in print and read by a magnifying device.
mi·cro·pyle (mī′krə pīl′), *n.* 1. *Zool.* any minute opening in the coverings of an ovum, through which spermatozoa may gain access to the interior. 2. *Bot.* the minute orifice or opening in the integuments of an ovule. [t. F, f. Gk.: *mīkro-* MICRO- + *pȳlē* gate, orifice] —**mi′cro·py′lar,** *adj.*
mi·cro·py·rom·e·ter (mī′krō pī rŏm′ə tər), *n.* an optical pyrometer for use with small glowing bodies.
micros., microscopy.

---

b., blend of, blended; c., cognate with; d., dialect, dialectal; der., derived from; f., formed from; g., going back to; m., modification of; r., replacing; s., stem of; t., taken from; ?, perhaps. See the full key on inside cover.

mi·cro·scope (mī′krə skōp′), *n.* an optical instrument having a magnifying lens or a combination of lenses for inspecting objects too small to be seen, or to be seen distinctly and in detail, by the naked eye. [t. NL: m.s. *microscopium*, f. *mikro-* MICRO- + s. Gk. *skopeîn* view + *-ium* -IUM]

mi·cro·scop·ic (mī′krə skŏp′ĭk), *adj.* 1. so small as to be invisible or indistinct without the use of the microscope. 2. very small; tiny. 3. of or pertaining to the microscope or its use. 4. performing the work of a microscope. 5. suggestive of the use of the microscope: *microscopic exactness.* Also, **mi′·cro·scop′i·cal.** —**mi′·cro·scop′i·cal·ly,** *adv.*

mi·cros·co·py (mī krŏs′kə pĭ, mī′krə skō′pĭ), *n.* 1. the use of the microscope. 2. microscopic investigation. —**mi·cros·co·pist** (mī krŏs′kə pĭst, mī′krə skō′pĭst), *n.*

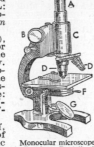

Monocular microscope
A. Eyepiece; B. Adjusting screw; C. Tube; D. Objective; E. Stage; F. Substage; G. Illuminating mirror

mi·cro·seism (mī′krō sī′zəm, -səm), *n. Geol.* a vibration of the ground recorded by seismographs but not believed to be due to an earthquake. [f. MICRO- + s. Gk. *seismós* earthquake] —**mi·cro·seis·mic** (mī′krō sĭz′mĭk, -sĭs′-), **mi′·cro·seis′mi·cal,** *adj.*

mi·cro·some (mī′krə sōm′), *n. Biol.* one of the minute granules in the protoplasm of animal and plant cells. [t. NL: m.s. *microsōma.* See MICRO-, -SOME³]

mi·cro·spo·ran·gi·um (mī′krō spō rǎn′jĭ əm), *n., pl.* **-gia** (-jĭ ə). *Bot.* a sporangium containing microspores. [t. NL. See MICRO-, SPORANGIUM]

mi·cro·spore (mī′krə spōr′), *n. Bot.* 1. the smaller of two kinds of spores produced by some pteridophytes. 2. a pollen grain.

mi·cro·spo·ro·phyll (mī′krə spōr′ə fĭl), *n. Bot.* a sporophyll bearing microsporangia.

mi·cro·stom·a·tous (mī′krə stŏm′ə təs, -stō′mə-), *adj.* having or pertaining to a very small mouth. Also, **mi·cros·to·mous** (mī krŏs′tə məs). [f. MICRO- + s. Gk. *stóma* mouth + -OUS]

mi·cro·tome (mī′krə tōm′), *n.* an instrument for cutting very thin sections, as of organic tissue, for microscopic examination.

mi·crot·o·my (mī krŏt′ə mĭ), *n.* the cutting of very thin sections, as with the microtome. —**mi·cro·tom·ic** (mī′krə tŏm′ĭk), **mi′·cro·tom′i·cal,** *adj.* —**mi·crot′o·mist,** *n.*

mi·cro·waves (mī′krō wāvz′), *n.pl. Electronics.* electromagnetic waves of extremely high frequency, approximately comprising the wavelength range from 50 cm. to 1 mm.

mic·tu·rate (mĭk′chə rāt′), *v.i.* **-rated, -rating.** to pass urine; urinate. [f. s. L *micturīre* desire to make water + -ATE¹]

mic·tu·ri·tion (mĭk′chə rĭsh′ən), *n.* act of passing urine. [f. s. L *micturītus,* pp. of *micturīre* desire to urinate + -ION]

mid¹ (mĭd), *adj.* 1. at or near its middle point: *in mid air.* 2. occupying a middle place or position: *in the mid-nineties of the last century.* 3. *Phonet.* having a tongue position intermediate between high and low: *beet, bet,* and *hot* have high, mid, and low vowels respectively. —*n.* 4. *Archaic.* the middle. [ME; OE *midd,* c. OHG *mitti,* Icel. *mithr,* Goth. *midjis* middle; akin to L *medius,* Gk. *mésos,* Skt. *madhya* middle]

mid² (mĭd), *prep.* amid. Also, **'mid.**

mid-, a combining form of "middle."

Mid., Midshipman.

mid., middle.

Mi·das (mī′dəs), *n.* 1. *Gk. Legend.* a Phrygian king, son of Gordius who was given by Dionysus the power of turning into gold whatever he touched. 2. a man of great wealth or great money-making ability.

mid·brain (mĭd′brān′), *n.* the mesencephalon.

mid·day (mĭd′dā′), *n.* 1. the middle of the day; noon. —*adj.* 2. of or pertaining to the middle part of the day. [ME; OE *middæg*]

mid·den (mĭd′ən), *n.* 1. *Archaic or Dial.* a dunghill or refuse heap. 2. *Brit.* a kitchen midden. [ME *myd(d)yng,* t. Scand.; cf. Dan. *mødding*]

mid·dle (mĭd′əl), *adj., n., v.,* **-dled, -dling.** —*adj.* 1. equally distant from extremes or limits: *the middle point of a line.* 2. intervening or intermediate: *the middle distance.* 3. medium: *a man of middle size.* 4. (*cap.*) (in the history of a language) intermediate between periods classified as old and new or modern: *Middle English.* 5. *Gram.* (in some languages) denoting a voice of verb inflection, in which the subject is represented as acting on or for itself, in contrast to the active voice in which the subject acts, and the passive, in which the subject is acted upon, as in Greek *gráphomai* "I write for myself," *gráphō* "I write." 6. *Rare.* at or near its middle. —*n.* 7. the point, part, etc., equidistant from extremes or limits. 8. the waist, or middle part of the human body. 9. something intermediate; a mean. —*v.t., v.i.* 10. *Chiefly Naut.* to fold in half. [ME and OE *middel,* c. G *mittel*]

—**Syn.** 7. MIDDLE, CENTER, MIDST indicate something from which two or more other things are (approximately or exactly) equally distant. MIDDLE denotes the point or part equidistant from or intermediate between extremes or limits in space or in time (activity): *the middle of a road.* CENTER, a more precise word, is ordinarily applied to a point within circular, globular, or regular bodies, or wherever a similar exactness appears to exist (*the center of the earth*): it may also be used metaphorically (still suggesting the core of a sphere): *center of interest.* MIDST usually suggests that a person or thing is closely surrounded or encompassed on all sides, esp. by that which is thick or dense: *the midst of a storm.*

middle age, the period between youth and old age.

mid·dle-aged (mĭd′əl ājd′), *adj.* 1. intermediate in age between youth and old age; commonly, from about 45 to about 60 years old. 2. characteristic of or suitable for middle-aged people.

Middle Ages, the time in European history between classical antiquity and the Italian renaissance (from the late 5th century to about A.D. 1350); sometimes restricted to the later part of this period (after 1100); sometimes extended to 1450 or 1500.

Middle Atlantic States, New York, New Jersey, and Pennsylvania.

mid·dle·break·er (mĭd′əl brā′kər), *n. Agric. Mach.* a lister. Also, **mid·dle·bust·er** (mĭd′əl bŭs′tər).

middle C, *Music.* the note indicated by the first ledger line above the bass staff and the first below the treble staff.

middle class, 1. the class of the people intermediate between the classes of higher and lower social rank or standing. 2. (in Great Britain) the class socially and conventionally intermediate between the aristocratic class and the laboring class. 3. an intermediate class.

mid·dle-class (mĭd′əl klǎs′, -kläs′), *adj.* belonging or pertaining to or characteristic of a middle class, esp., the social middle class; bourgeois.

Middle Congo, a colony in the SE part of French Equatorial Africa. 747,000 pop. (1936); 175,676 sq. mi. *Cap.:* Brazzaville.

middle distance, *Painting, etc.* the space between the foreground and the background or distance.

middle ear, *Anat.* the tympanum.

Middle East, 1. the lands from the E shores of the Mediterranean and Aegean to India: the Near East less the Balkan States. 2. (formerly) the area including Iran, Afghanistan, India, Tibet, and Burma.

Middle English, the English language of the period 1100–1500.

Middle French, the French language of the period 1400–1600.

Middle Greek, Medieval Greek.

Middle High German, the High German language from 1100 to 1450.

Middle Irish, the Irish language of the later Middle Ages.

Middle Kingdom, 1. Also, **Middle Empire.** the second great period in the history of the ancient Egyptian kingdom, about 2200 B.C. to 1890 B.C., comprising Dynasties XI–XIV. 2. the Chinese term for China proper (the eighteen inner provinces). 3. the Chinese Empire from its supposed position in the center of the earth.

mid·dle·man (mĭd′əl măn′), *n., pl.* **-men.** 1. an intermediary who distributes goods or securities from producer to consumer on his own account and risk. 2. one who acts as an intermediary between others.

mid·dle·most (mĭd′əl mōst′), *adj.* midmost.

Mid·dles·brough (mĭd′əlz brə), *n.* a seaport in NE England, on the Tees estuary. 138,400 (est. 1946).

Mid·dle·sex (mĭd′əl sĕks′), *n.* a county in SE England, bordering W and N London. 2,186,000 pop. (est. 1946); 232 sq. mi.

Middle Temple. See **Inns of Court.**

middle term, *Logic.* that term of a syllogism which appears twice in the premises, but is eliminated from the conclusion.

Mid·dle·ton (mĭd′əl tən), *n.* **Thomas,** c1570–1627, British dramatist.

Mid·dle·town (mĭd′əl toun′), *n.* 1. a city in SW Ohio, on the Miami river. 33,695 (1950). 2. a city in central Connecticut, on the Connecticut river. 29,711 (1950). 3. a city in SE New York. 22,586 (1950).

mid·dle·weight (mĭd′əl wāt′), *n.* 1. one of average weight. 2. a boxer or other contestant intermediate in weight between a light heavyweight and a welterweight, with a maximum weight of 160 pounds.

Middle West, that region of the United States bounded on the E and W by the Allegheny Mountains and the Rocky Mountains, and on the S by the Ohio river and the S extremities of Missouri and Kansas. —**Middle Western.** —**Middle Westerner.**

mid·dling (mĭd′lĭng), *adj.* 1. medium in size, quality, grade, rank, etc.; moderately large, good, etc. 2. *Colloq. or Dial.* in fairly good health. —*adv.* 3. *Colloq. or Dial.* moderately; fairly. —*n.* 4. (*pl.*) any of various products or commodities of intermediate quality, grade, etc., as the coarser particles of ground wheat mingled with bran. —**mid′dling·ly,** *adv.*

mid·dy (mĭd′ĭ), *n., pl.* **-dies.** 1. *Colloq.* a midshipman. 2. a middy blouse.

middy blouse, a loose blouse with a sailor collar, and often extending below the waistline to terminate in a broad band or fold, worn by children, young girls, etc.

Mid·gard (mĭd′gärd), *n. Scand. Myth.* the abode of humanity, joined to heaven by the rainbow bridge of the gods. Also, **Mid·garth** (mĭd′gärth), *Icelandic* **Mithgarthr.**

midge (mĭj), *n.* **1.** any of numerous minute flies (order *Diptera*), esp. those of the family *Chironomidae.* See **gnat. 2.** a small or diminutive person. [ME *mydge*, OE *mycg*, c. G *mücke*]

midg·et (mĭj′ĭt), *n.* **1.** a very small person. **2.** something very small of its kind. [f. MIDGE + -ET] —**Syn. 1.** See **dwarf.**

mid·gut (mĭd′gŭt′), *n.* the middle part of the alimentary canal.

Mi·di (mē dē′), *n.* **1.** the south. **2.** the south of France. [F: midday, the south, f. *mi* half (g. L *medius*) + *di* day (g. L *dies*)]

Mid·i·an (mĭd′ĭ·ən), *n.* the fourth son of Abraham by Keturah. Gen. 25:2.

Mid·i·an·ite (mĭd′ĭ·ən·īt′), *n.* a member of a desert tribe of northwest Arabia near the Gulf of Aqaba, descended from Midian. Ex. 2:15–22; Judges 6–8.

mid·i·ron (mĭd′ī′ərn), *n. Golf.* an iron club whose face has a medium degree of slope, used for far approaches.

mid·land (mĭd′lənd), *n.* **1.** the middle or interior part of a country. —*adj.* **2.** in or of the midland; inland. **Mid·lands** (mĭd′ləndz), *n., pl.* the central part of England; the midland counties.

mid·leg (*n.* mĭd′lĕg′; *adv.* -lĕg′), *n.* **1.** the middle part of the leg. **2.** one of the second pair of legs of an insect. —*adv.* **3.** at the middle of the leg.

Mid·lo·thi·an (mĭd′lō′thĭ·ən), *n.* a county in SE Scotland. 554,100 pop.(est. 1946); 366 sq. mi. *Co.* seat: Edinburgh. Formerly, **Edinburgh.**

mid·most (mĭd′mōst′), *adj.* **1.** being in the very middle; middlemost; middle. **2.** at or near its middle point. —*adv.* **3.** in the midmost part; in the midst.

mid·night (mĭd′nīt′), *n.* **1.** the middle of the night; 12 o'clock at night. —*adj.* **2.** of or pertaining to midnight. **3.** resembling midnight, as in darkness. **4. burn the midnight oil,** to study or work far into the night.

midnight sun, the sun visible at midnight in midsummer in arctic and antarctic regions.

mid·noon (mĭd′nōōn′), *n.* midday; noon.

mid·rash (mĭd′räsh), *n., pl.* **midrashim** (mĭd′rä′shĕm), **midrashoth** (mĭd′rä′shōth). *Hebrew Literature.* **1.** the traditional Jewish interpretation of Scripture, whether of its legal or its nonlegal portions. **2.** (*cap.*) a series of books, of various titles, containing the traditional Jewish interpretation of Scripture, arranged in the form of commentaries or homilies upon certain books of the Bible or upon selected passages from various books of the Bible. [t. Heb.: commentary]

mid·rib (mĭd′rĭb′), *n. Bot.* the central or middle rib of a leaf.

mid·riff (mĭd′rĭf), *n.* **1.** the diaphragm (in the body). **2.** a dress which exposes the middle part of the body. —*adj.* **3.** denoting or pertaining to such a dress. [ME *mydryf*, OE *midhrif*, f. *midd* mid + *hrif* belly]

mid·sag·it·tal plane (mĭd′săj′ə·təl), *Craniom., Cephalom.* a plane passing through the nasion at right angles to the biparionic or the bitragal plane, when the skull or head is oriented in the Frankfurt Horizontal.

mid·ship (mĭd′shĭp′), *adj.* in or belonging to the middle part of a ship.

mid·ship·man (mĭd′shĭp′mən), *n., pl.* **-men. 1.** *U.S. Navy and Coast Guard.* one of the rank held by young men while attending, and before graduation from, the service academies. **2.** *Brit. Navy.* **a.** an officer of the rank held by young men on leaving the government naval schools. **b.** (formerly) one of a class of boys or young men who had various minor duties and who formed the group from which officers were chosen.

mid·ship·mite (mĭd′shĭp′mīt′), *n.* (in humorous use) a midshipman.

mid·ships (mĭd′shĭps′), *adv.* amidships.

midst¹ (mĭdst), *n.* **1.** the position of anything surrounded by other things or parts, or occurring in the middle of a period of time, course of action, etc. **2.** the middle point, part, or stage. **3. in our (your, their) midst,** in the midst of us (you, them). [? f. *mids* middle + meaningless -*t*, or f. MID¹ + -EST] —**Syn. 1.** See **middle.**

midst² (mĭdst), *prep. Poetic.* amidst.

mid·stream (mĭd′strēm′), *n.* the middle of the stream.

mid·sum·mer (mĭd′sŭm′ər), *n.* the middle of summer.

Midsummer Night's Dream, a comedy (1595) by Shakespeare.

mid·Vic·to·ri·an (mĭd′vĭk·tôr′ĭ·ən), *adj.* **1.** of, pertaining to, or characteristic of the middle portion of the reign of Queen Victoria (reigned 1837–1901) in England: *mid-Victorian writers or ideas.* —*n.* **2.** a person, as a writer, belonging to the mid-Victorian time. **3.** a person of mid-Victorian ideas, tastes, etc.

mid·way (mĭd′wā′), *adv., adj.* **1.** in or to the middle of the way or distance; halfway. —*n.* **2.** a place or part situated midway. **3.** a place for side shows and other amusements at any fair or the like. [ME *mydwaye*, OE *midweg*]

Midway Islands, several islets in the N. Pacific, ab. 1200 mi. NW of and forming a part of the Territory of Hawaii: the Japanese were defeated in a naval engagement near here, June, 1942. 437 pop. (1940); 2 sq. mi.

mid·week (mĭd′wēk′), *n.* **1.** the middle of the week. **2.** (*cap.*) (among the Quakers) Wednesday. —*adj.* **3.** occurring in the middle of the week.

mid·week·ly (mĭd′wēk′lĭ), *adj.* **1.** midweekly. —*adv.* **2.** in the middle of the week.

Mid·west (mĭd′wĕst′), *U.S.* —*n.* **1.** Middle West. —*adj.* **2.** Middle Western. Also, **Mid·west·ern** (mĭd′wĕs′tərn). —**Mid·west′ern·er,** *n.*

mid·wife (mĭd′wīf′), *n., pl.* **-wives** (-wīvz′), a woman who assists women in childbirth. [ME, f. *mid* with, adv. (OE *mid*, c. G *mit*) + WIFE]

mid·wife·ry (mĭd′wīf′ər·ĭ, -wīf′rĭ), *n.* the art or practice of assisting women in childbirth.

mid·win·ter (mĭd′wĭn′tər), *n.* the middle of winter.

mid·year (mĭd′yĭr′), *n.* **1.** the middle of the year. **2.** (*pl.*) *Colloq.* midyear examinations. —*adj.* **3.** pertaining to or occurring in midyear.

mien (mēn), *n.* air, bearing, or aspect, as showing character, feeling, etc.: *a man of noble mien.* [der. *demean*, v., influenced by F *mine* aspect, t. Breton: m. *min* beak]

miff (mĭf), *Colloq.* —*n.* **1.** petulant displeasure; a petty quarrel. —*v.t.* **2.** to give offense to; offend. —*v.i.* **3.** to take offense; have a petty quarrel. [? imit. of an exclamation of disgust]

might¹ (mīt), *v.* pt. of **may.** [ME; OE *mihte*]

might² (mīt), *n.* **1.** power to do or accomplish; ability; effective power or force of any kind. **2.** superior power: *the doctrine that might makes right.* [ME *myghte*, OE *miht, meaht*, c. G *macht*] —**Syn. 2.** force, puissance. See **strength.** —**Ant. 2.** powerlessness.

might·i·ly (mī′tə·lĭ), *adv.* **1.** in a mighty manner; powerfully; vigorously. **2.** to a great extent or degree; very much.

might·y (mī′tĭ), *adj.*, **mightier, mightiest. 1.** having, characterized by, or showing might or power: *mighty rulers.* **2.** of great size; huge: *a mighty oak.* **3.** *Colloq.* great in amount, extent, degree, or importance. —*adv.* **4.** *Colloq.* very: *to be mighty pleased.* —**might′i·ness,** *n.* —**Syn. 1.** See **powerful.**

mi·gnon (mēn), *Fr.* mē·nyôn′), *adj. masc.* small and pretty; delicately pretty. [t. F, der. stem *mign-.* Cf. Celt. *mīno* tender, soft] —**mi·gnonne** (mĭn′yŏn; *Fr.* mē·nyôn′), *adj. fem.*

mi·gnon·ette (mĭn′yə·nĕt′), *n.* **1.** a plant, *Reseda odorata*, common in gardens, having racemes of small, fragrant, greenish-white flowers with prominent reddish-yellow or brownish anthers. **2.** light green as of reseda plants. [t. F: m. *mignonnette*, dim. of *mignon* MIGNON]

mi·graine (mī′grān, mĭ·grān′), *n.* a paroxysmal headache confined to one side of the head and usually associated with nausea; hemicrania. [t. F. See MEGRIM]

mi·grant (mī′grənt), *adj.* **1.** migrating; migratory. —*n.* **2.** one who or that which migrates, as a migratory bird. [t. L.: s. *migrans*, ppr.]

mi·grate (mī′grāt), *v.i.*, **-grated, -grating. 1.** to go from one country, region, or place of abode to settle in another. **2.** to pass periodically from one region to another, as certain birds, fishes, animals. **3.** (at English Universities) to change from one college to another. [t. L: m.s. *migrātus*, pp.] —**mi·gra·tor,** *n.* —**Syn. 1.** MIGRATE, EMIGRATE, IMMIGRATE are used of changing one's abode from one country or part of a country to another. To MIGRATE is to make such a move either once or repeatedly: *people emigrate from Ireland to the United States.* To EMIGRATE is to leave a country, usually one's own (and take up residence in another): *each year many people emigrate from Europe.* To IMMIGRATE is to enter and settle in a country not one's own: *there are many inducements to immigrate to South America.* MIGRATE is applied both to people or to animals that move from one region or habitat to another, esp. periodically; the other terms are generally applied to the movements of men.

mi·gra·tion (mī·grā′shən), *n.* **1.** the action of migrating: *the right of migration.* **2.** a migratory movement: *preparations for the migration.* **3.** a number or body of persons or animals migrating together. **4.** *Chem.* a movement or change of place of atoms within a molecule. [t. L: s. *migrātio*] —**mi·gra′tion·al,** *adj.*

migration of ions, *Chem.* the movement of ions toward an electrode, during electrolysis.

mi·gra·to·ry (mī′grə·tōr′ĭ), *adj.* **1.** migrating: *migratory species.* **2.** pertaining to a migration: *migratory movements of birds.* **3.** roving or nomad.

mi·ka·do (mĭ·kä′dō), *n., pl.* **-dos. 1.** (*often cap.*) a title of the emperor of Japan. **2.** (*cap.*) an operetta (1885) by Gilbert and Sullivan. [t. Jap.: lit., exalted gate]

mike (mīk), *n. Slang.* a microphone.

mi·kron (mī′krŏn), *n., pl.* **-kra, -kras.** micron.

mil (mĭl), *n.* **1.** a unit of length equal to .001 of an inch, used in measuring the diameter of wires. **2.** a military unit of angle equal to the angle subtended by an arc of 1/6400 of a circumference. This is the **artillery mil**; it has practically superseded the nearly equivalent **infantry mil** defined as the angle subtended by an arc of 1/1000 of the circumference. **3.** *Pharm.* a milliliter (.001 of a liter), or cubic centimeter. **4.** *Palestine.* a bronze coin equal to 0.001 of an English pound. [t. L: m. *mille* thousand]

mil., **1.** military. **2.** militia.

---

mi·la·dy (mĭ·lā'dĭ), *n.*, *pl.* **-dies.** a Continental rendering of English *my lady*, used in speaking to or of an English lady. Also, **mi·la'di.**

mil·age (mī'lĭj), *n.* mileage.

Mi·lan (mĭ·lăn', mī'lən), *n.* a city in N Italy, in Lombardy: famous cathedral. 1,255,026 (est. 1946). Italian, **Mi·la·no** (mē·lä'nō). —**Mil·an·ese** (mĭl'ə·nēz', -nēs'), *adj., n.*

Mi·laz·zo (mē·lät'tsō), *n.* a seaport in NE Sicily. 10,378 (1936).

milch (mĭlch), *adj.* denoting a cow, goat, or other milk-giving animal. [ME *milche*; akin to MILK]

mild (mīld), *adj.* **1.** amiably gentle or temperate in feeling or behavior toward others. **2.** characterized by or showing such gentleness, as manners, speech, etc. **3.** not cold, severe, or extreme, as air, weather, etc. **4.** gentle or moderate in force or effect: *mild penalties.* **5.** softly shining, as light, etc. **6.** not sharp, pungent, or strong: *mild flavor.* **7.** not acute, as disease, etc. **8.** moderate in intensity, degree, or character: *mild regret.* **9.** *Brit. Dial.* easily worked, as soil, stone, wood, etc. **10.** *Obs.* kind or gracious. [ME and OE, c. G *mild*] —**mild'ly,** *adv.* —**mild'ness,** *n.* —**Syn. 1.** See **gentle. 3.** temperate, moderate, clement. —**Ant. 1.** forceful. **3.** severe, harsh.

mil·dew (mĭl'dū', -dōō'), *n.* **1.** a plant disease usually characterized by a whitish coating or a discoloration on the surface caused by any of various parasitic fungi. **2.** any of these fungi. **3.** similar coating or discoloration, due to fungi, on cotton and linen fabrics, paper, leather, etc., when exposed to moisture. —*v.t., v.i.* **4.** to affect or become affected with mildew. [ME; OE *mildēaw, meledēaw,* lit., honey-dew] —**mil'dew'y,** *adj.*

mile (mīl), *n.* **1.** a unit of distance. **a.** the **statute mile,** used as a unit of distances on land in the English speaking countries, equal to 5280 ft. or 1760 yards. **b. nautical,** or **geographical, mile,** officially fixed in the U.S. at 6,080.20 feet, and in Great Britain at 6080 feet. **c.** the **international nautical** or **air mile,** a unit of distance in sea and air navigation, equal to 1.852 kilometers, (6,076.097 feet), recommended by the International Hydrographic Bureau for international adoption and adopted by a number of countries. **2.** other units of varying length at different periods and in different countries, e.g. the old **Roman mile** having been equivalent to about 1620 yds. or the present **Swedish mile** being equal to 10 km. [ME *myle,* OE *mīl,* t. L: m. *mīlia (passuum)* a thousand (paces)]

mile·age (mī'lĭj), *n.* **1.** the aggregate number of miles made or traveled over in a given time. **2.** length, extent, or distance in miles. **3.** an allowance for traveling expenses at a fixed rate per mile, esp. to a public official. **4.** a fixed charge per mile, as for railroad transportation. **5.** a mileage ticket. Also, **milage.**

mileage ticket, 1. a book or ticket of coupons good for a certain number of miles of transportation at a fixed rate per mile. **2.** one of the coupons.

mile·post (mĭl'pōst'), *n.* a post set up to mark distance by miles, as along a highway.

mil·er (mī'lər), *n.* one who is trained to race a mile.

mi·les glo·ri·o·sus (mī'lēz glōr'ĭ·ō'səs), *pl.* **milites gloriosi** (mĭl'ĭ tēz' glōr'ĭ·ō'sī). *Latin.* a braggart soldier.

mile·stone (mĭl'stōn'), *n.* **1.** a stone set up to mark distance by miles, as along a highway or other line of travel. **2.** a birthday or some event regarded as marking a stage in the journey of life.

Mi·le·tus (mī·lē'təs), *n.* an ancient city on the Aegean coast of Asia Minor. —**Mi·le·sian** (mī·lē'shən, -zhən), *adj., n.*

mil·foil (mĭl'foil'), *n.* the plant yarrow. [ME, t. OF, g. L *mīlifolium, millefolium,* lit., thousand leaves]

Mil·ford Haven (mĭl'fərd), **1.** a bay in SW Wales. **2.** a seaport on the N side of this bay. 10,017 (1939).

Mi·lhaud (mē·yō') *n.* **Darius** (dá·ryys'), born 1892, French composer, now living in the U.S.

mil·i·ar·i·a (mĭl'ĭ·âr'ĭ·ə), *n. Pathol.* an inflammatory disease of the skin, located about the sweat glands, marked by the formation of vesicles or papules resembling millet seeds; miliary fever. [t. NL, prop. fem. of L *mīliārius* MILIARY]

mil·i·ar·y (mĭl'ĭ·ĕr'ĭ, mĭl'yə·rĭ), *adj.* **1.** resembling a millet seed or seeds. **2.** *Pathol.* accompanied by spots (papules) or vesicles resembling millet seeds: *miliary fever.* [t. L: m.s. *mīliārius* of millet]

miliary tuberculosis, *Pathol.* tuberculosis in which the bacilli are spread by the blood from one point of infection, producing small tubercles in other parts of the body.

mi·lieu (mē·lyœ'), *n.* medium or environment. [t. F: f. *mi* (g. L *medius*) middle + *lieu* (g. L *locus*) place]

milit., military.

mil·i·tant (mĭl'ə·tənt), *adj.* **1.** combative; aggressive: *a militant reformer.* **2.** engaged in warfare; warring. —*n.* **3.** one engaged in warfare or strife; a militant person. [late ME, t. L: s. *mīlitans,* ppr., serving as a soldier] —**mil'i·tan·cy,** *n.* —**mil'i·tant·ly,** *adv.*

mil·i·ta·rism (mĭl'ə·tə·rĭz'əm), *n.* **1.** military spirit or policy. **2.** the principle of maintaining a large military establishment. **3.** the tendency to regard military efficiency as the supreme ideal of the state, and to subordinate all other interests to those of the military.

mil·i·ta·rist (mĭl'ə·tə·rĭst), *n.* **1.** one imbued with militarism. **2.** one skilled in the art of war. —**mil'i·ta·ris'tic,** *adj.* —**mil'i·ta·ris'ti·cal·ly,** *adv.*

mil·i·ta·rize (mĭl'ə·tə·rīz'), *v.t.,* **-rized, -rizing. 1.** to make military. **2.** to imbue with militarism. —**mil'i·ta·ri·za'tion,** *n.*

mil·i·tar·y (mĭl'ə·tĕr'ĭ), *adj.* **1.** of or pertaining to the army, armed forces, affairs of war, or a state of war. **2.** of or pertaining to soldiers. **3.** befitting a soldier. **4.** following the life of a soldier. **5.** having the characteristics of a soldier; soldierly. —*n.* **6.** soldiers generally; the army. [t. L: m. *mīlitāris*] —**mil'i·tar'i·ly,** *adv.* —**Ant. 1.** civilian.

military attaché, an army officer on the official staff of an ambassador or minister to a foreign country.

military law, rules and regulations applicable to persons in the military and naval services.

military police, soldiers who perform police duties within the Army.

mil·i·tate (mĭl'ə·tāt'), *v.i.,* **-tated, -tating.** to operate (*against* or *in favor of*); have effect or influence: *every fact militated against his argument.* [t. L: m.s. *mīlitātus,* pp.] —**mil'i·ta'tion,** *n.*

mi·li·tia (mĭ·lĭsh'ə), *n.* **1.** a body of men enrolled for military service, called out periodically for drill and exercise but for actual service only in emergencies. **2.** *U.S.* **a.** all able-bodied males who are or intend to become citizens, and are more than 18 and not more than 45 years of age. **b. unorganized** or **reserve militia,** that portion of the militia not belonging to the National Guard or the Organized Reserves, or the Naval or Marine Reserves. **3.** a body of citizen soldiers as distinguished from professional soldiers. [t. L: military service, soldiery]

mi·li·tia·man (mĭ·lĭsh'ə·mən), *n., pl.* **-men.** one serving in the militia.

mil·i·um (mĭl'ĭ·əm), *n., pl.* **milia** (mĭl'ĭ·ə). *Pathol.* a small white or yellowish nodule resembling a millet seed, produced in the skin by the retention of a sebaceous secretion. [t. L: millet]

milk (mĭlk), *n.* **1.** an opaque white or bluish-white liquid secreted by the mammary glands of female mammals, serving for the nourishment of their young, and, in the case of the cow and some other animals, used for food or as a source of dairy products. **2.** any liquid resembling this, as the liquid within a cocoanut, the juice or sap (latex) of certain plants, or various pharmaceutical preparations. —*v.t.* **3.** to press or draw milk by hand or machine from the udder of a cow or other animal. **4.** to extract as if by milking; draw (*out*). **5.** to extract something from as if by milking. **6.** to drain strength, information, wealth, etc., from; exploit. —*v.i.* **7.** to yield milk, as a cow. [ME; OE *milc, meolc,* c. G *milch*]

milk-and-wa·ter (mĭlk'ən wô'tər, wŏt'ər), *adj.* weak or insipid; wishy-washy.

milk bar, a place, often with an open front, where milk drinks, sandwiches, etc., are sold.

milk·er (mĭl'kər), *n.* **1.** one who milks. **2.** milking machine. **3.** a cow or other animal that gives milk.

milk fever, 1. *Pathol.* fever coinciding with the beginning of lactation, formerly believed to be due to lactation, but really due to infection. **2.** *Vet. Sci.* an acute condition often affecting dairy cows immediately after calving, causing somnolence and paralysis.

milk·fish (mĭlk'fĭsh'), *n., pl.* **-fishes,** (*esp. collectively*) **-fish.** a herringlike fish, *Chanos chanos,* extensively cultivated in southeastern Asia.

milking machine, a mechanical apparatus for milking cows.

milk leg, *Pathol.* a painful swelling of the leg, due to thrombosis of the large veins, occurring most frequently in connection with parturition.

milk·maid (mĭlk'mād'), *n.* a woman who milks cows or is employed in a dairy.

milk·man (mĭlk'măn'), *n., pl.,* **-men.** a man who sells or delivers milk.

milk of magnesia, *Pharm.* an antacid or laxative composed of a magnesium hydroxide, $Mg(OH)_2$, suspension in water.

milk punch, a beverage containing milk and alcoholic liquor with sugar, flavoring, etc.

milk shake, a frothy drink made of ice-cold milk, flavoring, and sometimes ice cream, shaken together.

milk sickness, a malignant disease of man, formerly common in some parts of middle western U.S., caused by consuming milk from cattle which had been poisoned by eating some kinds of snakeroot.

milk snake, a gray and black nonvenomous snake, *Lampropeltis triangulum,* with an arrow-shaped mark over the occiput, found widely in eastern North America.

milk·sop (mĭlk'sŏp'), *n.* a soft, unmanly fellow; an effeminate man or youth. —**milk'sop'ism,** *n.*

milk sugar, lactose, the largest solid constituent of milk.

milk tooth, one of the temporary teeth of a mammal which are replaced by the permanent teeth.

milk vetch, 1. a herb, esp. a European species *Astragalus Glycyphyllos,* of the fabaceous genus *Astragalus,* reputed to increase the secretion of milk in goats. **2.** any herb of certain allied genera.

milk·weed (mĭlk'wēd'), *n.* **1.** any of various plants (mostly with milky juice) of the family *Asclepiadaceae.*

esp. those of the genus *Asclepias*, as *A. syriaca* (the **common milkweed**). 2. any of various plants with a milky juice, as certain spurges.

milk·white (mĭlk′hwīt′), *adj.* of a white, or slightly blue-white color, such as that of milk.

milk·wort (mĭlk′wûrt′), *n.* 1. any of the herbs and shrubs constituting the genus *Polygala*, having (mostly) spikes or spikelike racemes of variously colored flowers, formerly reputed to increase the secretion of milk. 2. a primulaceous seaside plant, *Glaux maritima*, having small purplish-white flowers (**sea milkwort**).

milk·y (mĭl′kĭ), *adj.*, **milkier, milkiest.** 1. of or like milk. 2. of a chalky white. 3. giving a good supply of milk. 4. meek, tame, or spiritless. —**milk′i·ness,** *n.*

Milky Way, *Astron.* the faintly luminous band stretching across the heavens, composed of innumerable stars too faint for unassisted vision; the Galaxy. [trans. of L *via lactea*]

mill[1] (mĭl), *n.* 1. a building or establishment fitted with machinery, in which any of various mechanical operations or forms of manufacture is carried on: *a steel mill.* 2. a mechanical appliance or a building or establishment equipped with appliances for grinding grain into flour. 3. a machine for grinding, crushing, or pulverizing any solid substance: *a coffee mill.* 4. a steel roller for receiving and transferring an impressed design, as to a calico-printing cylinder or a banknote-printing plate. 5. a machine which does its work by rotary motion, as one used by a lapidary for cutting and polishing precious stones. 6. any of various other apparatuses for working materials into due form or performing other mechanical operations. 7. *Slang.* a boxing match or fist fight. —*v.t.* 8. to grind, work, treat, or shape in or with a mill. 9. to finish the edge of (a coin, etc.) with a series of fine notches or transverse grooves. 10. to beat or stir, as to a froth: *to mill chocolate.* 11. *Slang.* to beat or strike; fight; overcome. —*v.i.* 12. to move confusedly in a circle, as a herd of cattle. 13. *Slang.* to fight or box. [ME *mille, myln,* OE *mylen,* t. LL: m.s. *molīnum,* der. L *mola* millstone, mill]

mill[2] (mĭl), *n.* a U.S. money of account, equal to one thousandth of a dollar or one tenth of a cent. [short for L *millēsimus* thousandth, modeled on CENT]

Mill (mĭl), *n.* 1. **James,** 1773–1836, British philosopher, historian and economist. 2. his son, **John Stuart,** 1806–73, British philosopher and economist.

Mil·lais (mĭ lā′), *n.* **Sir John Everett,** 1829–96, British painter.

Mil·lay (mĭ lā′), *n.* **Edna St. Vincent,** (*Mrs. Eugen Jan Boissevain*) 1892–1950, U.S. poet.

mill·board (mĭl′bōrd′), *n.* *Bookbinding.* a strong, thick pasteboard used to make book covers.

mill·dam (mĭl′dăm′), *n.* a dam built in a stream to furnish a head of water for turning a mill wheel.

milled (mĭld), *adj.* having undergone the operations of a mill.

mil·le·nar·i·an (mĭl′ə nâr′Y ən), *adj.* 1. of or pertaining to a thousand, esp. the thousand years of the prophesied millennium. —*n.* 2. a believer in the millennium.

mil·le·nar·y (mĭl′ə nĕr′Y), *adj., n., pl.* **-naries.** —*adj.* 1. consisting of or pertaining to a thousand, esp. a thousand years. 2. pertaining to the millennium. —*n.* 3. an aggregate of a thousand. 4. millennium. 5. millenarian. [t. LL: m.s. *millēnārius* (def. 1)]

mil·len·ni·al (mĭ lĕn′Y əl), *adj.* 1. of or pertaining to a millennium or the millennium. 2. worthy or suggestive of the millennium. —**mil·len′ni·al·ly,** *adv.*

mil·len·ni·um (mĭ lĕn′Y əm), *n., pl.* **-niums, -nia** (-nY ə). 1. a period of a thousand years. 2. a thousandth anniversary. 3. the period of "a thousand years" (a phase variously interpreted) during which Christ is to reign on earth, according to the prophetic statement in Rev. 20:1–7. 4. a period of general righteousness and happiness, esp. in the indefinite future. [t. NL, f. L: *mille* thousand + *-ennium* as in BIENNIUM]

mil·le·pede (mĭl′ə pēd′), *n.* millipede.

mil·le·pore (mĭl′ə pōr′), *n.* a coralline hydrozoan of the genus *Millipora,* having a smooth calcareous surface with many perforations. [t. NL: m.s. *millepora,* f. L *mille* thousand + m. *porus* PORE[2]]

mill·er (mĭl′ər), *n.* 1. one who keeps or operates a mill, esp. a grain mill. 2. a milling machine. 3. any of various moths that look as if they were powdered with flour.

Mill·er (mĭl′ər), *n.* **Joaquin** (wä kēn′), (*Cincinnatus Heine Miller*) 1841–1913, U.S. poet.

Mille·rand (mēl rän′), *n.* **Alexandre** (à lĕk säN′dr), 1859–1943, president of France, 1920–24.

mill·er·ite (mĭl′ə rīt′), *n.* a mineral, nickel sulfide (NiS), occurring in bronze-colored slender crystals, a minor ore of nickel. [named after W. H. *Miller* (1801–80), British crystallographer. See -ITE[1]]

Mill·er·ite (mĭl′ə rīt′), *n.* a member of the Adventist church founded by William *Miller* (1782–1849), a U.S. preacher, who taught that the second advent of Christ and the beginning of the millennium were to occur in the immediate future (at first, about 1843).

mil·les·i·mal (mĭ lĕs′ə məl), *adj.* 1. thousandth. 2. consisting of thousandth parts. —*n.* 3. a thousandth part. [f. s. L *millēsimus* thousandth + -AL[1]]

mil·let (mĭl′Yt), *n.* 1. a cereal plant, *Setaria italica,* extensively cultivated in the East and in southern Europe for its small seed or grain (used as a food for man

and fowls), but in the U.S. grown chiefly for fodder. 2. any of various related or similar grasses cultivated as grain plants or forage plants, as **Indian millet,** and **pearl millet.** 3. the grain of any of these grasses. [late ME, t. F, dim. of *mil,* g. L *milium*]

Mil·let (mĭ lā′; Fr. mē lě′), *n.* **Jean François** (zhän frän swä′), 1814–75, French painter.

milli-, a word element meaning "thousand," used in the metric system for the division of the unit by 1,000. [t. L, comb. form of *mille*]

mil·liard (mĭl′yərd, -yärd), *n.* *Brit.* a thousand millions. [t. F, der. L *mille* thousand]

mil·li·ar·y (mĭl′Yĕr′Y), *adj.* 1. pertaining to the ancient Roman mile of a thousand paces. 2. marking a mile. [t. L: m.s. *milliārius* containing a thousand]

mil·li·bar (mĭl′ə bär′), *n.* *Meteorol.* a widely used unit of atmospheric pressure, equal to 1/1000 bar.

mil·lier (mē lyě′), *n.* 1000 kilograms; a metric ton. [F, der. L *mille* thousand]

mil·li·gram (mĭl′ə grăm′), *n.* a unit of one one-thousandth of a gram, equivalent to 0.0154 grain. Also, *esp. Brit.,* **mil′li·gramme′.**

Mil·li·kan (mĭl′ə kən), *n.* **Robert Andrews,** born 1868, U.S. physicist.

mil·li·li·ter (mĭl′ə lē′tər), *n.* a unit of capacity in the metric system, equal to one thousandth of a liter, and equivalent to 0.033815 fluid ounces, or 0.061025 cu. in. Also, *esp. Brit.,* **mil′li·li′tre.**

mil·li·me·ter (mĭl′ə mē′tər), *n.* a unit of length in the metric system equal to one thousandth of a meter, and equivalent to 0.03937 inch. Also, *esp. Brit.,* **mil′li·me′tre.** [t. F: m. *millimètre.* See MILLI-, METER[1]]

mil·li·mi·cron (mĭl′ə mī′krŏn), *n., pl.* **-cra** (-krə), a unit of length, the thousandth part of a micron. *Symbol:* μ.

mil·li·ner (mĭl′ə nər), *n.* one who makes or sells hats for women. [var. of obs. *Milaner* an inhabitant of Milan, a dealer in articles from Milan]

mil·li·ner·y (mĭl′ə nĕr′Y, -nə rY), *n.* 1. articles made or sold by milliners. 2. the business or trade of a milliner.

mill·ing (mĭl′Yng), *n.* 1. act of subjecting something to the operation of a mill. 2. the process of producing plane and formed surfaces. 3. the process of finishing the edge of a coin, etc., with fine notches or transverse grooves. 4. *Slang.* a thrashing.

milling machine, a machine tool used to produce plane and formed surfaces.

mil·lion (mĭl′yən), *n.* 1. one thousand times one thousand. 2. the amount of a thousand thousand units of money, as pounds, dollars, or francs. 3. a very great number. 4. the multitude, or the mass of the common people (prec. by *the*). —*adj.* 5. amounting to one million in numbers. [ME *millioun,* t. OF: m. *million,* t. It.: m. *milione,* aug. of *mille* thousand, g. L *mille*]

mil·lion·aire (mĭl′yə nâr′), *n.* 1. a person worth a million or millions, as of pounds, dollars, or francs. 2. a very rich person. Also **mil′lion·naire′.** [t. F: m. *millionnaire,* der. *million* MILLION]

mil·lionth (mĭl′yənth), *adj.* 1. coming last in a series of a million. 2. being one of a million equal parts. —*n.* 3. the millionth member of a series, a millionth part, esp. of one (1/1,000,000).

mil·li·pede (mĭl′ə pēd′), *n.* any one of the many arthropods belonging to the class *Diplopoda.* These are slow-moving, mostly herbivorous, myriapods having a cylindrical body of numerous segments, most of which bear two pairs of legs. Also, **millepede.** [t. L: m.s. *millepeda* wood louse, f. *mille* thousand + m.s. *pēs* foot]

Millipede, *Cambala annulata* (1 in. long)

mill·pond (mĭl′pŏnd′), *n.* a pond for supplying water to drive a mill wheel.

mill·race (mĭl′rās′), *n.* 1. the channel in which the current of water driving a mill wheel flows to the mill. 2. the current itself.

Mills grenade (mĭlz), *Mil.* a type of high-explosive grenade weighing about 1.5 pounds. [named after the inventor, Sir Wm. *Mills* (1856–1932)]

mill·stone (mĭl′stōn′), *n.* 1. either of a pair of circular stones between which grain or other substance is ground, as in a mill. 2. something that grinds or crushes. 3. a heavy burden (in allusion to Matt. 18:6).

mill·stream (mĭl′strēm′), *n.* the stream in a millrace.

mill wheel, a wheel, esp. a water wheel, used to drive a mill.

mill·work (mĭl′wûrk′), *n.* 1. ready-made carpentry work from a mill. 2. work done in a mill.

mill·wright (mĭl′rīt′), *n.* one who designs, builds, or sets up mills or mill machinery.

Milne (mĭln), *n.* **Alan Alexander,** born 1882, British writer of plays, books for children, and novels.

Mil·ner (mĭl′nər), *n.* **Alfred, 1st Viscount,** 1854–1925, British statesman and colonial administrator.

Mi·lo (mē′lō), *n.* Melos.

mi·lord (mĭ lôrd′), *n.* a Continental rendering of English *my lord,* used in speaking to or of an English lord or gentleman. [t. F, t. E: m. *my lord*]

milque·toast (mĭlk′tōst′), *n.* a timid, faint-hearted person. [named after Caspar *Milquetoast,* a comic-strip character]

mil·reis (mĭl′rās′; Port. mēl rās′), *n., pl.* **-reis.** 1. a Brazilian silver coin and monetary unit, equal to 1,000 reis, or about 5.3 U.S. cents at present.   **2.** a Portuguese gold coin and former monetary unit (superseded in 1911 by the escudo). [t. Pg.: a thousand reis, f. *mil* a thousand (g. L *mille*) + *reis*, pl. of *real*, lit., REGAL]

milt (mĭlt), *n.*   **1.** the secretion of the male generative organs of fishes.   **2.** the organs themselves. [ME and OE *milte*, c. G *milz*, etc.; akin to MELT]

milt·er (mĭl′tər), *n.* a male fish in breeding time.

Mil·ti·a·des (mĭl tī′ə dēz′), *n.* died c488 B.C., Athenian general who was victorious over the Persians in the battle of Marathon in 490 B.C.

Mil·ton (mĭl′tən), *n.* **John**, 1608–74, British poet.

Mil·ton·ic (mĭl tŏn′ĭk), *adj.* of or pertaining to the poet Milton or resembling his majestic style: *his poetry is Miltonic but completely uninspired.* Also, **Mil·to·ni·an** (mĭl tō′nĭ ən).

Mil·wau·kee (mĭl wô′kĭ), *n.* a city in SE Wisconsin: a port on Lake Michigan. 637,392 (1950).

Mi·lyu·kov (mĭ′lyŏŏ kôf′), *n.* **Pavel Nikolaevich** (pä′vĕl nĭ kŏ lä′yə vĭch), 1859–1943, Russian statesman and historian.

mime (mīm), *n., v.,* **mimed, miming.** —*n.* **1.** a comedian; jester; clown.   **2.** a player in an ancient Greek or Roman kind of farce which depended for effect largely upon ludicrous actions and gestures.   **3.** such a farce.   **4.** the dialogue for a classical mime.   —*v.t.* **5.** to mimic.   —*v.i.* **6.** to play a part by mimicry, esp. without words. [t. L: m.s. *mīmus*, t. Gk.: m. *mîmos*]   —**mim′er,** *n.*

mim·e·o·graph (mĭm′ē ə gräf′, -gräf′), *n.* **1.** a stencil device for duplicating letters, circulars, drawings, etc.   **2.** (*cap.*) a trademark for this device.   —*v.t.* **3.** to make copies using a mimeograph. [f. *mimeo-* (repr. Gk. *mīmé-omai* I imitate; cf. MIME) + -GRAPH]

mi·me·sis (mĭ mē′sĭs, mī-), *n.* **1.** *Rhet.* imitation or reproduction of the supposed words of another, as in order to represent his character.   **2.** *Biol.* imitation.   **3.** *Zool.* mimicry. [t. NL, t. Gk.: imitation]

mi·met·ic (mĭ mĕt′ĭk, mī-), *adj.* **1.** characterized by, exhibiting, or of the nature of mimicry: *mimetic gestures.*   **2.** mimic or make-believe. [t. Gk.: m.s. *mīmētikós*] —**mi·met′i·cal·ly,** *adv.*

mim·e·tite (mĭm′ə tīt′, mī′mə-), *n.* a mineral, lead chloro-arsenate, $Pb_5As_3O_{12}Cl$, occurring in yellow to brown prismatic crystals or globular masses, a minor ore of lead. [t. G: m. *mimetit,* f.s. Gk. *mīmētḗs* imitator + -*it* -ITE[1]]

mim·ic (mĭm′ĭk), *v.,* **-icked, -icking,** *n., adj.* —*v.t.* **1.** to imitate or copy in action, speech, etc., often playfully or derisively.   **2.** to imitate unintelligently or servilely; ape.   **3.** (of things) to be an imitation of; simulate.   —*n.* **4.** one apt at imitating or mimicking.   **5.** one who or that which imitates or mimics; an imitator or imitation.   **6.** *Obs.* a mime.   —*adj.* **7.** being merely an imitation or reproduction of the true thing, often on a smaller scale: *a mimic battle.*   **8.** apt at or given to imitating; imitative; simulative. [t. L: s. *mīmicus,* t. Gk.: m. *mīmikós* belonging to mimes]

mim·ic·ry (mĭm′ĭk rĭ), *n., pl.* **-ries.** **1.** the act, practice, or art of mimicking.   **2.** *Zool.* the close external resemblance, as if from imitation or simulation, of an animal to some different animal or to surrounding objects, esp. as serving for protection or concealment.   **3.** an instance, performance, or result of mimicking.

Mi·mir (mē′mĭr), *n. Scand. Myth.* the custodian of the spring of wisdom; his head, cut off by the Vanir, came into Odin's possession and gave him information and advice thenceforth.

mi·mo·sa (mĭ mō′sə, -zə), *n.* any plant of the genus *Mimosa,* native in tropical or warm regions, and comprising trees, shrubs, and plants having usually bipinnate and often sensitive leaves, and small flowers in globular heads or cylindrical spikes, esp., the sensitive plant, *M. pudica.* [t. NL, der. L *mīmus* MIME; apparently so named from seeming mimicry of animal life]

mim·o·sa·ceous (mĭm′ə sā′shəs, mī′mə-), *adj.* belonging to the *Mimosaceae,* or mimosa family of plants, usually treated as part of the larger family *Leguminosae.*

Mims (mĭmz), *n.* **Fort,** a stockade in SW Alabama, near the junction of the Alabama and Tombigbee rivers: Indian massacre, 1813.

min., **1.** mineralogical.   **2.** mineralogy.   **3.** minim.   **4.** minimum.   **5.** mining.   **6.** minor.   **7.** minute; minutes.

mi·na[1] (mī′nə), *n., pl.* **minae** (mī′nē), **minas.** an ancient unit of weight and value, equal to the sixtieth part of a talent. [t. L, t. Gk.: m. *mnâ;* prob. of Babylonian orig.]

mi·na[2] (mī′nə), *n.* myna.

mi·na·cious (mĭ nā′shəs), *adj.* menacing; threatening. [f. s. L *mināciae* threats + -OUS] —**mi·na′cious·ly,** *adv.* —**mi·na′cious·ness,** **mi·nac·i·ty** (mĭ năs′ə tĭ), *n.*

min·a·ret (mĭn′ə rĕt′, mĭn′ə rĕt′), *n.* a lofty, often slender, tower or turret attached to a Mohammedan mosque, surrounded by or furnished with one or more balconies, from which the muezzin calls the people to prayer. [t. Sp.: m. *minarete,* t. Ar.: m. *manāra(t),* orig., lighthouse]

Minaret

Mi·nas Basin (mī′nəs), the easternmost arm of the Bay of Fundy, in Nova Scotia: noted for high tides.

min·a·to·ry (mĭn′ə tōr′ĭ), *adj.* menacing; threatening. Also, **min′a·to′ri·al.** [t. LL: m.s. *minātōrius,* der. L *minārī* threaten] —**min′a·to′ri·ly,** *adv.*

mince (mĭns), *v.,* **minced, mincing,** *n.* —*v.t.* **1.** to cut or chop into very small pieces.   **2.** to subdivide minutely, as land, a subject, etc.   **3.** to soften or moderate (one's words, etc.) to a milder form.   **4.** to speak of (matters) in polite or euphemistic terms.   **5.** to perform or utter with affected elegance.   —*v.i.* **6.** to walk or move with short, affectedly dainty steps.   **7.** to act, behave, or speak with affected elegance.   —*n.* **8.** *Brit.* hash. [ME *mynce(n),* t. OF: m. *mincier* make small, ult. der. L *minūtus* small. Cf. MINISH]

mince·meat (mĭns′mēt′), *n.* **1.** a mixture composed of minced apples, suet (and sometimes meat), candied citron, etc., with raisins, currants, and other ingredients, for filling a pie (**mince pie**).   **2.** anything cut up very small.

minc·ing (mĭn′sĭng), *adj.* **1.** affectedly nice or elegant, as the gait, behavior, air, speech, etc.   **2.** walking, acting, or speaking in an affectedly nice or elegant manner. —**minc′ing·ly,** *adv.*

mind (mīnd), *n.* **1.** that which thinks, feels, and wills, exercises perception, judgment, reflection, etc., as in a human or other conscious being: *the processes of the mind.*   **2.** *Psychol.* the psyche; the totality of conscious and unconscious activities of the organism.   **3.** the intellect or understanding, as distinguished from the faculties of feeling and willing; the intelligence.   **4.** a particular instance of the intellect or intelligence, as in a person.   **5.** a person considered with reference to intellectual power: *the greatest minds of the time.*   **6.** intellectual power or ability.   **7.** reason, sanity, or sound mental condition: *to lose one's mind.*   **8.** way of thinking and feeling, disposition, or temper: *many men, many minds.*   **9.** opinion or sentiments: *to read someone's mind.*   **10.** inclination or desire.   **11.** purpose, intention, or will.   **12.** psychical or spiritual being, as opposed to matter.   **13.** a conscious or intelligent agency or being: *the doctrine of a mind pervading the universe.*   **14.** remembrance or recollection: *to keep in mind.*   **15. put in mind,** to remind.   **16.** commemoration.   —*v.t.* **17.** to pay attention to, heed, or obey (a person, advice, instructions, etc.).   **18.** to apply oneself or attend to: *to mind one's own business.*   **19.** to look after; take care of; tend: *to mind the baby.*   **20.** to be careful, cautious, or wary concerning: *mind what you say.*   **21.** to care about or feel concern at.   **22.** (in negative and interrogative expressions) to feel disturbed or inconvenienced by; object to: *would you mind handing me that book?*   **23.** to regard as concerning oneself or as mattering: *never mind what he does.*   **24.** *Dial.* to perceive or notice.   **25.** *Archaic or Dial.* to remember.   **26.** *Archaic or Dial.* to remind.   —*v.i.* **27.** to take notice, observe, or understand (chiefly in the imperative).   **28.** to obey.   **29.** to be careful or wary.   **30.** to care, feel concern, or object (often in negative and interrogative expressions): *mind if I go?*   **31.** to regard a thing as concerning oneself or as mattering: *never mind about them.* [ME *mind(e),* OE *gemynd* memory, thought, c. Goth. *gamunds* memory; akin to L *mens* mind]

—**Syn. 1.** MIND, INTELLECT, INTELLIGENCE refer to mental equipment or qualities. MIND is that part of man which thinks, feels, and wills, as contrasted with body: *his mind was capable of grasping the significance of the problem.* INTELLECT is reasoning power as distinguished from feeling; it is often used in a general sense to characterize high mental ability: *to appeal to the intellect, rather than the emotions.* INTELLIGENCE is ability to learn and to understand; it is also mental alertness or quickness of understanding: *a dog has more intelligence than many other animals.* **6.** MIND, BRAIN, BRAINS may refer to mental capacity. MIND is the philosophical and general term for the center of mental activity, and is therefore used of intellectual powers: *a brilliant mind.* BRAIN is properly the physiological term for the organic structure which makes mental activity possible (*the brain is the center of the nervous system*). but it is often applied, like MIND, to intellectual capacity: *a fertile brain.* The plural BRAINS is the anatomical word (*the brains of an animal used for food*) but, in popular usage, it is applied to intelligence (particularly of a shrewd, practical nature): *that takes brains.*

Min·da·na·o (mĭn′dä nä′ō, -nou′), *n.* the second largest of the Philippine Islands, in the S part of the group. 1,828,071 pop. (1939); 36,537 sq. mi.

mind·ed (mīn′dĭd), *adj.* **1.** having a certain kind of mind: *strong-minded.*   **2.** inclined or disposed.

mind·ful (mīnd′fəl), *adj.* keeping in mind; attentive; careful (usually fol. by *of*). —**mind′ful·ly,** *adv.* —**mind′-ful·ness,** *n.*

mind·less (mīnd′lĭs), *adj.* **1.** without intelligence; senseless.   **2.** unmindful, careless, or heedless. —**mind′-less·ly,** *adv.* —**mind′less·ness,** *n.*

Min·do·ro (mĭn dōr′ō; *Sp.* mēn dô′rō), *n.* one of the Philippine Islands, in the central part of the group. 116,988 pop. (1939); 3922 sq. mi.

mind reading, reading or discerning of the thoughts in the minds of others, esp. by some apparently supernormal power. —**mind reader.**

mind's eye, the imagination.

mine[1] (mīn), *pron.* **1.** possessive form of I, used predicatively or without a noun following.   **2.** the person(s) or thing(s) belonging to me: *that book is mine, a friend of mine.*   —*adj.* **2.** *Archaic.* my (used before a vowel or *h,* or after a noun): *mine eyes, lady mine.* [ME; OE *mīn,* poss. adj. and pron. of first person]

mine² (mīn), *n.*, *v.*, **mined, mining.** —*n.* **1.** an excavation made in the earth for the purpose of getting out ores, precious stones, coal, etc. **2.** a place where such minerals may be obtained, either by excavation or by washing the soil. **3.** a deposit of such minerals, either under the ground or at its surface. **4.** an abounding source or store of anything: *this book is a mine of information.* **5.** a subterranean passage made to extend under the enemy's works or position, as for the purpose of securing access or of depositing explosives for blowing up the position. **6.** a device containing a large charge of explosive in a watertight casing moored beneath the surface of the water for the purpose of blowing up an enemy vessel which passes in close proximity to it. **7.** a similar device used on land. —*v.i.* **8.** to dig in the earth for the purpose of extracting ores, coal, etc.; make a mine. **9.** to extract ores, etc. from mines. **10.** to make subterranean passages. **11.** to dig or lay mines, as in military operations. —*v.t.* **12.** to dig in (earth, etc.) in order to obtain ores, coal, etc. **13.** to extract (ores, coal, etc.) from a mine. **14.** to make subterranean passages in or under; burrow. **15.** to make (passages, etc.) by digging or burrowing. **16.** to dig away or remove the foundations of. **17.** to attack, ruin, or destroy by secret or slow methods. **18.** to dig or lay military mines under. [ME, t. OF, of Celtic orig.]

mine field, *Mil.*, *Naval.* an area on land or water throughout which mines have been laid.

mine layer, naval vessel with special equipment for laying underwater mines.

min·er (mī′nər), *n.* **1.** one who works in a mine. **2.** one who digs or lays military mines.

min·er·al (mĭn′ərəl, mĭn′rəl), *n.* **1.** a substance obtained by mining; ore. **2.** any of a class of substances occurring in nature, usually comprising inorganic substances (as quartz, feldspar, etc.) of definite chemical composition and definite crystal structure, but sometimes taken to include aggregations of these substances (more correctly called rocks) and also certain natural products of organic origin, as asphalt, coal, etc. **3.** any substance neither animal nor vegetable. **4.** (*pl.*) *Brit.* soft drinks. [ME, t. OF, t. ML: s. *minerāle,* prop. adj. neut.] —*adj.* **5.** of the nature of a mineral; pertaining to minerals. **6.** impregnated with a mineral or minerals. **7.** neither animal nor vegetable; inorganic: *the mineral kingdom.* [late ME, t. ML: s. *minerālis,* der. *minera* mine, t. OF: m. *miniere,* der. mine **MINE²**]

mineral., **1.** mineralogical. **2.** mineralogy.

min·er·al·ize (mĭn′ərəlīz′, mĭn′rə-), *v.t.*, **-ized, -izing.** **1.** to convert into a mineral substance. **2.** to transform (a metal) into an ore. **3.** to impregnate or supply with mineral substances. —**min′er·al·i·za′tion,** *n.* —**min′er·al·iz′er,** *n.*

mineral jelly, a gelatinous product made from petroleum which is used to stabilize some explosives.

min·er·al·o·gist (mĭn′ərăl′əjĭst, -rŏl′ə-), *n.* a specialist in mineralogy.

min·er·al·o·gy (mĭn′ərăl′əjĭ, -rŏl′ə-), *n.* the science of minerals. —**min·er·al·og·i·cal** (mĭn′ər ə lŏj′ə kəl), *adj.* —**min′er·al·og′i·cal·ly,** *adv.*

mineral oil, any of a class of oils of mineral origin, as petroleum, consisting of mixtures of hydrocarbons, and used as illuminants, fuels, etc., and in medicine.

mineral pitch, asphalt (bituminous substance).

mineral tar, bitumen of the consistency of tar; maltha.

mineral water, **1.** water containing dissolved mineral salts or gases, esp. such water for medicinal use. **2.** (*pl.*) *Brit.* soft drinks.

mineral wax, ozocerite.

mineral wool, an insulating material consisting of woolly fibers made from melted slag.

Mi·ner·va (mĭ nûr′və), *n.* **1.** *Rom. Myth.* the goddess of wisdom, the arts, and war, identified with the Greek Athena. **2.** a woman of great wisdom or learning.

min·e·stro·ne (mĭn′ə strō′nĭ; *It.* mē/nĕ strô′nĕ), *n.* *Italian.* a soup containing vegetables, herbs, etc., in a broth of chicken or meat. [It., aug. of *minestra* soup, der. *minestrare,* g. L *ministrāre* **MINISTER,** v.]

mine sweeper, *Naval.* a vessel or ship used for dragging a body of water in order to remove enemy mines.

Ming (mĭng), *n.* the dynasty which ruled China from 1368 to 1644, historically the last dynasty of true Chinese origin. In the Ming period art flourished and there were important revisions of Confucian philosophy. [t. Chinese (Pekin): lit., luminous]

min·gle (mĭng′gəl), *v.*, **-gled, -gling.** —*v.i.* **1.** to become mixed, blended, or united. **2.** to associate or mix in company. **3.** to take part with others; participate. —*v.t.* **4.** to mix or combine; put together in a mixture; blend. **5.** to unite, join, or conjoin: *joy mingled with pain.* **6.** to associate in company. **7.** to form by mixing, compound, or concoct. [ME *myngle, mengle,* freq. of *menge*(n), OE *mengan*] —**min′gler,** *n.* —**Syn.** **4.** See **mix, mixed.**

Mi·nho (mē′nyŏŏ), *n.* a river flowing from NW Spain along part of the N boundary of Portugal into the Atlantic. 171 mi. Spanish, **Miño.**

Min·how (mĭn′hō′), *n.* Foochow.

min·i·a·ture (mĭn′ĭ ə chər, mĭn′ə chər), *n.* **1.** a representation or image of anything on a very small scale.

2. greatly reduced or abridged form. **3.** a very small painting, esp. a portrait, on ivory, vellum, or the like. **4.** the art of executing such painting. **5.** illumination, as in manuscripts. —*adj.* **6.** on a very small scale; in a greatly reduced form. [t. It.: m. *miniatura,* der. L *miniāre* rubricate]

miniature camera, *Photog.* a small camera using film of 35 mm. width or less, esp. for taking candid photographs.

Min·ié ball (mĭn′ĭ, -ĭ ă′; *Fr.* mē nyĕ′), (formerly) a conical bullet with a hollow base, expanding, when fired, to fit the rifling. [named after C. E. *Minié* (1814–79), the (French) inventor]

min·i·fy (mĭn′ə fī′), *v.t.*, **-fied, -fying.** **1.** to make less. **2.** to minimize. [f. L *min*(*us*) less + -(I)FY]

min·i·kin (mĭn′ə kĭn), *n.* **1.** a person or object that is delicate or diminutive. —*adj.* **2.** delicate; dainty; mincing. [t. MD: m. *minnekijn,* dim. of *minne* love. See **-KIN**]

min·im (mĭn′əm), *n.* **1.** the smallest unit of liquid measure, the sixtieth part of a fluid dram, or about a drop. **2.** *Music.* a note, formerly the shortest in use, but now equivalent in time value to one half of a semibreve; half note. See illus. under **note.** **3.** the least quantity, or a jot, of anything. **4.** something very small n-significant. **5.** (*cap.*) a member of a mendicant religious order founded in the 15th century by St. Francis of Paula. —*adj.* **6.** smallest; very small. [ME, t. L: s. *minimus* least, smallest, superl. of *minor* **MINOR**]

min·i·mal (mĭn′ə məl), *adj.* **1.** pertaining to or being a minimum. **2.** least possible. **3.** smallest; very small. [f. s. L *minimus* least + -AL¹]

Min·i·mal·ist (mĭn′ə məl ĭst), *n.* a member of a less radical group of socialists, as of a faction of the Russian Social Revolutionary party. [f. MINIMAL + -IST]

min·i·mize (mĭn′ə mīz′), *v.t.*, **-mized, -mizing.** **1.** to reduce to the smallest possible amount or degree. **2.** to represent at the lowest possible estimate; to belittle. —**min′i·mi·za′tion,** *n.* —**min′i·miz′er,** *n.*

min·i·mum (mĭn′ə məm), *n.*, *pl.* **-ma** (-mə), **-mums,** *adj.* —*n.* **1.** the least quantity or amount possible, assignable, allowable, etc. **2.** the lowest amount, value, or degree attained or recorded (opposed to *maximum*). **3.** *Math.* a value of a function at a certain point which is less than or equal to the value attained at nearby points. —*adj.* **4.** that is a minimum. **5.** least possible. **6.** lowest: *a minimum rate.* **7.** pertaining to a minimum or minimums. [t. L, neut. of *minimus.* See **MINIM**]

minimum wage, the lowest wage, fixed by agreement with a union or by legal authority, payable to employees of a particular group.

min·ing (mī′nĭng), *n.* **1.** the action, process, or industry of extracting ores, etc., from mines. **2.** the action of laying explosive mines.

min·ion (mĭn′yən), *n.* **1.** a servile or base favorite of a prince or any patron. **2.** any favorite. **3.** *Print.* a size of type (7 point). —*adj.* **4.** dainty; elegant; trim; pretty. [t. F: m. *mignon* MIGNON]

min·ish (mĭn′ĭsh), *v.t.*, *v.i.* *Archaic.* to diminish or lessen. [ME *mynyssh*(en), t. OF: m. *menuisier* make small, g. Rom. *minūtiāre,* der. L *minūtus* MINUTE²]

min·is·ter (mĭn′ĭs tər), *n.* **1.** one authorized to conduct religious worship; a clergyman; a pastor. **2.** *Brit. and Continental.* one appointed by (or under the authority of) the sovereign or executive head of a government to some high office of state, esp. to that of head of an administrative department: *the Minister of Finance.* **3.** a diplomatic representative accredited by one government to another, esp. an envoy. See **envoy¹.** **4.** one acting as the agent or instrument of another. —*v.t.* **5.** to administer or apply. **6.** *Archaic.* to furnish; supply. —*v.i.* **7.** to give service, care, or aid; attend, as to wants, necessities, etc. **8.** to contribute, as to comfort, happiness, etc. [t. L: servant; r. ME *menistre,* t. OF]

min·is·te·ri·al (mĭn′ĭs tĭr′ĭ əl), *adj.* **1.** pertaining to the ministry of religion, or to a minister or clergyman. **2.** *Brit. and Continental.* pertaining to a ministry or minister of state. **3.** pertaining to or invested with delegated executive authority. **4.** of or pertaining to ministry or service. **5.** instrumental. —**min′is·te′ri·al·ly,** *adv.*

min·is·te·ri·al·ist (mĭn′ĭs tĭr′ĭ əl ĭst), *n.* *Brit. Pol.* a supporter of the ministry in office.

minister plenipotentiary, *pl.* **ministers plenipotentiary.** plenipotentiary.

min·is·trant (mĭn′ə strənt), *adj.* **1.** ministering. —*n.* **2.** one who ministers. [t. L: s. *ministrans,* ppr.]

min·is·tra·tion (mĭn′ə strā′shən), *n.* **1.** act of ministering care, aid, religious service, etc. **2.** an instance of it. —**min′is·tra′tive,** *adj.*

min·is·try (mĭn′ĭs trĭ), *n.*, *pl.* **-tries.** **1.** the service, functions, or profession of a minister of religion. **2.** the body or class of ministers of religion; the clergy. **3.** the service, function, or office of a minister of state. **4.** the policy-forming executive officials in a country, esp. England, taken collectively. **5.** *Brit.* any of the administrative departments of a country. **6.** *Brit.* the building which houses such a department. **7.** *Brit.* the term of office of a minister. **8.** act of ministering; ministration; service. [ME *ministerie,* t. L: s. *ministerium* office, service]

min·i·um (mĭn′ĭ əm), *n.* red lead, Pb₃O₄. [t. L: native cinnabar, red lead]

min·i·ver (mĭn′ə vər), *n.* (in medieval times) a fur of white or spotted white and gray used for linings or trimmings. [ME *meniver*, t. OF: m. *menu vair* small vair. See MENU, VAIR]

mink (mĭngk), *n.*, *pl.* **minks**, *(esp. collectively)* **mink.**
1. a semiaquatic weasellike animal of the genus *Mustela*, esp. of the North American *M. vison*. **2.** the valuable fur of this animal, brownish with lustrous outside hairs and thick, soft undercoat. [appar. t. Sw.: m. *mänk*]

Mink, *Mustela vison*
(Total length 2 ft., tail 8 in.)

Minn., Minnesota.
Min·ne·ap·o·lis (mĭn′Y-ăp′ə·lĭs), *n.* a city in SE Minnesota, on the Mississippi. 521,718 (1950).
min·ne·sing·er (mĭn′Y-sĭng′ər), *n.* one of a class of German lyric poets and singers of the 12th, 13th, and 14th centuries. [t. G: love singer]
Min·ne·so·ta (mĭn′ə·sō′tə), *n.* **1.** a State in the N central United States. 2,982,483 pop. (1950); 84,068 sq. mi. *Cap.:* St. Paul. *Abbr.:* Minn. **2.** a river flowing from the W border of Minnesota into the Mississippi near St. Paul. 332 mi. —**Min·ne·so·tan,** *adj., n.*
min·now (mĭn′ō), *n.*, *pl.* **-nows**, *(esp. collectively)* **-now.**
1. a small European cyprinoid fish, *Phoxinus phoxinus.* **2.** any fish of the family *Cyprinidae*, mostly small but including some large species, as the carp. **3.** (esp. in the U.S.) any of various other small silvery fishes. [ME *men(a)we*, late OE *myne* (for *mynu*), c. OHG *munewa* kind of fish]
Mi·ño (mē′nyō), *n.* Spanish name of **Minho.**
Mi·no·an (mĭ·nō′ən), *adj.* of or pertaining to the ancient advanced civilization of Crete, dating (approximately) from 3000 to 1100 B.C. [f. MINO(S) + -AN]
mi·nor (mī′nər), *adj.* **1.** lesser, as in size, extent, or importance, or being the lesser of two: *a minor share, minor faults.* **2.** under legal age. **3.** in English public schools, designating the younger of two students having the same name. **4.** *Music.* **a.** (of an interval) smaller by a half-step than the corresponding major interval. **b.** (of a chord) having a minor third between the root and the note next above it. **5.** *Logic.* less broad or extensive: **a. minor term** (of a syllogism) the term that is the subject of the conclusion. **b. minor premise,** the premise that contains the minor term. **6.** of or pertaining to the minority. **7.** *U.S. Educ.* noting or pertaining to educational minors: *a minor subject.* —*n.* **8.** a person under legal age. **9.** one of inferior rank or importance in a specified class. **10.** *U.S. Educ.* **a.** a subject or a course of study pursued by a student, esp. a candidate for a degree, subordinately or supplementarily to a major or principal subject or course. **b.** a subject for which less credit than a major is granted in colleges or occasionally in high school. **11.** *Music.* a minor interval, chord, scale, etc. **12.** *U.S. Sports.* a minor league. **13.** (*cap.*) a Minorite. —*v.i.* **14. minor in,** to study as a minor subject. [t. L: less, smaller, inferior, younger, a compar. form; r. ME *menour*, t. OF] —**Syn. 1.** smaller, inferior, secondary. —**Ant. 1.** major.
Mi·nor·ca (mĭ·nôr′kə), *n.* **1.** Spanish, **Menorca.** one of the Balearic Islands, in the W Mediterranean. 43,025 pop. (1940); 271 sq. mi. **2.** one of a Mediterranean breed of white-skinned domestic fowls of moderate size, notable for prolific laying. —**Mi·nor′can,** *adj., n.*
Mi·nor·ite (mī′nər·īt′), *n.* a Franciscan friar.
mi·nor·i·ty (mĭ′nôr′ə·tY, -nôr′-, mī-), *n.*, *pl.* **-ties. 1.** the smaller part or number: a number forming less than half of the whole. **2.** a smaller party or group opposed to a majority, as in voting or other action. **3.** the state or period of being a minor or under legal age.
minor key or **mode,** *Music.* a key or mode based on a minor scale.
minor league, *U.S.* any association of professional sports clubs other than the acknowledged major leagues.
minor orders, *Rom. Cath. Ch.* See **orders** (def. 15).
Minor Prophets. See **prophet** (def. 4c).
minor scale, *Music.* a scale whose third tone forms a minor third with the fundamental tone. See illus. under **scale.**
minor suit, *Bridge.* diamonds or clubs.
Mi·nos (mī′nəs, -nŏs), *n.* *Gk. Myth.* son of Zeus and king and lawgiver of Crete: after death, a judge in the lower world. Cf. **Aeacus, Rhadamanthus.**
Mi·not (mī′nət), *n.* a city in N North Dakota. 22,032 (1950).
Min·o·taur (mĭn′ə·tôr′), *n.* **1.** *Gk. Myth.* a fabulous monster, half bull and half man, confined in the Cretan labyrinth and fed with human flesh. It was killed by Theseus, with the help of Ariadne. **2.** any devouring or destroying agency. [t. L: s. *Mĭnōtaurus*, t. Gk.: m. *Mĭnōtauros*, f. *Mĭnō(s)* MINOS + *taûros* bull]
Minsk (mĕnsk), *n.* a city in the W Soviet Union: capital of the White Russian Republic. 238,772 (1939).
min·ster (mĭn′stər), *n.* *Chiefly Brit.* **1.** a church actually or originally connected with a monastic establishment. **2.** any large or important church, as a cathedral. [ME and OE *mynster*, c. G *münster*, of doubtful orig. Cf. LL *monastērium* MONASTERY]
min·strel (mĭn′strəl), *n.* **1.** one of a class of medieval musicians who sang or recited to the accompaniment of instruments. **2.** *Poetic.* any musician, singer, or poet.

3. one of a troupe of comedians, usually white men made up as Negroes, presenting songs, jokes, etc. [ME *menestral, minstral* t. OF: m. *menestrel*, orig., servant, g. LL *ministeriālis* ministerial]
min·strel·sy (mĭn′strəl·sY), *n.*, *pl.* **-sies. 1.** the art or practice of a minstrel. **2.** minstrels' songs, ballads, etc.: *a collection of Scottish minstrels.*
mint[1] (mĭnt), *n.* **1.** any plant of the labiate genus *Mentha*, comprising aromatic herbs with opposite leaves and small verticillate flowers, as the spearmint, the peppermint, and the horsemint. **2.** a soft or hard confection flavored with peppermint or other flavoring, often served after dinner. [ME and OE *minte* (c. OHG *minza*), t. L: m. *menta*, t. Gk.: m. *míntha*]
mint[2] (mĭnt), *n.* **1.** a place where money is coined by public authority. **2.** a vast amount, esp. of money. —*adj.* **3.** *Philately*, (of a stamp) as issued by the Post Office. —*v.t.* **4.** to make (coins) by stamping metal. **5.** to coin (money). **6.** to make or fabricate as if by coining: *to mint words.* [ME *mynt*, OE *mynet* coin (c. G *münze*), t. L: m. *monēta* mint, MONEY] —**mint′er,** *n.*
mint·age (mĭn′tYj), *n.* **1.** act or process of minting. **2.** the product or result of minting; coinage. **3.** the charge for or cost of minting or coining. **4.** the output of a mint. **5.** a stamp or character impressed.
mint julep, a frosted drink made of bourbon whiskey, sugar, crushed ice, and sprigs of fresh mint.
min·u·end (mĭn′yŏŏ·ĕnd′), *n.* *Math.* the number from which another (the subtrahend) is to be subtracted. [t. L: s. *minuendus*, ger. of *minuere* make smaller]
min·u·et (mĭn′yŏŏ·ĕt′), *n.* **1.** a slow stately dance of French origin. **2.** a piece of music for such a dance or in its rhythm. [t. F: m. *menuet*, orig. adj., very small (with reference to the small steps taken in the dance), dim. of *menu* small. See MENU]
Min·u·it (mĭn′yŏŏ·Yt), *n.* **Peter,** c1580–1638, first governor of the colony of New Netherland.
mi·nus (mī′nəs), *prep.* **1.** less by the subtraction of; decreased by: *ten minus six.* **2.** lacking or without: *a book minus its title page.* —*adj.* **3.** involving or denoting subtraction: *the minus sign.* **4.** negative: *a minus quantity.* **5.** *Colloq.* lacking: *the profits were minus.* **6.** *Bot.* (in heterothallic fungi) designating, in the absence of morphological differention, one of the two strains or mycelia which must unite in the sexual process. —*n.* **7.** the minus sign (−). **8.** a minus quantity. **9.** a deficiency or loss. [t. L, adj., neut. of *minor* MINOR]
mi·nus·cule (mĭ′nŭs′kūl), *adj.* **1.** small, as letters not capital or uncial. **2.** written in such letters (opposed to *majuscule*). —*n.* **3.** a minuscule letter. **4.** a small cursive script developed in the 7th century from the uncial, which it afterward superseded. [t. L: m.s. *minusculus* rather small, dim. of *minor* MINOR] —**mi·nus′cu·lar,** *adj.*
minus sign, *Math.* the symbol (−) denoting subtraction or a minus quantity.
min·ute[1] (mĭn′Yt), *n.*, *v.*, **-uted, -uting,** *adj.* —*n.* **1.** the sixtieth part of an hour; sixty seconds. **2.** an indefinitely short space of time: *wait a minute.* **3.** a point of time, an instant, or moment; *come here this minute!* **4.** a rough draft, as of a document. **5.** *Chiefly Brit.* a written summary, note or memorandum. **6.** (*pl.*) the official record of the proceedings at a meeting of a society, board, committee, council or other body. **7.** *Geom., etc.* the sixtieth part of a degree, or sixty seconds (often represented by the sign ′) 12°10′ (twelve degrees and ten minutes). —*v.t.* **8.** to time exactly, as movements, speed, etc. **9.** to make a draft of (a document, etc.). **10.** to record (something) in a memorandum; note (down). **11.** to enter in the minutes of a society or other body. —*adj.* **12.** prepared in a very short time: *minute steak.* [ME, t. OF, t. ML: m.s. *minūta* small part or division, prop. fem. of L *minūtus* MINUTE[2]]
—**Syn. 2.** MINUTE, INSTANT, MOMENT refer to infinitesimal amounts of time. A MINUTE, properly denoting sixty seconds, is often used loosely for any very short space of time (and may be interchangeable with *second*): *just a minute.* An INSTANT is practically a point in time, with no duration; though it is also used to mean a perceptible amount of time: *not an instant's delay.* MOMENT denotes much the same as INSTANT, though with a somewhat greater sense of duration (but somewhat less than MINUTE): *it will take a moment.*
mi·nute[2] (mĭ·nūt′, -nōōt′, mī′-), *adj.* **1.** extremely small, as in size, amount, extent, or degree: *minute differences.* **2.** of very small scope or individual importance: *minute particulars of a case.* **3.** attentive to or concerned with even very small details or particulars: *a minute observer or report.* [ME, t. L: m.s. *minūtus*, pp., made smaller] —**mi·nute′ness,** *n.* —**Syn. 1.** See **little.**
minute gun (mĭn′Yt), (formerly) a gun fired at intervals of a minute, as in token of mourning or of distress.
minute hand (mĭn′Yt), the hand that indicates the minutes on a clock or watch.
min·ute·ly[1] (mĭn′Yt·lY), *adj.* **1.** occurring every minute. —*adv.* **2.** every minute; minute by minute. [f. MINUTE[1] + -LY]
mi·nute·ly[2] (mĭ·nūt′lY, -nōōt′-, mī-), *adv.* in a minute manner, form, or degree; in minute detail. [f. MINUTE[2] + -LY]
min·ute·man (mĭn′Yt·măn′), *n.*, *pl.* **-men** (-mĕn′). one of a group of American militiamen just before and during the Revolutionary War who held themselves in readiness for instant military service.

mi·nu·ti·a (mĭ·nū′shĭ·ə, -shə, -nōō′-), *n.*, *pl.* **-tiae** (-shĭ·ē′). (*usually pl.*) a small or trivial detail; a trifling circumstance or matter. [t. L: smallness]

minx (mĭngks), *n.* a pert, impudent, or flirtatious girl. [? alter. of *minikins*, f. MINIKIN + hypocoristic -s]

Mi·o·cene (mī′ə·sēn′), *Stratig.* —*adj.* **1.** pertaining to a series of the Tertiary period or system. —*n.* **2.** a division of the Tertiary following Oligocene and preceding Pliocene. [f. *mio-* (repr. Gk. *meiŏn* less) + -CENE]

Miq·ue·lon (mĭk′ə·lŏn′; *Fr.* mē·klôN′), *n.* See **St. Pierre and Miquelon.**

mir (mĭr), *n.* *Russian.* a Russian village commune.

Mir·a·beau (mĭr′ə·bō′; *Fr.* mē·rà·bō′), *n.* **Honoré Gabriel Victor Riqueti** (ô·nô·rĕ′ gà·brē·ĕl′ vēk·tôr′ rēk·tē′), **Count de,** 1749–91, French Revolutionary statesman and orator.

mi·ra·bi·le dic·tu (mĭ·răb′ə·lē′ dĭk′tū, -tōō), *Latin.* strange to say; marvelous to relate.

mi·ra·bil·i·a (mĭr′ə·bĭl′ĭ·ə), *n.pl.* *Latin.* marvels; miracles.

mi·ra·cid·i·um (mī′rə·sĭd′ĭ·əm), *n.*, *pl.* **-cidia** (-sĭd′ĭ·ə). the larva that hatches from the egg of a trematode worm or fluke.

mir·a·cle (mĭr′ə·kəl), *n.* **1.** an effect in the physical world which surpasses all known human or natural powers and is therefore ascribed to supernatural agency. **2.** a wonderful thing: a marvel. **3.** a wonderful or surpassing example of some quality. **4.** a miracle play. [ME, t. OF, t. L: m.s. *mīrāculum*]

miracle play, a medieval dramatic form dealing with religious subjects such as Biblical stories or saints' lives, usually presented in a series or cycle by the craft guilds.

mi·rac·u·lous (mĭ·răk′yə·ləs), *adj.* **1.** of the nature of a miracle; marvelous. **2.** performed by or involving a supernatural power: *a miraculous cure.* **3.** having power to work miracles; wonder-working: *miraculous drugs.* [t. ML: m.s. *mīrāculōsus*, der. L *mīrāculum* miracle] —**mi·rac′u·lous·ly,** *adv.* —**mi·rac′u·lous·ness,** *n.*
—**Syn. 2.** MIRACULOUS, PRETERNATURAL, SUPERNATURAL refer to that which seems to transcend the laws of nature. MIRACULOUS usually refers to an individual event which apparently contravenes known laws governing the universe: *a miraculous answer*, or *success.* PRETERNATURAL suggests the possession of supernormal gifts or qualities: *dogs have a preternatural sense of smell, bats have a sense of hearing that is preternatural.* SUPERNATURAL suggests divine or superhuman properties: *supernatural aid in battle, a supernatural visitant.* —**Ant. 2.** normal.

Mi·ra·flo·res (mē′rä·flô′rĕs), *n.pl.* locks on the Panama Canal, near the Pacific entrance.

mi·rage (mĭ·räzh′), *n.* an optical illusion, due to atmospheric conditions, by which reflected images of distant objects are seen, often inverted. [t. F, der. (*se*) *mirer* look at (oneself) in a mirror, see reflected, g. VL *mīrāre.* See MIRROR, ADMIRE]

mire (mīr), *n.*, *v.*, **mired, miring.** —*n.* **1.** a piece of wet, swampy ground. **2.** ground of this kind; wet, slimy soil of some depth, or deep mud. —*v.t.* **3.** to plunge and fix in mire; cause to stick fast in mire. **4.** to involve in difficulties. **5.** to soil with mire or filth; bespatter with mire. —*v.i.* **6.** to sink in mire; stick in the mud. [ME *myre*, t. Scand.; cf. Icel. *mȳrr*]

mirk (mûrk), *n.*, *adj.* murk.

mirk·y (mûr′kĭ), *adj.*, **mirkier, mirkiest.** murky.

mir·ror (mĭr′ər), *n.* **1.** a reflecting surface, originally polished metal, now usually glass with a metallic or amalgam backing; a looking glass. **2.** *Optics.* a surface (plane, concave, or convex) for reflecting rays of light; a speculum. **3.** something that gives a faithful reflection or true picture of something else. **4.** a pattern for imitation; exemplar. **5.** *Archaic.* a glass, crystal, or the like used by magicians, etc. —*v.t.* **6.** to reflect in or as in a mirror, or as a mirror does. [ME *mirour*, t. OF, g. ML *mīrāre* wonder at, admire, r. L *mīrārī*]

mirth (mûrth), *n.* **1.** rejoicing; joyous gaiety; festive jollity. **2.** humorous amusement, as at something ludicrous, or laughter excited by it. [ME; OE *myr(g)th, myrigth,* der. *myrige* MERRY. See -TH¹]
—**Syn. 2.** MIRTH, GLEE, HILARITY, MERRIMENT refer to the gaiety characterizing people who are enjoying the companionship of others. MIRTH suggests spontaneous amusement or gaiety, manifested briefly in laughter: *uncontrolled outbursts of mirth.* GLEE suggests an effervescence of high spirits or exultation, often manifested in playful or ecstatic gestures; it may apply also to a malicious rejoicing over mishaps to others: *glee over the failure of a rival.* HILARITY implies noisy and boisterous mirth, often exceeding the limits of reason or propriety: *hilarity aroused by practical jokes.* MERRIMENT suggests fun, good spirits, and good nature rather than the kind of wit and sometimes artificial funmaking which cause hilarity: *the house resounded with music and sounds of merriment.* —**Ant. 1.** gloom.

mirth·ful (mûrth′fəl), *adj.* **1.** full of mirth; joyous; jolly; laughingly gay or amused. **2.** affording mirth; amusing. —**mirth′ful·ly,** *adv.* —**mirth′ful·ness,** *n.*

mirth·less (mûrth′lĭs), *adj.* without mirth; joyless; gloomy. —**mirth′less·ly,** *adv.* —**mirth′less·ness,** *n.*

mir·y (mīr′ĭ), *adj.*, **mirier, miriest. 1.** of the nature of mire; swampy: *miry ground.* **2.** abounding in mire; muddy. **3.** covered or bespattered with mire. **4.** dirty; filthy. —**mir′i·ness,** *n.*

mir·za (mûr′zə; *Pers.* mĭr′zä), *n.* (in Persia) **1.** a royal prince (as a title, placed after the name). **2.** a title of honor for men (prefixed to the name). [t. Pers., apocopa-

ted var. of *mīrzād*, f. *mīr* prince (t. Ar., m. *amīr* EMIR) + *zād* born]

mis-¹, a prefix applied to various parts of speech, meaning "ill," "mistaken," "wrong," or simply negating, as in *mistrial, misprint, mistrust.* [ME and OE *mis*(s)-, c. G *miss-* (see MISS, *v.*); often r. ME *mes-*, t. OF, g. L *minus* (see MINUS)]

mis-², var. of **miso-**, before some vowels, as in *misanthrope.*

mis·ad·ven·ture (mĭs′əd·vĕn′chər), *n.* **1.** a piece of ill fortune; a mishap. **2.** ill fortune.

mis·ad·vise (mĭs′əd·vīz′), *v.t.*, **-vised, -vising.** to advise wrongly.

mis·al·li·ance (mĭs′ə·lī′əns), *n.* an improper alliance or association, esp. in marriage; a mésalliance. [half adoption, half trans. of F *mésalliance*]

mis·al·ly (mĭs′ə·lī′), *v.t.*, **-lied, -lying.** to ally improperly or unsuitably.

mis·an·thrope (mĭs′ən·thrōp′, mĭz′-), *n.* a hater of mankind. Also, **mis·an·thro·pist** (mĭs·ăn′thrə·pĭst). [t. Gk.: m.s. *misánthrōpos* hating mankind]

mis·an·throp·ic (mĭs′ən·thrŏp′ĭk), *adj.* **1.** of, pertaining to, or characteristic of a misanthrope. **2.** having the character of, or resembling, a misanthrope. Also, **mis′an·throp′i·cal.** —**mis′an·throp′i·cal·ly,** *adv.*

mis·an·thro·py (mĭs·ăn′thrə·pĭ), *n.* hatred, dislike, or distrust of mankind.

mis·ap·plied (mĭs′ə·plīd′), *adj.* mistakenly applied; used wrongly.

mis·ap·ply (mĭs′ə·plī′), *v.t.*, **-plied, -plying.** to make a wrong application or use of. —**mis·ap·pli·ca·tion** (mĭs′ăp·lə·kā′shən), *n.*

mis·ap·pre·hend (mĭs′ăp·rĭ·hĕnd′), *v.t.* to misunderstand.

mis·ap·pre·hen·sion (mĭs′ăp·rĭ·hĕn′shən), *n.* misunderstanding.

mis·ap·pro·pri·ate (mĭs′ə·prō′prĭ·āt′), *v.t.*, **-ated, -ating. 1.** to put to a wrong use. **2.** to apply wrongfully or dishonestly to one's own use, as funds intrusted to one. —**mis′ap·pro′pri·a′tion,** *n.*

mis·ar·range (mĭs′ə·rānj′), *v.t.*, **-ranged, -ranging.** to arrange wrongly. —**mis′ar·range′ment,** *n.*

mis·be·come (mĭs′bĭ·kŭm′), *v.t.*, **-came, -come, -coming.** to be unsuitable, unbecoming, or unfit for.

mis·be·got·ten (mĭs′bĭ·gŏt′ən), *adj.* unlawfully or irregularly begotten; illegitimate. Also, **mis′be·got′.**

mis·be·have (mĭs′bĭ·hāv′), *v.t.*, *v.i.*, **-haved, -having.** to behave badly. —**mis′be·hav′ior,** *n.*

mis·be·lief (mĭs′bĭ·lēf′), *n.* **1.** erroneous belief; false opinion. **2.** erroneous or unorthodox religious belief.

mis·be·lieve (mĭs′bĭ·lēv′), *v.*, **-lieved, -lieving.** —*v.i.* **1.** to believe wrongly; hold an erroneous belief. —*v.t.* **2.** to disbelieve; doubt. —**mis′be·liev′er,** *n.*

mis·be·stow (mĭs′bĭ·stō′), *v.t.* to bestow improperly.

mis·brand (mĭs·brănd′), *v.t.* **1.** to brand or label erroneously. **2.** to brand with a simulated trademark or trade name.

misc., **1.** miscellaneous. **2.** miscellany.

mis·cal·cu·late (mĭs·kăl′kyə·lāt′), *v.t.*, *v.i.*, **-lated, -lating.** to calculate wrongly. —**mis′cal·cu·la′tion,** *n.*

mis·call (mĭs·kôl′), *v.t.* to call by a wrong name.

mis·car·riage (mĭs·kăr′ĭj), *n.* **1.** failure to attain the right or desired result: *a miscarriage of justice.* **2.** a transmission of goods not in accordance with the contract of shipment. **3.** failure of a letter, etc., to reach its destination. **4.** premature expulsion of a fetus from the uterus, esp. before it is viable.

mis·car·ry (mĭs·kăr′ĭ), *v.i.*, **-ried, -rying. 1.** to fail to attain the right end; be unsuccessful. **2.** to go astray or be lost in transit, as a letter. **3.** to have a miscarriage.

mis·ce·ge·na·tion (mĭs′ĭ·jə·nā′shən), *n.* **1.** mixture of races by sexual union. **2.** interbreeding between different races. [f. L *miscē(re)* mix + L *gen(us)* race + -ATION]

mis·cel·la·ne·a (mĭs′ə·lā′nĭ·ə), *n.pl.* a miscellaneous collection, esp. of literary compositions. [t. L, neut. pl. of *miscellāneus* MISCELLANEOUS]

mis·cel·la·ne·ous (mĭs′ə·lā′nĭ·əs), *adj.* **1.** consisting of members or elements of different kinds: *miscellaneous volumes.* **2.** of mixed character. **3.** having various qualities or aspects; dealing with various subjects. [t. L: m. *miscellāneus*, der. *miscellus* mixed] —**mis′cel·la′ne·ous·ly,** *adv.* —**mis′cel·la′ne·ous·ness,** *n.*
—**Syn. 1.** MISCELLANEOUS, INDISCRIMINATE, PROMISCUOUS refer to mixture and lack of order, and may imply lack of discernment or taste. MISCELLANEOUS emphasizes the idea of the mixture of things of different kinds or natures: *a miscellaneous assortment of furniture.* INDISCRIMINATE emphasizes lack of discrimination in choice (and consequent confusion): *indiscriminate praise.* PROMISCUOUS is even stronger than INDISCRIMINATE in its emphasis on complete absence of discrimination: *promiscuous flattery, promiscuous in his friendships.*

mis·cel·la·ny (mĭs′ə·lā′nĭ; *Brit.* mĭ·sĕl′ə·nĭ), *n.*, *pl.* **-nies. 1.** a miscellaneous collection by several authors, of literary compositions or pieces dealing with various topics, assembled in a volume or book. **2.** (*pl.*) miscellaneous collection of articles or entries, as in a book. [Anglicized var. of MISCELLANEA]

mis·chance (mĭs·chăns′, -chäns′), *n.* ill luck; a mishap or misfortune. [ME *meschance*, t. OF: m. *mescheance.* See MIS-¹, CHANCE]

---

b., blend of, blended; c., cognate with; d., dialect, dialectal; der., derived from; f., formed from; g., going back to; m., modification of; r., replacing; s., stem of; t., taken from; ?, perhaps. See the full key on inside cover.

mis·chief (mĭs′chĭf), *n.* **1.** harm or trouble, esp., as due to an agent or cause. **2.** an injury caused by a person or other agent, or an evil due to some cause. **3.** a cause or source of harm, evil, or annoyance. **4.** vexatious or annoying action. **5.** a tendency or disposition to tease, vex, or annoy. **6.** conduct such as to cause petty annoyance by way of sport. **7.** *Colloq.* the devil. [ME *meschief*, t. OF. der. *meschever* succeed ill, f. *mes-* MIS- + *chever* come to an end, der. *chef* head, end (see CHIEF)] —**Syn. 1.** See **damage.**

mis·chief-mak·er (mĭs′chĭf mā′kər), *n.* one who makes mischief; one who stirs up discord, as by talebearing. —**mis′chief-mak′ing,** *adj., n.*

mis·chie·vous (mĭs′chə vəs), *adj.* **1.** harmful or injurious. **2.** maliciously or playfully annoying, as persons, actions, etc. **3.** fond of mischief, as children. **4.** roguishly or archly teasing, as speeches, glances, etc. —**mis′chie·vous·ly,** *adv.* —**mis′chie·vous·ness,** *n.*

mis·ci·ble (mĭs′ə bəl), *adj.* capable of being mixed. [f. s. L *miscēre* mix + -IBLE] —**mis′ci·bil′i·ty,** *n.*

mis·col·or (mĭs kŭl′ər), *v.t.* **1.** to give a wrong color to. **2.** to misrepresent.

mis·con·ceive (mĭs′kən sēv′), *v.t., v.i.,* -**ceived,** -**ceiv·ing.** to conceive wrongly; misunderstand. —**mis′con·ceiv′er,** *n.*

mis·con·cep·tion (mĭs′kən sĕp′shən), *n.* erroneous conception; a mistaken notion.

mis·con·duct (*n.* mĭs kŏn′dŭkt; *v.* mĭs′kən dŭkt′), *n.* **1.** improper conduct; wrong behavior. **2.** unlawful conduct by an official in regard to his office, or by a person in the administration of justice, such as a lawyer, witness, or juror. —*v.t.* **3.** to mismanage. **4.** to misbehave (oneself).

mis·con·struc·tion (mĭs′kən strŭk′shən), *n.* **1.** wrong construction; misinterpretation. **2.** act of misconstruing.

mis·con·strue (mĭs′kən strōō′, mĭs kŏn′strōō), *v.t.,* -**strued,** -**stru·ing.** to construe wrongly; take in a wrong sense; misinterpret; misunderstand.

mis·count (mĭs kount′), *v.t., v.i.* **1.** to count erroneously; miscalculate. —*n.* **2.** an erroneous counting; a miscalculation.

mis·cre·ance (mĭs′krĭ əns), *n. Archaic.* wrong belief; misbelief; false religious faith.

mis·cre·an·cy (mĭs′krĭ ən sĭ), *n. Archaic.* **1.** miscreance. **2.** state or condition of a miscreant; turpitude.

mis·cre·ant (mĭs′krĭ ənt), *adj.* **1.** depraved, villainous, or base. **2.** *Archaic.* misbelieving; holding a false religious belief. —*n.* **3.** a vile wretch; villain. **4.** *Archaic.* a misbelieving person, as a heretic or an infidel. [ME *miscreaunt*, t. OF: m. *mescreant*, f. *mes-* MIS-[1] + *creant*, ppr. of *creire* believe, g. L *crēdere*]

mis·cre·ate (mĭs′krĭ āt′), *v.,* -**ated,** -**ating,** *adj.* —*v.t., v.i.* **1.** to create amiss; misform. —*adj.* **2.** *Archaic.* miscreated. —**mis′cre·a′tion,** *n.*

mis·cre·at·ed (mĭs′krĭ ā′tĭd), *adj.* wrongly created; misshapen; monstrous.

mis·cue (mĭs kū′), *n., v.,* -**cued,** -**cu·ing.** —*n.* **1.** *Billiards, etc.* a slip of the cue, causing it to strike the ball improperly or not at all. —*v.i.* **2.** to make a miscue. **3.** *Theat.* to fail to answer one's cue or to answer another's cue.

mis·date (mĭs dāt′), *v.,* -**dated,** -**dating,** *n.* —*v.t.* **1.** to date wrongly; assign or affix a wrong date to. —*n.* **2.** a wrong date.

mis·deal (mĭs dēl′), *v.,* -**dealt,** -**dealing,** *n.* —*v.t., v.i.* **1.** to deal wrongly, esp. at cards. —*n.* **2.** a wrong deal. —**mis·deal′er,** *n.*

mis·deed (mĭs dēd′), *n.* an ill deed; a wicked action.

mis·de·mean (mĭs′dĭ mēn′), *v.t., v.i.* to misbehave.

mis·de·mean·ant (mĭs′dĭ mē′nənt), *n.* **1.** one guilty of misbehavior. **2.** *Law.* one convicted of a misdemeanor.

mis·de·mean·or (mĭs′dĭ mē′nər), *n.* **1.** misbehavior; a misdeed. **2.** *Law.* an offense defined as less serious than a felony. Also, *esp. Brit.,* **mis′de·mean′our.**

mis·de·rive (mĭs′dĭ rīv′), *v.t., v.i.,* -**rived,** -**riv·ing.** to derive wrongly; assign a wrong derivation to.

mis·de·scribe (mĭs′dĭ skrīb′), *v.t., v.i.,* -**scribed,** -**scribing.** to describe incorrectly or falsely. —**mis·de·scrip·tion** (mĭs′dĭ skrĭp′shən), *n.*

mis·di·rect (mĭs′dĭ rĕkt′), *v.t.* to direct wrongly.

mis·di·rec·tion (mĭs′dĭ rĕk′shən), *n.* **1.** a wrong indication, guidance, or instruction. **2.** *Law.* an erroneous charge to the jury by a judge.

mis·do (mĭs dōō′), *v.t., v.i.,* -**did,** -**done,** -**do·ing.** to do wrongly. [ME *misdo(n)*, OE *misdōn*. See MIS-[1], DO[1]] —**mis·do′er,** *n.* —**mis·do′ing,** *n.*

mis·doubt (mĭs dout′), *Archaic.* —*v.t., v.i.* **1.** to doubt or suspect. —*n.* **2.** doubt or suspicion.

mise (mēz, mīz), *n.* a settlement or agreement. [t. OF, der. *mettre* put, set, g. L *mittere* send]

mis·ease (mĭs ēz′), *n. Archaic.* **1.** discomfort; distress, suffering. **2.** poverty.

mise en scène (mē zäṅ sĕn′), *French.* **1.** the equipment for a stage setting. **2.** stage setting, as of a play. **3.** the surroundings amid which anything is seen.

mis·em·ploy (mĭs′ĕm ploi′), *v.t., v.i.* to employ wrongly or improperly; misuse. —**mis′em·ploy′ment,** *n.*

Mi·se·no (mē zě′nô), *n.* a cape in SW Italy, on the N shore of the Bay of Naples: ruins of ancient **Mi·se·num** (mī sē′nəm), a Roman naval station and resort.

mi·ser (mī′zər), *n.* **1.** one who lives in wretched circumstances in order to save and hoard money. **2.** a niggardly, avaricious person. **3.** a wretched or unhappy person. [t. L: wretched, unhappy, sick, bad]

mis·er·a·ble (mĭz′ər ə bəl, mĭz′rə-), *adj.* **1.** wretchedly unhappy, uneasy, or uncomfortable. **2.** wretchedly poor; needy. **3.** *Colloq.* being in poor health; ailing. **4.** of wretched character or quality; contemptible; wretchedly bad. **5.** attended with or causing misery: *a miserable existence.* **6.** manifesting misery. **7.** worthy of pity; deplorable: *a miserable failure.* [t. L: m.s. *miserābilis* pitiable] —**mis′er·a·ble·ness,** *n.* —**mis′er·a·bly,** *adv.* —**Syn. 1.** forlorn, disconsolate, doleful. See **wretched. 5.** despicable, mean. **7.** pitiable; lamentable. —**Ant.** happy.

Mis·e·re·re (mĭz′ə râr′ĭ, -rĕr′ĭ), *n. Latin.* **1.** the 51st psalm (50th in the Vulgate and Douay versions), one of the penitential psalms. **2.** a musical setting for it. **3.** (*l.c.*) a prayer or expression asking for mercy. **4.** (*l.c.*) misericord (def. 3). [L: have pity; the first word of the psalm in the Vulgate]

mis·er·i·cord (mĭz′ər ə kôrd′, mĭ zĕr′ə kôrd′), *n.* **1.** a relaxation of a monastic rule. **2.** a room in a monastery where such relaxations were permitted. **3.** a small projection on the under side of a hinged seat of a church stall, which, when the seat was thrown back, gave support to a person standing in the stall. **4.** a medieval dagger, used for the mercy stroke to a wounded foe. Also, **mis′er·i·corde′.** [ME *misericorde*, t. OF, t. L: m.s. *misericordia* mercy]

mis·er·i·cor·di·a (mĭz′ər ə kôr′dĭə), *n. Latin.* compassion; mercy.

mi·ser·ly (mī′zər lĭ), *adj.* of, like, or befitting a miser; penurious; niggardly. —**mi′ser·li·ness,** *n.*

mis·er·y (mĭz′ə rĭ), *n., pl.* -**er·ies.** **1.** wretchedness of condition or circumstances. **2.** distress caused by privation or poverty. **3.** great distress of mind; extreme unhappiness. **4.** a cause or source of wretchedness. **5.** *Dial.* bodily pain. [ME *miserie*, t. L: m. *miseria*] —**Syn. 3.** grief, anguish, woe. See **sorrow.**

mis·es·teem (mĭs′ĕs tēm′), *v.t.* to esteem wrongly; fail to esteem or respect properly.

mis·es·ti·mate (*v.* mĭs ĕs′tə māt′; *n.* mĭs ĕs′tə mĭt), *v.,* -**mated,** -**mating,** *n.* —*v.t.* **1.** to estimate wrongly or incorrectly. —*n.* **2.** wrong estimate.

mis·fea·sance (mĭs fē′zəns), *n. Law.* **1.** wrong, actual or alleged, arising from or consisting of affirmative action (contrasted with *nonfeasance*). **2.** the wrongful performance of a normally lawful act; the wrongful and injurious exercise of lawful authority. [t. OF: m. *mesfaisance,* der. *mesfaire* misdo. See MIS-, FEASANCE, and cf. MALFEASANCE]

mis·fea·sor (mĭs fē′zər), *n. Law.* one guilty of misfeasance.

mis·fire (mĭs fīr′), *v.,* -**fired,** -**firing,** *n.* —*v.i.* **1.** to fail to be fired or exploded. —*n.* **2.** a failure in firing.

mis·fit (mĭs fĭt′; for 3 also mĭs′fĭt), *v.,* -**fitted,** -**fitting,** *n.* —*v.t., v.i.* **1.** to fit badly. —*n.* **2.** a bad fit; an illfitting garment, etc. **3.** a badly adjusted person.

mis·for·tune (mĭs fôr′chən), *n.* **1.** ill or adverse fortune; ill luck. **2.** an instance of this; a mischance or mishap. —**Syn. 2.** accident: disaster, calamity, catastrophe; reverse; blow. See **affliction.**

mis·give (mĭs gĭv′), *v.,* -**gave,** -**given,** -**giving.** —*v.t.* **1.** (of one's mind, heart, etc.) to give doubt or apprehension to. —*v.i.* **2.** to be apprehensive.

mis·giv·ing (mĭs gĭv′ĭng), *n.* a feeling of doubt, distrust, or apprehension. —**Syn.** See **apprehension.**

mis·gov·ern (mĭs gŭv′ərn), *v.t.* to govern or manage badly. —**mis·gov′ern·ment,** *n.* —**mis·gov′er·nor,** *n.*

mis·guide (mĭs gīd′), *v.t.,* -**guided,** -**guiding.** to guide wrongly; mislead. —**mis·guid′ance,** *n.* —**mis·guid′er,** *n.*

mis·guid·ed (mĭs gī′dĭd), *adj.* misled. —**mis·guid′ed·ly,** *adv.*

mis·han·dle (mĭs hăn′dəl), *v.t.,* -**dled,** -**dling.** to handle badly; maltreat.

mis·hap (mĭs′hăp, mĭs hăp′), *n.* an unfortunate accident.

Mish·a·wa·ka (mĭsh′ə wô′kə), *n.* a city in N Indiana, near South Bend. 32,913 (1950).

mis·hear (mĭs hĭr′), *v.t., v.i.,* -**heard,** -**hearing.** to hear incorrectly or imperfectly.

mish·mash (mĭsh′măsh′), *n.* a hodgepodge; a jumble.

Mish·nah (mĭsh′nə), *n., pl.* **Mishnayoth** (mĭsh′näyōth′). **1.** the collection of oral laws made by Judah ha-Nasi (A.D. c135–c220), which forms the basis of the Talmud. **2.** a paragraph of the Mishnah. Also, **Mish′na.** [t. Heb.: repetition, study] —**Mish·na·ic** (mĭsh-nā′ĭk), **Mish′nic, Mish′ni·cal,** *adj.*

mis·in·form (mĭs′ĭn fôrm′), *v.t.* to give false or misleading information to. —**mis′in·form′ant, mis′-in·form′er,** *n.* —**mis′in·for·ma′tion,** *n.*

mis·in·ter·pret (mĭs′ĭn tûr′prĭt), *v.t.* to interpret, explain, or understand incorrectly. —**mis′in·ter·pre·ta′tion,** *n.*

mis·join·der (mĭs join′dər), *n. Law.* a joining in one suit or action of causes or of parties not permitted to be so joined.

mis·judge (mĭs jŭj′), *v.t., v.i.,* -**judged,** -**judging.** to judge wrongly or unjustly. —**mis·judg′ment;** *esp. Brit.,* **mis·judge′ment,** *n.*

mis·lay (mĭsˈlāˈ), v.t., -laid, -laying. 1. to put in a place afterward forgotten. 2. to lay or place wrongly; misplace. —**mis·layˈer**, n.

mis·lead (mĭsˈlēdˈ), v.t., -led, -leading. 1. to lead or guide wrongly; lead astray. 2. to lead into error of conduct, thought, or judgment. —**mis·leadˈer**, n. —**mis·leadˈing**, adj. —**mis·leadˈing·ly**, adv.

mis·like (mĭsˈlīkˈ), v.t., -liked, -liking. 1. to dislike. 2. to displease. —**mis·likˈer**, n. —**mis·likˈing**, n.

mis·man·age (mĭsˈmănˈĬj), v.t., v.i., -aged, -aging. to manage badly. —**mis·manˈage·ment**, n.

mis·mar·riage (mĭsˈmărˈĬj), n. an unsuitable or unhappy marriage.

mis·match (mĭsˈmăchˈ), v.t. 1. to match badly or unsuitably. —n. 2. a bad or unsatisfactory match.

mis·mate (mĭsˈmātˈ), v.t., v.i., -mated, -mating. to mate amiss or unsuitably.

mis·move (mĭsˈmōōvˈ), n. a wrong move, as in a game or any course of procedure.

mis·name (mĭsˈnāmˈ), v.t., -named, -naming. to call by a wrong name.

mis·no·mer (mĭsˈnōˈmər), n. 1. a misapplied name or designation. 2. an error in naming a person or thing. [ME misnoumer, t. OF: m. mesnommer, n. use of inf., f. mes- MIS-[1] + nommer name, g. L nōmināre. See NOMINATE]

miso-, a word element referring to hate. [t. Gk., comb. form of mīsein to hate, mīsos hatred]

mi·sog·a·my (mĭˈsŏgˈə·mĬ, mī-), n. hatred of marriage. —**mi·sogˈa·mist**, n.

mi·sog·y·ny (mĭˈsŏjˈə·nĬ, mī-), n. hatred of women. [t. Gk.: m.s. mīsogynía] —**mi·sogˈy·nist**, n. —**mi·sogˈy·nous**, adj.

mi·sol·o·gy (mĭˈsŏlˈə·jĬ, mī-), n. hatred of reason or reasoning. [t. Gk.: m.s. mīsología hatred of argument] —**mi·solˈo·gist**, n.

mis·one·ism (mĭsˈōˈnēˈĬz·əm, mī·sō-), n. hatred or dislike of what is new. [t. It.: m. misoneismo, f. miso- MISO- + s. Gk. néos new + -ismo -ISM] —**mis·oˈne·ist**, n.

mis·pick·el (mĭsˈpĬkˈəl), n. arsenopyrite. [t. G]

mis·place (mĭsˈplāsˈ), v.t., -placed, -placing. 1. to put in a wrong place. 2. to place or bestow improperly, unsuitably, or unwisely. —**mis·placeˈment**, n. —Syn. 1. See displace.

mis·play (mĭsˈplāˈ), n. a wrong play.

mis·plead (mĭsˈplēdˈ), v.t., v.i. to plead incorrectly.

mis·plead·ing (mĭsˈplēˈdĬng), n. Law. a mistake in pleading as a misjoinder of parties, a misstatement of a cause of action, etc.

mis·print (n. mĭsˈprĬntˈ, mĭsˈprĬntˈ; v. mĭsˈprĬntˈ), n. 1. a mistake in printing. —v.t. 2. to print incorrectly.

mis·pri·sion (mĭsˈprĬzhˈən), n. 1. a wrongful action or commission, esp. of a public official. 2. neglect to give notice of an act of treason or felony. [ME, t. OF, der. mesprendre mistake, do wrong, f. mes- MIS-[1] + prendre take, g. L prehendre]

mis·prize (mĭsˈprīzˈ), v.t., -prized, -prizing. to despise; undervalue; slight; scorn. [t. OF: m. mesprisier, f. mes- MIS-[1] + prisier PRIZE[2]]

mis·pro·nounce (mĭsˈprə·nounsˈ), v.t., v.i., -nounced, -nouncing. to pronounce incorrectly. —**mis·pro·nun·ci·a·tion** (mĭsˈprə·nŭnˈsĬˈāˈshən), n.

mis·quote (mĭsˈkwōtˈ), v.t., v.i., -quoted, -quoting. to quote incorrectly. —**misˈquo·taˈtion**, n.

mis·read (mĭsˈrēdˈ), v.t., -read, -reading. to read wrongly; misinterpret.

mis·reck·on (mĭsˈrĕkˈən), v.t., v.i. to reckon incorrectly; miscalculate.

mis·re·mem·ber (mĭsˈrĬˈmĕmˈbər), v.t., v.i. 1. to remember incorrectly. 2. Dial. to fail to remember.

mis·re·port (mĭsˈrĬ·pōrtˈ), v.t. 1. to report incorrectly or falsely. —n. 2. an incorrect or false report. —**misˈre·portˈer**, n.

mis·rep·re·sent (mĭsˈrĕpˈrĬˈzĕntˈ), v.t. to represent incorrectly, improperly, or falsely. —**misˈrep·re·sen·taˈtion**, n. —**misˈrep·re·sentˈer**, n. —**misˈrep·re·senˈta·tive**, adj.

mis·rule (mĭsˈrōōlˈ), n., v., -ruled, -ruling. —n. 1. bad or unwise rule; misgovernment. 2. disorder or lawless tumult. —v.t. 3. to misgovern. —**mis·rulˈer**, n.

miss[1] (mĭs), v.t. 1. to fail to hit, light upon, meet, catch, receive, obtain, attain, accomplish, see, hear, etc.: to miss a train. 2. to fail to perform, attend to, be present at, etc.: to miss an appointment. 3. to perceive the absence or loss of, often with regret. 4. to escape or avoid: he just missed being caught. 5. to fail to perceive or understand: to miss the point of a remark. 6. miss fire, a. to fail to go off, as a firearm. b. to fail in any action; prove unsuccessful. —v.i. 7. to fail to hit, light upon, receive, or attain something. 8. to fail of effect or success; be unsuccessful. —n. 9. a failure to hit, meet, obtain, or accomplish something. 10. an omission. [ME misse, OE missan, c. D and G missen]

miss[2] (mĭs), n., pl. **misses**. 1. (cap.) the conventional title of respect for an unmarried woman, prefixed to the name. 2. (without the name) a term of address to an unmarried woman. 3. a young unmarried woman; a girl. [short for MISTRESS]

Miss., Mississippi.

mis·sal (mĭsˈəl), n. the book containing the prayers and rites for celebrating mass, used by the priest at the altar. [ME, t. ML: s. missāle, neut. of missālis, der. LL missa MASS[2]]

Mis·sa So·lem·nis (mĭsˈə sōlĕmˈnĬs). Mass in D, Op. 123 (1818–23, published 1827) by Beethoven.

mis·say (mĭsˈsāˈ), v., -said, -saying. Archaic. —v.t. 1. to say or speak ill of; abuse; slander. 2. to say wrongly. —v.i. 3. to speak wrongly.

mis·sel thrush (mĭsˈəl), a large European thrush, Turdus viscivorus, which is fond of the berries of the mistletoe. Also, **mis·sel**. [see MISTLE(TOE), THRUSH[1]]

mis·shape (mĭsˈshāpˈ), v.t., -shaped, -shaped or -shapen, -shaping. to shape ill; misform; deform.

mis·shap·en (mĭsˈshāˈpən), adj. badly shaped; deformed. —**mis·shapˈen·ly**, adv. —**mis·shapˈen·ness**, n.

mis·sile (mĭsˈəl), n. 1. an object or weapon that can be thrown, hurled, or shot, as a stone, a bullet, a lance, or an arrow. —adj. 2. capable of being thrown, hurled, or shot, as from the hand, a gun, etc. 3. that discharges missiles. [t. L: something which can be thrown]

miss·ing (mĭsˈĬng), adj. lacking; absent; not found.

missing link, 1. a hypothetical form of animal assumed to have constituted a connecting link between the anthropoid apes and man. 2. something lacking for the completion of a series or sequence of any kind.

mis·sion (mĭshˈən), n. 1. a body of persons sent to a foreign country to conduct negotiations, establish relations, or the like. 2. the business with which an agent, envoy, etc., is charged. 3. U.S. a permanent diplomatic establishment abroad: chief of mission. 4. Mil. an operation, by one or more war aircraft, against the enemy. 5. a body of persons sent into a foreign land for religious work among a heathen people, or into any region for the spiritual betterment of the inhabitants. 6. an establishment of missionaries in a foreign land; a missionary post or station. 7. a similar establishment in any region, designed for the spiritual betterment of its people. 8. the district assigned to a missionary priest. 9. missionary duty or work. 10. an organization for carrying on missionary work. 11. (pl.) organized missionary work or activities in any country, region, or field: foreign missions. 12. a church or a region with a minister or priest who lives near by but who is non-resident. 13. a series of special religious services for quickening piety and converting unbelievers: to preach a mission. 14. a self-imposed duty. 15. a sending or being sent for some duty or purpose. 16. those sent. [t. L: s. missio a sending] —**misˈsion·er**, n.

mis·sion·ar·y (mĭshˈən·ĕrˈĬ), n., pl. -aries, adj. —n. 1. a person sent to work for the propagation of his religious faith in a heathen land or a newly settled district. 2. any propagandist. 3. one sent on a mission. —adj. 4. pertaining to or connected with religious missions. 5. engaged in such a mission, or devoted to work connected with missions. 6. pertaining to any propaganda. 7. characteristic of a propagandist. [f. MISSION + -ARY[1]]

Missionary Ridge, a ridge in NW Georgia and SE Tennessee: Union victory near Chattanooga, 1863.

mis·sis (mĭsˈĬz, -Ĭs), n. Colloq. or Dial. 1. a man's wife. 2. the mistress of a household. Also, **missus**.

miss·ish (mĭsˈĬsh), adj. prim; affected; prudish.

Mis·sis·sip·pi (mĭsˈə·sĬpˈĬ), n. 1. a State in the S United States. 2,178,914 pop. (1950); 47,716 sq. mi. Cap.: Jackson. Abbr.: Miss. 2. a river flowing from N Minnesota S to the Gulf of Mexico: the principal river of the U.S. 2470 mi.; from the headwaters of the Missouri to the Gulf of Mexico, 3988 mi.

Mis·sis·sip·pi·an (mĭsˈə·sĬpˈĬ·ən), adj. 1. of or pertaining to the State of Mississippi or the Mississippi river. 2. Stratig. pertaining to a late Paleozoic geological period or a system equivalent to the Lower Carboniferous of usage outside of North America. —n. 3. a native or inhabitant of Mississippi. 4. Stratig. the period or system following Devonian and preceding Pennsylvanian.

mis·sive (mĭsˈĬv), n. 1. a written message; a letter. —adj. 2. sent, esp. from an official source. [late ME, t. ML: m.s. missivus, der. L missus, pp., sent]

Mis·so·lon·ghi (mĭsˈə·lŏngˈgĬ), n. a town in W Greece: Byron died here, 1824. 10,389 (1940). Also, **Mesolonghi**.

Mis·sou·la (mĭˈzōōˈlə), n. a city in W Montana. 22,485 (1950).

Mis·sou·ri (mĭˈzŏŏrˈĬ, -zŏŏrˈə), n. 1. a State in the central United States. 3,954,653 pop. (1950); 69,674 sq. mi. Cap.: Jefferson City. Abbr.: Mo. 2. from Missouri, Slang. skeptical; requiring proof. 3. a river flowing from SW Montana into the Mississippi N of St. Louis, Missouri. 2723 mi. 4. (pl.) a North American Indian tribe belonging to the Siouan linguistic stock, located on the Missouri river in early historic times; now extinct as a tribe. —**Mis·sourˈi·an**, adj., n.

mis·speak (mĭsˈspēkˈ), v.t., v.i., -spoke, -spoken, -speaking. to speak, utter, or pronounce incorrectly.

mis·spell (mĭsˈspĕlˈ), v.t., v.i., -spelled or -spelt, -spelling. to spell incorrectly. —**mis·spellˈing**, n.

mis·spend (mĭsˈspĕndˈ), v.t., -spent, -spending. to spend improperly; squander; waste.

mis·state (mĭsˈstātˈ), v.t., -stated, -stating. to state wrongly or misleadingly; make a wrong statement about. —**mis·stateˈment**, n.

mis·step (mĭsˈstĕpˈ), n. 1. a wrong step. 2. an error or slip in conduct.

mis·sus (mĭsˈəz, -əs), n. Colloq. or Dial. missis.

miss·y (mĭsˈĬ), n., pl. **missies**. Colloq. young miss.

mist (mĭst), n. 1. a cloudlike aggregation of minute

b., blend of, blended; c., cognate with; d., dialect, dialectal; der., derived from; f., formed from; g., going back to; m., modification of; r., replacing; s., stem of; t., taken from; ?, perhaps. See the full key on inside cover.

globules of water suspended in the atmosphere at or near the earth's surface. **2.** *Meteorol.* (by international agreement) a very thin fog in which the horizontal visibility is greater than 1 kilometer; in the U.S., synonymous with *drizzle.* **3.** a cloud of particles resembling a mist. **4.** something which dims, obscures, or blurs. **5.** a hazy appearance before the eyes, as due to tears or to bodily disorders. **6.** a suspension of a liquid in a gas. —*v.i.* **7.** to become misty. **8.** to rain in very fine drops; drizzle. —*v.t.* **9.** to make misty. [ME and OE, c. D, LG, and Sw. *mist*] —Syn. 1. See **cloud.**

mis·tak·a·ble (mĭs tā′kə bəl; *commonly* mə stā′-), *adj.* that may be mistaken, misapprehended, or misunderstood.

mis·take (mĭs tāk′; *commonly* mə stāk′), *n., v.,* -**took,** -**taken, -taking.** —*n.* **1.** an error in action, opinion, or judgment. **2.** a misconception or misapprehension. —*v.t.* **3.** to take or regard as something or somebody else. **4.** to conceive of or understand wrongly; misapprehend; misunderstand. —*v.i.* **5.** to be in error. [ME *mistake(n),* v., t. Scand.; cf. Icel. *mistaka* take by mistake. See MIS-[1], TAKE] —Syn. **1.** MISTAKE, BLUNDER, ERROR, SLIP refer to deviations from right, accuracy, correctness, or truth. A MISTAKE, grave or trivial, is caused by bad judgment or a disregard of rule or principle: *it was a mistake to argue.* A BLUNDER is a careless, stupid, or gross mistake in action or speech, suggesting awkwardness, heedlessness, or ignorance: *through his blunder the message was lost.* An ERROR (often interchanged with MISTAKE) is an unintentional wandering or deviation from accuracy, or right conduct: *an error in addition.* A SLIP is usually a minor mistake made through haste or carelessness: *a slip of the tongue.*

mis·tak·en (mĭs tā′kən; *commonly* mə stā′-), *adj.* **1.** wrongly conceived, entertained, or done: *a mistaken notion.* **2.** erroneous; wrong. **3.** having made a mistake; being in error. —**mis·tak′en·ly,** *adv.*

Mis·tas·si·ni (mĭs′tə sē′nĭ), *n.* a lake in E Canada, in Quebec province. ab. 100 mi. long; 975 sq. mi.

mis·teach (mĭs tēch′), *v.t.,* -**taught, -teaching.** to teach wrongly or badly.

mis·ter (mĭs′tər), *n.* **1.** (*cap.*) the conventional title of respect for a man, prefixed to the name and to certain official designations (usually written *Mr.*). **2.** *Colloq.* (in address, without the name) sir. **3.** the official title used in addressing: **a.** *Mil.* a warrant officer, or a cadet in the U.S. Military Academy. **b.** *Naval.* anyone of a rank lower than that of a commander. **c.** *Naut.* any officer other than the captain. —*v.t.* **4.** *Colloq.* to address or speak of as "mister" or "Mr." [var. of MASTER]

mist·flow·er (mĭst′flou′ər), *n.* a North American composite plant, *Eupatorium* (*Conoclinium*) *coelestinum,* with heads of blue flowers.

Mis·ti (mēs′tē), *n.* El Misti.

mis·time (mĭs tīm′), *v.t.,* -**timed, -timing.** to time wrongly; perform, say, etc., at a wrong time.

mis·tle·toe (mĭs′əl tō′), *n.* **1.** a European plant, *Viscum album* (family *Loranthaceae*), with yellowish flowers and white berries, growing parasitically on various trees, much used in Christmas decorations. **2.** any of various other plants of the same family, as *Phoradendron flavescens* of the U.S., also used in Christmas decorations. [ME *mistelto,* OE *misteltān* (c. Icel. *mistilteinn*), f. *mistel* mistletoe + *tān* twig]

mis·took (mĭs tŏŏk′), *v.* pt. of **mistake.**

mis·tral (mĭs′trəl, mĭs trăl′), *n.* a cold, dry northerly wind common in southern France and neighboring regions. [t. F: lit., master-wind, t. Pr.: important, g. L *magistrālis* MAGISTRAL]

Mis·tral (mēs trál′), *n.* **Frédéric** (frē dē rēk′), 1830–1914, French Provençal poet.

mis·trans·late (mĭs′trăns lāt′, -trănz-), *v.t., v.i.,* -**lated, -lating.** to translate incorrectly. —**mis·trans·la′tion,** *n.*

mis·treat (mĭs trēt′), *v.t.* to treat badly or wrongly. —**mis·treat′ment,** *n.*

mis·tress (mĭs′trĭs), *n.* **1.** a woman who has authority or control; the female head of a household or some other establishment. **2.** a woman employing, or in authority over, servants or attendants. **3.** a female owner, as of a slave, horse, dog, etc. **4.** a woman who has the power of controlling or disposing of something at pleasure. **5.** something regarded as feminine which has control or supremacy: *Great Britain, the mistress of the seas.* **6.** *Brit.* a female teacher; a schoolmistress. **7.** a woman who illicitly occupies the place of a wife. **8.** *Archaic or Poetic.* sweetheart. **9.** *Archaic or Dial.* a term of address for a woman. Cf. **Mrs.** and **Miss.** [ME *maistresse,* t. OF, fem. of *maistre* MASTER]

mis·tri·al (mĭs trī′əl), *n. Law.* **1.** a trial terminated without conclusion on the merits because of some error. **2.** an inconclusive trial, as where the jury cannot agree.

mis·trust (mĭs trŭst′), *n.* **1.** lack of trust or confidence; distrust. —*v.t.* **2.** to regard with mistrust; distrust. **3.** *Rare.* to suspect or surmise. —*v.i.* **4.** to be distrustful. —**mis·trust′ing·ly,** *adv.*

mis·trust·ful (mĭs trŭst′fəl), *adj.* full of mistrust; suspicious. —**mis·trust′ful·ly,** *adv.* —**mis·trust′-ful·ness,** *n.*

mist·y (mĭs′tĭ), *adj.,* **mistier, mistiest. 1.** abounding in or clouded by mist; of the nature of or consisting of mist. **2.** appearing as if seen through mist; indistinct in form or outline. **3.** obscure; vague. [ME; OE *mistig*] —**mist′i·ly,** *adv.* —**mist′i·ness,** *n.*

mis·un·der·stand (mĭs′ŭn dər stănd′), *v.t., v.i.,* -**stood, -standing. 1.** to misinterpret the words or actions of (a person). **2.** to understand wrongly; take (words, statements, etc.) in a wrong sense.

mis·un·der·stand·ing (mĭs′ŭn dər stăn′dĭng), *n.* **1.** disagreement or dissension. **2.** failure to understand; mistake as to meaning.

mis·un·der·stood (mĭs′ŭn dər stŏŏd′), *adj.* **1.** improperly interpreted. **2.** unappreciated.

mis·us·age (mĭs ū′sĭj, -zĭj), *n.* **1.** wrong or improper usage, as of words. **2.** ill usage; bad treatment.

mis·use (*n.* mĭs ūs′; *v.* mĭs ūz′), *n., v.,* -**used, -using.** —*n.* **1.** wrong or improper use; misapplication. **2.** *Obs.* ill-usage. —*v.t.* **3.** to use wrongly or improperly; misapply. **4.** to ill-use; maltreat.

mis·us·er (mĭs ū′zər), *n.* **1.** *Law.* abuse of a liberty or benefit or thing. **2.** one who misuses.

mis·val·ue (mĭs văl′ū), *v.t.,* -**ued, -uing.** to value wrongly.

mis·word (mĭs wûrd′), *v.t.* to word wrongly.

mis·write (mĭs rīt′), *v.t.,* -**wrote, -written, -writing.** to write incorrectly.

Mitch·ell (mĭch′əl), *n.* **1. Mount,** a mountain in W North Carolina: highest peak in the E United States. 6711 ft. **2. Maria,** 1818–89, U.S. astronomer. **3. Silas Weir** (wĭr), 1829–1914, U.S. physician and novelist. **4. William,** 1879–1936, U.S. Army officer in World War I: early advocate of strong air force.

mite[1] (mīt), *n.* any of various small arachnids (order *Acari*) with a saclike body, many being parasitic on plants and animals, others living in cheese, flour, unrefined sugar, etc. [ME *myte,* OE *mīte,* c. MD *mīte* (D *mijt*)]

mite[2] (mīt), *n.* **1.** a small contribution, but all that one can afford (in allusion to Mark 12:41–44): *to contribute one's mite.* **2.** a very small sum of money. **3.** a coin of very small value. See **lepton. 4.** a very small object. **5.** a very small creature. [ME, t. MD; ult. identical with MITE[1]]

mi·ter (mī′tər), *n.* **1.** the official headdress of a bishop in the Western Church, in its modern form a tall cap with a top deeply cleft crosswise, the outline of the front and back resembling that of a pointed arch. **2.** the office or rank of bishop; bishopric. **3.** the official headdress of the ancient Jewish high priest. **4.** a kind of headdress formerly worn by Asiatics. **5.** the abutting surface or bevel on either of the pieces joined in a miter joint. —*v.t.* **6.** to bestow a miter upon, or raise to a rank entitled to it. **7.** to join with a miter joint. **8.** to make a miter joint in; cut to a miter. Also, *esp. Brit.,* **mitre.** [ME *mitre,* t. L: m. *mitra,* t. Gk.: belt, headband, headdress]

miter box, a box or apparatus for use in cutting miters (def. 5).

mi·tered (mī′tərd), *adj.* **1.** shaped like a bishop's miter or having a miter-shaped apex. **2.** wearing, or entitled or privileged to wear, a miter. Also, **mitred.**

Bishop's miter. 14th century

miter joint, a joint formed when two pieces of identical cross section are joined at the ends, and where the joined ends are beveled at equal angles.

mi·ter·wort (mī′tər wûrt′), *n.* **1.** any of the low herbs which constitute the saxifragaceous genus *Mitella* (so called from the capsule, which resembles a bishop's miter). **2.** a low loganiaceous plant, *Cynoctonum Mitre-ola,* of the southeastern U.S. Also, *esp. Brit.,* **mitre-wort.**

Miter joint

Mit·ford (mĭt′fərd), *n.* **Mary Russell,** 1787–1855, British novelist and dramatist.

mith·er (mĭth′ər), *n. Scot. and N. Eng.* mother.

Mith·gar·thr (mĭth′gär′thər), *n.* Icelandic name for Midgard.

Mith·ras (mĭth′răs), *n. Persian Myth.* the god of light and truth, later of the sun. Also, **Mith·ra** (mĭth′rə). [t. L, t. Gk., t. OPers.: m. *Mithra*] —**Mith·ra·ic** (mĭth rā′ĭk), *adj.* —**Mith·ra·i·cism** (mĭth rā′ə sĭz′-əm), **Mith·ra·ism** (mĭth′rā ĭz′əm), *n.* —**Mith·ra·ist** (mĭth′rā ĭst), *n.* —**Mith·ra·is′tic,** *adj.*

Mith·ri·da·tes VI (mĭth′rə dā′tēz), ("*the Great*") c132–63 B.C., king of Pontus, 120?–63 B.C., and enemy of Rome.

mith·ri·da·tism (mĭth′rə dā′tĭz əm), *n.* the production of immunity against the action of a poison by taking the poison in gradually increased doses. [named after MITHRIDATES VI, said to have so immunized himself] —**mith·ri·dat·ic** (mĭth′rə dăt′ĭk), *adj.*

mit·i·gate (mĭt′ə gāt′), *v.,* -**gated, -gating.** —*v.t.* **1.** to lessen in force or intensity (wrath, grief, harshness, pain, etc.). **2.** to moderate the severity of (anything distressing). **3.** *Rare.* to make milder or more gentle; mollify. —*v.i.* **4.** to become milder; moderate in severity. [ME, t. L: m.s. *mitigātus,* pp.] —**mit′i·ga′tion,** *n.* —**mit′i·ga′tive, mit·i·ga·to·ry** (mĭt′ə gə tōr′ĭ), *adj.* —**mit′i·ga′tor,** *n.*

mi·tis (mī′tĭs, mē′-), *adj., n.* a name applied to a malleable iron (**mitis metal** or **mitis**) produced by fusing wrought iron with a small amount of aluminum rendering the product fluid enough to cast.

mi·to·sis (mĭ·tō′sĭs, mī-), *n. Biol.* the usual (indirect) method of cell division, characterized typically by the resolving of the chromatin of the nucleus into a thread-like form, which separates into segments or chromosomes, each of which separates longitudinally into two parts, one part of each chromosome being retained in each of two new cells resulting from the original cell. [t. NL, f. s. Gk. *mítos* a thread + *-osis* -OSIS] —**mi·tot·ic** (mĭ·tŏt′ĭk, mī-), *adj.* —**mi·tot′i·cal·ly,** *adv.*

mi·trail·leur (mē·trả·yœr′), *n. French.* one who operates a mitrailleuse.

mi·trail·leuse (mē·trả·yœz′), *n. French.* a machine gun. [F, der. *mitraille* scrap iron, der. OF *mitre, mite* small coin, fragment of metal]

mi·tral (mī′trəl), *adj.* of or resembling a miter.

mitral valve, *Anat.* the valve between the left auricle and ventricle of the heart which prevents the blood from flowing back into the auricle.

mi·tre (mī′tər), *n., v.t.,* **-tred, -tring.** *Chiefly Brit.* miter. —**mi′tred,** *adj.*

mi·tre·wort (mī′tər·wûrt′), *n. Chiefly Brit.* miterwort.

Mi·tro·pou·los (mĭ·trō′pōō·lŏs), *n.* **Dimitri** (dĭ′mē′trĭ), born 1897, Greek orchestra conductor, in U.S.

mitt (mĭt), *n.* **1.** a kind of long glove extending only to, or slightly over, the fingers, worn by women. **2.** *Baseball.* a kind of glove having the side next the palm of the hand protected by a large, thick mittenlike pad. **3.** a mitten. [apocopated var. of MITTEN]

mit·ten (mĭt′ən), *n.* **1.** a kind of hand covering enclosing the four fingers together and the thumb separately. **2.** a mitt (def. 1). **3.** (*pl.*) *Slang.* boxing gloves. [ME *myteyne,* t. OF: m. *mitaine,* g. Gallo-Rom. *medietāna* half (glove), der. L *medius* middle] —**mit′ten·like′,** *adj.*

mit·ti·mus (mĭt′ə·məs), *n. Law.* **1.** a warrant of commitment to prison. **2.** a writ for removing a suit or a record from one court to another. [t. L: we send]

mitz·vah (mĭts′vä), *n., pl.* **-voth** (-vōth). *Jewish Relig.* **1.** an order or commandment from the Bible or the rabbis. **2.** a religious act; a meritorious deed. Also, **mits′vah.** [t. Heb.: m. *miṣwāh* commandment]

mix (mĭks), *v.,* **mixed** or **mixt, mixing,** *n.* —*v.t.* **1.** to put together (substances or things, or one substance or thing with another) in one mass or assemblage with more or less thorough diffusion of the constituent elements among one another. **2.** to put together indiscriminately or confusedly (often fol. by *up*). **3.** to combine, unite, or join: *to mix business and pleasure.* **4.** to put in as an added element or ingredient: *to mix a little soda into the flour.* **5.** to form by combining ingredients: *to mix bread, to mix mortar.* **6.** to crossbreed. **7.** to confuse completely (fol. by *up*). —*v.i.* **8.** to become mixed: *oil and water will not mix.* **9.** to associate, as in company. **10.** to be crossbred, or of mixed breeding. —*n.* **11.** a mixing, or a mixed condition; a mixture. **12.** *Colloq.* a muddle or mess [back formation from *mixt* mixed, t. F: m. *mixte,* t. L: m. *mixtus,* pp.]. —**Syn. 1.** MIX, BLEND, COMBINE, MINGLE imply bringing two or more things into more or less intimate association. MIX is the general word for such association: *to mix fruit juices.* BLEND implies such a harmonious joining of two or more types of colors, feelings, etc., that the new product formed displays some of the qualities of each: *to blend fragrances or whiskeys.* COMBINE implies such a close or intimate union that distinction between the parts is lost: *to combine forces.* MINGLE usually suggests retained identity of the parts: *to mingle voices.* **2.** jumble, confuse, confound. **9.** consort, fraternize, mingle.

mixed (mĭkst), *adj.* **1.** put together or formed by mixing. **2.** composed of different constituents or elements; esp. in England, coeducational: *the children go to a mixed school.* **3.** of different kinds combined: *mixed candies.* **4.** comprising persons of different sexes, or of different classes, status, character, opinions, etc.: *mixed company.* **5.** *Law.* involving more than one issue or aspect: *a mixed question of law and fact.* **6.** *Colloq.* mentally confused. **7.** *Phonet.* (of a vowel) central. —**Syn. 1.** MIXED, MINGLED both refer to intimate association of two or more things. MIXED is generally applied to one noun, MINGLED commonly to two or more: *mixed feelings; mingled hope and fear.*

mixed metaphor. See *metaphor* (def. 2).

mixed number, a number consisting of a whole number and a fraction, as 4½.

mix·er (mĭk′sər), *n.* **1.** one who or that which mixes. **2.** *Colloq.* a person with reference to his sociability: *a good mixer.*

mix·ture (mĭks′chər), *n.* **1.** a product of mixing. **2.** any combination of differing elements, kinds, qualities, etc.: *a curious mixture of eagerness and terror.* **3.** *Chem., Physics.* an aggregate of two or more substances which are not chemically united, and which exist in no fixed proportion to each other. **4.** a fabric woven of yarns combining various colors: *a heather mixture.* **5.** act of mixing. **6.** state of being mixed. **7.** an added element or ingredient; an admixture. [t. L: m.s. *mixtūra*] —**Syn. 1.** blend, combination; compound. **2.** conglomeration, miscellany, jumble; medley; melange, potpourri, hodgepodge, hotchpotch.

mix-up (mĭks′ŭp′), *n.* **1.** a confused state of things; a muddle; a tangle. **2.** *Colloq.* a fight.

miz·zen (mĭz′ən), *Naut.* —*n.* **1.** the lower sail set on the mizzenmast. **2.** a mizzenmast. —*adj.* **3.** of, relating to, or set on, the mizzenmast. Also, **miz′en.** [ME *meseyn,* t. F: m. *misaine,* t. It.: m. *mezzana,* prop. fem. of *mezzano* middle, g. L *mediānus.* See MEDIAN]

miz·zen·mast (mĭz′ən·måst′, -mäst′; *Naut.* -məst), *n. Naut.* **1.** the aftermost mast of a three-masted vessel, or the third on a vessel with more than three masts. **2.** the after and shorter of the two masts of a yawl or ketch. Also, **miz′en·mast′.**

MKS system, the meter-kilogram-second system.

mkt., market.

ML, Medieval Latin. Also, **M.L.**

ml., **1.** mail. **2.** milliliter.

M.L.A., Modern Language Association.

Mlle., *pl.* **Mlles.** Mademoiselle.

M.L.S., Master of Library Science.

MM., Messieurs.

mm., **1.** (L *millia*) thousands. **2.** millimeter; millimeters.

Mme., *pl.* **Mmes.** madame.

m.m.f., magnetomotive force.

Mn, *Chem.* manganese.

mne·mon·ic (nē·mŏn′ĭk), *adj.* **1.** assisting, or intended to assist, the memory. **2.** pertaining to mnemonics or to memory. [t. Gk.: s. *mnēmonikós* of memory]

mne·mon·ics (nē·mŏn′ĭks), *n.* the art of improving or developing the memory. Also, **mne·mo·tech·nics** (nē′mō·tĕk′nĭks).

Mne·mos·y·ne (nē·mŏs′ə·nē′, -mŏz′-), *n. Gk. Myth.* the goddess of memory, daughter of Uranus and Gaea, and mother (by Zeus) of the Muses.

Mngr., Monsignor.

-mo, a final member of a series of compounds referring to book sizes by numbering the times the sheets are folded, e.g., 12*mo* or *duodecimo.*

Mo, *Chem.* molybdenum.

Mo., **1.** Missouri. **2.** Monday.

mo., **1.** *pl.* **mos.** month. **2.** months.

M.O., money order. Also, **m.o.**

mo·a (mō′ə), *n.* any of various extinct, flightless, birds of New Zealand, constituting the family *Dinornithidae,* allied to the apteryx but resembling an ostrich. [t. Maori]

Moa.
Dinornis maximus
(Ab. 10 ft. high)

Mo·ab (mō′ăb), *n.* an ancient kingdom E of the Dead Sea, in what is now Trans-Jordan. —**Mo·ab·ite** (mō′ə·bīt′), *n., adj.* —**Mo′ab·it′-ish,** *adj.*

moan (mōn), *n.* **1.** a prolonged, low, inarticulate sound uttered from or as if from physical or mental suffering. **2.** any similar sound: *the moan of the wind.* **3.** *Archaic.* complaint or lamentation. —*v.i.* **4.** to utter moans, as of pain or grief. **5.** (of the wind, sea, trees, etc.) to make any sound suggestive of such moans. **6.** to utter in lamentation. —*v.t.* **7.** to lament or bemoan: *to moan one's fate.* [ME *mone,* OE **mān* (inferred from its derivative, OE *mǣnan* complain of, lament)] —**moan′ing·ly,** *adv.* —**Syn. 1.** See groan.

moat (mōt), *Fort.* —*n.* **1.** a deep, wide trench surrounding a fortified place, as a town or a castle, and usually filled with water. See diag. under **bastion.** —*v.t.* **2.** to surround with, or as with, a moat. [ME *mote* moat, (earlier) mound, t. OF: mound, eminence; prob. from Celtic or Gmc.]

mob (mŏb), *n., v.,* **mobbed, mobbing.** —*n.* **1.** a disorderly or riotous assemblage of persons. **2.** a crowd bent on or engaged in lawless violence. **3.** *Sociol.* a group of persons stimulating one another to excitement and losing ordinary rational control over their activity. **4.** (often disparagingly) any assemblage or aggregation of persons, animals, or things; a crowd. **5.** the common mass of people; the populace or multitude. —*v.t.* **6.** to beset or crowd round tumultuously, as from rude curiosity or with hostile intent. **7.** to attack with riotous violence. [short for L *mōbile vulgus* the movable (i.e., excitable) common people]

mob·cap (mŏb′kăp′), *n.* a large, full cap fitting down over the ears, formerly much worn indoors by women.

mo·bile (mō′bəl, mō′bēl), *adj.* **1.** movable; moving readily. **2.** flowing freely, as a liquid. **3.** changing easily in expression, as features. **4.** quickly responding to impulses, emotions, etc., as the mind; facile; versatile. [t. L: movable (neut.)]

Mo·bile (mō·bēl′), *n.* a seaport in SW Alabama at the mouth of the **Mobile River,** a river (38 mi.) formed by the Alabama and Tombigbee rivers. 129,009 (1950).

Mo·bile Bay (mō′bēl), a bay of the Gulf of Mexico in SW Alabama: Civil War naval battle, 1864. 36 mi. long; 8–18 mi. wide.

mo·bil·i·ty (mō·bĭl′ə·tĭ), *n.* **1.** the quality of being mobile. **2.** *Sociol.* the movement of people in a population, as from place to place, or job to job, or social position to social position.

mo·bi·lize (mō′bə·līz′), *v.,* **-lized, -lizing.** —*v.t.* **1.** to put (armed forces) into readiness for active service. **2.** to organize or adapt (industries, etc.) for service to the government in time of war. **3.** to render mobile; put into motion, circulation, or active use: *to mobilize the wealth of a country.* —*v.i.* **4.** to be assembled, organized, etc., for war. [t. F: m.s. *mobiliser,* der. *mobile* MOBILE] —**mo/bi·li·za/tion,** *n.*

mob·oc·ra·cy (mŏb·ŏk′rə·sĭ), *n., pl.* **-cies. 1.** rule by the mob; political control by a mob. **2.** the mob as a ruling class. [f. MOB, n. + -(o)CRACY; modeled on DE-

MOCRACY, etc.] —**mob·o·crat·ic** (mŏb/ə krăt/ĭk), **mob/-o·crat/i·cal,** adj.

Mo·by Dick (mō/bĭ dĭk/), a novel (1851) by Herman Melville.

Mo·çam·bi·que (mō/səm bē/kə), n. Portuguese name of Mozambique.

moc·ca·sin (mŏk/ə sən, -zən), n. 1. a shoe made entirely of soft leather, as deerskin, worn originally by the American Indians. 2. a venomous snake, Ancistrodon piscivocrus, of the southern U.S., found in or near water (**water moccasin**). [t. Eastern Algonquian languages (Powhatan and Massachusetts); ? akin to makak small case or box]

moccasin flower, 1. the lady's-slipper. 2. a common cypripedium, Cypripedium reginae, of the U.S.

Mo·cha (mō/kə), n. 1. a seaport in Yemen, SW Arabia. ab. 5000. 2. (l.c.) a choice variety of coffee, originally coming from Mocha, Arabia. 3. (l.c.) a flavoring obtained from coffee infusion or combined chocolate and coffee infusion. 4. (l.c.) a glove leather, finer and thinner than doeskin, the best grades of which are made from Arabian goatskins.

mo·chi·la (mō chē/lä), n. Spanish. a flap of leather on the seat of a saddle.

mock (mŏk), v.t. 1. to assail or treat with ridicule or derision. 2. to ridicule by mimicry of action or speech; mimic derisively. 3. Poetic. to mimic, imitate, or counterfeit. 4. to defy; set at naught. 5. to deceive, delude, or disappoint. —v.i. 6. to use ridicule or derision; scoff; jeer (often fol. by at). —n. 7. a mocking or derisive action or speech; mockery or derision. 8. something mocked or derided; an object of derision. 9. imitation. —adj. 10. being an imitation or having merely the semblance of something: a mock battle. [ME mokken, t. OF: m. mocquer; orig. uncert.] —**mock/er,** n. —**mock/ing·ly,** adv. —**Syn.** 1. deride; taunt, flout, gibe; tease. See **ridicule.** 10. feigned, pretended, sham, counterfeit.

mock·er·y (mŏk/ər ĭ), n., pl. **-er·ies.** 1. ridicule or derision. 2. a derisive action or speech. 3. a subject or occasion of derision. 4. an imitation, esp. of a ridiculous or unsatisfactory kind. 5. a mere travesty, or mocking pretense. 6. something absurdly or offensively inadequate or unfitting.

mock-he·ro·ic (mŏk/hĭ rō/ĭk), adj. 1. imitating or burlesquing what is heroic, as in style, character, or action: mock-heroic dignity. —n. 2. an imitation or burlesque of what is heroic. —**mock/-he·ro/i·cal·ly,** adv.

mock·ing·bird (mŏk/ĭng bûrd/), n. 1. any of several gray, black, and white song birds of the genus Mimus, remarkable for their imitative powers, esp. the celebrated mocker, M. polyglottos, of the southern U.S. and Mexico. 2. any of various allied or similar birds, as the **blue mockingbird,** Melanotis caerulescens, of Mexico.

mock orange, the common syringa, Philadelphus coronarius.

mock turtle soup, a green soup prepared from a calf's head, or other meat, with seasonings.

mock-up (mŏk/ŭp/), n. model, built to scale, of a machine, apparatus, or weapon used in studying the construction and in testing a new development, or in teaching men how to operate the actual machine, apparatus, or weapon.

mod., 1. moderate. 2. Music. moderato. 3. modern.

mod·al (mō/dəl), adj. 1. of or pertaining to mode, manner, or form. 2. Music. a. pertaining to mode, as distinguished from key. b. based on a scale other than major or minor. 3. Gram. pertaining to mode, or producing varieties in meaning similar to those of different modes. 4. Philos. pertaining to mode as distinguished from substance, matter, or basic attribute. 5. Logic. exhibiting or expressing some phase of modality. [t. ML: s. modālis, der. L modus MODE[1]] —**mod/al·ly,** adv.

mo·dal·i·ty (mō dăl/ə tĭ), n., pl. **-ties.** 1. modal quality or state. 2. a modal attribute or circumstance. 3. Logic. that classification of propositions on the basis of whether what they assert is contingently true or false, possible, impossible, or necessary. 4. Med. the application of a therapeutic agent, usually a physical therapeutic agent.

mode[1] (mōd), n. 1. manner of acting or doing; a method; a way. 2. the natural disposition or the manner of existence or action of anything; a form: heat is a mode of motion. 3. Philos. appearance, form, or disposition taken by a single reality or by an essential property or attribute of it. 4. Logic. a. modality. b. any of the various forms of valid syllogism. See **mood**[2] (def. 2). 5. Music. any of various arrangements of the diatonic tones of an octave, differing from one another in the order of the whole steps and half steps; a scale. 6. Gram. Also, **mood. a.** (in many languages) a set of categories of verb inflection, whose selection depends either on the syntactic relation of the verb to other verbs in the sentence, or on difference in the speaker's attitude toward the action expressed by the verb (e.g., certainty vs. uncertainty, question vs. statement, wish vs. command, emphasis vs. hesitancy). Latin has indicative, imperative, and subjunctive; Greek adds optative; other languages have still others. **b.** (in some other languages, including English) a similar set of categories marked by the use of special auxiliary words (Eng. can, could, may, might, etc.) instead of by, or in addition to, inflection. **c.** any category of such a set. 7. Statistics. (in a statistical population) the category, value, or interval of the

variable having the greatest frequency. 8. Petrog. the actual mineral composition of a rock, expressed in percentages by weight. [ME, t. L: m.s. modus measure, due measure, manner] —**Syn.** 1. See **method.**

mode[2] (mōd), n. 1. customary or conventional usage in manners, dress, etc., esp. as observed by persons of fashion. 2. a prevailing style or fashion. 3. light gray, even drab. [t. F, t. L: m.s. modus MODE[1]]

mod·el (mŏd/əl), n., adj., v., **-eled, -eling** or (esp. Brit.) **-elled, -elling.** —n. 1. a standard for imitation or comparison; a pattern. 2. a representation, generally in miniature, to show the construction or serve as a copy of something. 3. an image in clay, wax, or the like to be reproduced in more durable material. 4. a person or thing that serves as a subject for an artist, etc. 5. one employed to put on articles of apparel to display them to customers. 6. mode of structure or formation. 7. a typical form or style. —adj. 8. serving as a model. 9. worthy to serve as a model; exemplary. —v.t. 10. to form or plan according to a model. 11. to give shape or form to; fashion. 12. to make a model or representation of. 13. to fashion in clay, wax, or the like. —v.i. 14. to make models. 15. to produce designs in some plastic material. 16. to assume a typical or natural appearance, as the parts of a drawing in progress. [t. F: m. modèle, t. It.: m. modello, dim. of modo, t. L: m. modus MODE[1]] —**mod/el·er,** esp. Brit. **mod·el·ler,** n. —**Syn.** 1. paragon; prototype. See **ideal.**

mod·el·ing (mŏd/əl ĭng, mŏd/lĭng), n. 1. act or art of one who models. 2. the process of producing sculptured form with plastic material, usually clay, as for reproduction in a more durable material. 3. Graphic Arts. the process of rendering the illusion of the third dimension. 4. the undulations of form in sculpture. Also, esp. Brit., **mod/el·ling.**

Mo·de·na (mō/dĕ nä/), n. a city in N Italy, in Emilia department. 111,219 (est. 1946).

mod·er·ate (adj., n. mŏd/ər ĭt, mŏd/rĭt; v. mŏd/ə rāt/), adj., n., v., **-at·ed, -at·ing.** —adj. 1. kept or keeping within due bounds; not extreme, excessive, or intense: a moderate request. 2. of medium quantity, extent, etc.: a moderate income. 3. mediocre; fair: moderate ability. 4. of or pertaining to moderates, as in politics or religion. —n. 5. one who is moderate in opinion or action, or opposed to extreme views and courses, esp. in politics or religion. 6. (usually cap.) a member of a political party advocating moderate reform. —v.t. 7. to reduce the excessiveness of; make less violent, severe, intense, or rigorous. 8. to preside over or at, as a deliberative body or a public meeting. —v.i. 9. to become less violent, severe, intense, or rigorous. 10. to act as moderator; preside. [ME, t. L: m.s. moderātus, pp.] —**mod/er·ate·ly,** adv. —**mod/er·ate·ness,** n. —**Syn.** 7. See **allay.**

moderate breeze, Meteorol. a wind of Beaufort scale #4, i.e. one within the range of 13–18 miles per hour.

moderate gale, Meteorol. a wind of Beaufort scale #7, i.e. one within the range of 32–38 miles per hour.

mod·er·a·tion (mŏd/ə rā/shən), n. 1. quality of being moderate; restraint; avoidance of extremes; temperance. 2. (pl.) Brit. (at Oxford University) the first public examinations for the B.A. degree. 3. **in moderation,** without excess; limited. 4. act of moderating.

mod·e·ra·to (mŏd/ə rä/tō), adj. Music. moderate; in moderate time. [It.]

mod·er·a·tor (mŏd/ə rā/tər), n. 1. one who or that which moderates. 2. a presiding officer, as over a public forum, a legislative body, or an ecclesiastical body in the Presbyterian Church. —**mod/er·a/tor·ship/,** n.

mod·ern (mŏd/ərn), adj. 1. of or pertaining to present and recent time; not ancient or remote. 2. characteristic of present and recent time; not antiquated or obsolete. —n. 3. a person of modern times. 4. one whose views and tastes are modern. 5. Print. a type style differentiated from old style by its heavy downstrokes and its straight serifs. [t. LL: s. modernus, der. L modo just now (orig. abl. of modus MODE[1])] —**mod/ern·ly,** adv. —**mod/ern·ness,** n.

—**Syn.** 1. MODERN, RECENT, LATE apply to that which is near to or characteristic of the present as contrasted with any other time. MODERN is applied to those things which exist in the present age, esp. in contrast to those of a former age or an age long past; hence the word sometimes has the connotation of up-to-date and, thus, good: modern ideas. That which is RECENT is separated from the present or the time of action by only a short interval; it is new, fresh, and novel: recent developments. LATE may mean nearest to the present moment: the latest news.

modern dance, a form of contemporary theatrical and concert dancing employing a special technique.

Modern English, the English language since c1500.

Modern Greats, at Oxford University, the course (or "school") of philosophy, politics, and economics.

modern history, history since the Renaissance.

mod·ern·ism (mŏd/ər nĭz/əm), n. 1. modern character; modern tendencies; sympathy with what is modern. 2. a modern usage or characteristic. 3. Theol. **a.** (cap.) movement in Roman Catholic thought which sought to interpret the teachings of the church in the light of philosophic and scientific conceptions prevalent in the late nineteenth and early twentieth centuries; condemned by Pope Pius in 1907. **b.** the liberal theological tendency in Protestantism (opposed to fundamentalism),

---

ăct, āble, dâre, ärt; ĕbb, ēqual; ĭf, īce; hŏt, ōver, ôrder, oil, bŏŏk, ōōze, out; ŭp, ūse, ûrge; ə = a in alone; ch, chief; g, give; ng, ring; sh, shoe; th, thin; ŧħ, that; zh, vision. See the full key on inside cover.

mod·ern·ist (mŏd′ər nĭst), *n.* **1.** one who follows or favors modern ways, tendencies, etc. **2.** one who advocates the study of modern subjects in preference to the ancient classics. **3.** an adherent of modernism in theological questions. —*adj.* **4.** pertaining to modernists or modernism.

mod·ern·is·tic (mŏd′ər nĭs′tĭk), *adj.* **1.** modern. **2.** of or pertaining to modernism or modernists: *a modernistic painting.*

mo·der·ni·ty (mŏ dûr′nə tĭ, mō-), *n., pl.* **-ties. 1.** the quality of being modern. **2.** something modern.

mod·ern·ize (mŏd′ər nīz′), *v.,* **-ized, -izing.** —*v.t.* **1.** to make modern; give a modern character or appearance to. —*v.i.* **2.** to become modern; adopt modern ways, views, etc. —**mod′ern·i·za′tion,** *n.* —**mod′·ern·iz′er,** *n.*

mod·est (mŏd′ĭst), *adj.* **1.** having or showing a moderate or humble estimate of one's merits, importance, etc.; free from vanity, egotism, boastfulness, or great pretensions. **2.** free from ostentation or showy extravagance: *a modest house.* **3.** moderate. **4.** having or showing regard for the decencies of behavior, speech, dress, etc.; decent. [t. L: s. *modestus* keeping due measure] —**mod′est·ly,** *adv.*
—**Syn. 4.** MODEST, DEMURE, PRUDISH imply conformity to propriety and decorum, and a distaste for anything coarse or loud. MODEST implies a becoming shyness, sobriety, and proper behavior: *a modest self-respecting person.* DEMURE implied originally a bashful, quiet simplicity, staidness and decorum; now a modesty either unconscious or cleverly assumed: *a demure young girl.* PRUDISH suggests an exaggeratedly self-conscious modesty or propriety in behavior or conversation of one who wishes to be thought of as easily shocked, and often is intolerant: *a prudish objection to a harmless remark.* —**Ant.** 4. bold, coarse.

mod·es·ty (mŏd′əs tĭ), *n., pl.,* **-ties. 1.** the quality of being modest; freedom from vanity, boastfulness, etc. **2.** regard for decency of behavior, speech, dress, etc. **3.** simplicity; moderation. **4.** modesty piece.

mod·i·cum (mŏd′ə kəm), *n.* a moderate or small quantity; a limited amount. [late ME, t. L, neut. of *modicus* moderate]

mod·i·fi·ca·tion (mŏd′ə fə kā′shən), *n.* **1.** act of modifying. **2.** state of being modified; partial alteration. **3.** a modified form; a variety. **4.** *Biol.* a change in a living organism acquired from its own activity or environment and not transmitted to its descendants. **5.** limitation or qualification. **6.** *Gram.* **a.** the use of a modifier in a construction, or of modifiers in a class of constructions or in a language. **b.** the meaning of a modifier, esp. as it affects the meaning of the word or other form modified: *limitation is one kind of modification.* **c.** a change in the phonemic shape of a morpheme, word, or other form when it functions as an element in a construction, e.g., the change of *not* to *-n't* in the phrase *doesn't.* **d.** the feature of a construction resulting from such a change, e.g., the phrases *doesn't* and *does not* differ in modification. **e.** an adjustment in the form of a word as it passes from one language to another.

mod·i·fi·ca·to·ry (mŏd′ə fə kā′tər ĭ), *adj.* modifying. Also, **mod′i·fi·ca′tive.**

mod·i·fi·er (mŏd′ə fī′ər), *n.* **1.** one who or that which modifies. **2.** *Gram.* a word, phrase, or sentence element which limits or qualifies the sense of another word, phrase, or element in the same construction: *adjectives are modifiers.*

mod·i·fy (mŏd′ə fī′), *v.,* **-fied, -fying.** —*v.t.* **1.** to change somewhat the form or qualities of; alter somewhat. **2.** *Gram.* (of a word or larger linguistic form) to stand in a subordinate relation to (another form called the *head*) usually with descriptive, limiting, or particularizing meaning, as in *a good man, good* modifies the head *man.* **3.** to be the modifier or attribute of. **4.** to change (a vowel) by umlaut. **5.** to reduce in degree; moderate; qualify. —*v.i.* **6.** to change; to become changed. [ME *modifie(n),* t. L: m. *modificāre, modificārī* set limits to] —**mod′i·fi·a·ble,** *adj.*
—**Syn. 1.** MODIFY, QUALIFY, TEMPER suggest altering an original statement, condition, or the like, so as to avoid anything excessive or extreme. To MODIFY is to alter in one or more particulars, generally in the direction of leniency or moderation: *to modify demands, rates.* To QUALIFY is to restrict or limit by exceptions or conditions: *to qualify one's praise, hopes.* To TEMPER is to alter the quality of something, generally so as to diminish its force or harshness: *to temper the wind to the shorn lamb.*

mo·dil·lion (mō dĭl′yən, mə-), *n. Archit.* one of a series of ornamental blocks or brackets placed under the corona of a cornice in the Corinthian and other orders. [t. It.: m. *modiglione,* ult. der. L *mutulus*]

mo·di·o·lus (mō dī′ō ləs, mə-), *n., pl.* **-li** (-lī′). *Anat.* the central conical axis round which the cochlea of the ear winds. [t. NL, dim. of L *modius* measure for grain]

mod·ish (mō′dĭsh), *adj.* in accordance with the prevailing mode, fashionable; stylish. —**mod′ish·ly,** *adv.* —**mod′ish·ness,** *n.*

Romanesque modillion

mo·diste (mō dēst′; *Fr.* mô-), *n.* a maker of or dealer in articles of fashionable attire, esp. women's dresses, millinery, etc. [t. F, der. *mode* MODE²]

Mo·djes·ka (mō jĕs′kə), *n.* **Helena** (hə lā′nə), (*Madame Modjeska*) 1840–1909, Polish actress, in America.

Mo·dred (mō′drĭd), *n. Arthurian Romance.* the nephew and treacherous killer of Arthur. Also, **Mordred.**

mod·u·late (mŏj′ə lāt′), *v.,* **-lated, -lating.** —*v.t.* **1.** to regulate by or adjust to a certain measure or proportion; soften; tone down. **2.** to alter or adapt (the voice) fittingly in utterance. **3.** *Music.* **a.** to attune to a certain pitch or key. **b.** to vary the volume of (tone). **4.** *Radio.* to cause the amplitude, frequency, phase, or intensity of (the carrier wave) to vary in accordance with the sound waves or other signals, the frequency of the signal wave usually being very much lower than that of the carrier: frequently applied to the application of sound wave signals to a microphone to change the characteristic of a transmitted radio wave. —*v.i.* **5.** *Radio.* to modulate a carrier wave. **6.** *Music.* to pass from one key to another. [t. L: m.s. *modulātus,* pp., having measured] —**mod′u·la′tive,** *adj.*

mod·u·la·tion (mŏj′ə lā′shən), *n.* **1.** act of modulating. **2.** state of being modulated. **3.** *Music.* transition from one key to another. **4.** *Gram.* **a.** the use of a particular distribution of stress or pitch in a construction, e.g., the use of rising pitch on the last word of *John is here?* **b.** the feature of a construction resulting from such a use, e.g., the question *John is here?* differs from the statement *John is here* only in modulation.

mod·u·la·tor (mŏj′ə lā′tər), *n.* **1.** one who or that which modulates. **2.** *Radio.* a device for modulating a carrier wave. Cf. **modulate** (def. 4).

mod·ule (mŏj′ool), *n.* **1.** a standard or unit for measuring. **2.** a selected unit of measure, ranging in size from a few inches to several feet, used as a basis for planning and standardization of building materials. **3.** *Archit.* the size of some part, as the semidiameter of a column at the base of the shaft, taken as a unit of measure. [t. L: m.s. *modulus,* dim. of *modus* measure, MODE¹]

mod·u·lus (mŏj′ə ləs), *n., pl.* **-li** (-lī′). *Physics.* a coefficient (def. 2), esp. of elasticity. [t. L: a small measure. See MODULE]

mo·dus op·e·ran·di (mō′dəs ŏp′ə răn′dī), *Latin.* mode of operating or working.

mo·dus vi·ven·di (mō′dəs vĭ věn′dī), *Latin.* **1.** mode of living. **2.** a temporary arrangement between persons or parties pending a settlement of matters in debate.

Moe·si·a (mē′shĭ ə), *n.* an ancient country in S Europe, S of the Danube and N of ancient Thrace and Macedonia: later a Roman province.

Moe·so·goth (mē′sō gŏth′, -sə-), *n.* one of the Christianized agricultural Goths who settled in Moesia in the 4th century. Also, **Moe′so-Goth′.** —**Moe′so·goth′ic,** *adj.*

mo·fette (mō fĕt′; *Fr.* mô-), *n.* **1.** a noxious emanation, consisting chiefly of carbon dioxide, escaping from the earth in regions of nearly extinct volcanic activity. **2.** one of the openings or fissures from which this emanation issues. Also, **mof·fette′.** [t. F, der. *moufir* rot, mold, der. *muffe* mould, t. G: m. *muff*]

Mo·ga·di·scio (It. mô′gä dē′shō), *n.* a seaport in E Africa: the capital of Italian Somaliland. ab. 45,000. Also, **Mo·ga·di·shu** (mô′gä dē′shoo).

Mog·a·dor (mŏg′ə dôr′; *Fr.* mô gà dôr′), *n.* a seaport in W Morocco, in the French Zone. 15,166 (1936).

Mo·gi·lëv (mō′gĭ lĕf′; *Russ.* mŏ gĭ lyŏf′), *n.* a city in the W Soviet Union, on the Dnieper river. 99,440 (1939).

Mo·gul (mō′gŭl, mō gŭl′), *n.* **1.** a Mongol or Mongolian. **2.** one of the Mongol conquerors of India in the 16th century. **3.** (*l.c.*) an important person. **4.** (*l.c.*) a steam locomotive, used for hauling heavy trains. [t. Ar. and Pers.: m. *Mughul* Mongol]

mo·hair (mō′hâr′), *n.* **1.** the coat or fleece of an Angora goat. **2.** a fabric of mohair yarn, in a plain weave for draperies and in a pile weave for upholstery. **3.** a garment made of mohair. [f. obs. *mo(cayare)* mohair (ult. t. Ar.: m. *mukhayyar*) + HAIR]

Moham., Mohammedan.

Mo·ham·med (mō hăm′ĭd), *n.,* A.D. 570?–632, Arabian prophet and founder of the Mohammedan religion. Also, **Mahomet, Muhammad.**

Mohammed II, 1430–81, sultan of Turkey, 1451–81; captured Constantinople in 1453.

Mohammed A·li (ä lē′, ä′lē), Mehemet Ali.

Mo·ham·med·an (mō hăm′ə dən), *adj.* **1.** of or pertaining to Mohammed or his religious system. —*n.* **2.** a follower of Mohammed; a believer in his religion. Also, **Mahometan, Muhammadan, Muhammedan.**

Mo·ham·med·an·ism (mō hăm′ə də nĭz′əm), *n.* the Mohammedan religion; Islam.

Mo·ha·ve (mō hä′vĭ), *n.* **1.** a North American Indian tribe belonging to the Yuman linguistic family, located on both sides of the Colorado river. —*adj.* **2.** of or pertaining to the Mohave tribe. Also, **Mojave.** [t. Amer. Ind., der. *hamok* three + *avi* mountain]

Mohave Desert, Mojave Desert.

Mo·hawk (mō′hôk), *n., pl.* **Mohawk, Mohawks. 1.** (*pl.*) a tribe of North American Indians, the most easterly of the Iroquois Five Nations, formerly resident along the Mohawk river, New York. **2.** a member of this tribe. [t. N Amer. Ind. (Narragansett): they eat animate things (hence, man-eaters)]

Mo·hawk (mō′hôk), *n.* a river flowing from central New York E to the Hudson. 148 mi.

Mo·he·gan (mō hē′gən), *n.* **1.** a tribe of Algonquian speaking North American Indians, dwelling chiefly

b., blend of, blended; c., cognate with; d., dialect, dialectal; der., derived from; f., formed from; g., going back to; m., modification of; r., replacing; s., stem of; t., taken from; ?, perhaps. See the full key on inside cover.

along the Thames river, Connecticut, in the 17th century. **2.** Mahican. [t. Amer. Ind. (Algonquian): m. *maingan* wolf]

Mo·hi·can (mō hē'kən), *n.* Mahican.

Mo·hock (mō'hŏk), *n.* one of a class of ruffians, often aristocrats, who infested the London streets at night in the early 18th century. [var. of MOHAWK. Cf. APACHE[2]]

Mohs scale (mōz), a scale of hardness used in mineralogy. Its degrees are: talc 1; gypsum 2; calcite 3; fluorite 4; apatite 5; feldspar 6; quartz 7; topaz 8; sapphire 9; diamond 10. Cf. **hardness.** [named after Friedrich *Mohs* (1773–1839), German mineralogist]

mo·hur (mō'hər), *n.* a former gold coin of India, in 1835 worth about $7.00: usually called **gold mohur.** [earlier *muhr,* t. Pers.: seal, gold coin]

moi·dore (moi'dōr), *n.* a former gold coin of Portugal and Brazil. [t. Pg.: m. *moeda d'ouro* coin of gold]

moi·e·ty (moi'ə tĭ), *n., pl.* **-ties. 1.** a half. **2.** an indefinite portion. **3.** *Anthropol.* one of two units into which a tribe is divided on the basis of unilateral descent. [ME *moit(i)e,* t. OF, g. LL *medietas* half, L the middle]

moil (moil), *v.i.* **1.** to work hard; toil; drudge. —*n.* **2.** toil or drudgery. **3.** confusion, turmoil, or trouble. [ME *moile(n),* t. OF: m. *moillier* wet, moisten, ult. der. L *mollis* soft] —**moil'er,** *n.*

moire (mwär, mōr), *n.* a watered fabric, as of silk or wool. [t. F, t. E: m. MOHAIR]

moi·ré (mwä rā', mōr'ā; Fr. mwà rē'), French. —*adj.* **1.** watered, as silk; having a wavelike pattern. —*n.* **2.** a design pressed on silk, rayon, etc., by engraved rollers. **3.** moire.

moist (moist), *adj.* **1.** moderately or slightly wet; damp; humid. **2.** (of the eyes) tearful. **3.** accompanied by or connected with liquid or moisture. [ME *moiste,* t. OF: moist, moldy. Cf. L *mūcidus* moldy, musty] —**moist'-ly,** *adv.* —**moist'ness,** *n.* —**Syn. 1.** See **damp.**

mois·ten (mois'ən), *v.t., v.i.* to make or become moist. —**moist'en·er,** *n.*

mois·ture (mois'chər), *n.* water or other liquid rendering anything moist. [ME, t. OF: m. *moistour*]

Mo·ja·ve (mō hä'vĭ), *n., adj.* Mohave.

Mo·ja·ve Desert (mō hä'vĭ), a desert in S California: part of the Great Basin. ab. 15,000 sq. mi. Also, **Mohave Desert.**

Mo·ji (mō'jē'), *n.* a seaport in SW Japan, on N Kyushu island. 101,540 (1946).

mol (mōl), *n. Chem.* the molecular weight of a substance expressed in grams; gram molecule. Also, **mole.** [t. G, der. *molekül* MOLECULE]

mo·lal (mō'lal), *adj. Chem.* **1.** pertaining to grammolecular weight, or containing a mol. **2.** pertaining to a solution containing one mol of solute per liter of solution.

mo·lar[1] (mō'lər), *n.* **1.** a tooth adapted for grinding with a broad biting surface as in human dentition. There are twelve molar teeth, three in each quadrant. —*adj.* **2.** adapted for grinding, as teeth, esp. those in man, with a broad biting surface, situated behind the bicuspids. **3.** pertaining to such teeth. [t. L: s. *molāris* a mill]

mo·lar[2] (mō'lər), *adj.* **1.** *Physics.* pertaining to a body of matter as a whole: contrasted with molecular and atomic. **2.** *Chem.* molal. [f. s. NL *mōles* mass + -AR[1]]

mo·las·ses (mə läs'ĭz), *n.* any of various thick, darkcolored syrups, as that produced during the refining of sugar, or that produced from sorghum. Cf. **treacle.** [t. Pg.: m. *melaço,* g. LL *mellāceum* must, der. *mel* honey]

mold[1] (mōld), *n.* **1.** a hollow form or matrix for giving a particular shape to something in a molten or plastic state. **2.** that on or about which something is formed or made. **3.** something formed in or on a mold: *a mold of jelly.* **4.** the shape imparted to a thing by a mold. **5.** shape or form. **6.** distinctive nature, or native character. **7.** *Archit.* **a.** a molding. **b.** a group of moldings. —*v.t.* **8.** to work into a required shape or form; shape. **9.** to shape or form in or on a mold. **10.** *Founding.* to form a mold of or from, in order to make a casting. **11.** to produce by or as if by molding or shaping material; form. **12.** to fashion; model the style or character of. **13.** to ornament with moldings. Also, *esp. Brit.* **mould.** [ME, t. OF: m. *modle,* g. L *modulus* MODULE] —**mold'a·ble,** *adj.*

mold[2] (mōld), *n.* **1.** a growth of minute fungi forming on vegetable or animal matter, commonly as a downy or furry coating, and associated with decay. **2.** any of the fungi that produce such a growth. —*v.t., v.i.* **3.** to make or become mold. Also, *esp. Brit.* **mould.** [ME *mowlde,* appar. var. of *mowled, mouled,* pp. of *moulen,* earlier ME *muwlen,* c. d. Dan. *mugle* grow moldy]

mold[3] (mōld), *n.* **1.** loose, friable earth, esp. such as is rich in organic matter and favorable to the growth of plants. **2.** *Archaic or Poetic.* the ground or earth. Also, *esp. Brit.* **mould.** [ME and OE *molde,* c. OHG *molta* mold, dust]

Mol·dau (mōl'dou), *n.* a river flowing from the Bohemian Forest N through W Czechoslovakia to the Elbe. ab. 270 mi. Czech, **Vltava.**

Mol·da·vi·a (mōl dā'vĭ ə, -vyə), *n.* **1.** a province in NE Rumania: formerly a principality which united with Walachia to form Rumania. 2,817,794 pop. (est. 1943); 14,562 sq. mi. *Cap.* Jassy. **2.** Official name, **Moldavian Soviet Socialist Republic.** a constituent republic of the Soviet Union, in the SW part: formed in 1940 of the former autonomous republic of Moldavia and the ceded Rumanian territory of Bessarabia. 2,700,000 pop. (est. 1947); 13,100 sq. mi. *Cap.:* Kishinev. —**Mol·da'vi·an,** *adj., n.*

mol·da·vite (mŏl'də vīt'), *n.* a natural green glass, found in Bohemia and thought to be of possible meteoritic origin. See **tektite.**

mold·board (mōld'bōrd'), *n.* the curved board or metal plate in a plow, which turns over the earth from the furrow. Also, *esp. Brit.,* **mouldboard.**

mold·er[1] (mōl'dər), *v.i.* **1.** to turn to dust by natural decay; crumble; waste away. —*v.t.* **2.** to cause to molder. Also, *esp. Brit.,* **moulder.** [freq. of obs. *mold,* v., molder, crumble away (v. use of MOLD[3]). See -ER[6]]

mold·er[2] (mōl'dər), *n.* **1.** one who molds; a maker of molds. **2.** *Print.* one of a set of electrotyped plates used only for making duplicate electrotypes. Also, *esp. Brit.,* **moulder.** [f. MOLD[1], v. + -ER[1]]

mold·ing (mōl'dĭng), *n.* **1.** act or process of one who or that which molds. **2.** something molded. **3.** *Archit., etc.* **a.** a decorative variety of contour or outline given to cornices, jambs, strips of woodwork, etc. **b.** a shaped member introduced into a structure to afford such variety or decoration. **4.** shaped material in the form of a strip, used for supporting pictures, covering electric wires, etc. Also, *esp. Brit.,* **moulding.**

molding board, the board upon which bread is kneaded, cookies prepared, etc.

mold·y (mōl'dĭ), *adj.,* **moldier, moldiest. 1.** overgrown or covered with mold. **2.** musty, as from decay or age. Also, *esp. Brit.,* **mouldy.** [f. MOLD[2] + -Y[1]] —**mold'i·ness,** *n.*

mole[1] (mōl), *n.* **1.** a small congenital spot or blemish on the human skin, usually of a dark color and slightly elevated, and often hairy. **2.** a pigmented naevus. [ME; OE *māl,* c. OHG *meil* wrinkle, blemish]

mole[2] (mōl), *n.* any of various small insectivore mammals, esp. of the family *Talpidae,* living chiefly underground, and having velvety fur, very small eyes, and strong, fossorial forefeet. [ME *molle,* c. MD and MLG *mol*]

Mole, *Scalopus aquaticus*
(Ab. 6½ to 7 in. long, tail 1 in.)

mole[3] (mōl), *n.* **1.** a massive structure, esp. of stone, set up in the water, as for a breakwater or a pier. **2.** an anchorage or harbor protected by such a structure. [t. L: m. *mōles* mass, dam]

mole[4] (mōl), *n.* mol.

mole[5] (mōl), *n. Pathol.* a fleshy mass in the uterus formed by a hemorrhagic dead ovum. [t. L: m.s. *mola* false conception, millstone]

Mo·lech (mō'lĕk), *n.* Moloch (defs. 1, 2).

mo·lec·u·lar (mə lĕk'yə lər), *adj.* pertaining to, caused by, or consisting of molecules. [f. s. NL *mōlecula* MOLECULE + -AR[1]] —**mo·lec'u·lar·ly,** *adv.*

molecular beam, a stream of molecules in a vacuum moving in directions almost parallel, produced experimentally by passing the molecules through a series of narrow openings. Also, **molecular rays.**

molecular film, a film or layer one molecule thick.

molecular weight, *Chem.* **1.** the average weight of a molecule of an element or compound measured in units, sixteen of which correspond to the average weight of the oxygen atom. **2.** the sum of the atomic weights of all the atoms in a molecule.

mol·e·cule (mŏl'ə kūl), *n.* **1.** *Chem., Physics.* the smallest physical unit of an element or compound, consisting of one or more like atoms in the first case, and two or more different atoms in the second case. **2.** a quantity of a substance, the weight of which, measured in any chosen unit, is numerically equal to the molecular weight; gram molecule. **3.** any very small particle. [t. NL: m. *mōlecula,* dim. of *mōles* mass. Cf. MOLE[3], MOL]

mole·hill (mōl'hĭl'), *n.* **1.** a small mound or ridge of earth raised up by moles burrowing under the ground. **2.** something insignificant, esp. an obstacle or difficulty.

mole·skin (mōl'skĭn'), *n.* **1.** the fur of the mole, soft, deep gray in color, and very fragile. **2.** a stout napped, twilled cotton fabric used for sportsmen's and laborers' clothing. **3.** (*pl.*) garments, esp. trousers, of this fabric.

mo·lest (mə lĕst'), *v.t.* to interfere with annoyingly, injuriously, or with hostile intent. [ME *moleste(n)* t. L: m. *molestāre*] —**mo·les·ta·tion** (mō'lĕs tā'shən, mŏl'ĕs-), *n.* —**mo·lest'er,** *n.* —**Syn.** See **attack.**

Mo·lière (mō lyĕr', *Fr.* mô lyâr'), (*Jean Baptiste Poquelin*) 1622–1673, French writer of comedies.

Mo·li·na (mō lē'nä), *n.* **Tirso de** (tĕr'sô dĕ), pen name of Gabriel Téllez.

Mo·line (mō lēn'), *n.* a city in NW Illinois, on the Mississippi. 37,397 (1950).

moll (mŏl), *n. Slang.* **1.** the unmarried female companion of a thief, vagrant, or gangster. **2.** a prostitute. [short for *Molly,* var. of MARY]

mol·les·cent (mə lĕs'ənt), *adj.* producing less hardness or firmness; softening. [t. L: s. *mollescens,* ppr.] —**mol·les'cence,** *n.*

mol·li·fy (mŏl'ə fī'), *v.t.,* **-fied, -fying. 1.** to soften in feeling or temper, as a person, the heart or mind, etc. **2.** to mitigate or appease, as rage. [ME *mollifie(n),* t.

L: m.s. *mollificāre* soften] —**mol/li·fi·ca/tion,** *n.*
—**mol/li·fi/er,** *n.* —**mol/li·fy/ing·ly,** *adv.* —**mol/li-fi/able,** *adj.*

Mol·lus·ca (məlŭs/kə), *n.* a large phylum of invertebrates including the chitins, snails, bivalves, squids, octopi, etc., characterized by the calcareous shell (sometimes lacking) of one, two, or more pieces that wholly or partly encloses the soft unsegmented body provided with gills, mantle, and foot. [see MOLLUSK.]

mol·lus·coid (məlŭs/koid), *adj., n.* denoting, or pertaining to, an animal group comprising the bryozoans and brachiopods. Also, **mol·lus·coi·dal** (mŏl/əskoi/dəl).

mol·lusk (mŏl/əsk), *n.* any of the *Mollusca.* Also, **mol/lusc.** [t. NL: m.s. *mollusca,* pl., in L neut. pl. of *molluscus* soft (applied to a thin-shelled nut)] —**mol·lus·can** (məlŭs/kən), *adj., n.* —**mol/lusk·like/,** *adj.*

mol·ly (mŏl/ĭ), *n., pl.* **mollies.** a live-bearing fish of the genus *Mollienisia,* often kept in home aquariums.

mol·ly·cod·dle (mŏl/ĭkŏd/əl), *n., v.., -dled, -dling.* —*n.* 1. a man or boy who is used to being coddled; a milksop. —*v.t., v.i.* 2. to coddle; pamper. [f. *Molly* (var. of MARY) + CODDLE] —**mol/ly·cod/dler,** *n.*

Mol·nár (mŏl/när), *n.* **Ferenc** (fĕ/rĕnts), born 1878, Hungarian dramatist and novelist.

Mo·loch (mō/lŏk), *n.* 1. a Semitic deity, mentioned in the Bible, whose worship was marked by the sacrifice by burning of children offered by their own parents. 2. anything conceived as requiring frightful sacrifice: *the Moloch of war.* 3. (*l.c.*) a spiny Australian lizard, *Moloch horridus.* Also, **Molech** for 1, 2. [t. L (Vulgate), t. Gk. (Septuagint), t. Heb.: m. *Mōlek,* orig. *melek* king]

Mo·lo·ka·i (mō/lōkä/ē), *n.* one of the Hawaiian Islands, in the central part of the group: leper colony. 4939 pop. (prelim. 1950); 259 sq. mi.

Mo·lo·tov (mō/lŏtôf), *n.* 1. **Viacheslav Mikhailovich** (vyä/chĕsläf/ mĭ hī/lō vĭch), born 1890, Soviet statesman: Commissar for Foreign Affairs 1939–1949. 2. a city in the W Soviet Union in Asia, on the Kama river. 255,196 (1939). Also, **Perm.**

molt (mōlt), *v.i.* 1. (of birds, insects, reptiles, etc.) to cast or shed the feathers, skin, or the like, to be succeeded by a new growth. —*v.t.* 2. to cast or shed (feathers, etc.) in the process of renewal. —*n.* 3. act or process of molting. 4. that which is dropped in molting. Also, *esp. Brit.,* **moult.** [ME *mout,* OE *-mūtian* change (in *bemūtian* exchange for), t. L: m. *mūtāre* change. Cf. MEW[4]] —**molt/er,** *n.*

mol·ten (mōl/tən), *v.* 1. pp. of **melt.** —*adj.* 2. liquefied by heat; in a state of fusion. 3. produced by melting and casting: *a molten image.*

Molt·ke (mōlt/kə), *n.* 1. **Helmuth Karl Bernhard** (hĕl/mōōt kärl bĕrn/härt), **Count von,** 1800–91, German field marshal. 2. **Helmuth Johannes Ludwig** (yō/hän/əs lōōt/vĭKH), **Count von,** 1848–1916, German general.

mol·to (mōl/tō), *adv. Music.* much; very. [It., g. L *multum*]

Mo·luc·cas (mōlŭk/əz, mə-), *n.pl.* a group of islands in the U.S. of Indonesia between Celebes and New Guinea. ab. 428,000 pop.; ab. 30,000 sq. mi. Also, **Spice Islands.**

mol. wt., molecular weight.

mo·ly (mō/lĭ), *n., pl.* **molies.** a fabulous herb with a milk-white flower and a black root, said by Homer to have been given by Hermes to Odysseus to counteract the spells of Circe. [t. L, t. Gk.]

mo·lyb·date (məlĭb/dāt), *n. Chem.* a salt of any molybdic acid.

mo·lyb·de·nite (məlĭb/dənīt/, mŏl/ĭb dē/nĭt), *n.* a soft, graphitelike mineral, molybdenum sulfide, MoS[2], occurring in foliated masses or scales, the principal ore of molybdenum. [f. obs. *molybdena* MOLYBDENUM + -ITE[1]]

mo·lyb·de·nous (məlĭb/dənəs, mŏl/ĭb dē/nəs), *adj. Chem.* containing divalent molybdenum (Mo+2).

mo·lyb·de·num (məlĭb/dənəm, mŏl/ĭb dē/nəm), *n. Chem.* a silver-white high-melting metalloid, alloyed with iron in making hard, high-speed cutting tools. *Symbol.:* Mo; *at. wt.:* 95.95; *at. no.:* 42; *sp. gr.:* 10.2. [t. NL, t. L: m. *molybdaena,* t. Gk.: m. *molýbdaina* galena]

mo·lyb·dic (məlĭb/dĭk), *adj. Chem.* of or containing molybdenum, esp. in the Mo+3 or Mo+6 state, as *molybdic acid,* H[2]MoO[4].

Mom·ba·sa (mŏm bä/sä, -bäs/ə), *n.* a seaport on Mombasa island in Kenya, British East Africa. 52,331 (est. 1938).

mo·ment (mō/mənt), *n.* 1. an indefinitely short space of time; an instant: *wait a moment.* 2. the present or other particular instant: *to recall his name at the moment.* 3. a definite stage, as in a course of events. 4. importance or consequence: *of great moment.* 5. *Statistics.* the average of a given power of the values of a set of variates. 6. *Philos.* an essential or constituent element or factor; momentum. 7. **a.** *Mech.* tendency to produce motion, esp. about an axis. **b.** (of a physical quantity) the product of the quantity and its perpendicular distance from an axis: *moment of area, moment of mass, etc.* [ME, t. L: s. *mōmentum* movement, moment of time, etc.] —**Syn.** 1. See minute[1].

mo·men·tar·i·ly (mō/məntĕr/əlĭ; *for emphasis* mō/məntĕr/ə lĭ), *adv.* 1. for a moment; *to hesitate momen-*

tarily. 2. every moment; from moment to moment: *danger momentarily increasing.* 3. at any moment: *momentarily liable to occur.*

mo·men·tar·y (mō/məntĕr/ĭ), *adj.* 1. lasting but a moment; of very short duration; very brief: *a momentary glimpse.* 2. occurring at any moment: *to live in fear of momentary exposure.* 3. *Rare.* constant. —**mo/men·tar/i·ness,** *n.*

mo·ment·ly (mō/məntlĭ), *adv.* 1. every moment; from moment to moment. 2. for a moment; momentarily.

mo·men·tous (mōmĕn/təs), *adj.* of great importance or consequence; fraught with serious or far-reaching consequences, as events, decisions, etc. —**mo·men/tous·ly,** *adv.* —**mo·men/tous·ness,** *n.* —**Syn.** See **heavy.**

mo·men·tum (mōmĕn/təm), *n., pl., -ta* (-tə) *-tums.* 1. *Mech.* the quantity of motion of a moving body, equal to the product of its mass and velocity. 2. impetus, as of a moving body. 3. *Philos.* a moment (def. 6). [t. L. See MOMENT]

Momm·sen (mŏm/sən; *Ger.* môm/zən), *n.* **Theodor** (tā/ō dōr/), 1817–1903, German historian and philologist.

Mo·mus (mō/məs), *n.* 1. *Gk. Myth.* the god of censure and ridicule. 2. (*sometimes l.c.*) a faultfinder; a carping critic. [t. L, t. Gk.: m. *mômos,* lit., blame, ridicule]

Mon (mŏn), *n.* one of the Mon-Khmer languages.

mon-, var. of **mono-,** before vowels.

Mon., 1. Monday. 2. Monsignor.

mon., 1. monastery. 2. monetary.

mon·a·chal (mŏn/ə kəl), *adj.* monastic. [t. ML: s. *monachālis,* der. LL *monachus* MONK]

mon·a·chism (mŏn/əkĭz/əm), *n.* monasticism.

Mon·a·co (mŏn/əkō/; *It.* mō/näkō/), *n.* 1. a principality on the Mediterranean coast, bordering SE France. 23,956 pop. (1938); ½ sq. mi. 2. the capital of this principality. 1936 pop. (1938).

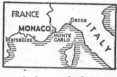

mon·ad (mŏn/ăd, mō/năd) *n.* 1. *Biol.* **a.** any simple, single-celled organism. **b.** a certain type of small flagellate, colorless, naked, amoeboid with one to three flagella. 2. *Chem.* an element, atom, or radical having a valence of one. 3. *Philos.* an entity, conceived after the fashion of the self, and regarded as the ultimate unit of being or as a microcosm. 4. unity. [t. LL: s. *monas,* t. Gk.: unit] —**mo·nad·ic** (mə năd/ĭk), **mo·nad/i·cal,** *adj.* —**mo·nad/i·cal·ly,** *adv.*

mon·a·del·phous (mŏn/ə dĕl/fəs), *adj. Bot.* 1. (of stamens) united into one bundle or set by their filaments. 2. (of a plant or flower) having the stamens so united. [f. MON- + s. Gk. *adelphôs* brother + -OUS]

mon·ad·ism (mŏn/ədĭz/əm, mō/năd ĭz/əm), *n. Philos.* 1. the doctrine of monads as ultimate units of being. 2. the philosophy of Leibnitz. Also, **mon·ad·ol·o·gy** (mŏn/ə dŏl/ə jĭ, mō/năd ŏl/-). —**mon·ad·is/tic,** *adj.*

Monadelphous flower

mo·nad·nock (mə năd/nŏk), *n.* 1. *Phys. Geog.* a residual hill or mountain standing well above the surface of a surrounding peneplain. [from def. 2] 2. (*cap.*) **Mount,** an isolated peak in SW New Hampshire. 3186 ft. [t. Amer. Ind.: prominent mountain]

Mon·a·ghan (mŏn/əgən), *n.* a county in NE Eire. 57,959 pop. (est. 1943); 498 sq. mi. *Co. seat:* Monaghan.

Mo·na Li·sa (mō/nə lē/zə), a famous portrait by da Vinci.

mo·nan·drous (mə năn/drəs), *adj.* 1. having but one husband at a time, as a woman. 2. characterized by or pertaining to monandry: *the monandrous system.* 3. *Bot.* **a.** (of a flower) having but one stamen. **b.** (of a plant) having such flowers. [t. Gk.: m. *mónandros* having one husband]

mo·nan·dry (mə năn/drĭ), *n.* the practice or the condition of having but one husband at a time.

Monandrous flower of mare's tail, *Hippuris vulgaris*

mo·nan·thous (mə năn/thəs), *adj. Bot.* one-flowered. [f. MON- + s. Gk. *ánthos* flower + -OUS]

Mo·na Passage (mō/nə; *Sp.* mô/nä), a strait between Hispaniola and Puerto Rico. ab. 80 mi. wide.

mon·arch (mŏn/ərk), *n.* 1. a hereditary sovereign with more or less limited powers, as a king or queen, an emperor or empress. 2. (*orig.*) a sole and absolute ruler of a state. 3. one who or that which holds a dominating or preëminent position. 4. a large black and red butterfly, *Danaus menippe,* whose larva feeds on milkweed. [late ME, t. LL: s. *monarcha,* t. Gk.: m. *monárchēs* ruling alone]

mo·nar·chal (mə när/kəl), *adj.* 1. pertaining to, characteristic of, or befitting a monarch. 2. having the status of a monarch. Also, **mo·nar·chi·al** (mə när/kĭ əl). —**mo·nar/chal·ly,** *adv.*

mo·nar·chi·cal (mə när/kə kəl), *adj.* 1. of or pertaining to a monarch or monarchy. 2. characterized by or favoring monarchy. Also, **mo·nar/chic.** —**mo·nar/-chi·cal·ly,** *adv.*

mon·ar·chism (mŏn/ərkĭz/əm), *n.* 1. the principles of monarchy. 2. advocacy of monarchical principles. —**mon/ar·chist,** *n., adj.* —**mon/ar·chis/tic,** *adj.*

---

b., blend of, blended; c., cognate with; d., dialect, dialectal; der., derived from; f., formed from; g., going back to; m., modification of; r., replacing; s., stem of; t., taken from; ?, perhaps. See the full key on inside cover.

mon·ar·chy (mŏn′ər kĭ), n., pl. **-chies.** 1. a government or state in which the supreme power is actually or nominally lodged in a monarch (known as an **absolute** or **despotic monarchy** when the monarch's authority is not limited by laws or a constitution and as a **limited** or **constitutional monarchy** when the monarch's authority is so limited). 2. supreme power or sovereignty wielded by a single person. [ME *monarchie*, t. LL: m. *monarchia*, t. Gk.] —**Syn.** 1. See **kingdom.**

mo·nar·da (mə när′də), n. any of the labiate genus, *Monarda*, of mintlike aromatic erect herbs of North America, including the horsemint, Oswego tea. [t. NL; named after N. *Monardès* (1493–1588), Spanish physician and botanist]

mon·as (mŏn′ăs, mō′năs), n., pl. **monades** (mŏn′ə dēz′.) monad. [t. LL]

mon·as·ter·y (mŏn′əs tĕr′ĭ), n., pl. **-teries.** 1. a house or place of residence occupied by a community of persons, esp. monks, living in seclusion from the world under religious vows. 2. the community of persons living in such a place. [ME, t. LL: m.s. *monasterium*, t. LGk.: m. *monastērion* solitary dwelling] —**mon·as·te·ri·al** (mŏn′ə stĭr′ĭ əl), adj.

mo·nas·tic (mə năs′tĭk), adj. Also, **mo·nas′ti·cal.** 1. of or pertaining to monasteries: *monastic architecture.* 2. of, pertaining to, or characteristic of monks, or other persons living in seclusion from the world under religious vows: *monastic vows of poverty, chastity, and obedience.* —n. 3. a member of a monastic community or order; a monk. [t. ML: s. *monasticus*, t. LGk.: m. *monastikós* living in solitude] —**mo·nas′ti·cal·ly,** adv.

mo·nas·ti·cism (mə năs′tə sĭz′əm), n. the monastic system, condition, or mode of life.

Mo·na·stir (mō′nä stēr′), n. Turkish name of **Bitolj.**

mon·a·tom·ic (mŏn′ə tŏm′ĭk), adj. Chem. 1. having one atom in the molecule. 2. containing one replaceable atom or group. 3. having a valence of one.

mon·ax·i·al (mŏn ăk′sĭ əl), adj. Bot. 1. uniaxial. 2. having flowers that grow on the primary axis.

mon·a·zite (mŏn′ə zīt′), n. a reddish- or yellowish-brown mineral, a phosphate of cerium and lanthanum, (Ce,La) PO₄, the principal ore of thorium. [t. G: m. *monazit*, f. s. Gk. *monázein* be alone + *-it* -ITE¹]

mon cher (môn shěr′), French. my dear (masc.).

Monck (mŭngk), n. **George.** See **Monk.**

Mon·day (mŭn′dĭ), n. the second day of the week, following Sunday. [ME *Mone(n)day*, OE *mōn(an)dæg* moon's day, used to render LL *Lūnae dies*]

monde (môNd), n. French. the world; people; society.

mo·ne·cious (mə nē′shəs, mō-), adj. monoecious.

Mo·nel metal (mō′nĕl′), n. 1. a nonrusting, silvery-white alloy containing about 67 percent nickel, 28 percent copper, and 5 percent other metals, produced from the nickeliferous ores of the Sudbury district in Canada, and used for a great number of purposes. 2. (cap.) a trademark for this metal. Also, **Mo·nell′.** [named after Ambrose *Monell* (d. 1921), of New York]

Mo·nes·sen (mə něs′ən, mō-), n. a city in SW Pennsylvania, on the Monongahela river. 17,896 (1950).

Mo·net (mô nĕ′), n. **Claude** (klōd), 1840–1926, French painter; a founder and leader of the impressionist school.

mon·e·tar·y (mŭn′ə tĕr′ĭ, mŏn′ə-), adj. 1. of or pertaining to the coinage or currency of a country. 2. of or pertaining to money, or pecuniary: *monetary consideration.* [t. L: m.s. *monētārius* pertaining to the mint] —**mon′e·tar′i·ly,** adv. —**Syn.** 1. See **financial.**

mon·e·tize (mŭn′ə tīz′, mŏn′ə-), v.t., **-tized, -tizing.** 1. to legalize as money. 2. to coin into money: *to monetize gold.* 3. to give the character of money to. —**mon′·e·ti·za′tion,** n.

mon·ey (mŭn′ĭ), n., pl. **moneys, monies.** 1. gold, silver, or other metal in pieces of convenient form stamped by public authority and issued as a medium of exchange and measure of value. 2. current coin. 3. coin or certificate (as banknotes, etc.) generally accepted in payment of debts and current transactions. 4. any article or substance similarly used, as checks on demand deposit, wampum, etc. 5. a particular form or denomination of currency. 6. a money of account. 7. property considered with reference to its pecuniary value. 8. (pl.) Archaic or Legal. pecuniary sums. 9. pecuniary profit. [ME *moneye*, t. OF: m. *moneie*, g. L *monēta* mint, money, der. *Jūno Monēta* Juno the Adviser, in whose temple at Rome money was coined] —**Syn.** 1. coin, cash, currency, specie, change. 7. funds, capital, assets.

mon·ey·bag (mŭn′ĭ băg′), n. 1. a bag for money. 2. (pl. construed as sing.) a wealthy person.

mon·ey·chang·er (mŭn′ĭ chān′jər), n. one whose business it is to change money at a fixed or authorized rate.

mon·eyed (mŭn′ĭd), adj. 1. having money; wealthy. 2. consisting of or representing money: *he denounced them as moneyed interests.*

mon·ey·lend·er (mŭn′ĭ lěn′dər), n. one whose business it is to lend money at interest.

mon·ey·mak·er (mŭn′ĭ mā′kər), n. 1. one engaged in or successful at gaining money. 2. something that yields pecuniary profit. —**mon′ey·mak′ing,** n., adj.

money of account, a monetary denomination used in reckoning, esp. one not issued as a coin, as the U.S. mill.

money order, an order for the payment of money, as one issued by one post office and payable at another.

mon·ey·wort (mŭn′ĭ wûrt′), n. a creeping primulaceous herb, *Lysimachia Nummularia,* with roundish leaves and yellow flowers.

mon·ger (mŭng′gər), n. (usually in compounds) 1. Brit. a dealer in some commodity: *a fishmonger.* 2. one who busies himself with something in a sordid or petty way: *a scandalmonger.* [ME *mongere,* OE *mangere* (c. Icel. *mangari,*) f. L *mang(o)* trader + *-ere* -ER¹] —**mon′·ger·ing,** n., adj.

Mon·gol (mŏng′gal, -gŏl, -gōl), n. 1. one of an Asiatic race now living chiefly in Mongolia. 2. a member of the Mongolian race. 3. any Mongolian language. —adj. 4. Mongolian.

Mongol Empire, A. D. 1200

Mongol Empire, an empire that under Genghis Khan, in the 13th century, encompassed the larger part of Asia and extended to the Dnieper river in E Europe: its capital was the vast tent city of Karakorum, in N Mongolia.

Mon·go·li·a (mŏng gō′lĭ ə), n. 1. a vast region in Asia, including Inner Mongolia, the Mongolian People's Republic, and Tannu Tuva. 2. **Inner,** the S part of Mongolia, under Chinese control, including the provinces of Jehol, Chahar, Suiyüan, and Ningsia. 3. **Outer,** former name of **Mongolian People's Republic.**

Mon·go·li·an (mŏng gō′lĭ ən), adj. 1. pertaining to Mongolia. 2. of or pertaining to the Mongol nationality of inner Asia. 3. denoting or pertaining to the so-called "yellow" race of Asia, characterized chiefly by yellowish complexion, prominent cheekbones, slant eyes, short broad nose, and straight black hair, and embracing the Mongols, Manchu, Chinese, Koreans, Japanese, Annamese, Siamese, Burmans, and Tibetans. 4. affected with Mongolism. —n. 5. a member of the Mongolian race. 6. a family of languages, including the languages of the Mongols, perhaps related to the Turkic and Tungusic families.

Mongolian People's Republic, a republic in E central Asia: the N part of Mongolia. ab. 850,000 pop.; ab. 600,000 sq. mi. Cap.: Ulan Bator Khoto. Formerly, **Outer Mongolia.**

Mon·gol·ic (mŏng gŏl′ĭk), adj. 1. Mongolian. —n. 2. the Mongolian language.

Mon·gol·ism (mŏng′gə lĭz′əm), n. abnormal condition of a child born with a wide, flattened skull, narrow, slanting eyes, and generally a mental deficiency.

Mon·gol·oid (mŏng′gə loid′), adj. 1. resembling the Mongols. 2. Anthropol. a. similar or related to the Mongols in physique. b. pertaining to the "yellow" race, which embraces Asiatic Mongolians, Indonesian-Malaysians, and American Indians. —n. 3. a person of a Mongoloid race.

mon·goose (mŏng′gōōs), n., pl. **-gooses.** a slender ferretlike carnivore, typified by *Herpestes edwardsii,* of India, of the same genus as the common ichneumon, used for destroying rats, etc., and noted for its ability to kill certain venomous snakes without being harmed. Also, **mon′goos.** [t. Marathi: m. *mangūs*]

Mongoose, *Herpestes ichneumon*
(Total length ab. 3 ft., tail 1½ ft.)

mon·grel (mŭng′grəl, mŏng′-), n. 1. any animal or plant resulting from the crossing of different breeds or varieties. 2. any cross between different things. —adj. 3. that is a mongrel; being of mixed breed, race, origin, nature, etc. [f. obs. *mong* mixture (OE *gemang*) + -REL] —**Syn.** 1. See **hybrid.** —**Ant.** 1. thoroughbred.

mongst (mŭngst), prep. Poetic. amongst.

Mon·i·er-Wil·liams (mŏn′ĭ ər wĭl′yəmz, mŏn′-), n. **Sir Monier,** 1819–99, British Sanskrit scholar.

mon·i·ker (mŏn′ə kər), n. 1. a symbol or mark used by a tramp to identify himself. 2. Slang. a person's name; a nickname. Also, **mon′ick·er.** [b. MONOGRAM and MARKER]

mo·nil·i·form (mō nĭl′ə fôrm′), adj. 1. Bot. and Zool. consisting of or characterized by a series of beadlike swellings alternating with contractions, as certain roots, stems, etc. 2. resembling a string of beads. [f. s. L *monīle* necklace + -(I)FORM]

mon·ism (mŏn′ĭzəm, mō′nĭz əm), n. Philos. 1. the doctrine of one ultimate substance or principle, as mind (*idealism*) or matter (*materialism*), or something that is neither mind nor matter but the ground of both. 2. the position that reality is one (op-

Moniliform fruits of sophora, *Sophora japonica*

posed to *pluralism*). [t. NL: s. *monismus*, der. Gk. *mónos* single] —**mon′ist**, *n.* —**mo·nis·tic** (mō-nĭs′tĭk), *adj.* —**mo·nis′ti·cal·ly**, *adv.*

mo·ni·tion (mō nĭsh′ən), *n.* 1. admonition; warning; caution. 2. an official or legal notice. 3. *Law.* a court order summoning a party, either to commence suit by appearance and answer or to answer contempt charges. 4. a formal notice from a bishop requiring the amendment of an ecclesiastical offense. [ME, t. L: s. *monitio* a reminding]

mon·i·tor (mŏn′ə tər), *n.* 1. a pupil appointed to assist in the conduct of a class or school, as to help keep order, etc. 2. one who admonishes, esp. with reference to conduct. 3. something that serves to remind or give warning. 4. an ironclad warship with a low freeboard and one or more revolving turrets, each containing one or more large calibre guns. The first such vessel, the **Monitor**, was used by Union forces during the Civil War against the Merrimac (1862). 5. an articulated mounting for a nozzle, usually mechanically operated, which permits a stream of water to be played in any desired direction, as in fire fighting. 6. any of the large lizards constituting the genus *Varanus* and family *Varanidae* of Africa, southern Asia, and Australia, fabled to give warning of the presence of crocodiles. —*v.t., v.i.* 7. *Radio.* **a.** to hear (transmitted signals) using a receiving set in order to check the quality of the transmission. **b.** to listen to (broadcasts) for operating compliance, censorship, propaganda analysis, and similar purposes. [t. L] —**mon′i·tor·ship′**, *n.*

mon·i·to·ri·al (mŏn′ə tōr′Ĭ əl), *adj.* 1. of or pertaining to a monitor. 2. monitory.

mon·i·to·ry (mŏn′ə tōr′Ĭ), *adj., n., pl.* **-ries.** —*adj.* 1. serving to admonish or warn; admonitory. 2. giving monition. —*n.* 3. Also, **monitory letter.** a letter, as one from a bishop, containing a monition. [late ME, t. L: m.s. *monitōrius*, adj.]

monk (mŭngk), *n.* a man who has withdrawn from the world from religious motives, either as an eremite or, esp., as a member of an order of cenobites living under vows of poverty, chastity, and obedience, according to a rule. [ME; OE *munuc*, ult. t. LL: m.s. *monachus*, t. LGk.: m. *monachós*, adj., solitary (as n., monk)] —**Syn.** MONK, FRIAR refer to special male groups in the Rom. Cath. Church whose lives are devoted to the service of the church. A MONK is properly a member of a monastery, under a superior; he is bound by a vow of stability, and is a co-owner of the community property of the monastery. Since the Reformation, MONK and FRIAR have been used as if they were the same. A FRIAR is, however, strictly speaking, a member of a mendicant order, whose members are not attached to a monastery and own no community property.

Monk (mŭngk), *n.* **George,** (*1st Duke of Albemarle*) 1608–70, British general who helped to restore Charles II to the throne of England. Also, **Monck.**

mon·key (mŭng′kĬ), *n., pl.* **-keys**, *v.,* **-keyed, -keying.** —*n.* 1. any member of the mammalian order *Primates,* except man, the anthropoid apes and, usually, the lemurs, e.g. the guenons, macaques, langurs, capuchins, etc. 2. a person likened to such an animal, as a mischievous child, a mimic, etc. 3. the fur of certain species of long-haired monkeys. 4. any of various mechanical devices, as the ram of a pile-driving apparatus. 5. *Coal Mining.* small passageway or opening. 6. *Brit. Slang.* five hundred pounds. —*v.i.* 7. *Colloq.* to play or trifle idly; fool (often fol. by *with*). —*v.t.* 8. to imitate as a monkey does; ape; mimic. 9. to mock. [appar. t. LG. Cf. MLG *Moneke* (name of son of Martin the Ape in story of Reynard), f. *mone-* (akin to Sp. and Pg. *mono* ape) + *-ke* (dim. suffix)]

Rhesus monkey, *Macacus rhesus* (Total length 30 in., tail 8 to 10 in.)

monkey bread, 1. the gourdlike fruit of the baobab, eaten by monkeys. 2. the tree itself.

mon·key-faced owl (mŭng′kĬ fāst′), the barn owl, *Tyto alba.*

monkey flower, any plant of the scrophulariaceous genus *Mimulus,* which includes species cultivated in gardens and greenhouses, as *M. cardinalis,* having a scarlet corolla.

monkey jacket, a short, close-fitting jacket or coat, formerly worn by sailors.

monkey nut, *Brit.* peanut.

mon·key·pot (mŭng′kĬ pŏt′), *n.* the woody, operculate seed vessel of any of certain large South American trees of the genus *Lecythis.*

monkey puzzle, a South American coniferous tree, *Araucaria arauna,* with candelabralike branches, stiff sharp leaves, and edible nuts.

mon·key·shine (mŭng′kĬ shĭn′), *n.* U.S. Slang. a mischievous or clownish trick or prank.

monkey wrench, a wrench with an adjustable jaw, for turning nuts of different sizes, etc.

Monkey wrench

Mon-Khmer (mŏn′kmĕr′), *adj.* designating a group of languages spoken chiefly in Indo-China.

monk·hood (mŭngk′hŏŏd), *n.* 1. the condition or profession of a monk. 2. monks collectively.

monk·ish (mŭngk′Ĭsh), *adj.* (often in depreciatory use) of or pertaining to, characteristic of, or resembling a monk. —**monk′ish·ly**, *adv.* —**monk′ish·ness**, *n.*

monk's cloth, a heavy cotton fabric in a basket weave, used for curtains.

monks·hood (mŭngks′hŏŏd), *n.* a plant of the genus *Aconitum,* esp. *A. Napellus* (so called from the hooded flowers). See **aconite.**

Mon·mouth (mŏn′məth), *n.* 1. **James Scott, Duke of,** 1649–85, leader of a rebellion against James II, reputed illegitimate son of Charles II. 2. Monmouthshire.

Mon·mouth·shire (mŏn′məth shĭr′, -shər), *n.* a county in SW England. 410,000 pop. (est. 1946); 543 sq. mi. *Co. seat:* Monmouth. Also, **Monmouth.**

mono-, a word element 1. meaning "alone," "single," "one." 2. denoting a monomolecular thickness, as in *monofilm, monolayer,* etc. 3. adapted in chemistry to apply to compounds containing one atom of a particular element, as in *monoxide.* Also, **mon-.** [t. Gk., comb. form of *mónos* alone]

mon·o·bas·ic (mŏn′ə bā′sĬk), *adj.* 1. *Chem.* (of an acid) containing one replaceable hydrogen atom. 2. *Biol.* monotypic.

mon·o·carp (mŏn′ə kärp′), *n. Bot.* a plant that dies after having once borne fruit.

mon·o·car·pel·lar·y (mŏn′ə kär′pə lĕr′Ĭ), *adj. Bot.* consisting of a single carpel.

mon·o·car·pic (mŏn′ə kär′pĬk), *adj. Bot.* producing fruit but once and then dying.

mon·o·car·pous (mŏn′ə kär′pəs), *adj. Bot.* 1. having a gynoecium which forms only a single ovary. 2. monocarpic.

mon·o·cha·si·um (mŏn′ə kā′zhĬ əm, -zĬ əm), *n., pl.* **-sia** (-zhĬ ə, -zĬ ə). *Bot.* a form of cymose inflorescence in which the main axis produces only a single branch. [t. NL: f. *mono-* MONO- + s. Gk. *chásis* separation + *-ium* -IUM] —**mon′o·cha′si·al**, *adj.*

mon·o·chord (mŏn′ə kôrd′), *n.* 1. an acoustical instrument, of ancient invention, consisting of an oblong wooden sounding box, usually with a single string, used for the mathematical determination of musical intervals. 2. *Rare.* harmony or agreement. [ME *monocorde,* t. OF, t. L: m. *monochordon,* t. Gk.: having a single string]

mon·o·chro·ic (mŏn′ə krō′Ĭk), *adj.* of one color. [f. s. Gk. *monóchroos* of one color + -IC]

mon·o·chro·mat·ic (mŏn′ə krō măt′Ĭk), *adj.* of, producing, or pertaining to one color or one wave length only. —**mon′o·chro·mat′i·cal·ly**, *adv.*

mon·o·chrome (mŏn′ə krōm′), *n.* 1. a painting or drawing in different shades of a single color. 2. the art or method of making these. [t. Gk.: m.s. *monóchrōmos* of one color] —**mon′o·chro′mic, mon′o·chro′mi·cal**, *adj.* —**mon′o·chrom′ist**, *n.*

mon·o·cle (mŏn′ə kəl), *n.* an eyeglass for one eye. [t. F, t. LL: m.s. *monoculus* one-eyed] —**mon′o·cled**, *adj.*

mon·o·cli·nal (mŏn′ə klĬ′nəl), *Geol.* —*adj.* 1. dipping in one direction, as strata. 2. pertaining to strata which dip in the same direction. —*n.* 3. monocline. —**mon′o·cli′nal·ly**, *adv.*

mon·o·cline (mŏn′ə klĬn′), *n. Geol.* a monoclinal structure or fold. [f. MONO- + m.s. Gk. *klīnein* incline]

mon·o·clin·ic (mŏn′ə klĬn′Ĭk), *adj. Crystall.* denoting or pertaining to crystallization in which the crystals have three unequal axes, with one oblique intersection.

mon·o·cli·nous (mŏn′ə klĬ′nəs, mŏn′ə klĬ′nəs), *adj. Bot.* (of a plant species, etc.) having both the stamens and pistils in the same flower.

mon·o·cot·y·le·don (mŏn′ə kŏt′ə lē′dən), *n. Bot.* 1. a plant with only one cotyledon. 2. a member of the group *Monocotyledonae,* one of the two subclasses of angiospermous plants, characterized in the main by producing seeds with a single cotyledon or seed leaf, and by an endogenous mode of growth. —**mon·o·cot·y·le·don·ous** (mŏn′ə kŏt′ə lē′dən əs, -lĕd′ən-), *adj.*

mo·noc·ra·cy (mō nŏk′rə sĬ), *n., pl.* **-cies.** government by a single person; autocracy. —**mon·o·crat·ic** (mŏn′ə krăt′Ĭk), *adj.*

mo·noc·u·lar (mə nŏk′yə lər), *adj.* 1. having only one eye. 2. pertaining to or intended for one eye: *a monocular microscope.* [f. s. LL *monoculus* one-eyed + -AR¹]

mon·o·cul·ture (mŏn′ə kŭl′chər), *n. Agric.* growing some single crop and not using the land in any other way.

mon·o·dac·ty·lous (mŏn′ə dăk′tə ləs), *adj. Zool.* having only one digit or claw. Also, **mon′o·dac′tyl.** [t. Gk.: m. *monodáktylos*]

mo·nod·ic (mə nŏd′Ĭk), *adj. Music.* pertaining to monody or homophony. Also, **mo·nod′i·cal.** [t. Gk.: m.s. *monōidikós*] —**mo·nod′i·cal·ly**, *adv.*

mon·o·dra·ma (mŏn′ə drä′mə, -drăm′ə), *n.* a dramatic piece for a single performer. —**mon·o·dra·mat·ic** (mŏn′ə drə măt′Ĭk), *adj.*

mon·o·dy (mŏn′ə dĬ), *n., pl.* **-dies.** 1. a Greek ode sung by a single voice, as in a tragedy; a lament. 2. a poem in which one person laments another's death. 3. *Music.* **a.** a style of composition in which one part or melody predominates; homophony, as distinguished from polyphony. **b.** a piece written in this style. [t. LL: m.s. *monōdia,* t. Gk.: m. *monōidía* a solo, lament] —**mon′o·dist**, *n.*

mo·noe·cious (mə nē′shəs), *adj.* **1.** *Biol.* having both male and female organs in the same individual; hermaphroditic. **2.** *Bot.* (of a plant species, etc.) having the stamens and the pistils in separate flowers on the same plant. Also, **monecious.** [f. MON- + m.s. Gk. *oikíon* house + -OUS]

Branch of monoecious tree A, Male catkins; B, Female catkins; C, Fruit

mo·nog·a·mist (mə nŏg′ə mĭst), *n.* one who practices or advocates monogamy. —**mo·nog′a·mis′tic,** *adj.*

mo·nog·a·mous (mə nŏg′ə məs), *adj.* **1.** practicing or advocating monogamy. **2.** pertaining to monogamy. [t. LL: m. *monogamus,* t. Gk.: m. *monógamos*]

mo·nog·a·my (mə nŏg′ə mĭ), *n.* **1.** marriage of one woman with one man. **2.** *Zool.* the habit of having only one mate. **3.** the practice of marrying only once during life.

mon·o·gen·e·sis (mŏn′ə jĕn′ə sĭs), *n.* **1.** the theoretical descent of all living things from a single ancestral organism. **2.** the theoretical descent of the whole human race from a single pair. **3.** *Biol.* development of an ovum into an organism similar to its parent, without metamorphosis. Also, **mo·nog·e·ny** (mə nŏj′ə nĭ).

mon·o·ge·net·ic (mŏn′ə jĭ nĕt′ĭk), *adj.* **1.** of or pertaining to monogenesis. **2.** having only one generation in the life cycle; without intermediate nonsexual generations: applied to trematode worms of the subclass *Monogenea.* **3.** *Geol.* resulting from one genetic process.

mon·o·gram (mŏn′ə gram), *n.* a character consisting of two or more letters combined or interlaced, commonly one's initials, often printed on stationery, embroidered on clothing, etc. [t. LL: m. *monogramma,* t. LGk.: m. *monógrammon* single-lettered character. See MONO-, GRAM-] —**mon·o·gram·mat·ic** (mŏn′ə grə măt′ĭk), *adj.*

mon·o·graph (mŏn′ə gräf′, -grăf′), *n.* **1.** a treatise on a particular subject. **2.** an account or description of a single thing or class of things, as of a species or genus of animals or plants. —**mon′o·graph′ic,** *adj.* —**mon′o·graph′i·cal·ly,** *adv.*

mo·nog·ra·pher (mə nŏg′rə fər), *n.* the writer of a monograph.

mo·nog·y·ny (mə nŏj′ə nĭ), *n.* the practice or the condition of having but one wife at a time. [f. MONO- + m.s. Gk. *gynía,* der. *gynḗ* woman]

mon·o·hy·dric (mŏn′ə hī′drĭk), *adj. Chem.* (of a compound, usually an alcohol) having a single hydroxyl radical.

mo·nol·a·try (mə nŏl′ə trĭ), *n.* the worship of but one god, when other gods are recognized as existing. [f. MONO- + m.s. Gk. *latreía* worship] —**mo·nol·a·ter** (mə nŏl′ə tər), **mo·nol′a·trist,** *n.* —**mo·nol′a·trous,** *adj.*

mon·o·lith (mŏn′ə lĭth), *n.* **1.** a single block or piece of stone of considerable size, esp. when used in architecture or sculpture. **2.** an obelisk, column, statue, etc., formed of a single block of stone. **3.** a stonelike material used for floors. **4.** (*cap.*) a trademark for this material. [t. LL: s. *monolithus,* t. Gk.: m. *monólithos* made of one stone] —**mon′o·lith′ic,** *adj.*

mon·o·logue (mŏn′ə lŏg′, -lôg′), *n.* **1.** a prolonged talk or discourse by a single speaker. **2.** any composition, as a poem, in which a single person speaks alone. **3.** a part of a drama in which a single actor speaks alone. **4.** a form of dramatic entertainment by a single speaker. Also, **mon′o·log′.** [t. F, t. Gk.: m.s. *monólogos* speaking alone] —**mon·o·log·ic** (mŏn′ə lŏj′ĭk), **mon′o·log′i·cal,** *adj.* —**mon·o·log·ist** (mŏn′ə lŏg′ĭst, -lŏg′-), *n.*

mo·nol·o·gy (mə nŏl′ə jĭ), *n., pl.* **-gies. 1.** the act or habit of soliloquizing. **2.** *Obs.* a monologue. [t. Gk.: m.s. *monología*]

mon·o·ma·ni·a (mŏn′ə mā′nĭ ə), *n.* **1.** insanity in which the patient is irrational on one subject only. **2.** an exaggerated zeal for, or interest in, some one thing; a craze. —**mon·o·ma·ni·ac** (mŏn′ə mā′nĭ ăk′), *n.* —**mon·o·ma·ni·a·cal** (mŏn′ə mə nī′ə kəl), *adj.*

mo·nom·er·ous (mə nŏm′ərəs), *adj. Bot.* (of flowers) having one member in each whorl. [f. s. Gk. *monomerḗs* consisting of one part + -OUS]

mon·o·me·tal·lic (mŏn′ə mə tăl′ĭk), *adj.* **1.** pertaining to or using one metal. **2.** pertaining to monometallism.

mon·o·met·al·lism (mŏn′ə mĕt′ə lĭz′əm), *n.* **1.** the use of one metal only (as gold or silver) as the monetary standard. **2.** the doctrine or actions supporting such a standard. —**mon′o·met′al·list,** *n.*

mo·no·mi·al (mō nō′mĭ əl), *adj.* **1.** *Alg.* consisting of one term only. **2.** *Biol.* denoting or pertaining to a name which consists of a single word or term. —*n.* **3.** *Alg.* a monomial expression or quantity. [irreg. f. MO(NO)- + -nomial, after BINOMIAL]

mon·o·mo·lec·u·lar (mŏn′ə mə lĕk′yə lər), *adj.* indicating a thickness of one molecule.

mon·o·mor·phic (mŏn′ə môr′fĭk), *adj.* **1.** *Biol.* having only one form. **2.** of the same or of an essentially similar type of structure. Also, **mon′o·mor′phous.**

Mo·non·ga·he·la (mə nŏng′gə hē′lə), *n.* a river flowing from N West Virginia through SW Pennsylvania into the Ohio river at Pittsburgh. 128 mi. (from junction of forks).

mon·o·pet·al·ous (mŏn′ə pĕt′ə ləs), *adj. Bot.* **1.** gamopetalous. **2.** having but one petal, as a corolla.

mon·o·pho·bi·a (mŏn′ə fō′bĭ ə), *n. Psychiatry.* morbid dread of being alone.

mon·o·phon·ic (mŏn′ə fŏn′ĭk), *adj.* monodic.

mon·oph·thong (mŏn′əf thông′, -thŏng′), *n.* a single, simple vowel sound; a monophthongal vowel. [t. Gk.: s. *monóphthongos* with one sound]

mon·oph·thon·gal (mŏn′əf thông′gəl, -thŏng′-), *adj. Phonet.* (of vowels) of unvarying quality; approximately the same from beginning to end.

mon·o·phy·let·ic (mŏn′ə fī lĕt′ĭk), *adj.* **1.** of or pertaining to a single tribe or stock. **2.** developed from a single ancestral type, as a group of animals. [f. MONO- + m.s. Gk. *phyletikós* belonging to a tribesman]

mon·o·phyl·lous (mŏn′ə fĭl′əs), *adj. Bot.* **1.** consisting of one leaf, as a calyx. **2.** having only one leaf. [t. Gk.: m. *monóphyllos*]

Mo·noph·y·site (mə nŏf′ə sĭt′), *n. Theol.* one holding that there is in Christ but a single nature, or one composite nature, partly divine and partly human, as the members of the Coptic Church of Egypt: used esp. with reference to the controversies of the 5th and 6th centuries. [t. LGk.: m.s. *monophysítēs,* f. Gk.: *mono-* MONO- + *phýs(is)* nature + -ítēs -ITE[1]] —**Mon·o·phy·sit·ic** (mŏn′ə fĭ sĭt′ĭk), *adj.* —**Mo·noph′y·sit·ism,** *n.*

mon·o·plane (mŏn′ə plān′), *n.* an airplane with a single sustaining plane.

mon·o·ple·gi·a (mŏn′ə plē′jĭ ə), *n. Pathol.* paralysis of only one extremity, upper or lower. [t. NL. See MONO-, -PLEGIA] —**mon·o·pleg·ic** (mŏn′ə plĕj′ĭk, -plē′jĭk), *adj.*

mon·o·pode (mŏn′ə pōd′), *adj.* **1.** having but one foot. —*n.* **2.** a creature having but one foot. **3.** one of a fabled race of men having but one leg. **4.** *Bot.* monopodium. [t. Gk.: m.s. *monópous* one-footed]

mon·o·po·di·um (mŏn′ə pō′dĭ əm), *n., pl.* **-dia** (-dĭ′ə). *Bot.* a single main axis which continues to extend at the apex in the original line of growth, giving off lateral branches beneath in acropetal succession. [NL, f. Gk.: *mono-* MONO- + m. *pódion* foot] —**mon·o·po′di·al,** *adj.*

mo·nop·o·lism (mə nŏp′ə lĭz′əm), *n.* the existence or prevalence of monopolies.

mo·nop·o·list (mə nŏp′ə lĭst), *n.* **1.** one who has a monopoly. **2.** an advocate of monopoly. —**mo·nop′o·lis′tic,** *adj.*

mo·nop·o·lize (mə nŏp′ə līz′), *v.t.,* **-lized, -lizing. 1.** to acquire, have, or exercise a monopoly of. **2.** to obtain exclusive possession of; keep entirely to oneself: *she tried to monopolize his time.* —**mo·nop′o·li·za′tion,** *n.* —**mo·nop′o·liz′er,** *n.*

mo·nop·o·ly (mə nŏp′ə lĭ), *n., pl.* **-lies. 1.** exclusive control of a commodity or service in a particular market, or a control that makes possible the manipulation of prices. **2.** an exclusive privilege to carry on a traffic or service, granted by a sovereign, state, etc. **3.** the exclusive possession or control of something. **4.** something which is the subject of a monopoly; a commodity, service, etc., which is exclusively controlled. **5.** a company or the like having a monopoly. [t. L: m.s. *monopólium,* t. Gk.: m. *monopólion* a right of exclusive sale]

mon·o·sac·cha·ride (mŏn′ə săk′ə rīd′, -rĭd), *n. Chem.* a simple sugar, such as glucose, fructose, arabinose, and ribose, occurring in nature or obtained by the hydrolysis of glucosides or polysaccharides.

mon·o·sep·al·ous (mŏn′ə sĕp′ələs), *adj. Bot.* **1.** gamosepalous. **2.** having but one sepal, as a calyx.

mon·o·sper·mous (mŏn′ə spûr′məs), *adj. Bot.* one-seeded. Also, **mon′o·sper′mal.**

mon·o·stich (mŏn′ə stĭk′), *n.* **1.** a poem or epigram consisting of a single metrical line. **2.** a single line of poetry. [t. LL: s. *monostichum,* t. Gk.: m. *monóstichon,* adj. neut., consisting of one line]

mon·o·stome (mŏn′ə stōm′), *adj.* having a single mouth, pore, or stoma. Also, **mo·nos·to·mous** (mə nŏs′tə məs). [t. Gk.: m. *monóstomos* with one mouth]

mon·o·stro·phe (mə nŏs′trə fĭ, mŏn′ə strōf′), *n.* a poem in which all the strophes or stanzas are of the same metrical form. [t. Gk.: m.s. *monóstrophos.* See MONO-, STROPHE] —**mon·o·stroph·ic** (mŏn′ə strŏf′ĭk), *adj.*

mon·o·sty·lous (mŏn′ə stī′ləs), *adj. Bot.* having but one style.

mon·o·syl·lab·ic (mŏn′ə sĭ lăb′ĭk), *adj.* **1.** having only one syllable, as the word *no.* **2.** having a vocabulary composed exclusively of monosyllables (formerly, erroneously said of Chinese). **3.** using or uttering monosyllables. —**mon′o·syl·lab′i·cal·ly,** *adv.*

mon·o·syl·la·bism (mŏn′ə sĭl′ə bĭz′əm), *n.* **1.** monosyllabic character. **2.** use of monosyllables.

mon·o·syl·la·ble (mŏn′ə sĭl′ə bəl), *n.* a word of one syllable, as *yes* and *no.* [f. MONO- + SYLLABLE. Cf. L *monosyllabon,* t. Gk.]

mon·o·the·ism (mŏn′ə thē′ĭz′əm), *n.* the doctrine or belief that there is but one God. [f. MONO- + s. Gk. *theós* god + -ISM] —**mon′o·the′ist,** *n.* —**mon′o·the·is′tic,** *adj.* —**mon′o·the·is′ti·cal·ly,** *adv.*

mon·o·tone (mŏn′ə tōn′), *n.* **1.** vocal utterance, or series of speech sounds. **2.** a single tone without harmony or variation in pitch. **3.** recitation or singing of words in such a tone. **4.** the person who sings in such manner. **5.** sameness of style, as in composition or writing. —*adj.* **6.** monotonous. [t. NL: m.s. *monotonus,* t. LGk.: m. *monótonos* of one tone]

mo·not·o·nous (mə nŏt′ə nəs), *adj.* **1.** unvarying in any respect, lacking in variety, or tiresomely uniform. **2.** characterizing a sound continuing on one note. **3.** having very little inflection; limited to a narrow pitch range. [f. MONOTONE + -OUS] —**mo·not′o·nous·ly,** *adv.* —**mo·not′o·nous·ness,** *n.* —**Syn. 1.** tedious, humdrum.

mo·not·o·ny (mə nŏt′ə nĭ), *n.* **1.** lack of variety, or wearisome uniformity, as in occupation, scenery, etc. **2.** the continuance of an unvarying sound; monotone. **3.** sameness of tone or pitch, as in utterance. [t. LGk.: m.s. *monotonía*]

mon·o·trem·a·tous (mŏn′ə trĕm′ə təs, -trē′mə-), *adj.* of or pertaining to a monotreme.

mon·o·treme (mŏn′ə trēm′), *n.* any of the *Monotremata,* the lowest order of mammals, restricted to the Australian region, and comprising only the duckbill and the echidnas, oviparous mammals in which the genital, urinary, and digestive organs have a common opening. [f. MONO- + m. Gk. *trêma* hole]

mo·not·ri·cha (mə nŏt′rə kə), *n.pl.* bacteria having the organs of locomotion at one pole. [f. MONO- + s. Gk. *thríx* hair + -*a* (repr. L and Gk. neut. pl. suffix -*a*)] —**mon·o·trich·ic** (mŏn′ə trĭk′ĭk), **mo·not′ri·chous,** *adj.*

mon·o·type (mŏn′ə tīp′), *n.* **1.** *Print.* **a.** type composed and cast on separate keyboarding and casting machines which produce each character on an individual body. **b.** (*cap.*) a trademark for a machine on which such type is set or cast. **2.** a print from a metal plate on which a picture is painted, as in oil color or printing ink. **3.** the method of producing such a print. **4.** *Biol.* the only or sole type of its group, as a single species constituting a genus. —**mon′o·typ′er,** *n.*

mon·o·typ·ic (mŏn′ə tĭp′ĭk), *adj.* **1.** having only one type. **2.** of the nature of a monotype. **3.** *Biol.* (of genera) established on the basis of a single species or genus.

mon·o·va·lent (mŏn′ə vā′lənt), *adj.* **1.** *Chem.* having a valence of one, as the cuprous ion (Cu¹). **2.** *Bacteriol.* (of a serum, tissue, etc.) capable of resisting a specific disease organism because of the presence of the proper antibodies or antigens. [f. MONO- + -VALENT] —**mon′·o·va′lence, mon′o·va′len·cy,** *n.*

mon·ox·ide (mŏn ŏk′sīd, mə nŏk′), *n. Chem.* an oxide containing one oxygen atom to the molecule.

Mon·roe (mən rō′), *n.* **1. Harriet,** 1861?–1936, U.S. editor and poet. **2. James,** 1758–1831, the 5th president of the United States, 1817–25. **3.** a city in N Louisiana. 38,572 (1950). **4. Fort,** a fort at the entrance to Hampton Roads, in SE Virginia.

Monroe Doctrine, the doctrine, based upon statements contained in the message of President Monroe to Congress (Dec. 2, 1823) that the interposition of any European power to control the destiny of a Spanish-American state should be looked upon as a manifestation of unfriendly disposition toward the U.S., and that the American continents should no longer be subjects for any new European political acquisition.

Mon·ro·vi·a (mən rō′vĭ ə), *n.* a seaport in, and the capital of, Liberia, in W Africa. ab. 10,000.

mons (mŏnz), *n. Anat.* a rounded eminence of fatty tissue, covered with hair, over the pubic symphysis of the adult human: called the **mons Veneris** in the female, the **mons pubis** in the male.

Mons (môns), *n.* a city in SW Belgium. 24,929 (est. 1944).

Mon·sei·gneur (môn sĕ nyœr′), *n., pl.* **Messeigneurs** (mĕ sĕ nyœr′). **1.** a French title of honor given to princes, bishops, and other persons of eminence. **2.** a person bearing this title. Also, **mon·sei·gneur′.** [t. F: my lord. See SEIGNEUR]

mon·sieur (mə syœ′), *n., pl.* **messieurs** (mĕ syœ′). the conventional French title of respect and term of address for a man, corresponding to *Mr.* and to *Sir.* [t. F: my lord (orig. applied to men of high station). See SIRE]

Mon·si·gnor (mŏn sē′nyər; *It.* môn′sē nyôr′), *n., pl.* **Monsignors, Monsignori** (mŏn′sē nyô′rē). *Rom. Cath. Ch.* **1.** a title conferred upon certain dignitaries. **2.** a person bearing this title. Also, **mon·si′gnor, Mon·si·gno·re** (mŏn′sē nyô′rĕ). [t. It.: f. F *mon* my + It. *signor*(e) lord]

mon·soon (mŏn sōōn′), *n.* **1.** the seasonal wind of the Indian Ocean and southern Asia, blowing from the southwest in summer, and from the northeast in winter. **2.** the season during which the southwest monsoon blows, commonly marked by heavy rains. **3.** any wind that reverses with the seasons. **4.** any persistent wind established between water and adjoining land. [t. early mod. D: m. *monssoen,* t. Pg.: m. *monçao,* t. Ar.: m. *mausim* time, season]

mon·ster (mŏn′stər), *n.* **1.** a fabulous animal compounded of brute and human shape or of the shapes of various brutes, as a centaur, a griffin, or a sphinx. **2.** an animal or a plant of abnormal form or structure, as from marked malformation, the absence of certain parts or organs, etc. **3.** something unnatural or monstrous. **4.** a person that excites horror, as by wickedness, cruelty, etc. **5.** any animal or thing of huge size. —*adj.* **6.** huge; enormous; monstrous. [ME *monstre,* t. OF, t. L: m.s. *monstrum* omen, prodigy, monster]

mon·strance (mŏn′strəns), *n. Rom. Cath. Ch.* a receptacle in which the consecrated host is exposed for adoration. [ME, t. ML: m.s. *monstrantia,* der. L *monstrāre* show]

mon·stros·i·ty (mŏn strŏs′ə tĭ), *n., pl.* **-ties. 1.** state or character of being monstrous. **2.** something monstrous, esp. in form or growth. **3.** a monster. [t. LL: m.s. *monstrōsitas*]

mon·strous (mŏn′strəs), *adj.* **1.** huge; prodigiously great: *a monstrous sum.* **2.** frightful or hideous; revolting; shocking: *a monstrous proposal.* **3.** deviating greatly from the natural or normal form or type. **4.** having the nature or appearance of a fabulous monster. [late ME, t. LL: m.s. *monstrōsus* strange] —**mon′strous·ly,** *adv.* —**mon′strous·ness,** *n.* —**Syn. 1.** colossal, stupendous, enormous, prodigious. See gigantic. **2.** horrible, atrocious.

Mont., Montana.

mon·tage (mŏn täzh′; *Fr.* môN täzh′), *n.* **1.** the art or method of arranging in one composition pictorial elements borrowed from several sources so that the elements are both distinct and blended into a whole, through techniques such as superimposition. **2.** a picture made in this way. **3.** *Motion Pictures.* **a.** a series of scenes, each of extreme brevity, following in rapid succession, used to present a stream of interconnected ideas. **b.** a type of process photography in which objects or other visual images are caused to whirl, flash or otherwise move into distinctness at one point. **c.** a section of a motion picture using either of these processes. [t. F: mounting, putting together]

Mon·ta·gu (mŏn′tə gū′), *n.* **Lady Mary Wortley** (wûrt′lĭ), (*Mary Pierrepont*) 1689–1762, British author.

Mon·ta·gue (mŏn′tə gū′), *n.* the family to which Romeo belongs in Shakespeare's *Romeo and Juliet.*

Mon·taigne (mŏn tān′; *Fr.* môN tĕn′y), *n.* **Michel Eyquem** (mē shĕl′ ĕ kĕm′), Seigneur de, 1533–92, French essayist.

Mon·tan·a (mŏn tăn′ə), *n.* a State in the NW United States. 591,024 pop. (1950); 147,138 sq. mi. *Cap.:* Helena. *Abbr.:* Mont. —**Mon·tan′an,** *adj., n.*

mon·tane (mŏn′tān), *Ecol.* —*adj.* **1.** pertaining to mountain conditions. —*n.* **2.** the lower vegetation belt on mountains. [t. L: m.s. *montānus* of a mountain]

mon·ta·ni sem·per li·be·ri (mŏn tā′nĭ sĕm′pər lĭb′ə rĭ′), *Latin.* mountaineers (are) always freemen (motto of West Virginia).

mon·tan wax (mŏn′tăn), a dark brown bituminous wax extracted from lignite and peat and often used for the original disk in phonograph recording. [f. *montan* (t. L: s. *montānus* of a mountain) + WAX¹]

Mon·tau·ban (môN tō bäN′), *n.* a city in S France. 36,281 (1946).

Mon·tauk Point (mŏn′tôk), the E end of Long Island, in SE New York.

Mont Blanc (môN bläN′). See **Blanc, Mont.**

Mont·calm (mŏnt käm′; *Fr.* môN kälm′), *n.* **Louis Joseph** (lwē zhō zĕf′), **Marquis de,** (*Louis Joseph, Marquis de Montcalm de Saint-Véran*) 1712–59, French general: defeated by the British under Wolfe at Quebec in 1759.

Mont·clair (mŏnt klâr′), *n.* a city in NE New Jersey. 43,927 (1950).

mont-de-pié·té (môN′də pyĕ tĕ′), *n., pl.* **monts-de-piété** (môN′-). a public pawnbroking establishment for lending money on reasonable terms, esp. to the poor. [F, t. It.: m. *monte di pietà,* lit., mountain (fund) of pity]

mon·te (mŏn′tĭ; *Sp.* môn′tĕ), *n.* a Spanish and Spanish-American gambling game at cards. [t. Sp.: mountain, heap (of cards), g. L *mons* MOUNT²]

Mon·te Car·lo (mŏn′tĭ kär′lō; *It.* môn′tĕ kär′lō), a town in Monaco principality, SE France: gambling resort. 10,681 (1938). See map under **Monaco.**

Mon·te Cas·si·no (mŏn′tĭ kä sē′nō). See **Cassino.**

mon·teith (mŏn tēth′), *n.* a large bowl commonly of silver, often with a rim for suspending drinking glasses in the cool water within the bowl. It is also used as a punch bowl. [orig. proper name]

Mon·te·ne·gro (mŏn′tə nē′grō; *It.* môn′tĕ nĕ′grō), *n.* a constituent republic of Yugoslavia, in the S part: formerly a kingdom. 360,000 pop. (1931); 5345 sq. mi. *Cap.:* Cetinje. —**Mon·te·ne·grin** (mŏn′tə nē′grĭn), *adj., n.*

Mon·te·rey (mŏn′tə rā′), *n.* a city in W California, on **Monterey Bay:** the capital of California until 1847. 16,205 (1950).

mon·te·ro (mŏn târ′ō; *Sp.* môn tĕ′rō), *n., pl.* **-ros** (-rōz; *Sp.* -rôs). a round huntsman's cap with a flap. [t. Sp.: m. *montera* hunting cap, der. *montero* huntsman, der. *monte* MOUNT²]

Mon·ter·rey (mŏn′tə rā′; *Sp.* môn′tĕr rĕ′), *n.* a city in NE Mexico: the capital of Nuevo León; battle, 1846. 185,833 (1940).

Mont·es·pan (mŏn′tĕs pän′; *Fr.* môN tĕs päN′), *n.* **Marquise de,** (*Françoise Athénaïs de Rochechouart*) 1641-1707, mistress of Louis XIV of France.

Mon·tes·quieu (mŏn′tĕs kiū′; *Fr.* môN tĕs kyœ′), *n.* (*Charles Louis de Secondat, Baron de la Brède et de Montesquieu*) 1689–1755, French philosophical writer on government and history.

Montenegro, 1871-1914

---

b., blend of, blended; c., cognate with; d., dialect, dialectal; der., derived from; f., formed from; g., going back to; m., modification of; r., replacing; s., stem of; t., taken from; ?, perhaps. See the full key on inside cover.

Mon·tes·so·ri (mŏn/tə sōr/ĭ; *It.* mŏn/tĕs sô/rē), *n.* **Maria**, born 1870, Italian educator.

Montessori method, a system for training and instructing young children, of which the fundamental aim is self-education by the children themselves, accompanied by special emphasis on the training of the senses. Also, **Montessori system.**

Mon·te·vi·de·o (mŏn/tə vĭ dā/ō, mŏn/tə vĭd/Ĭ ō′; *Sp.* mōn/tĕ vē dĕ/ō), *n.* a seaport in and the capital of Uruguay. 708,233 (est. 1943).

Mon·te·zu·ma II (mŏn/tə zōō/mə), c1477–1520, Aztec emperor of Mexico, 1503–20, conquered by Cortez and killed in a revolt by his own subjects.

Mont·fort (mŏnt/fərt; *Fr.* môn fôr′), *n.* **1. Simon de** (sē môn′ də), c1160–1218, French crusader. **2.** (*Earl of Leicester*) his son, **Simon de,** c1208–65, British soldier and statesman.

Mont·gol·fi·er (mŏnt gŏl/fĬ ər; *Fr.* môn gôl fyā′), *n.* **1. Jacques Étienne** (zhäk ĕ tyĕn′), 1745–99, French inventor. **2.** his brother, **Joseph Michel** (zhō zĕf′ mē shĕl′), 1740–1810, French inventor. The Montgolfier brothers invented the balloon and made the first successful flight in 1783. **3.** (*l.c.*) a balloon raised by heated air from a fire in the lower part.

Mont·gom·er·y (mŏnt gŭm/ər ĭ), *n.* **1. Sir Bernard Law,** born 1887, British general. **2. Richard,** 1736–75, American Revolutionary general. **3.** the capital of Alabama, in the central part, on the Alabama river. 106,525 (1950).

Mont·gom·er·y·shire (mŏnt gŭm/ər ĭ shĭr′, -shər), *n.* a county in central Wales. 46,000 pop. (est. 1946); 797 sq. mi. *Co. seat:* Montgomery. Also, **Montgomery.**

month (mŭnth), *n.* **1.** approximately one twelfth of a tropical or solar year (**solar month**). **2.** any of the twelve parts (January, February, etc.) into which the calendar year is divided (**calendar month**). **3.** the time from any day of one calendar month to the corresponding day of the next. **4.** a period of four weeks or 30 days. **5.** the period (**lunar month**) of a complete revolution of the moon with regard to some point, usually (**synodic month**) the interval from one new moon to the next, equivalent to 29 days, 12 hours, 44 minutes, and 2.7 seconds. [ME *mon(e)th,* OE *mōnath,* c. G *mond* MOON]

month·ly (mŭnth/lĭ), *adj., n., pl.* **-lies,** *adv.* —*adj.* **1.** pertaining to a month, or to each month. **2.** done, happening, appearing, etc., once a month, or every month. **3.** continuing or lasting for a month. —*n.* **4.** a periodical published once a month. **5.** (*pl.*) menses. —*adv.* **6.** once a month; by the month.

month's mind, *Rom. Cath. Ch.* the remembrance of a deceased person, by a requiem mass, a month after death.

Mon·ti·cel·lo (mŏn/tə sĕl/ō), *n.* the home of Thomas Jefferson, in central Virginia, near Charlottesville.

mon·ti·cule (mŏn/tĬ kūl′), *n.* **1.** a small mountain, hill, or mound. **2.** a subordinate volcano cone. [t. F, t. LL: m.s. *monticulus,* dim. of L *mons* MOUNT²]

Mont·mar·tre (môn mär′tr), *n.* a hilly section in the N part of Paris, France: artists' center; famous cafes.

Mont·mo·ren·cy (mŏnt/mə rĕn/sĭ; *Fr.* môn mô ränsē′), *n.* **Anne** (än), **Duc de,** 1493–1567, constable of France and French marshal.

Mont·pel·ier (mŏnt pēl/yər), *n.* the capital of Vermont, in the central part. 8599 (1950).

Mont·pel·lier (môn pĕ lyĕ′), *n.* a city in S France, near the Mediterranean. 93,102 (1946).

Mont·re·al (mŏnt/rĬ ôl′, mŭnt/-), *n.* a seaport in SE Canada, on an island in the St. Lawrence, in Quebec province. 903,007; with suburbs, 1,139,921 (1941).

Mon·treuil (môn trœ′y), *n.* a city in N France, near Paris. 69,838 (1946).

Mont·rose (mŏn trōz′), *n.* **James Graham, Marquis of,** 1612–50, Scottish supporter of Charles I.

Mont-Saint-Mi·chel (môn săn mē shĕl′), *n.* a rocky islet near the coast in NW France, in an inlet of the Gulf of St. Malo: famous abbey and fortress.

Mont·ser·rat (mŏnt/sə rät′), *n.* **1.** an island in the British West Indies: a presidency in the Leeward Islands colony. 12,895 pop. (est. 1942); 32½ sq. mi. *Cap.:* Plymouth. **2.** a mountain (4058 ft.) in NE Spain, NW of Barcelona: the site of **Monserrat Monastery.**

mon·u·ment (mŏn/yə mənt), *n.* **1.** something erected in memory of a person, event, etc., as a pillar, statue, or the like. **2.** a tomb. **3.** any building, megalith, etc., surviving from a past age, and regarded as of historical or archaeological importance. **4.** any work, writing, or the like by a person, regarded as a memorial of him after his death. **5.** any enduring evidence or notable example of something. **6.** an object, as a stone shaft, set in the ground to mark the boundaries of real property. **7.** *Obs.* a statue. [ME, t. L: s. *monumentum*]

mon·u·men·tal (mŏn/yə mĕn/təl), *adj.* **1.** resembling a monument; massive or imposing. **2.** *Fine arts.* of any size larger than that of life. **3.** historically prominent: *a monumental event.* **4.** *Colloq.* conspicuously great or gross: *monumental stupidity.* **5.** of or pertaining to a monument or monuments. **6.** serving as a monument. —**mon/u·men/tal·ly,** *adv.*

mon·u·men·tal·ize (mŏn/yə mĕn/tə līz′), *v.t.,* **-ized, -izing.** to establish an enduring memorial or record of.

mon·y (mŏn/ĭ), *adj., n.* *Scot. and N. Eng.* many.

-mony, a noun suffix indicating result or condition, as in *parsimony;* but sometimes having the same function as *-ment.* [t. L: m.s. *-mōnia, -mōnium*]

Mon·za (mōn/tsä), *n.* a city in N Italy, in Lombardy. 69,253 (est. 1946).

mon·zo·nite (mŏn/zə nīt′), *n.* any of a group of granular igneous rocks intermediate in composition between syenite and diorite. [t. G: m. *monzonit,* f. *Monzoni* (name of mountain in Tyrol) + *-it* -ITE¹] —**mon·zo·nit·ic** (mŏn/zə nĬt/Ĭk), *adj.*

moo (mōō), *v.,* **mooed, mooing,** *n., pl.* **moos.** —*v.i.* **1.** to utter the characteristic cry of a cow; low. —*n.* **2.** a mooing sound. [imit.]

mooch (mōōch), *Slang.* —*v.i.* **1.** to skulk or sneak. **2.** to hang or rove about. —*v.t.* **3.** to steal. **4.** to get without paying or at another's expense: *to mooch a cigarette.* Also, **mouch.** —**mooch/er,** *n.*

mood¹ (mōōd), *n.* **1.** frame of mind, or state of feeling, as at a particular time. **2.** (*pl.*) fits of uncertainty, gloominess, or sullenness. [ME; OE *mōd* mind, spirit, mood, c. G *mut* spirit, courage] —**Syn. 1.** temper, disposition, inclination.

mood² (mōōd), *n.* **1.** *Gram.* mode. **2.** *Logic.* any of the various forms of valid syllogisms, depending on the quantity and quality of their constituent propositions. [special use of MOOD¹ by contam. with MODE¹]

mood·y (mōō/dĭ), *adj.,* **moodier, moodiest. 1.** given to gloomy or sullen moods. **2.** proceeding from or showing such a mood: *a moody silence.* **3.** gloomy; sullen; ill-humored. —**mood/i·ly,** *adv.* —**mood/i·ness,** *n.*

Mood·y (mōō/dĭ), *n.* **1. Dwight Lyman,** 1837–99, U.S. evangelist. **2. William Vaughn,** 1869–1910, U.S. poet and dramatist.

moon (mōōn), *n.* **1.** the body which revolves around the earth monthly at a mean distance of 238,857 miles, accompanying the earth in its annual revolution about the sun. It is about 2160 miles in diameter. **2.** this heavenly body during a particular lunar month, or during a certain period of time, or at a certain point of time, regarded as a distinct object or entity. **a.** new moon, the moon when in conjunction with the sun and hence invisible, or the phase so represented, or the moon soon afterward when visible as a slender crescent. **b.** half-moon, the moon when half its disk is illuminated, occurring when at either quadrature, or quarter. **c.** full moon, the moon when the whole of its disk is illuminated, occurring when in opposition to the sun, or the phase so represented. **d.** old moon, the waning moon. **e.** waxing moon, the moon at any time before it is full, so called because its illuminated area is increasing. **f.** waning moon, the moon at any time after it has been full, so called because its illuminated area is decreasing. **3.** a lunar month, or, in general, a month. **4.** any planetary satellite. **5.** something shaped like an orb or a crescent. —*v.i.* **6.** *Colloq.* to wander about or gaze idly or listlessly. —*v.t.* **7.** to spend (time) idly. [ME *mone,* OE *mōna,* c. OHG *māno;* akin to Gk. *mḗne* moon, *mḗn* month, L *mensis* month]

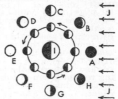

Phases of the moon
The figures on the inner circle show the moon in its orbit round the earth; those on the outer circle represent the moon's corresponding phases as seen from the earth. A, New moon (invisible); B, Waxing crescent; C, First quarter (half-moon); D, Gibbous; E, Full moon; F, Gibbous; G, Last quarter (half-moon); H, Waning crescent; I, Earth; J, Sun's rays

moon·beam (mōōn/bēm′), *n.* a ray of moonlight.

moon·blind (mōōn/blīnd′), *adj.* (of horses) afflicted with moon blindness. Also, **moon-eyed** (mōōn/īd′).

moon blindness, *Vet. Sci.* a specific, probably noninfectious disease of horses, of unknown cause, in which the eyes suffer from recurring attacks of inflammation, and which eventually results in opacity and blindness.

moon·calf (mōōn/kăf′, -käf′), *n.* a congenital imbecile. [lit., a person influenced by the moon]

mooned (mōōnd), *adj.* **1.** ornamented with moons or crescents. **2.** shaped like a moon or crescent.

Moo·ney (mōō/nĭ), *n.* **Thomas J. Zechariah** (zĕk/ə rī/ə), 1885–1942, U.S. labor leader.

moon·eye (mōōn/ī′), *n.* *Vet. Sci.* an eye of a horse affected with moon blindness.

moon·fish (mōōn/fĭsh′), *n., pl.* **-fishes,** (*esp. collectively*) **-fish. 1.** any of certain fishes having a deep, sharply compressed, silvery body, as of the carangoid genera *Selene* and *Vomer,* as *S. vomer* and *V. setipinnis* of the warmer coastal waters of North and South America. **2.** the opah. **3.** a minnow, *Platypoecilus maculatus.*

moon·flow·er (mōōn/flou/ər), *n.* a nightblooming convolvulaceous plant, *Calonyction aculeatum,* with fragrant white flowers.

moon·light (mōōn/līt′), *n.* **1.** the light of the moon. —*adj.* **2.** pertaining to moonlight. **3.** illuminated by moonlight. **4.** occurring by moonlight, or by night.

Moonlight Sonata, the title given to Beethoven's piano sonata, Op. 27 No. 2 (1801) after his death.

moon·lit (mōōn/lĭt′), *adj.* lighted by the moon.

moon·rise (mōōn/rīz′), *n.* **1.** the rising of the moon above the horizon. **2.** the time at which the moon rises above the horizon.

moon·seed (mōōn/sēd′), *n.* any of the climbing herbs constituting the genus *Menispermum* (family Meni-

spermaceae) with greenish-white flowers, so called from the crescent-shaped seeds.

moon·set (mōōn′sĕt′), *n.* **1.** the setting of the moon below the horizon. **2.** the time at which the moon disappears below the horizon.

moon·shine (mōōn′shīn′), *n.* **1.** the light of the moon. **2.** empty or foolish talk, ideas, etc.; nonsense. **3.** *U.S. Colloq.* smuggled or illicitly distilled liquor.

moon·shin·er (mōōn′shī′nər), *n.* *U.S. Colloq.* **1.** an illicit distiller. **2.** one who pursues an illegal trade at night.

moon·shin·y (mōōn′shī′nĭ), *adj.* **1.** like moonlight. **2.** moonlit. **3.** without sense; fictitious; visionary.

moon·stone (mōōn′stōn′), *n.* a white translucent variety of feldspar with a bluish pearly luster, used as a gem.

moon-struck (mōōn′strŭk′), *adj.* injuriously affected in mind (or otherwise), supposedly by the influence of the moon; dazed; crazed. Also, **moon-strick·en** (mōōn′strĭk′ən).

moon·wort (mōōn′wûrt′), *n.* **1.** any fern of the genus *Botrychium,* esp. *B. Lunaria* whose fronds have crescent-shaped pinnae. **2.** *Bot.* honesty (def. 5).

moon·y (mōō′nĭ), *adj.*, **moonier, mooniest. 1.** pertaining to or characteristic of the moon. **2.** resembling the moon in shape. **3.** moonlit. **4.** resembling moonlight. **5.** *Colloq.* mooning, listless, or silly.

moor[1] (mŏŏr), *n.* *Brit.* a tract of open, peaty, waste land, often overgrown with heath, common in high latitudes and altitudes where drainage is poor; a heath. **2.** a tract of land preserved for shooting game. [ME *more,* OE *mōr,* c. G *moor* marsh]

moor[2] (mŏŏr), *v.t.* **1.** to secure (a ship, etc.) in a particular place, as by cables and anchors (esp. two or more) or by lines. **2.** to secure, or fix firmly. —*v.i.* **3.** to moor a ship, etc. **4.** to take up a position or be made secure by means of anchors or the like, as a ship. [late ME *more,* OE (unrecorded, but cf. OE *mǣrels* mooring rope), c. MD *māren* moor, tie up]

Moor (mŏŏr), *n.* **1.** a Mohammedan of the mixed Berber and Arab race inhabiting NW Africa. **2.** one belonging to that group of this race which in the 8th century invaded and conquered Spain. [ME *More,* t. OF, var. of *Maure,* t. L: m. *Maurus,* t. Gk.: m. *Maûros*]

moor·age (mŏŏr′ĭj), *n.* **1.** act of mooring. **2.** state of being moored. **3.** a place for mooring. **4.** a charge or payment for the use of moorings.

moor cock, *Brit.* the male moorfowl.

Moore (mŏŏr, mōr), *n.* **1. George,** 1852–1933, Irish novelist, critic, and dramatist. **2. Sir John,** 1761–1809, British general. **3. John Bassett,** 1860–1947, U.S. jurist. **4. Thomas,** 1779–1852, Irish poet.

moor·fowl (mŏŏr′foul′), *n.* *Brit.* the red grouse, *Lagopus scoticus.* Also, **moorbird.**

moor hen, 1. *Brit.* the female moorfowl. **2.** a common European gallinule, *Gallinula chloropus.*

moor·ing (mŏŏr′ĭng), *n.* **1.** the act of one who or that which moors. **2.** (*usually pl.*) something by which a ship or the like is moored, as a cable, line, etc. **3.** (*pl.*) the place where a vessel is or may be moored.

mooring mast, the mast or tower to which a dirigible is moored. Also, **mooring tower.**

Moor·ish (mŏŏr′ĭsh), *adj.* **1.** of or pertaining to the Moors. **2.** in the style of the Moors, as architecture, decoration, etc.

moor·land (mŏŏr′lănd′), *n.* *Brit.* land consisting of a moor.

moor·wort (mŏŏr′wûrt′), *n.* a low, ericaceous shrub, *Andromeda Polifolia,* with white flowers, native to swamplands in the Northern Hemisphere.

moose (mōōs), *n., pl.* **moose. 1.** a large animal, *Alces americanus,* of the deer family, inhabiting Canada and the northern U.S., the male of which has enormous palmate antlers, long legs, and a large, unshapely head. **2.** a similar species, *A. gigas,* found in Alaska. **3.** the European elk, *A. machlis.* [t. N Amer. Ind.; cognate forms in Algonquian, Narragansett, Delaware, etc., meaning "he strips or eats off"]

Moose·head Lake (mōōs′hĕd′), a lake in central Maine. 36 mi. long; 120 sq. mi.

Moose Jaw, a city in SW Canada, in Saskatchewan. 20,753 (1941).

moot (mōōt), *adj.* **1.** subject to argument or discussion; debatable; doubtful: *a moot point.* —*v.t.* **2.** to argue (a case, etc.), esp. in a mock court. **3.** to bring forward (any point, subject, project, etc.) for discussion. —*n.* **4.** an early English assembly of the people, exercising political, administrative, and judicial powers. **5.** an argument or discussion, esp. of a hypothetical legal case. [ME *mote,* OE *mōt, gemōt* meeting, assembly, c. Icel. *mōt* D *gemoet*] —**moot′er,** *n.*

moot court, a mock court for the conduct of hypothetical legal cases, as for practice for students of law.

moot hall, (in an English village) a historic building where a moot (def. 4) was once held.

mop (mŏp), *n., v.,* **mopped, mopping.** —*n.* **1.** a bundle of coarse yarn, a piece of cloth, or the like, fastened at the end of a stick or handle, used for washing floors, dishes, etc. **2.** a thick mass, as of hair. —*v.t.* **3.** to rub, wipe, clean, or remove with a mop. **4.** to wipe: *to mop the face with a handkerchief.* **5.** *Mil.* to clear (ground, trenches, towns, etc.) of scattered or remaining enemy

combatants, after attacking forces have gone beyond the place (fol. by *up*). [earlier *map,* ME *mappe.* Cf. L *mappa* napkin, cloth, ? in ML mop]

mop-board (mŏp′bōrd′), *n.* a baseboard (def. 1).

mope (mōp), *v.,* **moped, moping,** *n.* —*v.i.* **1.** to be sunk in listless apathy or dull dejection. —*v.t.* **2.** to make listless and dispirited. —*n.* **3.** a person who mopes or is given to moping. **4.** (*pl.*) low spirits. [var. of obs. *mop* make a wry face. Cf. D *moppen* pout] —**mop′er,** *n.* —**mop′ing·ly,** *adv.*

mop·ish (mō′pĭsh), *adj.* given to moping; listless and dejected. —**mop·ish·ly,** *adv.* —**mop′ish·ness.** *n.*

mop·pet (mŏp′ĭt), *n.* **1.** *Obs. or Archaic.* a child or a young girl. **2.** *Colloq.* a doll. [f. (obs.) *mop* baby, rag doll + -ET]

mo·quette (mō·kĕt′), *n.* a kind of carpet with a thick velvety pile. [t. F; orig. uncert.]

mor., morocco.

mo·ra (mōr′ə), *n., pl.* **morae** (mōr′ē), **moras.** *Pros.* the unit of time, equivalent to the ordinary or normal short sound or syllable. [t. L: delay]

mo·ra·ceous (mō·rā′shəs), *adj.* belonging to the *Moraceae,* or mulberry family of plants, which includes the mulberry, breadfruit, fig, hemp, hop, Osage orange, etc. [f. s. L *mōrus* mulberry tree + -ACEOUS]

Mo·ra·da·bad (mō′rä·də·bäd′, mō′rä·dä·bäd′), *n.* a city in N India, in the United Provinces. 142,414 (1941).

mo·raine (mə·rān′), *n.* **1.** a ridge, mound, or irregular mass of boulders, gravel, sand, and clay transported in or on a glacier. **2.** a deposit of such material left on the ground by a glacier. [t. d. F, var. of *morêna* heap of earth, c. Pr. *mourreno* scree, der. *mourre* projection of rock, of pre-L orig.] —**mo·rain′al, mo·rain′ic,** *adj.*

mor·al (môr′əl, mŏr′əl), *adj.* **1.** pertaining to or concerned with right conduct or the distinction between right or wrong: *moral considerations.* **2.** concerned with the principles or rules of right conduct; ethical: *moral philosophy.* **3.** expressing or conveying truths or counsel as to right conduct, as a speaker, a literary work, etc.; moralizing. **4.** founded on the fundamental principles of right conduct rather than on enactment or custom: *moral rights.* **5.** capable of conforming to the rules of right conduct. **6.** conforming to the rules of right conduct (opposed to *immoral*): *a moral man.* **7.** sexually virtuous. **8.** being virtually or practically such through the effect on the mind or feelings or on results generally: *a moral victory; moral support.* **9.** depending upon what is observed of human nature and actions or of things generally, rather than upon demonstration: *moral evidence.* **10.** resting upon convincing grounds of probability: *a moral certainty.* —*n.* **11.** the moral teaching or practical lesson contained in a fable, tale, experience, etc. **12.** the embodiment or type of something. **13** (*pl.*) principles or habits with respect to right or wrong conduct; ethics. [ME, t. L: s. *mōrālis* relating to manners, customs]

—**Syn. 4.** righteous, just. **6.** virtuous, good. **13.** MORALS, ETHICS refer to rules and standards of conduct and practice. MORALS refers to generally accepted customs of conduct and right living in a society, and to the individual's practice in relation to these: *the morals of our civilization.* ETHICS now implies high standards of honest and honorable dealing, of methods used, and of quality of product, esp. in the professions or in business: *ethics of the medical profession.*

mo·rale (mə·răl′, -räl′), *n.* moral or mental condition with respect to cheerfulness, confidence, zeal, etc.: *the morale of troops.* [t. F, fem. of *moral,* adj. See MORAL]

moral hazard, *Insurance.* an insurance company risk as to the assured's trustworthiness and honesty.

mor·al·ism (môr′ə·lĭz′əm, mŏr′-), *n.* **1.** the habit of moralizing. **2.** a moral maxim. **3.** the practice of morality, as distinct from religion.

mor·al·ist (môr′ə·lĭst, mŏr′-), *n.* **1.** one who teaches or inculcates morality. **2.** one who practices morality. —**mor·al·is′tic,** *adj.*

mo·ral·i·ty (mə·răl′ə·tĭ, mō·răl′-), *n., pl.* **-ties. 1.** conformity to the rules of right conduct; moral or virtuous conduct. **2.** sexual virtue. **3.** moral quality or character. **4.** the doctrine or system of morals; ethics; duties. **5.** moral instruction; a moral lesson or precept; a moralizing discourse or utterance. **6.** morality play. —**Syn. 1.** See **goodness.**

morality play, a form of allegorical drama in vogue from the 14th to the 16th centuries, employing personifications of virtues and vices.

mor·al·ize (môr′ə·līz′, mŏr′-), *v.,* **-ized, -izing.** —*v.i.* **1.** to make moral reflections. —*v.t.* **2.** to explain in a moral sense, or draw a moral from. **3.** to improve the morals of. —**mor′al·i·za′tion,** *n.* —**mor′al·iz′er,** *n.* —**mor′al·iz′ing·ly,** *adv.*

mor·al·ly (môr′ə·lĭ, mŏr′-), *adv.* **1.** in a moral manner. **2.** from a moral point of view. **3.** virtuously. **4.** virtually; practically.

moral philosophy, ethics.

mo·rass (mə·răs′, mō-), *n.* **1.** a tract of low, soft, wet ground. **2.** a marsh or bog. **3.** marshy ground. [t. D: m. *moeras,* in MD *maras,* t. OF: m. *marais,* of Gmc. orig. See MARSH]

mor·a·to·ri·um (môr′ə·tōr′ĭ·əm, mŏr′-), *n., pl.* **-toria** (-tōr′ĭ·ə), **-toriums. 1.** a legal authorization to delay payment of money due, as in an emergency. **2.** the period during which such authorization is in effect. [t. NL, prop. neut. of LL *morātōrius* MORATORY]

---

mor·a·to·ry (môr′ə tōr′ĭ, môr′-), *adj.* authorizing delay of payment: *a moratory law.* [t. LL: m.s. *morātōrius* delaying, der. L *morārī* delay]

Mo·ra·va (mō′rä vä), *n.* **1.** German, **March.** a river flowing from N Czechoslovakia S to the Danube. ab. 210 mi. **2.** a river in E Yugoslavia, flowing N to the Danube. ab. 100 mi.

Mo·ra·vi·a (mō rā′vĭ ə), *n.* a province in central Czechoslovakia: a part of Bohemia-Moravia, 1939–45. Incl. Czech-Silesia, 3,634,300 pop. (est. 1936); 10,351 sq. mi. *Cap.*: Brno. Czech, **Morava.** German, **Mähren.**

Mo·ra·vi·an (mō rā′vĭ ən), *adj.* **1.** pertaining to Moravia or its inhabitants. **2.** of or pertaining to the religious body of Moravians. —*n.* **3.** a native or inhabitant of Moravia. **4.** a member of a Christian denomination, Unity of Brethren (also, **Moravian Brethren**), which traces its origin to John Huss. **5.** a dialect of Czech, spoken in Moravia.

Moravian Gate, a corridor between the Sudeten Mountains and the Tatra range of the Carpathians, leading from S Poland into Moravia, Czechoslovakia.

Mo·rav·ská Os·tra·va (mô′räf skä ôs′trä vä), a city in Czechoslovakia, in N Moravia. 125,307 (1930). German, **Mährisch-Ostrau.**

mo·ray (môr′ā, mō rā′), *n.*, *pl.* **-rays.** any of numerous eels of the family *Muraenidae*, esp. those of the genus *Muraena*, as *M. helena*, common in the Mediterranean and valued as a food fish, or *Gymnothorax moringa*, common in West Indian waters (**spotted moray**).

Mor·ay (mŭr′ĭ), *n.* a county in NE Scotland, on **Moray Firth,** an arm of the North Sea. 43,800 pop.; 476 sq. mi. *Co. seat*: Elgin. Formerly, **Elgin.**

mor·bid (môr′bĭd), *adj.* **1.** suggesting an unhealthy mental state; unwholesomely gloomy, sensitive, extreme, etc. **2.** affected by, proceeding from, or characteristic of disease. **3.** pertaining to diseased parts: *morbid anatomy.* [t. L: s. *morbidus* sickly] —**mor′bid·ly,** *adv.* —**mor′bid·ness,** *n.*

mor·bid·i·ty (môr bĭd′ə tĭ), *n.* **1.** morbid state or quality. **2.** the proportion of sickness in a locality.

mor·bif·ic (môr bĭf′ĭk), *adj.* causing disease. Also, **mor·bif′i·cal.** [t. NL: s. *morbificus*, der. L *morbus* disease] —**mor·bif′i·cal·ly,** *adv.*

mor·bil·li (môr bĭl′ī), *n.pl.* measles. [t. ML, pl. of *morbillus*, dim. of L *morbus* disease]

mor·ceau (môr sō′), *n.*, *pl.* **-ceaux** (sō′). *French.* **1.** morsel. **2.** an excerpt or passage of poetry or music.

mor·da·cious (môr dā′shəs), *adj.* biting; given to biting. [f. *mordaci*(ty) (t. L: m.s. *mordācitas* power of biting) + -ous] —**mor·da′cious·ly,** *adv.* **mor·dac·i·ty** (môr dăs′ə tĭ), *n.*

mor·dan·cy (môr′dən sĭ), *n.* mordant quality.

mor·dant (môr′dənt), *adj.* **1.** caustic or sarcastic, as wit, a speaker, etc. **2.** having the property of fixing colors, as in dyeing. —*n.* **3.** a substance used in dyeing to fix the coloring matter, esp. a metallic compound, as an oxide or hydroxide, which combines with the organic dye and forms an insoluble colored compound or lake in the fiber. **4.** an acid or other corrosive substance used in etching to eat out the lines, etc. —*v.t.* **5.** to impregnate or treat with a mordant. [ME, t. OF, ppr. of *mordre*, g. L *mordēre* bite] —**mor′dant·ly,** *adv.*

Mor·de·cai (môr′dĭ kī′, môr′dĭ kā′ī), *n.* (in the book of Esther) a cousin of Esther, who delivered Esther and the Jews from Haman. Cf. **Purim.**

mor·dent (môr′dənt), *n.* *Music.* **1.** a melodic embellishment consisting of a rapid alternation of a principal tone with a supplementary tone a half-step below it, called *single* or *short* when the supplementary tone occurs but once, and *double* or *long* when this occurs twice or oftener. **2.** See **inverted mordent.** [t. G, t. It.: m. *mordente*, prop. ppr. of *mordere*, g. L *mordēre* bite]

Written   Played
A
B

Mordents
A. Single; B. Double

Mor·dred (môr′drĕd), *n.* Modred.

more (mōr), *adj.*, *superl.* **most,** *n.*, *adv.* —*adj.* **1.** in greater quantity, amount, measure, degree, or number (as the comparative of *much* and *many*, with the superlative *most*): *more money.* **2.** additional or further: *do not lose any more time.* —*n.* **3.** an additional quantity, amount, or number. **4.** a greater quantity, amount, or degree. **5.** something of greater importance. **6.** (*construed as pl.*) a greater number of a class specified, or the greater number of persons. —*adv.* **7.** in or to a greater extent or degree: *more rapid.* **8.** in addition; further; longer; again. [ME; OE *māra*, c. OS and OHG *mēro*. See MOST]

More (mōr), *n.* **1. Hannah,** 1745–1833, British writer on religious subjects. **2. Paul Elmer,** 1864–1937, U.S. essayist, critic, and editor. **3. Sir Thomas,** 1478–1535, British statesman and author: canonized in 1935.

Mo·re·a (mō rē′ə), *n.* modern name sometimes used to designate the Peloponnesus.

Mo·reau (mô rō′), *n.* **Jean Victor** (zhäN vēk tôr′), 1763–1813, French general.

mo·reen (mə rēn′), *n.* a heavy fabric of wool, or wool and cotton, commonly watered, used for curtains, petticoats, etc. [? akin to MOIRE]

mo·rel (mə rĕl′), *n.* an edible mushroom of the genus *Morchella*, an ascomycetous group in which the fruit body has the aspect of a stalked sponge. [ME *morele*, t. OF, der. L *mōrum* a mulberry]

mo·rel·lo (mə rĕl′ō), *n.*, *pl.* **-los.** a sour cherry, *Prunus Cerasus*, var. *Austera*, with a dark-colored skin and juice. [t. It.: dark-colored (der. L *maurus* moor), ? b. with It. *amarello*, dim. of *amaro* bitter (g. L *amārus*)]

more·o·ver (mōr ō′vər), *adv.* beyond what has been said; further; besides. —**Syn.** See **besides.**

mo·res (mōr′ēz), *n.pl.* *Sociol.* folkways of central importance accepted without question and embodying the fundamental moral views of a group. [t. L: customs]

Mo·resque (mə rĕsk′), *adj.* Moorish. [t. F, t. It.: m. *moresco*, der. *Moro* MOOR]

Mor·gain le Fay (môr′gän lə fā′, môr′gən), Morgan le Fay.

Mor·gan (môr′gən), *n.* one of a breed of light carriage and saddle horses descended from the Morgan horse (see etymology). [named after their sire, a stallion owned by Justin *Morgan* (1747–1798), a New England teacher]

Mor·gan (môr′gən), *n.* **1. Daniel,** 1736–1802, American Revolutionary general. **2. Sir Henry,** c1635–1688, British buccaneer. **3. John Hunt,** 1826–64, Confederate general in the U.S. Civil War. **4. John Pierpont,** 1837–1913, U.S. financier and philanthropist. **5.** his son, **John Pierpont,** 1867–1943, U.S. financier. **6. Thomas Hunt,** 1866–1945, U.S. zoölogist.

mor·ga·nat·ic (môr′gə năt′ĭk), *adj.* designating or pertaining to a form of marriage in which a man of high rank takes to wife a woman of lower station with the stipulation that neither she nor the issue (if any) shall have any claim to his rank or property. Also, *Rare*, **mor·gan·ic** (môr găn′ĭk). [t. NL: s. *morganaticus*, from ML (*mātrimōnium ad*) *morganāticam* (marriage with) morning gift (in lieu of a share in the husband's possessions), der. OHG *morgan* morning. The morning gift was a gift from a husband to his wife the morning after their marriage] —**mor′ga·nat′i·cal·ly,** *adv.*

mor·gan·ite (môr′gə nīt′), *n.* rose beryl. [named after J. P. MORGAN. See -ITE[1]]

Mor·gan le Fay (môr′gən lə fā′), *Celtic and Arthurian Legend.* the fairy sister of King Arthur. Also, **Morgain le Fay, Morgana.**

Mor·gan·town (môr′gən toun′), *n.* a city in N West Virginia. 25,525 (1950).

mor·gen (môr′gən), *n.* **1.** a unit of land measure equal to about two acres, formerly in use in Holland and the Dutch colonies and still used in South Africa. **2.** a unit equal to about two thirds of an acre, formerly used in Prussia, Norway, and Denmark. [t. D and G]

Mor·gen·thau (môr′gən thô′), *n.* **Henry, Jr.,** born 1891, U.S. public official: secretary of the treasury, 1934–45.

morgue (môrg), *n.* **1.** a place in which the bodies of persons found dead are exposed for identification. **2.** *Journ.* **a.** the reference library of clippings, mats, books, etc., kept by a newspaper, etc. **b.** the room for it. [t. F; orig. name of building in Paris so used]

mor·i·bund (môr′ə bŭnd′, môr′-), *adj.* **1.** in a dying state. **2.** on the verge of extinction or termination: *a moribund political party.* [t. L: s. *moribundus*] —**mor′i·bun′di·ty,** *n.* —**mor′i·bund′ly,** *adv.*

mo·ri·on[1] (mōr′ĭ on′), *n.* an open helmet with a tall comb and a curved brim merging into a peak at front and back. [t. F, t. Sp.: m. *morrión*, der. *morra* crown of the head]

mo·ri·on[2] (môr′ĭ on′), *n.* a variety of smoky quartz of a dark-brown or nearly black color. [t. L, misreading (in early editions of Pliny's Nat. Hist.) of *mormorion*]

Spanish morion, 16th century

Mo·ris·co (mə rĭs′kō), *adj.*, *n.*, *pl.* **-cos, -coes.** —*adj.* **1.** Moorish. —*n.* **2.** a Moor. **3.** one of the Moors of Spain. [t. Sp., der. *Moro* MOOR]

mo·ri·tu·ri te sa·lu·ta·mus (môr′ĭ tyŏor′ī tē săl′ū tā′məs), *Latin.* we about to die salute thee: said by Roman gladiators as they marched by the Emperor.

Mor·ley (môr′lĭ), *n.* **1. Christopher Darlington,** born 1890, U.S. writer. **2. John,** (*Viscount Morley of Blackburn*) 1838–1923, British writer and statesman.

Mor·mon (môr′mən), *n.* **1.** a member of a religious body in the U.S., founded in 1830 by Joseph Smith and calling itself "The Church of Jesus Christ of Latter-day Saints." **2. The Book of Mormon,** a sacred book of the Mormon Church, supposed to be an abridgment by a prophet (**Mormon**) of a record of certain ancient peoples in America, written on golden plates, and discovered and translated (1827–30) by Joseph Smith. —*adj.* **3.** of or pertaining to the Mormons or their religious system. —**Mor′mon·ism,** *n.*

morn (môrn), *n. Poetic.* morning. [ME *morn(e),* OE *morne* (dat. of *morgen* morning), c. D and G *morgen*]

Mor·nay (môr nāʹ), *n.* **Philippe de** (fēlēpʹ də), (*Seigneur du Plessis-Marly*) 1549–1623, French Protestant leader and diplomat.

morn·ing (môrʹnĭng), *n.* **1.** the beginning of day; the dawn. **2.** the first part or period of the day, extending from dawn, or from midnight, to noon. **3.** the first or early period of anything. **4.** (*cap.*) the goddess Eos or Aurora. —*adj.* **5.** of or pertaining to morning: *the morning hours.* **6.** occurring, appearing, coming, used, etc., in the morning. [ME. See MORN, -ING[1], modeled on EVENING] —**Syn. 1.** morn, daybreak, sunrise.

morn·ing-glo·ry (môrʹnĭng glôrʹĭ), *n., pl.* **-ries.** any of various convolvulaceous plants, esp. of the genera *Ipomoea* and *Convolvulus,* as *I. purpurea,* a twining plant with cordate leaves and funnel-shaped flowers of various colors, common in cultivation.

morning sickness, nausea occurring in the early part of the day, as a characteristic symptom in the first months of pregnancy.

morning star, 1. a bright planet, seen in the east before sunrise. **2.** an annual plant, *Mentzelia Lindley,* with bright-yellow flowers, native to California.

Mo·ro (môrʹō), *n., pl.* **-ros. 1.** a member of any of various tribes of Mohammedan Malays in the southern Philippine Islands. **2.** Magindanao. [t. Sp.: a Moor]

Mo·roc·co (mə rŏkʹō), *n.* **1.** a sultanate in NW Africa (*traditional capitals:* Fez and Marrakech), divided into three administrative zones: **French Zone,** 6,296,136 pop. (1936); 153,910 sq. mi. (*cap.:* Rabat); **Spanish Zone,** 991,954 pop. (1940); 7589 sq. mi. (*cap.:* Tetuán); **Tangier Zone** (internationalized), 102,306 pop. (1941); 230 sq. mi. (*cap.:* Tangier). **2.** Marrakech. —**Mo·roc·can** (mə rŏkʹən), *adj., n.*

mo·roc·co (mə rŏkʹō), *n.* **1.** a fine leather made from goatskins tanned with sumac, orig. in Morocco. **2.** any leather made in imitation of this. Also, **morocco leather.**

mo·ron (môrʹŏn), *n.* a person of arrested intelligence whose mentality is judged incapable of developing beyond that of a normal child of 8 to 12 years of age. [t. Gk., neut. of *mōrós* dull, foolish] —**mo·ron·ic** (mə rŏnʹĭk), *adj.* —**mo·ron·ism, mo·ron·i·ty** (mə rŏnʹə tĭ), *n.*

mo·rose (mə rōsʹ), *adj.* gloomily or sullenly ill-humored, as a person, mood, etc. [t. L: m.s. *mōrōsus* fretful, morose, particular] —**mo·rose′ly,** *adv.* —**mo·rose′ness,** *n.* —**Ant.** good-natured.

morph-, var. of **morpho-** before vowels.

-morph, a word element meaning "form," as in *isomorph.* [t. Gk.: s. *morphē* form]

mor·pheme (môrʹfēm), *n. Gram.* any of the minimum meaningful elements in a language, not further divisible into smaller meaningful elements, usually recurring in various contexts with relatively constant meaning: either a word, as *girl, world,* or part of a word, as *-ish* or *-ly* in *girlish* and *worldly.* [f. MORPH(O)- + *-eme,* as in *phoneme*]

Mor·phe·us (môrʹfĭ əs, môrʹfūs), *n. Gk. Myth.* a minor deity, son of the god of sleep; the god of dreams. [ME, t. L, t. Gk., der. *morphē* form, in allusion to the forms seen in dreams] —**Mor′phe·an,** *adj.*

-morphic, a word element used as adjective termination corresponding to **-morph,** as in *anthropomorphic.* [f. s. Gk. *morphē* form + -IC]

mor·phine (môrʹfēn), *n.* a bitter crystalline alkaloid, $C_{17}H_{19}NO_3 \cdot H_2O$, the most important narcotic principle of opium, used in medicine (usually in the form of a sulfate or other salt) to dull pain, induce sleep, etc. Also, **mor·phi·a** (môrʹfĭ ə). [t. F, t. G: m. *morphin,* f. *Morph(eus)* MORPHEUS + *-in* -INE[2]]

mor·phin·ism (môrʹfĭ nĭzʹəm), *n. Pathol.* **1.** a morbid condition induced by the habitual use of morphine. **2.** the habit inducing it.

morpho-, initial word element answering to **-morph.**

mor·pho·gen·e·sis (môrʹfə jĕnʹə sĭs), *n. Embryol.* the structural development of an organism or part. —**mor·pho·ge·net·ic** (môrʹfō jə nĕtʹĭk), *adj.*

mor·pho·gen·ic (môrʹfə jĕnʹĭk), *adj. Embryol.* **1.** pertaining to morphogenesis. **2.** differentiation-inducing; form-producing: *morphogenic substances.*

mor·phol·o·gy (môrʹfŏlʹə jĭ), *n.* **1.** that branch of biology which deals with the form and structure of animals and plants, without regard to functions. **2.** the form of an organism considered as a whole. **3.** *Gram.* **a.** the patterns of word formation in a particular language, including inflection, derivation, and composition. **b.** the study and description thereof. See SYNTAX. **4.** *Phys. Geog.* the study of the form of lands. —**mor·pho·log·ic** (môrʹfə lŏjʹĭk), **mor·pho·log·i·cal,** *adj.* —**mor·pho·log′i·cal·ly,** *adv.* —**mor·phol′o·gist,** *n.*

-morphous, a word element used as adjective termination corresponding to **-morph,** as in *amorphous.* [t. Gk.: m. *-morphos,* der. *morphē* form]

Mor·ris (môrʹĭs, mŏrʹ-), *n.* **1. Gouverneur** (gŭvʹərnĭrʹ), 1752–1816, American statesman. **2. Robert,** 1734–1806, American patriot and financier. **3. William,** 1834–96, British poet, artist, and socialist writer.

Morris chair, a kind of large armchair having an adjustable back and loose cushions. [named after William MORRIS]

morris dance, a picturesque dance of English origin, performed by persons in costume, often representing personages of the Robin Hood legend, formerly common in England, esp. in May Day festivities. Also, **mor′ris.** [late ME *moreys daunce* Moorish dance]

Mor·ri·son (môrʹĭ sən, mŏrʹ-), *n.* **Herbert Stanley,** born 1888, British labor leader and statesman.

Morris Plan bank, a private banking organization in the U.S., originally designed primarily to grant small loans to industrial workers.

mor·ro (môrʹrō), *n., pl.* **-ros.** a rounded hill, hillock, or promontory. [Sp.: something round, der. stem *murr-round,* prob. of pre-L orig.]

Morro Castle, an old fort at the entrance to the harbor of Havana, Cuba.

mor·row (môrʹō, mŏrʹ-), *n. Archaic.* **1.** morning. **2.** the day next after this or after some other particular day or night. [ME *morwe,* apocopated var. of *morwen,* OE *morgen* morning. See MORN]

Mors (môrz), *n. Rom. Myth.* a deification of death. [t. L]

Morse (môrs), *n.* **1. Samuel Finley Breese,** 1791–1872, U.S. inventor (of the telegraph). **2.** the Morse code. —*adj.* **3.** noting or pertaining to the Morse code or the system of communications using it. **4.** pertaining to any code resembling the Morse, as the international.

Morse code, a system of dots, dashes, and spaces, or the corresponding sounds or the like, used in telegraphy and signaling to represent the letters of the alphabet, numerals, etc. Also, **Morse alphabet.**

mor·sel (môrʹsəl), *n.* **1.** a bite, mouthful, or small portion of food or the like. **2.** a small piece, quantity, or amount of anything; a scrap; a bit. —*v.t.* **3.** to distribute in or divide into tiny portions. [ME, t. OF, dim. of *mors* a bite, g. L *morsum,* pp. neut. of *mordēre* bite]

mort (môrt), *n. Obs.* death. [ME, t. OF, g. L *mors*]

mor·tal (môrʹtəl), *adj.* **1.** liable or subject to death: *all mortal creatures.* **2.** of or pertaining to man as subject to death; human: *this mortal life.* **3.** belonging to this world. **4.** pertaining to death: *mortal throes.* **5.** involving spiritual death (opposed to *venial*): *a mortal sin.* **6.** causing death; fatal: *a mortal wound.* **7.** to the death: *mortal combat.* **8.** deadly or implacable: *a mortal enemy.* **9.** dire, grievous, or bitter: *in mortal fear.* **10.** *Colloq.* long and wearisome. **11.** *Colloq.* extreme; very great: *in a mortal hurry.* **12.** *Colloq.* possible or conceivable: *of no mortal use.* —*n.* **13.** a being subject to death; a human being. [ME, t. L: s. *mortālis* subject to death] —**mor′tal·ly,** *adv.* —**Syn. 6.** See fatal.

mor·tal·i·ty (môr tălʹə tĭ), *n., pl.* **-ties. 1.** the condition of being mortal or subject to death; mortal character, nature, or existence. **2.** mortal beings collectively; humanity. **3.** relative frequency of death, or death rate, as in a district or community. **4.** death or destruction on a large scale, as from war, plague, famine, etc. **5.** *Obs.* death.

mortality table, *Insurance.* an actuarial table compiled from statistics on the life spans of an arbitrarily selected population group or of former policyholders.

mor·tar[1] (môrʹtər), *n.* **1.** a vessel of hard material, having a bowl-shaped cavity, in which drugs, etc., are reduced to powder with a pestle. **2.** any of various mechanical appliances in which substances are pounded or ground. **3.** a cannon very short in proportion to its bore, for throwing shells at high angles. **4.** some similar contrivance, as for throwing pyrotechnic bombs or a life line. [ME and OE *mortere,* t. L: m.s. *mortārium* vessel in which substances are pounded, or one in which MORTAR is made; in defs. 3 and 4, trans. of F *mortier*]

Mortar and pestle (def. 1)

mor·tar[2] (môrʹtər), *n.* **1.** a material which binds stones or the like into a compact mass. **2.** a mixture, as of quicklime, cement, etc., sand, and water which hardens in the air and is used for binding bricks, etc., together. —*v.t* **3.** to plaster or fix with mortar. [ME *morter,* t. F: m. *mortier,* g. L *mortārium.* See MORTAR[1]]

mor·tar·board (môrʹtər bōrd′), *n.* **1.** a board, commonly square, used by masons to hold mortar. **2.** a kind of academic cap with a close-fitting crown surmounted by a stiff, flat, cloth-covered square piece.

Morte d'Ar·thur (môrt′ där′thər), a compilation and translation of French Arthurian romances made by Sir Thomas Malory and printed by Caxton in 1485.

Mortarboard (def. 2)

mort·gage (môrʹgĭj), *n., v.,* **-gaged, -gaging.** *Law.* **1.** a conditional conveyance of property to a creditor as security, as for the repayment of money. **2.** the deed by which such a transaction is effected. **3.** the rights conferred by it, or the state of the property conveyed. —*v.t.* **4.** to convey or place (property, esp. houses or land) under a mortgage. **5.** to pledge. [ME *morgage,* t. OF: f. *mort* dead + *gage* pledge, GAGE[1], n.]

mort·ga·gee (môr′gĭ jēʹ), *n.* one to whom property is mortgaged.

mortgagee clause, a clause attached to a fire insurance policy, designed to protect the mortgagee against loss or damage.

mort·ga·gor (môr′gĭ jər), *n.* one who mortgages property. Also, **mort′gag·er.**

---

b., blend of, blended; c., cognate with; d., dialect, dialectal; der., derived from; f., formed from; g., going back to; m., modification of; r., replacing; s., stem of; t., taken from; ?, perhaps. See the full key on inside cover.

mor·tice (môr′tĭs), n., v.t. -ticed, -ticing. mortise.

mor·ti·cian (môr tĭsh′ən), n. an undertaker. [f. MOR-T(UARY) + -ICIAN, modeled on PHYSICIAN]

mor·ti·fi·ca·tion (môr′tə fə kā′shən), n. 1. humiliation in feeling, as by some wound to pride. 2. a cause or source of such humiliation. 3. the practice of asceticism by penitential discipline to overcome desire for sin and to strengthen the will. 4. Pathol. the death of one part of the body while the rest is alive; gangrene.

mor·ti·fy (môr′tə fī), v., -fied, -fying. —v.t. 1. to humiliate in feeling, as by a severe wound to the pride or self-complacency. 2. to bring (the body, passions, etc.) into subjection by abstinence, ascetic discipline, or rigorous austerities. 3. Pathol. to affect with gangrene or necrosis. —v.i. 4. to practice mortification or disciplinary austerities. 5. Pathol. to undergo mortification, or become gangrened or necrosed. [ME mortifie(n), t. OF: m. mortifier, t. LL: m. mortificare kill, destroy] —mor′ti·fi′er, n. —mor′ti·fy′ing·ly, adv. —Syn. 1. See ashamed.

Mor·ti·mer (môr′tə mər), n. Roger, (1st Earl of March) 1287?–1330, British soldier, the favorite of Queen Isabella, wife of Edward II of England.

mor·tise (môr′tĭs), n., v., -tised, -tising. —n. 1. a rectangular cavity of considerable depth in one piece of wood, etc., for receiving a corresponding projection (tenon) on another piece, so as to form a joint (**mortise and tenon joint**). —v.t. 2. to fasten by, or as by, a mortise. 3. to cut or otherwise form the mortise to fit a prescribed tenon. 4. to join securely. Also, **mortice**. [ME mortrays, t. OF: m. mortaise, ? t. Ar.: m. murtazz made fast]

A. Mortise; B, Tenon

mort·main (môrt′mān), n. Law. 1. the condition of lands or tenements held without right of alienation, as by an ecclesiastical corporation; inalionable ownership. 2. the holding of land by a corporation or charitable trust beyond the period of time or in violation of the conditions authorized by law. [ME mort(e)mayn(e), t. OF: m. mortemain, trans. of ML mortua manus dead hand]

Mor·ton (môr′tən), n. William Thomas Green, 1819–1868, U.S. dentist: introduced ether as an anesthetic.

mor·tu·ar·y (môr′chŏŏ ĕr′ĭ), n., pl. -aries, adj. —n. 1. a place for the temporary reception of the dead. 2. a customary gift formerly claimed by and due to the incumbent of a parish in England from the estate of a deceased parishioner. —adj. 3. of or pertaining to the burial of the dead. 4. pertaining to or connected with death. [ME, t. ML: m.s. mortuārium, prop. neut. of L mortuārius belonging to the dead]

mor·u·la (môr′yŏŏ lə, -ŏŏ-), n., pl. -lae (-lē′). Embryol. the mass of cells resulting from the cleavage of the ovum before the formation of a blastula. [t. NL, dim. of L mōrum mulberry] —mor′u·lar, adj.

mos., months.

mo·sa·ic (mō zā′ĭk), n. 1. a picture or decoration made of small pieces of stone, glass, etc., of different colors, inlaid to form a design. 2. the process of producing it. 3. something resembling a mosaic in composition. 4. Aerial Surveying. an assembly of aerial photographs taken vertically and matched in such a way as to show a continuous photographic representation of an area (**mosaic map**). 5. Also, **mosaic disease**. Plant Pathol. one of numerous plant diseases, caused by certain viruses, in which varicolored, mottled areas appear on the leaves. —adj. 6. pertaining to or resembling a mosaic or mosaic work. 7. composed of diverse elements combined. [ME, t. ML: s. mosaicus, var. of mūsaicus, lit., of the Muses, artistic]

Mo·sa·ic (mō zā′ĭk), adj. of or pertaining to Moses or the writings and institutions attributed to him. Also, **Mo·sa′i·cal**. [t. NL: s. Mosaicus, ? f. after Hebraicus]

mosaic gold, 1. stannic sulfide. 2. ormolu.

Mosaic Law, 1. the ancient law of the Hebrews, attributed to Moses. 2. the part of the Scripture containing this law; the Pentateuch.

Mos·by (mōz′bĭ), n. John Singleton, 1833–1916, Confederate cavalry colonel in the U.S. Civil War.

mos·chate (mŏs′kāt, -kĭt), adj. having a musky smell. [t. NL: m.s. moschātus, der. ML moschus musk]

mos·cha·tel (mŏs′kə tĕl′, mŏs′kə tĕl′), n. a small, inconspicuous plant, Adoxa moschatellina, having greenish or yellowish flowers with a musky odor. [t. F: m. moscatelle, t. It.: m. moscatella, der. moscato musk]

Mos·cow (mŏs′kou, -kō), n. the capital of the Soviet Union, in the central part of European Soviet Russia. 4,137,018 (1939). Russian, **Mos·kva** (mŏs kvä′).

Mo·sel (mō zĕl′), n. Moselle (def. 1).

Mo·selle (mō zĕl′), n. 1. a river flowing from the Vosges mountains in NE France into the Rhine in W Germany. 320 mi. 2. a light, sprightly white wine made along the Moselle in Germany.

Mo·ses (mō′zĭz, -zĭs), n. the liberator of the Hebrews from Egypt, leader throughout the years of the desert sojourn, founder of Israel's theocracy, and, according to tradition, its first lawgiver. Ex. 2, Deut. 34. [t. L, t. Gk., t. Heb.: m. Mōsheh]

Moses basket, Brit. a bassinet.

Moses boat, a ship's boat built with a keel. [orig. uncert.; ? named after Moses of Mass., boat-builder]

mo·sey (mō′zĭ), v.i., -seyed, -seying. U.S. Slang. 1. to move or go along or away; make off. 2. to shuffle along; stroll.

Mos·lem (mŏz′ləm, mŏs′-), adj., n., pl. -lems, -lem. —adj. 1. pertaining to the Mohammedan religion, law, or civilization. —n. 2. a Mohammedan. Also, **Muslem, Muslim**. [t. Ar.: m. muslim one submitting (i.e. accepting Islam, lit., submission)] —**Mos·lem·ic** (mŏz lĕm′ĭk, mŏs-), adj.

Mos·lem·ism (mŏz′lə mĭz′əm, mŏs-), n. Mohammedanism.

mosque (mŏsk, môsk), n. a Mohammedan temple or place of worship. Also, **mosk**. [t. F: m. mosquée, t. It.: m. moschea, t. Ar.: m. masjid, der. sajada prostrate oneself, worship]

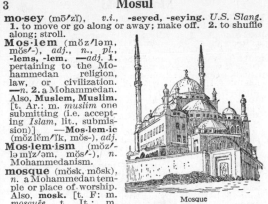

Mosque

mos·qui·to (mə skē′tō), n., pl. -toes, -tos. any of various dipterous insects of the family Culicidae (genera Culex, Anopheles, etc.), the females of which have a long proboscis, by means of which they puncture the skin of animals (including man) and draw blood, some species transmitting certain diseases, as malaria and yellow fever. [t. Sp., dim. of mosca, g. L musca a fly]

mosquito boat, a fast unarmored motorboat armed with torpedoes and small guns.

mosquito fleet, Naut. Slang. a group of small navy boats.

House mosquito,
Culex pipiens
(Body ¼ in. long)

mosquito hawk, a nighthawk.

mosquito net, a screen, curtain, or canopy of net, gauze, or the like (**mosquito netting**), for keeping out mosquitos.

moss (môs, mŏs), n. 1. any of the cryptogamic plants which belong to the class Musci, of the bryophytes, comprising small leafy-stemmed plants growing in tufts, sods, or mats on moist ground, tree trunks, rocks, etc. 2. a growth of such plants. 3. any of various similar plants, as certain lichens (see **Iceland moss**), the lycopods (see **club moss**), etc. 4. Chiefly Scot. and N. Eng. a swamp or peat bog. —v.t. 5. to cover with a growth of moss. [ME mos(se), OE mos bog, c. D mos moss, G moos bog, moss]

moss agate, a kind of agate or chalcedony containing brown or black mosslike dendritic markings from various impurities.

moss·back (môs′băk, mŏs′-), n. U.S. Slang. 1. a person attached to antiquated notions. 2. an extreme conservative.

moss·hunk·er (môs′bŭngk′ər, mŏs′-), n. the menhaden (fish). [t. D: m. marsbanker]

moss-grown (môs′grōn′, mŏs′-), adj. 1. overgrown with moss. 2. old-fashioned.

mos·so (mŏs′sō), adj. Music. moved; fast. [t. It., pp. of muovere move]

moss pink, a species of phlox, Phlox subulata, of the eastern U.S., with showy pink to purple flowers.

moss rose, a cultivated variety of rose with a mosslike growth on the calyx and stem.

moss-troop·er (môs′trōō′pər, mŏs′-), n. 1. one of a class of marauders who infested the mosses or bogs of the border between England and Scotland in the 17th century. 2. any marauder.

moss·y (môs′ĭ, mŏs′ĭ), adj., mossier, mossiest. 1. overgrown with, or abounding in, moss. 2. covered with a mosslike growth. 3. appearing as if covered with moss. 4. resembling moss. —**moss′i·ness**, n.

most (mōst), adj., superl. of more, n., adv. —adj. 1. in the greatest quantity, amount, measure, degree, or number (used as the superlative of much and many, with the comparative more): the most votes. 2. in the majority of instances: most exercise is beneficial. 3. greatest, as in size or extent: the most part. —n. 4. the greatest quantity, amount, or degree; the utmost. 5. the greatest number or the majority of a class specified. 6. the greatest number. 7. the majority of persons (construed as pl.). —adv. 8. in or to the greatest extent or degree (in this sense much used before adjectives and adverbs, and regularly before those of more than two syllables, to form superlative phrases having the same force and effect as the superlative degree formed by the termination -est): most rapid, most wisely. 9. Colloq. almost or nearly. [ME most(e), OE māst (r. ME mest(e), OE māst), c. G meist, etc.] —Syn. 9. See almost.

-most, a suffixal use of most found in a series of superlatives, e.g., utmost, foremost. [ME -most, r. ME and OE -mest, a double superl. suffix, f. -ma + -est, both forming superlatives]

most·ly (mōst′lĭ), adv. 1. for the most part; in the main: the work is mostly done. 2. chiefly. —Syn. 2. especially.

Mo·sul (mō sōōl′), n. a city in N Iraq on the Tigris, opposite the ruins of Nineveh. 108,593 (est. 1941).

Mosz·kow·ski (mŏsh kôf′skĭ), *n.* **Moritz** (mō′rĭts), 1854–1925, Polish composer and pianist.

mot (mō), *n.* 1. a pithy or witty remark. 2. *Archaic.* a note on a horn, bugle, etc. [t. F: word, saying, note of a horn, etc., g. L *muttum* a mutter, grunt]

mote[1] (mōt), *n.* a particle or speck, esp. of dust. [ME; OE *mot* speck, c. D *mot* grit, sawdust]

mote[2] (mōt), *v.t.*, *pt.* **moste** (mōst). *Archaic.* may or might. [ME *mot(e)*, OE *mōt*, pres. (c. G *muss*). See MUST, v.]

mo·tel (mō tĕl′), *n.* *U.S.* a roadside hotel providing both lodging, usually in individual cabins, for travelers and garage or parking space for their motor vehicles. [b. M(OTOR) and (H)OTEL]

mo·tet (mō tĕt′), *n.* *Music.* a vocal composition in polyphonic style, on a Biblical or similar prose text, intended for use in a church service. [ME, t. OF, dim. of *mot* word. See MOT]

moth (môth, mŏth), *n.*, *pl.* **moths** (môthz, mŏthz, môths, mŏths). 1. any of a very large group of lepidopterous insects, generally distinguished from the butterflies by not having their antennae clubbed and by their (mainly) nocturnal or crepuscular habits. 2. a clothes moth. [ME *motthe*, OE *moththe*, c. G *motte*]

moth ball, a small ball of naphthalene or (sometimes) camphor which repels moths and protects clothing.

Clothes moth.
Tinea pellionella
A. Adult; B. Larva

moth-eat·en (môth′ē′tən, mŏth′-), *adj.* 1. eaten or damaged by or as by moths. 2. decayed; out of fashion.

moth·er[1] (mŭth′ər), *n.* 1. a female parent. 2. (*often cap.*) one's own mother. 3. *Colloq.* a mother-in-law, stepmother, or adoptive mother. 4. a term of familiar address for an old or elderly woman. 5. the head or superior of a female religious community. 6. a woman looked upon as a mother, or exercising control or authority like that of a mother. 7. the qualities characteristic of a mother, or maternal affection. 8. something that gives rise to, or exercises protecting care over, something else. —*adj.* 9. that is a mother: *a mother bird.* 10. pertaining to or characteristic of a mother: *mother love.* 11. derived from one's mother; native: *mother tongue.* 12. bearing a relation like that of a mother, as in giving origin or rise, or in exercising protective care: *a mother church.* —*v.t.* 13. to be the mother of; give origin or rise to. 14. to acknowledge oneself the author of; assume as one's own. 15. to care for or protect as a mother does. [ME *moder*, OE *mōdor*, c. D *moeder*, G *mutter*, Icel. *mōdhir*; akin to L *māter*, Gk. *mētēr*, Skt. *mātar*-] —**moth′er·less**, *adj.*

moth·er[2] (mŭth′ər), *n.* a stringy, mucilaginous substance formed on the surface of a liquid undergoing acetous fermentation (as wine changing to vinegar), and consisting of the various bacteria, esp. *Mycoderma aceti*, which cause such fermentation. Also, **mother of vinegar**. [special use of MOTHER[1]]

Mother Car·ey's chicken (kâr′ĭz), any of various small petrels, esp. the stormy petrel, *Oceanites oceanicus.*

Mother Goose, the legendary author of the English folk nursery jingles called *Mother Goose's Melodies.*

moth·er·hood (mŭth′ər hood′), *n.* 1. the state of being a mother; maternity. 2. mothers collectively. 3. the qualities or spirit of a mother.

Mother Hub·bard (hŭb′ərd), 1. a kind of full, loose gown worn by women. 2. heroine of a nursery rhyme.

moth·er-in-law (mŭth′ər ĭn lô′), *n.*, *pl.* **mothers-in-law**. the mother of one's husband or wife.

moth·er·land (mŭth′ər land′), *n.* 1. one's native country. 2. the land of one's ancestors.

mother lode, *Mining.* a rich or principal lode.

moth·er·ly (mŭth′ər lĭ), *adj.* 1. pertaining to, characteristic of, or befitting a mother: *motherly affection.* 2. having the character, etc., of a mother. —*adv.* 3. in the manner of a mother. —**moth′er·li·ness**, *n.*

Mother of God, a designation of the Virgin Mary.

moth-er-of-pearl (mŭth′ər əv pûrl′), *n.* a hard, iridescent substance which forms the inner layer of certain shells, as that of the pearl oyster; nacre.

mother of vinegar, mother[2].

Mother's Day, *U.S.* a day for acts of grateful affection or remembrance by each person toward his mother, observed annually on the second Sunday in May (in schools, on the Friday preceding).

mother superior, the head of a female religious community.

mother tongue, 1. the language first learned by a person; native language. 2. a parent language.

Moth·er·well and Wish·aw (mŭth′ər wĕl′; wĭsh′-ô), a burgh in S Scotland. 65,391 (1939).

mother wit, common sense.

moth·er·wort (mŭth′ər wûrt′), *n.* a labiate European plant, *Leonurus cardiaca*, with cut leaves having a close whorl of flowers in the axils, a common U.S. weed.

moth·y (môth′ĭ, mŏth′-), *adj.*, **mothier, mothiest**. 1. containing moths. 2. moth-eaten.

mo·tif (mō tēf′), *n.* 1. a subject or theme for development or treatment, as in art, literature, or music. 2. a distinctive figure in a design, as of wallpaper. 3. a dominant idea or feature. [t. F. See MOTIVE]

mo·tile (mō′təl, -tĭl), *adj.* 1. *Biol.* moving, or capable of moving, spontaneously: *motile cells or spores.* —*n.* 2. *Psychol.* one in whose mind motor images are predominant or especially distinct. [f. s. L *mōtus*, pp., moved, + -ILE] —**mo·til·i·ty** (mō tĭl′ə tĭ), *n.*

mo·tion (mō′shən), *n.* 1. the process of moving, or changing place or position. 2. **in motion**, in active operation; moving. 3. a movement. 4. power of movement, as of a living body. 5. the action or manner of moving the body in walking, etc.; gait. 6. a bodily movement or change of posture; a gesture. 7. a proposal formally made to a deliberative assembly: *to make a motion to adjourn.* 8. *Law.* an application made to a court or judge for an order, ruling, or the like. 9. a suggestion or proposal. 10. an inward prompting or impulse; inclination: *of one's own motion.* 11. *Music.* melodic progression, as the change of a voice part from one pitch to another. 12. *Mach.* a. a piece of mechanism with a particular action or function. b. the action of such mechanism. —*v.t.* 13. to direct by a significant motion, or gesture, as with the hand: *to motion a person to a seat.* —*v.i.* 14. to make a significant motion; gesture, as with the hand for the purpose of directing or guiding: *to motion to a person.* [ME, t. L: s. *mōtio* a moving]

—**Syn.** 1. MOTION, MOVE, MOVEMENT refer to change of position in space. MOTION denotes change of position, either considered apart from, or as a characteristic of, that which moves; usually the former, in which case it is often a somewhat technical or scientific term: *perpetual motion.* The chief uses of MOVE are founded upon the idea of moving a piece, in chess or a similar game, for winning the game; and hence the word denotes any change of position, condition, or circumstances for the accomplishment of some end: *a shrewd move to win votes.* MOVEMENT is always connected with the person or thing moving, and is usually a definite or particular motion: *the movements of a dance.*

mo·tion·less (mō′shən lĭs), *adj.* without, or incapable of, motion. —**mo′tion·less·ly**, *adv.* —**mo′tion·less-ness**, *n.*

motion picture, 1. (*pl.*) consecutive pictures or photographs of objects in motion presented to the eye, esp. by being thrown on a screen by a projector (**motion picture projector**), so rapidly as to give the illusion that the objects are moving as they did in the original scenes. 2. a number of such pictures or photographs representing an event, play, or the like; a photoplay.

mo·ti·vate (mō′tə vāt′), *v.t.*, **-vated, -vating**. to provide with a motive or motives.

mo·ti·va·tion (mō′tə vā′shən), *n.* a motivating; a providing of a motive; inducement.

mo·tive (mō′tĭv), *n.*, *adj.*, *v.*, **-tived, -tiving**. —*n.* 1. something that prompts a person to act in a certain way or that determines volition; an incentive. 2. the goal or object of one's actions: *his motive was revenge.* 3. (in art, literature, and music) a motif. —*adj.* 4. causing, or tending to cause, motion. 5. pertaining to motion. 6. prompting to action. 7. constituting a motive or motives. —*v.t.* 8. to provide with a motive. 9. to motivate. 10. to relate to a motif or a principal theme or idea in a work of art. [t. ML: m.s. *mōtīvum* a moving cause, prop. neut. of *mōtīvus* serving to move, der. L *mōtus*, pp., moved; r. ME *motif*, t. OF]

—**Syn.** 1. MOTIVE, INCENTIVE, INDUCEMENT apply to whatever moves one to action. MOTIVE is, literally, that which moves a person; an INDUCEMENT, that which leads him on; an INCENTIVE that which inspires him. MOTIVE is applied mainly to an inner urge that moves or prompts a person to action, though it may also apply to a contemplated result, the desire for which moves the person: *his motive was a wish to be helpful.* INDUCEMENT is never applied to an inner urge, and seldom to a goal (*the pleasure of wielding authority may be an inducement to get ahead*); it is used mainly of opportunities offered by the acceptance of certain conditions, whether these are offered by a second person or by the factors of the situation: *the salary offered me was a great inducement.* INCENTIVE was once used of anything inspiring or stimulating the emotions or imagination (*incentives to piety*); it has retained of this its emotional connotations, but (rather like INDUCEMENT) is today applied only to something offered as a reward, and offered particularly to stimulate competitive activity: *incentives to greater production.* 2. See **reason**.

motive power, 1. any power used to impart motion. 2. a source of mechanical energy. 3. *Railroading.* locomotives, and other rolling equipment which supply tractive power for train operations.

mo·tiv·i·ty (mō tĭv′ə tĭ), *n.* the power of initiating or producing motion.

mot juste (mō zhyst′), *French.* the exact or appropriate word.

mot·ley (mŏt′lĭ), *adj.*, *n.*, *pl.* **-leys**. —*adj.* 1. exhibiting great diversity of elements; heterogeneous: *a motley crowd.* 2. being of different colors combined; particolored. 3. wearing a parti-colored garment: *a motley fool.* —*n.* 4. a combination of different colors. 5. a parti-colored effect of color. 6. the motley or parti-colored garment of the old-time professional fool or jester: *to wear the motley.* 7. a heterogeneous assemblage. 8. a medley. [ME, unexplained deriv. of MOTE[1]]

Mot·ley (mŏt′lĭ), *n.* **John Lothrop**, 1814–77, U.S. historian and diplomat.

mot-mot (mŏt′mŏt), *n.* any of the tropical and subtropical American birds constituting the family *Momotidae*, related to the kingfishers, and having a serrate bill and chiefly greenish and bluish plumage.

mo·to·cy·cle (mō′tō sī′kəl), *n.* motorcycle.

---

mo·tor (mō′tər), *n.* **1.** a comparatively small and powerful engine, esp. an internal-combustion engine in an automobile, motorboat, or the like. **2.** any self-powered vehicle. **3.** one who or that which imparts motion, esp. a contrivance (as a steam engine) which receives and modifies energy from some natural source in order to utilize it in driving machinery, etc. **4.** *Elect.* a machine which converts electrical energy into mechanical energy: *an electric motor.* **5.** (*pl.*) *Stock Exchange.* automobile securities. —*adj.* **6.** causing or imparting motion. **7.** pertaining to or operated by a motor. **8.** used in or for, or pertaining to, motor vehicles: *a motor highway.* **9.** *Physiol.* conveying an impulse that results or tends to result in motion, as a nerve. **10.** *Physiol., Psychol.* denoting the effect or phase of any mental process, as the innervation of muscles and glands. **11.** *Psychol.* pertaining to or involving action: *motor images.* —*v.i.* **12.** to ride or travel in an automobile. [t. L: *one who moves*]

mo·tor·boat (mō′tər bōt′), *n.* a boat propelled by its own mechanical power. —**mo′tor·boat′ing,** *n.*

mo·tor·bus (mō′tər bŭs′), *n.* a passenger bus powered by a motor. Also, **motor coach.**

mo·tor·cade (mō′tər kād′), *n.* a procession or parade of automobiles. [b. MOTOR(CAR) and (CAVAL)CADE]

mo·tor·car (mō′tər kär′), *n.* an automobile.

mo·tor·cy·cle (mō′tər sī′kəl), *n.* a self-propelled bicycle, tricycle, or the like. Also, **motocycle.** —**mo·tor·cy·clist** (mō′tər sī′klĭst), *n.*

motor drive, the mechanical system, including an electric motor, used to operate a machine or machines.

mo·tor·drome (mō′tər drōm′), *n.* a rounded course or track for automobile and motorcycle races.

mo·tored (mō′tərd), *adj.* having a motor or motors, esp. of specified number or type: *a bimotored airplane.*

mo·tor·ist (mō′tər ĭst), *n.* **1.** one who drives an automobile. **2.** the user of a privately owned automobile.

mo·tor·ize (mō′tə rīz′), *v.t.,* **-ized, -izing. 1.** to furnish with a motor or motors, as vehicles. **2.** to supply with motor-driven vehicles in the place of horses and horse-drawn vehicles. —**mo′tor·i·za′tion,** *n.*

motor lorry, *Chiefly Brit.* motor truck.

mo·tor·man (mō′tər mən), *n., pl.* **-men. 1.** one who operates the motor of an electric car or electric locomotive on a railway. **2.** one who operates a motor.

motor mimicry, *Psychol.* empathy.

motor ship, a ship driven by internal-combustion engines, usually Diesel engines.

motor truck, an automobile truck.

motor van, *Brit.* an automobile truck.

Mott (mŏt), *n.* **Mrs. Lucretia,** (*Lucretia Coffin*) 1793–1880, U.S. social reformer, advocate of women's rights.

motte (mŏt), *n.* *U.S. Dial.* a small patch of woods in prairie land. Also, **mott.** [t. F: mound]

mot·tle (mŏt′əl), *v.,* **-tled, -tling,** *n.* —*v.t.* **1.** to diversify with spots or blotches of a different color or shade. —*n.* **2.** a diversifying spot or blotch of color. **3.** mottled coloring or pattern. [back formation from MOTLEY]

mot·tled (mŏt′əld), *adj.* spotted or blotched in coloring.

mot·to (mŏt′ō), *n., pl.,* **-toes, -tos. 1.** a maxim adopted as expressing one's guiding principle. **2.** a sentence, phrase, or word attached to or inscribed on anything as appropriate to it. [t. It. See MOT]

mouch (mooch), *v.i., v.t.* *Slang.* mooch.

mou·choir (moo shwâr′), *n.* *French.* a handkerchief. [F, der. *moucher* wipe the nose, g. L *muccāre,* der. *muccus* MUCUS]

moue (moo), *n.* *French.* a pouting grimace. [see MOW³]

mouf·lon (moo′flŏn), *n.* a wild sheep, *Ovis musimon,* inhabiting the mountainous regions of Sardinia, Corsica, etc., the male of which has large curving horns. Also, **mouf′flon.** [t. F, t. Corsican; g. LL *mufron*]

mouil·lé (moo yā′), *adj.* *Phonet.* **1.** palatal or palatalized, esp. referring to sounds spelled *ll* and *ñ* in Spanish, *gl* and *gn* in Italian, etc. **2.** (of French sounds) spelled *l* or *ll* and pronounced as a *y* sound. [t. F, pp. of *mouiller* wet, moisten, der. L *mollis* soft]

mou·jik (moo zhĭk′, moo′zhĭk), *n.* muzhik.

Mouk·den (mook′dĕn′, mook′-), *n.* Mukden.

mou·lage (moo läzh′), *n.* **1.** the making of a mold in plaster of Paris, etc., of objects, footprints, tire tracks, etc., esp. for purposes of identification. **2.** the mold itself. [t. F]

mould (mōld), *n., v.t., v.i.* *Chiefly Brit.* mold. —**mould′er,** *n.* —**mould′ing,** *n.* —**mould′y,** *adj.* —**mould′i·ness,** *n.*

mould·board (mōld′bōrd′), *n.* *Chiefly Brit.* moldboard.

mould·er (mōl′dər), *n., v.i., v.t.* molder.

mou·lin (moo lăn′), *n.* a nearly vertical shaft or cavity worn in a glacier by surface water falling through a crack in the ice. [t. F, g. LL *molīnum* mill. See MILL¹]

Moul·mein (mool′mān′, mōl′-), *n.* a seaport in S Burma at the mouth of the Salween river. 65,506 (1931). Also, **Maulmain.**

moult (mōlt), *v.i., v.t., n.* *Chiefly Brit.* molt.

Moul·trie (moo′trĭ, mōl′trĭ), *n.* **Fort,** a fort at the entrance to the harbor of Charleston, South Carolina.

mound (mound), *n.* **1.** an elevation formed of earth or sand, debris, etc., overlaying ruins, a grave, etc. **2.** a tumulus or other raised work of earth dating from a prehistoric or long-past period. **3.** a natural elevation of earth; a hillock or knoll. **4.** an artificial elevation of earth, as for a defense work, a dam or barrier, or any other purpose; an embankment. **5.** a heap or raised mass: *a mound of hay.* **6.** *Baseball.* the slightly elevated ground from which the pitcher delivers the ball and which slopes gradually to the base lines. —*v.t.* **7.** to furnish with a mound of earth, as for a defense or barrier. **8.** to form into a mound; heap up. [OE *mund* hand, protection]

Mound Builders, the various Indian tribes who, in prehistoric and early historic times, erected the burial mounds and other earthworks of the Mississippi drainage basin and southeastern states.

mount¹ (mount), *v.t.* **1.** to go up or ascend: *to mount stairs.* **2.** to get up on (a platform, a horse, etc.). **3.** to set or place at an elevation: *to be mounted on stilts.* **4.** to furnish with a horse or other mount for riding. **5.** to set on horseback. **6.** to raise or put into position for use, as a gun. **7.** to have or carry (guns) in position for use, as a fortress or a vessel does. **8.** to go or put on (guard), as a sentry or watch. **9.** to fix on or in a support, backing, setting, etc.: *to mount a photograph.* **10.** to provide (a play, etc.) with scenery, costumes, and other appurtenances for production. **11.** to prepare (an animal body or skeleton) as a specimen. **12.** *Micros.* **a.** to prepare (a slide) for microscopic investigation. **b.** to prepare (a sample, etc.) for examination by a microscope, as by placing it on a slide. —*v.i.* **13.** to rise or go to a higher position, level, degree, etc.; ascend. **14.** to rise in amount (often fol. by *up*): *the costs are steadily mounting.* **15.** to get up on the back of a horse, etc., for riding. **16.** to get up on something, as a platform. —*n.* **17.** the act or manner of mounting. **18.** a horse or other animal (or sometimes a bicycle) used, provided, or available for riding. **19.** an act or occasion of riding a horse, esp. in a race. **20.** a support, backing, setting, or the like, on or in which something is, or is to be, mounted or fixed. **21.** *Micros.* the prepared slide. [ME *monte(n),* t. OF: m. *monter,* der. s. L *mons* mountain] —**Syn. 13.** rise, soar. See **climb.**

mount² (mount), *n.* a mountain or hill (now chiefly poetic, except in proper names, as *Mount Etna*). [ME *mont, munt,* OE *munt,* t. L: m.s. *mons*]

moun·tain (moun′tən, -tĭn), *n.* **1.** a natural elevation of the earth's surface rising more or less abruptly to a summit, and attaining an altitude greater than that of a hill. **2.** something resembling this, as in size: *a mountain of ice.* **3.** a huge amount. **4. the Mountain,** *French Hist.* a popular name for the extreme revolutionary party led by Danton and Robespierre in the legislatures of the French Revolution, whose members occupied the highest seats. It favored the ruthless prosecution of the Revolution and the Reign of Terror. —*adj.* **5.** of or pertaining to mountains: *mountain air.* **6.** living, growing, or found on mountains: *mountain people, mountain plants.* **7.** resembling or suggesting a mountain, as in size. [ME, t. OF: m. *montaigne,* der. *mont* mountain, g. L *mons*]

mountain ash, **1.** any of various small trees of the rosaceous genus *Sorbus,* as the European rowan, *S. Aucuparia,* and the American *S. americana,* both having pinnate leaves and bearing small white corymbose flowers succeeded by bright-red to orange berries. **2.** any of certain other trees, as several Australian species of eucalyptus.

mountain bluebird, a songbird, *Sialia arctica,* of western North America. The male is sky-blue.

mountain cat, 1. cougar. **2.** bobcat.

mountain chain, 1. a connected series of mountains. **2.** two or more mountain ranges of close geographical relation.

mountain cranberry, a vacciniaceous shrub, *Vaccinium Vitis-Idaea,* with evergreen leaves, prostrate stems, and acid red berries edible after cooking.

mountain damson, any of certain tropical American trees of the genus *Simaruba* (family *Simarubaceae*), the bark of whose root is used in medicine as a tonic and astringent, esp. *S. amara,* chiefly of the West Indies.

mountain dew, *Slang.* **1.** Scotch whiskey. **2.** any whiskey, esp. when illicitly distilled.

moun·tain·eer (moun′tə nĭr′), *n.* **1.** an inhabitant of a mountainous district. **2.** a climber of mountains. —*v.i.* **3.** to climb mountains. —**moun′tain·eer′ing,** *n.*

mountain goat, the Rocky Mountain goat, *Oreamnos montanus.*

mountain laurel, the American laurel, *Kalmia latifolia.*

mountain lion, the cougar.

moun·tain·ous (moun′tə nəs), *adj.* **1.** abounding in mountains. **2.** of the nature of a mountain. **3.** resembling a mountain or mountains; large and high; huge: *mountainous waves.* —**moun′tain·ous·ly,** *adv.*

Mountain goat, *Oreamnos montanus* (Ab. 3½ ft. high at the shoulder, total length 5½ ft.)

mountain range, 1. a series of more or less connected mountains ranged in a line. **2.** a series of mountains, or of more or less parallel lines of mountains, closely related in origin, etc. **3.** an area in which the greater part of the land surface is in considerable degree or slope, upland summits are small or narrow, and there are great differences in elevations within the area (commonly over 2000 feet).

mountain sheep, 1. the bighorn, *Ovis montana* (or *canadensis*), of the Rocky Mountains, with massive recurving horns. See illus. under **bighorn.** 2. any of various wild sheep inhabiting mountains.

mountain sickness, *Pathol.* a morbid condition characterized by difficult breathing, headache, nausea, etc., due to the rarefaction of the air at high altitudes.

Mountain time. See **standard time.**

Mount·bat·ten (mount·băt′ən), *n.* **Lord Louis,** born 1900, British admiral; Viceroy of India (1947); Governor General of India 1947–1948.

Mount De·sert Island (dĭ·zûrt′, dĕz′ərt), an island off the central coast of Maine: summer resort; Acadia National Park. 14 mi. long; 8 mi. wide.

moun·te·bank (moun′tə·băngk′), *n.* 1. one who sells quack medicines from a platform in public places, appealing to his audience by tricks, storytelling, etc. 2. any charlatan or quack. —*v.i.* 3. to play the mountebank. [t. It.: m. *montambanco,* contr. of *monta in banco* mount-on-(a)-bench] —**moun·te·bank·er·y** (moun′tə·băngk′ə·rĭ), *n.*

mount·ed (moun′tĭd), *adj.* 1. seated or riding on a horse or the like. 2. serving on horseback, or on some special mount, as soldiers, police, etc. 3. *Mil.* permanently equipped with trucks, tanks, or other vehicles, or horses as means of transportation. 4. fixed on or in a support, backing, setting, or the like: *mounted gems.* 5. put into position for use, as guns. —**Ant.** 1. afoot.

mount·er (moun′tər), *n.* one who or that which mounts.

mount·ing (moun′tĭng), *n.* 1. the act of one who or that which mounts. 2. something that serves as a mount, support, setting, or the like.

Mount Mc·Kin·ley National Park (mə·kĭn′lĭ), a national park in central Alaska, including Mounts McKinley and Foraker. 3030 sq. mi.

Mount Rai·nier National Park (rā·nĭr′, rā′nĭr), a national park in W Washington, including Mount Rainier. 378 sq. mi.

Mount Rob·son Park (rŏb′sən), a national park in the Rocky Mountains of E British Columbia, Canada.

Mount Ver·non (vûr′nən), 1. the home and tomb of George Washington in NE Virginia, on the Potomac, 15 mi. below Washington, D.C. 2. a city in SE New York, near New York City. 71,899 (1950).

mourn (mōrn), *v.i.* 1. to feel or express sorrow or grief. 2. to grieve or lament for the dead. 3. to display the conventional tokens of sorrow after a person's death. —*v.t.* 4. to feel or express sorrow or grief over (misfortune, loss, or anything regretted); deplore. 5. to grieve or lament over (the dead). 6. to utter in a sorrowful manner. [ME *mo(u)rne,* OE *murnan,* c. OHG *mornên*] —**Syn.** 1. bewail, bemoan. See **grieve.**

mourn·er (mōr′nər), *n.* 1. one who mourns. 2. one who attends a funeral as a mourning friend or relative of the deceased. 3. (at religious revival meetings) one who professes penitence for sin, with desire for salvation.

mourners' bench, (at religious revival meetings) a bench or seat at the front of the church or room, set apart for mourners or penitent sinners seeking salvation.

mourn·ful (mōrn′fəl), *adj.* 1. full of, expressing, or showing sorrow or grief, as persons, the tone, etc.; sorrowful; sad. 2. expressing, or used in, mourning for the dead. 3. causing, or attended with, sorrow or mourning: *a mournful occasion.* 4. gloomy, somber, or dreary, as in appearance or character: *mournful shadows.* —**mourn·ful·ly,** *adv.* —**mourn·ful·ness,** *n.*

mourn·ing (mōr′nĭng), *n.* 1. act of one who mourns; sorrowing or lamentation. 2. the conventional manifestation of sorrow for a person's death, esp. by the wearing of black, the hanging of flags at halfmast, etc. 3. the outward tokens of such sorrow, as black garments, etc. —*adj.* 4. of, pertaining to, or used in mourning. —**mourn·ing·ly,** *adv.* —**Ant.** 1. rejoicing.

Mourning Becomes Electra, a three-part tragedy (1931) by Eugene O'Neill.

mourning cloak, a European and American butterfly, *Nymphalis antiopa,* having dark wings with a yellow border.

mourning dove, a dove, *Zenaidura macroura,* of North America, so called from its plaintive cooing; regarded as a game bird in parts of the southern U.S.

mouse (*n.* mous; *v.* mouz), *n.,* *pl.* **mice** (mīs), *v.,* **moused,** **mousing.** —*n.* 1. any of various small rodents of the family *Muridae* and esp. of the introduced Old World genus *Mus,* as *M. musculus,* which infests houses. 2. any similar animal of some other family, as the *Cricetidae.* 3. *Slang.* a black eye. —*v.t.* 4. to hunt out, as a cat hunts out mice. 5. *Naut.* to secure with a mousing. —*v.i.* 6. to hunt for or catch mice. 7. to prowl (about, etc.), as if seeking something. 8. to seek or search stealthily or watchfully, as if for prey. [ME *mous,* OE *mūs* (pl. *mȳs*), c. G *maus,* L *mūs*]

Deer mouse,
Peromyscus leucopus
(Total length 6 to 7 in.,
tail 3 in.)

mouse-dun (mous′dŭn′), *n.* dark brownish gray.

mouse-ear (mous′ĭr′), *n.* any of various plants with

small hairy leaves, as the hawkweed, *Hieracium Pilosella,* the forget-me-not, *Myosotis palustris,* etc.

mous·er (mou′zər), *n.* 1. an animal that catches mice: commonly used with a qualifying term or with reference to the animal's ability to catch mice. 2. one who mouses, or seeks or prowls as if for prey.

mouse·tail (mous′tāl′), *n.* any plant of the ranunculaceous genus *Myosurus,* esp. *M. minimus,* the flowers of which have a taillike torus.

mous·ing (mou′zĭng), *n. Naut.* several turns of small rope or the like, uniting the shank and point of a hook.

mous·que·taire (mōōs′kə·târ′), *n.* musketeer. [F]

mousse (mōōs), *n.* any of various preparations of whipped cream, beaten eggs, gelatine, etc., sweetened and flavored and frozen without stirring. [t. F: moss, froth, of Gmc. orig. See MOSS]

mousse·line (mōōs·lēn′), *n. French.* muslin.

mousse·line de laine (mōōs·lēn′ də lĕn′), *French.* a thin woolen fabric, often having a printed pattern. [F: lit., woolen muslin]

mousse·line de soie (mōōs·lēn′ də swä′), *French.* a thin, stiff silk or rayon fabric. [F: lit., silken muslin]

Mous·sorg·sky (mōō·sôrg′skĭ), *n.* **Modest Petrovich** (mŏ′dĕst′ pĕ·trô′vĭch), 1839–81, Russian composer.

mous·tache (məs·tăsh′, mŭs′tăsh), *n. Chiefly Brit.* mustache.

Mous·te·ri·an (mōōs·tĭr′ĭ·ən), *adj. Anthropol.* pertaining to Paleolithic human relics having the workmanship, finish, and character of the flint scrapers found in the sands of Moustier, France. Also, **Mous·tie·ri·an.**

mous·y (mou′sĭ, mou′zĭ), *adj.,* **mousier,** **mousiest.** 1. resembling or suggesting a mouse, as in color, odor, etc. 2. drab and colorless. 3. quiet as a mouse. 4. infested with mice. Also, **mous/ey.**

mouth (*n.* mouth; *v.* mouth), *n.,* *pl.* **mouths** (mouthz), *v.* —*n.* 1. the opening through which an animal takes in food, or the cavity containing or the parts including the masticating apparatus. 2. the masticating and tasting apparatus. 3. a person or other animal as requiring food. 4. the oral opening or cavity considered as the source of vocal utterance. 5. utterance or expression: *to give mouth to one's thoughts.* 6. a grimace made with the lips. 7. an opening leading out of or into any cavity or hollow place or thing: *the mouth of a cave.* 8. a part of a river or the like where its waters are discharged into some other body of water: *the mouth of the Nile.* 9. the opening between the jaws of a vise or the like. 10. the lateral hole of an organ pipe. 11. the lateral blowhole of a flute. —*v.t.* 12. to utter in a sonorous, oratorical, or pompous manner, or with unnecessarily noticeable use of the mouth parts. 15. to put or take into the mouth, as food. 16. to press, rub, or mumble with the mouth or lips. 17. to accustom (a horse) to the use of the bit and bridle. —*v.i.* 18. to speak or declaim sonorously and oratorically, or with mouthing of the words. 19. to make a mouth; grimace with the lips. [ME; OE *mūth,* c. G *mund*]

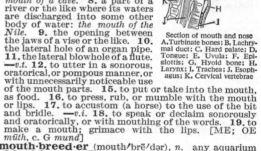

Section of mouth and nose
A, Turbinate bones; B, Lachrymal duct; C, Hard palate; D, Tongue; E, Uvula; F, Epiglottis; G, Hyoid bone; H, Larynx; I, Trachea; J, Esophagus; K, Cervical vertebrae

mouth·breed·er (mouth′brē′dər), *n.* any aquarium fish, of the genera *Tilapia* and *Haplochromis,* which care for their young by holding them in the mouth.

mouth·ful (mouth′fŏŏl′), *n., pl.* **-fuls.** 1. as much as a mouth can hold. 2. as much as is taken into the mouth at one time. 3. a small quantity.

mouth organ, a harmonica (def. 1).

mouth·piece (mouth′pēs′), *n.* 1. a piece placed at or forming the mouth, as of a receptacle, tube, or the like. 2. a piece or part, as of an instrument, to which the mouth is applied or which is held in the mouth: *the mouthpiece of a trumpet.* 3. the part of a bit or bridle, as for a horse, that passes through the animal's mouth. 4. a person, a newspaper, or the like that voices or communicates the sentiments, decisions, etc., of another or others; a spokesman.

mouth·y (mou′thĭ, mou′thĭ), *adj.,* **mouthier,** **mouthiest.** loud-mouthed; ranting; bombastic. —**mouth·i·ly,** *adv.* —**mouth·i·ness,** *n.*

mou·ton·née (mōō′tə·nā′), *adj. Phys. Geog.* designating scattered knobs of rock rounded and smoothed by glacial action. Also, **mou′ton·néed′.** [t. F: lit., rounded like a sheep's back, pp. fem. of *moutonner,* der. *mouton* sheep. See MUTTON]

mov·a·ble (mōō′və·bəl), *adj.* 1. capable of being moved; not fixed in one place, position, or posture. 2. *Law.* (of property) a. not permanent in place; capable of being moved without injury. b. personal, as distinguished from real. 3. changing from one date to another in different years. —*n.* 4. an article of furniture which is not fixed in place. 5. (*usually pl.*) *Law.* an article of personal property not attached to land. Also, **moveable.** —**mov·a·ble·ness,** **mov·a·bil·i·ty,** *n.* —**mov·a·bly,** *adv.*

move (mōōv), *v.,* **moved,** **moving,** *n.* —*v.i.* 1. to change place or position; pass from one place or situation to another. **2.** to change one's abode; go from one place of residence to another. **3.** to advance, progress, or make progress. **4.** to have a regular motion, as an implement or a machine; turn; revolve. **5.** *Com.* to be disposed of by sale, as goods in stock. **6.** *Colloq.* to start off, or depart: *it's time to be moving.* **7.** (of the bowels) to operate. **8.** to be active in a particular sphere: *to move in society.* **9.** to take action, or act, as in an affair. **10.** to make a formal request, application, or proposal: *to move for a new trial.* —*v.t.* **11.** to change the place or position of; take from one place, posture, or situation to another. **12.** to set or keep in motion; stir or shake. **13.** to prompt, actuate, or impel to some action: *what moved you to do this?* **14.** to cause (the bowels) to act or operate. **15.** to arouse or excite the feelings or passions of; affect with emotion; excite (to). **16.** to affect with tender or compassionate emotion; touch. **17.** to propose formally, as to a court or judge, or for consideration by a deliberative assembly. **18.** to submit a formal request or proposal to (a sovereign, a court, etc.). —*n.* **19.** act of moving; a movement. **20.** a change of abode or residence. **21.** an action toward an end; a step. **22.** *Games, etc.* the right or turn to move. [ME *move*(n), t. AF: m. *mover*, g. L *movēre*] —**mov′er**, *n.* —**Syn. 1.** See **advance. 11.** remove, transfer, shift. **13.** influence; induce, incite, instigate; lead. **19.** See **motion.** —**Ant. 11.** fix.

move·a·ble (mōōv′və bəl), *adj., n.* movable. —**move′a·ble·ness, move·a·bil′i·ty,** *n.* —**move′a·bly,** *adv.*

move·ment (mōōv′mənt), *n.* **1.** act or process of moving. **2.** a particular manner of moving. **3.** (*chiefly pl.*) an action or activity, as of a person or a body of persons. **4.** *Mil., Naval.* a change of position or location of troops or ships. **5.** rapid progress of events, or abundance of events or incidents. **6.** the progress of events, as in a narrative or drama. **7.** the suggestion of action, as in a painting or the like. **8.** a series of actions or activities directed or tending toward a particular end: *the antislavery movement.* **9.** the course of tendency, or trend, of affairs in a particular field. **10.** the price change in the market of some commodity or security. **11.** an evacuation of the bowels. **12.** the material evacuated. **13.** the works, or a distinct portion of the works, of a mechanism, as a watch. **14.** *Music.* **a.** a principal division or section of a sonata, symphony, or the like. **b.** motion; rhythm; time; tempo. **15.** *Pros.* rhythmical structure or character. —**Syn. 1.** See **motion.**

mov·ie (mōō′vĭ), *n. U.S. Colloq.* a motion picture.

mov·ing (mōō′vĭng), *adj.* **1.** that moves. **2.** causing or producing motion. **3.** actuating, instigating, or impelling: *the moving cause of a dispute.* **4.** that excites the feelings or affects with emotion, esp. touching or pathetic. —**mov′ing·ly,** *adv.* —**mov′ing·ness,** *n.*

moving picture, motion picture.

moving staircase, escalator.

mow[1] (mō), *v.,* **mowed, mowed** or **mown, mowing.** —*v.t.* **1.** to cut down (grass, grain, etc.) with a scythe or a machine. **2.** to cut grass, grain, etc. from. **3.** to cut down, destroy, or kill indiscriminately or in great numbers, as men in battle. —*v.i.* **4.** to cut down grass, grain, etc. **5.** to sweep down men in battle. [ME *mowe*(n), OE *māwan,* c. G *mähen*] —**mow′er,** *n.*

mow[2] (mou), *n.* **1.** the place in a barn where hay, sheaves of grain, etc., are stored. **2.** a heap or pile of hay or of sheaves of grain in a barn. [ME *mowe,* OE *mūga, mūha,* c. Icel. *mūgi* swath]

mow[3] (mou, mō), *Archaic.* —*n.* **1.** a wry or derisive grimace. —*v.i.* **2.** to make mows, mouths, or grimaces. [ME *mowe,* t. OF: m. *moe* a pouting grimace]

mowe (mou, mō), *n., v.,* **mowed, mowing.** *Archaic.* **mow**[3].

mow·ing (mō′ĭng), *n.* **1.** act of leveling or cutting down grass with a mowing machine or scythe. **2.** as much grass as is cut in any specified period.

mowing machine, a machine for mowing or cutting down standing grass, etc.

mown (mōn), *adj.* mowed; cut as if mowed.

mo·yen âge (mwȧ yě näzh′), *French.* the Middle Ages.

Mozamb., Mozambique.

Mo·zam·bique (mō′zəm bēk′), *n.* **1.** Also, **Portuguese East Africa.** a Portuguese colony in SE Africa. 5,085,630 pop. (1940); 297,731 sq. mi. *Cap.:* Lourenço Marques. **2.** a seaport on an island just off the NE coast of this colony. 9222 (1940). Portuguese, **Moçambique.**

Mozambique Channel, a channel between Mozambique and Madagascar. ab. 950 mi. long; 250–550 mi wide.

Mo·zart (mō′zärt; *Ger.* mō′tsärt), *n.* **Wolfgang Amadeus** (vôlf′gäng ä′mä dā′ŏŏs), 1756–91, Austrian composer.

moz·zet·ta (mō zět′ə; *It.* môt sět′tä), *n. Rom. Cath. Ch.* a short cape which covers the shoulders and can be buttoned over the breast, and to which a hood is attached, worn by the pope and by cardinals, bishops, abbots, and other dignitaries. Also, **mo·zet′ta.** [t. It. Cf. AMICE[1], MUTCH]

M.P., 1. melting point. **2.** Member of Parliament. **3.** Metropolitan police. **4.** Also, **MP,** Military Police. **5.** Also, **MP,** Mounted Police.

m.p., melting point.

m.p.h., miles per hour.

Mr. (mĭs′tər), *pl.* **Messrs.** mister: a title prefixed to a man's name or position, as in *Mr. Lawson, Mr. President.*

Mrs. (mĭs′ĭz, -ĭs, mĭz′-), *pl.* **Mmes.** mistress: a title prefixed to the name of a married woman, as in *Mrs. Jones.*

MS., *pl.* **MSS.** manuscript. Also, **ms.**

M.S., 1. Master of Science. **2.** Master in Surgery.

m.s., modification of the stem of.

M.Sc., Master of Science.

Msgr., Monsignor.

m′sieur (mə syœ′), *n. French.* contraction of *monsieur.*

m.s.t., mountain standard time.

Ms-Th, *Chem.* mesothorium.

Mt., *pl.* **Mts. 1.** mount: *Mt. Rainier.* **2.** mountain. Also, **mt.**

M.T., metric ton.

m.t., mountain time.

mtn., mountain.

Mt. Rev., Most Reverend.

mu (mū, mōō), *n.* the twelfth letter of the Greek alphabet (M, μ).

much (mŭch), *adj.,* **more, most,** *n., adv.* —*adj.* **1.** in great quantity, amount, measure, or degree: *much work.* —*n.* **2.** a great quantity or amount; a great deal: *much of this is true.* **3.** a great, important, or notable thing or matter: *the house is not much to look at.* **4. to make much of, a.** to treat, represent, or consider as of great importance. **b.** to treat (a person) with great, flattering, or fond consideration. —*adv.* **5.** to a great extent or degree; greatly; far: *much pleased.* **6.** nearly, approximately, or about: *this is much the same as the others.* [ME *muche, moche,* apocopated var. of *muchel, mochel,* OE *mycel*; r. ME *miche*(l), OE *micel* great, much, c. Icel. *mikill,* Goth. *mikils,* Gk. *megalo-* great]

Much Ado About Nothing, a comedy (about 1598) by Shakespeare.

much·ness (mŭch′nĭs), *n.* greatness, as in quantity, measure, or degree.

mu·cic acid (mū′sĭk), *Chem.* a dibasic crystalline acid, HOOC(CHOH)₄COOH, obtained by oxidizing certain gums, milk sugar, or galactose.

mu·cid (mū′sĭd), *adj.* moldy; musty. [t. L: s. *mūcidus*] —**mu′cid·ness,** *n.*

mu·ci·lage (mū′sə lĭj), *n.* **1.** any of various preparations of gum, glue, or the like, for causing adhesion. **2.** any of various gummy secretions or gelatinous substances present in plants. [ME, t. F, t. LL: m. *mucilāgo* a musty juice]

mu·ci·lag·i·nous (mū′sə lăj′ə nəs), *adj.* **1.** of, pertaining to, or secreting mucilage. **2.** of the nature of or resembling mucilage; moist, soft, and viscid.

mu·cin (mū′sĭn), *n. Biochem.* any of a group of nitrogenous substances found in mucous secretions, etc., and of varying composition according to their source. [f. s. L *mūcus* MUCUS + -IN[2]] —**mu′cin·ous,** *adj.*

muck (mŭk), *n.* **1.** farmyard dung, decaying vegetable matter, etc., in a moist state; manure. **2.** a highly organic soil, less than fifty per cent combustible, often used as manure. **3.** filth; dirt. **4.** *Brit. Colloq.* something of no value; trash. **5.** *Mining, etc.* earth, rock, or other useless matter to be removed in order to get out the mineral or other substances sought. —*v.t.* **6.** to manure. **7.** to make dirty; soil. **8.** to remove muck from. —*v.i.* **9. muck about,** *Brit.* to idle; putter. [ME *muk,* t. Scand.; cf. Icel. *myki* cow dung]

muck·er (mŭk′ər), *n.* **1.** *Brit. Slang.* a vulgar, ill-bred person. **2.** *Mining, etc.* one who removes muck.

muck·le (mŭk′əl), *n. U.S. Dial.* a wooden cudgel used to kill fish.

muck rake, a rake for use on muck or filth.

muck·rake (mŭk′rāk′), *v.i.,* **-raked, -raking.** *Colloq.* to expose, esp. in print, political or other corruption, real or alleged. [f. MUCK + RAKE] —**muck′rak′er,** *n.*

muck·y (mŭk′ĭ), *adj.,* **muckier, muckiest. 1.** of or like muck. **2.** filthy; dirty.

mu·coid (mū′koid), *n. Biochem.* any of a group of substances resembling the mucins, occurring in connective tissue, etc. [f. MUC(IN) + -OID]

mu·co·pro·te·in (mū′kō prō′tē′ĭn, -tēn), *n.* a compound, containing protein and a carbohydrate group.

mu·co·sa (mūkō′sə), *n., pl.* **-sae** (-sē). *Anat.* a mucous membrane. [t. NL, fem. of L *mūcōsus* MUCOUS]

mu·cous (mū′kəs), *adj.* **1.** pertaining to, consisting of, or resembling mucus. **2.** containing or secreting mucus: *the mucous membrane.* [t. L: m.s. *mūcōsus* slimy] —**mu·cos·i·ty** (mū kŏs′ə tĭ), *n.*

mucous membrane, a lubricating membrane lining an internal surface or an organ, such as the alimentary, respiratory, and genito-urinary canals.

mu·cro (mū′krō), *n., pl.* **mucrones** (mūkrō′-nēz). *Bot., Zool.* a short point projecting abruptly, as at the end of a leaf. [t. L: point]

mu·cro·nate (mū′krō nĭt, -nāt′), *adj. Bot.* having an abruptly projecting point, as a feather, leaf, etc. Also, **mu′cro·nat′ed.** [t. L: m.s. *mūcrōnātus* pointed]

Mucronate tail feather of chimney swift

mu·cus (mū′kəs), *n.* a viscid secretion of the mucous membranes. [t. L]

mud (mŭd), *n.* wet, soft earth or earthy matter, as on the ground after rain, at the bottom of a pond, or among the discharges from a volcano; mire. [ME *mudde, mode,* c. MLG *mudde*]

mud·cap (mŭd′kăp′), *v.t.,* **-capped, -capping. 1.** to cover with a cap of mud. **2.** (in blasting) to detonate (an explosive capped with mud), as on an exposed rock surface.

mud·cat (mŭd′kăt′), *n.* (in the Mississippi valley) a catfish grown to large size.

mud dauber, any of certain wasps of the family *Sphecidae,* which construct mud cells for their larvae and provision them with insects.

mud·dle (mŭd′əl), *v.,* **-dled, -dling,** *n.* — *v.t.* **1.** to mix up or jumble together in a confused or bungling way. **2.** to render confused mentally, or unable to think clearly. **3.** to render confused or stupid with drink, or as drink does. **4.** to mix or stir (chocolate, etc.). **5.** to make muddy or turbid, as water. **6. muddle through,** *Brit.* to come to a successful conclusion without planned direction. — *n.* **7.** a muddled condition; a confused mental state. **8.** a confused, disordered, or embarrassing state of affairs, or a mess. [f. MUD + *-le,* freq. and dim. suffix]

mud·dler (mŭd′lər), *n.* **1.** a stick for stirring drinks. **2.** one who muddles or muddles through.

mud·dy (mŭd′ĭ), *adj.,* **-dier, -diest,** *v.,* **-died, -dying.** — *adj.* **1.** abounding in or covered with mud. **2.** not clear or pure, as color. **3.** dull, as the complexion. **4.** not clear mentally. **5.** obscure or vague, as thought, expression, literary style, etc. — *v.t.* **6.** to make muddy; soil with mud. **7.** to make turbid. **8.** to render confused or obscure. — *v.i.* **9.** to become muddy. —**mud′di·ly,** *adv.* —**mud′di·ness,** *n.*

mud·guard (mŭd′gärd′), *n.* a guard or shield so placed as to protect riders or passengers from mud thrown by the wheel of a bicycle, automobile, or the like.

mud hen, any of various marsh-inhabiting birds, esp. the American coot.

mud puppy, 1. any of the large North American aquatic salamanders of the genus *Necturus,* which have bushy red gills and well developed limbs. **2.** any of various American salamanders of the genus *Ambystoma.*

mud·sill (mŭd′sĭl′), *n.* the lowest sill of a structure, usually placed in or on the ground.

mud·stone (mŭd′stōn′), *n.* a clayey rock of nearly uniform texture throughout, with little or no lamination.

mud·suck·er (mŭd′sŭk′ər), *n.* the long-jawed goby, *Gillichthys mirabilis,* a Californian fish much used as bait.

mud turtle, any of various fresh-water turtles of the U.S., as *Kinosternon subrubrum,* or *Chrysemys picta.*

mu·ez·zin (mū·ĕz′ĭn, mōō-), *n.* (in Mohammedan communities) the crier who, from a minaret or other part of a mosque, at stated hours five times daily, intones aloud the call summoning the Faithful to prayer. [t. Ar.: m. *muazzin,* d. var. of *muadhdhin*]

muff (mŭf), *n.* **1.** a kind of thick tubular case covered with fur or other material, in which the hands are placed for warmth. **2.** a tuft of feathers on the sides of the head of certain fowls. **3.** *Baseball.* a failure to hold a ball that comes into one's hands. — *v.t.* **4.** *Colloq.* to perform clumsily, or bungle. **5.** *Baseball.* to fail to hold (a ball that comes into one's hands). — *v.i.* **6.** *Colloq.* to bungle; make a muff. [t. D: m. *mof,* t. F: m. *moufle;* akin to MUFFLE, n.]

muf·fin (mŭf′ĭn), *n.* **1.** a small, round bread made with wheat flour, corn meal, or the like, eaten with butter and usually served hot. **2.** such a bread made from yeast dough. [orig. obscure]

muf·fle (mŭf′əl), *v.,* **-fled, -fling,** *n.* — *v.t.* **1.** to wrap or envelop in a cloak, shawl, scarf, or the like disposed about the person, esp. about the face and neck (often fol. by *up*). **2.** to wrap with something to deaden or prevent sound: *to muffle drums.* **3.** to deaden (sound) by wrappings or other means. — *v.i.* **4.** to muffle oneself (up) as in garments or other wrappings. — *n.* **5.** something that muffles. **6.** muffled sound. **7.** an oven or arched chamber in a furnace or kiln, used for heating substances without direct contact with the fire. **8.** the thick, bare part of the upper lip and nose of ruminants and rodents. [ME *mufle(n),* appar. t. OF. Cf. OF *em-mouflé* wrapped up]

muf·fler (mŭf′lər), *n.* **1.** a heavy neck scarf. **2.** any of various devices for deadening sound, as the sound of escaping gases of an internal-combustion engine. **3.** anything used for muffling.

muf·ti (mŭf′tĭ), *n., pl.* **-tis. 1.** civilian dress as opposed to military or other uniform, or as worn by one who usually wears a uniform. **2.** a Mohammedan legal adviser consulted in applying the religious law. **3.** (under the Ottoman Empire) the official head of the state religion, or one of his deputies. **4.** See **Grand Mufti.** [t. Ar.: lit., one who delivers a judgment; orig. Ar. meaning def. 2. Def. 1 from the fact that a mufti is a civil official]

mug (mŭg), *n., v.,* **mugged, mugging.** — *n.* **1.** a drinking cup, usually cylindrical and commonly with a handle. **2.** the quantity it holds. **3.** *Slang.* the face. **4.** *Slang.* the mouth. **5.** *Slang.* a grimace. — *v.t.* **6.** *Slang.* to take a photograph of (a person), esp. in compliance with an official or legal requirement. **7.** *Slang.* (of a thug, etc.)

to assault (a victim, etc.) from the rear by locking the forearm around the neck and throttling. — *v.i.* **8.** *Slang.* to grimace. [cf. Norw. *mugge,* Sw. *mugg;* drinking mugs shaped to resemble a face were formerly common, hence the slang meanings]

mug·ger (mŭg′ər), *n.* a broad-snouted crocodile, *Crocodilus palustris,* of India, etc., growing to about 12 feet in length. Also, **mug′gar, mug′gur.** [t. Hind.: m. *magar*]

mug·gins (mŭg′ĭnz), *n.* **1.** a convention in the card game of cribbage in which a player scores points overlooked by opponent. **2.** a game of dominoes in which any player, if he can make the sum of the two ends of the line equal five or a multiple of five, adds the number so made to his score. [? orig. surname *Muggins*]

mug·gy (mŭg′ĭ), *adj.,* **-gier, -giest.** (of the atmosphere, weather, etc.) damp and close; humid and oppressive. [f. d. *mug* mist (t. Scand.; cf. Icel. *mugga*) + *-y*[1]] —**mug′gi·ness,** *n.* —**Ant.** dry.

mug·wump (mŭg′wŭmp′), *n.* *U.S.* **1.** (in the presidential campaign of 1884) Republicans who refused to support the party nominee (J. G. Blaine). **2.** one who acts as an independent or affects superiority, esp. in politics. [t. Algonquian (Massachusetts): m. *mukquomp* leader, chief, great man, f. m. *moqki* great + *-omp* man] —**mug′wump′er·y,** *n.*

Mu·ham·mad (mōō·hăm′əd), *n.* Mohammed. —**Mu·ham′mad·an, Mu·ham′med·an,** *adj., n.*

Mühl·bach (myl′bäkh), *n.* **Luise** (lōō·ē′zə), (*Klara Muller Mundt*) 1814–73, German novelist.

Muir (myŏŏr), *n.* **John,** 1838–1914, U.S. naturalist, explorer, and writer.

Muir Glacier, a glacier in SE Alaska, flowing from the slopes of Mt. Fairweather into the ocean. ab. 350 sq. mi.

mu·jik (mōō zhĭk′, mōō′zhĭk), *n.* muzhik.

Muk·den (mŏŏk′dĕn′, mōōk′-), *n.* a city in NE China, in S Manchuria: the former capital of Manchuria; battle, 1905. 1,077,500 (est. 1941). Also, **Moukden** or **Fengtien.**

mu·lat·to (mə·lăt′ō, mū-), *n., pl.* **-toes,** *adj.* — *n.* **1.** the offspring of parents of whom one is white and the other a Negro. — *adj.* **2.** having a light-brown color (similar to the skin of a mulatto). [t. Sp. and Pg.: m. *mulato,* der. *mulo,* g. L *mūlus* MULE[1]; so called from the hybrid origin]

mul·ber·ry (mŭl′bĕr′ĭ, -bər ĭ), *n., pl.* **-ries. 1.** the edible, berrylike collective fruit of any tree of the genus *Morus.* **2.** a tree of this genus, as M. *rubra* (**red** or **American mulberry**), with dark-purple fruit, M. *nigra* (**black mulberry**), with dark-colored fruit, and M. *alba* (**white mulberry**), with fruit nearly white and with leaves especially valued as food for silkworms. **3.** a dull, dark reddish-purple color. [ME *mulberie,* dissimilated var. of *murberie,* OE *mōrberie,* f. s. L *mōrum* mulberry + *berie* BERRY]

mulch (mŭlch), *Hort.* — *n.* **1.** straw, leaves, loose earth, etc., spread on the ground or produced by tillage to protect the roots of newly planted trees, crops, etc. — *v.t.* **2.** to cover with mulch. [n. use of (obs.) *mulch,* adj., ME *molsh* soft, OE *myl(i)sc* mellow; akin to d. G *molsch* soft, overripe]

mulct (mŭlkt), *n.* **1.** a fine; a penalty. — *v.t.* **2.** to punish (a person, or formerly, an offense) by fine or forfeiture. **3.** to deprive of something as a penalty. **4.** to deprive of something by trickery. [t. L: s. *mulcta* fine]

mule[1] (mūl), *n.* **1.** the offspring of a male donkey and a mare, used esp. as a beast of burden because of its patience, sure-footedness, and hardiness. **2.** any hybrid between the donkey and the horse. **3.** *Colloq.* a stupid or stubborn person. **4.** *Biol.* a

Mule *Equus caballus x asinus* (ab. 5 ft. high at the shoulder)

hybrid, esp. a hybrid between the canary and some other finch. **5.** a machine which spins cotton, etc., into yarn and winds it on spindles. [ME *mule,* t. OF, g. L *mūla;* r. OE *mūl,* t. L: s. *mūlus*]

mule[2] (mūl), *n.* a kind of slipper which leaves the heel exposed. [ME, t. F.]

mule deer, a deer, *Odocoileus hemionus,* with large ears, common in western North America.

mule skinner, *U.S. Colloq.* a driver of mules.

mu·le·teer (mū′lə·tĭr′), *n.* a driver of mules. [t. F: m. *muletier,* der. *mulet,* dim. of OF *mul* MULE[1]]

mul·ey (mū′lĭ, mōōl′ĭ), *adj., n., pl.* **-leys.** — *adj.* **1.** (of cattle) hornless; polled. — *n.* **2.** any cow. Also, **mulley.** [var. of d. *moiley,* t. Irish: m. *maol,* or t. Welsh: m. *moel,* lit., bald]

Mule deer, *Odocoileus hemionus* (3½ ft. high at the shoulder, total length 5½ ft.)

muley saw, *U.S. Colloq.* a saw having a long, stiff blade which is not stretched in a gate but whose motion is directed by clamps at each end mounted on guide rails.

Mul·ha·cén (mōōl′ä·thĕn′), *n.* a mountain in S Spain: the highest peak in Spain. ab. 11,420 ft.

Mül·heim an der Ruhr (mȳl′hīm än dĕr rōōr′), a city in W Germany, near Essen. 137,540 (1939).

Mul·house (my lōōz′). *n.* a city in E France, near the Rhine. 87,655 (1946). German, **Mülhausen.**

mu·li·eb·ri·ty (mū′lĭ ĕb′rə tĭ), *n.* 1. womanly nature or qualities. 2. womanhood. [t. LL: m.s. *muliebritas*, der. L *muliebris* womanly]

mul·ish (mū′lĭsh), *adj.* like a mule; characteristic of a mule; stubborn, obstinate, or intractable. —**mul′ish·ly,** *adv.* —**mul′ish·ness,** *n.*

mull[1] (mŭl), *U.S. Colloq.* —*v.i.* 1. to study or ruminate (over), esp. in an ineffective way. —*v.t.* 2. to make a mess or failure of. [orig. obscure]

mull[2] (mŭl), *v.t.* to heat, sweeten, and spice for drinking, as ale, wine, etc.: *mulled cider.* [orig. uncert.]

mull[3] (mŭl), *n.* a soft, thin kind of muslin. [earlier *mulmul,* t. Hind.: m. *malmal*]

Mull (mŭl), *n.* an island in the Hebrides, in W Scotland. 3389 pop. (1931); ab. 351 sq. mi.

mul·lah (mŭl′ə, mōōl′ə), *n.* 1. (in Mohammedan countries) a title of respect for one who is learned in or teaches, or expounds, the sacred law. 2. (in Turkey) a provincial judge. Also, **mul′la.** [t. Turk., Pers., and Hind.: m. *mullā,* t. Ar.: m. *mawlā* patron, lord]

mul·lein (mŭl′ĭn), *n.* 1. a stout Old World weed, *Verbascum Thapsus,* with coarse woolly leaves and dense spikes of yellow flowers, locally common as a weed in North America. 2. any plant of the same genus, or any of various similar plants. Also, **mul′len.** [ME *moleyn,* t. AF: m. *moleine,* ? der. OF *mol,* g. L *mollis* soft]

mull·er (mŭl′ər), *n.* 1. an implement of stone or other substance with a flat base for grinding paints, powders, etc., on a slab of stone or the like. 2. any of various mechanical devices for grinding. [? orig. meaning powderer (der. ME *mul* powder, OE *myl* dust, c .G *müll*)]

Mül·ler (mŭl′ər; *Ger.* mȳ′lər), *n.* **Friedrich Max** (frē′drĭĸн mäks), 1823–1900, German Sanskrit scholar and philologist, in England.

mul·let (mŭl′ĭt), *n., pl.* **-lets,** (*esp. collectively*) **-let.** 1. any fish of the family *Mugilidae,* which includes various marine and fresh-water species with a nearly cylindrical body and generally gray coloration, as the wide-ranging striped mullet, *Mugil cephalus.* 2. a goatfish. 3. a sucker, particularly of the genus *Moxostoma.* 4. any of various other fishes. [ME *mulet,* t. OF, der. L *mullus* red mullet]

mul·ley (mōōl′ĭ), *adj., n., pl.* **-leys.** muley.

mul·li·gan (mŭl′ĭ gən), *n. U.S. Slang.* a kind of stew containing meat, vegetables, etc.

mul·li·ga·taw·ny (mŭl′ĭ gə tô′nĭ), *n.* a soup of East Indian origin, flavored with curry. [t. Tamil: m. *milagutannir* pepper water]

mul·lion (mŭl′yən), *Archit.* —*n.* 1. a vertical member, as of stone or wood, between the lights of a window, the panels in wainscoting, or the like. 2. one of the radiating bars of a rose window or the like. —*v.t.* 3. to furnish with, or to form into divisions by the use of mullions. [metathetic var. of *monial,* t. OF; orig. uncert.]

mul·lock (mŭl′ək), *n.* *Australasia.* mining refuse; muck. [f. d. *mull* rubbish (see MULLER) + -OCK]

Mu·lock (mū′lŏk), *n.* **Dinah Maria,** (*Mrs. Craik*) 1826–87, British novelist.

Mul·tan (mōōl′tän′), *n.* a city in Pakistan, in W Punjab. 142,768 (1941).

multi-, a word element meaning "many." [t. L, comb. form of *multus* much, many]

mul·ti·cel·lu·lar (mŭl′tĭ sĕl′yə lər), *adj.* composed of several to many cells.

mul·ti·coil (mŭl′tĭ koil′), *adj.* having more than one coil, as an electrical device.

mul·ti·col·ored (mŭl′tĭ kŭl′ərd), *adj.* of many colors.

mul·ti·cyl·in·der (mŭl′tĭ sĭl′ĭn dər), *adj.* having more than one cylinder, as an internal-combustion or steam engine. Also, **mul′ti·cyl′in·dered.**

mul·ti·den·tate (mŭl′tĭ dĕn′tāt), *adj.* having many teeth or toothlike processes.

mul·ti·far·i·ous (mŭl′tĭ fâr′ĭ əs), *adj.* 1. having many different parts, elements, forms, etc. 2. of many kinds, or numerous and varied; manifold (modifying a pl. n.): *multifarious activities.* [t. L: m. *multifārius* manifold] —**mul′ti·far′i·ous·ly,** *adv.* —**mul′ti·far′i·ous·ness,** *n.*

mul·ti·fid (mŭl′tĭ fĭd), *adj.* cleft into many parts, divisions, or lobes. Also, **mul·tif·i·dous** (mŭl tĭf′ə dəs). [t. L: s. *multifidus*]

mul·ti·flo·rous (mŭl′tĭ flôr′əs), *adj.* *Bot.* bearing many flowers, as a peduncle.

mul·ti·fold (mŭl′tĭ fōld′), *adj.* manifold.

mul·ti·fo·li·ate (mŭl′tĭ fō′lĭ ĭt, -āt′), *adj.* *Bot.* having many leaves or leaflets.

mul·ti·form (mŭl′tĭ fôrm′), *adj.* having many forms; of many different forms or kinds. [t. L: s. *multiformis*] —**mul′ti·for′mi·ty** (mŭl′tĭ fôr′mə tĭ), *n.*

mul·ti·graph (mŭl′tĭ grăf′, -gräf′), *n.* 1. a combined rotary typesetting and printing machine, commonly used to reproduce typewritten matter. 2. (*cap.*) a trademark for this machine. —*v.t., v.i.* 3. to reproduce (matter) with such a machine.

mul·ti·lam·i·nate (mŭl′tĭ lăm′ə nĭt, -nāt′), *adj.* having many laminae or layers.

mul·ti·lat·er·al (mŭl′tĭ lăt′ər əl), *adj.* 1. having many sides; many-sided. 2. *Govt.* multipartite. —**mul′ti·lat′er·al·ly,** *adv.*

mul·ti·lob·u·lar (mŭl′tĭ lŏb′yə lər), *adj.* having many lobules.

mul·ti·mil·lion·aire (mŭl′tə mĭl′yən âr′), *n.* one with property worth several millions, as of dollars.

mul·ti·mo·lec·u·lar (mŭl′tĭ mə lĕk′yə lər), *adj.* having many loculi, chambers, or cells.

mul·ti·mo·tored (mŭl′tĭ mō′tərd), *adj.* with a number of motors or engines.

mul·ti·nom·i·nal (mŭl′tĭ nŏm′ə nəl), *adj.* having many names.

mul·ti·nu·cle·ar (mŭl′tĭ nū′klĭ ər, -nōō′-), *adj.* having many or several nuclei, as a cell.

mul·tip·a·ra (mŭl tĭp′ə rə), *n., pl.* **-rae** (-rē′). *Obstet.* a woman who has borne two or more children, or who is parturient the second time. [t. NL, fem. of *multiparus* MULTIPAROUS]

mul·tip·a·rous (mŭl tĭp′ə rəs), *adj.* 1. producing many, or more than one, at a birth. 2. *Bot.* (of a cyme) having many lateral axes. [t. NL: m. *multiparus.* See MULTI-, -PAROUS]

mul·ti·par·tite (mŭl′tĭ pär′tīt), *adj.* 1. divided into many parts; having many divisions. 2. *Govt.* denoting an agreement or other instrument in which three or more states participate; multilateral. [t. L: m.s. *multipartītus* much-divided]

mul·ti·ped (mŭl′tə pĕd′), *adj.* having many feet. Also, **mul·ti·pede** (mŭl′tə pēd′). [t. L: s. *multipēs,* adj. and n., many-footed]

mul·ti·phase (mŭl′tə fāz′), *adj.* *Elect.* having many phases.

mul·ti·ple (mŭl′tə pəl), *adj.* 1. consisting of, having, or involving many individuals, parts, elements, relations, etc.; manifold. 2. *Elect.* denoting two or more circuits connected in parallel. 3. *Bot.* (of a fruit) collective. —*n.* 4. *Math.* a number which contains another number some number of times without a remainder: *12 is a multiple of 3.* 5. *Elect.* **a.** a group of terminals arranged to make a circuit or group of circuits accessible at a number of points at any one of which connection can be made. **b. in multiple,** in parallel. See **parallel** (def. 11). [t. F, t. LL: m. *multiplus* manifold]

multiple alleles, *Genetics.* a series of three or more alternative or allelic forms of a gene, only two of which can exist in any normal, diploid individual.

multiple cropping, *Agric.* the use of the same field for two or more separate crops, whether of the same or of different kinds, successively during a single year.

multiple factors, *Genetics.* a series of two or more pairs of genes responsible for the development of complex, quantitative characters such as size, yield, etc.

multiple neuritis, *Pathol.* inflammation of several nerves at the same time.

multiple star, *Astron.* three or more stars lying close together in the celestial sphere and usually united in a single gravitational system.

multiple voting, casting ballots in more than one constituency in one election, as in England before, and to some extent after, the franchise reform of 1918.

mul·ti·plex (mŭl′tə plĕks′), *adj.* 1. manifold; multiple: *multiplex telegraphy.* —*v.t.* 2. *Elect.* to arrange a circuit for use by multiplex telegraphy. [t. L: manifold]

multiplex telegraphy, a system for sending many messages in each direction, simultaneously, over the same wire or communications channel.

mul·ti·pli·a·ble (mŭl′tə plī′ə bəl), *adj.* that may be multiplied. Also, **mul·ti·pli·ca·ble** (mŭl′tə plĭ′kə bəl).

mul·ti·pli·cand (mŭl′tə plĭ′kănd′), *n.* *Math.* the number to be multiplied by another. [t. L: s. *multiplicandus,* gerundive of *multiplicāre* MULTIPLY]

mul·ti·pli·cate (mŭl′tə plĭ′kāt′), *adj.* multiple; manifold. [ME, t. L: m.s. *multiplicātus,* pp., multiplied]

mul·ti·pli·ca·tion (mŭl′tə plə kā′shən), *n.* 1. act or process of multiplying. 2. the state of being multiplied. 3. *Arith.* the process of finding the number (the product) resulting from the addition of a given number (the multiplicand) taken as many times as there are units in another given number (the multiplier). 4. *Math.* any generalization of this operation applicable to numbers other than integers, such as fractions, irrationals, vectors, etc. —**mul·ti·pli·ca′tion·al,** *adj.*

mul·ti·pli·ca·tive (mŭl′tə plə kā′tĭv), *adj.* 1. tending to multiply or increase. 2. having the power of multiplying. —**mul′ti·pli·ca′tive·ly,** *adv.*

mul·ti·plic·i·ty (mŭl′tə plĭs′ə tĭ), *n., pl.* **-ties.** 1. a multitide or great number. 2. state of being multiple or manifold; manifold variety. [t. LL: m.s. *multiplicitas*]

mul·ti·pli·er (mŭl′tə plī′ər), *n.* 1. one who or that which multiplies. 2. *Math.* the number by which another is to be multiplied. 3. *Physics.* a device for intensifying some phenomenon.

mul·ti·ply (mŭl′tə plī′), *v.,* **-plied, -plying.** —*v.t.* 1. to make many or manifold; increase the number, quantity, etc., of. 2. *Math.* to take by addition a given number of times; find the product by multiplication. 3. to produce (animals or plants) by propagation. 4. to increase by procreation. —*v.i.* 5. to grow in number, quantity, etc.; increase. 6. *Math.* to perform the process of multiplication. 7. to increase in number by procreation or natural generation. [ME *multiplie*(n), t. OF: m. *multiplier,* t. L: m. *multiplicāre*]

M. Mullion

mul·ti·po·lar (mŭl′tĭ pō′lər), *adj.* having many poles.

mul·ti·tude (mŭl′tə tūd′, -tōōd′), *n.* **1.** a great number; host: *a multitude of friends.* **2.** a great number of persons gathered together; a crowd or throng. **3. the multitude,** the common people. **4.** the state or character of being many, or numerousness. [ME, t. L: m. *multitūdo*] —Syn. 2. See **crowd.**

mul·ti·tu·di·nous (mŭl′tə tū′də nəs, -tōō′-), *adj.* **1.** forming a multitude or great number, or existing, occurring, or present in great numbers; very numerous. **2.** comprising many items, parts, or elements. **3.** *Poetic.* crowded or thronged. —**mul′ti·tu′di·nous·ly,** *adv.* —**mul′ti·tu′di·nous·ness,** *n.*

mul·ti·va·lent (mŭl′tə vā′lənt, mŭl tĭv′ə lənt), *adj. Chem.* having a valence of three or higher. Cf. **polyvalent.** —**mul·ti·va·lence** (mŭl′tə vā′ləns, mŭl tĭv′ə ləns), *n.*

mul·tum in par·vo (mŭl′təm ĭn pär′vō), *Latin.* much in little; a great deal in a small space or in brief.

mul·ture (mŭl′chər), *n.* a toll or fee given to the proprietor of a mill for the grinding of grain, usually consisting of a fixed proportion of the grain brought or of the flour made. [ME, t. OF: m. *molture*, g. L *molitūra* a grinding]

mum[1] (mŭm), *adj.* **1.** silent; not saying a word: *to keep mum.* —*interj.* **2.** Say nothing! Be silent! [ME; imit. Cf. G *mumm*]

mum[2] (mŭm), *v.i.,* **mummed, mumming. 1.** to say "mum" (with closed lips); call for silence. **2.** to act as a mummer. Also, **mumm.** [v. use of MUM[1]. Cf. OF *momer* mask oneself]

mum[3] (mŭm), *n. Colloq.* chrysanthemum.

mum[4] (mŭm), *n. Colloq.* mother.

mum·ble (mŭm′bəl), *v.,* **-bled, -bling,** *n.* —*v.i.* **1.** to speak indistinctly or unintelligibly, as with partly closed lips; mutter low, indistinct words. **2.** to chew ineffectively, as from loss of teeth: *to mumble on a crust.* —*v.t.* **3.** to utter indistinctly, as with partly closed lips. **4.** to chew, or try to eat, with difficulty, as from loss of teeth. —*n.* **5.** a low, indistinct utterance or sound. [ME *momele,* freq. of (obs.) *mum,* v., make inarticulate sound. Cf. G *mummeln*] —**mum′bler,** *n.* —**mum′bling·ly,** *adv.* —Syn. 1. See **murmur.**

mum·bo jum·bo (mŭm′bō jŭm′bō). **1.** meaningless incantation or ritual. **2.** an object of superstitious awe or reverence. **3.** (*cap.*) the guardian of western Sudan Negro villages symbolized by a masked man who combats evil and punishes women for breaches of tribal laws. Also, **mumm,** *v.i.* **mum**[2].

mum·mer (mŭm′ər), *n.* **1.** one who wears a mask or fantastic disguise, esp. as formerly and still locally at Christmas, New Year's, and other festive seasons. **2.** (in humorous use) an actor. [late ME, t. OF: m. *momeur,* der. *momer* MUM[2]]

mum·mer·y (mŭm′ə rĭ), *n., pl.* **-meries. 1.** performance of mummers. **2.** any mere theatrical performance or ceremony or empty spectacular pretense, or what is regarded as such. [t. OF: m. *mommerie*]

mum·mi·fy (mŭm′ə fī′), *v.,* **-fied, -fying.** —*v.t.* **1.** to make (a dead body) into a mummy, as by embalming and drying; to make like a mummy. —*v.i.* **2.** to dry or shrivel up. —**mum′mi·fi·ca′tion,** *n.*

mum·my (mŭm′ĭ), *n., pl.* **-mies,** *v.,* **-mied, -mying.** —*n.* **1.** the dead body of a human being or animal preserved by the ancient Egyptian (or some similar) method of embalming. **2.** a dead body dried and preserved by the agencies of nature. **3.** a withered or shrunken living being. —*v.t.* **4.** to make into or like a mummy; mummify. [ME *mumie,* t. ML: m. *mumia,* t. Ar.: m. *mūmiya,* from Pers. *mūmiyā* asphalt]

mumps (mŭmps) *n.pl.,* construed as *sing. Pathol.* a specific infectious disease characterized by inflammatory swelling of the parotid and (usually) other salivary glands, and sometimes by inflammation of the testicles, ovaries, etc. [orig. meaning "grimace"]

mun., municipal.

munch (mŭnch), *v.t.* **1.** to chew with steady or vigorous working of the jaws, and often audibly. —*v.i.* **2.** to chew steadily or vigorously, and often audibly. [ME *monche,* nasalized var. of obs. *mouch* eat, chew; orig. unknown] —**munch′er,** *n.*

Mün·chen (myn′кнən), *n.* German name of **Munich.**

Mün·chen-Glad·bach (myn′кнən glät′bäкн), *n.* a city in W Germany, in the Rhineland. 128,418 (1939).

Münch·hau·sen (mynкн′hou′zən), *n.* **Karl Friedrich Hieronymus** (kärl frē′drĭкн hē′ä rō′nymōōs′), **Baron von** (fən), 1720–97, German soldier, adventurer, and teller of unbelievable tales. English, **Mun·chau·sen** (mŭn chô′zən).

Mun·cie (mŭn′sĭ), *n.* a city in E Indiana. 58,479 (1950).

mun·dane (mŭn′dān), *adj.* **1.** of or pertaining to the world, universe, or earth. **2.** of or pertaining to this world or earth as contrasted with heaven; worldly; earthly: *mundane affairs.* [t. L: m.s. *mundānus* of the world; r. ME *mondeyne,* t. OF] —**mun′dane·ly,** *adv.* —Syn. 2. See **earthly.**

Mu·nich (mū′nĭk), *n.* **1.** a city in S Germany: the capital of Bavaria. 829,318 (1939). German, **München. 2.** any dishonorable appeasement. See **Munich Pact.**

Munich Pact, the pact signed by Germany, Great Britain, France, and Italy on September 29, 1938, by which the Sudetenland was ceded to Germany. Also, **Munich Agreement.**

mu·nic·i·pal (mū nĭs′ə pəl), *adj.* **1.** of or pertaining to the local government of a town or city: *municipal elections.* **2.** pertaining to the internal affairs of a state or nation rather than to international affairs. [t. L: s. *mūnicipālis,* der. *mūniceps* citizen of a privileged (sometimes self-governing) town standing in a certain relation to Rome] —**mu·nic′i·pal·ly,** *adv.*

mu·nic·i·pal·i·ty (mū nĭs′ə păl′ə tĭ), *n., pl.* **-ties. 1.** a city, town, or other district possessing corporate existence. **2.** a community under municipal jurisdiction. **3.** the governing body of such a district or community.

mu·nic·i·pal·ize (mū nĭs′ə pə līz′), *v.t.,* **-ized, -izing. 1.** to make a municipality of. **2.** to bring under municipal ownership or control. —**mu·nic′i·pal·i·za′tion,** *n.*

mu·nif·i·cent (mū nĭf′ə sənt), *adj.* **1.** extremely liberal in giving or bestowing; very generous. **2.** characterized by great generosity, as giving, a gift, etc. [back formation from L *mūnificentia* munificence] —**mu·nif′i·cence,** *n.* —**mu·nif′i·cent·ly,** *adv.* —Ant. 1. niggardly.

mu·ni·ment (mū′nə mənt), *n.* **1.** (*pl.*) *Law.* a document, as a title deed or a charter, by which rights or privileges are defended or maintained. **2.** a defense or protection. [ME, t. ML: s. *mūnimentum* document, title deed, L fortification]

mu·ni·tion (mū nĭsh′ən), *n.* **1.** (*usually pl.*) materials used in war, esp. weapons and ammunition. **2.** material or equipment for carrying on any undertaking. —*v.t.* **3.** to provide with munitions. [t. L: s. *mūnītio* fortification]

Mun·ká·csy (mōōn′kä chĭ), *n.* **Mihály von** (mĭ′häl′y fən), (*Michael Lieb*) 1844–1900, Hungarian painter.

mun·nion (mŭn′yən), *n.* mullion.

Mun·ro (mənrō′), *n.* **Hector Hugh,** (*Saki*) 1870–1916, British author, born in Burma.

Mun·ster (mŭn′stər), *n.* a province in SW Eire. 923,930 pop. (est. 1943); 9532 sq. mi.

Mün·ster (mŭn′stər), *n.* a city in NW Germany: the capital of Westphalia; treaty of Westphalia, 1648. 141,059 (1939).

Mün·ster·berg (mĭn′stər bûrg′; *Ger.* myn′stər bĕrкн′), *n.* **Hugo** (hū′gō; *Ger.* hōō′gō), 1863–1916, German psychologist and philosopher, in America.

munt·jac (mŭnt′jăk), *n.* **1.** any of various small deer constituting the genus *Muntiacus,* of southern and eastern Asia and the adjacent islands, esp. *M. muntjac,* of Java, India, etc., having well-developed horns on bony pedicels. **2.** any of the small deer of the related genus *Elaphodus,* of China and Tibet, having minute horns. Also, **munt′jak.** [t. Javanese]

Muntz metal (mŭnts), *Metall.* an alloy containing approximately 60% copper and 40% zinc, harder and stronger than brass.

mu·ral (myŏŏr′əl) *adj.* **1.** of or pertaining to a wall; resembling a wall. **2.** executed on or affixed to a wall. —*n.* **3.** a mural painting. [t. F, t. L: s. *mūrālis*]

mural crown, a golden crown formed with indentations to resemble a battlement, bestowed among the ancient Romans on the soldiers who first mounted the wall of a besieged place and there lodged a standard.

Mu·ra·sa·ki no Shi·ki·bu (mōō′rä sä′kē nō shē′kē bōō′), 11th cent., first Japanese writer of a novel. The English title of her novel is *The Tale of Genji.*

Mu·rat (myrà′), *n.* **Joachim** (zhô ä kēm′), 1767–1815, French general, marshal of France, brother-in-law of Napoleon I, and king of Naples, 1808–15.

Mu·rat (mōō rät′), *n.* a river in E Turkey, flowing W to the Euphrates. 425 mi. Also, **Mu·rad Su** (mōō-räd′ sōō′).

Mur·cia (mōōr′shə; *Sp.* mōōr′thyä, -syä), *n.* **1.** a region in SE Spain: formerly a kingdom. 1,094,173 pop. (1940); 10,108 sq. mi. **2.** a city in SE Spain. 193,731 (1940).

mur·der (mûr′dər), *n.* **1.** *Law.* the unlawful killing of another human being with malice aforethought. Special statutory definitions and degrees are common in the U.S. —*v.t.* **2.** *Law.* to kill by an act constituting murder. **3.** to kill or slaughter inhumanly or barbarously. **4.** to spoil or mar by bad execution, representation, pronunciation, etc. —*v.i.* **5.** to commit murder. [ME; var. of MURTHER] —**mur′der·er,** *n.* —**mur′der·ess,** *n.* —Syn. 2. See **kill**[1].

mur·der·ous (mûr′dər əs), *adj.* **1.** of the nature of or involving murder: *a murderous deed.* **2.** guilty of, bent on, or capable of murder. **3.** intentionally deadly. —**mur′der·ous·ly,** *adv.* —**mur′der·ous·ness,** *n.*

Mu·res (mōō′rĕsh), *n.* a river flowing from the Carpathian Mountains in central Rumania W to the Tisza river in S Hungary. ab. 400 mi. Hungarian, **Maros.**

mu·rex (myŏŏr′ĕks), *n., pl.* **murices** (myŏŏr′ə sēz′), **murexes. 1.** any of the marine gastropods, common in tropical seas, constituting the genus *Murex* or the family *Muricidae,* certain species of which yielded the celebrated purple dye of the ancients. **2.** a shell used as a trumpet, as in representations of Tritons in art. **3.** purplish red. [t. L: the purple fish]

Murex
*Murex
tenuispina*

Mur·frees·bor·o (mûr′frĭz bûr′ō), *n.* a city in central Tennessee: the battle of Stone River (or Murfreesboro) was fought near here, Dec. 31, 1862-Jan. 2, 1863. 13,052 (1950).

---

b., blend of, blended; c., cognate with; d., dialect, dialectal; der., derived from; f., formed from; g., going back to; m., modification of; r., replacing; s., stem of; t., taken from; ?, perhaps. See the full key on inside cover.

mu·ri·ate (myŏŏr′ĭ·āt′, -ĭt), n. (in industry) any chloride, esp. potassium chloride, KCl, used as a fertilizer. [f. s. L *muria* brine + -ATE²]

mu·ri·at·ed (myŏŏr′ĭ·ā′tĭd), adj. Obsolesc. charged with or containing a chloride or chlorides, as mineral waters.

mu·ri·at·ic acid (myŏŏr′ĭ·ăt′ĭk), the commercial name for hydrochloric acid.

Mu·ril·lo (myŏŏ·rĭl′ō; Sp. mōō·rē′lyō), n. **Bartolomé Esteban** (bär′tō·lō·mĕ′ ĕs·tĕ′bän), 1617–82, Spanish painter.

mu·rine (myŏŏr′īn, -ĭn), adj. belonging or pertaining to the *Muridae*, the family of rodents that includes the mice and rats, or to the *Murinae* the subfamily that includes the domestic species. —n. 2. a murine rodent. [t. L: m.s. *murinus* of a mouse]

murk (mûrk), n. 1. darkness. —adj. 2. dark, or with little light, as night, places, etc. Also, **mirk**. [ME *mirke*, t. Scand.; cf. Icel. *myrkr* gloom]

murk·y (mûr′kĭ), adj., **murkier**, **murkiest**. 1. intensely dark, gloomy, and cheerless. 2. obscure or thick with mist, haze, or the like, as the air, etc. Also, **mirky**. —**murk′i·ly**, adv. —**murk′i·ness**, n. —Syn. 1. See **dark**. —Ant. 2. clear.

Mur·man Coast (mŏŏr′män′), an Arctic coastal region in the NW Soviet Union in Europe, on the Kola Peninsula.

Mur·mansk (mŏŏr·mänsk′), n. a seaport (ice-free) and railroad terminus in the NW Soviet Union, on the Murman Coast. 117,054 (1939).

mur·mur (mûr′mər), n. 1. any low, continuous sound, as of a brook, the wind, trees, etc., or of low indistinct voices. 2. a mumbled or private expression of discontent. 3. Med. an abnormal sound heard on listening over the heart, usually through a stethoscope, produced by vibrations of the valves and walls of the heart and great vessels. [ME, t. L]
—v.i. 4. to make a low or indistinct continuous sound. 5. to speak in a low tone or indistinctly. 6. to complain in a low tone, or in private. 7. to sound by murmurs. —v.t. 8. to utter in a low tone. [ME, t. L: s. *murmurāre*] —**mur′mur·er**, n. —**mur′mur·ing**, adj., n. —**mur′mur·ing·ly**, adv.
—Syn. 5. MURMUR, MUMBLE, MUTTER mean to make sounds which are not fully intelligible. To MURMUR is to utter sounds or words in a low, almost inaudible tone, as in expressing blandishments, affection, dissatisfaction, etc.: *to murmur disagreement*. To MUMBLE is to utter imperfect or inarticulate sounds with the mouth partly closed, so that the words can be distinguished only with difficulty: *to mumble the answer to a question*. To MUTTER is to utter words in a low, grumbling way, often voicing complaint or discontent, not meant to be fully audible: *to mutter to oneself*. 6. See **complain**.

mur·mur·ous (mûr′mər·əs), adj. 1. abounding in or characterized by murmurs. 2. murmuring: *murmurous waters*. —**mur′mur·ous·ly**, adv.

mur·phy (mûr′fĭ), n., pl. **-phies**. Slang. an Irish or white potato. [from *Murphy*, Irish surname]

Mur·phy (mûr′fĭ), n. **Frank**, 1890–1949, U.S. public official: associate justice of U.S. Supreme Court from 1940–1949.

mur·rain (mûr′ĭn), n. 1. any of various diseases of cattle, as anthrax, foot-and-mouth disease, and Texas fever. 2. Archaic. a plague or pestilence (esp. in curses). [ME *moryne*, t. F: m. *morine* plague, der. L *mori* die]

Mur·ray (mûr′ĭ), n. 1. **Sir George Gilbert Aimé** (ā·mā′), born 1866, British classical scholar. 2. **Sir James Augustus Henry**, 1837–1915, British lexicographer and linguist. 3. **Lindley**, 1745–1826, British grammarian, born in America. 4. **Philip**, born 1886, U.S. labor leader, born in Scotland. 5. a river in SE Australia, flowing along the border between Victoria and New South Wales and through SE South Australia into the ocean. ab. 1500 mi.

murre (mûr), n. 1. either of two species of northern diving birds of the genus *Uria*, the thick-billed **Brunnich's murre** (*U. omvia*) or the slender-billed **common murre** (*U. aalge*). 2. Colloq. the razor-billed auk.

murre·let (mûr′lĕt), n. any of several small, chunky diving birds found principally about the islands and coasts of the north Pacific, as the **marbled murrelet**, *Brachyramphus marmoratus*.

mur·rey (mûr′ĭ), n. a dark purplish-red color. [ME *morrey*, t. OF: m. *more*, der. L *mōrum* mulberry]

mur·rhine (mûr′ĭn, -īn), adj. pertaining to a stone or substance of Roman times used for wine cups and other vessels. Also, **mur′rine**. [t. L: m.s. *murr(h)inus*]

murrhine glass, 1. any kind of glassware supposed to resemble the Roman cups of murrhine. 2. a ware composed of glass in which metals, precious stones, or the like are embedded.

Mur·rum·bidg·ee (mûr′əm·bĭj′ĭ), n. a river in SE Australia, flowing W through New South Wales to the Murray river. ab. 1350 mi.

mur·ther (mûr′thər), n., v.t., v.i. Obs. murder. [ME *morther*, OE *morthor*, c. Goth. *maurthr*]

Mus., 1. museum. 2. music. 3. musical. 4. musician.

mu·sa·ceous (mū·zā′shəs), adj. belonging to the *Musaceae*, or banana family of plants. [f. s. NL *Musāceae* (der. *Musa*, the typical genus, t. Ar.: m. *mawza* banana, prob. of East Ind. orig.) + -ous]

Mus.B., (L *Musicae Baccalaureus*) Bachelor of Music. Also, **Mus.Bac.**

mus·ca·delle (mŭs′kə·dĕl′), n. a grape variety of the aromatic muscat family grown in France. [ME, t. OF: m. *muscadel*, der. Pr. *muscat* MUSCAT]

mus·ca·dine (mŭs′kə·dĭn, -dīn′), n. a grape variety, *Vitis rotundifolia*, indigenous to America, esp. Scuppernong (white-skinned) and James (black-skinned).

mus·cae vo·li·tan·tes (mŭs′sē vŏl′ĭ·tăn′tēz), specks that seem to dance in the air before the eyes, due to defects in the vitreous humor of the eye or to other causes. [NL: flies flying about]

mus·cat (mŭs′kət, -kăt), n. a grape variety with pronounced pleasant sweet aroma and flavor, much used for making wine. [t. F, t. Pr., der. LL *muscus* MUSK]

Mus·cat (mŭs·kăt′), n. a seaport in SE Arabia: the capital of Oman. ab. 4200. Arabic, **Masqat**.

mus·ca·tel (mŭs′kə·tĕl′, mŭs′kə·tĕl′), n. 1. a sweet wine made from muscat grapes. 2. the muscat grape. [var. of MUSCADELLE. Cf. OF *muscatel*]

mus·cid (mŭs′ĭd), adj. 1. belonging or pertaining to the *Muscidae*, the family of dipterous insects that includes the common housefly. 2. any muscid fly. [t. NL: s. *Muscidae*, pl., der. L *musca* a fly]

mus·cle (mŭs′əl), n., v., **-cled**, **-cling**. —n. 1. a discrete bundle or sheet of contractile fibres having the function of producing movement in the animal body. 2. the tissue of such an organ. 3. muscular strength; brawn. —v.i. 4. Colloq. to make or shove one's way by sheer brawn or force. [t. F, t. L: m.s. *musculus* muscle, lit., little mouse (from the appearance of certain muscles)]

mus·cle-bound (mŭs′əl·bound′), adj. having muscles enlarged and inelastic, as from excessive athletics.

muscle plasma, the juice that can be expressed from fresh muscle.

muscle sense, Psychol., Physiol. a sense of movement derived from afferent nerves originating in tendons, muscle tissue, skin and joints.

Muscle Shoals, formerly rapids in the Tennessee river, in NW Alabama: now changed into a lake by Wilson Dam, part of the Tennessee Valley Authority.

muscle spindles, Anat. the sensory end organs in skeletal muscle.

mus·cone (mŭs′kōn), n. a large cyclic ketone, C₁₆H₃₀O, obtained from musk and used in the perfume industry.

mus·co·va·do (mŭs′kə·vā′dō), n. raw or unrefined sugar, obtained from the juice of the sugar cane by evaporation and draining off the molasses. [t. Pg.: m. (açucar) *mascavado* (sugar) of inferior quality, pp. of *mascavar* diminish]

mus·co·vite (mŭs′kə·vīt′), n. common light-colored mica, essentially KAl₃Si₃O₁₀(OH)₂, used as an electrical insulator. [formerly called Muscovy glass. See -ITE¹]

Mus·co·vy (mŭs′kə·vĭ), n. Archaic. Russia. —**Mus′co·vite′**, n., adj. —**Mus′co·vit′ic**, adj.

Muscovy duck, a large, crested neotropical duck, *Cairina moschata*, which has been widely domesticated. Wild birds are glossy-black with a large white patch on each wing. [erroneous var. of *musk-duck*]

mus·cu·lar (mŭs′kyə·lər), adj. 1. of or pertaining to muscle or the muscles. 2. dependent on or affected by the muscles: *muscular strength*. 3. having well-developed muscles; brawny. —**mus·cu·lar·i·ty** (mŭs′kyə·lăr′ə·tĭ), n. —**mus′cu·lar·ly**, adv. —Syn. 3. sinewy; strong, powerful; stalwart, sturdy.

mus·cu·la·ture (mŭs′kyə·lə·chər), n. the muscular system of the body or of its parts. [t. F, der. L *musculus* MUSCLE]

Mus.D., (L *Musicae Doctor*) Doctor of Music. Also, **Mus.Doc.**, **Mus.Dr.**

muse (mūz), v., **mused**, **musing**. —v.i. 1. to reflect or meditate in silence, as on some subject, often as in a reverie. 2. to gaze meditatively or wonderingly. —v.t. 3. to meditate on. [ME *muse(n)*, t. OF: m. *muser* ponder, loiter, trifle (cf. AMUSE) der. *muse* muzzle] —**mus′er**, n.

Muse (mūz), n. 1. Class. Myth. **a.** any of the nine sister goddesses, daughters of Zeus and Mnemosyne, presiding over poetry and song, the drama, dancing, astronomy, etc.: Calliope, Clio, Erato, Euterpe, Melpomene, Polyhymnia, Terpsichore, Thalia, Urania. **b.** some other goddess supposed to preside over a particular field. 2. (sometimes l.c.) the goddess or the power regarded as inspiring a poet. 3. (l.c.) a poet's characteristic genius or powers. [ME, t. OF, t. L: m. *mūsa*, t. Gk.: m. *Moûsa*]

muse·ful (mūz′fəl), adj. deeply thoughtful.

mu·sette bag (mū·zĕt′), a small leather or canvas bag for personal belongings of army officers, carried by a shoulder strap. [*musette*, t. F]

mu·se·um (mū·zē′əm), n. a building or place for the keeping and exhibition of works of art, scientific specimens, etc. [t. L, t. Gk.: m. *mouseion* seat of the Muses, place of study, library]

mush¹ (mŭsh), n. 1. U.S. meal, esp. corn meal, boiled in water or milk until it forms a thick, soft mass. 2. any thick, soft matter or mass. 3. anything unpleasantly lacking in firmness, force, dignity, etc. 4. Colloq. weak or maudlin sentiment or sentimental language. [b. (obs.) *moose* thick vegetable porridge (t. D: m. *moes*) and MASH, n.]

mush² (mŭsh), v.t. 1. to go or travel on foot, esp. over the snow with a dog team. —interj. 2. an order to start or speed up a dog team. —*n.* **3.** a march on foot, esp. over the snow with a dog team. [?. t. F: m. *marche* or *marchons*, impr. of *marcher* advance] —**mush′er**, *n.*

mush·room (mŭsh′rŏŏm, -rŏŏm), *n.* **1.** any of various fleshy fungi including the toadstools, puffballs, coral fungi, morels, etc. **2.** any of certain edible species belonging to the family *Agaricaceae*, usually of umbrella shape. Cf. **toadstool. 3.** the common **meadow mushroom**, *Agaricus campestris*, or related forms grown for the market. **4.** anything of similar shape or correspondingly rapid growth. —*adj.* **5.** of, pertaining to, or made of mushrooms. **6.** resembling or suggesting a mushroom in shape. **7.** of rapid growth and, often, brief duration: *mushroom fame.* —*v.i.* **8.** to gather mushrooms. **9.** to have or assume the shape of a mushroom. **10.** to spread or grow quickly, as mushrooms. [ME, t. F: m. *mousseron*, g. LL *mussiriōne*]

mush·y (mŭsh′ĭ), *adj.*, **mushier, mushiest. 1.** mushlike; pulpy. **2.** *Colloq.* weakly sentimental: *she was devoted to mushy radio programs.* —**mush′i·ly**, *adv.* —**mush′i·ness**, *n.*

mu·sic (mū′zĭk), *n.* **1.** an art of sound in time which expresses ideas and emotions in significant forms through the elements of rhythm, melody, harmony, and color. **2.** the tones or sounds employed, occurring in single line (melody) or multiple lines (harmony), and sounded or to be sounded by vo.ce(s) or/and instrument(s). **3.** musical work or compositions for singing or playing. **4.** the written or printed score of a musical composition. **5.** such scores collectively. **6.** any sweet, pleasing, or harmoniously effective sounds or sound: *the music of the waves.* **7.** appreciation of or responsiveness to musical sounds or harmonies. **8.** *Fox Hunting.* the cries of the hounds. [ME *musik*, t. L: m.s. *mūsica*, t. Gk.: m. *mousikē̇* (*téchnē*) orig., any art over which the Muses presided]

mu·si·cal (mū′zə kəl), *adj.* **1.** of, pertaining to, or producing music: *a musical instrument.* **2.** of the nature of or resembling music; melodious; harmonious. **3.** fond of or skilled in music. **4.** set to or accompanied by music: *a musical melodrama.* —*n.* **5.** musical comedy. —**mu′si·cal·ly**, *adv.* —**mu′si·cal·ness**, *n.*

musical comedy, a play with music, often of a whimsical or satirical nature, based on a slight plot with singing and dancing in solos and groups.

mu·si·cale (mū′zĭ kăl′), *n.* a program of music forming part of a social occasion. [t. F: (fem.) in phrase *soirée* (or *matinée*) *musicale* an evening (or afternoon) musical party]

music box, a box or case containing an apparatus for producing music mechanically, as by means of a comblike steel plate with tuned teeth sounded by small pegs or pins in the surface of a revolving cylinder or disk. Also, *Brit.*, **musical box.**

music hall, **1.** a hall for musical entertainments. **2.** *Chiefly Brit.* a hall or theater for vaudeville.

mu·si·cian (mū zĭsh′ən), *n.* **1.** one who makes music a profession, esp. as a performer on an instrument. **2.** one skilled in music. —**mu·si′cian·ly**, *adj.*

music of the spheres, a music, imperceptible to human ears, formerly supposed to be produced by the movements of the spheres or heavenly bodies.

mus·ing (mū′zĭng), *adj.* **1.** that muses; absorbed in thought; dreamy; meditative. —*n.* **2.** contemplation. —**mus′ing·ly**, *adv.*

mus·jid (mŭs′jĭd), *n.* masjid.

musk (mŭsk), *n.* **1.** a substance secreted in a glandular sac under the skin of the abdomen of the male musk deer, having a strong odor, and used in perfumery. **2.** an artificial imitation of the substance. **3.** a similar secretion of other animals, as the civet, muskrat, otter, etc. **4.** the odor, or some similar odor. **5.** *Bot.* any of several plants, as the monkey flower, having a musky fragrance. [ME *muske*, var. of *musco*, t. LL, abl. of *muscus*, t. LGk.: m. *móschos*, t. Pers.: m. *mushk*]

musk deer, a small, hornless animal of the deer kind, *Moschus moschiferus*, of central Asia, the male of which secretes musk and has large canine teeth.

musk duck, **1.** Muscovy duck. **2.** an Australian duck, *Biziura lobata.*

mus·keg (mŭs′kĕg), *n.* a bog formed in hollows or depressions of the land surface by the accumulation of water and growth of sphagnum mosses. [t. Amer. Ind. (Ojibwa, Kickapoo): grassy bog]

Mus·ke·gon (mŭs kē′gən), *n.* a city in W Michigan: a port on Lake Michigan. 48,429 (1950).

mus·kel·lunge (mŭs′kə lŭnj′), *n., pl.* **-lunge.** a large game fish, *Esox masquinongy*, of the pike family, of the lakes and rivers of eastern and middle western North America. Also, **maskalonge.** [appar. dissimilated var. of *muscanonge, maskinonge*, t. N Amer. Ind. (Ojibwa): m. *mashkinonge*, f. *mash* great + *kinonge* pike]

mus·ket (mŭs′kĭt), *n.* a hand gun for infantry soldiers, introduced in the 16th century, the predecessor of the modern rifle. [t. F: m. *mousquet*, t. It.: m. *moschetto*, orig. a kind of hawk, der. *mosca* a fly, g. L *musca*]

mus·ket·eer (mŭs′kə tĭr′), *n.* a soldier armed with a musket. [f. MUSKET + -EER, modeled on F *mousquetaire*]

mus·ket·ry (mŭs′kĭ trĭ), *n.* **1.** practice in group combat firing with rifles. **2.** muskets collectively. **3.** troops armed with muskets.

Mus·kho·ge·an (mŭs kō′gĭ ən), *n.* a family of Ameri-

can Indian languages of southeastern U.S., including Choctaw, Chickasaw and Creek (also called **Muskogee** in Oklahoma and **Seminole** in Florida). Also, **Mus·ko′ge·an.**

White-faced musk ox, *Ovibos moschatus*
(Ab. 5 ft. high at the shoulder, total length 8 ft.)

musk·mel·on (mŭsk′mĕl′ən), *n.* **1.** a kind of melon, of many varieties, a round or oblong fruit with a juicy, often aromatically sweet, edible flesh (yellow, white, or green). **2.** the plant, *Cucumis melo*, bearing it.

Mus·ko·gee (mŭs kō′gĭ), *n.* **1.** a city in E Oklahoma. 37,289 (1950). **2.** See **Muskhogean.**

musk ox, a bovine ruminant, *Ovibos moschatus*, intermediate between the ox and the sheep in size and anatomy, and having a musky odor. It is native to arctic America.

musk·rat (mŭsk′răt′), *n., pl.* **-rats**, (*esp. collectively*) **-rat. 1.** a large aquatic North American rodent, *Ondatra zibethica*, with a musky odor. **2.** its thick light-brown fur.

musk rose, a species of rose, *Rosa moschata*, having fragrant white flowers.

musk·y[1] (mŭs′kĭ), *adj.*, **muskier, muskiest.** of or like musk, as odors; having an odor like that of musk. [f. MUSK + -Y[1]]

Muskrat, *Ondatra zibethica*
(Total length 22 to 23 in., tail 10 in.)

mus·ky[2] (mŭs′kĭ), *n., pl.* **muskies.** *Colloq.* muskellunge.

Mus·lem (mŭz′ləm, mŭs′-), *n., adj.* Moslem. Also, **Mus·lim.**

mus·lin (mŭz′lĭn), *n.* **1.** a cotton fabric made in various degrees of fineness, and often printed, woven, or embroidered in patterns, esp. a cotton fabric of plain weave, used for sheets and for a variety of other purposes. **2.** *Naut. Slang.* sails. [t. F: m. *mousseline*, t. It.: m. *mussolina* muslin, der. *Mussolo* Mosul, city in Iraq]

mus·quash (mŭs′kwŏsh), *n.* muskrat. [t. Algonquian languages of Va. (Abnaki, Ojibwa): it is red]

muss (mŭs), *n. Colloq.* **1.** a state of disorder. **2.** an untidy or dirty mess. —*v.t.* **3.** *U.S. Dial.* to put into disorder; make untidy or messy; rumple. [alter. of MESS]

mus·sel (mŭs′əl). *n.* any bivalve mollusk, esp. an edible marine bivalve of the family *Mytilidae* and a freshwater clam of the family *Unionidae.* [ME and OE *muscle*, t. LL: m.s. *muscula*, var. of L *musculus* MUSCLE, mussel]

Mus·set (my sĕ′), *n.* **Alfred de** (ȧl frĕd′ də), (*Louis Charles Alfred de Musset*) 1810–57, French poet, dramatist, and writer of stories.

Mus·so·li·ni (mŏŏs′ə lē′nĭ; *It.* mŏŏs′sô lē′nē), *n.* **Benito** (bĕ nē′tô), (*Il Duce*) 1883–1945, Italian Fascist leader and prime minister of Italy, 1922–43.

Mus·sorg·sky (mŏŏ sôrg′skĭ), *n.* **Modest Petrovich** (mŏ dĕst′ pŏ trô′vĭch), 1835–81, Russian composer.

Mus·sul·man (mŭs′əl mən), *n., pl.* **-mans.** a Mohammedan. [t. Pers.: m. *musulmān*, der. *muslim* MOSLEM, t. Ar. (with the Pers. pl. ending -ān)]

muss·y (mŭs′ĭ), *adj.*, **mussier, mussiest.** *Colloq.* untidy, messy, or rumpled.

must[1] (mŭst), *aux. v.* **1.** to be bound by some imperative requirement to: *I must keep my word.* **2.** to be obliged or compelled to, as by some constraining force or necessity: *man must eat to live.* **3.** may reasonably be supposed to: *it must be a large sum now.* **4.** to be inevitably certain to: *it must seem strange.* **5.** to have to; ought to; should: *I must go soon.* **6.** (sometimes used with ellipsis of *go, get*, or some similar verb readily understood from the context): *we must away.* —*adj.* **7.** necessary; vital: *must legislation.* —*n.* **8.** anything necessary or vital: *this law is a must.* [ME *most*(*e*), OE *mōste*, pret. (pres. *mōt*); akin to D *moeten*, G *müssen* be obliged]

—**Syn. 5.** MUST, OUGHT, SHOULD express necessity or duty. MUST expresses necessity, or compulsion: *all men must die, I must answer this letter, soldiers must obey orders.* OUGHT (weaker than *must*) expresses obligation, duty, desirability: *you ought to tell your mother.* SHOULD expresses obligation, expectation, or probability (*you are not behaving as you should; children should be taught to speak the truth; they should arrive at one o'clock*); it also expresses the conditional (*I should be glad to play if I could*) and future intention (*I said I should be at home next week*).

must[2] (mŭst), *n.* new wine; the unfermented juice as pressed from the grape or other fruit. [ME and OE, t. L: s. *mustum*, short for *vinum mustum* fresh wine]

mus·tache (mŭs′tăsh, məs tăsh′), *n.* **1.** the hair growing on the upper lip, or on either half of the upper lip, of men. **2.** hairs or bristles growing near the mouth of an animal. **3.** a stripe of color, or elongated feathers, suggestive of a mustache on the side of the head of a bird. Also, *esp. Brit.*, **moustache.** [t. F: m. *moustache*, t. It.: m. *mostaccio*, ult. t. Gk.: m. *mýstax* upper lip, mustache]

mus·ta·chio (məs tä′shō), *n., pl.* **-chios.** a mustache.

Mus·ta·fa Ke·mal Pa·sha (mōōs′tä fä kə mäl′ pä-shä′), former name of **Kemal Atatürk.**

mus·tang (mŭs′tăng), n. the small, wild or half-wild horse of the American plains, descended from Spanish stock. [t. Sp.: m. *mestengo* wild]

mus·tard (mŭs′tərd), n. 1. a pungent powder or paste prepared from the seed of the mustard plant, much used as a food seasoning or condiment, and medicinally in plasters, poultices, etc. 2. any of various brassicaceous plants, esp. *Brassica hirta* (*B. alba*) (**white mustard**), *B. juncea* (**leaf mustard**), *B. nigra* (**black mustard**), and others cultivated for their seed. [ME, t. OF: m. *moustarde*, orig. powdered mustard seed and must, der. *moust*, g. L *mustum* MUST²]

mustard gas, a liquid chemical warfare agent, (ClCH₂CH₂)₂S, producing burns, blindness, and death, introduced by the Germans in World War I.

mustard oil, oil expressed from the seed of mustard, esp. a carbylamine, a drying oil, used in making soap.

mustard plaster, a powdered black mustard and rubber solution mixture placed on a cloth and used as a counterirritant.

mus·tee (mŭs tē′, mŭs′tē), n. 1. the offspring of a white person and a quadroon. 2. a half-breed. [t. Sp.: m. *mestizo*]

mus·te·line (mŭs′tə lĭn′, -lĭn), adj. 1. belonging or pertaining to the family *Mustelidae,* including the martens, skunks, minks, weasels, badgers, otters, etc. 2. weasellike. 3. tawny or brown, like a weasel in summer. [t. L: m.s. *mustēlīnus* belonging to a weasel]

mus·ter (mŭs′tər), v.t. 1. to assemble (troops, a ship's crew, etc.), as for battle, display, inspection, orders, discharge, etc. 2. to gather or summon: (often fol. by *up*): *he mustered up all his courage.* 3. Naut. to call the roll of. 4. **muster in** (or **out**), to enlist or discharge from military service. —v.i. 5. to assemble for inspection, service, etc., as troops or forces. 6. to come together, collect, or gather. —n. 7. an assembling of troops or men for inspection or other purposes. 8. an assemblage or collection. 9. act of mustering. 10. Also, **muster roll.** (formerly) a list of the men enrolled in a military or naval unit. 11. **pass muster,** to measure up to specified standards. [ME *mostre(n),* t. OF: m. *mostrer,* g. L *monstrāre* show] —**Syn. 1.** See **gather.**

mus·ty (mŭs′tĭ), adj., **-tier, -tiest.** 1. having an odor or flavor suggestive of mold, as old buildings, long-closed rooms, food, etc. 2. staled by time, or antiquated: *musty laws.* 3. dull; apathetic. [var. of *moisty* (f. MOIST + -Y¹), with loss of *i* before *s*] —**mus′ti·ly,** adv. —**mus′ti·ness,** n.

mut (mŭt), n. Slang. mutt.

mu·ta·ble (mū′tə bəl), adj. 1. liable or subject to change or alteration. 2. given to changing, or ever changing; fickle or inconstant. [ME, t. L: m.s. *mūtābilis*] —**mu′ta·bil′i·ty, mu′ta·ble·ness,** n. —**mu′ta·bly,** adv.

mu·tant (mū′tənt), adj. 1. undergoing mutation; resulting from mutation. —n. 2. a new type of organism produced as the result of mutation. [t. L: s. *mūtans,* ppr., changing]

mu·ta·ro·ta·tion (mū′tə rō tā′shən), n. Chem. a change in the optical rotation of fresh solutions of reducing sugars with time.

mu·tate (mū′tāt), v., **-tated, -tating.** —v.t. 1. to change; alter. 2. Phonet. to change by umlaut. —v.i. 3. to change; undergo mutation. —**mu·ta·tive** (mū′tə-tĭv), adj.

mu·ta·tion (mū tā′shən), n. 1. act or process of changing. 2. a change or alternation, as in form, qualities, or nature. 3. Biol. **a.** a sudden departure from the parent type, as when an individual differs from its parents in one or more heritable characteristics, caused by a change in a gene or a chromosome. **b.** an individual, species, or the like, resulting from such a departure. 4. Phonet. umlaut. [ME, t. L: m.s. *mūtātio*] —**mu·ta′tion·al,** adj. —**mu·ta·tive** (mū′tə tĭv), adj.

mu·ta·tis mu·tan·dis (mū tā′tĭs mū tăn′dĭs), Latin. with the necessary changes.

mutch (mŭch), n. Scot. and Brit. Dial. a cap worn by women and young children. [late ME, t. MD: m.s. *mutse,* c. G *mütze* cap]

mutch·kin (mŭch′kĭn), n. Scot. a unit of liquid measure equal to a little less than a U.S. liquid pint. [t. early mod. D: m. *mudseken* a measure]

mute (mūt), adj., n., v., **muted, muting.** —adj. 1. silent; refraining from speech or utterance. 2. not emitting or having sound of any kind. 3. incapable of speech; dumb. 4. Gram. (of letters) silent; not pronounced. 5. Law. making no response when arraigned, as a prisoner in **to stand mute,** now resulting in the entry of a plea of "not guilty." —n. 6. one unable to utter words. 7. an actor whose part is confined to dumb show. 8. Law. a person who makes no response when arraigned. 9. Brit. Obs. a hired attendant at a funeral. 10. a mechanical device of various shapes and materials for muffling the tone of a musical instrument. 11. Phonetics. a stop. 12. (of a letter) not pronounced. —v.t. 13. to deaden or muffle the sound of (a musical instrument, etc.). [t. L: m.s. *mūtus* silent, dumb; r. ME *muet,* t. OF] —**mute′ly,** adv. —**mute′ness,** n. —**Syn. 3.** See **dumb.**

mu·ti·late (mū′tə lāt′), v.t., **-lated, -lating.** 1. to deprive (a person or animal, the body, etc.) of a limb or other important part or parts. 2. to injure, disfigure, or make imperfect by removing or irreparably damaging

parts. [t. L: m.s. *mutilātus,* pp., cut off, maimed] —**mu′ti·la′tion,** n. —**mu′ti·la′tive,** adj. —**mu′ti·la′tor,** n. —**Syn. 1.** See **maim.**

mu·ti·neer (mū′tə nĭr′), n. one guilty of mutiny. [t. F (obs.): m. *mutinier,* der. *mutin* rebellious, der. OF *muete* rebellion, orig. pp., der. L *movēre* move]

mu·ti·nous (mū′tə nəs), adj. 1. disposed to, engaged in, or involving revolt against constituted authority. 2. characterized by mutiny; rebellious. —**mu′ti·nous·ly,** adv. —**mu′ti·nous·ness,** n.

mu·ti·ny (mū′tə nĭ), n., pl. **-nies,** v., **-nied, -nying.** —n. 1. revolt, or a revolt or rebellion, against constituted authority, esp. by soldiers or seamen. —v.i. 2. to commit the offense of mutiny; revolt against constituted authority. [f. (obs.) *mutin,* adj., mutinous (t. F) + -Y³]

mut·ism (mū′tĭz əm), n. Psychiatry. a conscious or unconscious refusal to respond verbally to interrogation, present in some mental disorders. [t. F: m. *mutisme,* der. L *mūtus* mute, adj.]

Mu·tsu·hi·to (mōō′tsŏŏ hē′tô), n. 1852–1912, emperor of Japan, 1867–1912.

mutt (mŭt), n. Slang. 1. a dog, esp. a mongrel. 2. a simpleton; a stupid person. Also, **mut.** [orig. obscure; ? shortened from *muttonhead*]

mut·ter (mŭt′ər), v.i. 1. to utter words indistinctly or in a low tone often in talking to oneself or in making obscure complaints, threats, etc.; murmur; grumble. 2. to make a low, rumbling sound. —v.t. 3. to utter indistinctly or in a low tone. —n. 4. the act or utterance of one that mutters. [ME *moter(e),* ? freq. of (obs.) *moot,* v., speak, murmur, OE *mōtian* speak in public. Cf. d. G *muttern* and L *mutīre*] —**mut′ter·er,** n. —**mut′ter·ing·ly,** adv. —**Syn. 1.** See **murmur.**

mut·ton (mŭt′ən), n. 1. the flesh of sheep, used as food. 2. the flesh of the well-grown or more mature sheep, as distinguished from lamb. [ME *moton* t. OF; of Celtic orig.] —**mut′ton·y,** adj.

mutton chop, 1. a rib piece of mutton having the bone chopped off at the small end, or some similar piece, for broiling or frying. 2. (pl.) side whiskers shaped like a mutton chop, narrow at the top, and broad and trimmed short at the bottom, the chin being shaved both in front and beneath.

Mut·tra (mŭt′rə), n. a city in N India, in the United Provinces: a Hindu shrine and holy city, being the reputed birthplace of Krishna; pilgrimages. 76,716 (1940).

mu·tu·al (mū′chŏŏ əl), adj. 1. possessed, experienced, performed, etc., by each of two or more with respect to the other or others; reciprocal: *mutual aid.* 2. having the same relation each toward the other or others: *mutual foes.* 3. of or pertaining to each of two or more, or common: *mutual acquaintance.* 4. pertaining to mutual insurance: *a mutual company.* [late ME, f. s. L *mūtuus* reciprocal + -AL¹] —**mu′tu·al·ly,** adv. —**Syn. 1.** MUTUAL, RECIPROCAL agree in the idea of an exchange or balance between two or more persons or groups. MUTUAL indicates an exchange of a feeling, obligation, etc. between two or more people, or an interchange of some kind between persons or things: *mutual esteem, in mutual agreement.* It is not properly a synonym for COMMON, though often used in that sense (shared by, or pertaining to two or more things), esp. in the phrase *a mutual friend* (a friend of each of two or more other persons). RECIPROCAL indicates a relation in which one act, thing, feeling, etc. balances or is given in return for another: *reciprocal promises or favors.*

mutual insurance, insurance in which those insured become members of a company who reciprocally engage, by payment of certain amounts into a common fund, to indemnify one another against loss.

mu·tu·al·i·ty (mū′chŏŏ ăl′ə tĭ), n. condition or quality of being mutual; reciprocity; mutual dependence.

mu·tu·al·ize (mū′chŏŏ ə līz′), v., **-ized, -izing.** —v.t. 1. to make mutual. 2. to incorporate with employee or customer ownership of the major or controlling portion of issued shares. —v.i. 3. to become mutual. —**mu′tu·al·i·za′tion,** n.

mutual savings bank, a noncapitalized savings bank distributing its profits to depositors.

mu·tule (mū′chōōl), n. Archit. a projecting flat block under the corona of the Doric cornice, corresponding to the modillion of other orders. [t. F, t. L: m.s. *mūtulus* modillion]

mu·zhik (mōō zhĭk′, mōō′zhĭk), n. a Russian peasant. Also, **moujik, mujik, mu·zjik′.** [t. Russ.]

M, Greek mutule

muz·zle (mŭz′əl), n., v., **-zled, -zling.** —n. 1. the mouth, or end for discharge, of the barrel of a gun, pistol, etc. 2. the projecting part of the head of an animal, including jaws, mouth, and nose. 3. a device, usually in arrangement of straps or wires placed over an animal's mouth to prevent the animal from biting, eating, etc. —v.t. 4. to put a muzzle on (an animal or its mouth) so as to prevent biting, eating, etc. 5. to restrain from speech or the expression of opinion; gag. [ME *mosel,* t. OF: m. *musel,* der. *muse* muzzle; orig. uncert.] —**muz′zler,** n.

muz·zle·load·er (mŭz′əl lō′dər), n. a firearm which is loaded through the muzzle. —**muz′zle·load′ing,** adj.

ăct, āble, dâre, ärt; ĕbb, ēqual; ĭf, īce; hŏt, ōver, ôrder, oil, bŏŏk, ōōze, out; ŭp, ūse, ûrge; ə = a in alone; ch, chief; g, give; ng, ring; sh, shoe; th, thin; ŧ̵h, that; zh, vision. See the full key on inside cover.

muzzle velocity, *Ordn.* the speed of a projectile in foot-seconds as it leaves a gun muzzle.

muz·zy (mŭz′ĭ), *adj.,* **-zier, -ziest.** *Colloq.* confused; indistinct. —**muz′zi·ly,** *adv.* —**muz′zi·ness,** *n.*

m.v., (It. *mezza voce*) *Music.* with half the power of the voice; softly.

M.W.A., Modern Woodmen of America.

Mwe·ru (mwā′rōō), *n.* a lake in S Africa between the Belgian Congo and Northern Rhodesia. 68 mi. long.

my (mī), *pron.* **1.** the possessive form corresponding to *I* and *me,* used before a noun: *my house.* —*interj.* **2.** *Colloq.* an exclamation of surprise: *Oh, my!* [ME *mī,* apocopated var. of *mīn,* OE *mīn.* See MINE¹]

my-, a word element meaning "muscle." Also, **myo-.** [t. Gk., comb. form of *mȳs*]

my·al·gi·a (mī·ăl′jĭ·ə), *n.* *Pathol.* pain in the muscles; muscular rheumatism.

my·as·the·ni·a (mī′ăs·thē′nĭ·ə), *n.* *Pathol.* muscle weakness.

myc-, a word element meaning "fungus." Also, **myco-.** [comb. form repr. Gk. *mȳkēs*]

my·ce·li·um (mī·sē′lĭ·əm), *n., pl.* **-lia** (-lĭ·ə). *Bot.* the vegetative part or thallus of the fungi, when composed of one or more filamentous elements, or hyphae. [t. NL, der. Gk. *mȳkēs*] —**my·ce·loid** (mī′sə·loid′), *adj.*

My·ce·nae (mī·sē′nē), *n.* an ancient city in S Greece, in Argolis: notable ruins.

My·ce·nae·an (mī′sĭ·nē′ən), *adj.* **1.** of or pertaining to the ancient city of Mycenae. **2.** denoting or pertaining to the Aegean civilization which flourished there (c1400 B.C. to c1100 B.C.).

-mycetes, *Bot.* a word element meaning "fungus," as in *myxomycetes.* [comb. form repr. pl. of Gk. *mȳkēs* fungus]

my·ce·to·zo·an (mī·sē′tə·zō′ən), *adj.* **1.** of or pertaining to the Mycetozoa. —*n.* **2.** any of the *Mycetozoa,* (*Myxomycetes,* slime molds), a group of very primitive organisms lying near the border line between the plant and animal worlds. [f. *myceto-,* var. of MYC- + -ZOAN]

myco-, var. of myc-, before consonants, as in *mycology.*

my·co·bac·te·ri·um (mī′kō·băk·tĭr′ĭ·əm), *n., pl.* **-teria** (-tĭr′ĭ·ə). any of a group of bacteria, difficult to stain but which, once stained, hold stain tenaciously and are acid and alcohol fast. Mycobacteria produce human and bovine or mammalian tuberculosis, avian tuberculosis, tuberculosis of cold-blooded animals, and leprosy. [t. NL. See MYCO-, BACTERIUM]

my·col·o·gy (mī·kŏl′ə·jĭ), *n.* **1.** the branch of botany that treats of fungi. **2.** the fungi found in an area. —**my·col′o·gist,** *n.*

my·co·sis (mī·kō′sĭs), *n.* **1.** *Pathol.* the presence of parasitic fungi in or on any part of the body. **2.** a disease caused by them. [t. NL. See MYC-, -OSIS] —**my·cot·ic** (mī·kŏt′ĭk), *adj.*

my·dri·a·sis (mĭ·drī′ə·sĭs, mī-), *n.* *Pathol.* excessive dilatation of the pupil of the eye, as the result of disease, drugs, or the like. [t. L, t. Gk.]

myd·ri·at·ic (mĭd′rĭ·ăt′ĭk), *adj.* **1.** pertaining to or producing mydriasis. —*n.* **2.** a mydriatic drug.

myel-, a word element meaning "marrow" or "of the spinal cord." [t. Gk., comb. form of *myelos* marrow]

my·e·len·ceph·a·lon (mī′ə·lĕn·sĕf′ə·lŏn′), *n.* *Anat.* the posterior segment of the brain, practically coextensive with the medulla oblongata; the afterbrain.

my·e·lin (mī′ə·lĭn), *n.* *Anat.* a soft, white, fatty substance encasing the axis cylinder of certain nerve fibers. Also, **my·e·line** (mī′ə·lēn′). [t. G. See MYEL-, -IN²]

my·e·li·tis (mī′ə·lī′tĭs), *n.* *Pathol.* inflammation of the substance of the spinal cord.

my·e·loid (mī′ə·loid′), *adj.* *Anat.* **1.** pertaining to the spinal cord. **2.** marrowlike. **3.** pertaining to marrow.

my·lo·nite (mī′lə·nīt′, mĭl′ə-), a rock which has been crushed and rolled out to such an extent that the original structure has been destroyed. [f. Gk. *mylōn* mill + -ITE¹]

my·na (mī′nə), *n.* any of various Asiatic birds of the starling family (*Sturnidae*), esp. those of the genera *Acridotheres* and *Eulabes,* some of which are well-known cage birds and learn to talk. Also, **mina, my′nah.** [t. Hind.: m. *mainā* a starling]

Myn·heer (mĭn·hâr′, -hĭr′), *n.* **1.** the Dutch term of address and title of respect corresponding to sir and Mr. **2.** (*l.c.*) *Colloq.* a Dutchman. [t. D: m. *mijnheer,* f. *mijn* my + *heer* lord, gentleman]

myo-, var. of my-, before consonants.

my·o·car·di·o·graph (mī′ō·kär′dĭ·ə·grăf′, -gräf′), *n.* *Physiol.* an apparatus which records the movements of the heart muscle.

my·o·car·di·tis (mī′ō·kär·dī′tĭs), *n.* *Pathol.* inflammation of the myocardium. [f. MYOCARD(IUM) + -ITIS]

my·o·car·di·um (mī′ō·kär′dĭ·əm), *n.* *Anat.* the muscular substance of the heart. [t. NL. See MYO-, CARDIO-]

my·o·graph (mī′ə·grăf′, -gräf′), *n.* *Physiol.* an instrument for taking tracings of muscular contractions and relaxations.

my·ol·o·gy (mī·ŏl′ə·jĭ), *n.* the science of muscles; the branch of anatomy that treats of muscles.

my·o·ma (mī·ō′mə), *n., pl.* **-mata** (-mə·tə), **-mas** (-məz). *Pathol.* a tumor composed of muscular tissue. [t. NL. See MY-, -OMA] —**my·om·a·tous** (mī·ŏm′ə·təs, -ō′mə-), *adj.*

my·o·pi·a (mī·ō′pĭ·ə), *n.* *Pathol.* a condition of the eye in which parallel rays are focused in front of the retina,

objects being seen distinctly only when near to the eye; near-sightedness (opposed to *hypermetropia*). [t. NL: f. s. Gk. *myōps* short-sighted + -ia -IA] —**my·op·ic** (mī·ŏp′ĭk), *adj.*

my·o·scope (mī′ə·skōp′), *n.* an apparatus or instrument for observing muscular contraction.

my·o·sin (mī′ə·sĭn), *n.* *Biochem.* a globulin occurring in muscle plasma. [f. MY- + -OS(E)² + -IN²]

my·o·sis (mī·ō′sĭs), *n.* *Pathol.* excessive contraction of the pupil of the eye, as the result of disease, drugs, or the like. [t. NL, f. Gk.: s. *myein* close (the eyes) + -ōsis -OSIS]

my·o·so·tis (mī′ə·sō′tĭs), *n.* any plant of the boraginaceous genus *Myosotis,* as the common forget-me-not. Also, **my·o·sote** (mī′ə·sōt′). [t. L, t. Gk.: the plant mouse-ear]

my·ot·ic (mī·ŏt′ĭk), *adj.* **1.** pertaining to, producing, or suffering from myosis. —*n.* **2.** a myotic drug.

My·ra (mī′rə), *n.* an ancient city in SW Asia Minor, in Lycia.

myr·i·ad (mĭr′ĭ·əd), *n.* **1.** an indefinitely great number. **2.** a very great number of persons or things. **3.** ten thousand. —*adj.* **4.** of an indefinitely great number; innumerable. **5.** having innumerable phases, aspects, etc.: *the myriad mind of Shakespeare.* **6.** ten thousand. [t. Gk.: s. *myriás* a number of ten thousand]

myr·i·a·pod (mĭr′ĭ·ə·pŏd′), *n.* **1.** any member of the *Myriapoda.* —*adj.* Also, **myr·i·ap·o·dous** (mĭr′ĭ·ăp′ə·dəs). **2.** belonging or pertaining to the *Myriapoda* or myriapods. **3.** having very numerous legs. [t. NL: s. *Myriapoda,* pl. See MYRIA-, -POD]

Myr·i·ap·o·da (mĭr′ĭ·ăp′ə·də), *n.pl.* a group of arthropods which have elongate bodies composed usually of many segments, most of which bear three-jointed legs; formerly treated as a class, embracing chiefly the centipedes and millipedes, or *Chilopoda* and *Diplopoda,* which were regarded as orders or subclasses. [NL, f. Gk.: *myriá*(*s*) MYRIAD + s. *poús* foot + -a, neut. pl. ending] —**myr′i·ap′o·dan,** *adj., n.*

my·ri·ca (mĭ·rī′kə), *n.* **1.** the bark of the wax myrtle. **2.** the bark of the bayberry. [t. L, t. Gk.: m. *myrīkē*]

myrmeco-, a word element meaning "ant." [t. Gk., comb. form of *myrmēx*]

myr·me·col·o·gy (mûr′mĭ·kŏl′ə·jĭ), *n.* the branch of entomology that treats of ants. —**myr·me·co·log·i·cal** (mûr′mĭ·kə·lŏj′ə·kəl), *adj.* —**myr′me·col′o·gist,** *n.*

myr·me·coph·a·gous (mûr′mĭ·kŏf′ə·gəs), *adj.* adapted for feeding on ants or termites, as the jaws, teeth, etc., of various anteaters.

myr·me·co·phile (mûr′mĭ·kō·fīl′, -fĭl), *n.* any species of foreign insect that lives more or less permanently in an ant colony.

myr·me·coph·i·lous (mûr′mĭ·kŏf′ə·ləs), *adj.* **1.** pertaining to myrmecophiles. **2.** pertaining to plants frequented by ants.

Myr·mi·don (mûr′mə·dŏn′, -dən), *n., pl.* **Myrmidons, Myrmidones** (mûr·mĭd′ə·nēz′). **1.** one of the warlike people of ancient Thessaly who accompanied Achilles, their king, to the Trojan War. **2.** (*l.c.*) one who executes without scruple his master's commands.

my·rob·a·lan (mī·rŏb′ə·lən, mĭ-), *n.* the dried plumlike fruit of certain tropical trees of the genus *Terminalia,* used in dyeing and making ink. [t. L: s. *myrobalanum,* t. Gk.: m. *myrobálanos* kind of fruit or nut]

My·ron (mī′rən), *n.* fl. c450 B.C., Greek sculptor.

myrrh (mûr), *n.* an aromatic resinous exudation from certain plants of the genus *Commibhora,* esp. *C. Myrrha,* a spiny shrub, used for incense, perfume, etc. [ME *mirre,* OE *myrre,* t. L: m. *myrrha, murra,* t. Gk.: m. *mýrra,* ult. from Akkadian *murrû*; cf. Heb. *mor,* akin to *mar* bitter]

myr·ta·ceous (mûr·tā′shəs), *adj.* **1.** belonging to the *Myrtaceae,* or myrtle family of plants, which includes the myrtle, the clove and allspice trees, the guava, the eucalyptus, etc. **2.** of, pertaining to, or resembling the myrtle. [t. LL: m. *myrtāceus* of myrtle]

myr·tle (mûr′təl), *n.* **1.** any plant of the genus *Myrtus,* esp. *M. communis,* a shrub of southern Europe with evergreen leaves, fragrant white flowers, and aromatic berries. This plant is used as an emblem of love and was anciently held sacred to Venus. **2.** *U.S.* any of certain plants of other families, as the common periwinkle, *Vinca minor,* and California laurel, *Umbellularia californica.* **3.** Also, **myrtle green.** dark green with bluish tinge. [ME, t. OF: m. *mirtile* myrtle berry, dim. of L *myrtus,* t. Gk.: m. *mýrtos* myrtle]

my·self (mī·sĕlf′), *pron., pl.* **ourselves. 1.** an intensifier of *me* or *I: I myself will go.* **2.** a reflexive substitute for *me: I burned myself.*

My·si·a (mĭsh′ĭ·ə), *n.* an ancient country in NW Asia Minor.

My·sore (mī·sōr′), *n.* **1.** a state in S India. 7,329,140 pop. (1941); 29,458 sq. mi. **2.** the capital of this state. 150,540 (1941).

mys·ta·gogue (mĭs′tə·gŏg′, -gŏg′), *n.* one who instructs persons before initiation into religious mysteries or before participation in the sacraments. [t. L: m.s. *mystagōgus,* t. Gk.: m. *mystagōgós*] —**mys·ta·go·gy** (mĭs′tə·gō′jĭ), *n.* —**mys·ta·gog·ic** (mĭs′tə·gŏj′ĭk), *adj.*

mys·te·ri·ous (mĭs·tĭr′ĭ·əs), *adj.* **1.** full of, characterized by, or involving mystery: *a mysterious stranger.* **2.** of obscure nature, meaning, origin, etc.; puzzling;

---

b., blend of, blended;   c., cognate with;   d., dialect, dialectal;   der., derived from;   f., formed from;   g., going back to; m., modification of;   r., replacing;   s., stem of;   t., taken from;   ?, perhaps.   See the full key on inside cover.

inexplicable. **3.** implying or suggesting a mystery: *a mysterious smile*. [f. s. L *mysterium* MYSTERY[1] + -OUS] —**mys·te′ri·ous·ly,** *adv.* —**mys·te′ri·ous·ness,** *n.*
—**Syn. 1.** secret, esoteric, occult, cryptic. MYSTERIOUS, INSCRUTABLE, MYSTICAL, OBSCURE refer to that which is not easily comprehended or explained. That which is MYSTERIOUS, by being unknown or puzzling, excites curiosity, amazement, or awe: *a mysterious disease.* INSCRUTABLE applies to that which is impenetrable, so enigmatic that one cannot interpret its significance: *an inscrutable smile.* That which is MYSTICAL has a secret significance, such as that attaching to certain rites, signs, and the like: *mystical symbols.* That which is OBSCURE is discovered or comprehended dimly or with difficulty: *obscure motives.* **2.** unfathomable; enigmatical.

mys·ter·y[1] (mĭs′tərĭ, -trĭ), *n., pl.* **-teries. 1.** anything that is kept secret or remains unexplained or unknown: *the mysteries of nature.* **2.** any affair, thing, or person that presents features or points so obscure as to arouse curiosity or speculation: *a mystery story.* **3.** obscurity, as of something unexplained or puzzling: *proceedings wrapped in mystery.* **4.** obscure, puzzling, or mysterious quality or character. **5.** any truth unknowable except by divine revelation. **6.** (in the Christian religion) **a.** a sacramental rite. **b.** (*pl.*) the eucharistic elements. **c.** the eucharist. **7.** an incident or scene in connection with the life of Christ, regarded as of special significance: *the mysteries of the Passion.* **8.** (*pl.*) ancient religions which admitted candidates by secret rites the meaning of which only the initiated might know. **9.** (*pl.*) rites or secrets known only to those specially initiated: *the mysteries of freemasonry.* **10.** a miracle play. [ME *mysterie*, t. L: m. *mysterium*, t. Gk.: m. *mystērion*]

mys·ter·y[2] (mĭs′tərĭ), *n., pl.* **-teries.** *Archaic.* **1.** a craft or trade. **2.** *Archaic or Hist.* a guild, as of craftsmen, merchants, or the like. [ME *misterye*, t. ML: m. *misterium*, L *ministerium* MINISTRY]

mys·tic (mĭs′tĭk), *adj.* **1.** spiritually significant or symbolic, as the *mystic dove* used in religious art to symbolize the Holy Ghost. **2.** of the nature of or pertaining to mysteries known only to the initiated: *mystic rites.* **3.** of occult character, power, or significance: *a mystic formula.* **4.** of obscure or mysterious character or significance. **5.** of or pertaining to mystics or mysticism. —*n.* **6.** one initiated into mysteries. **7.** one who claims to attain, or believes in the possibility of attaining, insight into mysteries transcending ordinary human knowledge, as by immediate intuition in a state of spiritual ecstasy. [ME *mystik*, t. L: m.s. *mysticus*, t. Gk.: m. *mystikós* mystic, secret]

mys·ti·cal (mĭs′tə kəl), *adj.* **1.** mystic; occult. **2.** of or pertaining to mystics or mysticism: *mystical doctrines.* **3.** spiritually symbolic. **4.** *Rare.* mysterious. —**mys′ti·cal·ly,** *adv.* —**mys′ti·cal·ness,** *n.* —**Syn. 1.** See mysterious.

mys·ti·cism (mĭs′tə sĭz′əm), *n.* **1.** the beliefs, ideas, or mode of thought of mystics. **2.** the doctrine of an immediate spiritual intuition of truths believed to transcend ordinary understanding, or of a direct, intimate union of the soul with the Divinity through contemplation and love. **3.** obscure thought or speculation.

mys·ti·fy (mĭs′tə fī′), *v.t.,* **-fied, -fying. 1.** to impose upon (a person) by playing upon his credulity; bewilder purposely. **2.** to involve (a subject, etc.) in mystery or obscurity. [t. F: m. *mystifier,* f. *mysti(que)* mystic + *-fier* -FY] —**mys′ti·fi·ca′tion,** *n.*

myth (mĭth), *n.* **1.** a traditional or legendary story, usually concerning some superhuman being or some alleged person or event, whether without or with a determinable basis of fact or a natural explanation; esp.

a traditional or legendary story usually concerning deities or demigods and the creation of the world and its inhabitants. **2.** stories or matter of this kind: *in the realm of myth.* **3.** any invented story. **4.** an imaginary or fictitious thing or person. **5.** *Sociol.* a collective belief that is built up in response to the wishes of the group instead of an analysis of what it pertains to. [t. NL: s. *mythus,* mod. var. of LL *mythos,* t. Gk.: word, speech, tale, legend, myth] —**Syn. 1.** See legend.

myth., **1.** mythological. **2.** mythology.

myth·i·cal (mĭth′ə kəl), *adj.* **1.** pertaining to, of the nature of, or involving a myth or myths. **2.** dealt with in myth, as a period. **3.** dealing with myths, as a writer. **4.** existing only in myth, as a person. **5.** having no foundation in fact; imaginary; fictitious: *his influence at the White House is completely mythical.* Also, **myth′ic.** —**myth′i·cal·ly,** *adv.*

myth·i·cize (mĭth′ə sīz′), *v.t.,* **-cized, -cizing.** to turn into, or treat or explain as, a myth.

mytho-, a word element meaning "myth." [t. Gk., comb. form of *mȳthos*]

mythol., **1.** mythological. **2.** mythology.

myth·o·log·i·cal (mĭth′ə lŏj′ə kəl), *adj.* of or pertaining to mythology. Also, **myth′o·log′ic.** —**myth′o·log′i·cal·ly,** *adv.*

my·thol·o·gist (mĭ thŏl′ə jĭst), *n.* **1.** an expert in mythology. **2.** a writer of myths.

my·thol·o·gize (mĭ thŏl′ə jīz′), *v.i.,* **-gized, -gizing. 1.** to classify, explain, or write about myths. **2.** to construct or relate myths. **3.** to make into or explain as a myth; make mythical. —**my·thol′o·giz′er,** *n.*

my·thol·o·gy (mĭ thŏl′ə jĭ), *n., pl.* **-gies. 1.** a body of myths, as that of a particular people, or that relating to a particular person: *Greek mythology.* **2.** myths collectively. **3.** the science of myths. [ME, t. LL: m.s. *mythologia,* t. Gk.: legend]

myth·o·ma·ni·a (mĭth′ə mā′nĭ ə), *n. Psychiatry.* lying or exaggerating to an abnormal degree. —**myth·o·ma·ni·ac** (mĭth′ə mā′nĭ ăk′), *n., adj.*

myth·o·poe·ic (mĭth′ə pē′ĭk), *adj.* mythmaking; pertaining to the making of myths. Also, **myth′o·pe′ic.** [f. m.s. Gk. *mȳthopoiós* making myths + -IC] —**myth′-o·poe′ism,** *n.* —**myth′o·poe′ist,** *n.*

Myt·i·le·ne (mĭt′ə lē′nĭ; *Gk.* mē′tē lē′nē), *n.* **1.** Also, **Lesbos.** a Greek island in the NE Aegean. 161,832 pop. (1940); 629 sq. mi. **2.** Also, **Kastro.** the capital of this island. 28,769 (1940).

myx-, a word element meaning "slimy." Also, **myxo-.** [t. Gk., comb. form of *mýxa* slime, mucus]

myx·e·de·ma (mĭk′sĭ dē′mə), *n. Pathol.* a disease characterized by thickening of the skin, blunting of the senses and intellect, labored speech, etc., associated with diminished functional activity of the thyroid gland. Also, **myx′oe·de′ma.** [t. NL. See MYX-, EDEMA] —**myx·e·dem·a·tous** (mĭk′sĭ dĕm′ə təs, -dē′mə təs), *adj.* —**myx·e·dem·ic** (mĭk′sĭ dĕm′ĭk), *adj.*

myx·o·my·cete (mĭk′sō mī sēt′), *n.* any one of the slime molds (*Myxomycetes, Mycetozoa*), primitive organisms whose characters place them at the border line between the plant and animal kingdoms.

myx·o·my·ce·tous (mĭk′sō mī sē′təs), *adj.* belonging or pertaining to the *Myxomycetes,* or slime molds (sometimes regarded as a distinct phylum, *Myxophyta,* and sometimes as a class of *Thallophyta*) having characteristics of both animals and plants. [f. s. NL *Myxomycētes,* pl. (see MYXO-, -MYCETES) + -OUS]

Myx·o·phyc·e·ae (mĭk′sō fĭs′ĭ ē′), *n.pl. Bot.* See blue-green algae.

N

N, n (ĕn), *n., pl.* **N's** or **Ns, n's** or **ns. 1.** a consonant, the 14th letter of the English alphabet. **2.** *Math.* an indefinite constant whole number, esp. the degree of a quantic or an equation, or the order of a curve. **3.** *Print.* an en.

N, 1. *Chem.* nitrogen. **2.** north. **3.** northern.

N., 1. Nationalist. **2.** Navy. **3.** New. **4.** Noon. **5.** *Chem.* Normal (strength solution). **6.** Norse. **7.** North. **8.** Northern. **9.** November.

n., 1. (L *natus*) born. **2.** nephew. **3.** neuter. **4.** new. **5.** nominative. **6.** noon. **7.** *Chem.* normal (strength solution). **8.** north. **9.** northern. **10.** noun. **11.** number.

na (nä, nə), *Obs. except Dial.* (*chiefly Scot.*). —*adv.* **1.** no. **2.** not. —*conj.* **3.** nor. [Scot. var. of NO]

Na, *Chem.* (L *natrium*) sodium.

N.A., 1. National Army. **2.** North America.

NAACP, National Association for the Advancement of Colored People. Also, **N.A.A.C.P.**

nab (năb), *v.t.,* **nabbed, nabbing.** *Colloq.* **1.** to catch or seize, esp. suddenly. **2.** to capture or arrest. [earlier *nap.* Cf. OE *hnæppan* strike]

Na·blus (nä blōos′), *n.* modern name of Shechem.

na·bob (nā′bŏb), *n.* **1.** an Englishman who has grown rich in India. **2.** any wealthy and luxurious person. **3.** nawab. [t. Hind.: m. *nawwab.* See NAWAB] —**na·bob·er·y** (nā′bŏb′ər ĭ, nā bŏb′ər ĭ), **na′bob·ism,** *n.* —**na′bob·ish,** *adj.*

Na·both (nā′bŏth, -bŏth), *n.* a man of Jezreel whose vineyard was secured for the covetous Ahab by the scheming of Jezebel. I Kings 21.

NACA, National Advisory Committee for Aeronautics.

na·celle (nə sĕl′), *n.* **1.** the enclosed part of an airplane, airship, or dirigible, in which the engine is housed or passengers, etc., are carried. **2.** the car of a balloon. [t. F, g. LL *nāvicella,* dim. of L *nāvis* ship]

na·cre (nā'kər), *n.* mother-of-pearl. [t. F. c. It. *nacchera*; prob. t. Pers. (Kurdish): m. *nakára* pearl oyster] —**na·cre·ous** (nā'krĭ əs), *adj.*

Na-Dene (nä dēn'), *n.* an American Indian linguistic phylum including Haida, Tlingit, and Athabascan.

na·dir (nā'dər; nā'dĭr), *n.* **1.** the point of the celestial sphere vertically beneath any place or observer, and diametrically opposite to the zenith. **2.** the lowest point, as of adversity. [ME, ult. t. Ar.: m. *naẓír* corresponding, opposite (i. e., to the zenith)]

nae (nā), *adj.*, *adv.* *Scot.* **1.** no. **2.** not. [var. of NO]

nae·thing (nā'thĭng), *n.*, *adv.* *Scot* nothing.

nae·vus (nē'vəs), *n.*, *pl.* **-vi** (-vī). *Dermatology.* any congenital anomaly, including various types of birthmarks and all types of moles. Also, **nevus.** [t. L] —**nae·void** (nē'void), *adj.*

nag[1] (năg), *v.*, **nagged, nagging.** —*v.t.* **1.** to torment by persistent faultfinding, complaints, or importunities. —*v.i.* **2.** to keep up an irritating or wearisome faultfinding, complaining, or the like (often fol. by *at*). [cf. MLG *naggen* irritate, provoke, Icel. *nagga* grumble, *nagg* grumbling] —**nag'ger**, *n.* —**nag'ging·ly**, *adv.*

nag[2] (năg), *n.* **1.** a small horse, or pony, esp. for riding. **2.** *Colloq.* a horse. **3.** an old or inferior horse. [ME *nagge*, c. D *negge*; akin to NEIGH]

na·ga·na (nə gä'nə), *n.* a disease of horses and other animals produced by the action of *Trypanosoma brucei* and carried by a variety of tsetse fly. It occurs only in certain parts of Africa. [native African name]

Na·ga·sa·ki (nä'gä sä'kē), *n.* a seaport in SW Japan, on Kyushu island: the second military use of the atomic bomb, Aug. 9, 1945. 174,141 (1946); 252,630 (1940).

Na·go·ya (nä'gō yä'), *n.* a city in central Japan, on Honshu island. 719,382 (1946).

Nag·pur (năg pŏor'), *n.* a city in central India: capital of the Central Provinces and Berar. 301,957 (1941).

Na·gy·vá·rad (nŏd'yə vä'rŏd), *n.* Hungarian name of **Oradea.**

Nah., Nahum.

Na·hua·tl (nä'wä'təl), *n.* any of a subgroup of Uto-Aztecan languages of central Mexico, including Aztec.

Na·hua·tlan (nä'wät'lən), *n.* the family of Uto-Aztecan languages which includes Aztec.

Na·hum (nā'həm), *n.* **1.** a Hebrew prophet of the late seventh century B.C. **2.** a book of the Old Testament, the seventh among the minor prophets. [t. Heb.]

nai·ad (nā'ăd, nī'-), *n.*, *pl.* **-ads, -ades** (-ə dēz'). **1.** (*also cap.*) *Class. Myth.* one of a class of water nymphs fabled to dwell in and preside over streams and springs. **2.** a girl swimmer. **3.** *Bot.* a plant of the genus *Naias*, or the family *Naiadaceae.* [t. L: s. *Nāias*, t. Gk.]

na·if (nä ēf'), *adj.* naïve. [t. F (masc.). See NAIVE]

nail (nāl), *n.* **1.** a slender piece of metal, usually with one end pointed and the other enlarged, for driving into or through wood, etc., as to hold separate pieces together. **2.** a thin, horny plate, consisting of modified epidermis, growing on the upper side of the end of a finger or toe. **3.** a measure of length for cloth, equal to 2¼ inches. **4. hit the nail on the head,** to say or do exactly the right thing. **5. on the nail,** *Colloq.* **a.** of present interest; under discussion. **b.** on the spot, or at once. —*v.t.* **6.** to fasten with a nail or nails: *to nail the cover on a box.* **7.** to stud with or as with nails driven in. **8.** to shut (up) within something by driving nails in: *to nail goods up in a box.* **9.** to make fast or keep firmly in one place or position: *surprise nailed him to the spot.* **10.** *Colloq.* to secure by prompt action, catch, or seize: *to nail a contract.* **11.** *Colloq.* to catch (a person) in some difficulty, a lie, etc. **12.** *Colloq.* to detect and expose (a lie, etc.). [ME; OE *nægl*, c. D and G *nagel*] —**nail'er**, *n.*

nail file, a small file for trimming fingernails.

nail set, a short rod of steel used to drive a nail below, or flush with, the surface.

nain·sook (nān'sŏok, nān'-), *n.* a fine, soft-finished cotton fabric, usually white, used for lingerie and infants' wear. [t. Hind.: m. *nainsukh*, lit., eye pleasure]

Nairn (nârn), *n.* a county in N Scotland. 8700 pop. (est. 1946); 163 sq. mi. *Co. seat:* Nairn. Also, **Nairn·shire** (nârn'shĭr, -shər).

Nai·ro·bi (nī rō'bĭ), *n.* the capital of Kenya, in British East Africa. ab. 65,000.

Nairobi disease, *Vet. Sci.* an infectious African disease of sheep, marked by severe gastroenteritis and caused by a specific virus.

na·ïve (nä ēv'), *adj.* having or showing natural simplicity of nature; unsophisticated; ingenuous. Also, **na·ive'.** [t. F, fem. of *naïf*, g. L *nātīvus* native, natural] —**na·ïve'ly**, *adv.* —**Syn.** simple, unaffected; unsuspecting.

na·ïve·té (nä ēv'tā'), *n.* **1.** the quality of being naïve; artless simplicity. **2.** a naïve action, remark, etc. Also, **na·ïve'te'.** [t. F, der. *naïve*]

na·ked (nā'kĭd), *adj.* **1.** without clothing or covering; nude. **2.** without adequate clothing. **3.** bare of any covering, overlying matter, vegetation, foliage, or the like: *naked fields.* **4.** bare, stripped, or destitute (of something specified): *trees naked of leaves.* **5.** without a sheath or customary covering: *a naked sword.* **6.** without carpets, hangings, or furnishings, as rooms, walls, etc. **7.** (of the eye, sight, etc.) unassisted by a microscope, telescope, or other instrument. **8.** defenseless or unprotected; unguarded; exposed, as to attack or harm.

9. simple; unadorned: *the naked truth.* **10.** not accompanied or supplemented by anything else: *a naked outline of facts.* **11.** exposed to view or plainly revealed: *a naked vein.* **12.** plain-spoken; blunt. **13.** *Law.* unsupported, as by authority or consideration: *a naked promise.* **14.** *Bot.* **a.** (of seeds) not enclosed in an ovary. **b.** (of flowers) without a calyx or perianth. **c.** (of stalks, etc.) without leaves. **d.** (of stalks, leaves, etc.) without hairs or pubescence. **15.** *Zool.* having no covering of hair, feathers, shell, etc. [ME *naked(e)*, OE *nacod*, c. G *nackt*] —**na'ked·ly**, *adv.* —**na'ked·ness**, *n.*

NAM, National Association of Manufacturers. Also, **N. A. M.**

nam·a·ble (nā'mə bəl), *adj.* that may be named. Also, **nameable.**

Na·man·gan (nä'mäng gän'), *n.* a city in the SW Soviet Union in Asia, in Uzbek Republic. 77,351 (1939).

Na·ma·qua·land (nə mä'kwə länd'), *n.* a coastal region in the S part of South-West Africa, extending into the Cape of Good Hope province of the Union of South Africa: inhabited by Hottentots.

nam·ay·cush (năm'ĭ kŭsh', -ā-), *n.* a lake trout. [t. Algonquian (Cree): m. *namekus*, dim. of *namew* fish]

nam·by-pam·by (năm'bĭ păm'bĭ), *adj.*, *n.*, *pl.* **-bies.** —*adj.* **1.** weakly simple or sentimental; insipid. —*n.* **2.** namby-pamby verse or prose. **3.** a namby-pamby person. **4.** namby-pamby sentiment. [orig. a nickname, *Namby Pamby*, for *Ambrose Philips* (d. 1749), British poet; first used by Henry Carey in 1726 as title of poem ridiculing Philips's verses]

name (nām), *n.*, *v.*, **named, naming.** —*n.* **1.** a word or a combination of words by which a person, place, or thing, a body or class, or any object of thought, is designated or known. **2.** mere designation as distinguished from fact: *king in name only.* **3.** an appellation, title, or epithet, applied descriptively, in honor, abuse, etc.: *to call him bad names.* **4.** a reputation of a particular kind given by common report: *a bad name.* **5.** a distinguished, famous, or great reputation; fame: *to seek name and fortune.* **6.** a widely known or famous person. **7.** a personal or family name as exercising influence or bringing distinction. **8.** a body of persons grouped under one name, as a family or race. **9.** the verbal or other symbolic representation of a thing, event, property, relation, or concept. A **proper name** represents some particular thing or event. A **common name** (e.g. "man") is the name of anything which satisfies certain indicated conditions. **10. in the name of, a.** with appeal to: *in the name of mercy, stop screaming!* **b.** by the authority of: *open in the name of the law.* **c.** on behalf of: *to vote in the name of others.* **d.** under the name of: *money deposited in the name of a son.* **e.** under the designation of; in the character of: *murder in the name of mercy.* **11. to one's name,** belonging to one: *not a nickel to my name.* —*v.t.* **12.** to give a name to: *name a baby.* **13.** to call by a specified name: *to name a child Regina.* **14.** to specify or mention by name: *three persons were named in the report.* **15.** to designate for some duty or office; nominate or appoint: *I have named you for the position.* **16.** to specify: *to name a price.* **17.** to tell the name of: *name the capital of Ohio.* **18.** to speak of. **19.** (in the English Parliament) to cite (a member) for contempt. [ME; OE *nama*, c. G *name*; akin to L *nōmen*, Gk. *ónoma*] —**nam'er**, *n.* —**Syn. 1.** NAME, TITLE both refer to the label by which a person is known. NAME is the simpler and more general word, for appellation: *the name is John.* A TITLE is an official or honorary term bestowed on a person or the specific designation of a book, article, etc.: *the title of Doctor, Treasure Island is the title of a book.*

name·a·ble (nā'mə bəl), *adj.* namable.

name·less (nām'lĭs), *adj.* **1.** unknown to fame; obscure. **2.** having no name. **3.** left unnamed: *a certain person who shall be nameless.* **4.** anonymous: *a nameless writer.* **5.** having no legitimate paternal name, as a child born out of wedlock. **6.** that cannot be specified or described: *a nameless charm.* **7.** too shocking or vile to be specified. —**name'less·ly**, *adv.* —**name'less·ness**, *n.*

name·ly (nām'lĭ), *adv.* that is to say; to wit: *two cities, namely, Paris and London.*

name·sake (nām'sāk'), *n.* **1.** one having the same name as another. **2.** one named after another. [alter. of *name's sake*]

Na·mur (nä mōor'; *Fr.* nå myr'), *n.* a city in S Belgium on the Sambre and Meuse rivers. 30,731 (est. 1944).

Nan·chang (nän'chäng'), *n.* a city in SE China: the capital of Kiangsi province. 206,400 (est. 1937).

Nan·cy (nän'sĭ'; *Fr.* nänsē'), *n.* a city in NE France: battles, 1477, 1914, 1944. 113,477 (1946).

Nan·da De·vi (nŭn'dä dā'vē), a peak of the Himalayas in N India, in the United Provinces. 25,661 ft.

nane (nān), *adj.*, *pron.*, *adv.* *Scot.* none.

Nan·ga Par·bat (nŭng'gə pŭr'bŭt), a peak of the Himalayas in NW Kashmir. 26,625 ft.

nan·keen (nän kēn'), *n.* **1.** a firm, durable, yellow or buff fabric, made orig. from a natural-colored Chinese cotton but now from other cotton and dyed. **2.** (*pl.*) garments made of this material. **3.** a yellow or buff color. **4.** a type of porcelain, blue on a white background. Also, **nan·kin.** [named after *Nankin* NANKING]

Nan·king (năn'kĭng'; *Chin.* nän'-), *n.* the capital of China, in the E part: a port on the Yangtze. 1,019,000 (est. 1940).

---

b., blend of, blended; c., cognate with; d., dialect, dialectal; der., derived from; f., formed from; g., going back to; m., modification of; r., replacing; s., stem of; t., taken from; ?, perhaps. See the full key on inside cover.

Nan Ling (nän′ lĭng′), a mountain range in S China. Also, **Nan Shan.**

Nan·ning (nän′nĭng′; *Chin.* nän′-), *n.* a city in S China, on the Si river: the capital of Kwangsi province. 80,300 (est. 1940).

nan·ny (nän′ĭ), *n.*, *pl.* -nies. *Brit.* a nurse for children, traditionally pictured as a loyal family retainer.

nanny goat, a female goat.

Nan·sen (nän′sən, nän′-), *n.* **Fridtjof** (frĭt′yŏf), 1861–1930, Norwegian arctic explorer, scientist, and diplomat.

Nan Shan (nän′ shän′), 1. broad mountain range in W China, in Chinghai and Kansu provinces. 2. Nan Ling.

Nantes (nänts; *Fr.* nänt), *n.* 1. a seaport in W France at the mouth of the Loire river. 200,265 (1946). 2. **Edict of,** a law promulgated by Henry IV of France in 1598, granting considerable religious and civil liberty to the Huguenots: revoked by Louis XIV, 1685.

Nan·ti·coke (nän′tə kōk′), *n.* a city in E Pennsylvania. 20,160 (1950).

Nan·tuck·et (nän tŭk′ĭt), *n.* an island off SE Massachusetts: summer resort. 3484 pop. (1950); 15 mi. long.

Na·o·mi (nā ō′mĭ, nā′ō mĭ′, -mĭ′), *n. Bible.* the mother-in-law of Ruth. Ruth 1:2, etc. [t. Heb.]

na·os (nā′ŏs), *n.* 1. a temple. 2. *Archit.* the central chamber, or cella, of an ancient temple. [t. Gk.: temple]

nap[1] (năp), *v.*, **napped, napping,** *n.* —*v.i.* 1. to have a short sleep; doze. 2. to be off one's guard: *I caught him napping.* —*n.* 3. a short sleep; a doze. [ME *nappe*(*n*), OE *hnappian*, c. MHG *napfen*]

nap[2] (năp), *n.*, *v.*, **napped, napping.** —*n.* 1. the short fuzzy ends of fibers on the surface of cloth drawn up in napping. 2. any downy coating, as on plants. —*v.t.* 3. to raise a nap on. [ME *noppe*, OE -*hnoppa* (in *wull-cnoppa*, mistake for *wullhnoppa* tuft of wool), c. MD and MLG *noppe*; akin to OE *hnoppian* pluck] —**nap′-less,** *adj.*

nap[3] (năp), *n.* napoleon (defs. 2, 3).

na·palm (nā′päm), *n. Mil.* a highly incendiary jellylike substance, used in bombs, flame throwers, etc.

nape (nāp, năp), *n.* the back (of the neck). [ME]

na·per·y (nā′pə rĭ), *n.* 1. table linen; tablecloths, napkins, etc. 2. linen for household use. [ME *naperie*, t. OF, der. *nape* tablecloth. See NAPKIN]

Naph·ta·li (năf′tə lī′), *n. Bible.* 1. a son of Jacob. Gen. 30:8. 2. one of the 12 tribes of Israel. Num. 1:15, 43.

naph·tha (năp′thə, năf′-), *n.* 1. a colorless, volatile liquid, a petroleum distillate (esp. a product intermediate between gasoline and benzine), used as a solvent, fuel, etc. 2. any of various similar liquids distilled from other products. 3. *Obs.* petroleum. [t. L, t. Gk.]

naph·tha·lene (năf′thə lēn′, năp′-), *n. Chem.* a white crystalline hydrocarbon, C₁₀H₈, usually prepared from coal tar, used in making dyes, as a moth repellant, etc. Also, **naph′tha·line,** **naph′tha·lin** (năf′thə-lĭn, năp′-). [f. NAPHTH(A) | AL(COHOL) + -ENE]

naph·thene (năf′thēn, năp′-), *n. Chem.* any of a group of hydrocarbon ring compounds of the general formula, CⁿH²ⁿ, derivatives of cyclopentane and cyclohexane, found in certain petroleums.

naph·thol (năf′thŏl, -thôl, năp′-), *n. Chem.* 1. either of two isomeric derivatives of naphthalene, having the formula C₁₀H₇OH, and occurring in coal tar, used as antiseptics and in dye manufacture. See betanaphthol. 2. any of certain hydroxyl derivatives of naphthalene. Also, **naph·tol** (năf′tŏl, -tôl, năp′-). [f. NAPHTH(A) +-OL²]

Na·pi·er (nā′pĭ′ər, nə pĭr′), *n.* 1. **Sir Charles James,** 1782–1853, British general. 2. **John,** 1550–1617, Scottish mathematician and inventor of logarithms.

Na·pier·i·an logarithm (nə pĭr′ĭ ən), *Math.* a logarithm using the number 2.718281828 + (*symbol: e*) as a base.

Napier of Mag·da·la (măg′də lə), **Robert Cornelis** (kôr nē′lĭs), **Napier, First Baron,** 1810–90, British field marshal.

na·pi·form (nā′pə fôrm′), *adj.* turnip-shaped, as a root. [f. s. L *nāpus* turnip + -(I)FORM]

nap·kin (năp′kĭn), *n.* 1. a rectangular piece of linen or cotton cloth used at table to wipe the lips and hands and to protect the clothes. 2. a square or oblong piece of linen or cotton cloth for some other purpose: **a.** a towel. **b.** *Chiefly Brit.* a diaper. **c.** *Now Scot.* a handkerchief. [late ME *napekyn*, dim. of *nape* tablecloth, t. F: m. *nappe*, g. L *mappa* cloth. Cf. MAP.]

Na·ples (nā′pəlz), *n.* 1. a seaport in SW Italy. 959,693 (est. 1946). 2. **Bay of,** the beautiful bay on which Naples is located. 22 mi. long. Italian, **Napoli.**

Na·po·le·on (nə pō′lĭ ən; *Fr.* nå pô lė ôn′), *n.* **Louis** (lwē), 1808–73, president of France, 1848–52; as **Napoleon III,** emperor of France, 1852–70 (son of Louis Bonaparte).

na·po·le·on (nə pō′lĭ ən), *n.* 1. a piece of pastry consisting of baked puff paste in layers with a cream filling. 2. a French gold coin, bearing a portrait of Napoleon (I or III), of the value of 20 francs, orig. about $3.86. 3. *Cards.* **a.** a game in which the players bid for the privilege of naming the trump, stating the number of tricks they propose to win. **b.** a bid in this game to take all five tricks of a hand. [named after NAPOLEON]

Napoleon I. See Bonaparte (def. 6).
Napoleon II. See Bonaparte (def. 7).
Napoleon III. See Napoleon, Louis.
Na·po·le·on·ic (nə pō′lĭ ŏn′ĭk), *adj.* pertaining to, re-

sembling, or suggestive of Napoleon I, or, less often, Napoleon III, or their dynasty.

Na·po·li (nä′pō lē′), *n.* Italian name of **Naples.**

nap·per[1] (năp′ər), *n.* 1. one who raises a nap on cloth. 2. a machine for putting a nap on cloth. [f. NAP² + -ER¹]

nap·per[2] (năp′ər), *n.* one who naps or dozes. [f. NAP¹ + -ER¹]

nap·py[1] (năp′ĭ), *adj.* 1. *Brit.* heady or strong, as ale. 2. *Chiefly Scot.* tipsy. —*n.* 3. *Chiefly Scot.* liquor, esp. ale. [prob. special use of NAPPY³]

nap·py[2] (năp′ĭ), *n.*, *pl.* -pies. a small dish, usually round and often of glass, with a flat bottom and sloping sides, for food, etc. Also, **nap′pie.** [orig. obscure]

nap·py[3] (năp′ĭ), *adj.* -pier, -piest. covered with nap; downy. [f. NAP² + -Y¹]

na·prap·a·thy (nə prăp′ə thĭ), *n.* a system of treatment based on the belief that all diseases are caused by connective tissue and ligament disorders and can be cured by massage. [f. Czech *napra(va)* correction (cf. Russ. *napravit′* direct, guide) + -PATHY] —**nap·ra·path** (năp′rə păth′), *n.*

Nar·ba·da (nər bŭd′ə), *n.* a river flowing from central India W to the Arabian Sea. ab. 800 mi. Also, **Nerbudda.**

Nar·bonne (nàr bôn′), *n.* a city in S France: an important port in Roman times. 29,975 (1946).

nar·ce·ine (när′sĭ ēn′, -ĭn), *n. Chem.* a bitter, white, crystalline alkaloid, C₂₃H₂₇NO₈, contained in opium, possessing a weak, smooth, muscle-relaxing action. Also, **nar·ce·in** (när′sĭ ĭn). [f. L *narcē* (t. Gk.: m. *nárkē* numbness, torpor) + -INE²]

nar·cis·sism (när sĭs′ĭz əm), *n. Psychoanal.* 1. sexual excitement through admiration of oneself. 2. self love; erotic gratification derived from admiration of one's own physical or mental attributes: a normal condition at the infantile level of personality development. Also, **nar·cism** (när′sĭz əm). [t. G: m. *Narzissismus.* See NARCISSUS, -ISM] —**nar·cis′sist,** *n.* —**nar′cis·sis′tic,** *adj.*

nar·cis·sus (när sĭs′əs), *n.*, *pl.* -cissuses, -cissi (-sĭs′ī). any plant of the amaryllidaceous genus *Narcissus*, which comprises bulbous plants bearing showy flowers with a cup-shaped corona, and includes the jonquil and the daffodil. [t. L, t. Gk.: m. *nárkissos* the plant (so named from its narcotic properties)]

Nar·cis·sus (när sĭs′əs), *n. Gk. Legend.* a beautiful youth who fell in love with his own image in water, pined away, and was metamorphosed into the narcissus.

nar·co·lep·sy (när′kə lĕp′sĭ), *n. Pathol.* a condition characterized by an uncontrollable desire for, and short attacks of sleep on all occasions. [b. NARCO(SIS) and (EPI)LEPSY] —**nar′co·lep′tic,** *adj.*

nar·co·sis (när kō′sĭs), *n.* 1. a state of sleep or drowsiness. 2. a temporary state of depression produced by a drug, or by heat, cold, or electricity. [t. NL, t. Gk.: m. *nárkōsis* a benumbing]

nar·co·syn·the·sis (när′kō sĭn′thə sĭs), *n.* a treatment for psychiatric disturbances which uses narcotics.

nar·cot·ic (när kŏt′ĭk), *adj.* 1. having the power to produce narcosis, as a drug. 2. pertaining to or of the nature of narcosis. 3. pertaining to narcotics or their use. 4. for the use or treatment of narcotic addicts. —*n.* 5. any of a class of substances that blunt the senses, relieving pain, etc., and inducing sleep, and in large quantities producing complete insensibility, often used habitually to satisfy morbid appetite. 6. an individual who is inclined toward the habitual use of narcotics. [t. Gk.: m.s. *narkōtikós* making stiff or numb]

nar·co·tism (när′kə tĭz′əm), *n.* 1. the habit of taking narcotics. 2. the action or influence of narcotics. 3. narcosis. 4. an abnormal inclination to sleep.

nar·co·tize (när′kə tīz′), *v.t.* -tized, -tizing. to subject to a narcotic; stupefy. —**nar′co·ti·za′tion,** *n.*

nard (närd), *n.* 1. an aromatic Himalayan plant, supposedly *Nardostachys Jatamansi* (spikenard), the source of an ointment used by the ancients. 2. the ointment. [ME, t. L: s. *nardus*, t. Gk.: m. *nárdos*]

nar·es (nâr′ēz), *n.pl.*, *sing.* naris (nâr′ĭs). *Anat.* the nostrils or the nasal passages. [t. L, pl. of *nāris*]

Na·rew (nä′rĕf), *n.* a river in NE Poland, flowing into the Bug river a little above its junction with the Vistula: battle, 1915. ab. 290 mi. Russian, **Na·rev** (nä′rĕf).

nar·ghi·le (när′gə lĭ′), *n.* an Oriental tobacco pipe in which the smoke is drawn through water before reaching the lips; a hookah. Also, **nar′gi·le, nar′gi·leh** (när′gə-lĕ). [t. Pers.: m. *nārgīlah*, der. *nārgīl* coconut]

nar·i·al (nâr′ĭ əl), *adj. Anat.* of or pertaining to the nares or nostrils. Also, **nar·ine** (nâr′ĭn, -īn).

nark (närk), *Brit. Slang.* —*n.* 1. a stool pigeon. —*v.i.* 2. to tell on someone else; act as a stool pigeon. 3. to criticize; irritate by vexing comment.

Nar·ra·gan·sett (năr′ə găn′sĭt), *n.pl.* a North American Indian tribe of the Algonquian family, formerly located on Rhode Island, now extinct. [f. Algonquian: *naiagans* very small point of land + -*et* on, in, along]

Narragansett Bay, an inlet of the Atlantic in E Rhode Island. 28 mi. long.

nar·rate (nă răt′, năr′āt), *v.*, -rated, -rating. —*v.t.* 1. to give an account of or tell the story of (events, experiences, etc.). —*v.i.* 2. to relate or recount events, etc., in speech or writing. [t. L: m.s. *narrātus,* pp.] —**nar·ra′tor, nar·rat′er,** *n.* —Syn. 1. See describe.

nar·ra·tion (nă rā′shən), *n.* 1. an account or story. 2. the act or process of narrating. 3. words or matter narrating something. **4.** *Rhet.* (in a classical speech) the third part, the exposition of the question.

nar·ra·tive (năr′ə tĭv), *n.* **1.** a story of events, experiences, or the like, whether true or fictitious. **2.** narrative matter, as in literary work. **3.** the act or process of narrating. —*adj.* **4.** that narrates: *a narrative poem.* **5.** of or pertaining to narration: *narrative skill.* —**nar′ra·tive·ly,** *adv.*
—**Syn. 1.** NARRATIVE, ACCOUNT, RECITAL, HISTORY are terms for a story of an event or events. NARRATIVE is the general term (for a story long or short; of past, present, or future; factual or imagined; told for any purpose; and with or without much detail). The other three terms apply primarily to factual stories of time already past. An ACCOUNT is usually told informally, often for entertainment with emphasis on details of action, whether about an incident or a series of happenings. A RECITAL, an extended narrative usually with an informative purpose, emphasizes accuracy and exhaustive details of facts and figures. A HISTORY, usually written and at some length, is characterized by a tracing of causes and effects, and by an attempt to estimate, evaluate, and interpret facts.

nar·row (năr′ō), *adj.* **1.** of little breadth or width; not broad or wide: *a narrow path.* **2.** limited in extent or space, or affording little room: *narrow quarters.* **3.** limited in range or scope. **4.** lacking breadth of view or sympathy, as persons, the mind, ideas, etc. **5.** limited in amount, small, or meager: *narrow resources.* **6.** straitened, as circumstances. **7.** barely sufficient or adequate, or being barely that: *a narrow escape.* **8.** careful; minute, as a scrutiny, search, or inquiry. **9.** *Brit. Dial. and Scot.* parsimonious or stingy. **10.** *Phonet.* tense. **11.** noting livestock feeds in which the proportion of protein is higher than ordinary. —*v.i.* **12.** to become narrower. —*v.t.* **13.** to make narrower. **14.** to limit or restrict. **15.** to make narrow-minded. —*n.* **16.** a narrow part, place, or thing. **17.** (*pl.*) a narrow part of a strait, river, ocean current, etc. **18. The Narrows,** the passage from upper to lower New York Bay, between Staten and Long Islands. Least width, 1¼ mi. **19.** a narrow part of a valley, of a passage between mountains, or of any road. [ME; OE *nearu,* c. OS *naru* narrow, D *naar* unpleasant] —**nar′row·ly,** *adv.* —**nar′row·ness,** *n.*

narrow gauge. See gauge (def. 10).

nar·row-gauge (năr′ō gāj′), *adj.* (of a railroad track) having less than 56½ inches between rails.

nar·row-mind·ed (năr′ō mīn′dĭd), *adj.* having or showing a prejudiced mind, as persons, opinions, etc. —**nar′row-mind′ed·ly,** *adv.* —**nar′row-mind′ed·ness,** *n.* —**Syn.** bigoted; intolerant.

nar·thex (när′thĕks), *n.* *Archit.* a vestibule along the facade of an early Christian or Byzantine church. [t. LGk.; in Gk., giant fennel]

Nar·va (när′vä), *n.* a seaport in the W Soviet Union, in the Estonian Republic: the Swedes defeated the Russians here, 1700. 23,512 (1934).

Nar·vá·ez (när vä′ĕth), *n.* **Pánfilo de** (päm′fē lō dě), c1478–1528, Spanish soldier and adventurer in America.

nar·whal (när′wəl), *n.* an arctic cetacean, *Monodon monoceros,* the male of which has a long, straight, spirally twisted tusk extending forward from the upper jaw. Also, **nar′wal,** **nar·whale** (när′hwāl). [t. Sw. or Dan.: m. *narhval* (f. *nar* + *hval* whale). Cf. Icel. *nāhvalr,* lit., corpse whale (from corpselike color of belly).]

Narwhal, *Monodon monoceros* (Body 12 ft. long, tusk ab. 9 ft.)

na·sal¹ (nā′zəl), *adj.* **1.** of or pertaining to the nose. **2.** *Phonet.* with the voice issuing through the nose, either partly (as in French nasal vowels) or entirely (as in *m, n,* or the *ng* of song). —*n.* **3.** *Phonet.* a nasal speech sound. [t. NL: s. *nāsālis,* der. L *nāsus* nose. See NOSE] —**na·sal·i·ty** (nā zăl′ə tĭ), *n.* —**na′sal·ly,** *adv.*

na·sal² (nā′zəl), *n.* a part of a helmet, protecting the nose and adjacent parts of the face. [ME, t. OF, der. L *nāsus* nose]

nasal index, **1.** *Craniom.* the ratio of the distance from nasion to the lower margin of the nasal aperture to that of the maximum breadth of the nasal aperture (on the skull). **2.** *Cephalom.* the ratio of the maximum breadth of the external nose to its height from nasal root to where the septum is confluent with the upper lip (on the head).

na·sal·ize (nā′zə līz′), *v.,* -ized, -izing. *Phonet.,* —*v.t.* **1.** to pronounce as a nasal sound by allowing some of the voice to issue through the nose. —*v.i.* **2.** to nasalize normally oral sounds. —**na′sal·i·za′tion,** *n.*

nas·cent (năs′ənt, nā′sənt), *adj.* **1.** beginning to exist or develop: *the nascent republic.* **2.** *Chem.* (of an element) being in the nascent state. [t. L: s. *nascens,* ppr., being born] —**nas′cence, nas′cen·cy,** *n.*

nascent state, *Chem.* the condition of an element at the instant it is set free from a combination in which it has previously existed. Also, **nascent condition.**

nase·ber·ry (nāz′bĕr′ĭ), *n., pl.* -ries. the fruit of the sapodilla, *Achras Zapota;* sapodilla. [t. Sp.: m. *nespera* medlar, g. L *mespila.* See MEDLAR]

Nase·by (nāz′bĭ), *n.* a village in central England, in Northamptonshire: Royalist defeat, 1645.

Nash (năsh), *n.* **1. Ogden,** born 1902, U.S. humorist. **2.** Also, **Nashe, Thomas,** 1567–1601, British poet, dramatist, and writer of pamphlets.

Nash·u·a (năsh′ōō ə), *n.* a city in S New Hampshire, on the Merrimack river. 34,669 (1950).

Nash·ville (năsh′vĭl), *n.* the capital of Tennessee, in the central part: battle, 1864. 174,307 (1950).

na·si·on (nā′zĭ ŏn′), *n.* *Craniom.* the intersection of the internasal suture with the nasofrontal suture, in the midsagittal plane. [t. NL, der. L *nāsus* nose] —**na′si·al,** *adj.*

na·so·fron·tal (nā′zō frŭn′təl), *adj.* of or pertaining to the nose and frontal bone.

na·so·phar·ynx (nā′zō făr′ĭngks), *n., pl.* -pharynges (-fə rĭn′jēz), -pharynxes. *Anat.* the part of the pharynx behind and above the soft palate, directly continuous with the nasal passages (distinguished from *oropharynx*).

Nas·sau (năs′ô; *for 2, 3, also Ger.* nä′sou, *Fr.* nȧ sō′), *n.* **1.** a seaport and the capital of the Bahama Islands. 29,391 (1943). **2.** a district in W Germany: formerly a duchy, now a part of Hesse-Nassau. **3.** a European royal family that has reigned in the Netherlands since 1815.

Nast (năst), *n.* **Thomas,** 1840–1902, U.S. cartoonist.

nas·tic (năs′tĭk), *adj.* *Plant Physiol.* of or showing sufficiently greater cellular force or growth on one side of an axis to change the form or position of an axis. [f. s. Gk. *nastós* squeezed together + -IC]

-nastic, a suffix forming adjectives of words ending in **-nasty.** [see NASTIC]

na·stur·tium (nă stûr′shəm, nə-), *n.* any of the garden plants constituting the genus *Tropaeolum,* much cultivated for their showy flowers of yellow, red, and other colors, and for their fruit, which is pickled and used like capers. [t. L: a kind of cress]

nas·ty (năs′tĭ), *adj.,* -tier, -tiest. **1.** physically filthy, or disgustingly unclean. **2.** offensive to taste or smell; nauseous. **3.** offensive; objectionable: *a nasty habit.* **4.** morally filthy; obscene. **5.** vicious, spiteful, or ugly: *a nasty dog.* **6.** bad to deal with, encounter, undergo, etc.: *a nasty cut.* **7.** very unpleasant: *nasty weather.* [ME, orig. uncert.] —**nas′ti·ly,** *adv.* —**nas′ti·ness,** *n.*

-nasty, a suffix indicating irregularity of cellular growth because of some pressure. [f. s. Gk. *nastós* squeezed together + -Y³]

nat., **1.** national. **2.** native. **3.** natural. **4.** naturalist.

na·tal (nā′təl), *adj.* **1.** of or pertaining to one's birth: *one's natal day.* **2.** presiding over or affecting one at birth: *natal influences.* **3.** *Chiefly Poetic.* (of places) native. [ME, t. L: s. *nātālis*]

Na·tal (nə tăl′, -täl′ *for 1;* nä täl′, -tôl′ *for 2*), *n.* **1.** a province of the Union of South Africa, in the E part. 2,182,733 pop. (1946); 35,284 sq. mi. (including Zululand). *Cap.:* Pietermaritzburg. **2.** a seaport in E Brazil. 51,896 (1940).

na·tal·i·ty (nā tăl′ə tĭ), *n.* birth rate.

na·tant (nā′tənt), *adj.* **1.** swimming; floating. **2.** *Bot.* floating on water, as the leaf of an aquatic plant. [t. L: s. *natans,* ppr.]

na·ta·tion (nā tā′shən), *n.* the act or art of swimming. [t. L: s. *natātio*] —**na·ta′tion·al,** *adj.*

na·ta·to·ri·al (nā′tə tōr′ĭ əl), *adj.* pertaining to, adapted for, or characterized by swimming: *natatorial birds.* Also, **na′ta·to′ry.** [f. s. LL *natātōrius* + -AL¹]

na·ta·to·ri·um (nā′tə tōr′ĭ əm), *n., pl.* -toriums, -toria (-tōr′ĭ ə). a swimming pool. [t. LL]

Natch·ez (năch′ĭz), *n.* **1.** a city in SW Mississippi: a port on the Mississippi. 22,740 (1950). **2.** (*sing. and pl.*) a member of an extinct Muskhogean Indian tribe once living on the lower Mississippi river.

na·tes (nā′tēz), *n.pl.* the buttocks. [t. L, pl. of *natis*]

Na·than (nā′thən), *n.* **George Jean,** born 1882, U.S. dramatic critic, author, and editor.

nathe·less (nāth′lĭs, năth′-), *Archaic.* —*adv.* **1.** nevertheless. —*prep.* **2.** notwithstanding. Also, **nath·less** (năth′lĭs). [ME *natheles,* OE *nāthēlæs,* var. of *nāthȳlæs,* f. *nā* never + *thȳ* the + *læs* less]

na·tion (nā′shən), *n.* **1.** an aggregation of persons of the same ethnic family, speaking the same language or cognate languages. **2.** a body of people associated with a particular territory who are sufficiently conscious of their unity to seek or to possess a government peculiarly their own. **3.** a member tribe of an Indian confederation. [ME, t. L: s. *nātio* race, people, nation, orig., birth] —**Syn. 2.** See RACE.

Na·tion (nā′shən), *n.* **Carry,** or **Carrie, Amelia,** (*Carry Amelia Moore*) 1846–1911, U.S. temperance leader.

na·tion·al (năsh′ən əl), *adj.* **1.** of, pertaining to, or maintained by a nation as an organized whole or independent political unit: *national affairs.* **2.** peculiar or common to the whole people of a country: *national customs.* **3.** devoted to one's own nation, its interests, etc.; patriotic. —*n.* **4.** a citizen or subject of a particular nation, entitled to its protection. —**na′tion·al·ly,** *adv.*

national bank, **1.** a central bank; a governmentally owned and administered bank. **2.** *U.S.* a bank chartered by the national government and formerly authorized to issue notes that served as money.

national church, the church established by law in a nation, generally the prevalent religion.

National Guard, State military forces, in part equipped, trained and quartered by the U.S. government, and paid by the U.S. government, which become an active component of the Army when called or ordered into federal service by the president under the authority of the Constitution and implementing laws.

National Guard of the United States, the officers who hold a dual commission, as officers of the National Guard and of the Army of the United States.

national income, *Econ.* the total net value of commodities produced and services rendered by all the people of a nation during a specified period.

na·tion·al·ism (năsh′ən əl ĭz′əm), *n.* **1.** national spirit or aspirations. **2.** devotion to the interests of one's own nation. **3.** desire for national advancement or independence. **4.** the policy of asserting the interests of a nation, viewed as separate from the interests of other nations or the common interests of all nations. **5.** an idiom or trait peculiar to a nation. **6.** a form of socialism which advocates the nationalizing of all industries.

na·tion·al·ist (năsh′ən əl ĭst), *n.* **1.** one inspired with nationalism. **2.** an advocate of national independence. —*adj.* **3.** Also, **na′tion·al·is′tic.** of or pertaining to nationalism or nationalists. —**na′tion·al·is′ti·cal·ly,** *adv.*

na·tion·al·i·ty (năsh′ə năl′ə tĭ), *n., pl.* **-ties. 1.** the quality of membership in a particular nation (original or acquired): *the nationality of an immigrant.* **2.** relationship of property, etc., to a particular nation, or to one or more of its members: *the nationality of a ship.* **3.** nationalism. **4.** existence as a distinct nation; national independence. **5.** a nation or people: *the various nationalities of America.* **6.** national quality or character.

na·tion·al·ize (năsh′ən əl īz′), *v.t.,* **-ized, -izing. 1.** to bring under the control or ownership of a nation, as industries, land, etc. **2.** to make nationwide: *to nationalize a holiday.* **3.** to naturalize. **4.** to make into a nation. Also, *Brit.,* **na′tion·al·ise′.** —**na′tion·al·i·za′tion,** *n.* —**na′tion·al·iz′er,** *n.*

national park, a tract of land maintained by the federal government for the use of the people.

National Socialism, the principles and practices of Hitler's National Socialist German Workers' (or Nazi) Party. See **Nazi.** —**National Socialist.**

na·tion·wide (nā′shən wīd′), *adj.* extending throughout the nation: *a nation-wide campaign against cancer.*

na·tive (nā′tĭv), *adj.* **1.** being the place or environment in which one was born or a thing came into being: *one's native land.* **2.** belonging to a person or thing by birth or nature; inborn; inherent; natural (often fol. by *to*). **3.** belonging by birth to a people regarded as natives, esp. outside of the general body of white peoples: *native policemen in India.* **4.** of indigenous origin, growth, or production; indigenous (fol. by *to*): *native pottery.* **5.** of, pertaining to, or characteristic of natives: *native customs in Java.* **6.** under the rule of natives: *the native states of India.* **7.** occupied by natives: *the native quarter of Algiers.* **8.** belonging or pertaining to one by reason of one's birthplace or nationality: *one's native language.* **9.** born in a particular place or country: *native American citizens.* **10.** remaining in a natural state; unadorned; untouched by art: *native beauty.* **11.** forming the source or origin of a person or thing. **12.** originating naturally in a particular country or region, as animals or plants. **13.** found in nature rather than produced artificially, as a mineral substance. **14.** occurring in nature pure or uncombined, as metals, etc.: *native copper.* **15.** belonging to one as a possession by virtue of his birth: *native rights.* **16.** *Archaic.* closely related, as by birth. —*n.* **17.** one of the original inhabitants of a place or country, esp. as distinguished from strangers, foreigners, colonizers, etc.: *the natives of Chile.* **18.** one born in a particular place or country: *a native of Milwaukee.* **19.** an animal or plant indigenous to a particular region. **20.** in England, an oyster. **21.** *Astrol.* one born under a particular planet. [t. L: m.s. *nātīvus* native, innate, natural; r. ME *natif,* t. OF] —**na′tive·ly,** *adv.* —**na′tive·ness,** *n.*

na·tive-born (nā′tĭv bôrn′), *adj.* born in a place or country indicated.

na·tiv·ism (nā′tĭ vĭz′əm), *n.* **1.** the policy of protecting the interests of native inhabitants against those of immigrants. **2.** *Philos.* the doctrine of innate ideas. —**na′tiv·ist,** *n.* —**na′tiv·is′tic,** *adj.*

na·tiv·i·ty (nā tĭv′ə tĭ, nə-), *n., pl.* **-ties. 1.** birth. **2.** birth with reference to place or attendant circumstances: *of Irish nativity.* **3.** (*cap.*) the birth of Christ. **4.** (*cap.*) the church festival commemorating the birth of Christ; Christmas. **5.** (*cap.*) a representation of the birth of Christ, as in art. **6.** *Astrol.* a horoscope. [ME *nativite,* t. LL: m.s. *nātīvitas*]

natl., national.

na·tri·um (nā′trĭ əm), *n.* an old pharmaceutical name for sodium.

nat·ro·lite (năt′rə līt′, nā′trə-), *n.* a zeolite mineral, a hydrous silicate of sodium and aluminum, $Na_2Al_2Si_3O_{10}\cdot 2H_2O$, occurring usually in white or colorless, often acicular crystals. [f. NATRO(N) + -LITE]

na·tron (nā′trŏn), *n.* a mineral, hydrated sodium carbonate, $Na_2CO_3\cdot 10H_2O$. [t. F, t. Sp., t. Ar.: m. *naṭrūn,* t. Gk.: m. *nítron* natron. See NITER]

nat·ty (năt′ĭ), *adj.,* **-tier, -tiest.** neatly smart in dress or appearance; spruce; trim: *a natty white uniform.* [? akin to NEAT[1]] —**nat′ti·ly,** *adv.* —**nat′ti·ness,** *n.*

nat·u·ral (năch′ər əl), *adj.* **1.** existing in or formed by nature; not artificial: *a natural bridge.* **2.** based on the state of things in nature; constituted by nature: *the natural day.* **3.** of or pertaining to nature or the created universe: *a natural science.* **4.** occupied with the study of natural science. **5.** in a state of nature; uncultivated, as land. **6.** growing spontaneously, as vegetation. **7.** having a real or physical existence, as opposed to one that is spiritual, intellectual, fictitious, etc. **8.** of, pertaining to, or proper to the nature or essential constitution: *natural ability.* **9.** proper to the circumstances of the case. **10.** free from affection or constraint: *a natural manner.* **11.** essentially pertaining; coming easily or spontaneously: *a manner natural to an aristocrat.* **12.** consonant with the nature or character of. **13.** in accordance with the nature of things: *it was natural that he should hit back.* **14.** based upon the innate moral feeling of mankind: *natural justice.* **15.** *Now Rare.* having or showing the nature, disposition, feelings, etc. befitting a person. **16.** in conformity with the ordinary course of nature; not unusual or exceptional. **17.** happening in the ordinary course of things, without the intervention of accident, violence, etc.: *a natural death.* **18.** by birth merely, and not legally recognized; illegitimate. **19.** based on what is learned from nature, rather than on revelation: *natural religion.* **20.** true to nature, or closely imitating nature. **21.** unenlightened or unregenerate: *the natural man.* **22.** being such by nature; born such: *a natural fool.* **23.** *Music.* **a.** neither sharp nor flat; without sharps or flats. **b.** changed in pitch by the sign ♮. —*n.* **24.** one naturally deficient in intellect; an idiot. **25.** *Colloq.* a thing or a person that is naturally or by nature notably satisfactory or a success. **26.** *Music.* **a.** a white key on the pianoforte, etc. **b.** the sign ♮, placed before a note canceling the effect of a previous sharp or flat. **c.** a note affected by a ♮, or a tone thus represented. [ME, t. L: s. *nātūrālis* by birth, in accordance with nature] —**nat′u·ral·ly,** *adv.* —**nat′u·ral·ness,** *n.*

Natural Bridge, a natural limestone bridge in W Virginia. 215 ft. high; 90 ft. span.

Natural Bridges, a national monument in SE Utah: three natural bridges; largest, 222 ft. high; 261 ft. span.

natural gas, combustible gas formed naturally in the earth, as in regions yielding petroleum, and consisting typically of methane with certain amounts of hydrogen and other gases, used as a fuel, etc.

natural history, **1.** the science or study dealing with all objects in nature. **2.** the aggregate of knowledge connected with such objects.

nat·u·ral·ism (năch′ər əl ĭz′əm), *n.* **1.** (in art or literature) **a.** an intention on the part of the artist to represent objects as nearly as possible under their natural and everyday forms. **b.** (esp. in literature) a theory, as practiced by Emile Zola, Stephen Crane and others, which applied scientific concepts and methods to such problems as plot development and characterization. **c.** the group of procedures derived from this theory. **2.** action arising from or based on natural instincts and desires alone. **3.** *Philos.* **a.** the view of the world which takes account only of natural elements and forces, excluding the supernatural or spiritual. **b.** the belief that all phenomena are covered by laws of science and that all teleological explanations are therefore without value. **c.** positivism or materialism. **4.** *Theol.* **a.** the doctrine that all religious truth is derived from a study of natural processes, and not from revelation. **b.** the doctrine that natural religion is sufficient for salvation. **5.** adherence or attachment to what is natural.

nat·u·ral·ist (năch′ər əl ĭst), *n.* **1.** one who is versed in or devoted to natural history, esp. a zoölogist or botanist. **2.** an adherent of naturalism.

nat·u·ral·is·tic (năch′ər əl ĭs′tĭk), *adj.* **1.** imitating nature or usual natural surroundings. **2.** pertaining to naturalists or natural history. **3.** pertaining to naturalism, esp. in art and literature.

nat·u·ral·ize (năch′ər əl īz′), *v.,* **-ized, -izing.** —*v.t.* **1.** to invest (an alien) with the rights and privileges of a subject or citizen; confer the rights and privileges of citizenship upon. **2.** to introduce (animals or plants) into a region and cause to flourish as if native. **3.** to introduce or adopt (foreign practices, words, etc.) into a country or into general use: *to naturalize a French expression.* **4.** bring into conformity with nature. **5.** to regard or explain as natural rather than supernatural: *to naturalize miracles.* **6.** to adapt or accustom to a place or to new surroundings. —*v.i.* **7.** to become naturalized, or as if native. —**nat′u·ral·i·za′tion,** *n.*

natural law, the expression of right reason or of religion, inhering in nature and man, and having ethically a binding force as a rule of civil conduct.

natural logarithm, Napierian logarithm.

natural philosophy, **1.** the study of nature in general. **2.** the branch of physical science which treats of those properties and phenomena of bodies which are unaccompanied by an essential change in the bodies themselves, including the sciences classed under physics.

natural resources, the wealth of a country consisting of land, forests, mines, water and energy resources.

natural science, science or knowledge dealing with objects in nature, as distinguished from mental or moral science, abstract mathematics, etc.

natural selection, the elimination of the unfit and the survival of the fit in the struggle for existence, depending upon the adjustment of an organism to a specific environment. Cf. **Darwinism.**

natural sine, tangent, etc., *Math.* the actual value, not the logarithm, of a sine (tangent, etc.).

na·ture (nā′chər), *n.* 1. the particular combination of qualities belonging to a person or thing by birth or constitution; native or inherent character: *the nature of atomic energy.* 2. the instincts or inherent tendencies directing conduct: *a man of good nature.* 3. character, kind, or sort: *a book of the same nature.* 4. a person of a particular character or disposition. 5. the material world, esp. as surrounding man and existing independently of his activities. 6. the universe, with all its phenomena. 7. the sum total of the forces at work throughout the universe. 8. reality, as distinguished from any effect of art: *true to nature.* 9. the physical being. 10. the vital powers: *food sufficient to sustain nature.* 11. a primitive, wild condition; an uncultivated state. 12. *Theol.* the moral state as unaffected by grace. 13. **by nature,** as a result of inherent qualities. 14. **of** or **in the nature of,** having the qualities of. [ME, t. OF, t. L: m.s. *nātūra* birth, natural character, nature]

nature study, the study of physical nature, esp. on the level of secondary schools.

Nau·cra·tis (nô′krə tĭs), *n.* an ancient Greek city in N Egypt, on the delta of the Nile. Greek, **Nau′kra·tis.**

naught (nôt), *n.* 1. a cipher (0); zero. 2. *Now Archaic or Literary.* nothing. 3. destruction, ruin, or complete failure: *to bring or come to naught.* 4. **set at naught,** to regard or treat as of no importance. —*adj. Obs. or Archaic.* 5. worthless; useless. 6. lost; ruined. 7. morally bad; wicked. —*adv.* 8. *Obs. or Archaic.* in no respect or degree. Also, **nought.** [ME; OE *nauht, nāwiht,* f. *nā* NO + *wiht* thing. See NOUGHT, WIGHT¹, WHIT]

naugh·ty (nô′tĭ), *adj.,* **-tier, -tiest.** 1. disobedient; m′schievous (esp. in speaking to or about children): *a naughty child.* 2. improper; obscene: *a naughty word.* 3. *Obs.* wicked; evil. [ME, f. NAUGHT (def. 7) + -Y¹] —**naugh′ti·ly,** *adv.* —**naugh′ti·ness,** *n.*

nau·ma·chi·a (nô mā′kĭ ə), *n., pl.* **-chiae** (-kĭ ē′), **-chias.** 1. a mock sea fight, given as a spectacle among the ancient Romans. 2. a place for presenting such spectacles. [t. L, t. Gk.]

nau·ma·chy (nô′mə kĭ), *n., pl.* **-chies.** naumachia.

nau·pli·us (nô′plĭ əs), *n., pl.* **-plii** (-plĭ ī′). (in many crustaceans) a larval form with three pairs of appendages, and a single median eye, occurring (usually) as the first stage of development after leaving the egg. [t. L: kind of shellfish]

Na·u·ru (nä ōō′rōō), *n.* a Pacific island near the equator, W of the Gilbert Islands: administered by Australia. 2672 pop. (1941); 8¼ sq. mi. Formerly, **Pleasant Island.**

nau·sea (nô′shə, -shĭ ə, -sĭ ə), *n.* 1. sickness at the stomach; a sensation of impending vomiting. 2. seasickness. 3. extreme disgust. [t. L, var. of *nausia,* t. Gk.]

nau·se·ate (nô′shĭ āt′, -sĭ-), *v.,* **-ated, -ating.** —*v.t.* 1. to affect with nausea; sicken. 2. to feel extreme disgust at; loathe. —*v.i.* 3. to become affected with nausea. [t. L: m.s. *nauseātus,* pp., having been seasick] —**nau′se·a′tion,** *n.*

nau·seous (nô′shəs, -shĭ əs), *adj.* 1. causing nausea, or sickening. 2. disgusting; loathsome. [t. L: m.s. *nauseōsus*] —**nau′seous·ly,** *adv.* —**nau′seous·ness,** *n.*

Nau·sic·a·ä (nô sĭk′ĭ ə, -ā ə, nou-), *n. Homeric Legend.* the daughter of Alcinoüs, king of the Phaeacians. She led the shipwrecked Ulysses to her father's court.

naut., nautical.

nautch (nôch), *n.* an East Indian exhibition of dancing by professional dancing girls (**nautch girls**). [t. Hind.: m. *nāch,* g. Prakrit *nachcha* dancing]

nau·ti·cal (nô′tə kəl), *adj.* of or pertaining to seamen, ships, or navigation: *nautical terms.* [f. s. L *nauticus* (t. Gk.: m. *nautikós* pertaining to ships or sailors) + -AL¹] —**nau′ti·cal·ly,** *adv.*

nautical mile, mile (def. 1b).

nau·ti·lus (nô′tə ləs), *n., pl.* **-luses, -li** (-lī). 1. any of the tetrabranchiate cephalopods that constitute the genus *Nautilus,* having a spiral, chambered shell with pearly septa; pearly nautilus. 2. the paper nautilus or argonaut. [t. L, t. Gk.: m. *nautílos,* lit., sailor]

nav., 1. naval. 2. navigation.

Nav·a·ho (năv′ə hō′), *n., pl.* **-hos, -hoes.** 1. the principal tribe of the southern division of the Athapascan stock of North American Indians, located in New Mexico and Arizona, and now constituting the largest tribal group in the U.S. 2. a member of this tribe. Also, **Nav·a·jo** (năv′ə hō′). [t. Sp.: m. *(Apaches de) Navajo,* t. Tewa: m. *Navahu* great fields, applied to former Tewa pueblo and by extension to the Navahos who intruded upon the agricultural pueblos]

na·val (nā′vəl), *adj.* 1. of or pertaining to ships, esp., and now only, ships of war: *a naval battle.* 2. belonging to, pertaining to, or connected with, a navy: *naval affairs.* 3. possessing a navy: *the great naval powers.* [t. L: s. *nāvālis* pertaining to a ship]

naval academy, a collegiate institution for training naval officers.

Na·va·ri·no (nä′vä rē′nō), *n.* a seaport in SW Greece, in the Peloponnesus: the Turkish and Egyptian fleets were defeated in a naval battle near here, 1827.

Na·varre (nə vär′), *n.* a former kingdom in SW France and N Spain. Spanish, **Na·var·ra** (nä-vär′rä).

Kingdom of Navarre, 1492

nave¹ (nāv), *n.* the main body, or middle part, lengthwise, of a church, flanked by the aisles and extending typically from the entrance to the apse or chancel. See diag. under **basilica.** [t. ML: m.s. *nāvis* nave of a church, L ship]

nave² (nāv), *n.* 1. the central part of a wheel; the hub. 2. *Obs.* the navel. [ME; OE *nafu,* c. G *nabe*]

na·vel (nā′vəl), *n.* 1. a pit or depression in the middle of the surface of the belly; the umbilicus. 2. the central point or middle of any thing or place. 3. *Her.* nombril. [ME; OE *nafela,* c. G *nabel*] —**na′vel·like′,** *adj.*

navel orange, a kind of orange having at the apex a navellike formation containing a small secondary fruit.

nav·i·cert (năv′ə sûrt′), *n.* a British consulate certificate, specif′ng the character of a ship's cargo, etc. [f. L *nāvi(s)* ship + CERT(IFICATE)]

na·vic·u·lar (nə vĭk′yə lər), *Anat.* —*adj.* 1. (of certain bones, etc.) boat-shaped. —*n.* Also, **na·vic·u·lar·e** (nə-vĭk′yə lâr′ĭ). 2. the bone at the radial end of the proximal row of the bones of the carpus. 3. the bone in front of the talus, or anklebone, on the inner side of the foot. [t. LL: s. *nāviculāris* relating to ships]

navig., navigation.

nav·i·ga·ble (năv′ə gə bəl), *adj.* that may be navigated, as waters, or vessels or a′rcraft. —**nav′i·ga·bil′-i·ty, nav′i·ga·ble·ness,** *n.* —**nav′i·ga·bly** *adv.*

nav·i·gate (năv′ə gāt′), *v.,* **-gated, -gating.** —*v.t.* 1. to traverse (the sea, a river, etc.) in a vessel, or (the air) in an aircraft. 2. to direct or manage (a ship or an aircraft) on its course. 3. to pass over (the sea, etc.), as a ship does. —*v.i.* 4. to direct or manage a ship or an aircraft on its course. 5. to travel by using a ship or boat, as over the water; sail. 6. to pass over the water, as a ship does. [t L: m.s. *nāvigātus,* pp.]

nav·i·ga·tion (năv′ə gā′shən), *n.* 1. act or process of navigating. 2. the art or science of directing the course of a ship or aircraft. —**nav′i·ga′tion·al,** *adj.*

nav·i·ga·tor (năv′ə gā′tər), *n.* 1. one who navigates. 2. one who practices, or is skilled in, navigation, whether of ships or aircraft. 3. one who conducts explorations by sea. 5. *Brit.* a navvy or laborer. [t. L]

Navigators Islands, former name of **Samoa.**

nav·vy (năv′ĭ), *n., pl.* **-vies.** *Brit.* a laborer employed in making canals, railroads, etc. [short for NAVIGATOR]

na·vy (nā′vĭ), *n., pl.* **-vies.** 1. the whole body of warships and auxiliaries belonging to a country or ruler. 2. the department of government charged with their management. 3. such a body of warships together with their officers and men, equipment, yards, etc. 4. Also, **navy blue.** a dark blue. 5. *Archaic.* a fleet of ships. [ME *navie,* t. OF, der. L *nāvis* ship]

navy bean, the common small white bean, used for food as dry beans.

navy yard, a government dockyard where naval vessels are built, repaired, and fitted out, and naval stores and munitions of war are laid up.

na·wab (nə wôb′), *n.* 1. a viceroy or deputy governor under the former Mogul empire in India. 2. an honorary title conferred upon Mohammedans of distinction in India. Cf. **rajah.** 3. nabob. [t. Hind.: m. *nawwāb,* t. Ar., pl. of *nā′ib* deputy, viceroy]

Nax·os (năk′sŏs; *Gk.* nä′ksôs), *n.* a Greek island in the S Aegean: the largest of the Cyclades group. 19,981 pop. (1928); 169 sq. mi.

nay (nā), *adv.* 1. no (used in dissent, denial, or refusal). 2. also, and not only so, but: *many good, nay, noble qualities.* —*n.* 3. a denial or refusal. 4. a negative vote or voter. [ME *nai, nei,* t. Scand.; cf. Icel. *nei* no, f. *ne* not + *ei* ever]

Naz·a·rene (năz′ə rēn′), *n.* 1. a native or inhabitant of the town of Nazareth, as Jesus Christ (**the Nazarene**). 2. a Christian (so called by the Jews, Mohammedans, etc.). 3. a member of a sect of early Jewish Christians who retained the Mosaic ritual. —*adj.* 4. of or pertaining to Nazareth or the Nazarenes. [ME *Nazaren,* t. LL: s. *Nazarēnus,* t. Gk.: m. *Nazarēnós,* der. *Nazarēt* Nazareth]

Naz·a·reth (năz′ə rəth, -rĭth), *n.* a town in N Israel: the childhood home of Jesus. 14,200 (est. 1944).

Naz·a·rite (năz′ə rīt′), *n.* 1. (among the ancient Hebrews) a religious devotee who had taken certain vows. Num. 6. 2. *Rare.* a Nazarene. 3. *Rare.* Christian. 4. *Rare.* Christ. Also, **Nazirite.** [f. L *Nazar(aeus)* (t. Gk.: m. *Nazaraîos,* der. Heb. *nāzar* consecrate) + -ITE¹]

Naze (nāz), *n.* **The,** Lindesnes.

Na·zi (nä′tsĭ, nät′sĭ), *n., pl.* **-zis,** *adj.* —*n.* 1. a member of the National Socialist German Workers party of Germany, which in 1933, under Adolf Hitler, obtained political control of the country, suppressing all opposition and establishing a dictatorship on the principles of one-party control over all cultural, economic, and political activities of the people, belief in the supremacy of

Hitler as Führer, anti-Semitism, and the establishment of Germany by superior force as a dominant world power. **2**. one who holds similar views elsewhere. —*adj.* **3**. of or pertaining to the Nazis. [t. G, short for *Nazi(onal-sozialist)* National Socia.ist]

Na·zi·mo·va (nä zē/mô vä), *n.* **Alla** (äl/lä), 1879–1945, Russian actress in America.

Naz·i·rite (năz/ə rīt/), *n.* Nazarite.

Na·zism (nä/tsYz əm, năt/sYz-), *n.* the principles or methods of the Nazis. Also, **Na·zi·ism** (nä/tsY Yz/əm, năt/sY-).

Nb, *Chem.* niobium.

N. B., **1**. New Brunswick. **2**. nota bene.

N. C., North Carolina.

N. C. O., Noncommissioned Officer.

Nd, *Chem.* neodymium.

n. d., no date.

N. Dak., North Dakota. Also, **N. D.**

Ne, *Chem.* neon.

NE, **1**. northeast. **2**. northeastern. Also, **n.e.**

N. E., **1**. New England. **2**. northeast. **3**. northeastern.

N. E. A., National Education Association.

Ne·an·der·thal (nY än/dər täl/; *Ger.* nä än/-), *adj.* *Anthropol.* of or pertaining to the Neanderthal man.

Neanderthal man, *Anthropol.* the species of primeval man widespread in Europe in the paleolithic period. [so called because earliest evidence was discovered at Neanderthal, a valley near Düsseldorf, Germany]

neap[1] (nēp), *adj.* **1**. designating those tides, midway between spring tides, which attain the least height. —*n.* **2**. neap tide. See diag. under **tide.** [ME *neep,* OE *nēp,* in *nēpflōd* neap flood]

neap[2] (nēp), *n.* *U.S. Dial.* the pole or tongue of a wagon, etc. [orig. uncert.]

Ne·a·pol·i·tan (nē/ə pŏl/ə tən), *adj.* **1**. of or pertaining to Naples. —*n.* **2**. a native or inhabitant of Naples. [ME, t. L: s. *Neāpolītānus*]

Neapolitan ice cream, variously flavored and colored ice cream and ice mixtures frozen in layers.

near (nYr), *adv.* **1**. close: *near by.* **2**. nigh; at, within, or to a short distance: *to stand near.* **3**. close at hand in time: *New Year's Day is near.* **4**. close in relation; closely with respect to connection, similarity, etc. **5**. *Now Chiefly Colloq. or Dial.* all but; almost: *a period of near thirty years.* **6**. *Naut.* close to the wind. —*adj.* **7**. being close by; not distant: *the near meadows.* **8**. less distant: *the near side.* **9**. short or direct: *the near road.* **10**. close in time: *the near future.* **11**. closely related or connected: *our nearest relation.* **12**. close to an original: *a near translation.* **13**. closely affecting one's interests or feelings: *a matter of near consequence to one.* **14**. intimate or familiar: *a near friend.* **15**. narrow: *a near escape.* **16**. parsimonious or niggardly: *a near man.* **17**. (in riding or driving) on the left (opposed to *off*): *the near wheel.* —*prep.* (strictly the adverb with "to" understood). **18**. at, within, or to a short distance, or no great distance, from: *regions near the equator.* **19**. close upon in time: *near the beginning of the year.* **20**. close upon (a condition, etc.): *a task near completion.* **21**. close to in similarity, resemblance, etc.: *near beer.* **22**. close to (doing something): *this act came near spoiling his chances.* —*v.t., v.i.* **23**. to come or draw near (to); approach. [ME *nere,* OE *nēar,* compar. of *nēah* NIGH] —**near/-ness,** *n.*

near·by (nYr/bī/), *adj.* close at hand; not far off; adjacent; neighboring: *a nearby village.*

Ne·arc·tic (nē ärk/tYk, -är/-), *adj.* (in zoögeography) belonging to the northern division of the New World (temperate and arctic North America, with Greenland).

Near East, **1**. *U.S.* the Balkan states, the Levant, and the countries of SW Asia. **2**. *Brit.* the Balkan States.

near-hand (nYr/hănd/), *adv.* *Now Brit. Dial. and Scot.* **1**. near at hand. **2**. nearly or almost.

near·ly (nYr/lY), *adv.* **1**. all but; almost: *nearly dead with cold.* **2**. with close approximation. **3**. with close agreement or resemblance: *a case nearly approaching this one.* **4**. with close kinship, interest, or connection; intimately. **5**. with parsimony. —**Syn. 1.** See **almost.**

near-sight·ed (nYr/sī/tYd), *adj.* seeing distinctly at a short distance only; myopic. —**near/-sight/ed·ly,** *adv.* —**near/-sight/ed·ness,** *n.*

neat[1] (nēt), *adj.* **1**. in a pleasingly orderly condition: *a neat room.* **2**. habitually orderly in appearance, etc. **3**. of a simple, pleasing appearance: *a neat cottage.* **4**. cleverly effective in character or execution: *a neat scheme.* **5**. clever, dexterous, or apt: *a neat characterization.* **6**. unadulterated or undiluted, as liquors. **7**. net: *neat profits.* [t. F: m. *net* clean, g. L *nitidus* bright, fine, neat] —**neat/ly,** *adv.* —**neat/ness,** *n.* —**Syn. 1.** NEAT, TIDY, TRIM describe orderliness and an attractive appearance. NEAT suggests order and absence of superfluous details: *a neat desk, dress.* TIDY has working class connotations and the idea of making humble things look their best; it suggests a painstaking orderliness, the result of effort and perhaps of habit: *the cottage looked cheerful and tidy.* TRIM suggests a combination of neatness and smartness or stylishness: *a trim new outfit.* —**Ant. 1.** slovenly.

neat[2] (nēt), *n., pl.* **neat.** *Obs.* cattle of the genus *Bos.* [ME *neet,* OE *nēat,* c. Icel. *naut*]

neath (nēth, nĕth), *prep.* *Poetic or Scot.* beneath. Also, **'neath.**

neat·herd (nēt/hûrd/), *n.* a cowherd.

neat's-foot oil (nēts/fŏŏt/), a pale-yellow fixed oil made by boiling the feet and shinbones of cattle, used chiefly as a dressing for leather. [see NEAT[2]]

neb (nĕb), *n.* **1**. a bill or beak, as of a bird. **2**. a person's mouth. **3**. the nose, esp. of an animal. **4**. the tip or pointed end of anything. **5**. the nib of a pen. [ME *nebbe,* OE *nebb,* c. MD and MLG *nebbe*]

Neb., Nebraska.

Ne·bi·im (nĕb/Y ēm/; *Heb.* nĕ vē/ēm/), *n.pl.* (in the Hebrew Bible) the Prophets, the books occurring after the Torah and before the Hagiographa. [t. Heb., pl of *nābhī* prophet]

Ne·bo (nē/bō), *n.* **Mount.** See **Pisgah, Mount.**

Nebr., Nebraska.

Ne·bras·ka (nə brăs/kə), *n.* a State in the central United States. 1,325,510 pop. (1950); 77,237 sq. mi. *Cap.:* Lincoln. *Abbr.:* Nebr. *or* Neb. —**Ne·bras/kan,** *adj., n.*

neb·ris (nĕb/rYs), *n.* *Gk. Antiq.* the skin of a fawn, esp. as worn by Bacchus and later, on festival occasions, by his priests and votaries. [t. L, t. Gk.]

Neb·u·chad·nez·zar (nĕb/yŏŏ kəd nĕz/ər, nĕb/ə-), *n.* a king of Babylonia, 604?–561? B.C., and conqueror of Jerusalem. II Kings 24–25. Also, **Neb·u·chad·rez·zar** (nĕb/yŏŏ kəd rĕz/ər, nĕb/ə-).

neb·u·la (nĕb/yə lə), *n., pl.* **-lae** (-lē/), **-las.** **1**. *Astron.* a cloudlike, luminous mass composed of gaseous matter or stars far beyond the solar system. **2**. *Pathol.* **a**. a faint opacity in the cornea. **b**. cloudiness in the urine. [t. L: mist, vapor, cloud] —**neb/u·lar,** *adj.*

nebular hypothesis, *Astron.* the theory that the solar system has been evolved from a mass of nebulous matter (a theory prominent in the 19th century following its precise formulation by Laplace).

neb·u·lize (nĕb/yə līz/), *v.t.,* **-lized, -lizing.** to reduce to fine spray; atomize. —**neb/u·liz/er,** *n.*

neb·u·lose (nĕb/yə lōs/), *adj.* **1**. nebulous; cloudlike. **2**. hazy or indistinct. **3**. having cloudlike markings.

neb·u·los·i·ty (nĕb/yə lŏs/ə tY), *n., pl.* **-ties.** **1**. nebulous or nebular matter. **2**. nebulous state.

neb·u·lous (nĕb/yə ləs), *adj.* **1**. hazy, vague, indistinct, or confused: *a nebulous recollection.* **2**. cloudy or cloudlike. **3**. nebular. [ME, t. L: m.s. *nebulōsus*] —**neb/u·lous·ly,** *adv.* —**neb/u·lous·ness,** *n.*

nec·es·sar·i·an (nĕs/ə sâr/Y ən), *n., adj.* necessitarian. —**nec/es·sar/i·an·ism,** *n.*

nec·es·sar·i·ly (nĕs/ə sĕr/ə lY), *adv.* **1**. by or of necessity: *you need not necessarily go to the party.* **2**. as a necessary result.

nec·es·sar·y (nĕs/ə sĕr/Y), *adj., n., pl.* **-saries.** —*adj.* **1**. that cannot be dispensed with: *a necessary law.* **2**. happening or existing by necessity. **3**. acting or proceeding from compulsion or necessity; not free; involuntary: *a necessary agent.* **4**. *Logic.* **a**. (of propositions) denoting that the denial of that proposition involves a self-contradiction (opp. to *contingent*). **b**. (of inferences or arguments) denoting that it is impossible for the premises of an inference or argument to be true and its conclusion false. **5**. *Archaic.* rendering indispensable or useful services. —*n.* **6**. something necessary, indispensable, or requisite. **7**. (*pl.*) *Law.* food, clothing, etc., required by a dependent or incompetent and varying with his social or economic position or that of the person upon whom he is dependent. **8**. a privy or water closet. [ME, t. L: m.s. *necessārius* unavoidable, indispensable] —**Syn. 1.** NECESSARY, ESSENTIAL, INDISPENSABLE, REQUISITE indicate something vital for the fulfillment of a need. NECESSARY applies to that which is inevitable to the fulfillment of a condition, or that which is the inevitable as a consequence to certain causes: *food is necessary to life, multiplicity is a necessary result of division.* INDISPENSABLE applies to that which cannot be done without or removed from the rest of a unitary condition: *food is indispensable to living things; he made himself indispensable as a companion.* That which is ESSENTIAL forms a vital necessary condition of something: *air is essential to redblooded animals, it is essential to understand the matter clearly.* REQUISITE applies to what is thought necessary to fill out, complete, or perfect something: *he had all the requisite qualifications for a position.*

ne·ces·si·tar·i·an (nə sĕs/ə târ/Y ən), *n.* **1**. one who maintains that the action of the will is a necessary effect of antecedent causes (opposed to *libertarian*). —*adj.* **2**. pertaining to necessitarians or necessitarianism.

ne·ces·si·tar·i·an·ism (nə sĕs/ə târ/Y ən Yz/əm), *n.* the doctrine of the determination of the will by antecedent causes, as opposed to that of the freedom of the will.

ne·ces·si·tate (nə sĕs/ə tāt/), *v.t.,* **-tated, -tating.** **1**. to make necessary: *the breakdown of the motor necessitated a halt.* **2**. to compel, oblige, or force: *the rise in prices necessitated greater thrift.* —**ne·ces/si·ta/tion,** *n.* —**ne·ces/si·ta/tive,** *adj.*

ne·ces·si·tous (nə sĕs/ə təs), *adj.* being in or involving necessity; needy; indigent. —**ne·ces/si·tous·ly,** *adv.* —**ne·ces/si·tous·ness,** *n.*

ne·ces·si·ty (nə sĕs/ə tY), *n., pl.* **-ties.** **1**. something necessary or indispensable: *the necessities of life.* **2**. the fact of being necessary or indispensable; indispensableness. **3**. an imperative requirement or need for something: *necessity for a decision.* **4**. state or fact of being necessary or inevitable. **5**. an unavoidable compulsion to do something. **6**. a state of being in difficulty or need; poverty. **7**. *Philos.* **a**. constraint viewed as a principle of universal causation, determining even the action of the will. **b.** the relation of the inevitable to the nature of its conditions; inevitable connection. [ME *necessite*, t. L: m.s. *necessitas* exigency] —**Syn. 3.** See **need.**

neck (nĕk), *n.* **1.** that part of an animal's body which is between the head and the trunk and connects these parts. **2.** the part of a garment covering the neck or extending about it. **3.** the length of the neck of a horse or other animal as a measure in racing. **4.** the slender part of a bottle, retort, or any similar object. **5.** any narrow, connecting or projecting part suggesting the neck of an animal. **6.** the longer slender part of a violin or the like, extending from the body to the head. **7.** *Anat.* a constricted part of a bone, organ, or the like. **8.** *Dentistry.* junction between enamel of crown and cementum of root of tooth. **9.** *Print.* a beard (def. 5). **10.** *Archit.* the lowest part of the capital of a column, above the astragal at the head of the shaft. See diag. under **column.** **11.** a narrow strip of land, as an isthmus or a cape. **12.** a strait. **13. neck and neck,** just even. **14. neck or nothing,** at every risk; desperately. **15. win by a neck,** *Racing.* to be first by a head and neck; finish closely. —*v.i.* **16.** *U.S. Slang.* to play amorously. —*v.t.* **17.** to strangle or behead. [ME *neck(e)*, OE *hnecca*, c. D *nek*; akin to G *nacken* nape of the neck]

neck·band (nĕk′bănd′), *n.* **1.** a band of cloth at the neck of a garment. **2.** band worn around the neck.

neck·cloth (nĕk′klôth′, -klŏth′), *n.* cravat.

Neck·er (nĕk′ər; *Fr.* nĕ ker′), *n.* **Jacques** (zhäk), 1732–1804, French statesman, born in Switzerland.

neck·er·chief (nĕk′ər chĭf), *n.* a cloth worn round the neck by women or men. [f. NECK + KERCHIEF]

neck·ing (nĕk′ĭng), *n.* **1.** *Archit.* **a.** a molding or group of moldings between the projecting part of a capital of a column and the shaft. **b.** a gorgerin. **2.** *Slang.* act of playing amorously.

neck·lace (nĕk′lĭs), *n.* an ornament of precious stones, beads, or the like, worn around the neck. Also, **neck·let** (nĕk′lĭt). [f. NECK + LACE string]

neck·piece (nĕk′pēs′), *n.* a scarf made of fur.

neck·tie (nĕk′tī′), *n.* **1.** a narrow band, as of silk or satin, worn around the neck, commonly under a collar, and tied in front. **2.** any band, scarf, or tie fastened at the front of the neck. **3.** *U.S. Slang.* a hangman's rope.

neck·wear (nĕk′wâr′), *n.* articles of dress worn round or at the neck.

necr-, a word element meaning "dead," "corpse," "death." Also, before consonants, **necro-.** [t. Gk.: m. *nekr-, nekro-*, comb. forms of *nekrós* body, dead]

nec·ro·ba·cil·lus (nĕk′rō ba sĭl′əs), *n.* any disease of cattle, horses, sheep and swine marked by necrotic areas in which a bacillus, *Actinomyces necrophorus*, is found.

nec·rol·a·try (nĕ krŏl′ə trĭ), *n.* worship of the dead.

ne·crol·o·gy (nĕ krŏl′ə jĭ), *n.*, *pl.* **-gies. 1.** an obituary notice. **2.** a list of persons who have died within a certain time. [t. ML: m.s. *necrologium*, f. Gk. (see NECRO-, -LOGY)] —**nec·ro·log·i·cal** (nĕk′rə lŏj′ə kəl), *adj.* —**nec′ro·log′i·cal·ly,** *adv.* —**ne·crol′o·gist,** *n.*

nec·ro·man·cy (nĕk′rə măn′sĭ), *n.* **1.** magic in general; enchantment; conjuration. **2.** the pretended art of divination through communication with the dead; the black art. [t. L: m.s. *necromantīa*, t. Gk.: m. *necromanteîa*; r. ME *nigromancie*, t. ML: m. *nigromantia*, alter. of L *necromantīa* by assoc. with L *niger* black. Cf. BLACK ART] —**nec′ro·man′cer,** *n.* —**nec′ro·man′tic,** *adj.* —**Syn. 2.** See **magic.**

nec·ro·ma·ni·a (nĕk′rə mā′nĭə), *n.* morbid attraction toward dead bodies.

ne·croph·i·lism (nĕ krŏf′ə lĭz′əm), *n.* morbid attraction to corpses. Also, **nec·ro·phil·i·a** (nĕk′rə fĭl′ĭə).

nec·ro·pho·bi·a (nĕk′rə fō′bĭə), *n.* **1.** morbid fear of death. **2.** a morbid aversion to, or fear of, dead bodies.

nec·rop·o·lis (nĕ krŏp′ə lĭs), *n.*, *pl.* **-lises. 1.** a cemetery, often of large size. **2.** an old or prehistoric burying ground, as of an ancient people. [t. NL, t. Gk.: m. *nekrópolis*, lit., city of the dead]

nec·rop·sy (nĕk′rŏp sĭ), *n.*, *pl.* **-sies.** the examination of a body after death; an autopsy. Also, **ne·cros·co·py** (nĕ krŏs′kə pĭ). [f. NECR- + s. Gk. *ópsis* sight + -Y³]

ne·crose (nĕ krōs′, nĕk′rōs), *v.t.*, *v.i.*, **-crosed, -crosing.** to affect or be affected with necrosis.

ne·cro·sis (nĕ krō′sĭs), *n.* **1.** *Pathol.* death of a circumscribed piece of tissue or of an organ. **2.** *Bot.* a diseased condition in plants resulting from the death of the tissue. [t. NL, t. Gk.: m. *nekrōsis* a killing] —**ne·crot·ic** (nĕ krŏt′ĭk), *adj.*

necrotic en·ter·i·tis (ĕn′tə rī′tĭs), a disease of swine characterized by extensive ulceration of the intestine.

ne·crot·o·my (nĕ krŏt′ə mĭ), *n.*, *pl.* **-mies. 1.** the excision of necrosed bone. **2.** dissection of dead bodies.

nec·tar (nĕk′tər), *n.* **1.** *Bot.* the saccharine secretion of a plant, which attracts the insects or birds that pollinate the flower, collected by bees, in whose body it is elaborated into honey. **2.** the drink, or, less properly, the food, of the gods of classical mythology. **3.** any delicious drink. [t. L, t. Gk.: m. *néktar*]

nec·tar·e·ous (nĕk târ′ĭəs), *adj.* **1.** of the nature of or resembling nectar. **2.** delicious; sweet. Also, **nec·tar′e·an,** [t. L: m. *nectareus*, t. Gk. m. *nektáreos*]

nec·tar·ine (nĕk′tə rēn′, nĕk′tə rēn′), *n.* a form of the common peach, having a skin destitute of down. [n. use of *nectarine*, adj., f. NECTAR + -INE¹]

nec·ta·ry (nĕk′tə rĭ), *n.*, *pl.* **-ries. 1.** *Bot.* an organ or part that secretes nectar. **2.** *Entomol.* one of a pair of small abdominal tubes from which aphids secrete honey dew. —**nec·tar·i·al** (nĕk târ′ĭəl), *adj.*

N.E.D., New English Dictionary (Oxford English Dictionary).

nee (nā), *adj.* born (placed after the name of a married woman to introduce her maiden name): *Madame de Staël, nee Necker.* Also, **née** (nā; *Fr.* nĕ). [t. F, fem. of *né*, pp. of *naître* to be born, g. L *nasci*]

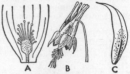

Nectaries (def. 1)
A, Grass of Parnassus, *Parnassia palustris*; B, Columbine, *Aquilegia canadensis*; C, Swamp lily, *Lilium superbum*

need (nēd), *n.* **1.** a case or instance in which some necessity or want exists; a requirement: *to meet the needs of the occasion.* **2.** urgent want, as of something requisite: *he has no need of your kindness.* **3.** necessity arising from the circumstances of a case: *there is no need to worry.* **4.** a situation or time of difficulty; exigency: *a friend in need.* **5.** a condition marked by the lack of something requisite: *the need for leadership.* **6.** destitution; extreme poverty. —*v.t.* **7.** to have need of; require: *to need money.* —*v.i.* **8.** to be necessary: *there needs no apology.* **9.** to be under a necessity (fol. by infinitive, in certain cases without *to*; in the 3d pers. sing. the form is *need*, not *needs*): *he need not go.* **10.** to be in need or want. [ME *nede*, d. OE *nēd*; r. ME *nud(e)*, OE *nȳd, nīed*; akin to G *not*] —**need′er,** *n.* —**Syn. 2.** NEED, NECESSITY imply a want, a lack, or a demand, which must be filled. NEED, a word of Old English origin, has connotations which make it strong in emotional appeal: *the need to be appreciated.* NECESSITY, a word of Latin origin, is more formal and impersonal or objective; though much stronger than NEED in expressing urgency or imperative demand, it is less effective in appealing to the emotions: *water is a necessity for living things.* **6.** See **poverty.**

need·ful (nēd′fəl), *adj.* **1.** necessary: *needful supplies of food and coal.* **2.** *Now Rare.* needy. —**need′ful·ly,** *adv.* —**need′ful·ness,** *n.*

need·i·ness (nē′dĭ nĭs), *n.* needy state; indigence.

nee·dle (nē′dəl), *n.*, *v.*, **-dled, -dling.** —*n.* **1.** a small, slender, pointed instrument, now usually of polished steel, with an eye or hole for thread, used in sewing. **2.** a slender, rodlike implement for use in knitting, or one hooked at the end for use in crocheting, etc. **3.** *Med.* a slender, pointed, steel instrument used in sewing or piercing tissues. **4.** any of various objects resembling or suggesting a needle. **5.** a small, slender, pointed instrument, usually of polished steel or some other material, used to transmit vibratory motions as from a phonograph record. **6.** magnetic needle. **7.** a pointed instrument used in engraving, etc. **8.** *Bot.* a needle-shaped leaf, as of conifer: *a pine needle.* **9.** *Zool.* a slender, sharp spicule. **10.** *Chem., Mineral.* a needlelike crystal. **11.** a sharp-pointed mass or pinnacle of rock. **12.** an obelisk, or tapering, four-sided shaft of stone. —*v.t.* **13.** to sew or pierce with or as with a needle. **14.** to prod or goad. **15.** to tease or heckle. —*v.i.* **16.** to form needles in crystallization. **17.** to work with a needle. [ME *nēdle*, d. OE *nǣdl*; r. OE *nǣdl*, c. G *nadel*] —**nee′dle-like,** *adj.*

nee·dle·fish (nē′dəl fĭsh′), *n.*, *pl.* **-fishes**, (*esp. collectively*) **-fish. 1.** any fish of the family *Belonidae*, with a long sharp beak and needlelike teeth, found in all warm seas and in some coastal fresh waters; agar. **2.** a pipefish.

nee·dle·ful (nē′dəl fŏŏl′), *n.*, *pl.* **-fuls.** a suitable length of thread for using at one time with a needle.

needle point, canvas which has been embroidered in a certain manner.

nee·dle·point (nē′dəl point′), *adj.* denoting a kind of lace (**needle-point lace**) in which a needle works out the design upon parchment or paper.

need·less (nēd′lĭs), *adj.* not needed or wanted; unnecessary: *a needless waste of food.* —**need′less·ly,** *adv.* —**need′less·ness,** *n.*

needle valve, *Mach., Eng., etc.* a valve with a needlelike part, a fine adjustment, or a small opening; esp., a valve in which the opening is controlled by a needlelike or conical point which fits into a conical seat.

nee·dle·wom·an (nē′dəl wŏŏm′ən), *n.*, *pl.* **-women**, a woman who does needlework.

nee·dle·work (nē′dəl wûrk′), *n.* the process or the product of working with a needle as in sewing or embroidery.

need·n't (nēd′ənt), contraction of *need not.*

needs (nēdz), *adv.* of necessity; necessarily (usually fol. by *must*). [ME *needes*, OE *nēdes*, orig. gen. of *nēd* NEED]

need·y (nē′dĭ), *adj.*, **needier, neediest.** in, or characterized by, need or want; very poor: *a needy family.*

neep (nēp), *n.* *Scot. and Brit. Dial.* a turnip. [ME *nepe*, d. OE *nǣp*; r. OE *nǣp*, t. L: m.s. *nāpus*]

ne'er (nâr), *adv.* *Chiefly Poetic.* contraction of *never.*

ne'er-do-well (nâr′dŏŏ wĕl′), *n.* **1.** a worthless person. —*adj.* **2.** worthless; good-for-nothing.

ne·far·i·ous (nĭ fâr′ĭəs), *adj.* extremely wicked; iniquitous: *nefarious practices.* [t. L: m.s. *nefārius* impious] —**ne·far′i·ous·ly,** *adv.* —**ne·far′i·ous·ness,** *n.*

neg., 1. negative. **2.** negatively.

ne·gate (nǐ gāt′, nē′gāt), *v.t.*, **-gated, -gating.** to deny; negative; nullify. [t. L: m.s. *negātus*, pp.]

ne·ga·tion (nǐ gā′shən), *n.* **1.** the act of denying. **2.** a denial. **3.** a negative thing; a nonentity. **4.** the absence or opposite of what is actual, positive, or affirmative. **5.** a thing, or object of thought, consisting in the absence of something positive.

neg·a·tive (nĕg′ə tǐv), *adj., n., v.,* **-tived, -tiving.** —*adj.* **1.** expressing or containing negation or denial: *a negative statement.* **2.** expressing refusal to do something. **3.** refusing consent, as to a proposal. **4.** prohibitory, as a command or order. **5.** characterized by the absence of distinguishing or marked qualities or features; lacking positive attributes: *a negative character.* **6.** *Math., Physics.* **a.** involving or denoting subtraction; minus. **b.** measured or proceeding in the opposite direction to that which is considered as positive. **7.** *Bacteriol.* failing to show a positive result in a test for a specific disease caused by either bacteria or viruses. **8.** *Photog.* denoting an image in which the gradations of light and shade are represented in reverse. **9.** *Physiol.* responding in a direction away from the stimulus. **10.** *Elect.* noting or pertaining to the kind of electricity developed on resin, amber, etc., when rubbed with flannel, or that present at the pole from which electrons leave an electric generator or battery, having an excess of electrons. **11.** *Chem.* (of an element or radical) tending to gain electrons and become negatively charged. **12.** *Logic.* (of a proposition) asserting a relation of exclusion between its subject and predicate. —*n.* **13.** a negative statement, answer, or word, etc. **14.** a refusal of assent. **15.** a veto. **16.** that side of a question which denies what the opposite side affirms. **17.** the negative form of statement (opposed to *affirmative*). **18.** a negative quality or characteristic. **19.** *Math.* a negative quantity or symbol. **20.** *Photog.* a negative image as on a film or plate, used chiefly for printing positive pictures. **21.** *Elect.* the negative plate or element in a voltaic cell. —*v.t.* **22.** to deny; contradict. **23.** to disprove. **24.** to refuse assent or consent to; pronounce against; to veto. **25.** to neutralize or counteract. [ME, t. L: m.s. *negātivus* that denies] —**neg′a·tive·ly,** *adv.* —**neg′a·tive·ness, neg′a·tiv′i·ty,** *n.*

neg·a·tiv·ism (nĕg′ə tǐ vǐz′əm), *n.* **1.** negativistic behavior. **2.** any system of negative philosophy, such as agnosticism, skepticism, etc. —**neg′a·tiv·ist,** *n.*

neg·a·tiv·is·tic (nĕg′ə tǐ vǐs′tǐk), *adj. Psychol.* marked by resistance to a stimulus; tending to react in the opposite way to any suggestion.

neg·a·to·ry (nĕg′ə tôr′ǐ), *adj.* denying; negative.

neg·a·tron (nĕg′ə trŏn′), *n. Physics, Chem. Rare.* an electron.

neg·lect (nǐ glĕkt′), *v.t.* **1.** to pay no attention to; disregard: *a neglected genius.* **2.** to be remiss in care for or treatment of: *to neglect one's family.* **3.** to omit (doing something), through indifference or carelessness. **4.** to fail to carry out or perform (orders, duties, etc.). **5.** to fail to take or use: *to neglect no precaution.* —*n.* **6.** the act or fact of neglecting; disregard. **7.** the fact or state of being neglected; negligence. [t. L: s. *neglectus,* pp., unheeded] —**neg·lect′er, neg·lec′tor,** *n.* —**Syn. 2.** See **slight. 6, 7.** NEGLECT, DERELICTION, NEGLIGENCE, REMISSNESS imply carelessness, failure, or some important omission in the performance of one's duty, a task, etc. NEGLECT and NEGLIGENCE are occasionally interchangeable, but NEGLECT commonly refers to the act, NEGLIGENCE to the habit or trait, of failing to attend to or perform what is expected or required: *gross neglect of duty, negligence in handling traffic problems.* DERELICTION implies culpable or reprehensible neglect or failure in the performance of duty: *dereliction in a position of responsibility.* REMISSNESS implies the omission or the careless or indifferent performance of a duty: *remissness was the cause for tardiness in reporting.* —**Ant. 6.** attention, care.

neg·lect·ful (nǐ glĕkt′fəl), *adj.* characterized by neglect; disregardful; careless; negligent (often fol. by *of*). —**neg·lect′ful·ly,** *adv.* —**neg·lect′ful·ness,** *n.*

neg·li·gee (nĕg′lə zhā′, nĕg′lə zhā′), *n.* **1.** a woman's dressing gown or robe. **2.** easy, informal attire. Also, French, **né·gli·gé** (nĕ glē zhā′). [t. F: m. *négligé,* orig. pp. of *négliger* neglect, t. L: m. *negligere*]

neg·li·gence (nĕg′lə jəns), *n.* **1.** state or fact of being negligent; neglect. **2.** an instance of being negligent; a defect due to carelessness. **3.** *Law.* the failure to exercise that degree of care which, under the circumstances, the law requires for the protection of those interests of other persons which may be injuriously affected by the want of such care. —**Syn. 1.** See **neglect.**

neg·li·gent (nĕg′lə jənt), *adj.* guilty of or characterized by neglect, as of duty: *negligent officials.* [ME, t. L: s. *negligens,* ppr., neglecting] —**neg′li·gent·ly,** *adv.*

neg·li·gi·ble (nĕg′lə jə bəl), *adj.* that may be neglected or disregarded. —**neg′li·gi·bil′i·ty, neg′li·gi·ble·ness,** *n.* —**neg′li·gi·bly,** *adv.*

ne·go·ti·a·ble (nǐ gō′shǐ ə bəl, -shə bəl), *adj.* **1.** capable of being negotiated. **2.** (of bills, etc.) transferable by delivery, with or without endorsement, according to the circumstances, the title passing to the transferee. —**ne·go′ti·a·bil′i·ty,** *n.*

ne·go·ti·ant (nǐ gō′shǐ ənt), *n.* one who negotiates.

ne·go·ti·ate (nǐ gō′shǐ āt′), *v.,* **-ated, -ating.** —*v.i.* **1.** to treat with another or others, as in the preparation of a treaty, or in preliminaries to a business deal. —*v.t.* **2.** to arrange for or bring about by discussion and settlement of terms: *to negotiate a loan.* **3.** to conduct (an affair, etc.). **4.** *Colloq.* to clear or pass (an obstacle, etc.). **5.** to circulate by endorsement: *to negotiate a bill of exchange.* **6.** to dispose of by sale or transfer: *to negotiate securities.* **7.** to transfer (a bill, etc.) by assignment or delivery. [t. L: m.s. *negōtiātus,* pp.] —**ne·go′ti·a′tor,** *n.*

ne·go·ti·a·tion (nǐ gō′shǐ ā′shən), *n.* mutual discussion and arrangement of the terms of a transaction or agreement: *the negotiation of a treaty.*

Ne·gri bodies (nā′grǐ), certain microscopic bodies found in the brain cells of animals affected with rabies.

Ne·gril·lo (nǐ grǐl′ō), *n., pl.* **-los.** a Negrito, esp. of the African division; a pygmy. [t. Sp., dim. of *negro* NEGRO]

Ne·gri Sem·bi·lan (nā′grē sĕm′ bē län′), a native state in the Federation of Malaya: formerly one of the Federated Malay States. 276,620 pop. (est. 1937); 2580 sq. mi. *Cap.:* Seremban.

Ne·grit·ic (nǐ grǐt′ǐk), *adj.* of or pertaining to Negroes or the Negritos.

Ne·gri·to (nǐ grē′tō), *n., pl.* **-tos, -toes.** a member of any of certain dwarfish Negroid peoples of southeastern Asia and of Africa, esp. of Malaya and the Andaman and Philippine Islands. [t. Sp., dim. of *negro* NEGRO]

Ne·gro (nē′grō), *n., pl.* **-groes,** *adj.* —*n.* **1.** a member of the Negro race. **2.** a person having more or less Negro blood. **3.** a member of any dark-skinned people. —*adj.* **4.** of, denoting or pertaining to the so-called "black" race of Africa and its descendants elsewhere, characterized by a brown-black complexion, broad and flat nose, projecting jaws, everted lips, and crisp or woolly hair. [t. Sp. and Pg.: a black person, Negro, g. L *niger* black] —**Ne·gress** (nē′grǐs), *n. fem.* (often used derogatorily).

Ne·gro (nā′grō; *Sp.* nĕ′grô), *n.* **Rí·o** (rē′ô). **1.** a river flowing from W Colombia through N Brazil into the Amazon. ab. 1400 mi. **2.** a river in S Argentina, flowing from the Andes E to the Atlantic. ab. 700 mi.

Ne·groid (nē′groid), *adj.* **1.** resembling, or akin to, the Negro race and presumably allied to it in origin, as shown by "black" skin and woolly hair. Included are African Negroes, Oceanic Negroes (Papuans and Melanesians), and Negritos, but excluded are Australian blackfellows on account of their non-woolly hair. —*n.* **2.** a person of a Negroid race.

ne·gro·phile (nē′grə fil′, -fǐl), *n.* one regarded as too friendly to Negroes. Also, **ne·gro·phil** (nē′grə fǐl).

ne·gro·phobe (nē′grə fōb′), *n.* one who fears, or has strong antipathy to, Negroes.

ne·gro·pho·bi·a (nē′grə fō′bǐ ə), *n.* fear of, or strong antipathy to, Negroes.

Neg·ro·pont (nĕg′rō pŏnt′), *n.* Euboea.

Ne·gros (nā′grōs; *Sp.* nĕ′grôs), *n.* one of the Philippine Islands, in the central part of the group. 1,218,710 pop. (1939); 5043 sq. mi.

ne·gus[1] (nē′gəs), *n.* **1.** a royal title in Ethiopia. **2.** (*cap.*) the emperor of Ethiopia. [t. Amharic: king]

ne·gus[2] (nē′gəs), *n. Chiefly Brit.* a beverage made of wine and hot water, with sugar, nutmeg, and lemon. [named after Colonel Francis *Negus* (d. 1732), its reputed inventor]

Neh., Nehemiah.

Ne·he·mi·ah (nē′ə mī′ə), *n.* **1.** a Hebrew leader of the 5th century B.C., returned to Jerusalem to rebuild its walls. **2.** a book of the Old Testament. [t. Heb.]

Neh·ru (nĕ′rōō), *n.* **Jawaharlal** (jə wə hər läl′), born 1889, Hindu political leader in India: prime minister of the republic of India since 1950.

neigh (nā), *v.i.* **1.** to utter the cry of a horse; whinny. —*n.* **2.** the cry of a horse; a whinny. [ME *neyghe,* OE *hnǣgan,* c. MHG *nēgen.* See NAG[2], n.]

neigh·bor (nā′bər), *n.* **1.** one who lives near another. **2.** a person or thing that is near another. **3.** a fellow being subject to the obligations of humanity. —*adj.* **4.** living or situated near to another. —*v.t.* **5.** to place or bring near. **6.** to live or be situated near to; adjoin; border on. —*v.i.* **7.** to associate on the terms of neighbors; be neighborly or friendly (fol. by *with*). **8.** to live or be situated near. Also, *Brit.,* **neigh′bour.** [ME *neighebour,* OE *nēahgebūr,* f. *nēah* nigh + *gebūr* dweller, countryman, c. G *nachbar*]

neigh·bor·hood (nā′bər hŏŏd′), *n.* **1.** the region near or about some place or thing; the vicinity. **2.** a district or locality, often with reference to its character or inhabitants: *a fashionable neighborhood.* **3.** a number of persons living near one another or in a particular locality: *the whole neighborhood was there.* **4.** *Now Rare.* neighborly feeling or conduct. **5.** nearness; proximity. **6. in the neighborhood of,** nearly; about.

neigh·bor·ing (nā′bər ǐng), *adj.* living or situated near; adjacent.

neigh·bor·ly (nā′bər lǐ), *adj.* befitting, or acting as befits, a neighbor; friendly. —**neigh′bor·li·ness,** *n.*

Neil·son (nēl′sən), *n.* **William Allan,** 1869–1946, U.S. educator and lexicographer, born in Scotland.

Neis·se (nīs′ə), *n.* a river flowing from NW Czechoslovakia N along part of the boundary between Germany and Poland to the Oder river. ab. 145 mi.

nei·ther (nē′t͟hər *or, esp. Brit.,* nī′t͟hər), *conj.* **1.** not either (a disjunctive connective preceding a series of two or more alternative words, etc., connected by the correlative *nor*); *neither you nor I nor anybody else knows the answer.* **2.** nor yet: *Ye shall not eat of it, neither shall ye touch it.* —*adj.* **3.** not either; not the one or the other: *neither statement is true.* [ME *neither* (f. *ne* not + EITHER); r. ME *nauther*, OE *nāwther*, contr. var. of *nāhwæther*, f. *nā* not + *hwæther* either, WHETHER]

Nejd (nĕzhd, nād), *n.* a former sultanate in central Arabia, forming (with dependencies) with Hejaz the kingdom of Saudi Arabia: inhabited by Wahabis. ab. 3,000,000 pop.; ab. 414,000 sq. mi. *Cap.*: Riyadh.

nek·ton (nĕk'tŏn), *n.* the aggregate of actively swimming organisms at the surface of the sea. [t. G, t. Gk.: (neut.) swimming] —**nek·ton'ic**, *adj.*

Nel·son (nĕl'sən), *n.* **1.** Viscount Horatio, 1758–1805, British admiral: famous victories over Napoleon I, esp. Trafalgar (1805). **2.** a river in central Canada, from Lake Winnipeg NE to Hudson Bay. ab. 390 mi.

ne·lum·bo (nĭ'lŭm'bō), *n., pl.* **-bos.** lotus (def. 3). [t. NL, t. Singhalese: m. *nelumbu*]

nemat-, a word element referring to threadlike things, especially to *nematodes*. Also, before consonants, **nemato-**. [t. Gk., comb. form of *nēma* thread]

nem·a·thel·minth (nĕm'ə thĕl'mĭnth), *n.* any of the *Nemathelminthes*, a phylum of worms (now usually broken up into several phyla), including the nematodes, etc., characterized by an elongated, unsegmented cylindrical body. Also, **nem·a·tel·minth** (nĕm'ə tĕl'mĭnth). [f. Gk.: s. *hĕlmins* worm]

nem·a·to·cyst (nĕm'ə tə sĭst'), *n. Zool.* an organ of offense and defense peculiar to coelenterates, consisting of a minute capsule containing a thread capable of being ejected and of causing a sting.

Nem·a·to·da (nĕm'ə tō'də), *n.pl.* the roundworms, a group variously considered a phylum or class. They are elongated smooth worms of cylindroid shape, parasitic or free-living, as ascarids, trichina, vinegar eel, etc.

nem·a·tode (nĕm'ə tōd'), *n.* any of the *Nematoda.*

Ne·me·a (nē'mĭ ə), *n.* a valley in SE Greece, in ancient Argolis. —**Ne·me·an** (nĭ mē'ən, nē'mĭ-), *adj.*

Nemean games, one of the four national festivals of the ancient Greeks. It was celebrated at Nemea in the 2d and 4th year of each Olympiad.

Nemean lion, *Gk. Legend.* a lion said to have been killed by Hercules.

ne·mer·te·an (nĭ mûr'tĭ ən), *n.* **1.** any of the *Nemertinea.* —*adj.* **2.** belonging or pertaining to the nemerteans. Also, **ne·mer·tine** (nĭ mûr'tĭn). [f. s. NL *Nemertea*, pl. (der. Gk. *Nēmertēs* name of a Nereid) + -AN]

Nem·er·tin·e·a (nĕm'ər tĭn'ĭ ə), *n.pl.* a group of unsegmented marine worms considered either a class of *Platyhelminthes* or an independent phylum, characterized by the long proboscis that can be shot out from the anterior end.

Nem·e·sis (nĕm'ə sĭs), *n., pl.* **-ses** (-sēz'). **1.** the goddess of retribution or vengeance. **2.** (*l.c.*) an agent of retribution or punishment. [t. L, t. Gk.]

ne·mi·ne con·tra·di·cen·te (nĕm'ə nē' kŏn'trə dĭ sĕn'tĭ), *Latin.* no one contradicting; unanimously.

ne·mi·ne dis·sen·ti·en·te (nĕm'ə nē' dĭ sĕn'shĭ ĕn'tĭ), *Latin.* no one dissenting; unanimously.

Ne·mu·nas (nyĕ'mŏŏ näs'), *n.* Lithuanian name of Niemen.

N. Eng., Northern England.

neo-, a word element meaning "new", "recent," used in combination, as in *Neo-Darwinism* (a new or modified form of Darwinism), *neo-Gothic* (Gothic after a new or modern style), *neo-Hebraic* (pertaining to Hebrew of the modern period), *neo-Hellenic*, *neo-Latin*, *neo-Persian*. [t. Gk., comb. form of *néos*]

ne·o·ars·phen·a·mine (nē'ō ärs'fĕn ə mēn', -fĭ năm'ĭn), *n., Pharm.* a yellow-orange medicinal powder, $H_2NC_6H_3(OH)As:C_6H_3(OH)NHCH_2OSONa$, prepared from, but less toxic than, salvarsan.

Ne·o-Cath·o·lic (nē'ō kăth'ə lĭk), *adj.* **1.** of or pertaining to those Anglicans who avowedly prefer the doctrines, rituals, etc., of the Roman Catholic Church to those of the Anglican communion. **2.** (in France) of or pertaining to a person who has left the Roman Catholic Church because of his belief in modernism (def. 3a). —*n.* **3.** a Neo-Catholic person. —**Ne·o-Ca·thol·i·cism** (nē'ō kə thŏl'ə sĭz'əm), *n.*

Ne·o·cene (nē'ə sēn'), *Stratig.* —*adj.* **1.** pertaining to a division of the Tertiary period or system that comprises Miocene and the Pliocene. —*n.* **2.** time or rocks comprising the later half of the Tertiary period or system.

ne·o·clas·sic (nē'ō klăs'ĭk), *adj.* belonging or pertaining to a revival of classic style, as in art or literature. Also, **ne·o·clas·si·cal**.

Ne·o-Dar·win·ism (nē'ō där'wĭ nĭz'əm), *n. Biol.* the theory of evolution as expounded by later students of Darwin, esp. Weismann, who hold that natural selection accounts for evolution, and deny the inheritance of acquired characteristics.

ne·o·dym·i·um (nē'ō dĭm'ĭ əm), *n. Chem.* a rare-earth, metallic, trivalent element occurring with cerium and other rare-earth metals, and having rose- to violet-colored salts. *Symbol:* Nd; *at. wt.*: 144.27; *at. no.*: 60; *sp. gr.*: 6.9 at 20° C. [t. NL; see NEO-, (DI)DYMIUM]

ne·o·im·pres·sion·ism (nē'ō ĭm prĕsh'ə nĭz'əm), *n.* the theory and methods of certain of the later impressionist painters (from about 1886), characterized by an attempt to make the impressionist methods strictly scientific by employment of the pointillist technique in

juxtaposing methodically small dots or squares of pure colors. —**ne·o·im·pres·sion·ist**, *n., adj.*

Ne·o-La·marck·ism (nē'ō lə märk'ĭz əm), *n. Biol.* Lamarckism as expounded by later biologists who hold especially that some acquired characters of organisms may be transmitted to descendants, but that natural selection also is a factor in evolution. —**Ne·o-La·marck·i·an** (nē'ō lə mär'kĭ ən), *adj., n.*

Ne·o-Lat·in (nē'ō lăt'ən), *n.* the Latin which became current (notably in scientific literature) after the Renaissance (approximately 1500). Also, New Latin.

ne·o·lith (nē'ə lĭth), *n.* a neolithic stone implement.

ne·o·lith·ic (nē'ə lĭth'ĭk), *adj. Anthropol.* noting or pertaining to the later part of the Old World stone age, characterized by the use of highly finished or polished stone implements and by food raising.

ne·ol·o·gism (nĭ ŏl'ə jĭz'əm), *n.* **1.** a new word or phrase. **2.** the introduction or use of new words, or new senses of words. **3.** a new doctrine. [t. F: m. *néologisme*, der. *néologie*. See NEO-, -LOGY] —**ne·ol'o·gist**, *n.* —**ne·ol·o·gis'tic, ne·ol·o·gis'ti·cal**, *adj.*

ne·ol·o·gy (nĭ ŏl'ə jĭ), *n., pl.* **-gies**. neologism. —**ne·o·log·i·cal** (nē'ə lŏj'ə kəl), *adj.*

ne·o·my·cin (nē'ō mī'sĭn), *n.* a recently developed antibiotic similar to streptomycin but more effective in combating certain microbic infections.

ne·on (nē'ŏn), *n. Chem.* a chemically inert gaseous element occurring in small amounts in the earth's atmosphere, and chiefly used in orange-red tubular electrical discharge lamps. *Symbol:* Ne; *at. wt.*: 20.183; *at. no.*: 10; *weight of one liter of the gas at 0°C. and at 760 mm. pressure:* 0.9002 g. [t. NL, t. Gk.: (neut.) new]

ne·o·or·tho·dox·y (nē'ō ôr'thə dŏk'sĭ), *n.* a recent movement in Protestant thought which revives and develops some of the leading doctrines of early theology, such as revelation, the fall, justification by faith.

ne·o·phyte (nē'ə fīt'), *n.* **1.** a converted heathen, heretic, etc. **2.** *Primitive Church.* one newly baptized. **3.** *Rom. Cath. Ch.* a novice. **4.** a beginner. [t. LL: m.s. *neophytus*, t. Gk.: m. *neóphytos* newly planted]

ne·o·plasm (nē'ə plăz'əm), *n. Pathol.* a new growth of different or abnormal tissue; a tumor. —**ne·o·plas·tic** (nē'ə plăs'tĭk), *adj.*

ne·o·plas·ty (nē'ə plăs'tĭ), *n.* the repairing or restoration of a part by plastic surgery.

Ne·o·pla·to·nism (nē'ō plā'tə nĭz'əm), *n.* a philosophical system founded chiefly on Platonic doctrine and Oriental mysticism, later influenced by Christianity. It originated in the 3rd century A.D. Also, **Ne'o-Pla'to·nism.** —**Ne·o·pla·ton·ic** (nē'ō plə tŏn'ĭk), *adj.* —**Ne'o·pla'to·nist**, *n.*

ne·o·prene (nē'ə prēn'), *n.* an oil-resistant synthetic rubber made by polymerizing chloroprene.

ne·o·sal·var·san (nē'ō săl'vər săn'), *n.* **1.** neoarsphenamine. **2.** (*cap.*) a trademark for it.

Ne·o-Scho·las·ti·cism (nē'ō skə lăs'tə sĭz'əm), *n.* a contemporary application of scholasticism to modern problems and life. —**Ne'o-Scho·las'tic**, *adj.*

ne·o·style (nē'ə stīl'), *n., v.*, **-styled, -styling.** —*n.* **1.** a type of cyclostyle. —*v.t.* **2.** to reproduce with a neostyle.

ne·ot·e·ny (nē ŏt'ə nĭ), *n. Zool.* the capacity or phenomenon of becoming sexually mature in the larval state. Cf. axolotl. [t. NL: m.s. *neotēnia*, f. Gk.: neo- NEO- + m.s. *teínein* extend + *-ia* -IA] —**ne·ot'e·nous**, *adj.*

ne·o·ter·ic (nē'ə tĕr'ĭk), *adj.* **1.** modern. —*n.* **2.** a modern writer, thinker, etc. [t. LL: s. *neōtericus*, t. Gk.: m. *neōterikós* youthful] —**ne·o·ter'i·cal·ly**, *adv.*

Ne·o·trop·i·cal (nē'ō trŏp'ə kəl), *adj. Zoogeog.* belonging to that part of the New World extending from the tropic of Cancer southward.

ne·o·yt·ter·bi·um (nē'ō ĭt'tûr'bĭ əm), *n.* ytterbium.

Ne·o·zo·ic (nē'ə zō'ĭk), *adj., n. Obs.* Cenozoic. [f. NEO- + s. Gk. *zōé* life + -IC]

NEP (nĕp), *n.* New Economic Policy. Also, **Nep, N.E.P.**

Ne·pal (nə pôl'), *n.* a kingdom in the Himalayas between N India and Tibet. ab. 5,600,000 pop.; ab. 54,000 sq. mi. *Cap.*: Katmandu.

ne·pen·the (nĭ pĕn'thĭ), *n.* **1.** a drug or draft (or the plant yielding it) mentioned by ancient writers as capable of bringing forgetfulness of sorrow or trouble. **2.** anything inducing easeful forgetfulness. Also, **ne·pen·thes** (nĭ pĕn'thēz). [t. L: m.s. *nēpenthes*, t. Gk.: (neut.) banishing sorrow] —**ne·pen'the·an**, *adj.*

neph·e·line (nĕf'ə lĭn), *n.* a mineral, essentially sodium aluminum silicate, $NaAlSiO_4$, occurring in alkali-rich volcanic rocks. Also, **neph·e·lite** (nĕf'ə līt'). [t. F, f. s. Gk. *nephélē* cloud + *-ine* -INE²]

neph·e·lin·ite (nĕf'ə lĭ nīt'), *n. Petrog.* a fine-grained, dark rock of volcanic origin, essentially a basalt containing nepheline but no feldspar and little or no olivine.

neph·e·lom·e·ter (nĕf'ə lŏm'ə tər), *n.* **1.** *Bacteriol.* an apparatus containing a series of barium chloride standards used to determine the number of bacteria in a suspension. **2.** *Chem., etc.* a device for studying the nature of suspensions using diffuse reflected light. [f. s. Gk. *nephélē* cloud + -(o)METER]

neph·ew (nĕf'ū *or, esp. Brit.*, nĕv'ū), *n.* **1.** a son of one's brother or sister. **2.** a son of one's husband's or wife's brother or sister. **3.** (in euphemistic use) an illegitimate son of an ecclesiastic. **4.** *Obs.* a grandson. **5.** *Obs.* a male descendant of more remote degree. [ME *nevew*, t. OF: m. *neveu*, g. s. L *nepos* grandson, nephew]

nepho-, a word element meaning "cloud." [t. Gk., comb. form of *nephos* cloud]

neph·o·gram (něf'ə grăm'), *n.* a photograph of a cloud or clouds.

neph·o·graph (něf'ə grăf', -gräf'), *n.* an instrument for photographing clouds.

ne·phol·o·gy (nǐ fŏl'ə jǐ), *n.* the branch of meteorology that treats of clouds. —**neph·o·log·i·cal** (něf'ə lŏj'ə kəl), *adj.*

neph·o·scope (něf'ə skōp'), *n.* an instrument for determining the altitude of clouds and the velocity and direction of their motion.

nephr-, var. of **nephro-**, before vowels.

ne·phral·gi·a (nǐ frăl'jǐ ə), *n. Pathol.* pain in the kidney or kidneys.

ne·phrec·to·my (nǐ frěk'tə mǐ), *n., pl.* -**mies.** *Surg.* excision or removal of a kidney.

neph·ric (něf'rǐk), *adj.* renal.

ne·phrid·i·um (nǐ frǐd'ǐ əm), *n., pl.* -**phridia** (-frǐd'ǐ ə). *Zool.* the excretory organ of invertebrates consisting of a tubule with an open or closed motile apparatus at its inner end. [t. NL, f. *nephr-* NEPHR- + -*idium* (dim. suffix)] —**ne·phrid'i·al,** *adj.*

neph·rism (něf'rǐzəm), *n. Pathol.* the unhealthy state produced by a chronic kidney disease.

neph·rite (něf'rīt), *n.* a mineral, a compact or fibrous variety of actinolite, varying from whitish to dark green. See **jade**[1] (def. 1). [t. G: m. *nephrit*, f. *nephr-* NEPHR- + -*it* -ITE[1]]

ne·phrit·ic (nǐ frǐt'ǐk), *adj.* of, pertaining to, or affected with nephritis. [t. LL: s. *nephriticus*, t. Gk.: m. *nephrītikós* affected with nephritis]

ne·phri·tis (nǐ frī'tǐs), *n. Pathol.* inflammation of the kidneys, esp. Bright's disease. [t. LL, t. Gk.]

nephro-, a word element referring to the kidneys. Also, **nephr-**. [t. Gk., comb. form of *nephrós* kidney]

neph·ro·lith (něf'rə lǐth), *n. Pathol.* a renal calculus.

ne·phrot·o·my (nǐ frŏt'ə mǐ), *n., pl.* -**mies.** *Surg.* incision into the kidney, as for the removal of a calculus.

ne plus ul·tra (nē' plŭs ŭl'trə), *Latin.* 1. no more beyond; no further (used in prohibiting). 2. the acme.

nep·man (něp'mən), *n., pl.* -**men.** (in the Soviet Union) one who, under the NEP, engaged in a private business.

Ne·pos (nē'pŏs, něp'ŏs), *n.* **Cornelius,** c99–c24 B.C., Roman biographer and historian.

nep·o·tism (něp'ə tǐz'əm), *n.* patronage bestowed in consideration of family relationship and not of merit. [t. F: m. *népotisme*, t. It.; m. *nepotismo*, ult. der. L *nepos* descendant. See -ISM] —**ne·pot·ic** (nǐ pŏt'ǐk), *adj.* —**nep'o·tist,** *n.*

Nep·tune (něp'tūn, -tōon), *n.* 1. *Rom. Myth.* the Roman god of the sea. Cf. **Poseidon.** 2. the sea or ocean. 3. *Astron.* the eighth planet in order from the sun. Its period of revolution is 164.8 years, its mean distance from the sun 2,793,500,000 miles and its diameter is 32,930 miles. It has one satellite. Symbol: ♆.

Nep·tu·ni·an (něp tū'nǐ ən, -tōo'-), *adj.* 1. pertaining to Neptune or the sea. 2. pertaining to the planet Neptune. 3. (*often l.c.*) *Geol.* formed by the action of water.

nep·tu·ni·um (něp tū'nǐ əm, -tōo'-), *n. Chem.* a radioactive transuranic element, not found in nature, produced artificially by the neutron bombardment of U-238. It decays rapidly to plutonium and then to U-235. *Symbol:* Np; *at. no.:* 93; *at. wt.:* 239.

Ner·bud·da (nər bŭd'ə), *n.* Narbada.

Ne·re·id (nǐr'ǐ ĭd), *n. Gk. Myth.* any one of the fifty daughters of the ancient sea god Nereus; a sea nymph. Also, **ne're·id.** [t. L: s. *Nēreis*, t. Gk.]

Ne·re·is (nǐr'ǐ ĭs), *n., pl.* **Nereides** (nǐ rē'ə dēz'). *Gk. Myth.* Nereid.

Ne·reus (nǐr'ōos), *n.* See **Nereid.**

Ne·ri (nâr'ǐ; *It.* nĕ'rē), *n.* **Saint Philip,** (*Filippo Neri*) 1515–95, Italian priest: founder of Congregation of the Oratory.

Ne·ro (nǐr'ō), *n.* (*Nero Claudius Caesar Drusus Germanicus, Lucius Domitius Ahenobarbus*) A.D. 37–68, Roman emperor, A.D. 54–68, notorious for his cruelty and corruption. —**Ne·ro·ni·an** (nǐ rō'nǐ ən), *adj.*

ne·rol (nǐr'ŏl), *n.* a colorless alcohol, $C_{10}H_{18}O$, contained in neroli oil.

ner·o·li oil (něr'ə lǐ, nǐr'-), an essential oil, brown in color, derived from orange blossoms, *Citrus bigardia*, consisting of citral, limonene, linalool, etc.; used in the perfume industry. [t. F, t. It.; named after an Italian Princess *Neroli*]

Ner·va (nûr'və), *n.* **Marcus Cocceius** (mär'kəs kŏk sē'yəs), A.D. 32?–98, Roman emperor, A.D. 96–98.

nerv·ate (nûr'vāt), *adj. Bot.* (of leaves) having nerves or veins; nerved.

ner·va·tion (nûr vā'shən), *n.* venation.

nerve (nûrv), *n., v.,* **nerved, nerving.** —*n.* 1. one or more bundles of fibers, forming part of a system which conveys impulses of sensation, motion, etc., between the brain or spinal cord and other parts of the body. 2. *Dentistry.* a. the nerve tissue in the pulp of a tooth. b. (popularly but incorrectly) pulp tissue of a tooth. 3. a sinew or tendon: *to strain every nerve.* 4. strength, vigor, or energy. 5. firmness or courage under trying circumstances: *a position requiring nerve.* 6. (*pl.*) nervousness: *a fit of nerves.* 7. get on one's nerves, to irritate.

8. *Slang.* impertinent assurance. 9. *Bot.* a vein, as in a leaf. 10. a line or one of a system of lines traversing something. —*v.t.* 11. to give strength, vigor, or courage to. [ME, t. L: m.s. *nervus*, akin to Gk. *neûron* sinew, tendon, nerve]

nerve cell, *Anat., Physiol.* 1. any of the cells constituting the cellular element of nervous tissue. 2. one of the essential cells of a nerve center.

nerve center, *Anat., Physiol.* a group of nerve cells closely connected with one another and acting together in the performance of some function.

nerve fiber, *Anat., Physiol.* a process, axone, or dendrite, of a nerve cell.

nerve impulse, *Physiol.* a wave of electrical and chemical activity progressing along nerve fibers and acting as a stimulus to muscle, gland or other nerve cells.

nerve·less (nûrv'lǐs), *adj.* 1. *Anat., Bot., etc.* without nerves. 2. lacking strength or vigor; feeble; weak. 3. lacking firmness or courage; spiritless; pusillanimous. —**nerve'less·ly,** *adv.* —**nerve'less·ness,** *n.*

ner·vine (nûr'vēn, -vīn), *adj.* 1. of or pertaining to the nerves. 2. acting on, or relieving disorders of, the nerves; strengthening or soothing the nerves. —*n.* 3. a nervine medicine.

nerv·ing (nûr'vǐng), *n. Vet. Sci.* the excision of part of a nerve trunk.

nerv·ous (nûr'vəs), *adj.* 1. of or pertaining to the nerves. 2. having or containing nerves of sensation, etc. 3. affecting the nerves, as diseases. 4. suffering from, characterized by, or proceeding from disordered nerves. 5. highly excitable; unnaturally or acutely uneasy or apprehensive. 6. characterized by or attended with acute uneasiness or apprehension. 7. sinewy or strong. [ME, t. L: m.s. *nervōsus* sinewy] —**nerv'ous·ly,** *adv.* —**nerv'ous·ness,** *n.*

nervous system, *Anat., Zool.* 1. the system of nerves and nerve centers in an animal. 2. a particular part of this system: a. the **central** or **cerebrospinal nervous system,** the brain and spinal cord. b. the **peripheral nervous system,** the system of nerves and ganglia derived from the central system, comprising the cranial nerves, the spinal nerves, the various sense organs, etc. c. the **autonomic nervous system,** the system of nerves and ganglia which supply the walls of the vascular system and the various viscera and glands.

ner·vure (nûr'vyōor), *n. Bot., Zool.* a vein, as of an insect's wing. [t. F, der. L *nervus* NERVE]

nerv·y (nûr'vǐ), *adj.,* **nervier, nerviest.** 1. *U.S. Slang.* audacious; bold. 2. requiring nerve. 3. having or showing courage. 4. strong or vigorous. 5. *Brit. Colloq.* nervous.

Nervures of wings in insects
A. Cockchafer, *Melolontha vulgaris*; B. Earwig, *Forficula auricularis*; C. Dragonfly, *Aeschna maculatissima*; D. Butterfly, *Parnassius apollo*; E. Fly, *Bibio marci*

n.e.s., not elsewhere specified.

nes·cience (něsh'əns, něsh'ǐ əns), *n.* 1. lack of knowledge; ignorance. 2. agnosticism. [t. LL: m.s. *nescientia*, der. L *nesciens*, ppr., being ignorant] —**nes'cient,** *adj.*

ness (něs), *n. Archaic., Dial., or in Place Names.* a headland; a promontory; a cape. [ME *nesse*, OE *ness*, c. MLG *ness*; akin to NOSE]

-ness, a suffix used to form, from adjectives and participles, nouns denoting quality or state (also often, by extension, something exemplifying a quality or state) as in *darkness, goodness, kindness, obligingness, preparedness.* [ME -*nes*(*se*), OE -*nes*(*s*), c. G -*niss*]

Nes·sel·rode (něs'əl rōd'), *n.* a mixture of preserved fruits, nuts, etc., used in pudding, pie, ice cream, or the like.

Nes·sel·rode (něs'əl rōd'; *Russ.* něs'sěl rō'dě), *n.* **Count Karl Robert** (kärl rŏ bĕrt' *or* rō'bĕrt), 1780–1862, Russian diplomat and statesman.

Nes·sus (něs'əs), *n. Gk. Legend.* a centaur shot by Hercules with a poisoned arrow. Hercules was himself fatally poisoned by a garment stained with the blood of Nessus, sent to him by Deianira, who thought that it would preserve his love for her.

nest (něst), *n.* 1. a structure formed or a place used by a bird for incubation and the rearing of its young. 2. a place used by insects, fishes, turtles, rabbits, or the like, for depositing their eggs or young. 3. a number of birds or other animals inhabiting one nest. 4. a snug retreat, or resting place. 5. an assemblage of things lying or set close together, as a series of boxes, trays, etc., that fit within each other. 6. a place where something bad is fostered or flourishes: *a nest of vice, a robbers' nest.* 7. the occupants or frequenters of such a place. —*v.t.* 8. to settle or place in or as in a nest. 9. to fit or place one within another. —*v.i.* 10. to build or have a nest: *the swallows nested under the eaves.* 11. to settle in or as in a nest. 12. to search for nests: *to go nesting.* [ME and OE, c. G *nest*; akin to L *nīdus*]

n'est-ce pas (něs pä'), *French.* isn't that so?

nest egg, 1. an egg (usually artificial) left in a nest to induce a hen to continue laying eggs there. 2. money saved as the basis of a fund or for emergencies.

nes·tle (nĕs/əl), v., **-tled, -tling.** —v.i. 1. to lie close and snug, like a bird in a nest; snuggle or cuddle. 2. to lie in a sheltered or pleasant situation. 3. Obs. to make or have a nest. —v.t. 4. to provide with or settle in a nest, as birds. 5. to settle or ensconce snugly. 6. to put or press confidingly or affectionately. [ME nestle(n), OE nestlian (c. D nestelen), der. nest NEST] —**nes/tler,** n.

nest·ling (nĕst/lĭng, nĕs/lĭng), n. 1. a young bird in the nest. 2. a young child.

Nes·tor (nĕs/tər), n. Gk. Legend. the wisest and oldest of the Greeks in the Trojan war.

Nes·to·ri·an (nĕs tōr/ĭ ən), n. one of a sect of Christians, followers of Nestorius, who denied the hypostatic union and was represented as maintaining the existence of two distinct persons in Christ. —**Nes·to/ri·an·ism,** n.

Nes·to·ri·us (nĕs tōr/ĭ əs), n. died A.D. c451, Syrian churchman; patriarch of Constantinople, A.D. 428–431.

net[1] (nĕt), n., v., **netted, netting.** —n. 1. a lacelike fabric with a uniform mesh of cotton, silk, rayon, or nylon, often forming the foundation of many kinds of lace. 2. a piece of meshed fabric for any purpose: a mosquito net. 3. a bag or other contrivance of strong thread or cord wrought into an open, meshed fabric, for catching fish, birds, or other animals. 4. anything serving to catch or ensnare. 5. any network or reticulated system of filaments, lines, veins, or the like. 6. Tennis, etc. a ball that hits the net. —v.t. 7. to cover, screen, or enclose with a net or netting. 8. to take with a net: to net fish. 9. to set or use nets in (a river, etc.), as for fish. 10. to catch or ensnare. 11. Tennis, etc. to hit (the ball) into the net. [ME net(te), OE net(t), c. G netz] —**net/like/,** adj.

net[2] (nĕt), adj., n., v., **netted, netting.** —adj. 1. exclusive of deductions, as for charges, expenses, loss, discount, etc.: net earnings. 2. sold at net prices. —n. 3. net income, profits, or the like. —v.t. 4. to gain or produce as clear profit. [t. F: clean, clear. See NEAT]

Neth., Netherlands.

neth·er (nĕth/ər), adj. 1. lying, or conceived as lying, beneath the earth's surface; infernal: the nether world. 2. lower or under: his nether lip. [ME; OE neothera, earlier ni(o)ther(r)a (c. G nieder), der. nither, adv., downward, down, a compar. form]

Neth·er·lands (nĕth/ər ləndz), n.pl. **The,** a kingdom in W Europe, bordering on the North Sea, Germany, and Belgium. 9,630,000 pop. (est. 1947); 13,433 sq. mi. Capitals: Amsterdam and The Hague. Also, **Holland.**

Netherlands Indies, Dutch East Indies.

neth·er·most (nĕth/ər mōst/, -məst), adj. lowest.

nether world, 1. hell. 2. the after world.

Né·thou (nĕ tōō/), n. **Pic de** (pēk də) a mountain in NE Spain: highest peak of the Pyrenees. 11,165 ft. Spanish, **Pico de Aneto.**

net·ting (nĕt/ĭng), n. any of various kinds of net fabric: fish netting, mosquito netting.

net·tle (nĕt/əl), n., v., **-tled, -tling.** —n. 1. any plant of the genus Urtica, comprising widely distributed herbs armed with stinging hairs. 2. any of various allied or similar plants. —v.t. 3. to irritate, provoke, or vex. 4. to sting as a nettle does. [ME; OE netele, c. G nessel]

nettle rash, Pathol. urticaria caused by contact with various plants causing local irritation.

net ton, a short ton.

net·work (nĕt/wûrk/), n. 1. any netlike combination of filaments, lines, veins, passages, or the like. 2. a netting or net. 3. Radio. a group of transmitting stations linked by wire so that the same program can be broadcast by all. 4. Elect. a system of interconnected admittances.

Neu·châ·tel (nœ shä tĕl/), n. 1. a canton in W Switzerland. 120,900 pop. (est. 1944); 309 sq. mi. 2. the capital of this canton, on the **Lake of Neuchâtel** (92 sq. mi.). 23,799 (est. 1941). German, **Neu·en·burg** (noi/-ĕn bōōrKH/).

Neuf·châ·tel cheese (nœ shä tĕl/), a soft, white cheese similar to cream cheese, made from whole or partly skimmed milk in Neufchâtel, a town in N France.

Neuil·ly-sur-Seine (nœ yē sɣr sĕn/), n. a city in N France, near Paris: treaty of peace between the Allies and Bulgaria, 1919. 60,172 (1946).

neur-, var. of neuro-, before vowels.

neu·ral (nyōōr/əl, nōōr/-), adj. of or pertaining to a nerve or the nervous system.

neu·ral·gia (nyōō răl/jə, nōō-), n. Pathol. sharp and paroxysmal pain along the course of a nerve. —**neu·ral/gic,** adj.

neu·ras·the·ni·a (nyōōr/əs thē/nĭ ə, nōōr/-), n. Pathol. nervous debility or exhaustion, as from overwork or prolonged mental strain, characterized by vague complaints of a physical nature in the absence of objectively present causes or lesions.

neu·ras·then·ic (nyōōr/əs thĕn/ĭk, nōōr/-), adj. 1. pertaining to or suffering from neurasthenia. —n. 2. a person suffering from neurasthenia.

neu·ra·tion (nyōō rā/shən, nōō-), n. venation.

neu·rec·to·my (nyōō rĕk/tə mĭ, nōō-), n., pl. **-mies.** Surg. the removal of a nerve or part thereof.

neu·ri·lem·ma (nyōōr/ə lĕm/ə, nōōr/-), n. Anat. (by assoc. with LEMMA[2] husk, outer layer) of neurilema, f. NEUR- + m. Gk. eílēma covering]

neu·ri·tis (nyōō rī/tĭs, nōō-), n. Pathol. 1. inflammation of a nerve. 2. continuous pain in a nerve associated with its paralysis and sensory disturbances. [NL. See NEUR-, -ITIS] —**neu·rit·ic** (nyōō rĭt/ĭk, nōō-), adj.

neuro-, a word element meaning "sinew," "tendon," "nerve." Also, **neur-.** [t. Gk., comb. form of neûron]

neu·ro·blast (nyōōr/ə blăst/, nōōr/-), n. Embryol. one of the cells in the embryonic brain and spinal cord of vertebrates, which are to give rise to nerve cells.

neu·ro·coele (nyōōr/ə sēl/, nōōr/-), n. Embryol. the cavity (ventricles and central canal) of the embryonic brain and spinal cord.

neu·rog·li·a (nyōō rŏg/lĭ ə, nōō-), n. Anat. the delicate connective tissue which supports and binds together the essential elements of nervous tissue in the central nervous system. [t. NL, f. Gk.: neu-ro- NEURO- + glía glue]

neu·rol·o·gy (nyōō rŏl/ə jĭ, nōō-), n. the science of the nerves or the nervous system, esp. the diseases thereof. —**neu·ro·log·i·cal** (nyōōr/ə lŏj/ə kəl, nōōr/-), adj. —**neu·rol/o·gist,** n.

neu·ro·ma (nyōō rō/mə, nōō-), n., pl. **-mata** (-mə tə), **-mas.** Pathol. a tumor formed of nervous tissue. [t. NL. See NEUR-, -OMA]

Diagram of a neuron
A, Cell; B, Nucleus; C, Dendrites; D, Axis

neu·ron (nyōōr/ŏn, nōōr/-), n. a nerve cell. Also, **neu·rone** (nyōōr/ŏn, nōōr/-). [t. Gk.: m. neûron nerve] —**neu·ron·ic** (nyōō-rŏn/ĭk, nōō-), adj.

neu·ro·path (nyōōr/ə păth/, nōōr/-), n. Psychiatry. a person subject to or affected with a functional nervous disease; a neurotic person.

neu·ro·path·ic (nyōōr/ə păth/ĭk, nōōr/-), adj. neurotic.

neu·ro·pa·thol·o·gy (nyōōr/ō pə thŏl/ə jĭ, nōōr/-), n. the pathology of the nervous system. —**neu·ro·pa·thol/o·gist,** n.

neu·rop·a·thy (nyōō rŏp/ə thĭ, nōō-), n. disease of the nervous system. [f. NEURO- + -PATHY]

neu·ro·psy·chi·a·try (nyōōr/ō sī kī/ə trĭ, nōōr/-), n. the branch of medicine dealing with diseases involving the mind and nervous system. —**neu·ro·psy·chi·at·ric** (nyōōr/ō sī/kĭ ăt/rĭk, nōōr/-), adj.

neu·ro·psy·cho·sis (nyōōr/ō sĭ kō/sĭs, nōōr-/), n., pl. **-ses** (-sēz). Pathol. mental derangement in association with nervous disease.

neu·rop·ter·ous (nyōō rŏp/tər əs, nōō-), adj. belonging to an order of insects, the Neuroptera, that includes the ant lions and lacewings, characterized by two pairs of membranous wings with netlike venation. [f. NEURO- + s. Gk. pterón wing + -OUS]

neu·ro·sis (nyōō rō/sĭs, nōō-), n., pl. **-ses** (-sēz). psychoneurosis.

neu·rot·ic (nyōō rŏt/ĭk, nōō-), adj. 1. having a psychoneurosis. 2. pertaining to the nerves or to nervous disease. —n. 3. a person affected with psychoneurosis. 4. Obs. a drug acting on the nerves.

neu·rot·o·my (nyōō rŏt/ə mĭ, nōō-), n., pl. **-mies.** surgical cutting of a nerve, as to relieve neuralgia.

Neu·satz (noi/zäts), n. German name of Novi Sad.

Neus·tri·a (nūs/trĭ ə, nōōs/-), n. the W part of the kingdom of the Franks, corresponding to N and NW France.

neut., neuter.

neu·ter (nū/tər, nōō/-), adj. 1. Gram. **a.** denoting or pertaining to one of the three genders of Latin, German, Greek, etc., or one of the two of Dutch, Swedish, etc.; so termed because few if any nouns denoting males or females belong to it, or (as in German) purely for traditional reasons. For example: Latin nōmen "name," cor "heart," bellum "war" are all neuter gender. **b.** (of verbs) intransitive. 2. Zool. having imperfectly developed sexual organs, as the workers among bees and ants. 3. Bot. having neither stamens nor pistils; asexual. 4. Archaic. neutral. —n. 5. Gram. **a.** the neuter gender. **b.** a noun of that gender. **c.** another element marking that gender. **d.** an intransitive verb. 6. an animal made sterile by castration. 7. a neuter insect. 8. Bot. a plant with neither stamens nor pistils. 9. a neutral. [t. L: neither; r. ME neutre, t. OF]

neu·tral (nū/trəl, nōō/-), adj. 1. (of a person or state) refraining from taking part in a controversy or war between others. 2. of no particular kind, color, characteristics, etc.; indefinite. 3. gray; without hue; zero chroma; achromatic. 4. Biol. neuter. 5. Chem. exhibiting neither acid nor alkaline qualities: neutral salts. 6. Elect., Magnetism. neither positive nor negative; not electrified; not magnetized. —n. 7. a person or a state that remains neutral, as in a war. 8. a citizen of a neutral nation. 9. Mach. the position or state of disengaged gears or other interconnecting parts: in neutral. [late ME, t. L: s. neutrālis neuter] —**neu/tral·ly,** adv.

neu·tral·i·ty (nū trăl/ə tĭ, nōō-), n. 1. the state of being neutral. 2. the attitude or status of a nation which does not participate in a war between other nations: the continuous neutrality of Switzerland. 3. neutral status, as of a seaport during a war.

---

b., blend of, blended; c., cognate with; d., dialect, dialectal; der., derived from; f., formed from; g., going back to; m., modification of; r., replacing; s., stem of; t., taken from; ?, perhaps. See the full key on inside cover.

neu·tral·ize (nū′trəlīz′, nōō′-), *v.t.*, **-ized**, **-izing**.
1. to make neutral. **2.** to render ineffective; counteract.
3. *Mil.* to put out of action or make incapable of action.
4. to declare neutral; invest with neutrality. **5.** *Chem.*
to render inert the peculiar properties of. **6.** *Elect.* to
render electrically neutral. **—neu′tral·i·za′tion,** *n.*
—neu′tral·iz′er, *n.*

neu·tri·no (nū trē′nō, nōō′-), *n., pl.* **-nos.** *Physics.* a
hypothetical neutral particle with less mass than the
electron.

neu·tron (nū′trŏn, nōō′-), *n. Physics.* a neutral parti-
cle with approximately the same mass as a proton. [f.
NEUTR(AL) neither positive nor negative + -on (after
ELECTRON, PROTON)]

Nev., Nevada.

Ne·va (nē′və; *Russ.* nĕ vä′), *n.* a river in the NW
Soviet Union, flowing from Lake Ladoga through
Leningrad into the Gulf of Finland: canalized for ships.
40 mi.

Ne·vad·a (nə văd′ə, -vä′də), *n.* a State in the W
United States. 160,083 pop. (1950); 110,540 sq. mi. *Cap.:*
Carson City. *Abbrev.:* Nev. **—Ne·vad′an,** *adj., n.*

né·vé (nä vā′; *Fr.* nĕ vĕ′), *n.* **1.** granular snow accumulated on high mountains and subsequently compacted
into glacial ice. **2.** a field of such snow. [t. F, through
Swiss F, der. O Southeastern F *neif*, g. s. L *nix* snow]

nev·er (nĕv′ər), *adv.* **1.** not ever; at no time. **2.** not
at all: absolutely not; not even. **3.** to no extent or degree. [ME; OE *næfre*, f. *ne* not + *æfre* EVER]

nev·er·more (nĕv′ər mōr′), *adv.* never again.

nev·er·the·less (nĕv′ər ᵺə lĕs′), *adv.* none the less;
notwithstanding; however. **—Syn.** See but[1].

Ne·vis (nĕv′ĭs, nēv′ĭs), *n.* one of the Leeward Islands
in the British West Indies. 14,597 pop. (est. 1942); 50
sq. mi.

Nev·ski (nĕv′skĭ, nĕf′-), *n.* **Alexander.** See **Alexander
Nevski.**

ne·vus (nē′vəs), *n., pl.* **-vi** (-vī). naevus. **— ne·void**
(nē′void), *adj.*

new (nū, nōō), *adj.* **1.** of recent origin or production,
or having but lately come or been brought into being: *a
new book.* **2.** of a kind now existing or appearing for the
first time; novel. **3.** having but lately or but now come
into knowledge: *a new chemical element.* **4.** unfamiliar
or strange (fol. by *to*): *ideas new to us.* **5.** having but
lately come to a place, position, status, etc.: *a new
minister.* **6.** unaccustomed (fol. by *to*): *men new to such
work.* **7.** coming or occurring afresh; further; additional: *new gains.* **8.** fresh or unused: *a new sheet.*
9. different and better, physically or morally: *the vacation made a new man of him.* **10.** other than the former
or the old: *a new era.* **11.** being the later or latest of
two or more things of the same kind: *the New Testament.*
12. (of a language) in its latest known period, esp. as a
living language at the present time: *New Latin.* **—adv.**
13. recently or lately. **14.** freshly; anew or afresh. **—n.**
15. something new. [ME and OE *newe*, c. G *neu*, L
novus, Gk. *néos*] **—new′ness,** *n.*
—Syn. 1. NEW, FRESH, NOVEL describe that which is not
old. NEW applies to that which has not been long in existence: *a new broom, dress* (one recently made or bought).
FRESH suggests a condition of newness, not yet affected by
use or the passage of time: *a fresh towel, dress* (newly clean).
NOVEL suggests newness which has an unexpected quality,
or is strange or striking, but generally pleasing: *a novel
experience, dress* (a dress of unusual material, of original
design, or the like).

New Al·ba·ny (ôl′bə nĭ), a city in S Indiana, on the
Ohio river. 29,346 (1950).

New Am·ster·dam (ăm′stər dăm′), a former Dutch
town on Manhattan Island: the capital of New Netherland; renamed New York by the British, 1664.

New·ark (nū′ərk, nōō′-), *n.* **1.** a city in NE New
Jersey, on **Newark Bay.** 438,776 (1950). **2.** a city in
central Ohio. 34,275 (1950).

New Bed·ford (bĕd′fərd), a seaport in SE Massachusetts: formerly a chief whaling port. 109,189 (1950).

New·ber·y Award (nū′bĕr′ĭ, -bərĭ, nōō′-), an annual award for the most distinguished book for juveniles.
[named after John Newbery, 1713–1767, noted British
publisher of books for children]

New·bolt (nū′bōlt, nōō′-), *n.* **Sir Henry John,** 1862–
1938, British poet and naval historian.

new·born (nū′bôrn′, nōō′-), *adj.* **1.** recently or only
just born. **2.** born anew; reborn.

New Brit·ain (brĭt′ən), **1.** a city in central Connecticut. 73,726 (1950). **2.** an island in the S Pacific, NE
of New Guinea: the largest island in the Bismark Archipelago. (Including nearby islands) 90,349 pop. (1940);
ab. 14,600 sq. mi. *Cap.:* Rabaul.

New Bruns·wick (brŭnz′wĭk), **1.** a province in SE
Canada, E of Maine. 457,401 pop. (1941); 27,985 sq. mi.
Cap.: Fredericton. **2.** a city in central New Jersey.
38,811 (1950).

New·burgh (nū′bûrg, nōō′-), *n.* a city in SE New
York, on the Hudson. 31,956 (1950).

New Cal·e·do·ni·a (kăl′ə dō′nĭ ə, -dōn′yə), **1.** an
island in the S Pacific, ab. 800 mi. E of Australia. 42,389
pop. (1936); 6224 sq. mi. **2.** a French colony comprising
this island and other small islands: formerly a penal
colony. 53,000 pop. (1936); 7200 sq. mi. *Cap.:* Nouméa.

New Cas·tile (kăs tēl′), a region in central Spain:
formerly a province. 3,129,170 pop. (1940); 27,933 sq. mi.

New·cas·tle (nū′kăs′əl, -käs′əl, nōō′-), *n.* **1.** Also,
Newcastle-upon-Tyne (-tīn). a seaport in NE England,
on the Tyne river: ship-building. 284,750 (est. 1946).
2. a seaport in SE Australia, in New South Wales.
104,485 (1933).

New Castle, a city in W Pennsylvania. 48,834 (1950).

Newcastle disease, a specific, virus-induced disease of chickens, etc., marked by loss of egg production
in old birds and by paralysis in chicks.

New Church, New Jerusalem Church.

New·chwang (nū′chwäng′, nōō′-), *n.* a city in NE
China: a river port ab. 30 mi. from the Gulf of Liaotung,
in S Manchuria. See **Yingkow.**

New·comb (nū′kəm, nōō′-), *n.* **Simon,** 1835–1909,
U.S. astronomer.

new·com·er (nū′kŭm′ər, nōō′-), *n.* one who has
newly come; a new arrival.

New Deal, 1. the principles of the progressive wing
of the Democratic party, esp. those advocated under the
leadership of President Franklin D. Roosevelt. **2.** the
Roosevelt administration. **—New Dealer.**

New Delhi, a city in N India, in Delhi province: the
capital of the Dominion of India. 93,733 (1941).

New Economic Policy, a Soviet Union program,
beginning in 1921, reviving the wage system and private
ownership of some factories and businesses, and abandoning grain requisitions.

new·el (nū′əl, nōō′-), *n.* **1.** a central pillar or upright
from which the steps of a winding stair radiate. **2.** a
post at the head or foot of a stair, supporting the hand-
rail. [ME *nowell*, t. OF: m. *noiel* kernel, newel (g. LL
nucāle, neut. of *nucālis* of or like a nut), b. with *noel* bud,
trickle-ornament, g. LL *nōdellus*, der. L *nōdus* knot]

New England, six States in the NE United States:
Connecticut, Massachusetts, Rhode Island, Vermont,
New Hampshire, and Maine. **—New Englander.**

New England aster, a tall aster, *Aster novae
angliae*, of the northeastern U.S., bearing heads with
deep-purple rays.

new·fan·gled (nū′făng′gəld, nōō′-), *adj.* **1.** new-
fashioned; of a new kind: *newfangled ideas.* **2.** fond of
novelty. [der. *newfangle*, ME *newefangel*, f. *newe* NEW +
fangel, der. ME *fangen* take]

new-fash·ioned (nū′făsh′ənd, nōō′-), *adj.* lately
come into fashion; of a
new fashion.

New Forest, a forest
region in S England, in
Hampshire: national park.
145 sq. mi.

New·found·land (nū′-
fənd lănd′, nōō′- *for 1*;
nū found′lənd, nōō- *for
2*), *n.* **1.** a large island
in the eastern part of Canada: became a Canadian
province on March 31, 1949. 312,889 pop. (1945);
42,734 sq. mi. (excluding Labrador). **2.** one of a breed
of large, shaggy dogs, orig. from
Newfoundland, noted for their
sagacity, docility, swimming
powers, etc.

New·found·land·er (nū-
found′lən dər, nōō-), *n.* a native
or inhabitant of Newfoundland.

New France, the name of
Canada while under French rule.

New·gate (nū′gāt, -gĭt, nōō′-),
n. a famous prison in London,
England: destroyed, 1902.

Newfoundland
(28 in. high at the shoulder)

New Gra·na·da (grə nä′də), **1.** a former Spanish
vice-royalty in NW South America, comprising the
present republics of Ecuador, Venezuela, Colombia, and
Panama. **2.** early name for Colombia (before the secession of Panama).

New Guin·ea (gĭn′ĭ), **1.** Also, **Papua.** a large island
N of Australia: divided into Dutch New Guinea and the
recently merged Australian territories of Papua and
New Guinea. ab. 900,000 pop.; ab. 316,000 sq. mi.
2. Territory of, a territory under the trusteeship of
Australia, including NE New Guinea, the Bismarck
Archipelago, Bougainville, and other islands: merged
with the Territory of Papua, 1945. 675,000 pop. (est.
1940); ab. 93,000 sq. mi. (ab. 69,700 sq. mi. mainland).

New Hamp·shire (hămp′shər, -shĭr), **1.** a State in
the NE United States. 533,242 pop. (1950); 9304 sq. mi.
Cap.: Concord. *Abbr.:* N.H. **2.** an American breed of
domestic fowl, mostly chestnut-red in color, early
maturing and fast-growing.

New Ha·ven (hā′vən), a seaport in S Connecticut,
on Long Island Sound. 164,443 (1950).

New Heb·ri·des (hĕb′rə dēz′), an island group in the
S Pacific, ab. 1000 mi. NE of Australia: under joint
British and French administration. ab. 43,000 pop.; ab.
5700 sq. mi. *Cap.:* Vila.

New Ireland, an island in the S Pacific, in the Bismarck Archipelago, NE of New Guinea. (With adjacent islands) 36,960 pop. (1940); ab. 3800 sq. mi.

new·ish (nū′ĭsh, nōō′-), *adj.* rather new.

New Jer·sey (jûr′zĭ), a State in the E United States.
on the Atlantic coast. 4,835,329 pop. (1950); 7836 sq. mi.
Cap.: Trenton. *Abbr.:* N.J. **—New Jer·sey·ite**
(jûr′zĭ īt′).

New Jerusalem, the heavenly city; the abode of God and His saints. Rev. 21:2.

New Jerusalem Church, the church composed of the followers of Swedenborg. See **Swedenborgian.**

New Kensington, a city in W Pennsylvania. 25,146 (1950).

New Latin, Neo-Latin.

New London, a seaport in SE Connecticut, on the Thames river: naval base. 30,551 (1950).

new·ly (nū′lǐ, nōō′-), *adv.* 1. recently; lately: *a newly wedded couple.* 2. anew or afresh: *a newly repeated slander.* 3. in a new manner or form. [OE *niwlic*]

New·man (nū′mən, nōō′-), *n.* **John Henry,** (*Cardinal Newman*) 1801–90, British theologian and author.

New·mar·ket (nū′mär′kǐt, nōō′-), *n.* 1. a town in E England, E of Cambridge: horse races. 20,943 (1939). 2. (*l.c.*) Also, **Newmarket coat.** a long, close-fitting outdoor coat worn by men and women. 3. (*l.c.*) a kind of card game of the stops family.

New Mexico, a State in the SW United States. 681,187 (1950); 121,666 sq. mi. *Cap.:* Santa Fe. *Abbr.:* N. Mex. or N.M. —**New Mexican.**

new moon. See moon (def. 2a).

New Netherland, a Dutch colony on the Hudson (1613) and Delaware rivers: after 1664, included by England in the New York, New Jersey, and Delaware colonies. *Cap.:* New Amsterdam.

New Or·le·ans (ôr′lǐ·ənz; *older* ôr lēnz′), a seaport in SE Louisiana, on the Mississippi: British defeated by the Americans under Andrew Jackson, 1815. 570,445 (1950).

New·port (nū′pōrt, nōō′-), *n.* 1. a seaport in SW England, near the Severn estuary. 100,340 (est. 1946). 2. a city in N Kentucky, on the Ohio river, opposite Cincinnati, Ohio. 31,044 (1950). 3. a seaport and summer resort in SE Rhode Island: naval base. 37,564 (1950). 4. a city on the Isle of Wight, in S England. 20,644 (1939).

Newport News, a seaport in SE Virginia. 42,358 (1950).

New Ro·chelle (rō shěl′, rə-), a city in SE New York, near New York City. 59,725 (1950).

news (nūz, nōōz), *n.pl.* (*now construed as sing.*) 1. a report of any recent event, situation, etc. 2. the report of events published in a newspaper. [ME *newes,* pl. of ME and OE *newe* that which is new, n. use of *newe,* adj.]

news·boy (nūz′boi′, nōōz′-), *n.* a boy who sells or delivers newspapers.

news·cast (nūz′kăst′, -käst′, nōōz′-), *n.* a radio broadcast of news reports. —**news′cast′er,** *n.*

news·deal·er (nūz′dē′lər, nōōz′-), *n.* U.S. a dealer in newspapers and often magazines, etc. Also, *Brit.,* **news agent.**

New Si·be·ri·an Is·lands (sī bǐr′ǐ·ən), a group of islands in the Arctic Ocean, N of the Soviet Union in Asia: part of the Yakut Autonomous Republic.

news·let·ter (nūz′lět′ər, nōōz′-), *n.* an informal or confidential report and analysis of the news.

news·man (nūz′măn′, -mən, nōōz′-), *n.* 1. one who sells or distributes newspapers, periodicals, etc. 2. a newspaper man; a reporter on a newspaper.

news·mon·ger (nūz′mŭng′gər, nōōz′-), *n.* a spreader of news by oral or written means, esp. a gossip.

New South Wales, a state in SE Australia. 2,924,-654 pop. (1946); 309,433 sq. mi. *Cap.:* Sydney.

New Spain, the former Spanish possessions in North America, at one time including Mexico, Central America, the West Indies, and parts of the United States.

news·pa·per (nūz′pā′pər, nōōz′-, nūs′-, nōōs′-), *n.* a printed publication issued at regular intervals, usually daily or weekly and commonly containing news, comment, features, and advertisements.

news·print (nūz′prǐnt′, nōōz′-), *n.* paper used or made to print newspapers on.

news·reel (nūz′rēl′, nōōz′-), *n.* a short motion picture presenting current news events.

news stall, *Brit.* a newsstand.

news·stand (nūz′stănd′, nōōz′-), *n.* U.S. a stand at which newspapers and often magazines, etc. are sold. Also, *Brit.,* **news stall.**

New Style. See style (def. 13).

news·wor·thy (nūz′wûr′thǐ, nōōz′-), *adj.* of sufficient interest to appear in a newspaper.

news·y (nū′zǐ, nōō′-), *adj.,* **newsier, newsiest,** *n.,* *pl.* **newsies.** —*adj.* 1. *Colloq.* full of news, as on various subjects. —*n.* 2. U.S. *Colloq.* a newsboy.

newt (nūt, nōōt), *n.* 1. the salamanders of the genus *Triturus* (or *Triton*), of North America, Europe, and northern Asia. 2. *Obs.* any of various small, tailed amphibians. [ME *newte,* for *ewte* (an *ewte* being taken as *a newte*), var. of *evet,* OE *efete.* Cf. EFT]

New Test., New Testament.

New Testament, those books in the Bible which were produced by the early Christian church, and were added to the Jewish scriptures (Old Testament).

New Thought, a system of doctrine and practice based on the theory that through the suggestion

Crested newt,
Triturus cristatus
(4 to 6 in. long)

of favorable and beneficial ideas all physical and mental circumstances of life may be regulated and controlled.

New·ton (nū′tən, nōō′tən), *n.* 1. **Sir Isaac,** 1642–1727, British scientist, mathematician, and philosopher, who formulated and proved the law of gravity. 2. a city in E Massachusetts, near Boston. 81,994 (1950). —**New·to·ni·an** (nū tō′nǐ·ən, nōō-), *adj., n.*

New Windsor, Windsor.

New World, the Western Hemisphere.

new year, 1. the year approaching or newly begun. 2. (*caps.*) the first day or days of a year. 3. (*caps.*) New Year's Day.

New Year's Day, January 1. Also, *esp.* U.S., **New Year's.**

New Year's Eve, the night of December 31, usually observed with merrymaking.

New York, 1. a State in the NE United States. 14,-830,192 pop. (1950); 49,576 sq. mi. *Cap.:* Albany. *Abbr.:* N.Y. 2. Also, **New York City.** a seaport in SE New York at the mouth of the Hudson: the largest city in the Western Hemisphere. 7,891,957 (1950); **Greater New York,** 12,831,914 (1950). —**New York′er.**

New York Bay, a bay of the Atlantic at the mouth of the Hudson, W of Long Island and E of Staten Island and New Jersey.

New York State Barge Canal, 1. a State waterway system in New York. 575 mi. long. 2. the main canal of this system, between the Hudson and Lake Erie, consisting of the rebuilt Erie Canal. 352 mi.

New Zea·land (zē′lənd), a dominion of the British Commonwealth of Nations, consisting of islands (principally North and South Islands) in the S Pacific. 1,761,259 pop. (est. 1946); 103,416 sq. mi. *Cap.:* Wellington. —**New Zea′land·er.**

Nex·ö (nǐk′sœ), *n.* **Martin Anderson** (mär′tēn än′ər-sən), born 1869, Danish novelist.

next (někst), *adj., superl.* of **nigh,** *adv.* —*adj.* 1. immediately following in time, order, mportance, etc.: *the next day.* 2. nearest in place or position: *the next room.* 3. nearest in relationship or kinship. —*adv.* 4. in the nearest place. time, importance, etc. 5. on the first subsequent occasion: *when next we meet.* [ME *nexte,* OE *nēxt,* var. of *nēhst,* superl. of *nēah* NIGH]

next friend, *Law.* a person who, as in a suit at law, acts or appears for the benefit of an infant or other person under legal disability.

next of kin, 1. a person's nearest relative or relatives. 2. *Law.* the nearest relative(s), to whom the personal property passes upon the death of an intestate.

nex·us (něk′səs), *n., pl.* **nexus.** 1. a tie or link; a means of connection. 2. a connected series. [t. L]

Ney (nā), *n.* **Michel** (mē shěl′), (*Duke of Elchingen, Prince of the Moskova*) 1769–1815, Marshal of France under Napoleon I.

Nez Per·cé (něz′ pûrs′; *Fr.* ně pěr sě′), *pl.* **Nez Per·cés** (pûr′sĭz; *Fr.* pěr sě′). 1. (*pl.*) a leading North American Indian tribe of the Sahaptian family. 2. (formerly as used by the French) a number of tribes, supposed to pierce the nasal septum for nose ornaments. 3. a member of one of these tribes. [t. F: lit., pierced nose]

NF, Norman French.

N.F., 1. Newfoundland. 2. *Banking.* no funds. Also, **n.f.** 3. Norman French.

N.G., 1. National Guard. 2. no good. Also, **n.g.**

Ngan·hwei (ngän′hwā′), *n.* Anhwei.

NGk., New Greek. Also, **N. Gk.**

N.H., New Hampshire.

Ni, *Chem.* nickel.

N.I., Northern Ireland.

ni·a·cin (nī′ə·sĭn), *n.* 1. nicotinic acid. 2. (*cap.*) the trademark for this acid. [f. NI(COTINIC) AC(ID) + -IN[2]]

Ni·ag·a·ra (nī ăg′rə, -ăg′ər·ə), *n.* 1. a river flowing from Lake Erie into Lake Ontario, on the boundary between W New York and Ontario, Canada. 34 mi. 2. Niagara Falls. 3. **Fort,** a fort at the mouth of the Niagara river, in W New York. 4. *Hort.* a widely grown eastern white grape.

Niagara Falls, 1. the falls of the Niagara river: Horseshoe Falls, in Canada, 158 ft. high; 2600 ft. wide; American Falls, 167 ft. high; 1400 ft. wide. 2. a city on the New York side of the falls. 90,872 (1950). 3. a city on the Canadian side. 20,589 (1940).

nib (nǐb), *n., v.,* **nibbed, nibbing.** —*n.* 1. a bill or beak, as of a bird; a neb. 2. *Brit.* a pen, for insertion into a penholder. 3. the point of a pen, or either of its divisions. 4. a point of anything. 5. any pointed extremity. —*v.t.* 6. *Brit.* to furnish with a nib or point. 7. to mend or trim the nib of. [OE *nybba* point (in a place name), c. Icel. *nibba* sharp point]

nib·ble (nǐb′əl), *v.,* **-bled, -bling,** *n.* —*v.i.* 1. to bite off small bits. 2. to eat or feed by biting off small pieces. 3. to bite slightly or gently (fol. by *at*). —*v.t.* 4. to bite off small bits of (a thing). 5. to eat by biting off small pieces. 6. to bite (off etc.) n small pieces. —*n.* 7. a small morsel or bit: *each nibble was eaten with the air of an epicure.* 8. act or an instance of nibbling. [late ME; cf. LG *nibbelen*] —**nib′bler,** *n.*

Ni·be·lung·en·lied (nē′bə lŏong′ən lēt′), *n.* a Middle High German epic, given .ts present form by an unknown author in South Germany during the first half of the 13th century. [t. G. See NIBELUNGS, LIED]

Ni·be·lungs (nē′bə lŏongz′), *n.pl., sing.* **Nibelung.**

Germanic. *Myth.* **1.** a race of Northern dwarfs who possessed the treasure later captured by Siegfried. They were named from their king, Nibelung. **2.** the followers of Siegfried, who captured the Nibelungs' hoard. **3.** (later, in the *Nibelungenlied*) the Burgundian kings. Also, **Ni·be·lung·en** (nē′bə lŏong′ən).

nib·lick (nĭb′lĭk), *n. Golf.* a club with a short, rounded, flat iron head whose face slopes greatly from the vertical.

Ni·cae·a (nī sē′ə), *n.* an ancient city in N W Asia Minor: Nicene Creed, A.D. 325.

Ni·cae·an (nī sē′ən), *adj.* Nicene.

Nic·a·ra·gua (nĭk′ə rä′gwə), *n.* **1.** a republic in Central America. 1,082,000 pop. (est. 1945); 57,143 sq. mi. *Cap.:* Managua. **2. Lake,** a lake in SW Nicaragua. 92 mi. long; 34 mi. wide; ab. 3000 sq. mi. —**Nic′a·ra′guan,** *adj., n.*

nic·co·lite (nĭk′ə līt′), *n.* a pale copper-red mineral of a metallic luster, nickel arsenide (Ni As), usually occurring massive. [f. s. NL *niccolum* nickel + -ITE¹]

nice (nīs), *adj., nicer, nicest.* **1.** pleasing; agreeable; delightful: *a nice visit.* **2.** amiably pleasant; kind: *they are always nice to strangers.* **3.** characterized by or requiring great accuracy, precision, skill or delicacy: *nice workmanship.* **4.** requiring or showing tact or care; delicate. **5.** showing minute differences; minutely accurate, as instruments. **6.** minute, fine, or subtle, as a distinction. **7.** having or showing delicate and accurate perception: *a nice sense of color.* **8.** refined as to manners, language, etc. **9.** suitable or proper: *not a nice song.* **10.** carefully neat as to dress, habits, etc. **11.** dainty or delicious, as food. **12.** dainty as to food. **13.** *Obs.* coy, shy, or reluctant. **14.** *Obs.* wanton. **15.** *Obs.* foolish. [ME, t. OF: simple, g. L *nescius* not knowing] —**nice′ly,** *adv.* —**nice′ness,** *n.*

Nice (nēs), *n.* a coastal resort in SE France. 211,165 (1946).

Ni·cene (nī sēn′, nī′sēn), *adj.* of or pertaining to Nicaea. Also, **Nicaean.** [ME, t. LL: m.s. *Nicēnus,* der *Nicea,* t. Gk.: m. *Nīkaia,* a town in Bithynia]

Nicene Council, either of two general ecclesiastical councils which met at Nicaea, the first in A.D. 325 to deal with the Arian heresy, the second in A.D. 787 to consider the question of images.

Nicene Creed, **1.** a formal statement of the chief tenets of Christian belief, adopted by the first Nicene Council. **2.** a later creed of closely similar form referred, perhaps erroneously, to the Council of Constantinople (A.D. 381) and hence sometimes known as the **Niceno-Constantinopolitan Creed,** received universally in the Eastern Church, and, with an addition introduced in the 6th century, accepted generally throughout western Christendom.

ni·ce·ty (nī′sə tĭ), *n., pl.* **-ties. 1.** a delicate or fine point: *niceties of protocol.* **2.** a fine distinction; subtlety. **3.** (*often pl.*) something nice; a refinement or elegance, as of manners or living. **4.** quality of being nice. **5.** delicacy of character, as of something requiring care or tact: *a matter of considerable nicety.* [ME *nycete,* t. OF: m. *nicete,* der. *nice* NICE]

niche (nĭch), *n., v.,* **niched, niching.** —*n.* **1.** an ornamental recess in a wall, etc., usually round in section and arched, as for a statue or other decorative object. **2.** a place or position suitable or appropriate for a person or thing. **3.** *Ecol.* the position or function of an organism in a community of plants and animals. —*v.t.* **4.** to place in a niche. [t. F, der. *nicher* to make a nest, g. Gallo-Rom. *nīdicāre,* der. L *nīdus* nest]

Nich·o·las (nĭk′ə ləs), *n.* **1.** name of five popes. **2. Grand Duke,** 1856–1929, Russian general in World War I. **3. Saint, a.** Santa Claus. **b.** fl. 4th cent., bishop in Asia Minor, patron saint of Russia, protector of children.

Nicholas I, 1. Saint, ("*the Great*") died A.D. 867, Italian ecclesiastic, pope, A.D. 858–867. **2.** 1796–1855, czar of Russia, 1825–55.

Nicholas II, 1868–1918, czar of Russia, 1894–1917, executed in the Russian Bolshevik Revolution.

ni·chrome (nī′krōm), *n.* a nickel-base alloy, containing chromium and iron, having high electrical resistance and stability at high temperatures.

Ni·ci·as (nĭsh′ĭ əs), *n.* died 414 B.C., Athenian aristocratic statesman and general.

nick (nĭk), *n.* **1.** a notch, groove, or the like, cut into or existing in a thing. **2.** a hollow place produced in an edge or surface, as of a dish, by breaking. **3.** a small groove on one side of the shank of a printing type, serving as a guide in setting or to distinguish different types. See diag. under **type.** **4.** the precise moment or time of some occurrence: *in the nick of time.* —*v.t.* **5.** to make a nick or nicks in; notch. **6.** to record by means of a notch or notches. **7.** to cut into or through; to cut short. **8.** to incise certain tendons at the root of (a horse's) tail when setting it, to cause him to carry it higher. **9.** to hit, guess, catch, etc., exactly. **10.** *Brit. Slang.* to capture or arrest. **11.** to trick, cheat, or defraud. [late ME; cf. OE *gehnycned* wrinkled]

Nick (nĭk), *n.* the devil (usually **Old Nick**). [familiar use of *Nicholas,* proper name]

nick·el (nĭk′əl), *n., v.,* **-eled, -eling** or (*esp. Brit.*) **-elled, -elling.** —*n.* **1.** *Chem.* a hard, silvery-white, ductile and malleable metallic element, allied to iron and cobalt, not readily oxidized, and much used in the arts, in making alloys, etc. *Symbol:* Ni; *at. wt.:* 58.6; *at. no.:*

28; *sp. gr.:* 8.9 at 20°C. **2.** *U.S.* a coin composed of or containing nickel, now a five-cent piece. —*v.t.* **3.** to cover or coat with nickel. [t. Sw., short for *kopparnickel* niccolite, t. G: half-trans., half-adoption of *kupfernickel,* said to mean copper demon, since it looks like copper but yields none]

nick·el·ic (nĭk′əl ĭk, nĭ kĕl′-), *adj. Chem.* of or containing nickel, esp. in the trivalent state (Ni+³).

nick·el·if·er·ous (nĭk′ə lĭf′ər əs), *adj.* containing or yielding nickel.

nick·el·o·de·on (nĭk′əl ō′dĭ ən), *n. U.S.* a place of amusement with motion pictures, etc. to which the price of admission is five cents. [f. NICKEL (def. 2) + *odeon,* var. of ODEUM]

nick·el·ous (nĭk′əl əs), *adj. Chem.* containing bivalent nickel (Ni+²).

nickel plate, thin coating of nickel deposited on the surface of a piece of metal by electroplating or otherwise.

nick·el-plate (nĭk′əl plāt′), *v.t.,* **-plated, -plating.** to coat with nickel by electroplating or otherwise.

nickel silver, German silver.

nick·er¹ (nĭk′ər), *n.* one who, or that which nicks. [f. NICK¹ + -ER¹]

nick·er² (nĭk′ər), *v.i., n. Chiefly Brit. Dial.* **1.** neigh. **2.** laugh; snicker. [appar. var. of *nicher, neigher,* freq. of NEIGH. Cf. LG *gnickern*]

nick·nack (nĭk′năk′), *n.* knickknack.

nick·name (nĭk′nām′), *n., v.,* **-named, -naming.** —*n.* **1.** a name added to or substituted for the proper name of a person, place, etc., as in ridicule or familiarity. **2.** a familiar form of a proper name, as *Jim* for *James.* —*v.t.* **3.** to give a nickname to, or call by a specified nickname. **4.** to call by an incorrect or improper name. [ME *nekename,* for *ekename* (an *ekename* being taken as *a nekename*). See EKE², NAME]

Nic·o·bar Islands (nĭk′ə bär′), a group of small islands in the Bay of Bengal, W of the Malay Peninsula: they form a part of the province of Andaman and Nicobar Islands. 12,452 pop. (1941); 635 sq. mi.

Nic·o·lay (nĭk′ə lā′), *n.* **John George,** 1832–1901, U.S. biographer.

nic·o·tine (nĭk′ə tēn′, -tĭn), *n.* a poisonous alkaloid, $C_{10}H_{14}N_2$, the active principle of tobacco, obtained as a colorless or nearly colorless, oily, acrid liquid. Also, **nic·o·tin** (nĭk′ə tĭn). [t. F, der. *Nicot,* who introduced tobacco into France in 1560]

nic·o·tin·ic ac·id (nĭk′ə tĭn′ĭk), *Chem.* an acid derived from the oxidation of nicotine, $C_6H_5NO_2$, found in fresh meat, yeast, etc. It is the component of the vitamin B complex which counteracts pellagra; niacin.

nic·o·tin·ism (nĭk′ə tēn ĭz′əm, -tĭn-), *n.* a condition due to excessive use of tobacco.

Nic·the·roy (nĭk′tĕ roi′), *n.* a seaport in SE Brazil, opposite Rio de Janeiro. 125,974 (1940). Also, **Niteroi.**

nic·ti·tate (nĭk′tə tāt′), *v.i.,* **-tated, -tating.** to wink. Also, **nic·tate** (nĭk′tāt). [t. ML: m.s. *nictitātus,* pp. of *nictitāre,* freq. of L *nictāre* wink] —**nic′ti·ta′tion,** *n.*

nictitating membrane, a thin membrane, or inner or third eyelid, present in many animals, capable of being drawn across the eyeball, as for protection.

Ni·da·ros (nē′därōs′), *n.* former name of **Trondheim.**

nid·der·ing (nĭd′ər ĭng), *Archaic.* —*n.* **1.** a cowardly or base person. —*adj.* **2.** cowardly; base. Also, **nid′er·ing.** [erroneous var. of *nithing,* t. Scand.; cf. Icel. *nidhingr*]

nide (nīd), *n.* a nest or brood, esp. of pheasants. [t. L: m.s. *nīdus* nest]

nid·i·fi·cate (nĭd′ə fə kāt′), *v.i.,* **-cated, -cating.** to build a nest. [t. L: m.s. *nīdificātus,* pp.] —**nid′i·fi·ca′tion,** *n.*

nid·i·fy (nĭd′ə fī′), *v.i.,* **-fied, -fying.** nidificate.

ni·dus (nī′dəs), *n., pl.* **-di** (-dī). **1.** a nest, esp. one in which insects, etc., deposit their eggs. **2.** a place or point in a living organism where a germ, whether proper or foreign to the organism, normal or morbid, may find means of development. [t. L. See NEST]

Nie·buhr (nē′bōor), *n.* **Barthold Georg** (bär′tôlt gā-ōrkh′), 1776–1831, German historian.

niece (nēs), *n.* **1.** a daughter of one's brother or sister. **2.** a daughter of one's husband's or wife's brother or sister. **3.** (in euphemistic use) an illegitimate daughter of an ecclesiastic. [ME *nece, nice,* t. OF: m. *niece,* g. VL *neptia,* r. L *neptis* granddaughter, niece]

ni·el·lo (nĭ ĕl′ō), *n., pl.* **nielli** (nĭ ĕl′ĭ), *v.,* **-loed, -loing.** —*n.* **1.** a black metallic composition, consisting of silver, copper, lead, and sulfur, with which an incised design or ground on metal is filled in to produce an ornamental effect. **2.** ornamental work so produced. **3.** a specimen of such work. —*v.t.* **4.** to decorate by means of niellowork; treat with niello or by the niello process. [t. It., g. L *nigellus* blackish]

Nie·men (nē′mən; *Pol.* nyĕ′mĕn), *n.* a river in the W Soviet Union, flowing into the Baltic: called **Memel** in its lower course. 565 mi. Lithuanian, **Nemunas.** Russian, **Nyeman.**

Nier·stein·er (nēr′stīnər, -shtīnər), *n.* a white Rhine wine. [t. G: f. *Nierstein* name of place near Mainz + -*er* -ER¹]

Nie·tzsche (nē′chə), *n.* **Friedrich Wilhelm** (frē′drĭkH vĭl′hĕlm), 1844–1900, German philosopher.

Nie·tzsche·ism (nē′chĭ ĭz′əm), *n.* the philosophy of Nietzsche, emphasizing self-aggrandizement, or the will to power, as the chief motivating force of both the individual and society. Also, **Nie/tzsche·an·ism.** —**Nie/-tzsche·an,** *n., adj.*

nieve (nēv), *n. Archaic except Scot. and Brit. Dial.* a fist. [ME *neve,* t. Scand.; cf. Icel. *hnefi* fist]

nif·fer (nĭf'ər), *v., n. Scot.* exchange; barter.

Ni·fl·heim (nĭv'əl hām'), *n.* (in Old Scand. cosmogony) the world of fog in the north. Also, **Ni/fel·heim/.** [t. Icel.]

nif·ty (nĭf'tĭ), *adj.,* **-tier, -tiest,** *n., pl.* **-ties.** *U.S. Slang.* —*adj.* **1.** smart; stylish; fine. —*n.* **2.** a smart or clever remark. [orig. theat. slang]

Ni·ger (nī'jər), *n.* **1.** a river in W Africa, flowing through French West Africa and Nigeria into the Gulf of Guinea. ab. 2600 mi. **2.** a colony in NE French West Africa. 1,902,000 pop. (1940); 499,540 sq. mi. *Cap.:* Niamey.

Ni·ge·ri·a (nī jĭr'ĭ ə), *n.* a British colony and protectorate in W Africa, including the Cameroons, under British trusteeship. 21,041,000 pop. (est. 1941); 372,599 sq. mi. *Cap.:* Lagos. —**Ni·ge/ri·an,** *adj., n.*

nig·gard (nĭg'ərd), *n.* **1.** an excessively parsimonious or stingy person. —*adj.* **2.** niggardly. [ME, f. (obs.) *nig* niggard (t. Scand.; cf. d. Sw. *nygg*) + **-ARD**]

nig·gard·ly (nĭg'ərd lĭ), *adj.* **1.** parsimonious; stingy. **2.** meanly small or scanty: *a niggardly allowance.* —*adv.* **3.** in the manner of a niggard. —**nig/gard·li·ness,** *n.*

nig·ger (nĭg'ər), *n. Offensive.* **1.** a Negro. **2.** a member of any dark-skinned race. [var. of *neger,* t. F: m. *nègre,* t. Sp.: m. *negro* NEGRO]

nig·gle (nĭg'əl), *v.i.,* **-gled, -gling.** to trifle; work ineffectively. [appar. t. Scand.; cf. Norw. *nigla*] —**nig/-gler,** *n.* —**nig/gling·ly,** *adv.*

nigh (nī), *adv., adj.,* **nigher, nighest** or **next,** *v., prep.* —*adv.* **1.** near in space, time, or relation. **2.** *Chiefly Archaic or Dial.* nearly or almost. —*adj.* **3.** being near; not distant; near in relationship. **4.** short or direct. **5.** (with reference to animals or vehicles) left or near. **6.** *Chiefly Archaic or Dial.* parsimonious. —*v.i., v.t.* **7.** *Archaic.* to approach. —*prep.* **8.** *Chiefly Archaic or Dial.* near to; near. [ME *nigh(e), neye,* OE *nēah, nēh,* c. G *nahe*]

night (nīt), *n.* **1.** the interval of darkness between sunset and sunrise. **2.** nightfall. **3.** the darkness of night; the dark. **4.** a state or time of obscurity, ignorance, misfortune, etc. [ME; OE *niht, neaht,* c. G *nacht*]

night blindness, nyctalopia (def. 1).

night-blooming cereus, a typical American species of the genus *Selenicereus* or *Cereus*), esp. *S grandiflorus,* bearing large fragrant flowers opening at night.

night·cap (nīt'kăp'), *n.* **1.** a cap for the head, intended primarily to be worn in bed. **2.** *Colloq.* an alcoholic drink taken before going to bed.

night clothes, garments designed to be worn in bed.

night club, a restaurant, open until very late, furnishing food, drink, entertainment, etc.

night crawler, *U.S. Dial.* the common large earthworm, which emerges from its burrow at night.

night·dress (nīt'drĕs'), *n.* **1.** dress or clothing for wearing in bed. **2.** a nightgown.

night·fall (nīt'fôl'), *n.* the coming of night.

night·gown (nīt'goun'), *n.* **1.** a loose gown, worn in bed by women or children. **2.** a man's nightshirt. **3.** *Obs.* a man's or woman's dressing gown.

night·hawk (nīt'hôk'), *n.* **1.** any of several long-winged American goatsuckers of the genus *Chordeiles,* all more or less nocturnal and differing from the whippoorwill in having no rictal bristles, as the **common nighthawk,** mosquito hawk, or bullbat (C *minor*). **2.** the European goatsucker or nightjar, *Caprimulgus europaeus.* **3.** *Colloq.* one who is habitually up or prowling about at night.

night heron, any of certain thick-billed herons of crepuscular or nocturnal habits, of the genus *Nycticorax* and allied genera, as the **black-crowned night heron** (*Nycticorax nycticorax*) of both New and Old Worlds, and the American **yellow-crowned night heron** (*Nyctanassa violocea*).

night·in·gale (nī'tən gāl', nī'-tǐng-), *n.* a small Old World migratory bird of the thrush family, esp. the common nightingale, *Luscinia megarhyncha,* of Europe, noted for the melodious song of the male given chiefly at night during the breeding season. [ME *nightyngale,* nasalized var. of *nightegale,* OE *nihtegale,* c. G *nachtigall,* lit., night singer (cf. OE *galan* sing)]

Nightingale,
Luscinia megarhyncha
(6½ in. long)

Night·in·gale (nī'tən gāl', nī'tǐng-), *n.* **Florence,** 1820-1910, British nurse, philanthropist, and reformer of hospital nursing.

night·jar (nīt'jär'), *n.* any Old World goatsucker, esp. the common species, *Caprimulgus europaeus* of England.

night latch, a spring latch for a door or the like, which when adjusted for use, as at night, prevents the door from being opened from outside except by a key.

night letter, a telegram, usually of greater length than an ordinary message, sent at a reduced rate of charge because subject to the priority in transmission and delivery of regular telegrams.

night·long (nīt'lông', -lŏng'), *adj.* **1.** lasting all night. —*adv.* **2.** throughout the whole night.

night·ly (nīt'lĭ), *adj.* **1.** coming, occurring, appearing, or active at night: *nightly revels.* **2.** coming or occurring each night. **3.** of, pertaining to, or characteristic of night. **4.** *Obs. or Rare.* resembling night. —*adv.* **5.** at or by night. **6.** every night: *performances given nightly.*

night·mare (nīt'mâr'), *n.* **1.** a condition during sleep, or a dream, marked by a feeling of suffocation or distress, with acute fear, anxiety, or other painful emotion. **2.** a condition, thought, or experience suggestive of a nightmare in sleep. **3.** a monster or evil spirit formerly supposed to oppress persons during sleep. [ME. See NIGHT, MARE[2]] —**night/mar/ish,** *adj.*

night owl, *Colloq.* a person given to staying up late at night.

night raven, **1.** *Now Poetic.* a bird that cries in the night. **2.** a night heron.

night-rid·er (nīt'rī'dər), *n. Southern U.S.* one of a band of mounted men committing deeds of violence at night, as for purposes of intimidation or vengeance. —**night/rid/ing,** *n.*

night robe, nightgown.

nights (nīts), *adv. Now Colloq. or Dial.* at night.

night school, a school held at night, esp. for those who cannot attend a day school.

night·shade (nīt'shād'), *n.* **1.** any of various plants of the genus *Solanum,* esp. *S. nigrum* (**black nightshade**) or *S. Dulcamara* (**woody nightshade,** or bittersweet). **2.** any of various other solanaceous plants, as the **deadly nightshade** (belladonna) or the **stinking nightshade** (henbane). [ME; OE *nihtscada.* See NIGHT, SHADE]

night·shirt (nīt'shûrt'), *n.* a knee-length shirt or loose garment worn in bed by men or boys.

night soil, the contents of privies, etc., removed at night and used as manure.

night stick, a heavy stick or long club carried by a policeman at night, and sometimes in the daytime.

night·time (nīt'tīm'), *n.* the time between evening and morning. Also, *Poetic,* **night·tide** (nīt'tīd').

night·walk·er (nīt'wô'kər), *n.* one who walks or roves about in the night, as a thief, a prostitute, etc.

night watch, **1.** a watch or guard kept during the night. **2.** the person or persons keeping such a watch. **3.** (*usually pl.*) a period or division of the night.

night·wear (nīt'wâr'), *n.* clothes for wearing in bed.

ni·gres·cent (nī grĕs'ənt), *adj.* blackish; somewhat black. [t. L: s. *nigrescens,* ppr., becoming black] —**ni·gres/cence,** *n.*

nig·ri·tude (nĭg'rə tūd', -tood'), *n.* **1.** blackness. **2.** something black. [t. L: m. *nigritūdo*]

ni·hil (nī'hĭl), *n.* nothing; a thing of no value. [t. L]

ni·hil·ism (nī'ə lĭz'əm), *n.* **1.** total disbelief in religion or moral principles and obligations, or in established laws and institutions. **2.** *Philos.* **a.** a belief that there is no objective basis of truth. **b.** an extreme form of skepticism, denying all real existence. **c.** nothingness or nonexistence. **3.** (*sometimes cap.*) the principles of a Russian revolutionary group, active in the latter half of the 19th century, holding that existing social and political institutions must be destroyed in order to clear the way for a new state of society, and in its extreme measures employing terrorism, assassination, etc. **4.** terrorism or revolutionary activity. [f. L *nihil* nothing + **-ISM**] —**ni/hil·ist,** *n.* —**ni/hil·is/tic,** *adj.*

ni·hil·i·ty (nī hĭl'ə tĭ), *n.* nothingness.

Ni·i·ga·ta (nyē'ē gä'tä), *n.* a seaport in central Japan, on NW Honshu island. 184,246 (1946).

Ni·jin·sky (nĭ zhĭn'skĭ; *Russ.* nĭ zhēn'-), *n.* **Waslaw** or **Vaslav** (väts'läf'), 1890-1950, Russian dancer.

Nij·me·gen (nī'mā'gən; *Du.* nī'mā'кнən), *n.* a city in E Netherlands, on the Waal river: peace treaty, 1678. 104,808 (est. 1946). Also, **Nimwegen.**

Ni·ke (nī'kē, nē'kā), *n. Gk. Myth.* **1.** the goddess of victory, called by the Romans Victoria and represented as a winged maiden, a palm branch in one hand and a garland in the other, or a fillet outstretched in both hands. **2.** the goddess Athena as the giver of victory.

Nik·ko (nyĭk'kô), *n.* a town in central Japan, on Honshu island: famous for its shrines and temples.

Ni·ko·la·ev (nĭ'kǒ lä'yĕf), *n.* a city in the SW Soviet Union, on the Bug river estuary. 167,108 (1939). Formerly, **Vernoleninsk.**

nil (nĭl), *n.* nothing. [t. L, contr. of *nihil*]

Nile (nīl), *n.* **1.** a river in E Africa, flowing N from Lake Victoria to the Mediterranean. 3473 mi. (from the headwaters of the Kagera river, ab. 4000 mi.). **2. Blue,** a tributary of the Nile, flowing from Lake Tana in Ethiopia into the Nile at Khartoum. **3. White,** a part of the Nile above Khartoum.

Nile blue, pale greenish blue.

Nile green, pale bluish green.

nil·gai (nĭl'gī), *n., pl.* **-gais,** (*esp. collectively*) **-gai.** a large East Indian antelope, *Boselaphus tragocamelus,* the male colored bluish-gray, the hornless female tawny. Also, **nylghau, nylghai.** [t. Hind.: lit., blue cow]

Nilgai,
Boselaphus tragocamelus
(4 ft. 4 in. to 4 ft. 8 in. high at the shoulder)

Nil·gi·ri Hills (nĭl'gĭ rĭ), a group of mountains in S India, in Madras province. Highest peak, Mt. Dodabetta, 8760 ft.

nill (nĭl), *v.t.*, *v.i.* *Archaic.* to be unwilling: *will he, nill he.* [ME *nille(n)*, OE *nyllan*, f. *ne* not + *willan* will]

Ni·lom·e·ter (nī lŏm′ə tər), *n.* a graduated column or the like used to measure the height of the floods of the Nile. [t. Gk.: m.s. *Neilométrion*]

Ni·lot·ic (nī lŏt′ĭk), *adj.* of or pertaining to the river Nile or the inhabitants of the Nile region. [t. L: s. *Nīlóticus*, t. Gk.: m. *Neilōtikós*]

nil si·ne nu·mi·ne (nĭl sī′nĭ nū′mĭ nĭ), *Latin.* nothing without the divine will (motto of Colorado).

nim·ble (nĭm′bəl), *adj.*, **-bler, -blest. 1.** quick and light in movement; moving with celerity and ease; agile; active; rapid: *nimble feet.* **2.** quick in apprehending, devising, etc.: *nimble wits.* **3.** cleverly contrived. [ME *nymel*, repr. OE var. (unrecorded) of *numol* quick at taking, der. *niman* take] **—nim′ble·ness,** *n.* **—nim′bly,** *adv.*

nim·bo·stra·tus (nĭm′bō strā′təs), *n.* *Meteorol.* a low, formless cloud layer, of a nearly uniform dark gray; a layer type of rain cloud. [f. *nimbo-* (comb. form of NIMBUS) + STRATUS]

nim·bus (nĭm′bəs), *n.*, *pl.* **-bi** (-bī), **-buses. 1.** a bright cloud anciently conceived of as surrounding a deity of the classical mythology when appearing on earth. **2.** a cloud or atmosphere of some kind surrounding a person or thing. **3.** *Art.* a disk or otherwise shaped figure representing a radiance about the head of a divine or sacred personage, a medieval sovereign, etc. **4.** *Obs.* the type of cloud or cloudmass, dense, with ragged edges, which yields rain or snow; a rain cloud. [t. L: rainstorm, cloud]

Nîmes (nēm), *n.* a city in S France: famous Roman ruins. 104,109 (1946).

ni·mi·e·ty (nĭ mī′ə tĭ), *n.* excess. [t. LL: m.s. *nimietas*]

nim·i·ny-pim·i·ny (nĭm′ə nĭ pĭm′ə nĭ), *adj.* mincing; affectedly nice or refined. [imit. of a mincing utterance]

Nim·itz (nĭm′ĭts), *n.* **Chester William,** born 1885, U.S. admiral.

n'im·porte (năN pôrt′), *French.* it does not matter.

Nim·rod (nĭm′rŏd), *n.* **1.** *Bible.* a "mighty hunter," the great-grandson of Noah. Gen. 10:8, 9. **2.** one expert in or devoted to hunting.

Nim·we·gen (nĭm′vā′KHən), *n.* Nijmegen.

nin·com·poop (nĭn′kəm pōōp′), *n.* a fool or simpleton.

nine (nīn), *n.* **1.** a cardinal number, eight plus one. **2.** a symbol for this number, as 9 or IX or VIIII. **3.** a set of nine persons or things. **4.** a team of baseball players. **5.** a playing card with nine pips. **6. The Nine,** the nine Muses. **—adj. 7.** amounting to nine in number. [ME; OE *nigen*, var. of *nigon*, c. G *neun*]

nine·fold (nīn′fōld′), *adj.* **1.** nine times as much. **2.** having nine parts. **—adv. 3.** nine times as much.

nine·pence (nīn′pəns), *n.* **1.** the sum of nine English pennies. **2.** a coin of this value.

nine·pins (nīn′pĭnz′), *n.pl.* **1.** (construed as *sing.*) a game played with nine wooden pins at which a ball is bowled to knock them down. **2.** (construed as *pl.*) the pins used in this game. **3.** (construed as *sing.*) tenpins played without using a head pin.

nine·teen (nīn′tēn′), *n.* **1.** a cardinal number, ten plus nine. **2.** a symbol for this number, as 19 or XIX or XVIIII. **—adj. 3.** amounting to nineteen in number. [ME *nintene*, repr. d. OE var. (unrecorded) of OE *nigontȳne*] **—nine′teenth′,** *adj.*, *n.*

nine·ty (nīn′tĭ), *n.*, *pl.* **-ties,** *adj.* **—n. 1.** a cardinal number, ten times nine. **2.** a symbol for this number, as 90 or XC or LXXXX. **—adj. 3.** amounting to ninety in number [ME *nineti*, OE *nigontig*] **—nine·ti·eth** (nīn′tĭ ĭth), *adj.*, *n.*

Nin·e·veh (nĭn′ə və), *n.* the ancient capital of Assyria: its ruins are opposite Mosul, on the Tigris river, in N Iraq. See map under **Babylon.**

Ning·po (nĭng′pô′), *n.* a seaport in E China, in Chekiang province. 218,800 (est. 1937).

Ning·sia (nĭng′shyä′), *n.* a province in NW China, in W Inner Mongolia. 723,700 pop. (est. 1944); 106,143 sq. mi. *Cap.:* Ningsia.

nin·ny (nĭn′ĭ), *n.*, *pl.* **-nies.** a fool; a simpleton.

ninth (nīnth), *adj.* **1.** next after the eighth. **2.** being one of nine equal parts. **—n. 3.** a ninth part, esp. one (1/9). **4.** the ninth member of a series. **5.** *Music.* **a.** a tone distant from another tone by an interval of an octave and a second. **b.** the interval between such tones. **c.** harmonic combination of such tones. **—ninth′ly,** *adv.*

ninth chord, *Music.* a chord formed by the superposition of four thirds.

Ni·nus (nī′nəs), *n.* *Gk. Legend.* the legendary founder of Nineveh: husband of Semiramis.

Ni·o·be (nī′ō bē′), *n.* *Gk. Myth.* the daughter of Tantalus and wife of Amphion of Thebes. She provoked Apollo and Artemis to vengeance by taunting their mother Leto with the number and beauty of her own children. Niobe's children were slain and after Zeus turned her into stone she continued to weep for them.

ni·o·bi·um (nī ō′bĭ əm), *n.* *Chem.* columbium. *Abbr.:* Nb. [t. NL; named after *Niobe*, daughter of Tantalus, because found with tantalum. See -IUM] **—ni·o·bic** (nī ō′bĭk, -ŏb′ĭk), **ni·o·bous** (nī ō′bəs), *adj.*

Ni·o·brar·a (nī′ə brär′ə), *n.* a river flowing from E Wyoming E through Nebraska to the Missouri. 431 mi.

nip[1] (nĭp), *v.*, **nipped, nipping,** *n.* **—v.t. 1.** to compress sharply between two surfaces or points; pinch or bite.

2. to take off by pinching, biting, or snipping (usually fol. by *off*). **3.** to check in growth or development: *to nip a plot.* **4.** to affect sharply and painfully or injuriously, as cold does. **5.** *Slang.* to snatch or take suddenly or quickly (fol. by *away, up,* etc.). **6.** *Slang.* to steal. **—v.i. 7.** *Brit. Colloq.* to move or go suddenly or quickly, or slip (fol. by *away, off, up,* etc.). **—n. 8.** the act of nipping; a pinch. **9.** a sharp or biting remark. **10.** a biting quality, as in cold or frosty air. **11.** sharp cold; a sharp touch of frost. **12.** the biting taste or tang in cheese. **13.** a small bit or quantity of anything. [ME *nyp(pen)*; akin to obs. *nipe*, c. D *nijpen*]

nip[2] (nĭp), *n.*, *v.*, **nipped, nipping. —n. 1.** a small drink of liquor; a sip. **2.** a small tankard of ale, about a half pint. **—v.t., v.i. 3.** to drink (liquor) in small sips, esp. repeatedly. [short for *nipperkin*, ? t. D or LG]

ni·pa (nē′pə, nĭ′pə), *n.* **1.** a palm, *Nipa fruticans,* of the East Indies, the Philippines, etc., whose foliage is much used for thatching, etc. **2.** the foliage itself. **3.** a thatch made of the foliage. [t. Malay: m. *nīpah*]

nip and tuck, *U.S.* (in a race or other contest) with one competitor equaling the speed or efforts of the other.

Nip·i·gon (nĭp′ə gŏn′), *n.* a lake in S Canada, in Ontario, N of Lake Superior. 1730 sq. mi.

Nip·is·sing (nĭp′ə sĭng), *n.* a lake in SE Canada, in Ontario, N of Georgian Bay. 330 sq. mi.

nip·per (nĭp′ər), *n.* **1.** one who or that which nips. **2.** (usually *pl.*) a device for nipping, as pincers or forceps. **3.** one of the large claws of a crustacean. **4.** (*pl.*) *Slang.* handcuffs. **5.** *Brit. Colloq.* a small boy.

nip·ping (nĭp′ĭng), *adj.* **1.** that nips. **2.** sharp or biting, as cold, etc. **3.** sarcastic. **—nip′ping·ly,** *adv.*

nip·ple (nĭp′əl), *n.* **1.** a protuberance of the mamma or breast where, in the female, the milk ducts discharge; a teat. **2.** something resembling it, as the mouthpiece of a nursing bottle. **3.** a short piece of pipe with threads on each end, used for joining valves, etc. [orig. uncert.]

Nip·pon (nĭp′pŏn′, nĭp′ŏn), *n.* Japanese name of **Japan.**

Nip·pon·ese (nĭp′ə nēz′, -nēs′), *n.*, *pl.* **-ese,** *adj.* Japanese. [f. *Nippon,* native name for Japan, + -ESE]

Nip·pur (nĭp pŏŏr′), *n.* an ancient city of Babylonia.

nip·py (nĭp′ĭ), *adj.* **-pier, -piest. 1.** apt to nip; sharp; biting. **2.** *Chiefly Brit. Colloq.* nimble; active.

nir·va·na (nĭr vä′na, -văn′ə, nər-), *n.* **1.** (often *cap.*) *Buddhism.* **a.** the extinguishment of the restlessness and heat of one's emotions. **b.** the passionless peace of imperturbability, attained through the annihilation of disturbing desires. **2.** freedom from pain, worry, and the external world. [t. Skt.: a blowing out (as of a light)]

Niš (nēsh), *n.* a city in E Yugoslavia: the capital of Serbia. 35,465 (1931). Also, **Nish.**

Ni·san (nī′săn; *Heb.* nē sän′), *n.* (in the Jewish calendar) the seventh month of the civil year and the first of the ecclesiastical year.

Ni·sei (nē′sā′), *n.*, *pl.* **-sei.** a person of Japanese descent, born in the U.S. and loyal to it. [t. Jap.]

Ni·sha·pur (nē′shä pŏŏr′), *n.* a town in NE Iran: the birthplace of Omar Khayyam. ab. 22,000.

ni·si (nī′sī), *conj.* unless (used esp. in law, as after *decree, order,* etc., to specify or suggest some contingency). [t. L]

ni·si pri·us (nī′sī prī′əs), *Law.* **1.** *U.S.* designating a court of first instance: *a nisi prius court.* **2.** *Brit.* unless before (a phrase formerly used in writs summoning the jurors to Westminster "unless before" that day justices came to the assizes). [t. L]

Nis·sen hut (nĭs′ən), a prefabricated shelter with the shape of a long, slightly flattened cylinder, insulated esp. for military troops in arctic regions; Quonset hut.

Nis·tru (nē′strōō), *n.* Rumanian name of **Dniester.**

ni·sus (nī′səs), *n.*, *pl.* **-sus.** effort; impulse. [t. L: effort]

nit (nĭt), *n.* **1.** the egg of a parasitic insect attached to a hair, or fiber of clothing, particularly the egg of a louse. **2.** the insect while young. [ME *nite,* OE *hnitu,* c. G *niss*]

ni·ter (nī′tər), *n.* **1.** nitrate of potassium, KNO_3. a white salt used in making gunpowder, etc.; saltpeter. **2.** nitrate of sodium, $NaNO_3$; Chile saltpeter. Also, *esp. Brit.,* **ni′tre.** [ME *nitre,* t. L: m. *nitrum,* t. Gk.: m. *nitron* natron, native sodium carbonate]

Ni·te·roi (nē′tĕ roi′), *n.* Nictheroy.

ni·ton (nī′tŏn), *n.* *Chem.* an early name for the element radon. *Symbol:* Nt [t. NL, der. L *nitēre* shine]

nitr-, var. of **nitro-,** before vowels.

ni·trate (nī′trāt), *n.*, *v.*, **-trated, -trating. —n. 1.** *Chem.* a salt or ester of nitric acid, or any compound containing the NO_3^{-1} radical. **2.** fertilizer consisting of potassium nitrate or sodium nitrate. **—v.t. 3.** to treat with nitric acid or a nitrate. **4.** to convert into a nitrate. [f. NITER + -ATE[2]] **—ni·tra′tion,** *n.*

ni·tric (nī′trĭk), *adj.* **1.** *Chem.* containing nitrogen, usually in the pentavalent state ($N+5$). **2.** of or pertaining to niter. [t. F: m. *nitrique.* See NITER, -IC]

nitric acid, a corrosive liquid, HNO_3, with powerful oxidizing properties.

nitric bacteria, nictrobacteria.

nitric oxide, a colorless gaseous compound of nitrogen and oxygen, NO, formed when copper is treated with dilute nitric acid.

ni·tride (nī′trīd, nī′trĭd), *n.* *Chem.* a compound, usually containing two elements only, of which the more electronegative one is nitrogen. Also, **ni·trid** (nī′trĭd). [f. NITER + -IDE]

ni·tri·fi·ca·tion (nī'trə fə kā'shən), n. **1.** act of nitrifying. **2.** the introduction of an NO_2 radical into an organic compound, usually by means of mixed nitric and sulfuric acids.

ni·tri·fy (nī'trə fī'), v.t., **-fied, -fying. 1.** to oxidize (ammonia compounds, etc.) to nitrites or nitrates, esp. by bacterial action. **2.** to impregnate (soil, etc.) with nitrates. **3.** to treat or combine with nitrogen or its compounds. **4.** *Obsolesc.* to convert into niter. [t. F: m. *nitrifier.* See NITER, -FY]

ni·trile (nī'trĭl, -trēl, -trīl), n. any of a class of organic compounds with the general formula RCN. Also, **ni·tril** (nī'trĭl). [f. NITR(OGEN) + -ILE]

ni·trite (nī'trīt), n. *Chem.* a salt of nitrous acid.

nitro-, *Chem.* **1.** a word element indicating the group NO_2. **2.** a misnomer for the nitrate group (NO_3), as in *nitrocellulose.* Also, **nitr-**. [t. Gk., comb. form of *nítron* native sodium carbonate]

ni·tro·bac·te·ri·a (nī'trō băk tĭr'ĭ ə), n.pl. certain bacteria of the soil, concerned in nitrifying processes.

ni·tro·ben·zene (nī'trō běn'zēn, -běn zēn'), n. *Chem.* a light-yellowish liquid, $C_6H_5NO_2$, a derivative of benzene, used in the manufacture of aniline.

ni·tro·cel·lu·lose (nī'trō sĕl'yə lōs'), n. cellulose nitrate.

ni·tro·gen (nī'trə jən), n. *Chem.* a colorless, odorless, gaseous element which forms about four fifths of the volume of the atmosphere and is present (combined) in animal and vegetable tissues chiefly in proteins. It is used in compounds, as fertilizer, in explosives, and in dyes. *Symbol:* N; *at. wt.:* 14.008; *at. no.:* 7. [t. F: m. *nitrogène.* See NITRO-, -GEN]

nitrogen fixation, 1. any process of combining free nitrogen from the air with other elements, either by chemical means or by bacterial action, used esp. in the preparation of fertilizers, industrial products, etc. **2.** this process as performed by bacteria (**nitrogen fixers**) found in the nodules of leguminous plants, which make the resulting nitrogenous compounds available to their host plants. **—ni·tro·gen-fix·ing** (nī'trə jən fĭk'sĭng), *adj.*

ni·tro·gen·ize (nī'trə jə nīz'), v.t., **-ized, -izing.** to combine with nitrogen or add nitrogenous material.

ni·trog·e·nous (nī trŏj'ə nəs), *adj.* containing nitrogen.

ni·tro·glyc·er·in (nī'trə glĭs'ər ĭn), n. a colorless, highly explosive oil, $C_3H_5(ONO_2)_3$, a principal constituent of dynamites and certain propellant and rocket powders: a nitration product of glycerin. Also, **ni·tro·glyc·er·ine** (nī'trə glĭs'ər ĭn, -ə rēn').

nitro group, the univalent $-NO_2$ radical.

ni·trol·ic (nī trŏl'ĭk), *adj. Chem.* of or denoting a series of acids of the type, RC(:NOH)NO_2, whose salts form deep-red solutions. [f. NITR- + -OL[1] + -IC]

ni·trom·e·ter (nī trŏm'ə tər), n. an apparatus for determining the amount of nitric acid or nitrates in a substance or mixture. [f. NITRO- + -METER]

ni·tro·par·af·fin (nī'trō par'ə fĭn), n. *Chem.* any of a class of compounds derived from the methane series replacing a hydrogen atom by the nitro group.

ni·tros·a·mine (nī trōs'ə mēn', nī'trōs ăm'ĭn), n. *Chem.* any of a series of oily compounds with the type formula R_2NNO. Also, **ni·tros·am·in** (nī'trōs ăm'ĭn).

ni·tro·syl (nī trō'sĭl, nī'trə sēl', nī'trə sĭl), n. *Chem.* the radical NO-. [f. *nitroso-* (comb. form repr. NL *nitrōsus* NITROUS) + -YL]

ni·trous (nī'trəs), *adj. Chem.* **1.** pertaining to compounds obtained from niter, usually containing less oxygen than the corresponding nitric compounds. **2.** containing nitrogen, usually trivalent (N[+3]). [t. NL: m.s. *nitrōsus* nitrous, L full of natron. See NITER]

nitrous acid, an acid, HNO_2, known only in solution.

nitrous bacteria, nitrobacteria which convert ammonia derivatives into nitrites by oxidation.

nitrous oxide, laughing gas.

Nit·ti (nēt'tē), n. **Francesco Saverio** (frän chĕs'kô sä vě'ryô), born 1868, Italian statesman and publicist.

nit·ty (nĭt'ĭ), *adj.* full of nits.

nit·wit (nĭt'wĭt'), n. a slow-witted or foolish person.

Ni·u·e (nĭ ōō'ā), n. an island in the S Pacific between the Tonga and Cook islands: a possession of New Zealand. 4200 pop. (est. 1944); ab. 100 sq. mi. Also, **Savage Island.**

Ni·ver·nais (nē vĕr nĕ'), n. a former province in central France. *Cap.:* Nevers.

Ni·vôse (nē vōz'), n. (in the French Revolutionary calendar) the fourth month of the year. [t. F, t. L: m.s. *nivōsus* snowy]

nix[1] (nĭks), *Slang.* —n. **1.** nothing. —adv. **2.** no. —interj. **3.** (used as a signal warning of someone's approach): *nix, the cops!* [t. G, var. of *nichts* nothing]

nix[2] (nĭks), n., pl. **nixes.** *Folklore.* a water spirit, usually small, and either good or bad. [t. G, var. of *nichs,* OHG *nichus,* c. OE *nicor* fabulous sea monster] —**nix·ie** (nĭk'sĭ), n. fem.

Ni·zam (nĭ zăm', nĭ zäm'), n. **1.** the title of the ruler of Hyderabad, India. **2.** (l.c.) a soldier of the Turkish regular army. [t. Hind. and Turk.]

Nizh·ni Nov·go·rod (nēzh'nĭ nŏv'gŏ rŏt), former name of Gorki.

Nizhni Ta·gil (tä gēl'), a city in the W Soviet Union in Asia, on the E slope of the Ural Mts. 159,864 (1939).

N.J., New Jersey.

Njord (nyôrd), n. *Scand. Myth.* the father of Frey and Freya: the dispenser of riches. Also, **Njorth** (nyôrth).

NL, New Latin or Neo-Latin. Also, **NL., N.L.**

n.l., 1. *Print.* new line. **2.** (L *non licet*) it is not permitted. **3.** (L *non liquet*) it is not clear or evident.

N. Lat., north latitude. Also, **N. lat.**

NLRB, National Labor Relations Board.

N.M., New Mexico. Also, **N. Mex.**

NNE, north-northeast. Also, **N.N.E.**

NNW, north-northwest. Also, **N.N.W.**

no[1] (nō), *adv., n., pl.* **noes,** *adj.* —*adv.* **1.** a word used: **a.** to express dissent, denial, or refusal, as in response (opposed to *yes*). **b.** to emphasize a previous negative or qualify a previous statement. **2.** not in any degree; not at all (used with a comparative): *he is no better.* **3.** not: *whether or no.* —n. **4.** an utterance of the word "no." **5.** a denial or refusal. **6.** a negative vote or voter. —*adj.* **7.** not any: *no money.* **8.** not at all; very far from being; not at all a: *he is no genius.* [ME; OE *nā* (c. Icel. *nei*), f. *ne* not + *ā* ever]

no[2] (nō), n., pl. **no.** a type of Japanese drama, originally religious, with dancing and singing. [t. Jap.]

No., 1. north. **2.** northern. **3.** number. Also, **no.**

No·a·chi·an (nō ā'kĭ ən), *adj.* **1.** of or pertaining to the patriarch Noah or his time: *the Noachian deluge.* **2.** extremely ancient. Also, **No·ach·ic** (nō ăk'ĭk, -ā'kĭk).

No·ah (nō'ə), n. a Hebrew patriarch, the builder of **Noah's Ark,** in which with his family and animals of every species, he survived the deluge. Gen. 5–9. [t. Heb.]

nob[1] (nŏb), n. **1.** *Slang.* the head. **2.** *Cribbage.* the knave of the same suit as the card turned up, counting one to the holder. [? var. of KNOB]

nob[2] (nŏb), n. *Brit. Slang.* a person of wealth or social distinction. [? special use of NOB[1]]

no-ball (nō'bôl'), n. *Cricket.* an unfairly thrown ball.

nob·ble (nŏb'əl), v.t., **-bled, -bling.** *Brit. Slang.* **1.** to disable (a horse), as by drugging it. **2.** to win (a person, etc.) over by underhand means. **3.** to swindle. **4.** to catch. [back formation from *nobbler,* var. of HOBBLER (an 'obbler being taken as a *nobbler*)] —**nob'bler,** n.

nob·by (nŏb'ĭ), *adj.,* **-bier, -biest.** *Chiefly Brit. Slang.* **1.** fashionable or elegant. **2.** first-rate. [f. NOB[2] + -Y[1]]

No·bel (nō bĕl'), n. **Alfred Bernhard** (ăl'frĕd bär'närd), 1833–96, Swedish inventor of dynamite and manufacturer of explosives: established Nobel prizes.

Nobel prizes, prizes awarded annually from the bequest of Alfred B. Nobel for achievement during the preceding year in physics, chemistry, medicine, literature, and the promotion of peace.

no·bil·i·ar·y (nō bĭl'ĭ ĕr'ĭ), *adj.* of or pertaining to the nobility. [t. F: m. *nobiliaire,* der. L *nōbilis* noble]

no·bil·i·ty (nō bĭl'ə tĭ), n., pl. **-ties. 1.** the noble class, or the body of nobles, in a country or state. **2.** (in Great Britain and Ireland) the peerage. **3.** the state or quality of being noble. **4.** noble birth or rank. **5.** exalted moral excellence. **6.** grandeur. [ME *nobilite,* t. OF, t. L: m.s. *nōbilitas*]

no·ble (nō'bəl), *adj.,* **nobler, noblest,** n. —*adj.* **1.** distinguished by birth, rank, or title. **2.** pertaining to persons so distinguished: *noble birth.* **3.** belonging to or constituting a class (the nobility) possessing a hereditary social or political preëminence in a country or state. **4.** of an exalted moral character or excellence: *a noble thought.* **5.** admirable in dignity of conception, or in the manner of expression, execution, or composition: *a noble poem.* **6.** imposing in appearance; stately; magnificent: *a noble monument.* **7.** of an admirably high quality; notably superior. **8.** *Chem.* inert; chemically inactive. **9.** (of some metals, as gold and platinum) that are not altered on exposure to the air, do not rust easily, and are much scarcer and more valuable than the so-called useful metals. **10.** *Falconry.* denoting the long-winged falcons which stoop to the quarry at a single swoop (opposed to *ignoble*). —n. **11.** a person of noble birth or rank; a nobleman. **12.** an old English gold coin, formerly current, for 6 shillings, 8 pence. **13.** (in Great Britain and Ireland) a peer. [ME, t. OF, g. L *nōbilis* well-known, highborn] —**no'ble·ness,** n.

—**Syn. 4.** NOBLE, HIGH-MINDED, MAGNANIMOUS agree in referring to lofty principles and loftiness of mind or spirit. NOBLE implies a loftiness of character or spirit that scorns the petty, mean, base, or dishonorable: *a noble deed.* HIGH-MINDED implies having elevated principles and consistently adhering to them: *a high-minded devotion to ideals.* MAGNANIMOUS suggests greatness of mind or soul, esp. as manifested in generosity or in overlooking injuries: *magnanimous toward his former enemies.* —**Ant. 4.** base, mean.

no·ble·man (nō'bəl mən), n., pl. **-men,** a man of noble birth or rank; a noble. —**no'ble·wom'an,** n. fem.

no·blesse (nō blĕs'), n. **1.** noble birth or condition. **2.** the nobility. [ME, t. OF, der. L *nōbilis* noble]

no·blesse o·blige (nō blĕs' ô blēzh'), *French.* noble rank requires honorable conduct.

no·bly (nō'blĭ), *adv.* **1.** in a noble manner. **2.** courageously. **3.** splendidly; superbly. **4.** of noble ancestry.

no·bod·y (nō'bŏd'ĭ, -bəd'ĭ), n., pl. **-bodies. 1.** no person. **2.** a person of no importance, esp. socially.

no·cent (nō'sənt), *adj. Now Rare.* **1.** hurtful; harmful; injurious. **2.** guilty. [t. L: m.s. *nocens,* ppr., harming]

nock (nŏk), n. **1.** a metal or plastic piece at the end of an arrow. **2.** a notch or groove at the end of an arrow into which the bowstring fits. **3.** a notch or groove at each end of the bow, to hold the bowstring in place. —*v.t.* **4.** to furnish (a bow or an arrow) with a nock. **5.** to adjust (the arrow) to the bowstring, in readiness to shoot. [ME *nocke*; ? t. D: m. *nok*, or LG: m. *nokk* tip or projection]

noc·tam·bu·lism (nŏk tăm′byə lῐz′əm), *n.* somnambulism. Also, **noc·tam′bu·la′tion.** [f. s. L *nox* night + s. *ambulāre* walk about + -ISM] **—noc·tam′bu·list,** *n.*

nocti-, a word element meaning "night." [t. L, comb. form of *nox*]

noc·ti·lu·ca (nŏk′tə lōō′kə), *n., pl.* **-cae** (-sē). a pelagic flagellate protozoan, genus *Noctiluca,* notable for its phosphorescence. [t. L: something that shines by night]

noc·ti·lu·cent (nŏk′tə lōō′sənt), *adj. Meteorol.* (of clouds) very high and cirruslike, visible during the short night of summer and believed to be of meteor dust shining with reflected sunlight.

noc·tu·id (nŏk′chŏŏ ῐd), *n.* **1.** any of the *Noctuidae,* a large family of dull-colored moths, the larvae of which include the highly injurious army worms and cutworms. —*adj.* **2.** belonging or pertaining to the *Noctuidae.* [t. NL: s. *Noctua* night owl]

noc·tule (nŏk′chōōl), *n.* a large reddish insectivorous bat, *Nyctalus noctula,* common to Europe and Asia. [t. F, t. It.: m. *nottola* bat, der. *notte* night, g. L *nox*]

noc·tur·nal (nŏk tûr′nəl), *adj.* **1.** of or pertaining to the night. **2.** done, occurring, or coming by night. **3.** active by night, as many animals. **4.** opening by night and closing by day, as certain flowers. [late ME, t. LL: s. *nocturnālis,* der. L *nocturnus* of or in the night] **—noc·tur′nal·ly,** *adv.*

noc·turne (nŏk′tûrn), *n. Music.* **1.** a piece appropriate to the night or evening. **2.** an instrumental composition of a dreamy or pensive character. [t. F, t. LL: m. *nocturna* (fem.) of the night]

noc·u·ous (nŏk′yŏŏ əs), *adj.* injurious; noxious: *nocuous vapors.* [t. L: m. *nocuus*] **—noc′u·ous·ly,** *adv.* **—noc′u·ous·ness,** *n.*

nod (nŏd), *v.,* **nodded, nodding.** —*v.i.* **1.** to make a slight, quick inclination of the head, as in assent, greeting, command, etc. **2.** to let the head fall forward with a sudden, involuntary movement when sleepy. **3.** to grow careless, inattentive, or dull. **4.** (of trees, flowers, plumes, etc.) to droop, bend, or incline with a swaying motion. —*v.t.* **5.** to incline (the head) in a short, quick movement, as of assent, greeting, etc. **6.** to express or signify by such a movement of the head: *to nod assent.* **7.** to summon, bring, or send by a nod of the head. **8.** to incline or cause to lean or sway. —*n.* **9.** a short, quick inclination of the head, as in assent, greeting, command, or drowsiness. **10.** a nap. **11.** a bending or swaying movement of anything. [ME, orig. obscure] **—nod′der,** *n.*

nod·al (nō′dəl), *adj.* pertaining to or of the nature of a node.

nod·dle[1] (nŏd′əl), *n. Colloq. and Humorous.* the head. [ME *nodel, nodul;* orig. uncert.]

nod·dle[2] (nŏd′əl), *v.t., v.i.,* **-dled, -dling.** to make light frequent nods. [freq. of NOD]

nod·dy (nŏd′ῐ), *n., pl.* **-dies. 1.** a white capped darkbrown tern, *Anous stolidus,* of warm seacoasts of both the New and the Old World common in the West Indies, usually so fearless of man as to seem stupid. **2.** a fool or simpleton. [t. use of *noddy,* adj., silly; orig. uncert.]

node (nōd), *n.* **1.** a knot, protuberance, or knob. **2.** a complication; difficulty. **3.** a centering point of component parts. **4.** *Bot.* **a.** a joint in a stem. **b.** a part of a stem which normally bears a leaf. **5.** *Geom.* a point on a curve or surface, at which there can be more than one tangent line or plane. **6.** *Physics.* a point, line, or region in a vibrating medium at which there is comparatively no variation of the disturbance which is being transmitted through the medium. **7.** *Astron.* either of the two points at which the orbit of a heavenly body cuts the plane of the ecliptic, equator, or other properly defined plane (that passed as the body goes to the north being called the **ascending node,** and that passed as it goes to the south being called the **descending node**). **8.** *Pathol.* circumscribed swelling. [t. L: m.s. *nōdus* knot]

N, Node on stem of polygonum

nod·i·cal (nŏd′ə kəl, nō′də-), *adj. Astron.* of or pertaining to the nodes: *the nodical month.*

no·dose (nō′dōs, nō dōs′), *adj.* having nodes. [t. L: m.s. *nōdōsus*] **—no·dos·i·ty** (nō dŏs′ə tῐ), *n.*

no·dous (nō′dəs), *adj.* full of knots. [t. L: m.s. *nōdōsus*]

nod·u·lar (nŏj′ə lər), *adj.* having, relating to, or shaped like nodules.

nod·ule (nŏj′ōōl), *n.* **1.** a small node, knot, or knob. **2.** a small rounded mass or lump. **3.** *Bot.* a tubercle. [t. L: m.s. *nōdulus,* dim. of *nōdus* node]

nod·u·lous (nŏj′ə ləs), *adj.* having nodules. Also, **nod·u·lose** (nŏj′ə lōs′), *adj.*

no·dus (nō′dəs), *n., pl.* **-di** (-dī). a difficult or intricate point, situation, plot, etc. [t. L: a knot]

No·el (nō ĕl′), *n.* **1.** Christmas. **2.** (*l.c.*) a Christmas song or carol. [t. F: *noël* Christmas carol, *Noël,* Christmas, g. L *nātālis* birthday, orig. adj.]

no·e·sis (nō ē′sῐs), *n.* **1.** *Philos.* a thing grasped by the intellect alone. **2.** *Psychol.* cognition; the functioning of the intellect. [t. Gk.: a perception]

no·et·ic (nō ĕt′ῐk), *adj.* **1.** of or pertaining to the mind. **2.** originating in and apprehended by the reason.

nog[1] (nŏg), *n.* **1.** *U.S.* any beverage made with beaten eggs, usually with alcoholic liquor; eggnog. **2.** a kind of strong ale. Also, **nogg.** [orig. uncert.]

nog[2] (nŏg), *n.* **1.** a brick-shaped piece of wood built into a wall. **2.** any wooden peg, pin, or block. [orig. uncert.; ? var. of obs. *knag,* ME *knagge* spur, peg]

nog·gin (nŏg′ῐn), *n.* **1.** a small cup or mug. **2.** a small amount of liquor, usually a gill.

nog·ging (nŏg′ῐng), *n. Brit.* brickwork serving to fill the interstices in a wooden frame. [f. NOG[2] + -ING[1]]

No·gu·chi (nō gōō′chῐ; *Jap.* nô′gōō chē′), *n.* **Hideyo** (hē′dē yō′), 1876–1928, Japanese physician and bacteriologist in America.

no·how (nō′hou′), *adv.* (in substandard use) in no manner; not at all.

noil (noil), *n.* a short fiber of wool or silk separated from the long fibers in combing.

noise (noiz), *n., v.,* **noised, noising.** —*n.* **1.** sound, esp. of a loud, harsh, or confused kind: *deafening noises.* **2.** *Physics.* the combination of a nonharmonious group of frequencies of very short duration. **3.** a sound of any kind. **4.** loud shouting, outcry, or clamor. **5.** *Archaic.* rumor. —*v.t.* **6.** to spread the report or rumor of. **7.** to spread (a report, rumor, etc.). —*v.i.* **8.** to talk much or publicly (fol. by *of.*). **9.** to make a noise, outcry, or clamor. [ME, t. OF, g. L *nausea* seasickness] **—Syn. 1.** NOISE, CLAMOR, DIN, HUBBUB, RACKET refer to (usually loud) unmusical or confused sounds. NOISE is the general word, though it may apply to soft, confused sounds as well: *street noises.* CLAMOR and HUBBUB are alike in referring to loud noises resulting from shouting, cries, animated or excited tones and the like; but in CLAMOR the emphasis is on the meaning of the shouting, and in HUBBUB the emphasis is on the confused mingling of sounds: *the clamor of an angry crowd, his voice could be heard above the hubbub.* DIN suggests a loud, resonant noise, painful if long continued: *the din of a boiler works.* RACKET suggests a loud, confused noise of the kind produced by clatter or percussion: *she always makes such a racket when she cleans up the dishes.* **3.** See **sound**[1].

noise·less (noiz′lῐs), *adj.* making, or attended with, no noise; silent; quiet: *a noiseless step.* **—noise′less·ly,** *adv.* **—noise′less·ness,** *n.* **—Syn.** See **still**[1].

noise·mak·er (noiz′mā′kər), *n.* a person or thing that makes noise, esp. a device used on Hallowe'en, New Year's Eve, etc.

noi·some (noi′səm), *adj.* **1.** offensive or disgusting, often as to odor. **2.** harmful, injurious, or noxious. [ME, f. obs. or prov. *noy* (aphetic var. of ANNOY) + -SOME[1]] **—noi′some·ly,** *adv.* **—noi′some·ness,** *n.*

nois·y (noi′zῐ), *adj.,* **noisier, noisiest. 1.** making much noise: *a noisy crowd.* **2.** abounding in noise: *a noisy street.* **—nois′i·ly,** *adv.* **—nois′i·ness,** *n.* **—Syn. 1.** See **loud.**

no·lens vo·lens (nō′lĕnz vō′lĕnz), *Latin.* willy-nilly.

no·li-me-tan·ge·re (nō′lῐ mē tăn′jə rῐ), *n. Latin.* **1.** one who or that which must not be touched or interfered with. **2.** a picture representing Jesus appearing to Mary Magdalene after his resurrection. John 20:17. **3.** the touch-me-not. [L: touch me not]

nol·le pros·e·qui (nŏl′ῐ prŏs′ə kwī′), *Law.* an entry made upon the records of a court when the plaintiff or prosecutor will proceed no further in a suit or action. [L: to be unwilling to pursue (prosecute)]

no·lo con·ten·de·re (nō′lō kən tĕn′də rῐ), *Law.* a defendant's pleading which does not admit guilt but which subjects him to punishment as though he had pleaded guilty, the determination of guilt remaining open in other proceedings. [L: I am unwilling to contend]

nol. pros., nolle prosequi.

nol-pros (nŏl′prŏs′), *v.t.,* **-prossed, -prossing.** *Law.* to determine by a nolle prosequi.

nom., nominative.

no·ma (nō′mə), *n. Pathol.* a gangrenous ulceration of the mouth and cheeks (and sometimes other parts), occurring mainly in debilitated children. [t. NL, t. Gk.: m. *nomē* a corroding sore]

no·mad (nō′măd, nŏm′ăd), *n.* **1.** one of a race or tribe without fixed abode, but moving about from place to place according to the state of the pasturage or food supply. **2.** any wanderer. —*adj.* **3.** nomadic. [t. L: s. *nomas,* t. Gk.: roaming (like cattle)] **—no′mad·ism,** *n.*

no·mad·ic (nō măd′ῐk), *adj.* of, pertaining to, or characteristic of nomads. **—no·mad′i·cal·ly,** *adv.*

no man's land, a tract of land under dispute, as one between opposing lines of trenches in war.

nom·arch (nŏm′ärk), *n.* the governor of a nome or a nomarchy. [t. Gk.: s. *nomárchēs*]

nom·ar·chy (nŏm′är kῐ), *n., pl.* **-chies.** one of the provinces into which modern Greece is divided.

nom·bles (nŭm′bəlz), *n.pl. Archaic.* numbles.

nom·bril (nŏm′brῐl), *n. Her.* the point in an escutcheon between the middle of the base and the fess point. See diag. under **escutcheon.**

nom de guerre (nôN də gĕr′), *French.* an assumed name; pseudonym. [F: war name]

nom de plume (nŏm′ də plōōm′; *Fr.* nôN də plŷm′), pen name. [coined in E from F words; lit., pen name]

nome (nōm), *n.* **1.** one of the provinces of ancient Egypt. **2.** nomarchy. [t. Gk.: m.s. *nomós* territorial division]

Nome (nōm), *n*. **1.** a seaport in W Alaska. 1852 (prelim. 1950). **2. Cape,** a cape on Seward Peninsula, W of Nome.

no·men·cla·tor (nō′mən klā′tər), *n*. **1.** one who calls or announces things or persons by their names. **2.** one who assigns names, as in scientific classification. [t. L]

no·men·cla·ture (nō′mən klā′chər, nō měn′klə-), *n*. **1.** a set or system of names or terms, as those used in a particular science or art, by an individual or community, etc. **2.** the names or terms forming a set or system. [t. L: m. *nōmenclātūra*]

nom·i·nal (nŏm′ə nəl), *adj*. **1.** being such in name only; so-called: *nominal peace*. **2.** (of a price, consideration, etc.) named as a mere matter of form, being trifling in comparison with the actual value. **3.** of, pertaining to, or consisting in a name or names. **4.** *Gram.* **a.** of, pertaining to, or producing a noun or nouns. **b.** used as or like a noun. **5.** assigned to a person by name: *nominal shares of stock*. **6.** containing, bearing, or giving a name or names. [ME, t. L: s. *nōminālis* pertaining to names]

nom·i·nal·ism (nŏm′ə nə lĭz′əm), *n*. *Philos.* the doctrine that universals are reducible to names without any objective existence corresponding to them. In the strict sense, there are no universals either in the mind or in the external world but words operate as symbols. It shades into conceptualism. **—nom′i·nal·ist,** *n*., *adj*. **—nom′i·nal·is′tic,** *adj*.

nom·i·nal·ly (nŏm′ə nə lĭ), *adv*. in a nominal manner; by or as regards name; in name; only in name; ostensibly.

nominal value, book or par value of a stock certificate; face value.

nominal wages, *Econ.* wages measured in terms of money and not by their ability to command goods and services. Cf. **real wages.**

nom·i·nate (*v*. nŏm′ə nāt′; *adj*. nŏm′ə nĭt), *v*., **-nat·ed, -nating,** *adj*. **—v.t. 1.** to propose as a proper person for appointment or election to an office. **2.** to appoint for a duty or office. **3.** *Rare.* to entitle; name. **4.** *Obs.* to specify. **—adj. 5.** having a particular name. [t. L: m.s. *nōminātus*, pp., named] **—nom′i·na′tor,** *n*.

nom·i·na·tion (nŏm′ə nā′shən), *n*. **1.** act of nominating, esp. to office. *the nomination of candidates for the governorship.* **2.** state of being nominated.

nom·i·na·tive (nŏm′ə nə tĭv, -nā′tĭv, nŏm′nə-), *adj*. **1.** *Gram.* **a.** denoting a case which by its form, position, or function indicates that it serves as the subject of a finite verb, as in Latin *nauta bonus est* "the sailor is good," *nauta* "sailor" is in the nominative case. **b.** similar to such a case form in function or meaning. **2.** nominated; appointed by nomination. **—n. 3.** *Gram.* the nominative case, a word in that case, or a form or construction of similar function or meaning. [t. L: m.s. *nōminātīvus* serving to name; r. ME *nominatif*, t. OF]

nominative absolute, *Gram.* a group of words including a substantive together with a participial modifier, not grammatically related to any other element in the sentence.

nominative of address, *Gram.* a noun naming the person to whom one is speaking. See **vocative.**

nom·i·nee (nŏm′ə nē′), *n*. one nominated, as to fill an office or stand for election. [f. NOMIN(ATE) + -EE]

no·mism (nō′mĭz əm), *n*. conduct in a religion based on a law or laws. [f. s. Gk. *nómos* law + -ISM] **—no·mis′tic,** *adj*.

no·mog·ra·phy (nō mŏg′rə fĭ), *n*. the art of drawing up laws. [t. Gk.: m. *nomographía* a writing of laws]

no·mol·o·gy (nō mŏl′ə jĭ), *n*. **1.** the science of law or laws. **2.** the science of the laws of the mind. [f. *nomo-* (t. Gk., comb. form of *nómos* law) + -LOGY] **—nom·o·log·i·cal** (nŏm′ə lŏj′ə kəl), *adj*.

no·mos (nō′mŏs), *n*. *Greek.* nome.

nom·o·thet·ic (nŏm′ə thět′ĭk), *adj*. **1.** lawgiving; legislative. **2.** nomistic. **3.** *Psychol.* pertaining to the search for general laws (opposed to *idiographic*). Also, **nom′o·thet′i·cal.** [t. Gk.: m.s. *nomothetikós*]

No·mu·ra (nō′mōō rä′), *n*. **Kichisaburo** (kē′chē sä′bōō rō′), born 1877, Japanese diplomat.

-nomy, a final word element meaning "distribution," "arrangement," "management," of having reference to laws or government, as in *astronomy, autonomy, bionomy, economy, isonomy, taxonomy*. [t. Gk.: m.s. *-nomia*, der. *nómos* custom, law. See -IA]

non-, a prefix meaning "not," freely used as an English formative, usually with a simple negative force as implying mere negation or absence of something (rather than the opposite or reverse of it, as often expressed by un-[1]), as in *nonadherence, noninterference, nonpayment,*

nonprofessional. Cf. *unprofessional*, and many other words, mostly self-explanatory, and formed at will to meet the needs. [repr. L *nōn* not; not a L prefix]

non·age (nŏn′ĭj, nō′nĭj), *n*. **1.** the period of legal minority. **2.** any period of immaturity. [ME *nounage*, t. AF, f. *noun-* NON- + *age* AGE]

non·a·ge·nar·i·an (nŏn′ə jə när′ĭ ən, nō′nə jə-), *adj*. **1.** of the age of 90 years, or between 90 and 100 years old. **—n. 2.** a nonagenarian person. [f. s. L *nōnāgēnāriu*[?] containing ninety + -AN]

non·a·gon (nŏn′ə gŏn′), *n*. a polygon having nine angles and nine sides. [f. s. L *nōnus* ninth + -*agon* (after HEXAGON)]

Nonagon

non·ap·pear·ance (nŏn′ə pĭr′əns), *n*. failure or neglect to appear, as in a court.

nonce (nŏns), *n*. the one or particular occasion or purpose (chiefly in *for the nonce*). [ME *nones*, in phrase *for the nones*, orig., *for then one*(*s*), lit., for the once]

nonce word, a word coined and used only for the particular occasion.

non·cha·lance (nŏn′shə ləns, nŏn′shə läns′), *n*. the quality of being nonchalant; cool unconcern or indifference; casualness. [t. F, der. *nonchalant* NONCHALANT]

non·cha·lant (nŏn′shə lənt, nŏn′shə länt′), *adj*. coolly unconcerned, indifferent, or unexcited; casual. [t. F: f. *non* NON- + *chalant* (ppr. of *chaloir* have concern for, g. L *calēre* be hot)] **—non′cha·lant·ly,** *adv*.

non·col·le·giate (nŏn′kə lē′jĭt, -jĭ ĭt), *adj*. **1.** *Brit.* belonging to the body of students in a university not attached to any particular college or hall. **2.** below the level usually associated with college or university study. **3.** (of a university) not composed of colleges. **4.** not belonging to a college.

non·com (nŏn′kŏm′), *n*. *Colloq.* a noncommissioned officer.

noncom., noncommissioned.

non·com·bat·ant (nŏn kŏm′bə tənt), *n*. **1.** one who is not a combatant; a civilian in time of war. **2.** one connected with a military or naval force in some capacity other than that of a fighter, as a surgeon, a chaplain, etc.

non·com·mis·sioned (nŏn′kə mĭsh′ənd), *adj*. not commissioned (applied esp. to military officers, as sergeants and corporals, ranking below warrant officer).

non·com·mit·tal (nŏn′kə mĭt′əl), *adj*. not committing oneself, or not involving committal, to a particular view, course, or the like: *a noncommittal answer*.

non·com·mu·ni·cant (nŏn′kə mū′nə kənt), *n*. **1.** one who is not a communicant. **2.** one who does not communicate.

non·com·pli·ance (nŏn′kəm plī′əns), *n*. failure or refusal to comply.

non·com·pli·ant (nŏn′kəm plī′ənt), *n*. one who fails or refuses to comply.

non com·pos men·tis (nŏn kŏm′pəs měn′tĭs), *Latin.* not of sound mind; mentally incapable.

non·con·duc·tor (nŏn′kən dŭk′tər), *n*. a substance which does not readily conduct or transmit heat, sound, electricity, etc.; an insulator. **—non′con·duc′ting,** *adj*.

non·con·form·ance (nŏn′kən fôr′məns), *n*. lack of conformity.

non·con·form·ist (nŏn′kən fôr′mĭst), *n*. **1.** one who refuses to conform, as to an established church. **2.** (*often cap.*) one who refuses to conform to the Church of England. **—non′con·form′ing,** *adj*.

non·con·form·i·ty (nŏn′kən fôr′mə tĭ), *n*. **1.** lack of conformity or agreement. **2.** failure or refusal to conform, as to an established church. **3.** (*often cap.*) refusal to conform to the Church of England.

non·co·öp·er·a·tion (nŏn′kō ŏp′ə rā′shən), *n*. **1.** failure or refusal to coöperate. **2.** a method or practice, established in India by Gandhi, of showing opposition to acts or policies of the government by refusing to participate in civic and political life or to obey governmental regulations. **—non′co·öp′er·a′tive,** *adj*. **—non′co·öp′er·a′tor,** *n*.

non·de·script (nŏn′dĭ skrĭpt′), *adj*. **1.** of no recognized, definite, or particular type or kind: *a nondescript garment*. **—n. 2.** a person or a thing of no particular type or kind. [f. NON- + s. L *dēscriptus*, pp., described]

non·dis·junc·tion (nŏn′dĭs jŭngk′shən), *n*. *Biol.* the failure of chromosomes to follow normal separation into daughter cells at division.

none[1] (nŭn), *pron*. **1.** no one; not one: *there is none to help*. **2.** not any, as of something indicated: *that is none of your business*. **3.** no part; nothing. **4.** (construed as *pl.*) no, or not any, persons or things: *none come to the*

non′ab·sorb′ent	non·Cath′o·lic	non′con·sec′u·tive	non·cu′mu·la′tive
non′ac·cept′ance	non·cel′lu·lar	non′con·sent′	non′de·cep′tive
non′ad·ja′cent	non·cen′tral	non′con·se·quence′	non′de·cid′u·ous
non′ag·gres′sion	non·Chris′tian	non′con·serv′a·tive	non′de·liv′er·y
non′ag·gres′sive	non·civ′i·lized′	non′con·sti·tu′tion·al	non′dem·o·crat′ic
non′al·co·hol′ic	non·cler′i·cal	non′con·ta′gious	non′de·struc′tive
non′al·lel′ic	non′col·laps′i·ble	non′con·tem′po·rar′y	non′dir′i·gi·ble
non′a·quat′ic	non·com′bat	non′con·tin′u·ance	non′dis·crim′i·na′tion
non′as·sess′a·ble	non′com·bust′i·ble	non·con·tin′u·ous	non′dis·pos′al
non′as·sim′i·la′tion	non′com·mer′cial	non′con·tra·band′	non′dis·tinc′tive
non′at·tend′ance	non′com·mu′ni·ca·ble	non′con·tra·dic′to·ry	non′di·ver′gent
non′be·liev′er	non′com·pet′i·tive	non′cor·ro′sive	non′di·vis′i·ble
non′bel·lig′er·ent	non′com·pul′sion	non′crit′i·cal	non′dog·mat′ic
non·break′a·ble	non′con·du′cive	non′crys′tal·line	non′dra·mat′ic

b., blend of, blended; c., cognate with; d., dialect, dialectal; der., derived from; f., formed from; g., going back to; m., modification of; r., replacing; s., stem of; t., taken from; ?, perhaps. See the full key on inside cover.

feasts. —*adv.* **5.** to no extent; in no way; not at all: *the supply is none too great.* —*adj.* **6.** not any; no (in later use only before a vowel or *h*): *Thou shalt have none other gods before me.* [ME *non*, OE *nān*, f. *ne* not + *ān* one]

none² (nōn), *n.* sing. of **nones¹**.

non·ef·fec·tive (nŏn′ə fĕk′tĭv), *adj.* **1.** not effective. **2.** not fit for duty or active service, as a soldier or sailor. —*n.* **3.** a noneffective person.

non·e·go (nŏn ē′gō, -ĕg′ō), *n. Metaphys.* all that is not the ego or conscious self; the object as opposed to the subject.

non·en·ti·ty (nŏn ĕn′tə tĭ), *n.*, *pl.* **-ties. 1.** a person or thing of no importance. **2.** something which does not exist, or exists only in imagination. **3.** nonexistence. [f. NON- + ENTITY]

nones¹ (nōnz), *n. Eccles.* the fifth of the seven canonical hours, or the service for it, orig. fixed for the ninth hour of the day (or 3 P.M.). [pl. of NONE², OE *nōn*, t. L: s. *nōna* (*hōra*). See NOON]

nones² (nōnz), *n.pl, sing.* **none.** (in the ancient Roman calendar) the ninth day before the ides, both days included, thus being the 7th of March, May, July, and October, and the 5th of the other months. [ME, t. L: m. *nōnae*, orig. fem. pl. of *nōnus* ninth]

non·es·sen·tial (nŏn′ə sĕn′shəl), *adj.* **1.** not essential; not necessary: *nonessential use of gasoline.* —*n.* **2.** a nonessential thing or person.

none·such (nŭn′sŭch′), *n.* **1.** a person or thing without equal; a paragon. **2.** *Bot.* black medic. Also, **nonsuch.**

non·ex·ist·ence (nŏn′ĭg zĭs′təns), *n.* **1.** absence of existence. **2.** a thing that has no existence. —**non′·ex·ist′ent,** *adj.*

non·ex·por·ta·tion (nŏn′ĕks pōr tā′shən), *n.* failure or refusal to export.

non·fea·sance (nŏn fē′zəns), *n. Law.* the omission of some act which ought to have been performed.

non·ful·fill·ment (nŏn′fŏŏl fĭl′mənt), *n.* neglect or failure to fulfill.

non·har·mon·ic tone (nŏn′här mŏn′ĭk), *Music.* a tone sounding with a chord of which it is not a chord tone.

no·nil·lion (nō nĭl′yən), *n.* **1.** a cardinal number represented in the U.S. and France by one followed by 30 zeros, and, in Great Britain and Germany, by one followed by 54 zeros. —*adj.* **2.** amounting to one nonillion in number. [t. F: f. *non-* (t. L: s. *nōnus* ninth) + (*m*)*illion* million] —**no·nil′lionth,** *n.*, *adj.*

non·im·por·ta·tion (nŏn′ĭm pōr tā′shən), *n.* failure or refusal to import.

non·in·duc·tive (nŏn′ĭn dŭk′tĭv), *adj. Elect.* not inductive: *a noninductive resistance.*

non·in·ter·ven·tion (nŏn′ĭn tər vĕn′shən), *n.* **1.** abstention by a state from interference in the affairs of other states or in those of its own political subdivisions. **2.** failure or refusal to intervene.

non·join·der (nŏn join′dər), *n. Law.* omission to join, as of one who should have been a party to an action.

non·ju·ror (nŏn jŏŏr′ər), *n.* **1.** one who refuses to take a required oath, as of allegiance. **2.** (*often cap.*) one of those clergymen of the Church of England who in 1689 refused to swear allegiance to William and Mary.

non·le·gal (nŏn lē′gəl), *adj.* not (definitely) legal; having no legal aspect (distinguished from *illegal*): *a completely nonlegal controversy.*

non·met·al (nŏn′mĕt′əl), *n. Chem.* **1.** an element not having the character of a metal, as carbon, nitrogen, etc. **2.** an element incapable of forming simple positive ions in solution.

non·me·tal·lic (nŏn′mə tăl′ĭk), *adj. Chem.* **1.** of or relating to nonmetal. **2.** not of a metallic quality: *a nonmetallic appearance.*

non·mor·al (nŏn mōr′əl, -mŏr′-), *adj.* having no relation to morality; neither moral nor immoral: *a completely nonmoral problem of society.*

non·ni·trog·e·nous (nŏn′nī trŏj′ə nəs), *adj.* containing no nitrogen.

non·ob·jec·tive (nŏn′əb jĕk′tĭv), *adj. Fine Arts.* not representing or containing objects known in physical nature; abstract or nonrepresentational.

non ob·stan·te (nŏn ŏb stăn′tĭ), *Latin.* notwithstanding.

non·pa·reil (nŏn′pə rĕl′), *adj.* **1.** having no equal; peerless. —*n.* **2.** a person or thing having no equal; something unique. **3.** a beautifully colored finch, *Passerina ciris*, of the southern U.S.; the painted bunting. **4.** *Print.* **a.** a size of type (6 point). **b.** a slug occupying 6 points of space between lines. [late ME, t. F: f. *non-* NON- + *pareil* equal (ult. der. L *pār*)]

non·par·ous (nŏn păr′əs), *adj. Physiol.* having borne no children.

non·par·tic·i·pat·ing (nŏn′pär tĭs′ə pā′tĭng), *adj. Insurance.* having no right to dividends or to a distribution of surplus.

non·par·ti·san (nŏn pär′tə zən), *adj.* **1.** not partisan; objective. **2.** not supporting any of the established or regular parties. Also, **non·par′ti·zan.**

Nonpartisan League, a political organization of farmers, founded in North Dakota, 1915, and extending to many States west of the Mississippi, with the aim of influencing agricultural legislation in State legislatures.

non·pay·ment (nŏn pā′mənt), *n.* condition of being unpaid; neglect to pay.

non·per·form·ance (nŏn′pər fôr′məns), *n.* failure or neglect to perform.

non·plus (nŏn plŭs′, nŏn′plŭs), *v.*, **-plused, -plusing** or (*esp. Brit.*) **-plussed, -plussing,** *n.* —*v.t.* **1.** to bring to a nonplus; puzzle completely. —*n.* **2.** a state of utter perplexity. [t. L: *nōn plus* not more, no further]

non pos·su·mus (nŏn pŏs′ə məs), *Latin.* we cannot.

non·pro (nŏn prō′), *n.*, *adj. Slang.* nonprofessional.

non·pro·duc·tive (nŏn′prə dŭk′tĭv), *adj.* **1.** not producing goods directly, as employees in charge of personnel, inspectors, etc. **2.** unproductive. —**non′·pro·duc′tive·ness,** *n.*

non·prof·it (nŏn prŏf′ĭt), *adj.* not yielding a return; not entered into for profit: *a nonprofit association.*

non pros., non prosequitur.

non·pros (nŏn′prŏs′), *v.t.*, **-prossed, -prossing.** *Law.* to adjudge (a plaintiff) in default.

non pro·se·qui·tur (nŏn prō sĕk′wə tər), *Law.* a judgment entered against the plaintiff in a suit when he does not appear to prosecute it. [L: he does not pursue (prosecute)]

non·rep·re·sen·ta·tion·al (nŏn′rĕp rĭ zĕn tā′shən əl), *adj.* not resembling any object in physical nature: *a nonrepresentational painting.*

non·res·i·dent (nŏn rĕz′ə dənt), *adj.* **1.** not resident in a particular place. **2.** not residing where official duties require one to reside. —*n.* **3.** one who is nonresident. —**non·res′i·dence,** **non·res′i·den·cy,** *n.*

non·re·sist·ant (nŏn′rĭ zĭs′tənt), *adj.* **1.** not resistant; passively obedient. —*n.* **2.** one who does not resist authority or force. **3.** one who maintains that violence should not be resisted by force. —**non′re·sist′ance,** *n.*

non·re·straint (nŏn′rĭ strānt′), *n.* **1.** *Psychiatry.* the treatment of the mentally ill without mechanical means of restraint. **2.** absence of restraint.

non·ed′i·ble	non·her′it·a·ble	non·mar′ry·ing	non′·per·pen·dic′u·lar
non·ed′u·ca·ble	non·his·tor′ic	non·mar′tial	non′·per·sist′ence
non·ed·u·ca′tion·al	non·hu′man	non·me·chan′i·cal	non′·phil·o·soph′i·cal
non·ef·fi′cient	non·hu′mor·ous	non·med′i·cal	non′pi·na′ceous
non·e·las′tic	non·i·den′ti·cal	non·me·dic′i·nal	non·po·et′ic
non·e·mo′tion·al	non·i·den′ti·ty	non·me·lo′di·ous	non·poi′son·ous
non·en·force′ment	non·id·i·o·mat′ic	non·mem′ber	non·po·lit′i·cal
non·e·quiv′a·lent	non·im·mu′ni·ty	non·met′ri·cal	non·po′rous
non·eth′i·cal	non′im·preg′nat·ed	non·mi′gra·to′ry	non·pred′a·to′ry
non′-Eu·clid′e·an	non·in·clu′sive	non·mil′i·tant	non·pre·dict′a·ble
non·ex·change′a·ble	non·in·dict′a·ble	non·mil′i·tar′y	non·pre·hen′si·le
non·ex·clu′sive	non·in·dict′ment	non·mor′tal	non·pre·scrip′tive
non·ex·ist′ing	non·in·dus′tri·al	non·mo′tile	non·pro·duc′ing
non·ex·plo′sive	non·in·fec′tion	non·nat′u·ral	non·pro·fes′sion·al
non·ex·port′a·ble	non·in·fec′tious	non·nav′i·ga·ble	non·prof·it·eer′ing
non·ex·tra·dit′a·ble	non·in·flam′ma·ble	non·ne·ces′si·ty	non·pro·gres′sive
non·fac′tu·al	non·in·form′a·tive	non·ne·go′ti·a·ble	non·pro·tec′tive
non·fad′ing	non·in·her′it·a·ble	non·neu′tral	non-Prot′es·tant
non·fed′er·al	non·in′ter·course′	non·nu·tri′tious	non·pun′ish·a·ble
non·fed′er·at·ed	non·in′ter·fer′ence	non·o·be′di·ence	non·ra′cial
non·fer′rous	non·in′ter·sect′ing	non·ob·lig′a·to′ry	non·re·al′i·ty
non·fes′tive	non·in·tox′i·cant	non·o′dor·ous	non·re·cip′ro·cal
non·fic′tion	non·in·tox′i·cat′ing	non·of·fi′cial	non·rec·og·ni′tion
non·fic′tion·al	non·ir′ri·ga·ble	non·or·tho·dox′	non·re·cur′rent
non·fis′cal	non·ir′ri·tant	non·pa·rish′ion·er	non·re·fill′a·ble
non·fis′sion·a·ble	non·ir′ri·tat′ing	non·par·lia·men′ta·ry	non·re·fu′el·ing
non·flam′ma·ble	non-Jew′	non·pa·ro′chi·al	non·re′gent
non·freez′ing	non-Jew′ish	non·par·tic′i·pa′tion	non·reg′i·ment·ed
non·func′tion·al	non′life	non·pas′ser·i·form′	non·reign′ing
non·gas′e·ous	non·lit′er·ar′y	non·pas′ser·ine	non·re·li′gious
non·green′	non·liv′ing	non·pay′ing	non·re·mu′ner·a′tive
non·hab′it·a·ble	non·lu′mi·nous	non·per′ma·nent	non·re·new′a·ble
non·he·red′i·tar′y	non·mag·net′ic	non·per′me·a·ble	non·res·i·den′tial

non·re·stric·tive (nŏn′rĭ strĭk′tĭv), *adj. Gram.* (of a word or clause) purely descriptive rather than limiting in its application to the sentence element it modifies. "Mr. Owen, *who was here yesterday*, is a farmer" illustrates a nonrestrictive clause. "The man who was here yesterday is a farmer" shows the same clause employed to restrict the meaning of *the man.*

non·rig·id (nŏn rĭj′ĭd), *adj.* 1. not rigid. 2. designating a type of airship having a flexible gas container without a supporting structure and held in shape only by the pressure of the gas within.

non·sec·tar·i·an (nŏn′sĕk târ′ĭ ən), *adj.* not affiliated with any specific religious denomination.

non·sense (nŏn′sĕns), *n.* 1. that which makes no sense or is lacking in sense. 2. words without sense or conveying absurd ideas. 3. senseless or absurd action; foolish conduct, notions, etc.: *to stand no nonsense from a person.* 4. absurdity: *the nonsense of an idea.* 5. stuff, trash, or anything useless. —**non·sen·si·cal** (nŏn-sĕn′sə kəl), *adj.* —**non·sen′si·cal·ly**, *adv.* —**non·sen′si·cal·ness,** *n.*

non seq., non sequitur.

non se·qui·tur (nŏn sĕk′wə tər), *Latin.* an inference or a conclusion which does not follow from the premises. [L: it does not follow]

non·skid (nŏn′skĭd′), *adj.* having the wheel rim or tire with a ridged or otherwise skid-resistant surface.

non·stop (nŏn′stŏp′), *adj., adv.* without a single stop: *a nonstop flight from New York to Paris.*

non·stri·a·ted (nŏn strī′ā tĭd), *adj.* not striated; unstriped, as muscular tissue.

non·such (nŭn′sŭch′), *n.* nonesuch.

non·suit (nŏn′sōōt′), *Law.* —*n.* 1. a judgment given against a plaintiff who neglects to prosecute, or who fails to show a legal cause of action or to bring sufficient evidence. —*v.t.* 2. to subject to a nonsuit.

non·sup·port (nŏn′sə pōrt′), *n. Law.* omission to support another, as a wife, child, or other dependent, as required by law.

non trop·po (nŏn trôp′pô), *Music.* not too much: *non troppo lento* (not too slow). [It.]

non·un·ion (nŏn ūn′yən), *adj.* 1. not belonging to, or not in accordance with the rules of, a trade union. 2. anti-union. —*n.* 3. failure of a broken bone to heal.

non·un·ion·ism (nŏn ūn′yə nĭz′əm), *n.* disregard of or opposition to trade unions. —**non·un′ion·ist,** *n.*

nonunion shop, a shop or business in which the employer fixes terms and conditions of employment unilaterally without recognizing or dealing with a union.

non·vot·er (nŏn vō′tər), *n.* one who does not vote.

noo·dle[1] (nōō′dəl), *n.* a strip or lump of dough or paste, served in soups, etc. [t. G: m. *nudel*]

noo·dle[2] (nōō′dəl), *n.* 1. *Slang.* the head. 2. a simpleton. [? var. of NODDLE[1] (with *oo* from FOOL)]

nook (nōōk), *n.* 1. a corner, as in a room. 2. any retired or obscure corner. 3. any small recess. 4. a remote spot. [ME *noke.* Cf. d. Norw. *nok* hook]

noon (nōōn), *n.* 1. midday. 2. twelve o'clock in the daytime. 3. the highest, brightest, or finest point or part. 4. *Poetic.* midnight. [ME *none,* OE *nōn,* t. L: s. *nōna* ninth hour. See NONES[1]]

noon·day (nōōn′dā′), *adj.* 1. of or at noonday. —*n.* 2. midday; noon.

no one, no person; nobody.

noon·ing (nōō′nĭng), *n.* 1. noontime. 2. an interval at noon for rest or food. 3. a rest or meal at noon.

noon·tide (nōōn′tīd′), *n.* 1. the time of noon; midday. 2. the highest or best point or part. 3. *Chiefly Poetic.* midnight. [ME *nonetyde,* OE *nōntīd*]

noon·time (nōōn′tīm′), *n.* the time of noon.

noose (nōōs), *n., v.,* **noosed, noosing.** —*n.* 1. a loop with a running knot, as in a snare, lasso, hangman's halter, etc., which tightens as the rope is pulled. 2. a tie or bond; a snare. —*v.t.* 3. to secure by or as by a noose. 4. to make a noose with or in (a rope, etc.). [prob. t. OF: m. *nos,* der. *noer* to knit, g. L *nōdāre,* der. *nōdus* knot]

Noot·ka (nōōt′kä), *n.* an American Indian language of Wakashan stock, spoken in Vancouver Island and Cape Flattery, a cape in NW Washington.

no·pal (nō′pəl), *n.* 1. any cactus or fruit of the genera *Opuntia* and *Nopalea.* 2. the prickly pear. [t. Sp., t. Mex.: m. *nopalli* cactus]

no-par (nō′pär′), *adj.* without par, or face, value.

No Plays (nō), the highly stylized Japanese classical drama, first developed in the 15th century, employing music, dancing, a chorus, symbolic scenery, and elaborate costumes and masks. Also, **Noh Plays.**

nor (nôr; *unstressed* nər), *conj.* 1. a negative conjunction used: **a.** as the correlative to a preceding *neither: he could neither read nor write.* **b.** *Archaic or Poetic.* with omission of a preceding *neither,* its negative force being understood: *he nor I was there.* **c.** *Now Chiefly Poetic.* instead of *neither,* as correlative to a following *nor: nor he nor I was there.* **d.** to continue the force of a negative, such as *not, no, never,* etc., occurring in a preceding clause: *He left and I never saw him again, nor did I regret it.* **e.** after an affirmative clause, or as a continuative, in the sense of *and . . . not.: they are happy; nor need we mourn.* 2. *Dial.* than. [ME *nor,* contr. of *nother.* OE *nōther,* f. *ne* not + *ōther* (contr. of *ōhwæther* either)]

nor-, *Chem.* a word element meaning "normal." [short for NORMAL]

Nor., 1. Norman. 2. North. 3. Norway. 4. Norwegian.

Nor·dau (nôr′dou), *n.* **Max Simon** (mäks zē′môn), 1849–1923, German writer and advocate of Zionism.

Nor·den·skjöld (nōōr′dən skhœld′), *n.* 1. **Nils Adolf Erik** (nĭls ä′dôlf ā′rĭk), **Baron,** 1832–1901, Swedish arctic explorer, born in Finland. 2. his nephew, **Nils Otto Gustaf** (nĭls ôt′tōō gŭs′tăv), 1869–1928, Swedish arctic and antarctic explorer.

Nordenskjöld Sea, an arm of the Arctic Ocean N of the Soviet Union in Asia, between Taimyr Peninsula and the New Siberian Islands. Also, **Laptev Sea.**

Nord·hau·sen (nôrt′hou′zən), *n.* a city in central Germany: site of a Nazi extermination camp during World War II. 42,576 (1939).

Nor·dic (nôr′dĭk), *adj.* 1. *Ethnol.* designating, or belonging or pertaining to, a race of men or a Caucasian racial subtype characterized by tall stature, blond hair, blue eyes, and elongated head, exemplified most markedly by Scandinavians and Britons and their descendants. —*n.* 2. a member of the Nordic race. [t. F: m. *nordique,* der. *nord* north, t. Gmc., and akin to NORTH. See -IC]

Nord·kyn Cape (nôr′kyn), a cape in N Norway: the northernmost point of the European mainland.

nor′·east·er (nôr ēs′tər), *n.* northeaster.

Nor·folk (nôr′fək), *n.* 1. a seaport in SE Virginia: naval base. 213,513 (1950). 2. a county in E England. 494,000 pop. (est. 1946); 2054 sq. mi. *Co. seat:* Norwich.

Norfolk Island, an island in the S Pacific between New Caledonia and New Zealand: a territory of Australia. 770 pop. (1943); 13 sq. mi.

Norfolk jacket, a loosely belted single-breasted jacket, with box pleats in front and back. Also, **Norfolk coat.**

Nor·ge (nôr′gə), *n.* Norwegian name of **Norway.**

no·ri·a (nôr′ĭ ə), *n.* a device consisting of a series of buckets on a wheel, used in Spain and the Orient for raising water. [t. Sp.; t. Ar.: m. *nā′ūra*]

Nor·i·cum (nôr′ĭ kəm, nŏr′-), *n.* an ancient Roman province in central Europe, roughly corresponding to the part of Austria S of the Danube.

nor·land (nôr′lənd), *n. Chiefly Poetic.* northland. [f. *nor* (apocopated var. of NORTH) + LAND]

norm (nôrm), *n.* 1. a standard, model, or pattern. 2. *Educ.* a designated standard of average performance of people of a given age, background, etc. [t. L: s. *norma* carpenter's square, rule, pattern]

nor·mal (nôr′məl), *adj.* 1. conforming to the standard or the common type; regular, usual, natural, or not abnormal: *the normal procedure.* 2. serving to fix a standard. 3. *Psychol.* **a.** approximately average in respect to any psychological trait, such as intelligence, personality, emotional adjustment, etc. **b.** without any mental aberrations; sane. 4. *Math.* **a.** being at right angles, as a line; perpendicular. **b.** of the nature of or pertaining to a mathematical normal. 5. *Chem.* **a.** (of a solution) containing one equivalent weight of the constituent in question in one liter of solution. **b.** pertaining to an aliphatic hydrocarbon having a straight unbranched carbon chain, each carbon atom of which is joined to no more than two other carbon atoms. **c. normal element,** a galvanic cell of known and reproducible voltage; standard cell. 6. *Biol., Med., etc.* **a.** free from any infection or experimental therapy. **b.** of natural occurrence. —*n.* 7. the standard or type. 8. the normal form or state; the average or mean. 9. *Math.* a perpendicular line or plane, esp. one perpendicular to a tangent line of a curve, or a tangent plane of a surface, at the point of contact. [t. L: s. *normālis* made according to a carpenter's square or rule] —**nor·mal·i·ty** (nôr măl′ə-tĭ), **nor′mal·ness,** *n.*

normal curve, *Statistics.* a bell-shaped curve giving

non′·re·strict′ed	non′·shrink′a·ble	non′·sub·mis′sive	non′·trib′u·tar′y
non′·re·turn′a·ble	non′·sig·nif′i·cant	non′·sub·scrib′er	non′·typ′i·cal
non′·re·vers′i·ble	non′·sink′a·ble	non′·sub·stan′tial	non′·u·nit′ed
non·rhym′ing	non′·slip′ping	non′·suc·ces′sive	non·us′er
non·rhyth′mic	non·smok′ing	non′·sup·port′er	non·ven′om·ous
non·ru′ral	non·so′cial	non′·sus·tain′ing	non·ver′ti·cal
non·sal′a·ble	non·spark′ling	non′·sym·met′ri·cal	non·vi′o·la′tion
non·sal′a·ried	non·spe′cial·ized′	non′·sys·tem·at′ic	non·vis′u·al
non′·sci·en·tif′ic	non·spir′it·u·al	non·tax′a·ble	non′·vo·cal′ic
non′·sea′son·al	non·spore′form′ing	non′·teach′a·ble	non′·vo·ca′tion·al
non·sec′tion·al	non·stain′a·ble	non·tech′ni·cal	non·vol′a·tile
non′·se·lec′tive	non′·stan′dard·ized′	non′·ter·ri·to′ri·al	non′·vol·un·tar′y
non·sen′si·tive	non·stim′u·lat′ing	non·tex′tu·al	non·vot′ing
non·shar′ing	non·strik′er	non·tox′ic	non·work′er
non·shat′ter	non·strik′ing	non′·trans·fer′a·ble	non·yield′ing

the distribution of probability associated with the different values of a variable.

nor·mal·cy (nôr′məl sĭ′), *n.* the character or state of being normal: *back to normalcy.*

nor·mal·ize (nôr′mə līz′), *v.t.,* **-ized, -izing.** to make normal. —**nor′mal·i·za′tion,** *n.* —**nor′mal·iz′er,** *n.*

nor·mal·ly (nôr′məl ĭ), *adv.* as a rule; regularly; according to rule; general custom, etc.

normal school, a school for the preliminary professional education of teachers. [after F *école normale*]

Nor·man (nôr′mən), *n.* **1.** a member of that branch of the Northmen or Scandinavians who in the 10th century conquered Normandy. **2.** one of the mixed Scandinavian and French (**Norman French**) race later inhabiting this region, which conquered England in 1066. **3.** a native or inhabitant of Normandy. **4.** Norman French (language). **5.** a city in central Oklahoma. 27,006 (1950). —*adj.* **6.** of or pertaining to the Normans. **7.** *Archit.* noting or pertaining to a variety of the Romanesque style of architecture which was introduced from Normandy into Great Britain before and at the time of the Norman conquest. [ME, back formation from OF *Normans,* pl. of *Normant.* See NORTHMAN]

Norman Conquest, the conquest of England by the Normans, under William the Conqueror, in 1066.

Nor·man·dy (nôr′mən dĭ), *n.* a region in N France along the English Channel: invaded and settled by Northmen in the 10th century; it became a duchy, and later a province; Allied invasion in World War II began June 6, 1944. Its capital was Rouen.

Norman French, 1. the French of the Normans or of Normandy. **2.** the legal jargon of England, now extinct except in phrases, orig. a dialect of Old French.

Nor·man·ize (nôr′mə nīz′), *v.i., v.t.,* **-ized, -izing.** to make or become Norman in customs, language, etc.

nor·mo·cyte (nôr′mə sīt′), *n. Anat.* a red blood cell of normal size.

Norn (nôrn), *n. Scand. Myth.* any one of the goddesses of fate, commonly represented as three in number, whose decrees were irrevocable. [t. Icel.]

Nor·ris (nôr′ĭs, nŏr′-), *n.* **1. Frank,** 1870–1902, U.S. novelist. **2. George William,** 1861–1944, U.S. senator.

Nor·ris·town (nôr′ĭs toun′, nŏr′-), *n.* a borough in SE Pennsylvania, near Philadelphia. 38,126 (1950).

Norr·kö·ping (nôr′chœ′pĭng), *n.* a seaport in SE Sweden. 75,792 (est. 1944).

Norse (nôrs), *adj.* **1.** belonging or pertaining to Norway, esp. ancient Norway with its colonies (as in Iceland), or to ancient Scandinavia generally. —*n.* **2.** (*construed as pl.*) **a.** the Norwegians. **b.** the ancient Norwegians. **c.** the Northmen or ancient Scandinavians generally. **3.** Norwegian (language) esp. in its older forms. See Old Norse. [prob. t. D: m. *noorsch,* var. of *noordsch,* der. *noord* north. Cf. Norw., Sw., Dan. *Norsk* Norwegian, Norse]

Norse·man (nôrs′mən), *n., pl.* **-men.** a Northman.

north (nôrth), *n.* **1.** a cardinal point of the compass lying in the plane of the meridian and to the right of a person facing the setting sun or west. **2.** the direction in which this point lies. **3.** (*l.c. or cap.*) a quarter or territory situated in this direction. **4.** (*cap.*) the northern area of the United States, esp. the States which fought with the Union in the Civil War, lying to the north of the Ohio river, Missouri, and Maryland. **5.** (*cap.*) North Country. **6.** *Chiefly Poetic.* the north wind. —*adj.* **7.** lying toward or situated in the north. **8.** directed or proceeding toward the north. **9.** coming from the north, as a wind. **10.** (*cap.*) designating the northern part of a region, nation, country, etc.: *North America.* —*adv.* **11.** in the direction which is to the right of a person facing the setting sun or west. **12.** toward or in the north. [ME and OE, c. G *nord*]

North (nôrth), *n.* **1. Christopher,** pen name of **John Wilson. 2. Lord Frederick,** (*2nd Earl of Guilford*) 1732–92, British statesman: prime minister, 1770–82. **3. Sir Thomas,** 1535?–1601?, British translator.

North Adams, a city in NW Mass. 21,567 (1950).

North America, the northernmost continent of the Western Hemisphere, extending from Central America to the Arctic Ocean. Highest point, Mt. McKinley, 20,300 ft.; lowest, Death Valley, 276 ft. below sea level. (Including Central America) ab. 183,000,000 pop.; ab. 8,440,000 sq. mi. —**North American.**

North·amp·ton (nôr thămp′tən, nôrth hămp′-), *n.* **1.** a city in central England. 103,240 (est. 1946). **2.** a city in central Massachusetts. 29,063 (1950).

North·amp·ton·shire (nôr thămp′tən shĭr′, -shər), *n.* a county in central England. 339,000 (est. 1946); 914 sq. mi. *Co. seat:* Northampton. Also, **Northampton.**

North Atlantic Treaty. See **Atlantic Pact.**

North Bor·ne·o (bôr′nĭ ō′), British North Borneo.

North Bra·bant (brə bănt′, brä′bənt), a province in S Netherlands. 1,150,432 pop. (est. 1946); 1965 sq. mi. *Cap.:* 's Hertogenbosch.

north by east, a point of direction on the mariner's compass, one point east of north.

north by west, a point of direction on the mariner's compass, one point west of north.

North Cape, 1. a point of land on an island at the N tip of Norway: the northernmost point of Europe. **2.** the northern end of North Island, New Zealand.

North Car·o·li·na (kăr′ə lī′nə), a State in the SE United States, on the Atlantic coast. 4,061,929 pop. (1950); 52,712 sq. mi. *Cap.:* Raleigh. *Abbr.:* N.C. —**North Car·o·lin·i·an** (kăr′ə lĭn′ĭ ən).

North Cau·ca·sus (kô′kə səs), a region in the S Soviet Union in Europe, E of the Black Sea.

North·cliffe (nôrth′klĭf), *n.* **Alfred Charles William Harmsworth, Viscount,** 1865–1922, British newspaper publisher.

North Country, 1. the part of England north of the Humber estuary. **2.** Alaska and the Yukon territory of Canada, considered as a geographical and economic unit.

North Da·ko·ta (də kō′tə), a State in the N central United States. 619,636 pop. (1950); 70,665 sq. mi. *Cap.:* Bismarck. *Abbr.:* N. Dak. —**North Da·ko′tan.**

north·east (nôrth′ēst′; *Naut.* nôr′-), *n.* **1.** the point or direction midway between north and east. **2.** a region in this direction. —*adv.* **3.** in the direction of a point midway between north and east. **4.** from this direction. —*adj.* **5.** lying toward or situated in the northeast. **6.** directed or proceeding toward the northeast. **7.** coming from the northeast, as a wind. —**north′east′ern,** *adj.*

northeast by east, a point of direction on the mariner's compass, one point east of northeast.

northeast by north, a point of direction on the mariner's compass, one point north of northeast.

north·east·er (nôrth′ēs′tər; *Naut.* nôr′-), *n.* a wind or gale from the northeast.

north·east·er·ly (nôrth′ēs′tər lĭ; *Naut.* nôr′-), *adj.* **1.** pertaining to, or located in, the northeast. **2.** toward or from the northeast. —*adv.* **3.** toward or from the northeast.

Northeast Passage, a route for ships along the N coast of Europe and Asia as a possible course for navigation between the Atlantic and Pacific.

north·east·ward (nôrth′ēst′wərd; *Naut.* nôr′-), *adv., adj.* **1.** Also, **north′east′ward·ly.** toward the northeast. —*n.* **2.** the northeast.

north·east·wards (nôrth′ēst′wərdz; *Naut.* nôr′-), *adv.* northeastward.

north·er (nôr′thər), *n.* **1.** (in the U.S. Gulf Coast region) a cold gale from the north, formed by a vigorous outbreak of continental polar air behind a cold front during the winter. **2.** a wind or storm from the north.

north·er·ly (nôr′thər lĭ), *adj.* **1.** moving, directed, or situated toward the north. **2.** coming from the north, as a wind. —*adv.* **3.** toward the north. **4.** from the north.

north·ern (nôr′thərn), *adj.* **1.** lying toward or situated in the north. **2.** directed or proceeding northward. **3.** coming from the north, as a wind. **4.** of or pertaining to the north, esp. (*cap.*) the North o. the U.S. **5.** *Astron.* north of the celestial equator or of the zodiac: *a northern constellation.* —*n.* **6.** one living in a northern region or country. [ME and OE *northerne.* See -ERN]

Northern Cir·cars (sər kärz′), the former name of a region along the E coast of India, in Madras province.

Northern Cross, *Astron.* (in the constellation Cygnus) six stars arranged in the form of a cross.

Northern Crown, *Astron.* Corona Borealis.

Northern Dvi·na (dvē nä′). See **Dvina, Northern.**

north·ern·er (nôr′thər nər), *n.* a native or inhabitant of the north, esp. (*cap.*) of the Northern U.S.

Northern Hemisphere, the half of the earth between the North Pole and the equator.

Northern Ireland, a political division of the United Kingdom, in the NE part of Ireland. 1,327,000 pop. (est. 1946); 5238 sq. mi. *Cap.:* Belfast.

northern lights, the aurora borealis.

north·ern·most (nôr′thərn mōst′, -məst), *adj.* furthest north.

Northern Rho·de·sia (rō dē′zhə, -zĭ ə), a British protectorate in S Africa. 1,382,000 pop. (est. 1940); 290,320 sq. mi. *Cap.:* Lusaka.

Northern Spy, a late-keeping, red-striped American apple.

Northern Territories, a British protectorate in W Africa, in the N part of the Gold Coast. 717,000 pop. (1931); 30,486 sq. mi. *Cap.:* Tamale.

Northern Territory, a territory in N Australia. 5250 pop. (1946); 523,620 sq. mi. *Cap.:* Darwin.

North Germanic, the Scandinavian subgroup of Germanic languages.

North Holland, a province in W Netherlands. 1,705,672 pop. (est. 1946); 1163 sq. mi. *Cap.:* Haarlem.

north·ing (nôr′thĭng, -thĭng), *n.* **1.** movement or deviation toward the north. **2.** distance due north. **3.** the distance due north made by a ship on any course tending northward.

North Island, the northernmost of the principal islands of New Zealand. 1,085,519 pop. (est. 1943); 44,281 sq. mi.

north·land (nôrth′lənd), *n.* **1.** the land or region in the north. **2.** the northern part of a country. **3.** (*cap.*) the peninsula containing Norway and Sweden. [ME and OE, c. G, Dan., Sw. *nordland*] —**north′land·er,** *n.*

North Little Rock, a city in central Arkansas, on the Arkansas river. 44,097 (1950).

North·man (nôrth′mən), *n., pl.* **-men.** a member of the Scandinavian group, which from about the 8th to the 11th century made many raids and settlements on Great Britain, Ireland, and other parts of Europe.

north-north·east (nôrth′nôrth′ēst′; *Naut.* nôr′nôr-ēst′), *adj.* **1.** lying or situated in the direction on the mariner's compass equidistant from north and north-east. —*n.* **2.** this direction. —*adv.* **3.** to or from this direction.

north-north·west (nôrth′nôrth′wĕst′; *Naut.* nôr′-nôr wĕst′), *adj.* **1.** lying or situated in the direction on the mariner's compass equidistant from north and north-west. —*n.* **2.** this direction. —*adv.* **3.** to or from this direction.

North Platte (plăt), a river flowing from N Colorado through SE Wyoming and W Nebraska into the Platte. 618 mi.

North Pole, 1. *Geog.* that end of the earth's axis of rotation marking the northernmost point on the earth. **2.** *Astron.* the zenith of the earth's north pole, about 1° distant from the North Star.

North Rid·ing (rī′dĭng), an administrative county in Yorkshire, England. 471,000 pop. (est. 1946); 2127 sq. mi. *Co. seat:* Northallerton.

North River, a name for that part of the Hudson river between New York City and New Jersey below the junction of Spuyten Duyvil Creek.

North Sea, an arm of the Atlantic between Great Britain and the European mainland. ab. 201,000 sq. mi.; greatest depth, 1998 ft. Formerly, **German Ocean.**

North Star, *Astron.* Polaris, the north polar star, situated near the north pole of the heavens.

North Ton·a·wan·da (tŏn′ə wŏn′də), a city in W New York. 24,731 (1950).

North·um·ber·land (nôr thŭm′bər lənd), *n.* a county in NE England. 762,000 pop. (est. 1946); 2019 sq. mi. *Co. Seat.:* Newcastle.

North·um·bri·a (nôr thŭm′brĭ ə), *n.* an early English kingdom extending from the Humber N to the Firth of Forth. See map under **Mercia.**

North·um·bri·an (nôr thŭm′brĭ ən), *adj.* **1.** of or pertaining to Northumbria, Northumberland, or the inhabitants or dialect of either. —*n.* **2.** a native or inhabitant of Northumbria or Northumberland. **3.** the English dialect of Northumbria or Northumberland.

north·ward (nôrth′wərd; *Naut.* nôr′thərd), *adv.* **1.** Also, **north′wards.** toward the north. —*adj.* **2.** moving, bearing, facing, or situated toward the north. —*n.* **3.** the northward part, direction, or point. —**north′-ward·ly,** *adj., adv.*

north·west (nôrth′wĕst′; *Naut.* nôr′-), *n.* **1.** the point or direction midway between north and west. **2.** a region in this direction. —*adj.* Also, **north′west′-ern. 3.** lying toward or situated in the northwest. **4.** directed or proceeding toward the northwest. **5.** coming from the northwest, as a wind. —*adv.* **6.** in the direction of a point midway between north and west. **7.** from this direction.

north·west·er (nôrth′wĕs′tər; *Naut.* nôr′-), *n.* a wind or gale from the northwest.

north·west·er·ly (nôrth′wĕs′tər lĭ; *Naut.* nôr′-), *adj., adv.* toward or from the northwest.

North-West Frontier Province, 1. a province in Pakistan, bordering the Punjab and Kashmir on the W. 3,038,000 pop. (1941); 14,263 sq. mi. *Cap.:* Peshawar. **2.** agencies and tribal areas between this province and the Afghanistan frontier. 2,378,000 pop.; 24,986 sq. mi.

Northwest Passage, ship route along the Arctic coast of Canada and Alaska, joining the Atlantic and Pacific oceans.

Northwest Territories, a territory of Canada lying north of the provinces and extending from Yukon territory E to Davis Strait. 12,028 pop. (1941); 1,304,903 sq. mi.

Northwest Territory, the region north of the Ohio river (Ohio, Indiana, Illinois, Michigan, Wisconsin, and part of Minnesota) organized by Congress in 1787.

Northwest Territory, 1787

north·west·ward (nôrth′-wĕst′wərd; *Naut.* nôr′-), *adv., adj.* **1.** Also, **north′-west′ward·ly.** toward the northwest. —*n.* **2.** the northwest.

north·west·wards (nôrth′wĕst′wərdz; *Naut.* nôr′-), *adv.* northward.

Nor·ton (nôr′tən), *n.* **1. Charles Eliot,** 1827–1908, U.S. scholar. **2. Thomas,** 1532–84, British author.

Norw., 1. Norway. **2.** Norwegian.

Nor·walk (nôr′wôk), *n.* a city in SW Connecticut. 49,460 (1950).

Nor·way (nôr′wā), *n.* a kingdom in N Europe, in the W part of the Scandinavian Peninsula. 3,105,000 pop. (est. 1946); 124,555 sq. mi. *Cap.:* Oslo. Norwegian, **Norge.**

Norway spruce, a spruce introduced from Europe, *Picea Abies,* widely grown as an ornamental.

Nor·we·gian (nôr wē′jən), *adj.* **1.** of or pertaining to

Norway, its inhabitants, or their language. —*n.* **2.** a native or inhabitant of Norway. **3.** the speech of Norway in any of its forms, whether Dano-Norwegian, or the local dialects, or the standard language based on these, all being closely related to one another and to the other Scandinavian languages.

nor′·west·er (nôr wĕs′tər), *n.* a seaman's oilskin raincoat.

Nor·wich (nôr′ĭch, -ĭj, nŏr′- *for 1*; nôr′wĭch *for 2*), *n.* **1.** a city in E England, in Norfolk: famous cathedral. 113,270 (est. 1946). **2.** a city in SE Connecticut, on the Thames river. 23,429 (1950).

Nor·wood (nôr′wŏŏd′), *n.* a city in SW Ohio, near Cincinnati. 35,001 (1950).

nos-, var. of noso-, before vowels.

Nos., numbers. Also, **nos.**

no·sce te ip·sum (nō′sē tē ĭp′səm), *Latin.* know thyself.

nose (nōz), *n., v.,* **nosed, nosing.** —*n.* **1.** the part of the face or head which contains the nostrils, affording passage for air in respiration, etc. **2.** this part as the organ of smell: *the aroma of coffee greeted his nose.* **3.** the sense of smell: *a dog with a good nose.* **4.** a faculty of perceiving or detecting: *a nose for news.* **5.** something regarded as resembling the nose of a person or animal, as a spout or nozzle. **6.** the prow of a ship. **7.** the forward end of an aircraft. **8.** a projecting part of any thing. —*v.t.* **9.** to perceive by or as by the nose or the sense of smell. **10.** to approach the nose to, as in smelling or examining; sniff. **11.** to move or push forward. **12.** to touch or rub with the nose; nuzzle. —*v.i.* **13.** to smell or sniff. **14.** to seek as if by smelling or scent (fol. by *after, for,* etc.); pry (fol. by *about, into,* etc.). **15.** to move or push forward: *the boat nosed in toward the shore.* **16.** to meddle. [ME; OE *nosu,* c. MD and MLG *nose.* Cf. L *nāsus*]

nose·band (nōz′bănd′), *n.* that part of a bridle or halter which passes over the animal's nose. See illus. under **harness.**

nose·bleed (nōz′blēd′), *n.* bleeding from the nose; epistaxis.

nose dive, 1. a dive or plunge of an airplane with the nose or fore part of the craft vertically downward. **2.** any sudden drop.

nose-dive (nōz′dīv′), *v.i.,* **-dived** or **-dove, -dived, -diving.** to execute a nose dive.

nose·gay (nōz′gā′), *n.* a bunch of flowers; a bouquet; a posy. [ME; lit., a *gay* (obs., something pretty) for the NOSE (i.e., to smell)]

nose·piece (nōz′pēs′), *n.* **1.** a protective cover for the nose. **2.** the part of a microscope where the object slide is attached. **3.** noseband.

nos·ey (nō′zĭ), *adj.,* **nosier, nosiest.** nosy.

nos·ing (nō′zĭng), *n.* a projecting edge, as the part of the tread of a step extending beyond the riser, or a projecting part of a buttress.

noso-, a word element meaning "disease." Also, **nos-.** [t. Gk., comb. form of *nósos*]

nos·o·ge·og·ra·phy (nŏs′ō jĭ ŏg′rə fĭ), *n.* the study of the causes and occurrence of diseases in terms of geography. —**nos·o·ge·o·graph·ic** (nŏs′ō jē′ə grăf′ĭk), **nos′o·ge′o·graph′i·cal,** *adj.*

no·sog·ra·phy (nō sŏg′rə fĭ), *n.* the systematic description of diseases.

no·sol·o·gy (nō sŏl′ə jĭ), *n.* **1.** the systematic classification of diseases. **2.** the knowledge of a disease. —**nos·o·log·i·cal** (nŏs′ə lŏj′ə kəl), *adj.* —**no·sol′o·gist,** *n.*

nos·tal·gia (nŏs tăl′jə, -jĭ ə), *n.* homesickness or strong desire for family and friends, in their severe forms producing derangement of mental and physical functions. [t. NL, f. Gk.: s. *nóstos* a return to home + *-algia* -ALGIA] —**nos·tal′gic,** *adj.*

nos·toc (nŏs′tŏk), *n.* any of the blue-green fresh-water algae constituting the genus *Nostoc,* often found in jelly-like colonies in moist places. [t. NL; coined by Paracelsus]

nos·tol·o·gy (nŏs tŏl′ə jĭ), *n.* geriatrics. —**nos·to·log·ic** (nŏs′tə lŏj′ĭk), *adj.*

nos·to·ma·ni·a (nŏs′tō mā′nĭ ə), *n. Psychiatry.* morbid nostalgia or homesickness; an irresistible compulsion to return home.

Nos·tra·da·mus (nŏs′trə dā′məs), *n.* 1503–66, French astrologer.

nos·tril (nŏs′trəl), *n.* an external opening of the nose. [ME *nostrill,* OE *nosterl,* var. of *nosthyrl,* f. *nosu* nose + *-thyrel* hole]

nos·trum (nŏs′trəm), *n.* **1.** a patent medicine. **2.** a quack medicine. **3.** a medicine made by the person who recommends it. **4.** a pet scheme or device for effecting something. [t. L, neut. of *noster* our, ours (cf. def. 3)]

nos·y (nō′zĭ), *adj.,* **nosier, nosiest.** *Colloq.* prying; inquisitive. Also, **nosey.**

not (nŏt), *adv.* a word expressing negation, denial, refusal, or prohibition: *not far, you must not do that.* [ME, reduced form of *noht, nouht.* See NOUGHT]

no·ta be·ne (nō′tə bē′nĭ), *Latin.* note well.

no·ta·bil·i·ty (nō′tə bĭl′ə tĭ), *n., pl.* **-ties. 1.** the quality of being notable. **2.** a notable person.

no·ta·ble (nō′tə bəl), *adj.* **1.** worthy of note or notice, noteworthy: *a notable success.* **2.** prominent, important, or distinguished, as persons. **3.** capable, thrifty, and industrious, as a housewife. —*n.* **4.** a notable person; a prominent or important person. **5.** (*often cap.*) *Fr. Hist.* one of a number of prominent men convoked by the king on extraordinary occasions. **6.** a notable thing. [ME. L: m.s. *notābilis*] —**no′ta·ble·ness**, *n.* —**no′ta·bly**, *adv.* —**Syn. 1.** conspicuous, memorable, great.

no·tar·i·al (nō târ′ĭ əl), *adj.* of or pertaining to, or drawn up or executed by, a notary.

no·ta·rize (nō′tə rīz′), *v.t.*, **-rized, -rizing.** to authenticate (a contract, etc.)

no·ta·ry (nō′tə rĭ), *n.*, *pl.* **-ries.** a notary public. [ME. t. L: m.s. *notārius* shorthand writer, clerk, secretary]

notary public, *pl.* **notaries public.** a public officer authorized to authenticate contracts, acknowledge deeds, take affidavits, protest bills of exchange, take depositions, etc.

no·ta·tion (nō tā′shən), *n.* **1.** a system of graphic symbols for a specialized use, other than ordinary writing: *musical notation.* **2.** the process of noting or setting down by means of a special system of signs or symbols. **3.** act of noting, marking, or setting down in writing, or a record or jotting. **4.** a note or record. [t. L: s. *notātio* a marking] —**no·ta′tion·al,** *adj.*

notch (nŏch), *n.* **1.** a more or less angular cut, indentation, or hollow in a narrow object or surface or an edge. **2.** *U.S.* a deep, narrow opening or pass between mountains. **3.** a cut or nick made in a stick or other object for record, as in keeping a score. **4.** *Colloq.* a step, degree, or grade. [n. use of v.] —*v.t.* **5.** to cut or make a notch or notches in. **6.** to make notches in by way of record. **7.** to record by a notch or notches. **8.** to score, as in a game. [t. AF: m. *anocher,* var. of OF *enocher,* der. *oche* notch]

note (nōt), *n.*, *v.*, **noted, noting.** —*n.* **1.** a brief record of something set down to assist the memory, or for reference or development. **2.** (*pl.*) a record of a speech, statement, testimony, etc., or of one's impressions of something. **3.** an explanatory or critical comment, or a reference to authority quoted, appended to a passage in a book or the like. **4.** a brief written or printed statement giving particulars or information. **5.** *Library Science.* additional information about a book, such as its special series or some other significant identification, entered on the library catalogue card. **6.** a short informal letter. **7.** a formal diplomatic or official communication in writing. **8.** a paper acknowledging a debt and promising payment; note of hand. **9.** a piece of paper money. **10.** a certificate, as of a government or a bank, passing current as money. **11.** eminence or distinction: *a man of note.* **12.** importance or consequence: *no other thing of note this year.* **13.** notice, observation, or heed. **14.** a characteristic or distinguishing feature. **15.** a mark, token, or indication of something, or from which something may be inferred. **16.** a musical sound or tone. **17.** *Music.* **a.** a sign or character used to represent a tone, its position and form indicating the pitch and duration of the tone. **b.** a key, as of a piano. **18.** *Archaic or Poetic.* a melody, tune, or song. **19.** a sound of musical quality uttered by a bird. **20.** any call, cry, or sound of a bird, fowl, etc. **21.** a tone sounded on a trumpet or other musical instrument as a signal. **22.** a signal, announcement, or intimation: *a note of warning.* **23.** *Colloq.* a new or unexpected element in a situation. **24.** way of speaking or thinking: *to change one's note.* **25.** a mark or sign, as of punctuation, used in writing or printing. —*v.t.* **26.** to mark down, as in writing; make a memorandum of. **27.** to make particular mention of in a writing. **28.** to annotate. **29.** to observe carefully; give attention or heed to. **30.** to take notice of; perceive. **31.** to set down in or furnish with musical notes. **32.** to indicate or designate; signify or denote. [ME. t. L: m. *nota* a mark] —**not′er,** *n.* —**Syn. 3.** See **remark.**

A, Breve; B, Whole note (semibreve); C, Half note (minim); D, Quarter note (crotchet); E, Eighth note (quaver); F, Sixteenth note (semiquaver); G, Thirty-second note (demisemiquaver); H, Sixty-fourth note (hemidemisemiquaver)

Notes (def. 17a)

note·book (nōt′bŏŏk′), *n.* **1.** a book of or for notes. **2.** a book in which notes of hand are registered.

not·ed (nō′tĭd), *adj.* **1.** conspicuous; celebrated; famous: *the room was full of noted scientists.* **2.** specially observed or noticed. —**not′ed·ly,** *adv.* —**not′ed·ness,** *n.*

note·less (nōt′lĭs), *adj.* **1.** of no note; undistinguished; unnoticed. **2.** unmusical or voiceless.

note of hand, a promissory note.

note paper, paper used for correspondence.

note·wor·thy (nōt′wûr′thĭ), *adj.* worthy of note or notice; notable. —**note′wor′thi·ly,** *adv.* —**note′wor′-thi·ness,** *n.*

noth·ing (nŭth′ĭng), *n.* **1.** no thing; not anything; naught: *say nothing.* **2.** no part, share, or trace (fol. by *of*): *the place shows nothing of its former magnificence.* **3.** that which is nonexistent. **4.** something of no importance or significance. **5.** a trivial action, matter, circumstance, thing, or remark. **6.** a person of no importance. **7.** that which is without quantity or magnitude. **8.** a cipher or naught. —*adv.* **9.** in no respect or degree; not at all: *it was nothing like what we expected.* [orig. two words. See NO, THING]

noth·ing·ness (nŭth′ĭng nĭs), *n.* **1.** state of being nothing. **2.** that which is nonexistent. **3.** nonexistence.

4. unconsciousness. **5.** utter insignificance, emptiness, or worthlessness; triviality. **6.** something insignificant.

no·tice (nō′tĭs), *n.*, *v.*, **-ticed, -ticing.** —*n.* **1.** information or intelligence: *to give notice of a thing.* **2.** an intimation or warning. **3.** a note, placard, or the like conveying information or warning. **4.** a notification of the termination, at a specified time, of an agreement, as for renting or employment, given by one of the parties to the agreement. **5.** observation, perception, attention, or heed: *worthy of notice.* **6.** interested or favorable attention. **7.** a single observation or perception. **8.** a brief written mention or account, as of a newly published book. —*v.t.* **9.** to pay attention to or take notice of. **10.** to perceive: *did you notice her hat?* **11.** to treat with attention, politeness, or favor. **12.** to acknowledge acquaintance with. **13.** to mention or refer to; point out, as to a person. **14.** to give notice to; serve with a notice. [late ME. t. OF. t. L: m.s. *nōtitia* a being known] —**Syn. 10.** NOTICE, DISCERN, PERCEIVE imply becoming aware of, and paying attention to, something. All are "point-action" verbs. To NOTICE is to become aware of something which has caught one's attention: *to notice the newspaper headline, I'm sorry I didn't notice it.* DISCERN suggests distinguishing (sometimes with difficulty) and recognizing a thing for what it is, discriminating it from its surroundings: *in spite of the fog we finally discerned the outline of the harbor.* PERCEIVE, often used as a formal substitute for "see" or "notice," may convey also the idea of understanding meanings and implications: *after examining the evidence he perceived its real meaning.* —**Ant. 9.** ignore. **10.** miss.

no·tice·a·ble (nō′tĭs ə bəl), *adj.* that may be noticed; such as to attract notice. —**no′tice·a·bly,** *adv.*

no·ti·fi·ca·tion (nō′tə fə kā′shən), *n.* **1.** act of notifying, making known, or giving notice. **2.** a formal notifying, or informing. **3.** a notice.

no·ti·fy (nō′tə fī′), *v.t.*, **-fied, -fying. 1.** to give notice to, or inform, of something. **2.** *Chiefly Brit.* to make known; give information of: *the sale was notified in the newspapers.* [ME *notifie(n),* t. OF: m. *notifier,* t. L: m. *nōtificāre* make known] —**no′ti·fi′er,** *n.*

no·tion (nō′shən), *n.* **1.** a more or less general, vague or imperfect conception or idea of something: *notions of beauty.* **2.** an opinion, view, or belief. **3.** conception or idea. **4.** a fanciful or foolish idea; whim. **5.** a device, contrivance, or ingenious article. **6.** (*pl.*) *U.S.* small wares, esp. pins, needles, thread, tapes, etc. [t. L: s. *nōtio* a becoming acquainted, conception, notion]

no·tion·al (nō′shən əl), *adj.* **1.** pertaining to or expressing a notion or idea. **2.** of the nature of a notion. **3.** abstract or speculative, as reflective thought. **4.** ideal or imaginary, as things. **5.** *U.S.* given to or full of notions, as a person; fanciful. **6.** *Gram.* **a.** relating to the meaning expressed by a linguistic form. **b.** having full lexical meaning, in contrast to relational. **7.** *Semantics.* presentive. —**no′tion·al·ly,** *adv.*

no·to·chord (nō′tə kôrd′), *n.* *Biol.* a rodlike stiffening structure found in the bodies of the protochordates, e.g. along the back of amphioxus, and also found in the embryos of the vertebrates, and presumed to represent an ancestral stage of the spinal column. [f. *noto-* (t. Gk., comb. form of *nōton* back) + CHORD]

No·to·gae·a (nō′tə jē′ə), *n.* *Zoogeog.* a great zoölogical division of the earth's land area, comprising the Austro-colombian, Australasian and Neotropical regions. [NL, f. Gk.: *nōto(s)* the south + m. *gaîa* land, earth] —**No′-to·gae′an,** *n.*, *adj.*

no·to·ri·e·ty (nō′tə rī′ə tĭ), *n.*, *pl.* **-ties. 1.** state or character of being notorious or widely known: *a craze for notoriety.* **2.** a widely known or well-known person.

no·to·ri·ous (nō tōr′ĭ əs), *adj.* **1.** widely but unfavorably known: *a notorious gambler.* **2.** publicly or generally known: *notorious crimes.* [t. ML: m. *nōtōrius,* der. L *nōtus,* pp., known] —**no·to′ri·ous·ly,** *adv.* —**no·to′ri·ous·ness,** *n.*

no·tor·nis (nō tôr′nĭs), *n.* any of the rare flightless birds constituting the genus *Notornis,* chiefly of New Zealand. [t. NL, f. Gk.: s. *nōtos* the south + *órnis* bird]

No·tre Dame (nō′trə dãm′, nō′tər; Fr. nô′tr dàm′), famous early Gothic cathedral in Paris (started 1163).

no-trump (nō′trŭmp′), *Bridge.* —*adj.* **1.** denoting a bid or play without any trump suit. —*n.* **2.** the play, or the bid to play without any trump suit.

no-trump·er (nō′trŭmp′ər), *n.* *Bridge.* a game or hand played in no-trump.

Not·ting·ham (nŏt′ĭng əm), *n.* **1.** a city in central England. 284,750 (est. 1946). **2.** Nottinghamshire.

Not·ting·ham·shire (nŏt′ĭng əm shĭr′, -shər), *n.* a county in central England. 782,000 pop. (est. 1946); 844 sq. mi. *Co. seat:* Nottingham. Also, **Nottingham** or **Notts** (nŏts).

no·tun·gu·late (nō tŭng′gyə lāt′), *adj.* *Paleontol.* of an order, *Notungulata,* of extinct herbivorous mammals.

not·with·stand·ing (nŏt′wĭth stăn′dĭng, -wĭth-), *prep.* **1.** without being withstood or prevented by; in spite of. —*adv.* **2.** nevertheless; yet. —*conj.* **3.** in spite of the fact that; although. [ME] —**Syn. 1.** NOTWITHSTANDING, DESPITE, IN SPITE OF imply that something is true even though there are obstacles or opposing conditions. The three expressions may be used practically interchangeably. NOTWITHSTANDING suggests, however, a hindrance of some kind: *notwithstanding the long delay, I shall still go.* DESPITE, now literary and somewhat archaic, indicates that there is an active opposition: *despite the circulation of slanderous stories about him, the candidate* *was elected.* In SPITE OF, the modern equivalent on an informal level, implies meeting strong opposing forces or circumstances which must be taken into account: *he succeeded in spite of all discouragements.*

nou·gat (noo̅′gət, noo̅′gä), *n.* a pastelike confection containing almonds or other nuts. [t. F, t. Pr., der. *noga*, g. LL *nuca* nut, r. L *nux*]

nought (nôt), *n., adj., adv.* naught. [ME *noht, nouht*, OE *nōht*, syncopated var. of *nōwiht*]

nou·me·non (noo̅′mənŏn′, nou′-), *n., pl.* **-na** (-nə). **1.** (in the Kantian philosophy) that which can be the object only of a purely intellectual (nonsensuous) intuition; essentially, a postulate. **2.** the transexperiential object to which a phenomenon is referred as to the basis or cause of its sense content. **3.** a thing in itself, as distinguished from a phenomenon or thing as it appears to us. [t. Gk.: m. *nooúmenon*, neut. ppr. pass., (anything) perceived] —**nou′me·nal**, *adj.* —**nou′me·nal·ly**, *adv.* —**nou′me·nal·ism**, *n.* —**nou′me·nal·ist**, *n.*

noun (noun), *n. Gram.* **1.** (in most languages) one of the major form classes, or "parts of speech," comprising words denoting person, places, things, and such other words as show similar grammatical behavior, as English *friend, city, desk, whiteness, virtue.* **2.** any such word. **3.** any word or construction of similar function or meaning. [ME *nowne*, t. AF: m. *noun*, g. L *nōmen* name] —**noun′al**, *adj.* —**noun′al·ly**, *adv.*

nou·rice (noo̅′rĭs), *n. Obs.* a nurse.

nour·ish (nûr′ĭsh), *v.t.* **1.** to sustain with food or nutriment; supply with what is necessary for maintaining life. **2.** to foster or promote. [ME *norische(n)*, t. OF: m. *noriss-*, s. *norir*, g. L *nūtrīre* suckle, feed, maintain] —**nour′ish·er**, *n.* —**nour′ish·ing·ly**, *adv.* —Syn. 2. See **nurse.**

nour·ish·ment (nûr′ĭshmənt), *n.* **1.** that which nourishes; food, nutriment, or sustenance. **2.** act of nourishing. **3.** state of being nourished.

nous (noo̅s, nous), *n. Gk. Philos.* mind or intellect. [t. Gk., contr. of *nóos*]

nou·veau riche (noo̅ vō rēsh′), *pl.* **nouveaux riches** (noo̅ vō rēsh′). *French.* one who has newly become rich.

Nov., November.

no·va (nō′və), *n., pl.* **-vae** (-vē), **-vas.** *Astron.* a new star which makes its appearance suddenly and then gradually grows fainter. [t. NL: (fem.) new]

No·va·chord (nō′vəkôrd′), *n.* a trademark for a keyboard instrument resembling in shape an upright piano, operating by electronic tone generation and providing a great variety of tone colors.

no·vac·u·lite (nō văk′yəlīt′), *n. Petrog.* a very hard, compact, siliceous rock, probably sedimentary, used for hones, etc. [f. s. L *novācula* sharp knife, razor + -ITE[1]]

No·va·lis (nō vä′lĭs), *n.* pen name of **Hardenberg, Friedrich von.**

No·va·ra (nō vä′rä), *n.* a city in NW Italy, in Piedmont. 52,269 (1936).

No·va Sco·tia (nō′və skō′shə), a peninsula and province in SE Canada: once a part of the French province of Acadia. 577,962 pop. (1941); 21,068 sq. mi. *Cap.:* Halifax. —**No′va Sco′tian.**

no·va·tion (nō vā′shən), *n.* **1.** *Law.* the substitution of a new obligation for an old one, usually by the substitution of a new debtor or of a new creditor. **2.** *Now Rare.* the introduction of something new; an innovation.

No·va·ya Zem·lya (nō′vä yä zĕm lyä′), two large islands in the Arctic Ocean, N of the Soviet Union in Europe. ab. 35,000 sq. mi. Also, **No·va Zem·bla** (nō′vä zĕm blä′).

nov·el[1] (nŏv′əl), *n.* **1.** a fictitious prose narrative of considerable length, portraying characters, actions, and scenes representative of real life in a plot of more or less intricacy. **2.** (formerly) a short story, as a novella. [t. It.: m.s. *novella*, t. L (appar. short for *novella narrātio* new kind of story)] —Syn. 1. NOVEL, ROMANCE are both long stories. A NOVEL is now a long fictitious story, picturing, in a series of evolving situations, characters and actions that represent real life: *a novel about a war veteran.* A ROMANCE (originally a story told in one of the Romance languages) came to mean a story laid especially in remote or unfamiliar times or places, describing unusual persons, customs, adventures and usually having love as a prominent theme: *a romance about the days of chivalry.*

nov·el[2] (nŏv′əl), *adj.* of a new kind, or different from anything seen or known before: *a novel experience.* [ME, t. LL: m.s. *novellus* new] —**nov′el·ly**, *adv.* —Syn. See **new.**

nov·el[3] (nŏv′əl), *n.* **1.** *Rom. Law.* **a.** a constitution with imperial authority, subsequent to publication of a code. **b.** *(pl., cap.)* constitutions of Justinian and later emperors before A.D. 582 issued after promulgation of the Justinian Code. **2.** *Civil Law.* an amendment to a statute. [t. LL: short for *novella (constitūtio)* new (regulation)]

nov·el·ette (nŏv′əlĕt′), *n.* a short novel.

nov·el·ist (nŏv′əlĭst), *n.* a writer of novels.

nov·el·is·tic (nŏv′əlĭs′tĭk), *adj.* of, pertaining to, or characteristic of novels. —**nov′el·is′ti·cal·ly**, *adv.*

nov·el·ize (nŏv′əlīz′), *v.t.* **-ized, -izing.** to put into the form of a novel. —**nov′el·i·za′tion**, *n.*

no·vel·la (nō vĕl′lä), *n., pl.* **-le** (-lĕ). **1.** a tale or short story of the type of those contained in the *Decameron* or Boccaccio, etc. **2.** a short story, usually domestic or middle-class in character. [t. It. See NOVEL[1]]

nov·el·ty (nŏv′əl tĭ), *n., pl.* **-ties.** **1.** novel character, newness, or strangeness. **2.** a novel thing, experience or proceeding. **3.** a new or novel article of trade; a variety of goods differing from the staple or ordinary kinds. [ME *novelte*, t. OF: m. *novelte*, g. LL *novellitas* newness]

No·vem·ber (nō vĕm′bər), *n.* the eleventh month of the year, containing 30 days. [t. L: the ninth month of the early Roman year; r. ME *Novembre*, t. OF]

no·ve·na (nō vē′nə), *n., pl.* **-nae** (-nē). *Rom. Cath. Ch.* a devotion consisting of prayers or services on nine consecutive days. [t. ML, prop. fem. of L *novēnus* nine each]

no·ver·cal (nō yûr′kəl), *adj.* of, like, or befitting a stepmother. [t. L: s. *novercālis*, der. *noverca* stepmother]

Nov·go·rod (nŏv′gŏ rŏt), *n.* a city in the NW Soviet Union: a former capital of Russia. 32,764 (1926).

nov·ice (nŏv′ĭs), *n.* **1.** one who is new to the circumstances, work, etc. in which he is placed; a tyro: *a novice in politics.* **2.** one who has been received into a religious order or congregation for a period of probation before taking vows. **3.** a person newly become a church member. **4.** a recent convert to Christianity. [ME *novise*, t. OF: m. *novice*, t. L: m.s. *novīcius* new]

No·vi Sad (nō′vĭ säd′), a city in NE Yugoslavia, on the Danube. 63,985 (1931). German, **Neusatz.**

no·vi·ti·ate (nō vĭsh′ĭ ĭt, -āt′), *n.* **1.** state or period of being a novice of a religious order or congregation. **2.** the quarters occupied by religious novices during probation. **3.** state or period of being a beginner in anything. **4.** a novice. Also, **no·vi′ci·ate.** [t. ML: s. *novītiātus*, der. L *novītius* new. See -ATE[3]]

no·vo·caine (nō′vəkān′), *n.* **1.** a nonirritant local anesthestic, $C_{13}H_{20}N_2O_2HCl$, a synthetic and much less toxic substitute for cocaine; procaine. **2.** *(cap.)* a trademark for this substance. Also, **no′vo·cain′.** [f. *novo-* (comb. form repr. L *novus* new) + (CO)CAINE]

No·vo·ros·siisk (nō′vŏ rŏ sēsk′), *n.* a seaport in the SW Soviet Union, on the Black Sea. 95,280 (1939).

No·vo·si·birsk (nō′vŏ sĭ bērsk′), *n.* a city in the W Soviet Union in Asia, on the Ob river. 405,589 (1939). Formerly, **No·vo·ni·ko·la·evsk** (nō′vŏ nĭ kŏ lä′yĕfsk).

no·vus or·do sc·clo·rum (nō′vəs ôr′dŏ sĕ klōr′əm), *Latin.* a new order of the ages (is born): motto on the great seal of the United States, adapted from Vergil's *Eclogues,* IV, 5.

now (nou), *adv.* **1.** at the present time or moment: *he is here now.* **2.** (more emphatically) immediately or at once: *now or never.* **3.** at this time or juncture in some period under consideration or in some course of proceedings described: *the case now passes to the jury.* **4.** at the time or moment only just past: *I saw him just now on the street.* **5.** in these present times; nowadays. **6.** under the present or existing circumstances; as matters stand. **7.** (often used as a preliminary word before some statement, question, or the like): *Now, what does he mean?* **8.** (to strengthen a command, entreaty, or the like): *come, now, stop that!* **9.** now and again or now and then, occasionally. **10.** now that, inasmuch as. —*conj.* **11.** now that; since, or seeing that: *now you are here, why not stay?* —*n.* **12.** the present time or moment. [ME; OE *nū*, c. D and G *nū*, Icel. and Goth. *nū*]

now·a·days (nou′ə dāz′), *adv.* **1.** at the present day; in these times. —*n.* **2.** the present. [ME; f. NOW + *adays* by day (f. *a* in + *days* by day, adv. gen.)]

no·way (nō′wā′), *adv.* in no way, respect, or degree; not at all. Also, **no′ways′.**

now·el (nō ĕl′), *n. Archaic.* Noel. [ME, t. OF: m. *no(u)el*, g. L *nātālis* natal]

no·where (nō′hwâr′), *adv.* in, at, or to no place; not anywhere. Also, *U.S. Dial.,* **no′wheres′.** [ME; OE *nāhwær* also *nōhwær*]

no·whith·er (nō′hwĭth′ər), *adv.* to no place; nowhere. [ME *nowhider*, OE *nāhwider* (also *nōhwider*)]

no·wise (nō′wīz′), *adv.* in no wise; noway; not at all.

nowt (nout), *n. Scot. and N. Eng.* cattle or oxen.

Nox (nŏks) *n. Rom. Myth.* the goddess of night. [t. L]

nox·ious (nŏk′shəs), *adj.* **1.** harmful or injurious to health or physical well-being: *noxious vapors.* **2.** morally harmful; pernicious. [t. L: m. *noxius* hurtful] —**nox′ious·ly**, *adv.* —**nox′ious·ness**, *n.*

no·yade (nwä yäd′; *Fr.* nwä yàd′), *n.* destruction or execution by drowning, esp. as practiced at Nantes, France, in 1793–94, during the Reign of Terror. [t. F, der. *noyer* drown, g. L *necāre* kill]

Noyes (noiz), *n.* **Alfred,** born 1880, British poet.

noz·zle (nŏz′əl), *n.* **1.** a projecting spout, terminal discharging pipe, or the like, as of a bellows or a hose. **2.** the socket of a candlestick. **3.** the spout of a teapot. **4.** *Slang.* the nose. [f. NOSE + -*le*, dim. suffix]

N.P., Notary Public.

nr., near.

NRA, National Recovery Administration. Also, **N.R.A.**

N.S., **1.** New Style. **2.** Nova Scotia.

n.s., not specified.

N.S.P.C.A., National Society for the Prevention of Cruelty to Animals.

N.S.P.C.C., National Society for the Prevention of Cruelty to Children.

N.S.W., New South Wales.

Nt, *Chem.* niton.

N.T., **1.** New Testament. **2.** Northern Territory.

b., blend of, blended; c., cognate with; d., dialect, dialectal; der., derived from; f., formed from; g., going back to; m., modification of; r., replacing; s., stem of; t., taken from; ?, perhaps. See the full key on inside cover.

nth (ĕnth), *adj.* **1.** the last in a series of infinitely decreasing or increasing values, amounts, etc. **2. the nth degree** or **power, a.** a high (sometimes, any) degree or power. **b.** the utmost extent.

nt. wt., net weight.

nu (nū, nōō), *n.* the thirteenth letter (N, *ν* = English N, n) of the Greek alphabet.

nu·ance (nūäns′, nōō-, nū′äns, nōō′-; *Fr.* nyäns′), *n.* a shade of color, expression, meaning, feeling, etc. [t. F, b. OF *muance* variation (der. *muer* to change, g. L *mūtāre*), and *nue* cloud]

nub (nŭb), *n.* **1.** a knob or protuberance. **2.** a lump or small piece. **3.** *U.S. Colloq.* the point or gist of anything. [var. of KNOB]

nub·bin (nŭb′ĭn), *n. U.S.* **1.** a small lump or piece. **2.** a small or imperfect ear of maize. **3.** an undeveloped fruit. [dim. of NUB]

nub·ble (nŭb′əl), *n.* **1.** a small lump or piece. **2.** a small knob or protuberance. [f. NUB + -*le*, dim. suffix]

nub·bly (nŭb′lĭ), *adj.* **1.** full of small protuberances. **2.** in the form of small lumps.

nu·bi·a (nū′bĭə, nōō′-), *n.* a woman's light knitted woolen scarf. [f. s. L *nūbes* cloud + -IA]

Nu·bi·a (nū′bĭə, nōō′-), *n.* a region in what is now S Egypt and the Anglo-Egyptian Sudan N of Khartoum, extending from the Nile to the Red Sea.

Nu·bi·an (nū′bĭən, nōō′-), *n.* Also, **Nu·ba** (nū′bə, nōō′-). **1.** one of a Negroid people, of mixed descent, inhabiting Nubia. **2.** a language of the Nile valley below Khartoum. **3.** a Nubian or Negro slave. **4.** a Nubian horse. —*adj.* **5.** of or pertaining to Nubia.

Nubian Desert, an arid region in the NE Anglo-Egyptian Sudan, E of the Nile.

nu·bile (nū′bĭl, nōō′-), *adj.* marriageable, esp. as to age or physical development. [t. L: m.s. *nūbilis*] —**nu·bil′i·ty,** *n.*

nu·bi·lous (nū′bələs, nōō′-), *adj.* **1.** cloudy or foggy. **2.** obscure; indefinite. [t. L: m. *nūbilus* cloudy]

nu·cel·lus (nū·sĕl′əs, nōō-), *n., pl.* **-celli** (-sĕl′ī). *Bot.* the central cellular mass of the body of the ovule, containing the embryo sac. [t. NL, dim. of L *nux nut*] —**nu·cel′lar,** *adj.*

nu·cha (nū′kə, nōō′-), *n., pl.* **-chae** (-kē). the nape of the neck. [ME, t. ML, t. Ar.: m. *nukhā* spinal marrow] —**nu′chal,** *adj.*

nu·cle·ar (nū′klĭər, nōō′-), *adj.* of, pertaining to, or forming a nucleus.

nuclear fission, the breakdown of an atomic nucleus of an element of relatively high atomic number into two or more nuclei of lower atomic number, with conversion of part of its mass into energy.

nuclear physics, the branch of physics dealing with the nature of atoms.

nu·cle·ate (nū′klĭ·ĭt, -āt′, nōō′), *adj.* having a nucleus. [t. L: m.s. *nucleātus* having a kernel or stone]

nu·cle·i (nū′klĭ·ī′, nōō′-), *n.* pl. of **nucleus.**

nu·cle·ic acid (nū·klē′ĭk, nōō′-), *Biochem.* any of a group of complex acids obtained from the proteins in the cell nucleus, composed of a phosphoric acid radical, carbohydrate, two purins and two pyrimidines.

nu·cle·in (nū′klĭ·ĭn, nōō′-), *n. Biochem.* any of a class of phosphorus-containing protein substances occurring in cell nuclei.

nu·cle·o·lar (nū·klē′ə·lər, nōō-), *adj. Biol.* relating or pertaining to the nucleolus.

nu·cle·o·lat·ed (nū·klē′ə·lā′tĭd, nōō′-), *adj.* containing a nucleolus or nucleoli. Also, **nu′cle·o·late′.**

nu·cle·o·lus (nū·klē′ə·ləs, nōō′-), *n., pl.* **-li** (-lī′). *Biol.* a conspicuous, often rounded body within the nucleus of a cell. Also, **nu·cle·ole** (nū′klĭ·ōl′, nōō′-). See diag. under **cell.** [t. L: little nut, dim. of *nūcleus.* See NUCLEUS]

nu·cle·o·plasm (nū′klĭ·ə·plăz′əm, nōō′-), *n. Biol.* karyoplasm. [f. *nucleo*- (comb. form of NUCLEUS) + -PLASM] —**nu′cle·o·plas′mic,** *adj.*

nu·cle·us (nū′klĭ·əs, nōō′-), *n., pl.* **-clei** (-klī′ī′), **-cle·uses. 1.** a central part or thing about which other parts or things are grouped. **2.** anything constituting a central part, foundation, or beginning. **3.** *Biol.* a differentiated mass (usually rounded) of protoplasm, encased in a delicate membrane, present in the interior of nearly all living cells and forming an essential element in their growth metabolism and reproduction. See diag. under **cell. 4.** *Anat.* a mass of gray matter in the brain and spinal cord in which incoming nerve fibers form connections with outgoing fibers. **5.** *Chem.* a fundamental arrangement of atoms, as the benzene ring, which may occur in many compounds by substitution of atoms without a change in structure. **6.** *Physics.* the central core of an atom, composed of protons and neutrons. It has a net positive charge equal to the number of protons. **7.** *Astron.* the more condensed portion of the head of a comet. **8.** *Meteorol.* a particle upon which condensation of water vapor occurs to form water drops. [t. L: nut, kernel, fruit stone]

nude (nūd, nōōd), *adj.* **1.** naked or unclothed, as a person, the body, etc. **2.** without the usual coverings, furnishings, etc.; bare. **3.** *Law.* unsupported; made without a consideration: *a nude pact.* —*n.* **4. the nude, a.** the condition of being undraped. **b.** the undraped human figure. **5.** a nude figure as represented in art. [t. L: m.s. *nūdus* bare] —**nude′ly,** *adv.* —**nude′-ness,** *n.*

nudge (nŭj), *v.,* **nudged, nudging,** *n.* —*v.t.* **1.** to push slightly or jog, esp. with the elbow, as in calling attention or giving a hint or with sly meaning. —*v.i.* **2.** to give a nudge. —*n.* **3.** a slight push or jog. [orig. obscure]

nudi-, a word element meaning "bare." [t. L, comb. form of *nūdus*]

nu·di·branch (nū′də·brăngk′, nōō′-), *n.* a shell-less type of marine snail with external respiratory appendages, noted for its beautiful coloring and graceful form. [t. F: m. *nudibranche,* f. nudi- NUDI- + *branche* gills, t. L: m. *branchia* BRANCHIA]

nu·di·caul (nū′də·kôl′, nōō′-), *adj. Bot.* having leafless stems. Also, **nu/di·cau′lous.** [f. NUDI- + s. L *caulus* stem]

nud·ism (nū′dĭz′əm, nōō′-), *n.* the practice of going nude or naked as a measure of healthful living, as by a company of persons. —**nud′ist,** *n., adj.*

nu·di·ty (nū′də·tĭ, nōō′-), *n., pl.* **-ties. 1.** state or fact of being nude; nakedness. **2.** something nude or naked. **3.** a nude figure, esp. as represented in art.

nu·dum pac·tum (nū′dəm păk′təm), *Latin.* a simple contract or promise with no consideration involved.

Nu·e·ces (nōō·ā′sās), *n.* a river in S Texas, flowing SE to Corpus Christi Bay, on the Gulf of Mexico. 388 mi.

Nue·vo Le·ón (nwĕ′vô lĕ·ôn′), a state in NE Mexico. 541,147 pop. (1940); 25,136 sq. mi. *Cap.:* Monterrey.

nu·gae (nū′jē), *n.pl. Latin.* jests; trifles.

nu·ga·to·ry (nū′gə·tôr′ĭ, nōō′-), *adj.* **1.** trifling; of no real value; worthless. **2.** of no force or effect; futile; vain. [t. L: m.s. *nūgātōrius* worthless]

nug·get (nŭg′ĭt), *n.* **1.** a lump of something. **2.** a lump of native gold. [appar. der. d. *nug* lump, block]

nui·sance (nū′səns, nōō′-), *n.* **1.** a highly obnoxious or annoying thing or person. **2.** something offensive or annoying to individuals or to the community, to the prejudice of their legal rights. [ME *nusance,* t. OF: m. *nuisance,* der. *nuire* harm, g. L *nocēre*]

nuisance tax, a tax paid in small amounts, usually by consumers.

null (nŭl), *adj.* **1.** of no effect, consequence, or significance. **2.** being none, lacking, or nonexistent. **3. null and void,** having no legal force or effect. **4.** zero. [t. L: s. *nullus* no, none]

nul·lah (nŭl′ə), *n.* (in the East Indies) **1.** the bed of a stream, whether with water, or dry; a ravine. **2.** a watercourse. [t. Hind.: m. *nālā*]

nulli-, a word element meaning "none." [t. L, comb. form of *nullus*]

nul·li·fi·ca·tion (nŭl′ə·fə·kā′shən), *n.* **1.** act of nullifying. **2.** state of being nullified. **3.** Also, **Nul′li·fi·ca′-tion.** *U.S.* the failure of a State to aid in the enforcement of Federal laws within its limits. —**nul′li·fi·ca′tion·ist,** *n.*

nul·li·fid·i·an (nŭl′ə·fĭd′ĭən), *n.* one who has no faith or religion; skeptic. [f. NULLI- + s. L *fides* faith + -IAN]

nul·li·fy (nŭl′ə·fī′), *v.t.,* **-fied, -fying. 1.** to make null; make ineffective, futile, or of no consequence. **2.** to render or declare legally void or inoperative: *to nullify a contract.* [t. LL: m *nullificāre* make null, dispose] —**nul′li·fi′er,** *n.*

nul·lip·a·ra (nə·lĭp′ə·rə), *n., pl.* **-rae** (-rē′). *Obstet.* a woman who has never borne a child. [t. NL: f. *nulli*-NULLI- + -*para,* fem. of *parus* -PAROUS] —**nul·lip′a·rous,** *adj.*

nul·li·pore (nŭl′ə·pōr′), *n. Bot.* any of the coralline algae with a crustlike plant body. [f. NULLI- + PORE[2]]

nul·li·ty (nŭl′ə·tĭ), *n., pl.* **-ties. 1.** state of being null; nothingness; invalidity. **2.** something null. **3.** something of no legal force or validity. [t. ML: m.s. *nullitas*]

Num., Numbers.

num., 1. numeral. **2.** numerals.

Nu·man·ti·a (nū·măn′shĭə, nōō-), *n.* an ancient city in N Spain: besieged and taken by Scipio the Younger, 134–133 B.C.

Nu·ma Pom·pil·i·us (nū′mə pŏm·pĭl′ĭ·əs, nōō′mə), d. 672? B.C., 2nd (legendary) king of Rome (715–672 B.C.), said to have introduced religious worship, having been instructed in it by a nymph, Egeria.

numb (nŭm), *adj.* **1.** deprived of or deficient in the power of sensation and movement: *fingers numb with cold.* **2.** of the nature of numbness: *a numb sensation.* —*v.t.* **3.** to make numb. [ME *nome,* lit., taken, seized, apocopated var. of ME *nomen, numen,* OE *numen,* pp. of *niman* take] —**numb′ly,** *adv.* —**numb′ness,** *n.*

num·ber (nŭm′bər), *n.* **1.** the sum, total, count, or aggregate of a collection of units or any generalization of this concept. **2.** a numeral. **3.** (*pl.*) *Obs.* arithmetic. **4.** the particular numeral assigned to anything in order to fix its place in a series: *a house number.* **5.** a word or symbol, or a combination of words or symbols, used in counting or to denote a total. **6.** one of a series of things distinguished by numerals. **7.** a single part of a book published in parts. **8.** a single issue of a periodical. **9.** any of a collection of poems or songs. **10.** a single part of a program made up of a number of parts. **11.** the full count of a collection or company. **12.** a collection or company. **13.** a quantity (large or small) of individuals. **14.** a certain collection, company, or quantity not precisely reckoned, but usually considerable or large. **15.** (*pl.*) considerable collections or quantities. **16.** numerical strength or superiority. **17.** quantity as composed of units. **18.** *Gram.* (in many languages) a cate-

gory of the inflection of nouns, verbs, and related word-classes, usually expressing the number of persons or objects referred to: comprising as subcategories the *singular* and *plural* and in some languages one or two intermediate subcategories (the *dual*, referring to two, and the *trial*, referring to three). **19.** (*pl.*) metrical feet, or verse. **20.** (*pl.*) musical periods, measures, or groups of notes. **21.** a distinct part of an extended musical work, or one in a sequence of compositions. **22.** conformity in music or verse to regular beat or measure; rhythm. **23. number one,** oneself. **24. without number,** of which the number is unknown or too great to be counted: *stars without number.* —*v.t.* **25.** to ascertain the number of. **26.** to mark with or distinguish by a number or numbers. **27.** to count over one by one. **28.** to mention one by one; enumerate. **29.** to fix the number of, limit in number, or make few in number. **30.** to reckon or include in a number. **31.** to mark with or distinguish with a number or numbers. **32.** to live or have lived (so many years). **33.** to have or comprise in number. **34.** to amount to in number: *a crew numbering fifty men.* **35.** *Obs.* to appoint or allot. —*v.i.* **36.** *Poetic.* to make enumeration; count. **37.** to be numbered or included. [ME *nombre*, t. OF, g. L *numerus*] —**num'ber·er,** *n.*
—**Syn. 1.** NUMBER, SUM both imply the total of two or more units. NUMBER applies to the result of a count or estimate in which the units are considered as individuals; it is used of groups of persons or things: *a number of persons before the house.* SUM applies to the result of addition, in which only the total is considered: *a large sum of money.*

num·ber·less (nŭm'bər lǐs), *adj.* **1.** innumerable; countless; myriad. **2.** without a number or numbers.

Num·bers (nŭm'bərz), *n.* the fourth book of the Old Testament (so called because it relates the numbering of the Israelites after the exodus from Egypt).

numbers pool, an illegal daily lottery in which money may be wagered on the appearance of certain numbers, usually obtained from daily racing totals.

number theory, *Math.* the study of numbers (integers) and of the relations which hold between them.

numb·fish (nŭm'fĭsh), *n., pl.* **-fishes,** (*esp. collectively*) **-fish.** an electric ray (fish); so called from its power of numbing its prey by means of electric shocks.

num·bles (nŭm'bəlz), *n.pl.* *Archaic.* certain of the inward parts of an animal, esp. of a deer, used as food. Also, **nom'bles.** [ME *noumbles,* t. OF: m. *nombles,* g. L *lumbulus,* dim. of *lumbus* loin]

nu·men (nū'mĭn, nōō'-), *n., pl.* **-mina** (-mə nə). a deity; a divine power or spirit. [t. L]

nu·mer·a·ble (nū'mər ə bəl, nōō'-), *adj.* that may be numbered or counted. [t. L: m.s. *numerābilis*]

nu·mer·al (nū'mər əl, nōō'-), *n.* **1.** a word or words expressing a number: *cardinal numerals.* **2.** a letter or figure, or a group of letters or figures, denoting a number: *the Roman numerals.* —*adj.* **3.** of or pertaining to number; consisting of numbers. **4.** expressing or denoting number. [t. LL: s. *numerālis,* der. L *numerus* number]

nu·mer·ar·y (nū'mər rĕr'ĭ, nōō'-), *adj.* of or pertaining to a number or numbers.

nu·mer·ate (nū'mə rāt', nōō'-), *v.t.,* **-ated, -ating. 1.** to number; count; enumerate. **2.** to read (an expression in numbers). [t. L: m.s. *numerātus,* pp.]

nu·mer·a·tion (nū'mə rā'shən, nōō'-), *n.* **1.** act, process, or result of numbering or counting. **2.** process or a method of reckoning or calculating. **3.** act, art, or method of reading numbers in numerals or figures.

nu·mer·a·tor (nū'mə rā'tər, nōō'-), *n.* **1.** *Math.* that term (usually written above the line) of a fraction which shows how many parts of a unit are taken. **2.** one who or that which numbers. [t. LL: a counter]

nu·mer·i·cal (nū mĕr'ə kəl, nōō'-), *adj.* **1.** of or pertaining to number; of the nature of number. **2.** denoting number or a number: *numerical symbols.* **3.** bearing or designated by, a number. **4.** expressed by a number or figure, or by figures, and not by a letter or letters. **5.** *Math.* denoting value or magnitude irrespective of sign: *the numerical value of -10 is greater than that of -5.* Also **nu·mer'ic.** —**nu·mer'i·cal·ly,** *adv.*

nu·mer·ol·o·gy (nū'mə rŏl'ə jĭ, nōō'-), *n.* the study of numbers (as one's birth year, etc.), supposedly to determine their influence on one's life and future. [f. s. L *numerus* number + -(o)LOGY] —**nu·mer·o·log·i·cal** (nū'mər ə lŏj'ə kəl, nōō'-), *adj.*

nu·mer·ous (nū'mə rəs, nōō'-), *adj.* **1.** very many, forming a great number. **2.** consisting of or comprising a great number of units or individuals. [t. L: m.s. *numerōsus*] —**nu'mer·ous·ly,** *adv.* —**nu'mer·ous·ness,** *n.* —**Syn. 1.** See **many.**

Nu·mid·i·a (nū mĭd'ĭ ə, nōō-), *n.* an ancient country in N Africa, corresponding generally to modern Algeria. —**Nu·mid'i·an,** *adj., n.*

Numidian crane, demoiselle (def. 2).

numis., **1.** numismatic. **2.** numismatics. Also, **numism.**

nu·mis·mat·ic (nū'mĭz măt'ĭk, -mĭs-, nōō'-), *adj.* **1.** of or pertaining to, or consisting of, coins and medals. **2.** pertaining to numismatics. Also, **nu'mis·mat'i·cal.** [t. F: m. *numismatique,* der. L *nomisma* coin, t. Gk.]

nu·mis·mat·ics (nū'mĭz măt'ĭks, -mĭs-, nōō'-), *n.* the science of coins and medals. —**nu·mis·ma·tist** (nū mĭz'mə tĭst, -mĭs'-, nōō'-), *n.*

nu·mis·ma·tol·o·gy (nū mĭz'mə tŏl'ə jĭ, -mĭs'-, nōō'-), *n.* numismatics. —**nu·mis'ma·tol'o·gist,** *n.*

num·ma·ry (nŭm'ə rĭ), *adj.* **1.** of or pertaining to coins or money. **2.** occupied with coins or money.

num·mu·lar (nŭm'yə lər), *adj.* **1.** pertaining to coins or money; nummary. **2.** coin-shaped. [f. s. L *nummulus* (dim. of *nummus* coin) + -AR[1]]

num·mu·lite (nŭm'yə līt'), *n.* any of the foraminifers (mostly fossil) that constitute the family *Nummulitidae,* having a somewhat coinlike shell. [t. NL: m.s. *nummulītes,* der. L *nummulus,* dim. of *nummus* coin] —**num·mu·lit·ic** (nŭm'yə lĭt'ĭk), *adj.*

num·skull (nŭm'skŭl'), *n.* *Colloq.* a dull-witted person; a dunce; a dolt. [f. NUMB + SKULL]

nun (nŭn), *n.* **1.** a woman devoted to a religious life under vows. **2.** a woman living in a convent under solemn vows of poverty, chastity, and obedience. [ME and OE *nunne,* t. LL: m. *nonna,* fem. of *nonnus* monk]

Nun (nōōn), *n.* the chief mouth of the Niger river, in W Africa.

Nunc Di·mit·tis (nŭngk' dĭ mĭt'ĭs), **1.** the canticle of Simeon (Luke 2:29–32), beginning "Lord, now lettest thou thy servant depart in peace." **2.** (*l.c.*) permission to depart; dismissal; departure. [t. L; the first words as given in the Vulgate]

nun·ci·a·ture (nŭn'shĭ ə chər), *n.* the office or the term of service of a papal nuncio. [t. It.: m. *nunziatura,* der. *nunzio* NUNCIO]

nun·ci·o (nŭn'shĭ ō'), *n., pl.* **-cios.** a permanent diplomatic representative of the Pope at a foreign court or capital. [t. It., g. L *nuntius* messenger]

nun·cle (nŭng'kəl), *n.* *Archaic and Brit. Dial.* uncle.

nun·cu·pa·tive (nŭng'kyə pā'tĭv, nŭng kū'pə tĭv), *adj.* (of wills etc.) oral, rather than written. [t. LL: m.s. *nuncupātīvus* nominal]

Nun·kiang (nōōn'jyäng'), *n.* a province in NE China, in Manchuria. 2,102,100 pop. (1946); 25,856 sq. mi. *Cap.:* Tsitsihar.

nun·ner·y (nŭn'ə rĭ), *n., pl.* **-neries.** a religious house for nuns; a convent.

nun's veiling, a thin, plain-woven, worsted fabric, orig. for nun's veils but now for dresses, etc.

nup·tial (nŭp'shəl), *adj.* **1.** of or pertaining to marriage or the marriage ceremony: *the nuptial day.* —*n.* **2.** (*usually pl.*) marriage; wedding. [t. L: s. *nuptiālis* pertaining to marriage] —**Syn. 2.** See **marriage.**

Nu·rem·berg (nyŏŏr'əm bûrg', noor'-), *n.* a city in S Germany, in Bavaria; war guilt trials of Nazis, 1945–46. 423,383 (1939). German, **Nürn·berg** (nyrn'bĕrκн).

nurse (nûrs), *n., v.,* **nursed, nursing.** —*n.* **1.** a person (woman or man) who has the care of the sick or infirm. **2.** a woman who has the general care of a child or children. **3.** a woman employed to suckle an infant; wet nurse. **4.** any fostering agency or influence. **5.** a worker that attends the young in a colony of social insects. **6.** *Billiards.* act of nursing the balls. —*v.t.* **7.** to tend in sickness or infirmity. **8.** to seek to cure (a cold, etc.) by taking care of oneself. **9.** to look after carefully so as to promote growth, development, etc.; foster; cherish (a feeling, etc.). **10.** to treat or handle with adroit care in order to further one's own interests. **11.** to bring up, train, or nurture. **12.** to clasp or handle as if fondly or tenderly. **13.** to suckle (an infant). **14.** to feed and tend in infancy. **15.** *Billiards.* to gather and keep (the balls) together for a series of caroms. —*v.i.* **16.** to act as nurse; tend the sick or infirm. **17.** to suckle a child. **18.** (of a child) to take the breast. [ME *nurse, nourice,* t. OF, g. LL *nūtrīcia* nurse, prop. fem of *nūtrīcius* that nourishes] —**nurs'er,** *n.*
—**Syn. 14.** NURSE, NOURISH, NURTURE may be used practically interchangeably to refer to bringing up the young. NURSE, however, suggests particularly attendance and service; NOURISH emphasizes providing whatever is needful for development; and NURTURE suggests tenderness and solicitude in training mind and manners.

nurse·ling (nûrs'lĭng), *n.* nursling.

nurse·maid (nûrs'mād'), *n.* a maidservant employed to take care of children. Also, **nurs'er·y·maid.**

nurs·er·y (nûr'sə rĭ), *n., pl.* **-eries. 1.** a room or place set apart for young children. **2.** a nursery school. **3.** any place in which something is bred, nourished, or fostered. **4.** any situation, condition, circumstances, practice, etc., serving to foster something. **5.** a place where young trees or other plants are raised for transplanting or for sale.

nurs·er·y·man (nûr'sə rĭ mən), *n., pl.* **-men.** one who owns or conducts a nursery for plants.

nursery rhyme, a short, simple poem or song for children.

nursery school, a prekindergarten school.

nurs·ing bottle (nûr'sĭng), a bottle with a rubber nipple, from which an infant sucks milk, water, etc.

nursing home, *Chiefly Brit.* a private convalescence hospital.

nurs·ling (nûrs'lĭng), *n.* **1.** an infant or child under a nurse's care. **2.** any person or thing under fostering care, influences, or conditions. Also, **nurseling.**

---

b., blend of, blended; **c.,** cognate with; **d.,** dialect, dialectal; **der.,** derived from; **f.,** formed from; **g.,** going back to; **m.,** modification of; **r.,** replacing; **s.,** stem of; **t.,** taken from; **?,** perhaps. See the full key on inside cover.

nur·ture (nûr′chər), v., **-tured, -turing,** n. —v.t. **1.** to feed, nourish, or support during the stages of growth, as children or young; rear. **2.** to bring up; train; educate. —n. **3.** upbringing or training. **4.** education; breeding. **5.** nourishment or food. [ME, t. OF, var. of *nourriture,* der. s. *nourrir* to nourish, g. L *nūtrīre*] —nur′tur·er, n. —Syn. **1.** See **nurse.**

nut (nŭt), n., v., **nutted, nutting.** —n. **1.** a dry fruit consisting of an edible kernel or meat enclosed in a woody or leathery shell. **2.** the kernel itself. **3.** *Bot.* a hard, indehiscent, one-seeded fruit, as the chestnut or the acorn. **4.** a difficult question, problem, or undertaking. **5.** any of various devices or parts supposed in some way to resemble a nut. **6.** *Slang.* the head. **7.** *Slang.* a person or fellow. **8.** *Slang.* a foolish or crazy person. **9.** a perforated block (usually of metal) with an internal thread or female screw, used to screw on the end of a bolt, etc. **10.** (in musical instruments of the violin type) **a.** the ledge, as of ebony, at the upper end of the finger board, over which the strings pass. **b.** the movable piece at the lower end of the bow, by means of which the hairs may be slackened or tightened. —v.i. **11.** to seek for or gather nuts. [ME *nute,* OE *hnutu,* c. G *nuss*] —nut′like′, adj.

N. Nut (def. 9); B, Bolt

nu·tant (nū′tənt, nōō′-), adj. *Bot.* drooping; nodding. [t. L: s. *nūtans,* ppr.]

nu·ta·tion (nū tā′shən, nōō-), n. **1.** a nodding. **2.** *Bot.* spontaneous movements of plant parts during growth. **3.** *Astron.* the periodic oscillation in the precessional motion of the earth's axis or of the equinoxes. [t. L: s. *nūtātio* a nodding]

nut-brown (nŭt′broun′), adj. brown, as many nuts when ripe.

nut cake, a doughnut or fried cake.

nut-crack·er (nŭt′krăk′ər), n. **1.** (often *pl.*) an instrument for cracking nuts. **2.** any of several corvine birds of the genus *Nucifraga* which feed on nuts, as the common nutcracker, *N. caryocatactes,* of Europe.

Nutcracker Suite, a ballet and concert suite (1892), by Tchaikovsky.

nut-gall (nŭt′gôl′), n. **1.** a nutlike gall or excrescence, esp. one formed on an oak. **2.** the Allepo nutgall.

nut grass, any of various sedges of the genus *Cyperus,* esp. *C. rotundus,* bearing small nutlike tubers.

nut-hatch (nŭt′hăch′), n. any of numerous small, short-tailed sharp-beaked birds constituting the family *Sittidae,* which creep on trees and feed on small nuts and insects. [ME *notehache, nuthage, nuthake,* lit., nut hacker]

nut-let (nŭt′lĭt), n. **1.** a small nut; a small nutlike fruit or seed. **2.** the stone of a drupe.

Nut-ley (nŭt′lĭ), n. a city in NE New Jersey. 26,992 (1950).

nut-meg (nŭt′mĕg), n. **1.** the hard, aromatic seed of the fruit of an East Indian tree, *Myristica fragrans,* used as a spice. **2.** the tree itself. **3.** the similar product of certain other trees of the same genus or other genera. [ME *notemuge,* f. *note* nut + OF *mug(u)e* musk, ult. der. LL *muscus*]

nut-pick (nŭt′pĭk′), n. a sharp-pointed table device for removing the meat from nuts.

nut pine, any of various trees of the southwestern U.S. and Rocky Mountains, as *Pinus monophylla, P. edulis,* etc., bearing edible nuts.

nu-tri-a (nū′trĭ ə, nōō′-), n. **1.** the coypu. **2.** the fur of this animal, resembling beaver. [t. Sp.: otter, g. L *lūtra* otter, b. with *enitria,* t. Gk.: m.s. *énydris*]

nu-tri-ent (nū′trĭ ənt, nōō′-), adj. **1.** containing or conveying nutriment, as solutions or vessels of the body. **2.** nourishing; affording nutriment. —n. **3.** a nutrient substance. [t. L: s. *nūtriens,* ppr., nourishing]

nu-tri-ment (nū′trə mənt, nōō′-), n. **1.** any matter that, taken into a living organism, serves to sustain it in its existence, promoting growth, replacing loss and providing energy. **2.** that which nourishes; nourishment, food, or aliment. [t. L: s. *nūtrīmentum*]

nu-tri-tion (nū trĭsh′ən, nōō-), n. **1.** act or process of nourishing or of being nourished. **2.** food; nutriment. **3.** the process by which the food material taken into an organism is converted into living tissue, etc. —nu-tri′tion-al, adj. —nu-tri′tion-al-ly, adv.

nu-tri-tion-ist (nū trĭsh′ən ĭst, nōō-), n. one who studies problems of food and nutrition.

nu-tri-tious (nū trĭsh′əs, nōō-), adj. nourishing, esp. in a high degree. [t. L: m. *nūtrīcius, nūtrītius*] —nu-tri′tious-ly, adv. —nu-tri′tious-ness, n.

nu-tri-tive (nū′trə tĭv, nōō′-), adj. **1.** serving to nourish; affording nutriment. **2.** of, pertaining to, or concerned in nutrition. —nu-tri-tive-ly, adv. —nu-tri-tive-ness, n.

nuts (nŭts), *Slang.* —interj. **1.** an expression of defiance, disgust, etc. —adj. **2.** crazy; insane.

nut-shell (nŭt′shĕl′), n. **1.** the shell of a nut. **2. in a nutshell,** in very brief form; in a few words: *Just tell me the story in a nutshell.*

nut-ter (nŭt′ər), n. one who gathers nuts.

nut-ting (nŭt′ĭng), n. act of seeking or gathering nuts.

nut-ty (nŭt′ĭ), adj., **-tier, -tiest. 1.** abounding in or producing nuts. **2.** nutlike, esp. in taste. **3.** full of flavor or zest. **4.** *Slang.* crazy. —nut′ti-ness. n.

nut-wood (nŭt′wŏŏd′), n. **1.** any one of various species of nut-bearing trees, as hickory, walnut, etc. **2.** a tree or the wood of a tree of such a species.

nux vom·i·ca (nŭks vŏm′ə kə), **1.** the strychnine-containing seed (used in medicine) of the orangelike fruit borne by an East Indian loganiaceous tree, *Strychnos nux-vomica.* **2.** the tree itself. [t. NL: vomiting nut, f. L *nux* nut + NL *vomica,* der. L *vomere* vomit]

nuz·zle¹ (nŭz′əl), v., **-zled, -zling.** —v.i. **1.** to burrow or root with the nose, as an animal does. **2.** to thrust the nose (fol. by *at, against, in,* etc.): *the pup nuzzled up close to the sick child.* —v.t. **3.** to root up with the nose. **4.** to touch or rub with the nose. **5.** to thrust the nose against or into. **6.** to thrust (the nose or head), as into something. [ME *nosele;* freq. of NOSE; to some extent confused with NESTLE]

nuz·zle² (nŭz′əl), v.t., v.i., **-zled, -zling.** to snuggle or cuddle. [? akin to NUZZLE¹]

NW, 1. northwest. **2.** northwestern. Also, **N. W., n.w.**

N.W.T., Northwest Territories (Canada).

N.Y., New York.

NYA, National Youth Administration. Also, **N.Y.A.**

Nya·sa (nyä′sä, nĭ ăs′ə), n. a lake in SE Africa. ab. 360 mi. long; ab. 11,000 sq. mi. Also, **Nyas′sa.**

Nya·sa·land (nyä′sä lănd′, nĭ ăs′ə-), n. a British protectorate on the W and S shores of Lake Nyasa, in SE Africa. 1,686,000 pop. (est. 1940); 37,596 sq. mi. *Cap.:* Zomba.

N.Y.C., New York City.

nyck·el·har·pa (nĭk′əl här′pə), n. an old-time Swedish stringed musical instrument, similar to the hurdy-gurdy but sounded with a bow instead of a wheel.

nyct-, a word element meaning "night." [t. Gk.; m. *nykt-,* comb. form of *nýx*]

nyc·ta·gi·na·ceous (nĭk′tə jə nā′shəs), adj. belonging to the *Nyctaginaceae,* or four-o'clock family of plants. [f. s. NL *Nyctago,* former name for genus *Mirabilis* (der. Gk. *nýx* night) + -ACEOUS]

nyc·ta·lo·pi·a (nĭk′tə lō′pĭ ə), n. **1.** a condition of the eyes in which sight is normal in the day or in a strong light, but is abnormally poor or wholly gone at night or in a dim light; night blindness. **2.** hemeralopia, a condition exactly opposite; day blindness. [t. LL, f. m.s. Gk. *nyktálops* blind by night + -ia -IA] —nyc·ta·lop·ic (nĭk′tə lŏp′ĭk), adj.

nyc·ti·trop·ic (nĭk′tə trŏp′ĭk), adj. *Bot.* tending to assume at or just before nightfall positions unlike those maintained during the day, as the leaves of certain plants. [f. *nycti-* (var. of NYCT-) + -TROPIC] —nyc·tit·ro·pism (nĭk tĭt′rə pĭz′əm), n.

Nye (nī), n. Edgar Wilson, ("Bill Nye") 1850–96, U.S. humorist.

Nye·man (nĕ′män), n. Russian name of **Nieman.**

nyl·ghau (nĭl′gô), n. nilgai. Also, **nyl·ghai** (nĭl′gī).

ny·lon (nī′lŏn), n. **1.** a synthetic polyamide capable of extrusion when molten into fibers, sheets, etc., of extreme toughness, strength, and elasticity: used for yarn (as for hosiery), for bristles (as for brushes), etc. It is a thermoplastic product, made by interaction of a dicarboxylic acid with a diamine. **2.** (*cap.*) a trademark for this material. **3.** (*pl.*) stockings made of nylon. [coined name]

nymph (nĭmf), n. **1.** one of a numerous class of inferior divinities of mythology, conceived as beautiful maidens inhabiting the sea, rivers, woods, trees, mountains, meadows, etc., and frequently mentioned as attending a superior deity. **2.** a beautiful or graceful young woman. **3.** *Chiefly Poetic or Playful.* a maiden. **4.** *Entomol.* **a.** the young of an insect without metamorphosis. **b.** a pupa. [ME *nimphe,* t. OF, t. L: m. *nympha,* t. Gk.: m. *nýmphē* nymph, pupa] —nymph′al, nym·phe·an (nĭm-fē′ən), adj. —Syn. **1.** See **sylph.**

nym·pha (nĭm′fə), n., pl. **-phae** (-fē). **1.** (*pl.*) *Anat.* the labia minora (see **labium** def. 2b). **2.** nymph (def. 4a).

nym·phae·a·ceous (nĭm′fĭ ā′shəs), adj. belonging to the *Nymphaeaceae,* or water-lily family of plants. [f. s. L *nymphaea,* t. Gk.: m. *nymphaía* water lily, prop. fem. of *nymphaîos* sacred to the nymphs) + -ACEOUS]

nym·pha·lid (nĭm′fə lĭd), n. any of the numerous butterflies of the family *Nymphalidae,* characterized by small useless forelegs, and including the fritillaries, etc. [t. NL: s. *nymphālis,* der. L *nympha* NYMPH + -idae -IDAE]

nym·pho·lep·sy (nĭm′fə lĕp′sĭ), n., pl. **-sies. 1.** an ecstasy supposed to be inspired by nymphs. **2.** a frenzy of emotion, as for something unattainable. [b. NYMPHOLEPT and EPILEPSY] —nym·pho·lep·tic (nĭm′fə-lĕp′tĭk), adj.

nym·pho·lept (nĭm′fə lĕpt′), n. one seized with nympholepsy. [t. Gk.: s. *nymphóleptos* caught by nymphs]

nym·pho·ma·ni·a (nĭm′fə mā′nĭ ə), n. *Pathol.* morbid and uncontrollable sexual desire in women. [f. Gk. *nympho-* NYMPH + MANIA] —nym·pho·ma·ni·ac (nĭm′-fə mā′nĭ ăk′), adj., n.

nys·tag·mus (nĭs tăg′məs), n. *Pathol.* an involuntary oscillation of the eyeball, usually lateral but sometimes rotatory or vertical: occurring esp. among miners and human albinos, and in certain diseases. [t. NL, t. Gk.: m. *nystagmós* nodding] —nys·tag·mic, adj.

Nyx (nĭks), n. Gk. Myth. a goddess, a personification of night.

N.Z., New Zealand. Also, **N. Zeal.**

O

O¹, o (ō), *n., pl.* **O's** or **Os, o's, os** or **oes. 1.** a vowel, the 15th letter of the English alphabet. **2.** something resembling the letter O in shape. **3.** the Arabic cipher; zero; naught (0). **4.** a mere nothing.

O² (ō), *interj., n., pl.* **O's.** —*interj.* **1.** a word used before the name in address, esp., as in solemn or poetic language, to lend earnestness to an appeal: *Praise the Lord, O Jerusalem.* **2.** an expression of surprise, pain, longing, gladness, etc. —*n.* **3.** the exclamation "O".

o' (ə, ō), *prep.* **1.** an abbreviated form of *of*, now chiefly *dial.* or *colloq.* except in *o'clock, will-o'-the-wisp,* etc. **2.** an abbreviated form of *on*.

O', a prefix meaning "descendant," in Irish family names: *O'Brien, O'Connor.* [repr. Irish ō descendant]

o-¹, *Chem.* an abridgment of ortho-.

o-², var. of **ob-,** before *m*, as in *omission*.

-o, an ending for the first element of many compounds, originally found in the combining forms of many Greek words, but often used in English as a connective irrespective of etymology, as in *Franco-Italian, speedometer,* etc.

O, 1. *Chem.* oxygen. **2.** Old.

o, ohm.

O., 1. Ocean. **2.** octavo. **3.** Ohio. **4.** Old. **5.** Ontario.

o., 1. (L *octavus*) pint. **2.** octavo. **3.** off. **4.** old. **5.** only **6.** order. **7.** *Baseball.* outs or put-outs.

oaf (ōf), *n.* **1.** a simpleton or blockhead. **2.** a lout. **3.** a deformed or idiotic child; an idiot. **4.** a changeling. [var. of *auf*, ME *alfe*, OE *ælf* elf, c. G *alp* nightmare] —**oaf'ish,** *adj.* —**oaf'ish·ly,** *adv.* —**oaf'ish·ness,** *n.*

O·a·hu (ō ä/hōō), *n.* the third largest and most important of the Hawaiian Islands: Honolulu is on Oahu. 345,000 pop. (est. 1950); 589 sq. mi.

oak (ōk), *n.* **1.** any tree or shrub of the large fagaceous genus *Quercus*, including many forest trees with hard, durable wood, bearing the acorn as fruit. **2.** the wood of on oak tree. **3.** the leaves of the oak tree, esp. as worn in a chaplet. **4.** anything made of oak, as furniture, a door, etc. **5. sport one's oak,** *Oxford and Cambridge Slang.* to indicate one is not at home to visitors by closing an outer door. [ME *ook,* OE *āc,* c. D *eik,* G *eiche*]

oak apple, any of various roundish galls produced on oaks. Also, **oak gall.**

oak·en (ō'kən), *adj.* **1.** made of oak: *the old oaken bucket.* **2.** of or pertaining to the oak.

Oak·land (ōk'lənd), *n.* a seaport in W California, on San Francisco Bay. 384,575 (1950).

oak leaf cluster, a small bronze decoration consisting of a twig bearing four oak leaves and three acorns. It is given to holders of medals for valor, wounds, or distinguished service, in recognition of some act justifying a second award of the same medal.

Oak·ley (ōk'lĭ), *n.* **Annie, 1.** (*Phoebe Anne Oakley Mozee*) 1860–1926, U.S. markswoman. **2.** *U.S. Slang.* a free ticket of admittance. [in allusion to the similarity between a punched ticket and a small target shot through by Annie Oakley]

Oak Park, a village in NE Illinois, near Chicago. 63,529 (1950).

Oak Ridge, a town in E Tennessee, near Knoxville: a center of atomic research. 30,229 (1950).

oa·kum (ō'kəm), *n.* loose fiber obtained by untwisting and picking apart old ropes, used for calking the seams of ships, etc. [ME *okom(e)*, OE *ācum(a)*, var. of *ācumba*, lit., offcombings. See COMB]

oar (ōr), *n.* **1.** an instrument for propelling a boat, sometimes used also for steering, consisting of a long shaft of wood with a blade at one end. **2.** something resembling this or used for a similar purpose. **3.** an oarsman. —*v.t.* **4.** to propel with or as with oars; row. **5.** to traverse (the sea, etc.), or make (one's way), by or as if by rowing. —*v.i.* **6.** to move or advance as if by rowing. [ME *ore,* OE *ār,* c. Icel. *ār*] —**oar'less,** *adj.* —**oar'like',** *adj.*

oared (ōrd), *adj.* furnished with oars.

oar·fish (ōr'fĭsh'), *n., pl.* **-fishes,** (*esp. collectively*) **-fish.** any of the pelagic fishes constituting the genus *Regalecus*, characterized by a compressed, tapelike body from 12 to over 20 feet long.

oar·lock (ōr'lŏk'), *n.* a contrivance on a boat's gunwale in or on which the oar rests and swings; rowlock. [ME *orlok,* OE *ārloc.* See OAR, LOCK¹]

Oarlock

oars·man (ōrz'mən), *n., pl.* **-men.** an expert in the use of oars. —**oars'man·ship',** *n.*

oar·y (ōr'ĭ), *adj.* *Chiefly Poetic.* oarlike.

o·a·sis (ō ā'sĭs, ō'ə sĭs). *n., pl.* **oases** (-sēz, -sēz'). a place in a desert region where ground water brought to the surface or surface water from other areas provides for humid vegetation. [t. L, t. Gk., ? t. Egyptian: m. *wāḥ*]

oast (ōst), *n.* *Chiefly Brit.* a kiln for drying hops or malt. [ME *ost,* OE *āst,* c. D *eest*]

oat (ōt), *n.* **1.** (*usually pl.*) a cereal grass, *Avena sativa*, cultivated for its edible seed, which is used in making oatmeal and as a food for horses, etc. **2.** (*pl.*) the seeds. **3.** any species of the same genus, as *A. fatua*, the common **wild oat. 4.** *Poetic.* a musical pipe made of an oat straw. **5. feel one's oats,** *U.S. Slang.* **a.** to feel gay or lively. **b.** to be aware of and use one's importance and power. **6. sow one's wild oats,** to indulge in the excesses or follies of youth. [ME *ote,* OE *āte*]

oat·cake (ōt'kāk'), *n.* a cake, usually thin and brittle, made of oatmeal.

oat·en (ō'tən), *adj.* **1.** made of oats or of oatmeal. **2.** of or pertaining to the oat. **3.** made of an oat straw.

oat grass, 1. any of certain oatlike grasses. **2.** any wild species of oat.

oath (ōth), *n., pl.* **oaths** (ōt̸hz). **1.** a solemn appeal to God, or to some revered person or thing, in attestation of the truth of a statement or the binding character of a promise: *to testify upon oath.* **2.** a statement or promise strengthened by such an appeal. **3.** a formally affirmed statement or promise accepted as an equivalent. **4.** the form of words in which such a statement or promise is made: *the Hippocratic oath.* **5.** a light or blasphemous use of the name of God or anything sacred. **6.** any profane expression; a curse. [ME *ooth,* OE *āth,* c. G *eid*]

oat·meal (ōt'mēl', ōt'mēl'), *n.* **1.** meal made from oats. **2.** porridge of this.

Oa·xa·ca (wä hä'kä), *n.* **1.** a state in S Mexico. 1,192,-794 pop. (1940); 36,375 sq. mi. **2.** the capital of this state. 29,306 (1940).

Ob (ôp), *n.* a river in the W Soviet Union in Asia, flowing NW to the **Gulf of Ob** (ab. 600 mi. long), an inlet of the Arctic Ocean. ab. 2600 mi.

ob-, a prefix meaning "toward," "to," "on," "over," "against," orig. occurring in words from the Latin, but now used also, with the sense of "reversely" or "inversely," to form Neo-Latin and English scientific terms. Also, **o-, oc-, of-, op-.** [t. L, repr. *ob,* prep., toward, to, about, before, on, over, against]

ob., 1. obiit. **2.** (L *obiter*) incidentally. **3.** oboe.

Obad., Obadiah.

O·ba·di·ah (ō'bə dī'ə), *n.* **1.** a Hebrew prophet. **2.** the Old Testament book which bears his name.

obb., obbligato.

ob·bli·ga·to (ŏb'lə gä'tō; *It.* ŏb'blē gä'tô), *adj., n., pl.* **-tos, -ti** (-tē). *Music.* —*adj.* **1.** obligatory or indispensable; so important that it cannot be omitted (opposed to *ad libitum*). —*n.* **2.** an obbligato part or accompaniment. Also, **obligato.** [t. It.: obliged]

ob·cor·date (ŏb kôr'dāt), *adj.* *Bot.* heart-shaped, with the attachment at the pointed end, as a leaf.

obdt., obedient.

ob·du·rate (ŏb'dyər ĭt, -də-), *adj.* **1.** hardened against persuasions or tender feelings; hard-hearted. **2.** hardened against moral influence; persistently impenitent: *an obdurate sinner.* [ME, t. L: m.s. *obdūrātus,* pp., hardened] —**ob·du·ra·cy** (ŏb'dyə rə sĭ), **ob·du·rate·ness,** *n.* —**ob'du·rate·ly,** *adj.*

o·be·ah (ō'bĭə), *n.* obi². [t. W Afr.]

o·be·di·ence (ō bē'dĭəns), *n.* **1.** state or fact of being obedient. **2.** act or practice of obeying; dutiful or submissive compliance (fol. by *to*). **3.** a sphere of authority, or a body of persons, etc., subject to some particular authority, esp. ecclesiastical. **4.** authority or rule, esp. ecclesiastical, as over those who should obey.

o·be·di·ent (ō bē'dĭənt), *adj.* obeying, or willing to obey; submissive to authority or constraint. [ME, t. L: m.s. *oboediens,* ppr.] —**o·be'di·ent·ly,** *adv.* —**Syn.** compliant, docile, tractable.

o·bei·sance (ō bā'səns, ō bē'-), *n.* **1.** a movement of the body expressing deep respect or deferential courtesy, as before a superior; a bow or curtsy. **2.** deference or homage. [ME *obeisaunce,* t. OF: m. *obeissance* obedience, der. *obeir* OBEY] —**o·bei'sant,** *adj.*

ob·e·lisk (ŏb'ə lĭsk), *n.* **1.** a tapering, four-sided shaft of stone, usually monolithic and having a pyramidal apex, of which notable examples are seen among the monuments of ancient Egypt. **2.** something resembling such a shaft. **3.** *Print.* the dagger (†), used esp. as a

Obelisk

b., blend of, blended; c., cognate with; d., dialect, dialectal; der., derived from; f., formed from; g., going back to; m., modification of; r., replacing; s., stem of; t., taken from; ?, perhaps. See the full key on inside cover.

reference mark. [t. L: m.s. *obeliscus*, t. Gk.: m. *obelískos*, dim. of *obelós* OBELUS] —**ob·e·lis/cal,** *adj.*

ob·e·lize (ŏb/ə līz/), *v.t.*, **-lized, -lizing.** to mark (a word or passage) with an obelus.

ob·e·lus (ŏb/ə ləs). *n., pl.* **-li** (-lī/). **1.** a mark (− or +) used in ancient manuscripts to point out spurious, corrupt, doubtful, or superfluous words or passages. **2.** *Print.* the obelisk or dagger (†). [t. LL, t. Gk.: m. *obelós* spit, pointed pillar, obelus]

O·ber·am·mer·gau (ō/bər äm/ər gou/), *n.* a village in S Germany, SW of Munich: famous for the Passion Play performed every ten years. 3022 (1939).

O·ber·hau·sen (ō/bər hou/zən), *n.* a city in W Germany, in the lower Ruhr valley. 191,829 (1939).

O·ber·land (ō/bər länt/), *n.* a mountain region in central Switzerland, mostly in S Berne canton.

O·ber·lin (ō/bər lĭn), *n.* a village in N Ohio. 7062 (1950).

O·ber·on (ō/bə rŏn/), *n.* in medieval folklore and in Shakespeare's *Midsummer Night's Dream*) the king of the fairies and husband of their queen, Titania. [var. of *Auberon*, t. F. Cf. G *Alberich*]

o·bese (ō bēs/), *adj.* excessively fat, as a person or animal, the body, etc.; corpulent. [t. L: m.s. *obēsus*, pp.] —**o·bese/ly,** *adv.* —**o·bese/ness, o·bes·i·ty** (ō bē/sə tĭ, ō bĕs/ə-), *n.*

o·bey (ō bā/), *v.t.* **1.** to comply with or fulfill the commands or instructions of; *obey your parents.* **2.** to comply with or fulfill (a command, etc.). **3.** (of things) to respond conformably in action to: *a ship obeys her helm.* **4.** to submit or conform in action to (some guiding principle, impulse, etc.). —*v.i.* **5.** to be obedient. [ME *obei(en)*, t. OF: m. *obeir*, g. L *oboedīre*] —**o·bey/er,** *n.*

ob·fus·cate (ŏb fŭs/kāt, ŏb/fəs kāt/), *v.t.*, **-cated, -cating. 1.** to confuse or stupefy. **2.** to darken or obscure. [t. LL: m.s. *obfuscātus*, pp.] —**ob/fus·ca/tion,** *n.*

o·bi¹ (ō/bĭ; *Jap.* ō/bē), *n., pl.* **obis.** a long, broad sash worn by Japanese women and children. [t. Jap.]

o·bi² (ō/bĭ), *n., pl.* **obis. 1.** a kind of sorcery practiced by the negroes of Africa, the West Indies, etc. **2.** a fetish or charm used in it. Also, **obeah.** [t. West African]

ob·i·it (ŏb/ĭ ĭt, ō/bĭ-), *Latin.* he (or she) died.

o·bit (ō/bĭt, ŏb/ĭt), *n.* the date of a person's death. **2.** an obituary notice. [ME, t. L: s. *obitus* death]

ob·i·ter dic·tum (ŏb/ə tər dĭk/təm), *pl.* **obiter dicta** (dĭk/tə). **1.** an incidental opinion; a passing remark. **2.** *Law.* an opinion by a judge in deciding a case, upon a matter not essential to the decision, and therefore not binding. [t. L: (something) said by the way]

o·bit·u·ar·y (ō bĭch/ŏŏ ĕr/ĭ), *n., pl.* **-aries,** *adj.* —*n.* **1.** a notice of the death of a person, often with a brief biographical sketch, as in a newspaper. —*adj.* **2.** pertaining to or recording a death: *an obituary notice.* [t. NL: m.s. *obituārius*, der. L *obitus* death]

obj., 1. object. **2.** objection. **3.** objective.

ob·ject (*n.* ŏb/jĭkt; *v.* əb jĕkt/), *n.* **1.** something that may be perceived by the senses, esp. by sight or touch; a visible or tangible thing. **2.** a thing or person to which attention or action is directed: *an object of study.* **3.** any thing that may be presented to the mind: *objects of thought.* **4.** a thing with reference to the impression it makes on the mind: *an object of curiosity.* **5.** the end toward which effort is directed: *the object of our visit.* **6.** a person or thing which arouses feelings of pity, disgust, etc. **7.** *Gram.* (in English and some other languages) the noun or its substitute which represents the goal of an action (in English either *direct* or *indirect*) or the ending point of a relation (in English expressed by a preposition). For example: In *John kicked the ball, ball* is the goal of the action. In *he came to Venice, Venice* is the ending point of the action. In *he gave the boy a coin, coin* is the direct object; *boy* is the indirect object. **8.** *Metaphys.* that toward which a cognitive act is directed; the nonego. —*v.i.* **9.** to offer a reason or argument in opposition. **10.** to express or feel disapproval; be averse. —*v.t.* **11.** to bring as a charge; attribute as a fault. **12.** *Obs.* or *Archaic.* to bring forward or adduce in opposition. [ME, t. ML: s. *objectum*, prop. neut. of L *objectus*, pp., thrown before, presented, exposed, opposed, reproached with] —**ob·jec/tor,** *n.* —**Syn. 5.** purpose, motive, intent. See **aim.**

object., 1. objection. **2.** objective.

object ball, *Billiards, etc.* the ball which the striker aims to hit with the cueball; any ball except the striker's.

object glass, objective (def.3).

ob·jec·ti·fy (əb jĕk/tə fī/), *v.t.*, **-fied, -fying.** to present as an object, esp. of sense; make objective; externalize. [f. s. ML *objectum* an object + -(I)FY] —**ob·jec/ti·fi·ca/tion,** *n.*

ob·jec·tion (əb jĕk/shən), *n.* **1.** something adduced or said in disagreement or disapproval; an adverse reason. **2.** the act of objecting. **3.** a ground or cause of objecting. **4.** a feeling of disapproval or dislike.

ob·jec·tion·a·ble (əb jĕk/shən ə bəl), *adj.* that may be objected to; offensive: *an objectionable passage.* —**ob·jec/tion·a·bly,** *adv.*

ob·jec·tive (əb jĕk/tĭv), *n.* **1.** an end toward which efforts are directed; something aimed at. **2.** *Gram.* **a.** the objective case. **b.** a word in that case. **3.** (in a telescope, microscope, etc.) the lens or combination of lenses which first receives the rays from the object and

forms the image viewed through the eyepiece or photographed. See diag. under **microscope.** —*adj.* **4.** being the object of perception or thought; belonging to the object of thought rather than to the thinking subject (opposed to *subjective*). **5.** free from personal feelings or prejudice; unbiased. **6.** being the object of one's endeavors or actions: *an objective point.* **7.** intent upon or dealing with things external to the mind rather than thoughts or feelings, as a person, a book, etc. **8.** of or pertaining to that which can be known, or to that which is an object or a part of an object. **9.** *Art.* **a.** of or pertaining to an object or objects (opposed to *nonobjective* and *nonrepresentational*). **b.** being, or pertaining to, the object whose perspective delineation is required: *an objective plane.* **10.** *Med.* (of a symptom) discernible to others as well as the patient. **11.** *Gram.* **a.** pertaining to the use of a form as object of a verb or preposition. **b.** (in English and some other languages) denoting a case specialized for that use: in *the boy hit him, him* is in the objective case. **c.** similar to such a case in meaning. [t. ML: m. *objectīvus*, adj.] —**ob·jec/tive·ly,** *adv.* —**ob·jec/tive·ness,** *n.*

objective complement, *Gram.* a word or a group of words predicated of a direct object or modifying it.

ob·jec·tiv·ism (əb jĕk/tĭ vĭz/əm), *n.* **1.** a tendency to lay stress on the objective or external elements of cognition. **2.** the tendency to deal with things external to the mind rather than thoughts or feelings, as in a writer. **3.** a doctrine characterized by this tendency. —**ob·jec/tiv·ist,** *n., adj.* —**ob·jec/ti·vis/tic,** *adj.*

ob·jec·tiv·i·ty (ŏb/jĕk tĭv/ə tĭ), *n.* **1.** the state or quality of being objective. **2.** intentness on objects external to the mind. **3.** external reality.

ob·ject·less (ŏb/jĭkt lĭs), *adj.* **1.** having no object. **2.** not directed toward any object; purposeless.

object lesson, 1. a lesson in which instruction is conveyed by means of a material object. **2.** a practical illustration of a principle.

ob·jet d'art (ŏb zhě där/), *pl.* **objets d'art** (ŏb zhě där/). *French.* an object of art.

ob·jur·gate (ŏb/jər gāt/, əb jûr/gāt). *v.t.*, **-gated, -gating.** to reproach vehemently; upbraid violently; berate. [t. L: m.s. *objurgātus*, pp.] —**ob/jur·ga/tion,** *n.* —**ob·jur·ga·to·ry** (əb jûr/gə tōr/ĭ), *adj.*

obl., 1. oblique. **2.** oblong.

ob·lan·ce·o·late (ŏb lăn/sĭ ə lĭt, -lāt/), *adj.* *Bot.* inversely lanceolate, as a leaf.

ob·late¹ (ŏb/lāt, ŏb lāt/), *adj.* flattened at the poles, as a spheroid generated by the revolution of an ellipse about its shorter axis (opposed to *prolate*). See diag. under **prolate.** [t. NL: m.s. *oblātus*, f. ob- OB- + -*lātus*, modeled on *prolātus* PROLATE] —**ob/late·ly,** *adv.*

ob·late² (ŏb/lāt, ŏb lāt/), *n.* **1.** a person offered to the service of a monastery, but not under monastic vows. **2.** a member of any of various Roman Catholic societies devoted to special religious work. [t. ML: m.s. *oblātus*, prop. pp. of *offerre* OFFER]

ob·la·tion (ŏb lā/shən), *n.* **1.** the offering to God of the elements of bread and wine in the Eucharist. **2.** the whole office of the Eucharist. **3.** the act of making an offering, now esp. to God or a deity. **4.** any offering for religious or charitable uses. [ME *oblacion*, t. LL: m.s. *oblātio*] —**ob·la·to·ry** (ŏb lā tōr/ĭ), *adj.*

ob·li·gate (*v.* ŏb/lə gāt/; *adj.* ŏb/lə gĭt, -gāt/), *v.*, **-gated, -gating,** *adj.* —*v.t.* **1.** to oblige or bind morally or legally: *to obligate oneself to fulfill certain conditions.* —*adj.* **2.** obligated, bound, or constrained. **3.** *Biol.* restricted to a particular condition of life, as certain parasites which must live in close association with their usual hosts in order to survive (opposed to *facultative*). [ME, t. L: m.s. *obligātus*, pp.] —**ob/li·ga/tor,** *n.*

ob·li·ga·tion (ŏb/lə gā/shən), *n.* **1.** a binding requirement as to action; duty: *to fulfill every obligation.* **2.** the binding power or force of a promise, law, duty, agreement, etc. **3.** a binding promise or the like made. **4.** act of binding oneself by a promise, contract, etc. **5.** *Law.* **a.** an agreement enforceable by law, originally applied to promises under seal. **b.** a document containing such an agreement. **c.** a bond containing a penalty, with a condition annexed for payment of money, performance of covenants, etc. **d.** any bond, note, bill, certificate, or the like, as of a government or a corporation, serving as security for payment of indebtedness. **6.** a benefit, favor, or service, for which gratitude is due. **7.** a debt of gratitude. **8.** the state or fact of being indebted for a benefit, favor, or service. —**Syn. 1.** See **duty.**

ob·li·ga·to (ŏb/lə gä/tō), *adj., n., pl.* **-tos, -ti** (-tē). obbligato.

ob·lig·a·to·ry (əb lĭg/ə tōr/ĭ, ŏb/lə gə-), *adj.* **1.** imposing obligation, morally or legally: binding: *an obligatory promise.* **2.** required as a matter of obligation: *a reply is expected but not obligatory.* **3.** incumbent or compulsory (fol. by *on* or *upon*): *duties obligatory on all.* **4.** creating or recording an obligation, as a writing. [ME, t. LL: m.s. *obligātōrius*] —**ob·lig/a·to/ri·ly,** *adv.*

o·blige (ə blīj/), *v.t.*, **obliged, obliging. 1.** to require or constrain, as the law, a command, duty, or necessity does. **2.** to bind (a person, etc.) by a promise, engagement, or contract. **3.** to bind (a person, etc.) morally or legally, as a promise, contract, or the like does. **4.** to make (an action, course, etc.) incumbent or obligatory. **5.** to place under a debt of gratitude for some benefit, favor, or service. **6.** to favor or accommodate (fol. by *with*): *he obliged us with a song.* [ME *oblige(n)*, t. OF: m. *obligier*, t. L: m. *obligāre* bind or tie around] **—o·blig′-er**, *n.*

—Syn. 6. OBLIGE, ACCOMMODATE imply making a gracious and welcome gesture of some kind. OBLIGE emphasizes the idea of conferring a favor or benefit (and often of taking some trouble to do it): *to oblige someone with a loan.* ACCOMMODATE emphasizes doing a service or furnishing a convenience: *to accommodate someone with lodgings and meals.*

ob·li·gee (ŏb′lə jē′), *n.* **1.** *Law.* a. one to whom another is bound. **b.** the person to whom a bond is given. **2.** one who is under obligation for a benefit or favor.

o·blig·ing (ə blī′jĭng), *adj.* **1.** disposed to do favors or services, as a person: *the clerk was most obliging.* **2.** that obliges. **—o·blig′ing·ly**, *adv.* **—o·blig′ing-ness**, *n.* **—Syn. 1.** helpful, kind, friendly, accommodating.

ob·li·gor (ŏb′lə gôr′, ŏb′lə gôr′), *n.* *Law.* **1.** one who is bound to another. **2.** the person who gives a bond.

ob·lique (ə blēk′; *military* ə blīk′), *adj.*, *v.*, **-liqued**, **-liquing.** **—adj. 1.** neither perpendicular nor parallel to a given line or surface; slanting; sloping. **2.** (of a solid) not having the axis perpendicular to the plane of the base. **3.** diverging from a given straight line or course. **4.** not straight or direct, as a course, etc. **5.** indirectly stated or expressed: *certain oblique hints.* **6.** indirectly aimed at or reached, as ends, results, etc. **7.** *Rhet.* indirect (applied to discourse in which the original words of a speaker or writer are assimilated to the language of the reporter). **8.** *Gram.* denoting or pertaining to any case of noun inflection except nominative and vocative, or except these two and accusative: *Latin genitive, dative, and ablative cases are said to be oblique.* **9.** morally or mentally wrong; perverse. **10.** *Anat.* pertaining to muscles running obliquely in the body as opposed to those running transversely or longitudinally. **11.** *Bot.* having unequal sides, as a leaf. **—v.i. 12.** to have or take an oblique direction; slant: *the wall obliques from the gate at a sharp angle.* **13.** *Mil.* to advance obliquely. [ME *oblike*, t. L: m.s. *oblīquus*] **—ob·lique′-ly**, *adv.* **—ob·lique′ness**, *n.*

oblique angle, an angle that is not a right angle.

oblique motion, *Music.* the relative motion of two melodic parts in which one remains in place while the other moves.

oblique sailing, navigation along a course other than directly north, south, east, or west.

ob·liq·ui·ty (ə blĭk′wə tĭ), *n.*, *pl.* **-ties.** **1.** the state of being oblique. **2.** divergence from moral rectitude. **3** a moral delinquency. **4.** mental perversity. **5.** an instance of it. **6.** inclination, or degree of inclination. **7.** *Astron.* **obliquity of the ecliptic**, the angle between the plane of the earth's orbit and that of the earth's equator, equal to about 23° 27′. **—ob·liq′ui·tous**, *adj.*

ob·lit·er·ate (ə blĭt′ə rāt′), *v.t.*, **-ated**, **-ating.** **1.** to remove all traces of; do away with; destroy. **2.** to blot out or render undecipherable (writing, marks, etc); cancel; efface. [t. L: m.s. *oblit(t)erātus*, pp., erased] **—ob·lit′er·a′tion**, *n.* **—ob·lit′er·a′tive**, *adj.* **—Syn. 2.** See **cancel.**

ob·liv·i·on (ə blĭv′ĭ ən), *n.* **1.** the state of being forgotten, as by the world. **2.** the forgetting, or forgetfulness, of something: *five minutes of oblivion.* **3.** disregard or overlooking: *oblivion of political offenses.* [ME, t. L: s. *oblīvio*]

ob·liv·i·ous (ə blĭv′ĭ əs), *adj.* **1.** forgetful; without remembrance: *oblivious of my former failure.* **2.** unmindful; unconscious (fol. by *of* or *to*): *she was oblivious of his adoration.* **3.** inducing forgetfulness. [ME, t. L: m.s. *oblīviōsus*] **—ob·liv′i·ous·ly**, *adv.* **—ob·liv′i·ous·ness**, *n.*

Oblong leaf

ob·long (ŏb′lông, -lŏng), *adj.* **1.** elongated, usually from the square or circular form. **2.** in the form of a rectangle of greater length than breadth. **—n. 3.** an oblong figure. [ME, t. L: s. *oblongus* rather long, oblong]

ob·lo·quy (ŏb′lə kwĭ), *n.*, *pl.* **-quies.** **1.** the discredit or disgrace resulting from public blame or revilement. **2.** censure, blame, or abusive language aimed at a person, etc., esp. by numbers of persons or by the public generally. [late ME *obloqui*, t. LL: s. *obloquium*, contradiction]

ob·nounce (ŏb nouns′), *v.i.* *Rom. Antiq.* to announce an unfavorable omen with reference to a proposed public action.

ob·nox·ious (əb nŏk′shəs), *adj.* **1.** objectionable; offensive; odious: *obnoxious remarks.* **2.** exposed or liable (to harm, evil, or anything objectionable). **3.** *Law.* responsible. **4.** *Obs.* liable to punishment or censure; reprehensible. [t. L: m. *obnoxius* exposed to harm] **—ob·nox′ious·ly**, *adv.* **—ob·nox′ious·ness**, *n.* **—Syn. 1.** See **hateful.**

Oboe

o·boe (ō′bō, ō′boi), *n.* **1.** a wooden wind instrument in the form of a slender conical tube, in which the tone is produced by a double reed. **2.** a reed stop in an organ which sounds like an oboe. [t. It., t. F: m. *hautbois* HAUTBOY]

o·bo·ist (ō′bō ĭst), *n.* a player on the oboe.

ob·ol (ŏb′əl), *n.* an ancient Greek silver coin and weight, ⅙ of a drachma. [see OBOLUS]

ob·o·lus (ŏb′ə ləs), *n.*, *pl.* **-li** (-lī′). **1.** an ancient Greek

unit of weight equal to about 11 grains. **2.** a modern Greek unit of weight equal to 0.1 gram. [t. L, t. Gk.: m. *obolós* a small coin, a weight]

ob·o·vate (ŏb ō′vāt), *adj.* inversely ovate; ovate with the narrow end at the base.

ob·o·void (ŏb ō′void), *adj.* inversely ovoid, ovoid with the narrow end at the base, as certain fruits.

Obovate leaf

O·bre·gón (ō′brĕ gôn′), *n.* **Álvaro** (äl′vä-rō′), 1880–1928, Mexican general and statesman: president of Mexico, 1920–24.

O·bre·no·vić (ō brĕ′nŏ vĕt′y), *n.* **1.** a former ruling family of Serbia. **2.** Alexander I of Serbia.

Obs. 1. observation. **2.** observatory. **3.** obsolete.

ob·scene (əb sēn′, ŏb-), *adj.* **1.** offensive to modesty or decency; indecent; lewd: *obscene pictures.* **2.** *Archaic.* abominable; disgusting; repulsive. [t. L: m.s. *obscēnus*, *obscaenus* of evil omen, offensive, disgusting] **—ob·scene′ly**, *adv.* **—ob·scene′ness**, *n.*

ob·scen·i·ty (əb sĕn′ə tĭ, -sē′nə-), *n.*, *pl.* **-ties.** **1.** obscene quality or character; indecency. **2.** something obscene, as language, a remark, an expression, etc.

ob·scur·ant (əb skyoor′ənt), *n.* **1.** one who strives to prevent inquiry and enlightenment. **2.** one who obscures. **—adj. 3.** pertaining to or characteristic of obscurants. [t. L: s. *obscūrans*, ppr.]

ob·scur·ant·ism (əb skyoor′ən tĭz′əm), *n.* **1.** opposition to inquiry and enlightenment. **2.** the principle or practice of obscurants. **—ob·scur′ant·ist**, *n.*, *adj.*

ob·scu·ra·tion (ŏb′skyoo rā′shən), *n.* **1.** act of obscuring. **2.** state of being obscured.

ob·scure (əb skyoor′), *adj.*, **-scurer**, **-scurest**, *v.*, **-scured**, **-scuring**, *n.* **—adj. 1.** (of meaning) not clear or plain; uncertain. **2.** (of language, style, a speaker, etc.) not expressing the meaning clearly or plainly. **3.** inconspicuous or unnoticeable: *the obscure beginnings of a great movement.* **4.** of no prominence, note, or distinction. **5.** not readily seen; remote; retired, as a place. **6.** indistinct to the sight, or to some other sense. **7.** dark, as from lack of light or illumination; murky; dim. **8.** enveloped in, concealed by, or frequenting darkness. **9.** dark, dull, or not bright or lustrous, as color or appearance. **10.** not perspicuous. **—v.t. 11.** to make obscure, dark, dim, indistinct, etc. **12.** to make obscure in sound, as a vowel in pronunciation. **—n. 13.** darkness or obscurity. [ME, t. L: m.s. *obscūrus* dark, dim, unknown, ignoble] **—ob·scure′ly**, *adv.* **—ob·scure′ness**, *n.* **—Syn. 1.** doubtful, dubious, ambiguous. See **mysterious. 9.** See **dark.**

ob·scu·ri·ty (əb skyoor′ə tĭ), *n.*, *pl.* **-ties.** **1.** the state or quality of being obscure. **2.** uncertainty of meaning or expression. **3.** the condition of being unknown. **4.** an unknown or unimportant person or thing. **5.** darkness; dimness; indistinctness.

ob·se·crate (ŏb′sə krāt′), *v.t.*, **-crated**, **-crating.** to entreat (a person, etc.) solemnly; beseech; supplicate. [t. L: m.s. *obsecrātus*, pp.] **—ob′se·cra′tion**, *n.*

ob·se·qui·ous (əb sē′kwĭ əs), *adj.* **1.** servilely compliant or deferential: *obsequious servants.* **2.** characterized by or showing servile complaisance or deference: *an obsequious bow.* **3.** *Now Rare.* compliant; obedient; dutiful. [ME, t. L: m.s. *obsequiōsus*] **—ob·se′qui·ous·ly**, *adv.* **—ob·se′qui·ous·ness**, *n.* **—Syn. 1.** See **servile.**

ob·se·quy (ŏb′sə kwĭ), *n.*, *pl.* **-quies.** (*usually pl.*) a funeral rite or ceremony. [ME *obsequies*, t. ML: m. *obsequiae*, pl., (L *exsequiae*) funeral rites]

ob·serv·a·ble (əb zûr′və bəl), *adj.* **1.** that may be or is to be noticed; noticeable; noteworthy. **2.** that may be or is to be followed or kept. **—ob·serv′a·bly**, *adv.*

ob·serv·ance (əb zûr′vəns), *n.* **1.** the action of conforming to or following: *observance of laws.* **2.** a keeping or celebration by appropriate procedure, ceremonies, etc. **3.** a procedure, ceremony, or rite, as for a particular occasion: *patriotic observances.* **4.** a rule or custom to be observed. **5.** *Rom. Cath. Ch.* **a.** a rule or discipline for a religious house or order. **b.** such a house or order. **6.** observation. **7.** respectful attention or service. **8.** *Archaic.* attentions or assiduities.

ob·serv·ant (əb zûr′vənt), *adj.* **1.** observing or regarding attentively; watchful. **2.** quick to notice or perceive; alert. **3.** careful in the observing of a law, custom, or the like (fol. by *of*). **—n. 4.** an observer of law or rule. **5.** Also, **Ob·ser·van·tine** (ŏb zûr′vən tĭn, -tēn′). (*cap.*) a member of a branch of the Franciscan order which in the 15th century separated from the Conventuals and observes strictly the rule of St. Francis. [ME, t. L: s. *observans*, ppr.] **—ob·serv′ant·ly**, *adv.*

ob·ser·va·tion (ŏb′zər vā′shən), *n.* **1.** the act of noticing or perceiving. **2.** the act of regarding attentively or watching. **3.** the faculty or habit of observing or noticing. **4.** notice: *to escape a person's observation.* **5.** act of viewing or noting something, for some scientific or other special purpose. **6.** the information or record secured thereby. **7.** that which is learned by observing. **8.** an utterance by way of remark or comment. **9.** *Naut.* **a.** the measurement of the altitude or azimuth of a celestial body to deduce a line of position for a vessel at sea. **b.** the result obtained. **10.** *Obs. or Rare.* observance, as of law, etc. **—Syn. 8.** See **remark.**

ob·ser·va·tion·al (ŏb′zər vā′shən əl), *adj.* of, pertaining to, or founded on observation, esp. as contrasted with experiment.

---

b., blend of, blended; c., cognate with; d., dialect, dialectal; der., derived from; f., formed from; g., going back to; m., modification of; r., replacing; s., stem of; t., taken from; ?, perhaps. See the full key on inside cover.

observation car, a railroad car usually attached to the rear end of a passenger train, designed to afford passengers an unobstructed view of passing scenery.

observation post, *Mil.* a lookout position from which targets may be observed.

observation train, a train run along a river, etc., to allow the passengers to watch a boat race.

ob·serv·a·to·ry (əb zûr′və tôr′ĭ), *n., pl.* **-ries. 1.** a place or building set apart and fitted up for making observations of astronomical, meteorological, or other natural phenomena. **2.** an institution which controls or carries on the work of an observatory. **3.** a place or structure for affording an extensive view.

ob·serve (əb zûrv′), *v.,* **-served, -serving.** —*v.t.* **1.** to see, perceive, or notice. **2.** to regard with attention, so as to see or learn something. **3.** to make or take an observation of; to watch, view, or note for some scientific, official, or other special purpose; *to observe an eclipse.* **4.** to remark; comment. **5.** to keep or maintain in one's action, conduct, etc.: *you must observe quiet.* **6.** to obey, comply with; conform to: *to observe a law.* **7.** to show regard for by some appropriate procedure, ceremonies, etc.: *to observe a holiday.* **8.** to perform duly, or solemnize (ceremonies, rites, etc.). —*v.i.* **9.** to notice. **10.** to act as an observer. **11.** to remark or comment (commonly fol. by *on* or *upon*). [ME *observe*(*n*), t. *observāre* watch, comply with, observe] —**ob·serv′er,** *n.* —**ob·serv′ing·ly,** *adv.*
—**Syn. 2.** OBSERVE, WITNESS imply paying strict attention to what one sees or perceives. Both are "continuative" in action. To OBSERVE is to mark or be attentive to something seen (heard, etc.); to consider carefully; to watch steadily: *to observe the behavior of birds, a person's pronunciation.* To WITNESS, formerly to be present when something was happening, has added the idea of having observed with sufficient care to be able to give an account as evidence: *to witness an accident.* —**Ant. 1.** disregard, overlook.

ob·sess (əb sĕs′), *v.t.* to beset, trouble, or dominate; haunt: *obsessed by a fear of doctors.* [t. L: s. *obsessus*, pp., besieged, beset] —**ob·ses′sive,** *adj.*

ob·ses·sion (əb sĕsh′ən), *n.* **1.** the besetting or dominating action or influence of a persistent feeling, idea, or the like, which the person cannot escape. **2.** the feeling or idea itself. **3.** the state of being obsessed. **4.** the act of obsessing.

ob·sid·i·an (əb sĭd′ĭ ən), *n.* a volcanic glass, usually of a very dark color and with a conchoidal fracture. [t. L: s. *Obsidiānus*, prop., *Obsiānus*, pertaining to *Obsius*, reputed discoverer of a similar mineral]

ob·so·les·cent (ŏb′sə lĕs′ənt), *adj.* **1.** becoming obsolete; passing out of use, as a word. **2.** tending to become out of date, as machinery, etc. **3.** *Biol.* gradually disappearing, or imperfectly developed as organs, marks, etc. [t. L: s. *obsolescens*, ppr.] —**ob·so·les′cence,** *n.* —**ob′so·les′cent·ly,** *adv.*

ob·so·lete (ŏb′sə lōt′), *adj.* **1.** fallen into disuse, or no longer in use: *an obsolete word.* **2.** of a discarded type; out of date: *an obsolete battleship.* **3.** effaced by wearing down or away. **4.** *Biol.* imperfectly developed or rudimentary in comparison with the corresponding character in other individuals, as of the opposite sex or of a related species. [t. L: m.s. *obsolētus*, pp.] —**ob′so·lete′·ly,** *adv.* —**ob′so·lete′ness,** *n.*

ob·sta·cle (ŏb′stə kəl), *n.* something that stands in the way or obstructs progress. [ME, t. OF, t. L: m.s. *obstāculum*]
—**Syn.** OBSTACLE, OBSTRUCTION, HINDRANCE, IMPEDIMENT refer to that which interferes with or prevents action or progress. An OBSTACLE is something, material or nonmaterial, which stands in the way of literal or figurative progress: *lack of imagination is an obstacle to one's advancement.* An OBSTRUCTION is something which more or less completely blocks a passage: *a blood clot is an obstruction to the circulation.* A HINDRANCE keeps back by interfering and delaying: *interruptions are a hindrance to one's work.* An IMPEDIMENT interferes with proper functioning: *an impediment in one's speech.* —**Ant.** help.

obstet., **1.** obstetric. **2.** obstetrics.

ob·stet·ric (əb stĕt′rĭk), *adj.* **1.** pertaining to the care and treatment of women in childbirth and during the period before and after delivery. **2.** of or pertaining to obstetrics. Also, **ob·stet′ri·cal.** [t. NL: s. *obstētrĭcus,* var. of L *obstētrĭcius* pertaining to a midwife] —**ob·stet′·ri·cal·ly,** *adv.*

ob·ste·tri·cian (ŏb′stə trĭsh′ən), *n.* one skilled in obstetrics.

ob·stet·rics (əb stĕt′rĭks), *n.* the branch of medical art or science concerned with caring for and treating woman in, before, and after childbirth; midwifery.

ob·sti·na·cy (ŏb′stə nə sĭ), *n., pl.* **-cies. 1.** the quality or state of being obstinate. **2.** obstinate adherence to purpose, opinion, etc. **3.** stubborn persistence: *the battle continued with incredible obstinacy.* **4.** unyielding nature, as of a disease. **5.** an obstinate action; an instance of being obstinate. [ME, t. ML: m.s. *obstinātia*]

ob·sti·nate (ŏb′stə nĭt), *adj.* **1.** firmly and often perversely adhering to one's purpose, opinion, etc.; not yielding to argument, persuasion, or entreaty. **2.** inflexibly persisted in or carried out: *obstinate resistance.* **3.** not easily controlled: *the obstinate growth of weeds.* **4.** not yielding readily to treatment, as a disease: *the obstinate,* t. L: s. *obstinātus,* pp., determined] —**ob′·sti·nate·ly,** *adv.* —**ob′sti·nate·ness,** *n.* —**Syn. 1.** mulish, obdurate, unyielding, unbending, intractable. See **stubborn.**

ob·sti·pant (ŏb′stə pənt), *n.* a substance that produces obstipation.

ob·sti·pa·tion (ŏb′stə pā′shən), *n.* obstinate constipation. [t. L: s. *obstipātio*]

ob·strep·er·ous (əb strĕp′ər əs), *adj.* **1.** resisting control in a noisy manner; unruly. **2.** noisy or clamorous; boisterous. [t. L: m. *obstreperus* clamorous] —**ob·strep′er·ous·ly,** *adv.* —**ob·strep′er·ous·ness,** *n.*

ob·struct (əb strŭkt′), *v.t.* **1.** to block or close up, or make difficult of passage, with obstacles, as a way, road, channel, or the like. **2.** to interrupt, make difficult, or oppose the passage, progress, course, etc. of. **3.** to come in the way of (a view, etc.). [t. L: s. *obstructus,* pp.] —**ob·struct′er, ob·struc′tor,** *n.* —**ob·struc′tive,** *adj.* —**ob·struc′tive·ly,** *adv.* —**ob·struc′tive·ness,** *n.* —**Syn. 1.** block, stop, close, choke, clog.

ob·struc·tion (əb strŭk′shən), *n.* **1.** something that obstructs; an obstacle or hindrance: *obstructions to navigation.* **2.** the act of obstructing. **3.** the retarding of business before a legislative group by parliamentary devices, or an attempt at such a retarding. **4.** the state of being obstructed. —**Syn. 1.** See **obstacle.**

ob·struc·tion·ist (əb strŭk′shən ĭst), *n.* a person who obstructs something, esp. legislative business. —**ob·struc′tion·ism,** *n.*

ob·stru·ent (ŏb′strōō ənt), *Med.* —*adj.* **1.** (of a substance) producing an obstruction. —*n.* **2.** a medicine that closes the natural passages of the body. [t. L: s. *obstruens,* ppr., blocking up]

ob·tain (əb tān′), *v.t.* **1.** to come into possession of; get or acquire; procure, as by effort or request: *he obtained a knowledge of Greek.* **2.** *Obs.* or *Archaic.* to attain or reach. —*v.i.* **3.** to be prevalent, customary, or in vogue: *the morals that obtained in Rome.* **4.** *Obs.* or *Archaic.* to succeed. [ME *obteine*(*n*), t. OF: m. *obtenir,* t. L: m. *obtinēre* take hold of, get, prevail, continue] —**ob·tain′a·ble,** *adj.* —**ob·tain′er,** *n.* —**ob·tain′ment,** *n.* —**Syn. 1.** See **get.**

ob·tect·ed (ŏb tĕk′tĭd), *adj. Entom.* denoting a pupa in which the antennae, legs, and wings are glued to the surface of the body by a hardened secretion. [f. s. L *obtectus,* pp., covered over + -ED[2]]

ob·test (ŏb tĕst′), *v.t.* **1.** to invoke as witness. **2.** to supplicate earnestly; beseech. —*v.i.* **3.** to protest. [t. L: s. *obtestārī* call as a witness] —**ob′tes·ta′tion,** *n.*

ob·trude (əb trōōd′), *v.,* **-truded, -truding.** —*v.t.* **1.** to thrust forward or upon a person, esp. without warrant or invitation: *to obtrude one's opinions upon others.* **2.** to thrust forth; push out. —*v.i.* **3.** to thrust oneself or itself forward, esp. unduly; intrude. [t. L: m.s. *obtrūdere* thrust upon or into] —**ob·trud′er,** *n.*

ob·tru·sion (əb trōō′zhən), *n.* **1.** the act of obtruding. **2.** something obtruded.

ob·tru·sive (əb trōō′sĭv), *adj.* **1.** having or showing a disposition to obtrude. **2.** (of a thing) obtruding itself: *an obtrusive error.* —**ob·tru′sive·ly,** *adv.* —**ob·tru′sive·ness,** *n.*

ob·tund (ŏb tŭnd′), *v.t.* to blunt; dull; deaden. [ME, t. L: s. *obtundere* beat, strike at] —**ob·tund′ent,** *adj.*

ob·tu·rate (ŏb′tyə rāt′, -tə-), *v.t.,* **-rated, -rating. 1.** to stop up; close. **2.** *Ordn.* to close (a hole, joint, or cavity) so as to prevent the flow of gas through it. [t. L: m.s. *obturātus,* pp.] —**ob′tu·ra′tion,** *n.* —**ob′tu·ra′tor,** *n.*

ob·tuse (əb tūs′, -tōōs′), *adj.* **1.** blunt in form; not sharp or acute. **2.** (of a leaf, petal, etc.) rounded at the extremity. **3.** not sensitive or observant; stupid; dull in perception, feeling, or intellect. **4.** indistinctly felt or perceived, as pain, sound, etc. [t. L: m.s. *obtūsus,* pp., dulled] —**ob·tuse′·ly,** *adv.* —**ob·tuse′ness,** *n.*

obtuse angle, an angle exceeding 90 degrees but less than 180 degrees.

ADE, Obtuse angle;
BDE, Right angle;
CDE, Straight angle

ob·verse (*adj.* ŏb vûrs′, ŏb′vûrs; *n.* ŏb′vûrs), *n.* **1.** that side of a coin, medal, etc., which bears the principal design (opposed to *reverse*). **2.** the front or principal face of anything. **3.** a counterpart. **4.** *Logic.* a proposition obtained from another by obversion. —*adj.* **5.** turned toward or facing one. **6.** corresponding to something else as a counterpart. **7.** having the base narrower than the top, as a leaf. [t. L: m.s. *obversus,* pp., turned toward or against] —**ob·verse′ly,** *adv.*

ob·ver·sion (ŏb vûr′shən, -zhən), *n.* **1.** the act or result of obverting. **2.** *Logic.* a form of inference in which a negative proposition is inferred from an affirmative or an affirmative from a negative.

ob·vert (ŏb vûrt′), *v.t.* **1.** to turn (something) toward an object. **2.** *Logic.* to change (a proposition) by obversion. [t. L: s. *obvertere* turn towards or against]

ob·vi·ate (ŏb′vĭ āt′), *v.t.,* **-ated, -ating.** to meet and dispose of or prevent (difficulties, objections, etc.) by effective measures: *to obviate the necessity of beginning again.* [t. LL: m.s. *obviātus,* pp., met, opposed, prevented] —**ob′vi·a′tion,** *n.*

ob·vi·ous (ŏb′vĭ əs), *adj.* **1.** open to view or knowledge: *an obvious advantage.* **2.** *Obs.* being or standing in the way. [t. L: m. *obvius* in the way, meeting] —**ob′vi·ous·ly,** *adv.* —**ob′vi·ous·ness,** *n.* —**Syn. 1.** plain, manifest, evident. See **apparent.**

ob·vo·lute (ŏb′və lōōt′), *adj.* **1.** rolled or turned in. **2.** *Bot.* noting or pertaining to a kind of vernation in which two leaves are folded together in the bud so that one half of each is exterior and the other interior. [t. L: m.s. *obvolūtus*, pp., wrapped up] —**ob′vo·lu′tion**, *n.* —**ob′vo·lu′tive**, *adj.*

oc-, var. of ob- (by assimilation) before *c*, as in *Occident*.

Oc., ocean. Also, **oc.**

oc·a·ri·na (ŏk′ə·rē′nə), *n.* a simple musical wind instrument shaped somewhat like an elongated egg, with finger holes. [prob. dim. of It. *oca* goose, with reference to the shape]

Ocarina

O′Ca·sey (ō·kā′sĭ), *n.* **Sean** (shôn), born 1884, Irish dramatist.

Oc·cam (ŏk′əm), *n.* **William of,** died 1349?, British scholastic philosopher. Also, **Ockham.**

occas., 1. occasional. 2. occasionally.

oc·ca·sion (ə·kā′zhən), *n.* 1. a particular time, esp. as marked by certain circumstances or occurrences: *on several occasions.* 2. a special or important time, event, or function. 3. a convenient or favorable juncture or time; opportunity. 4. **on occasion,** a. as occasion or opportunity arises; now and then. b. occasionally. 5. the ground, reason, or incidental cause of some action or result. 6. *Obs.* need or necessity. 7. (*pl.*) *Obs.* necessary business matters. —*v.t.* 8. to give occasion or cause for; bring about. [ME, t. L: s. *occāsio* opportunity, fit time] —**Syn.** 5. See **cause.**

oc·ca·sion·al (ə·kā′zhən·əl), *adj.* 1. occurring or appearing on one occasion or another or now and then: *an occasional visitor.* 2. intended for use whenever needed: *an occasional table.* 3. pertaining to, arising out of, or intended for the occasion: *occasional decrees.* 4. acting or serving for the occasion or on particular occasions. 5. serving as the occasion or incidental cause.

oc·ca·sion·al·ism (ə·kā′zhən·əl·ĭz′əm), *n. Philos.* the doctrine that the apparent interaction of mind and matter is to be explained by the supposition that God takes an act of the will as the occasion of producing a corresponding movement of the body, and a state of the body as the occasion of producing a corresponding mental state. —**oc·ca′sion·al·ist,** *n.*

oc·ca·sion·al·ly (ə·kā′zhən·əl·ĭ), *adv.* at times; now and then.

Oc·ci·dent (ŏk′sə·dənt), *n.* 1. countries in Europe and America (contrasted with the *Orient*). 2. the Western Hemisphere. 3. (*l.c.*) the west; the western regions. [ME, t. L: *occidens* the west, sunset, prop. ppr., going down]

oc·ci·den·tal (ŏk′sə·dĕn′təl), *adj.* 1. (*usually cap.*) of, pertaining to, or characteristic of the Occident. 2. western. —*n.* 3. (*usually cap.*) a native or inhabitant of the Occident. [ME, t. L: s. *occidentālis* western] —**oc′ci·den′tal·ly,** *adv.*

Oc·ci·den·tal·ism (ŏk′sə·dĕn′tə·lĭz′əm), *n.* Occidental character or characteristics. —**Oc′ci·den′tal·ist,** *n., adj.*

Oc·ci·den·tal·ize (ŏk′sə·dĕn′tə·līz′), *v.t.*, **-ized, -izing.** to make Occidental. —**Oc′ci·den′tal·i·za′tion,** *n.*

oc·cip·i·tal (ŏk·sĭp′ə·təl), *adj.* of or pertaining to the back of the head. [t. ML: s. *occipitālis,* der. *occiput* occiput]

occipital bone, a compound bone which forms the lower posterior part of the skull. See diag. under **cranium.**

occipito-, a word element meaning "occiput," as in *occipitofrontal* (pertaining to both occiput and forehead), *occipitohyoid* (pertaining to both the occipital and the hyoid bone), *occipitoparietal, occipitosphenoid.* [comb. form repr. L *occiput*]

oc·ci·put (ŏk′sə·pŭt′, -pət), *n., pl.* **occipita** (ŏk·sĭp′ə·tə). *Anat.* the back part of the head or skull. [ME, t. L]

oc·clude (ə·klōōd′), *v.,* **-cluded, -cluding.** —*v.t.* 1. to close, shut, or stop up (a passage, etc.). 2. to shut in, out, or off. 3. *Chem.* (of certain metals and other solids) to absorb and retain gases or liquids, in minute pores. —*v.i.* 4. *Dentistry.* to shut or close against each other, as the opposing teeth of the upper and lower jaws. [t. L: m.s. *occlūdere* shut up, close up] —**oc·clu·sion** (ə·klōō′zhən), *n.* —**oc·clu·sive** (ə·klōō′sĭv), *adj.*

oc·cult (ə·kŭlt′, ŏk′ŭlt), *adj.* 1. beyond the bounds of ordinary knowledge; mysterious. 2. not disclosed; secret; communicated only to the initiated. 3. (in early science) **a.** not apparent on mere inspection but discoverable by experimentation. **b.** of a nature not understood, as physical qualities. **c.** dealing with such qualities; experimental: *occult science.* 4. of the nature of, or pertaining to, certain reputed sciences, as magic, astrology, etc., involving the alleged knowledge or employment of secret or mysterious agencies. 5. having to do with such sciences. 6. *Obs.* or *Rare.* hidden from view. —*n.* 7. occult studies or sciences. 8. anything occult. —*v.t.* 9. to hide; shut off (an object) from view. 10. *Astron.* to hide (a body) by occultation. —*v.i.* 11. to become hidden or shut off from view. [t. L: s. *occultus,* pp., covered over, concealed] —**oc·cult′er,** *n.*

oc·cul·ta·tion (ŏk′ŭl·tā′shən), *n.* 1. *Astron.* the passage of one celestial body in front of a second, thus hiding the second from view (applied esp. to the moon's coming between us and a star or planet). 2. disappearance from view or notice. 3. act of occulting. 4. the resulting state.

oc·cult·ism (ə·kŭl′tĭz′əm), *n.* the doctrine or study of the occult. —**oc·cult′ist,** *n., adj.*

oc·cu·pan·cy (ŏk′yə·pən·sĭ), *n.* 1. the act of taking possession. 2. actual possession. 3. the term during which one is an occupant. 4. exercise of dominion over a thing which has no owner so as to become legal owner.

oc·cu·pant (ŏk′yə·pənt), *n.* 1. one who occupies. 2. a tenant of a house, estate, office, etc. 3. *Law.* an owner through occupancy. [t. L: s. *occupans,* ppr.].

oc·cu·pa·tion (ŏk′yə·pā′shən), *n.* 1. one's habitual employment; business, trade, or calling. 2. that in which one is engaged. 3. possession, as of a place. 4. act of occupying. 5. state of being occupied. 6. tenure, as of an office. 7. seizure, as by invasion. [ME *occupacion,* t. L: m.s. *occupātio* seizing, employment] —**Syn.** 1. OCCUPATION, BUSINESS, PROFESSION, TRADE refer to the activity to which one regularly devotes himself, esp. his regular work, or means of getting a living. OCCUPATION is the general word: *a pleasant or congenial occupation.* BUSINESS esp. suggests a commercial or mercantile occupation: *the printing business.* PROFESSION implies an occupation requiring special knowledge and training in some field of science or learning: *the profession of teaching.* TRADE suggests an occupation involving manual training and skill: *one of the building trades.*

oc·cu·pa·tion·al (ŏk′yə·pā′shən·əl), *adj.* 1. of or pertaining to occupation. 2. of or pertaining to an occupation, trade, or calling: *an occupational disease, occupational guidance.*

occupational therapy, *Med.* a method of treatment consisting of some kind of light work, such as basketry, carpentry, etc., which takes the mind of the patient off himself, and frequently serves to exercise an affected part or to give vocational training.

oc·cu·py (ŏk′yə·pī′), *v.,* **-pied, -pying.** —*v.t.* 1. to take up (space, time, etc.). 2. to engage or employ (the mind, attention, etc., or the person). 3. to take possession of (a place), as by invasion. 4. to hold (a position, office, etc.). 5. to be resident or established in. —*v.i.* 6. *Rare* or *Obs.* to take or hold possession. [ME *occupie*(n), t. OF: m. *occuper,* t. L: m. *occupāre* take possession of, take up, employ] —**oc′cu·pi′er,** *n.* —**Syn.** 1-4. See **have.**

oc·cur (ə·kûr′), *v.i.,* **-curred, -curring.** 1. to come to pass, take place, or happen. 2. to be met with or found; present itself; appear. 3. to suggest itself in thought (commonly fol. by *to*): *an idea occurred to me.* [t. L: s. *occurrere* run against, go up to, meet, befall] —**Syn.** 1. See **happen.**

oc·cur·rence (ə·kûr′əns), *n.* 1. the action or fact of occurring. 2. something that occurs; an event or incident: *a daily occurrence.* —**oc·cur′rent,** *adj.* —**Syn.** 2. See **event.**

o·cean (ō′shən), *n.* 1. the vast body of salt water which covers almost three fourths of the earth's surface. 2. any of the geographical divisions of this body (commonly given as five: the Atlantic, Pacific, Indian, Arctic, and Antarctic oceans). 3. a vast expanse or quantity: *an ocean of grass.* [t. L: s. *ōceanus,* t. Gk.: m. *ōkeanós* the ocean, orig. the great stream supposed to encompass the earth (see OCEANUS); r. ME *occean,* t. OF] —**o′cean-like′,** *adj.*

o·cean-gray (ō′shən·grā′), *n., adj.* light pearly gray: used by the U.S. Navy for warships in World War II.

O·ce·an·i·a (ō′shĭ·ăn′ĭ·ə, -ā′nĭ·ə), *n.* the islands of the central and S Pacific, including Micronesia, Melanesia, and Polynesia; sometimes also, Australia and the Malay Archipelago. Also, **O·ce·an·i·ca** (ō′shĭ·ăn′ə·kə). —**O·ce·an′i·an,** *adj., n.*

o·ce·an·ic (ō′shĭ·ăn′ĭk), *adj.* 1. of or belonging to the ocean; pelagic. 2. oceanlike; vast.

O·ce·a·nid (ō·sē′ə·nĭd), *n. Gk. Myth.* a daughter of Oceanus; an ocean nymph. [t. Gk.: m.s. *Okeanís*]

oceanog., oceanography.

o·ce·a·nog·ra·phy (ō′shĭ·ə·nŏg′rə·fĭ, ō′shən·ŏg′-), *n.* the branch of physical geography dealing with the ocean. —**o′ce·a·nog′ra·pher,** *n.* —**o·ce·a·no·graph·ic** (ō′shĭ·ə·nə·grăf′ĭk, ō′shə·nə-), **o′ce·a·no·graph′i·cal,** *adj.* —**o′ce·a·no·graph′i·cal·ly,** *adv.*

O·ce·a·nus (ō·sē′ə·nəs), *n. Gk. Myth.* 1. the ocean god, and father of the Oceanids. 2. the great body of water encircling the plain of the earth.

o·cel·lar (ō·sĕl′ər), *adj.* pertaining to an ocellus.

o·cel·lat·ed (ō′sə·lā′tĭd, ō·sĕl′ā·tĭd), *adj.* 1. (of a spot or marking) eyelike. 2. having ocelli, or eyelike spots. Also, **o·cel·late** (ō′sə·lāt′, ō·sĕl′īt, -āt). [f. s. L *ocellātus* having little eyes + -ED[2]]

o·cel·la·tion (ŏs′ə·lā′shən), *n.* an eyelike spot or marking.

o·cel·lus (ō·sĕl′əs), *n., pl.* **ocelli** (ō·sĕl′ī). 1. a type of eye common to invertebrates, consisting of retinal cells, pigments, and nerve fibers. 2. an eyelike spot, as on a peacock feather. [t. L, dim. of *oculus* eye]

Ocellated marking on feather of peacock

o·ce·lot (ō′sə·lŏt′, ŏs′ə-), *n.* a spotted, leopardlike cat, *Felis pardalis,* some 3 feet in length, ranging from Texas through South America. [t. F, t. Mex.: m. *ocelotl* field tiger]

Ocelot, *Felis pardalis* (Total length 3 ft. or more, tail 1 ft.)

o·cher (ō′kər), *n., adj., v.,* **ochered, ochering.** —*n.* 1. any of a class of natural earths, mixtures of hydrated oxide of iron with various earthy materials, ranging in color from pale yellow to orange, and red, and used as pigments. **2.** *Slang.* money, esp. gold coin. —*adj.* **3.** ranging from a pale-yellow to orange or reddish hue. —*v.t.* **4.** to color or mark with ocher. [ME *oker*, t. OF: m. *ocre*, t. L: m. *ōchra*, t. Gk.: yellow ocher] —**o′cher·ous**, *adj.*

och·loc·ra·cy (ŏk lŏk′rə sĭ), *n.*, *pl.* **-cies.** government by the mob; mobocracy; mob rule. [t. Gk.: m.s. *ochlokratía* mob rule] —**och·lo·crat** (ŏk′lə krăt′), *n.* —**och′-lo·crat′ic, och·lo·crat′i·cal,** *adj.*

och·one (ŏкн ōn′), *interj. Irish and Scot.* alas! [t. Irish and Gaelic: m. *ochóin*]

o·chre (ō′kər), *n.*, *adj.*, *v.t.* **ochred, ochring.** ocher. —**o·chre·ous** (ō′kər əs, ō′krĭ əs), *adj.*

och·re·a (ŏk′rĭ ə), *n.*, *pl.* **-reae** (-rĭ ē′). ocrea.

o·chroid (ō′kroid), *adj.* yellow as ochre. [t. Gk.: m.s. *ōchroeidḗs* pallid]

Ochs (ŏks), *n.* Adolph, 1858–1935, U.S. newspaper publisher.

-ock, a noun suffix used to make descriptive names, as in *ruddock* (lit., the red one); diminutives, as in *hillock*; etc. [ME *-ok*, OE *-oc, -uc*]

Ock·ham (ŏk′əm), *n.* William. See Occam.

o′clock (ə klŏk′), of or by the clock (used in specifying or inquiring the hour of the day): *It is now one o′clock.*

O′Con·nell (ō kŏn′əl), *n.* Daniel, 1775–1847, Irish political agitator and orator.

O′Con·nor (ō kŏn′ər), *n.* Thomas Power, 1848–1929, Irish journalist, author, and political leader.

o·co·til·lo (ō′kə tēl′yō; *Sp.* ō̍́kô tē̍́yō̍̍), *n.*, *pl.* **-los.** a spiny woody shrub, *Fouqueria splendens*, or candlewood, of arid Mexico and the southwestern U.S. [t. Mex. Sp., dim. of *ocote* kind of pine, t. Aztec: m. *ocotl*]

oc·re·a (ŏk′rĭ ə, ō′krĭ ə), *n.*, *pl.* **ocreae** (ŏk′-rĭ ē′, ō′krĭ-). *Bot. and Zool.* a sheathing part, as a pair of stipules united about a stem. Also, **ochrea.** [t. L: greave, legging]

o·cre·ate (ŏk′rĭ ĭt, -āt′, ō′krĭ-), *adj.* having an ocrea or ocreae; sheathed.

Ocrea

oct-, a word element meaning "eight." Also, **octa-.** [t. Gk., comb. form of *oktṓ*]

Oct., October.

oct., octavo.

oc·tad (ŏk′tăd), *n.* **1.** a group or series of eight. **2.** *Chem.* an element, atom, or radical having a valence of eight. [t. LL: s. *octas*, t. Gk.: m. *oktás*] —**oc·tad′ic,** *adj.*

oc·ta·gon (ŏk′ə gŏn′, -gən), *n.* a polygon having eight angles and eight sides. [t. Gk.: s. *oktágōnos* octangular. See OCTA-, -GON]

oc·tag·o·nal (ŏk tăg′ə nəl), *adj.* having eight angles and eight sides. —**oc·tag′-o·nal·ly,** *adv.*

oc·ta·he·dral (ŏk′tə hē′drəl), *adj.* having the form of an octahedron.

Octagon

oc·ta·he·drite (ŏk′tə hē′drīt), *n.* anatase.

oc·ta·he·dron (ŏk′tə hē′drən), *n.*, *pl.* **-drons, -dra** (-drə). a solid figure having eight faces. [t. Gk.: m. *oktáedron*. See OCT-, -HEDRON]

oc·tam·er·ous (ŏk tăm′ər əs), *adj.* **1.** consisting of or divided into eight parts. **2.** *Bot.* (of flowers) having eight members in each whorl. [f. s. Gk. *oktamerés* of eight parts + -OUS]

Regular octahedrons

oc·tam·e·ter (ŏk tăm′-ə tər), *Pros.* —*adj.* **1.** consisting of eight measures or feet. —*n.* **2.** an octameter verse. [t. LL, t. Gk.: m. *oktámetros* of eight measures]

oc·tane (ŏk′tān), *n. Chem.* any of eighteen isomeric saturated hydrocarbons, C₈H₁₈, some of which are obtained in the distillation and cracking of petroleum. [f. OCT- + -ANE]

octane number, (of gasoline) a designation of antiknock quality, numerically equal to the percentage of isooctane (2, 2, 4, trimethyl pentane) by volume in a mixture of isooctane and normal heptane that matches the given gasoline in antiknock characteristics. Also, **octane rating.**

oc·tan·gu·lar (ŏk tăng′gyə lər), *adj.* having eight angles. [f. s. L. *octangulus* eight-angled + -AR¹]

oc·tant (ŏk′tənt), *n.* **1.** the eighth part of a circle. **2.** *Math.* each of the eighths into which three mutually perpendicular planes with a common point divide space. **3.** an instrument having an arc of 45 degrees, used by navigators for measuring angles up to 90°. **4.** the position of one heavenly body when 45 degrees distant from another. [t. L: s. *octans*] —**oc·tan·tal** (ŏk tăn′təl), *adj.*

oc·tar·chy (ŏk′tär kĭ), *n.*, *pl.* **-chies.** **1.** a government by eight persons. **2.** a group of eight states or kingdoms.

oc·tave (ŏk′tĭv, -tāv), *n.* **1.** *Music.* **a.** a tone on the eighth degree from a given tone (counted as the first). **b.** the interval between such tones. **c.** the harmonic combination of such tones. **d.** a series of tones, or of keys of an instrument, extending through this interval. **2.** (in organ building) a stop whose pipes give tones an octave above the normal pitch of the keys used. **3.** a

series or group of eight. **4.** *Pros.* a group or a stanza of eight lines, as the first eight lines of a sonnet. **5.** the eighth of a series. **6.** *Eccles.* **a.** the eighth day from a feast day (counted as the first). **b.** the period of eight days beginning with a feast day. —*adj.* **7.** pitched an octave higher. [ME, t. L: m. *octāva* (fem.) eighth] —**oc·ta·val** (ŏk tā′vəl, ŏk′tə-), *adj.*

Oc·ta·vi·an (ŏk tā′vĭ ən), *n.* **1.** See Augustus. **2.** *Brit.* a supporter of Edward VIII, latterly Duke of Windsor.

oc·ta·vo (ŏk tā′vō, -tä′-), *n.*, *pl.* **-vos,** *adj.* —*n.* **1.** a book size (about 6 x 9 inches) determined by printing on sheets folded to form eight leaves or sixteen pages. *Abbr.:* 8vo or 8°. —*adj.* **2.** in octavo. [short for NL phrase *in octāvō* in an eighth (of a sheet)]

oc·ten·ni·al (ŏk tĕn′ĭ əl), *adj.* **1.** occurring every eight years. **2.** of or for eight years. [f. s. LL *octennium* a period of eight years + -AL¹] —**oc·ten′ni·al·ly,** *adv.*

oc·tet (ŏk tĕt′), *n.* **1.** a company of eight singers or players. **2.** a musical composition for eight voices or instruments. **3.** *Pros.* **a.** a group of eight lines of verse. **b.** the first eight lines (octave) of a sonnet. **4.** any group of eight. Also, **oc·tette′.** [f. OCT(O)- + -*et* as in *duet*]

oc·til·lion (ŏk tĭl′yən), *n.* **1.** a cardinal number represented (in the U.S. and France) by one followed by 27 zeros or (in England and Germany) by one followed by 48 zeros. —*adj.* **2.** amounting to one octillion in number. [t. F: f. *oct-* OCT- + (*m*)*illion* MILLION] —**oc·til′lionth,** *n.*, *adj.*

octo-, a word element meaning "eight." [t. L, Gk., comb. form of L *octo*, Gk. *oktṓ*]

Oc·to·ber (ŏk tō′bər), *n.* **1.** the tenth month of the year, containing 31 days. **2.** *Chiefly Brit.* ale brewed in this month. [t. L: the eighth month of the early Roman year; r. ME *Octobre*, t. OF]

oc·to·dec·i·mo (ŏk′tə dĕs′ə mō′), *n.*, *pl.* **-mos,** *adj.* —*n.* **1.** a book size (about 4 x 6¼ inches) determined by printing on sheets folded to form eighteen leaves or thirty-six pages; eighteenmo. *Abbr.:* 18mo or 18°. —*adj.* **2.** in octodecimo. [short for NL phrase *in octōdecimō* in an eighteenth (of a sheet)]

oc·to·ge·nar·i·an (ŏk′tə jə nâr′ĭ ən), *adj.* Also, **oc·tog·e·nar·y** (ŏk tŏj′ə nĕr′ĭ). **1.** of the age of 80 years. **2.** between 80 and 90 years old. —*n.* **3.** an octogenarian person. [f. s. L *octōgēnārius* containing eighty + -AN]

oc·to·nar·y (ŏk′tə nĕr′ĭ), *adj.*, *n.*, *pl.* **-naries.** —*adj.* **1.** pertaining to the number eight. **2.** consisting of eight. **3.** preceeding by eights. —*n.* **4.** a group of eight; an ogdoad. **5.** *Pros.* eight lines, as a stanza. [t. L: m.s. *octōnārius* containing eight]

oc·to·pod (ŏk′tə pŏd′), *n.* any of the *Octopoda*, an order or suborder of eight-armed dibranchiate cephalopods that includes the octopuses and paper nautiluses.

oc·to·pus (ŏk′tə pəs), *n.*, *pl.* **-puses, -pi** (-pī′). **1.** any animal of the genus *Octopus*, comprising octopods with a soft, oval body and eight sucker-bearing arms, and living mostly on the sea bottom. **2.** any octopod. **3.** a far-reaching and grasping organization, person, etc. [t. NL, t. Gk.: m. *óktōpous* eight-footed]

Octopus, *Octopus vulgaris*

oc·to·roon (ŏk′tə rōōn′), *n.* a person having one-eighth Negro blood; the offspring of a quadroon and a white. [f. OCTO- + -*roon*, modeled on QUADROON]

oc·to·syl·la·ble (ŏk′tə sĭl′ə bəl), *n.* a word or a line of verse of eight syllables. —**oc·to·syl·lab·ic** (ŏk′tə sĭ-lăb′ĭk), *adj.*

oc·troi (ŏk′troi; *Fr.* ôk trwȧ́), *n.* **1.** a local tax levied on certain articles, such as foodstuffs, on their admission into a city. **2.** the place at which the tax is collected. **3.** the officials collecting it. [F, der. *octroyer* grant, ult. der. L *auctor* granter, author]

oc·tu·ple (ŏk′tyŏŏ pəl, -tōō-; ŏk tū′pəl, -tōō′-), *adj.*, *v.*, **-pled, -pling.** —*adj.* **1.** eightfold; eight times as great. **2.** having eight effective units or elements. —*v.t.* **3.** to make eight times as great. [t. L: m.s. *octuplus* eightfold]

oc·u·lar (ŏk′yə lər), *adj.* **1.** of or pertaining to the eye: *ocular movements.* **2.** of the nature of an eye: *an ocular organ.* **3.** performed or perceived by the eye or eyesight. —*n.* **4.** the eyepiece of an optical instrument. [t. LL: s. *oculāris* of the eyes] —**oc′u·lar·ly,** *adv.*

oc·u·list (ŏk′yə lĭst), *n.* a doctor of medicine skilled in the examination and treatment of the eye; an ophthalmologist. [t. F: m. *oculiste*, f. s. L *oculus* eye + -*iste* -IST]

oc·u·lo·mo·tor (ŏk′yə lō mō′tər), *adj.* moving the eyeball. [f. *oculo-* (comb. form repr. L *oculus* eye) + MOTOR]

oculomotor nerve, *Anat.* either of the two cranial nerves which supply most of the muscles of the eyeball.

od (ŏd, ōd), *n.* a hypothetical force formerly held to pervade all nature and to manifest itself in magnetism, mesmerism, chemical action, etc. Also, **odyl, odyle.** [arbitrary name coined by Baron Karl von Reichenbach (1788–1869)]

Od (ŏd), *interj. Archaic or Dial.* reduced form of **God,** used interjectionally and in minced oaths. Also, **'Od, Odd.**

O.D., 1. Officer of the Day. **2.** (of military uniform) olive drab. **3.** overdraft. **4.** overdrawn.

o·da·lisque (ō′dəlĭsk), *n.* a female slave in a harem, esp. in that of the Sultan of Turkey. Also, **o′da·lisk.** [t. F, t. Turk.: m. *ŏdalik,* der. *ŏdah* room]

odd (ŏd), *adj.* **1.** differing in character from what is ordinary or usual: *an odd choice.* **2.** singular or peculiar in a freakish or eccentric way, as persons or their manners, etc. **3.** fantastic or bizarre, as things. **4.** out-of-the-way; secluded. **5.** additional to a whole mentioned in round numbers; being a surplus over a definite quantity. **6.** additional to what is taken into account. **7.** surplus of a lower denomination: *two dollars and some odd cents.* **8.** being part of a pair, set, or series of which the rest is lacking: *an odd glove.* **9.** leaving a remainder of 1 when divided by 2, as a number (opposed to *even*). **10.** remaining after a division into pairs, or into equal numbers or parts. **11.** occasional or casual: *odd jobs.* **12.** not forming part of any particular group, set, or class: *odd bits of information.* —*n.* **13.** that which is odd. **14.** *Golf.* **a.** a stroke more than the opponent has played. **b.** *Brit.* a stroke taken from a player's total score for a hole in order to give him odds. **15.** (*pl.*) odd things, bits, or scraps: *odds and ends.* See also **odds.** [ME *odde,* t. Scand.; cf. Icel. *odda-tala* odd number] —**odd′ly,** *adv.* —**odd′ness,** *n.* —**Syn. 1.** See **strange.**

Odd·fel·low (ŏd′fĕl′ō), *n.* a member of a secret social and benevolent society "Independent Order of Odd-fellows," originated in England in the 18th century.

odd·ish (ŏd′ĭsh), *adj.* rather odd; queer.

odd·i·ty (ŏd′ətĭ), *n., pl.* **-ties. 1.** the quality of being odd; singularity or strangeness. **2.** an odd characteristic or peculiarity. **3.** an odd person or thing.

odd·ment (ŏd′mənt), *n.* **1.** an odd article, bit, remnant, or the like. **2.** an article belonging to a broken or incomplete set. **3.** *Print.* any individual portion of a book excluding the text, as the frontispiece, index, etc.

odd-pin·nate (ŏd′pĭn′āt, -ĭt), *adj. Bot.* pinnate with an odd terminal leaflet.

odds (ŏdz), *n.pl. and sing.* **1.** an equalizing allowance, as that given to a weaker side in a contest. **2.** the amount by which the bet of one party to a wager exceeds that of the other. **3.** balance of probability in favor of something occurring or being the case. **4.** advantage or superiority on the side of one of two contending parties: *to strive against odds.* **5.** difference in the way of benefit or detriment. **6.** the amount of difference. **7.** disagreement or strife (chiefly in *at odds*).

ode (ōd), *n.* **1.** a lyric poem typically of elaborate or irregular metrical form and expressive of exalted or enthusiastic emotion. **2.** (*orig.*) a poem intended to be sung. **3. regular** or **Pindaric ode,** a complex poetic type, consisting of strophes, and antistrophes identical in form, with contrasting epodes, the three units being repeated in the poem. **4. irregular, pseudo-Pindaric,** or **Cowleian ode,** a poetic form in the general style of the regular ode, but lacking its strict complex form and written in a series of irregular strophes. **5. Horatian** or **Sapphic ode,** an ode in which one stanzaic form is repeated. [t. F, t. LL: m. *ōda,* t. Gk.: m. *ōidē,* contr. of *aoidē* song]

-ode[1], a suffix of nouns denoting something having some resemblance to what is indicated by the preceding part of the word as in *phyllode.* [t. Gk.: m. *-ōdēs* like, contr. of *-oeidēs* -OID]

-ode[2], a noun suffix meaning "way," as in *anode, electrode.* [t. Gk.: m. *-odos,* der. *hodós* way]

O·dels·thing (ō′dəlstĭng′), *n.* See **Storthing.**

O·den·se (ō′thən sā), *n.* a seaport in S Denmark, on Fyn island. 104,391 (1945).

O·der (ō′dər), *n.* a river flowing from the Carpathians in N Czechoslovakia through SW Poland and along the German-Polish border into the Baltic. ab. 550 mi.

O·des·sa (ō·dĕs′ə; *Russ.* ō′dĕs′sä), *n.* **1.** a seaport in the SW Soviet Union, on the Black Sea: the principal export center of Ukrainian grain. 604,223 (1939). **2.** a city in W Texas. 29,495 (1950).

O·dets (ō dĕts′), *n.* **Clifford,** born 1906, U.S. dramatist.

o·de·um (ō dē′əm), *n., pl.* **odea** (ō dē′ə). **1.** a hall or structure for musical or dramatic performances. **2.** (in ancient Greece and Rome) a roofed building for musical performances. [t. L, t. Gk.: m. *ōideîon* music hall]

od·ic[1] (ō′dĭk), *adj.* of an ode. [f. ODE + -IC]

od·ic[2] (ŏd′ĭk, ō′dĭk), *adj.* of or pertaining to the hypothetical force od. [f. OD + -IC]

O·din (ō′dĭn), *n. Scand. Myth.* the chief deity, being the god of wisdom, culture, war, and the dead. Also, **Othin.** [t. Icel.: m. *Odhinn,* c. E Woden, G *Wotan*]

o·di·ous (ō′dĭəs), *adj.* **1.** deserving of or exciting hatred; hateful or detestable. **2.** highly displeasing or offensive; disgusting: *an odious thought.* [ME, t. L: m.s. *odiōsus* hateful] —**o′di·ous·ly,** *adv.* —**o′di·ous·ness,** *n.* —**Syn. 1.** abominable, objectionable. See **hateful.**

o·di·um (ō′dĭəm), *n.* **1.** hatred; dislike. **2.** the reproach, discredit, or opprobrium attaching to something hated or odious. **3.** state of being hated. [t. L: hatred]

O·do·a·cer (ō′dō ä′sər), *n.* A.D. 434?-493, first barbarian ruler of Italy, A.D. 476-493. Also, **Odovacar.**

o·do·graph (ō′dəgrăf′, -gräf′), *n.* **1.** an odometer. **2.** a pedometer. **3.** a pedograph. [var. of *hodograph,* f. Gk. *hodó(s)* way + -GRAPH]

o·dom·e·ter (ō dŏm′ə tər), *n.* an instrument for meas-

uring distance passed over, as by an auto. [prop. *hodometer,* f. Gk. *hodó(s)* way + -METER] —**o·dom′e·try,** *n.*

odont-, a word element meaning "tooth." Also, **odonto-.** [t. Gk., comb. form of *odoús*]

-odont, terminal word element equivalent to **odont-.**

o·don·tal·gi·a (ō′dŏn tăl′jĭ ə), *n. Pathol.* toothache. —**o′don·tal′gic,** *adj.*

o·don·to·blast (ō dŏn′tə blăst′), *n. Anat.* one of a layer of cells which, in the development of a tooth, give rise to the dentin. —**o·don′to·blas′tic,** *adj.*

o·don·to·glos·sum (ō dŏn′tə glŏs′əm), *n.* any of the epiphytic orchids constituting the genus *Odontoglossum,* natives of the mountainous region from Bolivia to Mexico. [t. NL, f. Gk.: *odonto-* ODONTO- + m. *glōssa* tongue]

o·don·to·graph (ō dŏn′tə grăf′, -gräf′), *n.* an instrument for laying out the forms of geared teeth or ratchets.

o·don·toid (ō dŏn′toid), *adj.* **1.** noting a toothlike process, as that of the axis, or second cervical vertebra, upon which the atlas rotates. **2.** resembling a tooth. [t. Gk.: m.s. *odontoeidēs* toothlike]

o·don·tol·o·gy (ō′dŏn tŏl′ə jĭ, ŏd′ŏn-), *n.* **1.** the science or art which treats of the study of the teeth and their surrounding tissues, and of the prevention and cure of their diseases. **2.** dentistry. —**o·don·to·log·i·cal** (ō dŏn′tə lŏj′ə kəl), *adj.* —**o′don·tol′o·gist,** *n.*

o·don·to·phore (ō dŏn′tə fōr′), *n. Zool.* a structure in the mouth of most mollusks, over which the radula is drawn backward and forward in the process of breaking up food. [t. Gk.: m.s. *odontophóros* bearing teeth] —**o·don·toph·o·ral** (ō′dŏn tŏf′ə rəl), **o·don·toph·o·rine** (ō′dŏn tŏf′ə rin′, -rĭn), **o·don·toph·o·rous,** *adj.*

o·dor (ō′dər), *n.* **1.** that property of a substance which affects the sense of smell: *rank odors.* **2.** agreeable scent; fragrance. **3.** savor characteristic or suggestive of something: *an odor of suspicion.* **4.** repute or estimation: *in ill odor.* Also, *Brit.,* **o′dour.** [ME, t. OF, t. L] —**o′dor·less,** *adj.*

o·dor·if·er·ous (ō′də rĭf′ər əs), *adj.* yielding or diffusing an odor, esp. a fragrant one. [ME, f. L *odōrifer* bringing odors + -OUS] —**o′dor·if′er·ous·ly,** *adv.* —**o′dor·if′er·ous·ness,** *n.*

o·dor·ous (ō′dər əs), *adj.* having or diffusing an odor, esp. a fragrant odor. [t. L: m. *odōrus* emitting a scent] —**o′dor·ous·ly,** *adv.* —**o′dor·ous·ness,** *n.*

O·do·va·car (ō′dō vä′kər), *n.* Odoacer.

od·yl (ŏd′ĭl, ō′dĭl), *n.* od. Also, **od′yle.** [f. OD + -YL] —**o·dyl·ic** (ō dĭl′ĭk), *adj.*

-odynia, word element meaning "pain." [t. NL, t. Gk.]

O·dys·seus (ō dĭs′ūs, ō dĭs′ĭ əs), *n. Gk. Legend.* the son of Laertes, husband of Penelope, and father of Telemachus: wisest and wiliest of the Greek leaders. [t. Gk.]

Od·ys·sey (ŏd′ə sĭ), *n.* **1.** Homer's epic poem describing the ten years' wandering of Odysseus in returning to Ithaca after the Trojan War. **2.** (*also l.c.*) any long series of wanderings [t. Gk.: m.s. *Odýsseia,* der. *Odysseús* Odysseus, Ulysses] —**Od·ys·se·an** (ŏd′ə sē′ən), *adj.*

OE, Old English. Also, **OE., O.E.**

oec·u·men·i·cal (ĕk′yŏŏ mĕn′ə kəl or, *esp. Brit.,* ē′kyōō-), *adj.* ecumenical. Also, **oec′u·men′ic.**

O.E.D., Oxford English Dictionary.

Oed·i·pus (ĕd′ə pəs, ēd′ə-), *n. Gk. Legend.* a son of Laius and Jocasta. Reared by the king of Corinth, he slew his father involuntarily and solved the riddle of the Sphinx, thereby becoming King of Thebes and unwittingly winning the hand of his mother in marriage. When the nature of his deeds became apparent, Jocasta hanged herself, and Oedipus tore out his eyes.

Oedipus complex, *Psychoanal.* **1.** the unresolved desire of a child for sexual gratification through the parent of the opposite sex. This involves, first, identification with and, later, hatred for the parent of the same sex, who is considered by the child as a rival. **2.** sexual desire of the son for the mother. Cf. **Electra complex.**

oeil-de-boeuf (œ′y də bœf′), *n., pl.* **oeils-de-boeuf** (œ′y də-). *French.* a comparatively small round or oval window, as in a frieze. [F: eye of ox, bull's eye]

oeil·lade (œ yåd′), *n. French.* an amorous glance: ogle. [t. It.: m. *occhiata* glance (der. *occhio* eye, g. L *oculus*)]

oe·nol·o·gy (ē nŏl′ə jĭ), *n.* the science of viniculture. [f. m. Gk. *oîno(s)* wine + -LOGY] —**oe·no·log·i·cal** (ē′nə lŏj′ə kəl), *adj.* —**oe·nol′o·gist,** *n.*

oe·no·mel (ē′nə mĕl′, ĕn′ə-), *n.* **1.** a drink made of wine mixed with honey. **2.** something combining strength with sweetness. [t. LL: s. *oenomeli,* t. Gk.: m. *oinómeli* wine mixed with honey]

Oe·no·ne (ē nō′nĭ), *n. Gk. Myth.* a nymph living on Mount Ida near Troy. She was the lover of Paris, who later deserted her for Helen.

o′er (ōr), *prep., adv. Poetic or Dial.* over.

oer·sted (ûr′stĕd), *n.* **1.** a unit of magnetic intensity equal to the intensity produced by a magnetic pole of unit strength at a distance of one centimeter. **2.** *Obs.* the unit of magnetic reluctance equal to the reluctance of a centimeter cube of vacuum between parallel surfaces. [named after H. C. *Oersted* (1777-1851), Danish physicist]

oe·soph·a·gus (ē sŏf′ə gəs), *n., pl.* **-gi** (-jī). esophagus. —**oe·so·phag·e·al** (ē′sə făj′ĭ əl), *adj.*

oes·trin (ĕs′trĭn, ēs′trĭn), *n. Biochem.* estrone.

oes·tri·ol (ĕs′trĭ ōl′, -ŏl, ēs′trĭ′-), *n.* estriol.

oes·tro·gen (ĕs′trə jən, ēs′trə-), *n.* estrogen.

oes·trous (ĕs′trəs, ēs′trəs), *adj.* estrous.

---

b., blend of, blended; c., cognate with; d., dialect, dialectal; der., derived from; f., formed from; g., going back to; m., modification of; r., replacing; s., stem of; t., taken from; ?, perhaps. See the full key on inside cover.

oestrous cycle, estrous cycle.

oes·trus (ĕs′trəs, ēs′trəs), *n.* **1.** Also, **oes′trum.** estrus. **2.** passion or passionate impulse. **3.** a stimulus. [t. L, t. Gk.: m. *oîstros* gadfly, sting, frenzy]

oeu·vre (œ′vr), *n.*, *pl.* **oeuvres** (œ′vr). *French.* work.

of (ŏv, ŭv; *unstressed* əv), *prep.* a particle indicating: **1.** distance or direction from separation, deprivation, riddance, etc.: *within a mile of, to cure of.* **2.** derivation, origin, or source: *of good family, the plays of O'Neill.* **3.** cause, occasion, or reason: *to die of hunger.* **4.** material or substance: *a pound of sugar.* **5.** a relation of identity: *the city of Paris.* **6.** belonging or possession, connection, or association: *the property of all.* **7.** inclusion in a number, class, or whole: *one of us.* **8.** objective relation: *the ringing of bells.* **9.** reference or respect: *talk of peace.* **10.** qualities or attributes: *a man of tact.* **11.** time: *of an evening.* **12.** to or before (a designated hour of the clock): *twenty minutes of five.* **13.** *Chiefly Archaic.* the agent by whom something is done: *beloved of all.* [ME and OE *of*, prep. and adv. (see OFF), c. G *ab*]

of-, var. of **ob-,** (by assimilation) before *f*, as in *offend.*

OF, Old French. Also, **OF., O.F.**

off (ôf, ŏf), *adv.* **1.** away from a position occupied, or from contact, connection, or attachment: *take off one's hat.* **2.** to or at a distance from, or away from, a place: *to run off.* **3.** away from or out of association or relation: *to cast off a son.* **4.** deviating from, especially from what is normal or regular. **5.** as a deduction: *10 per cent off on all cash purchases.* **6.** away; distant (in future time): *summer is only a week off.* **7.** out of operation or effective existence. **8.** so as to interrupt continuity or cause discontinuance: *to break off negotiations.* **9.** away from employment or service: *to lay off workmen.* **10.** so as to exhaust, finish, or complete; completely: *to kill off vermin.* **11.** forthwith or immediately: *right off.* **12.** with prompt or ready performance: *to dash off a letter.* **13.** to fulfillment, or into execution or effect: *the contest came off on the day fixed.* **14.** so as to cause or undergo reduction or diminution: *to wear off.* **15.** on one's way or journey, as from a place: *to see a friend off on a journey.* **16.** *Naut.* away from the land, a ship, the wind, etc. **17. be** or **take off,** to depart; leave. **18. off and on, a.** intermittently: *to work off and on.* **b.** *Naut.* on alternate tacks. **19. off with** (anything specified), to remove; take or cut off: *off with his head.*
—*prep.* **20.** away from; so as no longer to be or rest on: *to fall off a horse.* **21.** deviating from (something normal or usual): *off one's balance.* **22.** from by subtraction or deduction: *25 per cent off the marked price.* **23.** away or disengaged from (duty, work, etc.). **24.** *Slang.* refraining from (some food, activity, etc.): *to be off gambling.* **25.** distant from: *a village some miles off the main road.* **26.** leading out of: *an alley off 12th Street.* **27.** *U.S. Colloq.* from, indicating source: *I bought it off him.* **28.** from, indicating material: *to make a meal off fish.* **29.** *Naut.* to seaward of.
—*adj.* **30.** *Now Colloq.* wide of the truth or fact, in error: *you are off on that point.* **31.** no longer in contemplation: *the agreement is off.* **32.** as to condition, circumstances, supplies, etc.: *better off.* **33.** (of time) on which work is suspended: *pastime for one's off hours.* **34.** not so good or satisfactory as usual: *an off year for apples.* **35.** of less than the ordinary activity, liveliness, or lively interest: *an off season in the woolen trade.* **36.** (of a chance) remote. **37.** more distant; farther: *the off side of a wall.* **38.** (with reference to animals or vehicles) right (opposed to *near* or *left*). **39.** *Naut.* farther from the shore. **40.** *Cricket.* noting that side of the wicket or of the field opposite which the batsman stands.
—*n.* **41.** state or fact of being off. **42.** *Cricket.* the off side.
—*interj.* **43.** be off! stand off! off with you!
[ME *of(f)*, OE *of.* See OF]

off., **1.** offered. **2.** office. **3.** officer. **4.** official.

of·fal (ôf′əl, ŏf′əl), *n.* **1.** the waste parts of a butchered animal, or the inedible portions of food animals, fowl, and fish. **2.** refuse in general. [ME, f. *of* off + *fal* fall]

off·cast (ôf′kăst′, -käst′, ŏf′-), *adj.* **1.** cast off; rejected. —*n.* **2.** a castoff person or thing.

off-chance (ôf′chăns′, -chäns′, ŏf′-), *n.* a remote chance or possibility.

off-col·or (ôf′kŭl′ər, ŏf′-), *adj.* **1.** defective in color, as a gem. **2.** of doubtful propriety: *an off-color story.* Also, *Brit.*, **off′-col′our.**

Of·fen·bach (ôf′ənbäk′, ŏf′-; *also Fr.* ô fĕnbàk′ *for 1; Ger.* ôf′ənbäкн′ *for 2*), *n.* **1. Jacques** (zhäk), 1819–80, French composer. **2.** a city in W Germany, on the Main river, near Frankfurt. 87,063 (1939).

of·fend (əfĕnd′), *v. t.* **1.** to irritate in mind or feelings; cause resentful displeasure in. **2.** to affect (the sense, taste, etc.) disagreeably. **3.** *Obs.* to violate or transgress. **4.** *Obs.* (in Biblical use) to cause to sin. —*v.i.* **5.** to give offense or cause displeasure. **6.** to err in conduct; commit a sin, crime, or fault. [ME *offende(n)*, t. OF: m. *offendre*, t. L: m. *offendere* strike against, displease] —**of·fend′er,** *n.* —**Syn. 1.** provoke, insult.

of·fense (əfĕns′), *n.* **1.** a transgression; a wrong; a sin. **2.** a transgression of law which is not indictable, but is punishable summarily or by the forfeiture of a penalty (**petty offense**). **3.** a cause of transgression or wrong. **4.** something that offends. **5.** act of offending or displeasing. **6.** the feeling of resentful displeasure caused: *to give offense.* **7.** act of attacking; attack or assault: *weapons of offense.* **8.** the persons, side, etc. attacking. **9.** *Obs.* injury, harm, or hurt. Also, *esp. Brit.*, **of·fence′.** —**Syn. 1.** See **crime.**

of·fense·less (əfĕns′lĭs), *adj.* **1.** without offense. **2.** incapable of offense or attack. **3.** unoffending.

of·fen·sive (əfĕn′sĭv), *adj.* **1.** causing offense or displeasure; irritating; highly annoying. **2.** disagreeable to the sense: *an offensive odor.* **3.** repugnant to the moral sense, good taste, or the like; insulting. **4.** pertaining to offense or attack: *offensive movements.* **5.** consisting in or characterized by attack: *offensive warfare.* —*n.* **6.** the position or attitude of offense or attack: *to take the offensive.* **7.** an offensive movement: *the big Russian offensive.* —**of·fen′sive·ly,** *adv.* —**of·fen′sive·ness,** *n.* —**Syn. 1.** See **hateful. 2.** disagreeable, distasteful, disgusting, repulsive, obnoxious. —**Ant. 1, 2.** pleasing.

of·fer (ôf′ər, ŏf′ər), *v.t.* **1.** to present for acceptance or rejection; proffer: *to offer someone a cigarette.* **2.** to put forward for consideration: *to offer a suggestion.* **3.** to make a show of intention (to do something): *we did not offer to go first.* **4.** to propose or volunteer (to do something): *she offered to accompany me.* **5.** to proffer (oneself) for marriage. **6.** to present solemnly as an act of worship or devotion, as to God, a deity, a saint, etc.; sacrifice. **7.** to present; put forward: *she offered no response.* **8.** to attempt to inflict, do, or make: *to offer battle.* **9.** to do or make (violence, resistance, etc.) actually. **10.** to present to sight or notice. **11.** to present for sale. **12.** to tender or bid as a price: *to offer ten dollars for a radio.* **13.** to render (homage, thanks, etc.). —*v.i.* **14.** to make an offer. **15.** to make an offer of marriage; propose. **16.** to present itself; occur: *whenever an occasion offered.* **17.** to make an offering as an act of worship or devotion; sacrifice. **18.** *Obs. or Rare.* to make an attempt (fol. by *at*). —*n.* **19.** act of offering: *an offer of assistance.* **20.** a proposal of marriage. **21.** a proposal to give or accept something as a price or equivalent for something else; a bid: *an offer of $10,000 for a house.* **22.** the condition of being offered: *an offer for sale.* **23.** something offered. **24.** *Law.* a proposal which requires only acceptance in order to create a contract. **25.** an attempt or endeavor. **26.** a show of intention. [ME *offre(n)*, OE *offrian*, t. L: m. *offerre*] —**of′fer·er, of′fer·or,** *n.*
—**Syn. 1.** OFFER, PROFFER, TENDER mean to present for acceptance or refusal. OFFER is a common word in general use for presenting something to be accepted or rejected: *to offer assistance.* PROFFER, with the same meaning, is now chiefly a literary word: *to proffer one's services.* TENDER (no longer used in reference to concrete objects) is a ceremonious term for a more or less formal or conventional act: *to tender one's resignation.* —**Ant. 1.** withdraw, withhold.

of·fer·ing (ôf′ərĭng, ŏf′ər-), *n.* **1.** something offered in worship or devotion, as to God, a deity, etc.; an oblation; a sacrifice. **2.** a contribution given to or through the church for a particular purpose, as at a service. **3.** anything offered; gift. **4.** act of one who offers.

of·fer·to·ry (ôf′ərtōr′ĭ, ŏf′ər-), *n.*, *pl.* **-ries. 1.** *Rom. Cath. Ch.* the oblation of the unconsecrated elements made by the celebrant at this part of the mass. **2.** *Eccles.* **a.** the verses, anthem, or music said, sung, or played while the offerings of the people are received at a religious service. **b.** that part of a service at which offerings are made. **c.** the offerings themselves. [ME *offertorie*, t. LL: m. *offertōrium* place to which offerings were brought, offering, oblation]

off·hand (ôf′hănd′, ŏf′-), *adv.* **1.** without previous thought or preparation; extempore: *to decide offhand.* **2.** cavalier, curt, or brusque. —*adj.* Also, **off′hand′ed. 3.** done or made offhand. **4.** informal or casual.

of·fice (ôf′ĭs, ŏf′ĭs), *n.* **1.** a room or place for the transaction of business, the discharge of professional duties, or the like: *the doctor's office.* **2.** the room or rooms in which the clerical work of an industrial or other establishment is done. **3.** the staff or body of persons carrying on work in a business or other office. **4.** a building or a set of rooms devoted to the business of a branch of a governmental organization: *the post office.* **5.** the body of persons occupying governmental offices. **6.** a position of duty, trust, or authority, esp. in the public services, or in some corporation, society, or the like. **7.** the duty, function, or part of a particular person or agency: *the office of adviser.* **8.** official employment or position: *to seek office.* **9.** a service or task to be performed: *little domestic offices.* **10.** *Slang.* (prec. by *the*) hint or signal. **11.** something (good, or occasionally bad) done for another. **12.** *Eccles.* **a.** the prescribed order or form for a service of the church, or for devotional use, or the services so prescribed. **b.** the prayers, readings from scripture, and psalms that must be recited every day by all who are in major orders. **c.** a ceremony or rite, esp. for the dead. **13.** (*pl.*) *Chiefly Brit.* the parts of a house, as the kitchen, pantry, laundry, etc., devoted to household work. **14.** *Chiefly Brit.* the stables, barns, cowhouses, etc., of a farm. [ME, t. OF, t. L: m.s. *officium* service, duty, ceremony] —**Syn. 8.** See **appointment.**

office boy, a boy employed in an office for errands, etc.

of·fice·hold·er (ôf′ĭshōl′dər, ŏf′ĭs-), *n.* a person filling a governmental position.

office hours, 1. the hours a person spends working in an office. **2.** the hours during which a professional man or an office conducts regular business.

of·fi·cer (ŏf'ə·sər, ŏf'ə-), *n.* **1.** one who holds a position of rank or authority in the army, navy, or any similar organization, esp. one who holds a commission in the army or navy. **2.** a policeman or constable. **3.** the master or captain of a merchant vessel or pleasure vessel, or any of his chief assistants. **4.** a person appointed or elected to some position of responsibility and authority in the public service, or in some corporation, society, or the like. **5.** (in some honorary orders) a member of higher rank than the lowest. **6.** *Obs.* an agent. —*v.t.* **7.** to furnish with officers. **8.** to command or direct as an officer does. **9.** to direct, conduct, or manage. [ME, t. OF: m. *officier*, t. ML: m.s. *officiārius*, der. L *officium* office]

officer of the day, *Mil.* an officer who has charge, for the day, of the guard and prisoners of a military force or camp.

officer of the guard, an officer, acting under the officer of the day, who is responsible for the instruction, discipline, and performance of duty of the guard in a post, camp, or station.

office seeker, one who seeks public office.

of·fi·cial (ə·fĭsh'əl), *n.* **1.** one who holds an office or is charged with some form of official duty: *police officials.* —*adj.* **2.** of or pertaining to an office or position of duty, trust, or authority: *official powers.* **3.** authorized or issued authoritatively: *an official report.* **4.** holding office. **5.** appointed or authorized to act in a special capacity: *an official representative.* **6.** formal or ceremonious: *an official dinner.* **7.** *Pharm.* authorized by the pharmacopoeia. [t. LL: s. *officiālis*, der. L *officium* office] —**of·fi'cial·ly,** *adv.*

of·fi·cial·dom (ə·fĭsh'əl·dəm), *n.* **1.** the position or domain of officials. **2.** the official class.

of·fi·cial·ism (ə·fĭsh'əl·ĭz'əm), *n.* **1.** official methods or system. **2.** excessive attention to official routine. **3.** officials collectively.

of·fi·ci·ant (ə·fĭsh'ĭ·ənt), *n.* one who officiates at a religious service or ceremony. [t. ML: s. *officians*, ppr. of *officiāre* OFFICIATE]

of·fi·ci·ar·y (ə·fĭsh'ĭ·ĕr'ĭ), *adj.* **1.** pertaining to or derived from an office, as a title. **2.** having a title or rank derived from an office, as a dignitary.

of·fi·ci·ate (ə·fĭsh'ĭ·āt'), *v.i.* -ated, -ating. **1.** to perform the duties of any office or position. **2.** to perform the office of a priest or minister, as at divine worship. [t. ML: m.s. *officiātus,* pp. of *officiāre,* der. L *officium* office] —**of·fi'ci·a'tion,** *n.* —**of·fi'ci·a'tor,** *n.*

of·fic·i·nal (ə·fĭs'ə·nəl), *adj.* **1.** kept in stock by apothecaries, as a drug. Cf. **magistral. 2.** recognized by the pharmacopoeia. —*n.* **3.** an officinal medicine. [t. ML: s. *officīnālis,* der. L *officina* workshop, laboratory]

of·fi·cious (ə·fĭsh'əs), *adj.* **1.** forward in tendering or obtruding one's services upon others. **2.** marked by or proceeding from such forwardness: *officious interference.* **3.** *Obs.* ready to serve. [t. L: m.s. *officiōsus* obliging, dutiful] —**of·fi'cious·ly,** *adv.* —**of·fi'cious·ness,** *n.*

off·ing (ôf'ĭng, ŏf'ĭng), *n.* **1.** the more distant part of the sea as seen from the shore, beyond the anchoring ground. **2.** position at a distance from the shore. **3. in the offing, a.** not very distant. **b.** close enough to be seen. **c.** ready or likely to happen, appear, etc.

off·ish (ôf'ĭsh, ŏf'ĭsh), *adj. Colloq.* aloof. —**off'ish·ness,** *n.*

off·print (ôf'prĭnt', ŏf'-), *n.* **1.** a reprint in separate form of an article which originally appeared as part of a larger publication. —*v.t.* **2.** to reprint separately, as an article from a larger publication.

off·scour·ing (ôf'skour'ĭng, ŏf'-), *n.* (*often pl.*) that which is scoured off; filth; refuse.

off·set (*v.* ôf'sĕt', ŏf'-, *n., adj.* ôf'sĕt', ŏf'-), *v.,* -set, -setting, *n., adj.* —*v.t.* **1.** to balance by something else as an equivalent: *to offset one thing by another.* **2.** to counterbalance as an equivalent does; compensate for: *the gains offset the losses.* **3.** *Print.* **a.** to make an offset of. **b.** to print by the process of offset lithography. **4.** *Archit.* to build with a setoff, as a wall. —*v.i.* **5.** to project as an offset or branch. **6.** *Print.* to make an offset. —*n.* **7.** something that offsets or counterbalances; a compensating equivalent. **8.** the start or outset. **9.** a short lateral shoot by which certain plants are propagated. **10.** any offshoot; branch. **11.** an offshoot from a family or race. **12.** a spur of a mountain range. **13.** *Lithog.* an impression from an inked design or the like on a lithographic stone or metal plate, made on another surface, as a rubber blanket, and then transferred to paper, instead of being made directly on the paper. **14.** *Print.* a faulty transfer of superabundant or undried ink on a printed sheet to any opposed surface, as the opposite page. **15.** *Mach.* a more or less abrupt bend in a pipe, bar, rod, or the like, to serve some particular purpose. **16.** *Archit.* a setoff. **17.** *Survey.* a short distance measured perpendicularly from a line. —*adj.* **18.** *Lithog.* pertaining to, or by, offset.

off·shoot (ôf'shoot', ŏf'-), *n.* **1.** a shoot from a main stem, as of a plant; a lateral shoot. **2.** a branch, or a descendant or scion, of a family or race. **3.** anything conceived as springing or proceeding from a main stock: *an offshoot of a mountain range, a railroad, etc.*

off·shore (ôf'shôr', ŏf'-), *adv.* **1.** off or away from the shore. **2.** at a distance from the shore. —*adj.* **3.** moving or tending away from the shore: *an offshore wind.* **4.** being or operating at a distance from the shore: *offshore fisheries or fishermen.*

off·side (ôf'sīd', ŏf'-), *adj. Football, Hockey, etc.* **1.** away from one's own or the proper side, as of the ball or of a player who last played or touched it (a position subject to restrictions or penalties in particular cases). **2.** being or done offside: *an offside play.*

off·spring (ôf'sprĭng', ŏf'-), *n.* **1.** children or young sprung from a particular parent or progenitor. **2.** a child or animal in relation to its parent or parents. **3.** a descendant. **4.** descendants collectively. **5.** the product, result, or effect of something: *the offspring of delirium.* [ME and OE *ofspring.* See OFF, SPRING, V.]

off·stage (ôf'stāj', ŏf'-), *adj.* not in view of the audience; backstage, in the wings, etc.

off·white (ôf'hwīt', ŏf'-), *adj.* white with a slight touch of gray in it.

Of Human Bondage, a novel (1915) by W. Somerset Maugham.

O'Fla·her·ty (ō·flă'hər·tĭ), *n.* **Liam** (lē'əm), born 1896, Irish novelist.

O.F.M., (L *Ordo Fratrum Minorum*) Order of Friars Minor (Franciscan).

oft (ôft, ŏft), *adv. Chiefly Poetic.* often; frequently. [ME *oft(e),* OE *oft,* c. G *oft*]

of·ten (ôf'ən, ŏf'ən), *adv.* **1.** many times; frequently. **2.** in many cases. —*adj.* **3.** *Archaic.* frequent. [ME *oftin,* var. (before vowels) of *ofte* OFT] —**Syn. 1, 2.** OFTEN, FREQUENTLY, GENERALLY, USUALLY refer to experiences which are customary. OFTEN and FREQUENTLY may be used interchangeably in most cases, but OFTEN implies numerous repetitions and, sometimes, regularity of recurrence (*we often go there*); FREQUENTLY suggests esp. repetition at comparatively short intervals: *it happens frequently.* GENERALLY refers to place and means "universally" (*it is generally understood; he is generally liked*), but is often used as a colloquial substitute for USUALLY. In this sense, GENERALLY, like USUALLY, refers to time, and means "in numerous instances." GENERALLY, however, extends in range from the merely numerous to a majority of possible instances; whereas USUALLY means "practically always": *the train is generally on time, we usually have hot summers.* —**Ant. 1.** seldom.

of·ten·times (ôf'ən·tĭmz', ŏf'ən-), *adv. Archaic.* often. Also, **oft'times'.**

O.G., Officer of the Guard.

o.g., *Philately.* a stamp with original gum; a mint stamp (having gum as issued by the post office).

O·ga·sa·wa·ra Ji·ma (ō'gä·sä·wä'rä jē'mä), Japanese name of the **Bonin Islands.**

Og·den (ŏg'dən), *n.* a city in N Utah. 57,112 (1950).

og·do·ad (ŏg'dō·ăd'), *n.* **1.** the number eight. **2.** group of eight. [t. LL: s. *ogdoas,* t. Gk.: the number eight]

o·gee (ō·jē', ō'jē), *n.* **1.** a double curve (like the letter S) formed by the union of a concave and a convex line. **2.** *Archit., etc.* a molding with such a curve for a profile; a cyma. [var. of OGIVE]

ogee arch, *Archit.* a form of pointed arch, each side of which has the curve of an ogee.

O·gil·vie (ō'gəl·vĭ), *n.* **John,** 1797–1867, Scottish lexicographer.

o·give (ō'jīv, ō·jīv'), *n. Archit.* **1.** a diagonal groin or rib of a vault. **2.** a pointed arch. **3.** *Statistics.* a curve such that the ordinate for any given value of the abscissa represents the frequency or relative frequency of values of the ordinate less than or equal to the given value. [ME, t. F, also formerly *augive;* orig. uncert.] —**o·gi'val,** *adj.*

Ogee arch
A, Convex curve;
B, Concave curve

o·gle (ō'gəl), *v.,* ogled, ogling, *n.* —*v.t.* **1.** to eye with amorous, ingratiating, or impertinently familiar glances. **2.** to eye; look at. —*v.i.* **3.** to cast amorous, ingratiating, or impertinently familiar glances. —*n.* **4.** an ogling glance. [appar. from a freq. (cf. LG *oegeln,* G *augeln*) of D *oogen* to eye, der. *oog* the eye] —**o'gler,** *n.*

O·gle·thorpe (ō'gəl·thôrp'), *n.* **James Edward,** 1696–1785, British general, founder of the colony of Georgia.

Og·pu (ŏg'poo), *n.* Gay-Pay-Oo.

o·gre (ō'gər), *n.* **1.** a monster, commonly represented as a hideous giant, of fairy tales and popular legends, supposed to live on human flesh. **2.** a person likened to such a monster. [t. F] —**o·gre·ish** (ō'gər·ĭsh), **o·grish** (ō'grĭsh), *adj.* —**o·gress** (ō'grĭs), *n. fem.*

oh (ō), *interj., n., pl.* **oh's, ohs,** *v.* —*interj.* **1.** an expression of surprise, pain, disappointment, etc. —*n.* **2.** the exclamation "oh." —*v.i.* **3.** to utter or exclaim "oh."

O'Har·a (ō·hâr'ə), *n.* **John,** born 1905, U. S. author.

O. Hen·ry (ō·hĕn'rĭ), pen name of **William Sydney Porter.**

OHG, Old High German. Also, **OHG., O.H.G.**

O·hi·o (ō·hī'ō), *n.* **1.** a State in the NE central United States: a part of the Midwest. 7,946,627 pop. (1950); 41.222 sq. mi. *Cap.:* Columbus. **2.** a river formed by the confluence of the Allegheny and Monongahela rivers at Pittsburgh, Pennsylvania, flowing SW to the Mississippi in S Illinois. 981 mi. —**O·hi'o·an,** *n., adj.*

ohm (ōm), *n. Elect.* the unit of resistance: the resistance of a conductor in which one volt produces a current of one ampere. [named after G. *S. Ohm* (1787–1854), German physicist] —**ohm·ic** (ō'mĭk), *adj.*

ohm·age (ō'mĭj), *n.* electrical resistance expressed in ohms.

ohm·me·ter (ōm′mē′tər), *n.* an instrument for measuring electrical resistance in ohms.

O.H.M.S., On His (or Her) Majesty's Service.

o·ho (ō hō′), *interj.* an exclamation expressing surprise, taunting, exultation, etc.

-oid, a suffix used to form adjectives meaning "like" or "resembling," and nouns meaning "something resembling" what is indicated by the preceding part of the word (and often implying an incomplete or imperfect resemblance), as in *alkaloid, anthropoid, cardioid, cuboid, lithoid, ovoid, planetoid.* [t. Gk.: m.s. *-oeidēs*, f. *-o-* (connective vowel from preceding word element) + *-eidēs* having the form of, like, der. *eîdos* form. Cf. -ODE¹]

-oidea, a suffix used in naming zoölogical classes or entomological superfamilies. [t. NL, der. *-oïdēs* -OID]

oil (oil), *n.* **1.** any of a large class of substances typically unctuous, viscous, combustible, liquid at ordinary temperatures, and soluble in ether or alcohol but not in water: used for anointing, perfuming, lubricating, illuminating, heating, smoothing waves at sea in a storm, etc. **2.** petroleum. **3.** some substance of oily consistency. **4.** *Painting.* **a.** an oil color. **b.** an oil painting. **5.** an oilskin garment. —*v.t.* **6.** to smear, lubricate, or supply with oil. **7.** to bribe. **8.** to make oily or smooth, as in speech. **9.** to convert (butter, etc.) into oil by melting. —*adj.* **10.** pertaining to or resembling oil. **11.** concerned with the production or use of oil. **12.** obtained from oil. [ME *olie, oile*, t. OF, g. L *oleum* (olive) oil]

oil·bird (oil′bûrd′), *n.* the guacharo.

oil cake, a cake or mass of linseed, cottonseed, etc., from which the oil has been expressed, used as a food for cattle or sheep, or as soil fertilizer.

Oil City, a city in NW Pennsylvania, on the Allegheny river. 19,581 (1950).

oil·cloth (oil′klôth′, -klŏth′), *n.* **1.** a cotton fabric made waterproof with oil and pigment, and used for table cloths, etc. **2.** a piece of it.

oil color, a color or paint made by grinding a pigment in oil, usually linseed oil.

oil·er (oi′lər), *n.* **1.** one who oils; a workman employed to oil machinery. **2.** any contrivance for lubricating with oil. **3.** a can with a long spout, used for oiling machinery. **4.** *U.S. Colloq.* an oilskin coat.

oil field, a place where oil is found.

oil of turpentine, a colorless, inflammable, volatile oil, a distillate of turpentine, having a penetrating odor and a pungent, bitterish taste: used in paints, varnishes, and the like, and in medicine as a stimulant, diuretic, rubefacient, etc.

oil of vitriol, sulfuric acid.

oil painting, 1. the art of painting with oil colors. **2.** a work executed in oil colors.

Oil Rivers, a region in W Africa, comprising the vast Niger river delta: formerly a British protectorate; now a part of Nigeria.

oil·skin (oil′skin′), *n.* **1.** a cotton fabric made waterproof by treatment with oil and used for fishermen's clothing and rain wear. **2.** a piece of this. **3.** (*often pl.*) a garment made of it.

oil slick, a slick or smooth place on the surface of water, due to the presence of oil.

oil·stone (oil′stōn′), *n.* a fine-grained whetstone, whose rubbing surface is lubricated with oil.

oil well, a well from which oil is obtained.

oil·y (oi′lĭ), *adj.*, **oilier, oiliest. 1.** pertaining to oil. **2.** full of or containing oil. **3.** smeared or covered with oil, or greasy. **4.** of the nature of or consisting of oil; resembling oil. **5.** smooth, as in manner or speech; bland; unctuous: *an oily hypocrite.* —*adv.* **6.** in an oily manner. —**oil′i·ly,** *adv.* —**oil′i·ness,** *n.*

oint·ment (oint′mənt), *n.* a soft, unctuous preparation, often medicated, for application to the skin; an unguent. [f. obs. *oint* (aphetic var. of ANOINT) + -MENT; r. ME *oignement*, t. OF]

Oir·each·tas (ĕr′əᴋ н thəs), *n.* **1.** the parliament of Eire (established Dec. 29, 1937), consisting of the President of Eire, the Dail Eireann (House of Representatives), and the Seanad Eireann (Senate). **2.** a national assembly or festival held annually in Ireland for the encouragement of the use of the Irish language as a literary medium. [t. Irish.: assembly, conference]

Oise (wäz), *n.* a river flowing from S Belgium SW through N France to the Seine near Paris. 186 mi.

O·jib·wa (ō jĭb′wä, -wə), *n., pl.* **-wa, -was. 1.** a large tribe of North American Indians of Algonquian family, divided between the United States and Canada in the Lake Superior region. **2.** a member of the Ojibwa tribe. **3.** their language. Also, **O·jib′way, Chippewa.** [t. Amer. Ind., *ojibway* (d.) to roast till puckered up, f. *ojib* to pucker up + *ub-way* to roast; with reference to the puckered seam on their moccasins]

O.K. (*adj., adv.* ō′kā′; *v., n.* ō′kā′), *adj., adv.* v. **O.K.'d, O. K'ing,** *n., pl.* **O.K.'s.** *Orig. U.S. Colloq.* —*adj., adv.* **1.** all right; correct. —*v.t.* **2.** to put "O.K." on (a bill, etc.); endorse; approve. —*n.* **3.** an approval or agreement. Also, **OK, okay.** [origin much debated, but prob. der. "O.K. Club," formed in 1840 by partisans of Martin Van Buren who allegedly named their organization in allusion to "Old Kinderhook," his birthplace being Kinderhook, N.Y.]

o·ka (ō′kə), *n.* **1.** a unit of weight in Turkey and neighboring countries, equal to about 2¾ lbs. **2.** a unit of

liquid measure, equal to about 1½ U.S. liquid quarts. Also, **oke.** [t. It.: m. *oc(c)a*, t. Turk.: m. ō*qa*, t. Ar.: m. *ūqiyya*, ult. t. Gk. m. *ounkĭa* = L *uncia*]

O·ka (ō kä′), *n.* a river in the central Soviet Union in Europe, flowing NE to the Volga at Gorki. ab. 950 mi.

o·ka·pi (ō kä′pĭ), *n., pl.* **-pis,** (*esp. collectively*), **-pi.** an African forest mammal, *Okapia johnstoni,* closely related to the giraffe, but smaller and with a much shorter neck. [from a Central Afr. language]

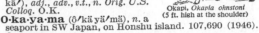

Okapi, Okapia ohnstoni
(5 ft. high at the shoulder)

o·kay (*adj., adv.* ō′kā′; *v., n.* ō′kā′), *adj., adv., v.t., n. Orig. U.S. Colloq.* O.K.

O·ka·ya·ma (ō′kä yä′mä), *n.* a seaport in SW Japan, on Honshu island. 107,690 (1946).

oke (ōk), *n.* oka.

O·kee·cho·bee (ō′kĭ chō′bē), *n.* a lake in the N part of the Everglades, in S Florida. ab. 40 mi. long; ab. 25 mi. wide.

O'Keeffe (ō kēf′), *n.* **Georgia,** born 1887, U.S. painter.

O'Kel·ley (ō kĕl′ĭ), *n.* **Seán Thomas** (shôn, shän), born 1883, Irish statesman; president of Ireland since 1945.

O·khotsk (ō kŏtsk′; *Russ.* ŏ hŏtsk′), *n.* **Sea of,** an arm of the N Pacific enclosed by Kamchatka Peninsula, the Kurile Islands, Sakhalin, and the Soviet Union in Asia. ab. 582,000 sq. mi.; greatest depth, 10,554 ft.

O·kie (ō′kĭ), *n. Colloq.* **1.** a native or inhabitant of Oklahoma. **2.** a migrant worker, orig. one from Oklahoma, who lost his land or was forced to move because of drought, insect plagues, etc.

O·ki·na·wa (ō′kə nä′wə; *Jap.* ō′kē nä′wä), *n.* the largest of the Ryukyu Islands, in the N Pacific, SW of Japan: taken by U.S. forces in the last major amphibious campaign of World War II, April-June, 1945. 435,681 pop. (1940); 485 sq. mi.

Okla., Oklahoma.

O·kla·ho·ma (ō′klə hō′mə), *n.* a State of the S central United States. 2,233,351 pop. (1950); 69,919 sq. mi. *Cap.:* Oklahoma City. *Abbr.:* Okla. —**O′kla·ho′man,** *adj., n.*

Oklahoma City, the capital of Oklahoma, in the central part. 243,504 (1950).

o·kra (ō′krə), *n.* **1.** a tall plant of the mallow family, *Hibiscus* or *Abelmoschus esculentus,* cultivated for its edible mucilaginous pods, used in soups, etc. **2.** the pod. **3.** the pods collectively. **4.** a dish made with the pods; gumbo. [t. d. West Afr.]

-ol¹, a noun suffix used in the names of chemical derivatives, pharmaceutical compounds, commercial products, etc. representing "alcohol," as in *glycerol, naphthol, phenol,* or sometimes "phenol" or less definitely assignable phenol derivatives. [short for ALCOHOL or PHENOL]

-ol², var. of **-ole.**

O·laf (ō′ləf; *Nor.* ō′läf), *n.* **Saint,** A.D. 995–1030, king of Norway, 1015–28.

Olaf Tryg·ves·son (tryg′věs sŏn′), A.D. 969?–1000, king of Norway, A.D. 995?–1000.

Ö·land (œ′länd′), *n.* an island in SE Sweden, separated from the mainland by Kalmar Sound. 27,295 pop. (1930); 519 sq. mi.

-olatry, a word element meaning "worship of," as in *demonolatry.* [see LATRIA]

old (ōld), *adj.,* **older, oldest** or **elder, eldest,** *n.* —*adj.* **1.** far advanced in years or life: *a venerable old man.* **2.** of or pertaining to advanced life or persons advanced in years: *to live to a good old age.* **3.** having the appearance or characteristics of advanced age: *prematurely old.* **4.** having reached a specified age: *a man thirty years old.* **5.** advanced in years, in comparison with others or relatively to a scale of age: *the oldest boy.* **6.** having existed long, or made long ago: *old wine.* **7.** long known or in use; familiar: *the same old excuse.* **8.** former, past, or ancient, as time, days, etc.: belonging to a past time: *old kingdoms.* **9.** being the earlier or earliest of two or more things of the same kind, or stages of a thing: *the Old Testament, Old Norse.* **10.** (of colors) dulled, faded or subdued: *old rose.* **11.** deteriorated through age or long use; worn, decayed, or dilapidated. **12.** *Phys. Geog.* (of topographical features) far advanced in reduction by erosion, etc. **13.** of long experience: *an old hand at the game.* **14.** sedate, sensible, or wise, as if from mature years: *an old head on young shoulders.* **15.** *Often Colloq. or Slang.* (implying long acquaintance or friendly feeling): *good old Henry.* **16.** *Colloq.* carried to great lengths; great. —*n.* **17.** old or former time, often time long past. [ME; OE *ald, eald,* c. D *oud,* G *alt;* orig. pp., and akin to Icel. *ala* nourish, bring up, and L *alere* nourish] —**old′ness,** *n.*

—**Syn. 1.** OLD, AGED, ELDERLY all mean well along in years. An OLD person has lived long, nearly to the end of the usual period of life. An AGED person is very far advanced in years, and is usually afflicted with the infirmities of age. An ELDERLY person is somewhat old, but usually has the mellowness, satisfactions, and joys of age before him. **8.** olden, early, primitive, primeval. —**Ant. 1.** young, youthful.

old age, the period of life (generally) after 65.

Old Bai·ley (bā′lĭ), the principal criminal court of London.

old boy, *Brit.* an alumnus of a "public school."

Old Cas·tile (kăs tēl′), a region in N Spain: formerly a province. 1,577,135 pop. (1940); 19,246 sq. mi.

Old·cas·tle (ōld′kăs·əl, -kăs·/əl), *n.* **John.** See **Cobham.**

Old Church Slavic, the extinct language (South Slavic) preserved in religious texts of the Russian Orthodox church. Also, **Old Church Slavonic.**

old country, the country from which an immigrant came, esp. Europe.

Old Curiosity Shop, a novel (1840–41) by Dickens.

Old Dominion, the State of Virginia.

old·en (ōl′dən), *adj. Archaic.* **1.** old. **2.** of old; ancient: *olden days.* **3.** of former days.

Ol·den·burg (ōl′dən bûrg′; *Ger.* -bŏŏrкн′), *n.* **1.** a state in Germany, including the three scattered provinces of Oldenburg in NW Germany, Birkenfeld in SW Germany, and Lübeck on the Baltic. 577,648 pop. (1939); 2083 sq. mi. **2.** the capital of this state, in NW Germany. 78,967 (1939).

Old English, 1. the English of periods before 1100; Anglo-Saxon. **2.** *Print.* the form of black letter used by English printers from the 15th to the 18th century.

old·er (ōl′dər), *adj.* of greater age, *compar. of* **old.** **—Syn.** OLDER, ELDER imply having greater age than something or someone else. OLDER is the usual form of the comparative of old: *this building is older than that one.* ELDER, now greatly restricted in application, is used chiefly to indicate seniority in age as between any two people but especially priority of birth as between children born of the same parents: *the elder brother became king.* **—Ant.** newer, younger.

old-fash·ioned (ōld′făsh′ənd), *adj.* **1.** of an old fashion or a style or type formerly in vogue. **2.** favored or prevalent in former period: *old-fashioned ideas.* **3.** (of persons) having the ways, ideas, or tastes of a former period; out of fashion. **—Syn. 1.** See **ancient.**

old-fo·gy·ish (ōld′fō′gYish), *adj.* of or like an old fogey; excessively conservative. Also, **old′-fo′gey·ish.**

Old French, the French language of periods before 1400.

Old Glory, the flag of the United States.

Old Guard, 1. the imperial guard created in 1804 by Napoleon. It made the last French charge at Waterloo. **2.** *U.S.* the ultraconservative element of the Republican party. **3.** (*usually l.c.*) the ultraconservative members of any group, country, etc. [trans. of F *Vieille Garde*]

Old·ham (ōl′dəm), *n.* a city in W England, near Manchester. 116,530 (est. 1946).

Old Hickory, nickname of Andrew Jackson.

Old High German, High German of before 1100.

Old Icelandic, the Icelandic of the Middle Ages.

Old Irish, the Irish language before the 11th century.

Old Ironsides, the old U.S. frigate *Constitution.*

old·ish (ōl′dYsh), *adj.* somewhat old: *an oldish man.*

old-line (ōld′līn′), *adj.* **1.** following or supporting conservative or traditional ideas, beliefs, customs, etc. **2.** long established; traditional.

old maid, 1. an elderly or confirmed spinster. **2.** *Colloq.* a person with the alleged characteristics of an old maid, such as primness, prudery, fastidiousness, etc. **3.** a game of cards in which the players draw from one another to match pairs. **—old′-maid′ish,** *adj.*

old master. See **master** (def. 14).

old moon. See **moon** (def. 2d).

Old Nick. See **Nick.**

Old Norse, 1. the language of Norway and Iceland in the Middle Ages. **2.** Old Icelandic.

Old Orchard Beach, a resort town in S Maine. 4593 (1950).

Old Persian, the ancient Iranian of the Persian cuneiforms.

Old Pretender, 1688–1776, James Francis Edward Stuart, son of James II of England.

Old Prussian, a Baltic language extinct since the 17th century.

old·rose (ōld′rōz′), *n., adj.* rose with a purplish or grayish cast.

Old Saxon, the Saxon dialect of Low German as spoken before 1100.

old school tie, *Brit.* **1.** a necktie of the colors of the "public school" that one attended. **2.** the influence wielded by the old public schools in English life.

old sledge, *Cards.* the game of seven-up.

old squaw, a lively, voluble sea duck, *clangula hyemalis,* of northern regions.

old·ster (ōld′stər), *n.* **1.** *Colloq.* an old or older person. **2.** (in the British Navy) a midshipman of four years' standing. [f. OLD + -STER, modeled on YOUNGSTER]

old style, 1. *Print.* a type style differentiated from *modern style* by the more or less uniform thickness of all strokes and the slanted serifs. **2.** (*cap.*) See **Style** (def. 13). **—old′-style′,** *adj.*

Old Test., Old Testament.

Old Testament, 1. the covenant between God and Israel on Mount Sinai (Ex. 19–24) constituting the basis of the Hebrew religion. See Jer. 31: 31–34; also II Cor. 3: 6, 14. **2.** the collection of Biblical books comprising the Scriptures of "the old covenant." In the Hebrew Bible the three main divisions are the Law, the Prophets, and the Writings. The order in other than Jewish translations follows the Septuagint. In the Vulgate (Latin) translation all but two books of the Apocrypha are included in the Old Testament.

old-time (ōld′tīm′), *adj.* belonging to or characteristic of old or former times: *old-time sailing ships.*

old-tim·er (ōld′tī′mər), *n. Colloq.* **1.** one whose residence, membership, or experience dates from old times. **2.** one who adheres to old-time ideas or ways.

old·wife (ōld′wīf′), *n., pl.* **-wives. 1.** any of various fishes, as the alewife, the menhaden, or a West Indian fish of the family Balistidae. **2.** the old squaw duck.

Old Wives' Tale, a novel (1908) by Arnold Bennett.

old-wom·an·ish (ōld′wŏŏm′ənYsh), *adj.* of or like an old woman; excessively fussy.

Old World, 1. Europe, Asia, and Africa. **2.** the Eastern Hemisphere.

old-world (ōld′wûrld′), *adj.* **1.** of or pertaining to the ancient world or to a former period of history. **2.** of or pertaining to the Old World.

-ole, a noun suffix meaning "oil." [repr. L *oleum*]

o·le·a·ceous (ō′lYā′shəs), *adj.* belonging to the *Oleaceae,* or olive family of plants, which includes the ash, jasmine, etc. [f. s. L *olea* olive + -ACEOUS]

o·le·ag·i·nous (ō′lYăj′ə nəs), *adj.* **1.** having the nature or qualities of oil. **2.** containing oil. **3.** producing oil. **4.** oily or unctuous. [t. L: m. *oleāginus* of the olive] **—o′le·ag′i·nous·ness,** *n.*

O·le·an (ō′lYăn′), *n.* a city in SW New York. 22,884 (1950).

o·le·an·der (ō′lYăn′dər), *n. Bot.* any plant of the apocynaceous genus *Nerium,* esp. *N. oleander,* a poisonous evergreen shrub with handsome rose-colored or white flowers, or *N. ordorum,* a species from India with fragrant flowers. [t. ML, ult. g. LL *lorandrum* (var. of L *rhododendron,* t. Gk.), influenced by *olea* oil, or *olea* olive]

o·le·as·ter (ō′lYăs′tər), *n.* an ornamental shrub or small tree, *Elaeagnus angustifolia,* of southern Europe and western Asia, with fragrant yellow flowers and an olivelike fruit. [ME, t. L: the wild olive]

o·le·ate (ō′lYāt′), *n. Chem.* an ester or a salt of oleic acid.

o·lec·ra·non (ō lĕk′rə nŏn′, ō′lə krā′nŏn), *n. Anat.* the part of the ulna beyond the elbow joint. [t. Gk.: m. *ōlékranon,* short for *ōlenókronon* the point of the elbow]

o·le·fin (ō′lə fYn′), *n. Chem.* any of a series of hydrocarbons homologous with ethylene, having the general formula, C_nH_{2n}, also known as alkenes. Also, **o·le·fine** (ō′lə fYn, -fēn′). [f. F *olef(iant)* oil-forming (der. L *oleum* oil) + -IN²] **—o′le·fin′ic,** *adj.*

o·le·ic (ō lē′Yk, ō′lYYk), *adj. Chem.* pertaining to or derived from oleic acid. [f. s. L *oleum* oil + -IC]

oleic acid, *Chem.* an oily liquid, $C_{17}H_{33}COOH$, one of the acids present in fats and oils as the glyceride ester.

o·le·in (ō′lYYn), *n. Chem.* **1.** a colorless oily compound, the glyceride of oleic acid and the component of olive oil. **2.** the oily or lower melting fractions of a fat as distinguished from the solid or higher melting constituents. [f. s. L *oleum* oil + -IN²]

o·le·o (ō′lYō′), *n.* shortened form of *oleomargarine.*

oleo-, a word element meaning "oil." [t. L, comb. form of *oleum*]

o·le·o·graph (ō′lYə grăf′, -gräf′), *n.* a kind of chromolithograph printed in oil colors. **—o′le·o·graph′ic,** *adj.* **—o·le·og′ra·phy** (ō′lY ŏg′rə fY), *n.*

o·le·o·mar·ga·rine (ō′lY ō mär′jə rēn′, -gə-), *n.* a cooking and table fat made by combining animal oils such as oleo oil and refined lard, and sometimes cottonseed oil, with milk. Also, **o·le·o·mar·ga·rin** (ō′lY ō mär′jə rĭn, -gə-).

oleo oil, a product obtained from beef fat, consisting mainly of a mixture of olein and palmitin: used for making butterlike foods.

o·le·o·res·in (ō′lY ō rĕz′ən), *n.* **1.** a natural mixture of an essential oil and a resin. **2.** *Pharm.* an oil holding resin in solution, extracted from a substance (as ginger) by means of alcohol, ether, or acetone.

ol·fac·tion (ŏl făk′shən), *n.* **1.** act of smelling. **2.** the sense of smell. [f. (obs.) *olfact* to smell (t. L: s. *olfactāre*) + -ION]

ol·fac·to·ry (ŏl făk′tər y, -trY), *adj., n., pl.* **-ries. —***adj.* **1.** of or pertaining to the sense of smell: *olfactory organs.* **—***n.* **2.** (*usually pl.*) an olfactory organ. [t. L: m.s. *olfactōrius,* adj.; only fem. occurs in n. use]

o·lib·a·num (ō lĭb′ə nəm), *n.* frankincense. [ME, t. ML, var. of LL *libanus,* t. Gk.: m. *libanos,* of Semitic orig.; cf. Heb. *lĕbhonāh*]

olig-, a word element meaning "few," "little." Also, before consonants, **oligo-.** [t. Gk., comb. form of *olígos* small, (pl.) few]

ol·i·garch (ŏl′ə gärk′), *n.* one of the rulers in an oligarchy.

ol·i·gar·chic (ŏl′ə gär′kYk), *adj.* of, pertaining to, or having the form of an oligarchy. Also, **ol′i·gar′chi·cal.**

ol·i·gar·chy (ŏl′ə gär′kY), *n., pl.* **-chies. 1.** a form of government in which the power is vested in a few, or in a dominant class or clique. **2.** a state so governed. **3.** the ruling few collectively. [t. Gk.: m.s. *oligarchía*]

ol·i·go·car·pous (ŏl′ə gō kär′pəs), *adj. Bot.* not bearing much fruit. [f. OLIGO- + -CARP + -OUS]

Ol·i·go·cene (ŏl′ə gō sēn′), *Stratig.* **—***adj.* **1.** pertaining to an early Tertiary epoch or series. **—***n.* **2.** a division of the Tertiary that follows Eocene and precedes Miocene. [f. OLIGO- + m.s. Gk. *kainós* new]

ol·i·go·chaete (ŏl′ə gō kēt′), *n.* any of a group of annelids that have locomotory setae sunk directly in the body wall. It includes earthworms and many small fresh-water annelids. —**ol′i·go·chae′tous,** *adj.*

ol·i·go·clase (ŏl′ə·gō·klās′), *n.* a kind of plagioclase feldspar occurring commonly in crystals of white color, sometimes shaded with gray, green, or red. [f. OLIGO- + m.s. Gk. *klásis* fracture]

ol·i·go·cy·the·mi·a (ŏl′ə·gō·sī·thē′mY·ə), *n.* *Pathol.* a form of anemia in which there is a reduction in the number of red corpuscles in the blood. Also, **ol′i·go·cy·thae′mi·a.** [f. OLIGO- + CYT- + -(H)EMIA]

ol·i·gu·ri·a (ŏl′ə·gyŏŏr′Y·ə), *n.* *Pathol.* scantiness of urine due to diminished secretion. Also, **ol·i·gu·re·sis** (ŏl′ə·gyŏŏ·rē′sYs). [f. OLIG- + URIA]

o·li·o (ō′lY·ō′), *n., pl.* **olios.** 1. a dish of many ingredients. 2. any mixture of heterogeneous elements. 3. a medley or potpourri (musical, literary, or the like); a miscellany. [t. Sp.: m. *olla* pot, stew. See OLLA]

Ol·i·phant (ŏl′ə·fənt), *n.* **Margaret,** (*Margaret Oliphant Wilson*) 1828–97, British novelist.

ol·i·va·ceous (ŏl′ə·vā′shəs), *adj.* of a deep shade of green; olive. [t. NL: m. *olīvāceus.* See OLIVE]

ol·i·var·y (ŏl′ə·vĕr′Y), *adj.* 1. shaped like an olive. 2. *Anat.* noting or pertaining to either of two oval bodies or prominences made up of nervous tissue (**olivary bodies**), one on each side of the anterior surface of the medulla oblongata. [t. L: m.s. *olīvārius* of olives]

ol·ive (ŏl′Yv), *n.* 1. an evergreen tree, *Olea europaea,* of Mediterranean and other warm regions, cultivated chiefly for its fruit, but yielding also a wood valued for ornamental work. 2. the fruit, a small oval drupe, esteemed as a relish (pickled in brine when either green or ripe), and valuable as a source of oil. 3. any of various related or similar trees. 4. the foliage of the olive tree (*Olea*). 5. an olive branch (an emblem of peace). 6. a wreath of it. 7. a shade of green or yellowish green. —*adj.* 8. of, pertaining to, or made of olives, their foliage or their fruit. 9. of a dull shade of green or yellowish green. 10. tinged with this color: *an olive complexion.* [ME, t. OF *olive*; t. L *olīva*; akin to Gk. *elaía* olive tree]

olive branch, 1. a branch of the olive tree (an emblem of peace). 2. anything offered in token of peace.

olive drab, 1. a deep yellowish green. 2. woolen cloth of this color used for U.S. Army uniforms.

ol·ive-green (ŏl′Yv·grēn′), *n., adj.* green with a yellowish or brownish tinge.

ol·iv·en·ite (ō·lYv′ə·nīt′, ŏl′ə·və·nīt′), *n.* a mineral, basic copper arsenate, Cu₄As₂O₈(OH)₂, occurring in crystals and in masses, usually olive-green in color. [f. G *oliven(erz)* olive ore + -ITE¹]

olive oil, an oil expressed from the olive fruit, used with food, in medicine, etc.

Ol·i·ver (ŏl′ə·vər), *n.* one of the 12 peers of Charlemagne. See **Roland.** [t. F: m. *Olivier*]

Oliver Twist (twYst), a novel (1838) by Dickens.

Ol·ives (ŏl′Yvz), *n.* **Mount of,** a small ridge E of Jerusalem, in Palestine. Highest point, 2680 ft. Also, **Ol·i·vet** (ŏl′ə·vĕt′, -vYt).

ol·i·vine (ŏl′ə·vēn′, ŏl′ə·vēn′), *n.* a very common mineral, magnesium iron silicate, (Mg, Fe)₂Si O₄, occurring commonly in olive-green to gray-green masses as an important constituent of basic igneous rocks; rarely, in the variety peridot, transparent and used as a gem. [f. s. L *olīva* olive + -INE²]

ol·la (ŏl′ə; *Sp.* ō′lyä, -yä), *n.* (in Spanish-speaking countries) 1. an earthen pot or jar for holding water or for cooking, etc. 2. a dish of meat and vegetables cooked in such a pot. [t. Sp.: pot. stew, in LL pot, jar]

ol·la-po·dri·da (ŏl′ə·pə·drē′də; *Sp.* ō′lyä·pō·drē′dä, ō′yä·), *n.* 1. a Spanish stew of meat and vegetables. 2. any incongruous mixture or miscellaneous collection. [t. Sp.: lit., rotten pot]

ol·o·gy (ŏl′ə·jY), *n., pl.* **-gies.** *Colloq.* any science or branch of knowledge. [abstracted from words like BIOLOGY, GEOLOGY where the element -LOGY is preceded by -o-. See -O-]

O·lo·mouc (ō′lō·mōts′), *n.* a city in central Czechoslovakia, in Moravia. 66,440 (1930). German, **Ol·mütz** (ŏl′myts).

O·lym·pi·a (ō·lYm′pY·ə), *n.* 1. a plain in ancient Elis, Greece, where the Olympic games were held. 2. the capital of Washington, in the W part, on Puget Sound. 15,819 (1950).

O·lym·pi·ad (ō·lYm′pY·ăd′), *n.* (*often l.c.*) 1. a period of four years reckoned from one celebration of the Olympic games to the next, by which the Greeks computed time from 776 B.C. 2. a celebration of the modern Olympic games. [ME, t. L: s. *olympias,* t. Gk.]

O·lym·pi·an (ō·lYm′pY·ən), *adj.* 1. pertaining to or dwelling on Mount Olympus, as the greater gods of Greece. 2. pertaining to Olympia in Elis. 3. like the gods of Olympus; grand; imposing. —*n.* 4. an Olympian deity. 5. a contender in the Olympic games.

O·lym·pic (ō·lYm′pYk), *adj.* 1. pertaining to the games held at Olympia in ancient Greece in honor of Zeus. 2. pertaining to Olympia, in Greece. —*n.* 3. an Olympic game. 4. **the Olympics,** the Olympic games.

Olympic games, 1. the greatest of the games or festivals of ancient Greece, held every four years in the plain of Olympia in Elis, in honor of Zeus. 2. a modern revival of these games consisting of international competitions in running, jumping, swimming, shooting, etc., held every four years, each time in a different country.

Olympic Mountains, a part of the Coast Range in NW Washington. Highest peak, Mt. Olympus, 8150 ft.

O·lym·pus (ō·lYm′pəs), *n.* **Mount, 1.** a mountain in NE Greece, on the boundary between Thessaly and Macedonia: fabled abode of the greater Grecian gods. 9730 ft. 2. heaven. 3. a peak of the Olympic Mountains in NW Washington. 8150 ft.

O·iyn·thus (ō·lYn′thəs), *n.* an ancient city in NE Greece, on Chalcidice Peninsula.

O.M., *Brit.* Order of Merit.

-oma, *pl.* **-omas, -omata.** a suffix of nouns denoting a morbid condition of growth (tumor), as in *carcinoma, glaucoma, sarcoma.* [t. Gk.]

O·ma·ha (ō′mə·hô′, -hä′), *n.* 1. a city in E Nebraska, on the Missouri river. 251,117 (1950). 2. an Indian of a Siouan tribe, formerly in Nebraska.

O·man (ō·män′), *n.* 1. Also, **Muscat and Oman.** a sultanate of SE Arabia. 830,000 pop. (est. 1946); ab. 82,000 sq. mi. *Cap.:* Muscat. 2. **Gulf of,** a NW arm of the Arabian Sea, at the entrance to the Persian Gulf.

O·mar Khay·yám (ō′mär kī·äm′, ō′mər), died 1123?, Persian poet, some of whose poems (*The Rubaiyat*) were translated by Edward Fitzgerald.

o·ma·sum (ō·mā′səm), *n., pl.* **-sa** (-sə). the third stomach of a ruminant, between the recticulum and the abomasum; the manyplies. See diag. under **ruminant.** [t. NL, in L bullock's tripe]

O·may·yad (ō·mī′ăd), *n.* 1. a caliph of the dynasty which ruled at Damascus, A.D. 661 to 750, claiming descent from Omayya, great-uncle of Mohammed the Prophet. 2. an emir (A.D. 756–929) or caliph (A.D. 929–1031) of the Omayyad dynasty of Spain. Also, **Ommiad.**

om·ber (ŏm′bər), *n.* 1. a game at cards, fashionable in the 17th and 18th centuries, played, usually by three persons, with forty cards. 2. the player who undertakes to win the pool in this game. Also, *esp. Brit.,* **om′bre.** [t. F: m. (*h*)*ombre,* t. Sp.: m. *hombre,* lit., man, g. s. L *homo*]

Om·dur·man (ŏm′dŏŏr·män′), *n.* a city in the Anglo-Egyptian Sudan, on the White Nile opposite Khartoum: British victory, 1898. 116,196 (est. 1941).

o·me·ga (ō·mē′gə, ō·mĕg′ə, ō′mĕg·ə), *n.* 1. the last letter (Ω, ω, English long O, o) of the Greek alphabet. 2. the last of any series; the end. [t. LGk.: ō *méga.* lit., great ō. Cf. OMICRON]

om·e·let (ŏm′ə·lYt, ŏm′lYt), *n.* eggs beaten with milk and fried or baked, often with other ingredients also, as chopped ham, cheese, or jelly. Also, **om′e·lette.** [t. F: m. *omelette,* b. *alemette* (var. of *alemelle,* ult. g. L *lāmella* thin plate) and *oeuf* egg (g. L *ōvum*)]

o·men (ō′mən), *n.* 1. anything perceived or happening that is regarded as portending good or evil or giving some indication as to the future; a prophetic sign. 2. a prognostic. 3. prophetic significance; presage: *a bird of ill omen.* —*v.t.* 4. to be an omen of; portend. 5. to divine, as if from omens. [t. L] —**Syn. 1.** See **sign.**

o·men·tum (ō·mĕn′təm), *n., pl.* **-ta** (-tə). *Anat.* a fold or duplication of the peritoneum passing between certain of the viscera: the **great omentum,** or epiploön (attached to and hanging down from the stomach and the transverse colon); the **lesser omentum** (between the stomach and the liver). [t. L] —**o·men′tal,** *adj.*

o·mer (ō′mər), *n.* a Hebrew unit of dry measure, the tenth part of an ephah. [t. Heb.: m. '*omer*]

om·i·cron (ŏm′ə·krŏn′, ō′mə-), *n.* the fifteenth letter (O, o, English short O, o) of the Greek alphabet. [t. LGk.: ō *mikrŏn,* lit., small O. Cf. OMEGA]

om·i·nous (ŏm′ə·nəs), *adj.* 1. portending evil; inauspicious; threatening: *a dull, ominous rumble.* 2. having the significance of an omen. [t. L: m.s. *ōminōsus* portentous] —**om′i·nous·ly,** *adv.* —**om′i·nous·ness,** *n.*

o·mis·si·ble (ō·mYs′ə·bəl), *adj.* that may be omitted.

o·mis·sion (ō·mYsh′ən), *n.* 1. act of omitting. 2. the state of being omitted. 3. something omitted. [ME, t. LL: s. *omissio*]

o·mis·sive (ō·mYs′Yv), *adj.* neglecting; leaving out.

o·mit (ō·mYt′), *v.t.,* **omitted, omitting.** 1. to leave out: *to omit passages of a text.* 2. to forbear or fail to do, make, use, send, etc.: *to omit a greeting.* [ME *omitte(n),* t. L: m. *omittere* let go, neglect, omit]

om·ma·te·um (ŏm′ə·tē′əm), *n.* *Zool.* a compound eye of arthropods.

om·ma·tid·i·um (ŏm′ə·tYd′Y·əm), *n., pl.* **-tidia** (-tYd′Y·ə). *Zool.* one of the radial elements which make up an ommateum. [Latinization of Gk. *ommatídion,* f. s. *ōmma* eye + -*idion* (dim. suffix)] —**om′ma·tid′i·al,** *adj.*

om·mat·o·phore (ə·măt′ə·fōr′), *n.* a tentacle or movable stalk bearing an eye, as in certain snails. [f. s. Gk. *ómma* eye + -(o)PHORE] —**om·ma·toph·o·rous** (ŏm′ə·tŏf′ə·rəs), *adj.*

Om·mi·ad (ŏ·mī′ăd), *n., pl.* **-ads, -ades** (-ə·dēz′). Omayyad.

omni-, a word element meaning "all," used in combination as in *omniactive* (all-active, active everywhere), *omnibenevolent, omnicompetent, omnicredulous, omniprevalent,* and various other words, mostly of obvious meaning. [t. L, comb. form of *omnis*]

om·ni·a vin·cit a·mor (ŏm′nY·ə vYn′sYt ā′môr), *Latin.* love conquers all.

om·ni·bus (ŏm′nə·bŭs′, -bəs), *n., pl.* **-buses,** *adj.* —*n.* 1. a bus. 2. a volume of reprinted works by a single author or related in interest or nature. —*adj.* 3. pertaining to or covering numerous objects or items at once: *an omnibus bill*. [t. L: lit., for all (dat. pl. of *omnis*)]

om·ni·far·i·ous (ŏm′nə·fâr′Ĭ·əs), *adj.* of all forms, varieties, or kinds. [t. L: m. *omnifārius* of all sorts] —om′ni·far′i·ous·ness, *n.*

om·nif·ic (ŏm·nĬf′Ĭk), *adj.* creating all things.

om·nip·o·tence (ŏm·nĬp′ə·təns), *n.* **1.** the quality of being omnipotent. **2.** (*cap.*) God.

om·nip·o·tent (ŏm·nĬp′ə·tənt), *adj.* **1.** almighty, or infinite in power, as God or a deity. **2.** having unlimited or very great authority. —*n.* **3.** an omnipotent being. **4. the Omnipotent**, God. [ME, t. L: s. *omnipotens* almighty] —om·nip′o·tent·ly, *adv.*

om·ni·pres·ent (ŏm′nə·prĕz′ənt), *adj.* present everywhere at the same time: *the omnipresent God*. [t. ML: m.s. *omnipraesens*. See OMNI-, PRESENT[1]] —om′ni·pres′ence, *n.*

—**Syn.** OMNIPRESENT, UBIQUITOUS refer to the quality of being everywhere. OMNIPRESENT emphasizes the power, usually divine, of being present everywhere at the same time, as though all-enveloping: *divine law is omnipresent*. UBIQUITOUS is applied to that which seems to appear in many and all sorts of places, or humorously is "all over the place," often when unwanted; it is now thus in contrast to the other lofty and dignified expression: *a bore seems to be ubiquitous*.

om·nis·cience (ŏm·nĬsh′əns), *n.* **1.** the quality of being omniscient. **2.** infinite knowledge. **3.** (*cap.*) God.

om·nis·cient (ŏm·nĬsh′ənt), *adj.* **1.** knowing all things, or having infinite knowledge. —*n.* **2.** an omniscient being. **3. the Omniscient**, God. [f. OMNI- + s. L *sciens*, ppr., knowing] —om·nis′cient·ly, *adv.*

om·ni·um-gath·er·um (ŏm′nĬ·əm·găth′ər·əm), *n.* a miscellaneous collection. [f. L *omnium* of all + *gatherum* a gathering, pseudo-L deriv. of GATHER]

om·niv·o·rous (ŏm·nĬv′ə·rəs), *adj.* **1.** eating all kinds of foods indiscriminately. **2.** eating both animal and plant foods. **3.** taking in everything, as with the mind. [t. L: m. *omnivorus*] —om·niv′o·rous·ly, *adv.* —om·niv′o·rous·ness, *n.*

o·mo·pha·gi·a (ō′mə·fā′jĬ·ə), *n.* the eating of raw flesh or raw food. [t.Gk.] —o·mo·phag·ic (ō′mə·făj′-Ĭk), **o·moph·a·gous** (ō·mŏf′ə·gəs), *adj.* —o·moph·a·gist (ō·mŏf′ə·jĬst), *n.*

Om·pha·le (ŏm′fə·lē′), *n.* Gk. *Legend.* a Lydian queen whom Hercules served in bondage for three years.

om·pha·los (ŏm′fə·ləs), *n.* **1.** the navel. **2.** the central point. **3.** Gk. *Antiq.* a rounded or conical stone in the temple of Apollo at Delphi, reputed to mark the center of the earth.

Omsk (ŏmsk), *n.* a city in the W Soviet Union in Asia, on the Irtish river. 280,716 (1939).

O·mu·ta (ō′mōō·tä′), *n.* a seaport in SW Japan, on W Kyushu island. 144,177 (1946). Also, **O·mu·da** (ō′mōō-dä′).

on (ŏn, ôn), *prep.* **1.** a particle expressing primarily: **a.** position above and in contact with a supporting surface: *on the table.* **b.** immediate proximity: *to border on absurdity.* **c.** situation, place, etc.: *a scar on the face.* **d.** support, suspension, dependence, or reliance: *on wheels.* **e.** state, condition, course, process, etc.: *on strike.* **f.** ground or basis: *a duty on silk.* **g.** risk or liability: *on pain of death.* **h.** time or occasion: *on Sunday.* **i.** direction or end of motion: *to march on the capital.* **j.** encounter: *to happen on a person.* **k.** object or end of action, thought, desire, etc.: *to gaze on a scene.* **l.** subject, reference, or respect: *views on public matters.* —*adv.* **2.** on a thing, place, or person: *put the coffee on.* **3.** on oneself or itself: *to put one's coat on.* **4.** fast to a thing, as for support: *to hold on.* **5.** toward a place, point, or object: *to look on.* **6.** forward, onward, or along, as in any course or process: *further on.* **7.** with continuous procedure: *to work on.* **8.** into or in active operation or performance: *to turn on the gas.* —*adj.* **9.** (of a brake) applied, and halting or slowing a vehicle, motor, etc. **10.** situated nearer; near. **11.** *Cricket.* noting that side of the wicket, or of the field, on which the batsman stands. —*n.* **12.** state or fact of being on. **13.** *Cricket.* the on side. [ME *on, an, o, a,* OE *on, an* on, in, to, c. D *aan*, G *an*, Icel. *ā*, Goth, *ana*; akin to Gk. *anā* up, upon. See ANA-]

On (ŏn), *n.* Biblical name of Heliopolis.

ON, Old Norse. Also, **ON.**, **O.N.**

on·a·ger (ŏn′ə·jər), *n.*, pl. **-gri** (-grī′), **-gers.** **1.** a wild ass, *Equus hemionus*, of southwestern Asia; kiang. **2.** an ancient and medieval engine of war for throwing stones. [ME, t. L, t. Gk.: m. *ōnagros* a wild ass]

on·a·gra·ceous (ŏn′ə·grā′-shəs), *adj.* belonging to the *Onagraceae* (or *Oenotheraceae, Ephilobiaceae*), the evening-primrose family, including the widespread ornamental fuchsia, the willow herb, etc.

Onager, *Equus hemionus*
(Ab. 4½ ft. high at the shoulder)

o·nan·ism (ō′nən·Ĭz′əm), *n.* **1.** *Psychiatry, Physiol.* withdrawal before occurrence of orgasm. **2.** masturbation. [from *Onan*, son of Judah: see Gen. 38:9. See -ISM] —o′nan·ist, *n.* —o′nan·is′tic, *adj.*

once (wŭns), *adv.* **1.** at one time in the past; formerly: *a once powerful nation.* **2.** a single time: *once a day.* **3.** even a single time; at any time; ever: *if the facts once become known.* **4.** once for all, finally and decisively.

5. once in a while, occasionally. **6. once upon a time**, long ago (a favorite beginning of a children's story, etc.). **7. once and again**, repeatedly. —*conj.* **8.** if or when at any time; if ever. **9.** whenever. —*n.* **10.** a single occasion: *once is enough.* **11. all at once**, suddenly. **12. at once**, **a.** immediately. **b.** at the same time: *do not all speak at once.* [ME *ones,* OE *ānes*, adv. (orig. genitive of *ān* ONE); r. ME *enes*, OE *ǣnes* once, f. *ǣne* once + -es, adv. suffix]

on·col·o·gy (ŏng·kŏl′ə·jĬ), *n.* the part of medical science that treats of tumors. [f. m. Gk. *ónko(s)* bulk, mass + -LOGY]

on·com·ing (ŏn′kŭm′Ĭng, ôn′-), *adj.* **1.** approaching: —*n.* **2.** the approach: *the oncoming of winter.*

on dit (ôN dē′), *French.* they say; it is said.

on·do·gram (ŏn′də·grăm′), *n.* an autographic record made on an ondograph.

on·do·graph (ŏn′də·grăf′, -gräf′), *n.* an instrument for graphically recording oscillatory variations, as in alternating currents. [irreg. f. F *onde* (g. L *unda*) wave + -o- + -GRAPH]

on·dom·e·ter (ŏn·dŏm′ə·tər), *n.* an instrument for measuring wave length of radio waves.

one (wŭn), *adj.* **1.** being a single unit or individual, rather than two or more; a single: *one apple.* **2.** being a person, thing, or individual instance of a number or kind indicated: *one member of the party.* **3.** some (day, etc., in the future): *you will see him one day.* **4.** single through union, agreement, or harmony: *all were of one mind.* **5.** of a single kind, nature, or character; the same: *all our pomp of yesterday is one with Nineveh and Tyre!* **6.** a certain (often used in naming a person otherwise unknown or undescribed): *one John Smith was chosen.* **7.** a particular day, night, time, etc., in the past: *one evening last week.* **8. all one,** (used predicatively) all the same, as in character, meaning, consequence, etc. —*n.* **9.** the first and lowest whole number, or a symbol, as 1, I, or i, representing it; unity. **10.** a unit; a single person or thing: *to come one at a time.* **11. at one**, in a state of unity, agreement, or accord: *hearts at one.* **12. one by one**, singly and in succession. —*pron.* **13.** a person or thing of number or kind indicated or understood: *one of the poets.* **14.** (in certain pronominal combinations) a person unless definitely specified otherwise: *every one.* **15.** (with a defining clause or other qualifying words) a person or a personified being or agency: *the evil one.* **16.** a person indefinitely; any one of us all: *as good as one would desire.* **17.** a person of the speaker's kind; such as the speaker himself: *to press one's own claims.* **18.** (to avoid repetition) a person or thing of the kind just mentioned: *the portraits are fine ones.* [ME *oon, oo, o,* OE *ān*, c. G *ein*]

-one, a noun suffix used in the names of chemical derivatives, esp. ketones. [t. Gk., abstracted from fem. patronymics]

O·ne·ga (ō·nē′gə; *Russ.* ŏ·nĕ′gä), *n.* a lake in the NW Soviet Union: second largest in Europe. 3764 sq. mi.

one-horse (wŭn′hôrs′), *adj.* **1.** using or having only a single horse. **2.** *U.S. Colloq.* unimportant; minor; petty.

O·nei·da (ō·nī′də), *n.* **1.** a tribe of the Iroquois confederacy, former inhabitants of the region east of **Oneida Lake,** a lake (20 mi. long; 6 mi. wide) in central New York. **2.** a member of the Oneida tribe. [t. Iroquois: m. *tiionenyote'* a rock which something set up and which is still standing (with reference to a boulder near an ancient village)]

O'Neill (ō·nēl′), *n.* **Eugene,** born 1888, U.S. dramatist.

o·nei·ro·crit·ic (ō·nī′rə·krĬt′Ĭk), *n.* **1.** an interpreter of dreams. **2.** oneirocriticism. [t. Gk.: m.s. *oneirokritikós*, adj., pertaining to the interpretation of dreams] —o·nei′ro·crit′i·cal, *adj.*

o·nei·ro·crit·i·cism (ō·nī′rə·krĬt′ə·sĬz′əm), *n.* the art of interpreting dreams.

o·nei·ro·man·cy (ō·nī′rə·măn′sĬ), *n.* divination through dreams. [f. Gk. *óneiro(s)* dream + -MANCY] —o·nei′ro·man′cer, *n.*

one·ness (wŭn′nĬs), *n.* **1.** the quality of being one; singleness; unity; sameness. **2.** agreement; concord; unity of thought, belief, aim, etc.

on·er·ous (ŏn′ər·əs), *adj.* burdensome, oppressive, or troublesome: *onerous duties.* [ME, t. L: m.s. *onerōsus*] —on′er·ous·ly, *adv.* —on′er·ous·ness, *n.*

one·self (wŭn·sĕlf′, wŭnz-), *pron.* a person's self (often used for emphasis or reflexively): *one hurts oneself by such methods.* Also, **one's self.**

one-sid·ed (wŭn′sī′dĬd), *adj.* **1.** considering but one side of a matter or question; partial, unjust, or unfair: *a one-sided judgment.* **2.** *Law.* unilateral, as a contract. **3.** unbalanced; unequal: *a one-sided fight.* **4.** existing or occurring on one side only. **5.** having but one side, or but one developed or finished side. **6.** having one side larger or more developed than the other. **7.** having the parts all on one side, as an inflorescence.

one-step (wŭn′stĕp′), *n.* **1.** a kind of round dance, danced by couples to ragtime. **2.** music for this dance.

one-time (wŭn′tīm′), *adj.* having been (as specified) at one time; former; quondam: *his one-time partner.*

one-track (wŭn′trăk′), *adj.* **1.** with but a single track. **2.** *Colloq.* restricted: *a one-track mind.*

one-way (wŭn′wā′), *adj.* moving, or allowing motion, in one direction only: *a one-way street.*

on·ion (ŭn′yən), *n.* **1.** a widely cultivated plant of the lily family, *Allium cepa*, having an edible succulent bulb of pungent taste and smell. **2.** the bulb. **3.** any of certain plants similar to the onion, as *A. Fistulosum* (**Welsh onion**). [ME *onyon*, t. OF: m. *oignon*, g. L *ūnio* large pearl, onion. See UNION]

On·ions (ŭn′yənz), *n.* **Charles Talbut**, born 1873, British lexicographer.

on·ion·skin (ŭn′yən skĭn′), *n.* a translucent, glazed paper.

on·look·er (ŏn′lŏŏk′ər, ôn′-), *n.* a spectator.

on·look·ing (ŏn′lŏŏk′ĭng, ôn′-), *adj.* **1.** looking on; observing; perceiving. **2.** looking onward or foreboding.

on·ly (ōn′lĭ), *adv.* **1.** without others or anything further; alone; solely; exclusively: *only he remained.* **2.** no more than; merely; but; just: *if you would only consent.* **3.** singly; as the only one: *the only begotten Son of God.* —*adj.* **4.** being the single one or the relatively few of the kind, or sole: *an only son.* **5.** single in superiority or distinction. —*conj.* **6.** but (introducing a single restriction, restraining circumstance, or the like): *I would have gone, only you objected.* **7.** *Now Colloq.* except that; but or except for: *only for him you would not be here.* [ME *oonli*(*ch*), OE *ānlīc*, var. of *ænlīc*, f. *ān* one + *-līc* -LY] —**Syn. 4.** ONLY, SOLE, SINGLE, UNIQUE are all used to refer to an object (or group of objects) as being without counterpart, alone of its kind, whether temporarily or permanently. SINGLE, SOLE, and ONLY all meant originally alone, unaccompanied, and this is still the meaning of SINGLE: *a huge load drawn by a single horse.* SOLE, however, and ONLY have come to refer to a single representative of a type of which no others exist, though this "type" may be very arbitrarily limited: *the only survivor of a disaster, I am his sole heir.* SOLE, today, is a very formal word and is infrequent outside of a few fixed phrases; in general, it is replaced by ONLY. UNIQUE has always meant existing alone of its kind; today, however, it is mainly used figuratively, to suggest that an object has no equal in excellence, importance, etc.: *a unique occasion.* —**Ant. 4.** plentiful, common.

on·o·mat·o·poe·ia (ŏn′ə măt′ə pē′ə, ō nŏm′ə tə-), *n.* **1.** the formation of a name or word by imitating sound associated with the thing designated, e.g., *cuckoo* and *whippoorwill* probably originated in onomatopoeia. **2.** *Obsolesc.* a word so formed. **3.** the use of imitative and naturally suggestive words for rhetorical effect. [t. LL, t. Gk. m. *onomatopoiía* the making of words] —**on′o·mat′o·poe′ic, on·o·mat·o·po·et·ic** (ŏn′ə măt′ə pō ĕt′ĭk), *adj.* —**on′o·mat′o·po·et′i·cal·ly,** *adv.*

On·on·da·ga (ŏn′ən dô′gə, -dä′-), *n.* **1.** a tribe of the Iroquois confederacy, former inhabitants of the region about **Onondaga Lake,** a salt lake (5 mi. long; 1 mi. wide) in central New York. **2.** a member of the Onondaga tribe. [t. Iroquois: m. *ononytáʔgeh* on top of hill]

on·rush (ŏn′rŭsh′, ôn′-), *n.* a strong forward rush, flow, etc.

on·set (ŏn′sĕt′, ôn′-), *n.* **1.** an assault or attack; a violent onset. **2.** a beginning or start.

on·shore (ŏn′shōr′, ôn′-), *adv., adj.* ashore.

on·side (ŏn′sīd′, ôn′-), *adj., adv.* not offside.

on·slaught (ŏn′slôt′, ôn′-), *n.* an onset, assault, or attack, esp. a vigorous or furious one.

Ont., Ontario.

On·tar·i·o (ŏn târ′ĭ ō′), *n.* **1.** a province in S Canada, bordering on the Great Lakes. 3,787,655 pop. (1941). 412,582 sq. mi. *Cap.:* Toronto. **2. Lake,** the smallest of the Great Lakes, between New York and Ontario. ab. 190 mi. long; ab. 7540 sq. mi. —**On·tar′i·an,** *adj., n.*

on·to (ŏn′tŏŏ, ŏn′-; *unstressed* -tə), *prep.* to a place or position on; upon; on: *to get onto a horse.*

on·tog·e·ny (ŏn tŏj′ə nĭ), *n.* *Biol.* the development of an individual organism (as contrasted with *phylogeny*). Also, **on·to·gen·e·sis** (ŏn′tō jĕn′ə sĭs). [f. Gk. *onto-* (comb. form of *ŏn* being) + -GENY] —**on·to·ge·net·ic** (ŏn′tō jə nĕt′ĭk), *adj.* —**on′tog′e·nist,** *n.*

ontological argument, *Metaphys.* the a priori argument for the being of God, founded on the assumption that existence is a property and one discoverable in the very concept of God.

on·tol·o·gism (ŏn tŏl′ə jĭz′əm), *n.* *Theol.* the doctrine that the human intellect has an immediate cognition of God as its proper object and the principle of all its cognitions.

on·tol·o·gy (ŏn tŏl′ə jĭ), *n.* **1.** the science of being, as such. **2.** the branch of metaphysics that investigates the nature of being and of the first principles, or categories involved. [t. NL: m. *ontologia*, f. Gk.: *onto-* (comb. form of *ŏn* being) + *-logia* -LOGY] —**on·to·log·i·cal** (ŏn′tə lŏj′ə kəl), *adj.* —**on·tol′o·gist,** *n.*

o·nus (ō′nəs), *n.* a burden; a responsibility. [t. L: load, burden]

o·nus pro·ban·di (ō′nəs prō băn′dī), *Latin.* the burden of proof.

on·ward (ŏn′wərd, ôn′-), *adv.* Also, **on′wards. 1.** toward a point ahead or in front; forward, as in space or time. **2.** at a position or point in advance. —*adj.* **3.** directed or moving onward or forward; forward. [ME. See ON, -WARD] —**Syn. 1.** See **forward.**

on·yx (ŏn′ĭks, ō′nĭks), *n.* a quartz consisting of straight layers or bands which differ in color, used for ornament. [ME *onix*, t. L: m. *onyx*, t. Gk.: nail, claw, veined gem]

oö-, a word element meaning "egg." [t. Gk., comb. form of *ōión*]

o·ö·cyte (ō′ə sīt′), *n.* *Biol.* a female germ cell in the maturation stage.

o·ö·gen·e·sis (ō′ə jĕn′ə sĭs), *n.* *Biol.* the genesis or origin and development of the ovum.

o·ö·go·ni·um (ō′ə gō′nĭ əm), *n., pl.* **-nia** (-nĭ ə), **-niums. 1.** *Biol.* one of the female germ cells at the multiplication stage, preceding the maturation or oöcyte stage. **2.** *Bot.* the one-celled female reproductive organ in certain thallophytic plants, usually a more or less spherical sac containing one or more eggs. [t. NL; see oö-, -GONIUM]

o·ö·lite (ō′ə līt′), *n.* *Geol.* **1.** a limestone composed of minute rounded concretions resembling fish roe, in some places altered to iron stone by replacement with iron oxide. **2.** (*cap.*) an upper division of the European Jurassic, largely composed of oölitic limestone. [t. F: m. *oolithe*, f. *oo-* oö- + *-lithe* -LITE] —**o·ö·lit·ic** (ō′ə lĭt′ĭk), *adj.*

o·öl·o·gy (ō ŏl′ə jĭ), *n.* the part of ornithology that treats of birds' eggs. —**o·ö·log·i·cal** (ō′ə lŏj′ə kəl), *adj.* —**o·öl′o·gist,** *n.*

oo·long (ōō′lông, -lŏng), *n.* a variety of semifermented brown or amber tea from Formosa. [t. Chinese: m. *wu-lung*, lit., black dragon]

oo·mi·ak (ōō′mĭ ăk′), *n.* umiak.

o·ö·pho·rec·to·my (ō′ə fə rĕk′tə mĭ), *n., pl.* **-mies.** *Surg.* the operation of removal of one or both ovaries. [f. *oöphor-* (t. NL, comb. form of *oöphoron* ovary, t. Gk.: lit., eggbearer) + -ECTOMY]

o·ö·pho·ri·tis (ō′ə fə rī′tĭs), *n.* *Pathol.* inflammation of an ovary, usually combined with an inflammation of the fallopian tubes; ovaritis.

oo·ra·li (ōō rä′lē), *n.* curare.

o·ö·sphere (ō′ə sfĭr′), *n.* *Bot.* an unfertilized egg within an oögonium.

o·ö·spore (ō′ə spōr′), *n.* *Bot.* a fertilized egg within an oögonium. Also, *Obs.*, **o·ö·sperm** (ō′ə spûrm′). —**o·ö·spor·ic** (ō′ə spōr′ĭk, -spôr′-), **o·ös·po·rous** (ō ŏs′pə rəs, ō′ə spōr′əs), *adj.*

Oost (ōst), *n.* **1. Jacob van** (yä′kôp vän), 1600?–71, Flemish painter. **2.** his son, **Jacob van,** 1639?–1713, Flemish painter.

o·ö·the·ca (ō′ə thē′kə), *n., pl.* **-cae** (-sē). a case or capsule containing eggs, as that of certain gastropods and insects. [t. NL, f. Gk.: ōo- oö- + m. *thēkē* case]

ooze¹ (ōōz), *v.,* **oozed, oozing,** *n.* —*v.i.* **1.** (of moisture, etc.) to percolate or exude, as through pores or small openings. **2.** (of air, etc.) to pass slowly or gradually as if through pores or small openings. **3.** (of a substance) to exude moisture, etc. **4.** (of information, courage, etc.) to leak or pass (out, etc.) slowly or imperceptibly. —*v.t.* **5.** to make by oozing. **6.** to exude (moisture, etc.). [ME *wose*(*n*), der. OOZE, n.] —*n.* **7.** act of oozing. **8.** that which oozes. **9.** an infusion of oak bark, sumac, etc., used in tanning. [ME *wos,* OE *wōs* juice, moisture]

ooze² (ōōz), *n.* **1.** a calcareous mud (chiefly the shells of small organisms) covering parts of the ocean bottom. **2.** soft mud, or slime. **3.** a marsh or bog. [ME *wose,* OE *wāse* mud]

ooze leather, leather prepared from calfskin or other skin with a soft, velvety finish on the flesh side.

ooz·y¹ (ōō′zĭ), *adj.* **1.** exuding moisture. **2.** damp with moisture. [f. OOZE¹ + -Y¹]

ooz·y² (ōō′zĭ), *adj.* of or like ooze, soft mud, or slime. [ME *wosie,* der. *wose* mud. See OOZE²] —**ooz′i·ness,** *n.*

op-, var. of ob-, (by assimilation) before *p,* as in *oppose.*

op., **1.** opera. **2.** operation. **3.** opposite. **4.** opus.

O.P., **1.** (L *Ordo Praedicatorum*) Order of Preachers (Dominican). **2.** Also, **o.p.** out of print.

OPA, Office of Price Administration.

o·pac·i·ty (ō păs′ə tĭ), *n., pl.* **-ties. 1.** state of being opaque. **2.** something opaque. **3.** *Photog.* the ratio of the incident light and that emerging from a photographic density. [t. L: s. *opācitas* shade]

o·pah (ō′pə), *n.* a large, deep-bodied brilliantly colored, oceanic food fish, *Lampris regius.* [t. West Afr.]

o·pal (ō′pəl), *n.* a mineral, an amorphous form of silica, (SiO₂ with some water), not as hard or as heavy as quartz, found in many varieties and colors (often a milky white), certain of which are iridescent and valued as gems. [t. L: s. *opalus,* t. Gk.: m. *opállios*]

o·pal·esce (ō′pə lĕs′), *v.i.,* **-esced, -escing.** to exhibit a play of colors like that of the opal.

o·pal·es·cent (ō′pə lĕs′ənt), *adj.* **1.** exhibiting a play of colors like that of the opal. **2.** having a milky iridescence. —**o′pal·es′cence,** *n.*

o·pal·ine (ō′pəl ĭn, -pə līn′), *adj.* of or like opal; opalescent.

o·paque (ō pāk′), *adj.* **1.** impenetrable to light; not able to transmit, or not transmitting light. **2.** not able to transmit, or not transmitting radiation, sound, heat, etc. **3.** not shining or bright; dark; dull. **4.** hard to understand; not clear or lucid; obscure. **5.** unintelligent; stupid. —*n.* **6.** something opaque. **7.** *Photog.* a coloring matter, usually black or red, used to darken a part of a negative. [ME *opake,* t. L: m.s. *opācus* shady, darkened] —**o·paque′ly,** *adv.* —**o·paque′ness,** *n.*

op. cit., opere citato.

ope (ōp), *adj., v.t., v.i.,* **oped, oping.** *Archaic.* open.

o·pen (ō′pən), *adj.* **1.** not shut, as a door, gate, etc. **2.** not closed, covered, or shut up, as a house, box, drawer, etc. **3.** not enclosed as by barriers, as a space. **4.** that may be entered, used, shared, competed for, etc., by all: *an open session.* **5.** accessible or available (often fol. by *to*): *the only course still open.* **6.** unfilled, as a position. **7.** not engaged, as time. **8.** without prohibition as to hunting or fishing: *open season.* **9.** *U.S. Colloq.* without legal restrictions, or not enforcing legal restrictions, as to saloons, gambling places, etc.: *an open town.* **10.** undecided, as a question. **11.** liable or subject to: *open to question.* **12.** accessible to appeals, ideas, offers, etc. (often fol. by *to*): *to be open to conviction.* **13.** having no cover, roof, etc.: *an open boat.* **14.** not covered or protected; exposed or bare: *to lay open internal parts with a knife.* **15.** unobstructed, as a passage, country, stretch of water, view, etc. **16.** free from ice: *open water in arctic regions.* **17.** free from frost; mild or moderate: *an open winter.* **18.** exposed to general view or knowledge; existing, carried on, etc., without concealment: *open disregard of rules.* **19.** acting publicly or without concealment, as a person. **20.** unreserved, candid, or frank, as persons or their speech, aspect, etc.: *an open face.* **21.** having openings or apertures: *open ranks.* **22.** perforated or porous: *an open texture.* **23.** expanded, extended, or spread out: *an open newspaper.* **24.** generous, liberal, or bounteous: *to give with an open hand.* **25.** *Print.* **a.** (of type) in outline form. **b.** widely spaced or leaded, as printed matter. **26.** not yet balanced or adjusted, as an account. **27.** *Music.* **a.** (of an organ pipe) not closed at the far end. **b.** (of a string) not stopped by a finger. **c.** (of a note) produced by such a pipe or string or, on a wind instrument, without the aid of a slide, key, etc. **28.** *Naut.* free from fog. **29.** not constipated, as the bowels. **30.** *Phonet.* **a.** pronounced with a relatively large opening above the tongue: *"cot" has a more open vowel than "caught."* **b.** (of a syllable) ending with its vowel.

—*v.t.* **31.** to move (a door, gate, etc.) from a shut or closed position so as to admit of passage. **32.** to make (a house, box, drawer, etc.) open (often fol. by *up*). **33.** to render (any enclosed space) open to passage or access. **34.** to give access to; make accessible or available, as for use. **35.** to recall or revoke, as a judgment or decree, for the purpose of allowing further contest or delay. **36.** to clear of obstructions, as a passage, etc. **37.** to make (bodily passages) clear. **38.** to uncover, lay bare, or expose to view. **39.** to disclose, reveal, or divulge: *to open one's mind.* **40.** to render accessible to knowledge, enlightenment, sympathy, etc. **41.** to expand, extend, or spread out: *to open a map.* **42.** to make less compact, less close together, or the like: *to open ranks.* **43.** to establish for the entrance or use of the public, customers, etc.: *to open an office.* **44.** to set in action, begin, start, or commence (sometimes fol. by *up*): *to open a campaign.* **45.** to cut or break into. **46.** to make an incision or opening in. **47.** to make or produce (an opening) by cutting or breaking, or by pushing aside or removing obstructions: *to open a way through a crowd.* **48.** *Naut.* to come in sight of, or get a view of, as by passing some intervening object. **49.** *Law.* to make the first statement of (a case) to the court or jury. —*v.i.* **50.** to become open, as a door, building, box, enclosure, etc. **51.** to afford access (into, to, etc.): *a door that opened into a garden.* **52.** (of a building, etc.) to open its doors. **53.** to begin a session or term, as a school. **54.** to begin a season or tour, as a theatrical company. **55.** to have an opening, passage, or outlet (into, upon, etc.): *a room that opens into a corridor.* **56.** to have its opening or outlet (fol. by *toward, to,* etc.). **57.** to come apart or asunder, or burst open, so as to admit of passage or display the interior. **58.** to become disclosed or revealed. **59.** to come into view, or become more visible or plain, as on nearer approach. **60.** to become receptive to knowledge, sympathy, etc., as the mind. **61.** to disclose or reveal one's knowledge, thoughts, feelings, etc. **62.** to spread out or expand, as the hand or a fan. **63.** to open a book, etc.: *open at page 32.* **64.** to become less compact, less close together, or the like: *ranks open.* **65.** to begin, start, or commence; start operations. **66.** to begin a season or tour, as a theatrical company. **67.** *Hunting.* (of hounds) to begin to bark, as on the scent of game.

—*n.* **68.** an open or clear space. **69.** the open air. **70.** the open water, as of the sea. **71.** the situation of one who does not use or seek concealment. **72.** an opening or aperture. **73.** an opening or opportunity. **74.** **the open,** the unenclosed or unobstructed country. [ME and OE, c. G *offen*] —**o′pen·er,** *n.* —**o′pen·ly,** *adv.* —**o′pen·ness,** *n.* —**Syn.** 20. See **frank.** —**Ant.** 20. reticent.

open air, the unconfined atmosphere; outdoor air.

o·pen-air (ō′pən âr′), *adj.* existing in, taking place in, or characteristic of the open air; outdoor.

o·pen-and-shut (ō′pən ən shŭt′), *adj.* obvious; easily decided.

open chain, *Chem.* a linking of atoms in an organic molecule which may be represented by a structural formula whose ends do not join to form a ring.

open city, *Mil.* a city which is officially declared to be of no military importance, either in battle or in the movement of troops and materiel, and is therefore not subject to military attack.

open door, 1. the policy of admitting all nations to a country upon equal terms, esp. for trade. **2.** free admission or access; admission to all upon equal terms.

o·pen-eyed (ō′pən īd′), *adj.* **1.** having the eyes open. **2.** having the eyes wide open as in wonder. **3.** watchful; alert. **4.** done or experienced with the eyes open.

o·pen-faced (ō′pən fāst′), *adj.* **1.** having a frank or ingenuous face. **2.** (of a watch) having the dial covered only by the crystal.

o·pen-hand·ed (ō′pən hăn′dĭd), *adj.* generous. —**o′pen-hand′ed·ly,** *adv.* —**o′pen-hand′ed·ness,** *n.*

o·pen-heart·ed (ō′pən här′tĭd), *adj.* **1.** unreserved, candid, or frank. **2.** kindly. —**o′pen-heart′ed·ly,** *adv.* —**o′pen-heart′ed·ness,** *n.*

o·pen-hearth (ō′pən härth′), *adj. Metall.* denoting a shallow-hearth reverberatory furnace for steelmaking, with two openings at each end to admit fuel and air. Combustion takes place over the molten metal charge.

open-hearth process, the steelmaking process using an open-hearth furnace.

open house, a house hospitably open to all friends who may wish to visit it or enjoy its entertainment.

o·pen·ing (ō′pən ĭng), *n.* **1.** a making or becoming open. **2.** act of one who or that which opens (in any sense). **3.** an unobstructed or unoccupied space or place. **4.** an open space in solid matter; a gap, hole, or aperture. **5.** *U.S.* a tract of land thinly wooded as compared with adjoining forest tracts. **6.** act of beginning, starting, or commencing. **7.** the first part or initial stage of anything. **8.** a vacancy. **9.** an opportunity. **10.** a formal beginning of a season's sale of goods. **11.** the first performance of a theatrical production. **12.** *Law.* the statement of the case made by counsel to the court or jury preliminary to adducing evidence. **13.** *Chess, etc.* a mode of beginning a game.

open letter, a letter made public by radio, newspaper, or such but in style written to a specific person.

o·pen-mind·ed (ō′pən mīn′dĭd), *adj.* having or showing a mind open to new arguments or ideas. —**o′pen-mind′ed·ly,** *adv.* —**o′pen-mind′ed·ness,** *n.*

o·pen-mouthed (ō′pən mouthd′, -moutht′), *adj.* **1.** having the mouth open. **2.** gaping with surprise or astonishment. **3.** greedy, ravenous, or rapacious. **4.** clamoring at the sight of game or prey, as hounds. **5.** vociferous or clamorous. **6.** having a wide mouth, as a vessel.

open policy, *Insurance.* a policy which covers a shifting quantity of goods and which usually requires a monthly computation of premium charges.

open position, *Music.* arrangement of a chord with wide spaces between the parts.

open primary, a direct primary election in which voters need not meet a test of party membership.

Open sesame!, a password or charm at which doors or barriers fly open (from the use of these words to open the door of the robbers' den in the tale of "Ali Baba and the Forty Thieves," in the *Arabian Nights' Entertainments*).

open shop, 1. a nonunion shop which may or may not employ union members together with nonmembers, but which does not recognize or deal with a union as the representative of the employees. Cf. **nonunion shop. 2.** an anti-union shop in which union members are not knowingly employed. **3.** a shop in which a union, because chosen by a majority of the employees, acts as representative of all the employees in making agreements with the employer, but in which union membership is not a condition of employment.

o·pen·work (ō′pən wûrk′), *n.* any kind of work, esp. ornamental, as of metal, stone, wood, embroidery, lace, etc., showing openings through its substance.

op·er·a[1] (ŏp′ər ə, ŏp′rə), *n.* **1.** an extended dramatic composition in which music is an essential and predominant factor, consisting of recitatives, arias, choruses, etc., with orchestral accompaniment, scenery, and acting, and sometimes dancing; a musical drama. **2.** the form or branch of musical and dramatic art represented by such compositions. **3.** the score or the words of a musical drama. **4.** a performance of one. **5.** *Colloq.* an opera house. See **grand opera, comic opera.** [t. It., t. L: service, work, a work]

o·pe·ra[2] (ŏp′ər ə), *n.* pl. of **opus.**

op·er·a·ble (ŏp′ər ə bəl), *adj.* **1.** that can be put into practice. **2.** admitting of a surgical operation.

o·pé·ra bouffe (ō′ə rə bōōf′; *Fr.* ō pĕ rä bōōf′), *French.* a comic opera, esp. of farcical character.

o·pé·ra co·mique (ō pĕ rä kō mēk′), *French.* comic opera.

opera glasses, a small, low-power binocular for use in theaters, etc. Also, **opera glass.**

opera hat, a man's collapsible tall hat, held open or in shape by springs.

opera house, a theater devoted chiefly to operas.

op·er·ant (ŏp′ər ənt), *adj.* **1.** operating; producing effects. —*n.* **2.** one who or that which operates. [t. L: s. *operans*]

op·er·ate (ŏp′ə rāt′), *v.,* **-ated, -ating.** —*v.i.* **1.** to work or run, as a machine does. **2.** to work or use a machine, apparatus, or the like. **3.** to act effectively; exert force or influence (often fol. by *on* or *upon*): *the same causes are operating for war.* **4.** to perform some process of work or treatment upon. **5.** *Surg.* to perform some manual act or series of acts upon the body of a patient, usually with instruments, to remedy deformity, injury, or disease. **6.** (of medicines, etc.) to produce the effect intended. **7.** *Mil., Naval.* **a.** to carry on operations in war. **b.** to give orders and accomplish military acts, as

---

b., blend of, blended; *c.,* cognate with; *d.,* dialect, dialectal; *der.,* derived from; *f.,* formed from; *g.,* going back to; *m.,* modification of; *r.,* replacing; *s.,* stem of; *t.,* taken from; *?,* perhaps.   See the full key on inside cover.

distinguished from doing staff work. **8.** to carry on transactions in securities, or some commodity, esp. speculatively or on a large scale. —*v.t.* **9.** to manage or use (a machine, etc.) at work: *to operate a switchboard.* **10.** to keep (a machine, apparatus, factory, industrial system, etc.) working or in operation. **11.** to bring about, effect, or produce, as by action or the exertion of force or influence. [t. L: m.s. *operātus*, pp., having done work, having had effect] —*op′er·at′a·ble, adj.*

op·er·at·ic (ŏp′ə·răt′ĭk), *adj.* of or pertaining to opera: *operatic music.* —**op′er·at′i·cal·ly**, *adv.*

op·er·a·tion (ŏp′ə·rā′shən), *n.* **1.** act, process, or manner of operating. **2.** state of being operative: *a rule no longer in operation.* **3.** the power of operating; efficacy, influence, or virtue. **4.** exertion of force or influence; agency. **5.** a process of a practical or mechanical nature in some form of work or production: *a delicate operation in watchmaking.* **6.** a course of productive or industrial activity: *building operations.* **7.** a particular course or process: *mental operations.* **8.** a business transaction, esp. one of a speculative nature or on a large scale: *operations in oil.* **9.** *Surg.* a process or method of operating on the body of a patient, as with instruments, to remedy injury, etc. **10.** *Math.* **a.** a process such as addition. **b.** the action of applying a mathematical process to a quantity or quantities. **11.** *Mil., Naval.* **a.** the conduct of a campaign. **b.** a campaign. —**op′er·a′tion·al,** *adj.*

op·er·a·tion·al·ism (ŏp′ə·rā′shən·ə·lĭz′əm), *n. Philos.* the doctrine that scientific concepts secure their meaning from the relevant set of operations involved, stimulated by the relativity theory of Einstein.

op·er·a·tive (ŏp′ə·rā′tĭv, -ər·ə·tĭv), *n.* **1.** a worker; one engaged, employed, or skilled in some branch of work, esp. productive or industrial work; a workman, artisan, or factory hand. **2.** a detective. —*adj.* **3.** operating, or exerting force or influence. **4.** having force, or being in effect or operation: *laws operative in a community.* **5.** effective or efficacious. **6.** engaged in, concerned with, or pertaining to work or productive activity. **7.** *Med.* concerned with, involving, or pertaining to remedial operations: *operative surgery.*

op·er·a·tor (ŏp′ə·rā′tər), *n.* **1.** a worker; one employed or skilled in operating a machine, apparatus, or the like: *a telegraph operator.* **2.** one who conducts some working or industrial establishment, enterprise, or system: *the operators of a mine.* **3.** one who operates in stocks, etc., esp. speculatively or on a large scale. **4.** one who performs a surgical operation.

o·per·cu·late (ō·pûr′kyə·lĭt, -lāt′), *adj.* having an operculum. Also, **o·per′cu·lat′ed.**

o·per·cu·lum (ō·pûr′kyə·ləm), *n., pl.* **-la** (-lə), **-lums. 1.** *Bot., Zool., etc.* a part or organ serving as a lid or cover, as a covering flap on a seed vessel. **2.** *Zool.* **a.** the gill cover of fishes and amphibians. **b.** (in many gastropods) a horny plate which closes the opening of the shell when the animal is retracted. [t. L: a cover, lid]

Oper-
culum
of cap-
sule of
moss

o·pe·re ci·ta·to (ō′pə·rē′ sĭ·tā′tō), *Latin.* in the work cited, or quoted. *Abbr.:* op. cit.

op·er·et·ta (ŏp′ə·rĕt′ə), *n., pl.* **-erettas, -erret·ti** (-ə·rĕt′ē). a short opera, commonly of a light character. [t. It., dim. of *opera* OPERA]

op·er·ose (ŏp′ə·rōs′), *adj.* **1.** industrious, as a person. **2.** done with or involving much labor. [t. L: m.s. *operōsus*] —**op′er·ose′ly,** *adv.* —**op′er·ose′ness,** *n.*

oph·i·cleide (ŏf′ə·klīd′), *n.* a musical wind instrument, a development of the old wooden serpent, consisting of a conical metal tube bent double. [t. F, f. Gk.: *ŏphi(s)* serpent + m.s. *kleĩs* key]

o·phid·i·an (ō·fĭd′ĭ·ən), *adj.* **1.** of, pertaining to, or belonging to the snakes. —*n.* **2.** a snake. [f. s. NL *Ophidia*, pl. (der. Gk. *ŏphis* serpent) + -AN]

oph·i·ol·a·try (ŏf′ĭ·ŏl′ə·trĭ, ō′fĭ-), *n.* serpent worship. [b. Gk. *ŏphi(s)* snake and (ID)OLATRY] —**oph′i·ol′a·trous,** *adj.*

O·phir (ō′fər), *n.* a country of uncertain location, possibly southern Arabia, or the Eastern coast of Africa, from which gold and precious stones and trees were brought for Solomon. I Kings 10:11. [t. Heb.]

oph·ite (ŏf′īt, ō′fīt), *n.* a greenish altered diabase. [t. L: m.s. *ophītēs*, t. Gk.: serpentlike, serpentine]

o·phit·ic (ō·fĭt′ĭk), *adj.* noting or pertaining to a rock texture exhibited by certain ophites (diabases), in which elongate feldspar crystals are embedded in a matrix.

ophthalm., ophthalmology.

oph·thal·mi·a (ŏf·thăl′mĭ·ə), *n. Pathol.* inflammation of the eye, esp. of its membranes or external structures. [t. LL, t. Gk.: a disease of eye]

oph·thal·mic (ŏf·thăl′mĭk), *adj.* of or pertaining to the eye; ocular.

oph·thal·mi·tis (ŏf′thăl·mī′tĭs), *n. Pathol.* inflammation of the eye, esp. of the eyeball in both its external and its internal structures. [t. NL]

ophthalmo-, a word element meaning "eye." [t. Gk., comb. form of *ophthalmós*]

oph·thal·mol·o·gist (ŏf′thăl·mŏl′ə·jĭst), *n.* a doctor of medicine skilled in ophthalmology.

oph·thal·mol·o·gy (ŏf′thăl·mŏl′ə·jĭ), *n.* the science dealing with the anatomy, functions, and diseases of the eye. —**oph·thal·mo·log·i·cal** (ŏf·thăl′mə·lŏj′ə·kəl), *adj.*

oph·thal·mo·scope (ŏf·thăl′mə·skōp′), *n.* an instrument for viewing the interior of the eye or examining the retina. —**oph·thal·mo·scop·ic** (ŏf·thăl′mə·skŏp′ĭk), **oph·thal·mo·scop·i·cal,** *adj.*

oph·thal·mos·co·py (ŏf′thăl·mŏs′kə·pĭ), *n.* the use of an opthalmoscope.

-opia, a word element of nouns denoting a condition of sight or of the visual organs, as in *amblyopia, diplopia, emmetropia, hemeralopia, myopia.* [t. Gk., der. *ŏps* eye]

o·pi·ate (*n., adj.* ō′pĭ·ĭt, -āt′; *v.* ō′pĭ·āt′), *n., adj., v.,* **-ated, -ating.** —*n.* **1.** a medicine that contains opium and hence has the quality of inducing sleep; a narcotic. **2.** anything that causes dullness or inaction, or that quiets the feelings. —*adj.* **3.** mixed or prepared with opium. **4.** inducing sleep; soporific; narcotic. —*v.t.* **5.** to subject to an opiate; stupefy. **6.** to dull or deaden. [t. ML: m.s. *opiātus*, der. L *opium* OPIUM]

o·pine (ō·pīn′), *v.t., v.i.,* **opined, opining.** *Obs. Except Humorously.* to think; deem; hold or express an opinion, or as one's opinion. [t. L: m.s. *opīnārī* think, deem]

o·pin·ion (ə·pĭn′yən), *n.* **1.** what is thought on any matter or subject; judgment or belief resting on grounds insufficient to produce certainty: *public opinion.* **2.** a particular judgment or belief of this kind; a view or notion (held or expressed): *to give an opinion on tariffs.* **3.** a formal or professional judgment expressed: *a medical opinion.* **4.** a judgment or estimate of a person or thing with respect to character, merit, etc. **5.** a favorable estimate; esteem. [ME, t. OF, t. L: s. *opīnio* supposition]
—**Syn. 1.** OPINION, SENTIMENT, VIEW are terms for one's conclusion about something. An OPINION is a belief or judgment which falls short of absolute conviction, certainty, or positive knowledge; it is a conclusion that certain facts, ideas, etc. are probably true or likely to prove so: *political opinions, an opinion about art, in my opinion this is true.* SENTIMENT (usually pl.) refers to an opinion or judgment arrived at as the result of deliberation and representing a rather fixed conviction; it usually has a tinge of emotion about it: *these are my sentiments.* VIEW is an estimate of something, an intellectual judgment, a critical survey based on a mental examination, particularly of a public matter: *views on governmental planning.* —**Ant. 1.** fact.

o·pin·ion·at·ed (ə·pĭn′yə·nā′tĭd), *adj.* obstinate or conceited with regard to one's opinions; conceitedly dogmatic. —**o·pin′ion·at′ed·ness,** *n.*

o·pin·ion·a·tive (ə·pĭn′yə·nā′tĭv), *adj.* **1.** of, pertaining to, or of the nature of opinion. **2.** opinionated. —**o·pin′ion·a·tive·ly,** *adv.* —**o·pin·ion·a·tive·ness,** *n.*

o·pi·um (ō′pĭ·əm), *n.* the inspissated juice of a poppy, *Papaver somniferum,* containing morphine and other alkaloids: a stimulant narcotic (in sufficient quantities a powerful narcotic poison) of great value in medicine to relieve pain, induce sleep, etc. [ME, t. L, t. Gk.: m. *ŏpion,* dim. of *opós* juice]

opium eating, the habitual use of opium in some form by eating or swallowing. —**opium eater.**

o·pi·um·ism (ō′pĭ·əm·ĭz′əm), *n. Pathol.* **1.** the habit of taking opium. **2.** a morbid condition induced by the habitual use of opium.

opium smoking, the practice or habit of smoking opium as a stimulant or intoxicant. —**opium smoker.**

op·o·del·doc (ŏp′ə·dĕl′dŏk), *n. Obs.* any of various liniments containing soap, camphor, alcohol, etc. [prob. coined by Paracelsus]

O·por·to (ō·pôr′tō), *n.* a city in NW Portugal: a port near the mouth of the Douro river. 258,548 (1940). Portuguese, **Porto.**

o·pos·sum (ə·pŏs′əm, pŏs′əm), *n.* **1.** a prehensile-tailed, pouched marsupial mammal, *Didelphis virginiana,* about the size of a large cat, common in the southern U.S., which feigns death when caught. **2.** any of many Neotropical genera of the same family. [t. Algonquian; cf. Renape (of Va.) *apásum* white beast, Ojibwa *wabäsim* white dog]

Opossum. *Didelphis virginiana*
(Total length 33 in., tail 12 in.)

opossum shrimp, any of the small, shrimplike schizopod crustaceans constituting the family *Mysidae.* The females carry their eggs in a pouch between the legs.

opp., 1. opposed. **2.** opposite.

Op·pen·heim (ŏp′ən·hīm′), *n.* E(dward) Phillips, 1866–1946, British novelist.

Op·pen·heim·er (ŏp′ən·hī′mər), *n.* J. Robert, born 1904, U.S. nuclear physicist.

op·pi·dan (ŏp′ə·dən), *adj.* **1.** of or pertaining to a town; urban. —*n.* **2.** a townsman. **3.** (at Eton College, England) a student not on the foundation, but boarding in the town. [t. L: s. *oppidānus* belonging to a town]

op·pi·late (ŏp′ə·lāt′), *v.t.,* **-lated, -lating.** to stop up; fill with obstructing matter; obstruct. [t. L: m.s. *oppīlātus,* pp.] —**op′pi·la′tion,** *n.*

op·po·nen·cy (ə·pō′nən·sĭ), *n.* **1.** act of opposing. **2.** state of being an opponent.

op·po·nent (ə·pō′nənt), *n.* **1.** one who is on the opposite side in a contest, controversy, or the like; an adversary. —*adj.* **2.** being opposite, as in position. **3.** opposing; adverse; contrary. **4.** *Anat.* bringing parts into opposition, as the muscles which set the thumb and little finger against each other. [t. L: s. *oppōnens,* ppr., opposing]
—**Syn. 1.** antagonist. OPPONENT, COMPETITOR, RIVAL refer

to persons engaged in a contest. OPPONENT is the most impersonal, meaning merely one who opposes; perhaps one who continually blocks and frustrates or one who happens to be on the opposite side in a temporary contest: *an opponent in a debate*. COMPETITOR emphasizes the action in striving against another, or others, for a definite, common goal: *competitors in business*. RIVAL has both personal and emotional connotations; it emphasizes the idea that (usually) two persons are struggling to attain the same object: *rivals for an office*.

op·por·tune (ŏp'ərtūn', -tōōn'), *adj.* **1.** appropriate or favorable: *an opportune moment*. **2.** occurring or coming at an appropriate time; timely: *an opportune warning*. [ME, t. L: m. *opportūnus*] **—op'por·tune'ly,** *adv.* **—op'por·tune'ness,** *n.*
—Syn. 2. OPPORTUNE, SEASONABLE, TIMELY refer to that which is particularly fitting or suitable for a certain time. OPPORTUNE refers to that which is well-timed and meets exactly the demands of the time or occasion: *an opportune remark*. That which is SEASONABLE is right or proper for the time or season or occasion: *seasonable weather*. That which is TIMELY occurs or is done at an appropriate time, esp. in time to meet some need: *timely intervention*. **—Ant. 1.** inappropriate.

op·por·tun·ism (ŏp'ərtū'nĭzəm, -tōō'-), *n.* **1.** the policy or practice, in politics or otherwise, of adapting actions, etc., to expediency or circumstances (often with implication of sacrifice of principle). **2.** an action or proceeding due to this policy. **—op'por·tun'ist,** *n.,* *adj.* **—op'por·tun·is'tic,** *adj.*

op·por·tu·ni·ty (ŏp'ərtū'nətĭ, -tōō'-), *n.,* *pl.* **-ties.** an appropriate or favorable time or occasion.

op·pos·a·ble (əpō'zəbəl), *adj.* **1.** capable of being placed opposite to something else. **2.** that may be opposed. **—op·pos'a·bil'i·ty,** *n.*

op·pose (əpōz'), *v.,* **-posed, -posing.** **—v.t. 1.** to act or contend in opposition to; drive against; resist; combat. **2.** to stand in the way of; hinder. **3.** to set as an opponent or adversary. **4.** be hostile or adverse to, as in opinion. **5.** to set as an obstacle or hindrance: *to oppose reason to force.* **6.** to set against in some relation, as of offsetting, antithesis, or contrast: *to oppose the advantages to the disadvantages.* **7.** to use or take as being opposite or contrary: *words opposed in meaning.* **8.** to set (something) over against something else in place, or so as to face or be opposite. **—v.i. 9.** to be or act in opposition. [ME, t. OF: m.s. *opposer*, b. L *opponere* set against and F *poser* POSE[1]] **—op·pos'er,** *n.*
—Syn. 1. OPPOSE, RESIST, WITHSTAND imply setting up a force against something. The difference between OPPOSE and RESIST is somewhat that between offensive and defensive action: to OPPOSE is mainly to fight against, in order to thwart certain tendencies, procedures, of which one does not approve: *he opposed the passage of the bill.* RESIST suggests that the subject is already threatened by the forces, or by the imminent possibility, against which he struggles: *to resist temptation.* Again, whereas OPPOSE always suggests an attitude of great disapproval, RESIST may imply an inner struggle in which the will is divided: *she tried unsuccessfully to resist his charm.* WITHSTAND generally implies successful resistance; it may refer to endurance that allows one to emerge unharmed (*to withstand a shock*), as well as to active resistance: *to withstand an attack.* **—Ant. 9.** comply, submit.

op·po·site (ŏp'əzĭt), *adj.* **1.** placed or lying over against something else or each other, or in a corresponding position from an intervening line, space, or thing: *opposite ends of a room*. **2.** contrary or diametrically different, as in nature, qualities, direction, result, or significance. **3.** *Bot.* **a.** situated on diametrically opposed sides of an axis, as leaves when there are two on one node. **b.** having one organ vertically above another; superposed. **4.** *Obs.* adverse or inimical. **—n. 5.** one who or that which is opposite or contrary. **6.** an antonym. **7.** *Rare.* an opponent. [ME, t. L: m. *oppositus*, pp., put before or against, opposed] **—op'po·site·ly,** *adv.* **—op'po·site·ness,** *n.*
—Syn. 2. OPPOSITE, CONTRARY, REVERSE imply that two things differ from each other in such a way as to indicate a definite kind of relationship. OPPOSITE suggests symmetrical antithesis in position, action, or character: *opposite ends of a pole, sides of a road, views*. CONTRARY sometimes adds to OPPOSITE the idea of conflict or antagonism: *contrary statements, beliefs*. REVERSE suggests that which faces or moves in the opposite direction: *the reverse side of a coin, a reverse gear*. **—Ant. 2.** same, like.

Opposite leaves (def. 3a)

opposite number, *Chiefly Brit.* a person who holds a corresponding position in another situation.

op·po·si·tion (ŏp'əzĭsh'ən), *n.* **1.** the action of opposing, resisting, or combating. **2.** antagonism or hostility. **3.** an opposing party or body. **4.** the political party opposed to the party in power. **5.** the act of placing opposite. **6.** the state or position of being placed opposite. **7.** the act of opposing or the state of being opposed by way of offset, antithesis, or contrast. **8.** *Logic.* **a.** the relation between two propositions which have the same subject and predicate, but which differ in quantity or quality, or in both. **b.** the relation between two propositions in virtue of which the truth or falsity of one of them determines the truth or falsity of the other. **9.** *Astron.* **a.** the situation of two heavenly bodies when their longitudes or right ascensions differ by 180°. **b.** the opposition of the moon or a planet and the sun, occurring when the earth is directly between them. [t.

L: s. *oppositio;* r. ME *opposicioun*, t. OF: m. *opposicion*] **—op'po·si'tion·al,** *adj.*

op·press (əprĕs'), *v.t.* **1.** to lie heavily upon (the mind, a person, etc.), as care, sorrow, or any disturbing thought does. **2.** to burden with cruel or unjust impositions or restraints; to subject to a burdensome or harsh exercise of authority or power. **3.** to weigh down, as sleep or weariness does. **4.** *Obs.* to put down, subdue or suppress. **5.** *Obs.* to press against or down. [ME *oppresse(n)*, t. ML: m. *oppressāre*, freq. of L *opprimere* press against, bear down, subdue] **—op·pres'sor,** *n.*
—Syn. 1, 2. OPPRESS, DEPRESS, both having the literal meaning to press down upon, to cause to sink, are today mainly limited to figurative applications. To OPPRESS is usually to subject (a people) to burdens, to undue exercise of authority, and the like; its chief application, therefore, is to a social or political situation: *the tyrant oppressed his subjects*. DEPRESS suggests mainly the psychological effect, upon the individual, of unpleasant conditions, situations, etc., which sadden and discourage: *depressed by the news*. When OPPRESS is sometimes used in this sense, it suggests a psychological attitude of more complete hopelessness: *oppressed by a sense of failure*. **—Ant. 1.** uphold, encourage.

op·pres·sion (əprĕsh'ən), *n.* **1.** the exercise of authority or power in a burdensome, cruel or unjust manner. **2.** act of oppressing. **3.** the state of being oppressed. **4.** the feeling of being oppressed by something weighing down the bodily powers or depressing the mind. **—Syn. 1.** tyranny, despotism, persecution.

op·pres·sive (əprĕs'ĭv), *adj.* **1.** burdensome, unjustly harsh, or tyrannical, as a king, taxes, measures, etc. **2.** causing discomfort because uncomfortably great, intense, elaborate, etc.: *oppressive heat*. **3.** distressing or grievous, as sorrows. **—op·pres'sive·ly,** *adv.* **—op·pres'sive·ness,** *n.*

op·pro·bri·ous (əprō'brĭəs), *adj.* **1.** conveying or expressing opprobrium, as language, a speaker, etc.: *opprobrious invectives*. **2.** disgraceful or shameful; contumelious. [ME, t. LL: m.s. *opprōbriōsus*] **—op·pro'bri·ous·ly,** *adv.* **—op·pro'bri·ous·ness,** *n.*

op·pro·bri·um (əprō'brĭəm), *n.* **1.** the disgrace or the reproach incurred by conduct considered shameful; infamy. **2.** a cause or object of such reproach. [t. L]

op·pugn (əpūn'), *v.t.* **1.** to assail by criticism, argument, or action. **2.** to call in question (rights, judgment, etc.); dispute (statements, etc.). [ME, t. F: s. *oppugner*, t. L: s. *oppugnāre* fight against] **—op·pugn'er,** *n.*

op·pug·nant (əpŭg'nənt), *adj.* opposing; antagonistic; contrary. **—op·pug'nan·cy,** *n.*

Ops (ŏps), *n.* *Rom. Myth.* the wife of Saturn and goddess of plenty. [t. L: lit., wealth]

-opsis, a word element indicating apparent likeness, as in *coreopsis*. [t. Gk.: appearance, sight]

op·son·ic (ŏpsŏn'ĭk), *adj.* *Bacteriol.* of, pertaining to, or influenced by opsonin.

opsonic index, the ratio of the number of bacteria taken up by phagocytes in the blood serum of a patient or test animal, to the number taken up in normal blood serum.

op·so·nin (ŏp'sənĭn), *n.* *Bacteriol.* a constituent of normal or immune blood serum which makes invading bacteria more susceptible to the destructive action of the phagocytes. [f. Gk. *opsŏn(ion)* provisions + -IN[2]]

op·so·nize (ŏp'sənīz'), *v.t.,* **-nized, -nizing.** *Immunol.* to increase the susceptibility of (bacteria) to ingestion by phagocytes. **—op'son·i·za'tion,** *n.*

opt (ŏpt), *v.i.* to make a choice; choose. [t. F: s. *opter*, t. L: m. *optāre* choose, wish]

opt., **1.** optative. **2.** optical. **3.** optician. **4.** optics.

op·ta·tive (ŏp'tətĭv), *Gram.* **—adj. 1.** designating or pertaining to a verb mood (as in Greek) having among its functions the expression of a wish, as Greek *ioimen* "may we (i.e., we wish we might) go." **—n. 2.** the optative mood. **3.** a verb in it. [t. LL: m.s. *optātīvus* serving to express a wish] **—op'ta·tive·ly,** *adv.*

op·tic (ŏp'tĭk), *adj.* **1.** pertaining to or connected with the eye as the organ of sight, or sight as a function of the brain. **2.** optical. **—n. 3.** (*usually pl.*) the eye. [t. ML: s. *opticus*, t. Gk.: m. *optikós* of sight]

op·ti·cal (ŏp'təkəl), *adj.* **1.** acting by means of sight or light, as instruments. **2.** constructed to assist the sight, as devices. **3.** pertaining to sight; visual: *an optical illusion*. **4.** pertaining to optics. **5.** dealing with or skilled in optics. **—op'ti·cal·ly,** *adv.*

optical activity, *Phys. Chem.* the property of compounds which consists of rotating the plane of vibration of polarized light.

optic axis, *Crystall.* the direction or directions, uniaxial or biaxial respectively, in a crystal exhibiting double refraction, along which this phenomenon does not occur.

op·ti·cian (ŏptĭsh'ən), *n.* **1.** one who makes glasses for remedying defects of vision, in accordance with the prescriptions of oculists. **2.** a maker or seller of optical glasses and instruments. [t. F: m. *opticien*, der. ML *optica* OPTICS. See -ICIAN]

optic nerve, the nerve of sight, connecting the eye with the brain. See diag. under **eye.**

op·tics (ŏp'tĭks), *n.* the branch of physical science that deals with the properties and phenomena of light and with vision. [pl. of OPTIC. See -ICS]

optic thalamus, thalamus (def. 1).

op·ti·me (ŏp'təmē'), *n.* (at Cambridge University, England) one of those in the second or third grade of honors in mathematics (**senior optimes** or **junior optimes**), the wranglers constituting the first rank. [t. L: adv., best, very well]

op·ti·mism (ŏp′tə·mĭz′əm), *n.* **1.** disposition to hope for the best; tendency to look on the bright side of things. **2.** the belief that good ultimately predominates over evil in the world. **3.** the doctrine that the existing world is the best of all possible worlds. **4.** the belief that goodness pervades reality. [t. NL: s. *optimismus*, der. L *optimus* best]

op·ti·mist (ŏp′tə·mĭst), *n.* one given to optimism.

op·ti·mis·tic (ŏp′tə·mĭs′tĭk), *adj.* **1.** disposed to take a favorable view of things. **2.** of or pertaining to optimism. Also, **op·ti·mis·ti·cal.** —**op′ti·mis′ti·cal·ly,** *adv.*

op·ti·mize (ŏp′tə·mīz′), *v.,* **-mized, -mizing.** —*v.i.* **1.** to be optimistic. —*v.t.* **2.** to make the best of.

op·ti·mum (ŏp′tə·məm), *n., pl.* **-ma** (-mə), **-mums,** *adj.* —*n.* **1.** the best or most favorable point, degree, amount, etc., for the purpose, as of temperature, light, moisture, etc., for the growth or reproduction of an organism. —*adj.* **2.** best or most favorable: *optimum conditions.* [t. L: (neut.) best (superl. of *bonus* good)]

op·tion (ŏp′shən), *n.* **1.** power or liberty of choosing; right of freedom of choice. **2.** something which may be or is chosen; choice. **3.** the act of choosing. **4.** a privilege acquired, as by the payment of a premium or consideration, of demanding, within a specified time, the carrying out of a transaction upon stipulated terms. [t. L: s. *optio* choice] —**Syn. 2.** See **choice.**

op·tion·al (ŏp′shən·əl), *adj.* **1.** left to one's choice: *attendance is optional.* **2.** leaving something to choice. —**op′tion·al·ly,** *adv.*

op·tom·e·ter (ŏp·tŏm′ə·tər), *n.* any of various instruments for measuring the refractive error of an eye. [f. OPT(IC) + -(O)METER]

op·tom·e·trist (ŏp·tŏm′ə·trĭst), *n.* one skilled in optometry.

op·tom·e·try (ŏp·tŏm′ə·trĭ), *n.* the practice or art of testing the eyes by means of suitable instruments or appliances (usually without the use of drugs), for defects of vision, in order to fit them with glasses.

op·u·lence (ŏp′yə·ləns), *n.* **1.** wealth, riches, or affluence. **2.** abundance, as of resources, etc. **3.** the state of being opulent. Also, **op′u·len·cy.**

op·u·lent (ŏp′yə·lənt), *adj.* **1.** wealthy, rich, or affluent, as persons or places. **2.** richly supplied; abundant or plentiful: *opulent sunshine.* [t. L: s. *opulens opulentus* rich, wealthy] —**op′u·lent·ly,** *adv.* —**Syn. 1.** See **rich.**

o·pun·ti·a (ō·pŭn′shĭ·ə), *n.* **1.** any plant of the cactaceous genus *Opuntia,* comprising fleshy herbs, shrubby plants, and sometimes trees, with branches usually composed of flattened or globose joints, and with (usually) yellow flowers and pear-shaped or ovoid, often edible fruit. **2.** a prickly pear. [t. NL, der. L *Opuntius* pertaining to *Opūs,* a town in Locris, Greece]

o·pus (ō′pəs), *n., pl.* **opera** (ŏp′ə·rə). **1.** a work or composition. **2.** a musical composition. **3.** one of the compositions of a composer as numbered according to date of publication. *Abbr.:* Op. [t. L: work, labor, a work]

o·pus·cule (ō·pŭs′kūl), *n.* **1.** a small work. **2.** a literary or musical work of small size. [t. L: m.s. *opusculum,* dim. of *opus* OPUS]

o·quas·sa (ō·kwăs′ə), *n.* a small trout, *Salvelinus oquassa,* with dark blue coloration, found in Maine. [said to be named after one of the Rangeley Lakes]

or[1] (ôr; *unstressed* ər), *conj.* a particle used: **1.** to connect words, phrases, or clauses representing alternatives: *to be or not to be.* **2.** to connect alternative terms: *the Hawaiian or Sandwich Islands.* **3.** often in correlation: *either . . . or; or . . . or; whether . . . or.* [ME *or,* orig. unstressed member of correlative *other . . . or,* earlier *other . . . other,* OE *āther oththe . . . oththe* either . . . or]

or[2] (ôr), *prep.. conj. Archaic* or *Dial.* before; ere. [ME *or* before, OE *ār* soon, early (c. Icel. *ār,* Goth. *air* early); akin to OE *ǣr* soon, before, ERE]

or[3] (ôr), *n. Her.* the tincture gold or yellow. [ME, t. F, g. L *aurum* gold]

-or[1], a suffix of nouns denoting action, state or condition, a quality or property, etc. as in *ardor, color, error, honor, labor, odor, tremor, valor, vigor.* [t. L; in some cases r. ME *-our,* t. AF (=F *-eur*), g. L *-or*]

-or[2], a suffix of nouns denoting who or that which does something, or has some particular function or office, as in *actor, confessor, creditor, distributor, elevator, emperor, governor, juror, refractor, tailor, traitor.* This suffix occurs chiefly in nouns originally Latin, or formed from Latin stems. In some cases it is used as an alternative or a substitute for **-er**[1] (a characteristically English suffix), esp. in legal terms (often correlative with forms in **-ee**) or with some other differentiation of use: *assignor, grantor, lessor, sailor, survivor, vendor.* [t. L; in some cases r. ME *-our,* t. AF: (m.) *-(e)our* (=F *-eur*), g. L *-or, -ātor,* etc.]

or·ach (ôr′əch, ŏr′-), *n.* any of the plants of the genus *Atriples,* esp. *A hortensis* (**garden orach**), cultivated for use like spinach. Also, **or′ache.** [ME *orage,* t. OF: m. *arache,* g. L *ātriplex,* t. Gk.: m.s. *atráphaxis*]

or·a·cle (ôr′ə·kəl, ŏr′-), *n.* **1.** (in ancient Greece and elsewhere) an utterance, often ambiguous or obscure, given by a priest or priestess at a shrine as the response of the god to an inquiry. **2.** the agency or medium giving such responses, or a shrine or place at which they were

given: *the oracle of Apollo at Delphi.* **3.** a divine communication or revelation. **4.** (*pl.*) the Scriptures. **5.** the holy of holies in the Jewish temple. See I Kings, 6:16, 19–23. **6.** any person or thing serving as an agency of divine communication. **7.** any utterance made or received as authoritative and infallible. **8.** a person who delivers authoritative or highly regarded pronouncements. [ME, t. OF, t. L: m.s. *ōrāculum*]

o·rac·u·lar (ō·răk′yə·lər), *adj.* **1.** of the nature of, resembling or suggesting an oracle: *an oracular response.* **2.** giving forth utterances or decisions as if by special inspiration or authority. **3.** uttered or delivered as if divinely inspired or infallible; sententious. **4.** ambiguous or obscure. **5.** portentous. —**o·rac′u·lar·ly,** *adv.*

O·ra·dea (ō·rä′dyä), *n.* a city in NW Rumania. 80,668 (est. 1940). Also, **Oradea Ma·re** (mä′rĕ). German, **Grosswardein.** Hungarian, **Nagyvárad.**

o·ral (ōr′əl), *adj.* **1.** uttered by the mouth; spoken: *oral testimony.* **2.** employing speech, as teachers or methods of teaching. **3.** of or pertaining to the mouth: *the oral cavity.* **4.** done, taken, or administered by the mouth: *an oral dose of medicine.* **5.** *Zool.* pertaining to that surface of polyps and marine animals which contains the mouth and tentacles. **6.** *Phonet.* with none of the voice issuing through the nose: *b* and *v* are oral consonants, and the normal English vowels are oral. —*n.* **7.** an oral examination in a college, school, etc. [f. s. L *ōs* mouth + -AL[1]] —**o′ral·ly,** *adv.*

—**Syn. 1.** ORAL, VERBAL are not properly synonyms. ORAL is properly applied to that which is uttered by word of mouth, as opposed to what is conveyed in writing: *oral message.* VERBAL is often used for oral: *a verbal agreement.* Literally, however, VERBAL applies to the words, spoken or written, in which thought or feeling is conveyed: *a verbal picture.* —**Ant. 6.** nasal.

oral interpretation, the study and practice of vocally expressing the meaning of the printed page, especially of literature.

O·ran (ō·rän′; *Fr.* ō·räN′), *n.* a seaport in NW Algeria. 200,671 (1936).

o·rang (ō·răng′), *n.* the orang-utan.

or·ange (ôr′ĭnj, ŏr′-), *n.* **1.** a globose reddish-yellow edible citrus fruit of which there are two principal kinds, the bitter and sweet, the latter comprising the most important of the citrus fruits. **2.** any of the white-flowered evergreen rutaceous trees yielding it, as *Citrus aurantium* (**bitter, Seville** or **sour orange**) and *C. sinensis* (**sweet orange**), cultivated in warm countries. **3.** any of several other citrus trees, as *Poncirus trifoliata* (**trifoliate orange**), a hardy Japanese species cultivated widely in the U.S., largely for hedges. **4.** any of certain trees of other genera, as *Maclura pomifera* (see **Osage orange**), or the fruit. **5.** reddish-yellow between yellow and red in the spectrum. —*adj.* **6.** of or pertaining to the orange. **7.** of a reddish-yellow color. [ME *orange,* t. OF, (b. with *or* gold), c. Sp. *naranja,* t. Ar.: m. *nāranj,* t. Pers.: m. *nārang,* prob. of East Indian orig.]

Or·ange (ôr′ĭnj, ŏr′-), *n.* **1.** a city in NE New Jersey, near Newark. 38,037 (1950). **2.** a river in the Union of South Africa, flowing from Basutoland W to the Atlantic. ab. 1300 mi. **3.** a former small principality of W Europe: now in the SE part of France. **4.** a princely family of Europe, rulers of the former principality of Orange. The present royal family of the Netherlands belong to this family. **5.** a town in SE France, near Avignon: Roman ruins. 7929 (1936). **6. Fort,** a former Dutch fort near the site of the present capitol in Albany, New York.

or·ange·ade (ôr′ĭnj·ād′, ŏr′-), *n.* a drink made of orange juice and water sweetened.

orange blossom, the flower of the orange, much worn in wreaths, etc., by brides.

Orange Free State, a central province of the Union of South Africa: a Boer republic, 1854–1900; a British colony (**Orange River Colony**), 1900–10. 872,545 pop. (1946); 49,647 sq. mi. *Cap.:* Bloemfontein.

Or·ange·ism (ôr′ĭnj·ĭz′əm, ŏr′-), *n.* the principles and practices of the Orangemen. —**Or′ange·ist,** *n.*

Or·ange·man (ôr′ĭnj·mən, ŏr′-), *n., pl.* **-men.** a member of a secret society formed in the north of Ireland in 1795, having for its object the maintenance of the Protestant religion and political ascendancy.

orange pekoe, **1.** a superior black tea composed of only the smallest top leaves and grown in India and Ceylon. **2.** any India or Ceylon tea of good quality.

or·ange·ry (ôr′ĭnj·rĭ, ŏr′-), *n., pl.* **-ries.** a place, as a glasshouse, in which orange trees are cultivated. [t. F: m. *orangerie,* der. *oranger* orange tree, der. *orange* ORANGE]

or·ange·wood (ôr′ĭnj·wŏŏd′, ŏr′-), *n.* the hard, finegrained, yellowish wood of the orange tree, used in inlaid work and fine turnery.

o·rang·u·tan (ō·răng′ŏŏ·tăn′), *n.* a large, long-armed anthropoid ape, *Pongo pygmaeus,* of arboreal habits, found in Borneo and Sumatra. It is less closely related to man than are the gorilla and chimpanzee. Also, **o·rang·ou·tang** (ō·răng′ŏŏ·tăng′), **orang.** [ult. t. Malay: man of the woods]

Orang-utan, *Pongo pygmaeus* (4½ ft. high, arm spread 7½ ft.)

o·ra pro no·bis (ōr′ə prō nō′bĭs), *Latin.* pray for us.

o·rate (ō rāt′, ōr′āt), *v.i.*, **orated, orating.** *Chiefly Humorous.* to make an oration; hold forth. [back formation from ORATION]

o·ra·tion (ō rā′shən), *n.* **1.** a formal speech, esp. one delivered on a special occasion, as on an anniversary, at a funeral, or at academic exercises. **2.** a speech whose style, diction, and delivery give a studied, even heightened effect. [ME *oracion,* t. L: m.s. *ōrātio* speech, discourse, prayer] —**Syn. 1.** See **speech.**

o·ra·tor (ōr′ə tər, ŏr′-), *n.* **1.** one who delivers an oration; a public speaker, esp. one of great eloquence. **2.** *Law.* one bringing suit; a plaintiff. [t. L: m. *ōrātor* speaker, suppliant; r. ME *oratour,* t. AF] —**or·a·tress** (ōr′ə trĭs, ŏr′-), *n. fem.*

or·a·tor·i·cal (ōr′ə tôr′ə kəl, ŏr′ə tŏr′-), *adj.* **1.** of, pertaining to, or characteristic of an orator or oratory. **2.** given to oratory. —**or·a·tor·i·cal·ly,** *adv.*

or·a·to·ri·o (ōr′ə tôr′ĭ ō, ŏr′-), *n., pl.* **-ri·os.** an extended musical composition, with a text more or less dramatic in character and usually based upon a religious theme, for solo voices, chorus, and orchestra, and performed without action, costume, or scenery. [t. It., g. LL *ōrātōrium* ORATORY²; so named from the musical services in the church of the Oratory of St. Philip Neri in Rome]

or·a·to·ry¹ (ōr′ə tôr′ĭ, ŏr′-), *n.* **1.** the exercise of eloquence; eloquent speaking. **2.** the art of an orator; the art of public speaking. [t. L: m.s. *ōrātōria,* prop. fem. of *ōrātōrius* of an orator]

or·a·to·ry² (ōr′ə tôr′ĭ, ŏr′-), *n., pl.* **-ries. 1.** a place of prayer, as a small chapel or a room for private devotions. **2.** (*cap.*) any of certain religious societies of the Roman Catholic Church, esp. one (**Oratory of St. Philip Neri**) composed of secular priests, not bound by vows, devoted to simple and familiar preaching. [ME, t. LL: m.s. *ōrātōrium* place of prayer, prop. neut. of L *ōrātōrius* oratorical]

orb (ôrb), *n.* **1.** *Chiefly Poetic.* any of the heavenly bodies: *the orb of day* (the sun). **2.** a sphere or globe. **3.** *Chiefly Poetic.* the eyeball or eye. **4.** a globe bearing a cross; the mound, or emblem of sovereignty, esp. as part of the regalia of England. **5.** *Now Rare.* a circle, or anything circular. **6.** *Astron. Obs.* the orbit of a heavenly body. **7.** *Astrol.* the space within which the influence of a planet, etc., is supposed to act. **8.** *Obs.* the earth. **9.** *Obs.* a range or area of action. —*v.t.* **10.** to form into a circle or a sphere. **11.** *Poetic.* to encircle; enclose. —*v.i.* **12.** to move in an orbit. **13.** *Obs.* to assume the shape of an orb. [t. L: s. *orbis* circle, disk, orb] —**Syn. 2.** See **ball¹.**

or·bic·u·lar (ôr bĭk′yə lər), *adj.* like an orb; circular; ringlike; spherical; rounded. [ME, t. LL: s. *orbiculāris,* der. L *orbiculus,* dim. of *orbis* ORB] —**or·bic·u·lar·i·ty,** *n.* —**or·bic·u·lar·ly,** *adv.*

or·bic·u·late (ôr bĭk′yə lĭt, -lāt′), *adj.* orbicular. Also, **or·bic·u·lat·ed.** [t. L: m.s. *orbiculātus,* der. *orbiculus.* See ORBICULAR]

Orbicular leaf

or·bit (ôr′bĭt), *n.* **1.** the elliptical or curved path described by a planet, etc., about another body, as the sun. **2.** a course regularly pursued, as in life. **3.** *Anat.* **a.** the bony cavity of the skull which contains the eye; the eye socket. **b.** the eye. **4.** *Zool.* the part surrounding the eye of a bird or insect. **5.** an orb or sphere. [t. L: s. *orbita* wheel track, course, circuit] —**or·bit·al,** *adj.*

or·bi·ta·le (ôr′bə tā′lĭ) *n.* **1.** *Craniom.* the lowermost point on the lower margin of the left orbit, located instrumentally on the skull. **2.** *Cephalom.* the lowermost point on the lower margin of the left orbit, located by palpation on the head. [t. L: of an orbit (neut.)]

orbital index, *Craniom.* the ratio of the maximum breadth to the maximum height of the orbital cavity.

orb·y (ôr′bĭ), *adj. Rare.* like or pertaining to an orb.

O.R.C., Officers' Reserve Corps.

or·ce·in (ôr′sĭ ĭn), *n. Chem.* a red dye obtained by oxidizing an ammoniacal solution of orcinol, and forming the principal coloring matter of cudbear and orchil. [arbitrary alter. of *orcin.* See ORCINOL]

orch., orchestra.

or·chard (ôr′chərd), *n.* **1.** a piece of ground, usually enclosed, devoted to the cultivation of fruit trees. **2.** a collection of such trees. [ME *orch(i)ard,* OE *orceard;* r. *ortyard,* ME *ortyerd,* OE *ortgeard* (cf. Goth. *aurtigards* garden), f. *ort-* (cf. L *hortus* garden) + *geard* YARD²]

or·chard·ist (ôr′chər dĭst), *n.* one who cultivates an orchard.

or·ches·tra (ôr′kĭs trə), *n.* **1.** a company of performers on various musical instruments, including esp. stringed instruments of the viol class, clarinets and flutes, cornets and trombones, drums, cymbals, etc., for playing concert music, as symphonies, operas, and other compositions. **2.** (in a modern theater, etc.) **a.** the space reserved for the musicians, usually the front part of the main floor, the orchestra pit. **b.** the entire main-floor space for spectators. **c.** the parquet. **3.** (in the ancient Greek theater) the circular space in front of the stage, alloted to the chorus. **4.** (in the Roman theater) a similar space reserved for persons of distinction. [t. L, t. Gk.: the space on which the chorus danced]

or·ches·tral (ôr kĕs′trəl), *adj.* **1.** of or pertaining to an orchestra. **2.** composed for or performed by an orchestra. —**or·ches·tral·ly,** *adv.*

or·ches·trate (ôr′kĭs trāt′), *v.t., v.i.,* **-trated, -trating.** to compose or arrange (music) for performance by an orchestra. —**or·ches·tra·tion,** *n.*

or·ches·tri·on (ôr kĕs′trĭ ən), *n.* a mechanical musical instrument, resembling a barrel organ but more elaborate, for producing the effect of an orchestra.

or·chid (ôr′kĭd), *n.* **1.** any plant of the family *Orchidaceae,* comprising terrestrial and epiphytic perennial herbs of temperate and tropical regions, with flowers which are usually beautiful and often singular in form. **2.** purple, varying from bluish to reddish. [t. NL: m.s. *Orchideae* (later *Orchidaceae*), der. L *orchis.* See ORCHIS]

or·chi·da·ceous (ôr′kĭ dā′shəs), *adj.* belonging to the *Orchidaceae,* or orchid family of plants, as the vanilla.

or·chid·ol·o·gy (ôr′kĭd ŏl′ə jĭ), *n.* the branch of botany or horticulture that deals with orchids.

or·chil (ôr′chĭl, -chĭl), *n.* **1.** a violet coloring matter obtained from certain lichens, chiefly species of *Roccella.* **2.** any such lichen. Cf. **litmus.**

or·chis (ôr′kĭs), *n.* **1.** any orchid. **2.** any of various terrestrial orchids (esp. of the genus *Orchis*) of temperate regions, with spicate flowers. **3.** any orchid of an allied genus, esp. *Blephariglottis,* including the fringed orchis. [t. L, t. Gk.: orig., testicle; so named with reference to the shape of the root]

or·ci·nol (ôr′sə nōl′, -nŏl′), *n. Chem.* a colorless crystalline compound found in many lichens, and also prepared synthetically. Also, **or·cin** (ôr′sĭn). [f. s. NL *orcina* (t. It.: m. *orcello* ORCHIL) + -OL²]

Or·cus (ôr′kəs), *n. Rom. Myth.* **1.** the world of the dead; Hades. **2.** the god of the underworld, Pluto.

ord., 1. order. **2.** ordinal. **3.** ordinance. **4.** ordinary. **5.** ordnance.

or·dain (ôr dān′), *v.t.* **1.** *Eccles.* to invest with ministerial or sacerdotal functions; confer holy orders upon. **2.** to appoint authoritatively. **3.** *Obs.* to select or appoint for an office. **4.** to decree; give orders for. **5.** (of God, fate, etc.) to destine or predestine. [ME *ordeine(n),* t. OF: m. *ordener,* t. L: m. *ordināre* order, arrange, appoint] —**or·dain′er,** *n.* —**or·dain′ment,** *n.*

or·deal (ôr dēl′, -dē′əl, ôr′dēl), *n.* **1.** any severe test or trial; a trying experience. **2.** a primitive form of trial to determine guilt or innocence, as by the effect of fire, poison, or water upon the accused, the result being regarded as a divine or preterhuman judgment. [var. (by correct etym. assoc. with DEAL¹) of *ordale,* ME and OE *ordāl,* var. of OE *ordēl,* c. G *urteil* judgment]

or·der (ôr′dər), *n.* **1.** an authoritative direction, injunction, or mandate. **2.** *Law.* a command of a court or judge. **3.** *Mil.* **a.** order arms: *at the order.* **b.** (*pl.*) commands or notices issued by the Army, Navy, Air Force, or a military commander to troops under him. **4.** the disposition of things following one after another, as in space, time, etc.; succession or sequence. **5.** a condition in which everything is in its proper place with reference to other things and to its purpose; methodical or harmonious arrangement. **6.** formal disposition or array: *set our men in order.* **7.** proper or satisfactory condition: *my watch is out of order.* **8.** state or condition generally: *affairs are in good order.* **9.** *Gram.* the arrangement of the elements of a construction in a particular sequence, e.g., the placing of *John* before and of *George* after the verb *saw* in the sentence *John saw George.* **b.** the feature of construction resulting from such an arrangement, e.g., the sentences *John saw George* and *George saw John* differ only in order. **10.** any class, kind, or sort, as of persons or things, distinguished from others by nature or character: *talents of a high order.* **11.** the usual major subdivision of a class or subclass, commonly comprising a plurality of families; e.g., the *Hymenoptera* (ants, bees, etc.). **12.** a rank, grade, or class of the community. **13.** a body of persons of the same profession, occupation, or pursuits: *the clerical order.* **14.** a body or society of persons living by common consent under the same religious, moral, or social regulations. **15.** any of the degrees or grades of the clerical office (the number of which varies in different churches, the Roman Catholic Church, for example, having the **major orders** of bishop, priest, deacon, and subdeacon, and the **minor orders** of acolyte, exorcist, lector, and ostiary, while the Anglican Church recognizes only the three grades of bishop, priest and deacon. **16.** any of the nine grades of angels in medieval angelology (see **angel,** def. 1). **17.** a monastic society or fraternity: *the Franciscan order.* **18.** (*usually pl.*) the rank or status of an ordained Christian minister. **19.** (*usually pl.*) the rite or sacrament of ordination. **20.** a prescribed form of divine service, or of administration of a rite or ceremony. **21.** the service itself. **22.** *Hist.* **a.** a society or fraternity of knights, of combined military and monastic character, as in the Middle Ages, as the Knights Templars, etc. **b.** an institution, partly an imitation of the medieval orders of military monks, having as its purpose the rewarding of meritorious service by the conferring of a dignity: *the Order of the Golden Fleece.* **23.** a modern organization or society more or less resembling the knightly orders: *fraternal orders.* **24.** conformity to law or established authority. **25.** absence of revolt, disturbance, turbulence, unruliness, etc. **26.** customary mode of procedure, or established usage. **27.** the customary or prescribed mode of proceeding in debates or the like, or in the conduct of deliberative or legislative bodies, public meetings, etc. **28.** conformity to this. **29.** prevailing course of things, or an established system or regime: *the old order* *changeth.* **30.** a direction or commission to make, provide or furnish something: *shoes made to order.* **31.** a quantity of goods purchased. **32.** *Chiefly Brit.* a pass for admission to a theater, museum or the like. **33.** *Archit.* **a.** a series of columns with their entablature arranged in given proportions. **b.** any one of the typical variations of such an arrangement distinguished by proportion, capital types and other characteristics: *the Doric, Ionic, Corinthian, Tuscan, and Composite orders.*

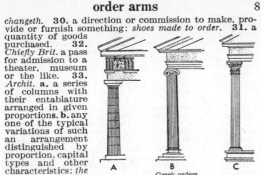

Greek orders
A, Doric; B Ionic; C, Corinthian

34. *Math.* degree, as in algebra. **35. in order,** permissible under the rules of parliamentary procedure. **36. in order that,** to the end that. **37. in order to,** as a means to. **38. in short order,** immediately. **39. on order, a.** subject to the order of buyer. **b.** ordered but not yet received. **40. on the order of,** resembling to some extent. **41. out of order,** not in accordance with recognized parliamentary rules.
—*v.t.* **42.** to give an order, direction, or command to. **43.** to direct or command to go or come (as specified): *to order a person out of one's house.* **44.** to give an order for. **45.** to prescribe: *a doctor orders a medicine for a patient.* **46.** to direct to be made, supplied, or furnished: *we ordered two steaks.* **47.** to regulate, conduct, or manage. **48.** to arrange methodically or suitably. **49.** to ordain, as God or fate does. **50.** *Eccles.* to invest with clerical rank or authority. —*v.i.* **51.** to issue orders.
[ME *ordre,* t. OF, t. L: m.s. *ordo* row, rank, regular arrangement] —**or′der·er,** *n.* —**Syn. 12.** See **direct.**

order arms, 1. a position in the manual of arms in close-order drill, in which the rifle is held at the right side, with the butt on the ground. **2.** (as an interjection) the command to move the rifle to this position.

or·der·ly (ôr′dər lĭ), *adj., adv., n., pl.* **-lies.** —*adj.* **1.** arranged or disposed in order, or regular sequence. **2.** observant of system or method, as persons, the mind, etc. **3.** characterized by or observant of order, rule, or discipline: *an orderly citizen.* **4.** charged with the communication or execution of orders. —*adv.* **5.** according to established order or rule. **6.** *Archaic.* methodically. —*n.* **7.** *Mil.* **a.** a private soldier or a noncommissioned officer attending on a superior officer to carry orders, etc. **b.** See **striker** (def. 5). **8.** an attendant in a hospital, charged with the maintenance of order, cleanliness, etc. —**or′der·li·ness,** *n.*
—**Syn. 1.** ORDERLY, METHODICAL, SYSTEMATIC characterize that which is neat, in order and planned. These three words are sometimes used interchangeably. However, ORDERLY emphasizes neatness of arrangement: *an orderly array of books.* METHODICAL suggests a logical plan, a definite order of actions or method from beginning to end: *a methodical examination of something.* SYSTEMATIC suggests thoroughness, an extensive and elaborately detailed plan or classification, together with regularity of action: *a systematic review.* —**Ant. 1.** chaotic, haphazard.

orderly officer, *Brit. Mil.* officer of the day.

or·di·nal[1] (ôr′də nəl), *adj.* **1.** pertaining to an order, as of animals or plants. —*n.* **2.** an ordinal number or numeral. [ME, t. LL: s. *ordinālis* der. L *ordo* order]

or·di·nal[2] (ôr′də nəl), *n.* **1.** a directory of ecclesiastical services. **2.** a book containing the forms for the ordination of priests, consecration of bishops, etc. [ME, t. ML: m. *ordināle.* See ORDINAL[1]]

ordinal number, any of the numbers *first, second, third,* etc. (in distinction from *one, two, three,* etc. which are called **cardinal numbers**). Also, **ordinal numeral.**

or·di·nance (ôr′də nəns), *n.* **1.** an authoritative rule or law; a decree or command. **2.** a public injunction or regulation. **3.** *Eccles.* **a.** an established rite or ceremony. **b.** a sacrament. **c.** the communion. [ME *ordinaunce,* t. OF: m. *ordenance,* der. *ordener* to order, t. L: m. *ordināre*]

or·di·nar·i·ly (ôr′də něr′ə lĭ; *emphatic* ôr′də nâr′ə lĭ), *adv.* **1.** in ordinary cases; usually: *ordinarily he sleeps until the last possible minute.* **2.** in the ordinary way. **3.** to the usual extent.

or·di·nar·y (ôr′də něr′ĭ), *adj., n., pl.* **-naries.** —*adj.* **1.** such as is commonly met with; of the usual kind. **2.** not above, but rather below, the average level of quality; somewhat inferior. **3.** customary; normal: *for all ordinary purposes.* **4.** (of jurisdiction etc.) immediate, as contrasted with that which is delegated. **5.** (of officials, etc.) belonging to the regular staff or the fully recognized class. —*n.* **6.** the ordinary condition, degree, run, or the like: *out of the ordinary.* **7.** something regular, customary, or usual. **8.** *Eccles.* **a.** an order or form for divine service, esp. that for saying mass. **b.** the service of the mass exclusive of the canon. **9.** *Obs. except Hist.* a clergyman appointed to prepare condemned prisoners for death. **10.** *Brit. Eccl. Law.* a bishop, archbishop, or other ecclesiastic or his deputy,

in his capacity as an *ex officio* ecclesiastical authority. **11.** (in some States of the U.S.) a judge of a court of probate. **12.** *Brit.* a meal regularly served at a fixed price in a restaurant or inn. **13.** *Obs.* a restaurant or inn, or its dining room. **14.** a high bicycle of an early type, with one large wheel in front and one small wheel behind. **15.** *Her.* **a.** any of the simplest and commonest heraldic charges or bearings, usually bounded by straight lines. **b.** any of the more important of these. **16. in ordinary,** (of officials, etc.) in regular service: *a physician in ordinary to a king.*
[ME, t. L: m.s. *ordinārius* of the usual order] —**or′di·nar′i·ness,** *n.*
—**Syn. 1.** See **common.**

or·di·nate (ôr′də nāt′, -nĭt), *n.* *Math.* the *y* Cartesian coördinate. [t. L: m.s. *ordinātus,* pp., ordained]

or·di·na·tion (ôr′də nā′shən), *n.* **1.** *Eccles.* act or ceremony of ordaining. **2.** the fact of being ordained. **3.** a decreeing. **4.** act of arranging. **5.** the resulting state. [ME *ordinacion,* t. L: m.s. *ordinātio* ordainment, an ordering]

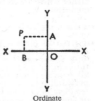

Ordinate
P, Any point; AO and PB,
Ordinate of P; YY, Axis
of ordinate; OB and AP,
Abscissa of P; XX, Axis
of abscissa

ordn., ordnance.

ord·nance (ôrd′nəns), *n.* **1.** cannon or artillery. **2.** military weapons of all kinds with their equipments, ammunition, etc. [var. of ORDINANCE]

or·do (ôr′dō), *n., pl.* **ordines** (ôr′də nēz′). *Rom. Cath. Ch.* a booklet containing short and abbreviated directions for the contents of the office and mass of each day in the year. [L: row, series, order]

or·don·nance (ôr′də nəns; *Fr.* ôr dô näns′), *n.* **1.** arrangement or disposition of parts, as of a building, a picture, or a literary composition. **2.** an ordinance, decree, or law. [t. F. See ORDINANCE]

Or·do·vi·cian (ôr′də vĭsh′ən), *Stratig.* —*adj.* **1.** pertaining to an early Paleozoic geological period or system equivalent to Lower Silurian of common usage before 1879. —*n.* **2.** the period or system following Cambrian and preceding Silurian. [f.s. L *Ordovicēs,* pl., an ancient British tribe in northern Wales + -IAN]

or·dure (ôr′jər, -dyŏŏr), *n.* filth; dung; excrement. [ME, t. OF, der. *ord* filthy, g. L *horridus* horrid]

Or·dzho·ni·kid·ze (ôr jŏ nĭ kēd′zĕ), *n.* a city in the S Soviet Union in Europe, in Caucasia. 127,172 (1939). Also, **Orjonikidze.** Formerly, **Vladikavkaz.**

ore (ōr), *n.* **1.** a metal-bearing mineral or rock, or a native metal, esp. when valuable enough to be mined. **2.** a mineral or natural product serving as a source of some nonmetallic substance, as sulfur. [ME (*o*)*or* metal, ore, OE *ār* brass]

ö·re (œ′rə), *n., pl.* **ö·re.** a bronze coin and money of account of Denmark, Norway, and Sweden, equal to one hundreth of a krone or krona.

Ore., Oregon.

o·re·ad (ōr′ĭ ăd′), *n.* *Class. Myth.* a mountain nymph. [t. L: s. *Oreas,* t. Gk.: m. *Oreiás,* der. *óros* mountain]

o·rec·tic (ô rĕk′tĭk), *adj.* *Philos.* of or pertaining to desire; appetitive. [t. Gk.: m.s. *orektikós*]

ore dressing, *Metall.* the art of separating the valuable minerals from an ore without chemical changes.

Oreg., Oregon.

Or·e·gon (ôr′ə gŏn′, -gən, ôr′-), *n.* a State in the NW United States, on the Pacific coast. 1,521,341 pop. (1950); 96,981 sq. mi. *Cap.:* Salem. *Abbr.:* Oreg. or Ore.
—**Or·e·go·ni·an** (ôr′ə gō′nĭ ən, ôr′-), *adj., n.*

Oregon grape, 1. a small, dark-blue berry of the western coast of the U.S. It is the official flower of Oregon. **2.** the evergreen shrub, *Mahonia aquifolia* (family *Berberidaceae*), on which the berry grows.

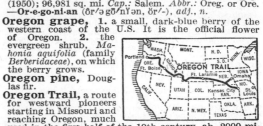

Oregon pine, Douglas fir.

Oregon Trail, a route for westward pioneers starting in Missouri and reaching Oregon, much used in the first half of the 19th century. ab. 2000 mi.

O·rel (ō rĕl′; *Russ.* ŏr yŏl′), *n.* a city in the central Soviet Union in Europe. 110,567 (1939).

O·ren·burg (ō′rĕn bŏŏrk′), *n.* a city in the E Soviet Union in Europe, on the Ural river. 172,925 (1939). Also, **Chkalov.**

O·res·tes (ō rĕs′tēz), *n.* *Gk. Legend.* son of Agamemnon and Clytemnestra, and brother of Electra: slew his mother and Aegisthus, who had slain Agamemnon.

Ö·re·sund (œ′rə sŏŏn′), *n.* Swedish and Danish name of **The Sound.**

org., **1.** organic. **2.** organized.

or·gan (ôr′gən), *n.* **1.** a musical instrument (**pipe organ**) consisting of one or more sets of pipes sounded by means of compressed air, played by means of keys arranged in one or more keyboards: in its full modern development the largest and most complicated of musical instruments. **2.** a reed organ, harmonium, or American organ. **3.** a barrel organ or hand organ. **4.** *Obs.* any of various musical instruments, esp. wind instruments. **5.** (in an animal or a plant) a part or member, as the heart, having some specific function. **6.** an instrument or means, as of performance. **7.** a means or medium of communicating thoughts, opinions, etc, as a newspaper serving as the mouthpiece of a political party. [ME, t. L: s. *organum,* t. Gk.: m. *órganon* instrument, tool, bodily organ, musical instrument]

or·gan·dy (ôr'gən dЎ), *n., pl.* **-dies.** a fine, thin, stiff cotton fabric usually having a durable crisp finish, and either white, dyed or printed; used for neckwear, dresses, curtains. Also, **or'gan·die.** [t. F: m. *organdi;* orig. uncert.]

organ grinder, a street musician who plays a hand organ by turning the crank.

or·gan·ic (ôr gǎn'Уk), *adj.* **1.** noting or pertaining to a class of chemical compounds which formerly comprised only those existing in or derived from living organisms (animal or plant), but which now includes these and all other compounds of carbon. **2.** characteristic of, pertaining to, or derived from living organisms: *organic remains found in rocks.* **3.** of or pertaining to an organ or the organs of an animal or a plant. **4.** *Philos.* having a physical organization similar in its complexity to that of living things. **5.** characterized by the systematic arrangement of parts; organized; systematic. **6.** of or pertaining to the constitution or structure of a thing; constitutional; structural. **7.** *Law.* of or pertaining to the constitutional or essential law or laws organizing the government of a state. [t. L: s. *organicus,* t. Gk.: m. *organikós*] —**Syn. 6.** inherent, fundamental, essential.

or·gan·i·cal·ly (ôr gǎn'Уk lЎ), *adv.* **1.** in an organic manner; by or with organs. **2.** with reference to organic structure. **3.** by or through organization.

organic chemistry, the branch of chemistry dealing with the compounds of carbon, originally thought to exist only in living organisms.

organic disease, a disease in which there is a structural alteration (opposed to *functional disease*).

or·gan·i·cism (ôr gǎn'ə sУz'əm), *n.* **1.** *Biol., Philos.* the theory that vital activities arise not from any one part of an organism but from its autonomous composition. **2.** *Neurol.* the doctrine that all or the majority of the diseases of the nervous system including those of the mind are organic, due to demonstrable changes in the brain or spinal cord. —**or·gan·i·cist** (ôr gǎn'ə sУst), *n.*

organic law. See law (def.2).

or·gan·ism (ôr'gə nУz'əm), *n.* **1.** an individual composed of mutually dependent parts constituted for subserving vital processes. **2.** any form of animal or plant life: *microscopic organisms.* **3.** any organized body or system analogous to a living being: *the Korean social organism.* **4.** *Philos.* any thing with a very complex structure and parts which function not only in terms of one another, but also in terms of the whole.

or·gan·ist (ôr'gən Уst), *n.* a player on an organ.

or·gan·i·za·tion (ôr'gən ə zā'shən), *n.* **1.** act or process of organizing. **2.** state or manner of being organized. **3.** that which is organized. **4.** organic structure. **5.** any organized whole. **6.** a body of persons organized for some end or work. **7.** the administrative personnel or apparatus of a business. **8.** the functionaries of a political party along with the offices, committees, etc. which they fill. **9.** an organism. —**or·gan·i·za'tion·al,** *adj.*

or·gan·ize (ôr'gə nīz'), *v.,* -ized, -izing. —*v.t.* **1.** to form as or into a whole consisting of interdependent or coördinated parts, esp. for harmonious or united action: *to organize a party.* **2.** to systematize: *to organize facts.* **3.** to give organic structure or character to. **4.** to build a trade union among: *to organize workers.* **5.** to enlist the employees of into a trade union: *to organize a factory.* —*v.i.* **6.** to combine in an organized company, party, or the like. **7.** to assume organic structure. Also, *esp. Brit.,* **or·gan·ise'.** [ME, t. ML: m.s. *organizāre,* der. L *organum* ORGAN] —**or·gan·iz'a·ble,** *adj.* —**or'gan·iz'er,** *n.*

organized ferment. See ferment (def. 1a).

organized labor, all workers who are organized in labor unions.

organo-, word element meaning "organ," usually used in the biological sense. [t. Gk., comb. form of *órganon*]

or·ga·nog·ra·phy (ôr'gə nŏg'rə fЎ), *n.* the description of the organs of animals or plants.

or·ga·nol·o·gy (ôr'gə nŏl'ə jЎ), *n.* **1.** the branch of biology that deals with the structure and functions of the organs of animals or plants. **2.** phrenology.

or·ga·non (ôr'gə nŏn'), *n., pl.* **-na** (-nə), **-nons. 1.** an instrument of thought or knowledge. **2.** *Philos.* a system of rules or principles of demonstration or investigation. [t. Gk. See ORGAN]

or·ga·no·ther·a·py (ôr'gə nō thĕr'ə pЎ), *n.* that branch of therapeutics which deals with the use of remedies prepared from the organs of animals, as the thyroid gland, the pancreas, the suprarenal bodies, etc. Also, **or·ga·no·ther·a·peu·tics** (ôr'gə nō thĕr'ə pū'tЎks).

organ pipe, **1.** one of the pipes of a pipe organ. **2.** something resembling such a pipe.

or·ga·num (ôr'gə nəm), *n., pl.* **-na** (-nə), **-nums. 1.** an organon. **2.** *Music.* **a.** the doubling, or simultaneous singing, of a melody at an interval of either a fourth, fifth, or octave. **b.** the second part in such singing. [t. L. See ORGAN]

or·gasm (ôr'gǎzəm), *n.* **1.** *Physiol.* a complex series of responses of the genital organs and skin at the culmination of a sexual act. **2.** immoderate excitement. [t. NL:

s. *orgasmus,* t. Gk.: m. *orgasmós,* der. *orgán* swell, be excited] —**or·gas·tic** (ôrgǎs'tЎk), *adj.*

or·geat (ôr'zhǎt; *Fr.* ôr zhà'), *n.* a syrup or drink made from almonds (orig. from barley), sugar, and a water prepared from orange flowers. [t. F, t. Pr., der. *orge,* g. L *hordeum* barley]

Or·get·o·rix (ôr jĕt'ərЎks), *n.* fl. c60 B.C., Helvetian chieftain.

or·gi·as·tic (ôr'jЎ ǎs'tЎk), *adj.* of, pertaining to, or of the nature of orgies. [t. Gk.: m.s. *orgiastikós*]

or·gy (ôr'jЎ), *n., pl.* **-gies. 1.** wild, drunken, or licentious festivities or revelry. **2.** any proceedings marked by unbridled indulgence of passions: *an orgy of killing.* **3.** *(pl.)* secret rites or ceremonies connected with the worship of certain deities of classical mythology, esp. the rites in honor of Dionysus, celebrated with wild dancing and singing, drinking, etc. [t. L: m.s. *orgia,* pl., t. Gk.]

o·ri·bi (ôr'ə bЎ, ôr'-), *n., pl.* **-bis.** a small tan-colored antelope, *Ourebia ourebi,* of South and East Africa, with spikelike horns. [t. S Afr. D, t. Hottentot]

o·ri·el (ôr'Ўəl), *n.* a bay window, usually semipolygonal, esp. in an upper story. [ME, t. OF: m. *oriol* porch, passage, gallery, ult. der. L *aureolus* gilded]

o·ri·ent (*n.; adj.* ôr'Ў ənt, ôr'Ў ĕnt'; *v.* ôr'Ў ĕnt'), *n.* **1.** the east; the eastern regions. **2. The Orient, a.** the East; the countries to the E (and SE) of the Mediterranean. **b.** the countries of Asia generally, especially E Asia. **3.** *Poetic.* shining brightness; radiance. **4.** the luster peculiar to the pearl. **5.** an orient pearl. —*adj.* **6.** rising; appearing as from beneath the horizon: *the orient sun.* **7.** *Now Poetic.* eastern or oriental. **8.** fine or precious, as gems, esp. pearls. —*v.t.* **9.** to place so as to face the east. **10.** to place in any definite position with reference to the points of the compass or other points: *to orient a building north and south.* **11.** to build (a church) with the chief altar to the east and the chief entrance to the west. **12.** to adjust with relation to, or bring into due relation to, surroundings, circumstances, facts, etc.: *to orient one's ideas to new conditions.* **13.** *Survey.* to turn a map or plane-table sheet so that the north direction on the map is parallel to the north direction on the ground. **14.** to direct to a particular object. —*v.i.* **15.** to turn toward the east, or in any specified direction. [ME, t. L: s. *oriens* the east, sunrise, n. use of ppr., rising]

Oriel

o·ri·en·tal (ôr'Ў ĕn'təl), *adj.* **1.** *(usually cap.)* of, pertaining to, or characteristic of the Orient or East. **2.** *(cap.)* *Zoogeog.* belonging to a division comprising southern Asia and the Malay Archipelago as far as and including the Philippines, Borneo, and Java. **3.** of the orient or east; eastern. **4.** (of gems) orient. **5.** designating sapphire varieties: *oriental amethyst.* —*n.* **6.** *(usually cap.)* a native or inhabitant of the Orient esp. one belonging to a yellow race. [ME, t. L: s. *orientālis*]

O·ri·en·tal·ism (ôr'Ў ĕn'tə lЎz'əm), *n.* **1.** an Oriental peculiarity. **2.** oriental character or characteristics. **3.** the knowledge and study of Oriental languages, literature, etc. Also, **orientalism.** —**O'·ri·en'tal·ist,** *n.*

O·ri·en·tal·ize (ôr'Ў ĕn'tə līz'), *v.t., v.i.,* -ized, -izing. to make or become oriental. Also, **orientalize.**

Oriental rug, any handmade rug or carpet woven, usually in one piece, in the Orient.

o·ri·en·tate (ôr'Ў ĕn tāt', ôr'Ў ĕn tāt'), *v.,* -tated, -tating. —*v.t.* **1.** to orient. —*v.i.* **2.** to face or turn toward the east, or in any specified direction; be oriented.

o·ri·en·ta·tion (ôr'Ў ĕn tā'shən), *n.* **1.** act or process of orienting. **2.** state of being oriented. **3.** *Psychol.* the ability to locate oneself in one's environment with reference to time, place, and people. **4.** the ascertainment of one's true position, as in a novel situation, with reference to new ideas, etc. **5.** *Chem.* **a.** the arrangement of atoms or radicals in a particular position due to electrical charges, etc. **b.** the determination of the position of substituted atoms or radicals in a compound.

O·ri·en·te (ô'rē ĕn'tĕ), *n.* a region in Ecuador, E of the Andes: a long-standing border dispute with Peru was declared settled in 1945.

or·i·fice (ôr'ə fЎs, ŏr'-), *n.* a mouth or aperture, as of a tube or pipe; a mouthlike opening or hole; a vent. [t. F, t. L: m.s. *ōrificium*]

or·i·flamme (ôr'ə flǎm', ŏr'-), *n.* **1.** the red banner of St. Denis, near Paris, carried before the early kings of France as a military ensign. **2.** any ensign or standard. [late ME *oriflam,* t. F: m. *oriflamme,* f. OF: *orie* golden (g. L *aureus*) + *flamme* FLAME]

orig., **1.** origin. **2.** original. **3.** originally.

or·i·gan (ôr'ə gən, ŏr'-), *n.* marjoram, esp. the Old World wild marjoram, *Origanum vulgare.* [ME, t. L: s. *orīganum,* t. Gk.: m. *orīganon*]

Or·i·gen (ôr'ə jĕn', -jən, ŏr'-), *n.* *(Origenes Adamantius),* A.D. c185–c254, Christian theologian, writer, and teacher, at Alexandria.

or·i·gin (ôr'ə jЎn, ŏr'-), *n.* **1.** that from which anything arises or is derived, the source: *to follow a stream to its origin.* **2.** rise or derivation from a particular source: *these and other reports of like origin.* **3.** the first stage of existence; the beginning: *the date of origin of a sect.* **4.** birth; parentage; extraction: *Scottish origin.* **5.** *Anat.* the point of derivation; the more fixed portion of a muscle. [t. L: s. *orīgo* beginning, source, rise]

o·rig·i·nal (ərĭj′ə nəl), *adj.* **1.** belonging or pertaining to the origin or beginning of something, or to a thing at its beginning: *the original binding.* **2.** new; fresh; novel: *an original way of advertising.* **3.** arising or proceeding from a thing itself, or independently of anything else. **4.** capable of or given to thinking or acting independently in self-suggested and individual ways: *an original thinker.* **5.** proceeding from a person as the inventor, maker, composer, or author: *original research.* **6.** being that from which a copy, a translation, or the like is made: *the original document is at Washington.* —*n.* **7.** a primary form or type from which varieties are derived. **8.** an original work, writing, or the like as opposed to any copy or imitation. **9.** the person or thing represented by a picture, description, etc. **10.** one who is original in his ways of thinking or acting. **11.** an eccentric person. **12.** *Archaic.* a source of being; an author or originator.

original gum, *Philately.* the mucilage put on the back of a stamp by the post office.

o·rig·i·nal·i·ty (ərĭj′ə nal′ə tĭ′), *n.*, *pl.* **-ties. 1.** the state or quality of being original. **2.** ability to think or act in an independent, individual manner. **3.** freshness or novelty, as of an idea, method, or performance.

o·rig·i·nal·ly (ərĭj′ə nəl′ĭ), *adv.* **1.** with respect to origin; by origin. **2.** at the origin; at first. **3.** in the first place; primarily. **4.** from the beginning. **5.** in an original, novel, or distinctively individual manner.

original sin, *Theol.* **1.** a depravity, or tendency to evil, held to be innate in mankind and transmitted from Adam to the race in consequence of his sin. **2.** *Rom. Cath. Theol.* the privation of sanctifying grace in consequence of Adam's sin.

o·rig·i·nate (ərĭj′ə nāt′), *v.*, **-nated, -nating.** —*v.i.* **1.** to take its origin or rise; arise; spring. —*v.t.* **2.** to give origin or rise to; initiate; invent. —**o·rig′i·na′tion,** *n.* —**o·rig′i·na′tor,** *n.* —**Syn. 2.** See **discover.**

o·rig·i·na·tive (ərĭj′ə nā′tĭv), *adj.* having or characterized by, the power of originating; creative. —**o·rig′i·na′tive·ly,** *adv.*

O·ri·no·co (ô/rē nō′kō), *n.* a large river in N South America, flowing from S Venezuela into the Atlantic. ab. 1600 mi.

o·ri·ole (ôr′Ĭ ōl′), *n.* **1.** any bird of the Old World passerine family *Oriolidae*, mostly bright-yellow with black on the head, wings and tail, as the golden oriole, *Oriolus oriolus*, of Europe and Africa. **2.** any of various brightly colored American passerine birds of the family *Iceridae*, not closely related to the true orioles of the Old World, as the Baltimore oriole, *Icterus galbula.* [t. ML: m.s. *oriolus*, var. of L *aureolus* golden]

O·ri·on (ō rī′ən), *n.*, *gen.* **Orionis** (ō rī′ō′nĭs, ōr′-). **1.** *Gk. Myth.* a giant and a hunter who pursued the Pleiades and was eventually slain by Artemis. He then became the giant constellation. **2.** *Astron.* a constellation, south of Gemini and Taurus, containing the bright supergiant stars Betelgeuse and Rigel, and a remarkable gaseous nebula.

O·ris·ka·ny (o rĭs′kə nĭ), *n.* a village in central New York, near Utica: battle, 1777. 1346 (1950).

o·ri·son (ôr′Ĭ zən, ōr′-), *n.* a prayer. [ME, t. OF, g. L *oratio* prayer. Cf. **oration.**]

O·ris·sa (ō rĭs′ə), *n.* a province in E India. 8,729,000 pop. (1941); 32,198 sq. mi. *Cap.:* Cuttack.

-orium. See **-ory**[2].

O·ri·za·ba (ō/rē sä′bä), *n.* **1.** a volcano in SE Mexico, in Veracruz state. 18,546 ft. **2.** a city near this peak. 47,910 (1940).

Or·jo·ni·kid·ze (ôr jô/nĭ kĕd′zĕ), *n.* Ordzhonikidze.

Ork·ney Islands (ôrk′nĭ), an island group off the NE tip of Scotland, comprising a county in Scotland. 21,600 pop. (est. 1946); 376 sq. mi. *Co. seat:* Kirkwall.

Or·lan·do (ôr län′dō; *for 1 also It.* ôr län′dô), *n.* **1.** **Vittorio Emanuele** (vĕt tô′ryô ĕ′mä nwĕ′lĕ), born 1860, Italian statesman. **2.** a city in central Florida: resort. 52,367 (1950).

orle (ôrl), *n. Her.* a narrow band within the shield and following the contour of its edge. [t. F, g. LL *ōrulum*, dim. of L *ōra* border]

Or·lé·a·nais (ôr lĕ ä nĕ′), *n.* a former province in N France. *Cap.:* Orléans.

Or·le·an·ist (ôr′lĬ ən ĭst), *n. French Hist.* an adherent of the Orleans family, which is descended from the younger brother of Louis XIV, and has furnished one sovereign, Louis Philippe (reigned 1830–48).

Or·lé·ans (ôr′lĬ ənz; *Fr.* ôr lĕ än′), *n.* **1.** a city in N France, on the Loire river: siege raised by Joan of Arc, 1428. 70,240 pop. (1946). **2. Louis Philippe Joseph** (lwē fē lēp′ zhō zĕf′), **Duc d',** (*Philippe Egalité*) 1747–1793, French political leader.

or·lon (ôr′lŏn), *n.* **1.** a synthetic fiber based on an acrylic resin, and woven from an extruded thermoplastic substance similar to nylon. It is more resistant to sunlight, heat, and chemical or fungicidal action than nylon. **2.** (*cap.*) a trademark for this material.

or·lop (ôr′lŏp), *n.* the lowest deck of a ship. [late ME, t. D: m. *overloop*, der. *overloopen* overrun, spread over; so called because it covers the ship's hold]

Or·mazd (ôr′məzd), *n. Zoroastrianism.* the cosmic principle, spirit, or person, in ceaseless conflict with the spirit of darkness and evil, Ahriman; Ahura Mazda.

Also, **Or′muzd.** [t. Pers., g. Avestan *Ahura Mazda* wise lord]

or·mer (ôr′mər), *n.* **1.** an ear shell, *Haliotis tuberculata*, a gastropod mollusk abundant in the Channel Islands. **2.** any ear shell. [t. F: m. *ormier* (g. L *auris maris* sea ear), b. with *mier* (g. L *merus* pure)]

or·mo·lu (ôr′mə lōō′), *n.* **1.** an alloy of copper and zinc, used to imitate gold. **2. a.** gold prepared for use in gilding. **b.** gilded metal. [t. F: m. *or moulu* ground gold, f. *or* (g. L *aurum* gold) + *moulu*, pp. of *moudre* grind (g. L *molere*)]

Or·muz (ôr′mŭz), *n.* Strait of. See **Hormuz.**

or·na·ment (*n.* ôr′nə mənt; *v.* ôr′nə mĕnt′), *n.* **1.** an accessory, article, or detail used to beautify the appearance or general effect: *architectural ornaments.* **2.** any adornment or means of adornment. **3.** a person who adds luster, as to surroundings, society, etc. **4.** act of adorning. **5.** state of being adorned. **6.** mere outward display. **7.** *Chiefly Eccles.* any accessory, adjunct, or equipment. **8.** *Music.* a tone or group of tones applied as decoration to a principal melodic tone. —*v.t.* **9.** to furnish with ornaments. **10.** to be an ornament to. t. L: s. *ornāmentum* equipment, ornament; r. ME *ornement*, t. OF]

or·na·men·tal (ôr′nə mĕn′təl), *adj.* **1.** used for ornament: *ornamental plants.* **2.** such as to ornament; decorative. **3.** of or pertaining to ornament. —*n.* **4.** something ornamental. **5.** a plant cultivated for decorative purposes. —**or′na·men·tal′i·ty,** *n.* —**or′na·men′tal·ly,** *adv.*

or·na·men·ta·tion (ôr′nə mĕn tā′shən), *n.* **1.** act of ornamenting. **2.** state of being ornamented. **3.** that with which a thing is ornamented.

or·nate (ôr nāt′), *adj.* **1.** elaborately adorned; sumptuously or showily splendid or fine. **2.** embellished with rhetoric, as a style or discourse. [ME, t. L: m.s. *ornātus*, pp., adorned] —**or·nate′ly,** *adv.* —**or·nate′ness,** *n.*

or·ner·y (ôr′nə rĬ), *adj. Chiefly U.S. Dial.* **1.** ugly in disposition or temper. **2.** stubborn. **3.** low or vile. **4.** ordinary; common. [contr. of **ordinary**]

or·nis (ôr′nĬs), *n.* an avifauna. [t. G, t. Gk.: bird]

ornith., 1. ornithological. **2.** ornithology.

or·nith·ic (ôr nĬth′ĭk), *adj.* of or pertaining to birds. [t. Gk.: m.s. *ornithikós* birdlike]

or·ni·thin (ôr′nə thĭn), *n.* an amino acid, $H_2N(CH_2)_3CH(NH)_2COOH$, obtained by hydrolysis of arginine.

ornitho-, a word element meaning "bird." Also, **or·nith-.** [t. Gk., comb. form of *órnis*]

or·ni·thoid (ôr′nə thoid′), *adj.* birdlike.

ornithol., 1. ornithological. **2.** ornithology.

or·ni·thol·o·gy (ôr′nə thŏl′ə jĬ), *n.* the branch of zoölogy that deals with birds. —**or·ni·tho·log·i·cal** (ôr′nə thə lŏj′ə kəl), *adj.* —**or·ni·thol′o·gist,** *n.*

or·ni·tho·pod (ôr′nə thə pŏd′, ôr nĭ′thə-), *n.* any of the *Ornithopoda*, a group of dinosaurs that walked erect on their hind feet. [t. NL: s. *Ornithopoda*, pl.; or f. ORNITHO- + -POD]

or·ni·thop·ter (ôr′nə thŏp′tər), *n.* a heavier-than-air craft sustained in and propelled through the air by flapping wings. [f. ORNITHO- + s. Gk. *pterón* wing]

or·ni·tho·rhyn·chus (ôr′nə thə rĭng′kəs), *n.* the duckbill. [t. NL, f. Gk.: *ornitho-* ORNITHO- + m. *rhýnchos* snout, beak]

or·ni·tho·sis (ôr′nə thō′sĬs), *n.* a disease of domestic pigeons and other birds, similar to psittacosis.

oro-, a word element meaning "mountain," as in *orography.* [t. Gk., comb. form of *óros*]

o·ro·ban·cha·ceous (ôr′ō băng kā′shəs, ŏr′ō-), *adj.* belonging to the *Orobanchaceae*, the widespread broom-rape family of parasitic herbs. [f. s. L *orobanchē* (t. Gk.: broom rape) + -ACEOUS]

o·rog·e·ny (ō rŏj′ə nĬ), *n. Geol.* the process of mountain-making or upheaval. —**or·o·gen·ic** (ôr′ə jĕn′Ĭk, ŏr′ə-), *adj.*

o·rog·ra·phy (ō rŏg′rə fĬ), *n.* that branch of physical geography that deals with mountains. —**or·o·graph·ic** (ôr′ə grăf′Ĭk, ŏr′ə-), **or·o·graph′i·cal,** *adj.*

o·ro·ide (ôr′ō′Ĭd′), *n.* an alloy containing copper, tin, etc., used to imitate gold. [t. F: f. *or* (g. L *aurum*) gold + -*oide* -OID]

o·rol·o·gy (ō rŏl′ə jĬ), *n.* the science of mountains. —**or·o·log·i·cal** (ôr′ə lŏj′ə kəl, ŏr′ə-), *adj.* —**o·rol′o·gist,** *n.*

o·rom·e·ter (ō rŏm′ə tər), *n.* an aneroid barometer with a scale giving elevations above sea level, used to determine altitudes of mountains, etc.

O·ron·tes (ō rŏn′tēz), *n.* a river flowing from the Lebanon valley N through NW Syria and SW past Antioch, Turkey into the Mediterranean. ab. 170 mi.

o·ro·phar·ynx (ôr′ō fâr′Ĭngks), *n.*, *pl.* **-pharynges** (-fə rĬn′jēz), **-pharynxes.** *Anat.* **1.** the space immediately beneath the mouth cavity. **2.** the pharynx as distinguished from the nasopharynx. [f. *oro-* (comb. form repr. L *ōs* mouth) + PHARYNX]

o·ro·tund (ôr′ə tŭnd′), *adj.* **1.** (of the voice or utterance) characterized by strength, fullness, richness, and clearness. **2.** (of a style of utterance) pompous or bombastic. [t. L: m. *ōre rotundō*, lit., with round mouth]

o·ro y pla·ta (ō′rō ē plä′tä), *Spanish.* gold and silver (motto of Montana).

O·roz·co (ō rôs′kō), *n.* **José Clemente** (hō sĕ′ klĕ mĕn′tĕ), 1883–1949, Mexican painter.

Or·pen (ôr′pən), *n.* **Sir William Newenham Montague,** 1878–1931, British painter.

or·phan (ôr′fən), *n.* **1.** a child bereaved by death of both parents, or, less commonly, of one parent. —*adj.* **2.** of or for orphans: *an orphan asylum.* **3.** bereaved of parents. —*v.t.* **4.** to bereave of parents or a parent. [late ME, t. LL: s. *orphanus,* t. Gk.: m. *orphanós* without parents, bereaved] —**or′phan·hood′,** *n.*

or·phan·age (ôr′fən ĭj), *n.* **1.** an institution for orphans. **2.** state of being an orphan. **3.** orphans collectively.

Or·phe·us (ôr′fī əs, -fūs), *n. Gk. Myth.* a son of Apollo and Calliope, a Thracian singer and player of the lyre. He followed his dead wife Eurydice to Hades and was allowed by Pluto, whom he had charmed by his music, to lead her out, provided that he did not look back. At the last moment he looked back and she was lost. —**Or·phe·an** (ôr fē′ən), *adj.*

Or·phic (ôr′fĭk), *adj.* **1.** of or pertaining to Orpheus. **2.** resembling the music attributed to Orpheus; entrancing. **3.** pertaining to a religious or philosophical school maintaining a form of the cult of Dionysus or Bacchus, ascribed to Orpheus as founder: *Orphic mysteries.* **4.** (*cap.* or *l.c.*) mystic; oracular.

Or·phism (ôr′fĭz əm), *n.* the religious or philosophical system of the Orphic school.

or·phrey (ôr′frĭ), *n., pl.* **-phreys. 1.** an ornamental band or border, esp. on an ecclesiastical vestment. **2.** *Now only Hist. or Archaic.* gold embroidery. **3.** *Now only Hist. or Archaic.* rich embroidery of any sort. **4.** a piece of richly embroidered stuff. [ME *orfreis,* t. OF, g. LL *aurifrisium,* for L *aurumphrygium* gold embroidery, lit., Phrygian gold]

or·pi·ment (ôr′pə mənt). *n.* a mineral, arsenic trisulfide, As_2S_3, found usually in soft yellow foliated masses, used as a pigment, etc. [ME, t. OF, t. L: m.s. *auripigmentum* gold pigment]

or·pine (ôr′pĭn), *n.* a crassulaceous perennial, *Sedum telephium,* bearing purplish flowers. Also, **or′pin.** [ME, t. F, back formation from *orpiment* ORPIMENT]

Or·ping·ton (ôr′pĭng tən), *n.* a modern breed of large white-skinned domestic fowls. [named after *Orpington,* town in Kent, southeastern England]

or·ra (ôr′ə, ŏr′ə), *adj. Scot.* odd; extra; occasional.

or·rer·y (ôr′ə rĭ, ŏr′-), *n., pl.* **-reries. 1.** an apparatus for representing the motions and phases of the planets, etc., in the solar system. **2.** any of certain similar machines, as a planetarium. [named after the Earl of *Orrery* (1676–1731), for whom it was first made]

or·ris (ôr′ĭs, ŏr′-), *n.* any of certain species of iris, as *Iris florentina,* with a fragrant rootstock. Also, **or′rice.** [unexplained var. of IRIS]

or·ris·root (ôr′ĭs rōōt′, -rŏŏt′, ŏr′-), *n.* the rootstock of the orris, used as a perfume, etc.

ort (ôrt), *n.* (*usually pl.*) a fragment of food left at a meal. [ME, c. LG *ort,* early mod. D *oorete,* f. *oor-* rejected (lit., out, from) + *ete* food. Cf. OE *or-,* *ǣt*]

Or·te·gal (ôr′tĕ gäl′), *n.* **Cape,** a cape in NW Spain, on the Bay of Biscay.

Or·te·ga y Gas·set (ôr tĕ′gä ē gäs sĕt′), **José** (hō-sě′), born 1883, Spanish philosopher and writer.

ortho-, **1.** a word element meaning "straight," "upright," "right," "correct," used in combination. **2.** *Chem.* **a.** a prefix indicating that acid of a series which contains most water. Cf. **meta-, pyro-.** **b.** a prefix applied to a salt of one of these acids: if the acid ends in *-ic,* the corresponding salt ends in *-ate,* as *orthoboric acid* (H_3BO_3) and *potassium orthoborate* (K_3BO_3); if the acid ends in *-ous,* the corresponding salt ends in *-ite,* as *orthoantimonous acid* (H_3SbO_3) and *potassium orthoantimonite* (K_3SbO_3). **c.** a prefix designating the 1.2 position in the benzene ring. [t. Gk., comb. form of *orthós* straight, upright, right, correct]

or·tho·bo·ric acid (ôr′thō bôr′ĭk). See **ortho-** (def. 2).

or·tho·cen·ter (ôr′thō sĕn′tər), *n. Geom.* the point of intersection of the altitudes of a triangle.

or·tho·ce·phal·ic (ôr′thō sə făl′ĭk), *adj.* having the relation between the height of the skull and the breadth or the length medium or intermediate. Also, **or·tho·ceph·a·lous** (ôr′thō sĕf′ə ləs). —**or′tho·ceph′a·ly,** *n.*

or·tho·chro·mat·ic (ôr′thō krō măt′ĭk), *adj. Photog.* **1.** pertaining to or representing the correct relations of colors, as in nature. **2.** designating a film or plate sensitive to yellow and green as well as to blue and violet.

or·tho·clase (ôr′thə klās′, -klāz′), *n.* a very common mineral of the feldspar group, potassium aluminum silicate, $KAlSi_3O_8$, occurring as an important constituent in many igneous rocks: used in the manufacture of porcelain. [f. ORTHO- + m.s. Gk. *klásis* cleavage]

or·tho·don·tia (ôr′thə dŏn′shə, -shĭ ə), *n.* the branch of dentistry that is concerned with the straightening of irregular teeth. [t. NL, f. Gk.: *ortho-* ORTHO- + s. *odoús* tooth + *-ia* -IA] —**or′tho·don′tic,** *adj.* —**or′tho·don′tist,** *n.*

or·tho·dox (ôr′thə dŏks′), *adj.* **1.** sound or correct in opinion or doctrine, esp. theological or religious doctrine. **2.** conforming to the Christian faith as represented in the primitive ecumenical creeds. **3.** (*cap.*) **a.** designating the Eastern or Greek Church. **b.** of or pertaining to the Greek Church. **4.** approved; conventional. [t. LL: s. *orthodoxus,* t. Gk.: m. *orthódoxos* right in opinion] —**or′tho·dox′ly,** *adv.*

Orthodox Church, the Christian church of the countries formerly comprised in the Eastern Roman Empire, and of countries evangelized from it, as Russia; the church or group of local and national Oriental churches in communion or doctrinal agreement with the Greek patriarchal see of Constantinople.

or·tho·dox·y (ôr′thə dŏk′sĭ), *n., pl.* **-doxies. 1.** orthodox belief or practice. **2.** orthodox character.

or·tho·ë·py (ôr thō′ə pĭ, ôr′thō-), *n.* the study of correct pronunciation. [t. Gk.: m.s. *orthoépeia* correctness of diction] —**or·tho·ëp·ic** (ôr′thō ĕp′ĭk), *adj.* —**or·tho′ë·pist,** *n.*

or·tho·gen·e·sis (ôr′thō jĕn′ə sĭs), *n.* **1.** *Biol.* the evolution of species in definite lines which are predetermined by the constitution of the germ plasm. **2.** *Sociol.* a hypothetical parallelism between the stages through which any culture necessarily passes, in spite of secondary conditioning factors. —**or·tho·ge·net·ic** (ôr′thō-jə nĕt′ĭk), *adj.*

or·thog·na·thous (ôr thŏg′nə thəs), *adj. Craniom.* straight-jawed; having the profile of the face vertical or nearly so; having a gnathic index below 98. See diag. under **facial angle.**

or·thog·o·nal (ôr thŏg′ə nəl), *adj.* **1.** *Math.* pertaining to or involving right angles or perpendicular lines: *an orthogonal projection.* **2.** *Crystall.* referable to a rectangular set of axes. [f. obs. *orthogon(ium)* (t. LL, t. Gk.: m. *orthogónion,* neut., right-angled) + -AL¹] —**or·thog′o·nal·ly,** *adv.*

or·thog·ra·pher (ôr thŏg′rə fər), *n.* **1.** one versed in orthography or spelling. **2.** one who spells correctly. Also, **or·thog′ra·phist.**

or·tho·graph·ic (ôr′thə grăf′ĭk), *adj.* **1.** pertaining to orthography. **2.** *Geom., etc.* orthogonal. Also, **or′tho·graph′i·cal.** —**or′tho·graph′i·cal·ly,** *adv.*

or·thog·ra·phy (ôr thŏg′rə fĭ), *n., pl.* **-phies. 1.** the art of writing words with the proper letters, according to accepted usage; correct spelling. **2.** that part of grammar which treats of letters and spelling. **3.** manner of spelling. **4.** an orthogonal projection, or an elevation drawn by means of it. [ME *orthographie,* t. L: m. *orthographia,* t. Gk.: correct writing]

or·tho·pe·dic (ôr′thə pē′dĭk), *adj.* pertaining to orthopedics. Also, **or′tho·pae′dic.**

or·tho·pe·dics (ôr′thə pē′dĭks), *n.* the correction or cure of deformities and diseases of the spine, bones, joints, muscles or other parts of the skeletal system in children or in persons of any age. Also, **or′tho·pae′dics, or·tho·pe′dy.** [f. *ortho-* + m.s. Gk. *país* child + -ICS]

or·tho·pe·dist (ôr′thə pē′dĭst), *n.* one skilled in orthopedics. Also, **or′tho·pae′dist.**

or·tho·phos·phor·ic acid (ôr′thō fŏs fôr′ĭk, -fŏr′ĭk), *Chem.* the tribasic acid of phosphorus in its valence of five, H_3PO_4, a colorless, crystalline compound, forming phosphates which are used in fertilizers.

or·tho·psy·chi·a·try (ôr′thō sī kī′ə trĭ), *n.* the science that concerns itself with the study and treatment of behavior disorders, esp., of young people. —**or·tho·psy·chi·at·ric** (ôr′thō sī kĭ ăt′rĭk), **or′tho·psy′chi·at′ri·cal,** *adj.* —**or′tho·psy·chi′a·trist,** *n.*

or·thop·ter (ôr thŏp′tər), *n.* ornithopter. [t. NL: s. *Orthoptera,* pl., f. Gk.: *ortho-* ORTHO- + *-pterá* wings]

or·thop·ter·on (ôr thŏp′tə rŏn′, -tə rən), *n.* an orthopterous insect.

or·thop·ter·ous (ôr thŏp′tər əs), *adj.* belonging or relating to the *Orthoptera,* an order of insects that includes the crickets, grasshoppers, cockroaches, etc., characterized usually by leathery fore wings and longitudinally folded, membranous hind wings. [t. NL: m. *orthopterus,* f. Gk.: *ortho-* ORTHO- + m. *-pteros* winged] —**or·thop′ter·an,** *adj., n.*

or·thop·tic (ôr thŏp′tĭk), *adj.* pertaining to or producing normal binocular vision.

orthoptic exercises, a method of exercising the eye and its muscles in order to cure strabismus or improve vision.

or·tho·rhom·bic (ôr′thə rŏm′bĭk), *adj. Crystall.* denoting or pertaining to a system of crystallization characterized by three unequal axes intersecting at right angles.

or·tho·scop·ic (ôr′thə skŏp′ĭk), *adj.* pertaining to, characterized by, or produced by normal vision; presenting objects correctly to the eye.

or·thos·ti·chy (ôr thŏs′tə kĭ), *n., pl.* **-chies.** *Bot.* **1.** a vertical rank or row. **2.** an arrangement of members, as leaves, at different heights on an axis so that their median planes coincide. [f. ORTHO- + m.s. Gk. *-stichía* alignment] —**or·thos′ti·chous,** *adj.*

or·tho·trop·ic (ôr′thə trŏp′ĭk), *adj. Bot.* noting, pertaining to, or exhibiting a mode of growth which is more or less vertical.

or·thot·ro·pism (ôr thŏt′rə pĭz′əm), *n. Bot.* orthotropic tendency or growth.

or·thot·ro·pous (ôr thŏt′rə pəs), *adj. Bot.* (of an ovule) straight and symmetrical, with the chalaza at the evident base and the micropyle at the opposite extremity.

Orthotropous ovule M. Micropyle; C. Chalaza; O. Ovule

Ort·ler (ôrt′lər), *n.* **1.** a range of the Alps in N Italy. **2.** the highest peak of this range and of the Eastern Alps. 12,802 ft.

or·to·lan (ôr′tə lən), *n.* **1.** an Old World bunting, *Emberiza hortulana,* esteemed as a table delicacy. **2.** the

---

b., blend of, blended; c., cognate with; d., dialect, dialectal; der., derived from; f., formed from; g., going back to; m., modification of; r., replacing; s., stem of; t., taken from; ?, perhaps. See the full key on inside cover.

bobolink. 3. the sora. [t. F, t. Pr.: lit. gardener (i.e. frequenting gardens), g. L *hortulānus* of gardens]

O·ru·ro (ô·rōō′rô), *n.* a city in W Bolivia: a former capital. 50,000 pop. (est. 1942); over 12,000 ft. high.

-ory[1], a suffix of adjectives meaning "having the function or effect of," as in *compulsory, contributory, declaratory, illusory.* [t. L: m.s. *-ōrius* (neut. *-ōrium;* see *-ORY*[2]), suffix of adjectives associated esp. with agent-nouns in *-or.* See *-OR*[2]]

-ory[2], a suffix of nouns denoting esp. a place or an instrument or thing for some purpose, as in *ambulatory, directory, dormitory, laboratory, purgatory.* [t. L: m. s. *-ōrium.* See *-ORY*[1]]

o·ryx (ôr′ĭks), *n., pl.* **oryxes,** (esp. *collectively*) **oryx.** a large African antelope, *Oryx beisa,* grayish with black markings, and having long, nearly straight horns. [ME, t. L, t. Gk.: pickax, oryx]

os[1] (ŏs), *n., pl.* **ossa** (ŏs′ə). *Anat., Zool.* a bone. [t. L]

os[2] (ŏs), *n., pl.* **ora** (ôr′ə). *Anat.* a mouth, opening, or entrance. [t. L: mouth]

os[3] (ōs), *n., pl.* **osar** (ō′sär). *Geol.* an esker, esp. when of great length. [t. Sw.: m. *as* (pl. *asar*) ridge]

Os, *Chem.* osmium.

OS, Old Saxon. Also, **OS., O.S.**

O/S, Old Style (calendar). Also, **o/s, O.S.**

o.s., out of stock.

O.S.A., Order of St. Augustine (Augustinian).

O·sage (ō′sāj), *n.* 1. a Siouan language closely related to Omaha. 2. a river flowing from E Kansas E to the Missouri river in central Missouri. ab. 500 mi.

Osage orange, 1. an ornamental moraceous tree, *Maclura pomifera,* native in Arkansas and adjacent regions, used for hedges. 2. its fruit, which resembles a warty orange.

O·sa·ka (ō·sä′kə; *Jap.* ô′säkä′), *n.* a seaport in S Japan, on Honshu island. 1,293,501 (1946).

O.S.B., Order of St. Benedict (Benedictine).

Os·born (ŏz′bərn), *n.* **Henry Fairfield,** 1857–1935, U.S. paleontologist and author.

Os·borne (ŏz′bərn), *n.* **Thomas Mott,** 1859–1926, U.S. prison reformer.

Os·can (ŏs′kən), *n.* 1. an ancient nationality of south-central Italy constituting a subdivision of the Italic branch (Oscan-Umbrians and Latins) of the Indo-European family. 2. their language, replaced by Latin.

Os·car II (ŏs′kər), 1829–1907, king of Sweden, 1872–1907, and of Norway, 1872–1905.

Os·ce·o·la (ŏs′ĭ·ō′lə), *n.* c1804–38, U. S. Indian chief, of the Seminole tribe.

os·cil·late (ŏs′ə·lāt′), *v.i.,* **-lated, -lating.** 1. to swing or move to and fro, as a pendulum does; vibrate. 2. to fluctuate between states, opinions, purposes, etc. 3. *Physics.* to have, produce, or generate oscillations: *a vacuum tube oscillates.* [t. L: m. s. *oscillātus,* pp., swung] —**Syn.** 1. See **swing**[1].

os·cil·la·tion (ŏs′ə·lā′shən), *n.* 1. act or fact of oscillating. 2. a single swing, or movement in one direction, of an oscillating body, etc. 3. fluctuation between states, opinions, etc. 4. *Physics.* **a.** a single forward and backward surge of electric charge. **b.** a rapid change in electromotive force. **c.** one complete cycle of an electric wave.

os·cil·la·tor (ŏs′ə·lā′tər), *n.* 1. a device or machine producing oscillations. 2. one who or that which oscillates.

os·cil·la·to·ry (ŏs′ə·lə·tōr′ĭ), *adj.* characterized by or involving oscillation.

os·cil·lo·graph (ə·sĭl′ə·grăf′, -gräf′), *n.* 1. an instrument for recording oscillations, esp. electric oscillations. 2. a device for recording the wave forms of changing currents, voltages or any other quantity which can be translated into electrical energy as, for example, sound waves. [f. s. L *oscillāre* swing + -(o)GRAPH]

os·cil·lo·scope (ə·sĭl′ə·skōp′), *n.* *Physics.* a device which makes the shape of a voltage or current wave visible on the screen of a cathode-ray tube, or other device.

os·cine (ŏs′ĭn, -īn), *adj.* of or pertaining to the *Oscines,* a large group of passerine birds, containing those with the most highly developed vocal organs, and commonly termed the singing birds. [back formation from *Oscines,* t.L (see def.)]

os·ci·tant (ŏs′ə·tənt), *adj.* 1. gaping; yawning. 2. drowsy; inattentive. [t. L: s. *oscitans,* ppr.] —**os·ci·tan·cy, os·ci·tance,** *n.*

os·cu·lant (ŏs′kyə·lənt), *adj.* 1. united by certain common characteristics. 2. *Zool.* adhering closely; embracing. [t. L: s. *osculans,* ppr., kissing]

os·cu·lar (ŏs′kyə·lər), *adj.* 1. pertaining to the mouth or kissing. [f. s. L *osculum* little mouth, kiss + -AR[1]]

os·cu·late (ŏs′kyə·lāt′), *v.,* **-lated, -lating.** —*v.t.* 1. to kiss. 2. to bring into close contact or union. 3. *Geom.* to touch so as to have three or more points in common at the point of contact. —*v.i.* 4. to kiss each other. 5. to come into close contact or union. 6. *Geom.* to osculate each other, as two curves. [t. L: m.s. *osculātus,* pp., kissed] —**os·cu·la·to·ry** (ŏs′kyə·lə·tōr′ĭ), *adj.*

os·cu·la·tion (ŏs′kyə·lā′shən), *n.* 1. kissing. 2. a kiss. 3. close contact. 4. *Geom.* the contact between two osculating curves or the like.

os·cu·lum (ŏs′kyə·ləm), *n., pl.* **-la** (-lə). a small mouth-like aperture, as of a sponge. [t. L, dim. of *ōs* mouth]

O.S.D., Order of St. Dominic (Dominican).

-ose[1], an adjective suffix meaning "full of," "abounding in," "given to," "like," as in *frondose, globose, jocose, otiose, verbose.* [t. L: m. *-ōsus.* Cf. *-OUS*]

-ose[2], a noun termination used to form chemical terms, esp. names of sugars and other carbohydrates, as *amylose, fructose, hexose, lactose,* and of proteid derivatives, as *proteose.* [abstracted from GLUCOSE]

Ö·sel (œ′zəl), *n.* German name of **Saaremaa.**

O.S.F., Order of St. Francis (Franciscan).

Osh·kosh (ŏsh′kŏsh), *n.* a city in E Wisconsin, on Lake Winnebago. 41,084 (1950).

o·sier (ō′zhər), *Chiefly Brit.* —*n.* 1. any of various willows, as *Salix viminalis* (the common **basket osier**) and *Salix purpurea* (**red osier**) with tough flexible twigs or branches which are used for wickerwork. 2. a twig from such a willow. —*adj.* 3. pertaining to or made of osiers. [ME, t. F]

O·si·ris (ō·sī′rĭs), *n.* one of the principal Egyptian gods, brother and husband of Isis, usually represented as a mummy wearing the crown of Upper Egypt.

-osis, *pl.* **-oses.** a noun suffix denoting action, process, state, condition, etc., as in *apotheosis, metamorphosis,* and in many pathological terms, as *necrosis, neurosis, sclerosis, tuberculosis.* [t. Gk., suffix forming nouns from verbs with infinitive in *-óein, -oûn*]

-osity, a noun suffix equivalent to **-ose** (or **-ous**) plus **-ity.** [f. **-OSE** + **-ITY,** repr. s. L *-ōsitas* and F *-osité*]

Os·ler (ōs′lər, ŏz′-), *n.* **Sir William,** 1849–1919, Canadian physician and professor of medicine.

Os·lo (ŏz′lō, ōs′-; *Nor.* ôōs′lōō), *n.* a seaport in and the capital of Norway, in the SE part at the head of **Oslo Fiord,** an inlet (ab. 75 mi. long) of the Skagerrak. 275,160 (est. 1939). Formerly, **Christiania.**

Os·man (ŏz′mən, ōs′-; *Turk.* ōs′män′), *n.* 1259–1326, Turkish sultan, founder of the Ottoman dynasty of rulers of Turkey. Also, **Othman.**

Os·man·li (ŏz·măn′lĭ, ōs-), *n., pl.* **-lis,** *adj.* —*n.* 1. an Ottoman. 2. Ottoman Turkish (language). —*adj.* 3. Ottoman. [t. Turk. See OTTOMAN]

os·mic (ŏz′mĭk), *adj.* *Chem.* of or containing osmium in its higher valences, esp. the tetravalent state.

os·mi·ous (ŏz′mĭ·əs), *adj.* *Chem.* of or containing osmium in its lower valences.

os·mi·um (ŏz′mĭ·əm), *n.* *Chem.* a hard, heavy metallic element used for electric-light filaments, etc., having the greatest density of any known material, and forming octavalent compounds, such as OsO_4, OsF_8. *Symbol:* Os; *at. wt.:* 190.2; *at. no.:* 76; *sp. gr.:* 22.48 at 20°C. [t. NL, der. Gk. *osmē* smell, odor; named from the penetrating odor of one of its oxides]

os·mo·sis (ŏz·mō′sĭs, ŏs-), *n.* *Phys. Chem., etc.* 1. the tendency of a fluid to pass through a semipermeable membrane into a solution where its concentration is lower, thus equalizing the conditions on either side of the membrane. 2. the diffusion of fluids through membranes or porous partitions. Cf. **endosmosis** and **exosmosis.** [t. NL, der. Gk. *ōsmós* a thrusting] —**os·mot·ic** (ŏz·mŏt′ĭk, ŏs-), *adj.* —**os·mot·i·cal·ly,** *adv.*

Os·na·brück (ŏz′nə·brŏŏk′; *Ger.* ōs′nä·brŷk′), *n.* a city in NW Germany, in Hanover. 107,081 (1939).

Os·na·burg (ŏz′nə·bûrg′), *n.* a heavy coarse cotton in a plain weave used for grain sacks and sports wear.

os·prey (ŏs′prĭ), *n., pl.* **-preys.** 1. a large hawk, *Pandion haliaetus,* which feeds on fish; the fish hawk. 2. a kind of feather used to trim hats. [ME *ospray(e),* t. F: m. *orfraie* (repr. L *ossifraga*), b. with L. See OSSIFRAGE]

Osprey, *Pandion haliaetus* (21 to 26 in. long, wingspread 4½ ft.)

OSS, Office of Strategic Services.

Os·sa (ŏs′ə), *n.* *Gk. Myth.* a mountain in E Greece, in Thessaly. When attacking the Olympian gods, the giants tried to reach heaven by piling Mount Pelion on Mount Olympus and Ossa on Pelion. 6405 ft.

os·se·in (ŏs′ĭn), *n.* *Biochem.* the organic basis of bone, which remains after the mineral matter has been removed by treatment with dilute acid. [f. s. L *osseus* bony + -IN[3]]

os·se·ous (ŏs′ĭ·əs), *adj.* 1. composed of, containing, or resembling bone; bony. 2. ossiferous. [t. L: m. *osseus* bony] —**os′se·ous·ly,** *adv.*

Os·se·tia (ō·sē′shə; *Russ.* ŏ·sĕt′ĭə), *n.* a region in the S Soviet Union in Europe, in Caucasia. —**Os·se′tian,** *adj.*

Os·sian (ŏsh′ən, ŏs′ĭ·ən), *n.* *Gaelic Legend.* a hero and poet of the third century.

Os·si·an·ic (ŏs′ĭ·ăn′ĭk, ŏsh′ĭ-), *adj.* 1. pertaining to, characteristic of, or resembling the poetry or rhythmic prose published by James Macpherson in 1762–63, as a translation of Ossian. 2. grandiloquent; bombastic.

os·si·cle (ŏs′ə·kəl), *n.* a little bone. [t. L: m.s. *ossiculum,* dim. of *os* bone]

Os·si·etz·ky (ŏs′ĭ·ĕts′kĭ), *n.* **Carl von** (kärl fən), 1889–1938, German pacifist leader.

os·sif·er·ous (ŏ·sĭf′ər·əs), *adj.* containing bones, as a deposit.

os·si·fi·ca·tion (ŏs′ə fə kā′shən), n. **1.** act or process of ossifying. **2.** the resulting state. **3.** that which is ossified.

os·si·frage (ŏs′ə frĭj), n. **1.** the osprey. **2.** the lammergeier. [t. L: m.s. *ossifragus*, masc., *ossifraga*, fem., lit., bonebreaker]

os·si·fy (ŏs′ə fī′), v., **-fied, -fying.** —v.t. **1.** to convert into, or harden like, bone. —v.i. **2.** to become bone or hard like bone. [f. s. L *os* bone + -(I)FY. Cf. F *ossifier*]

Os·si·ning (ŏs′ə nĭng), n. a village in SE New York, on the Hudson: the site of Sing Sing, a state prison. 16,098 (1950). Formerly, **Sing Sing.**

os·su·ar·y (ŏs′ŏ̄ ĕr′ĭ, ŏsh′-), n., pl. **-aries.** a place or receptacle for the bones of the dead. [t. LL: m.s. *ossuārium*, der. L *os* bone]

os·te·al (ŏs′tĭ əl), adj. osseous. [f. OSTE(O)- + -AL[1]]

os·te·i·tis (ŏs′tĭ ī′tĭs), n. Pathol. inflammation of the substance of bone. [f. OSTE(O)- + -ITIS]

Ost·end (ŏst ĕnd′), n. a seaport in NW Belgium. 44,303 (est. 1944). French, **Os·tende** (ŏs täNd′).

os·ten·si·ble (ŏs tĕn′sə bəl), adj. given out or outwardly appearing as such; professed; pretended. [t. F, f. s. L *ostensus*, pp., displayed + -*ible* -IBLE] —**os·ten′si·bly,** adv.

os·ten·sive (ŏs tĕn′sĭv), adj. **1.** manifestly demonstrative. **2.** ostensible. —**os·ten′sive·ly,** adv.

os·ten·ta·tion (ŏs′tĕn tā′shən), n. **1.** pretentious show; display intended to impress others. **2.** Obs. a show or display. Also, **os′ten·ta′tious·ness.** [ME, t. L: s. *ostentātio*.] —**Syn. 1.** See **show.**

os·ten·ta·tious (ŏs′tĕn tā′shəs), adj. **1.** characterized by or given to ostentation or pretentious show. **2.** (of actions, manner, qualities exhibited, etc.) intended to attract notice. —**os′ten·ta′tious·ly,** adv.

osteo-, a word element meaning "bone." Also, before vowels, **oste-.** [t. Gk., comb. form of *ostéon*]

os·te·o·blast (ŏs′tĭ ə blăst′), n. Anat. a bone-forming cell.

os·te·o·cla·sis (ŏs′tĭ ŏk′lə sĭs), n. **1.** Anat. the breaking down or absorption of osseous tissue. **2.** Surg. the fracturing of a bone to correct deformity. [t. NL, f. *osteo-* OSTEO- + m. Gk. *klásis* fracture]

os·te·o·clast (ŏs′tĭ ə klăst′), n. **1.** Anat. one of the large multinuclear cells in growing bone, and concerned in the absorption of osseous tissue, as in the formation of canals, etc. **2.** Surg. an instrument for effecting osteoclasis. [f. OSTEO- + m.s. Gk. *klastós* broken]

os·te·o·gen·e·sis (ŏs′tĭ ə jĕn′ə sĭs), n. Physiol. the formation of bone.

os·te·oid (ŏs′tĭ oid′), adj. bonelike. [f. OSTE(O)- + -OID]

os·te·ol·o·gy (ŏs′tĭ ŏl′ə jĭ), n. the branch of anatomy that treats of the skeleton and its parts. —**os·te·o·log·i·cal** (ŏs′tĭ ə lŏj′ə kəl), adj. —**os·te·ol′o·gist,** n.

os·te·o·ma (ŏs′tĭ ō′mə), n., pl. **-mas, -mata** (-mə tə). Pathol. a tumor composed of osseous tissue. [t. NL. See OSTEO-, -OMA]

os·te·o·my·e·li·tis (ŏs′tĭ ō mī′ə lī′tĭs), n. Pathol. a purulent inflammation of the bone.

os·te·o·path (ŏs′tĭ ə păth′), n. one who practices osteopathy. Also, **os·te·op·a·thist** (ŏs′tĭ ŏp′ə thĭst).

os·te·op·a·thy (ŏs′tĭ ŏp′ə thĭ), n. a theory of disease and a method of treatment resting upon the supposition that most diseases are due to deformation of some part of the body and can be cured by some kind of manipulation. —**os·te·o·path·ic** (ŏs′tĭ ə păth′ĭk), adj.

os·te·o·phyte (ŏs′tĭ ə fīt′), n. Pathol. a small osseous excrescence or outgrowth on bone. —**os·te·o·phyt·ic** (ŏs′tĭ ə fĭt′ĭk), adj.

os·te·o·plas·tic (ŏs′tĭ ə plăs′tĭk), adj. **1.** Surg. pertaining to osteoplasty. **2.** Physiol. pertaining to bone formation.

os·te·o·plas·ty (ŏs′tĭ ə plăs′tĭ), n. Surg. the transplanting or inserting of bone, or surgical reconstruction of bone to repair a defect or loss.

os·te·o·tome (ŏs′tĭ ə tōm′), n. Surg. a double-beveled chisellike instrument for cutting or dividing bone.

os·te·ot·o·my (ŏs′tĭ ŏt′ə mĭ), n., pl. **-mies.** Surg. the dividing of a bone, or the excision of part of it. —**os·te·ot′o·mist,** n.

Ös·ter·reich (œ′stər rīKH′), n. German name of **Austria.**

Os·ti·a (ŏs′tĭ ə; It. ô′styä), n. an ancient city of Latium at the mouth of the Tiber: the port of Rome.

os·ti·ar·y (ŏs′tĭ ĕr′ĭ), n., pl. **-aries. 1.** Rom. Cath. Ch. one ordained to the lowest of the four minor orders; a porter. **2.** a doorkeeper, as of a church. [ME, t. L: m. s. *ostiārius* doorkeeper]

os·ti·na·to (ŏs′tē nä′tō), n., pl. **-tos.** Music. a constantly recurring melodic fragment. [It.: lit., obstinate]

os·ti·ole (ŏs′tĭ ōl′), n. a small opening or orifice. [t. L: m.s. *ostiolum*, dim. of *ostium* door] —**os·ti·o·lar** (ŏs′tĭ ə lər), adj. or **os ti′-,** adj.

ost·ler (ŏs′lər), n. Now Rare. a hostler. [contr. of ME (h)osteler, t. OF. Cf. HOSTEL]

os·to·sis (ŏs tō′sĭs), n. Physiol. the formation of bone; ossification. [t. NL; see OST(EO)-, -OSIS]

Ost·preus·sen (ŏst′proi′sən), n. German name of **East Prussia.**

os·tra·cism (ŏs′trə sĭz′əm), n. **1.** the act of ostracizing. **2.** the fact or state of being ostracized. [t. Gk.: m.s. *ostrakismós*]

os·tra·cize (ŏs′trə sīz′), v.t., **-cized, -cizing. 1.** to banish (a person) from his native country; expatriate. **2.** to exclude by general consent from society, privileges, etc. **3.** Ancient Gk. Hist. to banish (a citizen) temporarily by public vote with ballots consisting of potsherds or tablets of earthenware. [t. Gk.: m.s. *ostrakizein* (def. 3), der. *óstrakon* potsherd]

os·trich (ŏs′trĭch, ôs′-), n. **1.** any of the large two-toed, swift-footed, flightless birds of the ratite genus *Struthio*, esp. the species *S. camelus*, the largest of existing birds, a native of Africa and Arabia, now extensively reared for the plumage. **2.** a rhea (**American ostrich**). [ME *ostrice*, t. OF: m. *ostruce*, g. LL *avi(s) strūthio*, f. *avis* bird + *strūthio* ostrich. t. Gk.: m. *strouthiōn*]

Os·tro·goth (ŏs′trə gŏth′), n. a member of the easterly division of the Goths, which maintained a monarchy in Italy from A.D. 493 to 555. [t. LL: s. *Ostrogothī*, pl., L *Austrogotī*, t. Goth.] —**Os′tro·goth′ic,** adj.

Ostrich. *Struthio camelus* (6 ft. long, including tail, 8 ft. high)

Os·ty·ak (ŏs′tĭ ăk′), n. a language of western Siberia, one of the Ugric languages of the Finno-Ugric family.

Os·we·go (ŏs wē′gō), n. a city in W New York: a port on Lake Ontario. 22,647 (1950).

Oswego tea, a North American labiate herb, *Monarda didyma*, bearing showy, bright red flowers.

OT, Old Testament. Also, **OT., O.T.**

ot-, var. of oto- before vowels.

o·tal·gi·a (ō tăl′jĭ ə), n. Pathol. earache. [t. NL, t. Gk.] —**o·tal′gic,** adj.

O·ta·ru (ō′tä rōō′), n. a seaport in N Japan, on Hokkaido island. 150,611 (1946).

O.T.C., 1. Officers' Training Camp. **2.** Brit. Officers' Training Corps.

O tem·po·ra! O mo·res! (ō tĕm′pə rə ō mōr′ēz), Latin. O the times! O the customs!

O·thel·lo (ō thĕl′ō, ə-), n. a tragedy by Shakespeare (acted 1604).

oth·er (ŭth′ər), adj. **1.** additional or further: *he and one other person.* **2.** different or distinct from the one or ones mentioned or implied: *in some other city.* **3.** different in nature or kind: *I would not have him other than he is.* **4.** being the remaining one of two or more: *the other hand.* **5.** (with plural nouns) being the remaining ones of a number: *the other men.* **6.** former: *men of other days.* **7. the other day** (night, etc.), a day (night, etc.) or two ago. **8. every other,** every alternate: *a meeting every other week.* —pron. **9.** the other one: *each praises the other.* **10.** another person or thing. **11. of all others,** above or beyond all others. **12.** some person or thing else: *some day or other.* **13.** otherwise. [ME; OE ōther, c. G ander; akin to Skt. antara] —**oth′er·ness,** n.

oth·er·guess (ŭth′ər gĕs′), adj. **1.** Archaic or Brit. Dial. of another kind. —adv. **2.** otherwise. [assimilatory var. of othergets, var. of othergates otherwise]

oth·er·where (ŭth′ər hwâr′), adv. Archaic or Dial. elsewhere.

oth·er·while (ŭth′ər hwīl′), adv. Archaic or Dial. **1.** at another time or other times. **2.** sometimes. Also, **oth′er·whiles′.**

oth·er·wise (ŭth′ər wīz′), adv. **1.** under other circumstances. **2.** in another manner; differently. **3.** in other respects: *an otherwise happy life.* —adj. **4.** other or different; of another nature or kind. **5.** that would otherwise be or exist. [ME other wis (two words), OE (on) ōthre wīsan in other manner. See OTHER, WISE[2]]

other world, the world of the dead; future world.

oth·er·world·ly (ŭth′ər wûrld′lĭ), adj. of, pertaining to, or devoted to another world, as the world of imagination, or the world to come. —**oth′er·world′li·ness,** n.

O·thin (ō′thĭn), n. Scand. Myth. Odin.

Oth·man (ŏth′mən; for 1 also Arab. ŏŏth män′), n., pl. **-mans. 1.** Osman. **2.** Ottoman (defs. 3, 4).

O·tho I (ō′thō), Otto I.

o·tic (ō′tĭk, ŏt′ĭk), adj. Anat., etc. of or pertaining to the ear; auricular. [t. Gk.: m.s. *ōtikós*]

-otic, an adjective suffix meaning: **1.** "suffering from," as in *neurotic.* **2.** "producing," as in *hypnotic.* **3.** "resembling," as in *Quixotic.* [t. Gk.: m.s. *-ōtikós*]

o·ti·ose (ō′shĭ ōs′, -tĭ-), adj. **1.** at leisure; idle; indolent. **2.** ineffective or futile. **3.** superfluous or useless. [t. L: m.s. *ōtiōsus*] —**o′ti·ose′ly,** adv. —**o·ti·os·i·ty** (ō′shĭ ŏs′ə tĭ, ō′tĭ-), n.

O·tis (ō′tĭs), n. **James,** 1725–83, American patriot.

o·ti·tis (ō tī′tĭs), n. Pathol. inflammation of the ear.

oto-, a word element meaning "ear." [t. Gk., comb. form of *oûs*]

o·to·cyst (ō′tə sĭst), n. a statocyst.

o·to·lar·yn·gol·o·gy (ō′tō lăr′ĭng gŏl′ə jĭ), n. the branch of medicine dealing with the ear and throat.

o·to·lith (ō′tə lĭth), n. Anat., Zool. a calcareous concretion in the internal ear of vertebrates and in the balancing organ of some invertebrates.

o·tol·o·gy (ō tŏl′ə jĭ), n. the science of the ear and its diseases. —**o·tol′o·gist,** n.

o·to·scope (ō'tə·skōp/), *n.* *Med.* **1.** an instrument for examining the external canal and tympanic membrane of the ear. **2.** an instrument for auscultation in the ear.

O·tran·to (ō·trän'tō; *It.* ô'trän·tō'), *n.* **Strait of,** a strait between SE Italy and Albania, connecting the Adriatic and the Mediterranean. 44 mi. wide.

ot·ta·va ri·ma (ŏt·tä'vä rē'mä), *Pros.* an Italian stanza of eight lines, each of eleven syllables (or, in the English adaptation, of ten or eleven syllables), the first six lines riming alternately and the last two forming a couplet with a different rime: used in Keats's *Isabella* and Byron's *Don Juan.* [It.: octave rime]

Ot·ta·wa (ŏt'ə·wə), *n.* **1.** the capital of Canada, in SE Ontario. 154,951; with suburbs, 215,022 (1941). **2.** a river in SE Canada, flowing generally SE along the boundary between Ontario and Quebec into the St. Lawrence at Montreal. 685 mi. **3.** a tribe of Algonquian Indians of Canada, forced into the Lake Superior and Lake Michigan regions by the Iroquois confederacy. **4.** a member of this tribe. [t. Canadian F: m. *Otana, Otawa,* t. d. Ojibwa (Cree, Ottawa, Chippewa): m. *adaawe* to trade]

ot·ter (ŏt'ər), *n., pl.* **-ters,** (*esp. collectively*) **-ter.** any of the various aquatic, fur-bearing, carnivorous musteline mammals of the genus *Lutra* and allied genera, with webbed feet, adapted for swimming, and a long tail slightly flattened horizontally, acting as a rudder, as *L. vulgaris,* of Europe, which in Great Britain is much hunted with dogs, and *L. canadensis,* of the U.S. and Canada, and the sea otter. [ME *oter,* OE *oter, ot(o)r,* c. D and G *otter*]

Otter, *Lutra canadensis*
(Total length 3½ ft., tail 1 ft.)

Ot·ter·burn (ŏt'ər·bûrn/), *n.* a village in NE England, in Northumberland: battle of Chevy Chase, 1388.

Ot·to I (ŏt'ō; *Ger.* ôt'ō), ("*the Great*") A.D. 912–973, German king, A.D. 936–973, and emperor of the Holy Roman Empire, A.D. 962–973. Also, **Otho I.**

Ot·to·man (ŏt'ə·mən), *adj. n., pl.* **-mans.** —*adj.* **1.** of or pertaining to the Turkish dynasty or empire founded about 1300 by Osman I, and replaced in 1922 by the republic of Turkey under Mustapha Kemal. **2.** of or pertaining to the lands, peoples, and possessions of the Ottoman Empire. —*n.* **3.** a Turk. **4.** a Turk of the family or tribe of Osman. **5.** (*l.c.*) a kind of divan or sofa, with or without a back. **6.** (*l.c.*) a low cushioned seat without back or arms. **7.** (*l.c.*) a cushioned footstool. **8.** (*l.c.*) a corded silk or rayon fabric with large cotton cord for filling. Also, **Othman** for 3, 4. [t. F, t. It.: named after the founder of the empire (Ar. *'Othmān*)]

Ottoman Empire, a former Turkish sultanate which held sway over large dominions in Asia, Africa, and Europe for more than six centuries until its collapse after World War I: at its most extensive it included (with Turkey) the Barbary States, Egypt, Arabia, the Balkan Peninsula, etc. *Cap.*: Constantinople. Also, **Turkish Empire.**

Ot·tum·wa (ə·tŭm'wə), *n.* a city in SE Iowa, on the Des Moines river. 33,631 (1950).

Ot·way (ŏt'wā), *n.* **Thomas,** 1652–85, British dramatist.

oua·ba·in (wä·bä'ĭn), *n.* *Pharm.* a cardiac glucoside derived from *Strophanthus gratus.*

Ouach·i·ta (wŏsh'ə·tô', wôsh'-), *n.* **1.** a river flowing from W Arkansas SE through NE Louisiana to the Red river. 605 mi. **2.** a former North American Indian tribe, apparently of the Caddoan stock, of NE Louisiana (not to be confused with the Wichita). Also, **Washita.**

oua·na·niche (wä/nə·nēsh/; *Fr.* wȧ·nä–), *n., pl.* **-niche.** a fresh-water salmon, *Salmo Salar ouananiche,* of the Saguenay River, Quebec, and neighboring waters. [t. Canadian F, f. Montagnais: *awanas* salmon + -*iš* little]

ou·bli·ette (ōō/blĭ·ĕt/), *n.* a secret dungeon with an opening only at the top, as in certain old castles. [t. F, der. *oublier* forget, g. Rom. *oblītāre,* der. L *oblīviscī*]

ouch¹ (ouch), *interj.* an exclamation expressing sudden pain. [t. G: m. *autsch*]

ouch² (ouch), *Archaic.* —*n.* **1.** a clasp, buckle, or brooch, esp. one worn for ornament. **2.** the setting of a precious stone. —*v.t.* **3.** to adorn with or as with ouches. [ME *ouche,* for *nouche* (*a nouche* being taken as *an ouche*). Cf. LL *nusca,* OHG *nuscha* buckle, ult. of Celtic orig.]

Oudh (oud), *n.* a part of the United Provinces of Agra and Oudh in N India. 14,114,000 pop. (1941); 24,071 sq. mi.

Oues·sant (wĕ·sän'), *n.* French name of **Ushant.**

ought¹ (ôt), *v. aux.* **1.** was (were) or am (is, are) bound in duty or moral obligation: *every citizen ought to help.* **2.** was (or am) bound or required on any ground, as of justice, propriety, probability, expediency, fitness, or the like (usually fol. by an infinitive with *to* or having the infinitive omitted but understood): *he ought to be punished.* —*n.* **3.** duty or obligation. [ME *ought, aught,* etc., OE *āhte,* pret. of *āgan* OWE] —**Syn. 1.** See **must¹.**

ought² (ôt), *n.* a cipher (0). [var. of NOUGHT, *a nought* being taken as *an ought*]

ought³ (ôt), *n., adv.* aught¹.

Oui·da (wē'də), *n.* pen name of **Louise de la Ramée.**

oui·ja (wē'jə), *n.* a device consisting of a small board on legs, which rests on a larger board marked with words, letters of the alphabet, etc., and which, by moving over the larger board and touching the words, letters, etc., while the fingers of mediums or others rest lightly upon it, is employed to give answers, messages, etc. [f. F *oui* yes + G *ja* yes]

ounce¹ (ouns), *n.* **1.** a unit of weight equal to 437.5 grains or ⅟₁₆ lb. avoirdupois. **2.** a unit of 480 grains, ⅟₁₂ lb. troy or apothecaries' weight. **3.** a fluid ounce. **4.** a small quantity or portion. [ME *unce,* t. OF, g. L *uncia* twelfth part, inch, ounce. Cf. INCH.]

ounce² (ouns), *n.* a long-haired leopardlike feline, *Panthera uncia,* inhabiting the mountain ranges of central Asia; snow leopard. [ME *once,* t. OF, var. of *lonce* (taken as *l'once* the ounce), g. L *lynx* LYNX]

Ounce, *Panthera uncia*
(6 to 6½ ft. long, tail 3 ft.)

our (our), *pron. or adj.* the possessive form corresponding to *we* and *us,* used before a noun. Cf. **ours.** [ME *oure,* OE *ūre,* gen. pl. See US]

ou·ra·ri (ōō·rä'rē), *n.* curare.

Our Lady, the Virgin Mary.

ours (ourz), *pron.* form of *our* used predicatively or without a noun following.

our·self (our·sĕlf'), *pron.* a form corresponding to *ourselves,* used of a single person, esp. (like *we* for *I*) in the regal or formal style.

our·selves (our·sĕlvz'), *pron. pl.* **1.** a substitute for reflexive of *us.* **2.** an intensifier of *we* or *us.*

-ous, 1. an adjective suffix meaning "full of," "abounding in," "given to," "characterized by," "having," "of the nature of," "like," etc.: *glorious, joyous, mucous, nervous, sonorous, wondrous.* **2.** a suffix used in chemical terms (as compared with -*ic,* -*ous*) to imply a larger proportion of the element indicated by the word, as *stannous chloride,* SnCl₂, and *stannic chloride,* SnCl₄. In other words, -*ous* implies a lower valence than in the case of a corresponding term in -*ic.* Also, **-eous, -ious.** [ME, t. OF, g. L -*ōsus;* often used to repr. L -*us,* adj., Gk. -*os,* adj.; in a few words (e.g. *wondrous*) it is attached to native stems]

Ouse (ōōz), *n.* **1.** a river in NE England, in Yorkshire, flowing SE to the Humber. 57 mi. **2.** a river in E England, flowing NE to the Wash. ab. 160 mi.

ou·sel (ōō'zəl), *n.* ouzel.

oust (oust), *v.t.* **1.** to expel from a place or position occupied. **2.** *Law.* to eject; dispossess. [t. AF: s. *ouster* remove, g. L *obstāre* be in the way, protect against]

oust·er (ous'tər), *n.* **1.** *Law.* a. ejection; dispossession. b. a wrongful exclusion from real property. **2.** one who ousts. [t. AF, n. use of inf. See OUST]

out (out), *adv.* **1.** forth from, away from, or not in a place, position, state, etc.: *out of fashion.* **2.** away from one's home, country, etc.: *to set out on a journey.* **3.** to exhaustion, extinction, or conclusion; to the end; so as to finish or exhaust or be exhausted; so as to bring to naught or render useless: *to pump out a well.* **4.** to or at an end or conclusion: *to fight it out.* **5.** no longer or not burning or furnishing light; extinguished: *the lamp went out.* **6.** not in vogue or fashion: *that style has gone out.* **7.** into or in public notice or knowledge: *the book came out in May.* **8.** seeking openly and energetically to do or have: *to try out for the team.* **9.** into or in society: *a young girl who came out last season.* **10.** not in present or personal possession or use; let for hire, or placed at interest: *let out for a year.* **11.** on strike: *the miners are going out.* **12.** so as to project or extend: *to stretch out.* **13.** into or in existence, activity, or outward manifestation: *fever broke out.* **14.** from a source, ground or cause, material, etc. (with *of*): *made out of scraps.* **15.** from a state of composure, satisfaction, or harmony: *to feel put out.* **16.** in or into a state of confusion, vexation, dispute, variance, or unfriendliness: *to fall out about trifles.* **17.** so as to deprive or be deprived (with *of*): *to cheat out of money.* **18.** having used the last (with *of*): *to run out of coal.* **19.** from a number, stock, or store: *to pick out.* **20.** aloud or loudly: *to call out.* **21.** with completeness or effectiveness: *to fit out.* **22.** thoroughly; completely; entirely. **23.** *Colloq.* out along; out on: *out Broadway.* **24.** *Baseball, Cricket, etc.* from a turn at bat: *he struck out.* **25. out and away,** in a preëminent degree; by far. —*adj.* **26.** external; exterior; outer. **27.** outlying. **28.** *Baseball, etc.* not having its inning: *the out side.* **29.** away from one's work: *to be out on account of illness.* **30.** exposed; made bare, as by tears in one's clothing: *out at the knees.* **31.** beyond fixed or regular limits: *the floods are out.* **32.** beyond the usual range: *an out size.* **33.** astray from what is correct: *out in one's calculations.* **34.** not in practice; unskilful from lack of practice: *your bow hand is out.* **35.** at a pecuniary loss: *to be out ten dollars.* **36.** removed from or not in effective operation, or play, a turn at bat, or the like, as in a game. **37.** not in office or employment; unemployed; disengaged: *a butler out of service.* **38.** at variance; at odds; unfriendly: *be not out with me.* **39. out of,** foaled by (a dam). **40. out of one's mind,** insane; crazed; crazy. —*prep.* **41.** out or forth from (now used chiefly after *from* or in certain expressions): *out the door, out the win-*

dow. **42.** outside of: on the exterior of; beyond (now chiefly in certain expressions): *out that wall*. —*interj.* **43.** Begone! away! **44.** *Archaic or Dial.* an exclamation of abhorrence, indignation, reproach, or grief: *out upon you!* —*n.* **45.** projection, or projecting corners: *ins and outs*. **46.** a means of escaping from a place, punishment, retribution, responsibility, etc.: *he always left himself an out*. **47.** *Baseball.* **a.** a putout. **b.** an outward curve. **48.** *Tennis.* a return which lands outside the court. **49.** *Polit.* a person not in office or political power (cf. *in*). **50.** *Colloq.* (*pl.*) odds; bad terms: *at outs with everyone*. **51.** *Printing.* **a.** the omission of a word or words. **b.** that which is omitted. **52.** *Colloq. or Dial.* an outing. —*v.i.* **53.** to go or come out: *murder will out*. **54.** to come out with; bring out; utter. —*v.t.* **55.** to put out; expel; discharge; oust. [ME; OE *ūt*, c. D *uit*, G *aus*, Icel. and Goth. *ūt*]

out-, prefixal use of **out**, *adv.*, *prep.*, or *adj.*, occurring in various senses in compounds, as in *outcast*, *outcome*, *outside*, and serving also to form many transitive verbs denoting a going beyond, surpassing, or outdoing in the particular action indicated, as in *outbid*, *outdo*, *outgeneral*, *outlast*, *outstay*, *outrate*, and many other words in which the meaning is readily perceived, the more important of these being entered below.

out·age (ou′tǐj), *n.* **1.** an outlet. **2.** a quantity lost or lacking, as from a container. [f. OUT + -AGE]

out-and-out (out′ənd out′), *adj.* thoroughgoing; thorough; complete; unqualified.

out·ar·gue (out är′gū), *v.t.*, **-gued, -guing.** to outdo or defeat in arguing.

out·bal·ance (out băl′əns), *v.t.*, **-anced, -ancing.** to outweigh.

out·bid (out bǐd′), *v.t.*, **-bid, -bidden** or **-bid, -bidding.** to outdo in bidding.

out·board (out′bōrd′), *adv.*, *adj.* *Naut.* on the outside, or away from the center, of a ship or boat.

outboard motor, a small portable gasoline engine with propeller and tiller, clamped on the stern of a boat.

out·bound (out′bound′), *adj.* outward bound.

out·brave (out brāv′), *v.t.*, **-braved, -braving.** **1.** to surpass in bravery or daring. **2.** to surpass in beauty, splendor, etc.

out·break (out′brāk′), *n.* **1.** a breaking out; an outburst. **2.** a sudden and active manifestation. **3.** a public disturbance; a riot; an insurrection.

out·breed (out brēd′), *v.t.*, **-bred, -breeding.** to breed outside the limits of the family, within a breed or variety. —**out′breed′ing,** *n.*

out·build (out bǐld′), *v.t.*, **-built, -building.** to exceed in building, or in durability of building.

out·build·ing (out′bǐl′dǐng), *n.* a detached building subordinate to a main building.

out·burst (out′bûrst′), *n.* **1.** a bursting forth. **2.** a sudden and violent outpouring: *an outburst of tears*.

out·cast (out′kăst′, -käst′), *n.* **1.** a person who is cast out, as from home or society. **2.** a vagabond; homeless wanderer. **3.** rejected matter; refuse. **4.** *Scot.* a falling out; quarrel. —*adj.* **5.** cast out, as from one's home or society. **6.** pertaining to or characteristic of an outcast: *outcast misery*. **7.** rejected or discarded.

out·caste (out′kăst′, -käst′), *n.* **1.** a person of no caste. **2.** (in India) one who has forfeited membership in his caste.

out·class (out klăs′, -kläs′), *v.t.* to surpass in class or grade; be distinctly ahead of (a competitor, etc.).

out·come (out′kŭm′), *n.* that which results from something; the consequence or issue. —**Syn.** See **end¹**.

out·crop (*n.* out′krŏp′; *v.* out krŏp′), *n.*, *v.*, **-cropped, -cropping.** —*n.* **1.** a cropping out, as of a stratum or vein at the surface of the earth. **2.** the emerging part. —*v.i.* **3.** to crop out, as strata.

out·cross·ing (out′krôs′ǐng, -krŏs′ǐng), *n.* breeding of unrelated animals or plants within a variety or breed.

out·cry (*n.* out′krī′; *v.* out krī′), *n.*, *pl.* **-cries,** *v.*, **-cried, -crying.** —*n.* **1.** a crying out. **2.** a cry of distress, indignation, or the like. **3.** loud clamor. **4.** an auction. —*v.t.* **5.** to outdo in crying; cry louder than.

out·curve (out′kûrv′), *n.* *Baseball.* an outshoot.

out·date (out dāt′), *v.t.*, **-dated, -dating.** to put out of date; make antiquated or obsolete. —**out·dat′ed,** *adj.*

out·dis·tance (out dǐs′təns), *v.t.*, **-tanced, -tancing.** to distance completely; leave far behind; outstrip.

out·do (out dōō′), *v.t.*, **-did, -done, -doing.** to surpass in doing or performance; surpass. —**Syn.** See **excel**.

out·door (out′dōr′), *adj.* **1.** occurring or used out of doors. **2.** *Brit.* outside of a poorhouse, hospital, etc.

out·doors (out dōrz′), *adv.* **1.** out of doors; in the open air. —*n.* **2.** the world outside of houses; open air.

out·er (ou′tər), *adj.* further out; exterior; external; of or pertaining to the outside. [compar. of OUT]

Outer Mongolia, former name of **Mongolian People's Republic.**

out·er·most (ou′tər mōst′, -məst), *adj.* furthest out; remotest from the interior or center. [f. OUTER + -MOST]

out·face (out fās′), *v.t.*, **-faced, -facing.** **1.** to face or stare down. **2.** to face or confront boldly; defy.

out·fall (out′fôl′), *n.* the outlet or place of discharge of a river, drain, sewer, etc.

out·field (out′fēld′), *n.* **1.** *Baseball.* **a.** the part of the field beyond the diamond or infield. **b.** the players stationed in it. **2.** *Cricket.* the part of the field farthest from the batsman. **3.** the outlying land of a farm, esp. beyond the enclosed land. **4.** an outlying region.

out·field·er (out′fēl′dər), *n.* *Baseball, Cricket.* one of the players stationed in the outfield.

out·fit (out′fǐt′), *n.*, *v.*, **-fitted, -fitting.** —*n.* **1.** an assemblage of articles for fitting out or equipping: *an explorer's outfit*. **2.** a set of articles for any purpose: *a cooking outfit*. **3.** *U.S. Colloq.* a group associated in any undertaking, as a military body, etc. **4.** *U.S. Colloq.* a party, company, or set. **5.** the act of fitting out or equipping, as for a voyage, journey, or expedition, or for any purpose. **6.** the mental or moral equipment. —*v.t.* **7.** to furnish with an outfit; fit out; equip. —*v.i.* **8.** to furnish oneself with an outfit. **—out′fit′ter,** *n.*

out·flank (out flăngk′), *v.t.* **1.** to go or extend beyond the flank of (an opposing army, etc.). **2.** to turn the flank of.

out·flow (out′flō′), *n.* **1.** the act of flowing out. **2.** that which flows out. **3.** any outward movement.

out·fly (out flī′), *v.t.*, **-flew, -flown, -flying.** **1.** to surpass or outstrip in flying. **2.** to fly out or forth.

out·foot (out fŏŏt′), *v.t.* **1.** (of one boat) to excel (another) in speed. **2.** to surpass in running, walking, dancing, etc.

out·frown (out froun′), *v.t.* to outdo in frowning; frown down.

out·gen·er·al (out jĕn′ər əl), *v.t.*, **-aled, -aling** or (*esp. Brit.*) **-alled, -alling.** to outdo in generalship.

out·go (*n.* out′gō′; *v.* out gō′), *n.*, *pl.* **-goes,** *v.*, **-went, gone, going.** —*n.* **1.** a going out. **2.** expenditure. **3.** that which goes out; outflow. —*v.t.* **4.** to outstrip in going; go faster than. **5.** to go beyond or exceed. **6.** to surpass, excel, or outdo. —*v.i.* **7.** *Obs.* to go out.

out·go·ing (out′gō′ǐng), *adj.* **1.** going out; departing: *outgoing trains.* —*n.* **2.** *Chiefly Brit.* (*usually pl.*) an amount of money expended. **3.** a going out. **4.** that which goes out; an effluence.

out·group (out′grŏŏp′), *n.* *Sociol.* everyone not belonging to an in-group.

out·grow (out grō′), *v.t.*, **-grew, -grown, -growing. 1.** to grow too large for. **2.** to leave behind or lose in the changes incident to development or the passage of time: *to outgrow a bad reputation.* **3.** to surpass in growing. —*v.i.* **4.** to grow out; protrude.

out·growth (out′grōth′), *n.* **1.** a natural development, product, or result. **2.** an additional, supplementary result. **3.** a growing out or forth. **4.** that which grows out; an offshoot; an excrescence.

out·guess (out gĕs′), *v.t.* to outwit.

out·haul (out′hôl′), *n.* *Naut.* a rope used for hauling out a sail on a boom, yard, etc.

out·her·od (out hĕr′əd), *v.t.* to outdo (Herod or any other person) in extravagance or excess.

out·house (out′hous′), *n.* **1.** an outbuilding. **2.** an outside privy.

out·ing (ou′tǐng), *n.* **1.** an excursion or pleasure trip. **2.** the part of the sea out from the shore.

outing flannel, a light cotton flannel with a short nap.

out·land (*n.* out′lănd′, *adj.* out′lănd′, -lənd), *n.* **1.** outlying land, as of an estate. **2.** *Archaic.* a foreign land. —*adj.* **3.** outlying, as districts. **4.** *Archaic.* foreign. [ME; OE *ūtland*]

out·land·er (out′lăn′dər), **1.** a foreigner; an alien. **2.** *Colloq.* an outsider.

out·land·ish (out lăn′dǐsh), *adj.* **1.** freakishly or grotesquely strange or odd, as appearance, dress, objects, ideas, practices, etc.; bizarre; barbarous. **2.** foreign-looking. **3.** out-of-the-way, as places. **4.** *Archaic.* foreign. —**out·land′ish·ly,** *adv.* —**out·land′ish·ness,** *n.*

out·last (out lăst′, -läst′), *v.t.* to last longer than.

out·law (out′lô′), *n.* **1.** one excluded from the benefits and protection of the law. **2.** one under sentence of outlawry. **3.** a habitual criminal. —*v.t.* **4.** to deprive of the benefits and protection of the law, as a person. **5.** to remove from legal jurisdiction; deprive of legal force. **6.** to prohibit. [ME *outlawe*, OE *ūtlage*, t. Scand.; cf. Icel. *ūtlagi*]

out·law·ry (out′lô′rǐ), *n.*, *pl.* **-ries. 1.** the act or process of outlawing. **2.** the state of being outlawed. **3.** disregard or defiance of the law.

out·lay (*n.* out′lā′; *v.* out lā′), *n.*, *v.t.*, **-laid, -laying.** —*n.* **1.** an expending; an expenditure. **2.** an amount expended. —*v.t.* **3.** to expend, as money.

out·let (out′lĕt), *n.* **1.** an opening or passage by which anything is let out; a vent or exit. **2.** *Elect.* **a.** a point on a wiring system at which current is taken to supply electrical devices. **b.** **outlet box,** the metal box or receptacle designed to facilitate connections to a wiring system. **3.** *Com.* **a.** a market for goods. **b.** (of a wholesaler or manufacturer) a store, merchant, or agency selling one's goods: *he has 50 good outlets.* **4.** a letting out or discharging.

out·li·er (out′lī′ər), *n.* **1.** one who or that which lies outside. **2.** one residing outside the place of his business, duty, etc. **3.** *Geol.* a part of a formation left detached through the removal of surrounding parts by denudation.

out·line (out′līn′), *n.*, *v.*, **-lined, -lining.** —*n.* **1.** the line, real or apparent, by which a figure or object is defined or bounded; the contour. **2.** a drawing or a style of drawing with merely lines of contour, without shading. **3.** a general sketch, account or report, indicating only the main features, as of a book, a subject, a project or work, facts, events, etc. —*v.t.* **4.** to draw the outline of, or draw in outline, as a figure or object. **5.** to give an outline of (a subject, etc.); sketch the main features of. —Syn. **1.** See **form.**

out·live (outlĭv′), *v.t.*, **-lived, -living. 1.** to live longer than; survive (a person, etc.). **2.** to outlast; live or last through: *the ship outlived the storm.* —Syn. **1.** See **survive.**

out·look (out′lŏok′), *n.* **1.** the view or prospect from a place. **2.** the mental view: *one's outlook upon life.* **3.** prospect of the future: *the political outlook.* **4.** the place from which an observer looks out; a lookout. **5.** a looking out. **6.** a watch kept.

out·ly·ing (out′lī′ĭng), *adj.* **1.** lying at a distance from the center or the main body; remote; out-of-the-way. **2.** lying outside the boundary or limit.

out·man (out·măn′), *v.t.*, **-manned, -manning. 1.** to surpass in manpower. **2.** to surpass in manliness.

out·ma·neu·ver (out′mə nōō′vər), *v.t.* to outdo in or get the better of by maneuvering.

out·march (out·märch′), *v.t.* to outstrip or outdo in marching.

out·match (out·măch′), *v.t.* to surpass; outdo.

out·mode (out·mōd′), *v.t.*, **-moded, -moding.** to cause to be out of style. —**out·mod′ed,** *adj.*

out·most (out′mōst′), *adj.* furthest out; outermost.

out·num·ber (out·nŭm′bər), *v.t.* to exceed in number.

out-of-date (out′əv dāt′), *adj.* of a previous style or fashion; obsolete.

out-of-doors (out′əv dōrz′), *adj.* **1.** Also, **out′-of-door′.** outdoor. —*adv., n.* **2.** outdoors.

out-of-the-way (out′əv thə wā′), *adj.* **1.** remote from much-traveled ways or frequented or populous regions; secluded. **2.** unusual. **3.** improper.

out·pa·tient (out′pā′shənt), *n.* a patient receiving treatment at a hospital but not being an inmate.

out·play (out·plā′), *v.t.* to play better than; defeat.

out·point (out·point′), *v.t.* **1.** to excel in number of points, as in a competition or contest. **2.** *Naut.* to sail closer to the wind than (another vessel).

out·post (out′pōst′), *n.* **1.** a station at a distance from the main body of an army to protect it from surprise attack. **2.** the body of troops stationed there.

out·pour (*n.* out′pōr′; *v.* out pōr′), *n.* **1.** an outflow or overflow; that which is poured out. —*v.t.* **2.** to pour out.

out·pour·ing (out′pōr′ĭng), *n.* outflow; effusion.

out·put (out′pŏot′), *n.* **1.** act of turning out; production. **2.** the quantity or amount produced, as in a given time. **3.** the product or yield, as of a mine.

out·rage (out′rāj), *n., v.*, **-raged, -raging.** —*n.* **1.** an act of wanton violence; any gross violation of law or decency. **2.** anything that outrages the feelings. **3.** *Obs.* a passionate or violent outbreak. —*v.t.* **4.** to subject to grievous violence or indignity. **5.** to affect with a sense of offended right or decency; shock. **6.** to offend against (right, decency, feelings, etc.) grossly or shamelessly. **7.** to ravish (a woman). [ME, t. OF, der. *outrer* push beyond bounds, der. *outre* beyond, g. L *ultra*]

out·ra·geous (out rā′jəs), *adj.* **1.** of the nature of or involving gross injury or wrong: *an outrageous slander.* **2.** grossly offensive to the sense of right or decency. **3.** passing reasonable bounds; intolerable or shocking: *an outrageous price.* **4.** violent in action or temper. —**out·ra′geous·ly,** *adv.* —**out·ra′geous·ness,** *n.*

ou·trance (ōō träns′), *n.* French. the utmost extremity, as in combat. [ME, t. OF, der. *outrer.* See **OUTRAGE**]

out·range (out rānj′), *v.t.*, **-ranged, -ranging.** to have a longer or greater range than.

out·rank (out·răngk′), *v.t.* to rank above.

ou·tré (ōō trā′), *adj.* French. passing the bounds of what is usual and considered proper. [F, pp. of *outrer.* See **OUTRAGE**]

out·reach (*v.* out rēch′; *n.* out′rēch′), *v.t.* **1.** to reach beyond; exceed. **2.** to reach out; extend. —*v.i.* **3.** to reach out. —*n.* **4.** a reaching out. **5.** length of reach.

ou·tre·mer (ōō′trə mer′), *adv.* French. beyond the sea.

out·ride (out rīd′), *v.*, **-rode, -ridden, -riding,** *n.* —*v.t.* **1.** to outdo or outstrip in riding. **2.** (of a ship) to last through a storm. —*v.i.* **3.** to ride out. —*n.* **4.** *Pros.* an unaccented syllable or syllables added to a metrical foot, esp. in sprung rhythm.

out·rid·er (out′rī′dər), *n.* **1.** a mounted attendant riding before or beside a carriage. **2.** one who rides out or forth.

out·rig·ger (out′rĭg′ər), *n.* **1.** a framework extended outboard from the side of a boat, esp., as in South Pacific canoes, supporting a float which gives stability. **2.** a bracket extending outward from the side of a racing shell, to support an oarlock. **3.** a spar rigged out from a ship's rail or the like, as for extending a sail. **4.** any of various projecting frames or parts on an airplane, as for supporting a rudder, etc.

Canoe with outrigger

out·right (*adj.* out′rīt′; *adv.* out·rīt′), *adj.* **1.** complete or total: *an outright loss.* **2.** downright or unqualified: *an outright refusal.* **3.** directed straight out or

on. —*adv.* **4.** completely; entirely. **5.** without restraint, reserve, or concealment; openly. **6.** at once. **7.** *Obs.* straight out or ahead.

out·root (out rōot′, -rŏot′), *v.t.* to root out; extirpate.

out·run (out rŭn′), *v.*, **-ran, -run, -running. 1.** to outstrip in running. **2.** to escape by or as by running. **3.** to exceed.

out·run·ner (out′rŭn′ər), *n.* **1.** one who or that which runs out or outside. **2.** an attendant who runs before or beside a carriage. **3.** the leader of a team of dogs. **4.** a forerunner.

out·sell (out sĕl′), *v.t.*, **-sold, -selling. 1.** to outdo in selling; sell more than. **2.** to sell or be sold for more than. **3.** to exceed in value.

out·set (out′sĕt′), *n.* the beginning or start.

out·shine (out shīn′), *v.*, **-shone, -shining.** —*v.t.* **1.** to surpass in shining. **2.** to surpass in splendor, excellence, etc. —*v.i.* **3.** to shine forth.

out·shoot (*v.* out shōot′; *n.* out′shōot′), *v.*, **-shot, -shooting,** *n.* —*v.t.* **1.** to surpass in shooting. **2.** to shoot beyond. **3.** to shoot or send forth. —*v.i.* **4.** to shoot forth; project. —*n.* **5.** a shooting out. **6.** something that shoots out. **7.** *Baseball.* a curve which shoots or bends out away from the batter as it approaches the home base.

out·side (*n., adj., adv.* out′sīd′; *prep.* out′sīd′), *n.* **1.** the outer side, surface, or part; the exterior. **2.** the external aspect or appearance. **3.** something merely external. **4.** the space without or beyond an enclosure, boundary, etc. **5.** *Chiefly Brit. Colloq.* an outside passenger or place on a coach, etc. **6. the outside,** *Colloq.* the utmost limit: *not more than ten at the outside.* —*adj.* **7.** being, acting, done, or originating beyond an enclosure, boundary, etc.: *outside noises.* **8.** situated on or pertaining to the outside; exterior; external. **9.** not belonging to or connected with an institution, society, etc.: *outside influences.* **10.** extreme: *an outside estimate.* —*adv.* **11.** on or to the outside, exterior, or space without. **12.** *U.S. Colloq.* with the exception (fol. by *of*). —*prep.* **13.** outside of. **14.** *Colloq.* except.

out·sid·er (out′sī′dər), *n.* **1.** one not within an enclosure, boundary, etc. **2.** one not belonging to a particular group, set, party, etc. **3.** one unconnected or unacquainted with the matter in question. **4.** a race horse, etc., not included among the favorites.

out·sing (out sĭng′), *v.*, **-sang, -sung, -singing.** —*v.t.* **1.** to sing better than. **2.** to sing louder than. —*v.i.* **3.** to sing out.

out sister, a nun, especially in a cenobite order, who works outside of the convent in its service.

out·sit (out sĭt′), *v.t.*, **-sat, -sitting. 1.** to sit longer than (another). **2.** to sit beyond the time of.

out·size (out′sīz′), *n.* **1.** an uncommon or irregular size. **2.** a garment of such a size, esp. when larger.

out·skirt (out′skûrt′), *n.* (*often pl.*) an outer or bordering part or district.

out·smart (out smärt′), *v.t. U.S. Colloq.* to prove too clever for.

out·soar (out sōr′), *v.t.* to soar beyond.

out·span (out spăn′), *v.*, **-spanned, -spanning,** *n. South African.* —*v.t.* **1.** to unyoke or unhitch, as oxen from a wagon. —*v.i.* **2.** to remove the yoke, harness, etc., from animals. —*n.* **3.** the act or place of outspanning. [t. S Afr. D: m. *uitspannen*]

out·speak (out spēk′), *v.*, **-spoke, -spoken, -speaking.** —*v.t.* **1.** to outdo or excel in speaking. **2.** to utter frankly or boldly. —*v.i.* **3.** to speak out.

out·spent (out spĕnt′), *adj.* exhausted.

out·spo·ken (out′spō′kən), *adj.* **1.** uttered or expressed with frankness or lack of reserve: *outspoken criticism.* **2.** free or unreserved in speech: *outspoken people.* —**out′spo′ken·ly,** *adv.* —**out′spo′ken·ness,** *n.* —Syn. **1.** See **frank.**

out·spread (*v.* out sprĕd′; *n., adj.* out′sprĕd′), *v.*, **-spread, -spreading,** *adj., n.* —*v.i., v.t.* **1.** to spread out; extend. —*adj.* **2.** spread out; stretched out. **3.** diffused abroad. —*n.* **4.** a spreading out. **5.** that which is spread out; an expanse.

out·stand (out stănd′), *v.*, **-stood, -standing.** *Now Rare.* —*v.i.* **1.** to be prominent. **2.** (of a ship) to sail out to sea. —*v.t.* **3.** to stay or remain beyond. **4.** to withstand.

out·stand·ing (out stăn′dĭng), *adj.* **1.** prominent; conspicuous; striking. **2.** that continues in existence; that remains unsettled, unpaid, etc. **3.** standing out; projecting; detached. **4.** that resists or opposes.

out·stare (out stâr′), *v.t.*, **-stared, -staring. 1.** to outdo in staring. **2.** to stare out of countenance.

out·sta·tion (out′stā′shən), *n.* an auxiliary station, esp. on the outskirts of a district.

out·stay (out stā′), *v.t.* **1.** to stay longer than. **2.** to stay beyond the time or duration of.

out·stretch (out strĕch′), *v.t.* **1.** to stretch forth; extend. **2.** to stretch beyond (a limit, etc.). **3.** to stretch out; expand. **4.** to strain.

out·strip (out strĭp′), *v.t.*, **-stripped, -stripping. 1.** to outdo; surpass; excel. **2.** to outdo or pass in running or swift travel. **3.** to get ahead of or leave behind in a race or in any course of competition.

out·stroke (out′strōk′), *n.* **1.** a stroke in an outward direction. **2.** (in an engine) the stroke during which the piston rod moves outward from the cylinder.

ăct, āble, dâre, ärt; ĕbb, ēqual; ĭf, īce; hŏt, ōver, ôrder, oil, bŏok, ōōze, out; ŭp, ūse, ûrge; ə = a in alone; ch, chief; g, give; ng, ring; sh, shoe; th, thin; ŧh, that; zh, vision. See the full key on inside cover.

out·talk (out·tôk′), *v.t.* to outdo or overcome in talking.

out·turn (out′tûrn′), *n.* the quantity produced; output.

out·vote (out·vōt′), *v.t.*, **-voted, -voting.** to outdo or defeat in voting.

out·wait (out·wāt′), *v.t.* 1. to lie in ambush longer than. 2. to surpass in waiting or expecting.

out·walk (out·wôk′), *v.t.* to outdo in walking.

out·ward (out′wərd), *adj.* 1. being, or pertaining to, what is seen or apparent, as distinguished from the underlying nature, facts, etc., or from what is in the mind: *the outward looks.* 2. pertaining to the outside of the body. 3. pertaining to the body as opposed to the mind or spirit: *our outward eyes.* 4. belonging or pertaining to the external world as opposed to the mind or spirit. 5. belonging or pertaining to what is external to oneself: *a man's outward relations.* 6. proceeding or directed toward the outside or exterior. 7. that lies toward the outside; that is on the outer side: *my outward room.* 8. of or pertaining to the outside, outer surface, or exterior. 9. not directly concerned or interested. —*n.* 11. the outward part; the outside or exterior. 12. that which is without; the external or material world. 13. outward appearance. 14. on the outside; without. —*adv.* Also, **out′wards.** 15. toward the outside; out. 16. away from port: *a ship bound outward.* 17. visibly; openly. [ME; OE *ūtweard*]

out·ward·ly (out′wərd·lĭ), *adv.* 1. as regards appearance or outward manifestation. 2. toward the outside. 3. on the outside or outer surface.

out·watch (out·wŏch′, -wôch′), *v.t.* 1. to outdo in watching. 2. to watch until the end of.

out·wear (out·wâr′), *v.t.*, **-wore, -worn, -wearing.** 1. to wear or last longer than; outlast. 2. to outlive or outgrow. 3. to wear out; consume by wearing. 4. to exhaust in strength or endurance. 5. to pass time.

out·weigh (out·wā′), *v.t.* 1. to exceed in value, importance, influence, etc.: *the advantages of the plan outweighed its defects.* 2. to be too heavy or burdensome for. 3. to exceed in weight.

out·wit (out·wĭt′), *v.t.*, **-witted, -witting.** 1. to get the better of by superior ingenuity or cleverness. 2. *Archaic.* to surpass in intelligence.

out·work (*v.* out·wûrk′, *n.* out′wûrk′), *v.t.*, **-worked or -wrought, -working,** *n.* —*v.t.* 1. to surpass in working; work harder or faster than. 2. to work out or carry on to a conclusion; finish. —*n.* 3. *Fort.* a part of the fortifications of a place lying outside the main work.

out·worn (out·wōrn′), *adj.* 1. outgrown, as opinions. 2. obsolete; out of date. 3. worn out, as clothes. 4. exhausted in strength or endurance, as persons.

ou·zel (ōō′zəl), *n.* 1. a name used in England for members of the thrush family, esp. the blackbird, *Turdus merula.* 2. water ouzel. Also, **ousel.** [ME *osel*, OE *ōsle*, c. G *amsel*]

o·va (ō′və), *n.* pl. of ovum.

o·val (ō′vəl), *adj.* 1. having the general form, shape, or outline of an egg; egg-shaped. 2. ellipsoidal or elliptical. —*n.* 3. any of various oval things. 4. a body or a plane figure oval in shape or outline. 5. an elliptical field, or a field on which an elliptical track is laid out, as for athletic contests. 6. *Colloq.* a football. [t. NL: s. *ōvālis,* der. L *ōvum* egg. See OVATE] —**o′val·ly,** *adv.* —**o′·val·ness,** *n.*

o·var·i·an (ō·vâr′Ĭ·ən), *adj.* of or pertaining to an ovary.

o·var·i·ot·o·my (ō·vâr′Ĭ·ŏt′ə·mĬ), *n.*, *pl.* **-mies.** *Surg.* incision into or removal of an ovary.

o·va·ri·tis (ō′və·rī′tĬs), *n. Pathol.* oöphoritis.

o·va·ry (ō′və·rĬ), *n.*, *pl.* **-ries.** 1. *Anat., Zool.* the female gonad or reproductive gland, in which the ova, or eggs, and the hormones that regulate female secondary sex characteristics develop. 2. *Bot.* the enlarged lower part of the pistil in angiospermous plants, enclosing the ovules or young seeds. [t. NL: *ōvārium,* der. L *ōvum* egg]

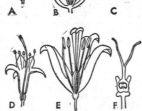

Longitudinal section of ovaries, with ovules
A. Larkspur, *Delphinium consolida*
B. Chickweed, *Stellaria media*; C. Buttercup, *Ranunculus bulbosus*; D. Fuchsia, *Fuchsia coccinea*; E. Lily, *Lilium superbum*; F. Maple, *Acer rubrum*

o·vate (ō′vāt), *adj.* 1. egg-shaped. 2. *Bot.* **a.** having a plane figure like the longitudinal section of an egg. **b.** having such a figure with the broader end at the base, as a leaf. [t. L: m.s. *ōvātus* egg-shaped]

o·va·tion (ō·vā′shən), *n.* 1. an enthusiastic public reception of a person; enthusiastic applause. 2. a lesser form of triumph accorded to an ancient Roman commander. [t. L: s. *ōvātio* rejoicing]

ov·en (ŭv′ən), *n.* a chamber or receptacle for baking or heating, or for drying with the aid of heat. [ME; OE *ofen*, c. G *ofen*]

Ovate Leaf

ov·en·bird (ŭv′ən·bûrd′), *n.* 1. a well-known American bird, *Seiurus aurocapillus,* which builds an oven-shaped nest of grasses, etc., on the forest floor. It belongs to the wood warbler family, *Compsothlypidae.* 2. any of the South American passerine birds of the genus *Furnarius.* 3. a North American warbler, *Seiurus auricapillus,* with a golden-brown color.

ov·en·wood (ŭv′ən·wŏŏd′), *n.* brushwood; dead wood fit only for burning.

o·ver (ō′vər), *prep.* 1. above in place or position; higher up than: *the roof over one's head.* 2. above and to the other side of: *to leap over a wall.* 3. above in authority, power, etc.; so as to govern, control, or conquer. 4. on or upon; so as to rest on or cover. 5. here and there on or in: *at various places over the country.* 6. through all parts of; all through: *to look over some papers.* 7. to and fro on or in: *to travel over Europe.* 8. from side to side of; to the other side of: *to go over a bridge.* 9. on the other side of: *lands over the sea.* 10. reaching higher than, so as to submerge. 11. in excess of, or more than: *over a mile.* 12. above in degree, etc. 13. in preference to. 14. from end to end of: *over the wire.* 15. until after the end of: *to adjourn over the holidays.* 16. during the duration of: *over a long term of years.* 17. in reference to, concerning, or about: *to quarrel over a matter.* 18. while engaged on or concerned with: *to fall asleep over one's work.* 19. **over all,** from one extremity of a thing to the other. 20. **over and above,** in addition to; besides. —*adv.* 21. over the top or upper surface or edge of something. 22. so as to cover the surface, or affect the whole surface: *to paint a thing over.* 23. through a region, area, etc.: *to travel all over.* 24. at some distance, as in a direction indicated: *over by the hill.* 25. from side to side, or to the other side: *to sail over.* 26. across any intervening space: *when are you coming over to see us?* 27. from beginning to end, or all through: *to read a thing over.* 28. from one person, party, etc., to another: *to make property over to others.* 29. on the other side, as of a sea, a river, or any space: *over in Europe.* 30. so as to bring the upper end or side down or under: *to throw a thing over.* 31. once more; again: *to do a thing over.* 32. in repetition: *twenty times over.* 33. in excess or addition: *to pay the full sum and something over.* 34. remaining beyond a certain amount: *five goes into seven once, with two over.* 35. throughout or beyond a period of time: *to stay over till Monday.* 36. Some adverbial phrases are: **all over, 1.** *U.S. Colloq.* everywhere. **2.** thoroughly; entirely. **3.** done with; finished.
all over with, done with; finished.
over again, once more; with repetition.
over against, 1. opposite to; in front of. **2.** as contrasted with or distinguished from: *to set truth over against falsehood.*
over and above, 1. in addition; besides. **2.** *Colloq.* overmuch; too much; too.
over and over, repeatedly.
over there, *U.S. Colloq.* in Europe.
—*adj.* 37. upper; higher up. 38. higher in authority, station, etc. 39. serving, or intended, as an outer covering: outer. 40. in excess or addition; surplus; extra. 41. too great; excessive. 42. at an end; done; past: *when the war was over.* —*n.* 43. an amount in excess or addition; an extra. 44. *Mil.* a shot which strikes or bursts beyond the target. 45. *Cricket.* **a.** the number of balls (now usually six) delivered between successive changes of bowlers. **b.** the part of the game played between such changes. —*v.t.* 46. *Rare.* to go or get over; leap over. —*v.i.* 47. *Rare.* to go or pass over. [ME; OE *ofer,* c. D *over,* G *über,* akin to Skt. *upari*]

over-, prefixal use of **over,** *prep., adv.,* or *adj.,* occurring in various senses in compounds, as in *overboard, overcoat, overhang, overlap, overlord, overrun, overthrow,* and especially employed, with the sense of "over the limit," "to excess," "too much," "too," to form verbs, adjectives, adverbs, and nouns, as *overact, overcapitalize, overcrowd, overfull, overmuch, oversupply, overweight,* and many others, mostly self-explanatory: a hyphen, which is commonly absent from old or well-established formations, being often used in new coinages, or in any words whose component parts it may be desirable to set off distinctly.

o·ver·a·bound (ō′vər·ə·bound′), *v.i.* to abound to excess.

o·ver·a·bun·dance (ō′vər·ə·bŭn′dəns), *n.* excessive abundance: *an overabundance of pie sent poor Tom to bed.* —**o′ver·a·bun′dant,** *adj.*

o·ver·act (ō′vər·ăkt′), *v.t.* to act (a part) in an exaggerated manner.

o·ver·ac·tive (ō′vər·ăk′tĬv), *adj.* active to excess; too active. —**o′ver·ac·tiv′i·ty,** *n.*

o·ver·age[1] (ō′vər·āj′), *adj.* beyond the proper age: *overage for the draft.* [f. OVER- + AGE, n.]

o·ver·age[2] (ō′vər·Ĭj), *n. Com.* 1. an excess supply of merchandise. 2. the value of goods in excess of amount called for by stock records; money in excess of the amount called for by sales records. [f. OVER- + -AGE]

o·ver·all (ō′vər·ôl′), *adj.* 1. from one extreme limit of a thing to the other: *the overall length of a bridge.* 2. covering or including everything. —*n.* 3. (*pl.*) loose, stout trousers, often with a part extending up over the breast, worn over the clothing to protect it, as by workmen and others. 4. (*pl.*) long waterproof leggings. 5. *Brit.* a smock or loose housedress.

o·ver·arch (ō′vər ärch′), *v.t.* **1.** to span with or like an arch. —*v.i.* **2.** to form an arch over something.

o·ver·arm (ō′vər ärm′), *adj. Baseball,* etc. delivered or executed with the arm raised above the shoulder.

o·ver·awe (ō′vər ô′), *v.t.,* **-awed, -awing.** to restrain or subdue by inspiring awe; cow.

o·ver·bal·ance (ō′vər bǎl′əns), *v.t.,* **-anced, -ancing,** *n.* **1.** to outweigh. **2.** to cause to lose balance or to fall or turn over. —*n.* **3.** overbalancing weight or amount. **4.** something that more than balances.

o·ver·bear (ō′vər bâr′), *v.,* **-bore, -borne, -bearing.** —*v.t.* **1.** to bear over or down by weight or force. **2.** to overcome. **3.** to prevail over or overrule (wishes, objections, etc.). **4.** to treat in a domineering way. —*v.i.* **5.** to produce fruit or progeny so abundantly as to impair the health.

o·ver·bear·ing (ō′vər bâr′ĭng), *adj.* domineering; dictatorial; haughtily or rudely arrogant. —*o′ver·bear′ing·ly, adv.*

o·ver·bid (*v.* ō′vər bĭd′; *n.* ō′vər bĭd′), *v.,* **-bid, -bidden** or **-bid, -bidding,** *n.* —*v.t., v.i.* **1.** to bid more than the value of (a thing). **2.** to outbid (a person, etc.). —*n.* **3.** a higher bid.

o·ver·bite (ō′vər bīt′), *n. Dentistry.* occlusion in which the upper incisor teeth overlap the lower.

o·ver·blow (ō′vər blō′), *v.,* **-blew, -blown, -blowing.** —*v.t.* **1.** to blow (clouds, etc.) over or away. **2.** to blow down. **3.** to blow over the surface of, as the wind, sand, or the like does. —*v.i.* **4.** to pass away, as a storm.

o·ver·blown (ō′vər blōn′), *adj.* more than full-blown.

o·ver·board (ō′vər bōrd′), *adv.* over the side of a ship or boat, esp. into or in the water: *to fall overboard.*

o·ver·build (ō′vər bĭld′), *v.t.,* **-built, -building. 1.** to cover or surmount with a building or structure. **2.** to erect too many buildings on (an area). **3.** to build (a structure) on too great or elaborate a scale.

o·ver·bur·den (ō′vər bûr′dən), *v.t.* to load with too great a burden; overload.

o·ver·bur·den·some (ō′vər bûr′dən səm), *adj.* excessively burdensome.

o·ver·buy (ō′vər bī′), *v.,* **-bought, -buying.** —*v.t.* **1.** to purchase in excessive quantities. **2.** *Finance.* to buy on margin in excess of one's ability to provide added security in an emergency, as in a falling market. —*v.i.* **3.** to buy regardless of one's financial ability.

o·ver·call (ō′vər kôl′), *v.t. Cards.* to bid higher than.

o·ver·cap·i·tal·ize (ō′vər kăp′ə tə līz′), *v.t.,* **-ized, -izing. 1.** to fix the nominal capital (total amount of securities) of a company in excess of the limits set by law or by sound financial policy. **2.** to overestimate the capital value (of a business property or enterprise). **3.** to provide an excessive amount of capital (for a business enterprise).—*o′ver·cap′i·tal·i·za′tion, n.*

o·ver·cast (ō′vər kăst′, -käst′, ō′vər kăst′, -käst′), *adj., v.,* **-cast, -casting.** —*adj.* **1.** overspread with clouds, as the sky; cloudy. **2.** dark; gloomy. **3.** *Sewing.* sewn by overcasting. —*v.t.* **4.** to overcloud, darken, or make gloomy. **5.** to sew with stitches passing successively over an edge, esp. long stitches set at intervals to prevent raveling. —*v.i.* **6.** to become cloudy or dark.

o·ver·cast·ing (ō′vər kăs′tĭng, -käs′-), *n.* **1.** act or practice of coating masonry with plaster. **2.** *Sewing.* the stitch used to overcast.

o·ver·cer·ti·fy (ō′vər sûr′tə fī′), *v.t.,* **-fied, -fying.** *Banking.* to issue (a bank check) for an amount greater than the drawer's balance in his account. —*o′ver·cer′ti·fi·ca′tion, n.*

o·ver·charge (*v.* ō′vər chärj′; *n.* ō′vər chärj′), *v.,* **-charged, -charging,** *n.* —*v.t.* **1.** to charge (a person) too high a price. **2.** to charge (an amount) in excess of what is due. **3.** to overload; fill too full. **4.** to exaggerate. —*n.* **5.** a charge in excess of a just price. **6.** an excessive load.

o·ver·check (ō′vər chĕk′), *n.* a checkrein passed over a horse's head between the ears.

o·ver·clothes (ō′vər klōz′, -klōŧħz′), *n.pl.* clothing worn outside other garments.

o·ver·cloud (ō′vər kloud′), *v.t.* **1.** to overspread with or as with clouds. **2.** to darken; obscure; make gloomy. —*v.i.* **3.** to become clouded over or overcast.

o·ver·coat (ō′vər kōt′), *n.* a coat worn over the ordinary clothing, as in cold weather; a greatcoat.

o·ver·come (ō′vər kŭm′), *v.,* **-came, -come, -coming.** —*v.t.* **1.** to get the better of in a struggle or conflict; conquer; defeat. **2.** to prevail over (opposition, objections, temptations, etc.). **3.** to surmount (difficulties, etc.). **4.** to overpower (a person, etc.) in body or mind, or affect in an overpowering or paralyzing way, as liquor, a drug, excessive exertion, violent emotion, or the like does. **5.** to overwhelm in feeling. **6.** *Archaic.* to overspread or overrun. —*v.i.* **7.** to gain the victory; conquer. [ME; OE *ofercuman*] —Syn. **1.** See **defeat.**

o·ver·com·pen·sa·tion (ō′vər kŏm′pən sā′shən), *n. Psychoanal.* the exaggerated striving for any trait to

neutralize and conceal strong feelings of an opposite kind.

o·ver·con·fi·dent (ō′vər kŏn′fə dənt), *adj.* too confident. —*o′ver·con′fi·dence, n.*

o·ver·crit·i·cal (ō′vər krĭt′ə kəl), *adj.* critical to excess; too critical; hypercritical.

o·ver·crop (ō′vər krŏp′), *v.t.,* **-cropped, -cropping.** *Agric.* to crop (land) to excess; exhaust the fertility of by continuous cropping.

o·ver·crowd (ō′vər kroud′), *v.t., v.i.* to crowd to excess.

o·ver·de·vel·op (ō′vər dĭ vĕl′əp), *v.t.* to develop to excess. —*o′ver·de·vel′op·ment, n.*

o·ver·do (ō′vər dōō′), *v.,* **-did, -done, -doing.** —*v.t.* **1.** to do to excess: *to overdo exercise.* **2.** to carry to excess or beyond the proper limit. **3.** to overact (a part); exaggerate. **4.** to overtax the strength of; fatigue; exhaust. —*v.i.* **5.** to do too much.

o·ver·done (ō′vər dŭn′), *v.* **1.** pp. of **overdo.** —*adj.* **2.** (of food, etc.) cooked too much.

o·ver·dose (*n.* ō′vər dōs′; *v.* ō′vər dōs′), *n., v.,* **-dosed, -dosing.** —*n.* **1.** an excessive dose. —*v.t.* **2.** to dose to excess.

o·ver·draft (ō′vər drăft′, -dräft′), *n.* **1.** a draft in excess of one's credit balance, or the amount of the excess. **2.** an excess draft or demand made on anything. **3.** the action of overdrawing an account, as at a bank. **4.** a draft made to pass over a fire, as in a furnace. **5.** a draft passing downward through a kiln.

o·ver·draw (ō′vər drô′), *v.,* **-drew, -drawn, -drawing.** —*v.t.* **1.** to draw upon (an account, allowance, etc.) in excess of the balance standing to one's credit or at one's disposal. **2.** to draw too far; strain, as a bow, by drawing. **3.** to exaggerate in drawing, depicting, or describing. —*v.i.* **4.** to overdraw an account or the like.

o·ver·dress (*v.* ō′vər drĕs′; *n.* ō′vər drĕs′), *v.t., v.i.* to dress to excess or with too much display.

o·ver·drive (*v.* ō′vər drīv′; *n.* ō′vər drīv′), *v.,* **-drove, -driven, -driving,** *n.* —*v.t.* **1.** to overwork; push or carry to excess. **2.** to drive too hard. —*n.* **3.** *Mach.* a device containing a gear set at such ratio and arrangement as to provide (when engaged) a propeller speed greater than the engine crankshaft speed.

o·ver·due (ō′vər dū′, -dōō′), *adj.* past due, as a belated train or a bill not paid by the assigned date.

o·ver·eat (ō′vər ēt′), *v.,* **-ate, -eaten, -eating.** —*v.i.* **1.** to eat too much. —*v.t.* **2.** to eat more than is good for (oneself).

o·ver·es·ti·mate (*v.* ō′vər ĕs′tə māt′; *n.* ō′vər ĕs′tə mĭt), *v.,* **-mated, -mating,** *n.* —*v.t.* **1.** to estimate at too high a value, amount, rate, or the like. —*n.* **2.** an estimate that is too high. —*o′ver·es′ti·ma′tion, n.*

o·ver·ex·cite (ō′vər ĭk sīt′), *v.t.,* **-cited, -citing.** to excite too much. —*o′ver·ex·cit′a·ble, adj.* —*o′ver·ex·cite′ment, n.*

o·ver·ex·ert (ō′vər ĭg zûrt′), *v.t.* to exert too much. —*o′ver·ex·er′tion, n.*

o·ver·ex·pose (ō′vər ĭk spōz′), *v.t.,* **-posed, -posing. 1.** to expose too much. **2.** *Photog.* to expose too long.

o·ver·feed (ō′vər fēd′), *v.t., v.i.,* **-fed, -feeding.** to feed to excess.

o·ver·fill (ō′vər fĭl′), *v.t.* **1.** to fill too full so as to cause overflowing. —*v.i.* **2.** to become too full.

o·ver·flow (*v.* ō′vər flō′; *n.* ō′vər flō′), *v.,* **-flowed, -flown, -flowing.** —*v.i.* **1.** to flow or run over, as rivers, water, etc. **2.** to have the contents flowing over, as an overfull vessel. **3.** to discharge a flow of something as from being overfull (fol. by *with*). **4.** to pass from one place or part to another as if flowing from an overfull space: *the population overflowed into the adjoining territory.* **5.** to be filled or supplied in overflowing measure (fol. by *with*): *a heart overflowing with gratitude.* —*v.t.* **6.** to flow over; flood; inundate. **7.** to flow over or beyond (the brim, banks, borders, etc.). **8.** to flow over the edge or brim of (a vessel, etc.). **9.** to fill to the point of running over. —*n.* **10.** an overflowing: *the annual overflow of the Nile.* **11.** that which flows or runs over: *to carry off the overflow from a fountain.* **12.** an excess or superabundance. **13.** a portion passing or crowded out from an overfilled place: *to house the overflow from a museum.* **14.** an outlet for excess liquid.

o·ver·gar·ment (ō′vər gär′mənt), *n.* outer garment.

o·ver·gild (ō′vər gĭld′), *v.t.,* **-gilded** or **-gilt, -gilding.** to cover with gilding.

o·ver·glance (ō′vər glăns′, -gläns′), *v.t.,* **-glanced, -glancing.** to glance over.

o·ver·glaze (ō′vər glāz′), *n.* a glaze or decoration applied over another glaze on pottery.

o·ver·grow (ō′vər grō′), *v.,* **-grew, -grown, -growing.** —*v.t.* **1.** to grow over; cover with a growth of something. **2.** to outdo in growing; choke or supplant by a more exuberant growth. **3.** to grow beyond, grow too large for, or outgrow. —*v.i.* **4.** to grow to excess; grow too large. —*o′ver·grown′, adj.*

o′ver·am·bi′tious	o′ver·cau′tious	o′ver·ea′ger	o′ver·fa·mil′iar
o′ver·anx·i′e·ty	o′ver·char′it·a·ble	o′ver·e·mo′tion·al	o′ver·fa·tigue′
o′ver·anx′ious	o′ver·child′ish	o′ver·em·pha·size′	o′ver·fit′
o′ver·bal′last	o′ver·con·serv′a·tive	o′ver·en·thu·si·as′tic	o′ver·fond′
o′ver·bold′	o′ver·cook′	o′ver·ex′er·cise′	o′ver·fre′quent
o′ver·bus′y	o′ver·cu′ri·ous	o′ver·ex·pand′	o′ver·full′
o′ver·care′ful	o′ver·del′i·cate	o′ver·ex·pan′sion	o′ver·gen′er·ous
o′ver·cau′tion	o′ver·dig′ni·fied′	o′ver·ex·po′sure	o′ver·greed′y

o·ver·growth (ō'vər grōth'), *n.* **1.** a growth overspreading or covering something. **2.** excessive or too exuberant growth.

o·ver·hand (ō'vər hănd'), *adj.* Also, **o'ver·hand'ed.** **1.** done or delivered overhand. **2.** *Cricket, etc.* overarm. —*adv.* **3.** with the hand over the object. **4.** with the hand raised above the shoulder, as in pitching a ball. **5.** *Sewing.* with close, shallow stitches over two selvages. —*n.* **6.** *Sports.* skill in the delivery of overhand strokes. —*v.t.* **7.** to sew overhand.

overhand knot, a simple knot of various uses which slips easily. See illus. under **knot.**

o·ver·hang (*v.* ō'vər hăng'; *n.* ō'vər hăng'), *v.,* **-hung, -hanging,** *n.* —*v.t.* **1.** to hang or be suspended over. **2.** to extend, project, or jut over: *a dark sky overhangs the earth.* **3.** to impend over, or threaten, as danger or evil: *the sadness which overhung him.* **4.** to adorn with hangings. —*v.i.* **5.** to hang over; project or jut out over something below. —*n.* **6.** an overhanging; a projection. **7.** the extent of projection, as of the bow of a vessel. **8.** *Archit.* a projecting upper part of a building as a roof or balcony. **9.** *Aeron.* the amount by which an upper wing of a biplane projects laterally beyond the corresponding lower wing.

o·ver·haul (ō'vər hôl'), *v.t.* **1.** to investigate or examine thoroughly, as for repair. **2.** to haul or turn over for examination. **3.** to gain upon or overtake. **4.** *Naut.* **a.** to slacken (a rope) by hauling in the opposite direction to that in which it was drawn taut. **b.** to release the blocks of (a tackle). —*n.* **5.** a thorough examination.

o·ver·head (*adv.* ō'vər hĕd'; *adj., n.* ō'vər hĕd'), *adv.* **1.** over one's head; aloft; up in the air or sky, esp. near the zenith: *overhead was a cloud.* **2.** so as to be completely submerged or deeply involved: *overhead in debt.* —*adj.* **3.** situated, operating, or passing overhead, aloft, or above. **4.** applicable to one and all; general; average. —*n.* **5.** the general cost of running a business. **6.** the general cost which cannot be assigned to particular products or orders.

overhead railway, *Brit.* an elevated railway.

o·ver·hear (ō'vər hĭr'), *v.t.,* **-heard, -hearing.** to hear (speech, etc., or a speaker) without the speaker's intention or knowledge. —**o'ver·hear'er,** *n.*

o·ver·heat (ō'vər hēt'), *v.t.* **1.** to heat to excess. —*n.* **2.** excessive heat; overheated condition.

o·ver·hung (ō'vər hŭng'), *v.* **1.** pt. and pp. of **overhang.** —*adj.* **2.** hung from above.

o·ver·in·dulge (ō'vər ĭn dŭlj'), *v.t., v.i.,* **-dulged, -dulging.** to indulge to excess. —**o'ver·in·dul'gence,** *n.* —**o'ver·in·dul'gent,** *adj.*

o·ver·is·sue (ō'vər ĭsh'ōō), *n.* an excessive issue of stocks or bonds, in excess of the needs of the business, or in excess of charter authorization.

o·ver·joyed (ō'vər joid'), *adj.* overcome with joy; made exceedingly joyful.

o·ver·lade (ō'vər lād'), *v.t.,* **-laded, -laded** or **-laden, -lading.** to overload (now chiefly in *overladen,* pp.).

o·ver·land (ō'vər lănd'), *adv.* **1.** over or across the land. **2.** by land. —*adj.* **3.** proceeding, performed, or carried on overland: *the overland route.*

overland stage, a stagecoach used in the western U.S. during the middle nineteenth century.

o·ver·lap (*v.* ō'vər lăp'; *n.* ō'vər lăp'), *v.,* **lapped, -lapping,** *n.* —*v.t.* **1.** to lap over (something else or each other); extend over and cover a part of. **2.** to cover and extend beyond (something else). —*v.i.* **3.** to lap over. —*n.* **4.** an overlapping. **5.** the extent or amount of overlapping. **6.** an overlapping part. **7.** the place of overlapping.

o·ver·lay¹ (*v.* ō'vər lā'; *n.* ō'vər lā'), *v.,* **-laid, -laying,** *n.* —*v.t.* **1.** to lay or place (one thing) over or upon another. **2.** to cover, overspread, or surmount with something. **3.** to finish with a layer or applied decoration of something: *wood richly overlaid with gold.* **4.** *Print.* to put an overlay upon. —*n.* **5.** something laid over something else; a covering. **6.** a layer or decoration of something applied: *an overlay of gold.* **7.** *Print.* a shaped piece of paper, or a sheet of paper reinforced at the proper places by shaped pieces, put on the tympan of a press to increase or equalize the impression. **8.** a transparent sheet giving special military information not ordinarily shown on maps, used by being placed over the map on which it is based. **9.** *Scot.* a neckcloth or cravat. [ME, f. OVER- + LAY¹]

o·ver·lay² (ō'vər lā'), *v.* pt. of **overlie.**

o·ver·leap (ō'vər lēp'), *v.t.* **1.** to leap farther than, or outleap. **2.** to overreach (oneself) by leaping too far. **3.** to pass over or omit. **4.** to leap over or across.

o·ver·lie (ō'vər lī'), *v.t.,* **-lay, -lain, -lying. 1.** to lie over or upon, as a covering, stratum, etc. **2.** to smother (an infant) by lying upon it, as in sleep.

o·ver·live (ō'vər lĭv'), *v.,* **-lived, -living.** —*v.t.* **1.** to live longer than; outlast. —*v.i.* **2.** to survive.

o·ver·load (*v.* ō'vər lōd'; *n.* ō'vər lōd'), *v.t.* **1.** to load to excess; overburden. —*n.* **2.** an excessive load.

o·ver·long (ō'vər lông', -lŏng'), *adj., adv.* too long.

o·ver·look (ō'vər lŏŏk'), *v.t.* **1.** to fail to notice, perceive, or consider: *to overlook a misspelled word.* **2.** to disregard or ignore indulgently, as faults, misconduct,

etc. **3.** to look over, as from a higher position. **4.** to afford a view down over: *a hill overlooking the sea.* **5.** to rise above. **6.** to take no notice of; ignore. **7.** to look over in inspection, examination, or perusal. **8.** to look after, oversee, or supervise. **9.** to look upon with the evil eye; bewitch. —**Syn. 1.** See **slight.**

o·ver·look·er (ō'vər lŏŏk'ər), *n. Brit.* overseer.

o·ver·lord (ō'vər lôrd'), *n.* one who is lord over another or over other lords. —**o'ver·lord'ship,** *n.*

o·ver·ly (ō'vər lĭ), *adv. Colloq.* overmuch; excessively; too: *a voyage not overly dangerous.*

o·ver·ly·ing (ō'vər lī'ĭng), *v.* ppr. of **overlie.**

o·ver·man (*n.* ō'vər mən *for 1 and 2,* ō'vər măn' *for 3; v.* ō'vər măn'), *n., pl.* **-men,** *v.,* **-manned, -manning.** —*n.* **1.** a foreman or overseer. **2.** an arbiter or umpire. **3.** a superman. —*v.t.* **4.** to oversupply with men, esp. for service. [ME]

o·ver·mas·ter (ō'vər măs'tər, -mäs'tər), *v.t.* to overcome; overpower.

o·ver·match (ō'vər măch'), *v.t.* to outmatch; surpass.

o·ver·much (ō'vər mŭch'), *adj., n., adv.* too much.

o·ver·nice (ō'vər nīs'), *adj.* too nice or fastidious.

o·ver·night (*adv.* ō'vər nīt'; *n., adj.* ō'vər nīt'), *adv.* **1.** during the night: *to stay overnight.* **2.** on the previous evening: *preparations were made overnight.* —*adj.* **3.** done, occurring, or continuing during the night: *an overnight stop.* **4.** designed to be used one night or very few nights: *overnight bag.* **5.** of or pertaining to the previous evening. —*n.* **6.** the previous evening.

o·ver·pass (*n.* ō'vər păs', -päs'; *v.* ō'vər păs', -päs'), *n., v.,* **-passed** or **-past, -passing.** —*n.* **1.** a highway or railway bridge crossing some barrier, as another highway. —*v.t.* **2.** to pass over or traverse (a region, space, etc.). **3.** to pass over (bounds, limits, etc.). **4.** to transgress. **5.** to get over (obstacles, etc.). **6.** to go beyond, exceed, or surpass. **7.** to pass through (time, experiences, etc.). **8.** to overlook; disregard; omit.

o·ver·pay (ō'vər pā'), *v.t.,* **-paid, -paying. 1.** to pay more than (an amount due). **2.** to pay in excess. —**o'ver·pay'ment,** *n.*

o·ver·peo·ple (ō'vər pē'pəl), *v.t.,* **-pled, -pling.** to overstock with people.

o·ver·per·suade (ō'vər pər swād'), *v.t.,* **-suaded, -suading. 1.** to bring over by persuasion. **2.** to persuade (a person) against his inclination or intention.

o·ver·play (ō'vər plā'), *v.t.* **1.** to play (a part, etc.) in an exaggerated manner. **2.** to defeat in playing. **3.** *Golf.* to hit (the ball) past the putting green.

o·ver·plus (ō'vər plŭs'), *n.* **1.** an excess over a particular amount, or a surplus. **2.** superabundance.

o·ver·pop·u·late (ō'vər pŏp'yə lāt'), *v.t.,* **-lated, -lating.** to overpeople. —**o'ver·pop·u·la'tion,** *n.*

o·ver·pow·er (ō'vər pou'ər), *v.t.* **1.** to overcome or overwhelm in feeling, or affect or impress excessively. **2.** to overcome, master, or subdue by superior force: *to overpower a maniac.* **3.** to overmaster the bodily powers or mental faculties of: *overpowered with wine.* **4.** to furnish or equip with excessive power. —**Syn. 1.** vanquish, overwhelm, subjugate.

o·ver·pow·er·ing (ō'vər pou'ər ĭng), *adj.* that overpowers; overwhelming. —**o'ver·pow'er·ing·ly,** *adv.*

o·ver·print (*v.* ō'vər prĭnt'; *n.* ō'vər prĭnt'), *v.t.* **1.** to print additional material or another color on a form or sheet previously printed. —*n.* **2.** a quantity of printing in excess of that desired; an overrun. **3.** *Philately.* **a.** any word, inscription or device printed across the face of a stamp altering its use or its locality, or overprinted for a special purpose. **b.** a stamp so marked.

o·ver·prize (ō'vər prīz'), *v.t.,* **-prized, -prizing.** to prize too highly; overvalue.

o·ver·pro·duce (ō'vər prə dūs', -dōōs'), *v.t., v.i.,* **-duced, -ducing.** to produce excessively or in excess of demand.

o·ver·pro·duc·tion (ō'vər prə dŭk'shən), *n.* excessive production; production in excess of the demand.

o·ver·proof (ō'vər prōōf'), *adj.* containing a greater proportion of alcohol than proof spirit does.

o·ver·proud (ō'vər proud'), *adj.* excessively proud.

o·ver·rate (ō'vər rāt'), *v.t.,* **-rated, -rating.** to rate too highly; overestimate: *his fortune has been overrated.*

o·ver·reach (ō'vər rēch'), *v.t.* **1.** to reach or extend over or beyond. **2.** to reach for or aim at but go beyond, as a thing sought, a mark, etc. **3.** to stretch (the arm, etc.) to excess, as by a straining effort. **4.** to defeat (oneself) by overdoing matters, often by excessive eagerness or cunning. **5.** to strain or exert (oneself) to the point of exceeding the purpose. **6.** to get the better of (a person, etc.); cheat. **7.** *Obs.* to overtake. —*v.i.* **8.** to reach or extend over something. **9.** to reach too far. **10.** to cheat others. **11.** (of horses, etc.) to strike, or strike and injure, the forefoot with the hind foot.

o·ver·ride (ō'vər rīd'), *v.t.,* **-rode, -ridden, -riding. 1.** to ride over or across (a region, etc.). **2.** to ride roughshod over. **3.** to pursue one's course in disregard of: *to override one's advisers.* **4.** to prevail over: *a decision that overrides all previous decisions.* **5.** to ride too much. **6.** to exhaust by excessive riding, as a horse. **7.** to pass or extend over. **8.** *Surg.* to overlap, as one piece of a fractured bone over another.

o'ver·hast'y	o'ver·mer'ry	o'ver·o·be'di·ent	o'ver·pow'er·ful
o'ver·high'	o'ver·mod'est	o'ver·plump'	o'ver·praise'
o'ver·jeal'ous	o'ver·mourn'ful	o'ver·plump'	o'ver·rash'
o'ver·meas'ure	o'ver·neg'li·gent	o'ver·pop'u·lous	o'ver·re·li'gious

b., blend of, blended; c., cognate with; d., dialect, dialectal; der., derived from; f., formed from; g., going back to; m., modification of; r., replacing; s., stem of; t., taken from; ?, perhaps. See the full key on inside cover.

o·ver·ripe (ō′vər rīp′), *adj.* too ripe; more than ripe.

o·ver·rule (ō′vər rōōl′), *v.t.*, **-ruled, -ruling.** **1.** to rule against or disallow the arguments of (a person). **2.** to rule or decide against (a plea, argument, etc.); disallow. **3.** to prevail over so as to change the purpose or action. **4.** to exercise rule or influence over.

o·ver·run (*v.* ō′vər run′; *n.* ō′vər run′), *v.*, **-ran, -run, -running,** *n.* —*v.t.* **1.** to rove over (a country, etc.), as hostile or ravaging invaders. **2.** to swarm over in great numbers, as animals, esp. vermin. **3.** to spread or grow rapidly over, as plants, esp. vines, weeds, etc. **4.** to run over so as to injure or overwhelm. **5.** to spread rapidly throughout, as a new idea, spirit, etc. **6.** to run beyond. **7.** to exceed. **8.** to run over; overflow. **9.** *Print.* **a.** to carry over (letters, words, or lines) to the next line, column, or page; to respace. **b.** to carry over words, etc., of. **10.** *Archaic.* to outrun; overtake in running. —*v.i.* **11.** to run over; overthrow. **12.** to extend beyond the proper or desired limit. —*n.* **13.** an overrunning. **14.** an amount overrunning or carried over.

o·ver·score (ō′vər skôr′), *v.t.*, **-scored, -scoring.** to score over, as with strokes or lines.

o·ver·seas (*adv.* ō′vər sēz′; *adj.* ō′vər sēz′), *adv.* **1.** over, across, or beyond the sea. —*adj.* **2.** of or pertaining to passage over the sea: *overseas travel.* **3.** situated beyond the sea: *overseas lands.* **4.** pertaining to countries beyond the sea; foreign: *overseas military service.* Also, **o·ver·sea** (*adv.* ō′vər sē′; *adj.* ō′vər sē′).

o·ver·see (ō′vər sē′), *v.t.*, **-saw, -seen, -seeing.** **1.** to direct (work or workers); supervise; manage. **2.** to survey; watch. **3.** *Obs.* to look over; inspect.

o·ver·se·er (ō′vər sē′ər), *n.* **1.** one who oversees; a supervisor. **2.** a minor official of a parish in England (in full, **overseer of the poor**).

o·ver·sell (ō′vər sel′), *v.t.*, **-sold, -selling.** **1.** to sell more of (a stock, etc.) than can be delivered. **2.** to sell to excess.

o·ver·set (*v.* ō′vər set′; *n.* ō′vər set′), *v.*, **-set, -setting,** *n.* —*v.t.* **1.** to upset or overturn; overthrow. **2.** to throw into confusion; disorder physically or mentally. —*v.i.* **3.** to become upset, overturned, or overthrown. **4.** *Print.* (of type or copy) **a.** to set in or to excess. **b.** (of space) to set too much type for. —*n.* **5.** act or fact of oversetting; overturn. **6.** *Print.* matter set up in excess of space.

o·ver·sew (ō′vər sō′, ō′vər sō′), *v.t.*, **-sewed, -sewed** or **-sewn, -sewing.** to sew with stitches passing successively over an edge, esp. closely, so as to cover the edge or make a firm seam.

o·ver·shade (ō′vər shād′), *v.t.*, **-shaded, -shading.** **1.** to cast a shade over. **2.** to make dark or gloomy.

o·ver·shad·ow (ō′vər shad′ō), *v.t.* **1.** to diminish the importance of, or render insignificant in comparison. **2.** to tower over so as to cast a shadow over. **3.** to cast a shadow over. **4.** to make dark or gloomy. **5.** to shelter or protect.

o·ver·shine (ō′vər shīn′), *v.t.*, **-shone, -shining. 1.** to outshine. **2.** to surpass in splendor, excellence, etc. **3.** to shine over or upon.

o·ver·shoe (ō′vər shōō′), *n.* **1.** a shoe worn over another shoe for protection against wet, cold, etc. **2.** a waterproof outer shoe of India rubber.

o·ver·shoot (ō′vər shōōt′), *v.*, **-shot, -shooting.** —*v.t.* **1.** to shoot or go over or above (something). **2.** to shoot or go beyond (a point, limit, etc.). **3.** to shoot a missile over or beyond (what is aimed at), thus missing: *to overshoot the mark.* **4.** to go further in any course or matter than is intended or proper, or go too far. **5.** to force or drive (a thing) beyond the proper limit. —*v.i.* **6.** to shoot or go beyond; fly beyond. **7.** to shoot over or too far.

o·ver·shot (ō′vər shot′), *adj.* **1.** driven by water passing over from above, as a vertical water wheel. **2.** having the upper jaw projecting beyond the lower, as a dog.

o·ver·side (ō′vər sīd′), *adv.* **1.** over the side, as of a ship. —*adj.* **2.** effected over the side of a ship. **3.** unloading or unloaded over the side.

Overshot water wheel

o·ver·sight (ō′vər sīt′), *n.* **1.** failure to notice or consider. **2.** an omission or error due to inadvertence. **3.** supervision; watchful care. —**Syn.** **1, 2.** mistake, blunder, slip. **3.** management, direction, control.

o·ver·size (ō′vər sīz′), *adj.* **1.** of excessive size. **2.** of a size larger than is necessary or required. —*n.* **3.** something that is oversize; an oversize article or object. **4.** a size larger than the proper or usual size.

o·ver·sized (ō′vər sīzd′), *adj.* of excessive size; over the average size; abnormally large.

o·ver·skirt (ō′vər skûrt′), *n.* **1.** an outer skirt. **2.** a drapery arranged over or upon a dress skirt.

o·ver·sleep (ō′vər slēp′), *v.*, **-slept, -sleeping.** —*v.i.* **1.** to sleep beyond the proper time of waking. —*v.t.* **2.** to sleep beyond (a certain hour).

o·ver·soul (ō′vər sōl′), *n.* a supreme reality or mind; the spiritual unity of all being; a Platonic concept developed esp. in transcendentalism (def. 2).

o·ver·spend (ō′vər spend′), *v.*, **-spent, -spending.** —*v.i.* **1.** to spend more than one can afford. —*v.t.* **2.** to spend in excess of. **3.** *Archaic.* to wear out.

o·ver·spread (ō′vər spred′), *v.t.*, **-spread, -spreading. 1.** to spread (one thing) over another. **2.** to cover (a thing) with something else. **3.** to be spread over (something else).

o·ver·state (ō′vər stāt′), *v.t.*, **-stated, -stating.** to state too strongly; exaggerate in statement: *to overstate one's case.* —**o′ver·state′ment,** *n.*

o·ver·stay (ō′vər stā′), *v.t.* **1.** to stay beyond the time or duration of. **2.** *Colloq. Finance.* to remain in (the market) beyond the point where a sale would have yielded the greatest profit.

o·ver·step (ō′vər step′), *v.t.*, **-stepped, -stepping.** to step or pass over or beyond.

o·ver·stock (*v.* ō′vər stok′; *n.* ō′vər stok′), *v.t.* **1.** to stock to excess. —*n.* **2.** a stock in excess of need.

o·ver·strain (ō′vər strān′), *v.* to strain to excess.

o·ver·stride (ō′vər strīd′), *v.t.*, **-strode, -stridden, -striding. 1.** to stride or step over or across. **2.** to stride beyond. **3.** to surpass. **4.** to bestride.

o·ver·strung (ō′vər strung′), *adj.* too highly strung.

o·ver·stud·y (*v.* ō′vər stud′ī; *n.* ō′vər stud′ī), *v.*, **-studied, -studying,** *n.* —*v.t., v.i.* **1.** to study too much or too hard. —*n.* **2.** excessive study.

o·ver·stuff (ō′vər stuf′), *v.t.* **1.** to force too much into. **2.** *Furnit.* to envelop completely with deep upholstery.

o·ver·stuffed (ō′vər stuft′), *adj.* *Furnit.* having the entire frame covered by stuffing and upholstery, so that only decorative woodwork or the like is exposed.

o·ver·sub·scribe (ō′vər səb skrīb′), *v.t.*, **-scribed, -scribing.** to subscribe for in excess of what is available or required. —**o′ver·sub·scrip′tion,** *n.*

o·ver·sup·ply (*n.* ō′vər sə plī′; *v.* ō′vər sə plī′), *n.*, *pl.* **-plies,** *v.*, **-plied, -plying.** —*n.* **1.** an excessive supply. —*v.t.* **2.** to supply in excess.

o·vert (ō′vûrt, ō vûrt′), *adj.* **1.** open to view or knowledge; not concealed or secret: *overt hostility.* **2.** *Her.* open, as a purse. [ME. t. OF. pp. of *ovrir* open, eg. L. *aperīre* open, with *o-* from *covrir* cover. See COVERT] —**Syn.** **1.** plain, manifest, apparent, open, public.

o·ver·take (ō′vər tāk′), *v.t.*, **-took, -taken, -taking. 1.** to catch up with in traveling or in pursuit. **2.** to come up with in any course of action. **3.** to come upon suddenly (said esp. of night, storm, death, etc.).

o·ver·task (ō′vər task′, -täsk′), *v.t.* to impose too heavy a task upon.

o·ver·tax (ō′vər taks′), *v.t.* **1.** to tax too heavily. **2.** to make too great demands on: *I had overtaxed my strength.*

o·ver·the·count·er (ō′vər ᴛͪə koun′tər), *adj.* having been sold or purchased other than on an exchange.

o·ver·throw (*v.* ō′vər thrō′; *n.* ō′vər thrō′), *v.*, **-threw, -thrown, -throwing,** *n.* —*v.t.* **1.** to cast down as from a position of power; overcome, defeat, or vanquish. **2.** to put an end to by force, as governments or institutions. **3.** to throw over; upset; overturn. **4.** to knock down and demolish. **5.** to subvert, ruin, or destroy. **6.** to destroy the sound condition of (the mind). —*n.* **7.** the act of overthrowing. **8.** the resulting state. **9.** deposition from power. **10.** defeat; destruction; ruin.

o·ver·time (*n., adv., adj.* ō′vər tīm′; *v.* ō′vər tīm′), *n., adv., adj., v.*, **-timed, -timing.** —*n.* **1.** time during which one works before or after regularly scheduled working hours; extra time. **2.** pay for such time. —*adv.* **3.** during extra time: *to work overtime.* —*adj.* **4.** of or pertaining to overtime: *overtime pay.* —*v.t.* **5.** to give too much time to, as in photographic exposure.

o·vert·ly (ō′vûrt lĭ, ō vûrt′lĭ), *adv.* openly; publicly.

o·ver·tone (ō′vər tōn′), *n.* **1.** *Acoustics.* any frequency emitted by an acoustical instrument that is higher in frequency than the fundamental. **2.** (*usually pl.*) additional meaning.

o·ver·top (ō′vər top′), *v.t.*, **-topped, -topping. 1.** to rise over or above the top of. **2.** to rise above in authority; override (law, etc.). **3.** to surpass or excel.

o·ver·trade (ō′vər trād′), *v.i.*, **-traded, -trading.** to trade in excess of one's capital or the requirements of the market.

o·ver·train (ō′vər trān′), *v.t., v.i.* to train to excess.

o·ver·trick (ō′vər trĭk′), *n. Cards.* an extra trick, one over the number necessary to win the game.

o·ver·trump (ō′vər trump′), *v.t., v.i. Cards.* to trump with a higher trump than has already been played.

o·ver·ture (ō′vər chər), *n., v.*, **-tured, -turing.** —*n.* **1.** an opening of negotiations, or a formal proposal or offer. **2.** *Music.* **a.** an orchestral composition forming the prelude or introduction to an opera, oratorio, etc. **b.** an independent piece of similar character. **3.** an introductory part, as of a poem. **4.** (in Presbyterian churches) **a.** the action of an ecclesiastical court in submitting a question or proposal to other judicatories for consideration. **b.** the proposal or question so submitted. —*v.t.* **5.** to submit as an overture or proposal.

o′ver·roast′	o′ver·sim·plic′i·ty	o′ver·stu′di·ous	o′ver·sweet′
o′ver·salt′	o′ver·sim′pli·fy′	o′ver·sub′tle	o′ver·talk′a·tive
o′ver·scru′pu·lous	o′ver·skep′ti·cal	o′ver·suf·fi′cient	o′ver·tech′ni·cal
o′ver·sen′si·tive	o′ver·stim′u·late′	o′ver·su′per·sti′tious	o′ver·thrust′ (n. or adj.)
o′ver·se′ri·ous	o′ver·strict′	o′ver·sus·pi′cious	o′ver·tire′

6. to make an overture or proposal to. [ME, t. OF, g. L *apertūra* opening, n., with -*o*- from *overt* OVERT] —Syn. **1.** See **proposal.**

o·ver·turn (*n.* ō′vər tûrn′; *n.* ō′vər tûrn′), *v.t.* **1.** to overthrow; destroy the power of, defeat or vanquish. **2.** to turn over on its side, face, or back; upset. —*v.i.* **3.** to turn on its side, face, or back; upset; capsize. —*n.* **4.** act of overturning. **5.** state of being overturned. **6.** *Com.* a turnover. —Syn. **1.** See **upset.**

o·ver·val·ue (ō′vər văl′ū), *v.t.*, -ued, -uing. to value too highly; put too high a value on.

o·ver·watch (ō′vər wŏch′, -wôch′), *v.t.* **1.** to watch over. **2.** to weary by watching.

o·ver·wear (ō′vər wâr′), *v.t.*, -wore, -worn, -wearing. **1.** to wear or use longer than necessary. **2.** to overuse; grow out of.

o·ver·wea·ry (ō′vər wîr′ĭ), *adj.*, *v.*, -ried, -rying. —*adj.* **1.** excessively weary; tired out. —*v.t.* **2.** to weary to excess; overcome with weariness.

o·ver·ween (ō′vər wēn′), *v.i.* to be conceited or arrogant.

o·ver·ween·ing (ō′vər wē′nĭng), *adj.* **1.** conceited, overconfident, or presumptuous: *overweening confidence.* **2.** that overweens. —**o′ver·ween′ing·ly,** *adv.*

o·ver·weigh (ō′vər wā′), *v.t.* **1.** to exceed in weight; overbalance or outweigh. **2.** to weigh down; oppress.

o·ver·weight (*n.* ō′vər wāt′; *adj.* ō′vər wāt′), *n.* **1.** extra weight; excess of weight. **2.** too great weight. **3.** greater weight; preponderance. —*adj.* **4.** weighing more than normally or necessarily required.

o·ver·whelm (ō′vər hwĕlm′), *v.t.*, **1.** to come, rest, or weigh upon overpoweringly; crush. **2.** to overcome completely in mind or feeling. **3.** to load, heap, treat, or address with an overpowering or excessive amount of anything. **4.** to cover or bury beneath a mass of something, a flood, or the like, or cover as a mass or flood does. **5.** *Obs. or Rare.* to overthrow.

o·ver·whelm·ing (ō′vər hwĕl′mĭng), *adj.* **1.** that overwhelms. **2.** so great as to render opposition useless: *an overwhelming majority.* —**o′ver·whelm′ing·ly,** *adv.*

o·ver·wind (ō′vər wīnd′), *v.t.*, -wound, -winding. to wind beyond the proper limit; wind too far.

o·ver·work (*v.* ō′vər wûrk′; *n.* ō′vər wûrk′), *v.*, -worked or -wrought, -working, *n.* —*v.t.* **1.** to cause to work too hard or too long; weary or exhaust with work (often reflexively). **2.** to fill (time) too full of work. **3.** to work up, stir up, or excite excessively. **4.** to elaborate to excess. **5.** to work or decorate all over; decorate the surface of. —*v.i.* **6.** to work too hard; work to excess. —*n.* **7.** work beyond one's strength or capacity. **8.** extra work.

o·ver·write (ō′vər rīt′), *v.t.*, *v.i.*, -wrote, -written, -writing. **1.** to write on top of other writing. **2.** to sacrifice quality to quantity in writing. **3.** to write in an ostentatious or flowery manner.

o·ver·wrought (ō′vər rôt′), *adj.* **1.** wearied or exhausted by overwork. **2.** worked up or excited excessively. **3.** overworked; elaborated to excess.

ovi-, a word element meaning "egg," as in *oviferous.* [t. L, comb. form of *ōvum*]

Ov·id (ŏv′ĭd), *n.* (*Publius Ovidius Naso*) 43 B.C.–A.D. 17?, Roman poet. —**O·vid·i·an** (ō vĭd′ĭ ən), *adj.*

o·vi·duct (ō′vĭ dŭkt′), *n.* *Anat., Zool.* one of a pair of ducts which lead from the body cavity to the exterior in the female and serve to transport and nourish the ova. In higher forms, the distal ends are fused to form the uterus and vagina. [t. NL: s. *ōviductus,* f. L: *ōvi-* ovi- + s. *ductus* DUCT]

O·vie·do (ô vyĕ′dŏ), *n.* a city in NW Spain. 82,548 (1940).

o·vif·er·ous (ō vĭf′ər əs), *adj. Anat., Zool.* bearing eggs.

o·vi·form (ō′vĭ fôrm′), *adj.* egg-shaped.

o·vine (ō′vīn, -vĭn), *adj.* pertaining to, of the nature of, or like sheep. [t. LL: m. s. *ovīnus,* der. L *ovis* sheep]

o·vip·a·ra (ō vĭp′ər ə), *n.pl.* egg-laying animals. [t. NL, t. L: (neut. pl.) egg-laying]

o·vip·a·rous (ō vĭp′ər əs), *adj. Zool.* producing ova or eggs which are matured or hatched after being expelled from the body, as birds, most reptiles and fishes, etc. [t. L: m. *ōviparus* egg-laying] —**o·vi·par·i·ty** (ō′vĭ păr′ə tĭ), *n.*

o·vi·pos·it (ō′vĭ pŏz′ĭt), *v.i.* to deposit or lay eggs, esp. by means of an ovipositor. [f. ovi- + s. L *positus,* pp., placed, put] —**o·vi·po·si·tion** (ō′vĭ pə zĭsh′ən), *n.*

o·vi·pos·i·tor (ō′vĭ pŏz′ə tər), *n.* (in certain insects) an organ at the end of the abdomen, by which eggs are deposited. [f. ovi- + L *positor* placer]

o·vi·sac (ō′vĭ săk′), *n. Zool.* a sac or capsule containing an ovum or ova.

O, Ovipositor of field cricket

o·void (ō′void), *adj.* **1.** egg-shaped; having the solid form of an egg. **2.** having such a form with the broader end at the base, as a fruit. Cf. **ovate.** —*n.* **3.** an ovoid body. [f. s. L *ōvum* egg + -OID]

o·vo·lo (ō′və lō′), *n., pl.* -li (-lē′). *Archit.* a convex molding forming or approximating in section a quarter of a circle or ellipse. See diag. under **column.** [t. It., var. (now obs.) of *uovolo,* dim. of *uovo,* g. L *ōvum* egg]

o·vo·vi·vip·a·rous (ō′vō vī vĭp′ə rəs), *adj. Zool.* producing eggs which are hatched within the body, so that the young are born alive but without placental attachment, as certain reptiles, fishes, etc. [f. *ovo-* (comb. form of OVUM) + VIVIPAROUS]

o·vu·lar (ō′vyə lər), *adj.* pertaining to or of the nature of an ovule. [t. NL: s. *ovulāris*]

o·vu·late (ō′vyə lāt), *v.i.*, -lated, -lating. *Biol.* to shed eggs from an ovary or ovarian follicle. [f. s. NL *ōvulum* little egg + -ATE[1]] —**o′vu·la′tion,** *n.*

o·vule (ō′vūl), *n.* **1.** *Biol.* a small egg. **2.** *Bot.* **a.** a rudimentary seed. **b.** the body which contains the embryosac and hence the female germ cell, and which after fertilization develops into a seed. [t. NL: m. *ōvulum,* dim. of L *ōvum* egg]

o·vum (ō′vəm), *n., pl.* ova (ō′və). **1.** *Biol.* **a.** an egg, in a broad biological sense. **b.** the female reproductive cell or gamete of plants. **c.** the female reproductive cell of animals, which (usually only after fertilization) is capable of developing into a new individual. **2.** *Archit.* an egg-shaped ornament. [t. L: egg]

owe (ō), *v.*, owed, owing. —*v.t.* **1.** to be indebted or beholden for (usually fol. by *to*). **2.** to be under obligation to pay or repay, or to render (often fol. by *to* or a simple dative): *to owe interest on a mortgage.* **3.** (by omission of the ordinary direct object) to be in debt to: *he owes not any man.* **4.** to have or cherish (a certain feeling) toward a person: *to owe one a grudge.* **5.** *Obs.* to own or possess. —*v.i.* **6.** to be in debt. [ME *owe*(n), OE *āgan,* c. OHG *eigan.* Cf. OWN, OUGHT[1]]

Ow·en (ō′ĭn), *n.* **1.** Robert, 1771–1858, British social reformer. **2.** Wilfred, 1893–1918, British poet.

Ow·ens·bor·o (ō′ĭnz bûr′ō), *n.* a city in NW Kentucky, on the Ohio river. 33,651 (1950).

Ow·en Stan·ley (ō′ĭn stăn′lĭ), a mountain range in SE New Guinea. Highest peak, Mt. Victoria. 13,030 ft.

OWI, Office of War Information.

ow·ing (ō′ĭng), *adj.* **1.** that owes. **2.** owed or due: *to pay what is owing.* **3.** *Obs.* indebted. **4. owing to, a.** on account of; because of. **b.** attributable to.

owl (oul), *n.* **1.** any of numerous birds of prey of the order *Strigiformes,* chiefly nocturnal, with a broad head and with large eyes which are usually surrounded by disks of modified feathers and directed forward. They feed on mice, small birds and reptiles, etc. **2.** a variety of domestic pigeons of owllike appearance. **3.** a person of nocturnal habits. **4.** a person of owllike solemnity of appearance. [ME *oule,* OE *ūle,* c. LG *ūle;* akin to G *eule,* Icel. *ugla*] —**owl′like′,** *adj.*

owl·et (ou′lĭt), *n.* **1.** a young owl. **2.** a small owl, esp. the **little owl,** *Athene noctua,* of Europe.

owl·ish (ou′lĭsh), *adj.* owllike: *an owlish air of wisdom.*

Horned owl,
Bubo virginianus
(23 in long)

owl's-clo·ver (oulz′klō′vər), *n.* a scrophulariaceous herb, *Orthocarpus erianthus,* native to California.

owl train, a railroad train which makes its trip during the night.

own (ōn), *adj.* **1.** belonging, pertaining, or relating to oneself or itself (usually used after a possessive to emphasize the idea of ownership, interest, or relation conveyed by the possessive): *his own money.* **2.** (absolutely, with a possessive preceding) own property, relatives, etc.: *to come into one's own.* **3. of one's own,** belonging to oneself. **4. on one's own,** *Colloq.* on one's own account, responsibility, resources, etc. **5. be one's own man,** to be independent. [ME *owen;* OE *āgen,* orig. pp. of *āgan* have, possess. See OWE] —*v.t.* **6.** to have or hold as one's own; possess. **7.** to acknowledge or admit: *to own a fault.* **8.** to acknowledge as one's own. —*v.i.* **9.** to confess: *to own to being uncertain.* [ME *ohnien,* OE *āgnian,* der. *āgen* OWN, adj.] —Syn. **6.** See have. —Ant. **6.** lack, need.

own·er (ō′nər), *n.* one who owns; a proprietor.

own·er·ship (ō′nər shĭp′), *n.* **1.** state or fact of being an owner. **2.** legal right of possession; proprietorship.

ox (ŏks), *n., pl.* oxen. the adult castrated male of the genus *Bos,* used as a draft animal and for food. [ME *oxe,* OE *oxa,* c. G *ochse*] —**ox′like′,** *adj.*

Ox., (L *Oxonia*) Oxford.

oxa-, a prefix meaning "oxygen when it replaces carbon."

ox·a·late (ŏk′sə lāt′), *n. Chem.* a salt or ester of oxalic acid. [f. OXAL(IC) + -ATE[2]]

ox·al·ic acid (ŏks ăl′ĭk), *Chem.* a white, crystalline, dibasic acid, $H_2C_2O_4 \cdot 2H_2O$, first discovered in the juice of a species of oxalis (wood sorrel), used in textile and dye manufacturing, in bleaching, etc. [*oxalic,* t. F: m. *oxalique,* der. L *oxalis* OXALIS]

ox·a·lis (ŏk′sə lĭs), *n.* any plant of the large genus *Oxalis,* as the common wood sorrel, *O. Acetosella,* a herb with leaves usually of three heart-shaped leaflets, and white or pink single flowers. [t. L, t. Gk.: sorrel]

---

o′ver·twist′	o′ver·ve′he·ment	o′ver·vi′gor·ous	o′ver·warmed′
o′ver·val′u·a′tion	o′ver·ven′ture·some	o′ver·vi′o·lent	o′ver·zeal′ous

---

ox·a·zine (ŏk/sə zēn′, -zĭn), *n. Chem.* any of a group of thirteen compounds, C_4H_5NO, containing four carbon atoms, one oxygen atom, and one nitrogen atom, arranged in a six-membered ring. Also, **ox·a·zin** (ŏk/sə zĭn). [f. ox(A)- + -AZINE]

ox·blood (ŏks/blŭd′), *n.* a deep dull red color.

ox·bow (ŏks/bō′), *n. U.S.* **1.** a bow-shaped piece of wood placed under and around the neck of an ox, with its upper ends inserted in the bar of the yoke. **2.** a bow-shaped bend in a river, or the land embraced by it.

ox·cart (ŏks/kärt′), *n.* an ox-drawn cart.

ox·en (ŏk/sən), *n.* pl. of **ox**.

Ox·en·stier·na (ōōk/sən shĕr′nä), *n.* **Count Axel,** (äk/səl), 1583–1654, Swedish statesman. Also, **Ox·en·stiern** (ŏk/sən stĭrn′).

ox·eye (ŏks/ī′), *n.* **1.** any of various plants with flowers composed of a disk with marginal rays, as the mayweed, the oxeye daisy, and the false sunflower (*Heliopsis*). **2.** any of several shore birds of the U.S., as the semi-palmated sandpiper (*Ereunetes pusillus*). [ME *oxie*, f. ox + *ie* EYE]

oxeye daisy. See **daisy** (def. 1).

ox·ford (ŏks/fərd), *n.* **1.** a low shoe laced or buttoned over the instep. **2.** shirting of cotton or rayon in a basket weave. [named after OXFORD, the city]

Ox·ford (ŏks/fərd), *n.* **1.** a city in S England: famous university (founded in the 12th century). 101,040 (est. 1946). **2.** Oxfordshire. **3.** Robert Harley, 1st Earl of, 1661–1724, British statesman. **4.** a large English breed of sheep, hornless, with dark brown face and legs, of the mutton type, noted for its relatively large, heavy market lambs, and heavy fleece of relatively coarse medium wool.

Oxford corners, *Print.* ruled borderlines about the text of a page, etc., that cross and project slightly at the corners.

Oxford gray, medium to dark gray.

Oxford group, Buchmanism.

Oxford movement, a movement toward High-Church principles in the Church of England, which originated at Oxford University about 1833.

Ox·ford·shire (ŏks/fərd shĭr′, -shər), *n.* a county in S England. 248,000 pop. (est. 1946); 749 sq. mi. *Co. seat:* Oxford. Also, **Oxford** or **Oxon.**

Oxford shoe, oxford (def. 1). Also, **Oxford tie.**

ox·heart (ŏks/härt′), *n.* any large, heart-shaped variety of sweet cherry.

ox·i·dase (ŏk/sə dās′, -dāz′), *n. Biochem.* any of a group of oxidizing enzymes. [f. OXID(E) + -ASE]

ox·i·date (ŏk/sə dāt′), *v.t., v.i.,* **-dated, -dating.** to oxidize. **—ox/i·da/tion,** *n.* **—ox/i·da/tive,** *adj.*

ox·ide (ŏk/sīd, -sĭd), *n. Chem.* a compound, usually containing two elements only, one of which is oxygen, as *mercuric oxide.* Also, **ox·id** (ŏk/sĭd). [t. F (now *oxyde*), f. *ox*(*ygène*) oxygen + (*ac*)*ide* acid]

ox·i·dim·e·try (ŏk/sə dĭm/ə trĭ), *n.* a technique of analytical chemistry which utilizes oxidizing agents for titrations.

ox·i·dize (ŏk/sə dīz′), *v.,* **-dized, -dizing.** *Chem.* **—***v.t.* **1.** to convert (an element) into its oxide; to combine with oxygen. **2.** to cover with a coating of oxide, or rust. **3.** to take away hydrogen from as by the action of oxygen; to add oxygen or any nonmetal to. **4.** to increase the valence of (an element) in the positive direction. **5.** to remove electrons. **—***v.i.* **6.** to become oxidized. Also, *esp. Brit.,* **ox/i·dise′.** **—ox/i·diz/a·ble,** *adj.* **—ox/i·di·za/tion,** *n.* **—ox/i·diz/er,** *n.*

ox·ime (ŏk/sēm, -sĭm), *n.* any of a group of compounds with the radical -C=NOH (**oxime group** or **radical**), prepared by the condensation of ketones or aldehydes with hydroxylamine. Also, **ox·im** (ŏk/sĭm). [f. OX(YGEN) + IM(IN)E]

ox·lip (ŏks/lĭp′), *n.* a species of primrose, *Primula elatior,* with pale-yellow flowers. [ME; OE *oxanslyppe,* f. *oxan* ox's + *slyppe* slime. See SLIP², and cf. COWSLIP]

Ox·on (ŏk/sŏn), *n.* Oxfordshire.

Oxon., **1.** (L *Oxonia*) Oxford. **2.** (L *Oxoniensis*) of Oxford.

Ox·o·ni·an (ŏk sō′nĭ ən), *adj.* **1.** of or pertaining to Oxford, England, or Oxford University. **—***n.* **2.** a member or graduate of Oxford University. **3.** a native or inhabitant of Oxford. [f. s. ML *Oxonia* Oxford + -AN]

oxonium compound, *Chem.* the product of reaction between an organic compound containing a basic oxygen atom, and a strong acid.

ox·peck·er (ŏks/pĕk′ər), *n.* either of two species of African starlings of the genus *Buphagus.*

ox·tail (ŏks/tāl′), *n.* the skinned tail of an ox used to make a soup.

ox·ter (ŏks/stər), *n. Scot.* the armpit. [appar. der. OE *ōxta* armpit]

ox·tongue (ŏks/tŭng′), *n.* any of various plants with rough, tongue-shaped leaves, as the bugloss, *Anchusa officinalis.*

Ox·us (ŏk/səs), *n.* ancient and modern name of **Amu Darya.**

oxy-¹, a word element meaning "sharp" or "acute." [t. Gk., comb. form of *oxýs* sharp, keen, acid]

oxy-², a combining form of **oxygen** sometimes used as an equivalent of *hydroxy-.*

ox·y·a·cet·y·lene (ŏk/sĭ ə sĕt/ə lēn′), *adj.* of or pertaining to a mixture of oxygen and acetylene, used in

a blowtorch (**oxyacetylene blowpipe**) at 3300°C., for cutting steel plates.

ox·y·ac·id (ŏk/sĭ ăs/ĭd), *n. Chem.* an inorganic acid containing oxygen. Also, **oxygen acid.**

ox·y·cal·ci·um (ŏk/sĭ kăl/sĭ əm), *adj.* pertaining to or produced by oxygen and calcium: *the oxycalcium light.*

ox·y·da·tion (ŏk/sə dā/shən), *n.* oxidation.

ox·y·gen (ŏk/sə jən), *n. Chem.* a colorless, odorless gaseous element, constituting about one fifth of the volume of the atmosphere and present in a combined state throughout nature. It is the supporter of combustion in air, and is the standard of atomic, combining, and molecular weights: *Weight of 1 liter at 0°C. and 760 mm. pressure:* 1.4290 grams. *Symbol:* O; *at. wt.:* 16.0; *at. no.:* 8. [t. F: m. *oxygène,* f. *oxy-* oxy-¹ + *-gène* -GEN]

ox·y·gen·ate (ŏk/sə jə nāt′), *v.t.,* **-ated, -ating.** to treat or combine, esp. to enrich, with oxygen. **—ox/y·gen·a/tion,** *n.*

oxygen-hydrogen welding, welding done at a temperature in excess of 5,000°F. with a blowpipe furnishing oxygen and hydrogen.

ox·y·gen·ize (ŏk/sə jə nīz′), *v.t.,* **-ized, -izing.** oxygenate.

oxygen mask, a masklike device worn by aviators at great altitudes when inhaling supplementary oxygen from an attached tank.

oxygen tent, a small tent for delivering oxygen to a sick person at critical periods.

ox·y·he·mo·glo·bin (ŏk/sĭ hē/mə glō/bĭn), *n.* the substance formed when hemoglobin proper unites loosely with oxygen, present in arterial blood. See **hemoglobin.**

ox·y·hy·dro·gen (ŏk/sĭ hī/drə jən), *n.* a mixture of oxygen and hydrogen, used in a blowtorch (**oxyhydrogen blowpipe**) at 2800°C. for cutting steel plates.

ox·y·mo·ron (ŏk/sĭ mōr/ŏn), *n., pl.* **-mora** (-mōr/ə). *Rhet.* a figure by which a locution produces an effect by a seeming self-contradiction, as in *cruel kindness* or *to make haste slowly.* [t. NL, t. Gk., neut. of *oxýmōros* pointedly foolish]

ox·y·salt (ŏk/sĭ sôlt′), *n. Chem.* any salt of an oxyacid. [f. oxy-² + SALT]

ox·y·sul·fide (ŏk/sĭ sŭl/fīd, -fĭd), *n. Chem.* a sulfide in which part of the sulfur is replaced by oxygen.

ox·y·to·cic (ŏk/sĭ tō/sĭk, -tŏs/ĭk), *Med.* **—***adj.* **1.** pertaining to or causing the stimulation of the involuntary muscle of the uterus. **2.** promoting or accelerating parturition. **—***n.* **3.** an oxytocic medicine or drug. [f. Gk.: m.s. *oxytókion* a medicine hastening childbirth + -IC]

ox·y·tone (ŏk/sĭ tōn′), *adj.* **1.** (in Greek grammar) having an acute accent on the last syllable. **—***n.* **2.** an oxytone word. [t. Gk.: m.s. *oxýtonos*]

O·ya·ma (ō/yä mä′), *n.* **Iwao** (ē/wä ō′), 1842–1916, Japanese field marshal.

o·yer (ō/yər, oi/ər), *n.* **1.** *Law.* a hearing or trial of (criminal) causes (chiefly in the phrase **oyer and terminer**). **2.** the production in court of some document pleaded by one party and demanded by the other (the party pleading it is said to *make profert* and the other is said to *crave oyer*). [ME, t. AF (prop. inf.), var. of *oir,* g. L *audire* hear]

oyer and ter·mi·ner (ûr/mə nər), *Law.* **1.** *U.S.* any of various higher criminal courts in some of the States. **2.** *Brit.* **a.** a commission or writ directing the holding of a court to try offenses. **b.** the court itself.

o·yez (ō/yĕs, ō/yĕz), *interj.* **1.** hear! attend! (a cry uttered, usually, thrice, by a public or court crier to command silence and attention before a proclamation, etc., is made). **—***n.* **2.** a cry of "oyez." Also, **o/yes.** [t. AF: hear ye, 2d pers. pl. impv. of *oyer.* See OYER]

oys·ter (ois/tər), *n.* **1.** any of various edible marine bivalve mollusks (family *Ostreidae*) with irregularly shaped shell, found on the bottom or adhering to rocks, etc., in shallow water, some species being extensively cultivated for the market. **2.** the oyster-shaped bit of dark meat in the front hollow of the side bone of a fowl. **3.** *Slang.* a close-mouthed person. **4.** something from which one may extract or derive advantage. **—***v.i.* **5.** to dredge for or otherwise take oysters. [ME *oistre,* t. OF, t. L: m.s. *ostrea, ostreum,* t. Gk.: m. *óstreon*]

oyster bed, a place where oysters breed or are cultivated.

oyster catcher, any of several long-billed, maritime wading birds constituting the genus *Haematopus,* with a plumage chiefly of black and white, as *H. ostralegus,* the common European species.

oyster crab, a crab, *Pinnotheres,* existing commensally in the mantle cavity of oysters.

oyster cracker, a small, round, (usually) salted cracker, served with oysters, soups, etc.

oyster farm, a place where oyster beds are kept.

oys·ter·man (ois/tər mən), *n., pl.* **-men.** **2.** a container for gathering oysters.

oyster plant, the salsify, whose root has an oyster-like flavor.

oyster white, very light gray with a greenish or yellowish tinge.

OZ., *pl.* **ozs.** **1.** ounce. **2.** ounces.

O·zark Mountains (ō/zärk), a group of low mountains in S Missouri, N Arkansas, and NE Oklahoma. Also, **O/zarks.**

o·zo·ce·rite (ō zō′kə rīt′, -sə rīt′, ō′zō sĭr′īt), n. mineral wax or waxlike mineral resin. [t. G: m. *ozokerit*, f. Gk. *ŏzō* I smell + s. Gk. *kērós* wax + -*it* -ITE[1]]

o·zone (ō′zōn, ō zōn′), n. **1.** a form of oxygen, O₃, having three atoms to the molecule, with a peculiar odor suggesting that of weak chlorine, which is produced when an electric spark is passed through air, and in several other ways. It is found in the atmosphere in minute quantities, esp. after a thunderstorm, and is a powerful oxidizing agent, used for bleaching, sterilizing water, etc. **2.** *Colloq.* clear, invigorating, fresh air. [t. F, f. s. Gk. *ŏzein* smell + -*one* -ONE] —**o·zon·ic** (ō zŏn′ĭk, ō zō′nĭk), adj.

ozone layer, *Meteorol.* a rather restricted region in the outer portion of the stratosphere at an elevation of about 20 miles, where much of the atmospheric ozone (O₃) is concentrated.

o·zo·nif·er·ous (ō′zə nĭf′ər əs), adj. containing ozone.

o·zo·ni·za·tion (ō′zə nə zā′shən), n. the treatment of a compound with ozone.

o·zo·nize (ō′zə nīz′), v.t., **-nized, -nizing. 1.** to impregnate or treat with ozone. **2.** to convert (oxygen) into ozone.

o·zo·nol·y·sis (ō′zə nŏl′ə sĭs), n. *Chem.* the reaction of ozone with hydrocarbons.

o·zo·nous (ō′zə nəs), adj. of or containing ozone.

ozs., ounces.

P

P, p (pē), n., pl. **P's** or **Ps, p's** or **ps. 1.** a consonant, the 16th letter of the English alphabet. **2.** *Genetics.* a symbol for the parental generation, P₁ indicating immediate parents, P₂ grandparents, etc. **3. mind one's P's and Q's,** to be careful, esp. in behavior. **4.** (in medieval Roman numerals) 400.

P, 1. *Chem.* phosphorus. **2.** *Physics.* pressure. **3.** *Chess.* pawn.

p-, *Chem.* para-[1].

P., 1. (L *Pater*) Father. **2.** (F *Père*) Father. **3.** President. **4.** Prince. **5.** Progressive.

p., 1. page. **2.** part. **3.** participle. **4.** past. **5.** (L *pater*) father. **6.** *Chess.* pawn. **7.** penny. **8.** peseta. **9.** peso. **10.** *Music.* (It. *piano*) softly. **11.** pint. **12.** *Baseball.* pitcher. **13.** population. **14.** (L *post*) after.

pa (pä), n. *Colloq.* papa.

Pa, protoactinium.

Pa., Pennsylvania.

P.A., 1. Passenger Agent. **2.** Post Adjutant. **3.** power of attorney. **4.** Purchasing Agent.

p.a., 1. participial adjective. **2.** per annum. **3.** press agent.

Paa·sen (pä′sən), n. **Pierre van** (pyĕr vän, văn), born 1895, U.S. journalist, author, and clergyman, born in the Netherlands.

pab·u·lum (păb′yə ləm), n. that which nourishes an animal or vegetable organism; food. [t. L: food, fodder]

Pac., Pacific.

P.A.C., Political Action Committee. Also, **PAC** (păk).

pa·ca (pä′kə, păk′ə), n. a large white-spotted, almost tailless hystricomorphic rodent, *Agouti paca*, of South and Central America; the spotted cavy. [t. Pg. or Sp., both t. Tupi]

Paca. *Agouti paca* (2½ ft. long, 1 ft. high)

pace[1] (pās), n., v., **paced, pacing.** —n. **1.** rate of stepping, or of movement in general: *a pace of ten miles an hour.* **2.** a lineal measure of variable extent, representing the space naturally measured by the movement of the foot in walking. The pace of a single step (**military pace**) is reckoned in the U.S. Army at 2½ feet for quick time and 3 feet for double time. The **geometrical** or **great pace** is 5 feet, representing the distance from the place where either foot is taken up, in walking, to that where the same foot is set down. The **Roman pace**, reckoned like the geometrical pace, was equal to 5 Roman feet, or about 58 English inches. **3.** a single step: *she made three paces across the room.* **4.** the distance covered in a step: *stand six paces inside the gates.* **5.** manner of stepping; gait. **6.** a gait of a horse, etc., in which the feet on the same side are lifted and put down together. **7.** any of the gaits of a horse, etc. **8.** a raised step or platform. —v.t. **9.** to set the pace for, as in racing. **10.** to traverse with paces or steps: *he paced the floor.* **11.** to measure by paces. **12.** to train to a certain pace; exercise in pacing: *to pace a horse.* —v.i. **13.** to take slow, regular steps. **14.** (of a horse) to go at a pace; amble. [ME *pas*, t. OF, g. L *passus* a step, lit., a stretch (of the leg)] —**Syn. 7.** step, gait, amble, rack, trot, canter, gallop, walk, run, singlefoot **10.** PACE, PLOD, TRUDGE refer to a steady and monotonous kind of walking. PACE suggests steady, measured steps as of one completely lost in thought or impelled by some distraction: *to pace up and down.* PLOD implies a slow, heavy, laborious, weary walk: *the ploughman homeward plods his weary way.* TRUDGE implies a spiritless but usually steady and doggedly persistent walk: *the farmer trudged to his village to buy his supplies.* —**Ant. 10.** scamper, scurry, skip.

pa·ce[2] (pā′sĭ), prep. *Latin.* with the permission of (a courteous form used to mention one who disagrees). [L, abl. of *pax* peace, pardon, leave]

paced (pāst), adj. **1.** having a specified pace: *slow-paced.* **2.** counted out or measured by paces. **3.** *Racing.* run at a pace determined by a pacemaker.

pace·mak·er (pās′mā′kər), n. one who sets the pace, as in racing. —**pace′mak′ing,** n.

pac·er (pā′sər), n. **1.** one who paces. **2.** a pacemaker. **3.** a horse that paces, or whose natural gait is a pace.

pa·cha (pə shä′, päsh′ə), n. pasha.

pa·cha·lic (pə shä′lĭk), n. pashalik.

pa·chi·si (pə chē′zĭ, pä-), n. parcheesi.

Pach·mann (päкн′män), n. **Vladimir de** (vlä dē′mĭr də), 1848–1933, Russian pianist.

pach·ou·li (păch′ŏŏ lĭ, pə chŏŏ′lĭ), n. patchouli.

Pa·chu·ca (pä chŏŏ′kä), n. a city in central Mexico: the capital of Hidalgo state; silver mines. 53,354 (1940).

pach·y·derm (păk′ə dûrm′), n. **1.** any of the thick-skinned nonruminant ungulates, as the elephant, hippopotamus, and rhinoceros. **2.** a person who is not sensitive to criticism, ridicule, etc. [t. F: m. *pachyderme*, t. Gk.: m.s. *pachýdermos* thick-skinned] —**pach′y·der′ma·tous, pach′y·der′mous,** adj.

pa·cif·ic (pə sĭf′ĭk), adj. **1.** tending to make peace; conciliatory: *pacific propositions.* **2.** peaceable; not warlike: *a pacific disposition.* **3.** peaceful; at peace: *pacific state of things.* **4.** (cap.) designating, or pertaining to, the Pacific Ocean. **5.** (cap.) of or pertaining to the region bordering on the Pacific Ocean: *the Pacific States.* —n. **6.** (cap.) the Pacific Ocean. Also, **pa·cif′i·cal** for 1–3. [t. L: s. *pācificus* peace-making] —**pa·cif′i·cal·ly,** adv.
—**Syn. 1.** PACIFIC, PEACEABLE, PEACEFUL describe that which is in a state of peace. That which is PACIFIC tends toward the making, promoting, or preserving of peace: *pacific intentions.* That which is PEACEABLE desires to be at peace or is free from the disposition to quarrel: *peaceable citizens.* That which is PEACEFUL is in a calm state, characteristic of, or characterized by peace: *a peaceful death.* —**Ant. 1** warlike, belligerent.

pa·cif·i·cate (pə sĭf′ə kāt′), v.t., **-cated, -cating.** to pacify. [t. L: m.s. *pācificātus*, pp.] —**pac·i·fi·ca·tion** (pās′ə fə kā′shən), n. —**pa·cif′i·ca′tor,** n. —**pa·cif·i·ca·to·ry** (pə sĭf′ə kə tōr′ĭ), adj.

pac·i·fism (păs′ə fĭz′əm), n. *Brit.* pacifism. —**pa·cif′i·cist,** n.

pa·ci·fi·co (pä sē′fē kô′), n., pl. **-cos** (-kôs′). *Spanish.* **1.** a peaceful person. **2.** a native of Cuba or the Philippine Islands not resisting Spanish occupation of his country. [Sp., t. L: m. *pācificus*]

Pacific Ocean, the largest ocean, between the American continents and Asia and Australia: divided by the equator into the **North Pacific** and the **South Pacific.** ab. 70,000,000 sq. mi.; greatest known depth, 35,433 ft.

Pacific time. See **standard time.**

pac·i·fi·er (păs′ə fī′ər), n. **1.** one who or that which pacifies. **2.** a rubber nipple, etc., given to a baby to suck. **3.** a teething ring.

pac·i·fism (păs′ə fĭz′əm), n. the principle or policy of establishing and maintaining universal peace or such relations among all nations that all differences may be adjusted without recourse to war. [f. PACIF(IC) + -ISM] —**pac′i·fist,** n., adj. —**pac′i·fis′tic,** adj.

pac·i·fy (păs′ə fī′), v.t., **-fied, -fying. 1.** to bring into a state of peace; quiet; calm: *pacify an angry man.* **2.** to appease: *pacify one's appetite.* [late ME, t. L: m. *pācificāre* make peace]

pack[1] (păk), n. **1.** a quantity of anything wrapped or tied up; parcel (sometimes of fixed amount as a measure): *a pack of cigarettes.* **2.** the quantity of anything, as food, packed or put up at one time or in one season: *salmon pack.* **3.** a set or gang (of people) or a group (of things): *a pack of thieves.* **4.** a company of animals: *a pack of wolves.* **5.** a complete set, as of playing cards, usually 52 in number. **6.** a considerable area of pieces of floating ice driven or packed together. **7.** *Med.* **a. a** wrapping of the body in wet or dry cloths for therapeutic purposes. **b.** the cloths used. **c.** state of being so wrapped. **8.** a cosmetic treatment similar to this. **9.** *Obs.* a worthless person.

—*v.t.* **10.** to make into a pack or bundle. **11.** to make into a group or compact mass, as animals, ice, etc. **12.** to fill with anything compactly arranged: *pack a trunk.* **13.** to press or crowd together; cram: *a packed gallery.* **14.** to put or arrange in suitable form for market: *pack fruit.* **15.** to make airtight, vaportight, or watertight by stuffing: *to pack the piston of a steam engine.* **16.** to cover or envelop with something pressed closely around. **17.** to load (a horse, etc.) with a pack. **18.** to carry, esp. as a load. **19.** to send off summarily (sometimes fol. by *off, away,* etc.): *packed off to her mother.* **20.** to put a load upon. **21.** *Boxing Slang.* to be able to make (a forceful blow). **22.** to treat with the therapeutic pack.
—*v.i.* **23.** to pack goods, etc., in compact form, as for transportation or storage (often fol. by *up*). **24.** to admit of being compactly stowed: *articles that pack well.* **25.** to crowd together, as persons, etc. **26.** to become compacted: *wet snow packs readily.* **27.** to collect into a pack: *grouse began to pack.* **28.** to leave hastily (generally fol. by *off, away,* etc.).
—*adj.* **29.** transporting, or used in transporting, a pack: *pack horse, pack animals.* **30.** made up of pack animals. **31.** *Chiefly Scot.* (of animals) tame. **32.** compressed into a pack; packed. **33.** used in or adapted for packing. [ME *packe, pakke,* t. Flem., D or LG] —**Syn. 1.** See **package. 4.** See **flock¹. 5.** *Now U.S. only.* deck.

pack² (păk), *v.t.* to collect, arrange, or manipulate (cards, persons, facts, etc.) so as to serve one's own purposes: *pack a jury.* [? var. of PACT]

pack·age (păk′ĭj), *n., v.,* **-aged, -aging.** —*n.* **1.** a bundle or parcel. **2.** that in which anything is packed, as a case, crate, etc. **3.** the packing of goods, etc. —*v.t.* **4.** to put into wrappings or a container.
—**Syn. 1.** PACKAGE, PACK, PACKET, PARCEL refer to a bundle or to something fastened together. A PACKAGE is a bundle of things packed and wrapped: *a package from the drug store.* A PACK is a large bundle or bale of things put or fastened together, usually wrapped up or in a bag, case, etc., to be carried by a person or a beast of burden: *a peddler's pack.* A PACKET, originally a package of letters or dispatches, is a small package or bundle: *a packet of gems.* A PARCEL is an object or objects wrapped up to form a single, small bundle: *a parcel containing two dresses.*

pack·er (păk′ər), *n.* **1.** one whose business is packing food for the market. **2.** one who or that which packs.

pack·et (păk′ĭt), *n.* **1.** a small pack or package of anything, orig. of letters. **2.** a boat that carries mail, passengers, and goods regularly on a fixed route. **3.** any ship. —*v.t.* **4.** to bind up in a package or parcel. [dim. of PACK¹] —**Syn. 1.** See **package.**

pack·ing (păk′ĭng), *n.* **1.** act or work of one who or that which packs. **2.** the preparing and packaging of foodstuffs. **3.** any material used for packing or making watertight, steamtight, etc., as a fibrous substance closing a joint, a metallic ring round a piston, etc.

packing effect, *Physics.* mass defect.

packing house, an establishment in which provisions, esp. beef and pork, are packed for the market.

pack·man (păk′mən), *n., pl.* **-men.** a peddler.

pack rat, *Zool.* a large, bushy-tailed rodent, *Neotoma cinerea,* of North America, noted for carrying away small articles which it keeps in its nest.

pack·sack (păk′săk′), *n.* a traveling bag, usually of canvas or leather, usually strapped over one's shoulders.

pack·sad·dle (păk′săd′əl), *n.* a saddle specially designed for supporting the load on a pack animal.

pack·thread (păk′thrĕd′), *n.* a strong thread or twine for sewing or tying up packages.

pact (păkt), *n.* an agreement; a compact. [ME, t. L: s. *pactum,* prop. pp. neut., agreed]

pac·tion (păk′shən), *n.* agreement.

Pac·to·lus (păk tō′ləs), *n.* a small river in ancient Lydia: famous for the gold washed from its sands.

pad¹ (păd), *n., v.,* **padded, padding.** —*n.* **1.** a cushionlike mass of some soft material, for comfort, protection, or stuffing. **2.** a cushion used as a saddle; saddle of leather and padding without a tree. **3.** a number of sheets of paper held together at the edge to form a tablet. **4.** a soft ink-soaked block of absorbent material for inking a rubber stamp. **5.** one of the cushionlike protuberances on the under side of the feet of dogs, foxes, and some other animals. **6.** the foot of a fox or other beast of the chase. **7.** *Zool.* a pulvillus on an insect's tarsus or pretarsus. **8.** the large floating leaf of the water lily. —*v.t.* **9.** to furnish, protect, fill out, or stuff with a pad or padding. **10.** to expand (writing or speech) with unnecessary words or matter. [special uses of obs. *pad* bundle to lie on, ? b. PACK¹ and BED]

pad² (păd), *n., v.,* **padded, padding.** —*n.* **1.** a dull sound, as of footsteps on the ground. **2.** a road horse, distinguished from a hunter or workhorse. **3.** a highwayman. **4.** *Brit. Dial.* a path or road. —*v.t.* **5.** to travel along on foot. **6.** to beat down by treading. —*v.i.* **7.** to travel on foot. **8.** to go with a dull sound of footsteps. [t. D or LG (c. PATH); orig. beggars' and thieves' slang]

Pa·dang (pä däng′), *n.* a seaport in the U.S. of Indonesia, in W Sumatra. 52,054 (1930).

pad·ding (păd′ĭng), *n.* **1.** material, as cotton or straw, with which to pad. **2.** unnecessary matter used to expand a speech, etc. **3.** act of one who or that which pads.

Pad·ding·ton (păd′ĭng tən), *n.* a W residential borough of London, England. 121,460 (est. 1946).

pad·dle¹ (păd′əl), *n., v.,* **-dled, -dling.** —*n.* **1.** a short oar held in the hands (not resting in the rowlock) and used esp. for propelling canoes. **2.** one of the broad boards on the circumference of a paddle wheel. **3.** a paddle wheel. **4.** one of the similar projecting blades by means of which a water wheel is turned. **5.** a flipper or limb of a penguin, turtle, whale, etc. **6.** an implement used for beating garments while washing them in running water, as in a stream. **7.** any of various similar implements used in industrial processes. **8.** act of padding. —*v.i.* **9.** to propel, or travel in, a canoe or the like by using a paddle. **10.** to row lightly or gently with oars. **11.** to move by means of paddle wheels, as a steamer. —*v.t.* **12.** to propel (a canoe, etc.) with a paddle. **13.** to stir. **14.** *U.S. Colloq.* to beat with or as with a paddle; spank. **15.** to convey by paddling, as in a canoe. [orig. obscure] —**pad′dler¹,** *n.*

pad·dle² (păd′əl), *v.i.,* **-dled, -dling. 1.** to dabble or play in or as in shallow water. **2.** to toy with the fingers. **3.** to toddle. [orig. uncert.] —**pad′dler²,** *n.*

paddle box, a box or casing covering the upper part of the paddle wheel of a vessel.

pad·dle·fish (păd′əl fĭsh′), *n., pl.* **-fishes,** (*esp. collectively*) **-fish.** a large ganoid fish, *Polyodon spathula,* remotely allied to the sturgeons, with a long, flat, paddlelike projection of the snout, abundant in the Mississippi river and its larger tributaries.

paddle wheel, a power-driven wheel with floatboards (paddles) on its circumference, for propelling a vessel over the water. —**pad′dle-wheel′,** *adj.*

pad·dock¹ (păd′ək), *n.* **1.** a small field or enclosure, esp. for pasture near a stable or house. **2.** a turfed enclosure for horses, esp. at a racecourse. **3.** *Australia.* any enclosed field or piece of land. —*v.t.* **4.** to confine or enclose in or as in a paddock. [var. of *parrock,* OE *pearroc* enclosure (orig. fence)]

pad·dock² (păd′ək), *n. Now Chiefly Dial. and Scot.* a frog or toad. [ME *paddoke,* f. *pad* toad + *-oke* -OCK]

pad·dy¹ (păd′ĭ), *n.* **1.** rice. **2.** rice in the husk, uncut or gathered. [t. Malay: m. *pādī*]

Pad·dy (păd′ĭ), *n., pl.* **-dies.** *Nickname.* an Irishman. [familiar var. of Irish *Padraig* Patrick]

pad·dy·whack (păd′ĭ hwăk′), *n.* **1.** *Brit. Colloq.* an intense anger; a rage. **2.** *U.S. Colloq.* a spanking.

Pa·de·rew·ski (pä′dĕ rĕf′skĭ, päd′ə-), *n. Fr.* **Ignace** (ē nyäs′) or *Pol.* **Ignacy** (ĭg nä′tsĭ) **Jan** (yän), 1860–1941, Polish pianist, composer, and statesman.

Pa·di·shah (pä′dĭ shä′), *n.* great king; emperor (a title applied esp. to the Shah of Iran, formerly also to the Sultan of Turkey, and in India, to the British sovereign as emperor). Also, **padishah.** [t. Pers. (poetical form), f. m. *pati* lord + *shāh* king]

pad·lock (păd′lŏk′), *n.* **1.** a portable or detachable lock having a pivoted or sliding hasp which passes through a staple, ring, or the like and is then made fast. —*v.t.* **2.** to fasten with or as with a padlock. [late ME, f. *pad,* var. of POD³, + LOCK¹]

pad·nag (păd′năg′), *n.* an ambling nag. [f. PAD¹+NAG²]

Pa·douk wood (pə dook′), *n.* an ornamental wood mottled in shades of yellowish red from a Malaysian tree, *Pterocarpus indicus:* used in inlaying and for making small articles; Amboina wood.

pa·dre (pä′drĭ; *Sp., It.* pä′drĕ), *n.* **1.** father (used esp. with reference to a priest). **2.** (among soldiers and sailors) a chaplain. [t. Sp., Pg., It., g. L *pater* father]

pa·dro·ne (pə drō′nĭ; *It.* pä drō′nĕ), *n., pl.* **-ni** (-nē). *Italian.* **1.** a master. **2.** one who controls and supplies Italian laborers, as in America. **3.** the master of a vessel. **4.** an innkeeper. [It., der. *padre* father]

Pad·u·a (păj′oo ə, păd′yoo ə), *n.* a city in NE Italy. 160,921 (est. 1946). **Italian, Pa·do·va** (pä′dō vä′).

pad·u·a·soy (păj′oo ə soi′), *n., pl.* **-soys. 1.** a smooth, strong, rich, silk fabric. **2.** a garment made of it. [appar. alter. of F *pou-de-soie,* by assoc. with *Padua* say serge of PADUA]

Pa·du·cah (pə dū′kə, -doo′-), *n.* a city in W Kentucky at the junction of the Tennessee and Ohio rivers. 33,828 (1950).

Pa·dus (pā′dəs), *n.* ancient name of **Po.**

pae·an (pē′ən), *n.* **1.** any song of praise, joy, or triumph. **2.** a hymn of invocation or thanksgiving to Apollo or some other Greek deity. Also, **pean.** [t. L, t. Gk.: m. *paiān* paean, *Paiān,* Homer's name for the physician of the gods, later Apollo]

paed-, var. of **ped-².** Also, **paedo-.**

pae·di·at·rics (pē′dĭ ăt′rĭks, pĕd′ĭ-), *adj. Chiefly Brit.* pediatrics.

pae·do·gen·e·sis (pē′dō jĕn′ə sĭs), *n.* reproduction by animals in the larval state, often by parthenogenesis.

pae·on (pē′ən), *n. Anc. Pros.* a foot of four syllables, one long (in any position) and three short. [t. L, t. Gk.: m. *paiōn* paeon, hymn, Attic var. of *paiān* PAEAN]

Paes·tum (pĕs′təm), *n.* an ancient coastal city of Lucania, in S Italy: the imposing ruins include three Greek temples and a Roman amphitheater.

pa·gan (pā′gən), *n.* **1.** one of a people or community professing some other than the Christian religion (applied to the ancient Romans, Greeks, etc., and sometimes the Jews). **2.** one who is not a Christian, a Jew, or a Mohammedan. **3.** an irreligious or heathenish person. —*adj.* **4.** pertaining to the worship or worshipers of any religion which is neither Christian, Jewish, nor Mohammedan. **5.** of, pertaining to, or characteristic of pagans. **6.** heathen; irreligious. [ME, t. L: s. *pāgānus* civilian; so called (by the Christians) because he was not a soldier of Christ] —**pa′gan·ish,** *adj.* —**Syn. 6.** See **heathen.**

pa·gan·dom (pā′gən dəm), *n.* **1.** the pagan world. **2.** pagans collectively.

Pa·ga·ni·ni (päg′ə nē′nē; *It.* pä′gä nē′nē), *n.* **Nicolò** (nē′kô lō′), 1784–1840, Italian violinist.

pa·gan·ism (pā′gən iz′əm), *n.* **1.** pagan spirit or attitude in religious or moral questions. **2.** the beliefs or practices of pagans. **3.** the state of being a pagan.

pa·gan·ize (pā′gə nīz′), *v.*, **-ized, -izing.** —*v.t.* **1.** to make pagan. —*v.i.* **2.** to become pagan.

page[1] (pāj), *n.*, *v.*, **paged, paging.** —*n.* **1.** one side of a leaf of a book, manuscript, letter, or the like. **2.** a record: *memory's page.* **3.** any event or period regarded as a matter of history: *a glorious page in Canadian history.* **4.** *Print.* the type set and arranged for a page. —*v.t.* **5.** to paginate. [t. F, g. L *pāgina*]

page[2] (pāj), *n.*, *v.*, **paged, paging.** —*n.* **1.** a boy servant or attendant. **2.** a youth in attendance on a person of rank, sometimes formerly in the course of training for knighthood. **3.** a young male attendant, usually in uniform, in a legislative hall, a hotel, etc. —*v.t.* **4.** *U.S.* to seek (a person) by calling out his name, as a hotel page does. **5.** to attend as a page. [ME, t. OF, t. It.: m. *paggio,* ult. t. Gk.: m.s. *paidion* boy, servant]

Page (pāj), *n.* **1. Thomas Nelson,** 1853–1922, U.S. novelist and diplomat. **2. Walter Hines,** 1855–1918, U.S. editor: ambassador to England, 1913–18.

pag·eant (păj′ənt), *n.* **1.** an elaborate public spectacle, whether processional or at some fitting spot, illustrative of the history of a place, institution, or other subject. **2.** a costumed procession, masque, allegorical tableau, or the like, in public or social festivities. **3.** a splendid or stately procession; a showy display. **4.** a specious show. **5.** *Obs. except Hist.* a platform or stage, usually moving on wheels, on which scenes from the medieval mystery plays were presented; or a stage bearing any kind of spectacle. [ME *pagent, pagyn;* orig. obscure]

pag·eant·ry (păj′ən trĭ), *n.*, *pl.* **-ries. 1.** spectacular display; pomp: *the pageantry of war.* **2.** mere show; empty display. **3.** *Obs.* pageants collectively.

Pag·et (păj′ĭt), *n.* **Sir James,** 1814–99, British surgeon and pathologist.

pag·i·nal (păj′ə nəl), *adj.* **1.** of or pertaining to pages. **2.** consisting of pages. **3.** page for page: *a paginal reprint.* [t. LL: s. *pāginālis,* der. L *pāgina* PAGE[1]]

pag·i·nate (păj′ə nāt′), *v.t.,* **-nated, -nating.** to indicate the sequence of (pages) by numbers or other characters on each leaf of the book.

pag·i·na·tion (păj′ə nā′shən), *n.* *Bibliog.* **1.** the number of pages or leaves (or both) of a book identified in bibliographical description or cataloging of the book. **2.** the figures by which pages are numbered. **3.** act of paging.

Pa·gliac·ci, I (ē pä lyät′chē), an opera (1892) by Leoncavallo.

pa·go·da (pə gō′də), *n.* (in India, Burma, China, etc.) a temple or sacred building, usually more or less pyramidal or forming a tower of many stories. Also, *Archaic,* **pag·od** (păg′əd, pə gŏd′). [t. Pg.: m. *pagode;* orig. uncert.]

Pa·go Pa·go (päng′ō päng′ō), the chief harbor and town of American Samoa, on Tutuila island: naval station. 1500(est. 1950). Also, **Pagopago.**

pa·gu·ri·an (pə gyŏŏr′ĭ ən), *adj.* *Zool.* **1.** belonging or pertaining to the hermit crab family *Paguridae,* esp. aquatic hermit crabs with short antennules. —*n.* **2.** a pagurian crab. [f. s. NL *Pagurus,* the typical genus (t. Gk.: m. *pãgouros* kind of crab) + -IAN]

pa·gu·rid (pə gyŏŏr′ĭd, păg′yə rĭd), *n.* a pagurian.

pah (pä, pă), *interj.* an exclamation of disgust.

Pa·hang (pä häng′), *n.* a native state in the Federation of Malaya: formerly one of the Federated Malay States. 205,758 pop. (est. 1937); 13,820 sq. mi. *Cap.:* Kuala Lipis.

Pah·la·vi (pä′lə vē′), *n.*, *pl.* **-vis. 1.** the dynasty now ruling in Iran, founded by Riza Shah Pahlavi in 1925. **2.** (*l.c.*) an Iranian gold coin worth 20 rials, in use since 1927. [t. Pers., named after Riza Shah *Pahlavi*]

Pah·la·vi (pä′lə vē′), *n.* the Iranian language of Zoroastrian books, written (3d–10th centuries) in a Semitic script. Also, **Pehlevi.** [t. Pers.: Parthian]

paid (pād), *v.* pt. and pp. of **pay**[1].

paid-in (pād′ĭn′), *adj.* having paid the dues, initiation fees, etc., required by any organization or association: *the union has a paid-in membership of 60,000.*

paid-in surplus, *Accounting.* surplus paid in by purchasers of stock certificates sold at a premium.

pail (pāl), *n.* a container of wood, metal, etc., nearly or quite cylindrical, with a bail or handle, for holding liquids, etc. [ME *payle,* OE *pægel* wine vessel, akin to G *pegel* water gauge] —**pail·ful** (pāl′fŏŏl′), *n.*

pail·lasse (păl′yăs′, păl′yăs), *n.* *Chiefly Brit.* a mattress of straw or the like. Also, **palliasse.** [t. F, der. *paille* straw, g. L *palea* chaff, straw]

pail·lette (păl′yĕt′), *n.* a spangle used in ornamenting a costume. [t. F, dim. of *paille* straw. See PALLET[1]]

pain (pān), *n.* **1.** bodily or mental suffering or distress (opposed to *pleasure*). **2.** a distressing sensation in a particular part of the body. **3.** (*pl.*) laborious or careful efforts; assiduous care: *great pains have been taken.* **4.** (*pl.*) the suffering of childbirth. **5. on pain of death,** liable to the penalty of death. —*v.t.* **6.** to inflict pain on; hurt; distress. —*v.i.* **7.** to cause pain or suffering. [ME *peine,* t. OF, g. L *poena* penalty. pain, t. Gk.: m. *poinē* fine] —**Syn. 1.** torture, misery. PAIN, ACHE, AGONY, ANGUISH are terms for sensations causing suffering or torment. PAIN and ACHE refer usually to physical sensations (except *heartache*); AGONY and ANGUISH may be physical or mental. PAIN suggests a sudden sharp twinge: *a pain in one's ankle.* ACHE applies to a continuous pain, whether acute or dull: *headache, muscular aches.* AGONY implies a continuous, excruciating, scarcely endurable pain: *in agony from a wound.* ANGUISH suggests not only extreme and long-continued pain, but also a feeling of despair. **3.** See **care. 6.** afflict, torture, torment.

Paine (pān), *n.* **1. Robert Treat,** 1731–1814, American jurist and statesman. **2. Thomas,** 1737–1809, American writer on government and religion, born in England.

pain·ful (pān′fəl), *adj.* **1.** affected with or causing pain: *painful thoughts.* **2.** laborious; difficult. **3.** *Obs.* or *Archaic.* painstaking. —**pain′ful·ly,** *adv.* —**pain′ful·ness,** *n.* —**Syn. 1.** distressing, torturing, agonizing.

pain·less (pān′lĭs), *adj.* without pain; causing no pain. —**pain′less·ly,** *adv.* —**pain′less·ness,** *n.*

pains·tak·ing (pānz′tā′kĭng), *adj.* **1.** assiduously careful: *painstaking work.* —*n.* **2.** careful and assiduous effort. —**pains′tak′ing·ly,** *adv.*

paint (pānt), *n.* **1.** a substance composed of solid coloring matter intimately mixed with a liquid vehicle, or medium, and applied as a coating. **2.** the dried surface pigment. **3.** the solid coloring matter alone; a pigment. **4.** color, as rouge, used on the face. **5.** application of color. —*v.t.* **6.** to represent (an object, etc.) or execute (a picture, design, etc.) in colors or pigment. **7.** to depict as if by painting; describe vividly in words. **8.** to coat, cover, or decorate (something) with color or pigment. **9.** to color as if by painting; adorn or variegate. **10.** to apply like paint, as a liquid medicine, etc. —*v.i.* **11.** to coat or cover anything with paint. **12.** to practice painting: *the Queen paints well.* **13.** to put or use artificial colors on the face. [ME *peint(en),* t. OF: m. *peint,* pp. of *peindre,* g. L *pingere* paint, adorn]

paint·brush (pānt′brŭsh′), *n.* **1.** a brush for applying paint. **2.** any of the figwort family of plants.

painted bunting, the nonpareil (def. 3).

painted cup, a plant of the genus *Castilleia,* primarily *C. coccinea,* the scarlet painted cup: so called from the highly colored dilated bracts about the flowers.

painted redstart, a brilliantly colored warbler, *Setophaga picta,* of the southwestern U.S. and Mexico.

paint·er[1] (pān′tər), *n.* **1.** an artist who paints pictures. **2.** a workman who coats surfaces with paint. [ME *peyntour,* t. AF: m. *peintour,* ult. g. L *pictor*]

paint·er[2] (pān′tər), *n.* a rope, usually at the bow, for fastening a boat to a ship, stake, etc. [? var. of d. *panter* noose, ult. t. Gk.: m.s. *panthēra* hunting net]

paint·er[3] (pān′tər), *n.* the American panther, or cougar. [var. of PANTHER]

painter's colic, lead poisoning causing intense pain in the intestines.

paint·ing (pān′tĭng), *n.* **1.** a picture or design executed in paints. **2.** act, art, or work of one who paints.

pair (pâr), *n.*, *pl.* **pairs, pair,** *v.* —*n.* **1.** two things of a kind, matched for use together: *a pair of gloves.* **2.** a combination of two parts joined together: *a pair of scissors.* **3.** a married or engaged couple. **4.** two mated animals; a span or team. **5.** *Govt.* **a.** two members on opposite sides in a deliberative body who for convenience (as to permit absence) arrange together to orgo voting on a given occasion. **b.** the arrangement thus made. **6.** *Cards.* **a.** two cards of the same denomination, without regard to suit or color. **b.** (*pl.*) two players who are matched together against different contestants. **7.** *Mech.* two parts or pieces so connected that they mutually constrain relative motion (**kinematic pair**). **8.** *Archaic or Dial.* a set or combination of more than two. —*v.t.* **9.** to arrange in pairs. **10.** to join in a pair; match; mate; couple. **11.** to cause to mate. —*v.i.* **12.** to separate into pairs (fol. by *off*). **13.** to form a pair or pairs. **14.** (in a deliberative body) to form a pair to forgo voting. [ME, t. OF: m. *paire,* g. L *pāria,* neut. pl. of *pār* equal] —**Syn. 1.** PAIR, BRACE, COUPLE, SPAN, YOKE are terms for groups of two. PAIR is used of two things naturally or habitually associated in use, or necessary to each other to make a complete set (*a pair of horses*). It is used also of one thing composed of two similar and complementary parts: *a pair of trousers.* BRACE is a hunter's term, used of a pair of dogs, ducks, etc. or a pair of pistols or slugs: *a brace of partridges.* In COUPLE the idea of combination or interdependence has become greatly weakened; it may be used loosely for two of anything (*a couple of apples*), and even for more than two (=several): *I have to see a couple of people.* SPAN is used of a matched pair of horses harnessed together side by side. YOKE applies to two animals hitched together under a yoke for drawing and pulling: *a yoke of oxen.*

pair-oared (pâr′ōrd′), *adj.* (in racing shells) having two oarsmen, with one oar each.

pair production, *Physics.* the simultaneous creation of a positron and an electron from a high energy gamma ray.

Pais·ley (pāz′lĭ), *n.* a city in SW Scotland, W of Glasgow: thread factories. 92,072 (1939).

pais·ley (pāz′lĭ), *n.*, *pl.* **-leys. 1.** a soft fabric made from wool and woven with a colorful and minutely detailed pattern. **2.** an article fashioned of paisley. —*adj.* **3.** made of paisley: *a paisley shawl.*

Pai·ute (pīōōt′), *n.* **1.** (*pl.*) a group of North American Indians of Uto-Aztecan family, dwelling in California, Nevada, Utah, and Arizona. **2.** a member of this group. [orig. name for Corn Creek tribe of Utah]

pa·jam·as (pə jăm′əz, pə jä′məz), *n.pl.* **1.** nightclothes consisting of loose trousers and jacket. **2.** loose trousers, usually of silk or cotton, worn by both sexes in India, etc. Also, *esp. Brit.,* **pyjamas.** [t. Hind., t. Pers.: m. *pāejāmah,* lit., leg garment]

Pa·ki·stan (pä′kĭ stän′), *n.* the predominantly Moslem areas of the peninsula of India (concentrated in the northeastern and northwestern parts) as contrasted to Hindustan, the predominantly Hindu areas. See **India.**

pal (păl), *n.*, *v.*, **palled, palling.** *Colloq.* —*n.* **1.** a comrade; a chum. **2.** an accomplice. —*v.i.* **3.** to associate as a pal or as pals. [t. Gypsy, dissimilated var. of *plal, pral* brother]

pa·la·bra (pä lä′brä), *n. Spanish.* **1.** a word. **2.** speech; talk. [see PALAVER]

pal·ace (păl′ĭs), *n.* **1.** the official residence of a sovereign, a bishop, or some other exalted personage. **2.** a stately mansion or building. **3.** a large place for exhibitions or entertainment. [ME *palais,* t. OF, g. L *palātium* palace, orig. the Palatine Hill in Rome (on which the emperors resided)]

Pa·la·cio Val·dés (pä lä′thyô väl dĕs′), **Armando** (är män′dô), 1853–1938, Spanish novelist and critic.

pal·a·din (păl′ə dĭn), *n.* **1.** one of the legendary twelve peers or knightly champions in attendance on Charlemagne. **2.** any knightly or heroic champion. [t. F, t. It.: m. *paladino,* g. L *palātīnus* PALATINE[1]]

palae-, var. of **pale-.** Also, before consonants, **palaeo-.** For words beginning with **palae-,** look under the more common spelling in **pale-.**

pa·laes·tra (pə lĕs′trə), *n.*, *pl.* **-tras, -trae** (trē). *Gk. Antiq.* palestra.

pal·an·quin (păl′ən kēn′), *n.* (in India and other Eastern countries) a covered or boxlike litter borne by means of poles resting on men's shoulders. Also, **pal′an·keen′.** [t. Pg. Cf. Skt. *palyanka, paryanka* couch, bed; prob. through Telegu]

pal·at·a·ble (păl′ət ə bəl), *adj.* **1.** agreeable to the palate or taste; savory. **2.** agreeable to the mind or feelings. —**pal′at·a·bil′i·ty, pal′at·a·ble·ness,** *n.* —**pal′at·a·bly,** *adv.*

Indian palanquin

pal·a·tal (păl′ə təl), *adj.* **1.** *Anat.* of or pertaining to the palate. **2.** *Phonet.* with the tongue held close to the hard palate: the *y* of *yield* is a palatal consonant. —*n.* **3.** *Phonet.* a palatal sound. [f. PALAT(E) + -AL[1]]

pal·a·tal·ize (păl′ə təl īz′), *v.t.*, **-ized, -izing.** *Phonet.* to pronounce with the tongue held close to the hard palate so that the sound acquires some of the quality of a *y:* in *million* the *l* sound may or may not be palatalized, but is always followed by a *y* sound. —**pal′a·tal·i·za′tion,** *n.*

pal·ate (păl′ĭt), *n.* **1.** the roof of the mouth, consisting of bone (**hard palate**) in front and of a fleshy structure (**soft palate**) at the back. See diag. under **mouth. 2.** this part of the mouth considered (popularly but erroneously) as the organ of taste. **3.** the sense of taste. **4.** mental taste or liking. [ME *palat,* t. L: s. *palātum*]

pa·la·tial (pə lā′shəl), *adj.* pertaining to, of the nature of, or befitting a palace: *palatial establishments.* [f. s. L *palātium* PALACE + -AL[1]] —**pa·la′tial·ly,** *adv.*

Pa·lat·i·nate (pə lăt′ə nāt′, -nĭt), *n.* **1.** The, Also **Lower** or **Rhine Palatinate.** German, **Pfalz.** a district in SW Germany, W of the Rhine, which belonged to Bavaria until 1945; formerly, with portions of the neighboring territory (the **Upper Palatinate**), it constituted an electorate of the Holy Roman Empire. 1,049,786 pop. (1939); 2121 sq. mi. *Cap.:* Speyer. **2.** a native or inhabitant of the Palatinate. **3.** (*l.c.*) the territory under the jurisdiction of a palatine.

pal·a·tine[1] (păl′ə tīn′, -tĭn), *adj.* **1.** possessing or characterized by royal privileges: *a count palatine.* **2.** pertaining to a count or earl palatine, or to a county palatine. **3.** of or pertaining to a palace; palatial. **4.** (*cap.*) of or pertaining to the Palatinate. —*n.* **5.** a vassal exercising royal privileges in a province; a count or earl palatine. **6.** an officer of an imperial palace. **7.** a high official of an empire. **8.** (*cap.*) a native or inhabitant of the Palatinate. **9.** (*cap.*) Palatine Hill. **10.** a shoulder cape formerly worn by women. [ME, t. L: m.s. *palātīnus* belonging to the palace, imperial (as n., a palace officer)]

pal·a·tine[2] (păl′ə tīn′, -tĭn), *adj.* palatal: *the palatine bones.* [t. F: m. *palatin,* der. L *palātum* PALATE]

Palatine Hill, one of the seven hills on which Rome was built.

Pa·lau Islands (pä lou′), a group of Pacific islands in the W part of the Caroline group: taken by U.S. forces after severe fighting, 1944; formerly a Japanese mandate, now under U.S. trusteeship. 12,764 pop. (1937); 171 sq. mi. Also, **Pelew Islands.**

pa·lav·er (pə lăv′ər, -lä′vər), *n.* **1.** a parley or conference, esp. with much talk, as between travelers and primitive natives. **2.** profuse and plausible talk; flattery. —*v.i.* **3.** to talk profusely and idly. —*v.t.* **4.** to cajole. [t. Pg.: m. *palavra,* g. L *parabola* PARABLE]

Pa·la·wan (pä lä′wän), *n.* one of the Philippine Islands, in the SW part of the group. 43,813 pop. (1939); 5697 sq. mi. *Cap.:* Puerto Princesa.

pale[1] (pāl), *adj.,* **paler, palest,** *v.,* **paled, paling.** —*adj.* **1.** of a whitish appearance; without intensity of color: *pale complexion.* **2.** of a low degree of chroma, saturation or purity; approaching white or gray: *pale yellow.* **3.** lacking in brightness; dim: *the pale moon.* **4.** faint; feeble; lacking vigor. —*v.i.,* *v.t.* **5.** to make or become pale. [ME, t. OF, g. L *pallidus* pallid] —**pale′ly,** *adv.* —**pale′ness,** *n.*
—**Syn. 1.** PALE, PALLID, WAN imply an absence of color, esp. from the human countenance. PALE implies a faintness or absence of color, which may be natural when applied to things (*the pale blue of a violet*) but when applied to the human face, usually unnatural and often temporary as arising from sickness or sudden emotion: *pale cheeks.* PALLID, limited mainly to the human countenance, implies an excessive paleness induced by intense emotion, disease, or death: *the pallid lips of the dying man.* WAN implies a sickly paleness, as after a long illness (*wan and thin*); the suggestion of weakness may be more prominent than that of lack of color: *a wan smile.* —**Ant. 1.** rosy, ruddy.

pale[2] (pāl), *n.,* *v.,* **paled, paling.** —*n.* **1.** a stake or picket, as of a fence. **2.** any enclosing or confining barrier. **3.** limits or bounds: *outside the pale of the church.* **4.** the area enclosed by a paling; any enclosed area. **5.** a district or region within fixed bounds. **6.** (*cap.*) a district in E Ireland included in the Angevin Empire of King Henry II and his successors. Also, **English Pale** or **Irish Pale. 7.** *Her.* a broad vertical stripe in the middle of an escutcheon and one third its width. —*v.t.* **8.** to enclose with pales; fence. **9.** to encircle or encompass. [ME, t. F: m. *pal,* g. L *pālus* stake]

pale-, var. of **paleo-,** before most vowels, as in *paleëthnology.*

pa·le·a (pā′lĭ ə), *n.,* *pl.* **-leae** (-lĭ ē′). *Bot.* **1.** a chafflike scale or bract. **2.** the scalelike, membranous organ in the flowers of grasses which is situated upon a secondary axis in the axil of the flowering glume and envelops the stamens and pistil. [t. L: chaff] —**pa·le·a·ceous** (pā′lĭ ā′shəs), *adj.*

pa·le·ëth·nol·o·gy (pā′lĭ ĕth nŏl′ə jĭ, păl′ĭ-), *n.* the branch of ethnology that treats of the earliest or most primitive races of mankind. [f. PALE- + ETHNOLOGY] —**pa·le·ëth·no·log·ic** (pā′lĭ ĕth′nə lŏj′ĭk, păl′ĭ-), **pa·le·ëth′no·log′i·cal,** *adj.* —**pa·le·ëth·nol′o·gist,** *n.*

pale·face (pāl′fās′), *n.* a white person (an expression attributed to the American Indians).

Pa·lem·bang (pä′lĕm bäng′), *n.* a city in the U.S. of Indonesia, in SE Sumatra. 108,145 (1930).

Pa·len·que (pä lĕng′kĕ), *n.* ruins of an ancient Mayan city in SE Mexico, in Chiapas state.

paleo-, a prefix meaning "old," "ancient." Also **pale-, palae-, palaeo-.** [t. Gk.: m. *palaio-,* comb. form of *palaiós*]

pa·le·o·bot·a·ny (pā′lĭ ō bŏt′ə nĭ, păl′ĭ-), *n.* the branch of paleontology that treats of fossil plants. —**pa·le·o·bo·tan·i·cal** (pā′lĭ ō bə tăn′ə kəl, păl′ĭ-), **pa·le·o·bo·tan′ic,** *adj.* —**pa·le·o·bot′a·nist,** *n.*

Pa·le·o·cene (pā′lĭ ə sēn′, păl′ĭ-), *Stratig.* —*adj.* **1.** pertaining to the oldest series or epoch of the Tertiary. —*n.* **2.** a division of the Tertiary period or system that precedes Eocene.

paleog., paleography.

pa·le·o·ge·og·ra·phy (pā′lĭ ō jĭ ŏg′rə fĭ, păl′ĭ-), *n.* representation of earth features belonging to any part of the geologic past. —**pa·le·o·ge·o·graph·ic** (pā′lĭ ō jē′ə grăf′ĭk, păl′ĭ-), **pa·le·o·ge·o·graph′i·cal,** *adj.*

pa·le·o·ge·ol·o·gy (pā′lĭ ō jĭ ŏl′ə jĭ, păl′ĭ-), *n.* the science of representing geologic conditions of some given time in past earth history. —**pa·le·o·ge·o·log·ic** (pā′lĭ ō jē′ə lŏj′ĭk, păl′ĭ-), *adj.*

pa·le·og·ra·phy (pā′lĭ ŏg′rə fĭ, păl′ĭ-), *n.* **1.** ancient forms of writing, as in documents and inscriptions. **2.** the study of ancient writing, including determination of origin and date, decipherment, etc. —**pa′le·og′ra·pher,** *n.* —**pa·le·o·graph·ic** (pā′lĭ ə grăf′ĭk, păl′ĭ-), **pa′le·o·graph′i·cal,** *adj.*

pa·le·o·lith (pā′lĭ ə lĭth, păl′ĭ-), *n.* a paleolithic stone implement.

pa·le·o·lith·ic (pā′lĭ ə lĭth′ĭk, păl′ĭ-), *adj.* noting or pertaining to the earlier part of the Old World Stone Age, marked by exclusive use of chipped stone implements.

paleolithic man, *Anthropol.* any of the primitive species of man (Piltdown, Neanderthal, etc.) living in the Paleolithic period.

paleontol., paleontology.

pa·le·on·tol·o·gy (pā′lĭ ən tŏl′ə jĭ, păl′ĭ-), *n.* the science of the forms of life existing in former geological periods, as represented by fossil animals and plants. [t. F: m. *paléontologie;* f. PALE- + ONTOLOGY] —**pa·le·on·to·log·ic** (pā′lĭ ən tə lŏj′ĭk, păl′ĭ-), **pa·le·on′to·log′i·cal,** *adj.* —**pa′le·on·tol′o·gist,** *n.*

Pa·le·o·zo·ic (pā/lῐ̄ ə zō/ῐ̄k, păl/ῐ̄-), *Stratig.* —*adj.* **1.** pertaining to the oldest geological era or rocks having abundant fossils; the age of ancient life. —*n.* **2.** the era or rocks comprising divisions from Cambrian to Permian. [f. PALEO- + s. Gk. *zōē̆* life + -IC]

pa·le·o·zo·öl·o·gy (pā/lῐ̄ ō zō öl/ə jῐ̄, păl/ῐ̄-), *n.* the branch of paleontology that treats of fossil animals. —**pa·le·o·zo·ö·log·i·cal** (pā/lῐ̄ ō zō/ə lŏj/ə kəl, păl/ῐ̄-), *adj.*

Pa·ler·mo (pä lĕr/mō), *n.* a seaport in and the capital of Sicily, in the NW part. 446,384 (est. 1946).

Pal·es·tine (păl/əs tīn/), *n.* a country in SW Asia, on the Mediterranean: now divided between the state of Israel and Arab Palestine; formerly a British mandate. 1,912,000 pop. (est. 1946); 10,429 sq. mi. Also, **Holy Land.** Biblical name, **Canaan.** —**Pal·es·tin·i·an** (păl/əs tῐ̆n/ῐ̄ ən), *adj., n.*

pa·les·tra (pə lĕs/trə), *n., pl.* **-tras, -trae** (-trē). *Gk. Antiq.* a public place for training or exercise in wrestling or athletics. Also, **palaestra.** [ME, t. L, t. Gk.: m. *palaístra*]

Pa·les·tri·na (păl/ə strē/nə; *It.* pä/lĕs trē/nä), *n.* Giovanni Pierluigi da (jō vän/nē pyĕr/loo ē/jē dä), 1526?–1594, Italian composer of church music.

pal·e·tot (păl/ə tō/, păl/tō), *n.* a loose outer garment or coat. [t. F; OF *paltoc*, of uncert. orig.]

pal·ette (păl/ῐ̆t), *n.* **1.** a thin, usually oval or oblong, board or tablet with a thumb hole at one end, used by painters to lay and mix colors on. **2.** the range of colors used by a particular artist. **3.** Also, **pallette.** *Armor.* a small armpit plate. See illustration under **armor.** [t. F: palette, flatbladed implement, ult. der. L *pāla* spade, shovel]

palette knife, a thin, flexible blade set in a handle, used for mixing painters' colors, etc.

pale·wise (pāl/wīz/), *adv. Her.* in the manner or direction of a pale (def. 7).

Pa·ley (pā/lῐ̄), *n.* **William,** 1743–1805, British theologian, philosopher, and clergyman.

pal·frey (pôl/frῐ̄), *n., pl.* **-freys. 1.** a riding horse, as distinguished from a war horse. **2.** a woman's saddle horse. [ME *palefrai*, t. OF: m. *palefrei*, g. LL *paraverēdus*, f. Gk. *parā* beside + L *verēdus* light horse, of Celtic orig.]

Pal·grave (pôl/grāv, păl/-), *n.* **Francis Turner,** 1824–97, British critic and poet.

Pa·li (pä/lῐ̄), *n.* the Prakrit language of the Buddhist scriptures. [t. Skt.: short for *pāli-bhāsā*, lit., canon language]

pal·i·kar (păl/ῐ̄ kär/), *n.* a Greek militiaman in the Greco-Turkish war of 1821–28. Also, **pellekar.** [t. NGk.: m. *palikári* lad, der. Gk. *pállax* youth]

pal·imp·sest (păl/ῐ̆mp sĕst/), *n.* a parchment or the like from which writing has been partially or completely erased to make room for another text. [t. L: s. *palimpsestus*, t. Gk.: m. *palímpsestos* scraped again]

pal·in·drome (păl/ῐ̄n drōm/), *n.* a word, verse, etc., reading the same backward as forward, as madam, I'm Adam. [t. Gk.: m.s. *palíndromos* running back]

pal·ing (pā/lῐ̄ng), *n.* **1.** a fence of pales. **2.** a pale, as in a fence. **3.** pales collectively. **4.** act of one who builds a fence with pales. [ME, f. PALE² + -ING¹]

pal·in·gen·e·sis (păl/ῐ̄n jĕn/ə sῐ̆s), *n.* **1.** rebirth; regeneration. **2.** *Biol.* **a.** that development of an individual which reproduces the ancestral features (opposed to cenogenesis). **b.** *Obs.* the supposed generation of organisms from others preformed in the germ cells. **3.** baptism in the Christian faith. **4.** the doctrine of transmigration of souls. [f. Gk. *pálin* back, again + -GENESIS]

pal·i·node (păl/ə nōd/), *n.* **1.** a poem in which the poet retracts something said in a former poem. **2.** a recantation. [t. LL: m.s. *palinōdia*, t. Gk.: m. *palinōidía*]

pal·i·sade (păl/ə sād/), *n., v.,* **-saded, -sading.** —*n.* **1.** a fence of pales or stakes set firmly in the ground, as for enclosure or defense. **2.** one of the pales or stakes, pointed at the top, set firmly in the ground in a close row with others, for defense. **3.** (*pl.*) a line of lofty cliffs. —*v.t.* **4.** to furnish or fortify with a palisade. [t. F: m. *palissade,* der. *palisser* furnish with a paling, der. *palis* paling, der. L *pālus* PALE²]

Pal·i·sades (păl/ə sādz/), *n.* the cliffs extending almost 40 mi. along the W bank of the lower Hudson river, in NE New Jersey and SE New York: partially included in the **Palisades Interstate Park.**

pal·ish (pā/lῐ̆sh), *adj.* somewhat pale.

pall¹ (pôl), *n.* **1.** a cloth, often of velvet, for spreading over a coffin, bier, or tomb. **2.** something that covers, shrouds, or overspreads, esp. with darkness or gloom. **3.** *Eccles.* **a.** a pallium (vestment). **b.** *Archaic.* a cloth spread upon the altar, esp. a corporal. **c.** a linen cloth, or now usually a square piece of cardboard covered with linen, used to cover the chalice. **4.** *Her.* a bearing representing the front of a pallium (vestment), consisting of a Y-shaped form charged with crosses. **5.** *Obs.* a cloak. —*v.t.* **6.** to cover with or as with a pall. [ME; OE *pæll,* t. L: m.s. *pallium* cloak, covering]

pall² (pôl), *v.i.* **1.** to have a wearying effect (fol. by *on* or *upon*). **2.** to become insipid, distasteful, or wearisome. **3.** to become satiated or cloyed with something. —*v.t.* **4.** to satiate or cloy. **5.** to make vapid, insipid, or distasteful. [ME *palle(n)*; appar. aphetic var. of APPALL]

Pal·la·di·an (pə lā/dῐ̄ ən), *adj.* pertaining to, introduced by, or in the style of Andrea Palladio.

Pal·la·di·an (pə lā/dῐ̄ ən), *adj.* **1.** of or pertaining to the goddess Pallas. **2.** pertaining to wisdom, knowledge, or study.

pal·lad·ic (pə lăd/ῐ̆k, -lā/dῐ̆k), *adj. Chem.* of or containing palladium, esp. in the tetravalent state (Pd+4).

Pal·la·dio (päl lä/dyō), *n.* **Andrea** (än drĕ/ä), 1518–80, Italian architect.

Pal·la·di·um (pə lā/dῐ̄ əm), *n., pl.* **-dia** (-dῐ̄ ə). **1.** a statue of Pallas Athene, esp. one on the citadel of Troy on which the safety of the city was supposed to depend. **2.** (*usually l.c.*) anything believed to afford effectual protection or safety. [ME, t. L, t. Gk.: m. *Palládion*]

pal·la·di·um (pə lā/dῐ̄ əm), *n. Chem.* a rare metallic element of the platinum group, silver-white, ductile and malleable, and harder than platinum and fusing more readily. *Symbol:* Pd; *at. wt.:* 106.7; *at. no.:* 46; *sp. gr.:* 12 at 20°C. [t. NL; named (1803) after the asteroid Pallas, then recently discovered]

pal·la·dous (pə lā/dəs, păl/ə dəs), *adj. Chem.* containing divalent palladium (Pd+2).

Pal·las (păl/əs), *n.* **1.** a name of Athena (often **Pallas Athene**). **2.** *Astron.* one of the asteroids. [t. L, t. Gk.]

pall·bear·er (pôl/bâr/ər), *n.* one of those who attend the coffin at a funeral.

pal·let¹ (păl/ῐ̆t), *n.* **1.** a bed or mattress of straw. **2.** a small or poor bed. [ME *pailet,* t. OF: dim. of *paille* straw, g. L *palea* chaff]

pal·let² (păl/ῐ̆t), *n.* **1.** an implement consisting of a flat blade or plate with a handle, used for shaping by potters, etc. **2.** a flat board or metal plate used to support ceramic articles during drying. **3.** *Horol.* a lever with three projections, two of which intermittently lock and receive impulses from the escape wheel, and one which transmits these impulses to the balance. **4.** a lip or projection on a pawl, that engages with the teeth of a ratchet wheel. **5.** *Gilding.* an instrument used to take up the gold leaves from the pillow, and to apply and extend them. **6.** a platform on which goods are placed for storage or transportation. **7.** a painter's palette. [t. F: m. *palette* PALETTE]

A, B, Pallets (def. 4); C, Pivot on which pawl oscillates

pal·lette (păl/ῐ̆t), *n. Armor.* palette.

pal·liasse (păl yăs/, păl/yăs), *n. Chiefly Brit.* paillasse.

pal·li·ate (păl/ῐ̄ āt/), *v.t.,* **-ated, -ating. 1.** to cause (an offense, etc.) to appear less grave or heinous; extenuate; excuse. **2.** to mitigate or alleviate: *to palliate a disease.* [t. L: m.s. *palliātus,* pp., covered with a cloak] —**pal/li·a/tion,** *n.* —**pal/li·a/tor,** *n.*

pal·li·a·tive (păl/ῐ̄ ā tῐ̆v), *adj.* **1.** serving to palliate. —*n.* **2.** something that palliates. —**pal/li·a·tive·ly,** *adv.*

pal·lid (păl/ῐ̆d), *adj.* pale; deficient in color; wan. [t. L: s. *pallidus*] —**pal/lid·ly,** *adv.* —**pal/lid·ness,** *n.* —Syn. See **pale¹.**

pal·li·um (păl/ῐ̄ əm), *n., pl.* **palia** (păl/ῐ̄ ə), **paliums. 1.** *Rom. Antiq.* a voluminous rectangular mantle worn by men, and esp. by philosophers. **2.** *Eccles.* **a.** a woolen vestment worn by the Pope and conferred by him on archbishops, consisting, in its present form, of a narrow ringlike band, which rests upon the shoulders, with two dependent bands or lappets, one in front and one behind. **b.** an altar cloth; a pall. **3.** *Anat.* the entire cortex of the cerebrum. **4.** *Zool.* a mantle. [OE, t. L. See PALL¹]

Pall Mall (pĕl/ mĕl/, păl/ măl/), a street in London, England, famed for its clubs. [see PALL-MALL (def. 2)]

pall-mall (pĕl/mĕl/), *n.* **1.** a game formerly played in which a ball of boxwood was struck with a mallet, the object being to drive it through a raised iron ring at the end of an alley. **2.** an alley in which this game was played. [t. F (obs.): m. *pallemaille,* t. It.: m. *pallamaglio* the game, f. *palla* ball (of Gmc. orig.; akin to BALL¹) + *maglio* mallet, g. L *malleus* hammer]

pal·lor (păl/ər), *n.* unnatural paleness, as from fear, ill health, or death; wanness. [t. L]

palm¹ (päm), *n.* **1.** that part of the inner surface of the hand which extends from the wrist to the bases of the fingers. **2.** the corresponding part of the forefoot of an animal. **3.** the part of a glove covering the palm. **4.** a metal shield worn over the palm of the hand by sailmakers to serve instead of a thimble. **5.** a linear measure based on either the breadth of the hand (3 to 4 inches) or its length from wrist to fingertips (7 to 10 inches). **6.** the flat, expanded part of the horn or antler of some deer. **7.** a flat, widened part at the end of an armlike projection. **8.** the blade of an oar. —*v.t.* **9.** to conceal in the palm, as in cheating at cards or dice or in juggling. **10.** to pass fraudulently or deceptively (fol. by *off*). **11.** to impose (something) fraudulently (fol. by *on* or *upon*). **12.** to touch or stroke with the palm or hand. **13.** to shake hands with. [t. L: s. *palma* palm, hand, blade of an oar; r. ME *paume,* t. OF, g. L]

---

palm[2] (päm), *n.* **1.** any of the plants constituting the large and important *Palmaceae* family, the majority of which are tall, unbranched trees surmounted by a crown of large pinnate or palmately cleft (fan-shaped) leaves. **2.** any of various other trees or shrubs which resemble the palm. **3.** a leaf or branch of a palm tree, esp. as formerly borne as an emblem of victory or as used on festal occasions. **4.** a representation of such a leaf or branch, as on a decoration of honor. **5.** the victor's reward of honor. **6.** victory; triumph. [ME and OE, t. L: s. *palma* palm tree, etymologically identical with PALM[1]] —**palm'like'**, *adj.*

Pal·ma (päl'mä), *n.* **1.** a seaport in and the capital of the Balearic Islands, on W Majorca. 114,405 (1940). **2.** one of the Canary Islands, off the NW coast of Africa. 64,049 pop. (1940); 281 sq. mi. *Cap.*: Santa Cruz de la Palma.

pal·ma·ceous (päl mā'shəs), *adj.* belonging to the palm family of plants.

Palma de Mallorca, Palma (def. 1).

pal·mar (päl'mər), *adj.* pertaining to the palm of the hand, or to the corresponding part of the fore foot of an animal. [t. L: s. *palmāris*.]

Pal·mas (päl'mäs), *n.* **Las** (läs). See **Las Palmas.**

pal·mate (päl'māt, -mȳt), *adj.* **1.** shaped like an open palm, or like a hand with the fingers extended, as a leaf or an antler. **2.** *Bot.* lobed or divided so that the sinuses point to or reach the apex of the petiole, somewhat irrespective of the number of lobes. **3.** *Zool.* web-footed. Also, **pal'·mat·ed.** [t. L: m.s. *palmātus*.] —**pal'·mate·ly,** *adv.*

Palmate leaf

pal·ma·tion (päl mā'shən), *n.* **1.** palmate state or formation. **2.** a palmate structure.

Palm Beach (päm), a town in SE Florida: seaside winter resort. 3886 (1950).

palm cat, any of various viverrine animals of southeastern Asia, the East Indies, etc., chiefly arboreal in habit, about the size of the domestic cat, and having a spotted or striped fur and a long curled tail. Also, **palm civet.**

palm·er[1] (pä'mər), *n.* a pilgrim who had returned from the Holy Land, in token of which he bore a palm branch. [ME *palmere*, der. PALM[2], translating AF *palmer*, ML *palmārius*, der. L *palma* PALM[2]]

palm·er[2] (pä'mər), *n.* one who palms something, as in cheating at cards. [f. PALM[1], v. + -ER[1]]

Palm·er (pä'mər), *n.* **George Herbert**, 1842–1933, U.S. educator, philosopher, and author.

Palmer Peninsula, a large peninsula of Antarctica, S of South America: a dependency of the Falkland Islands. Also, **Graham Land.**

Palm·er·ston (pä'mər stən), *n.* **Henry John Temple**, 3rd Viscount, 1784–1865, British statesman: prime minister, 1855–58 and 1859–65.

palmer worm, the larva of the tineid moth *Ypsilophus ligulellus*, which in eastern parts of the U.S. appears on the leaves of the apple in June, draws them together, and skeletonizes them. [f. PALMER[1] + WORM]

pal·met·to (päl mĕt'ō), *n., pl.* **-tos, -toes.** any of various species of palm with fan-shaped leaves such as *Sabal, Serenoa, Thrinax,* etc. [t. Sp.: m. *palmito*, dim. of *palma*, g. L *palma* PALM[2]]

palm·is·try (pä'mĭs trĭ), *n.* the art or practice of telling fortunes and interpreting character by the lines and configurations of the palm of the hand. [ME *pawmestry, palmestrie,* appar. der. *palmester* chiromancer, f. *palme* PALM[1] + -STER] —**palm·ist** (pä'mĭst), *n.*

pal·mi·tate (päl'mə tāt'), *n. Chem.* a salt or ester of palmitic acid.

pal·mit·ic acid (päl mĭt'ĭk), *Chem.* a white crystalline acid, $C_{15}H_{31}COOH$, occurring as a glyceride in palm oil and in most solid fats.

pal·mi·tin (päl'mə tĭn), *n.* a colorless fatty substance, $(C_{15}H_{31}COO)_3C_3H_5$, the glyceride of palmitic acid, occurring in palm oil and solid fats, and used in soap manufacture. [t. F: m. *palmitine*, der. L *palma* PALM[2]]

palm oil, 1. a yellow, butterlike oil from the fru't of *Elaeis guineensis*, of western Africa, used by the natives as food, and employed also for making soap and candles, etc. **2.** oil obtained from various species of palm.

palm sugar, sugar from the sap of certain palm trees.

Palm Sunday, the Sunday next before Easter, celebrated in commemoration of Christ's triumphal entry into Jerusalem.

palm·y (pä'mĭ), *adj.,* **palmier, palmiest. 1.** glorious, prosperous, or flourishing. **2.** abounding in or shaded with palms: *palmy islands.* **3.** palmlike.

pal·my·ra (päl mī'rə), *n.* a tropical Asian fan palm, *Borassus flabellifer.* Also, **palmyra palm.** [t. Pg.: m. *palmeira,* der. L *palma* PALM[2]]

Pal·my·ra (päl mī'rə), *n.* **1.** an ancient city in Syria, NE of Damascus: reputedly built by Solomon. Biblical name, **Tadmor. 2.** an atoll in the central Pacific, belonging to the U.S.: airfield. 32 pop. (1940); 1½ sq. mi.

Pal·o Al·to (päl'ō ăl'tō for 1; pä'lō äl'tō for 2). **1.** a city in W California, SE of San Francisco. 25,475 (1950). **2.** a battlefield in S Texas, near Brownsville: the first battle of the Mexican War was fought here, 1846.

pal·o·mi·no (păl'ə mē'nō), *n., pl.* **-nos.** a tan or cream-colored horse, bred chiefly in the SW United States. [t. Sp.]

Pa·los (pä'lōs), *n.* a seaport in SW Spain: starting point of Columbus' first voyage westward. 2201 (1930).

palp (pălp), *n.* a palpus. [t. F: m. *palpe,* t. L: m. *palpus* a feeler]

pal·pa·ble (păl'pə bəl), *adj.* **1.** readily or plainly seen, heard, perceived, etc.; obvious: *a palpable lie.* **2.** that can be touched or felt; tangible. **3.** *Med.* perceptible by palpation. [ME, t. LL: m.s. *palpābilis,* der. L *palpāre* touch] —**pal'pa·bil·i·ty,** *n.* —**pal'pa·bly,** *adv.*

pal·pate[1] (păl'pāt), *v.t.,* **-pated, -pating.** to examine by the sense of touch, esp. in medicine. [t. L: m.s. *palpātus,* pp., touched, stroked] —**pal·pa'tion,** *n.*

pal·pate[2] (păl'pāt), *adj. Zool.* having a palpus or palpi. [f. s. L *palpus* a feeler + -ATE[1]]

pal·pe·bral (păl'pə brəl), *adj.* of or pertaining to the eyelids. [t. LL: s. *palpebrālis.*]

pal·pi (păl'pī), *n.* pl. of **palpus.**

pal·pi·tant (păl'pə tənt), *adj.* palpitating. [t. L: s. *palpitans,* ppr.]

pal·pi·tate (păl'pə tāt'), *v.i.,* **-tated, -tating. 1.** to pulsate with unnatural rapidity, as the heart, from exertion, emotion, disease, etc. **2.** to quiver or tremble. [t. L: m.s. *palpitātus,* pp., moved quickly] —**Syn. 1.** See **pulsate.**

pal·pi·ta·tion (păl'pə tā'shən), *n.* **1.** act of palpitating. **2.** rapid or violent beating of the heart.

pal·pus (păl'pəs), *n., pl.* **-pi** (-pī). an appendage attached to an oral part, and serving as an organ of sense, in in ects, crustaceans, etc. [t. NL, t. L: a feeler]

pals·grave (pōlz'grāv', pălz'-), *n.* a German count palatine. [t. D: m. *paltsgrave* (now *paltsgraaf*), c. G *pfalzgraf* palace count]

pals·gra·vine (pōlz'grə vēn', pălz'-), *n.* the wife or widow of a pa sgrave.

pal·sy (pōl'zĭ), *n., pl.* **-sies,** *v.,* **-sied, -sying.** —*n.* **1.** paralysis. —*v.t.* **2.** to paralyze. [ME *parlesie,* t. OF: m. *paralisie,* g. L *paralysis* PARALYSIS] —**pal'sied,** *adj.*

pal·ter (pōl'tər), *v.i.* **1.** to talk or act insincerely; equivocate; deal crookedly. **2.** to haggle. **3.** to trifle. [cf. obs. *palter* mumble, shuffle, b. PALSY and FALTER]

pal·try (pōl'trĭ), *adj.,* **-trier, -triest. 1.** trifling; petty: *a paltry sum.* **2.** trashy or worthless: *paltry rags.* **3.** mean or contemptible: *a paltry coward.* [appar. der. d. *palt* rubbish. Cf. LG *paltrig*] —**pal'tri·ly,** *adv.* —**pal'tri·ness,** *n.* —**Syn. 1.** See **petty.**

pa·lu·dal (pə loo'dəl, păl'yə-), *adj.* **1.** of or pertaining to marshes. **2.** produced by marshes, as miasma or disease. [f. s. L *palus* marsh + -AL[1]]

pal·u·dism (păl'yə dĭz'əm), *n. Pathol.* malarial disease.

pal·y[1] (pā'lĭ), *adj. Chiefly Poetic.* palish; pale. [f. PALE[1] + -Y[1]]

pal·y[2] (pā'lĭ), *adj. Her.* divided palewise, or vertically, into equal parts of alternating tinctures. [t. F: m. *palé,* der. *pal* PALE[2] (see def. 7)]

pam (păm), *n. Cards.* **1.** the knave of clubs, esp. in a form of loo in which it is the best trump. **2.** the game. [for F *pamphile,* orig. proper name, t. Gk.: m. *Pámphilos,* lit., beloved of all]

pam., pamphlet.

Pam·e·la (păm'ə lə), *n.* a novel in letter form by Samuel Richardson, sometimes called the first English novel (1740).

Pa·mirs (pä mĭrz'), *n.pl.* **The,** a lofty plateau in central Asia, where the Hindu Kush, Tien Shan, and Himalayan mountain systems converge. Highest peaks, ab. 25,000 ft. Also, **I'amir.**

Pam·li·co Sound (păm'lĭ kō'), a sound between the North Carolina mainland and coastal islands.

pam·pas (păm'pəz; *attributively* păm'pəs; *Sp.* păm'-päs), *n. pl.* the vast grassy plains lying in the rain shadow of the Andes and south of the forested lowlands of the Amazon basin, esp. in Argentina. [t. Sp., pl. of *pampa,* t. Peruvian] —**pam·pe·an** (păm pē'ən, păm'pĭ ən), *adj.*

pampas grass, a tall ornamental grass, *Cortaderia Selloana,* native in South America but widely cultivated, having large, thick, feathery, silvery-white panicles.

Pam·pe·lu·na (păm'pĕ loo'nä), *n.* Pamplona.

pam·per (păm'pər), *v.t.* **1.** to indulge (a person, etc.) to the full or to excess: *to pamper a child, one's appetite, etc.* **2.** to indulge with rich food, comforts, etc. [ME *pampren.* Cf. Dan. *pamper,* G *pampen* cram] —**pam'per·er,** *n.* —**Syn. 1.** gratify, humor, coddle.

pam·pe·ro (päm pâr'ō; *Sp.* -pĕ'rô), *n., pl.* **-ros** (-rōz; *Sp.* -rôs). a cold and dry southwesterly wind that sweeps over the pampas of Argentina, and northeastward to the Brazilian coast, in the rear of barometric depression. [t. Sp.]

pamph., pamphlet.

pam·phlet (păm'flĭt), *n.* **1.** a short treatise or essay, generally controversial, on some subject of temporary interest: *a political pamphlet.* **2.** a complete publication generally less than 80 pages, stitched and usually enclosed in paper covers. [ME *pamflet,* syncopated var. of *Pamphilet,* popular name for ML poem formally entitled *Pamphilus, seu dē Amōre*]

pam·phlet·eer (păm'flə tĭr'), *n.* **1.** a writer of pamphlets. —*v.i.* **2.** to write and issue pamphlets.

Pam·phyl·i·a (păm fĭl′ĭ ə), *n.* an ancient country and Roman province in S Asia Minor.

Pam·plo·na (păm plô′nä), *n.* a city in N Spain. 61,188 (1940).

pan[1] (păn), *n., v.,* **panned, panning.** —*n.* **1.** a dish commonly of metal, usually broad and shallow and often open, used for domestic purposes: *a frying pan.* **2.** any dishlike receptacle or part, as the scales of a balance. **3.** any of various open or closed vessels used in industrial or mechanical processes. **4.** *Metall.* a vessel, usually of cast iron, in which the ores of silver are ground and amalgamated. **5.** a vessel in which gold or other heavy, valuable metals are separated from gravel, etc., by agitation with water. **6.** a depression in the ground, as a natural one containing water, mud or mineral salts, or an artificial one for evaporating salt water to make salt. **7.** hardpan. **8.** (in old guns) the depressed part of the lock, which holds the priming. —*v.t.* **9.** to wash (auriferous gravel, sand, etc.) in a pan to separate the gold or other heavy valuable metal. **10.** to separate by such washing. **11.** to cook (oysters, etc.) in a pan. **12.** *Colloq.* to criticize or reprimand severely. **13.** *U.S. Colloq.* to get or obtain. —*v.i.* **14.** *Colloq.* to succeed; turn out well (fol. by *out*). **15.** to wash gravel, etc., in a pan seeking for gold. **16.** to yield gold, as gravel washed in a pan. [ME and OE *panne,* c. G *pfanne*]

pan[2] (păn), *n.* **1.** the leaf of the betel. **2.** the masticatory of which the betel leaf comprises the wrapper. See **betel.** [t. Hind., g. Skt. *parna* feather, leaf]

Pan (păn), *n. Gk. Myth.* the god of forests, pastures, flocks, and shepherds, represented with the head, chest, and arms of a man, and the legs and sometimes the horns and ears of a goat.

pan-, a word element or prefix meaning "all," first occurring in words from the Greek, but now used freely as a general formative in English and other languages, esp. in terms implying the union, association, or consideration together, as forming a whole, of all the branches of a race, people, church, or other body, as in *Pan-Anglo-Saxon, Pan-Celtic, Pan-Christian, Pan-Presbyterian,* and other like words of obvious meaning, formed at will, and tending with longer use to lose the hyphen and the second capital, unless these are retained in order to set off clearly the component elements. [t. Gk., comb. form of *pâs* (neut. *pân*)]

Pan., Panama.

pan·a·ce·a (păn′ə sē′ə), *n.* a remedy for all diseases; cure-all. [t. L, t. Gk.: m. *panákeia*] —**pan′a·ce′an,** *adj.*

pa·nache (pə năsh′, -näsh′), *n.* an ornamental plume or tuft of feathers, esp. one worn on a helmet or on a cap. [t. F, t. It.: m. *pennacchio,* der. *penna,* g. L: feather]

pa·na·da (pə nä′də, -nā′-), *n.* a dish made of bread boiled and flavored. [t. Sp., Pr., ult. der. L *pānis* bread]

Pan·a·ma (păn′ə mä′; for. pä′nä mä′), *n.* **1.** a republic in S Central America, enclosing, but not including, the Panama Canal. 622,576 pop. (1940); 28,575 sq. mi. **2.** Also, **Panama City.** the capital of Panama, at the Pacific end of the Panama Canal, though not in the Canal Zone. 111,893 (1940). **3. Isthmus of,** (formerly, **Isthmus of Darien**) an isthmus between North and South America. Least width, ab. 30 mi. **4. Gulf of,** the portion of the Pacific in the bend of the Isthmus of Panama. **5.** (*l.c.*) Panama hat. —**Pan·a·ma·ni·an** (păn′ə mä′nĭ ən, -mä′-), *adj., n.*

Panama Canal, a canal extending SE from the Atlantic to the Pacific across the Isthmus of Panama. 40 mi. long.

Panama Canal Zone, Canal Zone.

Panama City, a city in NW Florida. 25,814 (1950).

Panama hat, a fine plaited hat made of the young leaves of a palmlike plant, *Carludovica palmata,* of Central and South America. [named after PANAMA]

Pan-A·mer·i·can (păn′ə mĕr′ə kən), *adj.* of all the countries or people of North, Central, and South America.

Pan-A·mer·i·can·ism (păn′ə mĕr′ə kə nĭz′əm), *n.* the idea or advocacy of a political alliance or union of all the countries of North, Central, and South America.

Pan American Union, an organization of the 21 American republics to further understanding and peace.

Pa·nay (pä nī′), *n.* one of the Philippine Islands, in the central part of the group. 1,291,548 pop. (1939); 4446 sq. mi. *Cap.:* Iloilo.

pan·cake (păn′kāk′), *n., v.,* **-caked, -caking.** —*n.* **1.** a flat cake of batter cooked in a pan or on a griddle; a griddlecake; a flapjack. **2.** an airplane landing made by pancaking. —*v.i.* **3.** (of an airplane, etc.) to drop flat to the ground after leveling off a few feet above the ground. —*v.t.* **4.** to cause (an airplane) to pancake.

pan·chro·mat·ic (păn′krō măt′ĭk), *adj.* sensitive to light of all colors, as a photographic film or plate.

pan·cra·ti·um (păn krā′shĭ əm), *n., pl.* **-tia** (-shĭ ə). *Gk. Antiq.* an athletic contest combining wrestling and boxing. [t. L, t. Gk.: m. *pankrátion* complete contest] —**pan·crat·ic** (păn krăt′ĭk), *adj.*

pan·cre·as (păn′krĭ əs, păng′-), *n. Anat., Zool.* a gland situated near the stomach, secreting an important digestive fluid (**pancreatic juice**), discharged into the intestine by one or more ducts. Certain groups of cells

(**Islets of Langerhans**) also produce a hormone, insulin. An animal's pancreas, used as food, is called **sweetbread.** [t. NL, t. Gk.: m. *pánkreas* sweetbread] —**pan·cre·at·ic** (păn′krĭ ăt′ĭk, păng′-), *adj.*

pan·cre·a·tin (păn′krĭ ə tĭn, păng′-), *n.* **1.** *Biochem.* a preparation containing all the enzymes of the pancreatic juice. **2.** a commercial preparation of the enzymes in the pancreas of animals, used as a digestive.

pan·cre·a·tot·o·my (păn′krĭ ə tŏt′ə mĭ, păng′-), *n., pl.* **-mies.** *Surg.* the operation of removing part or all of the pancreas.

pan·da (păn′də), *n.* **1.** Also, **lesser panda.** a carnivore, *Aelurus fulgens,* of the Himalayas, somewhat larger than a cat, and having reddish-brown fur darker beneath, face marked with white, and a long, bushy tail marked with pale rings. **2.** Also, **giant panda.** a large bearlike carnivore, *Ailuropoda melanoleuca,* of Tibet and southern China, white with black limbs, shoulders, and ears, and a black ring around each eye, little known in captivity before 1936. [said to be the name (for the animal) current in Nepal]

Giant panda, *Ailuropoda melanoleuca* (5 ft. long, 2 ft. high at the shoulder)

pan·da·na·ceous (păn′də nā′shəs), *adj.* belonging to the *Pandanaceae,* or pandanus family of trees and shrubs.

pan·da·nus (păn dā′nəs), *n.* any plant of the genus *Pandanus,* comprising tropical trees and shrubs, esp. of the islands of the Malay Archipelago and the Indian and Pacific oceans, having a palmlike or branched stem, long, narrow, rigid, spirally arranged leaves, and aerial roots, and bearing edible fruit; a screw pine. [t. NL, t. Malay: m. *pandan*]

Pan·da·rus (păn′də rəs), *n. Gk. Legend.* a leader of the Lycians and an ally of the Trojans in the siege of Troy. In Chaucer, other medieval accounts, and Shakespeare, he is represented as the procurer of Cressida for Troilus.

Pan·de·an (păn dē′ən), *adj.* of or pertaining to the god Pan: *Pandean pipes (Panpipe).*

pan·dect (păn′dĕkt), *n.* **1.** (*pl.*) a complete body or code of laws. **2.** a comprehensive digest. **3. Pandects,** *Rom. Law.* the Digest. [t. L: s. *pandecta, pandectēs,* t. Gk.: m. *pandēktēs,* lit., all-receiver]

pan·dem·ic (păn dĕm′ĭk), *adj.* **1.** (of a disease) prevalent throughout an entire country or continent, or the whole world. **2.** general; universal. —*n.* **3.** a pandemic disease. [f. s. Gk. *pandēmos* public, common + -IC]

pan·de·mo·ni·um (păn′də mō′nĭ əm), *n.* **1.** (*often cap.*) the abode of all the demons. **2.** hell. **3.** a place of riotous uproar or lawless confusion. **4.** wild lawlessness or uproar. [orig. *Pandaemonium,* Milton's name for the capital of hell. See PAN-, DEMON, -IUM]

pan·der (păn′dər), *n.* **1.** a go-between in intrigues of love; a pimp. **2.** one who ministers to the baser passions of others. —*v.t.* **3.** to act as a pander for. —*v.i.* **4.** to act as a pander; cater basely. [var. of *pandar,* generalized use of ME *Pandare* PANDARUS. Cf. Shakespeare's *Troilus and Cressida,* iii. 2. 210] —**pan′der·er,** *n.*

Pan·do·ra (păn dōr′ə), *n. Class. Myth.* the first mortal woman, on whom all the gods and goddesses bestowed gifts. She was given by Zeus to Epimetheus to bring misery to mankind because Prometheus had stolen fire from heaven. [t. L, t. Gk.: lit., all-gifted]

pan·do·ra (păn dōr′ə), *n.* bandore. Also, **pan·dore** (păn dōr′).

Pandora's box, *Class. Myth.* a box or jar, the gift of Zeus to Pandora, containing all human ills, which escaped when she opened it. According to a later version, the box contained all the blessings of the gods, which would have been preserved for the human race had not Pandora opened it, thus letting all the blessings escape, with the exception of hope.

pan·dour (păn′dōōr), *n.* **1.** one of a force of merciless soldiers raised in the 18th century in Croatia, later made a regiment in the Austrian army. **2.** a brutal, marauding soldier. [t. F, t. Hung.: m. *pandúr* infantryman]

pan·dow·dy (păn dou′dĭ), *n., pl.* **-dies.** *U.S.* a pudding or deep pie made with apples, and usually sweetened with molasses.

pan·du·rate (păn′dyə rāt′), *adj.* shaped like a fiddle, as a leaf. Also, **pan·du·ri·form** (păn dyōōr′ə fôrm′, -dyŏōr′). [f. s. LL *pandura* (see BANDORE) + -ATE[1]]

pan·dy (păn′dĭ), *n., pl.* **-dies,** *v.,* **-died, -dying.** *Chiefly Scot.* —*n.* **1.** a stroke on the palm with a cane or strap as a punishment in schools. —*v.t.* **2.** to strike thus. [said to be t. L: m. *pande,* impv., stretch out]

pane (pān), *n.* **1.** one of the divisions of a window, etc., consisting of a single plate of glass in a frame. **2.** a plate of glass for such a division. **3.** a panel, as of a wainscot, ceiling, door, etc. **4.** a flat section, side, or surface, as one of the sides of a bolthead. [ME *pan,* t. OF, g. L *pannus* a cloth, rag]

Pandurate leaf

paned (pānd), *adj.* having panes: *a diamond-paned window.*

pan·e·gyr·ic (păn′ə jĭr′ĭk), *n.* **1.** an oration, dis-

course, or writing in praise of a person or thing; a eulogy.
2. a formal or elaborate encomium. [t. L: s. *panēgyricus*,
t. Gk.: m. *panēgyrikós* festival oration, prop. adj.]
—**pan·e·gyr·i·cal,** *adj.* —**pan·e·gyr·i·cal·ly,** *adv.*

pan·e·gyr·ist (păn′ə·jĭr′ĭst, păn′ə·jĭr′ĭst), *n.* one
who panegyrizes; a eulogist.

pan·e·gy·rize (păn′ə·jə·rīz′), *v.,* **-rized, -rizing.** —*v.t.*
1. to pronounce or write a panegyric upon; eulogize.
—*v.i.* 2. to indulge in panegyric; bestow praises.

pan·el (păn′əl), *n.,* *v.,* **-eled, -eling** or (*esp. Brit.*)
-elled, -elling. —*n.* 1. a distinct portion or division of
a wainscot, ceiling, door, shutter, etc., or of any surface
sunk below or raised above the general level, or enclosed
by a frame or border. 2. a pane, as in a window. 3. a
comparatively thin, flat piece of wood or the like.
4. *Painting.* **a.** a flat piece of wood of varying kinds on
which a picture is painted. **b.** a picture painted on such
a piece of wood. 5. a photograph much longer in one
dimension than the other. 6. a broad strip of the same
or another material set vertically, as for ornament, in or
on a woman's skirt. 7. the section between the two
bands on the backstrip of a bound book. 8. *Elect.* a
division of a switchboard containing a set of related
cords, jacks, relays, etc. 9. the portion of a truss between adjacent chord joints. 10. *Law.* **a.** the list of
persons summoned for service as jurors. **b.** the body of
persons composing a jury. **c.** *Scot. Law.* the person or
persons indicted and brought to trial. 11. any list or
group of persons: *a panel to lead a public discussion.*
12. *Brit.* (in a system of health insurance) a list of
doctors to whom the patients may go. 13. *Aeron.* **a.** a
lateral subdivision of an airfoil with internal girder construction. **b.** a section of the hull of a rigid airship
marked off by a set of transverse and lateral girders.
14. *Mining.* an area of a coal seam, separated for mining
purposes from adjacent areas by extra thick masses or
ribs of coal. 15. a pad placed under a saddle. 16. a pad
or the like serving as a saddle. 17. a slip of parchment.
—*v.t.* 18. to arrange in, or furnish with, panels. 19. to
ornament with a panel or panels. 20. to set in a frame
as a panel. 21. to select (a jury). 22. *Scot. Law.* to
bring to trial. [ME *panel,* t. OF: piece (of anything),
ult. der. L *pannus* rag]

panel discussion, an organized discussion, the
topic, speakers, etc. being selected beforehand.

pan·el·ing (păn′əl·ĭng), *n.* 1. wood or other material
made into panels. 2. panels collectively. Also, *esp.
Brit.,* **pan·el·ling.**

pan·e·tel·la (păn′ə·tĕl′ə), *n.* a long slender cigar
pointed at the end intended for the mouth. [t. Sp.]

pan-fired tea (păn′fīrd′), a green Japanese tea of
small, tightly-twisted leaves.

pan fish, a fish suitable for frying whole in a pan.

pang (păng), *n.* 1. a sudden feeling of mental distress.
2. a sudden, brief, sharp pain, or a spasm or severe
twinge of pain: *the pangs of hunger.* [orig. uncert.]

pan·gen·e·sis (păn·jĕn′ə·sĭs), *n.* *Biol.* a theory advanced by Darwin, according to which a reproductive
cell or body contains gemmules or invisible germs which
were derived from the individual cells from every part
of the organism, and which are the bearers of hereditary
attributes. —**pan·ge·net·ic** (păn′jə·nĕt′ĭk), *adj.*

Pan-Ger·man·ism (păn′jûr′mə·nĭz′əm), *n.* the idea
or advocacy of a union of all the German peoples in one
political organization or state. —**Pan′-Ger′man,** *adj.,*
n. —**Pan-Ger·man·ic** (păn′jər·măn′ĭk), *adj.*

pan·go·lin (păng·gō′lĭn), *n.* any of the scaly anteaters
of Africa and tropical Asia, constituting an order of
mammals, *Pholidota,* having a
covering of broad, overlapping,
horny scales. [t. Malay: m.
penggōling roller]

pan·han·dle[1] (păn′hăn′dəl), *n.*
1. the handle of a pan. 2. *U.S.* a
narrow projecting strip of land,
esp. part of a State: *the Panhan-
dle of West Virginia, Texas,
Oklahoma, or Idaho.*

Pangolin, *Smutsia temminckii*
(Total length 30 in.,
tail 14 in.)

pan·han·dle[2] (păn′hăn′dəl),
v.i., **-dled, -dling.** *Colloq.* to beg (usually on the street).
—**pan′han′dler,** *n.*

Pan·hel·len·ic (păn′hə·lĕn′ĭk), *adj.* 1. pertaining to
all Greeks or to Panhellenism. 2. of or pertaining to
collegiate fraternities and sororities. Also, **pan′hel·len′ic.**

Pan·hel·len·ism (păn·hĕl′ə·nĭz′əm), *n.* the idea or
principle of a union of all Greeks in one political body.
—**Pan·hel′len·ist,** *n.*

pan·ic[1] (păn′ĭk), *n.,* *adj.,* *v.,* **-icked, -icking.** —*n.*
1. demoralizing terror, with or without clear cause, often
as affecting a group of persons or animals. 2. an instance, outbreak, or period of such fear. 3. *Finance.* a
sudden widespread fear concerning financial affairs leading to credit contraction and widespread sale of securities
at depressed prices in an effort to acquire cash. —*adj.*
4. (of fear, terror, etc.) suddenly destroying the self-control and impelling to some frantic action. 5. of the
nature of, due to, or showing panic: *panic haste.* 6. (*cap.*)
of or pertaining to the god Pan. —*v.t.* 7. *Theat. Slang.*
to keep (an audience or the like) highly amused. [t. F:
m. *panique,* t. L: m. *pānicus,* t. Gk.: m. *Panikós* pertaining to or caused by Pan] —**pan′ick·y,** *adj.* —**pan·ic-
strick·en** (păn′ĭk·strĭk′ən), **pan·ic-struck** (păn′ĭk-
strŭk′), *adj.* —**Syn. 1.** See **terror.**

pan·ic[2] (păn′ĭk), *n.* 1. any grass of the genus *Panicum,*
many species of which bear edible grain. 2. the grain.
Also, **panic grass.** [OE, t. L: s. *pānicum*]

pan·i·cle (păn′ə·kəl), *n.* *Bot.* 1. a compound raceme. 2. any loose, diversely
branching flower cluster. [t. L: m.s.
pānicula tuft on plants, dim. of *pānus*
swelling, ear of millet]

pa·nic·u·late (pə·nĭk′yə·lāt′, -lĭt), *adj.*
Bot. arranged in panicles. —**pa·nic′-
u·late′ly,** *adv.*

Pan-Is·lam·ism (păn′ĭs′lə·mĭz′əm),
n. the idea or advocacy of a union of all
Mohammedan nations in one political
body. —**Pan-Is·lam·ic** (păn′ĭs·lăm′ĭk,
-lä′mĭk), *adj.*

Branch with panicles

Pan·ja·bi (pŭn·jä′bĭ), *n.,* *pl.* **-bis.** 1.
Punjabi. 2. the Indic language used in the Punjab.

pan·jan·drum (păn·jăn′drəm), *n.* a mock title for any
important or pretentious official. [a made word, with
prefix PAN- and termination simulating Latin; appar.
first used by Samuel Foote (1720–77), English dramatist and actor]

panne (păn), *n.* a soft, lustrous, lightweight velvet
with flattened pile. [t. F, g. L *penna* feather]

pan·nier (păn′yər, -ĭ·ər), *n.* 1. a basket, esp. one of
considerable size, for carrying provisions, etc. 2. a basket for carrying on a person's back, or one of a pair to
be slung across the back of a beast of burden. 3. a
puffed arrangement of drapery about the hips. 4. a
framework formerly used for distending the skirt of a
woman's dress at the hips. [ME *panier,* t. OF, g. L
pānārium basket for bread]

pan·ni·kin (păn′ə·kĭn), *n.* *Chiefly Brit.* a small pan or
metal cup.

Pan·no·ni·a (pə·nō′nĭ·ə), *n.* an ancient country and
Roman province in central Europe, S and W of the
Danube: now mostly in Hungary and Yugoslavia.

pa·no·cha (pə·nō′chə), *n.* 1. a candy made of brown
sugar, butter, and milk, usually with nuts. 2. a coarse
grade of sugar made in Mexico. Also, **pa·no·che** (pə·nō′-
chĭ). [t. Mex. Sp.]

pan·o·ply (păn′ə·plĭ), *n.,* *pl.* **-plies.** 1. a complete suit
of armor. 2. a complete covering or array of something.
[t. Gk.: m.s. *panoplía* complete suit of armor] —**pan-
o·plied** (păn′ə·plĭd), *adj.*

pan·op·tic (păn·ŏp′tĭk), *adj.* containing all visible
objects within sight. Also, **pan·op′ti·cal.**

pan·o·ram·a (păn′ə·răm′ə, -rä′mə), *n.* 1. an unobstructed view or prospect over a wide area. 2. an
extended pictorial representation of a landscape or other
scene, often exhibited a part at a time and made to pass
continuously before the spectators. 3. a continuously
passing or changing scene. 4. a comprehensive survey,
as of a subject. [f. PAN- + m. Gk. *hórāma* view] —**pan′-
o·ram·ic,** *adj.* **pan′o·ram′i·cal·ly,** *adv.*

panoramic sight, a sight for guns that can be swung
in a complete circle.

Pan·pipe (păn′pīp′), *n.* a primitive wind instrument consisting
of a series of pipes of graduated
length, the tones being produced
by blowing across the upper
ends. Also, **Pan's pipes.**

Pan-Slav·ism (păn′släv′ĭz·əm,
-släv′-), *n.* the idea or advocacy
of a union of all the Slavic races
in one political body. —**Pan′-
Slav′, Pan′-Slav′ic,** *adj.*

pan·so·phism (păn′sə·fĭz′əm),
n. the claim or pretension to
pansophy. —**pan′so·phist,** *n.*

Panpipe

pan·so·phy (păn′sə·fĭ), *n.* universal wisdom or knowledge. [f. PAN- + m.s. Gk. *sophía* wisdom] —**pan·soph-
ic** (păn·sŏf′ĭk), **pan·soph′i·cal,** *adj.*

pan·sy (păn′zĭ), *n.,* *pl.* **-sies.** 1. the plant *Viola tricolor,* a species of violet having many cultivated varieties
with large, richly and variously colored flowers. 2. the
pansy blossom. [t. F: m. *pensée* pansy, lit., thought, der.
penser think. See PENSIVE]

pant (pănt), *v.i.* 1. to breathe hard and quickly, as
after exertion. 2. to emit steam or the like in loud puffs.
3. to gasp, as for air. 4. to long with breathless or intense eagerness: *he panted for revenge.* 5. to throb or
heave violently or rapidly; palpitate. —*v.t.* 6. to
breathe or utter gaspingly. —*n.* 7. act of panting. 8. a
short, quick, labored effort of breathing; a gasp. 9. a
puff, as of an engine. 10. a throb or heave, as of the
breast. [ME *panten;* appar. akin to OF *pantaisier,* prob.
(with ref. to the feeling of oppression in nightmare) ult.
der. L *phantasia* phantasm, idea, FANTASY] —**pant′-
ing·ly,** *adv.*
—**Syn. 1.** PANT, GASP suggest breathing with more effort
than usual. PANT suggests rapid, convulsive breathing, as
from violent exertion or excitement: *to pant after a run for
the train.* GASP suggests catching one's breath in a single
quick intake, as from amazement, terror, and the like or
a series of such quick intakes of breath as in painful breathing: *to gasp with horror, to gasp for breath* (as one having
asthma).

Pan·tag·ru·el (păn·tăg′rōō·ĕl′; *Fr.* päⁿ·tȧ·grȳ·ĕl′), *n.*
one of the characters of Rabelais, the huge son of
Gargantua, represented as dealing with serious matters

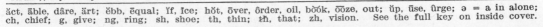

in a spirit of broad and somewhat cynical good humor. [t. F] —**Pan·ta·gru·el·i·an** (păn′tə grōō ĕl′ĭ ən), *adj.* —**Pan·ta·gru·el·ism** (păn′tə grōō′ə lĭz′əm, păn tăg′rōō ə lĭz′əm), *n.* —**Pan′ta·gru·el·ist**, *n.*

pan·ta·lets (păn′tə lĕts′), *n.pl.* **1.** long drawers with a frill or other finish at the bottom of each leg, and extending below the dress, commonly worn by women and girls in the 19th century. **2.** a pair of separate frilled or trimmed pieces for attaching to the legs of women's drawers. Also, **pan′ta·lettes′**. [alter. of PANTALOON, with dim. -ET(TE) substituted for -*oon*]

pan·ta·loon (păn′tə lōōn′), *n.* **1.** (*pl.*) *In U.S., Archaic except Hist.; in England, formal.* a man's closely fitting garment for the hips and legs, varying in form at different periods; trousers. **2.** (in the modern pantomime) a foolish, vicious old man, the butt and accomplice of the clown. **3.** (*cap. or l.c.*) (in the early Italian comedy) a lean and foolish old Venetian wearing pantaloons and slippers. [t. F: m. *pantalon*, t. It.: m. *pantalone* buffoon (see def. 3), *Pantalone* a Venetian, from St. *Pantaleone* patron of Venice]

pan·tech·ni·con (păn tĕk′nə kŏn′, -kən), *n. Brit.* **1.** a furniture van. **2.** a storage warehouse, esp. for furniture. **3.** *Obs.* a bazaar for everything artistic. [f. PAN- + m. Gk. *technikón* (neut. of *technikós* artistic; orig. def. 3)]

pan·tel·e·graph (păn tĕl′ə grăf′, -gräf′), *n.* a facsimile telegraph.

Pan·tel·le·ri·a (păn tĕl′lĕ rē′ä), *n.* an Italian island in the Mediterranean between Sicily and Tunisia. 10,209 pop. (1936); 32 sq. mi.

Pan-Teu·ton·ism (păn′tū′tən ĭz′əm, -tōō′-), *n.* Pan-Germanism.

pan·the·ism (păn′thē ĭz′əm), *n.* **1.** the doctrine that God is the transcendent reality of which the material universe and man are only manifestations. It involves a denial of God's personality, and expresses a tendency to identify God and nature. Cf. **theism, deism. 2.** any religious belief or philosophical doctrine which identifies the universe with God. [f. PAN- + s. Gk. *theós* god + -ISM] —**pan′the·ist**, *n.* —**pan′the·is′tic, pan′the·is′ti·cal**, *adj.* —**pan′the·is′ti·cal·ly**, *adv.*

Pan·the·on (păn′thĭ ŏn′, -ən, păn thē′ən), *n.* **1.** a domed circular temple at Rome, erected A.D. 120–124 by Hadrian using an older porch built by Agrippa 27 B.C., and used as a church since A.D. 609. **2.** (*l.c.*) a public building containing tombs or memorials of the illustrious dead of a nation. **3.** (*l.c.*) a temple dedicated to all the gods. **4.** (*l.c.*) the gods of a particular mythology considered collectively. [ME. t. L. t. Gk.: m. *pántheion*, prop. neut. of *pántheios* of all gods]

pan·ther (păn′thər), *n., pl.* -**thers**, (*esp. collectively*) -**ther**. **1.** the cougar or puma, *Felis concolor.* **2.** the leopard, *Panthera pardus.* [t. L: s. *panthēra*, t. Gk.: m. *pánthēr*; r. ME *pantere* (t. OF) and OE *pandher* (t. L)] —**pan·ther·ess** (păn′thər ĭs), *n. fem.*

pan·tile (păn′tīl′), *n.* a roofing tile straight in its length but curved in its width to overlap the next tile. [f. PAN[1] + TILE, n. Cf. G *pfannenziegel*]

Pantiles

panto-, synonymous with **pan-**. [t. Gk., comb. form of *pâs*, neut. *pân* all]

pan·to·fle (păn′tə fəl, păn tŏf′əl, -tōō′fəl), *n.* a slipper. Also, **pan′tof·fle**. [t. F: m. *pantoufle*, t. OIt.: m. *pantufola*, var. of Sicilian *pantofola*, t. Gk.: m. *pantóphellos* whole cork, through meaning of cork shoe]

pan·to·graph (păn′tə grăf′, -gräf′), *n.* **1.** an instrument for the mechanical copying of plans, diagrams, etc., upon any desired scale. **2.** *Elect.* a current collector transferring current from an overhead wire to a vehicle, usually consisting of two parallel hinged double-diamond frames with a rotatory bar between them.

pan·tol·o·gy (păn tŏl′ə jĭ), *n.* a systematic view of all human knowledge. —**pan·to·log·ic** (păn′tə lŏj′ĭk), **pan′to·log′i·cal**, *adj.* —**pan·tol′o·gist**, *n.*

pan·to·mime (păn′tə mīm′), *n., v.,* -**mimed**, -**miming**. —*n.* **1.** a play or entertainment in which the performers express themselves by mute gestures, often to the accompaniment of music. **2.** a form of theatrical spectacle, common in England during the Christmas season, a feature of which is a harlequinade (now sometimes omitted) including pranks of the clown and pantaloon and dancing of the harlequin and columbine. **3.** an actor in dumb show, as in ancient Rome. **4.** significant gesture without speech. —*v.t.* **5.** to represent or express by pantomime. —*v.i.* **6.** to express oneself by pantomime. [t. L: m.s. *pantomīmus*, t. Gk.: m. *pantómīmos*, lit., all-imitating] —**pan·to·mim′ic** (păn′tə mĭm′ĭk), *adj.*

pan·to·mim·ist (păn′tə mĭ′mĭst), *n.* **1.** one who acts in pantomime. **2.** the author of a pantomime.

pan·to·prag·mat·ic (păn′tə prăg măt′ĭk), *adj.* concerned or busied with all things; universally meddlesome.

pan·to·then·ic acid (păn′tə thĕn′ĭk), *Biochem.* an oily hydroxy acid, $HOCH_2C(CH_3)_2CHOHCONHCH_2$-$CH_2COOH$, found in plant and animal tissues, rice bran, etc. and essential for cell growth.

pan·try (păn′trĭ), *n., pl.* -**tries.** a room or closet in which bread and other provisions, or silverware, dishes, etc., are kept. [ME *panetrie*, t. AF, der. OF *panetier* servant in charge of bread, der. L *pānis* bread]

pants (pănts), *n.pl.* **1.** *U.S. Colloq.* trousers. **2.** *Brit.* drawers. [familiar abbr. of PANTALOONS]

pan·tun (păn tōōn′), *n.* a Malay verse form, usually of four lines, the third rhyming with the first, and the fourth with the second. Also, **pan·toum** (păn tōōm′). [t. Malay]

Pan·urge (păn ûrj′; *Fr.* på nyrzh′), *n.* (in Rabelais' *Gargantua and Pantagruel*) an irresistible rascal, companion of Pantagruel. [t. F, t. Gk.: m.s. *panoûrgos* ready to do anything]

Pan·za (păn′zə; *Sp.* pän′thä), *n.* See **Sancho Panza.**

pan·zer (păn′zər; *Ger.* pän′tsər), *adj.* German. armored: *a panzer division.*

Pao·shan (bou′shän′), *n.* a city in SW China, in Yünnan province, on the Burma Road.

Pao·ting (bou′tĭng′), *n.* a city in NE China, in Hopeh province. ab. 150,000.

pap[1] (păp), *n.* **1.** soft food for infants or invalids, as bread soaked in water or milk. **2.** *Slang.* profits or favors secured through official patronage. [ME. Cf. LG *pappe*, ML *pappa*]

pap[2] (păp), *n.* **1.** *Archaic or Dial.* a teat or nipple. **2.** something resembling a teat or nipple. [ME *pappe.* Cf. d. Norw. and Sw. *pappe*]

pa·pa[1] (pä′pə, pə pä′), *n.* father. [t. F, t. L. Cf. It. *pappa*, Gk. *páppas*]

pa·pa[2] (pä′pə), *n.* papas.

pa·pa·cy (pä′pə sĭ), *n., pl.* -**cies.** **1.** the office, dignity, or jurisdiction of the Pope (of Rome). **2.** the system of ecclesiastical government in which the Pope is recognized as the supreme head. **3.** the time during which a pope is in office. **4.** the succession or line of the popes. [ME, t. ML: m.s. *pāpātia,* der. *pāpa* pope. See PAPAS]

pa·pa·in (pə pä′ĭn, pä′pə-), *n.* **1.** *Chem.* a proteolytic enzyme contained in the fruit of the papaya tree, *Carica Papaya.* **2.** a commercial preparation of this, used as a digestant. [f. PAPA(YA) + -IN[2]]

pa·pal (pä′pəl), *adj.* of or pertaining to the Pope, the papacy, or the Roman Catholic Church. [ME, t. ML: s. *pāpālis,* der. *pāpa* pope. See PAPAS]

papal cross, a cross with three transoms. See illus. under **cross.**

Papal States, a large district in central Italy ruled as a temporal domain by the Popes from 755 until the final unification of Italy in 1870; partially annexed by Italy, 1860. Also, **States of the Church.**

pa·pas (pä′päs), *n.* **1.** *Gk. Ch.* a parish priest. **2.** the Pope (of Rome or Alexandria). Also, **papa.** [t. ML: pope, LL bishop, t. Gk.: m. *páppas* father (orig. in childish use). See POPE]

pa·pav·er·a·ceous (pə păv′ə rā′shəs), *adj.* belonging to the *Papaveraceae,* or poppy family of plants, a large group of medicinal importance as the source of opium. [f. L *papāver* poppy + -ACEOUS]

pa·pav·er·ine (pə păv′ə rēn′, -ər ĭn, pə pā′və-), *n.* a fine, odorless, crystalline, white alkaloid, $C_{20}H_{21}NO_4$, derived from opium, which relaxes the involuntary muscles of the gastrointestinal tract, and other smooth muscles. Also, **pa·pav·er·in** (pə păv′ər ĭn, pə pā′və-).

pa·paw (pô′pô, pə pô′), *n.* **1.** the small fleshy fruit of the temperate North American bush or small tree, *Asimina triloba.* **2.** the tree itself. Also, **pawpaw.** [t. Sp. See PAPAYA]

pa·pa·ya (pə pä′yə), *n.* **1.** the large yellow melonlike fruit of the tropical American shrub or small tree, *Carica Papaya,* of the family *Caricaceae,* much prized for its palatable fruits containing a digestive principle. **2.** the tree itself, which is herbaceous. [t. Sp.: *papaya* the fruit, m. *papayo* the tree; of Carib orig.]

Pa·pe·e·te (pä′pĭ ā′tĭ), *n.* a seaport in the Society Islands, on Tahiti: capital of the Society Islands and of French Oceania. 11,614 (1941).

pa·per (pä′pər), *n.* **1.** a substance made from rags, straw, wood, or other fibrous material, usually in thin sheets, for writing or printing on, wrapping things in, decorating walls, etc. **2.** something resembling this substance, as papyrus. **3.** a piece, sheet, or leaf of paper, esp. one bearing writing. **4.** a written or printed document or instrument. **5.** negotiable notes, bills, etc., collectively: *commercial paper.* **6.** a document establishing identity, status, or the like. **7.** (*pl.*) the documents required to be carried by a ship for the manifestation of her ownership, nationality, destination, etc. **8.** a set of questions for an examination, or an individual set of written answers to them. **9.** an essay, article, or dissertation on a particular topic. **10.** a newspaper or journal. **11.** a sheet or card of paper with pins or needles stuck through it in rows. **12.** *Slang.* a free pass to a place of entertainment. —*v.t.* **13.** to write or set down on paper. **14.** to describe in writing. **15.** to fold, enclose, or put up in paper. **16.** to decorate (a wall, room, etc.) with wallpaper. **17.** to supply with paper. —*adj.* **18.** made or consisting of paper: *a paper box.* **19.** paperlike; thin; flimsy; frail. **20.** pertaining to, or carried on by means of letters, articles, books, etc.: *a paper warfare.* **21.** written or printed on paper. **22.** existing on paper only and not in reality: *paper profits.* **23.** indicating the 1st event of a series, as a wedding anniversary. [ME and OE, t. L: m.s. *papȳrus* paper, PAPYRUS] —**pa′per·like′**, *adj.*

paper birch, the North American birch, *B. papyrifera*, a tall tree with tough, durable bark and valuable wood.

pa·per·er (pā′pər ər), *n.* 1. a paper hanger. 2. one who papers.

paper hanger, one whose business it is to cover or decorate walls with wallpaper. —**paper hanging.**

paper knife, a knifelike instrument with a blade of metal, ivory, wood, or the like, for cutting open the leaves of books, folded papers, etc.

paper money, currency in paper form, as government and bank notes.

paper nautilus, any dibranchiate cephalopod of the genus *Argonauta*, characterized by the delicate shell of the female; the argonaut.

pa·per·weight (pā′pər wāt′), *n.* a small heavy object laid on papers to keep them from being scattered.

pa·per·y (pā′pər ĭ), *adj.* like paper; thin or flimsy.

pap·e·terie (păp′ə trĭ; *Fr.* păp trē′). *n.* a case or box of paper and other materials for writing. [t. F, der. *papetier* one who makes or sells paper, der. *papier* PAPER]

Pa·phi·an (pā′fĭ an), *adj.* 1. of or pertaining to Paphos, an ancient city of Cyprus sacred to Aphrodite. 2. pertaining to love, esp. illicit love or sexual indulgence.

Paph·la·go·ni·a (păf′lə gō′nĭ ə), *n.* an ancient country and Roman province in N Asia Minor, on the S coast of the Black Sea.

Pa·phos (pā′fŏs), *n.* an ancient city in SW Cyprus.

Pa·pia·men·to (pā′pĭa měn′tō), *n.* the creolized Spanish of Curaçao, in the Dutch West Indies.

pa·pier col·lé (pá pyē′ kô lě′), *pl.* **papiers collés** (pá pyē′ kô lě′). *French.* an arrangement of various objects and materials pasted on a flat surface to achieve a formal design, used especially in cubism about 1912–14.

pa·pier-mâ·ché (pā′pər mə shā′; *Fr.* pá pyē′má shě′), *n.* a substance made of pulped paper or paper pulp mixed with glue and other materials, or of layers of paper glued and pressed together, molded when moist to form various articles, and becoming hard and strong when dry. [t. F: *papier mâché* chewed paper]

pa·pil·i·o·na·ceous (pə pĭl′ĭ a nā′shəs), *adj. Bot.* 1. having an irregular corolla shaped somewhat like a butterfly, as the pea and other leguminous plants. 2. belonging to the family *Papilionaceae* (*Fabaceae*), which is often currently treated as part of a *Leguminosae.* [t. NL: m. *pāpiliōnāceus*, der. L *pāpilio* butterfly]

pa·pil·la (pə pĭl′ə), *n., pl.* **-pillae** (-pĭl′ē). 1. any small nipplelike process or projection. 2. one of certain small protuberances concerned with the senses of touch, taste, and smell: *the papillae of the tongue.* 3. a small vascular process at the root of a hair. 4. a papule or pimple. 5. *Bot.* a small nipplelike projection. [t. L: nipple]

Papilionaceous flower of bean.
Phaseolus vulgaris
V, Vexillum; W, Wings;
K, Keel, or carina

pap·il·lar·y (păp′ə lĕr′ĭ, pə pĭl′ə rĭ), *adj.* 1. of or pertaining to, or of the nature of, a papilla or papillae. 2. provided or furnished with papillae.

pap·il·lo·ma (păp′ə lō′mə), *n., pl.* **-mata** (-mə tə), **-mas.** *Pathol.* a tumor of skin or mucous membrane, consisting of a hypertrophied papilla or group of papillae, as a wart or a corn. [f. PAPILLA + -OMA]

pap·il·lon (păp′ə lŏn′), *n.* a variety of toy spaniel.

pap·il·lose (păp′ə lōs′), *adj.* full of papillae. —**pap·il·los·i·ty** (păp′ə lŏs′ə tĭ), *n.*

pap·il·lote (păp′ə lōt′), *n.* a curled paper, put at the end of the bone of a cutlet or chop. [t. F, der. *papillon* butterfly, t. L: m.s. *pāpilio*]

pa·pist (pā′pĭst), *n.* 1. an adherent of the Pope. 2. a member of the Roman Catholic Church (usually in disparagement). —*adj.* 3. papistical. [t. NL: s. *pāpista*, der. L *pāpa* POPE]

pa·pis·ti·cal (pā pĭs′tə kəl, pə-), *adj.* of, pertaining to, or characteristic of papists or papistry (usually in disparagement). Also, **pa·pis′tic.**

pa·pist·ry (pā′pĭs trĭ), *n.* (usually in disparaging use) the systems, doctrines, or practices of papists.

pa·poose (pă pōōs′), *n.* a North American Indian baby or young child. Also, **pap·poose′.** [t. Algonquian (New England): m. *papeisses*, der. *peisses* child]

pap·pose (păp′ōs), *adj. Bot.* 1. having or forming a pappus. 2. downy. Also, **pap·pous** (păp′əs).

pap·pus (păp′əs), *n., pl.* **pappi** (păp′ī). *Bot.* a downy, bristly, or other appendage of the achene of certain plants, as the dandelion and the thistle. [t. L, t. Gk.: m. *páppos* down on seeds, orig. grandfather]

pap·py (păp′ĭ), *adj.,* **-pier, -piest.** like pap; mushy.

pap·ri·ka (pă prē′kə, păp′rə kə), *n.* the dried fruit of a cultivated form of *Capsicum frutescens* ground as a condiment, much less pungent than ordinary red pepper. [t. Hung.]

Pap·u·a (păp′yōō ə, pā′pōō ä′), *n.* 1. New Guinea. 2. Territory of, an Australian territory in SE New Guinea, including the adjacent islands: merged with the Territory of New Guinea, 1945. 303,000 pop. (est. 1941); 90,540 sq. mi. *Cap.:* Port Moresby. 3. Gulf of, a large gulf of the Coral Sea, on the SE coast of New Guinea. 4. a Papuan. [t. Malay: lit., frizzled]

Pap·u·an (păp′yōō ən), *adj.* 1. of or pertaining to Papua. 2. denoting or pertaining to the native Negroid race of New Guinea, characterized by a black or sooty-brown complexion and crisp, frizzled hair. —*n.* 3. a native or inhabitant of New Guinea. 4. any of a number of languages of the Southwest Pacific, particularly of New Guinea and New Caledonia.

pap·ule (păp′ūl), *n. Pathol.* a small, somewhat pointed elevation of the skin, usually inflammatory but not suppurative. [t. L: m.s. *papula* pustule, pimple]

pap·y·ra·ceous (păp′ə rā′shəs), *adj.* papery.

pa·py·rus (pə pī′rəs), *n., pl.* **-pyri** (-pī′rī). 1. a tall aquatic plant, *Cyperus Papyrus*, of the sedge family, found in Ethiopia, Palestine, etc., and formerly abundant in Egypt. 2. a material for writing on, prepared from thin strips of the pith of this plant laid together, soaked, pressed, and dried, used by the ancient Egyptians, Greeks, and Romans. 3. an ancient document or manuscript written on this material. [ME, t. L. t. Gk.: m. *pápyros* the plant papyrus, something made from papyrus. Cf. PAPER]

par (pär), *n.* 1. an equality in value or standing; a level of equality: *the gains and the losses are on a par.* 2. an average or normal amount, degree, quality, condition, or the like: *above par, below par.* 3. *Com.* **a.** the legally established value of the monetary unit of one country in terms of that of another using the same metal as a standard of value (**mint par of exchange**). **b.** the state of the shares of any business, undertaking, loan, etc., when they may be purchased at the original price (called **issue par**) or at their face value (called **nominal par**). Such shares or bonds are said to be **at par.** 4. *Golf.* the number of strokes allowed to a hole or course as representing a score made by expert playing. —*adj.* 5. average or normal. 6. *Com.* at or pertaining to par: *the par value of a bond.* [t. L: equal]

par., 1. paragraph. 2. parallel. 3. parenthesis. 4. parish.

pa·ra (pä rä′, pä′rä), *n., pl.* **-ras, -ra.** 1. a monetary unit of Turkey, equal to one fortieth of a piaster, or about .11 U.S. cent. 2. one hundredth of a dinar (of Yugoslavia). [t. Turk. (Pers.): m. *parah* piece, portion]

Pa·rá (pä rä′), *n.* Pará rubber.

Pa·rá (pä rä′), *n.* 1. Belém. 2. an estuary in N Brazil, receiving the Tocantins river and a branch of the Amazon. ab. 200 mi. long; ab. 40 mi. wide.

para-[1], a prefix meaning "beside," "near," "beyond," "aside," "amiss," and sometimes implying alteration or modification, occurring orig. in words from the Greek, but used also as a modern formative, chiefly in scientific words. Also, **par-.** [t. Gk., comb. form of *parā*, prep.]

para-[2], a prefix of a few words meaning "guard against," as in *parachute.* [t. F, t. It., impv. of *parāre* defend against, g. L: prepare]

Para., Paraguay.

par·a·bi·o·sis (păr′ə bī ō′sĭs), *n. Biol.* experimental or natural union of two individuals with exchange of blood. —**par·a·bi·ot·ic** (păr′ə bī ŏt′ĭk), *adj.*

par·a·blast (păr′ə blăst′), *n. Biol.* the nutritive yolk of an ovum or egg.

par·a·ble (păr′ə bəl), *n.* 1. a short allegorical story, designed to convey some truth or moral lesson. 2. a discourse or saying conveying the intended meaning by a comparison or under the likeness of something comparable or analogous. [ME *parabil*, t. LL: m.s. *parabola* comparison, parable, proverb, word, t. Gk.: m. *parabolē* a placing beside, comparison]

pa·rab·o·la (pə răb′ə lə), *n. Geom.* a plane curve formed by the intersection of a right circular cone with a plane parallel to a generator of the cone. See **conic section** diagram. [t. NL, t. Gk.: m. *parabolē.* See PARABLE]

par·a·bol·ic[1] (păr′ə bŏl′ĭk), *adj.* 1. having the form or outline of a parabola. 2. pertaining to, or resembling a parabola. [ME, t. LL: s. *parabolicus*, t. LGk.: m. *parabolikós* figurative]

par·a·bol·ic[2] (păr′ə bŏl′ĭk), *adj.* of, pertaining to, or involving a parable. Also, **par·a·bol·i·cal.** [see PARABOLIC[1], PARABLE] —**par′a·bol·i·cal·ly,** *adv.*

pa·rab·o·loid (pə răb′ə loid′), *n. Geom.* a solid or surface generated by the revolution of a parabola about its axis, or one of the second degree some of whose plane sections are parabolas. —**pa·rab·o·loi·dal** (pə răb′ə loi′dəl, păr′ə bə-), *adj.*

Common parabola
AB, Directrix; F, Focus; P, Point on parabola; PQ, Always equal to PF; XX, Axis

Par·a·cel·sus (păr′ə sĕl′səs), *n.* (Theophrastus Bombastus von Hohenheim) 1493?–1541, Swiss-German physician and alchemist.

par·a·chute (păr′ə shōōt′), *n., v.,* **-chuted, -chuting.** —*n.* 1. an apparatus used in descending safely through the air from a great height, esp. from an aircraft, being umbrellalike in form and rendered effective by the resistance of the air, which expands it during the descent and then reduces the velocity of its motion. —*v.t.* 2. to land (troops, equipment, etc.) by parachute. —*v.i.* 3. to descend by parachute. [t. F: f. *para-* PARA-[2] + *chute* a fall. See CHUTE] —**par′a·chut·ist,** *n.*

par·a·clete (păr′ə klēt′), *n.* 1. one called in to aid; an advocate or intercessor. 2. (*cap.*) the Holy Spirit, or Comforter. [t. LL: m.s. *paraclētus*, t. Gk.: m. *paráklētos*]

par·a·cy·mene (păr′ə sī′mēn), *n.* the most common

form of cymene, found in several essential oils, as oil of eucalyptus.

pa·rade (pərād/), *n., v.,* **-raded, -rading.** —*n.* **1.** a public procession for display: *a political parade.* **2.** a ceremony involving the marching of troop units and a mass salute at the lowering of the flag at the end of the day. **3.** the orderly assembly of troops for inspection or display. **4.** a place where troops regularly assemble for parade. **5.** show, display, or ostentation: *to make parade of pain.* **6.** *Chiefly Brit.* a promenade. **7.** *Chiefly Brit.* a body of promenaders. **8.** *Fort.* the level space forming the interior or enclosed area of a fortification. **9.** *Fencing.* a parry. —*v.i.* **10.** to walk up and down on or in. **11.** to make parade of; display ostentatiously. **12.** to cause to march or proceed for display. —*v.i.* **13.** to march or proceed with display. **14.** to promenade in a public place to show oneself. **15.** to assemble in military order for display. [t. F, t. Sp.: m. *parada,* der. *parar,* g. L *parāre* prepare] —**pa·rad/er,** *n.*

par·a·di·chlo·ro·ben·zene (păr/ə dī klôr/ō bĕn/zēn, -bĕn zēn/), *n. Chem.* a white crystalline compound, $C_6H_4Cl_2$, of the benzene series, used as moth repellent.

par·a·digm (păr/ə dĭm, -dīm/), *n.* **1.** *Gram.* **a.** the set of all forms containing a particular element, esp. the set of all inflected forms of a single root, stem, or theme. For example: *boy, boy's, boys, boys'* constitutes the paradigm of the noun *boy.* **b.** a display in fixed arrangement of such a set. **2.** a pattern; an example. [late ME, t. LL: s. *paradigma,* t. Gk.: m. *parádeigma* pattern] —**par·a·dig·mat·ic** (păr/ə dĭg măt/ĭk), *adj.*

par·a·di·sa·i·cal (păr/ə dĭ sā/ə kəl), *adj.* paradisiacal. Also, **par/a·di·sa/ic.** —**par/a·di·sa/i·cal·ly,** *adv.*

par·a·dise (păr/ə dīs/), *n.* **1.** heaven, as the final abode of the righteous. **2.** (according to some) an intermediate place for the departed souls of the righteous awaiting resurrection. **3.** the garden of Eden. **4.** a place of extreme beauty or delight. **5.** supreme felicity. [ME *paradis,* t. LL: s. *paradīsus,* t. Gk.: m. *parádeisos* park, t. OPers.: m. *pairidaēza* enclosure]

paradise fish, a beautiful fish of either of two species of *Macropodus,* often kept in aquariums.

Paradise Lost, an epic poem (1667) by John Milton.

par·a·di·si·a·cal (păr/ə dĭ sī/ə kəl), *adj.* of, like, or befitting paradise. Also, **par·a·dis·i·ac** (păr/ə dĭs/ĭ ăk/). [f. s. LL *paradīsiacus* of paradise + -AL¹] —**par/a·di·si/a·cal·ly,** *adv.*

par·a·dos (păr/ə dŏs/), *n. Fort.* the bank behind a trench that protects men from fire and from being seen against the skyline. [t. F: f. *para-* PARA-² + *dos* back]

par·a·dox (păr/ə dŏks/), *n.* **1.** a statement or proposition seemingly self-contradictory or absurd, and yet explicable as expressing a truth. **2.** a self-contradictory and false proposition. **3.** any person or thing exhibiting apparent contradictions. **4.** an opinion or statement contrary to received opinion. [t. L; s. *paradoxum,* t. Gk.: m. *parádoxon,* neut. of *parádoxos* contrary to received opinion, incredible] —**par/a·dox/i·cal,** *adj.* —**par/a·dox/i·cal·ly,** *adv.* —**par/a·dox/i·cal·ness,** *n.*

par·aes·the·sia (păr/əs thē/zhə, -zĭ/ə), *n. Pathol.* paresthesia. —**par·aes·thet·ic** (păr/əs thĕt/ĭk), *adj.*

par·af·fin (păr/ə fĭn), *n.* **1.** *U.S.* a white or colorless waxy substance (a mixture of hydrocarbons; see def. 2b below), not easily acted upon by reagents, obtained chiefly from crude petroleum, and used for making candles, forming preservative coatings, waterproofing paper, etc. **2.** *Chem.* **a.** any hydrocarbon of the methane series (or **paraffin series**). **b.** one of the higher members of the methane series, solid at ordinary temperatures, with boiling points above 300°C., which largely constitute commercial paraffin. **3.** *Brit.* kerosene. —*v.t.* **4.** to cover or impregnate with paraffin. [t. G, f. (by K. von Reichenbach) L *par(um)* not enough + L *affin(is)* related; so called from its lack of affinity for other substances]

par·af·fine (păr/ə fĭn, -fēn/), *n., v.t.,* **-fined, -fining.** paraffin.

paraffin wax, paraffin in its solid state.

par·a·form·al·de·hyde (păr/ə fôr măl/də hīd/), *n.* a colorless noncrystalline polymer of formaldehyde $(CH_2O)_3$, which is utilized as an antiseptic.

par·a·gen·e·sis (păr/ə jĕn/ə sĭs), *n. Geol.* the origin and associations of a mineral or a mineral deposit. Also, **par·a·ge·ne·si·a** (păr/ə jə nē/sĭ ə). [f. PARA-¹ + GENE-SIS] —**par·a·ge·net·ic** (păr/ə jə nĕt/ĭk), *adj.*

par·a·go·ge (păr/ə gō/jĭ), *n.* (in linguistic change) the addition of a syllable, phoneme, or other element not originally present, at the end of a word, as the substandard pronunciation of *height* as *height-th,* the standard showing no change. [t. LL, t. Gk.: a leading past] —**par·a·gog·ic** (păr/ə gŏj/ĭk), *adj.*

par·a·gon (păr/ə gŏn/, -gən), *n.* **1.** a model or pattern of excellence, or of a particular excellence. **2.** *Print.* a type size (20 points). **3.** an unusually large round pearl. —*v.t. Archaic or Poetic.* **4.** to match or parallel. **5.** to compare. **6.** to be a match for; equal; rival. **7.** to surpass. **8.** to regard as a paragon. [t. OF, t. It.: m. *paragone* touchstone, comparison, paragon]

par·a·graph (păr/ə grăf/, -grāf/), *n.* **1.** a distinct portion of written or printed matter dealing with a particular point, and usually beginning (commonly with indention) on a new line. **2.** a character (now usually ¶) used to indicate the beginning of a distinct or separate portion of a text, or as a mark of reference. **3.** a note, item, or brief article, as in a newspaper. —*v.t.* **4.** to divide into paragraphs. **5.** to write or publish paragraphs about. **6.** to express in a paragraph. [t. LL: s. *paragraphus,* t. Gk.: m. *parágraphos* line or mark in the margin]

par·a·graph·er (păr/ə grăf/ər, -grāf/ər), *n.* one who writes paragraphs, as for a newspaper. Also, *esp. Brit.,* **par/a·graph/ist.**

par·a·graph·i·a (păr/ə grăf/ĭə), *n. Psychiatry.* a cerebral disorder marked by the writing of words or letters other than those intended, or the loss of ability to express ideas in writing. [t. NL, f. Gk.: *para-* PARA-¹ + *-graphía* writing]

par·a·graph·ic (păr/ə grăf/ĭk), *adj.* **1.** of, pertaining to, or forming a paragraph. **2.** divided into paragraphs. **3.** of or pertaining to paragraphia. Also, **par/a·graph/i·cal.**

Par·a·guay (păr/ə gwā/, -gwī/; *Sp.* pä/rä gwī/), *n.* **1.** a republic in central South America between Bolivia, Brazil, and Argentina. 1,145,000 pop. (est. 1944); 150,515 sq. mi. *Cap.:* Asunción. **2.** a river flowing from W Brazil S through Paraguay to the Paraná. ab. 1500 mi. —**Par/a·guay/an,** *adj., n.*

Paraguay tea, maté.

par·a·keet (păr/ə kēt/), *n.* any of numerous small slender parrots, usually with long, pointed, graduated tail, as the **Australian grass parakeet,** *Melopsittacus undulatus.* Also, **paraquet, paroquet, parrakeet, parroket, parroquet.** [t. OF: m. *paroquet,* t. It.: m. *parrochetto,* dim. of *parroco* parson]

par·al·de·hyde (pər ăl/də hīd/), *n. Chem.* a colorless liquid, $(CH_3CHO)_3$, formed by polymerization of acetaldehyde, and used as a hypnotic. [f. PAR- + ALDEHYDE]

par·a·lip·sis (păr/ə lĭp/sĭs), *n., pl.* **-ses** (-sēz). *Rhetoric.* a pretended ignoring, for rhetorical effect, of something actually spoken of, as in "not to mention other faults." Also, **par·a·leip·sis** (păr/ə lĭp/sĭs). [t. NL, t. Gk.: m. *paráleipsis* a passing over]

Carolina parakeet, *Conuropsis carolinensis* (1 ft. long)

par·al·lax (păr/ə lăks/), *n.* **1.** the apparent displacement of an object observed, esp. a heavenly body, due to a change or difference in the position of the observer. **2. diurnal** or **geocentric parallax,** the displacement of a body owing to its being observed from the surface instead of from the center of the earth. **3. annual** or **heliocentric parallax,** the displacement of a star owing to its being observed from the earth instead of from the sun. **4.** apparent change in the position of cross hairs as viewed through a telescope, when the focusing is imperfect. [t. Gk.: s. *parállaxis* change] —**par·al·lac·tic** (păr/ə lăk/tĭk), *adj.*

Geocentric parallax of the moon
P, Parallax; O, Observer; E, Center of earth; M, Moon; E′, Image of E; O′, Image of O

par·al·lel (păr/ə lĕl/), *adj., n., v.,* **-leled, -leling** or (*esp. Brit.*) **-lelled, -lelling.** —*adj.* **1.** having the same direction, course, or tendency; corresponding; similar; analogous: *parallel forces.* **2.** *Geom.* **a.** (of straight lines) lying in the same plane but never meeting no matter how far extended. **b.** (of planes) having common perpendiculars. **c.** (of a single line, plane, etc.) equidistant from another or others at all corresponding points (fol. by *to* or *with*). **3.** *Music.* **a.** (of two voice parts) progressing so that the interval between them remains the same. **b.** (of a tonality or key), having the same tonic but differing in mode. —*n.* **4.** anything parallel in direction, course, or tendency. **5.** a parallel line or plane. **6.** *Geog.* **a.** a circle on the earth surface formed by the intersection of a plane parallel to the plane of the equator, bearing east and west and designated in degrees of latitude north or south of the equator along the arc of any meridian. **b.** the line representing this circle on a chart or map. **7.** a match or counterpart. **8.** correspondence or analogy. **9.** a comparison of things as if regarded side by side. **10.** *Print.* a pair of vertical parallel lines (||) used as a mark of reference. **11.** *Elect.* a connection of two or more circuits in which all ends having the same instantaneous polarity are electrically connected together, and all ends having the opposite polarity are similarly connected. The element circuits are said to be **in parallel** (opp. to *in series*). **12.** *Fort.* a trench cut in the ground before a fortress, parallel to its defenses, for the purpose of covering a besieging force. —*v.t.* **13.** to make parallel. **14.** to furnish a parallel for; find or provide a match for. **15.** to form a parallel to; be equivalent to; equal. **16.** to compare. [t. L: s. *parallēlus,* t. Gk.: m. *parállēlos* beside one another]

parallel bars, gymnasium apparatus consisting of two wooden bars on uprights, adjustable in height, and used for swinging, vaulting, balancing exercises, etc.

parallel cousin marriage, marriage between the children of two brothers or two sisters.

par·al·lel·e·pi·ped (păr′ə lĕl′ə pī′pĭd, -pĭp′ĭd), *n.* a prism with six faces, all parallelograms. Also, **par·al·lel·e·pip·e·don** (păr′ə lĕl′ə pĭp′ə dŏn′, -dən). [t. Gk.: s. *parallēlepīpedon* body with parallel surfaces]

par·al·lel·ism (păr′ə lĕl′ĭzəm), *n.* **1.** the position or relation of parallels. **2.** agreement in direction, tendency, or character. **3.** a parallel or comparison. **4.** *Metaphys.* the doctrine that mental and bodily processes are concomitant, each varying with variation of the other, but that there is no causal relation or relation of interaction between the two series of changes.

par·al·lel·o·gram (păr′ə lĕl′ə grăm′), *n.* a quadrilateral the opposite sides of which are parallel. [t. Gk.: s. *parallēlogrammon*, prop. neut. of *parallēlogrammos* bounded by parallel lines]

par·al·o·gism (pə răl′ə jĭz′əm), *n. Logic.* **1.** a piece of false or fallacious reasoning, esp. (as distinguished from *sophism*) one of whose falseness the reasoner is not conscious. **2.** reasoning of this kind. [t. Gk.: s. *paralogismós* false reasoning] —**pa·ral′o·gist**, *n.* —**pa·ral′o·gis′tic**, *adj.*

pa·ral·y·sis (pə răl′ə sĭs), *n., pl.* **-ses** (-sēz′). **1.** *Pathol.* **a.** loss of power of a voluntary muscular contraction. **b.** a disease characterized by this; palsy. **2.** a more or less complete crippling, as of powers or activities: *a paralysis of trade.* [t. L, t. Gk.: palsy]

par·a·lyt·ic (păr′ə lĭt′ĭk), *n.* **1.** one affected with general paralysis. —*adj.* **2.** affected with or subject to paralysis. **3.** pertaining to or of the nature of paralysis.

par·a·lyze (păr′ə līz′), *v.t.* **-lyzed, -lyzing. 1.** to affect with paralysis. **2.** to bring to a condition of helpless inactivity. Also, *esp. Brit.,* **par′a·lyse′.** —**Syn. 2.** stun. See **shock**[1]. —**par′a·ly·za′tion,** *n.* —**par′a·lyz′er,** *n.*

par·a·mag·net (păr′ə măg′nĭt), *n.* a body or substance having paramagnetic properties. —**par′a·mag′net·ism,** *n.*

par·a·mag·net·ic (păr′ə măg nĕt′ĭk), *adj.* denoting or pertaining to a class of substances (e.g. liquid oxygen) which are magnetic like iron, though in a much less degree (distinguished from *ferromagnetic* and opposed to *diamagnetic*). [f. PARA-[1] + MAGNETIC]

Par·a·mar·i·bo (păr′ə măr′ĭ bō′), *n.* a seaport in NE South America: capital of Surinam. 60,720 (est. 1944).

par·a·mat·ta (păr′ə măt′ə), *n.* a light, twilled dress fabric, having a silk or cotton warp and a woolen weft. Also, **parramatta.** [named after *Parramatta* in New South Wales]

par·a·me·ci·um (păr′ə mē′shī əm, -sǐ əm), *n., pl.* **-cia** (-shǐ ə, -sǐ ə). a ciliate infusorian having an oval body and deep long oral groove, inhabiting fresh water and widely distributed in a number of species, extensively used in experiments on protozoa. [t. NL, der. Gk. *paramēkēs* oblong]

pa·ram·e·ter (pə răm′ə tər), *n. Math.* a variable entering into the mathematical form of any distribution such that the possible values of the variable correspond to different distributions.

par·a·mo (păr′ə mō′; *Sp.* pä′rä mô′), *n., pl.* **-mos** (-mōz′; *Sp.* -môs′). a high plateau region in tropical South America, esp. one bare of trees. [t. Sp.]

par·a·morph (păr′ə môrf′), *n. Mineral.* a pseudomorph formed by a change in crystal structure but not in chemical composition. —**par′a·mor′phic,** *adj.*

par·a·mor·phism (păr′ə môr′fĭzəm), *n.* **1.** the process by which a paramorph is formed. **2.** the state of being a paramorph.

par·a·mount (păr′ə mount′), *adj.* **1.** above others in rank or authority; superior in power or jurisdiction. **2.** chief in importance; supreme; preëminent. —*n.* **3.** an overlord; a supreme ruler. [t. AF: m. *paramont* above, f. *par* by (g. L *per*) + *amont* upward, up (g. L *ad montem* to the mountain). Cf. AMOUNT] —**par′a·mount′cy,** *n.* —**Syn. 1.** See **dominant.**

par·a·mour (păr′ə mŏŏr′), *n.* **1.** an illicit lover, esp. of a married person. **2.** any lover. **3.** a beloved one. [ME, t. OF, orig. phrase *par amour* by love, by way of (sexual) love, f. *par* by (g. L *per*) + *amour* love (g. L *amor*)]

Pa·ra·ná (pä′rə nä′), *n.* **1.** a river flowing from S Brazil along the SE boundary of Uraguay and through E Argentina into the Río de la Plata. ab. 2450 mi. **2.** a city in E Argentina, on the Paraná river: the capital of Argentina, 1852–61. 76,600 (est. 1940).

pa·rang (pä′räng), *n.* a large, heavy knife used as a tool or a weapon by the Malays. [t. Malay]

par·a·noi·a (păr′ə noi′ə), *n. Psychiatry.* mental disorder characterized by systematized delusions and the projection of personal conflicts, which are ascribed to the supposed hostility of others. The disorder often exists for years without any disturbance of consciousness. Also, **par·a·noe·a** (păr′ə nē′ə). [t. NL, t. Gk.: derangement]

par·a·noi·ac (păr′ə noi′ăk), *adj.* **1.** pertaining to or affected with paranoia. —*n.* **2.** a person affected with paranoia. Also, **par·a·noe·ac** (păr′ə nē′ăk).

par·a·nymph (păr′ə nĭmf′), *n.* **1.** a groomsman or a bridesmaid. **2.** (in ancient Greece) **a.** a friend who accompanied the bridegroom when he went to bring home the bride. **b.** the bridesmaid who escorted the bride to the bridegroom. [ult. t. Gk.: s. *paránymphos,* masc., the best man, *paranýmphē,* fem., the bridesmaid]

par·a·pet (păr′ə pĭt, -pĕt′), *n.* **1.** *Fort.* **a.** a defensive wall or elevation, as of earth or stone, in a fortification. See diag. under **bastion. b.** an elevation raised above the main wall or rampart of a permanent fortification. See diag. under **machicolation. 2.** any protective wall or barrier at the edge of a balcony, roof, bridge, or the like. [t. It.: m. *parapetto,* f. *para-* PARA-[2] + *petto,* g. L *pectus* breast] —**par′a·pet·ed,** *adj.*

par·aph (păr′əf), *n.* a flourish made after a signature, as in a document, orig. as a precaution against forgery. [ME *paraf,* t. ML: m.s. *paraphus,* short for L *paragraphus* PARAGRAPH]

par·a·pher·nal·ia (păr′ə fər nāl′yə, -fə nāl′yə), *n.pl.* **1.** personal belongings. **2.** *Law.* the personal articles, apart from dower, reserved by law to a married woman. **3.** (sometimes construed as sing.) equipment; apparatus. [t. ML (prop. neut. pl.), der. LL *parapherna,* t. Gk.: bride's belongings other than dowry]

par·a·phrase (păr′ə frāz′), *n., v.,* **-phrased, -phrasing.** —*n.* **1.** a statement of the sense of a text or passage in other words, as for clearness; a free rendering or translation, as of a passage. **2.** the act or process of paraphrasing. —*v.t., v.i.* **3.** to restate; render in, or make, a paraphrase. [t. F, t. L: m.s. *paraphrasis,* t. Gk.] —**par′a·phras′er,** *n.* —**Syn. 1.** See **translation.**

par·a·phrast (păr′ə frăst′), *n.* one who paraphrases.

par·a·phras·tic (păr′ə frăs′tĭk), *adj.* having the nature of a paraphrase. —**par′a·phras′ti·cal·ly,** *adv.*

pa·raph·y·sis (pə răf′ə sĭs), *n., pl.* **-ses** (-sēz′). *Bot.* one of the sterile, usually filamentous, outgrowths often occurring among the reproductive organs in many cryptogamous plants. [t. NL, t. Gk.: offshoot]

par·a·ple·gi·a (păr′ə plē′jǐ ə), *n. Pathol.* paralysis of both lower or upper limbs. [t. NL, t. Gk.: paralysis on one side] —**par·a·pleg·ic** (păr′ə plĕj′ĭk, -plē′jĭk), *adj., n.*

par·a·po·di·um (păr′ə pō′dĭ əm), *n., pl.* **-dia** (-dĭ ə). *Zool.* one of the unjointed lateral locomotor processes or series of rudimentary limbs of many worms, as annelids. [t. NL. See PARA-, -PODIUM]

par·a·psy·chol·o·gy (păr′ə sī kŏl′ə jǐ), *n.* a division of psychology which investigates psychic phenomena, as clairvoyance, extrasensory perception, and the like.

par·a·quet (păr′ə kĕt′), *n.* parrakeet.

Pa·rá rubber (pä rä′), India rubber obtained from the euphorbiaceous tree *Hevea brasiliensis* and other species of the same genus, of tropical South America.

par·a·sang (păr′ə săng′), *n.* a Persian unit of distance, of varying length, anciently equal to about 3 2/5 miles. [t. L: s. *parasanga,* t. Gk.: m. *parasángēs;* of Pers. orig.]

par·a·se·le·ne (păr′ə sǐ lō′nǐ), *n., pl.* **-nae** (-nē). *Meteorol.* a bright moonlike spot on a lunar halo; a mock moon. Cf. **parhelion.** [t. NL, f. Gk.: *para-* PARA-[1] + *selēnē* moon]

par·a·shah (păr′ə shä′), *n., pl.* **parashoth** (păr′ə shōth′), **parashioth** (păr′ə shō′oth′). **1.** one of the lessons from the Torah or Law read in the Jewish synagogue on Sabbaths and festivals. **2.** one of the subsections into which the weekly lessons read on Sabbaths are divided. Cf. **haphtarah.** [t. Heb.: division]

Pa·ra·shu·ra·ma (păr′ə shŏŏ rä′mə), *n. Hindu Myth.* first of the three Ramas, and sixth incarnation of Vishnu.

par·a·site (păr′ə sīt′), *n.* **1.** an animal or plant which lives on or in an organism of another species (the host), from the body of which it obtains nutriment. **2.** one who lives on others or another without making any suitable return, esp. one who lives on the hospitality or patronage of others. **3.** (in ancient Greece) a professional diner-out, who got free meals in return for his amusing or impudent conversation. [t. L: m.s. *parasitus,* t. Gk.: m. *parásitos* one who eats at the table of another]

par·a·sit·ic (păr′ə sĭt′ĭk), *adj.* **1.** living or growing as a parasite; pertaining to or characteristic of parasites. **2.** (of diseases) due to parasites. Also, **par·a·sit′i·cal.** —**par′a·sit′i·cal·ly,** *adv.*

par·a·sit·i·cide (păr′ə sĭt′ə sīd′), *adj.* **1.** destructive to parasites. —*n.* **2.** an agent or preparation that destroys parasites.

par·a·sit·ism (păr′ə sī′tĭzəm), *n.* **1.** parasitic mode of life or existence. **2.** *Zool., Bot.* the vital relation which a parasite bears to its host; parasitic infestation. **3.** *Pathol.* diseased condition due to parasites.

par·a·sol (păr′ə sŏl′, -sôl′), *n.* a woman's small or light sun umbrella; a sunshade. [t. F, t. It.: m. *parasole,* f. *para-* PARA-[2] + *sole* (g. L *sōl* sun)]

pa·ras·ti·chy (pə răs′tə kĭ), *n., pl.* **-chies** (-kǐz). *Bot.* (in a spiral arrangement of leaves, scales, etc., where the internodes are short and the members closely crowded, as in the houseleek and the pine cone) one of a number of secondary spirals or oblique ranks seen to wind around the stem or axis to the right and left. [f. PARA-[1] + m.s. Gk. *-stichia* alignment]

par·a·sym·pa·thet·ic (păr′ə sĭm′pə thĕt′ĭk), *Anat., Physiol.* —*adj.* **1.** pertaining to that part of the autonomic nervous system which consists of nerves arising from the cranial and sacral regions, and which oppose the action of the sympathetic system, thus inhibiting heart beat, contracting the pupil of the eye, etc. —*n.* **2.** a nerve of the parasympathetic system.

par·a·syn·ap·sis (păr′ə sǐ năp′sǐs), *n. Embryol.* the conjugation of chromosomes, side by side; synapsis.

ăct, āble, dâre, ärt; ĕbb, ēqual; ĭf, īce; hŏt, ōver, ôrder, oil, bŏŏk, ōōze, out; ŭp, ūse, ûrge; ə = a in alone; ch, chief; g, give; ng, ring; sh, shoe; th, thin; ŧħ, that; zh, vision. See the full key on inside cover.

par·a·syn·the·sis (păr/ə sĭn/thə sĭs), *n. Gram.* the formation of a word by the addition of an affix to a phrase or compound, as *great-hearted*, which is *great heart* plus *-ed* (not *great* plus *hearted*). [f. PARA-[1] + SYNTHESIS] —**par·a·syn·thet·ic** (păr/ə sĭn thĕt/ĭk), *adj.*

par·a·tax·is (păr/ə tăk/sĭs), *n.* the placing together of sentences, clauses, or phrases without a conjunctive word, as *hurry up, it is getting late; I came—I saw—I conquered.* [t. NL, t. Gk.: a placing side by side] —**par·a·tac·tic** (păr/ə tăk/tĭk), **par·a·tac/ti·cal,** *adj.* —**par/a·tac/ti·cal·ly,** *adv.*

par·a·thy·roid (păr/ə thī/roid), *Anat.* —*adj.* **1.** situated near the thyroid gland. —*n.* **2.** a parathyroid gland.

parathyroid glands, *Anat.* several small glands or oval masses of epithelioid cells, lying near or embedded in the thyroid gland, whose internal secretion governs the calcium content of the blood.

par·a·troop (păr/ə trōōp/), *n.* a force or unit of paratroopers.

par·a·troop·er (păr/ə trōō/pər), *n.* a soldier who reaches battle by landing from a plane by parachute. [f. PARA(CHUTE) + TROOPER]

par·a·ty·phoid (păr/ə tī/foid), *adj.* noting or pertaining to paratyphoid fever.

paratyphoid fever, an infectious disease similar in some ways to typhoid fever but usually milder, and caused by different bacteria.

par·a·vane (păr/ə vān/), *n.* a device, usually torpedoshaped, for protecting a ship from moored mines. It is towed by a cable and has a device that cuts the mine cable, bringing the mine to the surface to be sunk by gunfire at a safe distance. Paravanes are always used in pairs, one towed from each bow. [f. PARA-[1] + VANE]

par a·vi·on (pårà vyôN/), *French.* by plane (a label for matter to be sent air mail).

par·boil (păr/boil/), *v.t.* to boil partially, or for a short time; precook. [ME *parboyle(n)* boil fully, t. OF: m. *parbouillir*, g. LL *perbullīre*. See PER-, BOIL[1]]

par·buck·le (păr/bŭk/əl), *n., v.,* -led, -ling. —*n.* **1.** a kind of purchase for raising or lowering a cask or similar object along an inclined plane or a vertical surface, consisting of a rope looped over a post or the like, with its two ends passing around the object to be moved. **2.** a kind of double sling made with a rope, as around a cask to be raised or lowered. —*v.t.* **3.** to raise, lower, or move with a parbuckle. [earlier *parbunkel;* orig. unknown]

Par·cae (păr/sē), *n.pl. Rom. Myth.* the Fates. [t. L]

par·cel (păr/səl), *n., v.,* -celed, -celing or (*Esp. Brit.*) -celled, -celling, *adv.* —*n.* **1.** a quantity of something wrapped or put up together; a package or bundle. **2.** a quantity of something, as of a commodity for sale; a lot. **3.** any group or assemblage of persons or things. **4.** a separable, separate, or distinct part or portion or section, as of land. **5.** *Chiefly Archaic except Law.* a part or portion of anything. —*v.t.* **6.** to divide into or distribute in parcels or portions (usually fol. by *out*). **7.** to make into a parcel, or put up in parcels, as goods. **8.** *Naut.* to cover or wrap (a rope, etc.) with strips of canvas. —*adv.* **9.** partly; in part; partially. [ME *parcelle*, t. OF, t. ML: m.s. *particella,* dim. of L *particula* particle] —**Syn. 1.** See **package.**

parcel post, a branch of a postal service charged with conveying parcels. Also, **parcels post.**

par·ce·nar·y (păr/sə nĕr/Y), *n. Law.* coheirship; the undivided holding of land by two or more coheirs.

par·ce·ner (păr/sə nər), *n. Law.* a joint heir; a coheir. [ME, t. AF, der. *parçon,* g. L *partītio* partition]

parch (părch), *v.t.* **1.** to make dry, esp. to excess, or dry up, as heat, the sun, or a hot wind does. **2.** to make (a person, the lips, throat, etc.) dry and hot, or thirsty, as heat, fever, or thirst does. **3.** to dry (peas, beans, grain, etc.) by exposure to heat without burning. **4.** (of cold, etc.) to dry or shrivel, like heat. —*v.i.* **5.** to become parched; undergo drying by heat. **6.** to dry (fol. by *up*). **7.** to suffer from heat or thirst. [ME *parche(n), perch(en);* orig. uncert.]

par·chee·si (păr chē/zY), *n.* **1.** a game somewhat resembling backgammon, played in India. **2.** a simplified form of this, played elsewhere. Also, **pachisi, par·che/si, par·chi/si.** [t. Hind.: alter. of *pachisi,* der. *pachīs* twenty-five (the highest throw in the game)]

parch·ment (părch/mənt), *n.* **1.** the skin of sheep, goats, etc., prepared for use as a writing material, etc. **2.** a manuscript or document on such material. **3.** a paper resembling this material. [ME *parchemin,* t. OF, b. LL *pergamēna* parchment (der. *Pergamum,* city in Mysia, Asia Minor, whence parchment was brought) and L *parthica (pellis)* Parthian (leather)]

parchment paper, a waterproof and grease-resistant paper obtained by treating a paper with concentrated sulfuric acid.

pard[1] (părd), *n. Archaic.* a leopard or panther. [ME, t. OF, t. L: s. *pardus,* t. Gk.: m. *párdos,* earlier *părdalis;* of Eastern orig.]

pard[2] (părd), *n. U.S. Slang.* partner. [alter. of PARTNER]

par·di (păr/dē), *adv., interj. Archaic.* verily; indeed. Also, **par·die/, pardy, perdie.** [ME *parde,* t. OF: by God]

par·don (păr/dən), *n.* **1.** courteous indulgence or allowance, as in excusing fault or seeming rudeness: *I beg your pardon* (a conventional form of apology). **2.** *Law.* **a.** a pardoning; a remission of penalty, as by an executive. **b.** the deed or warrant by which such remission is declared. **3.** forgiveness of an offense or offender. **4.** *Obs.* a papal indulgence. [ME, t. OF, der. *pardoner.* See below] —*v.t.* **5.** to remit the penalty of (an offense): *he will not pardon your transgressions.* **6.** to release (a person) from liability for an offense. **7.** to make courteous allowance for, or excuse (an action or circumstance, or a person): *pardon me, madam.* [ME *pardone(n),* t. OF: m. *pardoner,* t. LL: m. *perdōnāre* grant, concede, f. L *per-* PER- + *dōnāre* give] —**par/don·a·ble,** *adj.* —**par/don·a·bly,** *adv.* —**Syn. 3.** absolution, remission, amnesty. **5.** forgive, absolve, condone, overlook. **6.** See **excuse.**

par·don·er (păr/dən ər), *n.* **1.** one who pardons. **2.** an ecclesiastical official charged with the granting of indulgences.

par·dy (păr dē/), *adv., interj. Archaic.* pardi.

pare (pâr), *v.t.,* pared, paring. **1.** to cut off the outer coating, layer, or part of: *to pare potatoes.* **2.** to remove (an outer coating, layer, or part) by cutting (often fol. by *off* or *away*). **3.** to reduce or remove by, or as if by, cutting; diminish little by little: *to pare down one's expenses.* [ME *pare(n),* t. OF: m. *parer* prepare, trim, g. L *parāre*] —**Syn. 1.** See **peel**[1].

Pa·ré (pá rĕ/), *n.* Ambroise (äN brwáz/), 1510–90, French surgeon.

pa·re·cious (pə rē/shəs), *adj. Bot.* paroicous.

par·e·gor·ic (păr/ə gôr/Yk, -gŏr/Yk), *Pharm.* —*n.* **1.** a soothing medicine; an anodyne. **2.** a camphorated tincture of opium, intended primarily to check diarrhea in children. —*adj.* **3.** assuaging pain; soothing. [t. LL: s. *parēgoricus,* t. Gk.: m. *parēgorikós* encouraging, soothing]

pa·rei·ra (pə rār/ə), *n.* the root of a South American vine, *Chondodendron tomentosum,* used as a diuretic, etc.; a source of curare. [short for PAREIRA BRAVA]

pa·rei·ra bra·va (pə rār/ə brä/və, brä/və), pareira. [t. Pg.: m. *parreira brava,* lit., wild vine]

paren., parenthesis.

pa·ren·chy·ma (pə rĕng/kY mə), *n.* **1.** *Bot.* the fundamental (soft) cellular tissue of plants, as in the softer parts of leaves, the pulp of fruits, the pith of stems, etc. **2.** *Anat., Zool.* the proper tissue of an animal organ as distinguished from its connective or supporting tissue. **3.** *Zool.* a kind of connective tissue in which the cells are numerous. **4.** *Pathol.* the functional tissue of a morbid growth. [t. NL, t. Gk.: lit., something poured in beside] —**par·en·chym·a·tous** (păr/ĕng kĭm/ə təs), *adj.*

parens., parentheses.

par·ent (pâr/ənt), *n.* **1.** a father or a mother. **2.** a progenitor. **3.** an author or source. **4.** a protector or guardian. **5.** any organism that produces or generates another. [ME, t. L: s. *parens*]

par·ent·age (pâr/ən tĭj), *n.* **1.** derivation from parents; birth, lineage, or family; origin: *distinguished parentage.* **2.** parenthood.

pa·ren·tal (pə rĕn/təl), *adj.* **1.** of or pertaining to a parent: *the parental relation.* **2.** proper to or characteristic of a parent: *parental feelings.* **3.** having the relation of a parent. —**pa·ren/tal·ly,** *adv.*

par·en·ter·al (păr ĕn/tər əl), *adj. Anat., Med., Physiol.* in a manner other than through the digestive canal. [f. PAR(A)-[1] + s. Gk. *énteron* intestine + -AL[1]]

pa·ren·the·sis (pə rĕn/thə sĭs), *n., pl.* -ses (-sēz/). **1.** the upright curves ( ) collectively, or either of them separately, used to mark off an interjected explanatory or qualifying remark. **2.** *Gram.* a qualifying or explanatory word (e.g., an appositive), phrase, clause (e.g., a descriptive clause), sentence, or other sequence of forms which interrupts the syntactic construction without otherwise affecting it, having often a characteristic intonation, and shown in writing by commas, parentheses, or dashes. Example: *William Smith—you know him well—will be here soon.* **3.** an interval. [t. ML, t. Gk.: a putting in beside]

pa·ren·the·size (pə rĕn/thə sīz/), *v.t.,* -sized, -sizing. **1.** to insert as or in a parenthesis. **2.** to put between marks of parenthesis: *parenthesize the pronunciation.* **3.** to interlard with parenthesis.

par·en·thet·ic (păr/ən thĕt/Yk), *adj.* **1.** of, pertaining to, or of the nature of a parenthesis: *several unnecessary parenthetic remarks.* **2.** characterized by the use of parentheses. Also, **par·en·thet/i·cal.** —**par/en·thet/i·cal·ly,** *adv.*

par·ent·hood (pâr/ənt hŏŏd/), *n.* the position or relation of, or state of being, a parent.

pa·re·sis (pə rē/sĭs, păr/ə sĭs), *n. Pathol.* **1.** incomplete motor paralysis. **2.** See **general paralysis.** [t. NL, t. Gk.: a letting go]

par·es·the·sia (păr/əs thē/zhə, -zhĭ ə), *n. Pathol.* abnormal sensation, as prickling, itching, etc. Also, **paraesthesia.** [f. PAR(A)-[1] + m. Gk. *aisthēsía* sensation] —**par·es·thet·ic** (păr/əs thĕt/Yk), *adj.*

pa·ret·ic (pə rĕt/Yk, pə rē/tYk), *n.* **1.** one who has general paresis. —*adj.* **2.** pertaining to, or affected with, paresis.

Pa·re·to (pä rĕ/tô), *n.* **Vilfredo** (vēl frĕ/dô), 1848–1923, Italian sociologist and economist, in Switzerland.

par ex·cel·lence (păr ĕk/sə läns/; *Fr.* pår ĕk sĕ läNs/), *French.* by excellence or superiority; above all others; preëminently.

par ex·em·ple (pår ĕg zäN/pl), *French.* for example.

---

b., blend of, blended; c., cognate with; d., dialect, dialectal; der., derived from; f., formed from; g., going back to; m., modification of; r., replacing; s., stem of; t., taken from; ?, perhaps. See the full key on inside cover.

par·fait (pär fā′; *Fr.* pȧr fě′), *n.* a rich frozen preparation of whipped cream and egg, variously flavored. [t. F: lit., perfect]

par·get (pär′jĭt), *n.*, *v.*, **-geted, -geting** or (*esp. Brit.*) **-getted, -getting.** —*n.* **1.** gypsum or plaster stone. **2.** plaster, esp. a kind of mortar formed of lime, hair, and cowdung. **3.** plasterwork, esp. a more or less ornamental facing for exterior walls. —*v.t.* **4.** to cover or decorate with parget. [ME *pargette(n)*, t. OF: m. *parjeter* throw over a surface, f. *par* over + *jeter* throw]

par·get·ing (pär′jĭt Ĭng), *n.* **1.** act of one who pargets. **2.** parget. Also, *esp. Brit.*, **par′get·ting.**

par·he·li·a·cal (pär′hĭ lī′ə kəl), *adj.* of or pertaining to or constituting a parhelion or parhelia. Also, **par·he·lic** (pär hē′lĭk -hěl′ĭk).

parheliacal ring, *Meteorol.* a white horizontal band passing through the sun, either incomplete or extending round the horizon, produced by the reflection of the sun's rays from the vertical faces of ice prisms in the atmosphere. Also, **parhelic circle.**

par·he·li·on (pär hē′lĭ ən), *n.*, *pl.* **-lia** (-lĭ ə). *Meteorol.* a bright circular spot on a solar halo; a mock sun; usually one of two or more such spots seen on opposite sides of the sun, and often accompanied by additional luminous arcs and bands. Cf. **paraselene.** [t. L: m. *parēlion* (with etymological -*h*-), t. Gk., var. of *parēlios*, f. *para-* PARA-[1] + *hēlios* sun]

pa·ri·ah (pə rī′ə, pä′rĭ ə, pär′ĭ ə), *n.* **1.** any person or animal generally despised; an outcast. **2.** (*cap.*) a member of a low caste in southern India. [t. Tamil: m. *paraiyar*, pl. of *paraiyan*, lit., drummer (from a hereditary duty of the caste), der. *parai* a festival drum]

Par·i·an (pâr′ĭ ən), *adj.* **1.** of or pertaining to Paros, noted for its white marble. **2.** noting or pertaining to a fine unglazed porcelain resembling this marble. —*n.* **3.** a native or inhabitant of Paros. **4.** Parian porcelain.

par·i·es (pâr′ĭ ēz′), *n.*, *pl.* **parietes** (pə rī′ə tēz′). (*usually pl.*) *Biol.* a wall, as of a hollow organ; an investing part. [t. L: wall]

pa·ri·e·tal (pə rī′ə təl), *adj.* **1.** *Anat.* **a.** referring to the side of the skull, or to any wall or wall-like structure. **b.** noting or pertaining to the parietal bones. **2.** *Biol.* of or pertaining to parietes or structural walls. **3.** *Bot.* pertaining to or arising from a wall: usually applied to ovules when they proceed from or are borne on the walls or sides of the ovary. **4.** *U.S.* pertaining to, or having authority over, those within the walls or buildings of a college: *a parietal board.* [t. LL: s. *parietālis*, der. L *paries* wall]

parietal bones, *Anat.* a pair of bones of the cranium, right and left, developed in membrane, forming most of the top and sides of the skull vault, between the occipital and the frontal bones. See diag. under **cranium.**

parietal lobe, *Anat.* the middle lobe of the cerebrum.

par·i·mu·tu·el (pär′ĭ mū′chŏŏ əl), *n.* **1.** a form of betting, as on horseraces, in which those who bet on the winners divide the bets or stakes, less a percentage for the management, taxes, etc. **2.** the apparatus that records the bets. [t. F: mutual bet]

par·ing (pâr′ĭng), *n.* **1.** the act of one who or that which pares. **2.** a piece or part pared off.

pa·ri pas·su (pâr′ī păs′ŏŏ, pär′ī′), *Latin.* with equal pace or progress; side by side.

par·i·pin·nate (pär′ĭ pĭn′āt), *adj.* *Bot.* **1.** evenly pinnate. **2.** pinnate without an odd terminal leaflet.

Par·is (pär′ĭs; *Fr.* pȧ rē′), *n.* the capital of France, in the N part, on the Seine. 2,725,374 (1946). [in L *Lutetia Parīsiōrum*, in LL *Parīsiī*, orig. name of the Gallic tribe inhabiting the district] —**Pa·ri·sian** (pə rĭzh′ən, -rĭz′ĭ ən), *adj.*, *n.*

Par·is (pär′ĭs), *n.* *Gk. Legend.* a Trojan youth, son of King Priam and Hecuba. His abduction of Helen led to the Trojan War, at the end of which he was killed by Philoctetes. See **apple of discord.**

Paris green, an emerald-green pigment prepared from arsenic trioxide and acetate of copper, now used chiefly as an insecticide.

par·ish (pär′ĭsh), *n.* **1.** an ecclesiastical district having its own church and clergyman. **2.** a local church with its field of activity. **3.** *Chiefly Brit.* a civil district or administrative division. **4.** (in Louisiana) a county. **5.** the people of a parish (ecclesiastical or civil). [ME, t. OF: m. *paroisse*, g. LL *parochia*, var. of *paroecia*, t. Gk.: m. *paroikia*]

pa·rish·ion·er (pə rĭsh′ən ər), *n.* one of the community or inhabitants of a parish. [f. earlier *parishion* (t. OF: m. *parochien*) + -ER[1]]

par·i·ty[1] (pär′ə tĭ), *n.* **1.** equality, as in amount, status, or character. **2.** equivalence; correspondence; similarity or analogy. **3.** *Finance.* **a.** equivalence in value in the currency of another country. **b.** equivalence in value at a fixed ratio between moneys of different metals. [t. LL: m.s. *pāritas*, der. L *pār* equal]

par·i·ty[2] (pär′ə tĭ), *n.* *Obstet.* the condition or fact of having borne offspring. [f. s. L *parere* bring forth + -ITY]

park (pärk), *n.* **1.** a tract of land set apart, as by a city or a nation, for the benefit of the public: *Central Park, Yellowstone National Park.* **2.** a tract of land set apart for recreation, sports, etc.: *a baseball park.* **3.** a considerable extent of land forming the grounds of a country

house. **4.** *Brit.* an enclosed tract of land for wild beasts. **5.** *U.S.* a high plateaulike valley. **6.** a space where vehicles, esp. automobiles, may be assembled or stationed. **7.** *Mil.* **a.** the space occupied by the assembled guns. tanks, vehicles, stores, etc., of a body of soldiers. **b.** the assemblage formed. **c.** a complete equipment, as of guns, tools, etc. —*v.t.* **8.** to put or leave (an automobile, etc.) for a time in a particular place, as on the street. **9.** *U.S. Colloq.* to put or leave. **10.** to assemble (artillery, etc.) in compact arrangement. **11.** to enclose in or as in a park. —*v.i.* **12.** to park a car, bicycle, etc. [ME *parc*, t. OF; of Gmc. orig., akin to G *pferch* fold, pen, and OE *pearroc* enclosure, and to PADDOCK[1]]

Park (pärk), *n.* **Mungo** (mŭng′gō), 1771–1806?, Scottish explorer in Africa.

par·ka (pär′kə), *n.* **1.** a fur coat, cut like a shirt, worn in northeastern Asia and in Alaska. **2.** a long woolen shirtlike garment with an attached hood. [t. Russ.]

Park Avenue, a street in New York City which, because of its large, expensive apartment houses, has come to represent luxury, the height of fashion, etc.

Par·ker (pär′kər), *n.* **1.** **Sir Gilbert,** 1862–1932, Canadian novelist and politician in England. **2.** **Theodore,** 1810–60, U.S. preacher, theologian, and reformer.

Parker Ka·lon screw (kā′lŏn), **1.** a trademark for a self-tapping screw, widely used in airplane construction. **2.** (*l.c.*) this screw.

Par·kers·burg (pär′kərz bûrg′), *n.* a city in NW West Virginia, on the Ohio river. 29,684 (1950).

park·land (pärk′lănd′), *n.* a grassland region with isolated or grouped trees, usually in temperate regions.

Park·man (pärk′mən), *n.* **Francis,** 1823–93, U.S. historian.

Park Range, a range of the Rocky Mountains in central Colorado. Highest peak, Mt. Lincoln, 14,287 ft.

park·way (pärk′wā′), *n.* a broad thoroughfare with spaces planted with grass, trees, etc.

Parl., **1.** Parliament. **2.** (*also l.c.*) Parliamentary.

par·lance (pär′ləns), *n.* **1.** way of speaking, or language: *legal parlance.* **2.** *Archaic.* talk; parley. [t. OF, der. *parler* speak, der. L *parabola.* See PARABLE]

par·lay (pär′lĭ, pär lā′), *U.S.* —*v.t.*, *v.i.* **1.** to bet (an original amount and its winnings) on another race, contest, etc. —*n.* **2.** such a bet. [alter. of *paroli*, t. F, t. It., possibly der. Neapolitan *paro* pair]

par·ley (pär′lĭ), *n.*, *pl.* **-leys,** *v.,* **-leyed, -leying.** —*n.* **1.** a discussion; a conference. **2.** an informal conference with enemies under truce, to discuss terms, conditions of surrender, etc. —*v.i.* **3.** to hold an informal conference with an enemy, under a truce, as between active hostilities. **4.** to speak, talk, or confer. Also, *Archaic* or *Brit. Dial.*, **parle.** [t. OF: m. *parlēe* speech]

par·lia·ment (pär′lə mənt), *n.* **1.** (*usually cap.*) the legislature of Great Britain, historically the assembly of the three estates, now composed of lords spiritual and lords temporal (forming together the **House of Lords**), and representatives of the counties, cities, boroughs, and universities (forming the **House of Commons**). **2.** (*usually cap.*) the legislature of certain British colonies and possessions. **3.** any one of similar legislative bodies in other countries. **4.** (in pre-Revolutionary France) the highest court in each province, succeeding the feudal parlements, which were both courts and councils. **5.** a meeting or assembly for conference on public or national affairs. Also, *Obs.*, **parle·ment.** [ME *parlement*, t. OF, der. *parler* speak. See PARLANCE]

par·lia·men·tar·i·an (pär′lə měn târ′ĭ ən), *n.* **1.** one skilled in parliamentary procedure or debate. **2.** *Brit.* a member of Parliament. **3.** (*cap.*) a partisan of the British Parliament in opposition to Charles I.

par·lia·men·ta·ry (pär′lə měn′tə rĭ), *adj.* **1.** of or pertaining to a parliament. **2.** enacted or established by a parliament. **3.** characterized by the existence of a parliament. **4.** of the nature of a parliament. **5.** in accordance with the rules and usages of parliaments or deliberative bodies: *he insisted upon parliamentary procedure.*

par·lor (pär′lər), *n.* **1.** a room for the reception and entertainment of visitors; a living room. **2.** a semiprivate room in a hotel, club, or the like for relaxation, conversation, etc.; a lounge. **3.** *U.S.* a room more or less elegantly fitted up for the reception of business patrons or customers: *a tonsorial parlor.* Also, *Brit.*, **par′lour.** [ME *parlur*, t. AF, der. *parler* speak. See PARLANCE]

parlor car, a railroad passenger car for day or evening travel, fitted with individual reserved seats, and more comfortable than ordinary passenger cars.

par·lor·maid (pär′lər mād′), *n.* a maid who takes care of a parlor, waits on guests, etc.

par·lous (pär′ləs), *Archaic.* —*adj.* **1.** perilous; dangerous. **2.** terrible; very great. **3.** clever; shrewd. —*adv.* **4.** terribly; excessively. [ME; var. of PERILOUS] —**par′lous·ly,** *adv.*

parl. proc., parliamentary procedure.

Par·ma (pär′mä), *n.* **1.** a city in N Italy. 120,795 (est. 1946). **2.** a city in NE Ohio. 28,897 (1950).

Par·men·i·des (pär měn′ə dēz′), *n.* fl. c475 B.C., Greek Eleatic philosopher, born in Italy.

Par·me·san (pär′mə zăn′), *adj.* of or pertaining to the city, the province, or the former duchy of Parma in northern Italy. [t. F, t. It.: m. *parmigiano,* der. *Parma*]

ăct, āble, dâre, ärt; ĕbb, ēqual; ĭf, īce; hŏt, ōver, ôrder, oil, bŏŏk, ōoze, out; ŭp, ūse, ûrge; ə = a in alone; ch, chief; g, give; ng, ring; sh, shoe; th, thin; t͟h, that; zh, vision. See the full key on inside cover.

Parmesan cheese, a hard, dry, fine-flavored variety of Italian cheese, made from skim milk.

Par·na·hi·ba (pär/nəē/bə), *n.* a river in NE Brazil, flowing NE to the Atlantic. ab. 900 mi. Also, **Par/na·hy/ba.**

Par·nas·si·an (pärnăs/Yən), *adj.* **1.** pertaining to Mount Parnassus, or to poetry. **2.** noting or pertaining to a school of French poets, of the latter half of the 19th century, characterized esp. by emphasis of form and by repression of emotion (so called from *Le Parnasse Contemporain,* the title of their first collection of poems, published in 1866). —*n.* **3.** a member of the Parnassian school of French poets. [f. s. L *Parnās(s)ius,* (der. *Parnās(s)us*) + -AN. Cf. F *Parnassien*]

Par·nas·sus (pärnăs/əs), *n.* **1. Mount,** Modern, **Liakoura.** a mountain in central Greece, in ancient Phocis: sacred to Apollo and the Muses, and symbolic of poetic inspiration and achievement. 8068 ft. **2.** a collection of poems or of elegant literature.

Par·nell (pär/nəl, pärněl/), *n.* **Charles Stewart,** 1846–91, Irish political leader.

pa·ro·chi·al (pərō/kYəl), *adj.* **1.** of or pertaining to a parish or parishes. **2.** confined to or interested only in one's own parish, or some particular narrow district or field. [ME, t. LL: s. *parochiālis,* der. LL *parochia.* See PARISH] —**pa·ro/chi·al·ly,** *adv.*

pa·ro·chi·al·ism (pərō/kYəlYz/əm), *n.* parochial character, spirit, or tendency; narrowness of interests or view.

parochial school, an elementary or high school maintained and operated by an ecclesiastical organization.

par·o·dy (păr/ədY), *n., pl.* **-dies,** *v.,* **-died, -dying.** —*n.* **1.** a humorous imitation of a serious piece of literature or writing. **2.** the kind of literary composition represented by such imitations. **3.** a burlesque imitation of a musical composition. **4.** a poor imitation; a travesty. —*v.t.* **5.** to imitate (a composition, author, etc.) in such a way as to ridicule. **6.** to imitate poorly. [t. L: m.s. *parōdia,* t. Gk.: m. *parōidía* burlesque poem] —**par/o·dist,** *n.*

pa·roi·cous (pəroi/kəs), *adj. Bot.* (of certain mosses) having the male and female reproductive organs beside or near each other. Also, **parecious, pa·roe·cious** (pərē/shəs). [t. Gk.: m. *pároikos* dwelling beside]

pa·rol (pərōl/, pär/əl), *Law.* —*n.* **1.** the pleadings in a suit. —*adj.* **2.** given by word of mouth; oral; not written (opposed to *documentary,* or given by affidavit): *parol evidence.* [t. AF (legal): m. *parole.* See PAROLE]

pa·role (pərōl/), *n., v.* **-roled, -roling.** —*n.* **1.** *Penol.* **a.** the liberation of a person from prison, conditional upon good behavior, prior to the end of the maximum sentence imposed upon that person. **b.** such release or its duration. **2.** *Mil.* **a.** the promise of a prisoner of war to refrain from trying to escape, or, if released, to return to custody or to forbear taking up arms against his captors. **b.** a password given by authorized personnel in passing through a guard. **3.** word of honor given or pledged. **4.** *Law.* parol. —*v.t.* **5.** to put on parole. [t. F, g. L *parabola.* See PARABLE]

pa·rol·ee (pərō/lē/), *n. Penol.* one who is released on parole.

par·o·no·ma·si·a (păr/ənōmā/zhYə, -zYə), *n. Rhet.* **1.** a playing on words; punning. **2.** a pun. [t. L, t. Gk.] —**par·o·no·mas/tic** (/ənōmăs/tYk), *adj.*

par·o·nym (păr/ənYm), *n. Gram.* a paronymous word.

pa·ron·y·mous (pərŏn/əməs), *adj.* (of words) containing the same root or stem, as *wise* and *wisdom.* [t. Gk.: m. *parōnymos* derivative]

par·o·quet (păr/əkĕt/), *n.* parakeet.

Par·os (pär/ŏs; *Gk.* pä/rŏs), *n.* a Greek island in the S Aegean: one of the Cyclades; noted for its marble. 9369 pop. (1928); 77 sq. mi.

pa·ro·tic (pərō/tYk, pərŏt/Yk), *adj. Anat., Zool.* situated about or near the ear.

pa·rot·id (pərŏt/Yd), *Anat.* —*n.* **1.** either of two saliva-producing glands situated one at the base of each ear. —*adj.* **2.** noting, pertaining to, or situated near either parotid. [t. L: s. *parōtis,* t. Gk.: tumor near the ear]

par·o·tit·ic (păr/ətYt/Yk), *adj.* having the mumps.

par·o·ti·tis (păr/ətī/tYs), *n. Pathol.* mumps. Also, **pa·rot·i·di·tis** (pə rŏt/ə dī/tYs). [t. NL; see PAROT(ID), -ITIS]

pa·ro·toid (pərō/toid), *Zool.* —*adj.* **1.** resembling a parotid gland. **2.** denoting certain cutaneous glands forming warty masses or excrescences near the ear in certain salientians, as toads. —*n.* **3.** a parotoid gland. [f. Gk. *parōt(is)* (see PAROTID) + -OID]

-parous, an adjective termination meaning "bringing forth," "bearing," "producing," as in *biparous, oviparous, pupiparous, viviparous.* [t. L: m. *-parus,* der. *parere* bring forth]

par·ox·ysm (păr/əksYz/əm), *n.* **1.** any sudden, violent outburst; a fit of violent action or emotion: *paroxysms of rage.* **2.** *Pathol.* a severe attack, or increase in violence, of a disease, usually recurring periodically. [t. ML: s. *paroxysmus,* t. Gk.: m. *paroxysmós* irritation] —**par/ox·ys/mal,** *adj.*

par·ox·y·tone (păr ŏk/sə tōn/), *Greek Gram.* —*adj.* **1.** having an acute accent on the next to the last syllable. —*n.* **2.** a paroxytone word. [t. Gk.: m.s. *paroxýtonos.* See PARA-[1], OXYTONE]

par·quet (pär kā/, pär kĕt/), *n., v.,* **-queted, -queting** or (*esp. Brit.*) **-quetted, -quetting.** —*n.* **1.** a floor of inlaid design. **2.** the part of the main floor of a theater, etc., between the musicians' space and the parterre or rear division, or (*esp. U.S.*) the entire floor space for spectators. —*v.t.* **3.** to construct (a flooring, etc.) of parquetry. **4.** to furnish with a floor, etc., of parquetry. [t. F: part of a park, flooring, dim. of *parc* PARK]

parquet circle, a space with curving tiers of seats behind and around the parquet of a theater, etc.

par·quet·ry (pär/kYtrY), *n.* mosaic work of wood used for floors, wainscoting, etc. [t. F: m. *parqueterie*]

parr (pär), *n., pl.* **parrs,** (*esp. collectively*) **parr. 1.** a young salmon, having dark cross bars on its sides. **2.** the young of some other fishes, as the codfish. [orig. unknown]

Parquetry

Parr (pär), *n.* **Catherine,** 1512–48, sixth wife of Henry VIII of England.

par·ra·keet (păr/əkēt/), *n.* parakeet. Also, **par·ro·ket** (păr/əkĕt/), **par/ro·quet/.**

par·ra·mat·ta (păr/əmăt/ə), *n.* paramatta.

Par·ran (păr/ən), *n.* **Thomas,** born 1892, surgeon general of U.S. Public Health Service 1936–1948.

par·rel (păr/əl), *n. Naut.* a sliding ring or collar of rope or iron, which confines a yard or the jaws of a gaff to the mast but allows vertical movement. Also, **par/ral.** [ME *parail,* aphetic var. of *aparail* APPAREL]

par·ri·cide[1] (păr/əsīd/), *n.* one who kills either of his parents or any one else to whom he owes reverence. [t. F, t. L: m. *parricīda,* appar. der. *pater* father. See -CIDE[1], PATRICIDE] —**par/ri·cid/al,** *adj.*

par·ri·cide[2] (păr/əsīd/), *n.* the act or crime of killing one's father. [t. F, t. L: m. *parricīdium.* See -CIDE[2]]

Par·ring·ton (pär/Yngtən), *n.* **Vernon Louis,** 1871–1929, U.S. literary historian and critic.

Par·rish (păr/Ysh), *n.* **Maxfield,** born 1870, U.S. illustrator and painter.

par·rot (păr/ət), *n.* **1.** any of numerous hook-billed, fleshy-tongued, often gaily colored birds which constitute the order *Psittaciformes,* as the cockatoo, lory, macaw, parakeet, etc., valued as cage birds because they can be taught to talk. **2.** a person who unintelligently repeats the words or imitates the actions of another. —*v.t.* **3.** to repeat or imitate like a parrot. **4.** to teach to repeat or imitate thus. [t. F: m. *Perrot, Pierrot,* dim. of *Pierre* Peter]

parrot fever, psittacosis. Also, **parrot disease.**

parrot fish, any of various marine fishes so called because of their coloring or the shape of their jaws, mainly tropical, mostly of the family *Scaridae,* and certain species of the family *Labridae,* esp. *Labrichthys psittacula,* of Australasia and *Halichoeres radiatus* of Florida, the West Indies, etc.

par·ry (păr/Y), *v.,* **-ried, -rying,** *n., pl.* **-ries.** —*v.t.* **1.** to ward off (a thrust, stroke, weapon, etc.), as in fencing. **2.** to turn aside, evade, or avoid. —*v.i.* **3.** to parry a thrust, etc. —*n.* **4.** an act or mode of parrying as in fencing. **5.** a defensive movement in fencing. [prob. t. F: m. *parez,* impv. of *parer,* t. It.: m. *parare* ward off, protect, g. L: make ready, prepare]

Par·ry (păr/Y), *n.* **William Edward,** 1790–1855, British arctic explorer.

parse (pärs, pärz), *v.t.,* **parsed, parsing.** to describe (a word or series of words) grammatically, telling the part of speech, inflectional form, syntactic relations, etc. [t. L: m. *pars* part, as in *pars ōratiōnis* part of speech] —**pars/er,** *n.*

par·sec (pär/sĕk/), *n. Astron.* a unit of distance corresponding to a heliocentric parallax of one second of arc, being equal to 206,265 times the distance of the earth from the sun (or about 3.26 light years). [f. PAR(ALLAX) + SEC(OND)[2]]

Par·see (pär/sē, pär sē/), *n.* one of a Zoroastrian sect in India, descendants of the Persians who settled in India in the 8th century to escape Mohammedan persecution. Also, **Par/si.** [t. Pers. and Hind.: m. *Pārsī* a Persian]

Par·see·ism (pär/sē Yz/əm, pär sē/Yzəm), *n.* the religion and customs of the Parsees. Also, **Par/si·ism.**

Par·si·fal (pär/sə fəl, -fäl/), *n.* **1.** a music drama (composed 1877–82; premiere, 1882) by Wagner. **2.** *Germanic Myth.* Parzival.

par·si·mo·ni·ous (pär/sə mō/nYəs), *adj.* characterized by or showing parsimony; sparing or frugal, esp. to excess. —**par/si·mo/ni·ous·ly,** *adv.*

par·si·mo·ny (pär/sə mō/nY), *n.* extreme or excessive economy or frugality; niggardliness. [ME, t. L: m.s. *parsimōnia, parcimōnia,* lit., sparingness]

pars·ley (pärs/lY), *n.* **1.** a garden herb, *Petroselinum crispum,* with aromatic leaves which are much used to garnish or season food. **2.** any of certain allied or similar plants. [ME *persely,* b. OF *per(esil)* (g. LL *petrosilium*) and OE *(peter)silie,* t. LL]

pars·nip (pärs/nYp), *n.* **1.** a plant, *Pastinaca sativa,* cultivated varieties of which have a large whitish edible root. **2.** the root. [ME *pasnepe* (influenced by ME *nepe* NEEP), t. OF: m. *pasnaie,* g. L *pastināca*]

par·son (pär/sən), *n.* **1.** a clergyman, minister, or preacher. **2.** the holder or incumbent of a parochial benefice. [ME *persone,* t. ML: m. *persōna* parson, in L *person.* See PERSON]

---

par·son·age (pär′sən ĭj), *n.* **1.** the residence of a parson or clergyman, as provided by the parish or church. **2.** *Obs. or Legal.* the benefice of a parson.

part (pärt), *n.* **1.** a portion or division of a whole, separate in reality, or in thought only; a piece, fragment, fraction, or section; a constituent. **2.** an essential or integral portion. **3.** a portion, member, or organ of an animal body. **4.** each of a number of equal portions composing a whole: *a third part.* **5.** *Math.* an aliquot part or exact divisor. **6.** an allotted portion; a share. **7.** (*usually pl.*) a region, quarter, or district: *foreign parts.* **8.** one of the sides to a contest, question, agreement, etc. **9.** the dividing line formed in parting the hair. **10.** an extra piece for replacing worn out parts of a tool, machine, etc. **11.** *Music.* **a.** a voice, either vocal or instrumental. **b.** the written or printed matter extracted from the score which a single performer or section uses in the performance of concerted music: *a horn part.* **12.** participation, interest, or concern in something. **13.** one's share in some action; a duty, function, or office: *nature didn't do her part.* **14.** a character sustained in a play or in real life; a role. **15.** the words or lines assigned to an actor. **16.** (*usually pl.*) a personal or mental quality or endowment. **17.** Some special noun phrases are:
for my (**his**, etc.) **part**, so far as concerns me (him, etc.).
for the most part, as concerns the greatest part; mostly.
in good part, with favor; without offense.
in part, in some measure or degree; to some extent.
part and parcel, an essential part.
take part, to participate.
[ME and OE, t. L: s. *pars* piece, portion, share, role, region, party] —*v.t.* **18.** to divide (a thing) into parts; break; cleave; divide. **19.** to comb (the hair) away from a dividing line. **20.** to dissolve (a connection, etc.) by separation of the parts, persons, or things involved: *she parted company with her sisters.* **21.** to divide into shares; distribute in parts; apportion. **22.** to put or keep asunder (two or more parts, persons, etc., or one part, person, etc., from another); draw or hold apart; disunite; separate. **23.** *Obs.* to leave. —*v.i.* **24.** to be or become divided into parts; break or cleave: *the frigate parted amidships.* **25.** to go or come apart or asunder, or separate, as two or more things. **26.** to go apart from each other or one another, as persons: *we'll part no more.* **27.** to be or become separated from something else (usually fol. by *from*). **28.** *Naut.* to break or rend, as a cable. **29.** to depart. **30.** to die. **31. part with, a.** to give up; relinquish: *I parted with my gold.* **b.** to depart from. [ME *parte(n)*, t. F: m.s. *partir*, g. L *partīre*]
—**Syn. 1.** PART, PIECE, PORTION refer to that which is less than the whole. PART is the general word: *part of a house.* A PIECE suggests a part which is itself a complete unit, often of standardized form: *a piece of pie.* A PORTION is a part allotted or assigned to a person, purpose, etc.: *a portion of food.* —**Ant. 1.** whole.

part., **1.** participle. **2.** particular.

par·take (pär tāk′), *v.,* **-took, -taken, -taking.** —*v.i.* **1.** to take or have a part or share in common with others: participate (fol. by *in*). **2.** to receive, take, or have a share (fol. by *of*). **3.** to have something of the nature or character (fol. by *of*): *feelings partaking of both joy and regret.* —*v.t.* **4.** to take or have a part in; share. [back formation from *partaking, partaker,* for *part-taking, part-taker,* trans. of L *participātio, particeps*] —**par·tak′er,** *n.* —**Syn. 1.** See **share**[1].

par·tan (pär′tən), *n.* *Scot.* a crab. [t. Gael]

part·ed (pär′tĭd), *adj.* **1.** divided into parts; cleft. **2.** put or kept apart; separated. **3.** *Bot.* (of a leaf) separated into rather distinct portions by incisions which extend nearly to the midrib or the base. **4.** *Archaic.* deceased.

par·terre (pär târ′), *n.* **1.** the part of the main floor of a theater, etc., behind the orchestra or parquet, often under the galleries. **2.** an ornamental arrangement of flower beds of different shapes and sizes. [t. F, f. *par* by, on (g. L *per*) + *terre* earth (g. L *terra*)]

par·the·no·gen·e·sis (pär′thə nō jĕn′ə sĭs), *n.* *Biol.* development of an egg without fertilization. [f. Gk. *parthéno(s)* virgin + GENESIS] —**par·the·no·ge·net·ic** (pär′thə nō jə nĕt′ĭk), *adj.*

Par·the·non (pär′thə nŏn′, -nən), *n.* the temple of Athene on the Acropolis of Athens, completed (structurally) about 438 B.C., regarded as the finest example of Doric temple architecture. [t. L, t. Gk., der. *parthénos* virgin (*Athēnē Parthénos* Athene the Virgin)]

Par·then·o·pe (pär thĕn′ə pē′), *n.* *Gk. Legend.* a Siren who drowned herself when Ulysses remained adamant to her songs.

Par·the·nos (pär′thə nŏs′), *n.* maiden or virgin (applied to some Greek goddesses, esp. Athene).

Par·thi·a (pär′thĭ ə), *n.* an ancient country in W Asia, SE of the Caspian Sea: conquered by the Iranians, A.D. 226; now a part of NE Iran. —**Par′thi·an,** *adj., n.*

Parthian shot, 1. a rearward shot by a fleeing mounted archer. **2.** any sharp parting remark.

par·tial (pär′shəl), *adj.* **1.** pertaining to or affecting a part. **2.** being such in part only; not total or general; incomplete: *partial blindness.* **3.** *Bot.* secondary or subordinate: *a partial umbel.* **4.** being a part; component or constituent. **5.** biased or prejudiced in favor of

a person, group, side, etc. as in a controversy. **6.** particularly inclined in fondness or liking (fol. by *to*): *I'm partial to sodas.* [ME, t. LL: s. *partiālis,* der. L *pars* PART, n.] —**par′tial·ly,** *adv.* —**Syn. 5.** one-sided, unfair, unjust.

partial fractions, *Alg.* one of the fractions into which a given fraction can be resolved, the sum of such simpler fractions being equal to the given fraction.

par·tial·i·ty (pär shăl′ə tĭ, pär′shĭ ăl′-), *n., pl.* **-ties. 1.** the state or character of being partial. **2.** favorable bias or prejudice: *the partiality of parents for their own offspring.* **3.** a particular fondness or liking: *he had always shown a partiality for society.*

partial tone, *Chiefly Music.* one of the pure tones forming a part of a complex tone; the fundamental tone or a harmonic.

par·ti·ble (pär′tə bəl), *adj.* that may be parted or divided; divisible.

par·ti·ceps cri·mi·nis (pär′tə sĕps′ krĭm′ə nĭs), *Latin.* an accomplice in a crime.

par·tic·i·pant (pär tĭs′ə pənt), *n.* **1.** one who participates; a participator. —*adj.* **2.** participating; sharing.

par·tic·i·pate (pär tĭs′ə pāt′), *v.,* **-pated, -pating.** —*v.i.* **1.** to take or have a part or share, as with others; share (fol. by *in*): *to participate in profits.* —*v.t.* **2.** to take or have a part or share in; share. [t. L: m.s. *participātus,* pp.] —**par·tic′i·pa′tor,** *n.* —**Syn. 1.** See **share**[1].

par·tic·i·pa·tion (pär tĭs′ə pā′shən), *n.* **1.** the act or fact of participating. **2.** a taking part, as in some action or attempt. **3.** a sharing, as in benefits or profits.

par·ti·cip·i·al (pär′tə sĭp′ĭ əl), *Gram.* —*adj.* **1.** of or pertaining to a participle. **2.** similar to or formed from a participle. —*n.* **3.** a participle. [t. L: s. *participiālis*] —**par′ti·cip′i·al·ly,** *adv.*

par·ti·ci·ple (pär′tə sə pəl, -sĭp′əl), *n.* *Gram.* (in many languages) an adjective form derived from verbs, which ascribes to a noun participation in the action or state of the verb, without specifying person or number of the subject. For example: *burning* in *a burning candle* or *devoted* in *his devoted friend.* [ME, t. OF, der. *participe* (b. with ending *-ple*), t. L: m.s. *participium* a sharing]

par·ti·cle (pär′tə kəl), *n.* **1.** a minute portion, piece, or amount; a very small bit: *a particle of dust.* **2.** a clause or article, as of a document. **3.** *Rom. Cath. Ch.* **a.** a little piece of the Host. **b.** the small Host given to each lay communicant. **4.** *Gram.* **a.** (in some languages) one of the major form classes, or "parts of speech," consisting of words which are neither nouns nor verbs, or of all uninflected words, or the like. **b.** such a word. **c.** a small word of functional or relational use, such as an article, preposition, or conjunction, whether of a separate form class or not. [ME, t. L: m.s. *particula,* dim. of *pars* PART, n.] —**Syn. 1.** mite, whit, iota, jot, tittle.

par·ti·col·ored (pär′tĭ kŭl′ərd), *adj.* colored differently in different parts, or variegated: *parti-colored dress.* Also, **party-colored.**

par·tic·u·lar (pər tĭk′yə lər), *adj.* **1.** pertaining to some one person, thing, group, class, occasion, etc., rather than to others or all; special, not general: *one's particular interests.* **2.** being a definite one, individual, or single, or considered separately: *each particular item.* **3.** distinguished or different from others or from the ordinary; noteworthy; marked; unusual. **4.** exceptional or especial: *to take particular pains.* **5.** being such in an exceptional degree: *a particular friend of mine.* **6.** dealing with or giving details, as an account, description, etc., or a person; detailed; minute; circumstantial. **7.** attentive to or exacting about details or small points: *to be particular about one's food.* **8.** *Logic.* **a.** not general; not referring to the whole extent of a class, but only to an indefinite part of it: "*some men are wealthy*" is a particular proposition. **b.** partaking of the nature of the individual as opposed to the universal. **9.** *Law.* **a.** denoting an estate which precedes a future or ultimate ownership, as lands devised to a widow during her lifetime, and after that to her children. **b.** denoting the tenant of such an estate.
—*n.* **10.** an individual or distinct part, as an item of a list or enumeration. **11.** a point, detail, or circumstance: *a report complete in every particular.* **12.** *Logic.* an individual or a specific group subordinate to a general class or concept. **13. in particular,** particularly; especially: *one book in particular.*
[t. L: s. *particulāris* of a part, partial; r. ME *particuler,* t. OF]
—**Syn. 1.** See **special.** **7.** PARTICULAR, DAINTY, FASTIDIOUS imply great care, discrimination, and taste in choices, in details about one's person, etc. PARTICULAR implies esp. care and attention to details: *particular about one's clothes.* DAINTY implies delicate taste, and exquisite cleanliness: *a dainty dress.* FASTIDIOUS implies being difficult to please, and critical of small or minor points: *a fastidious taste in styles.* —**Ant. 7.** careless, slovenly, undiscriminating.

par·tic·u·lar·ism (pər tĭk′yə lə rĭz′əm), *n.* **1.** exclusive attention or devotion to one's own particular interests, party, etc. **2.** the principle of leaving each state of a federation free to retain its laws and promote its interests. **3.** *Theol.* the doctrine that divine grace is provided only for the elect. —**par·tic′u·lar·ist,** *n.* —**par·tic′u·lar·ist′ic,** *adj.*

par·tic·u·lar·i·ty (pər tĭk′yə lăr′ə tĭ), *n., pl.* **-ties. 1.** the quality or fact of being particular. **2.** special, peculiar, or individual character. **3.** detailed, minute, or circumstantial character, as of description or statement. **4.** attentiveness to details or small points, or special carefulness. **5.** fastidiousness. **6.** that which is particular; a particular or characteristic feature or trait.

par·tic·u·lar·ize (pər tĭk'yə lə rīz'), v., **-ized, -izing.** —v.t. **1.** to make particular (rather than general). **2.** to mention or indicate particularly. **3.** to state or treat in detail. —v.i. **4.** to speak or treat particularly or specifically; mention individuals. —**par·tic'u·lar·i·za'tion**, n. —**par·tic'u·lar·iz'er**, n.

par·tic·u·lar·ly (pər tĭk'yə lər lĭ'), adv. **1.** in a particular or exceptional degree; especially: *he read it with particularly great interest.* **2.** in a particular manner; specially; individually. **3.** in detail; minutely. —**Syn. 1.** See **especially.**

part·ing (pär'tĭng), n. **1.** the act of one who or that which parts. **2.** division; separation. **3.** leave-taking; departure. **4.** death. **5.** a place of division or separation. **6.** something that serves to part or separate things. —adj. **7.** given, taken, done, etc., at parting: *a parting shot.* **8.** of or pertaining to parting, leave-taking, departure, or death. **9.** departing: *the parting day.* **10.** dying. **11.** dividing; separating.

parting strip, a strip, as of wood, used to keep two parts separated, as one in each side of the frame of a window to keep the sashes apart when lowered or raised.

par·ti pris (pär tē' prē'), *French.* decision taken; foregone conclusion.

par·ti·san[1] (pär'tə zən), n. **1.** an adherent or supporter of a person, party, or cause. **2.** *Mil.* a member of a party of light or irregular troops engaged in harassing the enemy; a guerrilla. —adj. **3.** pertaining to or carried on by military partisans. **4.** of, pertaining to, or characteristic of partisans. Also, **partizan.** [t. F, t. It.: m. *partigiano,* der. *parte* part, n., g. L *pars*] —**par'ti·san·ship'**, n. —**Syn. 1, 2.** See **follower.**

par·ti·san[2] (pär'tə zən), n. a shafted weapon with broad blade and curved basal lobes, esp. carried by bodyguards. Also, **partizan.** [t. F: m. *partizane,* t. It.: m. *partigiana* fem., n. use of *partigiano,* adj., PARTISAN[1]]

par·tite (pär'tīt), adj. **1.** divided into parts. **2.** *Bot., etc.* parted. [t. L: m.s. *partītus,* pp.]

par·ti·tion (pär tĭsh'ən), n. **1.** division into or distribution in portions or shares. **2.** separation, as of two or more things. **3.** something that separates. **4.** a part, division, or section. **5.** an interior wall or barrier dividing a building, enclosure, etc. **6.** a septum or dissepiment, as in a plant or animal structure. **7.** *Law.* **a.** a division of property among joint owners or tenants in common, or a sale of such property followed by a division of the proceeds. **b.** a division of real property held in co-ownership. **8.** *Logic.* the separation of a whole into its integrant parts. **9.** *Math.* a mode of separating a positive whole number into a sum of positive whole numbers. **10.** (in a speech organized on classical principles) the second part, usually short, in which a speaker announces the chief lines of thought he proposes to discuss in support of his theme. —v.t. **11.** to divide into parts or portions. **12.** to divide or separate by a partition. **13.** *Law.* to divide property among several owners, either in specie or by sale and division of the proceeds. [ME, t. L: s. *partītio*] —**par·ti'·tion·er**, n. —**par·ti'tion·ment**, n. —**Syn. 1.** See **division.**

par·ti·tive (pär'tə tĭv), adj. **1.** serving to divide into parts. **2.** *Gram.* denoting part of a whole: *the Latin partitive genitive.* —n. **3.** *Gram.* a partitive word or formation, as of *the men* in *half of the men.* —**par'ti·tive·ly**, adv.

par·ti·zan (pär'tə zən), n., adj. partisan.

part·let (pärt'lĭt), n. *Obs.* a garment for the neck and shoulders, especially for women. [alter. of *patelet,* t. OF: m. *patelette* band of stuff]

part·ly (pärt'lĭ), adv. in part; in some measure; not wholly.

part music, music, esp. vocal music, with parts for two or more independent performers.

part·ner (pärt'nər), n. **1.** a sharer or partaker; an associate. **2.** *Law.* **a.** one associated with another or others as a principal or a contributor of capital in a business or a joint venture, usually sharing its risks and profits. **b.** See **special partner. 3.** See **silent partner. 4.** a husband or a wife. **5.** one's companion in a dance. **6.** a player on the same side with another in a game. **7.** (pl.) *Naut.* a framework of timber round a hole in a ship's deck, to support a mast, capstan, pump, etc. —v.t. **8.** to associate as a partner or partners. **9.** to be, or act as, the partner of. [ME *partener,* var. of PARCENER, appar. by assoc. with PART, n.] —**Syn. 1.** colleague, accessory, accomplice.

part·ner·ship (pärt'nər shĭp'), n. **1.** the state or condition of being a partner; participation; association; joint interest. **2.** *Law.* **a.** the relation subsisting between partners. **b.** the contract creating this relation. **c.** an association of persons joined as partners in business.

part of speech, *Gram.* any of the mutually exclusive major form classes of a language, which taken together include the entire vocabulary, e.g. in Latin, a word is either a *noun, verb, pronoun, adjective, adverb, preposition, conjunction,* or *interjection.*

par·took (pär tŏŏk'), v. pt. of **partake.**

par·tridge (pär'trĭj), n., pl. **-tridges,** (esp. collectively) **-tridge. 1.** any of various North American gallinaceous birds as, in New England, the ruffed grouse (*Bonasa umbellus*); in Virginia, the bob-white quail (*Colinus virginianus*), etc. **2.** any of various Old World gallinaceous gamebirds of the subfamily *Perdicinae,* esp. *Perdix perdix,* the common **gray partridge** of Europe. **3.** any of various South and Central American tinamous. [ME *pertrich,* t. OF: m. *perdriz, perdiz,* g. L *perdix,* t. Gk.]

Partridge,
Alectoris graeca
(14½ in. .ong)

par·tridge·ber·ry (pär'trĭj bĕr'ĭ), n., pl. **-ries.** a North American trailing rubiaceous perennial, *Mitchella repens,* having roundish evergreen leaves, fragrant white flowers, and scarlet berries.

part song, a song with parts for several voices, esp. one meant to be sung without accompaniment.

par·tu·ri·ent (pär tyŏŏr'ĭ ənt, -tŏŏr'-), adj. **1.** bringing forth or about to bring forth young; travailing. **2.** pertaining to parturition. **3.** bringing forth or about to produce something, as an idea. [t. L: s. *parturiens,* ppr., being in labor] —**par·tu'ri·en·cy**, n.

par·tu·ri·tion (pär'tyŏŏ rĭsh'ən, -chŏŏ-), n. the act of bringing forth young; childbirth.

par·ty (pär'tĭ), n., pl. **-ties,** adj. —n. **1.** a group gathered together for some purpose, as for amusement or entertainment. **2.** a social gathering or entertainment, as of invited guests at a private house or elsewhere: *to give a party.* **3.** a detachment of troops assigned to perform some particular service. **4.** a number or body of persons ranged on one side, or united in purpose or opinion, in opposition to others, as in politics, etc.: *the Republican party.* **5.** the system of taking sides on public questions or the like. **6.** attachment or devotion to a side or faction; partizanship. **7.** *Law.* **a.** one of the litigants in a legal proceeding; a plaintiff or defendant in a suit. **b.** a signatory to a legal instrument. **c.** one participating in or otherwise privy to a crime. **8.** one who participates in some action or affair. **9.** *U.S. Colloq.* **a.** the person under consideration. **b.** a person in general. —adj. **10.** of or pertaining to a party or faction; partisan: *party issues.* **11.** *Her.* divided into parts, usually two parts, as a shield. [ME *parti(e),* t. OF, pp. of *partir* PART, v.] —**Syn. 1.** See **company.**

par·ty-col·ored (pär'tĭ kŭl'ərd), adj. parti-colored.

party line, 1. a telephone line by which a number of subscribers are connected by one circuit to a central office. **2.** the bounding line between adjoining premises. **3.** the authoritatively announced policies and practices of a group, usually followed without exception: *the Communist party line.*

party man, a man belonging to a political party, esp. one who adheres strictly to the principles and policy of his party.

party wall, *Law.* a wall used, or usable, as a part of contiguous structures.

pa·rure (pə rŏŏr'; Fr. pà ryr'), n. a set of jewels or ornaments. [ME, t. F, der. *parer* prepare, adorn. See PARE]

par·ve·nu (pär'və nū', -nŏŏ'-), n. **1.** one who has risen above his class or to a position above his qualifications; an upstart. —adj. **2.** being or resembling a parvenu. **3.** characteristic of a parvenu. [t. F, prop. pp. of *parvenir* arrive, g. L *pervenīre*]

par·vis (pär'vĭs), n. **1.** a vacant enclosed area in front of a church. **2.** a colonnade or portico in front of a church. [ME *parvys,* t. OF: m. *parevis,* g. LL *paradīsus* PARADISE]

par·vo·line (pär'və lēn', -lĭn), n. *Chem.* any of several oily isomeric, organic bases, one occurring in coal tar and another in decaying mackerel. Also, **par·vo·lin** (pär'və lĭn). [f. s. L *parvus* small (with ref. to its relatively small volatility) + -OL[2] + -INE[2]; modeled on *quinoline*]

Par·zi·val (pär'tsĭ fäl'), n. the German counterpart of Percival. Also, **Parsifal.**

pas (pä), n. *French.* **1.** a step or movement in dancing, esp. in ballet. **2.** a dance. **3.** precedence; right of preceding. [see PACE[1]]

Pas·a·de·na (păs'ə dē'nə), n. a city in SW California, near Los Angeles. 104,577 (1950).

Pa·sar·ga·dae (pə sär'gə dē'), n. an ancient ruined city in S Iran, NE of Persepolis: an early capital of ancient Persia; tomb of Cyrus the Great.

Pas·cal (păs'kəl; Fr. pås kål'), n. Blaise (blĕz), 1623–1662, French philosopher, mathematician, and physicist.

Pasch (păsk), n. *Archaic.* **1.** the Passover. **2.** Easter. [ME *pasche,* t. LL: m. *pascha,* t. Gk., t. Heb.: m. *pesah* Passover. Pop. var. of PESACH]

pas·chal (păs'kəl), adj. pertaining to the Passover, or to Easter. [ME *paschall,* t. LL: m.s. *paschālis,* der. *pascha* PASCH]

paschal flower, pasqueflower.

paschal lamb, 1. (among the Jews, during the existence of the Temple) the lamb slain and eaten at the Passover. **2.** (cap.) Christ. **3.** (cap.) any of various symbolical representations of Christ. Cf. **Agnus Dei.**

Pas de Ca·lais (pä də kà lĕ'). See **Dover, Strait of.**

pas de deux (pä də dœ'), *French.* a dance by two persons.

pas du tout (pä dy tŏŏ'), *French.* not at all.

pash[1] (păsh), *Chiefly Dial.* —*v.t.* **1.** to hurl or dash. **2.** to smash or shatter. —*v.i.* **3.** to dash or strike violently. [ME *pas(s)he(n)*; appar. imit.]

pash[2] (păsh), *n.* *Chiefly Scot.* the head [orig. unknown]

pa·sha (pə shä′, păsh′ə, pā′shə), *n.* a title, placed after the name, formerly borne by civil and military officials of high rank in Turkish dominions, Also, **pacha.** [t. Turk., var of *bāshā*, der. *bash* head, chief]

pa·sha·lik (pə shä′lĭk), *n.* the territory governed by a pasha. Also, **pachalic, pa·sha′lic.** [t. Turk.: f. *pāshā* PASHA + -*lik*, suffix denoting quality or condition]

Pash·to (pŭsh′tō), *n.* Pushtu.

Pa·siph·a·ë (pə sĭf′ĭ ē′), *n.* *Gk. Legend.* wife of Minos, and mother of Ariadne. She was the mother of the Minotaur, by the white bull given to Minos by Poseidon.

pasque·flow·er (păsk′flou′ər), *n.* **1.** an Old World ranunculaceous plant, *Anemone Pulsatilla,* with purple flowers blooming about Easter. **2.** a similar plant, *A. ludoviciana,* whose flower is the State flower of South Dakota. [f. *Pasque* (var. spelling of PASCH) + flower (so named by the herbalist Gerarde in 1597); r. *passe-flower,* t. F: m. *passe-fleur.* See PASS, v., FLOWER]

pas·quil (păs′kwĭl), *n.* a pasquinade.

pas·quin·ade (păs′kwĭ nād′), *n., v.,* -**aded,** -**ading.** —*n.* **1.** a publicly posted lampoon. —*v.t.* **2.** to assail in a pasquinade or pasquinades. [t. F, t. It.: m. *pasquinata,* der. *Pasquino,* name given to an antique statue dug up in Rome (1501), which was decorated once a year and posted with verses] —**pas′quin·ad′er,** *n.*

pass (păs, päs), *v.,* **passed** or (*Rare*) **past; passed** or **past; passing;** *n.* —*v.t.* **1.** to go by or move past (something). **2.** to go by without acting upon or noticing; leave unmentioned. **3.** to omit payment of (a dividend, etc.). **4.** to go or get through (a channel, barrier, etc.). **5.** to go across or over (a stream, threshold, etc.); cross. **6.** to undergo successfully (an examination, etc.). **7.** to go beyond (a point, degree, stage, etc.); transcend; exceed; surpass. **8.** to cause to go or move onward; proceed: *to pass a rope through a hole.* **9.** to cause to go by or move past: *to pass troops in review.* **10.** to spend, as time. **11.** to cause to go about or circulate; give currency to. **12.** to cause to be accepted or received. **13.** to convey, transfer, or transmit; deliver. **14.** to pledge, as one's word. **15.** to cause or allow to go through something, as through a test, etc. **16.** to discharge or void, as excrement. **17.** to sanction or approve: *to pass a bill.* **18.** to obtain the approval or sanction of (a legislative body, etc.), as a bill. **19.** to express or pronounce, as an opinion or judgment. **20.** *Law.* to place legal title or interest in (another) by a conveyance, a will, or other transfer. **21.** *Magic.* to perform a pass on (a pack of cards, etc.). **22.** *Baseball.* to allow (a batter) to reach first base after four balls. —*v.i.* **23.** to go or move onward; proceed; make one's or its way. **24.** to go away or depart. **25.** to elapse or be spent, as time. **26.** to come to an end, as a thing in time. **27.** to die. **28.** *Colloq.* to faint (fol. by *out*). **29.** to go on or take place; happen; occur: *to learn what has passed.* **30.** to go by or move past, as a procession. **31.** to go about or circulate; be current. **32.** to be accepted or received (fol. by *for* or *as*): *material that passed for silk.* **33.** to be transferred or conveyed. **34.** to be interchanged, as between two persons: *sharp words passed between them.* **35.** to undergo transition or conversion: *to pass from a solid to a liquid state.* **36.** to go or get through something, such as a barrier, test, examination, etc. **37.** to go unheeded, uncensured, or unchallenged: *but let that pass.* **38.** to express or pronounce an opinion, judgment, verdict, etc. (usually fol. by *on* or *upon*). **39.** to be voided, as excrement. **40.** to be ratified or enacted, as a bill or law. **41.** *Law.* **a.** (of a member of an inquest or other deliberative body) to sit: *to pass on.* **b.** to adjudicate. **c.** to vest title or other legal interest in real or personal property in a new owner. **42.** *U.S.* to throw a ball from one to another; play catch. **43.** *U.S.* to make a pass, as in football. **44.** *Fencing.* to thrust or lunge. **45.** *Cards.* **a.** to forego one's opportunity to bid, play, etc. **b.** to throw up one's hand. **46.** Some special verb phrases are:

bring to pass, to cause to happen.
come to pass, to occur.
pass away, 1. to cease to be. **2.** to die.
pass off, 1. to put into circulation, or dispose of, esp. deceptively: *to pass off a bad dollar.* **2.** to cause to be accepted or received in a false character; *he passed himself off as my servant.*
pass over, 1. to disregard. **2.** to omit to notice.
[ME *passe(n),* t. OF: m. *passer,* ult. der. L *passus* a step] —*n.* **47.** a narrow route across a relatively low notch or depression in a mountain barrier separating the headwaters of approaching valleys from either side. **48.** a way affording passage, as through an obstructed region or any barrier. [ME *pas,* t. F, g. L *passus* PACE[1]] **49.** a navigable channel, as at the mouth or in the delta of a river. **50.** a permission or license to pass, go, come, or enter. **51.** *Mil.* **a.** a military document granting its bearer the right to cross lines, enter or leave a military or naval reservation, or other area or building. **b.** written authority given a soldier to leave a station or duty for a few hours or days. **52.** a free ticket. **53.** *Chiefly Brit.* (in a university, course, etc.) the passing of an examination or course, but without honors. **54.** the transference of a ball, etc., from one player to another, as in football. **55.** *Baseball.* the right to go to first base after four balls. **56.** a thrust or lunge, as in fencing. **57.** *Slang.* a jab with the arm, esp. one that misses its mark. **58.** *Cards.* an act of not bidding or raising another bid. **59.** *Magic, etc.* **a.** a passing of the hand over, along, or before anything. **b.** the transference or changing of objects by or as by sleight of hand; a manipulation, as of a juggler; a trick. **60.** a stage in procedure or experience; a particular stage or state of affairs: *things have come to a pretty pass.* **61.** the act of passing. **62.** *Archaic.* a sally of wit. **63. make a pass,** to make an amorous overture or gesture (usually fol. by *at*). [ME *passe;* partly n. use of PASS, v.; partly t. F, der. *passer*] —Syn. **27.** See die[1].

pass., 1. passenger. **2.** passive.

pass·a·ble (păs′ə bəl, päs′-), *adj.* **1.** that may be passed. **2.** that may be proceeded through or over, or traversed, penetrated, crossed, etc., as a road, forest, or stream. **3.** tolerable, fair, or moderate: *a passable knowledge of history.* **4.** that may be circulated, or has valid currency, as a coin. **5.** that may be ratified or enacted, as a bill. [ME, t. F, der. *passer* PASS, v.] —**pass′a·ble-ness,** *n.*

pass·a·bly (păs′ə blĭ, päs′-), *adv.* fairly; moderately: *the movie was passably good.*

pas·sade (pə säd′), *n.* *Manège.* a turn or course of a horse backward or forward on the same ground.

pas·sa·do (pə sä′dō), *n., pl.* -**dos,** -**does** (-dōz). *Fencing. Obs.* or *Archaic.* a forward thrust with the sword, one foot being advanced at the same time. [t. Sp.: m. *pasada,* t. It.: m. *passata,* der. *passare* PASS]

pas·sage[1] (păs′ĭj), *n., v.,* -**saged,** -**saging.** —*n.* **1.** an indefinite portion of a writing, speech, or the like, usually one of no great length; a paragraph, verse, etc.: *a passage of Scripture.* **2.** *Music.* **a.** a scalelike or arpeggiolike series of tones introduced as an embellishment; a run, roulade, or flourish. **b.** a phrase or other division of a piece. **3.** act of passing. **4.** liberty, leave, or right to pass: *to refuse passage through a territory.* **5.** that by which a person or thing passes; a means of passing; a way, route, avenue, channel, etc. **6.** *Chiefly Brit.* a hall, corridor, or the like. **7.** movement, transit, or transition, as from one place or state to another. **8.** a voyage across the sea from one port to another: *a rough passage.* **9.** the privilege of conveyance as a passenger: *to secure passage for Europe.* **10.** lapse, as of time. **11.** progress or course, as of events. **12.** the passing into law of a legislative measure. **13.** an interchange of communications, confidences, etc., between persons. **14.** an exchange of blows; an altercation or dispute: *a passage at arms.* **15.** the causing of something to pass; transference; transmission. **16.** an evacuation of the bowels. **17.** *Archaic.* an occurrence, incident, or event. —*v.i.* **18.** to make a passage; cross; pass; voyage. [ME, t. OF, der. *passer* PASS, v.]

pas·sage[2] (păs′ĭj), *v.,* -**saged,** -**saging,** *n.* —*v.i.* *Manège.* **1.** (of a horse) to move sideways, in obedience to pressure by the rider's leg on the opposite side. **2.** (of a rider) to cause a horse to do this. —*v.t.* **3.** to cause (a horse) to passage. —*n.* **4.** the act of passaging. [t. F: m. s. *passager,* t. It.: m. *passeggiare* to pace, walk, der. *passo* pace, g. L *passus* PACE]

Passage to India, A, a novel (1924) by E. M. Forster.

pas·sage·way (păs′ĭj wā′), *n.* a way for passage, as in a building or among buildings, etc.; a passage.

Pas·sa·ic (pə sā′ĭk), *n.* a city in NE New Jersey. 57,702 (1950).

Pas·sa·ma·quod·dy Bay (păs′ə mə kwŏd′ĭ), an inlet of the Bay of Fundy, between Maine and New Brunswick, Canada, at the mouth of the St. Croix river.

pas·sant (păs′ənt), *adj.* *Her.* (of a beast used as a bearing) walking with one paw raised, and looking forward to the dexter side of the escutcheon. [ME, t. F, ppr. of *passer* PASS, v.]

pass·book (păs′bŏŏk′, päs′-), *n.* **1.** *Chiefly Brit.* a bankbook. **2.** a customer's book in which a merchant or trader makes entries of goods sold on credit.

pas·sé (pă sā′, päs′ā; *Fr.* pȧ sā′), *adj.* **1.** antiquated, or out of date. **2.** past. **3.** past the prime; faded. [t. F, pp. of *passer* PASS, v.]

passed (păst, päst), *adj.* **1.** that has passed or has been passed. **2.** having passed an examination or test. **3.** *Naval.* having passed an examination for promotion, and awaiting a vacancy in the next grade. **4.** *Finance.* denoting a dividend not paid at the usual dividend date.

passed ball, *Baseball.* a pitched ball, not hit by the batsman, which the catcher fails to stop, though it is within his reach, his failure allowing a base runner or base runners to advance.

passe·men·terie (păs měn′trĭ; *Fr.* pȧs mäɴ trē′), *n.* trimming made of braid, cord, beads, etc., in various forms. [t. F, der. *passement,* der. *passer* PASS, v.]

pas·sen·ger (păs′ən jər), *n.* **1.** one who travels by some form of conveyance: *the passengers of a ship.* **2.** a wayfarer. [ME *passager,* t. OF: m. *passagier,* der. *passage* PASSAGE[1]; for -*n*-, cf. MESSENGER, etc.]

passenger pigeon, a wild pigeon, *Ectopistes migratorius,* once extraordinarily common in North America but now extinct.

passe partout (păs pär tōō′; *Fr.* pȧs pȧr tōō′), *French.* **1.** a kind of ornamental mat for a picture. **2.** a frame with such a mat, to receive a photograph or other representation. **3.** a picture frame consisting of a piece of glass, under which the picture is placed, affixed to a backing by means of adhesive strips of paper or other material. **4.** paper, etc., prepared for this purpose. **5.** that which passes, or by means of which one can pass, everywhere. **6.** a master key. [F: lit., pass-everywhere]

pass·er (păs/ər, päs/-), *n.* **1.** one that passes or causes something to pass. **2.** a passer-by.

pass·er-by (păs/ər bī/, päs/-), *n., pl.* **passers-by.** one who passes by.

pas·ser·ine (păs/ər ĭn, -ə rīn/), *adj.* **1.** belonging or pertaining to the *Passeriformes*, an order of birds, typically insessorial (perching), embracing more than half of all birds, and including the finches, thrushes, warblers, swallows, crows, larks, etc. —*n.* **2.** any bird of the order *Passeriformes*. [t. L: m.s. *passerīnus* of a sparrow]

pas seul (pä sœl/), *French.* a dance performed by one person.

pas·si·ble (păs/ə bəl), *adj.* capable of suffering or feeling; susceptible of sensation or emotion. [ME, t. LL: m.s. *passibilis*] —**pas/si·bil/i·ty,** *n.*

pas·si·flo·ra·ceous (păs/ĭ flô rā/shəs), *adj.* belonging to the *Passifloraceae*, or passionflower family of plants. [f. s. NL *Passiflora*, the typical genus, (f. L: *passi*(o) passion + -*flōra*, fem. adj., flowering) + -ACEOUS]

pas·sim (păs/ĭm), *adv. Latin.* here and there, as in books or writings.

pass·ing (păs/ĭng, päs/-), *adj.* **1.** that passes; going by; elapsing. **2.** fleeting or transitory. **3.** that is now happening; current. **4.** done, given, etc., in passing; cursory: *a passing mention.* **5.** surpassing, preëminent, or extreme. **6.** indicating that one has passed: *a passing grade on the test.* —*adv.* **7.** *Archaic.* surpassingly; exceedingly; very. —*n.* **8.** act of one that passes or causes something to pass. **9.** a means or place of passage; passage. **10. in passing,** in the course of passing, going on, or proceeding.

passing bell, 1. a bell tolled to announce a death or funeral. **2.** a portent or sign of the passing away of anything.

passing note, *Music.* a note foreign to the harmony, introduced between two successive chord tones in order to produce a melodic transition.

pas·sion (păsh/ən), *n.* **1.** any kind of feeling or emotion, as hope, fear, joy, grief, anger, love, desire, etc., esp. when of compelling force. **2.** strong amorous feeling or desire. **3.** passionate sexual love. **4.** an instance or experience of it. **5.** a person who is the object of such a feeling. **6.** a strong or extravagant fondness, enthusiasm, or desire for anything: *a passion for music.* **7.** the object of such a fondness or desire: *accuracy became a passion with him.* **8.** a passionate outburst: *she broke into a passion of tears.* **9.** violent anger. **10.** state or fact of being acted upon or affected by something external (opposed to *action*). **11.** (*often cap.*) **a.** the sufferings of Christ on the cross, or his sufferings subsequent to the Last Supper. **b.** the gospel narrative of the sufferings of Christ, as in Mark 14–15, and parallel passages in the other gospels. **c.** a musical setting of it. **d.** a pictorial representation of Christ's sufferings. **12.** *Archaic.* the sufferings of a martyr. [ME, t. OF, t. L: s. *passio* suffering] —**Syn. 1.** See **feeling.**

pas·sion·al (păsh/ən əl), *adj.* **1.** of or pertaining to passion or the passions. **2.** due to passion: *passional crimes.* —*n.* **3.** a book containing descriptions of the sufferings of saints and martyrs, for reading on their festivals.

pas·sion·ar·y (păsh/ə něr/ĭ), *n., pl.* -**aries.** passional.

pas·sion·ate (păsh/ən ĭt), *adj.* **1.** affected with or dominated by passion or vehement emotion: *a passionate advocate of socialism.* **2.** characterized by, expressing, or showing vehement emotion; impassioned: *passionate language.* **3.** vehement, as feelings or emotions: *passionate grief.* **4.** easily moved to anger; quick-tempered; irascible. [late ME *passionat*, t. ML: s. *passiōnātus*] —**pas/sion·ate·ly,** *adv.* —**pas/sion·ate·ness,** *n.*

pas·sion·flow·er (păsh/ən flou/ər), *n.* any plant of the genus *Passiflora*, which comprises climbing vines or shrubs, mainly American, bearing showy flowers and a pulpy berry or fruit which in some species is edible. [so named from a supposed resemblance of the flower to the wounds, crown of thorns, etc. of Christ]

pas·sion·fruit (păsh/ən frōot/), *n.* any edible fruit of a passionflower, as the maypop.

pas·sion·less (păsh/ən lĭs), *adj.* without passion; cold; unemotional.

passion play, a dramatic representation of the passion of Christ, such as that given every ten years at the Bavarian village of Oberammergau.

Passion Sunday, the fifth Sunday in Lent, being the second before Easter.

Passion Week, 1. the week preceding Easter; Holy Week. **2.** the week before Holy Week, beginning with Passion Sunday.

pas·sive (păs/ĭv), *adj.* **1.** not acting, or not attended with or manifested in open or positive action: *passive resistance.* **2.** inactive, quiescent, or inert. **3.** suffering action, acted upon, or being the object of action (opposed to *active*). **4.** receiving, or characterized by the reception of, impressions from without. **5.** produced by or due to external agency. **6.** suffering, receiving,

or submitting without resistance. **7.** characterized by or involving doing this: *passive obedience.* **8.** *Gram.* **a.** (in some languages) denoting a voice, or verb inflection, in which the subject is represented as being acted on. For example: Latin *portātur*, "(he, she, it) is carried," is in the passive voice. **b.** denoting a construction similar to this in meaning, as English *he is carried.* **9.** *Chem.* inactive, esp. under conditions in which chemical activity is to be expected. **10.** *Med.* pertaining to certain unhealthy conditions with insufficient strength; inactive (opp. to *active* or *spontaneous*). —*n.* **11.** *Gram.* **a.** the passive voice. **b.** a form or construction therein. [ME, t. L: m.s. *passīvus* capable of feeling] —**pas/-sive·ly,** *adv.* —**pas/sive·ness, pas·siv/i·ty,** *n.*

passive immunity, *Immunol.* immunity achieved by injecting immune serum from another organism.

passive resistance, the expression of disapproval of authority or of specific laws by various nonviolent acts, such as public demonstration or (in some cases) voluntary fasting.

pass·key (păs/kē/, päs/-), *n., pl.* -**keys. 1.** a master key. **2.** a private key. **3.** a latchkey.

Pass·o·ver (păs/ō/vər, päs/-), *n.* **1.** an annual feast of the Jews, instituted to commemorate the passing over or sparing of the Hebrews in Egypt when God smote the first-born of the Egyptians (see Ex. 12), but used in the general sense of the Feast of Unleavened Bread (Lev. 23: 5–6) in commemoration of the deliverance from Egypt, beginning on the eve of the 15th day of Nisan, and lasting originally seven days but in later Judaism eight days. **2.** (*l.c.*) the paschal lamb. **3.** (*l.c.*) Christ. [orig. verbal phrase *pass over*]

pass·port (păs/pôrt, päs/-), *n.* **1.** an official document granting permission to the person specified in it to travel, and authenticating his right to protection. **2.** an authorization to pass or go anywhere. **3.** a document issued to a ship, esp. to neutral merchant vessels in time of war, granting or requesting permission to proceed without molestation in certain waters. **4.** a certificate intended to secure admission. **5.** anything that gives admission or acceptance. [t. F: m. *passeport,* f. *passe*(r) PASS + *port* PORT[1] (def. 3)]

pas·sus (păs/əs), *n., pl.* -**sus,** -**suses.** a section or division of a story, poem, etc.; a canto. [t. ML, in L a step, PACE[2]]

pass·word (păs/wûrd/, päs/-), *n.* a secret word, made known only to authorized persons for their use in passing through a line of guards.

Pas·sy (pà sē/), *n.* **Paul Édouard** (pōl ĕdwâr/). 1859–1940, French phonetician.

past (păst, päst), *v.* **1.** pp. and occasional pt. of **pass.** —*adj.* **2.** gone by in time. **3.** belonging to, or having existed or occurred in, time previous to this. **4.** gone by just before the present time; just passed: *the past year.* **5.** ago. **6.** having served a term in an office: *past master.* **7.** *Gram.* designating a tense, or other verb formation or construction, which refers to events or states in time gone by. —*n.* **8.** the time gone by: *far back in the past.* **9.** the events of that time: *to forget the past.* **10.** a past history, life, career, etc.: *a glorious past.* **11.** a past career which is kept concealed: *a woman with a past.* **12.** *Gram.* **a.** the past tense, as *he ate, he smoked.* **b.** another verb formation or construction with past meaning. **c.** a form therein. —*adv.* **13.** so as to pass by or beyond; by: *the troops marched past.* —*prep.* **14.** beyond in time; after: *past noon.* **15.** beyond in position; further on than: *the house past the church.* **16.** beyond in amount, number, etc. **17.** beyond the reach, scope, influence, or power of: *past belief.* [see PASS, v.]

paste (pāst), *n., v.,* **pasted, pasting.** —*n.* **1.** a mixture of flour and water, often with starch, etc., used for causing paper, etc., to adhere. **2.** any material or preparation in a soft or plastic mass: *a tooth paste.* **3.** dough, esp. when prepared with shortening, as for making pie crust and other pastry: *puff paste.* **4.** any of the various food preparations, made from flour, of the macaroni and noodle kind. **5.** any of various sweet confections of doughlike consistence: *fig paste.* **6.** *Chiefly Brit.* a preparation of fish, tomatoes, or some other article of food reduced to a smooth, soft mass, as for a relish or for seasoning. **7.** a mixture of clay, water, etc., for making earthenware or porcelain. **8.** a brilliant, heavy glass, used for making artificial gems. **9.** an artificial gem of this material. **10.** *Slang.* a smart blow, esp. on the face. —*v.t.* **11.** to fasten or stick with paste or the like. **12.** to cover with something applied by means of paste. **13.** *Slang.* to strike with a smart blow, or beat soundly, as on the face or body. [ME, t. OF, g. LL *pasta,* t. Gk.: m. *pástē* barley porridge]

paste·board (pāst/bôrd/), *n.* **1.** a stiff, firm board made of sheets of paper pasted or layers of paper pulp pressed together, used for book covers. **2.** *Slang.* a card, as a visiting card or a playing card. **3.** *Slang.* a ticket, as for an entertainment. —*adj.* **4.** made of pasteboard. **5.** unsubstantial or flimsy; sham.

pas·tel[1] (păs těl/, păs/těl), *n.* **1.** a soft subdued shade. **2.** a kind of dried paste used for crayons, made of pigments ground with chalk and compounded with gum water. **3.** a crayon made with such paste. **4.** the art of drawing with such crayons. **5.** a drawing so made. **6.** a short, slight prose study or sketch. [t. F, t. Pr., der. LL *pasta* PASTE]

---

b., blend of, blended; **c.,** cognate with; **d.,** dialect, dialectal; **der.,** derived from; **f.,** formed from; **g.,** going back to; **m.,** modification of; **r.,** replacing; **s.,** stem of; **t.,** taken from; **?,** perhaps. See the full key on inside cover.

pas·tel² (păs′tĕl), *n.* **1.** the plant woad. **2.** the dye made from it. [t. F, t. It.: m. *pastello*, dim. der. LL *pasta* PASTE]

pas·tel·ist (păs′tĕl ĭst, păs tĕl′ĭst), *n.* an artist who draws with pastels. Also, *esp. Brit.,* **pas·tel·list.**

past·er (pās′tər), *n.* **1.** a slip of paper gummed on the back, to be pasted on or over something, as over a name on a ballot. **2.** one who or that which pastes.

pas·tern (păs′tərn), *n.* **1.** that part of the foot of a horse, etc., between the fetlock and the hoof. See illus. under **horse.** **2.** either of two bones of this part, the upper or first phalanx (**great pastern bone**) and the lower or second phalanx (**small pastern bone**), between which is a joint (**pastern joint**). [ME *pastron*, t. F: m. *pasturon*, der. *pasture* shackle for animal while pasturing]

Pas·teur (păs tœr′), *n.* **Louis** (lwē), 1822–95, French chemist and bacteriologist.

pas·teur·ism (păs′tə rĭz′əm), *n.* **1.** a treatment devised by Pasteur for preventing certain diseases, esp. hydrophobia, by inoculations with virus of gradually increasing strength. **2.** the act or process of pasteurizing milk, etc. [named after Louis PASTEUR. See -ISM]

pas·teur·ize (păs′tə rīz′, păs′chə rīz′), *v.t.,* **-ized, -iz·ing. 1.** to expose (milk, etc.) to a high temperature, usually about 140° F., in order to destroy certain microörganisms and prevent or arrest fermentation. **2.** to subject to pasteurism in order to prevent certain diseases, esp. hydrophobia. Also, *esp. Brit.,* **pas·teur·ise′. —pas′teur·i·za′tion,** *n.*

pas·tic·cio (păs tĕt′chō), *n., pl.* **-ci** (-chē). any work of art, literature, or music consisting of motifs borrowed from one or more masters or works of art. [t. It., der. *pasta* PASTE]

pas·tiche (păs tēsh′, päs-), *n.* a pasticcio. [t. F, t. It.: m. *pasticcio* PASTICCIO]

pas·tille (păs tēl′, -tĭl′), *n.* **1.** a flavored or medicated lozenge. **2.** a roll or cone of paste containing aromatic substances, burned as a perfume, disinfectant, etc. **3.** pastel for crayons. **4.** a crayon made of it. Also, **pas·til** (păs′tĭl). [t. F, t. Sp.: m. *pastilla,* dim. of *pasta* PASTE]

pas·time (păs′tīm′, päs′-), *n.* that which serves to make time pass agreeably; diversion, amusement, or sport: *to play cards for a pastime.* [late ME, f. PASS, v. + TIME]

past·i·ness (pās′tĭ nĭs), *n.* pasty quality.

past master, 1. one who has filled the office of master in a guild, lodge, etc. **2.** one who has ripe experience in any profession, art, etc.:

Pas·to (päs′tō), *n.* **1.** a city in SW Colombia. 57,637 pop. (est. 1943): ab. 8350 ft. high. **2.** a volcanic peak near this city. 13,990 ft.

pas·tor (păs′tər, päs′-), *n.* **1.** a minister or clergyman with reference to his flock. **2.** one having spiritual care of a number of persons. [t. L: shepherd; r. ME *pastour,* t. AF] **—pas′tor·ship′,** *n.*

pas·to·ral (păs′tə rəl, päs′-), *adj.* **1.** of or pertaining to shepherds. **2.** used for pasture, as land. **3.** having the simplicity or charm of such country, as scenery. **4.** pertaining to the country or life in the country. **5.** portraying the life of shepherds or of the country, as a work of literature, art, or music. **6.** pertaining to a minister or clergyman, or to his duties, etc. **—n. 7.** a poem, play, or the like, dealing with the life of shepherds, commonly in a conventional or artificial manner, or with simple rural life generally; a bucolic. **8.** a picture or work of art presenting shepherd life. **9.** a pastorale. **10.** a treatise on the duties of a minister or clergyman. **11.** a letter from a spiritual pastor to his people. **12.** a letter from a bishop to his clergy or people. **13.** a pastoral staff, or crozier. [ME, t. L: s. *pastorālis* pertaining to a shepherd] **—pas′to·ral·ism,** *n.* **—pas′to·ral·ist,** *n.* **—pas′to·ral·ly,** *adv.*

pas·to·ra·le (păs′tə rä′lĭ; *It.* päs′tô rä′lĕ), *n., pl.* **-li** (-lē), **-les.** *Music.* **1.** an opera, cantata, or the like, with a pastoral subject. **2.** a piece of music suggestive of pastoral life. [It., der. *pastore,* shepherd, der. L *pastor*]

pas·tor·ate (păs′tər ĭt, päs′-), *n.* **1.** the office, or the term of office, of a pastor. **2.** a body of pastors.

pas·to·ri·um (păs tōr′ĭ əm, päs-), *n. Southern U.S.* a parsonage. [t. NL, der. L *pastor* PASTOR]

pas·tor·ship (păs′tər shĭp′, päs′-), *n.* the dignity or office of a pastor.

past participle, *Gram.* a participle with past or perfect meaning; perfect participle, as *fallen, sung, defeated.*

past perfect, *Gram.* pluperfect.

pas·tra·mi (pə strä′mĭ), *n.* a highly seasoned shoulder cut of smoked beef. [t. Yiddish]

pas·try (pās′trĭ), *n., pl.* **-tries. 1.** food made of paste, esp. the shortened paste used for pie crust, etc. **2.** articles of food of which such paste forms an essential part, as pies, tarts, napoleons, etc. [f. PASTE + -(E)RY]

pas·tur·a·ble (păs′chər ə bəl, päs′-), *adj.* capable of affording pasture, as land.

pas·tur·age (păs′chər ĭj, päs′-), *n.* **1.** growing grass or herbage for cattle, etc. **2.** grazing ground. **3.** the act or business of pasturing cattle, etc. [t. F, der. *pasture* PASTURE]

pas·ture (păs′chər, päs′-), *n., v.,* **-tured, -tur·ing. —n. 1.** ground covered with grass or herbage, used or suitable for the grazing of cattle, etc.; grassland. **2.** grass or herbage for feeding cattle, etc. **—v.t. 3.** to feed (cattle,

etc.) by putting them to graze on pasture. **4.** (of land) to furnish pasturage for. **5.** (of cattle, etc.) to graze upon. **6.** to put cattle, etc., to graze upon (pasture). [ME, t. OF, g. LL *pastūra,* lit., feeding, grazing]

past·y¹ (pās′tĭ), *adj.,* **pastier, pastiest.** of or like paste in consistency, appearance, etc. [f. PASTE, n. + -Y¹]

past·y² (păs′tĭ, päs′-), *n., pl.* **pasties.** *Chiefly Brit.; Archaic or Hist. in U.S.* a pie filled with game, fish, or the like. [ME *pastee,* t. OF, der. *paste* PASTE]

pat¹ (păt), *v.,* **patted, patting.** *—v.t.* **1.** to strike lightly with something flat, as an implement, the palm of the hand, or the foot. **2.** to stroke gently with the palm or fingers as an expression of affection, approbation, etc. **3.** to strike (the floor, etc.) with lightly sounding footsteps. *—v.i.* **4.** to strike lightly or gently. **5.** to walk or run with lightly sounding footsteps. *—n.* **6.** a light stroke or blow with something flat. **7.** the sound of a light stroke, or of light footsteps. **8.** a small mass of something, as butter, shaped by patting or other manipulation. [ME; akin to PUTT]

pat² (păt), *adj.* **1.** exactly to the point or purpose. **2.** apt; opportune; ready. *—adv.* **3.** exactly or perfectly. **4.** aptly; opportunely. **5. stand pat,** *Colloq.* **a.** to stick to one's decision, policy, etc. **b.** (in poker) to play a hand as dealt, without drawing other cards. [appar. akin to PAT¹] **—pat′ness,** *n.* **—pat′ter,** *n.*

pat., **1.** patent. **2.** patented.

pa·ta·gi·um (pə tā′jĭ əm), *n., pl.* **-gia** (-jĭ ə). **1.** a wing membrane, as of a bat. **2.** the extensible fold of skin of a gliding mammal or reptile, as a flying squirrel. [t. NL, t. L: a gold border on a woman's tunic]

Pat·a·go·ni·a (păt′ə gō′nĭ ə), *n.* **1.** the tableland region constituting the S tip of Argentina. **2.** a region in the extreme S part of South America, extending from the Andes to the Atlantic: mostly in S Argentina, partly in S Chile. **—Pat′a·go′ni·an,** *adj., n.*

Patagonia (def. 1)

patch (păch), *n.* **1.** a piece of material used to mend a hole or break, or to strengthen a weak place: *a patch on a sail.* **2.** a piece of material used to cover or protect a wound, an injured part, etc.: *a patch over the eye.* **3.** any of the pieces of cloth sewed together to form patchwork. **4.** a small piece or scrap of anything. **5.** a piece or tract of land. **6.** a small piece of black silk or courtplaster worn on the face or elsewhere to hide a defect or to heighten the complexion by contrast. *—v.t.* **7.** to mend or strengthen with or as with a patch or patches. **8.** to repair or restore, esp. in a hasty or makeshift way (usually fol. by *up*). **9.** to make by joining patches or pieces together: *to patch a quilt.* **10.** to settle; smooth over: *they patched up their quarrel.* [ME *pacche;* orig. uncert.] **—patch′er,** *n.* **—Syn. 7.** See mend.

patch·ou·li (păch′ŏŏ lĭ, pə chŏŏ′lĭ), *n.* **1.** the East Indian menthaceous plants, *Pogostemon Heyneanus* and *P. Cablin,* which yield a fragrant oil. **2.** a penetrating perfume derived from it. Also, **pachouli, patch′ou·ly.** [t. vernacular of Madras region of India; orig. uncert.]

patch pocket, a pocket formed by sewing a piece of the material on the outside of a garment.

patch·work (păch′wûrk′), *n.* **1.** work made of pieces of cloth or leather of various colors or shapes sewed together, used esp. for covering quilts, cushions, etc. **2.** work or a product of any kind made up of various pieces or parts put together: *a patchwork of verses.*

patch·y (păch′ĭ), *adj.,* **patchier, patchiest. 1.** marked by patches. **2.** occurring in, forming, or like patches. **—patch′i·ly,** *adv.* **—patch′i·ness,** *n.*

patd., patented.

pate (pāt), *n. Humorous.* **1.** the head. **2.** the crown or top of the head. **3.** brains. [ME; orig. uncert.]

pâte (pät), *n. French.* **1.** paste. **2.** porcelain paste used in ceramic work. [see PASTE]

pâ·té (pä tĕ′), *n. French.* a form of pastry filled with chicken, sweetbreads, oysters, or the like. [see PASTY²]

pâ·té de foie gras (pä tĕ′ də fwä grä′), *French.* a paste made with the livers of specially fattened geese.

pa·tel·la (pə tĕl′ə), *n., pl.* **-tellae** (-tĕl′ē). **1.** *Anat.* the kneecap. See diag. under **skeleton. 2.** *Bot., Zool., etc.* a panlike or cuplike formation. **3.** *Archaeol.* a small pan or shallow vessel. [t. L: small pan, kneepan, dim. of *patina.* See PATINA²] **—pa·tel′lar,** *adj.*

pa·tel·late (pə tĕl′ĭt, -āt), *adj.* **1.** having a patella. **2.** patelliform.

pa·tel·li·form (pə tĕl′ə fôrm′), *adj.* having the form of a patella; shaped like a saucer, kneecap, or limpet shell. [f. s. L *patella* small pan + -(I)FORM]

pat·en (păt′ən), *n.* the plate on which the bread is placed in the celebration of the Eucharist. Also, **patin, patine.** [ME *patene,* t. OF, t. L, m. *patena, patina.* See PATINA²]

pa·ten·cy (pā′tən sĭ), *n.* **1.** the state of being patent. **2.** *Med.* the condition of not being blocked or obstructed. **3.** *Phonet.* openness of articulation, found more or less in all phonemes except plosives.

pat·ent (păt′ənt *or, esp. Brit.,* pā′tənt for 1–9, 14–18; *usually* pā′tənt for 10–13), *n.* **1.** a government grant to an inventor, his heirs or assigns, for a stated period of time, conferring upon him a monopoly of the exclusive right to make, use, and vend the invention or discovery. **2.** an invention, process, etc., which has been patented. **3.** an official document conferring some right, privilege, or the like. **4.** the instrument by which the United States conveys the legal fee-simple title to public land. —*adj.* **5.** of a kind specially protected by a patent. **6.** endowed with a patent, as persons. **7.** belonging as if by a proprietary claim; having a trademark. **8.** conferred by a patent, as a right or privilege. **9.** appointed by a patent, as a person. **10.** open to view or knowledge; manifest; evident; plain. **11.** lying open, or not shut in or enclosed, as a place. **12.** *Chiefly Bot.* expanded or spreading. **13.** open, as a door or a passage. **14.** *Phonet.* open, in various degrees, to the passage of the breath stream (opposed to *stopped* or *occlusive*). **15.** designating certain better grades of flour. —*v.t.* **16.** to take out a patent on; obtain the exclusive rights to (an invention) by a patent. **17.** to originate and establish as one's own. **18.** *Rare.* to grant the exclusive right to (an invention) by a patent. **19.** *Rare.* to grant by a patent (def. 4). [ME, t. L: s. *patens*, ppr., lying open; in some senses, through OF] —**pat'ent·a·ble,** *adj.* —**pat'ent·a·bil'i·ty,** *n.* —**pat'ent·ly,** *adv.* —**Syn. 10.** See **apparent.**

pat·ent·ee (păt'ən tē'), *n.* one to whom a patent is granted.

patent insides, newspaper sheets printed on one side of the sheet only, and thus sold to publishers, who fill the unprinted pages with matter of their own selection.

patent leather, a hard, glossy, smooth leather, usually finished in black.

patent log. See **log** (def. 2).

patent medicine, a medicine distributed by a company which has a patent on its manufacture.

pat·en·tor (păt'ən tər), *n.* one who grants a patent.

patent right, the exclusive right created by a patent.

pa·ter (pā'tər; *also for 2, 3* păt'ər), *n.* **1.** *Brit. Colloq.* father. **2.** the paternoster or Lord's Prayer. **3.** a recital of it. [ME, t. L: father]

Pa·ter (pā'tər), *n.* **Walter Horatio,** 1839–94, British critic, essayist, and novelist.

pa·ter·fa·mil·i·as (pā'tər fə mĭl'ĭ əs), *n.,* *pl.* **pa·tres·fa·mil·i·as** (pā'trēz fə mĭl'ĭ əs). **1.** the head of a family. **2.** *Roman Law.* a free male citizen who has been freed from patria potestas by death of his father or by emancipation. [t. L: f. *pater* father + *familias,* archaic gen. of *familia* family]

pa·ter·nal (pə tûr'nəl), *adj.* **1.** characteristic of or befitting a father; fatherly. **2.** of or pertaining to a father. **3.** related on the father's side. **4.** derived or inherited from a father. [f. s. L *paternus* fatherly + -AL¹] —**pa·ter'nal·ly,** *adv.* —**Syn. 1.** See **fatherly.**

pa·ter·nal·ism (pə tûr'nəl ĭz'əm), *n.* the principle or practice, on the part of a government or of any body or person in authority, of managing or regulating the affairs of a country or community, or of individuals, in the manner of a father dealing with his children. —**pa·ter'nal·is'tic,** *adj.* —**pa·ter'nal·is'ti·cal·ly,** *adv.*

pa·ter·ni·ty (pə tûr'nə tĭ), *n.* **1.** derivation from a father. **2.** the state of being a father; fatherhood. **3.** origin or authorship. [ME, t. LL: m.s. *paternitas,* der. L *paternus* fatherly]

pa·ter·nos·ter (pā'tər nŏs'tər, păt'ər-), *n.* **1.** Also, **Pater Noster,** the Lord's Prayer, esp. in the Latin form. **2.** a recital of this prayer as an act of worship. **3.** one of certain beads in a rosary, regularly every eleventh bead, differing in size or material from the rest, and indicating that a paternoster is to be said. **4.** any form of words used as a prayer or charm. [ME and OE, t. L: our father, the first words of the prayer in the Latin version]

Pat·er·son (păt'ər sən), *n.* a city in NE New Jersey. 139,336 (1950).

path (păth, päth), *n.* **1.** a way beaten or trodden by the feet of men or beasts. **2.** a walk in a garden or through grounds. **3.** a route, course, or track in which something moves. **4.** a course of action, conduct, or procedure. [ME; OE *pæth,* c. G *pfad*] —**Syn. 1.** PATH, LANE, TRAIL are passages or routes not so wide as a way or road. A PATH is a way for passing on foot; a track, beaten by feet, not specially constructed, often along the side of a road: *a path through a field.* A LANE is a narrow road or track, generally between fields, often enclosed with fences or trees; sometimes an alley or narrow road between buildings in towns: *a lane leading to a farmhouse, Drury Lane.* A TRAIL is a rough way made or worn through woods, or across mountains, prairies, or other untraveled regions: *an Indian trail.*

path., **1.** pathological. **2.** pathology.

Pa·than (pə tän', pə hän'), *n.* **1.** an Afghan. **2.** an Afghan dwelling in, or in the borderland of, India. [t. Pushtoo]

pa·thet·ic (pə thĕt'ĭk), *adj.* **1.** exciting pity or sympathetic sadness; full of pathos. **2.** affecting or moving the feelings. **3.** pertaining or due to the feelings. Also, **pa·thet'i·cal.** [t. LL: s. *patheticus,* t. Gk.: m. *pathētikós* sensitive] —**pa·thet'i·cal·ly,** *adv.*

pathetic fallacy, the attachment of human traits and feelings to nature.

path·find·er (păth'fīn'dər, päth'-), *n.* one who finds a path or way, as through a wilderness.

-pathia, an obsolete form of **-pathy.**

-pathic, a word element forming adjectives from nouns ending in *-pathy,* as *psychopathic.* [see -PATHY, -IC]

path·less (păth'lĭs, päth'-), *adj.* without paths; trackless. —**path'less·ness,** *n.*

patho-, a word element meaning "suffering," "disease," "feeling." [t. Gk., comb. form of *páthos*]

path·o·gen (păth'ə jən), *n.* a pathogenic or disease-producing organism. Also, **path·o·gene** (păth'ə jēn').

path·o·gen·e·sis (păth'ə jĕn'ĭs), *n.* the production and development of disease. Also, **pa·thog·e·ny** (pə thŏj'ə nĭ). —**path·o·ge·net·ic** (păth'ō jə nĕt'ĭk), *adj.*

path·o·gen·ic (păth'ə jĕn'ĭk), *adj.* disease-producing.

pathol., **1.** pathological. **2.** pathology.

path·o·log·i·cal (păth'ə lŏj'ə kəl), *adj.* **1.** of or pertaining to pathology. **2.** due to or involving disease; morbid. **3.** treating of or concerned with diseases. Also, **path'o·log'ic.** —**path'o·log'i·cal·ly,** *adv.*

pa·thol·o·gy (pə thŏl'ə jĭ), *n., pl.* **-gies.** **1.** the science of the origin, nature, and course of diseases. **2.** the conditions and processes of a disease. —**pa·thol'o·gist,** *n.*

pa·thos (pā'thŏs), *n.* **1.** the quality or power, as in speech, music, etc., of evoking a feeling of pity or sympathetic sadness; touching or pathetic character or effect (opposed to *ethos*). **2.** *Obs.* suffering. [t. Gk.: suffering, disease, feeling]

path·way (păth'wā', päth'-), *n.* a path.

-pathy, a noun element meaning "suffering," "feeling," as in *anthropopathy, antipathy, sympathy,* and often, esp. in words of modern formation, as "morbid affection," "disease," as in *anthropathy, deuteropathy, neuropathy, psychopathy,* and hence used also in names of systems or methods of treating disease, as in *allopathy, homeopathy, hydropathy, osteopathy.* [t. Gk.: m. *-pátheia*]

Pa·ti·a·la (pŭt'ĭ ä'lə), *n.* **1.** a state in NW India: foremost of the Punjab States. 1,936,000 pop. (1941); 5942 sq. mi. **2.** the capital of this state. 69,850 (1941).

pa·tience (pā'shəns), *n.* **1.** calm and uncomplaining endurance, as under pain, provocation, etc. **2.** calmness in waiting: *have patience a little longer.* **3.** quiet perseverance: *to labor with patience.* **4.** *Chiefly Brit.* a card game, usually played by one person alone. Cf. *U.S.* **solitaire** (def. 1). **5.** *Obs.* sufferance. [t. L: m.s. *patientia;* r. ME *pacience,* t. OF]
—**Syn. 1.** PATIENCE, ENDURANCE, FORTITUDE, STOICISM imply qualities of calmness, stability, and persistent courage in trying circumstances. PATIENCE may denote calm, self-possessed and unrepining bearing of pain, misfortune, annoyance, or delay; or painstaking and untiring industry or (less often) application in the doing of something: *to bear afflictions with patience.* ENDURANCE denotes the ability to bear exertion, hardship, or suffering (without implication of moral qualities required or shown): *running a marathon requires great endurance.* FORTITUDE implies not only patience but courage and strength of character in the midst of pain, affliction, or hardship: *to show fortitude in adversity.* STOICISM is calm fortitude, with such repression of emotion as to seem almost like indifference to pleasure or pain: *the American Indians were noted for stoicism under torture.*

pa·tient (pā'shənt), *n.* **1.** one who is under medical or surgical treatment. **2.** a person or thing that undergoes action (opposed to *agent*). **3.** *Obs.* or *Rare.* a sufferer. —*adj.* **4.** quietly persevering or diligent: *patient workers.* **5.** enduring pain, trouble, affliction, hardship, etc., with fortitude, calmness, or quiet submission. **6.** marked by such endurance. **7.** quietly enduring strain, annoyance, etc.: *patient in a traffic jam.* **8.** disposed to or characterized by such endurance. **9.** enduring delay with calmness or equanimity, or marked by such endurance: *be patient.* **10.** having or showing the capacity for endurance (fol. by *of*). **11.** susceptible (fol. by *of*). **12.** undergoing the action of another (opposed to *agent*). [t. L: s. *patiens,* ppr., suffering, enduring; r. ME *pacient,* t. OF] —**pa'tient·ly,** *adv.* —**Syn. 5.** uncomplaining, long-suffering, forbearing, resigned.

pat·in (păt'ən), *n.* paten. Also, **pat'ine.**

pat·i·na¹ (păt'ə nə), *n.* **1.** a film or incrustation, usually green, produced by oxidation on the surface of old bronze, and esteemed as ornamental. **2.** a similar film or coloring on some other substance. **3.** a surface calcification of implements, usually indicating great age. [t. It., t. L: dish, through meaning tarnish (on metal dish)]

pat·i·na² (păt'ə nə), *n., pl.* **-nae** (-nē'). a broad, shallow dish of the ancient Romans. [t. L]

pa·ti·o (pā'tĭ ō', păt'ĭ ō'; *Sp.* pä'tyō), *n., pl.* **-tios.** (in Spain and Spanish-American countries) a court, as of a house, esp. an inner court open to the sky. [t. Sp.]

Pat·more (păt'mōr), *n.* **Coventry** (kŏv'ən trĭ, kŭv'-), 1823–96, British poet.

Pat·mos (păt'mŏs, păt'mōs), *n.* one of the Dodecanese Islands, off the SW coast of Asia Minor: St. John is supposed to have been exiled on this island. Rev. 1:9. 3184 pop. (1936); 13 sq. mi. Italian, **Pat·mo** (pät'mō).

Pat·na (păt'nə, pŭt'nä'), *n.* a city in NE India, on the Ganges: the capital of Bihar province. 175,706 (1941).

Pat. Off., Patent Office.

pat·ois (păt'wä; *Fr.* pȧ twä'), *n., pl.* **patois** (păt'wäz; *Fr.* pȧ twä'). any peasant or provincial form of speech. [t. F, der. OF *patoier* handle clumsily, der. *pate* paw]

Pa·tras (pä träs'), *n.* a seaport in W Greece, on the **Gulf of Patras,** an inlet of the Ionian Sea in the NW Peloponnesus. 74,024 (1940). Greek, **Pa·trai** (pä'trē).